Congressional Quarterly's

POLITICS IN AMERICA 1992

THE 102nd CONGRESS

By CQ's Political Staff
Phil Duncan, Editor

A division of
CONGRESSIONAL QUARTERLY INC.
1414 22nd Street N.W., Washington D.C. 20037

Printed in the United States of America

Library of Congress Cataloging in Publication Data

Congressional Quarterly's Politics in America: 1992, the 102nd Congress / by CQ's political staff: Phil Duncan, editor.
p. cm.

Includes index.

1. United States. Congress — Biography. 2. United States. Congress — Committees. 3. United States. Congress — Election districts — Handbooks, manuals, etc. 4. Election districts — United States — Handbooks, manuals, etc. I. Duncan, Phil. II. Congressional Quarterly Inc. III. Title: Politics in America.
JK1010.C67 1991 328.73'073'45'0202—dc20 91-22082
ISBN 0-87187-641-8 CIP

Politics in America • 1992 • The 102nd Congress

Editor
Phil Duncan

Managing Editor
Virginia C. Armat

Contributing Editor
Ronald D. Elving

Principal Writers
Bob Benenson   Beth Donovan   Dave Kaplan

Major Contributors
John Schachter   Glen Craney   Holly Idelson   Charles Mahtesian

Other Contributors
Rhodes Cook, Elizabeth A. Palmer, Jennifer Silverman, Andrew Taylor, Christine M. Dixon, Philip Marwill, Paul L. Nyhan, Jennifer Seter, Ilyse J. Veron

Principal Researchers
Jennifer Silverman   Jeanne Kislitzin

Interns
Jennifer Seter   Hillary Bridgers

Contributing Researchers
Sharon Perkinson, Daniel D. Brown, Christine M. Dixon, Jacqueline R. Duobinis, Ernest James, Kenneth E. Jaques, Virginia Johnson, Philip Marwill, Julie F. Mattes, John Murawski, Paul L. Nyhan, Catherine Paler, Sharon M. Page, Celestine Rideout, Kevin Shanley, Dennis J. Smith, David W. Stewart, Ilyse J. Veron

Copy Editors
Colette Gergely, Virginia Cope, Eugene J. Gabler, Sandra Graziano, Kristin R. Kurtenbach, Charles Southwell

Cover Design
Ben Santora   Patt Chisholm

Photographers
R. Michael Jenkins (staff photographer)
Mickey Adair, Lisa Berg, Dennis Brock, Gordon Chibroski, Paul Conklin, Erike Fiske, Joe Gardner, Ken Heinen, Paul Indorf Jr., Sue Klemens, Marty LaVor, Joseph McCary, Eileen McClure, Brod Markel, Art Stein, Teresa Zabala

Phil Duncan came to Congressional Quarterly in 1979 and joined the politics staff of CQ's *Weekly Report* magazine in 1980. Since 1988, he has been CQ's politics editor and a contributing columnist to the *Weekly Report*. Duncan worked on the five previous editions of "Politics in America," and was editor of the 1990 edition. Born in Knoxville, Tenn., Duncan graduated from Davidson College in 1979 and worked for *The Charlotte Observer* and *The Knoxville News-Sentinel* before joining CQ. He lives in Falls Church, Va., with his wife Leslie and daughter Meredyth.

Virginia C. Armat came to CQ in 1990 as managing editor of "Politics in America." Before that, she worked for seven years as an editor in the magazine book department of *Reader's Digest*, and as a free-lance journalist in Paris for six years, where she was bureau chief for *The Washington Star*. A co-founder of *Mid-Atlantic Country* magazine, she is also co-author, with Rael Jean Isaac, of "Madness in the Streets," published in 1990 by Macmillan/Free Press. A native Washingtonian, Armat is an honors graduate of Vassar College and lives in the District of Columbia.

The chief editorial contributors to "Politics in America" are current or former members of the *Weekly Report*'s politics staff. Ronald D. Elving is deputy political editor; Bob Benenson, Beth Donovan and Dave Kaplan are political reporters. Glen Craney is editor of CQ's *Campaign Practices Report* newsletter. Holly Idelson covered politics for CQ in 1990 and now reports on legislative affairs. John Schachter wrote for CQ's "1990 Almanac," a compendium of legislative developments. Charles Mahtesian is a writer and researcher on the politics staff.

TABLE OF CONTENTS

NORTH CAROLINA

U.S. Senate

U.S. House of Representatives

NORTH DAKOTA

U.S. Senate

U.S. House of Representatives

OHIO

U.S. Senate

U.S. House of Representatives

OKLAHOMA

U.S. Senate

U.S. House of Representatives

OREGON

U.S. Senate

U.S. House of Representatives

PENNSYLVANIA

U.S. Senate

U.S. House of Representatives

Explanation of Statistics

Committees

Standing and select committees and subcommittees are listed for Senate and House members, as are joint committees. Seniority ranking is as of publication date. House seniority rankings include non-voting delegates and the resident commissioner, where applicable.

Elections

House

General election returns are given for House members for 1988 and 1990. Returns do not necessarily include candidates receiving less than 5 percent of the vote. Primary returns are given for House members for 1990. No primary results are listed if a candidate ran unopposed or was nominated by caucus or convention. Because percentages have been rounded to the nearest whole number, election totals do not always add up to exactly 100 percent.

Senate

Primary and general election returns are given for each senator's most recent election. No primary results are given if a candidate ran unopposed or was nominated by caucus or convention. For senators with previous service in the House, elections to the House are indicated with a footnote.

Key to Party Abbreviations

AM — American
AMI — American Independent
BAG — Better Affordable Government
C — Conservative
D — Democratic
GR — Grass Roots
I — Independent
IL SOL — Illinois Solidarity
L — Liberal
LIBERT — Libertarian
NA — New Alliance
PFP — Peace and Freedom
POP — Populist
R — Republican
RTL — Right to Life
SOC WORK — Socialist Workers
TIC — Tisch Independent Citizens
WW — Workers World
WWW — World Without War

Previous Winning Percentages

Winning election percentages are given for each member's entire congressional career. If no percentage is given, the member either did not run or lost the election that year. Percentages are included for both general elections and special elections.

District Vote for President

The vote presidential candidates received in each congressional district is given for 1976, 1980, 1984 and 1988. The tabulations are for the area within each current district, even though in most cases that area did not constitute a district until 1982.

Data for the district vote for president were compiled by Congressional Quarterly using state and county election agencies' official results. A few county results for 1988 were received from the Republican National Committee; the RNC's figures were taken directly from work sheets compiled by county officials. Results for selected counties in the following states were compiled in this manner: Arizona, Indiana, Mississippi, Missouri and New Jersey.

Some district totals will not correlate with state totals due to variances in tabulating absentee ballots by county election officials.

Vote totals for 1976 and 1980 were not available for Washington state. Vote totals included for independent (I) in 1980 are for John B. Anderson. The independent vote is included only if the candidate received 2 percent or more of the vote in the district. The vote for Anderson was not available for California.

Campaign Finance

Figures are given for all members of Congress and their general election challengers, if they filed reports with the Federal Election Commission (FEC). If no figures are listed, the candidate either did not file a report (reports are not required if receipts and expenditures are less than $5,000) or the reports listed receipts and expenditures of zero.

For House members, figures are given for the 1988 and 1990 elections. For senators, figures are given for the most recent election.

Campaign finance data cover the receipts and expenditures of each candidate during the two-year election cycle ending on Dec. 31 of the year the election was held. Data for 1988 cover the period Jan. 1, 1987 - Dec. 31, 1988. Data for 1990 cover the period Jan. 1, 1989 - Dec. 31, 1990. The data for 1990 used in "Politics in America" were compiled from Federal Election

Commission reports. Excluded are reports by candidate committees that exist solely to collect money for current or prior campaign debts.

Other candidate transactions, such as contributions to other campaigns, loan repayments, purchase and redemption of certificates of deposit, and debts owed to or by the campaign committees at the end of the election year, were not subtracted from the receipts and expenditures totals.

The figures for political action committee (PAC) receipts are based on the FEC summary report for each candidate. Amounts designated under this category include contributions from both PACs and candidate committees. PAC contributions received by a candidate but returned within 10 days are not reflected in the FEC compilation.

Key Votes

A series of significant votes has been selected from the roll-call votes taken during the 101st Congress, as well as one taken in the 102nd. The following captions give the number of the bill, the major sponsor, a brief description of the bill, a breakdown of the vote, the date the vote was taken and the president's position on the issue, if he took one. The following symbols are used:

Y, voted for (yea)
N, voted against (nay)
#, paired for
+, announced for
X, paired against
-, announced against
P, voted "present"
C, voted "present" to avoid possible conflict of interest
?, did not vote or otherwise make a position known.

SENATE KEY VOTES

1991

H J Res 77. Use of Force Against Iraq/Passage. Passage of the joint resolution to authorize the use of military force if Iraq has not withdrawn from Kuwait and complied with U.N. Security Council resolutions by Jan. 15. The resolution authorizes the use of force and the expenditure of funds under the War Powers act and requires the president to report to Congress every 60 days on the efforts to obtain Iraqi compliance with the U.N. resolutions. Passed 250-183: R 164-3; I 0-1; D 86-179 (ND 33-147, SD 53-32), Jan. 12, 1991. A "yea" was a vote supporting the president's position.

1990

S 1970. Omnibus Crime Package/Assault-Style Weapons. Hatch, R-Utah, amendment to strike provisions that would prohibit for three years making, selling and possessing nine types of semiautomatic assault-style weapons. Rejected 48-52: R 36-9; D 12-43 (ND 5-33, SD 7-10), May 23, 1990. A "yea" was a vote supporting the president's position.

S J Res 332. Constitutional Amendment on the Flag/Passage. Passage of the joint resolution to propose an amendment to the Constitution to prohibit the physical desecration of the U.S. flag. Rejected 58-42: R 38-7; D 20-35 (ND 10-28, SD 10-7), June 26, 1990. A two-thirds majority of those present and voting (67 in this case) of both houses is required for passage of a joint resolution proposing an amendment to the Constitution. A "yea" was a vote supporting the president's position.

HR 5257. Fiscal 1991 Labor, HHS and Education Appropriations/Abortion. Harkin, D-Iowa, motion to table (kill) the Armstrong, R-Colo., amendment to the committee amendment to permit federal funding of abortion in cases of rape or incest. The Armstrong amendment would require organizations receiving funds to notify a parent or legal guardian 48 hours before performing an abortion for a minor, unless there is a medical emergency. Motion rejected 48-48: R 8-34; D 40-14 (ND 31-6, SD 9-8), Oct. 12, 1990. (Subsequently, the Armstrong amendment was adopted by voice vote.)

S 3189. Fiscal 1991 Defense Appropriations/B-2 Bomber. Leahy, D-Vt., amendment to cut funds for the two additional B-2 bombers in the bill, thereby terminating the expansion of the program with the 15 bombers being produced and tested. Rejected 44-50: R 9-32; D 35-18 (ND 30-7, SD 5-11), Oct. 15, 1990. A "nay" was a vote supporting the president's position.

S 3209. Fiscal 1991 Budget Reconciliation Act/Passage. Passage of the bill to cut spending and raise revenues as required by the reconciliation instructions in the budget resolution and make changes in the budget process. Passed 54-46: R 23-22; D 31-24 (ND 20-18, SD 11-6), in the session that began, and the *Congressional Record* dated, Oct. 18, 1990. (The Senate subsequently passed HR 5835 by voice vote after striking everything after the enacting clause and inserting in lieu thereof the text of S 3209.)

S 2104. Civil Rights Act of 1990/Veto Override. Passage, over President Bush's Oct. 22 veto, of the bill to reverse or modify six recent Supreme Court decisions that narrowed the reach and remedies of job discrimination law and to authorize monetary damages under Title VII of the 1964 Civil Rights Act. Rejected 66-34: R 11-34; D 55-0 (ND 38-0, SD 17-0), Oct. 24, 1990. A two-thirds majority of those present and voting (67 in this case) of both houses is required to override a veto. A "nay" was a vote supporting the president's position.

1989

S 1352. Fiscal 1990-91 Defense Department Authorization/SDI Funding. Nunn, D-Ga., motion to table (kill) the Johnston, D-La., amendment to reduce to $3.95 billion appropriations for the strategic defense initiative (SDI) program. Motion agreed to 50-47: R 37-6; D 13-41 (ND 5-32, SD 8-9), July 27, 1989. A "yea" was a vote supporting the president's position.

HR 3072. Fiscal 1990 Defense Appropriations/National Endowment for the Arts Obscenity. Mitchell, D-Maine, motion to table (kill) the Helms, R-N.C., amendment to instruct the Senate conferees on the fiscal 1990 Interior Department appropriations bill (HR 2788) to insist on a Senate-passed provision barring the use of federal funds for artworks deemed "obscene or indecent." Motion agreed to 62-35: R 19-25; D 43-10 (ND 33-5, SD 10-5), Sept. 28, 1989.

HR 3628. Capital Gains Tax Cut/Cloture. Motion to invoke cloture (thus limiting debate) on the Packwood, R-Ore., substitute amendment to exclude capital gains from taxable income in the amount of 5 percent for each full year an asset is held (to a maximum of 35 percent) and to make individual retirement accounts available to all taxpayers with varying tax benefits. Motion rejected 51-47: R 45-0; D 6-47 (ND 2-34, SD 4-13), Nov. 14, 1989. A three-fifths majority vote (60) of the total Senate is required to invoke cloture. A "yea" was a vote supporting the president's position.

HOUSE KEY VOTES

1991

H J Res 77. Use of Force against Iraq/Passage. Passage of the joint resolution to authorize the use of military force if Iraq has not withdrawn from Kuwait and complied with U.N. Security Council resolutions by Jan. 15. The resolution authorizes the use of force and the expenditure of funds under the War Powers act and requires the president to report to Congress every 60 days on the efforts to obtain Iraqi compliance with the U.N. resolutions. Passed 250-183: R 164-3; I 0-1; D 86-179 (ND 33-147, SD 53-32), Jan. 12, 1991. A "yea" vote was a vote supporting the president's position.

1990

H J Res 350. Constitutional Amendment on the Flag/Passage. Brooks, D-Texas, motion to suspend the rules and pass the joint resolution to propose an amendment to the Constitution to prohibit the physical desecration of the U.S. flag. Rejected 254-177: R 159-17; D 95-160 (ND 43-130, SD 52-30), June 21, 1990. A two-thirds majority of those present and voting (288 in this case) of both houses is required for passage of a joint resolution proposing an amendment to the Constitution. A "yea" was a vote supporting the president's position.

HR 770. Family and Medical Leave Act/Veto Override. Passage, over President Bush's June 29 veto, of the bill to require public and private employers to give unpaid leave to care for a newborn child or a seriously ill child, parent or spouse, or to use as medical leave due to a serious health condition. Rejected 232-195: R 38-138; D 194-57 (ND 156-14, SD 38-43), July 25, 1990. A two-thirds majority or those present and voting (285 in this case) of both houses is required to override a veto. A "nay" was a vote supporting the president's position.

HR 4739. Fiscal 1991 Defense Authorization/SDI Funding. Bennett, D-Fla., amendment to reduce spending for the strategic defense initiative (SDI) by $600 million to a new level of $2.3 billion. Adopted 225-189: R 20-150; D 205-39 (ND 157-7, SD 48-32), Sept. 18, 1990. A "nay" was a vote supporting the president's position.

HR 4739. Fiscal 1991 Defense Authorization/Abortion Services. Fazio, D-Calif., amendment to provide military personnel and their dependents stationed overseas with reproductive health services, including privately paid abortions, at military hospitals. Rejected 200-216: R 35-139; D 165-77 (ND 113-50, SD 52-27), Sept. 18, 1990. A "nay" was a vote supporting the president's position.

HR 5835. Fiscal 1991 Omnibus Reconciliation Act/Democratic Alternative. Rostenkowski, D-Ill., en bloc amendment to provide smaller increases in the Medicare premium and deductible; delete revenue provisions, including the gas tax, the petroleum fuels tax, the extension of the Medicare tax to additional state and local employees, and the limit on itemized deductions; eliminate the "bubble" and lift the top marginal tax rate to 33 percent; create a 10 percent surtax on income above $1 million; increase the minimum tax rate; delay indexing for one year; provide a limited tax break for capital gains; and for other purposes. Adopted 238-192: R 10-164; D 228-28 (ND 157-16, SD 71-12), Oct. 16, 1990. A "nay" was a vote supporting the president's position.

S 2104. Civil Rights Act of 1990/Conference Report. Adoption of the conference report on the bill to reverse or modify six recent Supreme Court decisions that narrowed the reach and remedies of job discrimination laws and to authorize monetary damages under Title VII of the 1964 Civil Rights Act. Adopted 273-154: R 34-139; D 239-15 (ND 169-3, SD 70-12), Oct. 17, 1990. A "nay" was a vote supporting the president's position.

1989

HR 2461. Fiscal 1990-91 Defense Department Authorization/B-2 Bomber. Kasich, R-Ohio, substitute for the Synar, D-Okla., amendment, to allow the Air Force to complete a fleet of 13 B-2s already built or under construction and then to put the production line on hold while those 13 are used to test the new plane's exotic design. Rejected 144-279: R 28-144; D 116-135 (ND 102-68, SD 14-67), July 26, 1989. A "nay" was a vote supporting the president's position.

HR 3299. Fiscal 1990 Budget Reconciliation/Alternative Revenue Package. Rostenkowski, D-Ill., amendment to strike the Jenkins-Archer capital gains tax cut included in the reconciliation bill and substitute restored deductibility for individual retirement accounts, a deficit-reduction trust fund and an increase to 33 percent from 28 percent in the marginal tax rates for the highest incomes. Rejected 190-239: R 1-175; D 189-64 (ND 152-20, SD 37-44), Sept. 28, 1989. A "nay" was a vote supporting the president's position.

HR 2990. Fiscal 1990 Labor, HHS and Education Appropriations/Abortion Funding. Boxer, D-Calif., motion that the House recede from its disagreement to the Senate amendment to permit the use of federal funds to pay for abortions in cases of "promptly reported" rape or incest. Motion agreed to 216-206: R 41-134; D 175-72 (ND 124-44, SD 51-28), Oct. 11, 1989. A "nay" was a vote supporting the president's position.

HR 3660. Government Pay-and-Ethics Package/Passage. Passage of the bill to phase out honoraria, revise ethics rules and raise salaries for members of the House of Representatives and high officials of the executive and judicial branches. Passed 252-174: R 84-89; D 168-85 (ND 121-52, SD 47-33), Nov. 16, 1989.

HR 2. Minimum Wage Increase/Veto Override. Passage, over President Bush's June 13 veto, of the bill to raise the minimum wage from $3.35 an hour to $4.55 over three years, and to provide for a 60-day training wage — equal to 85 percent of the minimum — for workers who have not worked a total of 60 days. Rejected 247-178: R 20-150; D 227-28 (ND 171-3, SD 56-25), June 14, 1989. A two-thirds majority of those present and voting (284 in this case) of both houses is required to override a veto. A "nay" was a vote supporting the president's position.

Voting Studies

Voting studies prepared by Congressional Quarterly for the years since 1981 (97th Congress) indicate members' scores. The scores represent the percentage of the time a member of Congress has supported or opposed a given position. The votes are listed under two columns — S for support, O for opposition. For example, a score of 25 under the S column in the presidential support study would indicate that the member supported the president on 25 percent of the votes that were used in the study.

An explanation of the voting studies on roll-call votes follows.

Presidential Support

CQ tries to determine what the president personally, as distinct from other administration officials, does and does not want in the way of legislative action. This is done by analyzing his messages to Congress, press conference remarks and other public statements and documents.

Occasionally, important measures are so extensively amended that it is impossible to characterize final passage as a victory or defeat for the president. These votes have been excluded from the study.

Presidential support is determined by the position of the president at the time of a vote, even though that position may be different from an earlier one or may have been reversed after the vote was taken.

Votes on motions to recommit, to reconsider or to table often are key tests that govern the legislative outcome. Such votes are included in the presidential support tabulations. Failure to vote lowers both support and opposition scores equally. All presidential-issue votes have equal statistical weight in the analysis.

Party Unity

Party unity votes are defined as votes in the Senate and House that split the parties, a majority of voting Democrats opposing a majority of voting Republicans. Votes on which either party divides evenly are excluded.

Party unity scores represent the percentage of party unity votes on which a member voted "yea" or "nay" in agreement with a majority of his party. Failure to vote, even if a member announced his stand, lowers his score.

Opposition-to-party scores represent the percentage of party unity votes on which a member voted "yea" or "nay" in disagreement with a majority of his party. A member's party unity and opposition-to-party scores add up to 100 percent only if he participated on all party unity votes.

Conservative Coalition

As used in this study, the term "conservative coalition" means a voting alliance of Republicans and Southern Democrats against the non-Southern Democrats in Congress. This meaning, rather than any philosophical definition of the "conservative" position, provides the basis for CQ's selection of votes.

A conservative coalition vote is any vote in the Senate or House on which a majority of voting Southern Democrats and a majority of voting Republicans oppose the stand taken by a majority of voting non-Southern Democrats. Votes on which there is an even division within the ranks of voting Northern Democrats, Southern Democrats or Republicans are not included.

The Southern states are defined as Alabama, Arkansas, Florida, Georgia, Kentucky, Louisiana, Mississippi, North Carolina, Oklahoma, South

Carolina, Tennessee, Texas and Virginia.

The conservative coalition support score represents the percentage of conservative coalition votes on which a member voted "yea" or "nay" in agreement with the position of the conservative coalition. Failure to vote, even if a member announced a stand, lowers the score.

The conservative coalition opposition score represents the percentage of conservative coalition votes on which a member voted "yea" or "nay" in disagreement with the position of the conservative coalition.

Interest Group Ratings

Ratings of members of Congress by four interest groups are given for the years since 1981 (97th Congress). The groups were chosen to represent liberal, conservative, business and labor viewpoints. Following is a description of each group, along with notes regarding their ratings for particular years.

Americans for Democratic Action (ADA)

Americans for Democratic Action was founded in 1947 by a group of liberal Democrats that included Sen. Hubert H. Humphrey and Eleanor Roosevelt. In 1991 the president was Democratic Rep. Charles B. Rangel of New York.

American Conservative Union (ACU)

The American Conservative Union was founded in 1964 "to mobilize resources of responsible conservative thought across the country and further the general cause of conservatism." The organization intends to provide education in political activity, "prejudice in the press," foreign and military policy, domestic economic policy, the arts, professions and sciences. In 1991 the chairman was David A. Keene.

American Federation of Labor-Congress of Industrial Organizations (AFL-CIO)

The AFL-CIO was formed when the American Federation of Labor and the Congress of Industrial Organizations merged in 1955. With affiliates claiming more than 13 million members, the AFL-CIO accounts for approximately three-quarters of national union membership. In 1991 the president was Lane Kirkland.

Chamber of Commerce of the United States (CCUS)

The Chamber of Commerce of the United States represents local, regional and state chambers of commerce as well as trade and professional organizations. It was founded in 1912 to be "a voice for organized business." In 1991 the president was Richard L. Lesher.

Statistics and Maps

Each state profile contains figures on the population, area, presidential election vote and composition of the legislature. The U.S. congressional delegations reflect status as of June 1991 and the membership of the state legislatures indicates status as of March 1991. These numbers do not reflect later changes. Information on the makeup of the state legislatures was obtained from the National Conference of State Legislatures.

The following statistics and demographic data in each state profile section were obtained from the 1980 census:

- Demographic breakdown of settlement patterns and origin of birth;
- Work — occupations;
- Money — median family income;
- Education — persons with college degrees.

Racial demographic breakdown is taken from 1990 census figures. The three largest racial groups in each state are listed. Some persons are classified as both black and Hispanic, and some Hispanics are not classified by the Census Bureau as either black or white. Numbers are not intended to add up to 100 percent. The 1990 population and growth figures were taken from 1990 census figures. The populations of major cities are also 1990 census numbers.

The 1988 voter-turnout rate is based on the number of votes cast in the presidential contest; the 1986 and 1990 rates are based on the number of votes cast in House races. Figures were computed based on Census Bureau statistics.

Area and Land Use farm data were based on the 1982 reports of the Departments of Agriculture and Commerce. Forest land figures were taken from the 1987 U.S. Forest Service reports. The percentage of federally owned land is based on *Public Land Statistics 1987* from the Interior Department's Bureau of Land Management. The breakdown of state and local government workers is from the Census Bureau's *Public Employment in 1989.* Tax burden figures reflect 1985 Census Bureau reports. The amount of education spending came from the 1990 *Digest of Education Statistics*, published by the Department of Education; the data is based on 1987-88 figures, in current dollars. Violent crime figures are based on the FBI's 1989 report on *Crime in the United States.* The rankings for these categories were computed by Congressional Quarterly.

Ten states were redistricted prior to the beginning of the 99th Congress. Statistics for these states have been recalculated for the new districts, using census data. The 10 states are California, Hawaii, Louisiana, Maine, Mississippi, Montana, New Jersey, New York, Texas and Washington. In 1985 there was some minor redistricting in Ohio. Statistics have been recalculated to reflect the changes.

Explanation of Statistics

Each House district description contains statistics about the population, background and age of residents. Statistics are given for white, black and Spanish origin, and for other groups if they equal 1 percent or more of the total district population. Some persons are classified as both black and Hispanic, and some Hispanics are not classified by the Census Bureau as either black or white. All demographic data in the congressional district descriptions are based on the 1980 census; percentages were calculated by Congressional Quarterly.

Maps obtained from the Census Bureau are included for all states. All county names appear in capital letters. City names appear in upper and lower case.

Endangered Bases

Following is a list of the bases marked for closure in recommendations sent July 1, 1991, to President Bush by the Defense Base Closure and Realignment Commission; the House member representing the area is in parentheses. The list was subject to approval by President Bush and to a vote on Congress on whether to accept the entire list.

References in this book to military installations may not necessarily reflect the information on this list.

Arizona
Williams Air Force Base (John J. Rhodes III, R)

Arkansas
Eaker Air Force Base (Bill Alexander, D)

California
Fort Ord (Army) (Leon E. Panetta, D)
Sacramento Army Depot (Robert T. Matsui, D)
Long Beach Naval Station (Dana Rohrabacher, R)
Tustin Marine Corps Air Station (C. Christopher Cox, R)
Castle Air Force Base (Gary Condit, D)
Hunters Point Naval Annex (Nancy Pelosi, D)
Moffett Field Naval Air Station (Tom Campbell, R)

Colorado
Lowry Air Force Base (Patricia Schroeder, D)

Indiana
Fort Benjamin Harrison (Army) (Andrew Jacobs Jr., D)
Grissom Air Force Base (Jim Jontz, D)

Louisiana
England Air Force Base (Clyde C. Holloway, R)

Maine
Loring Air Force Base (Olympia J. Snowe, R)

Massachusetts
Fort Devens (Army) (Chester G. Atkins, D)

Michigan
Wurtsmith Air Force Base (Robert W. Davis, R)

Missouri
Richards-Gebaur Air Reserve Station (Ike Skelton, D; Alan Wheat, D)

Ohio
Rickenbacker Air Guard Base (Chalmers P. Wylie, R)

Pennsylvania
Philadelphia Naval Shipyard (Thomas M. Foglietta, D)
Philadelphia Naval Station (Foglietta)

South Carolina
Myrtle Beach Air Force Base (Robin Tallon, D)

Texas
Chase Field Naval Air Station (Greg Laughlin, D)
Bergstrom Air Force Base (J. J. Pickle, D)
Carswell Air Force Base (Pete Geren, D)

Washington
Sand Point (Puget Sound) Naval Station (John Miller, R)

Addenda

House Majority Whip William H. Gray III **(profile begins on page 1262)** announced June 20, 1991, that he would resign from the House in early September 1991 to become president of the United Negro College Fund. At press time, an election to replace Gray as majority whip was scheduled for July 11; the two candidates were David E. Bonior of Michigan **(page 754)** and Steny H. Hoyer of Maryland **(page 661)**. Gray planned to remain as whip until his departure from Congress. The outcome of the whip's contest will affect the lineup of Democratic partisan leaders **(page 1687)**.

Democratic Sen. Harris Wofford of Pennsylvania **(page 1258)** received his committee assignments in early June 1991. He was placed on the Environment and Public Works, Foreign Relations, and Small Business committees. Democratic majorities on all three panels were increased by one seat: the number of Democratic seats on Environment increased to 10, the number on Foreign Relations increased to 11 and the number on Small Business increased to 11. The changes should be reflected in the committee statistics of the following Democrats.

Environment (10 Democrats): Daniel Patrick Moynihan, N.Y. **(page 987)**; George J. Mitchell, Maine **(page 637)**; Max Baucus, Mont. **(page 870)**; Frank R. Lautenberg, N.J. **(page 929)**; Harry Reid, Nev. **(page 899)**; Bob Graham, Fla. **(page 292)**; Joseph I. Lieberman, Conn. **(page 259)**; Howard M. Metzenbaum, Ohio **(page 1144)**.

Foreign Relations (11 Democrats): Joseph R. Biden Jr., Del. **(page 283)**; Paul S. Sarbanes, Md. **(page 647)**; Alan Cranston, Calif. **(page 102)**; Christopher J. Dodd, Conn. **(page 257)**; John Kerry, Mass. **(page 679)**; Paul Simon, Ill. **(page 418)**; Terry Sanford, N.C. **(page 1091)**; Moynihan; Charles S. Robb, Va. **(page 1527)**.

Small Business (11 Democrats): Sam Nunn, Ga. **(page 353)**; Baucus; Carl Levin, Mich. **(page 722)**; Alan J. Dixon, Ill. **(page 415)**; Tom Harkin, Iowa **(page 527)**; Kerry; Barbara A. Mikulski, Md. **(page 650)**; Lieberman; Paul Wellstone, Minn. **(page 783)**.

The Senate Banking, Housing and Urban Affairs Committee organized its subcommittees too late in 1991 to be reflected on members' individual statistics pages in this book. The subcommittees listed on **pages 1657 and 1658** are correct for the 102nd Congress; the Banking subcommittees listed on members' pages are for the 101st Congress. Those senators whose subcommittees changed since the 101st Congress are noted below.

Page xvii. Americans for Democratic Action. Minnesota Democratic Sen. Paul Wellstone was elected president of the ADA in 1991.

Page 21. Statistics: Committees. On Banking, Shelby sits on the Housing and Urban Affairs and the Securities subcommittees.

Page 279. Statistics: Committees. On Banking, Roth sits on the Housing and Urban Affairs and the Securities subcommittees.

Page 292. Statistics: Committees. On Banking, Graham sits on the Housing and Urban Affairs and the International Finance and Monetary Policy subcommittees.

Page 295. Statistics: Committees. On Banking, Mack sits on the Housing and Urban Affairs, International Finance and Monetary Policy, and Securities subcommittees.

Page 410. U.S. House membership. With the July 2 election of Republican Thomas W. Ewing in the 15th District, Illinois' House delegation has 15 Democrats, seven Republicans and no vacancies.

Page 556. Statistics: Committees. On Banking, Kassebaum sits on the Housing and Urban Affairs and the International Finance and Monetary Policy subcommittees.

Page 680. Olver's office is in room 1116 of the Longworth Building; his telephone number is 225-5335. He was assigned to the Education and Labor and the Science, Space and Technology committees. At press time, he had not received subcommittee assignments.

Page 758. Statistics: Committees. Collins has joined the Post Office and Civil Service Committee and has left the Science, Space and Technology Committee.

Addenda

Page 839. Statistics: Committees. On Banking, Bond sits on the Consumer and Regulatory Affairs, Housing and Urban Affairs, and Securities subcommittees.

Page 901. First column, sixth paragraph. Bryan has left the Constituent Service task force.

Page 971. Statistics: Committees. On Banking, Domenici sits on the Housing and Urban Affairs and the International Finance and Monetary Policy subcommittees.

Page 973. Second column, second paragraph. Bingaman has left the Constituent Service task force.

Page 990. Statistics: Committees. On Banking, D'Amato sits on the Housing and Urban Affairs and the Securities subcommittees.

Page 1091. Statistics: Committees. On Banking, Sanford sits on the Housing and Urban Affairs and the Securities subcommittees.

Page 1333. Statistics: Committees. Chafee will sit on the Banking, Housing and Urban Affairs Committee through November 1991.

Page 1418. Statistics: Committees. On Banking, Gramm sits on the Housing and Urban Affairs and the Securities subcommittees.

Page 1426. Statistics: Committees. Johnson was assigned to the Banking, Finance and Urban Affairs and the Small Business committees. On Banking, where he ranks 20th of 20 Republicans, his subcommittees are: General Oversight; Housing and Community Development; International Development, Finance, Trade and Monetary Policy. On Small Business, he ranks 17th of 17 Republicans; at press time, he had not received subcommittee assignments.

Page 1500. Statistics: Committees. Hatch has joined the Finance Committee and has left the Foreign Relations Committee.

Page 1517. Statistics: Committees. Jeffords has joined the Foreign Relations Committee.

Page 1661. Governmental Affairs Committee. The vacant Republican seat that had been held by GOP Sen. John Heinz has been eliminated.

Introduction

As each new Congress descends on Washington, a new page in America's history is turned. The people keep sending their chosen representatives to the seat of government, the representatives keep coming, and the drama that is the country's political story keeps unfolding.

They come, these politicians, from the sod of rural America, from inner-city enclaves, from grassy and tree-lined suburbs, from the tidelands and highlands of the nation. And when they get here, they enter the swirl of political engagement that ultimately will determine the direction and definition of the country.

This process has been obscured a bit in recent years by a series of political scandals that have seized the headlines and rocked the political class in Washington. The 101st Congress, which folded its tents just before the 1990 elections, saw a House Speaker and Democratic whip leave office in midterm amid ethics accusations. Five senators came under investigation for allegedly bartering their legislative influence for campaign cash from a savings and loan tycoon. Another senator was "denounced" by his peers for violating Senate ethics rules.

And voters reacted angrily when members substantially increased their own pay. The 1990 elections, which sent the 102nd Congress to Washington, were characterized by voter anger at incumbents, by talk of term limits to break up the entrenched political caste, and by narrower margins of victory for both Democratic and Republican incumbents than many had ever seen.

And yet, for all the anger and frustration among voters and politicians alike, the process of lawmaking pushed forward, as it always does. Notable legislative achievements included a fundamental reordering of U.S. policy toward Nicaragua, passage of a landmark clean air bill and approval of a sweeping measure barring discrimination against those with physical or mental disabilities.

The 102nd Congress, convened under the clouds of war in the Mideast, stepped up to the challenge of a Great Debate in keeping with the gravity of the moment. The debate was passionate and unique, although the final floor balloting followed recent patterns of political sentiment on defense and foreign policy issues, with Republicans and Southern Democrats lining up for war and the vast majority of Democrats urging caution.

This book, the sixth biennial edition of "Politics in America," is an invitation to examine today's Congress in all of its capacity for accomplishment and tendency toward gridlock. The focus is on what motivates those whose ambitions bring them to Congress and what stirs those heartland Americans who send them here. In the process, some light is shed on why the national legislature often slows to a crawl when the tough issues loom, whether they be the budget or medical care, gun control or campaign finance. A large factor always is the personal experiences of the members and the collective sentiment of the people they represent.

This would seem self-evident, of course, and yet it sometimes gets overlooked in these times of ethical preoccupations and voter agitation over entrenched incumbency. Members are viewed widely these days as beholden to special interest contributors and chiefly motivated by desires for re-election. To a significant degree they are; but they are also products of the politics of their time and their place.

The debate over reauthorizing the Clean Air Act went on for nearly a decade, and millions of dollars were spent by industry and environmentalists to influence its course. Yet in the House, the issue boiled down to two stubborn and powerful men: Energy and Commerce Committee Chairman John D. Dingell, who comes from Michigan, where many people make a living building cars; and Health and Environment Subcommittee Chairman Henry A. Waxman, who hails from Southern California, where smog from auto emissions looms as a perennial hot issue. Not surprisingly, these men did not see eye to eye on what a new clean air bill should do.

Similarly, in the Senate, two strong-minded men were at the crux of the clean air clash: Appropriations Committee Chairman Robert C. Byrd of West Virginia, where coal mining puts the groceries on many tables; and Majority Leader George J. Mitchell of Maine, whose state's forests and lakes are plagued by the acid rain that stems from industrial use of coal for fuel. When the two senators went head-to-head on a key floor vote to amend the clean air bill, Byrd put the clash in simple terms. "Sen. Mitchell is fighting for what he believes in," he said, "and I'm fighting for what I believe in."

Enacting a new clean air law took years, and purists on neither side were happy with the final legislation passed in 1990. But finding a middle ground between strong personalities and legitimate competing interests is rarely quick and painless.

Congress offers such a variety of individual views and legislative styles that it is no wonder controversial legislation sits more than it moves. Consider Democrat David L. Boren of Oklahoma and Republican Mitch McConnell of Kentucky, who for the past two years have been the premier Senate combatants in the debate on overhauling campaign finance laws. Boren is a moderate-to-conservative on most issues, but he decries the excess and influence of money in modern-day politics and supports spending limits and public financing of campaigns. "How long are we going to wait to stop the money chase in American politics and return this government back to the people?" Boren asked in a May 1991 floor debate.

McConnell's world view on this issue is quite different, as was clear from his remarks in the same debate. "People do not go to the courthouse steps any more and listen to us [politicians] talk.... The way in which you participate today in the American political system is to make a small and disclosed contribution to your favorite candidate."

Reconciling these kinds of fundamental disagreements is ultimately the job of the various party and committee leaders in the House and Senate. Both chambers got new leaders at the top in 1989 — Mitchell in the Senate, and Thomas S. Foley of Washington as Speaker of the House — and their performance so far indicates that their leadership styles are significantly unalike.

Foley took over in June 1989 when Jim Wright of Texas resigned from the speakership and the House under an ethical cloud. Wright served as Speaker just a little over two years, but in that time he established a reputation as an agenda-setter, a man willing to use his position to enforce party discipline. He also, however, came across even to many Democrats as personally aloof and disinclined to consult on strategy.

Foley could not be more different. He grew up wanting to be a judge and providing a fair process for deliberation of issues is important to him — sometimes more important than seeing his viewpoint prevail. This was plainest in

May 1991, when the House was setting ground rules for debating the Brady bill (which would impose a seven-day waiting period for handgun purchases) and a competing measure backed by the National Rifle Association. Foley, from a rural district in eastern Washington, had been known as an opponent of gun control. But before the Brady debate, he said, "I want this to be decided by the members of the House without the imposition of any effort on my part to sway their decision" — a statement it is hard to imagine Wright making.

Foley is as collegial as Wright was a loner, and most House Democrats seem content to let their new Speaker define his job as he sees fit. But some grumble that the party needs more focused policy objectives, and there are signs that Democrats may be relying more on their committee chairmen to supply definition and discipline. In organizing for the 102nd Congress, the House Democratic Caucus dumped two aging committee chairmen — Glenn M. Anderson on Public Works and Frank Annunzio on House Administration — and replaced them with more activist members — Robert A. Roe and Charlie Rose. In May 1991, when health problems forced Morris K. Udall to resign, his job leading the Interior Committee went to George Miller, who is expected to wield the chairman's gavel less gently than Udall.

These new chairmen join a club that already has some hard-nosed members, including Dingell at Energy and Commerce, Jamie L. Whitten at Appropriations, Jack Brooks at Judiciary and Dan Rostenkowski at Ways and Means.

In the Senate, Mitchell's presence is not domineering, but his coolly delivered criticisms of President Bush are often sharp, and in his dealings with the media he is mindful of scoring partisan points for the Democratic Party. During the 101st Congress, Mitchell blunted Bush's drive for a capital gains tax cut after it had passed in the House, and he has ridiculed Bush's stance toward China. In his face-off with Byrd on the clean air amendment, Mitchell won by one vote — an important boost to his image as a power broker, given the influence Byrd has over his colleagues as Appropriations chairman.

The Republican Party's House and Senate leaders, Robert H. Michel and Bob Dole, both have made their careers as conservative but pragmatic legislators, men willing to cut a deal with Democrats. These days, though, Michel and Dole have their eyes trained rightward, looking for ways to placate an emerging generation of conservatives who are eager for a more confrontational approach toward the Democratic majority.

The conservative bloc is more visible in the House, having elected Newt Gingrich as minority whip in 1989. Gingrich cooperated reasonably well with Michel on several issues in the 101st, but the Georgian opposed the higher taxes that were part of the 1990 budget summit agreement, and he led his allies in a successful floor revolt against it.

When Senate Republicans organized for the 102nd Congress, Dole and Minority Whip Alan K. Simpson were unopposed for re-election to their leadership jobs, but four prominent party positions under them went to Southern conservatives. Phil Gramm won the chair of the National Republican Senatorial Committee, Don Nickles became chairman of the Policy Committee, Trent Lott emerged as chairman of the Committee on Committees and Thad Cochran ousted moderate John H. Chafee from his post as conference chairman. In addition to those changes, young conservative senators such as Robert C. Smith, Connie Mack and Daniel R. Coats are filtering up into plum committee positions.

Late in 1990, both Michel and Dole were rumored to be considering retirement after the 102nd Congress, but they seemed to get a second wind in early 1991, as the successful U.S. extraction of Iraq from Kuwait enhanced the popularity of Bush and the GOP. Still, internal tensions over the party's style and substance persist in both chambers.

In this edition of "Politics in America," as in the five preceding it, we have made our assessments of senators and representatives by watching them in action, by conducting interviews with their peers and by researching the public record. Dozens of members and key staff people — a cross-section of ideology, region and legislative interest — shared with us their observations about Congress. We drew upon the collective expertise of Congressional Quarterly's reporters and editors, whose knowledge of Capitol Hill is unmatched. Also, we asked each member of the House and Senate to provide information about his own work.

In writing our profiles, we do not try to decide what members ought to be for or against. Our aim is to explain how they go about expressing their views and to assess how effective they are at it. While there is considerable legislative information in these pages, this is primarily a book about people, so legislative detail is often truncated.

We cannot, of course, know all there is to know about each member, but many people at Congressional Quarterly have worked hard to make our book thorough, balanced and fair. Still, assessing members of Congress is an undeniably subjective process, and we take responsibility for all the judgments contained herein. If a reader feels that anything we have written is unfair or inaccurate, please contact me.

Phil Duncan
June 6, 1991

Redistricting: The Curtain Rises

In the opening months of 1991, numerous state legislatures began the task of redrawing congressional district lines for the decade ahead. The new district boundaries now being drawn will be in force for the 1992 election; until then, House members continue to represent the constituencies that elected them in 1990.

By mid-1991, only a handful of states had completed new maps. A number of state legislatures are expected to finish their redistricting work in the second half of 1991; in some cases the process will spill over into 1992. In addition, legal challenges to enacted plans — a frequent accompaniment to redistricting — could force states back to the drawing board at any time. The likelihood of legal action regarding the accuracy of the 1990 census also added an element of uncertainty to redistricting in many states.

On the following pages, Congressional Quarterly political reporter Bob Benenson surveys the states that approved redistricting plans before this edition of "Politics in America" went to press. Accompanying his report are data on 1980s population shifts in all 435 House districts, and a rundown of the 50 districts with the greatest rates of population change during the decade.

Continuing coverage of redistricting developments as they unfold will appear in Congressional Quarterly's *Weekly Report* magazine. A comprehensive roundup of redistricting action across the country, including descriptions of all newly drawn districts, will be published in the 1994 edition of "Politics in America."

Iowa

Reformers who want to "take politics out of redistricting" will point to Iowa's nonpartisan line-drawing process as Exhibit A. In April 1991, the state's Legislative Service Bureau presented a computer-generated congressional redistricting map that was passed overwhelmingly by both houses of the Democratic-controlled Legislature; in May, Republican Gov. Terry E. Branstad signed it into law.

The effort was nearly glitch-free, even though the map had to be radically redrawn to compensate for the loss of a House seat. The 3rd District, represented by Democratic Rep. Dave Nagle, and the 2nd, held by Republican Jim Nussle, were merged into a new 2nd District covering most of northeast Iowa. The other four incumbents — Republicans Jim Leach, Jim Ross Lightfoot and Fred Grandy, and Democrat Neal Smith — each gained thousands of new constituents.

Not everyone was thrilled with the bureau's handiwork. Some Democrats would have preferred that the plan merge two Republican districts, but they knew that would be bait for a Branstad veto. Lightfoot complained when his 5th District, which is concentrated in southwest Iowa, became the new 3rd District and was radically redrawn; his new constituency ranges across Iowa's southern tier to the eastern border, knifes into the central part of the state and picks up some Democratic territory on the way. Yet even the most burdened members of the delegation chose not to fight. "You can do better, you can do worse," said Nagle. "It's a fair plan."

Nagle appears to have a slight edge in a contest with Nussle. He has seniority on his side: While Nagle ran unopposed for a third term in 1990, Nussle (who at age 30 is the youngest member of the House) was winning the open 2nd District with barely 50 percent of the vote. Linn County (Cedar Rapids), the most populous in the 2nd District won by Nussle, is moved to Leach's 1st in the remap.

However, Nagle also made a sacrifice to the 1st, giving up Johnson County (Iowa City), seat of the University of Iowa and a center of liberal activism. While industrial Dubuque (from the current 2nd) has a Democratic lean, it also has a conservative, blue-collar constituency that could favor Nussle's anti-abortion views over Nagle's support of abortion rights. Potentially pivotal in a close election between Nagle and Nussle is Cerro Gordo County (Mason City), which was moved into the new 2nd from Grandy's 6th District. The county has a slight Democratic lean. Michael S. Dukakis carried it for president in 1988 by 3,500 votes; Democrat Tom Harkin defeated Republican Tom Tauke there in the 1990 Senate race by 124 votes.

Leach should not be unduly threatened by the additions of Johnson and Linn counties to his reshaped 1st District. Based in the industrial river city of Davenport, moderate Republican Leach has always run against a Democratic tide. His current 1st gave 55 percent of its vote to Dukakis; the new one went 56 percent for the Democrat. However, Leach is used to running in a district in which Davenport dominates various smaller cities and rural communities; Iowa City and Cedar Rapids may provide competing political power centers.

A look at election numbers shows why Lightfoot was aggrieved. In his current 5th, Dukakis took 52 percent; in the new 3rd, he received over 56 percent. Harkin, a southern Iowan with a populist pitch, took 59 percent in the new 3rd, his best district showing under the new map. Lightfoot will have to introduce himself to voters in such Democratic-oriented counties as Story (which includes the city of Ames and Iowa State University), Wapello (Ottumwa), Lee (Keokuk) and Des Moines (Burlington). However, Lightfoot now has a seat on the Appropriations Committee to brag about, and maintains much rural territory.

Smith, a 17-termer who is the third-ranking Democrat on Appropriations, also saw drastic changes wrought on his 4th District. For the past decade, Smith has represented a six-county triangle in the middle of Iowa, with a strong Democratic tilt; it includes Polk (Des Moines) and Story counties. His new district has 13 counties and runs west from Des Moines to the Missouri River, where it takes in GOP-leaning Pottawattamie County and the Council Bluffs suburbs of Omaha, Neb. Smith's hold on Polk County and his seniority should buffer him. However, if Smith, now past 70, retires during the 1990s, the district could be vulnerable to a Republican takeover.

Grandy appears to be the least affected incumbent. The plan mainly shifts a handful of rural counties to create the new 5th District in northwest Iowa. The major changes are the loss of Cerro Gordo County and the addition of Webster County (Fort Dodge).

Oklahoma

Oklahoma's redistricting act raced through the Democratic-dominated Legislature in late May 1991 and was immediately signed by Democratic Gov. David Walters.

Despite complete Democratic control of the process, the new district map contains few changes from its predecessor and appears to bolster all six members of the state's House delegation, including its two Republicans. This lessens the likelihood that the plan will face the kind of furious response engendered by the 1981 remap, which sought to preserve a 5-to-1 Democratic advantage; state Republicans tried to revoke that plan in a 1982 ballot initiative that barely lost.

The districts in the new map are just as oddly shaped as those in the 1981 plan. The 2nd District, held by Democrat Mike Synar, will swoop around the Republican-oriented city of Tulsa in a huge J-shape. The 3rd — the southeast Oklahoma district that is home to Democratic freshman Bill Brewster — reaches a finger north (as it did in the 1980s) to take in the college town of Sweetwater (Oklahoma State University). Republican Mickey Edwards' 5th District again begins in Oklahoma City, heads north to the Kansas border and then turns sharply east, taking in conservative farming and oil drilling areas along the way.

The changes in the 6th District, held by conservative Democrat Glenn English, drew the most flak during legislative proceedings. The rural 6th, which lost population during the past decade, gained people by reaching further into Oklahoma City and drawing most of its black population out of Edwards' 5th. Republicans viewed English's adoption of this heavily Democratic constituency as strengthening his hold on the 6th; state House GOP leader Joe Heaton criticized the new appendage as a "curved arthritic finger gouging into the belly of Oklahoma County."

However, the new map strengthens 1st District GOP Rep. James M. Inhofe. It restores to the 1st the staunchly Republican southeastern part of Tulsa, which had been moved to the 2nd in the last remapping to benefit then-1st District Democratic Rep. James R. Jones (who gave up the seat to run for the Senate in 1986 and was succeeded by Inhofe). Synar, a liberal (for Oklahoma) Democrat who took south Tulsa last time because he appeared electorally secure, has faced an increasing threat of conservative challenge in recent years; he benefits from losing south Tulsa in the new map.

Democratic Rep. Dave McCurdy, who has won easily in southwest Oklahoma's 4th District, is little affected by the remap.

Missouri

Also in May 1991, the Democratic-controlled Missouri Legislature overwhelmingly passed a plan that eschewed major changes in the state's nine House districts; the bill was then sent to Republican Gov. John Ashcroft, who had until July 15 to sign it.

The plan left intact the narrow black majority in the St. Louis-based 1st District, held by veteran black Democratic Rep. William L. Clay. It also had a relatively neutral effect on already vulnerable freshman Democratic Rep. Joan Kelly Horn, who in 1990 unseated GOP incumbent Jack Buechner by just 54 votes in the suburban 2nd District.

Redrawing the St. Louis-area districts was the biggest challenge for the legislators. Horn's 1990 win complicated matters for the dominant Democrats. Clay's 1st had lost 10 percent of its population; House Majority Leader Richard A. Gephardt's 3rd District, which takes in the south part of St. Louis and its southern suburbs, grew some, but slower than the state as a whole, requiring it also to pick up new constituents.

Had Buechner won, Clay and Gephardt could have picked off some of the 2nd's more Democratic areas and pushed the Republican into outlying conservative turf. But with Horn in office, the Democrats had to carve more carefully.

Clay's new district pushes somewhat farther into suburban St. Louis County, but maintains an overall black majority of 52 percent. Horn holds on to much of her St. Louis County base, while moving north into the growing suburban regions of St. Charles County. This is rather Republican-leaning turf, but it at least has the history of supporting a Democrat, conservative 9th District Rep. Harold L. Volkmer, from whom the territory was taken. Gephardt's district moves southward, adding rural St. Genevieve County to his current base in St. Louis and Jefferson counties.

Changes elsewhere are not extensive. Democrat Alan Wheat, whose Kansas City-centered 5th District lost about 5 percent of its population over the decade, picks up a bit more of Jackson County suburbia. However, Wheat, a black Democrat with biracial appeal, has won easily in his current district, which has a 3-to-1 white majority; the new district's black population, at 24 percent of the total, is actually minimally higher than he has represented.

Republican Tom Coleman, who in 1990 won with 52 percent of the vote in the 6th District, also adds more of Jackson County's suburbs to his mainly rural district. The changes in the rest of Missouri's districts, also heavily rural, involved the shifting of a handful of counties, without apparent major partisan impact.

Arkansas

The Democratic-dominated Arkansas Legislature in May 1991 approved a remap plan making minor changes in the state's four House districts and sent it on for the signature of Democratic Gov. Bill Clinton.

However, as the first of the Deep South states to complete redistricting, Arkansas may be the site of the first remap challenge from black activists seeking more "minority influence" districts. It may also provide a test of the nascent alliance between some of these activists and Republican officials, who see potential advantage for the GOP if loyally Democratic black constituencies previously divided among several districts held by white Democrats are concentrated into single districts.

As has been the pattern in Arkansas for decades, the new map consists of three districts surrounding a central district that includes the state's capital and largest city, Little Rock. The new plan would appear to have little partisan impact on the state's current House incumbents.

Northwest Arkansas' 3rd District, held by veteran Republican John Paul Hammerschmidt, saw its population grow by better than 10 percent during the 1980s. It sheds four counties in the remap, three to Democrat Beryl Anthony Jr.'s southern Arkansas 4th, and one to Democrat Bill Alexander's northeast Arkansas 1st. The Little Rock-based 2nd District, won in 1990 by Democrat Ray Thornton, gave up Lonoke County to the 1st, taking less populous Van Buren County in exchange.

However, the plan provoked the opposition of black state Rep. Ben McGee, who sought unsuccessfully to overturn it during legislative proceedings. McGee's alternative, which had support from some in the state Republican leadership, would have created a district in east and south Arkansas that would be 43 percent black. This plan would likely have the greatest effect on Anthony, whose district under the enacted plan has the highest black percentage (27 percent); under McGee's plan, he could face a competitive primary challenge from a black Democrat. The McGee plan also would shift the other three incumbents into some unfamiliar territory.

McGee said in May that he would await the results of an informal review by the U.S. Justice Department of the remap (Arkansas is not covered by Voting Rights Act regulations requiring Justice Department "pre-clearance" of any remap.) But the state Republican Party wasted no time before filing suit against the plan, naming five black voters as plaintiffs.

Indiana

The election in 1988 of Democrat Evan Bayh as governor gave state Democrats an apparent stranglehold on Indiana's congressional redistricting process. Under state law, a five-member commission was to be set up if the state Legislature failed to pass a redistricting plan before adjournment in May 1991; the members would be an appointee of the Democratic governor and two members each from the majority party in the state House (in which Democrats have a narrow majority) and state Senate (where Republicans are in control).

Thus assured of a 3-2 majority on the commission, the Legislature's Democrats had little incentive to push through a remap. Sure enough, the Legislature adjourned without much action on redistricting. The commission was then seated and quickly passed a plan drawn by the state Democratic leadership. Bayh signed an executive order accepting the plan.

Republicans assailed the rush to enactment, and some used a June special session of the Legislature — called to deal with budget issues — to push for changes in the new map. However, their efforts to reopen the issue drew little interest. A final plan, attached to a budget bill, made changes only to the border between the 6th and 7th districts, with no partisan effect on those heavily Republican seats.

Republican complaints about the remap centered on the 3rd and 5th districts, held by Democratic Reps. Tim Roemer and Jim Jontz. Roemer, who narrowly captured the 3rd District from GOP Rep. John Hiler in 1990, gets a more urban constituency that includes Michigan City (LaPorte County), which has been in the 1st District of Democrat Peter J. Visclosky. As redrawn, Jontz's 5th District no longer includes the Porter County city of Valparaiso, home to the GOP House candidate who gave Jontz a tough race in 1990. That part of Porter County goes to Visclosky's 1st, which as redrawn is still a solidly Democratic, Gary-based district.

Jontz said he got no special help in the remap, noting that his absorption of several rural counties in the new plan does little to offset the 5th District's overall Republican tone. He has won three terms in his mainly rural, conservative-minded 5th because of his personable brand of populism — especially on farm issues — and his aggressive constituent service.

There is an irony in the Republicans' complaints about gerrymandering. In 1981, the shoe was on the other foot, with Republicans in control of the governorship and the state Legislature. The resulting map was decried by Democrats as a gross gerrymander aimed at shifting House delegation control from a 6-5 Democratic majority to a 6-4 Republican edge (Indiana lost a seat in the 1980 reapportionment). As it turned out, though, the GOP mapmakers cut the lines too fine, resulting in the biggest redistricting backfire of the 1980s: By the end of the decade, Democrats held eight of the state's 10 House seats.

In addition, a Republican-drawn state legislative redistricting map resulted in the *Bandemer v. Davis* case that went to the Supreme Court in 1985. In its decision in that case, the court for the first time indicated that redistricting plans that unfairly dilute the voting impact of partisan communities may be justiciable. However, the court did not define the circumstances under which partisan redistricting might be ruled illegal. Since no further cases in the 1980s were decided under the *Bandemer* ruling, it is likely to get its first test in the 1990s.

Nebraska

After weeks of quibbling over relatively minor changes to Nebraska's three House districts, the state's unicameral Legislature on June 5 passed a redistricting plan; Democratic Gov. Ben Nelson signed the bill into law June 10.

There was little argument over the Omaha-based 2nd District, held by Democratic Rep. Peter Hoagland. The fastest-growing district in the state with a 7 percent population increase over the past decade, the 2nd gave up two Republican-leaning counties (Washington and Burt) and most of another (Cass) to GOP Rep. Doug Bereuter's Lincoln-centered 1st District.

However, the bill's progress was snagged over other changes in the 1st that would have made a marginal partisan difference. Democrats wanted to move strongly Republican Madison County to Republican Rep. Bill Barrett's heavily rural 3rd District (which lost 6 percent of its population over the past decade). Republicans wanted to keep Madison in the 1st, while moving Saline County, on Lincoln's outskirts and more Democratic in flavor, to the 3rd.

An amendment by a Democratic legislator resolved the issue. Both Madison and Saline counties were left in the 1st, while four rural counties (Fillmore, Knox, Jefferson and Pierce) were moved from the 1st to the 3rd. Bereuter, who wanted particularly to keep Knox County because of his work on issues involving its native American population and the Niobrara River, decried the plan as a Democratic gerrymander, but did not challenge the new map after its passage.

Nevada

Legislators in the Silver State had one of the easiest redistricting chores of all. The 1st District, held by Democrat Jim Bilbray, and the 2nd District, held by Republican Barbara F. Vucanovich, enjoyed population booms, with both growing at a nearly 50 percent pace in the past decade. Redistricting thus required the simple shifting of about 8,000 Nevadans from the slightly faster-growing 2nd to the 1st.

With Vucanovich and Bilbray cooperating on the remap, that task was easily completed. The 1st, which in the 1980s redistricting was given part of the city of Las Vegas and about half of Clark County's land area, as redrawn will conform roughly to the Las Vegas city limits. The redrawn 2nd takes in more of Las Vegas' suburbs and exurbs. As a result, the new 1st is a tiny island, completely surrounded by the vast and — outside of the Las Vegas and Reno areas — sparsely populated 2nd.

The demographics of the new districts should please the incumbents. The 1st will be 10 percent black, 12 percent Hispanic and 4 percent Asian; these minority constituencies help provide a dependable Democratic base. Overall, the 1st gives Democrats a 51-37 percent registration edge. The 2nd, on the other hand, is 84 percent white and less than 3 percent black; Republicans have a 48-40 percent registration edge.

District Change: Boom and Fade

Below is a listing of the 50 congressional districts that saw the greatest percentage of population change during the 1980s. The figures, based on the 1990 census, were released by the Census Bureau May 15, 1991.

FASTEST-GROWING DISTRICTS . . .

Calif. 37	Al McCandless, R	979,966	525,938	86.3
Calif. 35	Jerry Lewis, R	894,538	525,956	70.1
Texas 26	Dick Armey, R	894,930	526,598	69.9
Fla. 11	Jim Bacchus, D	838,330	512,691	63.5
Fla. 14	Harry A. Johnston, D	834,390	512,803	62.7
Calif. 43	Ron Packard, R	841,297	525,956	60.0
Fla. 13	Porter J. Goss, R	806,729	513,048	57.2
Ariz. 1	John J. Rhodes III, R	828,857	543,747	52.4
Nev. 2	Barbara F. Vucanovich, R	608,737	399,857	52.2
Fla. 4	Craig T. James, R	770,393	512,672	50.3
Fla. 12	Tom Lewis, R	766,527	513,121	49.4
Fla. 6	Cliff Stearns, R	765,397	512,950	49.2
Texas 7	Bill Archer, R	783,612	527,083	48.7
Fla. 9	Michael Bilirakis, R	759,792	513,191	48.1
Calif. 36	George E. Brown Jr., D	779,082	525,987	48.1
Nev. 1	James Bilbray, D	593,096	400,636	48.0
Calif. 20	Bill Thomas, R	759,419	525,750	44.4
Calif. 4	Vic Fazio, D	757,684	525,764	44.1
Calif. 14	John T. Doolittle, R	752,301	526,030	43.0
Ariz. 3	Bob Stump, R	778,301	544,870	42.8
Ga. 9	Ed Jenkins, D	776,911	551,782	40.8
Va. 8	James P. Moran Jr., D	747,324	534,366	39.9
Fla. 16	Lawrence J. Smith, D	716,058	513,365	39.5
Texas 10	J. J. Pickle, D	731,052	527,181	38.7
Fla. 5	Bill McCollum, R	705,724	513,005	37.6

. . . BIGGEST POPULATION LOSERS

Mich. 13	Barbara-Rose Collins, D	395,349	514,560	−23.2
Ill. 1	Charles A. Hayes, D	413,367	519,045	−20.4
Texas 18	Craig Washington, D	449,668	527,393	−14.7
Ill. 7	Cardiss Collins, D	445,232	519,034	−14.2
W.Va. 4	Nick J. Rahall II, D	421,256	487,526	−13.6
Mich. 1	John Conyers Jr., D	451,370	514,560	−12.3
Pa. 14	William J. Coyne, D	453,330	516,629	−12.3
Ill. 2	Gus Savage, D	459,387	518,931	−11.5
N.J. 10	Donald M. Payne, D	465,316	525,886	−11.5
W.Va. 1	Alan B. Mollohan, D	432,958	488,568	−11.4
La. 2	William J. Jefferson, D	467,234	525,331	−11.1
Ohio 21	Louis Stokes, D	458,125	514,169	−10.9
Ill. 17	Lane Evans, D	467,419	519,333	−10.0
Mo. 1	William L. Clay, D	491,614	546,208	−10.0
Ind. 1	Peter J. Visclosky, D	492,722	547,100	−9.9
Pa. 20	Joseph M. Gaydos, D	468,474	516,028	−9.2
Tenn. 9	Harold E. Ford, D	461,745	505,592	−8.7
Okla. 6	Glenn English, D	461,338	503,291	−8.3
Pa. 2	William H. Gray III, D	474,964	517,215	−8.2
Iowa 5	Jim Ross Lightfoot, R	447,544	485,639	−7.8
Iowa 6	Fred Grandy, R	448,516	485,491	−7.6
Ohio 17	James A. Traficant Jr., D	475,303	514,172	−7.6
N.Y. 33	Henry J. Nowak, D	478,652	516,392	−7.3
Ohio 20	Mary Rose Oakar, D	476,682	514,164	−7.3
Ohio 18	Douglas Applegate, D	477,614	514,173	−7.1

Official 1990 Count by District

The following population counts, released by the Census Bureau on May 15, 1991, are organized by congressional district. The table includes the House member who now represents the district, with Republicans in *italics*.

	1990	1980	% Chg.
UNITED STATES	248,709,873	226,545,805	9.8
ALABAMA	4,040,587	3,983,888	3.8
1 *Callahan*	593,911	563,905	5.3
2 *Dickinson*	569,423	549,505	3.6
3 Browder	565,135	555,321	1.8
4 Bevill	573,868	562,088	2.1
5 Cramer	603,726	549,884	9.8
6 Erdreich	537,179	554,156	−3.1
7 Harris	597,345	559,069	6.8
ALASKA			
AL *Young*	550,043	401,851	36.9
ARIZONA	3,665,228	2,718,215	34.8
1 *Rhodes*	828,857	543,747	52.4
2 Vacancy	626,308	543,187	15.3
3 *Stump*	778,301	544,870	42.8
4 *Kyl*	746,753	543,493	37.4
5 *Kolbe*	685,009	542,918	26.2
ARKANSAS	2,350,725	2,286,435	2.8
1 Alexander	555,487	573,551	−3.1
2 Thornton	612,672	569,116	7.7
3 *Hammerschmidt*	632,411	572,937	10.4
4 Anthony	550,155	570,831	−3.6
CALIFORNIA	29,760,021	23,667,902	25.7
1 *Riggs*	650,495	525,986	23.7
2 *Herger*	646,984	526,009	23.0
3 Matsui	660,388	525,774	25.6
4 Fazio	757,684	525,764	44.1
5 Pelosi	564,939	525,971	7.4
6 Boxer	580,737	526,020	10.4
7 Miller	665,903	525,990	26.6
8 Dellums	561,525	525,646	6.8
9 Stark	614,893	526,234	16.8
10 Edwards	692,321	525,882	31.6
11 Lantos	587,093	525,981	11.6
12 *Campbell*	585,472	525,731	11.4
13 Mineta	565,882	526,281	7.5
14 *Doolittle*	752,301	526,030	43.0
15 Condit	703,945	525,949	33.8
16 Panetta	653,067	526,120	24.1
17 Dooley	694,398	526,033	32.0
18 Lehman	693,002	525,990	31.8
19 *Lagomarsino*	647,217	526,032	23.0
20 *Thomas*	759,419	525,750	44.4
21 *Gallegly*	693,273	525,880	31.8
22 *Moorhead*	638,006	525,939	21.3
23 Beilenson	583,387	525,936	10.9
24 Waxman	633,793	525,918	20.5
25 Roybal	601,067	526,013	14.3
26 Berman	640,446	525,995	21.8
27 Levine	552,429	525,929	5.0
28 Dixon	600,050	525,993	14.1
29 Waters	642,498	525,938	22.2
30 Martinez	645,701	526,018	22.8

	1990	1980	% Chg.
31 Dymally	599,219	525,939	13.9
32 Anderson	619,159	525,922	17.7
33 *Dreier*	669,863	525,348	27.5
34 Torres	598,371	526,665	13.6
35 *Lewis*	894,538	525,956	70.1
36 Brown	779,082	525,987	48.1
37 *McCandless*	979,966	525,938	86.3
38 *Dornan*	647,517	525,919	23.1
39 *Dannemeyer*	624,575	525,858	18.8
40 *Cox*	691,175	525,935	31.4
41 *Lowery*	659,836	526,043	25.4
42 *Rohrabacher*	548,315	525,909	4.3
43 *Packard*	841,297	525,956	60.0
44 *Cunningham*	643,115	525,868	22.3
45 *Hunter*	695,678	525,927	32.3
COLORADO	3,294,394	2,889,964	14.0
1 Schroeder	453,337	481,672	−5.9
2 Skaggs	558,314	481,617	15.9
3 Campbell	525,645	481,854	9.1
4 *Allard*	528,789	481,512	9.8
5 *Hefley*	648,703	481,627	34.7
6 *Schaefer*	579,606	481,682	20.3
CONNECTICUT	3,287,116	3,107,576	5.8
1 Kennelly	541,237	516,232	4.8
2 Gejdenson	564,477	518,244	8.9
3 DeLauro	539,736	518,677	4.1
4 *Shays*	518,975	518,577	0.1
5 *Franks*	559,196	518,700	7.8
6 *Johnson*	563,495	517,146	9.0
DELAWARE			
AL Carper	666,168	594,338	12.1
FLORIDA	12,937,926	9,746,324	32.7
1 Hutto	631,859	512,821	23.2
2 Peterson	626,605	513,127	22.1
3 Bennett	568,815	512,692	10.9
4 *James*	770,393	512,672	50.3
5 *McCollum*	705,724	513,005	37.6
6 *Stearns*	765,397	512,950	49.2
7 Gibbons	608,097	512,905	18.6
8 *Young*	558,981	512,909	9.0
9 *Bilirakis*	759,792	513,191	48.1
10 *Ireland*	672,159	512,890	31.1
11 Bacchus	838,330	512,691	63.5
12 *Lewis*	766,527	513,121	49.4
13 *Goss*	806,729	513,048	57.2
14 Johnston	834,390	512,803	62.7
15 *Shaw*	543,682	512,950	6.0
16 Smith	716,058	513,365	39.5
17 Lehman	576,521	513,048	12.4
18 *Ros-Lehtinen*	534,364	513,250	4.1
19 Fascell	653,503	512,886	27.4
GEORGIA	6,478,216	5,463,105	18.6
1 Thomas	623,501	541,180	15.2
2 Hatcher	557,399	549,977	1.3
3 Ray	571,348	540,865	5.6
4 Jones	696,687	542,368	28.5
5 Lewis	539,904	550,070	−1.8
6 *Gingrich*	714,176	548,959	30.1

	1990	1980	% Chg.
7 Darden	721,100	545,913	32.1
8 Rowland	562,897	541,723	3.9
9 Jenkins	776,911	551,782	40.8
10 Barnard	714,293	550,268	29.8
HAWAII	1,108,229	964,691	14.9
1 Abercrombie	513,956	482,321	6.6
2 Mink	594,273	482,370	23.2
IDAHO	1,006,749	943,935	6.7
1 LaRocco	509,655	472,412	7.9
2 Stallings	497,094	471,523	5.4
ILLINOIS	11,430,602	11,426,518	—
1 Hayes	413,367	519,045	−20.4
2 Savage	459,387	518,931	−11.5
3 Russo	504,634	519,040	−2.8
4 Sangmeister	532,799	519,049	2.6
5 Lipinski	527,704	518,971	1.7
6 *Hyde*	538,201	519,015	3.7
7 Collins	445,232	519,034	−14.2
8 Rostenkowski	515,587	519,034	−0.7
9 Yates	527,012	519,120	1.5
10 *Porter*	566,396	519,660	9.0
11 Annunzio	515,195	518,995	−0.7
12 *Crane*	652,251	519,181	25.6
13 *Fawell*	610,450	519,441	17.5
14 *Hastert*	617,966	521,909	18.4
15 Vacancy	514,299	578,995	−0.9
16 Cox	509,900	519,035	−1.8
17 Evans	467,419	519,333	−10.0
18 *Michel*	487,093	519,026	−6.2
19 Bruce	504,392	518,350	−2.7
20 Durbin	490,307	519,015	−5.5
21 Costello	520,331	521,036	−0.1
22 Poshard	510,680	521,303	−2.0
INDIANA	5,544,159	5,490,224	1.0
1 Visclosky	492,722	547,100	−9.9
2 Sharp	556,191	553,510	0.5
3 Roemer	590,507	558,100	5.8
4 Long	572,593	553,698	3.4
5 Jontz	539,279	548,257	−1.6
6 *Burton*	608,272	540,939	12.4
7 *Myers*	561,680	555,192	1.2
8 McCloskey	551,150	546,744	0.8
9 Hamilton	561,347	544,873	3.0
10 Jacobs	510,418	541,811	−5.8
IOWA	2,776,755	2,913,808	−4.7
1 *Leach*	454,675	485,961	−6.4
2 *Nussle*	456,616	485,708	−6.0
3 Nagle	462,205	485,529	−4.8
4 Smith	507,199	485,480	4.5
5 *Lightfoot*	447,544	485,639	−7.8
6 *Grandy*	448,516	485,491	−7.6
KANSAS	2,477,574	2,363,679	4.8
1 *Roberts*	458,648	472,139	−2.9
2 Slattery	504,093	472,988	6.6
3 *Meyers*	548,767	472,456	16.2
4 Glickman	507,308	473,180	7.2
5 *Nichols*	458,758	472,916	−3.0
KENTUCKY	3,685,296	3,660,777	0.8
1 Hubbard	527,096	525,844	0.2
2 Natcher	534,216	520,634	2.6
3 Mazzoli	489,395	522,252	−6.3
4 *Bunning*	562,697	523,090	7.6
5 *Rogers*	524,626	523,664	0.2

	1990	1980	% Chg.
6 *Hopkins*	555,817	519,009	7.1
7 Perkins	491,449	526,284	−6.6
LOUISIANA	4,219,973	4,205,900	0.3
1 *Livingston*	540,730	525,883	2.8
2 Jefferson	467,234	525,331	−11.1
3 Tauzin	549,801	527,280	4.3
4 *McCrery*	528,964	525,194	0.7
5 Huckaby	507,120	527,220	−3.8
6 *Baker*	558,575	524,770	6.4
7 Hayes	545,602	525,361	3.9
8 *Holloway*	521,947	524,861	−0.6
MAINE	1,227,928	1,124,660	9.2
1 Andrews	636,486	563,073	13.0
2 *Snowe*	591,442	561,587	5.3
MARYLAND	4,781,468	4,216,975	13.4
1 *Gilchrest*	650,638	526,206	23.6
2 *Bentley*	575,337	526,354	9.3
3 Cardin	540,616	527,699	2.4
4 McMillen	610,454	525,453	16.2
5 Hoyer	583,666	527,469	10.7
6 Byron	669,998	528,168	26.9
7 Mfume	496,275	527,590	−5.9
8 *Morella*	654,484	528,036	23.9
MASSACHUSETTS	6,016,425	5,737,037	4.9
1 Olver	537,584	522,540	2.9
2 Neal	559,057	521,949	7.1
3 Early	570,063	521,354	9.3
4 Frank	544,459	521,995	4.3
5 Atkins	563,577	518,313	8.7
6 Mavroules	542,734	518,841	4.6
7 Markey	525,344	523,982	0.3
8 Kennedy	522,322	521,548	0.1
9 Moakley	536,081	519,226	3.2
10 Studds	592,571	522,200	13.5
11 Donnelly	522,633	525,089	−0.5
MICHIGAN	9,295,297	9,262,078	0.4
1 Conyers	451,370	514,560	−12.3
2 *Pursell*	535,849	514,560	4.1
3 Wolpe	517,277	514,560	0.5
4 *Upton*	530,372	514,560	3.1
5 *Henry*	578,779	514,560	12.5
6 Carr	540,077	514,559	5.0
7 Kildee	503,751	514,560	−2.1
8 Traxler	489,078	514,560	−5.0
9 *Vander Jagt*	556,218	514,560	8.1
10 *Camp*	537,245	514,560	4.4
11 *Davis*	521,218	514,560	1.3
12 Bonior	533,689	514,560	3.7
13 Collins	395,349	514,560	−23.2
14 Hertel	502,313	514,559	−2.4
15 Ford	507,452	514,560	−1.4
16 Dingell	496,939	514,560	−3.4
17 Levin	485,163	514,560	−5.7
18 *Broomfield*	613,158	514,560	19.2
MINNESOTA	4,375,099	4,075,970	7.3
1 Penny	527,423	509,460	3.5
2 *Weber*	480,079	509,500	−5.8
3 *Ramstad*	668,263	509,499	31.2
4 Vento	539,004	509,532	5.8
5 Sabo	498,387	509,506	−2.2
6 Sikorski	652,982	509,446	28.2
7 Peterson	518,213	509,521	1.7
8 Oberstar	490,748	509,506	−3.7

	1990	1980	% Chg.
MISSISSIPPI	2,573,216	2,520,638	2.1
1 Whitten	528,113	504,136	4.8
2 Espy	472,534	503,935	−6.2
3 Montgomery	530,348	505,169	5.0
4 Parker	506,790	503,297	0.7
5 Taylor	535,431	504,101	6.2
MISSOURI	5,117,073	4,916,686	4.1
1 Clay	491,614	546,208	−10.0
2 Horn	593,443	546,039	8.7
3 Gephardt	563,153	546,102	3.1
4 Skelton	615,381	546,637	12.6
5 Wheat	521,153	546,882	−4.7
6 *Coleman*	555,244	546,614	1.6
7 *Hancock*	609,862	545,921	11.7
8 *Emerson*	552,981	546,112	1.3
9 Volkmer	614,242	546,171	12.5
MONTANA	799,065	786,690	1.6
1 Williams	417,171	393,298	6.1
2 *Marlenee*	381,894	393,392	−2.9
NEBRASKA	1,578,385	1,569,825	0.5
1 *Bereuter*	526,107	523,079	0.6
2 Hoagland	559,980	522,919	7.1
3 *Barrett*	492,298	523,827	−6.0
NEVADA	1,201,833	800,493	50.1
1 Bilbray	593,096	400,636	48.0
2 *Vucanovich*	608,737	399,857	52.2
NEW HAMPSHIRE	1,109,252	920,610	20.5
1 *Zeliff*	571,811	460,863	24.1
2 Swett	537,441	459,747	16.9
NEW JERSEY	7,730,188	7,364,823	5.0
1 Andrews	567,461	526,069	7.9
2 Hughes	579,615	526,070	10.2
3 Pallone	562,026	562,074	6.8
4 *Smith*	615,288	526,080	17.0
5 *Roukema*	532,933	526,075	1.3
6 Dwyer	563,508	526,075	7.1
7 *Rinaldo*	520,431	526,076	−1.1
8 Roe	524,632	526,087	−0.3
9 Torricelli	512,375	526,066	−2.6
10 Payne	465,316	525,886	−11.5
11 *Gallo*	532,356	526,078	1.2
12 *Zimmer*	619,468	526,063	17.8
13 *Saxton*	612,710	526,062	16.5
14 Guarini	522,069	526,062	−0.8
NEW MEXICO	1,515,069	1,302,894	16.3
1 *Schiff*	497,270	434,141	14.5
2 *Skeen*	497,388	436,261	14.0
3 Richardson	520,411	432,492	20.3
NEW YORK	17,990,455	17,558,072	2.5
1 Hochbrueckner	567,257	516,407	9.8
2 Downey	513,292	515,595	−0.4
3 Mrazek	502,523	516,610	−2.7
4 *Lent*	490,448	516,641	−5.1
5 *McGrath*	513,201	516,712	−0.7
6 Flake	526,176	516,312	1.9
7 Ackerman	549,034	516,544	6.3
8 Scheuer	527,028	516,165	2.1
9 Manton	520,280	516,143	0.8
10 Schumer	508,998	516,471	−1.4
11 Towns	541,247	516,554	4.8
12 Owens	571,532	516,983	10.6
13 Solarz	521,518	516,512	1.0

	1990	1980	% Chg.
14 *Molinari*	536,346	516,537	3.8
15 *Green*	538,390	516,409	4.3
16 Rangel	533,834	516,405	3.4
17 Weiss	534,395	516,239	3.5
18 Serrano	554,401	517,278	7.2
19 Engel	511,587	516,498	−1.0
20 Lowey	517,269	516,507	0.1
21 *Fish*	561,079	516,778	8.6
22 *Gilman*	559,982	516,625	8.4
23 McNulty	519,492	516,943	0.5
24 *Solomon*	567,630	515,614	10.1
25 *Boehlert*	521,165	516,201	1.0
26 *Martin*	544,641	516,196	5.5
27 *Walsh*	525,046	516,364	1.7
28 McHugh	529,597	516,402	2.6
29 *Horton*	531,174	515,404	3.1
30 Slaughter	537,095	516,819	3.9
31 *Paxon*	528,419	516,271	2.4
32 LaFalce	499,203	516,387	−3.3
33 Nowak	478,652	516,392	−7.3
34 *Houghton*	508,524	516,154	−1.5
NORTH CAROLINA	6,628,637	5,881,766	12.7
1 Jones	587,399	536,219	9.5
2 Valentine	587,108	536,210	9.5
3 Lancaster	606,312	535,906	13.1
4 Price	698,950	533,580	31.0
5 Neal	569,605	535,212	6.4
6 *Coble*	582,310	529,635	9.9
7 Rose	600,601	539,055	11.4
8 Hefner	590,561	535,526	10.3
9 *McMillan*	662,778	536,325	23.6
10 *Ballenger*	571,903	532,954	7.3
11 *Taylor*	571,110	531,144	7.5
NORTH DAKOTA			
AL Dorgan	638,800	652,717	−2.1
OHIO	10,847,115	10,797,630	0.5
1 Luken	509,109	514,190	−1.0
2 *Gradison*	535,264	514,168	4.1
3 Hall	504,503	514,173	−1.9
4 *Oxley*	510,847	514,172	−0.6
5 *Gillmor*	514,936	514,173	0.1
6 *McEwen*	548,784	514,173	6.7
7 *Hobson*	527,006	514,170	2.5
8 *Boehner*	551,433	514,171	7.2
9 Kaptur	504,915	514,174	−1.8
10 *Miller*	526,475	514,173	2.4
11 Eckart	530,838	514,173	3.2
12 *Kasich*	569,755	514,173	10.8
13 Pease	521,359	514,176	1.4
14 Sawyer	503,390	514,172	−2.1
15 *Wylie*	573,234	514,176	11.5
16 *Regula*	510,736	514,171	−0.7
17 Traficant	475,303	514,172	−7.6
18 Applegate	477,614	514,173	−7.1
19 Feighan	516,807	514,174	0.5
20 Oakar	476,682	514,164	−7.3
21 Stokes	458,125	514,169	−10.9
OKLAHOMA	3,145,585	3,025,290	4.0
1 *Inhofe*	517,698	503,739	2.8
2 Synar	550,390	505,149	9.0
3 Brewster	505,870	504,268	0.3
4 McCurdy	552,990	505,869	9.3
5 *Edwards*	557,299	502,974	10.8
6 English	461,338	503,291	−8.3

	1990	1980	% Chg.
OREGON	2,842,321	2,633,105	7.9
1 AuCoin	616,851	526,840	17.1
2 *Smith*	556,663	526,968	5.6
3 Wyden	547,704	526,715	4.0
4 DeFazio	538,628	526,462	2.3
5 Kopetski	582,475	526,120	10.7
PENNSYLVANIA	11,881,643	11,863,895	0.1
1 Foglietta	481,479	515,145	−6.5
2 Gray	474,964	517,215	−8.2
3 Borski	498,064	516,154	−3.5
4 Kolter	490,740	515,572	−4.3
5 *Schulze*	580,602	515,528	12.6
6 Yatron	536,990	515,952	4.1
7 *Weldon*	506,260	515,766	−1.8
8 Kostmayer	577,811	516,902	11.8
9 *Shuster*	523,140	515,430	1.5
10 *McDade*	532,765	515,442	3.4
11 Kanjorski	507,151	515,729	−1.7
12 Murtha	481,264	515,915	−6.7
13 *Coughlin*	525,854	514,346	2.2
14 Coyne	453,330	516,629	−12.3
15 *Ritter*	566,189	515,259	9.9
16 *Walker*	587,226	514,585	14.1
17 *Gekas*	533,625	515,900	3.4
18 *Santorum*	504,738	516,050	−2.2
19 *Goodling*	564,138	516,605	9.2
20 Gaydos	468,474	516,028	−9.2
21 *Ridge*	502,207	516,645	−3.3
22 Murphy	481,931	515,122	−6.4
23 *Clinger*	502,701	515,976	−2.6
RHODE ISLAND	1,003,464	947,154	5.9
1 *Machtley*	490,853	474,429	3.5
2 Reed	512,611	472,725	8.4
SOUTH CAROLINA	3,486,703	3,121,820	11.7
1 *Ravenel*	616,219	520,338	18.4
2 *Spence*	567,789	522,688	8.6
3 Derrick	576,568	519,280	11.0
4 Patterson	577,304	520,525	10.9
5 Spratt	579,498	519,716	11.5
6 Tallon	569,325	519,273	9.6
SOUTH DAKOTA			
AL Johnson	696,004	690,768	0.8
TENNESSEE	4,877,185	4,591,120	6.2
1 *Quillen*	531,349	512,702	3.6
2 *Duncan*	539,540	510,197	5.8
3 Lloyd	520,980	516,692	0.8
4 Cooper	534,488	510,732	4.7
5 Clement	552,278	514,832	7.3
6 Gordon	607,033	511,805	18.6
7 *Sundquist*	628,167	503,611	24.7
8 Tanner	501,605	504,957	−0.7
9 Ford	461,745	505,592	−8.7
TEXAS	16,986,510	14,229,191	19.4
1 Chapman	568,553	527,016	7.9
2 Wilson	583,419	526,772	10.8
3 *Johnson*	713,800	527,023	35.4
4 Hall	620,260	526,991	17.7
5 Bryant	608,176	526,633	15.5
6 *Barton*	705,355	526,765	33.9
7 *Archer*	783,612	527,083	48.7
8 *Fields*	665,924	527,531	26.2

	1990	1980	% Chg.
9 Brooks	563,736	526,443	7.1
10 Pickle	731,052	527,181	38.7
11 Edwards	604,014	527,382	14.5
12 Geren	608,871	527,715	15.4
13 Sarpalius	521,876	526,840	−0.9
14 Laughlin	614,406	526,920	16.6
15 de la Garza	658,018	527,203	24.8
16 Coleman	637,578	527,401	20.9
17 Stenholm	560,433	526,913	6.4
18 Washington	449,668	527,393	−14.7
19 *Combest*	529,853	527,805	0.4
20 Gonzalez	497,833	526,333	−5.4
21 *Smith*	699,631	526,846	32.8
22 *DeLay*	684,620	526,602	30.0
23 Bustamante	700,926	526,746	33.1
24 Frost	635,137	527,267	20.5
25 Andrews	550,417	526,801	4.5
26 *Armey*	894,930	526,598	69.9
27 Ortiz	594,412	526,988	12.8
UTAH	1,722,850	1,461,037	17.9
1 *Hansen*	590,660	487,833	21.1
2 Owens	528,507	487,475	8.4
3 Orton	603,683	485,729	24.3
VERMONT			
AL ***Sanders (I)***	562,758	511,456	10.0
VIRGINIA	6,187,358	5,346,818	15.7
1 *Bateman*	615,085	535,092	14.9
2 Pickett	654,298	529,178	23.6
3 *Bliley*	622,061	533,668	16.6
4 Sisisky	578,193	535,703	7.9
5 Payne	543,751	531,308	2.3
6 Olin	553,857	538,360	2.9
7 *Slaughter*	672,775	535,147	25.7
8 Moran	747,324	534,366	39.9
9 Boucher	523,803	538,871	−2.8
10 *Wolf*	676,211	535,125	26.4
WASHINGTON	4,866,692	4,132,156	17.8
1 *Miller*	656,963	516,378	27.2
2 Swift	642,342	516,568	24.3
3 Unsoeld	603,588	516,473	16.9
4 *Morrison*	562,181	516,426	8.9
5 Foley	538,958	516,719	4.3
6 Dicks	608,115	516,561	17.7
7 McDermott	557,969	516,531	8.0
8 *Chandler*	696,576	516,500	34.9
WEST VIRGINIA	1,793,477	1,949,644	−8.0
1 Mollohan	432,958	488,568	−11.4
2 Staggers	487,596	487,438	—
3 Wise	451,667	486,112	−7.1
4 Rahall	421,256	487,526	−13.6
WISCONSIN	4,891,769	4,705,767	4.0
1 Aspin	533,391	522,838	2.0
2 *Klug*	571,746	523,011	9.3
3 *Gunderson*	544,605	522,909	4.1
4 Kleczka	537,144	522,880	2.7
5 Moody	516,838	522,854	−1.2
6 *Petri*	544,188	522,477	4.2
7 Obey	529,753	522,623	1.4
8 *Roth*	560,430	523,225	7.1
9 *Sensenbrenner*	553,674	522,950	5.9
WYOMING			
AL *Thomas*	453,588	469,557	−3.4

Alabama

U.S. CONGRESS

SENATE 2 D
HOUSE 5 D, 2 R

LEGISLATURE

Senate 28 D, 7 R
House 82 D, 23 R

ELECTIONS

1988 Presidential Vote	
Bush	59%
Dukakis	40%
1984 Presidential Vote	
Reagan	61%
Mondale	38%
1980 Presidential Vote	
Reagan	49%
Carter	48%
Anderson	1%
Turnout rate in 1986	38%
Turnout rate in 1988	46%
Turnout rate in 1990	33%

(as percentage of voting age population)

POPULATION AND GROWTH

1980 population	3,893,888
1990 population (22nd in the nation)	4,040,587
Percent change 1980-1990	+4%

DEMOGRAPHIC BREAKDOWN

White	74%
Black	25%
Asian or Pacific Islander	1%
(Hispanic origin)	1%
Urban	60%
Rural	40%
Born in state	79%
Foreign-born	1%

MAJOR CITIES

Birmingham	265,968
Mobile	196,278
Montgomery	187,106
Huntsville	159,789
Tuscaloosa	77,759

AREA AND LAND USE

Area	50,767 sq. miles (28th)
Farm	31%
Forest	67%
Federally owned	3%

Gov. Guy Hunt (R)
Of Holly Pond — Elected 1986

Born: June 17, 1933, Holly Pond, Ala.
Education: Graduated Holly Pond H.S., 1950.
Military Service: Army, 1954-56.
Occupation: Farmer.
Religion: Baptist.
Political Career: Cullman County probate judge, 1964-76; GOP candidate for Ala. Senate, 1962; GOP nominee for governor, 1978.
Next Election: 1994.

WORK

Occupations	
White-collar	47%
Blue-collar	39%
Service workers	12%
Government Workers	
Federal	58,443
State	87,931
Local	158,509

MONEY

Median family income	$ 16,347	(46th)
Tax burden per capita	$ 727	(41st)

EDUCATION

Spending per pupil through grade 12	$ 2,718	(47th)
Persons with college degrees	12%	(47th)

CRIME

Violent crime rate	591 per 100,000 (17th)

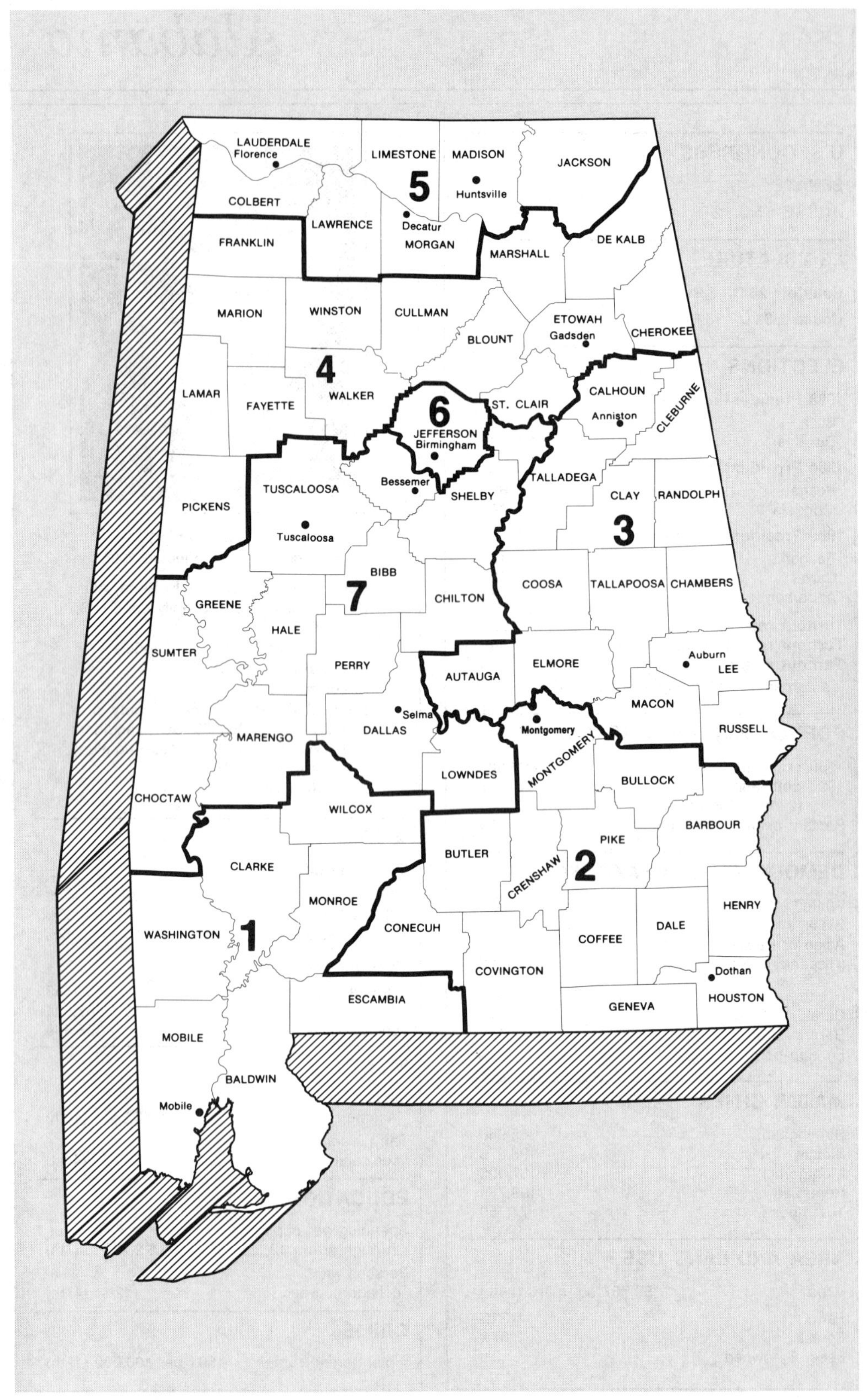
LAUDERDALE
Florence
LIMESTONE
MADISON
JACKSON
5
Huntsville
COLBERT
LAWRENCE
Decatur
MORGAN
FRANKLIN
MARSHALL
DE KALB
MARION
WINSTON
CULLMAN
ETOWAH
Gadsden
CHEROKEE
BLOUNT
4
LAMAR
FAYETTE
WALKER
6
ST. CLAIR
CALHOUN
Anniston
CLEBURNE
JEFFERSON
Birmingham
Bessemer
TALLADEGA
TUSCALOOSA
SHELBY
CLAY
RANDOLPH
PICKENS
Tuscaloosa
3
BIBB
COOSA
TALLAPOOSA
CHAMBERS
GREENE
7
CHILTON
HALE
SUMTER
PERRY
AUTAUGA
ELMORE
Auburn
LEE
Selma
DALLAS
MACON
Montgomery
RUSSELL
MARENGO
MONTGOMERY
LOWNDES
BULLOCK
CHOCTAW
WILCOX
BARBOUR
PIKE
CLARKE
BUTLER
CRENSHAW
2
MONROE
HENRY
WASHINGTON
1
CONECUH
COFFEE
DALE
COVINGTON
Dothan
ESCAMBIA
GENEVA
HOUSTON
MOBILE
BALDWIN
Mobile

Howell Heflin (D)

Of Tuscumbia — Elected 1978

Born: June 19, 1921, Poulan, Ga.
Education: Birmingham Southern College, B.A. 1942; U. of Alabama, J.D. 1948.
Military Service: Marine Corps, 1942-46.
Occupation: Judge; lawyer.
Family: Wife, Elizabeth Ann Carmichael; one child.
Religion: Methodist.
Political Career: Chief justice, Ala. Supreme Court, 1971-77.
Capitol Office: 728 Hart Bldg. 20510; 224-4124.

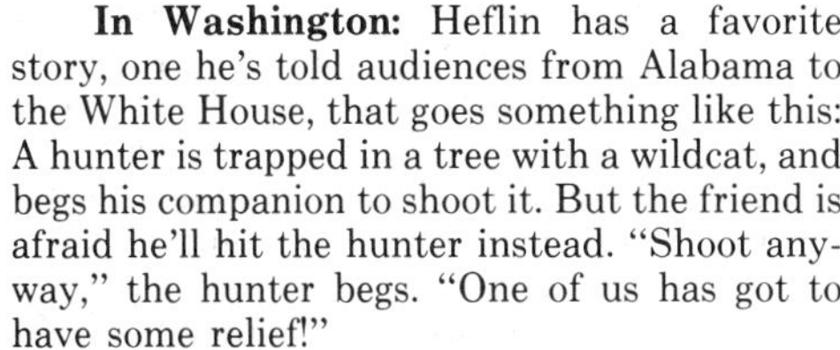

In Washington: Heflin has a favorite story, one he's told audiences from Alabama to the White House, that goes something like this: A hunter is trapped in a tree with a wildcat, and begs his companion to shoot it. But the friend is afraid he'll hit the hunter instead. "Shoot anyway," the hunter begs. "One of us has got to have some relief!"

As a political metaphor, that treed hunter is Heflin, trapped by one controversy or another. On questions large or commonplace, Heflin typically anguishes over the arguments and resists making decisions. He's known to members, staff and reporters as "the Judge," his preferred title from earlier days as chief justice of the Alabama Supreme Court. In fact, after two terms in the Senate, Heflin continues to see himself that way, not as a senator: "I just try to be the country judge," he said in late 1987. "I don't try to reach an early opinion on something. A judge is supposed to listen to the last argument before he makes up his mind."

But as a result, Heflin's reputation has shifted over time from judicious to indecisive. His nickname has lost some of its original, respectful connotation; it is not uncommon to hear it uttered in sarcasm. Even his jowlish, pear-shaped frame, generously described as imposing, makes him appear in his critics' eyes to be the caricature of an old-time Southern courthouse pol.

Heflin's ponderous approach to decision-making may frustrate senators seeking hints of his views on matters before the Judiciary Committee, where partisan splits arise frequently, particularly when judicial nominees are screened. But it is better suited to the Ethics Committee, where as chairman Heflin presides with all the deliberation expected of a former state Supreme Court chief justice.

Because of his background, Heflin was appointed Ethics chairman in 1979, the first freshman senator to head a committee since 1910. Typically, Heflin and GOP Vice Chairman Warren B. Rudman handle complaints against colleagues with informal bipartisanship.

In 1981, though Heflin had to forfeit the chair when Democrats lost their Senate majority, he was tapped to head the committee's investigation of New Jersey Democrat Harrison A. Williams Jr., who was caught in the FBI's Abscam bribery sting. In early 1982, he took the Senate floor to present the committee's recommendation that Williams be expelled. After Heflin's eloquent denunciation made an expulsion vote all but certain, Williams resigned.

The Ethics Committee put in long hours in the 101st Congress on two cases — one that produced the first Senate disciplinary action in a decade (against Minnesota Republican Dave Durenberger), and another that focused nationwide attention on the integrity of Congress (the Keating Five scandal).

One of the more popular members of the clubby Senate, Durenberger was "denounced" by the Senate for financial improprieties. He was also ordered to pay over $120,000 restitution for accepting speaking fees and housing reimbursements in violation of Senate rules.

On the Senate floor, Heflin walked the Senate through the charges, detailing how Durenberger "knowingly and willingly engaged in a pattern of unethical conduct." Though Durenberger called denouncement — one of the Senate's terms of punishment that falls short of expulsion — too harsh, he did not challenge the sanction or Heflin's account of events. The Senate voted 96-0 to denounce Durenberger.

The Keating Five affair stemmed from the collapse of the savings and loan industry in the late 1980s. Many failures were attributed to risky investments and fraudulent activities by high-flying thrift executives. One of the more notorious was Charles H. Keating Jr., chairman of American Continental Corp. in Phoenix, which owned the failed Lincoln Savings and Loan Association in Irvine, Calif.

Keating and his associates raised for or contributed $1.5 million to the campaign committees and other political causes of five senators: Republican John McCain of Arizona and Democrats Alan Cranston of California, Dennis DeConcini of Arizona, John Glenn of Ohio and Donald W. Riegle Jr. of Michigan. The senators were under scrutiny for intervening with federal thrift regulators on Keating's behalf. At issue was whether Keating's fundraising prompted their action and whether their intervention with regulators was undue political pressure.

The Ethics Committee's special counsel, Robert S. Bennett, maintained that Senate rules prohibiting members from engaging in "improper conduct which may reflect upon the Senate" meant that the appearance of impropriety was enough to breach that standard.

From the start, Heflin noted that the senators' actions failed that test in the public's eyes. In his opening statement, he addressed the five senators: "I need not tell you, for each of you know better than I, that . . . many of our fellow citizens apparently believe that your services were bought by Charles Keating, that you were bribed, that you sold your office, that you traded your honor and your good names for contributions and other benefits."

Though he directed penetrating questions to several witnesses as well as the five senators, Heflin provided little indication of his own view of the affair throughout the hearings. When he and Rudman in early 1991 issued the committee's findings — that Cranston likely violated the Senate standard against improper behavior and that the other four were guilty of poor judgment — the chairman and vice chairman said they neither accepted nor rejected Bennett's "appearance" standard. The committee recommended that further action be taken only against Cranston.

The burden of sitting in judgment of his brethren for more than a decade may have finally taken its toll on Heflin. After the completion of Cranston's case, Heflin planned to leave the Ethics Committee. Terry Sanford of North Carolina was named to replace him as chairman.

While deliberation and secrecy are hallmarks of an ideal Ethics Committee chairman, they do not necessarily translate readily into decision-making qualifications on legislative panels. As a result, Heflin has not availed himself of several opportunities for leadership. Regard for his probity earned Heflin a spot on the special Senate committee investigating the Reagan administration's Iran-contra scandal in 1987. Then, as a Southern conservative on the Judiciary Committee, he was poised to be the bellwether vote in the Senate showdown over confirmation of President Ronald Reagan's Supreme Court nominee, Robert H. Bork. In both controversies, however, many felt that Heflin fell short of the mark expected of a leader.

In Heflin's defense, he is in some ways a victim of others' high expectations. Elected in 1978, he was widely thought to represent the new, more moderate, racially tolerant South. But Heflin is not as moderate as many believed. In Reagan's last two years as president, Heflin supported him more often than any other Senate Democrat, a pattern he has continued with George Bush in the White House. In 1990, Heflin and Senate Minority Leader Bob Dole sponsored a constitutional amendment to ban physical desecration of the flag.

He seems provincial by choice, ducking the lead roles that outsiders expect of him. Moreover, now he is overshadowed by the newer, younger and truly moderate activists elected from his region in the 1980s.

On the Iran-contra committee, Heflin remained a backbencher and a clumsy interrogator throughout the three-month televised hearings. Perhaps his most memorable moment was outside the hearing room, when Heflin told reporters that former White House aide Lt. Col. Oliver L. North's secretary Fawn Hall had smuggled documents from the White House in her brassiere. "She's supposedly got some pretty good capacity to carry the documents," he said. Hall snapped that Heflin was "sexist," but later testified that she did smuggle papers — in her back waistband and boots.

As usual in controversial matters, Judiciary was split along party lines over Bork's nomination, with three undecided swing voters — Heflin, conservative DeConcini and liberal Republican Arlen Specter of Pennsylvania — holding both the balance of power and the media's attention. Heflin seemed to relish the attention most, and appeared regularly on the Sunday TV talk shows.

Bork opponents and some commentators suggested Heflin ultimately would lead other Southerners in voting against the conservative judge — out of concern that Bork would seek to reverse landmark civil rights rulings. Instead, Heflin stayed on the fence while a parade of Southern Democrats, including his junior Alabama colleague Richard C. Shelby, went to the Senate floor to state their opposition.

Reagan called Heflin to the White House (where the senator told his "treed hunter" tale) and he emerged still undecided. But already both Heflin and the committee were irrelevant; vote counts showed Bork would lose on the floor. All but ignored, the senator voted against confirmation.

But Heflin did play the decisive role in the rejection of Bush's nominee to the top civil rights post at the Justice Department, William Lucas, a black whose qualifications were questioned by leading civil rights advocates. After first winning a delay to study what he called new "information" about Lucas, Heflin voted to reject him.

Heflin was a pivotal swing voter on the Judiciary Committee for the six years the GOP controlled the Senate, before Democrats regained a majority in the 1986 elections. He frequently allied with Chairman Strom Thurmond and other GOP conservatives on major issues. Once, when Thurmond failed to notice Heflin among Democrats during a head count, Sen. Edward M. Kennedy protested, "I believe Mr. Heflin is a Democrat." Said Thurmond: "I always thought he was one of us."

Though Judiciary's province includes many of the legal issues Heflin knows best, he has not been a leading participant unless the subject deals with improvement of judicial operations, a favorite of his. Generally, Heflin seems uncomfortable with the legislative pace. Though coy when Republicans floated his name as a potential Supreme Court nominee in 1987, Heflin did express longing for the judiciary's more deliberative, thorough style.

At times, Heflin's public soul-searching is a self-parody. When the Senate in 1985 considered a bill naming the rose as the national flower, Heflin wavered between the rose, Alabama's marigold and its state flower, the camellia, in the longest speech of the day. "Roses are red, violets are blue, why must I choose between these two?" he asked. He finally chose the rose.

On the Agriculture Committee, Heflin has less trouble making choices. He is for cotton and whatever else grows in the South. So protective is he of the federal peanut subsidy program that Heflin has boasted he is the third senator from Georgia. He espoused a new subsidy program for Southern soybean farmers.

Heflin is an eager player in the committee's commodity-trading approach to legislation, in which members from one region ally with those from other regions to support subsidies for each others' products.

Frequently at odds with environmentalists back home, Heflin in 1988 joined with Republican Jesse Helms to oppose a pesticide regulation bill that was supported by environmentalists and cosponsored by Agriculture Committee Chairman Patrick J. Leahy and ranking Republican Richard G. Lugar. The Heflin-Helms version, backed by farmers and pesticide manufacturers, shifted the burden for paying regulatory costs from manufacturers to taxpayers, and limited farmers' liability. Some of its provisions were incorporated in the much-diluted bill that finally became law.

Heflin's record on environmental issues led Leahy to leave Heflin off the House-Senate conference on the 1990 farm bill. The chairman sought allies for his "circle of poison" proposal barring the export of pesticides proscribed for domestic use. Instead of choosing Heflin, fourth in seniority on the committee, Leahy picked the most junior Democrat, Nebraskan Bob Kerrey.

In the 101st Congress, Heflin joined a third legislative committee, Energy and Natural Resources. He lost his waiver to serve on three major committees for the 102nd Congress, however, and reluctantly left Energy. Outside his committee assignments, he is a leader in efforts to increase funding for NASA, along with other senators from states with NASA contractors and facilities.

At Home: Alabama Republicans had hoped in 1990 that Heflin had passed his prime, both as a campaigner and as a popular political figure. But the avuncular "country judge" proved to be as formidable a vote-getter as ever, winning a third Senate term with 61 percent of the vote.

His GOP challenger, state Sen. Bill Cabaniss, ran a scrappy campaign that tried to portray Heflin as soft on the environment, weak on ethics, and wrong on his support for the 1990 civil rights bill, which Cabaniss labeled a "quota" bill.

Cabaniss called on Heflin to step down as chairman of the Ethics Committee because Heflin's office accepted (and then returned) a $2,000 contribution in 1989 from a group formed by Sen. Cranston, then under investigation by the ethics committee.

Cabaniss also piggy-backed on criticism of Heflin by major environmental groups. The incumbent was the only Democrat named by Environmental Action to its 1990 "Dirty Dozen" list.

But Cabaniss lacked the resources to challenge Heflin dollar for dollar, and his swanky suburban Birmingham address and summertime vacations near President Bush's seacoast compound in Maine left Cabaniss open to charges of being a "country club" Republican.

The result: He carried only four of Alabama's 67 counties and failed to make a dent in Heflin's rural and small-town base that the incumbent had assiduously courted over the years by presenting himself as an honest, open, approachable public figure.

Cabaniss' showing was not much better than a more ideological challenger, former GOP Rep. Albert Lee Smith, made against Heflin in 1984. Smith had lost his Birmingham-based House seat in 1982 and was expected to try a House comeback. But he opted instead for the chance to spread his conservative message before a larger audience.

Known in the House as a zealous promoter of the New Right social agenda, Smith switched gears a little in his Senate campaign, talking more about economics and accusing Heflin of frustrating the Reagan agenda of tax and spending cuts. He also tried to make an issue of Heflin's ties to political action committees, which had given him more money in 1983 than any incumbent senator.

Heflin responded by calling himself an "independent, conservative to moderate" Democrat who backed Ronald Reagan more often than he had backed Jimmy Carter. The incumbent entered the final few weeks with a polling lead so awesome it defied belief, but presidential coattails eventually held Heflin to 63 percent of the vote.

Heflin's first campaign for the Senate was

not that much more suspenseful than his second. When Democratic Sen. John J. Sparkman announced his retirement in 1978, Gov. George C. Wallace was poised to replace him. But while the governor campaigned unofficially throughout 1977, he never announced, and for good reason. Polls showed Heflin far ahead of him.

One Democrat who did run against Heflin and came to regret it was Walter Flowers, a five-term U.S. House member. In a primary runoff that turned angry and unpleasant, Heflin took all but five counties in the state. Better organized and financed than the congressman, he blasted Flowers for being "part of the Washington crowd." The general election was a formality; the GOP had no candidate.

In his younger days, as a trial attorney in the northern Alabama town of Tuscumbia, Heflin was known as one of the best. He could cajole a jury with down-home stories, cry with them over his client's plight or delight them with an unexpected move. Once he lay down on the counsel's table to show the improbability of an alleged assault victim's story. History does not record whether the table survived.

Heflin's reputation as a lawyer led to his election as chief justice of the Alabama Supreme Court, where he streamlined the state judicial system, which had been hampered by a huge case backlog. To accomplish the task, he needed adoption of a state constitutional amendment, and the voters gave it to him. When political opponents criticized him because the amendment made him eligible for a $30,000 annual pension, Heflin pointed out that he could not receive the money if he served in the Senate or practiced law.

Heflin's uncle, "Cotton Tom" Heflin, served in the Senate from 1920 to 1931. He was an ardent segregationist and anti-Catholic who bolted the Democratic Party when Al Smith was nominated for president in 1928. Fifty-one years later, Howell Heflin made a speech welcoming Pope John Paul II to the United States.

Committees

Agriculture, Nutrition & Forestry (4th of 10 Democrats)
Rural Development & Rural Electrification (chairman); Agricultural Production & Stabilization of Prices; Conservation & Forestry

Judiciary (6th of 8 Democrats)
Antitrust, Monopolies & Business Rights; Courts & Administrative Practice (chairman); Patents, Copyrights & Trademarks

Elections

1990 General		
Howell Heflin (D)	717,814	(61%)
Bill Cabaniss (R)	467,190	(39%)
1990 Primary		
Howell Heflin (D)	540,876	(81%)
Mrs. Frank Ross Stewart (D)	123,508	(19%)

Previous Winning Percentages: 1984 (63%) **1978** (94%)

Campaign Finance

	Receipts	Receipts from PACs		Expend-itures
1990				
Heflin (D)	$3,422,129	$1,320,755	(39%)	$3,204,160
Cabaniss (R)	$1,757,312	$77,246	(4%)	$1,853,869

Key Votes

1991	
Authorize use of force against Iraq	Y
1990	
Oppose prohibition of certain semiautomatic weapons	Y
Support constitutional amendment on flag desecration	Y
Oppose requiring parental notice for minors' abortions	N
Halt production of B-2 stealth bomber at 13 planes	N
Approve budget that cut spending and raised revenues	N
Pass civil rights bill over Bush veto	Y
1989	
Oppose reduction of SDI funding	Y
Oppose barring federal funds for "obscene" art	N
Allow vote on capital gains tax cut	Y

Voting Studies

	Presidential Support		Party Unity		Conservative Coalition	
Year	**S**	**O**	**S**	**O**	**S**	**O**
1990	60	39	53	46	95	5
1989	71	29	39	61	92	8
1988	73	27	52	47	97	3
1987	54	46	50	50	94	6
1986	76	24	42	57	84	16
1985	54	45	56	43	88	12
1984	75	21	36	59	89	11
1983	42	52	57	41	77†	16†
1982	61	39	57	42	79	17
1981	68	30	64	34	81	15

† Not eligible for all recorded votes.

Interest Group Ratings

Year	ADA	ACU	AFL-CIO	CCUS
1990	28	55	78	64
1989	25	75	90	63
1988	30	58	64	50
1987	35	46	80	50
1986	25	65	53	58
1985	25	74	67	45
1984	20	91	45	67
1983	40	72	65	44
1982	25	75	65	75
1981	35	54	58	61

Richard C. Shelby (D)

Of Tuscaloosa — Elected 1986

Born: May 6, 1934, Birmingham, Ala.
Education: U. of Alabama, A.B. 1957, LL.B. 1963.
Occupation: Lawyer.
Family: Wife, Annette Nevin; two children.
Religion: Presbyterian.
Political Career: Ala. Senate, 1971-79; U.S. House, 1979-87.
Capitol Office: 313 Hart Bldg. 20510; 224-5744.

In Washington: When he moved from the House to the Senate, Shelby expressed a desire to join with senior Alabama colleague Howell Heflin to wield the kind of national influence the state once enjoyed under another Democratic Senate duo, postwar populists John Sparkman and Lister Hill. Shelby's young Senate career has indeed been entwined with Heflin's — so much so, in fact, that some wags refer to him as "Sheflin." But instead of melding into a powerful alliance by joining Heflin, Shelby completes a conservative pair that fits uneasily in the Democratic-controlled Senate, and plays a more parochial role than the earlier New Deal team.

Shelby's tendency to ally with Senate Republicans came as little surprise to those familiar with his four-term House career and his 1981 flirtation with the GOP. During the 100th and 101st Congresses, he defected from the Democratic line on numerous occasions. But he has toed that line when the issue was civil rights — reflecting his heightened sensitivity to the black voters who were crucial to his 1986 upset of GOP Sen. Jeremiah Denton.

Shelby's independence has had its cost. His bid for the Appropriations Committee in the 101st Congress was squashed in party deliberations. Senate Democratic leaders, while sympathetic to party conservatives' need to break ranks occasionally on issues unpopular back home, nonetheless saw no reason to reward someone who strays so frequently.

Shelby did not endear himself to the new Democratic regime, either, by his stance in the 1988 contest to succeed Majority Leader Robert C. Byrd of West Virginia. Though widely expected to support the conservative Southern candidate, J. Bennett Johnston of Louisiana, Shelby demurred until days before the vote, and then joined the bandwagon for Maine liberal George J. Mitchell. He thereby angered the Johnston camp, gained little in Mitchell's and burnished a reputation for being occasionally indecisive and opportunistic.

Early in the 101st Congress, Shelby redeemed himself a bit with party leaders — at no real political cost to himself in Alabama — by opposing former Sen. John Tower's nomination as defense secretary. Republicans had hoped for Shelby's support, so his surprise early announcement just before voting in the Armed Services Committee presaged Tower's ultimate rejection on the Senate floor. Shelby's decision may not have been all that difficult for him: He was concurring with Sam Nunn of Georgia, the Armed Services chairman he greatly admires, and in Alabama, Bible Belt concern over Tower's alleged drunkenness and womanizing was perceptible.

With the Cold War thawing and enthusiasm waning for expensive weapons systems to combat the Soviet threat, Shelby and New Mexico Democrat Jeff Bingaman offered an amendment to the fiscal 1991 defense authorization bill to redirect the administration's plans for the space-based strategic defense initiative. The amendment would slow development of the so-called "brilliant pebbles" — tens of thousands of heat-seeking guided missiles — and instead increase the emphasis within SDI for ground-based interceptor missiles and laser-armed satellites. The Senate adopted it 54-44.

Shelby claimed a measure of vindication over critics of the amendment following the favorable reports of the performance of the Patriot ground-based missile against Iraqi missiles in the Persian Gulf War. He was one of 10 Senate Democrats who voted to authorize President Bush to use force against Iraq. After the war ended, he worried that Democrats could suffer politically from the partisan breakdown of the vote. "This is not a party vote," he said. "If it is seen as a party vote, we're in deep trouble."

Shelby's stand with his party in support of civil rights issues marks a break from the pattern of his early congressional career. In 1987, he voted against the confirmation of Robert H. Bork, President Reagan's Supreme Court nominee, whose defeat was a top priority for civil rights groups. In 1988, Shelby joined all Democrats in voting to override Reagan's veto of a bill that aimed to overturn a Supreme Court decision limiting enforcement of four key civil rights laws. In 1990, he voted to override Bush's veto of a civil rights bill that Bush and other Republicans said would mandate racial hiring quotas.

Shelby's backing for the Republican president on other issues, however, remained high; during 1987, Shelby was second only to Heflin among Senate Democrats in his frequency of support for Reagan's legislative positions. Heflin and Shelby ranked first and second among Democrats bucking their party's position on votes in 1988, 1989 and 1990. Shelby has a political compass that steers a straight anti-communist course in defense and foreign policy, and a pro-business one in domestic affairs.

In the 101st Congress, Shelby joined Republicans Bob Kasten of Wisconsin and Connie Mack of Florida to sponsor a cut in the capital gains tax deeper than the one backed by Bush. They reintroduced their plan in the 102nd Congress. Shelby was one of six Democrats to vote in 1989 to thwart a threatened Democratic filibuster of Bush's capital gains cut.

Shelby led the Senate charge to keep the 1990 census from including illegal aliens in figures used for congressional reapportionment. Opponents argued that his amendment was unconstitutional, but the Senate attached it to an immigration bill and to the 1989 Commerce Department appropriations bill. "The basic rights of representation in our country are violated when voters in states with a large number of illegal aliens have a greater voice in choosing representatives in Congress," he said. But the House rejected the idea, and it was dropped off both bills.

Shelby has also devoted ample attention to home-state concerns. He has sponsored legislation to give states authority to regulate hazardous and solid waste disposal within their borders.

On the Banking Committee, Shelby was active in the 100th Congress in the long-running but inconclusive debate over corporate takeovers. Siding with Republicans, he opposed a Democratic bill aimed at restraining corporate raiders and the securities firms that finance their deals. Shelby argued the case against the bill in populist terms, saying small shareholders should be free to sell to raiders.

In the final weeks of the 100th Congress, Shelby allied with Republicans in successful filibusters of two bills central to Democrats' 1988 election agenda. He was one of only three Democrats to oppose a bill raising the minimum wage, and one of eight against Democrats' package of "family" issues — expanded child care subsidies, guaranteed job leave for parents with new or seriously ill children and toughened child-pornography sanctions.

As a House member, Shelby devoted much of his effort to the Energy and Commerce Committee. House Democratic leaders gave him a seat on the prestigious panel when he arrived in 1979, believing Shelby to be a Southern moderate. They came to regret their decision when he proved to be a reliable vote for the GOP and pro-industry positions on major issues. In the 102nd Congress, he replaced Heflin on the Senate Energy and Natural Resources Committee.

Shelby's conservative posture on economic and social issues complicated his statewide prospects in 1986, since he had alienated the party's labor and black constituencies. He frequently supported Reagan's initiatives during the early budget battles, and at times seemed receptive to GOP recruitment efforts. "If the Democratic Party continues to go to the left, it will destroy its Southern base," Shelby once warned.

He angered many black voters by opposing both the 1982 extension of the Voting Rights Act on the grounds that it unfairly penalized Southern states, and a national holiday honoring the Rev. Dr. Martin Luther King Jr. Once in the Senate, however, he supported a 1989 measure funding the King holiday commission.

At Home: For most of his 1986 campaign against Denton, Shelby seemed a certain victim of a political mess not of his making: An intraparty rift over the Democratic gubernatorial nomination that overshadowed Shelby's efforts. But with an aggressive closing strategy, he prevailed by just under 7,000 votes.

Denton led in public-opinion surveys throughout the campaign. He had a following among advocates of his staunchly conservative, pro-Reagan politics and those who viewed the former naval officer and longtime Vietnam prisoner of war as a national hero.

But in the Senate, Denton spent much time pursuing goals such as promoting chastity among teenagers — an agenda without strong appeal to the many voters concerned about economic issues. He was frequently ridiculed for being loose with his words (about spousal rape, for instance, he said, "Damn it, when you get married, you kind of expect you're going to get a little sex"). Denton, not skilled at personal politicking, also was criticized for not keeping in touch with his constituency.

But Shelby had problems of his own, caused by his cool relationship with Democratic liberals. The New South Coalition, a black organization headed by Birmingham Mayor Richard Arrington, endorsed Ted McLaughlin, an obscure former federal official, in the Democratic primary. Shelby had another serious primary foe in Jim Allen Jr., a state school board commissioner and son of former Sen. James Allen Sr. Shelby won just 51 percent in the primary, barely avoiding a runoff.

On the same day, Lt. Gov. William J. Baxley and state Atty. Gen. Charles Graddick finished one-two in the Democratic gubernatorial primary, setting up a runoff. After a bitter campaign, the runoff tally showed Graddick winning by 7,000 votes. But Baxley, a moderate, argued that Graddick, a conservative former Republican, had illegally recruited GOP voters to support him in the runoff. After a federal court agreed, a state party committee gave the nomination to Baxley. Eventually, many angry conservative Democrats helped elect Republican Guy Hunt as governor over Baxley.

The schism prompted Shelby to lay low for a while, but when it became clear the storm would not blow over, he started stumping, and made up ground quickly. He ran a TV commercial accusing Denton of voting to cut Social Security, and others portraying Denton as "out of touch and ineffective." Shelby was able to assuage his former foes on the Democratic left, partly because no matter how great their dissatisfaction with Shelby, black and union voters saw Denton as less desirable.

Shelby won with a strong boost from his 7th District base. He took Tuscaloosa County with 64 percent and carried several rural Black Belt counties by 3-to-1 margins. He also did well in traditionally Democratic counties in northwest and south-central Alabama.

Shelby's first election to the House was much less trying. In 1978, his former Tuscaloosa law partner, Democratic Rep. Walter Flowers, gave up the 7th for what turned out to be an unsuccessful Senate primary campaign. Shelby, whose support for such issues as the Equal Rights Amendment had typed him as a progressive Democrat during eight years in the state Legislature, went for Flowers' open seat.

Shelby's strong base in Tuscaloosa, where he had served as a prosecutor, helped him win 48 percent in the primary. In the runoff, he defeated black state Rep. Chris McNair by a 3-to-2 margin, in a campaign free of racial tensions. He easily won that November and never faced significant GOP opposition.

Dissatisfaction with Shelby's conservative House voting record led to a primary challenge from the left in 1982 that drew strong support from labor and blacks. But Shelby beat it back by a margin of nearly 2 to 1.

Committees

Special Aging (7th of 11 Democrats)

Armed Services (10th of 11 Democrats)
Conventional Forces & Alliance Defense; Projection Forces & Regional Defense; Readiness, Sustainability & Support

Banking, Housing & Urban Affairs (8th of 12 Democrats)
International Finance & Monetary Policy; Securities

Energy & Natural Resources (10th of 11 Democrats)
Energy Regulation & Conservation; Energy Research & Development (vice chairman); Mineral Resources Development & Production

Elections

1986 General		
Richard C. Shelby (D)	609,360	(50%)
Jeremiah Denton (R)	602,537	(50%)
1986 Primary		
Richard C. Shelby (D)	420,155	(51%)
Jim Allen Jr. (D)	284,206	(35%)
Ted McLaughlin (D)	70,784	(9%)
Mrs. Frank Ross Stewart (D)	26,723	(3%)
Steve Arnold (D)	16,722	(2%)

Previous Winning Percentages: **1984 *** (97%) **1982 *** (97%) **1980 *** (73%) **1978 *** (94%)

** House elections.*

Campaign Finance

	Receipts	Receipts from PACs	Expend-itures
1986			
Shelby (D)	$2,400,488	$882,686 (37%)	$2,259,167
Denton (R)	$4,682,587	$673,320 (14%)	$4,617,163

Key Votes

1991	
Authorize use of force against Iraq	Y
1990	
Oppose prohibition of certain semiautomatic weapons	Y
Support constitutional amendment on flag desecration	Y
Oppose requiring parental notice for minors' abortions	N
Halt production of B-2 stealth bomber at 13 planes	N
Approve budget that cut spending and raised revenues	N
Pass civil rights bill over Bush veto	Y
1989	
Oppose reduction of SDI funding	Y
Oppose barring federal funds for "obscene" art	N
Allow vote on capital gains tax cut	Y

Voting Studies

	Presidential Support		Party Unity		Conservative Coalition	
Year	**S**	**O**	**S**	**O**	**S**	**O**
1990	55	45	59	41	95	5
1989	68	32	46	54	95	5
1988	57	43	56	43	92	5
1987	47	50	61	36	75	16
House Service						
1986	44	49	58	33	84	8
1985	52	41	60	31	85	13
1984	43	45	44	45	78	12
1983	54	44	43	54	76	20
1982	60	40	35	63	86	10
1981	76	21	25	71	93	4

Interest Group Ratings

Year	ADA	ACU	AFL-CIO	CCUS
1990	33	48	78	50
1989	25	57	90	63
1988	35	60	71	57
1987	50	43	90	50
House Service				
1986	40	55	93	39
1985	25	67	50	57
1984	15	57	50	46
1983	25	74	53	55
1982	10	73	35	67
1981	0	93	27	89

1 Sonny Callahan (R)

Of Mobile — Elected 1984

Born: Sept. 11, 1932, Mobile, Ala.

Education: Graduated from McGill H.S. (Mobile), 1950.

Military Service: Navy, 1952-54.

Occupation: Moving and storage company executive.

Family: Wife, Karen Reed; six children.

Religion: Roman Catholic.

Political Career: Ala. House, served as Democrat, 1971-79; Ala. Senate, served as Democrat, 1979-83; sought Democratic nomination for lieutenant governor, 1982.

Capitol Office: 1330 Longworth Bldg. 20515; 225-4931.

In Washington: Still "Sonny" after all these years, the middle-aged Callahan is a gregarious, good-natured Southerner at ease with the personal give-and-take of the political process. He is the GOP version of a character type abundant in his region — the Democratic courthouse pol. That is not surprising, since Callahan himself was once a Democrat.

As a freshman on Public Works, Callahan was able to cultivate friendships and contacts enough to secure federal money for local projects. By the end of 1986, however, Callahan was aiming higher. He won one of two prize GOP vacancies on Energy and Commerce for the 100th Congress. A skeptic of government involvement in the marketplace, Callahan is typical of the panel's Republicans.

At the start of the 102nd Congress, he gained a seat on the Merchant Marine Committee, an important assignment for a member representing a district dominated by a port city — in Callahan's case, Mobile.

Serving a district with forests covering much of its rural areas, Callahan touts his sponsorship of the Forest Stewardship Program, enacted as part of the 1990 farm bill. The program reauthorizes and creates several programs to encourage better management of private forests and offers financial assistance for timber and conservation activities.

Callahan has had his share of mixed fortunes regarding a local Navy "homeport." His predecessor, GOP Rep. Jack Edwards, worked for years to get Mobile included in the Navy's homeporting force-dispersal strategy. Ground was finally broken for the facility in 1988, giving Callahan a well-timed publicity boost. In 1990, however, the Pentagon ordered a construction freeze on a number of homeports. Construction continued on the one in Mobile, pending an April 1991 decision.

Appropriate for a new member of the Merchant Marine Committee in whose district the major industry is shipbuilding, Callahan announced at the end of 1990 that he was moving out of his $1,300-a-month apartment in the Virginia suburbs to a 63-foot, three-bedroom, custom-built (in his district) houseboat anchored on the Potomac — his attempt to beat the Washington area's high cost of living.

At Home: When Edwards announced his retirement in late 1983, his endorsement went to Callahan. The only suspense in the race was over which party Callahan would choose. Elected to the Legislature as a Democrat, Callahan moved right. He formally joined the GOP in February 1984, and, confident of victory, waged a lackadaisical House campaign. Callahan's primary foe, Mobile lawyer Billy Stoudenmire, attacked him as a Democratic interloper. Callahan drew enough conservative Democrats across party lines to win the primary by a 60-40 percent margin. But his weakness rekindled hope among Democrats, who nominated Frank McRight, a Mobile trial lawyer.

McRight won his primary by attacking local government corruption. Then in the November campaign it was reported that Callahan had received an illegal campaign contribution two years earlier from a city official later indicted on other charges. In October, Callahan finally responded to the challenge. He reminded voters that McRight was twice the Carter-Mondale campaign chairman in Mobile, and he repeatedly asked how McRight would vote for president in 1984. In the end, though, Callahan owed much of his narrow margin to Reagan's smashing triumph in the 1st.

In 1986 and 1990, Democrats conceded without a fight. But in 1988, they recruited John M. Tyson Jr., a high-profile member of the state school board and member of a well-known political family. Tyson had the markings of a contender, but he ran a poorly organized, underfunded campaign and never seriously threatened the incumbent.

Alabama 1

Southwest — Mobile

The 1st, in the southwest corner of the state, is dominated by the outward-looking port city of Mobile, second-largest in the state, with a population of over 200,000. Perched on the state's tiny coastline, its location and Spanish and French heritage give the city a separate history.

Mobile County has been voting increasingly Republican in recent national elections. It gave Republican Jeremiah Denton more than 60 percent in his 1986 race for U.S. Senate. George Bush carried 61 percent of the Mobile vote in 1988, but in local elections, Democrats still have the edge.

On the eastern side of Mobile Bay is Baldwin County, the third-fastest growing county in Alabama; between 1980 and 1986 its population increased nearly 20 percent. Bush took 73 percent of the vote there.

The port is the area's largest employer. The 1985 completion of the Tennessee-Tombigbee Waterway, which connects Mobile Bay and the Tennessee River, eventually should help the port of Mobile compete with New Orleans in trade volume, although early trade on the massive waterway has been disappointing.

A continued federal involvement in port development was assured with the 1988 ground-breaking for the Mobile "homeport," part of the Reagan administration's strategy of dispersing U.S. naval forces.

Shipbuilding is a major industry. In addition, the salt domes north of the city have given rise to a chemical industry, and there are oil and gas drilling operations offshore. The other key industry in the 1st is pulp and paper; the raw material for the industry comes from the forests that cover much of the district's rural counties.

The strong GOP vote in Mobile and coastal Baldwin County often outstrips the Democratic strength in the rural, heavily black counties in the northern part of the district and in Prichard, a suburb of Mobile. Monroeville's racial climate (Monroe County) inspired the 1960 novel, "To Kill A Mockingbird," but now two of the six city council members are black. Wilcox County, more than two-thirds black, was one of 16 to back Michael S. Dukakis in 1988.

Population: 563,905. White 383,014 (68%), Black 174,657 (31%), Other 4,927(1%). Spanish origin 5,887 (1%). 18 and over 384,289 (68%), 65 and over 60,149 (11%). Median age: 28.

Committees

Energy & Commerce (12th of 16 Republicans)
Energy & Power; Transportation & Hazardous Materials

Merchant Marine & Fisheries (14th of 17 Republicans)
Coast Guard & Navigation; Merchant Marine

Elections

1990 General		
Sonny Callahan (R)	82,185	(100%)
1988 General		
Sonny Callahan (R)	115,173	(59%)
John M. Tyson Jr. (D)	77,670	(40%)

Previous Winning Percentages: **1986** (100%) **1984** (51%)

District Vote For President

	1988		1984		1980		1976	
D	73,312	(37%)	72,298	(35%)	77,758	(41%)	81,012	(48%)
R	121,510	(62%)	134,551	(64%)	107,679	(56%)	83,622	(50%)

Campaign Finance

	Receipts	Receipts from PACs		Expend-itures
1990				
Callahan (R)	$318,680	$169,350	(53%)	$183,910
1988				
Callahan (R)	$596,631	$253,301	(42%)	$651,127
Tyson (D)	$128,136	$52,400	(41%)	$125,029

Key Votes

1991	
Authorize use of force against Iraq	Y
1990	
Support constitutional amendment on flag desecration	Y
Pass family and medical leave bill over Bush veto	N
Reduce SDI funding	N
Allow abortions in overseas military facilities	N
Approve budget summit plan for spending and taxing	N
Approve civil rights bill	N
1989	
Halt production of B-2 stealth bomber at 13 planes	N
Oppose capital gains tax cut	N
Approve federal abortion funding in rape or incest cases	N
Approve pay raise and revision of ethics rules	N
Pass Democratic minimum wage plan over Bush veto	N

Voting Studies

	Presidential Support		Party Unity		Conservative Coalition	
Year	**S**	**O**	**S**	**O**	**S**	**O**
1990	63	32	73 †	20 †	96	0
1989	73	21	73	23	100	0
1988	63	37	79	17	100	0
1987	68	32	79	16	93	5
1986	73	21	75	21	98	0
1985	74	26	82	16	96	4

† Not eligible for all recorded votes.

Interest Group Ratings

Year	ADA	ACU	AFL-CIO	CCUS
1990	6	87	17	92
1989	0	93	9	100
1988	10	96	29	93
1987	4	78	19	87
1986	0	95	29	89
1985	0	86	12	86

2 Bill Dickinson (R)

Of Montgomery — Elected 1964

Born: June 5, 1925, Opelika, Ala.
Education: U. of Alabama, LL.B. 1950.
Military Service: Navy, 1943-46; Air Force Reserve.
Occupation: Railroad executive; judge; lawyer.
Family: Wife, Barbara Edwards; four children.
Religion: Methodist.
Political Career: Opelika city judge, 1951-53; Lee County Court of Common Pleas and Juvenile Court judge, 1953-59; 5th Judicial Circuit judge, 1959-63.
Capitol Office: 2406 Rayburn Bldg. 20515; 225-2901.

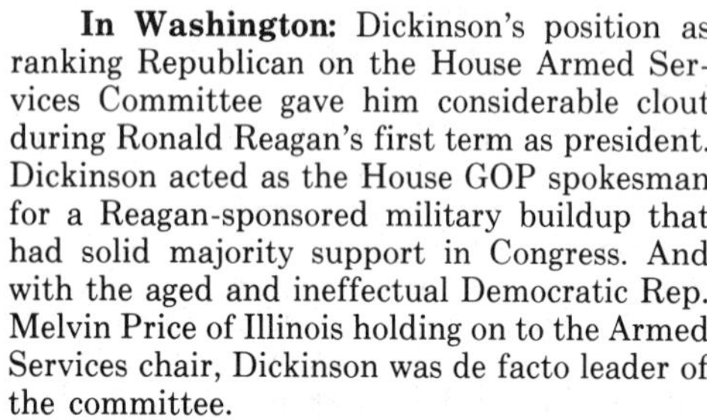

In Washington: Dickinson's position as ranking Republican on the House Armed Services Committee gave him considerable clout during Ronald Reagan's first term as president. Dickinson acted as the House GOP spokesman for a Reagan-sponsored military buildup that had solid majority support in Congress. And with the aged and ineffectual Democratic Rep. Melvin Price of Illinois holding on to the Armed Services chair, Dickinson was de facto leader of the committee.

But just as the defense buildup peaked in the mid-1980s, so did Dickinson's influence. A Democratic Caucus coup in 1985 removed Price as chairman and replaced him with Les Aspin of Wisconsin, an aggressive intellectual who quickly restored control of the committee to the majority party. Soon thereafter, the mushrooming fiscal crisis and a thaw in U.S.-Soviet relations stemmed the upward spiral in defense spending. Disoriented by the new demands of prioritizing between defense programs they favored, Dickinson and other "Old Guard" conservatives on Armed Services lost influence.

The 101st Congress was truly a valley in Dickinson's long political career. When passage of a conference report on a bill is stymied, the Democratic chairmen and ranking Republicans of the relevant House and Senate committees often huddle to work out the necessary compromises. But when final passage of the fiscal 1991 defense authorization bill stalled in October 1990, Aspin and his Senate counterparts, Armed Services Chairman Sam Nunn and ranking Republican John W. Warner, met in private, leaving Dickinson on the outside.

Dickinson protested, stating, "When so few politicians do all the final horse trading behind closed doors, you can never be certain that what they bring home is a nag or a filly." He was backed up by his cohorts; House Republican conferees on the bill refused to sign the conference report. Yet the incident symbolized what some of the younger conservatives on Armed Services see as the need for a leader who is more assertive — and more competitive with Aspin — than Dickinson.

At the same time he was suffering institutional setbacks, Dickinson faced serious trouble back home. News reports about Dickinson's financial transactions fueled the campaign of an aggressive Democratic challenger who held Dickinson to 51 percent of the vote. He thus entered the 102nd Congress politically weakened and pursued by speculation that he might soon retire.

None of this is to say that Dickinson has thrown in the towel on his legislative career. He showed even during the difficult 101st Congress that he can be a bulldog on defense issues.

Throughout the 1980s, Dickinson was a staunch supporter of the multi-warhead MX missile and its projected mobile rail-basing system, and he opposed its replacement with the more expensive, single-warhead Midgetman missile. In 1989, he parried a maneuver by MX opponents to give primacy to the Midgetman.

Dickinson and other MX backers made a deal with Aspin under which both MX and Midgetman would be funded in the fiscal 1990 budget. However, the House passed an amendment, proposed by Democrat John M. Spratt Jr., to cut MX funding nearly in half. Dickinson retaliated by joining in an odd coalition of conservative MX supporters and liberal arms control activists, who pushed through an amendment dropping funds for the Midgetman.

"I've only supported [Midgetman] as part of a package; the package is gone," Dickinson said. "Sometimes people get too cute." (The final defense bill that year provided relatively equal funding for the two programs. However, in 1990, Congress dropped funding for the development of the MX rail-basing mode.)

Also in 1989, President Bush and Defense Secretary Dick Cheney proposed to cut some popular, jobs-producing weapons systems in order to preserve funding for such "new generation" high-tech programs as the B-2 bomber and the strategic defense initiative (SDI). When some liberal Democrats sought to preserve defense contracts benefiting their districts, Dick-

Alabama 2

Southeast — Montgomery; Dothan

Most of the 2nd, which covers the southeast corner of Alabama, is rural territory. But half the population is concentrated in two urban centers at opposite corners of the district.

At the northwest edge is Montgomery County, with more than 200,000 people. The city of Montgomery has long been a national Republican stronghold in Alabama, voting for GOP presidential candidates as far back as 1956.

Montgomery was the first capital of the Confederacy, and to many the city represents the Fort Sumter of the civil rights movement. In 1955, when a black woman named Rosa Parks refused to give up her bus seat to a white man, her arrest resulted in a boycott led by the Rev. Dr. Martin Luther King Jr. and the end of bus segregation.

With the state Capitol crucial to its economy, Montgomery is largely a white-collar town with a government-oriented work force. Nearby Maxwell and Gunter Air Force bases employ nearly 10,000 people.

At the southeastern corner of the district, near the Florida and Georgia borders, is the Houston County seat of Dothan, a city of more than 50,000. Originally a cotton and peanut market town, Dothan has grown and diversified by attracting new industries, including large plants run by Michelin and Sony. Largely non-union, the Dothan plants represent most of the 2nd's large industry.

Although Houston County was always fiercely loyal to George C. Wallace, it has been voting regularly for conservative Republicans in other contests over the last decade. In 1986, GOP gubernatorial candidate Guy Hunt won it with 63 percent; in 1990, GOP Rep. Bill Dickinson won Houston County by roughly 4,000 votes, almost identical to his districtwide margin of victory.

Fort Rucker, where many Army and Air Force helicopter pilots and crews are trained, is northwest of Dothan in Dale County. More than 11,000 military and civilian personnel work at Fort Rucker. Pike County will be the site of a new Martin Marietta missile factory, expected to employ 200 employees when fully operational.

Between these two population centers are the Piney Woods of Alabama and a portion of the state's Black Belt. Sparsely populated, the area grows more peanuts than almost any other part of the country, although cotton is still cultivated. As a testament to the success of peanuts, the town of Enterprise in Coffee County erected a monument to the boll weevil, the insect whose destruction of the cotton crop in the early part of the century convinced farmers to switch to peanuts.

Rural Barbour and Bullock counties, George C. Wallace's original home base, have large black populations and are loyally Democratic. But farther south, the black population drops and chances for GOP success increase. The four mostly rural counties around Houston County went Republican in the close 1986 Senate and gubernatorial elections as well as in the 1988 presidential race.

Population: 549,505. White 376,259 (69%), Black 168,913 (31%), Other 2,879 (1%). Spanish origin 5,731 (1%). 18 and over 383,150 (70%), 65 and over 64,624 (12%). Median age: 29.

inson aimed a potshot at them.

"If your colleagues ... had been more supportive of defense budgets in the last few years, we might not be in the shape we're in now," he told Democratic Rep. George J. Hochbrueckner, who was trying to save the F-14 fighter built in his Long Island district.

Dickinson was strongly supportive of President Bush's decision to use military force in early 1991 to end Iraq's occupation of Kuwait. But during the Persian Gulf war, he complained about the seemingly slow pace at which U.S. allies were delivering their pledged financial contributions to the war effort. Noting that "Japan is a principal beneficiary" of the effort to protect Middle East oil fields from Iraqi aggression, Dickinson said, "People want to know what in hell [Japan is] paying."

Dickinson also continued to act on behalf of the military facilities and defense-related industries in his district. A list of his "major accomplishments" in the 101st Congress includes military construction projects at Maxwell and Gunter Air Force bases and the Army's Fort Rucker, totaling $71.5 million.

But Dickinson's continuing ability to secure those parochial gains does not match up to the broader swath he cut on Armed Services in the early 1980s. As Price struggled to hold onto the gavel, Dickinson took the lead and credit on many issues; during tours of bases and installations, military officials often thanked Dickinson first for his efforts to procure some new weapon or additional equipment.

Even as Aspin attempted to gain his footing as chairman, Dickinson appeared as a major member of the ruling committee coalition. At times, he joined Aspin in criticizing Reagan's priorities. In late 1986, Dickinson blasted Reagan's still-unreleased fiscal 1988 defense budget, complaining that "it shafts the Army" by slowing production of conventional weapons in order to pay for big-ticket items such as SDI, nuclear-powered naval aircraft carriers and state-of-the-art helicopters. He doggedly, and successfully, fought to restore funds for the M-1 tank, Bradley troop carriers and Apache and Blackhawk helicopters.

In 1987, Dickinson resisted Aspin's effort to cut the panel's own $306 billion alternative down to the $289 billion demanded by the Budget Committee. "We are cutting into the bone and sinew of our defense establishment," he complained. During a closed-door committee session, he reportedly grabbed an American flag and marched about the room in protest. Dickinson's viewpoint prevailed on the panel, but the House later made the cuts.

Dickinson's focus on defense in recent years has overshadowed all else. He also is the senior Republican in years of service on the House Administration Committee, but he has yielded the ranking seat there because party rules allow members to hold the top position on only one panel.

The committee's oversight of federal employee issues occasionally gives Dickinson an outlet for his fiscal and social conservatism. During consideration of the family leave bill in 1989, the House Administration Subcommittee on Personnel and Police passed a provision allowing leave of up to 18 weeks for mothers and fathers of newborn infants. Dickinson vigorously disagreed. "This is ludicrous in the extreme," he said. "I don't need 18 weeks off if my wife has a baby."

But if that sentiment seems old-fashioned, some of Dickinson's views have changed in the years since he came into office on the coattails of Barry Goldwater, the conservative Republican pioneer who carried Alabama for president in 1964 while losing a national landslide to President Lyndon B. Johnson. Dickinson was elected then on a pledge to combat the Great Society and the civil rights movement, and voted against Medicare when it was created in 1965. But in 1987, he publicly hailed passage of legislation extending coverage to catastrophic illnesses, the biggest expansion of the program since its creation (and one that was later rolled back because of public anger over its financing mechanisms).

His rhetoric of earlier days also has moderated. Though strong words still can obscure his good nature, Dickinson has never again invited the sort of furor that accompanied his 1965 House speech against the civil rights protestors on the Selma-to-Montgomery march. He called the marchers "human flotsam" and "communist dupes" for whom "drunkenness and sex orgies were the order of the day." Lawmakers walked off the floor in protest, some newspapers back home criticized him and Dickinson later conceded he may have erred and had none of the proof he had promised.

At Home: Probably few House members were helped more by the emergence of the Persian Gulf crisis in 1990 than Dickinson. It shifted voter attention in his district away from discussion of his personal financial dealings to the issue of national defense, much friendlier turf for Dickinson.

Yet he barely survived his bid for a 14th term. Dickinson faced a politically well-connected opponent in Faye Baggiano, a Cabinet-level official under both Democratic Govs. Fob James and George C. Wallace.

She mounted an aggressive challenge focusing on Dickinson's personal ethics. In the summer of 1989, *The Washington Post* reported that Dickinson had solicited contributions from defense contractors he oversees in order to fund a pro-defense institute.

That fall, Alabama regional newspapers owned by *The New York Times* reported that Dickinson offered to swap his contacts and "know-how" for a one-third interest in a $300,000 venture funded by a Montgomery businessman. The deal turned sour when the money was invested with a third party who turned out to be a swindler.

Dickinson denied any wrongdoing, but Baggiano maintained that the business venture was just the latest example of a cozy relationship between Dickinson and big-money contributors, many of them defense contractors.

Dickinson sought to refocus attention on his constituent service and the value of his congressional clout in a district heavily dependent on military dollars. He frequently appeared on local TV to discuss the Persian Gulf crisis.

Still, he narrowly won. Baggiano carried the populous Montgomery area and heavily black rural counties nearby. Dickinson scored heavily in the rest of the district, rolling up his decisive margin in the conservative Dothan area.

Before 1990, Dickinson's last close election was in 1982, when he faced Democrat Billy Joe Camp, Wallace's longtime press secretary and president of the state Public Service Commission. Camp was not an aggressive campaigner and did not have much money. But he had excellent name identification and benefited from Wallace's presence on the ballot as the gubernatorial nominee. That and a double-digit unemployment rate were nearly enough to send Camp to Congress.

With Camp carrying nine of the district's 13 counties, Dickinson had to run more than 10,000 votes ahead in the Montgomery and

Dothan areas to eke out a 1,386-vote victory.

There was real concern in Republican ranks that Camp would try again in 1984, and that a high black turnout generated by the presidential contest might take down Dickinson. Those fears turned out to be groundless. Camp, one of a handful of Wallace confidants with wide latitude in running the state, lost interest in coming to Washington.

No top-name Democrat stepped forward to replace him. And any increase in the black vote was more than canceled out by the Reagan surge among white voters. Dickinson won with a comfortable 60 percent. Easy victories in 1986 and 1988 followed; in 1988, he had no Democratic opposition.

A Democratic circuit judge in Lee County for four years, Dickinson quit the bench in 1963 to become assistant vice president of the Southern Railroad. But his stay in the business world was brief. He filed for the House just as Goldwater was launching his presidential campaign, and when Goldwater swept Alabama in 1964, Dickinson easily unseated Democratic Rep. George M. Grant.

Grant had a conservative record, but Dickinson managed to tie him to the national Democratic ticket, which not only was unpopular in the state but also was excluded from an official position at the top of the ballot.

Committees

Armed Services (Ranking)
Military Installations & Facilities; Procurement & Military Nuclear Systems (ranking)

House Administration (2nd of 9 Republicans)
Accounts; Office Systems; Personnel & Police

Elections

1990 General		
Bill Dickinson (R)	87,649	(51%)
Faye Baggiano (D)	83,243	(49%)
1988 General		
Bill Dickinson (R)	120,408	(94%)
Joel Brooke King (LIBERT)	7,352	(6%)

Previous Winning Percentages: **1986** (67%) **1984** (60%) **1982** (50%) **1980** (61%) **1978** (54%) **1976** (58%) **1974** (66%) **1972** (55%) **1970** (61%) **1968** (55%) **1966** (55%) **1964** (62%)

District Vote For President

	1988	1984	1980	1976
D	71,335 (37%)	73,603 (36%)	83,720 (44%)	88,208 (53%)
R	118,794 (62%)	130,370 (63%)	99,283 (53%)	75,528 (46%)

Campaign Finance

	Receipts	Receipts from PACs		Expend-itures
1990				
Dickinson (R)	$425,127	$218,921	(51%)	$596,096
Baggiano (D)	$169,109	$91,752	(54%)	$163,663
1988				
Dickinson (R)	$304,708	$168,639	(55%)	$234,923

Key Votes

1991	
Authorize use of force against Iraq	Y
1990	
Support constitutional amendment on flag desecration	Y
Pass family and medical leave bill over Bush veto	N
Reduce SDI funding	N
Allow abortions in overseas military facilities	N
Approve budget summit plan for spending and taxing	Y
Approve civil rights bill	N
1989	
Halt production of B-2 stealth bomber at 13 planes	N
Oppose capital gains tax cut	N
Approve federal abortion funding in rape or incest cases	Y
Approve pay raise and revision of ethics rules	N
Pass Democratic minimum wage plan over Bush veto	N

Voting Studies

	Presidential Support		Party Unity		Conservative Coalition	
Year	S	O	S	O	S	O
1990	66	31	82	12	94	4
1989	71	16	80	12	90	2
1988	63	34	83	9	95	3
1987	64	26	78	13	84	5
1986	71	22	78	14	88	2
1985	63	36	76	17	85	9
1984	64	26	72	18	90	5
1983	78	16	75	17	83	10
1982	75	14	76	11	89	4
1981	72	16	77	14	81	7

Interest Group Ratings

Year	ADA	ACU	AFL-CIO	CCUS
1990	0	88	17	79
1989	5	85	17	100
1988	20	92	38	100
1987	16	76	19	86
1986	15	86	38	73
1985	10	65	18	82
1984	10	84	23	60
1983	0	81	6	94
1982	0	100	0	84
1981	5	100	27	100

3 Glen Browder (D)

Of Jacksonville — Elected 1989

Born: Jan. 15, 1943, Sumter, S.C.

Education: Presbyterian College, B.A. 1965; Emory U., M.A., Ph.D. 1971.

Occupation: Professor of political science.

Family: Wife, Rebecca Moore; one child.

Religion: Methodist.

Political Career: Ala. House, 1983-87; Ala. secretary of state, 1987-89.

Capitol Office: 1221 Longworth Bldg. 20515; 225-3261.

In Washington: Browder did not have much time to plan for his first House race; he ran to fill the vacancy created by the December 1988 death of Democrat Bill Nichols. But Browder knew he wanted to serve in Congress, and knew what he wanted to do when he got there.

Not long after his arrival in the House, Browder lobbied the Democratic Steering and Policy Committee for an assignment on the Armed Services Committee, where Nichols had been a senior member. Although there were no openings on the committee when Browder arrived, he got a vacated slot in November 1989.

A soft-spoken political scientist with a knack for the rough-and-tumble of politics, Browder struck a rapport with Armed Services Chairman Les Aspin, a former economics professor. He persuaded Aspin to put him on the Military Installations Subcommittee, where he pursued the base-closing issue.

In January 1990, Defense Secretary Dick Cheney released a list of bases to be closed that included Fort McClellan, a chemical warfare training facility in Browder's district. Browder co-founded the "Fairness Network," a coalition of members whose districts would be affected by the base-closing plan.

Steering away from parochial appeals, Browder argued that the plan was not grounded in overall defense strategy. Noting that most of the targeted bases were in Democratic-held House districts, Browder said, "This is no time to risk America's capacity to protect her vital interests for partisan politics." He won adoption of his amendment to create a bipartisan commission modeled on the one that crafted the base-closing list enacted in 1989. But Fort McClellan remained on the base-closing list issued in early 1991.

Browder also has been active in the Democratic Leadership Council, a group of moderate and conservative Democrats who counter what Browder calls "the traditional liberal orthodoxy associated with our party."

At Home: Browder's special election victory in April 1989 was one of the year's most important, since it put to rest any Republican hopes of galloping realignment in the rural South. In a district that George Bush had won in 1988 with 60 percent, Browder beat GOP state Sen. John Rice by nearly 2 to 1. In 1990, Republicans offered only token opposition.

Browder came slowly to politics. After graduating from Presbyterian College in South Carolina in 1965, he moved to Atlanta, first working as a sportswriter for the *Atlanta Journal* and then as an investigator for the U.S. Civil Service Commission. But it was not long before Browder returned to college, earning his doctorate in political science at Emory University. With that, he landed a job on the faculty at Jacksonville State University in Alabama, where he found time to dabble in polling, research and political consulting.

In 1982, Browder ran for an open seat in the Alabama House, emerging victorious from a crowded primary field. He stayed four years, gaining attention for a controversial "career ladder" teacher pay and evaluation plan he promoted. The measure became law, but drew criticism for being too costly and time-consuming to administer; it was soon repealed.

In 1986 Browder ran for secretary of state against Annie Laurie Gunter, a George Wallace ally and the outgoing state treasurer. Out-organizing his better-known rival, Browder won the pivotal Democratic primary.

Once in office, he successfully lobbied the Legislature for stricter campaign-finance disclosure, which required candidates to make pre-election reports of campaign contributions.

When Nichols died of a heart attack, Browder was well positioned to run for his seat. The lone statewide official in the race, he had high name recognition across the rural, 13-county district. Browder's biggest test was the nine-man Democratic primary; with support from organized labor and help from an "attack" ad that portrayed his chief conservative rivals as proponents of big tax increases, he ran first with 25 percent of the vote. After that, Browder had few problems, easily winning a placid runoff against Tuskegee's black mayor, Johnny Ford, and the special election against Rice.

Alabama 3

East — Anniston; Auburn

Taking in the eastern side of the state from the outskirts of Montgomery to the hilly Piedmont Plateau, the 3rd is a conservative rural stronghold.

Textile mills dot the landscape, reflecting the traditional prominence of cotton in the area's agricultural economy. There is heavy industry in Anniston, the seat of Calhoun County and one of the 3rd's largest cities, with a population of 30,000. It is also home to two huge military facilities, Fort McClellan and the Anniston Army Depot. Several somewhat smaller cities are sprinkled in the southeastern corner of the 3rd, near the Georgia border. The best-known is Auburn (Lee County), home of Auburn University, the state's largest, with 21,000 students.

A notable monument of black culture is located in the 3rd's Macon County — Tuskegee University, founded in 1881 by Booker T. Washington as one of the nation's first black colleges. In 1968, the city of Tuskegee elected the first black sheriff in the South and the first two black members in the Alabama Legislature. Blacks make up 84 percent of the population in Macon County. But Macon is the only county in the 3rd with a black majority; districtwide, blacks are 28 percent of the population.

The towns in the southwestern part of the district, particularly in Elmore County, serve as bedroom communities for the state capital, Montgomery, just across the district line. Elmore was one of only four counties in the state that unsuccessful GOP Senate candidate Bill Cabaniss carried in 1990.

Although most voters in the 3rd consider themselves Democrats, statewide Republican candidates can do fairly well — especially in the more urbanized areas, such as Anniston in the north and Auburn in the south.

Population: 555,321. White 395,332 (71%), Black 156,665 (28%). Spanish origin 5,232 (1%). 18 and over 390,418 (70%), 65 and over 61,108 (11%). Median age: 28.

Committees

Armed Services (29th of 33 Democrats)
Military Installations & Facilities; Research & Development; Military Education

Science, Space & Technology (23rd of 32 Democrats)
Science; Space

Elections

1990 General		
Glen Browder (D)	101,923	(74%)
Don Sledge (R)	36,317	(26%)
1989 Special		
Glen Browder (D)	47,294	(65%)
John Rice (R)	25,142	(35%)
1989 Primary Runoff		
Glen Browder (D)	44,647	(63%)
Johnny Ford (D)	26,318	(37%)
1989 Special Primary		
Glen Browder (D)	14,715	(25%)
Johnny Ford (D)	14,440	(24%)
Jim Preuitt (D)	10,184	(17%)
Charles Adams (D)	9,851	(17%)
Gerald Dial (D)	5,882	(10%)
Donald Holmes (D)	3,908	(7%)

District Vote For President

	1988	1984	1980	1976
D	67,936 (38%)	70,024 (37%)	86,753 (50%)	90,034 (58%)
R	106,069 (60%)	113,641 (61%)	80,051 (46%)	62,198 (40%)

Campaign Finance

	Receipts	Receipts from PACs	Expend-itures
1990			
Browder (D)	$874,518	$547,750 (63%)	$754,106
Sledge (R)	$22,990	$100 (0%)	$22,989
1989 Special			
Browder (D)	$590,692	$354,100 (60%)	$573,964
Rice (R)	$450,221	$111,250 (25%)	$443,927

Key Votes

1991	
Authorize use of force against Iraq	Y
1990	
Support constitutional amendment on flag desecration	Y
Pass family and medical leave bill over Bush veto	N
Reduce SDI funding	N
Allow abortions in overseas military facilities	N
Approve budget summit plan for spending and taxing	N
Approve civil rights bill	Y
1989	
Halt production of B-2 stealth bomber at 13 planes	N
Oppose capital gains tax cut	N
Approve federal abortion funding in rape or incest cases	Y
Approve pay raise and revision of ethics rules	N
Pass Democratic minimum wage plan over Bush veto	Y

Voting Studies

	Presidential Support		Party Unity		Conservative Coalition	
Year	**S**	**O**	**S**	**O**	**S**	**O**
1990	41	59	74	25	93	7
1989	54 †	44 †	68 †	30 †	89 †	11 †

† Not eligible for all recorded votes.

Interest Group Ratings

Year	ADA	ACU	AFL-CIO	CCUS
1990	33	58	50	71
1989	44	58	63	70

4 Tom Bevill (D)

Of Jasper — Elected 1966

Born: March 27, 1921, Townley, Ala.
Education: U. of Alabama, B.S. 1943, LL.B. 1948.
Military Service: Army, 1943-46.
Occupation: Lawyer.
Family: Wife, Lou Betts; three children.
Religion: Baptist.
Political Career: Ala. House, 1959-67; sought Democratic nomination for U.S. House, 1964.
Capitol Office: 2302 Rayburn Bldg. 20515; 225-4876.

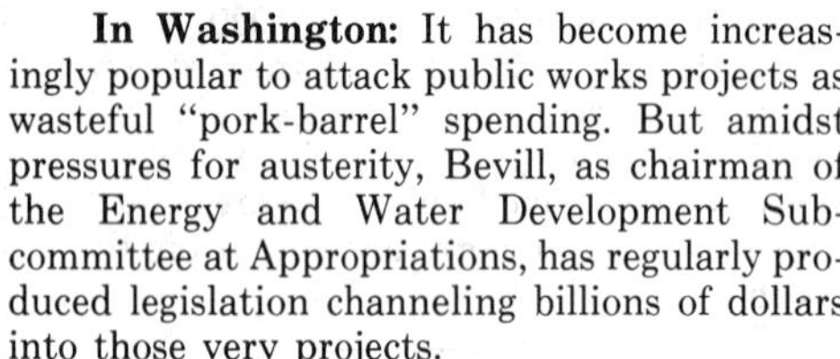

In Washington: It has become increasingly popular to attack public works projects as wasteful "pork-barrel" spending. But amidst pressures for austerity, Bevill, as chairman of the Energy and Water Development Subcommittee at Appropriations, has regularly produced legislation channeling billions of dollars into those very projects.

Bevill has always treated public works as a personal creed. This is understandable, since much of north Alabama was brought to economic health during the Depression by projects of the Tennessee Valley Authority (TVA). "There is no question," Bevill says, "that water-resources projects have helped develop the nation." He says every dollar invested in flood control has reaped benefits many times over.

When a new national issue seizes the public consciousness, Bevill looks for ways to tie it to the need for water projects. Usually he finds some, as he has in the case of trade. He talks about how important waterways and ports are to the nation's trading capacity.

However, Bevill has shown as chairman that he is more than a business-as-usual pork-barreler, taking a strong interest in the high-technology projects that fall under his jurisdiction.

His appropriations bill includes one of the most controversial high-tech projects, the $8 billion-plus giant atom smasher being built in Texas. Bevill was initially reluctant to begin building the superconducting super collider (SSC), which scientists want in order to study the building blocks of matter.

But he became a supporter after the administration assured him that foreign investors would help pay for its construction. Bevill's backing may also have been linked to an understanding with President Bush that the administration would not block new water projects being sought by members, although Bevill has denied there was any quid pro quo.

His support provided important momentum for the SSC project at a critical stage, while Bevill was able to help direct some of the super collider research to the University of Alabama. Bevill was still on board at the outset of the 102nd Congress, despite concerns about the project's mounting price tag and the paucity of foreign investors.

The Energy and Water appropriations bill also includes most of the Energy Department's budget, which came under renewed scrutiny in the 102nd due to energy concerns generated by the Persian Gulf War.

Here too, Bevill's district interests are evident; he supports federal programs to promote the use of coal, which is mined in his district. Bevill also advocated more federal research into renewable energy sources such as solar, wind and geothermal power.

Bevill has encountered some vocal opponents to his appropriations bills, but they are often louder than they are strong. In 1987, the energy and water bill was the first appropriations measure to reach the floor, and as such it was a prime target for budget-cutters. But when they attempted to trim 1.7 percent from every program in the bill, Bevill won 276-143.

Bevill also fended off another in a long series of attacks on the Appalachian Regional Commission (ARC). Only 82 members voted to cut $110 million from highways and projects under ARC, a remnant of the 1960s "War on Poverty" that has long pumped funds into the 4th District.

Bevill's success is not too surprising, given the nature of his legislation, which touches districts all around the country. Bevill is as gentlemanly as anyone in the House and not the type to make open threats of retaliation against opponents, but more than a few members are aware of the power that he has to deny funds that might otherwise come their way.

White Houses both Democratic and Republican have witnessed Bevill's power. In 1977, when the Carter administration tried to cancel 18 projects it said were too expensive and environmentally damaging, Bevill and his committee agreed to kill only one project and took the battle to the floor.

Carter eventually did stop funding for some of the least-popular projects. But in the

Alabama 4

North Central — Gadsden

Stretching across northern Alabama, the 4th is mostly rural, traditionally poor and overwhelmingly white. With a black population of only 7 percent, it has a different character from districts farther south.

The 4th has a long populist Democratic heritage. The "common man" rhetoric of former Gov. James E. Folsom Sr. (who grew up in the 4th's Cullman County) always played well in this region. When the racial tensions of the civil rights era caused Alabama politicians to emphasize segregation over agrarian populism, voters in this area went along, but race-baiting here was never as virulent as in other parts of Alabama because of the small black population.

Bevill's easy elections testify to the continuing dominance of the Democratic Party in the 4th, but recent developments point to some changes in the area's political complexion. During the 1970s, new residents moved into the 4th at a faster pace than into any other Alabama district, and many of the newcomers vote Republican. Two counties on the fringe of metropolitan Birmingham — Blount and St. Clair — supported Republican Jeremiah Denton in both his Senate races; even in his 1986 defeat, five other rural counties also backed Denton. George Bush carried 12 of the district's 14 counties in 1988. Another son of Cullman County now sits in the governor's chair — Republican Guy Hunt.

There is a GOP presence in the district dating to the Civil War. Winston County actually seceded from Alabama when the state seceded from the Union, and became the so-called "free state of Winston." The largest concentration of die-hard Democrats is in and around the district's largest city, Gadsden, an industrial center of 45,000 people in Etowah County. Smokestacks from Gulf States Steel and Goodyear Tire belch fumes, and the unionized labor force consistently votes Democratic; Etowah County was carried by unsuccessful 1990 Democratic nominee Paul Hubbert. In 1988, Michael S. Dukakis nearly carried Etowah over George Bush in the presidential contest. Blacks comprise about 25 percent of the county's population.

The western part of the 4th contains coal mines, and the United Mine Workers exerts a strong influence for Democratic candidates. The 1985 completion of the Tennessee-Tombigbee waterway — it cuts through Pickens County, in the district's southwestern corner — provides new transport from the mines to the port of Mobile.

Population: 562,088. White 519,706 (92%), Black 40,660 (7%). Spanish origin 3,200 (1%). 18 and over 397,076 (71%), 65 and over 71,872 (13%). Median age: 31.

long run, Bevill was the winner. The fight cost Carter enough political capital to cause any president to think hard about slashing the public works budget.

Although President Reagan was consistent in his efforts to reduce water-project funding, he was never willing to go to war with Congress over it.

There was some evidence of the more restrained budgetary climate in Bevill's water work in 1988. That year, he had to labor to repress members' desires to build new projects, and produced a bill that provided funding just for ongoing projects. "This has been the most difficult appropriations bill we have put together," Bevill said of the legislation, which was billed as the most austere energy and water bill in memory. With $17.8 billion in funding, it was also the biggest in memory.

The next year's energy and water appropriations bill was again laden with new projects. But in 1991, the stringent spending caps of a 1990 budget pact forced Bevill's subcommittee to pass a bill with no new water projects.

Bevill has become inured to the accusations that he is an advocate of "pork-barrel" legislation, but he is sensitive to the criticism. He changed the name of his subcommittee several years ago from "Public Works" to "Energy and Water Development" because the original name had such unpopular connotations.

"Energy was very popular. We thought we could pick up a few votes that way," Bevill said. "It worked. But I still like the term 'public works.' "

Bevill keeps an eye on his district's interests even when his subcommittee does not have jurisdiction. During the 1990 debate on the defense spending bill, for example, Bevill persuaded the House to spend $99 million for an anti-aircraft missile to be built in the 4th; the funding had been omitted from an earlier, more austere defense bill.

Bevill's most cherished project has probably been the Tennessee-Tombigbee, a massive barge canal that cuts through Alabama on its way to the Gulf of Mexico. Bevill was an emotional defender of the $3 billion waterway, which finally opened in 1985 after years of controversy.

Funding the canal demanded Bevill's eternal vigilance; opponents offered numerous amendments to delete money for the "Tenn-Tom." In 1980, an amendment to cancel funding for the project lost by 20 votes on the House floor; the next year it was 10 votes.

Tennessee-Tombigbee ultimately survived thanks to a trade-off with the embattled Clinch River nuclear breeder reactor in Tennessee, which Bevill long supported. For much of 1982, Bevill and his allies managed to stall floor votes on either project. Late in the year, however, the Bevill side agreed to a vote on Clinch River, and in return environmentalists did not press for one on Tennessee-Tombigbee. The House voted to block funding for Clinch River.

At Home: It was not a smooth political road that led Bevill to Congress, but he has been on easy street since arriving: Only in his first election in 1966 did he fall below 70 percent of the vote.

Bevill was elected to the Alabama Legislature in 1958, and served as a floor leader for first Gov. John Patterson and then Gov. George C. Wallace. But he lost his first congressional race in 1964, when incumbent Carl Elliott defeated him in the Democratic primary by more than 3-to-2.

Two years later, the district was open. Republican James D. Martin, who had defeated Elliott in November 1964, was running for governor. Bevill entered a four-way Democratic primary that included a popular state representative, Gary Burns, and a former Wallace press secretary, Bill Jones. Bevill led the first round with 36 percent of the vote, and his strength in the western part of the district gave him a runoff victory over Burns with 56 percent.

The general election was much simpler. Bevill beat Republican Wayman Sherrer, the little-known Blount County solicitor, by nearly 2-to-1 — a margin similar to the one by which Martin was losing the governorship to Lurleen B. Wallace.

Since then, Bevill has won every Democratic primary with at least 80 percent of the vote and every general election with at least 70 percent. Generally, his opposition has come from political novices. His only prominent challenger was Jim Folsom Jr., son of the colorful ex-governor, who made his political debut in 1976 by opposing Bevill for renomination. It was a flop. Bevill drew more than 80 percent.

Committees

Appropriations (8th of 37 Democrats)
Energy & Water Development (chairman); Interior; Military Construction

Elections

1990 General		
Tom Bevill (D)	129,872	(100%)
1988 General		
Tom Bevill (D)	131,880	(96%)
John Sebastian (LIBERT)	5,264	(4%)

Previous Winning Percentages: **1986** (78%) **1984** (100%) **1982** (100%) **1980** (98%) **1978** (100%) **1976** (80%) **1974** (100%) **1972** (70%) **1970** (100%) **1968** (76%) **1966** (64%)

District Vote For President

	1988	1984	1980	1976
D	83,042 (42%)	80,463 (40%)	104,802 (52%)	121,138 (65%)
R	111,528 (57%)	119,562 (59%)	91,768 (46%)	63,181 (34%)

Campaign Finance

	Receipts	Receipts from PACs	Expend-itures
1990			
Bevill (D)	$220,907	$106,550 (48%)	$168,054
1988			
Bevill (D)	$206,806	$94,850 (46%)	$130,642

Key Votes

1991	
Authorize use of force against Iraq	Y
1990	
Support constitutional amendment on flag desecration	Y
Pass family and medical leave bill over Bush veto	N
Reduce SDI funding	N
Allow abortions in overseas military facilities	N
Approve budget summit plan for spending and taxing	Y
Approve civil rights bill	Y
1989	
Halt production of B-2 stealth bomber at 13 planes	N
Oppose capital gains tax cut	Y
Approve federal abortion funding in rape or incest cases	N
Approve pay raise and revision of ethics rules	N
Pass Democratic minimum wage plan over Bush veto	Y

Voting Studies

	Presidential Support		Party Unity		Conservative Coalition	
Year	**S**	**O**	**S**	**O**	**S**	**O**
1990	42	56	71	23	85	11
1989	52	45	70	28	78	22
1988	31	58	71	19	71	11
1987	39	46	71	19	74	16
1986	40	58	67	26	82	18
1985	54	39	66	22	80	15
1984	53	35	55	29	83	7
1983	37	54	62	31	80	17
1982	55	44	70	26	75	19
1981	54	42	54	42	79	11

Interest Group Ratings

Year	ADA	ACU	AFL-CIO	CCUS
1990	22	58	50	57
1989	40	39	70	44
1988	45	50	100	46
1987	36	41	75	40
1986	40	50	79	29
1985	25	57	53	35
1984	35	50	58	43
1983	55	43	88	32
1982	20	59	74	47
1981	25	40	71	28

5 Bud Cramer (D)

Of Huntsville — Elected 1990

Born: Aug. 22, 1947, Huntsville, Ala.
Education: U. of Alabama, B.A. 1969, J.D. 1972.
Occupation: Lawyer.
Family: Widowed; one child.
Religion: Methodist.
Political Career: Madison County district attorney, 1981-91.
Capitol Office: 1431 Longworth Bldg. 20515; 225-4801.

The Path to Washington: A number of prosecuting attorneys have climbed the political ladder by portraying themselves as hard-charging crime fighters. But the mild-mannered Cramer made it from the Madison County courthouse to Congress by closely identifying himself with a relatively new and less macho issue — child abuse.

Cramer was drawn into child abuse cases as a prosecuting attorney in populous Madison County (Huntsville) during the 1980s; it did not take him long to become a nationally recognized expert.

The Children's Advocacy Center that he created as a shelter and counseling center for abused children became a nationwide model. From that came speaking engagements across the country, an annual conference on child abuse (the last of which drew 1,000 participants from 49 states and three foreign countries) and recognition from President Ronald Reagan at a White House ceremony in 1987.

When seven-term Democratic Rep. Ronnie G. Flippo indicated his intention to run for governor in 1990, Cramer was well positioned to run for the open 5th.

With Huntsville television stations reaching virtually every voter in the seven-county district, Cramer had high name identification and a favorable image as a "champion of the victim." That stemmed not just from his work on child abuse but from programs his office instituted to prosecute bad-check cases and spousal abuse.

Coupled with his strong base in the district's most populous county and an ample campaign treasury, Cramer ran far ahead of the crowded Democratic primary field, taking 44 percent of the vote.

In the runoff, state Public Service Commissioner Lynn Greer tried to paint Cramer as an upscale city slicker and liberal "national Democrat." "He's the country club crowd, and I'm just country," said Greer, before being trounced 3 to 2 by Cramer.

In the fall campaign, Cramer had the added advantage of being a Democrat in a district that had not elected a Republican this century. His GOP opponent was Albert McDonald, the state commissioner of agriculture and industries who had switched parties earlier in the year. But without the GOP making the race a high priority, McDonald was slow to raise money and could not find an issue that would woo voters from their historic Democratic bias.

Like Greer, McDonald sought to court support outside Huntsville with a "just folks" manner that contrasted with Cramer's more urbane deportment. He tried to portray Cramer as a liberal by focusing on the abortion issue. But Cramer mollified many anti-abortion voters by explaining his pro-abortion rights position in terms of his personal experience. As his late wife battled cancer several years ago, she needed an abortion to prolong her life.

In any case, voters in the 5th have usually been less concerned with ideology than with the flow of federal dollars into the district. Huntsville is heavily dependent on space and defense spending and the rest of the district on the Tennessee Valley Authority.

Both Flippo and his predecessor, Robert E. Jones, who rose to the chairmanship of the Public Works Committee, were consensus-seeking politicians who worked to keep the federal financial pipeline open. Cramer convinced voters that he was a dynamic innovator in Jones' mold, who would work to extend economic prosperity from the bustling Huntsville area to outlying counties in northern Alabama's Tennessee River Valley. He got an early start on this agenda. On his arrival in Congress he was named not only to Public Works but also to the Science, Space and Technology Committee.

Cramer was elected with more than two of every three votes and swept every county in the district. His percentage was even higher than what Flippo drew in 1988 when he ran against McDonald's, son, Stan.

In the process, Cramer becomes the district's first representative from Huntsville since Democrat John J. Sparkman held the seat from 1937 to 1946, when he was elected to the Senate.

Alabama 5

North — Huntsville

The Tennessee River runs through all seven counties of this district at the northern end of the state. Nearly half a century of resource development by the Tennessee Valley Authority (TVA) has contributed to the prosperity of this region, and the federal government is the largest employer.

With large federal installations in Huntsville and active labor unions in the metals, automobile and chemical plants along the Tennessee River, the 5th has more national Democratic sympathies than most other parts of Alabama. Because of the small black population (14 percent), race has rarely been a polarizing issue. In 1980 Jimmy Carter won 54 percent here, his best mark in the state. Even in 1988, as Michael S. Dukakis was being trounced statewide, he managed to carry three of the district's seven counties.

Huntsville, the seat of Madison County, was the only part of the district to side with Reagan against Carter in 1980, and that was by a very slim margin. But the GOP has picked up strength as Madison County's population has grown by nearly 20 percent since then. In 1986, Madison voted solidly Republican in the Senate and gubernatorial elections, and in 1988, the county went for George Bush by better than 2-to-1.

With just under 160,000 people, Huntsville is the state's fourth-largest city and has a predominantly white-collar work force. It went from cotton town to boom town during World War II when the Army, largely through the efforts of Sen. John J. Sparkman, a Huntsville native, built the Redstone Arsenal there to produce chemical-warfare matériel. After the Soviet Union launched Sputnik in October 1957, Wernher von Braun headed the Marshall Space Flight Center in Huntsville to perform the principal research for the fledgling National Aeronautics and Space Administration.

Companies that built plants in Huntsville — Boeing, International Business Machines and General Electric among them — stayed and diversified when the high-tech government contracts dwindled. Other industries moved in, including Dunlop and PPG.

As one moves downstream along the Tennessee River, blue-collar jobs begin to predominate. Towns such as Decatur, a chemical manufacturing center, and the Quad Cities of Florence, Sheffield, Tuscumbia and Muscle Shoals came into being as a result of the TVA. The Shoals area has been hurt by losses in its industrial base over the past decade, but unemployment rates dropped in the late 1980s to about 7 percent, down from 22 percent earlier in the decade. Muscle Shoals was originally selected as TVA headquarters; the site was later changed to Knoxville, Tenn.

The TVA has two huge nuclear complexes in the 5th — Browns Ferry at Decatur and Bellefonte at Scottsboro — but activity at both sites has been stalled by ongoing problems in the agency's nuclear energy program. Browns Ferry generated power from 1973 through 1985, when the reactors were shut down to correct safety deficiencies. One reactor is expected to become operational by the mid-1990s. Construction of the Bellefonte reactors has been indefinitely delayed.

Population: 549,844. White 466,851 (85%), Black 78,639 (14%), Other 2,901 (1%). Spanish origin 4,270 (1%). 18 and over 385,388 (70%), 65 and over 51,538 (9%). Median age: 29.

Committees

Public Works & Transportation (31st of 36 Democrats)
Economic Development; Surface Transportation; Water Resources

Science, Space & Technology (28th of 32 Democrats)
Energy; Space

Select Children, Youth & Families (22nd of 22 Democrats)

Campaign Finance

	Receipts	Receipts from PACs		Expend-itures
1990				
Cramer (D)	$662,457	$246,932	(37%)	$638,361
McDonald (R)	$184,089	$27,200	(15%)	$184,188

Key Vote

1991

Authorize use of force against Iraq	Y

Elections

1990 General		
Bud Cramer (D)	113,047	(67%)
Albert McDonald (R)	55,326	(33%)
1990 Primary Runoff		
Bud Cramer (D)	47,355	(60%)
Lynn Greer (D)	30,978	(40%)
1990 Primary		
Bud Cramer (D)	47,666	(44%)
Lynn Greer (D)	20,346	(19%)
Evelyn Pratt (D)	17,029	(16%)
Eddie Frost (D)	12,354	(11%)
Garland D. Terry (D)	8,659	(8%)

District Vote For President

	1988	1984	1980	1976
D	77,172 (40%)	80,039 (40%)	96,169 (54%)	106,191 (67%)
R	111,763 (59%)	119,034 (59%)	72,831 (41%)	50,039 (32%)
I			3,746 (2%)	

6 Ben Erdreich (D)

Of Birmingham — Elected 1982

Born: Dec. 9, 1938, Birmingham, Ala.
Education: Yale U., B.A. 1960; U. of Alabama, J.D. 1963.
Military Service: Army, 1963-65.
Occupation: Lawyer.
Family: Wife, Ellen Cooper; two children.
Religion: Jewish.
Political Career: Ala. House, 1971-75; Jefferson County Commission, 1975-83; Democratic nominee for U.S. House, 1972.
Capitol Office: 439 Cannon Bldg. 20515; 225-4921.

In Washington: As a junior member of the House, Erdreich was expected to follow the unwritten rules of the Alabama delegation: Vote a relatively conservative line, work behind the scenes and wait your turn for a position of influence. But Erdreich compiled a relatively moderate voting record and still wound up with such a position — a Banking subcommittee chairmanship — a bit ahead of schedule.

At the start of the 101st Congress, Erdreich became acting chairman of the new Policy Research and Insurance Subcommittee, with its mandate to review problem issues in banking, finance, housing and insurance.

Erdreich was not the senior Democrat on the panel. But Robert Garcia of New York — who had chaired one of the international subcommittees but lost out to a more senior member after the merger — was barred from serving as chairman because of his indictment in the Wedtech bribery case. The next two in line respectively opted to chair another panel's subcommittee and won a seat on the Budget Committee. The chairmanship thus fell to Erdreich. Garcia was convicted in October 1989 and resigned in January 1990; Erdreich remains at the helm of the panel.

Erdreich had served on Banking since his arrival in Congress. But the low-key Democrat had mainly stayed in the background during contentious committee debates on such issues as the savings and loan crisis and housing aid.

Erdreich also rarely grabs headlines back home unless in connection with a district-oriented issue. His most visible crusade in the 101st Congress centered on granting states more authority over imports of hazardous waste. Erdreich sought to give authority for Alabama to ban waste imports at a chemical landfill at Emelle, Ala., the nation's largest hazardous waste treatment facility. President Bush signed the measure into law in 1990.

During the 100th Congress, Erdreich pushed through funding to plan the Northern Beltline, a highway in suburban Birmingham.

Erdreich takes account of his large black constituency and the blue-collar workers in the district's steel industry. During the 101st Congress, he voted for controversial civil rights legislation that Bush and other opponents said would impose racial hiring quotas. In the 101st Congress, he sponsored legislation, signed into law in 1990, creating three regional metal casting technology centers.

This balance is reflected in ratings Erdreich receives from interest groups, often notching the most "liberal" ratings in the Alabama delegation from the Americans for Democratic Action — but also scores in the 50s and 60s from the American Conservative Union.

At Home: Beaten badly in his first House campaign in 1972, Erdreich waited a decade before trying again. But he chose the right moment. His victory over GOP Rep. Albert Lee Smith Jr. gave Democrats the Birmingham House seat for the first time in two decades.

A Birmingham native and a labor lawyer, Erdreich in 1972 challenged entrenched GOP Rep. John H. Buchanan Jr. after only two years in the state House. But Erdreich was thwarted by Buchanan's ability to win over Democrats with his moderate record.

When he launched his second House bid in 1982, Erdreich confronted a GOP incumbent quite unlike Buchanan. The very conservative Smith had ousted Buchanan in a 1980 primary, then barely won the general election. With Birmingham suffering from 15 percent unemployment in the fall of 1982, Erdreich charged that Reagan policies were leading to a depression. With black and labor support, he won by 12,000 votes.

In 1984, GOP leaders persuaded longtime Democratic state legislator J. T. "Jabo" Waggoner to switch parties and run. But Waggoner relied on robotlike Reagan loyalty to cover ineffective local efforts. Erdreich, who had locked up the votes of blacks, labor and the business community, won with enough ease to discourage tough GOP opposition since then.

Alabama 6

Birmingham and Suburbs

The steel industry remains the symbol of Birmingham — atop Red Mountain, overlooking the city, is a statue of Vulcan, the Roman god of fire hammering on an anvil. But the symbol is becoming misleading. The city's largest employer is the local branch of the University of Alabama (14,000 students, 1,700 faculty), one of the few college campuses that sprang from a medical school, rather than the other way around. The university has attracted medical and other research facilities, and Birmingham is beginning to depend on its reputation as a health center to move beyond its image as a declining steel town.

By far Alabama's largest city, with more than 266,000 people, Birmingham is 63 percent black. It has an early 20th-century industrial flavor that newer, white-collar Southern cities such as Atlanta lack. It also has problems of urban decay more often associated with the North, and accentuated by the 1980s recession. Birmingham always votes Democratic and has had a black mayor since 1979. But it casts little more than half the 6th District vote; candidates must pull suburban support to win.

The suburbs of the 6th are diverse. South of Red Mountain, which forms the southern edge of the city, are Mountain Brook, Homewood and Hoover, well-to-do bedroom communities that vote Republican. The areas to the north and east, home to conservative, middle-class professionals, are politically volatile — generally Republican, but not to be taken for granted.

Immediately southwest of Birmingham is the Democratic area called the Bessemer Cutoff. The district boundary stops just short of the largely black, labor-oriented steel town of Bessemer, but encloses six other blue-collar Democratic communities.

Population: 554,156. White 360,904 (65%), Black 190,417 (34%). Spanish origin 3,714 (1%). 18 and over 404,782 (73%), 65 and over 67,231 (12%). Median age: 30.

Committees

Banking, Finance & Urban Affairs (11th of 31 Democrats)
Consumer Affairs & Coinage; Housing & Community Development; Policy Research & Insurance ((chairman))

Government Operations (14th of 25 Democrats)
Commerce, Consumer & Monetary Affairs; Environment, Energy & Natural Resources

Select Aging (17th of 42 Democrats)
Health & Long-Term Care

Elections

1990 General		
Ben Erdreich (D)	134,412	(93%)
David A. Alvarez (I)	8,640	(6%)
Nathaniel Ivory (I)	1,745	(1%)
1988 General		
Ben Erdreich (D)	138,920	(66%)
Charles Caddis (R)	68,788	(33%)

Previous Winning Percentages: **1986** (73%) **1984** (60%) **1982** (53%)

District Vote For President

	1988		1984		1980		1976	
D	90,778	(42%)	88,340	(41%)	95,144	(44%)	83,381	(46%)
R	121,663	(57%)	125,716	(59%)	111,373	(51%)	96,737	(53%)

Campaign Finance

	Receipts	Receipts from PACs		Expend-itures
1990				
Erdreich (D)	$237,722	$172,819	(73%)	$113,168
1988				
Erdreich (D)	$251,841	$173,850	(69%)	$159,323
Caddis (R)	$8,604	0		$8,604

Key Votes

1991	
Authorize use of force against Iraq	Y
1990	
Support constitutional amendment on flag desecration	Y
Pass family and medical leave bill over Bush veto	Y
Reduce SDI funding	N
Allow abortions in overseas military facilities	Y
Approve budget summit plan for spending and taxing	Y
Approve civil rights bill	Y
1989	
Halt production of B-2 stealth bomber at 13 planes	N
Oppose capital gains tax cut	N
Approve federal abortion funding in rape or incest cases	Y
Approve pay raise and revision of ethics rules	N
Pass Democratic minimum wage plan over Bush veto	Y

Voting Studies

	Presidential Support		Party Unity		Conservative Coalition	
Year	**S**	**O**	**S**	**O**	**S**	**O**
1990	37	63	73	27	83	17
1989	49	50	71	29	85	15
1988	38	62	70	30	84	16
1987	40	60	66	33	91	9
1986	40	59	67	29	82	16
1985	52	48	68	28	76	22
1984	50	45	52	41	81	10
1983	37	63	56	40	78	21

Interest Group Ratings

Year	ADA	ACU	AFL-CIO	CCUS
1990	39	54	75	36
1989	55	46	67	50
1988	50	60	79	64
1987	40	30	63	53
1986	55	52	92	50
1985	35	52	59	45
1984	25	57	69	47
1983	50	52	76	40

7 Claude Harris (D)

Of Tuscaloosa — Elected 1986

Born: June 29, 1940, Bessemer, Ala.
Education: U. of Alabama, B.S. 1962, LL.B. 1965.
Military Service: Army National Guard, 1967-present.
Occupation: Judge; lawyer.
Family: Wife, Barbara Cork; two children.
Religion: Baptist.
Political Career: Ala. circuit judge, 1977-85.
Capitol Office: 1009 Longworth Bldg. 20515; 225-2665.

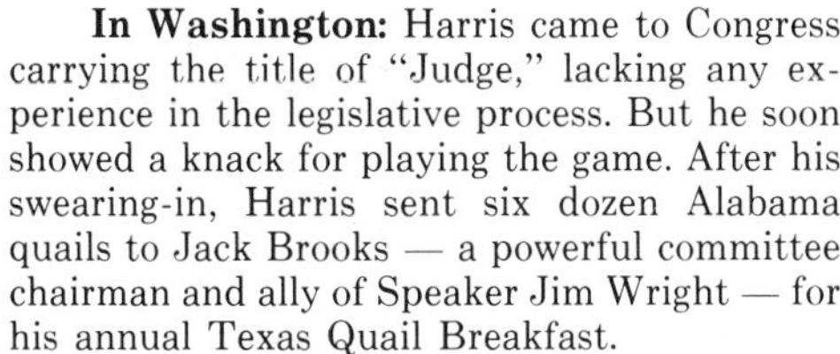

In Washington: Harris came to Congress carrying the title of "Judge," lacking any experience in the legislative process. But he soon showed a knack for playing the game. After his swearing-in, Harris sent six dozen Alabama quails to Jack Brooks — a powerful committee chairman and ally of Speaker Jim Wright — for his annual Texas Quail Breakfast.

It is with such personal gestures that Harris stays on good terms with the party leadership, even though he bucks their wishes on some key votes. In the 101st Congress, for instance, Harris opposed Democratic efforts to kill a capital gains tax cut, he voted for a constitutional amendment banning flag desecration and he opposed overriding President Bush's veto of the family and medical leave bill.

These apostasies, however, did not hurt Harris when party leaders were looking for a Southerner to fill an Energy and Commerce slot at the start of the 102nd Congress: He got a seat on the coveted panel.

Harris first ran for Congress as a business-oriented conservative Democrat. Like his predecessor, Richard C. Shelby, Harris regularly sides with home-state sentiments over the party's national thinking. But while Shelby had stormy relations with blacks and labor, Harris has sought a rapprochement with them.

In 1991, for example, he voted against giving Bush more flexibility in negotiating trade agreements with Mexico and other countries. The so-called fast-track bill — which labor warned would cost American jobs — passed anyway.

In the 100th Congress, the omnibus trade bill offered Harris another vehicle to meet labor partway. Backed by unions, the bill also appealed to local steel and textile industries hurting from foreign competition. In a rare floor speech, Harris used a box of candy canes produced in a communist country to illustrate the U.S. trade deficit problem. Harris supported the labor-backed Gephardt amendment, which mandated tariffs against countries with unfair trade practices, and he voted to override President Ronald Reagan's veto of the trade bill.

In 1990, Harris joined with the GOP leadership in opposing a provision in the omnibus crime bill that would have revamped the standards for death row prisoners appealing their cases to federal court. Harris warned that it would spur repetitive petitions.

At Home: Harris' efforts to reach out to labor and blacks helped broaden the conservative, business-oriented base established by Shelby. He has twice won re-election handily.

His initial campaign was a little more challenging. Harris began his 1986 race with a strong base in Tuscaloosa, where he had served more than two decades as a county assistant district attorney and then a state circuit judge. But he faced a potent primary rival in Shelby County District Attorney Billy Hill, whose roots were in populous suburban Birmingham.

Hill got a jump on Harris with an early series of TV ads, but he ran low on campaign funds just as Harris was gaining strength. Harris edged Hill in the primary, and his momentum continued to build in the runoff. Harris also was backed by the New South Coalition, a heavily black organization headed by Birmingham Mayor Richard Arrington. Harris' advantage in the predominantly black counties in the southern part of the 7th helped him win the nomination with 61 percent.

In the general election — usually a formality for local Democrats — Harris faced Republican Bill McFarland. A real estate developer and recent party-switcher, he was the GOP's most credible candidate in years. Harris was threatened by a schism in the state Democratic Party; it had awarded its disputed gubernatorial nomination to populist Lt. Gov. William J. Baxley over state Attorney General Charles Graddick, spurring a conservative Democratic revolt.

But while the backlash elected Republican Guy Hunt governor, it had little effect on the House contest. Harris was aided by Shelby's presence on the Senate ballot, and he also campaigned ably. He touted his support for the Nicaraguan contras, talked about his love for hunting, took time out to meet his National Guard duties and won by 20 percentage points.

Alabama 7

West Central — Tuscaloosa; Bessemer

The 7th moves southward from the outskirts of Birmingham, past the small industrial city of Bessemer and the college town of Tuscaloosa into the heart of the Alabama Black Belt, one of the poorest areas in the nation.

While the term Black Belt is said to refer not to the racial composition but to the rich, sticky cotton-growing soil, all but one of the eight rural counties in the Black Belt portion of the district have black majorities. These counties, which make up a quarter of the district's population, are staunchly Democratic: Even Michael S. Dukakis in 1988 neared 60 percent in many counties here.

Tuscaloosa, with 78,000 people, is the district's largest city. It has an industrial base that includes manufacturers of chemicals, fertilizer and rubber products, but it is more often identified as the home of the University of Alabama, which has 19,000 students. Tuscaloosa and Tuscaloosa County have become a swing area in Alabama politics.

Shelby and Chilton counties, closer to Birmingham and straddling I-65 on its way south to Montgomery, are growing rapidly and voting increasingly Republican.

The Jefferson County part of the 7th, mostly suburban in character, also has been leaning Republican in recent statewide contests. But there is one Democratic enclave — the city of Bessemer, blue-collar, largely black and weathering hard times in the steel industry.

Although Republicans run reasonably well through most of the district in national and statewide elections, the area has kept up its tradition of loyalty to conservative Democrats at the congressional level.

Population: 559,069. White 370,555 (66%), Black 186,384 (33%). Spanish origin 5,265 (1%). 18 and over 386,537 (69%), 65 and over 63,493 (11%). Median age: 28.

Committees

Energy & Commerce (27th of 27 Democrats)
Energy & Power; Telecommunications & Finance

Veterans' Affairs (9th of 21 Democrats)
Hospitals & Health Care; Housing & Memorial Affairs

Elections

1990 General		
Claude Harris (D)	127,490	(71%)
Michael D. Barker (R)	53,258	(29%)
1988 General		
Claude Harris (D)	136,074	(68%)
James E. "Jim" Bacon (R)	63,372	(32%)

Previous Winning Percentage: **1986** (60%)

District Vote For President

	1988	1984	1980	1976
D	84,638 (41%)	85,248 (40%)	92,384 (48%)	88,502 (55%)
R	123,074 (59%)	124,226 (59%)	91,267 (48%)	70,693 (44%)

Campaign Finance

	Receipts	Receipts from PACs		Expend-itures
1990				
Harris (D)	$237,577	$151,307	(64%)	$238,466
Barker (R)	$59,802	0		$58,952
1988				
Harris (D)	$405,426	$257,205	(63%)	$328,296
Bacon (R)	$9,842	0		$8,737

Key Votes

1991	
Authorize use of force against Iraq	Y
1990	
Support constitutional amendment on flag desecration	Y
Pass family and medical leave bill over Bush veto	N
Reduce SDI funding	N
Allow abortions in overseas military facilities	N
Approve budget summit plan for spending and taxing	N
Approve civil rights bill	Y
1989	
Halt production of B-2 stealth bomber at 13 planes	N
Oppose capital gains tax cut	N
Approve federal abortion funding in rape or incest cases	Y
Approve pay raise and revision of ethics rules	N
Pass Democratic minimum wage plan over Bush veto	Y

Voting Studies

	Presidential Support		Party Unity		Conservative Coalition	
Year	**S**	**O**	**S**	**O**	**S**	**O**
1990	39	59	73	26	93	7
1989	52	48	71	29	85	15
1988	39	60	68	32	87	13
1987	44	54	60	34	86	12

Interest Group Ratings

Year	ADA	ACU	AFL-CIO	CCUS
1990	33	58	50	57
1989	55	50	58	60
1988	40	68	79	64
1987	40	45	81	60

Alaska

U.S. CONGRESS

SENATE 2 R
HOUSE 1 R

LEGISLATURE

Senate 10 D, 10 R
House 24 D, 16 R

ELECTIONS

1988 Presidential Vote	
Bush	60%
Dukakis	36%
1984 Presidential Vote	
Reagan	67%
Mondale	30%
1980 Presidential Vote	
Reagan	54%
Carter	26%
Anderson	7%
Turnout rate in 1986	48%
Turnout rate in 1988	52%
Turnout rate in 1990	53%

(as percentage of voting age population)

POPULATION AND GROWTH

1980 population	401,851
1990 population (49th in the nation)	550,043
Percent change 1980-1990	+37%

DEMOGRAPHIC BREAKDOWN

White	76%
Black	4%
American Indian, Eskimo or Aleut	16%
(Hispanic origin)	3%
Urban	64%
Rural	36%
Born in state	32%
Foreign-born	4%

MAJOR CITIES

Anchorage	226,338
Fairbanks	30,843
Juneau	26,751
Sitka	8,588
Ketchikan	8,263

AREA AND LAND USE

Area	570,833 sq. miles (1st)
Farm	0.4%
Forest	36%
Federally owned	87%

Gov. Walter J. Hickel (I)
Of Anchorage — Elected 1990
(also served 1967-69)

Born: Aug. 18, 1919, Claflin, Kan.
Education: Graduated from Claflin H.S., 1936.
Occupation: Construction executive.
Religion: Roman Catholic.
Political Career: U.S. secretary of the interior, 1969-70; sought GOP nomination for governor, 1974.
Next Election: 1994.

WORK

Occupations	
White-collar	60%
Blue-collar	24%
Service workers	14%
Government Workers	
Federal	14,549
State	24,719
Local	24,502

MONEY

Median family income	$ 28,395	(1st)
Tax burden per capita	$ 3,620	(1st)

EDUCATION

Spending per pupil through grade 12	$ 7,971	(1st)
Persons with college degrees	21%	(2nd)

CRIME

Violent crime rate	498 per 100,000 (23rd)

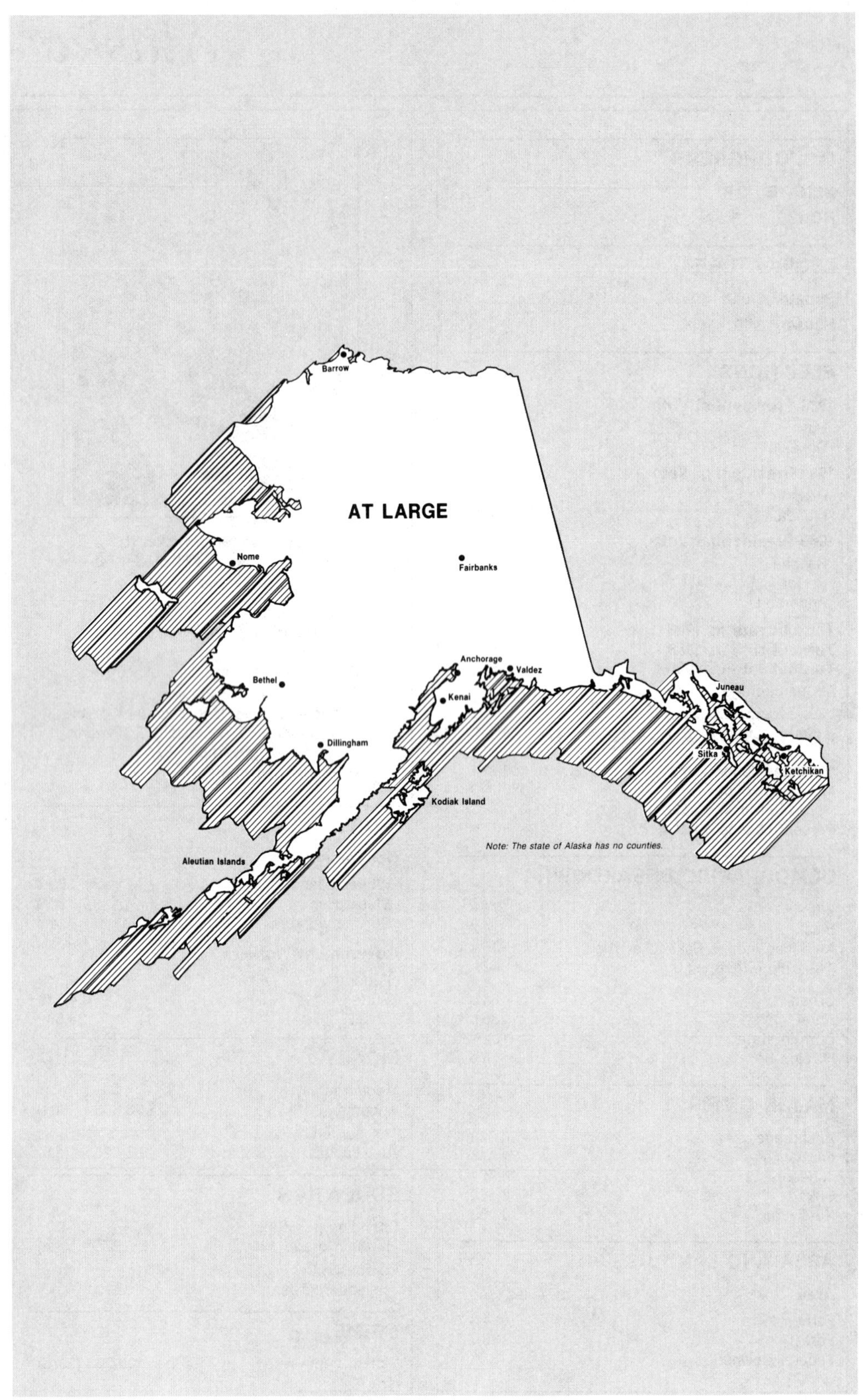
Barrow
AT LARGE
Nome
Fairbanks
Anchorage
Valdez
Bethel
Kenai
Juneau
Dillingham
Sitka
Ketchikan
Kodiak Island
Note: The state of Alaska has no counties.
Aleutian Islands

Ted Stevens (R)

Of Girdwood — Elected 1970

Appointed to the Senate 1968

Born: Nov. 18, 1923, Indianapolis, Ind.

Education: U. of California, Los Angeles, B.A. 1947; Harvard U., LL.B. 1950.

Military Service: Army Air Corps, 1943-46.

Occupation: Lawyer.

Family: Wife, Catherine Chandler; six children.

Religion: Episcopalian.

Political Career: Alaska House, 1965-68, majority leader and Speaker pro tempore, 1967-68; GOP nominee for U.S. Senate, 1962; sought GOP nomination for U.S. Senate, 1968.

Capitol Office: 522 Hart Bldg. 20510; 224-3004.

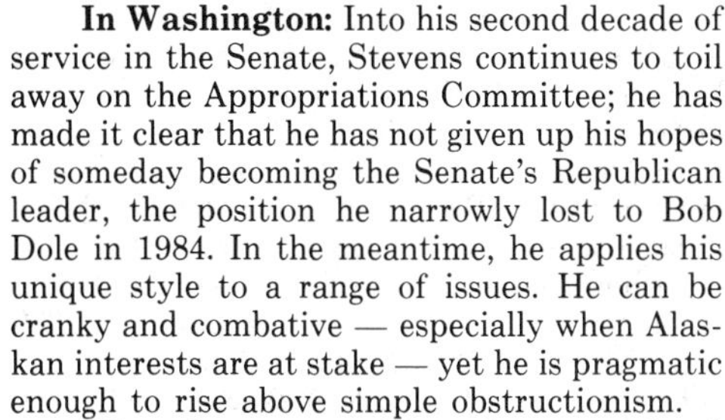

In Washington: Into his second decade of service in the Senate, Stevens continues to toil away on the Appropriations Committee; he has made it clear that he has not given up his hopes of someday becoming the Senate's Republican leader, the position he narrowly lost to Bob Dole in 1984. In the meantime, he applies his unique style to a range of issues. He can be cranky and combative — especially when Alaskan interests are at stake — yet he is pragmatic enough to rise above simple obstructionism.

When Stevens participated in a weekend retreat in March 1990 where GOP senators plotted strategy on campaign-finance legislation, his comment on the issue in many ways summed up his approach as a leader. "We need to stand on the positive side rather than just be against what the Democrats do," he said.

The intensity that Stevens displayed during eight years as assistant Republican leader, acting as the enforcer of party discipline and defender of congressional perquisites until 1985, has been focused since then on enhancing the power of the Defense Appropriations Subcommittee and, as always, on protecting Alaska against what he views as legislative intruders from the Lower 48.

A large number of environment-related issues dominated the agenda of Alaska lawmakers during the 101st Congress, especially in the wake of the oil spill of the tanker *Exxon Valdez* in Prince William Sound in March 1989 and the crisis and war in the Persian Gulf into 1991.

Stevens and his Alaska colleagues in Congress have fought for legislation to open portions of the vast Arctic National Wildlife Refuge (ANWR) to the oil industry. However, that uphill fight was shelved at least for the 101st Congress, in the wake of the *Valdez* oil spill. Stevens has renewed his calls to open ANWR to drilling, though in early 1991 he said he might oppose the measure unless the state and federal government could settle a multibillion-dollar disagreement over how to share revenues derived from the refuge. Current law gives Alaska 90 percent of the revenues and the federal government 10 percent; the Bush administration and Congress preferred a 50-50 split.

Stevens also played a role during congressional passage of oil-spill liability and cleanup legislation in the wake of the *Valdez* incident. He specifically backed some Alaska-related provisions, including the authorization of the Prince William Sound Oil Spill Recovery Institute at Cordova. He fought a provision in the measure, however, requiring congressional approval of the disbursement of funds from the $1 billion compensation fund. "An oil spill is like a fire," said Stevens, in opposing the time-consuming procedure. "Once it occurs, money has to be made available immediately."

In 1990, Stevens and fellow Alaska Republican Frank H. Murkowski were forced to accept a compromise in their efforts to prevent the end of an arrangement that guaranteed a steady supply of cheap timber from the 16.7 million-acre Tongass National Forest for mills in southeastern Alaska. Apparently more relieved than angered when the long battle — resulting in protection of over 1 million acres — was finally over, Stevens said, "After 19 years, we deserve a little peace."

On the controversial issue of forcing automakers to boost the fuel efficiency of passenger vehicles, Stevens brought the Alaska angle to the debate. After opposing the legislation in 1990, Stevens got bill sponsor Democrat Richard H. Bryan of Nevada to agree to an amendment that could relax fuel standards for four-wheel-drive vehicles — common on Alaska's rugged terrain. With the addition, Stevens voted for the bill.

Ever sensitive about the federal government trampling over the rights of less populous states such as Alaska, Stevens can strike a defensive pose. Of a 1989 federal measure mandating easier voter registration in the states, Stevens said, "It will become a sad day for small states if this bill becomes enacted. It runs roughshod and totally ignores the pleas of those administering these laws today." The measure ultimately stalled.

As subcommittee chairman in the 99th Congress and as ranking Republican on Defense Appropriations now, Stevens has been determined to establish the panel as an independent voice on military programs, rather than merely a bursar for the programs authorized by the Armed Services Committee. In doing so, he has faced opposition both from Armed Services and from the subcommittee's traditionally more powerful House counterpart.

He has been a loyal supporter of increases in military spending, and fought to defend high funding levels for the strategic defense initiative (SDI). In the 100th Congress, he opposed efforts to bar tests in space of any SDI weapons, which Democrats alleged would violate the 1972 U.S.-Soviet ABM treaty. Stevens also was one of the most aggressive proponents of the U.S.-Soviet intermediate-range nuclear-force (INF) treaty, helping the administration and Senate Democratic leaders thwart the small band of conservative opponents. As budget deficits climbed, Stevens has been a leader in promoting burden-sharing, which would require U.S. allies to pay more of NATO's defense costs.

Stevens was a prime Senate proponent of and point man for Reagan's policies toward Central America, both to defeat guerrillas in El Salvador and to assist the contras in overthrowing the leftist government of Nicaragua. By his prominence in key defense and foreign policy questions, Stevens previews for his party colleagues the sort of hard-charging floor leader he would make.

The same could be said of his high profile in the 100th Congress during Republicans' successful filibuster of a bill limiting campaign funds and introducing a system of public financing. He derided the bill as an "entitlement program for candidates for the Congress," and said, "I believe that the American taxpayer is not interested in putting up $95 [million] to $100 million to finance the campaigns of senators." He continued the fight in the 102nd Congress, succinctly summarizing the issue's main sticking point. "Our side of the aisle just cannot accept paying for campaigns out of the Treasury," said Stevens.

Stevens' near-miss at the majority leadership in December 1984 was one of the biggest surprises in recent Senate politics. Despite his long tenure as chief lieutenant to Majority Leader Howard H. Baker Jr., Stevens was considered by almost everyone as a sure loser in his bid to move up after Baker's retirement. Yet he outpolled three other contenders, losing to Dole on the final ballot by only three votes, 28-25.

That narrow defeat reflected the widespread ambivalence about Stevens. He is easily enraged and often confrontational. Yet many Republicans felt his militance might be needed to restore order to a Senate that had fallen into disarray under Baker's amiable stewardship. Moreover, they could forgive a lot in a man known as "Mr. Perk," who fought so unabashedly and tenaciously for the benefits they wanted but were afraid to pursue openly.

But in the end, Stevens could not overcome the simple fact that too many colleagues consider him a very difficult person to work with. Nevertheless, he seemed to take encouragement from the closeness of the outcome. Early on, he freely acknowledged he would seek the seat again if Dole gave it up.

From his first week in the chamber in 1969, when he tangled with Democrats over President Nixon's nomination of Alaska Gov. Walter J. Hickel as interior secretary, colleagues have known that debate with Stevens can quickly degenerate into a shouting match.

But for all his pugnacity, Stevens generally is not one to simmer and harbor grudges. His temper typically flares and just as quickly disappears. A moderate by GOP ideological standards, Stevens can deal effectively with Democrats as well as Republicans. He gets along fine in the collegial, horse-trading culture of Appropriations, where success can be measured by his catch for Alaska; an Anchorage paper in 1989 called Stevens "the six-billion-dollar man," estimating he has been worth at least that much to the state in federal largess.

Members in both parties appreciate his work for increased congressional salaries and benefits. While most members scurry for cover when the subject of pay raises comes up, Stevens brashly proclaims that Congress is underpaid.

Over his years as whip, Stevens pushed a variety of schemes to make congressional life more rewarding. The list of measures passed includes pay raises, a tax break for members' Washington, D.C., living expenses, expanded free mailing privileges, an end to limits on senators' outside income and an increased allowance for honoraria.

During the 101st Congress, Stevens fought to preserve mass mailings, defending them as an essential tool for members whose rural constituencies lack access to sophisticated media outlets. He worked out a proposal with Kentucky Democrat Wendell H. Ford to provide a 50 percent increase in the Senate's mail budget in fiscal 1991. Before final passage of the appropriations bill, the Senate adopted an amendment to reduce the amount included for Senate mail from the $35.5 million recommended by the Appropriations Committee to $30 million. Amendment sponsors initially sought a deeper cut — to $24 million — but compromised in the face of vigorous objections from Stevens.

His unflagging support for federal workers, an important constituency in Alaska, has made Stevens popular with public employee unions.

In fact, he is one of the few Senate Republicans to draw sizable campaign help from organized labor. As chairman of the Civil Service, Post Office and General Services Subcommittee at Governmental Affairs until 1987, he was ideally positioned to look out for federal workers.

He was once a federal employee himself, in the top ranks of the Interior Department in the 1950s, and he fights regularly against caps on federal pay raises, arguing that government workers should not have to suffer from inflation.

In 1990, Stevens was one of just 10 Republicans in the Senate who voted to override President Bush's veto of a measure to revise the Hatch Act, which prohibits federal employees from engaging in political activities. The override effort fell two votes short.

On the Commerce Committee, where he has served throughout his Senate career, Stevens mostly gets involved in shipping issues; while Republicans controlled the chamber, he was chairman of the Merchant Marine Subcommittee. He was a key player in the 98th Congress' approval of the first major changes in shipping law in 20 years. The legislation, strongly opposed by consumer groups, expanded the ocean-liner industry's antitrust immunity for setting prices and dividing routes.

In the late 1970s, one issue — Alaska lands legislation — dominated Stevens' agenda. He fought aggressively to open more state land for development, opposing those who stressed environmental protection and sought new parks.

During those years, Stevens was thoroughly alienated from his fellow Alaskan, Democratic Sen. Mike Gravel. The Stevens-Gravel feud was largely a question of style and tactics. Both wanted to keep the government from barring development in much of Alaska, but they disagreed vehemently on how to do so. Stevens felt the legislation was inevitable and wanted to make it as acceptable to Alaska as he could; Gravel sought to block it through filibusters and similar dilatory tactics, fighting with a showmanship Stevens and many others regarded as pure demagoguery.

"It's hard to do anything about Alaska with Mike Gravel in the Senate," he once complained. In 1980 he took the unusual step of backing Gravel's Democratic primary opponent, who defeated Gravel but then lost that fall to Murkowski. In contrast, Stevens works closely with Murkowski and Republican Don Young, Alaska's House member.

At Home: Stevens' careful defense of Alaska interests has made him invulnerable at the polls. Although he has not had his way on every issue, he always seems to have the right political approach — stubborn but pragmatic.

However, not everyone in Alaska is a Stevens fan. There are those who say his long years in the Senate have made him a remote figure to the average Alaskan and part of the "Washington crowd." Despite his record as a GOP loyalist, Stevens' focus on the economy and defense policy and lack of zeal on social issues has alienated some of the staunch conservatives — including a number of religious fundamentalists — who dominate the Alaska Republican Party. This mild dissent explains the sound but relatively modest victory margins run up by the heavily favored Stevens in the 1990 primary and general elections.

Stevens, who had been majority leader in the Alaska House, got to Washington by appointment when Democratic Sen. E. L. Bartlett died in 1968. He owed his promotion to Walter J. Hickel, then the state's GOP governor. Only months before, Stevens had failed to win the Senate GOP primary. Six years earlier, he had been nominated and drew only 41 percent of the vote.

Once in Washington, however, Stevens began digging in politically. In the 1970 contest to fill the final two years of Bartlett's term, he won with almost 60 percent while the GOP was losing the governorship. In that campaign, against liberal Democrat Wendell P. Kay, Stevens favored greater oil and mineral development; Kay was a firm conservationist.

Seeking a full term in 1972, Stevens crushed Democrat Gene Guess, the state House Speaker, whom he linked to presidential nominee George McGovern. Stevens also appealed to Alaska's hunters by calling Guess pro-gun control.

By 1978 Stevens had been elected to the Senate Republican leadership and no prominent Democrat even considered a serious campaign against him. An electrical contractor and an economics professor fought for the Democratic nomination. The contractor, Donald W. Hobbs, got it, but received less than a quarter of the vote against Stevens.

Though he had little difficulty beating Democrats, Stevens received a rebuke in 1980 from conservative elements in the Alaska GOP. Viewing Stevens as something of a moderate, the conservatives denied him the chairmanship of the Alaska delegation to the 1980 Republican National Convention. However, his strongly pro-Reagan voting record appeared to placate the opposition by 1984, when he was named delegation chairman.

In that same year, Stevens again coasted to re-election. John E. Havelock, a lawyer who served as the state's attorney general in the early 1970s, tried to convince voters that the incumbent was more interested in pursuing his own Senate ambitions than in Alaskan affairs. But Stevens paid his challenger little heed. Armed with a massive campaign treasury, he spent much of the time stumping for other GOP senators in pursuit of his party's Senate leader post. He crushed Havelock with 71 percent of the vote.

Stevens' electoral strength daunted prominent Democrats, who took a pass on the 1990 Senate campaign. But the fact that he was practically unchallenged did not stop the minority of Alaskans who had a gripe with Stevens from voting for his obscure challengers. In the primary, Robert M. Bird, a teacher and anti-abortion activist, took 30 percent of the Republican vote against Stevens.

In the general election, Stevens faced Democrat Michael Beasley. A political gadfly, Beasley had run in Democratic statewide primaries several times and never received more than 4 percent of the vote. But in 1990, he filed and won almost by default: His only primary opponent was an advocate of Alaskan secession from the United States.

Beasley rarely surfaced during the campaign and took some extreme positions when he did: At one point, he described abortion as an international plot to eradicate Americans. However, with Stevens mainly phoning in his campaign during the long congressional session, Beasley attracted some protest votes from those who were dissatisfied with Stevens or with Washington in general. Although Stevens' 66 percent tally was still impressive, his margin was down from his 1984 campaign against a more legitimate candidate.

Committees

Rules & Administration (Ranking)

Appropriations (2nd of 13 Republicans)
Commerce, Justice, State & Judiciary; Defense (ranking); Interior; Labor, Health & Human Services, Education; Military Construction

Commerce, Science & Transportation (4th of 9 Republicans)
Aviation; Communications; Merchant Marine; Science, Technology & Space; National Ocean Policy Study (ranking)

Governmental Affairs (2nd of 6 Republicans)
Federal Services, Post Office & Civil Service (ranking); General Services, Federalism & the District of Columbia; Oversight of Government Management; Permanent Subcommittee on Investigations

Small Business (6th of 8 Republicans)
Export Expansion; Innovation, Technology & Productivity (ranking)

Joint Library

Joint Printing

Elections

1990 General		
Ted Stevens (R)	125,806	(66%)
Michael Beasley (D)	61,152	(32%)
1990 Primary †		
Ted Stevens (R)	81,968	(59%)
Robert M. Bird (R)	34,824	(25%)
Michael Beasley (D)	12,371	(9%)
Tom Taggart (D)	9,329	(7%)

† In Alaska's "jungle primary," candidates of all parties are listed on one ballot.

Previous Winning Percentages: **1984** (71%) **1978** (76%) **1972** (77%) **1970 *** (60%)

** Special election. Stevens was appointed in 1968 to fill the vacancy caused by the death of Sen. E. L. Bartlett. The 1970 election was to fill the remainder of Bartlett's term.*

Campaign Finance

	Receipts	Receipts from PACs	Expend-itures
1990			
Stevens (R)	$1,380,780	$751,450 (54%)	$1,273,954
Beasley (D)	$1,000	0	$1,000

Key Votes

1991	
Authorize use of force against Iraq	Y
1990	
Oppose prohibition of certain semiautomatic weapons	Y
Support constitutional amendment on flag desecration	Y
Oppose requiring parental notice for minors' abortions	Y
Halt production of B-2 stealth bomber at 13 planes	N
Approve budget that cut spending and raised revenues	Y
Pass civil rights bill over Bush veto	N
1989	
Oppose reduction of SDI funding	Y
Oppose barring federal funds for "obscene" art	N
Allow vote on capital gains tax cut	Y

Voting Studies

	Presidential Support		Party Unity		Conservative Coalition	
Year	**S**	**O**	**S**	**O**	**S**	**O**
1990	72	23	66	31	84	5
1989	87	13	73	27	87	13
1988	67	30	71	27	78	19
1987	65	26	64	27	81	19
1986	83	11	83 †	15 †	88	9
1985	75	16	71	21	90	3
1984	84	12	85	8	94	4
1983	92	5	80	17	77	16
1982	74	18	85	8	90	4
1981	76	14	81	10	79	13

† Not eligible for all recorded votes.

Interest Group Ratings

Year	ADA	ACU	AFL-CIO	CCUS
1990	33	65	67	64
1989	20	64	40	75
1988	25	64	36	69
1987	25	65	60	67
1986	15	71	33	74
1985	10	64	25	78
1984	20	67	22	76
1983	15	44	13	74
1982	15	50	35	76
1981	15	53	17	100

Frank H. Murkowski (R)

Of Fairbanks — Elected 1980

Born: March 28, 1933, Seattle, Wash.

Education: Attended U. of Santa Clara, 1951-53; Seattle U., B.A. 1955.

Military Service: Coast Guard, 1955-56.

Occupation: Banker.

Family: Wife, Nancy Gore; six children.

Religion: Roman Catholic.

Political Career: Alaska commissioner of economic development, 1966-70; Republican nominee for U.S. House, 1970.

Capitol Office: 709 Hart Bldg. 20510; 224-6665.

In Washington: Murkowski is an Alaskan Horatius at the strait, ever striving to hold off the federal government, environmentalists, South Korean fishermen or whoever else would like to tell the state how to run its business.

Although his ascension in the 102nd Congress to ranking minority member on the Intelligence Committee provides Murkowski with an opportunity to broaden his focus, it is with home-state concerns that he will likely continue to be largely preoccupied.

A dogged advocate of tapping the state's vast oil and timber reserves, Murkowski has joined colleague Ted Stevens and Rep. Don Young in seeking to open up the coastal plain of Alaska's Arctic National Wildlife Refuge (ANWR) to oil exploration. Their effort was momentarily halted after the 1989 *Exxon Valdez* oil spill in Prince William Sound, but they gained new momentum after 1990 passage of a comprehensive oil-spill bill and renewed concern about crude oil supplies caused by the Persian Gulf War.

Murkowski rages against what he calls the "radical preservation ethic" of environmentalists who, he says, seek to treat Alaska as the national park of the 49 other states. During a 1991 speech at a conference of the Wilderness Society, Murkowski argued that less than 1 percent of ANWR would be affected if restrictions were lifted. Quipped one environmental advocate: "OK, I'll take 1 percent of the Mona Lisa — the smile. Some places need to be preserved." When the audience laughed and applauded, Murkowski walked out in protest; he was disgusted with their suggestions that the state was unfairly profiting from increased oil profits caused by the gulf war.

But he managed to catch environmentalists off guard in the 101st Congress when he attached a rider to a defense authorization bill that requires the president to list high-potential oil fields if imports hit 50 percent of U.S. oil use. By joint resolution, Congress could then permit the president to proceed with drilling without regard to endangered-species or wilderness laws. But Murkowski was less successful with the ANWR-drilling bill, backing off plans to attach it to a deficit-cutting reconciliation bill when defeat appeared certain.

The issue returned in the 102nd Congress. And when President Bush renewed his call in 1991 for ANWR drilling, Murkowski's battle saw a second front open. The White House, eyeing a potential infusion for the treasury, said that all the ANWR revenue should go to the federal government. Murkowski and Alaska officials cited a state law requiring 90 percent of the revenues to be returned to the state.

In 1990, Murkowski and Stevens were also forced to accept a compromise in their effort to prevent the end of an arrangement that guaranteed a steady supply of cheap timber from the 16.7 million-acre Tongass National Forest for mills in southeastern Alaska. Both senators seemed more relieved than angered when the 19-year battle was finally over, resulting in protection of over 1 million acres. "While this legislation errs too far on the side of preservation ... we have received assurances that it should bring some finality to the Tongass issue," said Murkowski.

The ranking Republican on the Veterans' Affairs Committee, Murkowski has used his clout with the Veterans Administration in a way that might surprise politicians in the Lower 48: He continually blocks construction of a VA hospital. This is quintessential Alaskan geopolitics, a decision dictated by the state's sprawling size and sparse population. In this case, it is simply easier for veterans to visit their local doctor.

He also has shown some signs of wanting to broaden his role within the Senate: In late 1988, he mounted a late and unsuccessful bid for a leadership post, the largely honorary chair of the GOP Conference, by arguing that its occupant, John H. Chafee of Rhode Island, had opposed President Reagan too frequently.

But on at least one prominent occasion

during the 100th Congress, it was Murkowski who crossed the president. He sided with Foreign Relations Committee Democrats on a measure to delay for a year the administration's plan to re-flag Kuwaiti oil tankers in the Persian Gulf as U.S. vessels, thus affording them U.S. military protection. Murkowski wanted mothballed U.S. tankers to be used.

Expanding Alaskan trade with the Far East is perhaps his chief pursuit as ranking member on the Foreign Relations Subcommittee on East Asian and Pacific Affairs, a panel he once chaired. He regularly leads trade delegations to Pacific Rim countries, encouraging them to buy more Alaskan coal, timber and other products. Frustrated with Japan's reluctance to allow increased imports, he sponsored legislation in 1985 to impose a 20 percent surcharge on Japanese goods.

Various such attempts to force reciprocal trade culminated in the 100th Congress with legislation that Murkowski sponsored with House Democrat Jack Brooks of Texas. The Brooks-Murkowski amendment denies foreign participation in all federally funded public works projects when the foreign firm's home market is closed to U.S. construction. In 1990, he sought to address growing concerns about foreign investment in the U.S. by removing a ban on the sharing of ownership data between the Bureau of Economic Analysis and the Census Bureau.

Another barrier to Murkowski's efforts comes from this side of the Pacific: the ban on export of Alaskan crude oil. Murkowski has pushed hard for years to end that export prohibition, but with very limited success, in part because U.S. maritime interests worry that the oil might be transported in foreign ships. The same interests tried to limit the export of refined oil during the 1988 debate over an omnibus trade bill. Murkowski teamed up with Stevens to strip the measure.

The Democrats' return to control of the Senate cost Murkowski the chair of the Veterans' Affairs Committee, which he had obtained because more-senior Republicans on the panel already were busy with more powerful assignments. The panel had provided Murkowski a career milestone that may be denied indefinitely to the other Republicans who came to the Senate in 1980. He was the first of the class to chair a standing committee. Until some future day when the GOP recaptures control of the chamber, he will be the only one ever to have been a chairman.

Once chairman, Murkowski played a significant role on veterans' issues. In some cases, he worked to protect funding for veterans' programs, and as ranking member he was active in establishing the Department of Veterans Affairs. But he also has sought to hold down costs of some veterans' programs through cost-saving legislative changes. One measure aimed at cutting health-care spending on veterans by encouraging the use of low-cost alternatives, such as halfway houses and private nursing homes. A former banker, he also wrote legislation to overhaul the veterans' home-loan program in order to bring down high foreclosure rates. He initially opposed, but ultimately supported, compensation for Vietnam War veterans exposed to the chemical defoliant Agent Orange.

At Home: When Murkowski was in his first term, a survey of the Capitol Hill press corps found him to be one of the least visible members of the Senate.

But if Murkowski's low-key approach to politics prompted smirks from the press corps then, it did not leave the Democrats laughing in Alaska. By eschewing the spotlight for a quiet focus on home-state concerns, Murkowski built a reputation as a formidable political figure back home. As a result, state Democratic leaders had difficulty finding anyone of stature willing to challenge his re-election in 1986.

The candidate who finally did emerge, Alaska Pacific University President Glenn Olds, began his campaign as a political unknown. He had never even been active in Democratic politics in Alaska, let alone run for public office.

Olds did boast a distinguished résumé. A Methodist minister who had taught college philosophy, Olds served in the U.S. delegation at the United Nations from 1969-71, then assumed the presidency of Ohio's Kent State University in the aftermath of the 1970 clash between students and National Guardsmen.

Olds sought to overcome his political anonymity by arguing that Murkowski had done little to stem the then-precipitous slide of Alaska's petroleum-based economy. But if voters were angry over the oil-price slump, most did not vent their frustrations on Murkowski. The incumbent, aided by his connections to the local banking industry, amassed a substantial campaign treasury, touted his efforts to remove a ban on exports of North Slope oil — and emerged with a 10-percentage-point victory.

Except for three years in state government and one failed campaign for the House, Murkowski had spent his entire adult life in banking before he announced for the Senate in June 1980.

His status as a relative newcomer to politics hardly seemed an advantage against Democrat Clark S. Gruening, a popular two-term state legislator and grandson of the legendary Ernest Gruening, a former Alaska senator and governor. But Democratic disunity and the Reagan tide enabled Murkowski to win, and with unexpected ease.

Throughout much of the early campaign season, Murkowski's effort was obscured by the bitter Democratic primary. To win the Democratic nomination, Gruening had to get past two-term incumbent Sen. Mike Gravel. It was a matter of revenge for Gruening; Gravel had ousted Gruening's grandfather from the Senate 12 years before.

Gravel's legislative behavior helped make Gruening's primary victory possible. Battling to prevent the Senate from enacting legislation restricting development of Alaska's lands, Gravel resorted to an obstructionism so strident and obnoxious that he did his cause more harm than good. A few days before the primary, the Senate succeeded in closing debate on a Gravel filibuster against the Alaska bill, lending credence to Gruening's charges that he had lost influence in the chamber. Although forecasters had predicted a tight race, Gruening won by a comfortable margin.

Gruening also outpolled Murkowski by more than 2-to-1 in Alaska's open primary, in which all candidates appear on the same ballot regardless of party affiliation. Although Murkowski easily won the GOP nomination, the comparison seemed significant — historically, the top vote-getter in the primary almost always has gone on to win the general election.

But Murkowski kept attention focused on Gruening's record in the Legislature. Accusing him of being too liberal for the state's electorate, Murkowski claimed the Democrat had supported the legalization of marijuana. He also tied Gruening to the environmentalist Sierra Club, anathema to pro-development Alaskans. Buoyed by national Republican help and a treasury exceeding $700,000 — nearly half of which came from political action committees — Murkowski did very well in his Fairbanks base and upset Gruening in the Democrat's hometown of Anchorage, Alaska's largest city.

A Seattle native who moved to Alaska while in high school, Murkowski got his first taste of elective politics in 1970. That year he defeated a member of the John Birch Society in a Republican primary for Alaska's at-large House seat, left vacant when Rep. Howard W. Pollock sought the governorship. He lost the general election to Democratic state Sen. Nick Begich, but the experience whetted his appetite. After serving for nine years as president of the Alaska National Bank of the North, at Fairbanks, he announced for the Senate.

Committees

Select Intelligence (Vice Chairman)

Energy & Natural Resources (4th of 9 Republicans)
Energy Regulation & Conservation; Mineral Resources Development & Production; Public Lands, National Parks & Forests (ranking)

Foreign Relations (5th of 8 Republicans)
East Asian & Pacific Affairs (ranking); International Economic Policy, Trade, Oceans & Environment; Near Eastern & South Asian Affairs

Select Indian Affairs (2nd of 7 Republicans)

Veterans' Affairs (2nd of 5 Republicans)

Elections

1986 General

Frank H. Murkowski (R)	97,674	(54%)
Glenn Olds (D)	79,727	(44%)

Previous Winning Percentages: 1980 (54%)

Campaign Finance

	Receipts	Receipts from PACs		Expenditures
1986				
Murkowski (R)	$1,423,961	$587,608	(41%)	$1,387,756
Olds (D)	$412,857	$150,772	(37%)	$412,074

Key Votes

1991	
Authorize use of force against Iraq	Y
1990	
Oppose prohibition of certain semiautomatic weapons	Y
Support constitutional amendment on flag desecration	Y
Oppose requiring parental notice for minors' abortions	N
Halt production of B-2 stealth bomber at 13 planes	N
Approve budget that cut spending and raised revenues	Y
Pass civil rights bill over Bush veto	N
1989	
Oppose reduction of SDI funding	Y
Oppose barring federal funds for "obscene" art	N
Allow vote on capital gains tax cut	Y

Voting Studies

	Presidential Support		Party Unity		Conservative Coalition	
Year	**S**	**O**	**S**	**O**	**S**	**O**
1990	75	22	85	14	92	0
1989	85	10	87	11	92	3
1988	65	18	81	7	89	3
1987	62	35	76	15	84	6
1986	80	17	81	15	88	5
1985	82	11	78	14	90	2
1984	84	12	90	5	94	2
1983	69	14	73	8	80	0
1982	79	11	91	5	89	1
1981	82	11	83	11	85	9

Interest Group Ratings

Year	ADA	ACU	AFL-CIO	CCUS
1990	11	76	44	83
1989	5	81	10	75
1988	15	79	23	85
1987	5	76	40	80
1986	20	78	36	65
1985	0	82	26	84
1984	10	86	18	88
1983	0	72	6	75
1982	10	63	24	70
1981	15	79	24	93

Alaska - At Large

AL Don Young (R)

Of Fort Yukon — Elected 1973

Born: June 9, 1933, Meridian, Calif.

Education: Yuba Junior College, A.A. 1952; Chico State College, B.A. 1958.

Military Service: Army, 1955-57.

Occupation: Elementary school teacher; riverboat captain.

Family: Wife, Lula Fredson; two children.

Religion: Episcopalian.

Political Career: Fort Yukon City Council, 1960-64; mayor of Fort Yukon, 1964-68; Alaska House, 1967-71; Alaska Senate, 1971-73; Republican nominee for U.S. House, 1972.

Capitol Office: 2331 Rayburn Bldg. 20515; 225-5765.

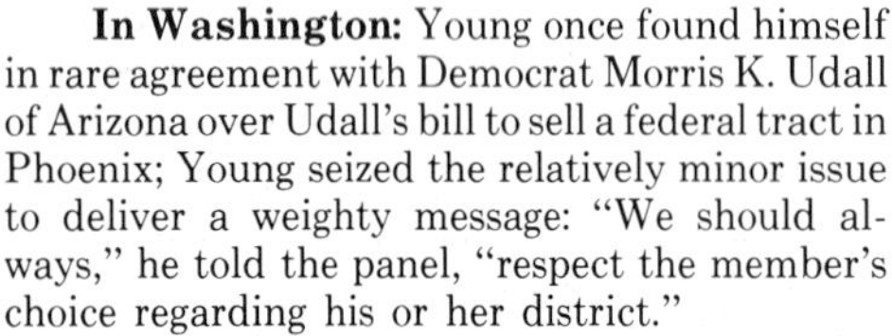

In Washington: Young once found himself in rare agreement with Democrat Morris K. Udall of Arizona over Udall's bill to sell a federal tract in Phoenix; Young seized the relatively minor issue to deliver a weighty message: "We should always," he told the panel, "respect the member's choice regarding his or her district."

The irony, as Young surely intended, is that many of his colleagues have done anything but respect his wishes for his gargantuan district, the state of Alaska. Since he came to the House in 1973 as an advocate of the trans-Alaska oil pipeline, Young has been making lonely, often losing stands against "outsiders" from the Lower 48 who want to preserve much of Alaska's unspoiled frontier from the miners, loggers, drillers and developers whose interests Young tenaciously promotes.

A former riverboat captain, Young is an individualist who regularly demands — often in angry bursts — that Washington stay out of his state's way. Since 1985, he has been well positioned to resist environmentalist legislation as ranking Republican on the Interior Committee. At the same time, the position's responsibility seems to have tempered the volatile Young somewhat.

Young is aggressively partisan, even though he is a product of Alaska's free-for-all, weak-party politics. As a member of the panel that makes House Republicans' committee assignments, Young has been known to grill applicants on party loyalty before supporting them for an Interior seat. His bluster is often tactical, used to intimidate foes, but Young's combativeness can complicate his dealings with fellow members, especially the Democratic majority on Interior.

Young may never stop seething about passage of a 1980 Alaska lands bill that reserved large portions of the state as federal wilderness. In his three-year fight against that bill, Young whittled down its wilderness acreage considerably and won provisions for development.

But when the bill was passed in the House in 1979, he complained, "People can sit on this floor and say it is all right to take what is already the people's of Alaska. That is immoral. . . . None of you has to go home to unemployment created by national legislation," Young added. Then he broke down in tears.

Young's work on that bill crystalized his role in the House as a scrappy underdog, and it still defines his attitude toward others. During committee action on unrelated legislation in 1987, for example, Young turned on Interior Chairman Udall, sitting beside him on the dais, and lashed out, "You screwed us in 1980 so royally. . . . You took land away from us."

The latest Alaska battles have been fought primarily on two fields. One involves a move, which Young supports, to open the Arctic National Wildlife Refuge (ANWR) to oil and gas development along its coastal plain. The second effort, which Young opposed, was to curb logging in the Tongass National Forest, a temperate-zone rain forest in Alaska's southeast panhandle.

Opponents of opening the wildlife refuge contend that development would threaten caribou, musk oxen, snow geese and polar bears. They were able to prevent bills from reaching the floor in either house during the 100th Congress. Young's bill was blocked in Interior by Udall, who countered with legislation to make the entire refuge a permanent wilderness. Young had somewhat better luck in the Merchant Marine Committee, where members are sympathetic to the shippers that would transport any new oil from ANWR.

But all efforts to pass an ANWR bill were suspended in the 101st Congress in response to public furor over the disastrous oil spill of the tanker *Exxon Valdez* off Alaska in early 1989.

The Persian Gulf War provoked a new spate of interest in domestic oil production. One of the most controversial features of President Bush's 1991 proposal to revamp energy policies was its plan to allow ANWR oil and gas drilling.

Alaska — At Large

Two years after the supertanker *Exxon Valdez* crashed into a reef in Alaska's Prince William Sound — spilling 10 million gallons of Alaskan crude into the fragile marine ecosystem — its repercussions are still being felt throughout the state.

Gone from the nation's television screens are the eerie images of dead, oil-soaked waterfowl and otters washing ashore, but scientists estimate that effects of the March 1989 disaster will linger for decades.

The oil spill, the worst in U.S. history, eventually fouled hundreds of miles of Alaskan coastline, disrupting two of the state's major industries — fishing and tourism. These industries have rebounded, though; fishermen in the sound reported record harvests within two years, and tourism is on the rise.

The accident was as untimely as it was devastating. The crash of oil prices in the mid-1980s caused rising unemployment and state budget shortfalls, ending nearly a decade of oil-fueled economic boom (which had enabled the state to build up a $1 billion reserve fund and sparked a wave of emigration that boosted state population by 33 percent between 1980 and 1986). The spill came just as stabilizing oil prices had eased the crisis atmosphere and just as the state's allies in Congress were readying a push to open Alaska's Arctic National Wildlife Refuge to oil exploration.

The spill also altered the state's political landscape. The pro-oil majority that controlled the state Legislature during the 1980s — associated with the GOP majority — has seen its influence wane; the Legislature passed a spate of environmentally protective measures within months of the wreck.

The nation's largest state in land area, it is also one of the least populated, with 550,000 residents. Despite Alaska's permafrost reputation, residents enjoy the state's breathtaking natural beauty and warm summers; in much of the state the summer solstice brings 24 hours of daylight. However, it still takes a hardy type to live this far north during the winter.

The pioneer spirit and sheer orneriness required to live in Alaska inspire political iconoclasm. Sixty percent of the state's voters are registered as neither Democrat nor Republican; in 1990, voters elected Gov. Walter J. Hickel, running on the Alaskan Independence ticket. (The party advocates secession from the United States, though Hickel does not.)

However, the tone of Alaska politics in recent years has been conservative because of the oil development (which drew many workers from the South), resentment toward "outsiders" who want restraints on development and anger over the federal control of much of Alaska's land. The GOP holds all three of the state's seats in Congress. In presidential elections, Democrats seldom contest Alaska.

Republican strength is considerable in the state's population nexus, Anchorage. The city has 226,000 residents, up 30 percent since 1980. More than 300 miles north of Anchorage is Fairbanks (population 31,000), the traditional trading center for the villages of inland Alaska. The city's role as the supply center for the Alaska oil pipeline promoted rapid growth and modernization.

Southeast Alaska is separated from the rest of the state by the St. Elias Mountains and the Gulf of Alaska. Juneau, the state capital, is inaccessible by land.

Alaska's vast "bush" region is dotted with towns that have evocative names but few people. Nome, on Alaska's west coast, has just over 8,000 residents. Native Indians and Eskimos predominate in remote Alaska, which includes the Aleutian Islands.

Population: 401,851. White 309,728 (77%), Black 13,643 (3%), American Indian, Eskimo and Aleut 64,103 (16%), Other 8,054 (2%). Spanish origin 9,507 (2%). 18 and over 271,106 (67%), 65 and over 11,547 (3%). Median age: 26.

The Tongass measure got as far as House passage in 1988 but the Senate took no action. Congress revisited it in the 101st Congress.

As introduced by New York Democrat Robert J. Mrazek, the bill would have designated 23 new wilderness areas in Tongass (about 1.8 million acres) as off limits to logging. It would also have repealed the timber-harvesting concessions made to that industry in the 1980 Alaska lands law; eliminated the federal subsidies for such costs as forest roads; and canceled long-term contracts with two troubled pulp mills that get federal timber at below-market prices.

During committee consideration, California Democrat George Miller offered a substitute amendment to change the bill to allow the Forest Service to abolish mandatory timber-sales quotas. Young called Miller's plan a "travesty of justice" that would eliminate thousands of jobs, but the committee adopted it by voice vote.

Young derided the Interior bill as the "Sierra Club's wish list." He favored a less restrictive version approved by the Agriculture Committee. On the floor, though, the Interior version soundly won the showdown with the Agriculture bill, despite Young's emotional plaint that it would cost 6,000 timber-industry jobs in Alaska.

In the Senate, however, Alaska's two senators had better luck. The final House-Senate compromise reduced the acreage to be protected to slightly more than 1 million acres. And while the compromise ended mandatory timber quotas and subsidies for roads, it did not terminate the pulp-mill contracts.

Young called the agreement "better than what passed the House," but he still said it was bad legislation and "a slap in the face to the local people of southeast Alaska." He castigated Democrats for protecting workers only if they are not "doing something their most pampered special interest group — the environmentalists — don't like." He warned, "They had better not come back at me again. I may be only one, but they had better not come back at me again. They had better leave my people alone and leave my state alone."

At one subcommittee hearing in the 100th Congress, Young so berated Mrazek that acting Chairman Sam Gejdenson recessed the panel and took Young aside to cool off. Later, on the House floor, Young erupted at Mrazek again, threatening political retribution while stabbing the air with his ever-present Buck knife.

Despite such contentiousness, the Tongass issue actually showed the slightly more temperate side of Young that has emerged in the years since he took Interior's top GOP seat. In the 100th Congress, he made a concerted effort to compromise with Miller, but their effort fell short. With the easygoing Udall, Young generally was less a lone wolf and more of a broker, representing the interests of panel Republicans, who are mostly partisan, pro-development Westerners like himself. That could change with Miller as chairman.

In 1989, Young led a Republican walkout during committee markup of a bill to set up a fund to buy land for parks, wildlife preserves, forests and historic sites. After two GOP amendments were defeated by lopsided votes, Young hotly warned Democrats to "quit stretching your muscles [and] ... look at the merits" of the GOP proposals. "In the long run, you're going to lose this baby," he said, threatening a presidential veto. When the next amendment failed by a similar margin, Young led the Republicans out of the room. The bill never made it to the floor.

Also in the 101st Congress, Young took a satirical approach to highlight what he perceives as liberals' interference in Western land matters. Young was peeved when Indiana Democratic Rep. Jim Jontz introduced legislation to curb logging in ancient Northwestern forests, which are the habitat of the threatened northern spotted owl. So Young introduced a bill to establish a 1.3 million acre national forest in northwestern Indiana, which is Jontz' habitat.

Among Young's bill's "findings" was that "the establishment of a national forest in northwestern Indiana would improve the environment and provide for weekend recreational opportunities for residents of Chicago and Indianapolis."

"Don's a funny guy," Jontz said. Young introduced the bill again in the 102nd Congress.

On Merchant Marine, Young has cooperated with liberal Massachusetts Democrat Gerry E. Studds to protect fishermen's interests and the Coast Guard's budget. He worked with Studds on a bill in the 101st Congress increasing oil spillers' federal liability limits.

Young, who claims to be the only trapper in Congress, has fought off repeated attempts to impose a ban on steel-jaw leghold traps, a move sought by animal-rights groups. Once, while testifying before Merchant Marine, he made his point by leaving his hand in a trap until his fingers turned blue.

On broader issues, Young fits the conservative label he claims. But like Ted Stevens, Alaska's senior Republican senator, he knows how to leaven his voting record with support for the construction unions and other labor interests important in state affairs.

At Home: Whatever the national issues at stake, each of Young's House campaigns turns into a debate over his personality. The contests seem to turn on whether Alaskans accept Young's portrayal of himself as a rough-hewn defender of home-state interests or see him as an obnoxious obstructionist who does more harm than good to Alaska.

Young thought he provided a definitive answer to that question in 1988, when he defeated a highly touted Democratic challenger, former state prosecutor Peter Gruenstein, with 62 percent of the vote. But in 1990, Young barely held off college president and former Valdez Mayor John E. Devens with 52 percent.

A co-founder of Prince William Sound Community College, Devens got state and national attention during the *Exxon Valdez* disaster. As Valdez mayor, Devens coordinated the city's response to the oil spill, appeared on national news shows and testified before congressional committees. He also set the stage for his House campaign, faulting Young for not quickly returning home to oversee the cleanup.

Devens' showing in the open August primary did not inspire hope among Democratic strategists. Young took 57 percent of the vote to 31 percent for Devens. But Devens found his footing in the campaign's final weeks. He saved his sparse dollars for a late TV ad blitz; in one ad, he appeared with mariners to underline his endorsement from the United Fishermen of Alaska, the state's largest commercial fishing organization.

Devens' closing rush coincided with Young's absence from the state during the long House session, and with a swell of public dissatisfaction at the status quo (which brought victory to former GOP Gov. Walter J. Hickel's late-starting independent gubernatorial bid).

Young was also the victim of a political hangover from his 1988 campaign. During it, Young tried to reinforce support from Alaska's pro-development majority by suggesting that Democrat Gruenstein may have received "laundered money" from environmental groups. Sued by Gruenstein for slander following the election, Young was ordered in October 1990 to stand trial. (In January 1991, Young reached an out-of-court settlement with Gruenstein just before trial.)

Young's narrow majority over Devens was his lowest percentage since his first House victory in a 1973 special election.

Young actually lost his first House bid in 1972 under extraordinary circumstances. His opponent, freshman Democratic Rep. Nick Begich, disappeared without a trace along with House Majority Leader Hale Boggs during an October plane flight from Anchorage to Juneau. However, the missing Begich was re-elected over Young by almost 12,000 votes.

The defeat was the only one of Young's political career, which includes stints in local office and the state Legislature. Born in California, Young moved to Alaska to teach, then became a licensed riverboat captain and a member of the Dog Mushers Association.

With his strong base in the Alaska "bush," Young rebounded quickly from his 1972 setback. He had hardly ended campaigning when Begich's seat was declared vacant in December. In the 1973 special election, Young edged out Emil Notti, the former state Democratic chairman. In 1974, Young weathered a vigorous challenge from state Sen. William L. Hensley. He won by comfortable margins in the next several elections.

Young then faced Pegge Begich, a former Democratic national committeewoman for Alaska and Nick Begich's widow. Begich criticized Young's attendance record, but Young brushed off the attacks, winning with 55 percent in 1984 and 57 percent in 1986. In 1988, Gruenstein was preceded into the House race by positive publicity for prosecuting several well-publicized murder cases. But Gruenstein's effort to portray himself as a moderate were blunted by Young, who cited the Democrat's New York roots and his work in the 1970s for a news service partially funded by consumer advocate Ralph Nader. Trumpeting his tireless work on crusades such as opening ANWR, Young even outpaced George Bush's strong Alaska performance.

Committees

Interior & Insular Affairs (Ranking)
Water, Power & Offshore Energy

Merchant Marine & Fisheries (2nd of 17 Republicans)
Fisheries & Wildlife Conservation & the Environment (ranking); Coast Guard & Navigation

Post Office & Civil Service (4th of 8 Republicans)
Postal Personnel & Modernization (ranking); Postal Operations & Services

Elections

1990 General		
Don Young (R)	99,003	(52%)
John E. Devens (D)	91,677	(48%)
1990 Primary †		
Don Young (R)	78,594	(57%)
John E. Devens (D)	43,420	(31%)
Gary L. Sinkola (R)	16,567	(11%)
1988 General		
Don Young (R)	120,595	(62%)
Peter Gruenstein (D)	71,881	(37%)

† In Alaska's "jungle primary," candidates of all parties are listed on one ballot.

Previous Winning Percentages: **1986** (57%) **1984** (55%) **1982** (71%) **1980** (74%) **1978** (55%) **1976** (71%) **1974** (54%) **1973 *** (51%)

** Special election.*

District Vote For President

	1988		1984		1980 †		1976	
D	72,105	(36%)	62,007	(30%)	41,842	(26%)	44,058	(36%)
R	118,817	(60%)	138,377	(67%)	86,112	(54%)	71,555	(58%)
I	5,459 *	(3%)			11,155	(7%)		

** Ron Paul, Libertarian Party.*
† Also, Ed Clark, Libertarian, received 18,389 votes (12%).

Campaign Finance

	Receipts	Receipts from PACs		Expend-itures
1990				
Young (R)	$560,908	$277,725	(50%)	$564,759
Devens (D)	$168,038	$13,150	(8%)	$164,732
1988				
Young (R)	$623,760	$296,950	(48%)	$626,377
Gruenstein (D)	$402,694	$99,084	(25%)	$402,477

Key Votes

1991	
Authorize use of force against Iraq	Y
1990	
Support constitutional amendment on flag desecration	Y
Pass family and medical leave bill over Bush veto	Y
Reduce SDI funding	N
Allow abortions in overseas military facilities	N
Approve budget summit plan for spending and taxing	Y
Approve civil rights bill	N
1989	
Halt production of B-2 stealth bomber at 13 planes	N
Oppose capital gains tax cut	N
Approve federal abortion funding in rape or incest cases	N
Approve pay raise and revision of ethics rules	Y
Pass Democratic minimum wage plan over Bush veto	N

Voting Studies

	Presidential Support		Party Unity		Conservative Coalition	
Year	**S**	**O**	**S**	**O**	**S**	**O**
1990	56	38	60	25	78	15
1989	70	27	71	21	78	17
1988	49	42	64	29	71	16
1987	52	37	58	30	81	16
1986	61	33	63	31	90	4
1985	51	46	62	32	82	18
1984	55	43	60	39	88	10
1983	52	34	57	21	78	7
1982	45	26	50	25	66	15
1981	67	17	61	14	89	1

Interest Group Ratings

Year	ADA	ACU	AFL-CIO	CCUS
1990	33	67	33	64
1989	15	77	50	60
1988	30	63	64	69
1987	16	63	50	57
1986	20	65	62	56
1985	30	62	53	45
1984	25	57	50	69
1983	20	52	50	56
1982	10	73	25	57
1981	10	92	36	88

Arizona

U.S. CONGRESS

SENATE 1 D, 1 R
HOUSE 4 R, 1 vacancy

LEGISLATURE

Senate 17 D, 13 R
House 27 D, 32 R, 1 vacancy

ELECTIONS

1988 Presidential Vote	
Bush	60%
Dukakis	39%
1984 Presidential Vote	
Reagan	66%
Mondale	33%
1980 Presidential Vote	
Reagan	61%
Carter	28%
Anderson	9%
Turnout rate in 1986	34%
Turnout rate in 1988	45%
Turnout rate in 1990	36%

(as percentage of voting age population)

POPULATION AND GROWTH

1980 population	2,718,215
1990 population (24th in the nation)	3,665,228
Percent change 1980-1990	+35%

DEMOGRAPHIC BREAKDOWN

White	81%
Black	3%
American Indian, Eskimo, or Aleut	6%
(Hispanic origin)	19%
Urban	84%
Rural	16%
Born in state	33%
Foreign-born	6%

MAJOR CITIES

Phoenix	983,403
Tucson	405,390
Mesa	288,091
Glendale	148,134
Tempe	141,865

AREA AND LAND USE

Area 113,508 sq. miles (6th)

Farm	52%
Forest	27%
Federally owned	44%

Gov. Fife Symington (R)
Of Phoenix — Elected 1991

Born: Aug. 12, 1945, New York, N.Y.
Education: Harvard U., B.A. 1968.
Military Service: Air Force, 1968-71.
Occupation: Real estate developer.
Religion: Episcopalian.
Political Career: No previous office.
Next Election: 1994.

WORK

Occupations	
White-collar	56%
Blue-collar	28%
Service workers	14%
Government Workers	
Federal	38,451
State	56,946
Local	153,745

MONEY

Median family income	$ 19,017	(30th)
Tax burden per capita	$ 924	(19th)

EDUCATION

Spending per pupil through grade 12	$ 3,744	(33rd)
Persons with college degrees	17%	(19th)

CRIME

Violent crime rate 600 per 100,000 (16th)

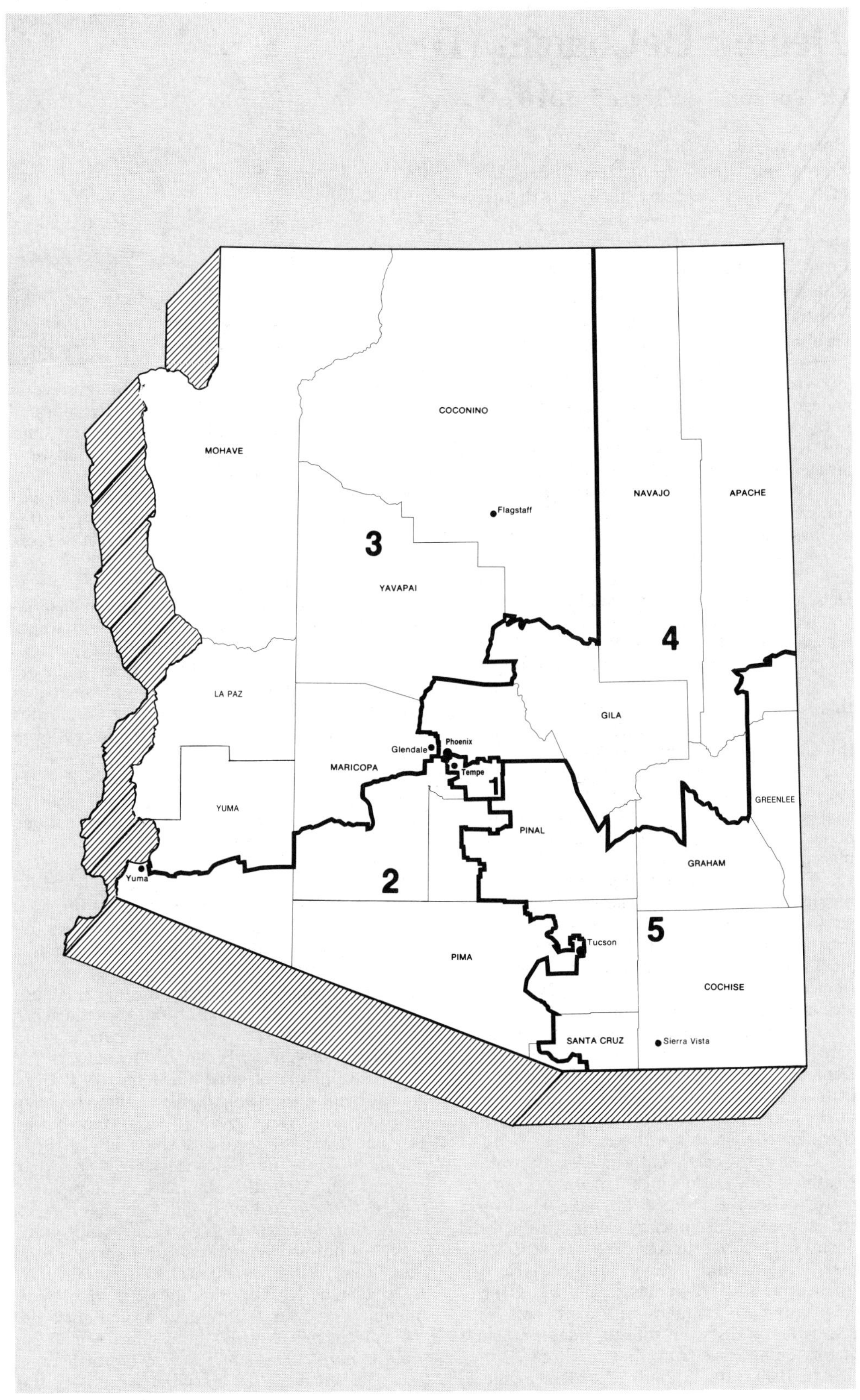
COCONINO
MOHAVE
NAVAJO
APACHE
Flagstaff
3
YAVAPAI
4
LA PAZ
GILA
Glendale
Phoenix
Tempe
MARICOPA
1
YUMA
PINAL
GREENLEE
GRAHAM
2
Yuma
5
Tucson
PIMA
COCHISE
SANTA CRUZ
Sierra Vista

Dennis DeConcini (D)

Of Tucson — Elected 1976

Born: May 8, 1937, Tucson, Ariz.
Education: U. of Arizona, B.A. 1959, LL.B. 1963.
Military Service: Army, 1959-60; Army Reserve, 1960-67.
Occupation: Lawyer.
Family: Wife, Susan Hurley; three children.
Religion: Roman Catholic.
Political Career: Pima County attorney, 1973-76.
Capitol Office: 328 Hart Bldg. 20510; 224-4521.

In Washington: DeConcini is just brazen enough to brush off an Ethics Committee rebuke of the improper appearance of his involvement in the Keating Five affair. "Aggressiveness has always been my hallmark," he said in early 1991.

Of the five senators investigated, DeConcini was perhaps the most militant in behalf of savings and loan magnate Charles H. Keating Jr., and the most combative in defending himself. Throughout the 14-month investigation, DeConcini was unapologetic for his efforts to get federal regulators to ease up on Lincoln Savings, and for his acceptance of $85,000 in campaign contributions raised by Keating.

"There is no improper conduct standard that says you cannot intervene for someone . . . who made a campaign contribution," he said as the 26-day televised hearing opened.

DeConcini took the investigating committee's recommendation that he not be punished as a full exoneration, and he did his utmost to make a virtue of the aggressive posture that placed him at the heart of the Keating affair.

DeConcini is nothing if not blunt about his mission as a senator and the way Capitol Hill works. "It's our job to get things done for our constituents," he said in 1989, defending earmarks in the bill approved by the Appropriations Subcommittee on Treasury, Postal Service and General Government, which he chairs.

The Keating episode tarnished the public perception of DeConcini as a law-and-order Democrat. But in the Senate, it seemed to have little effect. There DeConcini is known as a moderate conservative who votes carefully and is willing to deal to get things done.

Even at the height of the maelstrom over the Keating affair, DeConcini's moderate to conservative outlook continued to make his vote a crucial one on the Judiciary Committee and the Senate floor. He is often one of the last senators to make up his mind, and along the way he is courted by Democrats and Republicans. But if DeConcini frequently parts company with his party's leaders, he rarely casts the vote that denies them a victory on an issue truly dear to them.

In 1990, after Majority Leader George J. Mitchell of Maine, was defeated by three votes on a key clean air issue, he personally appealed to DeConcini to help him reverse the outcome. DeConcini had opposed Mitchell on that vote, as well as in the leadership race a year earlier. But he agreed to withhold his vote that day, pairing with an absent senator who supported Mitchell and helping the majority leader score an important victory.

DeConcini seems unbothered by the perception that his votes are often open to negotiation. In 1990, after Ohio Sen. Howard M. Metzenbaum dropped his effort to block DeConcini's bill to reform the federal racketeering statute known as RICO, DeConcini gave Metzenbaum the deciding vote on the Judiciary Committee for the Ohioan's vertical price fixing bill, even as DeConcini said he opposed it.

DeConcini's willingness to push RICO reform in the midst of the Keating hearing raised a few eyebrows. While the Arizonan is just one of many critics of the statute, the law was being widely used to bring charges against executives of failed S&Ls.

DeConcini's admirers saw his effort as a positive sign that his aggressive nature was unbent by the scandal. But his motivation was questioned at one 1989 Judiciary Committee meeting at which as much time was spent defending him as debating his bill. "I think everyone has entered this debate with clean hands," said Chairman Joseph R. Biden Jr. of Delaware.

DeConcini's original bill to narrow RICO's reach limited the triple damages allowed under current law, even though the government was seeking them to recoup a share of the S&L funds lost. While DeConcini stood by that amendment, he did eliminate a retroactive clause that would have applied the new law to cases already in court, including Keating's.

His bill had supporters ranging from President Bush to several Senate liberals. But the idea of weakening RICO during the S&L crisis made members queasy. After Metzenbaum took his hold off the bill, it passed the committee on a 12-2 vote in early 1990, but it moved no further.

DeConcini's 1989 amendment to block the

sale of certain military style assault weapons met a similar fate, but if that effort was also controversial, at least it had a wider audience of enthusiasts.

At the outset, DeConcini was torn between allies in the National Rifle Association, who opposed any restriction on weapons sales, and allies in law enforcement, who backed a far-reaching ban offered by Metzenbaum. DeConcini tried to split the difference with an amendment banning the sale of nine assault weapons, half as many as the Metzenbaum bill. But he wound up infuriating the NRA, which launched a brief recall drive against him.

That the conservative-minded DeConcini had introduced the amendment gave supporters of gun control a powerful boost. After months of furor, the Judiciary Committee on a tense 7-6 vote supported the amendment. (Because the bill also included an expansion of the federal death penalty, which DeConcini also supports, he was one of just two Judiciary Democrats to vote to send the package to the floor.) His assault weapon amendment was then sustained on a 52-48 vote of the full Senate, but no agreement could be reached with the House, and it was dropped.

The backdrop to these 101st Congress activities was the highly publicized Keating investigation. By late 1989, the $2 billion price tag on the failure of Keating's Lincoln Savings and Loan of California coupled with the Senate scandal emerged as emblems of the debacle. The Keating Five included Democratic Sens. Alan Cranston, Donald W. Riegle Jr. and John Glenn along with Arizona Republican John McCain.

DeConcini was forced to defend himself against charges that he acted more as a negotiator in Keating's behalf than as a senator asking legitimate questions of a regulator. During the 26 days of televised hearings in late 1990 and early 1991, he was singled out as the most aggressive of the five senators by two key witnesses, including former Federal Home Loan Bank Board Chairman Edwin J. Gray.

The case against the five senators hung on the nexus between their intervention and the political contributions they collected from Keating. Of the $1.3 million Keating raised for the five, a relatively small share went to DeConcini: $33,000 for his 1982 re-election, and $48,000 for 1988.

From his days as Pima County prosecutor in the mid-1970s, DeConcini knew of Keating as a Republican antipornography crusader and prominent businessman. The two met at a country club in 1981, the same year DeConcini unsuccessfully lobbied President Ronald Reagan to nominate Keating to be ambassador to the Bahamas.

After Keating's American Continental Corp., which employed 2,000 Arizonans, bought Lincoln in 1984, the two discussed Gray's efforts to clamp down on the thrift industry, which neither supported. In 1986, DeConcini urged Reagan to make a recess appointment of a Keating associate to the bank board. The president did, but the man resigned months later under the cloud of a Justice Department investigation of his ties to Keating.

In 1987, it was DeConcini who called Gray to schedule the pivotal April 2 meeting in his Senate office between Gray, four of the five senators, and no staff. Gray alleged that he was asked to refrain from enforcing a tough bank board regulation restricting Lincoln's investments and that DeConcini offered the government a deal on Keating's behalf. DeConcini disputed this.

A week later the five senators met with other regulators more intimately involved in the Lincoln case. Again, the meeting was in DeConcini's office, and again, DeConcini took the lead. No one disputed that he opened the session saying, "We wanted to meet with you because we have determined that potential actions of yours could injure a constituent." The meeting broke up when the regulators mentioned criminal referrals involving Lincoln.

DeConcini stopped inquiring about Lincoln until the end of 1988, when he made repeated calls to M. Danny Wall, who succeeded Gray as bank board chairman. DeConcini allegedly urged state and federal regulators not to seize Lincoln but to allow Keating to sell it.

But on April 13, 1989, American Continental filed for bankruptcy. The following day federal regulators seized Lincoln. That fall, the government sued Keating and American Continental, alleging among other things that Lincoln's money had been siphoned off into campaign contributions. With that action, DeConcini returned the contributions raised by Keating for his 1982 and 1988 campaigns.

Throughout the investigation and the hearings, DeConcini took issue with the actions of Robert S. Bennett, the special counsel assigned by the Ethics Committee to the case. DeConcini claimed that he was acting more as a prosecutor than an impartial investigator. DeConcini also got ensnared in an ugly dispute with fellow Arizonan McCain, who repeatedly contrasted his role with DeConcini's.

In the end, the Ethics Committee rebuked DeConcini and Riegle for the appearance of improper behavior but did not issue harsher sanctions, saying that the rules governing appearances of impropriety are unclear. In the cases of Glenn and McCain, the committee faulted their poor judgment, but did not even find the appearance of wrongdoing. In Cranston's case, the panel said he may have engaged in improper conduct and ordered further investigation.

While DeConcini does not appear to have suffered greatly among his colleagues as a result of the affair, it will likely disqualify him from being considered for a top law enforcement job. He was on Reagan's short list for the FBI directorship, a job he was said to be interested in, and in early 1989, Bush asked him to become the first drug czar, an offer DeConcini declined.

DeConcini came to the Senate after serving

as the administrator of the Arizona Drug Control District. Drug trafficking has become a bigger problem for Arizona, he says, because importers of Latin American narcotics have shifted their primary routes from Florida to the West. As vice chairman of the Senate Drug Enforcement Caucus, DeConcini was active in the 1986 movement to pressure foreign governments to curb the drug trade at its source. In the 101st Congress, he helped enact a pay hike for federal law enforcement officials, and unsuccessfully pushed to increase funding for antidrug programs by taking money from the Pentagon.

DeConcini's political position thrusts him into the spotlight during judicial confirmation hearings, when his vote can be pivotal. At the start of the 102nd Congress, he was the last member of the Judiciary Committee to announce his opposition to Bush's nomination of Kenneth L. Ryskamp to the federal appeals court; Ryskamp was rejected on a 7-6 vote.

In 1987, as the Senate weighed Reagan's nomination of Robert H. Bork to the Supreme Court, DeConcini was a key swing vote. Late in the process, he announced his opposition, saying Bork's record on discrimination was lacking. But he worried aloud about the political ramifications of the vote. In the end, it proved a savvy political move. The vote rallied Arizona Democrats frustrated by his relatively conservative record, without serious risk of riling many Republicans. Bork's strongest supporters in the state were arch-conservatives preoccupied with trying to keep Evan Mecham as governor during the events leading to his impeachment. While Bork campaigned for DeConcini's 1988 opponent, the vote never became a cutting issue.

The movement that provides refuge to Central American immigrants is strong in Arizona, and along with Massachusetts Democratic Rep. Joe Moakley, DeConcini favors legislation to grant Salvadorans and Nicaraguans special immigration status. He has managed to get the bill through a Judiciary subcommittee several times, but it has been blocked repeatedly by Republican Alan K. Simpson of Wyoming.

DeConcini has become a severe critic of U.S. missile sales if he thinks the weapons could end up in the hands of terrorists. This has put him at the forefront of efforts to block some arms sales to Arab nations, sometimes even after the pro-Israel lobby has compromised. In 1987, he sought to prevent the sale of shoulder-fired Stinger antiaircraft missiles to Bahrain. In 1988, he led the Senate forces opposed to the sale of Maverick air-to-ground and air-to-sea missiles. In both cases, he lost, although he did gain restrictions.

He is also a leading congressional supporter of Angolan guerrilla leader Jonas Savimbi. In the 101st Congress, the Senate approved his amendment conditioning aid to the U.N. peacekeeping forces in Angola on a certification that Cuba and Angola were living up to their part of the deal.

As a freshman, DeConcini became a major player during the Senate's bruising 1978 debate over the Panama Canal treaties. Just a year into his first term, he wound up playing the pivotal role in ratification of the two pacts. It was through his reservations to the treaties, assuring the United States the right to intervene to keep the canal open in case of trouble, that the leadership finally drew enough support to assure Senate approval.

At Home: The only Democrat to win a Senate election in Arizona in nearly 30 years, DeConcini puts considerable effort into securing himself against a conservative challenge at home. Coupled with a bit of luck — local GOP warfare in 1976 and 1988 and a good Democratic year in 1982 — his efforts have kept him from ever being seriously threatened.

In the two years leading up to his 1988 reelection, DeConcini stockpiled campaign funds and reinforced his well-regarded organization. The GOP, meanwhile, was caught up in a bitter feud sparked by Mecham's election to the governorship. After a stormy 15-month tenure, a messy impeachment fight and a threatened recall election, the GOP-controlled Legislature threw Mecham out of office in April 1988. Just when the GOP might have turned its attention to DeConcini, pro-Mecham forces ousted seven veteran GOP legislators in the September primary, further fracturing the party.

Virtually alone, 39-year-old businessman Keith DeGreen made scant progress against DeConcini, until he raised questions about the incumbent's personal finances; that issue prompted the National Republican Senatorial Committee to fund a $212,000 October TV advertising blitz on DeGreen's behalf.

In 1979, DeConcini — a multimillionaire with vast real estate holdings — together with his family bought 320 acres of land for $400,000. Before the purchase, the federal Bureau of Reclamation had been publicly considering part of the area as a possible route for a continuation of the Central Arizona Project (CAP), a massive aqueduct. The government chose the site in 1981 and five years later reached a $1.4 million settlement for 136 acres.

DeConcini also made a 1983 investment in a development group that was involved in a similar deal. Land purchased by the partnership for $13,000 per acre was condemned by the federal government in 1984 for construction of the New Waddell Dam, which is part of CAP. In a 1987 settlement, the partnership ceded about half of its original purchase for $20,000 per acre. DeConcini divested his 3.1 percent share of the partnership before the settlement when the U.S. attorney ruled that his involvement in a negotiated water rights settlement would violate a federal law barring contracts between the government and members of Congress. The senator gave his share to his siblings, though the U.S. attorney's decision in the case was subsequently overruled.

DeConcini said he had no privileged knowledge of the government's plans in either deal. He accused DeGreen of dirty campaign tactics and lashed out at GOP Sen. John McCain for tacitly condoning them. The episode added some drama to what was expected to be a walkaway win; some polls in the campaign's final weeks showed considerable volatility in the electorate. But most voters knew too little of DeGreen to switch to him. DeConcini won with a comfortable, if not spectacular, 57 percent.

Had DeConcini not paid such careful attention to his right flank over the years, the flap might have caused him more trouble. But ever since 1978, when enraged conservatives put up billboards across the state condemning his vote for the Panama Canal treaties, the Democrat has rarely strayed far from the center-right.

In his 1982 campaign, GOP challenger Pete Dunn, a three-term state legislator, used the Panama issue as part of his argument that DeConcini was a labor-backed liberal who "talks like Ronald Reagan in Arizona and votes like Ted Kennedy in Washington."

But by then, DeConcini had compiled a record that made it difficult to brand him a liberal. In 1981, he supported the conservative coalition of Republicans and Southern Democrats 63 percent of the time. He won re-election with 57 percent.

DeConcini campaigned for the Senate as a conservative in 1976, when he defeated GOP Rep. Sam Steiger. Stressing his law enforcement background as Pima County district attorney, he called for a crackdown on organized crime in Arizona. As it happened, neither crime nor any other policy issue had as much to do with the November outcome as a vicious Republican primary between Steiger and fellow Rep. John Conlan, longtime personal enemies.

Supporters of Steiger, a Jew, accused Conlan of pandering to anti-Semitism in a pitch for fundamentalist Christian votes. When Steiger won the primary, Conlan refused to endorse him, and Democrats rallied behind DeConcini in anticipation of a rare statewide victory.

DeConcini has his base in Tucson, the state's second-largest population center. It is where his family made a fortune in real estate. His father was a state Supreme Court justice and his mother a member of the Democratic National Committee. A brother, Dino, is a former Democratic chairman in Tucson.

Committees

Appropriations (8th of 16 Democrats)
Treasury, Postal Service & General Government (chairman); Defense; Energy & Water Development; Foreign Operations; Interior.

Judiciary (4th of 8 Democrats)
Patents, Copyrights & Trademarks (chairman); Antitrust, Monopolies & Business Rights; Constitution.

Rules & Administration (5th of 9 Democrats)

Select Indian Affairs (2nd of 9 Democrats)

Select Intelligence (6th of 8 Democrats)

Veterans' Affairs (2nd of 7 Democrats)

Joint Library

Joint Printing

Elections

1988 General

Dennis DeConcini (D)	660,403	(57%)
Keith DeGreen (R)	478,060	(41%)

Previous Winning Percentages: **1982** (57%) **1976** (54%)

Campaign Finance

	Receipts	Receipts from PACs		Expend-itures
1988				
DeConcini (D)	$2,818,427	$968,495	(34%)	$2,640,650
DeGreen (R)	$244,971	$20,350	(8%)	$238,369

Key Votes

1991	
Authorize use of force against Iraq	N
1990	
Oppose prohibition of certain semiautomatic weapons	N
Support constitutional amendment on flag desecration	Y
Oppose requiring parental notice for minors' abortions	N
Halt production of B-2 stealth bomber at 13 planes	Y
Approve budget that cut spending and raised revenues	N
Pass civil rights bill over Bush veto	Y
1989	
Oppose reduction of SDI funding	N
Oppose barring federal funds for "obscene" art	N
Allow vote on capital gains tax cut	Y

Voting Studies

	Presidential Support		Party Unity		Conservative Coalition	
Year	**S**	**O**	**S**	**O**	**S**	**O**
1990	40	57	74	21	35	59
1989	61	38	64	35	55	45
1988	52	36	61	30	65	30
1987	46	51	73	26	34	59
1986	43	53	62	35	61	37
1985	45	49	62	31	63	28
1984	42	39	50 †	24 †	45	21
1983	32	47	55	31	52	32
1982	61	34	52	36	74	20
1981	51 †	38 †	59 †	24 †	63 †	24 †

† Not eligible for all recorded votes.

Interest Group Ratings

Year	ADA	ACU	AFL-CIO	CCUS
1990	61	20	56	50
1989	60	32	80	50
1988	55	33	92	21
1987	60	27	80	33
1986	45	52	60	35
1985	45	38	62	45
1984	60	38	75	38
1983	45	43	60	41
1982	45	60	82	53
1981	45	57	50	53

John McCain (R)

Of Phoenix — Elected 1986

Born: Aug. 29, 1936, Panama Canal Zone.
Education: U.S. Naval Academy, B.S. 1958; attended National War College, 1973-74.
Military Service: Navy, 1958-81.
Occupation: Naval officer; Senate Navy liaison; beer distributor.
Family: Wife, Cindy Lou Hensley; six children.
Religion: Episcopalian.
Political Career: U.S. House, 1983-87.
Capitol Office: 111 Russell Bldg. 20510; 224-2235.

In Washington: For McCain, the Keating Five scandal — and particularly his lost composure under the accompanying scrutiny — has set a ceiling on his once-skyrocketing political fortunes. McCain's personal ties to savings and loan operator Charles H. Keating Jr. distinguished him from the other four senators, but he survived the scandal, receiving the mildest of rebukes. Still, he has tumbled considerably from the heights of 1988, when he was being actively discussed as a potential running mate for George Bush.

Generally, McCain is a voice of reason from the right, decidedly conservative but pragmatic enough to work with colleagues in both parties. Sometimes, though, an issue can seem to consume him, and on those occasions another McCain takes over — a man tightly wound rather than relaxed, blinded to foes' points of view and more shrill in his argument.

The most intense phase of the Keating inquiry provoked an extremely defensive reaction in McCain. He privately browbeat reporters over their coverage of his role in the affair, and used his status as a war hero to counter unflattering media accounts. He flared at hostile callers during a C-SPAN cable television call-in program.

Of the five senators (the others were Democrats Alan Cranston of California, Dennis DeConcini of Arizona, John Glenn of Ohio and Donald W. Riegle Jr. of Michigan), McCain was by far the closest to Keating. McCain is a former Vietnam POW who spent nearly six years in North Vietnamese prison camps; Keating is a former World War II pilot. They met in 1981 and hit it off immediately. Their families vacationed together at Keating's private resort in the Bahamas. McCain and his family often flew on planes owned or hired by Keating's Phoenix-based American Continental Corp. (ACC). Keating, his family and associates contributed a total of about $112,000 to McCain's 1982 and 1984 House campaigns and his 1986 Senate run.

When Keating complained in early 1987 that Federal Home Loan Bank Board regulators were harassing him in their examination of ACC-owned Lincoln Savings and Loan, McCain lent an ear. He and DeConcini discussed why the examination was taking so long. McCain received a letter from Lincoln's auditor (who later became an ACC executive) that supported Keating's plaint. When a meeting was set up with bank board chairman Edwin J. Gray, McCain agreed to come.

McCain refused, however, to negotiate in Keating's behalf. When DeConcini told Keating that McCain did not want to intervene improperly for him, Keating said McCain was a "wimp." McCain confronted Keating with the insult and informed him their friendship was over. Over Keating's protests, though, McCain went to the meeting with Gray, insisting on an obligation to ACC's employees — his constituents.

All but Riegle attended the meeting with Gray. McCain repeatedly expressed his concern about the propriety of the meeting, but Gray reassured him. Still, Gray was unable to answer questions about Lincoln, so he suggested that the senators meet with the regulators.

The following week, the five senators met with the regulators, who told them that Lincoln's mismanagement was so serious that it could face criminal investigation by the Justice Department. After the meeting, Riegle, Glenn and McCain stopped their inquiries into Lincoln; McCain told his banking aide he wanted nothing more to do with Lincoln.

In 1989, ACC went bankrupt, the government seized Lincoln, and the Internal Revenue Service began questioning the company's claimed tax deductions for the cost of nine plane trips to the Bahamas for McCain and his family in 1984-86. In May and June 1989, McCain, who insisted that he had intended to repay the company and thought he had, sent checks for $13,433 to ACC.

Robert S. Bennett, the Ethics Committee's special counsel in the Keating case, recommended after a preliminary investigation that the committee clear McCain and Glenn, because they had ended their involvement with Keating after learning that he could face criminal investigation. (The committee decided that because McCain had been a House member when he took the plane trips, they lacked jurisdiction to rule on their propriety.)

McCain told the committee that Keating had been a friend and supporter from 1981 to 1987, but when "he asked me to do something I thought was improper, I said no. . . . The only thing I said I could do was to inquire whether American Continental Corp. and Lincoln Savings were being treated properly."

The committee concluded that McCain "exercised poor judgment in intervening with the regulators," but that his actions "were not improper" and did not require further discipline. McCain said he was "relieved that I have been exonerated."

McCain will test the extent of the damage to his relationship with Arizona voters if he seeks a second term in 1992. One thing that may not recover, though, is the relationship between Arizona's two senators. In December 1990, a former ACC accountant testified about a letter he wrote to the Ethics Committee in which he expressed his belief McCain never intended to repay the company for the plane trips. Before the committee, the accountant backed off that assertion, but he also testified that DeConcini had asked for permission to release the letter to the media. The letter eventually was leaked. DeConcini also frequently griped that Bennett treated him more harshly than McCain.

The Keating affair checked McCain's rapid rise through Senate GOP ranks. His charm and genuine ability plus his war-hero background quickly made him a celebrity in Washington.

In late 1988, however, McCain's GOP Senate colleagues applied the first brake to his ambitions, rejecting his bid to chair their campaign fundraising committee.

McCain is most active on Armed Services, where he is now fourth in seniority among Republicans. He champions burden-sharing, a concept that calls on U.S. allies to increase spending for international security, and he favors mandatory national service.

The Senate adopted his amendment to the 1990 defense appropriations bill requiring a quarterly report by the president to Congress on contributions made by other countries to the military deployment against Iraq. But McCain did not back efforts that would have sharply cut U.S. troops in South Korea and Europe.

He and Illinois GOP Rep. John Porter coauthored a bill in the 101st Congress that would have created a voluntary part-time national service program and provided enhanced student aid for military volunteers.

Another issue that absorbed McCain over a longer period of time was aid to the Nicaraguan contras. Though a new senator in the 100th Congress, he was a leading proponent of President Ronald Reagan's policy. In early 1988, after the House defeated both Reagan's military aid package and Democratic leaders' humanitarian alternative, temporarily ending all aid, McCain gave $400 to a conservative group's fund for the rebels.

He was enraged by Speaker Jim Wright's intervention in the peace talks; when Wright, an opponent of Reagan's policy, met privately with representatives of the Nicaraguan government, McCain called his activities "at best unseemly and at worst unconstitutional." He welcomed the contra-aid accord reached between Bush and Congress early in Bush's administration; it gave the rebels non-military aid up through scheduled Nicaraguan elections in 1990. "I've detested the bitter partisan debate I've been in on . . . for the past six years," he said. "A lot of us felt a sense of relief."

Representing a state with a high number of retirees, McCain was swamped with complaints from Medicare beneficiaries angry with the 1988 catastrophic coverage law, which would have required about 40 percent of Medicare beneficiaries to fund the program by paying an income-based surtax. In 1989, he and Utah Republican Orrin G. Hatch sponsored an amendment to delay implementing the program. Unable to win with that proposal, and with calls mounting to repeal the entire catastrophic program, McCain offered a bill to repeal the surtax but keep unlimited coverage of hospital bills while eliminating most of the law's new benefits. The Senate passed it 99-0. But the House voted overwhelmingly to repeal all but the law's extended coverage for the poor. After weeks of contentious wrangling between the two chambers, the House position prevailed. McCain first vowed to filibuster the conference agreement but retracted that threat when repeal looked inevitable. "I'm not Jesse Helms," he said. "That's not my style."

McCain also sits on the Commerce, Science and Transportation Committee, where he pressed successfully in the 100th Congress for a bill requiring that federal agencies' phones be accessible to hearing-impaired callers. In the 101st Congress, Aviation Subcommittee Chairman Wendell H. Ford included in a catchall bill a McCain-sponsored proposal to give small airlines a chance to compete at the busiest air traffic hubs.

Criticized as a carpetbagger at the outset of his political career, McCain also has taken care to be attentive to state affairs. His assignment on the Select Indian Affairs Committee allows him to be active, as he was in the House, on a subject of great concern in Arizona.

In 1989, he and DeConcini co-chaired a special panel to investigate reports of federal mismanagement of Indian programs and corruption on reservations. In 1990, he won approval of a bill to prevent child abuse on Indian reservations.

On another local matter, in the 100th Congress he worked with Arizona Democratic Rep. Morris K. Udall, and against the administration, for a law restricting flights over the Grand Canyon to improve safety and decrease noise. In the 101st and 102nd Congresses, he sponsored bills to protect the Grand Canyon from damage caused by excessive water fluctuations released from the Glen Canyon Dam.

McCain prides himself on being a forceful advocate of a president's constitutional prerogatives in foreign policy, against what he sees as Congress' persistent and dangerous meddling. Yet he was hardly an uncritical, down-the-line supporter of Reagan's policies.

As a House member, he sharply took issue with the Marines' prolonged deployment in Lebanon, which ended in 1983 after a tragic barracks bombing. He criticized Defense Secretary Caspar W. Weinberger for rubber-stamping Pentagon funding requests. Even on the contra issue, McCain repeatedly urged the administration to quit trying to overthrow the Sandinistas and focus on pressing them to respect human rights and hold free elections.

In the Senate, he was openly skeptical when Reagan, heeding GOP political operatives, vetoed a defense bill to dramatize the parties' differences during the 1988 presidential campaign. When Reagan also that year vetoed the *Grove City* civil rights bill, calling instead for a more modest substitute, McCain snapped, "I hate to sound cynical, but where was the substitute when the issue was being debated?"

Despite his criticism of congressional foreign-policy making, in the 100th Congress McCain offered a dramatic initiative of his own over administration objections. With another Vietnam veteran, GOP Rep. Tom Ridge, he proposed a resolution calling for renewed, limited ties with Vietnam. Both men stressed that the proposal stopped short of full relations and was a means to advance U.S. interests. Ultimately McCain abandoned the resolution when Vietnam, citing the administration's "hostile policy," surprisingly suspended an agreement to help search for the remains of U.S. servicemen and to allow emigration of political detainees.

At Home: From the time Sen. Barry Goldwater announced plans not to run again in 1986, McCain was widely regarded as his likely successor.

McCain started with a strong pool of political capital. He had impressed Republican activists by winning election to the House in 1982, soon after his 1981 arrival in the state. Subsequent trips around Arizona as a member of Reagan's 1984 steering committee boosted his visibility. He became such a hot property that potential intraparty rivals backed away.

Democrats, too, were wary of his stature. Gov. Bruce Babbitt decided he would rather risk a run at the presidency than tangle with McCain for the Senate. After a host of other Democrats also passed up the race, party leaders were relieved when Richard Kimball declared his candidacy.

Kimball had served four years in the state Senate before his election in 1982 to the Corporation Commission, which regulates public utilities and charters corporations doing business with the state. But he never hit stride as a Senate candidate. He spent months holed up to research his stands on issues, which did not enhance his visibility.

McCain's campaign was not without hitches. His plans for a party unity ticket with gubernatorial candidate Burton S. Barr, longtime state House majority leader, faltered when Barr lost to conservative Evan Mecham in the primary.

McCain also stumbled by publicly referring to "Leisure World," an enormous senior citizens' center in Arizona, as "Seizure World." In a close race, that kind of gaffe could have proven fatal, but the race was not close. McCain swept all but three small counties.

McCain's initial opening to Congress came in 1982, when GOP Rep. John J. Rhodes decided to give up his 1st District seat. McCain won nomination by convincing voters that his experience as Navy liaison to the Senate gave him a knowledge of "how Washington works."

When rivals charged that he was a carpetbagger who would forget Arizona once in Washington, McCain said, "I went to Hanoi and I didn't forget about the United States of America."

There was never much question McCain would be a Navy man; his father commanded U.S. forces in the Pacific during the Vietnam War, and his grandfather was a Pacific aircraft carrier commander in World War II. In a Hanoi prison camp, his captors sarcastically called him the U.S. Navy's "crown prince."

The roots of McCain's political successes lie in his long ordeal in Vietnam, the years he spent tortured and in solitary confinement in Hanoi-area camps after his plane was shot down in 1967. At the 1988 GOP convention, McCain recounted his experiences for a prime-time national TV audience.

Committees

Select Indian Affairs (Vice Chairman)

Armed Services (4th of 9 Republicans)
Conventional Forces & Alliance Defense; Manpower & Personnel (ranking); Projection Forces & Regional Defense

Commerce, Science & Transportation (6th of 9 Republicans)
Aviation (ranking); Communications; Consumer

Special Aging (6th of 10 Republicans)

Elections

1986 General

John McCain (R)	521,850	(61%)
Richard Kimball (D)	340,965	(39%)

Previous Winning Percentages: **1984 *** (78%) **1982 *** (66%)

** House elections.*

Campaign Finance

	Receipts	Receipts from PACs		Expenditures
1986				
McCain (R)	$2,510,092	$773,152	(31%)	$2,189,510
Kimball (D)	$550,024	$190,187	(35%)	$531,698

Key Votes

1991	
Authorize use of force against Iraq	Y
1990	
Oppose prohibition of certain semiautomatic weapons	Y
Support constitutional amendment on flag desecration	Y
Oppose requiring parental notice for minors' abortions	N
Halt production of B-2 stealth bomber at 13 planes	Y
Approve budget that cut spending and raised revenues	N
Pass civil rights bill over Bush veto	N
1989	
Oppose reduction of SDI funding	Y
Oppose barring federal funds for "obscene" art	N
Allow vote on capital gains tax cut	Y

Voting Studies

	Presidential Support		Party Unity		Conservative Coalition	
Year	**S**	**O**	**S**	**O**	**S**	**O**
1990	74	25	78	19	76	22
1989	91	9	85	13	84	13
1988	70	23	84	13	78	16
1987	65	24	84	11	69	25
House Service						
1986	68	29	67	25	76	18
1985	68	25	81	13	84	13
1984	64	27	74 †	13 †	83	8
1983	80	17	83	9	90	7

† Not eligible for all recorded votes.

Interest Group Ratings

Year	ADA	ACU	AFL-CIO	CCUS
1990	11	87	22	83
1989	5	93	0	88
1988	10	80	14	64
1987	15	91	20	100
House Service				
1986	10	73	14	60
1985	5	81	18	91
1984	10	86	31	93
1983	10	96	6	85

1 John J. Rhodes III (R)

Of Mesa — Elected 1986

Born: Sept. 8, 1943, Mesa, Ariz.
Education: Yale U., B.A. 1965; U. of Arizona, J.D. 1968.
Military Service: Army, 1968-70.
Occupation: Lawyer.
Family: Wife, Ann Chase; four children.
Religion: Protestant.
Political Career: Mesa School Board, 1972-76; Republican district chairman, 1973-75; Central Ariz. Water Conservation District vice president, 1983-87.
Capitol Office: 326 Cannon Bldg. 20515; 225-2635.

In Washington: Any representative from Arizona's 1st would face comparison with high-profile John McCain, who held the seat for two terms before jumping to the Senate in 1986. But Rhodes has another tough act to follow: He is the son of former GOP House leader John J. Rhodes, who represented the district from 1953 to 1983.

Compared with his powerful father and McCain, Rhodes seems a bit bland, yet he is finding a niche for himself in the House. His overall voting record reveals his basic conservative instincts, though he has a more cautious nature than some of the brasher young members on the GOP right.

Rhodes was active in the 101st Congress on a number of issues before the Interior Committee. He sponsored legislation enacted in 1990 to strengthen the authority of Interior Department law enforcement officers on Indian land. His measure gave officials from the Bureau of Indian Affairs the right to carry guns and arrest people who commit crimes on Indian lands. The U.S. government has always been responsible for federal law enforcement on Indian reservations, but that authority had never been put into statutory language that carried the weight of law.

Rhodes brought his background as a water-rights attorney to the debate over designating vast tracts of Arizona and Nevada as wilderness. Rhodes wanted the law to require water-rights disputes to be settled in state courts (rather than federal). He lost his fight on the Nevada bill but achieved a limited compromise on the home state measure.

As a freshman, Rhodes had been part of a bipartisan conservative budget coalition that sought modest across-the-board cuts on most appropriations bills. In 1987, Rhodes unsuccessfully offered the group's amendment calling for a 0.9 percent cut from the military construction budget.

On home-state issues, Rhodes found that the political consequences of some budget cuts could loom quite large. When Appropriations' energy and water funding bill came to the full House in 1987, Rhodes' budget group offered an amendment to cut 1.7 percent from every program in the bill.

Amid rumors that the massive Central Arizona Water Project would be threatened if Rhodes and fellow Arizona freshman Jon Kyl supported the reduction, both backed the committee bill instead of the cut.

At Home: In his 1986 bid to succeed McCain, Rhodes offered more than just a famous name; he also had a formidable résumé that included a bronze star for service as an intelligence adviser in Vietnam. Active in local GOP affairs, he had been district chairman as well as president of the Mesa Chamber of Commerce and president of the Mesa Board of Education. In 1982, he was elected to the board of the Central Arizona Project.

But while Rhodes became the early front-runner, he proved neither entertaining nor inspirational on the stump. That gave an opening to primary challenger Ray Russell, a Mesa veterinarian who had run well against McCain in 1982. Russell began with a base of support among Mesa's politically active Mormons. His billboards proclaimed: "Vote for a leader, not a name." But whatever Rhodes' shortcomings as a campaigner, his experience and outlook made him acceptable to the mainstream Republicans who predominate in the 1st. He got 44 percent of the primary vote, with Russell 7 points back. That was tantamount to election in this GOP stronghold.

In 1988, Rhodes' father was mentioned as a possible contender in the scheduled recall election of GOP Gov. Evan Mecham. That angered Mecham's backers, who threatened to field a primary opponent to the younger Rhodes. But Mecham was impeached before the recall, and no one challenged Rhodes in the GOP primary.

Rhodes did have a Mechamite primary challenger in 1990, state Sen. John T. Wrzesinski. Rhodes handily turned back the maverick lawmaker and drew only token write-in opposition in the general election.

Arizona 1

Eastern Phoenix; Tempe; Mesa

Arizona's only truly urban district, the 1st is a collection of Sun Belt cities growing at a breakneck pace. According to one study done in 1984, some 40 percent of the population had lived there less than five years.

The balance of power clearly lies in the suburbs of Phoenix, where the bulk of the area's growth has occurred. Mesa expanded by almost 150 percent during the 1970s and by almost 90 percent in the 1990s. The city now has more than 280,000 residents. Tempe (142,000) and Chandler (90,500) add to the suburban totals.

Electronics and high-technology firms have thrived here in recent years, reinforcing the district's GOP tendencies. Managers and technicians flocking to the 1st have brought their Republican loyalties, augmenting those of the retirees who earlier had hastened the area's conservative shift.

Mesa is a reliable source of Republican votes. Founded by Mormons in 1878, it still has a politically active Mormon community and is the site of a large Mormon temple. It also has a McDonnell Douglas plant, and Williams Air Force Base is nearby.

The adjacent community of Tempe was developed around a flour mill built in 1871 and Tempe today has light industries, electronics plants and garment factories. The city usually votes Republican for state and local offices. But Tempe has a significant Democratic presence, thanks to the Arizona State University community with its 40,000 students and 1,700 faculty.

The 1st also takes in a politically diverse portion of southeastern Phoenix, a tabletop-flat area of the "Valley of the Sun" that includes upper-middle-class neighborhoods with a distinctly Republican bent as well as the district's only significant populations of blacks and Hispanics. Many of the minority voters live in neighborhoods around Sky Harbor Airport.

Democrats who avoid a liberal label in statewide elections sometimes win narrowly in the 1st. Sen. Dennis DeConcini has done so, as did former Gov. Bruce Babbitt. But in recent congressional and presidential contests, Republicans have had solid margins here.

Population: 543,747. White 474,724 (87%), Black 19,556 (4%), Other 12,582 (2%). Spanish origin 62,119 (11%). 18 and over 399,698 (74%), 65 and over 62,119 (11%). Median age: 29.

Committees

Interior & Insular Affairs (7th of 17 Republicans)
Energy & the Environment (ranking); Water, Power & Offshore Energy

Science, Space & Technology (16th of 19 Republicans)
Space

Elections

1990 General		
John J. Rhodes III (R)	166,223	(100%)
1990 Primary		
John J. Rhodes III (R)	58,763	(62%)
John T. Wrzesinski (R)	35,458	(38%)
1988 General		
John J. Rhodes III (R)	184,639	(72%)
John M. Fillmore (D)	71,388	(28%)

Previous Winning Percentage: **1986** (71%)

District Vote For President

	1988	1984	1980	1976
D	90,383 (34%)	58,492 (27%)	44,473 (25%)	57,839 (37%)
R	171,884 (65%)	154,845 (72%)	113,755 (63%)	93,155 (59%)
I			15,916 (9%)	

Campaign Finance

	Receipts	Receipts from PACs	Expend-itures
1990			
Rhodes (R)	$326,640	$170,339 (52%)	$323,328
1988			
Rhodes (R)	$293,044	$135,419 (46%)	$291,961
Fillmore (D)	$13,756	$1,250 (9%)	$11,855

Key Votes

1991	
Authorize use of force against Iraq	Y
1990	
Support constitutional amendment on flag desecration	Y
Pass family and medical leave bill over Bush veto	N
Reduce SDI funding	N
Allow abortions in overseas military facilities	N
Approve budget summit plan for spending and taxing	Y
Approve civil rights bill	N
1989	
Halt production of B-2 stealth bomber at 13 planes	N
Oppose capital gains tax cut	N
Approve federal abortion funding in rape or incest cases	N
Approve pay raise and revision of ethics rules	Y
Pass Democratic minimum wage plan over Bush veto	N

Voting Studies

	Presidential Support		Party Unity		Conservative Coalition	
Year	S	O	S	O	S	O
1990	77	22	90	9	93	7
1989	86	13	88	11	95	5
1988	70	29	93	5	95	5
1987	71	29	87	11	100	0

Interest Group Ratings

Year	ADA	ACU	AFL-CIO	CCUS
1990	17	63	17	71
1989	10	82	8	100
1988	10	96	7	100
1987	4	96	6	93

2 No Incumbent

Morris K. Udall
House Service: 1961-91

In Washington: Udall's physical health turned out to be the final and most uncompromising obstacle in a long career marked by unfailing grace, enormous creativity, unstinting humor and frequent and disappointing defeat.

Udall's career came to a melancholy close in early 1991 after a combination of Parkinson's disease and injuries he suffered from a fall in his home barred him from completing his final term. (He had already announced that he would retire at the end of the 102nd Congress.) In an April 19 letter to House Speaker Thomas S. Foley, Udall's wife announced that he would resign effective May 4.

Liberal reformer, presidential candidate, distinguished committee chairman, party raconteur: In his 30 years in Congress, Udall evolved from Young Turk to one of the House's most beloved elder statesmen. He used his assignment on the Interior Committee to make himself the chamber's most prolific author of environmental legislation, both before and after he became chairman in 1977.

Udall years ago gave up his House leadership ambitions, but if he had not suffered from Parkinson's disease, he might have become Speaker. No House Democrat could match Udall's combination of affection and respect among colleagues and sprightly wit; a healthy and ambitious Udall would have been the one credible rival to Jim Wright's 1986 accession as Speaker in the wake of the retirement of Thomas P. O'Neill Jr.

There was some irony in Udall's inability to claim the leadership role for which his long tenure in the House had prepared him. For most of his early career, he had the stamina and ambition to be a leader, but the House did not want to elect him.

In 1969, Udall was the Young Turk challenger to John W. McCormack for Speaker. While Udall never expected to oust McCormack, he did expect to become majority leader two years later, and most of his liberal allies expected it as well. But he lost badly to Hale Boggs of Louisiana, a man who had only recently recovered from the effects of a nervous collapse. Boggs offered no threat to the traditional power structure; Udall, a critic of seniority, did.

That defeat marked the turning point in Udall's career. It ended his leadership hopes and drove him deeper into the legislative process, in which he had come to excel.

Udall's legislative career was striking evidence that a member of Congress can find important work to do anywhere in the committee system. For 20 years, Udall never had anything resembling a major assignment — he joined Interior in 1961 to work on Arizona land and mining issues and also went on Post Office at the leadership's request.

But his proficiency at enacting environmental legislation cloaked the difficulty and frustration that the process engendered. The House passed strip-mine control legislation three times, and twice failed to override President Ford's vetoes, before a bill reasonably close to what Udall wanted became law in 1977. It took four years for Congress to enact legislation dividing Alaska lands between development and wilderness. Two years of struggle ended in deadlock on the last day of the 95th Congress in 1978; a compromise Alaska bill finally passed in 1980.

The 98th Congress saw enactment, after years of bickering, of a bill designating more than 8 million acres of new federal wilderness in 20 states — the first major addition to the wilderness system since 1964. The first wilderness bill to pass was for Arizona. In the 101st Congress, Udall ushered through bills designating more than 2 million acres in Arizona as wilderness.

Other major Udall ideas ran out of steam. His scheme to provide federal aid for local land-use planning as a solution to urban sprawl failed on the House floor amid charges that it smacked of socialism. As interest burgeoned in opening up the Arctic National Wildlife Refuge to oil and gas drilling, Udall steered in a resolutely opposite direction, backing a bill to de-

Arizona 2

Southwest — Western Tucson; Southern Phoenix; Yuma

The 2nd is Arizona's most Hispanic (36 percent) and most Democratic (60 percent) district. It stretches from downtown Phoenix to downtown Tucson and includes much of the classic desert landscape in between, dotted with the large saguaro cactus that is a hallmark of the American Southwest.

The Maricopa County (Phoenix) portion dominates the 2nd politically. Maricopa casts a majority of the district vote, most of it in Hispanic areas. The south side of Phoenix, included in the 2nd, traditionally has been the poorest and most faithfully Democratic part of the city.

The part of Tucson (Pima County) remaining in the district has the Hispanic neighborhoods in the city's western part, and the University of Arizona's 31,000 students, which along with the copper-mining town of Ajo and the San Xavier and Papago Indian reservations just south of the city favor Democrats.

Tucson, with a population that is almost 30 percent Hispanic, has a Democratic heritage that an influx of retirees and people attracted by high-tech firms has only lately begun to offset. Change is certain to continue, but at a slower rate. The 2nd was the slowest-growing congressional district in the state in the 1980s.

The bulk of Pima County's land area lies within the boundaries of the 2nd, although most of the county's residents live in eastern Tucson in the 5th District. North of Pima in the 2nd, Pinal County includes an important Cotton Belt.

The 2nd also takes in the southern tier of Yuma County, in which irrigated farm land grows citrus fruit and vegetables. The city of Yuma is famous for being America's hottest urbanized place.

The 2nd is typically in the Democratic column for state and congressional contests. Democrat Bruce Babbitt was extremely strong there in his 1978 and 1982 gubernatorial victories. In 1988, Democratic presidential nominee Michael S. Dukakis swamped George Bush in the 2nd.

Population: 543,187. White: 376,773 (69%), Black 30,548 (6%), American Indian, Eskimo and Aleut 28,327 (5%), Other 5,050 (1%). Spanish origin 192,632 (36%). 18 and over 372,734 (69%), 65 and over 52,322 (10%). Median age: 27.

clare ANWR permanently off limits to development.

The 100th Congress dealt a blow to a key Udall accomplishment of the early 1980s. After a three-year struggle, Congress in 1982 had approved legislation providing for orderly choice of nuclear-waste disposal sites based on safety and scientific criteria, not politics. That legislation was, in essence, reversed in 1987 when Congress voted to place the nuclear-waste dump in Nevada over the state's vociferous objections. Udall had sought unsuccessfully to delay the decision and to empower a high-level negotiator to find a willing state.

In his last few years as Interior chairman, Udall increasingly delegated responsibility for major bills to other senior members — particularly to his heir apparent, ranking Democrat George Miller of California. After Udall's fall, the Democratic Caucus elected Miller vice chairman of Interior, with all the powers of the chairman. When Udall resigned, Miller formally took the chairmanship.

Udall was never the kind of chairman who exacted retribution from members who crossed him. Indeed, he and Miller fought bitterly in 1988 — with no apparent long-term effect on their relationship — over a bill of great interest to the Arizona Democrat. The measure made a controversial land swap that gave a developer some downtown Phoenix real estate in exchange for Florida lands needed for a wildlife refuge. Miller said the deal was a bad bargain for the taxpayer.

While working on these issues, Udall was doing what Arizona expected him to do on Interior — protecting the Central Arizona Project, the massive water system for which Udall struggled throughout his career.

Udall had what amounted to a second legislative front on the Post Office Committee. A resting place for many of the less ambitious House members, Post Office turned out to be a perfect vehicle for many of Udall's interests. In his first decade there he worked to revise the federal pay system, including the one for Congress, and to make the Postal Service a semiprivate corporation. Much later, he won passage of President Carter's civil service reforms, to promote merit pay and more flexibility for managers.

Outside his committees, Udall spent more than 20 years pushing for changes in the political system, again with mixed results. He was chief sponsor of the 1971 bill that made the first real national rules for campaign finance, limiting expenditures and contributions and providing for voluminous disclosure. But he failed repeatedly with legislation to establish public financing of congressional campaigns.

Udall's own campaign for the 1976 Democratic presidential nomination, as the leading liberal alternative to Jimmy Carter, left a curious record: He gained wide respect within his party and survived through to the convention in New York without ever winning anything.

Udall finished second in seven primaries and was declared the Wisconsin winner prematurely by two networks, but he never had a first-place finish. He would almost certainly have won in New Hampshire had former Sen. Fred Harris not attracted liberal votes, but by the time Harris withdrew the next month, Carter was too strong to be headed off.

Udall eventually made his peace with Carter and was not one of the more outspoken critics during Carter's presidential term, but he endorsed Edward M. Kennedy's bid for the Democratic nomination in 1980. Eventually he receded into the elder statesman's role that allowed him to give the convention's keynote address. He thought about one more presidential campaign for himself in 1984, but gave the idea up to the realities of declining health.

Throughout his career, the lanky, soft-spoken Udall was distinguishable as one of the best-humored — and most humorous — figures in American politics. A favorite speaker at Democratic events, Udall wrote a book on political humor, published in 1988, titled "Too Funny to Be President."

"In the political arena," Udall has said, "laughter can be a tremendously powerful thing." He saw humor as a gentle way to disarm the opposition, gain a hearing for his own position and lighten up tense situations; he thought using sarcastic humor to devastate an opponent was a mistake.

"The best political humor, however sharp or pointed, has a little love behind it," he once said. "It's the spirit of the humor that counts.... Over the years it has served me when nothing else could."

At Home: Udall came to politics as a member of one of Arizona's best-known families. His father was a justice of the Arizona Supreme Court; his mother was a local Democratic activist.

A professional basketball player for the old Denver Nuggets despite the handicap of a glass eye, Udall entered law practice with his brother Stewart in 1949 and later was Pima County attorney while Stewart served in Congress. When Stewart Udall resigned from Congress in 1961 to become President Kennedy's interior secretary, Morris ran for the seat in a special election that drew attention as a test of Kennedy's first 100 days in office. Udall backed such Kennedy programs as federal aid to education and medical care for the aged. He won, but with only 51 percent. He was hurt by Stewart Udall's call for evacuation of farmers squatting on federal land along the Colorado River.

For years after that, Udall won easily. But in 1976 he drew less than 60 percent for the first time in a decade. His unsuccessful campaign for the Democratic presidential nomination that year had given high visibility to his liberal views. The presidential publicity generated expensive and bitterly fought House campaigns in 1978 and 1980, with Udall having to fight off heavy GOP spending — which he more than matched — and charges of "socialism" by his Republican challengers. In the 1980 campaign he admitted that he was suffering from Parkinson's disease, but still won by nearly 40,000 votes despite the Reagan presidential victory.

In 1982 Udall was faced with a difficult choice. Arizona's Republican Legislature divided his overpopulated 2nd District in half, with part of his hometown of Tucson in each half. Udall had the option of running either in the redrawn 2nd, which was safely Democratic but extended awkwardly all the way to Phoenix, where he had never run before; or in the 5th, which kept more of his familiar Tucson precincts but included a strong Republican vote.

Udall and his Tucson Democratic allies prepared to challenge the Legislature's district map for unfairly splintering the Hispanic vote. The Legislature compromised and placed more of Tucson in the 2nd. Udall won there easily.

Udall's 1986 primary challenge had its roots in 1982 redistricting, which made the 2nd District Arizona's most heavily Hispanic constituency. State Sen. Luis Gonzales decided it was time the district had Hispanic representation.

But he underestimated Udall's political strength. The incumbent, drawing on the strong support of top Hispanic leaders, many of whom regarded Gonzales' attempt merely as an effort to build name recognition for a future campaign, won going away.

No Democrat filed to run against Udall in 1988, and his perennial opponent, Joseph Sweeney, a former administrator of an unaccredited law school in Tucson, did not dent his typically huge general-election margin. Perhaps in deference to Udall's record and popularity, challengers stayed away in 1990. In his campaign swan song, Udall again crushed Sweeney.

District Vote For President

	1988	1984	1980	1976
D	77,470 (56%)	65,829 (48%)	46,830 (43%)	38,769 (41%)
R	60,582 (43%)	70,487 (51%)	48,700 (44%)	51,807 (55%)
I			11,726 (11%)	

3 Bob Stump (R)

Of Tolleson — Elected 1976

Born: April 4, 1927, Phoenix, Ariz.
Education: Arizona State U., B.S. 1951.
Military Service: Navy, 1943-46.
Occupation: Cotton farmer.
Family: Divorced; three children.
Religion: Seventh-day Adventist.
Political Career: Ariz. House, 1959-67; Ariz. Senate, 1967-77, Senate president, 1975-77.
Capitol Office: 211 Cannon Bldg. 20515; 225-4576.

In Washington: It was no great surprise in 1981 when Stump, one of the most conservative House Democrats, switched to the Republican Party of President Ronald Reagan. However, in doing so, this surpassingly low-profile member did something uncharacteristic: He made news.

His conversion placed Stump in the national headlines for the first and possibly the last time. Stump is rarely seen speaking in the well of the House and has little use for news conferences. He simply tends to his legislative business, which includes serving as ranking Republican on the Veterans Affairs Committee and maintaining a staunchly conservative line on the Armed Services Committee.

Although Republican strategists were boldly — if misguidedly — talking about "partisan realignment" in the early 1980s, Stump hardly made his switch because it was the thing to do. Stump felt he would be more comfortable — both politically and personally — in the conservative Republican caucus than on the liberal-dominated Democratic side.

Stump's crossover reflected the political evolution of voters in his 3rd District. Like many of his rural constituents, Stump, a cotton farmer, was raised as a "pinto Democrat," whose conservative philosophy closely matched that of the traditional Democrats of the South. During his early years in the House, Stump described himself as a Democrat who subscribed to "Thomas Jefferson's concept of limited government." Along with many in his district, he became increasingly alienated by the direction of the Democratic Party.

The degree of that disaffection was evident after his switch. Even though Reagan's overall support in the House faded during his second term, Stump backed the president's positions on floor votes over 80 percent of the time in each of his last four years in office. During the 101st Congress, Stump supported President Bush on more than 70 percent of House votes.

Stump can be unsparing of his liberal colleagues. After proposing a constitutional amendment to give the president a line-item appropriations veto in January 1991, Stump said, "It is said that old habits die hard; this is particularly true of the tax-and-spend habit of the liberals — their unrestrained desire to spend what we do not have and take from the taxpayers what they cannot afford." On Armed Services, where he is the third-most senior Republican, Stump is regarded as a near-automatic vote for weapons systems and other Defense Department priorities.

Stump's conservative proclivities go beyond his voting record to his relationships with other members. He is friendly with those whom he regards as "right-minded" but has little time for those with a liberal bent.

Fortunately for Stump, ideology and partisanship play little role in his main legislative bailiwick, the Veterans Affairs Committee. There is usually bipartisan consensus in support of the veterans' programs that come before the committee, and Stump works well with the chairman, conservative Democratic Rep. G. V. "Sonny" Montgomery of Mississippi.

Although he is less of a public figure than the chairman, Stump will fight for those educational, medical and other benefit programs he believes the nation's military veterans have coming to them. In 1990, he co-authored with Montgomery provisions to raise the pay of physicians, nurses and dentists employed by the Veterans Administration.

However, Stump is skeptical of new benefits for veterans suffering from illnesses not scientifically proven to have resulted from their military service. For this reason, Stump joined Montgomery in trying to block compensation for Vietnam veterans who claimed that their exposure to the herbicide Agent Orange had caused them to develop cancer.

The opponents of the benefits argued that studies had provided no definitive link between certain cancers and Agent Orange. However, after a four-year battle, Illinois Democratic Rep. Lane Evans got the Veterans Affairs Committee to attach an Agent Orange compensation amendment to a bill providing a cost-of-living adjustment (COLA) to recipients of veterans'

Arizona 3

North and West — Glendale; Flagstaff; Part of Phoenix

Once dominated almost entirely by "pinto Democrats" — ranchers and other conservative rural landowners — the 3rd has become prime GOP turf over the years.

Republicans have fared particularly well here in recent presidential elections. In 1984, it was Ronald Reagan's best district in the state; in 1988, the 3rd gave George Bush 64 percent.

The majority of the vote is cast in the Maricopa County suburbs west of Phoenix. Glendale, which produces wide GOP margins, grew by more than 52 percent in the 1980s. Bush won two-thirds of the vote in the Maricopa portion of the 3rd. In nearby Sun City, an affluent and largely Republican retirement community, political organizations among the retirees contribute to House election turnouts of 90 percent or higher.

Moving west, the 3rd takes in northern Yuma County, a sparsely populated mountainous area whose residents generally have a GOP point of view. Much of this portion of the county is occupied by a national wildlife refuge and an Army proving ground.

Residents of the northernmost portion of Yuma County moved to set up their own local government in June 1982, passing a ballot initiative that transformed northern Yuma into brand-new La Paz County. The La Paz community of Quartzsite swells during the winter, as travelers flock to take advantage of the warm climate and rock and mineral shows.

Mohave County, occupying the northwestern corner of the state, is home to three groups in constant political tension — Indians, pinto Democrats in Kingman and Republican retirees in Lake Havasu City. Though the county has been close in recent statewide elections, Republicans have gained a slight registration advantage over the Democrats; Bush carried Mohave with more than 60 percent of the vote.

To the east lies Coconino County, where partisan sentiments are mixed. The northern end, near the Utah border, includes "the Arizona strip," a heavily Mormon region that bears a staunch affinity for the GOP. Sedona, a city at the county's southern end, also votes Republican.

But old-time Democratic loyalties persist in Flagstaff, the seat of Coconino County and the commercial center of northern Arizona. Among Flagstaff's leading industries are lumber, mining and tourism — which is spurred by the proximity of ski resorts as well as the Grand Canyon to the north and the Oak Creek Canyon to the south.

A drive through Oak Creek Canyon brings one to Yavapai County, a mountainous area that includes ancient Indian ruins and ghost mining towns. The county centers on Prescott, the former territorial capital that hosted the first session of the Arizona Legislature in 1864. Yavapai County has been tough sledding for Democratic Sen. Dennis DeConcini in his last two elections; it was the only county in the state to go against him in 1982, and he just barely carried it in 1988.

Population: 544,870. White 468,924 (86%), Black 8,330 (2%), American Indian, Eskimo and Aleut 27,538 (5%), Other 3,845 (1%). Spanish origin 64,414 (12%). 18 and over 389,150 (71%), 65 and over 79,881 (15%). Median age: 31.

retirement and disability payments; Stump was on the losing side of a 16-14 committee vote.

Opponents of the Agent Orange provision raised objections on the Senate floor at the close of the 101st Congress and the bill died with adjournment. Stump then co-sponsored a "clean" COLA bill in January 1991. But Evans persisted as well and emerged with a compromise by which both the COLA and the Agent Orange provisions were enacted.

First elected as a Democrat in the year Jimmy Carter won the White House, Stump from the start voted more like a Republican. But he did not reach the party-breaking point until 1981, when House Democratic leaders threatened retaliation against those members — especially the conservative, mainly Southern "Boll Weevils" — who had bolted the party to support Reagan's landmark budget- and tax-cutting legislation.

In September 1981, Stump announced that he would run for re-election in 1982 as a Republican. "No pressure group in or out of Congress is going to dictate to me how I am going to vote on important issues," he said.

The GOP had the welcome mat out. Stump immediately got a GOP seat on Armed Services with no loss in seniority. His seniority also was guaranteed on Veterans' Affairs, though he took a leave from that committee to serve on Intelligence, a post he held from 1983 to 1987.

At Home: Secure after his first election to this northern Arizona seat in 1976, Stump had plenty of time to contemplate his party switch. When he finally filed on the Republican side in 1982, it caused barely a ripple back home.

Stump said his decision would not cost him any significant support in either party. He was right, at least initially. Conservative rural Democrats proved willing to move with him, while many of the retirees who had flocked to the region in recent years had brought Republican voting habits with them. Stump coasted to victory with 63 percent of the vote. His subsequent re-elections were uneventful until 1990, when a virtual unknown, Roger Hartstone, garnered 43 percent of the vote. A commercial photographer and self-described environmentalist, the Democrat launched a write-in effort after Stump successfully challenged his nomination petitions.

Hartstone ran an effective grass-roots campaign, searing Stump as "the Phantom of Congress" who rarely returned to the district. Stump was also criticized in the local press for listing his address in the 3rd (where he owns farmland) while actually living in a Phoenix condominium.

Hartstone attacked Stump's record on the environment and fiscal matters. Stump was also criticized for missing four important budget votes on a weekend when he attended an Arizona State football game; Stump said he had been assured by the House leadership that no crucial votes would occur.

Stump served 18 years in the state Legislature and rose to the presidency of the state Senate during the 1975-76 session. When GOP Rep. Sam Steiger tried for the U.S. Senate in 1976, Stump ran for his House seat.

In the 1976 Democratic primary, he defeated a more liberal, free-spending opponent, former state Assistant Attorney General Sid Rosen. Stump drew 31 percent to Rosen's 25 percent, with the rest scattered among three others. In the fall campaign, Stump's GOP opponent was fellow state Sen. Fred Koory, the Senate minority leader. Stump wooed conservative Democrats by criticizing his party's vice presidential nominee, Walter F. Mondale. He was helped in the election by the candidacy of state Sen. Bill McCune, a Republican who ran as an independent and drained GOP votes from Koory.

Committees

Veterans' Affairs (Ranking)
Compensation, Pension & Insurance (ranking); Hospitals & Health Care

Armed Services (3rd of 22 Republicans)
Investigations; Research & Development

Elections

1990 General		
Bob Stump (R)	134,279	(57%)
Roger Hartstone (D)	103,018	(43%)
1988 General		
Bob Stump (R)	174,453	(69%)
Dave Moss (D)	72,417	(29%)

Previous Winning Percentages: **1986** (100%) **1984** (72%) **1982** (63%) **1980** * (64%) **1978** * (85%) **1976** * (48%)

** Stump was elected as a Democrat in 1976-80.*

District Vote For President

	1988	1984	1980	1976
D	89,460 (35%)	61,884 (28%)	48,133 (24%)	63,232 (39%)
R	165,406 (64%)	158,767 (71%)	132,455 (67%)	95,078 (58%)
I			13,103 (7%)	

Campaign Finance

	Receipts	Receipts from PACs		Expend-itures
1990				
Stump (R)	$231,127	$132,850	(57%)	$225,149
Hartstone (D)	$9,735	$2,650	(27%)	$9,353
1988				
Stump (R)	$257,184	$115,046	(45%)	$319,690
Moss (D)	$26,551	0		$26,281

Key Votes

1991	
Authorize use of force against Iraq	Y
1990	
Support constitutional amendment on flag desecration	Y
Pass family and medical leave bill over Bush veto	N
Reduce SDI funding	N
Allow abortions in overseas military facilities	N
Approve budget summit plan for spending and taxing	N
Approve civil rights bill	N
1989	
Halt production of B-2 stealth bomber at 13 planes	N
Oppose capital gains tax cut	N
Approve federal abortion funding in rape or incest cases	N
Approve pay raise and revision of ethics rules	N
Pass Democratic minimum wage plan over Bush veto	N

Voting Studies

	Presidential Support		Party Unity		Conservative Coalition	
Year	S	O	S	O	S	O
1990	73 †	12 †	79	3	85 †	2 †
1989	72	27	96	2	90	5
1988	84	13	95	3	100	0
1987	81	19	95	3	98	2
1986	88	11	92	6	92	6
1985	84	16	93	6	96	4
1984	67	27	84	7	86	7
1983	77	18	91	6	92	7
1982	82	13	3	93	96	0
1981	74	18	17	81	97	0

† Not eligible for all recorded votes.

Interest Group Ratings

Year	ADA	ACU	AFL-CIO	CCUS
1990	6	100	9	80
1989	0	96	0	100
1988	0	100	0	85
1987	4	100	6	100
1986	0	100	8	100
1985	0	100	0	95
1984	5	86	17	79
1983	0	100	6	79
1982	0	100	0	89
1981	0	93	13	95

4 Jon Kyl (R)

Of Phoenix — Elected 1986

Born: April 25, 1942, Oakland, Neb.
Education: U. of Arizona, B.A. 1964, LL.B. 1966.
Occupation: Lawyer.
Family: Wife, Caryll Collins; two children.
Religion: Presbyterian.
Political Career: No previous office.
Capitol Office: 336 Cannon Bldg. 20515; 225-3361.

In Washington: With his specialty in defense issues and a busy agenda in other legislative areas, Kyl has quickly established himself in the House as a junior member to watch. While others in the class of 1986 are scrapping for a seat at the legislative table, Kyl not only has a place but has to be cautious about overextending himself.

As a House freshman, Kyl got a prime assignment to the Armed Services Committee, where he became an outspoken voice in support of many Reagan-era defense spending programs — particularly the strategic defense initiative (SDI). He allied himself with Georgia Republican Rep. Newt Gingrich and other aggressive younger Republicans who form the core of the Conservative Opportunity Society (COS). By the 101st Congress, his second House term, Kyl was serving as COS chairman.

The elevation of Gingrich to House minority whip in 1989 had benefits for Kyl: Gingrich tapped him as a deputy who, along with Nancy L. Johnson of Connecticut, oversaw the legislative strategy function of the whip operation. Kyl also attends to a full slate of home-state issues, particularly those that pertain to the 4th District. On top of all this, Kyl accepted a seat on the ethics committee at the start of the 102nd Congress.

Despite Kyl's diverse legislative interests, he has not forsaken his primary focus as a conservative stalwart on Armed Services. He is most closely identified with what has been a frustrating fight to defend the SDI program from budget cuts.

From its inception in 1983, President Reagan's concept of a high-tech, space-based anti-ballistic missile system met with widespread skepticism in Congress. Only the president's personal involvement and lobbying efforts enabled SDI supporters to obtain a series of funding increases through the mid-1980s.

However, by the time Kyl, an avid supporter of SDI, arrived in the House, dissent was already rising over the program's feasibility and cost. When Armed Services debated the fiscal 1989 military authorization bill, sentiment to cut back Reagan's full $4.9 billion request for the strategic defense initiative was strong among committee members. Kyl went against the tide, offering an amendment calling for full SDI funding; the motion failed by voice vote. With SDI targeted for a rollback to $4.1 billion, Kyl offered his amendment again on the House floor, where it lost in a 105-312 vote.

Kyl redoubled his efforts during the 101st Congress. He opposed the "balance of terror" theory behind prevailing U.S.-Soviet treaties barring anti-ballistic missile systems. "The fact is that survivable and effective defenses would strengthen deterrence and reduce the risk of war by significantly complicating the planning and execution of a first strike with strategic offensive forces," Kyl argued in a May 1990 statement.

But Kyl was shouting into an anti-SDI gale. Although President Bush gave strong verbal support to SDI, he also pledged to cut some defense spending as a response to the growing federal budget crisis; SDI opponents, more convinced than ever that it was a technological boondoggle, sent the program to the chopping block.

With the House moving a defense bill in July 1989 that limited fiscal 1990 SDI spending to $3.1 billion, Kyl proposed an amendment restoring the figure to $4.1 billion; it went down 117-299. When the next authorization bill hit the floor in September 1990, Kyl tried to stave off a slash in SDI spending to $2.3 billion; however, his amendment to provide $3.6 billion failed 141-273.

These setbacks hardly weakened Kyl's resolve. After war broke out between Iraq and a United States-led military coalition, Kyl linked SDI to the success of U.S. Patriot missiles in blunting Iraqi ballistic assaults. "It is time for the U.S. Congress to support President Bush for the development and ultimate deployment of strategic defenses against ballistic missiles," Kyl said in a January 1991 floor speech. He had to be heartened days later when Bush used a similar line of reasoning in his 1991 State of the Union address.

Voting a conservative line, Kyl supported

Arizona 4

Northeast — Northern Phoenix; Scottsdale

The wilds of northeastern Arizona provide most of the territory in the 4th, but most of the district's vote is cast in the comfortable confines of northern Phoenix. That white-collar area provides ample Republican majorities, as do Scottsdale and other Maricopa County suburbs. When the 4th was open in 1986, the Maricopa portion of the district cast nearly 80 percent of the vote and gave 69 percent of it to GOP nominee Kyl.

Scottsdale, an affluent resort community, attracts visitors with its warm, sunny climate, myriad golf courses and fashionable shops. The city grew by more than 46 percent between 1980 and 1990 and is now home to some 130,000 people. Many here are retirees; others commute to work at the management level in Phoenix corporations. Community names such as Paradise Valley and Carefree bespeak the lifestyle ideal.

The 4th went Republican upon its creation in 1972, and rapid growth has confirmed its conservative nature. The GOP vote for president has been consistently high, reaching 71 percent for President Reagan in 1984 and 65 percent for George Bush in 1988.

Democrats do rival the GOP in the region stretching north to the Utah border; where the population is concentrated in mining towns and Indian reservations. But while the Republican areas have prospered, the copper towns of Globe and Miami have not. In Navajo and Apache counties, on the New Mexico state line, the Navajo and Hopi Indian tribes make up almost half the population. Of the two, the Navajos show greater Democratic fealty. In Apache County, where the Navajo Indian influence is most dominant, Democrats outnumber Republicans by almost 4 to 1 and the 1990 Democratic gubernatorial nominee, Terry Goddard, won several precincts by 10-to-1 margins in November 1990. In 1988, Democratic presidential nominee Michael S. Dukakis carried the county with 58 percent of the vote.

Population: 543,493. White 442,730 (82%), Black 3,252 (1%), American Indian, Eskimo and Aleut 83,659 (15%), Other 3,264 (1%). Spanish origin 28,557 (5%). 18 and over 375,192 (69%), 65 and over 49,330 (9%). Median age: 30.

Bush's position on about 80 percent of House votes during the 101st Congress. But as COS chairman, Kyl nonetheless voiced some doubts about the president's adherence to conservative precepts.

For example, Kyl suggested that Bush's strong support for the Americans with Disabilities Act in 1990 led to his acceptance of several regulations and mandates opposed by congressional conservatives. "The other side always had the main bargaining leverage because they knew the president was going to sign the bill," Kyl said.

When not guarding conservative defense and fiscal principles, Kyl tends to Arizona affairs. Kyl supported passage of a 1990 bill that designated 1.1 million acres in Arizona as federally protected wilderness, after first working with Arizona GOP colleague John J. Rhodes III to ensure that state courts would have first say over federal water rights disputes.

The 4th includes more Indians living on reservations than any other House district, and Kyl pushed two measures through the 101st Congress that benefited local tribes. One law strengthened trademark protections for the artworks and crafts that are a major source of income for many Native Americans, and stiffened penalties for counterfeiting and misrepresentation of Indian art. The other restored to the San Carlos Apache Reservation 11,000 mineral-rich acres that had been under U.S. Forest Service jurisdiction since the late 1890s.

Kyl, who has a lower profile on the Government Operations Committee, took on a third assignment when he joined the ethics panel in 1991. Serving on ethics is generally regarded as a time-consuming, politically unrewarding task, but the assignment may actually have some benefits for Kyl's image in Arizona. The state has been plagued with a series of political scandals that have touched its two U.S. senators (in the savings-and-loan investigation), deposed GOP Gov. Evan Mecham (impeached in 1988), and most recently, seven state legislators indicted in February 1991 following a sting operation.

Kyl moved to protect himself from ethics problems in 1990, when he turned over to the U.S. Treasury $22,000 in campaign contributions he had received from savings-and-loan scandal figure Charles H. Keating Jr. and his associates. Keating's close link to five U.S. senators, including Democrat Dennis DeConcini and Republican John McCain of Arizona, was the focus of the Senate probe into the S&L crisis; Kyl is now regarded as a potential contender for DeConcini's seat in 1994.

At Home: Launching a House campaign against a well-known former incumbent can be daunting. But for Kyl, the reputation of ex-GOP Rep. John Conlan, his 1986 primary foe, was a blessing. Conlan was the longtime nemesis of Arizona's GOP establishment, which backed Kyl. After dispatching Conlan, Kyl had little trouble thrashing a well-financed Democratic foe in this traditionally GOP district. In 1988, Democrats did not field a candidate.

The 1986 campaign was Kyl's first, but he was no newcomer to politics. The son of former GOP Rep. John H. Kyl of Iowa, he had been active in party affairs and lobbied the state Legislature on behalf of highways, shopping centers and a local water project. A business-oriented attorney and former president of the Phoenix Chamber of Commerce, he won strong support from the corporate establishment.

But Kyl's success also depended on the specter of Conlan. A Religious Right activist, Conlan had alienated many Republicans in an acrimonious 1976 Senate primary. After losing that primary, Conlan refused to back nominee Sam Steiger, who then lost the general election. Buttressed by endorsements from a string of Republicans, Kyl trounced Conlan by a 2-to-1 margin and easily won the right to succeed retiring GOP Rep. Eldon Rudd.

In 1990, Kyl further firmed his political base and enhanced his reputation as a political comer in the state by easily defeating Mark Ivey, a country doctor who was a former president of the Arizona Medical Association.

Committees

Armed Services (14th of 22 Republicans)
Investigations; Research & Development

Government Operations (5th of 15 Republicans)
Employment & Housing; Legislation & National Security

Standards of Official Conduct (5th of 7 Republicans)

Elections

1990 General		
Jon Kyl (R)	141,843	(61%)
Mark Ivey Jr. (D)	89,395	(39%)
1988 General		
Jon Kyl (R)	206,248	(87%)
Gary Sprunk (LIBERT)	30,430	(13%)

Previous Winning Percentage: **1986** (65%)

District Vote For President

	1988	1984	1980	1976
D	88,773 (34%)	61,600 (28%)	46,274 (24%)	58,837 (36%)
R	167,264 (65%)	155,112 (71%)	130,172 (67%)	99,026 (61%)
I			14,461 (7%)	

Campaign Finance

	Receipts	Receipts from PACs		Expend-itures
1990				
Kyl (R)	$588,180	$171,389	(29%)	$442,366
Ivey (D)	$39,515	$4,500	(11%)	$38,851
1988				
Kyl (R)	$497,313	$178,114	(36%)	$316,476

Key Votes

1991	
Authorize use of force against Iraq	Y
1990	
Support constitutional amendment on flag desecration	Y
Pass family and medical leave bill over Bush veto	N
Reduce SDI funding	N
Allow abortions in overseas military facilities	N
Approve budget summit plan for spending and taxing	N
Approve civil rights bill	N
1989	
Halt production of B-2 stealth bomber at 13 planes	N
Oppose capital gains tax cut	N
Approve federal abortion funding in rape or incest cases	N
Approve pay raise and revision of ethics rules	Y
Pass Democratic minimum wage plan over Bush veto	N

Voting Studies

	Presidential Support		Party Unity		Conservative Coalition	
Year	**S**	**O**	**S**	**O**	**S**	**O**
1990	79	19	94	4	96	4
1989	80	20	96	3	95	5
1988	78	19	93	3	97	0
1987	76	24	94	3	98	2

Interest Group Ratings

Year	ADA	ACU	AFL-CIO	CCUS
1990	6	92	0	86
1989	0	96	8	100
1988	0	100	8	93
1987	0	96	0	93

5 Jim Kolbe (R)

Of Tucson — Elected 1984

Born: June 28, 1942, Evanston, Ill.
Education: Northwestern U., B.A. 1965; Stanford U., M.B.A. 1967.
Military Service: Navy, 1967-69.
Occupation: Real estate consultant.
Family: Wife, Sarah Dinham.
Religion: Methodist.
Political Career: Ariz. Senate, 1977-83; Republican nominee for U.S. House, 1982.
Capitol Office: 410 Cannon Bldg. 20515; 225-2542.

In Washington: Energetic and voluble, Kolbe is not a natural fit for the reserved and tradition-bound Appropriations Committee. But that may not matter much to Kolbe, who appears as interested in advancing himself at home as influencing legislation in Washington.

With Democratic Sen. Dennis DeConcini in political trouble as a result of the "Keating Five" investigation, Kolbe's name is being aggressively circulated as a potential 1994 challenger. Earlier, he looked seriously at a 1990 gubernatorial bid but decided against it.

On Appropriations, Kolbe primarily promotes projects important to Arizona, but in committee and on the House floor he is a loyal supporter of the GOP line, which helped him land a new assignment in the 102nd Congress: a seat on the Budget Committee. Like four of the five veteran Republicans appointed to the panel in 1991, he supported the controversial 1990 budget summit agreement negotiated by the White House and congressional Democrats.

Despite his consistently high party unity scores — he votes with the GOP majority more than 80 percent of the time — Kolbe goes his way on a few key issues that appeal to the more liberal elements of his constituency. He opposes the B-2 bomber, for instance, and is a long-time supporter of abortion rights. He also opposed the proposed constitutional amendment to ban flag burning in 1990, and in 1991, he boasted that Rep. Morris K. Udall was an original cosponsor of his bill to expand the Saguaro National Monument in the Sonora desert in the 5th.

Kolbe is best known for his support of improved relations with Mexico, and in the 102nd Congress, he is likely to be a leading supporter of a free trade agreement with Mexico, which shares a 100 mile border with his district.

"A North American Free Trade Agreement boils down to this: U.S. industries and specific firms will be able to offer a wider array of products — to a much larger number of people — at reduced prices, and American exports will increase substantially," he says, emphasizing that jobs will be created in both countries.

Earlier, he was one of Congress' most vocal advocates for the "maquiladora" assembly plant arrangement, by which U.S. companies manufacture components, then ship the items to Mexico, where they are assembled by Mexican workers; under current tariff laws, the assembled products can then be shipped back to the United States at modest cost for final packaging and distribution. Because of Mexico's lower labor costs and the favorable tariff provisions, goods produced under this arrangement can be sold at prices that are competitive with Asian-produced goods, Kolbe says. The maquiladora boom has been an important boost to southern Arizona's economy.

Critics of the "twin plant" method say it encourages U.S. companies to close their domestic manufacturing plants (often located in the East and Midwest) and transfer manufacturing to cheap-wage Mexico, costing American jobs. The "plant" on the U.S. side of the border, critics say, is often just a warehouse.

Another Kolbe issue is water, always a focal point in Arizona, where some places do not have enough of it, and some have too much. Although not on the Energy and Water Subcommittee, Kolbe, the only Arizonan on Appropriations, speaks out for funds aimed at flood control solutions, and for the Central Arizona Project, a massive system that brings water to Phoenix and other areas of the state.

In 1987, when the House debated the Energy and Water appropriations bill, Kolbe offered a successful floor amendment that settled a major controversy over the project. His amendment barred construction of Cliff Dam, which was opposed by a number of environmentalists. And in return, a coalition of environmentalists agreed to drop a lawsuit opposing other parts of the project.

Like other legislators from states along the nation's southern border, Kolbe has concerns about the influx of drugs into the United States. But on the Military Construction Sub-

Arizona 5

Southeast

In terms of registered voters, there are more Democrats than Republicans in the 5th. But that provides Democrats little comfort, because many of the district's Democrats are the rural, conservative, "pinto" variety; they have no qualms about casting GOP ballots. While two-thirds of Tucson is in the 5th, the part of the city most favorable to Democrats — the city's Hispanic neighborhoods — is mostly in the 2nd.

Largely a college town and resort center in the 1950s, Tucson today hosts an impressive number of high-technology firms; an IBM plant on Tucson's southern outskirts is among the most important high-tech employers. White-collar professional communities with firm GOP ties dominate the city's burgeoning east side.

Well-to-do residents of the Santa Catalina foothills and retirees from Davis-Monthan Air Force Base add to the GOP vote. Green Valley, an outlying Pima County town that rivals Sun City among the state's largest retirement communities, also has become a major GOP force. Democrats get some help in the Tucson portion of the 5th from the residential area around the University of Arizona, just across the border in the 2nd. The student body (31,000 in number) has become more conservative, but the faculty and staff retain a Democratic allegiance, and they are more likely than students to vote.

Outside Pima County, the 5th is largely desert.

In a landscape dominated by scrub oaks and cacti, the San Pedro River Valley provides the only relief, irrigating a fertile stretch planted in grain and pecans.

The Old West county of Cochise, anchoring southeastern Arizona, is the home of Tombstone, "the town too tough to die." Notorious for its lawlessness in the late 1800s, Tombstone still mines some silver, but relies mainly on tourism to boost the local economy. Heavily Hispanic Santa Cruz County on the Mexican border is solidly Democratic.

Late in 1988, Davis-Monthan Air Force Base in Tucson was slated for personnel reductions by the independent commission on base closings.

An Air Force study released in 1990 estimated that if Davis-Monthan were to close, the Pima County economy would lose more than 10,000 jobs and about $250 million .

Population: 542,918. White 477,610 (88%), Black 13,291 (2%), Other 10,512 (2%). Spanish origin 92,979 (17%). 18 and over 389,954 (72%), 65 and over 63,710 (12%). Median age: 31.

committee he also has raised concerns about the Defense Department's role. "I have deep reservations about the trend that is being set this year — that of expecting the Department of Defense to pay for other departments' work in the war on drugs," he said in 1988, pointing to funding that was going to boost the Coast Guard and Customs Service.

Kolbe's first term was spent on the Banking Committee, where then-chairman Fernand J. St Germain blocked him on a number of measures. But Kolbe did have some success with full-court legislative presses on the floor. He won passage of one floor amendment tightening training requirements for military procurement officers, and another cutting off aid to Lebanon until U.S. hostages were released.

At Home: Kolbe's 1984 victory did more than just avenge his narrow loss to Democrat James F. McNulty Jr. in 1982. It proved Kolbe had successfully convinced some rural 5th District residents that he was not as much a city slicker as they had once thought.

Polished, articulate and brimming with nervous energy, Kolbe does not evoke the laid-back image associated with the rural Southwest. He seems more comfortable with the bustle of high-growth Tucson than with the slower pace of the district's desert and mountain towns.

In the 1982 GOP primary, he devoted much attention to Republican-rich Tucson and surrounding Pima County to win a tight three-way nomination contest. For rural residents, that linked him firmly with the city. Democrat McNulty, a plain-spoken man with a folksy air, pulled enough support from them for a 2,407-vote edge in November.

In gearing up for the 1984 rematch, Kolbe was determined not to fall into the same trap. Free of any primary opposition, Kolbe canvassed the 5th's desert and mountain counties early in the campaign. He aired television advertisements showing him traversing the Arizona landscape on a horse. Kolbe reminded voters that he had spent much of his boyhood on a cattle ranch near the town of Sonoita — while McNulty was born and bred in Boston.

Kolbe's strategy paid off. Aided by a much better showing in the counties outside Pima, Kolbe ended with a 6,204-vote lead out of some

228,000 cast.

Kolbe's comeback victory also owed much to a change in the prevailing political conditions in the 5th. In 1982, McNulty had the advantage of running with two popular statewide Democrats at the top of the ticket. In 1984, Reagan's popularity helped Kolbe.

McNulty decided against a 1986 rematch, and local Democrats could not find a nominee of stature. Kolbe won with 65 percent.

In January 1988, Kolbe opened the door to a conservative primary challenge when he became the first Republican in Arizona's congressional delegation to call on embattled GOP Gov. Evan Mecham to resign. Mecham was ultimately removed from office by the GOP-controlled Legislature, but his conservative backers vowed revenge against Kolbe. Two Mecham supporters ran in the 5th District GOP primary; but most of the former governor's activists were bent on defeating state legislators — seven veterans were upset. Kolbe easily won both the primary and general election.

The far right threat may have enhanced Kolbe's position with independents. Their votes would be critical in a statewide race.

In 1990, potential legitimate Democratic candidates backed off to await the outcome of 1992 redistricting. As a result, Kolbe was blessed with an opponent whose major campaign splash occurred when he was jailed during the campaign on a charge of theft involving a purchase of a motor scooter. Chuck Phillips, a former social worker, had suffered previous clashes with the law, including serving three months for non-payment of child support. His campaign explanation: at least he had never been convicted of a felony.

During his six years in the Arizona Senate, Kolbe was known as a member of the state GOP's moderate-to-liberal wing and frustrated some of his more conservative colleagues, with whom he clashed on social service issues.

Kolbe played a key role in passing a state version of the Medicaid program, and was active in a overhaul of the state's groundwater-management plan. He helped establish a system for reviewing foster child-care cases.

Committees

Appropriations (19th of 22 Republicans)
Commerce, Justice, State & Judiciary

Budget (12th of 14 Republicans)
Human Resources; Urgent Fiscal Issues

Elections

1990 General		
Jim Kolbe (R)	138,975	(65%)
Chuck Phillips (D)	75,642	(35%)
1988 General		
Jim Kolbe (R)	164,462	(68%)
Judith E. Belcher (D)	78,115	(32%)

Previous Winning Percentages: **1986** (65%) **1984** (51%)

District Vote For President

	1988	1984	1980	1976
D	107,310 (44%)	86,049 (37%)	60,700 (32%)	76,224 (47%)
R	136,343 (55%)	142,205 (62%)	103,989 (55%)	79,013 (49%)
I			21,697 (11%)	

Campaign Finance

	Receipts	Receipts from PACs		Expend-itures
1990				
Kolbe (R)	$325,457	$133,605	(41%)	$250,642
1988				
Kolbe (R)	$419,090	$158,738	(38%)	$434,665

Key Votes

1991	
Authorize use of force against Iraq	Y
1990	
Support constitutional amendment on flag desecration	N
Pass family and medical leave bill over Bush veto	N
Reduce SDI funding	N
Allow abortions in overseas military facilities	Y
Approve budget summit plan for spending and taxing	Y
Approve civil rights bill	N
1989	
Halt production of B-2 stealth bomber at 13 planes	Y
Oppose capital gains tax cut	N
Approve federal abortion funding in rape or incest cases	Y
Approve pay raise and revision of ethics rules	Y
Pass Democratic minimum wage plan over Bush veto	N

Voting Studies

	Presidential Support		Party Unity		Conservative Coalition	
Year	**S**	**O**	**S**	**O**	**S**	**O**
1990	64	31	82	14	87	11
1989	69	28	81	17	85	15
1988	58	38	88	10	89	3
1987	67	31	84	13	93	7
1986	69	29	84	13	88	8
1985	78	23	86	11	91	9

Interest Group Ratings

Year	ADA	ACU	AFL-CIO	CCUS
1990	22	61	8	86
1989	15	85	0	100
1988	20	80	14	93
1987	8	87	6	93
1986	20	73	7	88
1985	0	76	6	95

Arkansas

U.S. CONGRESS

SENATE 2 D
HOUSE 3 D, 1 R

LEGISLATURE

Senate 31 D, 4 R
House 92 D, 8 R

ELECTIONS

1988 Presidential Vote	
Bush	56%
Dukakis	42%
1984 Presidential Vote	
Reagan	60%
Mondale	38%
1980 Presidential Vote	
Reagan	48%
Carter	48%
Anderson	3%
Turnout rate in 1986	39%
Turnout rate in 1988	47%
Turnout rate in 1990	37%

(as percentage of voting age population)

POPULATION AND GROWTH

1980 population	2,286,435
1990 population (33rd in the nation)	2,350,725
Percent change 1980-1990	+3%

DEMOGRAPHIC BREAKDOWN

White	83%
Black	16%
American Indian, Eskimo, or Aleut	1%
(Hispanic origin)	1%
Urban	52%
Rural	48%
Born in state	69%
Foreign-born	1%

MAJOR CITIES

Little Rock	175,795
Fort Smith	72,798
North Little Rock	61,741
Pine Bluff	57,140
Jonesboro	46,535

AREA AND LAND USE

Area	52,078 sq. miles (27th)
Farm	44%
Forest	51%
Federally owned	10%

Gov. Bill Clinton (D)
Of Little Rock — Elected 1982
(also served 1979-81)

Born: Aug. 19, 1946, Hope, Ark.
Education: Georgetown U., B.A. 1968; attended Oxford U., England, 1968-70; Yale U., J.D. 1973.
Occupation: Lawyer; law professor.
Religion: Baptist.
Political Career: Ark. attorney general, 1977-79; Democratic nominee for U.S. House, 1974; defeated for re-election as governor, 1980.
Next Election: 1994.

WORK

Occupations	
White-collar	44%
Blue-collar	38%
Service workers	12%
Government Workers	
Federal	19,432
State	48,423
Local	88,314

MONEY

Median family income	$ 14,641	(49th)
Tax burden per capita	$ 740	(38th)

EDUCATION

Spending per pupil through grade 12	$ 2,989	(46th)
Persons with college degrees	11%	(49th)

CRIME

Violent crime rate	474 per 100,000 (25th)

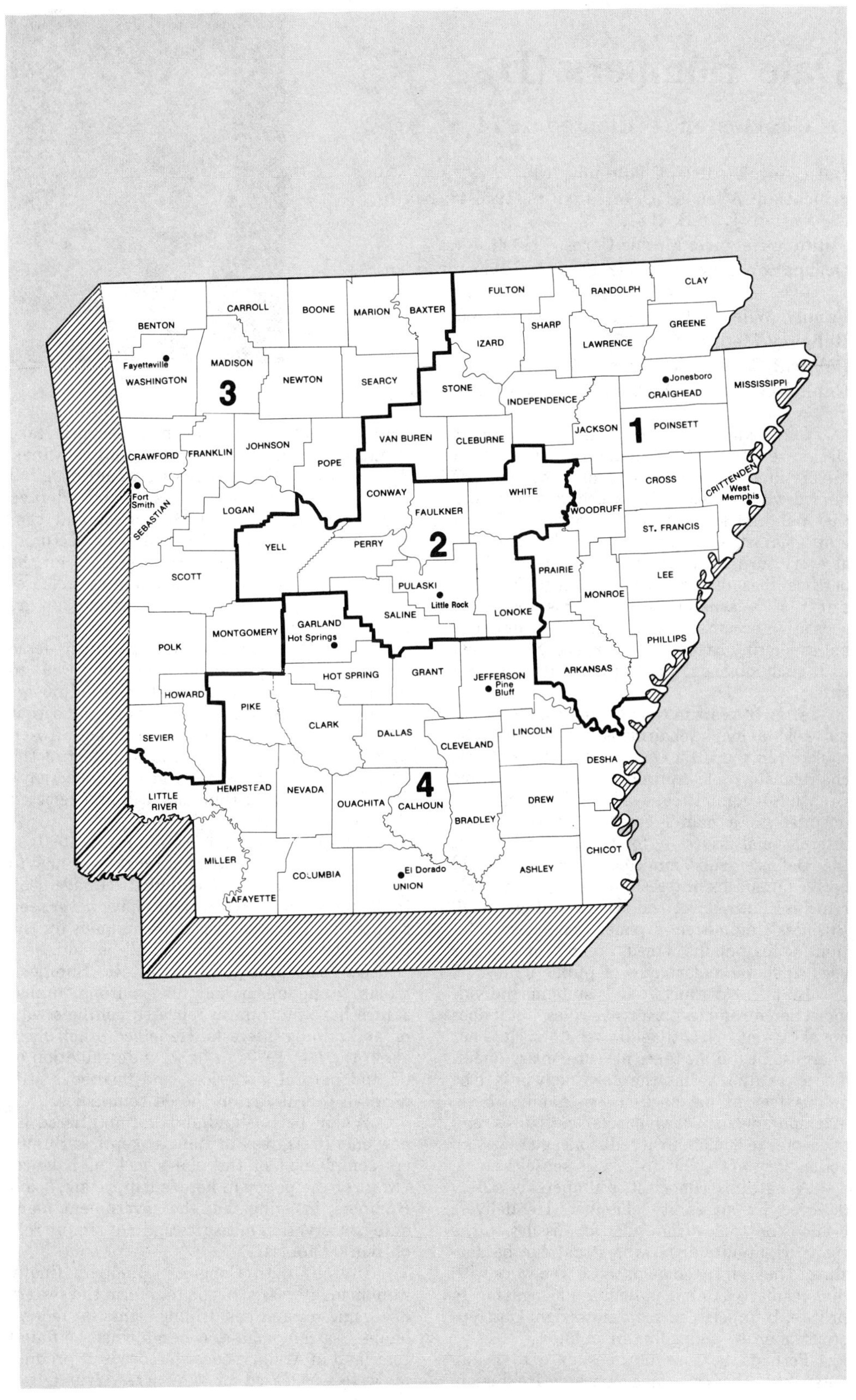
BENTON
CARROLL
BOONE
MARION
BAXTER
FULTON
RANDOLPH
CLAY
SHARP
IZARD
GREENE
LAWRENCE
Fayetteville
MADISON
WASHINGTON
3
NEWTON
SEARCY
STONE
INDEPENDENCE
Jonesboro
CRAIGHEAD
MISSISSIPPI
VAN BUREN
CLEBURNE
JACKSON
1
POINSETT
CRAWFORD
FRANKLIN
JOHNSON
POPE
CONWAY
WHITE
CROSS
CRITTENDEN
West Memphis
Fort Smith
SEBASTIAN
LOGAN
FAULKNER
WOODRUFF
ST. FRANCIS
YELL
PERRY
2
PRAIRIE
LEE
SCOTT
PULASKI
Little Rock
MONROE
SALINE
LONOKE
GARLAND
Hot Springs
MONTGOMERY
PHILLIPS
POLK
HOT SPRING
GRANT
JEFFERSON
Pine Bluff
ARKANSAS
HOWARD
PIKE
CLARK
DALLAS
LINCOLN
SEVIER
CLEVELAND
DESHA
4
LITTLE RIVER
HEMPSTEAD
NEVADA
OUACHITA
CALHOUN
DREW
BRADLEY
MILLER
CHICOT
El Dorado
COLUMBIA
UNION
ASHLEY
LAFAYETTE

Dale Bumpers (D)

Of Charleston — Elected 1974

Born: Aug. 12, 1925, Charleston, Ark.
Education: Attended U. of Arkansas, 1946-48; Northwestern U., J.D. 1951.
Military Service: Marine Corps, 1943-46.
Occupation: Lawyer; farmer; hardware company executive.
Family: Wife, Betty Flanagan; three children.
Religion: Methodist.
Political Career: Governor, 1971-75.
Capitol Office: 229 Dirksen Bldg. 20510; 224-4843.

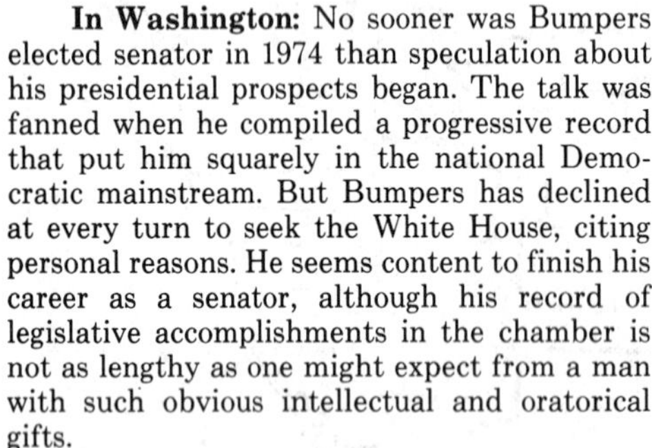

In Washington: No sooner was Bumpers elected senator in 1974 than speculation about his presidential prospects began. The talk was fanned when he compiled a progressive record that put him squarely in the national Democratic mainstream. But Bumpers has declined at every turn to seek the White House, citing personal reasons. He seems content to finish his career as a senator, although his record of legislative accomplishments in the chamber is not as lengthy as one might expect from a man with such obvious intellectual and oratorical gifts.

After 16 years in the Senate, Bumpers does not hold a major chairmanship. The best he could do in the 101st Congress was to trade his chairmanship of Appropriations' Legislative Branch Subcommittee — a housekeeping panel unsuited to a man focused on national and international issues — for the bottom seat at the Defense Subcommittee, where he could better pursue his interests in arms control. He remains chairman of the less important Small Business Committee, a panel that offers a forum for his populist creed, but not one he has used to shape major areas of public policy.

Bumpers' distinctive style suits the individualist Senate and its permissive rules, but it does not always sit well with fellow senators. He is not quarrelsome, but he takes pleasure in argument. The fewer allies he has, the more likely he is to be on his feet at his back-of-the-chamber desk, extemporaneously weaving facts, figures and anecdotes to explain to absent colleagues why an action they are about to take is senseless.

A natural iconoclast, Bumpers is rarely deterred by an empty chamber. He delivers orations on topics from nuclear missiles to the rights of satellite dish owners that can be dazzling to hear, if tiresome to those who work with him regularly. Calm, patient and engaging in private, Bumpers can seem downright obstreperous when he gets going in public.

Perhaps because he does dare to be an outspoken liberal from a conservative region, Bumpers gets vexed when colleagues take stands he sees as bending to the political winds. In 1988, as the Senate debated an antidrug bill timed for the campaign season, and adopted various penalties of arguable effect and constitutionality, a scornful Bumpers lectured, "Just to grow hair on your chest here on the Senate floor so you can put out press releases telling everyone back home how tough you are on drugs is no solution."

When North Carolina Republican Jesse Helms offered an amendment in 1989 to toughen language barring federal funding for obscene art, an indignant Bumpers noted that the obscenity issue "has had the Senate frozen with a great deal of terror and fear, fear of the 30-second spot when they run for re-election." The Senate heeded Bumpers' call and rejected the Helms proposal 62-35.

Bumpers was just as blunt in 1990 as Congress fell into political gridlock over how to reduce the growing budget deficit. "I have been in the Senate for 16 years, and I have never seen a time that I thought was more ominous for the future of the country than now," he said.

On the Energy Committee, Bumpers' streak of populism and his environmentalist stance have put him in repeated conflicts with oil and mining interests. He joined other liberals in the late 1970s in fighting deregulation of oil and natural gas prices, and favored a stiff windfall-profits tax on the oil companies.

When the Bush administration offered its new energy strategy in 1991, a skeptical Bumpers complained of the plan's lack of balance. "Most of the policy in here is happy talk," said Bumpers, insisting that the government mandate conservation measures and not simply rely on market forces.

In the 100th Congress, Bumpers finally won an eight-year struggle to reform the system of leasing oil and gas drilling rights on federal lands — a campaign that began when he found that land in Arkansas near hundreds of producing wells was leased for $1 an acre. Arguing that the lottery and over-the-counter lease systems in use were "a scandal . . . outmoded, susceptible to fraud and manipulation, and not designed to provide the government with a fair return," he passed a bill replacing them with a competitive bidding process.

He is also a critic of nuclear power, though he has failed in his effort to bar utilities from passing on to consumers the costs of closing nuclear power plants. Bumpers was the most vociferous Senate opponent of the Clinch River breeder reactor in Tennessee. He came within one vote of killing the expensive project in 1982, and finally won in 1984.

In the 1980s, Bumpers was perhaps best known as one of the Senate's most outspoken supporters of arms control, working at strengthening U.S. support for the unratified SALT II treaty. Bumpers and his allies urged the Reagan administration not to drop its policy of informally abiding by the treaty's arms limits. In 1986, Reagan finally decided to repudiate the treaty on the grounds of Soviet violations. The Senate in 1987 adopted Bumpers' amendment urging continued compliance, but a similar amendment fell by six votes the next year.

For Bumpers, who once accused Reagan of not wanting "to spend money on anything that does not explode," the MX missile was a special target. He offered repeated amendments to kill the MX, which finally was capped at 50 in a 1985 compromise.

Bumpers has also been a major opponent of the strategic defense initiative. While he was successful in getting Congress to vote to slow development of the SDI program, he failed in 1990 to pass an amendment to the defense authorization bill to cut overall spending on the program by $600 million.

During consideration of the defense bill in 1990, Bumpers unsuccessfully targeted Navy battleships and military base closings. His amendment to retire one of the two remaining *Iowa*-class ships equipped with cruise missiles fell by 11 votes. His amendment to nullify the secretary of Defense's list of bases to be closed suffered the same fate; among the bases slated for closure was Eaker Air Force Base in Blytheville, Ark.

A year earlier, the Senate rejected a Bumpers amendment requiring the withdrawal of 3,000 U.S. military personnel from South Korea. The move was an attempt to trim the military budget and send a message to allies that they were not spending enough on defense.

In the 100th Congress, Bumpers was a leading opponent of Reagan's policy of providing Navy escorts to Kuwaiti tankers in the Persian Gulf. Many members complained that Reagan had not properly consulted Congress before committing U.S. forces, but Bumpers was one of the few favoring legislative action against the policy. That idea met with fierce Republican opposition, and even many Democrats were reluctant to challenge an ongoing policy.

On Appropriations, Bumpers has used his various subcommittee posts to espouse health programs for the poor, aid for rural areas and the rice subsidies important to his state.

During consideration in 1989 of the Agriculture Department spending bill, Bumpers exhibited his dogged determination, though critics would call it stubbornness. The bill was stalled for weeks just short of final action in conference by an impasse between Bumpers and House Appropriations Committee Chairman Jamie L. Whitten of Mississippi.

Bumpers sought a $1.1 million grant for a private company located in Fayetteville, Ark., to provide farmers with information about reducing their use of chemicals on their crops. The Senate agreed to the grant, but in conference, Whitten insisted the money be removed. After a month of trying to wear Whitten down, Bumpers relented and the grant was stripped from the agreement.

As liberal as much of his work makes Bumpers sound, his iconoclasm makes him difficult to label. In 1978 he was the only senator to vote against popular "sunset" legislation for periodic reviews of all federal agencies. In 1987, as Small Business chairman, he allied with then-Sen. Dan Quayle of Indiana to oppose Labor Committee Chairman Edward M. Kennedy's bill requiring all employers to provide health insurance. And in 1988, he clashed with liberal House members over revamping the scandal-plagued program that reserves federal contracts for minority-owned firms. House negotiators felt Bumpers' bill was too tough on minority firms.

Unlike his counterpart in the House, Small Business Committee Chairman John J. LaFalce of New York, Bumpers has not changed the Senate's Small Business panel to give it a major role in the setting of tax and regulatory policy. Bumpers has championed small-business concerns about the burdens of government regulations. He also tried in March 1991 to provide assistance to Persian Gulf War veterans who owned small businesses; the Senate defeated the amendment 58-38.

At Home: "A smile and a shoeshine" was the phrase Winthrop Rockefeller used to describe the political phenomenon that removed him from the Arkansas governorship in 1970. It was a slur on Bumpers' intellectual substance, but it was not a bad description of the campaign that lifted him from a small-town law practice to the state Capitol in a remarkably short time.

Rockefeller had made Bumpers' accession possible by discrediting and retiring most of the segregationist "old guard" that had dominated the Democratic Party in Arkansas over the previous two decades. After four years of Republican rule under Rockefeller, the state was ready to go Democratic again under a modern leader. Bumpers was so clearly the right man that a smile, a shoeshine and a sophisticated set of TV ads were more than enough to give him a primary victory over the legendary race-baiter Orval E. Faubus in a Democratic runoff and an easy win over Rockefeller in the fall. Issues were beside the point.

Bumpers' gubernatorial campaign was so vague that the state had little reason to know what it was getting when he took office in January 1971. In fact, it was getting a man with a fair degree of liberal Yankee influence, a graduate of Northwestern University law school and a longtime admirer of Adlai E. Stevenson, who was governor of Illinois when Bumpers got his law degree. Bumpers came to the governorship without any political experience beyond the school board in Charleston, Ark., but with a clear sense of where he was going.

During four years in office, Bumpers presided over a modernization of state government, closing down many of the bureaucratic fiefdoms that old-guard Democrats had controlled. By early 1974, he was ready for national politics. State Democrats braced themselves for a titanic struggle between the governor and veteran Sen. J. William Fulbright, who had helped raise money for Bumpers in 1970.

As it turned out, the struggle failed to live up to its advance billing. Bumpers decided to run only after political consultant Deloss Walker showed him polls guaranteeing he could not lose. Bumpers defeated Fulbright by nearly 2-to-1 in the Democratic primary without offering a critical word or a divisive issue.

The 1980 election was nothing to worry about either. While other Arkansas Democrats were finally paying the price for a decade of too-easy liberal politics, Bumpers was winning a second term by 150,000 votes.

In 1986, Republicans nominated an aggressive challenger in Asa Hutchinson, who had served as U.S. attorney in Little Rock under the Reagan administration. But Bumpers took nothing for granted, turning up at hundreds of barbecues, fish-fries and other gatherings, re-establishing his roots by using the down-home style that had first vaulted him to success. Bumpers improved on his 1980 showing.

Committees

Small Business (Chairman)
Export Expansion; Rural Economy & Family Farming

Appropriations (9th of 16 Democrats)
Agriculture, Rural Development & Related Agencies; Commerce, Justice, State & Judiciary; Defense; Interior; Labor, Health & Human Services, Education

Energy & Natural Resources (2nd of 11 Democrats)
Energy Research & Development; Mineral Resources Development & Production; Public Lands, National Parks & Forests (chairman)

Elections

1986 General		
Dale Bumpers (D)	433,122	(62%)
Asa Hutchinson (R)	262,313	(38%)

Previous Winning Percentages: 1980 (59%) **1974** (85%)

Campaign Finance

	Receipts	Receipts from PACs	Expend- itures
1986			
Bumpers (D)	$1,726,383	$507,419 (29%)	$1,672,432
Hutchinson (R)	$916,436	$81,221 (9%)	$910,924

Key Votes

1991	
Authorize use of force against Iraq	N
1990	
Oppose prohibition of certain semiautomatic weapons	N
Support constitutional amendment on flag desecration	N
Oppose requiring parental notice for minors' abortions	Y
Halt production of B-2 stealth bomber at 13 planes	Y
Approve budget that cut spending and raised revenues	Y
Pass civil rights bill over Bush veto	Y
1989	
Oppose reduction of SDI funding	N
Oppose barring federal funds for "obscene" art	Y
Allow vote on capital gains tax cut	N

Voting Studies

	Presidential Support		Party Unity		Conservative Coalition	
Year	**S**	**O**	**S**	**O**	**S**	**O**
1990	35	62	84	14	57	43
1989	50	50	87	12	26	71
1988	44	50	84	7	41	57
1987	38	58	89	11	38	59
1986	39	59	77	20	49	47
1985	32	62	79	17	52	45
1984	36	53	76	14	45	51
1983	32	56	85	10	41	45
1982	30	63	86	11	20	74
1981	39	52	81	8	20	69

Interest Group Ratings

Year	ADA	ACU	AFL-CIO	CCUS
1990	72	23	56	33
1989	90	21	90	25
1988	80	12	79	33
1987	85	8	70	35
1986	70	22	64	47
1985	70	13	71	45
1984	75	18	60	42
1983	75	17	82	17
1982	85	26	81	21
1981	95	13	84	24

David Pryor (D)

Of Little Rock — Elected 1978

Born: Aug. 29, 1934, Camden, Ark.
Education: U. of Arkansas, B.A. 1957, LL.B. 1964.
Occupation: Lawyer; newspaper publisher.
Family: Wife, Barbara Lunsford; three children.
Religion: Presbyterian.
Political Career: Ark. House, 1961-67; U.S. House, 1967-73; governor, 1975-79; sought Democratic nomination for U.S. Senate, 1972.
Capitol Office: 267 Russell Bldg. 20510; 224-2353.

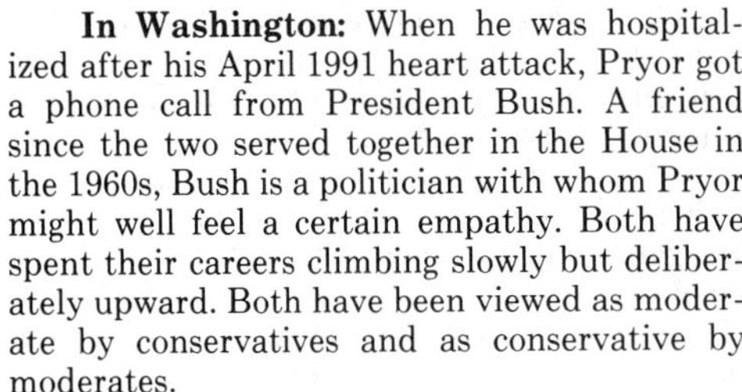

In Washington: When he was hospitalized after his April 1991 heart attack, Pryor got a phone call from President Bush. A friend since the two served together in the House in the 1960s, Bush is a politician with whom Pryor might well feel a certain empathy. Both have spent their careers climbing slowly but deliberately upward. Both have been viewed as moderate by conservatives and as conservative by moderates.

"I'm out of the woods, but I still need some rest," Pryor assured the president. Pryor's doctors called the heart attack moderate and counseled a cutback in his activities. He had been serving on five committees, as well as holding the No. 3 party leadership position as secretary of the Democratic Conference.

Few were surprised when Pryor responded to the medical advice by resigning from the Senate Ethics Committee, on which he had served for 11 years. Ethics is always a thankless task, even by this dutiful senator's standards.

Pryor's tour of Ethics duty had been especially stressful in 1990 and early 1991 as the committee weighed charges that five senators had used their influence to help savings and loan executive Charles H. Keating Jr., a major fundraiser.

Pryor's statements and questions during the proceedings suggested that he leaned toward relatively lenient treatment of his colleagues. In February, the committee decided that only Alan Cranston of California should be subject to further punishment by the full Senate; the other four received mild rebukes.

After years of relatively low-profile labors and middling success, Pryor began the 101st Congress not only as conference secretary but also as chairman of the Special Committee on Aging.

He had won the leadership post when Daniel K. Inouye of Hawaii left it to run unsuccessfully for majority leader. Pryor was elected easily in the same closed-door balloting that elected George J. Mitchell of Maine majority leader in November 1988.

Some of Pryor's colleagues indicated that, as the only Southerner on the new leadership team, he had won at least in part because of the regional and philosophical balance he lent to Mitchell and Democratic Whip Alan Cranston of California. (In 1990, Cranston left the whip's job and was replaced by Kentucky's Wendell H. Ford.)

But Pryor also seemed to have been more personally popular with his colleagues than his rival for conference secretary, Patrick J. Leahy of Vermont. Pryor seemed especially well regarded by younger members who admire his longstanding crusade against filibusters, dilatory floor tactics, quorum calls and extended roll call votes.

Pryor has long been one of the members most disturbed by the unreasonable demands the Senate schedule often puts on family life. He organized an informal panel of six senators who began pushing for changes aimed at restoring some measure of discipline to the way the Senate conducts its business. In 1985, his efforts helped produce an informal package of time-saving rules, such as limiting most votes to 15 minutes. The group's recommendation that the Senate work three weeks, then take a week off, has become the standard calendar.

The chair of the Aging panel fell to Pryor when predecessor Chairman John Melcher met unexpected defeat in Montana in 1988. Pryor has since set about re-establishing himself as a leader on the issue that helped vault him into prominence. As a young legislator in Little Rock in the 1960s, he showed an inspired knack for attracting public attention to the concerns of the elderly. Later, while serving in the House, Pryor ran a kind of rogue subcommittee on the needs of the elderly, operating out of trailers parked near the House office buildings.

Melcher's upset also raised Pryor to the No. 2 Democratic slot on the Agriculture Committee, behind Leahy. Here he had already proven an effective member, helping create a new "marketing loan" program for cotton and rice growers in the 1985 farm bill and protecting Southern soybean growers from a price-formula change in 1988.

On the 1990 farm bill, he worked with Republican Thad Cochran of Mississippi, a kindred spirit with whom he shared an interest in rice, cotton, soybeans and bipartisan cooperation. One staffer on the bill described the two working together "like brothers," but they could not match the success they had achieved for soybean producers five years earlier. Pryor complained that the fiscal squeeze was being misplaced. "It's hard for soybeans to contribute to deficit reduction when they don't contribute to the deficit," he said.

When it comes to Arkansas agriculture, Pryor will even reach for some of the procedural tools he generally decries. When a bill cutting federal farm-price supports came to the Senate floor in 1984, he and Arkansas colleague Dale Bumpers worried that the measure would harm their rice farmers. To delay action on the time-sensitive bill, they began to read their favorite rice recipes into the *Congressional Record.* "I think I know of about 1,000 dishes with rice in them," Pryor said, to the delight of the galleries and the chagrin of the leadership.

Pryor has been less active on the Finance Committee, taking a rather hands-off attitude toward most of the tax-reform upheaval of the 99th Congress. But as chairman of the subcommittee on Internal Revenue Service oversight, he has been a critic of the agency's "fearsome" powers and a voice for "taxpayers' rights" legislation. In 1990, a hearing he chaired received wide media play when a woman testified that the IRS had driven her husband to suicide.

When other committees' handiwork reaches the floor, Pryor sometimes pops up with difficult, even quixotic, amendments. In 1988, he amended the defense appropriations bill to require all consultants hired by the Pentagon to disclose their other clients. Passed by voice vote in the midst of publicity over alleged procurement fraud, Pryor's amendment was Congress' first response to the perceived scandal. But in the fall, House and Senate conferees quietly dropped it.

The military budget had previously attracted Pryor's eye, even before reports that the Pentagon had spent $600 for a toilet seat. But Pryor has had limited success with his efforts to impose stringent controls. One of his prime targets has been "sole source" defense contracts, by which the Pentagon certifies that only one company is qualified to produce a particular weapon. Pryor advocates competitive bidding to award contracts.

In 1983, citing some of the more elaborate examples of Pentagon hardware — such as a $40 million program to build an armored bulldozer to accompany the M-1 tank into battle — Pryor helped push through an amendment establishing an independent agency within the Pentagon to test weapons.

In 1985, Pryor went head-to-head with the Armed Services Committee in an effort to impose strict new procurement rules. He offered a comprehensive amendment to the defense authorization bill requiring that all weapons purchases be arranged through competition involving at least two bidders. In addition, the amendment barred Pentagon procurement officials from taking jobs with defense contractors for three years after they left the government. Preferring a milder alternative offered by the committee, the Senate rejected Pryor's effort, 22-67.

The next year, Pryor found himself defending his weapons-testing office. Armed Services members pushed to include the office under the authority of a new Pentagon procurement "czar" they were creating. Pryor sought to stop them, arguing that the move would undermine the independence of the testing office. He lost on the Senate floor, although the change was dropped in conference.

Pryor's biggest defense target has been the "binary" chemical weapons proposed by the Reagan administration. Although the weapons would be produced in Arkansas, creating jobs in the state, and have had the support of his pro-arms-control colleague, Bumpers, Pryor has been the most vocal opponent of the idea in the Senate. Ironically, Pryor's closest ally in the House on the issue was Rep. Ed Bethune, his 1984 Republican challenger.

Pryor opposes chemical weapons on both moral and economic grounds. Matching Soviet production of the lethal materials would "surrender the high ground as far as world opinion is concerned," he says, arguing also that the weapons would add little to U.S. defense capabilities.

In the 100th Congress, Pryor inserted a provision in the fiscal 1989 defense authorization bill by which the $99 million requested for "Bigeye" binary bombs would be unavailable pending further testing. Conferees later authorized only $15 million, all for bombs to be used in tests.

At Home: An impressive 1984 re-election performance and a foundering state GOP combined to ensure Pryor's re-election in 1990. His bid for a third Senate term was locked up when the GOP failed even to field a challenger. With his only opposition coming from an independent write-in candidate, Pryor was free to help former Democratic Rep. Ray Thornton, a one-time rival, who was seeking a comeback by running for the open 2nd District seat. Thornton won.

In 1984, in a convincing demonstration of the personal popularity he had built up over 21 years in office, Pryor easily defeated the strongest possible GOP challenger even as Arkansas went decisively for President Ronald Reagan.

Pryor's 1983 voting record — he opposed Reagan's positions more often than any other senator — encouraged national GOP officials to believe he could be turned out in a Reagan landslide, and they urged Bethune to make the race. Throughout the campaign, Bethune predicted that 1984 would bring a revolutionary change in Arkansas politics as traditional Democrats came to realize that the Democratic Party had been "taken over by the liberals."

But Pryor was well positioned to blunt Bethune's efforts at casting the race in ideological terms. In the eyes of most Arkansans, Pryor was not a liberal ogre who had "gone Washington"; he was a personable moderate who kept in touch with a large network of friends he had gained as a state legislator, congressman, governor and senator.

Pryor stressed the more conservative and populist aspects of his record, reminding voters of his support for a balanced-budget constitutional amendment and defense of the Rural Electrification Administration (REA) against Bethune's proposal to abolish the low-rate federal loans the REA grants to utility cooperatives.

Reagan campaigned in Arkansas the weekend before the election, but his presence was no aid to Bethune. Pryor won 58 percent, nearly matching Bumpers' 1980 re-election tally over a much weaker Republican foe.

Pryor has always had a talent for picking issues that bring favorable exposure in Arkansas. He was still in his 20s, struggling and outnumbered against the segregationist "Old Guard" in the state Legislature, when he began investigating abuses in nursing homes. That issue helped him win a House seat in 1966, when the 4th District was left vacant with the departure of veteran Democrat Oren Harris. Once settled in Washington, Pryor ran unopposed in 1968 and 1970.

In 1972 Pryor took on a challenge virtually every Democrat in the state told him he could not win — a primary campaign against the venerable senior senator, John L. McClellan. Pryor was determined, and he campaigned intensely all over the state for months, raising the issue of McClellan's age, which was 76. When he held the senator to 44 percent in the initial primary in May, forcing a runoff, Arkansas' startled Democrats assumed he had McClellan cornered. That was the second wrong assumption of the spring. The veteran fought back with surprising vigor in the runoff, seizing on Pryor's labor support to argue that union bosses wanted to get even for past McClellan corruption probes. On runoff night, Pryor found himself beaten by 18,000 votes.

Two years after his defeat, Pryor was elected governor, spoiling a comeback effort by Gov. Orval E. Faubus in that year's runoff. Faubus' once-vaunted political power had faded, along with the race issue that had fueled it, and his allies in the Arkansas business establishment deserted him for Pryor. Faubus called Pryor the "candidate of 52 millionaires" seeking to influence state policy, but the result was not even close. Pryor had no trouble winning the general election that fall, or a second two-year term in 1976.

Late in 1977, McClellan died. Pryor appointed Kaneaster Hodges to fill out the late senator's term. Under state law, Hodges was ineligible to succeed himself, and Pryor moved in on the seat in 1978.

This time he was no longer fighting the Old Guard. His competition in the primary came from two moderate representatives, Jim Guy Tucker of Little Rock and Thornton, who had succeeded Pryor in the 4th District House seat.

Pryor's pro-labor image had long since faded. As governor, he lost union support by sending in the National Guard to replace striking Pine Bluff firemen. In the two-man runoff, Tucker got the labor endorsement; Pryor made an issue of it.

Pryor won the runoff by a surprising 47,000 votes, picking up much of the southern Arkansas support that had gone at first to Thornton, a close third in the initial primary. The general election against Republican Thomas Kelly was easy; Pryor won by more than 3-to-1.

Committees

Special Aging (Chairman)

Agriculture, Nutrition & Forestry (2nd of 10 Democrats)
Agricultural Production & Stabilization of Prices (chairman); Domestic & Foreign Marketing & Product Promotion; Nutrition & Investigations; Rural Development & Rural Electrification

Finance (7th of 11 Democrats)
Private Retirement Plans & Oversight of the Internal Revenue Service (chairman);
Medicare & Long Term Care;
Taxation

Governmental Affairs (5th of 8 Democrats)
Federal Services, Post Office & Civil Service (chairman); Oversight of Government Management; Permanent Subcommittee on Investigations

Elections

1990 General

David Pryor (D)	493,910	(100%)

Previous Winning Percentages: **1984** (57%) **1978** (77%) **1970** * (100%) **1968** * (100%) **1966** * (65%)

* *House elections.*

Campaign Finance

	Receipts	Receipts from PACs		Expend-itures
1990				
Pryor (D)	$1,228,545	$485,067	(39%)	$368,579

Key Votes

1991

Authorize use of force against Iraq	N

1990

Oppose prohibition of certain semiautomatic weapons	N
Support constitutional amendment on flag desecration	N
Oppose requiring parental notice for minors' abortions	Y
Halt production of B-2 stealth bomber at 13 planes	Y
Approve budget that cut spending and raised revenues	Y
Pass civil rights bill over Bush veto	Y

1989

Oppose reduction of SDI funding	N
Oppose barring federal funds for "obscene" art	Y
Allow vote on capital gains tax cut	N

Voting Studies

	Presidential Support		Party Unity		Conservative Coalition	
Year	**S**	**O**	**S**	**O**	**S**	**O**
1990	34	62	85	13	65	32
1989	53	45	80	18	42	55
1988	48	47	85	11	49	43
1987	32	59	87	7	47	41
1986	35	60	70	24	55	38
1985	32	66	79	15	50	42
1984	45	47	60	25	72	23
1983	27	71	78	14	57	34
1982	45	49	73	23	56	35
1981	47	48	80	15	54	42

Interest Group Ratings

Year	ADA	ACU	AFL-CIO	CCUS
1990	67	18	56	25
1989	80	27	89	25
1988	75	16	79	43
1987	75	15	67	47
1986	60	33	40	53
1985	80	4	76	41
1984	55	38	60	50
1983	70	28	71	33
1982	70	55	69	45
1981	75	21	47	53

1 Bill Alexander (D)

Of Osceola — Elected 1968

Born: Jan. 16, 1934, Memphis, Tenn.
Education: Southwestern at Memphis, B.A. 1957; Vanderbilt U., LL.B. 1960.
Military Service: Army, 1951-53.
Occupation: Lawyer.
Family: Wife, Debi Drury; one child.
Religion: Episcopalian.
Political Career: No previous office.
Capitol Office: 233 Cannon Bldg. 20515; 225-4076.

In Washington: During his career in the House, Alexander has headed in several different directions — into party leadership circles, toward involvement in foreign policy, and down the pork-barrel politics route. But now in his third decade in Congress, Alexander finds that simply maintaining his electoral base is a time-consuming agenda item.

He was distracted in the mid-1980s by a stretch of bad publicity that contributed to his 1986 defeat in a bid for party whip, and a close call in the primary that year. Since the 1989 resignation of Speaker Jim Wright of Texas — who was once something of a mentor to Alexander — the Arkansan has rarely been a visible player in the legislative process. During the 1990 primary season, Alexander was back home fending off another vigorous challenger.

As the ethics charges that ultimately drove Wright from office gained momentum, Alexander was as loyal an ally as Wright had. He lodged ethics charges against Wright's chief accuser, Republican Newt Gingrich, in April 1989, a month after the Georgian won the No. 2 job in the GOP leadership. Mirroring questions raised about a book deal of Wright's, Alexander asked for an investigation of a partnership that raised some $105,000 — mostly from political supporters of Gingrich — to promote a book of his. But while the accusations irked Gingrich, they were widely viewed as a pro-Wright ploy and were dismissed after a yearlong ethics committee review.

While Alexander's position on Appropriations enables him to steer federal dollars to his east Arkansas district, the panel does not seem to offer Alexander any immediate avenues for advancement within the House that could return him to a position of broader influence. He is the No. 2 Democrat on two subcommittees — Military Construction and Commerce, Justice and State — but neither of the subcommittee chairmen Alexander serves behind appears on the verge of retiring.

Alexander lost his place in the party leadership when, after six years as chief deputy whip, he stumbled badly in his 1986 effort to move up to the No. 3 post of majority whip. Like other candidates for the job, which was being filled by a caucus election for the first time, Alexander was outdistanced early by the aggressive campaigning of Tony Coelho of California. Although Alexander had gotten his start in the leadership thanks to the man who was about to become Speaker, Wright, that did not translate into an advantage in the whip's race.

Alexander has a reputation as a somewhat unpredictable figure. Early in his career, he drew attention by engaging in a shoving match with a policeman outside Washington's National Airport. In 1985, he gained notoriety from a *Wall Street Journal* report that he waved an African spear and shouted "boogaloo" at a group of lobbyists in his office. Alexander said he actually had shouted a Kenyan greeting, "Jambo, Jambo."

In the summer of 1985, Alexander obtained a military jet to take a "congressional delegation" to Brazil and then turned out to be the only member on the trip. Alexander defended the $50,000 excursion as a useful energy fact-finding mission, but several colleagues criticized it as an abuse of congressional privileges.

The 1985 incidents stoked the fires of political opposition at home, giving him a startlingly close Democratic primary in 1986. Chastened, Alexander generally kept a lower profile for the next two years. But Alexander stumbled again in mid-1987 when he opened the way for critics to recycle the portrait of him as a misuser of taxpayer dollars. He inserted into the *Congressional Record* the text of four years of debate on the Boland amendment, a law central to the Iran-contra affair that was then engulfing the Reagan administration. Defenders called it a "must read" but others called it a waste of some $200,000 in printing costs.

During the Reagan years, Alexander's opposition to military aid for the contras in Nicaragua took considerable political courage in light of his traditional Southern district. He also took a risk opposing President Ronald Reagan's 1981 budget. His district strongly favored it, and influential Arkansas Democrats

Arkansas 1

East — Jonesboro

Covering most of the eastern third of the state and some hilly northern counties, the agricultural 1st is the part of Arkansas with the strongest Deep South tradition. Although it is the poorest district in the state, its flat, fertile Mississippi delta has traditionally supported large plantations, some running into tens of thousands of acres. Tied to the cotton trade long before the Civil War, the area now is heavily reliant on rice and soybeans.

Vestiges of the Old South still remain in places like Hughes, where plantations coexist with shantytowns, and where over a third of all blacks live below the poverty level. Jonesboro, the home of Arkansas State University (8,700 students) and West Memphis, a suburb of Memphis, Tenn., are the district's only major cities.

Despite agriculture's continued domination of the local economy, there is some new industry, and Helena, West Memphis and Osceola, all on the Mississippi River, are developing port cities. Blytheville, a Mississippi River town just south of the Missouri border, has attracted several new companies in recent years.

Over the past decade, retirees from Northern states have begun to settle in the 1st's hill country, populating retirement communities such as Cherokee Village in Sharp County. Many of these elderly newcomers are accustomed to voting for Republicans; Alexander carried Sharp by only 24 votes in November 1990. George Bush carried the 1st in 1988.

In most elections, the district remains solidly Democratic, especially in the Mississippi delta counties where there is a heavy concentration of blacks. Four of the seven Arkansas counties that the Rev. Jesse Jackson carried in Arkansas' 1988 Democratic presidential primary are in this area. But as the cotton economy has declined in the delta, the largely black delta counties have steadily lost population.

Population: 573,551. White 462,199 (81%), Black 107,604 (19%), Other 2,607(1%). Spanish origin 4,675 (1%). 18 and over 396,107 (69%), 65 and over 80,097 (14%). Median age: 30.

urged him to back Reagan to save his political career.

But that would have required breaking with Wright. Alexander worked hard for Wright in the 1976 contest for majority leader, and after the election was over, he was rewarded with Wright's old post in the middle ranks of the Democratic whip structure. In early 1981, when Chief Deputy Whip Dan Rostenkowski of Illinois took the Ways and Means Committee chairmanship, Wright chose Alexander to replace him.

While he has not abandoned his involvement in the kinds of foreign policy issues that have given fuel to opponents at home, Alexander is not as vocal as he once was. Joining the Democratic chorus for defense policy changes commensurate with the waning of the Cold War, he sponsored a 1990 amendment to halve the funding for Radio Martí, which broadcasts into Cuba. He also opposed U.S. funding of a new NATO base in Crotone, Italy.

At Home: Even after the Brazilian-junket controversy, Alexander showed few signs of concern when state Sen. Jim Wood launched a conservative challenge to him for 1986. The veteran Democrat had been challenged from the right before, by well-financed opponents, and had always won handsomely.

The previous challenges, however, were from Republicans, and they failed to ignite much enthusiasm in an old-fashioned Deep South district. Wood was a conservative Democrat, so he had access to a substantial bloc of votes previous challengers could not pry loose.

Wood, an amiable, cherubic state legislator, was not very amiable in his campaign. He called Alexander an "international jet-setter," and ran TV ads accusing him of taking 19 foreign trips at taxpayer expense. He attacked Alexander's support for improved U.S. relations with Cuba and referred darkly to his "affiliation and support for known communists." He said Alexander was too aloof and too arrogant to represent the 1st.

Alexander, slow to respond, spent little time campaigning until the final weeks before the primary. It was a near-fatal strategy: He retained only 52 percent of the primary vote. Primary day saw him lose substantial support in his usual strongholds along the Mississippi River, and he lost the white vote districtwide. But for strong backing from the 19 percent black minority in the 1st, Alexander would have lost.

Once past the primary, though, Alexander could afford to relax. Republicans tried to generate interest in their nominee, a 27-year-old radio station manager, but nearly all of Alexander's conservative Democratic critics came back to him in the fall, and he won by a wide margin.

Two years later, Darrell Glascock, the political consultant who had managed Wood's campaign, took on Alexander in the primary. Glascock raised all the same issues as Wood, but having lost the surprise factor, he was no match for Alexander, who prevailed by 2-to-1.

In 1990, Alexander faced an energetic, well-financed primary challenge from Mike Gibson, a little-known lawyer from Alexander's hometown, Osceola. Gibson attracted support from the monied business interests perennially keen on seeing Alexander ousted; he heavily outspent the incumbent on TV ads. Gibson also made a bid for votes in the black community.

But Alexander avoided repeating the mistakes of 1986. Even though he did not begin full-time campaigning until a month before primary day, he had returned to the district on most weekends in 1990. He reminded voters of the numerous public works projects he has channeled into the district over the years. He held on to win renomination with 54 percent of the vote. In November, Alexander took 64 percent against Republican real estate developer Terry Hayes.

Alexander was a young lawyer in Osceola when he entered the free-for-all 1968 Democratic primary to succeed Rep. Ezekiel "Took" Gathings, who was retiring.

There were nine candidates for the nomination, and Alexander had never held office before. But he was the front-runner from the start. As the son of an old east Arkansas political family, he had instant credentials with the network of large farmers and small-town courthouse Democrats that held great sway over politics in the area.

His main opponent called him "the hand-picked man of the big plantation owners and the political bosses." But that rival, Jack Files, a former aide to Sen. J. William Fulbright, ran a distant second to Alexander in the primary. In the runoff, Alexander drew 62 percent.

The resurgent Arkansas Republicans attempted to give Alexander a fight that November. Their candidate was Guy Newcomb, a pharmacist and farmer, also from Osceola. It was the first real general-election contest in the district since Reconstruction, but the Republican came out with only 31 percent of the vote.

Committee

Appropriations (9th of 37 Democrats)
Commerce, Justice, State & Judiciary; Legislative; Military Construction

Elections

1990 General		
Bill Alexander (D)	101,026	(64%)
Terry Hayes (R)	56,071	(36%)
1990 Primary		
Bill Alexander (D)	72,401	(54%)
Mike Gibson (D)	60,948	(46%)
1988 General		
Bill Alexander (D)		Unopposed

Previous Winning Percentages: **1986** (64%) **1984** (97%) **1982** (65%) **1980** (100%) **1978** (100%) **1976** (69%) **1974** (91%) **1972** (100%) **1970** (100%) **1968** (69%)

District Vote For President

	1988	1984	1980	1976
D	89,812 (48%)	86,743 (43%)	103,906 (52%)	135,001 (70%)
R	95,388 (51%)	114,091 (57%)	88,732 (45%)	57,776 (30%)
I			4,049 (2%)	

Campaign Finance

	Receipts	Receipts from PACs		Expend-itures
1990				
Alexander (D)	$773,016	$405,150	(52%)	$785,626
Hayes (R)	$36,792	$2,000	(5%)	$36,731
1988				
Alexander (D)	$674,287	$321,524	(48%)	$665,445

Key Votes

1991	
Authorize use of force against Iraq	N
1990	
Support constitutional amendment on flag desecration	Y
Pass family and medical leave bill over Bush veto	Y
Reduce SDI funding	Y
Allow abortions in overseas military facilities	Y
Approve budget summit plan for spending and taxing	N
Approve civil rights bill	Y
1989	
Halt production of B-2 stealth bomber at 13 planes	N
Oppose capital gains tax cut	N
Approve federal abortion funding in rape or incest cases	Y
Approve pay raise and revision of ethics rules	Y
Pass Democratic minimum wage plan over Bush veto	Y

Voting Studies

	Presidential Support		Party Unity		Conservative Coalition	
Year	S	O	S	O	S	O
1990	27	62	72	10	44	43
1989	34	63	88	9	37	59
1988	18	69	83	5	26	55
1987	22	68	84	5	42	44
1986	22	67	80	8	58	40
1985	25	68	84	7	36	56
1984	34	44	57	11	42	24
1983	34	52	68	10	39	44
1982	40	49	72	17	60	34
1981	49	42	67	24	60	28

Interest Group Ratings

Year	ADA	ACU	AFL-CIO	CCUS
1990	50	17	73	50
1989	60	22	91	30
1988	80	5	100	17
1987	64	0	94	13
1986	75	24	100	29
1985	70	5	82	23
1984	40	20	70	33
1983	65	9	88	39
1982	40	25	79	42
1981	45	20	87	24

2 Ray Thornton (D)

Of Little Rock — Elected 1990

Also served 1973-79.

Born: July 16, 1928, Conway, Ark.
Education: Yale U., B.A. 1950; U. of Arkansas, J.D. 1956.
Military Service: Navy, 1951-54.
Occupation: Lawyer.
Family: Wife, Betty Jo Mann; three children.
Religion: Church of Christ.
Political Career: Ark. attorney general, 1971-73; sought Democratic nomination for U.S. Senate, 1978.
Capitol Office: 1214 Longworth Bldg. 20515; 225-2506.

The Path to Washington: Thornton's return trip to Washington was remarkably smooth for someone seeking a seat held by a GOP party-switcher. National Republicans crowed about luring Tommy F. Robinson to their ranks in 1989, but when he left the 2nd to run for governor, Arkansas Republicans could not find a contender in the weight class of Thornton, a former three-term House member.

Robinson, who was thrice elected to the 2nd as a Democrat, switched to the GOP at a highly publicized White House ceremony in July 1989. But he could not secure the gubernatorial nomination of his new party: His primary campaign against Democrat-turned-Republican Sheffield Nelson — a caustic, rancorous fight — was the wildest show in Arkansas politics in 1990.

The race for the 2nd was much quieter. After former Democratic Rep. Jim Guy Tucker ended his flirtation with challenging Thornton in the primary, Thornton had the nomination to himself. (Tucker instead ran for lieutenant governor and won.) State Rep. Ron Fuller appeared to be the only Republican willing to take on the popular Democrat, but he inspired little enthusiasm among Republicans and decided to drop out of the race.

Freshman state Rep. Jim Keet took Fuller's place. A fast-food restaurant entrepreneur regarded as a rising star in the state GOP, Keet was widely seen as running for the House to gain experience for future campaigns. Keet largely avoided attacking Thornton, and the statewide newspapers paid little attention to the open-seat race. Thornton reclaimed the 2nd for the Democrats with 60 percent of the vote.

Thornton has been a statewide presence for two decades. After serving a two-year term as state attorney general, Thornton in 1972 won the House seat vacated by Democrat David Pryor, who failed in a challenge to Democratic Sen. John L. McClellan. In 1978, Pryor, then governor, ran against Thornton and then-Rep. Tucker in the Democratic Senate primary. Thornton came in a close third, splitting votes with Pryor. (Pryor won the runoff and the general election.) In 1990, Pryor, running unopposed for a new Senate term, was Thornton's House campaign chairman.

Through the years, Thornton's biggest benefactor has been his uncle, Little Rock financier W. R. "Witt" Stephens, a longtime kingmaker in Arkansas Democratic politics. Stephens' brother, Jackson T. "Jack" Stephens, backed Robinson for governor and played a prominent role in his campaign. The Stephens family's influence in state politics has long been controversial; Nelson scored points against Robinson by accusing him of being a puppet of the Stephenses.

In the race for the 2nd, though, Keet did not use the Stephens connection against Thornton, who has maintained an image for integrity and honesty.

Thornton represented southern Arkansas' 4th District from 1973 to 1979. As a freshman on the Judiciary Committee, he earned a reputation for caution and consideration that propelled him into a central role in the drafting of articles of impeachment of President Richard M. Nixon. Thornton was one of a seven-man swing coalition of Judiciary Republicans and Southern Democrats that emerged to draft the articles and form the strategy of the pro-impeachment forces. Two members of that coalition are still in Congress: New York Republican Rep. Hamilton Fish Jr. and Maine GOP Sen. William S. Cohen.

Thornton also served on the Science Committee, chairing its Domestic and International Scientific Planning and Analysis Subcommittee in his second term and the Science, Research and Technology Subcommittee in his third. At the end of 1975, Thornton left Judiciary to take a seat on the Agriculture Committee.

Arkansas 2

Central — Little Rock

The political and industrial capital of Arkansas and home of its only two statewide-circulation newspapers, Little Rock dominates the 2nd. The city and surrounding Pulaski County have 60 percent of the district's population, and their political weight is usually enough to determine the outcome of the district's elections.

Once a symbol of the resistance to desegregating public schools in the South, Little Rock today has shed much of its racial tension. One of the first cities in the country to make extensive use of urban renewal funds, the city has turned its attention to rebuilding the downtown and eradicating slum areas.

Little Rock's strong black vote and well-organized labor community, along with the liberal *Arkansas Gazette*, make the city a Democratic stronghold. But the Little Rock suburbs along the Arkansas River bluffs are home to a large managerial and professional community, which makes Pulaski County competitive. In 1984, it went for Republican Judy Petty over then-Democrat Tommy F. Robinson, and in 1988, Pulaski gave George Bush 55 percent of its vote. In the lopsided 1990 House race, Democrat Ray Thornton won Pulaski with 58 percent, just slightly weaker than his districtwide tally of 60 percent.

Most of the counties that surround Pulaski are more confirmed in their Democratic habits, although in presidential voting, only Conway County went Democratic in 1988. West of Pulaski are Saline County, the nation's sole domestic source of bauxite and home to a politically active union movement in the aluminum industry, and rural Yell and Perry counties, with traditional Southern Democratic loyalties. Lonoke County, just east of Pulaski, is farm country, although some industry has sprung up along Interstate 40, which connects Little Rock with Memphis, Tenn.

White County is a partial exception to the rural Democratic pattern. With one of the strongest GOP organizations in the state and a firmly conservative intellectual direction from the academic community at Harding College, the county tends to be more competitive in state elections than its rural neighbors.

Population: 569,116. White 467,430 (82%), Black 95,739 (17%), Other 3,833 (1%). Spanish origin 4,540 (1%). 18 and over 401,104 (70%), 65 and over 60,593 (11%). Median age: 29.

Committees

Government Operations (21st of 25 Democrats)
Government Activities & Transportation; Legislation & National Security

Science, Space & Technology (25th of 32 Democrats)
Investigations & Oversight; Science; Technology & Competitiveness

Campaign Finance

	Receipts	Receipts from PACs		Expend-itures
1990				
Thornton (D)	$697,067	$242,900	(35%)	$678,429
Keet (R)	$436,883	$24,157	(6%)	$430,932

Key Vote

1991

Authorize use of force against Iraq	Y

Elections

1990 General

Ray Thornton (D)	103,471	(60%)
Jim Keet (R)	67,800	(40%)

Previous Winning Percentages: **1976** (100%) **1974** (100%) **1972** (100%)

District Vote For President

	1988	1984	1980	1976
D	91,705 (43%)	87,447 (40%)	83,325 (44%)	120,683 (68%)
R	121,130 (56%)	133,093 (60%)	90,488 (48%)	57,936 (32%)
I			6,864 (4%)	

3 John Paul Hammerschmidt (R)

Of Harrison — Elected 1966

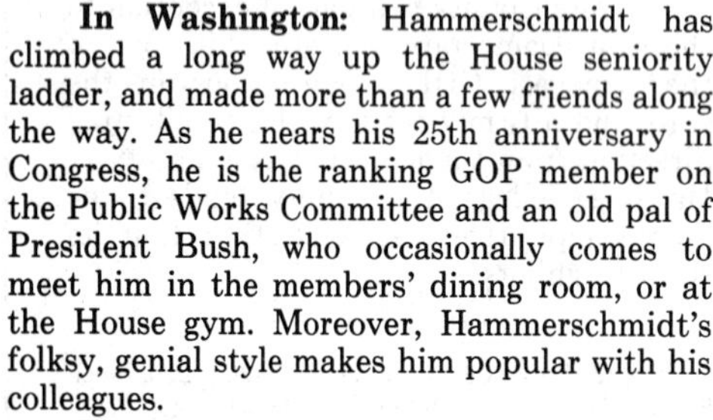

Born: May 4, 1922, Harrison, Ark.
Education: Attended The Citadel, 1938-39; U. of Arkansas, 1940-41; Oklahoma State U., 1945-46.
Military Service: Army, 1942-45; Ark. Army Reserve, 1945-60; D.C. Army Reserve, 1977-81.
Occupation: Lumber company executive.
Family: Wife, Virginia Sharp; one child.
Religion: Presbyterian.
Political Career: Ark. Republican Party chairman, 1964-66.
Capitol Office: 2110 Rayburn Bldg. 20515; 225-4301.

In Washington: Hammerschmidt has climbed a long way up the House seniority ladder, and made more than a few friends along the way. As he nears his 25th anniversary in Congress, he is the ranking GOP member on the Public Works Committee and an old pal of President Bush, who occasionally comes to meet him in the members' dining room, or at the House gym. Moreover, Hammerschmidt's folksy, genial style makes him popular with his colleagues.

This combination of seniority, access and personality imbues Hammerschmidt with considerable clout, but only rarely does he wield it publicly.

One of those rare instances came in March 1989, when Hammerschmidt gave a nominating speech on behalf of Georgian Newt Gingrich's bid for GOP whip. Gingrich's two-vote victory margin over Illinois' Edward Madigan was so narrow that it is impossible to isolate a single factor that put him over the top. But in a contest that turned in part on generational and stylistic considerations, it surely did not hurt that "young Turk" Gingrich had the support of Hammerschmidt, the third most-senior House Republican from the South and a man known to prefer collegiality over partisan confrontation.

Lately, Hammerschmidt has gotten behind another cause unusual for a member of his longevity and experience: term limitation. He is among those advocating a constitutional amendment limiting House members to six two-year terms and Senate members to two six-year terms. Hammerschmidt told the Arkansas Gazette that the proposal was needed to "shake up the institution" and change the leadership structure.

Not much "shaking up" goes on in the two committees where Hammerschmidt serves — Public Works and Veterans' Affairs. By and large, both panels still start from the old assumption that "more is better" — more public works projects, and more benefits for veterans.

The Democratic majority on Public Works knows that Hammerschmidt will rarely be an antagonist as ranking Republican. Though conservative on most issues of broad economic policy, he is strongly supportive of federal spending on public works, and has resisted White House budget-cutting efforts. But he can occasionally become feisty on geographical turf battles; in 1990, he sought to use mass transit funds to help pay for bus lifts for wheelchairs and other improvements in access for disabled persons that he felt would largely benefit urban areas.

At the outset of the 100th Congress, Hammerschmidt was the Republican floor manager for two major pieces of legislation: the Clean Water Act reauthorization and the omnibus highway reauthorization. It fell to Hammerschmidt to help guide the override of two presidential vetoes of the widely popular House measures.

Hammerschmidt has always been careful to look out for his home interests on Public Works. A decorated World War II pilot, he has sought to preserve federal subsidies that help cushion small airports, including several in his district, against the economic effects of deregulation. He has also sought to increase airline competition and improve passenger service in the midst of industry consolidation.

On Veterans' Affairs, where he was ranking Republican in the early 1980s, Hammerschmidt has sometimes frustrated Vietnam veterans because he places such emphasis on providing high benefit levels for World War II veterans. (His district is a mountain retirement mecca with more than 60,000 World War II vets.) But he has backed job-training measures for Vietnam veterans and compensation for victims of the chemical Agent Orange. Also, he has favored increased compensation to help draw

Arkansas 3

Northwest — Ozark Plateau; Fort Smith

The hilly 3rd, Arkansas' most reliably Republican constituency, is one of just three Southern districts that has been represented by the same Republican for two decades or longer. The roots of the allegiance go back to the Civil War, a conflict that struck many of the small-scale farmers here as one fought mostly on behalf of wealthy slaveholding plantation owners in the flatter parts of Arkansas. Ronald Reagan won the 3rd by more than 2-to-1 in 1984, and Democratic Gov. Bill Clinton lost nearly half of the district's 20 counties, although he carried every other county in the rest of the state. In 1988, George Bush swept the 3rd.

The district is overwhelmingly white and traditionally has had a poor economy dependent on relatively unproductive farmland. Vast pine forests have provided jobs in sawmills scattered throughout the rural counties.

In recent years, however, the Ozark economy has been boosted by a large influx of new residents. The area's mild climate and natural assets — such as Beaver Lake and Bull Shoals Lake, the Buffalo River and the Ozark and Ouachita national forests — have lured retirees to newly developed planned communities, and service industries, small businesses and tourism have provided work for job-hunting newcomers. Rapid growth has caused some consternation among lifelong residents, many of whom are descendants of the Scottish and Irish settlers who originally settled the Ozark hills.

Thousands still work in the Ozark's historic economic underpinnings — poultry, lumber and cattle. Tyson Food Inc., one of the nation's largest poultry-processing companies, has its headquarters in Springdale and numerous plants scattered around the 3rd. In the Ouachita Mountains, timber is a chief source of income, and the large livestock business in the western portion of the district gives the area around Fort Smith, near the Oklahoma border, a distinctly Western flavor.

There are about as many blacks in the northwest corner of Arkansas as in rural parts of Minnesota or Wisconsin. The 1990 census found many 3rd District counties with fewer than 100 black residents.

The district's two population centers are Fort Smith, the state's second-largest city, and Fayetteville, home of the University of Arkansas. In the past, both have supported Republicans against even popular Democrats. Clinton carried Sebastian County (Fort Smith) in his 1990 re-election, but by a lower percentage than his statewide tally. Fort Smith is a manufacturing center, with plants producing furniture and household appliances.

Population: 572,937. White 551,894 (96%), Black 11,794 (2%), Other 7,374 (1%). Spanish origin 4,382 (1%). 18 and over 414,806 (72%), 65 and over 85,231 (15%). Median age: 32.

more and better dental and medical staff to veterans' hospitals.

Hammerschmidt helped push legislation to elevate the Veterans Administration to a Cabinet-level department, a proposal that became law in 1988. Eleven of his colleagues on the Veterans' Affairs Committee wrote President Bush to urge that Hammerschmidt be appointed the first secretary of Veterans Affairs, but Bush chose former Rep. Edward J. Derwinski of Illinois.

Hammerschmidt is one of five current Republican members elected to the House with Bush in 1966. During the late 1960s, he and other junior Republicans were frequent guests aboard their Texas colleague's Formula speedboat on the Potomac. The two remained friends after Bush left the House, and in 1980, Hammerschmidt was an early supporter of Bush's first presidential bid.

At Home: Hammerschmidt, the first Republican elected to Congress from Arkansas in the 20th century, is the only consistent success story of the state's modern Republican Party, which established a foothold in 1966 but has performed spottily since then. Other contemporary Arkansas Republicans have flourished briefly — Winthrop Rockefeller and Frank White as governors, and Ed Bethune in the House — but Hammerschmidt alone remains in office today.

After returning from service in World War II, Hammerschmidt divided his time between Republican Party work and a lumber firm that had been in his family for three generations. From 1964-66 he was the state Republican chairman, helping lay groundwork that ultimately elected Rockefeller to the governorship.

In 1966, Hammerschmidt decided to try for Congress, and the move turned out to be perfectly timed. Two years earlier, the GOP challenger in the 3rd had softened up Democratic Rep. James Trimble, holding him to 55 percent, while Barry Goldwater was drawing a respectable 44 percent of the district's presidential vote. The 1966 election promised national Republican gains, and Hammerschmidt was in the right district to benefit.

Trimble had held the seat since 1944, when he succeeded J. William Fulbright. He was a moderate Democrat, closely identified with Arkansas River and Ozark development projects. Already 72 years old, Trimble had to fight off two strong primary challengers. He never really recovered politically. In November, Hammerschmidt won by almost 10,000 votes.

Since then, only two Democrats have drawn more than a third of the vote against Hammerschmidt. The first was Bill Clinton, who as a 28-year-old law professor in 1974 put on a yearlong campaign that came within 6,300 votes. Only Hammerschmidt's strong showing in Fort Smith, the district's largest city and a center of social and economic conservatism, saved him. Clinton has since won five terms as governor.

Democrats thought the time was right in 1982, and offered banker and one-time Fulbright aide Jim McDougal. An affable and tireless campaigner, he targeted blue-collar voters and tried to tie Hammerschmidt to GOP economic policies, which were unpopular with many senior citizens and retirees in the 3rd.

But McDougal was unable to dent Hammerschmidt's popularity. Fort Smith and surrounding Sebastian County, even with a high unemployment rate, gave the incumbent 79 percent, and Hammerschmidt won two-thirds of the districtwide vote.

In 1988, with Republicans talking openly of the possibility that Hammerschmidt would get a high-level job in the Bush administration, Democrats touted attorney David Stewart. But his challenge did not make an impression on voters; Hammerschmidt won with 75 percent. In 1990, he again topped 70 percent.

Committees

Public Works & Transportation (Ranking)

Select Aging (2nd of 27 Republicans)
Housing & Consumer Interests; Social Security and Women

Veterans' Affairs (2nd of 13 Republicans)
Hospitals & Health Care (ranking)

Elections

1990 General

John Paul Hammerschmidt (R)	129,876	(71%)
Dan Ivy (D)	54,332	(29%)

1988 General

John Paul Hammerschmidt (R)	161,623	(75%)
David Stewart (D)	54,767	(25%)

Previous Winning Percentages: **1986** (80%) **1984** (100%) **1982** (66%) **1980** (100%) **1978** (78%) **1976** (100%) **1974** (52%) **1972** (77%) **1970** (67%) **1968** (67%) **1966** (53%)

District Vote For President

	1988	1984	1980	1976
D	74,413 (33%)	69,972 (30%)	89,197 (39%)	111,118 (55%)
R	146,498 (66%)	165,217 (70%)	134,908 (58%)	89,063 (44%)
I			7,457 (3%)	

Campaign Finance

	Receipts	Receipts from PACs	Expend-itures
1990			
Hammerschmidt (R)	$266,438	$166,500 (62%)	$105,354
Ivy (D)	$15,876	$4,000 (25%)	$15,730
1988			
Hammerschmidt (R)	$330,387	$166,700 (50%)	$159,221
Stewart (D)	$60,059	$300 (0%)	$60,054

Key Votes

1991

Authorize use of force against Iraq	Y

1990

Support constitutional amendment on flag desecration	Y
Pass family and medical leave bill over Bush veto	N
Reduce SDI funding	N
Allow abortions in overseas military facilities	N
Approve budget summit plan for spending and taxing	Y
Approve civil rights bill	N

1989

Halt production of B-2 stealth bomber at 13 planes	N
Oppose capital gains tax cut	N
Approve federal abortion funding in rape or incest cases	N
Approve pay raise and revision of ethics rules	Y
Pass Democratic minimum wage plan over Bush veto	N

Voting Studies

	Presidential Support		Party Unity		Conservative Coalition	
Year	S	O	S	O	S	O
1990	59	36	72	21	93	2
1989	81	15	73	24	98	2
1988	64	32	72	25	97	3
1987	57	39	65	30	86	7
1986	69	31	69	29	90	10
1985	64	34	71	27	95	4
1984	58	32	67	22	92	3
1983	66	32	75	21	88	7
1982	65	32	79	20	99	1
1981	79	21	80	20	96	4

Interest Group Ratings

Year	ADA	ACU	AFL-CIO	CCUS
1990	6	82	8	77
1989	5	85	8	90
1988	10	96	29	86
1987	12	68	19	87
1986	5	82	14	78
1985	25	81	12	77
1984	15	91	8	60
1983	0	91	13	85
1982	5	73	15	86
1981	5	100	27	89

4 Beryl Anthony Jr. (D)

Of El Dorado — Elected 1978

Born: Feb. 21, 1938, El Dorado, Ark.
Education: U. of Arkansas, B.S., B.A. 1961, J.D. 1963.
Occupation: Lawyer.
Family: Wife, Sheila Foster; two children.
Religion: Episcopalian.
Political Career: Prosecuting attorney, Ark. 13th Judicial District, 1971-77.
Capitol Office: 1212 Longworth Bldg. 20515; 225-3772.

In Washington: While the 101st Congress brought Anthony more prominence than he had enjoyed in his first five terms, it dealt him enough setbacks to leave a bitter aftertaste.

Defeated in his attempt to move up the leadership ladder in 1989, Anthony stepped down as chairman of the Democratic Congressional Campaign Committee (DCCC) at the end of the 1990 election cycle. Democrats hold all the big jobs in Arkansas and a long queue stands ahead of him on Ways and Means, so new directions for Anthony's ambition are not readily apparent.

Anthony had reason to be proud of his four years at the DCCC. In 1988, the Democrats gained three seats despite losing the presidential election. In 1990, they added a net of nine. They also won eight of the eleven special elections held during the 101st.

Moreover, Anthony helped the committee survive a fundraising drought attributable to the 1989 resignations of Speaker Jim Wright of Texas and Democratic Whip Tony Coelho of California. Anthony used the tough times to cut costs and increase contributions from members with campaign funds to spare.

Yet these successes did not come without strains. And the Democrats' respectable election showing in 1990 seemed pale to those who had looked for a seat gain in the teens.

The 101st had begun with Anthony enviably positioned. He was in the leadership, but not entirely of the leadership. His identity remained rooted in the moderate-to-conservative South. Yet his rating by the liberal Americans for Democratic Action, which had crept steadily upwards through the decade, had just hit 80 percent. On Ways and Means he was a known insider, an ally and confidant of Chairman Dan Rostenkowski of Illinois who still often voted with the panel's bipartisan pro-business bloc.

The turning point for Anthony seemed to come in June 1989, when the House Democratic Caucus met to choose successors to Speaker Wright and Majority Whip Coelho. Anthony bid for Coelho's job, arguing that the leadership needed a Southerner.

But he did not corner the Southern vote in his campaign, winning support from only 30 members. William H. Gray III of Pennsylvania, who built up ties across regional and ideological lines as Budget chairman and in his successful campaign to be caucus chairman, finished with 134 votes. David E. Bonior of Michigan was second with 97.

Shortly after his loss, Anthony opened himself up for recriminations by publicly accusing Coelho of mismanaging the DCCC's fiscal affairs and saddling the committee with a debt problem. Anthony quickly stepped back from some of his comments, insisting that the DCCC debt of nearly $2 million was the result of many factors. But that did not erase the impression that Anthony was a sour-grapes loser in the whip's race, nor did it endear him to the many allies of Coelho who remain in Congress.

Anthony was also at odds with much of his party that same spring over the pre-eminent tax issue of 1989. Anthony had joined with several Southern colleagues on Ways and Means in supporting a cut in the tax on capital gains. It was a natural position for his district, which relies on tax-sensitive investment in timber, oil and gas. But Rostenkowski, after tolerating the notion temporarily, turned strongly against it. The division among committee Democrats spread to the caucus in general, and Republicans drove that wedge all the way through to a floor victory in the House in September.

The capital gains tax cut stalled in the Senate, but Anthony joined with GOP legislators in both chambers that fall to repeal the "Section 89" non-discrimination rules for private employee pensions. Rostenkowski had tried to save the rules, a legacy of the 1986 tax overhaul he had shepherded. But Anthony, saying, "The credibility of the committee is at stake," proved an effective advocate of businesses' objections.

Anthony became a prominent legislator without being responsible for much prominent legislation. Instead, during his career his political instincts have enabled him to promote oth-

Arkansas 4

South — Pine Bluff

When it comes to congressional elections, the voting habits of the 4th are like the flow of water from Hot Springs Mountain — very consistent. The 4th is so firmly Democratic that Republicans have offered a candidate for the House seat only six times since 1962; in no instance did their nominee top 35 percent of the vote.

Stretching across the southern third of Arkansas from the Texas border to the Mississippi River, the 4th is Deep South territory. It has more blacks than any other district in Arkansas, and its white electorate retains a Civil War-era allegiance to the Democratic Party even though the only recent Democratic presidential nominee it has found palatable was Jimmy Carter. George Bush carried the 4th in 1988, Ronald Reagan in 1984, Richard M. Nixon in 1972 and George C. Wallace in 1968.

Much of the district's economy depends on the timber industry. Georgia-Pacific has a paper mill and plant in Crossett that manufactures plywood, paper bags and chemicals. Growth in the swine industry has boosted the fortunes of several counties on the western fringe. Pine Bluff (population 57,100), the district's largest city, has several pulp and paper mills. With a 53 percent black population, Pine Bluff casts the highest minority vote of any city in Arkansas.

The Pine Bluff Arsenal once produced the nation's entire supply of anti-personnel biological weapons; after an 18-year moratorium on chemical weapons, in December 1987, assembly of binary nerve-gas weapons began at Pine Bluff, which employs more than 2,000 military and civilian personnel.

The district's second-largest city is Hot Springs (population 32,462), the seat of Garland County and a popular resort for more than a century. The bathhouses and spas of Hot Springs National Park are the center of a tourist economy that includes horse racing and theme parks. Hot Springs is becoming a Republican town, partly because it is acquiring a large population of retirees — a quarter of the city's residents are 65 or older. When redistricting in 1981 moved Garland County from the 3rd District of Republican John Paul Hammerschmidt, Hot Springs citizens tried to block the move in court.

Farther south is the "El Dorado fringe," Arkansas' narrow "oil band" running along the bottom of the state from Texarkana, on the Texas border, through El Dorado, Anthony's hometown and the place where H. L. Hunt got his start. El Dorado and surrounding Union County are the site of several oil refineries and chemical plants; a corps of politically active, conservative oil operators there makes the county a pocket of GOP strength. But Anthony, as a local product, has little trouble.

Population: 570,831. White 408,799 (72%), Black 158,631 (28%). Spanish origin 4,307 (1%). 18 and over 403,044 (71%), 65 and over 86,556 (15%). Median age: 31.

ers' concerns and himself at the same time.

Long before taking over the DCCC, Anthony proved he could court business interests as well as anyone in Congress. He has a social background that a number of corporate lobbyists can relate to, and he has never been one to shun the attention he has received from them as a member of Ways and Means. Even when he did not have a leadership position, Anthony acted as something of a fundraising entrepreneur for Democrats, arranging hunting and golfing outings at which lobbyists and members could socialize. His success at that informal role no doubt impressed many colleagues, particularly those eager to find a new DCCC chairman who could emulate Coelho's success at raising money from business political action committees.

Anthony won a spot on Ways and Means in his second term, helped by party leaders eager to cultivate an ambitious Southern Democrat with moderate political instincts. He has used that position not only to build his ties to business, but also to protect the interests of Arkansas timber, agriculture and oil.

During tax-revision efforts in the 99th Congress, Anthony took an interest in a variety of issues, including the taxing of thrift institutions and employee sponsored 401(k) tax-exempt savings plans. Mostly, however, he was interested in timber. He remains on the board of directors of his family business, Anthony Forest Products, and has strongly backed tax language that benefits the industry both directly and indirectly. During tax-revision efforts in the 99th Congress, Anthony led an informal group of members in crafting timber provisions adopted by the committee.

In 1983, Anthony played a part on Ways and Means in the effort to rescue the Social Security system. To address a deficit expected after the turn of the century, Anthony devised a plan calling for a 5 percent cut in initial benefits and an increase in payroll taxes in the year

2015. The committee accepted it. But the full House opted to save money in the next century by gradually raising the retirement age.

At Home: Nothing remotely challenging has happened in Anthony's electoral career since he got past his first hurdle in 1978. Most years, all he has to do is file his papers and he is guaranteed another term.

The 4th was open in 1978 because of Rep. Ray Thornton's Senate candidacy, and five major candidates entered the Democratic primary to succeed him. The overwhelming favorite was Arkansas Secretary of State Winston Bryant, an impressive vote-getter who had already been on district ballots several times.

Bryant had a 10,000-vote lead in the initial primary, but he was forced into a runoff against Anthony, then a businessman and prosecuting attorney in El Dorado, who portrayed himself as the "businessman's candidate" and campaigned against Bryant's identification with labor and teachers.

With a family name that was widely recognized and respected in the southern part of the district, Anthony was able to recruit traditional conservative Democrats against Bryant, who had a moderate-to-liberal reputation. Personal wealth from the Anthony family's lumber company and ties with the district's oil and gas producers gave Anthony a strong fundraising edge over Bryant, and he came from behind to win the runoff by 5,500 votes.

Anthony's only significant general-election contest came in 1982, when Republicans put up Bob Leslie, a Little Rock lawyer and legal counsel to the state GOP who went on to serve as state party chairman.

Leslie contrasted his own upbringing as a sharecropper's son with Anthony's more privileged background and argued that the average voter "needs a congressman who knows what it's like to work for a living." But Anthony was well prepared; on the way to taking 78 percent of the vote in his May primary, he spent weeks touring the district, polishing his down-home style of campaigning. Anthony easily dispatched Leslie, winning with 66 percent. He has not received less than two-thirds of the vote since.

Committees

Select Children, Youth & Families (6th of 22 Democrats)

Ways & Means (14th of 23 Democrats)
Oversight; Trade

Elections

1990 General		
Beryl Anthony Jr. (D)	110,365	(72%)
Roy Rood (R)	42,130	(28%)
1988 General		
Beryl Anthony Jr. (D)	129,508	(69%)
Roger N. Bell (R)	57,658	(31%)

Previous Winning Percentages: **1986** (78%) **1984** (98%) **1982** (66%) **1980** (100%) **1978** (100%)

District Vote For President

	1988	1984	1980	1976
D	93,307 (46%)	94,484 (44%)	111,613 (54%)	131,802 (68%)
R	103,562 (52%)	122,373 (56%)	89,036 (43%)	63,128 (32%)
I			4,080 (2%)	

Campaign Finance

	Receipts	Receipts from PACs		Expend-itures
1990				
Anthony (D)	$530,662	$374,300	(71%)	$480,853
Rood (R)	$520	0		$511
1988				
Anthony (D)	$547,244	$353,042	(65%)	$570,155
Bell (R)	$21,709	$880	(4%)	$21,538

Key Votes

1991	
Authorize use of force against Iraq	N
1990	
Support constitutional amendment on flag desecration	N
Pass family and medical leave bill over Bush veto	Y
Reduce SDI funding	Y
Allow abortions in overseas military facilities	Y
Approve budget summit plan for spending and taxing	N
Approve civil rights bill	Y
1989	
Halt production of B-2 stealth bomber at 13 planes	N
Oppose capital gains tax cut	N
Approve federal abortion funding in rape or incest cases	Y
Approve pay raise and revision of ethics rules	Y
Pass Democratic minimum wage plan over Bush veto	Y

Voting Studies

	Presidential Support		Party Unity		Conservative Coalition	
Year	**S**	**O**	**S**	**O**	**S**	**O**
1990	27	71	85	11	56	43
1989	38	57	79	14	54	29
1988	28	67	81	9	55	39
1987	24	69	85	5	47	37
1986	27	64	78	11	62	36
1985	28	71	81	14	58	36
1984	37	47	58	18	51	32
1983	45	51	69	25	64	36
1982	48	43	63	31	71	21
1981	61	38	61	30	76	15

Interest Group Ratings

Year	ADA	ACU	AFL-CIO	CCUS
1990	67	17	58	50
1989	60	23	70	44
1988	80	16	92	46
1987	68	5	88	27
1986	50	30	54	40
1985	55	33	59	32
1984	50	28	27	33
1983	50	24	69	65
1982	40	41	50	56
1981	30	40	73	33

California

U.S. CONGRESS

SENATE 1 D, 1 R
HOUSE 26 D, 19 R

LEGISLATURE

Senate 26 D, 11 R, 1 Independent, 2 vacancies
House 49 D, 31 R

ELECTIONS

1988 Presidential Vote

Bush	51%
Dukakis	48%

1984 Presidential Vote

Reagan	58%
Mondale	41%

1980 Presidential Vote

Reagan	53%
Carter	36%
Anderson	9%

Turnout rate in 1986	36%
Turnout rate in 1988	47%
Turnout rate in 1990	34%

(as percentage of voting age population)

POPULATION AND GROWTH

1980 population	23,667,902
1990 population (1st in the nation)	29,760,021
Percent change 1980-1990	+26%

DEMOGRAPHIC BREAKDOWN

White	69%
Black	7%
Asian or Pacific Islander	10%
(Hispanic origin)	26%
Urban	91%
Rural	9%
Born in state	45%
Foreign-born	15%

MAJOR CITIES

Los Angeles	3,485,398
San Diego	1,110,549
San Jose	782,248
San Francisco	723,959
Long Beach	429,433

AREA AND LAND USE

Area 156,299 sq. miles (3rd)

Farm	32%
Forest	39%
Federally owned	46%

Gov. Pete Wilson (R)
Of San Diego — Elected 1990

Born: Aug. 23, 1933, Lake Forest, Ill.
Education: Yale U., B.A. 1955; U. of California, Berkeley, LL.B. 1962.
Military Service: Marine Corps, 1955-58.
Occupation: Lawyer.
Religion: Protestant.
Political Career: Calif. Assembly, 1967-71; San Diego mayor, 1971-83; U.S. Senate, 1983-91.
Next Election: 1994.

WORK

Occupations

White-collar	58%
Blue-collar	27%
Service workers	13%

Government Workers

Federal	324,702
State	375,809
Local	1,264,720

MONEY

Median family income	$ 21,537	(10th)
Tax burden per capita	$ 1,098	(9th)

EDUCATION

Spending per pupil through grade 12	$ 3,840	(30th)
Persons with college degrees	20%	(8th)

CRIME

Violent crime rate 978 per 100,000 (3rd)

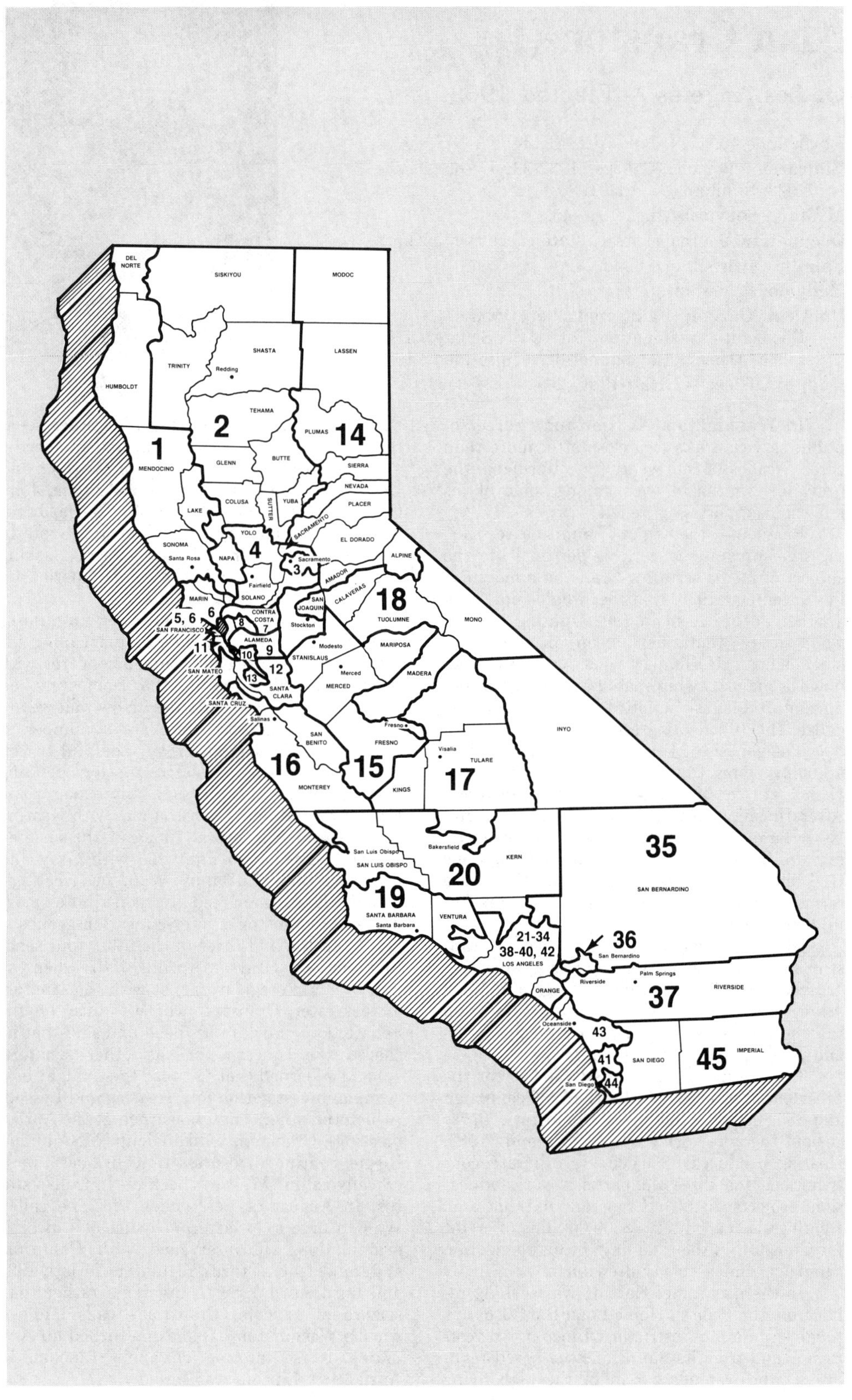
DEL NORTE
SISKIYOU
MODOC
SHASTA
LASSEN
TRINITY
Redding
HUMBOLDT
TEHAMA
2
PLUMAS
14
1
MENDOCINO
GLENN
BUTTE
SIERRA
NEVADA
COLUSA
SUTTER
YUBA
PLACER
LAKE
SACRAMENTO
YOLO
EL DORADO
SONOMA
Santa Rosa
4
NAPA
3
Sacramento
ALPINE
Fairfield
AMADOR
MARIN
SOLANO
CALAVERAS
18
5, 6
6
CONTRA COSTA
SAN JOAQUIN
TUOLUMNE
MONO
SAN FRANCISCO
8
7
Stockton
ALAMEDA
11
9
Modesto
MARIPOSA
SAN MATEO
10
STANISLAUS
12
Merced
MADERA
13
MERCED
SANTA CLARA
SANTA CRUZ
Fresno
Salinas
INYO
SAN BENITO
FRESNO
Visalia
16
15
TULARE
17
MONTEREY
KINGS
35
Bakersfield
KERN
San Luis Obispo
SAN LUIS OBISPO
20
SAN BERNARDINO
19
SANTA BARBARA
Santa Barbara
VENTURA
21-34
38-40, 42
LOS ANGELES
36
San Bernardino
Riverside
Palm Springs
RIVERSIDE
ORANGE
37
Oceanside
43
41
SAN DIEGO
45
IMPERIAL
San Diego
44

Alan Cranston (D)

Of Los Angeles — Elected 1968

Born: June 19, 1914, Palo Alto, Calif.

Education: Pomona College, 1932-33; U. of Mexico, 1933; Stanford U., A.B. 1936.

Military Service: Army, 1944-45.

Occupation: Journalist; real estate executive; author.

Family: Divorced; one child.

Religion: Protestant.

Political Career: Calif. controller, 1959-67; sought Democratic nomination for U.S. Senate, 1964; sought Democratic nomination for president, 1984.

Capitol Office: 112 Hart Bldg. 20510; 224-3553.

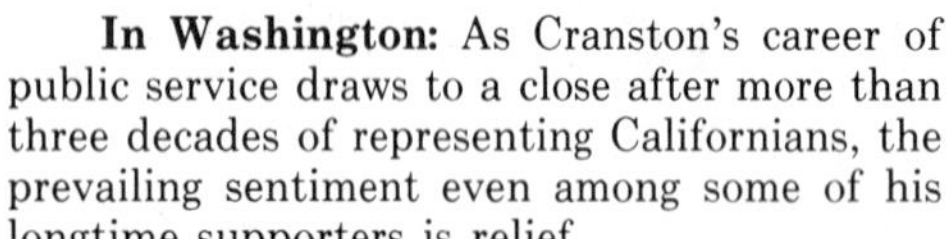

In Washington: As Cranston's career of public service draws to a close after more than three decades of representing Californians, the prevailing sentiment even among some of his longtime supporters is relief.

Pursued by the Ethics Committee, recovering from prostate cancer, his personal life the subject of media scrutiny, Cranston announced in November 1990 that he would not seek another Senate term in 1992, sparing himself what surely would have been an uphill re-election struggle. Similarly, his decision to step down as majority whip spared his colleagues the uncomfortable task of voting him out before the end of the 102nd Congress.

The genesis of Cranston's political decline arguably stems from his quixotic bid for the Democratic presidential nomination in 1984. After finishing near the bottom in Iowa and New Hampshire, Cranston saw his fundraising dry up. Two years later, he faced a vigorous GOP challenge to his bid for a fourth Senate term, a contest that ultimately cost him $11 million to win.

At a 1984 Democratic Party event, Cranston met the lobbyist for Charles H. Keating Jr., who owned the Lincoln Savings and Loan Association in Irvine, Calif. Cranston told him that he had worked hard for California S&Ls and Keating should support him.

Keating did. He generated $10,000 for the presidential race, $39,000 for the 1986 campaign and $85,000 for a California Democratic Party get-out-the-vote drive. In 1987 and 1988, Keating produced $850,000 in corporate contributions for three nonpartisan voter-education projects tied to Cranston and his son. Keating also expedited a $300,000 line of credit for Cranston in the final days of his re-election campaign, but he never drew on it.

In the meantime, Keating was seeking relief from the Federal Home Loan Bank Board's tough regulation restricting Lincoln's investments, and from its San Francisco-based regulators, who wanted to rein in the high-flying S&L. Keating also contacted four other senators whose campaigns he supported financially — Republican John McCain of Arizona and Democrats Dennis DeConcini of Arizona, John Glenn of Ohio and Donald W. Riegle Jr. of Michigan. In January 1985, Cranston wrote to bank board Chairman Edwin J. Gray, asking him to extend the public comment period on the proposed investment rule.

In January 1987, Cranston's fundraiser wrote the senator a memorandum calling his attention to Keating's continued concerns with the bank board and noting that Democrats had regained the Senate majority. "Now that we are back in the majority there are a number of individuals who have been very helpful to you who have cases or legislative matters pending with our office who will rightfully expect some kind of resolution." Cranston met with Keating and his lobbyist several times in the ensuing months, agreeing to intervene with Gray and his successor, M. Danny Wall, on Keating's behalf. Keating agreed to contribute more money to Cranston's voter-education groups.

Cranston and three of the other four senators met with Gray on April 2, 1987; when the San Francisco regulators met with the senators a week later, Cranston, who was busy on the Senate floor, stuck in his head and said that he shared the concerns of the other senators. When he learned that fall that there might be a criminal investigation into Keating and Lincoln (which the other senators learned at the April 9 meeting), Cranston, unlike Glenn, McCain and Riegle, continued to press Lincoln's case, periodically calling Wall to check on Lincoln's status. In August or September 1987, he called Wall to urge a speedy conclusion of Lincoln's examination. He intervened with California state and federal thrift regulators in late 1988 and until April 1989 to urge sale rather than seizure of Lincoln. Cranston's calls stopped when a Washington-based exam turned up even more adverse information about Lincoln. In April 1989, Lincoln was seized.

The Senate Ethics Committee began public hearings in November 1990 to determine if any of the so-called Keating Five violated Senate rules against exerting improper influence in return for compensation. A week before they started, Cranston announced that he would not seek re-election and would step down immediately as whip because he had been diagnosed as having prostate cancer. He underwent five weeks of radiation therapy in late 1990 and was unable to testify publicly in early 1991.

A tiering of the senators emerged early on in the proceedings. The committee's special counsel, Robert S. Bennett, suggested in his report that the committee should not proceed against Glenn or McCain, but should proceed against the other three. Bennett further separated Riegle — who backed off once he learned of the possible criminal investigation — from DeConcini and Cranston, who did not.

Cranston did not deny many of Bennett's basic assertions. But he sought to show that the complaints the regulators had against Keating were not airtight and that there was doubt that they were acting fairly toward Lincoln.

He vigorously defended his actions in behalf of Keating, condemning existing laws and Senate rules on campaign fundraising, which he said should be changed. "It is absurd to suggest that fundraising and substantive issues are separated in Senate offices by some kind of wall.... I submit that if you decide that it's improper to take a lawful and proper action at any time in behalf of someone who has contributed legally and properly, then every senator, including every member of this committee, had better run for cover — because every senator has done it; every senator must do it.

"How can you rationally refuse to give legal and proper help at any time to someone who seems to have a reasonable grievance just because he's contributed to your campaign?"

Cranston passionately defended his own prestige. "The situation has caused me deep anguish, because I cherish my reputation for integrity. I have a long and heretofore unquestioned record of sensitivity and adherence to the highest and strictest ethical standards throughout my 30 years in public office.... The notion, the notion, that I would risk my reputation and the reputation of this body which I love by raising money in any improper way is simply preposterous.

"All that any of us have after public office is our record and our reputation."

Bennett used Cranston's own candor to make his point that there was a connection between Keating's contributions and Cranston's actions in his behalf. He cited Cranston's sworn deposition: "A person who makes a contribution has a better chance to get access than someone who does not."

The committee ruled in February 1991 that the four other senators were guilty of poor judgment but warranted no further punishment. In Cranston's case, however, the committee said it was likely that he violated the Senate's general standard against improper behavior. Committee members left little doubt that they would probably recommend that the full Senate punish him. Cranston issued a one-sentence statement: "It is clear that I have been unfairly singled out, despite the evidence in all five cases." In a letter to the panel, he had tried to show that others among the five had engaged in practices no different from his.

In addition to losing his political standing at home because of the Keating affair, Cranston relinquished the party post in which he had excelled for so many years, Democratic whip.

Cranston started nose-counting in 1969, his first year in the Senate, when he was given a chance to help manage a Job Corps bill on the floor. He soon started helping round up votes on other measures crucial to his fellow liberals, having discovered a vacuum in the party's leadership of the early 1970s: Majority Leader Mike Mansfield of Montana was no arm-twister, and Robert C. Byrd of West Virginia, then the whip, was no liberal. Cranston was a liberal, one with a skill at building bridges to moderates and conservatives.

His trademark was his tally sheet, a piece of paper covered with scribbled pluses, minuses and question marks. In 1977, when Byrd became majority leader, Cranston easily won election as his deputy. Despite their ideological differences, which narrowed over the years, and Byrd's reluctance to delegate responsibilities, the two worked together with little friction. In 1984 and 1986, when Byrd faced real or threatened challengers, Cranston stuck by him.

In 1988, with the focus on the race to succeed Byrd, Cranston appeared unchallenged for a record seventh term as whip. Then two months before the Democrats would choose, moderate Wendell H. Ford of Kentucky announced his candidacy. Cranston insisted he had the votes. Indeed, when the tally reached 30-12, Ford moved to stop the count and make Cranston's election unanimous.

Ford immediately announced that he would run again for whip in 1990. If Cranston had not taken himself out of the running, Ford might have had the votes to unseat him.

Despite the time Cranston lost to the Ethics Committee investigation and his cancer treatment, he still managed a significant legislative achievement in the 101st Congress, shaping the first major overhaul of federal housing programs since 1974 from his post on the Banking Subcommittee on Housing, which he chairs.

In early 1987 he called for a "major reformation" of federal policy. "We cannot return to the costly and confusing programs of the past," Cranston said. "Neither can we abdicate federal responsibility." His first step was a modest but significant one. A yearlong effort in

1987 ended with a last-minute agreement on the first housing authorization bill since 1980.

In the 101st Congress, Cranston's more ambitious housing plans clashed with those of the new House Banking Committee chairman, Henry B. Gonzalez of Texas, who also chairs the Housing Subcommittee. Cranston wanted dramatically new programs with moderate spending increases, while Gonzalez wanted big increases for existing programs.

The two Housing subcommittees worked on their versions of the legislation. Cranston conferred frequently with Housing Secretary Jack F. Kemp, whose nomination he had welcomed, and crafted a bill with the ranking Republican on the panel, New York's Alfonse M. D'Amato. The Senate passed the bill in June 1990 by a vote of 96-1.

The centerpiece of Cranston's bill was a block grant program for new construction and renovation through public-private partnerships. The program was designed to increase affordable housing by giving matching grants to state and local governments. The Banking Committee shaved its price from $3 billion to $2 billion a year.

The House passed its bill more than a month later. Cranston set an early cordial tone for the imminent conference when he visited Gonzalez and ranking Republican Chalmers P. Wylie of Ohio on the House floor during the late-night housing debate prior to its passage.

Though Kemp preferred the Senate package, the administration objected strenuously to the new construction included in Cranston's plan, arguing that enough housing existed. Cranston countered that the program's emphasis was on rehabilitation, not construction. In negotiations with administration officials, however, the senators backed down, accepting limits on the number of communities that could use the money for construction.

As the bill was heading to final approval, it was almost toppled by Cranston's actions on an entirely unrelated matter: his proposal to redesign the nation's coins.

Diane Wolf, a prominent New York socialite, former member of the U.S. Commission on Fine Arts and a social companion of Cranston, had urged him to push coin redesign in 1987, and he has done so vigorously ever since. The housing conferees agreed to add Cranston's measure to require the federal Mint to redesign the backsides of the nation's five circulating coins, but a rank-and-file revolt forced House leaders to yank the bill from the floor. Despite Cranston's persistent lobbying on the House floor to retain the coin provision, Gonzalez, the chief House sponsor of the redesign, told him the housing bill would die unless the language was dropped. The conferees then met and issued a new conference report without the coin provision.

But Cranston was not through. Coin redesign measures were attached to several other bills speeding through the Senate in the waning days of the 101st Congress. "They've stuck it on everything but the Pledge of Allegiance," complained House Rules Committee Chairman Joe Moakley of Massachusetts. Members were unsure until the final *Congressional Record* was printed whether one of the bills cleared had managed to escape with a coin redesign aboard. (None had.)

On financial issues at Banking, Cranston has long been considered a friend of S&Ls. His state is home to the nation's largest firms, including many besides Lincoln that fell in the 1980s to mismanagement and fraud, thus draining the Federal Savings and Loan Insurance Corporation (FSLIC). Cranston opposed administration proposals in the 100th and 101st Congresses to bolster the FSLIC by raising S&Ls' premiums and tightening regulations, criticizing the plans as unfair and too costly for healthy firms.

On the question of banking deregulation, he has sided with the securities industry, which wants to keep banks from entering its field. In the debate over hostile corporate takeovers, he has generally opposed restricting the so-called raiders.

Cranston's work on behalf of his state's business interests has been a major element of his career, and a cornerstone of his success. That record is best symbolized by his support for the B-1 bomber, built in California, but he has also labored for growers, independent oil, savings and loans, Realtors, aerospace contractors and filmmakers. At the same time, he has been one of the foremost advocates of the liberal causes — civil rights, poverty programs, the environment and arms control — that have large constituencies in the state.

In the 101st and 102nd Congresses, Cranston led efforts to enact into law the Supreme Court's *Roe v. Wade* decision legalizing abortion. He was one of nine senators to vote against confirming David H. Souter as a Supreme Court justice; Souter ducked questions about his abortion position. Cranston said a vote for Souter placed "women's lives in jeopardy."

Cranston's reputed talent for coalition-building suffered from the Senate's polarization of the early 1980s, when Ronald Reagan was new in the White House, and then from Cranston's own preoccupations with running for president in 1984 and for Senate re-election in 1986. Still, back as whip full time in the 100th Congress, Cranston did some important work. He had a lead role in dealing his old California nemesis, Reagan, one of his biggest defeats — rejection of Supreme Court nominee Robert H. Bork — and he helped deliver one of Reagan's major triumphs — ratification of the intermediate-range nuclear-force (INF) treaty.

During the three-month fight over Bork in 1987, Cranston held numerous private meetings, and acted as a liaison between Northern and Southern Democrats. He helped persuade key senators to go public with their opposition to Bork's ideological conservatism, thus creating momentum toward rejection and providing cover for those hesitant to challenge Reagan.

Late in that year, he began strategy meetings for the INF debate, and then led the administration's lobbying for approval. It was a stunning irony. Cranston had been a Reagan antagonist since 1966, when, as state controller, he campaigned against Reagan's election as governor; Reagan, for his part, considered challenging Cranston in the 1974 Senate race. Now the two, in the twilight of their careers, were working for the same end.

Cranston's efforts for arms control predate his Senate career, going back to his postwar work in the United World Federalists. On the Foreign Relations Committee since 1981, he has worked not only to reduce the superpowers' arms, but also to block other nations from acquiring them. In the 101st Congress, he harshly criticized President Bush's decision to continue normalized trade status for China.

Cranston is not particularly active on Foreign Relations except when the subject is arms control or one other — Israel. He repeatedly led efforts to block Reagan's proposed arms sales to Arab nations. He also wrote a provision that has had a major impact on U.S. aid to Israel: Since 1984, foreign aid bills have included the so-called Cranston amendment, mandating that Israel get at least as much in economic aid each year as it must repay on past loans.

Cranston could have become chairman of Banking in 1989, but because that is a major committee, he would have had to forfeit the whip's job. (Despite leaving the whip's job in 1990, he again waived his right to chair Banking for the 102nd Congress.)

Party rules have allowed him to be chairman of the minor Veterans' Affairs Committee, a position he held from 1977-81 and regained in 1987 when Democrats retook the Senate. The 100th Congress was one of the most generous to veterans in recent years; as chairman, Cranston helped shepherd into law bills expanding health, education and housing benefits. And with House opposition finally dissolved, he won enactment on the fifth try of legislation giving veterans the right to appeal adverse benefits rulings to federal court. Also, the Veterans Administration was given a seat at the Cabinet table.

At Home: After a long run as a dominant political figure in California, Cranston saw his popularity plummet as the Keating Five scandal unfolded. In a California Poll taken in October 1989, 64 percent of the respondents reported a favorable opinion of Cranston. Just two months later, Cranston's positive rating had fallen to 33 percent.

Cranston had been on a downward slope — albeit a more gentle one — since his disastrous 1984 presidential campaign. Until that race, Cranston's career had been a picture of steady, if not unbroken, success.

The head of the Foreign Language Division of the Office of War Information during World War II, Cranston got involved with the United World Federalists and other peace groups following the war. In the late 1940s, he helped form the liberal California Democratic Council (CDC) and served as its first president.

In 1958, Cranston entered the political fray and became the first Democrat elected state controller in 72 years. Four years later, he won re-election by a record margin.

Thus emboldened, he ran for the Senate in 1964, but suffered a temporary setback. His primary foe, interim Democratic senator and former White House press secretary Pierre Salinger, charged that state inheritance tax appraisers were forced to give to the Cranston campaign. Salinger narrowly won the primary, but lost to Republican George Murphy.

The voters dealt Cranston another blow in the Republican year of 1966, turning him out of his controller's post.

But two years later, he tried for the Senate again, winning a five-way primary over a field that included state Sen. (and now U.S. Rep.) Anthony C. Beilenson.

That contest was gentle: The top contenders all were liberals and Vietnam doves. The general election, however, pitted Cranston against conservative Max Rafferty, the state superintendent of public instruction. Rafferty punched hard, attacking Cranston for ties to "left-wing radical groups" like the CDC and for advocating a Vietnam bombing halt — which he said would endanger U.S. troops.

But the GOP was badly divided, following an angry primary in which Rafferty had unseated moderate incumbent Thomas H. Kuchel, the Senate minority whip. In addition, a newspaper series tarnished Rafferty's super-patriot reputation by alleging that he was a World War II draft-dodger. Cranston won by 350,000 votes.

In 1974 Cranston won easily, taking 61 percent against state Sen. H. L. "Bill" Richardson, an early New Right activist and former John Birch Society field worker. At one point, when the Birch Society announced plans to circulate material linking Cranston to communists, it drew a rebuke from Gov. Reagan.

As he rose to prominence, Cranston became something of a paradox in California politics. He was a grass-roots politician in the ultimate media state, and a liberal on Reagan's home turf.

In 1980, Cranston had to run against the Reagan presidential tide, but he had the good fortune to draw as his GOP opponent Paul Gann. He had become known as the co-author of Proposition 13, which cut state property taxes in 1978. But the tax issue had faded some in two years, and Gann proved to be hopelessly inarticulate as a candidate. Cranston won with

57 percent of the vote.

After years of carefully courting centrist voters while not alienating his base, Cranston staked out a strongly liberal position in the 1984 presidential contest. That failed venture opened Cranston to attacks from Republicans, who said it exposed his true leftist colors. It also alienated many California voters, who said it distracted Cranston from his Senate duties.

Cranston might yet have survived those problems with little trouble in 1986 if California Republicans had stuck to their pattern of running hard-line conservatives against him. But instead, Rep. Ed Zschau, a one-time high-tech businessman with a moderate record and access to bundles of campaign cash, emerged from the GOP primary.

Although Cranston, a jogger and health buff, was vigorous for his 72 years, the 46-year-old Zschau had a youthful edge. Zschau also embodied the self-confident, forward-looking entrepreneurship that many Californians had come to consider the hallmark of their state.

Cranston did not take the threat lightly. He began running ads attacking the Republican for "flip-flops" on issues ranging from the MX missile and chemical weapons to child nutrition and apartheid in South Africa. At the same time, Cranston worked to repair what damage 1984 had done to his image. He emphasized his longevity in office, suggesting that he had an institutional weight in the Senate that Zschau could not hope to match.

Zschau only began to fight back in September, but he fought hard, with salvos accusing Cranston of being soft on drugs and terrorism. As the assaults continued, Zschau began to win over conservatives who had earlier been wary of him, and to pick up the support of independents and moderates who liked his free-market beliefs and liberal social outlook.

Cranston betrayed no outward signs of desperation. But as his lead in the polls slipped and the costs of campaigning mounted, Cranston began to scrap for sources of cash to refill his coffers. His efforts to tap one big-money contributor — Keating — would eventually lead to Cranston's political downfall.

At the time, though, Cranston's fundraising effort helped him stave off Zschau's late rush.

Out of more than 7 million votes cast, Cranston emerged just 105,000 votes ahead, with 49.3 percent of the vote.

Committees

Veterans' Affairs (Chairman)

Banking, Housing & Urban Affairs (2nd of 12 Democrats)
Housing & Urban Affairs (chairman); Securities

Foreign Relations (4th of 10 Democrats)
East Asian & Pacific Affairs (chairman); International Economic Policy, Trade, Oceans & Environment; Western Hemisphere & Peace Corps Affairs

Select Intelligence (5th of 8 Democrats)

Elections

1986 General		
Alan Cranston (D)	3,646,672	(49%)
Ed Zschau (R)	3,541,804	(48%)
1986 Primary		
Alan Cranston (D)	1,807,242	(81%)
Charles Greene (D)	165,594	(7%)
John Hancock Abbott (D)	124,218	(6%)
Robert J. Banuelos (D)	77,286	(3%)
Brian Lantz (D)	64,907	(3%)

Previous Winning Percentages: **1980** (57%) **1974** (61%) **1968** (52%)

Campaign Finance

	Receipts	Receipts from PACs		Expend-itures
1986				
Cranston (D)	$10,851,596	$1,366,173	(13%)	$11,037,707
Zschau (R)	$11,789,533	$1,239,898	(11%)	$11,781,316

Key Votes

1991	
Authorize use of force against Iraq	?
1990	
Oppose prohibition of certain semiautomatic weapons	N
Support constitutional amendment on flag desecration	N
Oppose requiring parental notice for minors' abortions	Y
Halt production of B-2 stealth bomber at 13 planes	Y
Approve budget that cut spending and raised revenues	Y
Pass civil rights bill over Bush veto	Y
1989	
Oppose reduction of SDI funding	N
Oppose barring federal funds for "obscene" art	Y
Allow vote on capital gains tax cut	N

Voting Studies

	Presidential Support		Party Unity		Conservative Coalition	
Year	**S**	**O**	**S**	**O**	**S**	**O**
1990	27	73	90	8	11	86
1989	50	50	95	4	13	87
1988	33	52	86	6	14	78
1987	36	58	93	4	9	88
1986	20	78	85	9	9	86
1985	25	73	80	16	18	78
1984	19	61	74	7	13	72
1983	28	40	55	7	7	52
1982	26	66	81	10	7	84
1981	38	48	77	10	10	74

Interest Group Ratings

Year	ADA	ACU	AFL-CIO	CCUS
1990	100	0	67	8
1989	85	4	90	50
1988	95	0	86	29
1987	75	0	89	33
1986	95	10	87	32
1985	100	4	80	21
1984	95	0	100	20
1983	75	0	100	18
1982	95	5	96	11
1981	85	0	100	13

John Seymour (R)

Of Anaheim — Appointed 1991

Born: Dec. 3, 1937, Chicago, Ill.
Education: U. of California, Los Angeles, B.S. 1962.
Military Service: Marine Corps, 1955-59.
Occupation: Real estate broker.
Family: Wife, Judy Thacker; six children.
Religion: Protestant.
Political Career: Anaheim City Council, 1974-78; mayor of Anaheim, 1978-82; Calif. Senate, 1983-91; sought GOP nomination for lieutenant governor, 1990.
Capitol Office: 361 Dirksen Bldg. 20510; 224-3841.

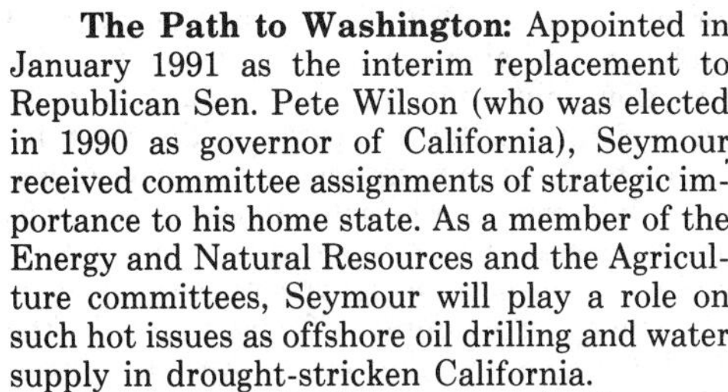

The Path to Washington: Appointed in January 1991 as the interim replacement to Republican Sen. Pete Wilson (who was elected in 1990 as governor of California), Seymour received committee assignments of strategic importance to his home state. As a member of the Energy and Natural Resources and the Agriculture committees, Seymour will play a role on such hot issues as offshore oil drilling and water supply in drought-stricken California.

Few members will ever enter the Senate at a more dramatic juncture than Seymour. Minutes after he was sworn in, the Senate began debate on the resolution authorizing President Bush to use force to end Iraq's occupation of Kuwait. Seymour's first Senate speech and vote were in favor of the war resolution.

But no matter what legislative priorities Seymour pursues in the Senate, no challenge will be greater than just holding on to his job. When Wilson gave up his Senate seat two years into his second term, he tapped Seymour — a state senator and a close political ally — to succeed him. But he also gave his friend a daunting task: building a statewide base and an ample campaign treasury in time for a 1992 special election to fill out the remaining two years of Wilson's unexpired term.

The appointment of Seymour came as a major surprise to the California political community: He was chosen over a lengthy list of better-known and more-often-mentioned Republicans. However, none of these Senate hopefuls could match Seymour's ties to Wilson. The two have known each other since the 1970s, when Wilson was mayor of San Diego and Seymour was mayor of Anaheim. Seymour — a retired owner of a successful real estate company and a former president of the California Association of Realtors — helped raise money for Wilson's first Senate bid in 1982 and chaired his re-election campaign committee in 1988.

Despite this high-level connection and his status as an interim incumbent, it quickly became clear that Seymour would not avoid vigorous competition for the seat in 1992. Like Wilson, Seymour is regarded as a conservative but pragmatic Republican, and is therefore viewed as too moderate by the large constituency of hard-right activists within the California Republican Party; one of them, Rep. William E. Dannemeyer, announced in February 1991 that he will challenge Seymour in the 1992 GOP Senate primary.

State Democratic leaders could hardly keep from salivating over the prospects of facing Seymour, who in 1990 was defeated in the Republican primary for lieutenant governor, his only previous try for statewide office. The Democratic field is led by former San Francisco Mayor Dianne Feinstein, who narrowly lost to Wilson in the heated 1990 contest for governor.

Seymour is faced with the prospect of raising the $20 million or more needed to run for Senate in the nation's most populous state, in a year when the fundraising competition will include candidates for president, California's other Senate seat (Democratic Sen. Alan Cranston is retiring) and at least 52 House seats that California will have following reapportionment. If he manages to survive this gantlet, his reward will be to do it over again in 1994, when his Senate seat will regularly be up for election.

Yet Seymour enters the maelstrom with strengths that would-be opponents ignore at their own risk. He has personal qualities — the toughness of an ex-Marine, the persistence and deal-making instincts of a successful real estate executive — that made him an effective state legislator and a popular figure in his home base, Anaheim (which is located in the suburban Los Angeles GOP heartland of Orange County).

In terms of philosophy, style and even appearance, Wilson and Seymour are so similar as to inspire "separated at birth" jokes. They are both middle-aged white males, slight of build and mild (some say bland) of temperament. Each describes himself as a "compassionate conservative," leaning right on such issues as defense, crime and fiscal responsibility, while taking a more moderate approach on education, aid to the disabled, environmental issues and such social concerns as abortion and gay rights.

As Wilson has proven in two successful races for Senate and one for governor, this profile could enable Seymour to develop a broad statewide electoral base. But it has also alienated conservatives of his own party, many of whom supported Marian Bergeson, a state Senate colleague from a neighboring Orange County district, when she defeated Seymour in the 1990 primary for lieutenant governor.

"A good question arises, what does this guy believe?" said Dannemeyer — who also shares Seymour's Orange County base — as he geared up to announce his Senate primary challenge.

Seymour has tried to assuage his conservative critics. "I think once the conservatives get to know John Seymour and are clear where he stands on issues, they'll be OK," Seymour said. As an example, he said would not go as far to profile himself as an environmentalist as Wilson did during his 1990 campaign. Even those to his right would have a hard time arguing Seymour's pro-business credentials. He is literally a "Chamber of Commerce Republican," having served as president of the Anaheim Chamber in 1973.

Seymour shares a common trait with most Californians: He is from somewhere else. Born in Chicago and graduated from a Pennsylvania high school, Seymour served four years in the Marine Corps. He then enrolled at U.C.L.A., stayed on in the Los Angeles area, and rode Southern California's real estate boom to financial success. Wilson, hailing Seymour's competence while announcing his appointment to the Senate, noted that Seymour had been "a millionaire in business before he was 30 years old."

Seymour entered politics by winning a seat on the Anaheim City Council in 1974, then moved up to mayor four years later. He supported development in the rapidly growing city; his best-known act as mayor was to lure the Rams pro football team from Los Angeles to Anaheim. (Anaheim is also home to Disneyland, which explains why Seymour frequently sports a Mickey Mouse watch.)

After winning a special election for state Senate in 1982, Seymour maneuvered his way within a year to the chairmanship of that body's Republican Caucus. He held that position until 1987, when he got swept up in a coup staged by conservative Republicans who complained about the leadership's lack of success at ending the GOP's minority status in the Senate. (Seymour was replaced by right-wing state Sen. John T. Doolittle, who is now a House freshman from California's 14th District.)

This setback did not deprive Seymour of a legislative role. He would become the chairman of the Senate Select Committee on Substance Abuse and the vice chairman of the Budget and Fiscal Review Committee.

In January 1987, the *California Journal* rated Seymour the sixth-most conservative out of the Senate's 40 members. But he proved adept at the art of the deal, obtaining funding for local transportation programs and education projects, as well as for law-enforcement efforts. "I'm not so rigid that I'm not willing to reach across the aisle to achieve a particular goal that benefits my constituents," Seymour would later tell the *Journal.*

Seymour's political flexibility became most pronounced in 1989. That year, he switched from an anti-abortion position to support for abortion rights, and came out against oil drilling off the California coastline. Seymour insisted he came to these views after long reflection. But critics, especially those on his right flank, accused him of opportunism, noting the upswing in abortion-rights activism following the June 1989 Supreme Court ruling in the *Webster* case and the outcry over the *Exxon Valdez* oil spill off Alaska that March.

The abortion debate loomed large in the 1990 lieutenant governor's primary. It was the only issue on which Seymour and Bergeson had significant disagreement. Bergeson won 60 percent of the Orange County vote, and took 55 percent statewide. (She went on to lose to incumbent Democrat Leo T. McCarthy.)

Despite his loss, Seymour exhibited his fundraising skills, amassing $1.2 million for the campaign. Along with past efforts on behalf of Wilson, Seymour raised money for Republican George Deukmejian's gubernatorial campaigns and for Bush's presidential effort in 1988.

One of Seymour's early fundraising efforts gave him a brush with controversy. During his 1982 state Senate campaign, Seymour accepted a $2,000 contribution from a fireworks manufacturer; that year, he voted for a law barring local fireworks ordinances. When the manufacturer was later convicted for bribing other public officials, his contribution to Seymour received media attention. However, no accusations of wrongdoing were lodged against Seymour, who denied any connection between the donation and his Senate vote.

Committees

Agriculture, Nutrition & Forestry (7th of 8 Republicans)
Agricultural Research & General Legislation (ranking); Agricultural Production & Stabilization of Prices; Domestic & Foreign Marketing & Product Promotion

Energy & Natural Resources (8th of 9 Republicans)
Energy Regulation & Conservation; Public Lands, National Parks & Forests; Water & Power

Governmental Affairs (5th of 6 Republicans)
General Services, Federalism & the District of Columbia (ranking); Government Information & Regulation; Oversight of Government Management; Permanent Investigations

Small Business (8th of 8 Republicans)
Innovation, Technology & Productivity; Urban & Minority-Owned Business Development

Key Vote

1991

Authorize use of force against Iraq	Y

1 Frank Riggs (R)

Of Windsor — Elected 1990

Born: Sept. 5, 1950, Louisville, Ky.
Education: Golden Gate U., B.A. 1980.
Military Service: Army, 1972-75.
Occupation: Real estate developer.
Family: Wife, Cathy Anne Maillard; three children.
Religion: Episcopalian.
Political Career: Windsor School Board, 1984-88.
Capitol Office: 1517 Longworth Bldg. 20515; 225-3311.

The Path to Washington: Every new class of House freshmen includes a few flukes, and Riggs will find it hard to avoid the tag. Little known outside his tiny hometown, he prevailed with a 43 percent plurality when a third-party candidate ran unexpectedly well on the left of the harried Democratic incumbent, Douglas H. Bosco.

It can be difficult for freshmen to be taken seriously in Washington, especially when people assume their tenure will be brief.

Riggs did not help his own case when, after the election, he appeared to hedge on a campaign promise not to accept the latest congressional pay raise.

In an interview with *The Santa Rosa Press-Democrat*, the new congressman indicated that he would take the full raise until he had retired his campaign debts (including his personal loans to the campaign). Mauled by the local news media for the perceived shift, Riggs said he had been misunderstood and would donate the amount of the pay raise (after taxes) to charity.

However shaky the beginning, the length of Riggs' run ultimately will depend on harmonizing the discords of coastal politics. Most immediately, these pose economic fears against environmental concerns.

The larger context is a cultural battle between conventional and alternative lifestyles that has been joined repeatedly through the past three decades of in-migration.

As a builder and developer in Sonoma County, the northern rim of the San Francisco Bay area, Riggs has been part of that growth and change. But the clean-cut and earnest Kentucky native is also a former policeman and deputy sheriff who fits in well with the older, more traditionally rural values found in the farther reaches of the district.

He had been active in the county GOP for years and had run the congressional district for the campaigns of Ronald Reagan in 1984 and of GOP Gov. George Deukmejian in 1982 and 1986. But he had also been president of the school board in Windsor and head of the Sonoma chapter of Habitat for Humanity, a home-building program for low-income families.

In his first days in office, Riggs signaled he would emphasize constituent services and seek a middle path on emotional issues. One of his first acts in office was a series of town hall hearings to sound out district opinion on the Persian Gulf crisis.

Riggs explicitly urged the district's sizable antiwar contingent to attend. "I want to represent every person in my district, whatever their point of view," he said.

Bosco had been known for attempting this feat, too. He once compared the delicacy of his job "to going through the Strait of Hormuz." After establishing a 63 percent share of the vote in the presidential year of 1988, Bosco was considered safe. But his luck changed with the 1990 "Redwood Summer" campaign by environmental activists bent on disrupting logging in old-growth forests.

Bosco opposed the demonstrations and refused to take an absolute position against offshore oil drilling.

Still, Bosco might have survived the sundering of his jobs-and-environment coalition had it not been for questions raised about his ties to the savings and loan industry and the substantial assets he had amassed while serving in Congress and the state Legislature. He was especially heavily criticized by some of the smaller local newspapers, such as Mendocino County's *Anderson Valley Advertiser*.

Some of the reporting helped Riggs put together a late mailing alleging that Bosco's business interests had profited from his public positions. Coming on the heels of defections among environmentalists, the S&L headlines helped convince many Bosco voters that they wanted an alternative.

More than 31,000 voters (about 15 percent of the November vote) turned to Darlene G. Comingore of the Peace and Freedom Party — enough to elect Riggs by about 2,000 votes.

California 1

Northern Coast — Santa Rosa; Eureka

With more than 300 miles of Pacific coastline and its majestic stands of redwood trees, the 1st has a bucolic quality. But partisan politics here can be contentious.

In presidential elections, this has become something of a swing district. Californian Ronald Reagan won here in 1984, but not by much. Democrat Michael S. Dukakis took the 1st in 1988 by a wider margin.

For many years this area was the exclusive province of fishermen, lumberjacks, and those who made their livings from the summer tourist trade. But from the 1970s on, these scenic environs drew a new class of immigrants — urban refugees from outside California who are determined to protect the environment at all costs.

The district has also been transformed by the population boom in Sonoma County, the famed wine-making region that reaches down toward the San Francisco metropolis. With housing tracts pressing in on the grapes, the city of Santa Rosa grew by 36 percent in the 1980s. About half the district's vote is cast in Sonoma County.

The liberal lean in Sonoma normally gives Democrats a leg up in carrying the district. Dukakis won 57 percent of the vote there, and in 1990, Democratic gubernatorial candidate Dianne Feinstein outran GOP foe Pete Wilson by almost 25,000 votes. However, in the section of neighboring Napa County that is in the district, Republicans are stronger.

Northward in the district, the bulk of the vote is cast in the coastal counties of Humboldt and Mendocino. This is primarily where the liberal transplants have settled, enjoying a serene rural lifestyle epitomized by herbal teas and organic farming. Dukakis carried both counties. Democratic Rep. Douglas H. Bosco took 67 percent of the vote in Humboldt County in 1988.

However, when Republican Frank Riggs ousted him in 1990, Bosco won Humboldt by only 66 votes; he was hurt in part by his opposition to anti-logging demonstrations.

Population: 525,986. White 483,984 (92%), Black 4,732 (1%), Other 20,466 (4%). Spanish origin 32,321 (6%). 18 and over 390,186 (74%), 65 and over 69,488 (13%). Median age: 32.

Committees

Banking, Finance & Urban Affairs (16th of 20 Republicans)
Consumer Affairs & Coinage; General Oversight; Housing & Community Development

Public Works & Transportation (17th of 21 Republicans)
Surface Transportation; Water Resources

Select Children, Youth & Families (13th of 14 Republicans)

Campaign Finance

	Receipts	Receipts from PACs		Expend-itures
1990				
Riggs (R)	$257,745	$8,000	(3%)	$251,662
Bosco (D)	$408,849	$190,421	(47%)	$413,213
Comingore (PFP)	$9,377	0		$7,291

Key Vote

1991

Authorize use of force against Iraq	N

Elections

1990 General		
Frank Riggs (R)	99,782	(43%)
Douglas H. Bosco (D)	96,468	(42%)
Darlene G. Comingore (PFP)	34,011	(15%)
1990 Primary		
Frank Riggs (R)	45,148	(77%)
Timothy Oliver Stoen (R)	13,244	(23%)

District Vote For President

	1988	1984	1980	1976
D	145,811 (55%)	119,330 (46%)	77,182 (36%)	80,635 (52%)
R	114,103 (43%)	134,358 (52%)	103,463 (49%)	72,082 (46%)

2 Wally Herger (R)

Of Rio Oso — Elected 1986

Born: May 20, 1945, Sutter County, Calif.
Education: American River Community College, A.A. 1967; attended California State U., 1968-69.
Occupation: Rancher; gas company president.
Family: Wife, Pamela Sargent; eight children.
Religion: Mormon.
Political Career: Calif. Assembly, 1981-87.
Capitol Office: 1108 Longworth Bldg. 20515; 225-3076.

In Washington: Herger is a conservative Northern California rancher whose friendly style helps explain the ease with which he first won and has since held his district — Democratic turf when the 1980s began.

Herger became vice president of his freshman Republican class, an early sign that his personality would wear well among his colleagues, too. None of them much doubt where he will end up on key floor votes: He takes a consistently conservative line.

On the Agriculture Committee, Herger seeks to protect his district's fruit and nut growers. His interest in averting a trade war with Europe stemmed from the threat of a European retaliatory tariff on U.S. walnuts. During consideration of the 1990 farm bill, Herger was especially keen on seeing the continuation of the Targeted Export Assistance program, which promotes exports of district products such as almonds and kiwi fruit.

From his seat on Agriculture's Forests Subcommittee, Herger fends for his district's loggers. He bristled at the Fish and Wildlife Service's 1990 decision to list the northern spotted owl as a threatened species, which would curtail lumbering in ancient forests in the Pacific Northwest.

In June he asked Interior Secretary Manuel Lujan Jr. to exempt Northern California from the listing, arguing that the service had ignored "important biological evidence." "Once again," Herger said, "we see that prudence and common sense have been sacrificed to appease the extremists."

Following the outcry over the federal government's "let-burn" policy toward fires that swept Yellowstone National Park and other public and private lands, Herger proposed a bill establishing a commission to recommend improvements in the government's management of wildfires. In May 1990, President Bush signed Herger's bill into law.

Herger has taken to the floor several times to decry alleged human rights abuses commit ted by the government of India against the Sikh minority in Punjab state. Members of the small Sikh community in Yuba City had told Herger of their concern for their relatives in the Punjab. Herger tried to amend the 1989 foreign aid authorization to bar development aid to India unless the president certified that India had prosecuted those responsible for several reported attacks on women in the Punjab in April 1989. His amendment lost 204-212.

At Home: Expected to face tough Democratic competition for the open 2nd District in 1986, Herger won by a wide margin. He has had little difficulty in his two elections since.

The north-central California district had been Democrat Harold T. Johnson's for 22 years before Republican Gene Chappie upset him in 1980. When Chappie decided to retire in 1986, a GOP succession was in doubt. District Democrats touted the chances of Shasta County Supervisor Stephen C. Swendiman.

However, Swendiman stumbled in the Democratic primary and barely held off a challenge from rancher Wayne Meyer.

Herger, on the other hand, got a boost for the general election with his easy GOP primary victory.

Herger, who was in his third term in the state Assembly, came in with a voter base that comprised nearly half the 2nd District, and complemented that asset with superior organizing and fundraising. He spent most of the fall campaign on the offensive, linking himself to President Reagan and Gov. George Deukmejian and calling Swendiman a "tax-and-spend Democrat." When Swendiman portrayed him as a "backbencher" in the Legislature, Herger highlighted his support of popular measures such as workfare and tougher sentencing for criminals.

Herger beat Swendiman in all 12 counties and took a solid 58 percent. Most Democrats declined to tackle Herger in 1988. Meyer, the 1986 Democratic primary runner-up, got the nomination unopposed, but found it tough to raise money against Herger; the incumbent won comfortably.

Democrats made even less of an effort in 1990, and Herger breezed past retired federal worker Erwin E. "Bill" Rush.

California 2

North Central — Chico; Redding

The 2nd, in the heart of Northern California, runs from the sparsely populated mountain counties on the Oregon border southward to the Napa Valley.

Its three northern counties — Siskiyou, Trinity and Shasta — make up a huge wilderness area where lumbering is the main occupation. Outdoors-lovers also contribute to the economy; 14,162-foot Mount Shasta and nearby Shasta Lake are tourist magnets.

Democrats have an edge in registration here, but there is more loyalty to the National Rifle Association than to the Democratic label; Ronald Reagan always did well here, as did George Bush in his 1988 race.

Heading south into the Sacramento River basin, the land flattens out and the vast forests give way to agricultural territory. Barley, rice and specialty crops such as olives, kiwi fruit and almonds are the main products. Many of the farmers here are members of families that arrived from the dust bowl during the Depression. They tend to be conservative.

The peach and tomato farmers of Sutter County reside in one of the district's most conservative areas. In 1988, Sutter gave Bush 67 percent of its vote and awarded GOP Sen. Pete Wilson one of his highest county percentages.

Across the low Vaca Mountains are the grape vineyards that cling to terraced hillsides in Napa County. Napa, the second most populous county in the district, is known worldwide for its wineries.

Population: 526,009. White 480,596 (91%), Black 6,235 (1%), Other 17,867 (3%). Spanish origin 34,320 (7%). 18 and over 384,601 (73%), 65 and over 69,055 (13%). Median age: 31.

Committees

Agriculture (11th of 18 Republicans)
Cotton, Rice & Sugar; Department Operations, Research & Foreign Agriculture; Domestic Marketing, Consumer Relations & Nutrition; Forests, Family Farms & Energy

Merchant Marine & Fisheries (10th of 17 Republicans)
Fisheries & Wildlife Conservation & the Environment; Oceanography, Great Lakes & Outer Continental Shelf

Select Narcotics Abuse & Control (8th of 14 Republicans)

Elections

1990 General		
Wally Herger (R)	133,315	(64%)
Erwin E. "Bill" Rush (D)	65,333	(31%)
Ross Crain (LIBERT)	10,753	(5%)
1988 General		
Wally Herger (R)	139,010	(59%)
Wayne Meyer (D)	91,088	(39%)

Previous Winning Percentage: **1986** (58%)

District Vote For President

	1988	1984	1980	1976
D	96,230 (40%)	83,085 (35%)	64,005 (31%)	61,220 (47%)
R	138,756 (58%)	150,641 (63%)	120,259 (58%)	68,548 (52%)

Campaign Finance

	Receipts	Receipts from PACs	Expend-itures
1990			
Herger (R)	$616,075	$212,749 (35%)	$515,020
Rush (D)	$6,118	$2,000 (33%)	$5,951
1988			
Herger (R)	$691,969	$258,675 (37%)	$696,748
Meyer (D)	$193,861	$58,900 (30%)	$193,915

Key Votes

1991	
Authorize use of force against Iraq	Y
1990	
Support constitutional amendment on flag desecration	Y
Pass family and medical leave bill over Bush veto	N
Reduce SDI funding	?
Allow abortions in overseas military facilities	N
Approve budget summit plan for spending and taxing	N
Approve civil rights bill	N
1989	
Halt production of B-2 stealth bomber at 13 planes	N
Oppose capital gains tax cut	N
Approve federal abortion funding in rape or incest cases	N
Approve pay raise and revision of ethics rules	N
Pass Democratic minimum wage plan over Bush veto	N

Voting Studies

	Presidential Support		Party Unity		Conservative Coalition	
Year	S	O	S	O	S	O
1990	69	30	94	4	94	6
1989	76	24	91	8	88	12
1988	68	32	91	8	92	5
1987	74	24	89	9	93	7

Interest Group Ratings

Year	ADA	ACU	AFL-CIO	CCUS
1990	6	96	8	79
1989	10	100	25	100
1988	0	92	29	93
1987	12	100	13	100

3 Robert T. Matsui (D)

Of Sacramento — Elected 1978

Born: Sept. 17, 1941, Sacramento, Calif.
Education: U. of California, Berkeley, A.B. 1963; U. of California, Hastings College of Law, J.D. 1966.
Occupation: Lawyer.
Family: Wife, Doris Okada; one child.
Religion: Methodist.
Political Career: Sacramento City Council, 1971-78.
Capitol Office: 2353 Rayburn Bldg. 20515; 225-7163.

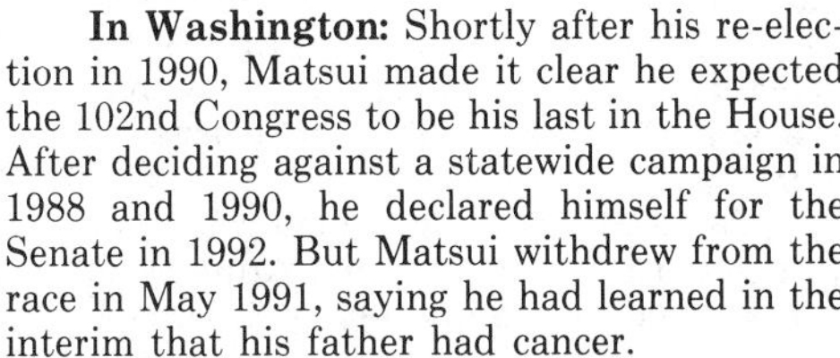

In Washington: Shortly after his re-election in 1990, Matsui made it clear he expected the 102nd Congress to be his last in the House. After deciding against a statewide campaign in 1988 and 1990, he declared himself for the Senate in 1992. But Matsui withdrew from the race in May 1991, saying he had learned in the interim that his father had cancer.

Matsui has always been known for his energy, driving himself and his staff hard from day to day and from issue to issue. He has also generally enjoyed the good will of the news media, who find him among the most accessible and quotable members. In the 101st Congress, Matsui also had added his first important leadership credential, ascending to the Democratic Steering and Policy Committee midway through 1989.

Through seven terms in the House, six of them on the Ways and Means Committee, Matsui has been remarkable in his ability to combine a thoughtful, generally liberal approach to tax policy with an intense interest in serving California business. While liberals can count on his votes on social-policy issues, Matsui has increasingly applied his capacity for hard work to the business side of the committee's ledger, especially where West Coast industries are concerned.

This avid solicitousness has been read as relating to Matsui's ambition: running statewide in California now requires funding in seven or eight digits. Of course, Matsui is also seen as currying public favor when he weighs in on behalf of consumers. And sometimes he seems to have played to both business and consumers on a single issue.

In 1989 he went after a provision in the 1986 tax overhaul that had allowed utilities to collect more tax-reserve money from customers than needed. This meant utilities could amass capital, avoid new debt for new plants and so hold down rates. But the extra withholding piled up embarrassingly fast, yielding a $19 billion windfall for utilities nationally by the midpoint of 1989. With Rep. Byron L. Dorgan, D-N.D., Matsui sought immediate repeal of the provision and a rebate of the reserves. Their effort failed in committee on a vote of 13-22.

On trade matters, Matsui has generally supported a free market across international borders. He argues that trade spurs growth, serving American interests as much as those of other nations. Cutting off trade when other countries displease us, he says, is tantamount to saying, "You improve your human rights behavior or we'll burn *our* house down."

Matsui rarely pursues a major legislative endeavor outside the purview of Ways and Means, but he did so in the 100th Congress on an issue especially close to his heart. With Rep. Norman Y. Mineta of California, Matsui was an important force behind passage of legislation to provide federal redress to the surviving Japanese-Americans who were interned during World War II.

In 1942, when he was six months old, Matsui and his family were ousted from their Sacramento home and sent to a detention camp, where they lived more than three years. "Just as the victim of a rape finds her chastity called into question, and finds that she cannot speak out to defend herself, so the Japanese-American community finds its loyalty called into question to such an extent that it could not speak out to protest," Matsui said during deliberations on the compensation bill.

The legislation, passed in 1987, formally apologized to those interned, and established a $1.25 billion fund to give $20,000 to each of the estimated 60,000 surviving victims, half the total number interned. Former detainees who accept the settlement agree to drop further claims against the government.

Ordinarily, Matsui focuses on Ways and Means, where he uses his seat on the Trade Subcommittee to watch out for California industries and to advocate knocking down foreign trade barriers to U.S. high-tech products, many of which are made in California. One trade measure Matsui offered — to mandate retaliation against countries that restrict markets for U.S. telecommunications equipment — was largely folded into the 1988 omnibus trade bill.

California 3

Most of Sacramento; Eastern Suburbs

Though it is the state capital and the metropolis of California's Central Valley, Sacramento typically has been overshadowed by the far larger and more glamorous coastal cities of Los Angeles, San Diego and San Francisco. In recent years, however, Sacramento has been emerging in its own right. A 34 percent increase between 1980 and 1990 boosted the city's population to 369,000.

The southern two-thirds of Sacramento make up the heart of the 3rd District, and provide much of the Democratic base that has made Matsui a dominant district figure. Its 50,000-plus state workers provide a strong pro-government constituency. Blacks and Hispanics make up over a quarter of the city's population.

There is a labor segment (Sacramento is a major inland port). The *Sacramento Bee*, the flagship newspaper of the McClatchy chain, takes a generally liberal editorial line.

The city vote has enabled Democrats to maintain their lock on Sacramento's House seat. Democrat John E. Moss represented the city and surrounding areas for years until he retired in 1978; Matsui has been in ever since.

But the balance of the 3rd is mainly suburban territory, with a Republican lean that often sways district results in contests above the House level. In 1988, George Bush carried the district Ronald Reagan won more comfortably in his two presidential contests. The district's Republican vote has been bolstered over the years by the military presence at Mather Air Force Base, located in Rancho Cordova to the east of Sacramento. However, this presence is soon to be sharply diminished; Mather is targeted for deep personnel cutbacks under the military base-closing plan enacted in April 1989.

The 1991 base-closing plan could hurt just as much; the Sacramento Army Depot is scheduled for closure, taking 3,100 civilian jobs with it.

Population: 525,774. White 413,400 (79%), Black 43,168 (8%), Asian and Pacific Islander 33,074 (6%), Other 5,290 (1%). Spanish origin 51,010 (10%). 18 and over 390,354 (74%), 65 and over 52,458 (10%). Median age: 30.

When the House took up legislation to carry out the 1988 U.S.-Canada trade pact, Matsui worked to protect not only California's telecommunications industry, but also its motion-picture industry. "Under the guise of protecting its cultural sovereignty, some officials in Canada have threatened to erect barriers against U.S. film companies," he said.

Tax legislation gives Matsui venues for both his business activism and his liberal social concerns. Both political strains were on display as Matsui helped draft the 99th Congress' overhaul of the federal tax code. He watched out for the high-tech industry and other local allies while supporting tax relief for the poor.

Matsui was an active and consistent supporter of the tax-code overhaul, which shifted a sizable share of the revenue burden from individuals to corporations.

But while he sometimes bristled at business' resistance to reform, he also championed protection for an important business concern: the tax-exempt bond market. No changes were proposed for municipal bonds used by governments, but the two-thirds of the bonds used to finance private development faced an end to exemptions.

As the pro-bond group gained strength, a personal appeal from Ways and Means Chairman Dan Rostenkowski of Illinois to Matsui kept the issue from being a stumbling block. "Mr. Chairman, I'm going to help you," Matsui was quoted as saying in "Showdown at Gucci Gulch," a book on the tax bill's passage. "I sure appreciate your asking me." In the end, a handful of bond-related exemptions were allowed, including one for an urban-redevelopment bond popular in California.

Before winning a post on Ways and Means, Matsui had to pay his dues in the House committee system.

He spent most of his first term on Judiciary, an assignment he accepted at the behest of House leaders. In 1980, he was rewarded with a spot on the Commerce Committee, where he joined the pro-consumer faction fighting against eased antitrust laws that would allow the American Telephone & Telegraph Co. to enter computer-related fields.

Matsui is a skilled fundraiser. He is often near the top of the receipt lists for congressional honoraria and for political action committee contributions.

At Home: One of several members of the California House delegation considered potential 1992 Senate candidates, Matsui was the first to announce his intentions to run, declaring in November 1990.

Yet there were doubters among state political insiders, who cited Matsui's withdrawal from the 1988 field of potential challengers to then-GOP Sen. Pete Wilson. Matsui also ruled out running in 1990 for the open governorship, which was eventually won by Wilson in a close contest with Democrat Dianne Feinstein, the former mayor of San Francisco.

Matsui would have entered a Senate campaign with a solid base in Sacramento, the state capital and one of California's booming growth areas. His business contacts and proven fundraising ability would also have benefited him in a year in which Senate contenders will have to compete for campaign funds against candidates for president, California's other Senate seat and at least 52 House seats.

Matsui's political career began on the local level. His experience in a World War II internment camp helped him establish a bond with Sacramento's large Asian community, and he won two elections for the City Council.

In 1972, the year after Matsui joined the council, he chaired U.S. Rep. John E. Moss' reelection campaign. His fundraising skills helped Moss win easily that year, and again in 1974 and 1976.

In 1978 Matsui was preparing to run for the county Board of Supervisors when Moss announced his retirement after 26 years. Matsui switched to a congressional campaign.

Two other prominent Sacramento Democrats also filed for the House, but Matsui's $225,000 primary campaign budget gave him a clear advantage. He ran television commercials identifying himself as "Citizen Matsui," setting himself apart from his rivals, both of whom had been heavily involved in state politics.

Matsui won the primary and then took the general election comfortably against Republican Sandy Smoley, considered the strongest candidate Sacramento Republicans had run for the House in many years. Moss repeatedly proclaimed his support for Matsui in a series of television commercials. Republicans have made no similar effort to capture the district since.

Committees

Budget (18th of 23 Democrats)
Defense, Foreign Policy & Space; Economic Policy, Projections & Revenues; Human Resources

Ways & Means (13th of 23 Democrats)
Trade

Elections

1990 General		
Robert T. Matsui (D)	132,143	(60%)
Lowell P. Landowski (R)	76,148	(35%)
David M. McCann (LIBERT)	10,797	(5%)
1990 Primary		
Robert T. Matsui (D)	71,562	(86%)
James J. Walsh (D)	11,857	(14%)
1988 General		
Robert T. Matsui (D)	183,470	(71%)
Lowell Landowski (R)	74,296	(29%)

Previous Winning Percentages: **1986** (76%) **1984** (100%) **1982** (90%) **1980** (71%) **1978** (53%)

District Vote For President

	1988	1984	1980	1976
D	130,495 (49%)	112,714 (44%)	86,618 (41%)	96,961 (53%)
R	132,533 (50%)	139,564 (55%)	97,854 (47%)	85,427 (46%)

Campaign Finance

	Receipts	Receipts from PACs		Expend-itures
1990				
Matsui (D)	$1,207,843	$582,964	(48%)	$734,005
Landowski (R)	$4,545	$250	(6%)	$4,628
1988				
Matsui (D)	$916,025	$475,366	(52%)	$638,688
Landowski (R)	$7,695	0		$7,695

Key Votes

1991	
Authorize use of force against Iraq	N
1990	
Support constitutional amendment on flag desecration	N
Pass family and medical leave bill over Bush veto	Y
Reduce SDI funding	Y
Allow abortions in overseas military facilities	Y
Approve budget summit plan for spending and taxing	Y
Approve civil rights bill	Y
1989	
Halt production of B-2 stealth bomber at 13 planes	N
Oppose capital gains tax cut	Y
Approve federal abortion funding in rape or incest cases	Y
Approve pay raise and revision of ethics rules	Y
Pass Democratic minimum wage plan over Bush veto	Y

Voting Studies

	Presidential Support		Party Unity		Conservative Coalition	
Year	**S**	**O**	**S**	**O**	**S**	**O**
1990	21	75	89	5	17	76
1989	33	66	94	3	15	85
1988	20	75	88	2	16	79
1987	20	80	95	2	14	79
1986	20	80	94	3	18	82
1985	20	80	94	2	9	89
1984	32	65	94	3	12	88
1983	32	67	93	6	24	76
1982	40	60	93	5	19	81
1981	45	53	80	17	32	63

Interest Group Ratings

Year	ADA	ACU	AFL-CIO	CCUS
1990	94	0	92	21
1989	95	4	92	10
1988	90	4	86	36
1987	92	9	87	20
1986	95	5	79	17
1985	90	5	94	18
1984	80	0	92	38
1983	85	4	94	25
1982	85	5	95	14
1981	70	0	87	17

4 Vic Fazio (D)

Of West Sacramento — Elected 1978

Born: Oct. 11, 1942, Winchester, Mass.
Education: Union College, B.A. 1965.
Occupation: Journalist; congressional and legislative consultant.
Family: Wife, Judy Kern; four children.
Religion: Episcopalian.
Political Career: Calif. Assembly, 1975-79.
Capitol Office: 2113 Rayburn Bldg. 20515; 225-5716.

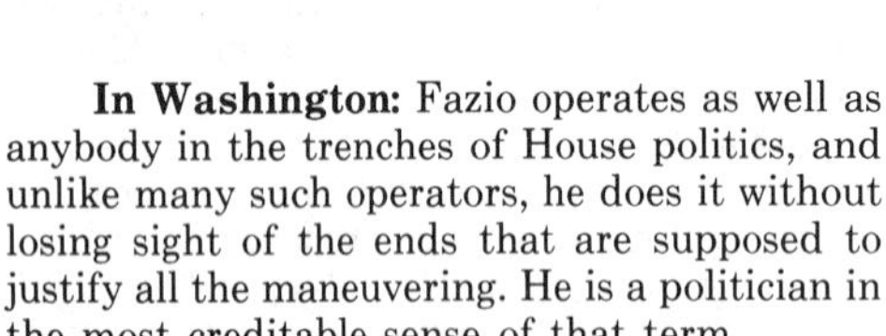

In Washington: Fazio operates as well as anybody in the trenches of House politics, and unlike many such operators, he does it without losing sight of the ends that are supposed to justify all the maneuvering. He is a politician in the most creditable sense of that term.

He has learned to negotiate with senior barons on the Appropriations Committee, as the youngest of the 13 subcommittee chairmen called the "College of Cardinals." He does unpleasant household tasks, such as advocating a congressional pay raise and serving on the ethics committee. One California magazine calls him "the Mr. Goodwrench of the Hill." Acknowledging his penchant for getting involved in controversial institutional issues, Fazio once described himself as a "heat-seeking missile."

His colleagues finally rewarded him by electing him vice chairman of the Democratic Caucus in mid-1989, when the party leadership was rebuilt after Speaker Jim Wright's resignation. The following year, they added the chairmanship of the Democratic Congressional Campaign Committee to his portfolio.

Fazio, who had earlier campaigned for the DCCC post under Wright's tenure, was initially cool to the opening the second time around, citing the need to spend more time with his family. (Fazio in 1990 publicly acknowledged that his teenage daughter has leukemia.)

But the Californian had already established formidable campaign credentials as head of IMPAC 2000, a leadership-sponsored group designed to advance Democratic prospects in upcoming redistricting. The organizing and fundraising prowess demonstrated there, along with Fazio's overall reputation for getting things done, made him the strong consensus pick for the job.

Fazio was waist-deep in controversial issues — congressional pay, perks and ethics — throughout the 101st Congress. He was the leadership's point man defending a controversial 51 percent pay raise for congressmen, a plan shot down by public criticism in early 1989. Fazio was generally admired for having defended a raise that many of his colleagues publicly denounced but privately coveted.

Fazio was chief author of an unsuccessful measure to outlaw honoraria — a major restriction on members' outside income that the Democratic leadership hoped, in vain, would make a pay raise more palatable to the public.

In another measure of the leadership's trust in his ability and willingness to take thankless jobs, Fazio was put in charge of a bipartisan task force to review House ethics standards.

Because of Fazio's close ties to the leadership, Republicans viewed with suspicion his role in the House ethics committee's investigation of Wright. Fazio was ranking Democrat on the ethics committee during that 1988-89 inquiry. Early in the investigation, the GOP passed a resolution calling on Fazio to disqualify himself because he invited Wright to a party fundraiser held in California after the ethics investigation had begun.

But Fazio remained in place, and while he was not as critical of Wright as some committee Democrats, neither was he an automatic pro-Wright vote; On several split committee votes over whether there was "reason to believe" Wright had violated House rules, Fazio joined all of the committee Republicans to vote the tougher line against Wright.

Thereafter, Fazio was named co-chairman of a bipartisan House task force on ethics along with then-Rep. Lynn Martin, an Illinois Republican. Fazio was charged with helping to craft, and rally support for, a second, 40 percent congressional pay raise and ethics package. The House passed that proposal 252-174 and it became law in November 1989.

Much of Congress' institutional dirty work has fallen to Fazio because he is chairman of the Appropriations Legislative Subcommittee, which is politically perhaps the least appealing of any of the Appropriations chairs. It handles the money Congress spends on itself, and members are always sensitive to criticism that they waste taxpayers' money by treating themselves too well.

California 4

Suburban Sacramento to Bay Area

Like a large jaw about to clamp down on the state capital, the 4th District surrounds Sacramento on three sides and takes in the northern part of the city as well. Nearly half the vote is cast in the suburban part of Sacramento County; the rest is split between Solano and Yolo counties to the west.

At the House level, Democrat Fazio has the 4th District firmly in hand. But in statewide contests, the district, though competitive, leans Republican. George Bush carried the 4th with 52 percent of the vote in 1988.

Though the city of Sacramento has a Democratic flavor, the Sacramento County suburbs to the north can be difficult for Democrats. The towns in this area have been growing rapidly — Folsom, with 30,000 residents, grew by over 171 percent between 1980 and 1990 — and their residents have little allegiance to the Sacramento Democratic establishment. The suburban voters also tend to be conservative on crime and other social issues.

Many local residents work in the high-tech industries. Folsom is home to Aerojet, an aerospace firm specializing in space shuttle technology. (The Folsom Prison, made famous by singer Johnny Cash, is just outside the district.)

Solano County, which provides about 30 percent of the 4th's vote, has also boomed, its population growing by 45 percent in the 1980s. Fairfield, with 77,000 people, is the dominant city. Democrats tend to have an edge in Solano, but not a huge one: Michael S. Dukakis carried the county with 52 percent of the vote in 1988; Democratic gubernatorial candidate Dianne Feinstein won 52 percent there in 1990.

The most liberal territory in the district is Yolo County, one of five counties in the state that went for Walter F. Mondale for president in 1984. Dukakis took 58 percent there in 1988, one of his best showings in California. The city of Davis (46,000 residents) is the county's Democratic bastion; a University of California campus is located there.

Population: 525,764. White 435,421 (83%), Black 30,224 (6%), Other 24,188 (5%). Spanish origin 60,417 (12%). 18 and over 374,278 (71%), 65 and over 41,017 (8%). Median age: 28.

Nevertheless, the subcommittee is Fazio's power base. Because of his work there, members all over the ideological spectrum feel indebted to him.

Fazio is unapologetic about the politics of politics. Discussing the possibility that Democrats were deliberately loading pet projects onto a funding bill that included one of President Bush's favorite projects, Fazio commented, "I wouldn't say there's a direct correlation, but if the administration is going to remain as committed as they are [to the super collider], obviously there's going to be some give and take."

But Fazio is also sensitive to public perceptions of Congress and its possible excesses. In the past he has defended congressional mailing privileges, but during the 101st, faced with perceived abuse of the system, Fazio moved for substantial reforms.

His proposal was sharply attacked by some Democratic colleagues as too drastic, but members did ultimately approve some new restrictions in late 1990.

In addition to giving him leverage over the internal workings of Congress, Fazio's subcommittee chairmanship allows him to leave his mark on a variety of appropriations bills, and he has done so to help the California delegation on issues such as protecting the coastline against offshore oil drilling and pushing for a fund to clean up toxic wastes at military installations, including several in the Sacramento area.

During the 101st Congress, he pleased local pear growers by persuading the Appropriations committee to delay banning red dye No. 3. Some groups believe the dye causes cancer, but critics say more study is needed. Growers complain that sales of fruit cocktail would plummet if it ceased to include the maraschino cherries that get their bright red color from the controversial dye.

At Home: Fazio's image as an ultimate Washington insider may have cost him a few points back home in 1990, a year marked by voter dissatisfaction in California. After winning with 70 percent of the vote in 1986, then running unopposed in 1988, Fazio slipped to 55 percent in 1990. He nonetheless won with a cushion of more than 32,000 votes over Republican Mark Baughman, a former aide to hard-line conservative GOP state Sen. John T. Doolittle (who was in the process of winning the open 14th District House seat).

Fazio began his career in politics not as a participant but as an observer: He followed the state Legislature as a journalist. He later served as an aide to the state Assembly Speaker, before winning an Assembly seat himself in a 1975 special election.

After winning that contest by just 472 votes, Fazio set about establishing a strong political base in Sacramento and Yolo counties with his activist approach to energy, consumer and environmental issues. Less than a year later, he won a full term with 74 percent.

That same day, Democratic U.S. Rep. Robert Leggett survived by just 651 votes against Albert Dehr, an obscure railroad worker. Leggett had been accused of taking bribes from South Korean government officials, and acknowledged going into debt to support a Capitol Hill secretary and their two illegitimate children. It was clear he would draw a more substantial challenge if he tried to run again.

But Leggett kept most Democratic aspirants out of the 1978 primary by insisting for months that he would run again despite the bad publicity. His retirement announcement, made two weeks before the filing deadline, surprised nearly every politician in the 4th except one — Fazio. The assemblyman was the only candidate ready with a campaign, and he coasted to the nomination.

The general election was not particularly close. Republican Rex Hime, a former aide to Ronald Reagan and a state-party staffer, could not match Fazio's fundraising skills. Fazio lost two agricultural counties in the northern part of the 4th, but carried the rest, most of which he had been representing in the Assembly. He did even better in 1980, winning all five counties against Dehr, who was making his third try.

Although the 1981 redistricting plan appeared to weaken Fazio slightly, he had no problems in the 1982 election. Republican nominee Roger Canfield, a former reapportionment consultant for the state GOP, expected substantial financial help from the political network of conservative state Sen. H. L. Richardson. But Canfield was never able to raise the money he needed to pose a threat, and Fazio walked off with better than 60 percent in all of the district's counties.

When Fazio stuck his neck out by working to pass the 1984 congressional pay raise the state GOP leadership considered sinking money into a challenge. But the Republican nomination that year went again to Canfield, who barely bettered his earlier showing.

Committees

Appropriations (19th of 37 Democrats)
Energy & Water Development; Legislative (chairman); Military Construction

Select Hunger (3rd of 22 Democrats)
International

Elections

1990 General		
Vic Fazio (D)	115,090	(55%)
Mark Baughman (R)	82,738	(39%)
Bryce Bigwood (LIBERT)	12,626	(6%)
1990 Primary		
Vic Fazio (D)	60,005	(79%)
Stan Warner (D)	16,097	(21%)
1988 General		
Vic Fazio (D)	181,184	(99%)

Previous Winning Percentages: **1986** (70%) **1984** (61%) **1982** (64%) **1980** (65%) **1978** (55%)

District Vote For President

	1988	1984	1980	1976
D	121,847 (48%)	96,775 (43%)	73,568 (41%)	77,887 (56%)
R	129,477 (51%)	127,252 (56%)	89,745 (50%)	59,567 (43%)

Campaign Finance

	Receipts	Receipts from PACs		Expend-itures
1990				
Fazio (D)	$845,622	$451,245	(53%)	$1,029,304
Baughman (R)	$40,439	$3,500	(9%)	$40,040
1988				
Fazio (D)	$752,357	$378,783	(50%)	$659,334

Key Votes

1991	
Authorize use of force against Iraq	N
1990	
Support constitutional amendment on flag desecration	N
Pass family and medical leave bill over Bush veto	Y
Reduce SDI funding	Y
Allow abortions in overseas military facilities	Y
Approve budget summit plan for spending and taxing	Y
Approve civil rights bill	Y
1989	
Halt production of B-2 stealth bomber at 13 planes	N
Oppose capital gains tax cut	Y
Approve federal abortion funding in rape or incest cases	Y
Approve pay raise and revision of ethics rules	Y
Pass Democratic minimum wage plan over Bush veto	Y

Voting Studies

	Presidential Support		Party Unity		Conservative Coalition	
Year	S	O	S	O	S	O
1990	19	81	91	5	26	72
1989	35	64	95	4	24	76
1988	19	73	92	2	16	74
1987	23	75	92	3	35	63
1986	20	80	93	5	30	64
1985	26	65	90	6	35	65
1984	31	64	88	8	25	68
1983	28	68	91	6	24	72
1982	36	58	92	7	29	67
1981	41	57	81	17	33	64

Interest Group Ratings

Year	ADA	ACU	AFL-CIO	CCUS
1990	89	4	100	21
1989	80	4	100	20
1988	85	0	100	29
1987	84	0	94	14
1986	80	9	93	24
1985	75	14	82	32
1984	75	4	85	38
1983	80	9	100	26
1982	80	5	90	14
1981	80	0	87	17

5 Nancy Pelosi (D)

Of San Francisco — Elected 1987

Born: March 26, 1940, Baltimore, Md.
Education: Trinity College, A.B. 1962.
Occupation: Public relations consultant.
Family: Husband, Paul Pelosi; five children.
Religion: Roman Catholic.
Political Career: Calif. Democratic Party Chairman, 1981-83.
Capitol Office: 109 Cannon Bldg. 20515; 225-4965.

In Washington: Though Pelosi did not hold public office before coming to Congress in 1987, she has the self-assurance one would expect from a woman born into the business. Her father, Thomas J. D'Alesandro Jr., was a New Deal-era House member and then mayor of Baltimore. She has also cut her own path, serving as California Democratic Party chairman and finance chairman of the Democratic Senatorial Campaign Committee.

That background gives her an understanding of the levers of power in Washington that compensates for her lack of legislative experience. On at least one occasion, when she appeared before the Rules Committee to make a request, her wishes were quickly granted because she had already made her case effectively behind the scenes.

Her ascent into the ranks of the respected continued at the start of the 102nd Congress when Pelosi won a seat on the powerful Appropriations Committee. She had unsuccessfully sought a seat on the panel in May 1990, but was apparently hindered then by the fact that there were already five Californians on the committee.

House leaders also drafted Pelosi in 1991 to sit on the House Committee on Standards of Official Conduct; she joins a number of other institutional loyalists who appear inclined to retain the ethics panel's historically cautious approach.

Despite impressive committee assignments and the initial respect she has earned from the party faithful, as a liberal Democrat from one of the nation's most liberal districts, Pelosi always runs the risk of being positioned on the political fringe.

Pelosi raised some eyebrows when she devoted a speech against war in the Persian Gulf to the environmental impact of the conflict. "While we are gravely concerned about the loss of life from combat in the Persian Gulf War, environmental consequences of the war are as important to the people there as the air they breathe and the water they drink," said Pelosi, as she circulated a letter among her colleagues asking the U.N. environmental agency to investigate the issue.

Her staunch environmentalism also was on display when she persuaded a Banking subcommittee to adopt an amendment to an international development measure. The provision sought to prevent U.S. representatives to the World Bank, International Monetary Fund and Inter-American Development Bank from approving loans for Third World development projects that had not been given a public environmental assessment from the president's Council on Environmental Quality.

Pelosi's actions reveal a tenacious junior legislator willing to tackle issues and pick fights as she sees fit. During the 101st Congress, Pelosi, whose San Francisco district includes thousands of Chinese-Americans, set her sights on China.

In 1989, Pelosi sponsored a bill to allow Chinese students caught in the United States at the time of the Chinese government's June crackdown on pro-democracy forces to seek permanent residency here without returning home first. Congress cleared the measure but President Bush vetoed the bill and the Senate sustained the veto early in 1990.

Pelosi, then on the Banking Committee, devoted serious effort in 1990 to restricting World Bank loans to China. "We are at a critical place in our relationship with China," she said.

At the start of the 102nd Congress, Pelosi was again at the forefront of those criticizing China's retention of most-favored-nation (MFN) trade status. "They're not acting in a way that I think would suggest they've been our friends," said Pelosi. "From that standpoint, they shouldn't have MFN."

Earlier in her term, Pelosi was particularly active in promoting legislation to fight AIDS, a serious problem in her district. One successful effort in 1988 involved adding a floor amendment to omnibus AIDS legislation to authorize funds for demonstration projects to provide mental-health services for victims and families who have "serious psychological reactions" af-

California 5

Most of San Francisco

San Francisco and the 5th District are liberal Democratic strongholds. The 5th has the highest percentage of registered Democrats — over 60 percent — of any district in the state without a black or Hispanic majority.

The 5th contains almost all of San Francisco. It is an ethnic, racial and sexual pastiche. A fifth of its residents are Asian, mostly Japanese and Chinese. Mexican-Americans live in the bustling Mission District. A large homosexual community is centered around Castro and Market streets.

The 5th starts at the northern end of the San Francisco peninsula, just east of the Presidio. Rising to the south is Pacific Heights, home to affluent professionals.

To the east are Nob and Russian hills, equally affluent but with pockets of students and elderly, and North Beach, which is both the city's Italian section and the spiritual home of the Beat Generation. Most of the voters have a socially conscious liberal streak that manifests itself in a solid Democratic vote.

From there, the district passes through Chinatown and the Financial District, into the workaday part of San Francisco south of Market Street. The 5th takes in the residential neighborhoods south of Market, including depressed Bayshore and Hunters Point, and the Hispanic neighborhoods of the Mission and Potrero Hill. It finishes in the middle- and working-class areas falling away from Twin Peaks and the neat, pastel-painted houses of the Sunset District.

In 1988, San Francisco County voted by a wide margin against requiring state officials to report the names of those infected with HIV, the AIDS-related virus. Voters there also gave overwhelming majorities to Democratic Senate challenger Leo T. McCarthy, and presidential candidate Michael S. Dukakis.

Population: 525,971. White 311,447 (59%), Black 56,892 (11%), Asian and Pacific Islander 113,295 (22%), Other 2,650 (1%). Spanish origin 75,368 (14%). 18 and over 434,190 (83%), 65 and over 83,827 (16%). Median age: 35.

ter a positive AIDS test is returned.

As the 101st Congress began, Pelosi was involved in a far different fight: She teamed with California Democrat Barbara Boxer to try to reverse a recommendation by a military base-closing commission that the Presidio in San Francisco be shut. The two argued that closing the base, which would then become part of the Golden Gate National Recreation area, would cost millions more per year than keeping it open. They said the commission failed to consider environmental cleanup costs and the expense of closing the base's medical center.

The commission's recommendations were to go into effect unless Congress rejected the entire plan, and the vast majority of the members did not have incentive to reopen the process. Pelosi vowed to try to block appropriators from committing funds for closing the Presidio.

In July 1989, Pelosi and Boxer secured a commitment from Pennsylvania Democrat John P. Murtha, the powerful chairman of the Defense Appropriations Subcommittee, to help them save their base. Murtha was to offer an amendment to tie base-shutdown funds to confirmation by the General Accounting Office (GAO) that the base closures it was studying would achieve promised savings.

When Murtha's provision was ruled out of order, though, Pelosi and Boxer were still ready to offer their own floor amendment that would specifically deny funds to close their base. Facing near-certain defeat, they decided against offering the amendment, saying they would wait for a final GAO report on base-closing savings due out in the fall. The California lawmakers, however, never acted and the Presidio remained slated for closure.

At Home: When she began her first House campaign, Pelosi was more familiar to national Democratic activists than to San Francisco voters. But the financial and political contacts she had developed over years of party service provided Pelosi with a critical edge in the special Democratic primary to succeed Democratic Rep. Sala Burton, who died in February 1987.

Winning that primary was tantamount to election for Pelosi. The 5th District is one of the Democrats' most loyal congressional districts.

Pelosi entered the contest backed by much of the city and state party establishment. Among those endorsing her were Sen. Alan Cranston, then-San Francisco Mayor Dianne Feinstein, and Lt. Gov. Leo T. McCarthy.

Pelosi also had powerful friends in the national Democratic hierarchy. While chairing the state party, she helped attract the 1984 Democratic National Convention to San Francisco. She lost a bid for national party chairman in 1985, but then directed money-raising efforts for the party's successful 1986 effort to retake the Senate.

The most important support for Pelosi was delivered, in dramatic fashion, just before the seat became vacant. Burton, a cancer victim, indicated several days prior to her death that she wanted Pelosi to be her successor. That backing was crucial because the 5th had long been dominated by the organization loyal to Sala Burton and her late husband, Rep. Phillip Burton.

Party backing did not clear the field for Pelosi. She faced a vigorous challenge from San Francisco Supervisor Harry Britt, the leading homosexual politician in San Francisco.

In a district where the gay vote was roughly one-fifth of the electorate, Britt started with a large base. He also aimed his campaign at a wider audience, citing his efforts on rent control and appealing to environmentalists with his opposition to new real-estate development.

But Pelosi was an energetic candidate who exhibited cool under fire. She fell short of 50 percent of the vote in the April primary contest, but took her GOP foe easily in a June runoff.

Pelosi quickly established her dominance in the district, winning a full term in 1988 with 76 percent. Further proof of her popularity was provided in 1990, when anti-incumbent sentiment was widespread: While most House members from California lost several percentage points off their normal showings, Pelosi scored a personal best with 77 percent against Republican lawyer Alan Nichols.

Committees

Appropriations (37th of 37 Democrats)
Commerce, Justice, State & Judiciary; Treasury, Postal Service & General Government

Standards of Official Conduct (6th of 7 Democrats)

Elections

1990 General		
Nancy Pelosi (D)	120,633	(77%)
Alan Nichols (R)	35,671	(23%)
1988 General		
Nancy Pelosi (D)	133,530	(76%)
Bruce M. O'Neill (R)	33,692	(19%)

Previous Winning Percentage: **1987** * (63%)

* *Special election.*

District Vote For President

	1988	1984	1980	1976
D	148,878 (71%)	142,282 (65%)	88,734 (52%)	95,035 (54%)
R	57,846 (28%)	72,437 (33%)	53,398 (32%)	74,062 (42%)

Campaign Finance

	Receipts	Receipts from PACs		Expend-itures
1990				
Pelosi (D)	$462,664	$262,900	(57%)	$440,973
Nichols (R)	$153,947	$5,190	(3%)	$154,858
1988				
Pelosi (D)	$1,865,268	$548,815	(29%)	$1,799,427
O'Neill (R)	$19,245	0		$19,245

Key Votes

1991	
Authorize use of force against Iraq	N
1990	
Support constitutional amendment on flag desecration	N
Pass family and medical leave bill over Bush veto	Y
Reduce SDI funding	Y
Allow abortions in overseas military facilities	Y
Approve budget summit plan for spending and taxing	N
Approve civil rights bill	Y
1989	
Halt production of B-2 stealth bomber at 13 planes	Y
Oppose capital gains tax cut	Y
Approve federal abortion funding in rape or incest cases	Y
Approve pay raise and revision of ethics rules	Y
Pass Democratic minimum wage plan over Bush veto	Y

Voting Studies

	Presidential Support		Party Unity		Conservative Coalition	
Year	**S**	**O**	**S**	**O**	**S**	**O**
1990	15	84	92	3	4	96
1989	26	70	93	1	0	98
1988	20	79	95	3	3	97
1987	15 †	84 †	90 †	3 †	0 †	88 †

† *Not eligible for all recorded votes.*

Interest Group Ratings

Year	ADA	ACU	AFL-CIO	CCUS
1990	100	4	92	15
1989	95	0	100	20
1988	100	0	93	21
1987	93	0	100	9

6 Barbara Boxer (D)

Of Greenbrae — Elected 1982

Born: Nov. 11, 1940, Brooklyn, N.Y.
Education: Brooklyn College, B.A. 1962.
Occupation: Congressional aide; journalist; stockbroker.
Family: Husband, Stewart Boxer; two children.
Religion: Jewish.
Political Career: Marin County Board of Supervisors, 1977-83; candidate for Marin County Board of Supervisors, 1972.
Capitol Office: 307 Cannon Bldg. 20515; 225-5161.

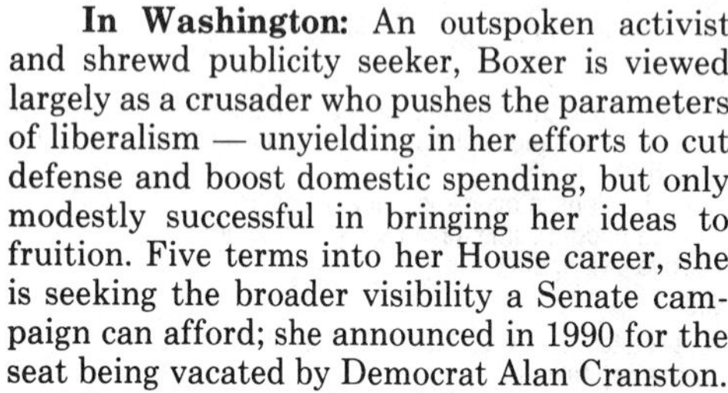

In Washington: An outspoken activist and shrewd publicity seeker, Boxer is viewed largely as a crusader who pushes the parameters of liberalism — unyielding in her efforts to cut defense and boost domestic spending, but only modestly successful in bringing her ideas to fruition. Five terms into her House career, she is seeking the broader visibility a Senate campaign can afford; she announced in 1990 for the seat being vacated by Democrat Alan Cranston.

Boxer serves on Armed Services, where her attacks on White House defense spending proposals put her in the committee's small group of hard-core liberals. In 1990, she unsuccessfully sought to cut defense by $6 billion, with the savings to be split between deficit reduction and domestic spending.

As a freshman, she was a caustic critic of Defense Department procurement policies, including overpayments for spare parts and other military equipment. In her second term, even before she won a seat on Armed Services, Boxer was appointed to an informal House task force to examine the purchasing problems. In September 1989, the House adopted an amendment by Boxer requiring the Pentagon to suspend progress payments to a contractor against whom there is "substantial evidence" of fraud.

In January 1991, Boxer opposed giving President Bush authority to use force against Iraq, quoting song lyrics by Bette Midler to make her case on the House floor. On a 390-0 vote, the House killed a Boxer resolution that would have required Bush to give the House documents concerning aspects of the war, such as forecasts of casualties and speculation on anticipated targets of terrorist attack and the long-term effects of exposure to Iraqi chemical or biological weapons.

Republicans condemned the so-called resolution of inquiry as a "fishing expedition," and even Democratic leaders worked to quash the measure, which they feared would lead to a clash with the White House in the middle of the war. Boxer was similarly rebuffed a year earlier during consideration of an intelligence authorization bill. Her effort then to require prior congressional approval of covert actions failed, 70-341.

During the Persian Gulf War, Boxer led unsuccessful efforts aimed at passing legislation to allow one spouse in a military couple or a single parent the option of obtaining a combat exemption. Boxer drew publicity when she wrote a letter reminding Defense Secretary Dick Cheney that he got a draft deferral during the Vietnam War on the grounds that he was about to become a father.

Boxer used her three terms on the Budget Committee to criticize Republican administration fiscal policies. In the 101st Congress, she headed Budget's Human Resources Task Force, which dealt with the health-care, child-care and education issues close to her heart.

It was in this social-issue arena that Boxer made her clearest legislative mark, helping orchestrate a major victory for abortion rights advocates in 1989. During consideration of an appropriations measure, the House agreed to a Boxer amendment to allow federal funding of abortions in cases involving rape and incest. Though the amendment was hailed as historic and would have reversed a decade-old federal policy, it provoked a veto that Congress could not override.

Boxer also serves on Government Operations, where in the 102nd Congress she assumed the chairmanship of the Subcommittee on Government Activities and Transportation. In her oversight capacity, she was among the harshest critics of the space station during floor debate in May 1991. Earlier, Boxer had held a hearing at which General Accounting Office (GAO) cost estimates were released that said the station would cost $40 billion to build, $10 billion more than NASA had estimated, and that the station's operating costs for its 30-year life would be close to $78 billion, $24 billion above NASA projections.

Boxer teamed with her Bay-area Democratic colleague Nancy Pelosi in the 101st Congress to try to reverse a recommendation by a

California 6

Northwest San Francisco; Marin County; Parts of Sonoma and Solano Counties

The 6th is no longer the bizarrely shaped district that earned a place in gerrymandering history in 1981. That version combined four detached pieces of territory connected only by water or a slim segment of railroad yard. But it is still an imaginative display of cartography. There are three sections of the district, two of them connected by the Golden Gate Bridge and the third by a narrow slip of land.

In land area and population, the largest of the three segments is Marin County. Marin has been stereotyped in fiction and journalism as the home of "mellow" — a uniquely California lifestyle enjoyed by the rich and characterized by a social and cultural permissiveness.

Yet Marin's staunchly liberal voting pattern is of fairly recent vintage: The county went for Gerald R. Ford in 1976 and for Ronald Reagan in 1980. But by 1984, it was one of five California counties that backed Democrat Walter F. Mondale; four years later, Democrat Michael S. Dukakis crossed the 60 percent mark.

Quality-of-life issues such as the environment are important here: In 1988, Marin voters endorsed a water safety and conservation ballot proposition, and they gave a cigarette-tax proposition its highest county vote in the state.

With about half of the district vote cast there, Marin gives Democratic candidates a big jump on capturing the 6th. But it is a slice of liberal San Francisco that cinches the district for the Democrats. The 6th includes Haight-Ashbury, made famous as a colony of hippie "flower children." Today, it is a funky mix of 1960s-retro and '80s yuppie.

The third section of the 6th consists of two areas that are geographically and psychologically distant from San Francisco — Solano County (Vallejo) and Sonoma County (Petaluma).

Vallejo is a blue-collar Democratic city that relies on a naval shipyard for its economic support. West of it are Petaluma and other fast-growing Sonoma County suburbs.

Population: 526,020. White 406,963 (77%), Black 51,007 (10%), Asian and Pacific Islander 50,800 (10%), Other 2,685 (1%). Spanish origin 28,187 (5%). 18 and over 409,204 (78%), 65 and over 59,593 (11%). Median age: 32.

military base-closing commission that the Presidio in San Francisco be closed. They stated that the commission had overlooked the high costs of making the site environmentally safe and of transferring it to the Interior Department, as required by law.

Boxer and Pelosi got Pennsylvania Democrat John P. Murtha, chairman of Appropriations' Defense Subcommittee, to agree in July 1989 to help them save their base. Murtha would offer an amendment to tie base-shutdown funds to confirmation by the GAO that the base closures would achieve promised savings.

Even after Murtha's provision was ruled out of order, the two Californians were ready to offer their own floor amendment to specifically deny funds to close their base. But seeing they would lose, they opted not to offer the amendment, deciding to wait for GAO's final report on base-closing savings due out that fall. The Presidio, however, remained slated for closure.

Reflecting consumer and congressional concern over tuna fishing practices that were killing dolphins in the eastern Pacific Ocean, Boxer sponsored legislation to require the labeling of tuna in accordance with the method used to catch it. Boxer won a partial victory in the 101st Congress, as legislation to regulate the labeling of "dolphin safe" tuna became law. The measure required that companies selling dolphin-safe tuna be able to prove that the fish was not caught with methods that killed dolphins. The bill also banned the use of large drift nets in U.S. waters and called on the administration to pursue an international agreement to end use of large drift nets on the high seas.

Though Boxer clearly has strongly held opinions, her colleagues were still startled by the stridency of her statements in support of the controversial 51 percent congressional payraise proposal in early 1989. Just before the final vote that scuttled the raise, she again excoriated critics of the proposal. But after all the strong language, Boxer surprised her colleagues once more, joining in the overwhelming House vote to kill the raise.

At Home: Boxer's 1990 House campaign was overshadowed by rumors that she was planning to run for senator in 1992. Just after breezing to re-election, Boxer confirmed the speculation, announcing that she would be a Senate candidate two years hence.

Boxer entered the House as the unintended beneficiary of one of the decade's more creative acts of district line-drawing. The 6th was the keystone of California's 1981 redistricting plan, drawn to shore up Democratic Rep. John Burton after his close 1980 re-election contest. It was a gift from his brother, Rep. Phillip Burton, who designed the California congressional map.

But three days before the filing deadline in 1982, John Burton decided to forgo another term in office. Boxer, then a Marin County supervisor who had worked for Burton in the mid-1970s, stepped up to take his place.

Her opponent in the primary was San Francisco Supervisor Louise Renne, who had the backing of her city's mayor, Dianne Feinstein. Boxer moved quickly to shore up her Democratic base in Marin, and with Burton's backing, lined up the support of San Francisco's liberal activists and the politically powerful gay community. That was enough for Boxer to edge Renne out for the nomination.

In the general election, Boxer ran against Republican Dennis McQuaid, who had made a strong showing against John Burton two years before. But Phillip Burton's lines did the trick for Boxer. She won overwhelmingly in the San Francisco portion of the 6th and ran up comfortable margins in outlying blue-collar communities, countering McQuaid's majority in Marin.

The district lines were modified slightly after the 1982 election, but with no negative impact on Boxer. In 1984 she easily defeated her Republican opponent, and by 1986 she was up to 74 percent of the vote. She nearly duplicated that showing in 1988.

As Cranston's popularity plummeted in the wake of the Keating Five scandal, Boxer dropped hints she might challenge the incumbent in the 1992 Democratic Senate primary. But on Nov. 8, 1990 — two days after Election Day — Cranston stated he would not seek a fifth term. Boxer, who had just won re-election over Republican banker Bill Boerum with 68 percent of the vote, then announced for the Senate.

Committees

Armed Services (21st of 33 Democrats)
Investigations; Military Personnel & Compensation; Research & Development

Government Operations (11th of 25 Democrats)
Government Activities & Transportation (chairman)

Select Children, Youth & Families (7th of 22 Democrats)

Elections

1990 General		
Barbara Boxer (D)	137,306	(68%)
Bill Boerum (R)	64,402	(32%)
1988 General		
Barbara Boxer (D)	176,645	(73%)
William Steinmetz (R)	64,174	(27%)

Previous Winning Percentages: **1986** (74%) **1984** (68%) **1982** (52%)

District Vote For President

	1988	1984	1980	1976
D	164,296 (64%)	141,884 (56%)	92,724 (44%)	91,399 (50%)
R	89,300 (35%)	106,610 (42%)	83,186 (39%)	85,144 (47%)

Campaign Finance

	Receipts	Receipts from PACs		Expend-itures
1990				
Boxer (D)	$921,666	$337,124	(37%)	$655,402
Boerum (R)	$32,788	$6,000	(18%)	$32,724
1988				
Boxer (D)	$450,306	$185,330	(41%)	$351,687
Steinmetz (R)	$50,955	$6,250	(12%)	$50,532

Key Votes

1991	
Authorize use of force against Iraq	N
1990	
Support constitutional amendment on flag desecration	N
Pass family and medical leave bill over Bush veto	Y
Reduce SDI funding	Y
Allow abortions in overseas military facilities	Y
Approve budget summit plan for spending and taxing	N
Approve civil rights bill	Y
1989	
Halt production of B-2 stealth bomber at 13 planes	Y
Oppose capital gains tax cut	Y
Approve federal abortion funding in rape or incest cases	Y
Approve pay raise and revision of ethics rules	Y
Pass Democratic minimum wage plan over Bush veto	Y

Voting Studies

	Presidential Support		Party Unity		Conservative Coalition	
Year	**S**	**O**	**S**	**O**	**S**	**O**
1990	14	81	86	4	11	83
1989	26	72	95	2	5	93
1988	17	69	86	5	8	87
1987	12	84	88	3	2	93
1986	13	78	84	4	12	82
1985	11	86	88	3	2	93
1984	20	68	86	3	2	92
1983	15	84	94	3	4	92

Interest Group Ratings

Year	ADA	ACU	AFL-CIO	CCUS
1990	94	4	83	8
1989	100	0	91	30
1988	80	5	93	27
1987	92	0	93	7
1986	90	5	100	13
1985	95	5	100	19
1984	95	0	92	46
1983	95	0	100	20

7 George Miller (D)

Of Martinez — Elected 1974

Born: May 17, 1945, Richmond, Calif.
Education: San Francisco State College, B.A. 1968; U. of California, Davis, J.D. 1972.
Occupation: Lawyer; legislative aide.
Family: Wife, Cynthia Caccavo; two children.
Religion: Roman Catholic.
Political Career: Democratic nominee for Calif. Senate, 1969.
Capitol Office: 2228 Rayburn Bldg. 20515; 225-2095.

In Washington: With Miller's ascension to the chairmanship of the Interior and Insular Affairs Committee, the partisan tenor on the panel is likely to change markedly. His predecessor, longtime Chairman Morris K. Udall of Arizona, was a conciliator who never sought retribution against committee members who crossed him. Miller is a gruff partisan whose stewardship should produce plenty of fireworks with the panel's aggressive Western Republicans, who have little use for Miller's environmentalist bent.

Since the 100th Congress, Miller had been regarded as heir apparent to the Interior chair once Udall retired. But Udall, who has Parkinson's disease, was injured in early 1991 when he fell in his home. In January, the Democratic Caucus elected Miller vice chairman of the panel, with all the duties of the chairman. Udall resigned May 4; Miller was elected chairman May 9.

Miller was never bashful about his imminent chairmanship (his office said he had become Udall's stand-in for much of the 101st Congress because of Udall's illness); when he was named vice chairman, he moved quickly to put his own stamp on the committee, replacing the panel's top two staff members. Miller, who is in his mid-40s, is apt to have a long time to imprint environmental legislation with his unusual combination of liberal passion and pay-as-you-go pragmatism.

He is a most unlikely Westerner to lead Interior. Representing a water-rich, suburban district, Miller, who retains his chairmanship of the Water Subcommittee, approaches water-policy debates from a perspective starkly different from that of colleagues — including Udall — from more arid Western areas. Miller acknowledges that in the area of Western water subsidies, the committee's leadership will undergo a "fundamental shift."

As a conservationist chairing what traditionally had been a pro-development subcommittee — the Water, Power and Offshore Energy Resources panel — Miller has worked to redefine the subcommittee's mission. Reflecting Miller's goals, the 100th Congress enacted legislation to supply water to 400,000 Southern Californians without building any dams and at no cost to the federal government.

Miller seeks to limit big farms' use of subsidized water. He also wants to divert water now going to farmers and use it to restore damaged breeding areas of fish and wildlife. "You have to start from the fundamental principle that these are the people's resources," he says. "This is not the farmer's water; it's the people's water."

For the most part, however, the change on Interior will be more stylistic than substantive. Like Udall, Miller is a liberal with strong environmental proclivities. But Miller's assertiveness is far more likely to rankle members of the GOP contingent, most of whom are driven by "Sagebrush Rebellion" antipathy toward federal land and water policy.

A May 1989 committee markup illustrated the partisan rift on Interior. Republicans came to the meeting with at least 10 amendments. When the first two were defeated on lopsided, mostly party-line votes, ranking Republican Don Young of Alaska hotly warned the Democrats to consider the amendments on their merits. Miller and other Democrats condemned the next amendment, and when it failed 14-24, the Republicans walked out. Noting the empty seats as he left, Montanan Ron Marlenee suggested that Democrats probably would "be more comfortable if the Sierra Club occupied our chairs on this side." "That's for damn sure," snapped Miller.

Still, opponents have noted that Miller can be a pragmatic negotiator. And Miller does not view himself as a throwback to the autocratic chairmen that his 1974 classmates ousted. "There's a difference between being a strong chairman and being a dictator, which is what we had back then," he says. "I also want to be open to new ideas and new agendas."

Miller does not always opt for confrontation. In the 100th Congress, debate over whether to limit logging in Alaska's Tongass National Forest allowed Miller to demonstrate his skill at attaining compromise. He shaved just enough off the conservationists' proposal to soften Young's criticism. This produced a lopsided House victory on the controversial legislation, but the bill died in the Senate.

California 7

Most of Contra Costa County; Richmond

Contra Costa County — about 80 percent of which is in the 7th District — is split almost evenly between the urbanized industrial areas along San Pablo Bay and the suburban tracts that have grown like crab grass farther east, behind the San Pablo mountain ridge.

In almost 50 years of unbridled expansion, the county's population has exploded from 100,000 to more than 800,000. The white-collar/blue-collar split in Contra Costa makes it one of California's more politically competitive counties.

Before Democrat Dianne Feinstein carried Contra Costa for governor in 1990, the county had sided with the GOP gubernatorial candidate in five of the previous six elections. But in 1988 Democratic presidential nominee Michael S. Dukakis carried the county with 52 percent of the vote.

The strongest Democratic area in the 7th is the industrial shoreline from Richmond to Pittsburg, a base for shipping, as well as oil and sugar refining. Oil refineries in the district provide many jobs, but not without environmental cost. Less than two years after sensitive wetlands in Martinez were soiled by a 1988 oil spill, an explosion at the Shell Oil refinery rocked the city with a blast that rattled windows seven miles away.

The Contra Costa shoreline looks more like northern New Jersey than like placid Marin County, just five miles across the bay. The blue-collar city of Richmond, 43 percent black, voted overwhelmingly for Walter F. Mondale in 1984 and Dukakis in 1988; the nearby industrial towns are nearly as strong for the Democrats.

The climate — both political and meteorological — is considerably different on the eastern side of the mountains that separate the sunny inland areas of the county from the fogbound coast. Once fertile agricultural area, the inland areas are largely occupied by housing tracts. Cities such as Concord — the 7th's largest with 111,000 residents — and Walnut Creek are home to thousands of white-collar professionals. A strong showing on this side of the mountains gave Reagan his 7th District win in 1984.

Population: 525,990. White 417,094 (79%), Black 56,929 (11%), Asian and Pacific Islander 23,204 (4%), Other 3,565 (1%). Spanish origin 51,165 (10%). 18 and over 379,409 (72%), 65 and over 49,389 (9%). Median age: 31.

When the Tongass bill came up again in the 101st Congress, Young protested Miller's substitute amendment, which changed the original bill to allow the Forest Service to take competitive bids on short contracts to log enough timber to meet market demand. The bill canceled two long-term, federally subsidized pulp-mill contracts and abolished mandatory timber-sales quotas in the Tongass. Young fought to no avail in Interior, which adopted Miller's plan by voice vote, and on the floor, where the House adopted it 356-60 and rejected a Young-backed alternative from the Agriculture Committee. But a House-Senate conference reduced the acreage protected in the bill and required the government to renegotiate (not cancel) the pulp-mill contracts. It became law in 1990.

In the 100th Congress, Udall delegated to Miller responsibility for legislation to permit oil drilling in the Arctic National Wildlife Refuge (ANWR). ANWR drilling is adamantly opposed by conservationists but supported by such powerful forces as President Bush. When the ANWR measure cleared the Merchant Marine Committee in 1988, Miller balked. He stalled on the bill, arguing the need for further study. In the wake of the 1989 *Exxon Valdez* oil spill, the bill was laid aside for the 101st Congress. Bush included ANWR drilling as part of his 1991 proposal to overhaul the energy policies.

The *Valdez* disaster cleared the way for enactment of a bill increasing the federal liability limits of oil spillers. Miller joined senior Merchant Marine Democrat Gerry E. Studds of Massachusetts, who sponsored such a bill in 1975, to push for tougher environmental amendments. The bill would compensate those harmed economically by accidents, enhance cleanup efforts and attempt to prevent spills.

Outside the Interior Committee, Miller had a high-visibility platform for advocating his social services agenda as chairman of the Select Committee on Children, Youth and Families. Miller ceded the chairmanship of the Children's panel in the 102nd Congress when he was named Interior vice chairman.

Miller can be quick to express his frustration at those who do not see the urgency of social problems the way he does. He was outraged at President Ronald Reagan's approach to domestic policy and only slightly gentler toward Democrats who showed an interest in compromising with the White House. He has been a prominent advocate for abortion rights.

In the 101st Congress, he and New York Democrat Thomas J. Downey co-authored legislation to increase federal aid for child care. Their plan competed with one approved by the

Education and Labor Committee, leading to jurisdictional battles throughout most of the Congress over how to finance it — by entitlement (as recommended by Downey and Miller) or by authorization. The final bill included some of both plans, adding a five-year, $1.5 billion entitlement program to help provide care for low-income families not quite poor enough to qualify for welfare.

During his tenure on the Budget Committee, Miller was one of the strongest union supporters in Congress. He also developed the "pay-as-you-go" budget-freeze concept. The 1990 budget agreement imposed strict pay-as-you-go limits on entitlement spending.

At Home: Not only is Miller a third-generation resident of his Northern California county — a fact that sets him apart in the state's mobile culture — he is also the third George Miller in his family to earn a living in government.

Miller's grandfather, George Sr., was the assistant civil engineer in Richmond. His father, George Jr., served 20 years from a state Senate constituency that resembled the current 7th. A football and swimming star in high school, George Miller III was a first-year law student in 1969 when his father died. Only 23, Miller won the Democratic nomination to succeed him but lost later in the year to Republican John Nejedly.

Miller went to work in the state Capitol as a legislative aide to state Sen. George Moscone, the Democratic floor leader. In 1974, when Democratic Rep. Jerome Waldie decided to run for governor, Miller sought Waldie's seat in Congress, challenging a local labor leader and the mayor of Concord, the largest city in the district.

Miller had the family name identification, plus the strong support of Assemblyman John T. Knox, who put his organization to work for him in Richmond, the district's second-largest city. He won the primary with 38 percent.

In the general election, against moderate Republican Gary Fernandez, Miller exploited Watergate, disclosing his campaign finances twice a month and chiding his opponent for not doing likewise. Miller won 56 percent of the vote. He has not drawn a threatening GOP opponent since and regularly wins two-thirds or more of the vote.

Committees

Interior & Insular Affairs (Chairman)
Water, Power & Offshore Energy (chairman); Insular & International Affairs

Select Children, Youth & Families (2nd of 22 Democrats)

Education & Labor (4th of 25 Democrats)
Elementary, Secondary & Vocational Education; Labor-Management Relations; Postsecondary Education

Elections

1990 General		
George Miller (D)	121,080	(61%)
Roger A. Payton (R)	79,031	(39%)
1988 General		
George Miller (D)	170,006	(68%)
Jean Last (R)	78,478	(32%)

Previous Winning Percentages: **1986** (67%) **1984** (66%) **1982** (67%) **1980** (63%) **1978** (63%) **1976** (75%) **1974** (56%)

District Vote For President

	1988	1984	1980	1976
D	136,163 (53%)	114,148 (47%)	84,310 (41%)	91,581 (54%)
R	116,314 (46%)	126,001 (52%)	96,340 (47%)	77,295 (45%)

Campaign Finance

	Receipts	Receipts from PACs	Expend-itures
1990			
Miller (D)	$469,400	$262,657 (56%)	$448,026
Payton (R)	$47,918	$1,150 (2%)	$47,912
1988			
Miller (D)	$429,305	$179,984 (42%)	$269,887
Last (R)	$14,818	0	$15,311

Key Votes

1991	
Authorize use of force against Iraq	N
1990	
Support constitutional amendment on flag desecration	N
Pass family and medical leave bill over Bush veto	Y
Reduce SDI funding	Y
Allow abortions in overseas military facilities	Y
Approve budget summit plan for spending and taxing	N
Approve civil rights bill	Y
1989	
Halt production of B-2 stealth bomber at 13 planes	Y
Oppose capital gains tax cut	Y
Approve federal abortion funding in rape or incest cases	Y
Approve pay raise and revision of ethics rules	Y
Pass Democratic minimum wage plan over Bush veto	Y

Voting Studies

	Presidential Support		Party Unity		Conservative Coalition	
Year	**S**	**O**	**S**	**O**	**S**	**O**
1990	16	81	89	6	6	93
1989	22	76	89	4	5	95
1988	18	69	85	6	5	82
1987	15	81	88	5	5	95
1986	14	80	84	4	8	80
1985	16	76	84	5	9	84
1984	22	69	85	6	7	86
1983	11	78	83	8	13	75
1982	26	71	92	4	7	90
1981	28	70	89	8	0	93

Interest Group Ratings

Year	ADA	ACU	AFL-CIO	CCUS
1990	100	4	83	21
1989	100	0	91	20
1988	95	4	93	31
1987	96	13	88	20
1986	90	6	91	15
1985	95	10	80	19
1984	100	4	85	31
1983	90	4	94	16
1982	95	0	95	20
1981	100	0	87	11

8 Ronald V. Dellums (D)

Of Oakland — Elected 1970

Born: Nov. 24, 1935, Oakland, Calif.
Education: San Francisco State College, B.A. 1960; U. of California, Berkeley, M.S.W. 1962.
Military Service: Marine Corps, 1954-56.
Occupation: Psychiatric social worker.
Family: Wife, Leola ' ' Roscoe ' ' Higgs; three children.
Religion: Protestant.
Political Career: Berkeley City Council, 1967-71.
Capitol Office: 2136 Rayburn Bldg. 20515; 225-2661.

In Washington: Dellums is a liberal activist to his core. The core still burns hot, two decades after his opposition to the Vietnam War carried him to Congress.

Dellums was a pre-eminent opponent of President Bush's 1990-91 Persian Gulf policy: He argued in favor of continued economic sanctions rather than military action to end Iraq's occupation of Kuwait, went to court in an attempt to require Bush to obtain congressional authorization before using force, and organized like-minded members to lobby Bush to stop the fighting once it started.

These actions fit well within Dellums' career pattern. Since his arrival in 1971, he has expressed the outrage of the left on the House floor, combining eloquent visions of world peace and angry charges of racism.

Dellums has consistently opposed U.S. military interventions and covert actions to aid insurgents fighting to overthrow leftist regimes. He staged a long and ultimately successful fight to impose sanctions on South Africa to protest its policy of apartheid. Long before the fall of the Berlin Wall forced even conservatives to think about defense spending cutbacks, Dellums wanted to divert much of the Pentagon's budget into domestic social welfare spending.

There is no artifice in Dellums' passion. Few who have watched him were surprised at reading in *The Washington Post* that when he first heard news reports of the U.S. bombing of Iraq in January 1991, Dellums sat on his bed and cried.

Yet Dellums has grown well beyond the image of radicalism that accompanied him when he arrived in Washington from the protest hotbeds of Oakland and Berkeley. Dellums has achieved enough House seniority and institutional power to join the establishment he came to challenge. While the system has not coopted Dellums, he has shown that he can work well within it.

Dellums' level-headed style as a legislator is evident in his role as a subcommittee chairman on the Armed Services Committee. In 1983, he took the helm of the subcommittee overseeing U.S. base construction. The low-profile assignment was a proving ground; Dellums showed he was not an obstructionist and would give fair treatment to Republicans and Democrats with whom he disagreed.

These traits muted opposition at the start of the 101st Congress, when Dellums became chairman of the Armed Services Research and Development Subcommittee, which has partial jurisdiction over weapons programs — such as the strategic defense initiative (SDI) and the B-2 "Stealth" bomber — he opposes.

Dellums tempers his ideological approach with a courtly manner and a dapper style. Dellums has in fact long tried to bury the "personally painful" perception that he is a '60s-style bomb-thrower. "I deliberately walked into the House well-groomed," he once said. "If they can relate to me and my clothes, they can relate to my ideas."

Dellums was elegance personified in October 1990, when he took to the House floor during an unusual Saturday session to call for a vote on a much-debated (and ultimately unsuccessful) effort to override Bush's veto of a budget resolution. Dressed in a tuxedo, Dellums was on his way to his son's wedding. "We know how we are going to vote," Dellums said. "Let us override this veto and let me love my son." His colleagues responded with a rousing round of applause.

This personal grace has enabled Dellums — long a pariah to House conservatives — to form ad hoc coalitions with a group of mainly younger Republican members who oppose some big-ticket defense items on the basis of cost. During the 101st Congress, Republican Rep. John R. Kasich, a leader of the "cheap hawks" faction, joined with Dellums in a crusade to kill the B-2 bomber project.

The two took sharply different approaches. To Dellums, the B-2's abilities to evade enemy radar, deliver nuclear weapons and return home safely apply to a military doctrine that nuclear war can be "winnable;" Dellums views such thinking as both impractical and immoral. Kasich focused on the extraordinary projected

California 8

Northern Alameda County — Oakland; Berkeley

The Black Panther Party, the "free-speech movement" and the Symbionese Liberation Army all were born within this district, a mixture of poverty and intellectual ferment. The East Bay cities of Oakland and Berkeley cast about 60 percent of the vote and form the economic, philosophical and political base.

The leftward-leaning constituency in these cities is fodder for Democratic candidates. Large margins there enabled Michael S. Dukakis to carry the 8th with 70 percent of the vote in 1988; Walter F. Mondale did even slightly better four years earlier.

However, even these liberal candidates were well to the right of many of Berkeley's political activists. Since 1977, the city of 103,000 has had self-described socialists as mayors, and their coalition, Berkeley Citizens' Action, has dominated the City Council since 1984.

The University of California's main campus at Berkeley is not the political hotbed it was in the 1960s, when it was a center for anti-war activism and student unrest. But occasionally, the university community appears frozen in time. In 1969, there were bloody confrontations between radical activists and police at "People's Park," a vacant lot on which the university had planned construction.

In May 1989, radicals and activists for the homeless, many of whom were living in the park, held a rally to mark the 20th anniversary and to protest another college building plan; it ended with a siege of vandalism and looting.

To the south is Oakland; with 372,000 residents, it is California's sixth-largest city. The city, which is about 44 percent black, is also one of the state's poorest. The 8th takes in most of Oakland, including some of its lowest-income black and Hispanic sections, near the Oakland/Alameda County Coliseum and the Oakland International Airport.

There is a marked contrast between Dellums' constituency in these cities and the mostly white, affluent voters in the Contra Costa County section of the 8th. Dellums' 1990 Republican opponent, Barbara Galewski, carried the Contra Costa County section by almost 20,000 votes in 1990. But Dellums took Alameda County by almost 65,000 votes, winning overall with 61 percent.

Population: 525,646. White 317,735 (60%), Black 139,730 (27%), Asian and Pacific Islander 43,148 (8%), Other 2,466 (1%). Spanish origin 34,394 (7%). 18 and over 409,168 (78%), 65 and over 63,941 (12%). Median age: 32.

cost of the B-2. He argued that the U.S. arsenal already contained much less expensive alternatives, such as the air-launched cruise missile, to accomplish the same objective.

Although they fell way short of a B-2 cutoff in 1989, the opponents gained ground the next year, as the imperative of cutting the overall defense budget grew stronger. Dellums ceaselessly lobbied his "arms control" allies for support; his victory in the House was assured when Armed Services Committee Chairman Les Aspin signed on. The amendment to end B-2 production after completion of the already authorized 15 planes passed Armed Services by a 34-20 vote in August 1990, and sailed through the House as part of the fiscal 1991 defense authorization bill.

Still, the anti-"Stealth" bomber coalition faced a formidable hurdle: Democrat Sam Nunn of Georgia, who as Senate Armed Services chairman is the guiding force on Senate defense policy, favored the B-2 and pushed through Bush's full request of $2.75 billion for production of the planes. In a conference in which Dellums was a major participant, a $2.35 billion figure was agreed to, accompanied by ambiguous language that left the future of the project to interpretation.

"As far as we're concerned, the B-2 is dead," said Dellums, who argued that the bill implicitly barred spending on anything but the 15 authorized planes. "The B-2 program is alive and well," said Nunn, who insisted that there was no language barring new production.

His alliance with Kasich aside, there are still Republican conservatives who bristle at the mention of Dellums' name. When House Speaker Thomas S. Foley picked Dellums in February 1991 for the House Intelligence Committee, conservative hardliners were angered; some implied that Dellums, a frequent critic of U.S. intelligence agencies, could not be trusted to keep classified information secret.

Dellums angrily rejected such assertions, pointing to his access to classified documents as a member of Armed Services. Dellums also found a defender in Minority Whip Newt Gingrich. Although the conservative GOP leader criticized the appointment on grounds that Dellums opposes most covert actions, he described his frequent adversary as an "honorable" member "who has kept secrets for years."

Dellums' appointment to Intelligence came as he was leading the faction opposing the U.S.-led war against Iraq. When Iraqi President Saddam Hussein, on the eve of the decisive ground offensive in late February 1991, suggested a conditional withdrawal of his troops from Kuwait, Dellums called for a temporary halt in U.S. bombing.

As early as October 1990, Dellums had lined up 83 House colleagues to sign a statement to Bush opposing offensive military action against Iraq. That December, he and 52 other members of Congress filed suit in federal court, arguing that Bush needed the permission of Congress to use force. Although District Judge Harold H. Greene ruled that he could not render a decision in a case brought by only 10 percent of the members, he affirmed that Congress had the constitutional responsibility to authorize war, a statement Dellums took as a victory.

In January, Dellums made a typically impassioned statement against a resolution authorizing Bush to use military force. The resolution passed and Bush used the authority days later to launch the air war. While nearly all House members — including many who had opposed the "war resolution" — rushed to back a resolution supporting Bush and the U.S. troops, Dellums voted "present."

This instance was far from the first time that Dellums had taken a stand that was more symbolic than successful. During the administrations of Ronald Reagan, Dellums sought a congressional inquiry into the 1983 U.S. invasion of Grenada, and filed a lawsuit to determine whether U.S. support for the Nicaraguan contras violated the Neutrality Act. His amendments to slash spending for SDI have consistently been drubbed, as have the alternative budget proposals, complete with deep defense spending cuts, that Dellums has supported as a leader of the Congressional Black Caucus (which he chaired during the 101st Congress).

However, Dellums has a landmark legislative achievement to his credit: In 1986, 15 years after he first proposed sanctions against South Africa, the House finally embraced his call for a trade cutoff and disinvestment by U.S. firms in that country. Dellums said it was an "exonerating" experience, adding, "It's been a long journey to this moment." His proposal formed the basis for a House-Senate compromise bill that was enacted over Reagan's veto.

In 1979, well before he received an Armed Services subcommittee gavel, Dellums had taken a leadership role as chairman of the House District of Columbia Committee. Still in that position, Dellums acts as an advocate for the District, which has no voting congressional representation and a resident population that is mainly black.

In 1990, two political events occurred that may ease Dellums' efforts to benefit the nation's capital. Sharon Pratt Dixon, who has ties to the national Democratic Party and to business, succeeded the controversial Marion Barry as mayor. Also, Republican Rep. Stan Parris of Virginia, the ranking Republican on Dellums' committee and a constant critic of the D.C. government, was defeated for re-election.

At Home: The politically divided 8th District has something of a love-hate relationship with Dellums. He is a hero in the dominant Alameda County part of his district, which includes the mainly black precincts of Oakland and the liberal university community in Berkeley. However, he usually loses in the Contra Costa County part of the 8th, which is more suburban, affluent and conservative.

In 1990, Dellums defeated Republican Barbara Galewski, a former professor, with 61 percent of the overall vote. He took 74 percent in Alameda County, but just 34 percent in Contra Costa.

Dellums wanted to be a professional baseball pitcher when he grew up, but he has said that encounters with racial prejudice spoiled that dream, leaving him with little ambition after high school. Following two years in the Marines, he went to college with the help of the GI Bill and six years later took a degrée in psychiatric social work.

He was a social worker in San Francisco, managing federally assisted poverty programs, when friends persuaded him to pursue his ideas about poverty and discrimination by running for the Berkeley City Council in 1967. He has since won every time he has run for office. In 1970, when Dellums launched a primary challenge to six-term Democratic Rep. Jeffery Cohelan, the East Bay region was in a state of turmoil. Student protest over the war in Vietnam was becoming increasingly intense and the Black Panther movement was gaining strength in Oakland's ghettos. Although his credentials as a liberal were solid, Cohelan was considered "old-fashioned" in his approach to politics. Dellums, by contrast, was usually described in the press as "angry and articulate" or "radical and militant."

Dellums put together a coalition of blacks, students and left-leaning intellectuals that has been the core of his support ever since. His major issue was Cohelan's tardiness in opposing the Vietnam War. Dellums registered nearly 15,000 new voters in the district and easily ousted Cohelan with 55 percent.

Attacks by Republican Vice President Spiro T. Agnew only brought out more support for Dellums among the district's Democrats. He easily defeated a 25-year-old political neophyte in the general election.

That victory ushered in a decade of political quiet in the district, in which Dellums rarely encountered more than minor opposition in either party. After a little-noticed Republican opponent held Dellums to 56 percent in 1980, however, the GOP put more effort into its attacks on him.

In 1982, Claude B. Hutchison Jr., a former bank president and the son of an ex-Berkeley mayor, launched a well-funded effort using campaign contributions from former business associates to help finance his campaign. The Republican pulled in more than $250,000 from donors eager to see Dellums retired.

With support among Republicans virtually guaranteed, Hutchison tried to win over moderate Democrats. He minimized his GOP ties and took positions similar to Dellums' in favor of funding for public education and against tuition tax credits for private schools.

Dellums fought back. Attacking "the madness of Reagan and Reaganomics," he drew on an impressive array of support from the national left to swamp Hutchison in raising funds. In the end, the results were like those of previous years. While Hutchison easily won the Contra Costa County portion of the 8th, Dellums more than made up the deficit in Oakland and Berkeley, winning with 56 percent.

In 1984, Eldridge Cleaver, the former Black Panther leader turned political conservative, announced that he would challenge Dellums as an independent. Republicans put up a black banker, Charles Connor, hoping that Cleaver, despite his ideological metamorphosis, would take enough votes from Dellums to elect Connor. But Cleaver dropped out of the contest at the end of the summer. Left on his own, Connor suffered from having to run in one of the few districts in the country where Reagan's coattails would be a liability. Dellums won 60 percent, a tally he matched two years later when his GOP foe was Piedmont City Councilman Steve Eigenberg. In 1988, Dellums won 67 percent.

Committees

District of Columbia (Chairman)
Fiscal Affairs & Health; Judiciary & Education

Armed Services (4th of 33 Democrats)
Research & Development (chairman)

Select Intelligence (9th of 12 Democrats)
Program & Budget Authorization

Elections

1990 General		
Ronald V. Dellums (D)	119,645	(61%)
Barbara Galewski (R)	75,544	(39%)
1988 General		
Ronald V. Dellums (D)	163,221	(67%)
John J. Cuddihy Jr. (R)	76,531	(31%)

Previous Winning Percentages: **1986** (60%) **1984** (60%) **1982** (56%) **1980** (56%) **1978** (57%) **1976** (62%) **1974** (57%) **1972** (56%) **1970** (57%)

District Vote For President

	1988	1984	1980	1976
D	178,864 (70%)	173,055 (65%)	113,944 (51%)	118,408 (59%)
R	74,437 (29%)	88,833 (34%)	73,632 (33%)	78,374 (39%)

Campaign Finance

	Receipts	Receipts from PACs		Expend-itures
1990				
Dellums (D)	$790,386	$71,935	(9%)	$840,029
1988				
Dellums (D)	$1,153,750	$87,299	(8%)	$1,174,676
Cuddihy (R)	$6,958	$200	(3%)	$7,071

Key Votes

1991	
Authorize use of force against Iraq	N
1990	
Support constitutional amendment on flag desecration	N
Pass family and medical leave bill over Bush veto	Y
Reduce SDI funding	Y
Allow abortions in overseas military facilities	Y
Approve budget summit plan for spending and taxing	N
Approve civil rights bill	Y
1989	
Halt production of B-2 stealth bomber at 13 planes	Y
Oppose capital gains tax cut	Y
Approve federal abortion funding in rape or incest cases	Y
Approve pay raise and revision of ethics rules	Y
Pass Democratic minimum wage plan over Bush veto	Y

Voting Studies

	Presidential Support		Party Unity		Conservative Coalition	
Year	S	O	S	O	S	O
1990	15	85	87	5	4	96
1989	23	76	93	2	0	100
1988	19	78	88	4	0	95
1987	10	86	91	2	5	95
1986	12	86	89	4	2	92
1985	16	83	91	3	5	91
1984	21	78	89	6	0	100
1983	7	83	82	7	2	91
1982	17	81	90	5	4	96
1981	21	66	83	6	8	87

Interest Group Ratings

Year	ADA	ACU	AFL-CIO	CCUS
1990	100	4	100	29
1989	100	0	100	20
1988	100	0	100	23
1987	100	0	100	0
1986	100	0	86	12
1985	95	5	100	19
1984	100	4	85	31
1983	95	5	94	22
1982	85	14	95	18
1981	95	7	80	0

9 Pete Stark (D)

Of Oakland — Elected 1972

Born: Nov. 11, 1931, Milwaukee, Wis.
Education: Massachusetts Institute of Technology, B.S. 1953; U. of California, Berkeley, M.B.A. 1960.
Military Service: Air Force, 1955-57.
Occupation: Banker.
Family: Wife, Carolyn Wente; four children.
Religion: Unitarian.
Political Career: Sought Democratic nomination for Calif. Senate, 1969.
Capitol Office: 239 Cannon Bldg. 20515; 225-5065.

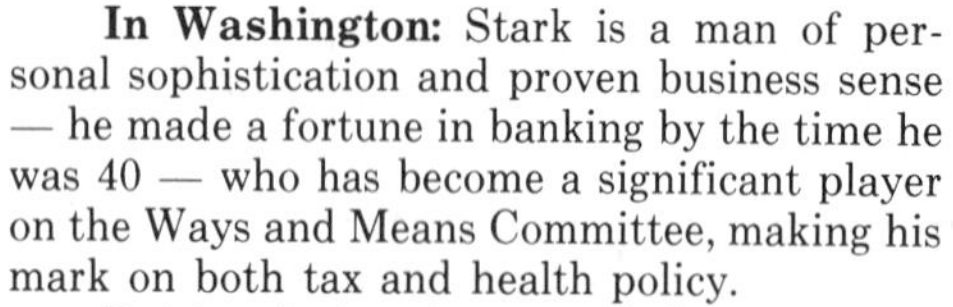

In Washington: Stark is a man of personal sophistication and proven business sense — he made a fortune in banking by the time he was 40 — who has become a significant player on the Ways and Means Committee, making his mark on both tax and health policy.

But in playing the part of the confrontational, outraged liberal, Stark seems prone to utter pronouncements that can sound supercilious and shocking. One such time came in 1990 when he attacked Louis W. Sullivan, the black secretary of Health and Human Services; another was in early 1991 when he singled out for criticism his "Jewish colleagues" who backed the use of force in the Persian Gulf.

At an August 1990 news conference, Stark erupted when a reporter's question mentioned Sullivan. "Lou Sullivan comes about as close to being a disgrace to his profession and his race as anyone I've ever seen."

Sullivan demanded an apology. "I don't live on Pete Stark's plantation," he said in a statement. "It's too bad ultraliberals like Pete Stark haven't progressed to the point that they can accept the independent thinking of a black man that does not conform to their own stereotyped views."

At first, Stark was unrepentant. "He's right, he doesn't live on my plantation," Stark said. "He lives on John Sununu's," referring to the White House chief of staff. But after House Republicans, including Bill Gradison of Ohio, who is ranking member on Stark's Health Subcommittee, rose to Sullivan's defense and denounced Stark for his remarks, Stark apologized — sort of.

"To the secretary, I have to say I blew it," Stark told the House. "I should not have brought into the discussion his race, because it obscures the fact that he is carrying a bankrupt policy for an administration which has been impacting the poor and the minorities of this country.... And to be led by the likes of John Sununu and [budget director] Mr. [Richard G.] Darman down the paths of darkness is wrong, and I apologize for obscuring that." Republicans hooted Stark; Democrats cheered. A few days later, though, Stark sent Sullivan a formal letter of apology.

Stark's remark was merely the most inflammatory of his many broadsides at the administration's health policies and at Sullivan, whom Democrats criticized for switching his abortion position and for failing to back up his anti-smoking rhetoric with support for anti-tobacco bills.

In January 1991, *The Alameda Journal*, a small semiweekly newspaper, reported that Stark told a town meeting that his "Jewish colleagues" agonized more than he had over supporting the resolution backing the use of force in the gulf. The newspaper said Stark criticized Democrats Stephen J. Solarz of New York, cosponsor of the resolution, and Tom Lantos of California, calling them "hostile, militant guys." He said Solarz was now known as "Field Marshal Solarz."

Reacting to the account, Solarz said: "One would have thought that we have gotten beyond the point of labeling people in terms of race, religion or ethnic background." A March editorial in *The New Republic* called Stark a "liberal bigot."

Stark said the newspaper took his remarks at the town meeting out of context. He wrote to the regional Anti-Defamation League of B'nai B'rith, explaining that he had observed that no group in Congress "seemed more torn than members who have led in supporting Israel." He added: "If I have in any way offended anyone by trying to describe this 'political science' lesson, I apologize."

While Stark's remarks may affect his relationships with some members, he remains an effective chairman of the Health Subcommittee, where he has shown an impressive aptitude for translating liberal goals into pragmatic legislative proposals.

Admitting that a comprehensive, British-style national health insurance system is not in the cards for the United States, Stark has won enactment of incremental measures to improve health services and insurance for those lacking coverage.

California 9

Suburban Alameda County — Hayward

The 9th is Democratic, but not nearly as liberal as the Democrat it sends to the House. A fast-growing suburban constituency helped Ronald Reagan carry the district in 1980 and 1984. But Michael S. Dukakis returned the 9th to the Democrats in 1988 by a comfortable margin.

Like most of the East Bay districts, the 9th has two separate sections. Working-class Democratic areas lie along the bay; a high-tech, suburban growth area is firmly established on the other side of the hills that form the eastern wall of the San Francisco basin.

The more densely populated bay-side area is dominated by warehouses and older factories that make motor-vehicle parts and office machines. This area includes San Leandro, an old Portuguese enclave that still has a strong blue-collar vote. Reagan's appeal to working-class ethnics enabled him to carry the city, though by just 100 votes in 1984. Dukakis easily prevailed there four years later.

To the north of San Leandro is Oakland. Although the bulk of the city is in the 8th District, Stark still represents about 70,000 residents of the city, most of them either black or Hispanic. Some parts of the city that have been hard-hit by drug-related crime are in the 9th.

Farther south, the district takes in all of Hayward, the district's largest city, with more than 111,000 residents. In the 1970s, Stark represented less than 10 percent of the city, but now he has the entire student population around Hayward's California State University, which works to the advantage of Stark and other Democrats.

The area of greatest concern to Democrats in the 9th is on the eastern side of the San Leandro Hills, where high-tech research industries centered around Livermore and Pleasanton have drawn thousands of affluent suburbanites. In the last 10 years, Livermore grew by 17 percent, while Pleasanton increased its population by 44 percent. Stark has overcome some early difficulties here — in 1980, both communities supported his opponent. But at the presidential level, Livermore and Pleasanton still go Republican.

Population: 526,234. White 393,257 (75%), Black 60,908 (12%), Asian and Pacific Islander 34,197 (6%), Other 3,845 (1%). Spanish origin 70,996 (14%). 18 and over 388,528 (74%), 65 and over 52,631 (10%). Median age: 31.

The 101st Congress, however, dealt Stark a supreme disappointment: It repealed virtually all of a landmark expansion of the Medicare program that had been enacted less than 17 months earlier. Stark and Gradison had co-authored the catastrophic coverage bill, which aimed to limit the amount for which beneficiaries could be held liable for Medicare-covered hospital and physician bills.

In winning passage in the 100th Congress, Stark and Gradison fended off attempts to derail it by a senior citizens' lobbying group and by prescription-drug manufacturers. The White House balked for a while, but President Reagan signed the bill, saying that the measure would "remove a terrible threat" from seniors' lives.

Many Medicare beneficiaries, however, did not believe they were at risk. Senior citizens' lobbying groups angrily protested that seniors were being forced to pay the entire costs of the new benefits. The complaints drowned out the explanations of those who put the program together, and by the end of 1989, catastrophic coverage was repealed.

Stark teamed with Gradison and California Democrat Henry A. Waxman, chairman of Energy and Commerce's Health Subcommittee, to make a last-ditch try to salvage a handful of the law's provisions. But Stark's amendment was rejected 156-269. "We are being stampeded by . . . a small group of the wealthiest seniors to deny needed benefits to a majority of seniors," Stark said, echoing comments of other erstwhile champions of catastrophic.

Unable to prevail, Stark found himself opposing his co-author, Gradison, in advocating repeal rather than accepting an alternative by Arizona GOP Sen. John McCain. The repeal measure, while scrapping virtually the entire law, left intact the 1988 law's expansions of Medicaid coverage for low-income elderly people and for pregnant women and infants.

Despite the catastrophic repeal, Stark still could point to some legislative successes in the 101st Congress. Over the strong objections of the American Medical Association, Congress overhauled the way Medicare paid doctors. The Health Subcommittee approved on an 11-3 vote Stark's package creating a national fee schedule for physician services. It takes into account the time, training and skill required to perform a given service. A controversial portion of the bill set targets for overall Medicare spending on doctor bills each year; breaching the targets in one year would result in smaller inflation increases in the following year. After a grueling House-Senate conference, the bill, with its spending targets on doctor bills, was attached to the fiscal 1990 budget reconciliation bill.

The physician payment reform battle produced another installment in one of Capitol Hill's more entertaining sideshows: the ongoing feud between Stark and the AMA. It is one in which Stark has usually maintained the upper hand. He rarely misses an opportunity to tweak the AMA, regularly referring to its members as "troglodytes."

At the beginning of the 100th Congress, Stark easily beat back a last-minute effort by senior Ways and Means member Charles B. Rangel to regain the Health Subcommittee, which Rangel once held. The AMA, which has devoted large sums of money to defeating Stark in the past, had wanted J. J. Pickle of Texas to challenge Stark, but he backed off after Stark quickly pocketed the commitments he needed to keep the seat.

On the physician payment bill, the AMA considered the targets on doctor bills anathema. When an AMA representative testified that limiting benefits through targets could result in "medically unacceptable results," Stark launched into a tirade. "That's always been the AMA's position: 'If we don't get what we want, we won't treat people.' I haven't heard one word about the doctors' being willing to take a little less." He warned that the AMA would be left out of the negotiating process if it did not moderate its position. "Does the AMA want to participate [in negotiations], or does it want to toddle off in its usual 19th-century mindset and have no part?" Stark asked.

From his subcommittee post, Stark is well positioned to reshape a variety of programs in the massive reconciliation bills, omnibus measures that make spending cuts dictated by the budget. When the budget calls for substantial reductions in Medicare, Stark is a major force in structuring the cuts and can quietly slip in changes in health policy.

Stark used the fiscal 1991 reconciliation bill to tighten significantly federal regulation of so-called Medigap insurance — private insurance plans sold to supplement Medicare coverage. Stark was one of the authors of the bill, which put teeth into a 1980 law to clamp down on reported abuse in the sales and marketing of Medigap policies.

In 1986, when LTV Corp. faced bankruptcy and members wanted laid-off workers to get their health benefits, they persuaded Stark to include language in a reconciliation bill requiring the company to pay the benefits.

But Stark and other liberal House Democrats, notably Waxman, found themselves outgunned on the reconciliation measure passed in late 1987. As part of the budget-summit agreement, Congress cut $2 billion from Medicare in fiscal 1988 and $3.5 billion in 1989. A united Senate and White House overpowered House negotiators to cut nearly half a billion dollars more than was mandated by the budget summit. House Democrats were furious at the Senate, and particularly Democrats on the Senate Finance Committee. "The Senate sold out to the White House," Stark fumed.

Stark spent part of the 101st Congress as one of four vice chairmen of the bipartisan Pepper Commission, which was charged with recommending improvements in the nation's health-care system. But the 15-member panel was cleaved by partisan and philosophical divisions, and it rendered split recommendations. The commission recommended creation of two programs at an annual cost of $66.2 billion to the federal government, but was vague on how to finance them. "I don't think we've done our job," Stark said. "We didn't figure out how to pay for it. There is no tax fairy out there who's going to pull it out from under a pillow."

Stark's experience with one of the most complex areas of tax law — dealing with insurance companies — assured him an influential role as Ways and Means sat down to overhaul the tax code in the 99th Congress. Stark earned Chairman Dan Rostenkowski's gratitude for his work on insurance issues and was a staunch enough loyalist that he was included in the circle of committee members handpicked to be conferees on the tax-overhaul bill.

When the 101st Congress assembled a package of tax changes, Stark added a provision broadening existing taxes on chemicals believed to damage the Earth's ozone layer to include additional compounds, including chlorofluorocarbons.

Some House members may still remember Stark for his quixotic 1975 effort to join the Black Caucus. Stark argued that although he was white, his constituency and personal sympathies made him eligible. The caucus said it had to "respectfully decline" the request.

Others may recall Stark's participation in an early movement to draft Sen. Edward M. Kennedy to run against President Jimmy Carter in 1980. Stark was one of a group of four House Democrats — led by Richard Nolan of Minnesota and including Edward P. Beard of Rhode Island and Richard L. Ottinger of New York — to press publicly in 1979 for Kennedy's candidacy. Stark was also a leader in the "open convention" drive against Carter after the primaries.

At Home: When Stark put an eight-foot-high neon peace symbol atop his bank in conservative Walnut Creek, people knew he was no ordinary banker. Ordinary California bankers did not protest the war in Vietnam or join the consumer movement. But Stark, who left Wisconsin to go to business school in California, relished his role as a maverick banker. And having founded his second bank at age 31, he had the money to play it.

Stark made his first political move in 1969, running for the state Senate. He finished third, losing the nomination to George Miller, now his colleague in the 7th District.

Three years later, Stark decided to take on another George Miller — the crusty old conservative Democrat who had represented Oakland in Congress for 28 years. Stark spent his money generously and used one of the state's top political consultants to convince the voters that they did not "have to settle for the 81-year-old Congressman George P. Miller anymore," as a campaign brochure put it. Miller's support for the Vietnam War was a major issue. Stark swept him aside easily, winning by 11,000 votes.

Only once since then has Stark had a close call. Lulled by years of easy re-election, he prepared for only a token effort in 1980. But conservative Republican William J. Kennedy, a tireless campaigner, galvanized a host of volunteers to back his challenge. Helped by Ronald Reagan's surprisingly strong showing in the district, Kennedy held Stark to 55 percent.

Kennedy never stopped running after that. He kept his campaign office open, and used his credentials from the 1980 contest to persuade donors and national GOP officials to support him more extensively in 1982. But Stark was ready for the rematch. He kept a high profile in the district, holding frequent meetings with constituents, and took advantage of the area's rising unemployment in that year of recession to woo back Democrats who had turned out for Reagan two years earlier.

After it was discovered that Kennedy had misrepresented his political background — telling audiences he had voted for a 1978 tax-cutting measure when he had not even been registered to vote — Stark's victory was sealed. He took 61 percent.

The flap over his rash criticism of Sullivan may have cost Stark some votes in 1990. He easily defeated GOP real estate agent Victor Romero, but his 58 percent of the vote was 15 points less than his 1988 tally.

Committees

District of Columbia (2nd of 8 Democrats)
Fiscal Affairs & Health (chairman); Government Operations & Metropolitan Affairs; Judiciary & Education

Select Narcotics Abuse & Control (3rd of 21 Democrats)

Ways & Means (5th of 23 Democrats)
Health (chairman); Select Revenue Measures

Joint Economic

Elections

1990 General		
Pete Stark (D)	94,739	(58%)
Victor Romero (R)	67,412	(42%)
1988 General		
Pete Stark (D)	152,866	(73%)
Howard Hertz (R)	56,656	(27%)

Previous Winning Percentages: **1986** (70%) **1984** (70%) **1982** (61%) **1980** (55%) **1978** (65%) **1976** (71%) **1974** (71%) **1972** (53%)

District Vote For President

	1988	1984	1980	1976
D	124,278 (57%)	106,640 (49%)	75,624 (42%)	98,624 (55%)
R	91,519 (42%)	107,925 (50%)	82,449 (46%)	77,320 (44%)

Campaign Finance

	Receipts	Receipts from PACs	Expend-itures
1990			
Stark (D)	$525,271	$270,170 (51%)	$300,996
Romero (R)	$206,798	$1,000 (0%)	$210,089
1988			
Stark (D)	$504,708	$325,428 (64%)	$410,540

Key Votes

1991	
Authorize use of force against Iraq	N
1990	
Support constitutional amendment on flag desecration	N
Pass family and medical leave bill over Bush veto	Y
Reduce SDI funding	Y
Allow abortions in overseas military facilities	Y
Approve budget summit plan for spending and taxing	N
Approve civil rights bill	Y
1989	
Halt production of B-2 stealth bomber at 13 planes	Y
Oppose capital gains tax cut	Y
Approve federal abortion funding in rape or incest cases	Y
Approve pay raise and revision of ethics rules	Y
Pass Democratic minimum wage plan over Bush veto	Y

Voting Studies

	Presidential Support		Party Unity		Conservative Coalition	
Year	S	O	S	O	S	O
1990	16	82	88	5	6	89
1989	24	73	90	3	2	93
1988	15	67	78	5	5	68
1987	12	81	86	4	2	88
1986	18	77	86	4	4	92
1985	18	73	89	3	2	91
1984	25	56	78	4	3	83
1983	21	72	83	7	12	83
1982	23	64	85	4	5	88
1981	29	64	84	8	11	83

Interest Group Ratings

Year	ADA	ACU	AFL-CIO	CCUS
1990	100	4	83	23
1989	95	0	100	20
1988	90	0	85	42
1987	96	13	88	20
1986	95	5	77	12
1985	90	11	94	14
1984	90	0	77	25
1983	90	9	93	26
1982	95	0	100	11
1981	95	13	87	11

10 Don Edwards (D)

Of San Jose — Elected 1962

Born: Jan. 6, 1915, San Jose, Calif.

Education: Stanford U., A.B. 1936; attended Stanford U. Law School, 1936-38.

Military Service: Navy, 1942-45.

Occupation: Title company executive; lawyer; FBI agent.

Family: Wife, Edith Wilkie; five children.

Religion: Unitarian.

Political Career: No previous office.

Capitol Office: 2307 Rayburn Bldg. 20515; 225-3072.

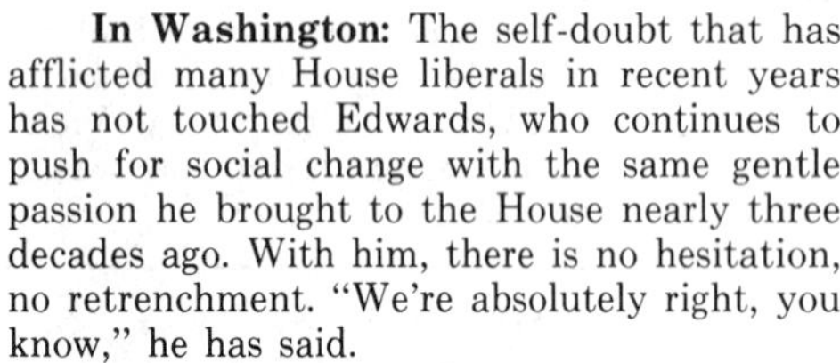

In Washington: The self-doubt that has afflicted many House liberals in recent years has not touched Edwards, who continues to push for social change with the same gentle passion he brought to the House nearly three decades ago. With him, there is no hesitation, no retrenchment. "We're absolutely right, you know," he has said.

For Edwards, liberalism means civil rights and civil liberties for everyone, including blacks, Mexican-Americans, women, children and dissenters of all kinds. He is a liberal first and a Democrat second; he has no qualms about opposing his party's leaders on what he considers a moral issue, such as Vietnam or the death penalty. Usually he has fought with restraint and bemused tolerance, although in recent years Edwards has taken to railing against Democratic colleagues' "gutlessness" in the face of conservative initiatives.

Edwards' ardent liberalism can leave him outside the inner circle of House Democrats, a crusader rather than an operator. But he is not uncompromising. In fact, Edwards likes to play the facilitator, as long as he can remain true to his fundamental principles. In 1988, he shepherded into law two of the most far-reaching civil rights bills since the 1960s. And while he had less luck guiding the 1990 civil rights bill to enactment, he was instrumental in defusing the furor for a constitutional amendment banning flag burning.

When the Judiciary Committee was reorganizing for the 102nd Congress, Edwards had a chance to take the chairmanship of a new subcommittee, but none were surprised when he stayed on at the helm of the Civil and Constitutional Rights Subcommittee, which perfectly suits his agenda. In the shuffle, however, Edwards picked up jurisdiction over death row inmate appeals. His vigorous defense of defendants' rights will complicate conservative bids to limit such appeals.

The final days of recent Congresses have found Edwards futilely battling election-season tides for punitive anti-drug bills, pleading that various law enforcement provisions are unconstitutional. "Drug legislation plus election-year posturing," he once told colleagues, "equals an assault on the Constitution."

While his frustration with the process remains, Edwards shifted tactics in 1990. Rather than cast lonely votes against crime bills, he worked to add language to further his cause: guaranteeing death row inmates competent legal counsel and restoring the chance to use new court rulings as the basis for appeal. Edwards acknowledged that it was "unique" for the Judiciary Committee to have attached the provisions to an anticrime bill that included sweeping capital punishment provisions. "Some of us have learned a lesson," he said. "The least we can do is make it fair."

The 101st Congress debate on whether to prohibit flag burning saw Edwards at his best. A staunch foe of a constitutional amendment, Edwards first worked to develop and enact a limited statute that gave cover to Democrats under pressure to halt flag burning. Then, as the new law was put to the test with a legal challenge, Edwards worked behind the scenes with liberal colleagues to develop a strategy to defeat an amendment if the courts struck down the statute.

The ad hoc task force used the Bill of Rights as both a legal argument and a symbol, writing letters to newspaper editors, meeting with grass-roots groups and appearing on television talk shows. By the time the Supreme Court declared the statute unconstitutional, the task force had laid down a foundation of skepticism about further action. Political interest in the matter waned, and the amendment died.

However, on civil rights, the issue most important to him, Edwards was not so successful. He entered the 101st Congress optimistic that President Bush would look more favorably upon such legislation than President Ronald Reagan had. A lead sponsor of the House bill designed to reverse recent Supreme Court decisions that made it more difficult to challenge discrimination in the workplace, he shepherded

California 10

Southeast Bay Area — Downtown San Jose; Fremont

Located at the southeastern end of the San Francisco Bay area, the 10th is split between Alameda and Santa Clara counties. It is the most industrial of the East Bay districts.

A large blue-collar Democratic base makes the 10th a safe haven for the prolabor Edwards. But the district is not nearly as dependable for statewide Democrats. With the votes of conservative, mainly white industrial workers in Fremont, President Ronald Reagan narrowly carried the 10th in 1984. However, Michael S. Dukakis won many of those voters back for the Democrats in 1988, enabling him to carry the district by a comfortable margin.

The Alameda County part of the 10th accounts for just over a third of the district's population. It is centered on Fremont, an automaking city of more than 173,000 that was once known as the Detroit of the West Coast. Today, its manufacturing has an international bent. General Motors Corp. has a joint venture with Toyota in Fremont; the plant turns out GM GEOs and Toyota Corollas.

Reagan's district victory in 1984 was largely the result of his 58 percent showing in Fremont. But in 1988, George Bush bested Dukakis in the city by only 500 votes.

The Santa Clara part of the district revolves around San Jose, which has surpassed San Francisco for the title of California's third-largest city. But the third of San Jose that is in the 10th, including its downtown area, faced a period of decline in the 1970s even as the rest of the city joined in the region's high-tech growth.

There are signs of revival in downtown San Jose, though. Several banks have moved in, and state and federal office buildings have brought more workers, restaurants and shops into the city. The construction of a light-rail system linking downtown with the northern suburbs and high-tech communities on the western edge of the bay has also stimulated development.

The rest of San Jose in the district has a working-class and ethnic flavor. There is a sizable contingent of Hispanic-Americans, who make up more than a quarter of the 10th's population. Growing communities of Asian-Americans, many of whom have opened up restaurants, groceries and other retail ventures, are having an impact on the city as well.

Population: 525,882. White 355,926 (68%), Black 29,537 (6%), Asian and Pacific Islander 51,517 (10%), Other 4,855 (1%). Spanish origin 147,361 (28%). 18 and over 360,334 (69%), 65 and over 33,111 (6%). Median age: 27.

the bill through the House. He unsuccessfully fought efforts to cap damage awards, and though his efforts to keep the burden of proof on employers rather than employees succeeded in Congress, the matter prompted a veto.

As the 102nd Congress opened, Edwards rejoined the battle. Pointing at the administration's claim that the bill would result in quotas, he said, "We'll name that for what it is. Politics and racism. It's to get votes."

Edwards had more luck in the late 1980s getting around Reagan administration opposition to civil rights legislation. Then, his eye for compromise carried the day. The grudging acceptance of an abortion provision by civil rights activists cleared the way for enactment, over Reagan's veto, of a law that not only overturned the Supreme Court's 1984 *Grove City* decision limiting the scope of four landmark civil rights laws, but also expanded those statutes. The contested abortion language specified that the law did not require hospitals to perform abortions just because they receive federal funds.

Edwards turned next to an even longer-lived stalemate, a 20-year-old fight to put teeth in the 1968 fair housing law. To appease the housing industry at the time, that law had left federal authorities virtually powerless to be anything more than mediators in discrimination disputes. Edwards wanted new administrative-law judges at the Department of Housing and Urban Development, empowered to levy fines and issue injunctions; Realtors and their Republican allies insisted on the option of a full jury trial.

After intense negotiations, including conference calls between civil rights advocates in Edwards' Capitol office and the Realtors' Chicago headquarters, a compromise was reached incorporating the housing representatives' demand for a trial option. The agreement, which Reagan belatedly endorsed, passed both the House and Senate overwhelmingly.

Edwards, however, is not always on the same side as his Democratic colleagues. He split with liberal ally Barney Frank of Massachusetts in the 100th Congress over Frank's ethics bill to limit lobbying by former lawmakers and senior staff. One of the few to oppose its passage, Edwards argued, "Lobbying Congress and the executive branch is an activity protected by the First Amendment. Getting paid for it doesn't make it any less protected."

When other Judiciary Democrats balked at pushing legislation to repeal insurance companies' antitrust exemption, complaining that too little time remained in the 100th Congress, Edwards lectured: "It shows how powerful a monopoly is in this country when it can intimidate Democrats into saying, 'Well, we have to be careful.' We've taken on a Goliath here, and this is what we get paid to do."

Edwards, however, is well placed to help House Democratic leaders bottle up conservatives' measures on volatile social issues. Only once, in 1979, did a House majority sign the necessary petition to wrest a measure from his subcommittee, a proposed anti-busing constitutional amendment. Edwards led the successful opposition on the floor. When criticized for being obstructive, he said, "Every member should use the rules any way he can."

Yet Republicans generally respect Edwards as fair and principled. Henry J. Hyde of Illinois, a frequent conservative foe, had complimentary words about Edwards even after the wars of the Reagan years: "He's a gentleman, he's honorable, he's extremely able. He's courteous, he's bright, he's a pleasure to work with. He's not arrogant or overbearing. He doesn't abuse the power he has."

In the past, Republicans have cooperated with Edwards to move bills they oppose out of his subcommittee, trusting his word that they will have an opportunity later to kill or amend the measures.

Edwards' role as the House's self-appointed guardian of constitutional rights overlaps with another — overseer of the FBI, his one-time employer. Infuriated that the FBI's Abscam sting may have amounted to entrapment of seven members of Congress, Edwards chaired a lengthy subcommittee investigation of the agency's undercover operations. Its 1984 report found "widespread deviation from avowed standards" resulting in "substantial harm to individuals and public institutions," and recommended advance judicial approval of undercover activities. Later, he used his subcommittee to probe both the FBI's two-year surveillance of citizens' groups opposed to U.S. military aid to Central America, and allegations of racism victimizing black and Hispanic agents.

Outside the civil rights arena, Edwards works on behalf of two industries important to California's economy: computers and movies. Also, he is dean of California's 27-member House Democratic delegation, coordinating strategy and information on issues of state interest.

In the 101st Congress, Edwards helped the entire California delegation come together in rare bipartisan form to win emergency aid after the Loma Prieta earthquake. And at the start of the 102nd, Edwards achieved a decade-long goal with the creation of the California Institute, a nonpartisan group to help the state make its case for federal largess. The need for such coordination crystallized in the late-1980s, when the state failed to make the list of finalists for the superconducting super collider. "One of the benefits of the institute will be to look ahead and tell us what might come up, so we will be far better prepared," he said.

At Home: Stories about Edwards inevitably emphasize his FBI background, citing it as rather unusual preparation for a career as a civil libertarian. Actually, Edwards was not only an FBI agent as a young man — he also was a Republican. He did not join the Democratic Party until he was 35, and on his way to a fortune as owner of the Valley Title Insurance Company in San Jose.

Wealth only seemed to make Edwards more liberal. He said he gave up on Republicans because they did not seem interested in the international agreements needed to preserve peace.

At the time, Edwards was beginning his long journey into activism. He joined the United World Federalists, the National Association for the Advancement of Colored People, the American Civil Liberties Union and the Americans for Democratic Action (ADA). He was national ADA chairman in 1965.

Most people in Edwards' district seem to care little about the causes that have preoccupied him all his life. What matters to them is that he is a friendly, open man whose staff takes care of their problems. With that combination, Edwards has been able to overcome a long string of challengers, candidates who have questioned his patriotism and warned voters he is too liberal for them.

Edwards had never sought any office before 1962, devoting most of his time to his business. But when a new district was drawn that year to include part of his home city of San Jose, Edwards decided to run.

His two major opponents for the Democratic nomination both had more political experience, but less personal charm. They fought bitterly with each other and Edwards won the Democratic primary by 726 votes, edging Fremont Mayor John Stevenson. It was an overwhelmingly Democratic district, and Edwards easily won in the fall.

Edwards' outspoken support for Eugene J. McCarthy's presidential campaign, and early reports of his possible retirement, gave him a difficult time in 1968. He faced two Santa Clara city councilmen, one in the Democratic primary and one in the general election. But Edwards still won both elections comfortably.

He has had no trouble since then. In 1982 and 1984, Republican candidate Bob Herriott, an airline pilot from his party's conservative wing, received a substantial amount of funding from GOP sources, but was unable to make a dent in Edwards' standing.

Edwards won his 1986 contest with 71 percent of the vote. In 1988, the GOP did not lift a finger against Edwards; his only opponents were a Hispanic challenger in the primary and a Libertarian in the general election. While his 1990 re-election contest was not quite so effortless, Edwards defeated Republican Mark Patrosso with 63 percent, a figure that was consistent with his totals in the early 1980s.

Committees

Judiciary (2nd of 21 Democrats)
Civil & Constitutional Rights (chairman); Administrative Law & Governmental Relations; Economic & Commercial Law

Veterans' Affairs (2nd of 21 Democrats)
Oversight & Investigations

Elections

1990 General		
Don Edwards (D)	81,875	(63%)
Mark Patrosso (R)	48,747	(37%)
1988 General		
Don Edwards (D)	142,500	(86%)
Kennita Watson (LIBERT)	22,801	(14%)

Previous Winning Percentages:				**1986**	(71%)	**1984**	(62%)
1982	(63%)	**1980**	(62%)	**1978**	(67%)	**1976**	(72%)
1974	(77%)	**1972**	(72%)	**1970**	(69%)	**1968**	(57%)
1966	(63%)	**1964**	(70%)	**1962**	(66%)		

District Vote For President

	1988	1984	1980	1976
D	101,702 (55%)	83,340 (48%)	57,017 (42%)	72,316 (59%)
R	80,515 (44%)	87,529 (51%)	61,367 (45%)	48,874 (40%)

Campaign Finance

	Receipts	Receipts from PACs		Expend-itures
1990				
Edwards (D)	$224,999	$171,050	(76%)	$209,243
Patrosso (R)	$2,702	0		$2,581
1988				
Edwards (D)	$166,689	$117,256	(70%)	$173,537

Key Votes

1991	
Authorize use of force against Iraq	N
1990	
Support constitutional amendment on flag desecration	N
Pass family and medical leave bill over Bush veto	Y
Reduce SDI funding	Y
Allow abortions in overseas military facilities	Y
Approve budget summit plan for spending and taxing	N
Approve civil rights bill	Y
1989	
Halt production of B-2 stealth bomber at 13 planes	Y
Oppose capital gains tax cut	Y
Approve federal abortion funding in rape or incest cases	Y
Approve pay raise and revision of ethics rules	Y
Pass Democratic minimum wage plan over Bush veto	Y

Voting Studies

	Presidential Support		Party Unity		Conservative Coalition	
Year	**S**	**O**	**S**	**O**	**S**	**O**
1990	17	82	92	3	7	89
1989	27	69	93	1	0	95
1988	18	80	94	3	5	87
1987	11	85	92	2	2	95
1986	16	84	95	3	4 †	94 †
1985	20	80	97	2	7	93
1984	24	75	94	5	2	98
1983	15	84	94	3	7	89
1982	27	68	93	4	7	93
1981	29	63	88	5	3	95

† Not eligible for all recorded votes.

Interest Group Ratings

Year	ADA	ACU	AFL-CIO	CCUS
1990	100	4	100	21
1989	100	0	100	20
1988	100	0	100	23
1987	100	0	100	0
1986	100	0	93	12
1985	100	0	100	18
1984	100	0	85	31
1983	100	0	100	20
1982	100	0	95	9
1981	95	0	93	12

11 Tom Lantos (D)

Of San Mateo — Elected 1980

Born: Feb. 1, 1928, Budapest, Hungary.
Education: U. of Washington, B.A. 1949, M.A. 1950; U. of California, Berkeley, Ph.D. 1953.
Occupation: Professor of economics.
Family: Wife, Annette Tillemann; two children.
Religion: Jewish.
Political Career: Millbrae Board of Education, 1958-66.
Capitol Office: 1526 Longworth Bldg. 20515; 225-3531.

In Washington: The traits Lantos exhibits in the House draw on a lifetime of varied experience. Born in Hungary, Lantos has the civilized air of a man bred in a pre-war Central European culture, and the stubbornness of a fighter in the anti-Nazi resistance in Budapest. He retains the intellectual self-assurance — some say arrogance — of the college professor he once was.

Those characteristics were on national display during the 101st Congress, when Lantos chaired high-profile hearings on alleged corruption at the Department of Housing and Urban Development. The hearings, held in 1989 in Lantos' Government Operations Subcommittee on Employment and Housing, centered on the alleged use of the Section 8 housing-rehabilitation program to benefit Republican consultants and developers, including some former Reagan administration officials.

During the hearings, Lantos won bipartisan praise for his courteous treatment of witnesses and committee members. But his sharp tongue ripped witnesses he found unhelpful. To a GOP fundraiser claiming innocence on the grounds that he lacked political influence, Lantos replied, "That is about as believable as Elvis' being seen in a K Mart store."

Of former Interior Secretary James Watt, a consultant for housing developers seeking HUD subsidies, Lantos said that Watt's only experience in housing was "making Bambi homeless." Harsher still, Lantos said, "What I find most obnoxious so far, is the unmitigated hypocrisy of people like James Watt who exude unction, piety and noble motives, who carry on a crusade to destroy these programs and at the same time shamelessly milk them." The hearings helped persuade Congress to pass legislation placing new restrictions on HUD managers and operating procedures, as well as on lobbyists.

Lantos extended some of his concern about political favoritism to Congress as well. That fall, he voted against $28 million worth of special projects legislators had tucked into the HUD appropriation bill, despite the fact that one of the projects was for his own district. Lantos did not go so far as to argue against the so-called earmarks on the floor, however, and the vote to remove them failed.

Prior to the HUD scandal, Lantos was best known for his interest in foreign affairs, particularly Eastern Europe and human rights. On those issues, Lantos can sometimes annoy colleagues with his thunderous denunciations of foreign totalitarianism.

Lantos makes no apologies for his boldness, nor his certitude that he is right. Few members would be so self-assured as to take being called "ignorant" and "arrogant" as a compliment. But Lantos beamed when his efforts on behalf of Tibetan human rights provoked those insults from Chinese Premier Deng Xiaoping in 1987.

Lantos, co-chairman of the Congressional Human Rights Caucus, had invited Tibet's exiled Dalai Lama to address the group. The Tibetan political and spiritual leader accused the Chinese government of human rights abuses and suppression of Tibetan dissent. Lantos' criticism of harsh Chinese efforts to quell Tibetan rioting later spurred the rebuke from Deng. Undeterred, Lantos visited China in 1988 to press the human rights cause. After the Chinese government's brutal crackdown on pro-democracy demonstrators in Tiananmen Square in June 1989, Lantos urged canceling favorable treatment for U.S.-China trade and strongly protested the administration's 1990 decision to renew those privileges.

Lantos takes a similarly critical line toward the Soviet Union, using human rights as the springboard to assail that nation's totalitarian nature. A strong supporter of the Jewish "refuseniks" seeking to emigrate from the Soviet Union to Israel, Lantos has also supported independence efforts by the Baltic republics of Lithuania, Latvia and Estonia, absorbed by the U.S.S.R. during World War II.

But while Lantos has widely broadcast his distrust of the Soviet Union, he has not joined with those House conservatives who warn against rapprochement. Prior to signs in early 1991 that the Soviet Union was moving away

California 11

Most of San Mateo County

The 11th District contains about 85 percent of the San Mateo County vote. But the 11th carefully skirts the most Republican areas of the county (located in the 12th District), which run down the middle of the San Mateo peninsula.

This cartography makes the 11th a Democratic stronghold. Michael S. Dukakis won it by a substantial margin in 1988; Democratic Senate candidate Leo T. McCarthy's strong showing here enabled him to carry San Mateo County as a whole. President Reagan did manage to carry the 11th in 1984, but with barely 50 percent of the vote.

The district reaches south from San Francisco, splitting into two distinct legs that straddle the San Mateo Mountains. Just below San Francisco is Daly City, a largely blue-collar suburb.

To the south are Pacifica, South San Francisco and San Bruno. A coastal, middle-class suburban town, Pacifica has drawn a number of teachers and other education professionals. South San Francisco is the home of Genentech, the gene-splicing firm.

The eastern leg of the 11th is tied together by 30 miles of the Bayshore Freeway. From Millbrae south to San Carlos are upper- and middle-class communities. All of them gave Reagan a majority in 1984, but many switched to Dukakis in 1988. At the southern end are East Palo Alto and the eastern part of Menlo Park, which are less affluent.

The western leg is primarily mist, fog and a smattering of small communities tucked into the mountains or perched on bluffs overlooking the sea. Half Moon Bay, at the far western end of the 11th, is a small fishing and agricultural community.

Population: 525,981. White 401,311 (76%), Black 35,104 (7%), Asian and Pacific Islander 53,751 (10%), Other 2,396 (1%). Spanish origin 70,909 (14%). 18 and over 400,549 (76%), 65 and over 53,599 (10%). Median age: 32.

from earlier reforms, Lantos advocated more robust U.S. support for democratization there.

During much of 1987, Lantos acted as chairman of Foreign Affairs' Europe and the Middle East Subcommittee because senior Democrat Lee H. Hamilton of Indiana was preoccupied with the Iran-contra investigation. An enthusiastic supporter of Israel and a critic of U.S. overtures to Israel's Arab adversaries, Lantos held hearings at which he criticized the commitment of U.S. naval forces to protect Kuwaiti oil tankers in the Persian Gulf.

In May 1989, Lantos worked to deter the World Health Organization (WHO) from admitting the Palestine Liberation Organization (PLO). Citing the WHO charter's requirement that members must be sovereign nations, Lantos insisted, "Whatever the PLO is, it isn't a sovereign nation-state." His proposal to cut off aid to WHO if it admitted the PLO passed the House by a wide margin.

More recently, Lantos backed the use of force to dislodge Iraq from Kuwait — despite earlier criticisms of administration policy toward Iraq and support for economic sanctions against that country. But Lantos sharply criticized U.S. allies, particularly Japan, for failing to shoulder a larger portion of the war's cost.

The California Democrat strongly opposed funding for the Nicaraguan contras, yet he collegially greeted then-Lt. Col. Oliver L. North when he was called before the Foreign Affairs Committee in late 1986. Lantos declared his "respect, affection and admiration" for the staunchly anti-communist North and contributed $250 to a fund that had been established to defray North's legal expenses.

Lantos gained an ally in the House with the 1990 election of his son-in-law, Democrat Dick Swett, from New Hampshire.

At Home: It took Lantos two difficult and expensive elections before he could settle securely into his district.

He was working on Capitol Hill as a consultant to the Senate Foreign Relations Committee when Republican Bill Royer won a 1979 special election to replace Democrat Leo J. Ryan, who had been assassinated the year before in Jonestown, Guyana.

Ryan's assassination brought out a host of Democrats who claimed to be his logical political heir, and by the time the primary was finished, the party was badly splintered. Royer picked his way through the Democratic debris to win the seat for the GOP.

But Lantos, well-known within local Democratic circles, left his job right after Royer's victory and began preparing a challenge for 1980. The one-time economics professor at San Francisco State University had held elective office only as a school board president in suburban Millbrae. But he had been active in party efforts and had built up name recognition as a foreign affairs commentator for a Bay-area TV station.

Royer, who had been a city councilman

and county supervisor for 23 years before moving on to Congress, went into the contest with a solid political foundation. He had tried to strengthen it over his term in office by taking a highly visible role in the investigation of the events surrounding Ryan's death.

Yet Lantos, who had held himself apart from the 1979 Democratic feuding, was able to unite his party around him for 1980. Although Lantos was less well-known than Royer and was short of campaign funds, he was politically astute and took advantage of the incumbent's overconfidence.

In the final weeks of the campaign, the Democrat filled the airwaves with advertising, while Royer, believing the election was his, yanked his own ads as an economy move. Royer ended up with a budget surplus, but a vote deficit: Lantos won by 3 percentage points.

Royer made it clear that he would be back two years later, and Lantos began raising money early. With typical single-mindedness, he pursued it not only at home, but within Jewish communities in the districts of other members — a habit that led initially to some hard feelings among his colleagues. By 1982, he was among the best-funded House candidates in the country. Royer argued that Lantos' interest in foreign affairs had come at the district's expense. He contrasted Lantos' actions with the local orientation of his own term in office. But Lantos was able to counter by stressing his work on local issues such as offshore drilling.

Lantos also responded strongly when Royer adopted the slogan "He's One of Us," a possible reference to Lantos' immigrant background. Lantos aired a five-minute television biography that outlined his early life, including his World War II efforts in the Hungarian resistance, and his accomplishments since immigrating. Lantos won comfortably.

In his last three contests, he has faced Republican G. M. "Bill" Quraishi, a nuclear and electrical engineer, who took 26 percent of the vote in 1986, 24 percent in 1988 and 29 percent in 1990. "At this rate," wrote the *California Journal* after that election, "he'll have Lantos out of office in 2002."

Committees

Foreign Affairs (8th of 28 Democrats)
Asian & Pacific Affairs; Europe & the Middle East; International Operations

Government Operations (9th of 25 Democrats)
Employment & Housing (chairman)

Select Aging (12th of 42 Democrats)
Retirement, Income & Employment

Elections

1990 General		
Tom Lantos (D)	105,029	(66%)
G. M. "Bill" Quraishi (R)	45,818	(29%)
June R. Genis (LIBERT)	8,518	(5%)
1988 General		
Tom Lantos (D)	145,484	(71%)
G. M. "Bill" Quraishi (R)	50,050	(24%)

Previous Winning Percentages: **1986** (74%) **1984** (70%) **1982** (57%) **1980** (46%)

District Vote For President

	1988	1984	1980	1976
D	126,351 (58%)	109,053 (49%)	74,797 (39%)	84,047 (50%)
R	89,063 (40%)	112,986 (50%)	88,313 (46%)	83,265 (49%)

Campaign Finance

	Receipts	Receipts from PACs	Expend-itures
1990			
Lantos (D)	$788,298	$120,550 (15%)	$620,782
Quraishi (R)	$97,638	$6,300 (6%)	$97,030
1988			
Lantos (D)	$386,453	$111,267 (29%)	$269,510
Quraishi (R)	$90,306	$8,100 (9%)	$95,575

Key Votes

1991	
Authorize use of force against Iraq	Y
1990	
Support constitutional amendment on flag desecration	N
Pass family and medical leave bill over Bush veto	Y
Reduce SDI funding	Y
Allow abortions in overseas military facilities	Y
Approve budget summit plan for spending and taxing	Y
Approve civil rights bill	Y
1989	
Halt production of B-2 stealth bomber at 13 planes	N
Oppose capital gains tax cut	Y
Approve federal abortion funding in rape or incest cases	Y
Approve pay raise and revision of ethics rules	Y
Pass Democratic minimum wage plan over Bush veto	Y

Voting Studies

	Presidential Support		Party Unity		Conservative Coalition	
Year	S	O	S	O	S	O
1990	26	74	89	6	30	70
1989	31	62	90	4	34	63
1988	27	71	89	6	42	55
1987	21	75	90	5	49	49
1986	23	76	89	5	40	60
1985	19	70	88	4	27	71
1984	27	69	83	4	14	81
1983	21	73	91	5	20	76
1982	31	57	87	4	29	66
1981	46	50	69	14	39	53

Interest Group Ratings

Year	ADA	ACU	AFL-CIO	CCUS
1990	78	17	92	21
1989	80	0	100	40
1988	85	8	100	31
1987	84	0	100	20
1986	70	18	100	31
1985	70	5	94	22
1984	85	5	100	43
1983	85	2	100	25
1982	80	10	89	11
1981	70	7	71	24

12 Tom Campbell (R)

Of Stanford — Elected 1988

Born: Aug. 14, 1952, Chicago, Ill.
Education: U. of Chicago, B.A., M.A. 1973, Ph.D. 1980; Harvard U., J.D. 1976.
Occupation: Professor of economics; federal official; lawyer.
Family: Wife, Susanne Martin.
Religion: Roman Catholic.
Political Career: No previous office.
Capitol Office: 313 Cannon Bldg. 20515; 225-5411.

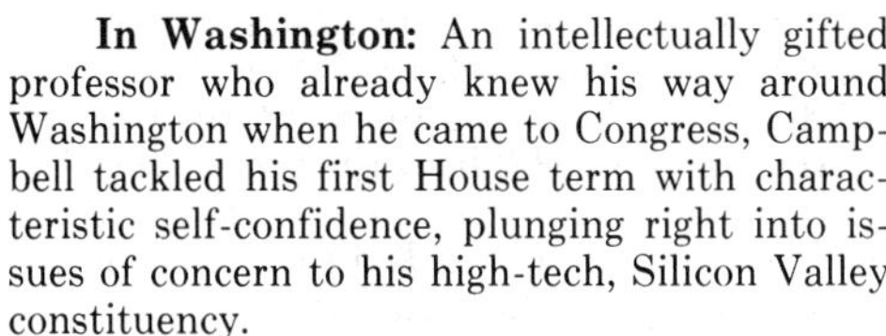

In Washington: An intellectually gifted professor who already knew his way around Washington when he came to Congress, Campbell tackled his first House term with characteristic self-confidence, plunging right into issues of concern to his high-tech, Silicon Valley constituency.

Campbell's aplomb, coupled with his moderate politics, stirred early talk of his potential to succeed as a legislative activist in the Democratic-controlled House. But Campbell instead hopes to take his talents to the Senate; early in his second term, he said he would try to move up in 1992.

As a House freshman, Campbell got a seat on the Science, Space and Technology Committee and weighed into the trade and competitiveness debate with two proposals. One sought to relax antitrust restrictions on some American industries, particularly high-tech firms, so they could pool some production resources and better keep pace with foreign competitors.

Another Campbell proposal was to require the United States to treat a foreign investor in the same manner that U.S. investors are treated in the foreigner's home country.

Campbell does not follow a straight ideological line. He is conservative on many economic issues, but supports abortion rights and environmental causes. The League of Conservation Voters has rated his voting record as perfect, and he has introduced legislation to give states more control over offshore oil drilling.

Campbell, who also sits on the Judiciary Committee, splits with many conservatives in the debate on civil rights legislation. He cosponsored a measure to reverse the effects of a Supreme Court ruling that made it harder to sue for job discrimination, and he voted for the 1990 Civil Rights Act, which was vetoed by President Bush. In the 102nd Congress, Campbell added a seat on the Banking Committee to his portfolio.

At Home: Campbell's first House victory was a bold stroke. He was one of only seven challengers to defeat a House incumbent in 1988, and the only one to unseat a member of his own party in a primary. After fending off a tough Democratic opponent that November, Campbell won with ease in 1990.

Campbell has always been an overachiever. He earned a Harvard law degree and a doctorate in economics from the University of Chicago before his 28th birthday. The son of a federal judge, Campbell was a law clerk for Supreme Court Justice Byron R. White. In 1980, he won a White House fellowship, then held several positions in the Reagan administration, including the post of director of the Federal Trade Commission's Bureau of Competition.

In 1983, Campbell moved to the 12th to teach at Stanford. In 1988, he challenged one-term GOP Rep. Ernie Konnyu. Konnyu had won the seat rather easily in 1986, succeeding GOP Rep. Ed Zschau, who lost a Senate bid.

But Konnyu's election did not thrill many Republicans. Zschau, a high-tech entrepreneur, was the kind of moderate Republican favored by Silicon Valley's affluent electorate.

Konnyu was a conservative activist in the state Assembly who won the 1986 House primary over two Republicans more typical of the district.

Campbell said his concern that Konnyu's hard-right posture would weaken the district's high-tech, tax and trade agenda motivated his challenge. His chances improved when *The San Jose Mercury-News* wrote articles detailing Konnyu's staff turnover and accusations of his boorish behavior toward women.

Campbell gained impressive backing for a primary challenger. Zschau, previous incumbent Paul N. McCloskey Jr. and former Deputy Secretary of Defense David Packard all supported him. Although the party officially supported Konnyu, Campbell was able to compete financially. He prevailed with 58 percent.

District Democrats nominated a capable candidate, San Mateo County Supervisor Anna G. Eshoo. The well-organized Eshoo spent more than $1 million, but Campbell spent more. Holding a series of "town hall" meetings and relying on the district's GOP leanings, Campbell won with 52 percent.

California 12

Parts of San Mateo and Santa Clara Counties

Used primarily by Democratic cartographers as a "dumping ground" for Republican votes in the 1980s round of redistricting, the 12th is dominated by a variety of towns with little in common except affluence and Republican inclination. The 12th has the highest median real-estate values in California.

Yet moderate voting tendencies guide many of the district's affluent voters, including a number of young professionals employed in high-tech industries. Though Californian Ronald Reagan won comfortably here, George Bush barely held the district for the Republicans in 1988. And while moderate Ed Zschau was a popular House member in the 12th, his successor, conservative Ernie Konnyu, was not; GOP primary voters dumped him after one term for Campbell, a more centrist figure.

The district begins along the beach in San Mateo County and moves east across the hills to Hillsborough and Woodside, the wealthiest parts of the Bay Area. Some residents commute to San Francisco by limousine.

But the heart of the 12th is in Santa Clara County, in the southern portion of the electronics and computer corridor known as Silicon Valley. Towns such as Los Altos, Los Altos Hills, Saratoga and Cupertino are home to such high-tech giants as Apple Computer, Hewlett-Packard and Ford Aerospace.

Palo Alto, the home of Stanford University, is a liberal bastion. The city of 56,000, which casts about 10 percent of the district vote, went for Democrat Michael S. Dukakis in 1988 by a 2-to-1 margin.

The 12th reaches into agricultural territory in southern Santa Clara County. Gilroy, which calls itself the "Garlic Capital of the World," is home to the yearly garlic festival. Morgan Hill has begun to see some housing spillover from Silicon Valley. To the east, the district holds a sliver of Santa Cruz County in the San Lorenzo Valley, taking in a chain of small Republican towns.

Population: 525,731. White 452,459 (86%), Black 9,033 (2%), Asian and Pacific Islander 34,163 (6%), Other 2,448 (1%). Spanish origin 51,848 (10%). 18 and over 397,900 (76%), 65 and over 48,834 (9%). Median age: 32.

Committees

Banking, Finance & Urban Affairs (14th of 20 Republicans)
Domestic Monetary Policy; Housing & Community Development; International Development, Finance, Trade & Monetary Policy

Judiciary (11th of 13 Republicans)
Intellectual Property & Judicial Administration; Economic & Commercial Law

Science, Space & Technology (15th of 19 Republicans)
Science; Technology & Competitiveness

Elections

1990 General		
Tom Campbell (R)	125,157	(61%)
Robert Palmer (D)	69,270	(34%)
Chuck Olson (LIBERT)	11,271	(5%)
1988 General		
Tom Campbell (R)	136,384	(52%)
Anna G. Eshoo (D)	121,523	(46%)

District Vote For President

	1988	1984	1980	1976
D	132,918 (49%)	108,069 (41%)	69,206 (31%)	76,856 (42%)
R	133,699 (49%)	148,724 (57%)	114,467 (51%)	102,809 (57%)

Campaign Finance

	Receipts	Receipts from PACs	Expend-itures
1990			
Campbell (R)	$1,286,200	$249,581 (19%)	$658,135
Palmer (D)	$109,410	$27,550 (25%)	$103,839
1988			
Campbell (R)	$1,445,770	$239,382 (17%)	$1,440,639
Eshoo (D)	$1,092,766	$422,547 (39%)	$1,089,570

Key Votes

1991	
Authorize use of force against Iraq	Y
1990	
Support constitutional amendment on flag desecration	Y
Pass family and medical leave bill over Bush veto	Y
Reduce SDI funding	Y
Allow abortions in overseas military facilities	Y
Approve budget summit plan for spending and taxing	N
Approve civil rights bill	Y
1989	
Halt production of B-2 stealth bomber at 13 planes	N
Oppose capital gains tax cut	N
Approve federal abortion funding in rape or incest cases	Y
Approve pay raise and revision of ethics rules	Y
Pass Democratic minimum wage plan over Bush veto	N

Voting Studies

	Presidential Support		Party Unity		Conservative Coalition	
Year	**S**	**O**	**S**	**O**	**S**	**O**
1990	50 †	47 †	69 †	28 †	48	43
1989	56	43	47	51	54	46

† Not eligible for all recorded votes.

Interest Group Ratings

Year	ADA	ACU	AFL-CIO	CCUS
1990	44	46	27	71
1989	40	50	17	100

13 Norman Y. Mineta (D)

Of San Jose — Elected 1974

Born: Nov. 12, 1931, San Jose, Calif.
Education: U. of California, Berkeley, B.S. 1953.
Military Service: Army, 1953-56.
Occupation: Insurance executive.
Family: Wife, Danealia Brantner; two children.
Religion: Methodist.
Political Career: San Jose City Council, 1967-71; mayor of San Jose, 1971-74.
Capitol Office: 2350 Rayburn Bldg. 20515; 225-2631.

In Washington: Mineta began the 102nd Congress with an attempted end run around the seniority system. Frustrated by the lack of leadership on the Public Works and Transportation Committee and spurred on by a cabal of younger members, Mineta toppled 77-year-old Chairman Glenn M. Anderson of California, only to lose the post to Robert A. Roe of New Jersey, the second-ranking Democrat.

Mineta's aborted coup ruffled some feathers in the California delegation. But he survived relatively unscathed because he retains the respect of many of his colleagues. "In the committee, in the Democratic Caucus, Mineta's leadership and stature have been enhanced," Georgia Rep. John Lewis told *The San Jose Mercury News*. "He was there when we needed him. The day will come when he will chair that committee," said Lewis, a middle-ranking Public Works Democrat.

Mineta began his House career as president of the rebellious 1974 freshman class, and for the next decade he was a key player in House politics who appeared headed for a rung on the leadership ladder. But after he slipped in a weak campaign for majority whip in the 99th Congress, Mineta refocused. He retained his deputy whip's post, but directed more energy toward his legislative base, the Public Works Subcommittee on Aviation.

By the end of the 100th Congress, his transition from the leadership to the legislative ladder was complete. After two years as the leading specialist and watchdog of the troubled airline industry, Mineta gave up the Aviation chairmanship for a more powerful subcommittee — Surface Transportation — in the 101st Congress. Now he has oversight of a far larger budget, and one that more directly serves his district.

Mineta's current post is one known for its locally oriented pork-barrel politics, but he tries to maintain a national perspective, just as he did on the Aviation panel, where he opposed the naming of specific projects in airport bills. In 1987, Mineta steered through the House a $20 billion, five-year airport reauthorization bill that was not adorned with pet-project add-ons.

In the 102nd Congress, Mineta is expected to shepherd a new five-year highway and mass transit bill that could produce the largest overhaul of U.S. transportation policy in the last 35 years. In early 1991 he gave notice that he was skeptical of Secretary of Transportation Samuel K. Skinner's call for stressing road repairs and gridlock relief rather than new highway construction. Mineta said he wanted balance between competing priorities.

A keen interest in protecting labor rights has been a hallmark of Mineta's work. In the 100th Congress, he championed a measure requiring airline carriers to pay benefits to workers hurt by mergers. The "labor-protection" provisions (LPPs) cleared the House as part of the transportation appropriations bill, but a veto threat knocked them off the bill in conference.

Mineta advocated a consumer-protection bill that included the LPPs as well as provisions requiring airlines to make extensive public disclosures about flight delays and lost baggage. After both chambers passed legislation in 1987, the Department of Transportation issued rules requiring on-time disclosure. With that accomplished, the bill got bogged down in debate over the LPPs and random drug testing of transportation workers, which Mineta vigorously opposed.

During the 100th Congress, he also pushed legislation to provide protection for aviation "whistleblowers" who call attention to safety violations. While the measure cruised through the House, it died in the Senate. Some suggested that Mineta's counterpart there, Aviation Subcommittee Chairman Wendell H. Ford of Kentucky, blocked the measure because he felt Mineta was foot-dragging on efforts to make the Federal Aviation Administration an independent agency. Mineta expressed concern that without the backing of the Department of Transportation, the FAA would lack the political clout to promote aviation needs.

In the 101st Congress, Mineta opposed President Bush's proposal to assess airline trav-

California 13

Santa Clara County — San Jose; Santa Clara

With its historic image as a working-class town and a market center for surrounding farm country, San Jose lived in the shadow of its more glamorous neighbor to the north, San Francisco. But with its explosive growth over the last four decades, San Jose finally surpassed San Francisco in size: It is now California's third-largest city, behind Los Angeles and San Diego.

San Jose's big burst began after World War II, with the sweep of suburbanization down both sides of San Francisco Bay, and was fueled by the high-tech growth in the "Silicon Valley." 1990 census figures estimate that San Jose — 50 miles south of San Francisco in Santa Clara County — has 782,000 residents.

The 13th, a relatively compact district contained entirely within Santa Clara County, includes just under two-thirds of San Jose (though not the downtown area, which is in the 10th). It takes in the adjoining suburban communities of Santa Clara, Campbell and Los Gatos.

As canneries and fruit-packing firms have given way to high-tech in Silicon Valley, San Jose's white-collar population has grown accordingly. The part of San Jose in the 13th is far more Anglo than the heavily Hispanic western side in the 10th.

Most of the voters in the 13th are the type who normally would consider voting Republican. Mineta's personal popularity has made the district comfortably Democratic, but Michael S. Dukakis carried it in 1988 with only 49 percent of the vote. Ronald Reagan won the 13th easily in 1980 and 1984.

When Democrats do win here, they usually benefit from a Democratic lean in Santa Clara. Many of the city's 90,000 residents work in the high-tech plants in Sunnyvale, located in the neighboring 12th District.

Population: 526,281. White 449,593 (85%), Black 11,881 (2%), Asian and Pacific Islander 33,182 (6%), Other 3,025 (1%). Spanish origin 61,057 (12%). 18 and over 380,270 (72%), 65 and over 35,614 (7%). Median age: 29.

elers a user fee to help pay for airport improvements, arguing that it amounted to double taxation, since a portion of current ticket prices goes to a trust fund that Mineta says should be used for airport improvements.

Perhaps Mineta's most significant accomplishment of recent years, however, had nothing to do with Public Works. He was a driving force behind passage of legislation to compensate Japanese-Americans interned by the U.S. government during World War II.

He described the internment as "an act born of racism," and the issue had topped his agenda for more than a decade. In 1978, he won passage of a bill to grant retirement benefits to interned Japanese-American civil servants. "Injustice does not dim with time," he said of the long wait for the 1987 bill.

Some 45 years earlier, Mineta and his family had been sent from their San Jose home to an internment camp in Wyoming, where they lived during the war. "Some say the internment was for our own good," he said. "But even as a boy of 10, I could see that the machine guns and the barbed wire faced inward."

When Congress passed legislation to provide a formal apology and $20,000 to each of the 60,000 surviving victims, Mineta signed the bill on behalf of the House.

In the 101st Congress, he also helped pass the Americans with Disabilities Act, which prohibits discrimination against the handicapped and requires increased accessibility of facilities for them.

Mineta's toughest legislative job in the 99th Congress involved the transfer of Dulles and National airports in suburban Virginia from federal ownership to control by a regional authority. Although the transfer had been recommended by various experts for more than 30 years, members of Congress balked at losing control of the airports they use to travel to and from their home districts.

To mollify numerous House critics, Mineta proposed leasing the airports for 50 years, rather than selling them, and creating a federal review board consisting of members of Congress to monitor the regional authority. That allowed a transfer bill to reach the House floor, and eventually to become law.

A member of the House Intelligence Committee from 1977 to 1984, Mineta was outspoken in his criticism of then-CIA Director William J. Casey for not informing Congress about certain agency activities. He was an early supporter of legislation to require advance congressional notice of covert intelligence activities.

Mineta also spent three terms on the Budget Committee, and when he rotated off the panel in 1983, he left behind a significant contribution: the concept of "credit accounting." The procedure created the first formal accounting of the money the federal government spends guaranteeing private loans.

At Home: San Jose's Japanese-American community was the springboard to Mineta's political career. Running an insurance business with his father in the 1960s, he became active in the city's Japanese American Citizens League. That led him to San Jose's Human Relations Commission, its housing authority and City Council and to the mayoralty in 1971.

The San Jose area was coming out of a decade of unprecedented suburban growth during Mineta's years as mayor, and he allied himself with those calling for limits on further development.

In 1974, the 13th District came open. It had been represented for over two decades by GOP Rep. Charles Gubser, and had voted Republican in every election since World War II. Gubser's retirement gave Democrats an opportunity to take advantage of the demographic changes that had swept the area. Mineta, who had been extremely popular as mayor, had no trouble winning the Democratic primary.

His GOP opponent was former state Rep. George W. Milias, who had lost an earlier primary for California secretary of state and gone on to work for the Defense Department in the Nixon administration. Challenged by more conservative opposition, Milias had only squeaked through to the nomination.

Milias was able to pick up campaign funds gathered earlier for Gubser. But as a GOP candidate in 1974, he was stuck with a difficult balancing act: reminding GOP conservatives of his service in the Nixon administration while distancing himself from the Watergate scandal. His absence from the district in the years before the election also hampered him.

Mineta, by contrast, was immensely strong within San Jose, and well recognized in the surrounding county. He won with 53 percent.

Since then, he has prevailed by solid margins, even though Democratic registration in the district has slipped below 50 percent. He topped out at 70 percent of the vote in 1986. Like most California House incumbents, he slipped a bit in 1990: His 58 percent was his lowest tally since 1978, but he still easily outdistanced Republican David E. Smith.

Committees

Public Works & Transportation (3rd of 36 Democrats)
Surface Transportation (chairman); Aviation; Investigations & Oversight

Science, Space & Technology (9th of 32 Democrats)
Space; Technology & Competitiveness

Elections

1990 General		
Norman Y. Mineta (D)	97,286	(58%)
David E. Smith (R)	59,773	(36%)
John H. Webster (LIBERT)	10,587	(6%)
1988 General		
Norman Y. Mineta (D)	143,980	(67%)
Luke Sommer (R)	63,959	(30%)

Previous Winning Percentages: **1986** (70%) **1984** (65%) **1982** (66%) **1980** (59%) **1978** (58%) **1976** (67%) **1974** (53%)

District Vote For President

	1988	1984	1980	1976
D	109,830 (49%)	89,789 (41%)	65,780 (34%)	79,060 (48%)
R	108,817 (49%)	126,585 (58%)	95,437 (50%)	83,744 (51%)

Campaign Finance

	Receipts	Receipts from PACs	Expend-itures
1990			
Mineta (D)	$666,915	$361,274 (54%)	$644,962
Smith (R)	$670	0	$624
1988			
Mineta (D)	$577,164	$277,450 (48%)	$521,674
Sommer (R)	$26,756	0	$25,511

Key Votes

1991	
Authorize use of force against Iraq	N
1990	
Support constitutional amendment on flag desecration	N
Pass family and medical leave bill over Bush veto	Y
Reduce SDI funding	Y
Allow abortions in overseas military facilities	Y
Approve budget summit plan for spending and taxing	Y
Approve civil rights bill	Y
1989	
Halt production of B-2 stealth bomber at 13 planes	Y
Oppose capital gains tax cut	N
Approve federal abortion funding in rape or incest cases	Y
Approve pay raise and revision of ethics rules	Y
Pass Democratic minimum wage plan over Bush veto	Y

Voting Studies

	Presidential Support		Party Unity		Conservative Coalition	
Year	**S**	**O**	**S**	**O**	**S**	**O**
1990	16	83	92	2	11	89
1989	29	64	93	2	7	93
1988	20	78	92	2	11	89
1987	13 †	83 †	93 †	4 †	12 †	79 †
1986	22	76	95	5	20	80
1985	21	76	95	3	13	85
1984	26	74	97	1	3	97
1983	16	84	95	4	8	88
1982	40	60	91	8	32	67
1981	50	47	84	13	25	71

† Not eligible for all recorded votes.

Interest Group Ratings

Year	ADA	ACU	AFL-CIO	CCUS
1990	94	0	92	15
1989	95	11	91	50
1988	95	4	93	31
1987	92	0	100	7
1986	95	5	79	18
1985	80	5	94	18
1984	90	0	100	38
1983	95	0	100	20
1982	80	0	90	23
1981	80	0	93	32

14 John T. Doolittle (R)

Of Rocklin — Elected 1990

Born: Oct. 30, 1950, Glendale, Calif.
Education: U. of California, Santa Cruz, B.A. 1972; U. of the Pacific, J.D. 1978.
Occupation: Lawyer.
Family: Wife, Julia Harlow; one child.
Religion: Mormon.
Political Career: Calif. Senate, 1981-91.
Capitol Office: 1223 Longworth Bldg. 20515; 225-2511.

The Path to Washington: Doolittle stands out as the most conservative member of the House class of 1990. A spokesman for conservative causes during a 10-year tenure in the California Senate, Doolittle has fervent supporters who view him as a future leader of the Republican Party.

Doolittle also has a number of detractors who see him as an ideologue and a hardball politician. The former group helped Doolittle win three state Senate elections and his 1990 election to succeed retiring Republican Rep. Norman D. Shumway, who served six terms. But the latter group lined up with Democratic candidate Patricia Malberg.

As a result, Doolittle carried the usually Republican 14th District with just 51 percent of the vote and a margin of 7,297 votes.

Doolittle, who was elected to the state Senate in 1980 at age 30, established himself as an outspoken conservative activist. He freely attacked "tax-and-spend liberals" and accused the Legislature's Democratic majority of having a zeal for burdensome regulation of business.

It was on social issues that Doolittle made his strongest impression. He became a leading opponent of abortion and of gay-rights legislation. He called for widespread testing for AIDS and advocated strict limits on confidentiality for those diagnosed as carrying the AIDS virus.

Doolittle's outspokenness made him a leader of the Republican right in the Senate, helping him win the chairmanship of the Senate Republican Caucus.

However, to many Democrats and even to more moderate members of his own party, Doolittle was seen as an ambitious demagogue.

In March 1990, the *California Journal* published an unscientific survey of state legislators and their staffs, lobbyists and journalists, who rated the legislators on a variety of qualities. Doolittle, by a wide margin, was rated the least flexible of the 40 Senate members.

Doolittle's campaign tactics were controversial. During his 1984 Senate campaign, a Doolittle campaign consultant lent assistance to the Democratic candidate in an effort to siphon votes from an independent who threatened Doolittle's re-election.

The California Fair Political Practices Commission found Doolittle negligent for overlooking the activities and fined him $3,000.

In 1988, Doolittle was criticized for blaming his Democratic opponent, a county sheriff, for the death of an alleged drug dealer who had jumped from a police car traveling 40 miles per hour.

Doolittle, who spent more than $1 million on that campaign, won re-election with 54 percent of the vote and entered the 1990 House contest with a large political base.

The Republican also benefited from the GOP tilt in the 14th, which gave 59 percent of its vote to George Bush in 1988.

However, Doolittle also faced a determined opponent in Malberg, who took 37 percent against Shumway in 1988 but never stopped campaigning.

Trying to catch a wave of anti-incumbent sentiment among voters, Malberg played up her extensive grass-roots effort, contrasting it with what she predicted would be a big-money, PAC-financed campaign by Doolittle.

Doolittle created a stir with his first campaign TV ad. Calling for a constitutional ban on flag-burning, Doolittle narrated that the American flag has been honored from "the Fourth of July parade to a place called Vietnam."

This angered some Vietnam veterans, who noted that Doolittle during the war had taken a student deferment, then served as a Mormon missionary in Argentina.

However, several veterans' groups, which had supported Doolittle's previous campaigns, came to his defense.

The district's conservative tone may have given Doolittle his ultimate edge. In debates Doolittle spoke out in favor of the death penalty, nuclear power, offshore oil drilling and construction of a dam near Auburn; he spoke against abortion. Malberg took the opposing position on each issue.

California 14

Northeastern California — Part of San Joaquin County

The 14th is California's most rural district, a long stretch of farmland, mountains, forests and lakes. It reaches 300 miles south from the Oregon border to San Joaquin County in the heart of California's Central Valley.

The district's rural nature gives it a Republican coloration. Ronald Reagan and George Bush swept all the district's counties in the presidential elections of the 1980s.

Republican Pete Wilson similarly dominated the 14th in his 1988 Senate reelection bid, and in his 1990 gubernatorial campaign.

The district is bottom-heavy, with San Joaquin County (part of which is in the 18th) providing a third of its vote. Stockton, an important inland port as well as a marketing center for the surrounding farm country, has been growing: Its population jumped by nearly 23 percent, to 183,000, between 1980 and 1986.

The rich delta lands of San Joaquin County raise asparagus, avocados, walnuts, artichokes, peaches and apricots. Some of this produce is processed and packaged in Lodi, a city of 44,000 that anchors the northern part of the county.

Just to the north are Amador and El Dorado counties, once the core of California's Gold Rush country. It was at Sutter's Sawmill, at what is now Coloma in El Dorado County, that gold was discovered in 1848, sparking the rise of numerous boom towns. Placerville, El Dorado's county seat, at one time rivaled San Francisco and Sacramento.

The boom ended long ago, and the towns faded. But some have recently revived, as refugees from the cities and suburbs, attracted by the Victorian houses and natural setting, moved in. Four of California's eight fastest growing counties — Amador, El Dorado, Nevada, and Placer — are located in the Sierra Nevada foothills at the southern end of the district. There is also a thriving recreational industry in the Lake Tahoe-Squaw Valley region near the Nevada border. Also in the area is Alpine County, which with 1,300 residents is by far the state's smallest.

Closer to Oregon, the counties are heavily forested and sparsely populated, given over largely to lumbering. Much of the land is in the national forest system.

Population: 526,030. White 476,228 (91%), Black 6,731 (1%), Other 18,546 (4%). Spanish origin 46,968 (9%). 18 and over 381,713 (73%), 65 and over 58,543 (11%). Median age: 32.

Committees

Interior & Insular Affairs (15th of 17 Republicans)
Energy & the Environment; General Oversight & California Desert Lands; Water, Power & Offshore Energy

Merchant Marine & Fisheries (16th of 17 Republicans)
Fisheries & Wildlife Conservation & the Environment; Merchant Marine

Elections

1990 General

John T. Doolittle (R)	128,039	(51%)
Patricia Malberg (D)	120,742	(49%)

District Vote For President

	1988	1984	1980	1976
D	111,570 (40%)	86,619 (34%)	61,102 (31%)	56,518 (48%)
R	165,850 (59%)	162,239 (64%)	112,499 (58%)	60,700 (51%)

Campaign Finance

	Receipts	Receipts from PACs	Expend-itures
1990			
Doolittle (R)	$529,813	$234,764 (44%)	$517,668
Malberg (D)	$222,011	$45,911 (21%)	$220,379

Key Vote

1991

Authorize use of force against Iraq Y

15 Gary Condit (D)

Of Ceres — Elected 1989

Born: April 21, 1948, Salina, Okla.

Education: California State College, Stanislaus, B.A. 1972.

Occupation: Public official.

Family: Wife, Carolyn Berry; two children.

Religion: Baptist.

Political Career: Ceres City Council, 1972-76, mayor of Ceres, 1974-76; Stanislaus County Board of Supervisors, 1976-82, chairman, 1980; Calif. Assembly, 1983-89.

Capitol Office: 1529 Longworth Bldg. 20515; 225-6131.

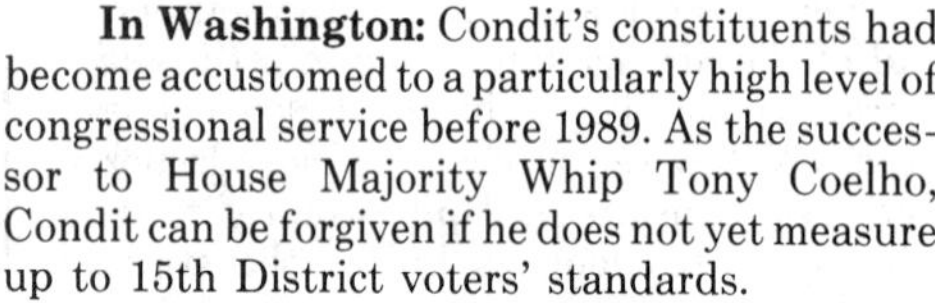

In Washington: Condit's constituents had become accustomed to a particularly high level of congressional service before 1989. As the successor to House Majority Whip Tony Coelho, Condit can be forgiven if he does not yet measure up to 15th District voters' standards.

Coelho had risen to the No. 3 post in the House Democratic hierarchy and was a prominent player on the Agriculture Committee, defending the Central Valley's dairy and water interests. But faced with questions about his personal finances, Coelho resigned his House seat in 1989. Condit lacks Coelho's clout, and he has yet to demonstrate a comparable grasp of the complicated issues under his purview.

Coelho's absence was palpable when the Agriculture Committee considered the 1990 farm bill. Livestock and Dairy Subcommittee leaders availed themselves of their newfound opportunity to skewer California's dairy industry and barred a generous subsidy available only in California. Coelho had repelled similar attacks during the 1985 farm bill, but in 1990, Condit's objections were dismissed.

Condit registered greater success elsewhere, winning House approval of his proposal to add seven miles of the Merced River to the federal Wild and Scenic River program. The legislation died; he planned to reintroduce it in the 102nd Congress. During consideration of a federal job-training program in 1990, Condit offered an amendment to increase the participation of migrant and seasonal farmworkers in the Job Training Partnership Act. The amendment was adopted by voice vote, but the bill perished in the Senate.

At Home: While Coelho's downfall led to a dramatic change in the House leadership, the succession in the 15th District was almost routine. Condit, a popular state assemblyman, was a logical choice for district Democrats and an easy winner in the September 1989 special election to succeed Coelho.

Candidates rarely have the best wishes of their political adversaries when they seek higher office. However, Democratic state Assembly Speaker Willie L. Brown Jr. was glad to see Condit — who had recently challenged his leadership — go to Washington.

Condit was a member of the "Gang of Five," a group of moderate-to-conservative Assembly Democrats who bridled at the liberal Brown's ironhanded rule. In May 1988, the "Gang" launched an effort to remove Brown as Speaker. But the move failed, and the rebels found themselves stripped of leadership positions, choice committee assignments and other perks.

Brown's retaliation appeared to short-circuit Condit's political rise. An Oklahoma native and the son of a Baptist preacher, Condit was first elected to local office in his conservative, farm-oriented home base at age 24, and served six years on the Stanislaus County Board of Supervisors prior to his 1982 election to the Assembly. By the end of his first term, Condit was named assistant Assembly majority leader; two years later, he became chairman of the Government Organization Committee.

The "Gang of Five" debacle cost Condit with the Assembly Democratic Caucus — but not in his conservative, mainly white Central Valley district. Condit ran unopposed for the Assembly in 1988, and became the frontrunner for the House following Coelho's resignation.

Condit faced seven other contenders in the open-ballot special election. His hold on his Democratic base was strengthened by support from Coelho, who remained locally popular despite his ethics problems. His main rival was Clare Berryhill, one of three Republicans on the ballot. A district farmer, former state legislator and a one-time director of the state Food and Agriculture Department, Berryhill tried to appeal to the district's farm constituency. But his efforts were blunted by the strength of Condit's personal base: The Democrat defeated Berryhill by 57 percent to 35 percent.

Condit's strong showing deterred Republicans from putting up much of a effort in 1990.

California 15

Mid-San Joaquin Valley — Modesto

The level, fertile fields of the 15th District connect two major farm centers of the San Joaquin Valley — Modesto in the north and Fresno in the south. The farmers of the valley have a Democratic heritage spawned in the Oklahoma Dust Bowl era and brought west to California more than a generation ago. In early 1989, voter registration in the 15th stood at 55 percent Democratic, 36 percent Republican.

But even as Coelho won re-election comfortably through the 1980s, the national Democratic Party was not doing so well in the 15th. The district voted for Ronald Reagan for president in 1980 and 1984, and George Bush won it 52-47 percent over Michael S. Dukakis in 1988.

At the northern end of the district are the 165,000 residents of Modesto. The largest city wholly within the district, Modesto is most often remembered for its restless teenagers in the movie "American Graffiti" and for its winery run by the Gallo Brothers. In the 1980s, the city become home for an increasing number of San Francisco Bay-area exurbanites; they helped boost Modesto's population by 54 percent in the 1980s.

The city has long been a processing and canning center for the crops flowing in from the surrounding fields. Although hard economic times in the early 1980s closed down some of the factories in the city, the opening of two tomato processing plants in nearby Los Banos compensated for much of the loss.

More than 100 miles south along Highway 99 is Fresno. Though nearly all the city is outside the 15th, it is the major media center for the southern part of the district. The 15th curves around the city from the south, taking in its outskirts on three sides.

Between Fresno and Modesto, the district is sparsely settled. Merced, with 56,000 people, is the only other major city. The influx of Hmong refugees from Laos into the Central Valley has strained Merced's services; but with the city's population now about one-fifth Hmong, it has also enjoyed a cultural flowering of Southeast Asian restaurants and craft fairs.

The rest of the 15th's population is scattered throughout the irrigated farm land, where more than 200 different commodities are grown. Besides large concentrations of agribusiness, the district is dotted with smaller dairy farms and vineyards. As in some other parts of the country, successive years of drought have caused problems for farmers. In addition to suffering lower crop yields, the agricultural sector has had to pay higher utility costs because of the need to pump water from increasingly drier wells. Grape growers have also been buffeted by imports of European wines and raisins.

Population: 525,949. White 425,244 (81%), Black 11,779 (2%), Other 16,082 (3%). Spanish origin 127,576 (24%). 18 and over 361,570 (69%), 65 and over 53,130 (10%). Median age: 28.

Committees

Agriculture (24th of 27 Democrats)
Cotton, Rice & Sugar; Livestock, Dairy & Poultry

Government Operations (19th of 25 Democrats)
Government Activities & Transportation; Government Information, Justice & Agriculture

Elections

1990 General		
Gary Condit (D)	97,147	(66%)
Cliff Burris (R)	49,634	(34%)
1989 Special		
Gary Condit (D)	51,543	(57%)
Clare Berryhill (R)	31,592	(35%)
Cliff Burris (R)	2,385	(3%)
Robert J. Weimer (R)	2,939	(3%)

District Vote For President

	1988		1984		1980		1976	
D	82,799	(47%)	70,069	(40%)	58,104	(41%)	63,302	(52%)
R	92,471	(52%)	101,657	(59%)	69,712	(49%)	55,963	(46%)

Campaign Finance

	Receipts	Receipts from PACs		Expend-itures
1990				
Condit (D)	$234,423	$74,970	(32%)	$212,430
Burris (R)	$31,920	0		$30,963

Key Votes

1991	
Authorize use of force against Iraq	Y
1990	
Support constitutional amendment on flag desecration	Y
Pass family and medical leave bill over Bush veto	Y
Reduce SDI funding	Y
Allow abortions in overseas military facilities	Y
Approve budget summit plan for spending and taxing	N
Approve civil rights bill	Y
1989	
Oppose capital gains tax cut	Y
Approve federal abortion funding in rape or incest cases	Y
Approve pay raise and revision of ethics rules	N

Voting Studies

	Presidential Support		Party Unity		Conservative Coalition	
Year	**S**	**O**	**S**	**O**	**S**	**O**
1990	25	70	70	24	54	44
1989	35 †	65 †	83 †	10 †	25 †	75 †

† Not eligible for all recorded votes.

Interest Group Ratings

Year	ADA	ACU	AFL-CIO	CCUS
1990	56	29	67	36
1989	-	33	100	50

16 Leon E. Panetta (D)

Of Carmel Valley — Elected 1976

Born: June 28, 1938, Monterey, Calif.
Education: U. of Santa Clara, B.A. 1960; J.D. 1963.
Military Service: Army, 1963-65.
Occupation: Lawyer.
Family: Wife, Sylvia Marie Varni; three children.
Religion: Roman Catholic.
Political Career: No previous office.
Capitol Office: 339 Cannon Bldg. 20515; 225-2861.

In Washington: With his reflexive laugh and ready smile, Panetta almost always seems to be in a good mood. Sometimes it's hard to figure why. Panetta serves as chairman of the House Budget Committee, a job for which he spent his first dozen years in Congress preparing. He presides over a budget process that, for all his hard and sincere work, yields mostly frustration and bad news.

Panetta invested monumental effort and personal prestige in the 1990 budget summit negotiations between congressional leaders and President Bush, a process that dragged on for four and a half months. When an agreement was reached late in September, angry House members from both parties — frustrated at having been left out of the process and furious over proposed Medicare cuts and tax increases — rejected the summit product on a floor vote of 179-254.

A successor agreement was cobbled together and cleared within a few days, but the sting of the rebuke remained. Panetta has said he believes the mechanism he and other summit negotiators crafted in 1990 will ultimately bring the deficit down, even if the immediate fiscal results were disheartening: deficits almost half again as high as the previous record.

Sometimes even an optimist can be overcome with gloom. "I never see the light at the end of the tunnel," he mused aloud at a House Budget hearing in January 1991. "Everybody predicts it, but we never get there. We never get there. There's something fundamentally wrong."

It was an uncharacteristically dark moment. Besides an unsurpassed knowledge of the budget process — what information he does not carry in his head is tucked within a bulging file that is a constant companion as he stalks the Capitol corridors — Panetta usually conveys the sense that somehow everything can eventually work out.

For all his self-effacement, Panetta knows well that all policy and politics these days must bow to the imperative of deficit reduction; the Budget chairmanship puts him at the center of congressional and Democratic Party action, just where he wants to be. "Through the budget," he once said, "you are making a statement about where the nation is at, and where you want it to go."

As a converted, moderate-to-liberal Democrat who was director of the Office of Civil Rights in Richard M. Nixon's administration, Panetta is a consensus-builder not generally known for partisanship. But the House is inescapably partisan, and the Budget Committee is the first place the Democrats' agenda gets set in the new legislative year. Committee Republicans say Panetta made overtures about putting together a bipartisan fiscal 1992 budget but soon broke off talks and produced a Democratic blueprint instead.

Panetta assumed the Budget chair in 1989, just as Democratic congressional leaders were joined at the negotiating table by a new and professedly more conciliatory Republican president. Panetta began by praising Bush's choice for budget director, Richard G. Darman, as a signal that the president was ready to deal.

But then he dismissed the first Bush budget, which proposed major cuts without specifying where reductions would come, as "a potential trap" that "left the tough choices to Congress." He insisted that Bush and Darman supply the politically painful details before Democrats would negotiate. The 1989 process dragged on into late November, complicated by a messy subplot concerning the tax on capital gains. In the end, an agreement was reached and ratified by the two chambers.

In 1990, however, the negotiating road took yet a new turn when Bush agreed to negotiate at the summit level with congressional leaders beginning in May. This time the sticking point was the general topic of new revenue, and in June, under heavy pressure from the Democratic leaders, Bush admitted that taxes would have to be raised. The shift, regarded as a reneging on his campaign antitax pledge, produced the sharpest division within the Republican Party in more than a decade.

But if House Republicans were incensed by

California 16

Central Coast — Salinas; Monterey

The 16th District follows a scenic highway, state Route 1, for 150 miles along the California coast. Tourism brings in much of the income in the coastal areas. As the district moves inland, agriculture is the major trade.

The 16th takes in San Benito County and part of San Luis Obispo County. But the population is centered in Monterey and Santa Cruz counties, where 80 percent of the district vote is cast.

Panetta has come to dominate through the entire district, easily sweeping all four counties in recent elections. Presidential contests are more competitive.

Though Santa Cruz County experienced considerable growth during the 1980s — population grew by 22 percent — its people will most likely remember its geological changes. In addition to the flooding and landslides of the early 1980s, Santa Cruz was devastated by the 1989 Loma Prieta earthquake; for the fifth time in 10 years, the county was declared a federal disaster area.

The county's Democratic tone is set by its namesake city, the site of a University of California campus. The student vote in Santa Cruz (population 49,000) is complemented by the city's long-lived countercultural community, a laid-back throwback to the 1960s.

Santa Cruz is located at the northern end of Monterey Bay. Moving south, the district picks up some more conservative territory, including Castroville. Just north of Monterey, Fort Ord, a major military base that employs a large civilian work force, was included in the 1991 base-closure plan.

Exclusive Monterey Peninsula has drawn liberal Democrats and upper-income Republicans. A little farther south is Big Sur, another gathering spot for the mellow. But life in the 16th District is not all fun and games. The vagaries of the coastal fishing industry were depicted by John Steinbeck in "Cannery Row."

Inland, lettuce fields and almond groves make agriculture king. Salinas, the Monterey County seat and the district's largest city with 109,000 residents, leans Republican for president, but not dramatically so: Bush won the city in 1988 by only 134 votes.

Population: 526,120. White 401,920 (76%), Black 20,897 (4%), Asian and Pacific Islander 26,169 (5%), Other 4,793 (1%). Spanish origin 115,776 (22%). 18 and over 391,002 (74%), 65 and over 58,955 (11%). Median age: 29.1

Bush's cave-in on taxes, House Democrats were displeased with the apportionment of the new taxes among income groups — as well as by the latest round of program cuts. So when the budget came to the floor in October, all the efforts of Panetta, his budget colleagues, the party leaders and the White House could not persuade a majority to approve it.

Panetta and the others went back to the drawing board in the final days of the session and brought forth the current "pay as you go" approach, which in the middle-to-long term should enforce a rough sort of discipline. In theory, at least, members now cannot propose spending without a corresponding spending cut or tax increase to finance it.

If it does, Panetta will be that rare specimen: the congressman who did his job well enough to lessen its importance in the future.

During his first stint on Budget, for six years until 1985, Panetta was a voice for deficit-conscious junior Democrats. That year he was a favorite to win the chairmanship, but his bid snagged on House Democratic rules and leadership politics. By a close vote, the Democratic Caucus decided against waiving its three-term limit on Budget Committee membership. The chairmanship went instead to Rep. William H. Gray III of Pennsylvania, who held it for two terms before moving on to be caucus chairman and then Democratic whip.

In the meantime, Panetta did not retreat. Over the next four years, he remained prominent in budget debates and did so largely as a sort of institutional minister without portfolio for House leaders.

In late 1985, he was a key House bargainer with the Senate and President Ronald Reagan in negotiating what became the Gramm-Rudman-Hollings budget-balancing law. Two years later, he helped draft the budget-summit agreement between Reagan and Congress that raised taxes and cut spending in both fiscal 1988 and 1989.

By that time, in late 1987, Panetta was the uncontested heir apparent to succeed Gray, although it was more than a year before House Democrats would vote. Two would-be rivals, liberal David R. Obey of Wisconsin and conservative Marvin Leath of Texas, had dropped their own bids after they plumbed and discovered the depth of Panetta's support.

Although Budget has been his focus, Panetta has made a mark as a senior member of the Agriculture Committee, which is important to the farming and processing industries in his district, and of the House Administration Committee, the institution's housekeeping arm.

In the 100th Congress, as chairman of the House Administration Subcommittee on Personnel, Panetta won House approval of rules extending civil rights laws to House employees. The action, limited as it was, constituted a first step toward eventual coverage of all congressional staff under other labor-protection laws governing wages, hours and conditions.

On Agriculture, he helped shape the five-year 1985 farm bill and, in 1986, a landmark immigration law. Representing California growers traditionally dependent on illegal alien workers, Panetta worked arduously with fellow Californian Howard L. Berman and New Yorker Charles E. Schumer to craft an immigration law providing for a continued flow of unskilled workers while protecting those laborers against abuse. Since then, the sponsors have cooperated to monitor and fine-tune the law's implementation.

His bipartisan work on the nutrition and food stamp provisions of the 1985 farm bill helped Panetta restore some bridges to Republicans that had been badly damaged in a bitter dispute over a 1984 Indiana House race. Democratic leaders, unwilling to seat Republican Richard D. McIntyre despite his apparent victory over Democratic incumbent Frank McCloskey, appointed Panetta to head a recount committee.

The panel ruled McCloskey the victor by four votes, contrary to Panetta's expectations. Nevertheless, Republicans aimed their fire at him; a task force member accused him of political "rape" and other Republicans questioned his integrity on the House floor. Perhaps the only consolation for Panetta was that the episode dispelled any lingering doubts among fellow Democrats about his party loyalty. Panetta has been a Democrat for two decades now, since shortly after he was dismissed from the Nixon administration's Office of Civil Rights for complaining about its slow desegregation efforts. Yet he is not so different from the liberal Republican he once was. His mix of liberal social policy and fiscal conservatism would easily win the approval of his political hero, California's former Republican governor and later U.S. Chief Justice Earl Warren, whose autographed picture hangs on Panetta's office wall.

He is also active on environmental issues, and during the Reagan years led the fight to protect California's coastal waters from oil and gas drilling. He has long espoused a national youth service and conservation corps. On defense and foreign policy, Panetta's views mesh easily with those of other House Democrats.

An opponent of the Reagan administration's military aid for the Nicaraguan contras, Panetta sponsored House resolutions in 1986 and 1988 calling for inquiries into how funds were spent. The first probe found millions of dollars unaccounted for; Panetta withdrew the 1988 resolution when federal officials satisfied him that aid was being spent according to law. Three years before, Panetta had been one of the first members of Congress to suggest publicly that White House aide Lt. Col. Oliver L. North was illegally providing aid to the contras — more than a year before the Iran-contra scandal broke.

At Home: Panetta's centrist politics, rising influence in Congress and attentions to his constituents have proved to be a formidable combination. Since he took 53 percent of the vote in ousting Republican incumbent Burt Talcott in 1976, Panetta has made his seat a safe one.

In 1990, a year that saw a general decline in vote margins for California House members, Panetta crushed his GOP opponent with 74 percent of the vote.

Although Panetta had been close to politics all his adult life — as an aide to GOP Sen. Thomas Kuchel, then with HEW, and later as an adviser to New York City Mayor John V. Lindsay — he did not run for public office until 1976.

By that time, Talcott had been in Washington for 14 years. In the previous two elections, a Hispanic candidate, Julian Camacho, had whittled Talcott's margin down to just 2,000 votes, making the incumbent a prime target for Democrats in 1976. Camacho opted against a third try, allowing Panetta to battle two other Democrats for the party's nomination.

Panetta was attacked for being a latecomer to the Democratic Party. But his most active primary opponent, John R. Bakalian, had serious problems of his own. He was viewed outside liberal Santa Cruz as being a bit too unconventional for the district's tastes. Bakalian wanted to impeach President Gerald R. Ford for allowing Secretary of State Henry A. Kissinger to threaten an invasion of Cuba.

Although Bakalian carried Santa Cruz County, Panetta won the nomination with a strong showing in Monterey. In the general election, Panetta kept Talcott on the defensive, saying the incumbent had little to show for his years in Congress. Stressing his roots in the Monterey area, Panetta narrowly defeated Talcott there, and beat him more decisively in Santa Cruz and San Luis Obispo counties.

Since then Panetta has continued to run far ahead of the district's Democratic registration.

Just before the 98th Congress began, Panetta caused a stir by jeopardizing the congressional remap Democrats had drawn up for the 1984 elections. The plan had to pass the state Legislature by the end of a special session in December 1982 if it was to be signed into law by Democratic Gov. Edmund G. Brown Jr. before he relinquished control to his Republican replacement. But Panetta was upset by the removal of the northern section of Santa Cruz County from his district and argued that the county should not be split.

Panetta prevailed upon the state senator from the area, Democrat Henry Mello, to try to amend the map; Mello's work in the Senate to accommodate Panetta helped hold up passage of the bill until the eleventh hour. However, the flap caused Panetta few lasting hard feelings among Democratic political insiders.

Committees

Budget (Chairman)

Agriculture (6th of 27 Democrats)
Department Operations, Research & Foreign Agriculture; Domestic Marketing, Consumer Relations & Nutrition; Forests, Family Farms & Energy

House Administration (4th of 15 Democrats)
Elections; Personnel & Police; Campaign Finance Reform

Select Hunger (2nd of 22 Democrats)
Domestic

Elections

1990 General		
Leon E. Panetta (D)	134,236	(74%)
Jerry M. Reiss (R)	39,885	(22%)
Brian H. Tucker (LIBERT)	6,881	(4%)
1990 Primary		
Leon E. Panetta (D)	65,159	(93%)
Arthur V. Dunn (D)	4,848	(7%)
1988 General		
Leon E. Panetta (D)	177,452	(79%)
Stanley Monteith (R)	48,375	(21%)

Previous Winning Percentages: **1986** (78%) **1984** (71%)
1982 (84%) **1980** (71%) **1978** (61%) **1976** (53%)

District Vote For President

	1988	1984	1980	1976
D	122,419 (54%)	98,292 (46%)	64,688 (36%)	75,713 (50%)
R	100,293 (44%)	111,375 (53%)	87,820 (49%)	73,818 (49%)

Campaign Finance

	Receipts	Receipts from PACs	Expend-itures
1990			
Panetta (D)	$295,399	$133,750 (45%)	$272,710
Reiss (R)	$23,939	0	$23,849
1988			
Panetta (D)	$318,076	$112,600 (35%)	$252,336
Monteith (R)	$71,035	0	$69,563

Key Votes

1991	
Authorize use of force against Iraq	N
1990	
Support constitutional amendment on flag desecration	N
Pass family and medical leave bill over Bush veto	Y
Reduce SDI funding	Y
Allow abortions in overseas military facilities	Y
Approve budget summit plan for spending and taxing	Y
Approve civil rights bill	Y
1989	
Halt production of B-2 stealth bomber at 13 planes	Y
Oppose capital gains tax cut	Y
Approve federal abortion funding in rape or incest cases	Y
Approve pay raise and revision of ethics rules	Y
Pass Democratic minimum wage plan over Bush veto	Y

Voting Studies

	Presidential Support		Party Unity		Conservative Coalition	
Year	**S**	**O**	**S**	**O**	**S**	**O**
1990	20	78	89	7	17	80
1989	31	67	91	7	15	85
1988	22	75	90	6	18	76
1987	16	81	91	4	21	79
1986	20	77	87	9	30	66
1985	20	79	88 †	8 †	25	71
1984	31	66	86	14	25	75
1983	20	79	85 †	10 †	21	78
1982	42	55	86	14	36	63
1981	50	50	78	22	45	55

† Not eligible for all recorded votes.

Interest Group Ratings

Year	ADA	ACU	AFL-CIO	CCUS
1990	83	8	83	21
1989	95	7	91	30
1988	90	4	93	33
1987	92	0	87	20
1986	85	11	85	31
1985	75	14	71	32
1984	75	8	54	50
1983	90	9	82	30
1982	75	5	90	18
1981	90	20	80	16

17 Calvin Dooley (D)

Of Visalia — Elected 1990

Born: Jan. 11, 1954, Visalia, Calif.
Education: U. of California, Davis, B.S. 1977; Stanford U., M.A. 1987.
Occupation: Farmer.
Family: Wife, Linda Phillips; two children.
Religion: Protestant.
Political Career: No previous office.
Capitol Office: 1022 Longworth Bldg. 20515; 225-3341.

The Path to Washington: Dooley's family has been farming in California's Central Valley for four generations, growing everything from alfalfa to cotton to walnuts. Most recently, the family has raised a fair crop of political activists.

Well before Dooley himself decided on 1990 as his year to seek elective office, his brother and sister-in-law had become senior aides to former Gov. Edmund G. Brown Jr. The family name has become familiar as Dooley's brother and parents have served on public boards and party committees.

Dooley had another important connection in politics as a former aide to state Sen. Rose Ann Vuich, a Fresno Democrat legendary for her constituent service. The Vuich persona helped him overcome the more liberal flavor of his relatives' politics, particularly their ties to Brown and Rose Bird, the former chief justice of the California Supreme Court whom voters ousted in 1986.

In 1990, Dooley sidestepped not only his personal associations with party liberals but also the issue at the heart of the coastal liberals' agenda: the "Big Green" environmental initiative. Dooley opposed the sweeping conservation measure, preferring the farmers' alternative that permitted wider use of pesticides.

Still, no one would have confused Dooley's campaign with that of a Republican. He regularly put forward the sociological sorrows of rural Tulare and Fresno counties, where even in good times the rates of unemployment, crime, pregnancy and disease run far ahead of state averages.

Well before committee assignments were made, Dooley knew his would include the Agriculture Committee. He got that assurance from no less a source than Speaker Thomas S. Foley, a man who knows firsthand how such a seat can help a Democrat hold a rural, Republican-flavored district. Dooley made considerable use of that promise in his campaign. But with all due respect to his family, Vuich and Foley, the man who helped Dooley most was the incumbent he defeated, Charles "Chip" Pashayan, Jr. The six-termer from Fresno committed two classic errors, and Dooley showed strong instincts in exploiting his openings on both.

Pashayan's first misstep followed his 71 percent-share victory in 1988. At last confident that he would not face major opposition for re-election, Pashayan left the Interior Committee, where he had been a mainstay of the subcommittee in charge of water projects critical to farming in the Central Valley.

Second, and far worse, Pashayan responded in low-key, "let it blow over" fashion to the festering savings and loan scandal in 1989. Instead of blowing over, the scandal blew up; and Pashayan's own limited involvement was made to look deep and damning.

Dooley made an issue of Pashayan's $26,000 in contributions from S&L kingpin Charles H. Keating Jr. and his family and associates. He made an issue of Pashayan's efforts to loosen regulations affecting a Keating institution. But the clinching factor may have been Pashayan's own less-than-complete explanations of his connections to Keating and efforts in his behalf.

Even with the overarching significance of the Keating matter, Dooley's victory owed much to basic campaigning. He concentrated on rural Tulare and Fresno counties, stressing his roots in the soil and his agribusiness degree. But he also presented himself well as a sophisticated alternative to Pashayan among the upwardly mobile swing voters of Fresno's more affluent neighborhoods, stressing his study at the Stanford Graduate School of Business.

As a freshman whose district borders on that of two more senior Democrats, Dooley will have his hands full preventing damage in the 1991 redistricting. But if he can keep his district lines roughly co-terminous with Vuich's and reproduce her coalition in his own style, he could become the latest symbol of the GOP's longstanding frustration in California.

California 17

Southern San Joaquin Valley

The 17th is the food basket of the nation's most agriculturally productive state. Driving the length of the district from Fresno in the north to Bakersfield in the south, a traveler encounters fields of virtually every kind of fruit and vegetable grown in the Temperate Zone.

Though the district abuts both Fresno and Bakersfield, the majority of the population lives in smaller communities, including farm centers like Tulare and Visalia, with fewer than 75,000 people, and dusty crossroads towns like Pixley and Lemoncove. But Fresno is the wellspring of money and power; prior to Dooley's election, the 17th had been represented by a Fresno-based congressman since the mid-1960s.

The irrigated farmland stretches almost to the eastern border of the district, where the Sierra Nevada Mountains climb steeply into Sequoia National Park. The mountains attract some recreational dollars into the district, but in minuscule amounts compared with the valley's farm income.

There is a rural, conservative Democratic tradition among some of those whose livelihoods depend on the farm economy. With an eye on water issues, they are notorious ticket-splitters; Dooley, a Kings County farmer, won every county in the 17th in 1990 while gubernatorial candidate GOP Sen. Pete Wilson beat Democrat Dianne Feinstein handily in each. Low-income Hispanics, based in Bakersfield, help keep Democrats competitive in the Kern County portion of the 17th.

But George Bush easily carried the 17th in 1988. In Tulare County — which competes with Fresno County for the largest share of the district vote — Bush took 60 percent of the vote. He was continuing a firmly established pattern in favor of Republican presidential candidates. Ronald Reagan carried the district in both 1980 and 1984, taking 63 percent of the vote in the latter campaign.

Population: 526,033. White 392,665 (75%), Black 10,974 (2%), Other 20,245 (4%). Spanish origin 146,304 (28%). 18 and over 356,229 (68%), 65 and over 50,303 (10%). Median age: 28.

Committees

Agriculture (26th of 27 Democrats)
Cotton, Rice & Sugar; Department Operations, Research & Foreign Agriculture; Domestic Marketing, Consumer Relations & Nutrition; Livestock, Dairy & Poultry

Small Business (26th of 27 Democrats)
Regulation, Business Opportunity & Energy

Campaign Finance

	Receipts	Receipts from PACs		Expend-itures
1990				
Dooley (D)	$547,763	$171,185	(31%)	$538,354
Pashayan (R)	$557,949	$283,684	(51%)	$622,184

Key Vote

1991

Authorize use of force against Iraq	N

Elections

1990 General		
Calvin Dooley (D)	82,611	(55%)
Charles "Chip" Pashayan Jr. (R)	68,848	(45%)
1990 Primary		
Calvin Dooley (D)	28,907	(59%)
Archie Nahigian (D)	13,736	(28%)
Paul M. Laygo (D)	6,641	(13%)

District Vote For President

	1988	1984	1980	1976
D	76,021 (40%)	65,892 (36%)	52,927 (36%)	52,327 (46%)
R	111,250 (59%)	116,975 (63%)	84,025 (57%)	61,548 (54%)

18 Richard H. Lehman (D)

Of Fresno — Elected 1982

Born: July 20, 1948, Sanger, Calif.
Education: Attended Fresno City College, 1968; California State U., Fresno, 1969; U. of California, Santa Cruz, B.A. 1970.
Military Service: Army National Guard, 1970-76.
Occupation: Legislative aide.
Family: Divorced.
Religion: Lutheran.
Political Career: Calif. Assembly, 1977-83.
Capitol Office: 1319 Longworth Bldg. 20515; 225-4540.

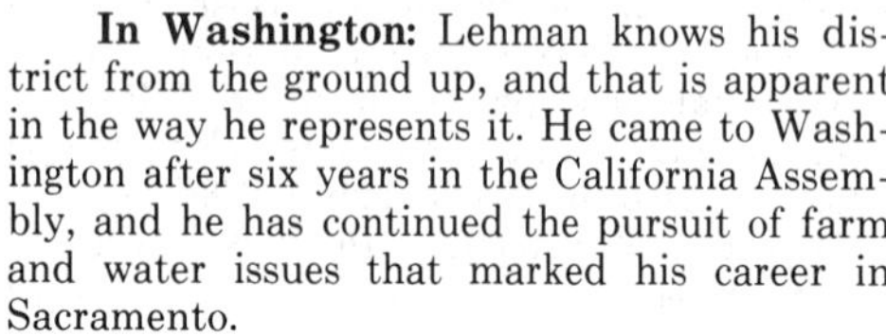

In Washington: Lehman knows his district from the ground up, and that is apparent in the way he represents it. He came to Washington after six years in the California Assembly, and he has continued the pursuit of farm and water issues that marked his career in Sacramento.

Now serving his fifth House term, Lehman has broadened his focus. In the 102nd Congress, he relinquished a Banking subcommittee chairmanship to take a seat on the powerful Energy and Commerce Committee. He also moved into an Interior subcommittee chair, and is serving as an at-large whip. (Lehman sticks with his party on partisan votes close to 90 percent of the time.)

Lehman has used his seat on the Interior Committee to advance legislation protecting his district's huge stretches of farmland and wilderness. He has proven adept at balancing the interests of growers and developers against those of farm workers and environmentalists.

During floor consideration in the 101st Congress of a bill authorizing water and power projects, the House adopted an amendment by California Democrat George Miller barring farm operations larger than 960 acres from receiving federally subsidized irrigation water. Lehman offered an amendment to specify that Miller's amendment would not apply to large farms run by family trusts. The House rejected it, 118-297.

On the Banking Committee, Lehman allied himself with the activist liberal, mid-tier committee Democrats who frequently clashed with Chairman Henry B. Gonzalez.

When the Financial Institutions Subcommittee considered a bill in 1989 to bail out and restructure the savings and loan industry, Lehman offered an amendment that would have preserved the rights of some 31 S&Ls to convert into banks and switch to banks' insurance fund. It was rejected, 17-28.

He and Wisconsin Democrat Gerald D. Kleczka introduced a deposit-insurance reform bill that would have limited insurance coverage to 100 percent of the first $50,000 put on deposit by an individual and 90 percent of the next $50,000. They reintroduced their bill in the 102nd Congress.

As chairman of the Consumer Affairs and Coinage Subcommittee in the 101st Congress, he pursued one of his favorite projects: the "Truth in Savings Act." The bill, which would set tougher standards for the disclosure of interest rates on savings accounts, passed the House in 1990. He introduced it for the sixth time in 1991. Also in the 101st Congress, Lehman opposed a move to redesign the back sides of the nation's coins.

At Home: Lehman's political rise was propelled by shrewd instincts worthy of a politician with twice his experience. During his years in the California Assembly, he showed the same ability to maneuver among competing interests that he has demonstrated in the House.

Lehman's style drew criticism: The *California Journal* once commented that he had "learned well the fine points of political one-upmanship, and thrives on its practice."

But his political agility also earned him the respect of his Democratic colleagues. The late Democratic Rep. Phillip Burton, who recast California's congressional map in 1981, drew the 18th with Lehman in mind — not so much because Lehman was a sure liberal ally, but because he would have been hard to stop.

Fueled by funding from local agribusiness, labor and education interests, and boasting an 80 percent approval rating from the California Farm Bureau, Lehman escaped even minor competition in the 1982 Democratic primary. He won easily that fall and has coasted since then. While other California House members worried about an "anti-incumbent" mood in 1990, Lehman was unopposed for re-election.

Lehman had been working for a Fresno-area state senator in 1975 when he joined with a small group of young political activists to run the successful Fresno City Council campaign of Dan Whitehurst. The following year, Lehman won his first of three state Assembly terms.

California 18

Central Valley; Fresno

A district of ungainly shape, the 18th's tentacles reach out in all directions for Democratic votes.

Most of the land is in four counties — Mono, Tuolumne, Calaveras and Madera — lightly populated and tilting Republican. The first three are in the southern gold country of the Sierra Nevadas; Madera County mixes timber and cattle raising.

But for Democratic map makers, these counties link two cities — Fresno and Stockton — that cast 70 percent of the 18th's vote and are reliably Democratic. The northeast corner of Fresno, in the 17th, tilts Republican.

Fresno, with a population of more than 354,000, is one of the most important agribusiness centers in the nation. Ever since a 1984 study ranked it as the least desirable place to live in America (largely due to its hot climate and high crime rate), civic boosters have been working to buff up the city's image. The efforts have achieved some success; Fresno posted a 63 percent population gain in the 1980s. Once a magnet for Armenians, Fresno is now absorbing Laotians, Vietnamese, Cambodians and Central Americans.

Stockton, in San Joaquin County, is split between the 18th and 14th districts, but the 18th has by far the larger portion. This city, too, is Democratic, but slightly less so than Fresno. It is the major canning and processing center for local crops.

Its odd shape does not make this an easy district in which to campaign. Stockton and Fresno, 115 miles apart and separated mainly by part of the 15th District, are served by different media markets.

Population: 525,990. White 379,833 (72%), Black 38,871 (7%), Other 24,853 (5%). Spanish origin 131,871 (25%). 18 and over 376,078 (71%), 65 and over 62,787 (12%). Median age: 29.

Committees

Energy & Commerce (26th of 27 Democrats)
Energy & Power; Telecommunications & Finance

Interior & Insular Affairs (12th of 29 Democrats)
General Oversight & California Desert Lands (chairman); Energy & the Environment

Elections

1990 General		
Richard H. Lehman (D)	98,804	(100%)
1988 General		
Richard H. Lehman (D)	125,715	(70%)
David A. Linn (R)	54,034	(30%)

Previous Winning Percentages: **1986** (71%) **1984** (67%) **1982** (60%)

District Vote For President

	1988	1984	1980	1976
D	101,146 (53%)	98,163 (48%)	72,927 (43%)	80,273 (55%)
R	88,016 (46%)	102,593 (51%)	81,436 (48%)	63,568 (44%)

Campaign Finance

	Receipts	Receipts from PACs	Expend-itures
1990			
Lehman (D)	$302,473	$201,780 (67%)	$299,728
1988			
Lehman (D)	$279,981	$131,276 (47%)	$193,681
Linn (R)	$89,428	$800 (1%)	$89,260

Key Votes

1991	
Authorize use of force against Iraq	Y
1990	
Support constitutional amendment on flag desecration	N
Pass family and medical leave bill over Bush veto	Y
Reduce SDI funding	Y
Allow abortions in overseas military facilities	Y
Approve budget summit plan for spending and taxing	N
Approve civil rights bill	Y
1989	
Halt production of B-2 stealth bomber at 13 planes	Y
Oppose capital gains tax cut	Y
Approve federal abortion funding in rape or incest cases	Y
Approve pay raise and revision of ethics rules	Y
Pass Democratic minimum wage plan over Bush veto	Y

Voting Studies

	Presidential Support		Party Unity		Conservative Coalition	
Year	S	O	S	O	S	O
1990	19	81	89	6	31	65
1989	29	63	92	3	12	83
1988	20	73	89	3	26	63
1987	16	83	91	3	19	79
1986	20	76	87	4	26	68
1985	16	74	83	3	20	71
1984	23	64	81	7	20	71
1983	22	76	91	4	15	79

Interest Group Ratings

Year	ADA	ACU	AFL-CIO	CCUS
1990	94	4	83	15
1989	90	0	100	40
1988	85	9	100	25
1987	92	0	94	7
1986	75	10	100	25
1985	80	0	88	15
1984	85	0	77	50
1983	80	0	100	30

19 Robert J. Lagomarsino (R)

Of Ventura — Elected 1974

Born: Sept. 4, 1926, Ventura, Calif.
Education: U. of California, Santa Barbara, B.A. 1950; U. of Santa Clara, LL.B. 1953.
Military Service: Navy, 1944-46.
Occupation: Lawyer.
Family: Wife, Norma Smith; three children.
Religion: Roman Catholic.
Political Career: Ojai City Council, 1958, mayor of Ojai, 1958-61; Calif. Senate, 1961-74.
Capitol Office: 2332 Rayburn Bldg. 20515; 225-3601.

In Washington: The ranch that was Ronald Reagan's second home during his White House years is located in the 19th District, represented by Lagomarsino. The conservative views held by these two local Republicans appear to be shared by the majority of district voters. GOP presidential candidates carry the 19th with regularity; for years, Lagomarsino too was an easy winner there.

However, there exists in the 19th a strong environmentalist movement that has its origins in a disastrous 1969 oil well blowout that fouled Santa Barbara's beaches. The increasing involvement of this "green" constituency in House politics caused Lagomarsino some anxiety in his last two House contests.

Democratic state Sen. Gary K. Hart held Lagomarsino to 51 percent of the vote in 1988. Two years later, against a much lesser-known Democratic candidate, Lagomarsino won with a modest 55 percent.

Since the 1960s, when he served in the California Senate, Lagomarsino has purveyed an image as environmentally conscious. After the 1969 oil spill, he called for a ban on drilling off Santa Barbara. After his election to the House, he got on the Interior Committee and worked to protect the Santa Barbara Channel against oil spills and shipping accidents.

However, Lagomarsino did not join with most of the California delegation in advocating total bans on federal oil leasing off the California coast. He said this position favors his district: A ban on oil drilling elsewhere would put pressure on the existing Santa Barbara offshore oil sites to produce, thus increasing the potential for accidents. However, to environmental activists who favored complete bans, including off Santa Barbara, the congressman's position was apostasy.

In 1988, Democratic candidate Hart enjoyed strong political and financial support from environmentalists. Meanwhile, Lagomarsino found himself under attack; the organization Environmental Action placed him on its "Dirty Dozen" list of the 12 worst members of Congress on their selected issues.

Lagomarsino survived, in part because he had some environmental achievements he could use to counter such criticisms. During the 100th Congress, he authored amendments to designate the Santa Barbara Channel on international shipping maps as an "area to be avoided." Lagomarsino also favored stricter regulation of air pollution given off by oil drilling platforms. As the second-ranking Republican on Interior, he has proposed wilderness and wild and scenic river designation for various 19th District locales.

Yet Lagomarsino was put on the spot once more on the oil drilling issue in 1990; President Bush issued an order placing a 10-year ban on new oil leasing off much of the nation's coastline. All of California was included — except for an area off Santa Barbara. Lagomarsino protested to Bush in private, but could not get the policy changed; Democrats used the issue against him that year.

Lagomarsino's rather moderate views on the environment cause him more political grief than his staunchly conservative views on foreign policy. When recent Democratic challengers looked for a secondary issue against Lagomarsino, they pointed at his opposition to abortion rights, not his foreign policy stands.

Now the third-ranking Republican on the Foreign Affairs Committee, Lagomarsino has been a steadfast backer of Reagan and Bush administration international policies. One of the most unshakable supporters of Reagan's Central America policy, Lagomarsino frequently called for loosening of human rights "conditions" on U.S. aid to El Salvador, and he dependably voted for the administration's proposals to aid the Nicaraguan contras.

Lagomarsino's assumption of the ranking

California 19

South Central Coast — Santa Barbara

The site of the ranch that was President Reagan's home away from home, the 19th has been dependable for GOP presidential candidates. But there are enough Democrats in this district, just beyond the northern fringe of metropolitan Los Angeles, to keep it from being safely Republican.

This was proved in the 1988 House election. Lagomarsino defeated his Democratic challenger by less than 2 percentage points. In the same election, however, George Bush carried the district with a healthy 54 percent of the vote.

The 19th is contained in two counties: Santa Barbara, which accounts for slightly more than 60 percent of the district vote, and Ventura. There are political, economic and social divisions within these areas. The affluent Santa Barbara voters whose hillside homes overlook offshore oil rigs tend to place environmental issues at the top of their priority lists. The water crisis is a volatile element in local politics; the 1990 drought led to a devastating fire that destroyed more than 600 homes. The oil workers in Oxnard, the ranchers in the foothills of the Coastal Range and the military families near Vandenberg Air Force Base are more interested in economic growth.

Overall, Santa Barbara County gives Republicans little to worry about. But there is a Democratic bloc around Santa Barbara's campus of the University of California.

Though Ventura County as a whole is a Republican stronghold, most of the county — and its most Republican parts — are in the neighboring 21st District. Oxnard's Mexican-American community is a source of Democratic votes in the Ventura portion of the 19th.

West of Santa Barbara, the Santa Ynez Valley is known as "The Valley of the Arabians" for the surfeit of Arabian horse ranches in the region.

Population: 526,032. White 405,581 (77%), Black 14,530 (3%), Other 21,409 (4%). Spanish origin 132,623 (25%). 18 and over 384,025 (73%), 65 and over 56,558 (11%). Median age: 29.

Republican position on the Foreign Affairs Subcommittee on Western Hemisphere Affairs during the 101st Congress tempered his advocacy role somewhat. After working to negotiate agreements on contentious Central America issues in 1989, he said he would be "bound to defend" his subcommittee's section of the fiscal 1990 foreign aid authorization bill.

Lagomarsino served for a time in the lower ranks of his party's leadership, as secretary of the House Republican Conference. But when he tried to move up to vice chairman in December 1988, he was defeated by Bill McCollum of Florida.

Generic factors may have contributed to this setback. Some members may have harbored a mild aversion to giving more power to California, since a member of that huge delegation, Jerry Lewis, had been elected Conference chairman, the third-ranking GOP House leader. But some of it had to do with Lagomarsino. Under the category of can't-win-for-losing, some hard-line conservatives may have been wary of Lagomarsino's reputation as a moderate on environmental issues. In choosing the younger McCollum, the Republicans also opted for his more aggressive manner over Lagomarsino's stolid, low-key style.

Lagomarsino did have an unusually blithe moment in 1990, after Bush publicly announced his dislike of broccoli. Lagomarsino, whose district includes a number of broccoli farms, then appeared on the House floor in a shirt depicting broccoli stalks marching from California to Washington, D.C. He said he wanted "to show that even the president can be wrong about some things — especially vegetables."

At Home: After outlasting Hart by fewer than 4,000 votes in 1988, Lagomarsino looked to be vulnerable heading into 1990. Given California voters' rather sour mood toward House incumbents that year, Lagomarsino might have been at serious risk had Hart run again.

But Hart, who had a "free ride" in 1988, chose instead to run for re-election to the state Senate in 1990. District Democrats substituted Anita Perez Ferguson, an educational administrator and former state Senate aide to Hart. Despite Ferguson's determined effort, she could not approach the popular state senator in either name recognition or fundraising ability.

Going into 1988, Lagomarsino was unaccustomed to having to fight for his seat. He had not received less than 64 percent of the vote since 1974.

Lagomarsino built his political security during his state legislative career by mixing conservatism on fiscal and social issues with a more moderate tone on the environment. In 1965 he was the first recipient of the Legislative Conservationist of the Year award from the California Wildlife Federation.

When veteran Republican Rep. Charles M. Teague died in 1974, Lagomarsino, with his 13 years in the state Senate, was heir apparent. Although the special election that March occurred amid the Watergate scandal, Lagomarsino steered the focus of the campaign away from the "mess in Washington" to the mess along the California coast: The district's beaches were still suffering the effects of the 1969 blowout. He won easily over seven Democratic candidates.

In the 1974 general election, Lagomarsino faced the special election's second-place finisher, Ojai Mayor James Loebl. But Lagomarsino had used his first few months in office to build support at home, and he won a larger percentage than he had in the special election. After one more serious effort to unseat him, in 1976, the Democrats virtually gave Lagomarsino a pass until Hart tired in 1988 of waiting for him to retire.

The Democrat campaigned as the superior environmentalist and as a liberal on issues of social and foreign policy. He benefited from his years of representing four-fifths of the district's population in the Legislature. The strong support he received from liberal activists, especially in the environmentalist community, helped Hart compete financially with the incumbent. But Lagomarsino countered Hart's attacks, and in the end, voters seemed happy enough with the status quo to keep both men in their relative places.

Ferguson tried to pick up where Hart left off. She too said she was more environmentally conscious than Lagomarsino, and contrasted her support for abortion rights with Lagomarsino's anti-abortion position. She made a pitch to the district's Hispanic population by noting that she was trying to become California's first female House member of Hispanic heritage.

However, Ferguson entered the contest without Hart's large personal constituency. And while Lagomarsino did not raise nearly the amount of money that he did in his previous contest, he still outspent Ferguson by a wide margin. He used his media money to restore his image as an environmental moderate while reminding his Republican base of his conservative record on most issues.

Committees

Foreign Affairs (3rd of 18 Republicans)
Asian & Pacific Affairs; Western Hemisphere Affairs (ranking)

Interior & Insular Affairs (2nd of 17 Republicans)
Insular & International Affairs (ranking); National Parks & Public Lands

Elections

1990 General		
Robert J. Lagomarsino (R)	94,599	(55%)
Anita Perez Ferguson (D)	76,991	(44%)
1990 Primary		
Robert J. Lagomarsino (R)	47,906	(89%)
Alan Winterbourne (R)	6,054	(11%)
1988 General		
Robert J. Lagomarsino (R)	116,026	(50%)
Gary K. Hart (D)	112,033	(49%)

Previous Winning Percentages: **1986** (72%) **1984** (67%) **1982** (61%) **1980** (78%) **1978** (72%) **1976** (64%) **1974** (56%) **1974 *** (54%)

* *Special election.*

District Vote For President

	1988	1984	1980	1976
D	101,934 (45%)	82,697 (37%)	63,570 (34%)	82,877 (48%)
R	123,145 (54%)	141,327 (62%)	99,908 (53%)	84,905 (50%)

Campaign Finance

	Receipts	Receipts from PACs		Expend-itures
1990				
Lagomarsino (R)	$643,444	$145,517	(23%)	$658,365
Ferguson (D)	$243,210	$72,875	(30%)	$241,815
1988				
Lagomarsino (R)	$1,226,229	$338,996	(28%)	$1,470,674
Hart (D)	$1,634,309	$511,277	(31%)	$1,633,020

Key Votes

1991	
Authorize use of force against Iraq	Y
1990	
Support constitutional amendment on flag desecration	Y
Pass family and medical leave bill over Bush veto	N
Reduce SDI funding	N
Allow abortions in overseas military facilities	N
Approve budget summit plan for spending and taxing	N
Approve civil rights bill	N
1989	
Halt production of B-2 stealth bomber at 13 planes	N
Oppose capital gains tax cut	N
Approve federal abortion funding in rape or incest cases	N
Approve pay raise and revision of ethics rules	N
Pass Democratic minimum wage plan over Bush veto	N

Voting Studies

	Presidential Support		Party Unity		Conservative Coalition	
Year	**S**	**O**	**S**	**O**	**S**	**O**
1990	70	30	89	11	93	7
1989	73	27	87	13	85	15
1988	63	38	91	9	95	5
1987	71	29	91	9	95	5
1986	80	19	92	7	88	12
1985	80	19	94	5	96	4
1984	68	32	89	11	93	7
1983	85	15	88	12	88	12
1982	83	16	90	10	93	7
1981	82	18	95	5	96	4

Interest Group Ratings

Year	ADA	ACU	AFL-CIO	CCUS
1990	11	92	0	79
1989	0	93	8	100
1988	35	80	36	93
1987	8	96	6	100
1986	5	86	7	89
1985	5	90	6	82
1984	5	79	15	94
1983	0	83	12	90
1982	5	86	5	77
1981	5	93	0	100

20 Bill Thomas (R)

Of Bakersfield — Elected 1978

Born: Dec. 6, 1941, Wallace, Idaho.
Education: San Francisco State U., B.A. 1963, M.A. 1965.
Occupation: Professor of political science.
Family: Wife, Sharon Lynn Hamilton; two children.
Religion: Baptist.
Political Career: Calif. Assembly, 1975-79.
Capitol Office: 2402 Rayburn Bldg. 20515; 225-2915.

In Washington: Thomas has a combative style that, while increasingly fashionable among House Republicans generally, has not been the norm among Republicans on the Ways and Means Committee. But Thomas relishes the role of partisan strategist; he is one of the best in the House at watching a floor debate or a committee meeting and taking in all the political implications. In his first term, he plotted strategy for his fellow freshmen in the contest that elected a new GOP leader; since then, he has sought to play a similar role as tactician for the California delegation.

Thomas' style does not suit all tastes. He can be snide to slower-witted colleagues, and quick to anger when he does not get his way. But in the the 101st Congress, cantankerousness seemed ascendant as Newt Gingrich of Georgia became the House GOP Whip and brought other impassioned conservatives to the spotlight. Thomas supported Gingrich's election: Roommates when they arrived in Washington in 1979, they are among the several former college professors who have risen in Congress as acerbic conservatives.

Thomas also comes into his own when there is a tough job to be done. A case in point is redistricting, the grueling enterprise of redrawing most of the nation's 435 House districts; incomprehensibly dull to the layman, redistricting is life and death to legislators. Thomas was chosen by his GOP peers to head their task force planning strategy and preparing ammunition for that struggle.

There is no doubt Thomas is positioned to be a significant legislative player. In the 100th Congress he won a spot on Budget, and he is sixth-ranking Republican on Ways and Means. On both committees, Thomas urges Republicans in their private councils to forge a united front, so the GOP can offer a clear alternative to the Democratic Party line.

Thomas' politically combative style stems in part from a watershed experience on House Administration. Early in the 99th Congress, Thomas was the lone Republican on that committee's task force that ruled that Democrat Frank McCloskey was the winner, by four votes, of the bitterly contested 8th District race in Indiana. Thomas furiously opposed the task force report, calling it a "rape" and "an arrogant use of raw power."

In the legislative arena, Thomas' partisan style can help rally the troops, but it sometimes hampers his ability to exercise influence.

Even though the massive tax-revision bill of the Reagan years was the Republican president's initiative, Thomas seemed to regard it largely as an example of misbehavior on the part of the House majority. Despite Thomas' clear mastery of the subject, his emotional speeches against the bill restricted his chance to alter it.

Thomas' experience on the tax bill contrasted with his first two years on Ways and Means, when he made his presence known on a variety of issues. Shortly after joining the committee, he agitated successfully for a higher Social Security retirement age as a way of keeping down future payroll tax increases.

Thomas serves on Ways and Means' Subcommittee on Trade, often crossing swords with the committee's free-trade bloc. As talk of a Mexican free trade agreement has intensified, Thomas has wanted to know how it will affect California farmers. He has lobbied to protect wine makers (particularly California vintners) and the pistachio growers in his district from imports, and he served as spokesman for his state's producers of highly viscous "heavy oil." He supported provisions of the 1987 omnibus trade bill providing import relief for perishable crops. In 1986 he supported an unsuccessful attempt to override Reagan's veto of legislation restricting textile imports (which compete with California textiles).

Thomas is more prominent on House Administration, where as the ranking Republican he is often his party's point man on highly political issues. He led the GOP effort on campaign finance reform in 1990, stressing such issues as a limit on political action committees (PACs) contributions to $1,000. Perhaps his favorite proposal has been a requirement that

California 20

Bakersfield; San Luis Obispo

Crossing the 20th District from east to west is like riding a roller coaster across Southern California. Beginning in the flat, bare desert lands of Inyo County on the Nevada border, the district rises through the southern end of the Sierra Nevada Mountains, dips down to Bakersfield in the Central Valley, lifts up again across the Coastal Range, then plunges to the Pacific Ocean near Pismo Beach in San Luis Obispo County.

The 20th includes the highest point (Mount Whitney) and the lowest (Death Valley) in the Lower 48 states. Kern County (Bakersfield) is one of the nation's leading agricultural counties.

Politically, however, there is not much variety in the area. It is uniformly conservative. The real power is in the agribusiness community, and the aerospace and defense industries.

The 1980s boom in the latter contributed to a population jump of nearly 66 percent in Bakersfield. East of the city is the China Lake Weapons Center, which makes Sidewinder missiles.

The core city of the district with 175,000 people, Bakersfield has a Southern flavor, a legacy of the Texans and Oklahomans who arrived in two migrations: first, to escape the "Dust Bowl" poverty of the Great Depression, as depicted in John Steinbeck's "The Grapes of Wrath," then later, in more prosperous times, to work in the region's oil fields. Bakersfield residents are sensitive to the gritty image affixed to the city, and to the stereotype that it is a cultural wasteland.

Though Kern County is heavily Republican — it gave 61 percent of its vote to George Bush in 1988 — the most conservative area of the district is at the northern end of Los Angeles County, in the Antelope Valley. Communities like Lancaster and Palmdale have relied economically on the aerospace industry that developed around Edwards Air Force Base. But the once-remote area is being drawn into Los Angeles' sphere, with bedroom suburbs expanding for commuters who do not mind the 50-mile drive across the San Gabriel Mountains.

Population: 525,750. White 440,375 (84%), Black 22,967 (4%), Other 17,043 (3%). Spanish origin 74,169 (14%). 18 and over 371,945 (71%), 65 and over 54,860 (10%). Median age: 30.

more than half of any member's funding come from his own constituents. Thomas also has pursued imposing new limits and reporting requirements on congressional franked mail. When a campaign finance reform bill was on the House floor in September 1990, Thomas got 194 votes for an instruction to the conferees to accept restrictions on franked mail proposed in the Senate's version of the legislation.

Despite the intense partisan wrangling on House Administration in early 1985, it also provided a forum for Thomas' more pragmatic side. On the Elections Subcommittee, Thomas worked with Washington Democrat Al Swift on legislation to prevent the TV networks from using election returns from Eastern states to forecast presidential winners before polls closed in the West. Their bill setting a uniform poll-closing time for presidential elections passed the House in the 100th and 101st Congresses, but died in the Senate both times. The same fate befell another Swift-Thomas effort in 1990: the "motor voter" bill allowing voters to register to vote as they apply for a driver's license.

At Home: Thomas has often described himself as a pragmatic conservative, a formula that has tended to work for him at the polls. However, some Republican hard-liners have come to view Thomas as more committed to pragmatism than conservatism. Thomas faced a 1990 primary challenge from the right. Although he won without difficulty, pool repairman Rod Gregory got 27 percent of the vote. In the general election, Thomas' 60 percent was his lowest since his first House election in 1978.

Leaving academia in 1974 to seek a state Assembly seat, Thomas ran as a staunch conservative; support for the death penalty was his central issue. But in 1978, when a House seat became available after GOP Rep. William Ketchum died following the June primary, Thomas positioned himself as the moderate Republican candidate. Although he was the ranking GOP legislator in the area, it took him seven ballots at a nominating convention to defeat two more conservative opponents.

Although Thomas and Ketchum had had some differences (Thomas backed Gerald R. Ford in the California primary in 1976 and Ketchum supported Ronald Reagan), Thomas won a general-election endorsement from Ketchum's widow. He easily defeated Democrat Bob Sogge, a former state Senate aide.

After establishing electoral security,

Thomas turned to the battle over the congressional redistricting maps drawn by California Democrats after the 1980 census. These artful plans were instrumental in increasing Democratic strength in the state's House delegation.

In 1981 Thomas was chosen by fellow members of the California Republican delegation to lead their fight against the new maps. He oversaw the successful effort to have the 1982 plan rejected by voters in a ballot referendum. The map was turned down decisively; a state court allowed it to remain in effect for 1982 only. Yet the Democrats who dominated the state Legislature passed a new map with only minor revisions, and sent it to outgoing Democratic Gov. Edmund G. Brown Jr. for signing just before Republican George Deukmejian succeeded him. Thomas launched a second challenge, but was thwarted by his colleagues' inability to agree on a course of action.

The issue died down after 1984, when voters rejected an initiative pushed by Deukmejian that would have thrown out the Democrats' map and set up a panel of judges to draw a new one. Legal challenges to the map continued, but ended when the U.S. Supreme Court refused further review early in 1989.

The issue revived as 1990s redistricting neared: Deukmejian decided not to seek a third term in 1990, creating a threat that Democrats might control the entire redistricting process again. Worried Republicans, including Thomas, pressed for a means of removing the redistricting process from the state Legislature, still under Democratic control.

However, this effort ended as badly or worse for the GOP than the earlier ones. Thomas and several House colleagues backed a June 1990 initiative to create a commission to judge competing remap plans. But many Republican state legislators wanted to retain some say over the remaps: They supported a ballot measure leaving redistricting in the Legislature, but requiring a two-thirds majority for passage.

While the Republicans were divided, Democratic initiative opponents staged an aggressive and well-funded campaign that helped defeat both measures by margins of 2-to-1. However, Republicans ended up with a redistricting firestop anyway, when GOP Sen. Pete Wilson defeated Democrat Dianne Feinstein for governor that November.

Committees

House Administration (Ranking)
Campaign Finance Reform (ranking)

Budget (3rd of 14 Republicans)
Budget Process, Reconciliation & Enforcement (ranking); Urgent Fiscal Issues

Ways & Means (6th of 13 Republicans)
Trade

Elections

1990 General		
Bill Thomas (R)	112,962	(60%)
Michael A. Thomas (D)	65,101	(34%)
William H. Dilbeck (LIBERT)	10,555	(6%)
1990 Primary		
Bill Thomas (R)	52,669	(73%)
Rod Gregory (R)	19,158	(27%)
1988 General		
Bill Thomas (R)	162,779	(71%)
Lita Reid (D)	62,037	(27%)

Previous Winning Percentages: **1986** (73%) **1984** (71%)
1982 (68%) **1980** (71%) **1978** (59%)

District Vote For President

	1988		1984		1980		1976	
D	79,866	(34%)	64,244	(30%)	49,807	(29%)	57,159	(44%)
R	150,366	(65%)	151,080	(69%)	106,733	(63%)	72,497	(55%)

Campaign Finance

	Receipts	Receipts from PACs		Expenditures
1990				
Thomas (R)	$430,525	$235,447	(55%)	$496,845
Thomas (D)	$696	0		$690
1988				
Thomas (R)	$335,586	$215,150	(64%)	$329,354
Reid (D)	$11,879	0		$15,914

Key Votes

1991	
Authorize use of force against Iraq	Y
1990	
Support constitutional amendment on flag desecration	Y
Pass family and medical leave bill over Bush veto	N
Reduce SDI funding	N
Allow abortions in overseas military facilities	Y
Approve budget summit plan for spending and taxing	N
Approve civil rights bill	N
1989	
Halt production of B-2 stealth bomber at 13 planes	N
Oppose capital gains tax cut	N
Approve federal abortion funding in rape or incest cases	Y
Approve pay raise and revision of ethics rules	Y
Pass Democratic minimum wage plan over Bush veto	N

Voting Studies

	Presidential Support		Party Unity		Conservative Coalition	
Year	**S**	**O**	**S**	**O**	**S**	**O**
1990	54	35	74	11	83	7
1989	72	28	81	15	90	7
1988	60	36	81	15	87	8
1987	64	25	81	8	88	9
1986	76	19	82	10	84	12
1985	61	33	79	15	84	11
1984	64	28	71	17	78	12
1983	74	21	81 †	10 †	84	10
1982	79	10	71	8	84	7
1981	76	14	69	11	75	11

† Not eligible for all recorded votes.

Interest Group Ratings

Year	ADA	ACU	AFL-CIO	CCUS
1990	17	74	9	91
1989	15	78	8	90
1988	25	78	43	100
1987	4	70	13	92
1986	10	85	21	93
1985	10	86	13	95
1984	15	64	9	82
1983	15	62	12	89
1982	5	86	0	85
1981	5	83	8	100

21 Elton Gallegly (R)

Of Simi Valley — Elected 1986

Born: March 7, 1944, Huntington Park, Calif.
Education: Attended Los Angeles State College, 1962-63.
Occupation: Real estate broker.
Family: Wife, Janice Shrader; four children.
Religion: Protestant.
Political Career: Simi Valley City Council, 1979-80; mayor of Simi Valley, 1980-86.
Capitol Office: 107 Cannon Bldg. 20515; 225-5811.

In Washington: Gallegly is an unassuming conservative who has used his unwavering loyalty to gain his leadership's attention. His reward came in the 101st Congress with a seat on Foreign Affairs.

Gallegly was at the forefront of congressional efforts to give President Bush authority to use force against Iraq. He made national headlines in December 1990 when after a White House meeting he quoted Bush referring to Iraqi President Saddam Hussein: "If we get into an armed situation, he's going to get his ass kicked." He introduced legislation in 1991 to cut off federal funds to states or cities offering sanctuary to members of the armed forces avoiding military service.

Gallegly drew notice in March 1991 when he and 11 other members who backed Bush's war policy ignored Speaker Thomas S. Foley's objections and visited Kuwait at the invitation of the Kuwaiti ambassador. The trip was paid by a company seeking business in Kuwait.

In July 1987, Gallegly made a high-profile venture into foreign policy, joining three other House members on the Capitol lawn to bash Toshiba products with sledgehammers. The Japanese firm had acknowledged selling restricted technology to the Soviets.

A member of a GOP task force on drugs, Gallegly talked tough on crime and advocated user accountability. After a Drug Enforcement Agency officer from Simi Valley was killed, Gallegly introduced legislation to reinstate a federal death penalty for anyone convicted of murdering a federal law-enforcement officer. He reintroduced it in the 102nd Congress.

At Home: Although Gallegly easily won a third term in 1990, the dropoff in his vote percentage exemplified the downward trend for California House incumbents that year.

After winning with 68 percent of the vote in 1986 and 69 percent in 1988, Gallegly slipped to 58 percent in 1990. That decline did not benefit Democratic challenger Richard D. Freiman, who received 34 percent, as much as Libertarian Peggy Christensen, who took 8 percent, a strong third-party showing in the 21st.

Gallegly first got a shot at this House seat in 1986, when Republican Rep. Bobbi Fiedler embarked on an unsuccessful bid for the GOP Senate nomination. But Gallegly had to fend off a primary opponent with some celebrity.

Tony Hope, son of comedian Bob Hope, had returned to the 21st after a 10-year stay in Washington, D.C., with seeming access to unlimited Hollywood money and glitter. But concerned he would be viewed as an election-buying carpetbagger, he played down his celebrity contacts and raised far less money than he might have.

Setting out to prove that he was not just "a pile of money from a distant planet," Hope stressed his background, including work for an accounting firm in Washington and service on the Grace commission on government waste.

Casting Hope as an interloper, Gallegly touted his record as mayor. He was well-known for having boosted economic development in Simi Valley, once derided in some parts as "Slimy Valley." Gallegly also pointed out that Hope had not even registered to vote during his sojourn in Washington, and had registered outside the 21st when he returned to California. Hope responded that Gallegly had switched his own registration from the GOP to independent in 1974, abandoning the party in the midst of Watergate. But party regulars backed Gallegly.

Gallegly did face the issue of heavy financial support from local real estate developers. Some of their projects needed approval by the City Council on which he sat. Hope wanted to raise questions of propriety, and also tap anti-development sentiment in the district.

But Hope's campaign organization was weaker than Gallegly's, and he neutralized his most important potential asset — money — with his squeamishness about using it. Gallegly, relatively unknown outside his Ventura County base when the campaign began, effectively used direct mail to spread his name and message across the populous San Fernando Valley portion of the district, resulting in an easy win.

California 21

Part of Ventura County; Western San Fernando Valley

The 21st District showed its conservative Republican colors in presidential elections throughout the 1980s. Ronald Reagan ran roughshod here both times; George Bush took 64 percent of the district vote in 1988.

Ten years earlier, voters in the territory of the 21st supported the property-tax revolt measure, Proposition 13, like those in no other part of the state. Fully 82 percent of the voters in such far-removed Los Angeles suburbs as Thousand Oaks and Simi Valley supported the plan to slash property taxes in half.

The 21st — which begins in Los Angeles County, skirts the San Fernando Valley, then knifes into Ventura County — was drawn to incorporate staunchly Republican areas while leaving out enough Democrats to populate two Democratic districts in between. This is the kind of territory where the Republican candidate with the strongest conservative credentials normally wins.

Though there is a diversified economy here, the aerospace industry is a primary employer. Raytheon, Northrop, Rockwell and Litton have facilities in the San Fernando Valley.

Population: 525,880. White 469,637 (89%), Black 8,866 (2%), Other 20,713 (4%). Spanish origin 54,584 (10%). 18 and over 367,604 (70%), 65 and over 34,644 (7%). Median age: 30.

Committees

Foreign Affairs (15th of 18 Republicans)
Arms Control, International Security & Science; Europe & the Middle East

Interior & Insular Affairs (8th of 17 Republicans)
Insular & International Affairs; National Parks & Public Lands

Elections

1990 General		
Elton Gallegly (R)	118,326	(58%)
Richard D. Freiman (D)	68,921	(34%)
Peggy Christensen (LIBERT)	15,364	(8%)
1990 Primary		
Elton Gallegly (R)	45,800	(68%)
Sang Korman (R)	21,256	(32%)
1988 General		
Elton Gallegly (R)	181,413	(69%)
Donald E. Stevens (D)	75,739	(29%)

Previous Winning Percentage: **1986** (68%)

District Vote For President

	1988	1984	1980	1976
D	95,910 (35%)	65,617 (27%)	48,825 (25%)	51,701 (40%)
R	178,542 (64%)	177,196 (72%)	127,042 (65%)	80,245 (60%)

Campaign Finance

	Receipts	Receipts from PACs		Expend-itures
1990				
Gallegly (R)	$599,454	$156,861	(26%)	$449,668
Freiman (D)	$13,706	$50	(0%)	$13,147
1988				
Gallegly (R)	$506,391	$163,825	(32%)	$465,310

Key Votes

1991	
Authorize use of force against Iraq	Y
1990	
Support constitutional amendment on flag desecration	Y
Pass family and medical leave bill over Bush veto	N
Reduce SDI funding	N
Allow abortions in overseas military facilities	N
Approve budget summit plan for spending and taxing	N
Approve civil rights bill	N
1989	
Halt production of B-2 stealth bomber at 13 planes	N
Oppose capital gains tax cut	N
Approve federal abortion funding in rape or incest cases	N
Approve pay raise and revision of ethics rules	Y
Pass Democratic minimum wage plan over Bush veto	N

Voting Studies

	Presidential Support		Party Unity		Conservative Coalition	
Year	**S**	**O**	**S**	**O**	**S**	**O**
1990	70	29	91	6	96	4
1989	76	24	90	8	93	7
1988	68	28	94	2	95	3
1987	71	29	94	5	88	12

Interest Group Ratings

Year	ADA	ACU	AFL-CIO	CCUS
1990	11	92	0	86
1989	5	89	18	100
1988	15	96	21	100
1987	4	96	6	100

22 Carlos J. Moorhead (R)

Of Glendale — Elected 1972

Born: May 6, 1922, Long Beach, Calif.
Education: U. of California, Los Angeles, B.A. 1943; U. of Southern California, J.D. 1949.
Military Service: Army, 1942-45; Army Reserve, 1945-82.
Occupation: Lawyer.
Family: Wife, Valery Joan Tyler; five children.
Religion: Presbyterian.
Political Career: Calif. Assembly, 1967-73.
Capitol Office: 2346 Rayburn Bldg. 20515; 225-4176.

In Washington: It would surprise some to learn that Moorhead is the second most senior Republican on both the Energy and Commerce and Judiciary committees. In an arena given to powerful wills, his legislative and personal styles are laid back.

But if Moorhead has not used these positions to the extent a more aggressive lawmaker might, he is no work-shirker. A friendly man who has no trouble cooperating with Democrats, he has managed to stake out a few areas of expertise.

On Energy and Commerce, Moorhead's willingness to collaborate with Democrats has helped move legislation on energy policy.

One such partnership was his work during the 99th Congress with Edward J. Markey of Massachusetts, then chairman of the Energy and Power Subcommittee of which Moorhead is the ranking Republican.

Markey and Moorhead worked together on legislation setting energy efficiency standards for appliances, a measure that was supported by a broad coalition of more than 40 groups. Though President Ronald Reagan pocket-vetoed the measure in the 99th Congress (saying it would interfere with the free market), early in the 100th he signed a nearly identical bill into law. In 1986, Moorhead and Markey won passage of a bill, sought by private utility companies, that disallowed the practice of giving public utilities preferences over private utilities in the relicensing of hydroelectric power plants.

Moorhead's relationship with Indiana Rep. Philip R. Sharp, who took over the subcommittee chair in the 100th, has been less fruitful. But the two men have joined forces on some energy measures, even where it meant crossing administration policy.

During the 101st Congress, Sharp and Moorhead successfully defied Bush administration objections to back creation of a federal reserve of refined petroleum products. They were also part of a congressional push to increase spending to help low-income families save energy by weatherizing their homes, a program the administration had proposed cutting.

During deliberations over the 1990 Clean Air Act, Moorhead joined with Markey to sponsor an amendment that would reward utilities for conservation or for using renewable energy sources.

When it comes to nuclear power, however, Moorhead has been more in tune with Republican administrations.

In the 100th Congress, Moorhead continued to represent the interests of the power industry; he pushed for renewal of the Price-Anderson nuclear insurance law, which protects nuclear power producers from the financial consequences of serious nuclear disasters, and he sponsored a provision allowing producers to pay their own legal fees from the insurance fund. Moorhead also opposed an unsuccessful effort by liberals to bar the Nuclear Regulatory Commission from relaxing its rules to allow the Shoreham (N.Y.) and Seabrook (N.H.) nuclear plants to open.

On the Judiciary Committee, Moorhead is typically a reliable vote for the administration and business interests.

When the panel debated legislation on vertical price fixing — which involves manufacturers or distributors setting a minimum price for their products — Moorhead sought unsuccessfully to limit the scope of proposed language that would make it easier for retailers to sue and win a price-fixing suit. Moorhead did win a floor vote to specify that the new legal standards would only apply to cases filed after enactment, however, the overall law did not clear Congress that year.

Moorhead had a similar concern with landmark civil rights legislation passed during the 101st, although it was ultimately vetoed; he narrowly lost a committee battle to make sure that the proposed law would not be retroactive.

Moorhead is the ranking Republican on Judiciary's Subcommittee on Intellectual Property and Judicial Administration, which oversees patent, trademark and copyright law.

California 22

Glendale; Part of Burbank; Part of Pasadena

This stretch of middle- and upper-middle-class communities flanking the San Gabriel Mountains is one of the most Republican districts in the state. George Bush took 64 percent of the 22nd's vote in 1988, one of his higher district percentages in California. Four years earlier, President Ronald Reagan topped 70 percent in the district. Other statewide Republicans, including Gov. George Deukmejian and his successor, former Sen. Pete Wilson, have thrived here.

The bulk of the district is in two legs on the southern flank of the mountains. With a population of 180,000, Glendale is the largest city entirely within the district. Formerly a rather homogeneous bedroom community, Glendale has received an influx of Armenian- and Mexican-Americans in recent years. It has been voting overwhelmingly for Moorhead since he began his political career by running for the state Legislature in 1966.

The vote for Republicans is equally enthusiastic in San Marino, named for a tiny European republic surrounded by Italy. The exclusive California community, with a 1985 per capita income of $33,000, is one of the most affluent in the state.

Arcadia and South Pasadena are more modest, but still well-to-do. Temple City and Monrovia, though, have working-class areas that provide some Democratic votes: Nearly 30 percent of Monrovia's 33,000 residents are black or Hispanic.

The 22nd also includes the more Republican parts of both Burbank and Pasadena. Some of the old mansions of Pasadena — including the Wrigley Mansion, now home office of the Tournament of Roses — are in the district. "Beautiful downtown Burbank" and the middle-class black and Mexican-American areas of Pasadena are not part of the 22nd.

As the district follows the San Gabriels' sweep toward the coast, it picks up the booming city of Santa Clarita, an incorporation of the developments of Newhall and Valencia, in the area whose ranches provided the backdrop for some of the earliest Hollywood westerns. The 22nd's northern end takes in the "high desert" for half of Palmdale, a city whose defense-related industries add to its conservative tone.

Population: 525,939. White 463,633 (88%), Black 9,710 (2%), Asian and Pacific Islander 23,523 (5%), Other 2,913 (1%). Spanish origin 64,641 (12%). 18 and over 403,471 (77%), 65 and over 74,460 (14%). Median age: 35.

During the 100th Congress, Moorhead sponsored the administration version of legislation to implement the Berne Convention, an international agreement protecting artists' intellectual property rights. Although a Democratic bill was passed in lieu of the measure Moorhead offered, the Republican was credited with playing a constructive role. Moorhead also sponsored legislation extending patent law to cover the importation of products made using U.S.-patented processes; provisions to that end ultimately were included in the omnibus trade bill.

In 1986 Moorhead played an important role in the drafting of the Electronic Privacy Act, which was designed to protect new forms of electronic communications, such as electronic mail, against improper interception.

The Justice Department initially opposed changes in wiretap law and was reluctant to participate in talks on the legislation. But Moorhead worked hard to win the administration over, stressing that protection of electronic privacy was important to the business community. The legislation ultimately became law, backed by a broad coalition that included members of both parties, business groups and the American Civil Liberties Union.

Other issues Moorhead has pressed on Judiciary include getting money to hire more border agents for the Justice Department and limiting the political activities of lawyers at the Legal Services Corporation.

During the 101st, Moorhead served on a 15-member study commission appointed by Chief Justice William Rehnquist to survey the heavily burdened federal court system. In April 1990, the committee presented Congress with more than 100 recommendations for change.

Moorhead will never be the most attention-grabbing spokesman for the pro-business philosophy. He rarely speaks in public without reading his material, and he has a tendency to do so with his head nearly touching the paper.

Early in his career, he had an opportunity to be in the spotlight as the Judiciary Committee debated the impeachment of President Richard Nixon in 1974. But he played only a minor role. A staunch defender of the president, he remarked in early 1974 that Nixon "has done a good job considering Congress has spent a million dollars trying to impeach him." When the time came for a vote, Moorhead backed Nixon on every impeachment count, changing his mind only with the release of the "smoking gun" tape.

At Home: Since entering the political arena in 1966, Moorhead has had an unsullied electoral record. Although a long series of landslide victories ended for Moorhead in 1990, he still won comfortably, with 60 percent of the vote.

Moorhead was raised in Glendale and worked as a lawyer there for 15 years before entering the Legislature. After three terms in Sacramento, he set his sights on Congress.

When eight-term Republican Rep. H. Allen Smith decided to retire from Congress in 1972, Robert H. Finch, a well-connected former adviser to Nixon, thought about running. But he opted against it, and nine candidates entered the GOP primary.

The contest quickly narrowed to two: Moorhead and Dr. Bill McColl, a Covina surgeon who had once played end for the Chicago Bears. Moorhead, who had carried the west side of the district in state Legislature elections, was the favorite of the local party apparatus over McColl, who had narrowly lost a primary to John H. Rousselot in the neighboring 24th District in 1970. The result was an easy nomination for Moorhead, and an even easier general election.

Moorhead's one moment of political concern came in 1982. After that year's redistricting plan dissolved Rousselot's neighboring district, giving part of it to Moorhead, Rousselot toyed with the idea of challenging Moorhead in a primary.

Rousselot was dean of the California Republican delegation, and with a nationwide network of loyal conservative supporters, he would have been a difficult opponent. But Rousselot decided instead to run in the heavily Democratic 30th, where he eventually lost. Moorhead was in the clear.

Committees

Energy & Commerce (2nd of 16 Republicans)
Energy & Power (ranking); Telecommunications & Finance

Judiciary (2nd of 13 Republicans)
Intellectual Property & Judicial Administration (ranking); Economic & Commercial Law

Elections

1990 General

Carlos J. Moorhead (R)	108,634	(60%)
David Bayer (D)	61,630	(34%)
William H. Wilson (LIBERT)	6,702	(4%)
Jan B. Tucker (PFP)	3,963	(2%)

1988 General

Carlos J. Moorhead (R)	164,699	(70%)
John G. Simmons (D)	61,555	(26%)

Previous Winning Percentages: **1986** (74%) **1984** (85%) **1982** (74%) **1980** (64%) **1978** (65%) **1976** (63%) **1974** (56%) **1972** (57%)

District Vote For President

	1988	1984	1980	1976
D	86,732 (35%)	63,874 (26%)	50,770 (23%)	63,493 (31%)
R	158,823 (64%)	175,164 (72%)	147,959 (68%)	137,401 (67%)

Campaign Finance

	Receipts	Receipts from PACs		Expenditures
1990				
Moorhead (R)	$444,157	$231,350	(52%)	$400,109
Bayer (D)	$40,872	$1,975	(5%)	$40,303
1988				
Moorhead (R)	$397,417	$215,165	(54%)	$234,920
Simmons (D)	$18,940	$503	(3%)	$18,046

Key Votes

1991	
Authorize use of force against Iraq	Y
1990	
Support constitutional amendment on flag desecration	Y
Pass family and medical leave bill over Bush veto	N
Reduce SDI funding	N
Allow abortions in overseas military facilities	N
Approve budget summit plan for spending and taxing	N
Approve civil rights bill	N
1989	
Halt production of B-2 stealth bomber at 13 planes	N
Oppose capital gains tax cut	N
Approve federal abortion funding in rape or incest cases	N
Approve pay raise and revision of ethics rules	Y
Pass Democratic minimum wage plan over Bush veto	N

Voting Studies

	Presidential Support		Party Unity		Conservative Coalition	
Year	S	O	S	O	S	O
1990	74	26	93	6	98	2
1989	72	24	88	10	95	2
1988	73	24	98	1	97	0
1987	71	27	91	6	86	12
1986	82	17	92	7	96	4
1985	80	20	96	3	93	5
1984	67	28	91	7	90	7
1983	78	16	92	3	96	2
1982	78	21	92	5	96	3
1981	75	18	91	4	92	4

Interest Group Ratings

Year	ADA	ACU	AFL-CIO	CCUS
1990	6	96	8	86
1989	0	93	0	100
1988	10	96	7	100
1987	4	96	0	100
1986	0	95	7	100
1985	5	90	0	95
1984	0	100	15	87
1983	0	100	0	85
1982	0	96	0	90
1981	5	100	0	94

23 Anthony C. Beilenson (D)

Of Los Angeles — Elected 1976

Born: Oct. 26, 1932, New Rochelle, N.Y.
Education: Harvard U., A.B. 1954, LL.B. 1957.
Occupation: Lawyer.
Family: Wife, Dolores Martin; three children.
Religion: Jewish.
Political Career: Calif. Assembly, 1963-67; Calif. Senate, 1967-77; sought Democratic nomination for U.S. Senate, 1968.
Capitol Office: 1025 Longworth Bldg. 20515; 225-5911.

In Washington: Beilenson is a thoughtful Democrat with a liberal outlook and a strong distaste for what he sees as wasteful government spending and parochial legislating.

His views lead him to challenge the status quo in ways that earn him some respect and some reproof from colleagues. Though Beilenson holds key positions on important committees — including the No. 3 Democratic spot on Rules — he is too independent-minded and iconoclastic to be an insider in the party leadership's power structure.

In the 101st Congress, Beilenson had two new forums. He was chairman of the Select Intelligence Committee and also took the Rules Committee seat on Budget, a position he used to continue to speak out on the federal debt.

His position on Intelligence thrust him into the congressional spotlight; the panel writes the annual multibillion-dollar authorizing legislation for the CIA and other intelligence agencies. In marking up the bill during 1990, the panel sought to place new limitations on covert aid programs in Afghanistan, Cambodia and Angola and establish new rules for presidential reporting of covert operations.

When President Bush unexpectedly vetoed the authorization measure — concerned that the notification requirement could have a "chilling effect" on the ability of diplomats to conduct important discussions — Beilenson reacted angrily, stating that the provision would have no such effect, and saying flatly that Bush had "received bad advice."

Beilenson almost did not have the chance to work on the 1990 authorization; his term as chairman had been due to expire at the start of 1990. Enforcement of the six-year limit on service on the Intelligence panel would have forced Beilenson from the post after just one year. When Thomas S. Foley took over as Speaker in mid-1989, he extended Beilenson's term through 1990. Committee members from both parties thought Beilenson had done well during his six months at the gavel and liked his deliberate style and avoidance of partisan confrontation.

As his term drew to a close at the end of the 101st Congress, Beilenson expressed some interest in serving even longer. Three former Intelligence Committee chairmen joined Beilenson in requesting a rules change to increase tenure on the committee to eight years and to allow chairmen to serve more than one term. Foley, however, never acted on the proposal, leading to Beilenson's departure from the panel at the start of the 102nd Congress.

During the 101st, Beilenson was also appointed by Bush to co-chair the commission that monitored the Nicaraguan elections in March 1990; he was one of 18 members of Congress chosen to consult with Bush on the crisis in the Persian Gulf while Congress was out of session late in 1990; and he traveled to the region in December 1990 as part of an official leadership delegation. Beilenson, once a peace candidate for a Senate seat, spoke out strongly against military action in the gulf.

Often critical of U.S. budget policy, Beilenson wrote in 1987, "Our failure to control the deficit is a failure of political will rather than of not knowing what to do or how to do it."

One plan Beilenson has continually pushed for lowering the deficit is to raise taxes on the wealthy and increase excise taxes on cigarettes, alcohol and gasoline. He offered legislation in 1989 once again to boost the gas tax, this time by 10 cents a year for five years. In the 102nd Congress, he assumed the chairmanship of the Budget Committee task force aimed at implementing the five-year deficit-reduction plan enacted in 1990.

Beilenson previously chaired a 1984 House Rules task force on the budget process, but House leaders declined to consider its proposals for procedural reforms and spending controls. They instead adopted the more drastic Gramm-Rudman-Hollings antideficit law that Beilenson criticizes for encouraging phony budgeting.

On the Rules Committee, he generally

California 23

Beverly Hills; Part of San Fernando Valley

The 23rd District is divided geographically and culturally by the Santa Monica Mountains. On the southern slope are the lush, well-tended neighborhoods of west Los Angeles, including Bel Air, the post-presidential residence of the Reagans, and Westwood, home of the U.C.L.A. campus.

To the east, at the foot of the mountains, is posh Beverly Hills, and to the south, Century City and Rancho Park. These are, for the most part, the provinces of wealthy, liberal families, many of them Jewish.

The district also holds about two-thirds of West Hollywood, which was incorporated as a separate city in 1984. It has a large homosexual population which is politically well-organized, and a large number of senior citizens.

Farther to the east, the 23rd reaches down to the beaches around Malibu, an ocean-front home for movie stars and a playground for partying surfers. Malibu tends to be somewhat less Democratic than other towns this side of the mountains. But it does have its share of activists, including actor Martin Sheen who, when appointed to the ceremonial post of mayor in 1989, declared Malibu a haven for the homeless.

On the other side of the mountains, where the ocean breezes seldom blow, is a different world. Here are such middle-class San Fernando Valley communities as Reseda, Tarzana, Canoga Park and Woodland Hills — indistinguishable suburbs linked together by commercial strips and shopping centers.

The willingness of many of this area's working-class residents to vote Republican for president counterbalances the liberal voting tendencies west of the mountains; President Reagan carried the district in 1984. But four years later, Michael S. Dukakis carried the 23rd for the Democrats.

Population: 525,936. White 467,002 (89%), Black 16,150 (3%), Other 21,238 (4%). Spanish origin 48,478 (9%). 18 and over 422,708 (80%), 65 and over 64,046 (12%). Median age: 34.

votes with his party, but is not an easy man for the leadership to persuade when he wants to go his own way. He is perhaps the panel's most independent Democrat.

Late in 1986, Beilenson clashed with incoming Speaker Jim Wright over antidrug legislation. Beilenson, at his independent best (but not politically smartest), criticized Wright as a television crew was filming Wright's appearance for a later documentary. The Speaker-to-be was furious that the film might show him being upbraided by one of his own Democratic members; the episode nearly kept Beilenson from gaining his Intelligence chairmanship, as Wright almost chose to skip over Beilenson in making the appointment in 1989.

Beilenson brought an interest in parkland and elephants with him from California. He helped create the Santa Monica Mountains National Recreation Area in 1978 and doggedly seeks more funding for it. He was able to help secure a $12 million appropriation for the park in 1990, bringing total funding for the site to more than $100 million.

In the 100th Congress, he succeeded in adding language to the Endangered Species Act to ban importation of ivory from African countries that do not have effective elephant-conservation programs. In the 101st Congress, he pushed Congress to approve $8.3 million in funds for fiscal 1990 and 1991 to help prevent extinction of the elephant.

At Home: Beilenson was a 14-year veteran of the state Legislature when Democratic Rep. Thomas M. Rees announced his retirement from Congress in 1976. The House district, which included some of the most liberal and heavily Jewish parts of Los Angeles, was ideal for Beilenson.

Beilenson's one major obstacle was cleared away when Howard L. Berman, then the Assembly's majority leader, chose to remain in the Legislature in 1976. Beilenson was the clear front-runner in the Democratic primary against five other candidates, none of whom held public office. His main competition came from Wallace Albertson, who headed the state's leading liberal organization, the California Democratic Council. Albertson criticized Beilenson for not being active enough in his support for a ballot proposition that would have restricted the development of nuclear power plants in the state. But the initiative fared poorly, and so did Albertson, who took 21 percent of the primary vote to Beilenson's 58 percent.

Beilenson won 60 percent of the general election vote that year and has never received less in seven subsequent contests. His only nervous moments came during the redistricting of 1982, but even that was less worrisome than had been expected.

In order to draw a favorable district for Berman, who now wanted to run for Congress, map makers removed part of the area near

Beverly Hills from the 23rd and added voters from a more conservative area in the western San Fernando Valley. When Beilenson complained that the change had hurt him badly, the Democrats who drew the district insisted he was panicking for no reason. "It's a good district for Tony," said Phillip Burton, the main architect of California's congressional district map. "He just doesn't know it. He's not a numbers guy."

It turned out Burton was right. Republicans hoped 1982 nominee David Armor — a former Rand Corp. analyst whose studies on school busing had been used by Los Angeles anti-busing forces in the late 1970s — would do well in the San Fernando section of the district, where anti-busing sentiment had been fierce. But Beilenson's Beverly Hills base was relatively secure, enabling him to put most of his effort into the communities that were new to him: He won with 60 percent.

Since he moved to the West Coast to practice law at age 25, Beilenson has met with only one political defeat. He was in the middle of his first state Senate term in 1968 when he decided to run for the Senate as a peace candidate, criticizing former state Controller Alan Cranston for what he said was a lukewarm antiwar position. Cranston won the Democratic nomination by more than a million votes.

Committees

Budget (8th of 23 Democrats)
Budget Process, Reconciliation & Enforcement (chairman); Defense, Foreign Policy & Space

Rules (3rd of 9 Democrats)
Rules of the House (chairman)

Elections

1990 General		
Anthony C. Beilenson (D)	103,141	(62%)
Jim Salomon (R)	57,118	(34%)
John Honigsfeld (PFP)	6,834	(4%)
1988 General		
Anthony C. Beilenson (D)	147,858	(63%)
Jim Salomon (R)	77,184	(33%)

Previous Winning Percentages: **1986** (66%) **1984** (62%) **1982** (60%) **1980** (63%) **1978** (66%) **1976** (60%)

District Vote For President

	1988	1984	1980	1976
D	138,264 (56%)	113,020 (46%)	83,218 (38%)	97,602 (50%)
R	106,610 (43%)	129,010 (53%)	109,736 (50%)	92,733 (48%)

Campaign Finance

	Receipts	Receipts from PACs		Expenditures
1990				
Beilenson (D)	$231,386	0		$201,404
Salomon (R)	$358,367	$15,100	(4%)	$360,389
1988				
Beilenson (D)	$150,275	0		$140,486
Salomon (R)	$130,438	$6,530	(5%)	$100,956

Key Votes

1991	
Authorize use of force against Iraq	N
1990	
Support constitutional amendment on flag desecration	N
Pass family and medical leave bill over Bush veto	Y
Reduce SDI funding	Y
Allow abortions in overseas military facilities	Y
Approve budget summit plan for spending and taxing	Y
Approve civil rights bill	Y
1989	
Halt production of B-2 stealth bomber at 13 planes	Y
Oppose capital gains tax cut	Y
Approve federal abortion funding in rape or incest cases	Y
Approve pay raise and revision of ethics rules	Y
Pass Democratic minimum wage plan over Bush veto	Y

Voting Studies

	Presidential Support		Party Unity		Conservative Coalition	
Year	**S**	**O**	**S**	**O**	**S**	**O**
1990	26	71	89	8	15	81
1989	33	64	84	9	17	80
1988	26	65	89	5	11	89
1987	23	72	86	6	5	84
1986	18	81	89	7	20	80
1985	23	69	88	4	11	84
1984	34	65	87	10	12	88
1983	29	66	91	7	16	84
1982	38	53	81	5	11	82
1981	30	64	79	8	8	80

Interest Group Ratings

Year	ADA	ACU	AFL-CIO	CCUS
1990	83	8	75	8
1989	85	4	67	30
1988	95	8	77	50
1987	84	13	63	20
1986	80	9	50	18
1985	95	5	88	24
1984	90	9	62	38
1983	85	9	76	40
1982	95	5	84	19
1981	90	0	80	6

24 Henry A. Waxman (D)

Of Los Angeles — Elected 1974

Born: Sept. 12, 1939, Los Angeles, Calif.
Education: U. of California, Los Angeles, B.A. 1961, J.D. 1964.
Occupation: Lawyer.
Family: Wife, Janet Kessler; two children.
Religion: Jewish.
Political Career: Calif. Assembly, 1969-75.
Capitol Office: 2418 Rayburn Bldg. 20515; 225-3976.

In Washington: Waxman is one of Congress' master legislators. Like a river forging a new path to the sea, he might take years to wear down the obstacles before him, or to find ways around them, but he nearly always reaches his goal in the end.

"God never meant liberals to be stupid," Waxman once said, and he lives to be proof of that. He sets such ambitious policy aims that colleagues might consider him a pie-in-the-sky fool if they were not by now so familiar with his technique of taking a small slice at a time until years later he is holding the whole pie — even in the face of spending retrenchment. Persistence and patience are his strengths. With Democrats back in charge of the Senate as well as the House after the 1986 elections, speculation was widespread that party liberals would embark on a spending spree to address the social demands pent up during the years of GOP White House and Senate control. Waxman knew better. "My time has not yet arrived," he said. Implied, of course, was his certainty that it would.

On the matter of air pollution, a critical issue in the smog-plagued 24th District, the 101st Congress was Waxman's time. After nearly a decade of delay, Congress finally passed sweeping clean air legislation that achieved many of Waxman's long-held goals.

A monumental accomplishment, the clean air legislation was just one of Waxman's triumphs in the 101st. He also passed bills to expand Medicaid coverage for poor women and children; to provide money for AIDS treatment; and to mandate nutrition labeling. But there was also the repeal of an earlier Waxman effort — catastrophic health insurance.

Like his California mentor, the late Phillip Burton, Waxman believes that power exists to be used, and that winning, rather than self-expression, is the ultimate liberal goal. Unlike Burton, he does not have the kind of explosive temper that alienates as many members as can be cultivated through personal favors. Waxman is privately passionate about his issues, and in pursuing them he takes on some of Congress' most formidable and exasperating members, such as GOP Sen. Jesse Helms of North Carolina or House Energy and Commerce Chairman John D. Dingell, Democrat of Michigan. Yet publicly, he is all but unflappable.

Waxman's base is Energy and Commerce's Health and the Environment Subcommittee, which he has chaired since 1979. From there he fended off Reagan-era attacks on the health budget and waged war for cleaner air.

Passage of the 1990 Clean Air Act culminated a longstanding battle between Waxman, who sought tougher measures against acid rain and urban smog, and Dingell, who represented the interests of Detroit's auto industry and, to a lesser extent, of Midwestern states with coal-burning power plants.

Their tussle dates to 1982, when the law was up for renewal. Dingell — along with the Reagan administration, utilities and heavy industry — sought to relax emission standards.

But Waxman shrewdly prolonged his subcommittee's work, and repeated the same stalling tactics after the bill finally reached the full committee. He offered scores of amendments, once wheeling them into the room in a shopping cart, and insisted they be read entirely and voted on. When Waxman actually won some rounds, Dingell abruptly adjourned the meetings, killing his chance to weaken the law.

But later Dingell employed similar tactics to thwart Waxman's efforts to move tougher air pollution rules. With Edward Madigan of Illinois, then the ranking Republican on Waxman's subcommittee, Dingell slowed his opponent with lack of quorums, hearings prolonged by dozens of opposition witnesses, lengthy questioning and, at bottom, too few votes.

As the 1980s progressed, however, Waxman took hope from growing voter concern about the environment. Political pressure for new air pollution laws mounted when President Bush proposed legislation to the 101st Congress. With passage of some new clean air bill looking increasingly certain, Dingell began to engage Waxman in a contest to shape the coming law.

There was competition, but also some occasion for collaboration. While many Demo-

California 24

Hollywood; Part of San Fernando Valley

More than any other district in the nation, the 24th depends on the entertainment industry for its economic well-being. It includes the symbolic center of the industry — the corner of Hollywood and Vine — as well as Universal Studios, Paramount Pictures, Samuel Goldwyn Studios and the West Coast headquarters of ABC and CBS.

Many of the heavily Jewish "bagel boroughs" of Los Angeles are also within the 24th District. Concentrated near the Wilshire Country Club, the many elderly voters in this area provide a solid core of support for virtually any Democratic candidate. The 24th gave Michael S. Dukakis almost two-thirds of its presidential vote in 1988.

Like the 23rd and 26th districts, the 24th District straddles the Santa Monica Mountains. It reaches into the San Fernando Valley to include the Valley Plaza section. Still, this territory, with its mostly middle-class, blue-collar residents, is not as conservative as the areas of the valley found farther to the west.

One of the few Republican-leaning communities in the 24th is Hancock Park, a favored home of Los Angeles' "old money." During the years preceding World War II, its residents' attitudes forced the newly affluent to look elsewhere for property; Beverly Hills thus became the address of choice for the arriving rich. Hancock Park now includes more modest neighborhoods, including a sizable black community, but its exclusive character still predominates.

The 24th's Democratic lean is reinforced by its Hispanics (who make up about a quarter of the 24th's population); it also has the largest concentration of Asian-American voters in the state outside San Francisco. Many of them are Koreans, concentrated at the southern end of the district, and Vietnamese, who have settled in and around Hollywood. There is a sizable homosexual community in Hollywood and West Hollywood, about a third of which is in the district.

Population: 525,918. White 348,566 (66%), Black 34,301 (7%), Asian and Pacific Islander 61,256 (12%), Other 2,763 (1%). Spanish origin 137,587 (26%). 18 and over 429,288 (82%), 65 and over 80,133 (15%). Median age: 33.

crats on Energy and Commerce walk on eggshells with Dingell, Waxman did not hesitate to gavel him down if, in the course of sitting in on subcommittee deliberations, the Michigan Democrat spoke beyond the fixed time limit. Waxman skillfully picked off members to build winning coalitions on several motor-vehicle provisions Dingell opposed.

Still, Waxman suffered some defeats at Dingell's hand and did not make a religion of opposing him. Both men stunned fellow committee members when, in October 1989, they reached a deal on auto emissions standards.

Waxman, who favored the stricter environmental standard, was seen as having a better chance of winning a floor vote. But Waxman gave some ground, recognizing the uncertainty of floor action and the value of having Dingell on board. "I've looked forward to this day for a long, long time," Waxman said as they announced the compromise.

Their agreement on that and several other key votes prevented a bitter showdown and enabled the bill to move toward passage. The end result was weaker than Waxman would have liked in areas such as alternative fuels for automobiles, but it was still considered landmark environmental legislation, tougher on pollution than the administration had proposed.

On Energy and Commerce, Waxman is most often associated with health-care issues.

One such cause is health insurance, a topic of increasing national concern. In 1987, Waxman joined his frequent partner, Massachusetts Sen. Edward M. Kennedy, to unveil grandiose legislation for national health insurance, to be paid by employers and the government for millions of now-uninsured Americans. He said what few other politicians would dare: "This will require new taxes. I wouldn't want to fool anybody into thinking we're going to be able to do these things without more money."

The health insurance battle, like so many that Waxman fights, will be a long one. But meanwhile, on that and other priorities, he will continue to take whatever small victories he can get in times of huge budget deficits and public skepticism about social welfare spending.

Over the past decade, Waxman has been instrumental in dramatically expanding Medicaid, mostly by tucking health-care provisions for poor women and infants into the massive "reconciliation" bills that have become part of Congress' budget-cutting routine. Such bills — by their size, importance and special protection under congressional rules — offer Waxman's initiatives safety from filibusters, killer amendments and vetoes.

In the 101st Congress, aided by some Senate Democrats, Waxman again used the budget bill to expand Medicaid coverage. One change raised from 6 to 18 the age to which states must cover all poor children. At Waxman's insistence, Medicaid coverage beginning in 1995 will also be expanded to cover people just above the official poverty line.

Waxman has seen his share of defeats. In late 1987, when he declared that he was not bound by health spending limits in a budget-summit agreement between President Ronald Reagan and Congress, House Democratic leaders bridled him into submission. The next month, in a budget conference, opponents swamped his far-reaching proposals to stem infant mortality.

The following year, he helped write the law providing the elderly with Medicare coverage against catastrophic illnesses. Waxman was largely responsible for major provisions such as granting first-time coverage for outpatient prescription drugs. But senior citizens soon wailed in protest over the new law, which increased premiums and imposed a surtax on wealthier recipients. Early in the 101st Congress, Waxman helped defeat an effort in his subcommittee to repeal the law's controversial surtax. The repeal movement grew more insistent, however. After a failed attempt to salvage portions of the law, Waxman, too, backed repeal rather than accept a replacement measure.

Waxman had better luck with another of his initiatives in the 100th Congress. During the landmark overhaul of the welfare system, he sponsored a crucial amendment providing continued Medicaid coverage for a year to those who leave the rolls to take jobs.

Many of Waxman's successes in the conservative climate of recent years have been defensive. But even on defense, Waxman is more interested in results than debating points. In 1985, he vehemently opposed the Gramm-Rudman anti-deficit law, but did not waste time trying to kill a bill sure to pass. Instead, he worked in the House and in conference with the Senate to exempt his favorite health programs from the law's threatened cuts.

In recent years Waxman has led the House effort against AIDS, but it is a fight that taxes his usual legislative patience, given the deadliness of the disease. He is stymied not only by budget pressures, but also by objections from members such as Helms and California Rep. William E. Dannemeyer, who moved into the ranking spot on Waxman's subcommittee in the 102nd Congress.

Waxman engineered passage in the 100th Congress of the first comprehensive AIDS bill, authorizing money for education, anonymous testing and treatment. But to achieve that, Waxman had to drop two top priorities — confidentiality for AIDS tests and a ban on discrimination against victims. Both were endorsed by Reagan's AIDS commission, but his refusal to go along prompted Waxman's retreat.

Waxman came back in the 101st Congress with an another AIDS bill, to provide emergency funds to the 13 hardest-hit U.S. cities.

Also in the 101st, Waxman won approval for laws to provide uniform nutrition labeling on many processed foods. Items that would have to be listed include the food's caloric, fat, cholesterol, sodium and fiber content.

Waxman originally won his subcommittee chairmanship in 1979 with hardball politics. He pioneered a practice that has since become routine in leadership contests, raising money from his wealthy campaign supporters and distributing it to Energy and Commerce Democrats who would choose the subcommittee chairmen. He was accused of trying to buy the chair, but he prevailed over highly respected Richardson Preyer of North Carolina, 15-12.

Like Dingell at the full committee level, Waxman has tried to broaden his panel's scope. When Ways and Means proposed a new Medicare payment policy in 1983, Waxman wanted to modify it even though the policy was not under his jurisdiction. Then-Speaker Thomas P. O'Neill Jr. of Massachusetts intervened, and Ways and Means amended the plan to Waxman's satisfaction.

With his own re-election campaigns mere formalities, Waxman has built political influence by helping others win elections. In 1982, the Los Angeles-based organization he co-founded with Rep. Howard L. Berman aided six of the California House delegation's eight new Democrats (including Berman).

The one sort of politics Waxman has typically avoided is the periodic maneuvering for top House leadership posts. In 1989 he did announce for majority whip after fellow California Rep. Tony Coelho quit the job and left the House in an ethics controversy. But Waxman soon withdrew his bid and went back to his work on Energy and Commerce.

At Home: One reason Waxman never has any trouble carrying the 24th District is that its heavily Jewish, liberal constituency fits him ideally. The other reason is the Waxman-Berman machine. Waxman says his organization is unlike the domineering big-city operations that gave the term "political machine" a pejorative meaning. "A machine traditionally is conservative and corrupt, and tied together by patronage," says Waxman. "We're none of those things."

But Waxman, Berman and their political allies do run an efficient, smoothly functioning operation that concentrates the vast financial resources of the Los Angeles liberal community, makes extensive use of computer technology and has substantial political power.

The Waxman-Berman alliance was originally forged during college days at U.C.L.A., when the two budding politicians became active in the state's Federation of Young Democrats. Their first visible success came in 1968, when Waxman challenged Democratic Assemblyman Lester McMillan in a primary.

McMillan had been in office 26 years and was nearing retirement. Rather than waiting until the seat opened up, Waxman decided to take on the incumbent. With massive volunteer help, much of it recruited from the ranks of the Young Democrats, Waxman beat McMillan with 64 percent of the vote.

That election saw the beginning of what has since become a Waxman-Berman trademark — computerized mailings. Each voter is identified by a variety of sociopolitical characteristics and given a campaign pitch specifically tailored to his or her interests.

The "machine" label was affixed in 1972, when Waxman, then a two-term assemblyman, lent his muscle to help Berman win an Assembly seat. Berman's brother, Michael, who was to become a leading Democratic political consultant, aided in the effort.

By 1974 the operation was functioning so smoothly that Waxman had little trouble winning a new U.S. House seat created with him in mind. He has had even less trouble retaining it.

In 1984, Waxman had political worries of a different sort. Ever since 1981, California Republicans had been trying to find a way to undo the redistricting plan drawn up by Democratic Rep. Burton, which gave Democrats 28 California seats in the House. The GOP efforts in 1984 centered on a ballot initiative put forward by Republican Gov. George Deukmejian to dissolve the existing map before the 1986 elections and place the task of drawing new lines in the hands of a commission of retired judges.

The Democratic campaign against the measure was largely financed through the efforts of Waxman and his west Los Angeles House allies Berman and Mel Levine. They tapped their extensive network of sources both locally and around the country, while other California Democrats approached friends in Washington.

The battle was revisited in 1990, when state Republicans backed a pair of initiatives aimed at restricting the influence of the Democratic-controlled Legislature in the post-1990 round of redistricting. Waxman again helped raise money for the Democrats' anti-initiative efforts, Michael Berman's firm again ran the media campaign, and both ballot proposals went down to resounding defeats.

Committees

Energy & Commerce (3rd of 27 Democrats)
Health & the Environment (chairman); Commerce, Consumer Protection & Competitiveness

Government Operations (4th of 25 Democrats)
Commerce, Consumer & Monetary Affairs; Human Resources & Intergovernmental Relations

Select Aging (8th of 42 Democrats)
Health & Long-Term Care; Social Security and Women

Elections

1990 General

Henry A. Waxman (D)	71,562	(69%)
John N. Cowles (R)	26,607	(26%)
Maggie Phair (PFP)	5,706	(5%)

1988 General

Henry A. Waxman (D)	112,038	(72%)
John N. Cowles (R)	36,835	(24%)

Previous Winning Percentages: **1986** (88%) **1984** (63%) **1982** (65%) **1980** (64%) **1978** (63%) **1976** (68%) **1974** (64%)

District Vote For President

	1988	1984	1980	1976
D	106,652 (65%)	88,680 (55%)	68,286 (46%)	84,403 (55%)
R	55,756 (34%)	70,370 (44%)	62,782 (42%)	66,304 (43%)

Campaign Finance

	Receipts	Receipts from PACs	Expend-itures
1990			
Waxman (D)	$500,847	$315,400 (63%)	$287,505
Cowles (R)	$1,835	0	$1,830
1988			
Waxman (D)	$345,006	$257,841 (75%)	$191,334
Cowles (R)	$15,835	$600 (4%)	$15,449

Key Votes

1991	
Authorize use of force against Iraq	N
1990	
Support constitutional amendment on flag desecration	N
Pass family and medical leave bill over Bush veto	Y
Reduce SDI funding	Y
Allow abortions in overseas military facilities	Y
Approve budget summit plan for spending and taxing	N
Approve civil rights bill	Y
1989	
Halt production of B-2 stealth bomber at 13 planes	Y
Oppose capital gains tax cut	Y
Approve federal abortion funding in rape or incest cases	Y
Approve pay raise and revision of ethics rules	Y
Pass Democratic minimum wage plan over Bush veto	Y

Voting Studies

	Presidential Support		Party Unity		Conservative Coalition	
Year	**S**	**O**	**S**	**O**	**S**	**O**
1990	20	75	90	4	6	93
1989	28	63	88	2	5	85
1988	21	66	79	4	11	71
1987	18	74	84	3	9	84
1986	12	86	87	4	2	92
1985	28	71	86	3	11	84
1984	25	66	80	5	5	93
1983	22	71	84	3	6	85
1982	36	58	87	7	12	86
1981	25	63	79	5	4	88

Interest Group Ratings

Year	ADA	ACU	AFL-CIO	CCUS
1990	100	4	92	21
1989	100	4	100	30
1988	90	0	93	21
1987	92	10	79	17
1986	95	5	92	20
1985	95	16	94	27
1984	100	10	77	42
1983	95	5	94	25
1982	95	5	90	14
1981	85	0	77	11

25 Edward R. Roybal (D)

Of Pasadena — Elected 1962

Born: Feb. 10, 1916, Albuquerque, N.M.
Education: Attended U. of California, Los Angeles, 1935; Southwestern U. Law School, 1952.
Military Service: Army, 1944-45.
Occupation: Public health educator; social worker.
Family: Wife, Lucille Beserra; three children.
Religion: Roman Catholic.
Political Career: Los Angeles City Council, 1949-62; Democratic nominee for lieutenant governor, 1954.
Capitol Office: 2211 Rayburn Bldg. 20515; 225-6235.

In Washington: As he nears the end of his third decade in Congress, Roybal holds a prestige position as an Appropriations subcommittee chairman. He also is chairman of the Select Aging Committee, a panel that provides a forum for drawing public attention to issues involving the elderly.

Yet Roybal, a reserved, almost dour figure, rarely makes a splash in these roles. And while he is a prolific generator of legislative proposals, particularly in the areas of health care and the elderly, he often lacks zeal for the horse-trading needed to get his plans enacted.

With the strong backing of senior citizens' and civil rights groups, Roybal did help enact legislation in the 101st Congress that reversed a 1989 Supreme Court ruling allowing age-based discrimination in employee benefits.

Saying the court had misconstrued the law, Roybal began drafting legislation to overturn the decision within weeks of the ruling. "Congress did not intend for older workers to go unprotected from age discrimination in an employment area as critical as employee benefits," said Roybal. A compromise drafted to attract sufficient GOP support and avoid a presidential veto made it through both chambers in 1990.

In 1987, Roybal had joined Rep. Claude Pepper of Florida, his predecessor as Aging Committee chairman, in unsuccessfully pushing a costly bill — $30 billion over five years — to provide funding for long-term health care for the chronically ill. This difficulty in obtaining authorization for large new programs has not forestalled Roybal from proposing them. He has promoted measures to greatly increase funding for Alzheimer's disease research and to offset a national nursing shortage by providing funds to recruit and raise the salaries of nurses.

In 1990, Roybal helped secure passage of legislation to renew pilot programs providing medical services for people with Alzheimer's disease and home health care for low-income people; a total of $7.5 million was authorized for each of the programs in fiscal 1991. Roybal and his cosponsors said the "aging of America" made it urgent that researchers find ways to prevent or treat Alzheimer's, which primarily affects the elderly, gradually sapping victims' memory, altering their behavior and eventually killing them.

Roybal has also taken on the cause of mental health treatment. In the 100th Congress, he achieved adoption of a pair of amendments, expanding demonstration projects for rural mental health care and establishing a national mental health education program.

The California Democrat works to obtain funds for these programs as a senior member of the Appropriations Committee. As chairman of the Subcommittee on Treasury, Postal Service and General Government, Roybal maintains his usual low profile. But that is fitting: The issues dealt with by the panel rarely are subject to heated debate.

During consideration of the panel's fiscal 1990 spending measure, Roybal briefly protested the inclusion during conference of $16 million in House earmarks for five university science projects; he said the new projects violated House rules against folding into a conference package items not originally in either the House or the Senate bill. But Roybal ultimately backed off, acknowledging that whether or not it was appropriate to add last-minute projects, "it's been done before."

The next year, Roybal was able to capitalize on massive displeasure with the savings and loan industry. During committee consideration of the fiscal 1991 bill, Roybal successfully offered an amendment allowing the U.S. Secret Service to investigate crimes committed by S&L officials. He also shot down an attempt to include a provision in the bill appropriating $3 million for Puerto Rico's three political parties to be used for lobbying activities.

Both on Appropriations and off, Roybal takes a particular interest in issues involving his fellow Hispanic-Americans. His ethnic concerns led him into his most public role, as an oppo-

California 25

Central and East Los Angeles

Hispanics dominate the 25th like no other district in California. Nearly two-thirds of its residents identified themselves as being of Hispanic ancestry in the 1980 census.

The district incorporates the shining glass-and-steel towers of downtown Los Angeles. The area is laced with L.A.'s legendary crowded expressways, all named for suburbs that house the district's daytime, white-collar population: Pasadena, Pomona, Ventura, Glendale, Santa Ana.

But those roads carry commuters past the barrios of Boyle Heights and East Los Angeles, home to many of the Hispanics who form the core of the district's permanent population. These are bustling communities with active businesses and large families seeking to work their way up to the middle class. But poverty and unemployment run high, and Democratic loyalty is virtually unshakable.

The district is actually less Hispanic than it was before the last redistricting. The western side of the district, nearly all Hispanic, was sheared off and replaced by middle-class, racially mixed neighborhoods in western and northern Pasadena. Even with the changes, only a quarter of the population was Anglo and 10 percent black following the remap.

Any group that votes in significant numbers can exert some influence here, because voting participation in the district is the lowest in the state. The 25th is the only constituency in California where fewer than 100,000 people voted for president in 1980 — less than half the statewide average. By 1988, participation was up a bit, to just over 110,000.

Population: 526,013. White 265,979 (51%), Black 50,592 (10%), Asian and Pacific Islander 40,207 (8%), Other 3,156 (1%). Spanish origin 332,862 (63%). 18 and over 358,659 (68%), 65 and over 48,881 (9%). Median age: 27.

nent of the Simpson-Mazzoli immigration bill that was enacted in the 99th Congress.

The bill faced such strong resistance that it had to be brought up in three Congresses before its final passage. The measure imposed sanctions on U.S. employers who hired illegal aliens, and national Hispanic organizations felt those sanctions would lead to discrimination against Hispanics falsely suspected of being illegal aliens. As chairman of the Hispanic Caucus in the 97th Congress, Roybal led the opposition the first time the bill was introduced in 1982, and he continued to oppose the measure on through its final passage in 1986.

Roybal played a notable role during consideration of the sweeping revision of legal-immigration laws that cleared Congress in 1990. He was one of a group of Hispanic members who fought to delete a proposed pilot program to create a forgery-proof driver's license that could be used by employers to screen illegal workers. They saw that as the first step toward a national identification card.

In floor debate, Roybal said, "It is ironic that South Africa has just abandoned its notorious pass-card identification program that has been an essential element of its hated apartheid system."

With Roybal and fellow Hispanic lawmakers aggressively working the chamber floor, the House removed the license proposal. The Senate did the same, and both chambers passed the bill.

Roybal's record as an ethnic spokesman was a help to him in 1978, when he and two other California colleagues were disciplined by the House in connection with the Korean vote-buying investigation. The ethics committee had recommended reprimands for Charles H. Wilson and John J. McFall, but urged that Roybal be censured, a more serious penalty, for lying to the committee about a $1,000 gift from South Korean lobbyist Tongsun Park.

Many of Roybal's allies considered the distinction a race-related insult. "Two of our white colleagues are brought down here to be slapped on the wrist," complained black California Democrat Ronald V. Dellums, "and one of my brown brothers is down here to be totally wiped out in the process."

Roybal called in chits from Hispanic leaders outside Congress, asking them to help reduce the penalty to a reprimand. When the House agreed, Roybal described the action as "not only a personal victory for me, but for all Hispanics throughout the nation.... [It] shows the potential strength of the Hispanic community when it unifies behind a cause."

At Home: Roybal is a durable man. Despite a style few would call dynamic, he has become a permanent part of the political landscape in the Hispanic neighborhoods of East Los Angeles.

Lately, Roybal has campaigned relatively little. An aide once said that the noisy Pomona Freeway running just a few yards from Roybal's Los Angeles home did not bother him, "because he is hardly ever there." But while there are younger, more aggressive Hispanic leaders in the East Los Angeles area, none have so far been willing to take on Roybal, who is viewed as a sort of community "elder."

Beginning with his first re-election in 1964, Roybal has never received less than 66 percent in a general election. He has won more than 80 percent the three times he has been challenged in a primary (1970, 1972 and 1976). Even the House reprimand of Roybal in 1978 had little political impact.

When Roybal was 4, he moved from New Mexico to the ethnically mixed Boyle Heights section of Los Angeles. Since then, the area has turned almost entirely Hispanic.

During the Depression he worked in the Civilian Conservation Corps and later became involved in public health for the California Tuberculosis Association. He was elected to the Los Angeles City Council from a Hispanic East Side district; he served four terms.

Roybal's first try for higher office, a 1954 bid for lieutenant governor, failed. But in 1962, he was elected to the House, where he has stayed ever since.

The 1962 campaign was a challenging one for Roybal. The state Legislature had just redrawn the congressional boundaries, pushing the district of nine-term Republican Rep. Gordon L. McDonough far into East Los Angeles. Given the lopsided Democratic registration, he looked so vulnerable that five Democrats, including Roybal, entered the 1962 primary.

Roybal had major primary opposition from William Fitzgerald, a Loyola University government professor, and G. Pappy Boyington, a World War II Marine flying ace who had become a hero as the commander of the "Black Sheep Squadron." But with his solid base in the Hispanic community, Roybal won three-fifths of the primary vote and went on to defeat McDonough easily in the general election.

As Roybal continued on to senior tenure in the House, his daughter, Lucille Roybal-Allard, built her own career in East Los Angeles politics. A member of the California Assembly, Roybal-Allard has been mentioned as a possible future successor to her father.

Committees

Select Aging (Chairman)
Health & Long-Term Care (chairman)

Appropriations (6th of 37 Democrats)
Treasury, Postal Service & General Government (chairman); Labor, Health & Human Services, and Education

Elections

1990 General		
Edward R. Roybal (D)	48,120	(70%)
Steven J. Renshaw (R)	17,021	(25%)
Robert H. Scott (LIBERT)	3,576	(5%)
1988 General		
Edward R. Roybal (D)	85,378	(85%)
Raul Reyes (PFP)	8,746	(9%)
John C. Thie (LIBERT)	5,752	(6%)

Previous Winning Percentages: **1986** (76%) **1984** (72%) **1982** (86%) **1980** (66%) **1978** (67%) **1976** (72%) **1974** (100%) **1972** (68%) **1970** (68%) **1968** (67%) **1966** (66%) **1964** (66%) **1962** (57%)

District Vote For President

	1988	1984	1980	1976
D	74,007 (67%)	65,974 (60%)	52,239 (57%)	57,998 (62%)
R	34,925 (32%)	42,375 (39%)	31,338 (34%)	33,920 (36%)

Campaign Finance

	Receipts	Receipts from PACs	Expend-itures
1990			
Roybal (D)	$144,260	$79,877 (55%)	$190,702
1988			
Roybal (D)	$86,724	$46,800 (54%)	$67,957

Key Votes

1991	
Authorize use of force against Iraq	N
1990	
Support constitutional amendment on flag desecration	N
Pass family and medical leave bill over Bush veto	Y
Reduce SDI funding	Y
Allow abortions in overseas military facilities	Y
Approve budget summit plan for spending and taxing	N
Approve civil rights bill	Y
1989	
Halt production of B-2 stealth bomber at 13 planes	Y
Oppose capital gains tax cut	Y
Approve federal abortion funding in rape or incest cases	Y
Approve pay raise and revision of ethics rules	Y
Pass Democratic minimum wage plan over Bush veto	Y

Voting Studies

	Presidential Support		Party Unity		Conservative Coalition	
Year	**S**	**O**	**S**	**O**	**S**	**O**
1990	16	81	92	4	15	81
1989	24	66	90	1	2	93
1988	20	77	89	3	5	95
1987	11	75	88	2	2	74
1986	16	80	88	5	16	74
1985	16	78	89	3	7	84
1984	24	67	85	4	5	90
1983	15	83	95	3	7	89
1982	23	71	95	2	8	92
1981	34	64	92	7	12	87

Interest Group Ratings

Year	ADA	ACU	AFL-CIO	CCUS
1990	100	4	100	36
1989	95	0	100	33
1988	95	0	100	23
1987	88	10	88	7
1986	95	5	85	19
1985	95	5	94	15
1984	100	4	92	38
1983	95	0	88	25
1982	95	9	100	9
1981	95	13	93	5

26 Howard L. Berman (D)

Of Panorama City — Elected 1982

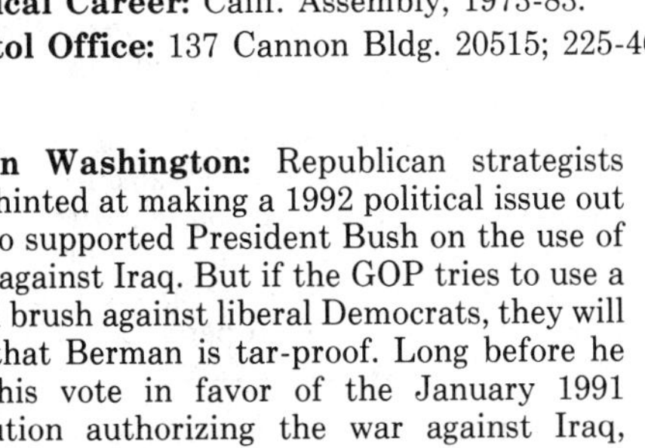

Born: April 15, 1941, Los Angeles, Calif.
Education: U. of California, Los Angeles, B.A. 1962, LL.B. 1965.
Occupation: Lawyer.
Family: Wife, Janis Schwartz; two children.
Religion: Jewish.
Political Career: Calif. Assembly, 1973-83.
Capitol Office: 137 Cannon Bldg. 20515; 225-4695.

In Washington: Republican strategists have hinted at making a 1992 political issue out of who supported President Bush on the use of force against Iraq. But if the GOP tries to use a broad brush against liberal Democrats, they will find that Berman is tar-proof. Long before he cast his vote in favor of the January 1991 resolution authorizing the war against Iraq, Berman was warning of the threat posed by that nation's dictator, Saddam Hussein.

From the time in 1988 when Iraq's troops used poison gas against that nation's Kurdish minority until the eve of the Iraqi invasion of Kuwait, Berman labored to pass a bill enacting economic sanctions against Iraq. But he was parried by opposition from officials in the Reagan and Bush administrations, who then viewed Iraq as a bulwark against Iran and as a key player in Middle East politics.

In the wake of the U.S. military action sparked by Iraq's aggression, Berman is certain to revisit Congress' role in shaping foreign policy: At the start of the 102nd Congress, he became chairman of the House Foreign Affairs Subcommittee on International Operations.

Berman's interest in Middle East affairs stems largely from his support for Israel. He consistently backs U.S. aid to Israel, opposes arms sales to Arab nations and favors strict trade limits on the radical Middle East states.

In 1988, Berman led the fight for a House bill barring U.S. oil purchases from Iraq and opposing U.S. trade credits and loans by international banking organizations to that nation unless its leaders swore off using chemical weapons. Though the Reagan administration said Iraq had given "reliable assurances" it would not use such weapons, the measure passed as part of a larger foreign aid bill. However, objections by Sen. Jesse Helms, R-N.C., to unrelated portions of the bill killed it at the end of the 100th Congress.

The issue was revived in April 1990, when an increasingly belligerent Saddam Hussein threatened to "burn up half of Israel" with chemical weapons if Israel attacked Iraq. Berman revived his sanctions bill, stating, "It is past time to deny this evil totalitarian the finance and materials he seeks to implement his threats." The Bush administration, still trying to keep open diplomatic channels to Iraq, succeeded at stalling the effort. The bill was reported by the Foreign Affairs Committee on Aug. 1, 1990; the next day, Iraqi troops overran Kuwait. The bill became law in November 1990.

The war resolution debate in January 1991 divided Jewish members of Congress, many of whom are liberal Democrats who opposed the U.S. intervention in Vietnam. Berman stuck by his anti-Saddam line and supported Bush, but not without an "I told you so."

"I was a longtime critic of this administration's policy toward Iraq, which I feel was partially responsible for the miscalculation on Saddam's part that the United States would tolerate any behavior by Iraq," Berman said. Just as on his Iraq bill, Berman ran into White House complaints about "micromanagment" when he proposed a bill instituting sanctions against countries and companies that sell chemical and biological weapons to other nations. The measure, attached as an amendment to the Export Administration Act of 1990, provoked a pocket veto by Bush.

One Berman-sponsored bill that became law during the 101st Congress tightened restrictions on arms sales to nations that sponsor terrorism. Berman and an ideological opposite, Illinois Republican Henry J. Hyde, first found common ground on the issue in 1986. But the law that resulted from their early efforts contained loopholes the Reagan White House exploited to sell arms to Iran in what would become the Iran-contra affair. After that scandal broke, Berman and Hyde proposed a tougher measure. It passed the House during the 100th Congress, but died in the Senate.

However, Berman and Hyde revived the bill. Its bans on U.S. aid and arms sales (government or commercial) to countries that the secretary of state has determined to be supporters of terrorism remained unchanged. But it contained a provision sought by the Bush administration which permits the president to

California 26

Santa Monica Mountains; Central San Fernando Valley

Clever Democratic map-making made Berman's House election a near-certainty. In picking up liberal territory that was part of Democratic Rep. Anthony C. Beilenson's old 23rd District, the 26th became a solidly Democratic district. Many of the former Beilenson voters live in the fashionable Mulholland Drive area north of Beverly Hills.

Farther west are Sherman Oaks and Studio City, in the San Fernando Valley at the base of the Santa Monica Mountains. Berman represented this area for a decade in the Assembly.

The less favorable part of the district for Democrats is in the heart of the San Fernando Valley — communities such as Van Nuys, Panorama City and Sepulveda. The ranch-style houses that line the endless straight streets here are home to the white-collar professionals and well-paid blue-collar workers who populate the valley.

The aviation and electronics industries are major employers. But Lockheed, which came here in 1928, announced plans in 1990 to shut down its huge facility in Burbank.

Nearly all the areas in the 26th have for years been under Democratic representation in the state Legislature. But the constituency occasionally shows a strong conservative streak on some social and economic issues. In 1988, the area voted for a ballot proposition to require mandatory AIDS testing for certain individuals.

The northernmost end of the district is the most industrialized portion; it has attracted large numbers of Mexican-Americans. Their migration to communities such as San Fernando City and Pacoima has helped boost the overall Hispanic population of the district to 25 percent.

Population: 525,995. White 417,569 (79%), Black 23,218 (4%), Other 21,880 (4%). Spanish origin 131,180 (25%). 18 and over 392,919 (75%), 65 and over 53,364 (10%). Median age: 31.

waive the bans if such action is in the national interest and if Congress is informed in advance. The bill became law in December 1989.

As a member of the Judiciary Committee, Berman has been active on immigration issues. He was one of the key negotiators in producing a new national immigration law in the 99th Congress. When the 101st Congress debated the first overhaul of the nation's immigration visa-allotment system since 1965, Berman called for a higher annual limit on the number of immigrants than that contained in the major proposal by Sens. Edward M. Kennedy, D-Mass., and Alan K. Simpson, R-Wyo.

It is on Judiciary, more so than on Foreign Affairs, that Berman's liberal instincts show. He opposed the 1989 law and the unsuccessful 1990 constitutional amendment to ban flag burning. Also, Berman has proposed a bill to ban the sale of assault rifles and pistols.

Berman retains the political skills that enabled him, along with House colleague and longtime friend Henry A. Waxman, to build a powerful Democratic organization in Los Angeles. At the start of the 101st Congress, Berman lobbied long and hard for a seat on the Budget Committee. "I made a real pest of myself," he later said. When the Democratic Steering and Policy Committee voted, Berman finished well ahead of the other 12 Democrats seeking the six open committee seats.

At Home: The "Berman-Waxman" organization dominates the West Los Angeles political scene. It is less a "machine" than a network of like-minded politicians who pool resources to back candidates — expected to be legislative allies — with money, organization, computer technology and the skills of Berman's brother, Michael, a political consultant.

Howard Berman's influence in Democratic politics stretches back to the late 1960s, when he and Waxman, students at UCLA, were involved in the Federation of Young Democrats. Berman succeeded Waxman in the presidency of the federation in 1967, and helped him win a seat in the state Assembly the following year.

In 1972 Berman again followed Waxman's lead, challenging veteran GOP Assemblyman Charles J. Conrad in a traditionally Republican district that had grown more Democratic with the migration of residents from inner-city Los Angeles. Pulling in funds from his by-then extensive contacts and mobilizing Young Democrats and students, Berman toppled Conrad.

Berman pursued his job in Sacramento with relish, building a following in the Legislature and allying himself with Speaker Leo T. McCarthy and Gov. Edmund G. Brown Jr. He was a consummate facilitator and tactician, with a relaxed style that made him approachable even to opponents.

Yet Berman's upward climb in the Assembly was derailed by his own ambitions. Despite his long alliance with McCarthy, Berman challenged him for Speaker in a 1980 contest that ended up poorly for both men.

Berman justified his move by contending that McCarthy's statewide ambitions — he planned to run for higher office in 1982 — were leading him to raise money for his own efforts instead of working to elect Democratic candidates to the Legislature. Both speakership contenders decided to use the 1980 elections to build their own strengths, funneling money to state legislative candidates who could be expected to back them in Sacramento. Once the air cleared in November, Berman, who already had support from most Assembly Democrats, had increased his forces by two members.

But even as McCarthy conceded defeat, his backers, bitterly opposed to a Berman speakership, threw their support to a third candidate, Willie L. Brown Jr. With the help of GOP members of the Assembly who feared Berman's leadership, Brown was elected Speaker, a position he would hold into the 1990s.

Redistricting offered the new Speaker an opportunity to help promote Berman out of Sacramento. When Rep. Phillip Burton's remap plan gave Berman a favorable congressional district, Brown was happy to ease its passage.

Still, Berman had to work for the House seat. The GOP nominated wealthy auto dealer Hal Phillips, who had strong financial backing. For the first time since his 1972 Assembly fight, Berman walked precincts and, with his brother's help, ran an extensive direct-mail campaign. He won with 60 percent of the vote.

Once in Congress, Berman worked to preserve the redistricting plan that had sent him there. In 1984, while coasting to re-election, he raised money to defeat GOP Gov. George Deukmejian's ballot initiative that would have undone the Democratic-tilted remap. In 1990, Berman campaigned against two ballot measures to limit the influence of the Democratic-controlled Legislature over 1990s redistricting. Michael Berman and his consulting partner Carl D'Agostino handled the media for the successful efforts against the initiatives.

Meanwhile, Berman has had no trouble at the polls. He topped out at 70 percent in 1988 before slipping to a more typical 61 percent in 1990 against GOP businessman Roy Dahlson.

Committees

Budget (12th of 23 Democrats)
Budget Process, Reconciliation & Enforcement; Defense, Foreign Policy & Space

Foreign Affairs (10th of 28 Democrats)
International Operations (chairman); Arms Control, International Security & Science

Judiciary (12th of 21 Democrats)
Economic & Commercial Law; International Law, Immigration & Refugees

Elections

1990 General		
Howard L. Berman (D)	78,031	(61%)
Roy Dahlson (R)	44,492	(35%)
Bernard Zimring (LIBERT)	5,268	(4%)
1990 Primary		
Howard L. Berman (D)	43,676	(86%)
Scott Gaulke (D)	6,912	(14%)
1988 General		
Howard L. Berman (D)	126,930	(70%)
G.C. Broderson (R)	53,518	(30%)

Previous Winning Percentages: **1986** (65%) **1984** (63%) **1982** (60%)

District Vote For President

	1988	1984	1980	1976
D	108,660 (55%)	90,429 (45%)	70,242 (38%)	83,316 (52%)
R	85,640 (44%)	108,528 (54%)	93,648 (51%)	74,919 (46%)

Campaign Finance

	Receipts	Receipts from PACs		Expend-itures
1990				
Berman (D)	$510,538	$181,500	(36%)	$450,401
Dahlson (R)	$83,775	$250	(0%)	$82,453
1988				
Berman (D)	$528,296	$209,317	(40%)	$409,233

Key Votes

1991	
Authorize use of force against Iraq	Y
1990	
Support constitutional amendment on flag desecration	N
Pass family and medical leave bill over Bush veto	Y
Reduce SDI funding	Y
Allow abortions in overseas military facilities	Y
Approve budget summit plan for spending and taxing	N
Approve civil rights bill	Y
1989	
Halt production of B-2 stealth bomber at 13 planes	Y
Oppose capital gains tax cut	Y
Approve federal abortion funding in rape or incest cases	Y
Approve pay raise and revision of ethics rules	‡
Pass Democratic minimum wage plan over Bush veto	Y

Voting Studies

	Presidential Support		Party Unity		Conservative Coalition	
Year	**S**	**O**	**S**	**O**	**S**	**O**
1990	20	77	93	3	7	93
1989	31	63	90	3	10	90
1988	23	66	90	4	5	84
1987	14	84	89	3	5	93
1986	18	80	89	5	12	82
1985	24	68	91	3	9	85
1984	29	62	84	6	7	88
1983	24	67	85	5	10	88

Interest Group Ratings

Year	ADA	ACU	AFL-CIO	CCUS
1990	100	4	92	23
1989	95	4	100	30
1988	95	4	85	36
1987	88	0	88	13
1986	95	5	92	19
1985	100	10	94	24
1984	95	9	77	43
1983	95	0	88	25

27 Mel Levine (D)

Of Los Angeles — Elected 1982

Born: June 7, 1943, Los Angeles, Calif.
Education: U. of California, Berkeley, A.B. 1964; Princeton U., M.P.A. 1966; Harvard U., J.D. 1969.
Occupation: Lawyer.
Family: Wife, Jan Greenberg; three children.
Religion: Jewish.
Political Career: Calif. Assembly, 1977-83.
Capitol Office: 2443 Rayburn Bldg. 20515; 225-6451.

In Washington: The decision on whether to support the resolution authorizing President Bush to use force against Iraq in January 1991 was a trying one for most liberal Democrats — especially Jewish members whose antiwar inclinations clashed with their support for Israel, an Iraqi adversary.

For Levine, however, the choice was not hard. A longtime critic of the Iraqi regime of Saddam Hussein, Levine favored using whatever means necessary to force Iraq's troops out of occupied Kuwait and to make Saddam give up his weapons of mass destruction.

In a speech favoring the "war resolution," Levine said his instincts favored diplomacy over force. "But what cannot be achieved by diplomacy or sanctions alone is our ability to defeat Saddam's increased ability to utilize chemical, biological and nuclear weapons," Levine said, adding that "we must be willing to act now or face the grave risk of Saddam's nuclear weapons to the nation and to the world."

Despite his support for the resolution and Bush's use of it to begin military action against Iraq, Levine did criticize the president during the Persian Gulf crisis for failing to anticipate Saddam's aggressive intentions. As a member of the Foreign Affairs Committee, Levine favored legislation to impose economic sanctions after the Iraqi government used poison gas against its Kurdish minority in 1988; the Reagan and Bush administrations opposed such moves as intrusions on their foreign policy prerogatives.

Levine's hawkish stance on Iraq was a far cry from his approach to some issues of war and peace in the 1980s: He was a persistent critic of President Ronald Reagan's Central America policies.

To these issues, Levine brought the passion of his days as an angry student activist at Berkeley and Harvard, as he attacked the "gunboat diplomacy" of the Reagan era. Levine was well ahead of most House members in early 1985, when he called for an investigation into alleged Reagan administration efforts to steer private aid to the Nicaraguan contras.

However, Levine's hard line against Iraq fit well within the context of his role as a leading supporter of Israel. He has consistently cautioned about linking the United States with Arab nations that are antagonistic to Israel. Even though Saudi Arabia was part of the anti-Iraq coalition and was the base for Operation "Desert Shield" (later "Desert Storm"), Levine was wary of Bush's plans to sell more U.S. arms to that nation. He said in August 1990 that he would be "very concerned if this crisis were used as a vehicle for transferring any sophisticated weapons to this region."

As a member of the Foreign Affairs Subcommittee on International Economic Policy and Trade, Levine has become a spokesman for those who say a federal investment is necessary if the U.S. high-technology industry is to win out over foreign competitors. In 1987, he co-founded Rebuild America, a Washington-based think tank that studies issues related to the nation's high-tech future.

Levine, whose suburban Los Angeles district contains a high-tech sector, says he favors a strategy by which the government promotes consortia of companies — which would research and develop new technologies — by easing antitrust restrictions and, in some cases, providing seed money to get the cooperative arrangements off the ground.

At the start of the 101st Congress, Levine acted on this concept by calling for a government-backed consortium to develop high-definition television (HDTV), an emerging technology that may produce sharper television images. Describing HDTV as the next commercial battlefield in a consumer electronics industry war now dominated by Japan, Levine said that a $1 billion federal investment might be necessary. "Ultimately, the countries that have this industry will find themselves in possession of the most important technologies of the 21st century," Levine said.

Levine's concern about competitiveness made him a staunch opponent of the FS-X project, a jet fighter based on the American F-16 to be jointly produced by Japan and the

California 27

Pacific Coast — Santa Monica

The 27th hugs the Pacific Coast for 20 miles, from Pacific Palisades in the north down to affluent Redondo Beach. Santa Monica is its political and geographic hub.

A city of 87,000, Santa Monica is a mixture of elderly middle-class residents and young families who like being close to both Los Angeles and the ocean. Political activism runs high here. It is the home base of Assemblyman and former 1960s radical Tom Hayden.

Although Hayden and his wife, activist actress Jane Fonda, separated in early 1989 and later divorced, they have left their mark on the local political scene. Their activities, along with the growth of a tenants' rights movement among its apartment-dwellers, have given Santa Monica a well-earned liberal reputation.

In 1984, the city gave Walter F. Mondale 55 percent of its vote. Michael S. Dukakis took 65 percent in 1988, enabling him to carry the 27th as a whole by a wide margin. That same year, Santa Monica voters gave a majority to a proposition, soundly defeated statewide, to use penalties against violators of housing and restaurant codes to increase funding for the hungry and the homeless.

Just east of Santa Monica is the Brentwood section of Los Angeles, an affluent, heavily Jewish area that has strongly supported Levine over the years. South of it is Venice, an artists' community that has been overrun by young "beach people."

South of Venice, the district runs in a narrow strip past Marina del Rey, taking in the sprawling Los Angeles International Airport and the upper-middle-class communities that run down the coastline to the South Bay area just north of the Palos Verdes Peninsula. There is more of a Republican vote here: The aerospace and defense industries compose the dominant economic forces in the South Bay area. Inland, even blue-collar towns like Lawndale have lost some of their Democratic loyalties in recent years.

The only pocket of true Democratic strength in the southern half of the 27th is in Inglewood, a heavily black community added to the district in 1983.

Population: 525,929. White 398,371 (76%), Black 57,636 (11%), Asian and Pacific Islander 29,949 (6%), Other 3,011 (1%). Spanish origin 75,261 (14%). 18 and over 415,975 (79%), 65 and over 50,212 (10%). Median age: 31.

United States. "We cannot ... prevent Japan from becoming a competitor in aerospace, but I do not see why we have to subsidize the development of our own competitors," said Levine.

Foreign policy is just one of the items on Levine's wide-ranging agenda, which befits a House member thought to have ambitions for higher office. In early 1991, Levine, a prolific campaign fundraiser, was viewed as a likely candidate for the Senate seat of Democrat Alan Cranston, who is not running for re-election in 1992.

Levine is a member of the Interior Committee, where he has worked over the last several years to resolve a long-stymied wilderness bill affecting the southern California desert. The anticipated prominence of this issue in the 102nd Congress was exhibited by the change in the name of a subcommittee Levine is on: General Oversight and Investigations became General Oversight and California Desert Lands.

In October 1989, Levine also gained a seat on the Judiciary Committee, replacing Maryland Democrat Benjamin L. Cardin (who moved to Ways and Means). One of his early marks was as a supporter of gun control. In early 1991, he backed the "Brady bill" to impose a seven-day waiting period for the purchase of a handgun.

Levine also has shown an interest in criminal justice issues as a member of the Select Committee on Narcotics Abuse and Control. He helped engineer the creation of a federal law-enforcement strike force to combat the violent street gangs involved in Los Angeles County's illegal drug trafficking.

At Home: Levine is a major partner in the west Los Angeles liberal Democratic organization founded by his House colleagues, Howard L. Berman and Henry A. Waxman. The issue of war with Iraq created a rare policy division within the organization: Levine and Berman favored the resolution authorizing the use of force, while Waxman opposed it.

Levine comes from a wealthy Los Angeles family with ties to both the Republican and Democratic parties. His own politics are marked by an ardent liberalism, tempered by his interest in high-tech industry and his support for Israel.

Eight years out of law school, with a mixed civil and public interest practice, he was tapped by a coalition of Jewish organizations to lobby the Legislature to prohibit businesses from complying with the Arab boycott of Israel. He developed a friendship with then-Assemblyman Berman. With the help of the Waxman-Berman organization, Levine won a 1977 special election for an Assembly seat. He spent five years in the Assembly, specializing in energy matters.

When Republican Rep. Robert K. Dornan decided to give up his coastal Los Angeles seat in 1982 to run for the Senate, Levine was ready to move on. The 27th was redrawn for him in 1981 redistricting, losing its more conservative southern communities. With Waxman-Berman help, Levine was a sure winner from the start. He had no primary opponent, and no Republican of any stature was willing to take him on. In the end, he faced country club owner Bart W. Christensen and won with 60 percent.

Two years later, Levine ran into unexpectedly tough opposition. Republican Robert Scribner, a former Los Angeles Rams running back and a conservative evangelical, mounted a well-funded effort to unseat him. Levine, perhaps too sure of easy victory, spent most of his time and money fighting a statewide redistricting initiative that would have hurt Democratic House members. He ended up with just 55 percent, enough of a drop to ensure that Scribner would be back for a return engagement.

But the rematch was no contest. Scribner raised eyebrows of Democrats and Republicans alike by sending a fundraising letter to local ministers in 1985, urging them to "agree to link arms with us as we literally 'take territory' for our Lord Jesus Christ." Levine, concentrating on his own campaign this time, won almost two-thirds of the vote.

After topping out at 68 percent in 1988, Levine faced a rather vigorous 1990 Republican opponent in 30-year-old lawyer David Barrett Cohen. Accusing Levine of supporting a "bankrupt liberal agenda," Cohen called for creation of a multiethnic, multiracial "Rainbow on the Right." Levine's performance slipped somewhat, but he still took 58 percent.

Committees

Foreign Affairs (11th of 28 Democrats)
Europe & the Middle East; International Economic Policy & Trade; International Operations

Interior & Insular Affairs (17th of 29 Democrats)
General Oversight & California Desert Lands; National Parks & Public Lands

Judiciary (16th of 21 Democrats)
Intellectual Property & Judicial Administration; Crime and Criminal Justice

Select Narcotics Abuse & Control (9th of 21 Democrats)

Elections

1990 General		
Mel Levine (D)	90,857	(58%)
David Barrett Cohen (R)	58,140	(37%)
Edward E. Ferrer (PFP)	7,101	(5%)
1988 General		
Mel Levine (D)	148,814	(68%)
Dennis Galbraith (R)	65,307	(30%)

Previous Winning Percentages: **1986** (64%) **1984** (55%) **1982** (60%)

District Vote For President

	1988	1984	1980	1976
D	126,695 (55%)	104,031 (46%)	80,285 (40%)	92,212 (49%)
R	102,897 (44%)	117,634 (52%)	92,964 (47%)	91,721 (49%)

Campaign Finance

	Receipts	Receipts from PACs		Expend-itures
1990				
Levine (D)	$1,496,790	$239,207	(16%)	$587,961
Cohen (R)	$148,295	$1,000	(1%)	$146,206
1988				
Levine (D)	$893,810	$153,500	(17%)	$398,597
Galbraith (R)	$17,392	$1,240	(7%)	$17,022

Key Votes

1991	
Authorize use of force against Iraq	Y
1990	
Support constitutional amendment on flag desecration	N
Pass family and medical leave bill over Bush veto	Y
Reduce SDI funding	Y
Allow abortions in overseas military facilities	Y
Approve budget summit plan for spending and taxing	N
Approve civil rights bill	Y
1989	
Halt production of B-2 stealth bomber at 13 planes	Y
Oppose capital gains tax cut	Y
Approve federal abortion funding in rape or incest cases	Y
Approve pay raise and revision of ethics rules	Y
Pass Democratic minimum wage plan over Bush veto	Y

Voting Studies

	Presidential Support		Party Unity		Conservative Coalition	
Year	**S**	**O**	**S**	**O**	**S**	**O**
1990	19	78	93	3	6	94
1989	31	65	96	0	10	88
1988	21	75	92	4	8	84
1987	17	79	96	3	7	91
1986	16	81	92	3	6	86
1985	24	75	94	3	7	91
1984	28	68	88	5	5	88
1983	21	77	86	6	20	76

Interest Group Ratings

Year	ADA	ACU	AFL-CIO	CCUS
1990	100	4	92	21
1989	90	0	100	40
1988	95	4	86	36
1987	96	9	88	20
1986	85	5	75	15
1985	100	10	94	27
1984	90	9	92	47
1983	90	0	94	30

28 Julian C. Dixon (D)

Of Culver City — Elected 1978

Born: Aug. 8, 1934, Washington, D.C.
Education: California State U., Los Angeles, B.S. 1962; Southwestern U., LL.B. 1967.
Military Service: Army, 1957-60.
Occupation: Legislative aide; lawyer.
Family: Wife, Betty Lee; one child.
Religion: Episcopalian.
Political Career: Calif. Assembly, 1973-79.
Capitol Office: 2400 Rayburn Bldg. 20515; 225-7084.

In Washington: Dixon earned his colleagues' respect in two unglamorous roles — the chairmanships of the House ethics committee and the Appropriations Subcommittee on the District of Columbia. At the start of the 101st Congress, he got a new role with more practical benefits — a seat on Appropriations' Defense Subcommittee. Dixon is the only member on that panel from defense-dependent California.

But before he could settle into enjoying the influence that position should bring him within the California delegation, Dixon had to endure time-consuming ethics committee tasks in the 101st Congress, the most onerous of which was the case of Speaker Jim Wright of Texas.

Dixon would have had just cause to borrow the Rev. Dr. Martin Luther King Jr.'s "free at last" quotation after his ethics committee tenure finally ended in 1991. When he joined the committee in 1983 and became its chairman in 1985, Dixon expected to serve the usual two-term rotation. However, he was asked by the Democratic leadership to stay on for a third term to handle an investigation of then-Banking Committee Chairman Fernand J. St Germain of Rhode Island; his stay was extended again when the probe of Wright carried over from the 100th Congress.

Like most Democratic members of the ethics committee, Dixon was chosen by the leadership because of his reputation as a reliable, low-key insider who could be counted on not to be a "hanging judge." These qualities led conservative Republicans — who were trying to make corruption an albatross issue for the Democratic Party — to complain in advance that Wright was likely to get off lightly in the investigation of his financial transactions.

However, Dixon's judicious conduct of the Wright case left little room to fault his impartiality. Dixon voted to pursue most of the charges against Wright. When Wright accused committee special counsel Richard J. Phelan of "a lack of professionalism" and "distortion," Dixon called the remarks "totally inaccurate, totally wrong, an exercise in bad judgment."

Wright resigned from the House in May 1989, precluding the need for the ethics committee to decide his fate. Although Dixon was praised for his handling of the affair, it was an experience he would not want to repeat. Earlier in 1989, Dixon had said, "You get burned out.... I've had it."

Dixon himself was discomfited by the glare of media scrutiny. In June 1989, he amended his 1986 financial-disclosure form to provide more information about his wife's investment in shops at Los Angeles International Airport. Some suspicion was cast on the deals following newspaper reports that the ethics committee had in 1986 retained a lawyer who at the time was the head of the Los Angeles airport commission. Dixon denied any wrongdoing.

Dixon avoided a potentially bloody partisan battle when a committee counsel recommended in August 1989 against pursuing an investigation of House Minority Whip Newt Gingrich of Georgia on charges stemming from a book-financing deal. However, the committee did have to settle the case of Massachusetts Democrat Barney Frank, who had admitted to a past relationship with a male prostitute, Steven Gobie, whom he hired as a personal assistant.

Some Republicans hoped to use any leniency toward Frank as evidence of Democratic libertinism. The committee investigation, while finding Frank guilty of such transgressions as fixing parking tickets, concluded he was blameless on more serious allegations, including permitting Gobie to use his residence for prostitution. After weeks of partisan wrangling, the committee voted in July 1990 for the relatively mild punishment of a House reprimand.

Rep. William E. Dannemeyer, an anti-homosexual activist, then proposed to expel Frank, and provoked Dixon's ire by raising charges on which the committee had cleared Frank. The usually mild-mannered Dixon furiously debunked Dannemeyer's statements as "edited, selective garbage." Dixon also turned the debate into a referendum on his and the committee's integrity, stating, "This case boils down to, really, who do you trust?"

The House trusted Dixon. Dannemeyer's

California 28

Southern Los Angeles; Culver City

Located directly south of Beverly Hills and Hollywood and stretching to the edge of downtown Los Angeles, the 28th is a racially mixed collection of neighborhoods, some middle-class and some poor, but nearly all Democratic. It was the second-best California district for Democratic presidential nominee Michael S. Dukakis in 1988, behind the neighboring 29th.

One reason for the Democratic strength is that the 28th has the second-highest percentage of blacks in California, trailing only the 29th. The district has been served by black Democrats — first, Yvonne Brathwaite Burke, then Dixon — since its creation in 1972.

The level of income in the 28th rises as the district moves west, away from central Los Angeles. The portions of the city in the district, centered around the Coliseum area, are largely poor and black.

Windsor Hills and Ladera Heights, west of the city limits, also have many black voters, but they are mainly middle- and upper-middle class. Many neighborhoods in these close-in suburbs have a generous ethnic mix, with whites, blacks, Hispanics and Asians living next to each other in single-family homes.

West of Ladera Heights is middle-class Culver City, a mostly white community that also has drawn well-to-do blacks, including Dixon. The home of MGM, Culver City will occasionally break from the district's Democratic path: In 1984, the city gave Ronald Reagan a majority. But in 1988, Dukakis took 62 percent in Culver City.

Population: 525,993. White 200,378 (38%), Black 202,809 (39%), Asian and Pacific Islander 39,985 (8%), Other 2,724 (1%). Spanish origin 146,604 (28%). 18 and over 395,349 (75%), 65 and over 52,395 (10%). Median age: 30.

amendment was trounced by a 30-390 vote; another Republican amendment to censure Frank was defeated by 141-287. The House then passed the committee's recommendation of a reprimand by 408-18.

The incident recalled a similar one in 1987, when the ethics panel recommended that Pennsylvania Democrat Austin J. Murphy be reprimanded for rules violations. Murphy portrayed himself as a sacrificial lamb being punished to quiet ethics committee critics. Then, too, Dixon made an impassioned speech defending the committee, and the reprimand passed.

Caught up in the turmoil of the 101st Congress, Dixon found no haven in his chairmanship of the D.C. Appropriations Subcommittee. Social-issue activists, using their leverage over the federal city's finances to advance their agendas, turned the debate on the routine funding bill into a battle over abortion.

The stage was set in 1988, when GOP Rep. Robert K. Dornan of California attached an amendment to the D.C. appropriations bill barring the District government from using federal or local monies to pay for abortions; although the House had passed such measures before, the Senate accepted the language for the first time.

Abortion-rights activists working to repeal the restrictions in 1989 were boosted by reaction to the Supreme Court's *Webster* ruling, which said states could decide for themselves how to regulate abortion. While opposing that decision, the activists argued it was unfair to give such power to the states but hinder the D.C. government's right to decide.

Dixon helped the Democratic leadership hold the anti-abortion side to its hard-line position. When New Jersey Republican Christopher H. Smith — hoping to avoid defections of lawmakers made nervous by the upswing in abortion-rights activism — tried to temper the 1989 amendment by permitting funding in cases where the woman's life was in danger, Dixon moved that such language would violate a House rule against legislating on appropriations bills. The House then voted down the abortion ban by a 206-219 vote.

The abortion-rights victory was short-lived, though. President Bush twice vetoed the bill; with time running out on the 1989 session, Dixon conceded to the restoration of the restrictive language. In 1990, anti-abortion lawmakers did not try to amend the D.C. appropriations bill, but instead worked to defeat the final bill, which excluded the funding restrictions. Although Dixon blamed the defeat in part to Washington, D.C.'s image problems — then-Mayor Marion S. Barry Jr. had been convicted of drug possession — he again agreed to restore the anti-abortion language.

Dixon's many distractions prevented him from playing a major role during his first term on the Defense Appropriations Subcommittee. With the defense budget in the early stages of a long-term decline, Dixon says his focus will be on keeping such facilities as the Los Angeles Air Force Base and the Long Beach Naval Shipyard open and providing economic assistance to communities hit hard by defense cutbacks.

Although Dixon's move from the Appropriations Foreign Operations Subcommittee to Defense was hailed even by some Republicans in the California delegation, some may wish he was a stronger Pentagon backer. Dixon is a longtime supporter of arms control efforts; he also opposed the January 1991 resolution authorizing use of force against Iraq. The chairman of the Congressional Black Caucus during the 98th Congress, Dixon has supported the caucus' budget alternatives that would have diverted defense dollars to domestic programs.

At Home: Dixon followed a political path blazed by Yvonne Brathwaite Burke, a prominent black official of the 1960s and '70s. When she first ran for the House in 1972, Dixon resigned as an aide to state Sen. (now U.S. Rep.) Mervyn M. Dymally and captured her open Assembly seat. In 1978, when Burke left to run what would be an unsuccessful bid for state attorney general, Dixon beat eight Democratic primary foes to win her House seat.

The primary was a power struggle among political brokers in Los Angeles' black community. Dixon's closest competitor, state Sen. Nate Holden, was backed by Kenneth Hahn, a white Los Angeles County supervisor with considerable popularity in the black areas of South Los Angeles. Another rival, City Councilman David S. Cunningham, was supported by Mayor Tom Bradley.

Dixon was the choice of Rep. Henry A. Waxman and then-state Rep. Howard L. Berman (now a House member). The Waxman-Berman machine helped Dixon win, 50-38 percent, over Holden in the primary. Dixon ran unopposed that November.

Committees

Appropriations (18th of 37 Democrats)
District of Columbia (chairman); Defense

Elections

1990 General		
Julian C. Dixon (D)	69,482	(73%)
George Z. Adams (R)	21,245	(22%)
William R. Williams (PFP)	2,723	(3%)
Bob Weber (LIBERT)	2,150	(2%)
1988 General		
Julian C. Dixon (D)	109,801	(76%)
George Adams (R)	28,645	(20%)

Previous Winning Percentages: **1986** (76%) **1984** (76%) **1982** (79%) **1980** (79%) **1978** (100%)

District Vote For President

	1988	1984	1980	1976
D	113,133 (73%)	108,287 (67%)	91,978 (64%)	91,936 (66%)
R	40,680 (26%)	51,069 (32%)	41,421 (29%)	44,835 (32%)

Campaign Finance

	Receipts	Receipts from PACs	Expend-itures
1990			
Dixon (D)	$161,900	$124,145 (77%)	$113,669
Adams (R)	$6,600	0	$3,799
1988			
Dixon (D)	$120,740	$70,980 (59%)	$114,523

Key Votes

1991	
Authorize use of force against Iraq	N
1990	
Support constitutional amendment on flag desecration	N
Pass family and medical leave bill over Bush veto	Y
Reduce SDI funding	Y
Allow abortions in overseas military facilities	Y
Approve budget summit plan for spending and taxing	N
Approve civil rights bill	Y
1989	
Halt production of B-2 stealth bomber at 13 planes	N
Oppose capital gains tax cut	Y
Approve federal abortion funding in rape or incest cases	Y
Approve pay raise and revision of ethics rules	Y
Pass Democratic minimum wage plan over Bush veto	Y

Voting Studies

	Presidential Support		Party Unity		Conservative Coalition	
Year	**S**	**O**	**S**	**O**	**S**	**O**
1990	20	78	89	3	17	83
1989	29	63	87	2	17	76
1988	17	71	85	0	3	92
1987	15	83	81	1	7	79
1986	13	74	80	2	12	70
1985	18	75	84	1	11	67
1984	25	61	79	4	12	75
1983	13	71	81	1	8	80
1982	32	55	79	7	15	73
1981	37	54	85	5	11	71

Interest Group Ratings

Year	ADA	ACU	AFL-CIO	CCUS
1990	100	4	100	23
1989	85	0	100	40
1988	85	0	100	25
1987	96	0	100	7
1986	85	0	100	25
1985	80	0	100	15
1984	95	5	83	38
1983	90	0	100	20
1982	85	20	100	32
1981	80	0	100	16

29 Maxine Waters (D)

Of Los Angeles — Elected 1990

Born: Aug. 31, 1938, St. Louis, Mo.
Education: California State U., Los Angeles, B.A. 1970.
Occupation: Head Start official.
Family: Husband, Sidney Williams; two children.
Religion: Christian.
Political Career: Calif. Assembly, 1977-91.
Capitol Office: 1207 Longworth Bldg. 20515; 225-2201.

The Path to Washington: Waters' agenda in the House will not greatly differ from that of her predecessor, 14-term Democratic Rep. Augustus F. Hawkins. Like Hawkins, Waters — whose mainly black-and-Hispanic state Assembly district formed the core of the 29th District — has devoted most of her efforts to improving the lot of the minority poor. Hawkins chaired the Education and Labor Committee; Waters is an advocate of federal school and employment programs.

However, there will be a marked change in style resulting from the turnover in the 29th. Whereas Hawkins was low-key, Waters is well-known for her outspoken, hard-nosed manner in pursuing her objectives. Although she angered many of her Assembly colleagues at one point or another, she also achieved respect for her determination.

As a state legislator, Waters also made her mark on national politics: She was a leading supporter of the Rev. Jesse Jackson's 1984 and 1988 bids for the Democratic presidential nomination (casting the lone vote against the 1988 party platform at the final drafting session). But as she maintained her image as a fiery liberal activist, Waters — a close ally of powerful state Assembly Speaker Willie L. Brown Jr. — also showed skill at insider politics. Waters was chairman of the California Assembly Democratic Caucus when she launched her bid for Congress.

Though she gave up some clout, Waters' move to Congress was one for which she had been preparing for years. During the last California redistricting in 1982, Waters maneuvered to remove from the 29th a blue-collar, mainly white suburban community, which she saw as unfriendly territory.

Although her legislative career and her marriage to a luxury automobile dealer have made Waters financially comfortable, she is no limousine liberal. Waters comes to her empathy for poor and working-class blacks from personal experience. Waters was born in St. Louis as one of 13 children in a welfare family and was raised in public housing projects. As a teenager, she bused tables in a segregated restaurant. Married just after high school, Waters moved in 1961 with her first husband and two children to Los Angeles, where she worked in a clothing factory and for the telephone company.

Waters' public career began in 1966, when she volunteered as an assistant teacher in the new Head Start program while pursuing a college degree. Her involvement in Head Start led Waters into other community-organizing activities and then into politics. After working as a volunteer and a consultant to several candidates, Waters ran and won an upset victory for a state Assembly seat in 1976.

Making her presence felt immediately, Waters, who had also emerged as a feminist spokeswoman, pushed to have the gender-neutral term "Assembly member" replace the official title of "assemblyman." Despite the derision of some male colleagues, Waters argued her case and won.

Waters sponsored a long list of successful legislation, including measures requiring state agencies to set minimum goals for awarding contracts to minority- and women-owned businesses; barring strip searches for those accused of non-violent misdemeanors; and creating a state child abuse prevention training program. During her House campaign, Waters touted her sponsorship of the Imperial Courts Learning Center, California's first public school within a public housing project.

Waters' most difficult legislative victory came in 1986. After a seven-year struggle, she persuaded the Legislature to pass a provision requiring state pension funds to divest stocks in companies doing business with South Africa.

Waters' election to the House was never in doubt. Running in a district that has an overwhelming Democratic majority, Waters defeated Republican Bill De Witt, a former South Gate City Council member, with 80 percent of the vote.

California 29

South-Central Los Angeles; Watts; Downey

More than four-fifths of the people in the 29th are either black or Hispanic. The district also provides the most overwhelming percentages for Democratic candidates in California.

The 29th's minority communities were once pretty well separated, blacks living in riot-scarred Watts, Hispanics in the adjacent suburbs of Huntington Park, Walnut Park and South Gate to the east. But in recent years, there has been more of a mixing. Only five years ago, the four high schools in Watts were majority-black; today, all are mostly Hispanic.

Watts has seen some improvement since the 1965 riots, with the growth of neighborhood centers and concerted attempts to organize residents around housing and health issues. A new light rail train line now runs through Watts. Despite those efforts and federal and state aid, poverty, high unemployment, blighted housing and crime persist.

More prosperous, middle-class Watts residents have moved north as their lot has improved. At the northern end of the district are the Los Angeles Coliseum, site of the 1984 (and 1932) Summer Olympics, and the Los Angeles Sports Arena, home of the L.A. Clippers basketball team and also the place where Democrats nominated John F. Kennedy for president in 1960.

In 1988, presidential nominee Michael S. Dukakis benefited from local blacks' Democratic allegiance, carrying better than 80 percent of the district vote. But the impact of this margin was tempered by the district's poor voter participation. Just over 114,000 29th District residents voted in the presidential contest — the second-lowest total in the state.

The district's Hispanics are not as staunchly Democratic as its blacks. Huntington Park and South Gate both supported Ronald Reagan for president in 1980 and 1984. But only South Gate went for George Bush in 1988.

South Gate and the portion of Downey in the district also house a number of conservative-minded white working-class voters. South Gate lost Firestone and General Motors plants, but has attracted small businesses and light manufacturing.

In the original 1980s redistricting, more of Downey's GOP voters were in the 29th. In the second round, Waters, then a state assemblywoman from the area and head of the redistricting committee, saw to it that this area, which she called "rednecky," was removed. About three-fourths of the city was cut from the district, leaving only a small Hispanic portion.

Population: 525,938. White 166,888 (32%), Black 263,190 (50%), Other 7,202 (1%). Spanish origin 192,059 (37%). 18 and over 339,585 (65%), 65 and over 46,391 (9%). Median age: 25.

Committees

Banking, Finance & Urban Affairs (23rd of 31 Democrats)
Consumer Affairs & Coinage; General Oversight; Housing & Community Development; International Development, Finance, Trade & Monetary Policy

Veterans' Affairs (17th of 21 Democrats)
Oversight & Investigations

Campaign Finance

	Receipts	Receipts from PACs	Expend-itures
1990			
Waters (D)	$740,793	$211,172 (29%)	$759,538

Key Vote

1991

Authorize use of force against Iraq	N

Elections

1990 General		
Maxine Waters (D)	51,350	(79%)
Bill DeWitt (R)	12,054	(19%)
Waheed R. Boctor (LIBERT)	1,268	(2%)
1990 Primary		
Maxine Waters (D)	36,182	(88%)
Lionel Allen (D)	2,666	(7%)
Twain M. Wilson (D)	1,115	(3%)
Ted Andromidas (D)	930	(2%)

District Vote For President

	1988	1984	1980	1976
D	92,086 (80%)	103,221 (77%)	86,730 (76%)	88,163 (77%)
R	22,052 (19%)	29,106 (22%)	23,478 (21%)	23,992 (21%)

30 Matthew G. Martinez (D)

Of Monterey Park — Elected 1982

Born: Feb. 14, 1929, Walsenburg, Colo.
Education: Graduated from Los Angeles Trade-Technical College, 1959.
Military Service: Marine Corps, 1947-50.
Occupation: Upholstery company owner.
Family: Wife, Elvira Yorba; five children.
Religion: Roman Catholic.
Political Career: Monterey Park City Council, 1974-80, mayor of Monterey Park, 1974-75; Calif. Assembly, 1981-82.
Capitol Office: 2446 Rayburn Bldg. 20515; 225-5464.

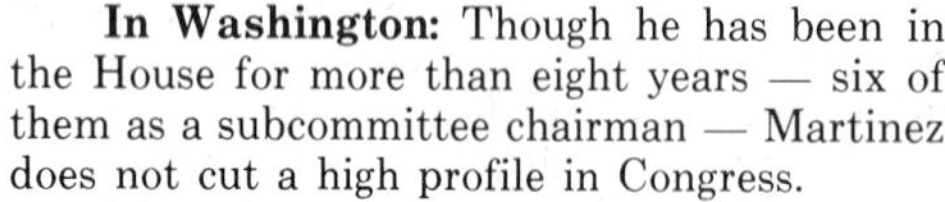

In Washington: Though he has been in the House for more than eight years — six of them as a subcommittee chairman — Martinez does not cut a high profile in Congress.

A number of Democrats in the large class of 1982 have become prominent players on hot issues and key committees, but the affable Martinez is not among them. He took over the Education and Labor Subcommittee on Employment Opportunities in 1985 but struggled with the arcane language and complex programs of the Job Training Partnership Act (JTPA), one of the laws under the panel's jurisdiction.

In 1990, during a full Education Committee markup of a bill to amend JTPA, GOP Rep. Steve Bartlett grilled Martinez repeatedly about details of the proposal. Clearly unnerved, Martinez had to rely on staff to hand him the answers to Bartlett's queries.

Martinez's trouble with the measure began at the subcommittee level. During his panel's markup, he called for a vote and reported out the bill. But the chairman had failed to notice that a quorum was not present. Though the JTPA bill died, Martinez was able to push through a measure to provide job training and counseling for displaced homemakers.

At the start of the 102nd Congress, Martinez moved to the chair of the Human Resources Subcommittee, where he has been active in field hearings across the country on legislation to reauthorize programs that aid the elderly.

At Home: Martinez's low profile has emboldened Republicans to make several forays against him. None has succeeded.

Martinez has a place of some prominence within the Hispanic population of the Los Angeles area. After winning re-election to the House in 1990, Martinez considered but declined a January 1991 run for the Los Angeles County Board of Supervisors from a district designed, under a court-ordered plan, to favor a Hispanic.

A former Republican, Martinez got his start on the Monterey Park City Council and served as mayor. He served briefly in the state Assembly after defeating veteran incumbent Jack R. Fenton in a 1980 Democratic primary.

In 1982, Democratic Rep. George E. Danielson resigned to accept a judgeship, and Martinez took a plurality in a special election to fill the vacancy. But he then barely survived a runoff with Republican business consultant Ralph Ramirez, who held him to 51 percent.

Seeking a full House term later that year, Martinez met GOP Rep. John H. Rousselot, whose vocal brand of conservatism had earned him a national following. Rousselot's district had been dismembered in redistricting, and he decided to run in the heavily Hispanic 30th rather than challenge another GOP incumbent.

Appealing to voters' conservative social instincts and to their ethnicity, Rousselot used $1,500 in campaign funds for Spanish lessons for his wife and appeared in a Mexican Independence Day parade. But the demographics were too tough; Martinez won with 54 percent.

In 1984, Martinez sank most of his campaign funding into a primary battle with Gladys C. Danielson, the wife of his Democratic predecessor. While her challenge fell far short, it did soften up Martinez for his GOP opponent, lawyer Richard Gomez, who attacked him for poor constituent service and sought a base in the district's growing Asian-American population. Martinez ended up taking 52 percent of the vote.

After this series of close calls, Martinez in 1986 drew a non-Hispanic opponent and finally topped 60 percent. In 1988, Martinez crushed what had been seen as a tough primary challenge from former Monterey Park Mayor Lily Chen, then in November deflected a comeback attempt by Republican Ramirez, taking 60 percent of the vote. In 1990, Martinez's percentage dropped slightly against 30-year-old Republican Reuben D. Franco, an account executive.

California 30

San Gabriel Valley — El Monte; Alhambra

As Los Angeles' Hispanic population has spiraled in the past 20 years, the Hispanic community has moved beyond the inner-city barrios to nearby suburbs such as those in the 30th District. The Hispanic population of the 30th — more than half the district total — is second in the state, behind only the 25th in East Los Angeles.

Once a garden spot of orange, lemon and walnut groves, the area in the 30th has become heavily industrialized. Tract houses and rows of palm trees sit alongside factories devoted to light industry and high-technology.

The district cuts a diagonal swath across the San Gabriel Valley. The largest Hispanic concentration — as much as 85 percent in some places — is at the southwestern end, adjoining East Los Angeles. Suburbs such as Maywood, Cudahy and Montebello all have substantial Hispanic majorities.

There is a greater ethnic mix in Martinez's hometown of Monterey Park, where Asian-Americans compete with Hispanics and Anglos for power, and in the former citrus-shipping center of Asuza.

El Monte (population 106,000) links the eastern and western parts of the district. It is the largest of the 14 independent municipalities in the 30th. For years, El Monte was a major hog-ranching center.

There are some distinctly Republican areas in the 30th, including Alhambra and San Gabriel, represented for years by conservative Republican John H. Rousselot.

Population: 526,018. White 353,519 (67%), Black 5,642 (1%), Asian and Pacific Islander 47,234 (9%), Other 4,800 (1%). Spanish origin 286,251 (54%). 18 and over 360,738 (69%), 65 and over 51,576 (10%). Median age: 27.

Committees

Education & Labor (8th of 25 Democrats)
Human Resources (chairman); Elementary, Secondary & Vocational Education; Labor-Management Relations

Government Operations (17th of 25 Democrats)
Commerce, Consumer & Monetary Affairs; Employment & Housing

Select Children, Youth & Families (12th of 22 Democrats)

Elections

1990 General		
Matthew G. Martinez (D)	45,456	(58%)
Reuben D. Franco (R)	28,914	(37%)
G. Curtis Feger (LIBERT)	3,713	(5%)
1988 General		
Matthew G. Martinez (D)	72,253	(60%)
Ralph R. Ramirez (R)	43,833	(36%)

Previous Winning Percentages: **1986** (63%) **1984** (52%) **1982** (54%) **1982 *** (51%)

** Special election.*

District Vote For President

	1988	1984	1980	1976
D	66,112 (53%)	56,598 (44%)	50,312 (43%)	58,162 (53%)
R	57,754 (46%)	71,658 (55%)	57,521 (49%)	48,584 (45%)

Campaign Finance

	Receipts	Receipts from PACs		Expend-itures
1990				
Martinez (D)	$209,495	$93,803	(45%)	$186,130
Franco (R)	$72,572	$15,950	(22%)	$72,867
1988				
Martinez (D)	$437,775	$226,400	(52%)	$460,622
Ramirez (R)	$381,587	$126,421	(33%)	$382,111

Key Votes

1991	
Authorize use of force against Iraq	N
1990	
Support constitutional amendment on flag desecration	Y
Pass family and medical leave bill over Bush veto	Y
Reduce SDI funding	Y
Allow abortions in overseas military facilities	Y
Approve budget summit plan for spending and taxing	N
Approve civil rights bill	Y
1989	
Halt production of B-2 stealth bomber at 13 planes	Y
Oppose capital gains tax cut	N
Approve federal abortion funding in rape or incest cases	Y
Approve pay raise and revision of ethics rules	Y
Pass Democratic minimum wage plan over Bush veto	Y

Voting Studies

	Presidential Support		Party Unity		Conservative Coalition	
Year	**S**	**O**	**S**	**O**	**S**	**O**
1990	18	79	81	6	31	63
1989	34	60	86	6	22	68
1988	14	72	90	2	13	74
1987	22	72	89	5	33	58
1986	18	76	82	5	16	70
1985	19	75	88	2	15	76
1984	27	71	93	5	10	85
1983	10	59	65	2	7	73
1982	32 †	55 †	82 †	6 †	10 †	73 †

† Not eligible for all recorded votes.

Interest Group Ratings

Year	ADA	ACU	AFL-CIO	CCUS
1990	78	9	92	38
1989	75	11	91	50
1988	90	0	100	23
1987	80	0	100	8
1986	85	10	100	7
1985	80	5	100	19
1984	95	9	92	38
1983	70	0	100	20
1982	80	19	100	24

31 Mervyn M. Dymally (D)

Of Compton — Elected 1980

Born: May 12, 1926, Cedros, Trinidad.

Education: California State U., Los Angeles, B.A. 1954; California State U., Sacramento, M.A. 1969; U.S. International U., Ph.D. 1978.

Occupation: Special education teacher; data-processing executive.

Family: Wife, Alice M. Gueno; two children.

Religion: Episcopalian.

Political Career: Calif. Assembly, 1963-67; Calif. Senate, 1967-75; lieutenant governor, 1975-79; defeated for re-election, 1978.

Capitol Office: 1717 Longworth Bldg. 20515; 225-5425.

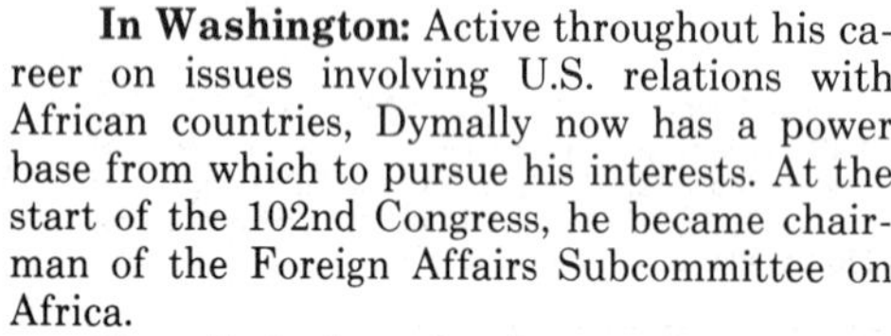

In Washington: Active throughout his career on issues involving U.S. relations with African countries, Dymally now has a power base from which to pursue his interests. At the start of the 102nd Congress, he became chairman of the Foreign Affairs Subcommittee on Africa.

Dymally had previously served on the Africa subcommittee for just one term. However, when the chairmanship came open, he jumped at it. He surrendered a similar position on the Foreign Affairs International Operations Subcommittee —which oversees U.S. diplomatic functions overseas — in the process.

Dymally succeeded Democratic Rep. Howard Wolpe of Michigan, who gave up the Africa post he had held for 10 years for a Science subcommittee chairmanship. There will little change in political direction with the turnover. Dymally was a strong supporter of the 1986 bill instituting sanctions against South Africa, on which Wolpe led the charge in the House. Both often posed strong opposition to the Reagan administration policy, continued by President Bush, of providing covert aid to anti-leftist armed insurgencies in such nations as Angola.

Where observers might see a difference is in approach to the issues. Although Wolpe is nearly as liberal as Dymally and could be even more fiery, his was the analytical manner of a former professor of African studies. Dymally, though also a former teacher, comes at Africa-related issues from the perspective of an African-American political activist and a leader in the Congressional Black Caucus.

Dymally established early on where he wanted to take the Africa subcommittee. In March 1991, he included a 25 percent increase in development aid for nations of sub-Saharan Africa in proposed foreign aid authorization legislation for fiscal 1992 and 1993.

His higher profile on African issues could create one political difficulty for Dymally. In recent years, he has come under attack from fringe political groups, which allege that Dymally is allied with the pro-Western but repressive regime of Zaire President Mobutu Sese Seko; Dymally strongly denies such links.

In 1989, the Rainbow Lobby and the U.S.-Congo Friendship Committee, affiliates of the leftist New Alliance Party (NAP), accused Dymally, who had taken fact-finding trips to Zaire, of having financial links to Mobutu; a $250,000 gift from Mobutu to a charity run by a Dymally associate was cited. The groups' rhetoric was, to say the least, severe: Dymally was described as "a bagman" and a "collaborator in the destruction of the African people."

In January 1990, *Washington Post* reporter Jim McGee wrote a pair of stories that highlighted Dymally's alleged links to Zaire. The stories also linked Dymally's support for easing diamond import restrictions embodied in South Africa sanctions legislation to a contribution made by a diamond merchant to a scholarship fund Dymally had founded.

Dymally denied the allegations, saying they had been planted by the Rainbow Lobby. (He also accused McGee, who had written critical articles about other black House members, of running a smear campaign against black political leaders.) Facing a 1990 primary challenge from an NAP-backed candidate, Dymally then went on the offensive, describing the group as a "cult" that, when founded in the 1970s, was aligned with the political movement of Lyndon H. LaRouche Jr.

Dymally appears an odd target for a left-fringe group. Dymally supported President Bush on just 11 percent of House votes in 1990. He not only opposed the resolution authorizing Bush to use military force against Iraq in January 1991 (though he missed the vote due to illness), but also opposed a resolution supporting the president after war broke out.

"I rise to state unequivocally that I support our forces who are currently deployed in the Persian Gulf . . . ," Dymally said. "In spite of

California 31

Southern Los Angeles County — Compton; Carson

This is a working-class suburban district with more ethnic and racial diversity than is found in almost any district in the state. When the district was shaped in the early 1980s, a third of the residents were black, a quarter were of Spanish origin, and nearly 10 percent were Oriental. Then, as now, most voted Democratic. Michael S. Dukakis carried the 31st in 1988 by close to a 2-to-1 margin.

The district's Democratic vote is anchored in lower-income working-class communities, such as Compton — which is almost all black and Hispanic — and Lynwood. Employment is not what it once was at nearby shipyards and auto plants, causing chronic economic problems.

Bellflower and Paramount, majority-white working-class communities at the district's eastern end, are somewhat better off. Hawthorne is another mostly white suburb at the western end, whose residents work largely in the aerospace industry. All of these communities supported President Reagan in 1984, but only Bellflower went for George Bush in 1988.

Carson, at the southern end, is a town of neat trailer parks and retirement communities. A large community of Samoans draws the attentions of candidates for U.S. delegate from American Samoa. Many of Carson's Samoans are still registered to vote on their native island.

The Asian vote in the district is located primarily in Gardenia, a tidy suburb just off the Harbor Freeway, which bisects the district. Japanese-Americans have been a major part of Gardenia's life and politics for several decades. On occasion, the Japanese-Americans will support Republicans of their own nationality, such as Paul T. Bannai, who represented the area in the state Assembly for eight years through 1980, when his district turned back to the Democrats.

Perhaps the district's most famous resident is the Goodyear blimp *Columbia,* whose permanent mooring is clearly visible from the intersection of the Harbor and San Diego freeways. Those two highways are important to the economy of the 31st District. Twice each day, they are filled with commuters from the 31st going to jobs in the defense and electronics industries. Throughout the rest of the day the highways are clogged with trucks hauling the products of the district: aircraft engines, semiconductors, and Mattel toys.

Population: 525,939. White 222,211 (42%), Black 177,923 (34%), Asian and Pacific Islander 41,668 (8%), Other 3,343 (1%). Spanish origin 131,121 (25%). 18 and over 354,360 (67%), 65 and over 37,104 (7%). Median age: 27.

my support for our troops, I feel their mission could have been averted if the president had continued to pursue our objectives through peaceful means."

Dymally also takes a strong interest in international human rights. Some of his criticisms over the years have been aimed at Israel, for its treatment of Palestinians and of Black Hebrews, a sect of black Americans who have tried to settle in that nation. But when some American Jewish organizations criticized him as anti-Israel, Dymally pointed to his efforts to gain emigration rights for Jews from the Soviet Union and Ethiopia.

Even on the low-profile Post Office and Civil Service Committee, Dymally has been engaged in some contentious debate. As chairman of the Census and Population Subcommittee in 1988, Dymally tried without success to push through legislation mandating an adjustment of the 1990 census to account for an expected "undercount" of minority-group Americans.

When tentative figures released in April 1991 by the Census Bureau indicated just such an undercount had occurred, Dymally — still a member of the Census subcommittee — renewed his calls for an adjustment.

Dymally is also on the District of Columbia Committee and is chairman of its Judiciary and Education Subcommittee.

At Home: The ease with which Dymally won re-election in 1990 masked a trying campaign year. Dogged by the *Washington Post* articles that raised questions about his financial dealings, Dymally had to fend off a noisy primary challenge from lawyer Lawrence A. Grigsby.

Dymally was never seriously threatened by Grigsby, who focused on the incumbent's alleged Zaire connection. But Dymally took no chances, assailing the integrity of his critics. He also quit the boards of education-related charities he had founded and which the *Post* articles had highlighted; Dymally blamed his decision on others' "hysteria about ethics and what constitutes a perception of impropriety."

Dymally ended up winning the June primary with 73 percent, while Grigsby took just 15 percent. In November, he coasted to a typically easy victory.

Dymally has proved his resiliency more than once in his political career. His smashing primary victory over Democratic Rep. Charles H. Wilson in 1980 resurrected a political future that looked bleak after a statewide loss only two years before.

Dymally had become California's leading black officeholder over a long career that began in 1962, when he won the state Assembly seat vacated by Democrat Augustus F. Hawkins, who moved to Congress.

In 1974, running with Edmund G. Brown Jr., Dymally was elected the state's first black lieutenant governor. But then his political career faltered. Unproven corruption charges, which eventually were investigated and dismissed by the FBI, led Brown to keep him at a distance. In 1978, seeking a second term in a job he himself said was not very enjoyable, Dymally received only 43 percent against Republican Mike Curb.

However, Wilson's own ethical problems provided Dymally with a hasty opportunity to return to elected office. Wilson was facing a House investigation into charges that included converting campaign funds to personal use. Dymally was initially reluctant to stage a primary challenge against an incumbent, but jumped in after former Democratic Rep. Mark Hannaford took the plunge first.

Demographics worked in Dymally's favor. The district was more than a third black, and Dymally was the only black candidate running against two well-known white candidates. Along with backing from the district's black leadership, Dymally had strong support from the liberal political machine run by U.S. Rep. Henry A. Waxman and then-Assemblyman Howard L. Berman. He was also helped during the primary campaign by the House ethics committee's recommendation of censure for Wilson.

Heavily outspending his opponents, Dymally kept up a constant stream of mailings to district voters and won an impressive 49 percent of the primary vote. He won that November's general election with 64 percent, and has taken at least 67 percent in each of his re-election bids.

Committees

District of Columbia (4th of 8 Democrats)
Judiciary & Education (chairman); Government Operations & Metropolitan Affairs

Foreign Affairs (7th of 28 Democrats)
Africa (chairman); International Operations

Post Office & Civil Service (8th of 15 Democrats)
Census & Population

Elections

1990 General		
Mervyn M. Dymally (D)	56,394	(67%)
Eunice N. Sato (R)	27,593	(33%)
1990 Primary		
Mervyn M. Dymally (D)	30,416	(73%)
Lawrence A. Grigsby (D)	6,426	(15%)
Carl E. Robinson Sr. (D)	4,965	(12%)
1988 General		
Mervyn M. Dymally (D)	100,919	(72%)
Arnold C. May (R)	36,017	(26%)

Previous Winning Percentages: **1986** (70%) **1984** (71%) **1982** (72%) **1980** (64%)

District Vote For President

	1988	1984	1980	1976
D	96,554 (64%)	87,740 (58%)	76,696 (59%)	79,682 (67%)
R	51,505 (34%)	61,006 (41%)	45,753 (35%)	37,317 (31%)

Campaign Finance

	Receipts	Receipts from PACs		Expend-itures
1990				
Dymally (D)	$434,143	$173,316	(40%)	$418,232
1988				
Dymally (D)	$488,149	$156,449	(32%)	$481,799
May (R)	$10,430	$745	(7%)	$10,169

Key Votes

1991	
Authorize use of force against Iraq	?
1990	
Support constitutional amendment on flag desecration	N
Pass family and medical leave bill over Bush veto	Y
Reduce SDI funding	Y
Allow abortions in overseas military facilities	Y
Approve budget summit plan for spending and taxing	N
Approve civil rights bill	Y
1989	
Halt production of B-2 stealth bomber at 13 planes	N
Oppose capital gains tax cut	Y
Approve federal abortion funding in rape or incest cases	Y
Approve pay raise and revision of ethics rules	Y
Pass Democratic minimum wage plan over Bush veto	Y

Voting Studies

	Presidential Support		Party Unity		Conservative Coalition	
Year	**S**	**O**	**S**	**O**	**S**	**O**
1990	11	87	87	3	11	87
1989	29	63	88	4	5	80
1988	16	69	83	3	0	87
1987	10	75	82	3	7	77
1986	13	83	92	2	8	86
1985	15	78	63	6	9	82
1984	24	55	65	5	10	66
1983	16	77	82	5	11	78
1982	22	56	78	4	11	74
1981	29	43	66	4	11	65

Interest Group Ratings

Year	ADA	ACU	AFL-CIO	CCUS
1990	100	4	100	36
1989	90	0	83	20
1988	90	0	100	23
1987	84	0	100	0
1986	100	0	93	19
1985	90	10	87	24
1984	85	6	92	33
1983	85	0	94	18
1982	65	17	100	30
1981	55	0	91	21

32 Glenn M. Anderson (D)

Of San Pedro — Elected 1968

Born: Feb. 21, 1913, Hawthorne, Calif.
Education: U. of California, Los Angeles, B.A. 1936.
Military Service: Army, 1943-45.
Occupation: Banker; home builder.
Family: Wife, Lee Dutton; three children.
Religion: Episcopalian.
Political Career: Mayor of Hawthorne, 1940-43; Calif. Assembly, 1943-51; lieutenant governor, 1959-67; defeated for re-election, 1966; Democratic nominee for Calif. Senate, 1950.
Capitol Office: 2329 Rayburn Bldg. 20515; 225-6676.

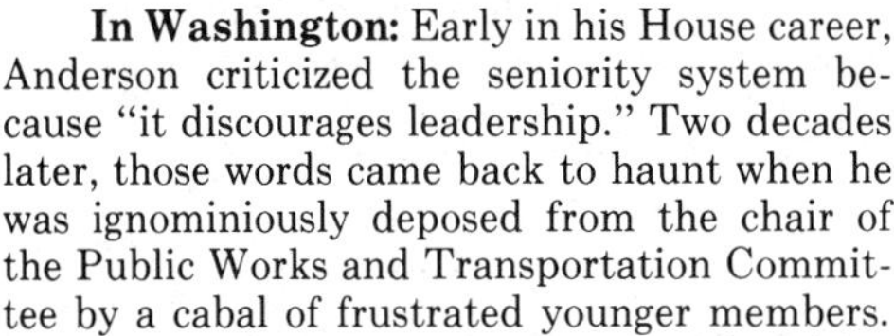

In Washington: Early in his House career, Anderson criticized the seniority system because "it discourages leadership." Two decades later, those words came back to haunt when he was ignominiously deposed from the chair of the Public Works and Transportation Committee by a cabal of frustrated younger members.

With support from the second-ranking committee Democrat, Robert A. Roe of New Jersey, Anderson had managed to stifle previous rumblings over his failure to prevent the panel from losing turf battles with other committees. But at the start of the 102nd Congress, Roe jumped ship and lobbied for the chairmanship when it became apparent that third-ranking Democrat Norman Y. Mineta of California would take Anderson's job if Roe failed to assert seniority.

Anderson tried to stave off the inevitable by promising to serve only one more term as chairman. But he lost the post and was not even given a subcommittee chair; he had to be satisfied with the honorary title of "chairman emeritus" of Public Works.

After nearly a half-century in local, state and federal offices, Anderson still leaves many baffled as to how and why he ever got into politics.

This withdrawn, quiet man seems to enjoy neither the camaraderie nor the combat of the political game. Some players thrive on personal alliances, while others relish confrontation, but few legislators are like Anderson in their apparent unease with both aspects of the job. Anderson also has gained the reputation of being overly reliant on staffers and his wife, who told *The Los Angeles Times* that she "always had to stand beside him and whisper him things."

For two decades in Congress, his reserved style and focus on home-state projects was of little matter to anyone else. But that changed with his ascent to the Public Works helm.

He inherited the seat after the sudden death of James J. Howard of New Jersey in March 1988. Months later, Anderson was re-elected chairman for the 101st Congress, but only after some committee Democrats determined that Roe was unwilling to be their candidate for a coup.

Anderson's weak position was obvious once the lineup of subcommittee chairmen was announced. Under pressure, he had given up the most coveted chair, of the Surface Transportation Subcommittee that he had headed since 1981, to Mineta, and settled instead for the Investigations and Oversight panel. Recent Public Works chairmen have not also held subcommittee chairs; Anderson's move after Howard's death to keep Surface Transportation, which has jurisdiction over all highway and mass-transit projects, antagonized some junior colleagues.

With Howard gone, Anderson not only inherited his chair but also the responsibility for defending the committee's turf. Public Works regularly butts heads with the Appropriations Committee, which routinely earmarks money for projects in its members' districts that Public Works has not authorized. In past years, Anderson had deferred to the scrappy Howard in conflicts involving his subcommittee's transportation jurisdiction.

Howard lost as often as not, but colleagues appreciated his doggedness. In contrast, Anderson — who likes to recall how he climbed the business success ladder from "foot messenger, then bicycle messenger, then motorcycle messenger" as a youth — never became more than a messenger of bad news to committee colleagues, who chafed under their diminishing clout.

An initial skirmish just weeks into Anderson's tenure foreshadowed his ultimate demise. Anderson was disregarded when he went to an Appropriations subcommittee, which was drafting the annual transportation spending bill, and objected to its inclusion of funds for the usual array of unauthorized projects.

The Rules Committee was only slightly more receptive when it set the ground rules for House debate on the transportation measure.

California 32

San Pedro; Long Beach

Though Anderson is not a national figure in Congress, his ability to deliver public works funding to his home district has truly put him on the map. Long Beach harbor has been named for Anderson, and he has been known to hand out gift bottles of wine labeled "Long Beach Port."

The shipyards are just part of the 32nd's industrial landscape. Aerospace and automotive plants extend along the flat, brown land, sharing space with fuel tanks and oil wells. In the older homes of Long Beach (population 429,000) are the descendants of the fishermen and sailors of many European nationalities who settled here.

Though there is a working-class Democratic tradition here, blue-collar conservatism often shifts the district to Republican presidential candidates. President Reagan won the 32nd easily in 1984, though George Bush eked out a narrow district victory.

Wilmington, at the district's western end, is the only solidly lower-income area, a home for Hispanics, blacks, Filipinos and other Pacific immigrants. In its snaking path through Long Beach, San Pedro and Lakewood, the 32nd strings together a hodgepodge of communities — quiet, middle-income suburbs, commercial downtown Long Beach, and slightly bedraggled stretches of poorer neighborhoods. Though only the inner harbor of the Port of Los Angeles is in the district, thousands of residents are involved in the transportation and shipping industries.

At its northern end, the 32nd sticks a two-block-wide finger past Bellflower to take in the southern two-thirds of Downey, which has a Republican lean. That city's huge Rockwell aerospace plant, where the space shuttle is manufactured, is in the district, as are many of the high-tech workers who are employed there.

Population: 525,922. White 384,734 (73%), Black 46,422 (9%), Asian and Pacific Islander 28,677 (5%), Other 4,527 (1%). Spanish origin 119,563 (23%). 18 and over 383,383 (73%), 65 and over 57,884 (11%). Median age: 30.

Unauthorized projects require waivers from Rules to be included in appropriations bills; Anderson, with surprising vigor, asked that the panel deny waivers for eight road projects. "I believe it is time to stop this deliberate evasion of the proper way to legislate," he said.

But one of his targeted projects was in the district of Rules member David E. Bonior, and missing from the hit list, it was noted, was a provision benefiting Long Beach Transit, included by Appropriations at Anderson's request. Rules denied waivers for just three of the items he opposed.

Months later, however, Appropriations members restored two of them during conference negotiations with the Senate, and they did so in a way he could not contest. They stipulated that if either project was stripped, Anderson's transit provision also would be deleted. "He can't have it both ways," said Democrat William Lehman, chairman of the Appropriations Subcommittee on Transportation.

On another controversial issue, drug testing of transportation workers, Anderson in the 100th Congress left observers scratching their heads. The Senate wanted mandatory random testing of workers in the rail, air, bus and truck industries, approving such requirements in its versions of a comprehensive anti-drug bill and a consumer-protection measure for air travelers.

Anderson seemed to resist. But the fight against testing was waged mainly by other House Democrats — labor and civil-liberties advocates — who called the tests unreliable and an invasion of workers' privacy.

Then, in an unexpected statement just before Congress adjourned, Anderson seemed to endorse drug testing. But his statement was a bid to break the impasse over the airline consumer bill, which also included a labor provision he wanted that protected workers' jobs in airline mergers. That bill, however, went nowhere, and ultimately, random-testing provisions were not included in the drug bill, either. Anderson subsequently said he strongly favored random testing, but felt legislative action was pointless because the Reagan administration was developing its own regulations.

Anderson was an ally of Howard in the long battle that led in 1982 to enactment of a $70 billion four-year highway and mass-transit program, financed by a gas-tax hike.

Anderson's personal priority in the bill was completion of the Interstate Highway System. He called it "the principal goal of our committee," rejecting complaints that 97 percent of the system had been built and much of the rest would be in costly, congested urban areas. His removal from the Public Works chair was particularly stinging because the committee was poised at the start of the 102nd Congress to consider a huge highway and mass transit reauthorization bill that would set the nation's future transportation policy.

Anderson's legislative priorities have reflected the work of two Public Works subcommittees he has chaired — Aviation and Surface Transportation — and of the Merchant Marine Committee, where he rose to the position of No. 2 Democrat before leaving at the end of the 100th Congress. Both panels address the interests of his coastal district, which is home to shipyards, ports and aerospace plants.

He has been a proponent of airline and intercity bus deregulation, safety regulations for the airline and trucking industries and limitations for safe transport of hazardous materials.

In the 98th Congress, Anderson succeeded in winning enactment of his long-sought legislation to promote the use of child-restraint seats in automobiles. Success resulted after his bill became the vehicle for a larger election-year issue — establishing a national drinking age to combat drunken driving.

In 1979, while still Aviation chairman, he pushed into law a bill limiting airport noise, with help from "anti-noise" Democrats and President Jimmy Carter. The Public Works Committee and the Senate approved a milder version of Anderson's subcommittee bill, one more to the aviation industry's liking. But pressured by his allies and backed by Carter's promise of a veto, Anderson opposed the diluted House-Senate compromise. Negotiators redrafted a tougher version, which became law.

At Home: Anderson's behind-the-scenes efforts to bring public works projects home to Long Beach have assured him of easy re-election victories. Complaints in Washington about his performance as Public Works chairman during the 101st Congress did not harm Anderson at the polls. After defeating Republican businessman Sanford W. Kahn with 67 percent of the vote in 1988, Anderson won a rematch with 62 percent in 1990.

It is not certain, though, whether voters back home will be so supportive in the wake of Anderson's removal as Public Works chairman in the 102nd Congress. Crowding 80 years old and facing a congressional remap that is likely to change the shape of the 32nd District, Anderson is a retirement question mark for 1992.

In a 1989 interview, Anderson proudly unfurled a navigation map of Los Angeles harbor and said, "In the history of our country, there are but two congressmen after whom ports have been named. Sam Houston of Houston and Glenn Anderson of Los Angeles."

Avidly attentive to the Long Beach harbor and other local matters, Anderson comes across in his district as a quiet, successful businessman who prefers the political background. His few moments in the limelight — as lieutenant governor during the Watts riots and as Public Works chairman — have not been pleasant.

Anderson entered politics early. At age 27 he was elected mayor of Hawthorne, a Los Angeles suburb. At that point, Anderson already was a prosperous businessman. After earning his college degree in political science and psychology, he had embarked on a profitable career selling automobiles, running a car-repair shop and operating a service station.

Anderson went from the Hawthorne City Hall to four terms in the state Assembly, where he wrote legislation abolishing segregated schools in California. He was defeated for a state Senate seat in 1950 and spent most of the 1950s expanding his home construction business. He served two years as state Democratic chairman.

In 1958, Anderson returned to public office on the coattails of Edmund G. "Pat" Brown, who was elected governor. For two terms as Brown's lieutenant governor, Anderson quietly and efficiently carried out the thankless tasks Brown gave him. He specialized in education and urban problems and was a ceaseless cheerleader for Brown's programs in the Legislature, where he presided benignly over the Senate.

He differed with Brown on only a few issues, one of which was Brown's support of John F. Kennedy for the 1960 Democratic nomination. Anderson backed Adlai E. Stevenson.

Brown frequently traveled outside California, leaving Anderson in charge, a practice that caused no problems until August 1965, when race riots broke out in the Watts area of Los Angeles while Brown was vacationing in Greece.

Anderson was not quick to respond, and by the time he sent in the National Guard the situation was out of control, with 35 dead, hundreds injured and millions of dollars in property damage. His hesitancy to act was used against him the next year as the Brown-Anderson ticket lost to Republicans Ronald Reagan and Robert H. Finch.

Once again, however, Anderson came back, this time in only two years. In 1968 Democrat Cecil R. King retired after serving more than 26 years in the House from the Torrance-San Pedro area. In both the Democratic primary and the general election, Anderson tried to convince voters he was "a conservative in economic matters and a liberal in human matters." His major primary opponent, Los Angeles City Councilman John S. Gibson Jr., and his Republican foe, Joseph Blatchford, both said Anderson was too liberal on all matters.

Anderson won the primary with 35 percent and was helped in the fall by a strong presidential vote in the district for Hubert H. Humphrey. The local Democratic strength allowed Anderson to edge past Blatchford with fewer than 4,000 votes to spare.

By 1970 the exciting days of Anderson's political career seemed to be over. He easily won re-election by lopsided margins throughout the rest of the decade.

In 1982, however, he faced a strong challenge. Previous redistricting had removed Anderson's original political base from his district; under the 1982 plan, Anderson picked up a huge number of voters from Republican Dan Lungren's neighboring Long Beach district and lost several Democratic towns.

Republicans felt they could take advantage of the new lines by nominating Brian Lungren, Dan's younger brother. Just under half the voters in the redrawn 32nd had been in Dan Lungren's old 34th District. Any possible confusion seemed likely to help the challenger.

With little in the way of political experience — he had left his job as a policeman at the end of 1981 to work for a county supervisor — Lungren was forced to rely on his brother's connections in building a political base. The two shared a campaign office, and the younger Lungren tried to tap into Dan's fund-raising network. Taking a leaf from his brother's successful 1978 effort, Brian campaigned door-to-door, stressing his law-and-order stance and branding Anderson as "tax and spend Glenn." He tried to resurrect the issue of Anderson's performance during the Watts riot.

But Anderson was not to be dislodged. He reminded Long Beach residents of his scrupulous attention to the harbor and community economic redevelopment, and lined up vocal support from businessmen of both parties. Returning to the district each weekend, he defended his stands against Lungren and reawakened the loyalty of conservative Democrats who had abandoned the party.

In the end, Anderson taught the Republicans a lesson, taking 58 percent of the vote, his lowest score since 1968 but still a comfortable showing for his first competitive election in a decade. In his four subsequent campaigns, Anderson has drawn lesser challengers and returned to winning with more than 60 percent.

Committees

Merchant Marine & Fisheries (25th of 29 Democrats)
Coast Guard & Navigation; Fisheries & Wildlife Conservation & the Environment

Public Works & Transportation (2nd of 36 Democrats)
Investigations & Oversight; Surface Transportation; Water Resources

Elections

1990 General

Glenn M. Anderson (D)	68,268	(62%)
Sanford W. Kahn (R)	42,692	(38%)

1988 General

Glenn M. Anderson (D)	114,666	(67%)
Sanford W. Kahn (R)	50,710	(30%)

Previous Winning Percentages: **1986** (69%) **1984** (61%) **1982** (58%) **1980** (66%) **1978** (71%) **1976** (72%) **1974** (88%) **1972** (75%) **1970** (62%) **1968** (51%)

District Vote For President

	1988	1984	1980	1976
D	87,998 (49%)	71,926 (40%)	61,523 (38%)	77,516 (51%)
R	89,411 (50%)	103,902 (58%)	84,461 (53%)	70,804 (47%)

Campaign Finance

	Receipts	Receipts from PACs	Expend-itures
1990			
Anderson (D)	$411,845	$257,766 (63%)	$462,503
Kahn (R)	$7,590	0	$7,579
1988			
Anderson (D)	$493,296	$276,785 (56%)	$457,410
Kahn (R)	$20,634	$400 (2%)	$20,608

Key Votes

1991

Authorize use of force against Iraq	Y

1990

Support constitutional amendment on flag desecration	N
Pass family and medical leave bill over Bush veto	Y
Reduce SDI funding	Y
Allow abortions in overseas military facilities	Y
Approve budget summit plan for spending and taxing	Y
Approve civil rights bill	Y

1989

Halt production of B-2 stealth bomber at 13 planes	N
Oppose capital gains tax cut	N
Approve federal abortion funding in rape or incest cases	Y
Approve pay raise and revision of ethics rules	N
Pass Democratic minimum wage plan over Bush veto	Y

Voting Studies

	Presidential Support		Party Unity		Conservative Coalition	
Year	**S**	**O**	**S**	**O**	**S**	**O**
1990	18	82	93	7	26	72
1989	36	58	85	11	37	61
1988	23	62	84	5	34	61
1987	23	69	84	11	40	53
1986	22	78	84	14	32	68
1985	39	60	84	12	36	62
1984	36	61	74	24	42	58
1983	29	70	76	21	45	54
1982	51	49	66	32	59	41
1981	46	50	77	21	47	51

Interest Group Ratings

Year	ADA	ACU	AFL-CIO	CCUS
1990	94	4	92	21
1989	65	27	82	50
1988	70	10	92	0
1987	72	14	69	29
1986	75	23	79	28
1985	70	38	88	19
1984	80	17	92	63
1983	75	26	88	10
1982	55	50	80	64
1981	50	13	80	17

33 David Dreier (R)

Of Claremont — Elected 1980

Born: July 5, 1952, Kansas City, Mo.
Education: Claremont McKenna College, B.A. 1975; Claremont Graduate School, M.A. 1976.
Occupation: Real estate developer; public relations executive.
Family: Single.
Religion: Christian Scientist.
Political Career: Republican nominee for U.S. House, 1978.
Capitol Office: 411 Cannon Bldg. 20515; 225-2305.

In Washington: After 10 years of waging a frustrating fight to scale back the federal government, Dreier was appointed to the Rules Committee in the 102nd Congress. His anti-government philosophy should mesh well with the confrontational conservatism of the new ranking Republican on Rules, Gerald B. H. Solomon of New York.

Dreier used his positions on the Banking and Small Business committees, where he served through the 101st Congress, to promote an agenda that includes privatization of government services and elimination of federal agencies he deems unnecessary. Dreier brought his distaste for bureaucracy to the 1988 debate over aid for the homeless. "We are creating a permanent homeless infrastructure in this country," he said. "What we essentially created is another grass-roots lobby that Congress will be unable to say 'no' to in the future."

Though he has made little headway with his proposals, he has been extraordinarily successful in another area of politics: fundraising. His seat on Banking enabled him to become the second-biggest recipient in the House of campaign contributions from savings and loan interests in the 1980s.

On the Banking Committee, Dreier advocated bank industry deregulation, supporting moves such as allowing banks to sell and underwrite insurance. On Small Business, he sought to eliminate the Small Business Administration.

Dreier's conservatism fits well into today's House GOP consensus. But a few years back, in the 97th Congress, he paid an unusual price for his ideological image, when a combination of retirements and re-election losses put him in line for the ranking GOP spot on the Banking subcommittee dealing with international lending institutions.

The panel's Republicans, who favored an internationalist approach, maneuvered like-minded Nebraskan Doug Bereuter into the job, for they feared Dreier would be hostile to the U.S. role in international lending. Retiring senior Republican J. William Stanton of Ohio gave up his subcommittee seat to Bereuter, who then used his overall seniority on Banking to claim the ranking position over Dreier.

At Home: Dreier's steadily mounting campaign treasury contained well over $1 million after his 1990 House race, a sum so eye-popping that it spawned some talk he might invest it in a Senate bid in 1992. Dreier has piled up so much cash because he raises money aggressively, but has had to spend relatively modestly in his routine re-elections. After his narrow victory over a Democratic incumbent in 1980, redistricting gave Dreier a safe GOP seat. He has not received less than 64 percent since.

Using the influential GOP establishment linked to the Claremont Colleges as his springboard, Dreier waged a four-year campaign against Democratic Rep. Jim Lloyd. In 1978, underfinanced and only 26 years old, Dreier came within 12,000 votes of Lloyd. Dreier's 1980 bid showed greater maturity and more effort to discuss issues. He followed much of the national GOP line, supporting the Kemp-Roth tax-cut and Reagan's presidential candidacy.

National GOP sources, rating Lloyd the most vulnerable Democratic incumbent in the state, helped Dreier outspend him by almost 2-to-1 and brought in Reagan to campaign for him. This time the 12,000-vote margin was Dreier's.

Dreier ended up in another fight two years later — with a fellow Republican. Redistricting had moved his Pomona political base out of the 35th, where he had won in 1980, into the neighboring 33rd. But the 33rd was also home to GOP Rep. Wayne Grisham.

The primary pitted a sedate, casual Grisham against an aggressive, dynamic Dreier. With voters offered different personalities, not different ideologies, Dreier's organization and fund-raising brought him a solid victory.

After averaging about 70 percent of the vote from 1984 to 1988, he slipped slightly to 63 percent in 1990.

California 33

Eastern Los Angeles — Pomona; Whittier

Most of the land in this sprawling outer suburban district is given over to uninhabitable mountains and hills. The majority of the people are at the southern end, where a mountain named after cornflakes king W. K. Kellogg separates working-class Covina from the white-collar communities of Pomona and Claremont, home of the Claremont Colleges. Farther west, the La Puente Hills isolate Whittier and La Mirada from the rest of the district.

Pomona, with 132,000 residents, is the largest city in the district. The 30 miles of freeway from Pomona to Los Angeles are packed each day with commuters; a smaller though substantial number of local residents opt for the shorter trips to San Bernardino and Riverside areas to the east.

The district combines two divergent elements of California's suburban culture. Voters south of the La Puente hills tend to be middle-aged homeowners with grown children. To the north, newer developments like Walnut and Diamond Bar, along the L.A. commuter routes, draw younger residents.

Though far from unified geographically or culturally, the district is united in its Republican leanings. George Bush topped 60 percent here in 1988, though he fell short of President Reagan's 70 percent in 1984. The only major GOP candidate to lose the 33rd in recent memory was Evelle Younger, who challenged Democratic Gov. Edmund G. Brown Jr. in 1978.

Population: 525,348. White 431,594 (82%), Black 28,402 (5%), Other 25,049 (5%). Spanish origin 100,478 (19%). 18 and over 370,470 (71%), 65 and over 42,959 (8%). Median age: 29.

Committees

Rules (3rd of 4 Republicans)
Rules of the House (ranking)

Elections

1990 General		
David Dreier (R)	101,336	(64%)
Georgia Houston Webb (D)	49,981	(31%)
Gail Lightfoot (LIBERT)	7,840	(5%)
1988 General		
David Dreier (R)	151,704	(69%)
Nelson Gentry (D)	57,586	(26%)

Previous Winning Percentages: **1986** (72%) **1984** (71%) **1982** (65%) **1980** (52%)

District Vote For President

	1988	1984	1980	1976
D	83,319 (37%)	63,307 (29%)	50,062 (27%)	60,050 (39%)
R	142,335 (62%)	152,606 (70%)	117,761 (64%)	89,237 (59%)

Campaign Finance

	Receipts	Receipts from PACs		Expend-itures
1990				
Dreier (R)	$591,313	$100,276	(17%)	$172,451
Webb (D)	$29,612	$2,950	(10%)	$29,177
1988				
Dreier (R)	$487,407	$101,850	(21%)	$186,183

Key Votes

1991	
Authorize use of force against Iraq	Y
1990	
Support constitutional amendment on flag desecration	Y
Pass family and medical leave bill over Bush veto	N
Reduce SDI funding	N
Allow abortions in overseas military facilities	N
Approve budget summit plan for spending and taxing	N
Approve civil rights bill	N
1989	
Halt production of B-2 stealth bomber at 13 planes	N
Oppose capital gains tax cut	N
Approve federal abortion funding in rape or incest cases	N
Approve pay raise and revision of ethics rules	N
Pass Democratic minimum wage plan over Bush veto	N

Voting Studies

	Presidential Support		Party Unity		Conservative Coalition	
Year	S	O	S	O	S	O
1990	73	27	94	6	94	6
1989	76	24	77	21	83	17
1988	76	18	89	4	89	5
1987	80	18	95	5	91	9
1986	83	16	95	4	94	2
1985	84	14	92	4	91	9
1984	73	25	95	4	88	8
1983	85	15	97	2	97	2
1982	78	17	87	2	95	1
1981	78	21	95	5	93	7

Interest Group Ratings

Year	ADA	ACU	AFL-CIO	CCUS
1990	17	83	8	79
1989	0	96	0	100
1988	5	100	0	92
1987	4	96	0	100
1986	0	95	0	100
1985	10	90	0	95
1984	5	92	8	81
1983	0	100	0	84
1982	0	100	0	95
1981	5	100	0	95

34 Esteban E. Torres (D)

Of West Covina — Elected 1982

Born: Jan. 27, 1930, Miami, Ariz.

Education: Attended East Los Angeles Community College, 1959-63; California State U., Los Angeles, 1963-64; U. of Maryland, 1965; American U., 1966.

Military Service: Army, 1949-53.

Occupation: International trade executive; autoworker; labor official.

Family: Wife, Arcy Sanchez; five children.

Religion: Roman Catholic.

Political Career: Sought Democratic nomination for U.S. House, 1974.

Capitol Office: 1740 Longworth Bldg. 20515; 225-5256.

In Washington: Torres has the background and the personal passion to be a high-profile leader among Hispanics in Congress. But in all his activities — on the Banking Committee, on Small Business and as chairman of the Congressional Hispanic Caucus in the 100th Congress — he has opted for a quieter role.

Torres is generally comfortable with the legislative agenda of the activist liberal Democrats who call the shots on Banking and Small Business. Where he can, the former ambassador to UNESCO works as a conciliator, smoothing out the rough edges of members' personal and philosophical conflicts to help keep legislation moving.

On Banking, Torres is in the diminishing community of Democrats who are on good terms with Chairman Henry B. Gonzalez. Despite Torres' relatively light participation in the construction of a sweeping bill overhauling federal housing programs in the 101st Congress, Gonzalez selected him to serve on the House-Senate conference committee. The bill included a Torres provision establishing a disaster-assistance program for low- and moderate-income people.

Early in the 102nd Congress, as the House debated a bill to provide an additional $30 billion to bail out savings and loan institutions, Torres clashed with the committee's ranking Republican, Chalmers P. Wylie. Wylie contended that the bill's minority-contracting provisions constituted mandatory minority hiring quotas; Torres rejected Wylie's contention as "ludicrous," saying that they were merely hiring goals.

In 1990, as the Banking Committee grappled with how to stop narcotics traffickers from using the wire-transfer system to launder drug money, Torres proposed requiring banks to maintain wire-transfer records. But he ran into opposition from several lawmakers who argued that such extensive recordkeeping would be too cumbersome and costly for banks.

The committee watered down his amendment to give the Treasury Department discretion over wire-transfer requirements. When Torres offered a House floor amendment to require Treasury to conduct a one-year pilot program, it was rejected, 127-283.

At Home: Torres, a former laborer, rose to serve as UNESCO ambassador and as a Hispanic-affairs adviser to President Jimmy Carter. His 1982 campaign slogan was "Autoworker to Ambassador, the American Dream."

Torres was an assembly-line welder in Los Angeles during the 1950s and became active in the United Auto Workers. In the 1960s, he was tapped by UAW President Walter Reuther to start a community action project in heavily Hispanic East Los Angeles. In 1968, Torres founded The East Los Angeles Community Union (TELACU), which grew into one of the country's largest anti-poverty agencies.

Torres developed Democratic contacts as an activist, but lost a 1974 primary in his initial bid for the House. He decided on another try in 1982, running in an open 34th District created by redistricting. This time Torres won, fending off former Democratic Rep. Jim Lloyd who had lost his seat to Republican David Dreier in 1980. Torres, with help from the political organization of Democratic Reps. Henry A. Waxman and Howard L. Berman, won easily.

While winning re-election with over 60 percent of the vote each time out, Torres has kept an eye on Los Angeles politics. In 1990, he hinted at a run for the Los Angeles County Board of Supervisors. However, Republican incumbent Pete Schabarum, instead of announcing that he would step down, simply failed to file as a candidate by the March 1990 deadline. By that time, Torres had filed to run again for the House: He defeated former Reagan administration official John Eastman with 61 percent.

California 34

Los Angeles Suburbs — Norwalk

This elongated slice of blue-collar suburbia twists through parts of Los Angeles County tourists see only if they are driving past on one of the four expressways that keep the area fragmented. The 34th more or less follows the San Gabriel River, a channelized concrete trough, through communities that have little contact with each other.

Torres' political success is stoked by two overlapping constituencies: Hispanics, who make up nearly half the district, and blue-collar workers, drawn to him by his labor background.

But a strong dose of working-class conservatism makes the 34th dicier for Democratic presidential candidates. Ronald Reagan easily carried the district in 1984; Michael S. Dukakis took it for the Democrats in 1988, but by a very narrow margin.

One of the Democrats' problems in the 34th is low voter participation by low-income voters. Turnout here was the sixth-lowest among California districts.

At each end of the district are two very different cities. On the southern border is Norwalk, an older working-class suburb with a modestly growing population; it is about 40 percent Hispanic. On the northern border is West Covina, a newer, faster-growing and significantly more affluent town.

Between are the district's most heavily Hispanic areas, around Pico Rivera and South El Monte, three-fourths of whose residents are of Hispanic origin; they are part of the constituency that in 1991 elected the first Hispanic to the county Board of Supervisors, Los Angeles City Councilwoman Gloria Molina. Overall, the 34th has the third-highest concentration of Hispanics among California's House districts.

Population: 526,665. White 392,988 (75%), Black 12,228 (2%), Other 25,863 (5%). Spanish origin 249,778 (47%). 18 and over 348,515 (66%), 65 and over 30,687 (6%). Median age: 26.

Committees

Banking, Finance & Urban Affairs (13th of 31 Democrats)
Consumer Affairs & Coinage (chairman); Housing & Community Development; International Development, Finance, Trade & Monetary Policy

Small Business (11th of 27 Democrats)
Environment & Employment; Procurement, Tourism & Rural Development

Elections

1990 General

Esteban E. Torres (D)	55,646	(61%)
John Eastman (R)	36,024	(39%)

1988 General

Esteban E. Torres (D)	92,087	(63%)
Charles M. House (R)	50,954	(35%)

Previous Winning Percentages: **1986** (60%) **1984** (60%) **1982** (57%)

District Vote For President

	1988	1984	1980	1976
D	76,154 (50%)	60,961 (40%)	52,931 (40%)	69,170 (55%)
R	73,409 (49%)	89,795 (59%)	69,202 (52%)	54,515 (43%)

Campaign Finance

	Receipts	Receipts from PACs	Expend-itures
1990			
Torres (D)	$241,635	$87,788 (36%)	$217,810
Eastman (R)	$75,581	$11,050 (15%)	$75,123
1988			
Torres (D)	$226,964	$108,280 (48%)	$227,098
House (R)	$167,419	$43,792 (26%)	$149,886

Key Votes

1991	
Authorize use of force against Iraq	N
1990	
Support constitutional amendment on flag desecration	N
Pass family and medical leave bill over Bush veto	Y
Reduce SDI funding	Y
Allow abortions in overseas military facilities	Y
Approve budget summit plan for spending and taxing	Y
Approve civil rights bill	Y
1989	
Halt production of B-2 stealth bomber at 13 planes	N
Oppose capital gains tax cut	Y
Approve federal abortion funding in rape or incest cases	Y
Approve pay raise and revision of ethics rules	Y
Pass Democratic minimum wage plan over Bush veto	Y

Voting Studies

	Presidential Support		Party Unity		Conservative Coalition	
Year	S	O	S	O	S	O
1990	17	81	94	2	20	78
1989	29	69	90	1	10	85
1988	16	76	90	2	11	76
1987	10	79	85	3	12	70
1986	18	80	91	2	10	84
1985	18	75	90	1	11	82
1984	26	73	94	2	5	95
1983	21	77	88	4	12	85

Interest Group Ratings

Year	ADA	ACU	AFL-CIO	CCUS
1990	89	0	100	21
1989	95	0	100	40
1988	90	0	100	23
1987	96	0	100	7
1986	90	5	93	18
1985	75	10	94	24
1984	95	0	100	38
1983	90	0	100	30

35 Jerry Lewis (R)

Of Redlands — Elected 1978

Born: Oct. 21, 1934, Seattle, Wash.

Education: U. of California, Los Angeles, B.A. 1956.

Occupation: Insurance executive.

Family: Wife, Arlene Willis; four children, three step-children.

Religion: Presbyterian.

Political Career: San Bernardino School Board, 1965-68; Calif. Assembly, 1969-79; Republican nominee for Calif. Senate, 1973.

Capitol Office: 2312 Rayburn Bldg. 20515; 225-5861.

In Washington: If the traditional process by which GOP House leaders are chosen were to hold, Lewis would have a good chance of succeeding Robert H. Michel as minority leader whenever Michel retires. But Republicans no longer necessarily pick their leaders the old-fashioned way, and that could spell trouble for any ambitions Lewis may have for moving up.

A member of the Appropriations Committee since his second term, Lewis has followed the customary path to prominence in the House GOP, diligently working his way up the ladder. He assumed his first formal leadership position in 1983, and now holds the No. 3 spot, Republican Conference chairman.

But none of that may count for much if the race to succeed Michel becomes a clash between Republicans bent on confronting Democrats and those, like Lewis, who are more willing to work with the House's majority party.

While somewhat more politically conservative than moderate, Lewis is nonetheless identified with the accommodationist wing of the House GOP — a position clearly displayed in late 1990, when he was one of just two members of the House GOP leadership voting with Michel for the bipartisan budget-summit agreement that included tax increases.

On that vote, Lewis parted ways with GOP Whip Newt Gingrich, leader of the party's confrontational faction and a likely contender for Republican leader after Michel retires. Lewis and Gingrich have been eyeing each other warily since 1989, when the Georgian stepped over Lewis to take the party's No. 2 job.

In early 1990, Gingrich backed a challenge to Lewis' re-election as conference chairman by Michigan's Carl Pursell. Lewis won, 98-64, and called his re-election "a disaster" for those in the leadership who tried to unseat him. But others noted that the fact an incumbent leader even drew a challenge was a bad sign for Lewis.

For such a high-ranking House member, Lewis remains something of an enigma. Colleagues laud his geniality, wit and purposeful approach to legislating, but few are close to him. He is not an inspiring speaker and does not command the kind of strong personal loyalty that would make his reach for a higher rung on the leadership ladder easier.

In early 1991, Lewis lost one of his power bases when the staunchly conservative element of California's 19-member GOP House delegation engineered him out of his seat on the panel that makes Republican committee assignments. California's seat on the Committee on Committees went instead to Ron Packard, a conservative with two terms' less seniority than Lewis.

While Lewis has expressed interest in being GOP leader someday, he has declined two recent opportunities to take on Gingrich directly. In late 1990, he formally announced that he would not challenge Gingrich's re-election as whip, citing "the need to be united." (Days later, the Pursell challenge to Lewis solidified.)

Similarly, when GOP Whip Dick Cheney left the House in early 1989 to become defense secretary, Lewis, who already held the No. 3 post, seemed a likely contender for the next rung up on the leadership ladder. But Michel and others helped convince Lewis that it would minimize party strife if he sat out the contest, which Gingrich eventually won. "We would have spent the next two months rearranging the chairs of our leadership and not moving forward on our programs," Lewis explained.

Talking up the importance of party unity is typical for Lewis. But another factor influencing his decision not to challenge Gingrich may have been his close showing in two earlier races for leadership jobs, with almost as many members opposing Lewis as supporting him.

When Lewis ran successfully for the chairmanship of the Republican Policy Committee in 1987, his main opponent was fellow Californian Duncan Hunter. Hunter, identified with the GOP's confrontational wing, ran a surprisingly strong race. Lewis eked out an 88-82 win.

The next year, when the chairmanship of the GOP Conference opened up, the contest was the most suspenseful leadership race of the year. Lewis, careful and organized, managed to

California 35

San Bernardino County

The 35th is basically a suburban district — with a huge and very dry backyard. Most of the population is packed into the southwestern corner of the district, surrounding the city of San Bernardino on three sides. But then the 35th ranges east to the Nevada border, taking in the vast and sparsely populated desert lands in between.

The Mojave Desert, Needles (the nation's hottest town), and the oddly named community of Zzyzx are places of Western lore, but they provide few votes. The areas that do, at the edge of the Los Angeles orbit, are well-to-do suburbs that give the 35th its conservative Republican tone. George Bush won nearly two-thirds of the district's vote in 1988.

West of San Bernardino, near the border with Los Angeles County, are communities such as Chino and Upland that have been experiencing exurban growth in recent years. Republicans are strong here, though a Hispanic population provides some Democratic votes. The cities of Redlands and Loma Linda, both university towns east of San Bernardino, are located in what was once a citrus-packing area at the edge of the nation's southern Citrus Belt. Some orange groves survive, but the area today is primarily suburban.

There is a scattering of moderately sized cities outside the suburban hub. Among them is rapidly-growing Victorville, whose proximity to George Air Force Base drew a number of military retirees. The military influence contributes to the 35th's conservative lean: The district reaches into Los Angeles County's northeast corner, picking up a part of Edwards Air Force Base, where the space shuttle lands, and most of Palmdale, which has a concentration of aerospace and defense plants.

Just south of Victorville is Hesperia, home to 50,000 residents. Once a quiet desert resort for movie stars, it posted an astonishing 268 percent population change in the 1980s.

Population: 525,956. White 457,891 (87%), Black 17,057 (3%), Other 15,770 (3%). Spanish origin 72,389 (14%). 18 and over 371,311 (71%), 65 and over 54,588 (10%). Median age: 29.

get past conference chairman Lynn Martin of Illinois on an 85-82 vote, but needed help from some conservatives who opposed Martin because of her pro-abortion rights stand.

Lewis' legislative career has been a mixture of institutional pragmatism and, in recent years, greater partisanship. As ranking minority member of the Appropriations Subcommittee on the Legislative Branch, Lewis has shown signs lately of downplaying his cordial legislative relationship with the panel's chairman, Vic Fazio, a California colleague and friend.

In the 101st Congress, Lewis and Fazio split on the issue of congressional mailing. Many GOP conservatives consider the frank an unfair advantage for incumbents and an obstacle to their mission of gaining a House majority. But when Lewis pushed the issue — proposing a reduction from six to two districtwide mailings and including town-meeting announcements in the count — he was too far in front of his troops. With Republicans balking at Lewis' plan, Fazio set a cap of four mailings with no limits on town meeting notices.

In the 100th Congress, Lewis pushed a floor amendment to stop the House TV cameras from panning the chamber during special order speeches. The panning practice had been ordered by Speaker Thomas P. O'Neill Jr. in 1984, to show an empty chamber when conservative Republicans were delivering aggressive and unanswered attacks on Democrats. The proposal was defeated on a party-line vote.

In 1988, Lewis was among the Republicans who urged Ronald Reagan to veto a defense bill that reshaped key arms programs and imposed certain arms control policies on the president. A fight, Lewis predicted, would allow the GOP to knock down the "charade" that the Democrats had put on at their presidential nominating convention that summer. "Those people are for less defense," he said, "not more defense."

But the pragmatist in Lewis has also been evident. Early in the 101st Congress he was visible as one of four members of a bipartisan leadership task force, which crafted legislation banning honoraria and developed tactics for promoting a congressional pay raise. The 51 percent pay raise became extremely controversial, and ultimately Lewis was among the overwhelming majority voting against it. Later, a smaller pay increase was approved.

Lewis has been active in fashioning the GOP position in recent anti-drug crusades. In the 100th Congress, as a co-chairman of the GOP's task force on drugs, he pushed legislation containing harsher penalties for users and dealers than the Democratic plan. In the 101st Congress, he offered the Drug War Bond Act, which would fund the fight against drugs with bonds like those sold in World War II.

Lewis has made much of his legislative

mark on the Appropriations subcommittee that handles foreign aid, and he has made it as an enduring critic of the World Bank and other international development agencies. Insisting that he is not dogmatic on the subject, Lewis says he simply wants this lending to be done on sound principles. "Nobody but nobody in my district is in favor of sending taxpayer largess overseas in the form of foreign aid," he says. "But they also want the United States to meet its responsibilities in the world."

His main target has been the International Development Association (IDA), the arm of the World Bank that lends money to the poorest nations. In 1989, Lewis' proposal to cut IDA's budget to protest the agency's numerous loans to China breached an agreement between the administration and House Democrats. Lewis said he had not been told of the agreement, and his proposal, which was supported by Democrats concerned about the crackdown on Chinese students in Tiananmen Square, derailed the agreement.

Over the years, he has worked to limit funding for the World Bank and the International Monetary Fund unless they urge Third World countries to adopt strategies Lewis deems vital to economic growth. In 1989, the House adopted a Lewis amendment to require that the Agency for International Development consider the extent of "economic freedom" in foreign countries before providing aid.

Lewis also served on the VA-HUD Subcommittee at Appropriations through the 101st Congress, where he had an opportunity to help oversee the Environmental Protection Agency. Like most Southern Californians, he favors stringent controls on automobile emissions. In the 101st Congress, he and Democrat Henry A. Waxman introduced a clean-air bill that won praise from environmentalists. The full House approved a Waxman-Lewis amendment providing for an EPA-administered pilot program in California promoting widespread commercial use of clean fuels and low-polluting cars.

Lewis parts ways with environmental advocates on the issue of wilderness designation for the California desert. While he calls the desert "one of the crown jewels of America's public lands," he offered legislation in the 101st Congress to provide wilderness designation for 2.1 million acres, compared with the 9 million acres environmentalists want to protect. Lewis' proposal also permits grazing and motor-vehicle access in certain areas. No agreement was reached in the 101st Congress and the matter will be revisited in the 102nd.

On Appropriations, Lewis plays the earmark game successfully, and in 1989 he was among those criticizing HUD Secretary Jack F. Kemp for his rebuke of the process. After Kemp balked at 40 projects earmarked in the housing appropriation bill — including $500,000 for a shelter for battered women in Lewis' district — Lewis implied that Kemp had better go along with Appropriations' wishes if he wanted sympathetic hearing for his own budget requests.

Although Lewis has expressed some qualms about the pork-barrel aspect of water projects, he seeks to bring water to his desert-dominated district. In 1990, the House approved $65 million for the Santa Ana flood control project. In 1986, he sponsored the successful the Lower Colorado Water Supply Act, to improve access to water for small desert communities. Lewis also has a strong interest in earthquake research and has worked on Appropriations to steer money to the Cajon Pass earthquake research site in California.

At Home: Lewis' rise to the Republican Conference chairmanship raised his profile in California, leading to speculation that he might aim for a Senate seat in 1992.

Yet in 1990, Lewis learned the unease that sometimes visits members of the leadership — especially when the electorate is feeling hostile toward Congress. While Lewis was never seriously threatened, he did face a primary challenge and a falloff from his normal general-election tally.

In the primary, lawyer and political neophyte Mark I. Blankenship ran as an outsider. Unabashedly ambitious — he told a reporter he had eyes on the White House — Blankenship received a spate of publicity: To highlight the effect on Republican candidates if President Bush was to back off his "no new taxes" pledge, *The New York Times* ran a feature story focusing on Blankenship's challenge to Lewis. The incumbent won easily, although Blankenship pulled off a fifth of the GOP vote.

Lewis was expected to have little trouble with Democrat Barry Norton, a welder: Stuck in Washington for most of the fall, Lewis applied part of his limited campaign time to the unsuccessful bid by Republican Bob Hammock to unseat Democratic Rep. George E. Brown Jr. in the neighboring 36th District.

However, Lewis faced a backlash after he publicly supported the unpopular budget summit agreement in October. Although he won comfortably, his 61 percent tally was his lowest since his first contest in 1978.

After the election, Lewis was mentioned among the possible candidates to succeed GOP Sen. Pete Wilson, who had won election as California governor with four years remaining on his Senate term. Lewis was bypassed — Wilson selected a more moderate appointee, state Sen. John Seymour — but he remained on the list of potential 1992 Senate candidates.

A successful insurance broker, Lewis entered GOP politics in the early 1960s and won a seat on the San Bernardino School Board. After three years there, he sought a state Assembly seat in 1968 and won the first of five terms.

In late 1973, Lewis barely missed winning a special election for the state Senate. He finished first in the special primary, taking 49 percent: Just 463 more votes would have given him the majority he needed to win the seat outright. But he was forced into a runoff with Democrat Ruben S. Ayala, who went on to win with 54 percent. Lewis was re-elected to the Assembly in 1974. In 1976, he not only got his usual Republican nomination, but also won the Democratic line in a write-in campaign.

With an Assembly constituency that covered more than half the 37th Congressional District, Lewis was an obvious choice for Republicans in 1978 when GOP Rep. Shirley N. Pettis retired. Earlier in his career, Lewis had worked as a field representative for Jerry Pettis, Shirley's husband, who represented the district for eight years before dying in a plane crash in 1975. Declaring himself a candidate in the "Pettis tradition," Lewis won the five-candidate GOP primary with 55 percent of the vote, then won the general election handily.

In 1982 the Democrats' redistricting plan gave Lewis a choice of two districts in which to run. The chief architect of the remap, Democratic Rep. Phillip Burton, had assumed Lewis would run in the 37th District, which took up most of heavily Republican Riverside County. But Lewis' home had been placed in the neighboring 35th, and he filed there.

His action forced GOP Rep. David Dreier, whose home was also in the new 35th, to look elsewhere. Dreier shifted to a nearby district and ousted GOP Rep. Wayne Grisham in a primary. Lewis made himself a fixture in the 35th, winning at least 70 percent three times in the 1980s.

Committees

Appropriations (11th of 22 Republicans)
Legislative (ranking); Defense

Elections

1990 General		
Jerry Lewis (R)	121,602	(61%)
Barry Norton (D)	66,100	(33%)
Jerry Johnson (LIBERT)	13,020	(6%)
1990 Primary		
Jerry Lewis (R)	53,806	(79%)
Mark I. Blankenship (R)	14,361	(21%)
1988 General		
Jerry Lewis (R)	181,203	(70%)
Paul Sweeney (D)	71,186	(28%)

Previous Winning Percentages: **1986** (77%) **1984** (85%) **1982** (68%) **1980** (72%) **1978** (61%)

District Vote For President

	1988	1984	1980	1976
D	88,126 (33%)	59,824 (28%)	45,868 (27%)	41,739 (43%)
R	172,872 (65%)	154,583 (71%)	111,606 (65%)	53,027 (55%)

Campaign Finance

	Receipts	Receipts from PACs	Expend-itures
1990			
Lewis (R)	$452,381	$292,014 (65%)	$211,940
Norton (D)	$2,266	0	$2,371
1988			
Lewis (R)	$212,905	$156,400 (73%)	$337,814

Key Votes

1991	
Authorize use of force against Iraq	Y
1990	
Support constitutional amendment on flag desecration	Y
Pass family and medical leave bill over Bush veto	N
Reduce SDI funding	N
Allow abortions in overseas military facilities	N
Approve budget summit plan for spending and taxing	Y
Approve civil rights bill	N
1989	
Halt production of B-2 stealth bomber at 13 planes	N
Oppose capital gains tax cut	N
Approve federal abortion funding in rape or incest cases	N
Approve pay raise and revision of ethics rules	Y
Pass Democratic minimum wage plan over Bush veto	N

Voting Studies

	Presidential Support		Party Unity		Conservative Coalition	
Year	S	O	S	O	S	O
1990	65	26	70	19	89	7
1989	78	21	80	17	83	17
1988	44	24	67	12	55	11
1987	68	30	81	12	91	2
1986	63	21	63	14	56	16
1985	65	28	75	18	84	11
1984	71	22	72	18	83	10
1983	70	20	74	17	74	8
1982	81	16	84	13	89	10
1981	72	20	75	15	81	15

Interest Group Ratings

Year	ADA	ACU	AFL-CIO	CCUS
1990	6	76	0	58
1989	10	79	25	78
1988	5	90	22	67
1987	8	83	13	93
1986	0	88	15	64
1985	10	76	27	62
1984	10	86	17	81
1983	5	88	13	89
1982	5	91	5	100
1981	5	79	0	100

36 George E. Brown Jr. (D)

Of Riverside — Elected 1962

Did not serve 1971-73.

Born: March 6, 1920, Holtville, Calif.

Education: El Centro Junior College, 1938; U. of California, Los Angeles, B.A. 1946.

Military Service: Army, 1942-46.

Occupation: Management consultant; physicist.

Family: Wife, Marta Macias; four children, three stepchildren.

Religion: Methodist.

Political Career: Monterey Park City Council, 1954-55, mayor, 1955-58; Calif. Assembly, 1959-63; sought Democratic nomination for U.S. Senate, 1970.

Capitol Office: 2300 Rayburn Bldg. 20515; 225-6161.

In Washington: With the start of the 102nd Congress, Brown finally shed the albatross of having served nearly three decades without gaining a full committee chairmanship.

When House Science Committee Chairman Robert A. Roe of New Jersey went to the head of the Public Works Committee, Brown took the Science mantle, a move that science advocates hope will usher in a new era of committee activism for high-tech programs.

Still, watching Brown today as he listens patiently to committee testimony on the science budget or shuffles from the House floor to enjoy another cigar in the members' lobby, it is hard to recall the spirited anti-war crusader that he was in the 1960s. But he is the same man; Brown has simply mellowed with the times, and been worn by years of political battles.

Brown, who is the No. 3 Democrat on the Agriculture Committee, has not ruled out a future bid to lead that panel, if its chair comes open. But he seems more suited to Science, where he says his new role is the "capstone of my career." Brown admits, however, that he will have to develop new horse-trading skills if he is to transform a reputation for being a thoughtful and articulate proponent of research and development programs into political clout.

With Roe at the helm, the committee was slow to move NASA's annual authorization bill, weakening the panel's influence in appropriations decisions. Brown will try to persuade his counterparts on the Senate Commerce and Science Committee and his colleagues on House Appropriations to return his panel to full partnership.

As chairman, Brown is likely to push NASA to shift its emphasis toward unmanned exploration, although he remains an advocate of one day establishing human settlements on the moon and possibly Mars. Because of budget constraints, Brown has spoken of a need to reassess every aspect of science policy, including big-ticket items such as the atom-smashing superconducting super collider planned for Texas. Other pet projects for Brown include improving science education, studying the effects of electric and magnetic fields and monitoring nutrition programs.

Brown has had, in effect, two separate House careers in which to pursue his liberal causes, broken by a one-term absence after his 1970 Senate defeat. Two issues — environmentalism and opposition to nuclear war — are the link between them.

When Brown returned to the House in 1973, U.S. activity in Vietnam was ending. He settled quietly into the Science and Agriculture committees and followed his issues, thoughtful but detached. Despite his seniority now on Agriculture, he seems engaged there mostly when the discussion turns from farm policy to the subject of pesticide regulation.

The old peace advocate — who voted against the January 1991 resolution authorizing use of force against Iraq — still surfaces in debates, particularly on space-based military programs. In the 1980s, Brown sponsored amendments imposing one-year bans on testing anti-satellite (ASAT) weapons against targets in space, contingent on Soviet abstention.

Brown is one of the more outspoken foes of the strategic defense initiative (SDI). He has supported efforts to cut its funding, and to commit the United States to continued observance of the 1972 anti-ballistic missile treaty — a document he says SDI would violate.

Brown's anti-military approach to space policy may have cost him a couple of key committee seats. In November 1987 he announced his resignation from the Intelligence Committee, calling it "a protest to the administration's use of the classification system to prevent members of Congress from engaging in vital national debates." However, Brown had come under pressure to resign from conserva-

California 36

San Bernardino; Riverside

Of the three districts covering the San Bernardino-Riverside metropolitan area, this is the only one a Democrat can win. Brown has done it in House elections by combining the votes of the blue-collar Anglo residents of San Bernardino and Riverside with those of San Bernardino's large Mexican-American population.

But no liberal candidate can rest comfortably here. This section of Southern California desert country is a conservative area where religious fundamentalism is an important factor.

This mixture makes the 36th one of the more competitive California districts in presidential elections. President Ronald Reagan carried the 36th with a comfortable 56 percent in 1984, but George Bush prevailed by a more modest margin.

About three-quarters of the district vote is cast in San Bernardino County. The county's "West Valley" area has drawn large numbers of middle-class newcomers pushed out of eastern Los Angeles and Orange counties by high real estate prices.

The city of San Bernardino (population 164,000) was a fruit-packing center in the 1930s. Today, its citrus industry shares space with the many electronics and aerospace firms in the area, as well as Kaiser Steel Corp.'s blast furnace in nearby Fontana.

Though the city has seen years of growth, San Bernardino suffered some blows in early 1989. That April, Congress ratified a military base-closing list that included Norton Air Force Base near the city.

Then, in May, a San Bernardino neighborhood was shattered by a pair of freak accidents. First, a runaway freight train crashed into a group of homes, causing several deaths. Just days later, a gas pipeline nicked by the train wreck erupted in flames, causing more death and destruction.

To the west of San Bernardino is burgeoning Ontario, which supports a major commercial airport and large Lockheed and General Electric plants. With the economy dependent on the local defense plants, Ontario voters have turned increasingly toward Republican candidates.

The 36th then reaches into Riverside County for a portion of the city of Riverside. Though parts of the city are in the 37th, Brown has the more Democratic northern neighborhoods, including blue-collar communities and the area around the University of California at Riverside.

Farther west is Glen Avon, site of the Stringfellow Acid Pits. A cleanup of toxic-contaminated groundwater is under way there.

Population: 525,987. White 402,029 (76%), Black 43,141 (8%), Other 13,913 (3%). Spanish origin 121,631 (23%). 18 and over 362,108 (69%), 65 and over 48,227 (9%). Median age: 27.

tive Democrats, who agreed with the Reagan administration that Brown had divulged classified information about U.S. military satellite capabilities. He insisted he relied only on published accounts.

Earlier, in 1985 and 1987, the chairmanship of the important Science Subcommittee on Space Science went to a colleague with far less seniority, Bill Nelson of Florida. Nelson's 1985 victory over Brown was explained in part in regional and generational terms: Nelson, whose district included the Kennedy Space Center, drew support from junior members and the panel's Floridians. But also, Brown's strong opinions about the use of space funds probably alienated some members who believe virtually any space expenditure is a good one.

Having lost the Science Subcommittee in 1985, Brown could have retained the chairmanship of the Agriculture Subcommittee on Department Operations and Research that he had held for four years. He chose not to, in part because he had just endured a frustrating and contentious battle over pesticide regulations. Nevertheless, in the 100th Congress, Brown not only regained the Agriculture subcommittee (after conceding the Science panel to Nelson), he also took responsibility for a pesticide bill and helped steer a stripped-down version into law.

On other issues, Brown casts liberal votes much as he did during the 1960s. Occasionally, however, he has cast pragmatic pro-defense votes he once might have denounced.

Early in the 101st Congress, he and Republican Jerry Lewis, from the neighboring 35th District, led the futile opposition to a package of proposed military base closures. The package, compiled by a blue-ribbon commission, had widespread support in Congress since most members' home-state bases escaped inclusion. But among the targets was Norton Air Force Base in Brown's district, employer of 4,520 military personnel and 2,133 civilians. Brown, however, did help keep a ballistic-missile section of the base from being relocated.

In 1980 he began voting for a California product, the B-1 bomber. "If the B-1 was being built in some other state," he once explained, "and I didn't have two Air Force bases and a lot of retired military people who feel strongly about the B-1, I'd probably have voted the other way."

This is the man, after all, who became a peace advocate as a scientist, and argued his cause from the start of his first term, in 1963. That year, he opposed extension of the draft as it passed the House 388-3. He voted against civil defense money, saying it "created a climate in which nuclear war becomes more credible."

By the spring of 1965, he had already begun speaking out against the Vietnam War, accusing President Lyndon B. Johnson of pretending "that the peace of mankind can be won by the slaughter of peasants in Vietnam." For the next five years he kept up such protests, refusing to vote for any military spending while the war continued; in 1966 his was the only House vote against the $58 billion defense bill.

Brown acquired a national reputation for his anti-war work during those years, but much of his legislative time was devoted to environmental issues. He supported a ban on offshore oil drilling along the California coast, backed federal land-use planning and proposed to outlaw production of internal combustion engines.

One intriguing legacy from the 1960s is Brown's relationship with President Bush, who served with him in the House late in the decade. Despite his liberalism, Brown was one of a number of Democrats whom Bush befriended. Both had to leave the House after 1970 Senate defeats, and Bush subsequently wrote to his former gym partner that he regretted the loss of "the paddleball earnings that you have made possible for me, my wife and my children."

At Home: The 1990 election proved either that Brown is one of the most marginal political veterans in the House, or that he has won the undying loyalty of a small but essential majority of his constituents.

Unlike most California House incumbents, Brown was not given a "safe" district in the 1980s redistricting: In four of his previous five elections, he faced John Paul Stark — a hard-right Republican with a base among religious fundamentalists — and won with relatively modest tallies ranging from 53 to 57 percent.

Yet GOP insistence on Brown's vulnerability was punctured in 1990. National Republican officials targeted Brown for defeat, and touted their candidate, San Bernardino County Supervisor Bob Hammock, as Brown's toughest challenger ever. Despite Hammock's supposed bipartisan appeal and his barrage of attacks on the incumbent's record, Brown won with 53 percent of the vote.

It was not a friendly campaign. After Hammock won the June Republican primary, Brown sent a "congratulatory" telegram that also called on the real-estate developer to release his business records. A mass mailing followed, detailing published allegations of potential Hammock conflicts of interest during his service on the county board. Hammock responded with a broadside about Brown's campaign fundraising from political action committees and his acceptance of honoraria.

After years of attacking Brown from the far right, GOP strategists hoped Hammock's moderate image would enable him to topple the liberal Brown. While taking anti-tax, anti-crime and strong-defense positions typical of Republican candidates, Hammock portrayed himself as an environmentalist and noted the strong support he had received at the local level from San Bernardino's Hispanic community.

However, Brown parried Hammock at every turn. He received crucial endorsements from the League of Conservation Voters and the Sierra Club, and held most of the Hispanic vote that is a crucial element of the Democratic base in the 36th District. While Hammock tried to blame the closure of Norton Air Force Base on Brown's record of arms control and anti-war activism, Brown touted his efforts, albeit unsuccessful, to save the base and his subsequent work to convert it to useful purposes.

With his 1990 win, Brown once again defied demographics that appeared to work against him. The 1982 remap gave him a district that was roughly balanced between the Democratic-leaning urban areas of San Bernardino and Riverside and the booming eastern Los Angeles suburbs that were more amenable to Republicans. Continued suburban growth during the decade appeared to make Brown's hold less secure; yet he survived.

Brown has persevered through even tougher political times. After serving as a local official and state assemblyman from a near-in Los Angeles suburb, Brown won a House seat in 1962 and held it for four terms. But he gave it up in 1970 for a Democratic Senate primary campaign that would deal him his only defeat.

The 1970 primary boiled down to Brown and Rep. John V. Tunney, son of former boxing champion Gene Tunney. Brown's opposition to the Vietnam War gave him an initial advantage: After American troops invaded Cambodia that spring, polls began to show Brown — who had called for the impeachment of President Richard M. Nixon because of the invasion — in front of Tunney, who had been much less outspoken against the war.

But Tunney then turned the tables on Brown, accusing him of being a radical and advocating student violence. Brown attempted to deflect what he termed Tunney's "dirty" tactics, but failed and lost by a 9-percentage-point margin.

Although Tunney went on to win the Senate seat, Brown exacted a revenge of sorts. His description of Tunney as the "lightweight son of the heavyweight champ" became part of California political folklore and helped end Tunney's career in 1976.

Brown's own political resurrection came quickly. In 1972, he moved to a newly created district in the San Bernardino-Riverside area. Brown prevailed in the eight-candidate primary field with 28 percent of the vote. Running in a district with a strong Democratic registration advantage, Brown won easily in November.

Brown topped 60 percent in three consecutive elections, even though 1974 redistricting put more of fast-growing and conservative Riverside County into the district.

But in the 1980 election, his first contest against Stark, Brown toppled to 53 percent. Stark, whose organization came largely from the Campus Crusade for Christ, benefited from a conservative tide that also helped carry Ronald Reagan to the White House that year.

Although Brown increased his margin over Stark in 1982, district Republicans hoped that Reagan's 1984 coattails might put the challenger over the top. But Brown had prepared carefully for the second rematch. His attention to the Stringfellow Acid Pits, a toxic-waste dump near Riverside, played well among middle-class voters susceptible to Stark's appeal.

In addition, Brown took his campaign onto Stark's home ground. He made the rounds of local churches — mainstream and fundamentalist — delivering his own arguments on the importance of extending "pro-life" views to take in nuclear-weapons issues and humanitarian concerns. He wound up taking 57 percent.

After a relatively easy 1986 contest against Republican businessman Bob Henley, Brown had to fend off Stark one more time. Despite speculation that the suburban boom would hurt him, Brown won by 54-42 percent.

Committees

Science, Space & Technology (Chairman)

Agriculture (3rd of 27 Democrats)
Department Operations, Research & Foreign Agriculture; Forests, Family Farms & Energy

Elections

1990 General

George E. Brown Jr. (D)	72,409	(53%)
Bob Hammock (R)	64,961	(47%)

1988 General

George E. Brown Jr. (D)	103,493	(54%)
John Paul Stark (R)	81,413	(42%)

Previous Winning Percentages: **1986** (57%) **1984** (57%) **1982** (54%) **1980** (53%) **1978** (63%) **1976** (62%) **1974** (63%) **1972** (56%) **1968** (52%) **1966** (51%) **1964** (59%) **1962** (56%)

District Vote For President

	1988	1984	1980	1976
D	92,521 (47%)	80,504 (43%)	58,623 (40%)	66,240 (58%)
R	100,291 (51%)	103,809 (56%)	74,963 (51%)	47,161 (41%)

Campaign Finance

	Receipts	Receipts from PACs	Expend-itures
1990			
Brown (D)	$818,181	$454,935 (56%)	$822,686
Hammock (R)	$538,381	$104,035 (19%)	$538,156
1988			
Brown (D)	$504,361	$276,543 (55%)	$532,897
Stark (R)	$219,019	$89,155 (41%)	$218,696

Key Votes

1991

Authorize use of force against Iraq	N

1990

Support constitutional amendment on flag desecration	N
Pass family and medical leave bill over Bush veto	Y
Reduce SDI funding	Y
Allow abortions in overseas military facilities	Y
Approve budget summit plan for spending and taxing	N
Approve civil rights bill	Y

1989

Halt production of B-2 stealth bomber at 13 planes	N
Oppose capital gains tax cut	Y
Approve federal abortion funding in rape or incest cases	Y
Approve pay raise and revision of ethics rules	Y
Pass Democratic minimum wage plan over Bush veto	Y

Voting Studies

	Presidential Support		Party Unity		Conservative Coalition	
Year	S	O	S	O	S	O
1990	19	76	79	5	31	61
1989	31	55	87	4	22	73
1988	13	65	80	3	8	76
1987	18	70	78	5	21	65
1986	18	71	82	3	16	76
1985	20	68	84	5	9	76
1984	27	69	91	5	12	81
1983	16	77	84	5	11	82
1982	32	51	85	5	12	79
1981	38	57	77	10	19	75

Interest Group Ratings

Year	ADA	ACU	AFL-CIO	CCUS
1990	89	4	83	31
1989	75	0	100	40
1988	80	5	100	25
1987	76	10	86	7
1986	95	0	92	21
1985	85	6	93	28
1984	95	0	82	33
1983	90	0	100	25
1982	75	5	94	29
1981	85	13	86	12

37 Al McCandless (R)

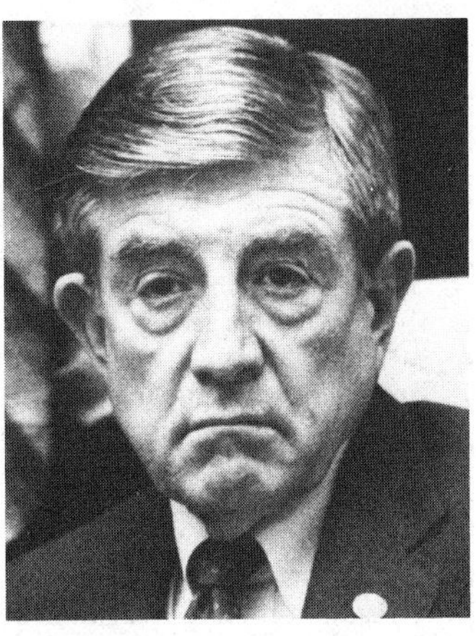

Of La Quinta — Elected 1982

Born: July 23, 1927, Brawley, Calif.
Education: U. of California, Los Angeles, B.A. 1951.
Military Service: Marine Corps, 1945-46, 1950-52.
Occupation: Automobile dealer.
Family: Wife, Gail Walmsley Glass; five children.
Religion: Protestant.
Political Career: Riverside County supervisor, 1970-82; candidate for Calif. Assembly, 1975.
Capitol Office: 2422 Rayburn Bldg. 20515; 225-5330.

In Washington: McCandless represented the 37th through most of the 1980s, a decade in which its population nearly doubled. With a shade under 1 million residents in 1990, it was the most populous district in the nation and the one with the highest growth rate (86 percent) since the census of 1980.

But watching McCandless in Congress gives one little sense of such dynamism. Now in his fifth term, he tries to convey the perspective of a businessman to his colleagues on the Banking and Government Operations committees. Despite this effort, he is probably best known for nearly losing to a former television actor in 1990.

Despite his relatively junior status, McCandless is the second-oldest Republican on Banking. Because of his age and his experiences in the automobile sales business, his views on government's proper role in the free enterprise system receive some note.

But McCandless' abiding resentment of federal regulation is so strong that it limits his ability to play a consensus-building role when disputes are being thrashed out. Even some conservative Republicans note that the Californian can be too opinionated to play a significant role in shaping legislation.

One cause McCandless has pursued for much of his House career is reform of the Social Security system. He has proposed legislation to remove Social Security trust funds from the federal budget, and to make the Social Security Administration an independent agency. In the 100th and 101st Congresses, McCandless introduced bills to repeal the limit on Social Security earnings. He calls the limitation "an unnecessary burden on the elderly."

McCandless sometimes comes to the defense of a federal program. For instance, he favors the mortgage guarantee programs of the Federal Housing Administration.

Occasionally, McCandless reaches back into his career in the car business to help him explain points in a policy debate. Arguing once against a nuclear-weapons freeze on the grounds that the United States had inferior weaponry, he complained that "we have Model Ts, and they have Thunderbirds."

At Home: McCandless' low profile almost cost him his seat in 1990, as the district's outnumbered Democrats put up the well-known actor Ralph Waite as their candidate.

Waite — who played the stalwart father of a rural Depression-era family in the long-running TV series "The Waltons" — was more familiar than McCandless to many voters, especially the thousands of new residents who flooded the 37th in recent years. To reinforce his local base, first-time candidate Waite emphasized his community activities, including his work with an alcohol-and-drug rehabilitation center he helped found.

The thrust of Waite's campaign, though, was an effort to tie McCandless' membership on the Banking Committee to the savings and loan crisis. While not accusing the incumbent of direct ethics violations, Waite said McCandless stood idly by while the scandal unfolded. McCandless countered that he had supported the 1987 bailout of the Federal Savings and Loan Insurance Corporation.

McCandless, who had never had to run a big-money House campaign, was somewhat slow to organize for the contest. But when polls showed Waite moving up, McCandless tapped the network of affluent Republicans in the district's desert communities: Former President Gerald R. Ford and comedian Bob Hope were among those who came to his aid.

McCandless hung on to win with a plurality of just under 50 percent, to 45 percent for Waite. This close call ended a string of three consecutive elections in which McCandless had taken 64 percent.

Although McCandless, a longtime Riverside County supervisor, was little known outside his Palm Springs area base when he embarked on his 1982 House bid, he emerged atop a multi-candidate Republican primary field with 25 percent of the vote. Running in a newly created district with a strong Republican tilt, McCandless easily got by the Democratic nominee in the fall with 59 percent.

California 37

Riverside County

This was the nation's fastest-growing House district during the 1980s. The booming subdivisions in Riverside County expanded by 86 percent, giving the 37th a population of nearly 1 million — much of which will be shed in the redistricting prior to the 1992 election.

McCandless' problem in 1990 was an aberration. This is a solidly Republican district, whose tone is set by the affluent neighborhoods of Riverside, and by Palm Springs, the desert playground of the wealthy. Both President Ronald Reagan in 1984 and George Bush in 1988 easily carried the 37th.

The district's population is dispersed over a huge expanse of Riverside County, from the Santa Ana Mountains in the west to the Colorado River at the Arizona border. But much of it is located near Orange County, the suburban L.A. area fabled for its Republican conservatism.

As it has grown, the city of Riverside has been shifted in and out of the Riverside County district. In the 1960s, it was completely included; in the '70s, it was completely removed. The most recent redistricting split the city, but in a manner beneficial to the already dominant GOP. The more-Democratic northern part of Riverside was placed in the 36th District, while the more upscale southern part went to the 37th.

The GOP edge is bolstered in such fast-growing Riverside suburbs as Norco and Corona. Farther east in the desert are the oasis resorts of Rancho Mirage and Palm Springs, where the leisure class contributes its ample wealth to the local economy. Although former President Gerald R. Ford has made his retirement home in this area, it is better known for its Hollywood set. Singer Sonny Bono, the mayor of Palm Springs, discussed the possibility that he might run for senator in 1992, but demurred.

Despite the growth of its suburbs and resorts, farmers continue to play a major role in the 37th's economy and politics. Irrigation ditches knife across Riverside County, and cotton and livestock growers battle to keep their scarce water resources from being diverted to the urbanized areas. Riverside was originally a trade center for the citrus ranches of the Santa Ana River basin; the first domestic navel orange was grown there in the 1870s.

Population: 525,938. White 439,899 (84%), Black 19,151 (4%), Other 12,338 (2%). Spanish origin 98,238 (19%). 18 and over 383,799 (73%), 65 and over 86,715 (16%). Median age: 33.

Committees

Banking, Finance & Urban Affairs (8th of 20 Republicans)
Consumer Affairs & Coinage (ranking); Financial Institutions Supervision, Regulation & Insurance; General Oversight; International Development, Finance, Trade & Monetary Policy

Government Operations (3rd of 15 Republicans)
Government Information, Justice & Agriculture (ranking)

Elections

1990 General		
Al McCandless (R)	115,469	(50%)
Ralph Waite (D)	103,961	(45%)
Bonnie Flickinger (LIBERT)	6,178	(3%)
Gary R. Odom (AMI)	6,474	(3%)
1990 Primary		
Al McCandless (R)	53,298	(74%)
Bud Mathewson (R)	19,128	(26%)
1988 General		
Al McCandless (R)	174,284	(64%)
Johnny Pearson (D)	89,666	(33%)

Previous Winning Percentages: **1986** (64%) **1984** (64%) **1982** (59%)

District Vote For President

	1988		1984		1980		1976	
D	108,106	(38%)	80,012	(34%)	55,950	(30%)	65,907	(48%)
R	172,644	(61%)	153,832	(65%)	113,408	(62%)	71,519	(52%)

Campaign Finance

	Receipts	Receipts from PACs		Expend-itures
1990				
McCandless (R)	$551,789	$179,600	(33%)	$602,444
Waite (D)	$622,159	$149,266	(24%)	$624,560
Flickinger (LIBERT)	$2,318	0		$2,318
1988				
McCandless (R)	$129,505	$75,500	(58%)	$122,839
Pearson (D)	$14,204	$8,000	(56%)	$13,767

Key Votes

1991	
Authorize use of force against Iraq	Y
1990	
Support constitutional amendment on flag desecration	Y
Pass family and medical leave bill over Bush veto	N
Reduce SDI funding	N
Allow abortions in overseas military facilities	Y
Approve budget summit plan for spending and taxing	N
Approve civil rights bill	N
1989	
Halt production of B-2 stealth bomber at 13 planes	N
Oppose capital gains tax cut	N
Approve federal abortion funding in rape or incest cases	Y
Approve pay raise and revision of ethics rules	N
Pass Democratic minimum wage plan over Bush veto	N

Voting Studies

	Presidential Support		Party Unity		Conservative Coalition	
Year	**S**	**O**	**S**	**O**	**S**	**O**
1990	71	29	92	7	98	2
1989	77	19	86	6	93	2
1988	67	27	84	5	95	3
1987	67	26	83	6	86	9
1986	77	18	84	11	94	6
1985	74	21	89	4	98	0
1984	71	27	90	8	92	8
1983	90	10	86	10	85	11

Interest Group Ratings

Year	ADA	ACU	AFL-CIO	CCUS
1990	6	92	8	79
1989	0	88	0	100
1988	10	95	0	92
1987	8	82	7	93
1986	5	95	7	94
1985	5	86	0	91
1984	5	92	0	71
1983	5	87	0	95

38 Robert K. Dornan (R)

Of Garden Grove — Elected 1976

Did not serve 1983-85.

Born: April 3, 1933, New York, N.Y.
Education: Attended Loyola U. (Los Angeles), 1950-53.
Military Service: Air Force, 1953-58; Air Force Reserve, 1958-75.
Occupation: Broadcast journalist and producer.
Family: Wife, Sallie Hansen; five children.
Religion: Roman Catholic.
Political Career: Candidate for mayor of Los Angeles, 1973; sought GOP nomination for U.S. Senate, 1982.
Capitol Office: 301 Cannon Bldg. 20515; 225-2965.

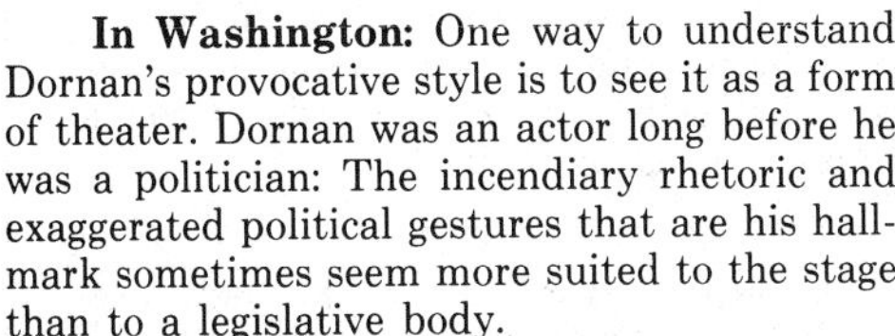

In Washington: One way to understand Dornan's provocative style is to see it as a form of theater. Dornan was an actor long before he was a politician: The incendiary rhetoric and exaggerated political gestures that are his hallmark sometimes seem more suited to the stage than to a legislative body.

Dornan promotes conservative causes with a flamboyance and lack of inhibition that give him a distinctive place in the House. To liberal opponents and more mild-mannered conservatives, Dornan can come off as too aggressive or too willing to question the patriotism or morality of others. But to his hardline followers, Dornan is something of a cultural hero: He is a frequent guest, and an occasional host, on nationally broadcast and televised political talk shows.

Because of his high profile, Dornan can become personally identified with the issues he advocates. His support throughout the 1980s for the B-1 bomber program earned the former Air Force pilot his lasting nickname of "B-1 Bob." During that decade, Dornan — then a member of the Foreign Affairs Committee — was one of the most vocal supporters of President Ronald Reagan's military buildup and a premier foe of all things communist.

Dornan serves on the Armed Services and Intelligence committees, and his role has changed slightly. Spurred by U.S. fiscal problems and the Soviet Union's preoccupation with its internal affairs, even the White House is supporting defense budget cuts: Dornan now warns against a too-precipitous defense retrenchment and a too-complacent attitude toward the communist world.

In 1990, Dornan fought against efforts to cap development of the B-2 stealth bomber. He also tried to block the House from diverting funds from the Strategic Defense Initiative (SDI) to other endangered weapons programs. But his amendment to increase SDI spending above the level recommended by the Armed Services Committee was defeated in the House by a 83-338 vote.

Dornan was a strong supporter of the January 1991 resolution authorizing President Bush to use military force to end Iraq's occupation of Kuwait. Less than two months later, as the U.S.-led military coalition closed in on victory, Dornan put on a vintage rhetorical performance in a House colloquy with conservative GOP Rep. Bob McEwen of Ohio.

Dornan laced into those who initially opposed the war ("How many more [Kuwaitis] would have been tortured if we had listened to the counsel of liberals in this chamber and wait for sanctions to stop [Iraqi dictator Saddam] Hussein"). And he faulted the media, which he regards as having a liberal bias and an anti-military attitude ("Did you note the media's fascination with body bags, body counts, this leftover Vietnam syndrome?").

Dornan also praised Bush as "a courageous commander in chief." These kind words for Bush are not unusual: While other conservatives doubted Bush as insufficiently ideological during his vice presidency, Dornan became a close ally and was an early and fervent supporter of Bush's 1988 presidential campaign.

On some issues, such as immigration, Dornan parts from some of the conservative rank and file. With a House district that includes a large population of Southeast Asian refugees, Dornan praises the role of immigrants in building the nation's economy.

On the other hand, there is hardly a member of Congress whose anti-abortion fervor exceeds Dornan's. Late in 1990, he made a series of anti-abortion speeches on the House floor, with a lifelike model of a 12-week-old fetus nearby. He calls for the reversal of the 1973 *Roe v. Wade* Supreme Court ruling that legalized abortion and works to mandate abortion limits in the only locality over which Congress has direct jurisdiction: the District of Columbia.

In 1988, Dornan scored a major victory for the anti-abortion movement; his amendment to a D.C. appropriations bill, barring city officials

California 38

Northwestern Orange County; Santa Ana; Garden Grove

The 38th ranges from coastal Orange County to the western half of Anaheim, where it takes in Disneyland and Anaheim Stadium, the home of baseball's California Angels. It is an older suburban area that is primarily home to young families.

As redrafted in the 1980s redistricting, the 38th was at first receptive to genial and moderate Democratic Rep. Jerry M. Patterson. But with many residents with roots in Texas and Oklahoma, the district had a profound conservative tilt that became evident in 1984, when Dornan sought his return to the House. Dornan — whose former 27th District had been dismembered by Democratic mapmakers, prompting his unsuccessful 1982 Senate effort — unseated Patterson with a modest percentage; he has won more solid majorities since.

Republicans also have a lock on the district at the presidential level. George Bush topped 60 percent there in 1988.

The district's vote is split nearly evenly between the middle-class suburban areas, such as Anaheim and Buena Park, in the northern part of the district, and Garden Grove and Santa Ana, working-class cities in the southern part of the 38th.

Santa Ana (population 294,000), the county seat, is about 65 percent Hispanic. The city is shared with the 39th and 40th districts, but most of the Hispanic neighborhoods are in the 38th, contributing to its Democratic vote.

Garden Grove (143,000 people), best known for the "positive thinking" television ministry of Robert Schuller and his Crystal Cathedral, has traditionally had a much smaller minority population. But in recent years, there has been a heavy influx of Indochinese refugees, spurring a conservative backlash by some of Garden Grove's white, blue-collar voters.

Population: 525,919. White 392,707 (75%), Black 13,438 (3%), Asian and Pacific Islander 36,819 (7%), Other 4,386 (1%). Spanish origin 149,578 (28%). 18 and over 364,684 (69%), 65 and over 36,462 (7%). Median age: 27.

from spending any federal or local funds to pay for abortions, became law.

The next August, anti-abortion forces endured a temporary setback, when the House defeated the "Dornan amendment" by 206-219. Abortion rights supporters were boosted by a surge in activism after the Supreme Court's *Webster* decision that June and by an argument that the amendment could cut off contraceptive funding (a claim Dornan denounced as distortion). However, Dornan came out on top in the end, as Bush vetoed the bill twice until the Dornan language was restored.

At Home: While a general anti-incumbent mood in 1990 cost many California House members several points off their usual margins, Dornan was down just 2 points from 1988. However, the election also proved that Dornan's hard-edged style will never win him landslide margins, even in conservative Orange County. Running against a Democratic candidate who dropped out even before the June primary, Dornan took 58 percent of the vote.

Dornan initially faced the prospect of a high-profile contest with wheelchair-bound antiwar activist Ron Kovic, whose recovery from paralyzing wounds suffered in Vietnam combat was the subject of the film "Born on the Fourth of July." But after strongly hinting that he would run, Kovic backed off just before the candidate filing deadline in March.

Local Planned Parenthood official Barbara Jackson then entered the contest but was discouraged from running by her employers, who were concerned about partisan links to their office. Jackson's name nonetheless remained on the ballot. Although she did not raise any money or campaign, Jackson took 42 percent.

Dornan supported the successful 1990 gubernatorial bid of GOP then-Sen. Pete Wilson, but sharply criticized Wilson's post-election choice of state Sen. John Seymour — an abortion rights supporter — as his interim replacement. But Dornan bypassed challenging Seymour in the June 1992 special primary election to pick a permanent successor to Wilson; in June 1991, he also decided not to run in the regularly scheduled contest for the Senate seat being vacated by retiring Democrat Alan Cranston.

His status as a conservative spokesman leads to frequent speculation about Dornan, who is no stranger to statewide politics. Dornan tried for an open Senate seat in 1982. But Wilson walked away with the nomination, as Dornan finished fourth in the primary, with just 8 percent.

Dornan entered politics after an eclectic career that included five years as an Air Force pilot, various journalism jobs, parts in TV dramas and several years as a TV talk show host. He spent much time on the road, registering black voters in Alabama in the 1960s and trying to ban objectionable textbooks in West Virginia in the 1970s. He also raised the visibility of the prisoner-of-war issue and invented the POW bracelet.

Dornan's first political bid was a losing

race for mayor of Los Angeles in 1973. But three years later, a vacancy occurred in the Republican-held 27th District. Running against two other Republicans Dornan solidified his conservative support base and won the GOP primary.

In the general election, Dornan called his opponent, Democratic businessman Gary Familian, a "warmed-over McGovernite," and he fended off Familian's efforts to link him to the John Birch Society and the Ku Klux Klan. Dornan won 55 percent of the vote.

Dornan then faced two tough contests against Democrat Carey Peck, the son of actor Gregory Peck. Although Dornan dismissed Peck as a rich political hobbyist, he won just 51 percent in 1978, then needed to spend nearly $2 million to achieve the same percentage in 1980.

A redistricting process controlled by state Democrats delivered a crueler blow to Dornan, stripping his district of its most Republican areas. Rather than run in a Democratic-oriented district or against another GOP incumbent, Dornan set out on his ill-fated Senate bid.

However, his hiatus from the House lasted just two years. In 1984, he moved from his previous base in Santa Monica to Orange County to make his House comeback.

Changing demographics in the 38th had made Democratic Rep. Jerry M. Patterson more vulnerable, and Dornan's national conservative credentials guaranteed him plenty of money.

The two fought fiercely. Patterson called Dornan "a far-right extremist" and "nearly a lunatic"; Dornan called him a "sneaky little dirt-bag." Dornan benefited from the unhappiness of the 38th's conservative electorate with the national Democratic ticket headed by Walter F. Mondale, winning with 53 percent.

Two years later, Dornan held on against a scrappy attack from state Assemblyman Richard Robinson, who accused Dornan of ignoring Orange County while pursuing his obsession with foreign policy.

Responding to accusations that he had falsified his military record, Dornan denied having done so, and he then charged that Robinson had misrepresented his own service as a Marine in Vietnam.

Committees

Armed Services (16th of 22 Republicans)
Research & Development; Seapower & Strategic & Critical Materials

Select Intelligence (4th of 7 Republicans)
Legislation; Oversight & Evaluation

Select Narcotics Abuse & Control (5th of 14 Republicans)

Elections

1990 General

Robert K. Dornan (R)	60,561	(58%)
Barbara Jackson (D)	43,693	(42%)

1988 General

Robert K. Dornan (R)	87,690	(60%)
Jerry Yudelson (D)	52,399	(36%)

Previous Winning Percentages: **1986** (55%) **1984** (53%) **1980** (51%) **1978** (51%) **1976** (55%)

District Vote For President

	1988	1984	1980	1976
D	58,068 (38%)	48,856 (30%)	43,851 (29%)	51,102 (46%)
R	93,697 (61%)	114,786 (69%)	93,281 (62%)	58,138 (53%)

Campaign Finance

	Receipts	Receipts from PACs		Expend-itures
1990				
Dornan (R)	$1,615,282	$35,234	(2%)	$1,445,577
1988				
Dornan (R)	$1,731,883	$83,231	(5%)	$1,755,892
Yudelson (D)	$250,191	$71,971	(29%)	$248,151

Key Votes

1991	
Authorize use of force against Iraq	Y
1990	
Support constitutional amendment on flag desecration	Y
Pass family and medical leave bill over Bush veto	N
Reduce SDI funding	N
Allow abortions in overseas military facilities	N
Approve budget summit plan for spending and taxing	N
Approve civil rights bill	N
1989	
Halt production of B-2 stealth bomber at 13 planes	N
Oppose capital gains tax cut	N
Approve federal abortion funding in rape or incest cases	N
Approve pay raise and revision of ethics rules	N
Pass Democratic minimum wage plan over Bush veto	?

Voting Studies

	Presidential Support		Party Unity		Conservative Coalition	
Year	**S**	**O**	**S**	**O**	**S**	**O**
1990	68	27	83	6	87	7
1989	70	23	81	9	85	12
1988	65	26	84	6	84	5
1987	73	21	82	8	88	9
1986	80	13	82	10	88	12
1985	80	16	79	10	82	13
1982	61	5	68	5	73	4
1981	57	26	67	9	63	8

Interest Group Ratings

Year	ADA	ACU	AFL-CIO	CCUS
1990	6	91	18	79
1989	0	96	10	100
1988	0	100	7	91
1987	0	100	7	100
1986	5	95	8	81
1985	10	95	12	81
1982	5	87	0	85
1981	10	93	8	93

39 William E. Dannemeyer (R)

Of Fullerton — Elected 1978

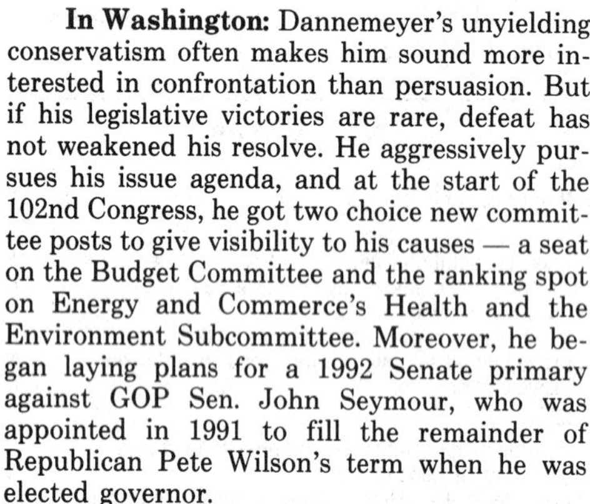

Born: Sept. 22, 1929, Los Angeles, Calif.

Education: Attended Santa Maria Junior College, 1946-47; Valparaiso U., B.A. 1950; U. of California, Hastings College of Law, J.D. 1952.

Military Service: Army, 1952-54.

Occupation: Lawyer.

Family: Wife, Evelyn Hoemann; three children.

Religion: Lutheran.

Political Career: Calif. Assembly, served as a Democrat, 1963-67, served as a Republican, 1977-79; Democratic nominee for Calif. Senate, 1966; Republican nominee for Calif. Assembly, 1972.

Capitol Office: 2234 Rayburn Bldg. 20515; 225-4111.

In Washington: Dannemeyer's unyielding conservatism often makes him sound more interested in confrontation than persuasion. But if his legislative victories are rare, defeat has not weakened his resolve. He aggressively pursues his issue agenda, and at the start of the 102nd Congress, he got two choice new committee posts to give visibility to his causes — a seat on the Budget Committee and the ranking spot on Energy and Commerce's Health and the Environment Subcommittee. Moreover, he began laying plans for a 1992 Senate primary against GOP Sen. John Seymour, who was appointed in 1991 to fill the remainder of Republican Pete Wilson's term when he was elected governor.

Dannemeyer leads the charge on a range of conservative issues, from reimposing the gold standard to instituting prayer in schools, but he pursues matters involving AIDS with unmatched zeal. He relentlessly offers amendments mandating AIDS testing and attacks any language that suggests AIDS victims have a right to confidentiality under the law. "I happen to believe as a matter of principle that the civil rights of the uninfected take precedence over the civil rights of the infected," he says.

Even Dannemeyer's critics concede that he argues from principle and with utter consistency, though they regularly quarrel with his facts and his suggested solutions. His opponents still cite with amazement the time Dannemeyer declared that restrictions should be placed on AIDS victims because they emit "spores" that can cause birth defects.

Dannemeyer brings to most discussions of AIDS an outspoken criticism of homosexuals. He reminds audiences that God created "Adam and Eve, not Adam and Steve." In mid-1989, he inserted a lengthy diatribe about homosexuals' influence on federal policy into the *Congressional Record.* A graphic, some said obscene, section titled "What Homosexuals Do" drew widespread outrage from all corners. In 1987, Dannemeyer complained, "Since the 1960s and the beginning of the sexual revolution, homosexuals have been striving to change American culture. These 'normaphobes' demand that the average American view their aberrant behavior as equal to heterosexuality."

In 1989, Dannemeyer demanded that Rep. Barney Frank of Massachusetts, who is homosexual, be expelled from the House for improperly using his office to help a male prostitute. The ethics committee had recommendmed that Frank be reprimanded, but Dannemeyer pursued his wish for explusion to the point where one GOP colleague called him "a zealot" and ethics Chairman Julian C. Dixon of California angrily called Dannemeyer's analysis of evidence "edited, selective garbage." The House voted 408-18 to reprimand Frank.

In the late 1980s, Dannemeyer's primary concern was mandatory AIDS testing and notification of public-health officials. As a member of the Energy and Commerce Committee, he pushed hopeless efforts to test the homeless and marriage-license applicants, and once he sought testing of the entire U.S. population for the virus that causes AIDS. He wanted physicians to be required to notify the spouses of anyone who tested positive.

During consideration of legislation to protect the civil rights of the disabled in 1990, Dannemeyer tried unsuccessfully to bar homosexuals and AIDS carriers from protection. He said he feared the Americans with Disabilities Act (ADA) would become "a homosexual bill of rights." He was one of just three members to oppose ADA in the Judiciary Committee, and one of 28 to do so when the bill came before the full House.

California 39

Northern Orange County — Anaheim; Fullerton

The hard-right conservative tradition in Orange County makes the 39th California's most Republican district. Ronald Reagan won 77 percent of the vote there in 1984, and it was the only California district where George Bush topped 70 percent in 1988.

A 1983 redistricting map that took the western part of Anaheim out of the 39th also deprived it of its most famous landmarks, Disneyland and Anaheim Stadium, the home of baseball's California Angels. But the remap left residential neighborhoods that are home to many of Anaheim's middle- and upper-class professionals, who set the district's Republican tone.

Thirty years ago, Anaheim was a sleepy community of 15,000 in the middle of the county's famous orange groves. Today, it is a city of more than 266,000 people (the 10th largest in California), with thriving electronics and defense-related industries. The 39th has Hughes, Rockwell and Northrop facilities, as well as Chevron and Unical energy research centers.

The fastest-growing communities in the 39th are to the east of Anaheim. Yorba Linda (52,000 residents), birthplace of Richard M. Nixon and site of his presidential library, grew by 86 percent in the 1980s, and has quadrupled in size since 1970.

Fullerton and Orange, both with just over 110,000 people, are the district's other population anchors. Fullerton, Dannemeyer's home base, has a campus of the University of California.

Population: 525,858. White 464,267 (88%), Black 5,472 (1%), Other 23,316 (4%). Spanish origin 70,716 (13%). 18 and over 380,058 (72%), 65 and over 35,906 (7%). Median age: 29.

His protracted fight on ADA was reminiscent of his unsuccessful 1988 battles to amend the fair-housing bill to state that those with contagious diseases, namely AIDS, were excluded from the definition of handicapped.

Dannemeyer scored a rare legislative victory during 1989 consideration of the District of Columbia funding bill. Appropriations leaders, including several Republicans, sought to block Dannemeyer from instructing House conferees to accept a Senate amendment exempting religious institutions from the District's anti-discrimination law, which covers homosexuals. But with Dannemeyer at the helm, House members rejected the leadership gambit and accepted his motion. The language was included in the final bill.

In the 100th Congress, a similar tactic helped Dannemeyer force a vote on language to outlaw telephone services that allow callers to dial a toll number to hear a pornographic message. With the measure blocked in Energy and Commerce, Dannemeyer outmaneuvered House leaders and won a vote instructing conferees on an education bill to outlaw "dial-a-porn."

In early 1989, Dannemeyer's parliamentary skill brought him perhaps his most significant political victory: defeat of the 51 percent congressional pay raise. House leaders hoped to adjourn the House quietly, thereby permitting the pay raise to go into effect without a vote. But Dannemeyer forced a last-minute roll call on the issue and defeated the Democratic leadership. The House voted against adjournment 88-238, and the following day defeated the pay raise by an even more lopsided vote.

Although some Republicans took a measure of delight in Dannemeyer's exposure of the Democratic leadership's pay raise ploy, GOP leaders have also been stung by his criticism: He often berates them for being too conciliatory toward the Democrats. His criticisms contributed to his horrible showing in a 1988 bid for the chairmanship of the House Republican Conference; he won just seven votes.

But Dannemeyer's appointment to the Budget Committee in early 1991 suggests that his confrontational tactics may be meeting with more acceptance, especially among younger-generation House Republicans. In late 1990, the GOP Conference came within two votes of accepting a Dannemeyer proposal to bar any Republican from serving as ranking member on more than one committee or subcommittee. The plan would have opened up 35 slots, and was a slap at ranking committee members, many of whom are more pragmatic and willing to work with Democrats.

Ironically, Dannemeyer's rigidity has won him some tactical Democratic favors. When a limited number of floor amendments are allowed on a bill, and some of them have to be offered by Republicans, Democratic leaders often look to Dannemeyer. They can count it as a gesture to the minority, knowing full well that his efforts usually fail. Dannemeyer regularly offers budget alternatives that lose overwhelmingly. In recent years, his efforts have drawn fewer than 50 votes.

Prior to leading the anti-AIDS crusade, Dannemeyer devoted considerable energy to returning the country to the gold standard. Having tracked down nearly every historical reference to back up his argument, he pointed out in a 1987 speech that Dante, in the "Divine Comedy," had a special hell for currency debasers. "Our own attitude is quite different," he complained. "We celebrate our own currency debasers in the Treasury and Federal Reserve. . . ."

At Home: Although Dannemeyer sometimes appears to push the outer limits of conservative discourse in the House, he is blessed with an Orange County constituency that more than tolerates his ideology. Dannemeyer's 65 percent of the vote in 1990 against Democrat Francis X. Hoffman was one of the lowest tallies of his House career: He often tops 70 percent.

Recently minted House colleagues might find it hard to believe, but Dannemeyer began his political career in 1962 by winning his first of two state Assembly terms as a Democrat. Even in those years, though, Dannemeyer was a staunch conservative. After an unsuccessful 1966 bid for state Senate, he switched to the Republican Party in 1967.

Dannemeyer lost his Republican debut as a candidate for State Senate in 1972. But in 1976 Dannemeyer was able to take back the Assembly seat he had won as a Democrat 14 years before, defeating an aide to the Republican who had replaced him.

Dannemeyer's victory was so convincing that when GOP Rep. Charles E. Wiggins retired from Congress two years later, nobody challenged Dannemeyer for the GOP nomination. Riding a wave of conservative activism and supporting the Proposition 13 tax-limitation initiative, he won the general election easily.

The only perturbation in Dannemeyer's career since then came in 1986, when he briefly ran for the GOP nomination to oppose Democratic Sen. Alan Cranston. Dannemeyer laid claim to the hard-line conservative vote in a large Republican field. He attracted some attention but too little money to keep his bid going, and dropped out early in February. That gave him time to file for his House seat, which he again won easily.

Committees

Budget (10th of 14 Republicans)
Economic Policy, Projections & Revenues; Urgent Fiscal Issues

Energy & Commerce (4th of 16 Republicans)
Health & the Environment (ranking); Energy & Power

Elections

1990 General		
William E. Dannemeyer (R)	113,849	(65%)
Francis X. Hoffman (D)	53,670	(31%)
Maxine B. Quirk (PFP)	6,709	(4%)
1988 General		
William E. Dannemeyer (R)	169,360	(74%)
Don E. Marquis (D)	52,162	(23%)

Previous Winning Percentages: **1986** (75%) **1984** (76%) **1982** (72%) **1980** (76%) **1978** (64%)

District Vote For President

	1988	1984	1980	1976
D	66,495 (28%)	52,591 (22%)	44,474 (21%)	52,802 (35%)
R	167,142 (71%)	185,491 (77%)	148,010 (70%)	97,978 (64%)

Campaign Finance

	Receipts	Receipts from PACs		Expend-itures
1990				
Dannemeyer (R)	$594,692	$129,250	(22%)	$627,842
1988				
Dannemeyer (R)	$300,156	$144,472	(48%)	$250,737
Marquis (D)	$1,432	0		$2,892

Key Votes

1991	
Authorize use of force against Iraq	Y
1990	
Support constitutional amendment on flag desecration	Y
Pass family and medical leave bill over Bush veto	N
Reduce SDI funding	N
Allow abortions in overseas military facilities	N
Approve budget summit plan for spending and taxing	N
Approve civil rights bill	N
1989	
Halt production of B-2 stealth bomber at 13 planes	X
Oppose capital gains tax cut	N
Approve federal abortion funding in rape or incest cases	N
Approve pay raise and revision of ethics rules	N
Pass Democratic minimum wage plan over Bush veto	N

Voting Studies

	Presidential Support		Party Unity		Conservative Coalition	
Year	**S**	**O**	**S**	**O**	**S**	**O**
1990	75	21	93	2	93	7
1989	70	26	87	4	80	5
1988	69	18	93	2	89	8
1987	74	22	89	4	88	12
1986	81	17	90	5	88	8
1985	78	16	89	3	87	7
1984	77	21	90	6	88	8
1983	77	15	91	4	84	9
1982	81	17	93	5	90	10
1981	74	24	92	5	85	11

Interest Group Ratings

Year	ADA	ACU	AFL-CIO	CCUS
1990	6	100	8	71
1989	5	100	0	89
1988	0	100	0	92
1987	12	100	7	100
1986	5	95	0	87
1985	10	90	6	95
1984	0	100	8	71
1983	5	95	0	89
1982	5	100	5	86
1981	10	100	0	100

40 C. Christopher Cox (R)

Of Newport Beach — Elected 1988

Born: Oct. 16, 1952, St. Paul, Minn.
Education: U. of Southern California, B.A. 1973; Harvard U., M.B.A., J.D. 1977.
Occupation: White House counsel.
Family: Single.
Religion: Roman Catholic.
Political Career: No previous office.
Capitol Office: 412 Cannon Bldg. 20515; 225-5611.

In Washington: Cox is every bit as conservative as you would expect a young Orange County Republican to be, but his style differs from that of his combative, higher-profile Class of 1988 California colleague, 42nd District Rep. Dana Rohrabacher. A one-time teacher at Harvard (where he received law and graduate business degrees), Cox usually goes after issues in a more low-key and erudite fashion.

Before coming to Congress, Cox worked in the White House as senior associate counsel to President Reagan. His duties included drafting reform proposals for the federal budget process, and Cox has carried on his interest in that area, serving as co-chairman of the GOP task force on Budget Process Reform. He has proposed requiring a binding budget before any spending legislation could be considered.

Cox's free-market bent showed up in 1989 when Congress looked into a rash of airline takeover bids. On the Public Works and Transportation Committee, Cox unsuccessfully offered amendments to weaken a measure designed to give the secretary of transportation additional power to disapprove takeovers financed by leveraged buyouts. Cox said the open market should determine the financial affairs of airlines. In response to the bitter Eastern Airlines strike, Cox tried to amend the Railway Labor Act to close what he said was a loophole enjoyed by airline and railway unions that permitted them to shut down businesses of neutral third parties.

Cox also has shown a keen interest in Eastern Europe. He joined a congressional delegation to observe Lithuanian elections, but only after the Soviet Union relented in its initial refusal to grant visas to the group. Cox called for official recognition of Lithuania, criticized Soviet President Michael Gorbachev's receipt of the Nobel Peace Prize and has sought to encourage the development of market economies in Poland and Hungary.

At Home: Many on Capitol Hill dream of moving down Pennsylvania Avenue to the White House. Cox spent 1988 making his move the other way — up that street to Congress.

Cox was working for Reagan in 1988 when 40th District GOP Rep. Robert E. Badham announced his plans to retire. Cox was no stranger to the Orange County district. A University of Southern California alumnus, he had signed on as a partner with a Newport Beach law firm following his graduation from Harvard and a clerkship with the U.S. Court of Appeals in San Francisco.

The odds of Cox winning to succeed Badham initially looked long: The 40th seemed likely to go to one of the well-known state legislators in the area. But when the prime prospects declined to run, Cox resigned from his White House job and joined a field of GOP primary candidates that eventually grew to 14.

The departing Badham had endorsed another Republican in the primary, Irvine city councilman Dave Baker. But Cox managed to enlist significant help from members of Orange County's prominent Irvine family.

More important to Cox's success, though, were his Washington connections. His literature pictured him with Reagan and then-Vice President George Bush in the White House. He got endorsements from 18 conservative members of Congress, and he benefited from campaign appearances by Robert H. Bork, Reagan's unsuccessful Supreme Court nominee, and retired Marine Lt. Col. Oliver L. North.

Cox pulled away from the field, winning 18 of the district's 20 municipalities in the primary. In November, he took 67 percent of the vote. Unlike many House members from California, Cox was unaffected by the general anti-incumbent mood of 1990: He again won two-thirds of the ballots cast.

Cox may be the first congressman who is an ex-publisher of *Pravda.* Cox, then working for the Newport Beach law firm, and his father (a retired publisher) produced an English-language version of the official Soviet newspaper to show how the Soviet government propagandizes its own people. The project was based in St. Paul, Minn., where Cox grew up, but the paper eventually folded after Cox turned his attention to running for Congress.

California 40

Coastal and Central Orange County

It is difficult for candidates to be too conservative for the voters of this central and coastal Orange County district. John G. Schmitz, who represented this area for a term in the early 1970s, was later removed from the executive council of the John Birch Society for extremism.

With more mainstream figures like Cox and his predecessor, Robert E. Badham, holding the seat, district voters have not had to think twice about sticking with the Republicans. The same applies in presidential contests. President Reagan won here by a 3-to-1 margin in 1984; George Bush carried the 40th by 2-to-1.

Newport Beach, a wealthy enclave noted for its luxurious housing, is the center of the district. A community of 67,000 people, Newport Beach regularly provides Republican candidates with tremendous margins. Reagan took 78 percent of the vote there in 1984; Bush won 72 percent in 1988.

Many of the residents of the 40th either commute to jobs in Los Angeles or are employed by high-technology companies scattered in gleaming "glass boxes" throughout the district. With the area's population growing and more people streaming onto the highways, traffic congestion has become a major local concern. That fact played a part in Cox's taking a seat on the Public Works Committee, which deals with surface transportation matters.

The University of California's Irvine campus is located in the 40th. But any liberal influence from this academic center is hardly noticed. The only incorporated areas in the district where Democrats have strength are Costa Mesa and Laguna Beach, two very different places.

Trendy Laguna Beach, which saw an influx of counterculture newcomers in the 1960s and 1970s, today is home for many single adults and couples without children. They live in comfortable condominium complexes along the ocean. Costa Mesa, whose airport is named for actor John Wayne, is not so chic. Just north of Newport Beach, it is home for young families in modest suburban homes. Both communities supported Bush by smaller margins than the rest of the district in 1988.

Population: 525,935. White 474,717 (90%), Black 7,078 (1%), Asian and Pacific Islander 23,814 (5%), Other 2,742 (1%). Spanish origin 40,133 (8%). 18 and over 399,759 (76%), 65 and over 54,692 (10%). Median age: 31.

Committees

Government Operations (8th of 15 Republicans)
Government Activities & Transportation (ranking)

Public Works & Transportation (14th of 21 Republicans)
Aviation; Public Buildings & Grounds; Surface Transportation

Elections

1990 General		
C. Christopher Cox (R)	142,299	(68%)
Eugene C. Gratz (D)	68,087	(32%)
1988 General		
C. Christopher Cox (R)	181,269	(67%)
Lida Lenney (D)	80,782	(30%)

District Vote For President

	1988	1984	1980	1976
D	87,331 (31%)	63,210 (24%)	47,255 (21%)	53,928 (32%)
R	191,392 (68%)	198,338 (75%)	152,430 (68%)	116,030 (68%)

Campaign Finance

	Receipts	Receipts from PACs		Expend-itures
1990				
Cox (R)	$688,836	$179,516	(26%)	$682,365
Gratz (D)	$43,277	$600	(1%)	$36,124
1988				
Cox (R)	$1,111,321	$198,786	(18%)	$1,110,126
Lenney (D)	$49,834	$2,475	(5%)	$47,746

Key Votes

1991	
Authorize use of force against Iraq	Y
1990	
Support constitutional amendment on flag desecration	Y
Pass family and medical leave bill over Bush veto	N
Reduce SDI funding	N
Allow abortions in overseas military facilities	N
Approve budget summit plan for spending and taxing	N
Approve civil rights bill	N
1989	
Halt production of B-2 stealth bomber at 13 planes	N
Oppose capital gains tax cut	N
Approve federal abortion funding in rape or incest cases	N
Approve pay raise and revision of ethics rules	N
Pass Democratic minimum wage plan over Bush veto	N

Voting Studies

	Presidential Support		Party Unity		Conservative Coalition	
Year	**S**	**O**	**S**	**O**	**S**	**O**
1990	75	24	86	8	83	13
1989	71	26	85	12	85	12

Interest Group Ratings

Year	ADA	ACU	AFL-CIO	CCUS
1990	11	88	0	85
1989	5	96	8	90

41 Bill Lowery (R)

Of San Diego — Elected 1980

Born: May 2, 1947, San Diego, Calif.
Education: Attended San Diego State U., 1965-69.
Occupation: Public relations executive.
Family: Wife, Kathleen Ellen Brown; three children.
Religion: Roman Catholic.
Political Career: San Diego City Council, 1977-80; deputy mayor of San Diego, 1979-80.
Capitol Office: 2433 Rayburn Bldg. 20515; 225-3201.

In Washington: Lowery cuts the typical profile of an Appropriations Committee member. The ranking Republican on the Military Construction Subcommittee, Lowery is likable and willing to work with members of both parties. Yet he is conservative enough to have made the early GOP list of potential 1992 Senate candidates.

That talk was interrupted by Lowery's brush with defeat in his 1990 House race. A former Banking Committee member, Lowery had raised money from savings-and-loan executives, including Texas financier Donald R. Dixon, who would be convicted on a variety of bank fraud charges. Although Lowery's involvement in the S&L scandal was tangential, Democratic opponent Dan Kripke hammered at the issue, holding the GOP incumbent to a record-low victory total.

Lowery was saved by the 41st District's GOP tendencies and by the benefits his Appropriations seat provides the district. He hailed the inclusion of $176 million in the fiscal 1991 military construction spending bill for the area's military facilities (including Miramar Naval Air Station in the 41st).

Lowery also continued his career-long effort to bar oil drilling off the California coast, calling for a 10-year ban; he took satisfaction when President Bush announced such a policy in June 1990. However, Lowery recently dropped his effort to codify the ban.

Lowery's voting record follows GOP convention: He supported Bush's positions on House votes about 70 percent of the time during the 101st Congress. He falls in more with the pragmatic wing of the California GOP delegation, symbolized by Republican Conference Chairman Jerry Lewis, than the hard-right faction of Reps. Robert K. Dornan and William E. Dannemeyer. Lowery is a co-founder of the California Institute, which promotes bipartisan efforts within California's huge House delegation to advance state interests.

At Home: Kripke, a psychiatry professor, has made three tries for Lowery's seat. In the first two contests Lowery took 68 percent of the vote in 1986, and 66 percent two years later, even as Kripke raised the issue of Lowery's fundraising from savings-and-loan figures.

But the S&L issue hit home with a vengeance in 1990, and almost cost Lowery his seat. Though underfinanced, Kripke staged a relentless assault. His commercials charged the incumbent with taking "criminal money." He even ran a TV ad in Washington, D.C., accusing Attorney General Dick Thornburgh of covering up Lowery's involvement in the S&L scandal.

Lowery denied unethical behavior, but remained on the defensive. Despite the 41st District's strong Republican bent, Lowery barely hung on by 49 percent to Kripke's 44 percent.

It was a precipitous slide for Lowery, whose only previous close race was his first in 1980, after Republican Rep. Bob Wilson announced his retirement plans. During his tenure as a San Diego city official, Lowery had laid the groundwork for a contest to succeed Wilson; he quickly emerged as the frontrunner.

Lowery had to survive a strong primary challenge from Dan McKinnon, the wealthy owner of a country music radio station. Positioning himself to Lowery's right, McKinnon wooed San Diego's pro-Reagan vote. Lowery won, but by fewer than 4 percentage points.

In the general election, Lowery's biggest problem was that his opponent had the same name as the retiring incumbent — Bob Wilson. Lowery attacked the conservative Democratic state senator for running on the "good name" of the incumbent. With national GOP backing and support from another popular Wilson — then-San Diego Mayor Pete Wilson — Lowery pulled out a 53 to 43 percent win.

His support climbed to 68 percent in 1982. Two years later, Lowery faced a spirited challenge from a blind University of San Diego law professor, Robert L. Simmons. With his disability guaranteeing him press attention, Simmons accused Lowery of having a poor environmental record. But Simmons was underfunded, and Lowery won with 63 percent. His three matchups with Kripke, two easy and one nearly fatal, followed.

California 41

North San Diego and Suburbs

The 41st is a predominantly white and affluent northern San Diego district where Republicans have a distinct edge.

The tone is set in strongly Republican Point Loma, on the peninsula guarding San Diego Harbor. From there, the district moves north through Ocean Beach and Banker Hill — mixed communities of students, older people and young professionals. Then come long stretches of middle-class and upper-middle-class neighborhoods such as Scripps Ranch and Rancho Bernardo, where GOP candidates regularly swamp their opposition. Pacific Beach and the posh La Jolla section are also in the 41st.

There is a Democratic presence at the northern end around Del Mar, contributed by the professors and students of University of California at San Diego. Mission Village, a blue-collar neighborhood farther south, is also amenable to Democratic overtures.

The 41st surrounds the huge Miramar Naval Air Station, the largest such base in the world. Rep. Randy "Duke" Cunningham, the freshman member from the nearby 44th District, is a former Navy pilot who taught at Miramar's "Top Gun" flight training school.

Miramar and other naval facilities here give the district a large military constituency. Aerospace and defense electronics firms also are in the area, and employ many of the professionals and executives who live in the district. But some local residents would like to see the base phased out as a military installation and made into a commercial airport serving San Diego.

District population growth has been steady during the 1980s. Most newcomers are young and middle-class who lean to the GOP. George Bush won nearly three-fifths of the district vote in 1988.

Population: 526,043. White 468,089 (89%), Black 12,331 (2%), Asian and Pacific Islander 26,067 (5%), Other 2,564 (1%). Spanish origin 37,897 (7%). 18 and over 412,731 (78%), 65 and over 56,650 (11%). Median age: 31.

Committees

Appropriations (16th of 22 Republicans)
Military Construction (ranking); Interior; Veterans Affairs, Housing & Urban Development, & Independent Agencies

District of Columbia (4th of 4 Republicans)
Judiciary & Education (ranking); Government Operations & Metropolitan Affairs

Elections

1990 General

Bill Lowery (R)	105,723	(49%)
Dan Kripke (D)	93,586	(44%)
Karen S.R. Works (PFP)	15,428	(7%)

1988 General

Bill Lowery (R)	187,380	(66%)
Dan Kripke (D)	88,192	(31%)

Previous Winning Percentages: **1986** (68%) **1984** (63%) **1982** (69%) **1980** (53%)

District Vote For President

	1988		1984		1980		1976	
D	121,278	(40%)	92,994	(35%)	64,634	(28%)	69,848	(41%)
R	175,588	(58%)	171,535	(64%)	135,569	(58%)	99,696	(58%)

Campaign Finance

	Receipts	Receipts from PACs		Expend-itures
1990				
Lowery (R)	$485,964	$205,165	(42%)	$575,637
Kripke (D)	$65,546	$5,000	(8%)	$72,261
1988				
Lowery (R)	$453,289	$182,415	(40%)	$407,025
Kripke (D)	$50,270	$8,050	(16%)	$45,311

Key Votes

1991	
Authorize use of force against Iraq	Y
1990	
Support constitutional amendment on flag desecration	Y
Pass family and medical leave bill over Bush veto	N
Reduce SDI funding	N
Allow abortions in overseas military facilities	N
Approve budget summit plan for spending and taxing	Y
Approve civil rights bill	N
1989	
Halt production of B-2 stealth bomber at 13 planes	N
Oppose capital gains tax cut	N
Approve federal abortion funding in rape or incest cases	N
Approve pay raise and revision of ethics rules	Y
Pass Democratic minimum wage plan over Bush veto	N

Voting Studies

	Presidential Support		Party Unity		Conservative Coalition	
Year	**S**	**O**	**S**	**O**	**S**	**O**
1990	67	29	68	19	89	4
1989	74	22	71	19	80	20
1988	62	30	81	9	79	11
1987	63	30	77	16	84	7
1986	76	21	68	22	80	18
1985	71	24	74	16	84	11
1984	69	28	76	16	86	7
1983	79	20	83	13	83	15
1982	78	17	88	10	93	7
1981	74	24	85	11	85	9

Interest Group Ratings

Year	ADA	ACU	AFL-CIO	CCUS
1990	11	70	8	77
1989	5	85	25	90
1988	15	92	14	100
1987	4	87	19	73
1986	5	74	8	75
1985	5	81	6	86
1984	5	83	15	80
1983	5	83	0	100
1982	0	91	5	100
1981	5	83	0	100

42 Dana Rohrabacher (R)

Of Long Beach — Elected 1988

Born: June 21, 1947, Coronado, Calif.
Education: Attended Los Angeles Harbor College, 1965-67; California State U., Long Beach, B.A. 1969; U. of Southern California, M.A. 1971.
Occupation: White House speechwriter; journalist.
Family: Single.
Religion: Baptist.
Political Career: No previous office.
Capitol Office: 1039 Longworth Bldg. 20515; 225-2415.

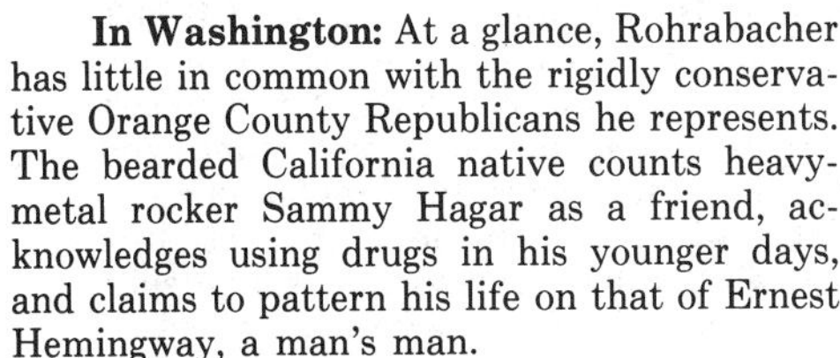

In Washington: At a glance, Rohrabacher has little in common with the rigidly conservative Orange County Republicans he represents. The bearded California native counts heavy-metal rocker Sammy Hagar as a friend, acknowledges using drugs in his younger days, and claims to pattern his life on that of Ernest Hemingway, a man's man.

But these eccentricities are little more than a stylistic generation gap. Rohrabacher's voting record is every bit as dynamically conservative as those of his older Orange County Republican colleagues, William E. Dannemeyer and Robert K. Dornan.

During his first House term, Rohrabacher led the fight against federal funding of "obscene" art. Denouncing controversial works funded by the National Endowment for the Arts, Rohrabacher said in 1989 that "censorship is not the solution; the answer is getting the government out of the arts." Rohrabacher sought to strike all NEA funding when the matter got to the full House. But parliamentary maneuvering by NEA supporters blocked Rohrabacher from offering his amendment; a token funding cut was passed instead. In 1990, he proposed far-reaching restrictions to prohibit the NEA from funding "obscene, indecent or sacrilegious" projects. But even some Republicans supportive of his intent said that Rohrabacher's ties to the arch-conservative American Family Association hurt his cause. Minimal restrictions were eventually approved.

Between taking office in January 1989 and his election the previous November, Rohrabacher made headlines for going to Afghanistan, where the White House had arranged for him to meet with Mujahedeen leaders.

At Home: Rohrabacher's high profile on the arts issue was bound to provoke criticism of him as a pro-censorship zealot. But the biggest glitch in his otherwise routine 1990 re-election campaign was a magazine article that portrayed him as a hypocrite.

In its issue dated Nov. 5, *The New Republic* published an article entitled "The Dope on Dana." The story said that although Rohrabacher had been a conservative Republican in his youth, he also experimented with drugs. Rohrabacher was also said to have declared himself an "anarchist" after his libertarian views cost him the chairmanship of a Young Americans for Freedom chapter.

Rohrabacher responded angrily, calling the article "character assassination." He said the magazine had timed its publication just prior to the election to punish him for his efforts against federal funding of obscene art.

But the flap had only a minor effect on Rohrabacher's campaign. In a rematch with Democratic college professor Guy C. Kimbrough, Rohrabacher won with 59 percent of the vote. That was five points less than he received in his 1988 contest with Kimbrough.

While Rohrabacher is rather new to the House, his ties to Ronald Reagan go back a long way. Active in GOP causes since his mid-teens, Rohrabacher was 19 when he camped out on Gov.-elect Reagan's lawn to protest the disbanding of the "Youth for Reagan" organization. Reagan reportedly came to the door half-shaven to promise to continue the group.

After stints as an editor for *The Orange County Register* and as a reporter for the City News Service of Los Angeles, Rohrabacher served as assistant press secretary for Reagan's 1976 and 1980 presidential campaigns. When Reagan won the White House, Rohrabacher joined his staff as a speechwriter, eventually becoming a special assistant to the president.

Rohrabacher decided to run for office when 42nd District GOP Rep. Daniel E. Lungren announced his retirement. He initially was regarded as an underdog in a crowded GOP primary field that included an Orange County supervisor who had Lungren's support. But with the front-runners beating each other up, Rohrabacher navigated his way through the field. A campaign fundraiser featuring former Marine Lt. Col. Oliver L. North raised Rohrabacher's standing among conservatives while adding $100,000 to his coffers. Rohrabacher ended up with 35 percent of the primary vote, well ahead of his nearest rival.

California 42

Coastal Los Angeles and Orange Counties

The oddly shaped and heavily Republican 42nd was one of the masterworks of the state's Democratic redistricters. Seeking to isolate as many Republicans in as few districts as possible, the map makers crafted the 42nd from parts of the old 27th, then held by GOP Rep. Robert K. Dornan, and the 34th, former Rep. Dan Lungren's previous district.

A strip of land only a few hundred feet wide runs along the Los Angeles and Long Beach waterfronts, joining the two segments. The Long Beach Naval Shipyard, the *Queen Mary* and Howard Hughes' "Spruce Goose" are all located here.

The 42nd is split fairly evenly between the established suburbs of Los Angeles County and the faster-growing environs of Orange County. The two areas are of equally Republican temperament. In his initial House campaign, Rohrabacher took 64 percent of the Los Angeles County vote, and 65 percent in Orange County. George Bush also did well in both areas, en route to carrying the 42nd with nearly two-thirds of the vote.

In Los Angeles County, at the northern and western end of the district, are Torrance and the lush, upper-income Palos Verdes Hills overlooking the Pacific Ocean. The hills contain four exclusive communities — Palos Verdes Estates, Rancho Palos Verdes, Rolling Hills and Rolling Hills Estates — whose voters are overwhelmingly Republican.

The Orange County portion of the 42nd takes in Cypress, Los Alamitos, Seal Beach, Rossmoor, part of Westminster and most of Huntington Beach, a city of 182,000 that forms the southern anchor of the district. A gathering spot for surfers who congregate around the city's pier, Huntington Beach is also a haven for Republican candidates, who can count on a large vote from the white-collar professionals whose split-level houses ring the area's many cul-de-sacs.

Population: 525,909. White 469,685 (89%), Black 6,927 (1%), Asian and Pacific Islander 29,804 (6%), Other 2,952 (1%). Spanish origin 38,446 (7%). 18 and over 400,256 (76%), 65 and over 52,744 (10%). Median age: 33.

Committees

District of Columbia (3rd of 4 Republicans)
Fiscal Affairs & Health (ranking); Judiciary & Education

Science, Space & Technology (13th of 19 Republicans)
Space; Technology & Competitiveness

Elections

1990 General		
Dana Rohrabacher (R)	109,353	(59%)
Guy C. Kimbrough (D)	67,189	(36%)
Richard Gibb Martin (LIBERT)	7,744	(4%)
1988 General		
Dana Rohrabacher (R)	153,280	(64%)
Guy C. Kimbrough (D)	78,778	(33%)

District Vote For President

	1988	1984	1980	1976
D	86,544 (34%)	67,480 (27%)	56,326 (24%)	66,602 (35%)
R	165,572 (65%)	183,392 (72%)	150,848 (65%)	123,946 (64%)

Campaign Finance

	Receipts	Receipts from PACs		Expend-itures
1990				
Rohrabacher (R)	$423,924	$119,075	(28%)	$398,963
Kimbrough (D)	$29,555	$7,950	(27%)	$28,350
1988				
Rohrabacher (R)	$521,565	$186,427	(36%)	$494,487
Kimbrough (D)	$11,911	$1,750	(15%)	$11,889

Key Votes

1991	
Authorize use of force against Iraq	Y
1990	
Support constitutional amendment on flag desecration	Y
Pass family and medical leave bill over Bush veto	N
Reduce SDI funding	N
Allow abortions in overseas military facilities	N
Approve budget summit plan for spending and taxing	N
Approve civil rights bill	N
1989	
Halt production of B-2 stealth bomber at 13 planes	N
Oppose capital gains tax cut	N
Approve federal abortion funding in rape or incest cases	N
Approve pay raise and revision of ethics rules	N
Pass Democratic minimum wage plan over Bush veto	N

Voting Studies

	Presidential Support		Party Unity		Conservative Coalition	
Year	S	O	S	O	S	O
1990	74	25	90	10	80	20
1989	70	29	82	15	93	7

Interest Group Ratings

Year	ADA	ACU	AFL-CIO	CCUS
1990	6	96	8	86
1989	10	96	9	90

43 Ron Packard (R)

Of Oceanside — Elected 1982

Born: Jan. 19, 1931, Meridian, Idaho.

Education: Attended Brigham Young U., 1948-50; Portland State U., 1952-53; U. of Oregon, D.M.D. 1957.

Military Service: Navy Dental Corps, 1957-59.

Occupation: Dentist.

Family: Wife, Roma Jean Sorenson; seven children.

Religion: Mormon.

Political Career: Carlsbad School Board, 1962-74; Carlsbad City Council, 1976-78; mayor of Carlsbad, 1978-82.

Capitol Office: 434 Cannon Bldg. 20515; 225-3906.

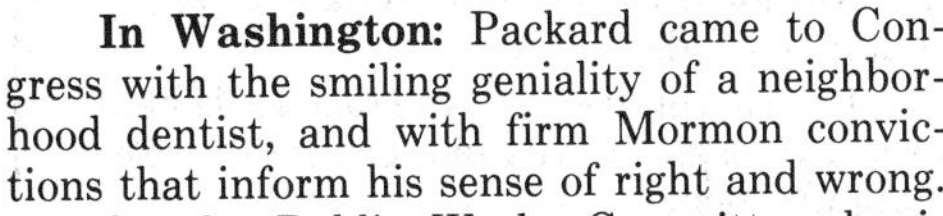

In Washington: Packard came to Congress with the smiling geniality of a neighborhood dentist, and with firm Mormon convictions that inform his sense of right and wrong.

On the Public Works Committee, he is developing skills in the old-fashioned art of horse-trading. In California's 19-man GOP House delegation, he is aligned with the state's more conservative members.

Although he did not gain a seat on the Appropriations Committee at the start of the 102nd Congress, he was installed as his state's representative on the GOP panel that makes committee assignments for all party members. Packard replaced Jerry Lewis, who is suspect among staunch conservatives because of his pragmatic legislative persona.

After years of effort on Public Works, Packard was able to add language to the 1987 omnibus highway bill providing $15 million to widen a 12-mile stretch of Highway 78 in his district. He also gained an amendment to the 1986 Clean Water Act authorizing filtering systems to defend against sewage seeping across the border from Mexico on the Tijuana River, and worked to secure authorization for $1.1 billion for Santa Ana River flood control.

In the 100th Congress, Packard used his seat on the Aviation Subcommittee to help lead the successful effort to require passenger aircraft to install collision-avoidance equipment. But he has opposed legislation limiting leveraged buyouts of airlines, trusting the market to determine the industry's financial affairs.

In the 102nd Congress, Packard cosponsored a bill to repeal the Social Security earnings test created during the Depression to discourage senior citizens from working.

During the 1987 debate over legislation to pay Japanese-Americans interned during World War II, Packard endorsed a federal apology, but opposed compensation. His father, who worked for a government contractor in the South Pacific, was imprisoned by the Japanese. Living on an Idaho farm, Packard and his 16 siblings became destitute during the war. Giving money to the internees, Packard said, "would demean a time when our family learned to work together, pull together and pray together."

At Home: Packard is one of the few members ever elected as a write-in candidate.

When GOP Rep. Clair W. Burgener announced his retirement in 1982, Packard and 17 other Republicans filed for the primary. Packard, a veteran of Carlsbad city politics, emerged as a front-runner. But he found himself in a pitched battle with recreational-vehicle tycoon Johnnie Crean.

A political neophyte, Crean sank close to $1 million into his bid, which consisted largely of personal attacks on his rivals, some wildly inaccurate. Afterward, Crean blamed his campaign's conduct on his consultants, whom he fired the day after the primary. Crean earned the abiding scorn of many Republicans, but won the nomination over Packard by 92 votes.

Many GOP partisans were unhappy with the outcome, and they helped persuade Packard to enter the general election as a write-in candidate. Crean tried to mend fences and reform his image. He argued that Republicans choosing Packard would split the GOP vote, electing the Democratic nominee, government professor Roy Pat Archer. Party officials came out for Crean, and Packard's funding dried up.

But Packard was still strong at the grass-roots level. While press coverage kept the Crean controversy fresh, Packard sent out 350,000 pieces of mail proclaiming himself the legitimate GOP alternative. On Election Day, his poll workers handed out pencils with Packard's name, urging their use. Packard edged Archer by 8,000 votes. Crean ran third.

Packard has not been seriously challenged since. But there was one interesting aspect of his 1990 House contest: Although district Democrats did not field a candidate, Packard got 68 percent of the vote, with 18 percent going to the nominee of the leftist Peace and Freedom Party and 13 percent to the Libertarian candidate.

California 43

Northern San Diego County; Southern Orange County

The current 43rd District is little different from the one that in 1980 gave its Republican incumbent 299,037 votes — more than any House candidate in U.S. history.

That total was somewhat inflated, coming at the end of a decade of population boom in the suburban/exurban sprawl between Los Angeles and San Diego that the district then covered. But while the last redistricting made the 43rd much more compact, it left the district just as Republican. George Bush received nearly 70 percent of the 1988 vote in the 43rd.

About two-thirds of the district vote is cast in San Diego County, with the rest in Orange County. The two segments are similar. Both are upper-middle-class residential areas, with little industry; Oceanside, Escondido and other fast-growing cities in the district consist mainly of suburban housing tracts.

San Marcos, in San Diego County, has burgeoned; its population (39,000 in 1990) more than tripled in the 1970s and grew by another 123 percent in the 1980s. Even the town of San Juan Capistrano, famous for the swallows that flock to its ancient Spanish mission each spring, is being transformed. But the town's historic nature remains unscathed; artifacts of California's Mission period were unearthed there recently.

The conservative lean of the area anchored by Oceanside, Carlsbad and San Marcos is influenced by the presence of Camp Pendleton, the Marine Corps base. To the north and east are exclusive Escondido and Rancho Santa Fe, with the citrus and avocado groves of Fallbrook and Valley Center beyond.

The southern end of the district is held down by coastal towns like Cardiff-by-the-Sea and Encinitas.

Population: 525,956. White 457,997 (87%), Black 13,458 (3%), Other 19,023 (4%). Spanish origin 68,102 (13%). 18 and over 387,050 (74%), 65 and over 61,760 (12%). Median age: 30.

Committees

Public Works & Transportation (5th of 21 Republicans)
Investigations & Oversight (ranking); Surface Transportation; Water Resources

Science, Space & Technology (7th of 19 Republicans)
Science (ranking); Space

Elections

1990 General		
Ron Packard (R)	151,206	(68%)
Doug Hansen (PFP)	40,212	(18%)
Richard L. Arnold (LIBERT)	30,720	(14%)
1988 General		
Ron Packard (R)	202,478	(72%)
Howard Greenebaum (D)	72,499	(26%)

Previous Winning Percentages: **1986** (73%) **1984** (74%)
1982 * (37%)

** Write-in candidate*

District Vote For President

	1988		1984		1980		1976	
D	90,746	(31%)	58,819	(25%)	39,452	(20%)	38,553	(35%)
R	199,744	(68%)	176,550	(74%)	136,966	(70%)	71,659	(64%)

Campaign Finance

	Receipts	Receipts from PACs		Expend-itures
1990				
Packard (R)	$167,017	$99,716	(60%)	$147,249
1988				
Packard (R)	$215,956	$114,538	(53%)	$160,267
Greenebaum (D)	$75,170	$1,500	(2%)	$74,087

Key Votes

1991	
Authorize use of force against Iraq	Y
1990	
Support constitutional amendment on flag desecration	Y
Pass family and medical leave bill over Bush veto	N
Reduce SDI funding	N
Allow abortions in overseas military facilities	N
Approve budget summit plan for spending and taxing	N
Approve civil rights bill	N
1989	
Halt production of B-2 stealth bomber at 13 planes	N
Oppose capital gains tax cut	N
Approve federal abortion funding in rape or incest cases	N
Approve pay raise and revision of ethics rules	Y
Pass Democratic minimum wage plan over Bush veto	N

Voting Studies

	Presidential Support		Party Unity		Conservative Coalition	
Year	**S**	**O**	**S**	**O**	**S**	**O**
1990	71	26	82	13	98	2
1989	81	15	69	27	93	7
1988	66	26	76	14	87	0
1987	70	27	81	14	88	12
1986	83	16	79	18	88	8
1985	75	24	85	10	91	9
1984	69	28	89	8	95	5
1983	83†	16†	92†	5†	91	2

† Not eligible for all recorded votes.

Interest Group Ratings

Year	ADA	ACU	AFL-CIO	CCUS
1990	11	88	8	93
1989	0	93	9	100
1988	5	100	15	92
1987	4	86	6	93
1986	5	91	7	94
1985	10	86	6	95
1984	0	83	8	75
1983	0	96	0	83

44 Randy "Duke" Cunningham (R)

Of Chula Vista — Elected 1990

Born: Dec. 8, 1941, Los Angeles, Calif.
Education: U. of Missouri, B.A. 1964, M.A. 1979; National U., M.B.A. 1985.
Military Service: Navy, 1967-87.
Occupation: Computer software company executive.
Family: Wife, Nancy Jones; three children.
Religion: Christian.
Political Career: No previous office.
Capitol Office: 1017 Longworth Bldg. 20515; 225-5452.

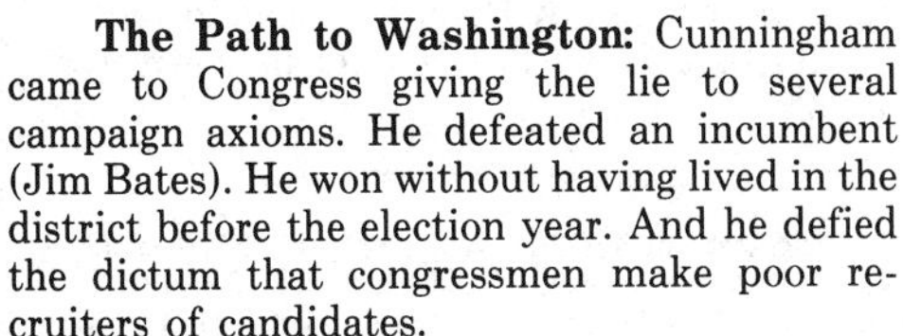

The Path to Washington: Cunningham came to Congress giving the lie to several campaign axioms. He defeated an incumbent (Jim Bates). He won without having lived in the district before the election year. And he defied the dictum that congressmen make poor recruiters of candidates.

Cunningham's entry into the race came at the urging of GOP Rep. Duncan Hunter, whose vast 45th District embraces the 44th on three sides. A lawyer who came to Congress at 32, Hunter has worked his way into leadership via a low-key and accommodating personality. Cunningham, by contrast, is a hard-driving career military man who will turn 50 in his freshman term. A former POW and air combat instructor with two Silver Stars and 10 Air Medals, Cunningham often speaks admiringly of the late actor John Wayne — another "Duke."

Born in Los Angeles the day after Pearl Harbor, Cunningham joined the Navy, trained as a fighter pilot and flew combat missions over Vietnam. On one such mission, his aircraft was disabled by a surface-to-air missile. He and his co-pilot ejected and were rescued at sea. Back in the United States, he turned to training new pilots at the Miramar Naval Station, the advanced training facility featured in the movie "Top Gun" (for which he was an adviser).

While still a naval officer, Cunningham received a business degree from National University, a small school in San Diego. After retiring from the Navy, he became dean of National's school of aviation. Later, he became a marketing specialist for the university. In the meantime, he sold flying instruction videos and computer software from his home and gave speeches across the country. "I've been a success at everything I've ever done," Cunningham often said during the campaign, including his record as a swimming coach. But his varied business ventures were not enough to keep him from agreeing to Hunter's suggestions that he jump into politics in 1990.

Cunningham moved from his beach home in exclusive Del Mar to Chula Vista, a middle-income suburb on the fringe of the 44th, to challenge Bates. Other GOP veterans had been discouraged by Bates' survival in 1988, after allegations of sexual harassment from women who had worked on Bates' staff became public.

Although a novice, Cunningham lined up party regulars and bankrollers and beat four rivals in the primary. In the fall, he clearly benefited from Bates' bruising in the sexual harassment case, which in 1989 led the House ethics committee to issue a reproval (the mildest form of disciplinary action).

Bates, meanwhile, had nearly emptied his campaign treasury in the primary, apparently convinced that he could handle anyone the GOP nominated. To many observers, despite the appeal of his military credentials in the Navy-oriented precincts of the 44th, Cunningham appeared too conservative for a district with just 34 percent GOP registration and most of the minority voters in the San Diego area.

But Bates' problems appeared to suppress turnout within his coalition — particularly among women. And he had trouble campaigning during the fall budget crisis in Washington. Cunningham also showed surprising savvy. He targeted both evangelical Christians and older, conservative Democrats to transcend the district's base GOP vote. He de-emphasized his stands against abortion and gun control, and highlighted his profile as a family man of personal integrity. His literature and broadcast ads spoke of "Christian family values" and "a congressman we can be proud of."

In the same vein, the victorious Cunningham announced he would base his congressional career on constituent services and other non-ideological pursuits. "I'm going to work so hard that people are not going to care whether I have an 'R' in front of my name or not," he said.

California 44

Central San Diego

As a whole, San Diego County has not voted for a Democratic presidential candidate in four decades; George Bush won there by nearly 200,000 votes in 1988. But the city of San Diego has usually had a large enough concentration of Democrats to support one safe Democratic House district.

In a 1980 upset, Republican Duncan Hunter won San Diego's Democratic seat, but in redistricting, a new inner-city district was created, the 44th, and Hunter's turf was moved out into the GOP suburbs and rural areas.

The 44th takes in white working-class neighborhoods near the center of town and farther east, the blue-collar, heavily minority suburb of National City to the south, and San Diego's black and Hispanic communities, including the San Ysidro barrio, less than a mile from the Mexican border.

The district also extends east into the GOP-leaning suburbs of Spring Valley, Lemon Grove, and the booming middle-income suburb of Chula Vista.

Much of Chula Vista's 61 percent growth during the 1980s occurred in the part located in the 44th; many newcomers are Republican. In 1990, first-time candidate Cunningham took 56 percent of the vote in Chula Vista, helping him win districtwide over a scandal-tainted Democratic incumbent.

Democratic mapmakers carefully excluded from the 44th San Diego's more Republican precincts, including the downtown business area and a section north of Balboa Park.

But the district's GOP tendencies have been enhanced by the importance of the military to San Diego's economy. The 44th, which includes the San Diego Naval Station, was carried by Ronald Reagan in 1984, and George Bush lost it only narrowly in 1988.

Population: 525,868. White 332,075 (63%), Black 73,400 (14%), Asian and Pacific Islander 42,490 (8%), Other 3,773 (1%). Spanish origin 141,823 (27%). 18 and over 379,593 (72%), 65 and over 44,081 (8%). Median age: 26.

Committees

Armed Services (21st of 22 Republicans)
Military Personnel & Compensation; Readiness; Research & Development

Merchant Marine & Fisheries (17th of 17 Republicans)
Merchant Marine; Oversight & Investigations

Elections

1990 General		
Randy "Duke" Cunningham (R)	50,377	(46%)
Jim Bates (D)	48,712	(45%)
Donna White (PFP)	5,237	(5%)
John Wallner (LIBERT)	4,385	(4%)
1990 Primary		
Randy "Duke" Cunningham (R)	11,350	(45%)
Joe Ghougassian (R)	7,459	(30%)
Jim Lantry (R)	3,968	(16%)
Kenny Harrell (R)	1,472	(6%)
Eric Epifano (R)	715	(3%)

District Vote For President

	1988	1984	1980	1976
D	80,893 (52%)	71,160 (47%)	52,841 (40%)	54,103 (56%)
R	74,236 (47%)	79,269 (52%)	64,434 (49%)	42,041 (43%)

Campaign Finance

	Receipts	Receipts from PACs		Expend-itures
1990				
Cunningham (R)	$539,721	$214,547	(40%)	$534,167
Bates (D)	$773,364	$360,800	(47%)	$744,463

Key Vote

1991	
Authorize use of force against Iraq	Y

45 Duncan Hunter (R)

Of Coronado — Elected 1980

Born: May 31, 1948, Riverside, Calif.
Education: Attended U. of Montana, 1966-67; U. of California, Santa Barbara, 1967-68; Western State U., B.S.L. 1976, J.D. 1976.
Military Service: Army, 1969-71.
Occupation: Lawyer.
Family: Wife, Lynne Layh; two children.
Religion: Baptist.
Political Career: No previous office.
Capitol Office: 133 Cannon Bldg. 20515; 225-5672.

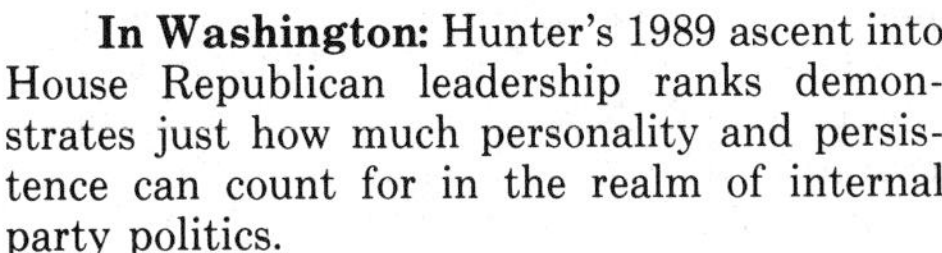

In Washington: Hunter's 1989 ascent into House Republican leadership ranks demonstrates just how much personality and persistence can count for in the realm of internal party politics.

Affable and self-effacing, this class of 1980 conservative is a difficult man not to like. Combined with the younger-generation, right-of-center pedigree that many House Republicans are now looking for in their leaders, Hunter's approachable nature allowed him to overcome qualms about his unfocused enthusiasm and intellectual depth.

His opponent in the race for chairman of the Republican Research Committee was Steve Bartlett of Texas, who resigned from the House in 1991 to run for mayor of Dallas. Similarly conservative, he was known for his keen mind, but not for being an unselfish team player like Hunter. On the strength of his personal qualities, Hunter won the Research post.

The Californian had worked hard to earn the job. He contributed generously to GOP House incumbents and challengers, and he devoted so much time to campaigning for colleagues that one San Diego newspaper speculated that through late October 1988, he had spent as much time trekking around the country as he had spent in his own district.

In mid-1987, Hunter had come surprisingly close to defeating fellow Californian Jerry Lewis in the race for Policy Committee chairman.

In many ways, Hunter's 1987 race foreshadowed the later GOP leadership changes of the 101st Congress, which featured the combative Newt Gingrich's elevation to minority whip. The 1987 contest between Hunter and Lewis was cast as a "young Turk" vs. "establishment man" choice. Hunter first gained notice when he chaired the Conservative Opportunity Society (COS), an insurgent faction of young Republicans (including Gingrich) that made its name by eschewing accommodation with the Democratic majority to underscore the differences between the parties.

While Lewis preceded Hunter in the House by just two years, he is a more traditional GOP player who has worked through the system for incremental change. Though clearly the underdog, Hunter mounted an energetic campaign and in the end, he held the favored Lewis to an 88-82 victory.

Subsequently, Hunter was among those Republicans involved with Gingrich in seeking to spotlight a number of ethical controversies involving House Democrats. Their efforts eventually led to Speaker Jim Wright's downfall in 1989, and helped elevate three former COS chairmen — Gingrich, Hunter and Vin Weber of Minnesota — to GOP leadership positions.

Hunter received a dose of media attention in July 1990 when he testified before a House Ways and Means subcommittee on the issue of tax avoidance by U.S. subsidiaries of foreign-controlled corporations. While federal regulations forbade the Internal Revenue Service (IRS) from publicly revealing information about specific companies' tax returns, such rules did not apply to Hunter.

He, in fact, had no apparent qualms about naming "a lot of famous names — Toshiba and Toyota, Sony and Sumitomo, Mitsubishi and Matsushita, which we know as Panasonic." He also showed the panel a longer list of U.S. subsidiaries of Japanese corporations being examined by the IRS.

Hunter and fellow Californian Tom Campbell — both representing districts with high-tech industries locked in global competition — had written congressional budget negotiators in June urging "a very close look at taxes owed by foreign-owned businesses." Hunter and Campbell cited IRS estimates that subsidiaries might owe as much as $50 billion.

Hunter introduced a bill in 1991 to impose a 5-percent tax of gross income on firms that do not provide information to accurately determine their taxable income.

Apart from his leadership endeavors, Hunter was best-known during the 1980s for his hard-line defense of Ronald Reagan's military

California 45

Imperial Valley; Part of San Diego

Crossing the entire southern border of the state from the Colorado River to San Diego's Sunset Cliffs, the 45th has much land that is sparsely populated and many voters who are devoutly Republican.

The 45th was created by redistricting just after Hunter entered the House. The remap gave Hunter a considerable amount of new territory, but he had no complaints. His original district, which he won in a 1980 upset, had large chunks of Democratic turf within the city of San Diego. The 45th, on the other hand, is mainly suburban and rural, and staunchly Republican. Ronald Reagan topped 70 percent here in 1984; George Bush took two-thirds of its vote in 1988.

The 45th has two distinct parts. One is the area around San Diego — the eastern suburbs of the city, such as Chula Vista, El Cajon and Lakeside, as well as the spit of land west of the city — Coronado — that separates the Pacific Ocean from San Diego Bay. Coronado is the home of many retired Navy officers. They give the area a decidedly pro-military, Republican flavor.

The other part of the district lies east of San Diego County — California's Imperial Valley. Below the level of both the Colorado River and the Pacific Ocean, the valley was relatively easy to irrigate at the turn of the century and has become one of the country's most productive farm areas.

As farmers and urban refugees have moved in with their house trailers, the valley has been experiencing its first substantial growth in several decades, with population rising by more than 15 percent in the early 1980s: More than 100,000 people now live there. The voting trend is conservative, but not so much as in the San Diego suburbs: Bush carried Imperial County with 55 percent of the vote.

Population: 525,927. White 447,436 (85%), Black 8,610 (2%), Other 18,518 (4%). Spanish origin 90,291 (17%). 18 and over 373,038 (71%), 65 and over 49,996 (10%). Median age: 29.

build-up and foreign policy. A staunch supporter of the Nicaraguan contras, Hunter spoke in apocalyptic terms of President Bush's 1989 contra accord with Congress, which did not seek renewal of military aid. "Nicaragua is lost," Hunter said. "The dark curtain of the Sandinista Gestapo has descended on Nicaragua."

Hunter's hyperbolic fears were disproven when the Sandinistas fell from power after the February 1990 elections. In the aftermath of the vote, Hunter focused his efforts on seeing U.S. aid properly channeled to the contras and their families for their repatriation.

From his seat on the Armed Services Committee, the intense Vietnam veteran brings his hawkish agenda to nearly every debate. In the 101st Congress he was a steadfast proponent of the B-2 stealth bomber and the MX missile. Despite the demise of the Cold War, Hunter remained wary of the Soviet Union. "I was disappointed when President Bush did not make the Soviet removal from the American hemisphere a major precondition to economic benefits flowing to the Soviet Union," he said late in 1989. Hunter also tried unsuccessfully to prohibit the sale of advanced telecommunications equipment to the Soviet Union.

In the 100th Congress, he was a prime sponsor of legislation to involve the military in drug interdiction. When the House approved a similar Hunter amendment in 1986, it was practically laughed off the Senate floor; in 1988, it won approval in both chambers.

Hunter stepped up efforts throughout 1990 to shut off the land border to drug smugglers; his district includes the entire Mexico-California border. His efforts bore some fruit by year's end when the California National Guard began a $1.2-million effort to build a major road to assist Border Patrol interception of drug-smuggling vehicles and when a branch of the U.S. Navy began repairing a large stretch of broken-down fence along the border.

At Home: Hunter has an unusual background for a conservative Republican. For the three years before his initial House campaign, he lived and worked in the Hispanic section of San Diego. Running his own storefront law office, Hunter often gave free legal advice to poor people. When President Reagan called for abolition of the Legal Services Corporation, Hunter was one of the dissenters.

Hunter's work in the usually Democratic inner city was one of the reasons for his 1980 upset victory over Democrat Lionel Van Deerlin, a nine-term House veteran. Running his campaign out of his law office, Hunter attracted volunteers and voters most GOP candidates would have had to write off.

Another reason was Hunter's ceaseless campaigning. He made endless rounds of the compact district, popping up at defense plants and on street corners, shaking 1,000 hands every day while Van Deerlin remained in Washington, assuming he would score a comfortable victory.

Hunter, who won a Bronze Star for participating in 25 helicopter combat assaults in Vietnam, blasted away at what he called Van Deerlin's "anti-defense" voting record. He promised his own pro-Pentagon stance would keep jobs in the district, which boasts the nation's largest naval base and numerous defense industries. "In San Diego," he said, "defense means jobs."

The message worked, as Hunter pulled off a stunning upset with 53 percent of the vote. Van Deerlin and other California Democrats complained that the television networks' election night projections of Ronald Reagan's victory over Jimmy Carter — while the polls in California were still open — discouraged thousands of Democrats from going to vote. But their hopes of proving that Hunter's victory was a fluke were quickly banished before the 1982 elections, when a redistricting plan gave Hunter a safely Republican district.

While that plan moved Hunter away from his original central San Diego base, it gave him a long strip of affluent suburbs and rural farmland along California's southern tier. The 45th District's Republican tendencies were evident in Hunter's first contest there: He took 69 percent in 1982. Hunter has topped 70 percent in each ensuing election.

District Democrats did not even field a candidate in 1990, leaving Hunter free to roam Southern California on behalf of Republican challenger candidates. His assistance provided a major boost for Republican Randy "Duke" Cunningham, a former Navy pilot who unseated four-term Democratic Rep. Jim Bates in the neighboring 44th District, which contains much of Hunter's original turf.

Hunter strongly endorsed and personally campaigned for Cunningham in the district, based in San Diego. Cunningham defeated the scandal-plagued Bates with a 46 percent plurality. Hunter, in the meantime, was running up 73 percent against Libertarian candidate Joe Shea.

Committees

Armed Services (6th of 22 Republicans)
Research & Development; Seapower & Strategic & Critical Materials

Select Hunger (8th of 12 Republicans)
International

Elections

1990 General

Duncan Hunter (R)	123,591	(73%)
Joe Shea (LIBERT)	46,068	(27%)

1988 General

Duncan Hunter (R)	166,451	(74%)
Pete Lepiscopo (D)	54,012	(24%)

Previous Winning Percentages: **1986** (77%) **1984** (75%) **1982** (69%) **1980** (53%)

District Vote For President

	1988	1984	1980	1976
D	76,206 (33%)	58,141 (28%)	45,726 (25%)	53,299 (42%)
R	153,368 (66%)	149,282 (71%)	120,516 (65%)	73,749 (57%)

Campaign Finance

	Receipts	Receipts from PACs		Expend-itures
1990				
Hunter (R)	$368,560	$110,465	(30%)	$376,408
1988				
Hunter (R)	$392,229	$150,718	(38%)	$489,395
Lepiscopo (D)	$8,618	$3,775	(44%)	$8,136

Key Votes

1991

Authorize use of force against Iraq	Y

1990

Support constitutional amendment on flag desecration	Y
Pass family and medical leave bill over Bush veto	N
Reduce SDI funding	N
Allow abortions in overseas military facilities	N
Approve budget summit plan for spending and taxing	N
Approve civil rights bill	N

1989

Halt production of B-2 stealth bomber at 13 planes	N
Oppose capital gains tax cut	N
Approve federal abortion funding in rape or incest cases	N
Approve pay raise and revision of ethics rules	Y
Pass Democratic minimum wage plan over Bush veto	N

Voting Studies

	Presidential Support		Party Unity		Conservative Coalition	
Year	**S**	**O**	**S**	**O**	**S**	**O**
1990	69	28	84	11	87	9
1989	76	22	85	7	90	7
1988	65	30	89	5	95	3
1987	72	22	86	6	88	7
1986	78	20	85	11	90	8
1985	74	20	75	12	87	11
1984	73	24	80	15	90	8
1983	74	24	88	10	93	7
1982	83	14	84	10	90	5
1981	74	25	89	11	95	5

Interest Group Ratings

Year	ADA	ACU	AFL-CIO	CCUS
1990	6	96	17	86
1989	10	96	18	100
1988	0	100	15	77
1987	4	91	13	93
1986	0	82	29	100
1985	10	86	19	76
1984	5	91	42	81
1983	15	91	12	80
1982	5	84	21	82
1981	10	100	27	89

Colorado

U.S. CONGRESS

SENATE 1 D, 1 R
HOUSE 3 D, 3 R

LEGISLATURE

Senate 12 D, 23 R
House 27 D, 38 R

ELECTIONS

1988 Presidential Vote	
Bush	53%
Dukakis	45%
1984 Presidential Vote	
Reagan	63%
Mondale	35%
1980 Presidential Vote	
Reagan	55%
Carter	31%
Anderson	11%
Turnout rate in 1986	42%
Turnout rate in 1988	55%
Turnout rate in 1990	40%

(as percentage of voting age population)

POPULATION AND GROWTH

1980 population	2,889,964
1990 population (26th in the nation)	3,294,394
Percent change 1980-1990	+14%

DEMOGRAPHIC BREAKDOWN

White	88%
Black	4%
Asian or Pacific Islander	2%
(Hispanic origin)	13%
Urban	81%
Rural	19%
Born in state	42%
Foreign-born	4%

MAJOR CITIES

Denver	467,610
Colorado Springs	281,140
Aurora	222,103
Lakewood	126,481
Pueblo	98,640

AREA AND LAND USE

Area	103,595 sq. miles (8th)
Farm	51%
Forest	32%
Federally owned	36%

Gov. Roy Romer (D)
Of Denver — Elected 1986

Born: Oct. 31, 1928, Garden City, Kan.
Education: Colorado State U., B.S., 1950; U. of Colorado, LL.B. 1952; Yale U., 1954.
Military Service: Air Force, 1952-53.
Occupation: Lawyer.
Religion: Presbyterian.
Political Career: Colo. House 1959-63; Colo. Senate, 1963-67; assistant minority leader, 1963-67; Colo. treasurer, 1977-87; Democratic nominee for U.S. Senate, 1966.
Next Election: 1994.

WORK

Occupations	
White-collar	58%
Blue-collar	27%
Service workers	13%
Government Workers	
Federal	52,980
State	68,375
Local	148,462

MONEY

Median family income	$ 21,279	(12th)
Tax burden per capita	$ 707	(42nd)

EDUCATION

Spending per pupil through grade 12	$ 4,462	(15th)
Persons with college degrees	23%	(1st)

CRIME

Violent crime rate	471 per 100,000 (27th)

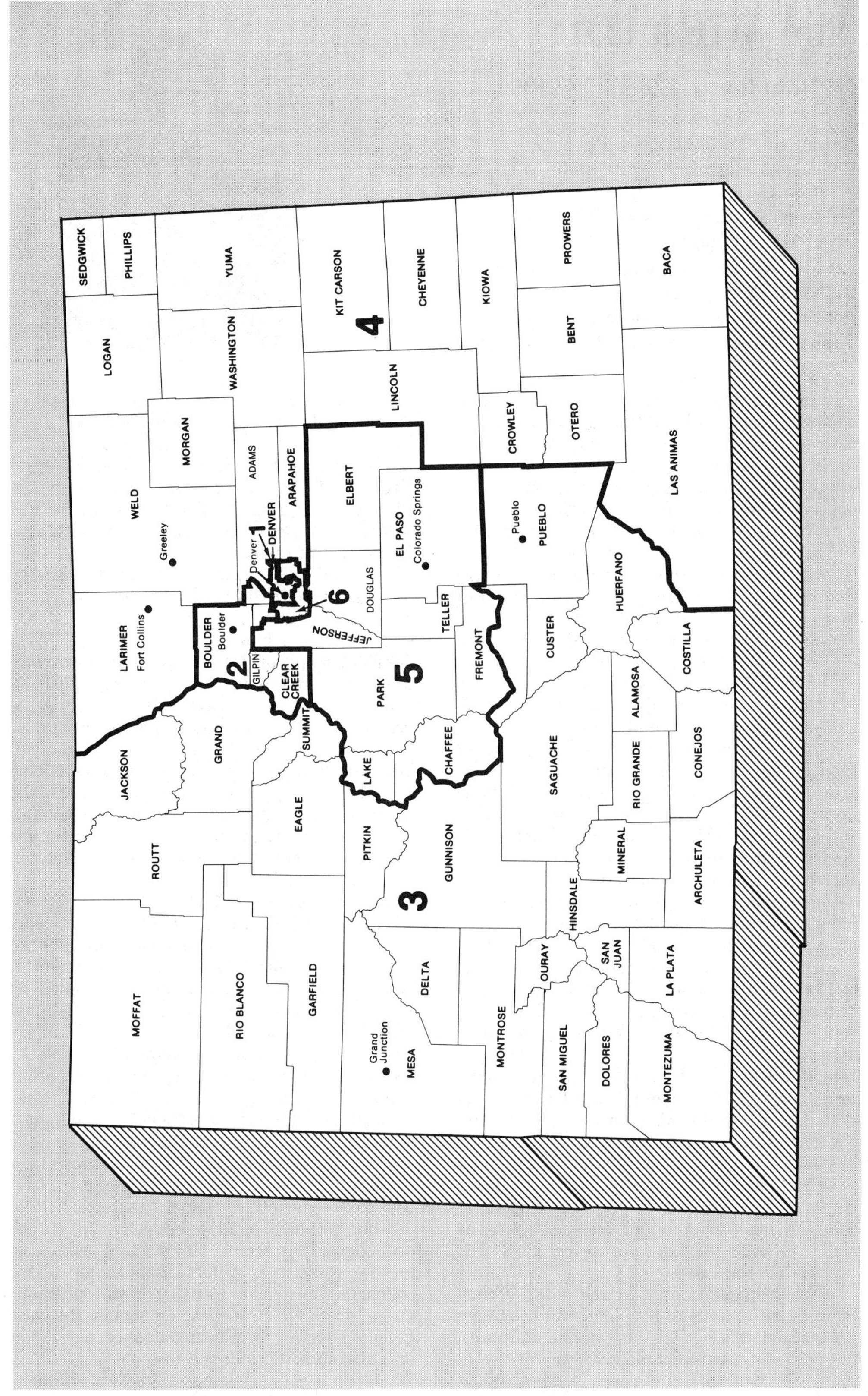
SEDGWICK
PHILLIPS
YUMA
KIT CARSON
CHEYENNE
KIOWA
PROWERS
BACA
LOGAN
WASHINGTON
4
LINCOLN
BENT
OTERO
CROWLEY
WELD
Greeley
MORGAN
ADAMS
ARAPAHOE
ELBERT
EL PASO
Colorado Springs
PUEBLO
Pueblo
LAS ANIMAS
1
DENVER
Denver
6
DOUGLAS
JEFFERSON
TELLER
LARIMER
Fort Collins
BOULDER
Boulder
2
GILPIN
CLEAR CREEK
PARK
5
FREMONT
CUSTER
HUERFANO
COSTILLA
ALAMOSA
JACKSON
GRAND
SUMMIT
LAKE
CHAFFEE
SAGUACHE
RIO GRANDE
CONEJOS
ROUTT
EAGLE
PITKIN
GUNNISON
MINERAL
ARCHULETA
HINSDALE
3
MOFFAT
RIO BLANCO
GARFIELD
MESA
Grand Junction
DELTA
MONTROSE
OURAY
SAN JUAN
LA PLATA
SAN MIGUEL
DOLORES
MONTEZUMA

Tim Wirth (D)

Of Boulder — Elected 1986

Born: Sept. 22, 1939, Santa Fe, N.M.
Education: Harvard U., A.B. 1961, M.Ed. 1964; Stanford U., Ph.D. 1973.
Military Service: Army Reserve, 1961-67.
Occupation: Education official; teacher.
Family: Wife, Wren Winslow; two children.
Religion: Episcopalian.
Political Career: U.S. House, 1975-87.
Capitol Office: 380 Russell Bldg. 20510; 224-5852.

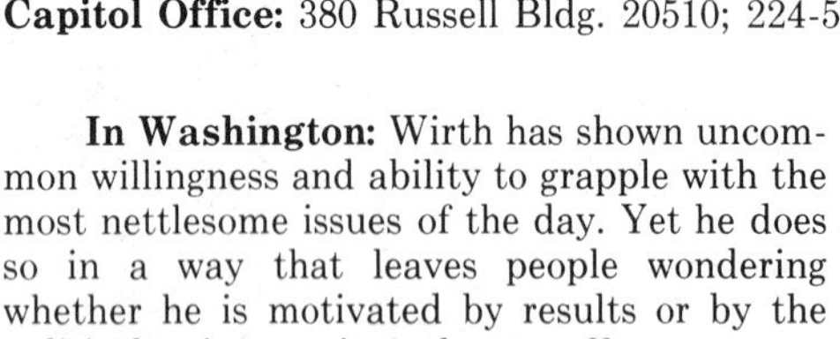

In Washington: Wirth has shown uncommon willingness and ability to grapple with the most nettlesome issues of the day. Yet he does so in a way that leaves people wondering whether he is motivated by results or by the political points an issue has to offer.

An intellectual standout in both the 1974 House Watergate class and the Democrats' large 1986 Senate crop — two activist groups that continue to change Congress as an institution — Wirth prides himself on a pragmatic, non-ideological legislative style. But he can be intolerant and does not belong to any coalition. He builds bridges to the other side of the aisle, only to lose ground by quarreling with liberals and moderates, his natural allies.

Never were these conflicts more evident than during Wirth's efforts in the 101st Congress to toughen the Clean Air Act. He teamed up with California Republican Pete Wilson to author a far-reaching amendment aimed at reducing auto emissions. The plan called for an aggressive alternative fuels program and an automatic second round of tailpipe emissions reductions, and it quickly became the No. 1 priority of environmental groups.

But the package was dubbed a deal-buster by Democratic Majority Leader George J. Mitchell, who had negotiated the bill with the White House. The Wirth-Wilson plan would drive up the cost, it was said, and guarantee a veto. In the end, Wirth lost the support of many well-known environmentalists, who worried that the bill would fall with the amendment, and gained the support of several conservatives, like Jesse Helms, who noisily denied mischief.

Wirth attributed the 46-52 defeat to White House and auto industry lobbying. "You could hear the arms snapping all the way down the mall," he said. "I know of seven guys who switched in the last hour."

Wirth spared himself trouble with Mitchell by being upfront about his plans. But the Clean Air conflict was not his first public split with the powerful environmentalist from Maine. In the 1989 contest for majority leader, Wirth endorsed not Mitchell but J. Bennett Johnston, the champion of oil and gas development from Louisiana. Wirth's vote suggested Johnston had support beyond Southerners and conservatives, and it cast doubt on the expectation that Mitchell would sweep the 1986 class he had helped elect. Both implications proved illusory; Mitchell won easily.

Wirth's allegiance to Johnston, the Energy and Natural Resources Committee chairman, reflected his gratitude for the free rein Johnston had given him on global warming. With Johnston's approval, Wirth presided over committee hearings and led the drafting of legislation to alleviate the "greenhouse effect" on the Earth caused by upper-atmospheric pollutants.

Early in the 102nd Congress, however, Wirth drew apart from Johnston by introducing a major energy policy package seen as the environmental alternative to the Louisianan's proposal. And Wirth now has a forum for his interests as chairman of the Energy Regulation and Conservation Subcommittee.

Among some of his Democratic colleagues, Wirth's pursuit of environmental issues appears to be the foundation of a future presidential campaign. But his alliance with environmentalists is occasionally an uneasy one. Though he opposes drilling in the vast Arctic National Wildlife Refuge and has a knack for finding a "green" angle on many seemingly unrelated issues, the Coloradan mixes his pro-environment votes with support for Western water projects and for measures benefiting oil-shale and energy industries back home.

On Armed Services, Wirth opposes steep funding increases for the strategic defense initiative (SDI) and other weapons systems, but in defense-minded Colorado, he bases that stance on budgetary concerns. However, his emphasis on the committee differs from many of his colleagues'. Instead of focusing on various weapons systems or strategies, he scours the vast defense complex for ways to advance his agenda on environmental and social issues.

With a major defense-related environmental problem in his back yard — at the Rocky Flats nuclear weapons plant outside Denver — Wirth offered a successful amendment in 1990 to shift $45 million from nuclear weapons programs to the Pentagon's environmental cleanup account.

Wirth also offered a controversial 1990 amendment to permit overseas military hospitals to perform abortions, and he held up consideration of the foreign aid bill in 1990 with an amendment to restore U.S. funding of international family planning groups providing abortion services and referrals. Though both proposals were supported by most senators, neither had enough support to end a filibuster or overturn a veto; both were eventually withdrawn.

Wirth is also an active member of the Banking and Budget committees, to which he brought previous experience from the House Budget Committee and from financial debates in his Energy and Commerce subcommittee. On Budget, he has supported increased funding for education and child care, though liberal activists find that he generally takes a more fiscally conservative line than they do. In late 1987, Wirth joined Republicans and just four other Senate Democrats in blocking floor action on a housing bill that violated budget limits.

From his post on Banking, Wirth drafted a compromise amendment with Pennsylvania Republican John Heinz (a friend since they attended the same preparatory school) to beef up federal investigations of thrift fraud and to increase the penalties for defendants. During consideration of the 1990 crime bill, which came up as Wirth and many others were under scrutiny for past campaign contributions from thrift executives, the amendment passed with the support of 99 senators.

Wirth brought over from the House his interest in telecommunications issues. He has had numerous clashes with the broadcast industry over his proposal to require that TV stations air educational children's shows and limit ads aimed at young viewers. His former allies in the House finally passed a compromise bill in the 100th and 101st Congresses, only to be frustrated by Wirth when it reached the Senate. He demanded more explicit requirements on broadcasters than most Democrats considered politically realistic. In 1988, Wirth relented just as the bill appeared doomed, but President Reagan vetoed it. The following year Wirth went back to pressing his old demands, and, after months of wrangling, managed to strike a compromise that was approved by President Bush.

Wirth, whose state is home to some of the nation's largest cable companies, is the cable industry's top defender in Congress. Deregulated by Congress in 1984, the industry has since resisted efforts to restore local control over rates and open the field to competition. Wirth blocked consideration of such legislation in 1990, though late in the year he struck a compromise to preserve some forms of exclusive agreements between cable operators and programmers; but it was struck too late to be taken up in the 101st Congress.

But, earlier in the House, Wirth was perhaps best known for his efforts to deregulate another segment of the telecommunications industry: His 1982 bill to clarify AT&T's roles after the Justice Department reached the antitrust agreement with the company prompted one of the largest mail-in campaigns in congressional history. His bill, which his subcommittee approved unanimously, was designed to restructure the company to guard against anticompetitive actions, to prevent unduly high telephone rates and to shore up the newly independent local phone companies. But when it reached full committee, AT&T backers stalled it with the help of a letter writing campaign by employees, stockholders and retirees of the communications giant. After much pain, Wirth finally withdrew the bill.

Early on, Wirth was viewed as a leader among those young House members variously described as neo-liberals or Atari Democrats. Outside his committee work, he tried to raise congressional interest in a national investment in high technology, arguing that it would make the United States more competitive in international markets.

At Home: Wirth's trek to the Senate proved a more harrowing journey than just about anybody would have predicted when he first announced he wanted to succeed Democrat Gary Hart. At the start of the campaign, even Republicans felt Wirth would probably stroll to victory. He shared the thoughtful, non-ideological manner that brought Hart two terms; it was a style that seemed more suited to Colorado than the ideological belligerence for which Rep. Ken Kramer, the GOP nominee, was known.

As it turned out, Wirth was the reliably smooth candidate he had always been. But Kramer confounded expectations. Though his conservatism was prominent in his campaign — he touted a constitutional amendment to balance the federal budget and backed spending on SDI — the GOP wild man many Democrats had expected was not in sight. Instead, Kramer was an affable campaigner with a confident manner. And his first major round of ads took a clever jab at Wirth's polished image, telling TV viewers, "I'm not slick. Just good."

Wirth, meanwhile, had more trouble latching onto a clear theme. His attempts to paint Kramer as an extremist were partially undercut by the Republican's moderate manner, and his effort to flesh out his own image for voters did not begin until late in the campaign.

But Wirth had strengths that made up for his diffuse campaign. He displayed such ease working crowds that some quipped that his peripheral vision was good enough to read name tags without breaking eye contact. His leadership of the so-called neo-liberals in his party gave him a base outside his district. Moreover, Wirth was interested in environmentalism as well as business competition and high-technology development, and could blend consumer advocacy with a sympathy for deregulation — stands that appealed to both GOP moderates and those in his own party.

And Wirth had an organization that ran circles around Kramer's — able to respond quickly to thrusts from Kramer or the state GOP and to keep Wirth's name in the news. Its field operations far outperformed Kramer's, especially in their party strongholds.

In the end, it was Wirth's almost 2-to-1 margin in Denver that helped him overcome a deficit elsewhere in the state and take the election by a little over 16,000 votes.

Wirth first rode into Congress in 1974 on a wave of enthusiasm for environmental safeguards and reaction against Watergate.

It was Wirth's political debut. A former White House fellow with a Ph.D. in education from Stanford, he began his campaign early and organized well. He combined an expertise on land, water and energy issues with sharp jabs at GOP Rep. Donald G. Brotzman for supporting President Richard M. Nixon. Building large margins in west Denver and Boulder, Wirth offset Brotzman's lead in Denver's Jefferson County suburbs to win the seat by 7,000 votes.

The district remained difficult for Wirth. Republican candidates criticized him as a big-spending liberal, and they spent a combined total of more than $1 million trying to oust him. Wirth drew over 56 percent only once, in 1982.

In 1984, Wirth's margin was down again, to 53 percent. His GOP challenger was Michael Norton, a former Jefferson County GOP chairman who tried to turn Wirth's national contacts and influence against him. He ran an ad that showed Wirth's face melting into Walter F. Mondale's. He pounded away at the AT&T breakup, charging that Wirth had led the fight for something his constituents did not want at the expense of more pressing district concerns.

The campaign ended on a sour note, with Norton charging that Wirth should be "strung up" for some of his views, and Wirth calling Norton the rudest challenger he had ever faced.

Committees

Armed Services (9th of 11 Democrats)
Conventional Forces & Alliance Defense; Defense Industry & Technology; Readiness, Sustainability & Support

Banking, Housing & Urban Affairs (10th of 12 Democrats)
International Finance & Monetary Policy; Securities

Budget (9th of 12 Democrats)

Energy & Natural Resources (6th of 11 Democrats)
Energy Regulation & Conservation (chairman); Public Lands, National Parks & Forests; Water & Power

Elections

1986 General

Tim Wirth (D)	529,449	(50%)
Ken Kramer (R)	512,994	(48%)

Previous Winning Percentages: **1984** * (53%) **1982** * (62%) **1980** * (56%) **1978** * (53%) **1976** * (51%) **1974** * (52%)

* *House elections.*

Campaign Finance

	Receipts	Receipts from PACs	Expend-itures
1986			
Wirth (D)	$3,819,308	$845,855 (22%)	$3,787,202
Kramer (R)	$3,829,927	$925,429 (25%)	$3,785,577

Key Votes

1991	
Authorize use of force against Iraq	N
1990	
Oppose prohibition of certain semiautomatic weapons	N
Support constitutional amendment on flag desecration	N
Oppose requiring parental notice for minors' abortions	Y
Halt production of B-2 stealth bomber at 13 planes	Y
Approve budget that cut spending and raised revenues	Y
Pass civil rights bill over Bush veto	Y
1989	
Oppose reduction of SDI funding	N
Oppose barring federal funds for "obscene" art	Y
Allow vote on capital gains tax cut	N

Voting Studies

	Presidential Support		Party Unity		Conservative Coalition	
Year	**S**	**O**	**S**	**O**	**S**	**O**
1990	37	60	88	10	14	81
1989	56	41	85	13	29	71
1988	47	52	86	11	27	68
1987	33	60	84	14	44	56
House Service						
1986	27	72	76	15	24	66
1985	21	71	81	10	20	73
1984	27	65	89	7	10	83
1983	18	78	82	7	16	81
1982	34	62	84	9	19	79
1981	38	51	78	14	23	61

Interest Group Ratings

Year	ADA	ACU	AFL-CIO	CCUS
1990	83	10	56	17
1989	95	7	90	57
1988	95	0	79	36
1987	85	0	90	41
House Service				
1986	75	14	92	54
1985	70	10	71	38
1984	85	4	92	40
1983	95	0	82	40
1982	95	0	84	14
1981	85	0	71	21

Hank Brown (R)

Of Greeley — Elected 1990

Born: Feb. 12, 1940, Denver, Colo.

Education: U. of Colorado, B.S. 1961, J.D. 1969; George Washington U., LL.M. 1986.

Military Service: Navy, 1962-66.

Occupation: Tax accountant; meatpacking company executive; lawyer.

Family: Wife, Nan Morrison; three children.

Religion: United Church of Christ.

Political Career: Colo. Senate, 1973-77; Republican nominee for lieutenant governor, 1978; U.S. House, 1981-91.

Capitol Office: 717 Hart Bldg. 20510; 224-5941.

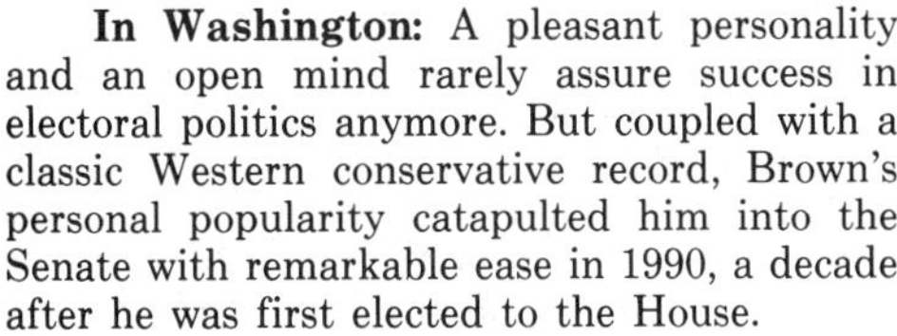

In Washington: A pleasant personality and an open mind rarely assure success in electoral politics anymore. But coupled with a classic Western conservative record, Brown's personal popularity catapulted him into the Senate with remarkable ease in 1990, a decade after he was first elected to the House.

Like many Western politicians, Brown combines party loyalty with a bit of iconoclasm. In the House, his reputation for independence earned him the respect of members on both sides of the aisle. Willing to do the dirty work required of junior members — he served two terms on the House ethics panel — Brown should have little trouble transferring that respect to the Senate.

Criticism of Brown focuses on his being perhaps too much of a gentleman, and some wondered if he would be tough enough for a rough Senate bid. While the Senate race never became close enough to test his mettle, part of the reason Brown won so comfortably was his emphasis on popular political issues during his last two years in the House: He was a leading foe of the congressional pay raise and defender of Social Security.

Brown won a seat on the Senate Budget Committee at the start of the 102nd Congress. In October 1990, he was among those who opposed the budget-summit agreement, and he is a well-known critic of deficit spending. Unlike many conservatives, however, his interest in cutting the deficit has at times extended to cuts in defense.

A member of the House Budget Committee during the mid-1980s, Brown was not an enthusiast for the massive defense buildup. He opposed deep cuts in the strategic defense initiative (SDI) — part of the SDI work is done in Colorado Springs — during the 101st Congress when he was running for the Senate, but in the past he had balked at the funding level sought by the Reagan administration.

Early in his tenure on the Senate Budget Committee, Brown teamed up with ranking Republican Pete V. Domenici of New Mexico to offer an amendment designed to limit tax increases. Conservatives on the Budget Committee wanted to eliminate provisions that allow other committees to make changes in entitlements and taxes on a pay-as-you-go basis. When that failed, Brown and Domenici offered an amendment that prohibits tax increases from funding program expansions unless three-fifths of the Senate concurs. While the Senate went along with the idea, the House balked.

During the 1991 debate on the budget, he also resumed a longtime fight against the honey price support program, which he calls "one of the silliest programs ever thought up in this nation or any nation in the history of the world." The Senate, however, defeated his measure to kill the program 57-38.

During his last two House terms, Brown served on the Ways and Means Committee. Ranking Republican on the Social Security Subcommittee in the 101st Congress, he supported removing Social Security from the budget and treating the Social Security Administration as an independent agency. Brown said this would prevent raids on the trust fund.

Though not generally known as a grandstander, Brown was a frequent critic of enforcement of ethical standards in the House, and in 1990, he became a leading foe of the pay raise. In August 1990, he held a high-visibility press conference with Ralph Nader and a coalition of self-described citizens' organizations to propose rolling back congressional salaries to the 1989 level and repealing the 1990 pay increase. At the time, Brown noted that it would be easier to accomplish this in the Senate where amendments can be offered to unrelated legislation.

Brown's challenges to House ethics enforcement quieted only modestly after the investigation of House Speaker Jim Wright of Texas. A member of the ethics panel, Brown kept a characteristically low profile, and then voted with the unanimous GOP bloc in finding that there was enough evidence to warrant further investigation of all 11 charges against Wright.

His critique of Congress as an institution goes further. Brown has tried to end Congress' practice of exempting itself from civil rights and other laws it imposes on others — a cause he will have the chance to champion as a member of the Senate Judiciary Committee. He has made several attempts over the years to cut funding for members' perks such as franked mail, elevator operators and leadership staff.

Brown also served on the ethics committee from 1981-84, when he demonstrated a willingness to dissent from the committee majority rather than go along with a conclusion he did not buy. Most notably, Brown in late 1984 filed a dissenting statement when ethics concluded that New York Democratic Rep. Geraldine A. Ferraro violated financial-disclosure requirements, but that the committee should take no further action because she was leaving the House at the end of the year. Brown argued that the decision set up a double standard, noting that Idaho Republican George Hansen had earlier been reprimanded for similar offenses.

When Brown won a coveted seat on the Ways and Means Committee in 1987, he was thrust immediately into a leadership role as ranking minority member of the Public Assistance Subcommittee just as Congress was gearing up for a major overhaul of the welfare system. That bill proved to be the most partisan issue before the committee in the 100th Congress, and Republicans' input in House deliberations was therefore limited. But Brown helped his fellow Republicans exert what leverage they could.

He put together a GOP alternative that struck a middle ground between a Democratic-drafted bill they deemed too costly, and a Reagan administration proposal that would have focused not on new federal money and mandates, but on allowing states to experiment with new welfare approaches.

Brown's efforts to mold the bill in committee fell victim to immovable party lines. And the Republican alternative did little better on the House floor, even though the Democratic leadership had a hard time holding onto its conservative flank.

But once the Senate passed a welfare bill with a lower cost and a more stringent work requirement for welfare recipients, Brown had an opening. Republicans won a rare victory when the House approved a Brown motion instructing its conferees to accept the Senate's price tag. Although the cost ultimately exceeded that, Brown's move helped pressure the House negotiators to move closer to the Senate position.

Although he was elected in 1980 with the huge class of Republicans swept into the House on Reagan's coattails, the independent-minded Brown was never a "Reagan robot." He was a solid backer of Reagan's economic policies, but voted against higher funding for SDI. In 1985, Brown was one of only two Budget Committee Republicans to vote with the Democratic majority on spending for defense. In the 100th Congress' debate on an omnibus trade bill, Brown was one of only 17 Republicans who voted for a controversial "fair trade" amendment sponsored by Missouri Democrat Richard A. Gephardt that critics called protectionist.

Brown is also the rare Republican first elected in 1980 who supports abortion rights. He describes his stand as classic conservatism, minimizing the federal government's role in private citizens' lives.

At Home: Few members of the Senate have had a smoother climb up the political ladder than Brown. He won election to the state Senate in 1972 and with a single exception has been winning ever since.

By 1974, he was assistant majority leader; in 1980, he was elected to the House, capturing the 4th District seat of retiring GOP Rep. Jim Johnson, whose campaign Brown had once managed. Brown won re-election throughout the 1980s with at least 70 percent of the vote. In 1990, he took the Senate seat being vacated by Republican William L. Armstrong with a comfortable 57 percent.

While Brown flirted with, but then shied away from, a run for governor in 1986, he jumped quickly into the 1990 Senate race. Barely a week after Armstrong indicated in early 1989 that he would not seek re-election, Brown announced his own candidacy.

He turned out to be a wire-to-wire leader in the polls. While Republicans quickly coalesced behind him, Democrats had to endure a bruising nominating battle among candidates who could ill afford the cost in money or stature.

Three of the state's most prominent Democrats — former Gov. Richard D. Lamm and Reps. Ben Nighthorse Campbell and David E. Skaggs — all skipped the race. With ardent support from environmentalists and feminists, former Boulder County Commissioner Josie Heath emerged as the Democratic nominee, but only after weathering a primary against lawyer Carlos Lucero, who was able to generate reams of free publicity by employing an investigative team to look into the collapse of the Colorado-based Silverado Banking, Savings and Loan Association.

Democrats tried to use the same issue to undermine Brown. President Bush came to a lucrative Brown fundraiser in December 1989 that was chaired by a controversial Denver developer with ties to Silverado. Democrats challenged Brown to return the money, which he declined to do. And with his "Boy Scout" image, he was able to ride out the criticism.

With few other issues to take advantage of, Heath was unable to offset Brown's long head start, his aura of quasi-incumbency and a feeling among many Colorado voters that one senator from the trendy college town of Boulder was enough (it is also home for Democratic Sen. Tim Wirth). She carried Boulder and Democratic Denver and Pueblo counties, but was trounced by Brown virtually everywhere else.

Even before running for public office Brown compiled an impressive résumé as student body president at the University of Colorado, as a decorated Vietnam War veteran, and as an executive with a meatpacking firm.

He has augmented this with an affable personality, a "Mr. Clean" image and a Main Street conservatism that combines a skinflint attitude on fiscal matters with a moderate stance on social issues. As a result Brown is usually able to draw votes from virtually every constituency.

He actually did lose one election, as the GOP nominee for lieutenant governor in 1978. But even that experience turned out to help more than hurt him. Brown won high marks for his vigorous campaigning and established solid name identification in the sprawling 4th District that paid off two years later when he routed veteran Democratic Party activist Polly Baca Barragan by more than 2-to-1 for the seat of the retiring Johnson.

Committees

Budget (9th of 9 Republicans)

Foreign Relations (7th of 8 Republicans)
East Asian & Pacific Affairs; European Affairs; Terrorism, Narcotics & International Operations (ranking)

Judiciary (6th of 6 Republicans)
Juvenile Justice (ranking); Technology & the Law (ranking)

Elections

1990 General

Hank Brown (R)	569,048	(56%)
Josie Heath (D)	425,746	(42%)

Previous Winning Percentages: **1988** * (73%) **1986** * (70%) **1984** * (71%) **1982** * (70%) **1980** * (68%)

* *House elections.*

Campaign Finance

	Receipts	Receipts from PACs		Expend-itures
1990				
Brown (R)	$4,179,746	$1,389,784	(33%)	$3,723,911
Heath (D)	$1,953,120	$314,413	(16%)	$1,943,422

Key Votes

1991

Authorize use of force against Iraq	Y

House Service

1990

Support constitutional amendment on flag desecration	Y
Pass family and medical leave bill over Bush veto	N
Reduce SDI funding	N
Allow abortions in overseas military facilities	Y
Approve budget summit plan for spending and taxing	N
Approve civil rights bill	N

1989

Halt production of B-2 stealth bomber at 13 planes	N
Oppose capital gains tax cut	N
Approve federal abortion funding in rape or incest cases	Y
Approve pay raise and revision of ethics rules	N
Pass Democratic minimum wage plan over Bush veto	N

Voting Studies

	Presidential Support		Party Unity		Conservative Coalition	
Year	**S**	**O**	**S**	**O**	**S**	**O**
House Service						
1990	70	29	87	11	87	13
1989	63	35	84	15	83	17
1988	68	29	85	12	87	11
1987	58	39	84	11	77	14
1986	67	32	92	7	84	16
1985	70	29	87	11	82	18
1984	65	35	85	15	83	17
1983	67	33	82	18	75	25
1982	68	32	89	11	75	25
1981	66	34	77	23	71	29

Interest Group Ratings

Year	ADA	ACU	AFL-CIO	CCUS
House Service				
1990	11	83	0	79
1989	20	86	17	100
1988	30	72	21	100
1987	16	73	19	85
1986	10	77	0	94
1985	30	67	12	82
1984	10	83	8	75
1983	25	61	12	90
1982	20	86	0	91
1981	20	100	13	89

1 Patricia Schroeder (D)

Of Denver — Elected 1972

Born: July 30, 1940, Portland, Ore.
Education: U. of Minnesota, B.A. 1961; Harvard U., J.D. 1964.
Occupation: Lawyer; law instructor.
Family: Husband, James Schroeder; two children.
Religion: United Church of Christ.
Political Career: No previous office.
Capitol Office: 2208 Rayburn Bldg. 20515; 225-4431.

In Washington: The chairmanship of the House Select Committee on Children, Youth and Families, which Schroeder succeeded to in February 1991, is a role she was cut out to play. A longtime liberal spokesman on federal programs for children — particularly those from low-income families — Schroeder has invested great energy trying to wrest the "pro-family" banner from conservative Republicans.

Schroeder took the top spot on the committee when the previous chairman, Democrat George Miller of California, replaced the ailing and soon-to-retire Morris K. Udall of Arizona at the helm of the Interior Committee. The select committee is not a congressional powerhouse; it has no legislative jurisdiction. But this should not be a big problem for Schroeder, whose success has been mainly as an activist, not a legislative craftsman.

Herein lies the overriding paradox of Schroeder's long House career. She is a celebrity on the national scene, whose status as a political star in liberal and feminist circles led her to consider a presidential campaign in 1988. She has used her committee positions to carry on a variety of high-profile crusades: for arms reduction as a member of Armed Services, for abortion rights and against sex discrimination on Judiciary, and for programs benefiting children on the committee she now chairs.

Yet the staunchly liberal nature of her politics circumscribes her effectiveness at passing legislation, as her history on Armed Services indicates. When she first joined Armed Services as an antiwar activist in 1973, Schroeder was practically ostracized by a dominant, conservative "Old Guard" that could justifiably be described as sexist. The committee's membership has since moderated and become more accepting of women's participation: Schroeder has been chairman of the Military Installations and Facilities Subcommittee since the start of the 101st Congress. Yet on major military issues, Schroeder remains on the committee's left flank; her bids to slash defense spending in order to fund domestic programs have consistently been rebuffed.

Schroeder's difficulties in the institution, though, go beyond mere ideology. Her style is also a factor. From the start, Schroeder sent contradictory signals, yearning to fit in while frequently invoking gender to draw distinctions or dramatize a point, such as referring to Pentagon war-planners' male glands. She is invitingly friendly, but the smile and exuberance come off as phony to members who know her as an independent operator.

She is as bright as her Harvard law degree would suggest, yet has a reputation as flaky. It was Schroeder who once wore a rabbit suit during an Armed Services trip to China at Eastertime and handed out jelly beans and candy eggs to the startled Chinese.

Irreverence and sharp wit enhance her stock on the speaking circuit: It was Schroeder who dubbed Ronald Reagan the "Teflon" president. When House completion of a child-care assistance bill was stalled in March 1990 because of a heated dispute over esoteric details, Schroeder quipped, "I think we're going to give everyone cookies and milk, put them down for a nap and then try again."

But Schroeder can also be sharp-tongued in a way that offends even her political allies. In May 1989, with Congress roiled by a scandal that would force the resignation of House Speaker Jim Wright, *Newsweek* magazine published a scathing critique of Congress as a "fortress of unreality." In that article, Schroeder was quoted as saying, "Everyone here checks their spines in the cloakroom."

The remark brought a rebuke from Democratic Rep. Thomas J. Downey of New York, a frequent ally of Schroeder on arms control and other issues. First, he challenged Schroeder at a weekly meeting of the Democratic whip organization. Downey then stated publicly, "Life is tough enough in this institution without other members dragging it down."

Still, Schroeder is recognized both inside and outside the House as brainy and articulate. Schroeder also has maintained her committed liberalism while others have flagged. She loses much of the time, but resiliently comes back.

For example, Schroeder is a leading advocate

Colorado 1

Denver

The 1st District, home to virtually all of Denver's half-million residents, is one of the few Democratic congressional strongholds in the Rocky Mountain region. Hispanics and blacks together make up about one-third of the district's population, and there is a strong liberal white-collar element.

A heavy Democratic vote in Denver often bails out the party's statewide candidates. In 1980 Sen. Gary Hart won the city by 50,000 votes, allowing him to lose the rest of the state by more than 30,000 and still hold his Senate seat. In 1990, Denver was one of the few jurisdictions that Democratic Senate candidate Josie Heath was able to carry in her unsuccessful challenge to Republican Hank Brown.

But with Denver's highly mobile population and the historic absence of a political machine, party roots are not deep and Democratic majorities are not always reliable. In 1988, Michael S. Dukakis became the first Democratic presidential candidate since 1964 to draw more than 51 percent of the Denver vote; he surpassed 60 percent. Ronald Reagan captured the city in 1980, as independent John B. Anderson took nearly 15 percent of the Denver vote, but Walter F. Mondale won it narrowly in 1984.

Denver's population dropped slightly in the 1980s, but the city retains its place as the Rocky Mountains' business center with its regional energy operations, federal government agencies and busy schedule of takeoffs and landings at Stapleton International Airport, which is soon to be replaced by a more modern facility.

Despite its scenic locale and casual, attractive lifestyle, Denver has serious problems. It is bedeviled by racial tensions, serious air pollution and an oil-dependent roller-coaster economy just beginning to climb out from the wreckage of the mid-1980s oil price crash. Local businessmen are hoping the new multibillion-dollar airport and a new 40,000-seat baseball stadium will help return the "Queen City of the Plains" to its full economic splendor.

Republican strength is concentrated in the middle- and upper-income neighborhoods of southeast Denver. Farther in that direction are newer subdivisions built in the hills along the Valley Highway (Interstate 25). Republicans also draw some votes downtown, where condominiums have mushroomed in the vicinity of Civil War-era Larimer Square.

Other parts of the city are reliably Democratic. Capitol Hills, perched on the eastern fringe of the downtown area, is home to a mixed population of students, young professionals and senior citizens. To the east and north are heavily black neighborhoods. Westward on the hills beyond the stockyards and the South Platte River live most of the city's Hispanics. The 1st also includes about 6,000 residents who live in Arapahoe County enclaves within the Denver city limits.

Population: 481,672. White 357,775 (74%), Black 59,330 (12%), Other 10,843 (2%). Spanish origin 91,194 (19%). 18 and over 373,579 (78%), 65 and over 61,524 (13%). Median age: 30.

of legislation that would require many employers to provide workers with unpaid leave time so they can care for newborns and relatives suffering from illness. In 1990, a family leave bill passed Congress, but was vetoed by President Bush, who called it burdensome for business. When the House upheld the veto, Schroeder — in a seeming reference to the song "We Shall Overcome" — said, "We shall override someday."

Even before gaining the chairmanship of Select Children, Schroeder had been trying to gain attention for a Democratic family agenda. She argues that Reagan established an image for Republicans as pro-family by opposing abortion and favoring "traditional" values, but cut nutrition, education and welfare programs that benefited children and families.

In early 1988, Schroeder led "The Great American Family Tour" through states with presidential primaries because, she said, no candidate "was really addressing these issues." As the 101st Congress began, she was promoting her book, "Champion of the Great American Family," which is part political discourse and part memoir about her experiences raising a family. With her long marriage and two clean-cut adult children, Schroeder's could be described as the traditional American family — except that Mom is the senior woman in the U.S. House of Representatives.

Schroeder's activist nature can be seen in her role on the Congressional Caucus on Women's Issues, which she co-chairs with GOP Rep. Olympia J. Snowe of Maine. In 1990, Schroeder and Snowe proposed a "women's health equity act" to create a Women's Health Research and Development office within the National Institutes of Health.

The caucus leaders also proposed in 1990

to expand federal research on contraception in what they described as an effort to find a middle ground on the divisive issue of family planning. However, this move did not signal a lessening of Schroeder's devotion to the abortion rights cause. During the 101st Congress, she asked the Supreme Court to uphold the 1973 *Roe v. Wade* decision that legalized abortion and asked the court to overturn restrictions, first instituted by Reagan, that bar federally funded family planning clinics from providing abortion counseling.

After the court's July 1989 *Webster* decision, which allowed states to limit access to abortions, Schroeder pledged to use her Judiciary Committee position to codify *Roe v. Wade*. "This is a wake-up call to all those Americans who didn't think they had to get involved," Schroeder said.

Also during the 101st Congress, Schroeder backed civil rights legislation seeking to expand protections against job discrimination and provide all women with some legal remedies currently available only to members of minority groups. Schroeder took a hardline position on the bill: When an amendment to cap monetary awards to job discrimination plaintiffs — a provision added in hopes of averting a Bush veto — was adopted in conference, Schroeder was one of four House Democrats to abstain in protest. Even with the cap, Bush vetoed the legislation anyway, calling it a "jobs quota" bill.

Schroeder's interest in women's issues extends to her activities on Armed Services. She is a longtime advocate of allowing women to serve in combat units, on grounds that current prohibitions against such service limit career advancement opportunities for women in the military. Although stymied for years, Schroeder gained some ground after a woman officer led a unit into combat during the 1989 Panama conflict. After a number of women performed dangerous assignments during the 1991 Persian Gulf War, Schroeder made a breakthrough.

During Armed Services deliberations on the fiscal 1992 defense authorization bill in May 1991, she proposed to allow women in the Air Force to volunteer to fly combat missions; she limited her amendment to the Air Force because that branch had expressed the most interest in such a move. But Democrat Beverly B. Byron of Maryland, the conservative chairman of the Military Personnel Subcommittee and a past opponent of women in combat, joined in and called for the amendment to include women in the Navy and the Marines. The amendment easily passed the committee.

This measure is an example of the more focused approach that may help Schroeder shed at least some of her reputation as a gadfly. She was ahead of most of her colleagues in calling for U.S. allies, including the NATO countries and Japan, to pick up more of the cost of their national defense. Under the currently straitened fiscal situation faced by Congress, the concept of burden-sharing has gained both currency and populist appeal.

But Schroeder remains active and best-known for her efforts as a representative of the Armed Services Committee's liberal wing. Since the beginnings of the military buildup under Reagan, Schroeder has been associated with such Democratic members as Downey, Ronald V. Dellums of California and Les AuCoin of Oregon in fights to institute nuclear test-ban laws and to end development of such controversial nuclear weapons systems as the MX missile. During the 101st Congress, she voted to slice funding for the strategic defense initiative and the B-2 bomber. In January 1991, she voted against authorizing the use of force to end Iraq's occupation of Kuwait.

Schroeder's strong advocacy role has made her relationship with Armed Services Chairman Les Aspin somewhat dicey. Both were anti-Vietnam War allies during the 1970s, and Schroeder supported Aspin when he led a successful coup to replace Democrat Melvin Price of Illinois, an aged "Old Guard" conservative, as chairman in 1985. Even after Aspin moved sharply to the center, supporting Reagan's position on MX missile deployment, Schroeder backed him in his successful 1987 defense against an intraparty revolt.

However, in 1989, Schroeder expressed the same complaint that drove the 1987 rebels: that Aspin was too willing to cut his own deals on defense issues with Republican administrations. During another debate over the MX missile in 1989, Schroeder complained, "People feel that they've been shut out of the loop." During the conference on the defense authorization bill later that year, Schroeder and Dellums persuaded the House Democratic leadership to give them a "veto" over any agreement that did not accommodate their views on at least some of the weapons systems in the bill.

The Military Installations Subcommittee that Schroeder chairs does not handle these big-picture defense issues. It does have jurisdiction, however, over military base closings. In 1989, Schroeder supported a base-closing list drawn up by a Defense Department commission as responsible and honest. Throughout the 101st Congress, she defended the procedure against efforts from members with affected districts to remove bases from the closing list.

However, in early 1991, another round of closings was proposed, and Schroeder took a more sanguine view: Denver's Lowry Air Force Base was slated for closure on the new list. "I will be scouring the Defense Department's submission to the commission to see if the decision to close Lowry is sound," Schroeder warned. "If I find anything wrong or questionable with what DOD did, and I expect to, I will raise it with the commission in the strongest way."

Schroeder's subcommittee chairmanship was hard won. Citing her seniority, she sought in 1985 to claim the Personnel Subcommittee chairmanship that Aspin vacated for the full committee chairmanship. But having criticized the seniority system throughout her career, she was hardly in a good position to take advantage of it. Resentful conservative Democrats on the panel threw their support to Byron, six years less senior than Schroeder.

Aspin then decided to keep the Personnel chair himself. When he gave it up two years later, Schroeder chose not to compete with Byron and kept the subcommittee chairmanship she held on the Post Office and Civil Service Committee. However, when Military Installations came open in 1989, she received Aspin's support and little opposition.

At Home: Schroeder was in the vanguard of the Democratic resurgence in Colorado in the early 1970s, scoring upset victories in the 1972 primary and general election to wrest the Denver House seat from Republican control.

Although she had been a practicing lawyer and women's rights activist, Schroeder was a political neophyte. She was encouraged to make the race by her lawyer husband, who had unsuccessfully sought a state House seat in 1970.

Cultivating support from liberals in Denver and feminists and environmentalists at the national level, Schroeder put together a strong grass-roots organization. She drew 55 percent of the vote against state Senate Minority Leader Arch Decker in the primary, and 52 percent in the fall against GOP Rep. James "Mike" McKevitt.

The GOP has fielded a variety of candidates against Schroeder since 1972, including an anti-busing leader, a veteran state legislator, a wealthy political newcomer, a prominent ex-Democrat, and in the last four elections, a succession of female women candidates.

The legislator, state Rep. Don Friedman, came the closest, in 1976. He sharply criticized Schroeder's liberal voting record and collected a campaign treasury that exceeded hers. He held her to 53 percent.

Since then, the Republican threat has subsided. Redistricting and population changes have tilted the district toward minority voters, and Schroeder draws on a coalition of liberals, young professionals, blacks and Hispanics.

Committees

Select Children, Youth & Families (Chairman)

Armed Services (5th of 33 Democrats)
Military Installations & Facilities (chairman); Research & Development

Judiciary (7th of 21 Democrats)
Civil & Constitutional Rights; Intellectual Property & Judicial Administration

Post Office & Civil Service (2nd of 15 Democrats)
Compensation & Employee Benefits

Elections

1990 General		
Patricia Schroeder (D)	82,176	(64%)
Gloria Gonzales Roemer (R)	46,802	(36%)
1988 General		
Patricia Schroeder (D)	133,922	(70%)
Joy Wood (R)	57,587	(30%)

Previous Winning Percentages: **1986** (68%) **1984** (62%) **1982** (60%) **1980** (60%) **1978** (62%) **1976** (53%) **1974** (59%) **1972** (52%)

District Vote For President

	1988	1984	1980	1976
D	124,659 (61%)	108,737 (51%)	81,640 (42%)	101,957 (48%)
R	73,915 (36%)	100,996 (47%)	81,196 (41%)	101,458 (48%)
I			27,128 (14%)	

Campaign Finance

	Receipts	Receipts from PACs	Expend-itures
1990			
Schroeder (D)	$441,609	$113,588 (26%)	$521,500
Roemer (R)	$162,502	$15,200 (9%)	$161,266
1988			
Schroeder (D)	$275,795	$131,785 (48%)	$217,503
Wood (R)	$26,529	$920 (3%)	$26,040

Key Votes

1991	
Authorize use of force against Iraq	N
1990	
Support constitutional amendment on flag desecration	N
Pass family and medical leave bill over Bush veto	Y
Reduce SDI funding	Y
Allow abortions in overseas military facilities	Y
Approve budget summit plan for spending and taxing	N
Approve civil rights bill	Y
1989	
Halt production of B-2 stealth bomber at 13 planes	Y
Oppose capital gains tax cut	Y
Approve federal abortion funding in rape or incest cases	Y
Approve pay raise and revision of ethics rules	N
Pass Democratic minimum wage plan over Bush veto	Y

Voting Studies

	Presidential Support		Party Unity		Conservative Coalition	
Year	**S**	**O**	**S**	**O**	**S**	**O**
1990	18	81	72	27	13	83
1989	19	79	67	31	17	80
1988	20	77	70	25	29	68
1987	13	81	68	25	23	70
1986	19	78	66	28	14	82
1985	30	69	58	39	24	76
1984	28	68	73	23	17	81
1983	11	84	81	16	18	78
1982	29	65	75	19	16	82
1981	29	70	76	21	12	85

Interest Group Ratings

Year	ADA	ACU	AFL-CIO	CCUS
1990	100	13	92	21
1989	100	11	92	40
1988	95	0	100	31
1987	76	9	64	27
1986	95	5	86	29
1985	80	19	71	55
1984	90	23	62	53
1983	85	17	76	20
1982	90	20	94	25
1981	95	13	80	6

2 David E. Skaggs (D)

Of Boulder — Elected 1986

Born: Feb. 22, 1943, Cincinnati, Ohio.

Education: Wesleyan U., B.A. 1964; Yale U., LL.B. 1967.

Military Service: Marine Corps, 1968-71; Marine Corps Reserve, 1971-77.

Occupation: Lawyer; congressional aide.

Family: Wife, Laura Locher; one child, two stepchildren.

Religion: Congregationalist.

Political Career: Colo. House, 1981-87, minority leader, 1983-85.

Capitol Office: 1507 Longworth Bldg. 20515; 225-2161.

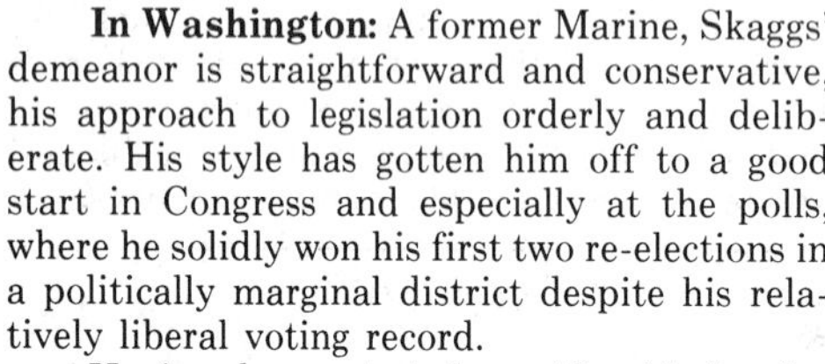

In Washington: A former Marine, Skaggs' demeanor is straightforward and conservative, his approach to legislation orderly and deliberate. His style has gotten him off to a good start in Congress and especially at the polls, where he solidly won his first two re-elections in a politically marginal district despite his relatively liberal voting record.

Having demonstrated considerable loyalty to the Democratic leadership, Skaggs snagged a plum in the 101st Congress — a seat on the Appropriations Committee. There he should be able to sustain the assiduous attention he gave to local concerns on his two prior committees, Science and Public Works.

He came to Washington with his sights set on Science, a valuable assignment because of the high-technology industry in his district. He lobbied for the seat and used it to help direct funds for superconductivity research at the National Bureau of Standards and for a new research laboratory of the National Oceanic and Atmospheric Administration in the 2nd.

In 1990, Skaggs worked to delay funding for plutonium processing at the Rocky Flats nuclear weapons plant pending a Department of Energy plan to improve safety. Environmentalists locally had backed a failed effort by Democrat Patricia Schroeder to cut funding outright.

On Public Works' Aviation Subcommittee, Skaggs was the point man in the House for Denver's proposed new airport, which is being built just outside his district. In the 100th Congress, he helped negotiate a deal allowing the city to sell some federally controlled land to help finance the project. He is also an advocate for building an annex of the Smithsonian Air and Space Museum on the site of Denver's Stapleton Airport, which is scheduled for closing in 1993.

At Home: After barely winning his first term in 1986, Skaggs has twice won re-election with more than 60 percent of the vote. Besides his own political skill, he has benefited from weak GOP opposition and perhaps an increasing comfort level among 2nd District voters who for years seemed iffy about sending Democrats to Congress.

In 1988 Skaggs faced GOP state Rep. David Bath, a conservative Christian activist and former Democrat; Jason Lewis, a self-described "William F. Buckley Republican" best known as the husband of a Denver TV anchorwoman, was Skaggs' opponent in 1990.

GOP foes have sought to pillory Skaggs as too liberal for the swing district's political mainstream. But as a Vietnam veteran, Skaggs has had considerable latitude in positioning himself, particularly on patriotic issues. He was the only member of the Colorado House delegation to join Democrat Pat Schroeder in opposing the proposed constitutional amendment banning desecration of the flag in 1990, and in opposing the use of military force in the Persian Gulf in January 1991.

Skaggs got into politics after moving to Colorado in 1971, becoming a precinct committeeman and then Democratic district chairman. That led him to Washington as the chief aide to Democratic Rep. Tim Wirth after the 1974 election. After a term, he moved back to Colorado and won a seat in the state House in 1980.

Skaggs' ties to Wirth and his high profile in the Boulder area made him a logical successor when Wirth ran for the Senate in 1986. He won the Democratic nomination handily, but went into the general election against Republican Mike Norton a 20-point underdog. Norton, a former regional administrator with the General Services Administration, had held Wirth to 53 percent of the vote in 1984 and had campaigned almost non-stop since. .

While quietly building an organization, Skaggs emulated Wirth's centrist approach to issues. In the fall he ran TV ads accusing Norton of inconsistency, gaining enough of a jump in the polls to help finance his final push.

Colorado 2

Northern Denver Suburbs; Boulder

The Colorado 2nd is rapidly emerging as a Rocky Mountain version of California's Silicon Valley. Nearly three-quarters of the district's voters live in Boulder County and in the populous portion of Adams County added in 1982 redistricting.

Broomfield, which sits on Boulder County's southern border, is bounded on one side by an AT&T research and manufacturing plant and the other by Storage Technology, which makes computer components. Fifteen miles due north is Longmont, a traditional market for sugar beet farmers that now has its fortunes linked to a large Hewlett-Packard plant nearby. Boulder itself, nestled against the Front Range of the Rockies, is the centerpiece of the county. While Boulder's population held steady between 1980 and 1986, Broomfield and Longmont each grew by nearly 20 percent.

An IBM research and manufacturing plant in Louisville, is a major employer, along with Ball Aerospace and government research outlets such as the National Oceanic and Atmospheric Administration. The academic community at the University of Colorado (23,000 students and 1,200 faculty) and the young professional work force create a strong vote in Boulder for liberal candidates.

Southeast of Boulder is suburban Adams County. Arvada is the most affluent of the county's suburbs in the 2nd District. The others, such as Westminster and Northglenn, tend to be blue-collar and have large Hispanic populations. About half of the district's land area — but little of its vote — is in the mountains west of Boulder in Clear Creek and Gilpin counties. Central City and the town of Black Hawk, two depressed small towns in Gilpin County, have instituted legalized gambling to escape their economic doldrums.

The Energy Department decided to abandon sections of the flawed Rocky Flats plutonium plant, shut down soon after its 1982 opening, and construct a new adjacent facility.

Population: 481,617. White 450,057 (94%), Black 3,919 (1%), Other 7,718 (2%). Spanish origin 41,944 (9%). 18 and over 339,617 (71%), 65 and over 25,890 (5%). Median age: 27.

Committees

Appropriations (35th of 37 Democrats)
Energy & Water Development; Treasury, Postal Service & General Government

Select Children, Youth & Families (15th of 22 Democrats)

Elections

1990 General		
David E. Skaggs (D)	105,248	(61%)
Jason Lewis (R)	68,226	(39%)
1988 General		
David E. Skaggs (D)	147,437	(63%)
David Bath (R)	87,578	(37%)

Previous Winning Percentage: **1986** (51%)

District Vote For President

	1988	1984	1980	1976
D	119,132 (50%)	83,357 (38%)	60,570 (33%)	76,702 (45%)
R	112,923 (48%)	130,543 (60%)	93,552 (50%)	84,997 (50%)
I			24,300 (13%)	

Campaign Finance

	Receipts	Receipts from PACs		Expenditures
1990				
Skaggs (D)	$415,235	$242,070	(58%)	$396,017
Lewis (R)	$49,679	$5,900	(12%)	$49,080
1988				
Skaggs (D)	$730,990	$452,772	(62%)	$721,647
Bath (R)	$93,581	$17,381	(19%)	$85,095

Key Votes

1991	
Authorize use of force against Iraq	N
1990	
Support constitutional amendment on flag desecration	N
Pass family and medical leave bill over Bush veto	Y
Reduce SDI funding	Y
Allow abortions in overseas military facilities	Y
Approve budget summit plan for spending and taxing	Y
Approve civil rights bill	Y
1989	
Halt production of B-2 stealth bomber at 13 planes	Y
Oppose capital gains tax cut	Y
Approve federal abortion funding in rape or incest cases	Y
Approve pay raise and revision of ethics rules	Y
Pass Democratic minimum wage plan over Bush veto	Y

Voting Studies

	Presidential Support		Party Unity		Conservative Coalition	
Year	**S**	**O**	**S**	**O**	**S**	**O**
1990	21	79	93	6	19	81
1989	35	65	94	6	22	78
1988	29	70	81	16	47	53
1987	24	76	91	9	35	65

Interest Group Ratings

Year	ADA	ACU	AFL-CIO	CCUS
1990	89	8	83	21
1989	85	7	83	30
1988	95	16	86	57
1987	84	9	81	33

3 Ben Nighthorse Campbell (D)

Of Ignacio — Elected 1986

Born: April 13, 1933, Auburn, Calif.

Education: San Jose State U., B.A. 1957; attended Meiji U., Tokyo, 1960-64.

Military Service: Air Force, 1952-54.

Occupation: Jewelry designer; rancher; horse trainer; teacher.

Family: Wife, Linda Price; two children.

Religion: Unspecified.

Political Career: Colo. House, 1983-87.

Capitol Office: 1530 Longworth Bldg. 20515; 225-4761.

In Washington: Campbell is an unconventional politician with an ample disrespect for conventional politics.

"People are sick and tired of plastic politicians — professional politicians who have done nothing else with their lives," Campbell said in his 1986 House campaign. Explaining in 1989 why he would not run for Colorado's open Senate seat in 1990, he told The Associated Press, "When you're honest, you get kicked in the teeth by special interests, and I'm not going to sell my integrity to raise the money." A daily reminder of his nonconformity is his attire: He has special permission to wear his trademark bolo tie on the House floor.

Campbell's unique personality showed through in an early 1991 encounter with a mugger near his Capitol Hill residence. Campbell had noticed a man following him for several blocks; when the mugger closed in and said he had a gun, Campbell demanded to see the weapon, then scuffled with the thief, who ran away. Campbell was slightly injured.

Legislatively speaking, Campbell's tenure in Washington has been less remarkable. He sits on Agriculture and Interior, good for the 3rd. His biggest first-term achievement was a bill to implement a settlement of Colorado Ute Indian water rights and pave the way for construction of the Animas-La Plata water project. It passed the House and became law.

Campbell says he will continue in the 102nd Congress to push for settlement of Colorado's decade-long dispute over designating wilderness areas. His acreage proposal in the 101st fell between those of Colorado's senators, Democrat Tim Wirth and now-retired Republican William L. Armstrong.

Campbell's father was Northern Cheyenne, making Campbell the first congressman to be half Indian since South Dakota Republican Ben Reifel left in 1971. "Indians have never had any political clout and very little voice in congressional matters," he has said.

Campbell was a member of the U.S. judo team at the 1964 Olympics and raises cattle on a Western Slope ranch. A craftsman of contemporary Indian jewelry, he is one of the few practicing artists in the Congressional Arts Caucus. Campbell has said he intends to serve only four House terms; he backed a 1990 Colorado ballot initiative to limit the terms of state and federal officeholders.

At Home: A narrow winner in 1986, Campbell quickly established himself and won in 1988 with three-fourths of the vote, a record for a Colorado Democratic House member. He was seriously discussed as a candidate for the Senate in 1990, but declined to run.

Campbell's vote fell just a shade in 1990, partly because of his opposition to the Nucla-Naturita Prairie Dog Shoot that summer. Many voters in western Montrose County, site of the event, began calling the incumbent "Ben Nightmare Campbell," and the precincts that included the tiny towns were the only ones in the 3rd to vote against him.

But if Campbell is persona non grata in Nucla and Naturita, he has the kind of individualist streak that often characterizes successful politicians on Colorado's Western Slope. In 1982, he ran for the state House from a conservative district while wearing a ponytail — and won. Two years later, he snipped it off and auctioned the hair to raise money.

In the Legislature, he was a dependable vote for farmers and ranchers on water rights issues. Though he occasionally sided with environmentalists, Campbell's views put him among conservatives in the Democratic Caucus.

That positioned Campbell well for his 1986 challenge to GOP Rep. Mike Strang. To win the 3rd, a Democrat must draw a big vote in blue-collar Pueblo, then hold his own on the conservative Western Slope; Campbell did that.

Strang geared up for a 1990 rematch, but instead sought the gubernatorial nomination, leaving Campbell with token opposition.

Colorado 3

Western Slope; Pueblo

This huge, mountainous district covers the Republican-oriented western half of the state and two predominantly Democratic areas to the east — populous Pueblo County and the largely Hispanic San Luis Valley.

Most of the votes are on the Western Slope of the Rockies, a booming energy center in the 1970s where growth has tapered off in recent years. The scenic Western Slope still contains the bulk of Colorado's vast mineral wealth. Democrats or independents have a registration advantage in many of the Western Slope counties, but there are more Republicans in the three most populous counties — Mesa, La Plata and Montrose. Scattered resort areas, such as Pitkin (Aspen) and San Miguel (Telluride) counties regularly supply Democratic candidates with votes.

As one moves north out of the forested mountains into open Western Slope ranch land, the GOP vote increases, as does the standard of living in good oil years. There are rich oil shale reserves in Colorado's northwest corner, and large coal deposits are located to the east. Grand Junction (population 29,000), the trade center for local energy operations, is the area's largest city.

Democrats are competitive in the 3rd because of the presence of Pueblo, the state's fifth-largest city (population 99,000); it casts one-quarter of the district's vote. Pueblo is a steel-producing town and the hub of union activity in Colorado. Climbing back after years of industrial decline, the city now has a more diversified economy that has wrestled unemployment rates down from a high of almost 20 percent in the early 1980s, to just over 8 percent by the end of the decade.

South of Pueblo is the San Luis Valley, an isolated lettuce- and potato-growing region that is the poorest part of the state. The area favors Democrats; two of the valley counties have Hispanic majorities.

Population: 481,854. White 436,299 (91%), Black 3,198 (1%), Other 6,648 (1%). Spanish origin 82,499 (17%). 18 and over 345,175 (72%), 65 and over 49,403 (10%). Median age: 29.

Committees

Agriculture (20th of 27 Democrats)
Department Operations, Research & Foreign Agriculture; Livestock, Dairy & Poultry

Interior & Insular Affairs (20th of 29 Democrats)
Mining & Natural Resources; National Parks & Public Lands; Water, Power & Offshore Energy

Elections

1990 General		
Ben Nighthorse Campbell (D)	124,487	(70%)
Bob Ellis (R)	49,961	(28%)
Howard E. Fields (POP Colorado)	2,859	(2%)
1988 General		
Ben Nighthorse Campbell (D)	169,284	(78%)
Jim Zartman (R)	47,625	(22%)

Previous Winning Percentage: **1986** (52%)

District Vote For President

	1988	1984	1980	1976
D	101,242 (46%)	76,712 (36%)	61,341 (33%)	74,039 (43%)
R	113,607 (52%)	132,109 (63%)	106,846 (57%)	92,478 (54%)
I			15,036 (8%)	

Campaign Finance

	Receipts	Receipts from PACs	Expend-itures
1990			
Campbell (D)	$310,176	$215,980 (70%)	$335,760
Ellis (R)	$27,049	$7,600 (28%)	$26,917
1988			
Campbell (D)	$519,957	$302,590 (58%)	$489,534
Zartman (R)	$17,937	0	$17,936

Key Votes

1991	
Authorize use of force against Iraq	Y
1990	
Support constitutional amendment on flag desecration	Y
Pass family and medical leave bill over Bush veto	N
Reduce SDI funding	Y
Allow abortions in overseas military facilities	Y
Approve budget summit plan for spending and taxing	N
Approve civil rights bill	Y
1989	
Halt production of B-2 stealth bomber at 13 planes	N
Oppose capital gains tax cut	N
Approve federal abortion funding in rape or incest cases	Y
Approve pay raise and revision of ethics rules	N
Pass Democratic minimum wage plan over Bush veto	N

Voting Studies

	Presidential Support		Party Unity		Conservative Coalition	
Year	S	O	S	O	S	O
1990	35	64	72	23	67	31
1989	45	50	70	25	66	32
1988	26	65	85	11	47	45
1987	34	66	78	18	65	33

Interest Group Ratings

Year	ADA	ACU	AFL-CIO	CCUS
1990	56	33	67	77
1989	50	36	64	60
1988	65	21	92	43
1987	64	9	88	40

4 Wayne Allard (R)

Of Loveland — Elected 1990

Born: Dec. 2, 1943, Fort Collins, Colo.
Education: Colorado State U., D.V.M. 1968.
Occupation: Veterinarian.
Family: Wife, Joan Malcolm; two children.
Religion: Protestant.
Political Career: Colo. Senate, 1983-91.
Capitol Office: 513 Cannon Bldg. 20515; 225-4676.

The Path to Washington: As Hank Brown's successor in the 4th, Allard may not be the new Republican senator's clone, but he should provide a similar type of representation.

Both are fairly conservative legislators with moderate temperaments. They share a common forte of quiet consensus-building rather than forceful presentation of issues.

Both Brown and Allard started their political careers in the Colorado Senate, and it did not take long for either man to climb the legislative ladder. Two years after Brown was elected to that body, he was its assistant majority leader. Two years after Allard took office, he was the GOP Senate caucus chairman (generally regarded as the No. 3 post in the party leadership).

As caucus chairman, Allard quietly marshaled support for party positions. But he was rarely out front on controversial issues himself. On Senate roll calls earlier this year, he often passed, leading Colorado legislative reporters to joke that he was waiting to commit himself until he had seen how state Sen. Jim Brandon, his rival in the GOP primary, would vote. Allard denied anything so Machiavellian, saying that with his name at the beginning of the roll call, he often needed more time to consider his vote.

Whatever the case, Allard has been publicly consistent in his support of efforts to limit government — from trimming regulations on small businesses to imposing term limits on legislators. One of the few high-profile issues he championed in the state Senate was a constitutional amendment to limit legislative sessions to 120 days (later approved by Colorado voters in a referendum).

During his eight years in the state Senate, Allard divided his time between the Legislature, his Loveland veterinary practice and constituent contact. According to his own tally, he held 130 "early bird" breakfasts with voters during his state Senate career, gatherings that often began at 6 a.m.

But quiet and mild-mannered, Allard was never particularly close to his peers and by all accounts was ready to quit the state Senate in 1990, even if that meant a temporary retirement from politics.

The situation changed, though, when Brown decided to risk his safe House seat for a run at the Senate. Allard had managed Brown's House re-election campaigns in 1984 and 1986 and was eager to run for Congress himself. He was well positioned for a House campaign. In both the primary against Brandon and the fall campaign against Democratic state Rep. Dick Bond, Allard had the advantage of geography. He had a strong base in populous Larimer County (Fort Collins), home to approximately one-third of the district population.

And he could appeal for votes in the far-flung rural areas of the district by pointing to his upbringing on a ranch, involvement in 4-H and service on the state Senate's Agriculture Committee. In addition, he stressed his fifth-generation Colorado roots and links to the popular Brown.

Still, neither the primary nor the general election was easy; in neither did Allard top 55 percent of the vote.

Brandon, a farmer and rancher, portrayed himself as a feisty legislative activist who would rattle some cages in Washington; he had strong support from a number of his legislative colleagues.

Bond, a professional biologist and former president of the University of Northern Colorado in Greeley, was strongly backed by the state and national Democratic parties, which saw him as ideally suited to win the normally Republican district.

In both contests, the clearest difference between Allard and his opponents arose over the abortion issue. Brandon and Bond both defended abortion rights; Allard maintained that abortion should be allowed only in cases of rape or incest or when the woman's life was at risk. That stance won him the support of anti-abortion activists, whose help was considered crucial in his primary victory.

Colorado 4

North and East — Fort Collins; Greeley

The 4th is Colorado's breadbasket, home of the state's agricultural heartland and its major farm markets.

Most of the voters live near the northern flank of the Front Range in Larimer (Fort Collins) and Weld (Greeley) counties. Both are educational and trade centers for agricultural northern Colorado, an area that was once one of the nation's top suppliers of sugar beets. As beet prices dropped, many farmers switched to corn or beans.

With nearly one-third of the district population, Larimer County is the larger, faster growing and more diverse of the two. Newcomers have been drawn by the spillover of high-tech firms from the Boulder area to Fort Collins and Loveland and the academic community at Colorado State University in Fort Collins (20,000 students).

To the east, on the fringe of the Great Plains, Weld County is more dependent on agriculture. Influenced by German and Russian immigration in the 19th century, it is also home to a large community of Hispanic truck farmers. Hispanics comprise nearly a fifth of the Weld County population.

The University of Northern Colorado (9,600 students) is in Greeley, but ranching is crucial to life in Weld County. Greeley is the home base of Montfort of Colorado, Brown's former employer and one of the largest feed lots and packing plants in the country. Small, family-run competitors dot the county.

The territorial heart of the 4th is the eastern plains, a vast agricultural region that covers one-third of the state but casts barely 30 percent of the district vote. Kit Carson and Cheyenne counties saw fortunes rise and fall in the 1980s; they were hit hard when the farm economy was down, but profited when local oil production doubled before leveling out again by the end of the decade. Like neighboring Nebraska and Kansas, this area is conservative and heavily Republican. But it has been a center of agrarian ferment — in the small community of Springfield, in Baca County, the American Agricultural Movement was born in the mid-1970s.

Most of the Democratic votes in the 4th are concentrated in the southern portion of the district. Las Animas County, which straddles the New Mexico border, is nearly half Hispanic, and is one of only two counties that went decisively for Democrat Dick Bond over Republican Wayne Allard in the 1990 House election.

Population: 481,512. White 441,718 (92%), Black 2,364 (1%), Other 5,429 (1%). Spanish origin 65,848 (14%). 18 and over 342,745 (71%), 65 and over 49,097 (10%). Median age: 28.

Committees

Agriculture (14th of 18 Republicans)
Conservation, Credit & Rural Development; Department Operations, Research & Foreign Agriculture; Livestock, Dairy & Poultry

Interior & Insular Affairs (16th of 17 Republicans)
Energy & the Environment; Water, Power & Offshore Energy

Small Business (15th of 17 Republicans)
Antitrust, Impact of Deregulation & Ecology; SBA, the General Economy & Minority Enterprise Development

Campaign Finance

	Receipts	Receipts from PACs		Expend-itures
1990				
Allard (R)	$363,633	$174,550	(48%)	$360,206
Bond (D)	$486,762	$255,580	(53%)	$481,666

Key Vote

1991

Authorize use of force against Iraq	Y

Elections

1990 General		
Wayne Allard (R)	89,285	(54%)
Dick Bond (D)	75,901	(46%)
1990 Primary		
Wayne Allard (R)	18,592	(56%)
Jim Brandon (R)	14,826	(44%)

District Vote For President

	1988	1984	1980	1976
D	95,025 (44%)	65,303 (31%)	58,221 (29%)	76,026 (42%)
R	119,554 (55%)	139,545 (67%)	115,469 (58%)	99,766 (55%)
I			20,455 (10%)	

5 Joel Hefley (R)

Of Colorado Springs — Elected 1986

Born: April 18, 1935, Ardmore, Okla.
Education: Oklahoma Baptist U., B.A. 1957; Oklahoma State U., M.S. 1962.
Occupation: Community planner.
Family: Wife, Lynn Christian; three children.
Religion: Presbyterian.
Political Career: Colo. House, 1977-79; Colo. Senate, 1979-87.
Capitol Office: 222 Cannon Bldg. 20515; 225-4422.

In Washington: Hefley is a pro-defense Republican from a district that includes the Air Force Academy and research facilities for the strategic defense initiative (SDI). His leanings were evident during debate on whether the United States should go to war with Iraq.

Hefley voted for the January 1991 resolution authorizing President Bush to use force to end Iraq's occupation of Kuwait. However, when the House Democratic leadership, after the outbreak of war, moved a resolution to support Bush and the U.S. troops in the Persian Gulf region, Hefley denounced it as a "gimmick." He said the Democrats were trying "to save their backsides because the majority of them failed to support the president" on the war resolution.

While others on the Armed Services Committee doubt SDI's feasibility and have targeted the program for cutbacks, Hefley — who took an Armed Services seat in the 101st Congress — has tried to hold the line. In 1987, Hefley's lobbying helped salvage funding for an SDI research center at Falcon Air Force Station in the 5th.

Hefley also obtained an Interior Committee seat for the 102nd Congress. He is trying to obtain federal money to treat water runoff from the Leadville Mine Drainage Tunnel, which contains such heavy metals as lead and iron.

On occasion, Hefley's views on social issues get a public airing. Following the 1989 massacre of pro-democracy protesters in Beijing, the House debated a bill lifting visa restrictions on Chinese students who wanted to remain in the United States. Although the measure was aimed at democracy movement activists, Hefley pushed through an amendment extending protections to students affected by China's "one child" policies, which at times require abortion.

Once an advocate of congressional term limits, Hefley now sees term limits as "un-American." He says, "I came here to give Americans more freedom, not less." But he plans to serve no more than 12 years in the House.

At Home: A business-oriented legislator who lists calf-roping as one of his hobbies, Hefley seems a good fit for the 5th, which combines affluent white-collar suburbs with cattle-ranching areas and mountain communities. But unlike his predecessor, Ken Kramer, Hefley is not known as a "movement conservative," which caused him some difficulty when he first sought this seat.

Hefley entered the 1986 contest as the front-runner. After 10 years in the Legislature, he was widely known in his Colorado Springs base, site of the Air Force Academy and other underpinnings of the "military-industrial complex." But while his legislative record satisfied his mainly conservative constituency, Hefley generally avoided lining up with the Legislature's ideological right. His display of what some considered "moderate tendencies" set the stage for a tough primary challenge from millionaire Harold A. Krause, a Republican national committeeman from the Denver suburbs. Hefley tried to portray himself as the candidate with "proven experience," and Krause as a novice "who's trying to buy his way to the top." But he found his years of experience being used against him. Krause maintained that if legislative experience alone could solve the country's problems, "we'd already have a balanced budget and no trade deficit."

Krause had one tactical advantage: money. It allowed him to wage a serious TV campaign in Colorado Springs, while the high cost of media in the Denver suburbs made it difficult for Hefley to raid Krause's suburban base. In the end, though, money was not enough. Hefley hit pay dirt by appealing to the parochialism of El Paso County voters, reminding them that electing Krause would give the Denver area four House members. In November, Hefley had no trouble with Democratic businessman Bill Story.

In 1988, Kramer threatened a comeback, vaguely complaining that Hefley was not a strong enough advocate of SDI. But he was persuaded to drop his challenge and offered a political appointment in the Department of the Army. Hefley was re-elected handily, as he was in 1990.

Colorado 5

South Central — Colorado Springs

The solidly Republican 5th revolves around Colorado Springs, the state's second-largest city and the southern anchor of the rapidly growing Front Range. Originally a resort whose sunny climate and proximity to Pikes Peak drew tourists from the East, the Front Range now has a more diversified economy and a fast-growing population that by 1990 had reached 280,000.

Tourism remains the keystone of the local economy. But after World War II, Colorado Springs emerged as a center of military operations in the Rocky Mountains. To the north is the Air Force Academy; east is Peterson Air Force Base; south is Fort Carson; and deep in a mountain to the west is NORAD (the North American Air Defense Command), maintaining a round-the-clock alert for an enemy attack.

To this impressive lineup of military installations, Colorado Springs has added the Air Force's new Space Command at Peterson and the Consolidated Space Operations Complex at the Falcon Air Force Station.

At the same time, electronics firms have been moving to the area in large numbers. Among the major employers are Hewlett-Packard and Digital Corp.

Yet while the economic base has broadened, the politics of Colorado Springs have remained consistently conservative. El Paso County (Colorado Springs) went 3-to-1 for George Bush in 1988.

The large military work force, augmented by a sizable number of military retirees, has made the Colorado Springs area one of the most reliable bastions of conservative Republicanism in the state.

North of El Paso County are suburban Denver communities in southwest Jefferson, southwest Arapahoe and Douglas counties. All have Republican voting habits. Jefferson County's major community within the district is Golden, the site of the Colorado School of Mines, the Adolph Coors brewery and Buffalo Bill's grave.

The rest of the 5th's voters live in Elbert County, a cattle-ranching area inhabited by rock-ribbed Republicans, and in sparsely populated mountain counties between Colorado Springs and the Continental Divide. Ranching, mining and tourism are mainstays of the mountain economy.

Population: 481,627. White: 436,996 (91%), Black 19,829 (4%), Other 8,472 (2%). Spanish origin 32,707 (7%). 18 and over 335,156 (70%), 65 and over 30,725 (6%). Median age: 28.

Committees

Armed Services (17th of 22 Republicans)
Investigations; Procurement & Military Nuclear Systems

Interior & Insular Affairs (13th of 17 Republicans)
Energy & the Environment; National Parks & Public Lands

Small Business (8th of 17 Republicans)
Antitrust, Impact of Deregulation & Ecology (ranking)

Elections

1990 General		
Joel Hefley (R)	127,740	(66%)
Cal Johnston (D)	57,776	(30%)
Keith L. Hamburger (LIBERT)	6,761	(4%)
1988 General		
Joel Hefley (R)	181,612	(75%)
John J. Mitchell (D)	60,116	(25%)

Previous Winning Percentages: **1986** (70%)

District Vote For President

	1988	1984	1980	1976
D	78,785 (31%)	50,683 (24%)	47,248 (25%)	64,460 (39%)
R	168,390 (67%)	155,688 (75%)	121,490 (64%)	94,920 (58%)
I			17,123 (9%)	

Campaign Finance

	Receipts	Receipts from PACs	Expend-itures
1990			
Hefley (R)	$135,707	$114,981 (85%)	$111,435
Johnston (D)	$15,313	$6,143 (40%)	$15,288
1988			
Hefley (R)	$228,896	$112,827 (49%)	$183,229
Mitchell (D)	$961	0	$930

Key Votes

1991	
Authorize use of force against Iraq	Y
1990	
Support constitutional amendment on flag desecration	Y
Pass family and medical leave bill over Bush veto	N
Reduce SDI funding	N
Allow abortions in overseas military facilities	N
Approve budget summit plan for spending and taxing	N
Approve civil rights bill	N
1989	
Halt production of B-2 stealth bomber at 13 planes	N
Oppose capital gains tax cut	N
Approve federal abortion funding in rape or incest cases	N
Approve pay raise and revision of ethics rules	N
Pass Democratic minimum wage plan over Bush veto	N

Voting Studies

	Presidential Support		Party Unity		Conservative Coalition	
Year	**S**	**O**	**S**	**O**	**S**	**O**
1990	71	29	90	6	91	9
1989	65	31	89	9	90	5
1988	60	35	91	8	92	3
1987	71	29	85	12	81	14

Interest Group Ratings

Year	ADA	ACU	AFL-CIO	CCUS
1990	6	92	0	79
1989	5	93	17	100
1988	5	100	7	100
1987	4	96	6	100

6 Dan Schaefer (R)

Of Lakewood — Elected 1983

Born: Jan. 25, 1936, Guttenberg, Iowa.
Education: Niagara U., B.A. 1961; attended State U. of New York at Potsdam, 1961-64.
Military Service: Marine Corps, 1955-57.
Occupation: Public relations consultant.
Family: Wife, Mary Lenney; four children.
Religion: Roman Catholic.
Political Career: Colo. House, 1977-79; Colo. Senate, 1979-83, president pro tempore, 1981-83.
Capitol Office: 1007 Longworth Bldg. 20515; 225-7882.

In Washington: Though Schaefer held an influential position in the Colorado Senate, in Washington he kept a fairly low profile on the very high-profile Energy and Commerce Committee, until the 102nd Congress.

When a bill to re-regulate the cable television industry emerged at the start of the session, Schaefer took a lead role on the committee in opposition. His district includes a number of headquarters for national cable operators; that, plus the urging of the Bush administration, led Schaefer to act. In the 101st Congress, Schaefer had warned that it was "clearly not in the public interest to reshackle this important source of information and entertainment."

Schaefer has a reputation as a party loyalist, if a rather diffident one. Home-state politics, however, forced him to part from Reagan-era GOP rhetoric on the clean air legislation. Late in 1988 Schaefer gave a rare speech on the House floor urging his colleagues to act on the bill and stressing the "need for a strong federal role in improving the environment." Air quality is a severe problem in the Denver metropolitan area and Schaefer backed alternative automotive fuels. In 1990, he was able to get language included in the bill to extend alternative fuel mandates for commercial fleet vehicles to Denver and other high-altitude cities.

With the other Denver-area House members, Schaefer also pushed for continued federal funding for the C-470 beltway being built around Denver. Schaefer saw the October 1990 completion of the 26-mile project following Congress' clearing of the final $9.1 million in funding for the beltway.

The 1988 collapse of Silverado, a Denver-based savings and loan, focused attention on the state's congressional delegation. In a decision aimed at distancing himself from S&L contributions and bolstering public confidence, Schaefer donated $3,600 in campaign funds to the federal government's debt-reduction fund.

At Home: Schaefer may lack star quality and a long list of legislative accomplishments, but he has proved a good fit for his suburban constituency. The 6th was a brand-new district in 1982, added as a result of reapportionment and carved for a Republican. Though interested, Schaefer deferred to Jack Swigert, the popular former Apollo astronaut. Swigert won but died of cancer before he was sworn in.

When Schaefer entered the special election to fill the vacancy, his biggest hurdle was the GOP nomination. Aided by national conservative GOP leaders, Schaefer won a fourth-ballot victory at a district convention in January 1983 and has won re-election ever since.

In 1988, the Democrats recruited a candidate they thought could wrest the 6th from Schaefer: former GOP state Sen. Martha Ezzard. A fiscal conservative, she was also known as an outspoken environmentalist and feminist. This appealed to her affluent Cherry Hills district, but not the Legislature's conservative GOP hierarchy, causing her to quit the party and the Legislature in 1987.

Against Schaefer, Ezzard quickly proved her prowess as a fundraiser and won headlines dubbing the incumbent "the invisible congressman." Schaefer defended his style as "quietly effective," championed his efforts to secure federal funds for local programs and claimed Ezzard would raise taxes. Ezzard badly underestimated the GOP loyalty of the district's voters and the draw of Schaefer's parochial focus; she lost by 60,000 votes. In 1990, he had only token Democratic opposition.

Schaefer came late to politics. The Iowa-born son of a construction worker, he was raised in North Dakota and educated in New York. After several years as a high school history teacher, he moved to Colorado and opened a public relations firm. Schaefer assisted the campaigns of other local GOP candidates and then successfully ran for the state House in 1976. Two years later he moved up to the state Senate. Personable and unflappable, he became its president pro tem in 1981. When he ran for Congress, he was assistant Senate majority leader.

Colorado 6

Denver Suburbs — Aurora; Lakewood

The 6th forms a "U" around Denver on the east, south and west, catching the homes of most white-collar commuters, while missing the working-class suburbs to the north. As electronics and engineering firms have moved to the suburbs, the population has ballooned and Republicans have thrived. In both 1980 and 1984, Reagan ran better in this district than he did statewide, as did George Bush in 1988. More than half the population of the 6th lives south and east of Denver in Arapahoe County. Another 40 percent lives west of the city in Jefferson County, with the remainder divided between part of Denver itself and a portion of Adams County northeast of the city.

The 6th's largest community is Aurora, which lies east of Denver, straddling the Adams-Arapahoe county line. The smaller Adams County portion of Aurora, one of the 6th's few minority enclaves, is the only part of the district that could be considered Democratic. Aurora's Arapahoe County portion, more affluent and Republican, has largely caused Aurora's 40 percent growth in the 1980s, bringing it to 222,000. Cheap land and an independent water supply have lured developers.

South of Denver are Cherry Hills Village and Greenwood Village, two affluent communities and the backbone of conservative Republicanism in the suburbs. Near Greenwood Village is the Denver Tech Center, a large complex of professional offices and leading commuter destination. To the west are Englewood and Sheridan, both older, politically marginal suburbs.

The areas west of Denver in Jefferson County are a mix of business executives, government employees and factory workers; most vote Republican even though not all are hard-line conservatives. The 6th also includes about 16,500 residents in southwest Denver, a center of 1970s anti-busing sentiment.

Population: 481,682. White 448,653 (93%), Black 13,063 (3%), Other 8,874 (2%). Spanish origin 25,525 (5%). 18 and over 344,879 (72%), 65 and over 30,686 (6%). Median age: 29.

Committees

Energy & Commerce (10th of 16 Republicans)
Oversight & Investigations; Telecommunications & Finance; Transportation & Hazardous Materials

Elections

1990 General		
Dan Schaefer (R)	105,312	(65%)
Don Jarrett (D)	57,961	(35%)
1988 General		
Dan Schaefer (R)	136,487	(63%)
Martha M. Ezzard (D)	77,158	(36%)

Previous Winning Percentages: **1986** (65%) **1984** (89%) **1983 *** (63%)

** Special election.*

District Vote For President

	1988		1984		1980		1976	
D	97,029	(42%)	65,615	(30%)	51,629	(26%)	60,365	(37%)
R	128,649	(56%)	148,388	(68%)	117,916	(60%)	100,216	(61%)
I					23,425	(12%)		

Campaign Finance

	Receipts	Receipts from PACs		Expend-itures
1990				
Schaefer (R)	$375,683	$229,103	(61%)	$280,103
Jarrett (D)	$2,295	0		$2,958
1988				
Schaefer (R)	$618,607	$335,747	(54%)	$636,204
Ezzard (D)	$493,515	$134,339	(27%)	$489,303

Key Votes

1991	
Authorize use of force against Iraq	Y
1990	
Support constitutional amendment on flag desecration	Y
Pass family and medical leave bill over Bush veto	N
Reduce SDI funding	N
Allow abortions in overseas military facilities	N
Approve budget summit plan for spending and taxing	N
Approve civil rights bill	N
1989	
Halt production of B-2 stealth bomber at 13 planes	N
Oppose capital gains tax cut	N
Approve federal abortion funding in rape or incest cases	N
Approve pay raise and revision of ethics rules	N
Pass Democratic minimum wage plan over Bush veto	N

Voting Studies

	Presidential Support		Party Unity		Conservative Coalition	
Year	S	O	S	O	S	O
1990	64	36	88	11	89	9
1989	69	29	84	12	88	2
1988	56	41	82	17	87	8
1987	65	27	89	7	79	12
1986	76	21	84	11	90	4
1985	76	20	84	10	91	4
1984	70	30	93	6	95	5
1983	74 †	20 †	93 †	5 †	92 †	7 †

† Not eligible for all recorded votes.

Interest Group Ratings

Year	ADA	ACU	AFL-CIO	CCUS
1990	11	79	25	79
1989	5	89	25	90
1988	15	83	50	71
1987	8	87	19	86
1986	0	95	15	88
1985	10	80	13	91
1984	10	92	8	81
1983	0	100	7	76

Connecticut

U.S. CONGRESS

SENATE 2 D
HOUSE 3 D, 3 R

LEGISLATURE

Senate 20 D, 16 R
House 89 D, 62 R

ELECTIONS

1988 Presidential Vote

Bush	52%
Dukakis	47%

1984 Presidential Vote

Reagan	61%
Mondale	39%

1980 Presidential Vote

Reagan	48%
Carter	39%
Anderson	12%

Turnout rate in 1986	40%
Turnout rate in 1988	58%
Turnout rate in 1990	41%

(as percentage of voting age population)

POPULATION AND GROWTH

1980 population	3,107,576
1990 population (27th in the nation)	3,287,116
Percent change 1980-1990	+6%

DEMOGRAPHIC BREAKDOWN

White	87%
Black	8%
Asian or Pacific Islander	2%
(Hispanic origin)	7%
Urban	79%
Rural	21%
Born in state	58%
Foreign-born	9%

MAJOR CITIES

Bridgeport	141,686
Hartford	139,739
New Haven	130,474
Waterbury	108,961
Stamford	108,056

AREA AND LAND USE

Area 4,872 sq. miles (48th)

Farm	14%
Forest	59%
Federally owned	0.4%

Gov. Lowell P. Weicker Jr. (I)
Of Greenwich — Elected 1990

Born: May 16, 1931, Paris, France.
Education: Yale U., B.A. 1953; U. of Virginia, LL.B. 1958.
Military Service: Army, 1953-55; Army Reserve, 1959-64.
Occupation: Lawyer.
Religion: Episcopalian.
Political Career: Conn. House, 1963-69; first selectman of Greenwich, 1963-67; U.S. House, 1969-71; U.S. Senate, 1971-1989.
Next Election: 1994.

WORK

Occupations

White-collar	58%
Blue-collar	30%
Service workers	11%

Government Workers

Federal	24,242
State	66,911
Local	110,161

MONEY

Median family income	$ 23,149	(2nd)
Tax burden per capita	$ 1,102	(8th)

EDUCATION

Spending per pupil through grade 12	$ 6,230	(4th)
Persons with college degrees	21%	(3rd)

CRIME

Violent crime rate 512 per 100,000 (22nd)

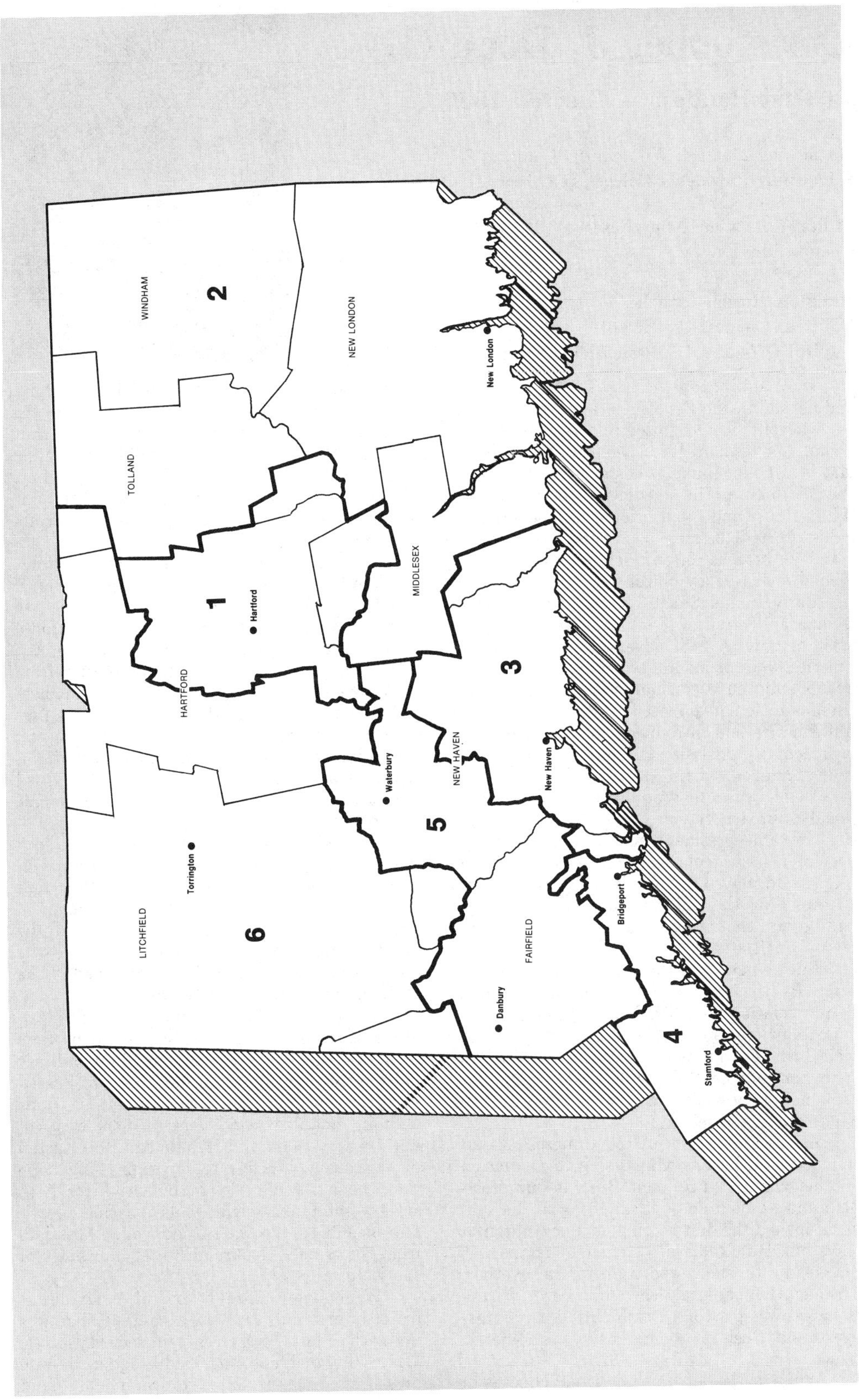
WINDHAM
2
NEW LONDON
New London
TOLLAND
MIDDLESEX
1
Hartford
HARTFORD
3
NEW HAVEN
New Haven
Waterbury
5
Torrington
LITCHFIELD
6
FAIRFIELD
Bridgeport
Danbury
4
Stamford

Christopher J. Dodd (D)

Of East Haddam — Elected 1980

Born: May 27, 1944, Willimantic, Conn.
Education: Providence College, B.A. 1966; U. of Louisville, J.D. 1972.
Military Service: Army Reserve, 1969-75.
Occupation: Lawyer.
Family: Divorced.
Religion: Roman Catholic.
Political Career: U.S. House, 1975-81.
Capitol Office: 444 Russell Bldg. 20510; 224-2823.

In Washington: As Dodd enters his second decade in the Senate, he appears eager to move beyond his recognized role as a thoughtful liberal spokesman to become a full-fledged player in policy-making. His strategy has been one of high-profile mediation between the White House and congressional Democrats, but in his efforts to be more conciliatory and statesmanlike, he has often yielded considerable ground in his policy objectives.

Early in his Senate career, Dodd was a leading and often strident spokesman against what he saw as U.S. adventurism in Central America, and for federal efforts to improve the lives of children. A constant critic of the Reagan administration, he opposed military aid to Central America and introduced some of the most far-reaching legislation to aid families with young children.

Dodd began to tone down his confrontational approach in early 1989, when George Bush became president and offered the prospect of a less ideological White House. That year, Dodd played a key role in Bush's victory on providing U.S. military aid to El Salvador and began negotiating toward passage of "pro-family" legislation.

But he never got the upper hand on either front: By the end of 1990, continued human rights violations in El Salvador pushed Dodd back to his opposition role on the issue; he had seen Bush veto a parental leave bill; and to win enactment of a child-care bill, Dodd stripped it of numerous provisions that were important to child-care advocates.

At the start of the 102nd Congress, Dodd sounded as if he was willing to give mediation another chance. "President Bush is our president and we hold no political grudges," he said as he opened the first hearing on a new parental leave bill. But Dodd also signaled that he was not ready to shelve partisanship altogether: Pushing the parental leave bill early in the Congress was part of a Democratic Party strategy to put Bush on the defensive on domestic issues.

Whatever leadership style Dodd chooses to employ, one thing about his work is consistent: He is a purposeful legislator who masters the details of issues important to him. That trait has helped minimize negative fallout stemming from his reputation as something of a playboy: Dodd is widely known on Capitol Hill for his after-hours merry-making with Massachusetts Sen. Edward M. Kennedy.

Dodd's interest in Central America dates back to his days as a Peace Corps volunteer in the Dominican Republic, where he learned to speak Spanish fluently. But his effort to find a middle ground on aid to El Salvador in the 101st Congress was a marked departure from his previous staunch opposition to U.S. involvement in the civil war there. In 1981, his first year in the Senate, he was the chief author of a law stipulating that the president could not continue aid to El Salvador unless he certified that the country was achieving social, economic and political reforms.

But when Bush needed an ally to block congressional Democrats from restricting military aid to newly elected Salvadoran President Alfredo Cristiani in 1989, Dodd, chairman of the Foreign Relations Subcommittee on the Western Hemisphere, was there. "To me the aid is a tactical question," he explained. "The strategic question is ending the conflict."

With a critical push from Dodd, Appropriations Committee language sponsored by Sen. Patrick J. Leahy of Vermont to limit military aid was defeated by a lopsided margin. Passed in its place was an amendment increasing funds without detailed conditions, which was co-authored by Dodd and Republican Bob Kasten of Wisconsin. While publicly expressing hope that the aid would be an incentive for both sides to end human rights violations and negotiate an end to the war, Dodd called Cristiani from the Senate cloakroom to let him know of the victory.

Weeks later, in mid-November, six Jesuit priests were murdered on a campus that was under the control of government security forces. While the incident put Dodd under intense pressure to break from his stance in favor of aid for the Cristiani government, he again opposed legislation to limit aid and instead backed a resolution warning the government to make a good-faith effort to find and prosecute those responsible for the killings.

But that would be the last time Dodd supported the administration on the issue. By mid-1990, with the investigation into the murders being criticized as badly flawed, Dodd came full circle, joining with Leahy to author an amendment adding complex restrictions to military aid to El Salvador. The measure was approved over strenuous Bush administration objections. Dodd planned to team up with Leahy again in 1991 to continue the conditions.

Still, Dodd in his current efforts is not known for the kind of intensely critical rhetoric that he used against the Reagan administration's Central America policies. Dodd's tone got him in trouble in 1983, when he was selected to respond to a Reagan speech on Central America. The senator delivered a blistering attack on the president's "formula for failure," accusing him of condoning Salvadoran police who murder "gangland style — the victim on bended knee, thumbs wired behind the back, a bullet through the brain."

The speech angered many Democrats, who thought Dodd had gone far beyond any party consensus on the issue. That reaction proved an important lesson to Dodd, who conceded that he alienated some people with his stridency. "You yourself can become the issue, and I did," he said.

Once, Dodd was dressed down by Secretary of State George P. Shultz for intruding in U.S. policy in an untoward manner; Shultz complained after Dodd requested a meeting with a Central American head of state that excluded the U.S. ambassador, a violation of protocol that Shultz said contributed to foreigners' confusion about policy.

Dodd's interest in children's issues is longstanding, and he is credited with being one of the first to focus legislative attention on the topic. With Pennsylvania Republican Arlen Specter, he founded the Senate Children's Caucus in 1983. When the Democrats regained control of the Senate after the 1986 elections, Dodd no longer needed this soapbox; he became chairman of the newly created Labor and Human Resources Subcommittee on Children, Family, Drugs and Alcoholism.

Dodd first introduced his Act for Better Child Care bill in 1987. The bill called for $2.5 billion in annual grants for states to subsidize care for low- and middle-income families, set federal health and safety standards, and directed funds into child-development training for teachers.

Despite bipartisan pledges of support for legislation to aid working families, it took long, painful months of negotiation to win White House approval of a bill far more modest than Democrats had hoped for. The final bill included $4.25 billion in grant authorizations over five years for low-income families, and a five-year, $18.3 billion expansion of tax credits for the working poor. It required states to adopt their own health and safety codes.

Dodd called 1990 "as good a year for children as any since 1965," when much of President Lyndon B. Johnson's War on Poverty legislation was enacted. But many Democrats, including a lead House sponsor of the child-care bill, expressed disappointment that Congress had "over-promised and under-delivered."

Advocates of children's issues had even less luck with the family leave bill, which sought to require businesses with more than 20 employees to allow time off to care for a newborn or adopted infant or to care for a sick family member. Though Dodd and others agreed to scale back the number of weeks allowed off and to reduce the number of businesses covered to those with more than 50 employees, the president refused to go along with any bill that made the requirements mandatory.

A family issue of another sort put Dodd on the spot as the 101st Congress began work. He was one of only three Democrats to vote for the nomination of John Tower as secretary of Defense. It did not escape attention that Tower had been one of only five senators to vote in 1967 against censuring Dodd's father, the late Thomas J. Dodd, for violating Senate rules against converting campaign funds to personal use.

The elder Dodd was a tough-talking, two-term senator who was among his party's most virulent anti-communists. When the younger Dodd took his Senate seat in 1981, his siblings gave him his father's pocket watch and chain. He hung a picture of his father in his office. And when he got the chance, he moved into office quarters that include part of his father's old office.

Dodd uses his post on the Banking Committee, where he chairs the Securities Subcommittee, to keep an eye on home-state matters. In the 100th Congress, Dodd played hardball to protect Connecticut insurance companies during markup sessions on legislation to deregulate the financial services industries, which pitted banks against insurers. He threatened to force votes on issues that senators did not want to take stands on unless the committee met his demands. After an intense day and a half, he apologized, but defended his right to protect his state's large insurance industry: "It's like hogs in Iowa," he said.

In even more dramatic fashion, Dodd temporarily joined with Republicans to kill a public housing measure in 1990 in order to persuade the chairman of the House Banking Committee to support a Dodd amendment allowing the Export-Import Bank to fund defense sales to NATO and Japan. That amendment was important to Dodd, because Sikorsky wanted to sell its Connecticut-made helicopters to Greece and Turkey.

During his tenure in the House from 1975-1981, Dodd was more liberal than most of his colleagues in the Democratic class of 1974, but he reflected his class' general distrust of bureaucracy and its interest in "good government" issues.

On the House Judiciary Committee, he supported gun control and lobby-disclosure bills. Later he was given a seat on the Rules Committee and was made an at-large whip. Arguing for his energy-poor Northeast constituency, Dodd opposed oil decontrol and tried to increase fuel aid for the poor.

At Home: From the day Democratic Sen. Abraham A. Ribicoff declared his retirement in 1979, Dodd was viewed as his heir apparent. Dodd was overwhelmingly popular in his 2nd District, and he bore one of the most potent names in Connecticut politics. His father was still revered by many voters, despite his 1967 Senate censure for personal use of campaign funds.

Dodd's only potential obstacle on the road to the Democratic Senate nomination was his fellow House member, Toby Moffett. When Moffett agreed to wait until 1982 to run for statewide office, Dodd's path was clear; he was nominated by acclamation at the state party convention.

His Republican opponent was former New York Sen. James L. Buckley, who carried the standard of the state Republican Party's newly resurgent conservative wing. The millionaire brother of columnist William F. Buckley Jr., James Buckley argued that his previous experience and national reputation would make him a significant force for conservatism in the Senate. With a strong constituency in Republican Fairfield County, he hoped to emulate Reagan by making inroads in normally Democratic blue-collar cities and towns to the east.

But Buckley's patrician style did not play well in those areas, and Dodd proved an exuberant campaigner, slipping into crowds with the comfort of a born politician, conversing both in English and fluent Spanish. He attacked Buckley as a conservative ideologue who, as a senator, had neglected the needs of the poor.

Dodd never forced the question of Buckley's carpetbagging; gentle references to it were enough. Dodd quipped that the Constitution mandates two senators for each state, not two states for each senator.

Dodd easily outdistanced Buckley, pulling votes from liberal Democrats on an issue basis and from older ethnic voters on the strength of their traditional Democratic habits. Carrying the major cities by huge margins, he earned a larger plurality than his father did in winning his first Senate term in 1958.

By 1984, Dodd felt politically secure enough at home to endorse the presidential candidacy of Colorado Sen. Gary Hart. The rest of Connecticut's Democratic establishment, including Gov. William A. O'Neill, backed Walter F. Mondale.

Hart won Connecticut's Democratic presidential primary convincingly. Dodd continued to advise and publicly support him even after it became clear that Mondale had enough delegates to win the nomination, and he placed Hart's name in nomination at the national convention in San Francisco.

Dodd's reputation as a rising star was enhanced by his landslide 1986 re-election. Initial Republican hopes of threatening Dodd were deflated by the refusal of high-profile personalities to challenge him. The GOP eventually awarded its nomination to 66-year-old Roger W. Eddy, a party national committeeman and former state representative. Though he was popular among party insiders, it turned out that Eddy was little known to voters outside his home area.

Eddy, inventor of the widely used Audubon birdcall, had an image as a "gentleman farmer," but his campaign style turned out to be surprisingly hard-hitting. He attacked Dodd's Central America stands, describing him as "the senator from communist Nicaragua," and implied that Dodd had inherited the Senate seat from his father.

In an appeal for labor votes, Eddy made an intemperate attack against Japan. He told a state AFL-CIO meeting that "Japan is sucking us dry," and implied that it is part of the Japanese culture to lie, cheat and steal in order to attain victory.

Eddy's brashness earned him headlines, but did not faze Dodd. He emphasized his support for programs in areas such as housing and higher education, defended his Central America record and brushed off Eddy's attacks as "disappointing." Dodd greatly outspent Eddy and amassed nearly 65 percent of the vote, the largest Senate vote percentage in state history.

Dodd grew up with Connecticut politics, and he went after public office himself at age 30. He was practicing law in New London in 1974 when Republican Rep. Robert H. Steele left his secure 2nd District seat to run for governor. Dodd attached himself to the camp of Democratic gubernatorial candidate Ella T. Grasso early in the spring and began making the rounds of delegates to the 2nd District Democratic convention.

By the time of the convention, he was the clear favorite over John M. Bailey Jr. — son of the state party chairman — and Douglas Bennet, a one-time aide to Ribicoff. Dodd locked up the party's endorsement on the first round of convention balloting, and went on to an easy victory in the general election.

Committees

Banking, Housing & Urban Affairs (4th of 12 Democrats)
Housing & Urban Affairs; Securities (chairman)

Budget (12th of 12 Democrats)

Foreign Relations (5th of 10 Democrats)
East Asian & Pacific Affairs; International Economic Policy, Trade, Oceans & Environment; Western Hemisphere & Peace Corps Affairs (chairman)

Labor & Human Resources (4th of 10 Democrats)
Aging; Children, Families, Drugs & Alcoholism (chairman); Education, Arts & Humanities; Labor

Rules & Administration (8th of 9 Democrats)

Elections

1986 General

Christopher J. Dodd (D)	632,695	(65%)
Roger W. Eddy (R)	340,438	(35%)

Previous Winning Percentages: **1980** (56%) **1978** * (70%) **1976** * (65%) **1974** * (59%)

** House elections.*

Campaign Finance

	Receipts	Receipts from PACs		Expend-itures
1986				
Dodd (D)	$2,395,798	$624,446	(26%)	$2,276,764
Eddy (R)	$466,915	$35,613	(8%)	$466,894

Key Votes

1991

Authorize use of force against Iraq	N

1990

Oppose prohibition of certain semiautomatic weapons	N
Support constitutional amendment on flag desecration	N
Oppose requiring parental notice for minors' abortions	Y
Halt production of B-2 stealth bomber at 13 planes	N
Approve budget that cut spending and raised revenues	Y
Pass civil rights bill over Bush veto	Y

1989

Oppose reduction of SDI funding	N
Oppose barring federal funds for "obscene" art	Y
Allow vote on capital gains tax cut	N

Voting Studies

	Presidential Support		Party Unity		Conservative Coalition	
Year	**S**	**O**	**S**	**O**	**S**	**O**
1990	39	58	89	8	30	65
1989	54	45	89	9	32	66
1988	49	40	86	9	38	54
1987	29	56	80	11	28	59
1986	25	73	71	28	29	70
1985	34	64	83	14	27	73
1984	32	61	85	8	6	89
1983	41	53	67	17	14	64
1982	35	61	82	12	5	85
1981	33	59	80	8	3	85

Interest Group Ratings

Year	ADA	ACU	AFL-CIO	CCUS
1990	61	9	78	9
1989	65	22	100	50
1988	85	8	86	36
1987	65	0	100	13
1986	85	17	73	44
1985	85	4	95	41
1984	100	10	91	42
1983	80	8	100	24
1982	100	8	96	16
1981	90	7	100	0

Joseph I. Lieberman (D)

Of New Haven — Elected 1988

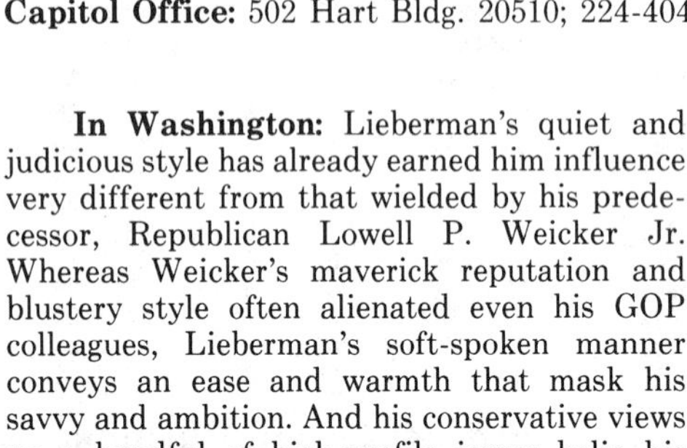

Born: Feb. 24, 1942, Stamford, Conn.
Education: Yale U., B.A. 1964, LL.B. 1967.
Occupation: Lawyer.
Family: Wife, Hadassah Freilich; four children.
Religion: Jewish.
Political Career: Conn. Senate, 1971-81, majority leader, 1975-81; Conn. attorney general, 1983-89; sought Democratic nomination for U.S. House, 1980;
Capitol Office: 502 Hart Bldg. 20510; 224-4041.

In Washington: Lieberman's quiet and judicious style has already earned him influence very different from that wielded by his predecessor, Republican Lowell P. Weicker Jr. Whereas Weicker's maverick reputation and blustery style often alienated even his GOP colleagues, Lieberman's soft-spoken manner conveys an ease and warmth that mask his savvy and ambition. And his conservative views on a handful of high-profile issues belie his generally liberal outlook.

Lieberman entered the Senate in a class of heavyweight Democratic freshmen that included three former governors, two of whom are Vietnam War veterans already being measured for presidential timber. Even if he does not rise to that level of star quality, Lieberman still has managed to draw his share of attention and lead some observers to say that he may be the standout of the class of '88.

Within his first two years in office, Lieberman began establishing an independent record. From his post on the Environment and Public Works Committee, he took a lead role in passing oil-spill liability legislation, helped lead a congressional effort to ban the chemical Alar from fruits and vegetables, and authored the act that greatly increased the number of investigators at the Environmental Protection Agency. He was also very active during consideration of the Clean Air Act extension, fighting unsuccessfully for stricter pollution controls than those in the compromise reached between Senate leaders and the administration.

Of more parochial interest, Lieberman sponsored legislation that created Connecticut's first national park site in 1990 and helped get the EPA to establish a Long Island Sound office to help restore and protect the sound.

Lieberman continues to build on the pro-consumer reputation he developed as Connecticut attorney general. He introduced legislation to allow state and local governments to re-regulate cable television rates, stopping only slightly short of arguing, among other things, for a constitutional right to watch baseball for free.

Following Iraq's invasion of Kuwait in August 1990, Lieberman promoted legislation to prevent oil companies from price gouging; he urged President Bush to tap the Strategic Petroleum Reserve and he pushed in early 1991 for a reimposition of the windfall profits tax.

Despite this seemingly traditional liberal record — he received higher ratings than Connecticut colleague Christopher J. Dodd in 1989 and 1990 from the liberal Americans for Democratic Action — Lieberman is not afraid to split from his party. He was one of just six Democrats to back a cut in the capital gains tax and one of only 10 Democratic senators (and the only one from the Northeast) to support the authorization of force in the Persian Gulf.

A staunch supporter of Israel and an activist foreign policy — during his 1988 campaign he stressed his support for the invasion of Grenada and the bombing of Libya — Lieberman was an early supporter of the administration's policy in the Persian Gulf. "I hope we'll return to the mainstream Democratic foreign policy of this century, represented by Wilson, Roosevelt and Kennedy," he said. "The Vietnam experience took us off that course." In October 1990, he had joined just five fellow Democrats in voting to authorize the president to use force to remove Panama's Gen. Manuel Antonio Noriega from power, two months before the U.S. invasion.

At Home: Lieberman was given little chance of ousting 18-year GOP Senate veteran Weicker in the 1988 race, but he wound up scoring the only Democratic upset of that year's Senate elections.

All year long, Lieberman had argued that it was a myth that Connecticut benefited from Weicker's maverick reputation. But the electoral appeal of the Republican's go-it-alone style had seemed impenetrable.

After months of trailing in opinion polls, Lieberman launched a series of animated ads late in the campaign that portrayed Weicker as a sleeping bear, dozing through important votes but awaking loud and ornery when personally piqued. The imagery of the bear ads clicked, and their appearance in the closing weeks of a yearlong campaign was perfectly timed. With Lieberman peaking late, Weicker did not have a chance to counterpunch.

He began the campaign well known from prior political service. Earlier in his career, he had given up a 10-year career in the state Senate (and his job there as majority leader) for a U.S. House bid, only to lose in the primary. But two years later, he bounced back, becoming the top state vote-getter in his election to attorney general.

During his nearly two terms in that office, he won many headlines for his pro-consumer lawsuits against car dealers, grocery stores and public utilities, as well as for his efforts toward stiffer enforcement of hazardous-waste disposal laws and child support payment requirements.

His visibility on these issues did not endear him to the "Old Guard" in Connecticut's Democratic Party, but his efforts had the liberal lilt needed to woo traditionally Democratic voters, and the party elected to unite behind him in his challenge to Weicker. Lieberman also raised doubts about Weicker's commitment to Social Security, a Democratic touchstone issue.

At the same time, Lieberman's profile also enabled him to court crossover voters. His demeanor is far more restrained than Weicker's; where the Republican campaigned with his sleeves rolled up and jacket slung over his shoulder, Lieberman seemed reluctant to loosen his tie. He stressed a family-man image, and is known as an Orthodox Jew whose avoidance of Saturday campaigning precluded him from attending even the convention that nominated him.

Lieberman also held the conservative ground on a few select issues. He supported allowing military involvement in drug interdiction, and backed the 1983 invasion of Grenada, both of which Weicker opposed. Lieberman also backed a moment of silence in schools, which may be used for prayer.

This combination won him an endorsement from noted conservative William F. Buckley Jr., who had long disdained Weicker for his social liberalism. Some conservatives concluded that a Lieberman victory would be no great catastrophe, so they sat out the Senate race. That deprived Weicker of crucial GOP support on Election Day, while Lieberman held his Democratic base and won enough independent votes to eke out a narrow victory.

While Democrats were pleased with his success, some liberals felt a twinge of remorse over the departure of Weicker, who so often had championed their causes in the Senate and in the national GOP. Some observers credit that voter guilt with helping Weicker in his successful 1990 bid, as an independent, for governor.

Committees

Environment & Public Works (8th of 9 Democrats)
Environmental Protection; Toxic Substances, Environmental Oversight, Research & Development; Water Resources, Transportation & Infrastructure

Governmental Affairs (7th of 8 Democrats)
General Services, Federalism & the District of Columbia; Government Information & Regulation; Oversight of Government Management; Permanent Subcommittee on Investigations

Small Business (9th of 10 Democrats)
Competitiveness & Economic Opportunity (chairman); Export Expansion; Government Contracting & Paperwork Reduction

Elections

1988 General

Joseph I. Lieberman (D)	688,499	(50%)
Lowell P. Weicker Jr. (R)	678,454	(49%)

Campaign Finance

	Receipts	Receipts from PACs		Expend-itures
1988				
Lieberman (D)	$2,647,603	$175,566	(7%)	$2,570,799
Weicker (R)	$2,519,961	$947,116	(38%)	$2,609,902

Key Votes

1991	
Authorize use of force against Iraq	Y
1990	
Oppose prohibition of certain semiautomatic weapons	N
Support constitutional amendment on flag desecration	N
Oppose requiring parental notice for minors' abortions	Y
Halt production of B-2 stealth bomber at 13 planes	Y
Approve budget that cut spending and raised revenues	N
Pass civil rights bill over Bush veto	Y
1989	
Oppose reduction of SDI funding	N
Oppose barring federal funds for "obscene" art	Y
Allow vote on capital gains tax cut	Y

Voting Studies

	Presidential Support		Party Unity		Conservative Coalition	
Year	**S**	**O**	**S**	**O**	**S**	**O**
1990	37	62	86	13	22	78
1989	56	44	81	19	32	68

Interest Group Ratings

Year	ADA	ACU	AFL-CIO	CCUS
1990	83	22	78	17
1989	75	32	90	38

1 Barbara B. Kennelly (D)

Of Hartford — Elected 1982

Born: July 10, 1936, Hartford, Conn.
Education: Trinity College (Washington, D.C.), B.A. 1958; Trinity College (Hartford, Conn.), M.A. 1973.
Occupation: Public official.
Family: Husband, James J. Kennelly; four children.
Religion: Roman Catholic.
Political Career: Hartford Court of Common Council, 1975-79; Conn. secretary of state, 1979-82.
Capitol Office: 204 Cannon Bldg. 20515; 225-2265.

In Washington: Kennelly is equal parts old pol and feminist. She moves easily between those roles, in one breath arguing forcefully for women's issues and in the next breath spinning a tale about "Danny" — Ways and Means Chairman Dan Rostenkowski — in a way that makes it clear the Chicago power broker is someone she likes and understands.

It is not surprising Kennelly feels at ease around old-fashioned Democrats. She grew up with them; her father was John Bailey, the legendary Connecticut party boss and chairman of the Democratic National Committee under Presidents Kennedy and Johnson. Kennelly's father also taught her an important skill that has helped her forge relationships with other members — golf. One way to crack any "old boy" network is to mix in socially, and the place Kennelly has mixed with members of Ways and Means is on the fairways and putting greens.

Kennelly's knack for getting along with the male-dominated House leadership has brought her a long way in a short time. She had been in the chamber less than a year when she won a seat on Ways and Means, and in December 1984, then-Speaker Thomas P. O'Neill Jr. appointed her to the Democratic Steering and Policy Committee, which makes committee assignments and helps design legislative and political strategies. In the 100th Congress, she became an at-large member of the majority whip organization, another means of having one's ticket punched on the road to leadership.

In the June 1989 Democratic leadership shake-up that followed Jim Wright's departure as Speaker, Kennelly made a long-shot bid for the open post of caucus chairman. She lost to Steny H. Hoyer of Maryland, who had been the caucus vice chairman. But Kennelly remains one to watch as leadership opportunities ripen in the 1990s, especially as relatively few of the contenders for promotion are women.

Meanwhile, back at the office, Kennelly rarely commands the spotlight at Ways and Means hearings. Even after eight years she remains in the bottom third of the Democrats by seniority, and she rarely gets to question headliner witnesses before most of the glitter has worn off. Moreover, by dint of Hartford's importance to the insurance industry, she has been typecast as an expert on the taxation of that industry. Widely respected for her erudition on the subject, she may also sense herself held back by it.

In working on legislation to overhaul the tax code in the 99th Congress, Kennelly specialized in the complex provisions affecting property- and casualty-insurance companies. In the 100th Congress, as Ways and Means worked on a bill to make technical corrections in the tax code, Kennelly displayed her legislative savvy by winning a surprising victory for the insurance industry over Rostenkowski's strong objections.

Rostenkowski, disturbed that certain types of life insurance were being used to dodge taxation, sought to rewrite the rules to discourage investors from dipping into certain insurance plans for tax-free earnings on premium payments. But Kennelly and New Jersey Democrat Frank J. Guarini felt Rostenkowski's plan was too stringent; they proposed a milder one and persuaded the committee to go along with it at a contentious meeting.

The insurance industry has had other occasions to thank Kennelly. In the 98th Congress, she helped shape a major revision of insurance tax laws, lowering the industry's tax burden.

In the 101st Congress, Kennelly was among those Democrats willing to discuss cutting the tax rate on capital gains as a short-term means of raising revenue for funding needs. But she returned to opposing such cuts when the battle lines were drawn in committee.

Kennelly has also been somewhat ambivalent on the issue of national service. A sponsor and cosponsor of national service bills in the 101st Congress, Kennelly supported student aid or home-buyer aid for veterans of military or civilian service. But she resisted making such service mandatory for all recipients of such aid. "I represent the fourth poorest city in America," she told one hearing. "I cannot force my constituents into national service by denying them . . . aid unless they serve."

Varying the program for Kennelly in re-

Connecticut 1

Central — Hartford

Hartford, the capital of Connecticut, is a city of contrast. The Travelers, Aetna, CIGNA and other insurance corporations hum with white-collar activity, and state government offers stable employment, yet many of the city's poor blacks and Hispanics stand idle.

Broadly speaking, the 1980s was a prosperous decade for the city, which benefited from a commercial real estate boom and the robust state economy. But in the shadows of downtown growth was a decaying inner-city. After the 1980 census, Hartford was rated the fourth-poorest city in the nation, with one-quarter of its residents living under the poverty line; a decade later, city officials concede that the ranking probably hasn't changed considerably.

The recession that gripped New England in the early 1990s marked the end of Hartford's boom. Two major hotels closed down, and one of the city's two department stores shut its doors for good. Even Aetna, the city's major employer, has moved some operations out of Hartford to surrounding towns.

In politics, the 1st used to be the fiefdom of state party boss John Bailey, Kennelly's father, who personally determined which Democrat would represent it in Congress every two years. The 1st has sent a Democrat to Congress in every election but one since 1948. In 1981, Hartford, which is about 39 percent black, became the first New England city to elect a black mayor, and it has had one ever since.

Bailey saw to it that all of Hartford's ethnic groups were welcomed under the Democratic banner, and Democratic candidates continue to do well among the city's ethnic and racial groups.

In 1988, support from Hartford's blacks helped Michael S. Dukakis carry the city with 76 percent. Many of the city's blacks are concentrated in the North End, with the Italian-American wards clustered in the South End. The North End is one of Hartford's most economically disadvantaged areas; estimates of local unemployment ran as high as 30 percent in 1990. Though Hartford now casts less than one-fifth of the total district vote, Dukakis still carried the 1st comfortably. It was the only Connecticut district to back him, and one of three to vote for Democratic Senate nominee Joseph I. Lieberman in 1988.

While Dukakis won the capital city's urbanized neighbors — East Hartford, West Hartford and Manchester — they are not immune to GOP entreaties. Lieberman carried Manchester by just 14 votes and narrowly lost West Hartford to GOP Sen. Lowell P. Weicker Jr. Reagan carried all three of these suburbs in 1984 on his way to winning a majority in the 1st.

Though United Technologies' Pratt & Whitney headquarters in East Hartford has made job cuts in recent years, it remains one of the larger sources of jobs in the district. Most of the employees are involved in skilled, high-technology work. Other aerospace and high-tech firms offering similar jobs helped build a well-paid work force throughout metropolitan Hartford.

Population: 516,232. White 429,260 (83%), Black 59,723 (12%), Other 4,056 (1%). Spanish origin 32,636 (6%). 18 and over 383,559 (74%), 65 and over 65,558 (13%). Median age: 32.

cent years has been her assignment to the Intelligence Committee, where she chairs the Subcommittee on Legislation. She is the first woman to serve on Intelligence.

Kennelly is a latecomer to feminist issues; she says her three daughters persuaded her to become active. When congressional feminists began pushing their "equity" agenda in 1983, Kennelly said, "Am I going to tell you I am going to change the world of Danny Rostenkowski? No. Am I going to try? Yes."

One of her first accomplishments was winning passage in 1984 of part of the "equity" package — a law to encourage payment of child support. It required states to see that money is withheld from the paychecks of parents who are delinquent in meeting court-ordered child-support payments. Four years later, when Ways and Means produced an overhaul of the welfare system, Kennelly and others pushed for even stricter enforcement requirements, forcing withholding even when payment is not in arrears.

Kennelly also brought the voice of the women's caucus to the tax-law rewrite, fighting to preserve the child-care deduction and to expand the standard deduction for single parents.

At Home: Even though she learned politics at her father's knee, Kennelly took her time getting into the business. She was almost 40, directing two large social-service agencies in Hartford, when she was appointed to fill a vacancy on the City Council in 1975. She easily won a full term soon after.

It took a strikingly independent move to win her next office. Gloria Schaffer, the Democratic secretary of state, decided to step down from her post in 1978. Party protocol called for replacing her with another Jewish woman to balance the ethnic makeup of the statewide ticket. Kennelly ignored precedent. At the state party convention she pieced together an organization that prompted comparisons with her father; she finagled the nomination from the party favorites and won easily in November.

In 1981, two weeks after six-term Democratic Rep. William R. Cotter died of cancer, Kennelly announced her candidacy to replace him. Other Democrats dropped out, and she was nominated by acclamation.

Kennelly had little trouble in the subsequent special election against GOP nominee Ann P. Uccello, a former mayor of Hartford. Although Uccello had been a strong vote-getter when she captured the mayoralty in 1969, her political visibility had faded after a narrowly unsuccessful 1970 campaign against Cotter.

Running in a Democratic stronghold, Kennelly also had a huge financial lead. The national Republican Party wrote off Uccello, and Kennelly won with nearly 60 percent.

Since then, Kennelly has rolled up huge tallies in each of her four re-election campaigns. The 1990 race was no different, despite the hopes of Republican nominee James P. Garvey.

Garvey, a political newcomer who quit his job as a credit analyst to campaign against Kennelly, said Kennelly had caught "Potomac fever" and forgotten the needs of the district. He got some campaign fodder from a taped television report that showed Kennelly and other members of the Ways and Means Committee romping on the beach during a taxpayer-paid trip to Barbados on congressional business in April 1990.

But Kennelly successfully defended her record and the trip, and won handily with 71 percent of the vote.

Kennelly shows no signs of tiring of the political life, although she has expressed interest in moving up a rung to statewide office. She was discussed as a possible candidate for governor in 1990 when Democratic incumbent William A. O'Neill announced his retirement, but she decided against making that race.

Committees

Select Intelligence (3rd of 12 Democrats)
Legislation (chairman); Oversight & Evaluation

Ways & Means (16th of 23 Democrats)
Human Resources; Select Revenue Measures

Elections

1990 General		
Barbara B. Kennelly (D)	126,566	(71%)
James P. Garvey (R)	50,690	(29%)
1988 General		
Barbara B. Kennelly (D)	176,463	(77%)
Mario Robles Jr. (R)	51,985	(23%)

Previous Winning Percentages: **1986** (74%) **1984** (62%) **1982** (68%) **1982 *** (59%)

* *Special election.*

District Vote For President

	1988	1984	1980	1976
D	133,867 (55%)	115,174 (47%)	109,702 (46%)	125,895 (52%)
R	106,890 (44%)	129,384 (53%)	93,750 (39%)	113,154 (47%)
I			34,942 (15%)	

Campaign Finance

	Receipts	Receipts from PACs	Expend-itures
1990			
Kennelly (D)	$483,041	$297,700 (62%)	$406,138
1988			
Kennelly (D)	$448,010	$269,603 (60%)	$471,530
Robles (R)	$11,522	0	$11,520

Key Votes

1991	
Authorize use of force against Iraq	N
1990	
Support constitutional amendment on flag desecration	N
Pass family and medical leave bill over Bush veto	Y
Reduce SDI funding	Y
Allow abortions in overseas military facilities	Y
Approve budget summit plan for spending and taxing	Y
Approve civil rights bill	Y
1989	
Halt production of B-2 stealth bomber at 13 planes	N
Oppose capital gains tax cut	Y
Approve federal abortion funding in rape or incest cases	Y
Approve pay raise and revision of ethics rules	Y
Pass Democratic minimum wage plan over Bush veto	Y

Voting Studies

	Presidential Support		Party Unity		Conservative Coalition	
Year	**S**	**O**	**S**	**O**	**S**	**O**
1990	22	78	92	6	17	83
1989	28	67	93	5	27	71
1988	28	71	92	6	32	68
1987	22	75	89	5	37	60
1986	20	78	91	4	20	74
1985	23	78	91	5	22	78
1984	31	65	88	7	15	78
1983	16	80	95	3	12	83
1982	34	66	92	8	26	74

Interest Group Ratings

Year	ADA	ACU	AFL-CIO	CCUS
1990	83	8	92	14
1989	95	7	92	30
1988	90	8	100	36
1987	84	0	88	21
1986	85	0	93	35
1985	90	10	94	27
1984	85	0	77	38
1983	90	4	94	25
1982	95	0	85	27

2 Sam Gejdenson (D)

Of Bozrah — Elected 1980

Born: May 20, 1948, Eschwege, Germany.
Education: Mitchell Junior College, A.S. 1968; U. of Connecticut, B.A. 1970.
Occupation: Dairy farmer.
Family: Wife, Karen Fleming; two children.
Religion: Jewish.
Political Career: Conn. House, 1975-79.
Capitol Office: 2416 Rayburn Bldg. 20515; 225-2076.

In Washington: During his early years in the House, Gejdenson was best known to many of his colleagues for his irreverent wit. While he still can be quick with a quip, seniority is bringing him greater responsibilities and a reputation as a serious legislator.

At the start of the 101st Congress, Gejdenson became chairman of the Foreign Affairs subcommittee that deals with international economic policy and trade. Later in 1989, he also gained a seat on the Democratic Steering and Policy Committee, which assigns Democratic members to the standing committees. Gejdenson's stature as a leadership insider was burnished early in 1991, when Speaker Thomas S. Foley of Washington tapped him to head a House Administration Committee subcommittee on congressional campaign finance reform.

These gains for Gejdenson were preceded by a minor setback. In January 1989, he fell short in his effort to obtain one of six open Democratic seats on the Budget Committee.

However, the New England seat on the Steering and Policy Committee opened that June, and Gejdenson — sponsored by new Rules Committee Chairman Joe Moakley of Massachusetts — got it. Ironically, it was Steering and Policy that had turned down Gejdenson's Budget Committee bid.

Gejdenson meanwhile had busied himself with trade subcommittee hearings on the Export Administration Act (EAA). When written in 1979 and revised in 1985, EAA strictly limited the export to communist nations of industrial goods and materials that had possible military applications; among the many prohibited items were high-speed personal computers, other electronic components, machine tools and satellite ground stations.

However, the five-year reauthorization of EAA came up at a time of drastically changed circumstance. Great geopolitical changes wrought from 1989 on — the replacement of communist rulers with pro-Western governments in much of Eastern Europe and the military retrenchment of the Soviet Union — created a rush for new export markets and a push to loosen restrictions on items without direct military use.

This new orientation was adopted by Gejdenson, who titled his reauthorization bill the "Export Facilitation Act." The bill would have shortened the list of restricted items, while maintaining "high fences" around those barred from trade. Gejdenson also emphasized a reorganization of the export licensing process in order to address complaints from exporters about bureaucratic red tape.

At first, Gejdenson looked to have a legislative success; the bill breezed through both houses of Congress. However, the Bush administration complained about various aspects of the bill, especially a Senate-crafted provision mandating sanctions against countries and companies involved in the international trade of chemical and biological weapons. Stating that the sanctions clause would "unduly interfere with the president's responsibility for carrying out foreign policy," Bush pocket-vetoed the bill in November 1990 — forcing Gejdenson to start the process over in the 102nd Congress.

Disagreements between Gejdenson and Republican administrations are not new. On the Foreign Affairs Western Hemisphere Subcommittee, Gejdenson was a sharp critic of President Ronald Reagan's Central American policies.

Gejdenson has faced one major quandary throughout his House career. His record on defense and foreign policy issues is mainly liberal: He opposed much of the 1980s military buildup and voted against the January 1991 resolution authorizing President Bush to use military force against Iraq. Yet his district's economy relies on defense contractors, including Electric Boat Co. which builds nuclear submarines.

Gejdenson takes a two-pronged approach. He lobbies hard on behalf of the Navy submarine program, describing it as "the most proven and effective component of our national security strategy." But Gejdenson also has promoted efforts to steer 2nd District economic development away from the defense sector. In 1987, he helped establish the Southeast Area Technology Development Center (SEATECH),

Connecticut 2

East — New London

Stretching from the shores of Long Island Sound to the state's upland hills, the 2nd District covers the least urbanized parts of Connecticut. Its vote varies with its geography. Along the coast, dependably Democratic shipbuilding towns and fishing villages border wealthy WASPish communities that provide Republican majorities. Inland, small manufacturing centers and college towns vote Democratic, while Yankee hill towns maintain the GOP tradition.

The fine balance among the areas helps give the 2nd a volatile voting pattern. When Gejdenson replaced Democrat Christopher J. Dodd in 1980, it marked the first time in nearly 50 years that the district had changed hands without changing parties. Between 1934 and 1950, it switched parties every two years. Historically a center for seafaring, the southern coast is the home of the Electric Boat shipbuilding installation in Groton. Construction site for the Trident nuclear submarine program, this is the district's largest industrial concern, employing 18,000 people.

Like Connecticut as a whole, the coastal area is heavily dependent on military spending and citizens there are nervously awaiting the effects of post-Cold War adjustments in Pentagon spending; local officials estimate that defense-related spending may account for up to half of the jobs in the district. The Groton maritime complex also features the Naval Underseas Research and Development Center, a Navy submarine port and a submarine training base.

Across the Thames River, in New London, is the U.S. Coast Guard Academy, which co-exists peacefully with Connecticut College and several small plastics and hardware plants. To the east is Mystic, a scenic old fishing town that served as a backdrop, and got title billing, for the movie "Mystic Pizza."

Farther inland, college towns and mill towns are neighbors on the hilly landscape. In Willimantic, Eastern Connecticut State College adjoins needle-and-thread and wire-cable firms. The town of Storrs is dominated by the 24,500 students at its University of Connecticut campus, while Middletown is home to Wesleyan University's 2,800 students.

Population: 518,244. White 493,893 (95%), Black 15,107 (3%), Other 4,710 (1%). Spanish origin 8,931 (2%). 18 and over 378,132 (73%), 65 and over 53,819 (10%). Median age: 30.

a nonprofit corporation aimed at finding ways to diversify his district's economy.

For several years, Gejdenson tried fruitlessly to expand this "economic diversification" concept by providing federal grants to defense-dependent communities. However, Gejdenson's idea caught on during the 101st Congress, which ushered in a new era of defense spending cutbacks spurred by post-Cold War and fiscal realities. An amendment to provide $200 million for community economic planning and for assistance to laid-off defense workers, co-authored by Gejdenson and Massachusetts Democrat Nicholas Mavroules, was attached to the fiscal 1991 defense authorization bill.

His efforts on district-related issues give Gejdenson the leeway to take on chores for the House Democratic leadership that may be less politically rewarding. These include his chairmanship of the campaign finance panel, created in an effort to untangle an issue on which there is division within Congress and little interest among the general electorate.

Gejdenson's busy agenda is rounded out by his assignment to the Interior Committee. He gained his first House experience with a gavel as the temporary chairman of the Interior Subcommittee on Energy and the Environment during the 100th Congress.

At Home: Gejdenson's district-focused work in Washington is not the only thing that has made him safe in a district with no clear preference for Democrats. The local media lavish praise on the incumbent for simply being a nice guy. After his 1988 announcement that he was running for re-election, the *New London Day* ran a glowing column about Gejdenson headlined, "Just a Farm Boy Who Spends His Week in Washington."

The story referred to the fact that Gejdenson had grown up on an eastern Connecticut dairy farm still owned by his parents, Lithuanian Jews who survived the World War II Holocaust. Gejdenson himself was born in the displaced persons' camp in Germany from which his family emigrated to America.

Leaving the farm behind to enter politics, Gejdenson served two terms in the state House, and prepared to run for Congress. He got his chance in 1980 when 2nd District Democratic Rep. Christopher J. Dodd vacated the seat to run for the Senate. Though John N. Dempsey Jr., the son of a former governor, won the party endorsement at the Democratic district convention, Gejdenson outcampaigned him in the primary, winning with 62 percent of the vote.

That fall, Gejdenson expected little trouble from Republican nominee Tony Guglielmo. But Guglielmo benefited from the national GOP trend. Reagan carried the 2nd by 18,000 votes, and Gejdenson emerged with just 53 percent. Guglielmo was back in 1982, but that year's economic downturn put him on the defensive, and Gejdenson won with 56 percent.

Gejdenson seemed safe by 1984, when the GOP put up a little-known botany professor, Roberta Koontz. But he was nearly caught off guard. Aided by voters' concerns about Gejdenson's liberalism and by Reagan's landslide victory in the 2nd, Koontz carried 23 of the district's 57 towns and held Gejdenson to 54 percent.

With three sub-60 percent tallies to Gejdenson's credit, analysts began saying he would always struggle in November. In 1986, he decisively proved them wrong. Republicans thought they had a strong challenger in Francis M. "Bud" Mullen, a former director of the federal Drug Enforcement Administration and former FBI official. Mullen faulted Gejdenson for not seeking a seat on Armed Services, and for opposing some Reagan defense programs. But Gejdenson countered with evidence that he had helped bring billions of dollars' worth of ship- and submarine-building contracts to the 2nd. He mauled Mullen that year, winning two-thirds of the vote, and went on to an easy 1988 win over political newcomer Glenn Carberry.

In 1990, Republicans put up another political novice, Mystic real estate developer John M. Ragsdale. Ragsdale recycled criticisms that Gejdenson should have sought a place on Armed Services to aid district defense contractors, and he attacked Gejdenson's opposition to a capital gains tax cut. Ragsdale had hoped that voter impatience with incumbents would help him crack Gejdenson's winning streak, but he had to settle for bringing the Democrat's victory tally down a few points to 60 percent.

Committees

Foreign Affairs (6th of 28 Democrats)
International Economic Policy & Trade (chairman); Western Hemisphere Affairs

House Administration (8th of 15 Democrats)
Accounts; Office Systems (chairman); Campaign Finance Reform (chairman)

Interior & Insular Affairs (10th of 29 Democrats)
Energy & the Environment; Water, Power & Offshore Energy

Joint Printing

Elections

1990 General		
Sam Gejdenson (D)	105,085	(60%)
John M. Ragsdale (R)	70,922	(40%)
1988 General		
Sam Gejdenson (D)	143,326	(64%)
Glenn Carberry (R)	81,965	(36%)

Previous Winning Percentages: **1986** (67%) **1984** (54%) **1982** (56%) **1980** (53%)

District Vote For President

	1988	1984	1980	1976
D	115,813 (49%)	90,869 (39%)	85,537 (38%)	106,788 (50%)
R	119,947 (50%)	141,593 (61%)	103,603 (46%)	105,737 (50%)
I			31,954 (14%)	

Campaign Finance

	Receipts	Receipts from PACs		Expenditures
1990				
Gejdenson (D)	$458,980	$185,950	(41%)	$464,500
Ragsdale (R)	$113,024	0		$112,881
1988				
Gejdenson (D)	$731,513	$208,800	(29%)	$727,919
Carberry (R)	$250,776	$30,354	(12%)	$246,903

Key Votes

1991	
Authorize use of force against Iraq	N
1990	
Support constitutional amendment on flag desecration	N
Pass family and medical leave bill over Bush veto	Y
Reduce SDI funding	Y
Allow abortions in overseas military facilities	Y
Approve budget summit plan for spending and taxing	Y
Approve civil rights bill	Y
1989	
Halt production of B-2 stealth bomber at 13 planes	Y
Oppose capital gains tax cut	Y
Approve federal abortion funding in rape or incest cases	Y
Approve pay raise and revision of ethics rules	Y
Pass Democratic minimum wage plan over Bush veto	Y

Voting Studies

	Presidential Support		Party Unity		Conservative Coalition	
Year	**S**	**O**	**S**	**O**	**S**	**O**
1990	19	81	95	4	7	89
1989	26	74	96	3	12	88
1988	19	78	93	3	8	92
1987	15	84	92	4	19	81
1986	13	87	96	3	12	88
1985	23	78	92	4	7	89
1984	27	69	91	7	5	95
1983	20	79	95	3	9	90
1982	36	60	92	4	15	82
1981	22	76	92	7	8	92

Interest Group Ratings

Year	ADA	ACU	AFL-CIO	CCUS
1990	94	4	100	14
1989	100	0	100	30
1988	95	0	92	29
1987	92	0	100	20
1986	95	0	100	41
1985	90	10	94	23
1984	95	0	100	50
1983	90	0	100	25
1982	100	0	95	23
1981	95	0	80	5

3 Rosa DeLauro (D)

Of New Haven — Elected 1990

Born: March 2, 1943, New Haven, Conn.
Education: Attended London School of Economics, 1962-63; Marymount College, B.A. 1964; Columbia U., M.A. 1966.
Occupation: Political activist.
Family: Husband, Stanley Greenberg; three children.
Religion: Roman Catholic.
Political Career: No previous office.
Capitol Office: 327 Cannon Bldg. 20515; 225-3661.

The Path to Washington: DeLauro's election to Congress came as welcome news to Democrats eager to regain the ideological offensive. In a district with only a slight leftward leaning, DeLauro campaigned as a progressive activist seeking to cut defense spending and win universal health care.

Politics is in DeLauro's blood; both parents served as aldermen in New Haven (her mother, Louisa DeLauro, is currently the longest-serving board member) and DeLauro frequently tagged along to political gatherings. She wasted little time beginning her own political work, and from the outset it had a liberal cast. Just out of graduate school in the mid-1960s, DeLauro became one of the earliest community organizers in the War on Poverty program. She continued her work on urban problems as assistant director of the National Urban Fellows program and as executive assistant to the mayor of New Haven.

Her energy caught the eye of Democrat Christopher J. Dodd, who recruited her to run his 1980 Senate campaign. They were successful, and she spent seven years as his chief of staff. That was followed by stints lobbying to end U.S. aid to the Nicaraguan contras and running EMILY's List, an organization that raises money for female candidates.

DeLauro left that job to seek the 3rd District seat being vacated by Democrat Bruce A. Morrison, who ran for governor. Though she had never before sought office, DeLauro's political contacts enabled her to raise money quickly and to shoo off intraparty competition. She had a ready-made consultant in husband Stanley Greenberg, a Democratic pollster.

Republicans put up state Sen. Thomas Scott, an energetic conservative opposed to gun control and abortion rights. He pulled close to DeLauro in the Democratic-leaning district, largely by painting her as a far-left radical. Scott also tried to turn DeLauro's Washington contacts against her, claiming that she was a Washington insider dependent on political action committees (PACs). DeLauro raised more than $300,000 from PACs and far outspent Scott.

But DeLauro was able to blunt those attacks by calling attention to her upbringing in Wooster Square, an Italian neighborhood of New Haven. Her father was an Italian immigrant and her mother a factory worker. Drawing on the connections and instincts of her background, DeLauro was able to forge a coalition that linked liberals drawn to her overall political philosophy with Democratic stalwarts such as labor leaders, who were more concerned with bread-and-butter issues. Scott outpolled her in many of the 3rd's smaller communities, but DeLauro won on the strength of a huge margin in New Haven.

Even as the Persian Gulf crisis got under way, DeLauro campaigned for cutting defense costs and channeling that money toward retraining defense workers and domestic programs.

DeLauro, who has a master's degree in international politics from Columbia University, has long been interested in foreign policy. But much of her platform focused on domestic issues such as child and health care.

DeLauro entered Congress amid expectations that she would hit the ground running. Not only is she familiar with the Hill from her days working for Dodd, but intensity appears to be a DeLauro trademark. She repeatedly told voters that, as a woman working in a field dominated by men, she had learned to be a fighter. During a campaign radio debate with Scott, the moderator had to pull the plug after the two candidates got into a shouting match. But Dodd and others have also said DeLauro understands the give and take of the political process and will be a pragmatic legislator. She will also have to be mindful of the centrist impulses in the 3rd; while she tagged Scott a hard-right conservative, he won about 48 percent of the vote.

Connecticut 3

South — New Haven

New Haven has slipped from its glory days as Connecticut's largest city and a premier industrial powerhouse of New England, but it is still the political heart of the 3rd; when a big political rally is planned, the New Haven Green is the only site considered.

New Haven was dominated in the 19th century by Yankee Republicans, and in the first half of the 20th, power was divided among the Italian, Polish and Irish communities. House members of Italian extraction held the 3rd from 1953 to 1983, and Italian-Americans still dominate local elections.

Democrat Bruce A. Morrison's 1982 House victory signaled the emergence of a new type of politics in the district — one in which age, income status and ideology are more important voting determinants than ethnicity. Rosa DeLauro's successful 1990 bid to replace Morrison, who ran for governor, showed that New Haven's Italian-Americans still carry political weight in the 3rd, although DeLauro is identified as much as a liberal politician (like Morrison) as an ethnic one. In 1989, New Haven elected a black mayor, John Daniels, even though blacks are not a majority of the city's population. He defeated an Italian-American for the job.

The fact that New Haven is about one-third black helps explain why its voting behavior is dramatically different from that of the surrounding communities. In 1988, Democratic presidential nominee Michael S. Dukakis carried New Haven with more than 70 percent of the vote, but narrowly lost the district to George Bush.

Because New Haven casts only about one-fifth of the total district vote, a Democrat cannot succeed in the 3rd without making a respectable showing outside the city. Democratic Senate nominee Joseph I. Lieberman carried the 3rd by winning New Haven with better than 60 percent of the vote, and winning both West Haven and Hamden, the two largest cities in the district outside New Haven.

The district's best-known institution is Yale University, in New Haven. Yale and City Hall have not always enjoyed a model town-gown relationship — there have been disputes over how the city should be compensated for the university's tax-exempt landholdings. But in recent years, Yale has helped the city promote and finance downtown redevelopment projects aimed at keeping shopping and entertainment from fleeing to the suburbs.

Population: 518,677. White 452,956 (87%), Black 53,767 (10%), Other 4,005 (1%). Spanish origin 15,171 (3%). 18 and over 387,740 (75%), 65 and over 64,393 (12%). Median age: 32.

Committees

Government Operations (23rd of 25 Democrats)
Employment & Housing; Human Resources & Intergovernmental Relations

Public Works & Transportation (32nd of 36 Democrats)
Economic Development; Investigations & Oversight; Water Resources

Select Aging (40th of 42 Democrats)
Human Services; Social Security and Women

Campaign Finance

	Receipts	Receipts from PACs		Expend-itures
1990				
DeLauro (D)	$973,625	$401,805	(41%)	$957,982
Scott (R)	$311,727	$64,937	(21%)	$304,258

Key Vote

1991

Authorize use of force against Iraq	N

Elections

1990 General

Rosa DeLauro (D)	90,772	(52%)
Thomas Scott (R)	83,440	(48%)

District Vote For President

	1988	1984	1980	1976
D	117,432 (49%)	101,877 (41%)	91,123 (39%)	106,441 (46%)
R	119,329 (50%)	146,171 (59%)	118,469 (50%)	122,995 (53%)
I			23,400 (10%)	

4 Christopher Shays (R)

Of Stamford — Elected 1987

Born: October 18, 1945, Stamford, Conn.
Education: Principia College, B.A. 1968; New York U., M.B.A. 1974, M.P.A. 1978.
Occupation: Real estate broker.
Family: Wife, Betsi de Raismes; one child.
Religion: Christian Scientist.
Political Career: Conn. House, 1975-87; Republican candidate for mayor of Stamford, 1983.
Capitol Office: 1531 Longworth House Office Building 20515; 225-5541.

In Washington: During his years in state politics, Shays honed an image as a maverick whose liberal views on many issues put him at odds with the state Republican hierarchy.

In the House, Shays is continuing to blaze a trail that sometimes unsettles GOP leaders. In the 101st Congress, as a member of the Government Operations subcommittee investigating Reagan-era misdeeds at the Department of Housing and Urban Development, Shays was among the first Republicans suggesting that the scandal might warrant a special prosecutor. And in his overall House voting record, Shays has sided with the White House only about one-third of the time, parting ways on such issues as parental leave and abortion rights, which he favors, and a constitutional amendment to ban flag desecration, which he opposes.

To GOP critics who say he shows an excess of independence, Shays notes that he is one of the few Republicans with a primarily urban constituency. And he says he is more conservative than many in his party on matters of federal spending. In the 102nd Congress, Shays sought a seat on the Budget Committee, arguing that he would be more in sync with the party line there. He got the job.

Soon upon arriving in Washington after his 1987 special-election victory, Shays surprised GOP leaders by turning down their offer of a seat on the Merchant Marine Committee; he said he had hoped for either Banking or Public Works. Shays sat without any committee assignments at all for two months, then finally got Government Operations and Science.

Government Operations became an unexpected publicity plum when, in 1989, the committee began hearings on charges of influence-peddling at HUD. The hearings were led by Democrat Tom Lantos of California, chairman of the Employment and Housing Subcommittee. Though less pointed and dramatic than Lantos in his questioning, Shays nevertheless was diligent and determined — too diligent, some GOP partisans thought — in grilling HUD officials.

In the fall of 1989, when some members tried to slip a few pet projects into the HUD spending bill, Shays joined a move to defeat these "earmarks." Likening the set-asides to preferential treatment within HUD, he said, "We cannot let this institution do exactly what we have criticized others for doing."

Shays has also been active in legislative efforts to re-regulate the cable industry and, following a 1987 Bridgeport building collapse that killed 28 workers, to improve safety for construction workers.

At Home: In the 1987 election held after veteran Republican Stewart B. McKinney died, Shays' personable style helped him overcome obstacles on his left and right. Campaigning from the center, Shays was positioned for success in the 4th, long a bastion of moderate Republicanism. As a result, he was virtually unopposed when he sought his first full term in 1988, and he had another easy race in 1990.

Shays stepped up to the House from the state Legislature, where he had a reputation as a stubbornly principled moderate-to-liberal. In 1985, after criticizing what he said were lax ethical standards in Connecticut's judicial system, Shays attempted to make a courtroom statement criticizing a judge for reducing charges against a lawyer who was accused of tampering with a will. Shays was slapped with a contempt citation and a short jail sentence, but he received plenty of favorable publicity.

Though that episode helped Shays expand his cadre of loyalists, it made some local Republicans wary. At the GOP nominating convention for the special election, Shays initially was denied a line on the ballot and qualified only after last-minute maneuvering. Nonetheless, with an extensive grass-roots network and tireless campaigning, Shays won with a 38 percent plurality.

In the general election, Shays' warm style contrasted favorably with that of Democrat Christine M. Niedermeier, who was widely known because she had run a strong 1986 campaign against McKinney. Seeking out voters at supermarkets, train stations and in movie theater queues, Shays won with 57 percent.

Connecticut 4

Southwest — Stamford; Bridgeport

Home to some of the wealthiest communities in the nation, the 4th is the best Republican territory in Connecticut. Towns such as Darien, Westport and New Canaan are symbols of upper-class New York City suburbia. Fairfield County is blanketed by newspapers and broadcasts that report the news of New York, not Connecticut.

Stamford, the largest of the suburban cities, has undergone a great change of character: What once was a small-business center whose outlying areas were dotted with country estates of the wealthy has become a haven for corporate headquarters, many of them fleeing New York's high tax rates. With Pitney-Bowes, GTE, Xerox and numerous others, Stamford by the mid-1980s had become one of the country's largest centers of corporate offices. Demand for more office space has put development pressure on places as far north as Fairfield, prompting distressed residents to organize to fight "commercial creep." Many of those suburbanites settled in the area 20 to 30 years ago.

However, even the 4th has not been spared the economic pain being felt statewide. After two decades of booming growth, for example, Stamford in 1989 began to experience a real estate slowdown.

Moderate Republicanism holds sway in the 4th. George Bush grew up in this area, and the 4th gave him 57 percent of the vote in 1988. This district was slow to embrace Ronald Reagan, though it voted for him over Jimmy Carter, and Shays won every town by a comfortable margin in 1990.

Despite the area's reputation as an enclave of white-collar Republican wealth, there are several dependably Democratic areas, including Bridgeport and some working-class areas of Stamford and Norwalk. In the 1988 Senate election, Democrat Joseph I. Lieberman's 7,200-vote margin in Bridgeport was by far his best showing in the 4th. Bridgeport (population 142,000), a workaday industrial city, is very much a part of Connecticut, quite apart from the more chic 4th District suburb-cities farther south, part of New York City's cultural orbit.

Now the largest city in Connecticut with 142,000 residents. Bridgeport actually lost 9 percent of its population between 1970 and 1980, but it surpassed Hartford in population because the decline in Hartford was far greater. However, Hartford registered a slight increase in the 1980s, while Bridgeport's population remained static.

Population: 518,577. White 437,190 (84%), Black 58,253 (11%), Other 4,793 (1%). Spanish origin 39,979 (8%). 18 and over 384,352 (74%), 65 and over 63,553 (12%). Median age: 34.

Committees

Budget (13th of 14 Republicans)
Budget Process, Reconciliation & Enforcement; Economic Policy, Projections & Revenues

Government Operations (6th of 15 Republicans)
Employment & Housing; Legislation & National Security

Select Narcotics Abuse & Control (9th of 14 Republicans)

Elections

1990 General		
Christopher Shays (R)	105,682	(77%)
Al Smith (D)	32,352	(23%)
1988 General		
Christopher Shays (R)	147,843	(72%)
Roger Pearson (D)	55,751	(27%)

Previous Winning Percentage: 1987 * (57%)

* *Special election.*

District Vote For President

	1988		1984		1980		1976	
D	96,177	(42%)	88,941	(36%)	82,004	(35%)	98,250	(41%)
R	128,702	(57%)	154,515	(63%)	124,209	(54%)	139,270	(58%)
I					23,186	(10%)		

Campaign Finance

	Receipts	Receipts from PACs	Expenditures
1990			
Shays (R)	$447,077	$58,000 (13%)	$395,892
Smith (D)	$90,780	$1,000 (1%)	$90,634
1988			
Shays (R)	$698,441	$151,617 (22%)	$675,079
Pearson (D)	$35,655	0	$46,147

Key Votes

1991	
Authorize use of force against Iraq	Y
1990	
Support constitutional amendment on flag desecration	N
Pass family and medical leave bill over Bush veto	Y
Reduce SDI funding	Y
Allow abortions in overseas military facilities	Y
Approve budget summit plan for spending and taxing	Y
Approve civil rights bill	Y
1989	
Halt production of B-2 stealth bomber at 13 planes	Y
Oppose capital gains tax cut	N
Approve federal abortion funding in rape or incest cases	Y
Approve pay raise and revision of ethics rules	Y
Pass Democratic minimum wage plan over Bush veto	Y

Voting Studies

	Presidential Support		Party Unity		Conservative Coalition	
Year	S	O	S	O	S	O
1990	34	66	60	40	41	59
1989	36	64	54	46	46	54
1988	42	58	59	41	61	39
1987	32 †	68 †	53 †	47 †	25 †	75 †

† *Not eligible for all recorded votes.*

Interest Group Ratings

Year	ADA	ACU	AFL-CIO	CCUS
1990	72	25	50	36
1989	85	29	67	70
1988	90	24	64	57
1987	89	67	78	40

5 Gary Franks (R)

Of Waterbury — Elected 1990

Born: Feb. 9, 1953, Waterbury, Conn.
Education: Yale U., B.A. 1975.
Occupation: Real estate investor.
Family: Wife, Donna Williams; one stepchild.
Religion: Baptist.
Political Career: Waterbury alderman, 1986-90.
Capitol Office: 1609 Longworth Bldg. 20515; 225-3822.

The Path to Washington: In an election cycle that left many Republicans wincing, Franks was one of the few smiles. His win gives the GOP its first black representative in 56 years, and strategists could hardly have scripted a better rainmaker to end that drought.

Franks, the son of a millworker, is a living realization of the political ideals of hard work and self-reliance. His father came north from North Carolina to work in the Waterbury brass mills, and his mother worked as a dietary aide at one of the city hospitals. Franks is one of six children, three of whom went on to earn doctorates.

Franks himself won a four-year scholarship to Yale, where he was captain of the basketball team. He was a labor and industrial relations specialist at several major corporations before beginning his own, successful real estate business.

Voters heard plenty about all this during the campaign against Democrat and former U.S. Rep. Toby Moffett for the seat vacated by John G. Rowland, a popular Republican.

Franks, whose political career includes 2½ terms on the Waterbury board of aldermen and an unsuccessful run for state comptroller, stressed his modest beginnings and subsequent successes.

Yet it remains difficult to predict Franks' future in Congress. Though active in Republican politics since the early 1980s, he did not have a particularly high political profile statewide. During the campaign, Moffett faulted Franks for missing meetings and dubbed him "Phantom Franks." Waterbury politicians sprang to Franks' defense, and friends praised him as a diligent, behind-the-scenes worker. But his low-key style made it easy to wonder about his political agenda, and, prior to his congressional campaign, he had not had occasion to speak widely on federal issues.

As reflected in campaign utterances, Franks' political philosophy seems well-steeped in '80s Reaganism: cut taxes, limit government, rely on private enterprise to drive the economy. He has taken this line even when it conflicts with the agenda of most black leaders: For example, Franks said he would have voted against the 1990 civil rights bill that Congress passed and President Bush vetoed, claiming that it would have led to hiring quotas. Franks does support abortion rights, but otherwise can be expected to vote on the right of the Connecticut delegation, as did Rowland.

Still, Franks appears unlikely to become part of the Republicans' vocal right wing in the House. Soft-spoken and personable, he has been known as a hard-working politician not given to grandstanding.

In fact, Franks probably owes his seat in Congress to his likability. He was one of five candidates competing at the July GOP district convention and finished last on the first round of balloting. But he moved ahead when other candidates fell to settling scores.

While each of his rivals had irrevocably alienated some delegates, Franks seemed an acceptable second choice to nearly all his rivals' partisans.

In his fall race, however, Franks did expend some of his "nice guy" capital to scuff up his opponent. He attacked Moffett (who had represented the 6th District and lived in the 3rd before moving to the 5th) as a liberal carpetbagger and faulted his attendance record while in Congress.

Franks finished only slightly behind Moffett in working-class Danbury and Waterbury, where Democrats had expected to do well, and outpolled him in many suburban areas (where GOP turnout was swelled by Rowland's gubernatorial candidacy).

Franks began his first term pledging attentiveness to district concerns, but for him the temptation of the larger stage will be stronger than for most. He drew the camera's eye as soon as he arrived, in part by breaking the party line in the Congressional Black Caucus. If Republican leaders have their way, Franks will be visible indeed.

Connecticut 5

West — Waterbury; Danbury

The rival industrial towns that cast most of the vote here tend to view each other with great wariness. It is said that when a federal grant goes to the Naugatuck Valley, Waterbury residents view the money as foreign aid.

Waterbury, at the northern end, is an old brass-making city where the once-powerful Democratic machine has been crumbling. Waterbury has had a GOP mayor since 1985, and in the 1990 House election, Democrat Toby Moffett won Waterbury by only 200 votes over Gary Franks, the GOP nominee. Franks was boosted by victories in seven of the eight predominately black wards in Waterbury.

The Naugatuck Valley, below Waterbury, has numerous small factories and conservative-minded working-class voters who are Democratic by registration but often not by practice. The majority-white GOP suburbs in New York City's orbit — Wilton, Weston and Ridgefield — gave Franks comfortable margins.

Not so very long ago, the 5th was a Democratic stronghold: In 1960, thousands of Waterburians waited long into the night for the arrival of John F. Kennedy, who concluded his campaign there with an election-eve rally. But the zeal of the Democratic faithful has slipped steadily. Hubert H. Humphrey was the last Democratic nominee to carry the 5th, and in 1984, there was another huge presidential campaign rally in Waterbury — for Ronald Reagan. Blue-collar Democrats continued to defect en masse in 1988 and the southern suburbs delivered their typically huge GOP margins. The 5th was George Bush's best Connecticut district, though Republican Lowell P. Weicker Jr. barely carried the district in his unsuccessful 1988 Senate re-election bid.

Though Waterbury's population has shrunk over the last 15 years as some factories folded or moved, it remains the district's largest city, with about 100,000 residents. Nearby Meriden, where business pursuits range from silverware to auto parts, remains more loyally Democratic than Waterbury. To the south, Danbury has seen the arrival of corporate headquarters and sophisticated industries seeking proximity to New York City. Union Carbide and Boehringer Ingelheim (a pharmaceuticals company) are major employers.

Population: 518,700. White 484,920 (94%), Black 21,582 (4%), Other 3,400 (1%). Spanish origin 17,244 (3%). 18 and over 372,002 (72%), 65 and over 57,224 (11%). Median age: 32.

Committees

Armed Services (22nd of 22 Republicans)
Investigations; Military Personnel & Compensation; Readiness

Select Aging (20th of 27 Republicans)
Retirement, Income & Employment

Small Business (14th of 17 Republicans)
Exports, Tax Policy & Special Problems; SBA, the General Economy & Minority Enterprise Development

Campaign Finance

	Receipts	Receipts from PACs		Expend-itures
1990				
Franks (R)	$587,045	$177,927	(30%)	$581,625
Moffett (D)	$880,726	$411,188	(47%)	$877,116

Key Vote

1991

Authorize use of force against Iraq	Y

Elections

1990 General

Gary A. Franks (R)	93,912	(52%)
Toby Moffett (D)	85,803	(47%)

District Vote For President

	1988	1984	1980	1976
D	97,553 (40%)	80,816 (33%)	80,411 (35%)	99,444 (45%)
R	141,664 (58%)	163,371 (67%)	123,976 (53%)	117,767 (54%)
I			25,577 (11%)	

6 Nancy L. Johnson (R)

Of New Britain — Elected 1982

Born: Jan. 5, 1935, Chicago, Ill.
Education: Radcliffe College, B.A. 1957; attended U. of London, 1957-58.
Occupation: Civic leader.
Family: Husband, Theodore Johnson; three children.
Religion: Unitarian.
Political Career: Conn. Senate, 1977-83; Republican candidate for New Britain Common Council, 1975.
Capitol Office: 227 Cannon Bldg. 20515; 225-4476.

In Washington: If she sometimes seems at the periphery of her party nationally, House Republicans regard Johnson as reliable enough to serve on the Committee on Standards of Official Conduct — a posting she took up early in 1991. And while she often votes with the Democrats, she can also be angrily partisan.

Johnson helped conservative firebrand Newt Gingrich become House GOP whip in 1989, and on the first day of the 1991 session she spoke so passionately against a perceived Democratic subterfuge on the budget that she ignored the Speaker's gavel and was threatened with removal by the House sergeant at arms.

Johnson endured some frustrations in the committee-assignment process during her first several years in Congress, losing bids to get on Armed Services, Energy and Commerce, and Ways and Means. She took a seat on Budget in the 100th Congress, but it was in the 101st Congress that she truly moved up to the big league, winning a place on Ways and Means.

In her first two years aboard the elite committee, she encountered predictable difficulty influencing its direction as the most junior member of the minority party. But by picking her spots on issues such as trade, Medicare, health and child care, she has made her voice heard.

In Connecticut, trade has become an increasingly sensitive issue as heavy industries have been battered by cheaper goods produced abroad. Johnson has been outspoken on a number of trade initiatives, and some of her concerns had been incorporated into trade legislation even before she joined the committee. Johnson is co-chairman of the Congressional Bearing Caucus, which looks out for the interests of the machine-tool and ball- and roller-bearing industry, an important employer in Connecticut. One of her efforts has been to speed governmental review of petitions brought by domestic industries seeking relief from imports on national security grounds. The bearing industry has sought such protections in recent years. She has also been instrumental in winning voluntary limits on imported machine-tools and a requirement that the Department of Defense buy American-made bearings.

But Johnson is wary of some measures aimed at U.S. competitors. She was opposed to the Gephardt "fair trade" amendment that was intended to force reductions in certain foreign trade surpluses. She warned that such an amendment would spark a trade war and ultimately hurt Connecticut.

"We can prevent our competitors from abusing American markets and consumers, and stealing jobs, without resorting to inflexible retaliation," she said.

Johnson was also an outspoken supporter of the Caribbean Basin Initiative, a program of lower tariffs begun in 1983 and renewed in 1990 to benefit Latin American economies.

On the broader economic front, Johnson likes to speak of compassion blended with conservatism, and she has looked for ways to present that mixture. Her record communicates traditional GOP business concerns and liberal social goals.

"Women have always been perceived as more open and more compassionate," she said when first campaigning for Congress. "I'm not sure a man could run as stridently as I have on economics and not be perceived as hard-hearted."

Johnson, the first Republican woman ever to serve on Ways and Means, has received some attention for her efforts to craft a comprehensive package of child-care initiatives. In the 100th Congress, one initiative that earned her praise from business groups and a supportive editorial from *The Washington Post* would have established vouchers to pay for child-care fees; revenue needed for the vouchers was to come from cutting back on child-care tax credits for families making over $60,000 per year. But the plan also had its share of opponents, in part because it allowed the vouchers to pay anyone caring for children, rather than just licensed day-care centers.

One reason Johnson had trouble getting

Connecticut 6

Northwest — New Britain

The 6th is diverse both geographically and politically. It includes the family home of William F. Buckley Jr., but it also produced Ralph Nader. Extending from quiet villages in the pastoral Litchfield Hills to the Hartford-Springfield, Mass., metropolitan area, the 6th is reliably Republican in presidential contests. But in other elections, it is unpredictable.

The "Nutmeggers" of rural Litchfield County, reflecting generations of small-town Yankee control, provide dependable GOP majorities. But that county also has mill towns, such as Torrington and Winsted, that often deliver Democratic margins.

To the southeast, the industrial city of New Britain, with its large Polish population, has been bedrock Democratic territory; Johnson lost it in 1982, but has carried it in her four re-elections. In 1988, Democratic Senate nominee Joseph I. Lieberman carried New Britain with 60 percent of the vote, on his way to a narrow victory in the 6th. The district's largest city, it lost population in the 1970s, but climbed slightly in the 1980s to 75,000.

Though much of the industry that once earned New Britain the moniker "the Hardware City" has left, there are still big job-providers in town, most notably The Stanley Works hardware company. Nearby Bristol, the second-largest city, has grown slightly in the last two decades and is catching up to New Britain in political clout; it produces a similar array of mechanical and electrical equipment and — except in Johnson's elections — votes heavily Democratic.

The 6th bumps up against the western side of Hartford, taking in strongly Republican upper-crust suburbs such as Farmington, Avon, Canton and Simsbury; Northeast of that area, the 6th includes Windsor Locks and Enfield, centers of large-scale industry along the Connecticut River. Democrats usually roll up their vote totals among Italian-American workers there. The district's largest employer, United Technologies' Hamilton-Standard aerospace division in Windsor Locks, provides 6,500 jobs.

Population: 517,146. White 501,201 (97%), Black 9,001 (2%), Other 2,539 (1%). Spanish origin 10,538 (2%). 18 and over 378,872 (73%), 65 and over 60,317 (12%). Median age: 32.

the committee posts she sought was her tendency to vote independently, both on committee and on the floor. On more than one occasion, her case-by-case decision-making approach has made her the target of some fierce lobbying. In 1985 she was pressed by the Reagan administration and the GOP leadership on the question of the MX missile. She had voted against the missile in 1984, but chief U.S. arms negotiator Max M. Kampelman and Defense Secretary Caspar W. Weinberger were among those urging her to change her mind and support spending $1.5 billion to buy 21 missiles. One member said Johnson "got the hell squeezed out of her," but she remained unconvinced, and voted against the funds. "I can honestly say I never considered switching my vote," she said. The House, however, voted 219-213 to approve the missiles.

As a member of the '92 Group, a coalition of moderate Republicans, and of the GOP platform committee in 1988, Johnson has tried to pull her party toward the political center. She has been particularly active working with '92 Group Republicans on ways to set budget priorities and reduce the deficit. She was a co-chairman of the group in the 100th Congress.

When the Republican Party was writing its national platform in 1988, Johnson joined with maverick Republican Lowell P. Weicker Jr., then the state's senior senator and in 1990 a successful independent candidate for governor, in challenging the document fashioned by the conservative majority. But the Nutmeggers' efforts, including a push to moderate the party's opposition to abortion rights and restore its support for the Equal Rights Amendment, were almost always rebuffed.

"If a party does not have diversity," Johnson says, "it isn't thinking."

At Home: Johnson was a rarity in 1982, a victorious Republican in an open district dominated by blue-collar Democrats. For her, that sort of victory was nothing new. In 1977 she became the first Republican in 30 years to represent the industrial city of New Britain in the state Senate, and she was re-elected easily.

Johnson's casual style gives her an appeal across class and party lines. "She can belly up to the toughest bar in town and captivate the customers," a local political reporter once wrote, "just as effectively as she can balance the teacups with totally proper ladies at any church social." That is just the right combination for the 6th, which encompasses lunch-bucket bastions such as New Britain and Bristol, and the Yankee towns of Litchfield County.

Johnson, the wife of an obstetrician, was a

longtime activist in New Britain community affairs. When the Republican town chairman asked her in 1976 to run for the state Senate, she agreed, and went on to defeat Democrat Paul S. Amenta by 150 votes.

When Democratic Rep. Toby Moffett announced at the end of 1981 that he was giving up the 6th to challenge incumbent Weicker for the Senate, Johnson moved eagerly to take his place. She quickly captured the backing of the party establishment and influential GOP donors, opening an early lead over her primary opponent, conservative Nicholas Schaus.

Johnson's Democratic opponent in the general election was a colleague from the state Senate, William E. Curry Jr. A liberal in the Moffett tradition, Curry had won a hard-fought primary battle by putting together an impressive grass-roots organization with the support of labor, environmentalists and consumer groups. But he was badly short of funds.

Most of Curry's campaigning was in New Britain, which he did carry by 3,000 votes. That effort cost him elsewhere, however; he won the district's other Democratic communities by much smaller margins than Moffett had.

Instead of squabbling over the nomination as they did in 1982, Democrats in 1984 agreed on insurance executive Art House, a candidate knowledgeable in the workings of Washington by virtue of his five years' service as a top aide to former Democratic Sen. Abraham Ribicoff. House accused Johnson of being a wishy-washy politician trying to give something to everyone, but her moderate pitch limited his options for specific attacks. She called Reagan's re-election "crucial," but complained about the administration's defense-spending levels, its cutbacks in education programs and its progress on arms control. House took only 36 percent of the vote.

In 1986, Johnson again faced Paul Amenta, whom she had narrowly beaten in her first state Senate race. This time, Johnson won easily. Two years later, Democrats put scant effort into the 6th, and Johnson won big.

Then, in 1990, Johnson took her highest congressional tally — a powerful 74 percent — against Suffield Selectman Paul A. Kulas.

Committees

Standards of Official Conduct (3rd of 7 Republicans)

Ways & Means (11th of 13 Republicans)
Health; Human Resources

Elections

1990 General

Nancy L. Johnson (R)	141,105	(74%)
Paul Kulas (D)	48,628	(26%)

1988 General

Nancy L. Johnson (R)	157,020	(66%)
James L. Griffin (D)	78,814	(33%)

Previous Winning Percentages: **1986** (64%) **1984** (64%) **1982** (52%)

District Vote For President

	1988	1984	1980	1976
D	115,742 (46%)	91,920 (37%)	92,955 (39%)	111,077 (48%)
R	133,709 (53%)	155,843 (63%)	113,203 (47%)	120,338 (52%)
I			32,748 (14%)	

Campaign Finance

	Receipts	Receipts from PACs		Expend-itures
1990				
Johnson (R)	$517,724	$252,737	(49%)	$556,718
Kulas (D)	$22,475	$4,000	(18%)	$22,211
1988				
Johnson (R)	$527,164	$135,322	(26%)	$399,370
Griffin (D)	$128,185	$30,175	(24%)	$128,853

Key Votes

1991

Authorize use of force against Iraq	Y

1990

Support constitutional amendment on flag desecration	N
Pass family and medical leave bill over Bush veto	Y
Reduce SDI funding	N
Allow abortions in overseas military facilities	Y
Approve budget summit plan for spending and taxing	Y
Approve civil rights bill	Y

1989

Halt production of B-2 stealth bomber at 13 planes	N
Oppose capital gains tax cut	N
Approve federal abortion funding in rape or incest cases	Y
Approve pay raise and revision of ethics rules	Y
Pass Democratic minimum wage plan over Bush veto	Y

Voting Studies

	Presidential Support		Party Unity		Conservative Coalition	
Year	**S**	**O**	**S**	**O**	**S**	**O**
1990	52	46	54	43	65	31
1989	60	38	43	53	71	27
1988	44	50	52	44	68	24
1987	47	52	53	42	65	28
1986	52	43	38	58	68	32
1985	50	50	45	51	67	33
1984	52	44	48	47	51	42
1983	51	46	43	49	54	46

Interest Group Ratings

Year	ADA	ACU	AFL-CIO	CCUS
1990	44	50	33	57
1989	30	50	33	80
1988	50	56	71	69
1987	48	35	50	73
1986	40	55	79	72
1985	40	48	47	64
1984	50	29	38	56
1983	45	26	44	50

Delaware

U.S. CONGRESS

SENATE 1 D, 1 R
HOUSE 1 D

LEGISLATURE

Senate 15 D, 6 R
House 17 D, 24 R

ELECTIONS

1988 Presidential Vote	
Bush	56%
Dukakis	44%
1984 Presidential Vote	
Reagan	60%
Mondale	40%
1980 Presidential Vote	
Reagan	47%
Carter	45%
Anderson	7%
Turnout rate in 1986	34%
Turnout rate in 1988	51%
Turnout rate in 1990	35%

(as percentage of voting age population)

POPULATION AND GROWTH

1980 population	594,338
1990 population (46th in the nation)	666,168
Percent change 1980-1990	+12%

DEMOGRAPHIC BREAKDOWN

White	80%
Black	17%
Asian or Pacific Islander	1%
(Hispanic origin)	2%
Urban	71%
Rural	29%
Born in state	52%
Foreign-born	3%

MAJOR CITIES

Wilmington	71,529
Dover	27,630
Newark	25,098
Milford	6,040
Elsmere	5,935

AREA AND LAND USE

Area 1,933 sq. miles (49th)

Farm	53%
Forest	33%
Federally owned	2%

Gov. Michael N. Castle (R)
Of Dover — Elected 1984

Born: July 2, 1939, Wilmington, Del.
Education: Hamilton College, B.A. 1961; Georgetown U., LL.B. 1964.
Occupation: Lawyer.
Religion: Roman Catholic.
Political Career: Del. deputy attorney general, 1965-66; Del. House, 1967-69; Del. Senate, 1969-77, minority leader, 1976-77; lieutenant governor, 1981-85.
Next Election: 1992.

WORK

Occupations	
White-collar	55%
Blue-collar	29%
Service workers	13%
Government Workers	
Federal	5,369
State	23,488
Local	17,870

MONEY

Median family income	$ 20,817	(17th)
Tax burden per capita	$ 1,312	(3rd)

EDUCATION

Spending per pupil through grade 12	$ 5,017	(10th)
Persons with college degrees	18%	(17th)

CRIME

Violent crime rate 557 per 100,000 (18th)

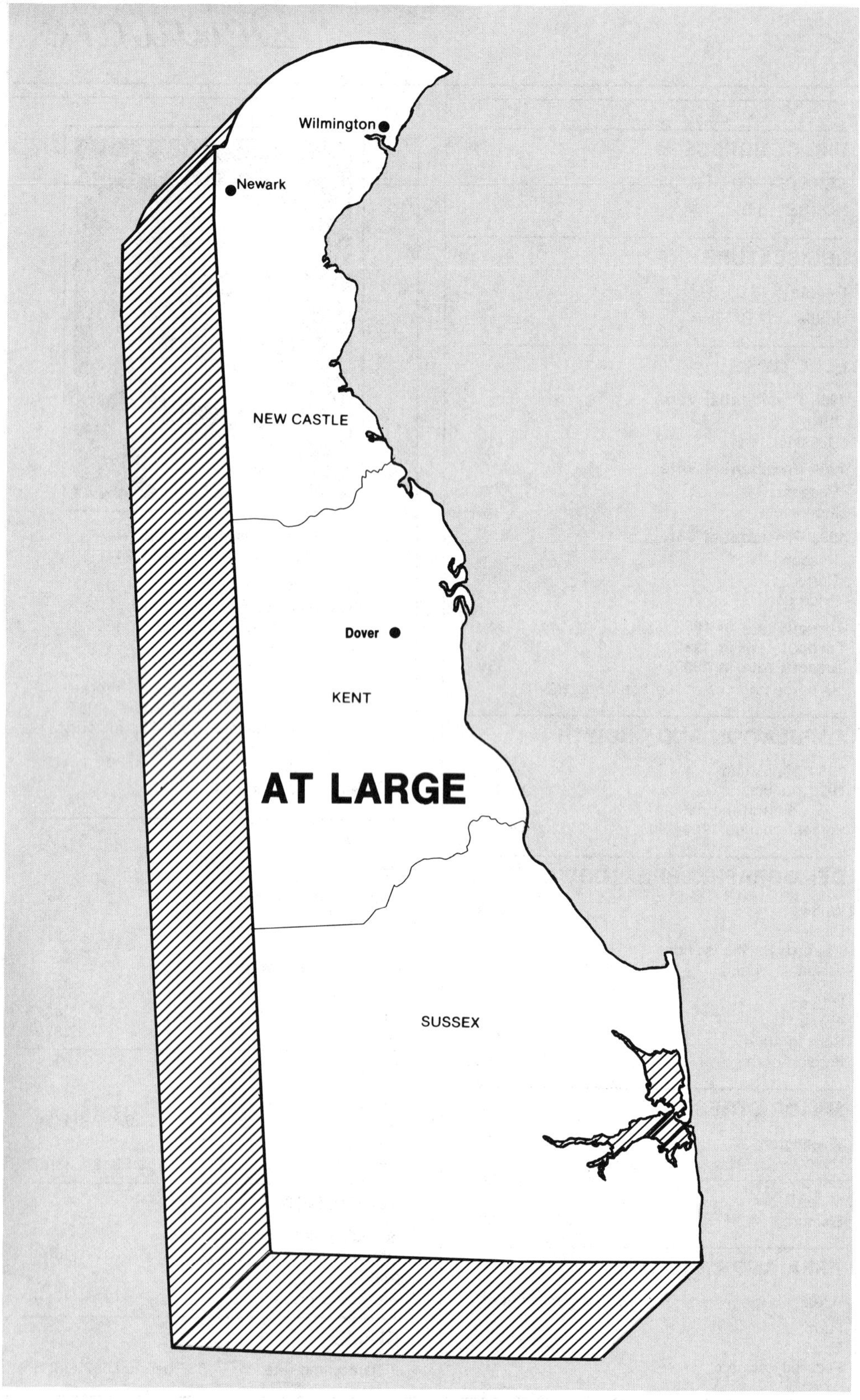
Wilmington
Newark
NEW CASTLE
Dover
KENT
AT LARGE
SUSSEX

William V. Roth Jr. (R)

Of Wilmington — Elected 1970

Born: July 22, 1921, Great Falls, Mont.
Education: U. of Oregon, B.A. 1944; Harvard U., M.B.A. 1947, LL.B. 1949.
Military Service: Army, 1943-46.
Occupation: Lawyer.
Family: Wife, Jane Richards; two children.
Religion: Episcopalian.
Political Career: U.S. House 1967-71; Republican nominee for lieutenant governor, 1960.
Capitol Office: 104 Hart Bldg. 20510; 224-2441.

In Washington: Roth is a legislator who likes grand ideas — massive tax cuts, huge new savings plans, sweeping revisions of government agencies. He has devoted most of his Senate career to drumming up support for such schemes, but outside that he sometimes has trouble making an impact; he is not a senator with an intense interest in the day-to-day chores of legislative life.

Roth has found himself in a defensive legislative posture in the late 1980s and early '90s — working to preserve the tax exemption for state and local bonds, to protect Individual Retirement Accounts (IRAs), to guard Delaware's franchise as a haven for corporate charters as the Congress examines the corporate takeover game, and to prevent the repeal of the Hatch Act, which prohibits federal workers from engaging in political activities.

An apparently visceral distaste for high taxes and excessive government spending put Roth in a new position in the 101st Congress — that of legislative naysayer. On a number of high-profile and high-cost issues, Roth voted against final passage, often being one of a mere handful of senators to do so.

Roth was the only senator to vote against the major overhaul of housing programs that Congress passed in 1990. He was joined by just three colleagues in opposing an emergency AIDS-relief measure and by just five in voting against an anticrime initiative. Roth also voted against final passage of the farm bill and campaign finance revisions — measures the Senate approved handily.

Roth did have a season in the national spotlight as an original co-author of President Reagan's 1981 tax cut. He had to settle for second billing, however. While he calls the legislation he sponsored "Roth-Kemp," virtually everyone else in America, at least outside his Senate office, refers to the income-tax cut — 25 percent across the board over three years — as "Kemp-Roth," after the younger and more dynamic co-author, Jack F. Kemp, the Housing and Urban Development secretary and former GOP House member from New York.

The importance of personal savings has been a recurring theme throughout Roth's career. When the Senate Finance Committee geared up in 1986 to produce a bill overhauling the federal tax code, Roth proposed a kind of value-added tax on gross business receipts to raise up to $115 billion over five years. Roth wanted to use that revenue to, among other things, pay for letting taxpayers establish tax-sheltered "Super Saver Accounts."

But after Finance Chairman Bob Packwood pushed a streamlined tax-overhaul bill through his committee in May 1986, Roth had his hands full just trying to save the deductibility of IRA contributions. The Senate heeded Packwood's pleas to keep his committee's bill basically intact, so Roth was reduced to lobbying for passage of a "sense of the Senate" resolution that instructed the chamber's conferees to assign "highest priority to maintaining maximum possible tax benefits for IRAs."

But in the House-Senate conference on the tax bill, neither the resolution nor Roth's pleas carried great weight. Some low- and middle-income taxpayers were allowed to continue deducting IRA contributions, but higher-income individuals and employees with pension plans were not. Roth attached another major IRA savings plan to President Bush's push for a capital gains tax cut during budget negotiations in 1989. His was a version of a "back-loaded" IRA, in which taxpayers could not deduct their IRA contribution, but they could exempt both the principal and earnings from taxes when they were withdrawn. Savers could also make limited withdrawals for a first home, a college education or catastrophic medical expenses.

The GOP tax plan — Roth's proposal plus the capital gains tax cut offered by Packwood — stirred Democrats to oppose the plan as a long range revenue loser. The Congressional

Budget Office (CBO) said Roth's plan would increase revenue at first but that "the short-term gain of $11.5 billion comes at the expense of about $22 billion in future revenues."

But Roth and Packwood argued that their plans, taken together, were revenue neutral over five years. Roth likened the proposal's potential impact to that of "Roth-Kemp," tax cuts he said had led to seven straight years of economic growth.

"My IRA is exactly what the economy needs for long-term growth," he said.

Despite having Bush's backing, a near-solid phalanx of GOP Senate support and some influential Democratic backers, the plan died. Bush asked Congress to strip the proposal from the deficit-reduction package and despite getting a majority of senators on record as supporting the tax cut and savings plan, two Senate tallies fell nine votes short of the 60 required to cut off debate on the measure.

Roth introduced a less-ambitious plan in 1990 to allow families to save up to $5,000 per year with tax-free withdrawal after seven years. And, early in the 102nd Congress, Roth joined Finance Committee Chairman Lloyd Bentsen of Texas in introducing a bill to restore the deductibility of deposits in IRAs and — like the 1989 Super IRA plan — allow non-penalized withdrawals for certain expenses. The proposal, like Roth's earlier one, also included the option of the back-loaded IRA.

On Governmental Affairs, Roth has been active in federal pay and procurement issues. He was a sponsor in 1990 of a major federal pay-overhaul proposal and also supported locality-based raises for federal workers in particularly expensive cities, a provision included in the final legislation and a significant change in the General Scale pay system.

Roth also took the lead in opposing efforts to revise the Hatch Act. Though Congress passed the revisions, Bush issued a veto that the Senate narrowly sustained. During deliberations throughout the 101st Congress, Roth argued against tampering with the 1939 law, insisting that the act provided protection for federal workers against political coercion and other abuses of the civil service system. "We can hardly afford further erosion of public confidence in our civil servants," he said.

To no great effect during the 101st Congress, Roth pushed for a measure to elevate the Environmental Protection Agency to Cabinet-level status. The measure ultimately stalled in 1990 over a standoff between Congress and the administration. Roth has also promoted, with a similar lack of success, a Cabinet-level Department of International Trade and Industry, composed of the Commerce Department, the Office of the U.S. Trade Representative and other trade-related federal agencies.

Concern about the changing global economy has at times led Roth to turn his attention beyond the domestic economic agenda. He narrowly lost a bid in December 1990 to become president of the North Atlantic Assembly, the legislative body of the North Atlantic Treaty Organization (NATO); he was completing a term as vice president. Some American and European lawmakers saw the assembly as a possible political replacement for NATO.

At Home: A mild-mannered man, Roth has never been able to generate a great deal of emotion among Delaware voters. But he has been doggedly attentive to state interests, and he has been rewarded for that service with victories in six statewide elections — two for the House and four for the Senate.

Born in Montana and educated at Harvard, Roth came to Delaware to work as a lawyer for a chemical firm and got involved in politics. After narrowly losing a 1960 bid for lieutenant governor, he became state Republican chairman. In 1966 Roth entered the race for Delaware's at-large U.S. House seat against veteran Democrat Harris B. McDowell Jr. He talked about Vietnam — backing U.S. efforts but berating the Johnson administration for not explaining the situation more fully — and about open-housing legislation (he opposed it but was willing to endorse state GOP convention language favoring it). Riding the coattails of GOP Sen. J. Caleb Boggs and a national Republican wave that carried 47 GOP freshmen to the House in 1966, Roth pulled off an upset.

McDowell tried for a comeback two years later. But he had alienated members of the state Democratic hierarchy by deploring their "old and tired leadership." Buoyed by his first-term record of strong constituent service, Roth pushed his margin of victory to nearly 60 percent of the statewide vote.

With the retirement of GOP Sen. John J. Williams in 1970, Roth became the uncontested choice of his party against the Democratic state House leader, Jacob W. Zimmerman. A Vietnam dove, Zimmerman had little money or statewide name recognition, and the contest was never much in doubt.

In 1976 Roth had a strong Democratic challenger — Wilmington Mayor Thomas C. Maloney. But Roth's efforts against busing had given him an excellent issue to run on, and Maloney was hurt by the coolness of organized labor. Roth's margin was down from 1970, but he was too strong in the suburbs for Maloney to have any chance to beat him.

Running for a third term in 1982, Roth faced his most difficult Senate test. As cosponsor of the supply-side tax cut, he was a visible target for complaints about the then-flagging economy: like other industrial states, Delaware had felt the effects of recession.

David N. Levinson, Roth's hard-charging Democratic opponent, encouraged voters to link Roth to Reagan's economic policies and the woes he claimed they had produced. Parodying

John Steinbeck's novel about the Great Depression, Levinson branded the administration's economic blueprint "The Grapes of Roth."

The incumbent did not hide his tax legislation; billboards advertising his candidacy read, "Bill Roth, the Taxpayer's Best Friend." But he was careful to evince his concern for Frost Belt economic needs, voting against 1981 reductions in three programs important to Delaware: Conrail, trade adjustment assistance to unemployed workers and energy subsidies for the poor.

Levinson campaigned for the seat for over two years; he got endorsements from labor and most of the other important groups Democrats need to be competitive statewide. But Roth suggested that the Democrat had come into the state just to challenge him. Though he lost Wilmington, Roth more than made it up in suburban New Castle County and rural territory to the south.

In 1988, Roth aimed to become the first Delaware senator to win a fourth term since Williams was re-elected in 1964. National Democratic officials called him vulnerable, noting that he had never reached the 60 percent mark denoting electoral security. In preparation for a tough campaign, Roth amassed a huge treasury.

Rep. Thomas R. Carper declined to challenge Roth. Democratic state party leaders scurried to the side of Samuel S. Beard, a wealthy civic activist and party fundraiser. But maverick Lt. Gov. S. B. Woo spoiled their plans for a smooth nomination. Woo, whose ties to the Chinese-American community guaranteed him a healthy campaign budget, defeated Beard by 71 votes in a bitter primary battle.

While Woo and Beard were slicing each other up, Roth was stressing his political assets, running a media campaign on his record of steering federal money to Delaware and his vaunted dedication to constituent service.

Because of Delaware's September primary date, Woo had little time to prepare for the general election. Roth surpassed 60 percent for the first time in his long career.

Committees

Governmental Affairs (Ranking)
Permanent Subcommittee on Investigations (ranking)

Banking, Housing & Urban Affairs (6th of 9 Republicans)
International Finance & Monetary Policy

Finance (3rd of 9 Republicans)
Health for Families & the Uninsured; International Trade; Taxation (ranking)

Joint Economic

Elections

1988 General

William V. Roth Jr. (R)	151,115	(62%)
S.B. Woo (D)	92,378	(38%)

Previous Winning Percentages: **1982** (55%) **1976** (56%) **1970** (59%) **1968** * (59%) **1966** * (56%)

** House elections.*

Campaign Finance

	Receipts	Receipts from PACs		Expenditures
1988				
Roth (R)	$1,887,995	$794,191	(42%)	$1,942,119
Woo (D)	$2,409,188	$91,810	(4%)	$2,385,414

Key Votes

1991

Authorize use of force against Iraq	Y

1990

Oppose prohibition of certain semiautomatic weapons	Y
Support constitutional amendment on flag desecration	Y
Oppose requiring parental notice for minors' abortions	N
Halt production of B-2 stealth bomber at 13 planes	Y
Approve budget that cut spending and raised revenues	N
Pass civil rights bill over Bush veto	N

1989

Oppose reduction of SDI funding	Y
Oppose barring federal funds for "obscene" art	Y
Allow vote on capital gains tax cut	Y

Voting Studies

	Presidential Support		Party Unity		Conservative Coalition	
Year	**S**	**O**	**S**	**O**	**S**	**O**
1990	72	28	80	20	76	24
1989	94	5	85	14	89	8
1988	72	27	51	47	70	30
1987	65 †	31 †	76 †	20 †	88 †	13 †
1986	83	16	83	13	80	17
1985	84	16	81	19	72	27
1984	74	18	85	10	83	15
1983	76	22	80	18	77	20
1982	77	20	76	22	83	16
1981	75	24	72	26	75	24

† Not eligible for all recorded votes.

Interest Group Ratings

Year	ADA	ACU	AFL-CIO	CCUS
1990	22	87	33	67
1989	0	81	0	88
1988	20	60	43	57
1987	20	80	50	94
1986	15	78	13	82
1985	20	70	14	83
1984	10	73	10	83
1983	30	56	13	50
1982	50	47	27	67
1981	20	67	32	78

Joseph R. Biden Jr. (D)

Of Wilmington — Elected 1972

Born: Nov. 20, 1942, Scranton, Pa.
Education: U. of Delaware, B.A. 1965; Syracuse U., J.D. 1968.
Occupation: Lawyer.
Family: Wife, Jill Jacobs; three children.
Religion: Roman Catholic.
Political Career: New Castle County Council, 1970-72.
Capitol Office: 221 Russell Bldg. 20510; 224-5042.

In Washington: Two personal crises — the humiliating end of his 1988 presidential bid, followed quickly by a life-threatening brain aneurysm — led Biden to examine his life in a most public manner as the 101st Congress opened in 1989. He acknowledged weaknesses and vowed reform. Critics, chastened by his trials, refocused on his many strengths. But now, more than two years later, the central question about Biden remains the same: Does he radiate more heat than light?

As chairman of the Judiciary Committee, Biden wrestles with some of the most high-profile and nettlesome issues facing Congress and the Democratic Party — crime and drugs, and in the 101st Congress, the flag. An Irish Catholic, middle-class son of a Scranton, Pa., auto dealer, Biden can strike the right note with his sincere, all-American rhetoric. "What we need," he said in a televised response to Bush's anti-drug speech in 1989, "is another D-Day, not another Vietnam, not a limited war, fought on the cheap, and destined for stalemate and human tragedy."

But Biden still has trouble matching his words with legislative muscle. His efforts to find a means to outlaw flag desecration in 1989 without amending the Constitution fell flat. And despite his willingness to compromise with Republicans on the death penalty and other matters (which troubled many Democrats), the 1990 crime bill conference fell apart. Instead of sweeping reform, a stripped-down bill was enacted.

Biden still speaks with the self-deprecation that is part of his charm — he often reminds witnesses before the Judiciary Committee that they did better in law school than he did. But he still talks too much. When members are given five minutes for opening remarks, Chairman Biden often takes 20 or 30.

None of this is new. From the time Biden arrived in the Senate, he struck observers as a man destined for big things, with the talent and charisma to be an influential Democrat for decades to come. He is legend for his ability to move audiences with his powerful oration. Intelligent and perceptive, he can quickly grasp and convey the essence of complex issues. Personable and conciliatory, he can be adept at legislative negotiations. These qualities, however, raise perhaps impossibly high expectations for him.

For all his potential, Biden can also be brash and impetuous. Early in his career, he was identified as something of an *enfant terrible* — a young man whose loquacity frequently outran his better judgment, impatient with the tedious details and sustained labors of legislating. But those traits, once dismissed as youthful excesses, remain with Biden as he has become a middle-aged senior senator.

Biden is apt to have many years to refine his public persona. As the second-youngest person ever elected to the Senate, with an apparently secure base in Delaware, he is set to have one of the longest careers in the institution's history. Already, he is 11th in seniority among Democrats, and at least 10 years younger than all but one member ahead of him.

Biden became chairman of the Judiciary Committee when the Democrats regained the Senate majority after the 1986 election, and in that role he has maintained a warm rapport with South Carolina Republican Strom Thurmond, the previous chairman. "My Henry Clay," Thurmond liked to call Biden, in recognition of his skill at bipartisan compromises. Biden still calls Thurmond "Mr. Chairman."

Confirmation hearings provide Biden with a highly visible forum, but one that places him in a delicate political position. Liberals and civil rights activists have complained that Biden was too tentative in opposing some of President Reagan's more controversial nominees — particularly the choices of William Bradford Reynolds to be associate attorney general in 1985 (he was rejected), and of Supreme Court Justice William H. Rehnquist to become chief justice in 1986. Conservatives, however, have accused Biden of leading a liberal lynch mob.

Biden was stung by a series of 1990 *Wall Street Journal* editorials during hearings to confirm Clarence Thomas to the U.S. appeals court. With a leaked copy of an extensive document request the committee had made of Thomas, the paper slammed the request as a "fishing expedition" and "little more than a trolling exercise." One editorial was entitled "The Next Lynching." (Biden and the Senate went on to support Thomas' nomination.)

Later, when David H. Souter's nomination to the Supreme Court came before Judiciary, Biden's treatment of him was solicitous. "While we may ask any questions we deem proper," Biden said in his opening statement, setting the tone for the hearing, "you are free to refuse to answer any questions you deem to be improper."

Souter was ultimately approved with scant controversy in late 1990, a stark contrast to the hearings that resulted in the October 1987 rejection of Reagan's nomination of Robert H. Bork to the Supreme Court.

Initially, Biden's handling of Bork's nomination showed the senator at his worst. He had once said he could accept Bork if Reagan nominated the conservative jurist. When Reagan did, Biden said he probably would oppose Bork. Then he announced he definitely would oppose Bork, but he would explain why later.

But Biden managed to rise above that and even put aside the plagiarism stories that broke in the second week of the Bork hearings and drove him from the 1988 presidential race. Ultimately, even Republicans and an embittered Bork would concede that Biden had been fair. He set a tone that was serious and respectful. He ably grilled Bork about the judge's controversial contention that the Constitution was silent about privacy rights, zeroing in for political effect on Bork's criticism of a 1965 case in which the court had cited privacy rights to strike down a state law making it a crime for married couples to use contraceptives.

When liberal dogma and public opinion collide, as they did in the flag desecration debate, few are as skilled as Biden at giving voice to the competing concerns. But in that instance, Biden's efforts to balance the competing forces left him out in the cold. Biden in 1989 sponsored a statutory means to outlaw flag desecration, in hopes of skirting the constitutional amendment sought by the president and anathema to liberals. While Biden moved the statutory bill quickly, he was repeatedly rebuffed by wide margins in his effort to block amendments that he feared would make the statute unconstitutional.

Indeed, the statute was struck down by the Supreme Court months later. While Biden came back to the table with a narrowly drawn constitutional amendment, key House liberals were working behind the scenes to fundamentally alter the debate. Ultimately, they succeeded: The public and politicians lost interest in the matter, the House defeated a constitutional amendment, and Biden glumly apologized for "wasting the taxpayers' money ... in discussing something that is going nowhere."

In both 1986 and 1988, Biden was a chief sponsor and key negotiator on sweeping anti-drug legislation. Early in the 101st Congress, he resisted offering another new anti-drug package, saying the government should fund the programs already in place.

But with President Bush and the GOP exerting political pressure to pass a crime bill, Biden and some fellow Democrats shifted their focus to issues such as the death penalty and gun control. After others had taken the lead on those fronts, Biden made an effort to reach a passable compromise, but the results pleased no one. The death penalty provisions in his crime bill, for instance, were an unwieldy combination of a broad federal death penalty measure sponsored by conservative Thurmond and an amendment added by liberal Sen. Edward M. Kennedy to bar the death sentence if it furthers a "racially discriminatory pattern."

Much of the crime package got through the Senate, but talks with the House collapsed. The issues will undoubtedly be revisited before the 1992 election, but Biden already feels his efforts have helped the Democratic Party's image on crime. "If you want the death penalty [for drug traffickers], we're for the death penalty," he said. "How many people do you want to kill, Mr. President?"

One of Biden's most significant legislative achievements was his role in the 1984 passage of legislation rewriting federal criminal statutes. The culmination of an 11-year effort, the legislation revised sentencing procedures to reduce the disparity in punishments imposed on persons who committed similar crimes, and allowed pretrial detention of some dangerous suspects. He was Democratic floor manager of the bill, and negotiated a deal with House leaders at the close of the 98th Congress.

Two years later, he was a guiding force behind enactment of tough new legislation against illegal drugs. His most important contribution came when the bill was deadlocked in conference, largely over a provision imposing the death penalty for certain drug crimes. Biden helped arrange the informal negotiations that cleared the way for final passage.

The drug bill's passage illustrated the two sides of Biden. In the final episode, he was the talented 11th-hour mediator, riding in to save the day. But as legislation unfolds in all its mind-numbing details, and slowly makes its way through a balky process, Biden often is hardly a presence. He is not a textbook legislator. With his glib tongue, people skills and penchant for quick action, his strength is at the podium, not the conference table.

With one major exception, Biden has been a reliable liberal vote on Judiciary. He broke ranks early and memorably over busing. A former participant in sit-ins to desegregate restaurants along U.S. Route 40, he surprised colleagues in 1975 when he won Senate approval of an anti-busing amendment. Suddenly he was allied with Southern conservatives on a wrenching national issue. "It is not a comfortable feeling for me," he said. But it was time, he argued, to admit that "busing does not work."

He has been consistently liberal on foreign policy issues. As a member of the Foreign Relations Committee — and of the Intelligence Committee until 1985 — Biden has pressed for arms control agreements, opposed military intervention in Central America and insisted that Congress be a full partner with the White House in decisions to send U.S. forces to hostile areas.

Biden combines his interest in foreign affairs and illegal drug trafficking with far-reaching proposals to provide debt relief to drug-producing Andean nations. In 1989, Congress approved a small piece of the program, forgiving $125 million in debts held by the U.S. government in exhange for drug eradication efforts by Bolivia, Columbia and Peru.

In the mid-1980s, Biden also served a stint on the Budget Committee, where he joined with Republicans Nancy Landon Kassebaum and Charles E. Grassley to propose a budget freeze. The so-called KGB Plan was rejected by the Senate, although it was something of a model for later deficit-reduction efforts.

Part of what makes Biden such a compelling political figure, and what commands such attention to his personal development, are the tragedies and dramas of his public life. Just weeks after his 1972 Senate election, Biden's wife and infant daughter were killed and his two sons seriously injured in an automobile accident. Biden said at first that he did not want to take the oath of office. Persuaded by Majority Leader Mike Mansfield to assume his seat, Biden was sworn in at his son's bedside.

After spending more than a decade rebuilding his life and career, Biden launched a long-awaited presidential campaign in June 1987. But in a season focused on candidates' character, he fell under the weight of reports that he had plagiarized passages in his speeches and a 1965 law school paper, and finally, that he had exaggerated his résumé. He withdrew from the race in September.

No sooner did the uncomfortable episode fade from public view than a brush with death put Biden back in the news. In February 1988, he had the first of two operations for a near-fatal brain aneurysm. By early 1989, however, Biden was back in action.

At Home: The collapse of Biden's 1988 presidential campaign amid allegations of plagiarism raised questions about his political future — not only his hopes for the White House, but also his future in the Senate.

With a number of his constituents admitting to some embarrassment over his campaign debacle, Biden looked potentially vulnerable to a Republican Senate challenge in 1990. Republican officials, including conservatives who sought to avenge Bork's Supreme Court defeat, began to shop for potential candidates.

However, Biden's home-state downturn did not last long. His triumph over life-threatening health problems in 1988 helped reinstate affections of supporters who had grown skeptical of him. His return to an assertive role in the Senate restored him to a position of dominance in Delaware politics.

Biden's quick rebound deterred high-level GOP competition as he bid for a fourth term. His Republican opponent was M. Jane Brady, a deputy state attorney general making her first try for elective office. Although Brady held frequent news conferences to attract free media attention, she failed to find an issue that would divert support from Biden.

Brady's strongest political credential was her anti-crime image as a prosecutor. But throughout the campaign, Biden made news with his efforts to craft a federal crime bill that included many tough new measures. Brady tried to make an issue out of Biden's receipt of campaign funds from savings-and-loan figures, including controversial Miami financier David L. Paul; Biden blunted that issue by sending the U.S. Treasury a check in an amount equal to the campaign funds he had received over the years from S&L sources.

Biden had taken a risk during an August appearance on the cable TV network C-SPAN by denying that he had committed plagiarism in law school. Brady — whose consultant was Donald Devine, a veteran of Republican campaign battles — unleashed a late campaign assault aimed at reminding voters of Biden's plagiarism problems. But she failed to revive the long-cooled issue. Biden cruised to victory with 62 percent of the vote, a career high.

Biden was in the underdog role himself when, at age 29, he made an audacious bid to unseat GOP Sen. J. Caleb Boggs. With service on the New Castle County Council his only electoral credential, Biden seemed a sure loser. But his celebrated brashness helped Biden pull off a major upset.

Biden ran hard on a dovish Vietnam platform and accused the Republican of being a do-nothing senator. He called for more spending on mass transit and health care services. The Biden campaign was essentially a family operation, without state-of-the-art media management, but it was sophisticated enough to cover a state with an electorate as small as Delaware's. Boggs awoke to the threat too late as his "safe" seat disappeared by 3,162 votes.

Delaware Democratic leaders, certain that a challenge to Boggs was hopeless, had given Biden little support in 1972. He gave them little attention in return for most of his first term. At the 1976 Democratic National Convention in

New York City, he stayed in one hotel, and the state delegation in another.

By 1978, Biden had made up with the party. Of greater importance in his re-election bid that year, however, was his opposition to busing. As he ran for re-election, a long-disputed busing plan was taking effect in New Castle County, outraging voters in suburban Wilmington.

With this anti-busing position offsetting his liberalism on some other social issues, Biden seemed unbeatable in 1978, and big-name Delaware Republicans refrained from taking him on. The task fell to an obscure southern Delaware poultry farmer, James H. Baxter, who gamely tried to paint the Democrat as too far left for the state. Biden easily beat him.

For a time, it appeared as though Biden might be seriously threatened in 1984. Republican Gov. Pierre S. "Pete" du Pont IV, ineligible to seek a third consecutive term, was pressured to challenge the incumbent by President Reagan and Senate Majority Leader Howard H. Baker Jr. But du Pont chose not to run.

The Republican who eventually emerged was John M. Burris, a businessman and former Republican leader of the Delaware House. While there, Burris was known as an articulate and faithful field general for du Pont.

Burris spent most of his time trying to brand Biden a fiscal profligate, echoing themes from Baxter's 1978 campaign. Burris chastised the incumbent for voting against the president's proposal for a constitutional amendment to balance the budget, and sought to remind voters of his role in helping to enact a state balanced-budget amendment under du Pont.

Burris succeeded in keeping the focus of the campaign on economic issues; Biden dwelt heavily on his "budget freeze" proposal. But that was the Republican's sole consolation. Biden crushed him in New Castle County and carried Delaware's two downstate counties en route to a 60 percent to 40 percent win.

Committees

Judiciary (Chairman)
Juvenile Justice

Foreign Relations (2nd of 10 Democrats)
East Asian & Pacific Affairs; European Affairs (chairman); International Economic Policy, Trade, Oceans & Environment

Elections

1990 General

Joseph R. Biden Jr. (D)	112,918	(63%)
M. Jane Brady (R)	64,554	(36%)
Lee Rosenbaum (LIBERT)	2,680	(1%)

Previous Winning Percentages: **1984** (60%) **1978** (58%) **1972** (51%)

Campaign Finance

	Receipts	Receipts from PACs	Expend-itures
1990			
Biden (D)	$1,898,297	$690,816 (36%)	$1,888,146
Brady (R)	$244,788	0	$240,669

Key Votes

1991	
Authorize use of force against Iraq	N
1990	
Oppose prohibition of certain semiautomatic weapons	N
Support constitutional amendment on flag desecration	N
Oppose requiring parental notice for minors' abortions	Y
Halt production of B-2 stealth bomber at 13 planes	Y
Approve budget that cut spending and raised revenues	N
Pass civil rights bill over Bush veto	Y
1989	
Oppose reduction of SDI funding	N
Oppose barring federal funds for "obscene" art	Y
Allow vote on capital gains tax cut	N

Voting Studies

	Presidential Support		Party Unity		Conservative Coalition	
Year	S	O	S	O	S	O
1990	33	67	83	16	16	84
1989	50	48	81	18	26	68
1988	13	3	13	1	3	5
1987	27	41	60	6	6	56
1986	27	67	83	12	25	71
1985	31	64	77	16	18	75
1984	35	65	79	21	28	72
1983	38	60	82	12	23	68
1982	34	61	79	17	28	67
1981	44	54	84	12	24	74

Interest Group Ratings

Year	ADA	ACU	AFL-CIO	CCUS
1990	83	17	67	36
1989	90	14	100	29
1988	15	0	80	67
1987	70	0	100	17
1986	80	5	87	38
1985	75	10	81	37
1984	85	18	82	44
1983	85	8	88	22
1982	80	32	84	38
1981	80	20	84	28

AL Thomas R. Carper (D)

Of Wilmington — Elected 1982

Born: Jan. 23, 1947, Beckley, W.Va.
Education: Ohio State U., B.A. 1968; U. of Delaware, M.B.A. 1975.
Military Service: Navy, 1968-73; Naval Reserve, 1973-present.
Occupation: Public official.
Family: Wife, Martha Ann Stacy; one child.
Religion: Presbyterian.
Political Career: Del. treasurer, 1977-83.
Capitol Office: 131 Cannon Bldg. 20515; 225-4165.

In Washington: For someone widely regarded as bright and affable, Carper has certainly had more than his share of scraps with party leaders. He is so pleasantly self-effacing and polite he has been known to ask staffers if they could spare him a minute. Yet he is not afraid to defy the chairman of the Banking Committee, the Ways and Means Committee or even the Speaker of the House to press for what he believes is right.

Such behavior suggests a confident young man who expects either to make his mark regardless of House protocol, or to pursue his political career elsewhere. In Carper's case, it is likely the latter. Having run statewide since 1976, first as state treasurer and then for his at-large House seat, Carper is a popular politician widely expected to run for governor in 1992.

Carper continued his pattern of defiance in the 101st Congress, opposing the new Banking Committee chairman, Henry B. Gonzalez, on a section of a bill overhauling federal housing programs. Carper and North Carolina Democrat David E. Price led a bloc of moderate and conservative Democrats in forging a compromise on a provision, sponsored by Texas Republican Steve Bartlett, designed to offer new incentives and requirements to persuade owners of federally subsidized housing to continue renting to low-income families.

But in order to do that, Carper and the Democrats first had to vote during Banking Committee consideration for Bartlett's amendment, which Gonzalez steadfastly opposed. Nevertheless, Carper and Price worked out a compromise and offered it on the floor. It was adopted 400-12; Gonzalez was one of the 12 voting against it. Carper paid a price for his independence, however: Gonzalez refused to appoint him to the House-Senate conference on the bill. Carper appealed Gonzalez' action to Speaker Thomas S. Foley, but Foley declined to intervene.

On a major issue confronting the nation — widespread bankruptcies in the savings and loan industry — Carper took a stand in the 100th Congress that ultimately proved correct. But in his determined effort to push through a package big enough to rescue the industry, he forced an embarrassing defeat on Speaker Jim Wright and Banking Committee Chairman Fernand J. St Germain, advocates of a smaller bailout package.

His confrontation with Wright over the S&L troubles began early in the 100th Congress. Carper won subcommittee approval for a plan (which had Reagan administration support) that called for higher S&L fees to bolster the faltering Federal Savings and Loan Insurance Corporation (FSLIC) by $15 billion over five years.

But Wright personally lobbied the full committee for a smaller package, fearing that a financially strong FSLIC would close the many Texas thrifts that were all but insolvent due to fraud and the state's economic collapse. The committee then adopted a $5 billion, two-year bailout by a single vote. Asked about Wright's influence, Carper replied, "I'll let today's vote and the broken arms speak for themselves."

But less than a month later, stung by negative publicity, Wright and St Germain reversed field and announced support for the $15 billion plan. Beforehand, Carper had gone to Wright to argue that the S&L problem would only grow, and future bailouts would aggravate the deficit, unless the FSLIC received a large infusion immediately.

Despite Wright's endorsement, the House rejected the larger proposal by an overwhelming 153-258, opting instead for the $5 billion plan favored by the S&L lobby. Ultimately the House and Senate compromised on a $10.8 billion plan. But as Carper predicted, the industry's problems burgeoned. In 1989, Congress passed a $50 billion S&L bailout bill. Many analysts estimate the ultimate cost of the bailout at $500 billion.

On Banking, which has been considering deregulation legislation to broaden banks' powers throughout the decade, Carper espouses giving banks wider latitude in the securities

Delaware — At Large

Delaware is divided by the Chesapeake and Delaware Canal. North of the canal, at the top of the Delmarva (Delaware-Maryland-Virginia) Peninsula, is Wilmington, in New Castle County, the state's only real metropolitan area. Wilmington is dominated economically by the Du Pont Co., its prime source of employment. Changes in banking law brought an influx of new corporations involved in international finance during the 1980s, but to a large extent Wilmington is still a one-company town.

The state's business roster reads like a who's who in the Fortune 500. Over 200,000 smaller corporations and more than half of the nation's largest industrial corporations are chartered here. Attracted by the liberal incorporation laws, most have no real presence in the state. The chemical industry has a more tangible affect on Delaware's economy, though, employing over 10 percent of the state's work force.

Forty years ago, almost half the state's people resided in Wilmington, but the city itself is down to a population under 72,000 and casts less than 15 percent of the state's vote.

A majority of Wilmington's population is black, but there are Italian, Irish and Polish neighborhoods as well. A Democratic candidate who hopes to win statewide must carry Wilmington by at least 10,000 votes. That means doing well among all the ethnic groups that make up the city's electorate.

While the city has been shrinking, the suburban areas around Wilmington have been growing steadily, so about 70 percent of Delaware's vote is still cast within New Castle County. The Republican voting habits of suburban New Castle are frequently strong enough to overcome the solid Democratic margin turned in by Wilmington.

Dover, the state capital, has some light industry, but the Dover Air Force Base has created a grim image for the city. Its huge mortuary has received thousands of dead servicemen over the past three decades, including casualties from the Persian Gulf War. The largest industries in the two southern counties are poultry and tourism; Sussex is the largest poultry-producing county in the United States. It also has Rehoboth Beach, which attracts thousands of sunbathers every summer; its year-round residents are firmly Republican.

Below the Chesapeake and Delaware Canal, changes in values, language and attitude emerge, similar to those of the border South. But if rural Kent and Sussex have similar cultures, they have slightly different voting habits. Sussex, which has experienced rapid development along the coastal plain, prefers conservative Republicans. It was the only one of the three counties to go for GOP Rep. Thomas B. Evans Jr. against Carper in 1982. Kent, in pure partisan terms, is the most Democratic part of Delaware. But these Democrats are conservative. Along with Sussex voters, they gave Ronald Reagan comfortable majorities in 1980 and 1984, and went solidly for George Bush in 1988.

Population: 594,338. White 487,817 (82%), Black 95,845 (16%), Other 5,440 (1%). Spanish origin 9,661 (2%). 18 and over 427,743 (72%), 65 and over 59,179 (10%). Median age: 30.

field, and favors letting states such as Delaware maintain their own liberal regulatory policies. Carper began the 102nd Congress as the new chairman of the Banking Subcommittee on Economic Stabilization.

In another defiant crusade in 1987, Carper went up against Ways and Means Committee Chairman Dan Rostenkowski, tenaciously advocating a less costly welfare-overhaul bill than the chairman and his panel favored — even though he did not sit on any of the four committees with jurisdiction.

Working with Delaware experts, he crafted a full-blown $2.5 billion alternative to the costlier version packaged in Ways and Means, and persuaded Democrats Charles W. Stenholm of Texas, Timothy J. Penny of Minnesota and John M. Spratt Jr. of South Carolina to join with him. But the Rules Committee refused to give Carper permission to offer his bill and approved instead Rostenkowski's request for a restrictive rule for debate on Ways and Means' proposal — "a gag rule," Carper called it.

He and his allies then mobilized opposition to the leadership's measure, forcing a delay in floor action. Rules finally drafted a new rule allowing consideration not of Carper's bill, but of an amendment to shave $500 million from the pending $6.2 billion five-year legislation. He protested at Rules, "We've heard a lot about *glasnost*. We're asking for a little House-nost." But many of his allies were satisfied; the rule was approved, and Carper voted for the bill. Months later, he was one of 65 Southern and conservative Democrats who helped pass a GOP motion calling on House welfare conferees to adopt the Senate's lower $2.8 billion five-year price tag. The final product cost $3.34 billion.

Off the Banking Committee, Carper joins with other fiscal conservatives — particularly those elected with him in the budget-conscious class of 1982 — to agitate for deficit reduction instead of increased social spending. Rather than build support within the more liberal Democratic Caucus for a given initiative, Carper and his allies seek backing from conservative Democrats and Republicans. That was true in 1987, when their bipartisan team sought across-the-board cuts in each appropriation bill that came to the floor, with mixed results. When deficit-reduction talks broke down in 1989 and automatic across-the-board cuts loomed, Carper said, "I don't fear it. In fact, I think it might be the tonic we need to throw in the face of the president and Congress so that maybe we do something about the deficit."

In 1990, Carper was a leader in the move to bring to the floor a constitutional amendment to balance the federal budget. But the joint resolution fell seven votes short of passage.

Carper again flouted party convention in 1990 when he recorded a campaign TV ad for the Banking Committee's ranking Republican, Chalmers P. Wylie, praising Wylie for having been a cosponsor of Carper's bill aimed at averting the S&L crisis. Although there was talk of disciplinary action by the Democratic Caucus, Carper was not punished.

If such tactics do not endear Carper to many Democrats, he gets on well generally with them because of his pleasant personality. He is respected, if grudgingly, as intelligent and earnest. After hours, he is part of the "gym caucus," joining with other athletic House activists for the basketball games that help make — or mend — legislative relationships.

On the Merchant Marine Committee, Carper looks out for Delaware's fishing and tourism industries and backs efforts against coastal pollution. In 1990 he was named to a House-Senate conference on a bill increasing oil spillers' federal liability limits and enhancing cleanup efforts.

Despite his reputation as a maverick, Carper has supported the House leadership on more than three-quarters of party-line votes. He backed the 1989 congressional pay raise package that revised ethics rules, and voted for the 1990 budget "summit" agreement. He also opposed a constitutional amendment to ban physical desecration of the flag.

At Home: A statewide officeholder since 1977 — as state treasurer and as an at-large House member — Carper is regarded as near-certain to run for governor of Delaware in 1992. As a warmup, Carper spent much of the 1990 election cycle flexing his political muscles.

By early 1989, Carper had come to view the scandal-plagued leadership of the New Castle County (Wilmington) Democratic organization as a potential albatross for party candidates, including himself. He helped organize a coup by Democratic reformists who ousted county Democratic Chairman Eugene T. Reed Sr.

During the 1990 House primary campaign, allies of Reed — who had been indicted on charges including campaign fraud — tried to even the score with Carper. Plumbing contractor Daniel D. Rappa, a regular in Reed's Democratic machine, entered the primary and spent heavily on a negative campaign against Carper.

Rappa tried to tie Carper's position on the Banking Committee to the savings and loan scandal, demanding that the incumbent return $150,000 in campaign contributions he had received over the years from the financial industry. But Carper batted the issue away, noting that he had received just $6,200 from S&L sources since 1987 and had tried unsuccessfully to convince House colleagues to tighten S&L regulation.

Rappa's campaign turned out to be as futile as it was furious. Carper ended up with 90 percent of the vote and a big boost for the general election. His Republican opponent, businessman Ralph O. Williams, tried to breathe life into the savings-and-loan issue, but was badly positioned to do so. Williams himself was a former chairman of a Delaware S&L — albeit a healthy one — and had once presented a campaign check to Carper on behalf of the U.S. League of Savings Institutions. Carper won by a 2-to-1 margin.

Carper's nonchalant entrance into politics gave no clue to his meteoric rise. He was lying on a beach in 1976 when he heard a radio report that his state's Democratic convention could not find a candidate for state treasurer. He jumped into the race and upset a strongly favored Republican.

In 1982, state Democrats again had recruiting problems, this time for the House contest against Republican Rep. Thomas B. Evans Jr. Although Carper stepped into the breach just 90 days before the vote, he went on to upset Evans, returning the state's House seat to Democratic control for the first time since 1966.

Carper's soft-spoken geniality and Delaware's economic problems in that recession year contributed to the outcome. But a scandal that tarred Evans' reputation was the biggest factor. The married Evans was damaged by revelations that linked him romantically to Paula Parkinson, a lobbyist who had posed nude for *Playboy*.

Carper never raised the Parkinson matter publicly, preferring to focus his fire on Reagan's economic policies and the administration's military buildup. But Evans was not as reluctant to discuss Carper's personal difficulties. When the *New York Post* printed a story accusing Carper of wife and child abuse, Evans called on his challenger to answer the "serious allegations."

The Wilmington *News-Journal* later reported that some Evans associates first tried to interest the Delaware press in the story, which grew out of a bitter child-custody fight over Carper's two stepchildren from his first marriage. The rumor-mongering ended up hurting Evans more than Carper. Although heavily outspent, Carper marshaled support from organized labor and volunteers. He overwhelmed Evans in Wilmington, and clinched victory by carving a narrow edge in its GOP suburbs.

Carper was not able to rest long on his laurels. He was challenged in 1984 by Elise R. W. du Pont, a former official at the Agency for International Development and wife of then-GOP Gov. Pierre S. "Pete" du Pont IV. The match was initially touted as one of the toughest House contests in the country.

Although she had never before sought elective office, Elise du Pont began her first campaign with the kind of assets that would turn most neophytes green with envy. Her marriage to Gov. du Pont — as well as her own record as an active participant in public affairs — made her well-known throughout the state. She also had a guaranteed ability to amass enormous sums of money. She used those advantages to try to cast Carper as a big-spending liberal lackey of the national Democratic Party.

But du Pont made some strategic errors that damaged her efforts to get that message across. She abandoned her ambitious pledge to make personal visits to 484 homes throughout the state by Election Day, and waffled on her husband's role in the campaign — seeking to minimize his influence early on, then actively involving him later.

Carper was well-positioned to take advantage of du Pont's problems, having carefully cultivated the district via a slew of town hall meetings. Further aided by the top-of-the-ticket presence of Democratic Sen. Joseph R. Biden Jr., he scored a resounding 59 percent to 41 percent victory. Carper's unexpectedly decisive margin of victory over du Pont helped discourage first-rate GOP competition in 1986. In 1988, the suspense among Delaware politicos was not whether Carper would defeat Republican contractor James P. Krapf Sr., but if his victory margin would exceed GOP Gov. Michael N. Castle's re-election mark. Castle's 71 percent tally just surpassed Carper's 68 percent.

Under Delaware's "two terms and out" law, Castle cannot seek re-election in 1992. Carper has made no secret of his intentions to run for governor that year. There has been some speculation that Carper and Castle might seek to execute a job switch, with Castle running for the House. However, many state politics watchers say Castle's ambitions point to the Senate, and they expect him to bypass the open House seat while he awaits Republican Sen. William V. Roth Jr.'s decision on whether to seek a fifth term in 1994.

Committees

Banking, Finance & Urban Affairs (12th of 31 Democrats)
Economic Stabilization (chairman); Housing & Community Development; Policy Research & Insurance

Merchant Marine & Fisheries (11th of 29 Democrats)
Coast Guard & Navigation; Fisheries & Wildlife Conservation & the Environment

Elections

1990 General		
Thomas R. Carper (D)	116,274	(66%)
Ralph O. Williams (R)	58,037	(33%)
Richard A. Cohen (LIBERT)	3,121	(2%)
1990 Primary		
Thomas R. Carper (D)	24,561	(90%)
Daniel D. Rappa (D)	2,676	(10%)
1988 General		
Thomas R. Carper (D)	158,338	(68%)
James P. Krapf Sr. (R)	76,179	(32%)

Previous Winning Percentages: **1986** (66%) **1984** (59%) **1982** (52%)

District Vote For President

	1988		1984		1980		1976	
D	108,647	(43%)	101,656	(40%)	105,700	(45%)	122,596	(52%)
R	139,639	(56%)	152,190	(60%)	111,185	(47%)	109,831	(47%)
I					16,275	(7%)		

Campaign Finance

	Receipts	Receipts from PACs		Expend-itures
1990				
Carper (D)	$548,682	$204,220	(37%)	$521,336
Williams (R)	$49,772	0		$49,770
1988				
Carper (D)	$365,432	$161,235	(44%)	$371,747
Krapf (R)	$188,584	$4,675	(2%)	$184,712

Key Votes

1991
Authorize use of force against Iraq Y

1990
Support constitutional amendment on flag desecration N
Pass family and medical leave bill over Bush veto Y
Reduce SDI funding Y
Allow abortions in overseas military facilities Y
Approve budget summit plan for spending and taxing Y
Approve civil rights bill Y

1989
Halt production of B-2 stealth bomber at 13 planes Y
Oppose capital gains tax cut Y
Approve federal abortion funding in rape or incest cases Y
Approve pay raise and revision of ethics rules Y
Pass Democratic minimum wage plan over Bush veto Y

Voting Studies

	Presidential Support		Party Unity		Conservative Coalition	
Year	**S**	**O**	**S**	**O**	**S**	**O**
1990	23	77	88	11	35	65
1989	41	58	85	14	54	46
1988	30	68	83	13	42	58
1987	31	68	74	22	58	42
1986	30	69	78	21	54	46
1985	43	58	75	22	51	49
1984	41	58	76	24	46	54
1983	33	66	76	23	35	65

Interest Group Ratings

Year	ADA	ACU	AFL-CIO	CCUS
1990	78	17	92	21
1989	80	21	83	50
1988	75	24	77	64
1987	72	9	75	53
1986	55	27	86	50
1985	55	24	71	50
1984	65	25	62	38
1983	80	13	59	53

Florida

U.S. CONGRESS

SENATE 1 D, 1 R
HOUSE 9 D, 10 R

LEGISLATURE

Senate 23 D, 17 R
House 74 D, 46 R

ELECTIONS

1988 Presidential Vote	
Bush	61%
Dukakis	39%
1984 Presidential Vote	
Reagan	65%
Mondale	35%
1980 Presidential Vote	
Reagan	56%
Carter	39%
Anderson	5%
Turnout rate in 1986	24%
Turnout rate in 1988	45%
Turnout rate in 1990	23%

(as percentage of voting age population)

POPULATION AND GROWTH

1980 population	9,746,324
1990 population (4th in the nation)	12,937,926
Percent change 1980-1990	+33%

DEMOGRAPHIC BREAKDOWN

White	83%
Black	14%
Asian or Pacific Islander	1%
(Hispanic origin)	12%
Urban	84%
Rural	16%
Born in state	31%
Foreign-born	11%

MAJOR CITIES

Jacksonville	672,971
Miami	358,548
Tampa	280,015
St. Petersburg	238,629
Hialeah	188,004

AREA AND LAND USE

Area	54,153 sq. miles (26th)
Farm	37%
Forest	48%
Federally owned	12%

Gov. Lawton Chiles (D)
Of Holmes Beach — Elected 1990

Born: April 3, 1930, Lakeland, Fla.
Education: U. of Florida, B.S. 1952, LL.B. 1955.
Occupation: Lawyer.
Religion: Presbyterian.
Political Career: Fla. House, 1959-67; Fla. Senate, 1967-71; U.S. Senate, 1971-1989.
Next Election: 1994.

WORK

Occupations	
White-collar	55%
Blue-collar	27%
Service workers	15%
Government Workers	
Federal	109,157
State	169,586
Local	521,658

MONEY

Median family income	$ 17,280	(39th)
Tax burden per capita	$ 694	(44th)

EDUCATION

Spending per pupil through grade 12	$ 4,092	(24th)
Persons with college degrees	15%	(29th)

CRIME

Violent crime rate	1,109 per 100,000 (2nd)

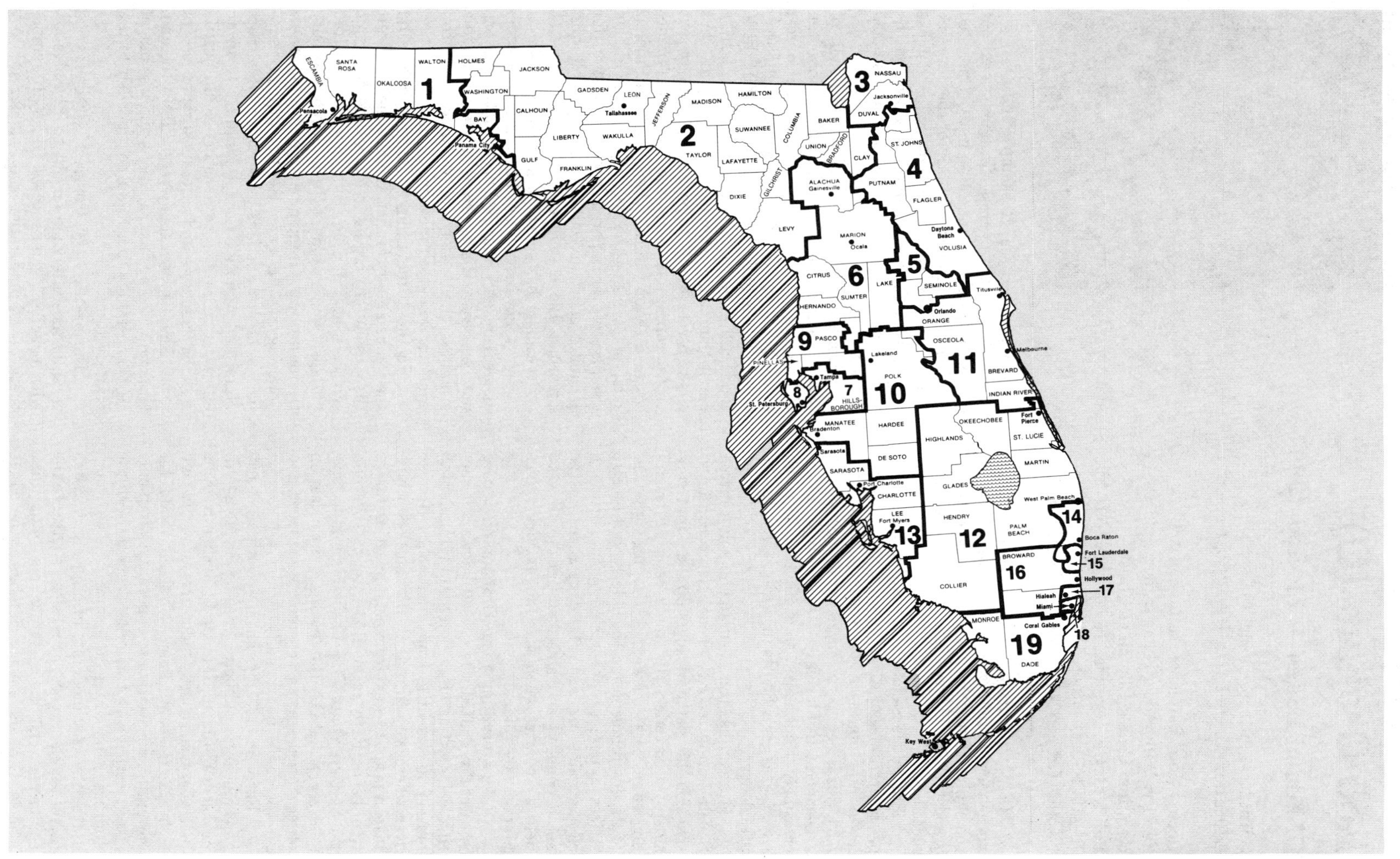

1
2
3
4
5
6
7
8
9
10
11
12
13
14
15
16
17
18
19
ESCAMBIA
SANTA ROSA
OKALOOSA
WALTON
HOLMES
WASHINGTON
BAY
JACKSON
CALHOUN
GULF
LIBERTY
FRANKLIN
GADSDEN
LEON
WAKULLA
JEFFERSON
MADISON
TAYLOR
HAMILTON
SUWANNEE
LAFAYETTE
DIXIE
COLUMBIA
GILCHRIST
LEVY
BAKER
UNION
BRADFORD
NASSAU
DUVAL
CLAY
ST. JOHNS
PUTNAM
FLAGLER
ALACHUA
MARION
VOLUSIA
SEMINOLE
LAKE
SUMTER
CITRUS
HERNANDO
PASCO
PINELLAS
HILLS-BOROUGH
POLK
ORANGE
OSCEOLA
BREVARD
INDIAN RIVER
ST. LUCIE
OKEECHOBEE
MARTIN
HIGHLANDS
HARDEE
DE SOTO
MANATEE
SARASOTA
CHARLOTTE
GLADES
LEE
HENDRY
PALM BEACH
BROWARD
COLLIER
MONROE
DADE
Pensacola
Panama City
Tallahassee
Jacksonville
Gainesville
Ocala
Daytona Beach
Orlando
Titusville
Melbourne
Lakeland
Tampa
St. Petersburg
Bradenton
Sarasota
Port Charlotte
Fort Myers
Fort Pierce
West Palm Beach
Boca Raton
Fort Lauderdale
Hollywood
Hialeah
Miami
Coral Gables
Key West

Bob Graham (D)

Of Miami Lakes — Elected 1986

Born: Nov. 9, 1936, Miami, Fla.
Education: U. of Florida, B.A. 1959; Harvard U., LL.B. 1962.
Occupation: Developer; cattleman.
Family: Wife, Adele Khoury; four children.
Religion: United Church of Christ.
Political Career: Fla. House, 1967-71; Fla. Senate, 1971-79; governor, 1979-87.
Capitol Office: 241 Dirksen Bldg. 20510; 224-3041.

In Washington: Graham does not fit the image most have of a politician with an eye on the White House. He is not pithy or prone to grandstanding; his style is cautious, his remarks measured.

But in the Senate, Graham has a position of stature unusual for a junior member with a low-profile approach to legislating. In large part, this is because of his electoral successes as a Democrat in Florida, a fast-growing and increasingly Republican state that soon could rival Texas as a Southern springboard to the presidency.

Graham has compiled a genuinely centrist Senate voting record. Though more conservative than his party's leadership, he is not considered a maverick. His stands reflect Florida's diverse electorate: Graham is a strong supporter of the environment and the elderly, but he also strikes a pose as pro-business (supporting a capital gains tax cut), anticrime (backing the death penalty) and anticommunist (voting to help the contras when they fought Nicaragua's Marxist government).

Like everything about Graham, his record is carefully crafted. He is well-known for methodically jotting down notes and reminders to himself in the little spiral notebooks that go everywhere with him. If Graham makes a mistake, it is apt to stem from belated action rather than haste. Early in his first term as governor, the *St. Petersburg Times* called him indecisive "Governor Jell-O." But by his fourth year in office, he was seen as a competent manager, and he won re-election handily.

Early in 1991, Graham's caution nearly kept him from publicly opposing Bush's nomination of Floridian Kenneth L. Ryskamp to the federal appeals court. Under pressure from civil rights activists at home, Graham made his eleventh-hour decision to oppose Ryskamp only after meeting with two swing Democrats on the Judiciary Committee to ensure that he would not be the only moderate in opposition. When he got that assurance, he released a letter to the committee chairman stating his opposition. Though Graham is not a member of the panel, his letter helped seal Ryskamp's fate.

In the 101st Congress, Graham stayed out of the spotlight during the hotly contested nominations of Robert H. Bork for the Supreme Court in 1987 and John Tower for defense secretary in 1989. Graham came down on the opposition side — but only after others had made the outcome clear.

Similarly, when George J. Mitchell of Maine was wrestling with J. Bennett Johnston of Louisiana for Southern votes in the contest for Senate majority leader, Graham's endorsement of Mitchell came late, doing him little good with either man. Mitchell put him on the panel that makes committee assignments, but Graham was unable to parlay that into an seat on Appropriations to replace his Florida predecessor, Lawton Chiles. When a seat on Finance came open during the 101st Congress, Graham was passed over in part because his support for a capital gains tax cut did not sit well with Chairman Lloyd Bentsen.

Graham has sought a moderating role on foreign policy issues, but finding the proper mix of idealism and pragmatism in that arena has not been easy. His efforts to stake out middle ground on the Persian Gulf War and on Central America wound up pleasing no one.

In the 102nd Congress, during debate on the Persian Gulf conflict, Graham helped draft the resolution urging reliance on economic sanctions against Iraq. But as talks with Iraq fell apart and President Bush moved the country toward war, Graham became uncomfortable opposing the president. He met with key supporters of the sanctions resolution — Sen. Sam Nunn and Majority Leader Mitchell — in an effort to redraft it so senators could justify backing sanctions and also authorizing use of force. The idea was coolly received. In the end, Graham voted against sanctions and was one of 10 Democrats voting to authorize Bush to use military force.

During the 101st Congress, Graham tried to split the difference on aid to El Salvador, with a similar lack of success. Generally sympathetic to administration requests for military aid to Central America, Graham offered a Bush-backed amendment in 1990 to stop U.S. funding only if the El Salvadoran government failed to continue negotiations with the rebels fighting it. However, in the wake of accusations that soldiers had murdered six Jesuit priests, Graham's amendment was rejected by a surprisingly wide vote of 39-58. Graham then supported an amendment to cut U.S. aid in half.

Graham had more luck on the minimum wage bill in 1989, when he was tapped for a leading role by Democratic leaders hoping to give cover to Southern Democrats. In a play for Southern votes, Graham offered the Democratic amendment, which lopped a dime from the $4.65-an-hour minimum wage backed by labor and incorporated a watered-down form of the subminimum "training wage" that labor bitterly opposed. The amendment was opposed by only two Southern Democrats and picked up the votes of eight moderate Republicans, but it still fell short of a veto-proof margin.

On the Banking Committee, Graham pushed a floor vote on Chairman Donald W. Riegle Jr.'s plan to put the financing of the savings-and-loan bailout on the federal books. Riegle had not wanted a floor showdown, and the Bush administration wanted to keep the cost from counting as part of the deficit, but Graham was unusually insistent. He fell well short of the votes needed for a procedural waiver. His objection to the off-budget financing eventually led him to become one of just seven senators to request they be counted in opposition to the bailout bill conference report as it passed by voice vote.

As governor, Graham earned the sobriquet "the killingest governor," and he carried his pro-death penalty stand to the Senate. He authored a successful amendment to strip the "racial justice provisions" from the crime bill in 1990. The language would have allowed those on death row to appeal convictions on the basis of discrimination. Graham later offered a successful amendment to authorize $2 million for a study of discrimination in capital punishment sentencing. But in the end, the capital punishment provisions were dropped from the bill.

On his other major assignment, Environment and Public Works, Graham is a fairly reliable green vote. His support for tougher tailpipe emission sanctions in the Clean Air bill was emblematic. He was one of 27 Democrats to vote against both Mitchell and Bush by supporting the amendment. In 1989, Graham won editorial accolades at home for his efforts to expand the Everglades National Park.

Graham has also developed a reputation as a free trader. In the 101st Congress, he was a leading supporter of expanding the Caribbean Basin Initiative. He made largely symbolic bids to reduce the import tariff for Caribbean rubber-soled shoes and fought to guarantee that the region's share of the U.S. sugar quota would hold steady. Neither proposal was approved, but Graham was satisfied that the legislation made the CBI permanent.

In 1988, when likely Democratic presidential nominee Michael S. Dukakis was running high in the polls, Graham let it be known that he was available for the No. 2 spot, suggesting that his Southern roots and moderate record would be a plus. Dukakis instead picked Bentsen, another candidate with those credentials.

At Home: In his 1986 challenge to GOP Sen. Paula Hawkins, Graham began the year substantially ahead, and he never lost his lead.

Graham had all the vital advantages. Though Hawkins was highly rated in voter surveys, he ranked higher. The governor maintained an image of vigor by performing muscular tasks as part of his "workdays" program, while Hawkins had to have surgery during the campaign to relieve painful back problems.

More important, Graham had an image of competence built on a record of accomplishment on environmental, economic and social issues. Hawkins was an early Senate advocate of action against drug trafficking and child abuse, but she had not played a visible role on major economic, foreign policy or defense issues. And she had committed several embarrassing and widely reported gaffes. This issue of substance was probably the decisive factor in Graham's comfortable 55 percent victory.

Graham inherited an interest in politics from his father, a wealthy dairy farmer who was a state senator in the 1930s and '40s and an unsuccessful candidate for governor in 1944. After graduating from the University of Florida and Harvard Law School, Graham joined his father in the real estate business. His projects, including development of the new town of Miami Lakes, helped him amass a fortune.

Graham was eased into politics by his half-brother Phil, publisher of *The Washington Post*. Before his suicide in 1963, Phil Graham had introduced his half-brother to many influential Democrats, including Lyndon B. Johnson, for whom Bob Graham worked at the 1960 Democratic National Convention.

Graham's victory in a 1966 state House campaign began his unbroken string of electoral successes. He moved up to the state Senate in 1970. Though Graham was popular in his own base, he was little known elsewhere when he entered the 1978 contest to succeed Democratic Gov. Reubin Askew. Regarded as rather bland, Graham was thought to have little chance in a field of bigger-name contenders.

But Graham came up with the "workdays" gimmick that became his trademark. He spent 100 days working at average, often menial, jobs in various regions of Florida; these efforts drew enormous publicity and gave the wealthy candidate a "common man" appeal. Graham finished a strong second in the primary, then raced past state Attorney General Robert L. Shevin in the runoff, gaining momentum for the general election. He defeated GOP drugstore magnate Jack M. Eckerd with 56 percent.

Graham was not overwhelmingly popular in his early years as governor. His support for capital punishment earned him conservative backing, but it also made him a target for anti-death penalty protesters. On other issues, Graham's caution and attention to detail gave rise to the "Governor Jell-O" nickname.

But beginning in 1982, Graham became more assertive. He hired staff members who promoted his agenda to the Legislature. He pushed his environmental initiatives, including the Save Our Rivers and Save Our Coasts projects. His high profile helped him sweep to re-election that year over GOP Rep. L. A. "Skip" Bafalis.

Graham's stature grew during his second term. He pushed for a balance between development and land-use planning to preserve the environment. Faced with a crime wave, Graham bolstered state law enforcement efforts and promoted an assault on illegal drug trafficking. He backed several tax increases, each one earmarked for a specific purpose, such as education or transportation.

By 1985, it was evident Graham would be a formidable challenger to Hawkins. Though she was known as a champion of family-oriented causes, her critics referred to her as a "lightweight." From her early Senate days, when she hosted a sirloin steak luncheon to announce a plan to jail food-stamp cheaters, Hawkins had a reputation for eccentricity.

Hawkins' campaign was put on hold for weeks after her April back surgery. When it resumed, the candidates largely ignored each other, running image-building TV ads produced by Bob Squier (Graham) and Robert Goodman (Hawkins). Goodman presented emotional tales of constituents rescued from serious trouble with the government by Hawkins' intervention. Graham was pictured riding with state police in a helicopter to spot drug smugglers.

Though Graham maintained his substantial lead in opinion polls, his advisers feared Hawkins' emotional ads might earn her a sentimental vote. So in October Graham went on the offensive, accusing Hawkins of exaggerating her anti-drug record and of "miniaturizing" the office of senator.

The Democrat's strategy succeeded in forcing Hawkins into an issues debate she could not win. She stirred up negative reactions with a pair of comments, one alleging that Graham had communist support, and another, in an appeal for Cuban-American support, that questioned the patriotism of Mexican-Americans. Graham scored a sweeping victory.

Committees

Banking, Housing & Urban Affairs (9th of 12 Democrats)
Consumer & Regulatory Affairs; International Finance & Monetary Policy

Environment & Public Works (7th of 9 Democrats)
Nuclear Regulation (chairman); Environmental Protection; Water Resources, Transportation & Infrastructure

Special Aging (9th of 11 Democrats)

Veterans' Affairs (5th of 7 Democrats)

Elections

1986 General		
Bob Graham (D)	1,877,543	(55%)
Paula Hawkins (R)	1,552,376	(45%)
1986 Primary		
Bob Graham (D)	851,586	(85%)
Robert P. Kunst (D)	149,797	(15%)

Campaign Finance

	Receipts	Receipts from PACs		Expend-itures
1986				
Graham (D)	$6,215,911	$887,337	(14%)	$6,173,663
Hawkins (R)	$6,566,447	$937,105	(14%)	$6,723,729

Key Votes

1991	
Authorize use of force against Iraq	Y
1990	
Oppose prohibition of certain semiautomatic weapons	N
Support constitutional amendment on flag desecration	Y
Oppose requiring parental notice for minors' abortions	Y
Halt production of B-2 stealth bomber at 13 planes	Y
Approve budget that cut spending and raised revenues	N
Pass civil rights bill over Bush veto	Y
1989	
Oppose reduction of SDI funding	Y
Oppose barring federal funds for "obscene" art	Y
Allow vote on capital gains tax cut	N

Voting Studies

	Presidential Support		Party Unity		Conservative Coalition	
Year	**S**	**O**	**S**	**O**	**S**	**O**
1990	53	47	76	23	59	41
1989	64	36	68	32	71	29
1988	60	40	83	16	65	35
1987	46	53	82	18	56	44

Interest Group Ratings

Year	ADA	ACU	AFL-CIO	CCUS
1990	67	30	44	36
1989	50	36	100	38
1988	55	28	71	38
1987	60	23	100	28

Connie Mack (R)

Of Cape Coral — Elected 1988

Born: Oct. 29, 1940, Philadelphia, Pa.
Education: U. of Florida, B.S. 1966.
Occupation: Banker.
Family: Wife, Priscilla Hobbs; two children.
Religion: Roman Catholic.
Political Career: U.S. House, 1983-89.
Capitol Office: 517 Hart Bldg. 20510; 224-5274.

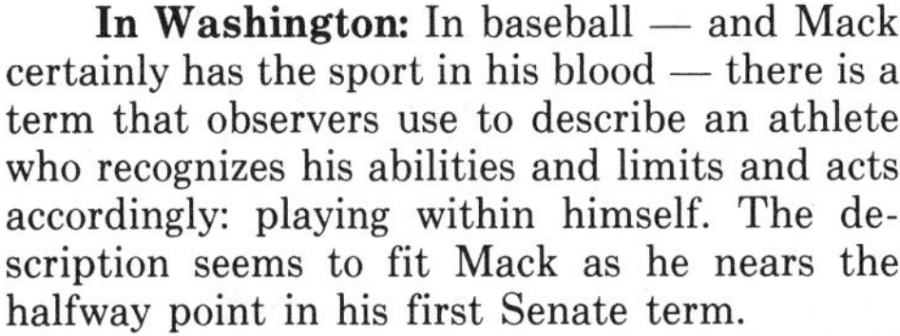

In Washington: In baseball — and Mack certainly has the sport in his blood — there is a term that observers use to describe an athlete who recognizes his abilities and limits and acts accordingly: playing within himself. The description seems to fit Mack as he nears the halfway point in his first Senate term.

Mack did not leave a long legislative trail on his way to the Senate, but he did leave a mark. In the House he made his reputation as an outspoken member of a group of Republicans with an aggressive approach to the Democratic majority. Like many younger-generation Republicans, he was far more prone to castigate the Democratic majority than to look for ways to cooperate with it. "In politics, you gain energy from confrontation," Mack once said, capsulizing the philosophy of the Conservative Opportunity Society (COS), in which he was active.

His early tenure in the Senate has shown him to be an ever-stalwart conservative, although a somewhat less strident and less obviously ambitious one.

Narrowly elected to the Senate in 1988 over a well-respected Democratic opponent, Mack faced a skeptical reception upon his entry into the chamber. He made his way to the Banking and Foreign Relations committees. The former gave him an opportunity to put to use his professional background — he was a bank president at age 35 — and the latter provided him a forum to air his hawkish views on the United States' role in world affairs. When Panama became engulfed in a political and economic crisis in early 1989, Mack introduced a resolution calling for an abrogation of the Panama Canal treaties. "We should not take one step further towards the transfer of the canal," he said.

After serving on Foreign Relations during his first two years, he relinquished the seat for one on Armed Services for the 102nd Congress; he used both panels to highlight his conservative views. He successfully pushed legislation in 1990 and 1991 tightening the economic embargo on Cuba — a position likely to curry favor with the large anti-Cuba segment of the Florida electorate. He also led the Senate's call on President Bush to suspend talks with the Palestine Liberation Organization — a popular stand in Florida's sizable Jewish community.

More than three months before Iraq invaded Kuwait in August 1990, Mack joined two Republican Senate colleagues in calling for the imposition of economic sanctions on that nation in hope of curtailing its chemical weapons capabilities. The Bush administration, however, opposed the efforts.

On Banking, Housing and Urban Affairs, Mack got involved in the effort to address the crisis in the savings and loan industry. When the Senate in early 1989 passed a bill overhauling the savings and loan regulatory structure, it adopted a Mack amendment requiring national standards for the selection of auditors by thrift institutions and for the conduct of such audits.

A staunch fiscal conservative, Mack was one of the most disappointed Republicans when Bush broke his no-new-taxes pledge in 1990. Within hours of Bush's announcement, Mack led a number of conservative Republicans in holding a news conference urging the president not to retreat from his promise. A consistent supply-sider, Mack also fought hard, and unsuccessfully, for inclusion of a capital gains tax cut in the budget legislation approved in 1990.

Mack has also used his position on Banking to play a role in cleaning up the scandal-ridden Department of Housing and Urban Development; Mack was ranking Republican on the HUD investigative subcommittee.

In the House, Mack worked hard to identify himself with the Gramm-Rudman balanced-budget law. He became its chief GOP sponsor and promoter in the House, though he was not noticeably involved in drafting it and did not play a significant role in the process by which members worked out their own language for conference with the Senate.

In 1986, Mack unsuccessfully tried to modify Gramm-Rudman. He introduced legislation to bar cuts in cost-of-living increases for beneficiaries of federal employee retirement programs. A similar protection already existed for Social Security recipients.

At Home: It is no small feat to win a Senate seat in a state as large and diverse as Florida, but if Mack's victory in 1988 had impressive elements, it was still a little surprising that the contest was so close given the factors working in his favor. Despite a significant head start, a financial advantage, Democratic infighting and an extremely strong GOP tide at the presidential level, Mack's victory was so narrow that the outcome was settled only by the count of absentee ballots.

Mack, a telegenic candidate in a state where media is extremely important, seemed to be charmed for much of the Senate contest. He entered the Senate race as an underdog against Democratic Sen. Lawton Chiles, but Chiles, who is now governor, surprised his party by announcing his retirement in late 1987. That boosted Mack, who had already nailed down enough Republican support to ward off a serious primary challenger. But it still did not make him the favorite; popular former Democratic Gov. Reubin Askew decided to make a comeback and was considered a likely winner. But then Askew got skittish and backed out, which helped create a Democratic nomination fight that lasted until a month before the general election. The winner, Democratic Rep. Buddy MacKay, emerged bruised, although with a degree of momentum.

While Mack avoided stiff primary competition, he did suffer some barbs from an aggressive Republican opponent, former U.S. Attorney Robert Merkle, who attacked him as a "packaged product." Merkle ran better than had been expected, and refused to endorse Mack afterwards.

Throughout the campaign — whether he was facing Chiles, Askew or MacKay — Mack framed the voters' choice as one between a conservative and a liberal. He maintained a theme of "less taxing, less spending, less government and more freedom." Even before the October runoff was settled, he ran ads with the tag line: "Hey Buddy, you're liberal."

But even some Republicans considered Mack's message too simplistic and narrow. MacKay was highly regarded among political insiders for his legislative work, both in the House and previously in the state Legislature, and his voting record put him closer to the center of the political spectrum than to the left. Some prominent environmentalists in the Republican Party said they could not support Mack because he had not addressed environmental issues crucial to fast-growing Florida. In his campaign, MacKay said the choice was "mainstream vs. extreme."

On election night and for a few days following, the race was too close to call, but absentee ballots ultimately put Mack over the top. MacKay considered challenging the results, suggesting that the state's computerized voting system might have failed in some key counties, but he soon abandoned that plan. Two years later, MacKay was elected lieutenant governor.

Mack may have inherited his desire to serve in Congress. His great-grandfather, John L. Sheppard, was a Democratic House member from Texas; his grandfather, Morris Sheppard, also served in the House, then moved on to a 28-year tenure in the Senate. Mack's step-grandfather, Tom Connally, also served Texas in the Senate, from 1929 to 1953.

But it was another forebear who provided Mack with enviable name recognition when he got into politics: His paternal grandfather was the original Connie Mack, the legendary owner and manager of the Philadelphia Athletics baseball team. Like his grandfather, Mack uses the familiar rather than the given version of his name: Cornelius McGillicuddy III.

After Republican Rep. L. A. "Skip" Bafalis decided to run for governor in 1982, Mack's name gave him a winning edge over four GOP primary opponents for the 13th District House seat. Once nominated, he was guaranteed election and re-election in the solidly Republican constituency.

Committees

Armed Services (8th of 9 Republicans)
Defense Industry & Technology; Projection Forces & Regional Defense; Readiness, Sustainability & Support

Banking, Housing & Urban Affairs (5th of 9 Republicans)
Housing & Urban Affairs; International Finance & Monetary Policy

Small Business (7th of 8 Republicans)
Competitiveness & Economic Opportunity (ranking); Rural Economy & Family Farming; Urban & Minority-Owned Business Development

Joint Economic

Elections

1988 General

Connie Mack (R)	2,051,071	(50%)
Buddy MacKay (D)	2,016,553	(50%)

1988 Primary

Connie Mack (R)	405,296	(62%)
Robert W. Merkle (R)	250,730	(38%)

Previous Winning Percentages: **1986** * (75%) **1984** * (100%) **1982** * (65%)

* *House elections.*

Campaign Finance

	Receipts	Receipts from PACs		Expend-itures
1988				
Mack (R)	$5,224,061	$1,018,745	(20%)	$5,181,639
MacKay (D)	$3,622,831	$899,385	(25%)	$3,714,852

Key Votes

1991

Authorize use of force against Iraq	Y

1990

Oppose prohibition of certain semiautomatic weapons	Y
Support constitutional amendment on flag desecration	Y
Oppose requiring parental notice for minors' abortions	N
Halt production of B-2 stealth bomber at 13 planes	N
Approve budget that cut spending and raised revenues	N
Pass civil rights bill over Bush veto	N

1989

Oppose reduction of SDI funding	Y
Oppose barring federal funds for "obscene" art	N
Allow vote on capital gains tax cut	Y

Voting Studies

	Presidential Support		Party Unity		Conservative Coalition	
Year	**S**	**O**	**S**	**O**	**S**	**O**
1990	88	12	86	14	95	5
1989	86	14	90	10	82	18
House Service						
1988	33	11	35	1	37	0
1987	77	19	91	3	91	5
1986	86	12	94	4	98	0
1985	85	15	91	7	91	9
1984	76	21	94	4	92	8
1983	77	20	94	4	92	6

Interest Group Ratings

Year	ADA	ACU	AFL-CIO	CCUS
1990	0	96	11	100
1989	5	96	10	88
House Service				
1988	0	100	0	86
1987	0	95	6	93
1986	0	100	7	100
1985	10	95	18	86
1984	5	96	15	94
1983	15	86	6	89

1 Earl Hutto (D)

Of Panama City — Elected 1978

Born: May 12, 1926, Midland City, Ala.
Education: Troy State U., B.S. 1949; attended Northwestern U., 1951.
Military Service: Navy, 1944-46.
Occupation: Advertising and broadcasting executive; high school English teacher; sportscaster.
Family: Wife, Nancy Myers; two children.
Religion: Baptist.
Political Career: Fla. House, 1973-79.
Capitol Office: 2435 Rayburn Bldg. 20515; 225-4136.

In Washington: Although Hutto was once a local sportscaster, his reserve as a House member makes it hard to imagine him as the Dick Vitale of western Florida. When Hutto faced his toughest House election campaign ever in 1990, youthful Republican challenger Terry Ketchel argued that he would be a more aggressive advocate for 1st District interests.

However, the GOP candidate's emphasis on style was a matter of necessity as well as opportunity. As the member from a right-leaning Panhandle district, Hutto's solid conservative House voting record gives district Republicans little room to maneuver on the issues.

During the 101st Congress, Hutto was among the House Democrats most willing to back the policies of President Bush. In 1989, he backed Bush on 70 percent of the roll-call votes in the House, and, in 1990, a bad year for Bush overall, 54 percent of the time. His presidential support scores far exceeded those of any other Democratic member of the Florida delegation.

This record continued the pattern Hutto had set during the presidency of Ronald Reagan. Hutto backed Reagan administration positions more than half the time in every year except 1988, Reagan's last in office. In fact, Hutto was seriously recruited to switch parties by national GOP officials.

Hutto's decision not to become a Republican was based at least as much on practicality as on party loyalty. While 1st District residents vote overwhelmingly Republican for president and support some GOP candidates for statewide office, their Southern Democratic traditions remain strong down the ballot.

The Republicans' hopes of converting Hutto — who had not publicly stated an interest in switching — may never have been much more than wishful thinking. Any such move would have cost Hutto his increasing seniority within the House Democratic majority, which in 1989 earned him the chairmanship of the Armed Services Subcommittee on Readiness.

During his early years in the House, Hutto concentrated on maintaining the flow of defense dollars to his district, which bristles with military facilities. His Readiness Subcommittee chairmanship could be of direct benefit to his district: The panel has jurisdiction over Special Operations Forces (SOF), such as the Green Berets and Delta Force, which have personnel based at Hurlburt and Duke fields in the 1st.

However, Hutto has shown signs that he would like a broader role in the defense strategy debate. A member of the pro-Pentagon "Old Guard" on Armed Services, Hutto counsels caution to members who cite the Soviet Union's military retrenchment as justification for deep cutbacks in military spending.

During the 101st Congress, Hutto appeared to be swimming against a strong tide: Even the Bush administration had conceded to a post-Cold War defense spending reduction of 25 percent over five years. However, Hutto and other defense conservatives claimed reinforcement from the events of late 1990, including the invasion of Kuwait by the forces of Iraq's President Saddam Hussein and the adoption of a less accommodating attitude by Soviet President Mikhail S. Gorbachev.

In January 1991, Hutto supported the resolution authorizing Bush to use force to end the occupation of Kuwait and the president's ensuing decision to launch the "Desert Storm" assault against Iraq. The next month, as the U.S.-led campaign neared its successful conclusion, Hutto called for a rethinking of the planned defense spending reduction. "In view of Mr. Gorbachev's backsliding and the advent of Desert Storm, the administration and the Congress should reassess that 25 percent drawdown and make sure that America will not be vulnerable to the future Saddam Husseins of this world," Hutto said.

Hutto had earlier signaled his aversion to budget-driven cutbacks in defense spending, especially those that affect conventional forces whose readiness is overseen by the subcommittee he chairs. In 1989, Armed Services Chairman Les Aspin had urged committee members to pass Bush's first defense budget as

Florida 1

Northwest — Pensacola; Panama City

Thanks to Hutto's predecessor, the legendary Robert L. F. Sikes, the 1st is packed with military bases, among them Pensacola's Naval Air Station, Tyndall Air Force Base in Panama City and Eglin Air Force Base, which spans three counties. Their political influence is significant: The bases provide jobs for civilians, and many of the enlisted personnel remain in the area after they leave the service.

This district has found little to love in the recent policies of the national Democratic Party. Escambia County (Pensacola) has voted Republican in the last five presidential elections; Bay County (Panama City) gave Jimmy Carter a slight edge in 1976, then swung decisively back to the Republican in subsequent elections. But like their neighbors in Alabama, many voters here still feel some guilt when they desert Old South traditions of voting Democratic. Hutto's Democratic conservatism just suits them.

In Pensacola, the district's largest city, the military's contribution to the economy is complemented by manufacturing of chemicals, plastics, textiles and paper. Despite its large natural harbor, its potential as a trading port is restricted because close-by Mobile and New Orleans have a lock on most of the gulf trade.

The 100-mile stretch of beach from Pensacola to Panama City, dubbed the "Miracle Strip" by civic boosters, also has been called the "Redneck Riviera" because it attracts many visitors from nearby Georgia, Alabama and other Southeastern states. Along the coastal strip, military retirees have settled in Fort Walton Beach and Destin, both in Okaloosa County just a few miles from Eglin Air Force Base. Okaloosa County gave George Bush about 80 percent in 1988.

Inland, the sparsely settled rural areas are occupied mostly by soybeans, corn, tomatoes, cantaloupes, cattle and pine trees.

Population: 512,821. White 428,075 (83%), Black 71,661 (14%), Other 9,351 (2%). Spanish origin 8,863 (2%). 18 and over 362,491 (71%), 65 and over 43,293 (8%). Median age: 29.

an honest first effort to trim spending. However, Hutto supported a committee-approved alternative that added funds for the National Guard and reserves and such threatened programs as the F-14 fighter plane and the Osprey hybrid airplane-helicopter.

In order to fund these programs, the amendment diverted some money from such big-ticket weapons systems as the B-2 "Stealth" bomber. However, Hutto's support for this maneuver was not a sign that he had lost faith in such programs: He voted during the 101st Congress against amendments to cap B-2 production and to slash funding for the strategic defense initiative.

Hutto's seat on Merchant Marine gives him some say over the Coast Guard, the only branch of the military not overseen by Armed Services. During the 100th Congress, Hutto served as chairman of the Merchant Marine Subcommittee on the Coast Guard. In that position, Hutto worked to expand Coast Guard participation in the war on illegal drug smuggling. His bill, providing $350 million for Coast Guard expenses, personnel and equipment, was attached to the 1988 omnibus drug law.

Given his own exertions to obtain funding for military installations in his district, Hutto was occasionally placed in the uncomfortable position as Coast Guard chairman of saying "no" to other members' pet projects. In 1987, Senate Commerce Committee Chairman Ernest F. Hollings of South Carolina set aside $10 million of a Coast Guard reauthorization to build a helicopter base near Charleston, S.C. Hutto initially took a stand against the project, stating the Coast Guard budget was too tight. However, when the bill was returned without Hollings' project, the Senate sat on it for months. Finally, in September 1988, the House relented, approving the Charleston base.

At Home: After a string of easy wins, Hutto got the scare of his congressional career on Election Day 1990, when Republican nominee Ketchel came within 7,566 votes of unseating him. Hutto had not been considered especially vulnerable, particularly after winning the two preceding elections with more than two-thirds of the vote.

But Ketchel, a Fort Walton Beach lawyer in his mid-30s, charged Hutto with lackadaisical job performance. He pledged to provide more energetic leadership at a time when budget cutbacks appeared to threaten jobs in the 1st's defense sector. As a former legislative aide to Michigan Rep. Guy Vander Jagt, who chairs the National Republican Congressional Committee, Ketchel also had the connections to help compete financially with Hutto.

Hutto maintained that his seniority on the Armed Services Committee would offer the best protection for district interests, such as helping along plans to make Pensacola a Navy homeport. Democrats initially appeared unworried by Ketchel. But with the fall budget crisis stoking anti-incumbent inclinations, the Republican began to surge in the polls. That push stopped just shy of toppling Hutto.

Ketchel may have been helped by turnout from the heavyweight gubernatorial race; incumbent Republican Gov. Bob Martinez carried the 1st, while losing statewide. But in the congressional race, most district voters stuck with their habit of voting Democratic, and voting for Hutto. The Democrat carried all but Okaloosa County, which went heavily for George Bush in 1988 and includes Ketchel's hometown of Fort Walton Beach.

Before his election to the state Legislature in 1972, Hutto was a television sportscaster in both Panama City and Pensacola, at opposite ends of the 1st. So when he began his 1978 congressional campaign, aiming to succeed the retiring Democratic Rep. Robert L. F. Sikes, his face was familiar to much of the district.

That was an enormous help to him in the Democratic primary. Rated no higher than third out of four candidates before the voting, Hutto finished a comfortable first in the initial primary, then won easily in the runoff.

With Sikes out of the picture, Republicans were optimistic that their candidate, former Pensacola Mayor Warren Briggs, could take the district in the fall. But Hutto gave Briggs no opening on the right. He promised to protect the 1st's military facilities — which had been well-tended by Armed Services Committee member Sikes — and stressed law enforcement and economy in government.

Hutto's involvement in Baptist church affairs was of special help in the district's rural areas, where Briggs' identification with Pensacola business interests was not an advantage. Hutto won 63 percent.

Briggs tried again in 1980, but Hutto was untouchable. Even though Reagan won the district's presidential vote, Briggs barely improved on his 1978 showing. Hutto then won easily for re-election, until Ketchel caught him by surprise in 1990.

Committees

Armed Services (8th of 33 Democrats)
Readiness (chairman); Military Installations & Facilities; Seapower & Strategic & Critical Materials

Merchant Marine & Fisheries (5th of 29 Democrats)
Coast Guard & Navigation; Fisheries & Wildlife Conservation & the Environment

Elections

1990 General		
Earl Hutto (D)	88,354	(52%)
Terry Ketchel (R)	80,788	(48%)
1990 Primary		
Earl Hutto (D)	53,648	(73%)
Steve Hudson (D)	19,779	(27%)
1988 General		
Earl Hutto (D)	142,449	(67%)
E.D. Armbruster (R)	70,534	(33%)

Previous Winning Percentages: **1986** (64%) **1984** (100%) **1982** (74%) **1980** (61%) **1978** (63%)

District Vote For President

	1988	1984	1980	1976
D	57,822 (27%)	49,401 (24%)	67,301 (35%)	79,481 (48%)
R	156,405 (73%)	155,842 (76%)	117,902 (61%)	85,395 (51%)
I			5,268 (3%)	

Campaign Finance

	Receipts	Receipts from PACs		Expend-itures
1990				
Hutto (D)	$184,405	$95,307	(52%)	$158,280
Ketchel (R)	$184,650	$8,198	(4%)	$182,229
1988				
Hutto (D)	$212,973	$109,186	(51%)	$210,940
Armbruster (R)	$23,912	$808	(3%)	$23,912

Key Votes

1991	
Authorize use of force against Iraq	Y
1990	
Support constitutional amendment on flag desecration	Y
Pass family and medical leave bill over Bush veto	N
Reduce SDI funding	N
Allow abortions in overseas military facilities	N
Approve budget summit plan for spending and taxing	N
Approve civil rights bill	N
1989	
Halt production of B-2 stealth bomber at 13 planes	N
Oppose capital gains tax cut	N
Approve federal abortion funding in rape or incest cases	N
Approve pay raise and revision of ethics rules	N
Pass Democratic minimum wage plan over Bush veto	N

Voting Studies

	Presidential Support		Party Unity		Conservative Coalition	
Year	**S**	**O**	**S**	**O**	**S**	**O**
1990	54	45	51	44	94	4
1989	70	29	54	43	93	7
1988	41	53	56	41	97	0
1987	53	46	55	40	91	7
1986	57	40	51	45	92	8
1985	56	43	56	40	93	7
1984	57	40	51	46	95	3
1983	61	37	45	51	96	2
1982	62	34	54	43	89	10
1981	74	25	46	53	93	5

Interest Group Ratings

Year	ADA	ACU	AFL-CIO	CCUS
1990	28	78	50	77
1989	10	85	45	100
1988	20	76	57	69
1987	24	68	27	64
1986	5	82	29	89
1985	15	76	25	86
1984	20	57	46	46
1983	10	91	24	75
1982	10	71	32	71
1981	10	93	40	78

2 Pete Peterson (D)

Of Marianna — Elected 1990

Born: June 26, 1935, Omaha, Neb.
Education: U. of Tampa, B.A. 1976; attended U. of Central Michigan, 1977.
Military Service: Air Force, 1954-80.
Occupation: Educational administrator.
Family: Wife, Carlotta Ann Neal; three children.
Religion: Roman Catholic.
Political Career: No previous office.
Capitol Office: 1415 Longworth Bldg. 20515; 225-5235.

The Path to Washington: Even in 1990, the year voters were supposed to "throw the bums out," ousting a House incumbent was no easy feat.

In the freshman class of the 102nd Congress, Peterson is among just 16 dragonslayers who managed to beat the odds and defeat a sitting representative.

In Peterson's case the victim was Republican Rep. Bill Grant, a two-termer whose own actions were the primary cause of his downfall. Though voter registration in the 2nd is heavily Democratic, Grant converted to the GOP just four months after winning his 1988 re-election campaign as a Democrat.

Grant's defection enraged Democratic activists, who nonetheless had trouble recruiting a well-known challenger. They settled on Peterson, whose prior political activity was limited to a seat on the Jackson County Democratic Executive Committee.

Peterson had assets to compensate for his political inexperience, however, and easily won a two-way primary.

Born in Nebraska, Peterson joined the Air Force just a year after finishing high school. Over his 27-year military career, he worked as a command pilot, instructor and base commander, and rose to the rank of colonel. Peterson volunteered for duty in Vietnam, where he was shot down and spent 6½ years as a prisoner of war.

After returning to the United States in 1973, Peterson earned a bachelor's degree in history at the University of Tampa and did graduate work in public administration.

After Peterson finished his military career in 1980, he settled in Florida with his wife, Carlotta Ann. The former Nebraskan started a general contracting firm and then co-founded a successful computer company.

Just before running for Congress, Peterson was headmaster of the Dozier School for Boys, a state institution for male juvenile offenders. Peterson was hired to install a new treatment program, run by faculty from Florida State University, aimed at rehabilitating the boys rather than simply punishing them.

Peterson had previously toyed with the idea of running for local office and said it was his work with Dozier that propelled him to enter politics. Trying to save money, GOP Gov. Bob Martinez in 1988 sought to close the school.

After looking around for someone else to fight the decision, Peterson said, "I recognized I was the only one who was going to do it." He began a fierce and ultimately successful lobbying effort to keep the school open.

That experience opened Peterson's eyes to the importance of political involvement. It also won him the support of some education groups who later backed him against Grant.

Though the conservative-minded Peterson admits he voted for Republican George Bush in 1988, he calls himself a lifelong Democrat.

Peterson's military career and reserved manner were not ideal preparation for the heavy public speaking and baby-kissing of a political campaign.

But his background did make him an ideal candidate to carry the integrity banner against Grant.

Peterson framed Grant's party-switching as a betrayal of voter trust. He chastised Grant for not resigning after his conversion to the GOP and then standing for office again as a Republican.

Peterson also hummed along with some of the anti-incumbent tunes prevalent in 1990, particularly with regard to congressional handling of the savings and loan scandal.

His military background became an asset in the general election campaign, as concerns over the Persian Gulf crisis focused attention on foreign policy and military matters.

Those strengths enabled the little-known Peterson to best Grant, despite the incumbent's financial edge and support from President Bush and other administration officials.

Florida 2

North — Tallahassee

This is the only Florida district where urban interests are secondary to rural concerns in politics. Natives consider North Florida to be the "real Florida," but some city dwellers outside the district think of the 2nd as the land of "rednecks" and "crackers." Some 30 percent of the district's people live in Leon County (Tallahassee), but the rest are scattered among 24 counties, none with a town of even 15,000 residents.

Two major Interstate highways intersect in Columbia County (Lake City): I-75, the route south for most Florida-bound tourists who live in the mid-South, and I-10, connecting Jacksonville with New Orleans and points west. But this is just a passing-through point for most visitors to Florida; the bulk of the 2nd is only beginning to see the changes that have transformed much of the rest of the state.

The "Big Bend" Gulf Coast from Gulf County to Levy County is mostly undeveloped. There are no military installations in the district and no large concentrations of elderly retirees. Pine trees cover endless acres, sustaining companies making paper, pulp and chemicals. Peanuts, tobacco and soybeans are among the important farm products; oystermen have plied their trade in Gulf and Franklin counties for generations. The district also includes the Cedar Key archipelago, a small group of 100 keys off the coast in Levy County. Though the islands once boasted a prosperous port and pencil-making industry, they are recognized more for their resemblance to Key West circa 1930.

The district's Democratic presidential vote has steadily slid — from 53 percent in 1980 to 40 percent in 1988 — and Republican voter registration has increased. But Democratic loyalties that were forged a century ago are still strong in local politics; one county, Liberty, has only 51 registered Republicans. By recapturing the 2nd District House seat in 1990, Democrats showed that incumbent Bill Grant had overestimated the district's tolerance for the GOP when he switched parties to become a Republican in 1989.

Aiding the Democratic cause are black voters, more numerous here than in all but two other Florida districts. The only Florida county to vote Democratic in the last two presidential elections was black-majority Gadsden County.

Tallahassee, Florida's capital, is economically sustained by state government and two universities, Florida State and Florida A&M. These institutions are diversifying forces, but the city's elegant antebellum homes and flower gardens reveal a Deep South influence that persists in the face of development and rapid population growth. A North Florida adage holds that the farther north you go from Miami, the farther South you get.

Population: 513,127. White 384,073 (75%), Black 124,421 (24%), Other 2,950 (1%). Spanish origin 6,515 (1%). 18 and over 363,447 (71%), 65 and over 54,766 (11%). Median age: 29.

Committees

Select Children, Youth & Families (21st of 22 Democrats)

Public Works & Transportation (35th of 36 Democrats)
Investigations & Oversight; Public Buildings & Grounds; Water Resources

Veterans' Affairs (15th of 21 Democrats)
Oversight & Investigations

Campaign Finance

	Receipts	Receipts from PACs		Expend-itures
1990				
Peterson (D)	$306,429	$133,170	(43%)	$306,104
Grant (R)	$801,238	$305,253	(38%)	$839,764

Key Vote

1991

Authorize use of force against Iraq — N

Elections

1990 General		
Pete Peterson (D)	103,007	(57%)
Bill Grant (R)	77,897	(43%)
1990 Primary		
Pete Peterson (D)	56,835	(60%)
Bob Boyd (D)	37,903	(40%)

District Vote For President

	1988	1984	1980	1976
D	82,000 (40%)	106,997 (47%)	96,530 (53%)	102,936 (60%)
R	120,995 (59%)	121,877 (53%)	79,208 (43%)	63,809 (37%)
I			5,035 (3%)	

3 Charles E. Bennett (D)

Of Jacksonville — Elected 1948

Born: Dec. 2, 1910, Canton, N.Y.
Education: U. of Florida, B.A., J.D. 1934.
Military Service: Army, 1942-47.
Occupation: Lawyer.
Family: Wife, Jean Fay; three children.
Religion: Disciples of Christ.
Political Career: Fla. House, 1941.
Capitol Office: 2107 Rayburn Bldg. 20515; 225-2501.

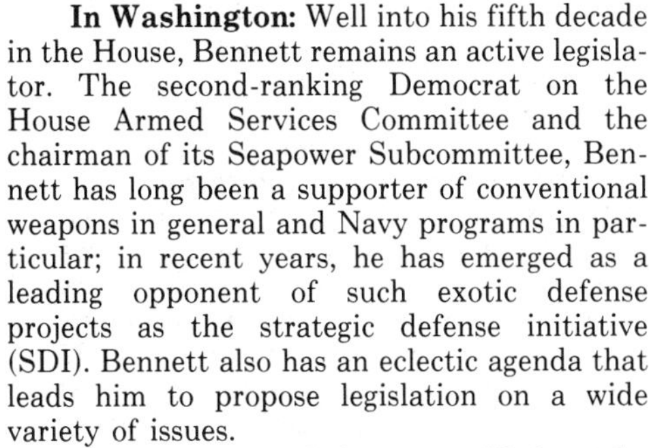

In Washington: Well into his fifth decade in the House, Bennett remains an active legislator. The second-ranking Democrat on the House Armed Services Committee and the chairman of its Seapower Subcommittee, Bennett has long been a supporter of conventional weapons in general and Navy programs in particular; in recent years, he has emerged as a leading opponent of such exotic defense projects as the strategic defense initiative (SDI). Bennett also has an eclectic agenda that leads him to propose legislation on a wide variety of issues.

Bennett is nonetheless more likely to be remembered for his resilience than for his legislative prowess. In his 80-plus years, Bennett has had to endure traumatic setbacks, including lower-body paralysis and the apparent suicide of a son in 1977. He also has bounced back from the humiliation of being rejected twice by the Democratic Caucus, in 1985 and 1987, for the Armed Services chairmanship.

No one could sum up Bennett's perseverance better than he did in a May 1990 speech supporting the Americans with Disabilities Act. Noting that he uses two canes to walk, Bennett related how he contracted polio during World War II service in the Philippines, and was told he might never walk again. "But two years later, with the assistance of canes like these, I was able to walk, and with these canes I have walked every step of the past 42 years," Bennett told the House.

Another sign of Bennett's deep well of optimism came in April 1991. Bennett released a statement that he would seek re-election in 1992 but would not run in 1994 "because that allows me a couple of decades to spend more closely with my beloved wife and children." If taken literally, Bennett was thus predicting that he would live past age 100.

It is ironic that concerns about Bennett's constancy weighed in his colleagues' decision to bypass him for the Armed Services helm, following the 1985 coup that displaced aged and declining Chairman Melvin Price of Illinois. But Bennett's bid was hurt by the fact that he had on occasion exhibited a streak of emotionality, which included outbursts of tears that were unnerving to colleagues. When Wisconsin Rep. Les Aspin, then 46 and the seventh-ranking Democrat on Armed Services, sought to leapfrog past Bennett, he attracted support from those who viewed him both as more vigorous and more steadfast.

Aspin also cultivated support from other members, while Bennett remained, as he had always been, something of an outsider. Though well-liked, Bennett never tried to be "one of the boys"; aside from a weekly prayer group, he did not socialize with other members.

Bennett pleaded that he had patiently waited for 36 years to be chairman. But the coup leaders, who had ignored the seniority system in pushing Price aside, were not swayed. Aspin defeated Bennett in the Democratic Caucus by a 125-103 vote.

Two years later, a coalition of liberals unhappy with Aspin's support for the MX missile program and conservative Democrats led by Rep. Marvin Leath of Texas sought to remove the chairman. After Aspin lost a no-confidence vote, Bennett decided to try again for the prize that eluded him. "It would be an absolute affront to me if they twice turned me down," he said. However, Aspin survived, Leath finished second, and Bennett lagged far behind in third.

Bennett recovered from these rejections, though, by finding a niche in the defense spending debate. His sponsorship of amendments during the 101st Congress to reduce SDI funding are among his signal legislative successes.

Although he was known through most of his career as a pro-Pentagon hawk, he established himself by the late 1980s as an opponent of strategic weapons systems that he viewed as draining money away from conventional programs. Beginning in 1982, he joined with more-liberal Democrats to oppose the multi-warhead MX. For several years his name was on the amendments to stop production, although he mainly served to lend his conservative credentials to the effort; he was not a leading tactician.

Florida 3

Northeast — Jacksonville

The 3rd, which is based in the city of Jacksonville, has grown less rapidly than many of Florida's other House districts. This has not caused much alarm among the business and political leaders of Jacksonville, who seem to prefer steady if unspectacular economic expansion based on the city's traditional economic foundations — shipping, insurance, banking and defense.

One sign that this strategy is working can be seen at the harbor, where hundreds of thousands of imported automobiles are unloaded and prepared for overland shipment. By touting its fine harbor and ready access to rail lines and roads that lead to dealers in the lucrative Southeastern market, Jacksonville has become a leading East Coast port of entry for foreign vehicles. When Japan bowed to U.S. pressure and agreed to curtail shipments of autos to the United States, Jacksonville was not hurt; the Japanese decided to abandon other smaller ports and consolidate their business in Jacksonville, where most of it had already been.

Workers handling cargo and building and repairing ships form a large segment of Jacksonville's blue-collar community. Prudential and Independent Life are among the prominent white-collar employers in the city, which has headquarters or regional offices for two dozen insurance companies. Several of Florida's top 25 financial institutions are based in Jacksonville; only Miami has a larger share. The city's three naval air stations contribute more than $500 million annually to the local economy.

When Jacksonville was developing into a major Atlantic port and land transportation hub earlier this century, its jobs lured farm boys from south Georgia, South Carolina and the Florida Panhandle. People of Deep South origin still dominate the work force and give Jacksonville an ambiance quite different from that of Florida cities that have witnessed large-scale migrations of Northerners or Cubans.

In presidential voting, the 3rd went for Southern Democrat Jimmy Carter in 1976 and 1980, but supported Ronald Reagan in 1984 and gave George Bush more than 60 percent in 1988. The district encompasses most of Jacksonville, including large black communities in the northern and northeastern parts of the city. Blacks account for 27 percent of the district's population, a larger proportion than in any other Florida district.

Population: 512,692. White 364,251 (71%), Black 139,997 (27%), Other 6,241 (1%). Spanish origin 9,195 (2%). 18 and over 362,272 (71%), 65 and over 49,479 (10%). Median age: 29.

Bennett then became one of the most outspoken critics of SDI, the experimental space-based anti-missile system that President Reagan began promoting in 1983. Joining with others who viewed SDI as too expensive, impractical and violative of the U.S.-Soviet anti-ballistic missile treaty, Bennett again placed his name on amendments to reduce spending on the program.

Although Reagan's sponsorship of SDI made the going slow for opponents, they began to make progress toward the end of his tenure. In 1988, the House passed Bennett's amendment to cut Reagan's $4.9 billion SDI request to $3.5 billion; a House-Senate conference settled on a middle-ground figure of $4 billion.

The anti-SDI cause then gained momentum with Reagan's departure. President Bush, while supporting the program, lacked Reagan's personal stake, and had promised to trim defense spending to try to reduce the deficit. When Bush proposed in 1989 to spend $4.9 billion on SDI research, the opposition had no trouble gaining a House majority to divert much of that money to other programs that were threatened with cuts.

An amendment by Bennett and Republican Tom Ridge of Pennsylvania to cut SDI funding to $3.1 billion passed the House, 248-175; after the Senate voted for $4.5 billion, a figure of $3.8 billion was adopted. The sentiment to trim SDI grew even stronger in 1990. A Bennett-Ridge amendment to cut Bush's $4.7 billion request by more than half — to $2.3 billion — passed the House by a 225-189 vote; House-Senate conferees agreed to $2.9 billion.

After a couple of years on the defensive, SDI supporters received a major boost in early 1991: They argued that the success of the Patriot missile system in shooting down Iraqi Scuds during the Persian Gulf War had proved the need and feasibility of an anti-ballistic missile program.

But Bennett took the contrary view. Among the points he made in an op-ed article titled "SDI Is No Patriot" was that the Patriot, a short-range weapon that shoots down missiles on their final approach, is a far cry from the unproven SDI technologies that would detect and knock down enemy missiles shortly after launch. "We can all be proud of the Patriot system . . .," Bennett said. "But those who are trying to piggyback their own pet programs on the back of this success story are sadly misinformed."

After Iraq occupied Kuwait in August 1990

and Bush responded with a deployment of U.S. troops to the Persian Gulf region, Bennett argued on constitutional grounds that the president needed the permission of Congress to wage war; in January 1991, he and Democrat Richard J. Durbin of Illinois proposed a resolution to that effect. But by the time the House took up the measure, it was overshadowed by a resolution authorizing Bush to use force. The Bennett-Durbin resolution passed by a 302-131 vote; the House then voted 250-183 to give Bush the war-making authority he sought.

Bennett opposed the war resolution. Like many Democrats, Bennett cited the failed U.S. military intervention in Vietnam as a reason for his worries. But unlike others, he cited regret over his own vote for the 1964 Gulf of Tonkin resolution that resulted in President Lyndon B. Johnson's escalation of the conflict.

But Bennett's anti-SDI agenda and antiwar vote hardly make him a dove. When Bush did commit U.S. forces to war, Bennett called for Americans to rally behind him. "Thank you, Mr. President, for your leadership," he said in a floor speech.

Bennett also used his speech to take a shot at House liberals who had been calling for post-Cold War defense cutbacks as a "peace dividend" to be used on domestic programs. "... [W]hen it becomes popular to destroy our defenses simply to make money available for something else, we ought to recognize that we are hurting the people who may be fighting for our country in the future," he said.

Bennett, whose Jacksonville-based district includes three naval air stations, promotes the Navy's role as head of the Seapower Subcommittee. He supported Reagan's goal of a 600-ship Navy (which has since been abandoned by Bush in the face of changing fiscal and strategic realities). Bennett was a promoter of the nuclear-powered submarine programs favored by the late Adm. Hyman G. Rickover, and was a key advocate of the Trident II submarine missile.

Bennett does disagree strongly with the Navy brass on the issue of "homeporting." Under this Reagan-era policy, the Navy fleet would be dispersed to several new homeports scattered along the U.S. coastlines. The rationale for this policy is that it would provide more strategic flexibility while making the fleet less vulnerable to attack. But to Bennett and other members from areas with established naval bases that stand to lose under the policy, homeporting is simply a job-creating tool that the Pentagon has used to build wider political support for the Navy.

Bennett has also been part of the movement to diminish waste and fraud in defense procurement. During the 100th Congress, he was co-chairman of the Military Reform Caucus. A strong advocate of "revolving door" legislation, Bennett has proposed to bar high-ranking uniformed and civilian military officials from taking employment with defense contractors for at least two years after leaving the government.

These issues tie in with Bennett's longtime interest in ethics: He was present at the start of the House Committee on Standards of Official Conduct, better known as the ethics committee. In 1966, House Speaker John W. McCormack named a special panel, with Bennett as its head, to investigate the activities of New York Democratic Rep. Adam Clayton Powell Jr. The committee called for establishing a permanent ethics panel, which was created the next year.

Bennett's preoccupation with ethics issues stemmed in part from his own strict code of personal conduct. "I don't drink, smoke or run around," he once said. "I'm a pretty simple guy." Over the years, Bennett has returned hundreds of thousands of dollars' worth of disability checks to the Treasury; he began releasing his financial records in the 1950s, long before disclosure was a political issue. Also, during that period, Bennett drafted the first ethics code for government workers, and wrote legislation that established "In God We Trust" as the nation's motto.

Yet his ethics quest would frustrate Bennett in a manner that presaged his later Armed Services setback. Although the House, with some reluctance, set up the ethics committee in 1967, the crusading Bennett was not put on the panel. Bennett called that action "the heaviest rebuke ever given in the Congress."

Bennett did get on ethics eight years later and rose to chairman. His tenure coincided with a rash of House scandals, including Abscam, and the panel issued recommendations that led to a series of House disciplinary actions, including the first-ever expulsion of a member — Pennsylvania Democrat Michael "Ozzie" Myers — on corruption charges.

However, after one term as chairman, Bennett was removed by Speaker Thomas P. O'Neill Jr. of Massachusetts. With the case of the last Abscam figure, leadership lieutenant John P. Murtha of Pennsylvania, pending before the committee, O'Neill replaced Bennett with Ohio Democrat Louis Stokes, a committee member who had been a voice for the accused. The committee ultimately recommended no action against Murtha, provoking its counsel to resign.

Aside from his assignments on Armed Services and the Merchant Marine Committee (a key post for a coastal member) and his ethics avocation, Bennett raises his voice on a variety of issues. At the beginning of the 102nd Congress, Bennett submitted election-related proposals to create a regional presidential primary procedure and to allow for voter registration by mail and at the polls for elections of federal officials.

Among Bennett's wide-ranging interests is the plight of young cows raised to produce veal. His proposed legislation, which is based on accusations by animal-rights activists of inhumane treatment of the calves, would impose new federal regulations on the veal industry.

Through much of his career, Bennett's

voting record differed little from that of other Southern Democrats. In the 1960s, he opposed major antipoverty programs, Medicare and the 1964 Civil Rights Act. But he supported the 1965 Voting Rights Act and the Equal Rights Amendment, and has backed sanctions against South Africa.

Today, Bennett's conservative heritage often shows through: He is a supporter of constitutional amendments to balance the federal budget, to give the president a line-item veto over appropriations, and to ban flag-burning. However, his overall voting record does not fall that far short of the House Democratic mean. In 1990, Bennett opposed Bush's position on House legislation two-thirds of the time.

At Home: The second-most senior member of the House — only Mississippi's Jamie L. Whitten has served longer — Bennett in early 1991 announced that a 1992 re-election bid probably would be his last.

His House career might have begun even earlier had not World War II intervened. Bennett launched his first campaign in late 1941, hoping to build on his political base as a state representative from Jacksonville. But he abandoned the race in 1942 to enlist in the infantry as a private, ignoring the draft deferment given to legislators.

When he returned home to practice law five years later, he was a war hero, leader of 1,000 guerrillas in the Philippines. But he was also disabled, a victim of polio he contracted during the jungle and mountain fighting.

He was no less determined to run for Congress. In 1948, he challenged Democratic Rep. Emory H. Price, who had been elected instead of him in 1942. Bennett ran on a platform of support for a military draft and opposition to the Truman civil rights program. He won the primary by less than 2,000 votes out of more than 75,000 cast, and took the general election with 91 percent. Price challenged Bennett in the 1950 primary, but his comeback attempt fell short. That year and throughout the 1950s, Bennett had no general-election opposition.

Republicans fired their best shot in 1964, when prominent Jacksonville businessman William T. Stockton Jr. opposed Bennett. Stockton drew 27 percent of the vote, higher than any GOP percentage before, but low enough to persuade the party to forget the idea of defeating the veteran Democrat. Bennett has been unopposed in eight of the 13 elections since. His 1990 opponent, Republican lawyer Rod Sullivan, made the best showing of the recent challengers and only matched Stockton's 27 percent.

Bennett was mentioned twice as a possible Senate candidate. In 1956 there was talk he would oppose first-term Democrat George A. Smathers. When Smathers retired in 1968, he was again considered. Neither rumor lasted long; his sphere has never been statewide.

Committees

Armed Services (2nd of 33 Democrats)
Seapower & Strategic & Critical Materials (chairman); Readiness; Research & Development

Merchant Marine & Fisheries (14th of 29 Democrats)
Merchant Marine

Elections

1990 General

Charles E. Bennett (D)	84,261	(73%)
Rod Sullivan (R)	31,703	(27%)

1988 General

Charles E. Bennett (D)	Unopposed

Previous Winning Percentages: 1986 (100%) 1984 (100%) 1982 (84%) 1980 (77%) 1978 (100%) 1976 (100%) 1974 (100%) 1972 (82%) 1970 (100%) 1968 (79%) 1966 (100%) 1964 (73%) 1962 (100%) 1960 (83%) 1958 (100%) 1956 (100%) 1954 (100%) 1952 (100%) 1950 (100%) 1948 (91%)

District Vote For President

	1988		1984		1980		1976	
D	65,309	(40%)	70,795	(41%)	69,230	(53%)	80,412	(64%)
R	97,579	(60%)	102,060	(59%)	58,864	(45%)	44,650	(35%)
I					2,655	(2%)		

Campaign Finance

	Receipts	Receipts from PACs	Expend-itures
1990			
Bennett (D)	$87,580	$30,450 (35%)	$108,953
Sullivan (R)	$15,336	0	$13,414
1988			
Bennett (D)	$104,518	$53,861 (52%)	$19,500

Key Votes

1991	
Authorize use of force against Iraq	N
1990	
Support constitutional amendment on flag desecration	Y
Pass family and medical leave bill over Bush veto	Y
Reduce SDI funding	Y
Allow abortions in overseas military facilities	Y
Approve budget summit plan for spending and taxing	Y
Approve civil rights bill	Y
1989	
Halt production of B-2 stealth bomber at 13 planes	Y
Oppose capital gains tax cut	Y
Approve federal abortion funding in rape or incest cases	Y
Approve pay raise and revision of ethics rules	N
Pass Democratic minimum wage plan over Bush veto	Y

Voting Studies

	Presidential Support		Party Unity		Conservative Coalition	
Year	S	O	S	O	S	O
1990	33	67	68	31	61	39
1989	43	57	80	20	61	39
1988	35	65	82	18	66	34
1987	34	66	79	21	58	42
1986	33	67	82	18	50	50
1985	35	65	82	18	51	49
1984	51	49	59	41	75	25
1983	41	59	61	39	72	28
1982	65	35	55	45	81	19
1981	59	41	48	52	80	20

Interest Group Ratings

Year	ADA	ACU	AFL-CIO	CCUS
1990	39	42	83	21
1989	70	46	75	60
1988	65	28	79	43
1987	48	22	50	60
1986	55	27	64	50
1985	70	19	88	32
1984	30	57	46	44
1983	50	57	53	55
1982	40	55	45	64
1981	25	47	40	58

4 Craig T. James (R)

Of DeLand — Elected 1988

Born: May 5, 1941, Augusta, Ga.
Education: Stetson U., B.S. 1963, J.D. 1967.
Military Service: Army National Guard, 1963-66; Army Reserve, 1966-69.
Occupation: Lawyer; businessman.
Family: Wife, Katherine Folks.
Religion: Baptist.
Political Career: No previous office.
Capitol Office: 1408 Longworth Bldg. 20515; 225-4035.

In Washington: James, who had been to Washington, D.C., only twice before his 1988 election, came across during his freshman House term as a feisty and prickly outsider not shy about speaking his mind or worried about fitting into "the club." He denounced pay raises for members, proposed barring former members from becoming lobbyists directly after leaving office and supported term limits, saying membership in the House "is not supposed to be a professional office."

But if charm is not James' long suit in Washington, voters in his 4th District were sufficiently satisfied with his performance to give him a solid re-election victory over a wealthy Democratic challenger.

James had become a top target of abortion rights groups after he seemed to suggest at a 1989 committee hearing that pregnant women may be too emotionally unstable to decide whether to have an abortion. "That is probably the most confusing point of any woman's life regardless of her economic or social status," James said. He also suggested that legalized abortion has led to greater promiscuity in women and has increased their exposure to AIDS.

James' overall voting record is generally conservative and strongly pro-business (the U.S. Chamber of Commerce gave him a perfect score for 1989). But he also wins moderately strong environmental ratings and voted to require a waiting period for handgun purchases.

James got some unusual publicity in 1990 during Judiciary Committee work on reauthorizing the Legal Services Corporation (LSC). During a subcommittee hearing, James questioned a witness about an LSC suit filed on behalf of migrant workers against a fern grower in his district — but without disclosing that he is co-owner of a family fernery. James, who was then ranking Republican on the subcommittee overseeing the legal aid agency, later recused himself from votes affecting the LSC.

At Home: James, who switched to the Republican Party to run for Congress in 1988, scored one of that year's biggest upsets over a longtime Democratic incumbent dogged by ethical questions. Democrats hoped to reclaim the seat in 1990, but James survived a nasty campaign to keep the 4th in GOP hands.

In 1988, Democrats initially had few worries about re-electing Bill Chappell Jr., a prodefense "Boll Weevil" who had drawn bipartisan support. But when summer brought news of Pentagon procurement irregularities, Chappell, chair of the Defense Appropriations Subcommittee, also drew unfavorable press scrutiny for his ties to Pentagon contractors.

James had no background in elective office, but his involvement in some well-publicized legal cases had earned fans who saw him as an advocate of taxpayers and critics who felt he was a conservative gadfly. In 1982, James led a successful effort to block a $40 million bond issue for a new jail in Volusia County (Daytona Beach); a less expensive jail was later built.

James made ethics the centerpiece of his campaign against Chappell. He also benefited from a strong Republican year statewide, and from a general anti-politician mood in north Florida. He won by just 791 votes.

Democrats contended that James' 1988 win was a fluke, but were unable to rally around a challenger in 1990. Reid Hughes, a wealthy former oil distributor and environmental activist, was the eventual winner of a bruising three-way Democratic primary in September.

In the general election, Hughes spent more than $400,000 of his own money to stress his abortion rights position and slam James for accepting substantial political action committee donations, despite having faulted Chappell for special-interest contributions in the 1988 race. One Hughes television ad showed a dog scratching itself while an announcer warned, "You lie down with dogs, you get up with fleas."

But James revived charges, first made in the primary, that Hughes had sold leaky gasoline tanks and was using "oil money to spread lies about Craig James." James' views on term limits and the congressional pay raise helped him rebut charges that he had become a Washington insider. He won with 56 percent.

Florida 4

Northeast — Daytona Beach

Daytona's beach at low tide is as wide as a superhighway, and the clutter sometimes makes it look like one. Ever since Florida's population began to boom in the 1950s, Daytona Beach has been the most popular resort on the state's east coast for vacationers who do not want to bother making a long trip down the peninsula.

Though the winter weather is sometimes cool, the city woos winter visitors from Canada, and the Daytona International Speedway schedules its Daytona 500 auto race in February to lure tourists.

Parts of Daytona, however, are less than elegant. The boardwalk and some of the city's motels built in earlier boom days are reaching middle age, and competition from neighboring beaches — and from inland tourist attractions such as Walt Disney World — has stepped up in recent years. Although Daytona's population increased by 14 percent in the 1980s, the rate of growth in Ormond Beach, just to the north, was much more substantial.

Flagler County, a few miles farther north, grew by 163 percent from 1980 to 1990. The boom has been fed by an influx of retirees to the area around Palm Coast.

Because of stiff competition from the nearby metropolitan areas of Jacksonville and Orlando, Daytona's success at attracting new jobs in recent years has been only modest, by Florida standards. Two of the largest employers are General Electric and Associated Coca-Cola Bottling Inc.

Daytona Beach and surrounding Volusia County cast about half the district vote. Although this was reliable Democratic territory for many years, Republicans recently have made significant inroads. A strong Baptist influence has helped give the district a conservative tilt.

Moving north from Volusia, the 4th flanks the St. Johns River as it flows toward Jacksonville and the Atlantic. On the coast, Spanish-founded St. Augustine trades on its tourist-drawing claim of being "the nation's oldest city"; inland, Palatka's economy and air quality bear the stamp of the large Georgia-Pacific paper mill there.

The southeast corner of Duval County, home to about one-fifth of the district's people, is in the 4th. It is a mostly white-collar, suburban-style area that supplies workers to downtown Jacksonville's offices.

Population: 512,672. White 451,306 (88%), Black 55,840 (11%), Other 3,602 (1%). Spanish origin 8,693 (2%). 18 and over 385,967 (75%), 65 and over 86,302 (17%). Median age: 35.

Committees

Judiciary (10th of 13 Republicans)
Intellectual Property & Judicial Administration; Economic & Commercial Law; International Law, Immigration & Refugees

Select Aging (18th of 27 Republicans)
Health & Long-Term Care

Veterans' Affairs (8th of 13 Republicans)
Hospitals & Health Care; Oversight & Investigations

Elections

1990 General		
Craig T. James (R)	120,804	(56%)
Reid Hughes (D)	95,293	(44%)
1988 General		
Craig T. James (R)	125,608	(50%)
Bill Chappell Jr. (D)	124,817	(50%)

District Vote For President

	1988		1984		1980		1976	
D	92,862	(36%)	75,495	(33%)	90,665	(40%)	101,649	(54%)
R	161,656	(63%)	151,283	(67%)	125,277	(56%)	85,485	(45%)
I					7,114	(3%)		

Campaign Finance

	Receipts	Receipts from PACs		Expend-itures
1990				
James (R)	$643,579	$211,951	(33%)	$634,891
Hughes (D)	$1,073,878	$103,400	(10%)	$1,067,366
1988				
James (R)	$314,634	$7,295	(2%)	$313,415
Chappell (D)	$955,540	$421,450	(44%)	$1,069,699

Key Votes

1991	
Authorize use of force against Iraq	Y
1990	
Support constitutional amendment on flag desecration	Y
Pass family and medical leave bill over Bush veto	N
Reduce SDI funding	N
Allow abortions in overseas military facilities	N
Approve budget summit plan for spending and taxing	N
Approve civil rights bill	Y
1989	
Halt production of B-2 stealth bomber at 13 planes	N
Oppose capital gains tax cut	N
Approve federal abortion funding in rape or incest cases	N
Approve pay raise and revision of ethics rules	N
Pass Democratic minimum wage plan over Bush veto	N

Voting Studies

	Presidential Support		Party Unity		Conservative Coalition	
Year	S	O	S	O	S	O
1990	58	41	83	16	94	4
1989	69	30	87	13	95	5

Interest Group Ratings

Year	ADA	ACU	AFL-CIO	CCUS
1990	17	71	8	79
1989	0	89	8	100

5 Bill McCollum (R)

Of Altamonte Springs — Elected 1980

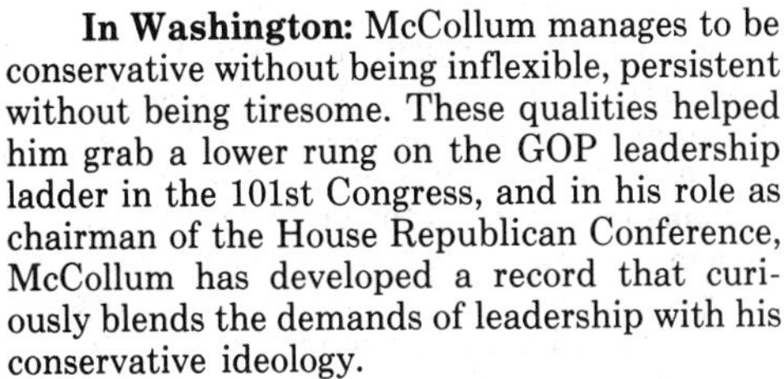

Born: July 12, 1944, Brooksville, Fla.
Education: U. of Florida, B.A. 1965, J.D. 1968.
Military Service: Navy, 1969-72; Navy Reserve, 1972-present.
Occupation: Lawyer.
Family: Wife, Ingrid Seebohm; three children.
Religion: Episcopalian.
Political Career: Seminole County Republican Executive Committee chairman, 1976-80.
Capitol Office: 2453 Rayburn Bldg. 20515; 225-2176.

In Washington: McCollum manages to be conservative without being inflexible, persistent without being tiresome. These qualities helped him grab a lower rung on the GOP leadership ladder in the 101st Congress, and in his role as chairman of the House Republican Conference, McCollum has developed a record that curiously blends the demands of leadership with his conservative ideology.

He voted against the 1990 budget summit because of its tax-increase provisions, even though the measure was a priority vote for the Bush administration and the GOP congressional leadership. Yet on another controversial leadership matter — the 1989 pay raise — McCollum served on the bipartisan ethics task force that recommended the raise and helped clear the way for its passage.

As McCollum juggles these demands and secures his place in the GOP hierarchy, the coming election presents him with a dilemma: Since his first election, he has supported a constitutional amendment for a 12-year House term limit and he is president of the Committee on Limiting Terms Lobby. His 12 years are up in 1992.

McCollum did not initially stand out among the Republican freshmen who came to Washington with Ronald Reagan in 1981. Neither his political background nor his physical presence was imposing; a lawyer who never had held public office, on first impression he seemed boy-scoutish in appearance and manner. But in 1988, when he defeated eight-term California veteran Robert J. Lagomarsino for Conference chair, McCollum proved that he had quietly established himself as one of the more influential junior Republicans.

Legislatively, McCollum's beachhead had been the Judiciary Subcommittee on Crime. After serving as ranking Republican there for six years, however, he was bumped from that role in the 102nd Congress. His ouster trickled down from Henry J. Hyde's decision to take the ranking spot on the Civil Rights Subcommittee when his term on Intelligence ended. That prompted F. James Sensenbrenner Jr. to take the Crime slot; McCollum shifted to the ranking post on Immigration.

While the loss irked McCollum, he has made an effort to move beyond his focus on crime in recent years. On Judiciary in the 101st Congress, he was a leading conservative critic of the Legal Services Corporation, and he repeatedly spoke up for business concerns during consideration of the Americans with Disabilities Act. On Banking, he went to bat for Florida's ailing thrift industry and offered numerous amendments to the savings and loan bailout bill seeking to relax capital standards.

But McCollum is best known for his role in shaping the nation's gun laws. In both 1988 and 1989, he gave opponents of a seven-day waiting period for handgun purchases, the Brady bill, a decisive advantage with a counterproposal directing the Justice Department to develop an instant background check to prevent felons from purchasing handguns.

In early 1991, before the Brady bill gained momentum, McCollum stuck with the idea. He proposed denying certain federal grants to states that do not ready their criminal records for an instant check. He dismissed criticism that he was obstructing the Brady bill, saying, "I'm interested in keeping guns out of felons' hands in a way that is least disruptive" to legitimate gun buyers.

A few years back, McCollum had worked with Crime Subcommittee Chairman William J. Hughes of New Jersey to draft a bill banning for 10 years the production, importation, sale or delivery of non-detectable firearms — those made mostly of plastic. The bill passed in the 100th Congress and was signed into law.

With the influx of refugees to Florida, McCollum has also played a role in immigration matters. His chief concern has been stemming the flow of illegal aliens. "We cannot accept all of those who seek to come to this country," he said as lead foe of a 1989 bill to protect from deportation Nicaraguans and Salvadorans residing here illegally.

Florida 5

North Central — Orlando and Northern Suburbs

In a state famous for its coastline, the 5th is the only Florida district without one. But that has been no hindrance to economic development or population growth in and around Orlando. In fact, metropolitan Orlando (encompassing Orange and Seminole counties) has a more diversified economic base than many of Florida's beach meccas, where the economy is skewed toward tourism, condo construction and real-estate speculation.

Orlando has its share of builders and bankers, but it also produces electronic equipment, boats, elevators and pharmaceuticals. It is the base of the Burger King empire and the site of numerous aerospace and defense contractors working on missiles and aircraft-control systems. Tourism is also a major contributor to the economy because the Orlando area is dotted with theme parks. Walt Disney World is across the border in the 11th District, but many of its employees live in the 5th.

When McCollum won the 5th in 1980, it was a much larger district, stretching from the Gulf almost to the Atlantic. But because it had nearly doubled in population during the 1970s, it was divided in redistricting. The part that McCollum kept contains all of downtown Orlando and the city's northern suburbs in Orange and southern Seminole counties.

The affluent Orange County communities of Winter Park and Maitland are home to Orlando's older, established elite, which provides strong support for Republican candidates. Another reliable source of Republican votes is Seminole County, north of Orlando, where many of the upper-level executives new to the area settle. In 1988, George Bush carried almost three-fourths of Seminole's vote. Most of the district's Democratic votes come out of working-class areas within the city of Orlando.

Growth has brought its share of problems to the Orlando area. The city's sewage threatens the health of Lake Tohopekaliga to the south, and paying for capital improvements to control the problem is costly. Demand for water has increased dramatically; lowering of the water table causes occasional sinkholes to open up, swallowing buildings, cars and swimming pools.

Population: 513,005. White 420,215 (82%), Black 84,264 (16%), Other 4,179 (1%). Spanish origin 15,041 (3%). 18 and over 373,987 (73%), 65 and over 61,889 (12%). Median age: 31.

Earlier, McCollum led the opposition in the 97th, 98th and 99th Congresses to provisions granting legal-resident status to millions of aliens living in the country illegally.

McCollum combines his assignments on Judiciary and Banking when it comes to legislation barring "money laundering," the practice by which criminals — particularly drug dealers — convert illegal profits into usable cash. In 1986, he and Hughes co-authored legislation to make a new federal crime of money laundering; it breezed through the House by voice vote during the 99th Congress' drive to enact major anti-drug legislation.

At the start of the 102nd Congress, when the Banking Committee began consideration of legislation to tighten money-laundering laws, McCollum won approval of an amendment requiring more detailed records on domestic wire transfers.

In the 100th Congress, McCollum served as one of six House Republicans on the committee investigating the Iran-contra affair. Although a staunch defender of Reagan's pro-contra policies who questioned the need for the hearings, he made news in June 1987 when he said that the testimony of a Justice Department lawyer showed that three central figures in the affair, William J. Casey, Rear Adm. John M. Poindexter and Lt. Col. Oliver L. North, had engaged in "criminal" behavior and had committed "one of the most treacherous" acts ever against a president. But he did not raise the subject when North and Poindexter testified.

An ardent supporter of the Nicaraguan contras, McCollum complained that the process had subjected private contra supporters to innuendoes and accusations. The message came back to haunt him for a moment in 1990, when an entry in North's notebooks suggested McCollum and three other House Republicans were briefed in 1985 about third country efforts to assist the contras. McCollum and the others called the allegation "patently untrue," while noting that third country aid is not illegal.

At Home: Spurred by Republican Rep. Richard Kelly's near defeat in 1978, McCollum was already campaigning for the 5th District GOP nomination in 1980 when the FBI snared Kelly in its Abscam investigation.

McCollum, a former Seminole County GOP chairman making his first bid for public office, used his early start to develop a stronger organization than either Kelly or state Sen. Vince Fechtel, who joined the field later. Since there were few issue differences among the men, image rather than substance dominated the campaign. McCollum portrayed himself as a morally upstanding family man qualified to fill a "leadership vacuum."

McCollum got 43 percent of the primary vote, running first in Seminole County and in the Orange County suburbs of Orlando, and also carrying the Gulf Coast GOP strongholds of Pasco and Pinellas counties. Kelly ran a poor third. In the runoff, McCollum again brought his organizational strength to bear against Fechtel, carrying six of the district's eight counties and winning 54 percent.

Democrats chose lawyer David Best, who had polled 49 percent against Kelly in 1978. McCollum, clearly more conservative than Best, caught the district's prevailing mood and was elected with 56 percent.

In 1982 McCollum's Democratic opponent was Dick Batchelor, a popular Orange County state representative considered a formidable, although underfunded, campaigner. Fearful of being dragged down by voter discontent with Reaganomics or concern over Social Security, McCollum did not emphasize his party label.

His main theme was repeated from the 1980 campaign — McCollum as the all-American husband and father (compared with the unmarried Batchelor) who had "restored integrity" to the district. With more money to buy media ads, McCollum succeeded in casting Batchelor as a liberal. He won 59 percent of the vote, and local Democrats did not challenge him again until 1990, when McCollum again prevailed with about 60 percent of the vote.

When Democrat Lawton Chiles announced his retirement from the Senate in 1988, McCollum considered running in the GOP primary against fellow Rep. Connie Mack. But Mack had gotten a significant head start securing commitments from state and national Republicans, some of whom publicly urged McCollum to stay in the House. After some thought, that is what he chose to do.

Committees

Banking, Finance & Urban Affairs (3rd of 20 Republicans)
General Oversight (ranking); Financial Institutions Supervision, Regulation & Insurance; International Development, Finance, Trade & Monetary Policy

Judiciary (5th of 13 Republicans)
International Law, Immigration & Refugees (ranking); Civil & Constitutional Rights; Crime and Criminal Justice

Elections

1990 General

Bill McCollum (R)	94,417	(60%)
Bob Fletcher (D)	63,243	(40%)

1988 General

Bill McCollum (R)	Unopposed

Previous Winning Percentages: **1986** (100%) **1984** (100%) **1982** (59%) **1980** (56%)

District Vote For President

	1988	1984	1980	1976
D	56,030 (31%)	50,693 (29%)	51,295 (34%)	59,891 (46%)
R	123,123 (68%)	125,106 (71%)	93,796 (62%)	68,991 (53%)
I			5,775 (4%)	

Campaign Finance

	Receipts	Receipts from PACs	Expend-itures
1990			
McCollum (R)	$427,325	$148,050 (35%)	$564,994
Fletcher (D)	$22,560	$2,371 (11%)	$18,635
1988			
McCollum (R)	$321,887	$117,835 (37%)	$304,853

Key Votes

1991	
Authorize use of force against Iraq	Y
1990	
Support constitutional amendment on flag desecration	Y
Pass family and medical leave bill over Bush veto	N
Reduce SDI funding	N
Allow abortions in overseas military facilities	N
Approve budget summit plan for spending and taxing	N
Approve civil rights bill	N
1989	
Halt production of B-2 stealth bomber at 13 planes	N
Oppose capital gains tax cut	N
Approve federal abortion funding in rape or incest cases	N
Approve pay raise and revision of ethics rules	Y
Pass Democratic minimum wage plan over Bush veto	N

Voting Studies

	Presidential Support		Party Unity		Conservative Coalition	
Year	S	O	S	O	S	O
1990	74	23	83	15	91	9
1989	72	26	76	19	90	5
1988	66	24	82	10	97	0
1987	69	26	82	12	95	2
1986	84	14	81	16	96	4
1985	80	19	82	13	91	9
1984	66	33	85	11	93	7
1983	78	17	89	6	94	3
1982	78	17	91	8	93	7
1981	67	28	83	14	85	12

Interest Group Ratings

Year	ADA	ACU	AFL-CIO	CCUS
1990	17	88	8	71
1989	0	96	9	100
1988	0	100	17	75
1987	4	87	0	100
1986	0	82	7	82
1985	5	90	6	90
1984	10	78	8	88
1983	0	100	0	89
1982	10	82	10	82
1981	0	93	13	94

6 Cliff Stearns (R)

Of Ocala — Elected 1988

Born: April 16, 1941, Washington, D.C.
Education: George Washington U., B.S. 1963.
Military Service: Air Force, 1963-67.
Occupation: Hotel executive.
Family: Wife, Joan Moore; three children.
Religion: Presbyterian.
Political Career: No previous office.
Capitol Office: 1123 Longworth Bldg. 20515; 225-5744.

In Washington: For a district that had never sent a Republican to Congress before, the 6th already looks surprisingly secure for second-termer Stearns. With careful attention to constituent needs and an ability to help find funding for some popular local projects, Stearns has established himself as a personable and competent representative.

The seat opened up when Rep. Buddy MacKay decided to run (unsuccessfully) for the Senate. MacKay had held the 6th for the Democrats since it was created after the 1980 census. After Stearns' surprise victory in 1988, he set about proving it had not been a fluke. In a textbook example of entrenchment, Stearns made sure he was home at every opportunity, sending out regular mailings and holding more than 80 town meetings.

A member of the Veterans' Affairs Committee, Stearns points to his work in getting money for a new psychiatric wing at a veterans' hospital and for a biotechnology center at the University of Florida, both located in Gainesville, the district's most Democratic territory.

A reliable conservative vote, Stearns established his loyal Republican credentials as a freshman, voting with a majority of his GOP colleagues in the House more than 85 percent of the time during his first term.

He also was active in the July 1989 debate over funding for the National Endowment for the Arts. Lawmakers agreed to cut funding for the NEA by $45,000 — the amount of two controversial grants that went to fund projects many found offensive.

Despite the compromise, Stearns pushed for further cuts in the agency's budget. The House overwhelmingly rejected his proposal to slash funding by 5 percent.

Stearns had earlier demonstrated some intraparty political acumen; when the freshman GOP class of 1988 gathered in Washington, he sought and won his class' spot on the influential House GOP panel that parcels out committee assignments to the party's members.

At Home: Stearns had no political experience when he launched his 1988 campaign in the open 6th. But his limited political background gave him a salient, populist theme, and he rode it home to victory.

From the outset, Stearns cast the 1988 election as a choice not between himself and a particular politician, but between himself and the entire concept of a politician. A heavy underdog to state House Speaker Jon Mills, the Democratic nominee, Stearns stressed that "the time has come for a 'citizen' congressman."

Stearns had developed some valuable contacts in the process of turning an investment in a dilapidated motel into a successful local motel and restaurant management company (called the House of Stearns). He was a director of the local chamber of commerce (where he was active in tourism development), served on the board of a major local hospital and was involved in church and civic groups. With those alliances and instinctive political savvy, Stearns was able to beat two better-connected candidates for the GOP nomination, and he went on to out-hustle Mills.

While Stearns campaigned tirelessly, an overconfident Mills spent time in Washington getting to know Democratic House leaders. Some Mills supporters had last-minute premonitions that the race was tightening, but none expected the shock they got on Election Day, when Stearns won handily, aided by George Bush's strong showing in the 6th.

Democrats began 1990 optimistic about regaining the 6th, but they failed to recruit a strong challenger.

Art Johnson, a Gainesville lawyer, won the nomination in a lightly attended primary. In his low-budget challenge, Johnson argued that Stearns, who opposes abortion rights and voted against the 1990 civil rights bill, was out of sync with the district.

But Stearns drew on a solid record in his first term, including obtaining the funds for the Gainesville veterans' psychiatric hospital and holding frequent town meetings. Stearns raised nearly $500,000, and won with 59 percent of the vote, an encouraging sign for his and GOP fortunes in the 6th.

Florida 6

North Central — Gainesville; Ocala

The 6th combines a moderate-to-liberal university city with conservative rural areas and a coastal region rapidly attracting Republican retirees. After the 1980 census, it was drawn to give an edge to Democrats in general and Buddy MacKay in particular. MacKay did not have any trouble holding the seat for the first half of the decade, but when he chose to leave, Republicans moved in and took over.

The University of Florida, with more than 35,000 students and 3,500 faculty, puts Gainesville and Alachua County clearly to the left of most of the Florida electorate. In 1988, Michael S. Dukakis ran 10 percentage points ahead of his 39 percent statewide tally there. Thirty percent of the people in the 6th live in Alachua.

From there, the district follows the southerly path of Interstate 75 to Ocala in Marion County. Motels, restaurants and gas stations strung along the highway cater to tourists drawn by the region's springs, rivers and lakes.

Some of central Florida's high-technology companies have been expanding operations north to Ocala in recent years, including Martin Marietta, Microdyne and others. Outside Ocala, Marion County is mostly citrus groves and range land for horse and cattle farms. While the newcomers to Marion County tend to vote Republican, most of its rural people are traditional Southern Democrats. Those two groups were closely matched in 1976, when Jimmy Carter barely carried Marion County over Gerald R. Ford, but in subsequent presidential elections the county has sided with the Republican ticket.

South of Marion, citrus groves continue into Sumter and Lake counties. Watermelons and berries are grown around Leesburg, the geographic center of Florida. Conservative retirees in Lake County make Republican candidates very strong here.

The 6th also takes in the Gulf Coast counties of Citrus and Hernando, which have grown by 71 percent and 127 percent, respectively, during the past decade. Retirees, responsible for much of the influx, generally help swing the vote to the right.

Population: 512,950. White 434,855 (85%), Black 71,182 (14%), Other 3,386 (1%). Spanish origin 11,761 (2%). 18 and over 394,134 (77%), 65 and over 94,663 (18%). Median age: 34.

Committees

Banking, Finance & Urban Affairs (10th of 20 Republicans)
Financial Institutions Supervision, Regulation & Insurance; Housing & Community Development; International Development, Finance, Trade & Monetary Policy

Select Aging (17th of 27 Republicans)
Health & Long-Term Care

Veterans' Affairs (9th of 13 Republicans)
Housing & Memorial Affairs; Oversight & Investigations

Elections

1990 General		
Cliff Stearns (R)	138,547	(59%)
Art Johnson (D)	95,410	(41%)
1990 Primary		
Cliff Stearns (R)	37,265	(78%)
Larry Gallagher (R)	10,556	(22%)
1988 General		
Cliff Stearns (R)	136,415	(53%)
Jon Mills (D)	118,756	(47%)

District Vote For President

	1988		1984		1980		1976	
D	101,003	(39%)	83,273	(35%)	79,547	(42%)	81,083	(55%)
R	157,184	(60%)	152,694	(65%)	101,489	(53%)	65,705	(44%)
I					8,380	(4%)		

Campaign Finance

	Receipts	Receipts from PACs		Expenditures
1990				
Stearns (R)	$497,703	$200,346	(40%)	$462,925
Johnson (D)	$27,844	0		$26,443
1988				
Stearns (R)	$421,198	$52,270	(12%)	$408,292
Mills (D)	$504,006	$200,800	(40%)	$503,654

Key Votes

1991	
Authorize use of force against Iraq	Y
1990	
Support constitutional amendment on flag desecration	Y
Pass family and medical leave bill over Bush veto	N
Reduce SDI funding	N
Allow abortions in overseas military facilities	N
Approve budget summit plan for spending and taxing	N
Approve civil rights bill	N
1989	
Halt production of B-2 stealth bomber at 13 planes	N
Oppose capital gains tax cut	N
Approve federal abortion funding in rape or incest cases	N
Approve pay raise and revision of ethics rules	N
Pass Democratic minimum wage plan over Bush veto	N

Voting Studies

	Presidential Support		Party Unity		Conservative Coalition	
Year	**S**	**O**	**S**	**O**	**S**	**O**
1990	71	29	89	10	91	7
1989	78	22	85	15	95	5

Interest Group Ratings

Year	ADA	ACU	AFL-CIO	CCUS
1990	17	83	8	71
1989	0	93	0	100

7 Sam M. Gibbons (D)

Of Tampa — Elected 1962

Born: Jan. 20, 1920, Tampa, Fla.
Education: U. of Florida, 1938-41, J.D. 1947.
Military Service: Army, 1941-45.
Occupation: Lawyer.
Family: Wife, Martha Hanley; three children.
Religion: Presbyterian.
Political Career: Fla. House, 1953-59; Fla. Senate, 1959-63.
Capitol Office: 2204 Rayburn Bldg. 20515; 225-3376.

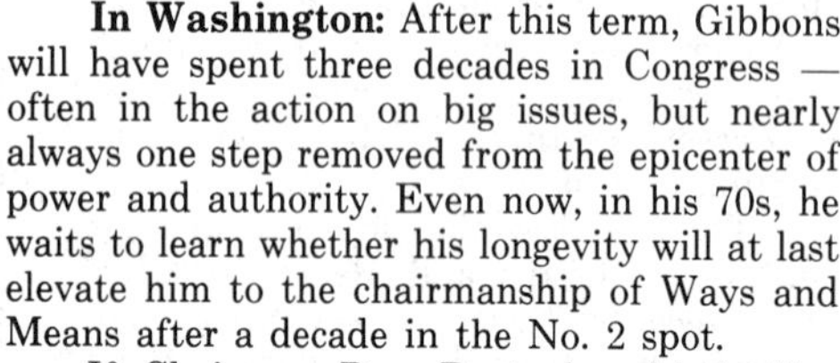

In Washington: After this term, Gibbons will have spent three decades in Congress — often in the action on big issues, but nearly always one step removed from the epicenter of power and authority. Even now, in his 70s, he waits to learn whether his longevity will at last elevate him to the chairmanship of Ways and Means after a decade in the No. 2 spot.

If Chairman Dan Rostenkowski decides not to retire after the 102nd Congress, Gibbons may consider doing so himself. Under current campaign finance law, he loses the right to convert about $575,000 in campaign funds to personal use if he returns for the 103rd Congress.

When still a junior member in the mid-1960s, Gibbons was tapped as floor manager of much of the Great Society program of President Lyndon B. Johnson, including Project Head Start. In those days he was at once a Florida liberal and a product of the Old South, a member who could vote for Great Society social programs and the Voting Rights Act of 1965 while opposing busing and the Civil Rights Acts of 1964 and 1968.

In the generation that has passed since, Gibbons has figuratively moved to the New South, and he has made the transition more easily than most. He has gone from opposing civil rights bills to co-sponsoring the Civil Rights Restoration bill of 1990. A veteran of the legendary 101st Airborne Division in World War II, he has come to regret his backing of the Vietnam War and he voted against authorizing the use of military force in the Persian Gulf in 1991 — giving a moving speech on the subject on the House floor.

Along the way, Gibbons has flirted with real power: as a marginal candidate for leadership posts, a subcommittee chairman on Ways and Means and as an heir apparent for the full committee chair. He has also emerged as one of Congress' leading spokesmen for an often unpopular principle: free trade.

In each of the last three Congresses, Gibbons has used his position as Trade Subcommittee chairman to resist and often moderate the forces that favor more aggressive trade policy. He has even carried to passage some modest improvements in the trade climate. In the 100th Congress there was the free trade agreement with Canada. And, in the 101st, Gibbons won permanent extension of the Caribbean Basin Initiative, a 1983 program giving products of that region favored access to U.S. markets. But Gibbons' efforts to expand the Caribbean effort were rebuffed by both the House and Senate. And on the whole, his mission is definitively a defensive one.

His devotion to trade has not always helped him make friends in the House. In fact, it led colleagues to snub him when the subcommittee chairmanship first became available to him more than a decade ago.

But for Gibbons, free trade is not just a political slogan; it is his creed. Raised in the Depression, and battle-scarred by world war, he is convinced that both catastrophes were born of the trade barriers nations had thrown up. "World War II had a tremendous impact on me," he has said. "I felt one reason it started was people didn't know how to work together .... My grand global goal is to make friends through commerce."

Gibbons has seen some progress toward that goal. In the 20 years he has been on Ways and Means, the volume of U.S. trade with the world has increased from about $50 billion to about $800 billion per annum. And in each Congress he seems to achieve something to further his cause.

At the same time, he has developed the skill of bending without breaking. In 1990 he acceded to a middle-course bill on China's trade status in the wake of the Tiananmen Square massacre. Gibbons helped strike a compromise between the Bush administration's desire for a free hand and House members' eagerness to cast Beijing's regime into the high-tariff darkness. The House passed the bill, but not before Gibbons and Rostenkowski had slowed it down and adjournment had precluded Senate consideration.

The China issue re-emerged early in the

Florida 7

West — Tampa

Ever since a Key West cigar factory moved to Tampa in 1886, this has been a city with a strong blue-collar orientation. Cubans came to work in the cigar business, and they were joined later by Georgians, Alabamans and other Southerners looking for jobs in factories around the harbor.

Tampa still makes cigars, and other traditional industries are strong, among them brewing, commercial fishing, steel-making and ship construction. The city is also a major port, giving it an interest in international markets that coincides with Gibbons' free-trade politics.

The large working-class community makes Tampa the Florida city that most closely approximates industrial cities of the North. The 7th is a Democratic district in most state and national elections, providing a sharp contrast to its neighbor across the bay, the Republican 8th District in St. Petersburg. But Tampa's traditional patterns have been less pronounced in the last two presidential elections; there were not enough Democratic votes in the city to prevent Ronald Reagan or George Bush from carrying surrounding Hillsborough County on a tide of suburban GOP support.

Unlike many Northern industrial cities, however, Tampa has been able to diversify beyond its industrial base to compete for the lucrative tourist trade. Busch Gardens, which started as a simple brewery tour, has been expanded into a 300-acre amusement park that is one of Florida's leading tourist attractions.

The district is 11 percent Hispanic. The influence of the Cuban and Spanish culture is most pronounced in Ybor City, a long-established community in southeast Tampa named after the man who brought his cigar factory here from Key West.

Blacks, who account for 15 percent of the district's population, live mostly in inner-city Tampa. In early 1987, the death of a black man in police custody spurred charges of brutality, and long before that, some black political leaders expressed the view that they had more in common with predominantly black areas of downtown St. Petersburg than with the rest of the 7th District. Early in 1982, the Tampa and St. Petersburg NAACP chapters proposed the creation of a congressional district that would have crossed Tampa Bay, uniting blacks in both cities. Legislators gave the proposal no serious consideration.

Population: 512,905. White 424,343 (83%), Black 76,610 (15%), Other 4,290 (1%). Spanish origin 58,176 (11%). 18 and over 376,478 (73%), 65 and over 62,422 (12%). Median age: 31.

102nd Congress, with even fewer members willing to defend that nation. Besides that, members were pressing for the right to amend the details of a free-trade agreement being discussed with Mexico. Beyond the cases of China and Mexico loomed the much broader implications of a prospective treaty renewing the General Agreement on Tariffs and Trade (GATT). And there remained the drumbeat of hostility toward the trade policies (and success) of the Japanese.

While Gibbons generally opposes using trade as a weapon, he does make exceptions. When Iraq occupied Kuwait in August 1990, Gibbons authored a measure empowering the president to bar imports from countries that continued to trade with Iraq. It passed the House by unanimous consent. And in both the 99th and 100th Congresses, his panel approved legislation from the Foreign Affairs Committee imposing trade sanctions on the apartheid regime of South Africa.

And, despite a stubborn streak, Gibbons reluctantly and perhaps unavoidably accepted the need for some congressional effort to get tough with U.S. trading partners. Beginning in 1985, he cooperated with Rostenkowski to help produce what became, three years later, the most far-reaching trade law in years.

Yet even as his subcommittee prepared to draft a bill early in the 100th Congress, Gibbons was ever mindful of perhaps the most famous trade law in history, the 1930 Smoot-Hawley Act, which dramatically boosted tariffs and contributed to the ensuing global Depression. Vowing a complete reversal of that approach, Gibbons fended off a variety of industry-specific protections.

Speaker Jim Wright and other House leaders preferred a tougher measure, however, and they got their wish on the floor: The House narrowly approved a controversial amendment by Rep. Richard A. Gephardt, D-Mo., to mandate limits on imports from nations such as Japan that maintain big surplus trade balances with the United States. Gibbons admitted he found the amended bill "a tough one to vote for," but he did so anyway, saying, "This is a bicameral organization, and there is hope that we can work out an acceptable bill before we are at the end of all this."

Other than the Gephardt amendment, the

House bill contained little Gibbons found objectionable. With the exception of telecommunications, it did not single out any industries for special treatment. And though it contained some threatening language, it still left the president considerable leeway on most trade matters. In the end, Gephardt's presidential campaign faltered and his trade amendment was dropped in House-Senate negotiations on the final bill.

In each of the past three Congresses, Gibbons had a more nettlesome role in producing a bill he wanted no part of — one limiting textile and apparel imports. Still, he did not use his position to kill it.

The bill had nearly 300 cosponsors in the 99th Congress, indicating enough support to pry it from Gibbons' subcommittee with a discharge petition had he chosen to play the obstructionist. He volunteered to take it up, but with a promise from the chief sponsor, Georgia Democrat Ed Jenkins, not to support amendments on the floor. That made it tough for Jenkins to broaden the bill's scope and expand his coalition. The measure passed easily, but fell short of the two-thirds needed to override President Reagan's veto.

In the 100th Congress, Gibbons again stood aside as his subcommittee originated a similar bill; when the House vote for passage fell short of two-thirds, presaging another successful veto, Gibbons could claim a species of victory. "No country in the world has ever extended its standard of living by closing its markets," he said. "It hasn't happened in 6,500 years of recorded history."

Jenkins and the other textile champions were back in the 101st Congress, but with somewhat fewer cosponsors. Gibbons again let the bill go by unmolested, observing, "If we want to stop the world and get off, this is the legislation we pass." The veto this time was delivered by President Bush, and again it was sustained.

Despite his more accommodating approach of late, Gibbons never will go as far toward trade protection as some Democrats would prefer. Consequently, he occasionally must worry about other committees and individuals encroaching on trade matters. In the 97th and 98th Congresses, the House, over his vigorous opposition, voted for labor-backed bills to protect U.S. automakers by imposing a "domestic content" requirement on autos sold domestically. Both bills died in the Senate.

Still, Gibbons' willingness not to block the trade bills has brought him closer to the House Democratic mainstream, which is where he would want to be should Rostenkowski decide to retire. If Gibbons were an unyielding free-trader, he might face opposition in moving up to the Ways and Means chair.

Gibbons has some experience with succession struggles. In 1977, his views probably prevented him from becoming chairman of the Trade Subcommittee. The chair was vacant then; he was the panel's senior Democrat and expected to inherit it. But his prospective leadership disturbed many committee Democrats, and Charles Vanik of Ohio, who had not even been on the Trade panel, exercised his full-committee seniority and snatched the chair.

By 1981, though, Gibbons was No. 2 on Ways and Means, and there was nobody to block him when the spot opened again. In fact, he was poised to assume the full-committee chairmanship that year. Retirements and surprise defeats left only Rostenkowski ahead of him, and Rostenkowski was more interested in being majority whip. But Speaker Thomas P. O'Neill Jr., a past rival of Gibbons, urged Rostenkowski to take the Ways and Means chair, preferring not to have Gibbons in it.

Gibbons' relations with Rostenkowski were strained in the 99th Congress when Gibbons emerged as a vocal critic of the committee's centerpiece legislation, a major revision of the tax code. On one occasion, he presided in the chairman's absence and lambasted the bill, prompting staffers to track down their boss, who returned fuming. According to a book on the bill's evolution, "Showdown at Gucci Gulch," one Ways and Means member consoled another who had bemoaned that he was "in a lot of shit" with Rostenkowski by telling him, "If you're in shit, you're standing on Sam Gibbons' shoulders."

In the late 1960s, Gibbons had espoused the very reforms the bill was aimed at — lower rates, fewer loopholes and simplicity. He has since had occasion to question even such sacrosanct tax breaks as the mortgage interest deduction. But in the midst of Rostenkowski's reform effort, Gibbons argued that raising business taxes to offset lower individual rates would hurt U.S. firms struggling to compete in world trade. Republicans in his district later claimed Gibbons was angling for contributions to build his campaign treasury, since his 1984 election had been the closest of his career. In the end, Gibbons voted for the tax bill, but Rostenkowski ignored his seniority and kept him off the House-Senate conference committee.

Gibbons is an affable man, but he can be volatile. During the tax bill deliberations, he would launch into tirades against the Ways and Means staff. That reflected not only his own quick temper, but also a general frustration among panel members with the sway Rostenkowski allows his professional minions.

Like many senior members, Gibbons has modified his early ideas about the House. "Secrecy and seniority," he once said, "are the twin vices of this House." But now, he favors the closed meetings that have become routine at Ways and Means. On the Education and Labor Committee in the 1960s, he crusaded to open sessions to the public. He helped draft new rules to restrict unrecorded voting on the House floor and to require confirmation votes on committee chairmen.

In such reformist efforts he was an ally of Arizona Democrat Morris K. Udall. Gibbons managed Udall's unsuccessful bid for majority leader in 1971 against Hale Boggs of Louisiana. Two years later, after Boggs' death, Gibbons launched a brief and futile campaign of his own. The overwhelming front-runner was O'Neill, who assumed that as majority whip he had the edge. O'Neill and Gibbons had been allies, so Gibbons' challenge was a curious one. He dropped out before the voting and O'Neill won unopposed, but the damage was done.

At Home: Gibbons, now in his 15th House term, is the only representative his Tampa-based district has ever had. He defeated a conservative Democrat to win it in 1962, the year it was created, then in 1968 held off another primary challenge from the right.

Only in the strong Republican year of 1984 did Gibbons' general-election tally fall below 60 percent, and then just barely. When that spurred talk of a serious challenge in the next election, Gibbons dusted off his campaign machinery, put a new emphasis on fundraising and hired a big-name consultant. He spent hundreds of thousands of dollars, but as it turned out, he was unopposed in 1986 and 1988 and only nominally challenged in 1990.

Before he came to Congress, Gibbons served 10 years in the Legislature, where he drafted his state's first successful urban-renewal measure and fought the "Pork Chop Gang" that wanted to preserve rural overrepresentation in legislative reapportionment.

Gibbons finished first in the five-way 1962 Democratic House primary, then faced a runoff with retired National Guard Lt. Gen. Sumter L. Lowry, a fervid segregationist and anti-communist. Lowry got contributions from wealthy conservatives all over the South, but Gibbons picked up the support of the moderate Democratic candidates who had failed to make the runoff. He defeated Lowry and won the general election handily.

Committees

Ways & Means (2nd of 23 Democrats)
Trade (chairman); Social Security

Joint Taxation

Elections

1990 General

Sam M. Gibbons (D)	99,454	(68%)
Charles D. Prout (R)	47,754	(32%)

1988 General

Sam M. Gibbons (D)	Unopposed

Previous Winning Percentages: **1986** (100%) **1984** (59%) **1982** (74%) **1980** (72%) **1978** (100%) **1976** (66%) **1974** (100%) **1972** (68%) **1970** (72%) **1968** (62%) **1966** (100%) **1964** (100%) **1962** (71%)

District Vote For President

	1988	1984	1980	1976
D	76,797 (41%)	70,645 (37%)	73,804 (43%)	79,593 (54%)
R	107,409 (58%)	119,135 (63%)	87,705 (51%)	66,684 (45%)
I			7,679 (5%)	

Campaign Finance

	Receipts	Receipts from PACs	Expend-itures
1990			
Gibbons (D)	$492,517	$316,125 (64%)	$825,795
1988			
Gibbons (D)	$604,570	$345,387 (57%)	$382,889

Key Votes

1991	
Authorize use of force against Iraq	N
1990	
Support constitutional amendment on flag desecration	N
Pass family and medical leave bill over Bush veto	Y
Reduce SDI funding	Y
Allow abortions in overseas military facilities	Y
Approve budget summit plan for spending and taxing	Y
Approve civil rights bill	Y
1989	
Halt production of B-2 stealth bomber at 13 planes	Y
Oppose capital gains tax cut	Y
Approve federal abortion funding in rape or incest cases	N
Approve pay raise and revision of ethics rules	Y
Pass Democratic minimum wage plan over Bush veto	Y

Voting Studies

	Presidential Support		Party Unity		Conservative Coalition	
Year	S	O	S	O	S	O
1990	32	66	82	14	48	52
1989	37	53	78	13	49	51
1988	35	54	74	20	55	32
1987	29	67	82	12	49	47
1986	33	62	71	19	56	34
1985	50	45	69	20	49	45
1984	45	47	59	24	51	36
1983	45	50	68	23	38	55
1982	65	29	62	35	64	32
1981	62	34	46	45	80	15

Interest Group Ratings

Year	ADA	ACU	AFL-CIO	CCUS
1990	61	27	55	31
1989	80	19	70	40
1988	60	35	71	64
1987	56	32	69	33
1986	50	45	31	57
1985	40	38	53	50
1984	35	29	33	25
1983	60	22	53	55
1982	50	41	40	48
1981	30	38	40	50

8 C.W. Bill Young (R)

Of Indian Rocks Beach — Elected 1970

Born: Dec. 16, 1930, Harmarville, Pa.
Education: Attended Pennsylvania public schools.
Military Service: National Guard, 1948-57.
Occupation: Insurance executive.
Family: Wife, Beverly F. Angelo; three children.
Religion: Methodist.
Political Career: Fla. Senate, 1961-71, minority leader, 1967-71.
Capitol Office: 2407 Rayburn Bldg. 20515; 225-5961.

In Washington: Young's thinning, blow-dried pompadour sometimes makes him look like a refugee from a country & western band, but he is in reality one of the more serious and effective conservatives in the House.

While Young plays his most substantive role as a GOP stalwart on the Appropriations Subcommittee on Defense, he gained an honorary title of symbolic significance early in the 101st Congress: dean of the majority party in Florida's 19-member House delegation.

When Young was first elected to the state Senate in 1960, he was its only Republican. A decade later, when he won a seat in the U.S. House, he was one of just three Republicans in the 12-member delegation. In the years since, Florida's House contingent and its Republican component have grown, but the GOP did not have a majority of House members until 2nd District Rep. Bill Grant switched parties in February 1989. The split went 10-9 for the GOP. "I have to admit," Young said, "this is the first time ever in my political career I'm in any kind of majority status." Though Grant lost to a Democrat in 1990, the GOP retained its delegation majority thanks to Ileana Ros-Lehtinen, who captured a Democratic district in a 1989 special election and held it in 1990.

Young is best known for expanding the purview of the Defense Appropriations Subcommittee. He has become the leading congressional advocate of the National Bone Marrow Donor Registry, and he has worked to fund it through the defense budget.

The money initially found its way into a defense funding bill in 1986, when then-Sen. Paul Laxalt of Nevada slipped it in. That same year, Laxalt announced his retirement, and Young came into contact with a 10-year-old girl from his district who was dying of cancer and could not find a bone-marrow donor. Since then, Young has guarded funding for the registry, eventually shifting it from the Navy (which contracted the registry out to the Red Cross) to the National Institutes of Health.

In the 101st Congress, Young secured $37 million for the program in four different appropriations bills, including the 1990 supplemental to fund Operation Desert Shield. He made the case that the threat of biological weapons increased the potential need for marrow transplants.

After years of championing this cause, Young learned in late 1990 that his eldest daughter had developed a form of leukemia treatable only through a marrow transplant. She received a transplant that year and is in remission.

While Young says the registry is his proudest achievement, he first made his mark as an advocate of the 1980s defense buildup. Though Young supported nearly all of President Ronald Reagan's individual defense initiatives, his seriousness and his willingness to work with Democrats earned him respect on both sides of the aisle. Young has suggested that his unyielding stance on some issues is just a strategy to offset the zeal of liberals bent on cutting defense. "I have become one of those who is the counterbalance on the right that makes it possible to compromise in the middle," he once said.

Young's 1989 support for denying funding for the Air Force's advanced tactical fighter plane (ATF) was seen as a sign of the times. "Money is getting tighter," he said. "We're more attentive to money issues, and this is a program with a lot of unanswered questions."

A member of the Intelligence Committee earlier in his House career, Young continued to pursue national security issues. He was a leading House proponent of expanding random polygraph testing for Defense Department and federal-contractor employees. Two years after approving a polygraph test program in the defense authorization bill, the 100th Congress approved language to permit annual random polygraph tests of up to 20,000 employees of the Defense Department and its contractors.

While the national security applications of polygraph testing have gained widespread support, Young's enthusiasm for testing in the private sector never caught on. In 1986 and 1987, the House passed legislation prohibiting most private employers from requiring employ-

Florida 8

West — St. Petersburg

The modern era of Florida politics began in this district a little over three decades ago, and the 8th is still a good signpost of political change statewide.

In 1954, this district made William C. Cramer the state's first Republican House member of the 20th century. Cramer owed his election to the influence of conservative retirees. In subsequent years, other Republican candidates prospered as the retirees' influence expanded elsewhere in Florida.

Today, the retirees are still crucial in the politics of the 8th, but no candidate can afford to ignore the growing numbers of young people drawn by its steadily diversifying economy. The young newcomers, like their peers flooding into other parts of Florida, are in some ways more conservative, which is good news for the GOP here.

Not too long ago, St. Petersburg was known almost exclusively as a retirement haven. The retirees who settled there — many of them storekeepers, office workers and civil servants from the small-town Midwest — brought their Republican preferences to Florida with them. The economy was mostly service oriented, geared to the needs of elderly residents and tourists. The morning rush hour saw many younger workers from St. Petersburg driving to jobs in Tampa, which provided employment in a greater variety of fields and a faster pace of life than in St. Pete, where the Shuffleboard Hall of Fame is a big attraction.

But during the last decade, St. Petersburg has sought to broaden its economic base by stressing that it offers a good climate for business investment. Now, St. Petersburg and Pinellas County firms such as Honeywell, Paradyne, E-Systems and General Electric are busy with research, development, production and marketing of computers, communications equipment and other high-technology items. A number of the major employers and subcontractors are engaged in defense-related work.

The median age of the Pinellas County population has dropped because so many young people attracted to good-paying jobs have moved into the area. Democrats are still competitive in some elections in the 8th, partly because many retirees identify the party as the founder and protector of Social Security. But Republicans have 25,000 more registered voters in Pinellas County, and in practice many of the registered Democrats vote Republican, especially at the national level.

Population: 512,909. White 463,124 (90%), Black 44,983 (9%), Other 3,161 (1%). Spanish origin 7,616 (2%). 18 and over 413,853 (81%), 65 and over 141,405 (28%). Median age: 45.

ees and job applicants to take lie-detector tests. During both debates, Young's amendments to permit testing under certain guidelines were defeated.

During his tenure on Intelligence, Young charted an independent course on some matters. He supported efforts to aid anti-communist insurgents, but he was critical of the agency following disclosures of the CIA role in helping elect Salvadoran President José Napoleón Duarte. "The CIA is not the place to run political campaigns," Young declared. He said he was bothered by the CIA's arrogance in refusing to keep Congress informed.

Young also plays a role in a number of issues closer to home. Together with Florida Democrat William Lehman, Young led the charge in the Appropriations Committee against lifting an existing moratorium on offshore oil drilling in the Gulf of Mexico. When an amendment challenging the drilling ban was offered, the committee turned it back. In the 101st Congress, he supported an amendment allowing states to enforce tougher oil liability laws than those on the federal books.

Young, who notes that his St. Petersburg-based district contains more Social Security recipients than any other, goes to considerable lengths to help them. In 1989, he was among the 44 Republican House members to reverse his earlier support for the catastrophic health care bill and helped repeal the act.

In 1985, he proposed a bill to prohibit employers from setting any mandatory retirement age; a similar measure became law in 1986. A member of the Appropriations subcommittee that sets spending levels for the Department of Health and Human Services, he has called for more expeditious health-care payments to Medicare recipients, and has proposed legislation guaranteeing that the cost-of-living adjustments for Social Security beneficiaries could not be cut back or eliminated.

At Home: A high school dropout from a Pennsylvania mining town, Young worked his way to success in the insurance business before going into politics in 1960. Ten years later, he inherited Florida's most dependable Republican seat from Rep. William C. Cramer, who left it when he ran for the U.S. Senate in 1970.

Young had known Cramer a long time. He had met the congressman at a Rotary Club barbecue in 1955, worked in his 1956 campaign and was hired as Cramer's district aide in 1957. In 1960 the Pinellas County GOP organization urged Young to challenge a veteran Democratic state senator. He won, and became the only Republican in the state Senate. By 1967, there were 20 others, and Young was minority leader.

When Cramer announced for the Senate in 1970, there was little question who would replace him. Young won 76 percent of the primary vote and 67 percent in the general election. Since then it has been even easier.

During the 1980s, Young drew Democratic opposition only twice. In 1984, he won 80 percent against Democrat Robert Kent, a former Sunshine Skyway toll collector. Kent, a Yugoslavian émigré and frequent congressional candidate from Indiana in the 1960s, changed his name from Ivan Korunek before running against Young, but the strategy failed to broaden his appeal. In 1988, Young got more than 70 percent of the vote against Democrat C. Bette Wimbish, a former St. Petersburg City Council president. Two years later, Democrats again did not bother to put up a challenger.

When prominent Republicans were looking for established politicians to challenge Democratic Gov. Bob Graham and Sen. Lawton Chiles in 1982, both Young and Rep. L. A. "Skip" Bafalis were intensively courted. Young pondered a statewide race, then ruled it out, a decision that seemed wise in retrospect. Bafalis took a chance and received a dismal 35 percent against Graham.

Committees

Appropriations (5th of 22 Republicans)
Defense; Labor, Health & Human Services, Education & Related Agencies

Select Intelligence (5th of 7 Republicans)
Program & Budget Authorization

Elections

1990 General		
C. W. Bill Young (R)	Unopposed	
1988 General		
C. W. Bill Young (R)	169,165	(73%)
C. Bette Wimbish (D)	62,539	(27%)

Previous Winning Percentages: **1986** (100%) **1984** (80%) **1982** (100%) **1980** (100%) **1978** (79%) **1976** (65%) **1974** (76%) **1972** (76%) **1970** (67%)

District Vote For President

	1988	1984	1980	1976
D	97,452 (45%)	91,393 (37%)	97,324 (41%)	98,426 (49%)
R	120,065 (55%)	153,584 (63%)	124,802 (53%)	100,586 (50%)
I			12,280 (5%)	

Campaign Finance

	Receipts	Receipts from PACs		Expenditures
1990				
Young (R)	$231,400	$132,900	(57%)	$201,188
1988				
Young (R)	$212,972	$109,600	(51%)	$208,320
Wimbish (D)	$37,501	$14,001	(37%)	$23,655

Key Votes

1991	
Authorize use of force against Iraq	Y
1990	
Support constitutional amendment on flag desecration	Y
Pass family and medical leave bill over Bush veto	N
Reduce SDI funding	N
Allow abortions in overseas military facilities	N
Approve budget summit plan for spending and taxing	Y
Approve civil rights bill	N
1989	
Halt production of B-2 stealth bomber at 13 planes	N
Oppose capital gains tax cut	N
Approve federal abortion funding in rape or incest cases	N
Approve pay raise and revision of ethics rules	Y
Pass Democratic minimum wage plan over Bush veto	N

Voting Studies

	Presidential Support		Party Unity		Conservative Coalition	
Year	**S**	**O**	**S**	**O**	**S**	**O**
1990	68	30	74	21	93	6
1989	71	26	83	13	95	2
1988	59	36	86	8	97	3
1987	59	36	76	17	84	9
1986	72	26	75	18	84	14
1985	74	25	80	14	87	9
1984	54	38	68	24	85	8
1983	74	23	77	18	87	11
1982	74	16	74 †	17 †	84	5
1981	72	24	83	12	88	7

† Not eligible for all recorded votes.

Interest Group Ratings

Year	ADA	ACU	AFL-CIO	CCUS
1990	17	79	8	57
1989	10	86	9	89
1988	10	88	36	79
1987	12	87	6	93
1986	5	95	8	67
1985	5	71	24	76
1984	25	58	15	60
1983	5	96	6	75
1982	10	86	5	80
1981	5	100	7	94

9 Michael Bilirakis (R)

Of Palm Harbor — Elected 1982

Born: July 16, 1930, Tarpon Springs, Fla.
Education: U. of Pittsburgh, B.S. 1959; Attended George Washington U., 1959-60; U. of Florida, J.D. 1963.
Military Service: Air Force, 1951-55.
Occupation: Lawyer; restaurant owner.
Family: Wife, Evelyn Miaoulis; two children.
Religion: Greek Orthodox.
Political Career: No previous office.
Capitol Office: 2432 Rayburn Bldg. 20515; 225-5755.

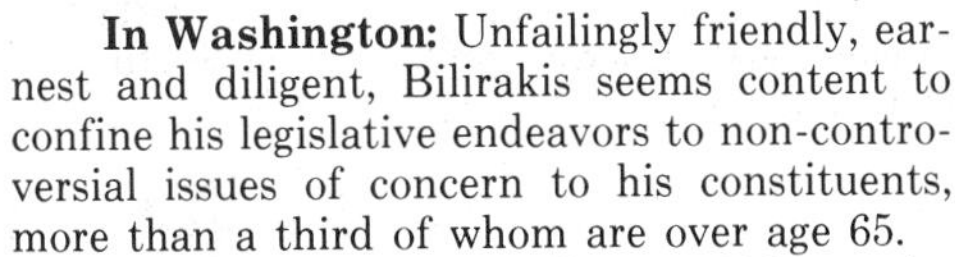

In Washington: Unfailingly friendly, earnest and diligent, Bilirakis seems content to confine his legislative endeavors to non-controversial issues of concern to his constituents, more than a third of whom are over age 65.

Generally a party loyalist — 1990 was the first time he voted with his party less than 84 percent of the time — Bilirakis parts company with the GOP when his constituency calls.

On the Energy and Commerce Committee, Bilirakis works cooperatively with liberal Health Subcommittee Chairman Henry A. Waxman when it serves his district. In the 101st Congress, Bilirakis was active on the environmental front, serving as a conferee on the Clean Air Act, helping to negotiate an agreement on automobile pollution standards and pushing legislation to help curb acid rain.

In the 99th Congress, Bilirakis had collaborated with Waxman to get five Medicare demonstration projects for victims of Alzheimer's disease included in a budget-reconciliation measure. In 1990, Congress passed a measure reauthorizing some of the programs — after adopting a Bilirakis amendment that set aside 10 percent of the funds for the very elderly.

Bilirakis supported the Republican alternative to the catastrophic-health insurance bill in the 100th Congress, but when it was rejected on a party-line vote Bilirakis was one of of 61 House Republicans willing to vote for the Democrats' version (ignoring the president's veto threat). In 1989, he tried unsuccessfully to get Congress to slow the phase-in of a new plan for paying physicians under Medicare, fearing that some doctors in his district might simply stop treating Medicare patients. Bilirakis' attentive concern for the elderly and his geniality earned him the chairmanship of the Republican Research Committee's Task Force on the Elderly.

A member of the Veterans' Affairs Committee, Bilirakis was among those calling for cost-of-living increases for disabled veterans, which Congress passed in January 1991. He has also maintained a keen interest in American servicemen missing in action or thought to be still held in Southeast Asia.

At Home: When Bilirakis announced plans to make his first political campaign in 1982, local GOP leaders were slightly bemused. But Bilirakis surprised the press, the party hierarchy and most supposed experts on Florida politics, turning innocence into a virtue and winning the newly created 9th.

A registered Democrat until 1970, Bilirakis had switched parties to back L. A. "Skip" Bafalis' bid for governor. Although he was intermittently active in local GOP campaigns during the next decade, he never considered running for office himself until 1982: "I found myself out of challenges," he explained.

In the GOP primary, Bilirakis was an underdog to state House Republican leader Curt Kiser. But while Kiser was taking his nomination for granted, Bilirakis was blanketing the district with signs saying that his was "a hard name to spell but an easy one to remember."

Using his own resources and contributions from the Tarpon Springs Greek community, Bilirakis flooded the airwaves with ads stressing his service to the area, as a judge in county and municipal courts and as president of several community organizations. Bilirakis finished well ahead of Kiser and Clearwater Mayor Charles LeCher, and beat Kiser in the runoff.

Bilirakis emphasized his personality in his general-election campaign against Democratic state Rep. George Sheldon. When he did speak out on issues, he espoused conservative positions — defending President Reagan's economic program and arguing for a constitutional ban on abortions — and he attacked Sheldon's more liberal voting record. Bilirakis won by 4,320 votes. He has quickly become entrenched, taking more than 70 percent in 1984 and 1986, and facing no opposition two years later.

His victory margin dipped to 58 percent in 1990, when he ran against Democrat Cheryl Davis Knapp, a liberal nurse from Safety Harbor. Knapp accused Bilirakis of doing too little for the environment, the homeless and women's rights, but she was not a serious political threat.

Florida 9

West — Clearwater; Parts of Pasco and Hillsborough Counties

Patching together pieces of three counties in the Tampa-St. Petersburg area, the 9th is a horseshoe-shaped district with a decidedly Republican bent. About 40 percent of the vote comes from Clearwater and nearby communities in Pinellas County, solidly Republican areas where a Democratic candidate is fortunate to win 45 percent of the vote. Clearwater, traditionally a beach resort, has benefited from the arrival of high-technology industry to metropolitan St. Petersburg. Just north of Clearwater, a substantial Greek community exists in Tarpon Springs, still vibrant a century after their ancestors first came to harvest the offshore sponge beds.

Republicans also hold the upper hand in Pasco County, which casts about one-third of the vote. But Democrats are more competitive there, since many of the retirees who have settled in the county in recent years come from working-class backgrounds and cling to Democratic voting habits. The eastern part of Pasco County, around Dade City, also has rural Democratic voters among the farm lands and citrus groves.

Of the three counties in the 9th, Hillsborough County, influenced by Tampa, is the friendliest to Democrats. But Hillsborough has only about one-fourth of the vote, none of that inside Tampa itself. Some of the residents of the rural eastern part of the county break party ranks when presented with a Democrat they perceive to be too liberal. To have much hope of winning in the 9th, a Democrat has to carry Hillsborough solidly and neutralize the GOP advantage in Pasco.

Population: 513,191. White 486,066 (95%), Black 21,774 (4%), Other 2,486 (1%). Spanish origin 12,787 (3%). 18 and over 404,361 (79%), 65 and over 123,085 (24%). Median age: 42.

Committees

Energy & Commerce (9th of 16 Republicans)
Commerce, Consumer Protection & Competitiveness; Health & the Environment; Telecommunications & Finance

Select Children, Youth & Families (9th of 14 Republicans)

Veterans' Affairs (6th of 13 Republicans)
Oversight & Investigations (ranking); Hospitals & Health Care

Elections

1990 General

Michael Bilirakis (R)	142,145	(58%)
Cheryl Davis Knapp (D)	102,495	(42%)

1990 Primary

Michael Bilirakis (R)	36,870	(83%)
John Freehafer (R)	7,316	(17%)

1988 General

Michael Bilirakis (R) Unopposed

Previous Winning Percentages: **1986** (71%) **1984** (79%) **1982** (51%)

District Vote For President

	1988	1984	1980	1976
D	112,844 (39%)	90,475 (33%)	82,783 (39%)	80,804 (51%)
R	172,473 (60%)	187,403 (67%)	119,229 (56%)	76,330 (48%)
I			9,795 (5%)	

Campaign Finance

	Receipts	Receipts from PACs	Expend-itures
1990			
Bilirakis (R)	$600,670	$234,430 (39%)	$815,366
Knapp (D)	$90,307	$36,915 (41%)	$89,852
1988			
Bilirakis (R)	$399,150	$149,975 (38%)	$193,901

Key Votes

1991	
Authorize use of force against Iraq	Y
1990	
Support constitutional amendment on flag desecration	Y
Pass family and medical leave bill over Bush veto	N
Reduce SDI funding	?
Allow abortions in overseas military facilities	?
Approve budget summit plan for spending and taxing	N
Approve civil rights bill	N
1989	
Halt production of B-2 stealth bomber at 13 planes	N
Oppose capital gains tax cut	N
Approve federal abortion funding in rape or incest cases	N
Approve pay raise and revision of ethics rules	Y
Pass Democratic minimum wage plan over Bush veto	N

Voting Studies

	Presidential Support		Party Unity		Conservative Coalition	
Year	**S**	**O**	**S**	**O**	**S**	**O**
1990	51	29	70	13	81	4
1989	60	36	86	11	85	12
1988	67	29	87	8	89	5
1987	66	32	86	10	91	9
1986	77	21	88	9	96	4
1985	75	24	84	10	87	11
1984	63	34	86	14	90	10
1983	79	20	90	9	93	4

Interest Group Ratings

Year	ADA	ACU	AFL-CIO	CCUS
1990	17	80	9	85
1989	10	86	25	100
1988	10	96	14	93
1987	16	78	13	87
1986	15	86	29	67
1985	10	71	29	77
1984	10	88	31	80
1983	10	87	18	85

10 Andy Ireland (R)

Of Winter Haven — Elected 1976

Born: Aug. 23, 1930, Cincinnati, Ohio.
Education: Yale U., B.S. 1952; attended Columbia U. School of Business, 1953-54; Louisiana State U. School of Banking, graduated 1959.
Occupation: Banker.
Family: Wife, Nancy Haydock; four children.
Religion: Episcopalian.
Political Career: Winter Haven City Commission, 1966-68; Democratic nominee for Fla. Senate, 1972.
Capitol Office: 2466 Rayburn Bldg. 20515; 225-5015.

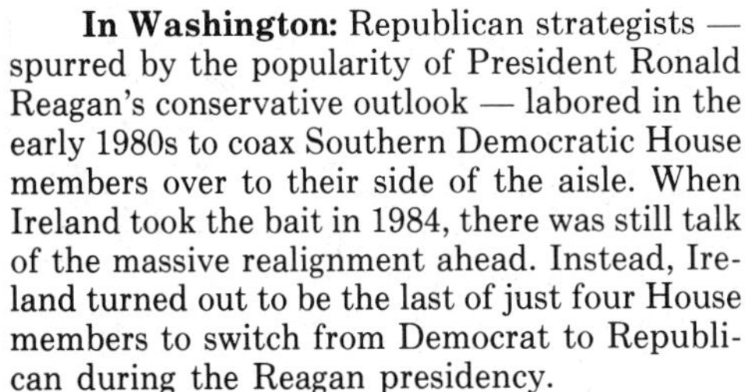

In Washington: Republican strategists — spurred by the popularity of President Ronald Reagan's conservative outlook — labored in the early 1980s to coax Southern Democratic House members over to their side of the aisle. When Ireland took the bait in 1984, there was still talk of the massive realignment ahead. Instead, Ireland turned out to be the last of just four House members to switch from Democrat to Republican during the Reagan presidency.

Although he was not in the vanguard of a great movement, things have not turned out badly for Ireland. One of a handful of House members devoted to small business issues, Ireland in February 1991 became the ranking Republican on the Small Business Committee (succeeding Joseph M. McDade of Pennsylvania, who took the ranking Republican spot on Appropriations).

Ireland has also achieved some prominence on the Armed Services Committee as an advocate of fiscal prudence in the Defense Department. He scored a coup in 1990 when he exposed cost overruns in the development of the A-12 attack plane; an ensuing Pentagon probe resulted in Defense Secretary Dick Cheney's decision to cancel the project.

Had Ireland remained a Democrat, he would likely have gotten lost amid the liberal Democrats for whom defense "waste, fraud and abuse" is something of a mantra. It is Ireland's perspective as a conservative Republican that makes him stand out. "I am a 'hawk' who has always believed that U.S. military superiority is our best chance for democracy and world peace," Ireland says. "However, I am also a fiscal conservative with a former banker's penchant for frugality."

Concerns about the Defense Department's accountability led him to target the A-12, a high-tech bomber slated to replace the carrier-based A-6 planes. Ireland, acting upon tips from "whistleblowers," met with Defense officials to suggest an investigation. After the probe found that the project was more than $1 billion over budget and that managers had withheld information from higher-ups, Cheney in January 1991 axed the program. Ireland shared the credit with Charlie Murphy, his aide for defense issues: A *Washington Post* story described them as the "A-12 giantkillers."

This incident was not Ireland's first run-in with Pentagon accountants. In April 1989, Ireland argued that a five-year spending plan presented by Cheney understated the amount of money actually needed by $45 billion. When Cheney was quoted as saying, "Andy doesn't know what he's talking about," Ireland set out to prove him wrong. Two weeks later, the Florida Republican released a General Accounting Office report he commissioned that appeared to back up his position.

Events also conspired to bolster Ireland's arguments in favor of getting U.S. allies to pick up a larger share of defense costs, a concept labeled "burden-sharing." He was the ranking Republican on a task force, chaired by Colorado Democrat Patricia Schroeder, that in early 1989 recommended reducing U.S. troop strength in Europe by 25,000.

With Soviet military strength apparently receding and Congress looking for ways to trim the defense budget, Ireland had some success toward that goal later in 1989. His proposal to bring home 15,000 defense employees — assigned to intermediate-range missile sites eliminated by a 1987 U.S.-Soviet treaty — was attached to the fiscal 1990 defense authorization bill.

Until he found his niche on Armed Services, Ireland devoted more time to his Small Business beat.

When a defense-procurement scandal broke into the news in mid-1988, Ireland used an Armed Services hearing on the issue to promote his favorite cause: "I believe that more involvement by small business in the procurement process would lead us away from a dangerous dependency on a handful of large defense contractors . . . ," Ireland said.

Ireland has pushed for permanent authorization of a White House Conference on Small

Florida 10

Central — Lakeland; Winter Haven; Bradenton

All over Florida, land once devoted to agriculture is being eaten away by shopping centers, motels and condominiums. But in Polk County, centerpiece of the 10th District, citrus is still king.

Thousands of area jobs are connected with the growing, picking, packing, processing and loading of oranges, orange concentrate and grapefruit. The biggest companies are well known — Tropicana and Minute Maid — but there are many lesser growers whose efforts combine to make the 10th the nation's foremost citrus-producing district.

Phosphate rock, the raw material of fertilizer, is another key element of the Polk County economy. Three-fourths of America's phosphate is strip-mined out of Polk, although demand for the product has been uneven in recent years.

In addition to work in the citrus and phosphate industries, Polk County's employment offerings include the Piper Aircraft Corp. and the Circus World and Cypress Gardens tourist attractions.

Polk County is home to 405,000 people, with the major concentration in the Lakeland-Winter Haven area. There is a remarkable disparity between party registration figures and election results. Registered Republicans are outnumbered by more than 40,000 in the county, yet Polk nearly always supports GOP presidential candidates and has given warm approval to Ireland since he left the Democratic Party to run as a Republican.

The 10th has one Gulf Coast county, Manatee, which is the only county in the 10th where registered Republicans outnumber Democrats. The Bradenton metropolitan area there grew by 43 percent in the 1980s, and the county as a whole also grew by 43 percent to 202,000. Manatee is a popular retirement area for people from Central and Midwestern states where GOP voting was a habit.

Democrats are competitive in local elections in Manatee, but federal elections are a different matter. In the 1984 House contest, Pat Glass, a popular Democratic officeholder in Manatee, challenged Ireland and lost decisively in her own home county. Ireland hasn't seen an opponent draw over 26 percent in the county since then.

De Soto and Hardee counties are also included in the 10th. Predominantly agricultural, they have cattle ranches, citrus groves, a scattering of small towns and conservative voters whose ties to the Democratic Party are stronger than in Polk.

Population: 512,890. White 435,256 (85%), Black 66,731 (13%), Other 2,514 (1%). Spanish origin 16,774 (3%). 18 and over 381,628 (74%), 65 and over 92,163 (18%). Median age: 35.

Business, to be held every four years. He favors giving the Small Business Administration (SBA) Cabinet-level status. SBA's fate was an issue on which Ireland, even after his partisan conversion, clashed with the Reagan administration, which wanted to eliminate the agency altogether.

Ireland also parts from conservative dogma on the issue of oil drilling off the Florida coast, which he strongly opposes. However, his overall record is in line with other Southern Republicans; he supported President Bush on 75 percent of House votes in 1990.

During his early years in the House, Ireland came across as a typical conservative Democrat and a genuine "good ol' boy" — a remarkable feat, considering that he was schooled at Phillips Academy and Yale and had served as treasurer of the Florida Bankers' Association.

But the longer Ireland stayed in Washington, the more ill at ease he felt calling himself a Democrat. "The House Democratic leadership uses the Solid South to sustain itself," he once complained, "but when it comes time for input, they say, 'Go take a hike.' " Finally, in March 1984, Ireland announced he would join the party he had been voting with all along.

At Home: Die-hard Democratic loyalists in the 10th were enraged when Ireland announced his party switch, and they vowed to exact revenge at the polls in 1984. But Ireland easily won a fifth term.

The first sign that Ireland would not have much trouble winning as a Republican in 1984 came July 20, the candidates' filing deadline. There had been talk after Ireland announced his switch that one or more moderate Democratic officeholders from Polk County, the district's largest, would run in the 10th. But none did, leaving the Democratic field to Manatee County Commissioner Patricia M. Glass and two others with no track records.

Glass had been a strong advocate of environmental protection, gaining publicity for fighting to protect the waters of Manatee County from pollution caused by phosphate mining. But she was not well known in Polk County, and her environmentalist record was not an aid to her there; phosphate mines are an important source of jobs in Polk.

To give herself more time and money to concentrate on Ireland, Glass hoped to win the nomination outright in the September primary. But she was held under 50 percent by Jack Carter, a retired field representative for the Social Security Administration who portrayed himself as more conservative than Glass. She defeated Carter in the October runoff, but by then Ireland was too far ahead.

Though he was campaigning for the first time under the GOP banner, Ireland needed to make few adjustments in his rhetoric. He had always talked about cutting government regulation, providing a strong defense and keeping taxes down. Republican officials in Washington made the race a priority, and he enjoyed a huge financial advantage over Glass. Aided by Reagan's showing, Ireland swept to an easy victory. By 1986, Democrats seemed resigned that Ireland's conversion had made the 10th a GOP seat.

Ireland's political career had begun in a 1976 Democratic House primary, as he and five others sought to replace retiring Democrat James A. Haley. As a wealthy banker, Ireland had the resources to compensate for his political inexperience. A runoff was expected, but Ireland won the nomination outright with 51 percent. His general-election foe was GOP state Rep. Robert Johnson, in the Legislature for six years but not well known outside his Sarasota home. Ireland won 58 percent of the vote.

Ireland's voting record was not popular with labor unions, minorities and others who found him too conservative, but he never had trouble in a Democratic primary. Republicans were so satisfied with Ireland that he met only one minor general-election challenge in his three re-election campaigns as a Democrat.

Committees

Small Business (Ranking)
SBA, the General Economy & Minority Enterprise Development (ranking)

Armed Services (11th of 22 Republicans)
Investigations; Procurement & Military Nuclear Systems

Elections

1990 General

Andy Ireland (R)	Unopposed	

1988 General

Andy Ireland (R)	156,563	(73%)
David Higginbottom (D)	56,536	(27%)

Previous Winning Percentages: **1986** (71%) **1984** (62%) **1982** * (100%) **1980** * (69%) **1978** * (100%) **1976** * (58%)

** Ireland was elected as a Democrat in 1976-82.*

District Vote For President

	1988	1984	1980	1976
D	69,725 (33%)	60,726 (29%)	71,059 (38%)	77,872 (49%)
R	137,911 (66%)	150,022 (71%)	107,348 (58%)	78,521 (50%)
I			5,857 (3%)	

Campaign Finance

	Receipts	Receipts from PACs	Expend-itures
1990			
Ireland (R)	$410,468	$169,683 (41%)	$384,555
1988			
Ireland (R)	$405,000	$164,389 (41%)	$460,468
Higginbottom (D)	$33,826	0	$33,823

Key Votes

1991	
Authorize use of force against Iraq	Y
1990	
Support constitutional amendment on flag desecration	Y
Pass family and medical leave bill over Bush veto	N
Reduce SDI funding	N
Allow abortions in overseas military facilities	N
Approve budget summit plan for spending and taxing	Y
Approve civil rights bill	N
1989	
Halt production of B-2 stealth bomber at 13 planes	Y
Oppose capital gains tax cut	N
Approve federal abortion funding in rape or incest cases	N
Approve pay raise and revision of ethics rules	Y
Pass Democratic minimum wage plan over Bush veto	N

Voting Studies

	Presidential Support		Party Unity		Conservative Coalition	
Year	S	O	S	O	S	O
1990	75	20	83	8	87	6
1989	65	22	82	9	85	7
1988	67	27	88	4	87	5
1987	68	28	85	6	91	5
1986	74	18	87	7	86	0
1985	80	19	88	6	89	7
1984	56	35	66 *	32 *	88	7
1983	72	23	31	62	89	7
1982	60	17	22	50	75	5
1981	74	16	29	56	87	7

** Ireland switched from the Democratic to the Republican party on July 5, 1984. Party Unity scores shown for 1984 are for Republican party membership. Ireland's scores as a Democrat were 24 percent party support and 62 percent opposition.*

Interest Group Ratings

Year	ADA	ACU	AFL-CIO	CCUS
1990	11	82	8	64
1989	10	88	8	100
1988	5	100	14	100
1987	0	96	0	100
1986	0	80	8	100
1985	5	90	6	82
1984	0	61	25	60
1983	10	91	6	89
1982	10	74	6	80
1981	5	87	29	100

11 Jim Bacchus (D)

Of Belle Isle — Elected 1990

Born: June 21, 1949, Nashville, Tenn.
Education: Vanderbilt U., B.A. 1971; Yale U., M.A. 1973; Florida State U., J.D. 1978.
Military Service: Army Reserve, 1971-77.
Occupation: Lawyer; journalist.
Family: Wife, Rebecca McMillan; two children.
Religion: Presbyterian.
Political Career: No previous office.
Capitol Office: 431 Cannon Bldg. 20515; 225-3671.

The Path to Washington: A textbook candidate who ran a textbook campaign, Orlando lawyer Bacchus won a real-life ticket to Washington in 1990.

When Democratic Rep. Bill Nelson announced that he would give up his 11th District post to run for governor, Democrats fretted that they might lose the seat. Republicans now outnumber registered Democrats in the district. But while six Republican candidates feuded for the party nomination, Bacchus became the unchallenged Democratic pick.

Bacchus came to the race with impressive credentials. Though he had never held elective office, he had a hefty track record in political and civic affairs. After first reporting on politics for *The Orlando Sentinel*, Bacchus became an active participant as an aide to then-Democratic Gov. Reubin Askew. He followed Askew to Washington when Askew was appointed U.S. trade representative, then returned to Florida to practice law.

Bacchus kept a hand in Democratic politics and an array of civic groups, including a space-business roundtable and the Greater Orlando Chamber of Commerce, and commissions on the arts, the environment, the homeless and growth.

Bacchus proceeded to run an impeccable campaign. He jumped in early and had raised more than $200,000 before 1990 began. Early on, Bacchus had also assembled campaign themes, position papers and endorsements.

Like many candidates in the 1990 cycle, Bacchus criticized the decay of modern politics and government. But Bacchus pointed a finger at voters as well as politicians, insisting that apathy is the root of the problem. If voters are unhappy with the result, Bacchus said, "we have no one to blame but ourselves."

Bacchus' initial solution was the campaign fixture of "Citizen Saturdays." He devoted each Saturday of the campaign to organizing volunteers to perform some community service, such as cleaning polluted beaches or building playgrounds.

Critics dismissed the Saturday programs as a campaign stunt, a knockoff of Lawton Chiles' walking tour of the state during his 1970 Senate campaign. But Bacchus insisted that the Citizen Saturdays were an end in themselves, an effort to get people mobilized within their own communities and the outgrowth of his "Jeffersonian" belief in participatory democracy.

Bacchus was helped by the fractious GOP primary and subsequent runoff, which kept the Republican nominee in doubt until early October. Bill Tolley, the eventual nominee, was a strong conservative from the right wing of the Republican Party. An opponent of abortion rights and taxes, Tolley blasted Bacchus as too liberal for the district.

But Bacchus spotlighted his business credentials and some conservative economic positions (such as support for a line-item veto and a constitutional balanced budget amendment) as proof that he is no free-spending liberal. Instead, Bacchus claimed that it was Tolley who was out of step, calling the contest a choice between "the mainstream and the extreme."

Bacchus was battling not only the Republicans' numerical advantage, but also a geographical disadvantage. Tolley came from Brevard County, which supplies more than half of the district's voters. But Bacchus, who carried Brevard by about 9,000 votes, fanned support there by waving a promise from the Democratic House leadership that he would be placed on the House Science, Space and Technology Committee.

The 11th is home to the Kennedy Space Center, and aerospace concerns are a critical component of district politics. Not surprisingly, Bacchus supports ambitious plans for NASA, such as a permanent moon base and possible mission to Mars.

Florida 11

East — Melbourne; Part of Orange County

The 11th fairly staggers with tourist attractions. It includes Walt Disney World, Circus World, Sea World, the Stars Hall of Fame and other diversions that provide low-skill, minimum-wage jobs and take in millions of visitors' dollars every year. Blue-collar support from people in Orange County who work in the tourist industry provides Democrats with an electoral cushion against Republican votes elsewhere.

Brevard County, home of the National Aeronautics and Space Administration's Kennedy Space Center, boomed during the era of space flights in the 1960s, then stalled when space exploration slipped from its status as a top-level national priority. The high-technology industries that had been lured to the area were forced to trim jobs, but a core group of engineers and other skilled workers remained. In the 1980s, the space shuttle program and President Reagan's increased military spending brought new opportunities for aerospace and defense-related work, which helped make Brevard County one of Florida's fastest-growing. The 1986 explosion of the *Challenger* cast an economic and psychological pall over Brevard that only began to lift when shuttle flights resumed in late 1988.

Brevard, casting just over half the district vote, has a slight Republican registration advantage. Engineers and other professionals make up a significant share of the electorate; they are mostly conservative and partial to Republicans in presidential elections, yet will vote for moderate Democrats in House contests. Jim Bacchus won the county by more than 9,000 votes in 1990.

The district also includes nearly all of Osceola and Indian River counties. Most of Osceola's people live in the northern half of the county, which lies on the outskirts of metropolitan Orlando. Southern Osceola has cattle ranches and citrus groves.

Retirees who have settled in Vero Beach and other coastal towns in Indian River County tend to come from North Central states — more Ohioans than New Yorkers. These older people are fairly affluent and accustomed to voting Republican. This area presents a problem for local Democrats, but it has a fairly small share of the district's population.

Population: 512,691. White 461,407 (90%), Black 40,318 (8%), Other 5,379 (1%). Spanish origin 17,537 (3%). 18 and over 380,011 (74%), 65 and over 59,741 (12%). Median age: 32.

Committees

Banking, Finance & Urban Affairs (26th of 31 Democrats)
Financial Institutions Supervision, Regulation & Insurance; International Development, Finance, Trade & Monetary Policy

Select Children, Youth & Families (20th of 22 Democrats)

Science, Space & Technology (26th of 32 Democrats)
Science; Space; Technology & Competitiveness

Campaign Finance

	Receipts	Receipts from PACs		Expend-itures
1990				
Bacchus (D)	$877,500	$412,573	(47%)	$875,386
Tolley (R)	$365,313	$106,100	(29%)	$364,926

Key Vote

1991

Authorize use of force against Iraq Y

Elections

1990 General

Jim Bacchus (D)	120,974	(52%)
Bill Tolley (R)	111,916	(48%)

District Vote For President

	1988	1984	1980	1976
D	72,912 (29%)	62,999 (26%)	65,216 (33%)	76,194 (47%)
R	178,859 (70%)	180,110 (74%)	120,144 (61%)	82,160 (51%)
I			8,877 (5%)	

12 Tom Lewis (R)

Of North Palm Beach — Elected 1982

Born: Oct. 26, 1924, Philadelphia, Pa.

Education: Attended Palm Beach Junior College, 1956-57; U. of Florida, 1958-59.

Military Service: Air Force, 1943-54.

Occupation: Real estate broker; aircraft testing specialist.

Family: Wife, Marian Vastine; three children.

Religion: Methodist.

Political Career: North Palm Beach City Council, 1964-71, mayor 1964-71; Fla. House, 1973-81, minority leader, 1979-81; Fla. Senate, 1981-83.

Capitol Office: 1216 Longworth Bldg. 20515; 225-5792.

In Washington: With seats on Agriculture and on Science, Space and Technology, Lewis has one committee assignment that suits the rural and traditional part of his district, and another that fits his personal expertise as well as the more modern and urbanized elements of his constituency.

Though the best-known parts of the 12th are its affluent bastions on the Atlantic and Gulf coasts, the sprawling expanse in between is mainly farmland that produces vegetables, sugar and livestock.

Lewis is now in the top half of the GOP contingent on Agriculture, but he is not one of the committee's more visible members, partly because of his low-key style and partly because most of the commodities grown in the 12th are not covered by federal programs. The 102nd Congress brought Lewis a new platform: the ranking position on the Domestic Marketing, Consumer Relations and Nutrition Subcommittee. He also sits on subcommittees that deal with sugar and livestock issues.

Lewis' professional background is in aviation, and he has made a bigger mark as a member of the Science Committee. A World War II flier and a longtime testing specialist for Pratt & Whitney, Lewis applies his experience to his duties as ranking Republican on the Technology and Competitiveness Subcommittee. Also, he holds the No. 2 GOP position on another subcommittee dealing with a key Florida issue, space.

Lewis has been a big booster of the National Aerospace Plane, a proposed $5 billion-plus superfast orbital plane. Pratt & Whitney is a contractor on the project.

Lewis has stepped out front on the topic of aviation safety. His National Air Safety Act of 1988, which breezed through both houses of Congress, orders the Federal Aviation Administration to spend a minimum of 15 percent of its annual research budget on a variety of safety issues. In the 101st Congress, Lewis wrote a law to require the FAA to perform additional research aimed at detecting problems that could lead to accidents involving aging airliners.

At Home: Lewis did not enter politics until he was nearly 40, and he was 58 by the time he came to Congress. But if he was slow to start, he has played the game well, never losing an election.

Lewis' chance for a House seat came when the 12th was created in 1981 redistricting. His two advantages were that his state Senate district encompassed most of the 12th, and that many conservative Democrats were displeased with their party's nominee, Brad Culverhouse, a labor-backed lawyer and rancher.

At one point in the campaign, construction workers angered by an ongoing economic downturn disrupted a Lewis rally featuring Vice President George Bush. Though Culverhouse disassociated himself from the protest, public reaction to the incident contributed to his defeat.

Culverhouse's active campaigning did enable him to hold Lewis to 53 percent of the vote, but Democrats since then have shown no interest in testing the incumbent; he has run unopposed in his general elections.

Born in Philadelphia, Lewis was a gunner aboard a B-25 bomber in World War II, flying out of India and China. During the Korean War, he was on the ground directing American warplanes to their targets. After leaving the military in 1954, he settled in Florida.

He worked 16 years with Pratt & Whitney as chief of rocket and jet engine testing. During this time, he served on the North Palm Beach City Council, where he was chosen mayor, a post he held throughout his municipal career. When he assumed the more time-consuming duties of the Legislature, he quit Pratt & Whitney and entered the real estate business. In the Legislature, Lewis' record earned him a 100 percent favorable rating from the American Conservative Union.

Florida 12

South Central — Parts of Palm Beach; West Palm Beach

The huge 12th encompasses much of inland South Florida and runs from the Gulf of Mexico to the Atlantic Ocean, but more than two-thirds of its people live in just three Atlantic Coast counties — Palm Beach, Martin and St. Lucie. The district's base Republican vote in statewide elections is over 55 percent.

The district line runs right through the most populous part of Palm Beach County, placing the northern part of Palm Beach and West Palm Beach in the 12th District, and the rest of each city in the 14th.

In wealthy Palm Beach, the spirit of noblesse oblige creates elaborate charity events but does not interfere with monolithic conservative politics. West Palm Beach, by contrast, is mostly middle class. Originally a railroad town and home for the Palm Beach servant community, it grew to dwarf the parent city. West Palm Beach today has some poor and minorities in its population and usually votes Democratic. North of West Palm Beach is Riviera Beach, which is two-thirds black.

At one time, Palm Beach was recognized as the northern limit of the densely populated "Gold Coast" region that begins near Miami. But development marches inexorably northward. In north Palm Beach County, Jupiter tripled in size during the 1970s, and grew another 153 percent in the first half of the '80s. Population in Martin County jumped 58 percent from 1980 to 1990; St. Lucie County grew 72 percent during the same period. Martin County is a GOP bastion; St. Lucie County has a Democratic majority by registration and a sizable liberal Democratic community.

At the other end of the state, on the Gulf Coast, the 12th includes about 39,000 residents of Collier County, a popular retirement area with twice as many registered Republicans as Democrats.

Although the inland areas of the 12th are lightly populated, their agricultural output makes an important contribution to the district's economy.

Population: 513,121. White 397,313 (77%), Black 98,038 (19%), Other 3,362 (1%). Spanish origin 26,625 (5%). 18 and over 384,221 (75%), 65 and over 97,027 (19%). Median age: 36.

Committees

Agriculture (8th of 18 Republicans)
Domestic Marketing, Consumer Relations & Nutrition (ranking); Cotton, Rice & Sugar; Livestock, Dairy & Poultry

Science, Space & Technology (4th of 19 Republicans)
Technology & Competitiveness (ranking); Space

Select Narcotics Abuse & Control (6th of 14 Republicans)

Elections

1990 General		
Tom Lewis (R)	Unopposed	
1990 Primary		
Tom Lewis (R)	33,826	(75%)
Kevan Boyles (R)	11,469	(25%)
1988 General		
Tom Lewis (R)	Unopposed	

Previous Winning Percentages: **1986** (99%) **1984** (100%) **1982** (53%)

District Vote For President

	1988		1984		1980		1976	
D	92,423	(35%)	81,535	(33%)	62,153	(34%)	66,662	(48%)
R	167,835	(64%)	168,472	(67%)	110,071	(61%)	70,289	(51%)
I					8,350	(5%)		

Campaign Finance

	Receipts	Receipts from PACs		Expend-itures
1990				
Lewis (R)	$336,333	$80,425	(24%)	$401,225
1988				
Lewis (R)	$288,963	$64,465	(22%)	$256,081

Key Votes

1991	
Authorize use of force against Iraq	Y
1990	
Support constitutional amendment on flag desecration	Y
Pass family and medical leave bill over Bush veto	N
Reduce SDI funding	N
Allow abortions in overseas military facilities	N
Approve budget summit plan for spending and taxing	N
Approve civil rights bill	N
1989	
Halt production of B-2 stealth bomber at 13 planes	N
Oppose capital gains tax cut	N
Approve federal abortion funding in rape or incest cases	N
Approve pay raise and revision of ethics rules	N
Pass Democratic minimum wage plan over Bush veto	N

Voting Studies

	Presidential Support		Party Unity		Conservative Coalition	
Year	**S**	**O**	**S**	**O**	**S**	**O**
1990	68	31	86	8	93	2
1989	72	28	93	5	100	0
1988	69	28	93	5	95	0
1987	63	34	88	8	88	9
1986	71	26	82	14	86	8
1985	66	34	85	12	87	11
1984	58	40	81	16	93	7
1983	67	32	78	18	91	8

Interest Group Ratings

Year	ADA	ACU	AFL-CIO	CCUS
1990	6	90	0	79
1989	5	93	17	100
1988	5	100	14	93
1987	8	83	6	93
1986	15	70	21	76
1985	5	81	6	86
1984	20	79	23	88
1983	20	70	18	75

13 Porter J. Goss (R)

Of Sanibel — Elected 1988

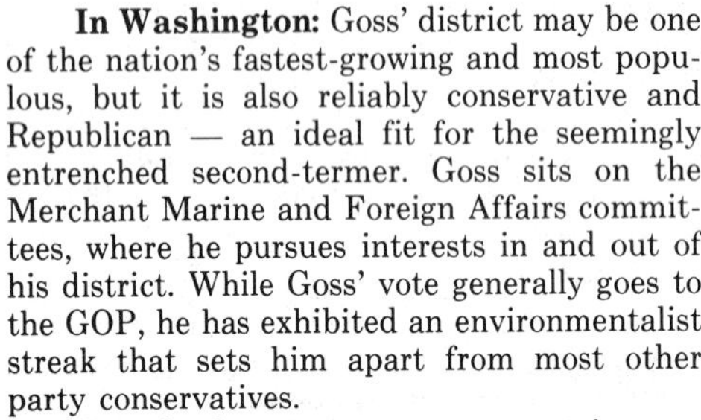

Born: Nov. 26, 1938, Waterbury, Conn.
Education: Yale U., B.A. 1960.
Military Service: Army, 1960-62.
Occupation: Small-businessman; newspaper founder; former CIA agent.
Family: Wife, Mariel Robinson; four children.
Religion: Presbyterian.
Political Career: Sanibel City Council, 1974-80, 1981-82, mayor of Sanibel, 1975-77, 1982; Lee County Commission, 1983-88, chairman, 1985-86.
Capitol Office: 224 Cannon Bldg. 20515; 225-2536.

In Washington: Goss' district may be one of the nation's fastest-growing and most populous, but it is also reliably conservative and Republican — an ideal fit for the seemingly entrenched second-termer. Goss sits on the Merchant Marine and Foreign Affairs committees, where he pursues interests in and out of his district. While Goss' vote generally goes to the GOP, he has exhibited an environmentalist streak that sets him apart from most other party conservatives.

Goss backs a permanent moratorium on offshore oil drilling in areas off Florida's coast and voted for the oil-spill liability measure passed in August 1990; he has sponsored legislation to allow a state to refuse the capture of dolphins in its waters.

On Foreign Affairs, Goss shows an interest in Central America, most notably serving on an Organization of American States delegation that observed the February 1990 elections in Nicaragua. Goss was successful earlier in attaching an amendment to a foreign aid measure criticizing Nicaragua's Sandinista government for failing to move toward democracy.

Representing a district with a huge elderly population, Goss predictably concentrates on health care. As a member of a GOP task force on catastrophic health care, Goss promoted the successful repeal in 1989 of the 1988 Medicare Catastrophic Coverage Act after senior citizens angrily protested paying for the new benefits.

At the start of the 102nd Congress, Goss asked to serve on the House ethics committee, a chore few members take on willingly. Goss wants to improve Congress' tattered image in the wake of recent ethics scandals, but has no plans for a throw-the-rascals-out charge up Capitol Hill. "I'm not a crusader and I'm not trying to change things," said Goss.

At Home: In 1988 Goss won his first bid for Congress with 71 percent of the vote, a signal that he was considered a good match for the 13th District. Two years in Washington did nothing to change that perception, and Goss ran unopposed in his first re-election race.

Local roots are not an obvious political selling point in fast-growing southwest Florida, where so many residents are new arrivals. But in 1988 Goss used his in local issues to convince voters that he would do the best job of protecting the environment that lured them there in the first place. A former employee of the CIA in Washington, D.C., and abroad, Goss moved to the district in 1971 and was drawn into politics by some of the same "quality-of-life" issues he stressed in the campaign. When picturesque Sanibel Island was hit by rapid development in the early 1970s, Goss played a major role in pushing for the town to incorporate and agree on growth-management laws. He became the small city's first mayor in 1975 and helped produce a development model that has been studied in public-policy schools and other localities.

Nearly a decade later, Goss was named to the Lee County Commission by then-Gov. Bob Graham, a Democrat. Goss, quickly tagged as the commission's environmentalist, got involved in controversial debates about managing growth countywide. But he easily won a full term, which positioned him to compete for the House seat when GOP Rep. Connie Mack decided to run for the Senate.

Goss had stiff competition for the GOP nomination: In particular, former Rep. L. A. "Skip" Bafalis, who had left the House for an unsuccessful gubernatorial bid in 1982, reappeared; among the three other GOP contenders was retired Army Brig. Gen. James Dozier, the victim of a well-publicized kidnapping by Italy's Red Brigades. Bafalis tried to label Goss a closet Democrat, saying Goss had contributed to Democratic candidates. But having moved back into the district shortly before launching his comeback bid, Bafalis found that his political strength had ebbed. His fundraising lagged (while Dozier's bid fizzled). Goss raised enough money to fund plenty of television and direct mail. He swept the October runoff and won the general election easily.

Florida 13

Southwest — Sarasota; Fort Myers

A glimpse at the 1988 presidential vote from the four counties in the 13th shows just how prohibitive the odds against a Democratic victory are. Michael S. Dukakis did not get more than 36 percent in any of the three counties wholly within the 13th — Lee, Sarasota and Charlotte. Collier County, with about half of its people in the district, gave Dukakis about 25 percent.

The political personality of the 13th is shaped by retirees from the small-town and suburban Midwest. These people changed their addresses but not their party registration, and they are a major contributor to the burgeoning strength of the GOP in Florida. From 1980-86, the 13th was the 10th fastest-growing district in the nation, bulging by more than 30 percent.

Sarasota and Lee counties each have about 40 percent of the district's residents, with the remaining 20 percent divided roughly evenly between Charlotte County and the section of Collier in the 13th.

Sarasota cultivates a refined image with its art museums, theaters and symphony performances, and it draws a wealthier class of retirees than most other west coast communities. It is also the traditional winter home of the Ringling Bros. and Barnum & Bailey Circus, although much of the entourage now spends the winter months a few miles south, at Venice. In Lee County, the city of Cape Coral, incorporated only in 1971, has grown at a rapid clip — to more than 30,000 people by decade's end, and to almost 80,000 by 1990.

Fort Myers, also in Lee County, is having some difficulty meeting the demands of its growing population. There are occasional calls for it to adopt a slow-growth policy, following the example of conservationists on the islands of Sanibel and Captiva located just offshore from Fort Myers. These islands enforce stringent restrictions on development in order to protect their natural beauty and animal population.

Naples first won the status of a small city with a 46 percent population explosion during the 1970s, gaining exclusive high-rise condominiums to mark its maturity. By the end of the 1980s the population was up to 18,000.

Population: 513,048. White 476,818 (93%), Black 29,190 (6%). Spanish origin 11,102 (2%). 18 and over 413,477 (81%), 65 and over (27%). Median age: 47.

Committees

Foreign Affairs (17th of 18 Republicans)
Arms Control, International Security & Science; Western Hemisphere Affairs; International Narcotics Control

Merchant Marine & Fisheries (12th of 17 Republicans)
Coast Guard & Navigation; Fisheries & Wildlife Conservation & the Environment

Standards of Official Conduct (6th of 7 Republicans)

Elections

1990 General		
Porter J. Goss (R)	Unopposed	
1988 General		
Porter J. Goss (R)	231,170	(71%)
Jack Conway (D)	93,700	(29%)

District Vote For President

	1988	1984	1980	1976
D	106,374 (32%)	73,407 (26%)	68,062 (28%)	72,886 (41%)
R	225,656 (68%)	207,548 (74%)	165,630 (67%)	102,769 (58%)
I			11,406 (5%)	

Campaign Finance

	Receipts	Receipts from PACs		Expenditures
1990				
Goss (R)	$303,600	$122,125	(40%)	$244,740
1988				
Goss (R)	$878,439	$141,976	(16%)	$836,224
Conway (D)	$216,711	$55,150	(25%)	$210,296

Key Votes

1991	
Authorize use of force against Iraq	Y
1990	
Support constitutional amendment on flag desecration	Y
Pass family and medical leave bill over Bush veto	N
Reduce SDI funding	N
Allow abortions in overseas military facilities	N
Approve budget summit plan for spending and taxing	N
Approve civil rights bill	N
1989	
Halt production of B-2 stealth bomber at 13 planes	N
Oppose capital gains tax cut	N
Approve federal abortion funding in rape or incest cases	Y
Approve pay raise and revision of ethics rules	N
Pass Democratic minimum wage plan over Bush veto	N

Voting Studies

	Presidential Support		Party Unity		Conservative Coalition	
Year	S	O	S	O	S	O
1990	72	28	88	11	85	15
1989	69	31	87	12	93	7

Interest Group Ratings

Year	ADA	ACU	AFL-CIO	CCUS
1990	33	79	8	86
1989	5	89	25	100

14 Harry A. Johnston (D)

Of West Palm Beach -- Elected 1988

Born: Dec. 2, 1931, West Palm Beach, Fla.
Education: Virginia Military Institute, B.A. 1953; U. of Florida, LL.B. 1958.
Military Service: Army, 1953-55.
Occupation: Lawyer.
Family: Wife, Mary Otley; two children.
Religion: Presbyterian.
Political Career: Fla. Senate, 1975-87, president, 1985-87; sought Democratic nomination for governor, 1986.
Capitol Office: 1028 Longworth Bldg. 20515; 225-3001.

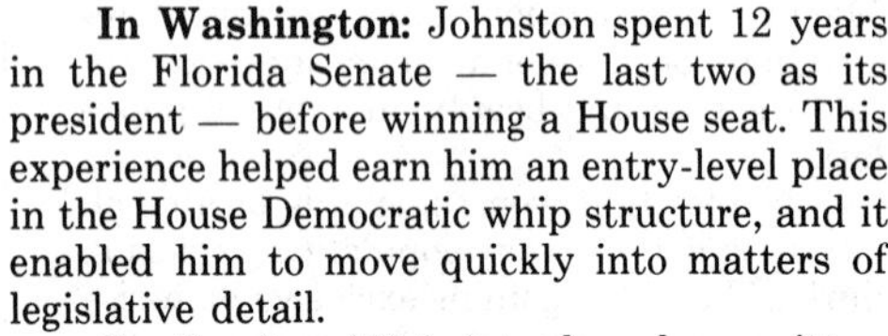

In Washington: Johnston spent 12 years in the Florida Senate — the last two as its president — before winning a House seat. This experience helped earn him an entry-level place in the House Democratic whip structure, and it enabled him to move quickly into matters of legislative detail.

On Foreign Affairs' trade subcommittee, Johnston has worked on the Export Administration Act, which restricts trade in goods of strategic importance. Responding to complaints of bureaucratic delays in obtaining trade permits, he favors streamlining the process.

Like most Florida members, Johnston voices concern about communism in Latin America. A member of Foreign Affairs' Western Hemisphere Subcommittee in the 101st Congress, he supported aid to the Nicaraguan contras; in 1990, he helped monitor elections that ousted Nicaragua's leftist government.

But while Johnston comes from a military school background (Virginia Military Institute), he is not hawkish: He favored sanctions in response to Iraq's invasion of Kuwait and opposed authorizing President Bush to use force against Iraq in January 1991.

Overall, Johnston has supported Bush's positions less often than most Florida members. His record reflects a constituency that has shifted less to the right than many others in Florida: Bush won the state with 61 percent in 1988, but took just 53 percent in the 14th.

In the 102nd Congress, Johnston moved to Foreign Affairs' Europe and Middle East Subcommittee, and took a seat on Interior, where his concerns include offshore oil drilling and the Everglades National Park.

At Home: Although Johnston has the bearing of a Southern patrician, his politics are hardly Old Florida. As a state legislator, he took on the clique of rural legislators who had long ruled the state, helping replace them with a more urban coalition committed to open government. As a House candidate in 1988, he combined that experience with a sophisticated campaign to win easily over popular rivals.

In 1988, Johnston told voters he could adapt quickly to congressional legislating. In Tallahassee, he had risen to become Senate president and pursued many initiatives, including tough growth-management legislation.

Still, there were doubts about Johnston's campaigning ability when he announced for the 14th, which came open as Democrat Daniel A. Mica ran for the Senate. Johnston's 1986 bid for governor — highly touted at the outset — failed to reach the runoff. He is not a natural campaigner, and once acknowledged worrying about invading voters' privacy.

In the Democratic House primary, he faced Dorothy Wilken, an outspoken Palm Beach County Commissioner who presented herself as the grass-roots candidate. But Johnston, a wealthy fifth-generation Floridian, used his establishment contacts to gain a significant financial edge and dominate the TV ad battle.

Johnston's unexpectedly strong primary victory made him a slight favorite over GOP nominee Ken Adams, a popular county commissioner. Adams billed himself a businessman with a conscience, noting his efforts to get funding for public housing and AIDS victims. He portrayed Johnston as "a liberal lawyer legislator," citing his votes for reducing penalties for criminals.

But Johnston forcefully dismissed Adams' charges as "a bucket of crap," and he played up some of his conservative stands, such as support for a presidential line-item veto. He won by 10 percentage points.

In 1990, Johnston faced even harsher GOP attacks from management consultant Scott Shore, who charged that Johnston faced too many conflicts of interest between his House duties and his partnership in a law firm. Johnston said his record was clean, but noted his plans to sever the law firm ties in compliance with new congressional ethics legislation, as he did in January 1991. Voters were deaf to Shore's pitch; Johnston romped.

Florida 14

Southeast — Parts of Palm Beach and West Palm Beach

The 14th is centered on West Palm Beach, a town that developed as the railroad terminus and supply center for the Palm Beach resorts but today is almost seven times larger. The area's pleasant environment has lured the headquarters of several international corporations, bringing in a cadre of well-paid business executives. This migration has altered the worldview of a community once dominated by leisure-minded socialites. Democrats still run well in West Palm Beach, but that is changing. Palm Beach itself is as affluent and Republican as ever.

South of Palm Beach, retirees living in the condominium communities of Boynton Beach and Delray Beach are a potent political force. Some in these complexes are Irish and Italian, but most are Jewish, and nearly all come from a Democratic background in the Northeast. The turnout rate among the condo residents is very high, thanks in part to "bosses" who have emerged in the turbulent world of condo politics.

Boca Raton, the next major city down the coast, is an upper-middle-class area that generally votes Republican. It is also home to electronics plants run by Sensormatic and International Business Machines.

In Broward County, the district takes in Coral Springs, Margate, Tamarac, North Lauderdale and parts of Lauderhill and Sunrise, all moderate-to-liberal Democratic areas. Population in each of these communities grew by 300 percent or more during the 1970s. Coral Springs, for example, jumped from 1,489 residents in 1970 to 37,349 in 1980 to an almost 80,000 in 1990.

Overall, the 14th grew by 32 percent from 1980-86; it was the ninth-fastest growing congressional district in the country. After Coral Springs, Sunrise notched the biggest estimated population increase from 1980 to 1990 — over 50 percent, topping 64,000.

Population: 512,803. White 484,198 (94%), Black 20,880 (4%), Other 2,682 (1%). Spanish origin 23,601 (5%). 18 and over 406,873 (79%), 65 and over 124,990 (24%). Median age: 42.

Committees

Foreign Affairs (17th of 28 Democrats)
Europe & the Middle East; International Economic Policy & Trade; International Narcotics Control; Western Hemisphere Affairs

Interior & Insular Affairs (27th of 29 Democrats)
National Parks & Public Lands; Water, Power & Offshore Energy

Elections

1990 General		
Harry A. Johnston (D)	156,050	(66%)
Scott Shore (R)	80,239	(34%)
1988 General		
Harry A. Johnston (D)	173,292	(55%)
Ken Adams (R)	142,635	(45%)

District Vote For President

	1988	1984	1980	1976
D	140,057 (47%)	110,773 (39%)	82,934 (37%)	85,922 (49%)
R	158,654 (53%)	171,663 (61%)	128,344 (57%)	86,375 (49%)
I			14,294 (6%)	

Campaign Finance

	Receipts	Receipts from PACs		Expend-itures
1990				
Johnston (D)	$508,525	$253,169	(50%)	$469,101
Shore (R)	$216,826	$9,800	(5%)	$213,139
1988				
Johnston (D)	$974,743	$296,636	(30%)	$971,883
Adams (R)	$752,874	$67,136	(9%)	$706,832

Key Votes

1991	
Authorize use of force against Iraq	N
1990	
Support constitutional amendment on flag desecration	N
Pass family and medical leave bill over Bush veto	Y
Reduce SDI funding	Y
Allow abortions in overseas military facilities	Y
Approve budget summit plan for spending and taxing	N
Approve civil rights bill	Y
1989	
Halt production of B-2 stealth bomber at 13 planes	Y
Oppose capital gains tax cut	Y
Approve federal abortion funding in rape or incest cases	Y
Approve pay raise and revision of ethics rules	N
Pass Democratic minimum wage plan over Bush veto	Y

Voting Studies

	Presidential Support		Party Unity		Conservative Coalition	
Year	**S**	**O**	**S**	**O**	**S**	**O**
1990	23	72	81	11	30	69
1989	34	64	88	8	37	59

Interest Group Ratings

Year	ADA	ACU	AFL-CIO	CCUS
1990	83	25	83	38
1989	70	7	83	50

15 E. Clay Shaw Jr. (R)

Of Fort Lauderdale — Elected 1980

Born: April 19, 1939, Miami, Fla.
Education: Stetson U., B.A. 1961, J.D. 1966; U. of Alabama, M.B.A. 1963.
Occupation: Nurseryman; lawyer.
Family: Wife, Emilie Costar; four children.
Religion: Roman Catholic.
Political Career: Fort Lauderdale assistant city attorney, 1968; chief city prosecutor, 1968-69; associate municipal judge, 1969-71; city commissioner, 1971-73; vice mayor, 1973-75; mayor of Fort Lauderdale, 1975-81.
Capitol Office: 2338 Rayburn Bldg. 20515; 225-3026.

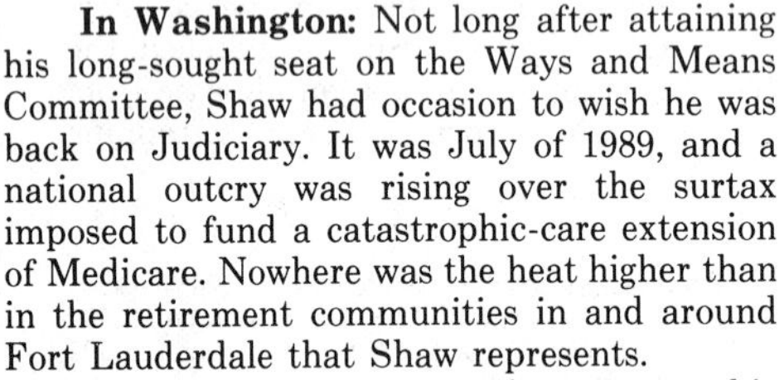

In Washington: Not long after attaining his long-sought seat on the Ways and Means Committee, Shaw had occasion to wish he was back on Judiciary. It was July of 1989, and a national outcry was rising over the surtax imposed to fund a catastrophic-care extension of Medicare. Nowhere was the heat higher than in the retirement communities in and around Fort Lauderdale that Shaw represents.

Shaw had voted for the catastrophic coverage in 1988, as had most of his Florida colleagues. But within months, Shaw had responded to constituent complaints by calling for outright repeal of the surtax. So when Ways and Means voted on a plan to cut the surtax in half, Shaw was in a quandary. If he voted yes, many would be spared the surtax but the drive for outright repeal might be weakened.

Shaw hesitated on the first round of voting. By the time his name was called again, his had become the deciding vote. "I held my nose and voted yes," Shaw said later. "The lesson I learned was never to pass again."

Later that year, Shaw joined in the overwhelming vote on the House floor to repeal the surtax and rescind nearly all the new benefits approved the year before.

Appointed to Ways and Means late in the 100th Congress, Shaw found himself in the 101st the ranking Republican on the Subcommittee on Human Resources. In that role, he successfully led resistance to increasing unemployment benefits (and raising employer taxes) as proposed by Democrat Thomas J. Downey of New York.

Shaw also drew notice during the 101st Congress by cosponsoring (with Texas Democrat Charles W. Stenholm) a comprehensive child-care package offered as an alternative to Downey's bill and a competing Democratic bill. Stenholm-Shaw, a somewhat leaner version of the main Democratic plans, won support from the Bush administration and the National Governors' Association. Although not enacted, it helped move Congress to resolve its child-care standoff.

Even as Shaw makes a name for himself on Ways and Means, most members still associate him with the drug issue. He remains chairman of the Republican Research Committee's task force on drug abuse — an issue of pre-eminent concern to his South Florida coastal constituency. It was at least partly as a reward for his work on drug matters that Shaw was given the coveted Ways and Means seat.

Shaw had tried for the seat at the start of the 100th Congress. Late to announce his intentions, he lost the endorsement of Florida Republicans to colleague Bill McCollum, who later lost his bid for a committee slot. When a committee vacancy occurred late in the Congress, Shaw declared his interest. His perseverance on the drug bill as well as his background as a tax attorney helped him win the state delegation's endorsement over McCollum, and he went on to victory.

Before moving to Ways and Means, Shaw was a member of the Judiciary Committee and the Select Narcotics Abuse and Control panel. In both the 99th and 100th Congresses, he was appointed to GOP drug task forces set up by Minority Leader Robert H. Michel, and a bill Shaw introduced became the basis of the 1988 Republican anti-drug legislative effort. His measure included several controversial provisions that were dropped two years earlier, but won approval in 1988 — a death penalty for major drug traffickers, a drug "czar" to coordinate federal efforts, and the use of the U.S. military for drug interdiction.

Shaw has met with considerably less success in his battle for widespread drug testing. While the House approved a Shaw amendment instructing conferees on the airline consumer protection bill to include mandatory testing provisions, controversy over the issue contributed to the political stalemate that killed the bill in the 100th Congress. Shaw did win

Florida 15

Southeast — Fort Lauderdale

Fort Lauderdale, once famous as a "where the boys are" student beach mecca, bills itself now as a stylish "American Venice." But one thing has not changed much — its habit of voting Republican. That habit started more than two decades ago, when conservative retirees from the Midwest started settling in Fort Lauderdale. Those sorts of people nowadays retire mostly to Florida's WASPier West Coast, but Fort Lauderdale still has a conservative flavor — it is less influenced by the liberal attitudes of Northeastern Jewish émigrés than are most other major South Florida cities.

Fort Lauderdale also has a substantial minority population; the blacks and Hispanics who walk some of its faded downtown streets live in a different world from the people who browse through the fashionable stores of Las Olas Boulevard on the waterfront a short distance away.

In recent years, some of Miami's drug traffic has migrated north to Fort Lauderdale, creating new fortunes for a few but causing many residents to fret about "creeping Miamism."

The Republicans' biggest obstacle at election time in the 15th District is the well-organized Democratic political movement based in the district's condominiums. These communities contain the district's heaviest concentration of Northeastern retirees, many of them attracted by advertising campaigns in the New York media. Their lifelong Democratic habits are tough for any Republican to crack.

Fort Lauderdale's manufacturing sector concentrates on production of computer software, electronic circuitry, aerospace components and communications equipment. Its deep-water port makes it a base for cruise ships, drawing a more affluent class of visitor than the Eastertime youth pilgrimage, which is no longer such an important part of Fort Lauderdale's tourism trade.

Population: 512,950. White 415,486 (81%), Black 91,511 (18%), Other 2,615 (1%). Spanish origin 17,532 (3%). 18 and over 411,582 (80%), 65 and over 116,583 (23%). Median age: 39.

passage of an amendment to a State Department authorization bill requiring drug tests for employees with access to secret information.

In the 99th Congress, Shaw asked his staff to participate in a voluntary drug-testing program, but House rules barred him from paying for the tests with his official allowance. In response, he submitted a bill in 1987 to change the rules. It did not pass.

The Florida Republican's anti-drug crusade began in earnest in the 99th Congress, just a week after then-Speaker Thomas P. O'Neill Jr. announced a major push for drug legislation. Shaw quickly offered a successful amendment to an appropriations bill to prohibit schools from receiving federal education funds unless they have drug-abuse-prevention programs.

As the issue gained national prominence, Shaw answered accusations that the 1986 drug bill represented an enormous new expense at a time of austerity. He insisted that the cost was outweighed by the urgency of the drug problem. "I think if we can pass a drug bill that's going to have a meaningful effect," he said, "then the price tag is of little consideration."

Shaw made a similar argument in voting to waive the Gramm-Rudman deficit reduction law to repeal the surtax for catastrophic care. "This one is so bad, there are a lot of things I'd do that are not fiscally sound."

Besides drug abuse, issues of interest to senior citizens have been the focus of Shaw's legislative zeal. In the 100th Congress, he drew some criticism for his persistent opposition to an amendment to the Fair Housing Act that barred discrimination against children. Though leading senior citizens' organizations signed off on the provision as workable, Shaw continued to claim that it would put an end to senior-citizen housing. His effort to strike the amendment lost 116-289.

Shaw dabbled in some high-stakes institutional politics during the 100th Congress when the House debated legislation to renew the special-prosecutor law. The Reagan administration opposed the law, calling it unconstitutional, but a chief point of controversy in the House involved the soon-to-be-deposed Speaker, Jim Wright, whose financial dealings were under investigation. When Shaw proposed an amendment to include members of Congress as potential subjects of independent-counsel investigations, House Democrats withdrew the bill from consideration. Wright subsequently put his financial holdings in a blind trust, and the House rebuffed Shaw's amendment on a largely party-line vote.

Also before his move to Ways and Means, Shaw served on the Public Works Committee, but he was often frustrated there. His pet issue was restricting billboards on federal highways and limiting federal support for billboards. In 1986, Shaw won a modest victory with the adoption of a compromise amendment freezing the total number of billboards allowed on federal highways while continuing to reimburse the billboard industry with federal funds for billboards that are taken down.

At Home: In the early 1980s, Democratic squabbling helped Shaw secure the 15th; now he seems to have a lock on it. In 1980, Democratic primary voters dumped 70-year-old Rep. Edward J. Stack for a younger candidate, former state Rep. Alan Becker. Shaw, who had been mayor of Fort Lauderdale since 1975, was unopposed for the GOP nomination.

Shaw launched a campaign denouncing Becker as a liberal carpetbagger; the Democrat had moved into the 15th in 1979 after four terms in the Legislature representing North Miami. Shaw bragged that real spending in Fort Lauderdale had decreased during his tenure, without cuts in fire or police protection. He claimed credit for broadening the city's economic base and changing its image from that of a beach town to that of a cosmopolitan city.

Shaw picked up support from some conservative Democrats who had liked Stack but not Becker's liberalism. Becker ran short of money after the primary, and Shaw won the seat with 55 percent.

In 1982 another intraparty fight divided the Democrats. Stack was back, hoping to avenge his 1980 loss, and engaged in a bitter primary battle with a former ally. Stack eked out 51 percent to become the nominee, while Shaw again enjoyed an uncontested primary.

Stack had strong union support and parts of his old condominium organization, but lingering Democratic disunity and his age dragged him down. Shaw, boosted by redrawn district lines that enhanced GOP strength in the 15th, won a second term with 57 percent.

No Democratic heavyweights ran in 1984, and Shaw swamped teacher Bill Humphrey that November. Shaw considered running for governor in 1986, but opted for the safety of his House seat. And it appears safe indeed; Shaw took 98 percent of the vote in 1990.

Committee

Ways & Means (9th of 13 Republicans)
Human Resources (ranking); Oversight

Elections

1990 General		
E. Clay Shaw (R)	104,273	(98%)
Charles Goodmon (Write-in)	2,374	(2%)
1988 General		
E. Clay Shaw Jr. (R)	132,090	(66%)
Mike Kuhle (D)	67,746	(34%)

Previous Winning Percentages: **1986** (100%) **1984** (66%) **1982** (57%) **1980** (55%)

District Vote For President

	1988	1984	1980	1976
D	83,311 (47%)	93,235 (41%)	77,192 (36%)	82,690 (51%)
R	94,061 (53%)	134,858 (59%)	123,753 (57%)	78,474 (48%)
I			13,190 (6%)	

Campaign Finance

	Receipts	Receipts from PACs	Expend-itures
1990			
Shaw (R)	$413,387	$245,760 (59%)	$120,632
1988			
Shaw (R)	$348,233	$153,750 (44%)	$455,578
Kuhle (D)	$48,633	$26,650 (55%)	$78,474

Key Votes

1991	
Authorize use of force against Iraq	Y
1990	
Support constitutional amendment on flag desecration	Y
Pass family and medical leave bill over Bush veto	N
Reduce SDI funding	N
Allow abortions in overseas military facilities	N
Approve budget summit plan for spending and taxing	Y
Approve civil rights bill	N
1989	
Halt production of B-2 stealth bomber at 13 planes	Y
Oppose capital gains tax cut	N
Approve federal abortion funding in rape or incest cases	N
Approve pay raise and revision of ethics rules	Y
Pass Democratic minimum wage plan over Bush veto	N

Voting Studies

	Presidential Support		Party Unity		Conservative Coalition	
Year	S	O	S	O	S	O
1990	75	24	75	21	91	7
1989	77	22	65	32	95	5
1988	65	32	70	23	100	0
1987	70	29	76	20	95	5
1986	79	19	86	10	90	6
1985	70	25	88	8	89	9
1984	61	37	82	14	90	5
1983	78	16	87	8	93	4
1982	77	23	84	16	90	10
1981	78	22	94	6	95	5

Interest Group Ratings

Year	ADA	ACU	AFL-CIO	CCUS
1990	6	83	8	57
1989	5	89	17	90
1988	5	96	21	92
1987	4	78	13	93
1986	5	82	7	87
1985	5	81	18	81
1984	5	73	8	86
1983	5	96	0	80
1982	15	77	15	82
1981	10	100	0	89

16 Lawrence J. Smith (D)

Of Hollywood — Elected 1982

Born: April 25, 1941, Brooklyn, N.Y.
Education: Attended New York U., 1958-61; Brooklyn Law School, LL.B. 1964, J.D. 1967.
Occupation: Lawyer.
Family: Wife, Sheila Cohen; two children.
Religion: Jewish.
Political Career: Fla. House, 1979-83.
Capitol Office: 113 Cannon Bldg. 20515; 225-7931.

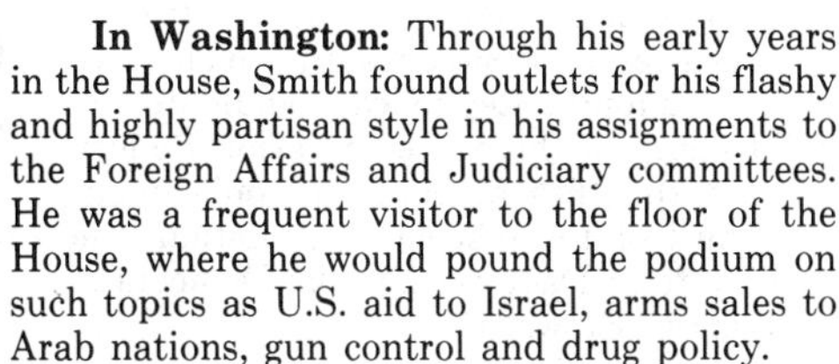

In Washington: Through his early years in the House, Smith found outlets for his flashy and highly partisan style in his assignments to the Foreign Affairs and Judiciary committees. He was a frequent visitor to the floor of the House, where he would pound the podium on such topics as U.S. aid to Israel, arms sales to Arab nations, gun control and drug policy.

However, at the start of the 102nd Congress, Smith gained a seat on Appropriations, a prestige committee but one known more for backroom dealmaking than for partisan speechifying. Smith may have to adapt his soapbox style a bit if he is to get along with the committee's go-along insiders.

Smith's adjustment will be eased by his appointment to the Appropriations Foreign Operations Subcommittee. From there, he can still pursue his foreign policy priorities, and he will have more real influence over how U.S. foreign aid is spent than he did on Foreign Affairs.

Smith, who is Jewish, is one of the most vocal House supporters of U.S. aid to Israel. Conversely, he has consistently derided White House initiatives to sell arms or otherwise cozy up to Arab countries as a way of encouraging them to accept the Jewish state.

Over the years, Smith fought U.S. arms sales to such nations as Jordan, Saudi Arabia and Kuwait. Smith also criticized Reagan and Bush administration attempts to woo Iraq, whose invasion of Kuwait in August 1990 exploded that policy. He pushed efforts, thwarted by Presidents Reagan and Bush, to impose sanctions after the 1988 incident in which Iraqi President Saddam Hussein's forces used poison gas against Iraq's Kurdish minority.

Since there was little direct arms trade between the United States and Iraq, Smith sought to punish other nations that provided arms or technology to Saddam Hussein. In 1990, he tried to bar the sale of nuclear weapon-related technology to countries, such as Brazil and China, suspected of transferring the technology to Iraq. He was among those who blew the whistle on Commerce Department efforts to license the sales of supercomputers, an aid in nuclear weapons research, to Brazil.

Despite his efforts to isolate Iraq, Smith opposed the January 1991 resolution authorizing Bush to take immediate military action to end the occupation of Kuwait. While stating that most House members wanted "to get rid of Saddam Hussein one way or the other," Smith called for Congress and the president to give sanctions and diplomacy more time to work.

When war between the U.S.-led coalition and Iraq did break out, relations between the United States and Israel — which had been chilled by Israel's harsh reaction to the ongoing Palestinian uprising — appeared to warm. Many of Israel's supporters in Congress cited the provision of U.S. Patriot missiles to help defend Israel against Iraqi SCUD attacks as a hopeful sign of rapprochement.

But Smith, who is convinced of a pro-Arab tilt in Bush's foreign policy, warned against too much optimism. "There is an institutional memory in the State Department that is not going to go away because of the closeness," said Smith, who added that the wartime help could later be used as a "chit" to force Israel into negotiations on the Palestinian issue.

Smith was wary of U.S. overtures to the Palestine Liberation Organization (PLO) in late 1988 and early 1989. Rather than accept PLO leader Yasir Arafat's statement renouncing terrorism, Smith said Bush "should have drawn a line in the sand, saying [to Arafat]: 'If there are any more terrorist incidents by anybody close to you, we will hold you responsible.' "

Although these ventures mark Smith as an internationalist, support for Israel is actually a local issue to the 16th District's large Jewish constituency. Likewise, Smith voices an opposition to Fidel Castro's regime in Cuba shared by the Miami area's large Cuban-American population. Although his overall record, on both foreign and domestic policies, conforms to that of the House Democrats' liberal majority, his staunchly pro-Israel and anti-Castro views gave him an image as one of the more "conservative" Democratic voices on the ideologically driven Foreign Affairs Committee.

Florida 16

Southeast — Hollywood; Part of Dade County

The 16th includes some of the most heavily Jewish precincts in South Florida — those in the condominium communities of Hollywood and other south Broward County cities such as Hallandale, Pembroke Pines and Miramar. Politics is a preoccupation of many of the retirees there; they are responsible for making the 16th a predominantly Democratic district.

This part of Broward County has a larger Jewish community than the neighboring Fort Lauderdale-based 15th, which drew many of its people from Midwestern Protestants and Irish Catholics in the first big postwar migration. The voters in the Broward part of the 16th tend to be Eastern, urban-oriented and liberal.

For years, Hollywood was overshadowed by larger Fort Lauderdale, a situation that had some positive benefits: Hollywood did not attract as much strip development, and it retained more areas of single-family homes that offer a feeling of community.

But in the late 1960s and early 1970s, rapid development of Hollywood's southern beachfront packed it with condominiums. A strain on roads and services induced a wave of anti-development sentiment that led local officials to restrict development of the city's northern beach.

The area that is mainly responsible for making the 16th politically competitive is the Dade County part of the district. It incorporates Westchester and Sweetwater, suburbs lying due west of Miami's S.W. 8th Street, the focal point of Cuban-American culture in South Florida. When upwardly mobile Cubans want to move from Miami to greener spaces, many of them settle in Westchester and Sweetwater, which have come to support Republican candidates by solid margins. But since the Dade County part of the 16th accounts for only about one-third of the district's population, the GOP vote in Dade is offset by Democratic margins in Broward.

Population: 513,365. White 476,065 (93%), Black 25,666 (5%), Other 3,867 (1%). Spanish origin 107,632 (21%). 18 and over 396,409 (77%), 65 and over 91,954 (18%). Median age: 37.

With Florida plagued by drug smuggling, Smith's chairmanship of the Foreign Affairs Task Force on International Narcotics Control also had a local angle. Though an advocate of "decertifying" nations viewed as uncooperative in battling drugs, Smith said in 1989 that the United States needed to first get its house in order: "How can I tell other countries that the United States disapproves of their anti-drug efforts when the United States government itself is neglecting to deal with its own failed policies?" He denounced Bush's Andean initiative, which emphasized military over economic aid to drug-producing nations.

On Judiciary, Smith made a mark as a gun control advocate, if little legislative headway. During 1990 debate on an omnibus crime bill, Smith's amendment to ban cheap handguns known as "Saturday Night Specials" lost on a 12-23 committee vote.

Not one to restrict himself to his committee assignments, Smith used his rhetorical flair to help shape the Democrats' "tax the rich" theme during the 1990 budget debate. Aiming at House Republicans, he said, "Whether you like it or not, and whether your president likes it or not, we are going to have a progressive tax policy that works for America." He also jumped in on the environment, opposing oil drilling off the Florida coast and calling for increased federal funding to preserve the Everglades.

Despite his busy national and international agendas, Smith nevers forgets to make a symbolic nod to his large elderly constituency. He annually submits legislation that declares the third Sunday in August as "National Senior Citizens Day."

At Home: After easily winning a first term in 1982, Smith suffered a slight setback in 1984 when former GOP state Rep. Tom Bush held him to 56 percent. Encouraged, Republicans claimed Smith was too liberal for the 16th and could be toppled by a coalition similar to the one Bush tried to mobilize — elderly conservatives and anti-communist Cuban-Americans.

But Smith's modest tally in 1984 had much more to do with Reagan's strong showing in the district than with any coalition Bush generated on his own. In 1986, GOP recruiting efforts faltered and Smith won 70 percent; he nearly matched that in 1988, as George Bush carried the 16th for president with 55 percent. In 1990, Smith had the luxury of running unopposed.

Smith's Brooklyn-born style sets him apart from Florida's Southern-oriented House members. But his manner is appropriate for the 16th, home to hundreds of thousands who moved from the Northeast to Florida in the past two decades. Many transplants grew up in the roisterous world of urban ward politics and are not put off by fast-talking candidates.

Smith moved to Florida in 1968, following

his parents, who had become active in local politics. He became known through civic work and his role in founding a temple, and in 1973 he got onto the Broward County Democratic executive committee. He served as chairman of the Hollywood Planning and Zoning Board and in 1978 was elected to the state House.

One of Florida's new House districts after the 1980 census was the 16th, including western Dade County and most of Broward County. It had in it the homes of Smith and former state Rep. Alan Becker, who in 1980 lost to Republican E. Clay Shaw Jr. in the 12th District. Becker and Smith met in a bitterly fought Democratic primary.

Smith, who was supported by the party establishment in Broward and by labor and business leaders, portrayed Becker as a carpetbagger. Becker, who represented condominium tenants in battles with developers, said Smith had sold out to business interests.

Becker enjoyed high name recognition from his 1980 House race and a 1978 campaign for state attorney general. But Smith overcame Becker's advantage by building his own condo network. Burdened by a less-than-obviously Jewish name in a district where the Jewish vote is crucial, Smith distributed pictures of his son's bar mitzvah and referred to his wife by her maiden name, Sheila Cohen. Smith lost the Dade portion of the 16th, but easily carried the more populous Broward County section.

Heavily outnumbered among registered voters in the 16th, local Republicans tried to tap the Jewish vote by nominating Maurice Berkowitz. But other districts in Florida offered better potential for Republican victory, so the 16th was not a priority for the national GOP.

In 1984, Republicans aimed in a new direction with Tom Bush, a native Floridian and fundamentalist Christian. The media played up Bush's efforts to ban abortion and to promote organized prayer and teaching of creationism in the schools. Bush dwelt on pocketbook issues and contended that Smith was too liberal, but fundraising problems hampered him.

Smith, with plenty of campaign cash, invested heavily in direct mail and media. To temper his liberal image, he stressed his anti-drug and anti-crime efforts.

Committees

Appropriations (34th of 37 Democrats)
Foreign Operations, Export Financing & Related Programs; Legislative

Select Narcotics Abuse & Control (11th of 21 Democrats)

Elections

1990 General

Lawrence J. Smith (D)	Unopposed	

1988 General

Lawrence J. Smith (D)	153,032	(69%)
Joseph Smith (R)	67,461	(31%)

Previous Winning Percentages: **1986** (70%) **1984** (56%) **1982** (68%)

District Vote For President

	1988	1984	1980	1976
D	92,263 (45%)	79,174 (39%)	65,583 (35%)	90,882 (55%)
R	113,360 (55%)	124,287 (61%)	107,954 (57%)	72,721 (44%)
I			14,631 (8%)	

Campaign Finance

	Receipts	Receipts from PACs	Expend-itures
1990			
Smith (D)	$527,994	$246,935 (47%)	$275,873
1988			
Smith (D)	$700,550	$280,493 (40%)	$606,334
Smith (R)	$15,325	0	$15,325

Key Votes

1991	
Authorize use of force against Iraq	N
1990	
Support constitutional amendment on flag desecration	N
Pass family and medical leave bill over Bush veto	Y
Reduce SDI funding	Y
Allow abortions in overseas military facilities	Y
Approve budget summit plan for spending and taxing	N
Approve civil rights bill	Y
1989	
Halt production of B-2 stealth bomber at 13 planes	N
Oppose capital gains tax cut	Y
Approve federal abortion funding in rape or incest cases	Y
Approve pay raise and revision of ethics rules	Y
Pass Democratic minimum wage plan over Bush veto	Y

Voting Studies

	Presidential Support		Party Unity		Conservative Coalition	
Year	**S**	**O**	**S**	**O**	**S**	**O**
1990	18	76	87	4	24	69
1989	34	64	89	3	20	76
1988	23	72	83	6	21	74
1987	19	74	86	3	33	67
1986	27	73	88	9	38	56
1985	30	61	88	5	27	65
1984	34	59	83	7	25	69
1983	23	74	89	6	26	72

Interest Group Ratings

Year	ADA	ACU	AFL-CIO	CCUS
1990	94	9	100	21
1989	90	0	100	20
1988	85	17	100	23
1987	80	9	100	20
1986	65	24	100	27
1985	55	35	94	33
1984	80	14	85	36
1983	85	4	94	25

17 William Lehman (D)

Of Biscayne Park — Elected 1972

Born: Oct. 5, 1913, Selma, Ala.
Education: U. of Alabama, B.S. 1934.
Occupation: Automobile dealer; high school English teacher.
Family: Wife, Joan Feibelman; two children.
Religion: Jewish.
Political Career: Dade County School Board, 1966-72, chairman, 1971-72.
Capitol Office: 2347 Rayburn Bldg. 20515; 225-4211.

In Washington: There *is* such a thing as a self-effacing, gentlemanly used-car dealer — meet Bill Lehman. When he addresses the House, smiling meekly and speaking in a soft drawl, it is hard to imagine he once sold Buicks in Miami under the name "Alabama Bill."

But watching him in action as chairman of the Appropriations Subcommittee on Transportation, it becomes clear how he succeeded. Lehman's rather benign style belies a canny talent for deal-making and power politicking. "I use automobile psychology," he says of his knack for getting his way.

Whenever possible, Lehman barters on the strength of the personal loyalty members of his subcommittee feel for him. He runs Transportation by consensus, and rarely tries to dictate policy decisions. Lehman's first line of defense, however, is his willingness to earmark funds for district projects. He wins members over by meeting a "mutuality of needs," and will fight in conference to protect any deal he has struck.

Should loyalty and earmarking fail, however, Lehman will employ other means to win. Sometimes he will quietly accept defeat on the House floor, then systematically restore his language in conference. And members who cross him, or the Democratic leadership, are likely to see funding for local highways and bridges clipped.

"The institution runs on a certain amount of discipline," he said, explaining the elimination of two projects in Pat Schroeder's Colorado district after she opposed the leadership on a funding bill. "Especially people as prominent as Pat have to accept a certain amount of responsibility for the institution."

An unbending liberal on most policy questions, Lehman practices what he preaches. When liberals and the leadership collided on the 1990 budget-summit agreement, Lehman went with the leadership and supported the package. But that was a rare instance in which he was forced to choose. His opposition to a constitutional amendment to protect the flag and to military aid to Nicaragua, while unpopular views in his district, square with the Democratic majority, as does his support for gun control and abortion rights.

The source of Lehman's strength — taking care of his members — also tests his skill in institutional wrangling. Lehman's willingness to fund unauthorized local projects directly leads him into perennial turf wars with the Public Works Committee.

With the election of Robert A. Roe of New Jersey to the Public Works chairmanship in 1991, Lehman faced the third chairman there in as many Congresses. While he lost his share of rhetorical showdowns with the aggressive James J. Howard of New Jersey in the mid-1980s and later lost a few procedural duels with the more docile Glenn M. Anderson of California, Lehman always managed to slip most of this programs through the legislative mill.

He secured a rather sweet truce with Public Works in 1990. Once Lehman agreed to send all unauthorized project requests to Anderson and Surface Transportation Subcommittee Chairman Norman Y. Mineta of California for approval before giving his own OK, they proceeded to accept virtually every program Lehman sent their way, apparently content not to be ignored.

In the previous two years, Public Works had made little headway in blocking Lehman from earmarking funds. In 1988, Anderson successfully appealed to the Rules Committee to deny Lehman's request to waive House rules banning funding of unauthorized projects. But when House and Senate conferees met, most of the projects were restored — and linked to an initiative Anderson wanted for his district. "He can't have it both ways," said Lehman, as the Public Works chairman dropped the campaign against the appropriations bill.

Anderson had even less luck in 1989: Lehman won a lopsided victory on a rule protecting some $70 million for unauthorized projects. But he was dealt a blow when the House voted to increase funding for the Coast Guard's drug-interdiction efforts. Lehman had adamantly opposed the amendment, and passage meant he had to cut other projects to offset the added cost.

Florida 17

Southeast — North Miami; Part of Hialeah

The 17th is the strongest Democratic district in Dade County, thanks in part to the overwhelming turnout among condominium residents who make this constituency the single most concentrated source of condominium votes in Florida.

All along the Dade County coast, from Golden Beach through North Miami Beach and North Miami down to Miami Shores, entire buildings seem to empty out as condominium residents flock to the polls on Election Day. Some condominiums turn out so many people they become precincts in themselves, with the voting machines placed in lobbies or recreation rooms.

Many of the condominium residents are middle-income retired people from the urban Northeast who maintain lifelong Democratic voting habits. A sizable number of them — about one-quarter of the district's overall population — are Jewish. About 80 percent of the condominium residents in the 17th vote a liberal Democratic line, and their combined tally can give a Democrat a lead of upwards of 30,000 votes in the district.

Also contributing to the Democratic majority in the 17th is the black population, which at 27 percent amounts to the second-largest concentration of blacks in any of the Florida districts. About one-quarter of the electorate is Hispanic, and the district's other "minority" group — WASPs — makes up about one-fifth of the population. In addition to the condominium-filled waterfront area, the district takes in the northern tip of Miami (down to Northwest 62nd Street) and suburban communities such as Carol City, Opa-Locka and most of Hialeah.

In the last redistricting, some Dade County territory in Lehman's old district was moved to the new 16th District, as was a corner of southern Broward County. The changes mean that the 17th is wholly contained within Dade County.

Population: 513,048. White 355,233 (69%), Black 136,887 (27%), Other 3,896 (1%). Spanish origin 126,485 (25%). 18 and over 385,199 (75%), 65 and over 80,913 (16%). Median age: 35.

When Lehman reviewed the vote, he found that a handful of members who opposed him on the Coast Guard vote had received funding for local projects, which solved his funding problem. In conference, Lehman dropped each and every project. "It wasn't exactly retribution," he said afterward. "We had to make cuts anyway. [And] we had to protect the integrity of the subcommittee — to see that our bill isn't rewritten on the floor."

The message got through, though: Most of the members involved were back on board in 1990 and their projects were back in the 1991 bill.

Nowhere is Lehman's project protection more vigilant than for mass transit and Miami's Metromover. A longtime booster of mass-transit programs, Lehman argues that expressways divide neighborhoods and lead to ecological "disaster." He has doggedly battled GOP administrations unsympathetic to mass transit, and for the most part he has prevailed. The Miami system is up and running.

Lehman takes as good care of his district as he does of his colleagues'. His home-state initiatives range from basic federal grant delivery to humanitarian legislating and daring adventures. In 1988, the $7.4 million federally funded William Lehman Aviation Center opened at Florida Memorial College, a historically black school.

Late in 1988, he personally chartered a plane and appealed to Cuban leader Fidel Castro for the release of three longtime political prisoners. Their return to Miami was greeted with triumphant headlines and high praise for Lehman, who has squabbled with local Cuban activists because of his opposition to aid to the Nicaraguan contras.

Lehman's Cuban mission recalled a 1984 episode, when he undertook a suspense-filled mercy mission to aid an ailing Soviet citizen. On an official visit to the Soviet Union, Lehman smuggled into the country a $2,000 artificial heart valve for a 22-year-old Soviet woman who needed the device for a life-saving heart operation. Lehman and an aide slipped away from their hotel and raced through the streets of Tbilisi to deliver the valve to the woman's family, all the while hoping that their taxi driver was not a KGB agent who would wreck the mission.

Although generally preoccupied with Transportation, Lehman uses his post on the Foreign Operations Subcommittee to promote restoration of U.S. involvement in international population control efforts. He also supports generous funding for Israel, and has devoted considerable attention to the plight of Jews in the Soviet Union.

In early 1991, Lehman was temporarily sidelined by a stroke. But, like earlier treatments for cancer of the salivary glands (which left his speech slightly slurred), his latest medical problems did not keep Lehman out of the legislative action for long.

At Home: Lehman was a surprise winner in 1972, and fellow Democrats gave him no peace for several years after that. His Dade County district, then the 13th, was brand new for the 1972 campaign, and seven Democrats ran there. The favorite was state Sen. Lee Weissenborn, a liberal legislator who had sponsored legislation on handgun control and a state kindergarten system.

Weissenborn finished first in the primary with 27 percent of the vote, but Lehman, who had gone from his successful auto business to the chairmanship of the Dade County School Board, forced a runoff by drawing 20 percent.

Lehman, more centrist by reputation than Weissenborn, said he would work in Congress for higher Social Security benefits and better rapid transit. He surprised many Democrats by winning the runoff easily with 57 percent of the vote. His general-election victory was comfortable, although no runaway.

In 1974 Lehman was thrown into a primary runoff against Dade County Commissioner Joyce Goldberg. But as in 1972, he showed surprising strength in the second round, winning by more than 2-to-1. The 1976 Democratic primary also was crowded, but Lehman won without a runoff and overwhelmed a Republican in the general election.

Since then, threats to Lehman's tenure have faded. In five of his 10 general-election contests, Lehman has faced no Republican opposition. Although he did face a challenger in 1990, his first in a decade, Lehman won handily with 78 percent of the vote.

In fact, Lehman's only real challenge in recent years has been fending off retirement rumors spurred by his age and occasional health problems. In 1984, Lehman made a major production of announcing his candidacy for reelection, something most secure incumbents do not bother to do. His office had been flooded with calls from people who thought he was retiring, partly because a local state legislator with the same last name had announced his retirement due to poor health. William Lehman, who the year before had had a cancerous tumor removed, wanted all to know that reports of his political demise were false.

Committees

Appropriations (16th of 37 Democrats)
Transportation (chairman); Foreign Operations, Export Financing & Related Programs

Select Children, Youth & Families (3rd of 22 Democrats)

Elections

1990 General

William Lehman (D)	79,560	(78%)
Earl Rodney (R)	22,027	(22%)

1988 General

William Lehman (D)	Unopposed

Previous Winning Percentages: **1986** (100%) **1984** (100%) **1982** (100%) **1980** (75%) **1978** (100%) **1976** (78%) **1974** (100%) **1972** (62%)

District Vote For President

	1988	1984	1980	1976
D	80,126 (59%)	89,283 (54%)	82,646 (51%)	114,887 (66%)
R	54,667 (40%)	76,081 (46%)	66,317 (41%)	57,720 (33%)
I			13,048 (8%)	

Campaign Finance

	Receipts	Receipts from PACs	Expend-itures
1990			
Lehman (D)	$425,117	$216,350 (51%)	$369,764
Rodney (R)	$37,812	$50 (0%)	$37,287
1988			
Lehman (D)	$324,062	$132,250 (41%)	$257,487

Key Votes

1991	
Authorize use of force against Iraq	N
1990	
Support constitutional amendment on flag desecration	N
Pass family and medical leave bill over Bush veto	Y
Reduce SDI funding	Y
Allow abortions in overseas military facilities	Y
Approve budget summit plan for spending and taxing	Y
Approve civil rights bill	Y
1989	
Halt production of B-2 stealth bomber at 13 planes	Y
Oppose capital gains tax cut	Y
Approve federal abortion funding in rape or incest cases	Y
Approve pay raise and revision of ethics rules	Y
Pass Democratic minimum wage plan over Bush veto	Y

Voting Studies

	Presidential Support		Party Unity		Conservative Coalition	
Year	S	O	S	O	S	O
1990	19	81	94	4	15	85
1989	24	71	95	1	5	93
1988	22	78	94	5	16	84
1987	14	83	95	2	9	86
1986	20 †	78 †	92	4	18	76
1985	23	78	95	2	11	85
1984	30	59	86	4	10	81
1983	17 †	78 †	85 †	5 †	18 †	77 †
1982	26	56	66 †	3 †	21 †	55 †
1981	39	53	77	8	19	71

† Not eligible for all recorded votes.

Interest Group Ratings

Year	ADA	ACU	AFL-CIO	CCUS
1990	89	0	92	21
1989	95	0	100	20
1988	100	8	93	36
1987	92	9	94	21
1986	100	0	83	20
1985	95	5	100	24
1984	85	0	92	42
1983	89	0	93	21
1982	89	6	92	15
1981	85	0	86	18

18 Ileana Ros-Lehtinen (R)

Of Miami — Elected 1989

Born: July 15, 1952, Havana, Cuba.
Education: Miami-Dade Community College, A.A. 1972; Florida International U., B.A. 1975, M.S. 1986.
Occupation: Teacher; private school administrator.
Family: Husband, Dexter Lehtinen; two children.
Religion: Roman Catholic.
Political Career: Fla. House, 1983-87; Fla. Senate, 1987-89.
Capitol Office: 416 Cannon Bldg. 20515; 225-3931.

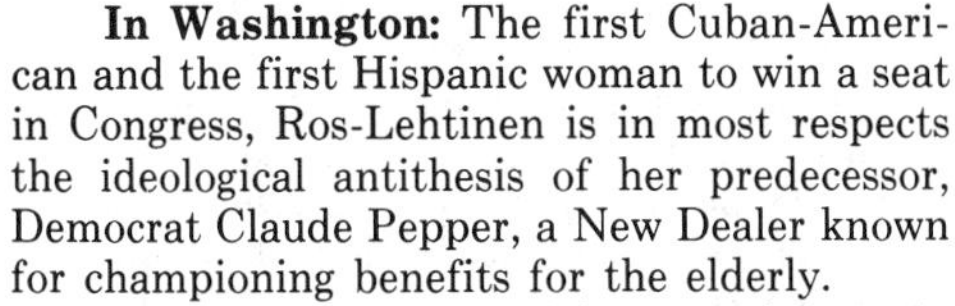

In Washington: The first Cuban-American and the first Hispanic woman to win a seat in Congress, Ros-Lehtinen is in most respects the ideological antithesis of her predecessor, Democrat Claude Pepper, a New Dealer known for championing benefits for the elderly.

But on two issues crucial to constituents in the 18th — U.S. policy toward Cuba and Israel — Ros-Lehtinen espouses the anti-Castro, pro-Israel line that Pepper followed.

The winner of an August 1989 special election following Pepper's death in May, Ros-Lehtinen got her dream assignment upon entering the House: a seat on the Foreign Affairs Committee. The Democratic leadership agreed to give the GOP another slot on the panel.

Hailing from a district that is 37 percent Cuban and vehemently opposed to Fidel Castro's communist regime, Ros-Lehtinen, a former Cuban refugee, also has a strong personal motivation to agitate for democracy in Cuba. She belongs to a "freedom caucus" in the House — a bipartisan group pressing the Cuban government to improve its human rights record and hold free elections.

Ros-Lehtinen's pro-Israel stance appeals to the sizable Jewish population in the 18th. When the United States supported a U.N. resolution criticizing Israel for the deaths of 19 Palestinians during a September 1990 Sukkot holiday confrontation in Bethlehem, Ros-Lehtinen opposed the measure, saying the United States "should not support a resolution unless there has been a complete investigation of this tragic situation." Ros-Lehtinen's overall conservative philosophy includes opposition to abortion and support for a constitutional amendment banning flag desecration.

At Home: From the moment she announced for Pepper's seat, Ros-Lehtinen was the leading contender for the GOP nomination.

She has stood out politically since 1982, when she became the first Hispanic elected to the state Legislature. Although not a major power broker in Tallahassee, Ros-Lehtinen was known as an articulate campaigner who tended to her home base, and as a leading member of South Florida's Cuban-American community.

That community tends to vote Republican, and national GOP strategists were itching to rally that vote and snatch the 18th from Democratic hands. Ros-Lehtinen easily beat three other candidates for the GOP nomination.

Democrats had hoped to build their own bridge to the Cuban-American vote, and many party insiders backed the candidacy of Rosario Kennedy, also a Cuban-American. But Gerald Richman, a Miami Beach attorney with limited political experience, ran an unexpectedly strong campaign and beat Kennedy in a runoff.

Richman's selection, just two weeks before the August special election, was a boon for Ros-Lehtinen. While the Democrats struggled to unify, she enjoyed generous GOP support, including visits from the likes of President Bush and Vice President Quayle. To reach the 18th's important bloc of Jewish voters, Ros-Lehtinen stressed her strong support for Israel, traveling there during the campaign. She also touted her crime-related work in the Legislature, including advocating drug testing for state employees and establishing a crime victim's bill of rights.

Richman, who is Jewish, reacted to GOP suggestions that Cuban-Americans deserved a voice in Congress by saying the 18th was "an American seat" that did not belong to any one group. Although Ros-Lehtinen and some media criticized Richman as bigoted, his approach did strike a chord with some voters. Ros-Lehtinen won the heavily attended special election, but by a smaller margin than anticipated.

Richman's showing led some to believe Ros-Lehtinen would be vulnerable when she sought a full term in 1990. But she had prepared well, opening district offices in heavily Democratic areas and amassing a formidable campaign treasury. Several Democratic heavyweights skipped the race, leaving the nomination to industrialist Bernard Anscher. Anscher, who had won just 703 votes in the 1989 Democratic primary for the 18th, lost by 20 points to Ros-Lehtinen.

Florida 18

Southeast — Miami and Miami Beach

With large constituencies of Cubans, Jews and blacks, the 18th is one of the state's more diverse districts. Democrat Pepper always won it comfortably, but it voted Republican in 1980s presidential elections, and after Pepper's death, Ros-Lehtinen's election certified the 18th's tilt to the GOP.

Many of the Cubans in Miami came to this country in the 1960s, fleeing Castro's takeover. They were well-educated professionals and business people in their homeland, and they have achieved positions of status here. Cubans, Puerto Ricans and Haitians who have arrived recently tend to be unskilled workers, and integrating them into society is more difficult. There are tensions between the middle-class and underclass Cuban communities.

The Cuban-American community for a time was consumed with discussing and plotting a military overthrow of Castro; American elections were not a focus. But in recent years, that has changed, and that has been good news for Republicans. There are some anti-Castro Cubans who have not trusted the Democratic Party since the Bay of Pigs invasion in 1961. The national GOP's more hawkish anti-communist stance has helped convince most Cuban voters to register Republican.

In the central part of the district is Liberty City, the black neighborhood plagued by economic despair and violence in the 1980s. A May 1980 riot that left 18 dead began when a restive black community was infuriated by an all-white jury's decision to acquit four white Miami police officers in the beating death of a black insurance executive. In 1989, riots again erupted following the shooting of a black motorcyclist by a policeman. The chamber of commerce has been pushing a program to create jobs for blacks and to promote black business ownership, but progress toward those goals is slow; the grim mood and appearance of Liberty City persist.

Miami Beach is the part of the district that accounts for its high median age — 44 years. Pepper's natural constituency was the lower, less affluent portion of Miami Beach, where there are no luxury hotels and few tourists. Some blacks and Hispanics live there, but the Jewish population is still very large. The Jewish community that gave Miami Beach its New York flavor usually prefers candidates who are moderately liberal on social issues, conservative on defense and strongly supportive of Israel.

Population: 513,250. White 395,634 (77%), Black 81,137 (16%), Other 3,151 (1%). Spanish origin 260,289 (51%). 18 and over 416,969 (81%), 65 and over 124,773 (24%). Median age: 44.

Committees

Foreign Affairs (18th of 18 Republicans)
Human Rights & International Organizations; Western Hemisphere Affairs

Government Operations (10th of 15 Republicans)
Employment & Housing (ranking)

Elections

1990 General		
Ileana Ros-Lehtinen (R)	56,354	(60%)
Bernard Anscher (D)	36,967	(40%)
1989 Special		
Ileana Ros-Lehtinen (R)	49,298	(53%)
Gerald Richman (D)	43,274	(47%)

District Vote For President

	1988	1984	1980	1976
D	47,474 (42%)	57,240 (40%)	58,549 (40%)	78,436 (55%)
R	65,621 (58%)	86,237 (60%)	75,799 (52%)	62,204 (44%)
I			10,006 (7%)	

Campaign Finance

	Receipts	Receipts from PACs	Expend-itures
1990			
Ros-Lehtinen (R)	$575,234	$168,784 (29%)	$560,847
Anscher (D)	$112,072	$750 (1%)	$112,071

Key Votes

1991	
Authorize use of force against Iraq	Y
1990	
Support constitutional amendment on flag desecration	Y
Pass family and medical leave bill over Bush veto	Y
Reduce SDI funding	N
Allow abortions in overseas military facilities	N
Approve budget summit plan for spending and taxing	N
Approve civil rights bill	Y
1989	
Oppose capital gains tax cut	N
Approve federal abortion funding in rape or incest cases	N
Approve pay raise and revision of ethics rules	N

Voting Studies

	Presidential Support		Party Unity		Conservative Coalition	
Year	S	O	S	O	S	O
1990	50	45	70	26	70	24
1989	66†	32†	74†	24†	82†	18†

† Not eligible for all recorded votes.

Interest Group Ratings

Year	ADA	ACU	AFL-CIO	CCUS
1990	33	65	8	54
1989	-	100	40	100

19 Dante B. Fascell (D)

Of Miami — Elected 1954

Born: March 9, 1917, Bridgehampton, N.Y.
Education: U. of Miami, J.D. 1938.
Military Service: Fla. National Guard, 1941-46.
Occupation: Lawyer.
Family: Wife, Jeanne-Marie Pelot; two children.
Religion: Protestant.
Political Career: Fla. House, 1951-54.
Capitol Office: 2354 Rayburn Bldg. 20515; 225-4506.

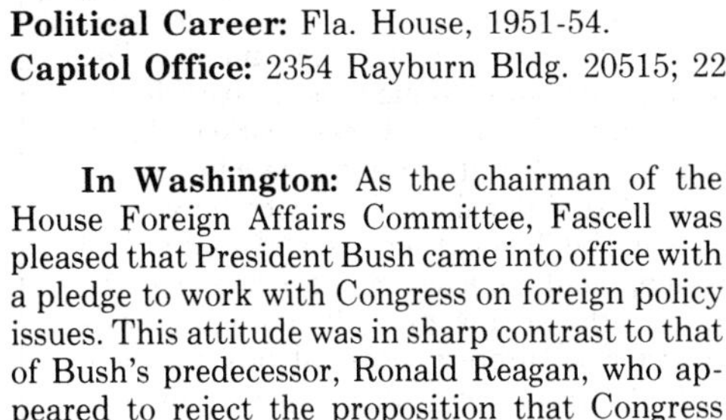

In Washington: As the chairman of the House Foreign Affairs Committee, Fascell was pleased that President Bush came into office with a pledge to work with Congress on foreign policy issues. This attitude was in sharp contrast to that of Bush's predecessor, Ronald Reagan, who appeared to reject the proposition that Congress had a meaningful role in U.S. foreign policy-making.

Early in the Persian Gulf crisis that followed Iraq's invasion of Kuwait, Fascell praised Bush for his outreach efforts. "The level of consultation has been excellent," he said.

For Fascell, meetings with Bush are far more than routine discussions. They are essential to any concrete role Fascell can have in shaping the nation's foreign policy. It is true that he chairs the House committee that has jurisdiction over foreign policy, and also responsibility for authorizing all foreign aid programs. But institutional problems within Congress, and conflicts between the legislative and executive branches, have severely crippled the influence of Foreign Affairs.

Few lay the blame on Fascell. When he became chairman in 1983, Fascell succeeded the late Clement J. Zablocki of Wisconsin, a caretaker who allowed the panel's liberal members — unyielding opponents of Reagan's policies on the Soviet Union and Central America — to dominate the Democratic side of the committee. Fascell took control, employed his moderate views to temper the committee's deep ideological divisions and tried to work out compromises with committee Republicans. More often than not, Fascell has been able to craft the committee's main legislative responsibility, an annual bill authorizing hundreds of foreign aid programs.

But in most years, Fascell's labors were lost. Resisting congressional efforts to place conditions on U.S. aid to certain countries, Reagan eschewed the authorization process, preferring to set aid levels in the annual must-pass appropriations bill. Despite his apparently greater willingness to consult with Congress, Bush has taken a similar approach to the foreign aid authorization bill.

Even more galling for Fascell than executive branch resistance is the chronic inability of his Democratic Senate counterpart, Foreign Relations Committee Chairman Claiborne Pell of Rhode Island, to produce an authorization bill that could at least get the process as far as conference: Pell is notoriously uncommanding as chairman. In addition, the Senate's rules, which allow unlimited debate and non-germane amendments, permit its more contrary members — including Foreign Relations' ranking Republican, Jesse Helms of North Carolina — to tie up the bill.

As a result, only one foreign-aid authorization bill (in 1985) has become law since Fascell took the Foreign Affairs gavel. With foreign policy being set by appropriations bills on an annual basis, Fascell complained in 1990 that the work of his committee had become "almost irrelevant."

The history of the foreign aid authorization bill in 1989 is descriptive of the problems Fascell has faced. That June, Fascell shepherded a fiscal 1990 bill to passage in the House. On certain contentious issues, such as aid to El Salvador, Fascell reined in some of his party's more liberal members to achieve compromise, while bluntly rejecting Bush administration complaints about policy details. Even though the administration would have further opportunities to amend the bill on the House floor, Fascell said, "They'll still have some other things that they'll cry and moan and bitch about. They always do."

The bill passed the House overwhelmingly, but the process went awry. As had happened so often in recent years, Senate Foreign Relations failed to act on the authorization bill, once again leaving the determination of the nation's foreign policy spending priorities to the House and Senate Appropriations committees.

The frequent failures of the foreign policy committees have given enormous clout to Democratic Rep. David R. Obey of Wisconsin, the chairman of the House Appropriations Subcommittee on Foreign Operations. However, Obey remained in favor of the textbook process authorizing foreign aid programs before funding

Florida 19

South — Coral Gables; Key West

Florida's southernmost district once included the whole Miami area. Now it has moved almost entirely out of the city and into the suburbs and rural country extending to the Florida Keys.

Redistricting in 1981 removed liberal areas of Miami as well as Miami Beach, replacing them with more conservative new territory. But there are still plenty of Democratic votes in the 19th.

Florida has taken in tens of thousands of Cuban and Haitian refugees in the 1980s, a frustrating experience for many residents in the 19th. The symbol of the problem is the Krome Avenue detention center, where many of the incoming have been held — often in overcrowded conditions. The Haitian community has been frustrated by the continued use of the detention center.

As the decade came to a close it was clear that the Latin community was being absorbed into the Miami political community, successfully working to elect Hispanic representatives to the state Legislature.

Much of the land in the district is taken up by the Everglades National Park, which has suffered for years because of climatic and manmade factors. Democratic Gov. Lawton Chiles elated environmentalists in early 1991 when he directed the state's powerful sugar cane industry to stop dumping pollutants into the Everglades system.

Coral Gables has liberal academics around the University of Miami, and there are poor and middle-class black neighborhoods, as well as a large Cuban community. The Jewish vote out of Kendall is sizable. Homestead and Florida City are markets for a vegetable and fruit-growing area and the domain of traditional rural Democratic voters.

In the Keys, there is a dispute over development policies. Some who have retired to the area want to discourage growth in order to preserve the islands in their current state. They are opposed by the Conchs, Keys' natives who see tourism and development as their livelihood and want to encourage growth.

Population: 512,886. White 430,795 (84%), Black 61,598 (12%), Other 6,581 (1%). Spanish origin 111,934 (22%). 18 and over 373,329 (73%), 65 and over 45,187 (9%). Median age: 30.

them, and he helped Fascell made a last stab at imposing his committee's authority.

During a conference on the fiscal 1990 foreign aid appropriations bill, Obey — backed by House Speaker Thomas S. Foley — called for a prohibition on spending any money on a foreign aid program that had not been authorized. Obey argued that the jurisdiction of the House Foreign Affairs Committee should not be jeopardized because the Senate Foreign Relations Committee "can't get its act together." However, Senate conferees sharply objected; after further negotiations, Obey and Foley gave in.

Fascell is hardly contrite about his ill will toward his Senate counterparts. In April 1990, Fascell said his committee would once again make the effort to craft a foreign aid authorization bill. "We're going to try our hardest," he said. "If it doesn't happen, it won't be our fault."

Fascell's frustration over this stymied process is rooted in his belief that Congress must be involved in the shaping of foreign policy. His insistence that the White House recognize Congress' constitutional role in matters of war and peace was reflected by his co-authorship in 1973 of the War Powers act.

His institutional prerogatives aside, Fascell was not a major antagonist of Reagan on most foreign policy issues, nor does he sharply disagree with the thrust of Bush's international agenda. Despite his place in the inner circle of House Democrats, Fascell backed Bush all the way on his deployment of troops to blunt Iraqi aggression in 1990 and his eventual decision to use military force to end Iraq's occupation of Kuwait.

Early on, Fascell was impressed by Bush's openness with Congress. But by the end of August, Fascell was showing concern about what he regarded as the president's constitutional obligation to advise Congress — and his political obligation to inform the public — on any actions that might lead to war. Calling on Bush to convene a joint session of Congress after the Labor Day recess, Fascell said, "The time has come to deepen and broaden the national dialogue on steps yet to be taken."

Even in the midst of the crisis, Fascell looked out for his committee's rights. He said Congress should pass a resolution authorizing the deployment of U.S. troops, rather than just appropriating money for troops already activated by Bush. "I don't want the appropriating committees making policy by indirection," he said. His panel passed such a resolution in September 1990, without giving Bush express authority to ensue hostilities against Iraq.

When Bush finally did ask Congress in January 1991 to authorize the use of force, Fascell was on board. Initially, he was set to have Foreign Affairs report a single resolution, proposed by Democratic Rep. Stephen J. Solarz of New York and Minority Leader Robert H. Michel of Illinois, backing the use of force. But Foley persuaded Fascell to allow a range of options to go to the floor.

Fascell voted against an alternative, sponsored by Democratic Reps. Richard A. Gephardt of Missouri and Lee H. Hamilton of Indiana, that would have continued economic sanctions against Iraq and forestalled the authorization of force. After the defeat of that measure, he spoke in favor of the Solarz-Michel resolution.

"If there is no credible threat of force because the Congress does not authorize the use of force, it will be impossible for the president or the United Nations to solve the problem," Fascell said. "Saddam Hussein will just stay put in Kuwait and extract a much higher price from the United States and the world community than he already has."

But even as he supported Bush on the policy question, Fascell praised Congress for invoking its role in the war-making process. "I want to express appreciation to those who had the resolve to start the movement to say that the Congress of the United States ought to share in the responsibility in a major decision of this kind," Fascell said.

As on the Persian Gulf War, Fascell went against the Democratic grain frequently on the contentious Central American issues of the 1980s. He often supported Reagan and Bush on providing aid to the contras fighting the then-Marxist government of Nicaragua and to the rightist government of El Salvador, which was battling insurgents of the left.

Still, Fascell's support for these policies was not unlimited. In 1985, he forced Senate conferees on the successful authorization bill to accept House language blocking the CIA or Pentagon from aiding the contras. When it was revealed the next year that the Reagan administration had sought to avoid an existing congressional ban on contra aid by covertly selling arms to Iran and diverting the proceeds to the rebels, Fascell was sharply critical.

Fascell had hoped to chair the special joint committee that in 1987 investigated the Iran-contra affair, but he became a victim of the age of television. The bulldog looks, gravelly voice and tough demeanor that had made Fascell a legislative force also made him ill-suited to act as the Democratic Party's front man in the highly publicized hearings. Fascell's previous support for the contras also discomfited some Democrats.

Then-Speaker Jim Wright instead tapped former Intelligence Committee Chairman Hamilton, a contra-aid opponent and a man with a more polished style, to chair the committee; Fascell served as vice chairman. Despite his hurt, Fascell was an active member. He concluded that "the administration went far astray from the democratic process," and "was so determined to pursue its policy that it ignored the normal checks and balances ... and said, 'We don't care what Congress thinks.' " Of Reagan, Fascell said, "The president knew, or he should have known."

Democratic opponents of contra aid generally did not resent Fascell going against them; most recognized that opposition to Latin American communism is mandatory for a south Florida congressman such as Fascell. Many of Fascell's Miami constituents are exiles from communist Cuba; like them, he has vehemently opposed any suggestion of warming toward Fidel Castro's regime.

Fascell is an avid supporter of Radio Martí and TV Martí, U.S. government-funded broadcasts that aim U.S. programming at Cuba. When some members in 1990 described TV Martí as a vestige of the Cold War and tried to cut its funding, Fascell helped fight them off. He compared the programs beamed into Cuba's controlled society as akin to "providing food to starving people."

Despite his frequent philosophical agreements with the White House, Fascell is no pushover for Republican presidents. Reacting to the epic changes in Eastern Europe, Fascell was in the forefront of a push during the 101st Congress to provide Poland and Hungary with more U.S. aid than Bush had proposed. He countered Republican concerns about the stability of the emerging democracies and partisan arguments that Democrats were trying to embarrass Bush. "Now with new democracies all over the world, we've got a new purpose that confronts the United States for which we must make money available," Fascell said. "It would be very shortsighted for us to ignore this opportunity."

Also chairman of the Foreign Affairs Subcommittee on Arms Control, International Security and Science, Fascell has often disagreed with Republican priorities on weapons of mass destruction. He has supported a nuclear test ban and the unratified SALT II treaty, and opposed the MX missile and deployment of the proposed strategic defense initiative.

Fascell has been one of the strongest advocates of international bans on chemical weapons. When Bush signed an agreement in June 1990 with Soviet President Mikhail S. Gorbachev to destroy chemical weapons and urge other nations to do the same, Fascell praised the pact as "real disarmament"; he also pointed to the ongoing congressional effort to limit funding for chemical weapons production as the spur for the U.S.-Soviet negotiations.

Since Reagan was in office, Fascell and others have tried to get the White House to accept a bill requiring economic sanctions against countries and individuals involved in the development or use of chemical weapons; Bush vetoed such a bill in 1990 as an encroachment on his foreign policy prerogatives.

In 1988, Fascell supported a more tightly focused bill to punish Iraq for its government's use of poison gas against its Kurdish minority; although it passed the House, Reagan administration objections blocked the bill. In 1990, Saddam Hussein's increasing belligerence resulted in the revival of the Iraqi sanctions bill: With Fascell as its chief sponsor, the bill passed the Foreign Affairs Committee on Aug. 1, 1990 — one day before Iraqi troops invaded and occupied Kuwait.

Outside foreign policy, Fascell earlier in his career specialized in reforming House procedures. The Democratic Caucus in 1973 adopted his amendment requiring committee sessions to be open unless members voted in public to close them. Later he moved successfully to open House-Senate conferences. On the Government Operations Committee until 1984, he helped enact the law to open executive agency meetings. Long before it was required, he disclosed his personal finances.

During the late 1960s and early 1970s Fascell used his membership on both Government Operations and Foreign Affairs to oppose what he saw as President Richard M. Nixon's usurpation of power. In addition to the War Powers act, which was enacted over Nixon's veto, he sponsored a bill curbing presidents' claims of executive privilege, and he cast the deciding vote in 1973 to pass legislation making it easier for Congress to force the executive branch to spend appropriated funds.

On domestic issues, Fascell has maintained a moderate-to-liberal record over the years. In 1965 he managed the bill creating the Department of Housing and Urban Development, and he also backed a federal consumer-protection agency and the Department of Education. He opposed the 1964 Civil Rights Act, but voted for later civil rights bills, including the 1965 Voting Rights Act, federal support for school integration and the 1970 Equal Rights Amendment.

Fascell has shown a strong law-and-order streak. He had little sympathy for 1960s protesters and sponsored legislation setting stiff penalties for inciting a riot. He has favored the death penalty for airline hijackers. In recent years, reflecting the concerns of Floridians, his thrust has been against drugs, seeking federal funds for law enforcement and education.

Despite his wide-ranging interests, Fascell tends to his home base. An opponent of oil drilling off the Florida coast, Fascell was not completely satisfied in 1990 when Bush announced a 10-year moratorium on most offshore oil leasing. "While the president's decision takes some of the annual pressure off, it does not go far enough," Fascell said. "Until a permanent prohibition is implemented, there is no satisfactory solution."

During the 101st Congress, Fascell spearheaded a successful effort to establish the area around the Florida Keys as a national marine sanctuary. The action was compelled by a series of accidents in which ships had run aground on the region's fragile coral reefs.

At Home: Like many of the people he represents, Fascell is not a native Southerner. His family moved to Florida from Long Island when he was 8. He earned his law degree from the University of Miami before leaving to fight in World War II.

After the war, he used the Dade County Young Democrats and the Italian-American club as an entry into politics, then ran successfully for the state Legislature in 1950.

Four years later, Rep. William Lantaff announced his retirement. With the slogan "Ring the bell for Dante Fascell," the 37-year-old lawyer won a majority in the five-man primary and was unopposed in November.

His first real re-election test was in 1962. Democratic state Rep. David C. Eldredge, a segregationist, criticized Fascell as a consistent supporter of an intrusive federal government and hinted that the incumbent was sympathetic to communism.

When President John F. Kennedy spoke at a Democratic fundraiser in Miami Beach, he made a point of endorsing Fascell. That hurt Eldredge; he protested Kennedy's intervention, but faded to receive only 35 percent of the primary vote.

Since then, Fascell generally has won well over 60 percent of the vote. Even in the infrequent instances when he has faced vigorous challengers, Fascell has never dropped below 57 percent.

National Republican strategists essentially left Fascell alone until 1982, when they were hopeful that redistricting had made the 19th promising territory for a candidate younger and more conservative than Fascell. In that year's remap, the 19th lost 20,000 solid Democratic votes in south Miami Beach, including poor, elderly people dependent on Social Security.

Fascell's admirers trembled in midsummer 1982, when pollster V. Lance Tarrance released a survey showing the veteran incumbent only 10 percentage points ahead of Republican Glenn Rinker, a TV news anchorman who had not even announced his House candidacy.

Rinker owed his strong showing in the survey to his name recognition, which was remarkably high for a challenger. Prior to his bid, Rinker had appeared regularly for six years on a Miami TV station. Fascell, meanwhile, had been gliding through quiet and easy re-elections; many of the district's residents had moved in after his last serious challenge, in 1972.

Fascell responded to Rinker with a campaign that had both positive and negative sides. He not only reminded voters of the federal largess he had brought the area during his years in the House, but he portrayed Rinker as a shallow ideologue, a tool of the national GOP who would be a Reagan puppet in Congress.

Fascell enjoyed a significant organizational advantage over Rinker, whose campaign started late. The Democrat raised and spent vastly more than he had in any of his previous campaigns — over $450,000. As Fascell's aggressive response became clear, Republican contributors backed out on Rinker, and in the end the challenger was badly outspent. As it turned out, Rinker's strength just about peaked at the time of that midsummer poll. Fascell scored a solid victory, taking 59 percent of the vote.

In both 1984 and 1986, district Republicans were embarrassed when primary voters nominated substitute teacher Bill Flanagan over party organization candidates. Flanagan, known in the media as "Shower Shoes" (a reference to his preferred footwear), was a recluse who made no organized public appearances and tersely, sometimes angrily, refused requests for interviews. Flanagan did not run again in 1988, but the GOP fared even more poorly without him. Fascell, improving on his 1986 tally, won 72 percent of the vote.

The 1990 GOP nominee, Bob Allen, a young lawyer with connections to Republican Gov. Bob Martinez, waged a more serious campaign and made a better showing. But Fascell still won with 62 percent of the vote.

Committees

Foreign Affairs (Chairman)
Arms Control, International Security & Science (chairman)

Select Narcotics Abuse & Control (7th of 21 Democrats)

Elections

1990 General

Dante B. Fascell (D)	87,677	(62%)
Bob Allen (R)	53,774	(38%)

1988 General

Dante B. Fascell (D)	135,355	(72%)
Ralph Carlos Rocheteau (R)	51,628	(28%)

Previous Winning Percentages: **1986** (69%) **1984** (64%) **1982** (59%) **1980** (65%) **1978** (74%) **1976** (70%) **1974** (71%) **1972** (57%) **1970** (72%) **1968** (57%) **1966** (57%) **1964** (64%) **1962** (65%) **1960** (71%) **1958** (100%) **1956** (61%) **1954** (100%)

District Vote For President

	1988	1984	1980	1976
D	74,323 (41%)	65,440 (36%)	56,728 (34%)	84,684 (54%)
R	105,860 (58%)	118,424 (64%)	90,859 (55%)	70,567 (45%)
I			17,626 (11%)	

Campaign Finance

	Receipts	Receipts from PACs	Expend-itures
1990			
Fascell (D)	$452,275	$164,116 (36%)	$500,117
Allen (R)	$162,658	$400 (0%)	$160,220
1988			
Fascell (D)	$490,976	$176,934 (36%)	$337,596
Rocheteau (R)	$4,600	0	$4,907

Key Votes

1991	
Authorize use of force against Iraq	Y
1990	
Support constitutional amendment on flag desecration	N
Pass family and medical leave bill over Bush veto	Y
Reduce SDI funding	Y
Allow abortions in overseas military facilities	Y
Approve budget summit plan for spending and taxing	Y
Approve civil rights bill	Y
1989	
Halt production of B-2 stealth bomber at 13 planes	N
Oppose capital gains tax cut	Y
Approve federal abortion funding in rape or incest cases	Y
Approve pay raise and revision of ethics rules	Y
Pass Democratic minimum wage plan over Bush veto	Y

Voting Studies

	Presidential Support		Party Unity		Conservative Coalition	
Year	**S**	**O**	**S**	**O**	**S**	**O**
1990	24	73	88	7	39	52
1989	40	59	89	6	34	59
1988	28	67	88	8	42	55
1987	23	77	94	3	33	67
1986	28	70	88	7	36	60
1985	34	63	88	6	40	58
1984	40	54	84	10	32	66
1983	33	62	86	11	31	66
1982	39	51	71	10	44	49
1981	41	54	83	10	19	73

Interest Group Ratings

Year	ADA	ACU	AFL-CIO	CCUS
1990	83	8	92	14
1989	60	4	92	20
1988	75	17	93	36
1987	80	9	100	20
1986	70	23	93	24
1985	60	24	94	11
1984	70	17	85	33
1983	85	9	88	30
1982	75	5	79	25
1981	80	7	87	21

Georgia

U.S. CONGRESS

SENATE 2 D
HOUSE 9 D, 1 R

LEGISLATURE

Senate 45 D, 11 R
House 145 D, 35 R

ELECTIONS

1988 Presidential Vote	
Bush	60%
Dukakis	40%
1984 Presidential Vote	
Reagan	60%
Mondale	40%
1980 Presidential Vote	
Reagan	41%
Carter	56%
Anderson	2%
Turnout rate in 1986	24%
Turnout rate in 1988	39%
Turnout rate in 1990	29%

(as percentage of voting age population)

POPULATION AND GROWTH

1980 population	5,463,105
1990 population (11th in the nation)	6,478,216
Percent change 1980-1990	+19%

DEMOGRAPHIC BREAKDOWN

White	71%
Black	27%
Asian or Pacific Islander	1%
(Hispanic origin)	1%
Urban	62%
Rural	38%
Born in state	71%
Foreign-born	2%

MAJOR CITIES

Atlanta	394,017
Columbus	179,278
Savannah	137,560
Macon	106,612
Albany	78,122

AREA AND LAND USE

Area	58,056 sq. miles (21st)
Farm	33%
Forest	65%
Federally owned	6%

Gov. Zell Miller (D)
Of Young Harris — Elected 1990

Born: Feb. 24, 1932, Towns Co., Ga.
Education: Young Harris Jr. College, 1951; U. of Georgia, A.B. 1957, M.A. 1958.
Military Service: Marine Corps, 1953-56.
Occupation: Educator.
Religion: Methodist.
Political Career: Ga. Senate, 1961-64; lieutenant governor, 1975-91.
Next Election: 1994.

WORK

Occupations	
White-collar	50%
Blue-collar	35%
Service workers	12%
Government Workers	
Federal	88,219
State	118,107
Local	286,757

MONEY

Median family income	$ 17,414 (37th)
Tax burden per capita	$ 757 (37th)

EDUCATION

Spending per pupil through grade 12	$ 3,434 (38th)
Persons with college degrees	15% (32nd)

CRIME

Violent crime rate	736 per 100,000 (8th)

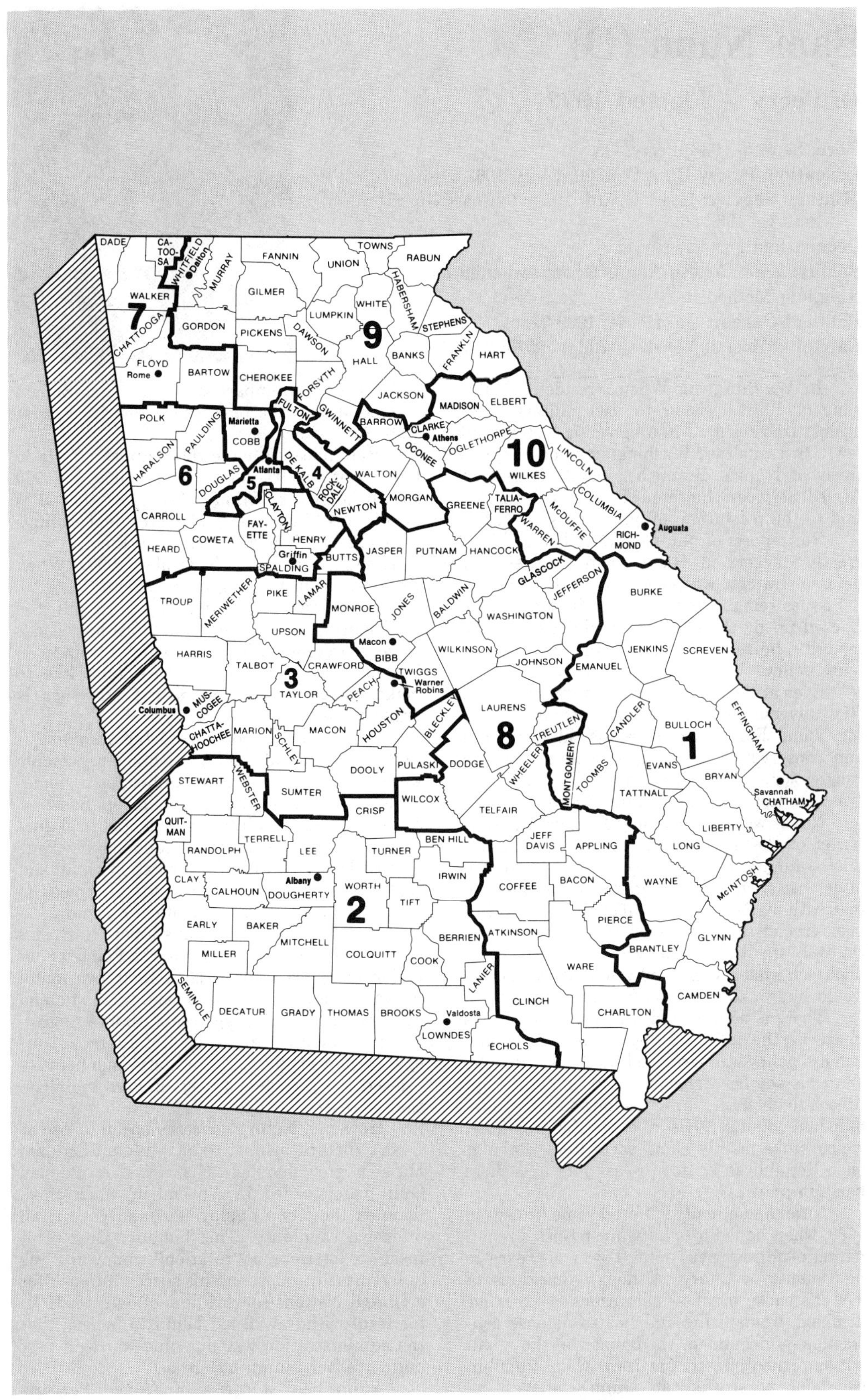

DADE
CA-TOO-SA
WHITFIELD
Dalton
MURRAY
FANNIN
UNION
TOWNS
RABUN
GILMER
WALKER
7
WHITE
HABERSHAM
LUMPKIN
9
STEPHENS
CHATTOOGA
GORDON
PICKENS
DAWSON
FRANKLIN
HART
HALL
BANKS
FLOYD
Rome
BARTOW
CHEROKEE
FORSYTH
JACKSON
ELBERT
MADISON
POLK
PAULDING
Marietta
COBB
FULTON
GWINNETT
BARROW
CLARKE
Athens
OCONEE
OGLETHORPE
10
WILKES
LINCOLN
HARALSON
6
DOUGLAS
Atlanta
DE KALB
4
ROCK-DALE
WALTON
5
CLAYTON
MORGAN
GREENE
TALIA-FERRO
COLUMBIA
McDUFFIE
CARROLL
NEWTON
FAY-ETTE
HENRY
WARREN
Augusta
RICH-MOND
HEARD
COWETA
Griffin
SPALDING
BUTTS
JASPER
PUTNAM
HANCOCK
GLASCOCK
JEFFERSON
BURKE
TROUP
MERIWETHER
PIKE
LAMAR
MONROE
JONES
BALDWIN
WASHINGTON
UPSON
Macon
BIBB
WILKINSON
JENKINS
SCREVEN
HARRIS
TALBOT
3
CRAWFORD
TWIGGS
JOHNSON
EMANUEL
TAYLOR
PEACH
Warner Robins
Columbus
MUS-COGEE
LAURENS
CANDLER
BULLOCH
EFFINGHAM
CHATTA-HOOCHEE
MARION
SCHLEY
MACON
HOUSTON
BLECKLEY
TREUTLEN
8
1
PULASKI
DODGE
WHEELER
MONTGOMERY
TOOMBS
EVANS
BRYAN
STEWART
WEBSTER
DOOLY
Savannah
CHATHAM
SUMTER
CRISP
WILCOX
TELFAIR
TATTNALL
QUIT-MAN
LIBERTY
TERRELL
BEN HILL
JEFF DAVIS
APPLING
LONG
RANDOLPH
LEE
TURNER
IRWIN
CLAY
Albany
COFFEE
BACON
WAYNE
McINTOSH
CALHOUN
DOUGHERTY
WORTH
TIFT
2
PIERCE
EARLY
BAKER
MITCHELL
BERRIEN
ATKINSON
GLYNN
BRANTLEY
MILLER
COLQUITT
COOK
WARE
LANIER
SEMINOLE
CLINCH
CAMDEN
DECATUR
GRADY
THOMAS
BROOKS
Valdosta
CHARLTON
LOWNDES
ECHOLS

Sam Nunn (D)

Of Perry — Elected 1972

Born: Sept. 8, 1938, Perry, Ga.
Education: Emory U., A.B. 1960, LL.B. 1962.
Military Service: Coast Guard, 1959-60; Coast Guard Reserve, 1960-66.
Occupation: Farmer; lawyer.
Family: Wife, Colleen Ann O'Brien; two children.
Religion: Methodist.
Political Career: Ga. House, 1969-72.
Capitol Office: 303 Dirksen Bldg. 20510; 224-3521.

In Washington: When President Bush's January 1991 decision to use military force against Iraq resulted in a lightning victory and few U.S. casualties, Washington pundits spoke freely of Nunn's diminished clout. As Senate Armed Services chairman, he had led opposition to the resolution authorizing use of force.

But reports of Nunn's reduced status were greatly exaggerated. His intricate knowledge of defense strategy, weapons systems and personnel issues remains without peer in the Senate. Backed up by the chamber's solid Democratic majority, he remains a dominant force on defense policy.

Even at the height of the postwar euphoria, GOP adversaries could go only so far in chastising Nunn. For nearly a decade, his influence and conservative views have helped preserve congressional majorities for the defense programs of Republican administrations.

Nunn was the leading Democratic supporter of the military buildup during the administration of Ronald Reagan. Now, in the era of defense spending retrenchment, Nunn is the man with his finger in the dike: His support has been crucial to saving such Bush priorities as the B-2 "stealth" bomber and other expensive, high-tech systems that more liberal Democrats would like to slash to the bone.

There is no question, though, that Nunn's image as the infallible high priest of Senate defense policy was tarnished by the war debate. With his somber demeanor and analytical approach to defense, Nunn was long seen as above mundane politics: His role on the war vote, which broke mainly along party lines, emboldened Republican critics to cast him as a mere partisan player.

Nunn had already suffered some bruises in 1989, when he led a fight against Bush's nomination of former Sen. John Tower of Texas to be Defense secretary. Although questions of Tower's background — allegations of excessive drinking, womanizing and ties to defense contractors — abounded, the debate on the nomination turned bitterly partisan. Many Republicans openly scoffed at Nunn's above-it-all reputation: "Nunnpartisan" was what Senate Democrats had become, said Minority Leader Bob Dole of Kansas.

Republicans charge that Nunn's efforts in the Tower and Iraq debates, as well as his 1990 switch to favor abortion rights, prove that he is positioning himself to run for president. Nunn's response: "When I agree with them, I'm a statesman," he said in November 1990. "When I don't . . . I'm running for president."

In March 1991, Nunn tried to put the presidential issue behind him. "I cannot visualize any circumstances under which I would run in 1992," he said. "Southerners don't like to make Sherman-like statements, but that is pretty close to one."

Despite his opposition to the administration's Persian Gulf policies, Nunn's arguments were, as usual, pedagogic rather than demagogic. They were grounded in opinions — widely shared by military and geopolitical analysts — that the ongoing economic blockade against Iraq could break that nation's will, and that war would cause thousands of American casualties and become a political quagmire.

Nunn actually gave full support to Bush's initial deployment of troops to the Persian Gulf region following Iraq's August 1990 invasion of Kuwait. The purpose, Bush said, was to defend against further Iraqi aggression. In late August, Nunn — an advocate of the "total force" strategy employed by U.S. military planners — praised the president for his limited mobilization of reserve troops.

However, Nunn's concerns began to rise as Bush's rhetoric against Iraqi President Saddam Hussein grew harsher. His views on Persian Gulf policy gelled in November, when Bush doubled the troop deployment and gave it an offensive capability. This buildup, Bush's refusal to institute a "rotation" policy for the desert-based troops, and his successful push for a United Nations-set deadline of Jan. 15, 1991, for Iraqi withdrawal, led Nunn to believe that the administration was pursuing war as a first option rather than a last resort.

Nunn held a series of Armed Services

Committee hearings, at which witnesses — including former chairmen of the Joint Chiefs of Staff — counseled against a rush to war with Iraq's huge and supposedly battle-seasoned army. During testimony by Defense Secretary Dick Cheney and Joint Chiefs Chairman Gen. Colin L. Powell Jr., Nunn laid out the case for continued sanctions. "If we have a war, we are never going to know whether [sanctions] would have worked, are we?" he asked.

Just before the U.N. deadline, Bush asked Congress to authorize the use of force against Iraq. Opponents crafted a resolution calling for continued sanctions. Although the measure was proposed by Majority Leader George J. Mitchell of Maine, Nunn's gravitas on defense made him the most influential voice against force.

If it came to war, Nunn said during his floor speech on the war resolution, "We know we can win, and we will win; no doubt about that." But he asked, "Will I be able to look at the parents and the wives and the husbands and the children in the eye and say that their loved ones sacrificed their lives for a cause vital to the United States, and that there was no other reasonable alternative?" Nunn's advocacy helped swing the votes of several moderate Democrats who look to him for guidance on military issues. But that just made it close: The Mitchell-Nunn resolution was defeated on a 46-53 vote, and the resolution authorizing Bush to use force passed, 52-47.

After Bush ordered an air campaign against Iraqi positions the following week, Nunn stated his support for the president and the troops. Yet he still held out hope for a diplomatic settlement that would forestall a ground war. When Saddam appeared to react favorably in February 1991 to peace feelers by the Soviet Union, Nunn said, "This could be the opening bid in Saddam's move toward diplomacy."

Instead, Bush launched a ground offensive that routed Iraqi forces. With Bush's popularity at an all-time high and Republican officials threatening to hold war-resolution opponents accountable, many Democrats took cover. But Nunn eschewed contrition. "There was a reasonable alternative . . ." to going to war, Nunn reiterated during a March 1991 TV interview. "I would not have voted the other way."

When Iraqi Kurdish and Shiite Muslim minorities, emboldened to revolt by Bush's anti-Saddam rhetoric, were crushed by forces loyal to Saddam, Nunn was among those who called for a massive U.S. relief effort and the use of U.S. military forces to help the refugees. "I do think we encouraged an awful lot of people to believe our policy was to support the overthrow of the government," Nunn said.

At first, Bush was reluctant to extend U.S. commitments to the region, noting obliquely that some of those urging a response to the refugee problem had been among the "severest critics" of his pre-war policy. But after a barrage of TV reports on the plight of the Kurds and a visit by Secretary of State James A. Baker III to the area, Bush instituted a relief and military protection program.

In any case, Nunn had already proven that he remains, in the words of Tennessee Democratic Sen. Al Gore, "the man to beat" on defense issues. In March 1991, he easily parried a Republican maneuver to advance a space-based Strategic Defense Inititiate (SDI) system that Nunn strongly opposes.

Playing off the highly publicized use of Patriot missiles to shoot down Iraq's ballistic Scuds during the Persian Gulf War, ranking Armed Services Republican John W. Warner of Virginia proposed an amendment to a supplemental appropriations bill to accelerate development and deployment of a space-based anti-ballistic missile (ABM) system. However, Nunn countered with his own amendment, which would have steered SDI strongly toward his own favored concept of a limited ground-based ABM program. Warner withdrew his amendment; had he pursued it, Nunn said, "We would have prevailed substantially."

Nunn is no anti-SDI liberal. In 1989, the Senate passed an amendment to cut Bush's $4.6 billion request for SDI research funding to $3.7 billion in fiscal 1990. However, Nunn argued that amount would give him no room to bargain with the House, which had set a $3.1 billion figure; the Senate then boosted its authorization to $4.3 billion. A House-Senate conference agreed to fund SDI at $3.8 billion.

Where Nunn has diverged from Republican administrations is on what type of ABM system to pursue. Since President Reagan unveiled the SDI program in 1983, the White House has pushed a vision of a space-based system of satellite-based or freely-orbiting rockets, which could shoot down at least some enemy ballistic missiles on launch. Nunn says such an approach is technologically unrealistic; moreover, he insists that it violates the 1972 U.S.-Soviet ABM treaty. Nunn favors a ground-based approach within the treaty's strictures.

In response to Reagan's efforts in 1987 to pursue the airborne testing of SDI technologies, Nunn gave three speeches outlining the history of the ABM pact. He concluded that its intent had been to ban the kind of tests Reagan sought.

In 1988, Nunn backed an amendment to the fiscal 1989 defense authorization bill to deter development of a system of thousands of small, orbiting ABM rockets (later titled Brilliant Pebbles); Reagan's veto blocked it from becoming law. But in 1990, two Nunn allies on Armed Services, Democrats Jeff Bingaman of New Mexico and Richard C. Shelby of Alabama, pushed through an amendment, which became law, diverting some funding from space-based to ground-based systems research.

The SDI split is, however, one of the few defense spending issues on which Nunn differs greatly from Bush and Cheney. He is a staunch advocate of the B-2, a radar-evading technological marvel but one whose huge price tag has made it the target of budget-cutters.

In 1990, the anti-B-2 forces scored a huge victory in the House, where Armed Services Chairman Les Aspin of Wisconsin signed on to a successful push to kill the program. Nunn held fast, however, pushing an authorization through the Senate and negotiating a conference deal to provide $2.35 billion to build the planes.

However, ambiguous language in the conference report presaged a continued battle in the 102nd Congress. Program opponents argued that the law allowed for construction of only the 15 B-2 bombers already authorized; "the B-2 is dead," said liberal Democratic Rep. Ronald V. Dellums of California. However, supporters argued that the law allowed for purchase of components for additional planes: "The B-2 program is alive and well," Nunn said.

Nunn's stature on defense issues continues traditions for both his family and his state. He is the grandnephew of Carl Vinson, a longtime chairman of the House Armed Services Committee, and he occupies the Senate seat once held by Georgia Democrat Richard Russell, who chaired Senate Armed Services.

Nunn did not leave the matter of committee assignments to chance when he came to Washington. He teamed up with his great-uncle Vinson, who by then had retired, and visited all the major Senate power brokers to win the Armed Services assignment.

Nunn's overall voting record is well to the right of the national Democratic Party. He supported Bush on 72 percent of Senate votes in 1989, and backed the president 57 percent of the time in 1990. Even so, his differences with the Democratic mainstream have narrowed some in recent years. "I'm still more conservative than most people in the Democratic Party," he says. "But it's not as wide a gap as it used to be, and I like to think that's because they're coming towards the middle."

Although the image of Nunn is justifiably that of a defense maven, he also has used his position as chairman of the Governmental Affairs Permanent Investigations Subcommittee to get involved in education policy, probing high default rates in student loan programs.

During the 101st Congress, Nunn held a yearlong investigation into outright fraud in such programs, particularly those that serve for-profit trade schools. Citing evidence of numerous trade-school scams, Nunn says the industry "attracted not just some bad apples, but bad orchards." Nunn's prominence on the issue was noted in March 1991 by Labor and Human Resources Chairman Edward M. Kennedy of Massachusetts, who informed new Education Secretary Lamar Alexander to "keep Sen. Nunn informed" about student loan programs.

In 1989, Nunn and Democratic Rep. Dave McCurdy of Oklahoma proposed a plan that would tie nearly all student aid programs to pledges by recipients to perform civilian or military "national service." The measure was blocked by criticism, even from national service supporters, that the student aid tie-in was too stringent and would put a burden on low-income students who most need assistance.

At Home: Republicans paid Nunn the ultimate political compliment in 1990, opting not to challenge his bid for a fourth term. One Republican unknown did try to run, but when she could not come up with the filing fee, the state GOP, far from chipping in, asked that her name be removed from the ballot.

That left Nunn free to run a re-election campaign that some speculated was as much geared toward a future presidential bid as to returning him to the Senate. In September 1990, when Nunn relaxed his longtime opposition to abortion rights, it was the latest in a series of signs that he is inching away from the conservative image he cultivated during his rise to dominance in Georgia politics.

In 1984, while running for a third Senate term, Nunn joined other state Democratic leaders in distancing himself from the doomed presidential campaign of liberal Democrat Walter F. Mondale. But Nunn's overwhelming re-election that year reaffirmed his position as Georgia's pre-eminent Democrat, and in the years since, he has been more generous about bestowing his stamp of approval on more liberal Democratic candidates.

In 1988, Nunn endorsed Michael S. Dukakis for president and made a well-publicized speech on his behalf at a rural Georgia rally in the last week of the campaign. (Dukakis won 40 percent in Georgia.) In 1986, Nunn gave a crucial boost to Democratic Rep. Wyche Fowler Jr.'s successful campaign against Republican Sen. Mack Mattingly. Nunn's imprimatur helped Fowler mitigate a liberal reputation, developed during a decade representing Atlanta's majority-black 5th District, as he sought the votes of rural and suburban Georgians. Nunn campaigned vigorously and appeared in commercials that portrayed Fowler as an urban representative who looked out for rural voters.

Nunn was a dark horse himself when he first decided to run for the Senate in 1972, but he turned out to be an ideal candidate against David H. Gambrell, the wealthy and urbane Atlanta lawyer whom Gov. Jimmy Carter named to the Senate after Russell's death.

Nunn also was a lawyer and state legislator, but his central Georgia roots and kinship with Carl Vinson allowed him to run as an old-fashioned rural Democrat. He called Gambrell a "fake conservative" who backed Democratic presidential nominee George McGovern, despite Gambrell's denials of any such link.

Though Gambrell finished first in the primary, he was forced into a runoff with Nunn, who intensified his attacks, all but saying Gambrell's wealthy family had bought the seat by contributing to Carter's gubernatorial campaign. It was enough to sink Gambrell.

The focus shifted in the general election, when Nunn encountered GOP Rep. Fletcher Thompson. This time, it was Thompson who used the McGovern issue. But Nunn countered by obtaining the blessing of Alabama Gov. George C. Wallace, then a conservative icon.

Despite his criticisms of busing and "welfare loafers," Nunn also got the support of black leaders, who claimed Thompson had not spoken to a black audience in four years, even though 40 percent of his Atlanta district was non-white. Further big-name help for Nunn came from Democratic Sen. Herman E. Talmadge, at the time an institution in state politics, whose critical support in rural areas helped Nunn offset his opponent's strength in the Atlanta suburbs. Nunn won with 54 percent.

Six years later, Nunn's fiscal conservatism and support for the military put him in such good position that no serious challenger emerged. The luckless Republican candidate, former U.S. Attorney John Stokes, had little money and ran a near-invisible campaign. Nunn's 83 percent was the highest vote any Senate candidate in the country received that fall against a major party opponent. In 1984, a banner year for Republican candidates in Georgia, Nunn took 80 percent of the vote.

Committees

Armed Services (Chairman)

Governmental Affairs (2nd of 8 Democrats)
Permanent Subcommittee on Investigations (chairman); Government Information & Regulation; Oversight of Government Management

Select Intelligence (2nd of 8 Democrats)

Small Business (2nd of 10 Democrats)
Government Contracting & Paperwork Reduction; Rural Economy & Family Farming; Urban & Minority-Owned Business Development

Elections

1990 General

Sam Nunn (D)	1,033,439	(100%)

Previous Winning Percentages: **1984** (80%) **1978** (83%) **1972** (54%)

Campaign Finance

	Receipts	Receipts from PACs		Expenditures
1990				
Nunn (D)	$1,978,221	$627,010	(32%)	$882,336

Key Votes

1991	
Authorize use of force against Iraq	N
1990	
Oppose prohibition of certain semiautomatic weapons	N
Support constitutional amendment on flag desecration	Y
Oppose requiring parental notice for minors' abortions	N
Halt production of B-2 stealth bomber at 13 planes	N
Approve budget that cut spending and raised revenues	Y
Pass civil rights bill over Bush veto	Y
1989	
Oppose reduction of SDI funding	Y
Oppose barring federal funds for "obscene" art	?
Allow vote on capital gains tax cut	N

Voting Studies

	Presidential Support		Party Unity		Conservative Coalition	
Year	**S**	**O**	**S**	**O**	**S**	**O**
1990	57	43	70	27	78	19
1989	72	28	68	30	87	11
1988	63	33	68	24	92	5
1987	46	53	77	22	91	6
1986	58	39	50	43	75	16
1985	58	42	57	41	88	10
1984	69	29	44	55	83	17
1983	64	33	49	48	84	11
1982	70	29	57	41	82	16
1981	59	31	59	39	84	15

Interest Group Ratings

Year	ADA	ACU	AFL-CIO	CCUS
1990	50	32	56	42
1989	35	37	80	63
1988	40	42	54	50
1987	55	23	100	28
1986	30	55	47	50
1985	30	57	43	59
1984	35	73	45	74
1983	40	28	35	42
1982	45	68	64	67
1981	35	47	32	72

Wyche Fowler Jr. (D)

Of Atlanta — Elected 1986

Born: Oct. 6, 1940, Atlanta, Ga.

Education: Davidson College, A.B. 1962; Emory U., J.D. 1969.

Military Service: Army, 1963-65.

Occupation: Lawyer.

Family: Wife, Donna Hulsizer; one child.

Religion: Presbyterian.

Political Career: Atlanta Board of Aldermen, 1970-74; president, Atlanta City Council, 1974-77; U.S. House, 1977-87; sought Democratic nomination for U.S. House, 1972.

Capitol Office: 204 Russell Bldg. 20510; 224-3643.

In Washington: Fowler has quickly become a Senate favorite, always ready to regale his colleagues with a joke or a story. Intelligent and politically shrewd, he has landed choice assignments thanks to his close association with Majority Leader George J. Mitchell.

Naturally gregarious, Fowler puts colleagues at ease by telling jokes and spinning yarns. He knows the words to more than one hymn. Once at a slack moment in the Senate schedule, while intense negotiations were taking place off the floor, he held forth on the pleasures of baseball.

But his most crucial speech may have been the one he gave to second the nomination of Mitchell for majority leader. Fowler was an early supporter of Mitchell, and as a Southerner, a most important one during the 1988 contest.

After his election, Mitchell named Fowler to the Democratic Steering Committee, which makes committee assignments. It was no surprise Fowler got a leg up on three other Southerners chasing a seat designated for the region on the powerful Appropriations Committee.

Mitchell later named Fowler assistant floor leader, a new post that put him visibly among the Senate's leaders.

Despite Fowler's junior status on the Budget and Appropriations committees, Mitchell named him to be his personal representative on the 1990 bipartisan budget summit. The discussions, involving House and Senate members and Bush administration officials, were held in seclusion at Andrews Air Force Base throughout the summer. Fowler was one of the lead negotiators for the Democrats.

After four and a half months of struggle, the summit negotiators reached an agreement, but it failed dramatically in the House, brought down by conservatives opposed to its tax increases and liberals unhappy with its spending cuts. Congress stayed in session over the Columbus Day weekend to put together a fallback budget resolution that left most of the details up to the House and Senate committees.

Fowler's voting record has moderated since his House days, but among Southerners he has been one of the most loyal to his party's line. He helped stake out the turf that made it safe for Southern Democrats to oppose the nomination of Robert H. Bork to the Supreme Court. It is not uncommon for Fowler to be on the opposite side of an issue from his conservative colleague, Sam Nunn, particularly on arms control votes.

Fowler left Energy and Natural Resources for the 101st Congress to move to Appropriations. But he kept a hand in one of his favorite issues — the conservation and stewardship of resources — by chairing Agriculture's Conservation and Forestry Subcommittee. He rejoined Energy in the 102nd.

His conservationist bent has shown up in his work on the Arctic National Wildlife Refuge issue, where oil exploration is at issue. He has introduced water-conservation legislation and angled to promote rural development with a revolving-loan program. But having to depend on conservative rural farmers for political support at home, Fowler must navigate a precarious course, steering between his environmental proclivities and the interests of farm organizations, which are hardly enthusiastic about efforts to impose environmental restrictions on farmers.

As early as 1988, Fowler proposed legislation to give farmers incentives to diversify their crops and use fewer chemicals and more environmentally sound farming methods. His legislation, promoting low-input sustainable agriculture, or LISA, won the strong support in 1989 of the committee's environmentalist chairman, Patrick J. Leahy, although many farm groups bitterly opposed it, particularly its requirement for mandatory testing of wells for pollutants.

During consideration of the 1990 farm bill, Fowler tried hard to satisfy environmentalists as well as farm commodity groups, but he ended up looking irresolute after sponsoring a commodity-backed pesticide conservation measure directly at odds with one he had backed weeks earlier.

In February 1990, Fowler stood alongside as a coalition of environmental groups unveiled tough proposals for getting farmers to reduce their pesticide and fertilizer use, for protecting wetlands from further encroachment by agriculture and for limiting soil erosion.

A month later, though, to the dismay of those environmental groups, Fowler's staff was preparing legislation that incorporated many suggestions by commodity organizations, which wanted instead to loosen and change existing environmental controls on farming.

Leahy and ranking Republican Richard G. Lugar moved to head off Fowler's measure, fearing it could undo a key conservation element of the 1985 farm bill, the wetland-protection program known as "swampbuster." The final bill reauthorized swampbuster and authorized $40 million for research into sustainable agriculture.

Fowler was on firmer political terrain when he championed another cause backed by conservationists, seeking in 1989 and 1990 to slash the Senate's appropriation for one of the timber industry's cherished federal subsidies: the forest road-building program that unlocks public lands for tree harvesting. The Senate adopted his amendment in 1989, but not only did House-Senate conferees drop it, they also made additional funds available at the last moment. In 1990, the Senate killed his proposal, 52-44.

Fowler's motives were not entirely ecological. The subsidy is a boon to timber companies in the Pacific Northwest, which harvest largely in federal forests. Logging companies in Georgia harvest primarily in private forests.

In a career that has reflected an interest in large ideas and discourse, Fowler has shown an occasional restlessness with the confining details of the legislative process. When he arrived in the House in 1977, he returned an official set of formal law books and lined his shelf with novels, poetry and best-sellers. Arriving in the Senate in 1987, he expressed a desire for "a little more time for reading and reflecting before meeting the demand for the day." He has constantly advocated a simpler society, one stripped of technological gadgetry and energy waste. He can work himself into a rage over the decadence of the electric toothbrush.

In the House, Fowler was consistently the leading opponent of President Ronald Reagan's policies in the Georgia delegation. To insulate himself from charges that he was a liberal, Fowler called himself "moderate in the extreme," and quoted Thomas Jefferson to the effect that government is best when it governs least.

At Home: Sheer political skill enabled Fowler to beat the odds in 1986, when he upset GOP Sen. Mack Mattingly. Widely regarded as too liberal and urban-oriented for Georgia's conservative Democratic yeomanry, Fowler proved a master campaigner with an extraordinary ability to tailor his style to his audience.

Fowler's main campaign asset was his multifaceted political personality. To Atlanta's 5th District, which he represented in the House for nearly 10 years, Fowler was the liberal critic of Reagan's domestic budget-cutting efforts. To voters in suburbs and college towns, the graduate of two of the South's most prestigious educational institutions was a deep-thinking intellectual.

But the persona that was decisive in the Senate contest was that of Good Ol' Wyche. To overcome his liberal image and the antipathy of many Georgians toward Atlanta pols — no Atlantan had ever before won a Senate seat — Fowler put on his best down-home accent and charmed audiences that were expected to be hostile. Though he did not run as well in outstate Georgia as more conservative predecessors, his totals there, combined with his Fulton County base, lifted him past Mattingly.

Many state Democratic officials believed Fowler could not win, and they had tried to recruit more conservative figures, including 9th District Rep. Ed Jenkins and then-University of Georgia football coach Vince Dooley, to seek the Senate nomination.

Fowler did face competition for the nomination, most notably from former Carter White House Chief of Staff Hamilton Jordan, who was coming off successful treatments for cancer. Jordan entered the race as the conservative alternative to Fowler. His earlier celebrity guaranteed him media attention, and he branded Fowler as a liberal in hopes of turning south Georgia voters against him. But Fowler, a south Georgia native, was able to mitigate his liberal image by peppering his speeches with jokes and folksy stories. And Jordan was burdened by a negative perception of the Carter administration. Winning 82 percent in Fulton County, carrying Atlanta's suburbs and holding down Jordan's rural margins, Fowler took a slim primary majority.

Fowler then turned to Mattingly. Since 1980, Democrats had predicted a short tenure for the Republican, who had won narrowly over veteran Democratic Sen. Herman E. Talmadge. The Indiana-born businessman won largely because Talmadge had been tainted by personal scandals and because metropolitan Atlanta voters had tired of his rural-oriented style.

In the Senate, Mattingly angered few voters, but did little to popularize himself. A backbencher with a wooden speaking style, he was a Reagan loyalist with one pet cause — giving the president line-item veto power.

But Mattingly was well-funded for 1986, and he staged a media blitz to undermine Fowler. His main line of attack was on Fowler's House attendance record, which had suffered during his primary campaign: Mattingly ads described Fowler as "Absent for Georgia."

Early polls showed Fowler with a double-digit deficit. But by October, his campaign jelled. Endorsements from previously reluctant Democrats helped Fowler temper his liberal image. Sam Nunn toured the state to praise Fowler's concern for rural interests.

The decisive factor was Fowler's ability to personalize the campaign. In one TV ad, a puppy enthusiastically licked Fowler's face. He stumped the state with a personal magnetism that mitigated the absenteeism charge.

The voting results differed sharply from 1980, when Mattingly ran up a huge margin in the Atlanta area to offset Talmadge's sweep elsewhere. Fowler carried Fulton County by 2-to-1, and also took suburban De Kalb County, which Mattingly won in 1980. Mattingly's conservatism helped him slice into the usual Democratic majorities in outstate Georgia, but Fowler still won more than half of those counties.

Fowler's countrified campaign was not a complete act; his family has deep roots in Georgia, and as a teenager he appeared as a country singer on an Atlanta talent show.

But basically, Fowler is a white-collar Atlantan. After graduating from Davidson College in 1962, he entered politics as an aide to 5th District Rep. Charles Weltner, a liberal Democrat who retired in 1966 after two terms rather than run on the same ticket with right-wing gubernatorial candidate Lester Maddox.

After graduating from Emory law school, Fowler returned to government in 1970, winning a seat on the Atlanta City Council. He made his initial try for Congress in 1972, badly losing the Democratic primary to civil rights activist Andrew Young. Fowler bounced back the next year, winning the City Council presidency over black activist Hosea L. Williams.

Fowler got another shot at the House in 1977, when Young was appointed to the United Nations by Carter. His main opposition came from another civil rights leader, John Lewis. The vote divided largely along racial lines. Fowler ran ahead in first-round voting and won the runoff with a nearly unanimous white vote.

Redistricting increased the black share of the 5th to 65 percent in 1982, but Fowler worked to prevent race-based voting. Quoting the Rev. Dr. Martin Luther King Jr., Fowler told blacks, "I know you're not going to judge me because of the color of my skin, but the content of my character." When Fowler left the 5th in 1986, Lewis won it.

Committees

Agriculture, Nutrition & Forestry (7th of 10 Democrats)
Conservation & Forestry (chairman); Domestic & Foreign Marketing & Product Promotion; Nutrition & Investigations

Appropriations (15th of 16 Democrats)
Agriculture, Rural Development & Related Agencies; District of Columbia; VA, HUD and Independent Agencies; Military Construction

Budget (10th of 12 Democrats)

Energy & Natural Resources (9th of 11 Democrats)
Energy Regulation & Conservation; Energy Research & Development; Public Lands, National Parks & Forests

Elections

1986 General		
Wyche Fowler Jr. (D)	623,707	(51%)
Mack Mattingly (R)	601,241	(49%)
1986 Primary		
Wyche Fowler Jr. (D)	314,787	(50%)
Hamilton Jordan (D)	196,307	(31%)
John D. Russell (D)	100,881	(16%)
Jerry Belsky (D)	14,365	(2%)

Previous Winning Percentages: **1984** * (100%) **1982** * (81%) **1980** * (74%) **1978** * (76%) **1977** † (62%)

** House elections.*
† Special House runoff election.

Campaign Finance

	Receipts	Receipts from PACs		Expend-itures
1986				
Fowler (D)	$2,912,638	$600,086	(21%)	$2,779,297
Mattingly (R)	$4,856,309	$990,313	(20%)	$5,119,249

Key Votes

1991	
Authorize use of force against Iraq	N
1990	
Oppose prohibition of certain semiautomatic weapons	N
Support constitutional amendment on flag desecration	Y
Oppose requiring parental notice for minors' abortions	Y
Halt production of B-2 stealth bomber at 13 planes	N
Approve budget that cut spending and raised revenues	Y
Pass civil rights bill over Bush veto	Y
1989	
Oppose reduction of SDI funding	N
Oppose barring federal funds for "obscene" art	Y
Allow vote on capital gains tax cut	N

Voting Studies

	Presidential Support		Party Unity		Conservative Coalition	
Year	**S**	**O**	**S**	**O**	**S**	**O**
1990	43	55	84	14	43	57
1989	61	38	72	27	71	29
1988	51	45	78	18	68	32
1987	35	62	85	13	53	47
House Service						
1986	17	42	30	8	24	16
1985	24	65	73	13	55	38
1984	40	45	66	21	51	42
1983	27	68	83	11	35	62
1982	45	48	70	17	48	44
1981	42	45	60 †	31 †	55	41

† Not eligible for all recorded votes.

Interest Group Ratings

Year	ADA	ACU	AFL-CIO	CCUS
1990	72	35	44	33
1989	60	15	89	50
1988	75	8	79	43
1987	90	8	100	22
House Service				
1986	15	44	43	50
1985	50	26	50	50
1984	70	35	69	27
1983	90	13	88	25
1982	65	10	74	35
1981	80	14	64	17

1 Lindsay Thomas (D)

Of Statesboro — Elected 1982

Born: Nov. 20, 1943, Patterson, Ga.
Education: U. of Georgia, B.A. 1965.
Military Service: Ga. Air National Guard, 1966-72.
Occupation: Farmer; investment banker.
Family: Wife, Melinda Ann Fry; three children.
Religion: Methodist.
Political Career: No previous office.
Capitol Office: 240 Cannon Bldg. 20515; 225-5831.

In Washington: Like most other Georgia Democrats, Thomas prefers a substantive role behind the scenes to prominent displays of oratory or political gamesmanship. While this style makes him one of the least visible members of Congress, it also makes him a good fit for the Appropriations Committee, where discretion is the order of the day.

Democratic leaders may also appreciate Thomas' low profile. Unlike other Southern conservatives, he sees little need to call attention to the differences between his votes and those of more liberal party elders.

Instead, Thomas has quietly carved a niche as a chamber of commerce Democrat. In the 100th Congress he stuck with his party on such matters as abortion funding and civil rights, but he went his own way on a host of other business priorities. He opposed overrides of presidential vetoes of the Family Leave Act and the minimum wage; he supported a capital gains tax cut and a conservative alternative to child-care legislation.

Thomas' subcommittees on Appropriations — Energy and Water and Military Construction — give him forums for addressing important home-state issues. In addition to helping secure funding for Kings Bay naval submarine base and the Fort Stewart Hunter Army Airfield complex in his district, Thomas is working to make himself a player in the debate on the classification and regulation of wetlands — a role he fosters as co-chairman of the Sunbelt Caucus.

Representing all of Georgia's seacoast, Thomas is caught between the push to protect the fragile ecology of the wetlands and the economic pull to develop the coast. "As a farmer who worked the land everyday," he says, "I learned that my livelihood depended on wetlands."

Thomas complains that the Bush plan to protect wetlands, however, goes too far. By protecting areas "no wetter than the average suburban backyard," he fears, the proposal will create a backlash against preservation. Thomas proposes a combination of tax and market incentives for landowners to protect wetlands on their property.

For much of his time in Congress, Thomas, an investment banker turned tobacco farmer, devoted himself to mastering the intricacies of farm issues. Until he joined Appropriations in 1987 — becoming the first Georgian on the committee since his predecessor in the 1st, Democratic Rep. Bo Ginn (1973-83) — Thomas was considered one of the more knowledgeable junior members of the Agriculture Committee.

Thomas put his knowledge of the machinations of the farm bill to work in the 101st Congress, however, when he teamed up with Georgia Sen. Wyche Fowler Jr. to protect the good name of Vidalia onions. The sweet onions are grown in a 19-county area of Georgia, where farmers pay a federal marketing order for promotion and quality control. Luscious Vidalias pump more than $25 million into Georgia's economy, but in recent years "counterfeit" onions from other parts of the country have captured as much as 25 percent of the market. The 1990 farm bill, however, will stop that practice by providing federal protection for Vidalias and other commodities that pay federal marketing orders.

When he was on the Agriculture Committee, Thomas' chief expertise was in tobacco, but he also worked in behalf of Georgia's sizable egg industry. In particular, he lobbied for a provision outlawing the Egg King, a machine used to crush hundreds of eggs and then separate the liquid from the shells. "It is a hazard to public health," Thomas argued. "Eggs are literally dumped into the machine along with traces of blood, chicken manure, dirt, rot and fragments of paper egg cartons." For egg processors, it was also an issue of economics: The Egg King was providing competition that could eventually put some of them out of business.

The Agriculture Committee agreed with Thomas, but on the floor, California Republican Robert E. Badham, whose district was home to the Egg King inventor, persuaded the House to reject the provision.

In his first term, Thomas was actively involved in revising the tobacco program. Farmers in Georgia had been agitating for years to change the allotment system, by which those with quotas to grow tobacco leased them to growers. Many felt this system was geared more

Georgia 1

Southeast — Savannah; Brunswick

The 1st is old Georgia, from Savannah and the Golden Isles — the state's only seacoast — to the inland rural counties, where the economy has not changed much in a century and a half.

Savannah, which celebrated its 257th anniversary in 1990, is Georgia's oldest city. Its tidy brick Georgian houses, moss-covered oaks and iron-grilled gateways give it a charm that tourists find irresistible. But the city of 137,560 is also a major Atlantic port, strongly unionized and with a black population above 50 percent. Like other cities of the coastal South, it is an ethnic melting pot, home to Irish Catholics, French Huguenots and a substantial Jewish community. The current mayor is of Greek descent.

Savannah provides statewide Democratic candidates with a 1st District base, but the burgeoning suburbs of surrounding Chatham County and neighboring Effingham County usually turn the tide in favor of Republicans. Chatham County as a whole gave 58 percent of its vote to George Bush in 1988; he took Effingham by a 2-to-1 margin. GOP Sen. Mack Mattingly carried both counties in his unsuccessful 1986 re-election bid. Effingham's rural complexion took on a new look after Fort Howard built a $700 million plant in 1986, and notched the region's highest employment growth from 1984 to 1989.

Bordering Chatham County to the south is fast-growing Bryan County, where suburbs are starting to encroach on the soybean, tobacco and peanut fields; the county grew by nearly 30 percent, to 13,000 residents, between 1980 and 1986. Statewide Republicans star here: Bush took 66 percent of the vote; Mattingly won with 60 percent.

The biggest burst of growth in the district has occurred in the southernmost county, Camden. Spurred by construction of the Kings Bay nuclear submarine base, Camden's population leaped by 127 percent in the 1980s. Recent statewide Republican margins have been fairly modest in Camden. But to the north, Glynn County, which contains the city of Brunswick and St. Simons Island, has been a GOP stronghold.

In between the Savannah and Brunswick areas is McIntosh County, a rural and coastal region that has maintained its Democratic leanings. Democratic presidential candidate Michael S. Dukakis took 54 percent in the county, the only one in the 1st District that he carried.

The inland 1st is rather sparsely populated farmland and forest country. Large black populations temper the Republican vote in many counties. But there are also some rural Republican bastions; Bush took 79 percent of the vote in Toombs County.

Population: 541,180. White 355,814 (66%), Black 179,817 (33%), Other 3,331 (1%). Spanish origin 6,510 (1%). 18 and over 375,257 (69%), 65 and over 55,349 (10%). Median age: 28.

to the interests of allotment holders than to the growers themselves. Thomas brought the subcommittee to his district to hold field hearings, then helped rewrite the law to place more leases in the hands of those farmers growing tobacco.

At Home: Thomas' varied career gave him an invaluable edge in bringing the disparate communities of his district together behind him when he first ran for Congress.

After college and training as an investment banker, Thomas spent six years with two Savannah investment-banking firms, becoming an assistant vice president of one of them. In 1973, however, he left the city for a small farming hamlet in Wayne County, deep in rural south Georgia. He began raising tobacco, corn and soybeans, and managing timberland.

A decade later, already active in various public-affairs groups related to agriculture, Thomas joined a crowd of congressional hopefuls when Democratic Rep. Ginn gave up his seat in an unsuccessful 1982 primary bid for governor. The early favorite to win the Democratic nomination was state Sen. Charles H. Wessels of Savannah, heir to a banking and insurance fortune, who had plenty of money to invest in the campaign and support from much of Savannah's black community.

But Thomas had money of his own, and he held several successful fundraising events, including an auction modeled after the famous Ducks Unlimited hunting auction.

In the crowded field, Thomas' background proved decisive. He drew on the ties to the Savannah business community he had developed during his investment-banking years, combining them with rural support that Wessels could not match. Thomas cited his farming experience to persuade rural voters he was one of them, taking quiet advantage of the antipathy toward urban Savannah interests traditional in the inland southern counties.

Thomas finished first in the primary, then buried Wessels in the runoff. He has had no trouble in any of his five general-election campaigns.

Committee

Appropriations (30th of 37 Democrats)
Energy & Water Development; Military Construction

Elections

1990 General

Lindsay Thomas (D)	80,515	(71%)
John Christian Meredith (R)	32,532	(29%)

1988 General

Lindsay Thomas (D)	94,531	(67%)
John Christian Meredith (R)	46,552	(33%)

Previous Winning Percentages: **1986** (100%) **1984** (82%) **1982** (64%)

District Vote For President

	1988	1984	1980	1976
D	62,529 (40%)	69,408 (41%)	82,446 (55%)	92,126 (66%)
R	94,646 (60%)	100,525 (59%)	63,003 (42%)	46,777 (34%)
I			2,363 (2%)	

Campaign Finance

	Receipts	Receipts from PACs		Expend-itures
1990				
Thomas (D)	$378,206	$167,765	(44%)	$399,035
Meredith (R)	$19,196	0		$10,130
1988				
Thomas (D)	$339,987	$149,969	(44%)	$337,048
Meredith (R)	$40,511	0		$40,461

Key Votes

1991	
Authorize use of force against Iraq	Y
1990	
Support constitutional amendment on flag desecration	Y
Pass family and medical leave bill over Bush veto	N
Reduce SDI funding	Y
Allow abortions in overseas military facilities	Y
Approve budget summit plan for spending and taxing	Y
Approve civil rights bill	Y
1989	
Halt production of B-2 stealth bomber at 13 planes	N
Oppose capital gains tax cut	N
Approve federal abortion funding in rape or incest cases	Y
Approve pay raise and revision of ethics rules	Y
Pass Democratic minimum wage plan over Bush veto	N

Voting Studies

	Presidential Support		Party Unity		Conservative Coalition	
Year	**S**	**O**	**S**	**O**	**S**	**O**
1990	43	56	76	23	94	4
1989	58	42	65	34	98	2
1988	38	61	77	23	95	5
1987	42	56	71	23	98	2
1986	47	53	72	28	96	4
1985	50	50	75	25	93	7
1984	54	46	70	29	86	14
1983	49	51	64	36	84	16

Interest Group Ratings

Year	ADA	ACU	AFL-CIO	CCUS
1990	28	50	42	69
1989	25	54	33	80
1988	50	48	64	64
1987	40	36	44	60
1986	25	68	43	61
1985	25	67	41	45
1984	45	16	69	50
1983	40	74	35	60

2 Charles Hatcher (D)

Of Newton — Elected 1980

Born: July 1, 1939, Doerun, Ga.
Education: Georgia Southern U., B.S. 1965; U. of Georgia, J.D. 1969.
Military Service: Air Force, 1958-62.
Occupation: Lawyer.
Family: Wife, Ellen Wilson; three children.
Religion: Episcopalian.
Political Career: Ga. House, 1973-81.
Capitol Office: 2434 Rayburn Bldg. 20515; 225-3631.

In Washington: Hatcher's friendly face and polite manner are well-known on the Agriculture Committee, but beyond that arena, Hatcher and his views are indistinct. He does not seem to mind. After chairing the Domestic Marketing, Consumer Relations and Nutrition Subcommittee for the 101st Congress as the committee assembled the 1990 farm bill, Hatcher has now taken over the subcommittee panel with the jurisdiction most relevant to his peanut-growing district.

As Domestic Marketing chairman, Hatcher was responsible for the sections of the farm bill concerning food stamps and marketing of agriculture products, such as fruits, nuts and vegetables.

Mostly, however, Hatcher sticks to peanuts. According to his office, his district grows 35 percent of the nation's goobers. When North Carolina Democrat Charlie Rose gave up the chairmanship of the Tobacco and Peanuts Subcommittee after the 101st Congress, Hatcher not only took the helm, but also changed the panel's name to the Peanuts and Tobacco Subcommittee. Tobacco is also important to his district, but the peanut reigns supreme.

The peanut title approved by the subcommittee for the 1990 farm bill continued the government's two-tier price-support program — one level for those grown under a nationally imposed quota system and a lower support level for "additional" peanuts sold overseas.

To peanut growers, the price-support program is vital. However, manufacturers — major candy and peanut butter companies — have long opposed it. The Bush administration also wanted to eliminate key elements of the peanut program, such as restrictions on the sale of quota peanuts, a cost-of-production escalator and the $631 per ton quota price-support rate.

Hatcher and Rose arranged a private meeting between national grower groups and the manufacturers, excluding Bush administration officials. But the marathon meeting failed to produce accord on several provisions. Hatcher offered a peanut title incorporating some points where the growers and manufacturers had reached a compromise, but the subcommittee rejected it by voice vote.

The pre-eminence of peanuts to south Georgia's economy forced Hatcher to learn his way around Capitol Hill quickly. As a freshman in 1981, he was lobbied heavily by the White House to vote for President Reagan's tax cut; he said he would like to vote with the president, but that he was especially anxious to see the federal peanut program preserved.

Hatcher voted for the tax bill and the Office of Management and Budget dropped its opposition to reauthorizing the bulk of the peanut program. Whether there was much of a connection is questionable. But Hatcher was able to return home and tell constituents that he had made a deal and contributed to the preservation of the program.

When the farm bill came up for renewal in 1985, Hatcher was not a visible presence in the committee's debates. But he made clear his opposition to any new effort to gut existing peanut and tobacco price-support programs.

In 1986, Hatcher backed Agriculture Chairman E. "Kika" de la Garza of Texas to pass emergency farm drought-relief legislation. The bill included $230 million to allow peanut and soybean farmers to receive disaster payments.

In the 100th Congress, Hatcher led a lower-profile subcommittee, the Small Business Committee's panel on Energy and Agriculture. There, he promoted his bill to expand a Small Business Administration (SBA) loan program in rural areas. The plan was signed into law as part of the SBA reauthorization bill.

Hatcher almost found himself displaced from his Small Business subcommittee chairmanship in the 100th Congress. He wanted to head an Agriculture panel, but he was beaten out by three more senior members. Meanwhile, the Small Business subcommittee he had chaired on Antitrust had been eliminated. But the committee reorganized and gave him the chairmanship of the new Energy and Agriculture Subcommittee.

A moderate Southern Democrat who sup-

Georgia 2

Southwest — Albany; Valdosta

There has been a constant refrain in recent years that the Peach State is developing into "two Georgias": booming Atlanta, and rural areas elsewhere that remain dependent on a struggling agricultural economy. The 2nd, in the southwest corner of the state, symbolizes the "other Georgia."

While thousands of new residents have poured into metro Atlanta, the population in the 2nd has remained stagnant. A bloc of rural counties near the Alabama border lost population in the early 1980s. The district's biggest city by far, Albany (Dougherty County) produces beer, soap and thread, and processes the pecans and peanuts grown by local farmers. The 1986 closure of a Firestone plant cost more than 2,200 jobs, but a flurry of new construction and a planned downtown redevelopment project has kept the local economy perking.

With its large blue-collar and black contingents, Dougherty County is crucial for statewide Democratic candidates hoping to carry the 2nd. But it has not been particularly dependable for them; George Bush took 51 percent of the county's vote in 1988.

Valdosta (Lowndes County), surrounded by the vast reaches of southern Georgia's piney woods, makes much of its living from the forests; turpentine, planing and paper mills, and sawmills anchor the local economy. Nearby Moody Air Force Base also gives the area a boost. Hatcher has maintained his support here, and Lowndes went narrowly for Democratic gubernatorial nominee Zell Miller in 1990, but Bush took 62 percent of the county's vote in 1988.

The rural counties, many of which have black majorities, continue to provide Democrats with a consistent, though diminishing, support base. Democrat Miller carried the 2nd in 1990, but of the seventeen counties he lost across the state, six were in the 2nd.

Population: 549,977. White 346,391 (63%), Black 200,556 (37%). Spanish origin 5,869 (1%). 18 and over 369,606 (67%), 65 and over 60,160 (11%). Median age: 28.

ports abortion rights, Hatcher is a fairly reliable vote for the Democratic leadership. In 1989, he voted for the ethics reform package that included a congressional pay raise. He also backed the use of federal funds to pay for abortions in cases of rape and incest, and supported the 1990 budget summit agreement.

On other issues, his votes reflect the interests of his conservative district. In the 101st Congress, he voted against a Democratic plan to kill a proposed cut in the capital gains tax. He also voted for proposed constitutional amendments to ban physical desecration of the flag and to require a balanced federal budget. In 1991, Hatcher voted to authorize President Bush to use force in the Persian Gulf against Iraq.

At Home: The 1988 Democratic primary put Hatcher in a rematch with former congressional aide Julian Holland, whom Hatcher had narrowly defeated in the 1980 primary that first earned him the seat. This time, though, Hatcher handled Holland with ease, and then went on to dismiss his most determined Republican challenger to date. That victory seems to have firmed up Hatcher's hold on the 2nd; in 1990, he faced no primary opposition, and coasted to an easy general election win.

Hatcher was assistant floor leader of the Georgia House when he entered the 1980 contest to succeed Democratic Rep. Dawson Mathis, who waged an unsuccessful primary challenge to Democratic Sen. Herman E. Talmadge. Though the experienced Hatcher was regarded as a primary favorite, he failed to win the majority needed to avoid a runoff with Holland, then Mathis' chief legislative aide.

Holland made a strong appeal to rural voters, portraying Hatcher as too liberal and not interested enough in farm issues. But residents of the district's small cities, especially Albany, who had preferred Hatcher in the primary, came through again for him in the runoff. Drawing on his strength in Albany and Valdosta, he won with 53 percent. Hatcher easily dispatched his GOP opponent.

But two years later, Hatcher had primary pressure again, this time from Mathis, who wanted his seat back. Concentrating on the 2nd's rural reaches, Mathis claimed he had done more than Hatcher for the peanut business. A strong campaigner, Mathis swept the district's rural counties, but Hatcher's showing in Albany and Valdosta once again pulled him through.

Hatcher then coasted until 1988, when Holland, who had spent the intervening years in Washington working mainly as a lobbyist, returned to the 2nd and announced a primary challenge to his old rival.

Holland tried to revive his rural base,

blaming Hatcher for failing to block a diesel-fuel tax increase, and stating that Hatcher had voted with the Democratic leadership during procedural votes on issues such as abortion and gun control. He also claimed there was a latent anti-Hatcher mood among businessmen skeptical of the incumbent's ability to boost the district's faltering economy.

But Holland never caught fire. Hatcher denied being a liberal on social issues, and noted his part in the move to roll back the diesel tax. He also cited his efforts to bring businesses, especially in the food-processing industry, to the 2nd. Hatcher won by a margin of nearly 2 to 1.

Businessman Ralph T. Hudgens, the vigorous GOP nominee, recycled the liberal characterization, and he tried to paint Hatcher as an elitist because he rode in a Mercedes during Albany's Pecan Festival. But Hatcher won 29 of the district's 30 counties, taking 62 percent of the vote.

Committees

Agriculture (11th of 27 Democrats)
Peanuts & Tobacco (chairman); Cotton, Rice & Sugar; Department Operations, Research & Foreign Agriculture; Domestic Marketing, Consumer Relations & Nutrition

Small Business (6th of 27 Democrats)
Exports, Tax Policy & Special Problems

Elections

1990 General		
Charles Hatcher (D)	77,910	(73%)
Jonathan Perry Waters (R)	28,781	(27%)
1988 General		
Charles Hatcher (D)	85,029	(62%)
Ralph T. Hudgens (R)	52,807	(38%)

Previous Winning Percentages: **1986** (100%) **1984** (100%) **1982** (100%) **1980** (74%)

District Vote For President

	1988	1984	1980	1976
D	57,423 (40%)	62,974 (42%)	82,687 (57%)	93,296 (70%)
R	83,163 (58%)	88,306 (58%)	60,378 (42%)	40,942 (30%)

Campaign Finance

	Receipts	Receipts from PACs	Expend-itures
1990			
Hatcher (D)	$328,506	$211,150 (64%)	$296,470
1988			
Hatcher (D)	$348,158	$200,458 (58%)	$368,470
Hudgens (R)	$132,230	$12,740 (10%)	$129,741

Key Votes

1991	
Authorize use of force against Iraq	Y
1990	
Support constitutional amendment on flag desecration	Y
Pass family and medical leave bill over Bush veto	N
Reduce SDI funding	Y
Allow abortions in overseas military facilities	Y
Approve budget summit plan for spending and taxing	Y
Approve civil rights bill	Y
1989	
Halt production of B-2 stealth bomber at 13 planes	N
Oppose capital gains tax cut	N
Approve federal abortion funding in rape or incest cases	Y
Approve pay raise and revision of ethics rules	Y
Pass Democratic minimum wage plan over Bush veto	Y

Voting Studies

	Presidential Support		Party Unity		Conservative Coalition	
Year	**S**	**O**	**S**	**O**	**S**	**O**
1990	37	59	76	19	85	13
1989	49	45	70	20	73	20
1988	31	55	72	19	84	5
1987	37	61	70	21	91	7
1986	34	54	67	18	78	16
1985	49	45	73	17	78	13
1984	43	41	58	20	66	10
1983	51	40	62	29	76	12
1982	43	42	53	35	79	8
1981	59	36	50	40	80	13

Interest Group Ratings

Year	ADA	ACU	AFL-CIO	CCUS
1990	28	50	42	57
1989	35	31	55	80
1988	50	43	62	64
1987	44	27	44	54
1986	30	56	64	69
1985	35	52	44	42
1984	25	20	67	58
1983	45	43	59	63
1982	25	56	61	65
1981	25	60	57	63

3 Richard Ray (D)

Of Perry — Elected 1982

Born: Feb. 2, 1927, Fort Valley, Ga.
Education: Graduated from Crawford County H.S.
Military Service: Navy, 1944-45.
Occupation: Pest control executive; Senate aide.
Family: Wife, Barbara Elizabeth Giles; three children.
Religion: Methodist.
Political Career: Perry City Council, 1962-64; mayor of Perry, 1964-70.
Capitol Office: 225 Cannon Bldg. 20515; 225-5901.

In Washington: More than two decades ago, small-town Mayor Ray gave Sam Nunn his first job in politics. Nunn rose faster, though, and Ray followed along, serving as the senior aide in Nunn's Senate office before winning the 3rd District in 1982.

Though Nunn is far more prominent as the Senate Armed Services Committee chairman, Ray is not regarded as merely a proxy for the senator in his role on House Armed Services. With his meticulous and methodical manner, Ray has earned respect for his expertise on various esoteric defense issues.

Ray is one of the strongest committee allies of Chairman Les Aspin of Wisconsin. Since Aspin took the helm at Armed Services in 1985, some more liberal Democrats have grumbled about his tendency to side with Reagan and Bush administration defense priorities. Ray is not in this group. A member and former deputy coordinator of the House Conservative Democratic Forum, Ray has several times gone along with Aspin and a majority of committee Republicans on close defense votes.

In 1989, Aspin praised Defense Secretary Dick Cheney's first budget proposal and asked the Armed Services Procurement Subcommittee to approve it. Ray went along; the measure passed the subcommittee by a 10-9 vote.

Ray's highest-profile split with Nunn on defense policy came in January 1991, on the question of authorizing the use of force to end Iraq's occupation of Kuwait. While Nunn counseled patience, Ray — whose district includes the Army's Fort Benning and the Robins Air Force Base — voted for the war resolution.

Ray also has doggedly pursued some specific defense-related issues. His current focus is environmental cleanup at Defense Department facilities, a long-term project with an enormous price tag. He chairs a special Armed Services panel on environmental restoration.

Ray has urged the Pentagon to increase payments to get the cleanup started. However, he also has tried to block efforts to allow states and localities to sue the federal government over past solid and hazardous waste disposal practices. In 1989, Ray argued that such a proposal would subject the Defense Department to huge, perhaps crippling, legal and settlement costs. He was unable to stop the bill in the House — his amendment to maintain federal "sovereign immunity" failed, 98-322 — but the measure was not enacted.

Ray is also on the Small Business Committee, where he reflects his district's rural nature. He favors greater federal efforts on rural development, and has worked on improving the provision of federal crop insurance to farmers.

At Home: As mayor of Perry in the 1960s, Ray appointed Nunn, a local lawyer, to an advisory panel on race relations. Nunn grew to admire Ray's organizational abilities, and signed him on as his administrative assistant after his Senate election in 1972.

By the time Democratic Rep. Jack Brinkley retired in 1982, Ray had firm ties to local officials throughout the 3rd. When Ray announced his candidacy, other Democratic aspirants stepped aside. The Democratic Congressional Campaign Committee passed word to Ray that a condition for receiving national money was to be a "loyal" — i.e., non-Boll Weevil — Democrat. Ray publicly denounced such a quid pro quo. The campaign committee ended up giving him just $250, but the publicity worked among his conservative constituents.

Republicans had hopes for their candidate, well-spoken lawyer Tyron Elliott. But Ray's Nunn connection provided him the mantle of Pentagon protector expected in the defense-oriented 3rd. Boosted by Nunn's active campaigning for him, Ray swept every county.

Ray was unopposed in his next two elections. And in 1990, he faced a Republican physician from Americus, Paul Broun Jr., who had never held elective office. Ray managed to top 60 percent.

Georgia 3

West Central — Columbus

The 3rd District's biggest VIP is former President Jimmy Carter, whose hometown of Plains is in Sumter County on the district's southern border. Voters here never deserted their favorite son. Even in 1980, when much of Georgia had soured on incumbent Carter, the 3rd gave him 60 percent of its vote. President Franklin Delano Roosevelt also found refuge in the 3rd, rejuvenating himself in the waters of Warm Springs before dying there in 1945.

The district, whose mainly rural and exurban expanse lies between the cities of Columbus and Warner Robins, remains loyal to its ascendant Democrats of the day, Sen. Sam Nunn and Rep. Ray. A solidly Democratic black population, over one-third of the total, bolsters that loyalty.

In 1988, George Bush carried the district's dominant counties, Muscogee (Columbus) and Houston (Warner Robins). Both of these counties have many residents who depend on nearby military installations for their economic well-being, and favor national GOP candidates.

Located on the Alabama border, Columbus (population 180,000) benefits from the Army's Fort Benning, the state's largest military base, which employs about 35,000 military and civilian staffers. Warner Robins (population 46,000), on the district's eastern border, is the site of Robins Air Force Base, a major air transport and Air Force supply center. The dominance of the military economy enabled Bush to carry Houston County with 64 percent of the vote. With more of a blue-collar Democratic base in Muscogee County, his total was a more modest but solid 55 percent.

Outside the cities are the peanut, peach and pecan farms characteristic of west-central Georgia. Though there are pockets of GOP strength, the rural region, with its substantial black population, went largely to the Democrats. In 1990, it and the urban Atlanta-based 5th were the only two districts in the state where unsuccessful GOP gubernatorial candidate Johnny Isakson did not win at least one county.

Population: 540,865. White 347,373 (64%), Black 185,763 (34%), Other 4,155 (1%). Spanish origin 8,810 (2%). 18 and over 376,128 (70%), 65 and over 53,146 (10%). Median age: 28.

Committees

Armed Services (15th of 33 Democrats)
Procurement & Military Nuclear Systems; Readiness

Small Business (13th of 27 Democrats)
Environment & Employment; Exports, Tax Policy & Special Problems

Elections

1990 General

Richard Ray (D)	72,961	(63%)
Paul Broun (R)	42,561	(37%)

1988 General

Richard Ray (D)	97,663	(100%)

Previous Winning Percentages: **1986** (100%) **1984** (81%) **1982** (71%)

District Vote For President

	1988		1984		1980		1976	
D	62,028	(42%)	68,149	(45%)	85,268	(60%)	92,186	(70%)
R	84,006	(57%)	83,658	(55%)	52,307	(37%)	39,699	(30%)
I					2,356	(2%)		

Campaign Finance

	Receipts	Receipts from PACs		Expend-itures
1990				
Ray (D)	$369,264	$155,950	(42%)	$378,774
Broun (R)	$70,271	$15,600	(22%)	$69,638
1988				
Ray (D)	$281,295	$131,117	(47%)	$256,751

Key Votes

1991

Authorize use of force against Iraq	Y
1990	
Support constitutional amendment on flag desecration	Y
Pass family and medical leave bill over Bush veto	N
Reduce SDI funding	Y
Allow abortions in overseas military facilities	N
Approve budget summit plan for spending and taxing	Y
Approve civil rights bill	Y
1989	
Halt production of B-2 stealth bomber at 13 planes	N
Oppose capital gains tax cut	N
Approve federal abortion funding in rape or incest cases	N
Approve pay raise and revision of ethics rules	Y
Pass Democratic minimum wage plan over Bush veto	N

Voting Studies

	Presidential Support		Party Unity		Conservative Coalition	
Year	**S**	**O**	**S**	**O**	**S**	**O**
1990	53	44	56	37	94	6
1989	69	28	48	48	95	2
1988	22	33	48	21	37	11
1987	32	35	42	27	51	7
1986	56	43	50	48	82	16
1985	56	43	54	44	98	2
1984	52	44	44	53	81	15
1983	66	33	37	62	91	8

Interest Group Ratings

Year	ADA	ACU	AFL-CIO	CCUS
1990	22	50	25	71
1989	15	65	9	100
1988	20	53	56	56
1987	28	63	23	73
1986	10	71	21	88
1985	15	71	25	82
1984	20	67	31	47
1983	20	91	24	74

4 Ben Jones (D)

Of Covington — Elected 1988

Born: Aug. 30, 1941, Tarboro, N.C.
Education: Attended U. of North Carolina, 1961-65.
Occupation: Actor.
Family: Wife, Vivian Walker; two children.
Religion: Baptist.
Political Career: Democratic nominee for U.S. House, 1986.
Capitol Office: 514 Cannon Bldg. 20515; 225-4272.

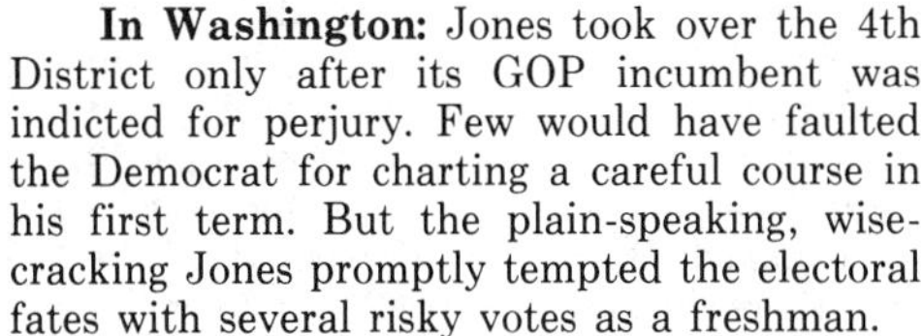

In Washington: Jones took over the 4th District only after its GOP incumbent was indicted for perjury. Few would have faulted the Democrat for charting a careful course in his first term. But the plain-speaking, wisecracking Jones promptly tempted the electoral fates with several risky votes as a freshman.

Most notable was Jones' vocal opposition to a constitutional amendment to ban flag desecration. Which is worse, Jones asked from the House floor, "the handful of demented malcontents who burn a flag and dishonor only themselves, or. . .to react to them by amending our Constitution, putting an asterisk on the Bill of Rights and changing the bedrock principles upon which our Nation was founded."

"Leave it alone, my colleagues," Jones concluded. "Leave it alone."

Jones also voted for the 1989 congressional pay raise package, controversial funding for the National Endowment for the Arts and, amid a competitive re-election campaign, for the budget agreement with tax increases.

After Atlanta Democratic Rep. John Lewis, Jones tends to have the most liberal record of the Georgia delegation. But he can also side with business interests; he advocated a capital gains tax cut and voted against mandatory parental leave legislation.

Jones arrived in Congress best-known for his portrayal of "Cooter," a hayseed auto mechanic, on "The Dukes of Hazzard" television series. He has tapped that persona for fundraisers, and his real-life folksy manner has helped make him popular with colleagues. His acting background may enliven his floor speeches, but Jones is still learning the legislative ropes. He offered modest initiatives in his first term, such as calling for a national charter for the National Association of Women Veterans. His district work included hearings to explain Medicare to senior citizens, and federal wetlands regulations to developers.

During the 102nd, Jones will continue to serve on the Public Works and Veterans' Affairs committees, and also as an at-large whip.

At Home: Jones won his first term by beating a scandal-plagued incumbent, prompting Republicans to label him a fluke. But two years later, Jones hung on against a credible and well-funded challenger, earning some breathing space in the politically divided 4th.

It took Jones two tries — first in 1986 and again in 1988 — to unseat GOP incumbent Pat Swindall. In 1986, despite being heavily outspent, Jones held Swindall to 53 percent by tarring him as a right-wing ideologue ready to cut the federal budget with a "chain-saw."

Though Jones spoke freely about his former alcohol abuse, his past only became a major campaign issue in 1988 when Swindall — whose alleged involvement in a money-laundering scheme led to an October 1988 indictment on federal perjury charges — tried to save his seat by attacking Jones. Jones himself conceded, "I have more bones in my closet than the Smithsonian Institution."

After a challenge from Swindall, Jones released records of his 1974 arrest on a simple-battery charge for shoving his second wife. Swindall also unearthed records of Jones' 1967 arrest in North Carolina for a trespassing incident involving his first wife. But Jones said those incidents only showed the damaging nature of alcoholism; he pointed to his successful fourth marriage as proof of his recovery.

Ultimately, voters were more troubled by Swindall's current problems than by Jones' past, electing Jones by a 20 percent margin.

Republicans insisted the result was merely an "anti-Swindall" mandate and vowed to recapture the seat in 1990. They rallied early around state Rep. John Linder, a dentist and businessman with a genteel demeanor and conservative views. Linder insisted that Jones' populist image was a front for liberal tendencies, citing Jones' opposition to the flag burning amendment. But Linder failed to rally the conservatives who had been so loyal to Swindall. And Jones was able to steal away the backing of some suburban Republicans on the issue of abortion rights, which he supports. Jones did well in the district's more urban areas.

Georgia 4

Atlanta Suburbs — De Kalb County

The removal of several black Atlanta precincts from the 4th in the redistricting of the early 1980s furthered the dominance of the district's affluent De Kalb County suburbs, and a growing GOP trend. Republican Pat Swindall unseated 4th District Democratic Rep. Elliott H. Levitas in 1984, while President Reagan took 66 percent of the district vote. However, in 1988 the scandal-plagued Swindall lost his seat to Democrat Jones in a landslide. George Bush kept the district in the GOP presidential column, but by a narrower margin than Reagan had four years earlier.

As Atlanta blossomed into the South's financial capital during the 1960s and 1970s, De Kalb County — with about two-thirds of the district's population — led the city's suburban growth. With over a half-million people, it is now Georgia's second most-populous county, though the boom has moderated somewhat as development expands farther out.

Affluence is prevalent in the 4th, with its well-manicured lawns in Dunwoody and Chamblee tended by corporate managers and young professionals. Many of these suburbanites came to booming Atlanta from other areas of the country — with Yankee accents, and without Southern Democratic loyalties.

However, Democrats have hardly become a negligible force in De Kalb. Democrats find their base in the central and southern parts of De Kalb. Decatur, the county seat, was a 19th-century commercial center until it lost out as a railroad center to Atlanta; it still has some industry, a sizable black population and a Democratic complexion. Emory University and the communities around it, many heavily Jewish or black, give local politics a liberal slant.

The two counties to the south continue to sprout subdivisions. Rockdale County has become solidly Republican: Bush won 74 percent of the vote there in 1988, and Jones held off Swindall by fewer than 50 votes. Newton County, Jones' home base, is more mixed. Bush took 65 percent of the vote there, but Jones carried 57 percent in his House race; Democrat Zell Miller carried the county in his successful 1990 gubernatorial bid. The 4th also has a slice of Fulton County, north of Atlanta. This section, mostly white-collar suburbia, contributes about 20 percent of the district vote.

Population: 542,368. White 463,338 (85%), Black 70,048 (13%), Other 6,131 (1%). Spanish origin 8,830 (2%). 18 and over 399,703 (74%), 65 and over 44,801 (8%). Median age: 30.

Committees

Public Works & Transportation (23rd of 36 Democrats)
Public Buildings & Grounds; Surface Transportation; Water Resources

Veterans' Affairs (13th of 21 Democrats)
Hospitals & Health Care; Housing & Memorial Affairs

Elections

1990 General		
Ben Jones (D)	96,526	(52%)
John Linder (R)	87,569	(48%)
1988 General		
Ben Jones (D)	148,394	(60%)
Pat Swindall (R)	97,745	(40%)

District Vote For President

	1988	1984	1980	1976
D	99,212 (41%)	77,481 (34%)	93,881 (51%)	116,288 (59%)
R	142,998 (59%)	148,469 (66%)	79,568 (43%)	79,894 (41%)
I			7,243 (4%)	

Campaign Finance

	Receipts	Receipts from PACs		Expend-itures
1990				
Jones (D)	$707,046	$416,333	(59%)	$711,015
Linder (R)	$696,858	$138,474	(20%)	$696,859
1988				
Jones (D)	$522,594	$265,606	(51%)	$516,737
Swindall (R)	$558,724	$193,042	(35%)	$696,301

Key Votes

1991	
Authorize use of force against Iraq	Y
1990	
Support constitutional amendment on flag desecration	N
Pass family and medical leave bill over Bush veto	N
Reduce SDI funding	Y
Allow abortions in overseas military facilities	Y
Approve budget summit plan for spending and taxing	N
Approve civil rights bill	Y
1989	
Halt production of B-2 stealth bomber at 13 planes	N
Oppose capital gains tax cut	N
Approve federal abortion funding in rape or incest cases	Y
Approve pay raise and revision of ethics rules	Y
Pass Democratic minimum wage plan over Bush veto	Y

Voting Studies

	Presidential Support		Party Unity		Conservative Coalition	
Year	S	O	S	O	S	O
1990	34	63	84	14	67	30
1989	38	59	86	13	59	41

Interest Group Ratings

Year	ADA	ACU	AFL-CIO	CCUS
1990	61	33	67	57
1989	70	14	67	60

5 John Lewis (D)

Of Atlanta — Elected 1986

Born: Feb. 21, 1940, Troy, Ala.
Education: American Baptist Theological Seminary, B.A. 1961; Fisk U., B.A. 1963.
Occupation: Civil rights activist.
Family: Wife, Lillian Miles; one child.
Religion: Baptist.
Political Career: Special-election candidate for U.S. House, 1977; Atlanta City Council, 1982-86.
Capitol Office: 329 Cannon Bldg. 20515; 225-3801.

In Washington: Those unfamiliar with Lewis' history are sometimes surprised by the deep respect many colleagues have for this junior legislator, who comes across as a perfectly unexceptional man when he speaks in committee or on the floor.

But many House members vividly recall the picture of a young Lewis being beaten by state troopers as he and other civil rights leaders crossed the Edmund Pettus bridge in Selma, Ala., in 1965. It was a seminal event in the civil rights movement, and Lewis' key role in the front lines of that struggle gives him a special status among his colleagues.

A glimpse of the esteem Lewis commands came in the 1987 debate on imposing sanctions on the apartheid government of South Africa. All seven other Georgia House Democrats made a surprise last-minute decision to vote for the sanctions as a tribute to Lewis, who had let them know that passage of the bill was important to him.

A small gesture, perhaps, but those seven Democrats strayed from the party line on several key votes in the 100th Congress, leaving Lewis the only Georgia House member voting to cut funds from the strategic defense initiative, to preserve plant-closing notification language, and to oppose the death penalty for drug-related murders.

During his first two terms, Lewis has stood out as a stalwart liberal in the traditionally conservative Georgia delegation, consistently earning 100 percent ADA ratings. His interests are often close to home, and he watches out for Atlanta's rapid transit system and airport. He has worked to designate as a National Historic Trail the route he marched from Selma to Montgomery, and has sought to clean up and limit construction of billboards on highways built with federal aid.

At Home: Lewis' 1986 victory in the 5th symbolized the rise of Southern blacks into the halls of political power. But to get to Congress, Lewis had to weather a bitter contest with a longtime ally, state Sen. Julian Bond.

The relationship between the civil rights leaders dated back to the early 1960s. Lewis, son of an Alabama sharecropper, was director of the Student Nonviolent Coordinating Committee (SNCC); Bond, from a middle-class Philadelphia background, was the group's spokesman.

Lewis spoke at the 1963 March on Washington. His fearlessness in the face of arrests and beatings was legendary. But when radical elements took over SNCC, Lewis moved on to head the Atlanta-based Voter Education Project.

Lewis lost his first political bid, a 1977 House primary, to Wyche Fowler Jr. In 1981, he won the first of two terms on the Atlanta City Council; he gained a following among blacks as well as whites in north Atlanta who appreciated his attention to neighborhood matters.

Bond, meanwhile, served 20 years in the Georgia Legislature, where he pushed through a redistricting plan that transformed the 5th District from nearly half white to almost two-thirds black. When Fowler announced his 1986 challenge to Republican Sen. Mack Mattingly, Bond became the favorite to succeed him in the 5th.

Bond did finish ahead in the primary. But Lewis, whose biracial appeal brought him a sizable white vote, forced Bond into a runoff. The campaign became nasty. Bond belittled Lewis' command of issues. But Lewis delivered sharper blows, implying that Bond had held a desk job in the civil rights revolution, and calling on Bond to join him in taking drug tests. Though he never accused Bond outright of using drugs, the implication was there for those who already saw Bond as a jet-setter.

Winning more than 80 percent of the vote in majority-white precincts, and cutting into Bond's margin among blacks, Lewis won nomination with 52 percent. The Democratic rift had little effect on Lewis in the general election; he prevailed by a 3-to-1 margin. By his first reelection, Lewis was a settled incumbent, running without primary opposition and winning with ease in the general election. That pattern was repeated in 1990.

Georgia 5

Atlanta

When the delegates poured into downtown Atlanta for the 1988 Democratic National Convention, they were greeted by symbols of prosperity: the steel-and-glass skyscrapers and towering hotels that make Atlanta the commercial center of the Southeast, and the symbolic capital of the New South.

However, in the shadows of those buildings is another Atlanta, a mostly black city struggling with typical urban social problems — unemployment, crime and drugs. While Atlanta's business boom spurred continued suburban sprawl through the early 1980s, the city's population dropped slightly, to just over 394,000.

But as host city for the 1996 Summer Olympics, Atlanta is on the cusp of another building boom; estimates of construction costs for Olympic venues have reached $500 million.

The 5th takes in most of Atlanta, as well as some suburban territory. Blacks are 65 percent of the population, and they make the district a Democratic bastion. Michael S. Dukakis took better than two-thirds of the vote here in 1988.

Lewis' 1986 victory to succeed Wyche Fowler Jr. returned the 5th to black representation. Fowler was preceded by Andrew Young, Atlanta's mayor from 1981-89.

Pockets of Republican strength can be found in the Fulton County suburbs to the north. Roswell used to be a cotton-milling center, but it is now a bedroom community booming with the white-collar, middle-level managers who are flocking to the Atlanta area. The 5th also contains the western half of Sandy Springs, another mostly white suburban community.

South of Atlanta, the district takes in East Point, a lower-middle-class community whose residents work in nearby factories and at Hartsfield Airport. The southwest corner of De Kalb County is also included in the 5th. It is overwhelmingly Democratic: In 1990, Lewis took 73 percent of the vote in the Fulton County part of the 5th, but won 93 percent in De Kalb.

Population: 550,070. White 188,204 (34%), Black 357,303 (65%), Other 2,608 (1%). Spanish origin 6,070 (1%). 18 and over 390,138 (71%), 65 and over 52,426 (10%). Median age: 28.

Committees

Interior & Insular Affairs (19th of 29 Democrats)
Insular & International Affairs; National Parks & Public Lands

Public Works & Transportation (16th of 36 Democrats)
Aviation; Public Buildings & Grounds; Surface Transportation

Select Aging (34th of 42 Democrats)
Human Services; Retirement, Income & Employment; Rural Elderly

Elections

1990 General		
John Lewis (D)	86,037	(76%)
J.W. Tibbs Jr. (R)	27,781	(24%)
1988 General		
John Lewis (D)	135,194	(78%)
J.W. Tibbs Jr. (R)	37,693	(22%)

Previous Winning Percentage: **1986** (75%)

District Vote For President

	1988	1984	1980	1976
D	113,308 (68%)	124,006 (67%)	111,457 (60%)	104,323 (68%)
R	52,118 (31%)	60,150 (33%)	65,506 (35%)	50,151 (32%)
I			6,768 (4%)	

Campaign Finance

	Receipts	Receipts from PACs	Expend-itures
1990			
Lewis (D)	$271,450	$175,510 (65%)	$108,118
Tibbs (R)	$1,992	0	$7,755
1988			
Lewis (D)	$193,584	$142,915 (74%)	$101,540
Tibbs (R)	$6,560	$1,000 (15%)	$6,047

Key Votes

1991	
Authorize use of force against Iraq	N
1990	
Support constitutional amendment on flag desecration	N
Pass family and medical leave bill over Bush veto	Y
Reduce SDI funding	Y
Allow abortions in overseas military facilities	Y
Approve budget summit plan for spending and taxing	N
Approve civil rights bill	Y
1989	
Halt production of B-2 stealth bomber at 13 planes	Y
Oppose capital gains tax cut	Y
Approve federal abortion funding in rape or incest cases	Y
Approve pay raise and revision of ethics rules	Y
Pass Democratic minimum wage plan over Bush veto	Y

Voting Studies

	Presidential Support		Party Unity		Conservative Coalition	
Year	**S**	**O**	**S**	**O**	**S**	**O**
1990	16	84	95	5	6	94
1989	28	72	98	2	0	100
1988	13	82	93	3	5	92
1987	13	85	93	4	12	88

Interest Group Ratings

Year	ADA	ACU	AFL-CIO	CCUS
1990	100	4	100	21
1989	100	4	100	40
1988	100	0	100	17
1987	96	0	100	20

6 Newt Gingrich (R)

Of Jonesboro — Elected 1978

Born: June 17, 1943, Harrisburg, Pa.
Education: Emory U., B.A. 1965; Tulane U., M.A. 1968, Ph.D. 1971.
Occupation: History professor.
Family: Wife, Marianne Ginther; two children.
Religion: Baptist.
Political Career: Republican nominee for U.S. House, 1974, 1976.
Capitol Office: 2438 Rayburn Bldg. 20515; 225-4501.

In Washington: If Gingrich were a professional athlete, he would be what is known as an "impact player," one whose presence in the game changes the style of play, disrupts the opposition and alters the outcome. From the time Gingrich arrived in the House it was clear he had such a role; his forceful, often fractious performance as Republican whip has simply carried it to a new level.

Throughout the Persian Gulf crisis, Gingrich goaded Democrats hesitant to support the use of military force. In the heady first days following the ouster of Iraqi troops from Kuwait, Gingrich crowed: "The last time they had a Democratic president they could not get eight helicopters across the desert" — an allusion to President Jimmy Carter's aborted effort to rescue U.S. hostages in Iran in 1980.

Gingrich's acerbic performance during the war and its aftermath served notice that his close call in the November 1990 election had not mellowed him.

The war helped Gingrich get back to scrapping with the Democrats after several months of being at odds with other power figures within the GOP. Late in the 101st Congress he had rallied conservative House Republicans against the budget-summit agreement that incorporated President Bush's capitulation on taxes. That earned him the enmity of Bush's chief of staff, John H. Sununu. Thereafter, Gingrich had criticized Bush's budget director, Richard G. Darman, for Darman's lack of enthusiasm about New Right social ideas (collectively called the "New Paradigm"). Gingrich had even suggested that Darman get with the program or resign.

While often a thorn in the sides of other Republicans, Gingrich has made his career as a scourge on Democrats. His 1988 complaint to the House ethics committee opened the inquiries that eventually toppled Speaker Jim Wright of Texas in 1989. It was Gingrich who also insisted the committee make a full disclosure of evidence gathered on Massachusetts Democrat Barney Frank's homosexuality.

So personal has Gingrich made his crusade against the liberal establishment that he could hardly have been surprised when his fire was returned. In 1989 he was accused of organizing various income streams that violated House rules, including a book deal some found comparable to the one that helped bring down Wright. But the ethics committee did not find enough merit in any of these allegations to justify any action.

A brainy and superarticulate former history professor, Gingrich popularized a more combative style for the House minority while still one of its backbenchers. Even as a freshman, he freely offered strategy advice to his party elders and drew scenarios for Republican dominance in crayon on a board in his office.

In the 1980s, Ronald Reagan became president, the Senate went Republican and a coalition of Republicans and Southern Democrats briefly controlled big votes on the floor of the House. But Gingrich remained at the outer edge of the guerrilla war. He co-founded the Conservative Opportunity Society in the House and inaugurated the late-afternoon floor speeches that addressed an empty chamber but reached millions of homes via cable television. He so provoked the Democrats as to induce Speaker Thomas P. O'Neill Jr. of Massachusetts to violate House rules in denouncing him. And, in his sixth term, he leaped into leadership as the House Republican whip by a margin of two votes.

Long dismissed by some as a personal fantast, Gingrich rode to institutional power on a wave of restlessness among House Republicans, frustrated by decades of minority status. And he was able to cash in on the new prominence he had gained as instigator of the historic ethics investigation of Wright.

Gingrich's promotion requires him to channel his boundless intellectual and political energy more carefully, now that he is a spokesman for the party and not just one of its gadflies.

"I've got to learn to make perfectly clear when I'm talking only about Newt Gingrich's view," he said in 1989.

Georgia 6

West Central — Atlanta Suburbs

When the decade began, Democrats hoped that the rural Democratic traditions of the 6th would reassert themselves, enabling them to topple Gingrich. Instead, demographic and political trends worked in the other direction. The booming growth of the suburbs to the south and west of Atlanta, along with growing tolerance for the GOP among rural conservatives, made the 6th a safe haven for Gingrich, and fertile ground for Republican presidential votes.

The biggest growth occurred in the suburbs abutting Atlanta to the south. Clayton County, the district's largest, grew by 21 percent between 1980 and 1990 to over 182,000 residents. The most explosive development was in Fayette County (population 62,000), which grew during that period by 115 percent.

The population boom was not limited to the close-in communities, though. Of the 11 counties entirely in the district, 10 had population growth rates in the early 1980s of over 10 percent. Only rural Polk County, in the district's northwest corner, lagged, with a modest increase of about 5 percent.

There is no real population center in the 6th. The growth has been divided up between such cities as Griffin, Carrollton, Forest Park, Newnan and College Park, which have populations ranging from 15,000 to 28,000.

These towns are in the shadow of Atlanta and within commuting range of the city. College Park is home to pilots, baggage handlers and others who work at Hartsfield International, the nation's second-busiest airport and the district's largest employer. The atmosphere changes to the southwest, although Republican habits do not. Newnan's wealth is tied less to Atlanta's recent growth than to the more distant past; spared during the Civil War, Newnan is known as "the City of Homes," for the stately antebellum mansions lining its streets.

The largest source of jobs in Griffin (Spalding County), located in the district's southeast corner, is the cotton mill industry. But the town's special claim is that it is the "pimento capital of the world," and pimento peppers are packed there.

The presidential vote throughout the more developed areas has become staunchly Republican. George Bush took 65 percent of the Clayton County vote, and won 78 percent in Fayette.

Though there has been some spillover growth in Atlanta's western exurbs, the landscape is still dominated by farms where cattle, pecans, peaches and corn are raised. Traditional Democratic tendencies remain fairly firm in some areas: Democrat Zell Miller carried all but Fayette County in his 1990 gubernatorial race, while House challenger David Worley took the four counties that border Alabama. However, the Republican vote for president is as sturdy as elsewhere in the district. Bush carried Douglas and Paulding counties with more than 70 percent of the vote.

Population: 548,959. White 462,791 (84%), Black 81,943 (15%), Other 2,752 (1%). Spanish origin 4,778 (1%). 18 and over 375,209 (68%), 65 and over 44,363 (8%). Median age: 29.

The lessons have come hard. He did show willingness to accept this yoke when he acceded to the pay-raise-and-ethics package of the 101st Congress, agreeing to foreswear its use as an issue in the 1990 campaign.

But he remains, at his core, a partisan activist who cares primarily about cutting a sharper profile for his party, and only secondarily about passing legislation and affecting policy in the interim.

The ultimate example of that came in the closing weeks of the 101st Congress, when Gingrich opposed the budget approved by Bush and by Gingrich's other putative boss: House Republican Leader Robert H. Michel of Illinois. Calling for aggressive tax cuts rather than compromise on the issue, Gingrich gave scores of House Republicans all the cover they needed to desert the president.

Some thought this highly visible defection had cost Gingrich support in his district when he nearly lost his seat the next month. But Gingrich took the opposite view. "I think had I voted for the tax increase I'd have been beaten," he said two months later.

Gingrich's 1989 move into the GOP leadership began within minutes of President Bush's announcement that he was nominating incumbent whip Dick Cheney of Wyoming to be secretary of Defense. At that moment, Gingrich had never held a leadership post and was regarded as a long-shot candidate.

His rival for the job, Edward Madigan of Illinois, had the consensus-building, bill-crafting skills traditionally associated with the whip's job. But Gingrich had what many House Republicans were looking for: something different.

Gingrich's victory was a narrow one — a change of two votes would have reversed the outcome — but it was read as a clear mandate for change.

His victory tapped into a growing feeling among Republicans that the Democratic majority was too heavy-handed in its use of power and that incumbent GOP leaders were too compliant. That disaffection ran so deep that some Republican moderates and even a few of the party's "Old Bulls" supported Gingrich.

Gingrich owes his election as much to Wright as to anyone. Wright, in his drive to establish a reputation as a strong Speaker, galvanized all elements of the Republican Conference to a more confrontational style.

And Gingrich's ethics crusade against Wright, once it resulted in an investigation of unprecedented breadth, gave him legitimacy he would not otherwise have had.

But Gingrich's crusade began as a lonely one. It was part of a broader effort to highlight the improprieties of powerful Democrats — such as former Banking Committee Chairman Fernand J. St Germain of Rhode Island — who had gotten off lightly at the hands of the ethics committee.

When he first called for an ethics investigation into published allegations of impropriety by Wright in 1987, Gingrich was easily dismissed by Democrats. But pressure built in May 1988, when his call was joined by the government-watchdog group Common Cause.

Once the ethics committee began its preliminary inquiry, the matter took on a life of its own and Gingrich kept a comparatively low profile. No jabs from this firebrand could be more devastating than the considered judgment of the bipartisan ethics committee.

Even as he assumed the mantle of leadership, Gingrich still had the freewheeling, undomesticated style of a newcomer. Despite some efforts to smooth his roughest edges, Gingrich has never shed his reputation as a bomb thrower.

Gingrich earned a permanent place in the conservative pantheon in 1984, when he took on the apotheosis of liberalism: then-Speaker O'Neill.

Addressing a nearly empty chamber one night in May, Gingrich complained about a letter that 10 House Democrats had written to Nicaraguan leader Daniel Ortega, addressing him as "Dear Commandante" and calling for a settlement between political factions in that country. Gingrich said the letter was undermining U.S. foreign policy and possibly was illegal because it constituted negotiation by private citizens with a foreign power.

A few days later, O'Neill took the floor to charge that Gingrich had "challenged the Americanism of several Democratic members" at a time when they were not present to respond. O'Neill called that "the lowest thing that I have ever seen in my 32 years in Congress."

Republican Whip Trent Lott of Mississippi moved that the Speaker's words be "taken down" — stricken from the record as inappropriate under House rules. Presiding officer Joe Moakley, a Massachusetts Democrat and close friend of O'Neill, had no choice but to accept Lott's motion — the first such embarrassment to a House Speaker since 1797.

Gingrich's record of legislative accomplishment is as sparse as a backbencher's — as befits someone who cares more about big ideas and grand strategies than about passing bills.

But in his campaign as whip, Gingrich said his ability to work with Democrats was abundantly in evidence in his work on two of the most bipartisan committees in Congress: Public Works and House Administration.

Before becoming whip, Gingrich served briefly as ranking Republican on House Administration, which oversees such housekeeping matters as committee staff budgets and office expense allowances. In that brief stint, Gingrich claimed a great triumph when he won for Republicans a larger share of committee staff jobs.

On Public Works, Gingrich could play the legislative game on the Aviation Subcommittee, where he became ranking minority member in 1987. That was a particularly useful spot for Gingrich, because Atlanta's huge Hartsfield International Airport is in his district.

When he became whip, Gingrich gave up both his ranking Republican committee posts and took a leave from the Public Works Committee.

At Home: After fighting hard to capture the 6th from Democratic hands in 1978, Gingrich appeared to have put his personal stamp on it. But complacence and a determined challenger dragged Gingrich to within 974 votes of a loss in 1990.

The man who almost retired Gingrich was Democrat David Worley, an aggressive young lawyer. Worley made his first run at Gingrich in 1988.

A party activist since his teens and a former aide to 4th District Democratic Rep. Elliott H. Levitas, Worley announced his plans to run in mid-1987. He soon drew the attention of national Democrats hoping to inflict some political wounds on one of their chief antagonists. For the next year and a half, Worley found something to criticize in nearly all of Gingrich's actions in Congress.

The main thrust of his campaign was a charge that Gingrich's proposed revamp of the nation's retirement system was actually a plot to destroy Social Security. He accused Gingrich of hypocrisy on ethics (pointing to, among other things, his efforts to have a political associate appointed a federal judge) and berated him for sympathizing with his scandal-plagued Georgia GOP colleague, Pat Swindall.

However, Gingrich proved again that he could give as good as he got. In countering Worley's depiction of his Social Security plan, Gingrich told campaign audiences, "This is a man so despicable and so desperate to be a congressman that he is deliberately scaring 80- and 90-year-old people with what he knows is a lie." He portrayed Worley, a Harvard-educated district native, as a Boston liberal, and frequently portrayed him as a stooge of the ethically tarnished Speaker Wright.

Gingrich ended up carrying all but one of the district's 12 counties; he took populous Clayton County, home base to both candidates, with 58 percent of the vote. Worley won only in the slice of Fulton County (Atlanta) that is in the 6th District.

Worley's 1988 showing, and his abrasive manner, left many Democrats unenthusiastic about 1990 — but not the candidate himself. Worley promptly announced he would try again and began an energetic campaign against Gingrich.

Worley's central argument in the rematch was that Gingrich had become enamored with national politics at the expense of district concerns. Thousands of Eastern Airlines workers live in the 6th, and Worley slammed the incumbent for opposing federal mediation for the Eastern strike and stepping down from the Aviation Subcommittee during the airline's troubles.

Worley also faulted Gingrich for supporting the 1989 congressional pay raise plan, although that stance appeared to cost him financial support from the Democratic Congressional Campaign Committee, due to a bipartisan agreement between party officials not to use the pay raise as a campaign issue.

That helped give Gingrich a vast fundraising edge. But budget battles kept Gingrich in Washington most of the fall, bolstering Worley's portrait of the incumbent as out of touch. And despite Gingrich's vocal opposition to the bipartisan, White House-sanctioned budget plan, the incumbent did not escape public disgust over the budget proceedings and taxes. Gingrich eked out a win, but acknowledged afterward he should have spent more time in the district.

Like many successful Republican politicians in the South, the Pennsylvania-born Gingrich is not a native. He spent his childhood in various military bases around the world before his family moved to Fort Benning, Ga. After receiving a graduate degree in European history, he taught history and geography at West Georgia College in Carrollton before launching his political career.

Gingrich set out after the 6th District seat with his trademark intensity. Though Gingrich's 1974 campaign was his first political candidacy, he used professional polling and a hired staff, commodities rarely seen before in rural Georgia congressional contests. He surprised veteran Democratic Rep. John J. Flynt Jr., coming within 2,800 votes of victory. Two years later, Gingrich had to contend with a beefed-up Flynt campaign and Georgian Jimmy Carter heading the Democratic ticket. He lost again, but still drew more than 48 percent of the vote.

Flynt retired in 1978, leaving Gingrich as the best-known contender. In previous campaigns, Gingrich had been considered relatively liberal for a Georgia Republican, drawing much of his support from environmentalists. But in 1978 he relied on the tax-cut issue and stressed his opposition to U.S. transfer of the Panama Canal. He swept the northern portion of the district, defeating wealthy Democratic state Sen. Virginia Shapard by 7,600 votes.

After winning easily in 1980, Gingrich faced some difficulty in 1982 against Jim Wood, a Forest Park newspaper publisher and Democratic state representative who urged voters to pin the blame for harsh economic conditions on the GOP in general — and Gingrich in particular.

But the race was overshadowed by other contests around the state, and Wood had trouble getting his message out; Gingrich's ability to outspend him by better than 2-to-1 made the difference.

Gingrich had little trouble with the next two general election campaigns, taking 60 percent or better each time. His 1988 defeat of Worley had seemed to be another Democratic flub, but that race laid the groundwork for Worley's near-upset two years later.

Committees

Minority Whip

House Administration (3rd of 9 Republicans)
Accounts; Procurement & Printing

Joint Printing

Elections

1990 General

Newt Gingrich (R)	78,768	(50%)
David Worley (D)	77,794	(50%)

1988 General

Newt Gingrich (R)	110,169	(59%)
David Worley (D)	76,824	(41%)

Previous Winning Percentages: **1986** (60%) **1984** (69%)
1982 (55%) **1980** (59%) **1978** (54%)

District Vote For President

	1988	1984	1980	1976
D	59,118 (33%)	53,929 (31%)	75,853 (52%)	87,232 (68%)
R	121,128 (67%)	117,764 (69%)	65,029 (45%)	41,333 (32%)
I			3,021 (2%)	

Campaign Finance

	Receipts	Receipts from PACs		Expend-itures
1990				
Gingrich (R)	$1,538,827	$433,421	(28%)	$1,538,945
Worley (D)	$342,310	$163,190	(48%)	$333,873
1988				
Gingrich (R)	$851,786	$262,976	(31%)	$838,708
Worley (D)	$354,847	$205,252	(58%)	$358,354

Key Votes

1991	
Authorize use of force against Iraq	Y
1990	
Support constitutional amendment on flag desecration	Y
Pass family and medical leave bill over Bush veto	N
Reduce SDI funding	N
Allow abortions in overseas military facilities	N
Approve budget summit plan for spending and taxing	N
Approve civil rights bill	N
1989	
Halt production of B-2 stealth bomber at 13 planes	N
Oppose capital gains tax cut	N
Approve federal abortion funding in rape or incest cases	N
Approve pay raise and revision of ethics rules	Y
Pass Democratic minimum wage plan over Bush veto	N

Voting Studies

	Presidential Support		Party Unity		Conservative Coalition	
Year	**S**	**O**	**S**	**O**	**S**	**O**
1990	66	29	83	8	94	4
1989	87	9	71	24	88	7
1988	62	32	80	6	92	3
1987	67	28	87	4	93	5
1986	72	23	85	8	80	14
1985	68	30	84	7	89	9
1984	60	29	83	9	86	8
1983	72	24	83	10	87	8
1982	70	26	78	18	75	12
1981	64	24	75	17	76	15

Interest Group Ratings

Year	ADA	ACU	AFL-CIO	CCUS
1990	17	86	25	92
1989	0	88	8	100
1988	5	100	15	100
1987	4	96	13	93
1986	0	81	14	94
1985	10	81	12	95
1984	5	78	8	60
1983	10	91	6	79
1982	5	86	10	75
1981	10	92	0	100

7 George "Buddy" Darden (D)

Of Marietta — Elected 1983

Born: Nov. 22, 1943, Hancock County, Ga.
Education: U. of Georgia, B.A. 1965, J.D. 1967.
Occupation: Lawyer.
Family: Wife, Lillian Budd; two children.
Religion: Methodist.
Political Career: Cobb County district attorney, 1973-77; Ga. House, 1981-83.
Capitol Office: 228 Cannon Bldg. 20515; 225-2931.

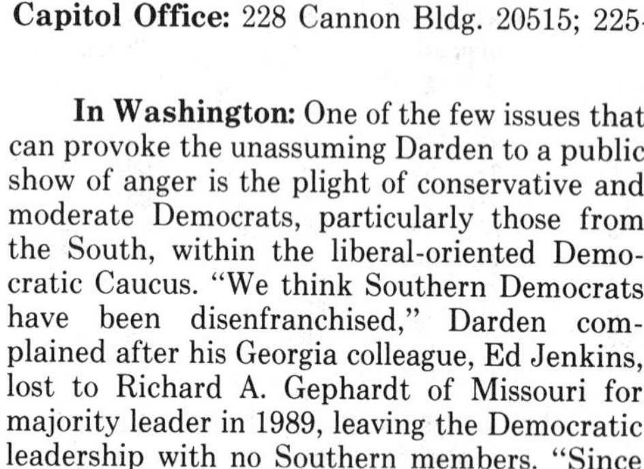

In Washington: One of the few issues that can provoke the unassuming Darden to a public show of anger is the plight of conservative and moderate Democrats, particularly those from the South, within the liberal-oriented Democratic Caucus. "We think Southern Democrats have been disenfranchised," Darden complained after his Georgia colleague, Ed Jenkins, lost to Richard A. Gephardt of Missouri for majority leader in 1989, leaving the Democratic leadership with no Southern members. "Since I've been here, the leadership has been more of a detriment to my electability than an asset."

Yet Darden has overcome his qualms about that leadership and has, in his quiet manner, worked himself into its outer circle: He serves as a Democratic at-large whip. At the start of the 102nd Congress, Darden also was given a seat on the House ethics committee, a position that typically goes to low-key and reliable party insiders.

Earlier, Darden had established himself on the Armed Services Committee as a key ally to its chairman, Democrat Les Aspin of Wisconsin. Darden has provided some important committee votes for Aspin, who has often disturbed more liberal Democrats by supporting weapons systems and other defense policies favored by the Republican administrations.

Darden's influence on Armed Services was boosted by the fortuitous choice he made during a 1987 challenge to Aspin's chairmanship. Darden was tugged to support the effort by fellow Southern Democrat Marvin Leath of Texas to unseat Aspin. But Darden cast his lot with Aspin and shared in the benefits of his victory: He strengthened his reputation for initiative and political savvy, while becoming one of the advisers who are part of what Darden refers to as "Aspin's team." Along with his subcommittee assignments, Darden is a member of the Defense Policy Panel, a task force that works on overall defense strategy issues.

During his first few years in the House, Darden was regarded as a cautious member who seemed wary of making too sharp a break from the right-wing record of his predecessor, Democrat Larry McDonald (who was killed in 1983 when the Korean Air Lines jet on which he was a passenger was shot down over the Soviet Union). Darden kept a low profile, establishing himself on Armed Services as a pro-defense Democrat and an advocate for programs directed at the Lockheed aircraft plant in the 7th District.

In fact, Darden made his first big mark in the House with his determined, though unsuccessful, effort to save a Lockheed defense project from extinction. Darden's experience in the C-5B debate during the 100th Congress can serve as solace to other House members who fear negative political consequences if the ongoing effort to trim the federal budget leads to cutbacks in their districts' defense projects.

The Defense Department, as part of its fiscal 1988 authorization request, had committed to replacing the hulking C-5B military cargo plane built at the Lockheed plant in Marietta with McDonnell Douglas' C-17, a smaller, more versatile plane to be built in California. After losing in committee, Darden made a last-ditch effort in May 1987 to convince the House that continued production of the C-5B would be more efficient than introducing a new plane.

With the Pentagon pushing hard in the other direction, Darden's amendment to scrap C-17 funding went down, 92-321. But he received praise from other House members for making a reasoned case for the C-5B, while earning the gratitude of his constituents for fighting, albeit fruitlessly, for a project that was a big local job-producer.

"They have no unrealistic expectations that when the president of the United States, the secretary of defense and the entire military-industrial complex are against [a project], that one relatively junior congressman will be able to reverse that," Darden later said. The downfall of the C-5B certainly did not hurt Darden at the polls: He won in 1988 with 65 percent of the

Georgia 7

Northwest — Rome; Marietta

Though the 7th runs 100 miles through seven counties — from the suburbs of Atlanta to those of Chattanooga, Tenn. — it is bottom-heavy. Cobb County, which borders Atlanta on the northwest, accounts for two-thirds of the district vote.

In recent statewide elections, Cobb has voted Republican. George Bush took 73 percent in 1988; it was the only county in the state to give unsuccessful GOP gubernatorial nominee Johnny Isakson more than 60 percent of its vote in 1990.

Though well within the Atlanta orbit, Marietta (population 44,100) provides Cobb County with its own population center. Marietta earned praise from *The Wall Street Journal* in 1989 as the nation's small business development capital. Darden's home city provides as much of a Democratic coloration as there is in Cobb.

The rest of the county, a collection of middle-income Atlanta suburbs, is largely white-collar. But it also has a military presence, with Dobbins Air Force Base and a large Lockheed aircraft plant, both in Marietta. The Lockheed facility, which sacked several thousand workers in the late 1980s, announced in May 1990 that two major aircraft production projects would be moved from California to Georgia.

To the north lie three rural counties — Bartow, Floyd and Chattooga — which are dotted with small textile-mill towns. There is more of a Democratic presence here; Democratic Rep. Wyche Fowler Jr. carried all three counties in his 1986 Senate election, though Bush took them with over 60 percent in 1988. Rome, a mill town in Floyd County, was once the district's largest city. Though eclipsed now by Marietta, it now serves as a regional health care center.

The northwestern corner of the district holds three counties that lie within Chattanooga's orbit. GOP tendencies, similar to those in the mountain Republican areas across the Tennessee border, are evident. Bush received 72 percent of the vote in Catoosa County in 1988.

Population: 545,913. White 509,303 (93%), Black 32,641 (6%), Other 2,773 (1%). Spanish origin 4,362 (1%). 18 and over 385,552 (71%), 65 and over 42,933 (8%). Median age: 30.

vote, even as George Bush was carrying the conservative-leaning district for president with 70 percent.

Darden has maintained his mainly pro-Pentagon demeanor. In January 1991, he voted for the resolution authorizing President Bush to use force to end Iraq's occupation of Kuwait. During the 101st Congress, Darden voted against floor amendments to slash funding for the strategic defense initiative and to sharply limit production of the B-2 stealth bomber.

He also expressed satisfaction with the fact that Dick Cheney, a former Republican House colleague from Wyoming, would be the one handling the scalpel during a period of defense budget cutbacks. "That doesn't make it more palatable, but at least we know that Cheney, having been a member, is sensitive to our concerns," Darden said.

However, Darden has on occasion spoken out against some of Cheney's priorities. He criticized the Defense Department in 1990 for going ahead with plans for a new NATO airbase in Italy while closing numerous military bases in the United States. Darden argued that with the pending massive cut in U.S. troop commitment to Europe, the Italy base would be "an absolute and total waste of money."

Darden is also on the House Interior Committee and is a member of its National Parks and Public Lands Subcommittee. During the 101st Congress, he was engaged in a pair of controversial issues involving land use in the western part of the United States.

One Darden proposal was aimed at ending the sweetheart arrangement, in existence since the 19th century, under which ranchers pay very low fees to graze their cattle on public rangelands. His bill to require ranchers to pay fair market value for grazing rights failed in the 101st Congress but was reintroduced in the 102nd.

Darden also made his own bid to settle a long-running dispute over Nevada wilderness legislation. His bill would have designated 1.4 million acres in 19 areas of Nevada for wilderness protection. A Senate bill, which covers 733,000 acres in 14 areas, was signed into law in 1989.

Darden also uses his position to focus on issues much closer to home. He is working to draw attention to the need to develop a water allocation strategy for the booming metropolitan Atlanta area, which includes much of his district.

Prior to his appointment to the Committee on Standards of Official Conduct, Darden did not cut an image as an ethical crusader (the cautious leadership almost never appoints members with that inclination to the ethics panel). However, he did indicate in 1990 that he was unwilling to allow violators of House rules to walk away with a slap on the wrist.

Darden expressed concern that Democratic Rep. Barney Frank of Massachusetts — who had admitted to minor infractions relating to his past relationship with a male prostitute — might get away too lightly; some of Frank's allies on the ethics committee had stated a preference for a letter of rebuke, the mildest form of punishment available. Frank's actions had "held the House up to a certain amount of public embarrassment," Darden said. "There's no other way to look at it." The committee eventually recommended a resolution of reprimand against Frank, a position supported by most House members, including Darden.

At Home: Darden's 1983 victory over McDonald's widow, Kathryn, was the first congressional victory in a decade for the 7th's mainstream Democrats. Larry McDonald, whose outspoken allegiance to the New Right made him a Democrat in name only, had his own bipartisan conservative network.

Elected in 1972 as Cobb County district attorney after five years as an assistant D.A., Darden developed a reputation as a law-and-order prosecutor. But his re-election effort in 1976 failed because he was dogged by charges he had bungled a 1971 murder investigation.

Darden went into private law practice. But in 1980, when one of Cobb County's seats in the state House opened up, he got the support of local Democratic officials and won easily.

After McDonald's death, Darden entered the nonpartisan special election. Calling himself a "responsible conservative," he promised to fight "big spenders in Congress." Though Darden earned a runoff position, he trailed Kathryn McDonald in first-round voting. However, McDonald's roughshod tactics — including an attempt to link Darden to gay rights through his ties to organized labor — alienated voters. Darden swept past her to win with 59 percent.

Again in 1984, Darden defended himself against charges of liberalism, this time from conservative airline pilot William Bronson. In the face of President Reagan's 1984 landslide, Darden won re-election with 55 percent of the vote. He has won comfortably in the three elections since.

Committees

Armed Services (19th of 33 Democrats)
Investigations; Research & Development

Interior & Insular Affairs (14th of 29 Democrats)
Energy & the Environment; Insular & International Affairs; National Parks & Public Lands

Standards of Official Conduct (4th of 7 Democrats)

Elections

1990 General		
George "Buddy" Darden (D)	95,817	(60%)
Al Beverly (R)	63,588	(40%)
1988 General		
George "Buddy" Darden (D)	135,056	(65%)
Robert Lamutt (R)	73,425	(35%)

Previous Winning Percentages: **1986** (66%) **1984** (55%) **1983** * (59%)

* *Special runoff election.*

District Vote For President

	1988	1984	1980	1976
D	64,396 (29%)	53,882 (27%)	78,101 (47%)	85,939 (61%)
R	155,367 (70%)	144,315 (73%)	81,442 (49%)	55,024 (39%)
I			4,177 (3%)	

Campaign Finance

	Receipts	Receipts from PACs	Expend-itures
1990			
Darden (D)	$463,055	$238,006 (51%)	$480,886
Beverly (R)	$19,028	0	$18,692
1988			
Darden (D)	$448,399	$241,375 (54%)	$382,281
Lamutt (R)	$60,926	0	$61,002

Key Votes

1991	
Authorize use of force against Iraq	Y
1990	
Support constitutional amendment on flag desecration	Y
Pass family and medical leave bill over Bush veto	N
Reduce SDI funding	N
Allow abortions in overseas military facilities	Y
Approve budget summit plan for spending and taxing	Y
Approve civil rights bill	N
1989	
Halt production of B-2 stealth bomber at 13 planes	N
Oppose capital gains tax cut	N
Approve federal abortion funding in rape or incest cases	N
Approve pay raise and revision of ethics rules	Y
Pass Democratic minimum wage plan over Bush veto	Y

Voting Studies

	Presidential Support		Party Unity		Conservative Coalition	
Year	**S**	**O**	**S**	**O**	**S**	**O**
1990	43	57	75	24	87	13
1989	56	42	72	28	90	7
1988	41	58	75	25	92	5
1987	43	57	68	30	91	9
1986	49	48	60	37	80	8
1985	51	46	67	31	87	13
1984	48	51	58	39	86	12
1983	40 †	60 †	48 †	48 †	100 †	0 †

† *Not eligible for all recorded votes.*

Interest Group Ratings

Year	ADA	ACU	AFL-CIO	CCUS
1990	28	58	50	57
1989	35	43	50	90
1988	45	50	64	64
1987	48	39	56	53
1986	10	79	31	82
1985	15	71	44	64
1984	30	54	38	44
1983	-	50	50	-

8 J. Roy Rowland (D)

Of Dublin — Elected 1982

Born: Feb. 3, 1926, Wrightsville, Ga.
Education: Attended Emory U. at Oxford, 1943; South Georgia College, 1946-47; U. of Georgia, 1947-48; Medical College of Georgia, M.D. 1952.
Military Service: Army, 1944-46.
Occupation: Physician.
Family: Wife, Luella Price; three children.
Religion: Methodist.
Political Career: Ga. House, 1977-83.
Capitol Office: 423 Cannon Bldg. 20515; 225-6531.

In Washington: Rowland was initially pegged as a kindly Georgia physician who would be content with a low-key role in the House, but he has emerged as an important Southern ally for the Democratic leadership. His work on the AIDS issue and on Nicaraguan contra funding helped win him a place in the hearts of the party hierarchy and a position in the 101st Congress on one of the most sought-after committees, Energy and Commerce.

Rowland predictably has directed most of his energy toward the health issues under Energy and Commerce's jurisdiction. But Rowland has also played a significant role in some non-health matters, including the laborious redrafting of the Clean Air Act.

Rowland's manner does not mark him as an ambitious politician. He has always approached politics on Capitol Hill with the same soft voice and courteous manner that won him the nickname of "Marcus Welby, M. D." in the Georgia Legislature. Even when addressing politically charged issues such as drug addiction or infant mortality, he speaks in matter-of-fact, almost clinical language.

But Rowland put himself in the thick of two difficult issues in the 100th Congress, serving on leadership task forces dealing with controversial AIDS legislation and with contra aid. On both, his contribution proved valuable in terms both of substance and of symbolism. As a Southern conservative, Rowland is just the kind of Democrat the leadership needs to enhance its credibility across the political spectrum on sensitive issues. And on AIDS in particular, Rowland — one of only two physicians in the House — brings specific knowledge and even more authority.

Before he joined Energy and Commerce, Rowland used his position on the Veterans' Affairs Committee as a route to enter the AIDS debate. There in the 100th Congress, he introduced legislation calling for the creation of a national AIDS advisory commission, to succeed a much-maligned presidential panel.

Although some critics argued that a second commission was not needed, supporters said that, unlike the presidential panel, the new advisory commission would be stocked with experts on the issue. The bill was approved by Veterans' Affairs unanimously, cleared the House 355-68, and later became law.

Rowland was among those in the House who felt the Reagan administration had not done enough to address the deadly disease. The administration's statements that much of the effort should be left to the states were "another indication that efforts to develop an effective national policy are in disarray," Rowland said. "The AIDS virus does not stop at state boundary lines. It is a national problem and we need a national strategy."

At the end of 1988, Congress moved closer to mapping that strategy, clearing legislation authorizing $650 million for education, anonymous testing, and home and community-based health care.

During the 101st Congress, Rowland continued to speak out on AIDS issues from his new berth on the Health subcommittee at Energy and Commerce. When some international scientists pledged to boycott an AIDS conference in San Francisco because of U.S. regulations forbidding entry to foreigners infected with the virus, Rowland introduced legislation to repeal the congressional mandate for the ban. His proposal passed as part of another bill, and the Bush administration subsequently lifted the restriction.

During debate on an AIDS bill in 1990, Rowland fended off a proposed amendment from California Republican William E. Dannemeyer requiring that the names and addresses of those who test positive for the HIV virus be reported to state health officials. Rowland won support for a substitute amendment that left the issue in the hands of the states.

On another medical issue, Rowland won passage in the 101st Congress for his bill to streamline claim processing for Medicare.

Georgia 8

South Central — Macon; Waycross

The oddly-shaped 8th twists nearly 300 miles from the black-majority counties just south of Athens to the Okefenokee Swamp on the Florida border. Covering 30 counties, it is one of the state's poorest areas; blacks are more than one-third of the population.

Most of this is rural territory, given over to tobacco and corn in the south, dairy farming and cotton farther north. The one large city is Macon, which together with surrounding Bibb County casts about one-third of the district's vote.

An old textile and railroad town, Macon has long been a trading and processing center for the agricultural lands of middle Georgia that surround it. Though Atlanta is little more than an hour up Interstate 75, the boom in the state capital region has not had a great effect on Macon, whose population dipped almost nine percent to 107,000 during the 1980s. Macon has undertaken an active redevelopment effort, although a strong preservationist spirit prevails as well; the city has renovated small houses dating from before the Civil War and turned them into low-cost housing.

Outside Macon, the 8th is largely rural, a land of antebellum homes, small country towns and open stretches of crop land. Washington, Wilkinson and Twiggs counties sit with Macon on Georgia's Fall Line between the red foothills of the Piedmont Plateau and the flat coastal plain; they are home to a large kaolin mining industry, which provides the white clay for use in white paint, china and stationery. Dublin and Milledgeville are textile towns.

Democratic traditions are sturdier in the 8th than in most rural districts in Georgia; Democratic presidential candidates remain competitive here. President Bush took 25 of the district's counties in 1988, but carried 60 percent of the vote or better in only five. Dukakis carried a bloc of three heavily black counties in the northeast section of the 8th, taking Hancock County with 75 percent, by far his best showing in the state. In the 1990 gubernatorial contest, only one county in the district (Glascock) sided with GOP candidate Johnny Isakson.

Population: 541,723. White 348,627 (64%), Black 191,182 (35%). Spanish origin 4,850 (1%). 18 and over 372,727 (69%), 65 and over 62,836 (12%). Median age: 29.

Rowland's 1986 vote to give military aid to the Nicaraguan contras was no surprise to most Democrats, who had come to expect that stand from their Georgia colleagues. But in 1988, Rowland stood apart from all but one of his state's House delegation — John Lewis, of Atlanta — and voted against President Reagan's request for $36 million in military and non-military aid. Later, Rowland helped fashion a non-military aid package that became law, altering his image in the eyes of more liberal members.

In late 1986, Rowland received scant backing when he first tried to get a seat on Energy and Commerce. But thanks to his subsequent work on AIDS and the contras, he was soon seen as a cinch to make the panel on his next try; two committee slots were open heading into the 101st Congress, and he got one.

Rowland arrived on the committee just in time for the complex negotiations over clean air legislation, which had been stalled for years.

Although the bill was at last moving, Dingell and Health and Environment subcommittee Chairman Henry A. Waxman had deadlocked over how much automakers should be required to do to limit auto emissions. Rowland worked behind the scenes to help fashion a compromise on that key provision, enabling the overall bill to move ahead. Chairman John D. Dingell named him to the conference committee on the bill, which passed at the close of the 101st Congress.

One of Rowland's more offbeat causes is his advocacy of "wayports," airports that would be built in remote areas to handle freight and transfer traffic and relieve overcrowded urban airports.

Mostly, however, Rowland's legislative interests flow out of his medical career. Rowland takes a special interest in research to reduce infant-mortality rates. A member of the Select Committee on Children, Youth and Families, Rowland has served on the National Commission to Prevent Infant Mortality and on a Congressional Sunbelt Council task force on that subject.

Rowland had been in the House less than a month in 1983 when he introduced legislation to make use of the drug methaqualone (Quaalude) illegal. It had been available as a prescription medicine for insomnia, but Rowland argued that it was being abused. A version of the bill became law in 1984.

Also during his first term, Rowland took the floor to argue for health benefits for the unemployed. He joined with Arkansas Republican John Paul Hammerschmidt to propose legislation compensating veterans exposed to ionizing radiation during atomic-bomb tests; the measure was included in the Agent Orange bill passed by the House early in 1984.

When the House took up a bill allowing doctors to use heroin to relieve pain in terminally ill cancer patients, Rowland said there were medically feasible alternatives. "We do not need to legitimize a drug that we know has been causing a great deal of problems in this country," he said. Coming from a medical man, Rowland's remarks helped defeat the bill.

At Home: Rowland grew up with politics as the common coin of dinner table conversations — his father was a district attorney and superior court judge, his grandfather and uncle were members of the state Legislature.

But Rowland himself opted for medicine. It was not until 1976, the year he turned 50, that he decided to run for office. He challenged his local Democratic state representative, with a coalition drawn largely from outside the area's political establishment, and won.

Six years later, he scored a similar victory for Congress. Democratic Rep. Billy Lee Evans had drawn embarrassing publicity when the Federal Election Commission fined his campaign for accepting illegal corporate contributions and illegal loans in 1980. The issue did its damage without much help from Rowland, who cited Evans' problems only indirectly; his TV ads urged viewers to "vote for an honest man."

Rowland's reluctance to hit hard served him well. Evans became more and more acerbic as the campaign wore on, and this only succeeded in alienating voters. Evans accused his opponent of performing abortions. Rowland acknowledged that he had and said he had done two such operations to save the women's lives.

While Rowland was taking the high road, another challenger, lawyer Edd Wheeler, was attacking Evans directly. He attracted less than 10 percent of the primary vote, but he softened Evans up for Rowland. Still, Wheeler's presence deprived Rowland of an immediate victory in the primary and forced a runoff.

Evans went after the black vote intensively during the runoff campaign. He did well in many black precincts, but it was not enough. Rowland increased his margin of victory the second time, carrying 20 of 30 counties, up from 13 in the primary. He has faced GOP opposition only twice, in 1986 and 1990, and won handily both times.

Committees

Energy & Commerce (20th of 27 Democrats)
Commerce, Consumer Protection & Competitiveness; Health & the Environment; Oversight & Investigations

Select Children, Youth & Families (9th of 22 Democrats)

Veterans' Affairs (7th of 21 Democrats)
Compensation, Pension & Insurance; Hospitals & Health Care

Elections

1990 General

J. Roy Rowland (D)	81,344	(69%)
Robert F. Cunningham (R)	36,980	(31%)

1988 General

J. Roy Rowland (D)	102,696	(100%)

Previous Winning Percentages: **1986** (86%) **1984** (100%) **1982** (100%)

District Vote For President

	1988	1984	1980	1976
D	73,518 (46%)	81,998 (48%)	107,718 (65%)	117,623 (73%)
R	85,540 (54%)	89,777 (52%)	55,844 (34%)	44,388 (27%)

Campaign Finance

	Receipts	Receipts from PACs		Expend-itures
1990				
Rowland (D)	$368,200	$228,050	(62%)	$365,513
Cunningham (R)	$106,278	$2,250	(2%)	$105,270
1988				
Rowland (D)	$261,545	$129,637	(50%)	$195,895

Key Votes

1991	
Authorize use of force against Iraq	Y
1990	
Support constitutional amendment on flag desecration	Y
Pass family and medical leave bill over Bush veto	N
Reduce SDI funding	Y
Allow abortions in overseas military facilities	Y
Approve budget summit plan for spending and taxing	Y
Approve civil rights bill	Y
1989	
Halt production of B-2 stealth bomber at 13 planes	N
Oppose capital gains tax cut	N
Approve federal abortion funding in rape or incest cases	Y
Approve pay raise and revision of ethics rules	Y
Pass Democratic minimum wage plan over Bush veto	N

Voting Studies

	Presidential Support		Party Unity		Conservative Coalition	
Year	S	O	S	O	S	O
1990	42	58	73	22	91	9
1989	52	45	73	25	98	2
1988	36	62	79	18	82	8
1987	43	57	71	25	93	7
1986	44	56	73	27	88	12
1985	50	50	75	25	96	4
1984	50	48	71	27	78	19
1983	44	55	60	38	88	12

Interest Group Ratings

Year	ADA	ACU	AFL-CIO	CCUS
1990	33	42	42	57
1989	30	54	42	90
1988	55	46	57	69
1987	40	30	44	67
1986	40	55	50	56
1985	30	67	41	45
1984	45	42	62	44
1983	40	65	31	55

9 Ed Jenkins (D)

Of Jasper — Elected 1976

Born: Jan. 4, 1933, Young Harris, Ga.
Education: Young Harris College, A.A. 1951; attended Emory U., 1957-59; U. of Georgia, LL.B. 1959.
Military Service: Coast Guard, 1952-55.
Occupation: Lawyer.
Family: Wife, Jo Thomasson; two children.
Religion: Baptist.
Political Career: No previous office.
Capitol Office: 2427 Rayburn Bldg. 20515; 225-5211.

In Washington: An unimposing expert in the quieter side of congressional dealmaking, Jenkins usually takes center stage only on the issue of restraining textile imports. But he stepped uncharacteristically to the forefront in the 101st Congress, not only on textiles but also on tax policy — and he even grabbed for the brass ring of a high leadership post. He fell short of his ultimate goal each time, but he carried his cause at least as far as could have been expected.

Conservative in manner as well as ideology, Jenkins has spent most of his career steadily gaining influence without appearing to be in pursuit of it. But after the 1989 fall of Speaker Jim Wright and the elevation of Thomas S. Foley to succeed him, Jenkins made a bid to succeed Foley as House majority leader. It was a remarkable move for one who had not been part of the leadership team (except as an ad hoc liaison between the leaders and their restive Southern colleagues). But Jenkins believed the South should have a dog in the fight and refused to accept the coronation of the favorite, Richard A. Gephardt of Missouri.

In another era, Jenkins' alliances might have been enough to secure a formal leadership post, but in this era, climbing the ladder requires extensive caucuswide campaigning. Until 1989, Jenkins had always been reluctant to launch such an effort, though frequently mentioned as a candidate. His earlier reluctance cost him; Gephardt's past experience as caucus chairman and presidential candidate had made him a familiar figure. Jenkins tried to reach outside the South to win over a number of liberals, but the contest never seemed winnable. Jenkins lost 76-181.

Among those supporting Jenkins was Ways and Means Chairman Dan Rostenkowski, a man with whom Jenkins has frequent differences but with whom he shares a special trust. Jenkins often dines with Rostenkowski at Morton's, a Georgetown restaurant where Democratic leadership loyalists tend to gather, and Rostenkowski usually seeks out Jenkins' opinion before making an important move. While Rostenkowski has some allies who speak *for* him, Jenkins is one who speaks *to* him.

All the same, soon after the majority leader vote, Jenkins and Rostenkowski were tussling over two issues that largely defined the Georgian's agenda in the 101st Congress.

The first was his proposed reduction in the tax on capital gains (the profit earned on appreciated assets). Jenkins led the Democratic revolt against Rostenkowski's opposition to such a cut on Ways and Means, cosponsoring the measure with the committee's senior Republican, Bill Archer of Texas. Jenkins recruited five other apostates, and this "Gang of Six," voting with the committee's 13 Republicans, was in control. The capital gains cut was approved in committee and sent to the floor, where Jenkins' rebellion rolled over not only the chairman but also Gephardt and Foley. Only the full use of parliamentary tactics and an expiring clock kept the cut from passage in the Senate in the fall of 1989.

Before the 101st Congress was out, Jenkins was back in the spotlight as a prime sponsor of the textile bill, a perennial piece of legislation seeking to limit the increase in textile imports. Jenkins' textile bill in the 99th Congress had been co-sponsored by nearly 300 members. And while he did not have quite that horde behind him in the 101st, he had enough to oblige both Rostenkowski and Trade Subcommittee Chairman Sam M. Gibbons of Florida to move the bill. Passage was also secured in the Senate, but President Bush vetoed the bill (as had President Ronald Reagan before him). An attempt to override the veto fell short.

Jenkins has not been without his successes in recent years. His "rural hospital initiative" improved the formula by which rural hospitals are reimbursed under federal programs. He also won another extension of the tax credit for businesses that invest in research and development, a feature of the tax code he would like to make permanent.

But on Jenkins' major fronts — capital gains and textiles — the 102nd Congress has yet to show much promise. Despite President

Georgia 9

Northeast — Gainesville

When it was drawn in the early 1980s, the 9th was oriented mainly toward the farms and factory towns of north Georgia. However, the district takes in a swath of Atlanta's booming outer suburbs, including those in the northern two-thirds of booming Gwinnett County. The portion of Gwinnett in the 9th provides far more votes than any of the other 21 counties. When growing Cherokee and Forsyth counties are added in, suburban Atlanta supplies about 40 percent of the district vote.

This affluent suburban growth, combined with the native conservatism of the district's rural reaches, helps make the 9th a GOP presidential stronghold. George Bush took 71 percent of the district vote in 1988, but in the House contest, conservative Democrat Jenkins managed to carry every county but Gwinnett. In 1990, he again lost Gwinnett, and Cherokee County also supported his GOP House challenger.

Locally, Gwinnett, which grew 112 percent between 1980 and 1990, tends to make the most news. But Forsyth County — with a black population of less than 1 percent — achieved national notoriety in early 1987, when black activists clashed with local whites during a civil rights march.

Though some residents of the central part of the 9th commute to Atlanta, most are employed locally. Textiles and tourism hold key places in the economy, but poultry is king in the rural reaches outside the Atlanta orbit. Chickens are raised and processed in Hall County and throughout the surrounding area. Gainesville, Hall's county seat, calls itself the "broiler capital of the world." In the center of town is the Georgia Poultry Federation's monument to the industry: an obelisk with a chicken statue on top. There is a new Mitsubishi plant near the sleepy Jackson County town of Braselton; the hamlet made headlines when it was purchased by movie starlet Kim Basinger. After Basinger shelled out $20 million for the town, developers began purchasing hundreds of acres along nearby I-85, anticipating a boom.

Development has begun to change the mountain region of northeast Georgia with the completion of I-575 running north from Atlanta. Weekend tourists are taking a toll on the unspoiled woods and streams of Gilmer, Fannin (the oldest GOP stronghold in the state), and Union counties, and retirees are making their mark on local politics. In 1990, unsuccessful GOP insurance commissioner candidate Billy Lovett played well in the 9th, winning ten counties outright and losing three others by a whisker.

The counties in the northwestern corner of the 9th are more industrialized than the rest of the district. Dalton, the seat of Whitfield County and the district's largest city, is one of the country's top carpet-making centers. Despite its blue-collar nature, Whitfield generally favors Republicans in competitive state races: It gave Bush 73 percent in 1988.

Population: 551,782. White 520,435 (94%), Black 28,607 (5%). Spanish origin 3,501 (1%). 18 and over 384,588 (70%), 65 and over 55,248 (10%). Median age: 30.

Bush's devotion to the idea, a capital gains cut did not emerge from the 1990 budget summit and has since been relegated to a study commission. Meanwhile, the push for a free-trade agreement with Mexico has raised a new threat to domestic textiles.

In the 100th Congress, Jenkins was chosen for the select committee investigating the Iran-contra scandal. Since he had neither Foreign Affairs nor Intelligence Committee experience, his appointment was surprising. But Jenkins, who had voted in favor of contra aid, supplied ideological and regional balance, and a matter-of-fact country lawyer manner that helped calm the sometimes-heated hearings.

"Whether one supports [the contras] is not the issue," Jenkins said at one point. "The issue is whether or not we have adherence to the rule of law by the executive branch, not the merits of the issue itself." Jenkins was the first member to question Marine Lt. Col. Oliver L. North after he had undergone intense probing by committee lawyers. The Georgian helped adjust the tone of the debate by calmly pointing out the pitfalls in North's behavior.

Jenkins does not always leave a lot of fingerprints on legislation, but there is rarely doubt that his hand has helped guide important work. Textiles took priority over tax reform for him in the 99th Congress, but Jenkins did aid Rostenkowski's efforts to keep the tax bill moving, and he got some key provisions he wanted. Much of the time, Jenkins concentrated on narrower provisions helpful to his district. He pushed to retain depletion allowances for marble, granite and farm-fertilizer materials. He also won tax breaks for small towns that rely on banks to support bond-financed municipal projects.

When Rostenkowski was embroiled in a fight with members from high-tax states over the deduction of state and local taxes, Jenkins' advice was a factor in getting the chairman to retain the provision. He warned that the deduction was favored even in low-tax states such as Georgia.

At Home: As a former aide to retiring Democratic Rep. Phil Landrum, and as a law partner of the veteran congressman's son, Jenkins had a relatively easy time winning this district when Landrum retired in 1976.

The early favorite in the contest was then-Lt. Gov. Zell Miller. But he decided not to run, and Jenkins' major hurdle was eliminated.

Benefiting from the Landrum connection, the Jasper lawyer finished first in a crowded Democratic primary field with 28 percent. Opponents complained that Jenkins should not have been practicing law and working for Landrum at the same time. But many voters knew Jenkins personally as Landrum's field representative and disregarded the criticism.

Jenkins took the runoff with 55 percent over an older foe, J. Albert Minish, who had once run a strong primary against Landrum. Jenkins overwhelmed minor GOP opposition in November. In 1978 he faced a primary challenge from a county official from suburban Atlanta. But Jenkins' strength in the rural counties brought him nearly two-thirds of the vote.

Jenkins has not faced a serious challenge since, although his victory margin has slipped in the last two elections. In 1988, Republican Joe Hoffman won 37 percent overall by taking a majority of the vote in his base, Gwinnett County, whose booming, affluent Atlanta suburbs are becoming increasingly Republican. But Jenkins swept the other 21 counties.

In a 1990 rematch, Hoffman, an architect, pulled Jenkins' tally below 60 percent. Some of the falloff was due to generalized anti-incumbent sentiment and to a long House session that constrained Jenkins' campaigning. But continued growth of GOP strength in the suburban part of the 9th also helped Hoffman.

In 1986, Jenkins was lobbied to run against GOP Sen. Mack Mattingly by Democrats who felt that only a conservative could unseat Mattingly. Jenkins declined, and 5th District Rep. Wyche Fowler Jr. of Atlanta overcame his liberal reputation and ousted Mattingly.

Committee

Ways & Means (8th of 23 Democrats)
Oversight; Trade

Elections

1990 General		
Ed Jenkins (D)	96,197	(56%)
Joe Hoffman (R)	76,121	(44%)
1988 General		
Ed Jenkins (D)	121,800	(63%)
Joe Hoffman (R)	71,905	(37%)

Previous Winning Percentages: **1986** (100%) **1984** (67%) **1982** (77%) **1980** (68%) **1978** (77%) **1976** (79%)

District Vote For President

	1988	1984	1980	1976
D	57,200 (29%)	52,706 (31%)	92,811 (57%)	106,905 (73%)
R	140,209 (71%)	118,505 (69%)	64,994 (40%)	38,570 (27%)
I			2,934 (2%)	

Campaign Finance

	Receipts	Receipts from PACs	Expend-itures
1990			
Jenkins (D)	$302,029	$186,000 (62%)	$318,247
Hoffman (R)	$139,652	$8,500 (6%)	$134,772
1988			
Jenkins (D)	$453,174	$310,897 (69%)	$405,040
Hoffman (R)	$64,419	0	$64,400

Key Votes

1991	
Authorize use of force against Iraq	N
1990	
Support constitutional amendment on flag desecration	Y
Pass family and medical leave bill over Bush veto	Y
Reduce SDI funding	Y
Allow abortions in overseas military facilities	N
Approve budget summit plan for spending and taxing	N
Approve civil rights bill	N
1989	
Halt production of B-2 stealth bomber at 13 planes	N
Oppose capital gains tax cut	N
Approve federal abortion funding in rape or incest cases	N
Approve pay raise and revision of ethics rules	Y
Pass Democratic minimum wage plan over Bush veto	Y

Voting Studies

	Presidential Support		Party Unity		Conservative Coalition	
Year	**S**	**O**	**S**	**O**	**S**	**O**
1990	44	51	62	30	87	9
1989	47	47	63	25	78	10
1988	38	59	68	26	87	11
1987	40	53	66	24	88	5
1986	41	52	65	28	70	16
1985	48	50	69	26	76	22
1984	42	46	57	33	66	19
1983	49	38	47	39	79	12
1982	40	49	47	44	77	15
1981	58	34	42	53	91	4

Interest Group Ratings

Year	ADA	ACU	AFL-CIO	CCUS
1990	39	54	42	67
1989	35	50	58	60
1988	45	54	64	71
1987	44	20	56	62
1986	35	58	36	53
1985	25	55	47	50
1984	35	39	54	56
1983	30	89	23	63
1982	30	60	37	57
1981	10	63	40	60

10 Doug Barnard Jr. (D)

Of Augusta — Elected 1976

Born: March 20, 1922, Augusta, Ga.
Education: Mercer U., B.A. 1942, LL.B. 1948.
Military Service: Army, 1943-45.
Occupation: Banker.
Family: Wife, Naomi Elizabeth Holt; three children.
Religion: Baptist.
Political Career: No previous office.
Capitol Office: 2227 Rayburn Bldg. 20515; 225-4101.

In Washington: As the 102nd Congress moved to reform the nation's fragile banking system, there was no doubt where Barnard would stand in the debate: He is a consistent and longtime advocate of removing the barriers that restrict banks from engaging in different areas of commerce.

Elected chairman of the Democratic caucus on Banking in the 101st Congress, Barnard is one of numerous Democrats on the committee whose relationship with Chairman Henry B. Gonzalez has been chilly. He complements his seat on Banking with his chairmanship of the Government Operations Subcommittee on Commerce, Consumer and Monetary Affairs, which he uses as another forum for his views on bank deregulation.

A banker by profession, Barnard has focused much of his legislative career on making policy to cover the arcane details of his industry — details that many of his colleagues prefer to ignore and most of his constituents fail to understand. In the House, many regard Barnard as the single most knowledgeable specialist in banking industry matters.

He favors lifting many of the prohibitions on bank activities that stem from the 1933 Glass-Steagall Act, the law that erected barriers between banking and securities firms.

In an 80-page treatise issued in 1987 by his Government Operations subcommittee, Barnard said, "The unnecessary and anti-competitive entry barriers in both commercial banking and securities markets should be entirely dismantled so that both banking and securities firms will face completely open competition." He views dismantling barriers as essential to preserving the stability of the banking system. The bank reform bill he introduced in 1991 closely tracked a proposal first put forward more than three years earlier by a coalition of diversified financial services corporations, including American Express Co. and Sears, Roebuck and Co.

In the 100th Congress, Congress worked on legislation to grant banks new authority to affiliate with securities firms. The Senate passed a bill, but the House Banking, Judiciary, and Energy and Commerce committees each approved differing versions of a second bill. Serious jurisdictional disagreements between Banking and the Energy and Commerce Committee scuttled the measures.

In 1984, when the Banking Committee was drawing up legislation to restrict banking activity, Barnard favored Senate legislation allowing banks to enter the fields of insurance, real estate and securities. Later that year, the House panel approved a Barnard proposal that preserved the ability of banks to provide discount brokerage services — taking customers' orders to buy stock without giving advice.

In recent years, Barnard has been the only banker on the Financial Institutions Subcommittee, which has worked on a variety of important bills involving the relationship between and solvency of savings and loan institutions and their competitors, the banks. The Financial Institutions panel was the first stop for the 1989 bill authorizing $50 billion to bail out insolvent S&Ls and restructure the thrift industry's deposit insurance system.

Barnard's Government Operations subcommittee cast an early negative light on savings and loan institutions in 1986. The panel issued a report that identified fraudulent real estate appraisal practices at one-fourth of the federally insured savings and loans, and blamed bad appraisals for the fiscal problems faced by many of these institutions. "Go-go lenders, get-rich-quick developers and compliant appraisers are equally to blame for this alarming situation," Barnard said.

Barnard captured headlines in 1989 with his subcommittee's investigation into corruption among top officials of the Internal Revenue Service. He ran into a wall, however, when he sought authority from the Ways and Means Committee to gain access to tax records: Chairman Dan Rostenkowski refused to cooperate. He wanted the Joint Taxation Committee, not Barnard's panel, to handle the inquiry.

In the 101st Congress, Barnard was part of a bloc of moderate and conservative Democrats

Georgia 10

North Central — Athens; Augusta

The 10th is a rambling swath of eastern Georgia anchored by Augusta on the east and metropolitan Atlanta on the west. In between is a stretch that has been touched by the ripple effect of Atlanta's booming growth, but remains mainly rural; the only population center is Athens, site of the University of Georgia.

Augusta (population 45,000), which sits on the Savannah River just across from South Carolina, has traditionally been the political heart of this district. It is Barnard's home base, and it provides him with the margins he needs to win re-election easily. In 1990, Barnard carried Augusta and surrounding Richmond County with 74 percent of the vote, and took suburban Columbia County with 62 percent.

But while the city itself has a majority-black population and a blue-collar work force yielding a reliable Democratic vote, its environs have a much more conservative — and GOP — tilt. The area has a sizable military population, and a number of military retirees, associated with nearby Fort Gordon, home of the Army Signal Corps.

The conservative, pro-defense spending attitude reflects the importance to the local economy of the Savannah River federal nuclear facility; located just downriver in Aiken, S.C., the plant processes tritium for use in nuclear weapons, though operations were suspended in late 1988 because of safety and environmental problems.

Military and civilian voters who work at these facilities give the Augusta metropolitan area a GOP edge in elections for high office. George Bush carried Richmond County with 57 percent, and suburban Columbia with 78 percent. Unsuccessful GOP candidates for governor, lieutenant governor and insurance commissioner all carried Columbia County in 1990.

The district rambles 150 miles west, through cotton, soybean, tobacco and corn-growing country that leans Republican for president. When the GOP bastions in suburban Atlanta's Gwinnett County are added in, the 10th becomes a GOP presidential stronghold. One of the country's fastest-growing areas, southern Gwinnett's affluent neighborhoods are filled with newcomers unbound by the region's traditional Democratic ties. Bush won in a landslide, and even Barnard trailed his opponent by a 61-39 percent margin in Gwinnett, the only county he lost in 1990.

Athens, in Clarke County at the center of the district, provides the only base for liberal activists, mainly derived from the university and its 26,000 students. When a nuclear freeze was being debated at the local level in the early 1980s, the Athens City Council endorsed it — the only civic body in the district to do so. Barnard took 65 percent of the Clarke County vote in 1990, and Michael S. Dukakis won the county in 1988 — by just four votes. Dukakis also carried Warren County, a mostly black rural county west of Augusta.

Population: 550,268. White 404,859 (74%), Black 137,321 (25%), Other 4,999 (1%). Spanish origin 7,680 (1%). 18 and over 388,067 (71%), 65 and over 45,469 (8%). Median age: 27.

who helped produce a compromise on a provision in the bill overhauling federal housing programs. The compromise offered new incentives and requirements to persuade owners of federally subsidized housing to continue renting to low-income families.

He also opposed an effort late in the 101st Congress to require the federal mint to redesign the back sides of the nation's coins.

Barnard's overall voting record places him to the right of the Democratic mainstream. He was one of only 15 House Democrats to oppose the 1990 civil rights act. He has regularly compiled one of the highest support scores for GOP presidents among House Democrats. In 1984 Barnard was one of a handful of Democrats who called publicly for liberal House Speaker Thomas P. O'Neill Jr. to step down.

At Home: For many years, Barnard enjoyed relatively easy re-elections. But in 1990, he struggled with one of the burdens of incumbency — affiliation with the savings and loan debacle. Barnard's role as chairman of a subcommittee overseeing thrifts encouraged Republicans to think he could become a target for voter outrage over the costly S&L bailout.

Political unknown Sam Jones won the GOP nomination to challenge Barnard, and made the S&L crisis the centerpiece of his campaign. He faulted Barnard for accepting $20,000 in 1986 from associates of Charles H. Keating Jr., a leading figure in the crisis. Beginning with billboards and moving to television, Jones insisted that Barnard return the money.

Jones' attacks did eventually prompt Barnard to give the money to several Georgia universities. But Barnard insisted he had done no wrong, and said he had sounded early warnings of the crisis. He also went on the attack, questioning why Jones, who was a pastoral counselor, had changed jobs frequently before running for Congress.

Although the GOP is gaining strength in the 10th, Barnard's conservative views have made him a comfortable choice for many Republicans over the years. That pattern held in 1990: Barnard won re-election with 58 percent of the vote.

Although Barnard had said in early 1989 that he planned to retire in 1992, he backed off that claim during the campaign and has not said whether he will seek a ninth term.

Barnard's 1976 House campaign marked his debut in elective politics after an extensive career in state government. A top aide to Gov. Carl Sanders in the mid-1960s, Barnard later turned to business, serving as executive vice president of the Georgia Railroad Bank.

Barnard thus had years' worth of contacts to call upon when Rep. Robert G. Stephens Jr.'s retirement opened the district in 1976. He was not helped in the district's rural counties by his ties to the Atlanta legal and business community, but he was well financed and had a strong base in Augusta.

That foundation enabled Barnard to run ahead of a large primary field, taking 27 percent of the vote. In the runoff he was slotted against Mike Padgett, a former key aide to Gov. Lester Maddox. Padgett had rural and conservative support, but also had made enemies during his years with Maddox. Coming out of Atlanta and Augusta with a 7,000-vote margin, Barnard won the contest by 2,800 votes. He was unopposed that November and in three of his first four re-election campaigns.

Committees

Banking, Finance & Urban Affairs (8th of 31 Democrats)
Consumer Affairs & Coinage; Domestic Monetary Policy; Financial Institutions Supervision, Regulation & Insurance; General Oversight

Government Operations (8th of 25 Democrats)
Commerce, Consumer & Monetary Affairs (chairman)

Elections

1990 General		
Doug Barnard Jr. (D)	89,683	(58%)
Sam Jones (R)	64,184	(42%)
1990 Primary		
Doug Barnard Jr. (D)	61,976	(71%)
Scott A. Starling (D)	25,276	(29%)
1988 General		
Doug Barnard Jr. (D)	118,156	(64%)
Mark Myers (R)	66,521	(36%)

Previous Winning Percentages: **1986** (67%) **1984** (100%) **1982** (100%) **1980** (80%) **1978** (100%) **1976** (100%)

District Vote For President

	1988	1984	1980	1976
D	66,060 (35%)	61,545 (35%)	80,511 (53%)	83,491 (64%)
R	122,156 (65%)	114,817 (65%)	66,097 (44%)	46,965 (36%)
I			3,590 (2%)	

Campaign Finance

	Receipts	Receipts from PACs		Expenditures
1990				
Barnard (D)	$778,139	$264,551	(34%)	$937,464
Jones (R)	$238,903	$21,750	(9%)	$154,326
1988				
Barnard (D)	$285,060	$148,371	(52%)	$193,123
Myers (R)	$7,375	$500	(7%)	$7,257

Key Votes

1991	
Authorize use of force against Iraq	Y
1990	
Support constitutional amendment on flag desecration	Y
Pass family and medical leave bill over Bush veto	N
Reduce SDI funding	?
Allow abortions in overseas military facilities	N
Approve budget summit plan for spending and taxing	N
Approve civil rights bill	N
1989	
Halt production of B-2 stealth bomber at 13 planes	N
Oppose capital gains tax cut	N
Approve federal abortion funding in rape or incest cases	N
Approve pay raise and revision of ethics rules	Y
Pass Democratic minimum wage plan over Bush veto	N

Voting Studies

	Presidential Support		Party Unity		Conservative Coalition	
Year	**S**	**O**	**S**	**O**	**S**	**O**
1990	49	40	52	37	89	6
1989	67	24	56	36	85	5
1988	38	43	56	26	82	0
1987	53	35	50	39	91	2
1986	54	32	52	33	70	4
1985	54	41	53	37	87	5
1984	44	39	48	34	69	8
1983	59	30	41	53	78	12
1982	60	31	46	47	88	5
1981	67	18	26	61	84	1

Interest Group Ratings

Year	ADA	ACU	AFL-CIO	CCUS
1990	22	81	50	86
1989	10	79	18	90
1988	25	64	54	67
1987	20	61	33	79
1986	25	72	23	79
1985	15	71	44	50
1984	15	56	50	38
1983	10	82	18	79
1982	10	79	21	63
1981	0	93	20	94

Hawaii

U.S. CONGRESS

SENATE 2 D
HOUSE 2 D

LEGISLATURE

Senate 22 D, 3 R
House 45 D, 6 R

ELECTIONS

1988 Presidential Vote

Bush	45%
Dukakis	54%

1984 Presidential Vote

Reagan	55%
Mondale	44%

1980 Presidential Vote

Reagan	43%
Carter	45%
Anderson	11%

Turnout rate in 1986	42%
Turnout rate in 1988	43%
Turnout rate in 1990	40%

(as percentage of voting age population)

POPULATION AND GROWTH

1980 population	964,691
1990 population (41st in the nation)	1,108,229
Percent change 1980-1990	+15%

DEMOGRAPHIC BREAKDOWN

White	33%
Black	3%
Asian or Pacific Islander	62%
(Hispanic origin)	7%
Urban	87%
Rural	13%
Born in state	58%
Foreign-born	14%

MAJOR POPULATION CENTERS

Honolulu	365,272
Hilo	37,808
Kailua	36,818
Kaneohe	35,448
Waipahu	31,435

AREA AND LAND USE

Area 6,425 sq. miles (47th)

Farm	48%
Forest	43%
Federally owned	17%

Gov. John Waihee III (D)
Of Honolulu — Elected 1986

Born: May 19, 1946, Honokaa, Hawaii.
Education: Andrews U., B.A. 1968; Central Michigan U., M.A. 1973; U. of Hawaii, J.D. 1976.
Occupation: Lawyer.
Religion: Christian.
Political Career: Hawaii House, 1981-83; lieutenant governor, 1983-87.
Next Election: 1994.

WORK

Occupations

White-collar	56%
Blue-collar	23%
Service workers	18%

Government Workers

Federal	26,973
State	53,839
Local	13,781

MONEY

Median family income	$ 22,750	(5th)
Tax burden per capita	$ 1,293	(4th)

EDUCATION

Spending per pupil through grade 12	$ 3,919	(28th)
Persons with college degrees	20%	(5th)

CRIME

Violent crime rate 270 per 100,000 (38th)

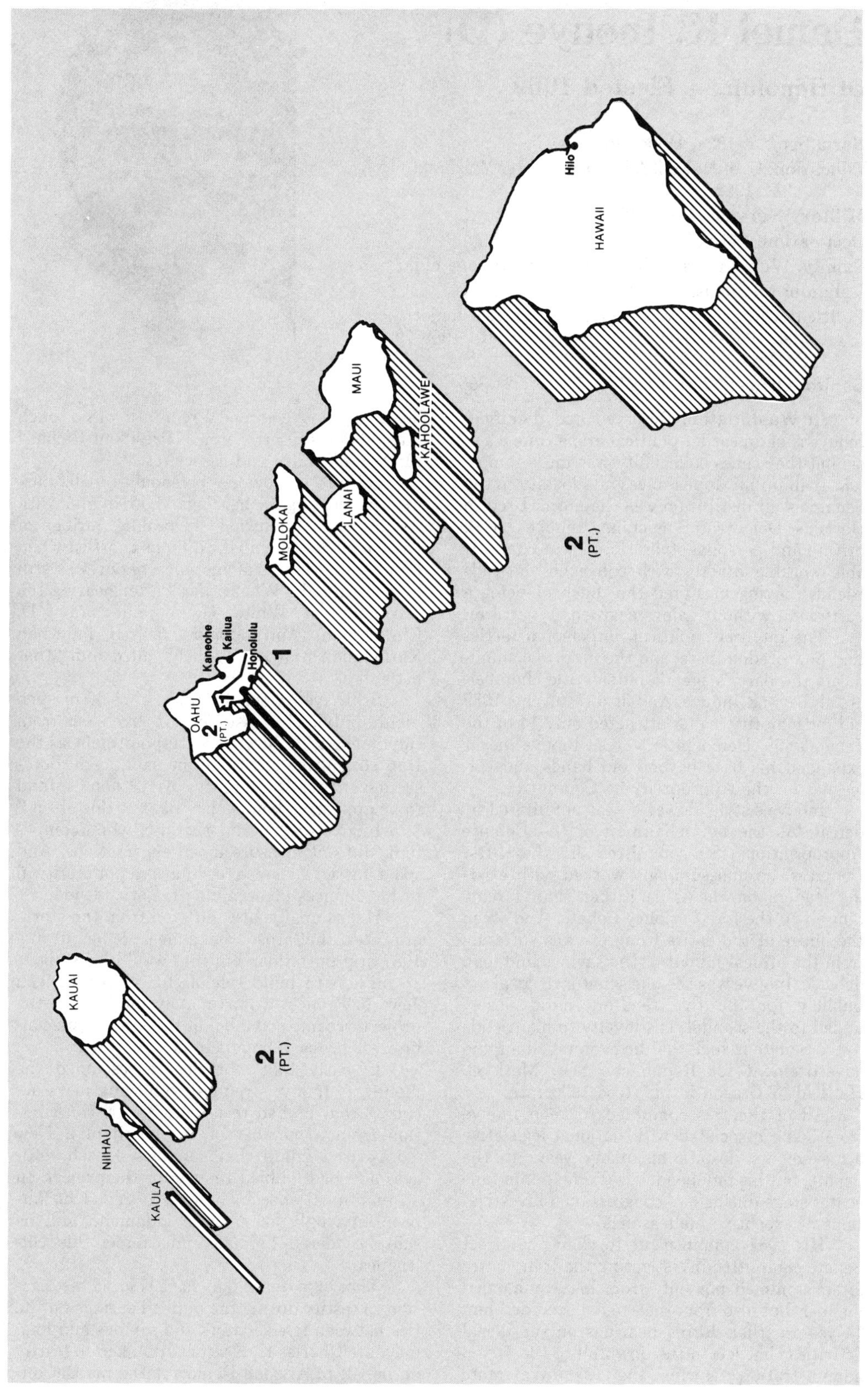
KAUAI
NIIHAU
KAULA
2 (PT.)
OAHU
2 (PT.)
1
Kaneohe
Kailua
Honolulu
1
MOLOKAI
LANAI
MAUI
KAHOOLAWE
2 (PT.)
HAWAII
Hilo

Daniel K. Inouye (D)

Of Honolulu — Elected 1962

Born: Sept. 7, 1924, Honolulu, Hawaii.

Education: U. of Hawaii, A.B. 1950; George Washington U., J.D. 1952.

Military Service: Army, 1943-47.

Occupation: Lawyer.

Family: Wife, Margaret Shinobu Awamura; one child.

Religion: Methodist.

Political Career: Hawaii Territorial House, majority leader, 1954-58; Hawaii Territorial Senate, 1958-59; U.S. House, 1959-63.

Capitol Office: 722 Hart Bldg. 20510; 224-3934.

In Washington: Reserved and dignified, Inouye is of an earlier political era, a time when behind-the-scenes collegiality was more important than public appearances and loyalty to the Senate as an institution was the norm. Bred in Hawaii's Democratic machine, Inouye has a private and personal style. He is most comfortable working quietly with colleagues he calls friends, having mastered the touch of being a party man without being regarded as partisan.

The intensely political, impersonal tactics that now predominate, and the need to communicate the party's agenda outside the chamber, are all beyond Inouye. And as a result, his 1989 bid for majority leader attracted only 14 of the Senate's 55 Democratic votes. Inouye never expanded his base beyond old hands and colleagues on the Appropriations Committee.

Inouye's style, however, was not altered by defeat. As the new chairman of the Defense Appropriations Subcommittee in the 101st Congress, he unassumingly worked with existing leaders on the issue rather than forcing himself to the fore of policy debate. And when the image of the entire Congress was suffering from the ethical fallout of the savings and loan debacle, Inouye was the one senator to speak up publicly for the five senators most closely linked to the scandal. His loyalty to his friends in the Senate is such that he even taped a radio advertisement for Republican Sen. Mark O. Hatfield of Oregon in his close 1990 race.

All of this has combined to keep Inouye from being associated with national legislative achievements despite his many years in the Senate, but his independence did help him take center stage during two congressional investigations of executive malfeasance.

His 1987 appointment to chair the select Senate committee investigating the Iran-contra affair stemmed not only from his evenhanded manner, but also from the esteem accorded him 14 years earlier during hearings on the illegal activities that led to the downfall of the Nixon administration. During the 1973 Watergate hearings, Inouye earned a reputation as a tough but judicious interrogator of President Richard M. Nixon's aides and associates.

Despite his low-key personality, polls during the Watergate hearings showed him with the highest nationwide "favorable" ratings of any committee member. Millions chortled when Inouye, unaware that his microphone was still live, muttered, "What a liar!" after hearing the testimony of White House aide John D. Ehrlichman. And support poured in when Ehrlichman's lawyer publicly called him "that little Jap."

Still, even when he finds himself in such highly public circumstances, Inouye shies from the limelight. Following his appointment as the Iran committee chairman, he said, "You don't see me at press conferences. And I don't intend to be appearing before the mike . . . this often."

Inouye's work and rhetoric, while competent, did not measure up to expectations. And so he missed a chance to shine at a point critical to his chances of becoming majority leader.

His campaign also suffered from the storm of protest that arose from a measure he put in a 1987 appropriations bill that would have spent $8 million to build schools for North African Jews in France. Unfortunately for Inouye, the project became a symbol of the kind of special-interest projects members favor.

In early 1988, the Senate rescinded the money at Inouye's request, following news accounts that he had received a $1,000 contribution from a member of the board of a New York-based group that supports Jewish refugees and had lobbied Inouye for the project. In an emotional speech, Inouye conceded no impropriety, only an error in judgment, and he said he feared he had embarrassed his colleagues.

That experience may have colored his decision to testify during the public hearings on the ties between five senators and savings and loan magnate Charles H. Keating Jr. Asked to testify on behalf of Arizona Democrat Dennis DeConcini, Inouye spoke passionately in defense of all five, suggesting that they had done nothing wrong, and were victims of changing mores. "I believe that what is on trial here are not five colleagues of mine but the United States Senate," he told the panel.

As a sign of how times have changed, Inouye found himself not praised at home for his actions but condemned. A few home-state pundits started referring to the case as the "Keating six."

Earlier in his career, Inouye came to the defense of another beleaguered colleague, Democrat Harrison A. Williams Jr. of New Jersey. When Williams was facing Senate expulsion for his role in the Abscam bribery scandal, Inouye acted as his lawyer. Describing the investigators' tactics as entrapment by the executive branch, Inouye said, "The integrity of the Senate is challenged by this investigation and the Constitution compels us to reject its advance." Williams eventually resigned before completion of the expulsion debate.

During the 101st Congress, Inouye found his good name mentioned in unsavory stories about a longtime aide, Henry K. Giugni, whom new Majority Leader George J. Mitchell of Maine permitted to remain for a term as Senate sergeant-at-arms. As secretary of the Senate Democratic Conference, the third-ranking position in the party hierarchy, Inouye had promoted Giugni for the job. During the 101st Congress, however, Giugni was publicly criticized for using official travel to pay for questionable trips to his native Hawaii.

Inouye gave up his party post to seek the majority leader job, but as part of Mitchell's campaign to unify Senate Democrats, he named Inouye chairman of the Democratic Steering Committee, the group that hands out committee assignments.

As chairman of the Appropriations Subcommittee on Defense, Inouye has shown firm command of defense numbers and held up well alongside such issue leaders as Sam Nunn of Georgia. Inouye was rarely out front on policy decisions, but when he was, he was often at odds with younger Democrats. He is a key spokesman against cutting funds for the B-2 bomber and maintaining U.S. troop strength in Europe. Inouye, a Cold War liberal, says that it is premature to assert that the Soviet Union has changed. "With all the pleasant speeches we've heard from Mr. Gorbachev, the facts just don't support it," he said in 1990.

Inouye also did his best to dodge the jurisdictional dogfights that often entangle defense appropriators and authorizers. In 1989, Inouye bundled into one amendment all of the procurement projects that had not been authorized in the Armed Services bill so as to give members of that panel a chance to debate them. "We want to do this upfront," he said.

Prior to the 101st Congress, Inouye chaired Appropriations' Foreign Operations Subcommittee. He occasionally had turf clashes with his House Appropriations counterpart, David R. Obey of Wisconsin, but Inouye generally earned good marks for his oversight of the foreign aid budget. He conducted a thorough line-by-line review of foreign aid programs before funding them. Subcommittee legislation generally reflected a consensus achieved by giving every party, including the minority and the administration, something to take home.

He is a consistent advocate for increased aid to Israel, and he often teams up with Wisconsin Republican Bob Kasten, who chaired Foreign Operations when the GOP controlled the Senate, to offer pro-Israel amendments. In 1990, the two authored a successful amendment authorizing the president to provide the Israelis $700 million worth of equipment from Department of Defense stockpiles.

On one foreign affairs issue, Inouye was well outside the Democratic mainstream. He spoke out in defense of Philippine President Ferdinand E. Marcos, even on the verge of his downfall and exile from the Philippines. Declaring an affinity for the Philippines, which like Hawaii had long been a territory of the United States, Inouye said that efforts to punish Marcos economically for corruption were hurting the Filipino people and that the hostility toward the Marcos regime was excessive.

Inouye also chairs the Commerce Subcommittee on Communications, although he usually lets others take the lead. During the 101st and 102nd Congresses, Inouye strongly opposed full committee Chairman Ernest F. Hollings' bill to allow the regional Bell companies into telecommunications equipment manufacturing, but he took no action to block consideration of the controversial bill. His pro-consumer views are consistent with his actions on deregulation of the cable industry.

In general, he has concentrated his Commerce work on helping his island home through shipping and tourism legislation. His work on the panel also prompted a rare reference to his service in the legendary Nisei regiment in World War II and the wound that took his right arm. In June 1986, as the committee was on its way to approving a $250,000 cap on certain court awards for pain and suffering, Inouye said, "I guess I can stand it, so I guess we can make [the cap] zilch. But I cannot speak for the rest of those who have lost their limbs."

The room had fallen silent. Support for the cap eroded, and the bill was doomed.

Although not a man of unusual legislative vigor, Inouye has brought energy and passion to the Senate Indian Affairs Committee, where he became chairman in 1987. "This committee has been known as the scrap heap of the Senate," he said. "I'm going to do everything in my power to change that."

Four comprehensive tribal bills are on tap

for the 102nd Congress, during which the panel is scheduled to hold 146 hearings, double the number in the 101st. He has made repeated trips west, particularly to the Northwest, to study Indian matters.

At Home: World War II cost Inouye his right arm, but it made him a hero and built the foundation for a political career of uninterrupted success.

Before the war, Inouye had wanted to become a surgeon. After he was wounded, while fighting in Europe with the all Japanese-American 442nd Regiment, he went into law and eventually into politics. He held several party posts, was majority leader in the territorial House of Representatives and then moved to the territorial Senate.

Inouye originally planned to run for the U.S. Senate when Hawaii was granted statehood in 1959. But he withdrew from that race and ran for the House instead, winning with the largest number of votes ever cast in Hawaii up to that time. He explained that he wanted to "give some elder statesman in our party a clear field" for the Senate.

This patience was rewarded. When Democratic Sen. Oren E. Long announced his decision in 1962 not to seek re-election, he endorsed Inouye to succeed him and promised his support. Inouye went on to defeat Republican Benjamin F. Dillingham, a member of one of Hawaii's pioneer families, by a landslide.

Since then, he has never fallen below 74 percent of the vote, his total against Republican Frank Hutchinson in 1986. Inouye's active support has provided a vital assist to Democratic candidates in Hawaii over the years. His backing of interim Sen. Daniel K. Akaka in the 1990 special Senate contest helped Akaka, a native Hawaiian, hold the crucial Japanese-American vote against Republican Rep. Patricia Saiki, who is of Japanese ancestry.

Committees

Select Indian Affairs (Chairman)

Appropriations (2nd of 16 Democrats)
Defense (chairman); Commerce, Justice, State & Judiciary; Foreign Operations; Labor, Health & Human Services, Education; Military Construction

Commerce, Science & Transportation (2nd of 11 Democrats)
Communications (chairman); Aviation; Merchant Marine; Surface Transportation; National Ocean Policy Study

Rules & Administration (4th of 9 Democrats)

Elections

1986 General		
Daniel K. Inouye (D)	241,887	(74%)
Frank Hutchinson (R)	86,910	(26%)

Previous Winning Percentages: **1980** (78%) **1974** (83%) **1968** (83%) **1962** (69%) **1960 *** (74%) **1959 †** (68%)

** House election.*
† Special House election.

Campaign Finance

	Receipts	Receipts from PACs	Expend-itures
1986			
Inouye (D)	$1,173,721	$540,455 (46%)	$1,039,418
Hutchinson (R)	$31,845	$3,450 (11%)	$31,843

Key Votes

1991	
Authorize use of force against Iraq	N
1990	
Oppose prohibition of certain semiautomatic weapons	N
Support constitutional amendment on flag desecration	N
Oppose requiring parental notice for minors' abortions	Y
Halt production of B-2 stealth bomber at 13 planes	N
Approve budget that cut spending and raised revenues	Y
Pass civil rights bill over Bush veto	Y
1989	
Oppose reduction of SDI funding	N
Oppose barring federal funds for "obscene" art	Y
Allow vote on capital gains tax cut	N

Voting Studies

	Presidential Support		Party Unity		Conservative Coalition	
Year	**S**	**O**	**S**	**O**	**S**	**O**
1990	45	53	84	15	59	38
1989	60	37	83	17	47	53
1988	42	44	87	7	24	62
1987	33	63	91	5	41	53
1986	17	70	72	16	18	66
1985	20	72	80	7	20	58
1984	39	52	78	14	30	62
1983	33	42	70	9	9	66
1982	28	66	74	14	17	65
1981	47	44	74	13	20	69

Interest Group Ratings

Year	ADA	ACU	AFL-CIO	CCUS
1990	72	13	89	17
1989	70	11	90	50
1988	85	4	92	38
1987	95	0	90	29
1986	90	5	100	38
1985	95	5	95	24
1984	85	19	100	29
1983	75	9	93	27
1982	70	24	88	22
1981	70	0	89	44

Daniel K. Akaka (D)

Of Honolulu — Elected 1990

Appointed to the Senate April 1990.

Born: Sept. 11, 1924, Honolulu, Hawaii.
Education: U. of Hawaii, B.Ed. 1952, M.Ed. 1966.
Military Service: Army Corps of Engineers, 1945-47.
Occupation: Elementary school teacher; principal; state program administrator.
Family: Wife, Mary Mildred Chong; five children.
Religion: Congregationalist.
Political Career: U.S. House, 1977-90; sought Democratic nomination for lieutenant governor, 1974.
Capitol Office: 720 Hart Bldg. 20510; 224-6361.

In Washington: When Democratic Sen. Spark M. Matsunaga died in April 1990, Akaka was a logical choice as his interim successor. Akaka had carried Hawaii's 2nd District by huge margins in seven House contests. A Native Hawaiian — the only one ever to serve in Congress — he was on good terms with Democratic Gov. John Waihee III, who made the appointment. Akaka was close to the leadership of the state Democratic Party, and had received support throughout his career from Japanese-Americans, a crucial Hawaii voting bloc.

However, with Akaka facing a special election in November 1990, there was a degree of trepidation about his ability to hold the seat. Akaka had been a rather sedate figure during his House career and was not readily identifiable to many Hawaiians. Some Democratic supporters feared that Akaka might be overwhelmed by his more aggressive opponent, 1st District Republican Rep. Patricia Saiki.

As it turned out, both Akaka and the state Democratic machine that backed him were underestimated. Akaka skillfully played to his strengths: his pleasing personality and his ability to deliver federal largess to Hawaii, proven as a member of the House Appropriations Committee. The Democratic organization got the party faithful to the polls: Akaka won by a surprisingly wide margin to fill out the final four years of Matsunaga's unexpired term.

During his House career, Akaka kept a low profile and a tight focus on Hawaiian interests. He delayed taking his Senate oath in order to ensure that funding for projects in Hawaii was advanced by House Appropriations.

Akaka sacrificed his seat on that committee when he moved to the Senate. However, he did get assignments to the Energy and Natural Resources, Governmental Affairs, Veterans' Affairs and Indian Affairs committees.

Toward the end of the 101st Congress, Akaka voted against the confirmation of Supreme Court nominee David H. Souter; a supporter of abortion rights, Akaka based his vote on Souter's refusal to state a position on abortion. He also took a First Amendment stand in June 1990 against the constitutional amendment to prohibit flag desecration. (Votes like these helped Akaka accrue a 100 percent rating from Americans for Democratic Action in 1990.)

In 1991, Akaka — a longtime supporter of Matsunaga's concept of a national peace institute — voted against authorizing use of military force to end Iraq's occupation of Kuwait. "What's the rush?" Akaka asked. "Sanctions and diplomacy are working.... They are the best weapon we can use to accomplish our objectives without resorting to war."

Yet despite his bolder posture on national issues, Akaka's primary interest remains Hawaii. In 1990, Akaka pushed through an amendment to a crime bill increasing penalties for purveyors of a methamphetamine known as "ice," which had become a problem in Hawaii; Akaka had pursued this issue as a member of House Select Committee on Narcotics Abuse. A protector of Hawaii's sugar industry, he fought an effort by Sen. Bill Bradley, D-N.J., to cut the federal sugar subsidy by 2 cents a pound; Akaka's motion to table Bradley's amendment to the 1990 farm bill passed by a 54-44 vote.

Akaka is slight of stature, a fact he makes light of himself. Discussing his battle with Bradley, a towering former pro basketball star, Akaka told a Honolulu newspaper, "I'm only 5-feet-7, but I slam-dunked him."

That comment recalls an incident earlier in Akaka's career. In 1984, the House Democratic leadership was one vote short on a crucial roll call as they sought to block President Reagan's request for production of the MX missile. With time running out, Illinois Democrat Marty Russo located Akaka, who had been recorded as a pro-MX vote, lifted him out of a phone booth and escorted — carried, said some witnesses — him into the chamber. Akaka then changed his vote, giving the anti-MX forces a key victory.

Daniel K. Akaka, D-Hawaii

At Home: On paper, Akaka had major advantages over Saiki. He had won seven House elections to her two. He had solid backing from such towering state Democratic figures as senior Sen. Daniel K. Inouye. He had demographics on his side: Population grew faster during the 1980s in his 2nd than in Saiki's 1st.

Yet the image persisted that Saiki, a Republican moderate with a more assertive personality and a base in the media center of Honolulu, was the favorite in the campaign. GOP strategists touted Hawaii as their best chance for a Senate "takeaway"; President Bush and other national Republican leaders took the long flight to campaign for Saiki.

However, Akaka ran a well-funded campaign highlighting his efforts to bring federal funds to Hawaii. Akaka also played upon the partisan themes of economic populism that developed during the 1990 federal budget impasse and resonated within the traditionally Democratic Hawaii electorate.

The long 1990 House session also played to Akaka's benefit. Saiki, like Akaka, was stuck in Washington until late October, and was never able to manifest her supposed advantage in personal campaign style. Akaka won with an unexpectedly hefty 54 percent of the vote.

The irony of Akaka's elevation to the Senate is that he was never regarded as one of the more upwardly mobile House members. Akaka had been viewed as far more likely to seek a seat on the board of the Bishop Trust, a Hawaii landholding estate, than to seek higher office.

Akaka rose through the Honolulu education bureaucracy before entering politics in 1971 as appointed head of the state Office of Economic Opportunity. In 1974, Democratic gubernatorial candidate George R. Ariyoshi tapped Akaka as his choice for lieutenant governor: Ariyoshi won but Akaka lost in the Democratic primary. As governor, Ariyoshi appointed Akaka as his special assistant for human resources.

In 1976 the 2nd District opened up with the unsuccessful Senate candidacy of Democratic Rep. Patsy T. Mink. Akaka faced formidable primary opposition from state Sen. Joe Kuroda, but won with a narrow plurality; he took the general election with 80 percent, and won subsequent elections with similar ease.

Politics in the 2nd District came full circle with Akaka's appointment to the Senate. Mink, his House predecessor, won the September 1990 special election to succeed Akaka and then won a full term in November.

Committees

Energy & Natural Resources (8th of 11 Democrats)
Energy Regulation & Conservation; Energy Research & Development; Public Lands, National Parks & Forests

Governmental Affairs (8th of 8 Democrats)
Federal Services, Post Office & Civil Service; General Services, Federalism & the District of Columbia; Oversight of Government Management

Select Indian Affairs (8th of 9 Democrats)

Veterans' Affairs (6th of 7 Democrats)

Elections

1990 Special Election		
Daniel K. Akaka (D)	188,901	(54%)
Patricia Saiki (R)	155,978	(45%)
1990 Special Primary		
Daniel K. Akaka (D)	180,235	(91%)
Paul Snider (D)	18,427	(8%)

Previous Winning Percentages: **1988 *** (89%) **1986 *** (76%) **1984 *** (82%) **1982 *** (89%) **1980 *** (90%) **1978 *** (86%) **1976 *** (80%)

** House elections.*

Interest Group Ratings

Year	ADA	ACU	AFL-CIO	CCUS
1990	100	11	88	10
House Service				
1989	85	7	100	30
1988	85	0	93	23
1987	64	0	88	0
1986	90	9	86	18
1985	65	14	88	22
1984	85	10	92	38
1983	85	4	100	35
1982	65	15	90	21
1981	65	7	100	16

Key Votes

1991	
Authorize use of force against Iraq	N
1990	
Oppose prohibition of certain semiautomatic weapons	N
Support constitutional amendment on flag desecration	N
Oppose requiring parental notice for minors' abortions	Y
Halt production of B-2 stealth bomber at 13 planes	Y
Approve budget that cut spending and raised revenues	N
Pass civil rights bill over Bush veto	Y
House Service	
1989	
Pass Democratic minimum wage plan over Bush veto	Y
Halt B-2 production at 13 planes	N
Oppose capital gains tax cut	Y
Approve federal funding of abortion in cases of rape or incest	Y
Approve pay raise and revision of ethics rules	Y

Voting Studies

	Presidential Support		Party Unity		Conservative Coalition	
Year	**S**	**O**	**S**	**O**	**S**	**O**
1990 *	23 †	75 †	88 †	10 †	23 †	73 †
House Service						
1989	35	62	96	2	22	78
1988	22	74	88	2	13	82
1987	23	67	87	4	37	58
1986	18	79	89	6	28	68
1985	26	68	86	7	35	58
1984	31	63	85	8	22	75
1983	28	66	86	9	42	56
1982	40	53	81	8	32	58
1981	46	54	81	17	52	48

** Akaka was sworn in May 16, 1990. For 1990, his Senate scores are shown. In the House, his presidential support score in 1990 was 17 percent; his opposition score was 74 percent. His party-unity support score was 86 percent; his opposition score was 0 percent. His conservative coalition support score was 17 percent; his opposition score was 83 percent.*
† Not eligible for all recorded votes.

Campaign Finance

	Receipts	Receipts from PACs		Expend-itures
1990				
Akaka (D)	$1,764,875	$854,107	(48%)	$1,760,839
Saiki (R)	$2,570,035	$902,829	(35%)	$2,398,961

1 Neil Abercrombie (D)

Of Honolulu — Elected 1990

Also served 1986-87.

Born: June 26, 1938, Buffalo, N.Y.

Education: Union College, B.A. 1959; U. of Hawaii, M.A. 1964, Ph.D. 1974.

Occupation: Community activist.

Family: Wife, Nancie Caraway.

Religion: Not specified.

Political Career: Hawaii House, 1975-79; Hawaii Senate, 1979-86; Honolulu City Council, 1988-90; sought Democratic nomination for U.S. Senate, 1970; sought Democratic nomination for U.S. House, 1986.

Capitol Office: 1440 Longworth Bldg. 20515; 225-2726.

The Path to Washington: Running in 1990 for a seat he held briefly four years earlier, Abercrombie easily defeated GOP state Rep. Mike Liu. He thus restored the 1st, held for two terms by Republican Patricia Saiki, to Democratic control.

Abercrombie's widely expected win was one of the few predictable events of his unconventional career. A veteran of protest politics — he took 13 percent of the vote in the 1970 Democratic Senate primary as an antiwar candidate — Abercrombie became a leading liberal activist in the state Legislature.

During his tenure in the Legislature, Abercrombie was an avid, sometimes unyielding advocate of aid to the underprivileged. His physical appearance — including a full beard and a mane of long hair — made him a widely recognized figure in Hawaii politics.

But Abercrombie's ideological cast and his often-abrasive manner in those days earned him his share of enemies. This cost Abercrombie dearly in 1986, when his House bid was ruined by a political fluke: He won and lost the 1st District seat on the same day.

Democratic Rep. Cecil Heftel's resignation to run for governor forced the scheduling of a special House election, which coincided with the regular September 1986 primary for a full term. Abercrombie was rated the front-runner in both contests. However, this status left him vulnerable to attacks from both Republican Saiki, his main competition in the open-ballot special election, and from Democratic businessman Mufi Hannemann, an aggressive political newcomer.

While Saiki predictably described Abercrombie as too liberal, Hannemann got personal: Playing off Abercrombie's iconoclastic image, he unearthed a 17-year-old newspaper article in which Abercrombie suggested what seemed to be a favorable attitude about decriminalizing marijuana. Although Abercrombie furiously denied that he countenanced drug use, the issue was damaging.

Abercrombie won the special election with 30 percent to 29 percent for Saiki and 28 percent for Hannemann. But he narrowly lost the primary to Hannemann. Several thousand voters who supported Saiki in the special election apparently voted for Hannemann in the primary (Saiki was unopposed for the nomination and won the general election).

Abercrombie did go to Congress, though, to fill out the remaining weeks of Heftel's term. During his 1990 campaign, Abercrombie emphasized that he was appointed in 1986 to the Armed Services Committee, a position that enabled him to speak for defense budget cuts while promoting Hawaii's importance as a military center in the Pacific.

Returning to Honolulu, Abercrombie won a City Council seat in 1988; Saiki won reelection to the House that year, establishing what looked to be a long-term hold on the seat. However, in April 1990, Democratic Sen. Spark M. Matsunaga died, and Saiki decided to take on interim Democratic Sen. Daniel K. Akaka in a November special Senate election.

Abercrombie jumped in, but with a somewhat tamer, less combative style. Better known than his primary foes — state Sen. Norman Mizuguchi and lawyer Matt Matsunaga (the son of the late senator) — Abercrombie won with 46 percent of the vote.

Although Abercrombie maintained a populist agenda, his cautious approach provided few opportunities for his GOP opponent. Liu, like Saiki, emphasized fiscal conservatism while espousing more moderate views on social issues. But he did not have the benefit, as there had been in 1986, of a Democratic split.

Hawaii 1

Honolulu

The 1st District is Honolulu, a diverse and cosmopolitan community that serves as a symbol both of Hawaii's natural splendor and of the perils of urban commercialization run amok. Visitors still thrill to the proud profile of Diamond Head and the inviting surf down below. But their enthusiasm is usually tempered by the sight of congested Waikiki Beach, whose skyscrapers and shopping centers make it look like an overdeveloped Pacific cousin to Miami Beach. Housing costs are a pressing problem: Honolulu has the highest median single-family home price of any city in the nation, far outdistancing its closest rival.

Honolulu is an active port city, and it hosts light food industries such as pineapple canning. Its status as the seat of state government also provides jobs. But tourism — hotels, restaurants and travel companies — is the city's economic staple.

The city is an elaborate ethnic patchwork, with substantial populations of Japanese, Chinese, Filipinos, Caucasians and those claiming pure or partial native Hawaiian blood. Neighborhoods such as Waialae-Kahala and the affluent Black Point, near Diamond Head, are largely Caucasian. Traditionally, Caucasians have voted Republican, while Japanese-Americans have gone Democratic; Filipino-Americans are considered more independent, unaffiliated with either party. Northwest of the central part of the city is Kalihi, the city's most impoverished area. It is home to a significant native Hawaiian community, as well as to immigrants from the Philippines, Korea and Southeast Asia.

Though no Republican had ever won Honolulu's House seat before Patricia Saiki in 1986, there had been some signs that the city's traditional Democratic bias was wavering. In 1984, the city backed Ronald Reagan, re-elected a Republican prosecutor and chose as mayor Frank F. Fasi, who had served in that post from 1969-81 as a Democrat. In 1988, Fasi won re-election, but the 1st voted solidly for Michael S. Dukakis for president; in 1990, when Saiki ran for the Senate, Democrat Neil Abercrombie easily recaptured the 1st.

Much of the GOP vote in the district comes from corporate managers, retirees from the mainland, and a group of Republican-voting Mormons connected with the Hawaiian branch of Brigham Young University, which lies in the 2nd. There are also GOP sentiments among members of the military, who are politically significant despite a Hawaii law mandating that anyone who registers to vote must pay state taxes. The entirety of the Pearl Harbor naval base is within the boundaries of the 1st.

Population: 482,321. White 143,597 (30%), Black 6,996 (2%), Asian and Pacific Islander 311,161 (65%). Spanish origin 27,882 (6%). 18 and over 362,478 (75%), 65 and over 42,643 (9%). Median age: 30.

Committees

Armed Services (31st of 33 Democrats)
Military Installations & Facilities; Readiness

Merchant Marine & Fisheries (26th of 29 Democrats)
Fisheries & Wildlife Conservation & the Environment; Merchant Marine; Oversight & Investigations

Select Aging (38th of 42 Democrats)
Housing & Consumer Interests; Human Services; Social Security and Women

Campaign Finance

	Receipts	Receipts from PACs		Expend-itures
1990				
Abercrombie (D)	$476,231	$143,600	(30%)	$442,211
Liu (R)	$271,319	$57,601	(21%)	$267,882

Key Vote

1991

Authorize use of force against Iraq	N

Elections

1990 General		
Neil Abercrombie (D)	97,622	(60%)
Mike Liu (R)	62,982	(39%)
1990 Primary		
Neil Abercrombie (D)	43,480	(46%)
Norman Mizuguchi (D)	30,942	(32%)
Matt Matsunaga (D)	21,128	(22%)

Previous Winning Percentage: **1986** * (30%)

** Special election.*

District Vote For President

	1988	1984	1980	1976
D	95,347 (54%)	74,912 (44%)	56,298 (43%)	65,216 (49%)
R	79,322 (45%)	93,894 (55%)	58,045 (44%)	67,080 (50%)
I			14,842 (11%)	

2 Patsy T. Mink (D)

Of Honolulu — Elected 1990

Also served 1965-77.

Born: Dec 6, 1927, Paia, Maui, Hawaii.

Education: U. of Hawaii, B.A. 1948; U. of Chicago, J.D. 1951.

Occupation: Lawyer.

Family: Husband, John Francis Mink; one child.

Religion: Protestant.

Political Career: Hawaii Territorial House, 1956-58; Hawaii Territorial Senate, 1958-59; Hawaii Senate, 1962-64; sought Democratic nomination for president, 1972; sought Democratic nomination for U.S. Senate, 1976; Honolulu City Council, 1983-87; sought Democratic nomination for governor, 1986; sought Democratic nomination for Honolulu mayor, 1988.

Capitol Office: 2135 Rayburn Bldg. 20515; 225-4906.

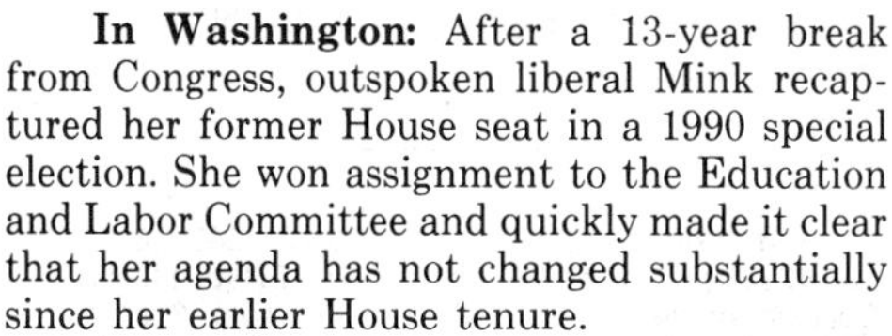

In Washington: After a 13-year break from Congress, outspoken liberal Mink recaptured her former House seat in a 1990 special election. She won assignment to the Education and Labor Committee and quickly made it clear that her agenda has not changed substantially since her earlier House tenure.

A staunch advocate of women's civil rights in employment, she warned Democratic colleagues as long ago as 1970 that "women are still the victims of discrimination [in the workplace]. I think we as a party must recognize our moral responsibility for this injustice."

Disappointed by President Bush's veto of a civil rights bill in 1990, she was infuriated in 1991 when leadership proponents of the legislation, in an effort to broaden its appeal, decided to write in language that would limit money damages for women and religious minorities who are the victims of job discrimination. She unsuccessfully tried to persuade other House members to oppose the limit, but after a civil rights measure without the cap failed on the House floor, she voted for the compromise.

Mink is also still as passionate about public health and environmental protection as she was in 1971, when she and 32 other members sued the Environmental Protection Agency and five other government agencies after they failed to disclose unclassified parts of a report on underground nuclear tests being conducted at the Alaskan Aleutian island of Amchitka.

In October 1990 she faced a similar incident closer to home. The Army had made plans to assemble, test and launch missiles at the Pacific Missile Range facility on the Hawaiian island of Kauai, in connection with work on the strategic defense initiative. In response, Mink and Sen. Daniel K. Akaka pushed a bill mandating that the Army do an environmental impact statement before proceeding with the program.

At Home: Mink is one of the hardiest figures on the Hawaii political scene. In 1956, she won a seat in the territorial House, then moved up to the Senate two years later. Mink was out of office during the early days of statehood, but won a state Senate seat in 1962.

In 1964, Mink narrowly won a primary for a U.S. House seat, then was elected with incumbent Democratic Rep. Spark M. Matsunaga (until 1970, both of Hawaii's House members were elected at large). Quickly establishing herself as an outspoken activist, Mink edged Matsunaga in total votes as both were elected in 1966; Matsunaga moved back ahead in 1968.

In her 1970 contest — her first in the newly created 2nd District — Mink ran unopposed. With President Richard M. Nixon scoring the first GOP presidential victory ever in Hawaii, Mink slipped to 57 percent of the vote in 1972. She rebounded to 63 percent in 1974.

However, Mink's rise was halted in 1976, when she bid for the seat of retiring Republican Sen. Hiram L. Fong. Her Democratic primary rival, House colleague Matsunaga, had backing from much of the state party leadership. Playing off his image as a conciliator against Mink's more ideological bearing, Matsunaga won with 51 percent to Mink's 41 percent.

Mink then signed on with the liberal Americans for Democratic Action, serving as president from 1978 to 1981. Returning to Hawaiian politics, she won two terms on the Honolulu City Council. In the ensuing years, though, Mink had more downs than ups, finishing third in the 1986 Democratic gubernatorial primary and failing in a 1988 primary bid for Honolulu mayor.

Thus, Mink's 1990 bid to succeed Akaka took the form of a comeback. In the September 1990 special election, her toughest foe was Mufi Hannemann, who had lost a 1986 House contest to Republican Patricia Saiki in the 1st District.

Hawaii 2

Honolulu Suburbs; Outer Islands

The 2nd encompasses virtually everything in Hawaii but the city of Honolulu. It includes all the islands outside of Oahu, where Honolulu is located, plus suburbs of the city itself. The fast-growing suburbs swelled the population of the 2nd in the 1970s, causing some turf to be transferred to the 1st in 1981 redistricting.

Although the Pearl Harbor naval base lies across district lines in the 1st, the 2nd retains many Oahu military installations, and these, along with wealthy residential neighborhoods in and around Kailua, have generated some respectable Republican showings in national elections, although Democrat Michael S. Dukakis carried the 2nd comfortably in 1988.

In other contests, the Democratic vote elsewhere overwhelms GOP candidates. Since its creation for the 1970 elections, the 2nd always has gone Democratic for the House, unlike the 1st, which the GOP held from 1987-91.

Oahu dominates the district politically. The island of Hawaii, at the chain's southeastern end, is known as "the Big Island," for it has two-thirds of the state's land area, but it contains only an eighth of Oahu's population. The island's main crop is sugar cane. Cattle, macadamia nuts, coffee beans and orchids also spur the economy.

The other islands of the chain contribute to the state's agricultural wealth but play only a minor part in its politics. The three populated islands of Maui County make up the state's richest pineapple-growing land. 98 percent of the island of Lanai, the sixth largest in the Hawaiian chain, is owned by a private pineapple-growing company. Sugar cane and beef cattle are important in Maui and in Kauai County, the lightly populated group of islands at the northernmost end of the archipelago. Kauai is home to Waialeale peak, considered the wettest spot on earth, with over 450 inches of rain annually.

Population: 482,370. White 175,173 (36%), Black 10,368 (2%), Asian and Pacific Islander 272,091 (56%). Spanish origin 43,381 (9%). 18 and over 326,630 (68%), 65 and over 33,507 (7%). Median age: 27.

A young, business-oriented candidate, Hannemann portrayed Mink as a candidate of a more liberal past. But touting her years of experience, Mink hung on, winning the special election by 2 percentage points, and the primary for a full term by a slightly larger margin.

The November campaign was much easier. Republican Andy Poepoe, a businessman and longtime state officeholder, had run a distant fourth in the special election. Mink won easily.

Committees

Education & Labor (18th of 25 Democrats)
Elementary, Secondary & Vocational Education; Labor-Management Relations; Postsecondary Education

Government Operations (20th of 25 Democrats)
Government Information, Justice & Agriculture; Human Resources & Intergovernmental Relations

Elections

1990 General		
Patsy T. Mink (D)	118,155	(66%)
Andy Poepoe (R)	54,625	(31%)
1990 Primary		
Patsy T. Mink (D)	47,998	(39%)
Mufi F. Hannemann (D)	44,536	(36%)
Ron Menor (D)	20,845	(17%)
1990 Special		
Patsy T. Mink (D)	51,841	(35%)
Mufi F. Hannemann (D)	50,164	(33%)
Ron Menor (D)	23,629	(16%)
Andy Poepoe (R)	8,872	(6%)

Previous Winning Percentages: **1974** (63%) **1972** (57%) **1970** (100%) **1964-68** †

† One of two Hawaii House members elected at large.

District Vote For President

	1988		1984		1980		1976	
D	97,017	(54%)	72,242	(44%)	79,581	(46%)	81,950	(52%)
R	79,302	(44%)	91,156	(55%)	72,067	(42%)	72,693	(46%)
I					17,179	(10%)		

Key Votes

1991	
Authorize use of force against Iraq	N
1990	
Approve budget summit plan for spending and taxing	N
Approve civil rights bill	Y

Voting Studies

	Presidential Support		Party Unity		Conservative Coalition	
Year	**S**	**O**	**S**	**O**	**S**	**O**
1990	22 †	78 †	81 †	5 †	21 †	75 †

† Not eligible for all recorded votes.

Interest Group Ratings

Year	ADA	ACU	AFL-CIO	CCUS
1990	-	20	100	50

Campaign Finance

	Receipts	Receipts from PACs		Expenditures
1990				
Mink (D)	$641,324	$147,784	(23%)	$641,037
Poepoe (R)	$191,641	$42,460	(22%)	$204,153

Idaho

U.S. CONGRESS

SENATE 2 R
HOUSE 2 D

LEGISLATURE

Senate 21 D, 21 R
House 28 D, 56 R

ELECTIONS

1988 Presidential Vote

Bush	62%
Dukakis	36%

1984 Presidential Vote

Reagan	72%
Mondale	26%

1980 Presidential Vote

Reagan	66%
Carter	25%
Anderson	6%

Turnout rate in 1986	53%
Turnout rate in 1988	58%
Turnout rate in 1990	44%

(as percentage of voting age population)

POPULATION AND GROWTH

1980 population	943,935
1990 population (42nd in the nation)	1,006,749
Percent change 1980-1990	+7%

DEMOGRAPHIC BREAKDOWN

White	94%
Black	0.3%
American Indian, Eskimo, or Aleut	1%
(Hispanic origin)	5%
Urban	54%
Rural	46%
Born in state	49%
Foreign-born	3%

MAJOR CITIES

Boise	125,738
Pocatello	46,080
Idaho Falls	43,929
Nampa	28,365
Lewiston	28,082

AREA AND LAND USE

Area	82,412 sq. miles (11th)
Farm	26%
Forest	41%
Federally owned	64%

Gov. Cecil D. Andrus (D)
Of Boise — Elected 1986
(also served 1971-77)

Born: Aug. 25, 1931, Hood River, Ore.
Education: Oregon State U., 1948-49.
Military Service: Navy, 1951-55.
Occupation: Lumberjack; sawmill manager; management consultant.
Religion: Lutheran.
Political Career: Idaho Senate, 1961-67, 1969-71; U.S. secretary of the interior, 1977-81; Democratic nominee for governor, 1966.
Next Election: 1994.

WORK

Occupations

White-collar	50%
Blue-collar	29%
Service workers	13%

Government Workers

Federal	9,880
State	20,794
Local	44,300

MONEY

Median family income	$ 17,492	(36th)
Tax burden per capita	$ 730	(40th)

EDUCATION

Spending per pupil through grade 12	$ 2,667	(48th)
Persons with college degrees	16%	(25th)

CRIME

Violent crime rate	255 per 100,000 (42nd)

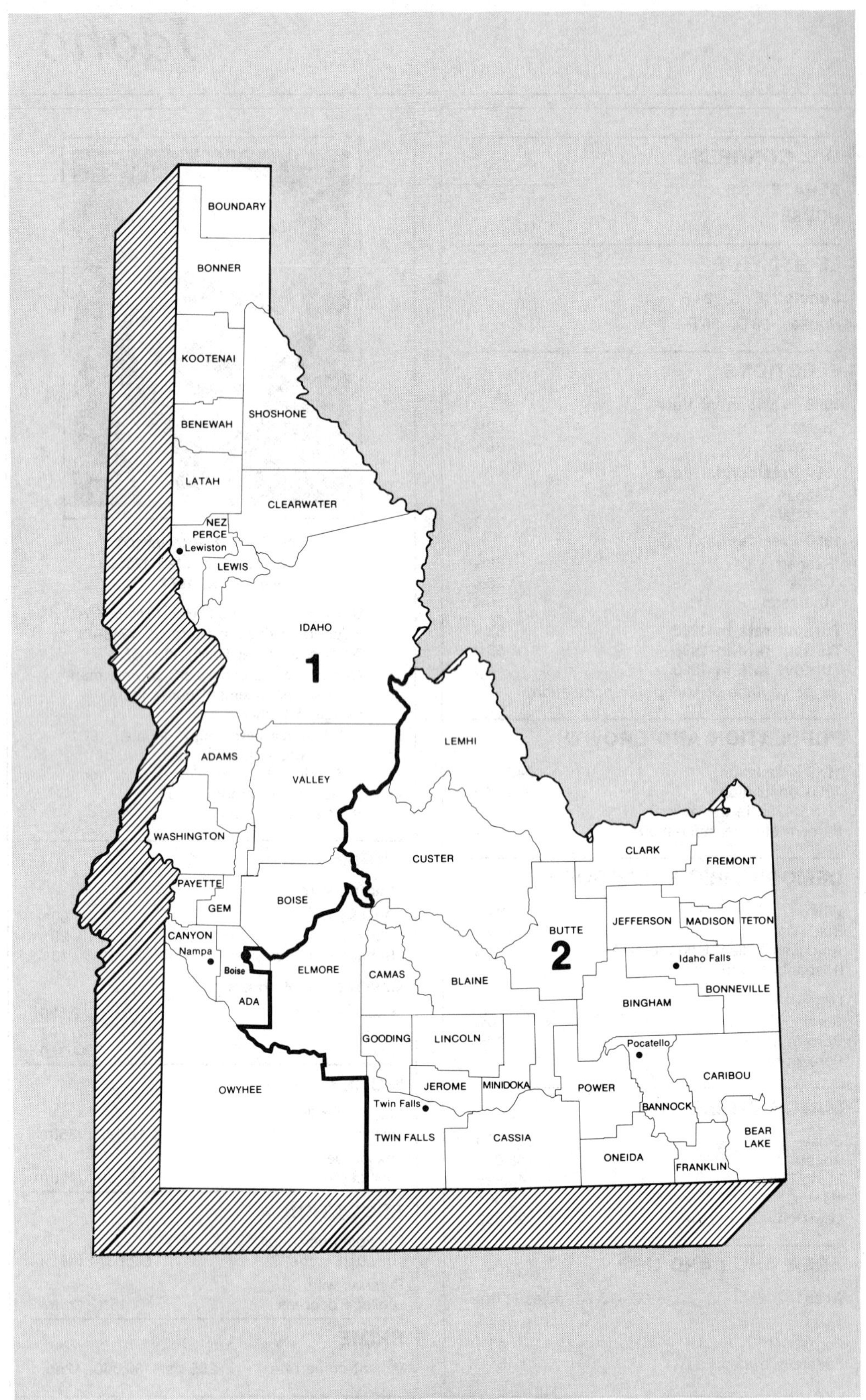
BOUNDARY
BONNER
KOOTENAI
SHOSHONE
BENEWAH
LATAH
CLEARWATER
NEZ PERCE
Lewiston
LEWIS
IDAHO
1
LEMHI
ADAMS
VALLEY
WASHINGTON
CUSTER
CLARK
FREMONT
PAYETTE
GEM
BOISE
JEFFERSON
MADISON
TETON
BUTTE
2
CANYON
Nampa
Boise
ELMORE
CAMAS
BLAINE
Idaho Falls
BONNEVILLE
BINGHAM
ADA
GOODING
LINCOLN
Pocatello
OWYHEE
JEROME
MINIDOKA
POWER
CARIBOU
Twin Falls
BANNOCK
TWIN FALLS
CASSIA
BEAR LAKE
ONEIDA
FRANKLIN

Steve Symms (R)

Of Caldwell — Elected 1980

Born: April 23, 1938, Nampa, Idaho.
Education: U. of Idaho, B.S. 1960.
Military Service: Marine Corps, 1960-63.
Occupation: Fruit grower; fitness club owner.
Family: Divorced; four children.
Religion: Methodist.
Political Career: U.S. House, 1973-81.
Capitol Office: 509 Hart Bldg. 20510; 224-6142.

In Washington: The boyish Symms who appeared in his 1972 TV campaign ads taking a bite from an apple is now in his 50s and has spent most of his adult life in Congress. Though he must increasingly confront the realization that he is now a part of the Establishment, he remains a conservative sentinel not infrequently to the right of the four Republican administrations he has served under since coming to Washington.

Symms came to the Senate from the House in 1981, one of 13 freshmen who had deposed incumbents the previous fall and delivered control of the chamber to the GOP. The ex-Marine was already a veteran of eight years of guerrilla warfare in the House, where he and his allies on the right used demands for roll call votes, frequent quorum calls and numerous amendments to tie up the Democratic leadership. Symms was not the group leader, but he was one of its most enthusiastic participants.

But with the Republicans in control of the Senate after the 1980 elections, he seemed to be moving from gadfly to serious legislator. He won high marks from other senators for his work on federal highway programs as chairman of the Environment Subcommittee on Transportation, a role in which he generally was credited with steadiness and diligence.

Although he did not achieve his goal of passing a long-term reauthorization for grants to states from the Highway Trust Fund in the 98th or 99th Congress, Symms was respected for his efforts. And, ironically, when the Democrats took control in 1987, they swiftly passed, over President Ronald Reagan's veto, the highway bill on which Symms had labored so long.

In 1990, Symms formed and chaired the GOP Conference Task Force on Transportation and Infrastructure, which he described as a strategy development group for the 1991 highway bill. He will seek to move the transportation trust funds off budget.

With Republicans no longer in the majority, some wondered whether Symms would resume the guerrilla-warfare approach that marked the earlier part of his career. The answer has been mixed. He has certainly not lost his ideological compass: 1990 would have been his eighth consecutive year of zero ratings from the liberal Americans for Democratic Action had he not supported an environmentalist-backed amendment to the Clean Air Act that promised to provoke a veto of the bill.

But Symms has also managed to have a serious impact on selected issues of importance to him or his state. He was, for example, an early advocate of a second production reactor for nuclear materials used in the nation's strategic weapons — a facility that fit his national security philosophy and could be built in Idaho. But the end of the Cold War has dampened the Energy Department's enthusiasm for the project.

Symms was also in the front lines of the 100th and 101st Congresses as an opponent of clean-air legislation. He and other Westerners viewed the bill as favoring Eastern high-sulfur coal, and Symms also said the bill would impose debilitating costs on businesses.

When the Environment Committee approved the bill for floor action, Symms' was the lone vote in opposition. He characterized it as a radical assault on industry and predicted it would offend other senators as they familiarized themselves with its details. "This bill is going to smell like a rotten bag of fish after two months," he said. He claimed vindication for his no vote when the Senate had to convene backroom talks with White House negotiators to craft a compromise package.

Unable to win adoption of amendments that would substantially mitigate business' burden, Symms set out to scuttle the clean-air bill. He voted for an amendment that would have made the bill's auto-emissions controls substantially tougher, knowing that it would likely sink the bill. His spokesman said Symms was not trying to kill the bill, but he freely admitted that his intention was to bust up the Senate-White House compromise.

Symms was poised to employ the same

strategy on the most fiercely contested amendment on the bill, West Virginia Democrat Robert C. Byrd's job-loss benefits plan for coal miners. The administration made clear its opposition to the amendment but was equivocal over whether its adoption would trigger a veto. White House Chief of Staff John H. Sununu told Delaware Democrat Joseph R. Biden Jr. that it was certain veto bait, but he led Symms to believe that it was not. Under heavy pressure from Republican leaders, Symms switched his vote during the roll call to a "nay"; the amendment was rejected 49-50. Later, Symms said, "If I were sure that . . . the amendment would have sunk the bill, I would have voted for it."

Earlier in the 101st Congress, Symms won passage of legislation that drew praise from environmental organizations. His bill, aimed at curbing the destruction of tropical rain forests and other fragile ecosystems, would require preparation and disclosure of environmental impact assessments on proposed multilateral bank projects before the United States could vote in favor of the project. It became law as part of a bill reauthorizing U.S. contributions to multilateral development banks.

Throughout his first Senate term, Symms often used his heated rhetoric to make things difficult for the Reagan administration and his party's Senate leadership. Whenever he saw a deviation from the strong conservative values he believed the president stood for personally, Symms did not hesitate to denounce it. Arms control was a target of many of Symms' attacks.

Symms is also a member of the Finance and Budget committees, but he has not been among their most active participants. Throughout much of the 99th Congress, he used his seat on Finance to question Reagan's tax-revision proposal ("a huge gamble with our economy"), although he voted for it in the end. In the 100th Congress, Symms had to leave Finance when its size was reduced. He rejoined at the start of the 101st Congress.

At Home: Even when Symms is not on the ballot, his unpredictable nature can generate election-year controversy. In 1988, he told a radio interviewer in Idaho that Kitty Dukakis, wife of the Democratic nominee for president, had been photographed burning an American flag. Challenged, he could produce no evidence. Symms also attracted some attention with a fundraising letter in 1988 that urged help in defeating Idaho Democratic Rep. Richard H. Stallings before he could become a threat to either of the state's GOP senators.

Stallings, who in 1990 turned down an opportunity to run for the open seat of retiring Sen. James A. McClure, is a prospective 1992 challenger to Symms.

Both of Symms' Senate elections have been close, but only one was as combative as the figures imply. That was in 1980, when he used his base in the House to launch a campaign against the state's most prestigious and durable liberal, Democrat Frank Church.

National conservative groups had targeted Church for defeat; an independent committee labeled ABC (Anybody But Church) ran television ads denouncing the senator's conciliatory stand on U.S. foreign policy issues. Symms charged that the Foreign Relations chairman was weak on national defense, supported too much government spending and hurt the state's economy with his bill to expand Idaho wilderness areas.

Church was a resourceful campaigner, however, and Symms had to deal with a number of side issues that emerged, including rumors that he was a womanizer and charges that he was involved in a conflict of interest through buying silver futures while serving on a House subcommittee overseeing the Commodity Futures Trading Commission. He denied the stories.

The conservative tide carried Symms to a narrow victory, helped along by the concession speech President Jimmy Carter delivered while the polls were still open in parts of the state. Symms' margin was less than 4,300 votes.

In 1986, it was Symms' turn for a challenge. His opponent was Gov. John V. Evans, who was constitutionally required to give up the governorship. At first glance, the contest had all the markings of a classic fight — two of the state's best-known politicians going head-to-head in a year in which control of the Senate was at stake. As it turned out, though, their race lacked the spark that marked other Senate contests that year.

For one thing, both candidates were so well-known that even before the campaign began in earnest, polls were showing most voters had already made up their minds between the two, dividing roughly in half.

But personality factors also made it unlikely from the start that the contest would ignite. Evans, who governed with a low-key, businesslike style, was not the sort to start any flame throwing. And Symms, whose freewheeling manner had been an issue in previous campaigns, seemed intent on projecting an aura of responsibility.

Policy issues had an ambiguous effect. Idaho was suffering through a depressing "triple recession," with mining, timber and agriculture struggling at the same time; Evans, as governor, was unable to lay all the blame for economic troubles on national GOP policies.

With Evans maintaining his typical low profile until relatively late in the campaign, Symms barnstormed the state, enthusiastic and affable, drawing crowds at county fairs and rodeos. He tried to counteract his flamboyant reputation with a series of ads offering testimonials from constituents and touting his work for farmers and lumbermen. By the time the election was drawing close, he had clearly strengthened his standing.

The one key uncertainty in the election was the effect of a ballot initiative to undo the state's right-to-work law. Unions, which are still strong in northern Idaho, were organizing fervently on its behalf, and Democrats believed that organized labor's efforts would help Evans.

But Evans never managed to put Symms on the defensive, and the right-to-work initiative provoked a strong turnout of voters who supported the right-to-work law. Evans won many of the counties in the blue-collar belt that runs from the center of the state north through the Panhandle. But he could not make enough inroads elsewhere. Voters happy with Symms' ideology were reassured by his efforts to convince them that he was not a flaky maverick, and he carried the bulk of the state's counties on his way to a 52 percent overall tally.

Symms' original campaign for Congress was the climax to a decade of operating around the conservative fringes of Idaho politics, developing a reputation as a genial and appealing man, but also a strident ideologue.

As a Marine in 1962, Symms served at the U.S. military base at Guantanamo during the Cuban missile crisis, and returned lamenting President John F. Kennedy's decision not to launch a full-scale invasion of the island. "It was just a matter of liberating the Cuban people," he said later. Back home in Idaho, he left his Presbyterian church when the parent body contributed to the legal defense of black activist Angela Davis, and became a Methodist instead. Then he began publishing an anti-government newsletter, the *Idaho Compass*, advocating leasing the University of Idaho forestry school to a paper company, and the school of mines to a copper company. He urged the university to permit students to major in capitalism.

By early 1972 Symms was so distressed by the liberal direction of the country — especially the Nixon administration's wage and price controls — that he talked about moving to Australia. But he ran for Congress instead, attracting voters with his enthusiasm and gimmicks such as a commercial in which he chomped on an apple, then asked viewers to elect him and "take a bite out of government."

Committees

Budget (2nd of 9 Republicans)

Environment & Public Works (3rd of 7 Republicans)
Water Resources, Transportation & Infrastructure (ranking); Environmental Protection; Nuclear Regulation

Finance (7th of 9 Republicans)
Energy & Agricultural Taxation (ranking); International Trade; Taxation

Joint Economic

Elections

1986 General		
Steve Symms (R)	196,958	(52%)
John V. Evans (D)	185,066	(48%)

Previous Winning Percentages: **1980** (50%) **1978 *** (60%) **1976 *** (55%) **1974 *** (58%) **1972 *** (56%)

* *House elections.*

Campaign Finance

	Receipts	Receipts from PACs		Expend-itures
1986				
Symms (R)	$3,387,726	$1,366,527	(40%)	$3,229,939
Evans (D)	$2,200,571	$690,398	(31%)	$2,128,223

Key Votes

1991	
Authorize use of force against Iraq	Y
1990	
Oppose prohibition of certain semiautomatic weapons	Y
Support constitutional amendment on flag desecration	Y
Oppose requiring parental notice for minors' abortions	N
Halt production of B-2 stealth bomber at 13 planes	N
Approve budget that cut spending and raised revenues	N
Pass civil rights bill over Bush veto	N
1989	
Oppose reduction of SDI funding	Y
Oppose barring federal funds for "obscene" art	N
Allow vote on capital gains tax cut	Y

Voting Studies

	Presidential Support		Party Unity		Conservative Coalition	
Year	**S**	**O**	**S**	**O**	**S**	**O**
1990	74	24	93	5	95	5
1989	82	14	94	4	92	5
1988	70	25	93	1	92	3
1987	74	19	92	4	97	0
1986	86	6	84	6	88	1
1985	81	18	91	7	92	7
1984	81	12	89	3	89	0
1983	62	35	84	12	86	9
1982	79	20	93	6	97	2
1981	80	13	90	7	91	4

Interest Group Ratings

Year	ADA	ACU	AFL-CIO	CCUS
1990	6	100	11	83
1989	0	96	0	88
1988	0	100	0	86
1987	0	88	11	94
1986	0	100	0	100
1985	0	100	0	90
1984	0	100	0	88
1983	0	100	0	84
1982	5	79	8	80
1981	0	100	6	100

Larry E. Craig (R)

Of Midvale — Elected 1990

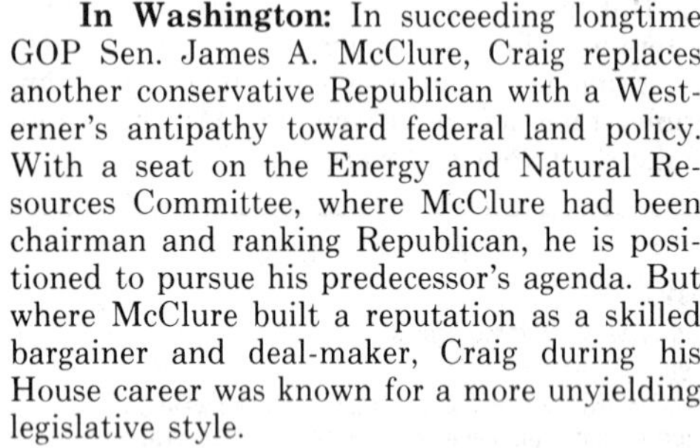

Born: July 20, 1945, Council, Idaho.
Education: U. of Idaho, B.A. 1969; attended George Washington U., 1970.
Military Service: Idaho National Guard, 1971-72.
Occupation: Farmer; real estate salesman.
Family: Wife, Suzanne Scott; three stepchildren.
Religion: Methodist.
Political Career: Idaho Senate, 1975-81; U.S. House, 1981-91.
Capitol Office: 302 Hart Bldg. 20510; 224-2752.

In Washington: In succeeding longtime GOP Sen. James A. McClure, Craig replaces another conservative Republican with a Westerner's antipathy toward federal land policy. With a seat on the Energy and Natural Resources Committee, where McClure had been chairman and ranking Republican, he is positioned to pursue his predecessor's agenda. But where McClure built a reputation as a skilled bargainer and deal-maker, Craig during his House career was known for a more unyielding legislative style.

On the House Interior Committee, Craig was a contentious and consistent critic of that panel's conservationist Democratic majority, which has placed millions of acres of federal land in wilderness status, beyond commercial development. For several years, Craig vehemently fought passage of a new Idaho wilderness bill that would increase federal holdings. He opposed the 1.4 million-acre compromise plan unveiled in 1987 by McClure and Democratic Gov. Cecil D. Andrus. That plan dissolved; professional negotiators in early 1990 began seeking a settlement between environmental and commercial interests. Craig says he supports the negotiation process.

In 1989, with many Northwesterners upset over proposed government intervention to protect the northern spotted owl, Craig introduced legislation aimed at weakening the Threatened and Endangered Species Act. His bill would have required public participation throughout the process of listing threatened and endangered species, rather than only after the Fish and Wildlife Service makes a proposed listing decision.

On one issue before the 100th Congress, Craig found himself on the environmental side of a development issue. He pushed a bill to prohibit the building of dams on portions of the Snake and lower Salmon rivers. Before the House unanimously endorsed the bill, which was later enacted, Craig heralded the effort to keep the free-flowing reaches of the rivers available to sportsmen.

In the 102nd Congress, Craig, concerned over a 1990 Supreme Court ruling that allowed the federal government to weigh in on water rights issues arising in hydroelectric power plants, introduced a bill to bolster the authority of states over water allocations. He tried to attach it to a comprehensive energy bill during Energy Committee consideration, but Chairman J. Bennett Johnston of Louisiana urged him to withdraw it and pursue another vehicle, saying that Energy Secretary James D. Watkins had called to argue against the amendment. Craig reluctantly withdrew it but left open the possibility of trying to add it later.

One of 52 House Republicans swept into office in 1980, Craig proudly counted himself a front-ranks leader in the "Reagan Revolution." He shared with the new president roots in the West, a conservative ideology and a confrontational approach to government. But by the end of Ronald Reagan's tenure in the White House, Craig was among those Republicans who seemed more ideologically consistent than Reagan himself.

Craig's years in Washington have little dimmed his philosophical certainty or quieted his rabble-rousing on the evils of federal debt. He talks in terms of a "war" against the deficit, and at times sounds dismayed that even after eight years under a president opposed to federal largess, the deficit has multiplied. Unlike many conservatives, however, Craig does not lay the blame squarely on Congress. He sees it as the "mutual responsibility" of the Congress and the president.

Craig is a crusader for a balanced-budget constitutional amendment, and he has carried that mission beyond the halls of Congress. Founder of CLUBB (Congressional Leaders United for a Balanced Budget), Craig urges state legislatures to demand that Congress enact a balanced-budget amendment or call a constitutional convention to draft one. Craig featured his call for a balanced-budget amendment in his 1990 Senate campaign.

The balanced-budget amendment came to the House floor in 1990, but it fell seven votes short of passage.

Craig's ardor for deficit reduction does not keep him from lobbying for home-state projects. But when he delivers, he seems to feel compelled to explain. In the 100th Congress, Craig helped secure the release of $300,000 to conduct a water-quality study in Idaho; he said it was "no pork barrel," but of "great importance" to several Western states. In a letter to constituents, Craig noted that a $1.35 million federal matching grant he helped secure for the Centennial Trail was "not one of the so-called budget-busting measures." The money was already set aside; he just earmarked it for Idaho.

In addition to Energy, Craig captured an assignment on the Agriculture Committee, where he is expected to embrace ranking Republican Richard G. Lugar's antagonism toward extensive government involvement in farming.

For the last four years of his House tenure, Craig served on the ethics committee. In the 101st Congress, he and Utah Republican James V. Hansen were the only committee members to vote for harsher punishment for Massachusetts Democratic Barney Frank when Georgia Republican Newt Gingrich proposed to censure Frank. The ethics committee reprimanded Frank for misusing his official position to help a male prostitute.

Craig regularly argues with the government of Canada on behalf of his timber-producing constituents. A member of the House Government Operations Committee until 1989, when he switched to Public Works, Craig voted against a bill to carry out the U.S.-Canada free-trade agreement to protest the low fee charged by the Canadians for timber removal from public land, which he said amounted to an unfair subsidy.

In 1985, Craig introduced legislation to restrain U.S. imports of Canadian timber. "I do not expect action from the Canadians," he said, "until we have the two-by-four with which we are preparing to hit them between the eyes squarely in hand." In late 1986, Canada agreed to impose a 15 percent tax on softwood exports.

Idaho historically has been a major producer of silver, but low prices in recent years have cost many miners their jobs. In the 100th Congress, Craig backed successful legislation to fund the Mining and Minerals Institute at the University of Idaho. As a freshman, Craig fought a Reagan administration plan to generate revenue by selling silver from the nation's strategic-minerals stockpile. He said this would depress prices.

A strong opponent of gun-control measures, Craig was one of only 21 House members to vote against a 1985 bill banning armor-piercing bullets. He claimed that the bill attempted to curb criminal behavior "by controlling little pieces of metal." He continued, "That approach is what gun control is all about — and this bill, like all other forms of gun control, will fail to achieve its stated objective." Craig strongly supported the 1986 legislation that rolled back some provisions of the Gun Control Act of 1968.

At Home: Craig's ascent to the Senate was a fairly smooth affair, as he mobilized the renowned statewide organization of retiring Sen. McClure to roll over his Democratic opponent, Ron Twilegar, a former state legislator and Boise City Council member.

Idaho Democrats also cooperated to some extent by failing to field a well-known candidate. Richard Stallings, the popular 2nd District representative, opted against the race. After prolonged consideration, former Gov. John V. Evans, the 1986 nominee against GOP Sen. Steve Symms, also decided not to run.

Craig, by contrast, declared that he would vacate his 1st District seat and enter the race less than a week after McClure's January 1990 retirement announcement. State Attorney General Jim Jones also filed for the Republican nomination. Jones ran a sparsely funded, populist campaign, hitting Craig as an ineffective legislator who had been inattentive to voters' concerns. But Jones was no match for the well-funded, well-organized Craig, who won 59 percent of the primary vote. Twilegar won his primary with 64 percent over an obscure Idaho Falls businessman.

Craig's reputation as a stalwart opponent of abortion produced one of the more awkward moments of his campaign. In a debate with Twilegar, Craig responded to a question by saying that if his wife were impregnated by rape, it would be up to her to decide if she should seek an abortion. Twilegar then archly asked whether Craig's wife should be the only woman in the country to have a choice.

But that was one of the few Twilegar shots that hit the mark. Mostly, his criticism of Craig's attendance record and votes on environmental issues had little visible effect. Craig's popularity in the 1st District, coupled with support in the more conservative 2nd, propelled him past the pro-abortion rights Democrat to a 61-39 percent victory.

In four re-election bids in the 1st, Craig was held below 65 percent only once. He had no trouble turning back the 1988 challenge of two-term state legislator Jeanne Givens, a member of the Coeur d'Alene tribe.

An eerie streak of bad fortune had befallen Craig's Democratic opponents in the two previous elections. In 1986, candidate Pete Busch, who two years before had mounted a spirited underdog campaign against McClure, died when the plane he was piloting crashed. Craig took 65 percent against Bill Currie, a former Boundary County commissioner who replaced Busch as the Democratic candidate.

In 1984, the man who initially decided to challenge Craig was killed in a car crash. Craig had won his first two House elections with just 54 percent, but he soared to 69 percent against Bill Hellar, who was named the substitute Democratic nominee after the fatal car crash.

That tally was the highest vote by any 1st District candidate in nearly 50 years. Neither McClure nor Symms, both of whom held the 1st before moving to the Senate, had ever surpassed 60 percent.

In the state Senate, Craig was known as something of a moderate, but in his 1980 House campaign, he tied himself to Symms, then campaigning for the Senate. After winning a tough primary, Craig was rated a solid favorite over underfinanced Democrat Glenn W. Nichols. Still, Nichols gave Craig trouble, drawing attention by walking the length of the 1st, from Canada to Nevada, criticizing Craig's "Sagebrush Rebellion" sympathies.

In 1982, Democrats nominated Larry LaRocco, who had worked as a field representative for former Democratic Sen. Frank Church. LaRocco said Craig favored wholesale privatization of federal lands. Craig complained he was the victim of "falsehoods, misrepresentations and misreporting." But strong support for LaRocco from the economically depressed northern part of the 1st did not derail Craig. In 1990, LaRocco ran again for Craig's seat and won with 53 percent.

Committees

Agriculture, Nutrition & Forestry (6th of 8 Republicans)
Conservation & Forestry (ranking); Agricultural Credit; Rural Development & Rural Electrification

Energy & Natural Resources (7th of 9 Republicans)
Mineral Resources Development & Production (ranking); Energy Research & Development; Public Lands, National Parks & Forests

Special Aging (8th of 10 Republicans)

Elections

1990 General		
Larry E. Craig (R)	193,641	(61%)
Ron J. Twilegar (D)	122,295	(39%)
1990 Primary		
Larry E. Craig (R)	65,830	(59%)
Jim Jones (R)	45,733	(41%)

Previous Winning Percentages: **1988** * (66%) **1986** * (65%) **1984** * (69%) **1982** * (54%) **1980** * (54%)

* *House elections.*

Campaign Finance

	Receipts	Receipts from PACs	Expend-itures
1990			
Craig (R)	$1,734,617	$811,026 (47%)	$1,652,532
Twilegar (D)	$544,516	$212,049 (39%)	$544,419

Key Votes

1991	
Authorize use of force against Iraq	Y
House Service	
1990	
Support constitutional amendment on flag desecration	Y
Pass family and medical leave bill over Bush veto	N
Reduce SDI funding	N
Allow abortions in overseas military facilities	N
Approve budget summit plan for spending and taxing	N
Approve civil rights bill	N
1989	
Halt production of B-2 stealth bomber at 13 planes	N
Oppose capital gains tax cut	N
Approve federal abortion funding in rape or incest cases	N
Approve pay raise and revision of ethics rules	N
Pass Democratic minimum wage plan over Bush veto	N

Voting Studies

	Presidential Support		Party Unity		Conservative Coalition	
Year	**S**	**O**	**S**	**O**	**S**	**O**
House Service						
1990	59	25	75	8	89	2
1989	78	22	93	6	93	7
1988	66	23	87	5	76	5
1987	65 †	28 †	83 †	8 †	93 †	5 †
1986	79	21	85	9	92	6
1985	75	24	91	5	96	2
1984	73	22	86	4	93	5
1983	73	16	86	4	93	3
1982	75	23	85	7	86	8
1981	72	24	91	5	91	4

† Not eligible for all recorded votes.

Interest Group Ratings

Year	ADA	ACU	AFL-CIO	CCUS
House Service				
1990	11	86	0	82
1989	0	96	0	100
1988	5	100	7	92
1987	8	86	13	93
1986	5	86	21	100
1985	0	90	0	91
1984	5	91	15	87
1983	0	100	0	84
1982	5	95	5	90
1981	0	100	13	95

1 Larry LaRocco (D)

Of Boise — Elected 1990

Born: Aug. 25, 1946, Van Nuys, Calif.
Education: U. of Portland, Ore., B.A. 1967; Boston U., M.S. 1969.
Military Service: Army, 1969-72.
Occupation: Stockbroker.
Family: Wife, Chris Bideganeta; two children.
Religion: Roman Catholic.
Political Career: Democratic nominee for U.S. House, 1982; Democratic nominee for Idaho Senate, 1986.
Capitol Office: 1117 Longworth Bldg. 20515; 225-6611.

The Path to Washington: LaRocco's election culminated an eight-year quest for public office that began with a 1982 challenge to GOP Rep. Larry E. Craig, then a freshman, who left the 1st for the Senate in 1990. His 46 percent tally was the best showing by a Democrat since 1966, the year the Democrats lost the seat once called Idaho's "Democratic district."

LaRocco was a familiar face in the western 1st when he announced his 1990 bid. He was Democratic Sen. Frank Church's north Idaho field representative from 1975 to 1981, tending to constituent matters throughout the logging areas in the north. (He also worked on Church's 1976 presidential campaign.) LaRocco points to his role in helping negotiate a settlement in the roadless Gospel Hump area as one of his most taxing and rewarding jobs as Church's aide.

The Church connection still reverberates in northern Idaho. Northern Panhandle counties remain the most favorable territory for Democrats in the state. Many locals recalled LaRocco's service in the north more than a decade ago in explaining why they supported the Democrat. Church's widow, Bethine Church, endorsed LaRocco during the Democratic primary campaign.

LaRocco supports abortion rights, opposes gun control and favors a compromise in the longstanding debate over the use of 5 million acres of pristine Idaho "wilderness" land. His Republican opponent, state Sen. C. A. "Skip" Smyser, used LaRocco's backing for a wilderness compromise as well as his support from environmental groups such as the Sierra Club to try to pry away votes in the north, where loggers shared Smyser's opposition to setting aside additional land as wilderness.

Smyser's northern strategy had limited success. In the logging towns in Benewah County (St. Maries), the message took hold: Smyser won 52 percent in Benewah, which had backed LaRocco in his 1982 race. But elsewhere in the north, LaRocco ran much stronger than he had against Craig. In the nine northernmost counties (which cast about 40 percent of the 1st's vote), LaRocco received 60 percent against Smyser; those counties gave LaRocco 53 percent in 1982. In the swing county of Kootenai (Coeur d'Alene), LaRocco captured 55 percent, 11 points better than in 1982.

LaRocco was also able to improve his previous support in the southern, more Republican counties. In the most populous county in the district, the part of Ada County (Boise) in the 1st, LaRocco only managed 41 percent against Craig. In 1990, he won Ada with 51 percent. In the 10 counties south of the Panhandle, LaRocco improved from a 17 percentage-point deficit against Craig to a 3-point disadvantage against Smyser.

LaRocco's strong showing in the south can be attributed to his high visibility throughout the 1980s. As vice president of the Boise office of a large brokerage firm, LaRocco was tapped for commentaries by Boise TV and radio stations. In 1988, LaRocco led a successful statewide effort to amend the state constitution to allow a lottery.

The lottery campaign boosted his profile on an issue popular in the 1st and gave his 1990 campaign a head start. Smyser, a little-known conservative legislator from the state's second most populous county, heavily Republican Canyon, started far behind LaRocco in familiarity. LaRocco was further aided by the high-profile three-way Democratic primary; Smyser had no GOP opposition.

In the primary, LaRocco faced two strong opponents: 1988 House nominee Jeanne Givens, a former state representative, and Dick Rush, who resigned as state agriculture director to run for Congress. LaRocco received 43 percent, 10 points more than Rush, his nearest competitor.

Idaho 1

North and West — Lewiston; Boise

LaRocco's 1990 House victory returned the 1st to the Democratic fold after a long absence. From the New Deal until the Great Society years, the 1st nearly always sent Democrats to Congress. It broke that habit in 1966, thanks to a redistricting that brought in more Republicans and to the House candidacy of then-state Sen. James A. McClure. LaRocco ended a 24-year streak of conservative GOP representation in the 1st, which used to be known as "Idaho's Democratic district."

LaRocco demonstrated that there is still significant Democratic strength in the 1st, based on labor influence in the mountainous northern Panhandle, where lumbermen and miners fought to organize unions early in this century. Also prone to go Democratic is a community of relatively liberal voters linked to the 9,900-student University of Idaho at Moscow in Latah County. In the 1980 Senate contest between liberal Democratic Sen. Frank Church and conservative Republican Steve Symms, Idaho's nine northernmost counties sided with Church. Even in 1988, when Michael S. Dukakis was struggling to win 37 percent of the statewide presidential vote, he got 50 percent or better in five of the nine Panhandle counties.

But the Democratic vote in the Panhandle is closely balanced with two urbanized areas at the southern end of the district that typically vote Republican — Canyon County and western Ada County — which together have more than 40 percent of the district's residents. In 1990, a key to LaRocco's victory was his ability to prevail in western Ada County, where he enjoyed higher name recognition than his GOP rival. Also, LaRocco got 43 percent of the vote in Canyon County, a respectable showing in a county George Bush carried by 2-to-1 in 1988 presidential voting.

The state capital, Boise, is in Ada County. Idaho's only city with more than 100,000 residents, Boise has a strong Republican vote cast by white-collar employees of the lumber, paper, food processing, electronics and construction corporations that have their headquarters there. Canyon County has the growing cities of Nampa and Caldwell — agricultural processing centers that usually vote Republican as well. Hispanic migrant farm workers, drawn to the work generated by a variety of crops produced every year in Canyon, are beginning to settle in larger numbers throughout the county, but their political impact is not yet much evident.

South of Canyon and Ada counties and spread across the southwestern corner is Owyhee County; though bigger in land area than New Jersey, it is populated with an average of just one person per mile.

Population: 472,412. White 454,305 (96%), Black 802 (0.2%), Other 7,982 (2%). Spanish origin 15,929 (3%). 18 and over 324,509 (69%), 65 and over 49,720 (11%). Median age: 29.

Committees

Banking, Finance & Urban Affairs (24th of 31 Democrats)
Consumer Affairs & Coinage; Financial Institutions Supervision, Regulation & Insurance; International Development, Finance, Trade & Monetary Policy

Interior & Insular Affairs (28th of 29 Democrats)
National Parks & Public Lands; Water, Power & Offshore Energy

Campaign Finance

1990	Receipts	Receipts from PACs		Expend-itures
LaRocco (D)	$449,419	$238,753	(53%)	$447,895
Smyser (R)	$487,424	$198,459	(41%)	$480,994

Key Vote

1991

Authorize use of force against Iraq	N

Elections

1990 General		
Larry LaRocco (D)	85,054	(53%)
C.A. "Skip" Smyser (R)	75,406	(47%)
1990 Primary		
Larry LaRocco (D)	14,001	(43%)
Jeanne Givens (D)	10,725	(33%)
Dick Rush (D)	7,472	(23%)

District Vote For President

	1988	1984	1980	1976
D	80,657 (39%)	62,588 (30%)	47,191 (31%)	65,243 (39%)
R	121,632 (59%)	141,459 (68%)	90,676 (59%)	96,377 (58%)
I			10,164 (7%)	

2 Richard Stallings (D)

Of Rexburg — Elected 1984

Born: Oct. 7, 1940, Ogden, Utah.
Education: Weber State College, B.S. 1965; Utah State U., M.A. 1968.
Occupation: History professor.
Family: Wife, Ranae Garner; three children.
Religion: Mormon.
Political Career: Democratic nominee for Idaho House, 1974, 1978; Democratic nominee for U.S. House, 1982.
Capitol Office: 1122 Longworth Bldg. 20515; 225-5531.

In Washington: Stallings left his career as a history professor to come to Congress, but every day he teaches Republicans a lesson about the task they face in building a House majority. As long as Democrats such as Stallings routinely win election in places as conservative as eastern Idaho, a GOP majority is almost certainly a distant dream.

Stallings' remarkable success in the 2nd — the more Republican of Idaho's two districts — has earned him frequent mention as a likely statewide candidate. He has announced that he will challenge GOP Sen. Steve Symms in 1992.

Representing a district that gave George Bush 65 percent of its vote in 1988, Stallings does not have the freedom to venture much outside issues that have a direct impact on his constituents. Yet he seems to feel freer to vote his conscience than some members from safer districts.

"If I can't stick my neck out for something that is right, perhaps the office isn't worth it," Stallings said after defying President Ronald Reagan on funding for the Nicaraguan contras in 1986.

Coming from most congressmen, that statement would sound like grandstanding. But it is believable in Stallings, a polite, workaday academician who, when asked by a colleague to cite the most memorable event of his young congressional career, mentioned a tour he took of the battlefield at Gettysburg.

But if Stallings sides with his party more often than many expected — an average of more than two-thirds of the time in his six years in office — his critics at home have had trouble painting him as being out of step with Idaho. His middle-of-the-road record includes votes against congressional pay raises (he says he donates his pay raise to fund college scholarships in his district), and support for a cut in the capital gains tax rate and for constitutional amendments to ban physical desecration of the flag and to balance the budget; he is no different from his GOP colleagues serving Idaho when it comes to gun control.

His opposition to abortion is well enough known that three anti-abortion activists at the 1988 Democratic National Convention voted to nominate Stallings, not Michael S. Dukakis, as the party's standard-bearer.

Stallings has said of the House Democratic leadership: "I think they recognize ... that I can give them 100 percent of the votes for two years, but that would be the end of it." Still, he manages to continue coming up with votes for the party line in risky situations: In January 1991, he voted against the congressional resolution authorizing the use of force against Iraq, favoring instead continued economic sanctions.

The Democratic leadership has gone out of its way to help Stallings hold his district. He got the committee assignments he wanted — Agriculture and Science — and has been given every chance to shine on them.

Stallings helped draft the section of the 1990 farm bill dealing with barley. During committee consideration, he won adoption of an amendment to require the Agriculture Department to recalculate the market price of barley for 1988 and 1989 taking into account malt as well as feed barley. The intent was to lower the amount of advance payments barley producers would have to repay the government.

Stallings was less successful in his efforts to gain funding for the special isotope separation project at the Idaho National Engineering Laboratory (INEL) in eastern Idaho. The project, estimated at $1.35 billion, would have brought thousands of new jobs, but the Energy Department grew less enthusiastic about it as the Cold War drew to an end. The fiscal 1991 energy appropriations bill did include money for a project Stallings supported at INEL that would convert its idle nuclear reactor into a brain cancer treatment facility.

At Home: Had he not decided to leave the 2nd to run statewide, Stallings probably would have continued to attract biennial GOP attentions. He won in 1984 because his opponent was a convicted felon; regardless of how long Stallings represented it, the 2nd District was

Idaho 2

East — Pocatello; Idaho Falls

Mormons migrating north from Utah first settled southeastern Idaho in the mid-1800s, and today their influence is pervasive in the area. Almost two-thirds of the people in southeastern Idaho are Mormon, and like their co-religionists elsewhere, they support conservative candidates and causes.

Bonneville County (Idaho Falls) is the largest county in the 2nd, and also the most conservative. Republican presidential candidates typically average well above 60 percent of the vote in Bonneville. George Bush won 75 percent there in 1988, well above his 63 percent statewide tally.

Idaho Falls processes potatoes grown in the surrounding upper Snake River Valley. It is 30 miles from the test site that pioneered commercial nuclear power in the 1950s, and nuclear energy retains considerable support. Bonneville and a handful of upper Snake River area counties on the eastern edge of the 2nd backed GOP Rep. George Hansen loyally throughout his career, voting strongly for him even in 1984.

On the western side of the district, the Republican voters are conservative, but less fervently so. Twin Falls County gave Bush 64 percent in 1988; it also was the base of an anti-Hansen group of Republicans who were crucial to Stallings in 1984. With their help, he carried the county by 698 votes.

Twin Falls is in the center of the Magic Valley farming area, so named because the sandy soils in this region, when irrigated with Snake River water, produce remarkable yields of potatoes, sugar beets and other cash crops.

The largest pocket of Democratic strength, which springs from a heavy labor vote and a sizable student vote from Idaho State University, is in Bannock County. The city of Pocatello there is a railroad and chemical center specializing in phosphate fertilizers.

Two other centers of Democratic support in the 2nd are Blaine County, home of the Sun Valley resorts, and the eastern section of Boise, around Boise State University.

Population: 471,523. White 447,336 (95%), Black 1,914 (0.4%), Other 8,487 (2%). Spanish origin 20,686 (4%). 18 and over 312,761 (66%), 65 and over 43,960 (9%). Median age: 26.

likely to remain one of the most conservative and Republican in the country.

But the GOP's last three efforts against him have scarcely left a scratch on Stallings, who has emerged as one of Idaho's most popular politicians. He is the only Democrat in Idaho history to win more than two consecutive terms in the eastern 2nd District.

In 1990, 27-year-old former Army Ranger Sean McDevitt, a first-time candidate, outworked a state senator and two others to win the GOP nomination. His strenuous toiling in a race that had been written off by many state Republicans netted favorable reviews in GOP circles, despite one comment he made that drew widespread criticism.

When House Speaker Thomas S. Foley campaigned for Stallings at an August 1990 fundraiser, McDevitt called Foley "un-American" for opposing a constitutional amendment to ban flag desecration. He said Stallings should "hunt up a more patriotic American" to stump for him. But McDevitt's attacks from the right did not dent Stallings' standing in the 2nd; the Democrat cruised to a career-best 64 percent.

In 1988, the GOP nominated former state Sen. Dane Watkins, an also-ran from the 1986 primary. Watkins' only rival for the 1988 nomination was a political neophyte who listed her occupation as poet and yet received more than 40 percent of the primary vote.

In the general election, Watkins tried to paint Stallings as a liberal national Democrat. But the Mormon incumbent's locally popular stands on a balanced budget, gun control and the 65 mph speed limit were widely known. In the end, Stallings won a stunning 63 percent, even as the district's presidential vote broke just as decisively for the GOP.

In 1986, the Republican champion was Idaho Falls sports announcer Mel Richardson. At first glance, he seemed an ideal candidate. Three decades in broadcasting had given him enormous recognition in the Idaho Falls area, and he had an easygoing, friendly manner.

But his campaign never progressed. High-profile Senate and gubernatorial contests soaked up much of Idaho's available funding. In the few direct encounters between the two, Stallings made the most of Richardson's legislative inexperience, accusing him of misunderstanding complex farm and government spending issues. Also, he worked to firm up the base he had built since 1984, paying close attention to the Boise area, where voters are more moderate than those farther east, and to farmers in the Magic Valley, around Twin Falls.

On Election Day, Stallings took 54 percent, carrying 15 of the district's 26 counties and losing only in the conservative upper Snake

River Valley and heavily Mormon southeast.

Stallings' 1984 success came after several disappointments. He lost two state legislative campaigns and also managed the 1976 House campaign of Democrat Stan Kress, who narrowly lost to GOP Rep. George Hansen. In 1982, Stallings was the Democratic nominee against Hansen. A late start hampered him, but he still got 48 percent.

For his second campaign against Hansen, Stallings started early, built a sizable organization and attracted ample funding. The accumulated weight of Hansen's legal and financial problems boosted Stallings. Hansen, who had been convicted in federal court of filing false financial disclosure reports, barely survived the primary. In June, he was sentenced to a five- to 15-month prison term and fined $40,000.

Stallings told voters he could put the district's needs first instead of being preoccupied with defending his personal integrity. He claimed that midyear polling data showed him leading by roughly 2-to-1.

But his luck began souring in July, when Democratic vice presidential nominee Geraldine A. Ferraro got embroiled in controversy over her financial-disclosure reports. Hansen exploited the issue expertly: When Democrats played down Ferraro's problems, Hansen railed at the double standard that he said excused a liberal Eastern Democrat while a conservative Western Republican was persecuted.

Stallings spent much of the fall on the defensive. At one point, he expressed reservations about voting for Mondale and Ferraro. Complaints from Democrats prompted him to pledge to support the ticket, but later, he voiced doubts about Ferraro's qualifications. In the end, Stallings finished on top by just 170 votes.

Now with three successful re-election campaigns behind him, Stallings is often projected as a candidate for statewide office. He has already prevailed in the half of the state that votes most heavily Republican. In 1990, he was the first choice of party recruiters for the open seat of retiring GOP Sen. James A. McClure. Having turned down that opportunity, he instantly became Sen. Symms' putative 1992 foe.

Committees

Agriculture (16th of 27 Democrats)
Conservation, Credit & Rural Development; Cotton, Rice & Sugar; Forests, Family Farms & Energy

Science, Space & Technology (14th of 32 Democrats)
Energy; Space

Select Aging (24th of 42 Democrats)
Retirement, Income & Employment; Rural Elderly

Elections

1990 General		
Richard Stallings (D)	98,008	(64%)
Sean McDevitt (R)	56,044	(36%)
1988 General		
Richard Stallings (D)	127,956	(63%)
Dane H. Watkins (R)	68,226	(34%)

Previous Winning Percentages: 1986 (54%) **1984** (50%)

District Vote For President

	1988	1984	1980	1976
D	66,615 (33%)	45,922 (23%)	63,001 (22%)	61,306 (35%)
R	132,249 (65%)	156,064 (77%)	200,023 (71%)	107,774 (62%)
I	5,313 * (3%)		16,894 (6%)	

** Ron Paul, Libertarian*

Campaign Finance

	Receipts	Receipts from PACs		Expend-itures
1990				
Stallings (D)	$405,115	$266,702	(66%)	$406,219
McDevitt (R)	$142,851	$1,900	(1%)	$141,681
1988				
Stallings (D)	$498,997	$266,739	(53%)	$502,083
Watkins (R)	$205,847	$26,450	(13%)	$206,960

Key Votes

1991	
Authorize use of force against Iraq	N
1990	
Support constitutional amendment on flag desecration	Y
Pass family and medical leave bill over Bush veto	N
Reduce SDI funding	Y
Allow abortions in overseas military facilities	N
Approve budget summit plan for spending and taxing	N
Approve civil rights bill	Y
1989	
Halt production of B-2 stealth bomber at 13 planes	N
Oppose capital gains tax cut	N
Approve federal abortion funding in rape or incest cases	N
Approve pay raise and revision of ethics rules	N
Pass Democratic minimum wage plan over Bush veto	Y

Voting Studies

	Presidential Support		Party Unity		Conservative Coalition	
Year	**S**	**O**	**S**	**O**	**S**	**O**
1990	42	56	67	29	81	19
1989	45	51	69	27	73	27
1988	35	58	71	24	79	11
1987	41	56	71	25	74	26
1986	42	58	62	34	72	26
1985	41	58	69	24	58	36

Interest Group Ratings

Year	ADA	ACU	AFL-CIO	CCUS
1990	39	46	27	79
1989	45	41	45	70
1988	55	48	71	71
1987	52	27	56	67
1986	45	32	57	71
1985	35	40	44	55

Illinois

U.S. CONGRESS

SENATE 2 D

HOUSE 15 D, 6 R, 1 vacancy

LEGISLATURE

Senate 31 D, 28 R

House 72 D, 46 R

ELECTIONS

1988 Presidential Vote

Bush	51%
Dukakis	49%

1984 Presidential Vote

Reagan	56%
Mondale	43%

1980 Presidential Vote

Reagan	50%
Carter	42%
Anderson	7%

Turnout rate in 1986	36%
Turnout rate in 1988	53%
Turnout rate in 1990	35%

(as percentage of voting age population)

POPULATION AND GROWTH

1980 population	11,426,518
1990 population (6th in the nation)	11,430,602
Percent change 1980-1990	0%

DEMOGRAPHIC BREAKDOWN

White	78%
Black	15%
Asian or Pacific Islander	3%
(Hispanic origin)	8%
Urban	83%
Rural	17%
Born in state	69%
Foreign-born	7%

MAJOR CITIES

Chicago	2,783,726
Rockford	139,426
Peoria	113,504
Springfield	105,227
Aurora	99,581

AREA AND LAND USE

Area 55,645 sq. miles (24th)

Farm	81%
Forest	12%
Federally owned	1%

Gov. Jim Edgar (R)
Of Charleston — Elected 1990

Born: July 22, 1946, Vinita, Okla.
Education: Eastern Illinois U., B.S. 1968.
Occupation: Legislative aide.
Religion: Baptist.
Political Career: Ill. House, 1977-79; Ill. secretary of state, 1981-91.
Next Election: 1994.

WORK

Occupations

White-collar	54%
Blue-collar	31%
Service workers	13%

Government Workers

Federal	106,976
State	163,787
Local	493,355

MONEY

Median family income	$ 22,746	(6th)
Tax burden per capita	$ 800	(32nd)

EDUCATION

Spending per pupil through grade 12	$ 4,369	(18th)
Persons with college degrees	16%	(24th)

CRIME

Violent crime rate 846 per 100,000 (5th)

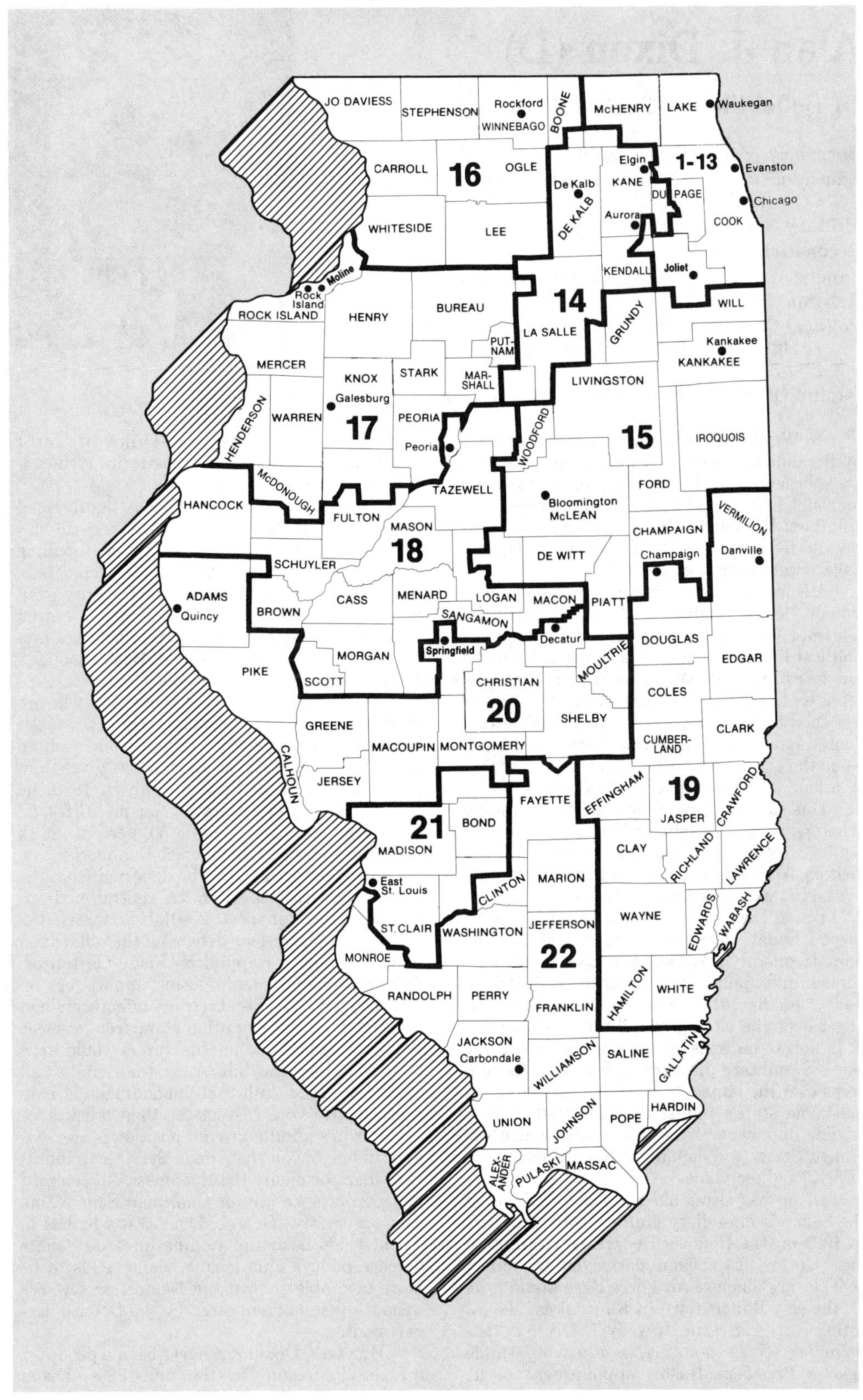
JO DAVIESS
STEPHENSON
Rockford
WINNEBAGO
BOONE
McHENRY
LAKE
Waukegan
CARROLL
16
OGLE
De Kalb
Elgin
KANE
1-13
Evanston
DU PAGE
Chicago
DE KALB
Aurora
COOK
WHITESIDE
LEE
KENDALL
Joliet
Moline
Rock Island
ROCK ISLAND
HENRY
BUREAU
14
LA SALLE
GRUNDY
WILL
PUT-NAM
Kankakee
KANKAKEE
MERCER
KNOX
STARK
MAR-SHALL
LIVINGSTON
HENDERSON
WARREN
Galesburg
17
PEORIA
Peoria
WOODFORD
15
IROQUOIS
McDONOUGH
TAZEWELL
FORD
HANCOCK
FULTON
Bloomington
McLEAN
MASON
VERMILION
CHAMPAIGN
18
DE WITT
SCHUYLER
Champaign
Danville
ADAMS
Quincy
BROWN
CASS
MENARD
LOGAN
MACON
PIATT
SANGAMON
Springfield
Decatur
DOUGLAS
MORGAN
EDGAR
PIKE
SCOTT
CHRISTIAN
MOULTRIE
COLES
20
SHELBY
GREENE
CLARK
CUMBER-LAND
MACOUPIN
MONTGOMERY
CALHOUN
JERSEY
EFFINGHAM
19
CRAWFORD
FAYETTE
JASPER
21
BOND
MADISON
CLAY
RICHLAND
LAWRENCE
East St. Louis
CLINTON
MARION
ST. CLAIR
WASHINGTON
JEFFERSON
WAYNE
EDWARDS
WABASH
22
MONROE
RANDOLPH
PERRY
FRANKLIN
HAMILTON
WHITE
JACKSON
Carbondale
WILLIAMSON
SALINE
GALLATIN
UNION
JOHNSON
POPE
HARDIN
ALEX-ANDER
PULASKI
MASSAC

Alan J. Dixon (D)

Of Belleville — Elected 1980

Born: July 7, 1927, Belleville, Ill.
Education: U. of Illinois, B.S. 1949; Washington U., LL.B. 1949.
Military Service: Navy, 1945-46.
Occupation: Lawyer.
Family: Wife, Joan Louise Fox; three children.
Religion: Presbyterian.
Political Career: Ill. House, 1951-63; Ill. Senate, 1963-71; Ill. treasurer, 1971-77; Ill. secretary of state, 1977-81.
Capitol Office: 331 Hart Bldg. 20510; 224-2854.

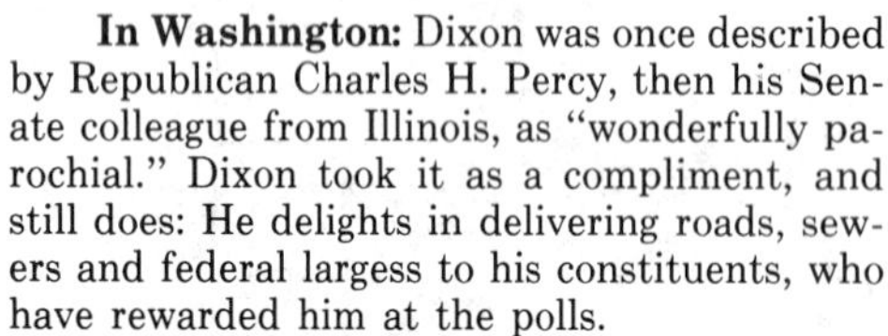

In Washington: Dixon was once described by Republican Charles H. Percy, then his Senate colleague from Illinois, as "wonderfully parochial." Dixon took it as a compliment, and still does: He delights in delivering roads, sewers and federal largess to his constituents, who have rewarded him at the polls.

His intellect is not dazzling, and only occasionally does he champion a broad policy initiative. But he has mastered the small devices of political life in the Senate as thoroughly as he did in Springfield. While he may appear less often on television talk shows than some other senators, he has few peers in the art of cutting deals, giving and demanding favors and even, when the occasion requires it, bringing business to a halt in order to get what he wants.

One of the more informal and accessible senators, he spends much of his time in Washington meeting with a steady stream of Illinois visitors, from auto dealers and insurance agents to sheriffs and sanitation officials.

But as Dixon — now nearing the end of his second Senate term — accrues seniority, he more frequently takes what he sees as good for Illinois, and applies it to larger areas of federal policy. In the 101st Congress, Dixon used his anger over the closing of military installations in Illinois to buttress his arguments for limiting the U.S. military presence in Europe. His concerns over the impact of foreign competition on his home state's industrial base made him a leading opponent of the deal under which the United States and Japan would co-produce the "FS-X" fighter plane.

Dixon has also staked his claim as one of the Senate's most fiery orators. During debate in 1989 on the Defense Department's military base closure list, Dixon portrayed the effect that closing Chanute Air Force Base would have on the east Illinois town of Rantoul as "devastating, an American tragedy." Dixon's fist-pounding, finger-pointing, arm-waving tirade against President Bush's appointment of T. Timothy Ryan to head the Office of Thrift Supervision (OTS) was a classic in 19th-century-style Senate oratory.

Yet the well-liked Dixon has hardly shed his persona of "Al the Pal." His accessibility and his peerless skill at legislative deal-making helped boost him into the Senate Democratic leadership — he was elected chief deputy whip at the start of the 101st Congress — even though his moderate voting record makes him more supportive of President Bush's policies than most of his partisan colleagues.

"I happen to think that those of us who are moderates, who are centrists, most often make the difference," he says. Dixon's outreach to both liberals and conservatives has given him across-the-board political appeal: In 1990, he received a 78 percent rating on an AFL-CIO legislative scorecard and a 50 percent mark from the national Chamber of Commerce.

In 1990, for example, he departed from the party line with respect to the central environmental legislation of the 101st Congress, the Clean Air Act. In floor debate on the bill, Dixon and Washington Republican Slade Gorton offered an amendment imposing import fees on foreign products when their manufacturers had not met the same pollution standards overseas that competing U.S. manufacturers would have to meet under the bill. After the Senate had voted 52-47 to kill that amendment, Dixon proceeded to vote against the final bill.

Dixon's middle-ground position is also evident in his role on the Armed Services Committee, where he chairs the Readiness Subcommittee. Dixon is an ally of Chairman Sam Nunn, the conservative Georgia Democrat who has in recent years been the guiding force on Senate defense policy. This means Dixon tends to be more favorable than many Democrats towards weapons systems requested by the Defense Department.

However, Dixon has never been a pushover for the Pentagon. In the mid-1980s, Dixon played a key role in killing the DIVAD antiaircraft gun, after learning firsthand that criticisms of the weapon's effectiveness were well-founded. Dixon wedged himself into the tight confines of an M-48 tank to test its DIVADs; one gun jammed and the other could not bring down the target, despite repeated tries.

Dixon's biggest rift with the Pentagon came in 1989, when Chanute turned up on a Defense Department commission's list of superfluous military bases to be closed. Dixon argued that many of the commission's recommendations, including that on Chanute, were based on faulty data.

That September, Dixon joined in a last-gasp effort to stop the closure plan: He supported an amendment, attached to the fiscal 1990 defense spending bill by the Appropriations Committee, that would have allowed the General Accounting Office (GAO) to block a shutdown if it would not save enough money within six years to offset the costs of closure. Dixon attacked the conclusions of the base closing commission with vitriol. "It would be an outrage if a fine community of 20,000 people in my state were torn asunder because of mistakes made by the government — by faceless, nameless people who have nothing to answer to." However, the provision was stripped from the bill by an 86-14 vote.

In 1990, Dixon led a charge against U.S. financing of a new NATO fighter base planned at Crotone, Italy. Dixon was among those who called the base an extravagance at a time when fiscal exigencies and a reduced Soviet threat were forcing an overall military downsizing. But it was also clear that Dixon was still rankled by the Chanute shutdown.

"I want the folks back home to know how good we do it overseas when we give up a hometown in Illinois," he said, pointing with obvious sarcasm to artists' depictions of the base. "Can they see the boulevard and the beautiful trees? Oh, Mr. President, a nice shopping center. . . ." Dixon's amendment to withhold funding was tabled by a 51-47 vote, but a similar provision was placed in the fiscal 1991 defense authorization bill by a conference committee. That bill also contained Dixon's proposal — approved by the Senate — to cut U.S. troop strength in Europe by 50,000.

Another area of disagreement between Dixon and the defense establishment was on the FS-X deal with Japan. He said the project to co-produce a version of the American F-16 fighter would give the Japanese access to U.S. aerospace technology, which they could eventually use to compete more effectively against U.S. aircraft manufacturers. "The building of the FS-X and the knowledge they gain from us will be like sending their engineers to college," said Dixon, who suggested that Japan should instead reduce its trade surplus with the United States by buying F-16s direct from the manufacturer. However, his resolution to disapprove the deal was defeated in May 1989 by a 47-52 vote.

Despite his generally conservative lean on defense issues, Dixon voted against the January 1991 resolution authorizing President Bush to use military force to end Iraq's occupation of Kuwait. However, it will probably be hard for Dixon's 1992 election opponent to argue that the incumbent is a white-flag pacifist.

In his speech during debate on the resolution, Dixon said he preferred continuation of the ongoing economic embargo against Iraq. But he also said he would favor use of American air power, and said he had sought assurance from the White House that any conflict would be fought from the air. Without that assurance, Dixon said, he had to vote against the resolution, because of the prevailing belief that thousands of Americans would be killed in ground combat. "I pray for peace; I fear war," Dixon said. "If it is war, I pray the president has heard my voice, and uses our massive air power to emerge successfully."

Much of Dixon's remaining legislative work is done on the Banking Committee; he chairs the Subcommittee on Consumer and Regulatory Affairs. Dixon was active in debate and negotiation on the savings and loan bailout bill.

The highlight of Dixon's S&L-related activities came in April 1990, when he made a last stand against Ryan's appointment to head OTS, the agency set up to handle the federal takeover and disposition of failed thrifts. Ryan was tabbed by Bush after a long search for a candidate to fill the rather unappealing job; with experience in federal regulation but little in banking, Ryan inspired little enthusiasm even from Republicans.

Dixon's Senate floor stemwinder against Ryan became known as the "small potatoes" speech; the broadly gesturing Dixon used that phrase to show how previous government scandals, such as Teapot Dome and Watergate, rated against the multibillion-dollar S&L collapse. He then argued that Ryan was the wrong man for the immense cleanup, and said approval of his nomination — which Dixon conceded was certain — would be a dark moment for the Senate.

"I'm saddened that we are finally asked to adopt a standard . . . that you better give the job to somebody, 'cause you can't find anybody to take it," Dixon said. "The lowest possible common denominator in public service now has finally been achieved this day by this vote." Despite Dixon's impassioned plea, Ryan was confirmed by a 62-37 vote.

Later that year, reports from the Congressional Budget Office and the GAO spurred concerns about the long-term prospects for the Federal Deposit Insurance Corporation's bank insurance fund. In September 1990, Dixon proposed a bank insurance reform package.

The bill, reintroduced in the 102nd Congress, would set risk-based deposit insurance premiums, with banks holding risky investments paying more than those that invest cautiously. The proposal would preserve the standard of $100,000 in insurance per bank account, but would not allow coverage of all deposits over $100,000 (a common FDIC practice in cases of large banks that are deemed "too big to fail"). Dixon's plan would also require the development of a private deposit insurance system that would cover 10 percent of the deposits held by the largest banks.

Dixon is one of the most steadfast Senate defenders of the Commodity Futures Trading Commission, which oversees Chicago-based futures markets. He has worked in recent years to fend off proposals to merge the CFTC with the Securities and Exchange Commission.

Unrelated to Dixon's committee assignments is his crusade to set up a system of regional primaries to select the major parties' presidential nominees. He calls the current patchwork system of state primaries and caucuses "archaic, chaotic, terribly flawed, ridiculous and unparalleled in a democratic society for its primitiveness."

At Home: Dixon's election to the Senate in 1980 lifted him out of a 30-year concentration on the nuts and bolts of Illinois politics. But while Dixon had coveted the broader forum, he waited for it patiently. And since attaining it, he has not let it alter his basic approach to politics: Cultivate your base, avoid divisive issues and show voters they are getting their share of government largess.

His background was something of a liability in his Senate contest, since he started out unfamiliar with major national issues. But by studying, holding press conferences and agreeing to debate his GOP opponent, Dixon erased the notion that he was a lightweight.

Democratic Sen. Adlai E. Stevenson III had chosen not to run for re-election in 1980, and Democrats turned to Dixon for one reason: He was a champion vote-getter. In his two races for the secretary of state's office, he led the state ticket, winning a phenomenal 74 percent in 1978. In his 1980 Senate primary, Dixon swamped Alex Seith, who had given Percy a strong challenge in 1978.

The favorite for the GOP nomination had been state Attorney General William J. Scott, but he became entangled in a long trial on income-tax evasion charges. So the GOP chose Lt. Gov. David E. O'Neal.

Although he was the No. 2 official in Illinois, O'Neal labored in the obscurity that usually accompanies the office of lieutenant governor. To shore up his name identity, he began running commercials in late summer introducing himself to the voters. But Dixon's higher name recognition, his personal popularity and his efforts to show himself as a substantive candidate kept him in the lead.

As in his other statewide races, Dixon was able to combine strong voter support in his downstate base with a typical Democratic margin in Chicago. He had always managed to stay on good terms with the Chicago Democratic organization without being seen as a creature of it.

This mixture of cooperation and independence earned him support from a broad spectrum of Illinois voters and brought him few enemies. It served him well in 1980, when bitter fighting broke out in the Chicago organization between then-Mayor Jane Byrne and Richard M. Daley, son of the late mayor. Both factions supported Dixon.

As 1986 drew near, Illinois Republicans went through a long public search for a candidate to oppose Dixon. The list of possibilities who bowed out included several House members, former Secretary of Defense Donald Rumsfeld and popular Illinois Secretary of State Jim Edgar. Former Rep. Tom Corcoran ran briefly and then — when he did not get the party's unified backing — dropped out.

In the end, the GOP nominated state Rep. Judy Koehler, a downstate conservative with a gadfly's role in the Legislature. She adopted the same posture during the campaign. She started off by running an ad labeling Dixon a "wimp" for remaining on the Democratic ticket with two statewide candidates allied with Lyndon H. LaRouche Jr. , who had won their nominations in a fluke. Then she made an issue of an article Dixon had written for *Playboy* magazine on terrorism. "The women of Illinois," she said, "have been insulted and disgraced."

But Koehler made little headway. The establishment wing of the GOP was clearly uncomfortable with her. Although Republicans had once hoped to take advantage of disarray in Democratic ranks caused by the LaRouche imbroglio, the party never gave Koehler its wholehearted support. Dixon took advantage of the disunity to make direct appeals to moderate Republicans, and he wound up winning 90 of the state's 102 counties.

Dixon's electoral clout has made his a sought-after endorsement for Illinois office-seekers. His strong backing helped Democrat Jerry F. Costello navigate his way through a tough 1988 campaign for the open House seat in the 21st District, which includes Dixon's home town of Belleville.

Committees

Armed Services (6th of 11 Democrats)
Readiness, Sustainability & Support (chairman); Conventional Forces & Alliance Defense; Projection Forces & Regional Defense

Banking, Housing & Urban Affairs (5th of 12 Democrats)
Consumer & Regulatory Affairs (chairman); International Finance & Monetary Policy

Small Business (5th of 10 Democrats)
Government Contracting & Paperwork Reduction (chairman); Rural Economy & Family Farming

Elections

1986 General		
Alan J. Dixon (D)	2,033,783	(65%)
Judy Koehler (R)	1,053,734	(34%)
1986 Primary		
Alan J. Dixon (D)	720,571	(85%)
Sheila Jones (D)	129,474	(15%)

Previous Winning Percentage: **1980** (56%)

Campaign Finance

	Receipts	Receipts from PACs		Expend-itures
1986				
Dixon (D)	$2,219,982	$984,408	(44%)	$1,928,750
Koehler (R)	$871,586	$74,178	(9%)	$851,305

Key Votes

1991	
Authorize use of force against Iraq	N
1990	
Oppose prohibition of certain semiautomatic weapons	N
Support constitutional amendment on flag desecration	Y
Oppose requiring parental notice for minors' abortions	N
Halt production of B-2 stealth bomber at 13 planes	N
Approve budget that cut spending and raised revenues	Y
Pass civil rights bill over Bush veto	Y
1989	
Oppose reduction of SDI funding	Y
Oppose barring federal funds for "obscene" art	Y
Allow vote on capital gains tax cut	N

Voting Studies

	Presidential Support		Party Unity		Conservative Coalition	
Year	**S**	**O**	**S**	**O**	**S**	**O**
1990	53	47	70	30	73	27
1989	72	28	62	38	58	42
1988	56	32	60	30	89	11
1987	41	55	75	23	84	16
1986	51	46	62	36	59	38
1985	46	50	69	29	50	47
1984	42	45	56	35	49	38
1983	54	41	70	26	55	43
1982	45	50	76	20	39	54
1981	57	41	73	26	57	38

Interest Group Ratings

Year	ADA	ACU	AFL-CIO	CCUS
1990	44	39	78	50
1989	55	32	90	50
1988	45	44	69	57
1987	60	20	80	41
1986	60	43	80	58
1985	60	41	81	43
1984	70	27	64	58
1983	60	29	76	32
1982	80	39	88	33
1981	65	20	61	61

Paul Simon (D)

Of Makanda — Elected 1984

Born: Nov. 29, 1928, Eugene, Ore.

Education: Attended U. of Oregon, 1945-46; Dana College, 1946-48.

Military Service: Army, 1951-53.

Occupation: Author; newspaper editor and publisher.

Family: Wife, Jeanne Hurley; two children.

Religion: Lutheran.

Political Career: Ill. House, 1955-63; Ill. Senate, 1963-69; lieutenant governor, 1969-73; U.S. House, 1975-85; sought Democratic nomination for governor, 1972; sought Democratic nomination for president, 1988.

Capitol Office: 462 Dirksen Bldg. 20510; 224-2152.

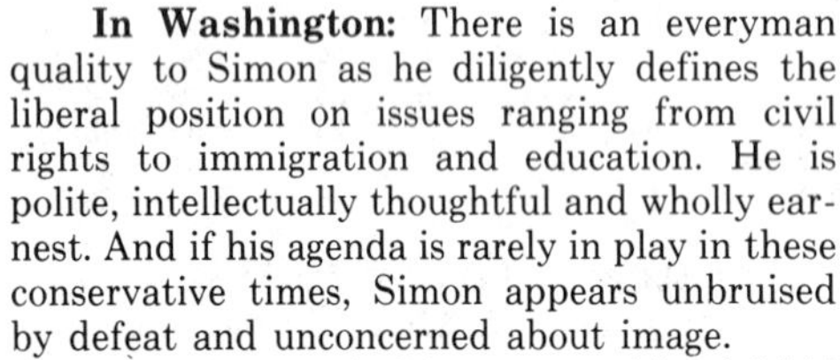

In Washington: There is an everyman quality to Simon as he diligently defines the liberal position on issues ranging from civil rights to immigration and education. He is polite, intellectually thoughtful and wholly earnest. And if his agenda is rarely in play in these conservative times, Simon appears unbruised by defeat and unconcerned about image.

All of this made his 1988 presidential bid rather quixotic. But the Senate not only tolerates quirky personalities, it embraces them. In the chamber, Simon has carved his niche as a respected spokesman for those who believe government should be active in social services at home and restrained in military activities abroad. While his role may not suit the national stage, Illinois voters gave it a seal of approval by re-electing Simon overwhelmingly in 1990.

Part of Simon's idiosyncratic vision is his support for a handful of conservative litmus test issues. The self-described liberal is also a former small-town newspaper publisher with an aversion to red ink. He is a leading Senate supporter of the balanced budget amendment and the line-item veto. In the 101st Congress, he was also a lead sponsor of legislation to waive antitrust laws to allow the networks to develop guidelines on TV violence. (He became involved in that issue after seeing someone cut in half by a chain saw on TV. "I am old enough to know it was not real, but it bothered me," he said.)

Simon is institutionally blocked from playing a larger role in major legislation in part because of the subcommittees he chairs. While he sits on four full committees and one select committee, he chairs the Judiciary Subcommittee on Constitutional Rights, long used as a graveyard for legislation antithetical to liberals, and the Foreign Relations Subcommittee on Africa, not a focus of strategic attention in recent years.

Sometimes it seems that Simon's goal is to quietly define the outer edge of debate. He is among the three most consistent supporters of minorities and women on Judiciary. But unlike Sen. Edward M. Kennedy, he lacks a powerful national profile, and unlike Sen. Howard M. Metzenbaum, he lacks sharp parliamentary prowess. As a result, Simon does not always find a place at the bargaining table. His 1989 bill that would have explicitly allowed municipalities to set aside a certain number of contracts for minority businesses was never seriously considered.

When it came to aid for Poland and Hungary, however, Simon was both persistent and on the popular side. He is widely credited with raising the funding level from the $146 million Bush had requested to $938 million. Simon had proposed a $1.2 billion bill.

On most issues, Simon will eventually set aside his intransigent liberalism and compromise, once he is given a hearing. During the 101st Congress' overhaul of legal immigration statutes, Simon offered a proposal that would have expanded rather than capped immigration, and kept the emphasis on family reunification, ensuring that the overwhelming majority of immigrants come from Mexico, Asia and Central America.

But on the Senate Immigration subcommittee, Simon took a realistic approach and bargained to raise the immigration cap, successfully fought an English-language preference proposal and used his knowledge of the House to help the bill's lead Senate sponsors succeed.

For all this, Simon's first love is education. He defended aid to education for a decade in the House and does so now on the Education and Labor Committee. In the 101st Congress, he championed efforts to end adult illiteracy, and with the support of a diverse coalition, including First Lady Barbara Bush, he helped secure increased funding for literacy training in the vocational education act.

When the committee debated a bill to

reauthorize the Higher Education Act in the 99th Congress, Simon promoted a number of causes, including aid to historically black colleges and a new limited program of federal support for graduate students — having more success with the former than the latter.

Simon is a lead sponsor of legislation reauthorizing the Jobs Training Partnership Act. The Senate approved Simon's proposal to make poverty over unemployment the chief determinate of funding in 1989, but the funding formula pitted urban areas against suburban and rural areas and the bill died. Simon reintroduced his bill in the 102nd Congress.

Simon highlights the fact that Chicago would be a big winner in his JTPA bill. Overall, he is careful to avoid being characterized in Illinois as a "national" senator; he touts his efforts to protect the interests of O'Hare International Airport outside Chicago and his work on other state transportation issues.

His local focus tightened after his 1988 presidential campaign failed. Simon was the candidate most willing to embrace his party and its history ("I am a not a neo-anything; I am a Democrat"), but his bid sputtered out after he got 5 percent in Wisconsin's Democratic primary. The highlight had been his home state's primary, which he won despite having to share favorite-son status with the Rev. Jesse Jackson.

Simon's White House bid began auspiciously, with a close-second finish in the Iowa precinct caucuses. In the end, though, Simon garnered about 1 million votes and 170.5 delegates (by The Associated Press' count), but most of both came from Illinois. He never raised the money the multi-state Super Tuesday primaries required. And his "unreconstructed Democrat" approach, apparently pitched to lunch-bucket voters, ironically showed more appeal among liberals in affluent suburbs and academic communities.

At Home: It will be little remembered in the wake of Simon's sweeping 1990 victory that he began his campaign near the top of the Republican target list. GOP optimism was based on the narrow margin of Simon's 1984 victory over three-term GOP Sen. Charles H. Percy, and on the failure of his presidential bid.

Simon was labeled "Senator No-Show" during his White House bid, as his Senate attendance record deteriorated. His liberal posture in 1988 also conflicted with the dour, moderate image he had crafted in his southern Illinois base.

The threat to Simon appeared fully deployed when GOP Rep. Lynn Martin announced against him. Martin was a fiscal conservative and liberal-basher, but her moderate record on social issues, including abortion and family leave, and her outgoing personality were expected to give her bipartisan appeal.

However, Simon proved he had not built a 35-year career in Illinois politics by being guileless. He lined up solid support from all elements of the Illinois Democratic Party (including blacks put off by his defeat of Jackson in the 1988 presidential primary) and raised an enormous campaign fund.

Then Simon stood back as Martin's campaign imploded. Martin blew her chances in downstate Illinois early on; in an interview, she used the word "rednecks" to describe voters who might oppose her because of her gender. Later, she offended Eastern European ethnics by referring to Simon's visit with Polish leader Lech Walesa as "crapola."

Simon, meanwhile, took full advantage of his incumbency, particularly his positions on the Judiciary and Foreign Relations committees. He dominated the airwaves, commenting on the confirmation of Supreme Court nominee David H. Souter and on the Persian Gulf crisis.

Simon ran into a couple of glitches. He signed a petition referring to the University of Illinois' "Chief Illiniwek" mascot as insensitive to American Indians, angering supporters of the mascot. Simon also faced reports that he had made a phone call to a savings-and-loan on behalf of an associate with foreclosure problems and had interceded with federal regulators on behalf of a pair of trade schools.

But Martin's furious effort to tie Simon's actions to the S&L scandal was a dud. Trailing badly in the polls, she ran short of money in late September. Then she had to apologize after her media consultant, Roger Ailes, called Simon "slimy" and "a weenie." Simon ended up taking a whopping 65 percent of the vote.

Since Simon began his political career in the early 1950s, his anti-charismatic appearance has not changed much. But neither has the strong reputation for honesty and candor that first made him popular. Simon first made a name for himself as editor of the *Troy Tribune* in southern Illinois in the early 1950s, crusading against local political corruption. In 1954, at age 25, he won a seat in the Illinois House. Eight years later, he moved to the state Senate, where gained note as a political reformer.

Democratic leaders picked Simon for lieutenant governor in 1968, hoping his reform reputation would help a state ticket struggling against reported scandal and an expected Republican tide. The gubernatorial and Senate candidates lost, but Simon won.

That victory made Simon the front-runner in the Democratic gubernatorial primary in 1972. But Daniel Walker, a wealthy corporate lawyer, convinced voters that Simon was a tool of Mayor Richard J. Daley's Chicago Democrats — even though the Daley machine was clinging to Simon, rather than the other way around.

Simon lost, then retired briefly to teach political science at a Springfield college. In 1974, however, a retirement opened a southern Illinois House district. Although Simon had to move south from his old base, he was favored and won easily. He went on to four more terms, struggling only in 1980, when Ronald Reagan's popularity boosted Simon's opponent.

Simon's base in a traditionally Democratic but conservative-leaning downstate area gave him a leg up when he jumped in against Percy in 1984. A business executive with a somewhat aristocratic manner, Percy had never achieved a large loyal following. Only his image as a moderate Republican had enabled him to outflank the more conservative Chicago Democrats who ran against him in 1972 and 1978.

By 1984, Percy was under fire from all sides. Conservatives thought him too liberal, while liberals disliked his support of the Reagan administration, especially as chairman of the Senate Foreign Relations Committee.

Simon was the best known of the Democrats' four Senate hopefuls. With support from organized labor and solid backing in Chicago's liberal lakefront wards and suburban areas, he took the nomination with 36 percent.

Percy had staved off a conservative primary challenge with an ad campaign stressing that he was "the Illinois advantage" in Washington. But he then took a rightward tack himself, portraying Simon as "ultraliberal."

The theme made it hard for Percy to hold his past coalition of blacks, suburbanites, and conservative downstaters. Simon got a heavy vote in both the black and white ethnic wards of Chicago. Combining that strength with a more-than-respectable showing downstate, Simon won by 2 points.

Illinois gave a temporary lift to Simon's 1988 presidential bid; under Illinois' modified winner-take-all system, Simon's 43 percent plurality earned him nearly 80 percent of the state's national convention delegates. But when it became obvious Simon would have to quit the race, Jackson backers urged him to withdraw before the state Democratic convention so primary runner-up Jackson could claim his delegates. Instead, Simon merely suspended his campaign, enabling his home-state loyalists to cinch their trips to Atlanta. Some blacks said the move would hurt Simon in future campaigns, but he won solid black support in 1990.

Committees

Budget (7th of 12 Democrats)

Foreign Relations (7th of 10 Democrats)
African Affairs (chairman); European Affairs; Terrorism, Narcotics & International Operations

Judiciary (7th of 8 Democrats)
Constitution (chairman); Antitrust, Monopolies & Business Rights; Immigration & Refugee Affairs

Labor & Human Resources (5th of 10 Democrats)
Employment & Productivity (chairman); Education, Arts & Humanities; Disability Policy

Select Indian Affairs (7th of 9 Democrats)

Elections

1990 General

Paul Simon (D)	2,115,377	(65%)
Lynn Martin (R)	1,135,628	(35%)

Previous Winning Percentages: **1984** (50%) **1982 *** (66%) **1980 *** (49%) **1978 *** (66%) **1976 *** (67%) **1974 *** (60%)

** House elections.*

Campaign Finance

	Receipts	Receipts from PACs		Expend-itures
1990				
Simon (D)	$8,462,209	$1,480,221	(17%)	$7,656,514
Martin (R)	$4,986,730	$1,193,942	(24%)	$4,921,613

Key Votes

1991	
Authorize use of force against Iraq	N
1990	
Oppose prohibition of certain semiautomatic weapons	N
Support constitutional amendment on flag desecration	N
Oppose requiring parental notice for minors' abortions	Y
Halt production of B-2 stealth bomber at 13 planes	Y
Approve budget that cut spending and raised revenues	N
Pass civil rights bill over Bush veto	Y
1989	
Oppose reduction of SDI funding	N
Oppose barring federal funds for "obscene" art	Y
Allow vote on capital gains tax cut	N

Voting Studies

	Presidential Support		Party Unity		Conservative Coalition	
Year	**S**	**O**	**S**	**O**	**S**	**O**
1990	20	80	90	8	8	92
1989	41	58	86	14	13	87
1988	31	42	70	1	0	54
1987	6	32	49	2	6	22
1986	19	78	89	11	13	86
1985	25	67	89	4	10	78
House Service						
1984	12	31	42	3	7	44
1983	15	59	74	4	17	56
1982	31	56	81	4	16	73
1981	36	59	76	11	28	64

Interest Group Ratings

Year	ADA	ACU	AFL-CIO	CCUS
1990	94	13	78	25
1989	100	14	90	25
1988	85	0	91	42
1987	35	0	100	13
1986	85	9	80	32
1985	85	5	95	34
House Service				
1984	45	13	100	67
1983	70	0	100	18
1982	75	6	95	15
1981	75	0	79	12

1 Charles A. Hayes (D)

Of Chicago — Elected 1983

Born: Feb. 17, 1918, Cairo, Ill.
Education: High school graduate.
Occupation: Labor official; packinghouse worker.
Family: Divorced; two children.
Religion: Baptist.
Political Career: No previous office.
Capitol Office: 1131 Longworth Bldg. 20515; 225-4372.

In Washington: Hayes spent nearly 50 years on the front lines of the labor movement in Illinois, and it shows. A burly, blunt-spoken man, he approaches his House work with the moral certainty that characterized most of his fellow Depression-era union organizers. "I do not have a problem of delineating justice from injustice or right from wrong," he once said on the House floor.

Early in the 101st Congress, Hayes felt he was the victim of injustice when he lost to a less-senior Democrat in his bid for a seat on the Post Office and Civil Service Committee. Paul E. Kanjorski, the candidate of Pennsylvania colleague and power broker John P. Murtha, won the post. It was the second time Hayes had lost a bid to a member with less seniority: In 1987, Ohio freshman Tom Sawyer beat him out.

Hayes, who said in 1989 that he had enough votes "until they got behind closed doors," said race was a factor in his defeat. "You have to be part of the 'in' crowd, and I feel that there was a little racism involved," he said. "When you meet all of the other requirements, what else could it be?"

Hayes finally got a seat on the panel in October 1989 after the death of Democrat Mickey Leland, one of the three black members already on the committee. The assignment came with an automatic subcommittee gavel; Hayes chairs the Postal Personnel and Modernization Subcommittee.

The activist fervor Hayes developed while organizing packinghouse workers in Chicago did not mellow when he began his second career as a House member at age 65. An outspoken opponent of South Africa's apartheid policies, Hayes was among the first members of Congress arrested for picketing that country's embassy in Washington. He was 40 years older than most of those with him on the picket line.

Hayes boasts proudly of his 100 percent lifetime House vote rating from the AFL-CIO. A staunch advocate of the Democrats' 1989 measure raising the minimum wage, Hayes worked the chamber door urging members to override President Bush's veto of the bill. "Let your conscience be your guide. Vote yes — to override," he bellowed over and over. In the 102nd Congress, Hayes promoted legislation protecting the jobs of striking workers.

In the 99th Congress, Hayes proposed a bill to provide state and local governments with $50 million over three years for projects aimed at reducing school dropout rates.

The bill stalled in the Senate, but in the 100th Congress, he successfully added it to the omnibus education bill during Elementary Education Subcommittee consideration. The 101st Congress reauthorized the program for two years.

Hayes was one of just six members to oppose a resolution backing the president and supporting U.S. troops in the Persian Gulf after the war started in January 1991.

At Home: Since winning a special election to succeed Democratic Rep. Harold Washington — who gave up the 1st District to become Chicago's first black mayor — Hayes has easily won re-election. Hayes did have to fight to win the seat in the first place, though. The 1983 special election contest revealed the first signs of strain within the coalition that had fueled Washington's successful mayoral bid that year.

Hayes, a machine operator turned union activist in the late 1930s, was an international vice president of the United Food and Commercial Workers Union when he helped organize labor backing for longtime friend Washington. But after Washington captured City Hall, two other prominent supporters — activist radio commentator Lu Palmer and civil rights leader Al Raby — also sought to succeed him.

Palmer was Hayes' chief threat. His constituency was mainly low-income residents of the city's public housing, and his organizing in the projects boosted Washington's mayoral campaign as much as Hayes' work with unions. But Washington endorsed Hayes, gaining him crucial get-out-the-vote assistance from the South Side organizations. Palmer by contrast, had a hard time turning out his supporters for the off-year special. Hayes won 45 percent of the vote in the 14-way primary.

Illinois 1

Chicago — South Side

The 1st contains the heart of Chicago's black South Side — an area that has been important in local politics since the 1920s, before most Northern cities even had substantial black populations. In the early 1980s, it became the political base for black political leader Harold Washington. After winning two elections as 1st District House member, Washington was elected in 1983 as Chicago's first black mayor. He died shortly after his re-election in 1987.

Although the 1st is a very poor area, with the decaying buildings common to inner cities everywhere, it also has had a stable black middle class. In the 1960s, when blacks on the more transient West Side rioted, this area was quiet.

Before World War II, most of the city's black population was concentrated here, just west of the wealthy residential areas on the Lake Michigan shore. But in recent years, as racial barriers fell in other parts of the city and its southern suburbs, many people have left the South Side. The 1st lost 20 percent of its people in the 1970s.

The 1st is overwhelmingly Democratic. More than 90 percent of its residents are black, and its small white population, centered around the University of Chicago, is nearly as Democratic as the black majority.

Some of the district's middle-class professionals live around the Michael Reese hospital complex on the district's northern border. Others live in Chatham, which established itself as a prosperous black residential neighborhood in the 1950s. Blue-collar workers profited for years from good-paying jobs at the steel mills of South Chicago; that industry's decline has caused economic hardship.

Many of the district's poorer black residents live in public housing projects, buildings seen as enlightened urban renewal when built in the 1950s but now derided as "vertical ghettos." One, the Robert Taylor Homes, is the country's largest such project.

Population: 519,045. White 33,477 (6%), Black 477,790 (92%), Other 4,077 (1%). Spanish origin, 5,467 (1%). 18 and over 358,925 (69%), 65 and over 53,927 (10%). Median age: 28.

Committees

Education & Labor (10th of 25 Democrats)
Elementary, Secondary & Vocational Education; Health & Safety; Labor-Management Relations; Postsecondary Education

Post Office & Civil Service (11th of 15 Democrats)
Postal Personnel & Modernization (chairman)

Elections

1990 General		
Charles A. Hayes (D)	100,890	(94%)
Babette Peyton (R)	6,708	(6%)
1990 Primary		
Charles A. Hayes (D)	83,098	(93%)
Gilbert S. Marchman (D)	6,676	(7%)
1988 General		
Charles A. Hayes (D)	164,125	(96%)
Stephen J. Evans (R)	6,753	(4%)

Previous Winning Percentages: **1986** (96%) **1984** (96%) **1983 *** (94%)

* *Special election.*

District Vote For President

	1988		1984		1980		1976	
D	174,793	(95%)	196,351	(94%)	177,491	(91%)	188,194	(90%)
R	7,168	(4%)	10,153	(5%)	10,912	(6%)	20,620	(10%)
I					3,991	(2%)		

Campaign Finance

	Receipts	Receipts from PACs		Expend-itures
1990				
Hayes (D)	$110,665	$85,250	(77%)	$125,509
Peyton (R)	$42,913	$1,000	(2%)	$42,901
1988				
Hayes (D)	$161,960	$115,634	(71%)	$156,905

Key Votes

1991	
Authorize use of force against Iraq	N
1990	
Support constitutional amendment on flag desecration	N
Pass family and medical leave bill over Bush veto	Y
Reduce SDI funding	Y
Allow abortions in overseas military facilities	Y
Approve budget summit plan for spending and taxing	N
Approve civil rights bill	Y
1989	
Halt production of B-2 stealth bomber at 13 planes	Y
Oppose capital gains tax cut	Y
Approve federal abortion funding in rape or incest cases	Y
Approve pay raise and revision of ethics rules	Y
Pass Democratic minimum wage plan over Bush veto	Y

Voting Studies

	Presidential Support		Party Unity		Conservative Coalition	
Year	**S**	**O**	**S**	**O**	**S**	**O**
1990	13	86	95	4	11	87
1989	27	73	98	2	0	100
1988	14	80	91	3	3	95
1987	10	90	95	2	2	98
1986	13	84	89	5	4	92
1985	15	84	93	1	4	93
1984	19	80	93	4	2	97
1983	7 †	86 †	87 †	7 †	9 †	85 †

† *Not eligible for all recorded votes.*

Interest Group Ratings

Year	ADA	ACU	AFL-CIO	CCUS
1990	100	4	100	29
1989	100	0	100	30
1988	95	0	100	14
1987	100	0	100	7
1986	95	0	100	6
1985	100	0	100	14
1984	100	4	100	38
1983	-	0	100	22

2 Gus Savage (D)

Of Chicago — Elected 1980

Born: Oct. 30, 1925, Detroit, Mich.
Education: Roosevelt U., B.A. 1951; attended Chicago-Kent College of Law, 1952-53.
Military Service: Army, 1943-46.
Occupation: Newspaper publisher.
Family: Widowed; two children.
Religion: Baptist.
Political Career: Sought Democratic nomination for U.S. House, 1968, 1970.
Capitol Office: 2419 Rayburn Bldg. 20515; 225-0773.

In Washington: Firebrand politicians like Savage run the same risk as trial lawyers who teach themselves to shed tears on cue — if not careful, they become uncontrollable caricatures of themselves.

During most of his first decade in Congress, Savage tried to advance his civil rights agenda mainly through angry denunciations of racial inequities instead of pursuing more traditional paths to power. He turned back criticisms of his style or agenda as "racist," but members at least understood his approach as calculated to further his goal of becoming a power broker in Chicago politics.

Recently, Savage has appeared to lose a grip on the act. As a subcommittee chairman on Public Works, he is positioned to exercise influence. But he still viscerally distrusts the establishment, so his increasing seniority in the House has not tempered his style. Although his weekly column, which appears in many black newspapers, gives Savage a large audience, he has little effectiveness in the House.

Perhaps his most significant contribution in the 101st Congress was a controversy he spurred over whether members should be permitted to delete floor remarks from the *Congressional Record*. After lashing out at Barney Frank of Massachusetts and two other colleagues for what he condemned as hypocrisy in their calling for his conduct to be investigated by the ethics committee, Savage removed the vituperative statements from the record. As a result, a task force later concluded that members should be able to delete "unparliamentary remarks" only with the consent of the House.

Savage's attack was in response to allegations that he made improper sexual advances to a young woman while on an official trip to Africa. The ethics committee, while recommending no formal punishment, ruled that Savage had acted contrary to a House rule requiring behavior to "reflect creditably" on the House. After first dismissing the charge as an "absolute lie," Savage eventually apologized to the woman, but boasted that he had avoided "even a slap on the wrist."

Savage's fiery rhetoric has always ensured him plenty of headlines. When Democratic Party Chairman Ronald H. Brown, who is black, said in 1989 that he would appear in Chicago with white Democratic mayoral candidate Richard M. Daley, who faced a black third-party foe, Savage attacked Brown: "When Ron Brown brings his Oreo you-know-what into Chicago, I'll guarantee I'm going to help organize a reception party for him at the airport and follow him all the way to some white hotel to denounce his coming in."

At the 1988 Democratic convention, he led a protest march against the vice presidential nomination of Lloyd Bentsen, whom Savage labeled a "reactionary Reaganite warhawk." Giving the keynote address at a Nation of Islam convention in 1985, he likened controversial Black Muslim leader Louis Farrakhan to the Rev. Dr. Martin Luther King Jr.

On the Small Business Committee, Savage tested his welcome when he provoked a shouting match with Chairman John J. LaFalce over legislation to revamp a federal program to foster minority business development.

At a 1987 meeting held to negotiate the final details of the overhaul, Savage angrily called the LaFalce plan a disaster. LaFalce, in turn, accused Savage of sending people to his Buffalo district to campaign against him, to which Savage replied that he did not need to send anyone — he would gladly campaign against LaFalce himself. As the dispute escalated, the committee's two black freshmen, Floyd H. Flake of New York and Kweisi Mfume of Maryland, sought to calm Savage. A deal that met with unanimous approval was ultimately worked out.

Late in 1988, Savage got some unwelcome publicity when allegations arose that his son Thomas was on the payroll of Washington, D.C., Del. Walter E. Fauntroy while the younger Savage was living in Chicago, a violation of House rules.

At Home: Although Savage never has seri-

Illinois 2

South Side Chicago; Harvey

The 2nd does not have the rich political history of its neighboring South Side district, which elected the nation's first black congressman of this century more than 60 years ago. Created only in 1971, the 2nd was represented by a white Democrat for eight years, even after its population was majority-black. Savage's election in 1980 marked its emergence as a black constituency.

Roughly U-shaped, the 2nd takes in Chicago's Far South Side and several of the southern Cook County suburbs. Blacks, both urban and suburban, make up more than two-thirds of the population. Harvey, an older industrial city, and Dixmoor, a suburb, are about two-thirds black. Phoenix, a village of about 3,000, has been nearly all black for the past 60 years.

The traditional economic base of the district is the vast industrial area around the Calumet River, where the sky, trees and grass long have been blackened with soot, but where factory workers could count on steady work and decent pay. These days the grass is still gray, but the mills are hulking shadows of their former selves.

The 2nd does have some middle-class black neighborhoods, toward its southern end and along its western fork, around Morgan Park. Unable to shake Savage's hold on lower-income voters, his primary challengers tend to focus their efforts here.

The Chicago portion of the district contains the 2nd's most politically significant white presence, although "white flight" has lowered it since the early 1970s. Chicago's 10th Ward, an ethnic blue-collar bastion near Lake Calumet, is the political base for Edward R. Vrdolyak, the former Cook County Democratic chairman who made a celebrated switch to the Republican Party. His efforts to galvanize an ethnic white surge to the GOP, of no great success citywide, have had no effect whatsoever on the black Democratic dominance in the 2nd; Savage's worries cease at the end of his Democratic primary campaigns.

The district's white suburban territory includes Riverdale and parts of Dolton and Calumet City, all blue-collar and less than 10 percent black in 1980. Many of the people here moved out from the Far South Side of the city in the past two decades.

Population: 518,931. White 131,211 (25%), Black 364,584 (70%). Spanish origin 38,249 (7%). 18 and over 340,827 (66%), 65 and over 35,955 (7%). Median age: 26.

ous Republican opposition in the mainly black 2nd District, he has faced fierce primary opposition in each of his six House campaigns from opponents who described him as an ineffective bully. Savage has survived each time with the support of a loyal bloc of voters who view him as a civil rights hero and a voice for the dispossessed.

Most of Savage's primaries have been heated battles not only for the House seat but for position in Chicago's black leadership. However, none were as rancorous as his rematch with educator Mel Reynolds in 1990.

When Reynolds, a former Rhodes Scholar, first ran in 1988, he received favorable notice from Chicago's major newspapers as an intelligent and consensus-minded alternative to the contentious Savage. But the incumbent dismissed Reynolds, who had grown up on Chicago's West Side, as an outsider and an intellectual elitist. Savage won with 52 percent of the vote to 25 percent for veteran state Sen. Emil Jones Jr.; Reynolds trailed with 14 percent.

Reynolds spent the next two years laying strong groundwork for a second challenge, and managed to fend off other major entrants, setting up the one-on-one match for which Savage's critics had hoped. Boosted by the controversy over Savage's Zaire incident, Reynolds looked to be a serious threat.

However, Savage responded with a barrage of invective unprecedented even for him. At a rally just before the March primary, Savage portrayed Reynolds as a tool of outside interests, especially Jewish contributors who opposed Savage's support for Arab causes and for Louis Farrakhan. Claiming that Reynolds had received 80 percent of his individual campaign contributions from members of the American-Israel Public Affairs Committee, Savage told his supporters, "He who pays the piper calls the tune."

The resulting flap caused some embarrassment for Democratic Reps. William H. Gray III of Pennsylvania and Charles B. Rangel of New York, who had appeared at the rally in Savage's behalf but had left before he made the controversial remarks. But the speech only bolstered Savage among his hard-core followers: He defeated Reynolds by 51 percent to 43 percent.

A fighter by nature — Savage admits to being in a street gang before joining the Army in World War II — Savage served on the front lines of the civil rights movement. In the late 1940s he organized sit-ins protesting discrimination against blacks in the hiring of department store clerks. Two decades later, he helped organize a wildcat strike of black bus drivers aimed at ending union discrimination.

Savage was also active in the Chicago League of Negro Voters, the first organization of black "independents" that fought the Democratic machine of Mayor Richard J. Daley. In 1967, Savage ran for alderman, but lost. His 1968 and 1970 bids for the House met with no more success.

But after a 10-year stint behind the scenes — he encouraged Harold Washington, later Chicago's first black mayor, to make his initial try for that office in 1977 — Savage's own political career took off.

In 1980, Democratic Rep. Morgan F. Murphy was retiring, and Savage became the focus of an effort to end machine control of the 2nd. The Democratic organization had tapped a black candidate, Reginald Brown, to succeed Murphy (who was white). But Savage, widely known as a political activist and publisher of a chain of community newspapers, was able to ride resentment over Brown's anointment to a primary victory, taking 45 percent of the vote.

In 1982 the machine tried another black candidate, former state legislator and Chicago Transit Authority Chairman Eugene M. Barnes. But even as Barnes was claiming that he could achieve more by working within the system than Savage did with his brash manner, a third candidate, state Rep. Monica Faith Stewart, was drawing off attention: She said straight out that Savage had embarrassed the 2nd District by behaving like a "clown." The result was a three-way split that enabled Savage to prevail with 39 percent.

In 1984, Leon Davis, an executive with the People's Gas Company, ran a woefully unorganized campaign. But Savage's modest 44 percent victory convinced his critics that he remained vulnerable. Two years later, Savage faced telephone company executive Raymond Arias, who drew Hispanic support, and the Rev. Al Sampson, a founder of the Chicago Council of Black Churches. But neither Arias nor Sampson could move beyond his base of support, and Savage took just under 50 percent.

Committees

Public Works & Transportation (9th of 36 Democrats)
Public Buildings & Grounds (chairman); Aviation; Economic Development

Small Business (9th of 27 Democrats)
Procurement, Tourism & Rural Development; SBA, the General Economy & Minority Enterprise Development

Elections

1990 General		
Gus Savage (D)	80,245	(78%)
William T. Hespel (R)	22,350	(22%)
1990 Primary		
Gus Savage (D)	41,837	(51%)
Mel Reynolds (D)	35,012	(43%)
Ernest Washington Jr. (D)	4,412	(5%)
1988 General		
Gus Savage (D)	138,256	(83%)
William T. Hespel (R)	28,831	(17%)

Previous Winning Percentages: **1986** (84%) **1984** (83%) **1982** (87%) **1980** (88%)

District Vote For President

	1988		1984		1980		1976	
D	150,387	(85%)	168,174	(83%)	151,227	(73%)	120,666	(73%)
R	25,896	(15%)	32,693	(16%)	47,347	(23%)	45,713	(27%)
I					4,853	(2%)		

Campaign Finance

	Receipts	Receipts from PACs		Expend-itures
1990				
Savage (D)	$196,926	$57,800	(29%)	$190,685
1988				
Savage (D)	$240,244	$116,218	(48%)	$242,487
Hespel (R)	$6,167	$220	(4%)	$6,392

Key Votes

1991	
Authorize use of force against Iraq	N
1990	
Support constitutional amendment on flag desecration	N
Pass family and medical leave bill over Bush veto	Y
Reduce SDI funding	Y
Allow abortions in overseas military facilities	Y
Approve budget summit plan for spending and taxing	N
Approve civil rights bill	Y
1989	
Halt production of B-2 stealth bomber at 13 planes	Y
Oppose capital gains tax cut	Y
Approve federal abortion funding in rape or incest cases	Y
Approve pay raise and revision of ethics rules	Y
Pass Democratic minimum wage plan over Bush veto	Y

Voting Studies

	Presidential Support		Party Unity		Conservative Coalition	
Year	**S**	**O**	**S**	**O**	**S**	**O**
1990	19	80	79	10	17	80
1989	23	70	88	2	2	93
1988	18	72	82	4	5	92
1987	10	88	87	3	5	88
1986	14	80	79	4	2	90
1985	13	84	85	3	2	87
1984	15	70	76	5	0	85
1983	7	87	88	4	4	84
1982	17	62	63	7	8	77
1981	14	49	57	5	5	49

Interest Group Ratings

Year	ADA	ACU	AFL-CIO	CCUS
1990	89	9	92	14
1989	100	0	91	22
1988	100	0	100	23
1987	100	0	100	0
1986	95	0	100	7
1985	100	5	100	18
1984	95	5	91	36
1983	95	0	100	16
1982	75	12	94	26
1981	65	7	100	0

3 Marty Russo (D)

Of South Holland — Elected 1974

Born: Jan. 23, 1944, Chicago, Ill.
Education: DePaul U., B.A. 1965, J.D. 1967.
Occupation: Lawyer.
Family: Wife, Karen Jorgenson; two children.
Religion: Roman Catholic.
Political Career: Cook County assistant state's attorney, 1971-73.
Capitol Office: 2233 Rayburn Bldg. 20515; 225-5736.

In Washington: Russo's boisterous and sometimes crude style has contributed to his image as a political hack for his mentor, Ways and Means Chairman Dan Rostenkowski, and for a combination of Chicago business and labor interests. But if he seems to treat the House as an oversized college fraternity, he is nonetheless a serious legislator capable of thinking and acting on his own. And in recent sessions he has developed a knack for being where the action is.

When the House in 1991 passed the seven-day waiting period for handgun purchases (the Brady bill), Russo made a crucial contribution by persuading a handful of fence-sitters not to vote for a de facto substitute.

In the 101st Congress, Russo was in the thick of the struggle over the budget summit, defense spending, the capital gains tax, trade with China and the surtax on seniors to pay for catastrophic Medicare coverage. Russo adamantly rejected the summit deal because it cut domestic programs but did not cut defense as much as he wanted. He pressed for tougher treatment of the Chinese, for higher taxes on the rich (serving as one of two key whips against the capital-gains tax cut) and for a repeal of the catastrophic-coverage surtax.

He was not always with the Democratic leadership, and he was not always with Rostenkowski. But when the votes were counted he was usually with the majority of the House. And, as if to forestall any break in the action, Russo, the second-ranking Democrat on the Ways and Means Subcommittee on Health, has introduced a national health-care plan in the 102nd Congress.

Russo will also be directing some of his renowned energy into a new committee in the 102nd, rotating off of Budget to House Administration, where he is expected to campaign for the needs of Ways and Means. The interests of his prime committee usually have priority with Russo. He went to the last Democratic Caucus meeting of 1990 arguing for restraint of the leadership "task forces" that tinker with the products of the traditional committees. His effort was beaten back, but Russo came away with something to show. Speaker Thomas S. Foley of Washington gave him a seat on the influential Democratic Steering and Policy Committee, which makes committee assignments.

Bringing Russo further into the fold (he was already a deputy whip) probably will not bring him to heel. He was one of only three Northern Democrats who voted against the civil rights bill in the 101st Congress, and repeated that stance early in the 102nd Congress. Similarly, after voting in early March 1988 for a bill overturning the Supreme Court's *Grove City* decision, which narrowed the scope of several civil rights laws, Russo three weeks later voted to sustain President Ronald Reagan's veto of the bill. He cited complaints about the bill in the intervening weeks from religious groups in his district.

And many members had been irritated in late 1987 over Russo's handling of a controversial budget bill that linked spending cuts, tax increases and a welfare-reform bill. Russo headed the leadership task force rounding up votes to bring the package to the floor. When the House blocked the bill on a procedural vote, the leadership dropped the welfare provisions and brought it back to the floor. It passed by a one-vote margin — with Russo voting against it.

Russo said he felt undercut by the leadership's change in strategy and called the final product a "totally different animal" from the bill he had agreed to round up votes for. But it galled some Democrats who had been whipped into voting the party line — despite personal reservations and political risks — to see Russo voting against it because it did not suit him.

Some members said that episode would hurt Russo in future efforts to round up votes. But he retains many of the attributes that have made him one of the most effective whips in the House. He has both persistence and a seat on Ways and Means, which gives him leverage with members looking for favors. Standing well over six feet, Russo also can be physically intimidating. In a moment of late-night raw nerves late in 1989, Russo took a swing at a colleague, Democrat Dennis E. Eckart of Ohio, on the House

Illinois 3

Southwest Chicago and Suburbs

The line between the 2nd and 3rd districts is also the line between black and white Chicago. Russo's district, concentrated on the west side of Western Avenue and in the suburbs just beyond the city, was 92 percent white when it was drawn in the early 1980s.

The city portions of the 3rd are dominated by blue-collar ethnics, many of Polish and Lithuanian origin. But Beverly, traditional home for Chicago's well-to-do Irish Catholics, is also included.

Most of the ethnics here retain fond memories of Mayor Richard J. Daley's Democratic Party in Chicago. With Daley's death in 1976 and the election of a black mayor in 1983, the party began to lose strength: Ronald Reagan carried the Chicago portion of the district in 1984 and Bush did well there in 1988. However, the 1989 election and 1991 re-election of Richard M. Daley to fill the position long owned by his late father has breathed new life into the remnants of the old Democratic organization.

The suburbs in the 3rd include Blue Island, developed for Illinois Central railroad workers, and Oak Lawn, a 19th-century suburb that now has a large Greek-American population. Midlothian and Oak Forest, built up in the 1960s, have drawn blue-collar workers from South Chicago. Most of the district's small black population is in Robbins, which has been majority-black for a generation, and Markham, which lost many of its white residents in the 1970s and is now about two-thirds black.

Russo lives in South Holland, which has a significant Dutch population but has also attracted Italians, Poles and others from Chicago's South Side. In many ways he is typical of the district. He grew up in an Italian neighborhood in the city and then lived in an apartment in Calumet Park before buying his South Holland home.

Many of the suburban ethnics became prosperous in the 1960s, when they left the city and began to vote Republican in some contests. The recessions of the 1970s shocked many of these people, threatening their fragile middle-class status. In 1974 the old 3rd District turned out Republican Rep. Robert Hanrahan for Russo, who has firmly established himself. But these communities have swung back and forth between the parties in state elections, while solidly favoring Republicans for president.

Population: 519,040. White 477,098 (92%), Black 29,518 (6%), Other 3,999 (1%). Spanish origin 18,049 (4%). 18 and over 379,396 (73%), 65 and over 65,329 (13%). Median age: 32.

floor. He missed.

Russo is perhaps best known for an uninhibited manner that often enlivens, if not ennobles, committee debates. At a Trade Subcommittee markup in 1990, Russo was in mid-tirade when Frank J. Guarini, D-N.J., tried to interrupt. "No," said Russo, "I'm on a roll." When Guarini replied that the "roll" was not "particularly good or productive," Russo shot back: "Look Frank, I listened to your idiotic comments for nearly half an hour."

But much of his reputation still stems from a single incident in 1984 when the leadership wanted to delay MX-missile production. As the final seconds of the roll call ticked away, party strategists gathered around a computer terminal indicating defeat by one vote. Russo raced into the Democratic cloakroom, where he found Daniel K. Akaka of Hawaii, a usual leadership loyalist who had been recorded on the pro-MX side. Russo lifted Akaka out of a telephone booth and carried him onto the House floor, where he arrived at the rostrum and reversed himself just as the presiding officer was banging down the gavel. The amendment carried by one vote.

As would be expected of a Rostenkowski protégé on Ways and Means, Russo was very active in the effort to overhaul the tax code in the 99th Congress. But he was not just a follower. Early in 1985, before drafting began on the basic tax-revision bill, Russo joined with New York Democrat Charles E. Schumer in pushing a new 25 percent minimum tax on corporations and on wealthy individuals making over $100,000 per year. They argued that preventing the affluent from escaping taxation would reduce the deficit and make the tax code fairer. Initially, Russo seemed to feel that a minimum tax might be the only reform needed.

There is no question that much of the work Russo does has a Chicago connection. During Ways and Means' efforts to cut Medicare costs in 1987, he was lead sponsor of an amendment backed by Illinois hospitals that would channel more money to industrial states. He said the change was needed to reflect regional variations in costs, but critics derided it as "pure pork."

At Home: When Russo launched his House candidacy in 1974 in a district drawn to favor a Republican, his credentials seemed modest. He had served as president of the

Young Democrats of Calumet Park, and was an assistant Cook County state's attorney from 1971 to 1973. Chosen by the Daley organization and unopposed for the nomination, he was looked upon as a long-shot candidate against freshman Republican Rep. Robert Hanrahan.

But he pulled off one of the sleeper upsets of 1974, coming from far behind in the closing weeks to surprise an overly confident incumbent who did little campaigning until mid-October. Russo had strong support from organized labor and the Cook County Democratic machine, and the advantage of the Watergate scandal, which contributed to a low Republican turnout.

Russo has steadily boosted his margins since then. He won 64 percent in 1984 and 62 percent in 1988 despite the district's heavy vote for the Republican presidential candidates in those years.

In 1990, no Republican candidate filed for the primary to run against Russo. Under state law, district Republicans were permitted to choose a nominee, and opted for 73-year-old former state Rep. Carl L. Klein. Russo won easily.

Russo's career was briefly threatened in 1982 by redistricting and his cool relations with then-Chicago Mayor Jane M. Byrne. The 1981 remap shifted the balance of power in his district's Democratic organization to ward and township leaders allied with Byrne.

When party slatemakers met in early 1982 to endorse a candidate for the primary, Russo lost out to state Sen. Frank Savickas, a Byrne ally. Russo vowed to challenge Savickas in the primary, but Byrne had a change of heart, and persuaded Savickas to drop out.

Committees

House Administration (12th of 15 Democrats)
Accounts; Office Systems; Personnel & Police

Ways & Means (11th of 23 Democrats)
Health; Oversight

Elections

1990 General

Marty Russo (D)	110,512	(71%)
Carl L. Klein (R)	45,299	(29%)

1988 General

Marty Russo (D)	132,111	(62%)
Joseph J. McCarthy (R)	80,181	(38%)

Previous Winning Percentages: **1986** (66%) **1984** (64%) **1982** (74%) **1980** (69%) **1978** (65%) **1976** (59%) **1974** (53%)

District Vote For President

	1988	1984	1980	1976
D	92,108 (41%)	84,752 (35%)	95,274 (44%)	79,792 (43%)
R	103,606 (59%)	158,281 (65%)	105,358 (49%)	104,166 (56%)
I			12,786 (6%)	

Campaign Finance

	Receipts	Receipts from PACs		Expend-itures
1990				
Russo (D)	$547,782	$382,966	(70%)	$541,279
1988				
Russo (D)	$558,458	$357,996	(64%)	$558,273
McCarthy (R)	$83,234	$25	(0%)	$81,325

Key Votes

1991	
Authorize use of force against Iraq	N
1990	
Support constitutional amendment on flag desecration	N
Pass family and medical leave bill over Bush veto	Y
Reduce SDI funding	Y
Allow abortions in overseas military facilities	N
Approve budget summit plan for spending and taxing	N
Approve civil rights bill	N
1989	
Halt production of B-2 stealth bomber at 13 planes	Y
Oppose capital gains tax cut	Y
Approve federal abortion funding in rape or incest cases	N
Approve pay raise and revision of ethics rules	Y
Pass Democratic minimum wage plan over Bush veto	Y

Voting Studies

	Presidential Support		Party Unity		Conservative Coalition	
Year	S	O	S	O	S	O
1990	29	70	82	16	24	74
1989	27	72	78	16	32	63
1988	29	63	78	15	39	58
1987	24	75	79	12	21	74
1986	18	79	81	13	26	64
1985	23	78	82	11	24	75
1984	27	63	74	18	22	69
1983	16	74	76 †	13 †	26	72
1982	30	62	81	15	32	68
1981	38	54	64	25	39	57

† Not eligible for all recorded votes.

Interest Group Ratings

Year	ADA	ACU	AFL-CIO	CCUS
1990	78	17	83	23
1989	80	11	83	30
1988	80	28	93	46
1987	84	17	93	33
1986	65	9	86	38
1985	70	14	82	36
1984	85	8	85	31
1983	75	30	69	20
1982	80	10	85	27
1981	55	14	73	25

4 George E. Sangmeister (D)

Of Mokena — Elected 1988

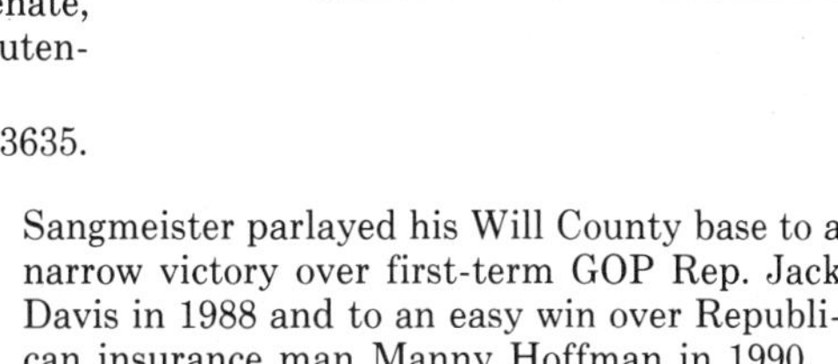

Born: Feb. 16, 1931, Joliet, Ill.
Education: Elmhurst College, B.A. 1957; John Marshall Law School, J.D. 1960.
Military Service: Army, 1951-53.
Occupation: Lawyer.
Family: Wife, Doris M. Hinspeter; two children.
Religion: United Church of Christ.
Political Career: Will County Justice of the Peace/Magistrate, 1961-64; Will County State's Attorney, 1964-68; Ill. House, 1973-77; Ill. Senate, 1977-87; sought Democratic nomination for lieutenant governor, 1986.
Capitol Office: 1032 Longworth Bldg. 20515; 225-3635.

In Washington: After serving as Judiciary Committee chairman in the Illinois Senate, Sangmeister had to adjust to life as a member of the 1988 House freshman class. The Democratic leadership did what it could to ease that transition, appointing Sangmeister to the Judiciary Committee. The low-key Sangmeister did not shine in debate on the omnibus crime bill that lurched to an inconclusive outcome in the 101st Congress. However, he displayed his years of experience on judicial affairs, packaging his ideas on such issues as habeas corpus reform, expedited death penalty appeals and the exclusionary rule into a legislative proposal.

Although not on an education-related committee, Sangmeister has made a cause of boosting geography and foreign language studies. In 1990 he sent a "Dear Colleague" letter in Chinese. "Chances are good you are not able to read or understand this passage," he wrote in the translation. "Yet if a similar passage in English were presented to the average Taiwanese high school student, he or she would be able to interpret the basic meaning."

During his first term, Sangmeister frequently opposed President Bush's stands. His 1990 GOP challenger tried to cast the laconic, white-haired incumbent as an ultra-liberal. But Sangmeister brushed off the label, pointing to his anti-crime work and support for a constitutional amendment banning flag burning.

Sangmeister also pushed local issues. In the debate over the location of a third Chicago-area airport, Sangmeister came out for a site near Kankakee, just south of the 4th; he fought a plan to put the airport in southeast Chicago, near his district's populous suburban part.

At Home: The Sangmeister name is a familiar one in Will County politics. His father (also George Sangmeister) is remembered on a plaque at the village hall in Frankfort, where he served as mayor for 32 years.

With a long political career of his own, Sangmeister parlayed his Will County base to a narrow victory over first-term GOP Rep. Jack Davis in 1988 and to an easy win over Republican insurance man Manny Hoffman in 1990.

By winning the House seat, Sangmeister rebounded from a terribly embarrassing 1986 defeat. That year, Sangmeister was the Democratic organization's choice for lieutenant governor. However, both he and the party-slated candidate for secretary of state lost in the Democratic primary to disciples of fringe politician Lyndon H. LaRouche Jr.

Sangmeister had never before tasted political defeat. At age 30, he served as a circuit court magistrate, then became state's attorney for Will County. He won a state House seat in 1972, then ousted a Republican state senator in 1976. His sturdy reputation helped him avoid most blame for the 1986 debacle, which was widely attributed to party complacency. When Davis, a combative state House member, barely won the open 4th in 1986, Democrats looked forward to a Sangmeister bid for the seat in 1988.

It was a nasty duel. Although Sangmeister remained rather taciturn, his well-financed operation portrayed Davis, a longtime GOP insider, as a shady pol. Davis returned fire, playing up the Democrat's ties to interest groups that Davis described as leftist. Sangmeister ended up on top by 1,039 votes. When Sangmeister entered the House, he was not quite 58, making him the oldest Democratic freshman elected in 1988. In 1990, Republicans offered Hoffman, the owner of a group of insurance brokerages. The mayor of the village of Homewood and a longtime civic activist, he had the support of a GOP machine that usually gives Republicans an edge in the suburban Cook County portion of the 4th.

But even Hoffman's tireless campaigning could not match Sangmeister's name recognition, especially in Will County. Sangmeister took 59 percent of the vote.

Illinois 4

Southern Chicago Suburbs; Joliet; Aurora

The 4th is a transitional district, one where metropolitan Chicago peters out into less heavily settled northern Illinois. In most maps of "Chicago and vicinity," the 4th's two largest cities, Aurora and Joliet, are just barely included. About 90 percent of the district's voting population is evenly divided between the northern part of Will County, centered on Joliet, and the southern suburbs of Cook County, including Chicago Heights. The 4th also takes in corners of Kane County, including part of the city of Aurora, and Kendall County.

The Will County part of the district has tended Republican over the years, especially at the presidential level. However, there is a base Democratic vote in the economically depressed Joliet area. Sangmeister, like his father, has proved that Democrats can win in Will County. His 7,500-vote margin there was crucial to his 1988 victory over GOP Rep. Jack Davis; his nearly 20,000-vote margin turned his 1990 contest into a runaway.

Joliet, a largely blue-collar city of about 77,000, has suffered from a decline in its heavy-industry base, including the 1979 shutdown of a U.S. Steel plant. Local officials have tried to attract federal defense projects to the long-dormant Joliet Arsenal.

The Republican vote is more dependable in Bloom Township, which includes the blue-collar Cook County communities around the old industrial city of Chicago Heights. That city's mayor, Charles Panici, founded an efficient Republican organization in the once-heavily Italian-American area, which now has a sizable black population. Davis' success in the Cook County suburbs won him the House seat in 1986, and nearly saved him in 1988.

However, Sangmeister won Cook County by nearly 2,000 votes in 1990. He benefited from his efforts to steer a projected third Chicago-area airport away from these densely populated areas of the 4th to a rural stretch south of the district.

Nestled in the district's northwest corner are Aurora, about 60 percent of which is in the 4th, and a section of Kendall County around the small town of Oswego. Aurora, a 19th-century industrial city on the Fox River, still has a heavy-equipment industry, but to draw high-tech firms it touts its proximity to the Fermi National Accelerator Laboratory located just outside the 4th.

Population: 519,049. White 439,484 (85%), Black 57,912 (11%), Other 4,529 (1%). Spanish origin 35,659 (7%). 18 and over 356,524 (69%), 65 and over 43,743 (8%). Median age: 28.

Committees

Judiciary (17th of 21 Democrats)
Intellectual Property & Judicial Administration; Crime and Criminal Justice

Public Works & Transportation (27th of 36 Democrats)
Aviation; Surface Transportation

Veterans' Affairs (12th of 21 Democrats)
Education, Training & Employment; Hospitals & Health Care

Elections

1990 General		
George E. Sangmeister (D)	77,290	(59%)
Manny Hoffman (R)	53,258	(41%)
1988 General		
George E. Sangmeister (D)	91,282	(50%)
Jack Davis (R)	90,243	(50%)

District Vote For President

	1988	1984	1980	1976
D	82,661 (44%)	77,291 (39%)	71,355 (36%)	111,214 (48%)
R	103,720 (56%)	120,290 (61%)	109,523 (56%)	118,762 (51%)
I			13,844 (7%)	

Campaign Finance

	Receipts	Receipts from PACs	Expend-itures
1990			
Sangmeister (D)	$477,551	$356,393 (75%)	$472,757
Hoffman (R)	$651,729	$87,725 (13%)	$642,391
1988			
Sangmeister (D)	$378,294	$144,294 (38%)	$359,942
Davis (R)	$388,118	$266,768 (69%)	$348,339

Key Votes

1991	
Authorize use of force against Iraq	N
1990	
Support constitutional amendment on flag desecration	Y
Pass family and medical leave bill over Bush veto	Y
Reduce SDI funding	Y
Allow abortions in overseas military facilities	N
Approve budget summit plan for spending and taxing	N
Approve civil rights bill	Y
1989	
Halt production of B-2 stealth bomber at 13 planes	Y
Oppose capital gains tax cut	Y
Approve federal abortion funding in rape or incest cases	Y
Approve pay raise and revision of ethics rules	N
Pass Democratic minimum wage plan over Bush veto	Y

Voting Studies

	Presidential Support		Party Unity		Conservative Coalition	
Year	S	O	S	O	S	O
1990	32	67	77	19	50	46
1989	21	78	86	11	41	56

Interest Group Ratings

Year	ADA	ACU	AFL-CIO	CCUS
1990	56	33	75	38
1989	90	14	92	50

5 William O. Lipinski (D)

Of Chicago — Elected 1982

Born: Dec. 22, 1937, Chicago, Ill.
Education: Attended Loras College, 1957-58.
Military Service: Army Reserve, 1961-67.
Occupation: Parks supervisor.
Family: Wife, Rose Marie Lapinski; two children.
Religion: Roman Catholic.
Political Career: Chicago city alderman, 1975-83.
Capitol Office: 1501 Longworth Bldg. 20515; 225-5701.

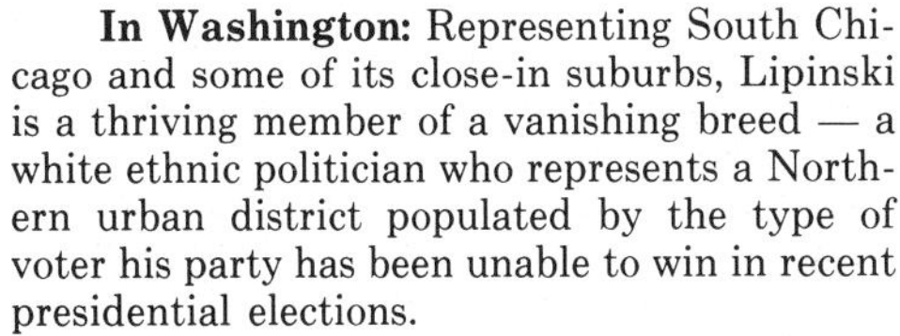

In Washington: Representing South Chicago and some of its close-in suburbs, Lipinski is a thriving member of a vanishing breed — a white ethnic politician who represents a Northern urban district populated by the type of voter his party has been unable to win in recent presidential elections.

Of Polish descent, he is the friend of organized labor and many New Deal-type programs — allegiances that have helped him emerge as a backroom traffic cop of competing Chicago delegation demands as well as the congressional liaison for the revitalized political machine of Chicago Mayor Richard M. Daley.

He also is a persistent and sometimes emotional spokesman for conservative ethnic values he thinks Democrats have discarded in recent years. The label "white ethnic," however, angers Lipinski. "These same political types who have made the term fashionable," he complains, "have at the same time tried to make it unfashionable to exhibit many of [the] beliefs real ethnics hold, implying that it's immoral to oppose all abortions, racist to support capital punishment...."

Lipinski finds some common ground with his party on family issues. In the 100th Congress, he criticized conservatives who, he says, base answers to current family problems on "an image of the family that no longer squares with the facts...." He wants Congress to enact legislation to establish IRA-type accounts for post-secondary education and for first-time home buyers, and he supports a day-care tax credit.

As one of the members of the Public Works Committee who helped oust Chairman Glenn M. Anderson of California at the start of of the 102nd Congress, he is well-positioned to look out for Chicago's needs. He was instrumental in passing legislation to assess airline passenger fees that could give the city financial leverage in its quest for a new airport. Lipinski was unsuccessful, however, in his effort to limit the scope of disabled-access requirements that commuter rail systems must meet.

Lipinski's training in old-school Chicago politics came into play in 1986 when he got an unexpected call from Ronald Reagan. The president wanted to know where Lipinski stood on aid to the Nicaraguan contras. Lipinski said there was "a need to stop communism" and he would be voting with the administration. Reagan then said to let the White House know if he could use any favors, a request that no politician who grew up in Mayor Richard J. Daley's machine could ever ignore.

"Have you ever heard of the Southwest Rapid Transit Line?" Lipinski asked. Reagan had not heard of it, but before the conversation was over he had promised to find out why money for it was delayed. Four months later, a federal contract for $496 million to start work on the line won approval.

A co-chairman of the Democratic National Committee's Council on Ethnic Americans, Lipinski is a watchdog for ethnic rights and an advocate for relaxing immigration restrictions, particularly for Eastern Europeans. In 1989, he argued for giving East German emigrants preference so the United States could tap that country's talent.

He also successfully pushed an amendment to the immigration bill that waived the need for asylum seekers to prove potential homeland persecution when applying for permanent residence.

And while he has failed to kick the habit himself, Lipinski worked behind the scenes in 1990 to ban smoking on domestic airline flights.

In the 101st Congress, Lipinski gained his first chairmanship — of the Oversight and Investigations Subcommittee of the Merchant Marine and Fisheries Committee .

At Home: When Cook County State's Attorney Richard M. Daley began his campaign for mayor of Chicago in 1989, Lipinski was one Democratic House member he knew he could count on for support. Lipinski owes his political career to Daley's late father.

In fact, Lipinski made it to Congress in 1982 as the result of an early skirmish in the younger Daley's unsuccessful first bid for mayor in 1983. Lipinski's House primary battle against Democratic Rep. John Fary was a bitter

Illinois 5

South Central Chicago and Suburbs

The 5th begins about a mile from Lake Michigan and, following the Adlai Stevenson Expressway, extends west to the split-levels of suburban Willow Springs.

It includes the home of the late Mayor Richard J. Daley and the political organization he dominated. Daley lived his entire life in Bridgeport, an almost exclusively Irish neighborhood. But Eastern Europeans, especially Poles, dominate the broader territory within the congressional district.

In local politics, the district has held to its traditions. The Daley machine stayed intact here even as it decayed elsewhere in Chicago, and local Democratic officials rejoiced when Richard M. Daley — also a Bridgeport resident — brought the legendary family name back to the mayor's office in 1989.

President Reagan made a breakthrough for the Republicans in 1984, winning 58 percent of the vote in the 5th, which had even stood by Jimmy Carter in 1980. The 1988 presidential contest was more competitive, but George Bush prevailed with 52 percent.

There are some longtime Republican pockets in the 5th. The Czech and Bohemian enclaves of Cicero and Berwyn have voted Republican in most recent contests, and the white-collar suburbs of Bridgeview and Hickory Hills lean to the GOP. But the inner suburban communities of McCook, Countryside, Hodgkins and Summit, all industrial, generally have echoed the Democratic tendencies of the Chicago part of the 5th.

At the district's eastern end, on Chicago's South Side, is the Union Stockyards, the setting for Upton Sinclair's "The Jungle," and a few blocks from the Daley home. Largely abandoned in the 1950s by the meatpacking industry, the huge stockyards area at one time employed 80 percent of the workers from surrounding neighborhoods; but as jobs dwindled, residents left for the suburbs. Even the Catholic churches that served as a cultural and religious hubs have been forced to close down.

Population: 518,971. White 413,301 (80%), Black 17,899 (3%), Other 9,358 (2%). Spanish origin 135,062 (26%). 18 and over 377,195 (73%), 65 and over 61,278 (12%). Median age: 30.

match that tested the remnants of Chicago's legendary political machine.

At the time of the 1982 House primary, the chief mayoral rivals were Daley and incumbent Jane M. Byrne (Harold Washington, the Democratic House member who would ride a wave of minority support to become Chicago's first black mayor, entered later). Fary, a longtime state legislator who had been tapped for Congress in 1975 as a reward for his devoted service to Mayor Daley, was being pressured to step down as early as 1980 by a group of South Side Democrats allied with Daley's son. Fary reportedly begged another term to boost his retirement benefits, and the Daley forces obliged him. Then, the 70-year-old Fary insisted on running yet again, denying he had made any commitment to retire. This time, the Daley organization endorsed Lipinski.

A lifelong Chicago resident and party loyalist, Lipinski had climbed through the ranks in the city Parks Department over 17 years. He began as a weekend athletic instructor and, thanks to his Daley machine contacts, rose to the position of area administrator managing personnel and programs at several local parks. He was elected to the City Council in 1975.

The 1982 primary was exceptionally tense despite the slight difference between the two candidates on most issues. Lipinski challenged Fary's ability to be an effective legislator at age 70, insisting that he would be a more vigorous representative. Fary accused his opponent of being a puppet for Richard M. Daley.

As the campaign drew to a close, Fary asked federal officials to monitor the polls on Election Day, saying he did not trust Daley to guard against voting irregularities — part of Daley's duties as state's attorney. In a joint appearance with Daley, Lipinski charged that Byrne had broken her vow of neutrality and was secretly working to help Fary, in hopes of embarrassing Daley.

The outcome was not even close. Although Fary drew support from Polish ethnic organizations and from some old-guard machine backers still loyal to Byrne, the mayor was unable to pull much weight in southwest Chicago's 23rd Ward, where Daley and Lipinski (the Democratic ward committeeman) turned out a huge vote. Lipinski drew over 60 percent of the vote to take the nomination, which was tantamount to election in the solidly Democratic 5th.

The election reflected increasing bitterness between Lipinski and Byrne. When Byrne won City Hall in 1979, Lipinski backed her on the City Council. But it was soon clear she would not grant Lipinski the clout he sought. The alderman then supported Daley's 1980 campaign for state's attorney against a Byrne-backed candidate.

Lipinski exasperated Byrne from his post as chairman of the Council's newly created Education Committee, a body Lipinski had fought to establish. When Byrne sought to restaff the Chicago Board of Education with her own appointees, Lipinski voted against virtually every Byrne nominee; he later pushed to make the school board an elective body. Although liberal Democrats deplored his votes against some black and Hispanic school board nominees, Lipinski was praised for conducting fair and open committee hearings on the matter. During his seven years on the Council, he gained a reputation for accessibility, straight talk and service to his home territory. Lipinski made a pet project of lobbying for the establishment of the Southwest Rapid Transit Line for the only part of the city that was without such service. He also sponsored a number of bills prohibiting mandatory busing.

Though his mainly white, ethnic constituency became openly skeptical of the Democratic Party and hostile to the city administrations of Washington and his black successor, Eugene Sawyer, Lipinski never suffered at the polls. With Richard M. Daley finally winning the mayoral office in 1989, Lipinski's constituents re-established links to the "new" Democratic machine in City Hall.

The revival of local Democratic strength emerged in Lipinski's 1990 House campaign. GOP officials touted their challenger, marketing executive David J. Shestokas. But the suburban-based Shestokas could not offset the the incumbent's disciplined urban precinct operation. Lipinski breezed in with 66 percent of the vote, up from 61 percent in 1988.

Committees

Merchant Marine & Fisheries (9th of 29 Democrats)
Oversight & Investigations (chairman); Oceanography, Great Lakes & Outer Continental Shelf

Public Works & Transportation (13th of 36 Democrats)
Aviation; Public Buildings & Grounds; Surface Transportation

Elections

1990 General		
William O. Lipinski (D)	73,805	(66%)
David J. Shestokas (R)	34,440	(31%)
Ronald Bartos (IL SOL)	3,001	(3%)
1988 General		
William O. Lipinski (D)	93,567	(61%)
John J. Holowinski (R)	59,128	(39%)

Previous Winning Percentages: **1986** (70%) **1984** (64%) **1982** (75%)

District Vote For President

	1988	1984	1980	1976
D	77,783 (48%)	76,570 (42%)	103,702 (52%)	99,925 (53%)
R	83,892 (52%)	107,199 (58%)	83,448 (42%)	87,259 (47%)
I			10,315 (5%)	

Campaign Finance

	Receipts	Receipts from PACs	Expend-itures
1990			
Lipinski (D)	$183,213	$137,317 (75%)	$171,746
Shestokas (R)	$43,950	0	$42,218
1988			
Lipinski (D)	$154,568	$96,464 (62%)	$165,144
Holowinski (R)	$55,457	$500 (1%)	$55,187

Key Votes

1991	
Authorize use of force against Iraq	N
1990	
Support constitutional amendment on flag desecration	Y
Pass family and medical leave bill over Bush veto	Y
Reduce SDI funding	N
Allow abortions in overseas military facilities	N
Approve budget summit plan for spending and taxing	N
Approve civil rights bill	N
1989	
Halt production of B-2 stealth bomber at 13 planes	N
Oppose capital gains tax cut	Y
Approve federal abortion funding in rape or incest cases	N
Approve pay raise and revision of ethics rules	Y
Pass Democratic minimum wage plan over Bush veto	Y

Voting Studies

	Presidential Support		Party Unity		Conservative Coalition	
Year	S	O	S	O	S	O
1990	41	57	76	20	56	43
1989	36	51	70	14	46	29
1988	33	56	68	20	47	42
1987	35	56	69	16	53	40
1986	42	54	74	18	52	42
1985	36	59	78	12	45	49
1984	45	46	71	14	46	41
1983	40	55	66	24	55	42

Interest Group Ratings

Year	ADA	ACU	AFL-CIO	CCUS
1990	44	54	75	54
1989	40	26	91	44
1988	55	35	100	45
1987	52	16	93	46
1986	45	45	92	27
1985	55	33	100	14
1984	60	35	92	33
1983	50	61	76	40

6 Henry J. Hyde (R)

Of Bensenville — Elected 1974

Born: April 18, 1924, Chicago, Ill.
Education: Attended Duke U., 1943-44; Georgetown U., B.S. 1947; Loyola U., J.D. 1949.
Military Service: Navy, 1942-46; Naval Reserve, 1946-68.
Occupation: Lawyer.
Family: Wife, Jeanne Simpson; four children.
Religion: Roman Catholic.
Political Career: Ill. House, 1967-75, majority leader, 1971-72; Republican nominee for U.S. House, 1962.
Capitol Office: 2262 Rayburn Bldg. 20515; 225-4561.

In Washington: It is increasingly hard to recall that Hyde once was typecast as a fringe conservative interested in one issue, abortion. He has become indispensable to Republicans as a point man on defense and foreign policy, and is widely considered a viable candidate for House GOP leader, whenever fellow Illinoisan Robert Michel retires.

Hyde would be a prominent presence even if he were not a hulk of a man with a luminous white mane. No matter who is the nominal sponsor of a conservative initiative, Hyde is likely to be its most impressive spokesman, waiting for flawed liberal arguments and then pouncing with all the wit and sarcasm he once used as a Chicago trial lawyer.

Though Hyde is criticized for having more zest for argument than for the less glamorous task of legislating, he says he is simply playing the proper role of a minority party member: "If you come to understand your role is to be a gadfly, a conscience factor, and try to work some influence in committee ... if that's enough and you don't need to be chairman of a subcommittee or see your name on a bill, this can be very rewarding."

Hyde is savvy about polishing his image in the media, and he takes care not to overexpose himself. "You have to husband your pearls before you cast them profligately about the chamber," he says. At the same time, Hyde takes pleasure in argument for its own sake: "Conflict and disputation are the heart and soul of drama, the heart and soul of literature and the heart and soul of the legislative process — if we're not all to die of boredom."

That spirit may allow Hyde to emerge as House GOP leader someday. He is confrontational enough to suit the brash, younger generation of House Republicans — and certainly a kindred conservative — yet his age and background link him to the "Old Bull" Republican who typically eschews confrontation to work with Democrats on legislation.

In 1989, when Minority Whip Dick Cheney left Congress to become Defense secretary, Hyde's name was briefly floated for the job by members unhappy with both leading contenders, pragmatist Edward Madigan and ideologue Newt Gingrich. Recognizing that many potential supporters were committed, and hesitating to challenge Illinoisans Madigan and Minority Leader Robert H. Michel, a Madigan backer, Hyde quashed the idea of running for whip. A former Illinois House majority leader, he had lost his first leadership bid in 1979, when he was defeated for House GOP Conference chairman by just three votes, and he was not about to be sidetracked again. If he makes another bid, it is likely to be for the No. 1 job.

Despite his high profile on foreign policy matters in recent years, Hyde still is best known for the Hyde amendment barring federal funding of abortion, which he passed as a freshman in 1976. It was Hyde's anti-abortion crusading that brought him attention beyond the reach of most of his colleagues. Hyde's famous amendment became his by legislative fluke; he was enlisted as sponsor by Maryland Republican Robert E. Bauman, who reckoned that the unknown freshman would draw less fire than a known conservative agitator. The House passed the amendment, though the Senate modified it to allow payment for abortions to save a woman's life. At that time, the government was paying for up to 300,000 abortions a year, mostly for poor Medicaid recipients; within a few years, the number had declined to about 2,000 annually.

During the 1980s, Hyde emerged as the most passionate anti-abortion spokesman in Congress, and his amendment became a routine part of annual appropriations legislation. But that began to change in 1988, when the Senate overwhelmingly voted to allow abortion funding for rape and incest victims. The House objected, and with backing from the White House, the Senate language was turned back. But the

Illinois 6

Far West Chicago Suburbs — Wheaton

The 6th is a white-collar suburban district in which any Republican could feel at home. Taking in parts of Cook and Du Page counties, it follows the route of two commuter rail lines that drew Chicagoans westward as early as the 1930s.

The southern part of the district is made up of such established suburbs as Elmhurst, Villa Park, Lombard, Glen Ellyn and Wheaton. It is the northern part, straddling the Du Page and Cook lines, that has enjoyed a big burst of suburban growth. Schaumburg, still rural in 1960, has seen its population soar to over 68,500, as condominiums and apartment complexes filled in around the enormous Woodfield shopping center. Roselle (population 21,000) has more than doubled in size since 1970. Itasca still has a modest population, but has seen a boom in commercial development because of its location near Interstate 290 in the O'Hare Airport corridor.

In between the boom towns in the north and the affluent older cities in the south are some more modest suburban areas, where most of whatever Democratic vote the district has can be found. Glendale Heights and Addison have some light industry and a blue-collar population. An industrial park is located near Elk Grove Village, another fast-growing suburb to the north. Bensenville, which years ago attracted migrant workers drawn by the farms of the area, still has a small Hispanic community.

On its northeastern border, the 6th hooks over to take in the older, prosperous suburbs of Des Plaines and Park Ridge. Des Plaines adjoins O'Hare, which is still the world's busiest airport, and is home to many airline employees.

Population: 519,015. White 494,144 (95%), Black 4,321 (1%), Other 14,812 (3%). Spanish origin 15,155 (3%). 18 and over 367,916 (71%), 65 and over 38,548 (7%). Median age: 30.

episode foreshadowed congressional setbacks for Hyde's cause in the 101st Congress.

Abortion foes found themselves on the defensive after the Supreme Court's 1989 *Webster* decision upheld state restrictions on access to the procedure. The first post-*Webster* House vote on abortion came in mid-1989 on the District of Columbia funding bill. For the first time in nine years, the House approved language to permit abortion funding in cases of rape and incest. The vote came as a surprise to all sides, and abortion foes attributed their defeat in part to the absence of Hyde, who was recuperating from prostate surgery.

When the issue came up weeks later during consideration of the Labor, Health and Human Services funding bill, Hyde was back, but there was little he could do to turn the tide. Congress approved the funding; only a presidential veto kept it from becoming law. "This debate is not about forcing people to have children, " he thundered before the House sustained the veto. "It is [about] forcing taxpayers to pay for the extermination of unborn children."

Comments such as that reflect the biting edge Hyde can put on his rhetoric. Though he is most often recognized for his erudite conservatism, his words occasionally foster the fringe image he has worked to shed. In 1990, when the Judiciary Committee was debating whether to cap damages awarded to victims of on-the-job harassment at $30,000, opponents of the limit cited the case of a Texas woman whose co-workers had repeatedly flashed their bare behinds at her. Hyde called the amendment to the civil rights bill fair, and angered many observers with his retort, "Someone can show me their buttocks all day long if I can get $30,000 per view."

Another quip nearly resulted in fisticuffs at the end of the 101st Congress, when nerves were frayed by endless budget negotiations. Angry over a sarcastic floor statement by liberal Barney Frank, Hyde suggested that the Massachusetts Democrat didn't know what he was talking about because he had been in the "gymnasium doing whatever he does in the gymnasium." The comment referred to an unsubstantiated charge by a male prostitute that he had had sex with Frank in the gym. After Hyde and Democrat Craig Washington of Texas came near to a scrap over the comment, Hyde publicly apologized to Frank and asked that his remark be stricken from the record.

For all the intensity of his conservatism, Hyde is not always ideologically predictable. He often forms odd-couple alliances with liberal House Democrats; for example, Hyde has cosponsored several measures with Henry A. Waxman to expand Medicaid coverage to more poor women and children. And in the 101st Congress he cosponsored legislation with Democrat Barbara Boxer, who authored the amendment undoing the Hyde amendment in 1990, to prohibit commercial surrogate mother contracts.

Hyde's votes can surprise his colleagues. In 1990, he voted to override Bush's veto of the Family and Medical Leave Act; earlier he had also helped lead the fight against a proposal to bar strikes by Legal Services Corporation lawyers, arguing that they had a constitutional right to strike. He also opposed a bill against child pornography, contending that it might be unconstitutional.

Although still the leader of the conservative forces on the Judiciary Committee, Hyde has devoted equal attention to the Foreign Affairs Committee, and, from 1985 through 1990, to the Intelligence panel. The ranking Republican on the latter in the 101st Congress, Hyde rotated off Intelligence after serving the maximum three terms.

During the 100th Congress, he was a member of the special Iran-contra investigating committee — where he emerged as President Reagan's leading defender. Hyde orchestrated the Republican strategy of using the hearings to promote Reagan's contra policy. He rarely questioned witnesses, instead favoring one-liners and long speeches. Hyde once asked a question, then told the witness, "I'd rather answer it myself," and did so.

Throughout the hearings Hyde derided the law against aiding the contras as "murky." And while he agreed the administration should not have lied to Congress, he implied Congress asked for it because of past leaks. He has been a zealot on the issue of secrecy since 1988, when he demanded an investigation after Speaker Jim Wright told reporters the CIA was fomenting unrest in Nicaragua. He accused Wright of leaking classified information, all the while denying such information existed. In an attempt to stop the alleged leaks, Hyde unsuccessfully promoted a bill during the 101st Congress to require members of the Intelligence panel to take an oath of secrecy.

A more successful foreign policy initiative during the 101st Congress grew out of the Iran-contra hearings: a new law to tighten controls on arms sales linked to terrorism. The author with California Democrat Howard L. Berman of a 1986 law requiring congressional notice of arms sales to terrorist nations, Hyde had criticized Reagan for not informing Congress about arms sales to Iran. In late 1989, a new Berman-Hyde measure to close the loopholes that allowed those sales was approved.

Release of Oliver North's notebooks in July 1990 caused a few uncomfortable moments for Hyde and three other House Republicans. The former National Security Council aide, who was found guilty of three felony charges in the case, had noted that the four members were briefed in 1985 about third-country efforts to aid the contras. Hyde had lamented after the reports of illegal aid to the contras that he was "in a considerable quandary, because I think saving the contras ... is a transcendent task. [But] the law is important, too."

While North wrote, "Hyde felt that we should expand private-sector and third-country assistance," Hyde said he had no recollection of the matter being discussed. "But even it if was, it wasn't illegal," he said.

Hyde is often noted for his appreciation of a worthy adversary. But at times in recent years, his intense feelings on foreign policy, especially contra aid, have made him less charitable toward those who disagree with him. He even has had harsh words for fellow Catholics who oppose U.S. policies in Central America, denouncing the "liberal clergy, the trendy vicars, the networking nuns."

In 1989, when President Bush quickly compromised with Democrats on a contra package limited to non-military aid, a disappointed Hyde said backing the plan was like chemotherapy: "It makes you sick to take it, but it just might save your life."

Hyde's quick and memorable ripostes can make for some effective sloganeering. He led the opposition in the early 1980s to a nuclear-weapons freeze, deriding it as "government by bumper sticker." The House passed a weakened freeze resolution in 1983, but Hyde was among those who turned a potent Democratic rallying point into a resolution without significance. In opposing a 1986 nuclear test-ban resolution, Hyde said, "If this is in our interest, I can't figure out why Gorbachev wants it."

Prominent in Hyde's office are both a bust and a portrait of St. Thomas More, the 16th-century English lord chancellor and Catholic martyr. By way of explaining, Hyde notes that More is the patron saint of lawyers, and a man who gave his life for his principles. More's career also reflected a mix of the secular and the religious that marks Hyde's own.

While Hyde believes it is appropriate to debate the morality of a public-policy decision, whether abortion or arms control, he tries to resist judging the morality of individuals.

In 1983 he opposed conservatives' motion to expel Illinois Republican Daniel B. Crane for sexual misconduct with a House page. "The Judeo-Christian tradition says, 'Hate the sin, love the sinner,' " Hyde said. "We are on record as hating the sin, some more ostentatiously than others. I think it is time to love the sinner." He also tried to help Bauman when his old ally in the abortion debate was defeated in 1980 after admitting to alcoholism and homosexuality; Hyde called numerous House Republicans, asking them to help find work for a fellow conservative who had suffered enough.

In 1990, however, he joined a majority of Republicans to reject the recommendation of the ethics committee that Frank be reprimanded for misuse of his office in connection with his involvement with the male prostitute. The GOP was unsuccessful in its effort to have Frank censured.

At Home: Hyde grew up as an Irish Catholic Democrat in Chicago, but began having doubts about the Democratic Party in the late 1940s. By 1952, he had switched parties and backed Dwight D. Eisenhower in his run for president.

After practicing law in the Chicago area for more than 10 years and serving as a Republican precinct committeeman, Hyde was chosen by the party organization in 1962 to challenge Democratic Rep. Roman Pucinski in a northwest Chicago House district. A Republican had represented the heavily ethnic district before Pucinski won it in 1958, and Hyde came within 10,000 votes of taking it back for the GOP.

Elected to the Illinois House in 1966, he was one of its most outspoken and articulate debaters. In 1971 Hyde became majority leader; he unsuccessfully ran for Speaker in 1973.

In 1974, longtime GOP Rep. Harold Collier retired from the suburban 6th District just west of Chicago. Much of the 6th was unfamiliar to Hyde, but he dominated the six-man GOP primary anyway.

The general election was tougher. Hyde's Democratic opponent was Edward V. Hanrahan, a former Cook County state's attorney. Hanrahan had been indicted for attempting to obstruct a federal investigation into a 1969 incident in which Chicago policemen, attached to his office, killed two Black Panther Party leaders. Hanrahan was acquitted but he was beaten for re-election in 1972.

Although Hanrahan's past exploits had made him a sort of folk hero among local blue-collar ethnics, he could not keep pace with Hyde in fund raising, organizing or personal campaigning. The Democrat used his record of antagonism to the Daley machine to tout his independence, but traditional sources of party funding were dry for him.

On Election Day, Hyde's superior resources won out. Using telephone banks and an army of precinct workers, his staff turned out enough voters to give him an 8,000-vote plurality over Hanrahan while GOP districts nationwide were falling to Democrats.

Hyde has since been invincible. The 1981 redistricting gave him an almost all-new constituency; an aggressive primary rival from the new area might have made Hyde work to hold the redrawn district. But no Republican bothered to challenge Hyde in 1982; by 1984 no one dared. He has swamped his Democratic opposition: The 67 percent of the vote Hyde received in 1990 was his lowest tally since 1980.

Committees

Foreign Affairs (8th of 18 Republicans)
Arms Control, International Security & Science; Human Rights & International Organizations

Judiciary (3rd of 13 Republicans)
Civil & Constitutional Rights (ranking)

Elections

1990 General

Henry J. Hyde (R)	96,410	(67%)
Robert J. Cassidy (D)	48,155	(33%)

1988 General

Henry J. Hyde (R)	153,425	(74%)
William J. Andrle (D)	54,804	(26%)

Previous Winning Percentages: **1986** (75%) **1984** (75%) **1982** (68%) **1980** (67%) **1978** (66%) **1976** (61%) **1974** (53%)

District Vote For President

	1988		1984		1980		1976	
D	67,356	(31%)	52,170	(24%)	51,049	(25%)	72,192	(33%)
R	147,387	(69%)	166,170	(76%)	126,318	(63%)	142,229	(65%)
I					21,069	(11%)		

Campaign Finance

	Receipts	Receipts from PACs		Expend-itures
1990				
Hyde (R)	$302,541	$130,648	(43%)	$270,435
Cassidy (D)	$1,520	0		$1,055
1988				
Hyde (R)	$303,395	$121,453	(40%)	$281,229
Andrle (D)	$27,274	$10,600	(39%)	$26,555

Key Votes

1991

Authorize use of force against Iraq	Y

1990

Support constitutional amendment on flag desecration	Y
Pass family and medical leave bill over Bush veto	Y
Reduce SDI funding	N
Allow abortions in overseas military facilities	N
Approve budget summit plan for spending and taxing	N
Approve civil rights bill	N

1989

Halt production of B-2 stealth bomber at 13 planes	?
Oppose capital gains tax cut	N
Approve federal abortion funding in rape or incest cases	N
Approve pay raise and revision of ethics rules	N
Pass Democratic minimum wage plan over Bush veto	N

Voting Studies

	Presidential Support		Party Unity		Conservative Coalition	
Year	**S**	**O**	**S**	**O**	**S**	**O**
1990	68	31	78	18	81	15
1989	66	16	58	12	61	10
1988	70	28	84	10	92	8
1987	65	32	76	18	86	9
1986	76	21	75	18	80	20
1985	71	19	75	17	85	9
1984	71	25	79	15	88	7
1983	89	10	83	15	88	12
1982	75	17	79 †	19 †	86	8
1981	79	20	77	19	81	16

† Not eligible for all recorded votes.

Interest Group Ratings

Year	ADA	ACU	AFL-CIO	CCUS
1990	11	88	17	64
1989	5	95	10	89
1988	15	92	14	100
1987	12	96	6	100
1986	5	90	7	75
1985	15	81	21	74
1984	10	88	8	87
1983	5	86	0	95
1982	15	85	11	81
1981	10	93	7	94

7 Cardiss Collins (D)

Of Chicago — Elected 1973

Born: Sept. 24, 1931, St. Louis, Mo.
Education: Attended Northwestern U., 1949-50.
Occupation: Auditor.
Family: Widow of Rep. George W. Collins; one child.
Religion: National Baptist.
Political Career: No previous office.
Capitol Office: 2264 Rayburn Bldg. 20515; 225-5006.

In Washington: When they were in the House, Shirley Chisholm of New York and Barbara C. Jordan of Texas earned considerable attention as black women influential in national policy debates. Collins, now in her ninth full term, has more House seniority than either Chisholm or Jordan accumulated, but unlike them, she has never drawn the spotlight for her quiet work on a handful of issues.

Collins gets a chance to raise her profile in the 102nd Congress, after recuperating from a series of illnesses that sidelined her during much of the 101st. In 1991, Collins became the new chairman of the Energy and Commerce Subcommittee on Commerce, Consumer Protection and Competitiveness. The subcommittee provides a platform for Collins to pursue some issues on which she already has worked, such as expanding business opportunities for minorities, and some issues mostly new to her, such as trade and the solvency of the insurance industry.

On the powerful Energy and Commerce Committee, the low-profile Collins is generally, though not automatically, a liberal vote. Her leanings in that direction are tempered by her desire to protect heavy industries in her district and to respond to the needs of the Chicago futures markets.

On the Clean Air bill, she focused on urban concerns, playing a role in ensuring that metropolitican areas, not just cities, would be penalized for failure to meet clean air standards.

On the Health Subcommittee in the 101st Congress, Collins was among those who argued successfully for Medicare coverage for two cancer-screening tests for women — Pap smears and mammograms.

From her post on the Telecommunications Subcommittee, Collins has criticized the Federal Communications Commission for not working to encourage minorities and women to enter the broadcasting industry. For the past several Congresses, she has introduced legislation to preserve preferences for minority and female applicants seeking broadcasting licenses from the FCC.

Collins has been somewhat more conspicuous on Government Operations, where she has risen to the position of No. 2 Democrat, just behind committee Chairman John Conyers Jr. of Michigan. From 1983 through 1991, Collins chaired the Subcommittee on Government Activities and Transportation. While that panel's legislative mandate is fairly limited, she has a strong personal commitment to air safety, having lost her husband in a 1973 airplane crash.

In early 1989, shortly after the bombing of Pan Am Flight 103 over Lockerbie, Scotland, it was Collins who made public the FAA security bulletins that had warned U.S. embassy personnel of a potential terrorist threat — a move that drew a rebuke from Transportation Secretary Samuel K. Skinner. While Collins offered to fashion a new process for sharing sensitive security information, she publicly criticized the bulletins as being ineffective and "dangerously inaccurate."

During the 100th Congress, Collins held oversight hearings on the Federal Aviation Administration's performance and criticized the FAA for failing "to rebuild the air-traffic controller work force, particularly at Chicago's O'Hare Airport," and for not doing enough to recruit minority and female controllers.

In her first years chairing the Government Activities Subcommittee, Collins used it as a platform to criticize the Reagan administration for its civil rights policies. She was particularly peeved by the refusal of three federal agencies, including the Justice Department, to comply with a directive of the Equal Employment Opportunity Commission that agencies set goals for hiring women and minorities. Administration officials said the EEOC had exceeded its authority; Collins said executive branch inaction was "a disgrace."

Collins was a novice at politics in 1973, when the Chicago organization placed her in the House as successor to her husband, George W. Collins, who was killed shortly after being elected to a second term. She soon became an active participant in the Congressional Black

Illinois 7

Chicago — Downtown; West Side

Only a few blocks west of Chicago's lakefront, with its elegant high-rises and nearby shops, the rank poverty of the West Side begins, with burned-out buildings and abandoned factories that stretch for miles. The West Side has traditionally been a port of entry for migrants to the city, Jews and Italians early in this century and blacks in the past generation. Roosevelt Road, the district's main artery running west from downtown out to the city limits, was the urban riot corridor in the 1960s. The 7th as a whole is nearly 70 percent black.

Once contained almost entirely within Chicago, the 7th now stretches from Lake Michigan more than a dozen miles west to suburban Bellwood. It mixes residential areas with industrial zones. The University of Illinois at Chicago is in the district, as is the West Side medical center complex.

But the heart of the 7th lies in the miles of low-income housing on the West Side. The picture is not one of unmitigated gloom; there are carefully tended houses sitting cheek-by-jowl with dusty lots and boarded-up buildings. But the West Side's poverty made it a target for the national civil rights movement as far back as the mid-1960s.

In national politics, the Chicago portion of the district is uniformly Democratic and liberal. On questions of Chicago politics, however, it is more complicated. The Daley machine held sway on the West Side longer than it did on the South Side, chiefly because the transient character of the West Side neighborhoods made organizing against the machine difficult. But the independent movement has made inroads over the last decade; Collins' roots in the traditional Democratic organization have caused her occasional problems with the independents.

Toward the western edge of the city, the 7th includes Austin, traditionally Eastern European in ethnic makeup but increasingly black. Farther west, it takes in some white-collar suburban territory, including generally liberal Oak Park, one of the city's oldest suburbs, and Republican River Forest. The suburbs of Maywood and Bellwood (one of the few district areas to see growth in the early 1980s, with the population up by nearly 10 percent) are predominantly black and vote Democratic.

Population: 519,034. White 150,445 (29%), Black 347,007 (67%), Other 7,409 (1%). Spanish origin 24,273 (5%). 18 and over 343,964 (66%), 65 and over 44,535 (9%). Median age: 26.

Caucus, and by 1979 was in line for the chairmanship. She took the post at a time of increasing black disillusionment with Jimmy Carter's administration, and she became a widely quoted voice of that discontent.

At Home: The movement that elected Harold Washington as the first black mayor of Chicago in 1983 put Collins in a difficult position. Caught in the cross-fire between Washington's allies and remnants of the Daley political machine that had promoted her, Collins faced serious primary challenges in 1984 and 1986.

Collins' husband, George, was a loyal lieutenant of longtime Mayor Richard J. Daley, for which he was awarded a city council seat and then a seat in Congress in 1970. A month after his 1972 re-election, however, he was killed in a plane crash near Chicago's Midway Airport. The organization that had sponsored him picked his widow as his successor. She won 93 percent in the special election.

Through the ensuing years, Collins kept her distance from the city's black independent movement. For a time, that created no problems for her. But after Daley's death in 1976, machine loyalties began unraveling in the black community; the independent movement, which had scored scattered successes earlier, began to pick up steam.

When Jane M. Byrne became mayor in 1979 and showed little apparent concern for black interests, a wave of independent activism began gathering force on the West Side, much of which Collins represents. Collins not only avoided the activists, she supported Byrne for renomination against Washington in 1983.

That gave the independents the basis for a challenge a year later. Alderman Danny K. Davis, a strong Washington supporter, launched a primary bid against Collins. By withholding her support from Washington, he said, she "ignored the hue and cry of the people and turned her back on those who were looking to her and to her office for leadership."

Davis tapped into the network of West Side ministers and grass-roots organizers who had supported Washington for mayor. Taking his campaign into storefront churches and community meetings, Davis tried to tie himself to the flood of "self-empowerment" sentiment that had fueled Washington's campaign.

But the fervor that had built up with the mayoral election had died down, and Davis' cash-strapped campaign had trouble stoking it up. While several members of Washington's staff took prominent roles in Davis' effort, the mayor himself did not endorse Davis until shortly before the election.

Collins, meanwhile, had help not only from old-line black machine Democrats, but also from labor unions and white liberals in Oak Park and lakefront Chicago who liked her environmentalist and feminist credentials. Collins took 49 percent to Davis' 38 percent.

Davis tried again in 1986, but the disgruntlement with Collins had peaked. Although Davis was somewhat better organized than in his first try, the non-presidential year ballot offered no other primaries to spark minority-group voters' interest. Black turnout was low, and Collins ended up with 60 percent.

Though Collins endorsed Washington in his 1987 re-election campaign against the comeback-minded Byrne, Davis again hinted at a challenge in the 1988 House primary.

However, he instead turned his attentions to the political turmoil that ensued in late 1987 after Washington's death and the controversial City Council choice of black Alderman Eugene Sawyer as his interim replacement. He announced plans to run in the 1989 special mayoral election before throwing his support to the unsuccessful independent bid of Washington ally Timothy Evans against Democrat Richard M. Daley. (Davis did go on to challenge Daley in 1991, but lost.)

Davis' preoccupation freed Collins for an easy 1988 re-election campaign. She coasted again in 1990.

Collins had numerous political contacts through her husband but had never been involved directly in politics before 1973. She worked as an auditor in the Illinois Revenue Department before her election to Congress.

Committees

Energy & Commerce (7th of 27 Democrats)
Commerce, Consumer Protection & Competitiveness (chairman); Transportation & Hazardous Materials

Government Operations (2nd of 25 Democrats)
Commerce, Consumer & Monetary Affairs; Legislation & National Security

Select Narcotics Abuse & Control (5th of 21 Democrats)

Elections

1990 General		
Cardiss Collins (D)	80,021	(80%)
Michael Dooley (R)	20,099	(20%)
1990 Primary		
Cardiss Collins (D)	52,763	(82%)
Sharon E. Butler (D)	7,005	(11%)
James Hammonds (D)	2,084	(3%)
Rosalind Collins (D)	1,529	(2%)
Earnest L. Thomas (D)	1,273	(2%)
1988 General		
Cardiss Collins (D)	135,331	(100%)

Previous Winning Percentages: **1986** (80%) **1984** (78%) **1982** (86%) **1980** (85%) **1978** (86%) **1976** (85%) **1974** (88%) **1973 *** (93%)

* *Special election.*

District Vote For President

	1988	1984	1980	1976
D	132,656 (77%)	141,185 (74%)	124,826 (70%)	117,450 (68%)
R	38,432 (22%)	47,301 (25%)	40,421 (23%)	53,344 (31%)
I			9,431 (5%)	

Campaign Finance

	Receipts	Receipts from PACs		Expend-itures
1990				
Collins (D)	$278,392	$229,648	(82%)	$399,748
1988				
Collins (D)	$235,058	$199,043	(85%)	$127,487

Key Votes

1991	
Authorize use of force against Iraq	N
1990	
Support constitutional amendment on flag desecration	N
Pass family and medical leave bill over Bush veto	Y
Reduce SDI funding	Y
Allow abortions in overseas military facilities	Y
Approve budget summit plan for spending and taxing	N
Approve civil rights bill	Y
1989	
Halt production of B-2 stealth bomber at 13 planes	?
Oppose capital gains tax cut	Y
Approve federal abortion funding in rape or incest cases	?
Approve pay raise and revision of ethics rules	Y
Pass Democratic minimum wage plan over Bush veto	?

Voting Studies

	Presidential Support		Party Unity		Conservative Coalition	
Year	**S**	**O**	**S**	**O**	**S**	**O**
1990	10	82	87	3	9	81
1989	14	38	51	0	2	51
1988	16	70	87	2	3	84
1987	8	85	85	2	0	86
1986	12	71	78	3	6	84
1985	16	76	87	1	2	89
1984	21	65	82	5	5	83
1983	5	80	85	3	7	88
1982	25	65	86	6	7	85
1981	28	70	83	7	4	85

Interest Group Ratings

Year	ADA	ACU	AFL-CIO	CCUS
1990	94	5	100	31
1989	40	0	100	57
1988	90	0	100	21
1987	92	0	100	0
1986	95	0	100	13
1985	95	5	100	10
1984	95	4	92	36
1983	90	0	100	15
1982	90	0	100	33
1981	85	0	87	6

8 Dan Rostenkowski (D)

Of Chicago — Elected 1958

Born: Jan. 2, 1928, Chicago, Ill.
Education: Attended Loyola U., 1948-51.
Military Service: Army, 1946-48.
Occupation: Insurance executive.
Family: Wife, LaVerne Pirkins; four children.
Religion: Roman Catholic.
Political Career: Ill. House, 1953-55; Ill. Senate, 1955-59.
Capitol Office: 2111 Rayburn Bldg. 20515; 225-4061.

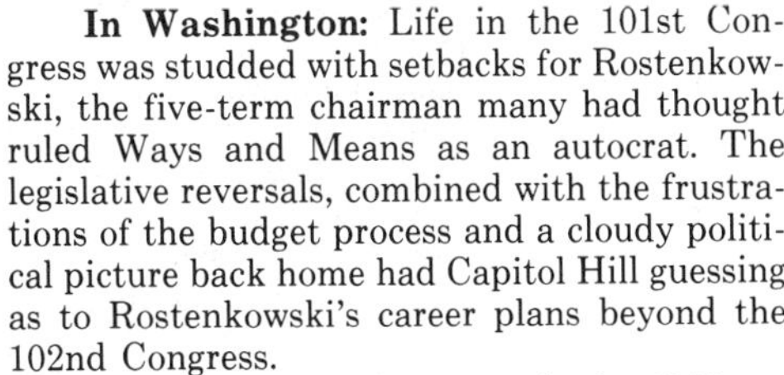

In Washington: Life in the 101st Congress was studded with setbacks for Rostenkowski, the five-term chairman many had thought ruled Ways and Means as an autocrat. The legislative reversals, combined with the frustrations of the budget process and a cloudy political picture back home had Capitol Hill guessing as to Rostenkowski's career plans beyond the 102nd Congress.

Retirement talk began early in 1989, as Rostenkowski privately complained of the deterioration he saw in the quality of congressional life. Then, in rapid succession, he was slapped with defeats in committee on the capital gains tax, the extension of Medicare to catastrophic illness and the requirement that businesses distribute pension benefits equally among their employees. He could not keep a limit on textile imports, which he opposed, from reaching the floor. In each case, Rostenkowski saw his coalition on the panel pulled apart by pressures greater than any he himself could bring to bear.

A close Rostenkowski associate, Ed Jenkins of Georgia, led five other Democrats and all 13 Ways and Means Republicans in backing a cut in the capital gains tax. At first, it was not clear whether or not Rostenkowski himself wanted to use such a cut as a bargaining chip with his old friend and former committee colleague, President Bush. By the time the chairman had committed himself to fighting it, the die was cast. Jenkins prevailed in committee and again on the floor, even after the Democratic leadership had thrown in behind Rostenkowski.

The battle over catastrophic coverage, and the surtax passed in 1988 to pay for it, was even more disheartening. Rostenkowski was stunned by the vehemence of seniors' objection to the surtax, especially when he found his car pursued down a Chicago thoroughfare by elderly constituents shouting "Impeach Rottenkowski!"

Small wonder, then, that Rostenkowski led the list of senior members considered potential retirees in 1993. Under the "grandfather clause" of current campaign finance law, members elected before 1980 may convert campaign funds to personal use if they retire no later than the end of the 102nd Congress. That would mean about $1 million to Rostenkowski, a man who has repeatedly complained about the House's unwillingness to pay members a salary commensurate with their managerial responsibilities.

But the betting odds shifted as the 102nd got under way and Rostenkowski seemed as firmly ensconced in the chair as ever. Although the ever-tightening constraints of the budget deficit seemed to corset Ways and Means to an unprecedented degree, Rostenkowski seemed unwilling to hang up his spikes just yet. One reason might be that the chairman still hopes to revive the satisfaction he found in his job during the momentous tax overhaul of the 99th Congress.

It was then that Rostenkowski seemed to discover that government can be just as much fun as politics. After nearly three decades in the House accumulating political power as if it were an end in itself, he began applying himself to larger legislative purposes, such as overhauling U.S. trade law and the welfare system.

He has a reputation both in Chicago and Washington as a rather unsubtle ward politician. But it has become increasingly clear that Rostenkowski wants to be known by the end of his career for something beyond the hoarding of influence.

Such resolve to enlarge his legacy seemed evident in Rostenkowski's comprehensive March 1990 proposal for attacking the budget deficit. Few believed meaningful budget moves could be made in an election year, yet Rostenkowski proposed a deal of heroic proportions. It raised taxes on gasoline and alcohol as well as on income. It carved deep into defense spending and froze domestic spending (including Social Security benefits) for a year to slow long-range spending growth. Widely praised by editorialists, Rostenkowski's plan received a surprisingly cordial nod from the White House, a precursor of later flexibility on taxes. The Ros-

Illinois 8

Chicago — North and Northwest Sides

The 8th District is exactly the right kind of constituency for Rostenkowski. It stretches out along Milwaukee Avenue, Chicago's traditional "Polish corridor," taking in such symbolic places as St. Hyacinth Parish, still a first stop for Polish immigrants and a spot where a question asked in Polish may draw a ready response. The lines of the 8th essentially chart the movement of Rostenkowski's lifelong political allies as they have made their way northwest from the inner city, out Milwaukee Avenue. Even Rostenkowski's suburban constituents, in communities such as River Grove and Elmwood Park, are largely ethnic and transplanted from the city.

Nearly any statewide Democratic candidate can still carry the 8th comfortably. However, there have been changes wrought by the political tensions between white ethnics and blacks, stemming from the 1983 election of black Mayor Harold Washington. Ronald Reagan also provided an unusual appeal to 8th District ethnics; he narrowly won there in 1984, after getting just 34 percent four years earlier. But in 1988, Rostenkowski helped bring the district back to the Democratic fold; Michael S. Dukakis took the 8th with 59 percent of the vote.

The strength of Democratic loyalty appears inversely proportional to distance from the heart of the city. The three wards farthest from downtown voted for Reagan in 1984, with the heaviest GOP vote in the Italian 36th Ward at the western edge. Closer to downtown, political loyalties are still decidedly Democratic. Rostenkowski's own ward, the 32nd, gave just 34 percent of its vote to Reagan in 1984.

The 8th's Hispanic population, somewhat more than 30 percent of the total, lives mainly along lower Milwaukee Avenue, and generally provides a Democratic cushion. The 31st and 26th wards in particular have strong Hispanic political organizations.

Population: 519,034. White 392,337 (76%), Black 22,464 (4%), Other 13,318 (3%). Spanish origin 164,164 (32%). 18 and over 375,186 (72%), 65 and over 64,532 (12%). Median age: 30.

tenkowski plan did not become anyone's blueprint, but the chairman took satisfaction in the belief that he had raised everyone's sights.

Whatever the future holds, it seems likely that Rostenkowski's chief legacy will be his remarkable achievement of the 99th Congress, when he maneuvered a new federal tax code through a reluctant House and on into law. Many others played key roles in that drama, but none did quite what he did.

"I've had a reputation as a gut politician, a total political animal from the city of Chicago," he said early in 1985. "But I'm also trying . . . to do the responsible thing."

Still, Rostenkowski has a pride in his raw political skills that is rare in an institution coming to be dominated by new-breed Democrats who are more inclined to distance themselves from their party and the institution. Both his pride and his irritation were on display in early 1989, when he chastised the House for lacking the self-respect to accept a pay raise.

"In my hometown of Chicago they call politics a blood sport," he said. "I have been pretty successful at it. I don't apologize for getting in the arena and I'll be damned if I'll apologize for winning."

The key to Rostenkowski's legislative success has been the horse-trading skills he learned under Chicago Mayor Richard J. Daley. Indeed, Rostenkowski has managed to turn the Ways and Means Committee into a well-oiled political machine of its own. He has treated his committee like a big-city ward, where personal loyalty counts far more than ideology. He has built members' allegiance the old-fashioned way, by doing favors, keeping his word, and taking down the names of those who do not go along.

Despite his background in Democratic machine politics, Rostenkowski's preferred mode of legislating is bipartisan. He is willing to deal with Republicans as well as Democrats in his patented way of building coalitions within the committee: Give everyone an opportunity to participate in the decision-making process, but exact a stiff price for participation.

On any important bill, Rostenkowski's subcommittee chairmen are given a relatively free hand at preparing provisions under their jurisdiction. Rostenkowski backs them in full committee, on the floor and in conference. They are expected to pledge loyalty to the entire bill and maintain it until the legislation is signed.

His grip on the committee and its products is not always firm, as the capital gains defeat of 1989 showed. Previously, his chairmanship was tarnished in the early years of the Reagan administration when House Democrats were either ignored or ambushed on important tax matters.

In 1981, his first year as Ways and Means

chairman, Rostenkowski suffered an acutely embarrassing defeat when he laced a tax bill with special-interest provisions so he could beat President Ronald Reagan on the House floor, and ended up losing. "If we accept the president's substitute," he said on the floor, "we accept his dominance of the House in the months ahead." The House accepted the Reagan substitute by a vote of 238-195.

In his second year as chairman, Rostenkowski had to stand by helplessly as his committee's Democrats refused even to write a tax bill, thus giving up Ways and Means' traditional leverage in negotiating with the Senate in revenue matters.

In the Congress after that, Rostenkowski won some notable legislative victories — his committee moved through a bill keeping the Social Security system solvent for the foreseeable future — but he seemed most concerned with achieving control over his committee. He gradually restored the power of the Ways and Means chair, which had ebbed under the tenure of his predecessor, the well-informed but ineffectual Al Ullman of Oregon.

Rostenkowski's power-building efforts paid off handsomely when Reagan made overhauling the tax code the top domestic priority of his second term.

At first, Rostenkowski saw political danger for Democrats if they stood in the way of a popular president who wanted to see the tax code rewritten. But most of the pressures turned out to be in the opposite direction. There never was much grass-roots support for tax revision; what there was in great quantities was resistance from economic interests that stood to lose through its enactment. And throughout the process, liberal House Democrats continued to insist that some of the revenues generated by eliminating tax subsidies be used to reduce the federal deficit — a sure-fire way to lose Reagan's crucial support.

In drafting the tax-overhaul bill, Rostenkowski asked members of both parties what it would take to win their support for the massive project. He agreed to consider meeting those demands only if the member, in return, would give an ironclad commitment to support the final product. If not, he saw no reason to deal. "You might as well kick a guy's brains out if he's not for you," he said at one point.

Before going to conference with the Senate on the tax-overhaul bill, Rostenkowski did a thorough loyalty check of his troops. Only tested and reliable allies were named to the conference committee. The basic role of House conferees was to keep quiet and support the chairman. Indeed, Rostenkowski negotiated many of the most difficult provisions of the final bill himself, head-to-head with Senate Finance Committee Chairman Bob Packwood of Oregon.

The new federal revenue code that became law on Jan. 1, 1987, reduced the top individual tax rate to 28 percent — far below the 38 percent recommended in the House bill. But in many ways, it represented a triumph for Rostenkowski and the House position. The bill written by Rostenkowski's committee recouped an estimated $140 billion over five years through the cancellation of business-tax subsidies enacted over a long period of time. The final bill incorporated the vast majority of those changes.

Ironically, Rostenkowski's very success in overhauling the tax code made his job tougher in subsequent years. The growing deficit and the new presumption against adding new tax breaks left Rostenkowski with less of the currency of influence he had used to round up votes in the past: special tax breaks.

By the 101st Congress, Rostenkowski was explicitly hostile to virtually any change in the tax code unless it could be accomplished with a minimum of disruption and no cost in revenue.

Whether he retires in the short run or not, the odds are now overwhelming that Rostenkowski will close his House career in the job he now holds. There is some irony in that. Rostenkowski never planned to be a tax specialist. For more than 20 years he played pure House politics, trading votes and committee assignments and angling for a top leadership position.

The success of Rostenkowski's tax-revision crusade in 1986 rekindled speculation that he might mount a campaign for Speaker in 1987. His opponent then would have been Jim Wright of Texas, whom he had helped make majority leader in 1976, but with whom he had since been at odds.

Rostenkowski never made the move. Wright had actively courted the junior members who cast most of the votes in leadership contests. Rostenkowski, on the other hand, lacked close ties to many of the younger members not on Ways and Means. Moreover, the ethnic machine Democrats, his natural constituency, were dwindling.

When Wright resigned under fire over ethics in 1989, Rostenkowski was not among those scrambling for a new job. He stood by while the uppermost echelon of leadership was occupied by a new generation, including a man with whom his relations have been ambiguous, Rep. Richard A. Gephardt of Missouri. Rostenkowski had backed Gephardt's bid for president in 1988, but wags had said he did so to get Gephardt off of Ways and Means. When the Missourian ran for majority leader in 1989, Rostenkowski backed the long-shot candidacy of Jenkins, his nemesis on capital gains. Gephardt won as expected; but when his acceptance speech dragged on, Rostenkowski made a show of walking out — complaining as he left about the "filibuster."

By then it seemed hard to believe that when Rostenkowski took the Ways and Means chair in 1981 he still entertained thoughts of being Speaker. At that juncture he had also been in line to be whip, the third-ranking position in the leadership and steppingstone for the last two Speakers. Rostenkowski agonized and consulted friends for weeks before taking the committee chair.

Becoming Ways and Means chairman meant a major change in the tempo of Rostenkowski's life. Until then, he had shown little interest in haggling over the details of the revenue code. And for most of the late 1970s, he was not one of the hardest workers in the House. He had joined Ways and Means in 1965 mainly because it then made the committee assignments for all House Democrats and offered endless opportunities for politicking. When Ways and Means lost that function in 1975, Rostenkowski's interest largely lapsed.

Rostenkowski had once hoped the 1970s would see his career flower. But he was haunted by an event in 1968 that blocked what had seemed to be a steady rise in the party leadership. Rostenkowski stepped in at the command of President Lyndon B. Johnson to restore order at the tumultuous 1968 Democratic National Convention in Chicago. He physically took the gavel from House Majority Leader Carl Albert of Oklahoma, who had lost control of the situation. Later Rostenkowski talked openly about having done it, and Albert was insulted. In 1971 Albert moved up from majority leader to Speaker of the House. Rostenkowski threw his influence behind Hale Boggs of Louisiana for majority leader, in exchange for a Boggs promise to appoint Rostenkowski as Democratic whip. Boggs was elected leader.

But Albert was still angry over the convention squabble, and his attitude did not improve when Rostenkowski took his time endorsing him for Speaker. That lapse was costly: Albert vetoed Rostenkowski as whip. The man chosen instead was Thomas P. O'Neill Jr. of Massachusetts.

In all the maneuvering that year, Rostenkowski failed to protect the position he already held as Democratic Caucus chairman. Texans quietly rounded up the votes to elect their candidate, Olin E. "Tiger" Teague. Some Northern liberals cooperated with them, feeling Rostenkowski had banged his gavel a little too quickly on anti-war speakers while presiding over the House. It took six years for Rostenkowski to make it back into the leadership. By that time, O'Neill was the newly elected Speaker. Rostenkowski had endorsed dark horse Wright for majority leader, and Wright and O'Neill agreed that a place should be found for him. They made him chief deputy whip.

At Home: Before deciding his future, Rostenkowski may well wait to see the shape of the district designed for him by Democrats in the Illinois Legislature and GOP Gov. Jim Edgar. One Chicago area seat is going to be lost to reapportionment, and a second is likely to go to a Hispanic candidate.

In 1990, deterred by Rostenkowski's sturdy dominance of his district, Republicans hung their hopes for local inroads on rumors that he might retire in 1992; Rostenkowski had no Republican opponent in 1990.

The steadfast core of anti-Rosty voters in the district sent him a message anyway, giving 21 percent of the vote to Libertarian candidate Robert Marshall. But Rostenkowski's 79 percent matched his tally in the 1986 midterm election.

Rostenkowski's early role as "Mayor Daley's man in Congress" helped make him a force in House politics. It also stamped him as a leader among Chicago Democrats at an unusually early age. He was barely 30 when the city's politicians began talking about him as a successor to Richard J. Daley in City Hall — someday. That day never came. By the time the office opened up in 1977, Rostenkowski was a comfortable and influential 18-year House veteran.

Still, Rostenkowski's political life was focused to an extraordinary degree on Chicago. Until he became Ways and Means chairman in 1981, he spent much of his time in the city, working on strategy with the regular Democratic faction that opposed Mayor Jane Byrne.

Rostenkowski worked hard to defeat Byrne in 1983 and replace her with Richard M. Daley, son of the late mayor. He got half his wish: Byrne was beaten, but by Harold Washington, a black House member to whom neither Rostenkowski nor anyone else in the Daley machine had ever been close.

After more than a decade in eclipse, Rostenkowski's longtime allies from the Daley days surged back in the 1989 special mayoral election that came as a result of Washington's death. In the Democratic primary, the younger Daley defeated controversial interim Chicago Mayor Eugene Sawyer, then swept to an easy general election victory. But Rostenkowski's responsibilities in Washington kept him from playing as strong a role in that mayoral race as he would have in the past.

It must have been difficult for Rostenkowski to keep from being distracted by the turmoil back home. He has spent his entire adult life in the thick of Chicago politics. At 24, he became the youngest member of the Illinois House. At 26, he was the youngest in the Illinois Senate. And at 30, he was a member of Congress. When Rostenkowski went to the Legislature, the elder Daley was Cook County clerk, and they developed the relationship that proved fruitful for both for a quarter-century.

It was not just youth and talent that brought Rostenkowski so far so fast; it was family. The Rostenkowskis were a sort of political elite on the city's Polish Northwest Side. The congressman's father, Joseph, was a Chicago alderman and ward committeeman for 20 years and later U.S. collector of customs.

Joe Rostenkowski was influential in launching his son's political career and dissuading him from professional baseball. At one point, the younger Rostenkowski turned down an offer from Connie Mack, owner of the Philadelphia Athletics.

In 1958, Democratic Rep. Thomas Gordon of Chicago, chairman of the House Foreign Affairs Committee, decided to retire. Daley was mayor by then and it was his task to pick a successor. He anointed Rostenkowski. At that point, the average age of the Chicago Democratic delegation in the House was 72. Daley felt some youth was needed.

Rostenkowski remained a committed loyalist, even when he was chastised, as he was by a Chicago judge in 1963, for paying constituents' traffic tickets out of Democratic Party funds.

In 1966, a year of high racial tension and strong white backlash in Chicago, Rostenkowski ran his only "scared" race. His opponent was John Leszynski, a cab driver who openly appealed to the backlash against open-housing demonstrations. Rostenkowski was re-elected, but his percentage fell below 60 percent for the only time in his career.

Since then, his position has been impregnable. Even the drift of many of his district's white ethnics away from their traditional Democratic moorings in the 1980s has done him little harm: In each of his last four elections, he has topped 70 percent of the vote.

Committees

Ways & Means (Chairman)
Trade

Joint Taxation

Elections

1990 General

Dan Rostenkowski (D)	70,151	(79%)
Robert Marshall (LIBERT)	18,529	(21%)

1988 General

Dan Rostenkowski (D)	107,728	(75%)
V. Stephen Vetter (R)	34,659	(24%)

Previous Winning Percentages: **1986** (79%) **1984** (71%) **1982** (83%) **1980** (85%) **1978** (86%) **1976** (81%) **1974** (87%) **1972** (74%) **1970** (74%) **1968** (63%) **1966** (60%) **1964** (66%) **1962** (61%) **1960** (67%) **1958** (75%)

District Vote For President

	1988	1984	1980	1976
D	92,135 (59%)	85,928 (48%)	111,965 (59%)	122,652 (60%)
R	63,885 (41%)	90,875 (51%)	65,215 (34%)	80,327 (39%)
I			10,043 (5%)	

Campaign Finance

	Receipts	Receipts from PACs	Expend-itures
1990			
Rostenkowski (D)	$378,282	$197,700 (52%)	$298,653
1988			
Rostenkowski (D)	$866,341	$444,698 (51%)	$428,607

Key Votes

1991

Authorize use of force against Iraq	Y

1990

Support constitutional amendment on flag desecration	N
Pass family and medical leave bill over Bush veto	Y
Reduce SDI funding	Y
Allow abortions in overseas military facilities	N
Approve budget summit plan for spending and taxing	Y
Approve civil rights bill	Y

1989

Halt production of B-2 stealth bomber at 13 planes	N
Oppose capital gains tax cut	Y
Approve federal abortion funding in rape or incest cases	N
Approve pay raise and revision of ethics rules	Y
Pass Democratic minimum wage plan over Bush veto	Y

Voting Studies

	Presidential Support		Party Unity		Conservative Coalition	
Year	**S**	**O**	**S**	**O**	**S**	**O**
1990	33	59	76	12	33	56
1989	36	59	85	10	39	54
1988	29	58	80	9	32	58
1987	20	66	73	5	37	47
1986	19	66	84	5	36	58
1985	28	61	82	6	18	73
1984	39	42	68	11	34	46
1983	41	52	77	12	33	64
1982	44	44	80	14	42	56
1981	50	49	77	18	44	52

Interest Group Ratings

Year	ADA	ACU	AFL-CIO	CCUS
1990	67	14	83	17
1989	70	19	100	10
1988	65	19	85	50
1987	68	18	77	22
1986	65	15	86	35
1985	75	20	81	36
1984	65	10	83	36
1983	65	9	81	39
1982	85	10	85	35
1981	55	14	73	26

9 Sidney R. Yates (D)

Of Chicago — Elected 1948

Did not serve 1963-65.

Born: Aug. 27, 1909, Chicago, Ill.
Education: U. of Chicago, Ph.B. 1931, J.D. 1933.
Military Service: Navy, 1944-46.
Occupation: Lawyer.
Family: Wife, Adeline Holleb; one child.
Religion: Jewish.
Political Career: Democratic nominee for U.S. Senate, 1962.
Capitol Office: 2109 Rayburn Bldg. 20515; 225-2111.

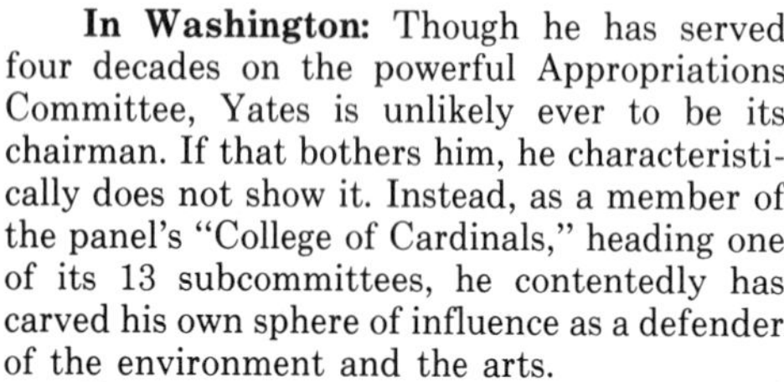

In Washington: Though he has served four decades on the powerful Appropriations Committee, Yates is unlikely ever to be its chairman. If that bothers him, he characteristically does not show it. Instead, as a member of the panel's "College of Cardinals," heading one of its 13 subcommittees, he contentedly has carved his own sphere of influence as a defender of the environment and the arts.

Yates is now the oldest member of the House. He has served under nine presidents. But he continues to fend off budget cuts with all the vigor he brought to past crusades for public housing in the 1950s and against the SST in the 1970s. Generally Yates works behind the scenes as chairman of the Interior Subcommittee, but he was often provoked into the spotlight during the Reagan years — from 1981, when he blocked a proposed 50 percent funding reduction for the National Endowment for the Arts (NEA), to 1988, when he engineered a far-reaching moratorium against administration plans to lease offshore lands for oil drilling. He found himself back in the spotlight in the first two years of the Bush administration over NEA funding, although this time, the president was not leading the assault.

Yates has a reputation as one of Appropriations' toughest subcommittee chairmen. His hearings are among the most detailed in the House; he does much of his own research on issues and always seems familiar with each budget item. He employs the probing style of a crafty lawyer to corner administration witnesses, and to nudge his own colleagues — from Chairman Jamie L. Whitten on down — toward his position. But he is also personable and witty, and respected both for the grace of his argument and the quality of his work.

Yates is fourth-ranking on Appropriations, but nowhere near so close to the chair as his proximity would suggest. He is older than all three men ahead of him, including Whitten, who in any case is expected to remain in Congress a few more years. So Yates' fiefdom probably will remain limited to his subcommittee, which itself holds broad sway over the budgets for the Interior Department, national parks, mines, Indian affairs, the national endowments for the arts and humanities and the Smithsonian Institution.

Within the House, Yates is one of the committee's most loyal advocates in protesting the limitations imposed on it by the 1985 Gramm-Rudman-Hollings law; he detests what he sees as the phoniness of the law's budget-balancing targets and the arbitrariness of its threatened cuts. He is equally outspoken within the committee, and has concurred with junior colleagues who chafe at the panel's traditional stricture against offering amendments.

He stakes out the liberal ground, at times too liberal in some fellow Democrats' view. On the floor, however, he occasionally seems to lose his taste for a good fight. In 1985, he went more than halfway to accommodate conservative Republicans who proposed a 10 percent cut in an arts budget because they said the agency supported authors of sexually explicit poems. Rather than try to defeat the amendment outright, Yates agreed to a smaller reduction.

But his 1981 skirmish over arts spending was more typical. His subcommittee simply ignored Reagan's requested cuts. The president finally signed the measure, and never again sought such major bites from arts funding.

The issue resurfaced, however, in 1989, when conservatives — upset by two photographs by NEA grant recipients deemed by many members pornographic or sacrilegious — sought to cut the art agency's budget. Texas Republican Dick Armey proposed a 10 percent cut in the agency's appropriation. But Yates outmaneuvered Armey and enlisted Texas Democrat Charles W. Stenholm, head of the Boll Weevils, to offer a substitute amendment cutting the NEA's appropriation by the amount of the two photographs. The House adopted it overwhelmingly, rejecting another attempt to cut the NEA.

Yates' next task was to hold the line in the House-Senate conference; the Senate had adop-

Illinois 9

Chicago — North Side Lakefront; Northern Suburbs

Narrow at its base along Lake Michigan, the 9th District widens and turns westward once it reaches Chicago's northern limits, ending in a hook around the suburbs of Glenview and Northbrook. The purpose of the elaborate cartography, performed in the 1981 redistricting, was to make a secure district for Yates by including liberal areas within the city and heavily Jewish communities in the suburbs.

The 9th is anchored on the North Side of Chicago, but it runs north along the lake all the way to Evanston, and its western portion takes in parts of Skokie, Wilmette, Morton Grove and Northfield township.

The city portion of the 9th includes a mixture of neighborhoods from the opulent lakefront high-rises to the two- and three-story walk-ups just a few blocks west. These apartments house many of the prosperous singles and couples who work in professional jobs in downtown Chicago. There is an urban-restoration contingent living in older homes in the area. The city portion of the 9th also contains some of Chicago's few Republican wards.

The large Jewish population in the urban lakefront part of the district is predominantly middle-aged, well-to-do and politically active. While most white voters in Chicago rejected black Democratic mayoral candidate Harold Washington, many liberal Jewish voters from this area went with him and provided him with margins crucial to his victories in 1983 and 1987.

The two wards west of the more prosperous neighborhoods are made up mostly of Hispanics, who comprise about 10 percent of the overall population of the district. The 9th is also about 10 percent black.

The parts of the 9th that lie beyond Chicago are not typically suburban in their political outlook. Evanston, once a bastion of conservative Republicanism, has a large liberal community around Northwestern University; it has also attracted young married professionals from Chicago, who tend to vote Democratic. Aiding the Democrats in Evanston is the racial makeup — the city of about 73,000 is almost a quarter black.

West of Evanston are Morton Grove and Skokie, two heavily Jewish towns that made headlines in recent years. Morton Grove was in the news for passing a stringent gun-control law. Skokie gained attention because of efforts by its Jewish population, including some survivors of World War II concentration camps, to prevent American Nazis from rallying in their town.

Population 519,120. White 407,592 (79%), Black 50,716 (10%), Asian and Pacific Islander 30,708 (6%). Spanish origin 49,558 (10%). 18 and over 422,900 (81%), 65 and over 70,023 (13%). Median age: 32.

ted language by North Carolina GOP Sen. Jesse Helms prohibiting federal funding of obscene, indecent or antireligious art. California Republican Dana Rohrabacher sought to put the House on record in support of Helms' amendment. But Yates trumped again: He had Ralph Regula, the subcommittee's ranking Republican, block Rohrabacher through a parliamentary ploy. His procedural move enabled the House to avoid having to vote on Helms' language. The conferees watered down Helms' amendment; the bill barred the NEA and National Endowment for the Humanities from funding works that the endowments might find obscene or without merit.

That did not end the NEA controversy for the 101st Congress. In 1990, the Education and Labor Committee, which authorizes NEA money, toiled toward compromise language governing grants for controversial projects. Yates agreed with Montana Democrat Pat Williams, a staunch opponent of restrictions and chairman of the Education panel with jurisdiction over the arts agency, that the issue belonged to the authorizing committee.

Chairman Whitten, however, had other ideas. He made a surprise appearance at an Interior panel closed markup and submitted a handwritten amendment to Yates, requesting a prohibition on funding "filthy pictures." Yates deferred discussion on the proposal to the full committee. But Whitten inserted arts funding restrictions in a report on a short-term emergency funding measure. Yates complained that it would be useless and disruptive to impose a standard for less than a month. His motion to delete the language was approved by voice vote.

Yates is a dedicated environmentalist, and his subcommittee is one of the few on Appropriations that regularly grapples with controversial policy issues, not just budget numbers. He played a key role in blocking some of the Reagan administration's more controversial resource-development policies, including leasing of federal lands for coal mining and offshore oil and gas drilling. Annually, over administration objections, Yates' panel would include more funding for energy conservation, park land acquisition and Indian health programs.

In recent years, his subcommittee has sired

moratoriums on oil and gas drilling in selective offshore areas from Alaska to Massachusetts. In the 100th Congress, Yates raised a procedural challenge that helped obstruct a bill to open Alaska's vast Arctic National Wildlife Refuge for oil and gas exploration. Efforts in the 101st Congress to pass an ANWR bill were suspended following the *Exxon Valdez* oil spill in early 1989, but President Bush proposed ANWR drilling as an element of his 1991 energy proposal.

Yates has been a jealous guardian of congressional spending prerogatives. In the 99th Congress, he led a drive to revoke the president's authority to defer appropriations by Congress — a power he felt Reagan had abused. Although Congress did not enact Yates' amendment, subsequent federal court rulings circumscribed the president's deferral authority.

Yates' low-key style masks a stubbornness that allows him to stick with an issue for years, if necessary, to get what he wants. That was true in the long debate over the supersonic transport plane, which was first proposed in 1963 at an estimated cost of $1.5 billion, but was sidelined until President Richard M. Nixon came into office in 1969.

Yates had opposed the idea from the beginning, complaining that it was an "incredible distortion of our national priorities" to spend that much public money for a private purpose. Throughout the 1960s, his amendments to eliminate SST funds had been defeated regularly, always on non-recorded votes. Millions of dollars already had been spent on preliminary planning when, in 1971, the House finally confronted the issue directly.

Newly adopted rules forced an on-the-record vote for the first time, and Yates was ready with stacks of facts and figures. Backing him was a well-organized environmental lobby and a carefully orchestrated publicity campaign. In the roll-call vote, he won, 217-203.

Yates was just a freshman when he won a place on Appropriations in 1949. An energetic urban liberal in the 1950s, he became a leading advocate for the government's efforts to provide aid to older cities like Chicago.

When the GOP-controlled House sought to kill the public housing program in 1953, Yates fought back. "We need a program that will satisfy the housing needs of all Americans, of every economic level," he said, "not just those who can afford to buy their own houses." In the end, a compromise authorized 20,000 new housing units (compared with the 75,000 President Harry S. Truman sought before leaving office). Yates also advocated legislation in those days to make mortgage credit money more easily available.

In his second term, he took up a different kind of campaign, to convince the Navy it should promote Hyman G. Rickover to admiral. The renowned advocate of nuclear submarines had been bypassed and was about to leave the service. Yates thought that was wrong and said so, repeatedly. The resulting congressional hearings and public attention brought the desired result. Rickover was promoted, and remained on active duty until 1982.

Yates was out of Congress for two years in the 1960s, after an unsuccessful Senate campaign. When he came back to the House in 1965, he returned to Appropriations. This time he was placed on the Transportation Subcommittee, where he was drawn into the SST fight. Later, Yates switched to the Interior Subcommittee; he became its chairman in 1975.

He also serves on Appropriations' Foreign Operations Subcommittee, where he is a strong supporter of aid to Israel. Otherwise, he does not invest much time or attention on the panel.

At Home: After 40 years in Congress, interrupted by one failed Senate bid and a two-year hiatus, Yates had good reason to believe his electoral problems were behind him. Yet he found himself in 1990 facing a primary battle with a young man in a hurry.

While other Democrats viewed as more likely successors to Yates deferred to the incumbent, Chicago Alderman Edwin Eisendrath staged a noisy challenge. A former school teacher from a wealthy family, Eisendrath spent $250,000 in his successful 1987 City Council race and said he intended to spend big in his effort to unseat Yates.

Eisendrath released a pile of position papers to establish himself as an issues-oriented candidate. He got more attention, however, for his blasts at Yates. He said Yates had focused on national issues, including his arts bailiwick, at the expense of local needs. Eisendrath also accused Yates of campaign-finance irregularities, citing a fundraising letter for Yates from an official of the American Association of Museums which the challenger described as a "shakedown."

Yates angrily rejected that charge, stating he had no prior knowledge of the letter. Yates also burst any illusions Eisendrath might have had that he would be complacent. Yates made personal campaign appearances, ran newspaper ads signed by hundreds of well-known Chicagoans and engaged the support of most district Democratic officials. When the primary vote was tallied, Yates had flattened Eisendrath, winning with 70 percent.

That November, Yates won with 71 percent over Herbert Sohn, a physician-lawyer who is a hardy perennial of Illinois politics. Sohn has now lost four straight House contests to Yates. In fact, Yates has not had a close House race since 1956, when he won with 54 percent.

Only one member of the current House — Mississippi's Whitten — entered it before Yates did in January 1949. Had Yates not ventured for the Senate in 1962, when he challenged then-Minority Leader Everett M. Dirksen, he would have the full measure of that seniority.

Yates' Senate campaign had the backing of Chicago Mayor Richard J. Daley and the Democratic organization. But some Democrats thought Yates was undercut by his party's top leadership: They contended that President John F. Kennedy secretly favored Dirksen, considering him the friendliest Republican Senate leader he was likely to get. The Cuban missile crisis took place in the final month of the campaign, and Dirksen was consulted often and openly by the White House.

But Yates, who received 47 percent of the vote, rejected rumors of a Kennedy-Dirksen compact. In 1963, Kennedy appointed him U.S. representative to the United Nations Trusteeship Council, a post he held for more than a year.

In the fall of 1964, the Chicago Democratic organization suddenly found a judgeship for Rep. Edward Finnegan, whom it had chosen to replace Yates in the House. Since Finnegan had already been renominated, the local party had the right to designate a candidate for the vacancy, and to no one's surprise, Yates was the choice. Spared the trouble of a primary, Yates easily won his way back to the House.

Yates originally won his seat as a last-minute organization choice, though under much different circumstances. In 1948, recently returned to his Chicago law practice after World War II, he had been drafted to run against Republican Rep. Robert J. Twyman, who was expected to win re-election easily. But the Democratic ticket swept Illinois that year, and Yates came in with an 18,000-vote majority. He kept his seat narrowly in 1950 and 1952 before establishing electoral security.

In 1982, Yates batted away district Republicans' only recent effort to challenge him. GOP recruiters found an articulate moderate, 32-year-old Catherine Bertini, and launched a vigorous campaign with a "time for a change" theme. But the veteran incumbent took the challenge seriously, and worked to introduce himself to the thousands of new constituents redistricting had given him that year. Yates won re-election with 67 percent.

Committee

Appropriations (4th of 37 Democrats)
Foreign Operations, Export Financing & Related Programs; Interior (chairman); Treasury, Postal Service & General Government

Elections

1990 General

Sidney R. Yates (D)	96,557	(71%)
Herbert Sohn (R)	39,031	(29%)

1990 Primary

Sidney R. Yates (D)	53,758	(70%)
Edwin W. Eisendrath (D)	20,821	(27%)
James Newport-Chiakulas (D)	2,289	(3%)

1988 General

Sidney R. Yates (D)	135,583	(66%)
Herbert Sohn (R)	67,604	(33%)

Previous Winning Percentages: **1986** (72%) **1984** (68%) **1982** (67%) **1980** (73%) **1978** (75%) **1976** (72%) **1974** (100%) **1972** (68%) **1970** (76%) **1968** (64%) **1966** (60%) **1964** (64%) **1960** (60%) **1958** (67%) **1956** (54%) **1954** (60%) **1952** (52%) **1950** (52%) **1948** (55%)

District Vote For President

	1988	1984	1980	1976
D	137,259 (61%)	129,644 (55%)	110,744 (49%)	129,098 (51%)
R	85,855 (38%)	106,151 (45%)	83,961 (37%)	121,293 (48%)
I			28,537 (13%)	

Campaign Finance

	Receipts	Receipts from PACs	Expend-itures
1990			
Yates (D)	$779,125	$267,746 (34%)	$839,106
Sohn (R)	$11,545	$2,000 (17%)	$15,164
1988			
Yates (D)	$126,705	$25,250 (20%)	$122,900
Sohn (R)	$41,986	0	$36,837

Key Votes

1991	
Authorize use of force against Iraq	N
1990	
Support constitutional amendment on flag desecration	N
Pass family and medical leave bill over Bush veto	Y
Reduce SDI funding	Y
Allow abortions in overseas military facilities	Y
Approve budget summit plan for spending and taxing	N
Approve civil rights bill	Y
1989	
Halt production of B-2 stealth bomber at 13 planes	Y
Oppose capital gains tax cut	Y
Approve federal abortion funding in rape or incest cases	Y
Approve pay raise and revision of ethics rules	N
Pass Democratic minimum wage plan over Bush veto	Y

Voting Studies

	Presidential Support		Party Unity		Conservative Coalition	
Year	S	O	S	O	S	O
1990	17	79	88	4	6	89
1989	27	72	93	4	7	90
1988	17	66	81	5	8	71
1987	12	86	95	2	2	95
1986	18	77	88	3	2	86
1985	31	68	93	4	7	91
1984	28	71	91	8	5	93
1983	17	77	95	4	7	87
1982	19	53	75	4	4	70
1981	26	71	90	9	5	95

Interest Group Ratings

Year	ADA	ACU	AFL-CIO	CCUS
1990	100	5	92	17
1989	100	4	83	20
1988	80	5	100	36
1987	96	9	87	7
1986	90	0	85	12
1985	100	10	88	20
1984	95	0	92	31
1983	95	4	100	10
1982	75	0	100	13
1981	100	0	80	11

10 John Porter (R)

Of Wilmette — Elected 1980

Born: June 1, 1935, Evanston, Ill.

Education: Attended Massachusetts Institute of Technology, 1953-54; Northwestern U., B.S., B.A. 1957; U. of Michigan, J.D. 1961.

Military Service: Army Reserve, 1958-64.

Occupation: Lawyer.

Family: Wife, Kathryn Cameron; five children.

Religion: Presbyterian.

Political Career: Ill. House, 1973-79; Republican nominee for Cook County circuit court judge, 1970; Republican nominee for U.S. House, 1978.

Capitol Office: 1026 Longworth Bldg. 20515; 225-4835.

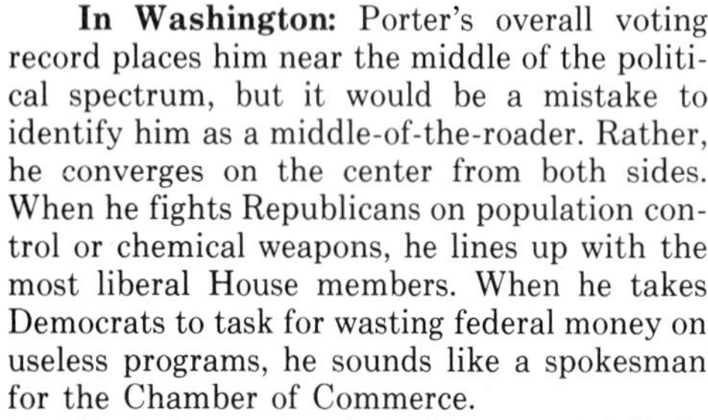

In Washington: Porter's overall voting record places him near the middle of the political spectrum, but it would be a mistake to identify him as a middle-of-the-roader. Rather, he converges on the center from both sides. When he fights Republicans on population control or chemical weapons, he lines up with the most liberal House members. When he takes Democrats to task for wasting federal money on useless programs, he sounds like a spokesman for the Chamber of Commerce.

Porter's conservative side emerged fully in early 1990 when a wide-ranging debate on Social Security arose from New York Sen. Daniel Patrick Moynihan's proposal to roll back the withholding tax for the program. A longtime advocate of major change in the system, Porter took the opportunity to promote his plan to privatize Social Security gradually.

In an opinion piece in *The Wall Street Journal*, he suggested that the government refund Social Security taxes not needed to pay current benefits to mandatory Individual Social Security Retirement Accounts (ISSRA) for each wage earner. When workers with ISSRAs retired, Porter proposed that the government adjust their federal Social Security benefit to reflect the income from their privately held ISSRA. The plan won Porter editorial praise from *Forbes* magazine and William F. Buckley, but it did not get off the ground in Washington.

Porter has the freedom to pursue such provocative ideas in part because he is in an unusually comfortable political position. He represents a firmly Republican and relatively affluent district north of Chicago; most of his constituents do not have a pressing need for federal goods and services. Like Porter, they tend to be relatively liberal on many social issues, but conservative on fiscal matters.

True to his district, Porter's approach to the federal budget deficit is pure conservative. In each year of the last three Congresses, he has co-authored alternative budgets that would freeze most spending, including cost-of-living adjustments in entitlement programs. Porter decries Congress' reliance on continuing resolutions to keep the government afloat. During the contentious 1990 budget debate, which required two CRs, Porter said passage of the bills "further cements in the minds of the American people the catastrophic failure of this Congress to behave responsibly."

Though rather reserved, Porter is no stranger to strong rhetoric. He has referred to the effect of the federal debt on future generations as "fiscal child abuse." And earlier in his career, he gave a floor speech chastising Democrats for the state of the economy: "Ladies and gentlemen of the far left, you are the problem.... The stagnation and unemployment we are suffering you have caused. Not President Reagan. Not supply-side economics. Not tax cuts. You."

When it comes to gun control, however, Porter comfortably crosses the political aisle to stand shoulder-to-shoulder with liberals. Even before 1989 — when a mentally ill woman opened fire on a classroom in Porter's district, killing one child and wounding five others — Porter was a leading GOP supporter of a waiting period preceding handgun purchases. In 1989, he offered legislation to allow seven to 30 days for federally mandated criminal background checks for all handgun purchases. During the 1988 debate to require a seven-day waiting period for handgun purchases, Porter implored his colleagues to show "the courage to do something to stop the handgun carnage in America." The measure was soundly defeated.

He also joined liberals in denouncing the proposed constitutional amendment to ban flag desecration in 1990. Although he opposes federal funding for abortion, he believes it should remain a legal option and is a strong supporter of family planning domestically and abroad. In both 1990 and 1991, Porter introduced legislation to overturn federal regulations that bar

Illinois 10

North and Northwest Chicago Suburbs — Waukegan

Although Porter's roots are in Evanston, he has no political complaints about the redistricting of the early 1980s that removed that mainly Democratic city from his district. The 10th begins in the affluent northern Chicago suburbs in Cook County, crosses into Lake County and extends all the way to the Wisconsin border. It is firmly Republican.

The district's closest-in towns — Kenilworth, Winnetka, Glencoe — along Lake Michigan are Illinois' wealthiest, and among Chicago's oldest suburbs. They are solidly Republican: Porter took 72 percent of the Cook County vote in 1988.

Lake County, most of which votes in the 10th, is a GOP stronghold. George Bush carried it with 63 percent in 1988, Republican Gov. Jim Edgar won Lake with well over 60 percent of the vote in 1990, and unsuccessful GOP attorney general candidate Jim Ryan scored a 31,000 vote plurality the same year.

The only major Democratic enclave in the county — or in the district — is the old port city of Waukegan. Now a manufacturing center producing pharmaceuticals, hospital supplies and outboard motors, Waukegan has a population that is about 15 percent Hispanic.

Though the traditional commuting pattern from the district is to downtown Chicago, corporate outposts have sprung up among the bedroom communities in recent years. Allstate, Kraft, Walgreen's and Household Finance are major employers in the district, as well as the Great Lakes Naval Training Center, on the lake near North Chicago: The largest such operation in the country, it employs well over 30,000.

Residential and commercial development in the high-growth areas of southern Lake and northern Cook counties are major local issues in the 10th, as communities struggle to maintain a balance between economic growth and quality of life.

Population: 519,660. White 469,474 (90%), Black 29,339 (6%), Other 10,315 (2%). Spanish origin 22,202 (4%). 18 and over 368,611 (71%), 65 and over 40,566 (8%). Median age: 30.

federally funded family planning groups from discussing abortion. In his role as a member of the Appropriations Subcommittee on Foreign Operations, he is a leading advocate of restoring U.S. funding of the United Nations Family Planning Agency.

Porter first made a name for himself in the 1980s as a harsh critic of the Pentagon's contention that chemical weapons could be quickly deployed in Europe in the event of armed confrontation with the Soviet Union. In 1989, he offered a successful amendment to the defense authorization bill expressing the sense of Congress that the president should intensify efforts to reach a non-proliferation treaty on chemical weapons with the Soviet Union.

Consistent with the Bush administration's emphasis on volunteerism — and the noblesse oblige attitudes of his wealthy constituents — Porter is one of many members to author national service legislation. He is a leading advocate of a "good samaritan" law to encourage states to change liability statutes to protect volunteers from lawsuits.

As a result of Porter's conservative position on most budget questions, some of his colleagues bristle when he lobbies the Appropriations Committee to provide funds for projects in his district. But so far, little revenge seems to have been exacted. In October 1988, he was on hand for the dedication of a new air-traffic-control tower at Waukegan Regional Airport in his district. Porter was credited with winning federal funding for it.

Like many members of Congress, Porter is not a modest man — he points out that he was an honors graduate from law school. And he occasionally sees a future president in the mirror in the morning. "I realize how difficult it is to achieve," he once said. "Still, I'm aiming for the office. I'd like nothing better than to continue my programs for human rights, conservation and debt reduction, among others, from the White House. Meanwhile, I'll continue my work at the lower level."

At Home: The son of a well-known judge in Evanston, Porter returned to the affluent suburbs north of Chicago after a stint in Washington with the Kennedy Justice Department in the early 1960s. He set up a law practice and worked to build a political base.

Porter's first goal was to follow in his father's footsteps to a judgeship. The path he chose, though — work in the Young Republicans organization — was not necessarily the best for an ambitious young lawyer in an area dominated at a countywide level by Chicago Democrats. In 1970, he lost the election for Cook County circuit court judge on a GOP slate dubbed "the suicide squad."

But the bid helped boost his credentials within GOP circles. Immersed in Evanston Republican affairs, Porter had no trouble winning a state House seat in 1972, and re-election twice.

Meanwhile, Democrat Abner J. Mikva, one of the most liberal Democrats in the House, had won the old 10th District by scanty margins in 1974 and 1976. Porter was one of seven Republicans who wanted to take him on in 1978.

During his six years in the state Legislature, Porter had been viewed as a moderate, at least on social issues, and had received high ratings from the liberal Independent Voters of Illinois. His chief opponent in the 1978 primary, Daniel Hales, had support from national New Right organizations. The crucial asset for Porter was the backing of the local GOP apparatus, including the two key Republican township organizations in the district. He won the primary comfortably.

His contest with Mikva proved rougher. Porter raised more money from political action committees than any other House candidate in the country that year, and spent it freely. But Mikva, no mean fundraiser himself, had a slight edge in organization, and nudged Porter out by 650 votes.

Mikva was appointed to a federal judgeship only a few months later, and both parties realized that the seat probably would not remain Democratic without him. This time, Porter had no trouble securing the nomination. In his 1980 special election against Democrat Robert Weinberger, a former Commerce Department aide, he had a massive spending advantage and emerged with 54 percent. Seeking a full term in November 1980, he was returned to office by a convincing margin.

It seemed at first that he would have no chance to rest. In the 1981 remap, Porter's Evanston home was placed in the heavily Democratic 9th District. Porter announced he would move north to challenge GOP Rep. Robert McClory in the newly drawn 10th, where Republican loyalties were solid. But the showdown between the GOP incumbents never happened. The 74-year-old McClory, after filing for an 11th term, decided in January 1982 that he would step down for his younger colleague.

Though only one-fifth of the people in the new 10th came from Porter's old district, he met no challenge in the primary and won easily in November against an experienced Democratic state legislator, Eugenia S. Chapman. His elections since have been routine.

Committees

Appropriations (12th of 22 Republicans)
Foreign Operations, Export Financing & Related Programs; Labor, Health & Human Services, Education & Related Agencies; Legislative

Select Aging (15th of 27 Republicans)
Housing & Consumer Interests; Retirement, Income & Employment

Elections

1990 General		
John Porter (R)	104,070	(68%)
Peg McNamara (D)	47,286	(31%)
1988 General		
John Porter (R)	158,519	(72%)
Eugene F. Friedman (D)	60,187	(28%)

Previous Winning Percentages: **1986** (75%) **1984** (73%) **1982** (59%) **1980** (61%) **1980 *** (54%)

* *Special election.*

District Vote For President

	1988	1984	1980	1976
D	86,280 (38%)	70,881 (31%)	60,308 (28%)	70,251 (33%)
R	143,022 (62%)	154,106 (68%)	129,386 (59%)	139,680 (65%)
I			25,273 (12%)	

Campaign Finance

	Receipts	Receipts from PACs	Expend-itures
1990			
Porter (R)	$255,970	$110,025 (43%)	$313,498
1988			
Porter (R)	$245,366	$115,321 (47%)	$212,630
Friedman (D)	$62,786	$21,800 (35%)	$62,560

Key Votes

1991	
Authorize use of force against Iraq	Y
1990	
Support constitutional amendment on flag desecration	N
Pass family and medical leave bill over Bush veto	N
Reduce SDI funding	N
Allow abortions in overseas military facilities	Y
Approve budget summit plan for spending and taxing	Y
Approve civil rights bill	N
1989	
Halt production of B-2 stealth bomber at 13 planes	Y
Oppose capital gains tax cut	N
Approve federal abortion funding in rape or incest cases	N
Approve pay raise and revision of ethics rules	Y
Pass Democratic minimum wage plan over Bush veto	N

Voting Studies

	Presidential Support		Party Unity		Conservative Coalition	
Year	**S**	**O**	**S**	**O**	**S**	**O**
1990	65	33	69	29	70	30
1989	65	35	54	41	71	24
1988	57	42	71	22	82	18
1987	54	41	69	25	81	19
1986	59	39	68	28	68	32
1985	68	30	71	25	73	25
1984	58	40	65	31	80	19
1983	73	22	69	29	67	30
1982	60	32	66	28	62	32
1981	68	32	65	33	61	36

Interest Group Ratings

Year	ADA	ACU	AFL-CIO	CCUS
1990	22	67	17	79
1989	30	63	8	100
1988	30	68	15	100
1987	20	62	6	100
1986	15	64	7	94
1985	20	71	24	82
1984	40	42	23	81
1983	25	52	6	95
1982	35	67	17	81
1981	30	67	7	89

11 Frank Annunzio (D)

Of Chicago — Elected 1964

Born: Jan. 12, 1915, Chicago, Ill.
Education: DePaul U., B.S. 1940, M.A. 1942.
Occupation: High school teacher; labor official.
Family: Wife, Angeline Alesia; three children.
Religion: Roman Catholic.
Political Career: Ill. labor director, 1949-52.
Capitol Office: 2303 Rayburn Bldg. 20515; 225-6661.

In Washington: As his 1990 campaign for a 14th House term approached, Annunzio clearly had problems stemming from his connections with the savings-and-loan industry. His longtime advocacy of savings-and-loans as friends of the working class — which had been a political strength in his blue-collar urban district — threatened to become a liability with the collapse of the scandal-plagued industry.

As chairman of the Banking Subcommittee on Financial Institutions, Annunzio had played a role in crafting the mega-billion S&L bailout legislation that had little support from the general public. GOP officials recruited a tough young candidate to drive home this point.

Though never a center-stage player and further slowed in recent years by the advance of age, Annunzio remained a street-hardened remnant of Chicago's Democratic machine and he responded to his political dilemma with agility. With the help of his aides, Annunzio repackaged himself as the savings-and-loan lawman, with a "Jail the S&L Crooks" button as his badge. He took the spotlight at a series of Banking hearings: It was Annunzio who made a federal case of the role of Neil Bush, son of President Bush, in the collapse of a Colorado savings-and-loan.

This activist mode helped him win in November 1990, but it did not alter the consensus within the House that Annunzio's star was fading. Less than a month later, Annunzio was removed as chairman of the House Administration Committee, and replaced with a younger Democrat, Charlie Rose of North Carolina. Also, Annunzio had to work to stem rumblings against him as chairman of the Banking Financial Institutions Subcommittee.

"Here's a man that, though he ran successfully for re-election, probably is going to serve as a poster child for the problems we have out there," said Oklahoma Democratic Rep. Dave McCurdy after Annunzio's defeat in the Democratic Caucus, by a 125-127 vote, for House Administration chairman.

Annunzio's critics belabor his ties to the S&L industry. They note that in 1985, Annunzio sought to delay a rule by the Federal Home Loan Bank Board that restricted direct investments by savings-and-loans in commercial ventures. During 1990 debate on the bailout bill, Annunzio favored looser capital requirements for S&Ls than those eventually enacted. Even as he was talking tough about the S&L situation in 1990, Annunzio faced questioning about the past employment of his sons-in-law in the savings-and-loan industry and campaign contributions from executives of a Maryland S&L.

Annunzio rejects implications that he bears some responsibility for the S&L crisis. He says his affections for S&Ls are based on their traditional role in financing home mortgages, particularly for wage-earners who had trouble getting loans from commercial banks. "Savings and loans are institutions that belong to the average American, the common American, the middle-class American," Annunzio says.

Throughout his last campaign, Annunzio pointed out that he was one of only 13 House members who in 1980 voted against a bill that he says resulted in the deregulation of the industry. During debate on the bailout bail, he pushed for stronger penalties for S&L fraud, including an amendment that instituted civil penalties of at least $1 million a day for violations. Later in the 101st Congress, he advocated funding for stepped-up Justice Department investigations of financial fraud.

Annunzio also stood out as a tough critic of the Office of Thrift Supervision (OTS), the agency founded to handle the federal takeover and disposition of failed thrifts. Arguing that OTS was moving too slowly in selling off the assets of these S&Ls, Annunzio at the end of the 101st Congress blocked a unanimous consent motion to provide more money for the bailout — forcing the House to take up the unwanted issue again in the 102nd Congress.

Annunzio was thrust into the S&L limelight just after taking over the Financial Institutions chairmanship. For 14 years prior, Annunzio had headed the low-profile Subcommittee on Consumer Affairs and Coinage, where he oversaw the minting of coins —

Illinois 11

Northwest Chicago and Suburbs

Despite a Republican trend in statewide elections, the 11th was until 1990 a secure home base for Annunzio. His enduring appeal was not hard to explain. Many of his constituents moved out during the 1970s from the old West Side 7th; like other Chicago Democrats, Annunzio simply followed them to the suburbs. "These are my people," he once said. "Lincolnwood? My daughter lives in Lincolnwood. Stone Park? There's a seminary there for Italian priests, and an Italian-American cultural center. Northlake? That's where we have an Italian old folks' home."

But these suburbs are not so kind to other Democrats. Stretching north to Niles and west to O'Hare Airport, the district takes in a collection of middle-class suburban developments built in the 1950s and early 1960s. Most of the residents of this area are ethnic in background, but they have moved beyond their blue-collar roots; many of them have voted for Republican candidates in statewide elections regularly during the past decade. President Reagan easily carried the 11th in 1984 with 61 percent of the vote; George Bush won with a more modest 54 percent four years later. Republican Sen. Charles H. Percy put in a strong showing there as well in his losing 1984 bid for re-election.

The city part of Annunzio's district is not all that different politically. Middle-class ethnic wards such as the 41st and 45th, in the northwest corner of the city, went heavily for Reagan and Percy in 1984. A Republican candidate dwelling on law and order and fiscal conservatism could expect to do well there in any battle following Annunzio's retirement.

A somewhat more liberal vote comes out of the 50th Ward, at the northeast end of the city, which has a substantial Jewish presence around Rogers Park.

The 39th Ward, which is generally conservative and ethnic, also has a Jewish vote that tempers its Republican nature; Reagan carried the 39th in 1984, but Democrat Paul Simon edged out Percy in the Senate contest there.

The district is overwhelmingly white. About 6 percent of the population is Hispanic; less than 1 percent is black. The Chicago Jewish communities are reinforced by a large Jewish population in Skokie, which is split between the 11th and the 9th.

Population: 518,995. White 475,460 (92%), Black 2,010 (0.4%), Asian and Pacific Islander 24,400 (5%). Spanish origin 31,425 (6%). 18 and over 409,539 (79%), 65 and over 86,119 (17%). Median age: 37.

both legal tender and commemoratives — and fought a long but fruitless battle to cap credit card interest rates.

Annunzio's interest in coins hardly ceased when he gave up the subcommittee's gavel. Known earlier in his House career as "Mr. Ethnic," Annunzio has proposed striking a coin in 1992 to commemorate the 500th anniversary of Christopher Columbus' landing in America, with proceeds of the sale to go for scholarships.

During his years as House Administration chairman, Annunzio oversaw the internecine squabbles over House committee budgets and took credit for upgrading the Capitol police force. But critics, including those who led the coup against him, said Annunzio allowed staff members to run the committee.

At Home: Though never a legislative wizard, Annunzio had a working-class manner that firmly established him in the 11th District. But even as Annunzio was swatting aside weak challengers during the 1980s, Republican officials insisted they could compete in the 11th, a conservative, ethnic-dominated stretch across the north side of Chicago and its near-in suburbs that has for years favored GOP presidents.

In 1990, the Republicans came up with a candidate qualified to test their theory: state Sen. Walter W. Dudycz. A son of Ukrainian immigrants, a Vietnam veteran and a former Chicago police officer, Dudycz appeared to perfectly fit the district. Dudycz expected to focus his campaign on his devotion to blue-collar values. He had earlier made a name for himself by leading protests against a Chicago art exhibit in which an American flag was trod upon, and by staging rallies against state tax increases.

However, by January 1990, Dudycz' campaign became fixated on Annunzio's ties to the savings and loan industry. Dudycz blasted Annunzio for receiving a $3,000 campaign contribution in 1986 from Charles Keating, and proceeded to dump blame for the S&L crisis on the high-ranking Banking Committee member.

Annunzio — who had not faced a tough race since 1972 — first defended himself against charges of wrongdoing, then went on the offensive; "Jail the S&L Crooks" became his slogan.

Dudycz' efforts to take advantage of the S&L issue were blunted by his own bad press.

In August, a newspaper reported that Dudycz had a lucrative second job as a Cook County deputy sheriff while serving as a state senator. Although Dudycz denied ever taking money he had not earned, Annunzio's campaign consultants dubbed him "double-dipping Dudycz."

Annunzio hung on with 54 percent of the vote. But his worries are hardly over. Illinois is losing two House seats in reapportionment, one of which is certain to come from Democratic turf in Chicago. Annunzio's district, is considered a likely target.

Annunzio, who began his House career in a downtown Chicago district, is on the Northwest Side today because of redistricting drawn for the 1972 election. Annunzio and black Rep. George Collins were placed in the 7th district, setting up a possible intraparty battle. But the 11th District had become open, and the Democratic organization, headed by Democratic Mayor Richard J. Daley, convinced Annunzio to move northwest.

The move to the 11th was another sign of Annunzio's loyalty to the Daley machine. A former school teacher turned union activist, Annunzio was serving as Democratic Gov. Adlai E. Stevenson's secretary of labor in the early 1950s when he met Daley, then state revenue director. Annunzio was forced from his job in 1952, following unconfirmed allegations that he was using his position to steer business to an insurance company he had founded. But his alliance with Daley remained strong.

After years in ward politics, Annunzio got a red-carpet opportunity to run for the House himself in 1964. Rumors of organized crime connections forced Democratic Rep. Roland Libonati to retire; Daley's organization turned to Annunzio to replace him. Annunzio won easily that year and was not seriously challenged in three ensuing 7th District contests.

When he shifted to the 11th in 1972, Annunzio found voters who were less solidly Democratic than his former constituents and were disaffected by the presidential candidacy of liberal George McGovern. However, Annunzio was able to fend off Republican Chicago Alderman John Hoellen with 53 percent.

Committees

Banking, Finance & Urban Affairs (2nd of 31 Democrats)
Financial Institutions Supervision, Regulation & Insurance (chairman); Consumer Affairs & Coinage; General Oversight

House Administration (2nd of 15 Democrats)
Procurement & Printing (chairman); Accounts

Elections

1990 General		
Frank Annunzio (D)	82,703	(54%)
Walter W. Dudycz (R)	68,850	(45%)
1988 General		
Frank Annunzio (D)	131,753	(65%)
George S. Gottlieb (R)	72,489	(35%)

Previous Winning Percentages: **1986** (71%) **1984** (63%) **1982** (73%) **1980** (70%) **1978** (74%) **1976** (67%) **1974** (72%) **1972** (53%) **1970** (87%) **1968** (83%) **1966** (81%) **1964** (86%)

District Vote For President

	1988	1984	1980	1976
D	101,346 (46%)	93,584 (38%)	111,641 (45%)	123,612 (48%)
R	117,883 (54%)	149,521 (61%)	114,691 (46%)	135,612 (52%)
I			19,979 (8%)	

Campaign Finance

	Receipts	Receipts from PACs		Expend-itures
1990				
Annunzio (D)	$723,159	$478,891	(66%)	$855,952
Dudycz (R)	$408,470	$217,755	(53%)	$407,617
1988				
Annunzio (D)	$260,514	$158,200	(61%)	$239,158
Gottlieb (R)	$39,882	$1,730	(4%)	$41,259

Key Votes

1991	
Authorize use of force against Iraq	N
1990	
Support constitutional amendment on flag desecration	Y
Pass family and medical leave bill over Bush veto	Y
Reduce SDI funding	Y
Allow abortions in overseas military facilities	N
Approve budget summit plan for spending and taxing	N
Approve civil rights bill	N
1989	
Halt production of B-2 stealth bomber at 13 planes	N
Oppose capital gains tax cut	Y
Approve federal abortion funding in rape or incest cases	N
Approve pay raise and revision of ethics rules	Y
Pass Democratic minimum wage plan over Bush veto	Y

Voting Studies

	Presidential Support		Party Unity		Conservative Coalition	
Year	S	O	S	O	S	O
1990	35	65	83	14	52	48
1989	37	60	89	8	34	63
1988	27	69	90	8	50	47
1987	14	42	66	3	28	30
1986	23	73	90	5	32	66
1985	29	71	89	7	33	62
1984	42	57	86	12	39	58
1983	29	62	83	12	38	56
1982	51	43	85	11	47	52
1981	55	45	77	22	59	41

Interest Group Ratings

Year	ADA	ACU	AFL-CIO	CCUS
1990	56	38	75	43
1989	75	7	100	44
1988	75	17	100	25
1987	48	9	93	20
1986	70	5	93	39
1985	75	5	100	23
1984	70	25	92	31
1983	70	14	94	21
1982	65	19	95	24
1981	45	0	80	21

12 Philip M. Crane (R)

Of Mount Prospect — Elected 1969

Born: Nov. 3, 1930, Chicago, Ill.

Education: Attended DePauw U., 1948-50; Hillsdale College, B.A. 1952; attended U. of Michigan, 1952-54; U. of Vienna, Austria, 1953, 1956; Indiana U., M.A. 1961, Ph.D. 1963.

Military Service: Army, 1954-56.

Occupation: History professor; author; advertising manager.

Family: Wife, Arlene Catherine Johnson; eight children.

Religion: Protestant.

Political Career: Sought Republican nomination for president, 1980.

Capitol Office: 1035 Longworth Bldg. 20515; 225-3711.

In Washington: Crane's 1980 presidential bid has faded to a footnote in the history of that watershed election year. Yet, like others who stride the presidential stage, however briefly, he retains some enhanced stature years later.

Crane once thought Ronald Reagan might pass the torch of conservative leadership to him. But more than a decade has passed since, and Crane's name is not heard. In the House, the torch has been seized by combative House conservatives who elected Newt Gingrich as minority whip early in the 101st Congress. The Georgian is 13 years younger than Crane, and 10 years his junior in the House.

Few question Crane's intellectual abilities or his oratorical skills. He received a perfect 100 percent rating from the American Conservative Union in all but one year from 1981 to 1990. But he has never displayed the mindset needed for the give and take of legislating. Even Crane describes some of his rigidly conservative legislative endeavors as "spitting in the wind."

Crane often acts to define the ideologically pure frontier. When funding of the National Endowment for the Arts became controversial in the 101st Congress, Crane called for the NEA's outright abolition, attracting the votes of less than one-third of his own party's colleagues. In June 1990, with Congress in high dudgeon over the S&L crisis, Crane stood alone against 420 members in a floor vote appropriating an extra $75 million for investigating and prosecuting S&L fraud cases.

In the 100th Congress, there were 11 floor votes in which only one Republican in the entire House voted "no." On six occasions, Crane was that lone dissenter. He twice cast the solo vote against an education bill, and once was the only holdout on a housing bill.

Of all his solitary votes, the one Crane says he remembers best is his 1984 vote against easing a Reagan administration policy that had purged thousands of disabled Social Security beneficiaries from government rolls.

Now in his third decade of House service, Crane has not found the national visibility he wanted. But he has earned seniority on the powerful Ways and Means Committee, a forum he could use to enhance his profile.

In the 101st Congress, Crane united with members who united against Chairman Dan Rostenkowski to repeal the funding mechanism for catastrophic health care and "Section 89" rules against discriminatory pension arrangements.

Crane was a fairly low-profile member of Ways and Means for a number of years, but in the 99th Congress, he assumed the ranking position on the Trade Subcommittee. He has emerged as a vocal proponent of free trade, battling other members' efforts to protect domestic industries from imports.

Many other members share his concern about protectionist attempts to reduce the U.S. trade deficit, but few feel as strongly as Crane. Early in 1987, he was one of only two Ways and Means members to vote against reporting an omnibus trade bill to the floor. Although others complained about various parts of the legislation, Crane was virtually alone in questioning the need for any bill at all.

More than once in his career, Crane's opinions on tax policy have been ahead of the curve of debate on the subject. But when the ideas he was espousing began working their way through the legislative process, Crane was not known for fighting in the trenches for their passage.

He was one of the earliest congressional supporters of tax indexing, introducing legislation as far back as 1974. But while he could claim victory with its passage in 1981, he was not prominent in the key negotiations on the issue.

Well before tax-code revision became a

Illinois 12

Far Northwest Cook County Suburbs — Palatine

When Crane won his first term in 1969, his district came in all the way to the Chicago city limits. Not an inch of that original territory remains within the 12th District boundaries today.

Crane still has a chunk of the suburban territory that he represented during the 1970s. But the 12th is now a demographic hodgepodge, dominated by the affluent and rapidly growing outer Cook County suburbs, yet taking in a mix of blue-collar towns and rural areas as well.

The one thing the various district constituencies share is their Republican orientation; this is rock-solid GOP territory. President Reagan won the 12th by a 3-to-1 margin in 1984; George Bush also topped 70 percent four years later.

The population center of the district is in the suburban towns of northwest Cook County. These communities, populated largely by younger professionals, have grown dramatically in the past 20 years. Arlington Heights, the largest, now has over 75,000 residents. Hoffman Estates has more than 40,000. Inverness is still an affluent village, though its population — 5,400 in 1986 — was up over 33 percent in the early part of the decade.

Just below, in the southwest corner of Crane's Cook County territory, are blue-collar suburbs, settled by people who work in Chicago or in small industrial cities such as Elgin. There are pockets of Democratic votes here, but they rarely have an impact on the district vote for statewide office.

Crane's constituency also extends beyond metropolitan Chicago, taking in most of semi-rural McHenry County and part of Lake County.

Southern Lake County, like northern Cook County, is populated by professionals and wealthy executives who commute to Chicago or to the offices springing up in the suburbs to the south. But as its name suggests, the county has several large recreational lakes; in the summer, its population explodes as Chicagoans and suburbanites converge on it to go fishing or boating or spend their time in summer homes.

Heavily Republican McHenry County has about a third of the voters in the 12th. McHenry has seen some development spillover from Lake, but is still mainly dairy farms and small market towns. Its largest city, Woodstock, has about 13,000 residents. Harvard, in western McHenry, bills itself as the "Milk Capital of the World."

Population: 519,181. White 500,456 (96%), Black 4,078 (1%), Other 7,779 (2%). Spanish origin 15,651 (3%). 18 and over 356,939 (69%), 65 and over 35,082 (7%). Median age: 29.

major issue, Crane proposed a flat-rate tax of 10 percent on income, with no deductions or credits, and a $2,000 personal exemption. But in 1985, when Ways and Means produced a tax-revision bill incorporating some of his ideas, he described the bill — which had White House backing — as "poorly and thoughtlessly crafted" and burdensome on business. Unlike President Reagan and most House members, Crane did not want a revenue-neutral bill but one that would greatly lower the tax burden.

Preferential treatment for capital gains was another Crane cause of longstanding. But that treatment succumbed to tax reform in the 99th Congress, and, when the issue returned in 1989, other committee members took the lead in pushing for its restoration.

On the expenditures side of the federal ledger, Crane is a sure vote to cut spending for domestic programs. Neither education, housing, mail service nor a variety of other programs are mandatory federal functions, according to him.

Crane did score two legislative successes in the 100th Congress. In 1988, he successfully offered an amendment on the floor to bar federal employees earning more than $72,500 (including members of Congress) from receiving a 4 percent cost-of-living raise. He also succeeded in amending the McKinney homeless-aid bill to allow certain transitional housing facilities to pay residents to maintain the structures or to transport residents to other jobs.

Matters of broad fiscal impact do not occupy all of Crane's time. In the 99th Congress he lobbied for easier parking for members of Congress at Washington's National Airport. Crane, with 37 other members, asked the Federal Aviation Administration to prohibit Supreme Court justices and diplomats from using the airport's free "officials" parking lot. There were not enough spaces in the lot, he argued, and members of Congress were forced to cope with "irregular and unpredictable time constraints." The FAA refused.

Throughout his years in the House, Crane has kept up a busy schedule outside the institution, speaking on free enterprise and the need for a strong national defense to groups across the country. His efforts generally place him on the high end of House honoraria-earners.

Crane launched his 1980 presidential campaign from his base as chairman of the American Conservative Union. After Crane spent a year trying to organize support for the New Hampshire primary, William Loeb, then the acerbic Manchester Union Leader publisher and political baron, ran articles accusing Crane of heavy drinking and womanizing. By the time New Hampshire voted, Crane was a minor candidate and received just 1.8 percent of the vote. He won five convention delegates, but withdrew and endorsed Reagan.

At Home: Crane's conservative political philosophy was formed early, and the principal catalyst was his father, Dr. George Washington Crane III, a psychologist and writer. The senior Crane emphasized self-reliance, free enterprise and the wisdom of the Founding Fathers.

George Crane's sons may not make up a political dynasty, but they have generated a long series of congressional campaigns. Philip's younger brother Daniel B. Crane served three terms from a southern Illinois district before being unseated in 1984. David Crane lost three House races in Indiana's old 6th District.

The Cranes lived in modest circumstances in a working-class neighborhood on the South Side of Chicago. After the death of an older brother in an airplane crash, Philip Crane abandoned his early career in advertising and went back to school. In 1967, he became director of Westminster Academy, a private, conservative-oriented school north of Chicago.

In 1969 Crane entered the GOP House primary in a special election held after Donald Rumsfeld resigned from Congress to become head of the Office of Economic Opportunity in the Nixon administration. Among seven GOP candidates, Crane's meticulous organization of conservative activists put him over the top with 22 percent of the vote.

Crane's Democratic opponent, Edward A. Warman, used the election as a referendum on the Vietnam War. Soft-spoken and articulate, Crane rebuffed Warman's attempt to paint him as an extremist: He won with 58 percent.

The 1980 presidential bid was Crane's one political failure. He has easily won 11 re-election contests. In 1990, with no Democratic opponent, he won with a career-best 82 percent against Illinois Solidarity Party candidate Steve Pedersen.

Committees

Ways & Means (3rd of 13 Republicans)
Social Security; Trade (ranking)

Elections

1990 General

Philip M. Crane (R)	113,081	(82%)
Steve Pedersen (IL SOL)	24,450	(18%)

1988 General

Philip M. Crane (R)	165,913	(75%)
John A. Leonardi (D)	54,769	(25%)

Previous Winning Percentages: **1986** (78%) **1984** (78%) **1982** (66%) **1980** (74%) **1978** (80%) **1976** (73%) **1974** (61%) **1972** (74%) **1970** (58%) **1969** * (58%)

* *Special election.*

District Vote For President

	1988	1984	1980	1976
D	66,474 (29%)	49,605 (23%)	50,189 (24%)	66,018 (31%)
R	161,488 (71%)	163,832 (76%)	131,495 (64%)	146,331 (68%)
I			20,394 (10%)	

Campaign Finance

	Receipts	Receipts from PACs	Expend-itures
1990			
Crane (R)	$163,442	0	$163,376
1988			
Crane (R)	$466,894	0	$480,460
Leonardi (D)	$11,798	$7,150 (61%)	$11,955

Key Votes

1991	
Authorize use of force against Iraq	Y
1990	
Support constitutional amendment on flag desecration	Y
Pass family and medical leave bill over Bush veto	N
Reduce SDI funding	N
Allow abortions in overseas military facilities	N
Approve budget summit plan for spending and taxing	N
Approve civil rights bill	N
1989	
Halt production of B-2 stealth bomber at 13 planes	N
Oppose capital gains tax cut	N
Approve federal abortion funding in rape or incest cases	N
Approve pay raise and revision of ethics rules	N
Pass Democratic minimum wage plan over Bush veto	N

Voting Studies

	Presidential Support		Party Unity		Conservative Coalition	
Year	S	O	S	O	S	O
1990	84	12	89	2	87	7
1989	63	30	86	5	90	5
1988	79	15	91	2	92	3
1987	71	16	83	2	72	9
1986	82	16	87	4	90	4
1985	80	11	79	5	76	9
1984	73	21	86	7	85	10
1983	76	16	92	4	92	6
1982	79	18	81	5	89	7
1981	64	28	81	9	80	13

Interest Group Ratings

Year	ADA	ACU	AFL-CIO	CCUS
1990	11	100	0	79
1989	5	100	0	90
1988	0	100	0	93
1987	4	100	0	92
1986	0	100	0	93
1985	5	95	6	82
1984	0	100	15	93
1983	5	100	6	85
1982	0	100	0	85
1981	10	100	0	89

13 Harris W. Fawell (R)

Of Naperville — Elected 1984

Born: March 25, 1929, West Chicago, Ill.
Education: Attended North Central College, 1947-49; Chicago-Kent College of Law, J.D. 1952.
Occupation: Lawyer.
Family: Wife, Ruth Johnson; three children.
Religion: Methodist.
Political Career: Ill. Senate, 1963-77; candidate for Ill. Supreme Court, 1976.
Capitol Office: 435 Cannon Bldg. 20515; 225-3515.

In Washington: By the time a bill comes before one of Fawell's committees, he not only has read it line by line, he is likely to have underlined and highlighted the document and scribbled notes in the margins about questions he wants to raise.

But for all his preparation, Fawell can come across as a rambling inquisitor of witnesses before the Education and Labor Committee. At a 1991 hearing on striker protection legislation, he used his entire time allotment trying to articulate a question for AFL-CIO chief Lane Kirkland. When Fawell attempted to follow-up on the answer, an exasperated chairman cut him off for exceeding the time limit.

Fawell reflects the aptitudes and opinions of his affluent, suburban Republican district. On most issues, he quietly pursues the anti-tax, pro-business orientation of his constituents. It is not unusual for his voting record to earn a perfect score from the U.S. Chamber of Commerce.

But while Fawell supports most of the Bush administration economic and defense policies, his voting record does not place him in the ranks of House hard-liners: He opposed Bush's position on roughly a third of House legislation in the 100th Congress. Notably, Fawell parts company with Republican orthodoxy in his support of environmental legislation and his backing for funding of abortion in cases of rape and incest.

When affluent seniors began grumbling about the costs of the 1988 "catastrophic" health insurance bill, Fawell became their champion. A foe of the initial bill, he co-chaired the GOP task force pushing for its repeal, and entered the discharge petition that helped shake the bill out of the Ways and Means Committee, which was blocking action. In late 1989, Fawell claimed victory when Congress repealed the bill.

Fawell is something of a bug on esoteric funding issues that most House members overlook. Though a few of these matters have turned into legislative victories, his nitpicking tends to amplify a less than weighty image. In the 100th Congress, Fawell led a successful effort to overturn an $8 million appropriation to build schools in Paris for Jewish refugees from North Africa. Also in 1988, Fawell opposed a bill to allow Boston College to write off $12 million on a loan it obtained to build a library named after former House Speaker Thomas P. O'Neill Jr. Though Fawell was one of only two members to speak against the bill on the House floor, it was defeated, 158-239. In the 101st Congress, he made an unsuccessful attempt to delete funding to renovate the House beauty shop.

At Home: Fawell can afford to talk about the need to assess issues from a "businessman's point of view." The political mainstream in the 13th ranges from the moderate to far right within the Republican Party. Fawell's only electoral worries would arise within his own party, and those are unlikely; he has rolled over his Democratic opponents.

As the campaign treasurer for his longtime friend, veteran Rep. John N. Erlenborn, Fawell was well-positioned in 1984 when Erlenborn announced his retirement after 20 years of service. Fawell picked up most of the veteran incumbent's political network; Erlenborn's chief aide became his campaign manager.

That help proved invaluable in winning the GOP primary. Fawell, who as a state legislator had promoted measures to aid the handicapped, faced two conservative opponents — state Sen. George Ray Hudson and former state Sen. Mark Rhoads — who tried to portray him as a liberal.

With backing from the formal Du Page and Cook County GOP organizations as well as conservative contacts, Hudson seemed at least an even bet to defeat Fawell. But he lost time and momentum after falling off a campaign stage and breaking a leg.

Fawell took the nomination over Hudson by more than 3,000 votes, and coasted through November. He has not been threatened since, defeating all Democratic comers with at least two-thirds of the district vote.

Illinois 13

Southwest Chicago Suburbs — Downers Grove

The affluent, suburban 13th is one of the most Republican constituencies in the country. Once set almost entirely within Du Page County, the 13th was redrawn in the early 1980s to include the southwest Cook County suburbs of Chicago, which account for over 40 percent of the population.

The section of Du Page in the district casts a little over half the 13th's vote. Rapid growth there in Naperville has boosted the city's population to 85,000 — an increase of 100 percent between 1980 and 1990. Naperville (part of which is in the neighboring 14th District) is strategically located on the East-West Tollway to the north and near Interstate 55 in the south.

Closer to Chicago are the more established suburbs clustered along the Burlington Northern railroad tracks that extend from the Cook County towns of Riverside and Western Springs to Hinsdale, Clarendon and Downers Grove in Du Page. The cul-de-sacs of Riverside, one of the area's first planned suburban developments, were copied again and again as suburbia crept along the railroad line out from Cook County into Du Page.

The only blue-collar territory in the 13th is in prewar industrial suburbs such as Broadview. But even Lisle, a traditional working-class town, saw its per capita income double in the early 1980s. Any Democratic votes here are canceled out by those of the affluent communities surrounding them.

In the center of the district is the Argonne National Laboratory, a federal energy research center. At the southern end of Cook County, the 13th opens up to rolling countryside with pockets of newer residential developments; several forest preserves and lakes in the Cook County park system are in this area. The district also includes a corner of Will County, between Joliet and Chicago. About seven percent of the vote is cast in Will County.

Population: 519,441. White 494,504 (95%), Black 7,925 (2%), Other 13,078 (3%). Spanish origin 9,184 (2%). 18 and over 370,153 (71%), 65 and over 44,505 (9%). Median age: 31.

Committees

Education & Labor (7th of 14 Republicans)
Human Resources (ranking); Labor-Management Relations; Labor Standards

Science, Space & Technology (9th of 19 Republicans)
Energy; Science

Select Aging (9th of 27 Republicans)
Human Services

Elections

1990 General		
Harris W. Fawell (R)	116,048	(66%)
Steven K. Thomas (D)	60,305	(34%)
1988 General		
Harris W. Fawell (R)	174,992	(70%)
Evelyn E. Craig (D)	74,424	(30%)

Previous Winning Percentages: **1986** (73%) **1984** (67%)

District Vote For President

	1988	1984	1980	1976
D	81,899 (31%)	62,647 (25%)	68,726 (26%)	69,653 (29%)
R	179,221 (69%)	184,195 (74%)	164,990 (62%)	164,699 (69%)
I			25,915 (10%)	

Campaign Finance

	Receipts	Receipts from PACs		Expend-itures
1990				
Fawell (R)	$336,789	$119,570	(36%)	$271,913
1988				
Fawell (R)	$292,896	$98,171	(34%)	$289,190
Craig (D)	$45,825	$18,700	(41%)	$45,760

Key Votes

1991	
Authorize use of force against Iraq	Y
1990	
Support constitutional amendment on flag desecration	Y
Pass family and medical leave bill over Bush veto	N
Reduce SDI funding	N
Allow abortions in overseas military facilities	Y
Approve budget summit plan for spending and taxing	N
Approve civil rights bill	N
1989	
Halt production of B-2 stealth bomber at 13 planes	N
Oppose capital gains tax cut	N
Approve federal abortion funding in rape or incest cases	Y
Approve pay raise and revision of ethics rules	N
Pass Democratic minimum wage plan over Bush veto	N

Voting Studies

	Presidential Support		Party Unity		Conservative Coalition	
Year	**S**	**O**	**S**	**O**	**S**	**O**
1990	70	30	88	11	81	19
1989	60	40	73	25	88	10
1988	61	36	80	18	92	8
1987	64	34	74	23	84	16
1986	69	30	83	17	78	22
1985	85	15	79	18	78	22

Interest Group Ratings

Year	ADA	ACU	AFL-CIO	CCUS
1990	11	88	8	93
1989	10	93	0	100
1988	40	64	14	92
1987	24	70	0	100
1986	20	73	14	89
1985	15	81	6	95

14 Dennis Hastert (R)

Of Yorkville — Elected 1986

Born: Jan. 2, 1942, Aurora, Ill.
Education: Wheaton College, A.B. 1964; Northern Illinois U., M.A. 1967.
Occupation: Teacher; restaurateur.
Family: Wife, Jean Kahl; two children.
Religion: Protestant.
Political Career: Ill. House, 1981-87.
Capitol Office: 515 Cannon Bldg. 20515; 225-2976.

In Washington: Hastert is a beefy former wrestling coach who once headed the National Wrestling Congress, but he is not a stereotypical jock. He is a serious legislator who came to Washington to serve as ombudsman for his constituents, just as he did for six years in the Illinois Legislature.

In the process, Hastert has capitalized on his political skills and sensibilities to become an effective player inside House GOP politics. He mixes with the Republican troops and has the reputation of being eyes and ears for Minority Leader Robert H. Michel. Hastert holds a seat on the GOP's Committee on Committees, which makes party committee assignments.

At the start of the 102nd Congress, Hastert parlayed his contacts into a committee move of his own: He switched from Public Works to Energy and Commerce, where his interests are expected to include development of home-grown, renewable fuels such as ethanol.

Among the issues of direct concern to his constituents is the cleanup of low-level nuclear waste. West Chicago is home to many in the 14th and also to a site where a now-defunct plant once buried low-level nuclear waste. In his first term, Hastert tried to pass an amendment blocking the Nuclear Regulatory Commission (NRC) from designating a permanent waste site in the district until other alternatives had been studied.

"Certainly small communities should not be asked to gamble with the lives of their residents if better and safer solutions exist," Hastert said when he pushed for an amendment to the NRC authorization bill on the House floor. The amendment was accepted, but did not become law.

Hastert also has repeatedly sought to remove penalties in the form of decreased Social Security benefits that are levied on senior citizens between 65 and 69 who continue to work after retirement.

At Home: Hastert went a long way in politics without breaking a sweat. Appointed to the Illinois House in 1981 to fill a vacancy, Hastert was selected in 1986 as the 14th District nominee by a Republican convention after GOP Rep. John E. Grotberg was forced to retire because of a terminal illness.

But in the general election, Hastert had to struggle to maintain the Republican hold on the district. His Democratic foe, Kane County coroner Mary Lou Kearns, enjoyed some advantages that made the election close.

Whereas Kearns was an official in the district's largest county, Hastert came from the southeast corner of the 14th, away from its population centers. And while Kearns had begun to campaign in summer 1985, Hastert was not nominated until June 1986, leaving him just a little more than four months to summon the district's normal GOP loyalties.

Hastert was hindered in that effort by the bruised feelings left over from the convention that nominated him. The backers of two other candidates -- West Chicago lawyer Tom Johnson and Elgin Mayor Richard Verbic -- complained the convention was stacked in Hastert's favor. The hard-working Kearns added to Hastert's troubles, attacking him for supporting a utility measure in the Legislature that she claimed would result in rate increases.

In the final weeks, amid widespread GOP concern that a safe seat might be at risk, Hastert's sluggish effort finally came together. He promoted his experience in Springfield, where he was GOP spokesman on the state House Appropriations Committee.

Hastert also went after Kearns, reminding district Republicans that she was a presidential convention delegate in 1984 for Walter F. Mondale. He received a late boost when Johnson put aside his resentment and publicly backed the Republican nominee. Hastert won with 52 percent. Kearns considered a rematch in 1988, but declined, and Hastert has twice coasted to reelection.

An evangelical Christian, Hastert has a reputation as a conservative, but not an ideologue. He was respected for his knowledge of budget matters during his tenure in the state House, where he was an ally of GOP Gov. James R. Thompson.

Illinois 14

North Central — De Kalb; Elgin

The 14th stretches from Naperville, whose commuters hop the train for Chicago, south to Wenona, a crossroads farm town that serves the surrounding agricultural community in Marshall County. In between, in the valleys of the Illinois and Fox rivers, are a host of light industrial plants in such LaSalle County towns as Ottawa and Streator.

The semi-industrial character of the district does not interfere with its solid GOP majorities — recorded in most of the nine counties that are all or part in the district. The only Democratic bloc of any size is in LaSalle, where Michael S. Dukakis won in 1988 by 105 votes. That outcome drowned in George Bush's strong showing in Kane County, which provides nearly 40 percent of the district's vote: Bush won there by almost 30,000 votes.

The Kane County population is largely in Elgin (part of which is in the 12th District) and Aurora (shared with the 4th). Located on the Fox River in the northern part of Kane, Elgin is a longtime industrial center; its name is on much of the country's street-sweeping equipment. In recent years, it has also become a suburban outpost for white-collar Chicagoans who have settled on its east side, near the Cook County line. The city's population rose by 13 percent from 1980-86, and now numbers 77,000. The 14th also includes industrial Aurora in southern Kane County and the city's white-collar residential section.

Outside Kane County, the 14th begins to move the Illinois congressional map out of the Chicago metropolitan area. Corn and soybeans remain important to the economy in De Kalb and La Salle counties, where the farm land is among the richest in the country.

The largest city in the 14th's more rural reaches is De Kalb. An agricultural research center, it is the site of Northern Illinois University, which has about 25,500 students. Independent candidate John B. Anderson's strong showing hindered Ronald Reagan's 1980 effort in De Kalb County, but Reagan won by 2-to-1 in 1984. Bush's 1988 tally was 58 percent.

Population: 521,909. White 496,962 (95%), Black 9,991 (2%), Other 5,150 (1%). Spanish origin 20,362 (4%). 18 and over 367,441 (70%), 65 and over 49,852 (10%). Median age: 29.

Committees

Energy & Commerce (14th of 16 Republicans)
Energy & Power; Health & the Environment

Government Operations (4th of 15 Republicans)
Commerce, Consumer & Monetary Affairs (ranking)

Select Children, Youth & Families (2nd of 14 Republicans)

Elections

1990 General		
Dennis Hastert (R)	112,383	(67%)
Donald J. Westphal (D)	55,592	(33%)
1988 General		
Dennis Hastert (R)	161,146	(74%)
Stephen Youhanaie (D)	57,482	(26%)

Previous Winning Percentage: **1986** (52%)

District Vote For President

	1988	1984	1980	1976
D	81,320 (36%)	69,139 (33%)	61,516 (28%)	76,024 (38%)
R	144,966 (64%)	153,315 (69%)	136,573 (61%)	118,335 (60%)
I			21,114 (10%)	

Campaign Finance

	Receipts	Receipts from PACs		Expend-itures
1990				
Hastert (R)	$461,002	$181,074	(39%)	$312,555
1988				
Hastert (R)	$373,879	$148,608	(40%)	$346,785

Key Votes

1991	
Authorize use of force against Iraq	Y
1990	
Support constitutional amendment on flag desecration	Y
Pass family and medical leave bill over Bush veto	N
Reduce SDI funding	N
Allow abortions in overseas military facilities	N
Approve budget summit plan for spending and taxing	Y
Approve civil rights bill	N
1989	
Halt production of B-2 stealth bomber at 13 planes	N
Oppose capital gains tax cut	N
Approve federal abortion funding in rape or incest cases	N
Approve pay raise and revision of ethics rules	N
Pass Democratic minimum wage plan over Bush veto	N

Voting Studies

	Presidential Support		Party Unity		Conservative Coalition	
Year	**S**	**O**	**S**	**O**	**S**	**O**
1990	67	31	91	6	91	9
1989	76	23	90	9	90	10
1988	62	34	92	6	95	3
1987	66	33	90	7	91	9

Interest Group Ratings

Year	ADA	ACU	AFL-CIO	CCUS
1990	6	79	0	86
1989	10	85	17	100
1988	10	92	21	86
1987	8	87	13	87

15 Thomas W. Ewing (R)

Of Pontiac — Elected 1991

Born: Sept. 19, 1935, Atlanta, Ill.
Education: Millikin U., B.S. 1957; John Marshall Law School, J.D. 1968.
Military Career: Army, 1957; Army Reserve, 1957-63.
Occupation: Lawyer.
Family: Wife, Connie Lupo; six children.
Religion: Methodist.
Political Career: Ill. House, 1975-91.

The Path to Washington: Ewing's victory in a July 1991 special election restored the 15th District's voice in the House; he filled the vacancy created by the February appointment and March confirmation of longtime Republican Rep. Edward Madigan as President Bush's secretary of Agriculture.

Ewing, the deputy Republican leader in the state House at the time of Madigan's resignation, was unopposed for the GOP nomination in the 15th's special election; former Democratic state Rep. Gerald Bradley won a lightly attended primary to oppose him. With nine state House victories under his belt, a strong base in the south-central part of the 15th, and a Republican tradition in the heavily rural House district working for him, Ewing was heavily favored to win.

Bradley staked his hopes for an upset on the potential for a low turnout. Local corn and soybean growers, the core of the Republican base in the 15th, were busy in the fields during the campaign; also, the July 2 election date came as many were gearing up for the Fourth of July holiday.

But Ewing, who had a huge fundraising advantage over Bradley, ran an extensive media campaign and employed phone banks to get the vote out. His efforts paid off: Unofficial returns gave Ewing 25,675 votes (66.4 percent) to 13,011 (33.6 percent) for Bradley.

A member of local Young Republican organizations, Ewing entered the public arena in 1968 as an assistant state's attorney for Livingston County. His elective career began with his 1974 win for the state House. As he rose through the leadership ranks, to assistant House minority leader and then to the deputy's position, Ewing remained a partisan activist. He was a delegate to the 1980, 1984 and 1988 Republican national conventions, and was elected treasurer of the state GOP in 1990.

In replacing Madigan, Ewing is not expected to present a sharp contrast in style or approach. Although his record was mainly conservative, Madigan during his House tenure was a consensus-oriented member with many friends across the aisle. While Ewing's strong streak of partisanship brought him fewer Democratic allies in the state House than Madigan had in Congress, he too is regarded as a low-key, results-oriented legislator.

Ewing will undoubtedly feel the pull and tug of the intraparty debate on House Republican strategy. In the 1989 contest for House Republican whip, Madigan — the epitome of the Midwestern "Main Street" Republican — faced off against Georgia Republican Rep. Newt Gingrich, leader of a more confrontational conservative faction; Gingrich won narrowly.

However, Ewing would fit within a regional tradition of conservative pragmatism if he were to maintain Madigan's approach. Central Illinois was kind to Madigan, who ran unopposed in two of his last three House contests, and is home to a Republican of similar demeanor, House Minority Leader Robert H. Michel.

At the same time, Ewing's views on issues will enable him to fit in comfortably as a junior member of the House Republican Conference. A business-oriented conservative who once served as president of his hometown Chamber of Commerce, Ewing received a rating of 85 out of 100 in 1989 from the state Chamber of Commerce. His AFL-CIO rating was 20.

During the 86th Illinois General Assembly (1989-91), Ewing voted against an increase in the state income tax (pushed by then-Republican Gov. James R. Thompson), legislation requiring some businesses to provide eight weeks of "family leave," and an assault weapons ban. He voted for a bill to set fetal viability standards as part of abortion law.

Ewing will be watched to see if he maintains his predecessor's strong legislative interest in farm issues. Madigan served as ranking Republican on the Agriculture Committee prior to his Cabinet appointment.

Ewing served four terms (1975-83) on the state House Agriculture Committee. However, in recent years, his legislative agenda has focused on broader economic concerns. He has served on the Labor and Commerce and Public Utilities committees. He also was co-chairman of the Legislature's Economic and Fiscal Commission.

Illinois 15

Central — Bloomington; Kankakee

The spacious 15th ranges from Kankakee, just beyond the fringe of metropolitan Chicago, south to the outskirts of Champaign, then west to Lincoln, former Rep. Madigan's hometown, squarely in the center of Illinois. In between is a great expanse of black-soil farmland, fertile territory for corn, soybeans — and Republicans.

Rural Republicanism is the chief political thread in the 15th; Democrats rarely make a pretense about competing here. Corn and soybean counties such as Iroquois and Ford are among the most Republican in the state. Both gave President Ronald Reagan about three-fourths of their 1984 vote; George Bush, who entered the 1988 contest without a natural base in farm country, took better than two-thirds in each county. In his successful run for governor in 1990, Republican nominee Jim Edgar carried every county in the 15th.

The district's largest urban region is the Bloomington-Normal area in the west. Bloomington, with over 52,000 residents, is home to the national headquarters of State Farm Insurance, the largest auto insurer in the world.

Normal (population 40,000) is best known as the site of Illinois State University, which has 23,000 students; the city's name refers to the school's origins as a teachers' college, or "normal" school.

In the eastern sections of the district, the economic picture is mixed. Although neither Champaign nor Urbana is in the district, some of their northern suburban areas that are in the 15th have benefited from the growth of the University of Illinois and the high-tech industry that is blooming around it. However, the shutdown of Chanute Air Force Base at nearby Rantoul, under the base-closure plan enacted in April 1989, could cost the area over 3,000 military and civilian jobs.

Hard times came several years ago to the district's other urban locale, Kankakee, whose population declined by 7 percent to just over 27,600 between 1980 and 1990. The city is struggling to replace the blue-collar jobs lost when Roper Appliance, A. O. Smith and other industrial firms closed down factories. Many local officials have lined up behind efforts to build a third Chicago-area airport south of Chicago — preferably in Kankakee County — in hope that it will provide jobs and spur economic development.

Though still mainly farmland, parts of Will County at the northern edge of the 15th are being drawn into the Chicago exurbs. For instance, the farm community of Peotone has sprouted single-family subdivisions that have boosted its population to nearly 3,000.

Population: 518,995. White 482,975 (93%), Black 29,524 (6%), Other 2,925 (1%). Spanish origin 6,364 (1%). 18 and over 370,509 (71%), 65 and over 56,330 (11%). Median age: 29.

District Vote For President

	1988	1984	1980	1976
D	74,315 (37%)	66,325 (32%)	60,415 (29%)	81,858 (39%)
R	124,923 (63%)	140,964 (68%)	134,660 (64%)	123,957 (59%)
I			13,070 (6%)	

16 John W. Cox Jr. (D)

Of Galena — Elected 1990

Born: July 10, 1947, Hazel Green, Wis.

Education: U. of Wisconsin, Platteville, B.S. 1969; John Marshall School of Law, J.D. 1975.

Military Service: Army, 1969-70.

Occupation: Lawyer.

Family: Wife, Bonnie Aide; three children.

Religion: Roman Catholic.

Political Career: Jo Daviess County state's attorney, 1977-85.

Capitol Office: 501 Cannon Bldg. 20515; 225-5676.

The Path to Washington: If Cox's grandfather were still alive, he might well enjoy the irony of seeing his descendant become the first Democrat to represent this district in Congress, filling the seat left open when Lynn Martin ran for the Senate.

The elder Cox was a Republican, but he was also a follower of Robert "Fighting Bob" La Follette, a Republican senator from Wisconsin and a symbol of the Progressive movement. La Follette's wing of the party failed, and the elder Cox became a Democrat. When his grandson followed that lead, he seemed to accept a lonely existence in this district, but in 1990 he attracted enough company to win this seat with 55 percent.

At first glance one would guess Cox made electoral history by striking a conservative pose that appealed to this conservative stronghold. But Cox was noted for his outspoken liberal views. An active Catholic, Cox expressed qualms about the morality of abortion but nevertheless supported abortion rights. He also opposed requiring minors to get parental consent for abortions. Although he had been the state prosecutor in Jo Daviess County, Cox opposed the death penalty. When asked several years ago what he would do if his personal view conflicted with his duty to prosecute, Cox vowed that he would resign (no murder cases were filed while Cox had the job in the rural county).

The secret of Cox's success may have been his forthrightness, but he also owed much to his opponent, GOP state Rep. John W. Hallock Jr. Although he had represented Rockford, the heart of the district, for a dozen years, Hallock was unable to shake a spate of bad publicity. He seemed to be in the newspapers less often for his campaign than for his highly public divorce and his run-in with state police (he was stopped for allegedly driving his jeep at nearly 100 mph). Cox was repeatedly urged to attack Hallock on these grounds but he refused, even after Hallock accused him of planning to lend Social Security trust funds to central cities with poor credit ratings.

But if Cox seemed too reticent to his advisers, voters seemed to warm to his mild manner — a demeanor that reflected the gentility of his historic (and carefully preserved) hometown of Galena. Cox's own home is only blocks from the house given by the townspeople to Gen. Ulysses S. Grant on his return from the Civil War.

Cox arrived in Congress and immediately was confronted by two familiar issues: war and taxes. He opposed the Vietnam War as a student but felt it his duty to serve and tried unsuccessfully to enlist in the Navy before he was drafted.

Once in the Army, his Vietnam assignment was rescinded when he was sidelined by stomach ulcers (he received an honorable discharge). In the campaign, Cox said he supported President Bush's actions in the Persian Gulf to date but wanted to see sanctions given more of a chance. He voted against the use of force against Iraq.

Cox has also gone on record supporting at least considering tax increases to reduce the national budget deficit and finance the thrift-industry bailout.

He has mentioned excise taxes, an income-tax surcharge, a tax increase on the wealthy and a national sales tax. But when Hallock tried to label him a tax-and-spend liberal, Cox said he advocated only an increase in the income tax rate from 28 percent to 35 percent for people earning more than $150,000 a year.

To retain this seat, Cox will be pressured to move to his right. But he is familiar with surviving in Republican territory. In 1977, he ousted a GOP incumbent for state's attorney, becoming the first Democrat to hold the seat since 1933. Local Republican leaders were impressed enough not to bother fielding a challenger in 1980.

Illinois 16

Northwest — Rockford

Although the 16th, nestled snugly in the northwest corner of Illinois, has a mainly rural feel, the presence of blue-collar Rockford in the district long made it a temptation for Democrats. But throughout this century, the city seemed an island in a sea of rural Republicanism, as the GOP prevailed in House elections here. That finally changed in 1990, with Cox's upset victory.

Rockford — the state's second-largest city, with 135,000 residents — and surrounding Winnebago County account for some 50 percent of the district's vote. From its early days as a sawmill town, the city has been an industrial center, making farm implements, machine tools, furniture, automotive parts and aviation equipment.

Recent recessions hit the city hard, with unemployment soaring to the 20 percent level in the early 1980s. Yet the city's park system and other amenities have kept it more livable than many factory towns, helping prevent a steep decline: Rockford's 3 percent population loss from 1980 to 1986 was minimal compared with that of many Midwestern cities.

Despite the economic instability, a majority of Winnebago voters leaned Republican in the 1980s; George Bush took 55 percent of the county vote in 1988, and former GOP Rep. Lynn Martin always ran well there. But when Martin left for a Senate bid in 1990, Cox shook the county loose from its GOP moorings.

Other nearby cities, such as Belvidere (Boone County) to the east and Freeport (Stephenson County) to the west, also have a heavy-manufacturing base. There, also, Republicans tend to hold the upper hand. The rest of the district is largely rural, settled by Germans, Swedes and Yankees transplanted from New England. Their labors help make the 16th the state's leading district for dairy farming.

The northwest corner of the 16th is a vacation area, with antique stores and state parks scattered throughout hilly, GOP-leaning Jo Daviess County. The terrain, villages and history of the county has given the region the nickname "Little New England."

The home of President Ulysses S. Grant is a historical site in Galena, considered to be the bed-and-breakfast capital of the Midwest. Ronald Reagan's boyhood homes are at the southern edge of the district, at Dixon and Tampico.

Population: 519,035. White 484,432 (93%), Black 24,906 (5%), Other 2,728 (1%). Spanish origin 13,405 (3%). 18 and over 364,824 (70%), 65 and over 58,988 (11%). Median age: 30.

Committees

Banking, Finance & Urban Affairs (28th of 31 Democrats)
Financial Institutions Supervision, Regulation & Insurance; Housing & Community Development; International Development, Finance, Trade & Monetary Policy

Government Operations (25th of 25 Democrats)
Environment, Energy & Natural Resources; Government Information, Justice & Agriculture

Campaign Finance

	Receipts	Receipts from PACs		Expend- itures
1990				
Cox (D)	$377,421	$191,666	(51%)	$371,114
Hallock (R)	$495,061	$205,507	(42%)	$491,287

Key Vote

1991

Authorize use of force against Iraq	N

Elections

1990 General		
John W. Cox Jr. (D)	83,061	(55%)
John W. Hallock Jr. (R)	69,105	(45%)
1990 Primary		
John W. Cox Jr. (D)	6,778	(33%)
Stephen J. Eytalis (D)	6,205	(31%)
James E. Dixon (D)	4,990	(25%)
Robert E. Brinkmeier (D)	2,299	(11%)

District Vote For President

	1988	1984	1980	1976
D	85,552 (42%)	80,648 (37%)	60,910 (28%)	84,993 (42%)
R	116,627 (58%)	138,250 (63%)	117,600 (55%)	115,618 (57%)
I			33,015 (15%)	

17 Lane Evans (D)

Of Rock Island — Elected 1982

Born: Aug. 4, 1951, Rock Island, Ill.
Education: Augustana College (Ill.), B.A. 1974; Georgetown U., J.D. 1978.
Military Service: Marine Corps, 1969-71.
Occupation: Lawyer.
Family: Single.
Religion: Roman Catholic.
Political Career: No previous office.
Capitol Office: 1121 Longworth Bldg. 20515; 225-5905.

In Washington: Given the 17th District's previous Republican tendencies, Evans' House voting record would seem to place him to the left of much of his constituency. In 1990, Evans opposed President Bush's position on House legislation 84 percent of the time, a figure that matched his record during much of the Reagan administration.

However, Evans may well be closer to his district's mainstream than these numbers might indicate. His theme of economic populism strikes a chord in a district whose economy, dependent on heavy industry, has declined in recent years. In October 1990, Evans joined other Democrats who accused Bush of trying to solve the federal budget crisis by soaking the middle class. The next month, Evans won a fifth House term with 67 percent of the vote.

Evans has described himself as a "card-carrying capitalist," but argues that the economy should be organized with the interests of the average American in mind. "We're always consulted by corporations when they want something," he once complained. "When they want to leave town, they do it overnight."

While he holds strong views, Evans conducts himself in an engaging manner that makes it difficult for even conservative critics to dislike him. His high energy and hometown-boy style endear him to 17th District voters.

Evans' image is also tempered by his role as an activist on veterans' issues. Although he was not assigned to Vietnam, Evans was in the Marine Corps during the U.S. military action there; as a member of the House Veterans Affairs Committee, he has become an advocate for programs benefiting Vietnam veterans.

Evans stands out as the premier House crusader to compensate victims of diseases linked to Agent Orange, a defoliant used during the Vietnam conflict. His four-year effort, which put him at loggerheads with Veterans Affairs Committee Chairman G.V. "Sonny" Montgomery, D-Miss., paid off in his biggest legislative success: the enactment of Agent Orange legislation at the start of the 102nd Congress.

Vietnam veterans' groups have claimed for years that several diseases contracted by some of their constituents were caused by exposure to Agent Orange. However, succeeding administrations blocked efforts to provide benefits to these veterans, citing a lack of a scientific link between the herbicide and the diseases. This position was adopted by Montgomery, who said that providing benefits on this basis could set a dangerous precedent and drain the budget for veterans' programs.

However, benefit supporters presented studies showing a link and portrayed Montgomery, a military officer in World War II and the Korean War, as an obstructionist intent on protecting his generation's programs at the expense of Vietnam veterans. These activists lined up behind Evans' legislation, which initially would have provided benefits for victims of four forms of cancer, as well as for chloracne, a skin condition already acknowledged to have a link to Agent Orange.

Strong opposition from the Reagan administration and Montgomery stymied Evans' early efforts. However, by the 101st Congress, the wave of public openness to Vietnam veterans and the growing political clout of that group gave momentum to the benefits cause.

The Senate in October 1989 included an Agent Orange provision in a routine bill providing a cost of living allowance (COLA) for recipients of veterans' disability payments. Although Montgomery tried to thwart similar efforts in the House, Evans pressed on. "People are frustrated, and meanwhile veterans are out there literally dying," Evans said.

In early 1990, Bush administration Veterans Affairs Secretary Edward J. Derwinski announced that his department would provide benefits to victims of soft-tissue sarcomas and non-Hodgkins lymphoma who had been exposed to Agent Orange. However, Evans pressed ahead, adapting his proposal to codify Derwinski's policy and to mandate a National Academy of Sciences review of Agent Orange-related studies.

Illinois 17

West — Rock Island; Moline; Galesburg

Cradled between the Mississippi and Illinois rivers, the 17th is prime farm land where most corn and soybean growers can survive even bad years. But it is also a troubled region of small industrial cities.

At the northwestern edge in Rock Island County, Rock Island and Moline join with Iowa's Davenport and Bettendorf to make up the "Quad Cities." The Davenport, Moline and Rock Island metropolitan area is home to 351,000 residents.

However, the population has dropped somewhat in recent years, a result of a decline in the region's heavy industrial base. With one of the country's most intensive concentrations of farm equipment manufacturing — the John Deere company is headquartered at Moline — the region's economy suffered when several International Harvester factories closed down in 1983 following a corporate buyout.

That move and other problems — such as layoffs at the Caterpillar plant across the river in Davenport — had devastating effects on the area's economy. Though the situation has eased somewhat, double-digit unemployment was a fact of life in the Illinois portion of the Quad Cities, in rural Rock Island County and in the city of Galesburg through much of the 1980s.

Hard times have provided an opening to Democratic candidates that is unavailable to them in most downstate locations. Though Republicans continue to insist the 17th should be their district, the 1988 results may have finally disillusioned them: Michael S. Dukakis took the district with 53 percent of the vote — winning 59 percent in Rock Island County — and Evans ran up a personal-best percentage. Evans took 65 percent in the county in 1990.

Traditionally, rural areas such as Bureau and Henry counties — the self-proclaimed "Hog Capital of the World" — could outvote the cities of Rock Island, Moline and Galesburg in congressional elections. However, Evans has even won many of his district's rural voters: he swept all 14 counties in the district his last time out.

Population: 519,333. White 496,650 (96%), Black 14,261 (3%), Other 2,566 (1%). Spanish origin 11,662 (2%). 18 and over 372,502 (72%), 65 and over 66,095 (13%). Median age: 30.

Evans' amendment to the House COLA bill failed in the Veterans Affairs Compensation Subcommittee, but the full committee passed the the proposal by a 16-14 vote. The bill then passed the House by voice vote.

The victory for Evans' side would not be immediate. Senate opponents stalled the bill, while Montgomery tried but failed with a separate proposal including only the COLA. Montgomery tried to focus the veterans' anger over the failure of the COLA against those promoting the Agent Orange benefits. However, when the 102nd Congress opened, Montgomery's proposal of a "clean" bill was countered by Evans' COLA bill that included Agent Orange language. Montgomery then yielded to a compromise, under which his bill would first pass, followed by Agent Orange legislation.

Unlike on Veterans Affairs, Evans has not yet found a major niche on the Armed Services Committee. His record on defense is generally as liberal as on economic issues. He opposed the January 1991 resolution authorizing President Bush to use force to end Iraq's occupation of Kuwait. During the 101st Congress, Evans voted to cut funding for the strategic defense initiative and to limit production of the B-2 "Stealth" bomber.

At Home: Although his capture of the traditionally Republican seat in 1982 was regarded at the time as a stunning upset, the hard-working and personable Evans quickly became a fixture. In his first two re-election campaigns, district Republicans tried, but failed, to convince voters that Evans was an undesirable liberal extremist. By 1988, a less aggressive GOP watched in frustration as Evans ran up 65 percent of the vote.

Evans wins in part because he works tirelessly at home — conducting meetings to study the district's economic problems, popping up at every county fair and small-town celebration, making himself available to the local media, and putting in countless hours helping constituents.

In 1982, Evans emerged from his community legal clinic in Rock Island to make his first run for public office. It was an effort that seemed futile until primary day in March of that year, when former state Sen. Kenneth G. McMillan, a New Right stalwart, defeated Rep. Tom Railsback, a moderate eight-term Republican who always enjoyed broad bipartisan support.

Railsback's defeat set up a clear ideological choice for the voters. McMillan, who had castigated Railsback for not giving President Reagan enough support, asked that the administration's program be given more time to prove itself.

Evans, who had worked in the presidential campaign of Sen. Edward M. Kennedy in 1980, managed to deflect the "Kennedy liberal" label and focus the contest on McMillan and Reagan. He urged voters in the economically troubled district to use his candidacy as a way to "send Reagan a message," and forced McMillan to vow, somewhat defensively, that he would not vote to cut farm subsidies.

By Election Day, Evans had successfully framed his foe as a right-winger. With crucial help from the United Auto Workers he won decisively in Rock Island and Moline, offsetting McMillan's rural strength.

The 1984 election brought a rematch. McMillan moderated his rhetoric, trying to appeal both to conservative voters in the rural counties of the district and to blue-collar voters in the industrial cities to the north. But Evans carried nine of the district's 14 counties.

In 1986, the GOP offered Rock Island lawyer Sam McHard, who had strengths where McMillan was weak. McHard came out of the party's moderate wing and had been an active supporter of Railsback in 1982. Railsback's support gave McHard the unified backing of the district's GOP establishment, and greater credibility in the Rock Island area, which is crucial to any Republican hoping to cut into Evans' base.

Like McMillan before him, McHard tried to paint Evans as ideologically unfit. But he was unable to dent Evans' personal popularity — he cut slightly into Evans' margin in Rock Island County, but not enough to pose much of a threat. Evans carried the same nine counties he had carried two years before.

With his position firmly established, Evans faced less serious Republican challenges in his last two contests. In 1988, the Republicans put up William E. Stewart, a low-key attorney from the small Henry County city of Kewanee. Evans swept all of the district's counties, running away in Rock Island County with 70 percent of the vote. He blew by Republican professor Dan Lee in 1990 with a career-high 67 percent.

Evans' next challenge may not be at the polls but in the state Legislature, where a new district map will be drawn for 1992. Illinois is losing two seats, and Evans' current 17th District — where population declined over the past decade — may be reshaped.

Committees

Armed Services (25th of 33 Democrats)
Investigations; Procurement & Military Nuclear Systems; Readiness

Select Children, Youth & Families (13th of 22 Democrats)

Veterans' Affairs (4th of 21 Democrats)
Oversight & Investigations (chairman); Compensation, Pension & Insurance

Elections

1990 General		
Lane Evans (D)	102,062	(67%)
Dan Lee (R)	51,380	(33%)
1988 General		
Lane Evans (D)	132,130	(65%)
William E. Stewart (R)	71,560	(35%)

Previous Winning Percentages: **1986** (56%) **1984** (57%) **1982** (53%)

District Vote For President

	1988	1984	1980	1976
D	107,639 (53%)	103,510 (46%)	80,889 (36%)	100,760 (45%)
R	95,672 (47%)	123,117 (54%)	125,591 (56%)	119,970 (54%)
I			15,447 (7%)	

Campaign Finance

	Receipts	Receipts from PACs	Expend-itures
1990			
Evans (D)	$417,626	$228,998 (55%)	$390,401
Lee (R)	$116,755	$26,830 (23%)	$115,495
1988			
Evans (D)	$461,211	$211,218 (46%)	$471,233
Stewart (R)	$125,065	$14,951 (12%)	$124,133

Key Votes

1991	
Authorize use of force against Iraq	N
1990	
Support constitutional amendment on flag desecration	N
Pass family and medical leave bill over Bush veto	Y
Reduce SDI funding	Y
Allow abortions in overseas military facilities	Y
Approve budget summit plan for spending and taxing	N
Approve civil rights bill	Y
1989	
Halt production of B-2 stealth bomber at 13 planes	Y
Oppose capital gains tax cut	Y
Approve federal abortion funding in rape or incest cases	Y
Approve pay raise and revision of ethics rules	N
Pass Democratic minimum wage plan over Bush veto	Y

Voting Studies

	Presidential Support		Party Unity		Conservative Coalition	
Year	**S**	**O**	**S**	**O**	**S**	**O**
1990	16	84	97	3	9	91
1989	23	77	97	3	5	95
1988	17	83	97	2	8	92
1987	11	87	94	3	2	93
1986	13	86	95	4	6	92
1985	14	86	96	1	5	93
1984	24	73	94	6	7	92
1983	9	90	91	6	13	84

Interest Group Ratings

Year	ADA	ACU	AFL-CIO	CCUS
1990	100	4	100	21
1989	100	7	92	40
1988	100	0	100	14
1987	100	0	94	0
1986	100	0	93	11
1985	100	5	100	18
1984	90	0	85	38
1983	95	4	94	10

18 Robert H. Michel (R)

Of Peoria — Elected 1956

Born: March 2, 1923, Peoria, Ill.
Education: Bradley U., B.S. 1948.
Military Service: Army, 1942-46.
Occupation: Congressional aide.
Family: Wife, Corinne Woodruff; four children.
Religion: Apostolic Christian.
Political Career: No previous office.
Capitol Office: 2112 Rayburn Bldg. 20515; 225-6201.

In Washington: To borrow from Michelese, the House Republican leader is one doggone decent son of a gun. That sentiment goes a long way toward explaining how this amiable son of Peoria has survived as leader for a decade, even though unity within the GOP ranks is threatened by a younger generation of restless conservatives.

Like many House leaders before him, Michel patiently waited years to reach the top, only to be accused once there of being wrong for the times. He is one of the "Old Bulls," a traditional Republican from the small-town chamber of commerce set. He is a conservative, to be sure, but also a pragmatist, a man who can tangle with a Democrat but then cut a deal with him and go out for a bipartisan round of golf. Yet since he came to power in 1981, Michel has had to come to terms with a new wave of more confrontational, more ideologically motivated Reagan-era House Republicans.

Michel has tried to keep pace with the times. As he said in early 1989, after the latest and most serious challenge to his style of leadership, "From time to time you have to go with the flow. I think that part of my success has been the fact that I have been able to accommodate some of the vicissitudes of life that come up." Indeed, Michel has been eminently adaptable, although sometimes at the expense of a forceful image and clear direction.

The 101st Congress was a particularly turbulent one for Michel, as upheaval in the GOP ranks was followed soon after by a purge of the Democrats' leadership. In the March 1989 race for the open post of GOP whip, right-wing agitator Newt Gingrich of Georgia defeated Old Bull Edward Madigan of Illinois, whom Michel had backed. Within a few months, the Democrats' most assertive leaders, Speaker Jim Wright and Whip Tony Coelho, resigned amid scandal, and the more conciliatory Thomas S. Foley became Speaker.

The 1989 changes planted a burr on Michel's right flank while another was removed from his left. They have produced an uneasy mutual accommodation between Michel and Gingrich, and a competitive but relatively harmonious working relationship with Foley — the kind of bipartisan spirit that usually characterized Michel's dealings with Wright's predecessor as Speaker, Thomas P. O'Neill Jr.

Michel's adaptability, together with members' affection for him and his own instinct for House politics, have combined to carry him into a sixth term as leader. Among many Republicans — fellow bulls and devoted moderates — Michel is secure; the young Turks on the right, meanwhile, have thus far chosen to battle for lower leadership jobs, partly from a sense that Michel will retire from his post before long.

At several points in the 101st Congress, Michel did seem to be tiring of the chase — when the Republican Conference picked Gingrich for whip, signaling impatience with Michel's more accommodating brand of legislating; in the fall of 1990, when he confronted deep divisions within his party over taxes and a president weakened by the budget battle; in November, when the GOP lost House seats in the election; and at the end of 1990, when Illinois lost two House seats in reapportionment, and it appeared that his constituency could disappear in redistricting.

But the belief that Michel would retire at the end of the 102nd Congress — a view once widely held on Capitol Hill — began to wane in the early months of 1991.

Michel's redistricting worry was eased when President Bush selected Madigan to be Agriculture secretary. Michel had told his good friend Madigan that if a remap combined their neighboring seats, he would retire rather than oppose his younger colleague.

Most importantly, Michel was buoyed by the U.S. military triumph in the Middle East and Bush's resurgent popularity. "I'm certainly not in a discouraging mood," he said in March 1991. He confessed that at the end of 1990, "I was really in the downers. What's the use? We're so divided. Will we be able to pull this thing together? Lo and behold! Here comes Desert Shield and Storm!"

The World War II combat veteran had

Illinois 18

Central — Peoria

The 18th zigs and zags from Peoria south to the outskirts of Decatur and Springfield and west to Hancock County on the Mississippi. A mostly rural area, it is linked by the broad Illinois River basin, ideal for growing corn.

The district's troubled industrial base, centered in Peoria, is the 18th's dominant economic issue, however. The region has staged a modest comeback since the depths of the recession in the early 1980s. But many of the high-paying blue-collar jobs lost then have not returned.

Massive layoffs in the early 1980s by the Caterpillar Tractor Co., which has its international headquarters in Peoria and has several large plants in the district, caused severe economic dislocation. Michel had to fight to keep his seat during the 1982 recession.

His opponent that year, Democrat G. Douglas Stephens, staked a 1988 comeback attempt on the long-term effects of the industrial decline: Peoria's population had dropped about 9 percent, to under 115,000, since 1980. But Michel effectively presented his own sets of numbers, showing a slippage in unemployment and increased hiring by Caterpillar. There had also been an upswing in agricultural research, funded by federal money that Michel had channeled to the district.

Michel's 1988 victory over Stephens, as well as Ronald Reagan's and George Bush's success in the district, indicate that hard times have not had a lasting effect on the district's Republican tendencies. Bolstered by the GOP base in the district's more rural areas, Reagan captured 60 percent in the 18th in 1984; Bush took 55 percent four years later.

Peoria is the constant in a district whose lines have changed often during Michel's long tenure. In the 1960s Peoria anchored the southern end of the district; in the '70s it was in the center. Since 1982, it has been perched at the northern tip. Peoria and Tazewell (Pekin) counties are the only territories remaining from the district that elected Michel in 1970. The 18th now is a particularly fragmented constituency. Michel once represented eight counties and most of a ninth; now he is responsible not only for eight complete counties but also parts of eight more.

Population: 519,026. White 490,556 (95%), Black 23,919 (5%), Other 2,764 (1%). Spanish origin 3,728 (1%). 18 and over 368,659 (71%), 65 and over 62,341 (12%). Median age: 30.

joined New York Democrat Stephen J. Solarz to lead the House campaign for giving Bush authorization to use military force against Iraq. During debate over the joint resolution, Michel made an emotional plea to members not to forget the lessons of the past: "Those of our generation know from bloody experience that unchecked aggression against a small nation is a prelude to international disaster.... Patience at any price is not a policy. It is a cop-out." The House passed the Solarz-Michel joint resolution 250-183. Michel was the first member of Congress Bush notified when the U.S. bombing of Iraq started.

The success of the war resolution, along with a perception that Foley gives the House minority a fairer shake than it got under Wright, have helped Michel counter criticism of his legislative style from junior GOP firebrands. In the mid-1980s they began winning national media attention under the banner of the Conservative Opportunity Society (COS). COS leaders Gingrich and Vin Weber of Minnesota argued that Republicans should turn the House floor into a theater for partisan warfare, televised live on cable TV.

Michel's initial advice to the militants was to calm down. "It's one thing to be out there on the stump, flapping your gums," he said, "and it is another thing to put something together. Some of the greatest talkers around here can't legislate their way out of a paper bag." In 1984, when Gingrich lambasted 10 Democrats for advocating talks with Nicaragua, and O'Neill responded with a rare outburst that brought a rebuke from the presiding officer, many Republicans gave Gingrich a standing ovation. Michel kept his seat.

Though Michel had a poor personal relationship with Wright before and after he took over as Speaker in 1987, Michel remained aloof from Gingrich's crusade for the ethics inquiry that ultimately brought Wright down. As Wright's leadership crumbled in the opening months of the 101st Congress, Michel was mostly quiet.

What the COS began in the mid-1980s culminated in 1989 with Gingrich's election as GOP whip. It was a wake-up call to Michel that a majority of his House colleagues felt the need for more partisan zip at the top of GOP leadership ranks.

Michel is hardly one of the House's best orators, and he has no special policy expertise. His parliamentary skills are good, but not unusual. He is neither charismatic nor intimidating. This is how he once described his method for rounding up votes from colleagues: "You can't treat two alike," he once explained. "I know what I can get and what I can't, when to back off and when to push harder. It's not a matter of twisting arms. It's bringing them along by gentle persuasion."

The election of Gingrich as whip seemed to augur anything but "gentle persuasion" on the GOP side. "What that says to me," Michel said after Gingrich's defeat of Madigan, "is that they want us to be more activated and more visible and more aggressive, and that we can't be content with business as usual."

But instead of having to endure Gingrich and Wright putting the House through a daily partisan slugout, Michel has been able to deal with Speaker Foley, whose instincts are more judicial than partisan. As for Gingrich, he has on occasion played the part of loyal leadership man, but still seems more comfortable as an agitator of the right.

The late 1989 pay raise and ethics reform package was an early example of the new party leadership teams coexisting more peacefully. Congress had begun the year by rejecting a 51 percent pay raise. Then Foley and Michel put the full weight and prestige of their offices behind their pay raise package. It was a show of bipartisanship and leadership force missing in the first pay-raise drive, about which Wright had seemed lukewarm.

To build support for the new package, Democratic leaders attended a GOP party caucus; Republican leaders, including Gingrich, attended the Democratic caucus. The party's four campaign committee chairmen signed a letter to Foley and Michel promising to oppose using the pay-raise vote as a campaign issue. The House passed the bill 252-174, with 84 Republicans joining 168 Democrats to approve it.

Earlier in the year, Michel had given Gingrich a scolding after the Georgian appeared to announce unilaterally a party strategy at odds with Michel's on the sensitive topics of campaign-finance and ethics reform. "He, by his own admission, says he is still getting used to the ropes," Michel said. "I accept that." Gingrich added: "If I were Bob Michel, I'd be irritated, too."

Oddly, though, it was Michel who next stepped beyond the GOP consensus on campaign finance. A few months after the GOP Conference adopted a reform package negotiated between the young Turks and Old Bulls, Michel announced that he would consider agreeing to spending limits for House races if they were set high enough, perhaps at $1 million. The GOP agreement had specifically rejected spending caps, and few Republicans followed him.

The most drastic rent in the GOP quilt came in 1990, as Congress and the White House sought to craft an agreement on the fiscal 1991 budget. As the economic and deficit outlook worsened, pressure grew for high-level talks between congressional leaders and the White House to resolve basic tax and spending differences.

Bush retracted his key 1988 campaign promise, saying he would consider a tax increase, but he also wanted a cut in the capital gains tax. However, Gingrich, a member of the budget summit team, remained firmly opposed to new taxes; he was unwilling to relinquish such a central GOP theme.

After four and a half months of struggle, summit negotiators reached an accord. Michel was one of five members of Congress who negotiated the final deal with the White House. A pivotal moment in the talks came when Michel backed away from including a capital gains proposal in the agreement, saying that Democrats were demanding too much in exchange for it. "The doggone price is too steep," he said. Since Michel was regarded as the president's most loyal soldier on the Hill, his comments were considered devastating to Bush's chances for a capital gains tax cut.

But when the budget summit plan came to the floor, Gingrich defected along with most of the party's whip organization, leading a GOP revolt; the plan was rejected 179-254, and the federal government shut down. Congress stayed in session over the Columbus Day weekend to put together a fallback budget resolution.

For all the debate among House Republicans about the level of combat with Democrats, at times the greater frustration for Michel and his minions has been with fellow Republicans in the administration and Senate — especially during the six years the GOP held the Senate. Time after time in the Reagan years, Michel would object that House Republicans had not been consulted, but were expected to fall docilely in line.

In 1981, the White House had depended on Michel for a sense of strategy and timing in passing its budget and tax bills through the Democratic House; the virtual unanimity of the GOP vote, a combined 568-3 on the trio of measures, was partly a tribute to his skills. But Michel's job got harder as the Republicans' numbers declined with succeeding elections and as Democrats reunited; he no longer had the working majority of Republicans and Boll Weevil Democrats he enjoyed in his first term as leader. Also complicating Michel's work was Reagan's waning influence in the face of recession, flagging legislative ingenuity and finally the Iran-contra scandal.

With Democrats back in control of the Senate since 1987, Republicans in both chambers have sometimes felt like the odd men out in an agenda-setting process dominated by the White House and the Democrats' congressional leadership. But because GOP senators have larger individual platforms than Republican House members, the anxiety is more acute among Michel's troops in the House.

The current image of Michel as a moderate

coming to terms with militant conservatism would surprise anyone familiar with the House in the 1960s, when he was clearly on the GOP right, an orthodox Midwestern Republican decrying wasteful government.

Back then, the GOP was split between conservatives of his stripe and Northeastern moderates. Since that time, the moderates have declined while a Sun Belt-based power bloc, committed to a New Right social agenda and supply-side economics, has emerged. Michel votes with this new group on social issues, though he does not stress them. To carry out Reagan's economic program, he had to shelve his traditional conservative view that reducing deficits is a higher priority than reducing taxes. But as Michel's district hit hard times, some of the Reaganomics votes popular among Southern and Western Republicans did not play well in Peoria, as Michel's near-loss in 1982 proved.

Michel's ties to the moderate wing of the GOP brought him their support when he ran for party leader in 1981, and they reluctantly backed Reagan's first budget partly as a favor to him. Late that year, he dissuaded some conservatives from forming a pro-Reagan group to counter the moderate Gypsy Moths, saying of them, "They're too good as people to dismiss. I love those guys, even if we've been voting on opposite sides for years."

Most Reaganites had backed Guy Vander Jagt of Michigan for House GOP leader in 1981. But Michel won the 103-87 decision on the same qualities that until recent years traditionally won GOP leadership races — cloakroom companionship, homespun Midwestern conservatism, aptitude for legislative detail and a grasp of the rules.

Like his immediate predecessors, John J. Rhodes and Gerald R. Ford, Michel is a product of the collegial Appropriations Committee. He spent a quarter-century there focused on details rather than broad policy, but became an able negotiator in the process. On its Labor-Health, Education and Welfare Subcommittee, for years he opposed a working majority of liberals and Republicans; annually, he complained that the subcommittee's bill cost too much.

The Michel-Vander Jagt race began in December 1979, when Rhodes announced his impending retirement. Michel had an advantage among senior members and moderates, but Vander Jagt, as chairman of the campaign committee that donated money to GOP candidates, had the edge among those recently elected.

The sparring extended to the 1980 GOP convention. When Vander Jagt was selected as keynote speaker, Michel's forces complained and their man was made Reagan's floor manager. The election brought 52 new Republicans, more than even Vander Jagt had imagined. But by giving Republicans control of the White House and Senate, the election actually helped Michel; he argued successfully that Reagan needed a legislative tactician in the House, not a fiery speaker. Vander Jagt got most of the newcomers, but Michel got the leadership job.

At Home: Serious economic problems in Michel's district during the 1980s resulted in threatening challenges by Democratic labor lawyer G. Douglas Stephens in 1982 and 1988. But after Stephens' two failed efforts, district Democrats opted to await the outcome of redistricting: He ran without Democratic opposition in 1990.

Michel's position at the top of the Republican leadership has earned him the respect, but not the awe, of his constituents. Michel was often called to task for supporting Reagan administration policies that many voters believed were hurtful, or at least less than helpful, to the district's industrial workers and farmers.

Running at the height of the 1982 recession, Democrat Stephens held Michel to 52 percent, his closest call ever. But while Stephens was equally relentless and better funded in 1988, the stabilized local economy and an attentive campaign brought Michel a more comfortable 55 percent.

Stephens' 1982 surge caught Michel by surprise. The Democrat, then 31, was making his first bid for elective office. But Stephens told voters that Michel's role as chief mover of Reagan programs in the House put him at odds with the district's factory workers, farmers, small-business people, poor and elderly, all of whom Stephens said had been hurt.

The Democrat criticized Michel particularly for failing to persuade Reagan to lift U.S. sanctions on selling natural gas pipeline equipment to the Soviet Union. Those sanctions cost Caterpillar Tractor Co. and other Illinois equipment companies lucrative contracts, exacerbating already high unemployment.

Michel's task was complicated by redistricting: some 45 percent of his district's residents were new to him. Initially slow to counterattack, Michel began to cast Stephens as a puppet of organized labor and a negativist foe with a limited record of community involvement. Reagan appeared in the district in Michel's behalf and hinted at the forthcoming removal of sanctions on the pipeline equipment sales.

In the two most populous counties of the district — Peoria and Tazewell — Stephens held Michel to 51 percent, and he finished first in four other counties. But Michel's slim margins in the 10 remaining counties pulled him to victory by 6,125 votes.

By 1984, circumstances had shifted in Michel's favor. Although the national economic recovery had not enveloped the 18th, the worst of the recession was over, and Reagan was more popular. Michel changed his political style, setting up a campaign organization early and dropping his long-held aversion to trumpeting federal projects he had attained for the district. With Stephens bypassing the contest, Michel went over 60 percent, and stayed there in 1986.

Hoping that the end of the Reagan era would portend a Democratic year, Stephens tried again in 1988. He insisted that declining unemployment figures masked the downfall of the region's industries and exodus of their blue-collar workers from the area.

But Michel was ready for Stephens' challenge. He presented statistics showing how the district economy had improved, and pointed to Caterpillar's modest rehiring. He also boasted of the public works and agricultural research projects he had obtained. Michel's win in Peoria County was marginal and he lost Tazewell, but he swept nearly all the remaining counties.

Michel was born in Peoria, the son of a French immigrant factory worker. Shortly after graduating from Bradley University in Peoria, he went to work for the district's new representative, Republican Harold Velde.

Velde became chairman of the old House Un-American Activities Committee during the Republican-dominated 83rd Congress (1953-55) and received much publicity for his hunt for communist subversives. Michel rose to become Velde's administrative assistant.

In 1956 Velde retired, and Michel ran for the seat. Not very well-known in the district, Michel still had the support of many county organizations, for whom he had been a political contact in Washington. He won the primary with 48 percent against four opponents.

Ironically, Michel's predecessor was among the last House Republican committee chairmen. Democrats recaptured a House majority in the 1954 election and have held it ever since. Michel and Republican colleague William S. Broomfield hold the all-time record for continuous House membership without ever being in the majority.

Minority Leader

Elections

1990 General		
Robert H. Michel (R)	105,693	(98%)
1988 General		
Robert H. Michel (R)	114,458	(55%)
G. Douglas Stephens (D)	94,763	(45%)

Previous Winning Percentages: **1986** (63%) **1984** (61%) **1982** (52%) **1980** (62%) **1978** (66%) **1976** (58%) **1974** (55%) **1972** (65%) **1970** (66%) **1968** (61%) **1966** (58%) **1964** (54%) **1962** (61%) **1960** (59%) **1958** (60%) **1956** (59%)

District Vote For President

	1988	1984	1980	1976
D	94,732 (45%)	89,490 (40%)	71,861 (32%)	92,613 (44%)
R	114,841 (55%)	135,170 (60%)	137,198 (61%)	114,120 (55%)
I			12,710 (6%)	

Campaign Finance

	Receipts	Receipts from PACs	Expend-itures
1990			
Michel (R)	$705,878	$519,161 (74%)	$579,258
1988			
Michel (R)	$874,026	$555,417 (64%)	$861,969
Stephens (D)	$242,764	$80,600 (33%)	$231,511

Key Votes

1991	
Authorize use of force against Iraq	Y
1990	
Support constitutional amendment on flag desecration	Y
Pass family and medical leave bill over Bush veto	N
Reduce SDI funding	N
Allow abortions in overseas military facilities	N
Approve budget summit plan for spending and taxing	Y
Approve civil rights bill	N
1989	
Halt production of B-2 stealth bomber at 13 planes	N
Oppose capital gains tax cut	N
Approve federal abortion funding in rape or incest cases	N
Approve pay raise and revision of ethics rules	Y
Pass Democratic minimum wage plan over Bush veto	N

Voting Studies

	Presidential Support		Party Unity		Conservative Coalition	
Year	S	O	S	O	S	O
1990	75	18	78	15	91	6
1989	88	9	75 †	17 †	90	7
1988	64	30	76	14	82	8
1987	77 †	17 †	85 †	9 †	93 †	2 †
1986	74	18	73	20	76	18
1985	85	11	78 †	15 †	91	7
1984	75	20	80	11	90	3
1983	84	7	71 †	20 †	81	15
1982	83	12	81	16	89	10
1981	80	17	82 †	11 †	83	13

† Not eligible for all recorded votes.

Interest Group Ratings

Year	ADA	ACU	AFL-CIO	CCUS
1990	11	76	0	71
1989	10	84	18	89
1988	10	92	31	85
1987	0	86	6	86
1986	5	86	8	88
1985	5	86	6	81
1984	5	82	8	81
1983	5	81	12	100
1982	5	82	10	80
1981	10	86	0	100

19 Terry L. Bruce (D)

Of Olney — Elected 1984

Born: March 25, 1944, Olney, Ill.
Education: U. of Illinois, B.S. 1966, J.D. 1969.
Occupation: Lawyer; farmer.
Family: Wife, Charlotte Roberts; two children.
Religion: Methodist.
Political Career: Ill. Senate, 1971-85; Democratic nominee for U.S. House, 1978.
Capitol Office: 419 Cannon Bldg. 20515; 225-5001.

In Washington: The legislative know-how acquired over 14 years in the Illinois Senate helped ensure that, among the freshman class of 1984, Bruce would be one of the quickest out of the blocks. After just one term, Bruce won a much-coveted seat on the Energy and Commerce Committee, where he was soon in the thick of deliberations over clean-air legislation.

But Bruce stumbled during the 101st Congress, when his deal-making on clean air riled committee Chairman John D. Dingell. That tiff may slow his progress on the committee, although it does not appear to have curbed Bruce's legislative energies overall.

It was Bruce's deft courtship of Dingell that got him on the Energy and Commerce panel so swiftly. Bruce made it clear he was the sort Dingell wanted — a liberal team player on most issues, but not a down-the-line environmentalist who would fight the chairman over controversial clean-air legislation.

While Bruce represents a sizable liberal academic community at the University of Illinois at Champaign-Urbana, he must balance their concerns against those of constituents who work in the coal and auto industries and could be hurt by tough environmental legislation.

Bruce got a fast start on the committee, hooking up with an ad hoc caucus of key moderate-to-conservative Democrats who worked behind the scenes to try to break a six-year deadlock on reauthorizing the Clean Air Act. On the full Energy and Commerce Committee, Dingell and more industry-oriented members had been at odds with California Democrat Henry A. Waxman and an environmentalist faction for years over anti-smog and anti-acid rain measures. The so-called "group of nine," to which Bruce belonged, hoped to find some acceptable compromise in the 101st Congress.

When dealing on the bill began in earnest, Bruce was generally aligned with Dingell. By siding with Dingell on certain key issues, Bruce expected to get the chairman's aid in crafting acid rain provisions that would not unduly harm his Illinois district.

By late 1989, however, Bruce felt Dingell was not living up to his end of the bargain and he began to cut his own deals with Waxman and others. Bruce's maneuverings did help win committee votes allowing Midwestern utilities to sell pollution "credits" and to promote ethanol, which is made from corn grown in districts such as the 19th, as a car fuel.

But Bruce's moves alienated Dingell, who left him off the conference committee for the clean-air bill. And Bruce likely did not improve his standing with the chairman or some colleagues by sharing the whole saga with *The Washington Post.* Reflecting on Dingell's decision to leave him off the conference committee, Bruce told the *Post*, "I played by one set of rules, and he played by another. Good deeds do not get rewarded unless they're his good deeds."

But if Dingell plans to clip Bruce's wings on Energy and Commerce, Bruce himself appears undaunted.

Early in the 102nd Congress, he introduced a bill to provide tax credits for pollution equipment for coal-burning facilities. Bruce said the Clean Air Act had not done enough to promote coal, an important alternative to imported oil.

Bruce, who strongly backs organized labor, has also been outspoken on several trade issues. During the 101st, he fought administration plans to build the FS-X fighter jet jointly with Japan, saying the deal would give away valuable American technological know-how.

He was also an early skeptic of President Bush's proposed free trade pact with Mexico, wary that such an agreement would jeopardize American jobs. He stepped up those criticisms in 1991, urging that any agreement include a "social charter" that commits both countries to enforcing certain environmental, labor and consumer protections.

Bruce is a member of the Rural Health Care Caucus, and during the 101st Congress backed successful legislation to fund research projects on Alzheimer's disease and home health care.

During the 100th Congress, Bruce had worked to place limits on the advertising that

Illinois 19

Southeast — Danville; Champaign-Urbana

The Republican tradition in the Corn Belt counties that make up much of the 19th has not changed. However, the addition of the university town of Champaign in the redistricting of the 1980s made Democratic candidates for national office somewhat more competitive, and has helped make Democrat Bruce a dominant figure in the district.

Before the last redistricting, the largest city in the 19th was Danville (population 34,000). But the remap brought in three-quarters of Champaign County, including the University of Illinois. Champaign and its twin city of Urbana together have about 100,000 people, and the university influence leads them into the Democratic column in many statewide contests. When he toppled GOP incumbent Crane in 1984, Democrat Bruce took almost two-thirds in Champaign County. But in 1988, George Bush carried the county (part of which is in the 15th District) with 53 percent of the vote.

Danville, in Vermillion County, has deep Republican roots: It sent autocratic Republican Speaker Joseph G. Cannon to Congress for 30 years, around the beginning of this century. But it is also an aging industrial center whose blue-collar population provides a Democratic tinge. Democrat Michael S. Dukakis took Vermillion County with 52 percent in 1988.

Dukakis fell just short in the southernmost counties, where oil and coal are the major industries. Hamilton and White counties are laced with stripper oil wells. White has been the major oil-producing county in the state, with Hamilton not far behind. Bush carried Hamilton County by just four votes, and won White County with 51 percent.

However, the Republican built his winning edge in the 19th by sweeping through the farm counties in between. He carried Effingham, one of the larger rural counties, with 65 percent.

Population: 518,350. White 491,245 (95%), Black 20,051 (4%), Other 4,403 (1%). Spanish origin 4,254 (1%). 18 and over 386,732 (75%), 65 and over 68,713 (13%). Median age: 29.

can be shown on children's television, and to encourage broadcasters to provide educational programming for children. The Federal Communications Commission had abolished limits in 1984, and Bruce, along with Democrats John Bryant of Texas and Edward J. Markey of Massachusetts, felt new restrictions were necessary. Congress passed legislation that was somewhat softer than Bruce had pushed, but President Reagan, citing concerns about freedom of speech, killed it with a pocket veto. However, a version of the bill did pass and become law during the 101st.

At Home: Bruce lost his first House bid to Republican Daniel B. Crane in 1978, but evened the score by unseating Crane in 1984.

When Crane won the open-seat House race in 1978, he took the 19th District out of Democratic hands for the first time in two decades. Crane won re-election twice, but in 1983 he was censured by the House for an affair with a female congressional page several years earlier. For a conservative "family advocate" like Crane, the episode was devastating; yet his defeat was no foregone conclusion. He spent the summer campaigning, and he went on TV early with hard-hitting ads attacking Bruce for "flip-flopping" on issues such as the Equal Rights Amendment, which Bruce belatedly had come to support.

When Bruce's ads hit the airwaves, however, they made their point. Crane's 1982 foe had aggressively attacked the incumbent as ineffective, and Bruce pursued the same issue. He scored Crane for never having passed a bill, for missing committee hearings, for his mention in the *Washington Monthly* as one of the House's worst members, and for the censure.

Crane had tried hard to minimize the impact of the scandal, tearfully apologizing to his colleagues and making the rounds of the 19th to plead for his constituents' forgiveness. For a time, the issue seemed to die down. But Bruce's ads reawakened it and tied it to the matter of Crane's general performance in the House. With the help of organized labor and liberal activists, Bruce swamped Crane in Champaign, offsetting his deficit elsewhere in the district; he won with 52 percent.

Bruce quickly established himself, winning with 66 percent of the vote in 1986. Two years later, district Republicans put up Robert F. Kerans, a staunchly conservative aviation consultant: Bruce won with 64 percent, even as George Bush was winning the 19th District's presidential vote by a wide margin.

Republicans held out some hope for the 1990 House contest against Bruce, touting lawyer Lane Harvey as an up-and-coming candidate. But Harvey failed to get past a Republican primary with a comeback-minded Kerans, who took 52 percent of the GOP vote. Bruce had even less trouble with Kerans the second time around, winning with 66 percent.

Committees

Energy & Commerce (19th of 27 Democrats)
Commerce, Consumer Protection & Competitiveness; Energy & Power; Health & the Environment

Science, Space & Technology (13th of 32 Democrats)
Energy; Science

Elections

1990 General		
Terry L. Bruce (D)	113,958	(66%)
Robert F. Kerans (R)	55,680	(32%)
Brian James O'Neill II (IL SOL)	2,250	(1%)
1988 General		
Terry L. Bruce (D)	132,889	(64%)
Robert F. Kerans (R)	73,981	(36%)

Previous Winning Percentages: **1986** (66%) **1984** (52%)

District Vote For President

	1988	1984	1980	1976
D	95,599 (45%)	86,323 (38%)	78,359 (34%)	101,969 (46%)
R	114,212 (54%)	141,611 (62%)	131,504 (57%)	117,017 (53%)
I			16,801 (7%)	

Campaign Finance

	Receipts	Receipts from PACs		Expend-itures
1990				
Bruce (D)	$471,745	$306,491	(65%)	$258,093
Kerans (R)	$3,418	$250	(7%)	$3,581
1988				
Bruce (D)	$457,955	$276,182	(60%)	$193,205
Kerans (R)	$16,445	$1,250	(8%)	$16,241

Key Votes

1991	
Authorize use of force against Iraq	N
1990	
Support constitutional amendment on flag desecration	N
Pass family and medical leave bill over Bush veto	Y
Reduce SDI funding	Y
Allow abortions in overseas military facilities	N
Approve budget summit plan for spending and taxing	N
Approve civil rights bill	Y
1989	
Halt production of B-2 stealth bomber at 13 planes	Y
Oppose capital gains tax cut	Y
Approve federal abortion funding in rape or incest cases	N
Approve pay raise and revision of ethics rules	N
Pass Democratic minimum wage plan over Bush veto	Y

Voting Studies

	Presidential Support		Party Unity		Conservative Coalition	
Year	**S**	**O**	**S**	**O**	**S**	**O**
1990	20	80	90	9	33	67
1989	33	67	86	14	34	66
1988	23	77	89	9	39	61
1987	14	79	88	5	23	67
1986	20	80	88	12	34	66
1985	29	71	89	10	25	75

Interest Group Ratings

Year	ADA	ACU	AFL-CIO	CCUS
1990	83	8	100	36
1989	75	14	83	30
1988	75	24	100	36
1987	80	9	94	13
1986	80	9	100	33
1985	70	19	76	36

20 Richard J. Durbin (D)

Of Springfield — Elected 1982

Born: Nov. 21, 1944, East St. Louis, Ill.
Education: Georgetown U., B.S. 1966, J.D. 1969.
Occupation: Lawyer; congressional and legislative aide.
Family: Wife, Loretta Schaefer; three children.
Religion: Roman Catholic.
Political Career: Democratic nominee for Ill. Senate, 1976; Democratic nominee for lieutenant governor, 1978.
Capitol Office: 129 Cannon Bldg. 20515; 225-5271.

In Washington: Durbin came to Congress with an understanding of its rules and a knack for playing its internal politics — a combination that has given him the savvy and self-assurance to act the parts of both insider and insurgent.

An amiable man with the face of an aging choirboy, he is well-acquainted with legislative procedure, having been a parliamentarian of the Illinois Senate; from the start, House leaders tapped him to preside over the chamber even during controversial debates. Like a number of Democrats first elected in the 1982 recession, he is a budget-conscious liberal trying to rebuild his party's fiscal credibility. He quickly emerged as a popular figure among younger House members, while forging ties with current leaders that got him a prize seat on Appropriations in his second term.

At the same time, Durbin has challenged Appropriations' hierarchy, bucking its stricture against controversial amendments and otherwise opposing the powerful "College of Cardinals" subcommittee chairmen. Durbin escapes harsh judgment thanks to his geniality, articulate argument and sense of fair play, but those qualities have not yet been enough to earn him a place on the party leadership ladder. He finished last in a four-way race for Democratic Caucus vice chairman in June 1989. He was mentioned in 1990 as a possible candidate for the chairmanship of the Democratic Congressional Campaign Committee, but did not run.

Legislatively, however, the 101st Congress brought Durbin the victory of a lifetime when Congress approved a permanent ban on cigarette smoking on domestic airline flights. The battle pitted him against two Appropriations subcommittee chairmen, the tobacco lobby and conventional wisdom. But Durbin succeeded in putting Congress on record for the first time proscribing smoking for health reasons.

Durbin, whose chain-smoking father died of lung cancer when Durbin was 14, was roused to action in 1987 after taking a Phoenix-to-Chicago flight on which he had to sit between two smokers. He first tried to get the Appropriations Committee to approve an amendment to ban smoking on all flights. When that was defeated, he limited the ban and carried the battle to the House floor, a step akin to airing family laundry for an Appropriations member.

After an emotional debate, the House passed Durbin's measure, 198-193, surprising even him. With support from New Jersey Sen. Frank R. Lautenberg, chairman of the Senate's Transportation Appropriations Subcommittee, a similar measure passed in the Senate. The compromise that became law banned smoking on flights of two hours or less for a two-year trial period.

In the 101st Congress, Durbin bypassed the Appropriations Committee altogether, going instead to the Rules Committee with a request to offer a floor amendment to the transportation spending bill for a total ban. Rules rejected his bid, but with the acquiescence of the tobacco lobby — which was hoping to limit its losses — Durbin was allowed to offer an amendment making the existing ban permanent. It passed the House handily, while the Senate passed a total ban. Conferees agreed to the tougher language, excluding only a small number of flights, after Durbin threatened to bring his fight back to the floor. The ban went into effect Feb. 25, 1991.

Two in particular who will never forget his victory are Appropriations "Cardinals" William H. Natcher and W. G. "Bill" Hefner, from the tobacco states of Kentucky and North Carolina, respectively. "It was clear to me from the start that there were political risks involved ... because of the grudges that might result," said Durbin afterward. But so far, broad public support for his efforts has tempered any retribution.

Durbin also made national headlines when he took to the floor, as colleagues intoned about a proposed constitutional amendment to ban flag desecration, to decry "the desecration of a great American symbol ... the baseball bat." His lampooning referred to baseball purists against the shift away from wooden bats toward aluminum bats. "Are we ready to see the Louisville Slugger replaced by the aluminum ping

Illinois 20

Central — Springfield; Decatur; Quincy

The 20th District sweeps across Illinois at mid-state, starting in traditionally Democratic counties and working its way west to Republican territory along the Missouri border. Redistricting in 1981 took away the suburbs of Springfield and other good GOP areas, boosting the prospects of statewide Democratic candidates in the 20th, and providing a cushion for Durbin once he established himself as the district's Democratic House member.

But while Democrat Michael S. Dukakis was quite competitive in the 20th, George Bush kept it in the Republican presidential column with 51 percent of the vote in 1988. Four years earlier, Ronald Reagan took the district with 58 percent.

The 20th has the Mississippi River port of Quincy and the inner-city section of Springfield, with the state Capitol and a substantial bloc of white-collar workers in state government. Springfield and surrounding Sangamon County cast more than 30 percent of the district vote.

Agriculture remains the economic base of the district, thanks to the rich bottom lands of the Illinois and Mississippi rivers. Hogs, corn and soybeans are important; the soybean market in Decatur sets prices for a large area of the Midwest. But coal has more importance in the 20th than it once did, with the addition in 1981 redistricting of the mining counties of Christian, Shelby and Moultrie. The third-largest coal mine in the world is in Macoupin County.

The Southern Democratic traditions of these southern Illinois counties have shifted somewhat. Reagan carried all three counties easily both in 1980 and 1984, and Bush carried Shelby and Moultrie. However, Democrat Neil Hartigan won Christian and Shelby counties in his unsuccessful 1990 gubernatorial bid.

The industrial city of Decatur (population 84,000), can be counted on to vote Democratic in most elections. For more than half a century, one of Decatur's leading employers has been the Staley company, a soybean processing firm; the Decatur Staleys were one of the original teams in the National Football League.

Population: 519,015. White 489,038 (94%), Black 26,679 (5%). Spanish origin 2,666 (1%). 18 and over 375,764 (72%), 65 and over 75,365 (15%). Median age: 32.

dinger?" he asked. "Is nothing sacred?"

Humor aside, Durbin's vocal opposition to the flag amendment was consistent with his increasingly outspoken partisanship. He is among those who complain that congressional Democrats negotiate too long and too much with the Republican administration. Early in 1990, as the party leadership debated whether to proceed with a budget summit, Durbin said no. "I, for one, would rather see us do battle with the Republicans over budget priorities," he said. "If we as a party can't stand together and say what we are for, then why are we here?"

In that vein, he joined with Florida Democrat Charles E. Bennett in early 1991, as the country headed toward war with Iraq, to introduce a resolution asserting congressional war-making powers. "The decision to go to war should not be left to one man," the two wrote. With little controversy, the resolution passed 302-131. While Durbin argued passionately against the use of force, he said the subsequent congressional vote on that issue demonstrated that "the Constitution prevailed."

At the same time, early in 1991, Durbin called on the Bush administration to exert more pressure on the Soviet Union to withdraw from the Baltic states. A first-generation Lithuanian-American, Durbin a year earlier had led a congressional delegation to Lithuania; the delegation had hoped to observe the elections, but visa problems delayed their arrival until after the voting. In June 1990, the House approved a Durbin amendment to the Export Administration bill to prohibit the easing of economic restrictions on exports to the U.S.S.R. until the Soviet government began negotiations toward Lithuanian self-determination.

Durbin opposes abortion on demand, and he had opposed federal funding of abortion even in cases of rape and incest. But in 1989, with heightened attention on the issue, Durbin said his past votes had "haunted" him. After meeting with victims of incest in his district, he supported federal abortion funding for poor women who are victims of rape or incest, or whose lives are in danger.

Durbin is well-placed on Appropriations to look after his district, which has both farmland and urban areas such as Springfield. Combining his roles on the Agriculture and Transportation Subcommittees, Durbin is a spokesman for ethanol-based fuels, which are made from corn.

In the 100th Congress, he joined the Budget Committee, taking one of the slots reserved for an Appropriations representative. Appropriations Chairman Jamie L. Whitten reminded Durbin that he was an Appropriations member on Budget, and not the other way around. Still, Durbin joined with other junior Appropriations members to coax Whitten to comply with the non-binding budget resolution — or face threats of across-the-board cuts on the floor. Whitten reluctantly did so.

At Home: Just as he rose rapidly to become a key player in the House, Durbin quickly became ensconced in the 20th. In 1982, Durbin unseated 11-term GOP Rep. Paul N. Findley by 1,410 votes; two years later, Durbin was already over 60 percent.

Redistricting helped Durbin in his bid to unseat Findley. A Democratic-oriented remap had transformed the 20th from about 53 percent Republican to about 53 percent Democratic, and gave Findley more than 175,000 new and unfamiliar constituents.

That was only one of several factors favoring Durbin. The district's agricultural economy was dismal in 1982; layoffs in the slumping farm-implement industry burdened the blue-collar work force and damaged Findley.

Durbin also benefited from generous financing by pro-Israel groups offended by Findley's liaisons with the Palestine Liberation Organization. Findley would later write a book excoriating the influence of the "Israel lobby," which he blamed in large part for his defeat.

Though Durbin barely edged the veteran incumbent, within two years he was clearly in charge. Republican Richard Austin, chairman of the Sangamon County (Springfield) Board, ran in 1984, but was hopelessly overmatched. Durbin's visible efforts to funnel redevelopment funds to depressed communities paid political dividends. He carried every county.

By 1986 the GOP appeared to have given up. Then and since, Durbin has won easily.

Durbin's political mentor was Democrat Paul Simon, now Illinois' junior senator. When Simon became lieutenant governor in 1969, he hired Durbin as an adviser. Following Simon's loss in the 1972 gubernatorial primary, Durbin became chief Democratic staff aide on the Illinois Senate Judiciary Committee, and then Senate parliamentarian. Although he lost for state Senate in 1976 and for lieutenant governor in 1978, those contests turned out to be training for Durbin's successful House runs.

Committees

Appropriations (27th of 37 Democrats)
Rural Development, Agriculture & Related Agencies; Transportation

Budget (5th of 23 Democrats)
Defense, Foreign Policy & Space (chairman); Economic Policy, Projections & Revenues; Human Resources

Select Children, Youth & Families (14th of 22 Democrats)

Elections

1990 General		
Richard J. Durbin (D)	130,114	(66%)
Paul E. Jurgens (R)	66,433	(34%)
1988 General		
Richard J. Durbin (D)	153,341	(69%)
Paul E. Jurgens (R)	69,303	(31%)

Previous Winning Percentages: **1986** (68%) **1984** (61%) **1982** (50%)

District Vote For President

	1988	1984	1980	1976
D	109,922 (49%)	99,163 (42%)	89,095 (38%)	114,032 (48%)
R	113,401 (51%)	135,523 (58%)	132,407 (57%)	119,329 (51%)
I			11,303 (5%)	

Campaign Finance

	Receipts	Receipts from PACs		Expend-itures
1990				
Durbin (D)	$338,066	$207,978	(62%)	$209,360
Jurgens (R)	$44,565	$10,500	(24%)	$44,861
1988				
Durbin (D)	$367,468	$220,605	(60%)	$251,634
Jurgens (R)	$58,532	$8,300	(14%)	$57,708

Key Votes

1991	
Authorize use of force against Iraq	N
1990	
Support constitutional amendment on flag desecration	N
Pass family and medical leave bill over Bush veto	Y
Reduce SDI funding	Y
Allow abortions in overseas military facilities	N
Approve budget summit plan for spending and taxing	N
Approve civil rights bill	Y
1989	
Halt production of B-2 stealth bomber at 13 planes	Y
Oppose capital gains tax cut	Y
Approve federal abortion funding in rape or incest cases	N
Approve pay raise and revision of ethics rules	N
Pass Democratic minimum wage plan over Bush veto	Y

Voting Studies

	Presidential Support		Party Unity		Conservative Coalition	
Year	**S**	**O**	**S**	**O**	**S**	**O**
1990	16	83	91	6	26	74
1989	24	76	95	4	12	88
1988	24	76	88	9	18	82
1987	13	84	91	5	19	77
1986	17	82	90	9	22	78
1985	28	73	79	19	20	78
1984	32	66	82	18	29	69
1983	13	85	77	17	31	69

Interest Group Ratings

Year	ADA	ACU	AFL-CIO	CCUS
1990	83	4	92	31
1989	95	4	83	30
1988	90	16	100	36
1987	92	4	94	0
1986	85	14	93	22
1985	65	19	82	36
1984	70	13	85	31
1983	85	13	76	20

21 Jerry F. Costello (D)

Of Belleville — Elected 1988

Born: Sept. 25, 1949, East St. Louis, Ill.
Education: Belleville Area College, A.A. 1970; Maryville College of the Sacred Heart, B.A. 1972.
Occupation: Law enforcement administrator.
Family: Wife, Georgia Cockrum; three children.
Religion: Roman Catholic.
Political Career: St. Clair County Board chairman, 1980-88.
Capitol Office: 119 Cannon Bldg. 20515; 225-5661.

In Washington: As an executive officer weaned in the smoky backrooms of St. Clair County, Costello came to Washington in 1988 well-schooled in the adage that all politics are local. What he soon discovered was that national politics can also become intensely personal.

When President Bush sent U.S. troops to the Persian Gulf, Costello was one of only two members to have sons or daughters on the line. While his 21-year-old son prepared for war with the 82nd Airborne Division near the Kuwait border, Costello agonized over his vote on a resolution to sanction the use of force. He voted against the resolution, telling The *Washington Post* that "if every member of Congress had a son or daughter in the Middle East, if the president had his son or his daughter in the Middle East in combat now, it might change their attitude to some extent. . . ."

Costello's wrestling with the global issue contrasted sharply with his usual concern — pursuing projects for a southwestern Illinois home front suffering from industrial decline. Gaining a politically helpful committee assignment on Public Works, he issued a stream of news releases on grants for the 21st, many of which had been in the pipeline during the tenure of his predecessor, Democratic Rep. Melvin Price, who died in office in 1988.

Entering his second full term, Costello has developed a reputation as an effective inside player in his own right, pursuing such local projects as a light-rail system linking his district to the job market on the St. Louis side of the Mississippi. In the 101st Congress, Costello also got seats on the Science and Select Aging committees.

At Home: In winning for the House, Costello has written the last three chapters of Republican Robert H. Gaffner's political odyssey. Gaffner has been the unsuccessful GOP candidate for the southwest Illinois House seat in six consecutive elections.

Most frustrating for Gaffner is that three times he came close to winning the seat. After twice losing soundly to Price, Gaffner nearly upset the aged incumbent in 1986. He then gave Costello fits in a 1988 special election and in the general election later that year. However, Costello secured the district by 1990. With Gaffner a reluctant stand-in for the candidate-poor district GOP, Costello won overwhelmingly.

Costello had huge advantages entering the 1988 House campaign to succeed Price, who had announced his retirement. The member of a prominent political family — his father served in the Illinois Legislature and as sheriff and later treasurer of St. Clair County — Costello was elected chairman of the county commission in 1980. He emerged as a dominant figure in his heavily Democratic region, serving at one point as chairman of the metropolitan St. Louis Council of Governments.

However, Costello wielded clout, critics said, in the hardball tradition of an urban-based St. Clair County Democratic machine.

In the March 1988 primary, Madison County Auditor Pete Fields tried to use Costello's image as a machine boss against him. Costello survived, but with a 46 percent plurality that turned out to be an omen for the August 1988 special election forced by Price's death that April.

Gaffner, a college official, copied the line of attack used by Costello's Democratic opponents. He ran ads suggesting that voters call Costello and quiz him about ethics questions.

Costello won the special election with 51.5 percent. In November with Gaffner belaboring the ethics issue to some effect, Costello again held on, winning just under 53 percent.

The 1990 contest was a different story. Gaffner entered only after no other Republican candidate came forward, and was distracted by an illness in his family. Costello, meanwhile, received positive publicity for his Public Works efforts, while avoiding the muddy waters of St. Clair County politics.

His improved standing was symbolized by a warm endorsement he received from the Belleville News Democrat, a longtime adversary that Costello had once sued for libel. The incumbent won with 66 percent.

Illinois 21

Southwest — East St. Louis; Alton

The southwestern Illinois region covered by the 21st has long been identified by the grimy industrial cities across the Mississippi River from St. Louis. But while the grime remains, much of the industry has left; the district's steel, petroleum-refining and glass industries have declined.

East St. Louis, formerly the district's dominant city, has suffered the most. A national meatpacking center as recently as the late 1960s, the city has been abandoned by manufacturing firms, and has also lost much of its retail base. A population decline of 21 percent in the 1970s, and another 10 percent drop between 1980 and 1986, have left East St. Louis with just under 50,000 residents, 95 percent of whom are black. Unemployment rates have lingered between 15 and 20 percent for the past five years; 60 percent of the city's residents are on welfare. One bright spot remains amid the despair — the East St. Louis High School Flyers have won the state football championship five of the last ten years.

Though the economic problems carry over to neighboring Belleville (population 43,000), the St. Clair County seat has weathered the vagaries somewhat better. The city includes a number of St. Louis commuters and a segment of minority poor.

With its blue-collar and minority populations (and an active coal-mining industry in its southern reaches), St. Clair remains one of the most dependable Democratic bastions south of Chicago. It is the home base of Democratic Sen. Alan J. Dixon; Democratic presidential candidate Michael S. Dukakis took 57 percent of its vote in 1988. However, with East St. Louis' decline and stagnant population growth elsewhere, St. Clair does not carry the weight it once did. Madison County to the north, which includes such industrial cities as Alton and Granite City, provides slightly more votes than St. Clair in most statewide elections. But Madison usually bolsters St. Clair's partisan direction: Dukakis won the county with 55 percent.

Three mainly rural counties — Bond, Montgomery and Clinton — fill out the balance of the district, and provide it with a Republican counterweight. Bond, the only one of the three entirely within the 21st, gave a slight edge to George Bush in 1988.

Population: 521,036. White 439,188 (84%), Black 76,733 (15%), Other 2,821 (1%). Spanish origin 5,779 (1%). 18 and over 367,291 (71%), 65 and over 62,217 (12%). Median age: 30.

Committees

Public Works & Transportation (21st of 36 Democrats)
Aviation; Surface Transportation; Water Resources

Science, Space & Technology (21st of 32 Democrats)
Energy; Science

Select Aging (29th of 42 Democrats)
Housing & Consumer Interests; Retirement, Income & Employment

Elections

1990 General		
Jerry F. Costello (D)	95,208	(66%)
Robert H. Gaffner (R)	48,949	(34%)
1988 General		
Jerry F. Costello (D)	105,836	(53%)
Robert H. Gaffner (R)	95,385	(47%)

Previous Winning Percentage: **1988** * (51%)

* *Special election.*

District Vote For President

	1988	1984	1980	1976
D	110,653 (54%)	100,109 (46%)	93,309 (45%)	120,941 (56%)
R	92,956 (46%)	114,839 (53%)	104,414 (50%)	92,047 (43%)
I			8,437 (4%)	

Campaign Finance

	Receipts	Receipts from PACs	Expend-itures
1990			
Costello (D)	$654,131	$231,550 (35%)	$380,559
Gaffner (R)	$24,670	0	$26,230
1988			
Costello (D)	$1,106,495	$329,661 (30%)	$1,106,233
Gaffner (R)	$159,271	$33,798 (21%)	$157,171

Key Votes

1991	
Authorize use of force against Iraq	N
1990	
Support constitutional amendment on flag desecration	Y
Pass family and medical leave bill over Bush veto	Y
Reduce SDI funding	Y
Allow abortions in overseas military facilities	N
Approve budget summit plan for spending and taxing	N
Approve civil rights bill	Y
1989	
Halt production of B-2 stealth bomber at 13 planes	N
Oppose capital gains tax cut	Y
Approve federal abortion funding in rape or incest cases	N
Approve pay raise and revision of ethics rules	N
Pass Democratic minimum wage plan over Bush veto	Y

Voting Studies

	Presidential Support		Party Unity		Conservative Coalition	
Year	**S**	**O**	**S**	**O**	**S**	**O**
1990	26	73	86	14	48	52
1989	36	63	79	20	59	41
1988	24 †	76 †	86 †	11 †	67 †	33 †

† *Not eligible for all recorded votes.*

Interest Group Ratings

Year	ADA	ACU	AFL-CIO	CCUS
1990	67	29	92	36
1989	70	18	92	40
1988	-	57	100	-

22 Glenn Poshard (D)

Of Carterville — Elected 1988

Born: Oct. 30, 1945, Herald, Ill.
Education: Southern Illinois U., B.S. 1970, M.S. 1974, Ph.D. 1984.
Military Service: Army, 1962-65.
Occupation: Educator.
Family: Wife, Jo Roetzel; two children.
Religion: Baptist.
Political Career: Sought nomination for Ill. Senate, 1982; Ill. Senate, 1984-89.
Capitol Office: 314 Cannon Bldg. 20515; 225-5201.

In Washington: An intellectual with working-class roots, Poshard is engaging and earnest. He has a conservative demeanor and outlook, but his rural southern Illinois constituency has pressing needs, and he usually votes like a traditional labor Democrat.

As a freshman, he supported Democratic efforts to increase the minimum wage, and unsuccessful bids to enact the Family and Medical Leave Act and the 1990 civil rights bill.

Poshard's background made him a natural for a spot on the Education and Labor Committee. He was one of four freshmen named to that committee for the 101st Congress, and he also took a seat on Small Business. Although he endorses such conservative budgetary tools as the line-item veto and the balanced budget amendment, overall in his first term, Poshard voted with a majority of Democrats more than 80 percent, and against President Bush more than 70 percent, of the time.

Poshard initially backed a constitutional amendment to ban flag desecration, but later said that trips to Philadelphia and Gettysburg led him to conclude that First Amendment protection of freedom of speech extended to flag burning. He voted against the amendment.

One of his rare high-profile votes against the Democratic leadership was Clean Air. Stressing the devastating effect the legislation would have on his coal-mining district, he was one of 20 House members to oppose the bill.

Poshard drew national attention when he queried the Navy's handling of the investigation of the April 1989 explosion aboard the USS *Iowa*. Unofficial news leaks from the Navy implicated Petty Officer Kendall Truitt, a 22nd District resident, in a murder-suicide pact with Clayton Hartwig, a sailor who died in the blast. Poshard questioned the source of the leaks and cited the need to protect Truitt's rights. After much publicity, the inquiry into Truitt's role was dropped and his name cleared.

At Home: Poshard made a smooth transition from the state Legislature to the House. Using his state Senate district — which covered about half of the 22nd — as a springboard, Poshard won easily in 1988 to succeed retiring Democratic Rep. Kenneth J. Gray.

There were sharp contrasts between Poshard and his predecessor. Gray, known for his flashy clothes and boisterous personality, never attended college, and had worked as a car dealer and auctioneer. Poshard has a doctorate in educational administration, and he headed a regional program for gifted students.

However, Poshard has working-class roots. Like Gray, he exhibits a populist style that has appeal in the 22nd's coal-mining communities and Ohio River towns. It was Poshard's ability to address blue-collar concerns that first caught the eye of the local and state Democratic leadership. Although his 1982 primary challenge to a veteran Democratic state senator fell short, Poshard impressed party officials.

When the senator died in mid-1984, district Democratic leaders unanimously picked Poshard for the vacancy. Within months, Poshard defended the seat in a tough campaign against a Republican state House member. He coasted to re-election in 1986.

Poshard specialized in education, labor, rural health care and coal-related issues in Springfield. Some colleagues complained that Poshard was too much a young man in a hurry. But he was named keynote speaker for the 1986 state party convention and chairman of the Senate Labor and Commerce Committee.

When Poshard decided he would try to fill Gray's place, no Democrat stood in his way. His GOP foe, law professor Patrick Kelley, was articulate, but little-known outside Carbondale, where he had served two terms on the City Council. Kelley's efforts to frame the election as an ideological contest were easily deflected by Poshard, who is opposed to abortion and supportive of school prayer. Poshard won with 65 percent of the vote. In 1990, Poshard faced only an independent challenger, Jim Wham, who was unhappy with the incumbent's vote against the constitutional amendment to ban flag-burning. Poshard won with 84 percent.

Illinois 22

South — Carbondale

In the southern part of Illinois the prairies give way to hills, and coal mining replaces large-scale farming as a dominant economic activity. About 5,100 miners work in the Illinois Basin, a coal vein that runs under Franklin, Randolph, Williamson, Saline, Perry and Jefferson counties.

The people here are descendants of 19th-century settlers from places such as Kentucky and Tennessee. And like their peers farther south, the voters here have slipped from their conservative Democratic traditions: President Reagan won the 22nd with 56 percent of the vote in 1984. However, continued hard economic times in the coal country and in the fading Ohio River port towns have stemmed the Republican tide somewhat.

Carbondale (population 27,000) is the largest of the small cities that lie along the Main Street of the district: state Route 13. Carbondale is dominated by Southern Illinois University, with 24,000 students.

At the southern tip of the district is Alexander County, in the region called "Little Egypt." Situated at the confluence of the Mississippi and Ohio Rivers, the depressed river town of Cairo, the Alexander County seat, has as bitter a history of racial confrontation as almost any community in the Deep South. The underlying anger that culminated in the race riots of the 1960s has given way to a new resentment; over sixty-five percent of blacks between the ages of 20 and 30 are unemployed. Cairo is now majority black, and its vote helped Dukakis carry Alexander County with nearly 58 percent of its vote. Overall, Dukakis carried 10 district counties, including eight across the center of the district, for a total of 52 percent.

The Republican vote is most consistent in the farm territory toward the northern end of the district. In 1984, Washington County gave Reagan nearly 70 percent of its vote, and was one of only three counties in the district carried by Republican Jim Edgar in the 1990 gubernatorial contest. George Bush took 61 percent in 1988.

Population: 521,303. White 483,298 (93%), Black 33,771 (7%). Spanish origin 3,284 (1%). 18 and over 381,684 (73%), 65 and over 77,842 (15%). Median age: 31.

Committees

Public Works & Transportation (28th of 36 Democrats)
Aviation; Public Buildings & Grounds; Surface Transportation

Small Business (21st of 27 Democrats)
Environment & Employment; Procurement, Tourism & Rural Development

Elections

1990 General		
Glenn Poshard (D)	138,425	(84%)
Jim Wham (Jim Wham Party)	26,896	(16%)
1988 General		
Glenn Poshard (D)	139,392	(65%)
Patrick J. Kelley (R)	75,462	(35%)

District Vote For President

	1988	1984	1980	1976
D	113,071 (52%)	103,010 (43%)	95,562 (42%)	127,388 (54%)
R	104,886 (48%)	133,547 (56%)	125,032 (54%)	103,843 (44%)
I			8,427 (4%)	

Campaign Finance

	Receipts	Receipts from PACs		Expend-itures
1990				
Poshard (D)	$68,078	$5,150	(8%)	$103,396
Wham (Jim Wham)	$26,137	0		$16,737
1988				
Poshard (D)	$430,240	$248,970	(58%)	$392,791
Kelley (R)	$81,763	$15,872	(19%)	$80,675

Key Votes

1991	
Authorize use of force against Iraq	N
1990	
Support constitutional amendment on flag desecration	N
Pass family and medical leave bill over Bush veto	Y
Reduce SDI funding	Y
Allow abortions in overseas military facilities	N
Approve budget summit plan for spending and taxing	N
Approve civil rights bill	Y
1989	
Halt production of B-2 stealth bomber at 13 planes	Y
Oppose capital gains tax cut	Y
Approve federal abortion funding in rape or incest cases	N
Approve pay raise and revision of ethics rules	N
Pass Democratic minimum wage plan over Bush veto	Y

Voting Studies

	Presidential Support		Party Unity		Conservative Coalition	
Year	S	O	S	O	S	O
1990	23	77	85	14	43	57
1989	35	65	79	20	41	59

Interest Group Ratings

Year	ADA	ACU	AFL-CIO	CCUS
1990	78	29	92	29
1989	80	21	92	40

Indiana

U.S. CONGRESS

SENATE 2 R
HOUSE 8 D, 2 R

LEGISLATURE

Senate 24 D, 26 R
House 52 D, 48 R

ELECTIONS

1988 Presidential Vote

Bush	60%
Dukakis	40%

1984 Presidential Vote

Reagan	62%
Mondale	38%

1980 Presidential Vote

Reagan	56%
Carter	38%
Anderson	5%

Turnout rate in 1986	39%
Turnout rate in 1988	53%
Turnout rate in 1990	36%

(as percentage of voting age population)

POPULATION AND GROWTH

1980 population	5,490,224
1990 population (14th in the nation)	5,554,159
Percent change 1980-1990	+1%

DEMOGRAPHIC BREAKDOWN

White	91%
Black	8%
Asian or Pacific Islander	1%
(Hispanic origin)	2%
Urban	64%
Rural	36%
Born in state	71%
Foreign-born	2%

MAJOR CITIES

Indianapolis	731,327
Fort Wayne	173,072
Evansville	126,272
Gary	116,646
South Bend	105,511

AREA AND LAND USE

Area 35,932 sq. miles (38th)

Farm	71%
Forest	19%
Federally owned	2%

Gov. Evan Bayh (D)
Of Indianapolis — Elected 1988

Born: Dec. 26, 1955, Terre Haute, Ind.
Education: Indiana U., B.S. 1978; U. of Virginia, J.D. 1981.
Occupation: Lawyer.
Religion: Christian.
Political Career: Ind. secretary of state, 1986-89.
Next Election: 1992.

WORK

Occupations

White-collar	47%
Blue-collar	38%
Service workers	13%

Government Workers

Federal	41,639
State	104,612
Local	221,316

MONEY

Median family income	$ 20,535 (18th)
Tax burden per capita	$ 789 (33rd)

EDUCATION

Spending per pupil through grade 12	$ 3,794 (31st)
Persons with college degrees	13% (45th)

CRIME

Violent crime rate	407 per 100,000 (29th)

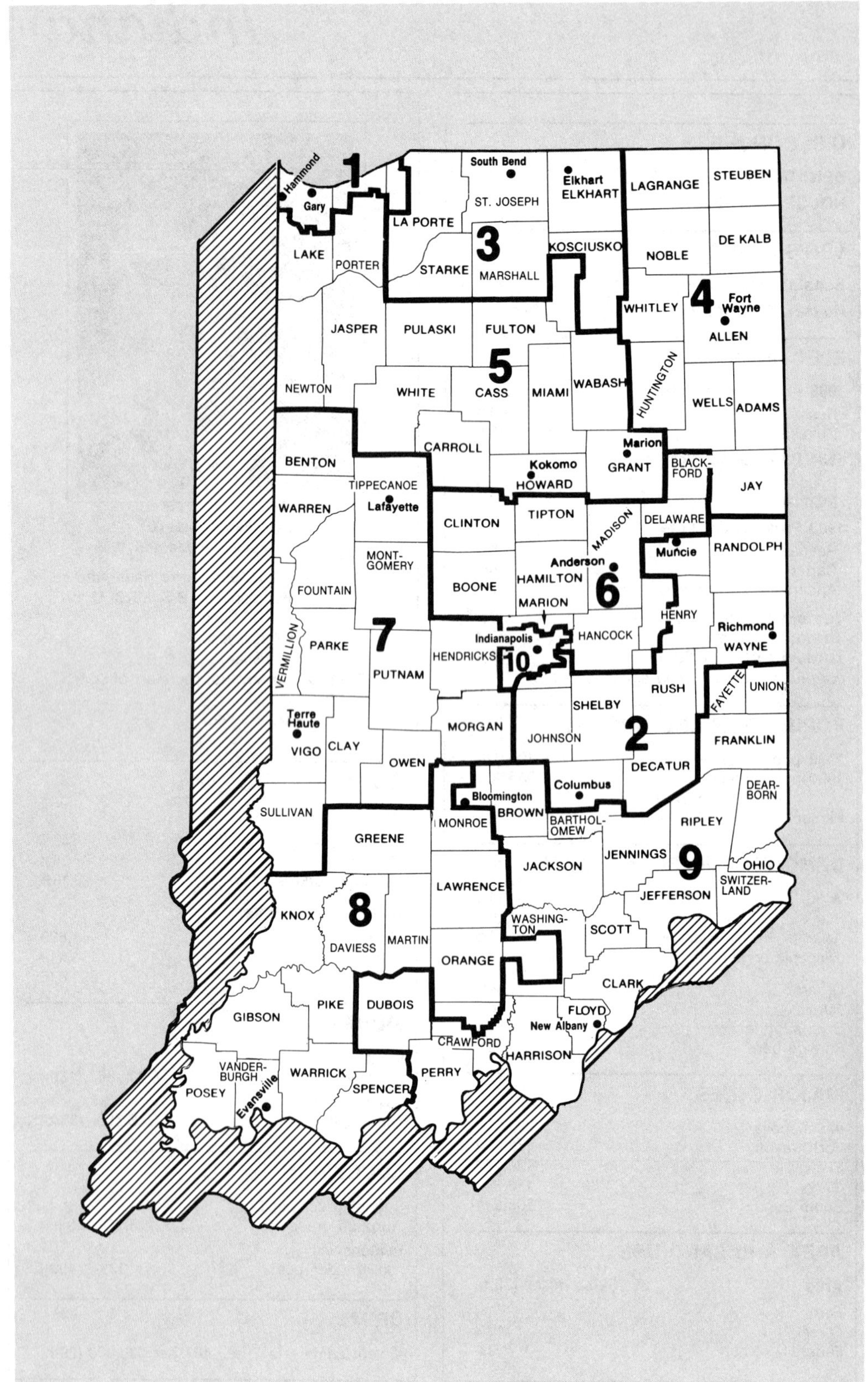
1
Hammond
Gary
LAKE
PORTER
LA PORTE
South Bend
ST. JOSEPH
Elkhart
ELKHART
LAGRANGE
STEUBEN
3
STARKE
MARSHALL
KOSCIUSKO
NOBLE
DE KALB
4
WHITLEY
Fort Wayne
ALLEN
JASPER
PULASKI
FULTON
5
NEWTON
WHITE
CASS
MIAMI
WABASH
HUNTINGTON
WELLS
ADAMS
CARROLL
Marion
GRANT
BLACK-FORD
JAY
BENTON
TIPPECANOE
Kokomo
HOWARD
WARREN
Lafayette
CLINTON
TIPTON
MADISON
DELAWARE
Muncie
RANDOLPH
MONT-GOMERY
FOUNTAIN
BOONE
Anderson
HAMILTON
6
MARION
HENRY
Richmond
WAYNE
VERMILLION
PARKE
7
Indianapolis
HANCOCK
HENDRICKS
10
PUTNAM
RUSH
FAYETTE
UNION
SHELBY
Terre Haute
VIGO
CLAY
MORGAN
JOHNSON
2
FRANKLIN
OWEN
DECATUR
Columbus
DEAR-BORN
Bloomington
BROWN
SULLIVAN
MONROE
BARTHOL-OMEW
RIPLEY
GREENE
JENNINGS
9
JACKSON
OHIO
SWITZER-LAND
LAWRENCE
JEFFERSON
KNOX
8
WASHING-TON
SCOTT
DAVIESS
MARTIN
ORANGE
CLARK
GIBSON
PIKE
DUBOIS
FLOYD
New Albany
CRAWFORD
HARRISON
VANDER-BURGH
WARRICK
PERRY
POSEY
SPENCER
Evansville

Richard G. Lugar (R)

Of Indianapolis — Elected 1976

Born: April 4, 1932, Indianapolis, Ind.

Education: Denison U., B.A. 1954; Oxford U., B.A., M.A. 1956.

Military Service: Navy, 1957-60.

Occupation: Agricultural industries executive.

Family: Wife, Charlene Smeltzer; four children.

Religion: Methodist.

Political Career: Indianapolis School Board, 1964-67; mayor of Indianapolis, 1968-75; Republican nominee for U.S. Senate, 1974.

Capitol Office: 306 Hart Bldg. 20510; 224-4814.

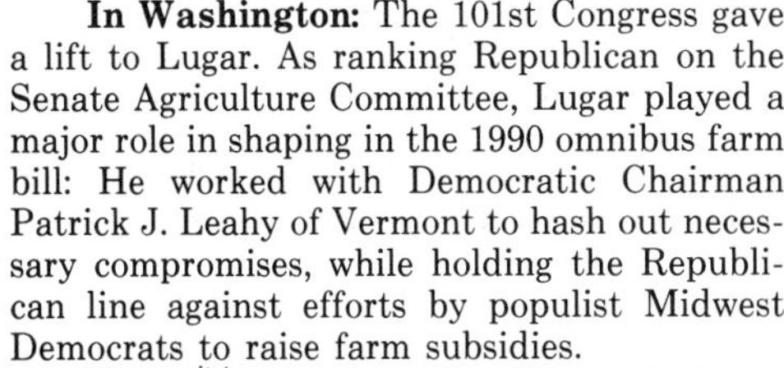

In Washington: The 101st Congress gave a lift to Lugar. As ranking Republican on the Senate Agriculture Committee, Lugar played a major role in shaping in the 1990 omnibus farm bill: He worked with Democratic Chairman Patrick J. Leahy of Vermont to hash out necessary compromises, while holding the Republican line against efforts by populist Midwest Democrats to raise farm subsidies.

Well-spoken and comfortable on television, Lugar — who served as chairman of the Senate Foreign Relations Committee from 1985 to 1987 — also acted as a Republican spokesman on the Persian Gulf crisis that followed Iraq's 1990 invasion of Kuwait. He obtained that role in lieu of North Carolina Sen. Jesse Helms, the current ranking Republican on Foreign Relations, who has an adversarial relationship with the media and is much more of a conservative polemicist than Lugar.

His prominence on these issues provided something of a revival for Lugar, whose political rise had been temporarily interrupted. The Republicans' loss of the Senate majority in 1986 deprived Lugar of his chairmanship. He even lost his ranking position on Foreign Relations to Helms who, having fulfilled a campaign pledge to chair Agriculture during consideration of the 1985 farm bill, used his seniority to claim the foreign policy soapbox.

Lugar then had to swallow hard in 1988 when George Bush reached past him and tapped his Indiana Senate colleague Dan Quayle for vice president. Although the two had gotten along, Quayle had less seniority and less stature among his fellow senators than Lugar. As one who first stated his desire for the presidency while he was mayor of Indianapolis, Lugar suddenly had a younger home-state rival complicating the hopes he held of one day seeking the White House.

Lugar proved resilient, though, brushing off whatever disappointment he might have felt and continuing his role as an active legislator. His chief assignment during the 101st Congress was the five-year reauthorization of the federal government's agriculture, soil-conservation and nutrition programs.

Lugar had already developed a close working relationship with Leahy. Before becoming Agriculture chairman in 1987, Leahy had devoted much of his time to other assignments, and was happy to tap Lugar's detailed knowledge of agriculture policy. The bill passed in 1987 to bail out the nation's farm credit system bore Lugar's strong imprint. Leahy and Lugar took joint credit in 1990 for a bill reauthorizing the Commodity Futures Trading Commission.

Despite their differing partisan perspectives, Leahy and Lugar had the same basic goal: to produce a fiscally lean farm bill. Leahy looked to fashion agreements that could draw bipartisan support and avert the threat of a veto by President Bush; Lugar, who is philosophically opposed to farm-income subsidies, was determined to block efforts to boost spending on the programs.

Lugar's free-market approach is unusual on a committee whose members — Republicans and Democrats alike — tend to favor increased subsidies and trade favors for their constituents' programs. Given the integral role of the federal government in farm-income support, which was reinforced by the 1985 farm bill, Lugar recognized that his hope for a strictly market-based farm economy was a far-off goal. Still, he worked around the edges, and scored a point in 1990 when the Senate passed his amendment to end a controversial honey-subsidy program, which provides large payments to a small number of beekeepers.

Those seeking increased subsidies were also kept off balance by Lugar's hints that he might stage a debate over the very nature of farm-subsidy programs, which he regards as akin to welfare. "At some point, maybe we should acknowledge that we are simply making transfer payments from one taxpayer to another," Lugar said.

Lugar's efforts benefited Leahy; the chairman had to fight off an insurgency from some liberal farm-state Democrats, who were not only determined to increase farm subsidies but viewed the issue as an effective one to use against Republicans back home. While Leahy gathered a group of moderate Democrats to freeze subsidy levels, Lugar maintained a solid bloc of GOP members on most votes.

Though overall a strong supporter of President Bush's policies, Lugar expressed anger when administration officials, who had stayed on the sidelines during much of the deliberations, criticized the farm bill as not austere enough. "Without a great deal of assistance, I've managed to achieve a freeze of target prices and loan rates," Lugar said in July 1990. "And the failure of the administration to acknowledge this strikes me as curious."

Lugar's environmentalist tendencies are stronger than most Senate Republicans, and many Agriculture Committee members of either party. He worked with Leahy to block changes sought by farm organizations in environmental restrictions in the 1985 farm bill, including the "swampbuster" provisions requiring cutoffs in federal payments to farmers who drain protected wetlands.

Despite their overriding attempts at cooperation, there were instances of partisan misunderstanding during the bill's birthing process. In May 1990, Leahy proposed a plan that included 1 percent increases in subsidy levels for certain crops. Although the chairman viewed the bill as a marker and not a hard proposal, Lugar saw it as an end run around the committee's Republicans. "This plan is a nonstarter," said Lugar, who temporarily took a more adversarial approach to the process.

The tables turned as the final bill moved to passage that October. Leahy had put a high priority on a provision limiting export of pesticides that are banned for use on U.S. crops; he did so in support of those who decried "the circle of poison," by which these banned chemicals were applied by foreign growers whose produce was then imported back into the United States. But during a House-Senate conference, Lugar pushed through an amendment severely weakening the provision, which was eventually dropped.

In the end, though, the fiscal crisis forced Leahy and Lugar to work together to make the unpalatable cuts that would be needed for the farm bill to meet budget guidelines and avoid a veto. The conference committee sliced nearly $14 billion out of the farm programs, though the cuts would be accounted for in a separate budget-reconciliation measure.

Apart from their lead roles on Agriculture, Lugar and Leahy have much in common. Both speak in moderate tones that mask strong ideological bearings: Lugar as a conservative and Leahy as a liberal. Both are highly accessible to the media. Like Leahy, who served as ranking Democrat on the Senate Intelligence Committee in the mid-1980s, Lugar has a strong interest in foreign policy issues.

Lugar took the lead among Foreign Relations Republicans on the U.S. response to the August 1990 occupation of Kuwait by forces of Iraqi President Saddam Hussein. After the invasion, Lugar raced out ahead of Bush, whose stated goal was simply to get Iraq to give up Kuwait. Lugar said that even if that occurred, the continued danger of a heavily armed Iraq "leaves us in a very unsatisfactory situation.... It seems to me important that Saddam Hussein must either leave or be removed."

Lugar also insisted that Congress needed to fulfill what he viewed as its constitutional responsibility to authorize the use of military force. Even before the 101st Congress adjourned in late October, Lugar said, "Congress ought to come back into session to entertain a declaration of war."

Still, Lugar emerged as a Senate point man for Bush's Persian Gulf policy. Lugar spoke frequently, in the Senate and during national television interviews, in favor of the January 1991 resolution authorizing Bush to employ military force against Iraq and Bush's decision to use that authority a few days later.

Despite the U.S.-led military rout that liberated Kuwait, Lugar's hopes for Saddam Hussein's immediate downfall were not met; instead, the Iraqi strongman used what military might he had left to crush revolts among his nation's Kurdish and Shiite Moslem populations. Lugar nonetheless defended Bush against criticisms that he had stopped short of Saddam's removal and had reacted slowly to the plight of Iraq's minority groups.

"We did not betray the Kurds nor did we make a designed approach here that Saddam Hussein ... should stay ...," Lugar said during an April 1991 television interview. "We had a basic choice, and that is if we wanted to occupy Iraq, wring out its government, and make a new start for Iraq, that was one thing. We chose not to do that, and I think so wisely."

Lugar was much more visible during the war than the laconic Foreign Relations chairman, Democrat Claiborne Pell of Rhode Island, or Helms, who uses the Foreign Relations post mainly to sustain his anti-communist crusades. Lugar, whose proactive role during his chairmanship gave him a reputation as something of a shadow secretary of State, has hardly let Helms' dibs on the Republican top spot blunt his ambitions to influence foreign policy.

The conflicting approaches of the two Republicans had brought them to loggerheads even before Helms, by a 24-17 vote, pre-empted Lugar for the ranking position in 1987. They had clashed during deliberations on a 1986 bill mandating economic sanctions against South Africa, which Lugar had a key role in crafting.

Although Lugar was a strong supporter

and promoter of President Ronald Reagan's policies, he tried without success to get the administration to accommodate the overwhelming sentiment in Congress against South Africa's policy of apartheid (racial separation). Faced with losing control of the issue to Democrats, Lugar pushed his own sanctions bill. He crafted a compromise with broad support in Foreign Relations, and held off stringent Democratic amendments on the floor. Then he got House leaders to accept the Senate bill unchanged to avoid a conservative filibuster against the conference report.

Reagan nonetheless vetoed the bill, setting the stage for Lugar's blowup with Helms. At Helms' behest, the South African foreign minister lobbied two senators and warned of retaliation against U.S. farm products if sanctions were enacted. Outraged, Lugar denounced the attempts as "despicable," and condemned Helms' move as "an affront to the decency of the American people."

Although Lugar worked to engineer the veto override, he expressed regret over his disagreement with Reagan and chagrin that he had been unable to get the president to change his mind. However, Lugar did manage to convince a reluctant Reagan to accede to the ouster of a longtime U.S. ally, scandal-plagued President Ferdinand E. Marcos of the Phillipines.

Early in 1986, Reagan asked Lugar to head a U.S. delegation monitoring the election between Marcos and challenger Corazon Aquino. Lugar quickly concluded that Marcos was stealing the election. Privately he implored Reagan to denounce Marcos, but Reagan argued instead that there had been fraud on both sides.

Lugar persisted. Eventually the administration pressured Marcos to leave office peacefully, in what came to be regarded as one of Reagan's chief foreign policy achievements. But in 1989, Aquino gave the credit to Lugar. "Without him," she said, "there would be no Philippine-U.S. relations to speak of by now." That year, Lugar was a chief sponsor of a measure that authorized U.S. participation in a multinational economic assistance program for the Philippines.

When Lugar ran for Senate Republican leader in 1984 — finishing third in a field of five candidates — some colleagues expressed concern that he was too pleasant and accommodating to be a strong leader. But Lugar has since shown that he can be a hard-hitting partisan when the situation prevails.

In 1990, Lugar voted against a Democratic-crafted civil rights package that Bush vetoed as a "quota bill." When Democrats threatened to revive the bill in early 1991, Lugar rejected their arguments that Republicans were engaging in racially divisive rhetoric. "Republicans say [the quota issue] is a live issue out in the country," Lugar said. "So if Democrats want to keep pushing the same old bill, bring it on."

At Home: Lugar's long record of electoral success is remarkable given his modest gifts as a campaigner. He meets crowds woodenly and his style borders on lecturing. But he has always managed to impress the Indiana electorate as a man of substance.

Even in 1974, running for the Senate in a Watergate-dominated year with a reputation as "Richard Nixon's favorite mayor," he came within a respectable 75,000 votes against Democrat Birch Bayh. Two years later, against a much weaker Democrat, Sen. Vance Hartke, he won handily. In his 1982 re-election bid, Lugar's personal popularity — and massive campaign treasury — put him out of reach of his Democratic challenger, Rep. Floyd Fithian.

Lugar's record as mayor of Indianapolis still stands as the foundation of his political career. His conservative, efficiency-minded administration won him favorable notices all over Indiana, and he attracted national attention by defeating John V. Lindsay of New York City for vice president of the National League of Cities in 1970.

A Rhodes scholar, Lugar served in the Navy as a briefing officer at the Pentagon before returning home to run the family tool business. He won his first election in 1964, to the Indianapolis School Board.

Three years later, he saw an opportunity to take over the mayor's office. The Democrats were divided, and with the help of powerful Marion County GOP Chairman Keith Bulen, he beat incumbent Democrat John Barton.

Lugar's foremost accomplishment as Indianapolis mayor was creation of Uni-Gov, the consolidation of the city and its suburbs, which he lobbied through the state Legislature.

Lugar's election over Lindsay was national news because he won it in an electorate of big-city mayors, most of whom were Democrats. He was a spokesman for Nixon administration policies, and from that time on the president began to take an interest in him.

He came to regret those ties in 1974, when he was saddled with the Nixon connection. In an attempt to deal with it, he declared that the Oval Office tape transcripts "revealed a moral tragedy" in the White House. But this alienated segments of the Republican right in Indiana and made his campaign against Bayh even more difficult.

Still, he came close enough to be the logical contender in 1976 against Hartke. Hartke had nearly been beaten six years earlier and was severely damaged by a primary challenger who charged him with foreign junketing and slavish loyalty to the communications industry. Lugar coasted to an easy win.

Working to ensure the same result in 1982, Lugar began preparing two years in advance. By the time the election drew near, he had organizations in every county. By contrast, Democrat Fithian got off to a slow start. After his old 2nd District was dismembered in redistricting, Fithian initially announced plans to run for Indiana secretary of state, then switched to the Senate contest — angering other Democrats already in the race and prompting some observers to brand him "Flip-Flop Floyd."

Seeking to make up lost ground, Fithian attacked Lugar's record on Social Security, charging that the incumbent voted 16 times to reduce minimum benefits. He tied Lugar to Reagan policies Fithian claimed were responsible for Indiana's economic woes. Lugar acknowledged the troubled economic climate — billing himself as a "good man for tough times" — but put the blame on previous Democratic administrations. Lugar did not go to great lengths to identify himself with the White House, however. He criticized the president for vetoing the supplemental appropriation that included his own emergency housing legislation.

Fithian did manage to shore up support in predominantly Democratic southern Indiana, taking 14 counties in this region. In most areas, though, Lugar was a comfortable winner, and he finished with 54 percent statewide.

In 1988, with Hoosier Democrats on the march (they captured the governorship and gained parity in the Legislature), Lugar essentially drew a pass.

The only Democrat who filed to oppose him was Jack Wickes, an Indianapolis lawyer who had never run for office. Personable and energetic as Wickes was, his principal credential was that he had run Gary Hart's successful presidential primary campaign in Indiana in 1984. Wickes never raised nearly enough money to make a serious race against Lugar. He was not even able to run television advertisements. Lugar got more votes (1.43 million) and a wider victory margin (761,747 votes) than any previous candidate in Indiana history. His vote share (68 percent) easily eclipsed the previous record for a Senate race in the state.

Committees

Agriculture, Nutrition & Forestry (Ranking)

Foreign Relations (2nd of 8 Republicans)
Western Hemisphere & Peace Corps Affairs (ranking); East Asian & Pacific Affairs; International Economic Policy, Trade, Oceans & Environment

Elections

1988 General		
Richard G. Lugar (R)	1,430,525	(68%)
Jack Wickes (D)	668,778	(32%)

Previous Winning Percentages: **1982** (54%) **1976** (59%)

Campaign Finance

	Receipts	Receipts from PACs		Expend-itures
1988				
Lugar (R)	$3,029,708	$775,836	(26%)	$3,022,597
Wickes (D)	$338,465	$119,150	(35%)	$314,233

Key Votes

1991	
Authorize use of force against Iraq	Y
1990	
Oppose prohibition of certain semiautomatic weapons	Y
Support constitutional amendment on flag desecration	Y
Oppose requiring parental notice for minors' abortions	N
Halt production of B-2 stealth bomber at 13 planes	N
Approve budget that cut spending and raised revenues	Y
Pass civil rights bill over Bush veto	N
1989	
Oppose reduction of SDI funding	Y
Oppose barring federal funds for "obscene" art	Y
Allow vote on capital gains tax cut	Y

Voting Studies

	Presidential Support		Party Unity		Conservative Coalition	
Year	**S**	**O**	**S**	**O**	**S**	**O**
1990	86	11	86	12	97	3
1989	93	2	83	15	89	11
1988	86	13	76	19	86	14
1987	76	21	77	20	78	13
1986	88	11	89	10	88	9
1985	89	10	92	8	88	12
1984	92	8	94	6	87	13
1983	95	5	92	8	95	5
1982	83	15	85	14	84	16
1981	90	9	93	7	90	10

Interest Group Ratings

Year	ADA	ACU	AFL-CIO	CCUS
1990	6	83	11	75
1989	10	75	0	100
1988	10	88	21	92
1987	5	72	20	88
1986	10	78	0	89
1985	5	74	10	90
1984	10	82	18	79
1983	15	44	12	68
1982	15	63	28	70
1981	5	100	0	94

Daniel R. Coats (R)

Of Fort Wayne — Elected 1990

Appointed to the Senate 1988.

Born: May 16, 1943, Jackson, Mich.
Education: Wheaton College, B.A. 1965; Indiana U., J.D. 1971.
Military Service: Army Corps of Engineers, 1966-68.
Occupation: Lawyer.
Family: Wife, Marcia Anne Crawford; three children.
Religion: Presbyterian.
Political Career: U.S. House, 1981-89.
Capitol Office: 411 Russell Bldg. 20510; 224-5623.

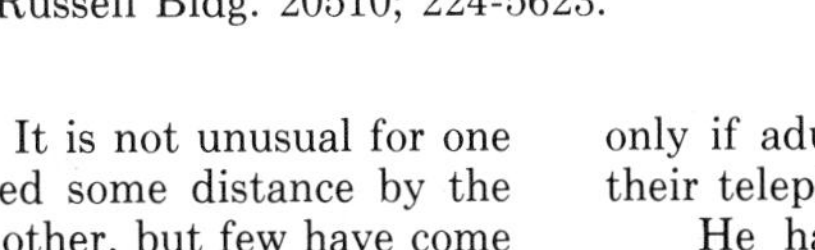

In Washington: It is not unusual for one politician to be carried some distance by the career successes of another, but few have come as far this way as Coats.

Starting as a staff aide to Dan Quayle when Quayle represented northeast Indiana in the House, Coats has moved up behind his boss. When Quayle went to the Senate in 1980, Coats ran for and won his House seat. And after Quayle was elected vice president in 1988, Indiana's retiring GOP Gov. Robert D. Orr appointed Coats to succeed Quayle in the Senate.

There is nothing wrong with being appointed to the Senate in place of one's political mentor. That was how Senate Majority Leader George J. Mitchell of Maine first arrived in 1980. The key is how one proceeds from there.

Coats' appointment, lasting only through the 101st Congress, had to be ratified by the voters in November 1990, and he must defend the seat in its regular re-election cycle in 1992 (Quayle was re-elected in 1986). Two campaigns in four years leave little time to cut a legislative swath. But with his first Senate win behind him, Coats — who inherited Quayle's committee assignments, including Armed Services — has moved past the appointment bugaboo.

During his short tenure, Coats has shown a particular zest for attacking trash — whether it be New Jersey tin cans or sexually explicit telephone messages. During the 101st Congress, Coats irritated Frank R. Lautenberg and Bill Bradley of New Jersey when he obtained Senate passage of a bill allowing state bans or limits on solid waste from other states. Coats, who ran campaign ads lampooning New Jerseyites dumping their garbage on a horrified Hoosier couple's lawn, denied political motivations for the provision (dropped in conference).

Known primarily as a serious social conservative given to pondering the implications of his Christian-based, "pro-family" politics, Coats also introduced legislation in 1990 to outlaw so-called "Dial-a-Porn" and to allow the sale of sexually explicit telephone messages only if adults specifically seek access through their telephone company.

He has urged the like-minded to move beyond such issues as school prayer and abortion to a concern for the material welfare of children and the poor. But his role is limited by his reluctance to depart from the conservative orthodoxy and suspicion of government he brought with him to Congress.

As a result, he often finds himself attempting the difficult balancing act of offering economic incentives without spawning government interference. He has called for doubling the personal tax exemption and creating tax credits for low-income families with children younger than 6. He also won adoption of several amendments in the 1989 child care legislation to permit in-home care and to allow requirements that care-providers adhere to certain religious beliefs.

Coats, like Quayle, is a fiscal conservative, and he champions the cause of the line-item veto. Still, he has been one of the House class of 1980 who not only survived electorally but built a détente with the government he opposed in getting elected. Many of his classmates who had ridden Ronald Reagan's 1980 coattails came a cropper in the recession of 1982; Coats actually ran stronger that year than in either of Reagan's landslides. He did it, in part, by watching out for his Fort Wayne-based 4th District's economic interests.

In the House, Coats spent much of his time at the Select Committee on Children, Youth and Families, where he was ranking Republican. He defended programs for underprivileged families that some conservatives assail as too expensive. In 1985, Coats argued for eight controversial education and health programs for the poor. "These strands of the social safety net — from the Head Start program to prenatal care to education for the handicapped — are working as intended," Coats said.

At Home: When Orr named Coats to replace Quayle in the Senate a month after the

1988 presidential election, he was formalizing what many Indiana observers had considered a fait accompli. Coats was presumed to be Quayle's choice, just as he had been when Quayle left the House eight years earlier.

As Quayle's district representative from 1978 through 1980, Coats cultivated the role of surrogate congressman. He handled constituents' problems personally, and sometimes stepped in for Quayle to give a "government is too big" speech. When Quayle ran for the Senate in 1980, Coats had a spot on the ballot just below him and shared the highly effective organization both had helped build. Coats actually bested Quayle that November in the 4th.

By tradition, appointed senators have not fared well before the voters. And the timing of Coats' ascent might have been better. Among the more reliably GOP states in recent years, Indiana has shown signs of restiveness of late. In 1988 it elected its first Democratic governor in two decades and gave Democrats a share of control in the Legislature.

But Democrats in 1990 tried and failed to recruit a front-line candidate such as Rep. Lee Hamilton. Instead, they nominated little-known state Rep. Baron P. Hill, a former high school basketball star. Hill gained ground with clever television ads depicting the state as being flooded by Coats' franked mail. He also took a walking tour of the length of the state. Voters warmed to Hill's fiery stump style, which contrasted with Coats' stiff presence in crowds and reliance on television ads and mailings. In the end, Hill did not have enough money and name recognition to overtake the incumbent, but he did do well enough to merit being mentioned as a possible repeat challenger in 1992.

When he first ran for Congress in 1980, Coats was still a relative newcomer to the district. But he easily surmounted a bitter GOP primary against two candidates with much stronger local roots, winning the primary by carrying every county. In November, Coats smashed Democrat John D. Walda in Walda's second try. Four re-election campaigns produced no surprises.

Committees

Armed Services (7th of 9 Republicans)
Defense Industry & Technology (ranking); Conventional Forces & Alliance Defense; Readiness, Sustainability & Support

Labor & Human Resources (4th of 7 Republicans)
Children, Families, Drugs & Alcoholism (ranking); Aging; Education, Arts & Humanities; Employment & Productivity

Elections

1990 General

Daniel R. Coats (R)	806,048	(54%)
Baron P. Hill (D)	696,639	(46%)

Previous Winning Percentages: **1988** * (62%) **1986** * (70%) **1984** * (61%) **1982** * (64%) **1980** * (61%)

* *House elections.*

Campaign Finance

	Receipts	Receipts from PACs	Expend-itures
1990			
Coats (R)	$4,082,803	$1,113,664 (27%)	$3,718,903
Hill (D)	$1,082,402	$488,461 (45%)	$1,077,074

Key Votes

1991	
Authorize use of force against Iraq	Y
1990	
Oppose prohibition of certain semiautomatic weapons	Y
Support constitutional amendment on flag desecration	Y
Oppose requiring parental notice for minors' abortions	N
Halt production of B-2 stealth bomber at 13 planes	N
Approve budget that cut spending and raised revenues	N
Pass civil rights bill over Bush veto	N
1989	
Oppose reduction of SDI funding	Y
Oppose barring federal funds for "obscene" art	Y
Allow vote on capital gains tax cut	Y

Voting Studies

	Presidential Support		Party Unity		Conservative Coalition	
Year	**S**	**O**	**S**	**O**	**S**	**O**
1990	77	18	87	11	92	8
1989	81	19	92	8	92	8
House Service						
1988	59	38	77	20	84	11
1987	64	36	83	16	86	12
1986	70	29	84	15	84	16
1985	74	26	81	17	80	20
1984	67	30	92	8	90	10
1983	78	21	88 †	12 †	84	16
1982	71	29	84	13	82	18
1981	74	26	86	14	91	9

† *Not eligible for all recorded votes.*

Interest Group Ratings

Year	ADA	ACU	AFL-CIO	CCUS
1990	0	96	22	83
1989	10	86	20	88
House Service				
1988	10	92	29	93
1987	8	91	0	100
1986	10	82	14	94
1985	20	86	18	86
1984	5	92	0	69
1983	10	87	6	85
1982	30	73	15	73
1981	10	93	20	100

1 Peter J. Visclosky (D)

Of Merrillville — Elected 1984

Born: Aug. 13, 1949, Gary, Ind.
Education: Indiana U., B.S. 1970; U. of Notre Dame, J.D. 1973; Georgetown U., LL.M. 1982.
Occupation: Lawyer.
Family: Wife, Ann Marie O'Keefe; two children.
Religion: Roman Catholic.
Political Career: No previous office.
Capitol Office: 330 Cannon Bldg. 20515; 225-2461.

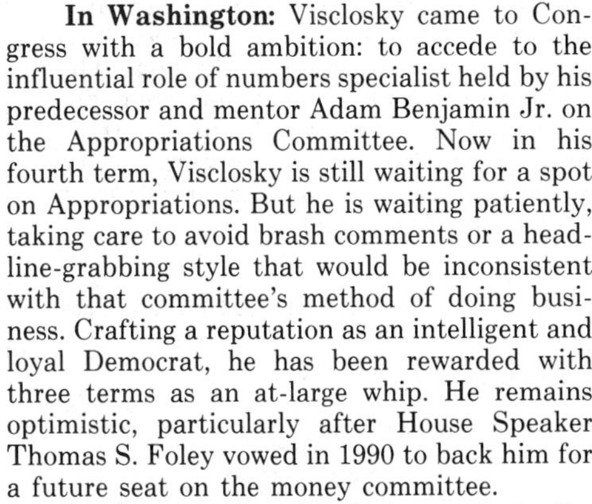

In Washington: Visclosky came to Congress with a bold ambition: to accede to the influential role of numbers specialist held by his predecessor and mentor Adam Benjamin Jr. on the Appropriations Committee. Now in his fourth term, Visclosky is still waiting for a spot on Appropriations. But he is waiting patiently, taking care to avoid brash comments or a headline-grabbing style that would be inconsistent with that committee's method of doing business. Crafting a reputation as an intelligent and loyal Democrat, he has been rewarded with three terms as an at-large whip. He remains optimistic, particularly after House Speaker Thomas S. Foley vowed in 1990 to back him for a future seat on the money committee.

In the meantime, Visclosky tends to the home front, working for such projects as a new airport in Gary. His floor statements honoring veterans, Lithuanians and the Rev. Dr. Martin Luther King Jr. reflect the roots and concerns of his solidly Democratic, but diverse district. Steel is the common ground for many Visclosky constituents, and he serves the industry and its workers from his committee posts on Education and Labor, Interior and Insular Affairs, and Public Works.

Indiana's 1st produces more steel than any other district, and it has suffered devastating economic losses in the last two decades. Visclosky rarely misses an opportunity to speak out for American steel. When the omnibus highway bill was debated on the floor, Visclosky reminded his colleagues how important highway projects are for the steel industry.

A member of the executive committee of the Congressional Steel Caucus, Visclosky advocated provisions in the 1988 trade bill to increase the U.S. trade representative's enforcement authority. The new law clarifies that foreign countries' voluntary steel import restrictions cannot be circumvented by processing the steel in a third country. In the 101st Congress, Visclosky worked to extend the voluntary restraint agreements on steel imports.

Visclosky has become well-versed on pension issues and is an advocate for increasing employee input on investment decisions. He also successfully promoted legislation enlarging the Indiana Dunes National Lakeshore, a longtime *cause célèbre* for Midwest environmentalists and one of the few tourist attractions in northwest Indiana.

At Home: After finishing law school in 1973, Visclosky linked his fortunes to Benjamin, then a state senator and rising star. Visclosky coordinated Benjamin's successful campaign for Congress in 1976 and worked with him in Washington for the next six years.

When Benjamin died in September 1982, Gary's longtime black mayor, Richard G. Hatcher, was the 1st District Democratic chairman, and thus had the legal right to choose the Democratic nominee. He picked Katie Hall, a black state senator and loyal ally. She survived the general election and sought renomination in 1984. Visclosky and Jack Crawford, the Lake County prosecutor, challenged her, and at first, Crawford seemed the more formidable of the two white candidates.

In the end, though, Visclosky had greater appeal. To contrast his modestly funded bid with Crawford's high-budget operation, Visclosky put on dozens of "dog-and-bean" $2 dinners aimed at attracting the young, the elderly and the unemployed. His Eastern European background also helped him (he called himself "the Slovak Kid"), and older voters responded favorably because they remembered his father, John, who had served as Gary's comptroller and mayor.

Visclosky won over late-deciding white voters whose first priority was defeating Hall. She finished second, Crawford a close third. Visclosky swamped Republican Joseph B. Grenchik, the mayor of Whiting, in November.

In 1986, Hall tried a comeback. She retained her support in the black community, where Visclosky had alienated some voters by failing to close his congressional office on the Martin Luther King Jr. holiday in 1985. But with Hall as his only serious foe in this white-majority district, Visclosky's renomination was all but assured. Hall's 1990 primary bid fell flat.

Indiana 1

Industrial Belt — Gary; Hammond

The 1st stretches from the Illinois line at Hammond through Gary all the way to Michigan City, 40 miles to the east, covering almost the entire Indiana shoreline along Lake Michigan. It extends inland only slightly beyond the congested, polluted lakefront industrial area.

Crossing through the heart of the 1st on the Indiana Toll Road, one sees the maze of refineries and steel plants that form the district's economic base. A generation ago, Gary was dominated by Eastern European ethnic factory workers; today it is 81 percent black. Indiana's third-largest city with a population of about 117,000, it remains heavily unionized and was the political base for former Mayor Richard G. Hatcher, whose two decades of service made him one of the nation's most durable black officeholders. He was defeated for renomination in 1987.

Gary, nearby industrial Hammond and the surrounding northern half of Lake County provide the bulk of Democratic strength in the 1st. More than four-fifths of the vote is cast in the district's Lake County portion.

The remaining fifth of the voters live in LaPorte and Porter counties. This side of the district is neither as Democratic nor as industrial as Lake County. There are pockets of Democratic strength, however, in northern Porter County and in Michigan City, located in agricultural LaPorte County. Michigan City, once a larger lake port than Chicago, is now a depressed industrial town. Porter County contains the state's only active shipping port, at Burns Harbor, and there are several steel mills and a large state prison in the area. The suburban tracts of Porter County are populated by many Eastern European ethnic steelworkers and oil refinery workers who moved out of the depressed inner-city areas of Gary and Hammond.

Population: 547,100. White 390,290 (71%), Black 132,650 (24%), Other 2,945 (1%). Spanish origin 44,985 (8%). 18 and over 375,863 (69%), 65 and over 47,696 (9%). Median age: 28.

Committees

Education & Labor (23rd of 25 Democrats)
Employment Opportunities

Interior & Insular Affairs (15th of 29 Democrats)
National Parks & Public Lands

Public Works & Transportation (14th of 36 Democrats)
Investigations & Oversight; Surface Transportation; Water Resources

Elections

1990 General		
Peter J. Visclosky (D)	68,920	(66%)
William B. Costas (R)	35,450	(34%)
1990 Primary		
Peter J. Visclosky (D)	37,286	(51%)
Katie B. Hall (D)	21,749	(30%)
Gregory S. Reising (D)	9,712	(13%)
Sandra K. Smith (D)	3,754	(5%)
1988 General		
Peter J. Visclosky (D)	138,251	(77%)
Owen W. Crumpacker (R)	41,076	(23%)

Previous Winning Percentages: **1986** (73%) **1984** (71%)

District Vote For President

	1988		1984		1980		1976	
D	112,133	(59%)	125,803	(56%)	106,716	(50%)	127,309	(57%)
R	78,440	(41%)	95,657	(43%)	95,848	(45%)	94,741	(42%)
I					8,712	(4%)		

Campaign Finance

	Receipts	Receipts from PACs		Expend-itures
1990				
Visclosky (D)	$248,272	$168,020	(68%)	$299,280
Costas (R)	$21,358	0		$21,355
1988				
Visclosky (D)	$222,620	$157,250	(71%)	$141,855

Key Votes

1991	
Authorize use of force against Iraq	N
1990	
Support constitutional amendment on flag desecration	N
Pass family and medical leave bill over Bush veto	Y
Reduce SDI funding	Y
Allow abortions in overseas military facilities	Y
Approve budget summit plan for spending and taxing	Y
Approve civil rights bill	Y
1989	
Halt production of B-2 stealth bomber at 13 planes	Y
Oppose capital gains tax cut	Y
Approve federal abortion funding in rape or incest cases	Y
Approve pay raise and revision of ethics rules	N
Pass Democratic minimum wage plan over Bush veto	Y

Voting Studies

	Presidential Support		Party Unity		Conservative Coalition	
Year	**S**	**O**	**S**	**O**	**S**	**O**
1990	22	76	90	8	30	69
1989	30	67	89	9	32	66
1988	22	78	91	9	18	82
1987	19	81	94	6	28	72
1986	19	81	93	7	20	80
1985	30	70	90	9	33	67

Interest Group Ratings

Year	ADA	ACU	AFL-CIO	CCUS
1990	72	13	92	14
1989	100	7	83	40
1988	100	0	100	36
1987	92	0	94	13
1986	90	0	93	33
1985	80	5	71	36

2 Philip R. Sharp (D)

Of Muncie — Elected 1974

Born: July 15, 1942, Baltimore, Md.
Education: Georgetown U., B.S. 1964; Attended Oxford U., 1966; Georgetown U., Ph.D. 1974.
Occupation: Political science professor.
Family: Wife, Marilyn Augburn; two children.
Religion: Methodist.
Political Career: Democratic nominee for U.S. House, 1970, 1972.
Capitol Office: 2217 Rayburn Bldg. 20515; 225-3021.

In Washington: Sharp became known to many of his House colleagues through his work guiding President Jimmy Carter's energy package through Congress in the late 1970s, and for his unfolding expertise in the field.

Interest in energy policy waned during the 1980s, muting Sharp's legislative profile as well. But Sharp did not change his focus, and when the issue re-emerged with a vengeance following the 1990 Iraqi invasion of Kuwait, he was ready. As Chairman of the Energy and Power Subcommittee of Energy and Commerce, he entered the 102nd Congress with a chance to play a leading role in the energy debate — provided his habitual caution does not leave him behind the political curve.

Sharp, a former political science professor, was a quick standout in the large Democratic class of 1974: hard-working, sober and intellectually curious. Nevertheless, he took over what had been a Republican district and is one of the few House members who often has to fight hard to stay in office.

He is by nature careful and slow to step out front, and his insecure electoral standing amplifies that deliberative streak. Sharp's overall record is moderate to liberal, despite some concessions to his more conservative constituency.

As chairman of Energy and Power, Sharp is committed to finding consensus but reluctant to pressure wavering Democrats. Reflecting his academic bent, he conducts hearings like seminars and explores all sides of an issue.

The subcommittee provides a wide legislative field within the Energy and Commerce Committee; in the 100th Congress, it was formed by consolidating the old Fossil Fuels panel, which Sharp had led since 1981, and another subcommittee responsible for nuclear power and conservation. Sharp's influence over such issues is enhanced by the fact that he also is a senior member of the two Interior subcommittees that oversee energy.

During the 101st Congress, much of Sharp's energies were directed toward protecting Midwest interests in negotiations over the new clean air legislation.

The home-state pressures Sharp faces on the clean air issue are great: The auto industry is important in Indiana; the state ranks high in emissions of sulfur dioxide (a precursor of acid rain); and state utilities rely on high-sulfur coal. In some early skirmishes, Sharp favored relaxing auto-emission standards, though not by as much as industry would like.

When the clean air bill finally began to move in the 101st, Sharp fought desperately to win help for Midwestern utilities expected to face demanding cleanup requirements. Sharp stalled the acid rain provisions of the bill in his subcommittee, insisting that the "clean" states share in the costs of stopping pollution from the coal-fired Midwest power plants.

The politics of the bill ran against Sharp, and despite the initial backing of Energy and Commerce Chairman John D. Dingell on cost-sharing, he could not obtain direct financial aid for the utilities. But he was instrumental in winning them some relief in the form of an emission "allowances" swap system. Under the trading scheme, utilities that exceeded cleanup requirements for sulfur dioxide emissions could sell the resulting credit to utilities in other areas that needed to expand.

A personable and approachable man, Sharp is liked and admired by colleagues of both parties. Yet at the outset of the 101st, some Democrats were restive, complaining that he lacked aggressiveness and that his subcommittee was all but dormant. Energy was no longer at the top of the congressional agenda and Sharp had been distracted by a family illness in the 100th Congress.

That dynamic changed with the Iraqi invasion of Kuwait, which sent politicians scrambling in search of ways to cut U.S. dependence on foreign oil.

When members reassembled for the 102nd Congress, Sharp was ready with five bills designed to cut oil consumption. They included measures to promote energy efficiency, natural gas and renewable energy sources such as solar or wind power.

Indiana 2

East Central — Muncie; Richmond

Shaped like the letter "J," this district runs through a collection of areas with little in common — Indianapolis suburbs, lightly populated farmlands and three widely dispersed industrial cities.

Two-thirds of the vote is cast in the vicinities of Indianapolis, Muncie, Richmond and Columbus. Voters in those cities read different newspapers and watch different television stations. The only economic thread common to the cities is a dependence on the automobile industry.

Muncie, the model for "Middletown," the sociological study of small-town American life in the 1920s, is the largest city in the district, with a population of about 71,000. It was settled largely by Southerners and tends to be more Democratic than the other cities in the district.

In addition to auto-parts factories, the Ball Corporation (of canning jar fame) is a major employer, although the jars are now made elsewhere. Muncie and surrounding Delaware County strongly support Democrat Sharp; even in close House contests it has not been unusual for him to approach the 70 percent level in Delaware County. In 1988, when Sharp was held to 53 percent districtwide, he still won the county by 2 to 1.

Wayne County (Richmond) and Bartholomew County (Columbus) both went for George Bush in 1988, but Wayne County voted Democratic for governor and for the House, while Bartholomew went Republican in those elections. The city of Columbus is the home of the Cummins Engine Company, manufacturers of diesel engines.

The portions of metropolitan Indianapolis (Marion County) in the 2nd are primarily conservative, middle-income suburban areas. The suburban part of the 2nd also extends south of Indianapolis into Johnson County, which is almost as conservative. Those counties were added to the 2nd in 1981 redistricting in order to give Sharp trouble, and they have. In 1988, Republican House nominee Mike Pence won handily in Marion County and also carried Johnson County. In 1990, Marion was the only county in the 2nd that was carried by Pence.

The corn and hog farmers of the district usually prefer Republicans; all the smaller counties in the 2nd went Republican in the 1988 presidential and Senate races, but they voted for Sharp and successful Democratic gubernatorial candidate Evan Bayh by smaller margins.

Population: 553,510. White 535,065 (97%), Black 14,576 (3%). Spanish origin 3,225 (1%). 18 and over 390,981 (71%), 65 and over 58,462 (11%). Median age: 30.

Two of the bills would also enlarge the size of the nation's Strategic Petroleum Reserve, loosen the conditions under which the president could tap the reserve, and require oil importers to donate a certain portion of their imports to the reserve. During the 101st, Sharp had already won passage of legislation requiring the administration to stockpile refined oil products as well as crude oil.

Sharp also launched an exhaustive series of hearings on virtually every aspect of energy policy, from electric utility regulation to global warming.

But his caution remained in evidence. Sharp was content to let Democratic Sen. J. Bennett Johnston, who chairs the Senate Energy Committee, take the lead with an omnibus energy bill. And he hung back on some of the most controversial energy issues under discussion, particularly increased auto fuel efficiency standards, which had been opposed by Dingell.

Sharp's involvement with energy policy dates to the 1970s, when he had pushed for expansive energy and environmental initiatives. But by the mid 1980s the sparse energy agenda consisted largely of dismantling those policies as the energy crisis became overshadowed by an economic crisis in the oil states.

In the 100th Congress, Sharp's subcommittee successfully sponsored the repeal of a 1978 law aimed at encouraging industries and utilities to burn coal instead of oil or gas. Sharp also backed the drive to kill the Synthetic Fuels Corporation, established in 1980 to develop petroleum substitutes. He had reassessed his past support in light of the budget deficit, declining oil prices and the corporation's management problems.

During his years as Fossil Fuels chairman, Sharp was at the center of debate over natural gas prices. When prices shot up in late 1982, liberal Democrats and some Midwestern Republicans began agitating for tighter regulation while President Ronald Reagan proposed eliminating all existing controls to boost supply.

Maneuvering between pro-producer and pro-consumer factions on his subcommittee, Sharp steered through a bill that forced producers to lower their prices in some contracts in exchange for eased regulations. Neither side was happy, and the bill stalled in the Rules Committee.

Still, he demonstrated political skill simply by getting the bill through Energy and Commerce, given the committee's factions and the opposition of Chairman Dingell. And gas producers began exercising some voluntary price restraint. By 1989, after several years of low and stable gas prices, Sharp easily won congressional approval of price decontrol.

In the 100th Congress, Sharp guided into law two conservation bills that reflected both his and Congress' more modest aims.

A bill to set energy efficiency standards for large appliances, which Reagan had vetoed the Congress before, was enacted after a minor change. The second measure established pilot projects to promote alternative vehicle fuels, such as ethanol and methanol.

On Interior, Sharp generally takes an environmentalist view, but his record and style are conciliatory enough that he sometimes served as a bridge between liberal Chairman Morris K. Udall of Arizona and more conservative Democrats.

His pragmatic drive for solutions was evident in the 100th Congress' effort to overhaul the 1957 Price-Anderson Act, which limited utilities' liability for nuclear reactor accidents. With Udall, Sharp cosponsored a bill to raise utilities' joint liability tenfold, to $7 billion — still far below estimates of what a major accident would cost.

He helped Udall manage the bill on the House floor, calling it "a bargain" providing greater certainty of victims' compensation. Foes disagreed. One called the bill "a K-mart blue-light special for the nuclear power industry." In the end, the bill passed the House overwhelmingly; a House-Senate compromise version later became law.

On a non-energy issue in 1988, legislation for a federal product liability law, Sharp was one of the few Energy and Commerce Democrats to support a GOP amendment limiting manufacturers' liability in cases where consumers alter or misuse a product. He also voted for the bill, to the dismay of consumer groups and trial lawyers. But the measure went no further.

During the 101st Congress, Sharp and Democratic Sen. Jim Exon of Nebraska brokered a compromise with the administration over legislation to improve the collection and analysis of government information about foreign investment in the United States. Administration officials had complained that other versions of the bill would chill foreign investment and damage the economy.

Sharp had not been in the House long before he conceded that his experiences had deeply affected his attitude toward government. "In many cases we've gone toward excessive regulation," he said in late 1979. "I have a greater appreciation for the market than I did when I first ran." At times, his tilt toward business has led to conflict with the United Auto Workers (UAW), the strongest labor presence in Sharp's district.

At Home: When Sharp began his initial campaign for Congress in 1970, he was a 28-year-old political science professor with little campaign experience and limited contacts in the district. He out-organized most of his six rivals to win the Democratic nomination with 22 percent of the vote. In November, with recession worrying people in the industrial cities of central Indiana, Sharp came within 2,500 votes against Republican David W. Dennis.

Sharp was better known and even better prepared in 1972, but President Richard M. Nixon won Indiana by 2 to 1, helping Dennis boost his share of the vote to 57 percent.

On his third try, Sharp had all the name recognition he needed, and it was the right year. Even in Indiana, Republicans were on the run in 1974; Sharp won with 54 percent.

In the next three elections, Sharp faced the same opponent — farmer William G. Frazier. A gregarious campaigner with a devoted core of rural followers, Frazier was unable to broaden his base for general elections. Sharp helped himself by assuming a high personal profile and by tending to the needs of constituents regardless of their partisan affiliation.

In the 1981 redistricting, Indiana's Republican Legislature placed him in a redrawn district with clear Republican leanings. The GOP thought it had a good candidate in Ralph Van Natta, a former Shelbyville mayor who had gained further visibility as head of the state Bureau of Motor Vehicles under popular GOP Gov. Otis R. Bowen. But Van Natta did not live up to expectations. Economic troubles were causing many to fear for their jobs, and Van Natta was encumbered by publicity about investigations of the state's patronage-controlled motor vehicle bureaus. Sharp outspent Van Natta by nearly $100,000, carried his Democratic base of Muncie by 2 to 1, and won easily.

Kenneth MacKenzie, the 1984 GOP nominee, was different from Frazier and Van Natta. He was able to compete with Sharp in debating ability and fundraising. A former congressional aide on leave from his job as public affairs director for Muncie's Ball Corp., MacKenzie stressed his support for Reagan's efforts to give free enterprise a larger role in the economy.

Sharp accused MacKenzie of placing his loyalty to Reagan above the district; he called MacKenzie one of the few Midwest Republicans favoring full decontrol of natural gas prices. But Sharp's constituent service did far more for him than any of the issues he stressed. "The reason for my success is my service," he said as returns gave him a comfortable win on election night. "A lot of people who consider themselves Republicans voted for me."

The 1986 campaign provided an entirely

new experience for Sharp, and a welcome one. In the aftermath of MacKenzie's costly failure, no prominent Republican wanted to bother challenging the incumbent. Donald Lynch, a 31-year-old minister with no political experience, won the GOP nomination, and Sharp broke 60 percent for the first time.

But the security was short-lived. In 1988, with neighbor Dan Quayle on the national GOP ticket, Sharp had to contend with another outpouring of Republican votes in the 2nd. His hope was that his underfinanced opponent, Mike Pence, would not be strong enough to ride the tide.

But Pence, a 29-year-old attorney from the Indianapolis area, turned his weakness to advantage. He not only ran his own campaign without any political action committee (PAC) money, he succeeded in making PACs the central issue of the local campaign by taking the incumbent to task for his heavy PAC reliance.

For this Pence received favorable press both locally and nationally. He still came up short (47 percent).

Pence vowed to repeat his challenge, and in 1990 the national GOP had high hopes. But Pence, who again made campaign finance an issue, was hoist with his own petard when it was revealed that he was living on his campaign funds. The practice was not illegal, but even Republicans conceded that it was bad judgment. Pence, who could not grasp presidential coattails this time around, stalled and never recovered.

Both candidates levied charges of campaign improprieties; Pence ran TV ads accusing Sharp's staff of fomenting a Federal Election Commission complaint filed by a Democratic county prosecutor. The prosecutor charged that Pence had accepted illegal corporate contributions solicited by a supporter, who inserted written requests with the paychecks of her company's employees. The GOP in turn charged that the prosecutor made an illegal in-kind contribution to Sharp by using his law firm to bring the complaint and issue a press release.

Committees

Energy & Commerce (4th of 27 Democrats)
Energy & Power (chairman); Transportation & Hazardous Materials

Interior & Insular Affairs (2nd of 29 Democrats)
Energy & the Environment; Water, Power & Offshore Energy

Elections

1990 General		
Philip R. Sharp (D)	93,495	(59%)
Mike Pence (R)	63,980	(41%)
1988 General		
Philip R. Sharp (D)	116,915	(53%)
Mike Pence (R)	102,846	(47%)

Previous Winning Percentages: **1986** (62%) **1984** (53%) **1982** (56%) **1980** (53%) **1978** (56%) **1976** (60%) **1974** (54%)

District Vote For President

	1988	1984	1980	1976
D	83,849 (38%)	72,085 (32%)	76,120 (34%)	92,744 (42%)
R	137,236 (62%)	151,136 (67%)	138,118 (61%)	126,543 (57%)
I			10,143 (5%)	

Campaign Finance

	Receipts	Receipts from PACs	Expend-itures
1990			
Sharp (D)	$714,491	$498,599 (70%)	$773,178
Pence (R)	$590,467	0	$595,457
1988			
Sharp (D)	$465,414	$311,581 (67%)	$444,422
Pence (R)	$380,667	0	$332,880

Key Votes

1991	
Authorize use of force against Iraq	N
1990	
Support constitutional amendment on flag desecration	Y
Pass family and medical leave bill over Bush veto	Y
Reduce SDI funding	?
Allow abortions in overseas military facilities	Y
Approve budget summit plan for spending and taxing	N
Approve civil rights bill	Y
1989	
Halt production of B-2 stealth bomber at 13 planes	Y
Oppose capital gains tax cut	Y
Approve federal abortion funding in rape or incest cases	Y
Approve pay raise and revision of ethics rules	N
Pass Democratic minimum wage plan over Bush veto	Y

Voting Studies

	Presidential Support		Party Unity		Conservative Coalition	
Year	**S**	**O**	**S**	**O**	**S**	**O**
1990	20	74	79	17	41	56
1989	28	66	76	17	39	51
1988	31	64	79	19	61	39
1987	25	73	81	14	47	51
1986	24	73	81	16	42	56
1985	43	56	76	21	36	62
1984	38	50	63	31	47	36
1983	22	77	79	20	35	64
1982	42	57	69	28	36	64
1981	43	57	70	27	52	47

Interest Group Ratings

Year	ADA	ACU	AFL-CIO	CCUS
1990	67	22	83	46
1989	80	20	83	33
1988	75	20	100	50
1987	72	4	93	38
1986	65	10	86	41
1985	65	38	71	50
1984	50	43	54	14
1983	80	18	88	25
1982	80	14	95	41
1981	65	20	57	21

3 Tim Roemer (D)

Of South Bend — Elected 1990

Born: Oct. 30, 1956, South Bend, Ind.
Education: U. of California, San Diego, B.A. 1979; U. of Notre Dame, M.A. 1982, Ph.D. 1986.
Occupation: Congressional aide.
Family: Wife, Sally Johnston.
Religion: Roman Catholic.
Political Career: No previous office.
Capitol Office: 415 Cannon Bldg. 20515; 225-3915.

The Path to Washington: Roemer's arrival in Washington will be a homecoming of sorts; he served as an aide to both former Democratic House Majority Whip John Brademas of Indiana and Democratic Sen. Dennis DeConcini of Arizona.

Shaking off early primary criticism from some fellow Democrats that he was a carpetbagger from the East Coast, Roemer (who was born in South Bend and raised in Mishawaka) took aim at Republican Rep. John Hiler, a veteran of four hard-fought re-elections since upsetting Brademas as part of the 1980 Reagan conservative youth corps.

This swing district — which encompasses industrial, Democratic-leaning St. Joseph County — has a history of adopting youthful political upstarts. The Democrats had long targeted Hiler, most recently in 1988, when they poured in money in a doomed bid to tip the balance of repeat candidate Thomas W. Ward's 1986 razor-close loss.

A son-in-law of Democratic Sen. J. Bennett Johnston of Louisiana, Roemer shook the Beltway money tree and set in place a sophisticated campaign with the help of Johnston's research and media consultants. Bearing a striking physical resemblance to Indiana Democratic Gov. Evan Bayh, the youthful Roemer raised his name recognition in the district with groups of volunteers called "Roemer's Roamers," who donned T-shirts and performed public services such as picking up trash and playing bingo with the elderly.

Roemer also benefited from the emergence of the savings and loan scandal. The issue wounded Hiler, who during his tenure championed the Reagan passion for government deregulation and who sat on the House committee that oversees the thrift and banking industries.

Meanwhile, Roemer managed to dodge criticism of his connection with DeConcini, one of the "Keating Five" senators who have been subjected to a public ethics hearing on their roles in attempting to interfere with federal thrift regulators in behalf of a contributor. Although he called on Hiler to decline thrift-industry contributions, Roemer refused Hiler's proposal for a mutual ban on contributions from all political action committees.

Effectively steering a middle course during the campaign, Roemer sprinkled a traditional populism with occasional dashes of conservatism; one day he would hold a news conference at a plant rumored to be closing to lambaste the plight of the middle class; the next day he would out-Republican some Republicans by calling for a balanced budget and criticizing President Bush for backing away from his no-taxes pledge.

On the abortion issue, for example, Roemer — a Roman Catholic and a graduate of the University of Notre Dame — left the conservative Hiler no room to maneuver. Although Hiler opposed abortion, at least one anti-abortion group endorsed Roemer, arguing that he supported legislation that went beyond protecting the unborn by providing education, job training and health care for mothers. Roemer opposes abortion, except in the cases of rape, incest or to save the woman's life.

Roemer's openness about his financial condition during the campaign reinforced the perception that he was fighting for the average Joe. He reminded voters that he was living on $15,000 in savings while his wife moonlighted as a clerk in a department store after putting in a full day on the campaign. In contrast, Hiler reported assets of more than $1 million.

Roemer's only previous political effort was an unsuccessful primary bid for state representative while he was a graduate student. A holder of master's and doctoral degrees in international affairs and government and a former instructor at The American University, Roemer got a spot on the Education and Labor Committee, where he says he will support national service legislation that would encourage student participation in service projects in exchange for financial assistance for their education.

Indiana 3

North Central — South Bend

Anchored by the industrial cities of South Bend and Elkhart, the 3rd has long been a swing district. Democrat Tim Roemer got just 51 percent of its vote in ousting Republican incumbent John Hiler in 1990; Hiler never won more than 55 percent in the five elections he won. His Democratic predecessor, John Brademas, held the seat for 11 terms, but reached 60 percent only twice.

South Bend, besides being the home of the University of Notre Dame, has several Bendix facilities that make automobile and airplane parts, and an AM General plant that once claimed to be the largest military truck-assembly facility outside of the Soviet Union. South Bend's population of 105,000 is a mixture of blue-collar workers and university-related professionals.

St. Joseph County, which includes South Bend, often supports Democrats at the state and local levels: Democrat Roemer's districtwide victory in 1990 was due in no small part to a strong showing in St. Joseph County. In 1988, Democratic presidential nominee Michael S. Dukakis received 49 percent of the county's vote, well above his 40 percent statewide tally.

The city of Elkhart's economy is less closely tied to the auto industry, and therefore more resilient than South Bend's. Elkhart depends more on the manufactured housing and recreational-vehicle industries, which are responsible for over 50,000 jobs in the 3rd. It is also headquarters for Miles Laboratories and is the band instrument capital of the United States. At one time nearly 60 percent of the world's band instruments came from there.

Republicans routinely draw more than 60 percent of the Elkhart County vote in local and statewide elections. Elkhart County and neighboring LaGrange County (in the 4th District) contain the second-largest concentration of Amish people in the United States.

Elkhart County casts about a fifth of the district's vote, and St. Joseph County a little less than half. But the large GOP pluralities from Elkhart frequently offset the smaller Democratic margins from St. Joseph, particularly when combined with the GOP strength of the district's farmers.

About a third of the vote comes from four rural counties to the south and west of South Bend and Elkhart. The cattle and dairy farmers of Kosciusko and Marshall counties traditionally vote a strong Republican ticket. In Starke County, where potatoes are a major crop, the voters sometimes side with the Democrats. Roemer and unsuccessful Democratic Senate candidate Baron Hill both won Starke in 1990.

Population: 558,100. White 521,400 (93%), Black 29,558 (5%), Other 3,139 (1%). Spanish origin 7,746 (1%). 18 and over 395,121 (71%), 65 and over 62,682 (11%). Median age: 30.

Committees

Education & Labor (22nd of 25 Democrats)
Elementary, Secondary & Vocational Education; Postsecondary Education

Science, Space & Technology (27th of 32 Democrats)
Energy; Science; Technology & Competitiveness

Campaign Finance

	Receipts	Receipts from PACs		Expend-itures
1990				
Roemer (D)	$504,884	$269,313	(53%)	$473,055
Hiler (R)	$776,009	$257,112	(33%)	$745,145

Key Vote

1991

Authorize use of force against Iraq	N

Elections

1990 General		
Tim Roemer (D)	80,740	(51%)
John Hiler (R)	77,911	(49%)
1990 Primary		
Tim Roemer (D)	22,898	(64%)
Daniel T. Durham (D)	8,101	(23%)
Sally Lou Croff (D)	2,357	(7%)
Samuel E. Lehman (D)	1,362	(4%)
Christopher A. Mikulak (D)	1,107	(3%)

District Vote For President

	1988	1984	1980	1976
D	87,080 (40%)	82,107 (38%)	81,627 (37%)	95,289 (44%)
R	128,039 (59%)	135,263 (62%)	124,750 (56%)	118,782 (55%)
I			13,777 (6%)	

4 Jill L. Long (D)

Of Larwill — Elected 1989

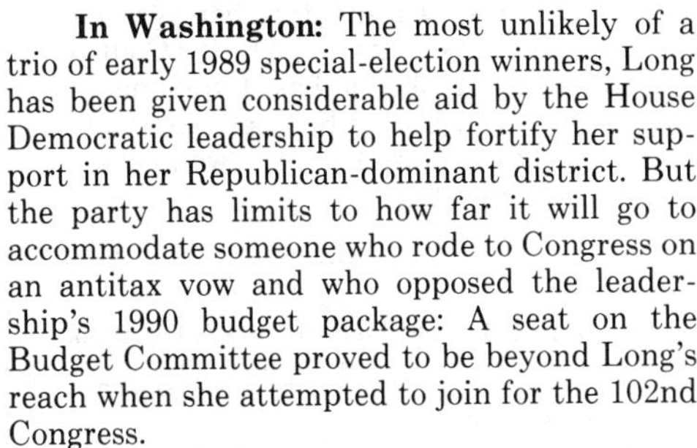

Born: July 15, 1952, Warsaw, Ind.

Education: Valparaiso U., B.S. 1974; Indiana U., M.B.A. 1978, Ph.D. 1984.

Occupation: Professor.

Family: Single.

Religion: Methodist.

Political Career: Valparaiso City Council, 1983-86; Democratic nominee for U.S. Senate, 1986; Democratic nominee for U.S. House, 1988.

Capitol Office: 1513 Longworth Bldg. 20515; 225-4436.

In Washington: The most unlikely of a trio of early 1989 special-election winners, Long has been given considerable aid by the House Democratic leadership to help fortify her support in her Republican-dominant district. But the party has limits to how far it will go to accommodate someone who rode to Congress on an antitax vow and who opposed the leadership's 1990 budget package: A seat on the Budget Committee proved to be beyond Long's reach when she attempted to join for the 102nd Congress.

Her fiscal conservatism aside, Long is no party maverick. In her first two years, she backed the Democratic position on roll-call votes more than three-quarters of the time. She voted to allow federal funds for abortions in cases of rape and incest, and supported raising the minimum wage and requiring employers to give workers unpaid family leave. In 1991, a surprisingly comfortable re-election behind her, she voted against authorizing President Bush to use force in the Persian Gulf.

In her first term, members helped Long fend off an attack on a provision in the 1990 defense authorization bill that had been added for her. Over strenuous GOP objections, the Armed Services Committee included $357,000 for North American Van Lines, headquartered in Fort Wayne, to reimburse the company for the destruction of a subsidiary's offices in the December 1989 U.S. invasion of Panama.

Kentucky Republican Larry J. Hopkins tried to delete the provision, blasting it as flagrant favoritism. But Democrats rallied around Long, and Hopkins' amendment was rejected 189-228. Some members said Long was the kind of friendly, agreeable colleague whom they routinely support on such matters.

At Home: In winning the 4th District in a March 1989 special election, Long finally found a "Dan" she could beat. She had been routed by Dan Quayle in a 1986 Senate bid and by Dan Coats in a 1988 House race. But those campaigns gave her high name recognition and a volunteer network — crucial ingredients in her narrow victory over Fort Wayne lawyer and city administrator Dan Heath.

She did learn some valuable lessons from her earlier campaigns. In her 1986 Senate race, she laid out a liberal agenda. Since then, she has done her best to avoid ideological typecasting while calling on Democrats with more moderate reputations to campaign for her, such as Tennessee Sen. Al Gore and Indiana Gov. Evan Bayh.

Her 1989 House victory was an embarrassment to the state and national Republican Party. The seat had been held by both Quayle and Coats, whose appointment to Quayle's Senate seat in December 1988 created the need for the special election.

When Long sought her first full term in 1990, infighting among Republicans helped her. GOP front-runner state Rep. Dan Stephan dropped out of the race just days before the primary after failing to energize the "Quayle-Coats" faction. Rick Hawks, a locally televised pastor, stepped in, delighting conservatives.

Hawks attempted to portray the race as a contest between ideologies, but Long dismissed him as a member of his party's "fringe element." Nor did revelations that Hawks was living on his campaign funds ease concerns of some residents about his religious fundraising background, despite the fact that he resigned his Baptist ministry to run for office. Long won easily with 61 percent.

Until 1989, politics had been an avocation for her rather than a career. Most of her paychecks have come from college teaching. Long has a doctorate in business from Indiana University and had to balance her campaign schedule in 1989 with two business courses at Indiana University/Purdue University-Fort Wayne. Even on Election Day, she had to break away from greeting voters to teach a noontime class. After teaching and politics, the third facet of Long's background is farming. She grew up on a farm, and before her election to Congress, she lived on an 80-acre farm in Whitley County, and helped her parents run their farm nearby.

Indiana 4

Northeast — Fort Wayne

Planted in the northeastern corner of the state, the 4th is dominated politically and economically by Fort Wayne, Indiana's second-largest city. Allen County, which includes Fort Wayne, has more than half of the district's population. With about 173,000 people, Fort Wayne is where voters in the surrounding nine counties look for news and commercial needs.

Located where the St. Mary's and St. Joseph rivers meet to form the Maumee, Fort Wayne has been a transportation and manufacturing center since the first half of the 19th century. General Electric, General Motors and Magnavox are currently among its major employers.

With a large German ethnic population, Fort Wayne is a strongly Republican town. Only once in the last 40 years — in 1964 — has Allen County failed to support the GOP presidential nominee. George Bush won the county by nearly 2-to-1 in 1988. The surrounding farm counties usually vote as consistently for the GOP as Fort Wayne does. The small town of Huntington, about 25 miles southwest of Fort Wayne, is the home of Vice President Dan Quayle; LaGrange County is home to a large concentration of Amish people. Yet while Republican voting habits in the district may be strong, they are not cast in stone. In winning the Indiana governorship in 1988, Democrat Evan Bayh carried six of the district's 10 counties; Long won every county in 1990.

Long not only took Allen County in 1988 and 1990, but also broke the expected grip of her GOP opponents on the rural vote by effectively promoting her agrarian roots — she owns a farm in Whitley County — against Fort Wayne-based opponents. Republican Sen. Daniel R. Coats and GOP state Auditor Ann DeVore won every county here in 1990.

Population: 553,698. White 520,079 (94%), Black 26,628 (5%), Other 2,670 (1%). Spanish origin 7,128 (1%). 18 and over 382,150 (69%), 65 and over 58,015 (10%). Median age: 29.

Committees

Agriculture (23rd of 27 Democrats)
Conservation, Credit & Rural Development; Livestock, Dairy & Poultry; Wheat, Soybeans & Feed Grains

Select Hunger (19th of 22 Democrats)
Domestic

Veterans' Affairs (14th of 21 Democrats)
Hospitals & Health Care; Oversight & Investigations

Elections

1990 General		
Jill L. Long (D)	99,347	(61%)
Rick Hawks (R)	64,415	(39%)
1990 Primary		
Jill L. Long (D)	30,505	(94%)
J. Carolyn Williams (D)	2,914	(6%)
1989 Special		
Jill L. Long (D)	65,272	(51%)
Dan Heath (R)	63,494	(49%)

District Vote For President

	1988	1984	1980	1976
D	71,156 (33%)	70,300 (33%)	73,699 (33%)	88,170 (40%)
R	143,461 (66%)	144,009 (67%)	128,189 (58%)	127,446 (58%)
I			16,699 (8%)	

Campaign Finance

	Receipts	Receipts from PACs	Expend-itures
1990			
Long (D)	$753,725	$448,381 (59%)	$752,362
Hawks (R)	$580,037	$79,448 (14%)	$575,363
1989			
Long (D)	$326,025	$182,763 (56%)	$313,724
Heath (R)	$393,716	$131,200 (33%)	$378,441

Key Votes

1991	
Authorize use of force against Iraq	N
1990	
Support constitutional amendment on flag desecration	Y
Pass family and medical leave bill over Bush veto	Y
Reduce SDI funding	Y
Allow abortions in overseas military facilities	Y
Approve budget summit plan for spending and taxing	N
Approve civil rights bill	Y
1989	
Halt production of B-2 stealth bomber at 13 planes	N
Oppose capital gains tax cut	N
Approve federal abortion funding in rape or incest cases	Y
Approve pay raise and revision of ethics rules	N
Pass Democratic minimum wage plan over Bush veto	Y

Voting Studies

	Presidential Support		Party Unity		Conservative Coalition	
Year	S	O	S	O	S	O
1990	29	71	78	22	67	33
1989	33 †	67 †	89 †	11 †	35 †	65 †

† Not eligible for all recorded votes.

Interest Group Ratings

Year	ADA	ACU	AFL-CIO	CCUS
1990	50	38	67	43
1989	68	25	80	50

5 Jim Jontz (D)

Of Monticello — Elected 1986

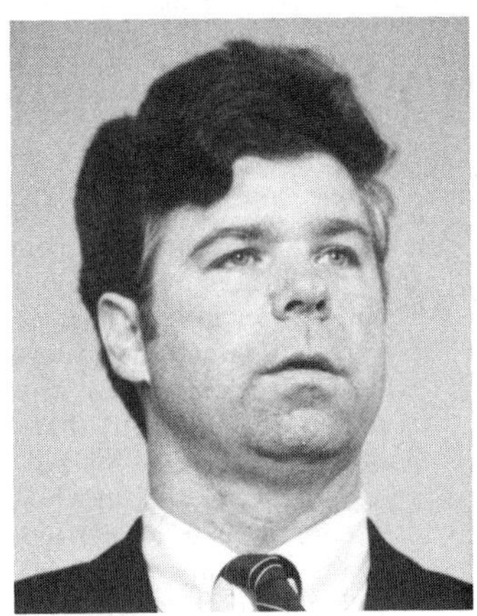

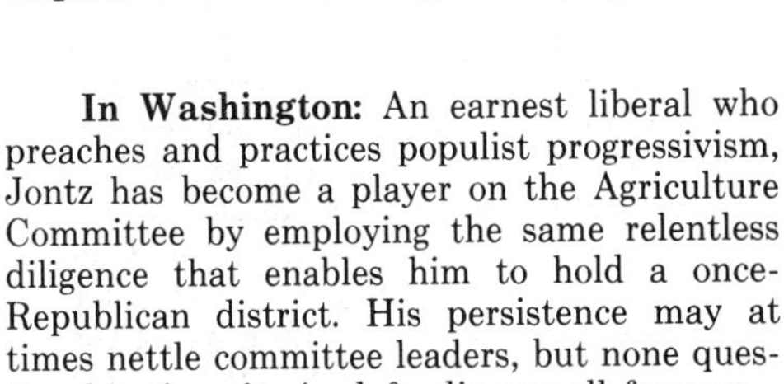

Born: Dec. 18, 1951, Indianapolis, Ind.
Education: Indiana U., B.S. 1973.
Occupation: State legislator.
Family: Single.
Religion: Methodist.
Political Career: Ind. House, 1975-85; Ind. Senate, 1985-87.
Capitol Office: 1317 Longworth Bldg. 20515; 225-5037.

In Washington: An earnest liberal who preaches and practices populist progressivism, Jontz has become a player on the Agriculture Committee by employing the same relentless diligence that enables him to hold a once-Republican district. His persistence may at times nettle committee leaders, but none question his sincerity in defending small farmers.

Working on the farm bill in 1990, Jontz' ubiquity earned him a reputation as something of a troublemaker. The Agriculture Committee staff honored him with the first question of their 1990 Farm Bill Trivia Quiz: To which of the 17 sections of the bill did Jontz not attach an amendment? The answer, as near as they could determine, was two minor sections.

Jontz is a vigorous advocate of higher farm subsidies, but he also believes Congress can help preserve the family farmer by encouraging producers to steward land better. His environmentalist perspective sets him apart from most committee members, who resent attempts to reduce farmers' use of chemicals. "I think there can be an alliance between environmentalists and family farmers," Jontz once said.

But his amendment to the research title of the farm bill, which said government research should investigate ways to "strengthen the family-farm system" and "protect the natural environment," irritated other farm-state legislators. Texas Democrat Charles W. Stenholm said, "We are being asked to believe that our method of production agriculture is faulty, and I am not prepared to do that." Committee members fuzzed it up and adopted it.

Jontz was a leading advocate of allowing farmers some freedom from planting the same mix of crops every year. A flexible planting plan was adopted as part of the farm bill.

Jontz' environmental concerns are not confined to Indiana. In 1990 he injected himself into one of the nation's most contentious debates and made himself a household name 2,000 miles from Kokomo. In 1990 the Fish and Wildlife Service listed the northern spotted owl as a threatened species. Seeking not only to protect the owl but to preserve their habitat of ancient "old-growth" forests, Jontz introduced a bill to ban logging in old-growth forests. Most such forests are in the Pacific Northwest, where loggers were apoplectic over what they considered an assault on their livelihood. Jontz was burned in effigy before a huge crowd of angry loggers in Washington state.

Jontz' old-growth bill and his support for banning development of another 1.8 million acres of the Tongass National Forest in Alaska prompted Alaska GOP Rep. Don Young to introduce a bill to establish a 1.3 million acre national forest in northwestern Indiana, in part to "provide for weekend recreational opportunities for residents of Chicago and Indianapolis." "Don's a funny guy," Jontz said.

Jontz can pursue his environmental interests on the Interior Committee, where he took a seat in the 102nd Congress. He left his post on Veterans' Affairs, but says he will continue to push for legislation to improve the treatment for the mostly Vietnam-era veterans afflicted by post-traumatic stress disorder.

With a temporary assignment on the Education and Labor Committee in the 101st Congress, Jontz pushed successfully for a six-month amnesty for student-loan defaulters. His bill, which aimed to save up to $20 million in the first year, became law as part of the 1989 year-end deficit-reduction bill.

Soon upon arriving in Washington in 1987, Jontz got busy. He secured construction-project money for Grissom Air Force Base in the 5th, and he was principal sponsor of five bills that passed the House. One expanded veterans benefits, one allowed communities to repay federal loans at a lower interest rate, and another lowered loan rates for small agriculture cooperatives hurt by drought. Jontz refused the 1987 pay raise and used the funds to sponsor scholarships in his district.

At Home: Jontz lives happily in one party while appealing aggressively to voters in the other. "I don't walk away from the party," he says. "At the same time I must have an independent appeal. The biggest point on my literature is not that I'm a Democrat."

Indiana 5

North — Kokomo

The 5th travels northwest from Kokomo, a small industrial center, to the suburbs of Chicago in Lake County. In between is mile upon mile of flat farmland. There once was a time when these three distinct political worlds shared one trait — they voted Republican. But that was before Jim Jontz. In 1988, he carried all but one of the 14 counties included in whole or part in the 5th, and in 1990, he carried all but two.

Traditionally, the part of the district friendliest to Republicans has been the southeast corner, in and around Kokomo (Howard County) and Marion (Grant County), another industrial city. Both have numerous small factories and a few very large ones, most of them related to the automobile industry. They also serve as major distribution points for the area's agricultural output. About 30 percent of the district's vote comes from these two counties.

The downturn in the auto industry during the last recession had as serious an effect on these communities as on any in the nation, with unemployment exceeding 15 percent in several places. In 1986, frustration over continuing industrial malaise helped Jontz overcome the straight-ticket GOP voting habits that usually prevail in Howard County and Grant County. By 1988, the employment picture in most factories was better, if not rosy, and George Bush took more than 60 percent in both Howard and Grant. That did not, however, deter Jontz from winning the counties in both 1988 and 1990.

Ninety miles to the northwest are the residents of southern Lake and Porter counties. These fast-growing suburban areas are attracting some employees from the steel mills along Lake Michigan, as well as former Chicago residents seeking a slower-paced life. More than one-fourth of the district vote comes out of Lake and Porter counties, which are separated from the rest of the district psychologically as well as geographically. Voters there watch Chicago TV stations and read newspapers from Chicago and Gary. Jontz carried both in 1988, though he lost Porter in 1990. Linking the small industrial cities and the burgeoning outer suburban fringe are expanses of corn and soybeans. All 10 of the predominantly rural counties voted for Bush in 1988, but nearly all also went for Jontz. Jontz won nine of the ten in 1990.

Population: 548,257. White 530,879 (97%), Black 11,875 (2%), Other 2,820 (1%). Spanish origin 6,106 (1%). 18 and over 380,248 (69%), 65 and over 55,952 (10%). Median age: 29.

Since the beginning of his political career, Jontz has won in basically GOP territory through a mix of energy, attentiveness and careful positioning. He can pay such persuasive attention to a group that it often will overlook some of his "wrong" votes.

Some thought it an incredible gaffe when Jontz told *USA Today* in 1988 that his hero was Eugene Debs, the Indiana-born union organizer who was five times the Socialist candidate for president. Yet in the same election cycle, Jontz was a cosponsor of the resolution calling for a balanced-budget constitutional amendment. And when courting voters personally, he concentrates on those who would consider Debs a radical. He rarely wastes time on Democrats he knows will support him if he can find Republicans who, someday, just might.

In the spring of 1989, Jontz was seriously considering a 1990 challenge to appointive GOP Sen. Daniel R. Coats. Jontz had urged the race on Rep. Lee H. Hamilton, the state's senior Democrat. When Hamilton said no, Jontz emerged as the party's next choice. In May, however, he opted out, saying he wanted to establish himself in his sprawling district.

Jontz found himself in a tougher-than-anticipated 1990 re-election battle against Republican John A. Johnson, a millionaire businessman, lawyer and physicist who fueled his campaign with about $350,000 in personal money. A political neophyte, Johnson espoused congressional term limitations and rode an anti-incumbent backlash. He also tried to capitalize on the fuss Jontz stirred in the Pacific Northwest with his forest-protection bill. Johnson invited himself to speak before the Northwest Timber Association, where he took in contributions.

In the end, Jontz managed to portray himself as a defender of the common man against a wealthy foe, despite criticism he faced when a local newspapers reported that Jontz had purchased a home in the District of Columbia. Jontz won by 53-47 percent.

Jontz' remarkable rise began when, at age 22, he challenged the Republican leader of the Indiana House and unseated him by two votes. A decade later, he ran for the state Senate in the midst of the Reagan presidential tide, and took a seat out of GOP hands.

Despite that track record, many Republicans seemed unaware of the threat he posed in 1986, when GOP Rep. Elwood Hillis was retiring from the 5th. As late as two weeks before the November election, GOP strategists boasted of a 20-point lead.

Jontz is not only good, he is lucky. His 1974 upset victory was made possible by the Watergate malaise that hurt Republicans everywhere. His election to Congress was in part the result of an angry primary that pitted the district's GOP establishment against an energetic group of conservative Christian activists.

The winner of that 1986 GOP primary was James Butcher, a Kokomo lawyer and state senator and a favorite of evangelical Christians. After winning nomination, Butcher moved to the center, stressing his work as a legislator and insisting he was no religious zealot.

But while Butcher was repositioning, Jontz was pressing on with the campaign he began in the fall of 1985, shortly after Hillis made his retirement announcement. It was a full-time, person-to-person effort in all 14 of the district's counties, augmented by fund-raising that brought in a surprising sum for a Democrat in a district long in GOP hands.

Butcher eventually went after Jontz, calling him a liberal in camouflage and reminding voters that while Jontz trumpeted family values and jobs, he was a bachelor and professional officeholder. But the charges never stuck, and Jontz won with 51 percent.

In 1988, the GOP offered Patricia Williams, who was running the Kokomo Board of Realtors and had worked in Hillis' office for 16 years. Williams banked on a big turnout for the GOP presidential ticket, in part because Dan Quayle hailed from a county bordering the 5th. The turnout was large, but many GOP voters split their tickets, and Jontz won 56 percent.

Committees

Agriculture (18th of 27 Democrats)
Department Operations, Research & Foreign Agriculture; Forests, Family Farms & Energy

Interior & Insular Affairs (25th of 29 Democrats)
Energy & the Environment; Mining & Natural Resources; National Parks & Public Lands

Select Aging (28th of 42 Democrats)
Retirement, Income & Employment

Elections

1990 General		
Jim Jontz (D)	81,373	(53%)
John A. Johnson (R)	71,750	(47%)
1988 General		
Jim Jontz (D)	116,240	(56%)
Patricia L. Williams (R)	90,163	(44%)

Previous Winning Percentage: **1986** (51%)

District Vote For President

	1988	1984	1980	1976
D	73,065 (35%)	67,224 (31%)	68,760 (31%)	81,118 (44%)
R	136,223 (65%)	150,354 (69%)	140,368 (63%)	114,774 (58%)
I			9,677 (4%)	

Campaign Finance

	Receipts	Receipts from PACs	Expenditures
1990			
Jontz (D)	$620,713	$405,145 (65%)	$652,280
Johnson (R)	$783,818	$33,600 (4%)	$781,224
1988			
Jontz (D)	$721,637	$471,725 (65%)	$689,086
Williams (R)	$247,010	$90,262 (37%)	$244,985

Key Votes

1991	
Authorize use of force against Iraq	N
1990	
Support constitutional amendment on flag desecration	N
Pass family and medical leave bill over Bush veto	Y
Reduce SDI funding	Y
Allow abortions in overseas military facilities	Y
Approve budget summit plan for spending and taxing	N
Approve civil rights bill	Y
1989	
Halt production of B-2 stealth bomber at 13 planes	Y
Oppose capital gains tax cut	Y
Approve federal abortion funding in rape or incest cases	Y
Approve pay raise and revision of ethics rules	N
Pass Democratic minimum wage plan over Bush veto	Y

Voting Studies

	Presidential Support		Party Unity		Conservative Coalition	
Year	**S**	**O**	**S**	**O**	**S**	**O**
1990	14	85	90	10	28	72
1989	22	78	94	6	7	93
1988	16	84	91	8	26	74
1987	11	89	93	7	12	88

Interest Group Ratings

Year	ADA	ACU	AFL-CIO	CCUS
1990	89	17	83	36
1989	100	4	83	20
1988	95	4	100	21
1987	100	0	94	20

6 Dan Burton (R)

Of Indianapolis — Elected 1982

Born: June 21, 1938, Indianapolis, Ind.

Education: Attended Indiana U., 1958-59; Cincinnati Bible Seminary, 1959-60.

Military Service: Army, 1956-57; Army Reserve, 1957-62.

Occupation: Real estate and insurance agent.

Family: Wife, Barbara Logan; three children.

Religion: Protestant.

Political Career: Ind. House, 1967-69, 1977-81; Ind. Senate, 1969-71, 1981-83; Republican nominee for U.S. House, 1970; sought Republican nomination for U.S. House, 1972.

Capitol Office: 120 Cannon Bldg. 20515; 225-2276.

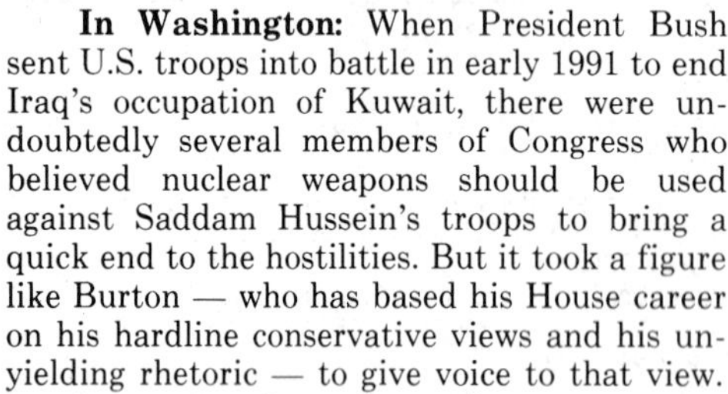

In Washington: When President Bush sent U.S. troops into battle in early 1991 to end Iraq's occupation of Kuwait, there were undoubtedly several members of Congress who believed nuclear weapons should be used against Saddam Hussein's troops to bring a quick end to the hostilities. But it took a figure like Burton — who has based his House career on his hardline conservative views and his unyielding rhetoric — to give voice to that view.

In a series of speeches and appearances on television news programs, Burton promoted the use of tactical nuclear weapons against Iraqi military targets. "A surgical strike with extremely low-yield nuclear weapons would not endanger civilian areas, and would probably save thousands of U.S. lives," he said. Bush, however, had expressly stated that the United States would not use nuclear or any other unconventional weapons in the Persian Gulf War, and Burton's proposal did not move him.

Although Burton's critics branded him an extremist for proposing the use of nuclear weapons, he was certainly not the first member of Congress to do so in times of war: Lloyd Bentsen, the respected chairman of the Senate Finance Committee and the 1988 Democratic vice presidential candidate, made just such a proposal as a young House member during the Korean War. Still, Burton's stand reconfirmed his image as a stalwart of the hard-right flank on the Foreign Affairs Committee and in the House overall.

It is somewhat ironic that the reasoning underlying Burton's nuclear strike proposal was similar to that used by many of the Democrats who opposed Bush's initial decision to go to war: Both sides cited the then-prevailing wisdom that the United States would suffer large numbers of casualties in a land war against Iraq's massive concentrations of supposedly battle-hardened forces. Burton said that if conventional bombing did not draw Saddam Hussein's elite troops from their fortifications, then U.S. bombers should "dislodge them with everything at our disposal before we send our young Americans into a meat grinder."

Burton had already shown in his performance on Foreign Affairs that there are no shades of gray in his worldview. He regards communist governments and movements — even those with which Republican administrations have sought rapprochement — with unstinting hostility. He is not much kinder to fellow House members who do not see things his way.

Burton unloosed one of his harshest attacks during a 1987 debate over U.S. aid to the contra rebels then fighting the leftist Sandinista government of Nicaragua. "My colleagues on the left," Burton said, "need to admit forthrightly that they support the communist government of Nicaragua and quit this charade that they try to put forth on the American people."

Although it has no obvious political benefit to a member from the Indiana heartland, Burton's position as ranking Republican on the Foreign Affairs Africa Subcommittee is pivotal to his anti-communist crusade. He sponsors U.S. aid to anti-leftist insurgents — whom he describes as "freedom-fighters" — on that continent, but strongly opposes the use of sanctions to modify the behavior of African rulers known for anti-democratic practices but pro-Western sympathies.

During subcommittee debate on a foreign aid authorization bill in April 1989, Burton opposed placing conditions on U.S. aid to Kenya and Liberia, while calling for a cutoff of aid to Marxist-led Mozambique. Although Burton said the panel was "singling out our friends for specific criticism" while supporting a "communist dictatorship," his amendments were defeated. His attempt the next month to place strict conditions on aid to Mozambique was

Indiana 6

Northern Indianapolis; Anderson

No Democrat need apply in the 6th, a "lifetime appointment" for any GOP incumbent who stays clear of primary trouble.

One-fourth of the vote is cast in the affluent Washington Township area of Indianapolis, some of Indiana's most Republican turf. A Democratic candidate does well to top 25 percent here.

Hamilton County, north of Indianapolis, outdoes even Washington Township in its partisan loyalty. It is the single most Republican county in Indiana, as well as the fastest-growing in recent years. In 1990, GOP Sen. Dan Coats and Burton both notched over 70 percent.

After Indianapolis, the only other sizable city is Anderson, with just over 59,000 people. It and surrounding Madison County contribute another quarter of the district's vote. General Motors has been crucial to Anderson's economy since the 1920s; the city has a large group of United Auto Workers and a hard-core Democratic vote. During economic downturns, Anderson's vote is almost enough to tip Madison County away from the GOP. Unemployment rates have dipped since record highs in the early 1980s, but tough times in Anderson have made the county more amenable to Democratic advances; Burton and Coats squeaked by in 1990 while every other GOP statewide candidate lost Madison. Usually, though, Republican votes outside Anderson keep the county in the GOP column; since 1948, the county has voted Democratic for president only once, in 1964.

The remaining third of the district is primarily rural. Farmers in the counties north and east of Indianapolis dislike being part of a mostly urban and suburban district, but they have enough in common with conservative suburbanites to make for a relatively homogeneous district politics.

Population: 540,939. White 520,429 (96%), Black 16,369 (3%), Other 2,849 (1%). Spanish origin 3,445 (1%). 18 and over 381,833 (71%), 65 and over 54,972 (10%). Median age: 31.

defeated on a 5-26 vote by the full committee.

During debate on that amendment, Burton said Mozambique's anti-government guerrilla group Renamo was backed by South Africa, which he said was "allied" with the United States. The comment earned Burton a rebuke from Democratic Rep. Howard Wolpe of Michigan, then the Africa subcommittee chairman, who said no such alliance existed with South Africa, which faced U.S. economic sanctions for its policy of racial separation, or apartheid.

Burton has long been a staunch opponent of such sanctions, which he says are counterproductive. In 1988, Burton presented a "black empowerment" alternative to a bill to impose stiff sanctions against South Africa. His amendment promised U.S. aid for black-owned businesses in South Africa, and provided tax benefits for American companies that followed nondiscriminatory practices in South Africa.

Burton said his measure would enable blacks to gain economic and political power, while sanctions would create an economic crisis "that will lead to an escalating spiral of violence and repression." But while Burton got some credit for shaping his anti-sanctions position into a politically palatable form, the House defeated the proposal by a wide margin.

Although Burton appears preoccupied with foreign policy issues, he does not ignore his other assignments. These include the ranking Republican positions on the Post Office and Civil Service Subcommittee on Human Resources and on the Veterans Affairs Subcommittee on Housing and Memorial Affairs.

During the run-up to the 1990 census, Burton fought to prevent the counting of illegal aliens. Burton claimed that the inclusion of this group cost Indiana (which has few such immigrants) a House seat after the 1980 census.

"I won't let this happen again," he said during a 1988 Post Office and Civil Service Committee debate on a bill aimed at adjusting the 1990 census to offset an expected "undercount" of minorities. "Illegal aliens are not citizens, so they should not be counted." Burton won passage of an amendment barring the counting of illegal aliens, leading committee Democrats to scuttle the whole bill. However, the Census Bureau ultimately did include illegal aliens in the 1990 headcount.

Burton's overall voting record is supportive of the Bush administration. In 1990, he backed Bush on 77 percent of House votes. But like most conservative Republicans, Burton fumed in June 1990 when Bush took his first step back from his "no new taxes" pledge. Joining in a news conference with like-minded GOP House members, Burton said, "If the president calls me and says, 'I need you on this,' I'll say, 'I have to stick to my pledge to the American people not to raise taxes.' "

Burton also stands out as a fervent opponent of gay rights legislation. In October 1989, he spoke in support of an amendment by Rep. William E. Dannemeyer, R-Calif., providing religious-based schools with a waiver from a District of Columbia law barring discrimination on the basis of sexual orientation. Countering opponents of the amendment, Burton said, "How far do we go down the slippery road of homosexual rights?" Burton, who has also proposed universal annual blood testing for the AIDS virus, may emerge as the leading House opponent of gay rights after Dannemeyer, who is running for the Senate in 1992, departs.

One issue on which Burton does demur from conservative orthodoxy is free trade. Burton takes a more protectionist position than many Republicans, a reflection of the difficulties foreign competition has caused many of Indiana's blue-collar industries. Burton is a co-chairman of the Congressional Auto Caucus and is a member of the Steel Caucus.

At Home: Burton settled an old intraparty score by winning his 1982 primary.

A decade earlier he had lost to William Hudnut by 81 votes for the nomination in a nearby district; Hudnut served a term in the House and later became mayor of Indianapolis. When the new 6th was created in 1981, Mayor Hudnut hoped to secure the nomination for his GOP ally, state party Chairman Bruce Melchert. Against Melchert, however, Burton won.

Burton and Melchert agreed on most issues, and the competition was mostly amiable. But the Burton-Hudnut feud surfaced at one point, when Burton suggested that the mayor had engineered the last-minute candidacy of political unknown Ricky Bartl to deprive Burton of first position on the alphabetical ballot.

Burton won the primary by 5,260 votes of over 72,000 cast, and in November he began what seems sure to be a long streak of decisive general-election victories by taking 65 percent.

Burton served 10 years in the state Legislature, his tenure interrupted by two congressional campaigns — the losing 1972 primary against Hudnut, and an unsuccessful 1970 bid against Democratic Rep. Andrew Jacobs Jr.

Committees

Foreign Affairs (11th of 18 Republicans)
Africa (ranking); Western Hemisphere Affairs

Post Office & Civil Service (5th of 8 Republicans)
Human Resources (ranking)

Veterans' Affairs (5th of 13 Republicans)
Housing & Memorial Affairs (ranking); Hospitals & Health Care

Elections

1990 General		
Dan Burton (R)	116,470	(63%)
James P. Fadely (D)	67,024	(37%)
1988 General		
Dan Burton (R)	192,064	(73%)
George Thomas Holland (D)	71,447	(27%)

Previous Winning Percentages: **1986** (68%) **1984** (73%) **1982** (65%)

District Vote For President

	1988	1984	1980	1976
D	81,466 (31%)	80,918 (33%)	73,070 (29%)	86,898 (38%)
R	183,075 (69%)	160,491 (66%)	161,358 (65%)	139,352 (61%)
I			12,404 (5%)	

Campaign Finance

	Receipts	Receipts from PACs		Expend-itures
1990				
Burton (R)	$526,451	$203,426	(39%)	$311,727
Fadely (D)	$41,866	$9,000	(21%)	$41,180
1988				
Burton (R)	$383,170	$141,170	(37%)	$333,723
Holland (D)	$12,319	$5,000	(41%)	$11,743

Key Votes

1991	
Authorize use of force against Iraq	Y
1990	
Support constitutional amendment on flag desecration	Y
Pass family and medical leave bill over Bush veto	N
Reduce SDI funding	N
Allow abortions in overseas military facilities	N
Approve budget summit plan for spending and taxing	N
Approve civil rights bill	N
1989	
Halt production of B-2 stealth bomber at 13 planes	N
Oppose capital gains tax cut	N
Approve federal abortion funding in rape or incest cases	N
Approve pay raise and revision of ethics rules	Y
Pass Democratic minimum wage plan over Bush veto	N

Voting Studies

	Presidential Support		Party Unity		Conservative Coalition	
Year	**S**	**O**	**S**	**O**	**S**	**O**
1990	77	22	95	2	94	2
1989	60	28	85	6	85	7
1988	84	16	96	2	95	0
1987	76	19	93	3	93	7
1986	81	18	94	4	96	4
1985	80	16	94	2	100	0
1984	73	20	93	3	90	5
1983	83	16	92	4	93	6

Interest Group Ratings

Year	ADA	ACU	AFL-CIO	CCUS
1990	11	96	17	85
1989	5	96	17	90
1988	0	100	0	93
1987	8	100	0	93
1986	5	100	21	89
1985	5	100	0	86
1984	0	83	23	86
1983	10	91	13	80

7 John T. Myers (R)

Of Covington — Elected 1966

Born: Feb. 8, 1927, Covington, Ind.
Education: Indiana State U., B.S. 1951.
Military Service: Army, 1945-46.
Occupation: Banker; farmer.
Family: Wife, Carol Carruthers; two children.
Religion: Episcopalian.
Political Career: No previous office.
Capitol Office: 2372 Rayburn Bldg. 20515; 225-5805.

In Washington: Myers is the kind of old-fashioned, middle-American moderate Republican traditionally found within the inner circle of the House GOP leadership. His insider status served Myers well over the years, earning him his seat on the Appropriations Committee, where he is now the No. 2 Republican in seniority.

A banker, a farmer, a Mason, an Elk and a Lion, Myers shares with other Appropriations members a pragmatic worldview in which deal-making skills are valued over ideology.

This philosophy, however, has spurred distrust among some of his party's House conservatives, who think Myers and other senior GOP appropriators are more loyal to their committee's products than to party principles of fiscal conservatism. Myers may well have fewer sharp critics across the aisle than within the Republican Conference.

But Myers has never left any doubt about his affiliation with Appropriations politics. The ranking Republican on the Energy and Water Development Subcommittee, he likes to describe the panel's spending measure as "an All-American bill" that would "touch every congressional district in our country directly."

He once said the provisions of the bill would help ensure the supply of electricity Americans use when they "plug the toaster in and turn on the electric stove and use our electric razors or the curling irons for the ladies," and the water "we drew this morning for our showers, that we use daily in our consumption, not only in our homes, but also in industry."

In 1990, as the fiscal 1991 energy and water appropriations bill breezed through the full committee, Myers took note of the lack of substantive amendments. "How can you improve upon perfection?" he joked.

Myers emerged in the 101st Congress as a supporter of the super-conducting supercollider (SSC), a giant atom smasher to be built in Texas by the Department of Energy. Defending the first-stage appropriation for the multi-billion-dollar project, Myers pointed to the predicted technological spinoffs of the basic research to be done by SSC scientists. "We don't know exactly where we're going," Myers said in July 1989. "But it's time to make an investment in our future."

It is the subcommittee's control over the science research and water projects that many members covet for their districts — and conservatives deride as "pork" — that makes the panel an important power base for Myers. He also gets his share for the 7th District: The fiscal 1991 bill included Energy Department funding for a research center at Indiana State University in Terre Haute.

Myers can be a genial jokester in the Republican cloakroom, but is noted for playing hardball on bills he has a hand in: He tracks closely those who vote with and against him. Once in a private meeting with Republicans, Myers pulled just such a list of names from his suit pocket and brandished it for all to see.

Myers can be sharp toward Republicans who try to demonstrate their fiscal conservatism by cutting the energy and water bill. In mid-1987, he told some members they would lose pet projects if they supported efforts to cut the bill on the House floor. Saying it would be hard in a House-Senate conference to defend projects of members who did not support the whole bill, Myers later explained, "It's not a threat. It's a fact of life."

The antagonism between Republican pragmatists like Myers and the more confrontational conservative activists led by Georgia Republican Newt Gingrich boiled up in 1989. At issue was whether Myers, then ranking Republican on the House ethics committee, and the other traditional Republican insiders on that panel would be tough enough in the investigation of Jim Wright, who was then still Speaker.

Myers had moved up to the ranking position when South Carolina Republican Floyd D. Spence resigned from the committee for health reasons. Some matters — such as the selection of the outside attorney to head the probe — were delegated almost entirely to Myers and Julian C. Dixon of California, the Democrat

Indiana 7

West Central — Terre Haute; Lafayette

The 7th is the district of the Wabash River, a broad tributary of the Ohio that Hoosier chauvinists still rhapsodize about when they sing "My Indiana Home." The Wabash flows through six of the 14 counties in the district. It is the state's longest river and was responsible for the rapid development of the area in the early 19th century, when newcomers arrived in western Indiana via flatboats and steamers.

The Wabash crosses some of the richest glaciated farmland in the Midwest, land used primarily for grain and livestock farming. The voters here are the kind of solid Republican farmers whose opinions have determined the course of state politics over most of this century.

The 7th is Indiana's second-largest district in area, with only two real population centers — Terre Haute and Lafayette — at opposite ends of the district. Vigo County (Terre Haute) and Tippecanoe County (Lafayette) each account for about a fifth of the district's population.

Terre Haute, once part of a small coal-mining region that has since turned to light industry and food processing, has Democratic roots. Many of its citizens came originally from Indiana's southern hill country, rather than from the more prosperous Republican farmland to the north. Flanking Vigo County on the north and south are Vermillion and Sullivan counties, also supporting Democrats.

Lafayette, with its smaller twin, West Lafayette, rests comfortably in the Republican heartland, 85 miles north of Terre Haute. Tippecanoe County voters rarely swing to the Democratic Party. With its emphasis on agriculture and engineering, Purdue University, the economic mainstay of West Lafayette, has spawned a conservative, GOP-leaning academic community. The economy of the area is diversifying; a Subaru-Isuzu plant was built in Lafayette in 1989, employing 1,900 people.

The most Republican counties in the 7th District, however, are Hendricks and Morgan, near Indianapolis. Here almost any GOP candidate can expect to receive at least twice as many votes as any Democrat. And as conservative homeowners move out of Indianapolis to outlying suburbs and small towns in these counties, the GOP margins continue to grow.

Population: 555,192. White 540,436 (97%), Black 9,381 (2%), Other 3,507 (1%). Spanish origin 3,483 (1%). 18 and over 403,139 (73%), 65 and over 62,715 (11%). Median age: 29.

who was then the committee's chairman.

Yet Myers was put on the spot in February 1989 by Gingrich. Expressing concern that the ethics committee might "issue a whitewash," Gingrich asked a Republican leadership panel to call for the committee to release all of its testimony and documents. Myers headed off that suggestion, convincing his colleagues that the probe would be thorough. And he took umbrage at the interference. "If we don't hang somebody the first day of the trial, some people complain," he said in an interview.

The concerns of the Republican right proved unjustified. When the ethics committee voted to pursue charges against Wright in a trial-like proceeding, Myers voted "yes" on every count. He defended his Republican colleagues against an implication by Wright's lawyers that they were trying to get even for the Senate's 1989 rejection of John Tower's nomination to be secretary of defense. "To accuse members of this committee that we were party to a political vendetta ... is an insult," Myers said. The controversy unleashed by the ethics committee report resulted in Wright's resignation in May 1989.

Myers also took a tough line on Democratic Rep. Barney Frank of Massachusetts, whose past relationship with a male prostitute was under investigation in 1990. When some committee Democrats suggested letting Frank off with the lightest punishment, a letter of reproval, Myers held out for a stricter sentence. The committee eventually compromised on a reprimand for Frank, which the House passed.

At the start of 102nd Congress, Myers finished his three-term rotation on ethics, and returned full time to his more comfortable assignments on Appropriations and on the Post Office and Civil Service Committee, where he is ranking Republican on the Compensation and Employee Benefits Subcommittee.

In the 101st Congress, he backed a bill by Indiana Democrat Frank McCloskey to crack down on deceptive mailings. The bill, enacted in 1990, requires direct-mail fundraisers to include disclaimers on solicitations that appear to be government documents. Myers said deceptive mailers "prey upon senior citizens and others ... easily taken in."

At Home: Myers began his winning ways in 1966, when redistricting produced a 7th District without an incumbent. Myers had long had been active in the party, mostly on the local level in Covington and in the Young Republicans. His 29 percent was enough for the GOP nomination over five opponents, one of whom, Daniel B. Crane, later served in the House from Illinois.

For years, Democrats helped Myers by nominating candidates of limited appeal. In 1966, Myers defeated Elden C. Tipton, a former naval officer and farmer who had already been beaten twice before. Tipton tried two more campaigns against Myers but never came close. His son, J. Elden Tipton, ran a similarly weak campaign against Myers in 1976.

By 1978, many Democrats in the 7th were saying that Myers' only real strength was his ability to draw the Tiptons as his opposition. That year, Democrat Charlotte Zietlow, a former Bloomington City Council president, ran a spirited race against Myers, basing her campaign on the claim that consumers were being bilked by utility-rate increases. But Myers' rural support canceled out Democratic strength in Bloomington, and he won comfortably.

Redistricting in 1981 significantly altered Myers' constituency, but not to his detriment. Democratic Bloomington was removed from the 7th and the more conservative city of Lafayette was added, as well as GOP turf near Indianapolis. Running in the reshaped district in 1982, Myers faced a credible but underfinanced foe, Stephen S. Bonney, a former Purdue University professor. Myers got 62 percent.

Democrats had a vigorous challenger in 1984 in Art Smith, a 29-year-old former congressional aide. But when Smith's lopsided loss scared away significant opposition in 1986 and made Democratic leaders pessimistic about their prospects in 1988. Their nominee, 27-year-old attorney Mark R. Waterfill, wound up running the strongest Democratic campaign of the 1980s. Even so, he failed to reach 40 percent. In the anti-incumbent wave of 1990, Myers slipped to 58 percent against John W. Riley, a school bus driver and former carpenter.

Committees

Appropriations (2nd of 22 Republicans)
Energy & Water Development (ranking); Rural Development, Agriculture & Related Agencies

Post Office & Civil Service (3rd of 8 Republicans)
Compensation & Employee Benefits (ranking); Postal Personnel & Modernization

Elections

1990 General

John T. Myers (R)	88,598	(58%)
John W. Riley Sr. (D)	65,248	(42%)

1988 General

John T. Myers (R)	130,578	(62%)
Mark R. Waterfill (D)	80,738	(38%)

Previous Winning Percentages: **1986** (67%) **1984** (67%) **1982** (62%) **1980** (66%) **1978** (56%) **1976** (63%) **1974** (57%) **1972** (62%) **1970** (57%) **1968** (60%) **1966** (54%)

District Vote For President

	1988	1984	1980	1976
D	79,244 (37%)	73,751 (33%)	77,802 (34%)	98,966 (44%)
R	136,233 (63%)	147,763 (66%)	136,445 (59%)	126,314 (56%)
I			12,080 (5%)	

Campaign Finance

	Receipts	Receipts from PACs		Expend-itures
1990				
Myers (R)	$198,891	$98,870	(50%)	$228,556
1988				
Myers (R)	$171,287	$96,500	(56%)	$163,280
Waterfill (D)	$67,889	$34,800	(51%)	$67,591

Key Votes

1991	
Authorize use of force against Iraq	Y
1990	
Support constitutional amendment on flag desecration	Y
Pass family and medical leave bill over Bush veto	N
Reduce SDI funding	N
Allow abortions in overseas military facilities	N
Approve budget summit plan for spending and taxing	N
Approve civil rights bill	N
1989	
Halt production of B-2 stealth bomber at 13 planes	N
Oppose capital gains tax cut	N
Approve federal abortion funding in rape or incest cases	N
Approve pay raise and revision of ethics rules	Y
Pass Democratic minimum wage plan over Bush veto	N

Voting Studies

	Presidential Support		Party Unity		Conservative Coalition	
Year	**S**	**O**	**S**	**O**	**S**	**O**
1990	69	29	65	33	94	6
1989	73	27	56	40	88	10
1988	57	33	60	34	82	13
1987	65	29	59	36	88	7
1986	67	31	54	45	82	18
1985	69	28	58	39	91	9
1984	59	40	69	26	93	7
1983	68	27	72	25	88	8
1982	70	27	84	16	89	11
1981	75	25	77	21	91	9

Interest Group Ratings

Year	ADA	ACU	AFL-CIO	CCUS
1990	11	83	0	86
1989	20	74	25	100
1988	15	83	15	92
1987	8	87	19	60
1986	20	91	36	50
1985	20	71	18	73
1984	15	74	15	50
1983	10	83	0	90
1982	5	85	15	86
1981	0	93	29	83

8 Frank McCloskey (D)

Of Smithville — Elected 1982

Born: June 12, 1939, Philadelphia, Pa.
Education: Indiana U., A.B. 1968, J.D. 1971.
Military Service: Air Force, 1957-61.
Occupation: Lawyer; journalist.
Family: Wife, Roberta Ann Barker; two children.
Religion: Roman Catholic.
Political Career: Democratic nominee for Ind. House, 1970; mayor of Bloomington, 1972-83.
Capitol Office: 127 Cannon Bldg. 20515; 225-4636.

In Washington: In his assignments on the Armed Services and Foreign Affairs committees and his senior position on the lower-profile Post Office and Civil Service Committee, McCloskey's legislative pursuits have earned him some attention. He has thus made headway in distancing himself from his reputation as "the four-vote wonder," a millstone since his controversial 1984 re-election campaign.

McCloskey had won an apparent narrow victory in 1984, but a recount gave the edge to Republican Richard D. McIntyre, who was certified the winner by Indiana's Republican secretary of state. The House Democratic leadership then pushed through a measure ordering a recount by the U.S. General Accounting Office (GAO), which declared McCloskey the winner by four votes. The outcome prompted a mass walkout by House Republicans, and still today, some among them harbor a grudge over what they saw as a "railroad" job by the Democratic majority.

For his part, McCloskey shook off the near-defeat and has worked hard to establish a role for himself in Armed Services policy-making, speaking out on issues ranging from the prominent to the esoteric.

During the latter days of the Reagan administration, McCloskey became a leading critic of one of the president's pet projects: the strategic defense initiative (SDI). McCloskey was not unalterably opposed to SDI research: The $3.85 billion he proposed in a 1987 amendment was higher than the $3.2 billion approved by a subcommittee. But like many Democrats, McCloskey was skeptical of SDI's value and worried about its effect on arms control negotiations.

He took particular umbrage at strategies for early deployment of SDI. This sentiment moved McCloskey to attempt to block development of a heat-seeking rocket then seen as a linchpin for any near-term SDI deployment. McCloskey joined South Carolina Democrat John M. Spratt Jr. in trying to bar development and testing of the rocket; they lost on 203-216 vote.

Most Armed Services members have favored weapons programs, and McCloskey is no exception. He is opposed to the budget-based effort by Defense Secretary Dick Cheney to eliminate development of the V-22 Osprey, a hybrid airplane-helicopter. McCloskey concedes that his interest in the project is based partially on the fact that the Osprey's engines are built in Indiana.

McCloskey has described himself as an ally of centrist Armed Services Chairman Les Aspin. But he strongly disagreed with Aspin's support for an early military response to Iraq's invasion of Kuwait. "The sanctions are working," McCloskey said in opposing the 1991 resolution authorizing use of force against Iraq. "Are the problems of jobs, productivity, health care, deficit reduction, the environment and a truly peaceful new world order not more important than jumping the gun in the sands of the Middle East?"

Overall, McCloskey's House voting record might appear somewhat liberal for southern Indiana. However, he has maintained his base by attending to 8th District issues, including those related to agriculture and coal mining.

McCloskey has also applied himself to the more mundane work of the Post Office Committee. He is chairman of the Postal Operations and Services Subcommittee, succeeding Democratic Rep. Mickey Leland of Texas, who died in an August 1990 plane crash.

The 101st Congress enacted a bill, authored and promoted by McCloskey, aimed at barring deceptive mailings by fundraising or advocacy organizations. The law requires a disclaimer on any non-governmental mailing that uses an emblem or other insignia that might give the impression it is a government document. McCloskey also sponsored a successful measure that requires potentially harmful drugs and household products sent through the mail to be packaged in child-proof containers.

At Home: After an easy 1988 victory, McCloskey took 55 percent of the vote in 1990, a slide back toward the narrow margins he won in his first three House elections.

The closest of those three, of course, was his 1984 contest with McIntyre. The GOP challenger

Indiana 8

Southwest — Evansville

The Democrats have now held the 8th in five straight elections, and McCloskey's solid victory in 1988 marked the first time since 1972 that a candidate for the 8th has received more than 60 percent of the vote. The Democrat seems to be bringing electoral stability to a district that was once among the nation's most politically marginal. It was Republican until 1974, Democratic for the next four years, and then Republican for four years before switching back to the Democrats in 1982.

Evansville, with 126,000 people, is the economic center of southern Indiana. The state's third-largest city, it has a diversified industrial base and a largely middle-class population. From the time when former U.S. Sen. Vance Hartke was mayor in the 1950s, the city has tried to entice new industry to replace major corporations that pulled out after World War II. In recent years, Evansville has taken an interest in its history as an important Ohio River port; commercial and cultural offerings are envisioned in a redeveloped riverbank sector.

Evansville's political influence extends over the southern half of the 8th. More than half the district's voters watch Evansville television stations, and the city provides jobs for a large area along the Ohio River. The Democratic heritage of the river counties, which dates back to their original settlement 150 years ago, remains strong. McCloskey's margin in Vanderburgh County (Evansville) dropped from 68 percent in 1988 to 53 percent in 1990, but he carried every county except Lawrence.

Though the district has only one town larger than 25,000, it boasts several famous native sons. French Lick (Orange County) was the boyhood home to basketball star Larry Bird; Abraham Lincoln spent his youth in Spencer County.

The 8th stretches north all the way to Bloomington, taking in the southern, most prosperous third of the city and most of the surrounding Monroe County suburbs. This area normally votes Republican, although it does include some students and faculty from Indiana University.

In the last round of redistricting, the GOP-controlled Legislature deliberately placed most of the university community in the neighboring 9th, an unsuccessful effort to help keep the district Republican in 1982.

Population: 546,744. White 528,659 (97%), Black 14,832 (3%). Spanish origin 2,461 (1%). 18 and over 395,151 (72%), 65 and over 70,673 (13%). Median age: 31.

hoped to ride Ronald Reagan's long coattails that year by attacking McCloskey as much too liberal for the 8th. The tally on election night showed that McIntyre had fallen just short: McCloskey led by 72 votes. However, a recount by state officials showed McIntyre with a 418-vote lead; more than 4,800 ballots were discarded for technical reasons.

But McIntyre was headed off at the pass: Before his formal swearing-in, the House Democratic leadership asked him to step aside. They argued that the election results from the 8th were such a tangle that the real winner was not yet known; their proposal to hold the seat vacant passed on a party-line vote.

The House Administration Committee appointed a task force of two Democrats and one Republican to oversee an April 1985 recount by the GAO, whose auditors were directed to ignore many of the technicalities that resulted in the original ballot disqualifications. When the final count was announced, McCloskey had won by four votes.

Republican leaders threatened retribution; some members even proposed physically blocking McCloskey from taking the oath of office. Their ultimate response was symbolic: House Republicans staged a brief walkout when McCloskey was sworn in that May.

However, Republicans did try to carry out their vow of revenge at the polls. National GOP strategists felt voters in the 8th were sufficiently convinced of Democratic misconduct to make McIntyre a rematch winner in 1986. McIntyre was not so sure; he delayed announcing for a second House campaign and toyed with running instead for statewide office. Eventually, though, he agreed to take on McCloskey.

In retrospect, it is easy to see why McIntyre hesitated. He did not have the Reagan coattails that boosted him in 1984, and he still had the disadvantage of coming from small Lawrence County, in the 8th's northeast corner. McCloskey won in 1984 largely thanks to support in populous Evansville, and there was little cause for him to be much weaker there, or McIntyre much stronger, in 1986.

And as it turned out, the recount issue was not much on voters' minds when they went to the polls. McIntyre himself said people were weary of the dispute. He looked for another issue, but never found a good one.

McIntyre chose to play hardball, reaching back into the Democrat's record as Bloomington mayor in the 1970s to argue that McCloskey had been irresponsible in his denunciations of the Vietnam War and soft in dealing with drug offenses. But he probably went too far in charging that McCloskey had smoked opium; no convincing evidence was ever found.

McCloskey, meanwhile, played effective incumbent politics, talking up his work for the Crane Naval Weapons Center and bringing Armed Services Chairman Aspin to promise that the center would not be closed. McCloskey also reaped valuable publicity investigating possible PCB contamination from a Union Carbide plant on the district border. The incumbent won Evansville overwhelmingly and that propelled him to a 53 percent victory.

McCloskey climbed above 60 percent against a weak foe in 1988, but ran into anti-incumbent sentiment in 1990 and saw his margin slip against Republican Richard E. Mourdock, an Evansville coal mining executive. Mourdock hit McCloskey on his votes for a congressional pay raise and for a federal deficit-reduction package that included some tax increases.

Were it not for an auto accident, McCloskey might never have made it to the House. The Indiana Legislature redrew the 8th in 1981 to make it secure for GOP Rep. Joel Deckard, and at the outset of his 1982 campaign, he was favored over challenger McCloskey. But Deckard drove his car into a tree in early October and admitted he had been drinking. That incident, combined with Depression-level unemployment in parts of the 8th, boosted McCloskey to a 51 percent win.

A former newspaper reporter, McCloskey was first elected Bloomington's mayor in 1971, the year he finished law school. He won that race with the help of students at Indiana University, who were attracted by his liberal politics. But after his 1975 re-election campaign, which he won by a narrower margin against a weaker opponent, he modified some of his more liberal positions and emphasized economic development and neighborhood restoration in Bloomington. Those efforts broadened his base beyond the academic community, and he was re-elected in 1979.

Committees

Armed Services (17th of 33 Democrats)
Investigations; Procurement & Military Nuclear Systems

Foreign Affairs (24th of 28 Democrats)
Arms Control, International Security & Science

Post Office & Civil Service (6th of 15 Democrats)
Postal Operations & Services (chairman); Investigations

Elections

1990 General		
Frank McCloskey (D)	97,465	(55%)
Richard E. Mourdock (R)	80,645	(45%)
1990 Primary		
Frank McCloskey (D)	44,906	(89%)
John W. Taylor (D)	5,814	(11%)
1988 General		
Frank McCloskey (D)	141,355	(62%)
John L. Myers (R)	87,321	(38%)

Previous Winning Percentages: **1986** (53%) **1984** (50%) **1982** (51%)

District Vote For President

	1988	1984	1980	1976
D	97,530 (42%)	88,851 (38%)	95,833 (40%)	115,188 (49%)
R	133,017 (57%)	143,526 (61%)	127,427 (54%)	118,212 (50%)
I			10,846 (5%)	

Campaign Finance

	Receipts	Receipts from PACs	Expend-itures
1990			
McCloskey (D)	$467,981	$322,320 (69%)	$446,040
Mourdock (R)	$147,535	$13,125 (9%)	$146,961
1988			
McCloskey (D)	$549,096	$342,058 (62%)	$551,484
Myers (R)	$132,638	$19,665 (15%)	$130,243

Key Votes

1991	
Authorize use of force against Iraq	N
1990	
Support constitutional amendment on flag desecration	N
Pass family and medical leave bill over Bush veto	Y
Reduce SDI funding	Y
Allow abortions in overseas military facilities	Y
Approve budget summit plan for spending and taxing	N
Approve civil rights bill	Y
1989	
Halt production of B-2 stealth bomber at 13 planes	N
Oppose capital gains tax cut	Y
Approve federal abortion funding in rape or incest cases	Y
Approve pay raise and revision of ethics rules	Y
Pass Democratic minimum wage plan over Bush veto	Y

Voting Studies

	Presidential Support		Party Unity		Conservative Coalition	
Year	**S**	**O**	**S**	**O**	**S**	**O**
1990	20	78	93	6	26	72
1989	31	69	89	7	22	78
1988	20	78	91	7	29	71
1987	20	79	90	5	28	72
1986	24	76	84	13	52	48
1985	29 †	71 †	89 †	10 †	27 †	73 †
1984	37	59	84	9	25	69
1983	17	82	89	10	29	69

† Not eligible for all recorded votes.

Interest Group Ratings

Year	ADA	ACU	AFL-CIO	CCUS
1990	83	8	92	21
1989	85	7	92	30
1988	75	16	100	21
1987	80	4	94	14
1986	55	18	86	50
1985	68	28	76	30
1984	75	13	85	31
1983	85	22	94	20

9 Lee H. Hamilton (D)

Of Nashville — Elected 1964

Born: April 20, 1931, Daytona Beach, Fla.

Education: DePauw U., B.A. 1952; attended Goethe U., Frankfurt, Germany, 1952-53; Indiana U., J.D. 1956.

Occupation: Lawyer.

Family: Wife, Nancy Nelson; three children.

Religion: Methodist.

Political Career: No previous office.

Capitol Office: 2187 Rayburn Bldg. 20515; 225-5315.

In Washington: To a number of Democrats hoping to regain broad appeal for their national party, Hamilton has stood out as a symbol. Hamilton is nearly as liberal as the average House Democrat; but with his moderate tone, square looks and squeaky-clean reputation, Hamilton is Middle American to his core.

This image helped Hamilton win some prestige assignments — he chaired the committee in 1987 that investigated the Iran-contra affair — and even rated him consideration for vice president in 1988. The second-ranking Democrat on the Foreign Affairs Committee, Hamilton appears certain someday to succeed Chairman Dante B. Fascell of Florida, who is 14 years his senior.

But at the start of the 102nd Congress, Hamilton's status as a national figure appeared closely linked to the ultimate outcome of the Persian Gulf crisis. Hamilton was a leader in the fight against authorizing President Bush to use military force against Iraq (which since August 1990 had occupied Kuwait); the lightning-fast U.S. military victory in early 1991 initially appeared to diminish Hamilton. But ensuing events involving Kurdish refugees in the war's aftermath took some glory out of the victory and partially vindicated Hamilton's prewar warnings of "unintended consequences."

When he entered the debate, Hamilton knew he could not be labeled as "soft" on Iraq. As chairman of the Foreign Affairs Subcommittee on Europe and the Middle East, he supported economic sanctions after the Iraqi regime of Saddam Hussein used poison gas in 1988 against the Kurdish minority. The Reagan and Bush administrations blocked such sanctions, favoring continued attempts to improve relations with Baghdad. "In this instance, Congress led the administration," Hamilton said after Iraq invaded Kuwait.

But Hamilton expressed concern about the large deployment of U.S. troops to contain Iraqi aggression. His opposition to Bush's policy became manifest by November 1990, when the president doubled the deployment and created the potential for offensive action against Iraq.

In December, Hamilton engaged in an exchange with Secretary of State James A. Baker III. Stating that the existing policy of economic blockade had contributed to Iraq's release of Western hostages, Hamilton said, "If the present strategy of sanctions, diplomacy, threat of military force is working, they then give us an opportunity ... to achieve our objectives without war and without casualties...." Baker responded, "What's working, Mr. Hamilton ... is the fact that we are beginning, finally, to get the clear message across to Saddam Hussein that if he doesn't withdraw peacefully, he will be forced out."

Bush insisted throughout the crisis that he had the constitutional authority to commit U.S. troops to war against Iraq without prior congressional approval. But as the Jan. 15, 1991, deadline set by the United Nations for Iraqi withdrawal from Kuwait closed in, Bush asked Congress to authorize the use of force. Hamilton and House Majority Leader Richard A. Gephardt of Missouri countered with a resolution that, while not foreclosing future military action, called for continued use of sanctions and diplomacy.

During his floor speech favoring his resolution, Hamilton spoke with certitude of the consequences war might bring. "War will: Split the [anti-Iraq] coalition; estrange us from our closest allies; make us the object of Arab hostility; endanger friendly governments in the region; and not be easy to end, once started," he said. He also noted that American troops, who made up more than three-quarters of the coalition forces, were greatly at risk. But the House defeated the Hamilton-Gephardt resolution, 183-250, a mirror image of the vote that ratified the resolution approving force.

Like most members who opposed the authorization, Hamilton stated his backing for the president and troops once war ensued. But just after the war's end — with Bush riding high in the polls and Republican officials threatening to hold war opponents accountable — Hamilton discomfited some Democrats by defending his

Indiana 9

Southeast — Bloomington; New Albany

This is the largest and least urbanized district in the state. The hilly forests and farmlands are more akin to Kentucky and parts of southern Ohio and Illinois than to the flat Hoosier farmlands farther north. Many of those who settled here came from the South and brought with them their Democratic allegiances.

Poultry and cattle are the major agricultural commodities of the area, which is also the center of some of the nation's finest and most abundant limestone quarries. Stone cutters, like those portrayed in the movie "Breaking Away," regularly excavate rock that is used for building material throughout the country.

The Indiana suburbs of Louisville, Ky., along the Ohio River, make up the district's largest concentration of voters. The focal point of this mostly middle-income area is New Albany, which lies just across the Ohio River from Louisville and is the district's largest city, with 36,000 people.

In the days of the steamboats, when Indiana's economy depended upon the cargoes that came up the Ohio River, New Albany was the state's largest city. Although the river's contribution to the local livelihood has dropped off considerably in the last hundred years, the 9th still depends upon river traffic and industries located along the river bank for many jobs.

In its northwest corner, the 9th takes in most of the Democratic parts of Bloomington, the home of Indiana University (enrollment 32,000). The district boundary runs along 3rd Street in Bloomington, placing the northern two-thirds of the city's 61,000 residents in the 9th. Included in that area is all of Indiana University's campus as well as most of the off-campus housing and faculty neighborhoods.

Population: 544,873. White 530,291 (97%), Black 10,205 (2%). Spanish origin 3,180 (1%). 18 and over 383,018 (70%), 65 and over 56,470 (10%). Median age: 28.

vote. "How do you calculate the cost [of U.S. and Iraqi casualties]?" Hamilton wrote in *The Washington Post*. "Were we wrong to support a policy that might have spared these lives and that damage?"

However, events shortly after the war made it appear that any political damage to Hamilton might be short-lived. Saddam Hussein remained in power, and engaged in a bloody repression of internal revolts by the nation's Kurdish and Shiite Moslem populations; a reluctant President Bush extended U.S. financial and military commitments to protect refugees in the region. Hamilton could refer critics to a passage from his January war resolution speech, in which he said, "Bringing stability to the Middle East after a war will be protracted and difficult."

His risky leadership role in the anti-war resolution movement was the boldest move of Hamilton's career. The one complaint that his Democratic colleagues had previously voiced about Hamilton was that he shied from steps that might antagonize one faction or another. Judicious caution, the key to Hamilton's influence and credibility, can also be his handicap. Never was that more clear than in the evolution of the Iran-contra scandal.

Revelations that the Reagan administration had secretly sold arms to Iran and diverted the profits to the Nicaraguan contras burst into the news in November 1986. But the facts might have emerged sooner if Hamilton, as Intelligence Committee chairman in 1985 and 1986, had not held back from probing early reports of illegal White House activity. "One of the emerging lessons from these events," Hamilton conceded as the scandal unfolded, "is that we did not have sufficient oversight."

But, as he was to ask over and over, what can Congress do — what can he do — if questions are met with administration lies? The initial lie was told to Hamilton directly. In September 1985, he had called then-national security adviser Robert C. McFarlane before Intelligence; McFarlane assured Hamilton that National Security Council aide Lt. Col. Oliver L. North had not "in any way been involved with funds for the contras." "I for one am willing to take you at your word," Hamilton replied, and the matter was dropped.

Hamilton did go on to do a much-commended job as House chairman of the special committee that investigated the affair. He was an ideal choice for Democratic leaders: Moderate and conservative Democrats saw in Hamilton an image they wanted to project for the party, while liberals appreciated his steadfast opposition of U.S. aid to the contras.

He asked few questions through the summer hearings, but gave lengthy summations following key figures' testimony that laid calm emphasis on their evidence of lies and subversion of foreign policy. In impassioned remarks to North, Hamilton said, "I don't have any doubt at all, Colonel North, that you are a patriot.... But there is another form of patriotism that is unique to democracy. It resides in those who have a deep respect for the rule of law and faith in America's democratic traditions."

Hamilton pursued answers to his Iran-contra questions into the 101st Congress. Documents disclosed in North's 1989 criminal trial provided new evidence to contradict Reagan's and then-Vice President Bush's denials of their involvement, and raised questions about why the Iran-contra committee did not get the documents. Hamilton asked Bush for explanations and urged Intelligence, of which he was no longer a member, to investigate.

Before the Iraqi invasion, Hamilton had been largely preoccupied during the 101st Congress with the thaw in U.S.-Soviet relations and the collapse of communism in Eastern Europe. He was a lead sponsor of the Support for East European Democracy (SEED) acts that provided U.S. funds for countries in that region in 1989 and 1990.

Hamilton also urged Bush to reciprocate for Soviet President Mikhail S. Gorbachev's efforts to reverse Soviet imperialism and to warm relations with the United States. He said the Bush-Gorbachev summit at Malta in December 1989 "fundamentally changed the tone and psychology of U.S.-Soviet relations," adding, "We put aside questions of motives ... and made it clear that it's in our interest to help Gorbachev."

By the following December, enthusiasm for Gorbachev had faded, in large part because of his resistance to demands for independence by the Soviet Baltic States. Hamilton remained adamant that continued ties with the Soviet leader remained the best course. Citing growing unrest throughout the Soviet Union, Hamilton said, "We have to help them get through this immediate crisis.... It is not in our interest to see the country break apart at the seams."

Hamilton believes emphatically that Congress should be consulted as an equal partner in foreign policy. However, he has shared with Republican administrations the view that the structure of U.S. foreign aid programs has gotten too complicated.

Along with New York Republican Rep. Benjamin A. Gilman, Hamilton co-chaired a Foreign Affairs task force that studied ways to reform a foreign aid program that had become a bureaucratic nightmare. Hamilton agreed with the thrust of the panel's report, released in February 1989, which said that foreign aid programs were "hamstrung by too many conflicting objectives, legislative conditions, earmarks [of aid to specific nations] and bureaucratic red tape."

Hamilton said he envisioned a deal between Congress and the president under which "the executive branch will pay attention to the initiatives of the Congress and not ignore them, and the Congress will not try to micromanage" the president's foreign policy.

Hamilton did get the Foreign Affairs leadership to include many task force ideas in a draft bill, but found he could do little to rein in his colleagues' zeal for setting foreign aid priorities. When the Europe and Middle East Subcommittee marked up its part of a foreign aid authorization bill in April 1989, it contained numerous earmarks, including traditional ones for the largest recipients of U.S. funds: Israel, Egypt, Greece and Turkey.

Hamilton's mild manner and willingness to work with Republicans for achievable goals was evident during the 101st Congress, when he chaired the Joint Economic Committee (JEC). In 1989, the JEC issued a bipartisan report — the first time that had been accomplished by the committee since 1980 — and did so again in 1990. However, consensus was reached by avoiding contentious issues. "We don't deal with the specifics of how you reduce the deficit," Hamilton said. "But we all agree that the deficit is a very serious problem."

From the start of his House career, Hamilton has enjoyed his colleagues' high regard. He was president of the huge freshman Democratic class elected in 1964.

In 1972, Hamilton sponsored the first measure that Foreign Affairs adopted to stop the Vietnam War. The proposal, which called for a U.S. withdrawal contingent on release of all prisoners of war and on a cease-fire plan with North Vietnam, later was killed on the House floor, but it helped set the stage for later congressional actions to end the war.

In the post-Watergate period of concern for government integrity, Hamilton's image of rectitude made him a leader on ethics issues. In 1977 he chaired a task force that recommended new House rules limiting members' outside income and honoraria. During 1979-80, he served on the House ethics committee.

At Home: In the early months of 1989, Hamilton was contemplating an unexpected and momentous question in Indiana. Party leaders were urging him to challenge junior GOP Sen. Daniel R. Coats in the 1990 special election to fill the remainder of Vice President Dan Quayle's Senate term.

Despite the limits of his base in the state's rural southeast, Indiana political observers considered him the party's most promising candidate against Coats. So great was the respect for Hamilton in both the state and national party structures that the nomination was almost literally his to refuse.

But refuse it he did. Hamilton would have been forced to sacrifice his seat and House seniority to take on Coats. Even if he won, he would have faced another campaign just two years later, when the Quayle term expired. For a cautious man like Hamilton, that was a venture worth walking away from.

Lee H. Hamilton, D-Ind.

The son and brother of ministers, Hamilton has a devotion to work that comes out of his traditional Methodist family. From his days in Evansville High School in 1948, when he helped propel the basketball team to the state finals, to his race for Congress in 1964, he displayed a quiet, consistent determination.

When he graduated from DePauw University in 1952, he received an award as the outstanding senior. He accepted a scholarship to Goethe University in Germany for further study.

Hamilton practiced law for a while in Chicago, but soon decided to settle in Columbus, Ind., where his interest in politics led him into the local Democratic Party.

In 1960 he was chairman of the Bartholomew County (Columbus) Citizens for Kennedy. Two years later he managed Birch Bayh's Senate campaign in Columbus.

He was the consensus choice of the local Democratic organization for the 9th District House nomination in 1964, and won the primary with 46 percent of the vote in a field of five candidates. He went on to defeat longtime Republican Rep. Earl Wilson, a crusty fiscal watchdog who had represented the district for almost a quarter of a century.

Hamilton has been re-elected easily ever since. After a few years, Republicans gave up on defeating him and added Democrats to his district to give GOP candidates a better chance elsewhere in the state.

Committees

Joint Economic (Vice Chairman)

Foreign Affairs (2nd of 28 Democrats)
Europe & the Middle East (chairman); Human Rights & International Organizations

Elections

1990 General		
Lee H. Hamilton (D)	107,526	(69%)
Floyd Eugene Coates (R)	48,325	(31%)
1990 Primary		
Lee H. Hamilton (D)	67,056	(92%)
Lendall B. Terry (D)	5,930	(8%)
1988 General		
Lee H. Hamilton (D)	147,193	(71%)
Floyd Eugene Coates (R)	60,946	(29%)

Previous Winning Percentages: **1986** (72%) **1984** (65%) **1982** (67%) **1980** (64%) **1978** (66%) **1976** (100%) **1974** (71%) **1972** (63%) **1970** (63%) **1968** (54%) **1966** (54%) **1964** (54%)

District Vote For President

	1988	1984	1980	1976
D	89,744 (42%)	93,283 (40%)	92,931 (43%)	109,023 (52%)
R	123,198 (58%)	139,901 (60%)	112,568 (52%)	98,908 (47%)
I			8,747 (4%)	

Campaign Finance

	Receipts	Receipts from PACs	Expend-itures
1990			
Hamilton (D)	$399,758	$188,824 (47%)	$392,606
1988			
Hamilton (D)	$369,547	$152,066 (41%)	$333,957

Key Votes

1991	
Authorize use of force against Iraq	N
1990	
Support constitutional amendment on flag desecration	N
Pass family and medical leave bill over Bush veto	N
Reduce SDI funding	Y
Allow abortions in overseas military facilities	Y
Approve budget summit plan for spending and taxing	Y
Approve civil rights bill	Y
1989	
Halt production of B-2 stealth bomber at 13 planes	N
Oppose capital gains tax cut	Y
Approve federal abortion funding in rape or incest cases	N
Approve pay raise and revision of ethics rules	N
Pass Democratic minimum wage plan over Bush veto	Y

Voting Studies

	Presidential Support		Party Unity		Conservative Coalition	
Year	**S**	**O**	**S**	**O**	**S**	**O**
1990	27	73	78	22	43	57
1989	42	58	77	23	54	46
1988	25	74	88	12	47	50
1987	26	74	84	16	51	49
1986	33	67	83	17	48	52
1985	38	63	82	18	42	56
1984	49	51	71	29	54	46
1983	35	65	82	17	42	58
1982	47	52	66	33	58	42
1981	47	51	71	27	56	44

Interest Group Ratings

Year	ADA	ACU	AFL-CIO	CCUS
1990	67	13	58	43
1989	60	21	67	60
1988	85	8	100	36
1987	72	9	69	47
1986	55	23	57	56
1985	60	33	69	57
1984	55	42	54	38
1983	75	17	71	45
1982	70	18	80	45
1981	65	20	67	28

10 Andrew Jacobs Jr. (D)

Of Indianapolis — Elected 1964

Did not serve 1973-75.

Born: Feb. 24, 1932, Indianapolis, Ind.
Education: Indiana U., B.S. 1955, LL.B. 1958.
Military Service: Marine Corps, 1950-52.
Occupation: Lawyer; police officer.
Family: Wife, Kimberly Hood; two children.
Religion: Roman Catholic.
Political Career: Ind. House, 1959-61; Democratic nominee for U.S. House, 1962; defeated for re-election to U.S. House, 1972; re-elected, 1974.
Capitol Office: 2313 Rayburn Bldg. 20515; 225-4011.

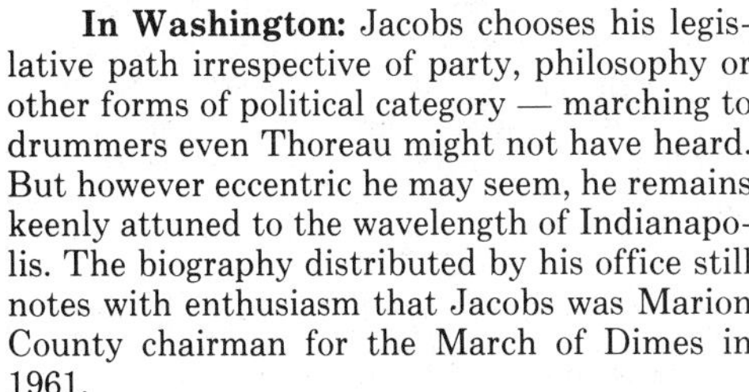

In Washington: Jacobs chooses his legislative path irrespective of party, philosophy or other forms of political category — marching to drummers even Thoreau might not have heard. But however eccentric he may seem, he remains keenly attuned to the wavelength of Indianapolis. The biography distributed by his office still notes with enthusiasm that Jacobs was Marion County chairman for the March of Dimes in 1961.

The special relationship Jacobs maintains with his home folks frees him from the fear that tyrannizes some other incumbents whose tenure has been interrupted (Jacobs was out of the House for two years after losing in 1972). Some who have known such setbacks hoard massive campaign treasuries to discourage challengers; Jacobs refuses political action committee (PAC) money and speaking fees and spends little on his campaigns.

Yet Indianans seem attracted by the same traits that have kept Jacobs an outsider in House politics. He is outspoken to the point of showmanship in his fiscal conservatism and attention to federal waste.

He has long opposed lawmakers' salary increases, and after two rounds of raises were approved in the 101st Congress, he launched a noisy crusade for their repeal that grated even on some colleagues who had opposed the raises in the first place.

Being generally liberal on social questions and dovish on defense has not made Jacobs predictable. He usually votes against spending both for defense and public works projects. Like the most conservative Republicans, he supports a constitutional amendment requiring a balanced budget.

In 1989, Jacobs supplied the deciding vote on Ways and Means for a capital-gains tax cut, contributing to his party leadership's biggest defeat in the 101st Congress.

Some observers were surprised at Jacobs' capital-gains vote, given his usual rhetoric about taxes and the rich. But Jacobs said he liked the proposal because it allowed capital gains (profits on appreciated assets) to be adjusted for inflation. "I can gargle the lower rates," he said, adding that the Democratic Caucus had not taken an official position. "I don't know how you can be an apostate from a religion that does not exist," he said.

Not that Jacobs has hesitated to defy party doctrine on other occasions. In 1981, he voted against the Democratic leadership's package of House rules at the beginning of the 97th Congress and was threatened with ouster from his seat on Ways and Means. Nothing was done, and Jacobs' reputation as a misfit was reinforced.

Jacobs looked like a target again in 1990 when the full Democratic Caucus decided it would henceforth choose the subcommittee chairmen on Ways and Means (as it does for Appropriations). But no challenge to Jacobs materialized.

Before becoming chairman of the Ways and Means Social Security Subcommittee, he had held the gavel for the Health Subcommittee. When the Social Security reform bill reached Ways and Means in 1983, Jacobs added a Medicare payment plan setting fixed costs for inpatient treatment of various diseases.

Jacobs also pushed to freeze Medicare payments to physicians and to prevent the charging of extra fees beyond those Medicare paid. "Vote for the canes, not for the stethoscopes," he said. That provoked the American Medical Association to mount a $300,000 independent effort to defeat him in 1986. (He won with 58 percent.)

But in the 100th Congress, Jacobs took another tack when a corporate constituent's interests were at stake. When Ways and Means drafted a bill expanding Medicare to cover catastrophic illness and outpatient prescription drugs, Jacobs succeeded in deleting a provision promoting generic drugs over more expensive name-brand versions.

The provision would save the government $400 million, it was estimated, but it would cost

Indiana 10

Indianapolis

Indianapolis has a larger population than Boston or Washington, D.C., but it has retained a small-city flavor. It does not have the ethnic mixture of other areas in the industrial Midwest; most of its white residents are Protestants with small-town roots in Indiana or neighboring states, and they still reflect those roots after a generation or more of urban life.

The city's diversified economy ranges from pharmaceuticals (Eli Lilly) and grocery store chains (Kroger) to automotive plants (Ford, General Motors and Chrysler). Also contributing to the local economy are state government and the Fort Benjamin Harrison Army base.

The 10th includes about 70 percent of Indianapolis' population, leaving out the heavily Republican section in northern Washington Township. The major Democratic strength in the district lies in Center Township, which is about 40 percent black and contributes more than a third of the district's vote. Center Township is large enough to tilt the 10th Democratic even though Indianapolis' white population is more conservative than in most cities of comparable size. In 1988, the 10th was one of just two districts in Dan Quayle's Indiana to vote for the Democratic White House ticket.

North of the downtown area, behind the old mansions that line Meridian Street, are middle-income, integrated neighborhoods with large trees and broad streets. This area, in the southern part of Washington Township, has been loyal to Democratic House candidates, particularly Jacobs, who grew up here.

The western side of the district features the nationally famous town of Speedway and its Memorial Day classic, the Indianapolis 500. When not overrun with race-car enthusiasts, this is a white-collar, middle-income area that often votes Republican.

Population: 541,811. White 386,866 (71%), Black 148,711 (27%), Other 3,428 (1%). Spanish origin 5,288 (1%). 18 and over 384,402 (71%), 65 and over 57,747 (11%). Median age: 28.

drug manufacturers such as Indianapolis-based Eli Lilly. When another committee restored the generic drug requirement, Jacobs tried again to strike it. The House rejected his move, 161-265, despite drug companies' intense lobbying.

When Ways and Means devoted most of its attention to overhauling the tax code in the 99th Congress, Jacobs dealt himself out of the major action by opposing the entire enterprise. He called the first proposal from the Reagan administration "the emperor's new cut," a guileful bid to reduce taxes on the wealthy.

He was not much kinder to Congress' version, which sought to eliminate deductions and raise business taxes while phasing in lower individual tax rates. "The mother lode on this bill," he said in late 1986, "is to give people with over $200,000 in income a year a walloping tax cut."

Ways and Means provides Jacobs with a platform to rail about the dangers of smoking. He was a sponsor of the laws that established separate smoking sections on commercial airliners and later banned smoking on virtually all domestic flights. He has also been a consistent advocate of doubling the cigarette tax and earmarking extra revenues for the Social Security hospital insurance trust fund.

Many members know Jacobs for his longstanding war on the perquisites of congressional office. Over the years he has returned tens of thousands of dollars to the Treasury from his salary, veterans' disability payments, mileage reimbursements and office allowances.

He issued dire pronouncements before the latest round of House salary increases (to $125,000) although members cut off their speaking fees in exchange. Jacobs had long depicted such honoraria as barely legal bribery ("The only reason it is not bribery is because Congress gets to say what bribery is," he says).

He is prolific in drafting bills and amendments. Some pass. The 101st Congress' welfare reform package included Jacobs' pilot program for college students to serve as "aunts and uncles" to welfare children. Another Jacobs effort made the Social Security system available to help blood banks find donors suspected of carrying the AIDS virus.

Jacobs' portfolio has also included animal-rights measures, a resolution aimed at providing meatless federal school lunches (he is a vegetarian) and a proposed anti-abortion constitutional amendment.

Early in his career, he was best known as a critic of the Vietnam War. Later, he vocally opposed military aid to the contras fighting Nicaragua's leftist rulers, insisting that either side would rule as dictators, resulting in a flood of illegal immigrants to the United States.

At Home: In August 1989, 57-year-old Jacobs and his wife had their first child, an 11-

pound boy named Andy. The name was no surprise: The congressman's father, Andrew Jacobs Sr., was elected to Congress from Indianapolis in 1948 but was turned out of office after one term. The younger Jacobs began moving early toward the congressional career his father never got to carry out.

In 1958, at the age of 26, Jacobs won a seat in the state House. Four years later he tried for Congress but was defeated by GOP Rep. Donald Bruce. In 1964 Bruce announced plans to retire, and Jacobs ran again. With the help of the national Democratic landslide, he edged into office by 3,000 votes out of 295,000 cast.

It would have been difficult for Jacobs to win re-election in 1966 within the same district boundaries. But under court mandate the lines were redrawn, and, with Democrats controlling that process, Jacobs got a more favorable district. He was re-elected regularly until 1972, when Republican redistricting, combined with Richard M. Nixon's presidential landslide, temporarily cost him his seat. He lost that year to Republican William Hudnut, a Presbyterian minister. But he came back to beat Hudnut and reclaim his seat in the 1974 Democratic Watergate surge.

Redistricting following the 1980 census brought Jacobs new headaches. With Republicans again in control of the process, the remap eliminated Democrat David W. Evans' 6th District. Rather than run in one of several heavily Republican constituencies or launch a statewide campaign in 1982, Evans took the risk of a primary challenge to Jacobs, his fellow Democrat and friend.

Jacobs began with a geographic advantage: He had represented just over half the redrawn district. But Evans' tenuous political career — comprising four narrow House elections — had taught him how to fight. A near-fanatic on the campaign trail, Evans went after voters with everything from computerized direct mail to doorbell-ringing. Jacobs, however, had the party's endorsement and financial help. He outpolled Evans by as much as 4-to-1 in some black precincts, won the primary with 60 percent and had no trouble in November.

In 1986, Jacobs ran against the combined fundraising effort of his GOP oppponent, Jim Eynon, a 40-year-old Indianapolis real estate manager, and the American Medical Association, which ran an independent barrage of ads. Jacobs, running with his usual low-budget ($40,000) nonchalance, took 58 percent.

In 1988 and 1990, the GOP was back to its less ambitious program against Jacobs, who skated to easy wins.

Committees

Ways & Means (6th of 23 Democrats)
Social Security (chairman); Oversight

Elections

1990 General		
Andrew Jacobs Jr. (D)	69,362	(66%)
Janos Horvath (R)	35,049	(34%)
1990 Primary		
Andrew Jacobs Jr. (D)	21,554	(90%)
Jocelyn E. Tandy (D)	2,482	(10%)
1988 General		
Andrew Jacobs Jr. (D)	105,846	(61%)
James C. Cummings (R)	68,978	(39%)

Previous Winning Percentages: **1986** (58%) **1984** (59%) **1982** (67%) **1980** (57%) **1978** (57%) **1976** (60%) **1974** (53%) **1970** (58%) **1968** (53%) **1966** (56%) **1964** (51%)

District Vote For President

	1988		1984		1980		1976	
D	91,726	(51%)	87,159	(44%)	97,427	(49%)	120,009	(50%)
R	85,967	(48%)	109,130	(55%)	90,132	(45%)	118,886	(49%)
I					8,493	(4%)		

Campaign Finance

	Receipts	Receipts from PACs		Expend-itures
1990				
Jacobs (D)	$28,712	0		$14,816
Horvath (R)	$21,644	0		$13,201
1988				
Jacobs (D)	$35,731	0		$35,786
Cummings (R)	$45,743	$2,800	(6%)	$42,857

Key Votes

1991	
Authorize use of force against Iraq	N
1990	
Support constitutional amendment on flag desecration	Y
Pass family and medical leave bill over Bush veto	Y
Reduce SDI funding	Y
Allow abortions in overseas military facilities	Y
Approve budget summit plan for spending and taxing	N
Approve civil rights bill	Y
1989	
Halt production of B-2 stealth bomber at 13 planes	Y
Oppose capital gains tax cut	N
Approve federal abortion funding in rape or incest cases	Y
Approve pay raise and revision of ethics rules	N
Pass Democratic minimum wage plan over Bush veto	Y

Voting Studies

	Presidential Support		Party Unity		Conservative Coalition	
Year	**S**	**O**	**S**	**O**	**S**	**O**
1990	23	76	55	41	30	67
1989	27	67	48	47	37	61
1988	26 †	68 †	58 †	35 †	26 †	68 †
1987	18	82	61	36	19	81
1986	17	80	61	38	26	74
1985	35	65	53	44	27	71
1984	27	68	65	29	15	80
1983	23	68	61	31	31	64
1982	39	60	62	29	26	74
1981	34	64	73	24	25	75

† Not eligible for all recorded votes.

Interest Group Ratings

Year	ADA	ACU	AFL-CIO	CCUS
1990	78	25	83	43
1989	85	33	83	50
1988	95	12	100	42
1987	96	4	94	33
1986	85	0	79	50
1985	80	24	65	59
1984	80	25	69	44
1983	75	19	87	29
1982	85	32	90	41
1981	90	36	67	16

Iowa

U.S. CONGRESS

SENATE 1 D, 1 R
HOUSE 2 D, 4 R

LEGISLATURE

Senate 28 D, 22 R
House 55 D, 45 R

ELECTIONS

1988 Presidential Vote

Bush	45%
Dukakis	55%

1984 Presidential Vote

Reagan	53%
Mondale	46%

1980 Presidential Vote

Reagan	51%
Carter	39%
Anderson	9%

Turnout rate in 1986	42%
Turnout rate in 1988	59%
Turnout rate in 1990	38%

(as percentage of voting age population)

POPULATION AND GROWTH

1980 population	2,913,808
1990 population (30th in the nation)	2,776,755
Percent change 1980-1990	−5%

DEMOGRAPHIC BREAKDOWN

White	97%
Black	2%
Asian or Pacific Islander	1%
(Hispanic origin)	1%
Urban	59%
Rural	41%
Born in state	78%
Foreign-born	2%

MAJOR CITIES

Des Moines	193,187
Cedar Rapids	108,751
Davenport	95,333
Sioux City	80,505
Waterloo	66,467

AREA AND LAND USE

Area 55,966 sq. miles (23rd)

Farm	91%
Forest	4%
Federally owned	0.4%

Gov. Terry E. Branstad (R)
Of Des Moines — Elected 1982

Born: Nov. 17, 1946, Leland, Iowa.
Education: U. of Iowa, B.A. 1969; Drake U., J.D. 1974.
Military Service: Army, 1969-71.
Occupation: Lawyer; farmer.
Religion: Roman Catholic.
Political Career: Iowa House, 1973-79; lieutenant governor, 1979-83.
Next Election: 1994.

WORK

Occupations

White-collar	47%
Blue-collar	30%
Service workers	14%

Government Workers

Federal	18,515
State	60,608
Local	133,376

MONEY

Median family income	$ 20,052	(20th)
Tax burden per capita	$ 800	(31st)

EDUCATION

Spending per pupil through grade 12	$ 4,124	(23rd)
Persons with college degrees	14%	(37th)

CRIME

Violent crime rate 266 per 100,000 (39th)

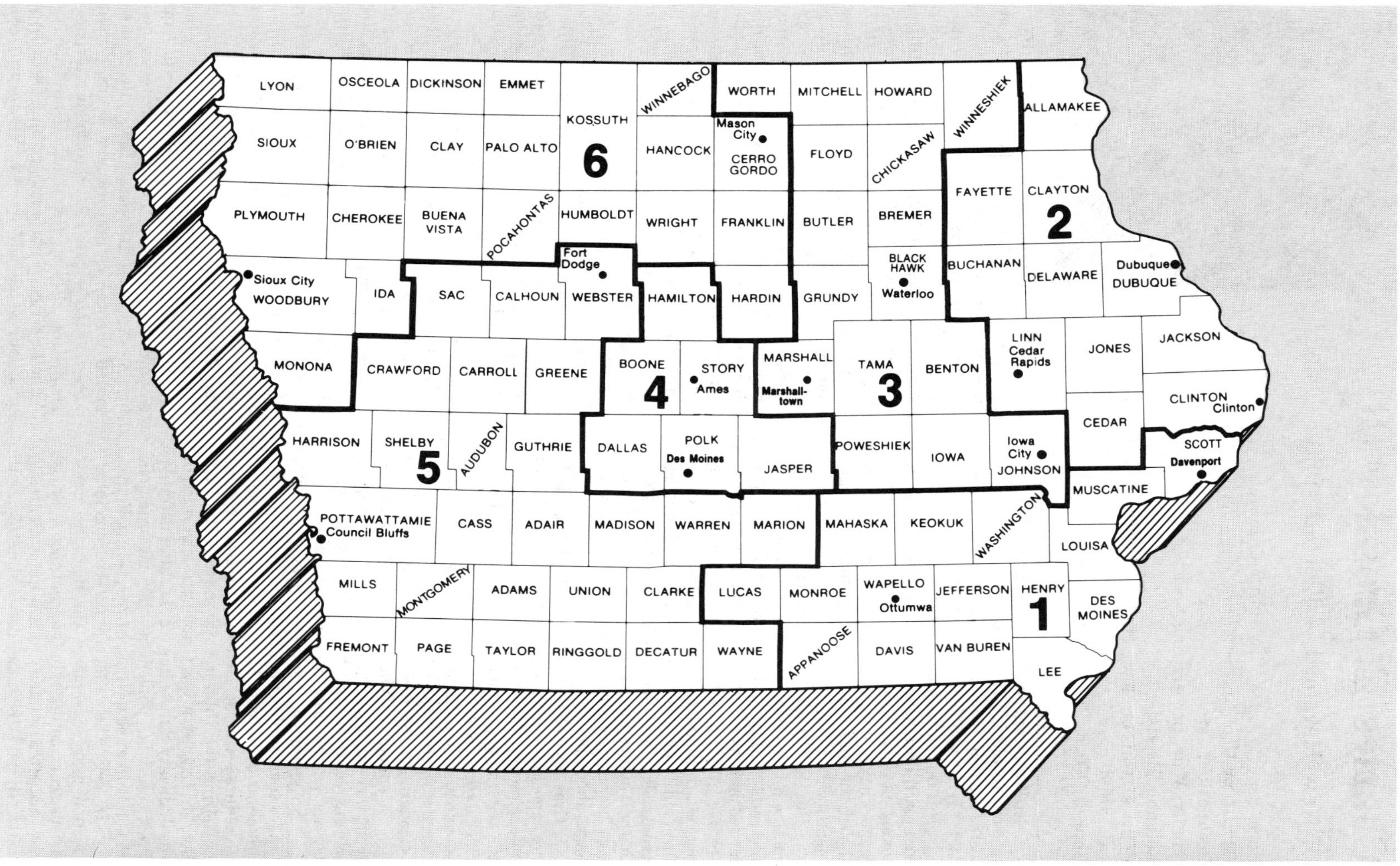

LYON
OSCEOLA
DICKINSON
EMMET
KOSSUTH
WINNEBAGO
WORTH
MITCHELL
HOWARD
WINNESHIEK
ALLAMAKEE
SIOUX
O'BRIEN
CLAY
PALO ALTO
6
HANCOCK
Mason City
CERRO GORDO
FLOYD
CHICKASAW
FAYETTE
CLAYTON
2
PLYMOUTH
CHEROKEE
BUENA VISTA
POCAHONTAS
HUMBOLDT
WRIGHT
FRANKLIN
BUTLER
BREMER
Fort Dodge
BLACK HAWK
Waterloo
BUCHANAN
DELAWARE
Dubuque
DUBUQUE
Sioux City
WOODBURY
IDA
SAC
CALHOUN
WEBSTER
HAMILTON
HARDIN
GRUNDY
MONONA
CRAWFORD
CARROLL
GREENE
BOONE
4
STORY
Ames
MARSHALL
Marshall-town
TAMA
3
BENTON
LINN
Cedar Rapids
JONES
JACKSON
CLINTON
Clinton
HARRISON
SHELBY
5
AUDUBON
GUTHRIE
DALLAS
POLK
Des Moines
JASPER
POWESHIEK
IOWA
Iowa City
JOHNSON
CEDAR
SCOTT
Davenport
MUSCATINE
POTTAWATTAMIE
Council Bluffs
CASS
ADAIR
MADISON
WARREN
MARION
MAHASKA
KEOKUK
WASHINGTON
LOUISA
MILLS
MONTGOMERY
ADAMS
UNION
CLARKE
LUCAS
MONROE
WAPELLO
Ottumwa
JEFFERSON
HENRY
1
DES MOINES
FREMONT
PAGE
TAYLOR
RINGGOLD
DECATUR
WAYNE
APPANOOSE
DAVIS
VAN BUREN
LEE

Charles E. Grassley (R)

Of New Hartford — Elected 1980

Born: Sept. 17, 1933, New Hartford, Iowa.
Education: U. of Northern Iowa, B.A. 1955, M.A. 1956.
Occupation: Farmer.
Family: Wife, Barbara Ann Speicher; five children.
Religion: Baptist.
Political Career: Iowa House, 1959-75; U.S. House, 1975-81.
Capitol Office: 135 Hart Bldg. 20510; 224-3744.

In Washington: Grassley has made a career out of playing the country bumpkin. "I'm just a farmer from Butler County," he once said. "What you see is what you get."

It is not entirely an act. Grassley's intellectual reach does have its limits. And aside from taking on obvious evils, his Senate accomplishments have not been broad-ranging, even though he has important committee assignments.

But if Grassley's slow-talking, farm-boy routine reinforces all the Eastern stereotypes of the rural Midwest, the liberals who once dismissed him as a right-wing rube now call him sly like a fox. The conservative Grassley may not be a brilliant theorist, but he has a knack for identifying federal infractions that outrage people all across the political spectrum. Back on the Finance Committee in 1991 after a four-year hiatus, Grassley is positioned to tap voter angst about taxes.

Grassley got to the Senate and has made his name there by demonstrating unusual skill at exploiting the widespread perception that the federal government is a spendthrift. His chief target, however, has not been welfare spending, as one might expect from a conservative, but waste at the Pentagon — a good choice considering most Iowans' skepticism of heavy defense spending. While Pentagon mismanagement was one of the most popular bandwagons in Congress in the last half of the 1980s, Grassley was on the case from the beginning.

No specialist in defense policy, Grassley strikes some professionals as simplistic with his criticisms of Defense Department procurement procedures. But he captured public attention by seizing the subject with the tenacity of a bulldog. In 1984, it was Grassley, as chairman of the Judiciary Subcommittee on Administrative Practices, who publicized the now-infamous $7,600 coffee maker bought by the Air Force.

In 1988, when a federal prosecutor's investigation dragged some of the nation's largest defense contractors onto the front pages, Grassley was often quoted as a leading Pentagon critic. In mid-1990, he drew attention with revelations of further procurement follies: Pentagon purchases of $999 pliers, $1,868 toilet seat covers and a mystifying $343 altar vase. No sweeping congressional investigation followed, but Grassley got his headlines. "Unfortunately sometimes it takes a $999 pair of pliers to get anyone's attention that the bureaucracy is winning the battle against the taxpayers," he said.

His endeavors have led to a few serious scrapes with those in his own party, but Grassley does not mind advertising that to Iowa's independent-minded electorate. After resisting President Reagan's pleas to support the MX missile in a 1985 vote, Grassley revealed that a White House operative had summed up his feelings for the senator by saying, "I hope that son-of-a-bitchin' Grassley dies."

Grassley was far more circumspect in his decision to oppose President Bush with a vote against authorizing the use of force in the Persian Gulf in early 1991. He announced his decision in Iowa, a few days before the vote. But he did not make a statement before the Senate until after Bush had his victory in hand. He was the only GOP senator to oppose the resolution.

In recent years, Grassley's concern with defense fraud has made him a major sponsor of legislation to protect workers who blow the whistle on abuse of tax dollars. After Reagan issued a surprise veto of the bill near the end of his term, Grassley said the administration "hasn't exactly a sterling record where whistleblowers are concerned." Grassley helped smooth out compromises that let Bush sign a similar measure in 1989.

In the 101st Congress, he tried with less success to protect workers in the private sector who disclose unlawful or dangerous activities that threaten public health.

Grassley's first serious legislative attack on defense waste came in the 99th Congress, when he and Arkansas Democrat David Pryor promoted Pentagon procurement reforms that were resisted not only by the Defense Department, but also by Republican Dan Quayle's Armed Services Subcommittee on Defense Acquisition, which had its own reform proposal.

Quayle won, and the Iowan was the lone Republican to support the Grassley-Pryor bill.

But Grassley succeeded in a 1986 attack on dishonest military contractors. He won passage of a bill updating the penalties and enforcement procedures of the federal False Claims Act, a law passed during the Civil War to crack down on suppliers who bilked the Union Army. In 1988, Grassley and Ohio Democrat Howard M. Metzenbaum succeeded in creating a new crime statute to deal specifically with fraud in government contracts, with possible penalties of 10 years' imprisonment and fines up to $5 million.

Another of Grassley's protect-the-taxpayers crusades that eventually ripened concerned congressional pay. In 1987 and 1988 he sponsored a provision to require roll-call votes in both chambers for a pay raise to take effect, a reaction to a hands-off procedure that brought a 16 percent raise in early 1987. The Senate backed Grassley's proposal several times, but each time House leaders jettisoned it. In early 1989, however, public outrage over a proposed 51 percent pay increase forced floor votes that killed it.

In a pay-raise/ethics reform bill that came later that year, Grassley wanted the Senate to ban honoraria and the practice of allowing members to give speaking fees to charity. "Except for allowing you to pocket the money, that maintains every other bad aspect of honoraria," he said. "You're still indebted to the organization and traveling around still detracts from the time we ought to be giving to the job." The Senate refused to ban either practice.

Grassley has met similar resistance in seeking to provide civil rights protections to Senate workers. During consideration of legislation to protect handicapped workers from discrimination in 1990, Grassley's amendment to permit Senate workers to sue in federal court gummed up the bill's expected smooth path to passage. "Two hundred years ago, James Madison wrote that it was essential that Congress make no law which would not fully apply to itself and also the great mass of society," Grassley argued.

But Senate Democrats contended that allowing courts to second-guess congressional actions would be a dangerous violation of the Constitution's separation of power between the branches. After much debate, the Senate codified existing Senate rules providing civil rights protection to its workers.

Grassley has been talking about the curse of federal deficits ever since his first days in the House in 1975. In recent years, he has favored an overall budget freeze to bring the deficit under control. In the 101st Congress, he ignored White House pressure and became the lone Republican on the Budget Committee to support the initial Senate budget in 1990, which included substantial cuts in defense. Acknowledging that his support was also partly due to an exemption from cuts provided for agricultural programs, Grassley said he did not want to abandon the congressional budget process for summit talks.

It was not the first time he had parted company from his party brethren on the budget. When Reagan issued a 1986 budget seeking more for defense and less for domestic programs, Grassley balked. "People are finding it difficult to justify a big increase in defense when we're cutting Social Security," he said.

A belief in fiscal restraint is by no means Grassley's only motive for slowing defense spending. As he has demonstrated many times, he wants some of that money to go instead to farmers, especially those facing foreclosure. In 1987 Grassley teamed with Minority Leader Bob Dole to try to speed up some income payments to corn farmers, but the attempt failed. The corn connection held in the 1988 presidential nominating race, as Grassley helped Dole win the Iowa caucuses.

Looking out for Iowa interests was Grassley's chief role during the Finance Committee's 1986 debate on tax-code revision. He won a tax break for farmers who are forced into bankruptcy, and another benefiting a Des Moines trucking firm run by one of his campaign contributors. But he was not a significant player in the broader debate over tax policy. Earlier on Finance, Grassley was active in the 1982 passage of "revenue-enhancing" legislation. He helped develop provisions aimed at raising more money by increasing penalties for tax evasion and strengthening enforcement powers of the Internal Revenue Service.

In the committee shuffle after the Democrats' 1987 Senate takeover, Grassley lost his seats on Finance and on Labor, but he won assignment to Appropriations and its Agriculture Subcommittee. At the start of the 102nd Congress, he gave up his seat on Appropriations to return to Finance.

Grassley also serves on the Judiciary Committee. During the 1987 debate over Reagan's appointment of Robert H. Bork to the Supreme Court, Grassley directed his frustration at both the left and the right. He stuck with Bork and charged that the nominee's detractors "spent millions to willfully smear an American citizen." But some of his bitterest comments were directed at Reagan for vacationing when the Bork battle was joined.

At Home: Grassley plays to the Iowa audience with understated artistry, blending shrewd political positioning with the homespun simplicity of the farm country he grew up in. This skill has made him unstoppable since he entered politics at the age of 25.

Grassley joined the Iowa House in 1959, rose to become chairman of its Appropriations Committee and developed a reputation for personal integrity and suspicion of government.

When veteran GOP Rep. H. R. Gross announced his retirement from Congress in 1974, Grassley organized the 3rd District's most conservative elements and won the GOP nomination with 42 percent of the vote against four opponents. In November, he eked out 51 percent against an aggressive young Democrat in a Democratic year.

After conservative Republicans helped Roger W. Jepsen to victory over liberal Democratic Sen. Dick Clark in 1978, attention focused on Grassley as a 1980 challenger to Clark's liberal Senate colleague, John C. Culver.

Grassley's announcement of his Senate candidacy mobilized conservatives, who built a strong grass-roots organization across Iowa. Against a well-financed, moderate GOP primary opponent who was endorsed by popular Gov. Robert Ray, Grassley won 90 of the state's 99 counties.

Then Grassley ran head-on into Culver, who conducted an insistent and impassioned defense of his liberal Senate voting record and characterized Grassley's legislative accomplishments as mediocre. Targeted for defeat by the Moral Majority and the National Conservative Political Action Committee, Culver lashed out at Grassley's New Right supporters, calling them a "poison in the political bloodstream."

But Grassley, an earnest, easygoing farmer, did not fit the part of a fanatic. He disassociated himself from New Right tactics without losing conservative support, and he turned voters' attention to pocketbook issues by charging that Democratic economic policies brought high inflation. Outpolling Reagan in Iowa, Grassley won 54 percent of the vote. (Reagan carried Iowa with 51 percent.)

By 1986, Grassley's crusades against federal waste had built him a constituency that was unaffected by Iowa's massive farm discontent and anti-Reagan feelings. No prominent Democrat wanted to run against him, and the candidate who did, Des Moines lawyer John Roehrick, was never really in the contest. Grassley won a second Senate term with two-thirds of the vote.

Committees

Agriculture, Nutrition & Forestry (8th of 8 Republicans)
Agricultural Credit (ranking); Agricultural Production & Stabilization of Prices; Domestic & Foreign Marketing & Product Promotion

Budget (3rd of 9 Republicans)

Finance (8th of 9 Republicans)
Deficits, Debt Management & International Debt (ranking); International Trade; Private Retirement Plans & Oversight of the Internal Revenue Service

Judiciary (4th of 6 Republicans)
Courts & Administrative Practice (ranking); Patents, Copyrights & Trademarks

Special Aging (3rd of 10 Republicans)

Elections

1986 General

Charles E. Grassley (R)	588,880	(66%)
John Roehrick (D)	299,406	(34%)

Previous Winning Percentages: **1980** (54%) **1978 *** (75%) **1976 *** (57%) **1974 *** (51%)

** House elections.*

Campaign Finance

	Receipts	Receipts from PACs		Expend-itures
1986				
Grassley (R)	$2,749,564	$971,730	(35%)	$2,513,319
Roehrick (D)	$256,057	$88,672	(35%)	$255,673

Key Votes

1991

Authorize use of force against Iraq	N

1990

Oppose prohibition of certain semiautomatic weapons	Y
Support constitutional amendment on flag desecration	Y
Oppose requiring parental notice for minors' abortions	N
Halt production of B-2 stealth bomber at 13 planes	Y
Approve budget that cut spending and raised revenues	N
Pass civil rights bill over Bush veto	N

1989

Oppose reduction of SDI funding	N
Oppose barring federal funds for "obscene" art	N
Allow vote on capital gains tax cut	Y

Voting Studies

	Presidential Support		Party Unity		Conservative Coalition	
Year	**S**	**O**	**S**	**O**	**S**	**O**
1990	70	30	85	15	70	30
1989	79	21	91	9	84	16
1988	78	20	87	13	86	14
1987	58	40	77	22	69	31
1986	67	31	72	28	82	18
1985	66	34	64	35	78	22
1984	74	25	79	18	89	11
1983	74	26	81	19	77	23
1982	84	16	82	17	86	12
1981	81	16	84	15	91	7

Interest Group Ratings

Year	ADA	ACU	AFL-CIO	CCUS
1990	17	87	33	83
1989	25	86	10	75
1988	5	88	21	93
1987	25	81	30	83
1986	30	70	27	74
1985	10	57	33	69
1984	15	73	9	79
1983	15	64	12	58
1982	30	60	19	62
1981	5	87	6	94

Tom Harkin (D)

Of Cumming — Elected 1984

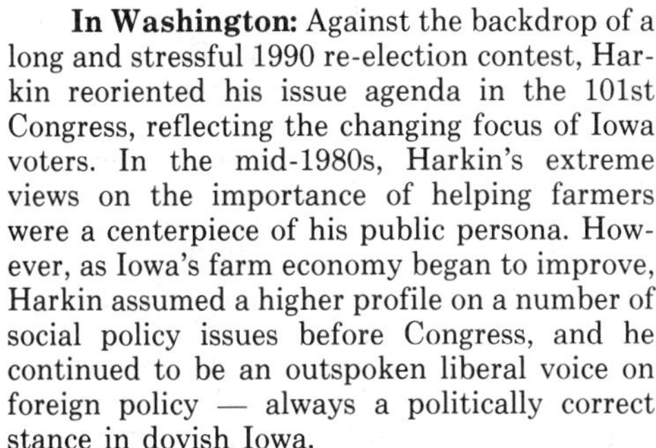

Born: Nov. 19, 1939, Cumming, Iowa.

Education: Iowa State U., B.S. 1962; Catholic U., J.D. 1972.

Military Service: Navy, 1962-67; Naval Reserve, 1968-74.

Occupation: Lawyer.

Family: Wife, Ruth Raduenz; two children.

Religion: Roman Catholic.

Political Career: U.S. House, 1975-85; Democratic nominee for U.S. House, 1972.

Capitol Office: 531 Hart Bldg. 20510; 224-3254.

In Washington: Against the backdrop of a long and stressful 1990 re-election contest, Harkin reoriented his issue agenda in the 101st Congress, reflecting the changing focus of Iowa voters. In the mid-1980s, Harkin's extreme views on the importance of helping farmers were a centerpiece of his public persona. However, as Iowa's farm economy began to improve, Harkin assumed a higher profile on a number of social policy issues before Congress, and he continued to be an outspoken liberal voice on foreign policy — always a politically correct stance in dovish Iowa.

But one thing about Harkin has remained the same over the years: his fiery, sometimes grating, populist rhetoric. In early 1991, just as he started his second Senate term, Harkin began publicly exploring a run for president in 1992. "Bush thinks the threat to the United States is halfway around the world — but the real threat is right down the street," Harkin told *The Boston Globe* in late May, saying Bush has come up short on solving domestic problems. Although not committing to seeking the White House, Harkin said, "I don't think Bush is that popular. He's got feet of clay and I'm going to go after him."

Harkin has tried to create the political bonds and debts back home that help extend one term into another while clinging to his belief that a majority of Iowa voters will accept even the most liberal ideological record if it is explained with conviction.

His annual rating from the liberal Americans for Democratic Action has been at least 90 percent all six years he has served in the Senate. In 1989 and 1990, Harkin opposed President Bush on floor votes in the chamber more than all but one other senator. And on controversial issues, Harkin can be adamant in his views, as exemplified by his strong opposition to a constitutional amendment to ban flag desecration. He has a reputation for taking positions and promoting ideas that are distinctive enough to divide people.

Harkin views himself as a defender of the interests of the common folk against the rich and powerful. The appeal of Harkin's legislative ideas tends to be to farmers and the disabled, and to those who have little personal clout and distrust those who have. He can be blunt in his language. "In a free economic system," he once said, "there come times when too few people have too much wealth and too much power, and too many people have neither of both. It's the primary purpose of government to redress that imbalance."

Harkin was successful in 1990 with one of his foremost legislative priorities — the Americans With Disabilities Act. Harkin says the day Bush signed the bill (PL 101-336) was the proudest moment of his 16 years in Congress. The law, passed after years of effort and negotiations, extends broad civil rights protections to an estimated 43 million Americans with mental and physical disabilities.

During final consideration, Harkin delivered a portion of his floor speech in sign language; that was, he said, a message to his brother Frank, who is deaf. "I told him that today Congress opens the doors to all Americans with disabilities — that today we say no to ignorance, no to fear, no to prejudice."

Harkin also sponsored successful legislation that increased the accessibility of closed-captioned television broadcasts for hearing-impaired viewers; a bill that reauthorized programs aimed at protecting the rights of people with developmental disabilities; and another measure that authorized $10 million for states to work on health-objective plans. On the last bill, though, Harkin piqued Senate colleagues when he held up consideration of an appropriations measure trying to get the program funded.

In contrast with those achievements, Harkin has had little success in advancing his theories on agriculture policy since the farm crisis began to ease in late 1987.

In 1985, he introduced the Save the Family Farm Act, a radically different approach to farm programs. He reintroduced it in 1987 with Democratic Rep. Richard A. Gephardt of Missouri. In essence, the plan would replace existing farm-subsidy programs with stringent federal controls on production and marketing of farm products. The aim would be to reduce supplies enough to cause much higher prices, perhaps as much as doubling them. Production controls would be implemented if approved by referendum among farmers.

Harkin was defeated, 36-56, when he offered the plan as an amendment to the 1985 farm bill. His cause had not been helped by the fact that, shortly after he came to the Senate in 1985, Harkin began lecturing his colleagues on farm problems in a way that seemed to imply they had scarcely heard of the issue before.

By 1990, Harkin was no longer loudly preaching the gospel of supply management and touting mandatory production controls. He was not an active player in shaping the 1990 farm bill, and even broke with some prairie populist Democrats, such as South Dakota's Tom Daschle and Montana's Max Baucus, when he voted for the farm bill in committee and on the floor when it was first considered. Harkin did vote against final passage of the measure in October 1990.

During his five House terms and now in the Senate, Harkin has been known for his outspokenness on U.S. foreign policies, especially those involving Central America and the human rights records of other countries.

His vigorous opposition to U.S. military involvement in Central America stems in part from his experiences as a Vietnam veteran, and his stand reflected majority sentiment in Iowa. Harkin's interest in human rights came out of an experience in 1970, when, as an investigator for a House committee, he traveled to Vietnam and discovered the "tiger cages" in which prisoners of war were being kept. He has never served on the Foreign Affairs or Foreign Relations committees, but his has been one of the loudest foreign policy voices on the floor.

When the 102nd Congress convened and turned its attention to the crisis in the Persian Gulf, Harkin led the liberals' charge. Less than two months before, in November 1990, Harkin joined 53 Democratic House members in a lawsuit seeking to prevent Bush from launching a military attack without Congress' approval.

Within minutes after the Senate went into session in 1991, Harkin sought to introduce a resolution demanding that Bush seek "explicit authorization" from Congress before acting militarily. The move surprised and visibly angered Majority Leader George J. Mitchell of Maine, who opposed immediate congressional action.

Harkin's virulent opposition to the contras led him to criticize Bush's proposal late in 1989 to send aid to Nicaragua to assist that country in its democratic elections. Harkin insisted that by giving some money directly to the opposition coalition led by Violetta Chamorro, the United States risked making her coalition look like a Washington puppet. "Do we really want Mrs. Chamorro to be known as the best candidate American money can buy?" Harkin asked.

In his first House term, Harkin introduced a successful amendment that became a national issue during the Carter administration. It barred U.S. aid to any country engaging in a consistent pattern of violations of human rights.

At Home: Although Harkin was widely considered one of the senators least likely to survive the 1990 elections, he pulled off an historic win to become the first Iowa Democrat to be returned to the Senate.

Harkin took nothing for granted en route to a second term. He opened his re-election battle early in 1989 by announcing his county-by-county campaign chairmen and stockpiled a sizable campaign fund.

That was not enough to scare off Rep. Tom Tauke, perhaps the strongest candidate the Republicans could have nominated other than GOP Gov. Terry Branstad. Tauke also began early, raising money and seeking to build on his bipartisan base in the 2nd District.

Tauke pecked away at Harkin on a variety of issues, accusing him of franking abuses, for example, and of voting for excessive federal spending. But none of the attacks truly took hold, while Harkin called attention to his popular work on landmark legislation to help people with disabilities.

The two men also clashed over abortion — Harkin supports abortion rights, Tauke does not — although voters also appeared divided on the issue, possibly making it a political wash.

Given the seeming competitiveness of the race, and its priority among national party leaders, it was little surprise that the "Battle of the Toms" turned negative. Yet in the end Harkin won by a rather comfortable 10 percentage points.

Harkin was no stranger to hard-fought campaigns; his 1984 race against Republican Sen. Roger W. Jepsen was one of that year's heavyweight bouts, with all the civility of a mud-wrestling match.

Six years earlier, Jepsen had stunned Iowa Democrats by unseating Sen. Dick Clark. There never was much doubt that Clark would be vulnerable in 1984, and Harkin, as a strong campaigner who had proven his popularity by securing a Republican House district, was the logical challenger. By early 1983, having preempted much of the party establishment's support, he was the acknowledged Democratic candidate.

Jepsen had a serious problem: Most of the events by which he had distinguished himself in office reflected badly on him. In 1983, for example, he had cited constitutional immunity to escape paying a traffic ticket while driving to work.

National conservative organizations flocked to Jepsen's defense, giving him the money he needed for a barrage of television and radio ads skewering Harkin for opposing a balanced-budget constitutional amendment and favoring higher taxes. Harkin came back with charges that Jepsen was freer with tax dollars than any other recent Iowa senator, dubbing him "Red Ink Roger."

As the campaign wore on, the candidates traded charges, quarreling over who had a combat record in the military and whose views on nuclear arms were more dangerous.

Polls showed a close race, but Harkin easily outdistanced Jepsen in the cities and carried much of the countryside, winning even in 55 counties that went for Reagan for president.

Republicans saw little cause for worry when Harkin first announced for Congress in 1972 against a well-entrenched GOP incumbent in a solidly conservative district. But they soon found themselves up against one of the more resourceful Democrats in recent Iowa politics.

Harkin projected his concern for agriculture in rural west Iowa and drew publicity with his gimmick of "work days," spending a day at a time as a truck driver, as a gas station attendant and in other blue-collar work to convince voters of his empathy with their concerns. Republican Rep. William Scherle defeated him, but by the lowest percentage of his House career.

Harkin launched his 1974 bid early, built a stronger organization and raised more money. Scherle, activated by his unimpressive 1972 showing, made more appearances and tried to distance himself from the unpopular Republican administration.

But Harkin won on the strength of his showing in Story County (Ames), which he took by 6,195 votes.

Committees

Agriculture, Nutrition & Forestry (5th of 10 Democrats)
Nutrition & Investigations (chairman); Agricultural Production & Stabilization of Prices; Domestic & Foreign Marketing & Product Promotion;

Appropriations (11th of 16 Democrats)
Labor, Health & Human Services, Education (chairman); Agriculture, Rural Development & Related Agencies; Defense; Foreign Operations; Transportation

Labor & Human Resources (6th of 10 Democrats)
Disability Policy (chairman); Children, Families, Drugs & Alcoholism; Employment & Productivity; Labor

Small Business (6th of 10 Democrats)
Competitiveness & Economic Opportunity; Export Expansion

Elections

1990 General

Tom Harkin (D)	535,975	(54%)
Tom Tauke (R)	446,869	(45%)

Previous Winning Percentages: **1984** (56%) **1982 *** (59%) **1980 *** (60%) **1978 *** (59%) **1976 *** (65%) **1974 *** (51%)

** House elections.*

Campaign Finance

	Receipts	Receipts from PACs		Expend-itures
1990				
Harkin (D)	$4,983,819	$1,546,535	(31%)	$5,263,568
Tauke (R)	$4,941,809	$1,374,706	(28%)	$5,060,104

Key Votes

1991	
Authorize use of force against Iraq	N
1990	
Oppose prohibition of certain semiautomatic weapons	N
Support constitutional amendment on flag desecration	N
Oppose requiring parental notice for minors' abortions	Y
Halt production of B-2 stealth bomber at 13 planes	Y
Approve budget that cut spending and raised revenues	N
Pass civil rights bill over Bush veto	Y
1989	
Oppose reduction of SDI funding	N
Oppose barring federal funds for "obscene" art	Y
Allow vote on capital gains tax cut	N

Voting Studies

	Presidential Support		Party Unity		Conservative Coalition	
Year	**S**	**O**	**S**	**O**	**S**	**O**
1990	22	78	85	15	8	92
1989	38	58	77	22	26	71
1988	42	57	89	6	8	86
1987	31	65	87	8	16	81
1986	19	78	91	5	5	91
1985	22	77	90	8	17	82
House Service						
1984	29	66	79	14	17	80
1983	7	85	82	10	16	81
1982	26	69	83	12	12	86
1981	25	70	81	14	21	73

Interest Group Ratings

Year	ADA	ACU	AFL-CIO	CCUS
1990	94	22	78	17
1989	95	14	100	38
1988	95	0	92	36
1987	95	4	90	44
1986	90	14	93	28
1985	100	5	90	24
House Service				
1984	75	21	46	33
1983	90	5	88	20
1982	95	0	95	24
1981	85	7	73	5

1 Jim Leach (R)

Of Davenport — Elected 1976

Born: Oct. 15, 1942, Davenport, Iowa.

Education: Princeton U., B.A. 1964; Johns Hopkins U., M.A. 1966; attended London School of Economics, 1966-68.

Occupation: Propane gas company executive; foreign service officer.

Family: Wife, Elisabeth Ann "Deba" Foxley; two children.

Religion: Episcopalian.

Political Career: Republican nominee for U.S. House, 1974.

Capitol Office: 1514 Longworth Bldg. 20515; 225-6576.

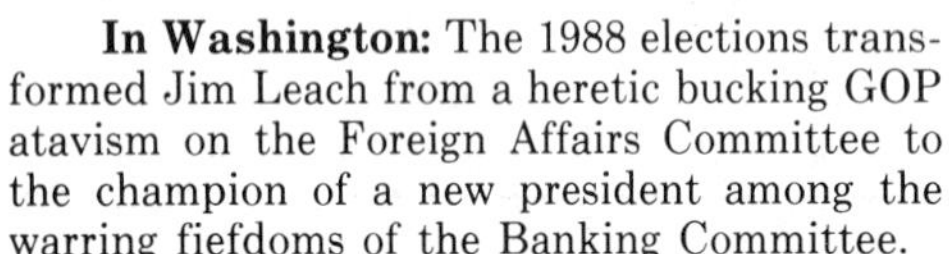

In Washington: The 1988 elections transformed Jim Leach from a heretic bucking GOP atavism on the Foreign Affairs Committee to the champion of a new president among the warring fiefdoms of the Banking Committee.

Leach has changed neither his outlook nor his assignments, but the splintering of the Banking Committee following the defeat of its longtime warlord and the ascendancy of his friend George Bush have given him new authority.

Leach's association with Bush dates to the early 1970s, when Bush was United Nations ambassador and Leach was a young foreign service officer there. In 1980, Leach helped Bush win the Iowa caucuses — a turning point in Bush's ascension to Ronald Reagan's running mate and successor.

Despite his professorial demeanor, some of Leach's outspoken foreign policy views have made him a pariah to his party's dominant right wing. It does not seem to bother Leach, who often relishes the chance to demonstrate his iconoclasm and prove that policy is more important to him than party.

Leach's independence has found room to operate on the Banking Committee following the surprise 1988 defeat of its chairman, Fernand J. St Germain of Rhode Island. St Germain's secretive autocracy has been replaced by the more tenuous grip of Henry B. Gonzalez of Texas, and policy is set by shifting alliances that transcend seniority and party.

Intellectually, Leach often outshines Banking's uninventive senior Republican, Chalmers P. Wylie of Ohio. Still, it is Gonzalez's alliance with Wylie that spurred passage of the panel's most important legislation in the 101st Congress. While Leach gets along with Wylie, he has a tendency to free-lance instead of consulting with his GOP colleagues.

In the past, he has shown a preference for going down in flames for what he considers right. His dire prophecies on the thrift industry were validated in the 101st Congress. But prophets are not given to consensus building, and Leach is willing to breach convention in pursuit of his cause.

For years, Leach's cause has been to require financial institutions to keep more capital on hand and to make safer investments. He was among the first to warn of an impending crisis in the nation's savings and loan industry, and when it finally burst into public view, he cast blame widely on Congress, the Reagan administration, the industry and state regulators.

Eventually, the House came around to Leach's views. In 1987, a Leach amendment to restrict speculative investments by thrifts was defeated on the floor 17-391. That did not deter Leach. In 1988, he tried a slightly different tack, suggesting that regulators use the same rules on risky investments for thrifts as for banks; that lost 20-29 in committee. But in the 1989 thrift bailout, he won as a leading proponent of the administration's plan to toughen up on the industry: The committee adopted 28-23 his amendment to apply federal restrictions on direct investments to all thrifts, even if they are state-chartered.

Leach cast one of two votes against the bailout bill in committee, saying it was not tough enough. "The issue," he said during subcommittee consideration of an amendment to weaken the capital standards, "is whether we want a business-as-usual approach to the industry and a Congress-as-usual approach to this business."

But he supported the House bill on the floor after winning a surprise victory with a 412-7 stampede for his proposal to strike a list of special-interest provisions. Nevertheless, he voted against the final conference agreement — "not because the legislation should necessarily be vetoed by the president," he said, "but because of my profound disappointment that Congress did not do better." He predicted that Congress would have to enact another bailout

Iowa 1

Southeast — Davenport

The 1st stretches west from a string of manufacturing cities along the Mississippi River — Bettendorf, Davenport, Muscatine and Burlington — across almost half of southern Iowa. It takes in 16 southeastern Iowa counties. But more than half of the vote is cast in its urban areas.

Both parts of the district have been hurting. Like most industrialized areas, the 1st suffered badly in the economic slump of the early 1980s, when unemployment districtwide hovered around 15 percent. Many of the jobless have left; every county in the district except Henry lost population during the 1980s.

The depression and drought that have hit the farm economy have left their mark on the cities; Davenport lost its Caterpillar facility, and Iowans who worked at International Harvester across the river in Illinois lost their jobs when the farm implement division was closed down.

With a population of 151,000, Scott County (Davenport) is by far the 1st District's largest population center. Despite the loss of Caterpillar, Davenport remains a heavy-industry town: Alcoa's aluminum plant there is one of the largest in the world.

While it has a large blue-collar vote, however, Scott County can be agreeable territory for Republicans. In the last three House elections, Leach has taken no less than 62 percent of the county's vote. In 1990, GOP Gov. Terry E. Branstad carried Scott with 64 percent, but Democratic Sen. Tom Harkin drew 53 percent. In 1988 presidential voting, Michael S. Dukakis edged George Bush in Scott County by 3,390 votes.

Downriver from Davenport are Muscatine (Muscatine County) and Burlington (Des Moines County). Muscatine is usually Republican (it supported Republican Sen. Roger W. Jepsen in his weak re-election campaign in 1984), but Democrats running statewide often win Burlington. Dukakis carried it by nearly 3,000 votes in 1988. Leach has no trouble in either place.

The northern rural portions of the district have shown steady allegiance to the GOP. But in the southern tier of rural counties along the Missouri border, the soil is poorer, cropland gives way to grazing land, and Democratic loyalties are stronger. Partly because the GOP establishment in this area is weaker, presidential hopeful Pat Robertson ran well here in the 1988 GOP caucuses; he won six of the 16 counties in the 1st.

Though there are signs that economic conditions are stabilizing, the farm crisis has had an effect on politics throughout the district, boosting the visibility of groups with a liberal outlook, such as the Iowa Farm Unity Coalition, Rural America and the American Agriculture Movement.

Population: 485,961. White 469,441 (97%), Black 9,732 (2%), Other 2,408 (1%). Spanish origin 7,886 (2%). 18 and over 345,540 (71%), 65 and over 64,556 (13%). Median age: 30.

bill in the next 18 to 36 months; the next installment, a $30 billion bill to refinance the thrift salvage agency, was indeed signed into law less than two years later.

Leach also would apply stricter standards and stiffer regulation to banks. He is among the most vocal advocates of making bank owners increase the amount of money they have invested in their institutions. He was prepared to push for tougher standards as the committee began considering plans to reform bank deposit insurance in the 102nd Congress.

Leach's background at the London School of Economics and his assignment on Foreign Affairs has made him one of the few members active on international debt issues, in contrast with the Main Street focus of most in Congress.

Leach was the author of a 1983 law that was intended to require banks to maintain sizable cash reserves against Third World loans that were not likely to be repaid. In the 101st Congress, he pressed commercial banks to cooperate with the Bush administration's proposals for reducing Third World debt. But he resisted a measure that would have forced private banks either to cooperate or set aside more cash reserves against potential losses on their loans.

In past years, he has tried to preserve funding for the Export-Import Bank, a tool he says is under-used in helping American industry sell its products abroad.

The thrift crisis drew Leach from the cul-de-sac of Foreign Affairs, where the growing conservatism of the Republican contingent had left him isolated. Conservative Republicans resented the aura of bipartisanship he sometimes lent to Democrats by cosponsoring their bills or joining their initiatives, such as a trip to Cuba in 1984 with Rep. Bill Alexander of Arkansas.

In Reagan's second term, Leach was often the leading Republican critic of Reagan's policies on issues such as Central America, arms control and South Africa. In supporting sanctions against the apartheid regime in South Africa, he said, "All we ask of this Republican president is that he advance a foreign policy consistent with the views of the first Republican president, Abraham Lincoln."

Leach was a consistent opponent of U.S. aid to the Nicaraguan contras. When the Iran-contra affair began to unfold, Leach was harshly critical of the Reagan administration as well as Congress; he said that by watering down restrictions on covert involvement in 1985, Congress invited mischief. Democrats, he said, had buried their heads in the sand when reports of that mischief began to surface, out of fear that they would be blamed for "losing Central America" to communism. "The issue is backbone, not oversight," he said.

Occasionally Leach finds himself criticizing even the Democrats on Foreign Affairs as practicing too blatant an interventionism — as when he opposed the first proposals to give aid to rebels fighting the communist regime in Cambodia. But when Bush sought authority in 1991 to use military force in the Persian Gulf, Leach voted to give it to him. He praised Bush for working through the United Nations to line up international condemnation of Iraqi President Saddam Hussein's invasion and occupation of Kuwait.

Leach is not uninterested in being a party man. He simply wants the party to come to him. He has tried to use organizations such as the Ripon Society, which he chaired, and the Republican Mainstream Committee, which he founded, to raise a moderate voice in GOP politics.

But even with the White House coming into the hands of Bush — a man Leach feels much closer to than he did to Reagan — Leach still is a party maverick. Only five other Republicans opposed Bush's positions on roll call votes more often than Leach in 1989, and only eight others in 1990. He was one of 17 Republicans to vote against approving a constitutional amendment to ban desecration of the flag. He favors abortion rights and voted for federal funds for abortions in cases of rape or incest. Some elements of his domestic policy voting record are not liberal; he rarely draws even a mediocre rating, for example, from the AFL-CIO.

Early in his career, Leach often sounded more conservative than he does now. As a freshman, for example, he amended the 1978 Civil Service Act to place a ceiling on the number of federal workers. It was an idea that struck a popular anti-bureaucratic theme, and it sailed through the House on a 251-96 vote. It gave President Carter a year to shrink the work force to 1977 levels — a reduction of 68,000 employees — and made Leach a target of criticism from the bureaucracy for years.

His restiveness with the domination of conservatives came to flower in 1981, when he was installed as president of the Ripon Society, a moderate GOP group that had fallen into quiescence during the 1970s. Leach all but declared war on the party's conservative social-issue activists. Leach said he had no intention of being "lashed to the guillotine of the New Right's social and security agenda." He declared a "moderate manifesto" touting the need for arms control and the Equal Rights Amendment.

In 1984, Leach formed the Republican Mainstream Committee, a loose coalition of moderates, to fight on the GOP platform.

Leach recognizes that moderates have been outflanked in fundraising and publicity. "The temper and tone of [moderates'] position-taking is not best suited to the harsh appeals of direct mail or best suited to get the attention of the media," he said. He has advised that moderates "must cease being moderate if they are going to recapture public leadership."

At Home: Since Leach took the 1st District out of Democratic hands in 1976, his moderate House voting record and high visibility at home have enabled him to choke off challenges with ease. He carried every county in the district in 1978 and 1980; in 1986, with a devastated farm economy cutting into Republican strength, he still carried all but one. The 1st District registered distinct disenchantment with the GOP national ticket in 1988, but Leach still carried 14 out of 16 counties. And in 1990, Democrats did not bother to challenge Leach at all.

Leach brought a varied background to his first campaign, in 1974, against first-term Democrat Edward Mezvinsky. Leach had studied at Princeton and at the London School of Economics, worked in the Office of Economic Opportunity and in the Foreign Service, was assigned to the Arms Control and Disarmament Agency, then returned to Iowa to run the propane gas manufacturing firm owned by his family.

He lost to Mezvinsky in 1974 by 12,147 votes, but that was a good showing for a Republican newcomer in a Democratic year. During the next two years, he spoke regularly in the district, held his organization together and built a $200,000 campaign fund.

In 1976 Leach stressed his ties to Robert Ray, Iowa's moderate Republican governor. He described himself as a "Bob Ray Republican" and called Mezvinsky "a Bella Abzug Democrat." Leach won by carrying his home base of Scott County (Davenport), which Mezvinsky had taken in 1974. The Democrat carried Iowa City, Burlington and Keokuk, but they were not enough.

In 1978 Leach's courting of the voters in the areas where he had run poorly two years earlier paid off. He drew 64 percent, the first time in 16 years that any House candidate in the 1st had won more than 55 percent.

The only Democrat who has given Leach any trouble since he won the seat was the 1982 nominee, former Scott County Supervisor William E. Gluba, a forceful campaigner with a populist flair and over 10 years of political involvement in the 1st's most populous county.

But Gluba was so little known outside his home county that he gave up 37 percent of the Democratic primary vote to a candidate who had spent several years in prison for a variety of offenses, including burglary and armed robbery.

That embarrassment made it difficult for Gluba to convince potential contributors he could win, and he never obtained the resources necessary to match Leach's organization. Also, Gluba was unsuccessful at tying Leach to Reaganomics. Leach could point to his role as a leading Republican critic of Reagan's priorities for defense, education and social services. Gluba ended up with two counties.

Gluba was back in 1988, winning the nomination after former gubernatorial nominee Lowell Junkins had passed on it. But Gluba was even more woefully underfunded than in 1982. He again carried just two counties, and his share of the districtwide vote slipped below 40 percent.

Committees

Banking, Finance & Urban Affairs (2nd of 20 Republicans)
International Development, Finance, Trade and Monetary Policy (ranking); Financial Institutions Supervision, Regulation & Insurance

Foreign Affairs (5th of 18 Republicans)
Asian & Pacific Affairs (ranking); Europe & the Middle East

Elections

1990 General		
Jim Leach (R)	90,042	(100%)
1988 General		
Jim Leach (R)	112,746	(61%)
Bill Gluba (D)	71,280	(38%)

Previous Winning Percentages: **1986** (66%) **1984** (67%) **1982** (59%) **1980** (64%) **1978** (64%) **1976** (52%)

District Vote For President

	1988	1984	1980	1976
D	106,756 (55%)	99,112 (47%)	85,545 (41%)	100,738 (50%)
R	86,724 (44%)	110,057 (52%)	104,062 (50%)	99,128 (49%)
I			14,763 (7%)	

Campaign Finance

	Receipts	Receipts from PACs	Expend-itures
1990			
Leach (R)	$115,051	0	$87,489
1988			
Leach (R)	$206,618	0	$218,707
Gluba (D)	$62,395	$36,151 (58%)	$59,204

Key Votes

1991	
Authorize use of force against Iraq	Y
1990	
Support constitutional amendment on flag desecration	N
Pass family and medical leave bill over Bush veto	N
Reduce SDI funding	Y
Allow abortions in overseas military facilities	Y
Approve budget summit plan for spending and taxing	Y
Approve civil rights bill	Y
1989	
Halt production of B-2 stealth bomber at 13 planes	Y
Oppose capital gains tax cut	N
Approve federal abortion funding in rape or incest cases	Y
Approve pay raise and revision of ethics rules	N
Pass Democratic minimum wage plan over Bush veto	Y

Voting Studies

	Presidential Support		Party Unity		Conservative Coalition	
Year	**S**	**O**	**S**	**O**	**S**	**O**
1990	38	59	62	37	52	48
1989	45	52	59	34	51	44
1988	35	65	62	35	61	39
1987	38	59	58	32	42	58
1986	47	52	58	39	37 †	63 †
1985	34	64	53	40	22	78
1984	42	53	51	42	36	58
1983	39	55	40	51	28	71
1982	45	52	43	54	36	62
1981	58	42	54	45	48	51

† Not eligible for all recorded votes.

Interest Group Ratings

Year	ADA	ACU	AFL-CIO	CCUS
1990	61	21	42	57
1989	65	46	25	67
1988	75	32	79	64
1987	52	38	31	79
1986	55	32	21	61
1985	60	33	53	50
1984	50	30	8	67
1983	50	18	33	65
1982	65	23	45	45
1981	55	73	20	79

2 Jim Nussle (R)

Of Manchester — Elected 1990

Born: June 27, 1960, Des Moines, Iowa.
Education: Luther College, B.A. 1983; Drake U., J.D. 1985.
Occupation: Lawyer.
Family: Wife, Leslie Harbison; one child.
Religion: Lutheran.
Political Career: Delaware County attorney, 1986-90.
Capitol Office: 507 Cannon Bldg. 20515; 225-2911.

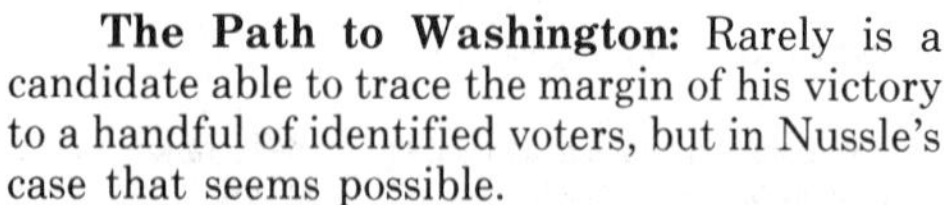

The Path to Washington: Rarely is a candidate able to trace the margin of his victory to a handful of identified voters, but in Nussle's case that seems possible.

The 30-year-old Republican entered the homestretch of the 1990 campaign as an underdog against Democrat Eric Tabor, who had gained a degree of name recognition from two prior unsuccessful efforts to unseat GOP Rep. Tom Tauke. Tauke left open the seat he had held since 1979 when he opted for a bid against Democratic Sen. Tom Harkin.

But Tabor's campaign blew up in his face just days before the election when it was revealed that an aide had registered his father, mother and sister as Democrats to vote absentee ballots in the district even though they lived in the 4th District, which sits in the middle of the state and is not even adjacent to the 2nd.

Tabor moved quickly to staunch the damage by firing the aide, but local GOP officials questioned whether there might be other such examples yet uncovered.

They observed that Tabor's sister and her husband, claiming temporary residence, had voted absentee in the 2nd even though their home was in the 3rd District. The incidents may have reminded voters of a controversy involving Tabor in 1988, when the Iowa Democratic Party mailed letters signed only "Jim" and attacking Tauke's record.

In the end, 2nd District voters — by a 1,642-vote margin — chose a man who could philosophically mirror the popular Tauke, who like Nussle came to Congress at a tender age (28).

Nussle, a lawyer and former Delaware County attorney, was an assistant in Washington for Tauke, whose strong grass-roots organization helped Nussle carry six of the eleven counties in the district, including Dubuque County — where Democrats hold a 3-to-1 registration advantage.

Nussle, however, did not escape controversy of his own during an extremely negative campaign. Tabor charged that Nussle had exaggerated work experience on his résumé, which said he had served as a "staff assistant, legal counsel" for Gov. Terry E. Branstad in 1985 and was an "attorney at law" the same year.

In fact, Nussle did not receive his law degree from Drake University until 1985, and he served only as an unpaid intern in Branstad's office.

Nussle touts his Danish heritage and stresses conservative themes such as individualism and family values, criticizing what he says is over-reliance on government to cure social ills. He campaigned against strict government controls mandating soil conservation, and drew criticism from environmentalists after he admitted that, until a few years ago, he was unaware where his garbage went.

His anti-abortion stand — which contrasted sharply with Tabor's pro-abortion rights position — boosted him, perhaps in part because he also supported aid to expectant mothers. In heavily Catholic Dubuque County, parishioners on the Sunday before the election were read a letter from the National Conference of Catholic Bishops reminding them of the church's position on the issue.

Nussle gained seats on the Agriculture and Banking committees. He will also likely be interested in family issues; he was adopted, and his daughter has Down's syndrome.

His new colleagues should also be on notice that Nussle has said that one of his first pieces of legislation will try to tie members' salaries to Congress' performance in cutting the deficit.

Not long after taking office in Washington, however, Nussle came face to face with the harsh realities of redistricting. In May 1991, Iowa's Legislature approved a remap that lumped Nussle with Democratic Rep. Dave Nagle in a new, Democratic-tilted 2nd District covering most of northeastern Iowa.

Iowa 2

Northeast — Cedar Rapids

The 2nd remains what it has been for decades: a triangle of interdependent industrial cities amid corn, livestock and dairy farms. The points of the triangle — and the district's population centers — are the cities of Cedar Rapids, Dubuque and Clinton.

Cedar Rapids is the second-largest city in Iowa and one of the country's leading manufacturers of goods for export. It is a center for meatpacking, grain processing and production of pumps, valves and electronic and telecommunication equipment. Eastman Kodak Co. announced in 1990 that it would build a $50 million biotechnology complex there. Once firmly Republican, Linn County (Cedar Rapids) swung to the Democratic side in statewide contests during the 1970s. In 1988, Michael S. Dukakis won Linn County's county's presidential vote by nearly 10,000 votes, but in 1990, GOP Gov. Terry E. Branstad carried it by 11,000 votes.

Dubuque, which sits on the west bank of the Mississippi River, is largely Catholic and historically friendlier to Democrats than Cedar Rapids. The city's Democratic leanings made Dubuque County one of only four Iowa counties carried by Jimmy Carter in 1980, but its Catholic tilt gives a boost to candidates opposed to abortion. Former GOP Rep. Tom Tauke's opposition to abortion earned him a following among local abortion foes; in 1990, GOP House candidate Jim Nussle's opposition to abortion helped him edge an abortion-rights supporter in Dubuque County.

On the Dubuque and Delaware County border is Dyersville, formerly known as the Farm Toy Capital of the World, but fast becoming a tourist trap for those making a pilgrimage to the baseball site featured in the movie, "Field of Dreams."

Dubuque grew up as a processing center for the dairy and meat industries; it also builds tractors and heavy industrial machinery. The area's economy was hit particularly hard in the early 1980s, as unemployment rates hit 14 percent. The economic situation has improved since then, but depends in part on farm prices and remains volatile. Years of industrial decline have taken their toll on Dubuque, but local boosters hope tourism will increase now that legalized gambling has begun on 19th century paddle-wheel riverboats.

Clinton, about half the size of Dubuque, is another manufacturing center on the west bank of the Mississippi. Democratic strength in Clinton County has dropped dramatically during the past decade, though unsuccessful Democratic House challenger Eric Tabor managed a 1,500-vote victory there in 1990.

Population: 485,708. White 478,593 (99%), Black 3,734 (1%). Spanish origin 2,755 (1%). 18 and over 338,272 (70%), 65 and over 58,801 (12%). Median age: 29.

Committees

Agriculture (16th of 18 Republicans)
Conservation, Credit & Rural Development; Cotton, Rice & Sugar; Wheat, Soybeans & Feed Grains

Banking, Finance & Urban Affairs (17th of 20 Republicans)
Economic Stabilization; General Oversight; Policy Research & Insurance

Select Aging (26th of 27 Republicans)
Human Services; Social Security and Women

Campaign Finance

	Receipts	Receipts from PACs		Expend-itures
1990				
Nussle (R)	$469,933	$146,558	(31%)	$466,259
Tabor (D)	$567,456	$389,847	(69%)	$568,659

Key Vote

1991

Authorize use of force against Iraq	Y

Elections

1990 General		
Jim Nussle (R)	82,650	(50%)
Eric Tabor (D)	81,008	(49%)
Jan J. Zonneveld (I)	2,325	(1%)
1990 Primary		
Jim Nussle (R)	8,209	(40%)
Joe Ertl (R)	7,455	(36%)
Wayne A. Moldenhauer (R)	4,845	(24%)

District Vote For President

	1988	1984	1980	1976
D	113,993 (56%)	100,647 (47%)	86,085 (40%)	101,630 (49%)
R	86,874 (43%)	113,814 (53%)	106,157 (49%)	103,412 (49%)
I			19,774 (9%)	

3 Dave Nagle (D)

Of Cedar Falls — Elected 1986

Born: April 15, 1943, Grinnell, Iowa.

Education: Attended U. of Northern Iowa, 1961-65; U. of Iowa, LL.B. 1968.

Occupation: Lawyer.

Family: Wife, Diane Lewis; one child.

Religion: Roman Catholic.

Political Career: Black Hawk County Democratic chairman, 1978-82; Iowa Democratic chairman, 1982-85.

Capitol Office: 214 Cannon Bldg. 20515; 225-3301.

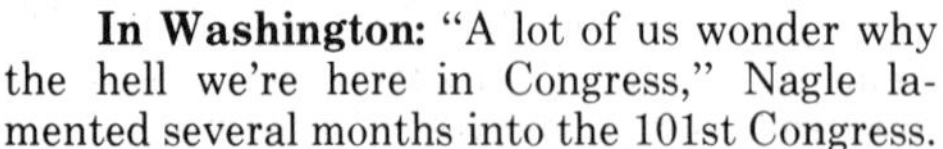

In Washington: "A lot of us wonder why the hell we're here in Congress," Nagle lamented several months into the 101st Congress.

That expression of gloom came as Nagle found himself caught up in the fall of Speaker Jim Wright in the spring of 1989. Nagle, a leadership loyalist, had been enlisted to control political damage done to Wright as questions about his business dealings intensified.

If those were not happy times for Nagle, things did not get much better for him as time wore on. He failed in an effort to amend the 1990 farm bill to assist soybean growers, and, unlike nearly all Agriculture Committee members, did not get appointed to the conference committee on the measure. He offered himself for the chairmanship of the Democratic Congressional Campaign Committee in 1990, but that post went to another member. In May 1991, the state Legislature approved a congressional redistricting plan that put Nagle and GOP Rep. Jim Nussle in the same district. Even before that occurred, Nagle suggested after his 1990 re-election that he might retire from Congress.

But it would not be surprising if Nagle stayed on to fight for his seat. Politics is a passion for him; in fact, he is given more to politics than to legislating. A former state Democratic chairman, in the House he has become known as an ambitious trooper for the party, eager to help the whip organization and interested in a place in the power structure.

After Wright's departure, Nagle was quick to display his loyalty to the new leadership. He jumped to defend new Speaker Thomas S. Foley when he was attacked by the Republican National Committee. And in the 101st and 102nd Congresses, Nagle followed the party line in a number of controversies, supporting the congressional pay raise and the budget summit agreement and opposing the authorization for use of force in the Persian Gulf.

In his drive for influence in the House, Nagle faces the challenge of matching his love of politics with substantive legislative accomplishments.

But on his major committee, Agriculture, Nagle's penchant for making partisan waves is not well-received by Chairman Kika de la Garza of Texas. During consideration of the 1990 farm bill, Nagle backed a proposal formulated by the American Soybean Association to greatly increase the soybean loan rate above the world market price. It was a direct attempt to redirect the thrust of U.S. farm policy since 1985 by making the government, rather than the international marketplace, the main repository of surplus commodities. A bloc of senior Democrats on the panel joined Republicans to defeat the plan, which the Congressional Budget Office had estimated would have cost $9.2 billion over five years.

When the farm bill went to conference, Nagle was conspicuously missing from the negotiating team picked by de la Garza. All committee Republicans were appointed to the conference committee, along with 24 of the 27 Democrats. Nagle was one of the missing three and the only one who had played a major role throughout the bill's earlier consideration.

When the Bush administration hinted in May 1991 that it might not offer $1.5 billion in agriculture credit guarantees to the Soviet Union, Nagle objected. "To me it's incredible," he said, standing up for his Iowa farmers. "What we have is the equivalent of a grain embargo."

On the Science Committee's Space Subcommittee, Nagle is known as the "pit bull" because of his inclination to quarrel with Republicans. He has also emerged as a sharp critic of NASA, even though he professes support for many of the agency's goals. In mid-1990, as NASA continued to be plagued by expensive and embarrassing equipment failures, Nagle commented, "The damn agency is dying of a thousand nicks."

Nagle has opposed funding the Advanced Shuttle Rocket Motor (ASRM), the next generation of booster rockets for the space shuttle. He said that the ASRM would make the shuttle

Iowa 3

North Central — Waterloo; Iowa City

The votes of liberal Johnson County (Iowa City) helped swing the 3rd into Democratic hands in 1986 and keep it there in 1988. Home to the University of Iowa (29,000 students, 1,600 faculty), Johnson County went for Nagle by 2-to-1 in both elections. The county's left-of-center tendencies were obvious throughout the 1980s: Ronald Reagan won only 32 percent of the Johnson vote in 1980; eight years later, George Bush got 35 percent there. Johnson County was added to the 3rd after the 1980 census, transforming a secure GOP constituency into a battleground. But Nagle would not have prevailed in 1986 had he not won also in Black Hawk County, which casts the district's largest single bloc of votes, nearly 30 percent.

With two major towns — Waterloo (population 66,000) and Cedar Falls (population 34,000) — Black Hawk is Iowa's fourth-largest metropolitan area. Meatpacking and the farm-implement industry are crucial, and labor unions have demonstrated political strength here, although there has been a long Republican tradition in House voting. Until the 100th Congress, Waterloo was the only major city in Iowa that had not been represented by a Democrat since World War II. But as is the case all across Iowa, Democrats have been more successful in Black Hawk County in recent years: Michael S. Dukakis carried it in 1988 presidential voting.

The 3rd stretches from Johnson County all the way north to the Minnesota border, and much of it is made up of rural counties that have a long Republican tradition. The land in most of the 3rd is flatter and richer than it is farther south, and until recently, farmers were comparatively well off. But hard times in agriculture during the 1980s loosened GOP allegiances; Nagle in 1988 carried every county in the district but one, and Dukakis won all but three.

Population: 485,529. White 469,3[illegible] Black 10,319 (2%), Other 3,838 (1%). Spanish origin 2,783 (1%). 18 and over 352,455 (73%), 65 and over 60,717 (13%). Median age: 29.

only marginally safer and that NASA's money would be better spent fixing the existing shuttle. "You should fix what you've got before you build something new," Nagle said in 1989. He never offered his amendment to halt the ASRM project, but did get the committee to adopt an amendment calling for a series of reports on the cost and the need for the ASRM.

On the full committee, Nagle did battle with the panel's senior Republican, Pennsylvanian Robert S. Walker, when he championed the cause of a drug-free workplace. Nagle frequently gave Walker fits, often with sarcastic remarks, by trying to thwart his amendment prohibiting the spending of federal money in any workplace if there is proof that illegal drugs were ever used there. Nagle called Walker's idea ridiculous and said the Republican was trying to create a "police state" at federally funded laboratories.

While other foes of Walker's proposal worked to fashion some kind of compromise, Nagle dug in. In the end, however, Nagle found himself on the sidelines. Walker got his drug-free workplace amendment through Congress, and Democrats more pragmatic than Nagle succeeded in loading the amendment with enough language to render it fairly innocuous.

At Home: Prior to 1986, Republicans won 26 consecutive elections in the 3rd. Whenever a competitive situation developed, Democrats squandered it by running an urban liberal with no appeal to the district's rural majority. By those standards of history, Nagle was the wrong man to nominate when GOP Rep. Cooper Evans retired in 1986.

But Nagle seized an opportunity and made thorough use of it. A tough, serious, intense Waterloo lawyer, he came out of a background in party organization, and his closest ties were to labor unions and the liberal activists who now play a crucial role in Iowa's Democratic ranks.

Two accidents befell the GOP. First, the candidate with the strongest ties to Evans, attorney Donald Redfern, failed to file his nomination papers on time. That gave the GOP nomination to former state Rep. John McIntee, whose claim on rural votes was even weaker than Nagle's.

McIntee, a real estate developer, began his fall campaign with a howling blunder. He wrote President Reagan a letter in which he suggested that farmers might relieve the shortage of storage space by keeping their crop in the ground all winter. Those knowledgeable about farming guffawed (the Iowa Corn Growers said most of the crop would rot in the fields).

Nagle told audiences that unlike McIntee, he not only knew how to plant corn, but also when to take it out of the ground. McIntee admitted his error, but never recovered his momentum.

Nagle was a strong candidate in his own right, despite his urban image and Type-A style. He began with a solid network of contacts in all the district's counties, including the rural ones, built during three hard-working years as state party chairman.

Nagle took pains to note that he was raised in a community of fewer than 3,000 people, and that he owned a 100-acre wildlife preserve on the Wapsipinicon River in Chickasaw County.

Equally important, the 3rd had been changed significantly by redistricting in 1981. Map makers that year added Johnson County, home to a liberally oriented population centered around the University of Iowa in Iowa City. Nagle courted this vote by decrying Reagan cutbacks in aid to education, and he also played up his opposition to U.S. aid to the Nicaraguan contras. He won by 10 points.

In 1988, Nagle had to prove his claim to the 3rd against Redfern. A former chairman of the party in Black Hawk County, Redfern seemed ideal to retake what was once the province of the legendary anti-government champion H.R. Gross (1949-75). Redfern cast Nagle as a profligate, high-spending national Democrat out of touch with Iowans. After Speaker Wright came to the district for Nagle, Redfern campaigned against his ethical conduct.

But Nagle had worked the small towns and farmlands of his district well, and had made sure his contributions to bills such as the farm credit legislation of 1987 were widely known. So well had Nagle insulated himself against Redfern's attacks that he pushed his winning tally well over 60 percent. Republicans did not challenge Nagle in 1990.

Nagle entered Democratic politics as a young lawyer in Waterloo in the early 1970s, spent four years as county chairman there, and then took over the state Democratic Party in 1982. His tenure in the state post coincided with the caucuses that launched the Democrats' national nominating process in 1984. Nagle had the responsibility for running those caucuses, and the publicity they received guaranteed him name recognition unusual for a non-elected state party official.

Committees

Agriculture (17th of 27 Democrats)
Conservation, Credit & Rural Development; Livestock, Dairy & Poultry; Wheat, Soybeans & Feed Grains

Science, Space & Technology (19th of 32 Democrats)
Investigations & Oversight; Science; Space

Elections

1990 General		
Dave Nagle (D)	100,947	(99%)
1988 General		
Dave Nagle (D)	129,204	(63%)
Donald B. Redfern (R)	74,682	(37%)

Previous Winning Percentage: **1986** (55%)

District Vote For President

	1988	1984	1980	1976
D	118,602 (57%)	108,563 (47%)	91,217 (40%)	105,877 (48%)
R	89,365 (43%)	118,411 (52%)	111,226 (49%)	108,818 (49%)
I			23,484 (10%)	

Campaign Finance

	Receipts	Receipts from PACs	Expend-itures
1990			
Nagle (D)	$360,951	$264,001 (73%)	$345,154
1988			
Nagle (D)	$608,264	$406,018 (67%)	$596,950
Redfern (R)	$262,188	$39,753 (15%)	$261,911

Key Votes

1991	
Authorize use of force against Iraq	N
1990	
Support constitutional amendment on flag desecration	N
Pass family and medical leave bill over Bush veto	N
Reduce SDI funding	Y
Allow abortions in overseas military facilities	Y
Approve budget summit plan for spending and taxing	Y
Approve civil rights bill	Y
1989	
Halt production of B-2 stealth bomber at 13 planes	N
Oppose capital gains tax cut	Y
Approve federal abortion funding in rape or incest cases	Y
Approve pay raise and revision of ethics rules	Y
Pass Democratic minimum wage plan over Bush veto	Y

Voting Studies

	Presidential Support		Party Unity		Conservative Coalition	
Year	S	O	S	O	S	O
1990	20	78	88	7	22	76
1989	41	58	88	7	29	68
1988	21	76	86	8	45	55
1987	22	77	89	5	26	74

Interest Group Ratings

Year	ADA	ACU	AFL-CIO	CCUS
1990	83	8	75	36
1989	80	7	92	40
1988	80	8	100	36
1987	88	0	94	7

4 Neal Smith (D)

Of Altoona — Elected 1958

Born: March 23, 1920, Martinsburg, Iowa.
Education: Attended U. of Missouri, 1945-46; Syracuse U., 1946-47; Drake U., LL.B. 1950.
Military Service: Army Air Corps, 1941-45.
Occupation: Lawyer; farmer.
Family: Wife, Beatrix Havens; two children.
Religion: Methodist.
Political Career: Sought Democratic nomination for U.S. House, 1956.
Capitol Office: 2373 Rayburn Bldg. 20515; 225-4426.

In Washington: Smith's long House career is one of contrasts. His name would not appear on any short list of prominent activists in Congress, yet he has seized a few issues with the determination of a crusader. He is an institutionalist, as befits his seniority, yet he occasionally tilts at the House system and its leaders with the rebelliousness of a maverick.

Like most effective appropriators, Smith spends the bulk of his time outside the spotlight, tending to his chairmanship of the Appropriations Subcommittee on Commerce, Justice, State and the Judiciary. He tenaciously defends programs under his jurisdiction against budget assaults, and tinkers with crop subsidies, dam construction and other Appropriations business that affects his district.

But in the 101st Congress, Smith's bullheaded approach to two issues — support for drug program funding and opposition to razing the U.S. embassy in Moscow — raised his visibility considerably.

As third in line at Appropriations behind two octogenarians, Smith always has in mind the possibility that he could eventually chair the powerful panel. Though past 70 himself, Smith acknowledged as far back as 1986 that he thinks about running the show someday. "I can't help it," he said. "Everyone keeps telling me I'll be chairman."

Though he is a fair and honest broker as subcommittee chairman — he is known to keep debate going until agreement can be reached without resorting to votes — Smith has the political strength and personal willpower to fight to the end for ideas dear to him. A man of liberal instincts rooted in Depression-era Iowa, he cannot fathom how other members, particularly Democrats, can put deficit reduction ahead of addressing society's needs.

The spending bill under his jurisdiction is diverse enough to give Smith entrée to a host of areas, and he is intimately familiar with the details of the bill, which funds three disparate Cabinet departments, the federal courts and 23 agencies, including the Federal Trade, Communications and Securities and Exchange commissions and the Small Business Administration.

Perhaps more than any other subcommittee chairman in Appropriations' "College of Cardinals," Smith resists the strictures imposed on appropriations bills by 1980s budget laws and by free-lance attacks from junior budget-cutters on the House floor.

During 1989 consideration of the legislative spending bill, he went as far as offering an amendment to cut off funding for the House Budget Committee staff if the budget process were not revamped by January 1990. While that idea was not treated seriously, the Budget Committee did, ironically, lose some influence as a result of the 1990 budget summit. The summit fixed overall spending limits through fiscal 1995, but appropriators have leeway to operate within those limits.

Typically quiet and understated — "bland and boring," a GOP foe once said — Smith can turn fierce when his priorities are challenged. He angrily protests what he sees as some colleagues' politically opportunistic attempts to have it both ways — voting to authorize new initiatives but later opposing appropriations for them in the name of deficit reduction. "Some members that talk big about wanting to control deficits, they also want all these things — drug abuse, homeless money," he once groused.

In 1989, Smith put Congress and the administration to the test. Arguing that it was time to pay for the ballyhooed $2.8 billion anti-drug bill of 1988 (for which just $500 million had been appropriated), he ignored requests from the administration and the Budget Committee to keep the cost of the supplemental appropriation bill down, and inserted $822 million for anti-drug programs. Smith was way out in front of the newly installed House Democratic leadership on the issue, but he would not budge. After a month-long standoff, the House finally approved his amendment. This led to a 90-day delay as Senate negotiators and the White House refused to consider the funding. Smith dug in, but finally had to settle for $75

Iowa 4

Central — Des Moines; Ames

More than 60 percent of the 4th District's voters are in Polk County, and most of them are in Des Moines. Surrounding farm counties and smaller industrial towns in the 4th look to Des Moines as the region's commercial, financial and governmental center.

Predominantly white, Protestant and middle class, Des Moines has little of the ethnic flavor of other Midwestern industrial cities such as Chicago or Omaha. More than 50 insurance companies have their headquarters there, making it the nation's second-largest insurance city. A sizable group of government workers live in and around the capital city, adding to its white-collar work force. The city also depends on grain marketing, publishing and the manufacture of farm equipment.

With about 4,000 members and a regional office in Des Moines, the United Auto Workers is a significant political presence. Workers in the farm equipment business are UAW members, and were hard hit by the 1980s farm depression, but the city's unemployment dropped to under 4 percent by 1990. The UAW has been important to past Democratic successes in the Des Moines area.

In 1980 presidential voting, a growing preference for the GOP was evident in the suburbs of Des Moines. That enabled Ronald Reagan to win Polk County by a slim margin over Jimmy Carter. But over the course of the Reagan administration, many more of Polk's voters turned away from the GOP than toward it. Walter F. Mondale narrowly carried the county in 1984, and Michael S. Dukakis decisively defeated George Bush there in 1988. The 4th, in fact, was Dukakis' best district in Iowa, giving him nearly 60 percent of its vote.

North of Polk, in Story County, is Ames (population 47,000), the home of Iowa State University's 25,000 students. In the 1980 presidential election, Story gave independent John B. Anderson more than 19 percent, his fifth-best county showing in the nation. Four years later, it was narrowly in Reagan's corner, but Story voted for Dukakis in 1988.

Population: 485,480. White 461,514 (95%), Black 14,645 (3%), Other 4,601 (1%). Spanish origin 5,722 (1%). 18 and over 356,227 (73%), 65 and over 53,382 (11%). Median age: 29.

million for the programs.

Smith's contrary streak also emerged when Congress considered the "dire emergency" 1990 supplemental spending bill. After members had spent months debating what pork-barrel projects to add on to it, Smith suggested that the words "dire" and "emergency" be stripped off the title of the measure. "I think we hold ourselves open to a little bit of ridicule with those words in there," he said. "We shouldn't pretend that it's a dire emergency."

House and Senate conferees informally agreed, but House chairman Jamie L. Whitten remained notably quiet. Whitten eventually decided that because conferees had not voted, the words should remain in place.

Smith's battles with the Budget Committee began in earnest in the 100th Congress, when he so opposed the House-passed budget resolutions in 1987 and 1988 that he devised a way for his subcommittee to ignore the budget's limits when drafting his panel's annual appropriations bill. His subcommittee omitted funding for some programs that either had not been authorized, or were so popular that members would surely cough up more money for his panel to allocate to them.

In both years, he took his bill to the full committee and acted as both its manager and chief critic. In 1987 he told Appropriations his measure was "woefully inadequate" because of the "crazy accounting" of Congress' budget process. In 1988, he presented his bill saying, "Everyone should oppose this bill on its merits. There just isn't enough money."

For several years, Smith has used his position on appropriations to almost singlehandedly block the government from tearing down the unfinished, bug-riddled U.S. embassy in Moscow. During construction, the building was seeded with listening devices by Soviet operatives, and the State Department and many members of Congress — including Smith's counterpart on the Senate Appropriations Committee, Ernest F. Hollings — favored razing the building and starting over again.

Smith adamantly opposed that idea, estimated to cost $300 million, and year after year foiled attempts to fund demolition. In early 1990 he opposed proceeding with new design work unless it included an option beyond the raze-and-rebuild plan. The State Department finally gave in; in 1991, the Bush administration threw its support to a less costly plan, under which new secure floors would be built on top of the bugged building. But critics of the "top hat" plan vowed to resist it.

Outside Appropriations, Smith was active

in the late 1980s in fighting for tougher poultry inspection laws, a drive that recalls a crusade early in his House career that resulted in perhaps his single most notable achievement.

That effort began in 1961, characteristically low-key, and it ended with passage of the 1967 Wholesome Meat Act and the 1968 Wholesome Poultry Products Act. The legislation was the first major overhaul of the law regulating the meatpacking industry since its passage during the Theodore Roosevelt administration, in the wake of the exposé "The Jungle." Similarly, Smith's long-sought success in the 1960s followed reports of scandalous conditions in meatpacking houses, this time by *The Des Moines Register*, which won a Pulitzer Prize.

Though his quiet persistence had been largely responsible for forcing the issue, the 1967 law did not go nearly as far as Smith wanted. He tried to amend it to impose federal standards on the industry, but failed in the House by six votes. Congress eventually cleared a bill simply providing funds for states to upgrade their facilities.

In recent Congresses, Smith has rejoined the battle to improve poultry processing. He has helped block an industry push for more lenient federal supervision, and took the offensive by proposing increased inspections in response to reports of growing incidents of poultry contamination. Though he is not on the Agriculture Committee, which has jurisdiction, Smith testifies there as a sort of expert witness.

He does play a role in farm policy as a member of Appropriations' Agriculture Subcommittee. In 1986, Smith worked with Republican Silvio O. Conte of Massachusetts on an amendment to limit federal subsidies to $250,000 per individual producer after news reports that some large cotton and rice producers had received as much as $20 million under the 1985 farm law.

Smith's reformist approach to agriculture has been a consistent theme in his career. He was instrumental in creating the Commodity Futures Trading Commission to guard against grain trading abuses, and in setting up strict federal procedures for grain inspection. He has fought White House efforts to turn grain inspection back to private enterprise.

"They cheated before," he said of private grain interests, "and there's no indication they wouldn't cheat again."

One of his landmark reforms, however, had nothing to do with agriculture. It was a rule against nepotism on congressional payrolls. As of the late 1960s, more than 50 members had hired relatives as aides. Smith's measure prevented that, although it "grandfathered" those already employed.

To get his rule past the House, Smith had to offer it as an amendment to a related bill, and he found a vehicle in legislation increasing federal salaries. Before most members knew what had happened, the House had passed it.

That bit of parliamentary gamesmanship demonstrated the fascination Smith always has had with House procedure. He has proposed a variety of rules changes over the years, including the one in 1973 that reduced the dominance of the seniority system by making all committee chairmen subject to a Democratic Caucus vote at the start of each Congress.

Despite his parliamentary skill and the wide respect he enjoys, Smith never has excelled at internal politics. In 1975, he tried to become Budget Committee chairman, but lost to Brock Adams of Washington, 148-119. In the 99th Congress, he mounted a quixotic challenge to a member of the Democratic Steering and Policy Committee, though no incumbent on that leadership panel had ever been defeated that way. Eventually Smith gave up.

At Home: Smith has always won votes beyond the normal Democratic constituency in Iowa. His long run of easy re-elections was interrupted by a poor showing in 1980, but he rebounded convincingly two years later, and has had no problems since.

Until 1980, Smith had not seen tough elections since the early years of his political career. After serving as national president of the Young Democrats of America, he first ran for Congress in 1956, losing the Democratic primary to state Rep. William Denman, who nearly unseated GOP Rep. Paul Cunningham in the general election.

In 1958 Smith finished first in a five-man Democratic primary. But he fell short of winning the 35 percent plurality required by state party rules, so the party's district convention was left to choose the nominee. Although Smith had to overcome some opposition from Des Moines labor unions, he won the nomination easily at the convention.

Cunningham's narrow 1956 victory marked him as vulnerable in 1958, but Democratic unity had been damaged by the bitter nomination fight. Smith had to struggle to win with 52 percent, aided by a national Democratic tide that took three Iowa congressional seats from Republican control.

In 1960 Smith was the sole survivor among the state's three first-term Democrats. His GOP opponent, Des Moines physician Floyd Burgeson, was a forceful speaker but an inexperienced politician. Smith prevailed with 53 percent and won easily during the next decade.

Redistricting after the 1970 census threw Smith into the same district with Republican Rep. John Kyl. The national Democratic Party and labor groups gave Smith extra support, and he easily overcame Kyl (whose son Jon now serves in the House from Arizona). Smith coasted through subsequent elections until he met Republican Don Young in 1980.

Smith's close call against Young capped a year of unusual activity among 4th District

Republicans. A Des Moines physician, Young used financial and organizational help from the national GOP to build a respectable campaign organization and raise about $250,000. He called the congressman an entrenched fixture of a Democratic Congress that had weakened the nation's economy and defense.

Disquieted by polls showing a sharp drop in his popularity, Smith fought back with radio, television and billboard advertisements in the closing weeks of the campaign. He won just over 55 percent in Polk County (Des Moines) and Wapello County (Ottumwa), but lost two rural, small-town counties and was held to a bare majority in six others. For the first time in 20 years, Smith was held below 60 percent.

The strong showing by Young generated considerable optimism among Republicans that Smith could be toppled in 1982. The optimism faded, however, when Young announced in late 1981 that he would forgo a rematch and concentrate on running his medical clinic.

Des Moines state Sen. Dave Readinger stepped in to take the GOP nomination. He blanketed the district with billboards to increase his name recognition and tried to portray Smith as having spent too much time in Washington to be attuned to Iowa concerns.

But the conservative mood that aided Young in 1980 had passed. Smith won two-thirds of the vote, and since then, Republicans have invested little in the 4th.

Committees

Appropriations (3rd of 37 Democrats)
Commerce, Justice, State & Judiciary (chairman); Labor, Health & Human Services, Education & Related Agencies; Rural Development, Agriculture & Related Agencies

Small Business (2nd of 27 Democrats)
SBA, the General Economy & Minority Enterprise Development

Elections

1990 General		
Neal Smith (D)	127,812	(98%)
1988 General		
Neal Smith (D)	157,065	(72%)
Paul Lunde (R)	62,056	(28%)

Previous Winning Percentages: **1986** (68%) **1984** (61%) **1982** (66%) **1980** (54%) **1978** (65%) **1976** (69%) **1974** (64%) **1972** (60%) **1970** (65%) **1968** (62%) **1966** (60%) **1964** (70%) **1962** (63%) **1960** (53%) **1958** (52%)

District Vote For President

	1988	1984	1980	1976
D	131,356 (59%)	118,092 (50%)	95,948 (42%)	113,687 (51%)
R	90,855 (41%)	115,898 (49%)	105,044 (45%)	103,091 (46%)
I			27,252 (12%)	

Campaign Finance

	Receipts	Receipts from PACs	Expend-itures
1990			
Smith (D)	$167,829	$116,970 (70%)	$56,903
1988			
Smith (D)	$205,035	$162,585 (79%)	$83,474

Key Votes

1991	
Authorize use of force against Iraq	N
1990	
Support constitutional amendment on flag desecration	N
Pass family and medical leave bill over Bush veto	Y
Reduce SDI funding	N
Allow abortions in overseas military facilities	Y
Approve budget summit plan for spending and taxing	Y
Approve civil rights bill	Y
1989	
Halt production of B-2 stealth bomber at 13 planes	N
Oppose capital gains tax cut	N
Approve federal abortion funding in rape or incest cases	Y
Approve pay raise and revision of ethics rules	Y
Pass Democratic minimum wage plan over Bush veto	Y

Voting Studies

	Presidential Support		Party Unity		Conservative Coalition	
Year	S	O	S	O	S	O
1990	27	72	88	10	41	59
1989	31	56	82	8	22	59
1988	30	63	79	12	37	53
1987	27	69	87	8	47	49
1986	22	70	80	13	44	52
1985	30	66	85	11	35	62
1984	38	55	71	17	42	47
1983	30	68	84	13	29	66
1982	40	56	83	17	30	67
1981	42	55	76	20	40	55

Interest Group Ratings

Year	ADA	ACU	AFL-CIO	CCUS
1990	83	8	83	29
1989	70	11	75	40
1988	80	16	86	46
1987	76	9	81	14
1986	70	14	83	22
1985	75	10	75	24
1984	70	21	62	53
1983	70	17	76	61
1982	80	19	70	45
1981	55	20	64	18

5 Jim Ross Lightfoot (R)

Of Shenandoah — Elected 1984

Born: Sept. 27, 1938, Sioux City, Iowa.
Education: Attended U. of Iowa; U. of Tulsa.
Military Service: Army, 1955-56; Army Reserve, 1956-63.
Occupation: Radio broadcaster; store owner; police officer.
Family: Wife, Nancy Harrison; four children.
Religion: Roman Catholic.
Political Career: Corsicana, Texas, City Commission, 1974-76.
Capitol Office: 1222 Longworth Bldg. 20515; 225-3806.

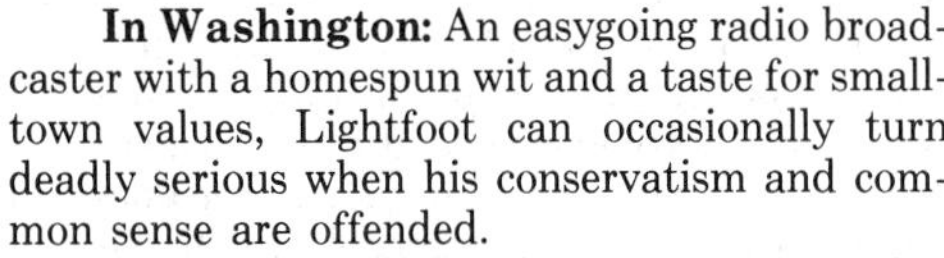

In Washington: An easygoing radio broadcaster with a homespun wit and a taste for small-town values, Lightfoot can occasionally turn deadly serious when his conservatism and common sense are offended.

During the 1990 budget quagmire, Lightfoot took to the floor for a rare emotional display of member-bashing, calling Congress "the only insane asylum run by its own inmates."

"I would suggest to my colleagues that many Republicans and good conservative Democrats are sick and tired of being cast and forced into the role of playing the clown," said Lightfoot. "It is time that this circus closed and left town."

And during the debate in the 101st Congress over increasing federal funding for abortion, Lightfoot took up the cause for "a bunch of people whose natural mothers decided to let us live." Lightfoot, who was adopted as an infant and who has a daughter born with spina bifida, debated the issue with Rep. Barbara Boxer, D-Calif., on the Phil Donahue show. "So they'll never call him a wimp, this guy Lightfoot," said Donahue after the show. "Nobody's going to accuse him of waffling."

Some critics nevertheless say Lightfoot is stronger on anecdotes than on evidence. But he won two convincing re-elections in his agriculture-dependent district at a time when many had criticized the GOP for turning breadbasket Iowa into an economic basket case.

And he sufficiently impressed GOP House leaders to earn, on his second try, a coveted seat on the Appropriations Committee in the 102nd Congress. The move required him to give up his spots on Interior and Public Works.

In a state where GOP House members such as Jim Leach and former Rep. Tom Tauke carved out niches well to the left of the Reagan administration, Lightfoot has usually followed a conservative line, not only on agricultural issues, where he stresses reliance on the free market, but also on many of the defense and foreign policy questions that excite Iowa's dovish, quasi-isolationist instincts.

Lightfoot's views are well received by those farmers in the 5th not battling bankruptcy and who remain suspicious of the federal role in agriculture despite benefiting from some programs. Still, Lightfoot — formerly chairman of the House Rural Communities Task Force — voted against the 1990 farm bill because, he said, "it contained $13 billion in cuts in farm programs as mandated by the budget deal."

His first major vote in the 99th Congress was for the MX missile; no other Iowan in the House or Senate supported it. He also has voted for the strategic defense initiative, chemical weapons and aid to anti-communist rebels in Angola. In each of his six years in Washington, he supported the Reagan and Bush administrations' position on House floor votes more often than any other Iowa House member.

But Lightfoot did register a conspicuous difference with the administration in 1986 by opposing aid to the Nicaraguan contras.

After being turned away from the Agriculture Committee upon arriving in Washington — with two Iowans on the panel, the state was thought to have its share of seats — Lightfoot took a seat on Public Works, where he was briefly, before moving to Appropriations, ranking minority member on the Public Buildings panel.

When a seat on Agriculture opened up in his second term, he decided to keep Public Works, "because it's where the money is." There, he lobbied for a flood-control project as well as for a federal buy-out of farmers' land flooded by a lake in the district. He has also pushed for local bridge improvements, airport projects and a highway demonstration project.

A pilot and certified flight instructor, Lightfoot devoted a good deal of attention to aviation matters from the Aviation Subcommittee at Public Works. He called for moving back the mandatory retirement age of pilots and for requiring child safety seats on airplanes — an issue spurred by the deaths of five infants in the 1989 crash of a United flight in Sioux City.

Iowa 5

Southwest — Council Bluffs; Fort Dodge

The 5th is farm country, a sprawling patch of southwest Iowa whose health is measured in dollars-per-bushel and debt-to-asset ratios. Its small towns, some a main street lined by worn, wood-planked sidewalks and faded storefronts, live off the agricultural economy. Only one other district in the country has a higher percentage of its population living on farms.

The rural counties of the 5th are divided by a line that roughly follows Interstate 80 between Council Bluffs and Des Moines. To the north, the land is flatter, the soil richer, and the farms — until recent years — more prosperous. The land to the south is rocky and pocked with gullies, more suitable for raising livestock than for growing crops. The counties along the Missouri border have historically been among the poorest in the state; the farm-debt crisis and three years of drought followed by 1984 flooding devastated many farms in the area.

Even so, the district's southwest corner is staunchly Republican. Pottawattamie County and those counties to the south, east and northwest of it voted solidly Republican in 1984 and in 1988; there are twice as many registered Republicans than Democrats in Cass, Mills, Montgomery and Page counties.

There are only two cities of any size, Council Bluffs and Fort Dodge. Council Bluffs, the seat of Pottawattamie County, is the larger, with about 54,000 people. An old trading settlement built against the Missouri River bluffs across from Omaha, it makes its living from meatpacking, railroads and light manufacturing. Council Bluffs has a good-sized union population, but it also has a middle class, almost suburban character that has made it resistant to major Democratic inroads.

At the northern end of the district, Fort Dodge, (population 27,000), the Webster County seat, is much more reliable Democratic territory. An industrial center near large gypsum deposits, the city is in the heart of a region settled by Irish Catholics. Webster County and its heavily Catholic neighbor, Greene County, were two of the three counties in the 5th that voted Democratic for president in 1984. In 1988, Democratic Party fortunes soared in the 5th, with Michael S. Dukakis carrying 19 of the district's 27 counties.

At its eastern end, the district holds southern suburbs of Des Moines in Warren County. This county was the state's fastest growing in the 1970s, but the growth has leveled off in recent years.

Population: 485,639. White 480,799 (99%), Black 1,649 (0.3%). Spanish origin 3,071 (1%). 18 and over 346,800 (71%), 65 and over 75,869 (16%). Median age: 32.

At a 1989 hearing on airport and airline safety following the December 1988 terrorist bombing of an airliner over Scotland, Lightfoot noted that he had a special perspective on the tragedy, since he had worked as a policeman and charter plane operator as well as a pilot.

Lightfoot gained one of his legislative goals in 1990 when Congress created the Western Historic Trails Center in Council Bluffs to commemorate the the westward expansion in the 19th century along a system of trails.

The 100th Congress was a rough time for Lightfoot. In late 1987, he broke two toes rushing down some stairs. Later quizzed on the open shoe he wore, he explained, "I went to the Gerald Ford School of Walking, where you have to fall down and break something to graduate." Lightfoot spent the first three months of 1988 recovering from double-bypass heart surgery.

At Home: Affable and unassuming, Lightfoot fits his district like a comfortable pair of dungarees. "I've been involved in agriculture for many years," he has said, "and involved in a business on Main Street. I was a blue-collar worker.... That's what this district is made of — small business, blue-collar workers and farms." In 1984, he brought the GOP its first victory in the 5th in a decade.

When Democrat Tom Harkin left the 5th to run for the Senate, Lightfoot was an obvious contender for the Republican nomination. For 16 years, off and on, he had been a farm editor and announcer for KMA, the major farm station in southwest Iowa. With his highly personal delivery of market and weather reports, farm news and comments on local and national affairs a daily feature of life for farm families, he had developed a big following. His appearances at hog roasts, county fairs, rodeos and charity events cemented his celebrity status.

In addition, after years of farm reporting and quiet support for various Republican causes, Lightfoot had ready access to county-by-county networks of pork producers and cattlemen, and to GOP regulars. Urged to run for Congress after returning from a well-publicized trip to the Far East with President Reagan in 1983, Lightfoot agreed. He proved his potency in a primary against four Republicans.

The general election proved much tougher. Lightfoot was no longer selling himself just to the faithful. Southern Iowa's farm economy was in wretched shape, and voters were in no mood to accept generic GOP assurances.

Moreover, Democrat Jerry Fitzgerald was no average candidate himself. A former state House majority leader, he had run twice for governor, in 1978 and 1982. Well-known in the district's northern counties, he had extensive ties to Democratic activists and the added strength of Harkin on the Senate ballot to pull him along.

Lightfoot's campaign cultivated an image of neighbors getting together to help a friend — on the back of the campaign cards he handed out was a recipe for "Florence Falk's sour cream apple pie."

Fitzgerald, more cerebral and reserved, could not compete on the level of personality but came across as the more substantive. He attacked Lightfoot as ill-informed about federal policy.

Fitzgerald's tactics paid off where neither candidate was known, especially in the southeastern counties outside of KMA's listening radius. But Lightfoot built up huge support in his home territory, and he won by just over 3,000 votes districtwide.

Democrats were optimistic they could unseat Lightfoot in 1986 amid the deepening farm discontent, but they never quite came together on how to do it. The preferred candidate of many of the Harkin Democrats was state Sen. Leonard Boswell, a farmer and former military officer. But Boswell ran sluggishly and lost the nomination to Scott Hughes, a little-known Council Bluffs lawyer.

Hughes had some credibility with farmers from his work in fighting foreclosures, and he tried to paint Lightfoot as insensitive to the rural crisis. He accused Lightfoot, who had voted for the 1985 farm bill, of placing his Reagan loyalties ahead of agricultural needs.

But Lightfoot's years of contact with the farm community made that case difficult to sell. As depressed as conditions were in southwest Iowa, voters seemed unwilling to blame Lightfoot. He won every county for a victory margin exceeding 25,000 votes. He took the next two elections by an even larger margin.

Committees

Appropriations (22nd of 22 Republicans)
Military Construction; Treasury, Postal Service & General Government

Elections

1990 General		
Jim Ross Lightfoot (R)	99,978	(68%)
Rod Powell (D)	47,022	(32%)
1988 General		
Jim Ross Lightfoot (R)	117,761	(64%)
Gene Freund (D)	66,599	(36%)

Previous Winning Percentages: 1986 (59%) **1984** (51%)

District Vote For President

	1988	1984	1980	1976
D	100,734 (52%)	88,949 (42%)	74,675 (35%)	101,119 (49%)
R	92,323 (47%)	123,243 (58%)	123,622 (58%)	103,428 (50%)
I			14,128 (7%)	

Campaign Finance

	Receipts	Receipts from PACs		Expend-itures
1990				
Lightfoot (R)	$497,363	$146,243	(29%)	$418,134
Powell (D)	$67,655	$34,920	(52%)	$63,591
1988				
Lightfoot (R)	$478,842	$166,077	(35%)	$420,730
Freund (D)	$133,183	$68,275	(51%)	$131,599

Key Votes

1991	
Authorize use of force against Iraq	Y
1990	
Support constitutional amendment on flag desecration	Y
Pass family and medical leave bill over Bush veto	N
Reduce SDI funding	N
Allow abortions in overseas military facilities	N
Approve budget summit plan for spending and taxing	N
Approve civil rights bill	N
1989	
Halt production of B-2 stealth bomber at 13 planes	N
Oppose capital gains tax cut	N
Approve federal abortion funding in rape or incest cases	N
Approve pay raise and revision of ethics rules	N
Pass Democratic minimum wage plan over Bush veto	N

Voting Studies

	Presidential Support		Party Unity		Conservative Coalition	
Year	S	O	S	O	S	O
1990	68	30	90	7	98	2
1989	72	27	91	7	98	2
1988	63	26	76	8	92	3
1987	65	34	89	10	88	12
1986	70	30	83	16	84	16
1985	63	38	85	14	84	16

Interest Group Ratings

Year	ADA	ACU	AFL-CIO	CCUS
1990	6	92	0	93
1989	5	79	0	90
1988	10	90	15	85
1987	8	74	6	87
1986	10	64	14	94
1985	10	81	24	82

6 Fred Grandy (R)

Of Sioux City — Elected 1986

Born: June 29, 1948, Sioux City, Iowa.
Education: Harvard U., B.A. 1970.
Occupation: Actor; congressional aide.
Family: Wife, Catherine Mann; three children.
Religion: Episcopalian.
Political Career: No previous office.
Capitol Office: 418 Cannon Bldg. 20515; 225-5476.

In Washington: Grandy has distinguished himself as one of the most able of the younger generation of House Republicans. Should he choose to make a career out of it, he could rise to a position of considerable influence in the House. He has a good place to start the climb: a seat on the Ways and Means Committee that he got at the beginning of his third term.

A onetime congressional aide, Grandy already had a working knowledge of the House when he arrived in 1987. In his first two terms, he primarily focused on the Agriculture Committee, where he earned a reputation for intelligence, incisiveness and homework. He was named to the House-Senate conference committee on the 1987 farm-credit bill, the most important agriculture legislation of the 100th Congress. He was also a co-author of the Drought Assistance Act of 1988.

Grandy does not react to farm issues reflexively. Where the majority of Agriculture Committee members are committed to getting the most for the farmers in their districts, Grandy casts an eye toward the programs' cost, seeing growing reluctance among House members to support generous farm payouts.

When the committee considered a disaster-relief bill in 1989, Grandy won approval of an amendment that limited outlays to the amount of money saved by the government that year because of the adverse weather. With the drought raising commodity prices, the government paid less in farm price and income supports. Only such savings could be used for disaster payments.

During work on the 1990 farm bill, members from states that grow soybeans and oilseeds (such as sunflowers) sought new subsidies. But Grandy warned that the added cost would never fly on the House floor. He proposed that any additional subsidies be paid by taking money from other crops' subsidies. "We cannot spend more than we have, or we will be decimated on the floor," he said. But his "zero-sum" approach to subsidies was not approved.

Grandy began working on enacting groundwater-protection legislation in his first term; he was one of the GOP floor managers for the groundwater-research bill that passed the House in 1987. The bill died in the Senate. Frustrated over what he saw as the Department of Agriculture's inaction on the issue, he introduced a sweeping bill in 1989 to specify how the department should coordinate groundwater policy. Some groundwater-control language became law in the 1990 farm bill. Grandy was a member of the House-Senate conference committee that worked out the details of that bill.

In the middle of 1989, Grandy was appointed to the House ethics committee. Ethics is generally considered a thankless assignment; Grandy's place there demonstrates his willingness to do some heavy lifting for GOP leaders.

In his two terms on Education and Labor, Grandy was usually allied with the committee's more combative conservative Republicans against such labor-endorsed initiatives as mandatory parental leave. He regularly earns high marks from business organizations and low scores from organized labor.

One Education and Labor fight that led Grandy to break with committee conservatives was the effort to restrict the funding discretion of the National Endowment for the Arts. Conservatives urged restricting — or abolishing — the NEA following an uproar over projects by grant recipients that some members considered obscene or sacrilegious. Defending the NEA, Grandy said, "I defy anyone in this chamber to find me a federal agency that has a better record of success." He added that conservative groups lobbying for restrictions "do not necessarily speak for all of the families of America."

The NEA debate was but one example of how difficult Grandy is to typecast ideologically. An opponent of abortion, Grandy votes with his party more often than the average Republican. But he was one of only 17 House Republicans to oppose a constitutional amendment to ban flag desecration in 1990. Less than a week after that vote, he chastised delegates at his state's GOP convention after they backed a flag-burning amendment. "You can't trash the First Amendment to protect our flag," he said.

Iowa 6

Northwest — Sioux City

Northwestern Iowa's flat, rich soil makes it one of the most agriculturally productive areas of the nation, with consistently impressive yields for both corn and soybeans. But as farming has become a more costly, technologically complex business, many small-scale farmers have sold their land to agribusiness operations, eliminating jobs and causing migration from the district. Of the 23 counties in the 6th, every county lost population in the last decade.

Some of the more industrialized pockets of the district were hit hard by the 1982 recession and have yet to recover; Emmet County, in the north-central part, saw its unemployment soar to 16 percent that year, the result of meatpacking plant closings.

There are troubles in the rural counties as well. In the western part of the district, where farmers expanded considerably in the 1970s, some counties have seen scores of farms go on the market with no purchasers.

Sioux City, western Iowa's largest city (population 80,000), is the political core of the 6th. An old meatpacking town on the Missouri River, Sioux City has grown into an urban center with a massive downtown urban renewal project that includes a regional shopping center. The city ran into troubles a bit earlier than its neighbors, due to the closing of a large Zenith electronics plant in 1978. Since then, its condition has stabilized with the influx of some small industries.

The city and surrounding Woodbury County have about a fifth of the district's population and generally vote Republican.

Notwithstanding Grandy's easy reelections, his district is becoming somewhat less enamored of the national Republican Party. Democratic nominee Michael S. Dukakis won 15 of the district's 23 counties in 1988, but still lost the district by a tenth of a percentage point. Four years earlier, Ronald Reagan carried the district comfortably, but even he lost Cerro Gordo County, the second most populous in the 6th. Mason City, the county seat, is a producer of ice machines and building materials and a processor of meat and dairy products. It is also the town that inspired Meredith Willson, a native son, to write "The Music Man."

Population: 485,491. White 479,511 (99%), Black 1,621 (0.3%), Other 2,510 (1%). Spanish origin 3,319 (1%). 18 and over 348,641 (72%), 65 and over 74,259 (15%). Median age: 32.

A former actor, Grandy is known to TV trivia buffs as "Gopher Smith," the bumbling and likable ship's purser on the "Love Boat" series, which made Grandy famous. As Grandy has gained acceptance as a serious player on Capitol Hill, most members have allowed Grandy to progress beyond sitcom. But a few of his colleagues still dwell on the past.

According to *The Des Moines Register*, during Agriculture Committee consideration of a Grandy amendment to the farm bill, North Carolina Democrat Charlie Rose remarked that his state's senior senator, Jesse Helms, would consider Grandy's idea a "communist plot." "No pun intended," Rose said, "but this Love Boat should be stopped at the dock."

Grandy was not amused. "I assure you this proposal contains no homoerotic content," he said, alluding to Helms' efforts to muzzle the NEA. "Don't you speak about my senator like that," said Rose, his voice rising. "I'll tell him you said that," Grandy replied. He ended up withdrawing his amendment, however.

At Home: Grandy left college divided between ambitions in government and theater. He first chose the former, becoming a legislative aide and speechwriter to Wiley Mayne, then the GOP representative for northwest Iowa. But show business beckoned. Grandy was soon appearing in off-Broadway productions and films, and in 1975 his run with "Love Boat" began.

As that commercial success wound down, Grandy looked again to Washington. The road to Congress lay through Sioux City, where luck gave him a shot at an open seat in 1986.

When Grandy first started running for Congress in 1985, his bid was viewed as just a curiosity. An actor from California who had left Iowa as a young teenager, he returned to an area where he had never even voted to take on popular six-term Rep. Berkley Bedell (who had defeated Mayne in 1974). But early in 1986, Bedell decided not to run.

Left in the lurch, Democrats nominated Clayton Hodgson, Bedell's longtime chief agricultural aide in the district. Despite his late start and low name recognition, Hodgson had strengths Grandy lacked: a solid agricultural background, lifelong residency in the state and strong support from Bedell.

But Grandy proved surprisingly successful at deflecting carpetbagger charges and jokes about his show business career. An articulate graduate of Exeter and Harvard, Grandy set out early to, as he put it, "make people understand that there is a long-pants version of Fred Grandy, not just Gopher Smith in short pants." He worked hard to master issues of importance to Iowa, and built a large campaign treasury.

While Hodgson stressed that he was an Iowan and Grandy was not, Grandy noted that his father's name still graced an insurance company in Sioux City, the 6th's largest city. He criticized his former home state of California as a "superficial environment." Grandy praised Iowa's sense of community and thanked residents for welcoming him back.

Ideological differences between the candidates were largely overshadowed by questions of background and style, but they did exist. Grandy tried to have the best of both worlds, appearing with President Reagan at the signing of the 1985 farm bill, but taking care not to defend the administration's agricultural policies. To troubled farmers he stressed the need to expand exports, with federal subsidies if necessary. Hodgson called Grandy's farm proposals "a welfare check for farmers" and pushed for production controls.

Grandy's victory was far from overwhelming. He carried only 11 of 23 counties in the district. But those who expected him to fall in his first re-election bid were soon surprised by both the job he did in Washington and his high-profile presence back home.

Democrats had thought Grandy vulnerable for his vote on contra aid and for the time he had spent campaigning for other GOP candidates or visiting in California. But the party was unable to field a strong candidate.

Their nominee was 30-year-old lawyer David O'Brien of Sioux Falls. Although he had excellent political contacts in the district, O'Brien was far outspent, and made no headway with his attacks on Grandy for being less attuned to the district than Bedell. Grandy easily carried every county and won by an even larger margin two years later.

Committees

Standards of Official Conduct (2nd of 7 Republicans)

Ways & Means (13th of 13 Republicans)
Human Resources; Select Revenue Measures

Elections

1990 General		
Fred Grandy (R)	112,333	(72%)
Mike D. Earll (D)	44,063	(28%)
1988 General		
Fred Grandy (R)	125,859	(64%)
Dave O'Brien (D)	69,614	(36%)

Previous Winning Percentage: **1986** (51%)

District Vote For President

	1988	1984	1980	1976
D	99,116 (50%)	90,257 (42%)	75,202 (34%)	96,880 (45%)
R	99,214 (50%)	121,665 (57%)	125,915 (57%)	114,986 (53%)
I			16,232 (7%)	

Campaign Finance

	Receipts	Receipts from PACs		Expend-itures
1990				
Grandy (R)	$409,067	$251,675	(62%)	$322,563
Earll (D)	$44,250	$17,350	(39%)	$42,597
1988				
Grandy (R)	$527,487	$294,944	(56%)	$523,108
O'Brien (D)	$174,475	$74,825	(43%)	$175,951

Key Votes

1991	
Authorize use of force against Iraq	Y
1990	
Support constitutional amendment on flag desecration	N
Pass family and medical leave bill over Bush veto	N
Reduce SDI funding	Y
Allow abortions in overseas military facilities	N
Approve budget summit plan for spending and taxing	Y
Approve civil rights bill	N
1989	
Halt production of B-2 stealth bomber at 13 planes	Y
Oppose capital gains tax cut	N
Approve federal abortion funding in rape or incest cases	N
Approve pay raise and revision of ethics rules	N
Pass Democratic minimum wage plan over Bush veto	N

Voting Studies

	Presidential Support		Party Unity		Conservative Coalition	
Year	S	O	S	O	S	O
1990	63	37	81	17	76	22
1989	74	26	86	13	90	10
1988	52	43	70	27	87	11
1987	63	37	77	20	86	14

Interest Group Ratings

Year	ADA	ACU	AFL-CIO	CCUS
1990	28	42	0	86
1989	25	64	8	100
1988	40	64	57	86
1987	20	57	19	80

Kansas

U.S. CONGRESS

SENATE 2 R

HOUSE 2 D, 3 R

LEGISLATURE

Senate 18 D, 22 R

House 63 D, 62 R

ELECTIONS

1988 Presidential Vote

Bush	56%
Dukakis	43%

1984 Presidential Vote

Reagan	66%
Mondale	33%

1980 Presidential Vote

Reagan	58%
Carter	33%
Anderson	7%

Turnout rate in 1986	44%
Turnout rate in 1988	54%
Turnout rate in 1990	42%

(as percentage of voting age population)

POPULATION AND GROWTH

1980 population	2,363,679
1990 population (32nd in the nation)	2,477,574
Percent change 1980-1990	+5%

DEMOGRAPHIC BREAKDOWN

White	90%
Black	6%
Asian or Pacific Islander	1%
(Hispanic origin)	4%
Urban	67%
Rural	33%
Born in state	63%
Foreign-born	2%

MAJOR CITIES

Wichita	304,011
Kansas City	149,767
Topeka	119,883
Overland Park	111,790
Lawrence	65,608

AREA AND LAND USE

Area 81,778 sq. miles (13th)

Farm	90%
Forest	3%
Federally owned	1%

Gov. Joan Finney (D)
Of Topeka — Elected 1990

Born: Feb. 12, 1925, Topeka, Kan.
Education: Kansas City Conservatory of Music, 1946; College of St. Theresa, 1950; Washburn U., B.A. 1981.
Occupation: Legislative aide.
Religion: Roman Catholic.
Political Career: Kan. state treasurer, 1975-91.
Next Election: 1994.

WORK

Occupations

White-collar	51%
Blue-collar	30%
Service workers	13%

Government Workers

Federal	24,826
State	57,216
Local	127,617

MONEY

Median family income	$ 19,707	(26th)
Tax burden per capita	$ 782	(35th)

EDUCATION

Spending per pupil through grade 12	$ 4,076	(25th)
Persons with college degrees	17%	(22nd)

CRIME

Violent crime rate	401 per 100,000	(30th)

Kansas - Congressional Districts

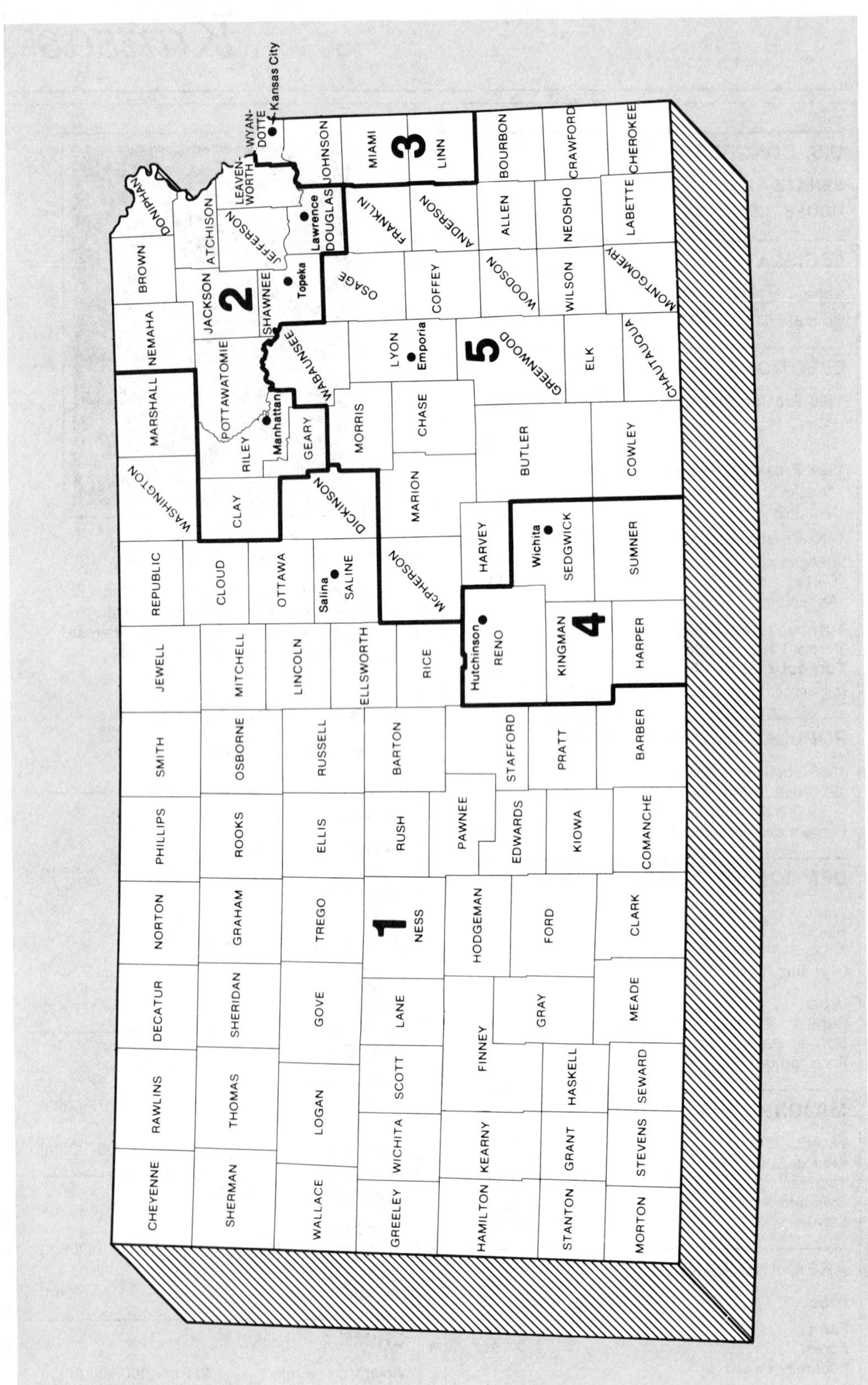

Bob Dole (R)

Of Russell — Elected 1968

Born: July 22, 1923, Russell, Kan.
Education: Attended U. of Kansas, 1941-43; Washburn U., A.B., LL.B. 1952.
Military Service: Army, 1943-48.
Occupation: Lawyer.
Family: Wife, Mary Elizabeth Hanford; one child.
Religion: Methodist.
Political Career: Kan. House, 1951-53; Russell County attorney, 1953-61; U.S. House, 1961-69; Republican nominee for vice president, 1976; sought Republican nomination for president, 1980, 1988.
Capitol Office: 141 Hart Bldg. 20510; 224-6521.

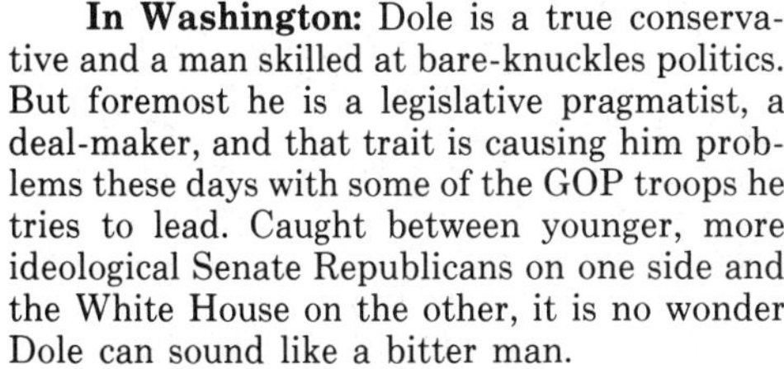

In Washington: Dole is a true conservative and a man skilled at bare-knuckles politics. But foremost he is a legislative pragmatist, a deal-maker, and that trait is causing him problems these days with some of the GOP troops he tries to lead. Caught between younger, more ideological Senate Republicans on one side and the White House on the other, it is no wonder Dole can sound like a bitter man.

"Party discipline is not a problem on this side of the aisle," he carped at one point in 1990. "We never had it. We are all free spirits. We are all leaders on this side."

Dole always has seen himself as the personification of the American ideal, proof certain that hard work and determination can lift a man from humble roots and carry him through adversity to great success. Dole's belief in that ethic drove him with unbroken success from the Kansas House to the top job in the U.S. Senate.

But in 1980 and again in 1988, he was defeated as he tried to move up to the presidency, and as the 1990s opened, Dole found himself struggling to get his Senate GOP colleagues to toe a party line. He faces the twin frustrations of serving as chief congressional advocate for his erstwhile rival for the presidency — a job Dole has carried out with remarkable loyalty — and swatting away brickbats directed at him from within the GOP Conference.

In anger and frustration, Dole twice in the 101st Congress sardonically suggested that Republicans find a new Senate leader. Then, in the 1990 elections, the GOP lost a seat, dimming prospects that Dole would ever again lead the Senate as he had in 1985 and 1986. Rumors began circulating that he would retire in 1992 or perhaps resign sooner. By the start of the 102nd Congress, in the glow of the Persian Gulf War, that speculation subsided. But little else had changed to ease Dole's frustration.

Elected in 1968, after eight years in the House, he is the Senate's fourth most senior Republican, and he is coping with a Congress far different from the one he entered a generation ago. As Senate GOP leader, Dole has shown a will and a capacity to exercise power and exert control, but he now finds around him a greater number of younger conservative activists who are impatient with their elders' more pragmatic approach. In the Senate, this internal Republican rift is not as wide or as public as it has been in the House, but in organizing for the 102nd Congress, several conservatives won GOP leadership positions over more moderate competition.

The political crosscurrents Dole fights to tame roiled during the protracted budget debate of 1990. Recession finally had forced legislators to make a more concerted effort to reduce the deficit, and with Democrats scoring political points with demands for "tax fairness," President Bush dropped his 1988 campaign pledge not to raise taxes.

A fierce partisan, Dole quickly defended Bush's new line, saying he was merely trying to get Democrats to bargain seriously. But politically and personally, it was a tough sell for the minority leader because Bush's "read my lips, no new taxes" rhetoric had been echoed by countless Republicans after it blistered Dole in the 1988 New Hampshire presidential primary.

Less than a day after defending Bush, Dole reverted to his characteristic dark humor. When asked how GOP candidates should react to Bush's change in signals, he quipped, "Tell them to get some lip balm; it's good for cracked lips."

But from there, Dole went on to be perhaps Bush's most relentless ally in the budget summit process. During weeks of congressional-White House negotiations, Dole propelled the talks forward at several tense junctures. When the final agreement failed to gain congressional approval, it was not for a lack of a fight by Dole — liberals had balked at its program cuts and conservatives at its tax increases.

Dole then joined with Senate Majority

Leader George J. Mitchell to put up a united front for a budget much like the summit agreement. Both leaders heard complaints from senators unhappy with the post-summit compromise; conservatives chafed when Dole blocked consideration of an amendment to eliminate a proposed increase in gasoline taxes. But arguing that any amendment would unravel the deal, Mitchell and Dole managed to keep reluctant troops in line.

During conference negotiations with the House, Dole stared down House Democrats pushing a budget that placed a politically potent tax on millionaires. "I wish we would stop all this rich-poor argument," groused Dole, who has worked to give the GOP a more egalitarian image and deeply resents attempts to portray his party as the millionaires' playground. "We all want fairness in the tax code."

When prospects for a House-Senate conference deal seemed bleak, Dole and Senate Finance Committee ranking member Bob Packwood resuscitated the talks with a complicated arrangement whereby personal exemptions for the wealthy would be phased out. The agreement was bland enough not to offend the White House and hard enough to explain to keep it out of the Democratic slogan book. Its enactment ended one of the most difficult budget battles in years.

The episode illustrated Dole's frustration with the White House and some of his Republican colleagues, as well as his relatively cordial relationship with Mitchell. After becoming majority leader in 1989, Mitchell made a point of keeping Dole informed of scheduling plans, easing Republican fears of procedural sneak attacks. The two worked as a team during the Senate's long debate on clean air legislation in early 1990, sharing strategy and vote counts to defeat amendments to a successful compromise they had negotiated with the White House.

While the relationship strained when Dole complained that Republicans were providing a disproportionate share of the votes needed to kill politically popular amendments to the clean air bill, the honeymoon lasted until mid-1990, when Democrats forced a partisan showdown Dole had hoped to avoid on civil rights.

Throughout the 1980s, Dole was a key broker on civil rights legislation. He overrode Reagan administration objections and formulated a compromise that allowed the 1982 Voting Rights Act extension to emerge from a divided Judiciary Committee with provisions making it easier to prove violations. In 1990, he had expressed reservations about whether a new law was needed to address employment discrimination, but civil rights activists appeared to believe that Dole eventually would come around.

When Democrats fast-tracked the employment discrimination legislation, however, Dole unleashed a tirade that was unusually biting even for a man renowned for his caustic wit. Voice trembling, he complained that the vote to end debate was a partisan ploy designed to cast Republicans as opposing civil rights even as negotiations with the White House were close to an agreement. "This senator's never voted against a civil rights bill," he said. "But he has never had one shoved down his throat before."

Dole's outburst, however, was also directed at some wayward Republicans — this time not conservatives, but moderates — who helped Mitchell win the pivotal 62-38 cloture vote. In a closed meeting just before the vote, Republican senators had been urged to oppose cloture. No head count was taken, but none of the eight who would defect spoke up. "If we are going to let Democrats run the Senate and throw away eight or nine Republican votes to help them, then I don't want any part of it," Dole said afterward. "Maybe we should get together and elect another leader."

He made a similar threat during the budget debate. As conservatives balked at the package he had labored to produce, Dole challenged Malcolm Wallop of Wyoming to run against him for leader. "If you feel that way, fine," one senator quoted Dole saying in a private meeting. "Let's have a ballot right here."

All of this is a far cry from the days when Dole led the Senate with his unique blend of go-it-alone determination and deal-cutting savvy. Though his stint as majority leader was brief, it proved a point that badly needed proving at the time: The Senate could be led.

"You have to produce, and you have to prove leadership," he said shortly after Republicans elected him over four contenders in late 1984. Dole did both, even if he failed to achieve a number of his most important goals.

Beyond the major bills that passed with his help — tax revision, a new immigration law, a five-year farm bill and aid to the Nicaraguan contras, among others — Dole's chief accomplishment was to undermine the ability of small groups of senators to bring the chamber regularly to a standstill. His success rested on the palpable sense of his will to use power. "I did not become majority leader to lose," he once said.

Dole's style contrasted with that of his predecessor, the amiable Howard H. Baker Jr. of Tennessee, who tended to let his colleagues fight it out in hopes that eventually, exhausted, they would agree to something. "I don't wait for the consensus," Dole said. "I try to help build it."

His aggressive use of power occasionally embittered colleagues, mostly Democrats. During consideration of South Africa sanctions in 1985, Dole had the official legislation locked in a safe, preventing further action on it. In 1986, Dole averted defeat on a vote to confirm a bitterly contested judicial nominee, Daniel A. Manion, by persuading two opponents to withhold their votes as a traditional courtesy to two Republican supporters who were absent. When it was learned that the absent Republicans had not made up their minds, Democrats and some Republicans complained they had been misled.

At one point in 1986, Dole got into an unusually heated confrontation with Democratic leader Robert C. Byrd, who accused him of trying to suppress senators' rights. Dole was typically defiant: "I don't intend to be intimidated by anyone in the Senate."

Dole's use of force is vividly remembered by Democrats, who also know that unlike most recent Senate leaders, Dole does not let his floor duties prevent him from being actively involved in committee work, particularly on major bills. He was virtually chairman of the Agriculture Committee during work on the 1985 farm bill, since titular Chairman Jesse Helms of North Carolina was politically isolated and preoccupied with foreign policy controversies. On the floor, Dole's leadership was severely tested when differences over price supports for farmers threatened to kill the bill, but he put together a compromise with enough sweeteners for different commodities to secure a majority.

His success that year was much in the minds of those responsible for putting together the 1990 farm bill. Agriculture Chairman Patrick J. Leahy and ranking Republican Richard G. Lugar labored to put together a bill that came within strict budget limits, while meeting the varied needs of farm state legislators. A crack in their coalition, they continually feared, would allow Dole to move in and take over. "If we arrive at a point where progress on the committee bill stalls," Dole warned in mid-1990, "I believe my substitute ... can be supported by a bipartisan cast of senators."

But throughout much of the debate on the farm bill, Dole was preoccupied by the budget negotiations, and he may have been chastened by his defeat in a 1989 clash with Leahy. Dole had aggressively pushed a winter-wheat drought relief bill, similar to one his rival, Kansas Democrat Dan Glickman, was moving through the House. But Leahy had other priorities, and before he would agree to move the bill he got Dole to agree to move a rural development bill in tandem. The Democrat then delayed consideration of the drought relief bill and allowed the aid to be divided among all farmers suffering from dry weather, handing Dole an embarrassing defeat.

When work began on the farm bill months later, Dole remained in the background, and only during floor debate did he attempt to regain influence over the final product. In an unusual role reversal, Dole faulted the bill as over budget, complaining that Lugar had given in to too many Democratic spending demands. In the past, it had been Lugar who upheld the administration's budget principles while Dole relished cutting deals with Democrats. While Dole and the administration had hoped for a one-year reauthorization, Leahy and Lugar managed to get the full five-year plan through.

One mission Dole accomplished in the 101st Congress was putting to rest questions about his willingness to wage Bush's wars on Capitol Hill after their bitter presidential feud. However deep Dole's resentments, he is also a staunch Republican partisan, and a fighter who fights to win. As he had done with President Ronald Reagan, Dole sometimes took up the White House cause reluctantly, only to become totally committed once engaged.

In the first test of Bush's presidency, the Senate rejected the nomination of former Sen. John Tower to be Defense secretary, after months of allegations about Tower's womanizing, drunkenness and financial conflicts. Tower was not popular among senators. But his defeat — and, more important, Bush's — came only after Dole turned in a vintage performance in defense of the nomination.

He vigorously argued that a president has the benefit of the doubt in choosing aides. But on a lower plane, Dole also got personal, exchanging hostilities on the floor with outspoken Democratic Sen. Ernest F. Hollings, and accusing Armed Services Committee Chairman Sam Nunn of a power grab in leading the opposition to Tower. Finally, with Tower's defeat looming, Dole proposed an extraordinary tactic typical of his no-holds-barred drive to win. He suggested that Tower be approved for a probationary six months, after which time the Texan would be judged again. Democrats dismissed the idea as "a desperation move."

Given his immediate past with Bush, Dole's performance was remarkable. In 1988, the two men were the main combatants in a six-man GOP presidential field, fighting what came to resemble class conflict more than any political or ideological battle. In Dole's eyes, it was Dole the self-made son of the heartland against Bush the son of Eastern privilege. Both men competed for Reagan's mantle, but Dole cast himself as the man who helped shape it legislatively while Bush merely stood by for ceremonial occasions.

Just before the Iowa caucuses, when Bush happened to be presiding over the Senate, Dole confronted him audibly for his "lowdown, nasty, mean politics." Dole won that pivotal first contest, proving his farm-state appeal. But then he went on to New Hampshire, where he set up such high expectations of his victory and eventual nomination that he looked all the more foolish when he lost. Worse, he looked like a sore loser; that night on network television, he snapped to Bush, "Stop lying about my record."

Dole has never been a visionary or an idealist, and by so revealing his occasionally caustic side he lost voters seeking inspiration, intimacy and a message conveying what his election would mean for them. Weeks later, on Super Tuesday, his campaign was effectively over when he failed to win a single one of the 17

GOP events held that day, most in the South. Still, he persisted for three embarrassing weeks before conceding at the end of March. Through the November election, the only time he and Bush would speak to each other was at the time of the New Orleans convention, when Bush called to say that Dole was not his choice for vice president. Despite their feuding, Dole had plainly wanted the job.

Finally, weeks after the election, they met and pledged cooperation. "We've both been in politics for quite a while," Dole said. "We understand that when the election is over, it's over." Later, Bush named Dole's wife, Elizabeth, to be Labor secretary.

Much has been made of the impact on Dole of his handicap — a nearly useless right arm and an impaired left one resulting from combat in Italy late in World War II — and of the years the once-athletic farm boy spent recovering. Clearly his character was indelibly marked. "I do try harder," he once said. "If I didn't, I'd be sitting in a rest home, in a rocker, drawing disability."

Dole's partisanship, and his loyal support for Republican presidents, is consistent with the man who first arrived in the Senate two decades ago. If anything, leadership has tempered him. He was President Richard M. Nixon's most staunch Senate backer, defending in often abrasive terms his Vietnam policies, his Supreme Court nominations, his ABM program and almost every other move Nixon made.

Dole's performance did not sit well with some Senate colleagues; in 1971, Ohio Republican William B. Saxbe said Dole was a "hatchet man" who "couldn't sell beer on a troopship." But Nixon rewarded Dole in 1971 by naming him national party chairman. Dole never got along with the White House staff, however, and was pushed from the party leadership in January 1973 — a stroke of good fortune because he escaped the subsequent Watergate scandal. Although he had been GOP chairman when the June 1972 burglary occurred, Dole never knew what was going on at the Nixon re-election committee. "Watergate happened on my night off," he later said.

He re-emerged as Gerald R. Ford's vice presidential running mate in 1976, but his subsequent denunciation of the 20th century's "Democrat wars" gave national circulation to the hatchet-man label that haunts Dole still. Only after days of controversy did Dole grudgingly back away from the remark.

That campaign may have been a turning point. While Dole never accepted the notion that his negative style cost Ford the presidency, he has rarely sounded so strident since. Some attribute this to the influence of his wife, whom he married in 1975 when she was a federal trade commissioner.

When she appeared before a Senate committee before her confirmation as Reagan's Transportation secretary in 1983, Dole said, "I regret that I have but one wife to give for my country's infrastructure."

Dole is often as funny as that, but most of the time there is more bite to his humor. Early in 1982, he told listeners he had good news and bad news. "The good news," he said, "is that a bus full of supply-siders went off a cliff. The bad news is that two seats were empty."

That joke symbolized Dole's doubts about the philosophy behind Reagan's 1981 tax cut. Dole wanted targeted tax incentives aimed at boosting savings, investment and productivity, rather than across-the-board reduction. But as Finance chairman he loyally shepherded the Reagan plan through the Senate, though he did persuade Reagan to scale back the cut from 30 percent to 25 percent over three years.

On Finance, Dole was also at the center of debate on Social Security. As a member of a special national commission, he played a key role in the compromise that led to the commission's recommendations on saving the system, which Congress used as the basis for its 1983 rescue bill.

In 1985, this gave him credibility to cajole GOP colleagues to support a freeze in Social Security in order to pass a budget. Dole still hails that budget, with its estimated $50 billion in deficit reduction, as one of his proudest achievements. It reflected his old-line Republican fealty to balanced budgets, a goal for which Dole was willing to raise taxes until his 1988 presidential campaign made him a subscriber to anti-tax rhetoric. To his lasting chagrin, Reagan later disowned the budget, and it was said to have contributed to the Republicans' 1986 loss of the Senate.

As a member of Agriculture, and of Judiciary until 1985, Dole has built a supportive record on two issues — civil rights and food stamps — that stands out from his otherwise consistent conservatism. He has also been a crusader for federal aid to the handicapped. He routinely has broken conservative ranks to protect and enlarge the food stamp program, popular among Kansas farmers as well as the poor.

At Home: While his presidential ambitions were twice thwarted, Kansas voters were good to Dole in the 1980s, giving him two decisive re-election victories that established him as the state's foremost political figure.

But the road to political security was rough. He faced a series of contests early in his career in which the swing of not many votes would have sent him home to Russell.

Dole emerged from his World War II ordeal with ambition and an ample share of discipline. Before completing his law degree, he won a term in the Kansas House. Two years later, he became Russell County prosecutor.

In 1960, Dole ran in the Republican primary for an open House seat against Keith G. Sebelius. Dole defeated him by 982 votes, forcing Sebelius to wait eight years for a House vacancy. In the fall, Dole was an easy winner, keeping the old 6th District in its traditionally

Republican hands.

In 1962 the state's two western districts were combined, and Dole had to run against a Democratic incumbent, J. Floyd Breeding. He beat him by more than 20,000 votes. But he had a more difficult time coping with the 1964 national Democratic landslide and with Bill Bork, a farmers' co-op official. Democrat Bork said he would be a better friend of agriculture than Dole, who was a small-town lawyer, not a farmer. Dole won by 5,126 votes.

In 1968, Republican Frank Carlson announced his retirement from the Senate, and Dole competed with former Gov. William H. Avery for the GOP nomination to succeed him. Avery had been ousted from the governorship two years earlier by Democrat Robert Docking, and he seemed preoccupied during much of the primary campaign with Docking rather than Dole. The result was an easy Dole victory.

That fall, Dole also had an easy time against Democrat William I. Robinson, a Wichita attorney who criticized him for opposing federal aid to schools. Dole talked about the social unrest of that year and blamed much of it on the Johnson administration.

The 1974 campaign was different. Dole was burdened by his earlier Nixon connections, which were played up, probably to an unwise degree, by Democratic challenger William Roy, a two-term House member. Roy continued to refer to Nixon and Watergate even though he had built a comfortable lead against Dole. This enabled Dole to strike back with an ad in which a mud-splattered poster of himself was gradually wiped clean as he insisted on his honesty. Dole came from behind to win.

Since then, he has had nothing to worry about. He met only weak opposition for a third term in 1980. In 1986, as the defeats of several Senate GOP colleagues cost him the job of majority leader, Dole coasted.

The futures of several Kansas politicians will hinge on Dole's decision whether to seek a fifth Senate term in 1992. Among others, GOP Reps. Pat Roberts and Jan Meyers and Democratic Reps. Dan Glickman and Jim Slattery have all been mentioned as potential Senate candidates.

Committees

Minority Leader

Agriculture, Nutrition & Forestry (2nd of 8 Republicans)
Agricultural Production & Stabilization of Prices; Agricultural Research & General Legislation; Nutrition & Investigations

Finance (2nd of 9 Republicans)
Social Security & Family Policy (ranking); Energy & Agricultural Taxation; Medicare & Long Term Care

Rules & Administration (5th of 7 Republicans)

Joint Taxation

Elections

1986 General		
Bob Dole (R)	576,902	(70%)
Guy MacDonald (D)	246,664	(30%)
1986 Primary		
Bob Dole (R)	228,301	(84%)
Shirley J. Ashley Landis (R)	42,237	(16%)

Previous Winning Percentages: **1980** (64%) **1974** (51%) **1968** (60%) **1966 *** (69%) **1964 *** (51%) **1962 *** (56%) **1960 *** (59%)

** House elections.*

Campaign Finance

	Receipts	Receipts from PACs		Expend-itures
1986				
Dole (R)	$2,640,050	$1,034,324	(39%)	$1,517,585

Key Votes

1991	
Authorize use of force against Iraq	Y
1990	
Oppose prohibition of certain semiautomatic weapons	N
Support constitutional amendment on flag desecration	Y
Oppose requiring parental notice for minors' abortions	N
Halt production of B-2 stealth bomber at 13 planes	N
Approve budget that cut spending and raised revenues	Y
Pass civil rights bill over Bush veto	N
1989	
Oppose reduction of SDI funding	Y
Oppose barring federal funds for "obscene" art	N
Allow vote on capital gains tax cut	Y

Voting Studies

	Presidential Support		Party Unity		Conservative Coalition	
Year	**S**	**O**	**S**	**O**	**S**	**O**
1990	80	20	86	14	95	5
1989	94	4	89	11	87	13
1988	68	19	70	12	86	5
1987	71	24	85	10	81	6
1986	92	8	92	7	95	4
1985	92	7	92	6	92	5
1984	90	9	90	8	96	2
1983	78	21	88	8	89	7
1982	86	13	91	8	85	10
1981	85	7	94	5	92	5

Interest Group Ratings

Year	ADA	ACU	AFL-CIO	CCUS
1990	0	83	33	75
1989	5	86	0	88
1988	15	91	33	91
1987	5	77	20	83
1986	0	91	0	89
1985	0	91	10	90
1984	10	86	0	83
1983	5	64	19	56
1982	15	80	20	62
1981	5	76	11	100

Nancy Landon Kassebaum (R)

Of Burdick — Elected 1978

Born: July 29, 1932, Topeka, Kan.
Education: U. of Kansas, B.A. 1954; U. of Michigan, M.A. 1956.
Occupation: Broadcasting executive.
Family: Divorced; four children.
Religion: Episcopalian.
Political Career: Maize School Board, 1973-75.
Capitol Office: 302 Russell Bldg. 20510; 224-4774.

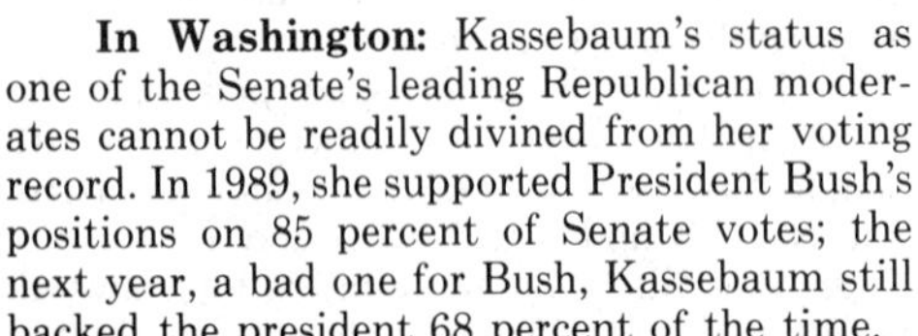

In Washington: Kassebaum's status as one of the Senate's leading Republican moderates cannot be readily divined from her voting record. In 1989, she supported President Bush's positions on 85 percent of Senate votes; the next year, a bad one for Bush, Kassebaum still backed the president 68 percent of the time.

Yet Kassebaum's mild tone and her willingness to buck the GOP line on some high-profile issues make her stand out from more aggressively partisan colleagues — including a fellow Kansan, Minority Leader Bob Dole. Kassebaum's support for abortion rights is often noted. A reputation as a maverick follows Kassebaum; in 1989, for example, she was the only Republican to vote against confirming former Sen. John Tower as defense secretary.

Her independent thinking and pleasant manner have given Kassebaum bipartisan appeal in Kansas. When she backed off a pledge — made in her first Senate campaign in 1978 — not to seek a third term in 1990, Kassebaum felt no voter backlash; she won overwhelmingly.

Her decision to run again cheered Republicans, who knew they risked losing the Kansas seat if she bowed out. But some Democrats were not unhappy, either, since they can expect Kassebaum occasionally to break GOP ranks and bestow on their position a semblance of bipartisanship. Party loyalties aside, she is widely regarded as a quiet, positive force within the institution.

Most others who come to Congress promising to be short-term "citizen legislators" soon become just as concerned about partisan advantage as the professional politicians they once reviled. But a dozen years in the Senate has not worked that change on Kassebaum. Perhaps more than anyone else there, she still has the plain-spoken honesty and common sense she had when she arrived in 1979 as an almost complete political neophyte.

Kassebaum's style has not changed much over the years. She still appears on occasion to be shy and uneasy in a public role. "Someday I'm going to hit someone over the head for calling me diminutive and soft-spoken," she once said. "But I am." She chafes at comparisons to Dorothy in "The Wizard of Oz," yet has enough humor about her image that her staff felt free to include representations of the film in a patchwork quilt they made her.

Kassebaum also continues to suffer angst when she feels compelled to resist the tidal pull of party loyalty. This was evident during the Tower debate. While the Senate was roiled for weeks by bitter partisan debate over reports of Tower's drinking, womanizing and financial conflicts of interest, Kassebaum was typically quiet. She told few except Bush about her qualms, so it was a surprise to many when she cast her singular "no" vote. However, she had made it clear to Bush that she would have backed Tower if hers had been the deciding vote.

Kassebaum eschews harsh partisan rhetoric and tries to act as a mediator on some of the Senate's more contentious issues. As a member of the Foreign Relations and Labor and Human Resources committees, she finds no shortage of opportunities to employ her conciliatory nature.

In 1990, members sharply divided over a bill to provide legal remedies for certain instances of job discrimination: Democratic leaders defined the bill as a civil rights act, while Bush described it as a "jobs quota bill" and threatened to veto it.

Kassebaum sought middle ground. Her alternative would have established an easier test than in the Democratic bill for employers to prove they had not discriminated, and it would have lowered the maximum monetary payments that courts could order employers to pay to victims of intentional discrimination.

Her efforts went for naught, though. With the 1990 elections looming, the civil rights debate had taken on a partisan dimension that dwarfed the details of the legislation; Kassebaum's proposal died without a vote in the Senate. It had a brief life in the House: Democrat John J. LaFalce of New York, chairman of the Small Business Committee, picked up on Kassebaum's plan, which was then co-opted by Minority Leader Robert H. Michel as a GOP alternative. However, the proposal was defeated in the House on a 188-238 vote.

Kassebaum, whose political experience prior to the Senate was on her hometown school board, has supported programs Bush has promoted in his self-proclaimed role as the "education president." Yet as ranking Republican on the Labor and Human Resources Subcommittee on Education, Kassebaum shows a Republican's wariness of programs that expand the federal bureaucracy. In 1989, she persuaded Democratic Sen. Paul Simon to drop provisions for a new federal office on literacy and an advisory council from his bill to expand federal literacy programs.

On Foreign Relations, Kassebaum's moderate approach clashes with that of the ranking Republican, conservative confrontationalist Jesse Helms of North Carolina. The contrast was sharply cast during the presidency of Ronald Reagan. While Helms drew an ideological line in the sand on such issues as U.S. aid to the Nicaraguan contras, Kassebaum sought to steer an independent course between Reagan and his mainly Democratic critics.

While Kassebaum supported military aid for the contras, she grew increasingly critical of both the rebels and the president as Nicaragua's civil war dragged on. In 1986, she was a principal architect of a $100 million military aid package that included Reagan's promises to push contra leaders to curb human rights abuses and to end their internal disunity. She lambasted aid supporters for portraying the issue as "a disagreement between Republicans in white hats and Democrats in red banners."

From the Africa Subcommittee, which she chaired when Republicans controlled the Senate, Kassebaum has influenced the debate on policy toward South Africa. She was initially skeptical about the value of sanctions, warning they could harm oppressed blacks. But in 1986, a campaign of repression by South Africa's government allayed Kassebaum's doubts. She prodded Reagan to take action. When he did not, she backed sanctions and opposed his veto in order to "send a decisive message" of U.S. condemnation.

Still the ranking Republican on the Africa subcommittee, Kassebaum continues to take a human rights-oriented approach to U.S. policy. In 1989, reports of political repression by Zaire President Mobutu Sese Seko brought an effort led by Foreign Relations Democrats to cap American aid to that nation. Helms, citing Mobutu's pro-Western sympathies, offered an amendment to remove the cap, but it was defeated by a 7-12 committee vote; Kassebaum was one of two Republicans voting against it.

On the most critical foreign policy issue of her Senate tenure — the U.S. military response to Iraq's August 1990 invasion of Kuwait — Kassebaum stood solidly behind Bush. In her speech during the January 1991 debate on the resolution authorizing the president to use force against Iraq, Kassebaum praised the international coalition mobilized by Bush as a "landmark achievement."

However, Kassebaum had not been satisfied with U.S policy toward Iraq prior to its invasion of Kuwait. Viewing Iraq as a bulwark against Iran, the Reagan and Bush administrations sought better relations with Iraqi President Saddam Hussein and blocked congressional efforts to mandate economic sanctions in response to reports of Saddam's human rights violations. Kassebaum favored sanctions, even though they would have affected Kansas farmers who had found an export market in Iraq.

When a sanctions bill reached Foreign Relations in July 1990, administration officials said ending farm credit guarantees to Iraq would hurt American farmers more than Iraq. "I cannot believe that any farmer in this nation would want to send his products . . . to a country that has used chemical weapons and to a country that has tortured and injured their children," Kassebaum responded.

Despite her status as one of only two women in the Senate, Kassebaum has refused to be used by her party as a symbol. When officials of the 1984 GOP convention sought to have her appear on the podium with other prominent Republican women, she pointedly declined. "I'd be happy to speak on substantive issues," she said, "but to be treated as a bauble on a tree is not particularly constructive."

Kassebaum likewise has charted her own course on economic issues. As a member of the Budget Committee, Kassebaum opposed the 1985 Gramm-Rudman-Hollings budget-balancing law after sponsors exempted Social Security and other programs from its strictures. It could not work, she said, if Congress singled out sacred cows for special protection.

Kassebaum became so frustrated by the ongoing deficit impasse that she not only considered leaving the Budget Committee but proposed dissolving it. She stayed on Budget only at the urging of GOP leaders, who did not want to open a spot for strong-willed Texas Republican Phil Gramm. Finally, however, she had had enough; for the 101st Congress, Kassebaum left and Gramm took her seat.

She also left the Commerce Committee, and instead joined the Labor and Banking panels. On Commerce, where she once was chairman of the Aviation Subcommittee, Kassebaum helped enact a complex airport development and tax bill in 1982. She was less successful with legislation to limit small plane manufacturers' accident liability (Kansas is home to Cessna and Beech), a cause she continues to pursue.

At Home: Kassebaum's modesty and moderate philosophy made her an overwhelming favorite for re-election in 1990. In a way, it was fitting that she ended up being opposed in November by the *loser* of the Democratic Senate primary.

Kassebaum was no sure bet to run for a third term. But Republican officials lobbied Kassebaum to run again and she assented, noting that she had tried without success to get Congress to consider term limits.

Prominent Democrats backed off, and it seemed that Kassebaum would face Dick Williams, a little-known college instructor and an opponent of U.S. policies in Central America. But on the last day for candidate filing, former Democratic Rep. Bill Roy Sr. walked into the race. One week later, the 64-year-old Roy, who had lost to Kassebaum in 1978, walked back out, saying he lacked the stamina for campaigning. However, his name remained on the ballot, and was so much better known than Williams' that Roy won the primary.

A physician who said he wanted to emphasize health care issues, Roy reconsidered his withdrawal, but finally renounced the nomination. Williams was then chosen by a state party committee. He never made a dent in Kassebaum's support; she won with 74 percent.

The Landon in Kassebaum's name marks her deep roots in Kansas politics. Her father, Alfred M. Landon, was a governor of Kansas and the 1936 GOP presidential nominee. (He died in 1987, just after his 100th birthday.)

Before 1978, Kassebaum's political activity had been confined to the school board in a town of 785 people and one year as an aide to GOP Sen. James B. Pearson. But when Pearson announced plans to retire, she joined eight other contestants in the Republican primary. Kassebaum's middle name helped her stand out in the crowded field. She built upon that advantage with a series of TV ads featuring her father. The result was a clear victory.

That fall, she faced Roy, who had nearly ousted Sen. Dole in 1974. However, the Watergate backlash that helped Roy against Dole had faded. Kassebaum had no record for Roy to aim at, and her gentle style made attacks on her inexperience seem unmannerly. She beat Roy more comfortably than had Dole.

By 1984, Kassebaum was entrenched. Any re-election worries she had ended when Democratic Rep. Dan Glickman decided not to run against her. The Democratic line went to investment executive Jim Maher, loser in two earlier Senate bids. Kassebaum won 76 percent.

Committees

Banking, Housing & Urban Affairs (8th of 9 Republicans)
Housing & Urban Affairs; Securities

Foreign Relations (3rd of 8 Republicans)
African Affairs (ranking); International Economic Policy, Trade, Oceans & Environment; Western Hemisphere & Peace Corps Affairs

Labor & Human Resources (2nd of 7 Republicans)
Education, Arts & Humanities (ranking); Children, Families, Drugs & Alcoholism; Employment & Productivity

Select Indian Affairs (6th of 7 Republicans)

Elections

1990 General

Nancy Landon Kassebaum (R)	578,605	(74%)
Dick Williams (D)	207,491	(26%)

1990 Primary

Nancy Landon Kassebaum (R)	267,946	(87%)
R. Gregory Walstrom (R)	39,379	(13%)

Previous Winning Percentages: **1984** (76%) **1978** (54%)

Campaign Finance

	Receipts	Receipts from PACs	Expend-itures
1990			
Kassebaum (R)	$481,852	$187,858 (39%)	$407,387
Williams (D)	$16,827	$500 (3%)	$16,627

Key Votes

1991	
Authorize use of force against Iraq	Y
1990	
Oppose prohibition of certain semiautomatic weapons	N
Support constitutional amendment on flag desecration	Y
Oppose requiring parental notice for minors' abortions	N
Halt production of B-2 stealth bomber at 13 planes	?
Approve budget that cut spending and raised revenues	Y
Pass civil rights bill over Bush veto	N
1989	
Oppose reduction of SDI funding	Y
Oppose barring federal funds for "obscene" art	Y
Allow vote on capital gains tax cut	Y

Voting Studies

	Presidential Support		Party Unity		Conservative Coalition	
Year	**S**	**O**	**S**	**O**	**S**	**O**
1990	68	29	67	31	76	16
1989	85	14	71	27	84	16
1988	69	28	61	32	81	8
1987	59	28	65	22	72	22
1986	70	24	77	21	80	13
1985	76	19	79	17	75	22
1984	79	19	75	24	81	17
1983	78	20	71	25	59	36
1982	78	19	74	24	77	21
1981	82	17	77	20	80	18

Interest Group Ratings

Year	ADA	ACU	AFL-CIO	CCUS
1990	44	64	22	67
1989	20	57	0	63
1988	30	61	23	71
1987	30	60	20	71
1986	45	41	21	58
1985	35	48	10	69
1984	45	55	45	61
1983	35	36	24	42
1982	50	42	29	53
1981	35	60	5	88

1 Pat Roberts (R)

Of Dodge City — Elected 1980

Born: April 20, 1936, Topeka, Kan.
Education: Kansas State U., B.A. 1958.
Military Service: Marine Corps, 1958-62.
Occupation: Journalist; congressional aide.
Family: Wife, Franki Fann; three children.
Religion: Methodist.
Political Career: No previous office.
Capitol Office: 1110 Longworth Bldg. 20515; 225-2715.

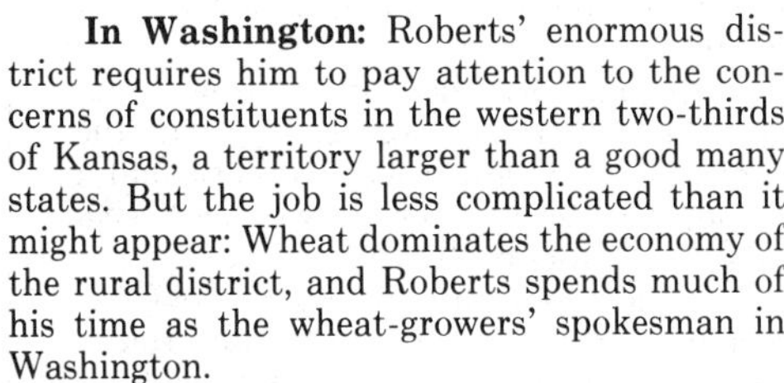

In Washington: Roberts' enormous district requires him to pay attention to the concerns of constituents in the western two-thirds of Kansas, a territory larger than a good many states. But the job is less complicated than it might appear: Wheat dominates the economy of the rural district, and Roberts spends much of his time as the wheat-growers' spokesman in Washington.

And he does speak out. He has been an active player on the Agriculture Committee, where he is viewed not only as an advocate for Kansas farmers, but also as the resident wit. Pleasantly irascible, Roberts has a sarcastic sense of humor similar to that of Kansas' senior senator, Republican Bob Dole, who represented the 1st in the 1960s. Sometimes, deliberately or not, he even projects inflections and mannerisms similar to Dole's.

Colleagues also compare Roberts to Dole in another way. He is widely viewed as a man with both the interest and ability to serve in the other chamber of Congress in the event Dole or GOP Sen. Nancy Landon Kassebaum moves on.

Committee members consider Roberts' working knowledge of farm programs as voluminous as anyone's on the panel. His instincts may be conservative, but he is an unwavering defender of programs that help his state's farmers. His outlook is nearly always a reflection more of his rural district than of his partisan label. During the debate over the 1985 farm bill in the 99th Congress he freely attacked the unpopular Reagan farm policy — which he described as a "so-called" policy. Expressing farmers' frustration, he once warned that Air Force One would get a "pitchfork in the belly" if it flew too low over Kansas.

The centerpiece of the 1990 farm bill was a plan, long backed by Roberts and Texas Democrat Charles W. Stenholm, to reduce the amount of cropland eligible for government income-support payments. The change, known as "triple base," would allow every farmer who participates in government crop programs to plant whatever he wanted (except for fruits and vegetables) on 15 percent of the land on which he usually raises subsidized crops, such as wheat, corn, cotton and rice. Triple base was touted as reintroducing market forces into the farm economy.

Construction of the 1990 farm bill took place amid palpable pressure to cut spending. When the farm economy was in a near depression during the 1985 farm bill debate, Roberts was uncomfortable about killing a plan that would have imposed production controls on farmers — and forced prices up. But with the mood on the farm comparatively tranquil in the 101st Congress, Roberts was willing to argue for some fiscal restraint in farm programs.

He spoke against a proposal by a group of junior Democrats, led by Iowan Dave Nagle, that would have sharply increased crop price support levels; Roberts said the proposal would bring back the high-surplus days of the mid-1980s. "If you raise loan rates above the market price, guess who gets the grain. Uncle Sam," he said. The Democrats' amendment was rejected.

Roberts was less concerned about budget stringencies when Kansas farmers were hit by drought in 1988 and 1989. His district bore the brunt of the drought, and he sought disaster relief for his constituents. When the committee considered a disaster-relief bill in 1989, Roberts added an amendment exempting winter-wheat farmers from the bill's provisions requiring virtually all farmers receiving aid under the bill to buy crop insurance for 1990.

He was not enthralled with an amendment added by Iowa Republican Fred Grandy that limited disaster-relief outlays to government savings that year as a result of adverse weather. The amendment was designed to win the favor of Budget Committee Chairman (and Agriculture Committee member) Leon E. Panetta, whose support was crucial if the committee was to secure a budget act waiver. Roberts described Grandy's amendment as a "suppository to the repository of Mr. Panetta."

Roberts is ranking member on the Agriculture Subcommittee on Department Operations, Research and Foreign Agriculture, and that has involved him in efforts to write pesticide laws.

Kansas 1

West — Salina; Dodge City

The farmlands of western Kansas used to be populous enough to support two congressional districts. By the 1960s, however, the exodus of farmers from the land had cost the region a seat. And as population continued its fall with each census, the lines of the remaining district — the 1st — moved farther to the east. The "Big First" now stretches across 58 counties, two time zones, and two-thirds of the state's land area.

Though the population continues to slip in many of the grain-growing areas — more than half the district's counties had a net loss in the first half of the 1980s — the 1st continues to produce the huge harvests of winter wheat that help make Kansas the nation's leading wheat-producing state. And industrial expansions by several of southwest Kansas' major meatpackers have actually brought a flush of fresh growth to such cities as Garden City and Dodge City.

The district has a solidly rural character and a conservative political outlook. The farmers and ranchers are traditionally suspicious of federal involvement in agriculture, and Republican registrants far outnumber Democrats.

An occasional wave of prairie populism will sweep through the 1st, as in 1976, when a protest against President Gerald R. Ford's farm policies limited the Republican to 52 percent of the district vote. But in 1984, in the midst of a supposed "farm crisis," President Reagan took 74 percent in the 1st. George Bush won in 1988 with a somewhat more modest 60 percent.

For years, the district's only sizable city was Salina, near the eastern edge of the 1st. Once the place where farmers flocked for Saturday marketing and entertainment, Salina evolved into a source of jobs for some of those who gave up full-time farming. The city's population jumped by about 11 percent in the 1970s, thanks to plant expansion by such companies as Westinghouse and Beech Aircraft. But growth was fairly flat through the 1980s.

It is not a great distance from Salina to Russell County, home base of senior Sen. Bob Dole. But just to the west is Ellis County (Hays), home of Fort Hays State University, which helps give it a Democratic flavor unusual for western Kansas. Ellis was one of three Kansas counties to go for Democrat Michael S. Dukakis for president in 1988.

Moving west, the ranches grow larger and the population more sparse. But the endless horizons are broken by that handful of industrial towns whose growth has been a bright spot for the 1st.

Lying about 50 miles apart along the Arkansas River, Garden City and Dodge City were rivals in the late 19th century; Garden City was founded as a center for farming, while Dodge City was a stopover for cowboys driving cattle that needed to eat the grass the farmers were plowing up.

Today, the two towns compete for the title of southwest Kansas' biggest city. Garden City has the lead with about 33,000 people. Dodge City, best known for its recreation of the "Old West" Front Street, is pushing 27,000.

The only other southwest city of any size is Liberal, in Seward County near the Oklahoma border. The city's name has little to do with its politics, which are generally as GOP as the surrounding country; Seward gave 71 percent of its 1988 vote to Bush.

Population: 472,139. White 456,427 (97%), Black 4,280 (1%), Other 2,611 (1%). Spanish origin 14,643 (3%). 18 and over 342,439 (73%), 65 and over 75,593 (16%). Median age: 32.

He fought efforts during deliberations over the 1990 farm bill to lessen farmers' use of chemicals and he opposed provisions designed to break the "circle of poison" by greatly restricting the export of pesticides banned in the United States.

In the 99th and 100th Congresses, much of Roberts' activity centered on an overhaul of the Federal Insecticide, Fungicide and Rodenticide Act (FIFRA).

In 1986, after a long delay in reaching some consensus on FIFRA legislation, Roberts worked to help craft a bill that won support from farmers, farm chemical manufacturers, environmentalists, public-health groups and labor unions. The bill would have accelerated health testing and registration of pesticides and required manufacturers to help pay for it.

There was considerable disagreement over one provision that Roberts pushed passionately. On the House floor he won a fight over an amendment to set uniform national limits on the amount of pesticide residue allowed in foods. He said that differing standards around the country would make it more difficult for farmers to market their products.

But Roberts' strong desire for uniform standards was surpassed by pragmatism. "We have those who will prefer an issue," he said in 1987, "and we have those who will prefer a bill. It is time we had a FIFRA bill." By the end of the 100th Congress that was what they had. The bill, dubbed "FIFRA Lite" by some, dropped many controversial issues, including the question of uniform limits nationwide.

Roberts has other rural interests outside the Agriculture Committee. In the 100th Congress he was a member of the bipartisan Rural Health Care Coalition, a group that worked to make changes in the Medicare system, which many legislators consider unfair and harmful to rural health services. Just before the 102nd Congress began, he and Stenholm were named co-chairmen of the caucus.

At Home: As the long-tenured member from the sprawling 1st District, Roberts is often mentioned as a potential Senate contender. But with Dole and Kassebaum holding fast through 1990, he has not had a chance to bid for the Senate.

Roberts understudied his House role for 12 years as top aide to GOP Rep. Keith G. Sebelius. When Sebelius retired in 1980, Roberts was ready. Most GOP county chairmen backed Roberts in the primary, and he won with 56 percent.

Roberts' victory in November was scarcely in doubt. Capitalizing on the popularity of Sebelius, Roberts referred to "our record" so frequently that he sounded like an incumbent. He defeated Democratic state Rep. Phil Martin with 62 percent of the vote.

In 1984, Roberts faced some loud opposition: Democrat Darrell Ringer, who declared that the government would neglect the nation's agricultural problems unless more farmers went to Congress. But most voters concluded that Ringer, an activist in the American Agricultural Movement, would be more strident than successful; Roberts won by 3 to 1.

After a similar Roberts performance in 1986, Democrats left him unopposed in 1988.

In 1990, state Democrats initially failed to find a volunteer to run against Roberts, and Democratic state chairman James W. Parrish entered himself as a candidate. But he withdrew after the primary and was replaced by lawyer Duane West, who was the prosecutor in the 1958 murder case that inspired Truman Capote's book "In Cold Blood." Although West did better than past 1st District Democratic challengers, Roberts still won with 62 percent.

Roberts' father, C. Wesley Roberts, was the state GOP chairman in the late 1940s. In 1953, he was chosen chairman of the Republican National Committee. But the Kansas City *Star* accused him of having improperly used his influence as a state party leader to affect an appropriation by the state Legislature. Nine weeks after taking his GOP post, he resigned.

Committees

Agriculture (4th of 18 Republicans)
Department Operations, Research & Foreign Agriculture (ranking); Livestock, Dairy & Poultry; Wheat, Soybeans & Feed Grains

House Administration (4th of 9 Republicans)
Personnel & Police (ranking); Libraries & Memorials

Joint Library

Joint Printing

Elections

1990 General		
Pat Roberts (R)	102,974	(63%)
Duane West (D)	61,396	(37%)
1988 General		
Pat Roberts (R)	168,700	(100%)

Previous Winning Percentages: **1986** (77%) **1984** (76%) **1982** (68%) **1980** (62%)

District Vote For President

	1988		1984		1980		1976	
D	74,713	(38%)	54,565	(25%)	56,219	(26%)	96,421	(45%)
R	120,325	(60%)	161,439	(74%)	140,375	(66%)	111,433	(52%)
I					12,501	(6%)		

Campaign Finance

	Receipts	Receipts from PACs		Expend-itures
1990				
Roberts (R)	$222,760	$132,250	(59%)	$152,249
West (D)	$16,965	$250	(1%)	$16,701
1988				
Roberts (R)	$191,584	$99,600	(52%)	$81,140

Key Votes

1991	
Authorize use of force against Iraq	Y
1990	
Support constitutional amendment on flag desecration	Y
Pass family and medical leave bill over Bush veto	N
Reduce SDI funding	N
Allow abortions in overseas military facilities	N
Approve budget summit plan for spending and taxing	Y
Approve civil rights bill	N
1989	
Halt production of B-2 stealth bomber at 13 planes	N
Oppose capital gains tax cut	N
Approve federal abortion funding in rape or incest cases	N
Approve pay raise and revision of ethics rules	Y
Pass Democratic minimum wage plan over Bush veto	N

Voting Studies

	Presidential Support		Party Unity		Conservative Coalition	
Year	S	O	S	O	S	O
1990	71	27	87	11	87	9
1989	79	21	86	12	93	5
1988	62	33	86	10	95	3
1987	63	31	83	10	81	9
1986	69	31	87	11	90	8
1985	63	38	83	10	80	16
1984	63	35	84	8	85	10
1983	73	27	87	11	85	13
1982	62	36	86	11	84	14
1981	67	30	86	11	91	5

Interest Group Ratings

Year	ADA	ACU	AFL-CIO	CCUS
1990	6	75	0	79
1989	5	79	0	100
1988	10	79	25	100
1987	4	86	0	100
1986	0	82	7	94
1985	15	71	12	95
1984	5	96	8	80
1983	10	91	6	90
1982	15	82	0	90
1981	10	100	0	84

2 Jim Slattery (D)

Of Topeka — Elected 1982

Born: Aug. 4, 1948, Good Intent, Kan.
Education: Attended Netherlands School of International Economics and Business, 1969-70; Washburn U., B.S. 1970, J.D. 1974.
Military Service: Army National Guard, 1970-75.
Occupation: Realtor.
Family: Wife, Linda Smith; two children.
Religion: Roman Catholic.
Political Career: Kan. House, 1973-79.
Capitol Office: 1512 Longworth Bldg. 20515; 225-6601.

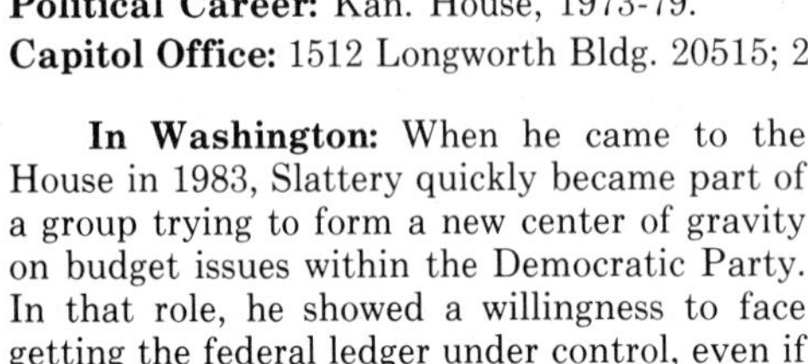

In Washington: When he came to the House in 1983, Slattery quickly became part of a group trying to form a new center of gravity on budget issues within the Democratic Party. In that role, he showed a willingness to face getting the federal ledger under control, even if it meant bucking the Democratic leadership.

Now in his fifth term, Slattery has served long enough to get onto the Budget Committee and then be forced to leave the panel, which has a three-term limit. And for all his deficit-cutting efforts, Slattery has seen little significant progress in reducing red ink. His frustration over the budget appears to be mounting, so much so that many expected him to abandon Congress for a 1990 gubernatorial bid. Instead, Slattery successfully sought another House term — one that will challenge him to find new tactics for his budget crusade, or new crusades.

Slattery was one of three moderate-to-conservative Democrats appointed to the Budget Committee in 1985 when Speaker Thomas P. O'Neill Jr. was under pressure to change its liberal tilt. In 1985 the group proposed a budget that called for a freeze on most federal programs, domestic as well as military, and included Social Security among those eligible to be frozen. It lost on the floor, 56-372.

Slattery pressed on, and during the 101st Congress his fiscal concerns inspired a battle against the B-2 Stealth bomber. Slattery had earlier supported the bomber, but changed his mind after its cost overruns mounted. In early 1990, he joined with 13 Armed Services Committee members seeking to stop production of the B-2. The House did ultimately vote to cap funding for the plane, although the ultimate size of the B-2 fleet is uncertain.

Slattery is prepared to cut other costly items in the budget, such as the strategic defense initiative and the superconducting super collider. Newly appointed to the Banking Committee in the 102nd Congress, he and Democratic Rep. Joseph Kennedy sponsored legislation requiring the government to pay off future costs of the savings-and-loan bailout through a tax increase or with budget cuts, to avoid adding to the federal deficit.

But Slattery lost that vote, and there are signs he is losing patience with such battles. During the summer of 1990, he voted against a proposed constitutional amendment requiring a balanced budget. But he warned that he might jump sides on the issue should Congress fail to make real progress on deficit reduction.

Slattery has also shown a willingness to go after smaller expenditures, even at the expense of embarrassing colleagues. Near the end of the 101st Congress, he set his sights on a $500,000 appropriation for a German-Russian interpretive center at the North Dakota birthplace of bandleader Lawrence Welk. Slattery's move to rescind the funding prevailed in the House, but the well-publicized crusade angered North Dakota Democratic Rep. Byron Dorgan, an advocate for the project.

Slattery is prepared to spend more on some of his own priorities, such as health care; During the 101st Congress, he successfully advocated expanding Medicaid coverage to certain poor children.

In addition to his budget efforts, Slattery has put considerable time into his work on the Energy and Commerce Committee, an influential panel that allows him to pursue a variety of interests, most of them important to his home state. He was able to get that choice committee spot as a freshman because he had something to offer nearly all the factions in his party. Liberals could look at his pro-consumer record in the Kansas Legislature; energy interests could reasonably assume that, as a member from an oil-and-gas state, he would listen to them on issues they cared about.

Slattery does have a middle-of-the-road view on many issues before the committee. He is considered close to business, but supports measures pushed by environmental groups a little more often than he opposes them.

In the 100th Congress, Slattery was part of an informal caucus of moderate-to-conservative Democrats, the so-called "group of nine," who

Kansas 2

Topeka; Lawrence

Slattery has gained firm control of the 2nd since taking it from the GOP in 1982. But the district still trends Republican in statewide contests. George Bush's 53 percent in 1988 was well off President Reagan's 63 percent four years earlier, and he won two counties with less than 50 percent of the total vote. But he did manage to carry all 13 of the district's counties.

Topeka, Kansas' capital and third-largest city (about 120,000), is the heart of the 2nd. In addition to state government's crucial role in Topeka and surrounding Shawnee County, there is a substantial manufacturing base as well. One of several large health-care facilities in Topeka is the prominent Menninger Foundation, which specializes in psychiatric care.

There is more Democratic strength in Shawnee County than in less-urbanized parts of the state. The county has voted Democratic in the last four gubernatorial contests, giving 1990 Democratic nominee Joan Finney 60 percent in her victory over GOP incumbent Mike Hayden. But Bush edged Democrat Michael S. Dukakis with 51 percent of the vote, and Reagan won Shawnee easily.

Dukakis did slightly better in Douglas County (Lawrence), site of the University of Kansas and its 26,000 students; Bush won there by under 400 votes. Douglas has been a source of strength for Slattery, whose House prospects were boosted by the addition of the county to the 2nd in the last redistricting. Finney drew only 42 percent here in 1990.

The district's other major academic center, Riley County (Manhattan), is a counterweight to the liberal lean of Douglas County. Manhattan is home to Kansas State University, an agriculture-oriented school with 18,000 students that has a more conservative atmosphere than the University of Kansas. Riley County went solidly for Bush in 1988 and Hayden in 1990. Clay County, at the district's western edge, is an even stronger GOP bastion; Bush took 72 percent there.

Federal installations are a considerable presence in the 2nd. In Leavenworth, along with the federal prison, the Army maintains the Command and General Staff College at Fort Leavenworth, the military's largest tactical training center. Junction City has Fort Riley, an Army base.

Population: 472,988. White 418,516 (88%), Black 34,559 (7%), Other 10,392 (2%). Spanish origin 14,179 (3%). 18 and over 348,994 (74%), 65 and over 51,790 (11%). Median age: 28.

banded together to try to break a six-year deadlock on reauthorizing the Clean Air Act. Their work formed the basis of many of the clean air revisions finally enacted in the 101st Congress. In those deliberations, Slattery worked with others in the Kansas delegation to get favorable treatment in the clean air bill for Kansas City, which had made significant progress meeting air pollution controls, but had not demonstrated strict compliance.

Another example of Slattery's attentiveness to district concerns was his bill pertaining to greyhound racing. The National Greyhound Association is based in Kansas, and Slattery's bill sought to give dog owners a share of the profits when races are simulcast across state lines. Slattery got the bill through Energy and Commerce, but it died at the end of the 101st Congress. It was reintroduced at the beginning of the 102nd Congress in the House and the Senate.

Slattery sits on the Telecommunications Subcommittee of Energy and Commerce, and early in the 102nd Congress he joined the push to let the regional Bell companies manufacture telecommunications equipment.

During the mid-1980s, Slattery tried to help mediate the dispute in his party over aid to the Nicaraguan contras, which he had opposed. As a key swing vote on the issue, Slattery worked with other moderates to try to push the White House to use diplomacy rather than force in Nicaragua; at the same time, he was a supporter of sending non-military aid to the contras. "We are not abandoning the contras," he said of Democratic efforts to end military aid. "We are simply giving them a rest."

In addition to joining Banking in the 102nd, Slattery also reclaimed his old seat on the Veterans' Affairs Committee, from which he had been on leave during his Budget Committee service.

At Home: Although Slattery won re-election easily in 1990, the campaign cycle was somewhat frustrating for him. Long regarded as a rising star in Kansas politics, Slattery moved tentatively toward seeking the governorship, but backed off tackling GOP Gov. Mike Hayden — only to see the beleaguered incumbent defeated by a less-highly regarded Democrat, state Treasurer Joan Finney.

Slattery won his fifth House term in a

breeze, defeating Republican Scott Morgan, a former Hayden aide, with 63 percent. Soon he was being mentioned as a possible 1992 Senate candidate, pending GOP Sen. Bob Dole's decision on whether to run for a fifth term.

Slattery has never made a secret of his political ambitions. He was 24 and still in law school when he defeated a Republican state representative. In the Legislature, Slattery and his allies pushed through the first major revision of the state's income-tax code in 30 years, and led a drive to make workers' compensation laws more to labor's liking.

In 1978 Slattery left the Legislature to develop his Topeka real-estate business and prepare a run for Congress. Democrats had lost the 2nd to Republican Jim Jeffries in 1978, but by 1982, Jeffries' reputation as a blustery, tactless ideologue had eroded his support. Slattery launched his campaign before Jeffries had decided whether to run again. An unfavorable remap helped persuade Jeffries to retire.

In his place, the GOP chose former legislator and state party Chairman Morris Kay. He tied himself to President Reagan and called Slattery "another Boston liberal." Slattery's retort was effective: "This isn't a race between Tip O'Neill and Ronald Reagan," he said. "It's between Jim Slattery and Morris Kay."

Slattery appealed to Republicans by stressing his farm background and his ties to the Topeka business community. He carried all but two of the district's 13 counties. Despite continued Republican efforts to profile him as a liberal, Slattery easily won in 1984 and 1986.

With speculation already rife about Slattery's potential 1990 plans, the GOP hoped to slow him by running a high-profile candidate in 1988. They even tried to recruit David Eisenhower, son-in-law of former President Richard M. Nixon and grandson of the late President Dwight D. Eisenhower, a Kansas native.

When Eisenhower demurred, the GOP settled on Phil Meinhardt, a recently retired Air Force lieutenant colonel who originally hailed from Kansas. But Meinhardt, who returned to his home state in 1988 after a military career of more than three decades, lacked the name identification or financial backing to make a serious run at Slattery, who won with 73 percent.

Committees

Banking, Finance & Urban Affairs (30th of 31 Democrats)

Energy & Commerce (14th of 27 Democrats)
Oversight & Investigations; Telecommunications & Finance; Transportation & Hazardous Materials

Veterans' Affairs (8th of 21 Democrats)
Education, Training & Employment; Hospitals & Health Care

Elections

1990 General		
Jim Slattery (D)	99,093	(63%)
Scott Morgan (R)	58,643	(37%)
1990 Primary		
Jim Slattery (D)	30,287	(86%)
Mark Creamer (D)	5,020	(14%)
1988 General		
Jim Slattery (D)	135,694	(73%)
Phil Meinhardt (R)	49,498	(27%)

Previous Winning Percentages: **1986** (71%) **1984** (60%) **1982** (57%)

District Vote For President

	1988	1984	1980	1976
D	85,689 (46%)	66,539 (36%)	61,150 (34%)	76,297 (43%)
R	99,411 (53%)	117,971 (63%)	100,343 (56%)	97,716 (55%)
I			16,303 (9%)	

Campaign Finance

	Receipts	Receipts from PACs		Expend-itures
1990				
Slattery (D)	$467,018	$327,550	(70%)	$504,861
Morgan (R)	$87,021	$8,054	(9%)	$84,568
1988				
Slattery (D)	$453,832	$266,122	(59%)	$388,866
Meinhardt (R)	$86,328	$7,577	(9%)	$86,273

Key Votes

1991	
Authorize use of force against Iraq	Y
1990	
Support constitutional amendment on flag desecration	N
Pass family and medical leave bill over Bush veto	N
Reduce SDI funding	Y
Allow abortions in overseas military facilities	Y
Approve budget summit plan for spending and taxing	Y
Approve civil rights bill	Y
1989	
Halt production of B-2 stealth bomber at 13 planes	N
Oppose capital gains tax cut	Y
Approve federal abortion funding in rape or incest cases	N
Approve pay raise and revision of ethics rules	N
Pass Democratic minimum wage plan over Bush veto	Y

Voting Studies

	Presidential Support		Party Unity		Conservative Coalition	
Year	**S**	**O**	**S**	**O**	**S**	**O**
1990	32	67	73	25	48	48
1989	45	55	74	24	59	41
1988	32	61	78	19	61	29
1987	38	60	73	24	63	33
1986	34	66	68	30	62	38
1985	43	58	71	27	65	35
1984	39	61	60	39	49	51
1983	39	61	57	38	58	38

Interest Group Ratings

Year	ADA	ACU	AFL-CIO	CCUS
1990	61	22	67	43
1989	55	21	75	60
1988	55	33	85	38
1987	68	4	69	47
1986	45	27	57	56
1985	55	33	53	36
1984	50	38	38	44
1983	55	36	71	55

3 Jan Meyers (R)

Of Overland Park — Elected 1984

Born: July 20, 1928, Lincoln, Neb.

Education: William Woods College, A.F.A. 1948; U. of Nebraska, B.A. 1951.

Occupation: Homemaker; community volunteer.

Family: Husband, Louis "Dutch" Meyers; two children.

Religion: Methodist.

Political Career: Overland Park City Council, 1967-72, council president, 1970-72; Kan. Senate, 1973-85; sought Republican nomination for U.S. Senate, 1978.

Capitol Office: 1230 Longworth Bldg. 20515; 225-2865.

In Washington: When she came to the House from a position of some influence in the Kansas Legislature, Meyers had high hopes for a prestige committee post. However, a seat on a high-profile panel has eluded Meyers, as did her bid to be House Republican Conference secretary at the start of the 101st Congress. Instead, she has busied herself with work on Foreign Affairs and Small Business, and with the '92 Group, established in the 1980s to work toward a GOP House majority in 1992. In the 102nd Congress, she co-chairs the group.

Meyers tried the traditional route up the party ladder, taking on low-visibility party housekeeping tasks for GOP leader Robert H. Michel, with whom she shares a proclivity for legislative compromise. But by the time Meyers ran for conference secretary, a more confrontational style was ascendant among House Republicans, embodied by Newt Gingrich and his Conservative Opportunity Society. The genteel Meyers was swept aside by COS member Vin Weber of Minnesota. However, after his 1989 election as GOP whip, Gingrich appointed her deputy whip for theme development.

On Small Business, Meyers has focused on such issues as extending the health insurance deduction for the self-employed, while maintaining the GOP line against federal mandates on employers. She has not been a highly visible player on Foreign Affairs.

Instead, Meyers has made a semi-career of serving on various task forces and policy bodies, such as the Republican Task Force on Health Care Policy. Besides her post in the '92 Group, she was elected in 1989 as vice chairman of the Environmental and Energy Study Conference.

Meyers' other efforts typically have a home-base angle. In 1990, her bill to study improvements in firefighter safety became law; she came to the issue after a 1988 incident in Kansas City, Mo., in which a trailer containing volatile materials exploded, killing six firefighters. Meyers also successfully lobbied for funding of a federal building and courthouse in Kansas City, Kan. Drug-abuse prevention is another Meyers priority. She proposed increasing criminal penalties for operators of common carriers, who, while under the influence of drugs or alcohol, are involved in accidents that cause death and injury; provisions of her bill were attached to the 1988 omnibus drug act.

At Home: One of Kansas' three House Republicans, Meyers has been mentioned as a possible statewide candidate. Her name came up when GOP Sen. Nancy Landon Kassebaum looked iffy about seeking re-election in 1990. But Kassebaum ran again and won easily.

Meyers has already made one attempt for statewide office, which failed. In the 1978 GOP Senate primary, won by Kassebaum, she ran fourth with just under 10 percent of the vote.

However, she did much better in 1984, when Republican Larry Winn Jr.'s retirement opened the 3rd. Meyers' 17 years as a city and state officeholder enabled her to fend off four GOP primary challengers. While Meyers' image as a fiscal conservative satisfied GOP stalwarts, her moderate reputation in the state Senate — where she was involved in issues such as care for the elderly, and prevention of child abuse and drunken driving — gave her wider appeal.

Although her Democratic opponent, Kansas City Mayor Jack Reardon, was a colorful campaigner, Meyers's political experience and slogan, "Jan Can," brought her 55 percent. Meyers solidified her position, ran without opposition in 1986 and won by 3-to-1 in 1988.

The 1990 campaign was a little tougher. Ill-fated GOP Gov. Mike Hayden became a burden at the top of the ticket: A state property tax increase sparked an anti-Hayden reaction in affluent Johnson County, which contains most of the 3rd District's population. However, Meyers' base held; she defeated Democrat Leroy Jones, a locomotive engineer, with 60 percent.

Kansas 3

East — Kansas City

When Rodgers and Hammerstein wrote "Everything's up-to-date in Kansas City," they meant Kansas City, Mo. Kansas City, Kan., on the western bank of the Missouri River, lives on in the shadow of its larger, more bustling namesake. The 3rd, centered around blue-collar Kansas City, Kan., and the Johnson County suburbs to the south, remains within the orbit of Missouri's economy, though it is developing an economic identity all its own.

Booming Johnson County boasts over 60 percent of the district's population; the county grew by more than 31 percent in the 1980s. One of the nation's top counties in per-capita income, Johnson County is reliably Republican. George Bush took 63 percent of the county vote in 1988, running up a 40,000-vote margin on Democrat Michael S. Dukakis.

Though the dominant image of Johnson County is one of stately homes and manicured lawns, there are more modest, older suburban towns, such as Lenexa, many of them settled by immigrants who worked in the various industries of the two Kansas Citys. Sprawling south and farther west is the county's boom corridor, reaching to Olathe and beyond — a mix of farm land and new office buildings and shopping centers.

There is little in common between suburban Johnson County and urban, industrial Wyandotte County (Kansas City) to the north. Kansas City, once one of the Great Plains' major stockyard centers, suffered from years of decline. Efforts to diversify the economy have been moderately successful, as Monsanto and Ciba-Geigy have located laboratories in the area, complementing the existing biotech firms.

The city maintains the Democratic tradition dating back to the halcyon days of its ethnic-oriented political machine. The city's sizable black population — almost 30 percent of the total — is dependably Democratic. Wyandotte gave Dukakis 66 percent of its vote in 1988; it was one of three Kansas counties won by the Democrat.

Population: 472,456. White 416,244 (88%), Black 45,319 (10%), Other 4,490 (1%). Spanish origin 12,360 (3%). 18 and over 334,153 (71%), 65 and over 45,786 (10%). Median age: 30.

Committees

Foreign Affairs (12th of 18 Republicans)
Europe & the Middle East; International Narcotics Control; Western Hemisphere Affairs

Select Aging (10th of 27 Republicans)
Retirement, Income & Employment; Rural Elderly

Small Business (5th of 17 Republicans)
Regulation, Business Opportunity & Energy (ranking)

Elections

1990 General		
Jan Meyers (R)	88,725	(60%)
Leroy Jones (D)	58,923	(40%)
1988 General		
Jan Meyers (R)	150,223	(74%)
Lionel Kunst (D)	53,959	(26%)

Previous Winning Percentages: **1986** (100%) **1984** (55%)

District Vote For President

	1988	1984	1980	1976
D	99,785 (45%)	78,289 (36%)	70,201 (36%)	78,764 (42%)
R	121,658 (54%)	138,118 (63%)	108,207 (55%)	104,811 (56%)
I			14,436 (7%)	

Campaign Finance

	Receipts	Receipts from PACs	Expend-itures
1990			
Meyers (R)	$211,505	$110,641 (52%)	$209,986
Jones (D)	$78,289	$51,299 (66%)	$76,007
1988			
Meyers (R)	$201,229	$110,395 (55%)	$234,583
Kunst (D)	$13,483	0	$13,483

Key Votes

1991	
Authorize use of force against Iraq	Y
1990	
Support constitutional amendment on flag desecration	Y
Pass family and medical leave bill over Bush veto	N
Reduce SDI funding	N
Allow abortions in overseas military facilities	Y
Approve budget summit plan for spending and taxing	Y
Approve civil rights bill	Y
1989	
Halt production of B-2 stealth bomber at 13 planes	N
Oppose capital gains tax cut	N
Approve federal abortion funding in rape or incest cases	Y
Approve pay raise and revision of ethics rules	N
Pass Democratic minimum wage plan over Bush veto	N

Voting Studies

	Presidential Support		Party Unity		Conservative Coalition	
Year	S	O	S	O	S	O
1990	65	35	70	29	78	22
1989	69	31	53	46	88	12
1988	52	45	71	24	87	13
1987	59	41	71	26	77	21
1986	59	39	73	27	70	30
1985	68	31	68	26	78	18

Interest Group Ratings

Year	ADA	ACU	AFL-CIO	CCUS
1990	22	67	0	57
1989	15	64	17	100
1988	35	58	23	85
1987	12	61	6	93
1986	25	55	14	78
1985	15	71	19	86

4 Dan Glickman (D)

Of Wichita — Elected 1976

Born: Nov. 24, 1944, Wichita, Kan.
Education: U. of Michigan, B.A. 1966; George Washington U., J.D. 1969.
Occupation: Lawyer.
Family: Wife, Rhoda Yura; two children.
Religion: Jewish.
Political Career: Wichita Board of Education, 1973-76, president, 1975-76.
Capitol Office: 2311 Rayburn Bldg. 20515; 225-6216.

In Washington: Unfettered by the House's tendency to specialize, Glickman has extended his concerns from farm policy to television violence to campaign finance reform. Whether he ever reaches the Senate — his well-known goal — his legislative résumé already matches those of many senators.

The Kansas Democrat serves on four committees — Agriculture, Judiciary, Science, and Intelligence, and manages to be a serious player on each. He seems to have an amendment for nearly every major bill those committees bring to the floor, and every subcommittee he chairs becomes a legislative mill. This industry has helped Glickman move past his early reputation as merely a media-seeking maverick. Glickman's legislative ubiquity was noted in a headline in *The Hutchinson News* at the start of his 1990 campaign: "God Rested — Dan Won't."

A central player on the 1985 farm bill, Glickman was one of a group of younger House Democrats who wanted Congress to try new approaches for federal price-support program. At the start of the 100th Congress, he inherited a powerful new position, the chairmanship of the Agriculture Subcommittee on Wheat, Soybeans and Feed Grains. That guaranteed him a pivotal role in the committee's most important pieces of legislation, such as the 1990 farm bill.

Glickman was sensitive to the intensified budget-cutting atmosphere that prevailed in the 101st Congress, and to the diminishing sympathy for farm programs among members not from farm states. "The antipathy toward higher spending ... is higher than it has ever been before," he said. "And it is particularly going to afflict us in agriculture." Glickman favored the concept of "flexibility" included in the bill — allowing farmers to plant whatever they wanted on a portion of their land without government involvement or subsidy.

Several members circulated ideas to boost subsidies to soybean growers by creating a so-called marketing loan, a market-oriented price-support mechanism, for soybeans and other oilseeds. U.S. soybean growers were beleaguered by high production costs and foreign competition. Glickman proposed setting a loan level of $5.50 per bushel, modest compared with some of the other plans being advanced. The Wheat Subcommittee adopted his plan, which gave the Agriculture secretary authority to reduce the support rate by 5 percent a year. But deliberations in committee and later in the House-Senate conference reduced loan levels to $5.02 and included an assessment that would make the effective rate $4.92.

Glickman and Kansas' senior senator, Republican Bob Dole, have long battled for preeminence in their state's political arena, particularly among the state's farmers. Two politically astute operators with senior positions on Agriculture panels, each has contrived to outmaneuver the other on high-profile issues.

In 1989, the two dueled on a disaster-relief bill for farmers. Glickman engineered the House plan, which sailed through virtually unopposed. It extended eligibilty for aid to virtually any farmer who suffered a significant loss. Dole focused his efforts on getting more benefits for winter wheat farmers, threatening to obstruct the bill if his proposal was not accepted. "We're going to keep fighting for Kansas farmers, whether Dan likes it or not," Dole chided in *The Kansas City Times*.

But Dole was pressed to release the bill; he was constrained by the Bush administration to keep the cost of the bill to $875 million. Senate Agriculture Committee politics also complicated Dole's efforts. "Let our drought bill go," Glickman urged. Dole relented, and Glickman was credited with outflanking the Senate minority leader.

Glickman navigates potentially rough waters in working with Agriculture Chairman E. "Kika" de la Garza of Texas. In 1980, Glickman helped lead a group of dissident committee Democrats who tried to deny de la Garza the chairmanship.

Kansas 4

Central — Wichita

Aircraft workers with Southern roots give a blue-collar Democratic presence to Wichita and surrounding Sedgwick County, where more than three of every four votes in the 4th are cast. Wichita was the base of unsuccessful 1986 Democratic gubernatorial nominee Tom Docking, and in the governor's race of 1982, Democratic incumbent John Carlin won Sedgwick County's vote even though his opponent came from Wichita. Sedgwick's working-class voters have been the backbone of Glickman's strength, although Glickman also runs well among the county's suburban and rural voters.

This Democratic cast has become less and less evident at the presidential level, though. In 1976, President Ford edged Democrat Jimmy Carter in Sedgwick. In 1984, President Reagan won the county with 63 percent. George Bush took a comfortable 55 percent victory over Democrat Michael S. Dukakis.

The Republican lean at the national level is partly due to the beneficial local effect of the increased defense spending levels of the Reagan years. Boeing's military aviation works in Wichita enjoyed a boom during the period, cushioning the region's economy even from the recession of the early 1980s. McConnell Air Force Base, outside Wichita, which has facilities for basing B-1 bombers, also provides economic benefits for the district.

Civilian aviation is the other economic mainstay of Wichita, a city of more than 304,000 people that includes some of the state's largest minority communities outside Kansas City. Thousands are employed on the assembly lines of Boeing's commercial divisions, Cessna, Beech and Gates-Learjet, and by their subcontractors. However, the commercial-aviation business tends to be more cyclical and more subject to foreign competition than the military aircraft industry.

In addition to the aviation industry, Wichita retains an identity as a corporate base for Kansas' oil industry, which played an important role in the city's early development. The mid-1980s oil bust took a considerable toll in Kansas, costing jobs from the executive suites to the oil fields, but the industry is once again showing signs of life.

Outside of Wichita, farming remains the mainstay of the five-county district. The only other city of size in the 4th is Hutchinson (Reno County), with about 39,000 people.

Population: 473,180. White 421,885 (89%), Black 33,405 (7%), Other 8,356 (2%). Spanish origin 14,288 (3%). 18 and over 341,718 (72%), 65 and over 51,611 (11%). Median age: 29.

Though considered an expert on commodity futures, Glickman has not endeared himself to some of his colleagues by going up against the powerful financial interests in the futures markets, an important source of honoraria for Agriculture Committee members. But with recent federal investigations into trading fraud in the two largest markets, Glickman, a former attorney with the Securities and Exchange Commission (SEC), has reasserted himself. He joined with Ohio Democrat Dennis E. Eckart in the 101st Congress to propose merging the activities of the SEC and the Commodity Futures Trading Commission, creating a Markets and Trading Commission. They reintroduced their bill in the 102nd Congress.

From his seat on Judiciary, Glickman introduced legislation in the 101st Congress to exempt television-industry officials from antitrust laws if they get together to discuss reducing TV violence. It became law at the end of 1990. He also added an amendment to the 1990 anticrime bill that increased jail sentences for those convicted of using sawed-off shotguns, bombs or grenades in drug crimes.

Glickman has played a key role in the thorny debate over campaign finance reform. In the 101st and 102nd Congresses, he and Oklahoma Democrat Mike Synar advanced a plan to wean candidates from political action committees and replace lost dollars with public funds.

At Home: With his prominence on Kansas-related issues and his strength in a district that includes populous Wichita, Glickman faces speculation about his ambitions every time one of the state's Senate seats comes up. But through 1990, neither of the state's formidably popular Republican senators — Bob Dole and Nancy Landon Kassebaum — had stepped down, and Glickman was not inclined to give up his safe House seat to challenge either of them.

Nonetheless, with Dole facing a decision about whether to run for a fifth term in 1992, Glickman will once again lead the list of potential Democratic Senate contenders.

Although his district is a Republican stronghold in presidential contests, Glickman has frustrated all GOP challenges. Bolstered politically by his senior positions on district-relevant committees, Glickman amplifies his visibility by making himself accessible to the Wichita media. "I am never too busy to talk to local TV, period, exclamation point," Glickman has said.

Glickman's only tough House contest was his first one in 1976, when he became the first Democrat to win this Wichita-based district in 36 years. A member of a wealthy and prominent local family, Glickman was the youthful president of the Wichita school board when he decided to challenge veteran GOP Rep. Garner E. Shriver, who had been re-elected by a surprisingly small margin in 1974.

Campaigning as a fiscal conservative and a moderate on other issues, Glickman worked vigorously to paint Shriver as a tired, inactive House member. "You've had 16 years of a professional politician. Now is the time for a citizen congressman," Glickman's campaign literature urged; Glickman himself called for six-term limits on House tenure. The 64-year-old Shriver was slow to respond. Glickman won by 3,235 votes.

Just two years later, Glickman was winning re-election with 70 percent of the vote; his work on behalf of district interests had quickly made him a popular figure. In six House contests since, he has never taken less than 64 percent of the vote.

Glickman received that figure in 1988. After running a series of staunchly conservative challengers, district Republicans nominated attorney Lee Thompson, a moderate with political ties to Kassebaum.

Thompson tried to hold Glickman to an old campaign promise: He centered his campaign on the "six terms and out" idea Glickman advocated in 1976. But Glickman easily deflected this thrust, noting that he had tried with no success as a House freshman to push his limited-tenure plan. He also reminded voters that his departure would weaken their influence on the then-pending farm bill revision.

After bypassing challenges to Dole in 1980 and 1986 and to Kassebaum in 1984, Glickman looked poised to move up in 1990. Kassebaum, like Glickman, had promised to serve no more than 12 years when she first ran for Congress. However, Kassebaum was correctly presumed as a sure bet for re-election, and also used seniority-based arguments when she announced for another term. Glickman stayed in the 4th.

Committees

Agriculture (8th of 27 Democrats)
Wheat, Soybeans & Feed Grains (chairman); Conservation, Credit & Rural Development; Department Operations, Research & Foreign Agriculture

Judiciary (8th of 21 Democrats)
Economic & Commercial Law; Intellectual Property & Judicial Administration

Science, Space & Technology (4th of 32 Democrats)
Technology & Competitiveness

Select Intelligence (4th of 12 Democrats)
Oversight & Evaluation; Program & Budget Authorization

Elections

1990 General		
Dan Glickman (D)	112,015	(71%)
Roger M. Grund (R)	46,283	(29%)
1988 General		
Dan Glickman (D)	122,777	(64%)
Lee Thompson (R)	69,165	(36%)

Previous Winning Percentages: **1986** (65%) **1984** (74%) **1982** (74%) **1980** (69%) **1978** (70%) **1976** (50%)

District Vote For President

	1988	1984	1980	1976
D	84,235 (43%)	70,140 (36%)	70,871 (37%)	87,817 (48%)
R	108,417 (55%)	124,731 (63%)	100,757 (53%)	89,301 (49%)
I			13,477 (8%)	

Campaign Finance

	Receipts	Receipts from PACs	Expend-itures
1990			
Glickman (D)	$520,945	$294,865 (57%)	$355,581
Grund (R)	$4,227	$300 (7%)	$4,317
1988			
Glickman (D)	$562,266	$280,540 (50%)	$545,755
Thompson (R)	$149,704	$8,400 (6%)	$149,035

Key Votes

1991	
Authorize use of force against Iraq	Y
1990	
Support constitutional amendment on flag desecration	N
Pass family and medical leave bill over Bush veto	N
Reduce SDI funding	Y
Allow abortions in overseas military facilities	Y
Approve budget summit plan for spending and taxing	Y
Approve civil rights bill	Y
1989	
Halt production of B-2 stealth bomber at 13 planes	N
Oppose capital gains tax cut	Y
Approve federal abortion funding in rape or incest cases	Y
Approve pay raise and revision of ethics rules	Y
Pass Democratic minimum wage plan over Bush veto	Y

Voting Studies

	Presidential Support		Party Unity		Conservative Coalition	
Year	S	O	S	O	S	O
1990	27	72	81	17	37	61
1989	37	60	80	18	59	34
1988	32	65	75	20	61	39
1987	26	74	80	17	58	42
1986	28	70	76	21	60	40
1985	36	63	76	22	53	45
1984	40	59	69	29	44	53
1983	43	57	73	23	46	53
1982	47	53	74	26	45	53
1981	47	53	70	30	48	51

Interest Group Ratings

Year	ADA	ACU	AFL-CIO	CCUS
1990	72	17	67	31
1989	80	18	67	50
1988	80	16	86	43
1987	80	9	75	47
1986	55	32	64	50
1985	55	35	59	41
1984	60	29	62	38
1983	70	22	63	55
1982	70	18	80	24
1981	75	27	60	26

5 Dick Nichols (R)

Of McPherson — Elected 1990

Born: April 29, 1926, Fort Scott, Kan.
Education: Kansas State U., B.S. 1951.
Military Service: Navy, 1944-46.
Occupation: Banker.
Family: Wife, Constance Weinbrenner; three children.
Religion: Methodist.
Political Career: No previous office.
Capitol Office: 1605 Longworth Bldg. 20515; 225-3911.

The Path to Washington: The minute Nichols was sworn in, the clock began to run out on him. The oldest of the 44 freshmen in his class, he was elected at an age (64) when most people are about to retire — and his advocacy of term limits suggests that he expects to return soon to southeastern Kansas. But age and inclination may be beside the point: Kansas is losing one of its five seats to reapportionment after 1992, and Nichols' district was the only one in the state to lose population between 1980-86. The likelihood of the 5th being dismembered helped persuade Republican Rep. Bob Whittaker, Nichols' predecessor for six terms, to retire in 1990.

Nichols entered a six-way primary and won with a polished and savvy campaign. He poured in more than $165,000 of his own money, bought extensive television and radio time, and made a flying tour of 11 district cities just before the primary. He also made the most of the edge he had as former chairman of the Republican Party in the district and benefited from the business contacts he had built as a small-town banker and past president of the Kansas Bankers Association.

Although Nichols hails from the far western edge of the district and won the primary vote outright in just four of the district's 25 counties, he outran the field and kept fences well enough mended in the process to corral the endorsements of all five of his rivals.

After the primary, in which Nichols bettered his nearest opponent by fewer than 900 votes, the general election proved anticlimactic. Unlike other open-seat races across the country, there was little rancor.

The rhetoric was muted partly because Nichols' Democratic opponent, George Wingert, had little to offer voters aside from his former service as a state legislator and the contrast between his imposing height and Nichols' slight build.

Nichols took care to stress his small-town roots in this heavily rural district, and he displayed a personal touch — even playing the piano in some appearances. He also pointed to his knowledge of agriculture, gained not only through his lifelong residence in the 5th but through his work as a farm broadcaster and as a member of the state Board of Agriculture. He also put forward his background in economic development as good preparation for jump-starting the region's farm and energy sectors.

A mainstream conservative, Nichols preached fiscal responsibility and favored cutting congressional salaries and other federal spending to reduce the deficit. He advocated a strong national defense but called for economies such as canceling new orders for B-2 bombers.

That message proved well-tailored to the times and the district: Nichols took 22 of 25 counties, losing populous Lyon County (Emporia) but chalking up a 2-to-1 advantage in Butler, Cowley, Harvey and McPherson counties.

Nichols is something of an oddity, seeking public office for the first time in his seventh decade. But candidacy had long been on his mind. He had a tussle with Whittaker in 1986 when he ran against Whittaker's chosen candidate for 5th District Republican chairman.

Winning that race, Nichols served in the job for nearly four years. Some thought Nichols might challenge Whittaker in 1988, but the rift healed, and Whittaker endorsed Nichols against Wingert.

Nichols' varied experiences include one in 1986 far more harrowing than any he is likely to encounter in Congress.

While in New York City celebrating the rededication of the Statue of Liberty, Nichols and his wife sustained serious stomach wounds when attacked by a deranged man with a sword who killed two and wounded five on the Staten Island Ferry.

Nichols kept his spirits throughout the ordeal. After visiting Nichols in the hospital, then-New York City Mayor Edward I. Koch said: "He ended up comforting me instead of me comforting him."

Kansas 5

Southeast — Emporia; Pittsburg

Economic slumps in two of southeast Kansas' leading industries — agriculture and energy resource production — brought hard times to wide areas of the 5th District in the 1980s. Of the district's 25 counties, 19 lost population from 1980-86, with seven incurring losses of 5 percent or more.

The problems in the local economy have not shaken district voters from their conservative tendencies, however. George Bush took 56 percent of the district vote in 1988, his second-highest figure in the state, and carried all but one county.

Though no Democrat has held the 5th since 1960, the region used to have some appeal for Democrats. Numerous Southerners moved north to work in the wheat and oil fields of southeast Kansas, and so many Eastern Europeans migrated to work in the coal mines of the area that it took on the name of "the Balkans." That name is also a reference to the region's hilly landscape, which belies the image of Kansas as a flat, arid expanse of wheat.

Lingering Democratic sympathies are most evident in Crawford County, site of the depressed industrial city of Pittsburg. The city has a population of just over 18,000, and includes a sizable blue-collar work force, but is economically isolated due to the lack of a major highway to southeast Kansas. In 1988, Democrat Michael S. Dukakis took 52 percent of the vote in Crawford County, one of three counties in he won statewide. In 1990, it was one of only three counties that went for unsuccessful Democratic House candidate George Wingert over Nichols.

The Republican tilt in Lyon County — which includes Emporia, the district's largest city with about 24,600 residents — is much more standard for the district. Located at the center of the Flint Hills, which run the length of eastern Kansas, and midway between Topeka and Wichita on the Kansas Turnpike, Emporia is the 5th's major commercial hub. The local agricultural industry is augmented by several manufacturing and processing interests, including an Iowa Beef Processors Inc. (IBP) slaughterhouse that employs 2,200. Some of Emporia's large population of Welsh extraction still celebrate St. David's Day, honoring the patron saint of Wales.

The region once boasted booming ore mines. Now the 5th's economy depends on agriculture, primarily soybeans and wheat.

Population: 472,916. White 455,149 (96%), Black 8,564 (2%), Other 4,602 (1%). Spanish origin 7,869 (2%). 18 and over 347,340 (74%), 65 and over 81,483 (17%). Median age: 33.

Committees

Public Works & Transportation (19th of 21 Republicans)
Aviation; Surface Transportation

Select Aging (25th of 27 Republicans)
Retirement, Income & Employment

Veterans' Affairs (12th of 13 Republicans)
Housing & Memorial Affairs

Campaign Finance

	Receipts	Receipts from PACs		Expend-itures
1990				
Nichols (R)	$573,188	$100,125	(17%)	$565,410
Wingert (D)	$69,450	$12,950	(19%)	$68,281

Key Vote

1991

Authorize use of force against Iraq	Y

Elections

1990 General		
Dick Nichols (R)	90,555	(59%)
George D. Wingert (D)	62,244	(41%)
1990 Primary		
Dick Nichols (R)	18,599	(29%)
Sheila C. Bair (R)	17,839	(28%)
Doyle Talkington (R)	11,686	(18%)
Ed Roitz (R)	7,614	(12%)
Kent Hodges (R)	6,133	(9%)
Bill Otto (R)	2,290	(4%)

District Vote For President

	1988	1984	1980	1976
D	78,214 (42%)	63,616 (32%)	67,709 (34%)	91,122 (47%)
R	104,238 (56%)	135,037 (67%)	117,130 (59%)	99,491 (51%)
I			11,514 (6%)	

Kentucky

U.S. CONGRESS

SENATE 1 D, 1 R
HOUSE 4 D, 3 R

LEGISLATURE

Senate 27 D, 11 R
House 68 D, 32 R

ELECTIONS

1988 Presidential Vote	
Bush	56%
Dukakis	44%
1984 Presidential Vote	
Reagan	60%
Mondale	39%
1980 Presidential Vote	
Reagan	49%
Carter	48%
Anderson	2%
Turnout rate in 1986	23%
Turnout rate in 1988	48%
Turnout rate in 1990	28%

(as percentage of voting age population)

POPULATION AND GROWTH

1980 population	3,660,777
1990 population (23rd in the nation)	3,685,296
Percent change 1980-1990	+1%

DEMOGRAPHIC BREAKDOWN

White	92%
Black	7%
Asian or Pacific Islander	1%
(Hispanic origin)	1%
Urban	51%
Rural	49%
Born in state	79%
Foreign-born	1%

MAJOR CITIES

Louisville	269,063
Lexington-Fayette	225,366
Owensboro	53,549
Covington	43,264
Bowling Green	40,641

AREA AND LAND USE

Area 39,669 sq. miles (37th)

Farm	56%
Forest	48%
Federally owned	5%

Gov. Wallace G. Wilkinson (D)
Of Lexington — Elected 1987

Born: Dec. 12, 1941, Liberty, Ky.
Education: Attended U. of Kentucky, 1961.
Occupation: Businessman.
Religion: Christian.
Political Career: No previous office.
Next Election: 1991.

WORK

Occupations	
White-collar	46%
Blue-collar	37%
Service workers	13%
Government Workers	
Federal	35,423
State	80,685
Local	120,340

MONEY

Median family income	$ 16,444	(45th)
Tax burden per capita	$ 809	(28th)

EDUCATION

Spending per pupil through grade 12	$ 3,011	(45th)
Persons with college degrees	11%	(48th)

CRIME

Violent crime rate 357 per 100,000 (33rd)

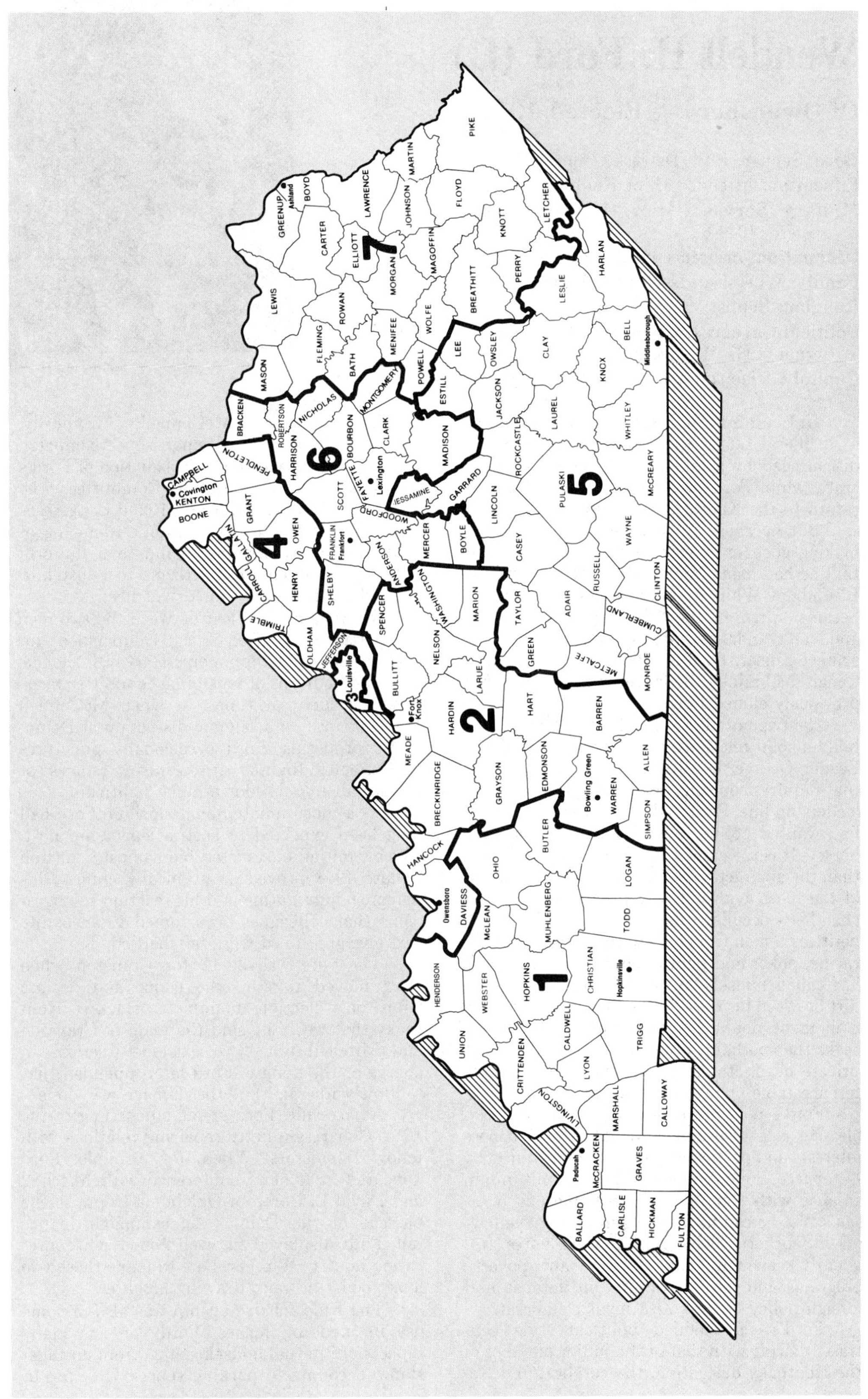
PIKE
MARTIN
FLOYD
JOHNSON
LAWRENCE
BOYD
Ashland
GREENUP
CARTER
ELLIOTT
7
MORGAN
MAGOFFIN
KNOTT
LETCHER
HARLAN
LESLIE
PERRY
BREATHITT
WOLFE
MENIFEE
ROWAN
LEWIS
FLEMING
BATH
MASON
POWELL
LEE
OWSLEY
CLAY
BELL
Middlesborough
KNOX
LAUREL
JACKSON
ESTILL
MONTGOMERY
NICHOLAS
ROBERTSON
BRACKEN
HARRISON
BOURBON
CLARK
MADISON
WHITLEY
McCREARY
PULASKI
5
ROCKCASTLE
LINCOLN
GARRARD
JESSAMINE
FAYETTE
Lexington
6
SCOTT
PENDLETON
CAMPBELL
Covington
KENTON
BOONE
GRANT
OWEN
GALLATIN
CARROLL
4
HENRY
TRIMBLE
OLDHAM
SHELBY
FRANKLIN
Frankfort
WOODFORD
ANDERSON
MERCER
BOYLE
CASEY
WAYNE
RUSSELL
CLINTON
ADAIR
TAYLOR
MARION
WASHINGTON
SPENCER
JEFFERSON
Louisville
3
BULLITT
NELSON
LARUE
GREEN
CUMBERLAND
METCALFE
MONROE
HART
BARREN
HARDIN
2
Fort Knox
MEADE
BRECKINRIDGE
GRAYSON
EDMONSON
ALLEN
WARREN
Bowling Green
SIMPSON
BUTLER
LOGAN
HANCOCK
OHIO
Owensboro
DAVIESS
McLEAN
MUHLENBERG
TODD
CHRISTIAN
Hopkinsville
HOPKINS
1
HENDERSON
WEBSTER
UNION
CALDWELL
TRIGG
CRITTENDEN
LYON
LIVINGSTON
MARSHALL
CALLOWAY
Paducah
McCRACKEN
GRAVES
BALLARD
CARLISLE
HICKMAN
FULTON

Wendell H. Ford (D)

Of Owensboro — Elected 1974

Born: Sept. 8, 1924, Daviess County, Ky.
Education: Attended U. of Kentucky, 1942-43.
Military Service: Army, 1944-46; Army National Guard, 1949-62.
Occupation: Insurance executive.
Family: Wife, Jean Neel; two children.
Religion: Baptist.
Political Career: Ky. Senate, 1965-67; lieutenant governor, 1967-71; governor, 1971-74.
Capitol Office: 173A Russell Bldg. 20510; 224-4343.

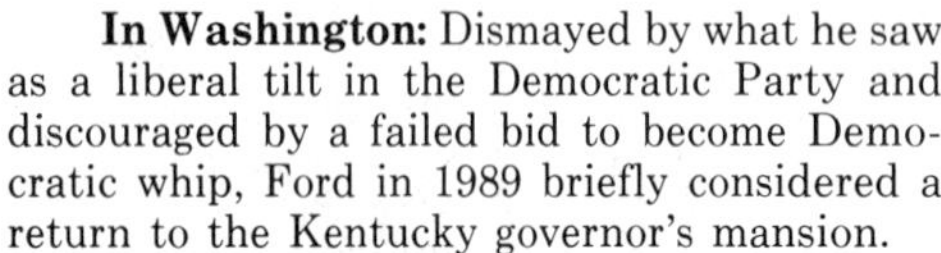

In Washington: Dismayed by what he saw as a liberal tilt in the Democratic Party and discouraged by a failed bid to become Democratic whip, Ford in 1989 briefly considered a return to the Kentucky governor's mansion.

But he chose to persevere in the Senate, making good on a vow to run again for whip that he had made immediately after his rebuff. Incumbent Whip Alan Cranston of California became mired in the "Keating Five" savings and loan scandal and preoccupied with his fight against cancer; Ford at the start of the 102nd Congress obtained the leadership post that had previously eluded him.

Reinvigorated, Ford seemed determined to build a solid relationship with Senate Majority Leader George J. Mitchell of Maine in a job that requires counting votes and promoting the leadership line. Ford told fellow Democrats that he "wanted to be a workhorse, not a show horse." It is the game that fascinates Ford more than the abstractions of public policy. He is one of the most avid and wily practitioners of the chamber's peculiar rules, with a gambler's style befitting a man from a state that takes its horse racing, poker and politics equally seriously. He has called himself "a dumb country boy with dirt between his toes," but colleagues do not for a moment doubt his shrewdness. He seldom seeks the spotlight, preferring to work through private negotiations in committee, at the conference table or in the cloakroom.

Ford's politics are nothing if not negotiable. He is a deal-maker, usually for business interests and particularly for those in Kentucky — tobacco, liquor and coal. That has put him in alliance with Republicans on numerous occasions. Yet he can be as partisan as any "yellow-dog" Southern Democrat, and he votes frequently enough for labor, anti-poverty programs and party positions on defense and foreign policy to rank as a loyal Democrat.

Ford's clay-clodded political style contrasts sharply with that of the junior member of the Kentucky delegation, the cerebral and Republican Mitch McConnell. Ironically, McConnell's developed expertise — campaign finance — falls within the jurisdiction of Ford's Rules and Administration Committee, the springboard in the 101st and 102nd Congresses for bills that would create public financing of congressional campaigns, mandate a uniform poll closing and permit citizens to register to vote when they apply for driver licenses.

There is no love lost between the two men — particularly after Ford campaigned for McConnell's 1990 opponent, Harvey I. Sloane. The undercurrent of tension in committee hearings is evident at times, as when McConnell launches into an academic dissection of Democratic proposals, Ford occasionally punctures McConnell's flights with a raspy remark or lecture about real, down-home politickin'.

As a consummate Senate insider, Ford had long been expected to seek a leadership post. But his initial unexpected bid against Cranston in late 1988 proved so atypically clumsy, his defeat so humiliating and his reaction so ungracious that colleagues accustomed to an astute and engaging Ford were left baffled.

The vote was 30-12 for Cranston when Ford moved to stop the count and declare Cranston's election unanimous. Back in Kentucky that week, he said the team of Cranston and Mitchell put "two extreme liberals" in charge of the Senate. Ford later amended that to "fairly liberal," but the damage was done.

As a result, Ford spent much time in the 101st Congress quietly repairing relations with fellow Democrats. When, for example, Ford appeared at a news conference with Mitchell and David L. Boren of Oklahoma to praise the passage of the Democratic campaign-finance bill, Ford displayed his well-honed self-deprecating humor. "I'm just here to make these two look good," he said, drawing laughter.

The Rules chairmanship was also of some use in mending fences. Ford controls many aspects of internal housekeeping, from postage-stamp accounts to parking spaces; they are of little consequence to the public, but of great importance to his colleagues.

Ford's relations with some Republicans remain frosty. Some expressed outrage and even threatened to put holds on his bills when Ford traveled to South Dakota in 1990 to campaign for Larry Pressler's Democratic opponent, Ted Muenster. "He doesn't work. He doesn't mingle. He doesn't prepare for anything," Ford said of Pressler in comments appearing in *The Washington Post.*

Ford and the controlled Mitchell are an odd political team, and how they will pull in harness remains to be seen. But in the 101st Congress Ford demonstrated that he was willing to submerge parochial interests to work with Mitchell: Ford backed the 1990 budget package that imposed higher taxes on tobacco and liquor. He also rushed to Mitchell's defense when Republicans criticized his handling of civil rights legislation.

Ford is most active on two other committees — Commerce, Science and Transportation; and Energy and Natural Resources — where his close ties to business have made him one of the Senate's top fundraisers. In recognition of his money-raising prowess, Ford's colleagues chose him to head the Democratic Senatorial Campaign Committee from 1976 through 1982.

In 1987, Ford became chairman of Commerce's Aviation Subcommittee. There, he worked to steer grants to small airports, such as those common in Kentucky, and to base awards not only on an airport's passenger traffic but on cargo: Louisville is home to United Parcel Service's air-freight business. He opposed Bush administration proposals to increase aviation taxes — which he warned would be used to reduce the federal budget deficit — and favors removing the Federal Aviation Administration from the Transportation Department.

On Commerce, Ford also has been a critic of federal business regulation; he sponsored the legislation enacted in 1980 to trim the authority of the Federal Trade Commission. He also opposes efforts to restrict billboards, a position that allies Ford not only with the wealthy billboard lobby but also with his home-state liquor and cigarette interests, which rely on outdoor advertising.

Insurance is the business Ford is closest to — so close, in fact, that opponents have lodged conflict-of-interest complaints against him. Ford owned two Kentucky insurance companies during most of his first decade in the Senate, and recused himself when insurance issues came before Commerce. He completed the sale of his interests to family members in 1985.

Once those ties were cut, Ford began working openly on the industry's behalf. In 1986, he fought to weaken a provision requiring insurance companies to report certain information to the federal government, and opposed a bill making it easier for other businesses to form their own liability insurance pools.

Ford is also one of the tobacco family, and he fits the part with his ever-present cigarette, a ruddily handsome face with skin like smoked-leather and a raspy drawl. In 1984 he temporarily blocked a bill mandating new health warnings on cigarettes; the bill eventually moved, but only after Ford secured an agreement to drop some language critical of tobacco.

The next year, along with North Carolina Republican Jesse Helms, he helped engineer a complex deal establishing a new tobacco price-support program in return for tobacco interests' agreement to a permanent extension of the 16-cents-a-pack cigarette tax. Ford lobbied Democrats on the Finance Committee to attach the compromise to a deficit-reduction bill, thus easing the controversial tobacco program's way past floor opposition. The package became law early in 1986.

Having long helped bury legislation requiring warning labels on liquor, Ford joined in Commerce's unanimous approval of a labeling bill in 1988. The industry publicly objected, but privately it favored the federal warning as a potential defense against liability lawsuits and as a uniform standard to prevent a proliferation of state-passed requirements.

On Energy, Ford is in a good position to defend Kentucky's coal producers. He has repeatedly sought repeal of tough federal strip-mining regulations, and in 1986 killed a provision imposing penalties on states that failed to enforce federal requirements for the restoration of strip-mined land. In 1987, he agreed to a repeal of the 1978 law requiring utilities to use coal rather than oil and gas, which was enacted during an oil shortage, but he did add language stipulating that new power plants must not be unadaptable to coal use. Ford has fought Western coal producers' push for a coal-slurry pipeline to transport their coal more cheaply and make it competitive with Appalachian coal in Eastern and Southern markets.

In 1990, Ford held up Senate confirmation of three White House nominees to the Energy Department until he got the Bush administration's to notice his proposal to revamp the Energy Department's uranium enrichment enterprise. The Paducah, Ky., plant sells fuel to nuclear power producers and is the second largest employer in western Kentucky. But Ford was unable to overcome House opposition to the bill in conference.

At Home: Ford plays Kentucky politics to win, and he plays it just about full time. Faced with the likelihood of weak opposition in his first Senate re-election (in 1980), Ford still amassed a huge campaign treasury in case of a serious challenger. None did, but he conducted an exhausting campaign anyway and crushed long-shot Republican Mary Louise Foust.

In 1986, he actually had a reason to be cautious. Two years before, his Democratic colleague, Walter D. Huddleston, had been ousted in a surprise GOP victory, and Republicans hoped for a repeat performance.

But in the wake of Huddleston's defeat, Ford commissioned a series of polls to test where in the state he might be in danger. He then set about shoring up his support there. He again began raising money early, and by the end of 1985 had more than enough to give any prospective GOP candidate pause. As it turned out, Ford's opponent was a Louisville lawyer named Jackson M. Andrews, an unknown who asked voters not to confuse him with "a dead president." Ford won 74 percent of the vote.

While building his insurance business, Ford started in politics as a protégé of Democratic Gov. Bert Combs, for whom he worked as an aide from 1959-63. But that relationship turned sour. By 1971, after a term in the state Senate and one as lieutenant governor, Ford was ready for the governorship. Combs, however, decided on a comeback the same year.

Their contest for the Democratic nomination was rough. Ford said Combs was the candidate of the "fat cats and the courthouse crowd." Combs said Ford was a "punchless promiser with both hands tied behind him by special interests." Combs had his traditional base in eastern Kentucky, but Ford did better in Louisville and the counties to the west and defeated his old mentor soundly. He had little trouble beating Republican Tom Emberton that fall.

As governor, Ford earned popularity by cutting taxes imposed under his Republican predecessor, Louie B. Nunn. This left him in good stead when he ran for the Senate in 1974 against one-term GOP incumbent Marlow W. Cook. The Ford-Cook race was no more pleasant than the earlier gubernatorial contest. Cook accused Ford of using state contracts as governor to reward his political allies. Ford labeled Cook "marvelous Marlow, the wonderful wobbler." Cook was hurt by his earlier defense of Richard M. Nixon. In a Democratic year, Ford won comfortably.

After deciding not to run for governor in 1983, Ford conducted the race vicariously by helping an ally, Lt. Gov. Martha Layne Collins, win. In 1984, he was notably less successful. He volunteered to chair the state campaign for Democratic presidential nominee Walter F. Mondale, hoping to hold down Reagan's margin and thereby protect Huddleston. Mondale lost badly, and Huddleston fell with him.

Committees

Rules & Administration (Chairman)

Commerce, Science & Transportation (3rd of 11 Democrats)
Aviation (chairman); Communications; Consumer; National Ocean Policy Study

Energy & Natural Resources (3rd of 11 Democrats)
Energy Research & Development (chairman); Mineral Resources Development & Production; Water & Power

Joint Printing (Vice Chairman)

Elections

1986 General

Wendell H. Ford (D)	503,775	(74%)
Jackson M. Andrews (R)	173,330	(26%)

Previous Winning Percentages: **1980** (65%) **1974** (54%)

Campaign Finance

	Receipts	Receipts from PACs		Expend-itures
1986				
Ford (D)	$1,519,672	$843,282	(55%)	$1,201,624
Andrews (R)	$58,616	$3,500	(6%)	$58,572

Key Votes

1991	
Authorize use of force against Iraq	N
1990	
Oppose prohibition of certain semiautomatic weapons	Y
Support constitutional amendment on flag desecration	Y
Oppose requiring parental notice for minors' abortions	N
Halt production of B-2 stealth bomber at 13 planes	N
Approve budget that cut spending and raised revenues	Y
Pass civil rights bill over Bush veto	Y
1989	
Oppose reduction of SDI funding	N
Oppose barring federal funds for "obscene" art	N
Allow vote on capital gains tax cut	N

Voting Studies

	Presidential Support		Party Unity		Conservative Coalition	
Year	**S**	**O**	**S**	**O**	**S**	**O**
1990	55	45	69	30	86	14
1989	60	39	64	35	71	29
1988	64	33	70	29	78	22
1987	35	64	85	13	66	34
1986	34	66	74	25	47	53
1985	39	60	76	23	68	28
1984	45	51	76 †	22 †	55	38
1983	40	56	81	17	52	43
1982	32	60	75	24	66	33
1981	56	44	84	14	58	41

† Not eligible for all recorded votes.

Interest Group Ratings

Year	ADA	ACU	AFL-CIO	CCUS
1990	39	35	89	33
1989	45	25	100	25
1988	65	24	93	21
1987	75	19	100	22
1986	55	35	67	53
1985	50	43	81	48
1984	80	23	82	39
1983	70	20	88	32
1982	70	55	81	55
1981	70	13	63	50

Mitch McConnell (R)

Of Louisville — Elected 1984

Born: Feb. 20, 1942, Sheffield, Ala.
Education: U. of Louisville, B.A. 1964; U. of Kentucky, J.D. 1967.
Occupation: Lawyer.
Family: Divorced; three children.
Religion: Baptist.
Political Career: Jefferson County judge/executive, 1978-85.
Capitol Office: 120 Russell Bldg. 20510; 224-2541.

In Washington: Kentuckians may know thoroughbred racing, but when it comes to legislative plowing, they could not have picked a more mismatched team of draft horses to pull their load in the Senate.

The cerebral, methodical McConnell clashes sharply in both style and personality with backslapping, down-home Democrat Wendell H. Ford. Neither has any love lost for the other, particularly after Ford actively campaigned for McConnell's Democratic opponent in 1990. Ironically, Ford must put up with his upstart junior colleague in his own back yard — the Rules and Administration Committee — where McConnell has developed the reputation as an expert on campaign finance and the leading GOP obstructionist of Democratic proposals to pay for congressional campaigns with public funds.

McConnell got into the Senate by ambushing a veteran Democrat whom he dubbed a "shadow senator." But he has proven to be no dynamo himself, in part by calculation. He has approached the job in a studied fashion, searching for a few issues like campaign finance and tort reform on which he can learn and lead.

Considered somewhat of an icy loner, McConnell lacks Ford's old-boys-club cachet. But he has honed a superb constituent-service operation and is one of the better practitioners of finding and pushing the hot buttons back home with television ads and franked mail. In 1990, he was singled out by *The Wall Street Journal* as one of the best examples of a member who has solidified his base with the tools of incumbency while having accomplished relatively little legislatively.

He is also perceived as having some influence with President Bush; McConnell was one of the few senators who supported Bush over Senate Minority Leader Bob Dole of Kansas during the 1988 presidential primary.

McConnell's political antenna, as good as it is, has on occasion been known to malfunction. In 1989, McConnell proposed allowing federal law enforcement agents to shoot down planes suspected of drug-trafficking. But the proposal, after being initially adopted, was ultimately rejected after Democrat John Glenn of Ohio took to the floor to argue, "If I have ever seen anything that I thought was posturing on behalf of the U.S. Senate, this is it."

A former political science professor, McConnell compensates for his lack of charm by studying an issue to the point where he knows more about it than most of his colleagues.

In the 100th Congress, he found a chance to move down the learning curve with one of the most divisive issues to come before the Senate by helping to lead the Republican filibuster against Democratic campaign finance legislation. The Democrats tried, and failed, to shut off debate a record eight times.

McConnell's stance has become the GOP line in the Senate, and as the ethics of public office became a hot political issue in early 1989, his role seemed ready to widen further. Late in the 100th Congress, Dole named McConnell to head a task force on campaign finance law.

McConnell has proposed banning political action committee (PAC) contributions and decreasing out-of-state individual contributions, and he seeks to enhance the role of party committees by letting them spend more on campaigns. In essence, the finance system he envisions plays to the strengths of the GOP, which has a large individual donor base and a sophisticated party operation, but a worsening record of collecting PAC money. McConnell's opposition to Democratic plans stems first from their attempt to limit campaign spending, and second from their reliance on various public financing schemes to induce adherence to the spending limit.

In the 101st Congress, McConnell, the floor manager of the GOP bill, could not prevent passage of a Democratic measure that offered incentives such as reduced television and mail costs, as well as public funds in some instances, to candidates who limited their spending. But the measure died in conference along with a Democratic House bill. McConnell continued his resistance to similar Democratic proposals in the 102nd Congress.

In 1990, McConnell tried to parlay his success in protecting GOP fundraising into the chairmanship of the National Republican Senatorial Committee. But he suffered the first electoral defeat of his career when colleagues chose Phil Gramm of Texas.

On Agriculture, McConnell's guiding philosophy has been, in his own words: "When it comes to tobacco, I'm prepared to wheel and deal." He did just that in 1985, helping Democrats get a farm bill out of the Agriculture Committee in exchange for Democratic backing of a revamped tobacco price-support system that was being considered in Finance.

Democratic Sens. David Pryor of Arkansas and David L. Boren of Oklahoma — both members of Agriculture as well as Finance — agreed to support tobacco in the Finance Committee if McConnell would back their farm bill in Agriculture. The Republican agreed, even though during three previous months of farm bill markups he had voted faithfully with GOP farm proposals pushed by Jesse Helms and Dole.

"My only interest is in the 150,000 people in Kentucky who grow tobacco," McConnell said after the September 1985 committee vote, although he added that his commitment to the Democratic measure was only temporary. "I have cooperated in getting the farm bill out on the floor. I'm not bound by that vote on the floor." Later, McConnell voted with nearly every other GOP senator for a Dole-drafted compromise farm bill that passed the Senate.

But on U.S. policy toward South Africa, McConnell quickly made it clear he was not comfortable with the party line. "I think the administration is not in touch with reality on this issue," he said in June 1985. "We don't want young people in this country to think that only liberal senators are interested in doing something about a 17th-century society."

McConnell joined with Delaware Republican William V. Roth Jr. to offer a package of sanctions against South Africa that struck a middle ground between the White House position and stiffer penalties sought by Sens. Edward M. Kennedy, Democrat of Massachusetts and Lowell P. Weicker Jr., Republican of Connecticut. This bill served as a starting point for the Foreign Relations Committee as it went on to write the sanctions bill that eventually became law over President Ronald Reagan's veto.

The venture seemed to whet McConnell's appetite for the foreign policy realm; at the beginning of the 100th Congress, he left his seats on the Judiciary and Intelligence committees and took a spot on Foreign Relations. McConnell has shown himself open-minded and amenable to argument, but he tries to be a GOP loyalist. During the 101st Congress, he successfully led the fight for confirmation of Bush appointee Donald Gregg to be ambassador of South Korea. Democrats had reservations about the role of Gregg, a former CIA official and Bush aide, during the Iran-contra scandal.

At Home: Three things brought McConnell to Congress: bloodhounds, Reagan and dogged persistence in the face of daunting odds.

And three things have kept him there: bloodhounds, infighting between state Democrats and a record of looking out for Kentucky's interests that spurred even some Democrats to move into his camp in 1990.

For much of 1984, few people believed McConnell had much chance of defeating two-term Democratic Sen. Walter D. Huddleston. Even some GOP leaders complained that McConnell had a "citified" image that would not play well in most parts of Kentucky; his base was metropolitan Louisville, where he had twice been elected Jefferson County judge, the county's top administrative post.

McConnell's campaign struggled for quite a long time; he even lost the endorsement of Marlow Cook, the last Republican to win a Senate election in Kentucky and McConnell's boss when he was a Senate aide in the 1960s. At times, it seemed that McConnell's bid was surviving on little more than the candidate's fierce ambition to be a senator, a goal he admitted having harbored for two decades.

Then the challenger hit upon a clever, homey gimmick to get across his claim that Huddleston was a senator of limited influence who was often absent from committee meetings. McConnell aired TV ads showing bloodhounds sniffing frantically around Washington in search of the incumbent.

The hound dog gimmick got people talking about a race they had ignored, and many concluded McConnell had a point — they were not exactly sure what Huddleston had been doing since he went to Congress in 1973. The incumbent, an easygoing mainstream Democrat, had worked behind the scenes on Kentucky issues, such as tobacco and coal, never causing much controversy and never earning much publicity.

Huddleston's overconfident campaign failed to devise an imaginative counter to McConnell's ads, and with Reagan crushing Walter F. Mondale by more than 280,000 votes statewide, McConnell had long coattails to latch onto. He won by four-tenths of a percentage point.

In 1990, McConnell — confronting a 2-1 Democratic registration ratio -- was tabbed as one of the most vulnerable Republicans up for re-election. But, unlike his predecessor, McConnell came out early and tough. He brought back the TV bloodhounds, this time to bark up the fact that he had made 99 percent of the votes cast during his first term, and was thus no Huddleston.

Former Louisville Mayor Harvey I. Sloane emerged from a bloody Democratic primary as one of the best-heeled Senate challengers in the country. But McConnell, a polished debater with a flair for cutting, sometimes snide repartee, kept Sloane on the defensive from the start. He needled Sloane about his Yale University schooling, his vacation home in Canada and his wealth — particularly his holdings in Exxon Corp. stock, which Sloane declined to sell and which McConnell suggested had increased in value during the Persian Gulf crisis.

Sloane, a non-practicing physician, was also plagued throughout the campaign by revelations that he had once prescribed himself sleeping pills during a 20-month period, contrary to accepted medical practice and without renewing his permit for prescribing drugs.

McConnell effectively portrayed himself as the defender of the common man against what he said was the East Coast liberalism of Sloane. Although several local Democratic officials endorsed McConnell, Sloane belatedly managed to rally top Democrats into his fold, including Ford and Louisville Mayor Jerry Abramson, who agreed to appear in television spots.

The campaign became increasingly negative; Sloane and the Louisville *Courier-Journal* accused McConnell of exaggerating his record. Both candidates also levied charges that each had connections to troubled savings and loan institutions.

In the final days of the campaign, Sloane appeared to ride the wave of anti-incumbent sentiment to close the gap, but he came up short with 48 percent.

A lifelong political overachiever, McConnell was student body president in high school and college, and president of the student bar association at law school. After earning his law degree in 1967, he worked for Cook and then served as deputy assistant U.S. attorney general in the Ford administration. In his 1977 campaign for Jefferson County judge, McConnell defeated a Democratic incumbent; four years later, he won re-election by a narrow margin and started laying the groundwork for a statewide campaign.

Committees

Agriculture, Nutrition & Forestry (5th of 8 Republicans)
Nutrition & Investigations (ranking); Agricultural Production & Stabilization of Prices; Domestic & Foreign Marketing & Product Promotion

Foreign Relations (6th of 8 Republicans)
International Economic Policy, Trade, Oceans & Environment (ranking); East Asian & Pacific Affairs; Terrorism, Narcotics & International Operations

Rules & Administration (7th of 7 Republicans)

Elections

1990 General		
Mitch McConnell (R)	478,034	(52%)
Harvey I. Sloane (D)	437,976	(48%)
1990 Primary		
Mitch McConnell (R)	64,063	(89%)
Tommy Klein (R)	8,310	(11%)

Previous Winning Percentage: **1984** (50%)

Campaign Finance

	Receipts	Receipts from PACs		Expend-itures
1990				
McConnell (R)	$4,073,583	$1,076,029	(26%)	$5,074,187
Sloane (D)	$2,571,559	$518,688	(20%)	$2,927,624

Key Votes

1991	
Authorize use of force against Iraq	Y
1990	
Oppose prohibition of certain semiautomatic weapons	Y
Support constitutional amendment on flag desecration	Y
Oppose requiring parental notice for minors' abortions	N
Halt production of B-2 stealth bomber at 13 planes	N
Approve budget that cut spending and raised revenues	N
Pass civil rights bill over Bush veto	N
1989	
Oppose reduction of SDI funding	Y
Oppose barring federal funds for "obscene" art	N
Allow vote on capital gains tax cut	Y

Voting Studies

	Presidential Support		Party Unity		Conservative Coalition	
Year	**S**	**O**	**S**	**O**	**S**	**O**
1990	78	22	84	15	92	5
1989	82	18	94	6	97	3
1988	85	15	80	18	92	8
1987	65	32	85	13	91	6
1986	87	13	90	10	92	8
1985	85	14	82	16	90	8

Interest Group Ratings

Year	ADA	ACU	AFL-CIO	CCUS
1990	0	87	33	92
1989	10	89	20	75
1988	5	92	29	93
1987	10	80	33	89
1986	0	83	7	89
1985	5	78	10	79

1 Carroll Hubbard Jr. (D)

Of Mayfield — Elected 1974

Born: July 7, 1937, Murray, Ky.

Education: Georgetown College, B.S. 1959; U. of Louisville, J.D. 1962.

Military Service: Ky. Air National Guard, 1962-67; Ky. Army National Guard, 1968-70.

Occupation: Lawyer.

Family: Wife, Carol Brown; two children, three stepchildren.

Religion: Baptist.

Political Career: Ky. Senate, 1968-75; sought Democratic nomination for governor, 1979.

Capitol Office: 2268 Rayburn Bldg. 20515; 225-3115.

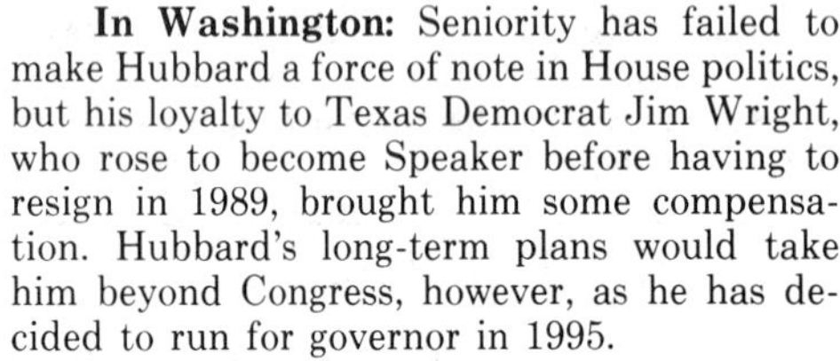

In Washington: Seniority has failed to make Hubbard a force of note in House politics, but his loyalty to Texas Democrat Jim Wright, who rose to become Speaker before having to resign in 1989, brought him some compensation. Hubbard's long-term plans would take him beyond Congress, however, as he has decided to run for governor in 1995.

At Wright's behest, Hubbard served as an at-large party whip for five consecutive terms. Since the 100th Congress, he has been a regional whip, responsible for lining up Democrats in his state and four others.

In the early 1980s, Hubbard found it easier to find a place as a party insider in the Wright regime than to establish a position of legislative influence.

In 1983, Hubbard was in line for a Banking subcommittee chairmanship when the important Economic Stabilization panel came open. However, John J. LaFalce of New York, who was one place behind Hubbard in seniority on Banking, got that chairmanship instead.

At the time, there was talk Hubbard had been asked to stand aside by colleagues who viewed LaFalce as better equipped intellectually for the post. Hubbard insists he never was interested in the job and never pursued it. Hubbard did not go after the Economic Stabilization chairmanship at the start of the 100th Congress, when LaFalce moved on to become chairman of the Small Business Committee.

Instead, Hubbard kept his chairmanship of the Banking Subcommittee on General Oversight and Investigations, which he had assumed at the start of the 99th Congress. His panel held hearings on several issues related to the savings and loan crisis in the 100th Congress.

But unlike Banking Chairman Henry B. Gonzalez of Texas, who became an aggressive inquisitor into the S&L crisis and the collapse of the $5.7 billion Lincoln Savings and Loan Association of California, Hubbard sympathized with the federal regulators who were accused of delaying action against Lincoln, defending his longtime friend, M. Danny Wall, who was the top thrift regulator. Wall was a target of House Democrats in general, and Gonzalez in particular, who pressured him to resign.

Hubbard also defended the senators who were charged with improperly intervening with thrift regulators in Lincoln's behalf. Hubbard himself had called Wall, who was chairman of the Federal Home Loan Bank Board, seeking a "status report" on a proposal to sell Lincoln and avoid its seizure by the government. Wall said there was nothing improper about Hubbard's call.

Hubbard is a champion of "little" banks. During the House-Senate conference on the 1989 S&L bailout bill, he joined Democrats Gerald D. Kleczka of Wisconsin and Nancy Pelosi of California in engineering the removal of a provision opposed by smaller banks that would have required all banks to have annual, outside audits.

The 101st Congress saw Hubbard rescind two longstanding positions: his opposition to abortion and to gun control. Following the Supreme Court's 1989 *Webster* decision, Hubbard, whose wife, a possible congressional candidate in 1992, supports abortion rights, voted to allow federal funds to be used for abortions in cases of rape or incest. He had opposed a similar amendment in 1988. He later voted for an amendment that would have allowed privately paid abortions to be performed at overseas military hospitals.

"I admit to you I've voted wrong on this issue in the past years," he told the House in 1989. He said during a Lexington TV public affairs program that Congress should uphold the 1973 *Roe v. Wade* decision that legalized abortion if the Supreme Court changes or reverses it. "If the vote comes in the Congress, where the issue is 'pro-choice' for women in the first three months [of pregnancy], I would vote

Kentucky 1

West — Paducah

The birthplace of Jefferson Davis, Kentucky's 1st District has a stronger Deep South flavor than any other part of the state.

In contests for governor and for the U.S. Senate, the 1st usually turns in solid Democratic majorities. Democratic Senate candidate Harvey Sloane carried 13 of the 24 counties in the 1st in his 1990 statewide loss to GOP Sen. Mitch McConnell. Jimmy Carter won the district in 1976 and 1980, and even Massachusetts Democrat Michael S. Dukakis nearly won it in 1988. Year in and year out, the only district in the state as faithfully Democratic as the 1st is eastern Kentucky's 7th District, which also is influenced by the United Mine Workers. Registration is over 80 percent Democratic.

The 1st is the only part of Kentucky where cotton is grown. The western lowlands near the Mississippi River — known as the Jackson Purchase — were once slaveholding territory. Today, the 1st does not have a massive black population; only one of the 24 counties in the district is over 20 percent black. But the heritage of the 1st and its relative poverty made it fertile ground for the rural populism of George C. Wallace. Four of the five Kentucky counties Wallace carried in his 1968 presidential campaign are in the 1st.

Like Wallace's success in 1968, the presidential victories by Ronald Reagan and George Bush in the 1st indicated that voters there are not so bound by tradition that they will accept any Democratic presidential nominee.

Four TV markets reach western Kentucky, but no city in the 1st has more than 30,000 people. Most of the area is closely tied to agriculture; soybeans and dark-fired (or smokeless) tobacco are major crops. Coal fields provide employment in the northeastern part of the district. Relatively small factories producing textiles and chemicals are prominent in cities such as Paducah and Hopkinsville.

The Ohio River port of Paducah (McCracken County) long has been the population center and political capital of western Kentucky. It was the home of Alben W. Barkley, longtime Democratic senator and vice president under Harry S Truman. Barkley helped provide an economic shot in the arm to Paducah by steering an Atomic Energy Commission plant to the area.

Southeast of Paducah is Hopkinsville (Christian County), an agricultural market and trade center for the nearby Fort Campbell military base. With its mobile population, the Hopkinsville area has more independent voting habits than the rest of the 1st.

Population: 525,844. White 475,701 (90%), Black 46,405 (9%). Spanish origin 4,662 (1%). 18 and over 379,011 (72%), 65 and over 72,755 (14%). Median age: 31.

the 'pro-choice' viewpoint."

Also in 1989, Hubbard tempered his adamant aversion to gun-control measures. After highly publicized shooting sprees in Stockton, Calif., and Louisville, Hubbard signed on as a cosponsor to a bill that would have limited the importation and domestic manufacture of certain semiautomatic assault weapons. And after voting in 1988 against a seven-day waiting period for handgun purchases — known as the Brady bill — Hubbard in 1989 said that he would vote for it. He voted for the Brady bill in 1991.

Hubbard has always put great stock in the prevailing public opinion in his district. He publicizes the results of his "Hubbard poll," a yearly questionnaire on issues that he sends to his constituents. He told the Louisville *Courier-Journal* that his constituents supported a ban on assault weapons and that since *Webster*, "the tide seems to be turning" in favor of abortion rights.

Most of Hubbard's legislative activities have a district orientation. He has worked to secure projects for the Department of Energy's gaseous diffusion plant in West Paducah. In 1986, Hubbard spoke out on behalf of his district's satellite television dish owners, who were upset by signal-scrambling that had been instituted by some TV program providers. "Today the No. 1 issue here in Washington is aid to the contras in Nicaragua," Hubbard told the Energy and Commerce Subcommittee on Telecommunications. "But in portions of western Kentucky, aid to satellite-dish owners is also important."

At Home: Hubbard's political enemies hoped his political career had come full circle in 1988. His aggressive primary challenger attacked him as a generally lethargic legislator and a chronic absentee from congressional committee meetings — a line of assault that Hubbard had generally followed in ousting veteran Democratic

Rep. Frank Stubblefield in 1974. But on primary night, the only similarity with that earlier campaign was that Hubbard had won.

Challenger Lacey T. Smith had the resources to defeat Hubbard in 1988. A wealthy lawyer, businessman and former state senator, Smith pumped roughly $500,000 of his own money into a high-profile campaign portraying the incumbent as a "pen pal" more effective at sending calendars and congratulatory letters to his constituents than at promoting the district's economic development.

But Smith was stung by media accounts of his controversial past, which included an indictment for influence-peddling while an aide to Louisville Mayor Harvey Sloane in the mid-1970s (he was later acquitted) and a reputation for high living when he resided in south Florida in the mid-1980s.

Meanwhile, Hubbard ran effective advertising that twitted Smith as a well-to-do carpetbagger whose interest in economically beleaguered western Kentucky was limited to its House seat. The final result was not even close: Hubbard swept all 24 counties in the district and outpolled Smith by a margin of nearly 3-to-1.

In the staunchly Democratic 1st, Hubbard's only serious contests have come in the 1974 and 1988 primaries. And organized labor, led by the United Mine Workers, was in his corner both times. In 1974, labor backing helped Hubbard overcome Stubblefield's support from farmers and the official courthouse organizations to win by 629 votes out of nearly 60,000 cast.

In contrast to Hubbard's firm grip on his House seat, his one attempt to broaden his appeal statewide — a 1979 gubernatorial bid — ended in defeat. His campaign, based on his brand of personal politics, got lost in the confusion of a nine-candidate field, forcing him to try to use his House office to gain publicity. Without large-scale funding or the support of any significant party bloc, he was never really a factor. He finished a distant fourth with only 12 percent of the vote, carrying his home district but little else.

Hubbard announced after his landslide 1990 re-election that he planned to seek the governorship in 1995, but that he would seek re-election to Congress in 1992 and 1994.

Committees

Banking, Finance & Urban Affairs (4th of 31 Democrats)
General Oversight (chairman); Consumer Affairs & Coinage; Financial Institutions Supervision, Regulation & Insurance; Housing & Community Development

Merchant Marine & Fisheries (3rd of 29 Democrats)
Merchant Marine

Elections

1990 General		
Carroll Hubbard Jr. (D)	85,323	(87%)
Marvin H. Seat (POP)	12,879	(13%)
1988 General		
Carroll Hubbard Jr. (D)	117,288	(95%)
Charles K. Hatchett (I)	6,106	(5%)

Previous Winning Percentages: **1986** (100%) **1984** (100%) **1982** (100%) **1980** (100%) **1978** (100%) **1976** (82%) **1974** (78%)

District Vote For President

	1988		1984		1980		1976	
D	92,391	(49%)	87,339	(45%)	102,503	(54%)	114,194	(65%)
R	96,150	(51%)	104,613	(54%)	83,296	(44%)	59,226	(34%)

Campaign Finance

	Receipts	Receipts from PACs		Expend-itures
1990				
Hubbard (D)	$351,966	$271,327	(77%)	$239,620
1988				
Hubbard (D)	$518,338	$356,663	(69%)	$546,908

Key Votes

1991	
Authorize use of force against Iraq	Y
1990	
Support constitutional amendment on flag desecration	Y
Pass family and medical leave bill over Bush veto	N
Reduce SDI funding	Y
Allow abortions in overseas military facilities	Y
Approve budget summit plan for spending and taxing	N
Approve civil rights bill	Y
1989	
Halt production of B-2 stealth bomber at 13 planes	N
Oppose capital gains tax cut	N
Approve federal abortion funding in rape or incest cases	Y
Approve pay raise and revision of ethics rules	Y
Pass Democratic minimum wage plan over Bush veto	?

Voting Studies

	Presidential Support		Party Unity		Conservative Coalition	
Year	**S**	**O**	**S**	**O**	**S**	**O**
1990	42	57	59	40	83	13
1989	49	50	64	35	83	17
1988	39	58	67	30	68	24
1987	36	53	57	33	74	12
1986	52	48	49	49	94	6
1985	59	36	48	44	76	15
1984	46	43	37	52	73	20
1983	46	35	44	46	70	25
1982	55	42	43	47	86	11
1981	58	41	49	48	87	13

Interest Group Ratings

Year	ADA	ACU	AFL-CIO	CCUS
1990	39	52	42	79
1989	50	58	64	89
1988	50	54	86	50
1987	52	19	81	53
1986	35	59	86	50
1985	20	63	63	68
1984	30	67	82	55
1983	50	55	82	42
1982	25	64	50	71
1981	25	40	71	37

2 William H. Natcher (D)

Of Bowling Green — Elected 1953

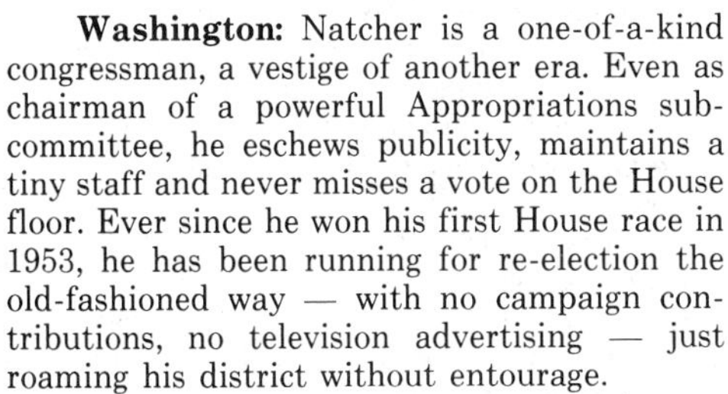

Born: Sept. 11, 1909, Bowling Green, Ky.

Education: Western Kentucky U., B.A. 1930; Ohio State U., LL.B. 1933.

Military Service: Navy, 1942-45.

Occupation: Lawyer.

Family: Widowed; two children.

Religion: Baptist.

Political Career: Federal conciliation commissioner of western Kentucky, 1936-37; Warren County attorney, 1937-49; commonwealth attorney, 8th judicial district, 1951-53.

Capitol Office: 2333 Rayburn Bldg. 20515; 225-3501.

Washington: Natcher is a one-of-a-kind congressman, a vestige of another era. Even as chairman of a powerful Appropriations subcommittee, he eschews publicity, maintains a tiny staff and never misses a vote on the House floor. Ever since he won his first House race in 1953, he has been running for re-election the old-fashioned way — with no campaign contributions, no television advertising — just roaming his district without entourage.

Natcher's gentlemanly manner and commitment to the House as an institution has earned him respect even from the most partisan Republicans. "He reminds you of the world that once was, in which politics happens in your district and governing happens in Washington," Republican firebrand Newt Gingrich of Georgia once said.

When contentious floor debates are imminent, Natcher is often called to the speaker's chair. Respected for his evenhanded, controlled judgment, Natcher keeps partisans in order with legendary parliamentary precision. He memorized Roberts Rules of Order while in law school in 1933, and first presided over the House in 1954, just four months after arriving in Congress.

Natcher's exacting nature carries over to many aspects of his life. He dresses carefully, votes carefully and keeps a detailed diary of his everyday life.

Of Natcher's many accomplishments, one is listed in the "Guinness Book of World Records": his 16,900 — and counting — consecutive votes. Natcher says he didn't notice his perfect record until five years into his term, when a House clerk pointed it out. While he made up his mind to keep the record, Natcher has sacrificed personally and professionally to sustain it, and he advises junior members to miss a vote early on. For two weeks some years ago, he flew between Kentucky and Washington daily to be with his ill wife, and in 1979 he missed a trip to his district by President Jimmy Carter — all to keep his streak unbroken.

A member of the Appropriations Committee since his second year in the House, Natcher helped set the standard of collegiality that for decades has defined the panel. While his refusal to fund unauthorized projects and his great reluctance to earmark funds for specific projects now seem out of step, he is not a man to bend with the times. But whether Natcher — the No. 2 Democrat on the committee - ever gets a chance to impose the old order beyond his subcommittee depends on whether his close friend, Democratic Chairman Jamie L. Whitten of Mississippi, relinquishes the gavel any time soon.

In the meantime, Natcher already has more power than most full committee chairmen. Whitten trusts Natcher implicitly and often defers to his judgment. And the Appropriations Subcommittee on Labor, Health and Human Services, and Education, which Natcher chairs, has more expansive jurisdiction than any other subcommittee but Defense.

Natcher's share of the budget pie has grown to more than $170 billion, even after a decade of budget cuts. But the percentage left to discretionary funds has fallen to just a little more than a quarter of that budget, as demands on the untouchable entitlements have grown. Even so, Natcher proudly points out that funding for the National Institutes of Health has grown from $73 million when he was first elected to more than $8.3 billion today.

"I have always believed that if you take care of the health of your people and educate your children, you continue living in the strongest country in the world," he says time and again.

While Natcher has had an increasingly difficult time stifling efforts to use his bill for social policy debate — particularly on abortion — he is not a man to be stampeded, either by the Senate or by his more aggressive House colleagues. When he wants to, Natcher can sit

Kentucky 2

West Central — Owensboro

Perched between the staunchly Democratic 1st and the reliably Republican 5th, the 2nd is a swing district in state and national elections.

Republicans are consistent winners in only three small counties — Allen, Edmonson and Grayson, hotbeds of Union support during the Civil War. But in good Republican years, statewide GOP candidates also have a chance to carry the three major population centers — Daviess County (Owensboro), Hardin County (Elizabethtown) and Warren County (Bowling Green), which together cast nearly half the district's vote. In 1990, GOP Sen. Mitch McConnell won all three counties.

The district includes parts of three distinct areas: the Bluegrass region in the east, the Louisville suburbs in the north and the rolling hill country of the Pennyrile in the southwest. The geographic heart of the 2nd is the Knobs area, a region of sinkholes and caves that includes the Mammoth Cave National Park. Although primarily agricultural, the district has some light industry in Owensboro and Bowling Green.

Warren County (Bowling Green) grew 24 percent in the 1970s, marking the largest increase in any of the district's major population centers, and another seven percent in the 1980s. Bowling Green is the home of Western Kentucky University, with almost 12,000 students, the largest college in the state west of Louisville.

Outside the population centers, the fastest growth has been in Bullitt County, a part of the Louisville suburbs. A busing plan in metropolitan Louisville helped fuel a 66 percent growth rate in neighboring Bullitt during the 1970s, although the growth rate has slowed markedly during the more placid 1980s. With a sizable blue-collar element that frequently bolts the Democratic ticket, Bullitt was the only Kentucky county outside the 1st to vote for George C. Wallace for president in 1968. Both Reagan and McConnell won it in 1984. In the 1988 presidential contest, George Bush clobbered Democratic nominee Michael S. Dukakis.

Along the Ohio River in the northwest corner of the district is Owensboro, the largest city in the 2nd and the third-largest in the state. Nearby oil and coal fields and a large General Electric plant provide an industrial base.

Between Owensboro and Louisville is Hardin County, the home of Fort Knox. The rest of the district is rural. Tobacco and livestock are mainstays of the economy. Republicans are strongest in the poorer farm counties in the center of the district; Democrats run best in the outer Bluegrass counties to the northeast.

Population: 520,634. White 483,696 (93%), Black 31,693 (6%), Other 2,752 (1%). Spanish origin 5,441 (1%). 18 and over 361,229 (69%), 65 and over 52,022 (10%). Median age: 27.

in meetings for day after day waiting for others to meet his terms. But sometimes Natcher seems to care more about getting his bill signed into law than about the details of what it contains.

After assertive abortion rights members stripped decade-old language prohibiting abortion in cases of rape and incest in 1989, Natcher was caught between his desire to pass his appropriation bill and his opposition to abortion. He wound up voting for the bill on final passage, despite the abortion amendment he had opposed, and then voted to override President Bush's veto. When the override failed, Natcher introduced a bill that was identical except for lacking the abortion language, and the House quickly passed it.

All the while he is overseeing a huge slice of the federal budget, Natcher makes sure his predominantly rural Kentucky district gets its share. He has secured local funding for programs from flood control to education of the disadvantaged.

Despite a tooth-and-nail fight, though, even the respected Natcher could not prevent a major defeat for his district's powerful tobacco interests in 1987, when Congress passed an amendment banning smoking on airplane flights of at least two hours' duration. After Natcher blocked the ban in subcommittee and full committee, it passed on the House floor, and in 1989 was made permanent.

Natcher inherited the Labor-HHS Subcommittee chair in 1979 from Daniel J. Flood. And he soon attracted attention by announcing that he wanted to close the subcommittee's markup session and then presiding over an 8-4 vote that closed it for the first time in many years. Lobbyists swarmed outside the committee room, and Natcher said it would be difficult to produce a fiscally responsible bill had they been allowed to record how the members voted. Natcher has kept his subcommittee markups closed ever since.

Before that, he spent 18 years as chairman of one of the least politically appealing Appropriations subcommittees, on the District of Columbia. Natcher clashed often with Washington city officials — particularly over the subway system then on the drawing boards. Three years in a row he delayed the D.C. budget for months while he pressured local officials to finish their highway projects before demanding subway money. Natcher got much of what he wanted.

Natcher's response to media criticism is to ignore it. He seldom grants interviews. He refuses to allow reporters to accompany him on campaign trips. Natcher does issue one press release a year. It announces the new record he has set for attendance at roll calls on the House floor.

At Home: Nearly as important to Natcher as his perfect voting record is his persistent refusal to accept campaign contributions. The small political bills he incurs, seldom more than $5,000 per election, he pays himself. "Some people are spending $1 million on House races," Natcher once lamented. "That's wrong. It's morally wrong. I don't believe they can really represent their people if they are taking money from these groups [political action committees]."

It was no great burden for Natcher to pay his campaign expenses; he usually escaped serious opposition. But in 1982 and 1984, Natcher faced primary fights that would have induced most other incumbents to collect and spend bundles of cash. Natcher stuck to his old ways; he spent only about $21,000 in both years combined, all from his own pocket.

In 1982, three major challengers felt that Natcher was aging and might be ripe for an upset. They contended that he was too eccentric and too liberal for the rural 2nd. His personal frugality, they said, masked a liberal big spender who voted for all major appropriations bills. Altogether, Natcher's foes spent more than $400,000 on the campaign, not including thousands of dollars that the National Conservative Political Action Committee pumped into an independent anti-Natcher ad campaign.

To Natcher's advantage, his primary rivals came from the three corners of the far-flung district; none was well-known outside his home area. With a low turnout and a regional split in the anti-Natcher vote, the incumbent carried all but one of the district's 18 counties, winning renomination with 60 percent.

In 1984, Natcher was challenged by Democratic state Sen. Frank Miller, who as chairman of the Senate Banking and Insurance Committee had access to ample funding. Miller, copying the 1982 attempt to portray Natcher as penny-wise but pound-foolish, complained that he had not used his leadership position on Appropriations to curb the federal deficit. But Natcher won with 70 percent of the vote.

No matter who challenges him, Natcher campaigns in his same old-fashioned manner. He shuns "media events," reporters and other campaign entourage, preferring to drive through the district unaccompanied and stop to chat with people in courthouses and Main Street stores, delivering a simple message: "I'm Bill Natcher, up there in Washington trying to do a good job for you."

Though Natcher does not command a formidable political machine — many of those who helped him secure the district in the 1950s are no longer politically active — he still keeps in touch with a few influential people in most towns. And most average voters know about his refusal to accept campaign contributions, about his attendance record, and about the millions of dollars in federal money he has brought the district. Also, the accumulated weight of nearly four decades of constituent service means that Natcher's work has touched just about every family in the 2nd.

Natcher had congressional ambitions even as a teenager. After serving in several local political offices in Warren County (Bowling Green) and as president of the Kentucky Young Democrats, he got his chance in 1953, when Democratic Rep. Garrett L. Withers died. Party leaders united behind him, and he won without opposition in a special election.

Since then, the success of GOP presidential and statewide candidates in the 2nd has occasionally encouraged the party to make bids to unseat Natcher. But Republicans came close to beating him only once, in 1956, when Dwight D. Eisenhower's coattails pulled the GOP candidate to within 3,000 votes of victory.

Committee

Appropriations (2nd of 37 Democrats)
Labor, Health & Human Services, Education & Related Agencies (chairman); District of Columbia; Rural Development, Agriculture & Related Agencies

Elections

1990 General

William H. Natcher (D)	77,057	(66%)
Martin Tori (R)	39,624	(34%)

1988 General

William H. Natcher (D)	92,184	(61%)
Martin A. Tori (R)	59,907	(39%)

Previous Winning Percentages: **1986** (100%) **1984** (62%)

1982	(74%)	**1980**	(66%)	**1978**	(100%)	**1976**	(60%)
1974	(73%)	**1972**	(62%)	**1970**	(100%)	**1968**	(56%)
1966	(59%)	**1964**	(68%)	**1962**	(100%)	**1960**	(100%)
1958	(76%)	**1956**	(52%)	**1954**	(100%)	**1953** *	(100%)

* *Special election.*

District Vote For President

	1988	1984	1980	1976
D	72,768 (41%)	64,163 (36%)	78,356 (47%)	75,633 (55%)
R	102,721 (58%)	112,019 (63%)	83,861 (50%)	60,030 (44%)
I			3,009 (2%)	

Campaign Finance

	Receipts	Receipts from PACs		Expend-itures
1990				
Natcher (D)	$6,768	0		$6,766
Tori (R)	$144,166	$1,600	(1%)	$144,315
1988				
Natcher (D)	$8,397	0		$8,397
Tori (R)	$84,270	$1,950	(2%)	$84,102

Key Votes

1991

Authorize use of force against Iraq	N

1990

Support constitutional amendment on flag desecration	Y
Pass family and medical leave bill over Bush veto	Y
Reduce SDI funding	Y
Allow abortions in overseas military facilities	N
Approve budget summit plan for spending and taxing	N
Approve civil rights bill	Y

1989

Halt production of B-2 stealth bomber at 13 planes	N
Oppose capital gains tax cut	N
Approve federal abortion funding in rape or incest cases	N
Approve pay raise and revision of ethics rules	Y
Pass Democratic minimum wage plan over Bush veto	Y

Voting Studies

	Presidential Support		Party Unity		Conservative Coalition	
Year	**S**	**O**	**S**	**O**	**S**	**O**
1990	29	71	86	14	67	33
1989	49	51	83	17	61	39
1988	26	74	94	6	42	58
1987	34	66	91	9	65	35
1986	29	71	89	11	58	42
1985	30	70	87	13	56	44
1984	34	66	85	15	46	54
1983	32	68	83	17	53	47
1982	48	52	74	26	63	37
1981	54	46	69	31	75	25

Interest Group Ratings

Year	ADA	ACU	AFL-CIO	CCUS
1990	61	25	75	36
1989	65	25	83	50
1988	75	16	100	21
1987	76	13	94	13
1986	65	23	93	28
1985	60	24	76	23
1984	60	29	69	44
1983	65	26	82	25
1982	55	41	80	55
1981	35	20	80	26

3 Romano L. Mazzoli (D)

Of Louisville — Elected 1970

Born: Nov. 2, 1932, Louisville, Ky.

Education: U. of Notre Dame, B.S. 1954; U. of Louisville, J.D. 1960.

Military Service: Army, 1954-56.

Occupation: Lawyer; law professor.

Family: Wife, Helen Dillon; two children.

Religion: Roman Catholic.

Political Career: Ky. Senate, 1968-70; sought Democratic nomination for mayor of Louisville, 1969.

Capitol Office: 2246 Rayburn Bldg. 20515; 225-5401.

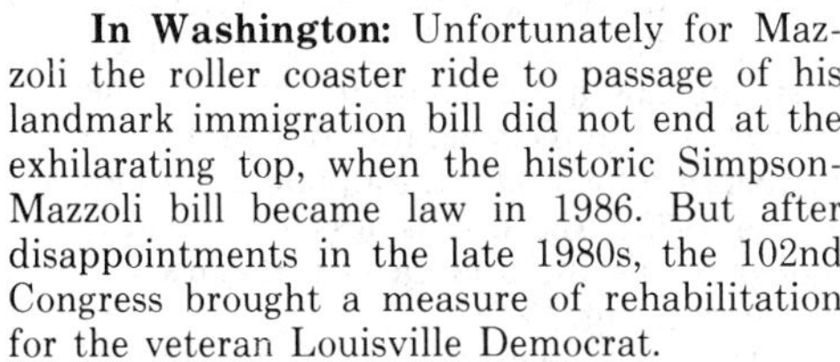

In Washington: Unfortunately for Mazzoli the roller coaster ride to passage of his landmark immigration bill did not end at the exhilarating top, when the historic Simpson-Mazzoli bill became law in 1986. But after disappointments in the late 1980s, the 102nd Congress brought a measure of rehabilitation for the veteran Louisville Democrat.

In 1991 — two years after Democrats on the Judiciary Committee ousted Mazzoli from the chairmanship of the Immigration Subcommittee — they returned him to the chair, which had been vacated by a member who unsuccessfully sought statewide office.

The seeds of Mazzoli's 1989 rejection were sown during the long, stormy legislative battle over the immigration bill, when he was alternately contentious and withdrawn. He became even more isolated and stolid in the two years after final passage. But at bottom, Mazzoli lost his chairmanship for being a Republican sympathizer on a committee dominated by activist liberal Democrats.

Days before Judiciary Democrats met to ratify their leaders at the outset of the 101st Congress, Mazzoli got word of the impending coup and tried to head it off. But it was too late; the committee voted 16-5 to strip him of the job he had held for eight years. Mazzoli conceded in an interview afterward, "The subcommittee did kind of get a little bit sloppy, a little directionless." Because of his preoccupation with a tough 1988 primary race, Mazzoli said, "I was a bit of an absentee landlord." But he was bitter nonetheless, so much so that there was some speculation he would defect to the GOP.

Mazzoli's views and votes span the political spectrum, which is perhaps not surprising for a member from an urban district in the border South. He first won election in 1970 as an antiwar candidate, he is a strong opponent of abortion, he supports handgun controls, and he often votes with conservatives on budget issues. In the eyes of many Democrats, his most offensive departure from the party script came on the party-line 1985 vote to seat Democratic incumbent Frank McCloskey rather than his GOP rival in a disputed Indiana election. Mazzoli sided with the GOP.

But instead of switching parties after losing his Judiciary chairmanship in 1989, Mazzoli set out to emphasize those aspects of his record that are consistent with Democratic orthodoxy. In the 101st Congress, he sharply criticized President Bush for his reluctance to ban assault rifles, he joined the Democratic chorus for a surtax on millionaires, and he championed campaign finance reform, renouncing political action committee (PAC) money. He kept a low profile as the Immigration Subcommittee steered a legal immigration bill through the 101st Congress, and he shied away from close, public association with Republicans, especially on the controversial issue of abortion policy.

All these efforts help explain why Judiciary's liberal bloc was willing to let Mazzoli retake the subcommittee chair in 1991; he got his gavel back on an 18-3 vote. Also contributing to the liberals' generosity was the fact that little action was slated for the Immigration panel in the 102nd Congress. Mazzoli also has picked up a seat on the panel that makes Democratic committee assignments, which should help him further his fence-mending efforts.

Mazzoli now has a chance to settle back into the style of his early House years, when he was known as hard-working and lawyerlike, a man who quietly tended to details many found too technical to bother with. "We have a lot of wonderful orators here," he once said. "A lot of bright, overwhelmingly intelligent people. But sometimes the modern Demosthenes doesn't carry the day . . . Sometimes those gray drudges can carry the day."

Mazzoli's day was Oct. 17, 1986, when Congress cleared the Simpson-Mazzoli immigration bill. The law penalizes employers who knowingly hire illegal aliens, and offered amnesty to illegal aliens who could prove that they had been in the United States before 1982.

By the time of final passage, however,

Kentucky 3

Louisville and Suburbs

To many rural and small-town Kentuckians, Louisville (population 269,000) is something strange, an influence to be guarded against. In a state where blacks make up just 7 percent of the population, Louisville is almost 30 percent black. It also has an exceptionally large Catholic population, a legacy of massive German immigration in the mid-19th century. And Louisville's *Courier-Journal* newspaper is a leading liberal voice in a state that generally prefers moderate-to-conservative politicians.

Louisville's reputation in the hinterlands seems a bit undeserved, since, in its social history, the city has faced South. Its public places were not fully desegregated until well after World War II. In recent years court-ordered busing has been a major problem, particularly in blue-collar neighborhoods in the South End and in neighboring Shively. The anti-abortion movement is strong within the conservative Catholic constituency.

Louisville's South End is predominantly white, blue-collar and Democratic. Most blacks live near downtown in the West End, an area that regularly turns in heavy Democratic majorities. The affluent, Republican East End includes mansions on the bluffs overlooking the Ohio River.

Louisville Republicans elected two mayors in a row in the 1960s, partly by appealing to black voters against a decayed Democratic organization. But Democrats swept back into City Hall in 1969 and have held it since then. One recent mayor, Harvey I. Sloane, felt the sting of the state's anti-Louisville sentiment three times; he was runner-up in both the 1979 and 1983 Democratic gubernatorial primaries, and lost in the 1990 Senate general election.

The Louisvillian most recently elected to statewide office was not a liberal Democrat, but a conservative Republican — Mitch McConnell, who moved from his job as Jefferson County executive to the U.S. Senate in 1984.

McConnell won a second Senate term in 1990, defeating Sloane.

Prior to 1982 redistricting, the 3rd took in Louisville and only a few of the city's inner suburbs, a combination that made the district reliably Democratic. As redrawn to compensate for Louisville's population loss in the 1970s, the 3rd is less Democratic, though Louisville still casts a majority of the district vote.

Most of the voters added in the remap live south and southeast of the city in such blue-collar communities as Buechel, Fern Creek and Jeffersontown. Many work in suburban Louisville's General Electric and Ford plants. While a large share are registered Democrats, they are swing voters. Their support for Republican candidates frequently puts metropolitan Jefferson County in the GOP column.

Population: 522,252. White 413,605 (79%), Black 104,573 (20%), Other 2,493 (1%). Spanish origin 3,265 (1%). 18 and over 381,792 (73%), 65 and over 63,347 (12%). Median age: 30.

Mazzoli had relinquished the leadership role he had played for most of the process. Emotionally spent from polarizing fights in the two past Congresses, he contented himself with working behind the scenes, lending technical expertise to the debate while others stepped into the spotlight. "The fight's gone out of the dog," one House Democrat said of Mazzoli.

Picking up the mantle of leadership that Mazzoli had let fall were three younger House Democrats: Judiciary's Charles E. Schumer of New York and Howard L. Berman of California, and Californian Leon E. Panetta of the Agriculture Committee. In 1989, Schumer and Berman would be among the leaders of the successful move to unseat Mazzoli, and to install in the Immigration chair a liberal colleague, Bruce A. Morrison of Connecticut.

If Mazzoli sometimes seemed like the forgotten man in the final stages of the immigration bill, GOP Sen. Alan K. Simpson of Wyoming and others who conducted the concluding negotiations left no doubt that Mazzoli had helped make it all possible. Moreover, the Kentucky Democrat had emerged in the end to deal with one of the bill's most controversial aspects — the proposal to establish a permanent "guest worker" program for growers who rely on foreign labor. He helped draft a compromise between growers, who said they needed the help, and organized labor, which insisted the program was exploitative, just when the dispute threatened to sink the entire bill for the third consecutive time.

The first time, during the 97th Congress, the immigration bill had passed the Senate, but did not reach the House floor until the closing days in 1982. At that point, Hispanic Caucus Chairman Edward R. Roybal of California killed it by threatening to demand roll-call votes on more than 100 amendments. When Mazzoli reluctantly pulled the bill, his colleagues gave him a standing ovation for his efforts.

Early in the 98th Congress, the Senate again passed an immigration bill, but Speaker O'Neill refused to bring the issue to the House floor in 1983. The next year, stung by criticism that he was stifling a needed reform for political purposes, O'Neill relented. Mazzoli orchestrated a week of debate on dozens of amendments; he went out of his way to lavish praise on virtually everyone who addressed the subject, even opponents, for making a constructive contribution.

The House narrowly passed the bill, 216-211, after the balance had seesawed until the last seconds. "I begged those guys," Mazzoli said later. "I said, 'For God's sake, don't let us come up empty-handed.' " But as he suspected even then, it was to prove impossible to reach agreement with the Senate. Also, immigration had become an issue in the Democratic Party's presidential campaign, with nominee Walter F. Mondale and the national party leadership joining Hispanics in opposing the bill. Victory would have to wait for the 99th Congress.

Once the bill was law in the 100th Congress, immigration experts monitored implementation. By its first anniversary in late 1987, Mazzoli would proudly say, "Even the most implacable foes of the bill have had to eat some crow."

Meanwhile, his Judiciary colleagues were restless to do more than savor past successes. In 1987, Mazzoli was the only Democrat on his subcommittee and the full committee to join Republicans in opposing a bill to allow extended stays in the United States for refugees of El Salvador and Nicaragua until conditions at home improved. Then Mazzoli proposed an alternative safe-haven bill for refugees of armed conflict or environmental disaster, but it died in the Senate.

His subcommittee Democrats also wanted to extend the 1986 immigration law's amnesty period for another year, to ensure that all eligible aliens took advantage of the opening. And having successfully tackled illegal immigration, they wanted to begin work on revising the legal-immigration system, with its country-by-country quotas and eligibility standards that are widely considered outdated. Mazzoli wanted to undertake neither effort.

Pressed by a majority of his panel, however, Mazzoli finally agreed to a vote on the proposed amnesty extension just weeks before the law's May 1988 deadline. He proposed a six-month extension as a compromise; the full committee, acting within an hour of the subcommittee, settled on seven months. The measure narrowly was passed by the House, but died in a Senate filibuster. The amnesty deadline passed, leaving committee Democrats resentful that Mazzoli had waited until it was too late for action.

At Home: Whether in Washington or Louisville, Mazzoli sometimes seems to encounter as much opposition from fellow Democrats as he does Republicans. Republicans tried to make a run at Mazzoli in 1990, but it has been years since the GOP has seriously tested him at the polls. But on four occasions since 1976 he has drawn significant primary opposition.

A furor over school busing provided the ammunition for the 1976 challenge. Mazzoli at first accepted busing as a means of desegregating the Louisville schools, then switched to an antibusing position after the city's turmoil began. But the shift in positions came too late and was too mild for vocal busing foes. He was held to 56 percent of the primary vote.

The second primary challenge came in 1982, fueled by lingering resentment over the busing crisis and an unfavorable 1982 remap that extended his district deep into the Republican suburbs of Louisville. His opponent, state Rep. Mark O'Brien, sought to tie the busing issue to a controversial school-tax referendum, saying that if there were no busing, the proposed county surtax on the state income tax would be unnecessary. But because O'Brien's campaign was underfinanced and starting late, it turned out to be more smoke than fire; Mazzoli comfortably surpassed the 60 percent mark.

The third primary challenge came in 1988, from Jeffrey Hutter, administrative director of the Humana Heart Institute and a former Louisville TV reporter. He was not especially well financed either, but made up for it with brashness. He accused Mazzoli of ignoring Louisville and voting against its interests. The incumbent "isn't dopey," Hutter said, "but he has been voting like Sleepy."

Hutter had support from the 80,000-member Greater Louisville Central Labor Council, which was upset with Mazzoli for his support of a smoking ban on domestic airplane flights of two hours or less (a vote labor saw as a threat to jobs in the state's lucrative tobacco industry) and his opposition to the Gephardt "fair trade" amendment.

Yet while Hutter carried blue-collar precincts, he could not crack the base that Mazzoli had constructed over nine terms among the district's many Catholic and elderly voters. Mazzoli got 61 percent of the vote.

Hutter tried again in 1990, this time with the backing of several district and city officials. But Mazzoli, who swore off contributions from PACs, had a surprisingly easy time in turning back both Hutter and city alderman Paul Bather in the primary.

In the general election, Mazzoli faced Al Brown, a black labor-relations consultant and a member of the Kentucky Lottery Commission. Brown early on gained the attention and blessing of the national GOP, always eager to promote its black candidates. But Brown had stumbled unexpectedly in the primary, barely defeating a little-known white businessman who had been outspent 10-to-1 and who tapped the political and racial frustrations of blue-collar residents in the south and west ends of Louisville.

Brown, like Hutter, argued that Mazzoli was ineffective in bringing federal projects to the district. Although he described himself as moderate-to-conservative, Brown supported abortion rights, contrasting himself to Mazzoli and his staunch anti-abortion position. Yet Brown, plagued by a lack of funds, could manage only 39 percent of the vote.

Mazzoli's base has shifted a bit since he first ran for the House in 1970. Then, he was an opponent of the Vietnam War, with a strong base among blacks, young liberals and blue-collar Catholics. But the decisive factor in his House victory that year was the bitter intraparty feud between GOP incumbent William O. Cowger and Republican Gov. Louie B. Nunn over local patronage.

Cowger had challenged the governor to run a candidate for Congress against him in the primary. Nunn responded by saying Cowger was in need of a "psychiatric examination." The breach never healed and Mazzoli took advantage of it to win a 211-vote victory.

Since then, Republicans have held Mazzoli below 60 percent only once, in 1976 when Louisville was at the height of the busing furor. The GOP was optimistic about unseating him after the state's 1982 remap expanded the 3rd further into Jefferson County.

However, the GOP challenge was short-circuited by Mazzoli's aggressive efforts to court his new constituents. By a margin of 2-to-1, he overwhelmed GOP nominee Carl Brown, a Jefferson County commissioner, who had trouble raising money and building an organization.

Committees

Judiciary (4th of 21 Democrats)
International Law, Immigration & Refugees (chairman); Administrative Law & Governmental Relations; Economic & Commercial Law

Select Narcotics Abuse & Control (17th of 21 Democrats)

Small Business (4th of 27 Democrats)
Antitrust, Impact of Deregulation & Ecology; SBA, the General Economy & Minority Enterprise Development

Elections

1990 General		
Romano L. Mazzoli (D)	84,750	(61%)
Al Brown (R)	55,188	(39%)
1990 Primary		
Romano L. Mazzoli (D)	28,103	(45%)
Jeffrey Hutter (D)	20,152	(32%)
Paul Bather (D)	13,768	(22%)
1988 General		
Romano L. Mazzoli (D)	131,981	(70%)
Philip Dunnagan (R)	57,387	(30%)

Previous Winning Percentages: **1986** (73%) **1984** (68%) **1982** (65%) **1980** (64%) **1978** (66%) **1976** (57%) **1974** (70%) **1972** (62%) **1970** (49%)

District Vote For President

	1988	1984	1980	1976
D	102,383 (53%)	99,200 (48%)	101,315 (52%)	106,071 (54%)
R	90,291 (47%)	109,042 (52%)	83,848 (43%)	83,972 (43%)
I			6,699 (4%)	

Campaign Finance

	Receipts	Receipts from PACs	Expend-itures
1990			
Mazzoli (D)	$301,713	0	$333,885
Brown (R)	$329,060	$33,675 (10%)	$327,390
1988			
Mazzoli (D)	$378,438	$196,650 (52%)	$371,431
Dunnagan (R)	$6,916	0	$4,931

Key Votes

1991	
Authorize use of force against Iraq	N
1990	
Support constitutional amendment on flag desecration	Y
Pass family and medical leave bill over Bush veto	Y
Reduce SDI funding	Y
Allow abortions in overseas military facilities	N
Approve budget summit plan for spending and taxing	N
Approve civil rights bill	Y
1989	
Halt production of B-2 stealth bomber at 13 planes	N
Oppose capital gains tax cut	N
Approve federal abortion funding in rape or incest cases	N
Approve pay raise and revision of ethics rules	Y
Pass Democratic minimum wage plan over Bush veto	N

Voting Studies

	Presidential Support		Party Unity		Conservative Coalition	
Year	**S**	**O**	**S**	**O**	**S**	**O**
1990	31	68	87	12	44	52
1989	50	50	80	19	59	41
1988	33	62	84	14	42	50
1987	42	57	84	15	74	26
1986	40	58	78	20	62	38
1985	48	52	74	25	62	36
1984	40	57	79	20	47	53
1983	40	59	78	20	51	48
1982	44	53	75	22	49	49
1981	47	43	62	29	49	36

Interest Group Ratings

Year	ADA	ACU	AFL-CIO	CCUS
1990	78	13	83	29
1989	40	32	25	80
1988	75	21	77	54
1987	52	30	56	33
1986	50	32	64	24
1985	55	33	47	50
1984	65	38	38	38
1983	65	35	53	55
1982	70	27	90	41
1981	60	36	64	44

4 Jim Bunning (R)

Of Southgate — Elected 1986

Born: Oct. 23, 1931, Campbell County, Ky.
Education: Xavier U., B.S. 1953.
Occupation: Investment broker; professional baseball player.
Family: Wife, Mary Catherine Theis; nine children.
Religion: Roman Catholic.
Political Career: Fort Thomas City Council, 1977-79; Ky. Senate, 1979-83; Republican nominee for governor, 1983.
Capitol Office: 116 Cannon Bldg. 20515; 225-3465.

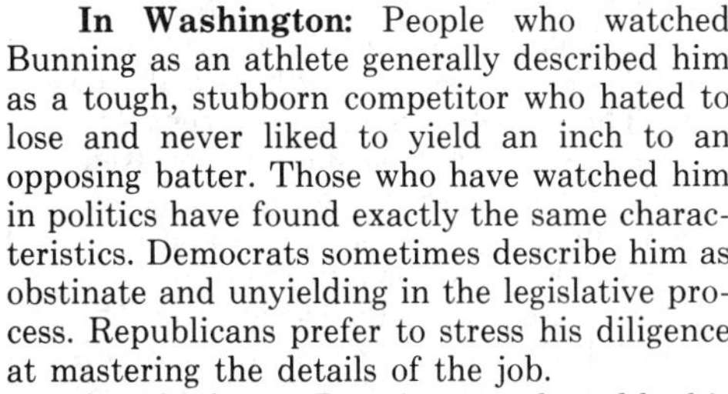

In Washington: People who watched Bunning as an athlete generally described him as a tough, stubborn competitor who hated to lose and never liked to yield an inch to an opposing batter. Those who have watched him in politics have found exactly the same characteristics. Democrats sometimes describe him as obstinate and unyielding in the legislative process. Republicans prefer to stress his diligence at mastering the details of the job.

As a freshman, Bunning was elected by his classmates to be their representative on the GOP Committee on Committees, which determines committee assignments. Bunning made some useful contacts there with more senior Republicans, enabling him to secure a seat on the highly coveted Ways and Means Committee for the 102nd Congress after falling short in a prior bid. He was also assigned to the House ethics committee.

Bunning's unyielding legislative style is entirely in keeping with the confrontational conservatives who populate a wing of the House GOP. In an interview with *The Louisville Courier-Journal*, Bunning said, "I think there comes a time you have to take a stand on an issue even if you know you're going to lose. . . . I am waiting to see that kind of leadership." The House conservatives evidently like his approach: They elected him chairman of the Conservative Opportunity Society for the 102nd Congress.

His combative nature carries over into electoral politics. In a 1989 fundraising letter that discussed impending redistricting, he exhorted supporters not to "cave in to the plots and schemes of the Frankfort Democrats who want to change our district."

Bunning's presence offers House Republicans a chance for guaranteed supremacy in one of the few areas of partisan competition they have dominated in recent years — the congressional baseball game. Not since 1975 has there been a major league player in the House, and there has never been one like Bunning, who pitched two no-hitters and won 224 games over a 15-year big-league career.

At Home: After retiring as an active player in 1971, Bunning tried minor league managing for a while, then returned to his native Kentucky, where he set up as an investment broker and agent to professional athletes.

He also got involved in civic activities that led him to a seat on the Fort Thomas City Council, where in 1977 he began his rapid political rise. After just two years, Bunning unseated a longtime Democratic state senator. He quickly became the minority leader for the small group of Senate Republicans.

In 1983, Kentucky Republicans, searching for a viable gubernatorial candidate, recruited Bunning. In his uphill campaign against Democrat Martha Layne Collins, he claimed the state's economy had stagnated during a long period of Democratic rule. He also took a "tough man" approach that seemed designed for voters uncomfortable with the idea of a woman governor. Bunning got a respectable 44 percent.

He initially had planned on another try for the governorship in 1987. But GOP Rep. Gene Snyder announced his retirement in 1986, and GOP officials were worried about holding the 4th. They needed a strong candidate, and enlisted Bunning.

His opponent was Democratic state Rep. Terry Mann, who had lost to Snyder by only 12,000 votes in 1982 and had considerable strength in Bunning's Campbell County political base, just across the Ohio River from Cincinnati. Mann contrasted his 14 years in the Legislature to Bunning's four. But Mann drew negative press in March, when it was reported that he had rigged his state House voting lever with a rubber band so he would be recorded as present while he was absent from a session.

That episode, coupled with Bunning's image as a conservative in Snyder's mold and a big GOP financial edge, helped Bunning build a winning margin in the Cincinnati-area counties of Kenton and Boone and in the populous Louisville suburbs of Jefferson County.

Kentucky 4

Louisville Suburbs; Covington; Newport

A full 80 percent of the 4th's vote is cast either in the suburbs of Louisville, at the western end of the district, or in those of Cincinnati, at the eastern end. Both areas lean Republican and have made the district the state's best GOP territory outside the mountainous 5th. Along the Ohio River between the two population centers are four predominantly rural Democratic counties.

Redistricting in 1982 shifted the focus of the district more toward the eastern end of the district. Roughly half of the population now lives in Boone, Campbell (Newport) and Kenton (Covington) counties near Cincinnati. This suburban territory is largely blue-collar, but it has never had strong Democratic ties. The Cincinnati commuters and factory workers who live here regularly turn in Republican majorities.

Covington and Newport are old factory towns directly across the Ohio River from Cincinnati. Like the Louisville area, they have a large Catholic population of German extraction. Anti-abortion candidate Ellen McCormack ran a close second to Jimmy Carter there in the 1976 Democratic presidential primary.

The major population growth in the Kentucky suburbs of Cincinnati has been in Boone County. Attracting spillover from Campbell and Kenton counties, its population grew more than 50 percent from 1970-86.

The suburban Louisville portion of the district is diverse. Communities at the southern end of Jefferson County are largely blue-collar. But in the northeastern sector are some of the wealthiest suburbs in the country, and it is here that most of the county's GOP loyalists live. Their support helped Bunning carry Jefferson with 63 percent of the vote in 1986.

Oldham County, just north of Jefferson, is a magnet for people seeking to escape the crowding closer to Louisville. Oldham's population boomed by 91 percent in the 1970s, the largest growth rate in the state. The influx slowed to 19 percent during the 1980s, but remains one of Kentucky's fastest-growing counties. Like Jefferson, Oldham backs Bunning solidly.

The other seven counties in the 4th are rural and predominantly Democratic. Unsuccessful Democratic presidential candidate Michael S. Dukakis carried all but two of them in 1988.

Population: 523,090. White 507,366 (97%), Black 12,547 (2%). Spanish origin 2,885 (1%). 18 and over 363,075 (69%), 65 and over 50,877 (10%). Median age: 30.

Committees

Standards of Official Conduct (4th of 7 Republicans)

Ways & Means (12th of 13 Republicans)
Social Security (ranking); Oversight

Elections

1990 General		
Jim Bunning (R)	101,680	(69%)
Galen Martin (D)	44,979	(31%)
1988 General		
Jim Bunning (R)	145,609	(74%)
Richard V. Beliles (D)	50,575	(26%)

Previous Winning Percentages: **1986** (55%)

District Vote For President

	1988		1984		1980		1976	
D	71,505	(35%)	62,253	(30%)	77,599	(40%)	71,300	(41%)
R	133,660	(65%)	143,262	(69%)	108,825	(56%)	99,199	(58%)
I					6,657	(3%)		

Campaign Finance

	Receipts	Receipts from PACs		Expend-itures
1990				
Bunning (R)	$532,775	$225,900	(42%)	$563,409
Martin (D)	$76,407	$32,900	(43%)	$76,580
1988				
Bunning (R)	$593,585	$236,184	(40%)	$468,870
Beliles (D)	$23,752	$16,425	(69%)	$23,636

Key Votes

1991	
Authorize use of force against Iraq	Y
1990	
Support constitutional amendment on flag desecration	Y
Pass family and medical leave bill over Bush veto	N
Reduce SDI funding	N
Allow abortions in overseas military facilities	N
Approve budget summit plan for spending and taxing	N
Approve civil rights bill	N
1989	
Halt production of B-2 stealth bomber at 13 planes	N
Oppose capital gains tax cut	N
Approve federal abortion funding in rape or incest cases	N
Approve pay raise and revision of ethics rules	N
Pass Democratic minimum wage plan over Bush veto	N

Voting Studies

	Presidential Support		Party Unity		Conservative Coalition	
Year	**S**	**O**	**S**	**O**	**S**	**O**
1990	71	28	94	2	96	2
1989	78	17	95	3	88	10
1988	65	29	92	3	97	0
1987	74	24	95	4	95	5

Interest Group Ratings

Year	ADA	ACU	AFL-CIO	CCUS
1990	6	87	8	79
1989	5	96	17	100
1988	0	100	8	100
1987	4	87	6	93

5 Harold Rogers (R)

Of Somerset — Elected 1980

Born: Dec. 31, 1937, Barrier, Ky.
Education: U. of Kentucky, B.A. 1962, LL.B. 1964.
Military Service: Army National Guard, 1956-64.
Occupation: Lawyer.
Family: Wife, Shirley McDowell; three children.
Religion: Baptist.
Political Career: Commonwealth attorney, Pulaski and Rockcastle counties, 1969-79; Republican nominee for lieutenant governor, 1979.
Capitol Office: 343 Cannon Bldg. 20515; 225-4601.

In Washington: Leaving the White House after a contentious meeting about the collapsing budget summit agreement in late 1990, Rogers said: "The main concerns we raised were ... strategic." Rogers was undecided about whether it was a good idea for the GOP to be associated with the tax-raising summit agreement, and he advised that "The president needs to make this case to the American public."

As this episode suggests, Rogers is a man interested in political tactics, and one who usually operates comfortably within the system from his seat on the Appropriations Committee. But his subsequent vote against the Bush-backed summit plan highlighted another fact about Rogers: He is not just a loyal soldier of the system. In the factionalized House GOP, he stands somewhere between the confrontational "New Guard" and the old-line advocates of legislative compromise.

With a largely parochial agenda during the 1980s, Rogers seldom attracted much publicity as he threaded his way through the institution, finding the appropriate levers to pull to land good committee assignments. Now entering his second decade in the House, Rogers has worked his way up to Appropriations and Budget, and he holds a seat on the coveted Committee on Committees, which assigns GOP members to House panels.

On Appropriations, Rogers follows the panel's ethic of bipartisan cooperation and picks up plums for his district. On Budget, he puts enough of an edge on his anti-deficit rhetoric to win friends among the brasher Republicans, who chafe at the way Democrats control the budget debate in Congress.

At the start of the 102nd Congress, Rogers made a bid for the ranking spot on Budget. Though his effort was a solid one, he ended up losing to Bill Gradison of Ohio, a supreme legislative pragmatist and the preferred choice of GOP Minority Leader Robert H. Michel.

Rogers' assignment on Budget can be frustrating. Democrats there routinely thwart Republican initiatives, and fiscally conservative GOP members complain that even President Bush has undermined their cause. In 1990, Rogers was one of 96 House Republicans to write Bush that they were "stunned" by his reversal on his no-new-taxes pledge. A year earlier, after Bush and congressional leaders had announced a bipartisan budget accord, Rogers balked at the pact's underlying economic assumptions and its accounting maneuvers aimed at achieving short-term savings.

When the Budget Committee considered that accord, Rogers joined with New Jersey Democrat Frank J. Guarini to propose an amendment adding $1 billion to drug treatment and education programs, to be offset with an across-the-board cut in all discretionary spending, including defense and foreign aid. With committee leaders from both parties arguing against any change in the basic agreement with the White House, that amendment and several others were rejected in committee by margins of 2-to-1. Later, Rogers was one of 61 Republicans voting against the budget resolution when it passed the House.

Rogers' behind-the-scenes skills are well suited to Appropriations, where Democrats and Republicans usually work together closely to draft money bills that all panel members can support. Rogers is ranking Republican on the Commerce, Justice and State Appropriations Subcommittee. In the 101st Congress, budget constraints limited debate on the subcommittee's bill mostly to lamentations about how little money was available. Rogers called the 1989 bill "bare-bones" and as "puny as can be."

In 1987, he successfully argued for an uptick in funds for federal prosecutors and agents fighting illegal immigration and drugs. He also helped the Reagan administration by fighting against a determined effort to reimpose rules requiring broadcasters to air all sides of controversial issues (the "fairness doctrine").

While such subjects offer only tangential

Kentucky 5

Southeast — Middlesboro

Eastern Kentucky's mountain counties have been voting Republican since the 1860s, when their small-scale farmers opposed the slaveholding secessionist Democrats elsewhere in the state. Republican Alfred M. Landon carried the 5th against Franklin D. Roosevelt in 1936; Barry Goldwater won it in 1964.

Democratic votes here are found in the coal-producing southeast corner of the district. Only Harlan and Letcher (the southern portion of which is in the 5th) counties in the district backed Michael S. Dukakis in 1988, and also unsuccessful Democratic Senate nominee Harvey Sloane in 1990, while the 26 other counties in the 5th went for GOP Sen. Mitch McConnell.

In spite of some of the richest coal deposits in the nation along the district's eastern border, the 5th is the poorest district in Kentucky, and one of the poorest in the nation. In 1980, it was ranked last among all congressional districts in percentage of residents 25 or older who were high school graduates. Coal mining can be a good provider, but the boom-and-bust cycle of the industry leaves many without a reliable source of income.

None of the counties in the 5th has a per capita income that approaches the statewide level; six of the 25 counties in the U.S. with the lowest personal income per capita in the mid-80's were located within the 5th. McCreary and Wayne, two economically disadvantaged counties on the Tennessee border, hope to reap tourism and business development dollars from newly-opened Big South Fork National River and Recreation Area.

Tobacco, apples, poultry and livestock are mainstays of the farm economy in the rolling hill country in the central and western parts of the district. Poor transportation and the absence of major population centers have hampered industrial development; textile mills are the biggest employers. The 5th is the only district in the state without a city of 15,000 people. Its largest community, Nicholasville, has just over 13,000 residents.

Population: 523,664. White 511,632 (98%), Black 10,751 (2%). Spanish origin 4,275 (1%). 18 and over 359,513 (69%), 65 and over 63,341 (12%). Median age: 29.

benefits to his district, the top spot on the subcommittee puts Rogers in a position to influence other spending bills, particularly those that might benefit his economically struggling southeastern Kentucky district. A major flood control project on the Upper Cumberland River, a tunnel at the Cumberland Gap and the Southern Kentucky Rural Development project attest to Rogers' skill as an appropriator.

But Rogers' press releases announcing new federal funds pair with those proclaiming his staunch opposition to tax increases, and that has drawn some critical press at home. One 1990 headline read, "Rep Rogers' dilemma: Pet Projects vs. Tax Hikes." Rogers says he is just trying to make up for years of neglect his area suffered from the federal government. "Just because [my constituents] have been ignored all these years, it's no reason to say, 'Sorry, you're out of the picture. We don't have the money,'' he says.

Tobacco is a subject that can get the normally easygoing Rogers excited: He is a smoker, and he views the "right to smoke" as an issue of personal liberty. That is good politics, since tobacco sustains the 5th District's rural economy. There are 40,000 allotments in the district, most of them held by small-scale farmers.

In 1985, perturbed by administration proposals to phase out parts of the tobacco price-support system, Rogers "took a walk" during a high-profile Appropriations Committee vote on the MX missile. His refusal to vote on the issue had the intended effect — it attracted attention at the White House. Quickly, a meeting was arranged for Rogers with Chief of Staff Donald T. Regan. The Kentucky Republican fully vented his tobacco concerns before agreeing to back President Reagan on the MX.

Fighting to protect tobacco, however, has increasingly been a rear-guard action. In 1987, Rogers helped snuff out in subcommittee a plan by Illinois Democrat Richard J. Durbin to ban smoking on airplane flights — only to have Durbin win on the House floor and in conference. The trend is not lost on Rogers, who has been seeking funds for aquaculture and crop diversification to broaden his district's economic base. He also sponsored a task force to entice vacationers to southeastern Kentucky's parks and lakes.

At Home: Rogers, a protégé of GOP Rep. Tim Lee Carter, who retired in 1980, is generally identified as a moderate on the Kentucky GOP spectrum. In 1976, when most of the state party backed Reagan, Rogers ran Gerald R. Ford's primary campaign.

Rogers made his name locally in the 1960s

as a civic activist promoting industrial development in Somerset. He took over as the commonwealth's attorney in 1969 and continued to play a conspicuous role in politics as the prosecutor for Pulaski and Rockcastle counties.

He was unsuccessful as the GOP nominee for lieutenant governor in 1979, but the race helped him build name recognition, and that paid off in the House campaign. Carter's retirement touched off a scramble, but Rogers quickly moved to the front of the 11-candidate GOP field. The primary revolved around personalities, geography and political alliances, not issues. Although Carter remained neutral, Rogers capitalized on their past association. He chaired Carter's re-election committee in 1978.

Rogers drew barely one-fifth of the vote, but carried 11 of the district's 28 counties, most of them around his home base in the center of the 5th. Fall elections are Rogers' runaways in the Republican 5th; Democrats have not even fielded a candidate in the last three elections.

Committees

Appropriations (13th of 22 Republicans)
Commerce, Justice, State & Judiciary (ranking); Treasury, Postal Service & General Government

Budget (4th of 14 Republicans)
Economic Policy, Projections & Revenues (ranking); Budget Process, Reconciliation & Enforcement

Elections

1990 General

Harold Rogers (R)	64,660	(100%)

1988 General

Harold Rogers (R)	104,467	(100%)

Previous Winning Percentages: **1986** (100%) **1984** (76%) **1982** (65%) **1980** (68%)

District Vote For President

	1988	1984	1980	1976
D	59,941 (33%)	58,788 (30%)	69,640 (37%)	67,794 (42%)
R	121,651 (67%)	134,073 (69%)	116,015 (61%)	92,134 (57%)

Campaign Finance

	Receipts	Receipts from PACs	Expend-itures
1990			
Rogers (R)	$180,606	$71,025 (39%)	$103,286
1988			
Rogers (R)	$177,242	$69,566 (39%)	$119,720

Key Votes

1991	
Authorize use of force against Iraq	Y
1990	
Support constitutional amendment on flag desecration	Y
Pass family and medical leave bill over Bush veto	N
Reduce SDI funding	N
Allow abortions in overseas military facilities	N
Approve budget summit plan for spending and taxing	N
Approve civil rights bill	N
1989	
Halt production of B-2 stealth bomber at 13 planes	N
Oppose capital gains tax cut	N
Approve federal abortion funding in rape or incest cases	N
Approve pay raise and revision of ethics rules	N
Pass Democratic minimum wage plan over Bush veto	N

Voting Studies

	Presidential Support		Party Unity		Conservative Coalition	
Year	**S**	**O**	**S**	**O**	**S**	**O**
1990	69	31	85	14	94	2
1989	80	20	83	16	95	5
1988	62	38	85	11	87	11
1987	62	34	77	18	91	5
1986	70	29	76	23	92	8
1985	64	34	75	21	89	9
1984	54	41	66	28	92	7
1983	70	29	80	19	89	10
1982	70	29	73	20	86	12
1981	72	28	81	18	88	9

Interest Group Ratings

Year	ADA	ACU	AFL-CIO	CCUS
1990	6	83	17	86
1989	10	71	25	80
1988	5	96	21	100
1987	4	78	13	80
1986	10	86	43	67
1985	10	76	18	76
1984	25	71	38	73
1983	5	87	12	74
1982	15	76	30	77
1981	10	93	40	84

6 Larry J. Hopkins (R)

Of Lexington — Elected 1978

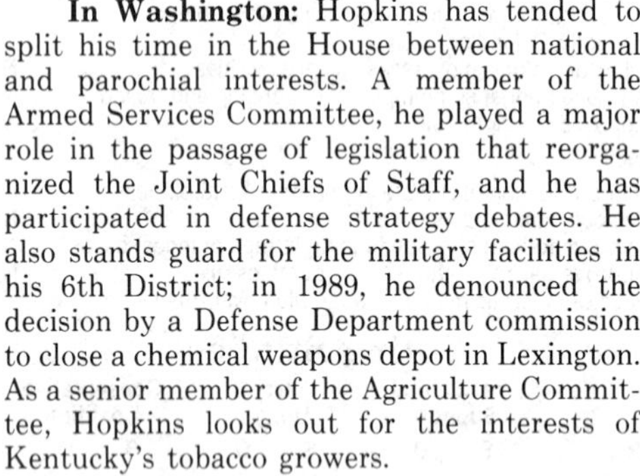

Born: Oct. 25, 1933, Detroit, Mich.
Education: Attended Murray State U., 1952-54.
Military Service: Marine Corps, 1954-56.
Occupation: Stockbroker.
Family: Wife, Carolyn Pennebaker; three children.
Religion: Methodist.
Political Career: Republican nominee for Fayette County Commission, 1970; Ky. House, 1972-78; Ky. Senate, 1978-79.
Capitol Office: 2437 Rayburn Bldg. 20515; 225-4706.

In Washington: Hopkins has tended to split his time in the House between national and parochial interests. A member of the Armed Services Committee, he played a major role in the passage of legislation that reorganized the Joint Chiefs of Staff, and he has participated in defense strategy debates. He also stands guard for the military facilities in his 6th District; in 1989, he denounced the decision by a Defense Department commission to close a chemical weapons depot in Lexington. As a senior member of the Agriculture Committee, Hopkins looks out for the interests of Kentucky's tobacco growers.

In 1991, Hopkins decided to let his home-state side go full flower, seeking the Kentucky governorship. In May, he won a narrow victory with 51 percent of the vote in the Republican primary for that office. Should he not succeed in his November 1991 bid for governor, he would return to his House seat and his key subcommittee assignments. Hopkins is ranking Republican on Armed Services' Investigations Subcommittee, and holds the No. 2 GOP spot on the Procurement and Military Nuclear Systems Subcommittee. He maintains the senior GOP position on the Agriculture Subcommittee on Peanuts and Tobacco.

If Hopkins does win for governor, he will probably be most remembered in Washington for his work on the Joint Chiefs reform bill in the 99th Congress. The legislation gave more bureaucratic and command control to the chairman of the Joint Chiefs of Staff at the expense of the heads of the separate armed services, and took other measures to enhance interservice coordination. There are military analysts who attribute the smooth operation of U.S. forces during the 1991 war with Iraq, at least in part, to these changes.

The final bill bore the names of two senior members who guided it: GOP Sen. Barry Goldwater of Arizona (now retired) and Democratic Rep. Bill Nichols of Alabama (who died in 1988). But Hopkins was one of the leading activists on Armed Services and on the House floor who overcame fierce resistance from the Defense Department bureaucracy. At one point, Hopkins sounded off against "a sustained frontal assault orchestrated by opponents at the Pentagon who are determined to maintain the status quo."

In general, Hopkins is a "strong defense" Republican who supported much of the Reagan-era military buildup. Although fiscal problems and Soviet military retrenchment have since caused the Defense Department to plan a major downsizing, Hopkins colorfully noted during the Persian Gulf War that such talk had been temporarily deferred. "America doesn't have on its green eyeshade," he said. "It has on its helmet."

Still, Hopkins was never an automatic vote for the Pentagon. He was no fan of the multiwarhead MX missile or the rail-basing mode that defense planners had in mind for it. During Armed Services deliberations on the fiscal 1990 defense authorization bill, an amendment to eliminate the rail-mobile version of the MX, proposed by liberal Democrat Ronald V. Dellums of California, was defeated 10-42. Hopkins was the only Republican voting in favor.

Hopkins made a particular cause of eliminating the LH, a new missile-equipped tank-hunting helicopter favored by Defense Secretary Dick Cheney. Hopkins disliked everything about the project — its high cost, its surfeit of high-tech equipment, and, some wags said, even its initials (which matched his own). He argued that the Army would be better off just upgrading its fleet of AHIP helicopters. Though Hopkins' vigorous efforts in 1990 resulted in a leaner program and stricter testing requirements (and a new name) for the LH, he failed to kill off the aircraft.

As ranking Republican on the Investigations Subcommittee, Hopkins typically works well with its chairman, Democrat Nicholas Mavroules of Massachusetts. However, Hopkins in 1990 fought one of Mavroules' projects: a $200 million program providing assistance to communities and workers affected by the shut-

Kentucky 6

North Central — Lexington; Frankfort

The 6th is Kentucky as the rest of the nation pictures it. Horses, tobacco and whiskey are the mainstays of its culture and economy. Its centerpiece is Lexington (Fayette County), de facto capital of the Bluegrass even though the 6th also contains the state capital of Frankfort.

Lexington is best known for its thoroughbred horse farms that regularly produce Kentucky Derby champions, but the University of Kentucky (enrollment 22,000) and the city's pleasant setting have attracted high-technology industry there, and Lexington's rapid growth has generated employment in engineering and other white-collar jobs.

The boom has swung Lexington into the Republican column. In his competitive early elections, Hopkins depended on Fayette to offset the Democratic vote in the district's farm counties. In 1990, Fayette gave GOP Senate candidate Mitch McConnell 54 percent; in 1988, George Bush took it by a margin of 3-to-2.

There also has been significant population and manufacturing growth in rural Bluegrass counties within commuting distance of Lexington. The largest of the adjoining counties is Madison (Richmond). Madison County, although nominally more Democratic than Fayette County, voted just like its larger neighbor — for Reagan and McConnell in 1984; for Bush in 1988. The northern portion of Madison County is dotted with bedroom communities whose residents work in Lexington. The southern portion revolves around Richmond, a tobacco market and site of Eastern Kentucky University (12,500 students). Ten percent of the district population lives in Madison, making it the second most populous county in the 6th.

Frankfort (Franklin County) is the district's other major population center. Chosen as the state capital in a 1792 compromise between competing Lexington and Louisville, it has never grown into a metropolis and today remains a small city of 26,000 people with picturesque old buildings. The long heritage of Democratic governors has produced a loyal pool of state workers who help keep Franklin County in the Democratic column. It voted solidly for Democrat Harvey Sloane in his unsuccessful 1990 Senate bid.

Population: 519,009. White 467,159 (90%), Black 48,249 (9%). Spanish origin 3,325 (1%). 18 and over 377,249 (73%), 65 and over 53,093 (10%). Median age: 29.

down of defense facilities. Hopkins said the program would give defense workers a cushion unavailable to those in other industries.

"It grants special status and benefits to a limited category of our work force without regard to the millions of other civilian employees who perform similar work," Hopkins said. But with members worried about the economic impact of the proposed build-down, the measure had momentum and passed as part of the fiscal 1991 defense authorization bill.

Meanwhile, on the Agriculture Committee, Hopkins champions the cause of tobacco growers in general, and of Kentucky's burley leaf growers in particular. It is a responsibility he takes on for his constituents and pursues with dedication, but with no personal zeal.

A non-smoker, Hopkins says he does not promote the practice, but that he is put in the position of defending it. Asked on one television program if smoking caused cancer, he responded: "How would I know that? I'm not a physician or a scientist. I can't actually say — I don't think it's good for you."

At Home: Hopkins' string of victories in the politically marginal 6th had long made him attractive to GOP leaders as a potential statewide candidate, and in 1991 he took the gubernatorial plunge after rejecting party overtures to run for the nomination in 1983 and again in 1987.

Confronted with the specter of being thrown into one district with 4th District Rep. Jim Bunning in the coming round of redistricting, Hopkins announced after his unopposed 1990 re-election that he would seek the governorship in 1991.

In a bitter and much closer primary race than expected, Hopkins — who held nearly a 4-to-1 fundraising edge — slipped past Lexington lawyer Larry Forgy for the right to meet Democratic Lt. Gov. Brereton Jones. Forgy did not go down without drawing blood; he skewered Hopkins for implying on his resume that he served in the Korean War. Hopkins in fact did not join the Marine Corps until the fighting in Korea was over, and he did not visit that country until much later, as a congressman.

Hopkins has said he will seek reelection to Congress if he is not elected governor.

The surprising defeat of Rep. John B. Breckinridge in the 1978 Democratic House primary gave Republicans and Hopkins an opportunity in the 6th they had not expected. Hopkins capitalized on that opportunity, becoming the first Republican in 50 years to win the district. Since then, prodigious fund raising and an ability to draw Democratic votes have helped Hopkins dig in.

Going into 1978, Breckinridge was considered unbeatable, so neither Hopkins nor any other formidable Republican candidates entered the GOP primary. But when Breckinridge lost to a more liberal Democrat, Republican leaders met and substituted Hopkins for the GOP's token candidate, a 68-year-old former state auditor. Hopkins, a popular state senator from Lexington, the district's largest city, was able to mount an expensive television campaign to make up for his late start.

Over the previous decade, he had built a strong electoral base in his hometown. After running unsuccessfully for the county commission, he was appointed county clerk of courts and then elected to the Legislature.

Hopkins' well-organized congressional campaign aimed its appeal at conservative farmers and blue-collar workers. He portrayed his opponent, maverick state Sen. Tom Easterly, as a pawn of the unions. In return, Easterly labeled the shuffling that put Hopkins in the contest a Watergate-style maneuver.

But the Democrat was unable to heal the party divisions that resulted from his campaign against Breckinridge, and Hopkins outspent him by more than 2-to-1. Winning Fayette County (Lexington) by nearly 12,000 votes, Hopkins captured the seat with 51 percent.

Easterly tried again in 1980, but the rematch with Hopkins was anticlimactic. The incumbent won re-election by nearly 3-to-2.

In 1982 Democrats counted on favorable redistricting and the recession to give Hopkins a scare. They nominated Democrat Don Mills, a former editor of the Lexington *Herald,* who shared Hopkins' home base. A one-time press secretary to Gov. Edward T. Breathitt and an aide to Gov. John Y. Brown, Mills drew the primary-eve endorsement of three former Kentucky governors to win the Democratic nomination easily. But his general election campaign was woefully underfinanced.

Committees

Agriculture (3rd of 18 Republicans)
Peanuts & Tobacco (ranking); Livestock, Dairy & Poultry

Armed Services (4th of 22 Republicans)
Investigations (ranking); Procurement & Military Nuclear Systems

Elections

1990 General		
Larry J. Hopkins (R)	76,859	(100%)
1988 General		
Larry J. Hopkins (R)	128,898	(74%)
Milton Patton (D)	45,339	(26%)

Previous Winning Percentages: **1986** (74%) **1984** (71%) **1982** (57%) **1980** (59%) **1978** (51%)

District Vote For President

	1988	1984	1980	1976
D	82,755 (42%)	72,942 (37%)	90,271 (49%)	83,835 (52%)
R	112,162 (57%)	123,859 (62%)	83,127 (45%)	74,110 (46%)
I			8,031 (4%)	

Campaign Finance

	Receipts	Receipts from PACs	Expend-itures
1990			
Hopkins (R)	$203,286	$92,200 (45%)	$120,647
1988			
Hopkins (R)	$356,281	$134,335 (38%)	$295,333
Patton (D)	$41,638	$10,000 (24%)	$41,610

Key Votes

1991	
Authorize use of force against Iraq	Y
1990	
Support constitutional amendment on flag desecration	Y
Pass family and medical leave bill over Bush veto	N
Reduce SDI funding	N
Allow abortions in overseas military facilities	N
Approve budget summit plan for spending and taxing	N
Approve civil rights bill	N
1989	
Halt production of B-2 stealth bomber at 13 planes	Y
Oppose capital gains tax cut	N
Approve federal abortion funding in rape or incest cases	N
Approve pay raise and revision of ethics rules	N
Pass Democratic minimum wage plan over Bush veto	N

Voting Studies

	Presidential Support		Party Unity		Conservative Coalition	
Year	**S**	**O**	**S**	**O**	**S**	**O**
1990	66	33	90	9	94	2
1989	72	28	87	12	85	12
1988	63	37	80	20	92	8
1987	70	29	91	6	98	2
1986	72	27	82	16	96	4
1985	61	38	71	25	84	15
1984	60	39	77	22	80	20
1983	65	34	84	14	85	12
1982	58	39	77	22	78	21
1981	68	29	79	20	80	16

Interest Group Ratings

Year	ADA	ACU	AFL-CIO	CCUS
1990	11	83	17	79
1989	20	82	17	100
1988	20	76	36	93
1987	0	77	13	93
1986	10	73	21	94
1985	10	71	24	81
1984	20	75	31	69
1983	20	74	12	80
1982	20	67	40	68
1981	20	93	40	76

7 Carl C. Perkins (D)

Of Hindman — Elected 1984

Born: Aug. 6, 1954, Washington, D.C.
Education: Davidson College, B.A. 1976; U. of Louisville, J.D. 1979.
Occupation: Lawyer.
Family: Wife, Janet Neville; two children.
Religion: Baptist.
Political Career: Ky. House, 1982-84.
Capitol Office: 1004 Longworth Bldg. 20515; 225-4935.

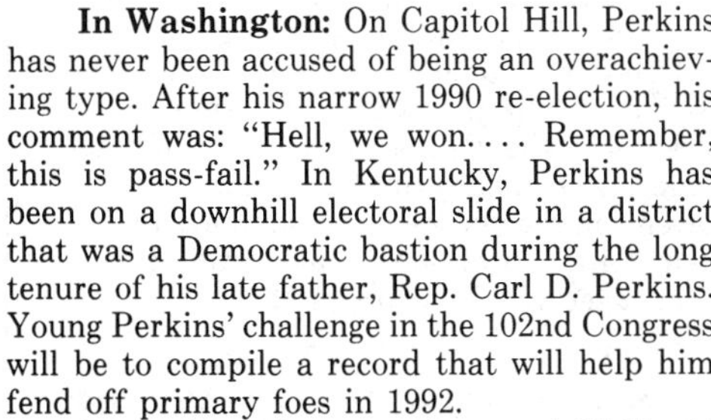

In Washington: On Capitol Hill, Perkins has never been accused of being an overachieving type. After his narrow 1990 re-election, his comment was: "Hell, we won.... Remember, this is pass-fail." In Kentucky, Perkins has been on a downhill electoral slide in a district that was a Democratic bastion during the long tenure of his late father, Rep. Carl D. Perkins. Young Perkins' challenge in the 102nd Congress will be to compile a record that will help him fend off primary foes in 1992.

Succeeding the most famous hillbilly in Congress was not easy. The elder Perkins, who served 35 years until his death in 1984 and whom many fondly called "Uncle Carl," was devoted to federal anti-poverty programs as chairman of the Education and Labor Committee.

Despite his establishment education, son Chris does a convincing hillbilly routine. But after he won the special election to succeed his father, he became known as a member struggling to adapt to the demands and pressures of congressional life. He was divorced, remarried and had a son in the space of three months in 1987. On the 1988 Democratic Caucus retreat to Greenbrier, W.Va., Perkins and his new wife were involved in an early-morning commotion at a bar. In 1990, it was disclosed that he owed $1,300 in delinquent 1988 property taxes and had defaulted on a $200,000 loan. Both financial matters were settled, but only after another series of embarrassing headlines.

In the 101st Congress, Perkins showed some signs of settling into legislative duties on Education and Labor. He unassumingly worked to increase funding for updating equipment and facilities during debate on the Carl D. Perkins Vocational Education Act. In the 102nd Congress, Perkins has a new forum to prove himself, as he takes the chair of the Employment Opportunities Subcommittee, which has jurisdiction over the Job Training Partnership Act and the Jobs Corps.

At Home: Perkins should be braced for an all-out assault in 1992 after nearly being upset in 1990 by repeat GOP challenger Will T. Scott, a former circuit judge who came up about 2,000 votes short.

The political vultures are already circling. Carol Brown Hubbard, wife of 1st District Democratic Rep. Carroll Hubbard Jr., announced after the election that she would purchase a home in her childhood 7th to take on Perkins. Outwardly unperturbed, Perkins said that new residents were always welcome in the district and expressed hope that Mrs. Hubbard would bring new dollars into the coalfield region.

After the 1990 election, the National Republican Congressional Committee conceded that it blundered by not giving more money to Scott's campaign. Scott, a former paratrooper, used creative techniques to gain publicity, such as parachuting from an airplane to highlight the lack of facilities for veterans.

Scott may have been helped by wounds inflicted on Perkins in the Democratic primary by challenger Jerry Cecil, a tenacious Vietnam War veteran who said he was disgusted that Perkins seemed to treat the 7th District seat as his due legacy. Though Cecil was a political neophyte, he took about one of every three votes in the Democratic primary.

Perkins' biggest political asset has clearly been his name. Although he goes by Chris, he invites voters to recall his father by listing himself on ballots as Carl C. Perkins. The family name and party were enough to put down early challenges, but Scott's 1990 showing suggests that voters are beginning to distinguish between Perkins and his father.

Perkins did not face a stern test at the polls until Scott's entry in 1988. Scott spoke glowingly of the elder Perkins, but dismissed his Washington-raised son as a stranger in his own district. Scott's slogan — "Winning Respect in Washington" — questioned the younger Perkins' effectiveness and implicitly recalled controversies in his personal life.

Perkins focused on Scott's GOP label, blaming the Reagan administration for stymieing highway and bridge construction in Appalachia. Though helped by the United Mine Workers, Perkins polled under 60 percent, a foreshadowing of his closer race in 1990.

Kentucky 7

East — Ashland

Coal booms come and go, but the Appalachian 7th remains one of the nation's poorest districts. The 1970s were a boom time here; a coal revival and the decline of industry in the urban Midwest brought many former residents back to their hometowns in the hills and hollows. But demand for coal has slackened, and the 1980s were grim. "What I see ... in some places in my district [is that] 20, 30, 35, 40 percent unemployment exists," Perkins said on the House floor in 1986. "You say that is unbelievable, but it is true."

With the United Mine Workers (UMW) a major force in politics, the 7th is a Democratic bastion in most elections. It has supported the party's presidential nominee in seven of the last eight elections, failing only in 1972. Michael S. Dukakis carried it easily in 1988.

Democratic strength is greatest in the southern two-thirds of the district, a rugged area that is one of the nation's leading producers of bituminous coal. Since the New Deal and the UMW transformed politics here, the coal counties have turned in some of the highest Democratic percentages in the state.

The northern portion of the 7th, stretching from the West Virginia boundary northwestward into the Ohio River Valley, is primarily agricultural. Major products include tobacco, cattle and fruit. But compared with Kentucky's fertile Bluegrass region farther west, it is mediocre land dominated by small-scale and subsistence farming.

The urbanized exception in the north is the area around Ashland, the Ohio River city that is headquarters for the Ashland Oil Co. Strong unions kept the Ashland area — industrialized Boyd and Greenup counties — in the Democratic column for decades, but their grip has weakened; the seven counties in the north supported GOP Sen. Mitch McConnell and GOP House challenger Will T. Scott in 1990.

Population: 526,284. White 519,847 (99%), Black 5,259 (1%). Spanish origin 3,553 (1%). 18 and over 356,178 (68%), 65 and over 54,393 (10%). Median age: 28.

Committees

Education & Labor (11th of 25 Democrats)
Employment Opportunities (chairman); Elementary, Secondary & Vocational Education; Labor Standards

Science, Space & Technology (17th of 32 Democrats)
Science; Space

Elections

1990 General		
Carl C. Perkins (D)	61,330	(51%)
Will T. Scott (R)	59,377	(49%)
1990 Primary		
Carl C. Perkins (D)	30,748	(68%)
Jerry Cecil (D)	14,195	(32%)
1988 General		
Carl C. Perkins (D)	96,946	(59%)
Will T. Scott (R)	68,165	(41%)

Previous Winning Percentages: **1986** (80%) **1984 †** (74%)

† Elected to a full term and to fill a vacancy at the same time.

District Vote For President

	1988	1984	1980	1976
D	98,314 (56%)	91,955 (51%)	97,733 (55%)	97,090 (60%)
R	77,474 (44%)	88,477 (49%)	76,302 (43%)	62,781 (39%)

Campaign Finance

	Receipts	Receipts from PACs		Expend-itures
1990				
Perkins (D)	$340,047	$267,575	(79%)	$344,561
Scott (R)	$170,784	$9,500	(6%)	$172,257
1988				
Perkins (D)	$418,749	$264,300	(63%)	$411,699
Scott (R)	$435,370	$37,330	(9%)	$432,403

Key Votes

1991	
Authorize use of force against Iraq	N
1990	
Support constitutional amendment on flag desecration	Y
Pass family and medical leave bill over Bush veto	Y
Reduce SDI funding	Y
Allow abortions in overseas military facilities	N
Approve budget summit plan for spending and taxing	N
Approve civil rights bill	Y
1989	
Halt production of B-2 stealth bomber at 13 planes	Y
Oppose capital gains tax cut	N
Approve federal abortion funding in rape or incest cases	N
Approve pay raise and revision of ethics rules	Y
Pass Democratic minimum wage plan over Bush veto	Y

Voting Studies

	Presidential Support		Party Unity		Conservative Coalition	
Year	**S**	**O**	**S**	**O**	**S**	**O**
1990	24	76	88	12	41	59
1989	37	62	88	12	34	66
1988	20	80	95	5	26	74
1987	19	81	95	5	19	81
1986	22	78	89	10	40	60
1985	20	80	94	6	27	73

Interest Group Ratings

Year	ADA	ACU	AFL-CIO	CCUS
1990	78	13	100	21
1989	85	21	83	40
1988	85	12	100	14
1987	84	4	100	7
1986	80	9	93	17
1985	85	10	88	23

Louisiana

U.S. CONGRESS

SENATE 2 D

HOUSE 4 D, 4 R

LEGISLATURE

Senate 33 D, 6 R

House 86 D, 18 R, 1 Independent

ELECTIONS

1988 Presidential Vote

Bush	54%
Dukakis	44%

1984 Presidential Vote

Reagan	61%
Mondale	38%

1980 Presidential Vote

Reagan	51%
Carter	46%
Anderson	2%

Turnout rate in 1986	12%
Turnout rate in 1988	51%
Turnout rate in 1990	3%

(as percentage of voting age population)

POPULATION AND GROWTH

1980 population	4,205,900
1990 population (21st in the nation)	4,219,973
Percent change 1980-1990	0%

DEMOGRAPHIC BREAKDOWN

White	67%
Black	31%
Asian or Pacific Islander	1%
(Hispanic origin)	2%
Urban	69%
Rural	31%
Born in state	78%
Foreign-born	2%

MAJOR CITIES

New Orleans	496,938
Baton Rouge	219,511
Shreveport	198,525
Lafayette	94,440
Kenner	72,033

AREA AND LAND USE

Area	44,522 sq. miles (33rd)
Farm	31%
Forest	49%
Federally owned	4%

Gov. Buddy Roemer (R)
Of Bossier City — Elected 1987

Born: Oct. 4, 1943, Shreveport, La.
Education: Harvard U., B.A. 1964, M.B.A. 1967.
Occupation: Banker; political consultant; data processing executive.
Religion: Methodist.
Political Career: U.S. House, 1981-88; Democratic nominee for U.S. House, 1978.
Next Election: 1991.

WORK

Occupations

White-collar	50%
Blue-collar	34%
Service workers	13%

Government Workers

Federal	33,915
State	97,319
Local	165,522

MONEY

Median family income	$ 18,088 (33rd)
Tax burden per capita	$ 860 (23rd)

EDUCATION

Spending per pupil through grade 12	$ 3,138 (42nd)
Persons with college degrees	14% (38th)

CRIME

Violent crime rate	782 per 100,000 (7th)

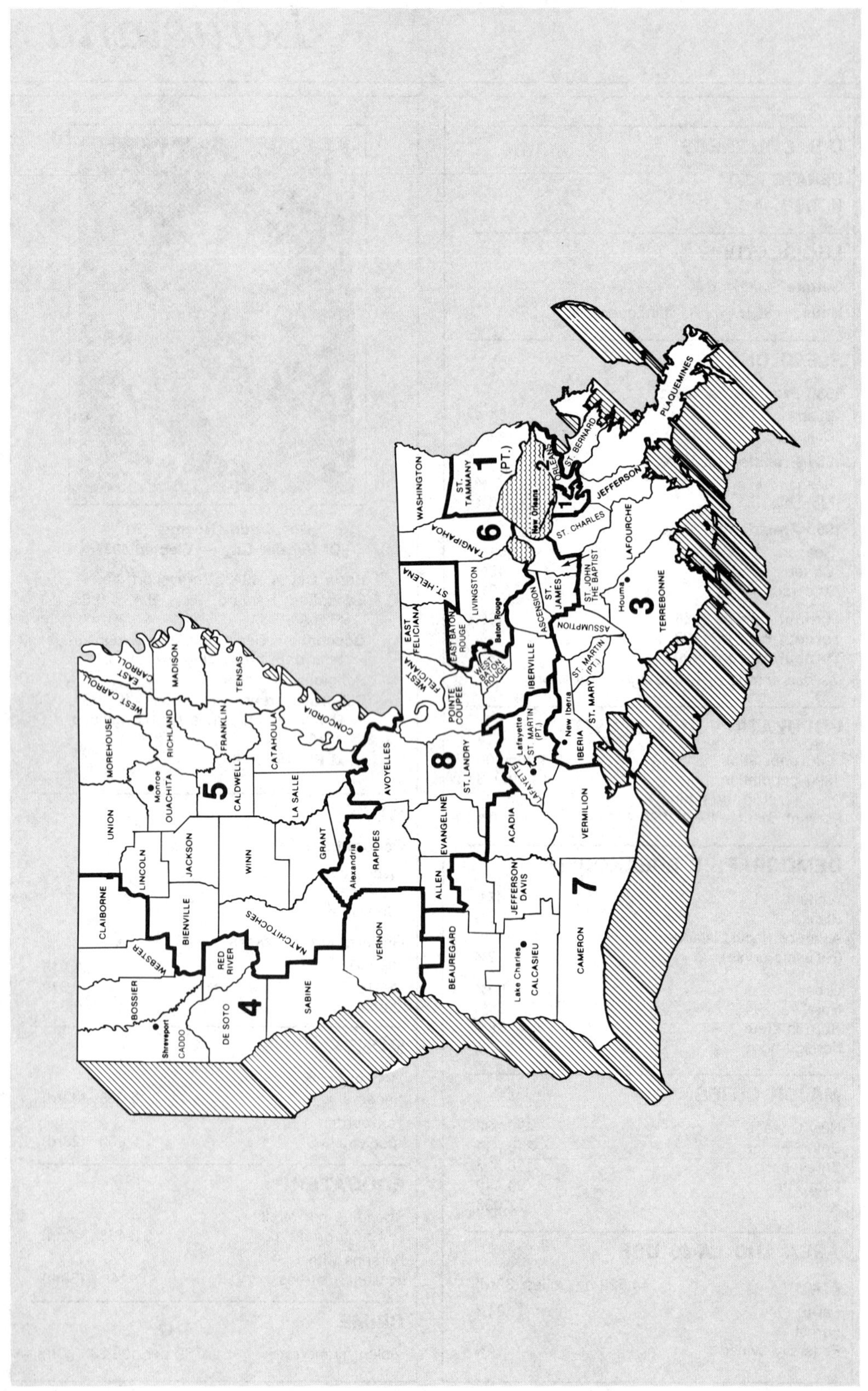
CADDO
Shreveport
BOSSIER
WEBSTER
CLAIBORNE
DE SOTO
4
RED RIVER
BIENVILLE
LINCOLN
UNION
MOREHOUSE
WEST CARROLL
EAST CARROLL
MADISON
TENSAS
RICHLAND
FRANKLIN
OUACHITA
Monroe
JACKSON
WINN
CALDWELL
5
CATAHOULA
CONCORDIA
LA SALLE
GRANT
NATCHITOCHES
SABINE
VERNON
RAPIDES
Alexandria
AVOYELLES
8
ST. LANDRY
EVANGELINE
ALLEN
BEAUREGARD
JEFFERSON DAVIS
CALCASIEU
Lake Charles
CAMERON
7
VERMILION
ACADIA
LAFAYETTE
Lafayette
ST. MARTIN (PT.)
IBERIA
New Iberia
ST. MARY
ST. MARTIN (PT.)
IBERVILLE
POINTE COUPEE
WEST FELICIANA
EAST FELICIANA
WEST BATON ROUGE
EAST BATON ROUGE
Baton Rouge
ST. HELENA
LIVINGSTON
TANGIPAHOA
6
WASHINGTON
ST. TAMMANY
1 (PT.)
2
ORLEANS
New Orleans
1
ST. BERNARD
PLAQUEMINES
JEFFERSON
ST. CHARLES
LAFOURCHE
ST. JOHN THE BAPTIST
ST. JAMES
ASCENSION
ASSUMPTION
Houma
3
TERREBONNE

J. Bennett Johnston (D)

Of Shreveport — Elected 1972

Born: June 10, 1932, Shreveport, La.
Education: Attended Washington and Lee U., 1950-51, 1952-53; U.S. Military Academy, 1951-52; Louisiana State U., LL.B. 1956.
Military Service: Army, 1956-59.
Occupation: Lawyer.
Family: Wife, Mary Gunn; four children.
Religion: Baptist.
Political Career: La. House, 1964-68; La. Senate, 1968-72; sought Democratic nomination for governor, 1971.
Capitol Office: 136 Hart Bldg. 20510; 224-5824.

In Washington: The late 1980s were not very kind to Johnston. His reputation as the Senate's consummate wheeler-dealer was not the image Democrats wanted to project, so they rejected his bids for majority leader in 1986 and 1988.

After the second loss, Johnston's influence also slipped a notch on the Appropriations Committee, where former Majority Leader Robert C. Byrd of West Virginia assumed the chairmanship in 1989, determined to assert his authority.

As 1991 rolled around and Johnston began his fourth term in the Senate, however, the outlook brightened somewhat for him. Not without considerable clout, Johnston chairs the Energy and Natural Resources Committee as well as the Appropriations Subcommittee on Energy and Water, giving him leviathan power on issues important to his economically troubled oil-patch state. At the outset of the 102nd Congress, he became the Senate's point man on national energy policy.

When Johnston gets involved in an issue, he tends to take charge. Whether working in a closed conference or managing a bill on the floor, he absorbs the legislative fine points and then bargains with aplomb. A master crafter of the pragmatic coalition, he can cut a deal that gives something to everyone — or at least to everyone who stays alert.

Some find Johnston's horse-trading unsavory, but he gladly acts the part. Waiting for other senators to bring amendments to the floor, he will open his arms and flash a big grin as he says: "We're open for business here."

For those unwilling to do business, Johnston has sharp elbows and no qualms about bruising his way past a foe. This method gets things done, but it does not facilitate formation of the kind of personal relationships that are paramount in leadership races.

On Energy, Johnston predictably has looked out for the oil and gas industries vital to Louisiana, although by 1991 he was seeking to play on the national stage. With events in the Persian Gulf in 1990 and 1991 stirring renewed debate over national energy policy, Johnston and ranking Energy Republican Malcolm Wallop offered an omnibus energy package that was quickly seen as the legislative slate on which other measures would be added or subtracted.

The plan paired two opposing issues: allowing oil drilling in the Arctic National Wildlife Refuge (ANWR) and increasing automakers' corporate average fuel economy (CAFE) standards. By linking them, Johnston hoped to forge a consensus. "We need a national energy policy that integrates the tradeoffs of energy, the economy and the environment," he said.

Johnston praised the Bush administration's energy effort, but said its package could not pass without a stronger conservation component such as higher fuel economy standards. He held up his own bill as a more palatable mix. But even Johnston's bill was considered unacceptable to many environmental groups; they adamantly opposed its drilling and nuclear provisions and were skeptical that it would really mandate higher fuel efficiency. Other aspects of Johnston's plan — changes in regulation of electricity and nuclear power, a de facto oil import fee and alternative fuel mandates — also stirred controversy.

Although Johnston was able to win relatively quick approval of his plan in his own committee, which is dominated by senators from energy producing states, the bill was expected to receive a more critical reception in the full Senate, which has stronger environmental leanings. Also, by the time the bill cleared committee in late May, the receding images of the Persian Gulf War and stable gasoline prices had combined to shift the spotlight away from the complex, often dry issue of energy policy.

One of Johnston's biggest legislative victories came in 1989 when Congress lifted price controls from natural gas. In contrast to previous years, when it was one of the most contentious issues on Capitol Hill, gas decontrol moved easily through the 101st Congress, as members from gas-producing and gas-consuming states alike agreed that controls kept very little gas below market prices and had thus become largely irrelevant to consumers.

Johnston introduced his bill in April, encountering opposition from a longtime gas-decontrol foe, Ohio Democrat Howard M. Metzenbaum. The committee, however, shrugged off amendments in May and voted overwhelmingly to approve Johnston's bill for floor action.

Metzenbaum continued to oppose the bill on the floor, issuing attacks on the Energy Committee and oil-and-gas state senators supporting the bill that drew an angry response from Johnston. "I would be severely and personally resentful of the remarks of my distinguished colleague from Ohio had I not heard this story before. It is the same old tired rhetoric," Johnston said. The Senate passed the measure easily in June.

Emboldened by Iraq's invasion of Kuwait in August 1990 — and the resulting worldwide embargo against Iraq that crimped oil supplies, raised gas prices and renewed concerns over the country's dependence on foreign fuel — Johnston was a prime mover behind a bill that expanded the nation's rainy-day supply of crude oil. The bill forced the administration to expand its plan to fill the strategic petroleum reserve to 1 billion barrels, up from the existing goal of 750 million.

Arguing that the nation needed a bigger fuel cushion in case of another embargo, Johnston had pushed for a billion-barrel reserve for some time. The Louisiana Land and Exploration Co., a large oil and gas producer, wanted Congress to increase the 750 million-barrel cap so it could lease the government some of its extra salt domes for storage, a deal that could be worth millions of dollars a year.

Johnston also crafted compromise legislation in 1990 that withheld from timber-cutting more than 1 million additional acres of Alaska's Tongass National Forest.

He worked hard to draft a compromise Tongass bill that could bring together the two wings of his committee: the environmentalists and those such as Alaska Republican Sen. Frank H. Murkowski, who wanted to protect the sectors of the economy in the southeastern Alaskan Panhandle dependent on Tongass timber. Alaska lawmakers sought to prevent the end of an arrangement that guaranteed a steady supply of cheap timber from the 16.7 million-acre forest. The Senate passed Johnston's Tongass bill in June by a 99-0 vote.

Johnston's panel also has jurisdiction over the status of Puerto Rico, an issue Johnston has personally adopted. Legislation to give Puerto Ricans the right to determine their future relationship with the United States stalled at the end of the 101st Congress. The measure died after Johnston announced that there was not enough time to resolve fundamental differences between his bill — which made it through his committee in 1989 — and the House version.

Johnston sought to assure Puerto Ricans that quick action was possible in 1991. But in February, his committee on a 10-10 vote killed the plebiscite bill he had introduced at the start of the 102nd Congress.

Energy Appropriations is another important legislative showcase for Johnston, one where he boldly flexes his muscle. As usual, the panel's fiscal 1991 money bill was full of home-state projects for well-placed senators, who stripped House projects to make room for their own. As subcommittee chairman, Johnston oversaw the bill and inserted money for Louisiana. The bill included nearly $150 million for Louisiana water projects (much more than President Bush or the House had recommended); $12.5 million for Louisiana State University's Biomedical Research Institute; and $750,000 for Louisiana Tech University.

If there is a Louisiana angle on a piece of legislation, Johnston will find it. He joins his fellow Louisiana lawmakers in seeking federal funds for the state's wetlands. And though he once seemed skeptical of the Texas-based superconducting super collider (SSC), Johnston now backs it; two companies bidding to build the massive magnets for the SSC promised to set up factories in Louisiana.

From his Appropriations subcommittee chair, Johnston in July 1990 pushed through Bush's full 1991 request of $318 million for the SSC; a highly favorable committee report contained no mention of the projected $2 billion cost increase for the project. In early 1991, General Dynamics was awarded a $240 million contract to build the collider's magnets and announced that it would do much of the assembly in Louisiana.

Divide and conquer is another well-known Johnston legislative device. He employed this tactic in 1987, when he almost single-handedly rammed a nuclear-waste plan through Congress. Johnston's initial plan was to abandon a search for an Eastern disposal site and put all waste in one of three Western states. He assembled a Senate majority by uniting states with one thing in common: None wanted to host the nation's permanent radioactive-waste dump.

In tense negotiations on a variety of details, Johnston engineered a plan to put all the waste in Nevada. Angry Nevadans cried foul, but the plan passed, and Johnston calmly noted, "If I were a Nevadan living in the real world, I would be happy with this bill. I would bet that in a very few years, Nevada will deem this one of their most treasured industries."

Also a member of the Budget Committee — now its third-ranking Democrat — Johnston dropped out of active participation in the panel's work in 1988 when it recommended less spending for energy programs than he wanted. Johnston even publicly questioned the relevance of the committee in 1991 during the panel's consideration of the budget resolution, saying it made "absolutely no difference" what the committee did.

Generally conservative on defense and foreign policy issues — he was one of just 10 Senate Democrats to vote in January 1991 to authorize the use of force in the Persian Gulf — Johnston has emerged as a leading Senate critic of the strategic defense initiative (SDI). In pursuit of limiting the program, he characteristically has proven to be a powerful player. In the 99th Congress, Johnston offered a floor amendment that came within one vote, 49-50, of cutting SDI funding below the amount recommended by the Armed Services Committee.

The Senate in July 1989 narrowly turned back a Johnston proposal that would have trimmed the program by an additional $558 million. The bill already called for a $366 million reduction in President Bush's $4.9 billion request; Johnston said his proposal would have left SDI funding at the existing level.

Johnston said the program was poorly planned, and he faulted the Pentagon for never clearly stating SDI's mission. Suspecting a close vote, the administration pulled out the stops; the final vote on the motion to kill Johnston's amendment was 50-47.

During consideration of the defense appropriations measure two months later, Johnston again failed to get the chamber to slice the SDI budget. Conferees on the bill ultimately approved $3.8 billion for SDI, almost the precise midpoint between the amounts authorized by the House and the Senate.

Johnston's role in 1987 in leading the opposition to archconservative Supreme Court nominee Robert H. Bork surprised those who remembered him as a young lawyer defending segregation. As late as 1981, when a controversy raged over busing to achieve integration in Baton Rouge schools, he took the lead on a Senate proposal to bar the courts from ordering busing except in limited cases. After a protracted floor struggle, he got the measure through the Senate, though the House balked.

In mid-1986, Johnston announced his challenge to then-Minority Leader Byrd, hoping to transform inchoate dissatisfaction with his leadership into an insurgency. But when the Democrats regained the Senate majority that November, Byrd was widely interviewed in post-election analysis as the new majority leader, with nary a mention of his challenger. Days later, Johnston quit the race, saying he could not dissolve Byrd's "aura of electability."

Johnston's second try began late in 1987 when rumors flourished that Byrd would step down as majority leader to take over Appropriations. Johnston immediately set up a political action committee, Pelican PAC, to raise money for colleagues facing re-election in 1988, and to offset the reputed fundraising prowess of anticipated rivals George J. Mitchell of Maine and Daniel K. Inouye of Hawaii.

A master of the poker-faced political bluff, Johnston brought that game to his bid, working hard to create a perception in the media and in Democratic ranks that his success was assured. The job, however, went easily to Mitchell, whose campaign for the post was as low-key as Johnston's was brash.

At Home: Another 5,000 votes would have made Johnston governor of Louisiana in 1972. Rather than slowing him down, however, Johnston's near-miss in the Democratic runoff against Edwin W. Edwards brought him the public attention he needed for a successful Senate campaign a few months later.

Still, it took an unexpected turn of events to bring Johnston to Washington. After losing the governor's race, he decided on a primary challenge to veteran Sen. Allen J. Ellender, who despite his age (81), was a man of remarkable vigor; he also was chairman of the Appropriations Committee and a master at providing federal money for Louisiana. But three weeks before the primary, Ellender died of a heart attack. Johnston had a clear path to election.

Before his 1971 campaign for governor, Johnston had been just a moderately visible conservative state legislator from northern Louisiana and a lawyer practicing with his father in Shreveport. In the Legislature, his major issue was completion of an Interstate highway linking his home city with New Orleans.

Campaigning against each other in the Democratic runoff, Johnston and Edwards differed politically, regionally and personally. Edwards, a Catholic from Cajun southern Louisiana, had moderate social views and a flamboyant manner. Johnston called for racial moderation, but was more aloof in style, and, as a Baptist from the Protestant north, was universally perceived as being to Edwards' right.

There was little anyone could do to stop Johnston in 1972 once Ellender died. Former Gov. John J. McKeithen tried a last-minute move to reopen filing for the August primary, but the state Democratic committee turned him down. Johnston easily won nomination.

In the fall, McKeithen ran as an independent, bidding for the votes of blacks and low-income whites by characterizing Johnston as the candidate of the wealthy. The former governor had a problem, however, in the well-publicized indictments of key members of his administration. McKeithen himself was never accused of wrongdoing, but Johnston campaigned on the need for a return to honest government.

The GOP nominee was Ben C. Toledano, who had run unsuccessfully for mayor of New Orleans in 1970. He sought to link Johnston to Democratic presidential nominee George Mc-

Govern, but Johnston sloughed off that charge and won 55 percent of the vote.

By 1978, Johnston had some problems at home. He had a reputation among some local Democrats as being aloof and Washington-oriented, and among others as insufficiently conservative. He drew a serious challenge from Democratic state Rep. Louis "Woody" Jenkins, who had worked for George C. Wallace in national politics.

Jenkins labeled the senator a devotee of high taxes and spending, and seemed to be making inroads. But after a slow start, Johnston put on an aggressive drive for renomination. He had taken away Jenkins' best issue earlier in the year by voting against ratification of the Panama Canal treaties. Johnston won 59 percent of the primary vote, assuring him reelection under Louisiana law.

Johnston had clear sailing in 1984, yet in 1990 there were renewed complaints that Johnston had "Potomac fever." But Republicans, after failing to draft a top-drawer candidate, ended up scrambling just to avoid national embarrassment. The sanctioned GOP candidate, little-known state Sen. Ben Bagert, could not raise the money needed to run a credible campaign. Pressured by some Republicans, Bagert dropped out of the race just days before the state's open primary, a move that may have averted a November runoff between Johnston and rogue GOP candidate David Duke.

Duke, a state representative and former Ku Klux Klan leader, ran stronger than expected in a heavy primary turnout, gaining 44 percent against Johnston. Many Republicans — including eight GOP senators — campaigned for Johnston, fearing a Duke upset.

Before Bagert withdrew, Johnston had stayed above the fray, allowing former boxer Bagert to bloody Duke on the hustings. But as the primary approached, Johnston reversed his strategy, stumping the parishes in the populist tradition of the state while running ads showing Duke at cross burnings and giving white power salutes. Despite Johnston's win, Democrats and traditional Republicans were clearly shaken by Duke's strong showing.

Committees

Energy & Natural Resources (Chairman)

Appropriations (4th of 16 Democrats)
Defense; Energy & Water Development (chairman); Foreign Operations; VA, HUD and Independent Agencies; Interior

Budget (3rd of 12 Democrats)

Special Aging (5th of 11 Democrats)

Elections

1990 Primary †

J. Bennett Johnston (D)	752,902	(54%)
David Duke (R)	607,391	(44%)

† In Louisiana the primary is open to candidates of all parties. If a candidate wins 50 percent or more of the vote in the primary, no general election is held.

Previous Winning Percentages: 1984 (86%) **1978** (59%) **1972** (55%)

Campaign Finance

	Receipts	Receipts from PACs		Expend-itures
1990				
Johnston (D)	$4,167,111	$1,416,331	(34%)	$4,989,521
Duke (R)	$2,670,311	0		$2,615,267

Key Votes

1991	
Authorize use of force against Iraq	Y
1990	
Oppose prohibition of certain semiautomatic weapons	Y
Support constitutional amendment on flag desecration	Y
Oppose requiring parental notice for minors' abortions	N
Halt production of B-2 stealth bomber at 13 planes	N
Approve budget that cut spending and raised revenues	N
Pass civil rights bill over Bush veto	Y
1989	
Oppose reduction of SDI funding	N
Oppose barring federal funds for "obscene" art	Y
Allow vote on capital gains tax cut	Y

Voting Studies

	Presidential Support		Party Unity		Conservative Coalition	
Year	**S**	**O**	**S**	**O**	**S**	**O**
1990	53	41	65	29	84	11
1989	70	30	71	29	63	37
1988	63	35	77	20	86	11
1987	44	54	82	17	88	13
1986	58	42	61	37	67	30
1985	45	53	63	33	68	27
1984	61	30	51	44	83	11
1983	55	44	54	40	82	5
1982	61	37	47	48	93	6
1981	68	26	49	45	93	3

Interest Group Ratings

Year	ADA	ACU	AFL-CIO	CCUS
1990	39	38	86	33
1989	30	32	70	63
1988	55	36	86	50
1987	70	20	90	33
1986	50	35	67	44
1985	60	45	80	28
1984	55	59	56	47
1983	20	56	43	67
1982	35	63	50	67
1981	25	27	35	82

John B. Breaux (D)

Of Crowley — Elected 1986

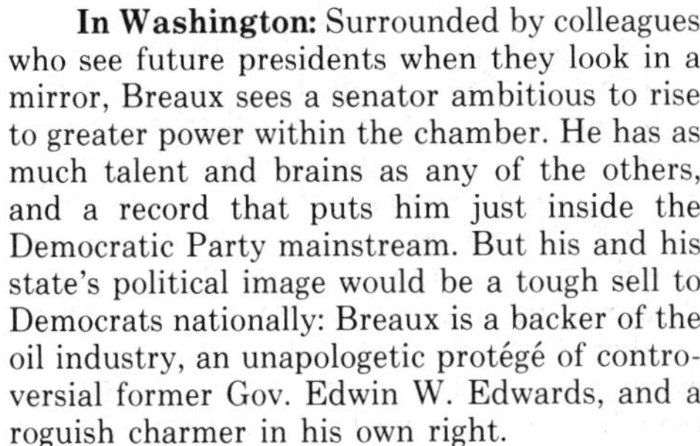

Born: March 1, 1944, Crowley, La.
Education: U. of Southwestern Louisiana, B.A. 1964; Louisiana State U., J.D. 1967.
Occupation: Lawyer.
Family: Wife, Lois Daigle; four children.
Religion: Roman Catholic.
Political Career: U.S. House, 1972-87.
Capitol Office: 516 Hart Bldg. 20510; 224-4623.

In Washington: Surrounded by colleagues who see future presidents when they look in a mirror, Breaux sees a senator ambitious to rise to greater power within the chamber. He has as much talent and brains as any of the others, and a record that puts him just inside the Democratic Party mainstream. But his and his state's political image would be a tough sell to Democrats nationally: Breaux is a backer of the oil industry, an unapologetic protégé of controversial former Gov. Edwin W. Edwards, and a roguish charmer in his own right.

He already has begun an impressive ascent in the Senate. With more congressional experience (seven House terms) than any of the 13 freshman senators who arrived in 1987, Breaux had the rare privilege of immediately becoming chairman of two subcommittees. Then late in 1988, newly elected Majority Leader George J. Mitchell of Maine picked Breaux for the position that Mitchell himself had parlayed into his leadership victory: chairman of the fundraising Democratic Senatorial Campaign Committee (DSCC).

During the 101st Congress, the Democratic Steering Committee awarded Breaux a coveted seat on the Finance Committee, the same panel where former Louisiana Democrat Russell B. Long wielded great institutional power as chairman for 14 years.

Breaux was chosen to head the DSCC even though he had been campaign manager for Mitchell's rival for majority leader, senior Louisiana Sen. J. Bennett Johnston. The choice appeared to be an olive branch from Mitchell, but the fact was, no one was better for the job than Breaux. He cannot get enough of politics, whether fundraising, strategizing or legislating. And, true to the Cajun let-the-good-times-roll tradition, he makes it look like great fun.

Breaux could look back with satisfaction when he completed his DSCC term after the 1990 election. While Republicans had spoken of using 1990 as a springboard for retaking Senate control in 1992 — Breaux said in 1989 that "my goal is to hold the line" — the Democrats actually increased their majority by one seat, with Breaux raising record amounts of money for his party's candidates.

As one who simply loves the legislative game for its own sake, Breaux does not bring ideology or great policy aims to the table. However, like other moderate-to-conservative Southerners, he has called for the Democratic Party to move rightward. He was one of 10 Democratic senators to support the January 1991 resolution authorizing the president to use force in the Persian Gulf.

Two years earlier, he opposed the selection of a black, Ronald H. Brown, as national party chairman, frankly arguing that Democrats needed to court white males who had left the party. Breaux's objections sparked some controversy, given his status as a party campaign spokesman and the fact that he owed his 1986 election in part to overwhelming black support.

Breaux is similarly unabashed about courting business. His shrewd pragmatism is almost shameless, although endearingly so, as illustrated by his now-legendary remark in 1981 explaining that he would support President Ronald Reagan's proposed social spending cuts in return for concessions on natural gas policy and sugar subsidies. Breaux quipped that while his vote could not be bought, "it can be rented."

Above all, Breaux is an advocate for Louisiana's interests, especially energy and commercial fishing. On Commerce, Science and Transportation, he chairs the Merchant Marine panel. On Environment and Public Works, he headed the Nuclear Regulation Subcommittee before leaving the committee to join Finance.

Calling the Finance panel "a whole new world" for him, Breaux said of its jurisdiction: "The power to tax is the power to destroy, but it is also the power to do a lot of good things." Breaux sought the seat in part to push for a cut in the capital gains tax, a top business priority.

In 1990, he used his position to secure funding to help Louisiana address its coastal erosion problems, a concern not only of environmentalists, but also of business. Late in the 101st Congress, during consideration of the deficit-reduction package, Breaux persuaded his colleagues on Finance to include in the measure a $50 million "wetlands preservation" trust fund, with about $35 million of the total going to Louisiana.

Earlier, he had proposed a bill to restore eroding wetlands — like his state's shrimp-rich coast — by using a share of federal oil-leasing revenues. To further protect Louisiana shrimpers, Breaux joined with Johnston in 1989 to gain approval of a measure to bar shrimp imports from any country that does not take actions to protect endangered sea turtles. With American shrimpers subject to turtle-protection regulations, Breaux and Johnston said foreign imports had an unfair advantage. The senators successfully attached the provision to a spending measure approved by Congress in October.

Despite a dedication to nuclear power and the petrochemical industry, Breaux also has to balance the safety and environmental concerns of Louisianans. When Environment Committee members offered their first rewrite of the Clean Air Act in April 1989, Breaux was considered a pivotal backer. "Those of us in Louisiana want not only jobs, we want to be able to breathe the air and breathe it safely," he said. While his state is home to many oil refineries and chemical manufacturers affected by the bill, it is also hard-hit by air-toxics emissions and has a high incidence of health problems suspected to be caused by those emissions.

During committee debate on strengthening the act, Breaux generally represented industry viewpoints, but early in 1989 he cosponsored legislation against toxic emissions. When Bush administration and congressional representatives bogged down in early 1990 over a number of the bill's provisions, Breaux participated in three weeks of backroom negotiations that produced a compromise aimed at satisfying environmentalists without forfeiting administration support. Breaux fought on the floor to prevent the adoption of amendments designed to tighten controls on toxic air pollution even further, fearing such stringent regulations would unduly burden industry and would lead the administration to oppose the measure.

Breaux also played a role in oil-spill liability legislation during the 101st Congress. When the Senate considered an amendment to raise significantly the liability limits approved by the Environment Committee, an angry Breaux argued that the higher insurance costs mandated by higher liability limits would bring higher oil prices. In part to accommodate Breaux, the limits were scaled back and the legislation was enacted in 1990.

On the Nuclear Regulation Subcommittee he chaired, Breaux worked closely with ranking Republican Alan K. Simpson of Wyoming. They had a lead role in the effort that renewed the Price-Anderson law on nuclear accident insurance, cosponsoring legislation to raise utilities' liability tenfold to about $7 billion. The committee approved the bill unanimously in 1987, but jurisdictional tiffs with Johnston's Energy Committee prevented final action until the next year, when the Senate acted on a House-passed bill.

It was not surprising that Breaux hit the Senate running, given his long House experience. First elected at 28, he became a power broker while most of his contemporaries were still learning the process. He might have risen higher, if not for his 1981 defection to Reaganomics. In 1983, House leaders dispensed prize committee seats as rewards for party loyalty, and denied Breaux a Budget Committee spot he wanted.

He built his House career in part by filling a power vacuum. Finding that most members of the Merchant Marine and Fisheries Committee paid little attention to it, he chose to concentrate there, not only for his district's fishing interests but also for the panel's potential role in energy and environmental policy. As chairman of the Subcommittee on Fisheries and Wildlife Conservation and the Environment, Breaux helped force the committee's way into a number of important legislative battles, such as development on the outer continental shelf and the effort by some coastal states to get a larger share of the revenues from offshore drilling leases.

At Home: Breaux learned his trade from one of Louisiana's masters — Edwards, the state's three-term governor and a former U.S. representative. Breaux was Edwards' junior law partner and served for four years as one of his top congressional aides.

When Edwards first won the governorship in February 1972, he pushed for Breaux to be his successor in the House. With Edwards' organization, Breaux easily paced the field of six Democratic primary candidates, then won the September runoff with 55 percent of the vote over TV newscaster Gary Tyler, the same man Edwards had defeated to win his first congressional term seven years earlier.

Breaux does not, however, owe his ascent to the Senate to Edwards' influence. If anything, his one-time mentor made his 1986 bid to replace retiring Democrat Long more difficult.

During Edwards' third term, Louisiana's oil industry had foundered, and by the time of the 1986 Senate contest the state's economy was reeling. Many voters were in a mood to blame the Democrats. Moreover, Edwards' image had suffered during two trials on corruption charges, even though he was eventually acquitted.

Those circumstances gave the Republicans one of their best openings in years. Early in 1986, GOP Rep. W. Henson Moore began airing ads designed to exploit voters' restlessness. "The party is over," they said. "It's time to go back to work." Democrats, Moore charged, had squandered the state's resources and prostituted the political system to their own advantage. Republicans, Moore argued, were the party of reform. He quickly took the lead.

If Moore had continued on the same tack, he might have won. But as the nonpartisan September primary approached, he pushed to win more than 50 percent of the vote and avoid a runoff. He shifted his emphasis, beginning a wave of ads and mailings that attacked Breaux directly. "The politician's politician, always putting himself first," one mailer called the Democrat. At the same time, the national GOP mounted a program to purge ineligible voters from the rolls in black precincts.

None of those tactics sat well with Louisiana's basically Democratic electorate. Moore seemed mean-spirited, especially in contrast with Breaux's roguish Cajun charm. And the "ballot security" program infuriated black voters — a boost for Breaux, since many blacks had considered him too conservative.

The primary was a turning point. Moore came in first, but he did not run as strongly as many had expected. Over the next month, Breaux worked to take the high ground Moore had squandered, arguing that the state's problems stemmed not from the state government, but from a Republican administration in Washington that had followed misguided trade and farm policies. Moore's first allegiance, he charged, was to his party and to Reagan, not to Louisiana. Moore tried to recoup, softening his message, but Breaux carried 42 of 64 parishes.

Committees

Commerce, Science & Transportation (9th of 11 Democrats)
Merchant Marine (chairman); Communications; Surface Transportation; National Ocean Policy Study

Finance (11th of 11 Democrats)
Energy & Agricultural Taxation; International Trade; Social Security & Family Policy

Special Aging (6th of 11 Democrats)

Elections

1986 General		
John B. Breaux (D)	723,586	(53%)
W. Henson Moore (R)	646,311	(47%)
1986 Primary †		
W. Henson Moore (R)	529,433	(44%)
John B. Breaux (D)	447,328	(37%)
Samuel B. Nunez (D)	73,505	(6%)
J.E. Jumonville Jr. (D)	53,394	(5%)
Sherman A. Bernard (D)	52,479	(4%)
Others	41,102	(3%)

† In Louisiana the primary is open to candidates of all parties. If a candidate wins 50 percent or more of the vote in the primary, no general election is held.

Previous Winning Percentages: **1984 *** (86%) **1982 *** (79%) **1980 *** (100%) **1978 *** (60%) **1976 *** (83%) **1974 *** (89%) **1972 †** (100%)

** House elections.*
† Special House election.

Campaign Finance

	Receipts	Receipts from PACs		Expenditures
1986				
Breaux (D)	$2,990,614	$898,173	(30%)	$2,948,313
Moore (R)	$6,002,459	$1,204,936	(20%)	$5,986,460

Key Votes

1991	
Authorize use of force against Iraq	Y
1990	
Oppose prohibition of certain semiautomatic weapons	Y
Support constitutional amendment on flag desecration	Y
Oppose requiring parental notice for minors' abortions	N
Halt production of B-2 stealth bomber at 13 planes	N
Approve budget that cut spending and raised revenues	Y
Pass civil rights bill over Bush veto	Y
1989	
Oppose reduction of SDI funding	N
Oppose barring federal funds for "obscene" art	N
Allow vote on capital gains tax cut	N

Voting Studies

	Presidential Support		Party Unity		Conservative Coalition	
Year	**S**	**O**	**S**	**O**	**S**	**O**
1990	57	41	68	31	95	5
1989	71	28	62	38	87	13
1988	61	36	73	25	92	5
1987	42	58	84	15	81	19
House Service						
1986	21	28	24	11	32	0
1985	49	44	53	36	89	5
1984	50	38	49	36	80	8
1983	52	40	41	50	85	9
1982	58	27	44	42	64	14
1981	61	24	35	42	63	7

Interest Group Ratings

Year	ADA	ACU	AFL-CIO	CCUS
1990	33	39	78	33
1989	40	30	100	50
1988	50	44	85	43
1987	70	19	90	28
House Service				
1986	30	63	100	25
1985	35	62	53	62
1984	15	52	25	40
1983	20	70	31	65
1982	15	71	22	67
1981	0	69	20	84

1 Robert L. Livingston (R)

Of Metairie — Elected 1977

Born: April 30, 1943, Colorado Springs, Colo.
Education: Tulane U., B.A. 1967, J.D. 1968.
Military Service: Navy, 1961-63; Naval Reserve, 1963-67.
Occupation: Lawyer.
Family: Wife, Bonnie Robichaux; four children.
Religion: Episcopalian.
Political Career: Republican nominee for U.S. House, 1976; Republican candidate for governor, 1987.
Capitol Office: 2368 Rayburn Bldg. 20515; 225-3015.

In Washington: A former prosecutor, Livingston brings conservative fervor and an adversarial style to his House assignments. The Appropriations Committee gives Livingston a forum for his staunch support of big weapons systems, and a chance to deliver defense dollars to his economically struggling state. On House Administration, which Livingston joined in the 102nd Congress, he waves the GOP flag on issues such as public financing of campaigns, which he stoutly opposes.

Livingston's ideology and legislative temperament give him much in common with the younger generation of House GOP confrontationalists, led by party whip Newt Gingrich. But Livingston came to Congress in 1977, a bit before the New Wave-conservative Republicans hit Washington in 1979, and, in greater numbers, in 1981. Livingston at times seems to have a foot in the "Old Bull" camp of veteran Republicans, who are more accommodating in their legislative dealings with Democrats, and more loyal to the White House line.

When President Bush and Minority Leader Robert H. Michel pleaded with conservatives to stick with the 1990 budget summit agreement despite its tax increases, Livingston was with them. After a White House meeting, he said, "For us Republicans, we owe it to our president to listen to his fears." He supported the agreement on the House floor, where Gingrich was busily — and successfully — mobilizing his GOP allies to defeat it.

In early 1989, Livingston took a moderate stand when he called on the United States to return to the bargaining table with Gen. Manuel Antonio Noriega in Panama, and offer to drop drug charges against him in exchange for his relinquishing power. In that case, the administration took the hard line, using military force to overthrow Noriega.

On Appropriations, Livingston has been a leading supporter of the strategic defense initiative and of military aid to Central America. During the Reagan-era battles over contra aid, Livingston seemed to view each vote on the issue as a test of patriotism. Democrats usually failed the test by advancing what he saw as a policy of appeasement. After the House narrowly defeated a "humanitarian" contra-aid package in 1988, Livingston took to the House well to warn, "We might ultimately have to send our boys to some Central America front before very long because we have given peace a chance."

When not battling liberals on matters of foreign policy, Livingston spends his time looking for ways to bring defense dollars home. He also works to protect the state's offshore oil drilling industry. With plans to ban the drilling moving in Congress and supported by the Bush administration in 1990, Livingston complained that Congress had succumbed to "environmental hysteria."

Livingston has championed protection for the Pelican State's shrimpers. In the 1987 supplemental appropriations bill, he attached an amendment telling the federal government to back off regulations requiring shrimpers to equip their nets with "turtle-excluder devices" (TEDs). The controversial TEDs are 50-pound metal frames, each equipped with a trapdoor that opens when a netted turtle presses against it. While they usually work fine in clear-water areas, TEDs get jammed with sticks and mud in Louisiana's less pristine waters, and shrimpers can lose much of their catch. After a battle with the Rules Committee — where the chairman of the fisheries committee complained that the issue was far more complex than Livingston presented — a delay in the regulation was approved.

When neither Louisiana nor favored military projects are involved, Livingston hews to a cost-cutting approach to appropriating. Of his willingness to cut social programs and boost defense spending, he once said: "I happen to think that none of our social programs will function too well under the red boot."

Earlier in his career, Livingston was a

Louisiana 1

Southeast — Jefferson Parish

The 1st is a largely suburban and decidedly conservative constituency. The only part of New Orleans in the district is the wealthy Lakeview section of the city.

The heart of the 1st is the heavily populated northern half of Jefferson Parish. Known for decades as the "Free State of Jefferson" because of its tolerance for casinos, slot machines and cockfights, the parish has undergone a whitewashing in the public mind as suburbanization has cleaned it up. Gambling in recent years has been restricted to horse races.

The populous east bank of Jefferson Parish is more white-collar, affluent and Republican than the areas on the west bank of the Mississippi. Elegant homes are concentrated near the shore of Lake Pontchartrain, in communities like Metairie, New Orleans' original suburb. Metairie's politics received national attention in early 1989 when Republican David Duke, a former leader of the Ku Klux Klan, was elected to the Louisiana Legislature. National Republican leaders blasted Duke as a bigot, but that did not prevent his narrow runoff victory over John Treen, brother of former GOP Gov. David C. Treen. Duke went on to wage a surprisingly strong, although losing, campaign for the Senate in 1990.

The west bank tends to be blue-collar, although its voters like Livingston's conservative orientation on defense and foreign policy issues. Shipbuilding and offshore oil supply companies line the Harvey Canal on the west bank. At Avondale is one of the largest shipyards in the country, the district's largest employer. Hard times in the maritime industry have forced it to rely heavily on Navy contracts for survival. Many ship workers live in nearby Gretna and Westwego, the most populous towns on the west bank.

From Jefferson Parish, the 1st jumps some 25 miles across Lake Pontchartrain to take in St. Tammany Parish — which Livingston considered so important to his political survival that he threatened to run for the U.S. Senate in 1984 if the Legislature removed it from the 1st. Once an isolated vacation area for residents escaping the heat and humidity of New Orleans, St. Tammany Parish now is a booming suburban haven.

St. Tammany has been the fastest growing parish in the state in the last two decades. In the 1970s it had a 74 percent increase; in the 1980s it grew more than 30 percent. Many of the newcomers are transplants from the East and Midwest who have maintained Republican voting habits. St. Tammany gave George Bush roughly 70 percent of its vote in 1988.

Population: 525,883. White 457,630 (87%), Black 58,073 (11%), Other 6,215 (1%). Spanish origin 22,817 (4%). 18 and over 367,724 (70%), 65 and over 43,197 (8%). Median age: 29.

congressional ethics specialist, spending much of his time on business before the Committee on Standards of Official Conduct. He was one of the hard-line members of the committee, arguing strongly for the expulsion of Pennsylvania Democrat Michael "Ozzie" Myers in an Abscam bribery case and for censure of Charles H. Wilson, a California Democrat accused of several kickback charges. In the 101st Congress, Livingston was appointed to a special bipartisan panel reviewing ethics standards.

At Home: The 1st District did not come close to electing a Republican to the House for a century after Reconstruction, but now that it has one, it seems quite satisfied. Livingston has had no difficulty holding the seat he won in a 1977 special election.

But Livingston has shown some restlessness in Congress. Late in 1986 he told the Baton Rouge magazine *Gris Gris*, "I've been here 10 years and I'm 43 years old. In all likelihood, in 10 years I'll be 53 years old and still broke and the only thing I can say then is that I've been here 20 years."

That led in part to his decision to run for governor in 1987. Livingston's visibility among Republicans in the New Orleans area put him in a strong position to finish near the top of a field of five major candidates, which included colorful and scandal-tainted Democratic Gov. Edwin W. Edwards, and Democratic Reps. W. J. "Billy" Tauzin and Buddy Roemer.

All candidates appear on the same primary ballot in Louisiana, and as the only major Republican, Livingston had an inside track to the runoff. Many felt he could win the governorship if his runoff foe was the troubled incumbent, Edwards.

But Roemer, the eventual winner, was a dynamic candidate who successfully appealed to many conservatives who might have voted Republican. Meanwhile, Livingston proved to be a somewhat plodding candidate; during one televised debate he lost his train of thought and fell silent during a statement on education. Livingston finished third, behind both Roemer and Edwards. Roemer won the governorship, and in 1991 switched to the GOP.

A prosperous New Orleans lawyer, former assistant U.S. attorney and veteran party worker, Livingston made his first bid for Congress in 1976, when Democrat F. Edward Hebert retired. He lost narrowly to a labor-backed Democrat, state Rep. Richard A. Tonry.

Livingston did not have to wait long, however, for a second try. Tonry's 1976 primary opponent succeeded in pressing a vote-fraud case against him, and Tonry resigned from the House in May 1977. He sought vindication in a second Democratic primary that June, but lost to state Rep. Ron Faucheux. Tonry later pleaded guilty to violations of federal campaign finance law and went to prison.

Livingston was ready to run as soon as Tonry resigned. He mounted a well-financed campaign against Faucheux that drew significant blue-collar support as well as backing from more traditional GOP voters in white-collar areas. Spending over $500,000, Livingston launched an ad blitz that showed him in his earlier job as a welder, and as a devoted family man (in contrast to Faucheux, a young bachelor). With organized labor refusing to support Faucheux, Livingston won easily, and he has met no formidable Democratic challenger since.

The only threat to his House career was posed in 1981 by the Democratic Legislature, which passed a redistricting bill that would have forced Livingston to run in a new district heavily weighted with blue-collar sections of Jefferson Parish. When Republican Gov. David C. Treen threatened a veto, the Legislature backed off.

Court-ordered redistricting in 1983 further strengthened Livingston's position, when the Legislature shifted most of New Orleans out of the 1st in exchange for the affluent "east bank" of Jefferson Parish.

Committees

Appropriations (9th of 22 Republicans)
Defense; Foreign Operations, Export Financing & Related Programs

House Administration (8th of 9 Republicans)
Elections (ranking); Personnel & Police

Elections

1990 Primary †		
Bob Livingston (R)	132,855	(84%)
Vincent J. Bruno (R)	25,494	(16%)
1988 Primary †		
Bob Livingston (R)	67,679	(78%)
George Mustakas (D)	13,091	(15%)
Eric Honig (D)	5,457	(6%)

† In Louisiana the primary is open to candidates of all parties. If a candidate wins 50 percent or more of the vote in the primary, no general election is held.

Previous Winning Percentages: **1986** (100%) **1984** (88%) **1982** (86%) **1980** (88%) **1978** (86%) **1977 *** (51%)

** Special election.*

District Vote For President

	1988	1984	1980	1976
D	61,017 (29%)	45,633 (22%)	59,716 (30%)	63,032 (39%)
R	147,346 (70%)	157,865 (77%)	130,452 (66%)	94,430 (59%)
I			4,726 (2%)	

Campaign Finance

	Receipts	Receipts from PACs	Expend-itures
1990			
Livingston (R)	$279,603	$140,878 (50%)	$108,207
1988			
Livingston (R)	$262,408	$127,834 (49%)	$555,058
Mustakas (D)	$102,880	0	$99,065
Honig (D)	$27,006	$854 (3%)	$26,106

Key Votes

1991	
Authorize use of force against Iraq	Y
1990	
Support constitutional amendment on flag desecration	Y
Pass family and medical leave bill over Bush veto	N
Reduce SDI funding	N
Allow abortions in overseas military facilities	N
Approve budget summit plan for spending and taxing	Y
Approve civil rights bill	N
1989	
Halt production of B-2 stealth bomber at 13 planes	N
Oppose capital gains tax cut	N
Approve federal abortion funding in rape or incest cases	N
Approve pay raise and revision of ethics rules	Y
Pass Democratic minimum wage plan over Bush veto	N

Voting Studies

	Presidential Support		Party Unity		Conservative Coalition	
Year	**S**	**O**	**S**	**O**	**S**	**O**
1990	75	23	71	23	87	7
1989	79	21	68	29	98	2
1988	63	26	78	11	95	3
1987	43	22	41	16	70	2
1986	76	19	71	21	92	6
1985	74	24	81	15	96	4
1984	75	24	86	12	95	5
1983	77	18	76	17	85	12
1982	79	14	76	20	84	11
1981	76	21	71	20	76	17

Interest Group Ratings

Year	ADA	ACU	AFL-CIO	CCUS
1990	6	83	8	79
1989	5	93	17	90
1988	5	100	8	100
1987	0	73	7	78
1986	0	82	21	78
1985	0	86	12	86
1984	5	96	15	81
1983	5	90	6	95
1982	5	80	5	82
1981	20	71	27	94

2 William J. Jefferson (D)

Of New Orleans — Elected 1990

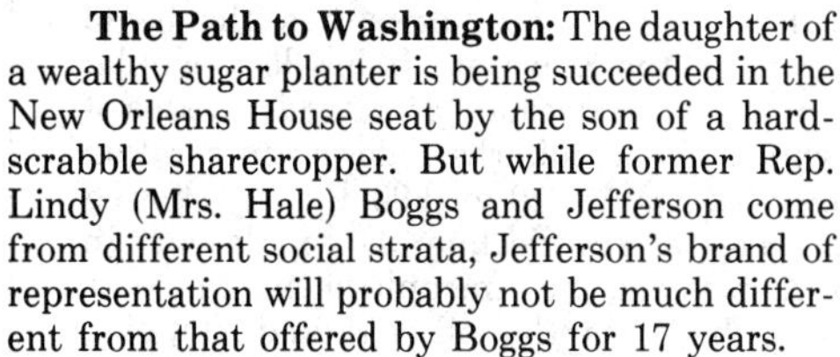

Born: March 14, 1947, Lake Providence, La.
Education: Southern U., B.A. 1969; Harvard U., J.D. 1972.
Military Service: Army, 1969-75.
Occupation: Lawyer.
Family: Wife, Andrea Green; five children.
Religion: Baptist.
Political Career: La. Senate, 1980-91; candidate for mayor of New Orleans, 1982, 1986.
Capitol Office: 506 Cannon Bldg. 20515; 225-6636.

The Path to Washington: The daughter of a wealthy sugar planter is being succeeded in the New Orleans House seat by the son of a hard-scrabble sharecropper. But while former Rep. Lindy (Mrs. Hale) Boggs and Jefferson come from different social strata, Jefferson's brand of representation will probably not be much different from that offered by Boggs for 17 years.

Like Boggs, he is regarded as a liberal Democrat; and like the politically well-connected widow of a one-time House majority leader, Jefferson boasts of being a coalition-builder who can steer federal largess to economically slumping New Orleans.

Jefferson's election was notable on several counts. He is Louisiana's first black congressman since Reconstruction, and his constituency is the last black-majority House district in the country to gain black representation.

In Jefferson, it will have a representative whose life has almost literally been a rags-to-riches story. Raised in poverty in rural northeast Louisiana as one of 10 children, he quickly showed brains and ambition. He was student body president at Southern University in Baton Rouge, winner of a scholarship to Harvard Law School, a law clerk in New Orleans for veteran federal appellate court Judge Alvin Rubin and then a legislative assistant to Louisiana Democratic Sen. J. Bennett Johnston.

In 1979, Jefferson launched his political career by winning a seat in the Louisiana Senate, ousting a white incumbent in a racially mixed New Orleans district that included much of the affluent Uptown area.

Jefferson was a major player in the Legislature. While he chaired the Senate Governmental Affairs Committee that has jurisdiction over reapportionment, he considered economic development and budget matters his specialty.

Jefferson served on the Senate Finance Committee for much of the 1980s and headed the special Budget Stabilization Committee created to cut state spending and find new revenue sources when Louisiana's oil-based economy nose-dived several years ago.

When Boggs announced her retirement in 1990, Jefferson was well-positioned to succeed her. With the backing of Mayor Sidney Barthelemy, many of the city's white officials and the Interdenominational Ministerial Alliance (the city's largest organization of black clergy), he ran first in the crowded Oct. 6 voting, then beat attorney Marc H. Morial by roughly 5,000 votes in the November runoff

On issues, there was little difference between Jefferson and Morial, the 32-year-old son of the city's first black mayor, Ernest N. "Dutch" Morial.

But their runoff turned bitter as the candidates focused on personality and questions of competence. To Jefferson, the choice was between an experienced legislator and an untried young man trying to win office on his father's name. To Morial, the choice was an energetic, reform-minded community servant or a tainted pol.

Morial mocked Jefferson's experience in the Legislature ("We don't want to take Baton Rouge shenanigans to Washington," he said) and hit hard at questions surrounding Jefferson's personal finances.

Jefferson had done lucrative legal work for the state while serving in the Legislature and was dogged by reports that he owed tens of thousands of dollars in outstanding loans and back taxes on struggling business ventures. Jefferson disputed the size of his financial obligations, which he blamed on the city's slumping economy, and said his legal work for the state had been approved by the state's ethics board and the state attorney general.

The 2nd is nearly 60 percent black, and the two candidates ran virtually neck and neck in the city's black precincts. Jefferson won on the strength of his showing on the largely white, working-class West Bank.

Some think Jefferson ultimately has his eye on City Hall; he lost bids for the New Orleans mayoralty in 1982 and 1986.

Louisiana 2

Jefferson Parish — New Orleans

New Orleans seems slightly exotic to most Americans, but it is a patchwork of ethnic neighborhoods, just like every other large industrial city in the country. Besides the black community that makes up more than half the city's population, there are large numbers of Italians, Irish, Cubans and the largest group of Hondurans outside Central America. These groups are not as separate from each other as they might be in other cities; the ethnic communities are scattered throughout the city in "marble cake" fashion.

The Algiers section, which sits on the west bank of the Mississippi River, is a microcosm of the city as a whole, a blend of high- and low-income residents, new condominiums and well-tended historic buildings. On the east bank, between the Mississippi and Lake Pontchartrain, is a fascinating variety of neighborhoods: comfortable Carrolton, an area of middle-class whites on the west side of the city; the wealthy Uptown section, with its professionals and academics clustered around Tulane and Loyola universities; the predominantly black Lower 9th Ward; and fast-growing New Orleans East, reaching into the city's marshland, with its middle-class black and white families.

The district also holds all of the New Orleans that tourists expect to see: the French Quarter, which includes former Rep. Lindy (Mrs. Hale) Boggs' home on Bourbon Street; the Garden District and its historic mansions; and downtown New Orleans.

The 75,000-seat Louisiana Superdome — site of the 1988 Republican National Convention and numerous Super Bowls — is the centerpiece of the construction boom that has transformed the downtown area. Along nearby Poydras Avenue, most of the major oil companies have built large office towers. Not far away is the site of the 1984 World's Fair; it has been turned into a convention center and a food and shopping emporium called Riverwalk.

Still, in spite of the development, New Orleans sometimes seems more like the older cities of the North than the boom towns of the Sun Belt. It has lost population in recent decades, as a steady exodus of whites to the suburbs followed integration in 1960. From 1980 to 1990, the city showed an 11 percent decline in population. In recent years, its unemployment rate has been high, as the oil, gas and shipping industries declined and the building boom of previous years slowed down.

Since 1980, the city has had a black majority. A 1983 redistricting plan, which by court order had to create a majority-black congressional district, placed the 2nd entirely within New Orleans. With its new shape, the district is 59 percent black.

Population: 525,331. White 205,407 (39%), Black 307,865 (59%), Other 7,697 (2%). Spanish origin 17,732 (3%). 18 and over 370,324 (71%), 65 and over 58,513 (11%). Median age: 28.

Committees

Education & Labor (20th of 25 Democrats)
Elementary, Secondary & Vocational Education; Postsecondary Education; Select Education

Merchant Marine & Fisheries (28th of 29 Democrats)
Fisheries & Wildlife Conservation & the Environment; Merchant Marine

Campaign Finance

	Receipts	Receipts from PACs		Expend-itures
1990				
Jefferson (D)	$448,100	$104,950	(23%)	$446,743
Morial (D)	$492,323	$26,500	(5%)	$487,171

Key Vote

1991

Authorize use of force against Iraq	N

Elections

1990 General		
William J. Jefferson (D)	55,621	(53%)
Marc H. Morial (D)	50,232	(47%)
1990 Primary		
William J. Jefferson (D)	32,237	(24%)
Marc H. Morial (D)	29,366	(22%)
Jon D. Johnson (D)	25,468	(19%)
Harwood "Woody" Koppel (D)	24,175	(18%)
Edgar "Dooky" Chase (D)	9,017	(7%)
Michael G. Bagneris (D)	4,742	(4%)

District Vote For President

	1988	1984	1980	1976
D	111,706 (68%)	116,744 (62%)	102,723 (61%)	98,378 (62%)
R	50,134 (31%)	70,886 (38%)	60,105 (36%)	57,593 (36%)
I			3,653 (2%)	

3 W.J. "Billy" Tauzin (D)

Of Thibodaux — Elected 1980

Born: June 14, 1943, Chackbay, La.
Education: Nicholls State U., B.A. 1964; Louisiana State U., J.D. 1967.
Occupation: Lawyer.
Family: Wife, Gayle Clement; five children.
Religion: Roman Catholic.
Political Career: La. House, 1971-80; Democratic candidate for governor, 1987.
Capitol Office: 2342 Rayburn Bldg. 20515; 225-4031.

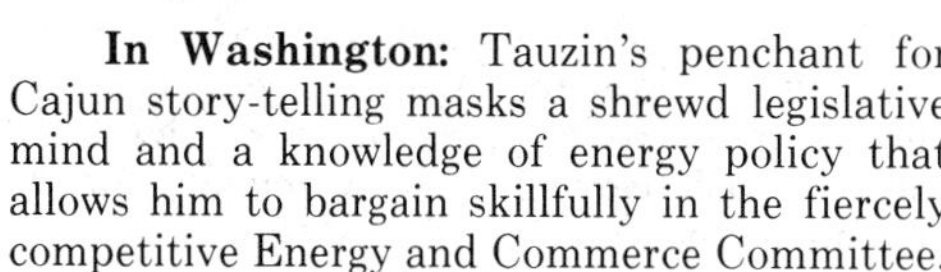

In Washington: Tauzin's penchant for Cajun story-telling masks a shrewd legislative mind and a knowledge of energy policy that allows him to bargain skillfully in the fiercely competitive Energy and Commerce Committee.

Tauzin's hopes to move beyond the House were dashed in 1987 when his gubernatorial bid flopped. But he quickly rebounded and plunged back into the familiar bayous of his committee.

Energy and Commerce is a good spot for this truck driver's son, who made his way to Washington with unusual purpose. By the age of 10 his grandfather was referring to him as "the lawyer," but he had to overcome a rustic naïveté and a lisp before becoming student body president in high school. He went to law school at Louisiana State, where he was a classmate of John B. Breaux, now the state's junior senator. At ease in the recondite world of Louisiana politics, Tauzin is able to think on several planes at once — a valuable asset when operating in the shadow of the vulpine John D. Dingell, chairman of Energy and Commerce.

Tauzin is more than just a player on Energy and Commerce. He is a play-maker, building coalitions to win support for his point of view. His involvement is usually a signal that a given proposal must be taken seriously.

In the 101st Congress, for example, Tauzin was instrumental in mobilizing support for a pipeline safety bill. In October 1989, 11 fishermen died off the Louisiana-Texas coast after their ship hit an uncovered natural gas pipeline in an inland waterway. Tauzin responded with a bill requiring pipeline owners to inspect their underwater pipelines in the Gulf of Mexico and inland waterways to ensure they were properly buried. He had initially proposed even broader rules, but scaled them back and persuaded fishing groups to agree to the compromise version as well. As a result, the bill moved through Congress with the basic assent of the industry.

Energy and Commerce is a key committee for Louisiana's oil and gas industry, and Tauzin is one of the industry's most knowledgeable allies. In typical Tauzin fashion, his major influence lately was behind the scenes, on an issue crucial to the state's economy: rewriting the Clean Air Act. During the 100th Congress, he was a member of the so-called "group of nine." The group was composed of Energy and Commerce members trying to forge a compromise between Dingell's protection of the automobile industry and Midwestern utilities, on one hand, and the environmentalists led by California's Henry A. Waxman, chairman of the Health and the Environment Subcommittee, on the other.

Tauzin's district makes him sensitive both to job and environmental concerns, and he offered a key compromise on toxic air pollutants that won support from both camps. But not enough breakthroughs were made on other aspects of the issue during the 100th, and the controversial legislation did not move until the next Congress.

Tauzin's expertise kept him in the thick of clean-air negotiations in the 101st Congress, but he was unable to stop two House members from Texas from diluting an alternative fuels requirement for automobiles. Louisiana's natural gas is one of the alternative fuels that would have been promoted more forcefully under the original provision.

Tauzin took over the Coast Guard and Navigation Subcommittee of the Merchant Marine Committee in early 1989, just in time for the *Exxon Valdez* oil spill in Alaska.

Tauzin held the first congressional hearing on the spill and began prodding his colleagues to pass federal oil spill prevention and compensation legislation. They did, but not the version he had hoped for; Tauzin, whose pro-industry views sometimes leave him outside the more environmentally tilted mainstream in the House, complained that the bill did not limit liability for shippers and would make it impossible for some to get liability insurance.

Tauzin also successfully used the subcommittee post to argue for a heftier Coast Guard budget, winning an extra $64 million for its operations and projects in the 101st Congress. At the same time, he was not shy about calling for Coast Guard assistance. When the Commerce Department required shrimpers to

Louisiana 3

South Central — Houma; New Iberia

Just west of New Orleans, Cajun Louisiana begins. The Cajuns — the word is a slurring of "Acadians" — are descendants of 15,000 French settlers who moved south from Acadia (Nova Scotia) in the 18th century. Their territory roughly covers the southern half of Louisiana. This is a predominantly Catholic area, one of the few in the Deep South, and there is a historic antipathy to the hard-shell Protestantism of north Louisiana and neighboring states.

The area is different from most of the state politically as well as culturally. There are relatively few blacks, and race is less of an issue than in other regions. There has been more loyalty to the national Democratic Party than elsewhere in Louisiana.

Most of the people in the 3rd live along a corridor that parallels U.S. 90, the thoroughfare that connects New Orleans and Lafayette. Houma, Morgan City and New Iberia are the major towns along this corridor. Dotted with marshland and bayous, this part of Louisiana has traditionally been valued for its salt, sugar cane and shrimp. But the dominant feature of the economy in recent years has been oil. Deposits are centered in St. Mary and Terrebonne parishes, as well as offshore.

High-paying oil jobs once drew thousands of workers from outside Louisiana to the coastal parishes. But with the oil boom's ebb, the region has had some of its tranquility restored. Because jobs here required few references, the "oil patch" became a haven for fugitives, runaways and illegal aliens; many of the "foreigners" who flocked here in the 1970s and early '80s, however, have moved off in search of jobs elsewhere.

At the eastern end of the district is the low, flat marshland of Plaquemines and St. Bernard parishes. For generations Plaquemines had been a world of its own, ruled with an iron hand by segregationist Leander Perez until his death in 1969. Reflecting Perez' wishes, Plaquemines cast more than 75 percent of its presidential ballots for Dixiecrat Strom Thurmond in 1948, Barry Goldwater in 1964 and George C. Wallace in 1968. But Perez' descendants have not matched his influence; they have played only a minor role in recent campaigns. George Bush carried it with roughly 60 percent of the vote in 1988.

Lying closer to New Orleans, St. Bernard has a growing blue-collar population; many of its residents work in large Kaiser Aluminum and Tenneco plants. The blue-collar element often votes Democratic in closely contested statewide races. But the GOP's presidential vote surpassed 70 percent in 1984 and 60 percent in 1988.

In the 1980s round of redistricting, the district picked up some working-class suburban territory in Jefferson Parish. In these suburbs, oil field service companies and boating and fishing firms line the intracoastal waterway feeding into the Mississippi.

Population: 527,280. White 413,383 (78%), Black 103,379 (20%), Other 8,689 (2%). Spanish origin 17,100 (3%). 18 and over 346,013 (66%), 65 and over 36,606 (7%). Median age: 26.

rig their boats with devices to protect sea turtles, there were loud objections. Violent confrontations between shrimpers and the Coast Guard led Tauzin to ask the Coast Guard to moderate its enforcement.

In recent years, Tauzin has worked hard to make the "superfund" hazardous-waste cleanup program less of a problem for Louisiana industry. For petrochemical companies, the overriding issue in the 99th Congress was superfund's financing. But when Tauzin and others tried to broaden the base of superfund taxes (and lessen the relative burden on petrochemical firms) in 1985, they were defeated on a floor vote of 206-220. In the final 1986 legislation, a compromise tax was adopted, and Tauzin saw the domestic oil industry get some relief: higher fees were placed on imported oil than on domestic oil.

On non-industry issues that come before Energy and Commerce, Tauzin is often a crucial swing vote, reluctant to take sides in advance and eager to negotiate.

When he does take a stand, it often has a populist flavor, as with his championing of the cause of satellite-dish owners. For several years he pushed to force cable companies to make unscrambled signals available to dish owners, who often live in rural areas not served by either regular or cable TV. In 1988 he succeeded in getting such a bill approved by an Energy and Commerce subcommittee on a 13-11 vote. That helped pressure the industry to accommodate dish owners.

At Home: Tauzin won his House seat in 1980 with the help of an influential ally, Edwin W. Edwards, who was then between terms as governor. Seven years later the two ended up as rivals in a hot gubernatorial contest.

Tauzin's decision to run for governor in 1987 came as no great surprise; many expected him to be a strong contender for statewide office someday. But his bid was greatly complicated by Edwards, a colorful figure whose political stock had plummeted as a result of well-publicized indictments (he was eventually acquitted). Even when Edwards insisted he would seek another term, many suspected he would eventually drop out of the race.

He did not. And in a field of five major candidates, that spelled trouble for Tauzin. Both Edwards and Tauzin were popular among southern Louisiana Cajuns and blacks. And while Tauzin was critical of Edwards' candidacy, he also had difficulty distancing himself from his one-time mentor. In the end there was a surge for Democratic Rep. Buddy Roemer, and Tauzin ran a poor fourth. Edwards finished second, while GOP Rep. Bob Livingston, who competed on the same ballot, was third.

Most of Tauzin's political outings have been more successful. His victory in a 1980 special election restored control of the 3rd District to French-speaking, Democratic south Louisiana, after nearly a decade under a Republican from suburban New Orleans, David C. Treen.

When Treen vacated the seat after winning the governorship, he tried to pick a successor, James J. Donelon, a Democrat-turned-Republican. Edwards campaigned ardently for Tauzin.

Like Edwards, Tauzin is as comfortable speaking French as English. After practicing law in the bayou towns of Houma and Thibodaux, he won a state legislative seat in 1971. In eight years in the Legislature he emerged as Edwards' protégé, serving as his floor leader in the lower chamber.

Again with Edwards' help, Tauzin finished a strong second in the first round of the special election to fill Treen's House vacancy. Donelon led the four-man field, but not by a large enough margin to avoid a runoff. The second round was bitter and expensive. Tauzin won by more than 7,000 votes, building a big lead in the Cajun parishes to offset Donelon's home-base advantage in New Orleans' suburbs. The margin discouraged GOP leaders, who have not fielded a candidate against Tauzin since.

Committees

Energy & Commerce (9th of 27 Democrats)
Energy & Power; Telecommunications & Finance; Transportation & Hazardous Materials

Merchant Marine & Fisheries (6th of 29 Democrats)
Coast Guard & Navigation (chairman); Oceanography, Great Lakes & Outer Continental Shelf

Elections

1990 Primary †		
W.J. "Billy" Tauzin (D)	155,351	(88%)
Ronald P. Duplantis (I)	14,909	(8%)
Millard F. Clement (I)	6,562	(4%)
1988 Primary †		
W.J. "Billy" Tauzin (D)	72,110	(89%)
Millard F. Clement (I)	8,602	(11%)

† In Louisiana the primary is open to candidates of all parties. If a candidate wins 50 percent or more of the vote in the primary, no general election is held.

Previous Winning Percentages: **1986** (100%) **1984** (100%) **1982** (100%) **1980** (85%) **1980** * (53%)

* *Special election.*

District Vote For President

	1988	1984	1980	1976
D	90,163 (43%)	71,890 (33%)	84,048 (43%)	81,155 (50%)
R	113,371 (55%)	142,625 (66%)	102,882 (53%)	76,767 (47%)
I	3,963 * (2%)		3,604 (2%)	

* *David Duke, Independent Populist.*

Campaign Finance

	Receipts	Receipts from PACs	Expend-itures
1990			
Tauzin (D)	$460,418	$243,922 (53%)	$474,224
1988			
Tauzin (D)	$347,890	$263,228 (76%)	$707,085

Key Votes

1991	
Authorize use of force against Iraq	Y
1990	
Support constitutional amendment on flag desecration	Y
Pass family and medical leave bill over Bush veto	N
Reduce SDI funding	N
Allow abortions in overseas military facilities	N
Approve budget summit plan for spending and taxing	N
Approve civil rights bill	Y
1989	
Halt production of B-2 stealth bomber at 13 planes	N
Oppose capital gains tax cut	N
Approve federal abortion funding in rape or incest cases	N
Approve pay raise and revision of ethics rules	N
Pass Democratic minimum wage plan over Bush veto	N

Voting Studies

	Presidential Support		Party Unity		Conservative Coalition	
Year	**S**	**O**	**S**	**O**	**S**	**O**
1990	46	49	56	40	100	0
1989	69	29	48	48	93	5
1988	45	54	61	37	97	3
1987	19	24	36	20	37	5
1986	49	51	56	44	98	2
1985	54	43	55	37	91	5
1984	44	53	46	47	83	17
1983	54	45	35	60	90	10
1982	57	36	35	63	82	15
1981	67	28	36	60	91	7

Interest Group Ratings

Year	ADA	ACU	AFL-CIO	CCUS
1990	22	58	25	85
1989	20	74	25	80
1988	45	64	86	62
1987	20	53	75	56
1986	20	64	50	72
1985	25	65	53	65
1984	15	67	31	53
1983	25	74	35	70
1982	5	73	20	73
1981	0	71	21	79

4 Jim McCrery (R)

Of Shreveport — Elected 1988

Born: Sept. 18, 1949, Shreveport, La.
Education: Louisiana Tech U., B.A. 1971; Louisiana State U., J.D. 1975.
Occupation: Lawyer; congressional aide.
Family: Single.
Religion: Methodist.
Political Career: Candidate for Leesville City Council, 1978.
Capitol Office: 429 Cannon Bldg. 20515; 225-2777.

In Washington: With his low-key approach, McCrery is not one of the more attention-grabbing junior members of the House. When he does speak up, though, he leaves no doubt about his conservative Republican credentials.

The former Democrat was once an aide to 4th District Rep. Buddy Roemer, whose 1987 election as Louisiana governor opened the seat for McCrery. But even as he followed in the footsteps of his one-time boss, McCrery was a step ahead in one respect: Democrat Roemer switched to the Republican Party in 1991.

McCrery, a Budget Committee member and a former business lobbyist, voted in October 1990 against the federal budget compromise crafted by President Bush and the congressional leadership. He also expressed distaste for the final budget plan, but said he would vote for it, saying, " I will hold my nose and eat skunk for dinner. . . ."

Blaming Democratic "tax-and-spend" policies for the budget morass, McCrery said that voters ". . .cannot continue to elect a Republican to the White House to keep their taxes low and to do the right thing for the country, and then send Democrats to Congress to fatten all of the federal programs they think are important, and even to create new ones."

A member of Budget since his arrival in the House, McCrery gained a seat on the Armed Services Committee during the 101st Congress. In 1989, he played a role in floor debate on the nation's intercontinental ballistic missile strategy, calling for continued funding of both the MX and Midgetman programs.

McCrery's methodical manner is helping him live down the unusual splash he made when he first came to Congress. A 1989 article in the Capitol Hill newspaper *Roll Call* described McCrery's visit to a topless club in South Carolina, where he wore a dancer's bra on his head. "I'm not going to live like a monk while I'm in Congress," said McCrery.

At Home: Of all the candidates vying to succeed Roemer, McCrery was best positioned to campaign on the departing incumbent's record: only he had worked as his aide.

McCrery's GOP label, acquired in late 1987 before his House bid began, helped his victory. Originally from Leesville, in the southern end of the 4th, he served at one time as assistant city attorney in Shreveport. In recent years he had worked in Baton Rouge, the state capital, as a lobbyist for Georgia-Pacific Corp.

This background, and his work for Roemer, did not make him well-known in the 4th; he stood out in the 10-person March-primary field largely because he was the only Republican, and he impressed many with his knowledge of legislative issues.

And while linking himself to Roemer, he also associated himself with Republican figures, running ads featuring President Reagan. In a district that tends to favor Republicans in national and state elections, McCrery's conservative ties helped him outdistance the large field; Democratic state Sen. Foster Campbell ran second, earning a place in the April runoff.

Campbell was a flamboyant, populist-style campaigner, and his base was in the 4th's northern rural parishes. But a month before the election, Campbell was seriously injured in a car crash while driving on a closed highway.

After the special election, McCrery had little time to prepare for November. Fortunately for him, the Democratic effort in the 4th fizzled. Potential challengers stopped in their tracks when Roemer's mother, Adeline, entered the race. She lost badly.

Campbell, having just paid off debts from his previous campaign, came back unexpectedly strong in 1990, buoyed by polls late in the race suggesting that he could beat McCrery. McCrery lost valuable campaign time because he was shuttling back and forth from Washington while the House was debating the budget. He also took heat for his opposition to plant-closing notification and parental-leave bills, and his support for a constitutional amendment permitting abortion only for rape or incest.

But McCrery got his campaign back on track in the final days of the race and won re-election.

Louisiana 4

Northwest — Shreveport

The 4th District is dominated by Shreveport, the conservative stronghold that fought Huey P. Long in the 1930s and became a center of Republican voting in the 1970s. It still offers the economic and social conservatism for which it long has been known.

Shreveport once conducted its battles against the rest of the state from a position of wealth and prominence made possible by the presence of the oil industry. But the oil and gas boom in northwest Louisiana has long since faded, and while Shreveport remains a branch-office town for oil companies, it has relatively few new high-paying jobs to attract people. The population growth in Shreveport and surrounding up-country parishes has been quite slow.

The city has helped itself some by diversifying. AT&T Consumer Products (formerly Western Electric) is the major employer now, and General Motors has opened a large plant to produce light trucks. Diversification has maintained the influence of non-Southerners that began with the oil boom early this century.

Blacks constitute 45 percent of Shreveport's population and industrialization has given organized labor a toehold, but their influence is far outweighed by conservative sentiments.

Across the Red River from Shreveport is Bossier City (population 53,000), the site of Barksdale Air Force Base, headquarters for a unit of the Strategic Air Command. Many military retirees have settled here, drawn by low taxes and nearby lakes.

Nearly half of the district population lives in Caddo Parish. Another 15 percent resides in Bossier Parish. The rest are in rural parishes to the south and east.

The district's six southern parishes, with nearly one-quarter of the vote, form a transitional area between the Cajun parishes of the south and the Louisiana up-country. They usually vote Democratic. Timber and cattle are important here, with cotton still grown in the bottomlands of the Red River. Along the Texas border is the 70-mile-long Toledo Bend Reservoir, a source of recreational dollars for Vernon and Sabine parishes.

Population: 525,194. White 352,137 (67%), Black 166,040 (32%), Other 4,030 (1%). Spanish origin 10,682 (2%). 18 and over 363,684 (69%), 65 and over 58,547 (11%). Median age: 28.

Committees

Armed Services (18th of 22 Republicans)
Military Installations & Facilities; Military Personnel & Compensation; Research & Development

Budget (7th of 14 Republicans)
Defense, Foreign Policy & Space (ranking); Urgent Fiscal Issues

Elections

1990 Primary †		
Jim McCrery (R)	89,859	(55%)
Foster L. Campbell (D)	74,388	(45%)
1988 Primary †		
Jim McCrery (R)	72,228	(69%)
Adeline Roemer (D)	28,027	(27%)
Robert "Bob" Briggs (D)	5,103	(5%)

† In Louisiana the primary is open to candidates of all parties. If a candidate wins 50 percent or more of the vote in the primary, no general election is held.

Previous Winning Percentage: **1988 *** (51%)

** Special election.*

District Vote For President

	1988		1984		1980		1976	
D	77,042	(40%)	67,788	(34%)	81,619	(44%)	68,747	(45%)
R	111,878	(59%)	130,400	(65%)	99,476	(54%)	80,311	(53%)

Campaign Finance

	Receipts	Receipts from PACs		Expend-itures
1990				
McCrery (R)	$469,766	$190,623	(41%)	$481,504
Campbell (D)	$316,703	$139,450	(44%)	$305,348
1988				
McCrery (R)	$791,895	$287,341	(36%)	$742,158
Roemer (D)	$176,655	$6,500	(4%)	$175,450
Briggs (D)	$50	0		$127

Key Votes

1991	
Authorize use of force against Iraq	Y
1990	
Support constitutional amendment on flag desecration	Y
Pass family and medical leave bill over Bush veto	N
Reduce SDI funding	N
Allow abortions in overseas military facilities	N
Approve budget summit plan for spending and taxing	N
Approve civil rights bill	N
1989	
Halt production of B-2 stealth bomber at 13 planes	N
Oppose capital gains tax cut	N
Approve federal abortion funding in rape or incest cases	N
Approve pay raise and revision of ethics rules	Y
Pass Democratic minimum wage plan over Bush veto	N

Voting Studies

	Presidential Support		Party Unity		Conservative Coalition	
Year	**S**	**O**	**S**	**O**	**S**	**O**
1990	68	25	62	23	87	7
1989	85	15	71	21	95	2
1988	61 †	35 †	80 †	18 †	94 †	0 †

† Not eligible for all recorded votes.

Interest Group Ratings

Year	ADA	ACU	AFL-CIO	CCUS
1990	17	88	8	86
1989	0	86	8	90
1988	12	94	20	100

5 Jerry Huckaby (D)

Of Ringgold — Elected 1976

Born: July 19, 1941, Hodge, La.
Education: Louisiana State U., B.S. 1963; Georgia State U., M.B.A. 1968.
Occupation: Farmer; engineer.
Family: Wife, Suzanna Woodard; two children.
Religion: Methodist.
Political Career: No previous office.
Capitol Office: 2182 Rayburn Bldg. 20515; 225-2376.

In Washington: Huckaby takes his political bearings from his rural Louisiana home, using the Agriculture Committee to defend his and his state's interests — cotton, sugar, soybeans and rice. He does not shy from highly technical issues and is not afraid to cut deals. He is a cagey legislator who can fool those who underestimate his profound knowledge of farm programs or his negotiating prowess.

He was the Boll Weevils' choice in 1989 for a slot informally designated for a Southern Democrat on the Budget Committee. In his first (unsuccessful) try for the Budget Committee in 1985, he had argued that no one was representing farmers' point of view in budget deliberations. In addition to his spot on the Budget Committee, Huckaby chairs the Agriculture Subcommittee on Cotton, Rice and Sugar.

The large growers that Huckaby speaks for on Agriculture are sophisticated players in the legislative process, adept at using lobbying, campaign contributions and honoraria to make sure their voices are heard. Huckaby helps them make decisions about which members need to be courted at which times.

Still, Huckaby has displayed some sensitivity toward the public perception of farm programs as costly giveaways to "fat cat" farmers. In 1987, he worked on the compromise in the year-end budget reconciliation bill that capped farm income payments at $100,000 and further tightened the loopholes.

In the 101st Congress, two Mississippi cotton farmers captured attention in Washington for their success at circumventing federal limits on farm program subsidies. By creating an elaborate financial empire called a "Mississippi Christmas tree," the two families stood to gain about $1.3 million a year in government crop-subsidy payments. (Individual farmers are not supposed to get more than $50,000 a year in direct income support, nor more than $250,000 in federal payments combined with loans and disaster relief.)

In December 1989, Huckaby complained to Agriculture Secretary Clayton Yeutter about the scheme. "It was clearly not the intent of Congress that operations would qualify for such vast sums," he wrote. "This type of publicity could be very harmful to farm programs." It did give ammunition to a coalition of urban liberals and suburban conservatives intent on denying payments to farmers with incomes greater than $100,000 a year.

During House consideration of the farm bill, Huckaby sought to head off farm program opponents by offering an amendment that lowered the total benefits allowed for most government program crops to $200,000. The House adopted his proposal on a 375-45 vote, but the House-Senate conference raised it back to $250,000. However, the conference limited total marketing loan payments to $75,000, a drop from the $100,000 in Huckaby's amendment.

Meanwhile, the Agriculture Department (USDA) in June 1990 disqualified the two Mississippi cotton farmers from receiving farm subsidies. But in February 1991, a federal judge ordered USDA to reinstate their subsidy payments, ruling that Huckaby and his staff had "exerted impermissible influence" on USDA officials to deny the payments. That ruling was appealed.

Huckaby had an important hand in the sugar provisions of the 1985 farm bill. When an attempt was made on the floor to reduce sugar price supports to help consumers and open U.S. markets to sugar-producing nations that needed money to repay debts to U.S. banks, Huckaby and his allies on Agriculture argued that the price supports were protecting U.S. jobs. Louisiana is a major sugar-producing state, although Huckaby's district does not produce sugar.

When the farm bill came up for reauthorization in 1990, Huckaby attempted to craft a deal to loosen the tight restrictions on sugar imports that Congress forced on the administration in the 1985 farm bill, while raising the federal price-support levels for domestic sugar — even though U.S. prices were well above world prices. He assembled a fragile coalition that included the usually protectionist cane and sugar-beet industries and their longtime

Louisiana 5

North — Monroe

The rural 5th is one of the poorest areas of Louisiana. Incomes are less than half the level of those in Louisiana's major urban centers, and the area has been losing population. Forests cover much of the district, and what little industry exists is timber-related. Lumber mills are scattered throughout the 5th.

Small farmers backed the populism embodied by Gov. Huey P. Long, a native of Winn Parish, in the 5th District. But after World War II, the region became a segregationist bulwark. Both Barry Goldwater in 1964 and George C. Wallace in 1968 drew a higher vote here than in any other Louisiana district; in 1990, unsuccessful GOP Senate candidate David Duke carried 13 of the 19 parishes wholly within the 5th. In recent years, most of the parishes here have been reliably Republican in presidential elections. One of them — LaSalle — gave George Bush almost 75 percent of its vote in 1988.

GOP strength is concentrated in the district's only major population center, Ouachita Parish (Monroe), home for about one-quarter of the district's voters. Monroe (population 55,000) is at the center of a large gas field and long has been the trading hub of northeast Louisiana. The opening of Interstate 20 pumped new life into the city, making it a convention center and overnight stop along the heavily traveled thoroughfare from Atlanta to Dallas. Monroe is over one-half black. Ouachita Parish gave Bush more about 69 percent in 1988.

The Democratic areas in the 5th are along the Mississippi and Red rivers; blacks comprise a majority of the population in three of the four parishes adjoining those waterways. Two of them — East Carroll and Madison — were the only parishes in north Louisiana to buck the local Wallace tide and vote for Hubert H. Humphrey for president in 1968. Both voted for Michael S. Dukakis in 1988.

Population: 527,220. White 359,467 (68%), Black 164,664 (31%). Spanish origin 5,361 (1%). 18 and over 360,687 (68%), 65 and over 66,071 (13%). Median age: 28.

rivals, the Caribbean and Central American nations. The Bush administration bitterly opposed his plan, however, fearing that its new measures to protect U.S. sugar, including an annual import-quota level of 1.25 million tons of sugar, would undermine negotiations on the General Agreement on Tariffs and Trade. The final package dropped the import quota but required domestic marketing controls if sugar imports fell below 1.25 million tons.

Huckaby also had to contend with an effort by New York Democrat Thomas J. Downey and Ohio Republican Bill Gradison to impose a 2-cent-per-pound cut in the 18-cents-per-pound sugar price support. The administration voiced support for their amendment, but with some Republicans facing tough election contests in the cane- and beet-growing states of Hawaii, Michigan and Minnesota, its lobbying was lukewarm. Huckaby and Agriculture Committee Chairman E. "Kika" de la Garza of Texas rounded up votes among Democrats. The result was not close: The House rejected the Downey amendment 150-271.

Although cotton and rice growers make up a relatively small group compared with other commodity interests, Huckaby and other members representing Southern states where cotton and rice are grown played a proportionately larger role in the 1985 farm bill. With a significant amount of help from Southerners in the Senate, Huckaby worked for cotton and rice programs that contained some of the boldest — and possibly most expensive — provisions in the entire farm package.

Those provisions included a new market-oriented price-support mechanism for cotton and rice growers called a "marketing loan." Rather than allow growers to default on their price-support loans if prices failed to rise above the loan rate (as happened under the existing system), the Agriculture secretary must allow rice growers, and has the option to allow cotton growers, the chance to repay the loan at the lower rate commodities bring on the market. The cotton and rice marketing loan plans were renewed in the 1990 farm bill.

Although much of Huckaby's focus has been on crop subsidies, agriculture is not his only interest. Huckaby, once a farmer, is also an electrical engineer. In the 100th Congress, he again showed a penchant for plunging into the work of the Interior Subcommittee on Energy.

He continued work begun in the 99th Congress to settle a fight in the Interior Committee over nuclear liability. Huckaby helped negotiate the successor to the Price-Anderson Act, raising the nuclear power industry's liability to $7 billion in an accident. He pressed the industry's position in the debate over how to compensate lawyers in liability suits.

Shell Oil Co. became his cause when it

appeared that legislation to sanction South Africa for its apartheid society would prevent Shell, because of the activities in South Africa of its parent corporation, from bidding on new U.S. oil leases in the Gulf of Mexico. Shell is the largest wildcat driller in the gulf and employs thousands in Louisiana. Huckaby led the fight against the measure in Interior and on the floor, joining forces with conservative Republicans against the bill. It is one reason liberals on the committee are not unhappy to see him take a leave from Interior while he serves on Budget.

At Home: While ambitious young politicians waited for veteran Rep. Otto E. Passman to retire, Huckaby took the risk of challenging him in 1976, defeated him in the Democratic primary and won the seat. It was Huckaby's first campaign. But the wealthy dairy farmer mounted an aggressive, well-financed challenge that capitalized on Passman's age (76) and political problems.

The 15-term incumbent had been beset with charges of irregularities in his congressional travel expenses. And he had been criticized for his 1971 vote against a constitutional amendment to permit prayer in public schools.

With Passman's defeat, Republicans had high hopes of capturing the seat. Their candidate, Monroe businessman Frank Spooner, had a large treasury.

But Spooner was unable to document his basic campaign theme — that Huckaby was a liberal Democrat out of step with the conservative district. Huckaby offset the Republican's 7,000-vote plurality in the district's major population center, Ouachita Parish (Monroe), and repeated his strong primary showing in the rural parishes to win the seat by 8,000 votes.

Some Democratic politicians were annoyed that the upstart Huckaby had taken the prize for which so many of them had waited. One of them, state Sen. James H. Brown Jr., challenged Huckaby in 1978. But Huckaby won easily and has had no trouble since.

Committees

Agriculture (7th of 27 Democrats)
Conservation, Credit & Rural Development; Cotton, Rice & Sugar (chairman); Department Operations, Research & Foreign Agriculture; Forests, Family Farms & Energy

Budget (9th of 23 Democrats)
Defense, Foreign Policy & Space; Urgent Fiscal Issues

Elections

1990 Primary †		
Jerry Huckaby (D)	128,137	(74%)
Carl Batey (D)	24,050	(14%)
Bradley T. Roark (R)	16,331	(9%)
1988 Primary †		
Jerry Huckaby (D)	96,200	(68%)
Jack Wright (D)	32,284	(23%)
Bradley T. Roark (R)	6,403	(9%)

† In Louisiana the primary is open to candidates of all parties. If a candidate wins 50 percent or more of the vote in the primary, no general election is held.

Previous Winning Percentages: **1986** (68%) **1984** (100%) **1982** (83%) **1980** (89%) **1978** (52%) **1976** (53%)

District Vote For President

	1988	1984	1980	1976
D	70,477 (36%)	69,254 (32%)	83,040 (42%)	83,034 (48%)
R	122,309 (62%)	140,427 (66%)	110,824 (56%)	85,900 (50%)
I	3,771 * (2%)		3,604 (2%)	

** David Duke, Independent Populist*

Campaign Finance

	Receipts	Receipts from PACs	Expend-itures
1990			
Huckaby (D)	$218,774	$106,498 (49%)	$240,832
Batey (D)	$5,000	0	$4,415
1988			
Huckaby (D)	$266,854	$131,650 (49%)	$194,021
Wright (D)	$9,021	0	$9,007

Key Votes

1991	
Authorize use of force against Iraq	Y
1990	
Support constitutional amendment on flag desecration	Y
Pass family and medical leave bill over Bush veto	N
Reduce SDI funding	N
Allow abortions in overseas military facilities	N
Approve budget summit plan for spending and taxing	N
Approve civil rights bill	N
1989	
Halt production of B-2 stealth bomber at 13 planes	N
Oppose capital gains tax cut	N
Approve federal abortion funding in rape or incest cases	N
Approve pay raise and revision of ethics rules	N
Pass Democratic minimum wage plan over Bush veto	N

Voting Studies

	Presidential Support		Party Unity		Conservative Coalition	
Year	**S**	**O**	**S**	**O**	**S**	**O**
1990	50	44	54	40	94	0
1989	74	22	50	43	88	10
1988	44	45	56	35	84	5
1987	43	55	61	32	91	5
1986	41	49	53	31	80	4
1985	49	49	51	38	89	7
1984	49	46	48	42	80	14
1983	54	45	44	51	85	13
1982	51	38	46	46	75	14
1981	67	25	33	61	83	9

Interest Group Ratings

Year	ADA	ACU	AFL-CIO	CCUS
1990	22	71	25	79
1989	15	62	27	100
1988	40	65	57	77
1987	44	35	50	64
1986	20	65	31	73
1985	35	57	41	71
1984	25	57	15	57
1983	35	70	35	65
1982	25	48	32	45
1981	10	93	27	76

6 Richard H. Baker (R)

Of Baton Rouge — Elected 1986

Born: May 22, 1948, New Orleans, La.
Education: Louisiana State U., B.A. 1971.
Occupation: Real estate broker.
Family: Wife, Kay Carpenter; two children.
Religion: Methodist.
Political Career: La. House, 1973-87; Democratic candidate for La. Senate, 1980.
Capitol Office: 404 Cannon Bldg. 20515; 225-3901.

In Washington: Despite his relative youth, Baker is a seasoned veteran of Bayou politics. By the time he was 24, he had already made it to the state House, where he spent most of his 14 years as a labor-oriented Democrat. But when he switched parties and made his way to Congress, he showed a calculated ability to maneuver in Louisiana politics. Baker's name is now routinely included when talk turns to possible statewide candidates.

Baker has proved to be one of the most low-key members of his class in Washington. He spent his first two years on the Interior Committee, but in the 101st Congress he moved onto the Banking Committee, where he can better pursue business-oriented interests. He also serves on the Small Business Committee. A conservative party loyalist, he sided with the leadership on two especially contentious votes in the 101st Congress, backing the 1989 pay raise and ethics reform package and the 1990 budget "summit" agreement.

Baker was probably more visible in Louisiana. In addition to regular political and constituent work, he chaired George Bush's 1988 Louisiana campaign and led the state's delegation at the convention in New Orleans.

In the 101st Congress, Baker fueled speculation that he was moderating his voting record to appeal to a statewide audience. After voting in 1988 to bar federal funds for abortions in cases of rape and incest, Baker voted in 1989 to permit the use of funds in those cases — three months after the Supreme Court's landmark *Webster* ruling.

Baker said that earlier votes on the issue "were reflections of my own personal judgment. Now I have a better feel" for the opinions of his constituents through "heightened public awareness of the issue.... My vote is a reflection of public sentiment that abortion in cases of rape and incest is very different from abortion for the convenience of the woman."

He opposed a 1990 amendment that would have allowed privately paid abortions at military hospitals for overseas military personnel.

At Home: After GOP Rep. W. Henson Moore announced plans to run for the Senate in 1986, Baker put together an unusual coalition of country-club Republicans and blue-collar Democrats to defeat a better-financed Democratic opponent, state Senate president pro tempore Thomas Hudson.

It was an odd election. Baker had spent 12 years in the Legislature as a Democrat, switching parties in 1985 at the urging of GOP leaders who saw him as the only candidate capable of stopping Hudson. Representing a blue-collar Baton Rouge district, he had been identified for most of his career as a labor-oriented lawmaker. Hudson, on the other hand, represented a white-collar constituency.

Baker could not compete with Hudson when it came to endorsements from the district's organized political forces. His 1976 stand against right-to-work legislation cost him important business backing, and his party switch cost him support from the previously supportive AFL-CIO. Only in the rural parishes, where he had Farm Bureau backing, did Baker receive help from a significant pressure group.

But Baker did have a core of committed GOP volunteers, many of them affluent suburbanites who had supported Moore. TV ads linked Baker to the popular Republican incumbent and he benefited from his reputation as a "clean government" reformer.

Baker also developed an effective appeal to diverse religious groups. He had been a Methodist lay preacher, and he expanded his support among fundamentalists with an endorsement from Baton Rouge-based TV evangelist Jimmy Swaggart, then still an influential figure. Many Catholics appreciated Baker's opposition to abortion and his support for state aid to parochial schools.

TV advertisements showing him with his wife and children contrasted Baker with his twice-divorced foe. And Baker made many personal appearances, especially in blue-collar areas where he needed to reinforce his popularity. On Election Day, Baker nearly carried Hudson's Senate district, and did carry Hudson's own precinct.

Louisiana 6

East Central — Baton Rouge

The 6th extends from the state capital and university community of Baton Rouge on the west to Bogalusa, a town by the Pearl River known for its past racial turmoil, on the east. The territory in between is primarily rural, with pine forests and small farms providing the base for lumbering and agriculture. But there has been increasing suburbanization by commuters from Baton Rouge and New Orleans.

Baton Rouge now has a population of 219,500 and has surpassed Shreveport as the second-largest city in Louisiana. State government employees and service workers in Baton Rouge provide a large white-collar base that has made Republicans dominant here in state and national elections. But the large academic communities at Louisiana State University (30,000 students) and predominantly black Southern University (9,100 students), the extensive labor presence and the city's 44 percent black population keep Democrats competitive.

About two-thirds of the voters in the 6th reside in the Baton Rouge area. The rest live to the east, in the Florida parishes, so named because they were part of Spanish Florida until 1810. Culturally, this area resembles more neighboring Mississippi than the rest of Louisiana. Locally, the Democratic Party reigns, although suburbanization has strengthened the GOP in Livingston Parish.

Farther east is Tangipahoa Parish. Hammond, at the junction of two Interstate highways, is the trade center for the Florida parishes. The Hammond area, home to a large Italian-American community, is a leading supplier of the nation's strawberries. Washington Parish at the district's eastern end is a heavily forested rural backwater bounded on the north and east by Mississippi. All three parishes east of Baton Rouge voted for unsuccessful GOP Senate candidate David Duke in 1990.

Population: 524,770. White 387,238 (74%), Black 131,746 (25%), Other 3,406 (1%). Spanish origin 8,268 (2%). 18 and over 362,252 (69%), 65 and over 41,937 (8%). Median age: 27.

Committees

Banking, Finance & Urban Affairs (9th of 20 Republicans)
Consumer Affairs & Coinage; Financial Institutions Supervision, Regulation & Insurance; Housing & Community Development

Small Business (7th of 17 Republicans)
Environment & Employment (ranking)

Elections

1990 Primary ‡

Richard H. Baker (R)	Unopposed

1988 Primary ‡

Richard H. Baker (R)	Unopposed

‡ In Louisiana a candidate unopposed in the primary and general elections is declared elected. His name does not appear on the ballot in either election.

Previous Winning Percentage: **1986** (51%)

District Vote For President

	1988	1984	1980	1976
D	82,815 (39%)	77,570 (35%)	85,067 (44%)	73,695 (53%)
R	125,710 (60%)	141,115 (64%)	103,932 (53%)	61,253 (44%)
I			4,192 (2%)	

Campaign Finance

	Receipts	Receipts from PACs	Expend-itures
1990			
Baker (R)	$382,622	$153,761 (40%)	$332,905
1988			
Baker (R)	$287,230	$124,525 (43%)	$270,899

Key Votes

1991

Authorize use of force against Iraq	Y

1990

Support constitutional amendment on flag desecration	Y
Pass family and medical leave bill over Bush veto	N
Reduce SDI funding	N
Allow abortions in overseas military facilities	N
Approve budget summit plan for spending and taxing	Y
Approve civil rights bill	N

1989

Halt production of B-2 stealth bomber at 13 planes	N
Oppose capital gains tax cut	N
Approve federal abortion funding in rape or incest cases	Y
Approve pay raise and revision of ethics rules	Y
Pass Democratic minimum wage plan over Bush veto	N

Voting Studies

	Presidential Support		Party Unity		Conservative Coalition	
Year	S	O	S	O	S	O
1990	69	27	81	7	85	7
1989	70	27	87	11	98	2
1988	63	32	80	10	97	3
1987	66	30	76	16	84	5

Interest Group Ratings

Year	ADA	ACU	AFL-CIO	CCUS
1990	0	86	18	83
1989	5	79	17	90
1988	5	100	15	100
1987	4	81	6	100

7 Jimmy Hayes (D)

Of Lafayette — Elected 1986

Born: Dec. 21, 1946, Lafayette, La.
Education: U. of Southwestern Louisiana, B.S. 1967; Tulane U., J.D. 1970.
Military Service: La. Air National Guard, 1968-74.
Occupation: Lawyer; real estate developer.
Family: Wife, Leslie Owen; three children.
Religion: Methodist.
Political Career: No previous office.
Capitol Office: 503 Cannon Bldg. 20515; 225-2031.

In Washington: House Democratic leaders hunting alliances with shrewd Southern Democrats thought they had found in Hayes a Boll Weevil able to deliver votes for the party line.

As a freshman, Hayes made a name for himself by emerging as the party point man in a battle over controversial drug-related amendments. He impressed colleagues with his acumen and amused them with his wit. When it came time to orient new freshmen in 1988, Hayes was asked to help them learn the ropes, and he was tapped as a whip for four Southern states. But after his initial successes, Hayes has become frustrated with the Democratic leadership, which bypassed him when filling openings on the both the Ways and Means and Appropriations Committees. In 1990, Hayes complained to the New Orleans *Times Picayune* that the leadership had left Louisiana Democrats no voice on those key panels. "I'm a moderate Southern Democrat and it appears there's no place for me or voters like me," Hayes said. "Every four years presidential candidates are chosen with the same liberal bias and we really lose big."

That bitter-sounding Hayes is a far cry from the man who gained notice for deftly dealing with Rep. Robert S. Walker, a Pennsylvania Republican, in the 1988 "drug-free work place" controversy. Walker, like Hayes a member of the Science Committee, began pushing amendments to bills barring spending for any grant or contract "until the recipient shall certify to the government that they will provide a drug-free work place."

Democrats cried that the amendment could wreak havoc on contracts and create a police-state mentality, but they were clearly in a political pinch. Hayes volunteered to try to forge a compromise. Working with Walker, Hayes helped hammer out a softer version that prevented the government from withholding payments for a single violation.

One of Hayes' top priorities has been to save coastal wetlands without overregulation. In the 102nd Congress, he introduced a bill that would decrease protection of low-level wetlands by tightening definitions, prioritizing based on ecological and productive value and compensating owners for land taken by preservation.

At Home: Hayes had never run for office when he began his 1986 House campaign, and he was not the clear choice of Democratic regulars. But thanks to his loyalty to traditional Democratic issues, he benefited from the same coalition of unions, blacks and courthouse politicians that lifted his predecessor John B. Breaux to victory in the 1986 Senate contest.

Hayes, an investor and developer, had the money to court any audience. The son of a prominent independent oilman, he launched his campaign with a flurry of ads stressing his concerns about two issues crucial to troubled south Louisiana: jobs and agriculture.

But Hayes, who resigned his appointed job as state commissioner of financial institutions to campaign, was challenged from the right and left: On the right was state Rep. Margaret Lowenthal, a wealthy pro-business Democrat; on the left was state Rep. James David Cain, a labor-oriented legislator backed by many blacks and blue-collar workers.

Hayes' strong personality initially put off some, but he improved steadily as a campaigner, and built support in his hometown of Lafayette. That, added to his media effort, put him in a runoff with Lowenthal.

Despite the blue-collar tilt of her legislative district, Lowenthal was regarded as anti-labor by many Cain supporters. Hayes seized the center, won Cain's backing and made a special effort to woo his labor and rural allies. Lowenthal, known as a maverick in the Legislature, stressed her independence and reformist image: Noting Hayes' state job, she tried to tie him to scandal-tainted Democratic Gov. Edwin W. Edwards. Hayes won with 57 percent.

In 1990, Hayes turned back David Thibodaux, who ran third in the 1986 open primary. A professor at the University of Southwestern Louisiana and a conservative GOP activist, Thibodaux got campaign help from former Marine Lt. Col. Oliver L. North.

Louisiana 7

Southwest — Lake Charles; Lafayette

The *bon temps* Cajun ethic is thoroughly a part of the 7th's identity. But economically, the district has had a rough time. It suffered after the bust of southern Louisiana's oil boom.

Founded by Acadian refugees, Lafayette is the traditional center of Cajun culture. Many of the street signs are in French, and the radio station at the University of Southwest Louisiana broadcasts in both French and English. But the offshore oil discoveries that drew oil company branch offices transformed Lafayette from a Cajun market town into a mini-Houston during the 1970s. At its peak in the early 1980s, the city was becoming a stronghold of white-collar Republicanism. Though it still retains the strongest concentration of GOP voters in the district, many of the risk-taking businessmen who helped the the boom get started have departed, as have many of the workers. Republican candidates still do well in the southern half of the city, home to executives for the corporations that remain.

Despite the slight upturn in the oil economy in the early 1990s, local officials are looking to tourism revenues to boost the economy.

In the smaller towns dotting the rest of this part of Acadiana, the Cajun heritage has always remained strong. To the east of Lafayette in St. Martin Parish is St. Martinville, once known as Le Petit Paris because it was a haven for Royalists after the French Revolution. The farmland west of Crowley is one of the nation's leading sources of rice.

Beyond the rice fields lies a much different part of the 7th, a grimy fist of heavy industry that centers on Lake Charles and extends into Texas. Blue-collar workers are a more dominant influence in this region. With a heavy concentration of petrochemical plants, Lake Charles is one of the most unionized cities in Louisiana, and it is strongly Democratic. Michael S. Dukakis drew more than 53 percent of the vote in 1988 in Lake Charles and surrounding Calcasieu Parish; he got less than 40 percent in Lafayette, and was neck and neck with George Bush in Acadia Parish.

Population: 525,361. White 415,979 (79%), Black 105,508 (20%). Spanish origin 8,920 (2%). 18 and over 355,571 (68%), 65 and over 46,188 (9%). Median age: 27.

Committees

Public Works & Transportation (18th of 36 Democrats)
Aviation; Investigations & Oversight; Water Resources

Science, Space & Technology (20th of 32 Democrats)
Science; Space

Elections

1990 Primary †

Jimmy Hayes (D)	103,308	(58%)
David Thibodaux (R)	68,530	(38%)
Johnny Myers (D)	7,369	(4%)

1988 Primary ‡

Jimmy Hayes (D)	Unopposed

† In Louisiana the primary is open to candidates of all parties. If a candidate wins 50 percent or more of the vote in the primary, no general election is held.

‡ In Louisiana a candidate unopposed in the primary and general elections is declared elected. His name does not appear on the ballot in either election.

Previous Winning Percentage: **1986** (57%)

District Vote For President

	1988		1984		1980		1976	
D	105,717	(49%)	91,106	(40%)	96,448	(48%)	95,887	(59%)
R	106,169	(49%)	132,813	(59%)	98,749	(49%)	62,691	(38%)
I					4,097	(2%)		

Campaign Finance

	Receipts	Receipts from PACs		Expend-itures
1990				
Hayes (D)	$317,295	$164,850	(52%)	$309,229
Thibodaux (R)	$158,918	$7,957	(5%)	$157,656
1988				
Hayes (D)	$304,917	$206,100	(68%)	$268,116

Key Votes

1991	
Authorize use of force against Iraq	Y
1990	
Support constitutional amendment on flag desecration	Y
Pass family and medical leave bill over Bush veto	N
Reduce SDI funding	N
Allow abortions in overseas military facilities	N
Approve budget summit plan for spending and taxing	N
Approve civil rights bill	Y
1989	
Halt production of B-2 stealth bomber at 13 planes	N
Oppose capital gains tax cut	N
Approve federal abortion funding in rape or incest cases	N
Approve pay raise and revision of ethics rules	Y
Pass Democratic minimum wage plan over Bush veto	Y

Voting Studies

	Presidential Support		Party Unity		Conservative Coalition	
Year	**S**	**O**	**S**	**O**	**S**	**O**
1990	38	49	63	24	85	6
1989	59 †	38 †	64 †	33 †	88 †	10 †
1988	35	57	70	23	87	13
1987	36	57	72	19	79	19

† Not eligible for all recorded votes.

Interest Group Ratings

Year	ADA	ACU	AFL-CIO	CCUS
1990	22	55	45	75
1989	30	56	67	60
1988	55	52	92	62
1987	48	22	69	53

8 Clyde C. Holloway (R)

Of Forest Hill — Elected 1986

Born: Nov. 28, 1943, Lecompte, La.
Education: Attended National School of Aeronautics, Kansas City, Mo., 1966.
Occupation: Nursery owner.
Family: Wife, Cathie Kohlhepp; four children.
Religion: Baptist.
Political Career: Republican candidate for U.S. House, 1980, 1985.
Capitol Office: 1206 Longworth Bldg. 20515; 225-4926.

In Washington: In his third term of being a GOP House anomaly — winning in a district that is roughly 85 percent Democratic, even while siding with his party more than 80 percent of the time — Holloway set his sights higher early in the 102nd Congress: He decided to seek the Louisiana governorship in 1991.

Unknown statewide, Holloway announced that he would run in the state's October primary only if he won the endorsement of the GOP state convention in June. The convention did endorse Holloway, but the value of that endorsement was lessened because Gov. Buddy Roemer did not participate in the balloting. Roemer had switched to the GOP in March 1990 in hopes of avoiding an intraparty fight for re-election.

If Holloway fails in his bid for governor and tries to keep his House seat in 1992, he faces the prospect of losing his district; Louisiana lost a seat in reapportionment, and the gerrymandered 8th — which sits precariously in the jaws of the state's other districts — is a likely target for the Democratic Legislature. If the seat somehow survives, Holloway faces the unpleasant prospect of a difficult and competitive re-election race every two years.

Despite his precarious position, Holloway has never run scared in Washington; he seems to run happy, simply enjoying the opportunity to serve from a district so heavily stacked against his party that by any logic it should not elect him. Day in and day out, he supports President Bush, as he did President Ronald Reagan, voting with a majority of Republicans as often as many members from solidly Republican districts.

Despite his deep-seated commitment to reducing the level of federal intrusion, Holloway is not blind to political realities, and on some high-profile issues he has departed from the party line. He voted to override Bush's veto in 1990 of a textile bill that would have mandated stiff new quotas on imports to shore up domestic producers. In the 100th Congress, he voted to override Reagan's vetoes of an omnibus trade bill that included plant-closing notification provisions and of a highway bill that had funding earmarked for Louisiana.

But, Holloway said in 1987, referring to his GOP colleague's 1st District, "I wouldn't vote for a few of the bills that I vote for if I was in Bob Livingston's district in Louisiana, because it is a conservative district, and they don't have the very, very, very hard times that we have in my district."

For the 102nd Congress, Holloway gave up his seats on the Agriculture and Small Business committees — where he made no big impressions — to take a seat on the influential Energy and Commerce Committee.

In 1990, Holloway received some notoriety when he was named by Environmental Action as one of the year's "Dirty Dozen" in Congress for his votes on bills involving clean air and oil spills. Holloway defended his record, arguing that much of the legislation would have threatened jobs in the district. "I consider myself to be an environmentalist, but I don't consider myself one of the fruits or nuts hanging from the tree," the affable nurseryman told the New Orleans *Times-Picayune.*

Holloway also received some attention on the subject of day care, a hot issue in the 100th Congress. His alternative to a Democratic day-care bill proposed giving a refundable tax credit to all parents with preschool children, not just to parents who pay for day care. The bill never went anywhere, but some conservatives, including Education Secretary William J. Bennett, latched onto it.

Necessarily attentive to district concerns, Holloway has established a strong constituent service record and looked out for local economic interests, taking the lead in efforts to prevent the closing of the local England Air Force Base.

At Home: There is such a thing as being in the wrong place at the right time.

In 1986, a crowd of Democrats lined up to succeed retiring Rep. Cathy (Mrs. Gillis) Long, but Holloway was the only Republican on the nonpartisan primary ballot. His narrow political base was firm enough to send him into a November runoff against attorney Faye Williams, a liberal black Democrat whose base was

Louisiana 8

Central — Alexandria

In some ways, the 8th is a microcosm of Louisiana. It starts in the piney woods of the north, moves southeast through Cajun country, crosses the Mississippi River and ends up on the outskirts of metropolitan New Orleans.

But the district is poorer, more rural, and more loyally Democratic than the state as a whole. The 8th went for Ronald Reagan in the 1984 presidential race, but Holloway's three election victories still cut against the usual political grain. Democrat Michael S. Dukakis carried the district for president in 1988.

The 8th is centered on Rapides Parish, including Alexandria (population 49,000), the district's major population center and its biggest outpost of conservative thinking. With neighboring Pineville, Alexandria is the commercial and military center of central Louisiana. Nearby forests fuel lumber mills. Just outside town is England Air Force Base, fingered by the Pentagon for closure.

Rapides, Avoyelles and Evangeline parishes together cast about 40 percent of the district vote. These three parishes constitute a border between Louisiana's Protestant north and its Cajun Catholic south. Cotton, a leading crop of north Louisiana, is grown along the Red River. Rice and sugar cane are grown nearby.

The 8th takes in the northern tip of Cajun country, which begins just below Rapides Parish and extends south and east toward Baton Rouge. This area is racially more tolerant than the rest of the district, and it is reliably Democratic in most elections; however, unsuccessful GOP Senate candidate David Duke carried Avoyelles and Evangeline parishes in 1990.

Farther east are the Mississippi River parishes, the center of Louisiana's productive "sugar bowl." Along the river south of Baton Rouge are a number of old plantations, a reminder of the wealth and power of the antebellum planters. The plantation buildings coexist incongruously with modern petrochemical plants, a source of pollution, jobs and working-class voters. The combination of organized labor and blacks — about 40 percent of the population in the six river parishes — makes this area one of the most Democratic in the state.

Population: 524,861. White 320,931 (61%), Black 200,966 (38%). Spanish origin 8,254 (2%). 18 and over 349,177 (67%), 65 and over 53,220 (10%). Median age: 27.

equally narrow. Had any of several white Democrats made it to the runoff against Holloway, the Republican would have had little chance.

He had entered the contest with a reputation as something of a political bumpkin, stemming from two clumsy and ill-fated congressional campaigns — one in 1980 against Democratic Rep. Gillis W. Long and another in 1985 against Cathy Long, who won the 8th in a special election following her husband's death.

Despite the impression given by those efforts, Holloway's involvement in local issues had left him with a dedicated following and demonstrated that he possessed some degree of political skill. He first appeared on the scene in 1980, when he was point man in a protest against busing to achieve integration in Alexandria and surrounding Rapides Parish. Holloway led efforts to create a private school as an alternative for anti-busing parents in his hometown of Forest Hill, and he became the school's chairman of the board.

There was never any doubt that race would be a crucial factor in a contest between a black woman and a white Republican known for his anti-busing activism. But Holloway did not directly raise the issue and sought to dispel any impression that he was racist by arguing that he had fought busing, not integration. "I believe it is an evil," he said of busing at one point. "I believe blacks think it is an evil." His campaign brochures pictured him in a schoolroom with several black children.

Holloway tried to put Williams on the defensive by making her ideology and background the issues. Williams' résumé was more than reasonable for a congressional candidate; she was a lawyer and former U.S. House aide who spent several years working with the Michigan Education Association. But in gathering her experience, Williams had spent most of her adult life outside Louisiana. While questioning Williams' roots, Holloway stressed that he was a local nurseryman.

Holloway also ran ads claiming that Williams was "ultra-liberal, pro-abortion, for gay rights, for gun control" — an attempt to create the impression that she was far more unacceptably liberal than he was unacceptably conservative to the average voter. He had some help from Williams, who did little to distance herself from those issues or personally ingratiate herself with many white courthouse Democrats. Holloway won over enough rural and blue-collar Democrats to win narrowly.

Although some immediately dubbed him "two-year Clyde," Holloway's political stock rose considerably in 1988 when it became clear that local Democrats had not learned from history and were preparing to repeat it. Williams competed with two prominent white Democrats and again made it into the runoff with Holloway.

Williams, blaming some of her 1986 defeat on opposition to her race and sex, hoped to win greater acceptance in her second campaign. But some usually loyal Democrats who had supported her first effort backed away the second time, finding her views too liberal and her personality wearing. Many had learned that they could live with Holloway, an approachable man who impressed even some hard-core Democrats with his attention to the district.

It was evident in the primary that Holloway would be tough to oust: He came within several points of winning a majority of the vote. In November he took an amazing 57 percent of the vote.

In 1990, Holloway again avoided a runoff by gaining 56 percent against two Democratic state lawmakers in the primary. Democrats again split the primary vote, with liberals and blacks in one camp and traditional courthouse types in the other. State Sen. Cleo Fields, a black law school graduate from Baton Rouge, ran a better campaign than had Williams. But state Sen. Joe McPherson, an environmentalist who enjoyed the support of district sportspeople, finished with 14 percent — enough to prevent Fields from forcing a runoff.

Committees

Energy & Commerce (15th of 16 Republicans)
Energy & Power; Health & the Environment

Select Children, Youth & Families (3rd of 14 Republicans)

Elections

1990 Primary †		
Clyde C. Holloway (R)	113,607	(56%)
Cleo Fields (D)	59,511	(30%)
Joe McPherson (D)	28,170	(14%)
1988 General		
Clyde C. Holloway (R)	116,241	(57%)
Faye Williams (D)	88,564	(43%)

† In Louisiana the primary is open to candidates of all parties. If a candidate wins 50 percent or more of the vote in the primary, no general election is held.

Previous Winning Percentage: **1986** (51%)

District Vote For President

	1988	1984	1980	1976
D	114,647 (53%)	109,857 (49%)	116,443 (56%)	107,574 (59%)
R	97,428 (45%)	113,154 (50%)	86,624 (42%)	69,186 (38%)

Campaign Finance

	Receipts	Receipts from PACs		Expend-itures
1990				
Holloway (R)	$383,701	$144,263	(38%)	$385,877
Fields (D)	$120,070	$8,500	(7%)	$111,828
McPherson (D)	$181,505	$30,550	(17%)	$180,288
1988				
Holloway (R)	$690,080	$315,886	(46%)	$629,950
Williams (D)	$518,494	$182,683	(35%)	$434,854

Key Votes

1991	
Authorize use of force against Iraq	Y
1990	
Support constitutional amendment on flag desecration	Y
Pass family and medical leave bill over Bush veto	N
Reduce SDI funding	N
Allow abortions in overseas military facilities	N
Approve budget summit plan for spending and taxing	N
Approve civil rights bill	N
1989	
Halt production of B-2 stealth bomber at 13 planes	N
Oppose capital gains tax cut	N
Approve federal abortion funding in rape or incest cases	N
Approve pay raise and revision of ethics rules	N
Pass Democratic minimum wage plan over Bush veto	N

Voting Studies

	Presidential Support		Party Unity		Conservative Coalition	
Year	**S**	**O**	**S**	**O**	**S**	**O**
1990	67	29	84	8	91	6
1989	66	26	88	7	90	10
1988	65	27	76	11	92	3
1987	66	26	77	15	95	5

Interest Group Ratings

Year	ADA	ACU	AFL-CIO	CCUS
1990	11	91	18	92
1989	15	93	33	90
1988	0	96	36	92
1987	0	82	20	93

Maine

U.S. CONGRESS

SENATE 1 D, 1 R
HOUSE 1 D, 1 R

LEGISLATURE

Senate 22 D, 13 R
House 97 D, 54 R

ELECTIONS

1988 Presidential Vote	
Bush	55%
Dukakis	44%
1984 Presidential Vote	
Reagan	61%
Mondale	39%
1980 Presidential Vote	
Reagan	46%
Carter	42%
Anderson	10%
Turnout rate in 1986	48%
Turnout rate in 1988	62%
Turnout rate in 1990	56%

(as percentage of voting age population)

POPULATION AND GROWTH

1980 population	1,124,660
1990 population (38th in the nation)	1,227,928
Percent change 1980-1990	+9%

DEMOGRAPHIC BREAKDOWN

White	98%
Black	0.4%
Asian or Pacific Islander	1%
(Hispanic origin)	1%
Urban	47%
Rural	53%
Born in state	73%
Foreign-born	4%

MAJOR CITIES

Portland	64,358
Lewiston	39,757
Bangor	33,181
Auburn	24,309
South Portland	23,163

AREA AND LAND USE

Area	30,995 sq. miles (39th)
Farm	7%
Forest	90%
Federally owned	1%

Gov. John R. McKernan Jr. (R)
Of Cumberland — Elected 1986

Born: May 20, 1948, Bangor, Maine.
Education: Dartmouth College, A.B. 1970; U. of Maine, J.D. 1974.
Military Service: Army National Guard, 1970-73.
Occupation: Lawyer.
Religion: Protestant.
Political Career: Maine House, 1973-77, assistant minority leader, 1975-76; U.S. House, 1983-87.
Next Election: 1994.

WORK

Occupations	
White-collar	46%
Blue-collar	37%
Service workers	13%
Government Workers	
Federal	17,659
State	27,122
Local	50,878

MONEY

Median family income	$ 16,167 (47th)
Tax burden per capita	$ 864 (22nd)

EDUCATION

Spending per pupil through grade 12	$ 4,258 (19th)
Persons with college degrees	14% (34th)

CRIME

Violent crime rate	137 per 100,000 (46th)

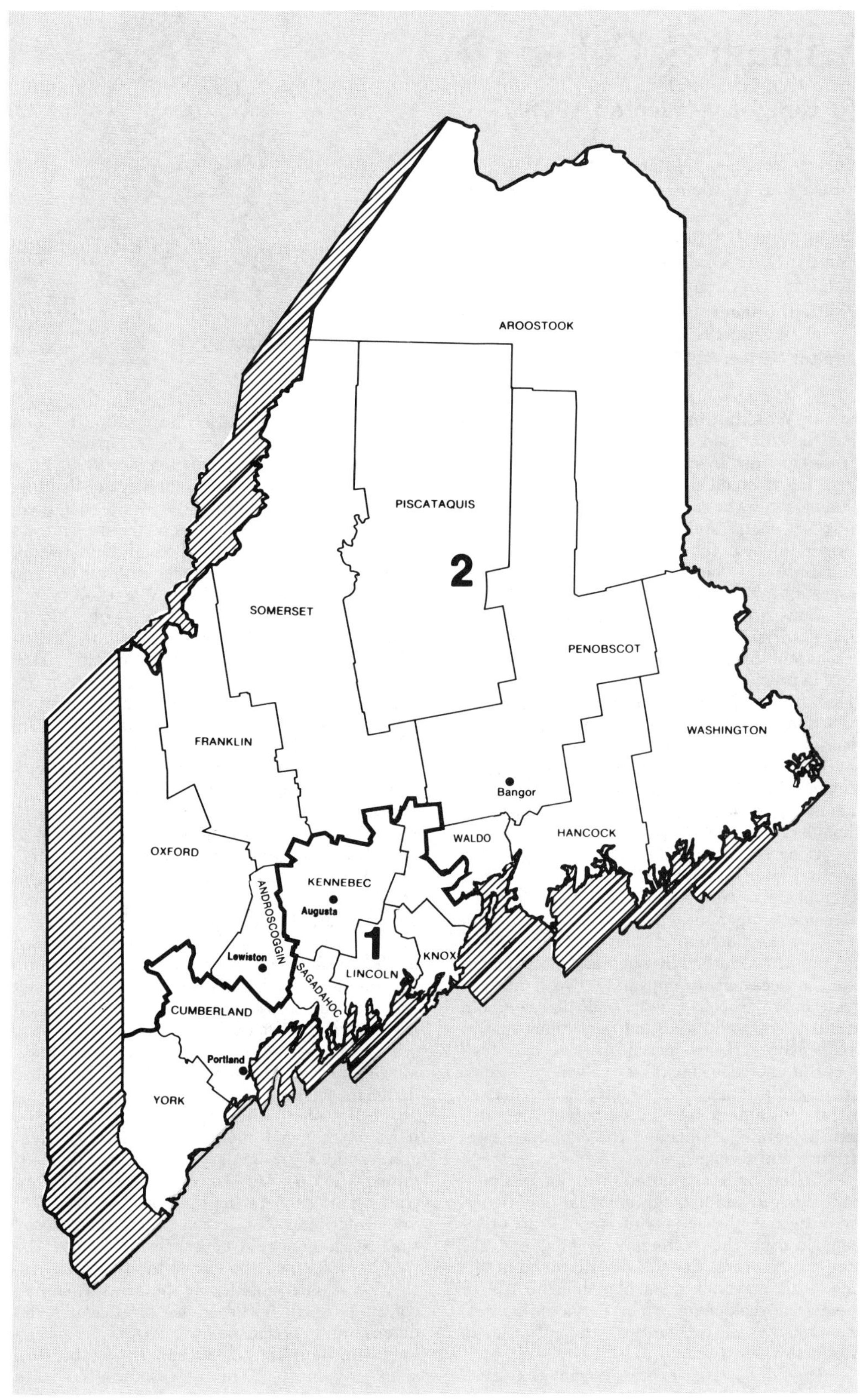
AROOSTOOK
PISCATAQUIS
2
SOMERSET
PENOBSCOT
WASHINGTON
FRANKLIN
Bangor
WALDO
HANCOCK
OXFORD
KENNEBEC
ANDROSCOGGIN
Augusta
1
KNOX
Lewiston
SAGADAHOC
LINCOLN
CUMBERLAND
Portland
YORK

William S. Cohen (R)

Of Bangor — Elected 1978

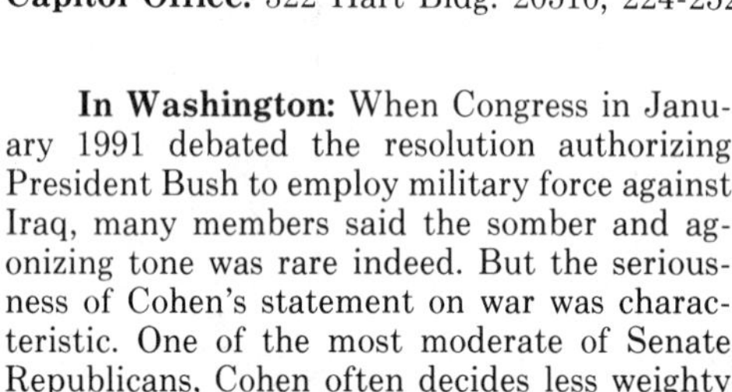

Born: Aug. 28, 1940, Bangor, Maine.
Education: Bowdoin College, B.A. 1962; Boston U., LL.B. 1965.
Occupation: Lawyer.
Family: Divorced; two children.
Religion: Unitarian.
Political Career: Bangor City Council, 1969-72; mayor of Bangor, 1971-72; U.S. House, 1973-79.
Capitol Office: 322 Hart Bldg. 20510; 224-2523.

In Washington: When Congress in January 1991 debated the resolution authorizing President Bush to employ military force against Iraq, many members said the somber and agonizing tone was rare indeed. But the seriousness of Cohen's statement on war was characteristic. One of the most moderate of Senate Republicans, Cohen often decides less weighty issues after deep thought.

Cohen noted that other members had drawn different conclusions about the "war resolution" based on the United States' experience in previous conflicts. "They remind us that there are no absolutes, no blueprints from the past that will provide a clear guide to the right decisions," Cohen said. A poet and author of seven books (including several spy mysteries), Cohen added: "So we are left to make judgments while doubt sits like a raven on our shoulders and taunts us."

Congress does not always provoke such serious public soul-searching in Cohen. At times he appears to view it with bemused and fascinated detachment as a living drama, as grist for his writings. The impression that Cohen is less than totally absorbed by Congress' daily doings, that he occasionally appears above it all, can grate on some colleagues. So do the self-conscious literary allusions and recitations that so frequently mark his speeches.

But no one mistakes Cohen for some dreamy dilettante. He is widely respected as an artful legislator conversant equally in the most tedious details of bills and the complexities of defense and foreign policy.

Cohen built a reputation as an independent thinker, and had become a national figure, by criticizing the actions of Republican presidents during the Watergate scandal and the Iran-contra affair. The war debate would not be one of his maverick moments, though. A GOP member of the Senate Armed Services Committee, Cohen voted to give Bush the authority to use force against Iraq.

He did, however, express dismay that Bush had not consulted with Congress earlier and more often about the course of the crisis. Cohen had urged as early as September 1990, little more than a month after Iraqi dictator Saddam Hussein's troops conquered Kuwait, that Bush seek Congress' approval for his decision to deploy U.S. troops to the Persian Gulf region.

Although Cohen disagrees with the 60- and 90-day deadlines in the 1973 War Powers Act, he called on the congressional leadership to demand that Bush follow its mandates to obtain Congress' permission to continue a U.S. military commitment.

This demand for consultation reflected an issue that drove Cohen during the latter years of his tenure (1983-91) on the Intelligence Committee. As the ranking Republican, or vice chairman, of the committee, Cohen attempted to pass legislation requiring the president to notify Congress within 48 hours of the start of any covert military or intelligence operation.

Cohen's bill was a result of the Iran-contra affair that occurred during the presidency of Ronald Reagan. Cohen had served as minority vice chairman of the Senate-House committee of the 100th Congress that investigated efforts by the Reagan administration to secretly sell arms to Iran and then divert the proceeds to aid the contras in Nicaragua.

Cohen — who examined the Watergate allegations as a freshman member of the House Judiciary Committee in 1974 and voted to impeach President Richard M. Nixon — was the most outspoken Republican detractor of Reagan's actions. In January 1987 he resisted administration pressure to release an Intelligence staff report exonerating the president of direct knowledge, and took to the Senate floor to say that Reagan "should have known."

By July, near the end of the panel's investigation, Cohen noted that the arms sales had continued against the advice of Reagan's top defense and foreign policy advisers. "You can only conclude that that had to be because somebody in the White House wanted it to continue," he said, "somebody being the president of the United States."

Cohen was one of only three Republicans to sign the majority report that held Reagan responsible for his "cabal of zealots." He also introduced his "48-hour notice" bill, which he said would close loopholes that permitted the covert Iran-contra policies to develop.

Despite opposition from Reagan, who complained the bill would impede the president's authority to conduct foreign policy, the Senate overwhelmingly approved the measure. But House Republicans forced Democratic leaders there to shelve it late in 1988.

Although Bush came into office in 1989 with a promise to be forthcoming in his relationship with Congress, Cohen said the Intelligence Committee still hoped to get a notification understanding in writing. "What we can't have is a return to the days when the administration says that 'timely notice' means whatever the president says it means," he said.

After a series of negotiations between Cohen, Intelligence Committee Chairman David L. Boren of Oklahoma, and administration officials, Bush agreed in October 1989 to give notice of covert action "in a fashion sensitive to congressional concerns." Bush said he would notify Congress in advance of such actions, except in rare instances when he might withhold information for a few days.

Cohen said he would have preferred the 48-hour provision but conceded that Bush would have vetoed any bill containing it. He did support efforts to codify a requirement that the president submit a written "finding" to Congress prior to a covert action except under "extraordinary circumstances." The provision was attached as an amendment to the fiscal 1991 intelligence authorization bill, which Bush vetoed.

Cohen's willingness to buck his own party's hierarchy is also evident in his role on Armed Services. He is one of the sharpest critics of the B-2 stealth bomber program, describing it as too expensive and unnecessary given the existence of less costly options such as the air-launched cruise missile.

In 1989, Cohen was one of just 29 senators to support a bill capping B-2 production at 13 planes. But the Soviet Union's military retrenchment and the ongoing U.S. fiscal crunch gave B-2 opponents momentum in 1990: Cohen's amendment to eliminate funding for two additional planes was defeated narrowly on a 45-53 vote (despite strong support for the program by the Democratic chairman of Armed Services, Sam Nunn of Georgia).

Cohen had earlier criticized the Bush administration for opening the first "post-Cold War" defense budget debate without a game plan for future defense strategy. "By waiting another year, without arriving at a consensus as to what the shape of the budget ought to be, we run the risk of having numbers plucked out of the air arbitrarily," Cohen said in April 1990.

Despite these disagreements, Cohen is no liberal on military matters; he mainly votes a pro-defense line on Armed Services, where he is the third-ranking Republican. He supports Navy projects, particularly those that pertain to such Maine facilities as the Bath Iron Works shipbuilding company and the Portsmouth Naval Shipyard.

Cohen's image as a political moderate is actually based more on domestic than defense issues. During the 101st Congress, Cohen voted to override Bush's veto of a Democratic-backed minimum wage bill, and in 1990 was the only Republican senator to be endorsed by the League of Conservation Voters. As a guardian for Maine's shoe industry, Cohen supported a textile trade bill opposed by Bush and succeeded at tabling several amendments aimed at loosening restrictions on footwear imports. He works cooperatively on Maine issues with Democratic colleague George J. Mitchell, the Senate majority leader (with whom Cohen co-authored a book on the Iran-contra investigation).

Along with his Armed Services assignment, Cohen is ranking Republican on the Governmental Affairs Oversight Subcommittee. Even here, his interest in the Pentagon intrudes: He has sponsored proposals to place stricter controls on government contracting and procurement, especially for defense, and to protect "whistleblowers," federal employees who risk their jobs by reporting acts of fraud or waste.

At Home: Cohen's image as a moderate, independent Republican and his support of Maine industries have made him a political force. In fact, Cohen was thought early in his 1990 campaign to have a chance to best Mitchell's state record of 81 percent of the vote, run up against a hard-right opponent in 1988.

However, Cohen ended up facing an unexpectedly game challenge from Democratic state Rep. Neil Rolde. Although he won easily, Cohen fell way short of Mitchell's mark.

Cohen entered the campaign with huge advantages, including a statewide base built in his two previous Senate campaigns. He also had the benefits of incumbency: He received front-page coverage for his late summer visit to U.S. forces deployed to Saudi Arabia following Iraq's August 1990 invasion of Kuwait.

But Rolde spent more than $1 million, much of it his own money, on TV ads that focused on the need for a national health care policy. Rolde widely touted his proposal for a universal health care plan based on the system in Canada, which finances all medical costs with government tax dollars but allows individuals to choose their own doctors.

Cohen criticized the concept, citing reports that Canada's system was plagued by debt and service delays; he countered with his own plan to provide incentives to insurers to supply inexpensive "no frills" coverage. But the issue gained Rolde a share of news media attention. Cohen won, but the 61 percent he received was well below his 1984 figure.

When then-Gov. Joseph E. Brennan declined to run against Cohen in 1984, the Democratic nomination went to state House Majority Leader Elizabeth H. Mitchell. Although Mitchell was well-grounded on state-level issues, she took a misguidedly strident approach that centered on her support for a nuclear weapons freeze. Her rejection of political action committees' money led much of the Democratic establishment to write off her campaign as hopelessly quixotic. Cohen ran away with 73 percent.

Cohen has been a political star in Maine since the day he spoke out for Nixon's impeachment, carving an image as a Republican of conscience. His good looks, easygoing manner and careful questioning were perfect for TV.

Cohen had risen quickly from local to national politics. After three years as a Bangor City Council member and one as mayor, Cohen won easily for the 2nd District House seat vacated by Democratic Rep. William D. Hathaway for a successful Senate bid.

After the 1974 period of Watergate celebrity, Cohen spent nearly a year considering a 1976 campaign against Maine's senior Democratic senator, Edmund S. Muskie. But while private polls showed it might be a close contest, prudence dictated a two-year wait and a campaign against Hathaway, more liberal and less of an institution than Muskie.

Hathaway worked hard to save himself in 1978, but Cohen had almost no weaknesses. The personal glamour of 1974 had never really worn off, and state and national media refurbished it for the campaign.

Cohen shifted slightly to the right, arguing that Hathaway was too liberal for most of Maine. At the same time, he worked for Democratic votes, concentrating his efforts in such places as Portland's Irish-Catholic Munjoy Hill section. Although the incumbent had done nothing in particular to offend the voters, Cohen swamped him, winning 57 percent to Hathaway's 34 percent.

Committees

Special Aging (Ranking)

Armed Services (3rd of 9 Republicans)
Projection Forces & Regional Defense (ranking); Conventional Forces & Alliance Defense; Strategic Forces & Nuclear Deterrence

Governmental Affairs (3rd of 6 Republicans)
Oversight of Government Management (ranking); Government Information & Regulation; Permanent Subcommittee on Investigations

Elections

1990 General

William S. Cohen (R)	319,167	(61%)
Neil Rolde (D)	201,053	(39%)

Previous Winning Percentages: **1984** (73%) **1978** (57%) **1976 *** (77%) **1974 *** (71%) **1972 *** (54%)

** House elections.*

Campaign Finance

	Receipts	Receipts from PACs		Expend-itures
1990				
Cohen (R)	$1,452,273	$549,194	(38%)	$1,572,195
Rolde (D)	$1,635,717	$29,647	(2%)	$1,630,894

Key Votes

1991	
Authorize use of force against Iraq	Y
1990	
Oppose prohibition of certain semiautomatic weapons	Y
Support constitutional amendment on flag desecration	Y
Oppose requiring parental notice for minors' abortions	Y
Halt production of B-2 stealth bomber at 13 planes	Y
Approve budget that cut spending and raised revenues	N
Pass civil rights bill over Bush veto	Y
1989	
Oppose reduction of SDI funding	Y
Oppose barring federal funds for "obscene" art	Y
Allow vote on capital gains tax cut	Y

Voting Studies

	Presidential Support		Party Unity		Conservative Coalition	
Year	**S**	**O**	**S**	**O**	**S**	**O**
1990	44	56	47	53	30	70
1989	74	26	52	48	71	29
1988	52	43	39	59	41	54
1987	55	42	57	42	63	38
1986	78	22	63	33	74	25
1985	63	27	55	38	55	32
1984	62	30	42	53	53	47
1983	66	29	60	36	73	23
1982	67	31	62	36	47	52
1981	76	19	69	25	59	36

Interest Group Ratings

Year	ADA	ACU	AFL-CIO	CCUS
1990	61	48	33	42
1989	45	50	30	75
1988	35	46	57	57
1987	55	58	40	67
1986	50	52	20	63
1985	35	55	45	68
1984	80	45	73	28
1983	45	30	47	33
1982	55	50	27	42
1981	35	47	33	76

George J. Mitchell (D)

Of Portland — Elected 1982

Appointed to the Senate 1980

Born: Aug. 20, 1933, Waterville, Maine.

Education: Bowdoin College, B.A. 1954; Georgetown U., LL.B. 1960.

Military Service: Army, 1954-56.

Occupation: Lawyer; judge.

Family: Divorced; one child.

Religion: Roman Catholic.

Political Career: Maine Democratic Party chairman, 1966-68; Democratic National Committee, 1969-77; assistant county attorney, 1971-77; U.S. attorney, 1977-79; U.S. District Court Judge, 1979-80; Democratic nominee for governor, 1974.

Capitol Office: 176 Russell Bldg. 20510; 224-5344.

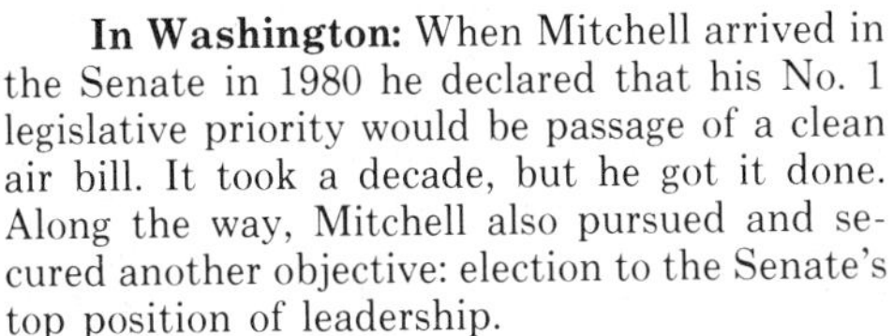

In Washington: When Mitchell arrived in the Senate in 1980 he declared that his No. 1 legislative priority would be passage of a clean air bill. It took a decade, but he got it done. Along the way, Mitchell also pursued and secured another objective: election to the Senate's top position of leadership.

It was not coincidental that long-pending clean air legislation finally was enacted in the 101st Congress, the first in which Mitchell was Senate majority leader. In that job, he could control the chamber's schedule, influence its deliberations and swing deals with both the House and the Bush administration.

Mitchell's predecessor, Robert C. Byrd of West Virginia, had blocked clean air bills as threats to jobs in his coal-mining state. Byrd took one last poke at the 1990 bill on the Senate floor, proposing a compensation package for unemployed miners. Mitchell opposed the amendment as a deal-buster that would kill the bill. He prevailed by a single vote.

Even after he had bested Byrd, Mitchell left much of his natural constituency disappointed when he opposed an amendment to strengthen car-pollution controls and clean-fuel provisions. That was the price, Mitchell said, for avoiding a veto.

"We've had 13 years of speeches on the subject," Mitchell would say. "The question is: Do we want to continue to make statements or do we want to make law?"

Mitchell is no stranger to making statements. He is often at his rhetorical best when he is protesting an impending defeat — as on the 1991 vote authorizing military force in the Persian Gulf. But he shows a marked preference for making law.

In the 101st Congress, Mitchell applied his new power not only to clean air but also to shepherding a flock of bills touching health and other human services. Perhaps most visibly of all, he sidetracked (and eventually derailed) Bush's No. 1 tax policy: the capital gains tax cut.

All in all, it was an impressive rookie season for a man who had held only an honorific leadership post before the 101st Congress — a man some had thought too cerebral for the job. So successful has Mitchell been as majority leader that unfriendly editorialists compare him with Lyndon B. Johnson, the legendary cloakroom bully.

And in these times of short lists and wide nets, he is even mentioned as a potential Democratic candidate for president in 1996 — if not sooner. Mitchell has acknowledged interest, saying "I'd like to be president" in a network TV interview in 1991. But he always sets the timetable well in the future.

Most people do not hear "Hail to the Chief" when they look at Mitchell, whose appearance and demeanor rather suggest a business accountant or the federal judge he in fact used to be. But in his leadership tour to date, Mitchell has caused many an ally and adversary to recall instead his years as a wiry point guard for the Bowdoin College basketball team. Mitchell is reputed to have personified the terrier-like tenacity demanded by his position, and he continues to do so in the Senate.

As a lawyer, a judge and a determined politician, Mitchell relates to interviews as debates and treats questions as three-dimensional traps. He often responds to questions not by answering them but by questioning their premises — usually with a few words of courteous preface such as "with all due respect."

For example, asked why Democrats opposed the fast-track procedure for approving trade agreements, Mitchell will cite the names of several prominent Democrat leaders who do not oppose such procedures. But if asked why Democrats are not doing more to assert the rights of the Congress over trade, he can argue that he and others like him are doing everything they can to protect the livelihoods of American workers.

Mitchell can, as the old joke goes, "preach it both ways." But he is at his most effective on issues he feels most deeply. In January 1991 he delivered one of the most riveting of all the solemn speeches preceding the vote on military force in the Persian Gulf.

"Just this morning I heard it said that there may be only a few thousand American casualties. For the families of those few thousand — the fathers and mothers, husbands and wives, daughters and sons — the word 'only' will have no meaning," said Mitchell. With the chamber hushed, Mitchell went on to state the case for sanctions: "If we go to war now, no one will ever know if sanctions would have worked if given a full and fair chance."

Once the Senate had voted 52-47 to authorize the use of force, Mitchell swiftly switched modes. He made sure the resolution supporting the troops was so written that all Democrats could support it. And when the package of benefits for returning Persian Gulf veterans was put together in March, Mitchell made sure every Democratic senator would be on board for the vote. He also reintroduced what had been controversial legislation to compensate Vietnam veterans who had been exposed to Agent Orange. Previous efforts to compose House and Senate bills on the issue had failed. In the January 1991 atmosphere, an agreement was reached with remarkable ease.

It was, in a sense, a victory for Mitchell and other congressional leaders just to have a meaningful vote on the use of military force in the Gulf crisis. Through much of the period between Iraq's invasion of Kuwait and the onset of hostilities, the Bush administration intimated that it did not need congressional authority to act under the authority of a United Nations mandate.

Mitchell was also at his sharpest in the 1990 debate over withdrawing favorable trade status for China in reaction to the Tiananmen Square massacre. In another memorable floor speech, Mitchell said allowing China full trading-partner status would "sacrifice our principles to temporary dictators." Pronouncing Bush's efforts at conciliation "a dismal failure," he called on the president not to "compound the mistake."

The administration, however, did renew China's trade status, and the Senate adjourned in the fall before acting on a House measure linking that status to China's human rights policies.

Mitchell can also become exercised on the subject of taxes. In fall 1989, when the House had passed a substantial cut in capital gains taxes and the Senate was thought likely to follow suit, Mitchell seemed almost alone in resisting the tide.

But when Finance Chairman Lloyd Bentsen of Texas kept the cut out of his committee's version of the relevant legislation, Mitchell had the parliamentary tool he needed. Senate Republicans needed 60 votes to insert the tax cut on the floor, and Mitchell kept enough Democrats behind him to deny the president the up-or-down vote that would have favored the cut.

In the 102nd Congress, the Maine Democrat says, his No. 1 priority is health care. More to the point, he wants to find a way to restructure the health-care system to provide insurance for those without it, long-term care for those who cannot afford it and cost controls for the employers, insurers and families who must pay the bills.

"We get the best of care, but only for those who can afford it," Mitchell says.

Mitchell's emphasis on health care reflects an abiding interest pursued as a top health policy-maker on the Finance Committee. But it also implicitly suggested the gloomier prospects for bills on civil rights and campaign finance reform. The Senate debated and passed a campaign finance measure in May 1991. To the surprise of some, the bill included a ban on honoraria. But it still needed to be reconciled with a House version. And, in any event, it attracted just five Republican votes. President Bush was considered unlikely to sign any campaign plan that so many Republicans opposed.

Also in spring 1991, Mitchell was in the thick of negotiations toward a civil rights bill that could either avoid or survive a veto. Similarly, he sought to amend the seven-day waiting period for handguns (the Brady bill) so it, too, could become law. Indeed, Mitchell seems to have been involved in the substance and strategy of nearly every piece of important legislation brought to the floor since he was elected leader at the end of the 100th Congress.

That election on Nov. 29, 1988, was declared unanimous after he had dominated two rivals on the first ballot. The victory capped a remarkable seven-month campaign in which Mitchell overcame seniority, regional rivalry, and reservations about his liberal views and low-key style.

In the end, he won with a certain flair, not just because he got more votes but because he had held his coalition together under intense pressures — both internal and external. His competitors, J. Bennett Johnston of Louisiana and Daniel K. Inouye of Hawaii, both attempted to declare themselves the winners in advance and create momentum — with Inouye making his pitch in the cloakroom and Johnston making his in the media.

But Mitchell, who probably led the race wire to wire, was cautious in public statements while pursuing his votes systematically in private. Not until a few days before the secret ballot did he discuss his own vote tally —

which, in the end, proved accurate.

Mitchell's coalition was based on liberals, Easterners, senators elected in the 1980s and senators with strong interest in the environment. But he supplemented these categories with votes from all levels of seniority, every region and most of the Senate Democrats' ideological range. Mitchell divided the spoils of his triumph, both the real positions of power and the more honorific posts, with generosity to the defeated and their supporters.

In the early months of 1989, Mitchell assumed his new power with what might be called due deliberate speed. He ceded often to others, as he had promised to do. He had Bentsen deliver the Senate Democrats' TV response to President Bush's first address to Congress. He stepped aside while Sen. Sam Nunn of Georgia led the first battle with Bush, the rejection of former Sen. John G. Tower, Bush's nominee for secretary of Defense. He did the same later when Nunn led the Democratic opposition to Bush's use of force resolution in the gulf in 1991.

He seemed intent on rationalizing the Senate floor routine, as he had promised. This particular effort has met with mixed success. He has generally hewn to a schedule in which every fourth week is either a recess or a light-work session without recorded votes. He has tried to encourage senators not to put formal "holds" on bills, a traditional practice that contributes to the logjam of legislative business at the end of a session. But he has found, as all other reformers have before him, that much of the Senate's obfuscation endures because it serves the purposes of too many senators too well.

Mitchell's own demeanor remains one of almost exaggerated dignity. Even after hours of floor maneuvering and off-the-floor negotiating, he strives for an even temper and a moderate tone. In fall 1989, the press of the budget battle kept the Senate in late sessions for weeks, much as it always had. But at least the Senate concluded its business before the end of November. During the negotiations over the myriad clean-air provisions, Mitchell was able to forestall filibusters and complete the process without the kind of marathon nocturnal sessions often used to force bills to completion in the 1980s.

Mitchell did have one sharp test in the early months of 1989: the proposed 51 percent congressional pay raise. Initially, Mitchell said he would prefer a smaller increase but that some increase was needed. When the moment of truth came, he voted "no" (as did all but five senators).

Meanwhile, in the House, Speaker Jim Wright was alienating colleagues by scheduling a vote when he was supposed to let the raise take effect automatically. Mitchell's matador-style handling of the issue was equally disappointing to some, but it attracted far less attention.

When Mitchell came to town as an appointed senator in 1980, he struck colleagues as a fellow with a judicial temperament who generally kept partisan rhetoric out of his speeches. Few could have imagined then that he would soon chair the Democratic Senatorial Campaign Committee and lead his party's 1986 charge to retake control of the Senate.

But Mitchell's long public career has been as much politics as it has law — he was a Democratic state chairman years before he was a judge — and it did not take him much time in the Senate to show that there was a vocal and aggressive politician lurking behind the soft-spoken intellectual façade.

During the 1986 campaign, Mitchell's combative side was often in evidence. The son of a janitor and a strong believer in the Democratic Party's working-class roots, he sometimes seemed personally offended by the philosophy and style of the Reagan administration.

Responding to Reagan's 1986 State of the Union speech, Mitchell portrayed Reagan as a man who relied on "rhetoric that refuses to face the real world." After the Iran-contra arms revelations convinced many Americans that Reagan was, at best, absent-minded, Mitchell all but gloated. "Never again will there be the period of the dominant Reagan presidency of the first six years," he said.

Mitchell took the campaign committee job for 1986 knowing that history clearly favored Democratic chances of toppling the GOP's 53-47 Senate majority. Ever since popular Senate elections began in 1914, an administration's sixth-year election had cost the president's party an average of seven Senate seats.

But with the GOP enjoying its typically large financial advantage and Reagan campaigning all-out to protect vulnerable GOP incumbents, no one expected the Democrats to retake the chamber so decisively, with 55 seats.

To reward Mitchell when they organized the 100th Congress, Senate Democrats gave him the position of deputy president pro tempore, a job that was created for Hubert H. Humphrey in 1977 and had not been occupied since Humphrey's death. Winning such a prestigious post clearly marked Mitchell as a man on the move, but another role lay ahead — one that would add a critical dimension to his drive for majority leader: He became one of six Democrats on the special Senate committee investigating the Iran-contra affair.

In July 1987, Mitchell took over the public questioning of North and walked the former Marine through a series of lawyerly questions. He cut off the show-stealing answers North had given other interrogators on the panel, and delivered one of the most memorable lines of the hearings. " . . . Recognize that it is possible for an American to disagree with you on aid to the contras and still love God and still love this country just as much as you do," he told North.

Later, when Reagan delivered his national address on the subject in August, Mitchell was chosen to give the Democrats' response. It was a measured, serious performance that made little effort to charm. But it was a hit. Mitchell blends his partisanship with a keen memory for detail and an ability to pursue several complicated tasks at once.

On the Finance Committee, Mitchell did not play a prominent role in shaping tax bills in the 97th and 98th Congresses, but he was active in the tax-code overhaul enacted by the 99th Congress. Mitchell argued that middle-income taxpayers should benefit as much from revision as those in high- and low-income groups, and he sought to ensure that new restrictions on real-estate tax shelters would not eliminate the incentive to build and maintain low-income housing.

The tax bill that came out of Finance also called for a two-tiered rate structure for individuals. On the Senate floor, Mitchell tried to add a third tier, an effort to get more tax revenue from the highest-income taxpayers. In the end, Mitchell's plan lost by 71-29; the decisive margin sent a signal that the Senate would resist all major changes in the tax rates and basic reform elements of the Finance Committee's bill.

Later, Mitchell did get the Senate to approve a tax credit that preserved incentives for investing in low-income housing.

Mitchell has fought in Finance and elsewhere to protect Maine's declining shoe industry from cheap foreign competition. He was a member of the congressional coalition that fought successfully to ensure that the administration's Caribbean Basin Initiative, cleared by Congress in 1983, did not go too far in easing barriers against the importing of shoes and other products from the region. That issue was back at the forefront in 1990, when supporters of Caribbean trade were seeking to authorize CBI permanently and expand its scope. Mitchell once again stood in the breach, arguing that what was left of Maine's shoe and clothing industry was still worth preserving. The Congress made CBI permanent, but only within its previous limitations.

At Home: Mitchell's feats on the national stage are matched by his political accomplishments in Maine in the 1980s. He started the decade as an appointed senator scrapping to win election on his own; by 1988, he was the holder of the state record for the most lopsided Senate victory.

Mitchell was assured an easy re-election campaign in 1988 when GOP Rep. Olympia J. Snowe decided not to challenge him. Instead, he faced Jasper Wyman, a leader in the 1986 anti-pornography state referendum campaign and head of the state's Christian Civic League.

For the Senate contest, Wyman stepped back from his conservative social agenda and focused on taxes and national defense. But he was no match for Mitchell, who won 81 percent of the vote, the highest percentage for any 1988 Senate candidate.

As resounding a victory as that was, the thrill was much greater for Mitchell when he won in 1982. A year before that election, appointee Mitchell had looked like a sitting duck: He had failed in his only previous attempt to win statewide office, and he trailed by 36 points in a poll released by Republican David F. Emery, a four-term House member with designs on Mitchell's seat.

Yet on Election Day, Mitchell crushed Emery with 61 percent of the vote, a stronger showing than even the invincible Edmund S. Muskie had posted when winning his fourth Senate election in 1976.

A share of the credit went to Emery, whose campaign was guilty of some well-publicized blunders. One of the worst was a letter Emery sent to veterans in which he boasted that the Veterans of Foreign Wars (VFW) had rated his voting record at 92, while giving a zero to Mitchell. The VFW statistics were compiled in June 1980, just a month after Mitchell took office. They contained no votes in which the senator could have participated. That incident prompted newspaper editorials criticizing Emery for practicing the "politics of distortion," an especially unkind cut in Maine, where voters disdain negative campaigning.

Mitchell, meanwhile, came home often and impressed many. He won support from millworkers and other working-class voters who had been laid off or feared for their jobs during the recession of 1982. They were consoled less by Emery's Reaganomics than by Mitchell's promise that Democrats would not accept high unemployment.

In the end, Mitchell won all but one county, derailing the political career of Emery (who attempted a House comeback in 1990 but lost to Democrat Thomas H. Andrews in Maine's 1st District).

Mitchell's move into national politics in 1980 came out of his longstanding relationship with Muskie. The two had been allies since the early 1960s, when Mitchell worked as Muskie's administrative assistant. After Muskie moved to the State Department in 1980, he suggested that Mitchell be named to succeed him in the Senate. Democratic Gov. Joseph E. Brennan agreed.

Mitchell had few enemies and seemed the perfect compromise, allowing Brennan to bypass the more prominent but more controversial contenders. Mitchell had defeated Brennan in the 1974 gubernatorial primary, but that contest had left no ill feelings.

The campaign for governor in 1974 had been Mitchell's one statewide effort, and it had been an embarrassing defeat. Widely considered the favorite that fall, he underestimated the independent candidacy of James Longley, a Lewiston businessman running on a platform of reduced state spending. Longley drew thousands of blue-collar votes that Mitchell took for granted, and he won by 15,000 votes.

From working-class roots, Mitchell worked his way through law school as an insurance adjuster and spent two years in the Justice Department's antitrust division before joining Muskie's staff. He returned to Maine to practice law in 1965, later serving as Democratic state chairman and national committeeman. In the wake of the 1972 McGovern defeat, he staged an unsuccessful drive to become chairman of the Democratic National Committee. As the choice of the party's liberal faction, he lost to Robert S. Strauss of Texas.

On Muskie's recommendation, President Jimmy Carter named Mitchell U.S. attorney for Maine in 1977. Two years later the same connection won Mitchell the federal judgeship he gave up after only a few months to accept the Senate appointment.

Committees

Majority Leader

Environment & Public Works (3rd of 9 Democrats)
Environmental Protection; Superfund, Ocean & Water Protection; Water Resources, Transportation & Infrastructure

Finance (6th of 11 Democrats)
Health for Families & the Uninsured; International Trade; Medicare & Long Term Care

Veterans' Affairs (3rd of 7 Democrats)

Elections

1988 General

George J. Mitchell (D)	452,590	(81%)
Jasper S. Wyman (R)	104,758	(19%)

Previous Winning Percentage: **1982** (61%)

Campaign Finance

	Receipts	Receipts from PACs		Expenditures
1988				
Mitchell (D)	$1,810,602	$724,547	(40%)	$1,340,157
Wyman (R)	$147,981	$2,599	(2%)	$147,760

Key Votes

1991

Authorize use of force against Iraq	N

1990

Oppose prohibition of certain semiautomatic weapons	N
Support constitutional amendment on flag desecration	N
Oppose requiring parental notice for minors' abortions	Y
Halt production of B-2 stealth bomber at 13 planes	Y
Approve budget that cut spending and raised revenues	Y
Pass civil rights bill over Bush veto	Y

1989

Oppose reduction of SDI funding	N
Oppose barring federal funds for "obscene" art	Y
Allow vote on capital gains tax cut	N

Voting Studies

	Presidential Support		Party Unity		Conservative Coalition	
Year	S	O	S	O	S	O
1990	34	66	89	11	22	78
1989	57	43	86	14	37	63
1988	43	57	95	4	5	95
1987	36	64	90	10	31	69
1986	31	66	84	14	25	74
1985	33	67	87	13	30	70
1984	36	61	84	15	15	85
1983	40	60	84	15	30	70
1982	35	63	89	11	16	84
1981	45	51	88	10	24	75

Interest Group Ratings

Year	ADA	ACU	AFL-CIO	CCUS
1990	83	9	56	17
1989	80	11	100	50
1988	95	0	100	21
1987	95	8	90	28
1986	85	14	87	32
1985	65	17	86	31
1984	90	9	73	37
1983	80	12	76	42
1982	95	40	88	30
1981	90	7	95	35

1 Thomas H. Andrews (D)

Of Portland — Elected 1990

Born: March 22, 1953, North Easton, Mass.
Education: Bowdoin College, B.A. 1976.
Occupation: Association director; political activist.
Family: Wife, Debra Johnson.
Religion: Unitarian.
Political Career: Maine House, 1983-85; Maine Senate, 1985-90.
Capitol Office: 1724 Longworth Bldg. 20515; 225-6116.

The Path to Washington: The themes of economic populism, such as "tax equity" and "fairness," have long been staples for Andrews, liberal activist turned legislator. But the adoption of these themes by the national Democratic leadership during the 1990 budget debate gave a boost to Andrews' bid for the open 1st.

Locked in a tight battle with former GOP Rep. David F. Emery, Andrews gained momentum in the closing weeks of the campaign and ended up winning easily. Andrews ended the comeback hopes of Emery, who served the 1st from 1975 to 1983, and held for Democrats the seat vacated by Democratic Rep. Joseph E. Brennan, who lost for governor.

While Andrews' economic views struck a nerve with voters, it was another aspect of his activist past that ensured his success. A veteran grass-roots organizer, Andrews built a districtwide network of volunteers whose get-out-the-vote work brought him victory.

Andrews says he organized efforts in behalf of the disadvantaged while a high school student. While in college, he served as director of a center for mentally handicapped adults.

It was a personal trauma, though, that set Andrews on the activist path. When he was 15, Andrews learned he had cancer on one knee; seven years later, that leg had to be amputated. Says Andrews, who is fitted with a prosthesis, "When you lie there in bed and wonder whether you'll live or die, it makes you rethink your priorities." After several years of working on causes related to the poor, Andrews signed on in 1981 as executive director of the Maine Association of Handicapped Persons.

Andrews was also involved in a variety of environmentalist campaigns in the early 1980s. He took his causes to the legislative arena when he won a state House seat in 1982. After just one term, he ran in 1984 for an open state Senate seat, using his strong personal base to overcome an opponent with Democratic organization backing.

As chairman of the Legislature's Taxation Committee, Andrews struck a populist note by advocating middle-class property tax relief. He also moved into a variety of mainstream roles, including the chairmanship of the Economic Development Committee. In 1987, Andrews co-founded the Maine Studies Center at the University of Southern Maine, which encourages the study of current affairs.

Andrews nonetheless entered the 1990 House primary as an underdog. He faced four other candidates, including state Attorney General James E. Tierney, the 1986 Democratic nominee for governor. Yet Andrews again outorganized his competition, winning with a 36 percent plurality.

Emery, remembered from four House campaigns and his failed 1982 challenge to Democratic Sen. George J. Mitchell, had an initial name recognition advantage over Andrews. The public interest in such international issues as the Persian Gulf crisis played to an Emery strength: He was assistant director of the Arms Control and Disarmament Agency under President Ronald Reagan.

But Andrews had a more zealous following than Emery, who alienated some longtime backers with his switch from an anti-abortion position to support for abortion rights. And economics, not foreign policy, came to dominate the campaign agenda; Emery was damaged by the turn of events.

Late in the campaign, Emery cast Andrews as an extreme liberal whose call for a 50 percent reduction in military spending would cost jobs at Maine defense facilities, including the Bath Iron Works (BIW) shipbuilding company. But Andrews — who insisted that his proposed post-Cold War cutbacks would come from nuclear forces, not the conventional weapons in which Maine specializes — had cover: He was endorsed by BIW's president, with whom he had worked as chairman of the Economic Development Committee.

Maine 1

South — Portland; Augusta

Maine's industrial Democratic core follows Interstate 95 from Biddeford in the south to Waterville in the north, right through the heart of the 1st. With the exception of Androscoggin County (Lewiston), all the state's most populous and Democratic counties lie in the district. The 1st is made competitive for Republicans by the small coastal towns that stretch northeast from Portland.

Powered by the waters of Maine's rivers, industries here have made shoes, ships, textiles, lumber and paper throughout the 20th century. Low wages and high unemployment in the area in the postwar years made southern Maine a fertile recruiting ground for Edmund S. Muskie and other Democratic leaders in the 1950s.

Portland is Maine's largest city with 63,000 people, and its Irish and Franco-American communities, combined with an environmentalist white-collar vote, has kept surrounding Cumberland County in the Democratic column in most contests. In 1990 House voting, Democrat Thomas H. Andrews drew 64 percent in the county.

The spread of high-technology industry up the coast from Boston brought a modest boom to Portland in the 1980s; high-rise office buildings have sprouted, and its downtown streets boast trendy boutiques and restaurants. A hike in prices for upscale housing displaced many native Mainers and even jolted yuppies moving into the Portland area from out of state.

Maine's southernmost county, York, is home to the Democratic strongholds of Biddeford and Saco, heavily Franco-American factory towns south of Portland. York County's pulse quickened in the mid-1980's, as the region's economy boomed, only to see the growth peter out by the end of the decade. The planned closing of Pease Air Force base (just across the New Hampshire border) and cutbacks at the naval shipyard in Kittery will not help the economy. Waterville, a textile city at the northern edge of Kennebec County, is another Democratic bastion; Andrews won it with 69 percent.

Nearby Augusta, the state capital, has a smaller Franco-American population and is more evenly split between factory workers and white-collar government workers.

The district's Republican heartland lies along the coast. Lincoln, Knox, and Waldo counties consist mainly of coastal Republican towns that help make Maine the No. 1 lobster state, as well as the "Vacation State."

In 1988, George Bush was considered something of a native son — his family has long owned a vacation compound in Kennebunkport — which helped him win every county in the state.

Population: 563,073. White 557,507 (99%), Black 1,636 (0.3%), Other 2,667 (1%). Spanish origin 2,683 (1%). 18 and over 405,831 (72%), 65 and over 72,456 (13%). Median age: 31.

Committees

Armed Services (32nd of 33 Democrats)
Research & Development; Seapower & Strategic & Critical Materials

Small Business (25th of 27 Democrats)
Exports, Tax Policy & Special Problems

Campaign Finance

	Receipts	Receipts from PACs		Expend-itures
1990				
Andrews (D)	$696,604	$244,473	(35%)	$693,165
Emery (R)	$465,551	$162,121	(35%)	$463,873

Key Vote

1991

Authorize use of force against Iraq	N

Elections

1990 General		
Thomas H. Andrews (D)	167,623	(60%)
David F. Emery (R)	110,836	(40%)
1990 Primary		
Thomas H. Andrews (D)	16,158	(36%)
James E. Tierney (D)	14,995	(34%)
Elizabeth H. Mitchell (D)	7,634	(17%)
Linda Elowitch Abromson (D)	4,957	(11%)
Ralph W. Conant (D)	762	(2%)

District Vote For President

	1988	1984	1980	1976
D	131,078 (43%)	120,708 (40%)	114,661 (42%)	120,645 (48%)
R	169,292 (56%)	180,808 (60%)	122,193 (45%)	123,020 (49%)
I			30,118 (11%)	

2 Olympia J. Snowe (R)

Of Auburn — Elected 1978

Born: Feb. 21, 1947, Augusta, Maine.
Education: U. of Maine, B.A. 1969.
Occupation: Concrete company executive; public official.
Family: Husband, John R. McKernan Jr.
Religion: Greek Orthodox.
Political Career: Maine House, 1973-77; Maine Senate, 1977-79.
Capitol Office: 2464 Rayburn Bldg. 20515; 225-6306.

In Washington: As Snowe rose in seniority through the 1980s, her interests ranged beyond the borders of the 2nd District. She applied herself to foreign policy issues as a member of the Foreign Affairs Committee, and to women's health and pay concerns as co-chairman of the Congressional Caucus for Women's Issues.

An early enrollee in the 1988 presidential campaign of part-time Maine resident George Bush, Snowe had a high-profile role at the Republican National Convention that year. She also gained visibility as part of Maine's "power couple": in 1989, she married Republican Gov. John R. McKernan Jr., a former House colleague.

Yet the same criteria that made Snowe one of the nation's better-known woman politicians also made her susceptible to criticism from her 1990 Democratic opponent that she had lost touch with her home base. Somewhat slow to react to these attacks, Snowe found herself in a dangerously close re-election contest.

Snowe has never been one to ignore her district; in fact, for much of her House career, she had a reputation for being cautious and overly responsive to her constituents' views. How well Snowe impresses voters with her district-oriented activities during the 102nd Congress will bear on whether she returns to her usually robust victory margins.

But Snowe — who, with the 1991 retirement of Nebraska Rep. Virginia Smith, is the senior GOP woman in the House — is unlikely to eschew her broader agenda. As the ranking Republican on the Foreign Affairs Subcommittee on International Operations, she has been in the middle of the debate over the fate of the bugged U.S. embassy in Moscow.

Early in 1987, U.S. officials revealed that the unfinished embassy had been seeded with listening devices by Soviet operatives. Snowe traveled to the embassy site with then-subcommittee Chairman Daniel A. Mica and soon became adamant that the building was unsalvageable and should be torn down; that position was adopted first by President Ronald Reagan in 1988 and then by President Bush in 1989.

However, a stalemate developed between those, such as Snowe, who emphasized the embassy's security and others who focused on the cost (estimated at more than $300 million) of razing and rebuilding the embassy. The need for fiscal austerity forced the Bush administration in March 1991 to throw its support to a less expensive plan, under which new secure floors would be built on top of the bugged building.

Snowe usually supports Bush on foreign policy issues: She backed the January 1991 resolution authorizing the president to use military force against Iraq. The two did part ways in 1989, though, on the issues of U.S. aid to Greece and Turkey.

Bush, like Reagan before him, sought to increase aid to Turkey, which has had a more consistently pro-U.S. line than Greece in recent years. But Snowe, a Greek-American, argued for continuation of a formula providing Greece with $7 in aid for every $10 that went to Turkey, which had been in effect since Turkey occupied part of Cyprus in the mid-1970s. Abandoning the ratio, Snowe said, "will be seen as an indication that America has grown weary of the Cyprus issue."

Despite Snowe's generally conservative views on foreign affairs and fiscal issues, her more liberal leanings on domestic social issues have earned her a reputation as one of the leading GOP moderates in the House. During the latter years of the Reagan administration, Snowe backed the Republican president on well under half of House votes; during the 101st Congress, she supported Bush just about half the time.

A supporter of abortion rights, Snowe cochairs the women's caucus with Democratic Rep. Patricia Schroeder of Colorado. Snowe is a strong advocate of expanded federal health care efforts for the elderly (she is ranking Republican on the Aging Subcommittee on Human Services) and for women in general.

Like many Republican moderates, Snowe has had to search for a policy-making role within the conservative-oriented GOP. Snowe helped establish the '92 Group — a caucus of GOP moderates dedicated to developing programs and strategies to gain the Republicans a

Maine 2

North — Lewiston; Auburn; Bangor

America's largest congressional district east of the Mississippi, the 2nd accounts for the vast bulk of Maine's territory. Across its northern reaches stretch the pine forests that have fueled the northwoods economy since the 18th century. Its people are clustered at the southern end, closer to the state's industrial core.

The one portion of the district actually within Maine's industrial belt is Androscoggin County, anchored by the twin cities of Lewiston (population 40,000) and Auburn (population 24,000). Ancient factory towns — Auburn claims to be the birthplace of the shoe industry in Maine — the cities traditionally anchor the Democratic vote in the district. Lewiston, the state's second-largest city, is the more Democratic of the two — there are four times as many registered Democrats than Republicans. Unsuccessful Democratic House challenger Patrick McGowan carried Lewiston in 1990 with 62 percent. Auburn — which voted for Jimmy Carter in 1976 — has gone Republican for president ever since. Both cities, however, tend to abandon any Democratic tradition to vote for Republican Sen. William S. Cohen. The only other city of significant size in the 2nd is Bangor (Penobscot County), the third-largest in the state. Bangor's heyday as a ship-making center is over, as are the days when woodsmen from the north would come to squander their paychecks in the neighborhood known as the "Devil's Half-Acre." But its wood-products industry and modest port remain in operation, and its international airport is a refueling station for transoceanic flights.

Though still Democratic in local elections, Bangor is a more dependable Republican vote at the national level than the two cities farther south. Like Reagan in 1980 and 1984, George Bush narrowly carried Bangor.

The rest of the district is rural, much of it covered with the forests that supply trees for huge lumber and paper mills. The land that is left produces apples, blueberries, corn, chickens and Maine's biggest cash crop, potatoes. The potatoes are grown largely in Aroostook County, the huge northern tract that is bigger than four states.

Yankee Republican farmers form a solid majority outside the industrial cities, and their votes keep the district Republican in most elections; outside of Androscoggin, Snowe took all but one of the district's ten counties in 1990. Still, the chronic poverty that afflicts the area is gradually bringing some of its residents into the Democratic column as they turn to the government for assistance. Pockets of severe poverty are found in the woodlands in Aroostook County and in coastal Washington County, which lacks the tourist attraction of the more accessible coastal regions. With its large Franco-American population, Democrats often prevail in Washington County, though Bush carried it with 56 percent in 1988.

Population: 561,587. White 552,343 (98%), Black 1,492 (0.3%), Other 4,367 (1%). Spanish origin 2,322 (0.4%). 18 and over 397,442 (71%), 65 and over 68,462 (12%). Median age: 30.

House majority by 1992. But Snowe in 1989 joined with a group of moderate and conservative Republican House members, who showed their dissatisfaction with the status quo under the establishment "Old Bull" Republicans by electing conservative activist Rep. Newt Gingrich of Georgia as party whip.

At Home: Before 1990, Snowe had been an overpowering force in the 2nd District. Three times, in presidential election years, Snowe received better than three-quarters of the House vote; in two other re-election campaigns, she took at least two-thirds.

By contrast, her 1990 opponent, five-term state Rep. Patrick K. McGowan, began the campaign little-known outside his home base. However, McGowan was a young political veteran (he won his first state House term at age 23) and turned out to be a savvy challenger.

The mainly inland 2nd — always the poorer of the two Maine districts — was being hit by the effects of a recession, and McGowan used populist themes to his advantage. He criticized Snowe for spending so much of her time on foreign policy issues, stating, "I want to be an advocate for the 2nd District."

Polls throughout the campaign gave Snowe a generous lead, and she was expected to spend most of her time working for McKernan in his tough re-election campaign. But when Snowe took a break from the long 1990 House session to debate McGowan, she engaged in a series of heated exchanges — surprising pundits who expected Snowe to ignore McGowan.

It turned out Snowe had reason for concern. She won with 51 percent and a plurality of just over 4,000 votes. Her percentage brought her to a level she had not approached since her first House contest.

That 1978 win culminated a political rise that Snowe had not meant to happen. Snowe did not even begin life as a Republican. Orphaned at age 9 and raised by an aunt and uncle in blue-collar surroundings, she worked as an intern for Democratic Gov. Kenneth M. Curtis. But Olympia Bouchles met and, in 1969, married Peter Snowe, an Auburn businessman involved in Republican politics.

The next year, Peter Snowe won a state House seat. But in 1973, he was killed in an automobile accident. Olympia Snowe — who recently had taken a job in the district office of then-Republican Rep. William S. Cohen — was elected to fill his vacant seat. After winning another term on her own, Snowe was elected in 1976 to the state Senate. Two years later, Cohen gave up his 2nd District seat to run for Senate, and Snowe moved up again.

Snowe had to fight to win the seat. Her Democratic foe, Maine Secretary of State Markham L. Gartley, had taken just 29 percent in a 1974 House race against Cohen, but the Vietnam veteran had the distinction of being the first prisoner of war released by the North Vietnamese.

Snowe moved skillfully through the campaign, though. To coarsen a fashionable image she had developed, Snowe traded her designer clothes for a wool shirt and hiking boots and walked across the district — a tactic Cohen had used successfully. While Snowe won with a bare majority, she had a 10-point edge on Gartley, with the remainder going to other candidates.

Snowe's quick rise to district dominance encouraged talk of statewide possibilities. However, she bypassed challenges to Democratic Sen. George J. Mitchell in 1982 and 1988.

Republican officials were able to recruit Snowe for one new role in 1988 — deputy permanent chairman of the GOP national convention, a job that frequently put her in front of the TV cameras in New Orleans. As a woman of Greek extraction, Snowe was an ideal choice to give the party a more inclusive image and counter Michael S. Dukakis' ethnic appeal.

Committees

Foreign Affairs (7th of 18 Republicans)
International Operations (ranking); Arms Control, International Security & Science

Select Aging (4th of 27 Republicans)
Human Services (ranking); Rural Elderly; Social Security and Women

Joint Economic

Elections

1990 General		
Olympia J. Snowe (R)	121,704	(51%)
Patrick K. McGowan (D)	116,798	(49%)
1988 General		
Olympia J. Snowe (R)	167,226	(66%)
Kenneth P. Hayes (D)	85,346	(34%)

Previous Winning Percentages: **1986** (77%) **1984** (76%) **1982** (67%) **1980** (79%) **1978** (51%)

District Vote For President

	1988	1984	1980	1976
D	112,491 (45%)	93,807 (37%)	106,383 (42%)	111,634 (48%)
R	137,839 (55%)	155,692 (62%)	116,329 (46%)	113,300 (49%)
I			23,209 (9%)	

Campaign Finance

	Receipts	Receipts from PACs	Expend-itures
1990			
Snowe (R)	$278,223	$97,655 (35%)	$306,289
McGowan (D)	$229,478	$65,903 (29%)	$228,344
1988			
Snowe (R)	$229,929	$72,300 (31%)	$202,317
Hayes (D)	$69,218	$26,772 (39%)	$68,857

Key Votes

1991	
Authorize use of force against Iraq	Y
1990	
Support constitutional amendment on flag desecration	Y
Pass family and medical leave bill over Bush veto	Y
Reduce SDI funding	Y
Allow abortions in overseas military facilities	Y
Approve budget summit plan for spending and taxing	N
Approve civil rights bill	Y
1989	
Halt production of B-2 stealth bomber at 13 planes	N
Oppose capital gains tax cut	N
Approve federal abortion funding in rape or incest cases	Y
Approve pay raise and revision of ethics rules	N
Pass Democratic minimum wage plan over Bush veto	N

Voting Studies

	Presidential Support		Party Unity		Conservative Coalition	
Year	**S**	**O**	**S**	**O**	**S**	**O**
1990	48	51	57	43	67	33
1989	51	48	47	52	76	22
1988	37	63	54	46	82	18
1987	38	58	48	50	65	35
1986	44	54	53	47	64	36
1985	48	52	56	43	69	31
1984	49	51	47	53	64	36
1983	50	50	46	53	49	49
1982	47	52	53	46	58	40
1981	67	33	68	32	69	31

Interest Group Ratings

Year	ADA	ACU	AFL-CIO	CCUS
1990	28	54	33	43
1989	35	54	25	90
1988	60	40	86	50
1987	56	22	44	73
1986	50	48	64	61
1985	35	48	53	59
1984	55	25	38	38
1983	35	43	29	75
1982	50	36	35	57
1981	45	87	40	89

Maryland

U.S. CONGRESS

SENATE 2 D
HOUSE 5 D, 3 R

LEGISLATURE

Senate 38 D, 9 R
House 116 D, 25 R

ELECTIONS

1988 Presidential Vote

Bush	51%
Dukakis	48%

1984 Presidential Vote

Reagan	53%
Mondale	47%

1980 Presidential Vote

Reagan	44%
Carter	47%
Anderson	8%

Turnout rate in 1986	32%
Turnout rate in 1988	49%
Turnout rate in 1990	30%

(as percentage of voting age population)

POPULATION AND GROWTH

1980 population	4,216,975
1990 population (19th in the nation)	4,781,468
Percent change 1980-1990	+13%

DEMOGRAPHIC BREAKDOWN

White	71%
Black	25%
Asian or Pacific Islander	3%
(Hispanic origin)	3%
Urban	80%
Rural	20%
Born in state	54%
Foreign-born	5%

MAJOR CITIES

Baltimore	736,014
Rockville	44,835
Frederick	40,148
Gaithersburg	39,542
Bowie	37,589

AREA AND LAND USE

Area	9,837 sq. miles (42nd)
Farm	41%
Forest	42%
Federally owned	3%

Gov. William Donald Schaefer (D)
Of Baltimore — Elected 1986

Born: Nov. 2, 1921, West Baltimore, Md.
Education: Baltimore City College, B.A. 1939; U. of Baltimore, LL.B. 1942, LL.M. 1951.
Military Service: Army, 1942-45; Army Reserve, 1945-79.
Occupation: Lawyer.
Religion: Episcopalian.
Political Career: Baltimore City Council, 1955-71, president, 1967-71; Baltimore mayor, 1971-87.
Next Election: 1994.

WORK

Occupations

White-collar	61%
Blue-collar	25%
Service workers	13%

Government Workers

Federal	132,277
State	99,732
Local	177,045

MONEY

Median family income	$ 23,112	(3rd)
Tax burden per capita	$ 984	(16th)

EDUCATION

Spending per pupil through grade 12	$ 5,201	(8th)
Persons with college degrees	20%	(4th)

CRIME

Violent crime rate	855 per 100,000 (4th)

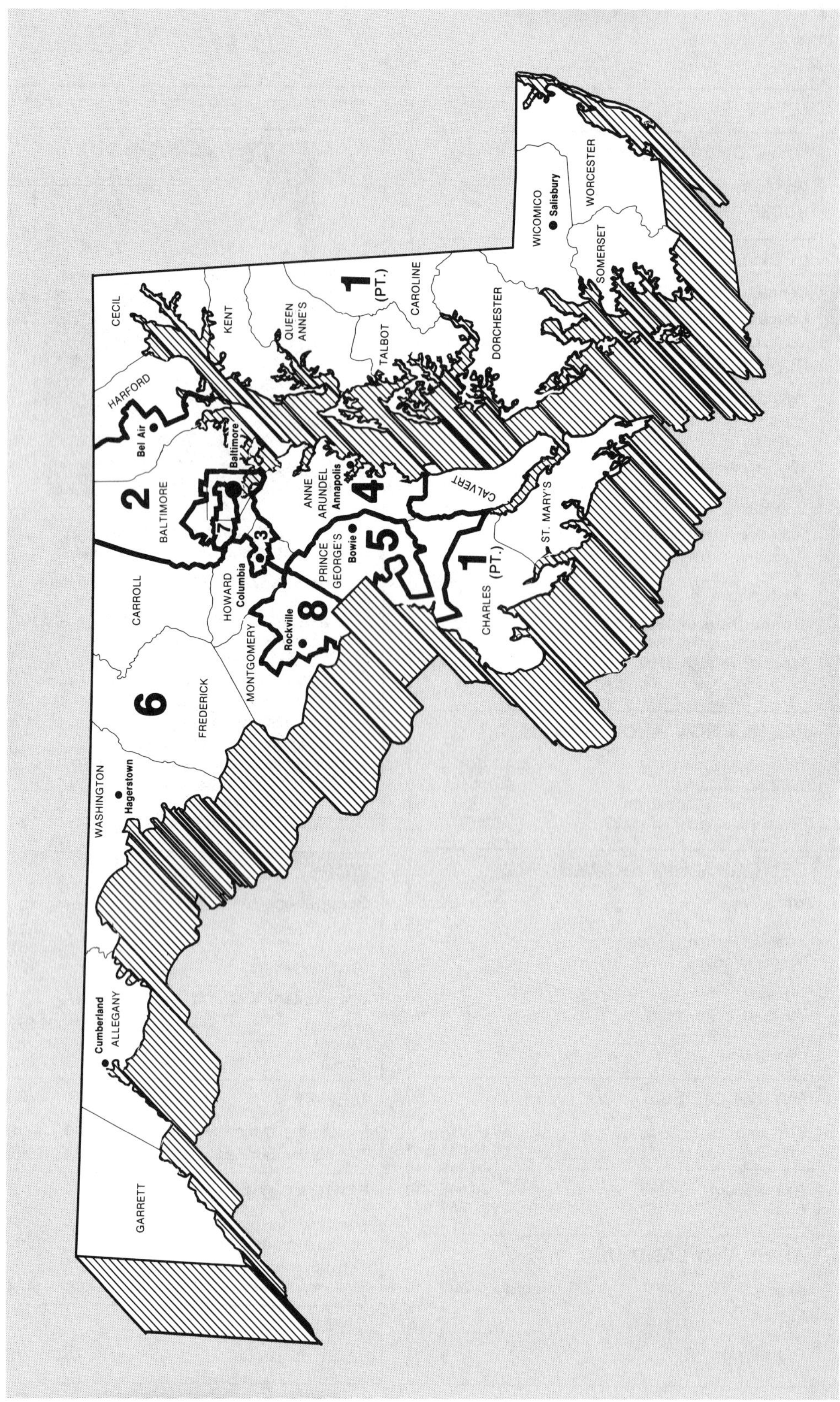
GARRETT
ALLEGANY
Cumberland
WASHINGTON
Hagerstown
6
FREDERICK
CARROLL
MONTGOMERY
Rockville
8
HOWARD
Columbia
BALTIMORE
2
7
3
Baltimore
Bel Air
HARFORD
CECIL
KENT
QUEEN ANNE'S
ANNE ARUNDEL
Annapolis
4
PRINCE GEORGE'S
Bowie
5
1 (PT.)
CHARLES
ST. MARY'S
CALVERT
TALBOT
CAROLINE
1 (PT.)
DORCHESTER
WICOMICO
Salisbury
WORCESTER
SOMERSET

Paul S. Sarbanes (D)

Of Baltimore — Elected 1976

Born: Feb. 3, 1933, Salisbury, Md.
Education: Princeton U., A.B. 1954; Oxford U., B.A. 1957; Harvard U., LL.B. 1960.
Occupation: Lawyer; law clerk.
Family: Wife, Christine Dunbar; three children.
Religion: Greek Orthodox.
Political Career: Md. House, 1967-71; U.S. House, 1971-77.
Capitol Office: 309 Hart Bldg. 20510; 224-4524.

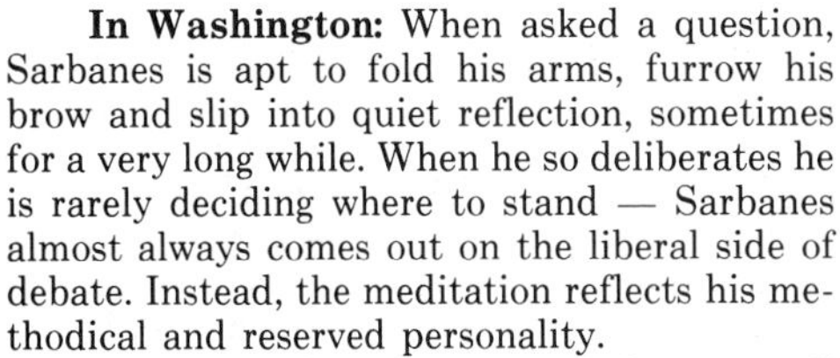

In Washington: When asked a question, Sarbanes is apt to fold his arms, furrow his brow and slip into quiet reflection, sometimes for a very long while. When he so deliberates he is rarely deciding where to stand — Sarbanes almost always comes out on the liberal side of debate. Instead, the meditation reflects his methodical and reserved personality.

"It is quite true I don't make decisions off the top of my head," he once explained. "I don't think important decisions ought to be made that way."

Legislatively, Sarbanes' agenda meshes with his style: He is a leader on Third World debt, an arcane subject with worldwide economic implications. Politically, Democratic leaders turn to Sarbanes when they need a spokesman resistant to partisan fire: In 1987, he was selected to serve on the panel investigating the Iran-contra scandal.

But Sarbanes' painstaking approach and narrow legislative focus frustrate his admirers, who feel he could be a leader. One of the Senate's most penetrating intellects, he has the skills to leave opponents sputtering, but he is not a provocateur.

Sarbanes vexes colleagues by targeting minor issues, leading some to conclude that his judgment on the importance of subjects does not always equal his thoroughness in examining them. When he spars at length with witnesses over technicalities, he sometimes seems to miss the big picture nit-picking minutiae.

For a man who has made politics his life's work, Sarbanes has a curious, if refreshing, distaste for publicity. When he does make headlines, it is generally because he has unearthed a detail offensive to good-government sensibilities. This was the case in 1989, when Sarbanes held up the consideration of ambassadorial nominees who were major contributors to the GOP. Acknowledging that the practice of rewarding political supporters with ambassadorships has a long bipartisan history, Sarbanes argued that the Bush administration had pursued the practice to excess.

The nomination of Florida real estate magnate Joseph Zappala to be ambassador to Spain was Sarbanes' test case. "We propose to send as ambassador to Spain [a man] with no particular interest or knowledge of Spain," he said, adding that Mr. Zappala's $145,000 in contributions "appear to be the sole reason" for his selection. While many senators concurred that Zappala's résumé was thin, the Foreign Relations Committee narrowly approved his nomination, as did the full Senate.

When Donald P. Gregg was nominated to be ambassador to South Korea, Sarbanes dwelt not on political connections, but on the Iran-contra affair. Sarbanes grilled Gregg, the former national security adviser to then-Vice President Bush, about his knowledge of the diversion of funds to the contras. But after a heated debate, the Senate approved his nomination 66-33.

On the select committee investigating the Iran-contra affair in 1987, Sarbanes' performance drew mixed reviews in part because expectations for him were high. His cool, legalistic approach seemed perfect to untangle the complex web of evidence. Many recalled his critical role in the 1974 hearings to impeach President Richard M. Nixon; then a member of the House Judiciary Committee, Sarbanes drafted the most important article of impeachment, charging the president with obstruction of justice.

But what was overlooked about Sarbanes' role in the Watergate hearings was that he had taken center stage for a time precisely because of his cautious nature. The case he built against Nixon was tightly constructed and cogently argued, but he was selected for the job in part because he had avoided the spotlight and withheld an opinion until the committee's work was well under way.

During the Iran-contra hearings, Sarbanes was a diligent and detailed questioner, but not a central player. He spent much of his time trying to shed light on a scheme to generate funds for covert activities through a complex transfer of high-technology items and weapons among the United States, Israel and China.

A member of Foreign Relations and chairman of the Banking Subcommittee on International Finance, Sarbanes is an expert on the problem of Third World debt. After Congress rebuffed his amendment to the 1988 omnibus trade bill requiring the U.S. to seek establishment of an international debt-management facility to buy and sell Third World loans at a discount, he helped draft a successful compromise requiring the Treasury to report on the desirability of such a program.

Sarbanes later took satisfaction in the inclusion of loan-discounting in the Treasury Department's 1989 plan for Third World debt. But he also acknowledges Congress' limited role in the issue. "We have to prod the administration," he says. "They have to negotiate this at an international level."

In the 100th and 101st Congress, Sarbanes also served as chairman of the Joint Economic Committee, which in recent years has released two annual economic reports — a majority report featuring a gloomy forecast and a minority report with a rosy view. Sarbanes and the Democrats contended that short-term success "is taking place in the context of long-run trends that ought to be of very deep concern" — the federal deficit and the trade imbalance.

Sarbanes described the 1988 report as aimed neither at Congress nor the White House, but at the public. "This is an effort to forewarn, to say, 'If we don't address this, it's all going to come home to roost on us,'" he said.

Although Sarbanes may never match Maryland's junior Senator, Barbara A. Mikulski, when it comes to bringing home the bacon — she chairs an Appropriations subcommittee — he nonetheless makes an effort to tout his role as leader of the state delegation. In the 101st Congress, he was the chief Senate sponsor of legislation to clean up the Chesapeake Bay. In 1986, he launched the first filibuster of his career over legislation that would have transferred control over two major Washington airports from the federal government to a regional authority. Marylanders saw the bill as an economic threat to their state's major airport. Sarbanes talked for five days, with an uncharacteristic enthusiasm that won concessions aimed at providing some protection for Maryland's interests.

At Home: In winning three terms in the House and three more in the Senate, Sarbanes has yet to break into a serious sweat. His 1988 win with 62 percent of the vote over Republican Alan L. Keyes, a former diplomat, was typical.

The son of Greek immigrant parents, Sarbanes grew up on Maryland's Eastern Shore, attended Princeton, won a Rhodes scholarship and graduated from Harvard Law School magna cum laude. He settled into Baltimore's legal community, but soon began to consider a bid for the state Legislature. In 1966 he won a seat in the House of Delegates.

During his four-year tenure there, Sarbanes developed the quiet, meticulous approach to problem-solving that has marked his Washington career. He left the Legislature in 1970 to challenge veteran Democratic Rep. George H. Fallon, the chairman of the House Public Works Committee. Running as an anti-war, anti-machine insurgent, Sarbanes defeated the aging Fallon for the Democratic nomination in Baltimore's multi-ethnic 4th District. With Democrats enjoying nearly a 4-to-1 registration advantage in the 4th, he had no general-election trouble.

Two years later, redistricting threw him together with another old-time Democrat, Rep. Edward Garmatz, but Garmatz retired.

By 1976 Sarbanes was ready to move to the Senate, and one-term Republican J. Glenn Beall Jr. was ready to be taken. Sarbanes first had to dispose of former Sen. Joseph D. Tydings, trying for a comeback in the Democratic primary. He did that easily, deflecting Tydings' charges that he was too liberal. In the fall, Beall called him an inactive legislator, and Sarbanes responded with television spots playing up his Judiciary Committee role during Watergate. Sarbanes beat Beall by nearly a quarter-million votes.

There were early signs that his 1982 reelection campaign might be more difficult. After the Republican success in the 1980 elections, Sarbanes' name was at the top of GOP target lists. The National Conservative Political Action Committee (NCPAC) launched a half-million-dollar advertising attack in 1981.

But by early 1982, Sarbanes' opponents had lost their confidence. Many felt the NCPAC campaign had backfired: The Democrat had stepped up his schedule of personal appearances, lashed out at NCPAC as "an alien force" and raised money aggressively.

Meanwhile, the GOP was having trouble finding a prominent candidate willing to challenge the incumbent. After state party leaders failed in their attempts to enlist several big names, the nomination went to Prince George's County Executive Lawrence J. Hogan — whose criticism when he served in the U.S. House of President Nixon had chilled his relationship with many Maryland Republicans.

Hogan called Sarbanes "the phantom," a do-nothing senator whose complaints about the Reagan administration's economic program were not backed up by alternative proposals. But Sarbanes was unfazed. Sweeping all but three counties, he won 64 percent of the vote.

Approaching 1988, state Republicans again talked a good game, describing Sarbanes' liberal politics as out of step in a state that had voted for Ronald Reagan in 1984. The GOP eventually fielded an aggressive candidate in Keyes, who drew additional attention as one of two black Senate contenders in 1988. But Sarbanes still won easily.

Keyes was hindered by a very late start. Not only was he not the first Republican choice for the seat, he was not even in the running when the GOP first picked a nominee. The party's March Senate primary had featured nine little-known contenders. Wealthy businessman Thomas L. Blair spent freely and easily won nomination. But he withdrew in May, citing business obligations.

At a state party convention to replace Blair on the ballot, conservatives lobbied for Keyes, a former State Department official who had served as a top assistant to U.N. Representative Jeane J. Kirkpatrick. Though Keyes had not previously been active in the state party, he gained the nomination.

Keyes, one of a still-small group of black conservative leaders, gained some national media attention at the Republican National Convention and also in the fall. In a basically liberal-voting state with a large urban black population, he denounced "welfare-state" policies that he said promoted dependency, and he opposed anti-apartheid sanctions against South Africa.

But Keyes also exhibited an independent streak that alienated some Republicans. He rejected a draft of a convention speech, suggested by the Bush campaign, as tokenistic, and called on the state GOP chairman to resign after the mailing of a party fundraising letter linking Democratic presidential nominee Michael S. Dukakis with furloughed rapist Willie Horton.

Meanwhile, Sarbanes raised a large treasury and kept a big lead in the polls. With the incumbent campaigning confidently — he spent nearly as much time plugging for Dukakis as for himself — Keyes could not reverse the impression that the outcome was predetermined. Though his 38 percent was not bad considering his low name recognition, Keyes lagged far behind Bush, who carried the state.

Committees

Banking, Housing & Urban Affairs (3rd of 12 Democrats)
International Finance & Monetary Policy (chairman); Housing & Urban Affairs

Foreign Relations (3rd of 10 Democrats)
International Economic Policy, Trade, Oceans & Environment (chairman); European Affairs; Near Eastern & South Asian Affairs

Joint Economic (Chairman)

Elections

1988 General

Paul S. Sarbanes (D)	999,166	(62%)
Alan L. Keyes (R)	617,537	(38%)

1988 Primary

Paul S. Sarbanes (D)	309,919	(86%)
B. Emerson Sweatt (D)	25,932	(7%)
A. Robert Kaufman (D)	25,450	(7%)

Previous Winning Percentages: **1982** (64%) **1976** (57%) **1974 *** (84%) **1972 *** (70%) **1970 *** (70%)

** House elections.*

Campaign Finance

	Receipts	Receipts from PACs		Expend-itures
1988				
Sarbanes (D)	$1,477,516	$604,799	(41%)	$1,466,477
Keyes (R)	$684,383	$63,352	(9%)	$662,651

Key Votes

1991

Authorize use of force against Iraq	N

1990

Oppose prohibition of certain semiautomatic weapons	N
Support constitutional amendment on flag desecration	N
Oppose requiring parental notice for minors' abortions	Y
Halt production of B-2 stealth bomber at 13 planes	Y
Approve budget that cut spending and raised revenues	Y
Pass civil rights bill over Bush veto	Y

1989

Oppose reduction of SDI funding	N
Oppose barring federal funds for "obscene" art	Y
Allow vote on capital gains tax cut	N

Voting Studies

	Presidential Support		Party Unity		Conservative Coalition	
Year	**S**	**O**	**S**	**O**	**S**	**O**
1990	31	69	93	7	11	89
1989	45	53	95	4	11	87
1988	40	59	96	4	8	92
1987	31	67	95	4	6	94
1986	18	81	96	3	3	95
1985	22	74	90	5	8	87
1984	30	64	94	2	0	98
1983	41	58	88	9	11	84
1982	25	65	91	3	2	78
1981	38	61	93	6	7	93

Interest Group Ratings

Year	ADA	ACU	AFL-CIO	CCUS
1990	83	4	67	8
1989	85	7	100	25
1988	90	4	100	29
1987	100	0	90	28
1986	100	0	100	16
1985	100	0	100	25
1984	100	0	100	21
1983	95	0	100	16
1982	85	28	92	15
1981	95	0	95	11

Barbara A. Mikulski (D)

Of Baltimore — Elected 1986

Born: July 20, 1936, Baltimore, Md.
Education: Mount Saint Agnes College, B.A. 1958; U. of Maryland, M.S.W. 1965.
Occupation: Social worker.
Family: Single.
Religion: Roman Catholic.
Political Career: Baltimore City Council, 1971-77; U.S. House, 1977-87; Democratic nominee for U.S. Senate, 1974.
Capitol Office: 320 Hart Bldg. 20510; 224-4654.

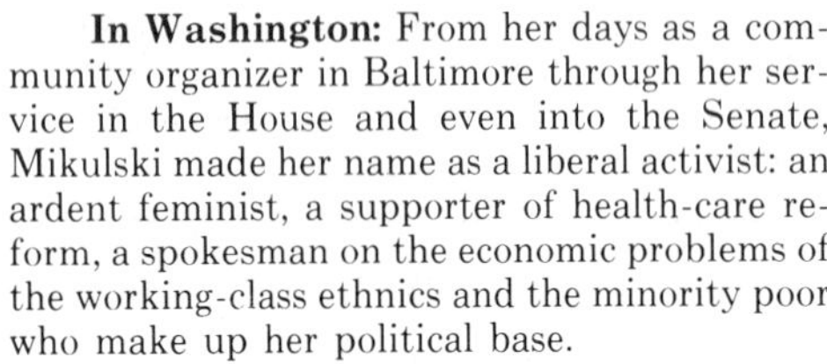

In Washington: From her days as a community organizer in Baltimore through her service in the House and even into the Senate, Mikulski made her name as a liberal activist: an ardent feminist, a supporter of health-care reform, a spokesman on the economic problems of the working-class ethnics and the minority poor who make up her political base.

But since gaining the chairmanship of a Senate Appropriations subcommittee at the start of the 101st Congress, Mikulski has proved that she can take a stand and also make a deal.

Even more than on most Appropriations panels, crafting compromise is a vital skill on Mikulski's Veterans' Affairs, Housing and Urban Development and Independent Agencies subcommittee. As the wordy title suggests, the panel sets spending levels for an amalgam of federal programs in such unrelated areas as housing, veterans' benefits, environmental protection and space exploration.

Mikulski, who calls herself "an idealist and a pragmatist," established early on her strategy for balancing the competing constituencies within her jurisdiction: She would try to get them to work together in efforts to obtain a bigger pot of money for the subcommittee as a whole.

"Let's make sure we have an alliance for the veterans, who fought to save our planet, the homeless, who have a right to live on it with dignity, the environmentalists, who take care of it, and you, who explore it," Mikulski said in a 1989 speech to the American Institute of Aeronautics and Astronautics.

But the 101st Congress was not the most fortuitous one in which to become an Appropriations subcommittee chairman. The crisis atmosphere surrounding the huge federal budget deficit was roiling, and Mikulski found herself arguing that her subcommittee's programs were being shortchanged.

"I thought I'd have the federal checkbook," she said in September 1989. "They gave me the federal change purse."

Mikulski's dilemma has deepened in the 102nd Congress, thanks to the deficit-cutting legislation passed in late 1990. It assures that supporters of her subcommittee's programs will be fighting over a smaller pie, and this predicament will test her fortitude as a chairman.

But mettle is something that Mikulski has never lacked. She is as tough and street-hardened a fighter as there is in the mannerly Senate. Mikulski may not be the most popular legislator: She can be abrupt and dismissive, particularly toward those whose opinions she does not share. But her fighting spirit has enabled her to maintain the loyalty of the blue-collar ethnics whom she champions, at a time when most of them spurn other Democrats with views as liberal as Mikulski's.

Mikulski stands toe-to-toe with administration officials, including Housing and Urban Development Secretary Jack F. Kemp. During the 101st Congress, Kemp argued for an end to the congressional practice of "earmarking" housing funds for specific projects. But Mikulski, who opposed eliminating earmarks, used one of Kemp's pet projects to send a message.

In September 1990, Mikulski and her House Appropriations subcommittee counterpart, Bob Traxler of Michigan, moved to block a $9 million subsidy for Washington, D.C.'s Kenilworth-Parkside project, a model of Kemp's program to allow low-income residents of public housing to buy their homes. Under pressure from Kemp, who was to appear at a ribbon-cutting ceremony for the project, Mikulski relented: Her Senate subcommittee approved $18.9 million for Kenilworth-Parkside. But the appropriation was placed in a new account that revived the Senate earmarks Kemp aimed to kill.

While the low-income housing programs within her purview appeal most to Mikulski's idealistic side, she is not an uninterested observer of the subcommittee's other activities. Its jurisdiction over the Environmental Protection

Agency enables Mikulski to oversee programs to clean up the Chesapeake Bay. Veterans' programs have particular appeal among Mikulski's original blue-collar base.

Mikulski is also not among those liberals who favor gutting space programs to pay for other domestic needs. In part, her interest is parochial. The National Aeronautics and Space Administration's Goddard Space Flight Center in Greenbelt, Md., is a major employer. Mikulski has come out strongly in favor of the proposed space station and the so-called Mission to Planet Earth, which would deploy a series of satellites to study the Earth's environment.

Mikulski is hardly an uncritical NASA advocate, though. When it was revealed in June 1990 that the Hubble Space Telescope had been deployed with a faulty lens, Mikulski fumed. "They have had 10 years to put this together," she said. "They spent $2.8 billion to be able to get it right, and now we find out that the Hubble telescope has a cataract."

The range of subjects Mikulski has pursued as a chairman has not chilled the activist instincts of this former social worker. She was a leading supporter of the child-care assistance bill passed by Congress but vetoed by President Reagan in 1988. As a member of the Labor and Human Resources Committee in 1989, she played a key role in negotiating a compromise bill that President Bush signed into law.

Mikulski is also a staunch supporter of abortion rights. She was one of nine senators who voted in September 1990 against the Supreme Court confirmation of David H. Souter, who had declined to state his views on abortion.

One of Mikulski's biggest disputes with the Bush administration was on an abortion-related issue. Mikulski tried to get around a ban, in effect since 1985, on U.S. contributions to the U.N. population fund; anti-abortion activists accused the U.N. agency of supporting China's "one child per couple" policies, which they claimed included forced abortions.

In 1989, Mikulski won passage of an amendment to a foreign aid spending bill providing $15 million for the population fund, while barring use of any of the money for programs in China. However, Bush vetoed the bill, singling out the "Mikulski amendment" as the reason; the amendment was then dropped.

Mikulski's interest in women's issues extends to the area of health care. In 1990, she proposed successful legislation that created a women's health research office within the National Institutes of Health.

While advocating another health-care program in March 1987, Mikulski showed a personal side. A supporter of long-term health-care legislation, she testified for a proposal to mitigate rules that required individuals to exhaust virtually all their assets before receiving Medicaid assistance for expensive nursing home care, and tapped her family's experience for illustration: Her father, the longtime owner of a Baltimore grocery, was then confined to a nursing home with Alzheimer's disease (from which he died in 1988).

"We were able to grapple with that because of the resources within my own family," Mikulski said. "But not every family has a daughter who is a United States senator who can help when this crisis occurs."

At Home: When veteran GOP Sen. Charles McC. Mathias Jr. decided to retire in 1986, Mikulski jumped into the fray to succeed him. Many questioned whether the pudgy, 4-foot-11 Mikulski would strike voters as "senatorial"; the appeal of her urban image to suburbanites also was suspect. But Mikulski proved that the political skills that elected her in Baltimore transferred to the statewide level.

Mikulski's vibrant campaign style gave her a big edge in the primary against two prominent Democrats, 8th District Rep. Michael D. Barnes and outgoing Gov. Harry R. Hughes. Barnes was expected to earn some liberal backing with his strong opposition to Reagan's Central America policies, but his colorless campaign was unable to attract much support outside his Montgomery County turf. The taciturn Hughes, undercut by a state savings and loan crisis, was almost invisible. Mikulski outpolled Barnes by 100,000 votes; Hughes was a distant third.

Mikulski then had to overcome a negative campaign by Republican Linda Chavez. A longtime Democrat, Chavez had lived only briefly in Maryland. But she had gained a conservative following during her tenure as staff director of the U.S. Commission on Civil Rights, where she angered some minority activists with her stands against affirmative action and busing.

Chavez was never more than a long shot against Mikulski. But the Republican did not go quietly, describing Mikulski as a "San Francisco-style" liberal. The Democrat's supporters accused Chavez of raising that city's image as a haven for homosexuals as part of a campaign of innuendo against Mikulski, who is single.

But Mikulski managed to keep her own legendary temper in check, resisting the bait to engage in battle with an opponent who was no electoral threat. Winning 83 percent of the vote in her home city of Baltimore, and carrying better than 60 percent in Baltimore County and the Washington, D.C., suburbs of Montgomery and Prince George's counties, Mikulski coasted to victory.

During the presidential campaign of 1988, Mikulski found herself a symbol for both the Democratic and Republican parties. In his nomination acceptance speech, Democrat Michael S. Dukakis mentioned Mikulski and several other ethnic- and minority-group Democrats as examples of his party's diversity. But right-wing religious broadcaster Pat Robertson, in a speech to the Republican convention, portrayed Mikulski as a symbol of big-spending social liberalism and regulatory intrusion. He said Democrats want America to be "one big family," with "Jim Wright as the daddy, Barbara Mikulski as the momma and Teddy Kennedy as Big Brother."

Mikulski has been brushing aside liberal-bashing remarks like those throughout her political career. Having made a name for herself as a civic activist and a Baltimore City Council member, she had no trouble winning a 1976 Democratic House primary to succeed Democrat Paul S. Sarbanes, then running in his first Senate election. In five House general elections, she faced no serious Republican opposition.

Mikulski is the granddaughter of Polish immigrants, and her interest in her ethnic roots first gained her a political following. In 1970, Mikulski, then a social worker, wrote a *New York Times* opinion piece about the "forgotten" ethnic American, whose interests were neglected by urban planners. Mikulski accused government officials of polarizing black and ethnic communities when they should be co-operating on a working-class agenda.

At the time, Mikulski was a community organizer fighting against a highway that would have leveled several Baltimore neighborhoods. Her campaign preserved the communities and saved a tract that later became Harborplace, the hub of Baltimore's downtown revival.

Mikulski's activism propelled her into the City Council in 1971. She also established herself in the feminist movement. She was appointed by Democratic National Committee Chairman Jean Westwood in 1972 to serve on a commission to review the party's delegate-selection rules, and later became commission chairman.

When no prominent Maryland Democrat stepped forward to challenge Mathias in 1974, Mikulski filled the vacuum. She had little money, and Mathias pre-empted much of her natural base by winning the support of the state AFL-CIO. Still, the energetic Mikulski drew a respectable 43 percent of the vote, carrying Baltimore city and Baltimore County.

Committees

Appropriations (12th of 16 Democrats)
VA, HUD and Independent Agencies (chairman); Foreign Operations; Legislative Branch; Transportation; Treasury, Postal Service & General Government

Labor & Human Resources (8th of 10 Democrats)
Children, Families, Drugs & Alcoholism; Education, Arts & Humanities; Employment & Productivity; Labor

Small Business (8th of 10 Democrats)
Export Expansion (chairman); Urban & Minority-Owned Business Development

Elections

1986 General		
Barbara A. Mikulski (D)	675,225	(61%)
Linda Chavez (R)	437,411	(39%)
1986 Primary		
Barbara A. Mikulski (D)	307,876	(50%)
Michael D. Barnes (D)	195,086	(31%)
Harry Hughes (D)	88,908	(14%)
Debra Hanania Freeman (D)	9,350	(2%)
Edward M. Olszewski (D)	7,877	(1%)
A. Robert Kaufmann (D)	6,505	(1%)
Others (D)	6,322	(1%)

Previous Winning Percentages: **1984 *** (68%) **1982 *** (74%) **1980 *** (76%) **1978 *** (100%) **1976 *** (75%)

* *House elections.*

Campaign Finance

	Receipts	Receipts from PACs		Expend-itures
1986				
Mikulski (D)	$2,160,812	$660,260	(31%)	$2,057,216
Chavez (R)	$1,716,192	$285,253	(17%)	$1,699,175

Key Votes

1991	
Authorize use of force against Iraq	N
1990	
Oppose prohibition of certain semiautomatic weapons	N
Support constitutional amendment on flag desecration	N
Oppose requiring parental notice for minors' abortions	Y
Halt production of B-2 stealth bomber at 13 planes	Y
Approve budget that cut spending and raised revenues	Y
Pass civil rights bill over Bush veto	Y
1989	
Oppose reduction of SDI funding	N
Oppose barring federal funds for "obscene" art	Y
Allow vote on capital gains tax cut	N

Voting Studies

	Presidential Support		Party Unity		Conservative Coalition	
Year	**S**	**O**	**S**	**O**	**S**	**O**
1990	26	73	89	6	16	81
1989	41	56	94	5	11	89
1988	40	58	93	3	5	92
1987	28	64	93	4	13	84
House Service						
1986	11	80	75	4	10	64
1985	18	83	89	4	18	82
1984	24	65	84	6	12	75
1983	15	84	90	6	18	76
1982	31	68	90	7	18	79
1981	32	68	84	9	11	87

Interest Group Ratings

Year	ADA	ACU	AFL-CIO	CCUS
1990	94	5	75	10
1989	90	8	100	38
1988	95	0	100	29
1987	100	4	100	28
House Service				
1986	90	5	93	20
1985	80	10	100	32
1984	85	0	83	21
1983	90	9	94	11
1982	90	23	100	19
1981	100	7	87	16

1 Wayne T. Gilchrest (R)

Of Kennedyville — Elected 1990

Born: April 15, 1946, Rahway, N.J.
Education: Wesley College (Del.), A.A. 1971; Delaware State U., B.A. 1973.
Military Service: Marine Corps, 1964-68.
Occupation: High school teacher.
Family: Wife, Barbara Rawley; three children.
Religion: Methodist.
Political Career: Republican nominee for U.S. House, 1988.
Capitol Office: 502 Cannon Bldg. 20515; 225-5311.

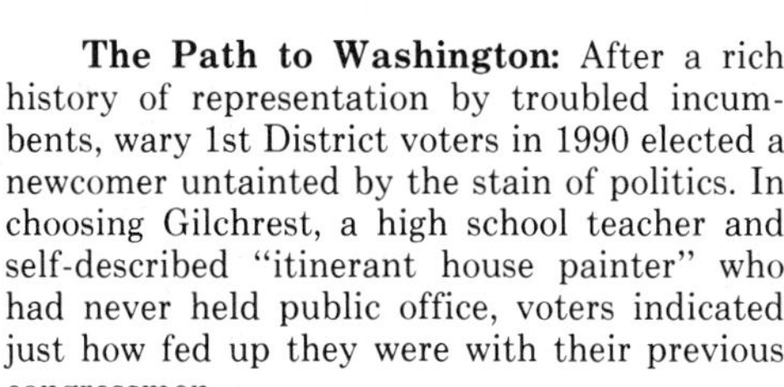

The Path to Washington: After a rich history of representation by troubled incumbents, wary 1st District voters in 1990 elected a newcomer untainted by the stain of politics. In choosing Gilchrest, a high school teacher and self-described "itinerant house painter" who had never held public office, voters indicated just how fed up they were with their previous congressmen.

Beginning with his first run for Congress in 1988, Gilchrest has enjoyed positive publicity, having been portrayed as the sincere and idealistic "Mr. Smith Goes to Washington" character of movie lore. The Eastern Shore media likened Gilchrest to Jimmy Stewart's character, Sen. Jefferson Smith, for his unpolished ways, unassuming style and supposedly naive approach to government.

More likely to engage in a discourse on philosophy than to give a partisan speech, Gilchrest truly has taken the road less traveled to office. Among other occupations, he has labored as a barn builder, forest ranger and chicken slaughterhouse employee. Voters identified with his common-man background, and found appealing the contrast to Democratic Rep. Roy Dyson and his scandal-plagued predecessors.

Gilchrest would have had to be naive to expect to win the 1st in his first try, in 1988. After spending about $300 to win a low-turnout primary, he faced Dyson, the scion of a politically prominent southern Maryland family. Dyson was sitting on a huge treasury and had won re-election with 67 percent of the vote in 1986.

Running a shoestring campaign, Gilchrest was given virtually no shot of beating Dyson. But shortly after the primary, the incumbent was hit by a wave of negative publicity about his connections to contractors involved in the Pentagon procurement scandal, and about the suicide of his top House aide, whose personnel management practices were under scrutiny.

As Dyson's popularity began to plummet, local GOP officials tried to persuade Gilchrest to bow out in favor of a better-known challenger. But Gilchrest refused, and he came within 1,540 votes of an upset, though outspent nearly 6-to-1.

The 1988 effort took a heavy financial toll on Gilchrest. The time spent campaigning drained his family's savings, and Gilchrest was forced to claim state unemployment benefits. He also worked at a sawmill until returning to teaching.

Gilchrest decided to make another run in 1990, joining seven others vying to take on the wounded incumbent. Although he was the most liberal of the eight Republicans, he won easily, mainly on the strength of name recognition from his 1988 run.

Dyson was well-prepared for the rematch. He paid close attention to the district after his close call in 1988, and accumulated a formidable campaign account. He ran well against a strong primary challenger, despite revelations in the final weeks of the race that the hawkish Dyson had been a conscientious objector during the Vietnam War.

In the rematch, Gilchrest's determination to arrive in Washington with no strings attached led him to eschew much of the money and resources available from the National Republican Congressional Committee and other party sources.

His relatively meager fundraising and reluctance to use negative ads led some party officials to wonder if Gilchrest was tough enough to overtake Dyson.

But just as many were beginning to question Gilchrest's moxie, his campaign went on the offensive. Discarding his "Mr. Smith" cloak, Gilchrest, a decorated veteran, ran ads focusing on his Vietnam War record, and clashed with Dyson in televised debates. Buoyed by a last-minute cash infusion, he saturated the airwaves with ads, including one that questioned Dyson's veracity.

Maryland 1

Eastern Shore; Southern Maryland

The remote fishing villages and farm towns of the Chesapeake Bay region long took pride in their semi-isolation. Some of the watermen living on the small islands of the Bay speak with the Elizabethan twang of their ancestors who landed here over three centuries ago. However, modern suburbs from the Washington, D.C., and Baltimore areas have spread to the 1st, along with vacation home subdivisions near the Bay and the Atlantic Ocean.

Pollution caused by rapid growth in the Philadelphia-Washington megalopolis threatens the Bay's aquatic life and has heightened environmental awareness. Yet while these problems have led district voters to demand environmental consciousness of their officials, their overall tone remains conservative. This is true throughout the 1st, even though it is a discontiguous mass running from the northeastern edge of the state down through the entire Eastern Shore, then west across the Bay to three Southern Maryland counties.

The district, especially the rural Eastern Shore, long held Southern Democratic sympathies. But a swelling of GOP registration during the 1980s has given the 1st a more Republican tone, as became clear in 1990 when Wayne T. Gilchrest captured the 1st for the GOP. Two years earlier, George Bush had taken 63 percent of the district's presidential vote, winning every county.

The once-isolated Eastern Shore has experienced substantial growth in the three decades since the Chesapeake Bay Bridge linked it conveniently to the rest of Maryland. But despite the high-rise growth in the vacation capital of Ocean City, the region on the whole remains farm country; Frank Perdue's chicken business is headquartered here. The Eastern Shore is home to more than half the district vote.

The Choptank River serves as a dividing line for the mainly Protestant Eastern Shore. The upper shore, which includes the cities of Easton, Aberdeen and Elkton, takes in a portion of Harford County, which is being absorbed into Baltimore's orbit. The district's strongest GOP county, Talbot, has seen its population expand with an influx of yuppies, some of them fleeing Washington, D.C.

The Democratic strongholds of Worcester and Somerset counties are found on the lower shore, which consists of the four counties south of the Choptank. The small cities of the lower shore, including Salisbury and Cambridge, contain much of the district's black population.

Southern Maryland, on the western side of the Bay, has long had the same rural ambience as the Eastern Shore, but that is fading in the face of urban sprawl and the declining use of its mainstay product, tobacco. Shopping centers and subdivisions have sprung up in Charles County, fast becoming an outer suburb of Washington. St. Mary's County has retained much of its rural, Catholic influence despite the encroachment of development. Along with Harford's Aberdeen Proving Ground, southern Maryland provides the district with a strong military presence. The Patuxent Naval Air Center and the Indian Head Naval Ordnance Station are both located there.

Population: 526,206. White 422,847 (80%), Black 97,779 (19%), Other 3,911 (1%). Spanish origin 5,170 (1%). 18 and over 369,721 (70%), 65 and over 54,049 (10%). Median age: 30.

Committees

Merchant Marine & Fisheries (15th of 17 Republicans)
Coast Guard & Navigation; Fisheries & Wildlife Conservation & the Environment

Science, Space & Technology (19th of 19 Republicans)
Science; Technology & Competitiveness

Select Aging (23rd of 27 Republicans)
Health & Long-Term Care; Housing & Consumer Interests

Select Hunger (11th of 12 Republicans)
Domestic

Campaign Finance

	Receipts	Receipts from PACs		Expend-itures
1990				
Gilchrest (R)	$266,930	$60,074	(23%)	$264,932
Dyson (D)	$759,213	$497,700	(66%)	$771,809

Key Vote

1991

Authorize use of force against Iraq	Y

Elections

1990 General		
Wayne T. Gilchrest (R)	88,920	(57%)
Roy Dyson (D)	67,518	(43%)
1990 Primary		
Wayne T. Gilchrest (R)	9,095	(29%)
Barry J. Sullivan (R)	4,330	(14%)
Mark R. Frazer (R)	3,996	(13%)
Richard F. Colburn (R)	3,894	(12%)
Raymond J. Briscuso (R)	3,700	(12%)
Luis A. Luna (R)	3,623	(11%)
Perry Weed (R)	2,114	(7%)
Charles G. Grace (R)	1,104	(3%)

District Vote For President

	1988		1984		1980		1976	
D	75,575	(36%)	64,381	(35%)	75,300	(42%)	76,207	(49%)
R	131,161	(63%)	121,294	(65%)	94,343	(52%)	78,180	(51%)
I					9,912	(6%)		

2 Helen Delich Bentley (R)

Of Lutherville — Elected 1984

Born: Nov. 28, 1923, Ruth, Nev.

Education: Attended U. of Nevada, 1941-42; George Washington U.,1943; U. of Missouri, B.A. 1944.

Occupation: International trade consultant; journalist.

Family: Husband, William Roy Bentley.

Religion: Greek Orthodox.

Political Career: Republican nominee for U.S. House, 1980, 1982.

Capitol Office: 1610 Longworth Bldg. 20515; 225-3061.

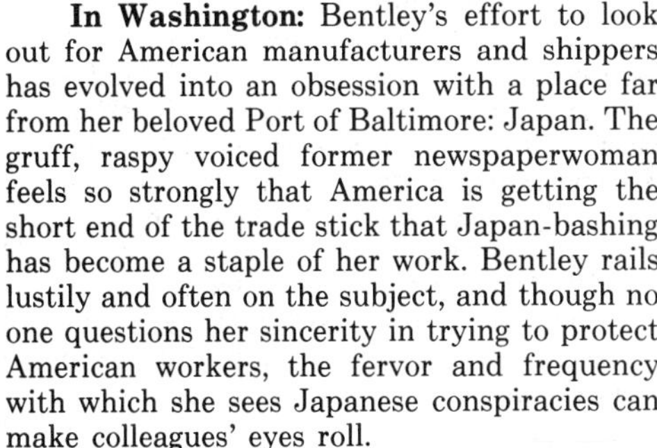

In Washington: Bentley's effort to look out for American manufacturers and shippers has evolved into an obsession with a place far from her beloved Port of Baltimore: Japan. The gruff, raspy voiced former newspaperwoman feels so strongly that America is getting the short end of the trade stick that Japan-bashing has become a staple of her work. Bentley rails lustily and often on the subject, and though no one questions her sincerity in trying to protect American workers, the fervor and frequency with which she sees Japanese conspiracies can make colleagues' eyes roll.

A constant critic of Japanese influence over the U.S. economy, she loudly criticized the 1989 purchase of Columbia Pictures by Sony Corp., having warned that the Japanese were trying to buy into the movie industry. She called for an antitrust investigation into the deal, arguing that it would stifle competition within the industry.

Not one to mince words or thoughts, Bentley wrote late in 1989 that Japanese foreign investment in the United States "is the modern Pearl Harbor." She also took to the House floor on a number of occasions early in the 102nd Congress to lament further Japanese inroads into staples of American culture and life. In March 1991, she criticized the Japanese for their purchase of the Pebble Beach golf course. "Instead of crying fore, golfers can cry bonsai," she complained. "Will we have to plant a flag with the Rising Sun on each green?"

Bentley led unsuccessful efforts in early 1990 to try to keep the luxury cruise ship S.S. *Monterey* under domestic control in case it was needed for troop transit. She also cited foreign trade as a reason for keeping the *Monterey* in the United States, saying the ship was expected to earn at least $100 million. "I'm tired of employing foreigners all the time in foreign countries and helping them out. I want to help out Americans," said Bentley.

In the summer of 1987, Bentley gained attention when she organized a media event on the steps of the Capitol in which she and several Republican members used sledgehammers to destroy a Toshiba radio. It was intended as a symbolic denouncement of the Japanese firm's sale of sensitive technology to the Soviet Union.

Bentley has been an avid supporter of a range of "Buy American" amendments — requiring government purchase of U.S. goods and monitoring the loss of American jobs as the result of foreign imports.

Bentley also received some unusual attention in June 1990 when a process server accused her of assaulting him as he was handing her a subpoena as a potential witness in a murder trial. Although the assault charges were dropped within a month, those who know Bentley well did not think it completely ridiculous that this feisty five-foot-two, 66-year-old woman could have wrangled with the process server, a tall 230-pound, former policeman.

Now in her fourth term, Bentley was elected on a promise to pry loose funds for dredging the Port of Baltimore. She used her seat on Public Works to lobby for inclusion of the project in a water resources bill, and then fought to get the funds into a 1986 supplemental appropriation. As a former chairman of the Federal Maritime Commission, Bentley has valuable contacts in the executive branch and the maritime agency. Even if she does not know a bureaucrat personally, she is not shy about calling to let him know in very clear terms what she wants done for her district.

During heated negotiations between waterfront management and dockworkers at the port in late 1989, Bentley volunteered to serve as mediator. She devoted long hours and risked her reputation, but emerged with the respect of those on both sides in the dispute.

When Bentley has ventured into broader political terrain, her success has been mixed. She caught flak from environmentalists for an apparent flip-flop on oil drilling in Alaska. In 1986, Bentley supported legislation that would have barred oil and gas production in an Alaskan wildlife refuge. The next year she cosponsored a bill to invite bids for such exploration. Bentley defended the switch, saying that she did not recall the original bill including the ban

Maryland 2

Baltimore Suburbs

Baltimore County, which constitutes the bulk of the 2nd, is affluent and Republican as it reaches north, away from the city of Baltimore: In such prosperous towns as Towson, Lutherville and Cockeysville sit the spacious homes of Baltimore's business establishment. To the east of the city (which is not in the district), the 2nd is more blue-collar and traditionally Democratic.

This mix kept Democrats in competition in the 2nd through the early 1980s. In 1980, Ronald Reagan bested President Carter here by only 3 percentage points; Democratic Rep. Clarence D. Long held off two determined challenges by Bentley. However, Bentley's 1984 victory and subsequent success, combined with Reagan's popularity, have made the 2nd more dependably Republican. Reagan scored a 2-to-1 victory in the district in 1984; George Bush took it with 62 percent in 1988.

Residents of northern Baltimore County are careful to point out that their area has nothing to do with the urban Democratic politics of Baltimore city. However, not many today are anxious to hail a figure who was once a local hero: Republican Spiro T. Agnew, who began his political career in Towson and rose to county executive and governor, prior to his ill-fated tenure as vice president.

The southern area of the county inside the Baltimore Beltway is a demographic extension of the city. Dundalk, just east of the city, is heavily Polish. The Bethlehem Steel mill at Sparrows Point has been a fixture there for years, but the industry's hard times have led to decline and layoffs. Bentley's tough-talking image and protectionist trade stance have enabled her to erode the Democratic base there.

The most important change in the district for the 1980s — and the one that helped bring about Long's eventual demise — was the addition of burgeoning western Harford County, northeast of Baltimore. This portion of Harford favors Republicans, especially for president: Bush took 68 percent of its vote.

Western Harford used to be farm land, but people have followed Interstate 95 out of Baltimore and turned the pastures into subdivisions.

Population: 526,354. White 488,860 (93%), Black 28,590 (5%), Other 7,227 (1%). Spanish origin 4,446 (1%). 18 and over 388,788 (74%), 65 and over 46,971 (9%). Median age: 31.

on oil production.

She also faced charges of flip-flopping on abortion votes in the 101st Congress. First, Bentley was one of 26 House members who switched their votes on Medicaid funding of abortions from a more-restrictive stance in 1988 to a less-restrictive stance in 1989. Then, on two abortion-related House votes in October 1989, Bentley was one of just four members in the chamber to vote differently on the two motions. Bentley defended her votes, saying she believed the first was on policy and the second on funding.

At Home: Persistence paid big dividends for Bentley. It took her three tries to convince suburban Baltimore voters that veteran Democrat Clarence D. Long had overstayed his welcome. But within two years of her 1984 victory, Bentley was rising to state and national prominence, beating back a $1 million challenge by Democrat Kathleen Kennedy Townsend, the eldest child of the late Sen. Robert F. Kennedy.

Bentley, who dubbed herself "the fighting lady," lost to Long in 1980 and 1982, but she improved with each campaign. Her theme was that Long had mishandled Baltimore's harbor economy.

Her cause was aided by the recognition that she had expertise on harbor issues. Bentley worked for 25 years as a maritime reporter and editor for The Sun of Baltimore. She also produced a local weekly TV program on the harbor that ran for 15 years. In 1969, Bentley was appointed chairman of the Federal Maritime Commission by President Nixon, becoming the highest-ranking woman in federal government at that time. She was also active in GOP politics.

In her first two campaigns against Long, Bentley contended that his opposition to dredging the Baltimore harbor had cost jobs; she won 43 percent the first time, 47 percent the second. To earn the chance for a third try, she had to weather a 1984 primary challenge from Dave Smick, a former aide to GOP Rep. Jack F. Kemp.

That fall, Bentley did little to alter her previous campaign pitch, even though the 11-term incumbent had backed off his opposition to the harbor-dredging project. Long, meanwhile, ran the most professional campaign of his career. But Bentley was aided by a redistricting change that bolstered the GOP presence in the 2nd and by Reagan's strong showing there. By registering solid margins in GOP strongholds along Baltimore County's central corridor and cutting into Long's strength in such Democratic towns as Dundalk and Essex, Bentley won with 51 percent.

Bentley's first-term emphasis on harbor dredging and trade issues helped secure her base, but they did not earn her respite from a vigorous re-election challenge.

The Democratic candidate was a relative newcomer to the district, but had no name identification problem. Townsend, a 35-year-old attorney, quickly drew media attention, both locally and from national and foreign journalists. Many reports highlighted the "two siblings" angle — Townsend's brother, Joseph P. Kennedy II, was running to succeed retiring House Speaker Thomas P. O'Neill Jr. in Massachusetts.

While Bentley was slowed with a kidney ailment, Townsend campaigned vigorously. Many observers speculated that Townsend's broad smile and cheerleader-like enthusiasm would contrast well with Bentley's gruff persona.

Townsend, who had recently moved to the district from Boston, campaigned under the name of her husband, a district native and a college teacher in Annapolis. But Bentley, who chafed at the publicity the newcomer was receiving, ran hard on the carpetbagger issue. Despite Townsend's upbringing in the Virginia suburbs of Washington, D.C., Bentley referred to her as "the money machine from Massachusetts." Townsend tried to portray herself as a "new ideas" Democrat, but Bentley saw her as an heir to her family's liberal agenda.

Bentley's strongest card was her record of constituent service; she focused heavily on the largess she had brought to the 2nd. Her incumbency also helped her raise more money than the heavily financed Democrat. Bentley won an impressive 59 percent victory.

Bentley had an easy time in the next two elections, taking more than 70 percent.

Committees

Budget (9th of 14 Republicans)
Community Development & Natural Resources (ranking); Defense, Foreign Policy & Space; Human Resources

Merchant Marine & Fisheries (7th of 17 Republicans)

Public Works & Transportation (7th of 21 Republicans)
Economic Development (ranking); Public Buildings & Grounds; Water Resources

Select Aging (8th of 27 Republicans)
Health & Long-Term Care; Rural Elderly

Elections

1990 General		
Helen Delich Bentley (R)	115,398	(74%)
Ronald P. Bowers (D)	39,785	(26%)
1988 General		
Helen Delich Bentley (R)	157,956	(71%)
Joseph Bartenfelder (D)	63,114	(29%)

Previous Winning Percentages: **1986** (59%) **1984** (51%)

District Vote For President

	1988	1984	1980	1976
D	85,451 (37%)	74,102 (34%)	98,946 (44%)	87,259 (46%)
R	141,948 (62%)	145,320 (66%)	107,701 (47%)	102,243 (54%)
I			18,513 (8%)	

Campaign Finance

	Receipts	Receipts from PACs		Expend-itures
1990				
Bentley (R)	$781,008	$214,305	(27%)	$730,852
1988				
Bentley (R)	$850,900	$293,984	(35%)	$782,796
Bartenfelder (D)	$69,042	$17,865	(26%)	$65,023

Key Votes

1991	
Authorize use of force against Iraq	Y
1990	
Support constitutional amendment on flag desecration	Y
Pass family and medical leave bill over Bush veto	N
Reduce SDI funding	N
Allow abortions in overseas military facilities	N
Approve budget summit plan for spending and taxing	N
Approve civil rights bill	N
1989	
Halt production of B-2 stealth bomber at 13 planes	N
Oppose capital gains tax cut	N
Approve federal abortion funding in rape or incest cases	Y
Approve pay raise and revision of ethics rules	N
Pass Democratic minimum wage plan over Bush veto	N

Voting Studies

	Presidential Support		Party Unity		Conservative Coalition	
Year	**S**	**O**	**S**	**O**	**S**	**O**
1990	61	36	76	17	87	11
1989	51	40	74	17	80	5
1988	46	45	74	16	87	11
1987	49	48	68	25	84	16
1986	57	38	60	30	80	14
1985	64	34	74	19	85	13

Interest Group Ratings

Year	ADA	ACU	AFL-CIO	CCUS
1990	11	83	25	77
1989	20	86	50	90
1988	10	86	69	79
1987	32	57	63	73
1986	15	62	67	63
1985	20	76	24	73

3 Benjamin L. Cardin (D)

Of Baltimore — Elected 1986

Born: Oct. 5, 1943, Baltimore, Md.
Education: U. of Pittsburgh, B.A. 1964; U. of Maryland, LL.B. 1967.
Occupation: Lawyer.
Family: Wife, Myrna Edelman; two children.
Religion: Jewish.
Political Career: Md. House, 1967-87, Speaker, 1979-87.
Capitol Office: 117 Cannon Bldg. 20515; 225-4016.

In Washington: The quintessential young man in a hurry, Cardin has come a long way in a short time, exuding impatience with his pace all the while. A state legislator before he had finished law school, a powerful committee chairman at 32 and Speaker of the Maryland House at 35, Cardin arrived in Washington with uncommon momentum. Elevated to a coveted seat on Ways and Means before the end of his third year in Congress, Cardin soon seemed to chafe at his junior status there.

A frustrated Cardin stood outside a closed session of the budget summit in September 1990, protesting on behalf of committee members left out of the deal-making. "Even if we weren't happy with what was going on," he said, "we'd be a lot more comfortable if we knew *what* was going on."

As the 102nd Congress got under way, however, Cardin's energy seemed to be finding channels. He was named to the Committee on Standards of Official Conduct, the panel that passes judgment on colleagues' ethics. Though far from sought after, the assignment generally indicates that a member has won the confidence of the leadership.

Cardin already had a vote of confidence from Ways and Means Chairman Dan Rostenkowski. As an at-large whip in 1988, Cardin was part of the task force apparatus organized under Democratic Whip Tony Coelho that helped pass Rostenkowski's catastrophic health insurance plan (since repealed). Cardin also had a key ally in fellow Marylander Steny H. Hoyer, who moved up to House Democratic Caucus chairman when William H. Gray III took over Coelho's whip post in the leadership shake-up of 1989.

Since arriving on Ways and Means, he has learned that being 22nd among 23 Democrats means waiting a long time to take a crack at administration witnesses or corporate captains summoned before the panel. He has generally joined with the committee's bloc of younger, more liberal members who believe the federal tax structure became unacceptably regressive during the 1980s. He has supported changes in that structure that would roll back Reagan-era tax cuts for the highest income groups and opposed tax cuts (such as the partial exclusion of capital gains income) that would principally benefit the wealthy.

In his first term, the Baltimore Democrat arrived in Congress brimming with confidence that his reputation as a legislative deal-maker and budgetary expert would win him a coveted seat on Budget, if not Ways and Means. Though those committees are usually unreachable for a freshman, Cardin lobbied hard — a bit too hard, perhaps — and in the end, he had to settle for Judiciary and Public Works.

But Cardin did not waste time sulking over missing out on a top committee assignment. He spent considerable time on the floor, listening to the proceedings and talking with members one-on-one. Despite his evident ambitions, he managed to stay on friendly personal terms with most colleagues. When he did rise to speak during the 100th Congress, it was often about the plight of individual Soviet Jewish "refuseniks," an important concern in his district.

Most of all, he dug into the work of his two panels, and carried the water for his party when needed. On Judiciary, he offered an amendment to the 1988 drug bill to strike "user accountability" language. Like many liberals, Cardin maintained that convicted drug users who had gone to jail had paid their debt to society and should not be disqualified from federal benefits, such as education and job training. His amendment was rejected in favor of one requiring drug offenders to complete rehabilitation programs.

Nonetheless, Cardin's understanding of the legislative process and his willingness to help the Democratic leadership was soon noted by senior members, who named him an at-large whip and sped his progress toward Ways and Means.

For all his ambition, Cardin has not been one to forget the home folk. In his few years in Congress thus far he has compiled a creditable record of service — including not just the usual

Maryland 3

Baltimore; Northern and Southern Suburbs

Blue-collar neighborhoods in East Baltimore dominate this district and provide most of its Democratic vote. In Little Italy, Greektown, Canton and Hamilton, the "Bawlamer" accent is strong and the attachment to the baseball Orioles deep.

East Baltimore is the state's industrial core. It includes the city's busy port, which handles everything from delicate electronic parts to coal. But the area's most celebrated aspect is Harborplace, a complex of shops and restaurants that replaced a stretch of decaying warehouses and became the hub of Baltimore's vaunted downtown revitalization.

This project has been accompanied by the renewal of the adjacent Otterbein neighborhood. To the south is the district's largest community of blacks, in the Cherry Hill section.

Unlike his predecessor Barbara A. Mikulski, who was a symbol of ethnic Baltimore, Cardin finds his base in the upscale communities in Baltimore's northwest corner, and the suburbs added in the 1980s' redistricting. Pikesville, northwest of the city, absorbed much of the Jewish population that fled northwest Baltimore as the city's black ghetto expanded.

Southwest of the city, the district takes in most of Catonsville, a middle-class ethnic town. When radicals poured blood on the files of the Catonsville draft board during the Vietnam War, the resulting trial brought national attention to the quiet community.

The district also includes the planned community of Columbia, in Howard County. It was designed in the mid-1960s by James W. Rouse — also the developer of Harborplace — whose idealistic social goals for Columbia attracted liberal-minded people to the town. About one-fifth black, Columbia has subsidized housing scattered about to avoid segregation.

While the 3rd is predominately Democratic, its residents are not totally averse to supporting Republican candidates; the 3rd went narrowly to President Reagan in 1984. Michael S. Dukakis brought it back to the Democrats in 1988, winning 54 percent of the vote.

Population: 527,699. White 433,741 (82%), Black 84,523 (16%), Other 6,957 (1%). Spanish origin 5,674 (1%). 18 and over 399,019 (76%), 65 and over 73,372 (14%). Median age: 33.

constituent errands but chief sponsorship of the Chesapeake Bay Restoration Act and active defense of Maryland's unusual system for reimbursing hospitals under Medicare.

He has also brought home such classic bacon as the preservation of the Coast Guard base at Curtis Bay, the restoration of Fort McHenry in Baltimore and development funds for a light rail system in Baltimore.

At Home: Like most state legislators, Cardin was perceived as having taken a step up when he moved to Congress from the Maryland House. But Cardin gave up considerable power in doing so. He had served as House Speaker in Annapolis for almost a decade, growing accustomed to calling the legislative shots.

Cardin's legislative talents helped him acquire a leadership role in the Maryland House at an extraordinarily young age. He was 23 when first elected to the Legislature and in 1975 he was chairman of the House Ways and Means Committee. Four years later, Cardin became the youngest Speaker in the history of the Maryland House.

Cardin was generally popular among his colleagues in Annapolis. Those who viewed him as tough but fair far outnumbered critics who complained that he planted pliable allies in chairmanships, and rushed favored bills through without debate. On such difficult issues as pension laws and bank deregulation, Cardin adopted a conciliatory and bipartisan approach. Though he opposed extreme tax-limitation measures, Cardin established a Spending Affordability Committee to restrain the growth in state spending.

Cardin initially hoped that his strong legislative record would earn him his party's nomination in 1986 to succeed outgoing Democratic Gov. Harry Hughes. But William Donald Schaefer, the popular Democratic mayor of Baltimore, also decided to run for governor. Cardin recognized that Schaefer would overshadow him, so he opted to seek the 3rd District House seat that Democrat Barbara A. Mikulski was leaving to run for the Senate.

Cardin's reserved demeanor is in sharp contrast to Mikulski's pugnacity. But the strength of his credentials easily offsets the relative mildness of his personality. His House elections have been non-events: He drew no significant primary opposition in 1986, and he twice brushed aside perennial GOP candidate Ross Z. Pierpont.

Committees

Standards of Official Conduct (5th of 7 Democrats)

Ways & Means (22nd of 23 Democrats)
Health; Social Security

Elections

1990 General

Benjamin L. Cardin (D)	82,545	(70%)
Harwood Nichols (R)	35,841	(30%)

1990 Primary

Benjamin L. Cardin (D)	43,496	(83%)
Martin Glaser (D)	8,788	(17%)

1988 General

Benjamin L. Cardin (D)	133,779	(73%)
Ross Z. Pierpont (R)	49,733	(27%)

Previous Winning Percentage: **1986** (79%)

District Vote For President

	1988	1984	1980	1976
D	113,869 (54%)	108,399 (49%)	105,804 (54%)	108,801 (51%)
R	95,071 (45%)	110,231 (50%)	72,565 (37%)	102,500 (49%)
I			15,537 (8%)	

Campaign Finance

	Receipts	Receipts from PACs		Expend-itures
1990				
Cardin (D)	$532,752	$200,790	(38%)	$363,847
Nichols (R)	$4,325	0		$4,234
1988				
Cardin (D)	$405,789	$208,148	(51%)	$354,701
Pierpont (R)	$50,364	0		$48,101

Key Votes

1991

Authorize use of force against Iraq	N

1990

Support constitutional amendment on flag desecration	N
Pass family and medical leave bill over Bush veto	Y
Reduce SDI funding	Y
Allow abortions in overseas military facilities	Y
Approve budget summit plan for spending and taxing	Y
Approve civil rights bill	Y

1989

Halt production of B-2 stealth bomber at 13 planes	Y
Oppose capital gains tax cut	Y
Approve federal abortion funding in rape or incest cases	Y
Approve pay raise and revision of ethics rules	Y
Pass Democratic minimum wage plan over Bush veto	Y

Voting Studies

	Presidential Support		Party Unity		Conservative Coalition	
Year	**S**	**O**	**S**	**O**	**S**	**O**
1990	21	79	95	4	13	87
1989	36	63	94	5	22	76
1988	22	76	93	4	18	79
1987	22	75	90	3	19	81

Interest Group Ratings

Year	ADA	ACU	AFL-CIO	CCUS
1990	83	4	92	14
1989	90	7	100	30
1988	90	4	93	36
1987	88	0	94	13

4 Tom McMillen (D)

Of Crofton — Elected 1986

Born: May 26, 1952, Elmira, N.Y.
Education: U. of Maryland, B.S. 1974; Oxford U., M.A. 1978.
Occupation: Professional basketball player; communications equipment distributor.
Family: Single.
Religion: Roman Catholic.
Political Career: No previous office.
Capitol Office: 420 Cannon Bldg. 20515; 225-8090.

In Washington: McMillen has established for himself a point in the Democratic Party that is not quite conservative but definitely not liberal. That gives him room to maneuver should he ever choose to run for higher office, a course, given his visibility and broad agenda, that is widely assumed to be in his future.

McMillen balances the concerns of his conservative district with solid support for the Democratic leadership on most party-line votes. When the House considered President Bush's plan to cut the capital gains tax, for example, McMillen bucked the leadership and backed the tax cut.

"The Democratic Party should try to find some consensus on this," he said. It's as important "for the woman who sells her hair salon . . . as to a millionaire."

In the 101st Congress, McMillen backed aid to the Nicaraguan contras and amending the Constitution to ban physical desecration of the flag. But he also voted for the 1990 budget-summit agreement, and to raise the minimum wage, fund abortions, require employers to provide family and medical leave, and to give Congress a pay raise and revise its ethics rules.

In early 1990, after steady campaigning, McMillen won a seat on the Energy and Commerce Committee, which should fulfill his quest for visibility and a wide issue agenda. He added an amendment to the Clean Air Act reauthorization requiring the Environmental Protection Agency to investigate the sources of toxic air pollutants in the Chesapeake Bay region.

In the 101st Congress, McMillen and Maryland Democratic Rep. Steny H. Hoyer successfully lobbied to transfer 7,600 acres of surplus land at Fort George G. Meade to the Interior Department for wildlife use. The Army had intended to sell the land for development, but area residents objected.

Along with Democratic Rep. Edolphus Towns of New York and New Jersey Democratic Sen. Bill Bradley, McMillen cosponsored legislation to require colleges and universities to report annually the graduation rates of athletes attending school on athletic scholarships. Bush signed it into law in 1990.

Elected president of his party's freshman class, McMillen created Class PAC, which gave campaign funds to freshman Democrats. He also campaigned for some of his freshman colleagues in 1988, capitalizing on his celebrity as a former pro basketball player to draw crowds.

At Home: McMillen proved how quickly incumbency can dispel insecurity. In 1986, rookie McMillen won by just 428 votes against a GOP state legislator. In 1988, McMillen coasted to re-election over an unknown.

The 6-foot-11 McMillen starred in basketball at the University of Maryland — where he earned a Rhodes scholarship — then played 11 years in the National Basketball Association. Though he spent most of his career with Atlanta, he was traded in 1983 to the Washington Bullets, who play in Landover, Md. After the trade, McMillen ran a communications equipment company, engaged in civic work and prepared to run in the 4th.

McMillen left sports for politics when seven-term GOP Rep. Marjorie S. Holt announced in 1986 she would retire. Holt's success had shown that the 4th, with its many defense-related employers, leaned right despite a Democratic registration edge. So McMillen billed himself as a moderate, bringing in such prominent Southerners as Georgia Sen. Sam Nunn and former Virginia Gov. Charles S. Robb to campaign for him. He also spent over $650,000 to boost his already high name recognition.

McMillen gained a big lead in polls over Republican Robert Neall, who had little exposure as leader of the small GOP contingent in the state House. But Neall made a late charge. A lifelong district resident and father of four, he said McMillen, a wealthy bachelor, was not in touch with the average voter's concerns.

McMillen had to wait two weeks — after absentee ballots were counted — to declare victory. Neall had no stomach for a rematch, and McMillen won the 1988 race and his succeeding re-election campaign by solid margins.

Maryland 4

Anne Arundel, Southern Prince George's Counties

The 4th begins at the suburbs of Baltimore and ends at the suburbs of Washington, D.C., with Annapolis in the middle. Like most Maryland districts, the 4th has a large Democratic registration advantage. But with its military presence — symbolized by the U.S. Naval Academy in Annapolis — and its defense-related industries, the district also has a conservative bent. Republican Marjorie S. Holt held it for 14 years before McMillen's election; Ronald Reagan and George Bush easily won there in the last two elections.

Anne Arundel County is the core of the district. Annapolis, the county seat and state capital, has an electorate heavy with government workers. It has a black community that dates back three centuries and composes a third of the town.

Just north of Annapolis, suburban Baltimore begins and the Republican vote increases. The GOP is in firm control in Severna Park, where corporate executives live in homes fronting Chesapeake Bay. Closer to Baltimore, the suburbs tend to be less affluent. A band of blue-collar, Democratic-leaning towns occupies the northernmost end of the district.

Back toward Washington, Crofton, a bedroom community founded in the late 1960s, usually tilts Republican, although it is McMillen's home base. Northwest of Crofton is Fort George G. Meade, which faces a phase-out, with the loss of some 500 jobs, under a base realignment plan enacted in 1989.

The suburban-and-exurban Republican vote in Anne Arundel goes a long way toward offsetting the Democratic lean in Annapolis. Bush carried the county with 64 percent of the vote in 1988.

Southern Prince George's County, with a large contingent of federal workers and blacks, is the more liberal part of the 4th. But the military vote near Andrews Air Force Base provides the area with some Republican turf. The district also contains a small chunk of outer-suburban Howard County, which generally goes Republican.

Population: 525,453. White 404,506 (77%), Black 108,571 (21%), Other 9,207 (2%). Spanish origin 7,393 (1%). 18 and over 372,900 (71%), 65 and over 32,775 (6%). Median age: 29.

Committees

Energy & Commerce (23rd of 27 Democrats)
Commerce, Consumer Protection & Competitiveness; Energy & Power; Telecommunications & Finance

Science, Space & Technology (18th of 32 Democrats)
Environment; Space; Technology & Competitiveness

Elections

1990 General		
Tom McMilllen (D)	85,601	(59%)
Robert P. Duckworth (R)	59,846	(41%)
1990 Primary		
Tom McMillen (D)	47,863	(83%)
Jack A. Blum (D)	6,636	(12%)
John W. Dotterweich (D)	2,956	(5%)
1988 General		
Tom McMillen (D)	128,624	(68%)
Bradlyn McClanahan (R)	59,688	(32%)

Previous Winning Percentage: **1986** (50%)

District Vote For President

	1988	1984	1980	1976
D	87,650 (42%)	79,144 (40%)	73,667 (41%)	80,239 (50%)
R	120,027 (57%)	115,669 (59%)	89,510 (50%)	80,601 (50%)
I			12,927 (7%)	

Campaign Finance

	Receipts	Receipts from PACs	Expend-itures
1990			
McMillen (D)	$757,145	$423,275 (56%)	$560,909
Duckworth (R)	$41,205	0	$41,129
1988			
McMillen (D)	$730,652	$392,892 (54%)	$599,881

Key Votes

1991	
Authorize use of force against Iraq	Y
1990	
Support constitutional amendment on flag desecration	Y
Pass family and medical leave bill over Bush veto	Y
Reduce SDI funding	Y
Allow abortions in overseas military facilities	Y
Approve budget summit plan for spending and taxing	Y
Approve civil rights bill	Y
1989	
Halt production of B-2 stealth bomber at 13 planes	N
Oppose capital gains tax cut	N
Approve federal abortion funding in rape or incest cases	Y
Approve pay raise and revision of ethics rules	Y
Pass Democratic minimum wage plan over Bush veto	Y

Voting Studies

	Presidential Support		Party Unity		Conservative Coalition	
Year	**S**	**O**	**S**	**O**	**S**	**O**
1990	27	73	92	8	44	56
1989	45	55	86	14	68	32
1988	27	73	90	10	58	42
1987	32	68	92	8	60	40

Interest Group Ratings

Year	ADA	ACU	AFL-CIO	CCUS
1990	56	17	83	29
1989	60	29	92	40
1988	75	12	100	36
1987	80	4	100	27

5 Steny H. Hoyer (D)

Of Berkshire — Elected 1981

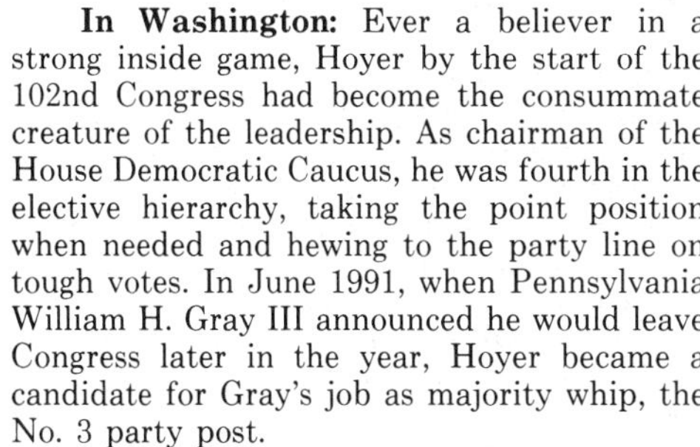

Born: June 14, 1939, New York, N.Y.

Education: U. of Maryland, B.S. 1963; Georgetown U., J.D. 1966.

Occupation: Lawyer.

Family: Wife, Judith Pickett; three children.

Religion: Baptist.

Political Career: Md. Senate, 1967-79, president, 1975-79; sought Democratic nomination for lieutenant governor, 1978.

Capitol Office: 1705 Longworth Bldg. 20515; 225-4131.

In Washington: Ever a believer in a strong inside game, Hoyer by the start of the 102nd Congress had become the consummate creature of the leadership. As chairman of the House Democratic Caucus, he was fourth in the elective hierarchy, taking the point position when needed and hewing to the party line on tough votes. In June 1991, when Pennsylvania William H. Gray III announced he would leave Congress later in the year, Hoyer became a candidate for Gray's job as majority whip, the No. 3 party post.

Hoyer has become the rarest of species: a member whose future in the House seems surer than his survival at home. Hoyer might be Speaker someday, but before looking to such heights he must assure himself a base. And the demographics of his increasingly black district pose a problem with each redistricting cycle.

Hoyer has proved adept at maintaining the loyalty of black voters in the heart of his district: the middle-class Washington suburbs of Prince George's County. He has maneuvered on the Appropriations Committee to ensure funding for subway transit and to pull federal jobs in his district's direction.

But the Supreme Court has directed legislatures to create, wherever practicable, districts where minority voters predominate. The Democratic Legislature in Maryland will in 1991 seek to draw districts accommodating both Hoyer and fellow Democratic Rep. Tom McMillen, who represents the neighboring 4th District. But a lawsuit may follow, and a court may order the black populations of both districts combined. Under that scenario, there might not be room for more than one white Democrat.

Whatever uneasiness that prospect may cause Hoyer, he has kept his focus on the House and on moving up within its structure. As early as the 100th Congress, he was being tapped to direct leadership task forces on AIDS and on welfare reform. He endured a setback at the outset of that Congress when the deputy whip job he had hoped for went instead to David E. Bonior of Michigan. Hoyer reset his clock, waiting for his next chance to move up and busying himself with the Helsinki commission, an international human rights organization (of which he was chairman in the 102nd Congress).

Hoyer got back in the leadership scramble sooner than expected. He became vice chairman of the caucus in the 101st Congress and moved up in June 1989 after Gray succeeded Tony Coelho as majority whip. Coelho, who had resigned facing ethics charges, had also been the prime sponsor of the Americans with Disabilities Act. Hoyer soon became that bill's designated shepherd.

It was an unfamiliar assignment for Hoyer, steeped as he was in the different customs and politics of the Appropriations Committee. But his work on the disabilities bill may have enhanced his reputation as much as his new office. The legislation was submitted to seven subcommittee and full committee markups, and Hoyer was present and pacing like an expectant father at each.

Hoyer now enters the legislative process more often by appointing task forces on issues. These ad hoc groups may discuss ideas or act as last-minute make-up artists, touching up committee products for floor presentation. Task forces were used by preceding caucus chairmen, including Gray and Majority Leader Richard A. Gephardt. But at least some of the traditional committee chairmen have become restive with the concept as practiced by Hoyer. Ways and Means Chairman Dan Rostenkowski referred to it as a contagious disease.

One apparent sign of Hoyer's ever-deepening loyalty to the leadership was his vote in January 1991 favoring sanctions over military force in the Persian Gulf crisis. Hoyer previously had warned his party about its national security posture. Early in 1985, when the House debated the MX missile program, Hoyer urged Democrats to change their soft-on-defense image. He voted for the MX, angering liberals and breaking with party leadership.

Hoyer has never been shy about getting ahead. Defeated in a statewide race at

Maryland 5

Northern Prince George's County

The federal bureaucracy provides a secure, if modest, standard of living for the thousands of white and black residents of "P.G." County. Prince George's County is a few status rungs down from its neighbor, Montgomery County, one of the nation's wealthiest jurisdictions. But Prince George's has a relatively high median income and some comfortable neighborhoods that belie its middle-brow reputation.

This was where Washington's white working class moved after World War II as the city became increasingly black. In the past 15 years there has been a second migration, as middle-class blacks have left D.C. for the suburbs.

The black population of Prince George's County doubled during the 1970s; today, more than a third of the 5th's residents are black. Years of black activism for integration of housing and schools spawned a generation of assertive black politicians who are gaining recognition as powerful members of the reigning Democratic coalition in Prince George's County.

The black vote has remained the solid base for Hoyer's House wins and for Democratic presidential victories; Michael S. Dukakis carried the 5th with 59 percent. Strong black support earlier had enabled the Rev. Jesse Jackson to win the 5th in the 1988 Maryland Democratic primary, as he did in 1984.

However, these gains do not represent an unbroken line of progress for county blacks. While many residents of both races find suburban tranquility in Prince George's County, some lower-income residents have found urban violence following them to the suburbs. An exploding illegal drug trade, centered in the Landover area, sparked a rash of murders beginning in 1988 that coincided with D.C.'s surge of drug-related violence.

There is a core of conservative whites who see black gains as their losses. But this conservative backlash was more evident in an older version of the 5th, which elected a Republican in 1968, 1970 and 1972. By the mid-1970s, the black population was so large that Democratic victory was almost assured.

Despite GOP efforts to appeal to working-class voters in the inner suburbs and to more affluent residents of such eastern Prince George's County towns as Bowie and Laurel, no GOP presidential candidate has received more than 42 percent in the 5th in the 1980s.

The district also includes College Park, site of the University of Maryland's main campus.

Population: 527,469. White 323,052 (61%), Black 183,887 (35%), Other 14,206 (3%). Spanish origin 11,862 (2%). 18 and over 374,737 (71%), 65 and over 29,585 (6%). Median age: 28.

the age of 39, he got back on track when an incumbent's illness vacated a House seat. After just a year in the House, he scratched his way to a seat on Appropriations, succeeding despite the opposition of a senior Maryland colleague already on the panel.

Hoyer's most consistent issue concerns have related to the federal employees who populate his district in the Washington, D.C., suburbs. In the 100th Congress, he bucked the tide on drug testing for federal employees, fighting random testing as unconstitutional. Early in 1989, Hoyer was an outspoken supporter of the 51 percent pay increase for Congress set in motion by a presidential commission; many federal employees expected the raise to ripple through the rank and file.

In the 100th and 101st Congresses, Hoyer was co-chairman of the Federal Government Service Task Force, which seeks to convince other members that more should be spent on federal employee pay and benefits.

But Hoyer has been able to do more for federal workers as a member of Appropriations. His base of operations has been the Subcommittee on Treasury, Postal Service and General Government — a secondary assignment that many members ignore, but for Hoyer a gold mine of constituent service.

When the House and Senate and White House finally agreed on a federal pay package late in 1990, Hoyer brokered the deal. It will give federal workers pay increases calibrated to private-sector increases beginning in 1992. And in 1994, it will provide federal workers in high-cost cities an extra boost.

At Home: From the presidency of his state's Young Democrats to the presidency of the Maryland Senate to his House career, Hoyer has been preoccupied with politics nearly all his adult life. A losing bid for lieutenant governor stalled him in 1978, but after a three-year hiatus, he was back on the road.

Hoyer was barely out of law school when he was first elected to the state Senate in 1966. After two terms he was chosen Senate president with the help of Gov. Marvin Mandel, becoming the youngest person to occupy that post in

Maryland history. Hoyer's rise to power coincided with the growing influence of the Prince George's County Democratic organization, which he helped build and lead.

Hoyer declared as a candidate for governor in 1978, but later opted to campaign as running mate to Acting Gov. Blair Lee III, who failed to win the gubernatorial nomination.

In February 1981, the 5th District House seat held by Democrat Gladys Noon Spellman was declared vacant. Spellman had never regained consciousness after suffering a heart attack the previous October.

The special-election primary to succeed Spellman drew 31 candidates, the largest number in any congressional primary in the nation in 20 years. Hoyer's chief competition came from Spellman's husband, Reuben, who was backed by his wife's loyal supporters. But with the help of most of the coalition of liberals, labor and blacks that had been instrumental in his earlier rise to power, Hoyer emerged on top.

In the general election that May, Hoyer faced the Republican mayor of Bowie, Audrey Scott. The Reagan economic program was the campaign's central issue, and both candidates had help from their national parties, but Hoyer had by far the more united party support locally. Hoyer took 55 percent of the vote.

Since then, he has trounced weak GOP challengers. His bigger political concerns have been within his own party. Leaders of the 5th's large and increasingly assertive black constituency were disturbed in both 1984 and 1988 by Hoyer's reluctance to endorse the Rev. Jesse Jackson, who carried the district in the Democratic presidential primary in both those years.

In 1990, that dissatisfaction led to a primary challenge from Abdul Alim Muhammad, a spokesman for Nation of Islam leader Louis Farrakhan. Muhammad campaigned on black empowerment and the Nation of Islam's record of cleaning up drug-infested neighborhoods. Hoyer took the threat seriously enough to run his first campaign television commercials ever, touting his work on rights for the disabled and subway service from the district to downtown Washington. Hoyer swamped Muhammad, taking almost 80 percent of the primary vote, and coasted to an easy November win.

Committees

Appropriations (24th of 37 Democrats)
District of Columbia; Labor, Health & Human Services, Education & Related Agencies; Treasury, Postal Service & General Government

House Administration (14th of 15 Democrats)
Elections; Libraries & Memorials; Procurement & Printing

Elections

1990 General		
Steny H. Hoyer (D)	84,747	(81%)
Lee F. Breuer (R)	20,314	(19%)
1990 Primary		
Steny H. Hoyer (D)	49,473	(79%)
Abdul Alim Muhammad (D)	13,141	(21%)
1988 General		
Steny H. Hoyer (D)	128,437	(79%)
John Eugene Sellner (R)	34,909	(21%)

Previous Winning Percentages: **1986** (82%) **1984** (72%) **1982** (80%) **1981 *** (55%)

** Special election.*

District Vote For President

	1988	1984	1980	1976
D	107,195 (59%)	108,074 (58%)	78,156 (51%)	88,033 (58%)
R	72,873 (40%)	79,134 (42%)	61,644 (40%)	63,897 (42%)
I			12,215 (8%)	

Campaign Finance

	Receipts	Receipts from PACs	Expend-itures
1990			
Hoyer (D)	$725,418	$417,235 (58%)	$716,469
Breuer (R)	$9,084	0	$8,709
1988			
Hoyer (D)	$490,736	$239,828 (49%)	$416,187

Key Votes

1991	
Authorize use of force against Iraq	N
1990	
Support constitutional amendment on flag desecration	N
Pass family and medical leave bill over Bush veto	Y
Reduce SDI funding	Y
Allow abortions in overseas military facilities	Y
Approve budget summit plan for spending and taxing	Y
Approve civil rights bill	Y
1989	
Halt production of B-2 stealth bomber at 13 planes	N
Oppose capital gains tax cut	Y
Approve federal abortion funding in rape or incest cases	Y
Approve pay raise and revision of ethics rules	Y
Pass Democratic minimum wage plan over Bush veto	Y

Voting Studies

	Presidential Support		Party Unity		Conservative Coalition	
Year	**S**	**O**	**S**	**O**	**S**	**O**
1990	19	79	96	2	22	76
1989	35	63	93	3	29	68
1988	23	77	98	1	18	82
1987	25	75	93	3	28	72
1986	21	79	95	3	26	72
1985	29	71	93	5	29	71
1984	42	57	89	9	32	63
1983	32	67	91	6	29	70
1982	38	57	92	5	25	71
1981	40 †	55 †	86 †	11 †	32 †	67 †

† Not eligible for all recorded votes.

Interest Group Ratings

Year	ADA	ACU	AFL-CIO	CCUS
1990	89	0	100	14
1989	80	0	100	20
1988	95	0	100	21
1987	84	0	100	7
1986	95	5	93	22
1985	75	14	94	32
1984	75	8	92	33
1983	80	9	100	25
1982	75	18	85	32
1981	72	0	92	12

6 Beverly B. Byron (D)

Of Frederick — Elected 1978

Born: July 27, 1932, Baltimore, Md.
Education: Attended Hood College, 1963-64.
Occupation: Civic leader; homemaker.
Family: Husband, Kirk Walsh; three children.
Religion: Episcopalian.
Political Career: No previous office.
Capitol Office: 2430 Rayburn Bldg. 20515; 225-2721.

In Washington: Despite her Democratic label, Byron's conservative leanings place her leagues apart from the party liberals who dominate Maryland politics. With her staunch pro-defense posture on the House Armed Services Committee, Byron also cuts a distinctly different profile from most of the women in the Democratic Caucus.

In fact, there is a role reversal between Byron and her Republican neighbor to the south, 8th District Rep. Constance A. Morella. Despite her GOP affiliation, Morella exhibits the liberal leanings of the Washington, D.C., suburbs. Byron's district reaches down to the affluent Washington suburb of Potomac, but her record clearly reflects the political tenor of the mill towns, mines and mountain communities of rural western Maryland.

When voting on House legislation, Byron has been one of the leading Democratic supporters of President Bush's policies; she held a similar status during the Reagan administrations. Her philosophy is most evident on defense issues; she is a member of the Armed Services Committee's pro-Pentagon "Old Guard." As chairman of the Armed Services Subcommittee on Military Personnel and Compensation, Byron has fought drastic cuts in manpower as part of the post-Cold War downsizing of the U.S. military.

Military issues are close to home for Byron. Her father was an aide to Gen. Dwight D. Eisenhower in World War II; her son is an Air Force captain who served during the 1990-91 conflict with Iraq. When Byron succeeded her late husband, Goodloe Byron, in the 6th District in 1979, she took his Armed Services seat.

Although her subcommittee handles programs that make up about 40 percent of the Defense Department budget, it is regarded as unglamorous compared to the panels that deal with big-ticket weapons systems. Her subcommittee deals with such issues as formulas for retirement benefits and the amounts military retirees can be charged under the Defense Department hospitalization plan. However, the prospects of long-term cutbacks and the personnel-related exigencies of the Persian Gulf War have raised the profile of the Personnel subcommittee and of its chairman.

When the rapid change in U.S.-Soviet relations prompted a reduction in troop strength during the 101st Congress, Byron pushed for assistance to personnel who had been involuntarily separated from the service. In 1990, she joined Armed Services Chairman Les Aspin in developing a defense policy plan that would cut military hardware programs before personnel.

In November 1990, Byron noted that fewer young members of Congress these days have military service in their background. "As we wrestle with budget issues, it's going to be difficult, and we're going to have to educate these new members," she told a meeting of the National Association of Uniformed Services.

However, those worries were allayed, at least temporarily, by the rush to provide benefits to troops who served during the Persian Gulf crisis. Byron, who supported the January 1991 resolution authorizing Bush to use force to end Iraq's occupation of Kuwait, submitted a bill providing added compensation and benefits for troops in the conflict.

Byron also proposed a bill prohibiting separation of enlisted mothers, or fathers with sole custody, from their infant children; it passed the House as part of a veterans' benefits package but was dropped in conference. The measure resulted from numerous stories of reservists who left children behind during the rapid deployment to the Persian Gulf region.

Although hardly a "movement" feminist — she is opposed to abortion, for instance — Byron takes an active interest in the role of women in the military. When she visited U.S. troops in Saudi Arabia in September 1990, Byron made a point of visiting with female soldiers.

The high-profile role played during the Persian Gulf War by women soldiers — some of whom faced dangerous assignments — tempered Byron's longstanding opposition to women in combat. In May 1991, she joined Colorado Democrat Patricia Schroeder on an

Maryland 6

West — Hagerstown; Cumberland

Democrat Byron is so strong in the 6th that district Republicans rarely bother to challenge her. Her strength is due to her conservative leanings and famous last name, not her party line. The western 6th, rivaling the eastern 1st District for the title of Maryland's most rural, has a strong conservative flavor.

Aside from Byron, that conservatism is beneficial to GOP candidates, especially at the national level. George Bush took 65 percent of the district's vote in 1988, just below President Reagan's 69 percent in 1984. Although the 6th has the smallest black population percentage of any Maryland district, black conservative Republican Alan L. Keyes ran well there in his 1988 challenge to Democratic Sen. Paul S. Sarbanes, losing to Sarbanes by fewer than 1,000 votes out of more than 225,000 cast.

The district stretches from the Baltimore and Washington suburbs over rolling farm land to the Appalachian Mountains. Though it takes in the wealthy Montgomery County suburb of Potomac and some of the county's more rural areas, the 6th rarely gets much play in the Washington media.

District affairs provoke much more interest in Frederick, an 18th-century museum piece that arrested its earlier economic decline by crafting a new identity as a restaurant and boutique center, and by courting high-technology industry. Now the district's largest city with over 40,000 people, Frederick grew by more than 30 percent in the 1980s. Many residents commute to work in the high-tech corridor that sprouted along Interstates 70 and 270.

Just east of Frederick, Baltimore's suburban sprawl has moved out into Carroll County, bringing a surge of subdivisions to once sleepy towns. The county also saw its population jump by 28 percent in the 1980s.

While the economies of these areas thrive, job losses at a Fairchild Industries aircraft plant and a Mack Trucks factory in the early 1980s caused some problems in the Hagerstown area in Washington County.

But the problems of industrial decline have been most marked in Allegany County, located in the Appalachian foothills. The population in the manufacturing city of Cumberland fell by 10 percent in the 1980s, as major factories shut their doors and the county suffered double digit unemployment. Rates dropped in the early 1990s, but there is slim hope that many of the high-paying, heavy-industry jobs will return; local optimists are staking their hopes on attracting smaller-scale manufacturers and boosting tourism in the scenic area.

At the far western end lies rural Garrett County, whose fealty to the GOP is rivaled only by Allegany. Garrett, home to Deep Creek Lake and Backbone Mountain, has a year-round tourist economy, hosting skiers in winter and boaters in summer. A common political thread for the district's counties is their bias in presidential voting: Bush swept the five counties totally within the district, all by wide margins. Unsuccessful gubernatorial candidate William Shepard carried four of these five counties in 1990, losing only Allegany.

Population: 528,168. White 502,767 (95%), Black 19,829 (4%), Other 4,138 (1%). Spanish origin 3,983 (1%). 18 and over 376,405 (71%), 65 and over 54,034 (10%). Median age: 31.

amendment, which passed Armed Services, allowing women to volunteer for air-combat duty.

On issues involving defense strategy, Byron has generally supported Republican administrations' positions. She joined with Reagan in the mid-1980s to fight efforts by liberal Democrats to accelerate nuclear test-ban talks between the United States and the Soviet Union.

However, the era of defense cutbacks ushered in by Bush made Byron wary of giving the White House free rein to eliminate programs. In 1989, Aspin asked Armed Services members to pass Bush's first defense authorization plan as an effort to deal with fiscal realities. However, Byron joined with a committee majority in voting for an alternative that restored money to the National Guard and reserves and to such endangered programs as the F-14D fighter and the Osprey helicopter/airplane.

Byron was the first woman to hold an Armed Services subcommittee chairmanship. She struggled to gain the post: In 1985, Aspin held the Personnel chairmanship himself to forestall a fight between Byron and Schroeder, whose liberal politics often put her at cross-purposes with committee conservatives. However, in 1987, Schroeder opted to head another subcommittee, and Byron claimed Personnel.

Byron also is a member of the Interior Committee, which abets her interest in recreational facilities. A physical fitness buff, Byron has lobbied to improve hiking trails in Maryland and to make a federal inventory of hiking trails in the United States. During the 101st Congress, Byron helped obtain $2.3 million to improve the C & O National Historic Park, which runs from Washington, D.C., to West Virginia, and $8 million for another Washington-area trail.

At Home: Family history repeated itself in 1978 when Byron succeeded her late husband in the House. In 1941, Goodloe Byron's father, U.S. Rep. William D. Byron, was killed in an airplane crash. The elder Byron's widow won the election that year to fill out his term.

Goodloe Byron collapsed while jogging along the Chesapeake and Ohio Canal near Washington, and died at age 49. District Democratic leaders instantly offered Beverly Byron the nomination; she accepted it within 24 hours.

Mrs. Byron had met her husband while she was in high school. She got into politics when he first ran for the Maryland House in 1962 because, she said, "It meant I either stayed at home by myself or joined him." She helped organize Byron's campaigns, and shared his interest in exercise and national parks.

Winning the 1978 election posed little problem for her. Republican officials had not offered an opponent against her husband, letting a perennial office-seeker, Melvin Perkins, win the GOP line. A self-described pauper, Perkins spent part of the fall campaign in jail in Baltimore County, where he had been charged with assaulting a woman bus driver.

Two years later, Byron's constituent work and conservative voting record proved effective in defusing serious opposition. She triumphed easily over a lackluster primary field, and in the general election registered a landslide victory.

Byron's conservative views have meant she cannot take the Democratic nomination for granted; in both 1988 and 1990, furniture executive Anthony Patrick Puca won some primary support as a liberal alternative to Byron.

But Byron, who took 64 percent of the 1990 primary vote, has yet to face a serious nomination threat. And in her seven general election campaigns, Byron's conservative tilt has been a consistent formula for easy victories.

Committees

Armed Services (6th of 33 Democrats)
Military Personnel & Compensation (chairman); Research & Development

Interior & Insular Affairs (8th of 29 Democrats)
National Parks & Public Lands; Water, Power & Offshore Energy

Select Aging (7th of 42 Democrats)
Housing & Consumer Interests

Elections

1990 General		
Beverly B. Byron (D)	106,502	(65%)
Christopher P. Fiotes Jr. (R)	56,479	(35%)
1990 Primary		
Beverly B. Byron (D)	31,384	(64%)
Anthony Patrick Puca (D)	17,512	(36%)
1988 General		
Beverly B. Byron (D)	166,753	(75%)
Kenneth W. Halsey (R)	54,528	(25%)

Previous Winning Percentages: **1986** (72%) **1984** (65%) **1982** (74%) **1980** (70%) **1978** (90%)

District Vote For President

	1988	1984	1980	1976
D	82,781 (34%)	66,062 (31%)	64,800 (35%)	71,206 (44%)
R	158,808 (65%)	146,543 (69%)	108,821 (58%)	91,657 (56%)
I			11,896 (6%)	

Campaign Finance

	Receipts	Receipts from PACs	Expend-itures
1990			
Byron (D)	$282,337	$165,245 (59%)	$325,997
Fiotes (R)	$3,559	0	$3,557
1988			
Byron (D)	$218,098	$142,722 (65%)	$213,554

Key Votes

1991	
Authorize use of force against Iraq	Y
1990	
Support constitutional amendment on flag desecration	Y
Pass family and medical leave bill over Bush veto	N
Reduce SDI funding	N
Allow abortions in overseas military facilities	N
Approve budget summit plan for spending and taxing	Y
Approve civil rights bill	Y
1989	
Halt production of B-2 stealth bomber at 13 planes	N
Oppose capital gains tax cut	N
Approve federal abortion funding in rape or incest cases	N
Approve pay raise and revision of ethics rules	Y
Pass Democratic minimum wage plan over Bush veto	N

Voting Studies

	Presidential Support		Party Unity		Conservative Coalition	
Year	**S**	**O**	**S**	**O**	**S**	**O**
1990	48	49	59	35	87	13
1989	71	29	54	43	98	2
1988	49	46	61	34	100	0
1987	44	54	58	34	86	12
1986	50	50	55	37	78	18
1985	52	43	63	30	80	13
1984	50	48	47	45	81	17
1983	57	40	43	51	87	10
1982	56	40	44	49	79	15
1981	62	33	38	56	93	4

Interest Group Ratings

Year	ADA	ACU	AFL-CIO	CCUS
1990	33	48	50	57
1989	15	64	25	100
1988	30	68	77	69
1987	48	35	63	60
1986	20	71	46	63
1985	10	65	47	59
1984	20	65	46	38
1983	25	74	59	58
1982	30	55	45	52
1981	15	73	50	65

7 Kweisi Mfume (D)

Of Baltimore — Elected 1986

Born: Oct. 24, 1948, Baltimore, Md.
Education: Morgan State U., B.S. 1976; Johns Hopkins U., M.A. 1984.
Occupation: College professor; radio station program director; talk show host.
Family: Divorced; five children.
Religion: Baptist.
Political Career: Baltimore City Council, 1979-87.
Capitol Office: 217 Cannon Bldg. 20515; 225-4741.

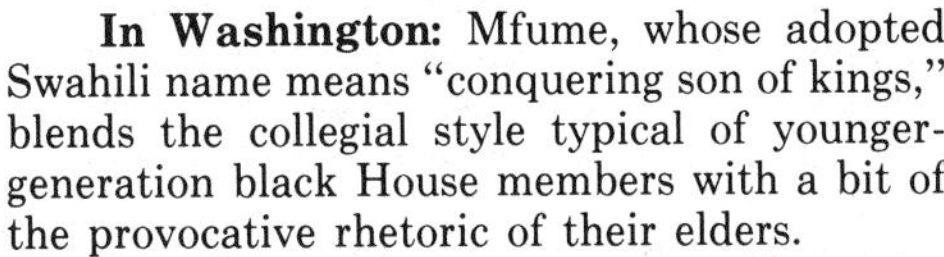

In Washington: Mfume, whose adopted Swahili name means "conquering son of kings," blends the collegial style typical of younger-generation black House members with a bit of the provocative rhetoric of their elders.

Representing a 73 percent black-majority district with many poor residents, Mfume could succeed politically simply by voicing anger and frustration with "the system." Instead, he has come to be known as a thoughtful lawmaker who tries to help the needy by making legislative allies. Mfume is outspoken in his support for civil rights legislation, but sees his role primarily as one of fostering "economic development and economic empowerment" for his minority constituents. He is a strong advocate of so-called minority set-asides — provisions that set goals for minority business participation in federal contracts.

On the Banking, Finance and Urban Affairs Committee, Mfume gave voice to the concerns of public housing residents during debate in the Housing Subcommittee. In 1990, the panel approved a Mfume amendment to change the way tenants calculate their rents, allowing them to pay according to their actual income, not their estimated income, which could include alimony or child support payments that do not come through. At the start of the 102nd Congress, he gave up his seat on the Education and Labor Committee and took a post on the Joint Economic Committee.

Amid the chorus of voices expressing concern over drug abuse and proposing grand plans to combat it, Mfume has tried to make a dent in the problem by focusing on a small corner of the issue. In 1989, he began pushing to curb sales of electronic beepers to minors, who, he says, use them to arrange drug deals. Mfume said a curb could "make it a little more difficult" for dealers to do business. He reintroduced his bill in the 102nd Congress.

At Home: Prior to his 1986 House election, Mfume was well known in Baltimore for his careers in broadcasting and on the City Council. But his background is not that of a typical congressional candidate.

Mfume was born Frizzell Gray in the slums of West Baltimore. After his mother died when he was 16, he quit high school, drifted through a series of jobs and, between the ages of 17 and 22, fathered five sons by four different women. But in his early 20s, he adopted a new name and way of life, climbing the career ladder at Morgan State University's radio station. Mfume finished high school, graduated from Morgan State at 27, and earned an advanced degree from Johns Hopkins University.

After achieving popularity as a radio talk show host, Mfume won a seat on the Baltimore City Council, where he promoted the causes of his inner-city constituents and established a maverick image.

Criticized early on by some colleagues for his confrontational style, Mfume developed a more temperate approach that helped win some victories, including a new law ordering the city to divest itself of investments in companies doing business with South Africa.

Even so, Mfume entered the 1986 Democratic House as an underdog. But the favorite, state Sen. Clarence M. Mitchell (the nephew of retiring Rep. Parren J. Mitchell) was damaged by reports on his personal finances and his alleged relationship with a jailed drug dealer.

Another prominent contender, the Rev. Wendell H. Phillips, a veteran of the civil rights movement, was hurt by accusations that he was cozy with the city's white power structure.

Mfume quietly promoted himself as the compromise candidate. Assisted by a group of black clergy, Mfume swept to an easy primary victory.

Though Mfume was seemingly unbeatable in the heavily Democratic 7th, his GOP opponent, Saint George I. B. Crosse III, harassed him by making an issue of his children born out of wedlock. Mfume stated that he supported his sons financially and emotionally, and the local press portrayed his rise from poverty in a positive light. He won with 87 percent of the vote and has faced little or no opposition since.

Maryland 7

Baltimore — West and Central

Anchored in inner-city Baltimore, the 7th is overwhelmingly Democratic and overwhelmingly black. Its 73 percent black population is exceeded by only three districts nationwide. Baltimore has had a significant black population dating back to the early 1800s. But it was not until the 1980 census that a majority of the city's population was shown to be black.

To compensate for the stream of people leaving the city during the 1970s, the district as redrawn for the '80s had to reach into the western suburbs. Baltimore has continued to lose population, dropping about 6 percent since 1980. These changes, however, have hardly altered the 7th's Democratic cast. Michael S. Dukakis in 1988 and Walter F. Mondale in 1984 both carried the district with over 80 percent of the vote.

The only problem Democrats have here is getting people to the polls. Although Baltimore now has a black mayor, Kurt Schmoke, many low-income blacks are disenchanted with Baltimore's "power structure," which they see as favoring downtown development over neighborhood revitalization, and with the national Democratic Party, which they regard as taking them for granted. These sentiments manifested themselves in Democratic primary wins for the Rev. Jesse Jackson in 1984 and 1988.

The 7th spreads out from downtown Baltimore, past tenement neighborhoods that were Jewish before World War II, then turned black in the 1950s. Moving west, the tenements give way to neat row houses owned by Baltimore's black middle class. The district also includes the gentrified areas of Bolton Hill and, a step down the ladder of upward mobility, Druid Hill Park. It takes in Johns Hopkins University and the working-class neighborhoods around Memorial Stadium, home of the baseball Orioles through the 1991 season. The Orioles will move to a new downtown stadium in 1992.

Outside the city, the 7th reaches into suburban Woodlawn, taking in the huge Social Security complex. The rest of the district's suburban territory has a handful of Republican loyalists, but their votes are drowned by the urban Democrats.

Population: 527,590. White 134,200 (25%), Black 386,759 (73%), Other 4,396 (1%). Spanish origin 4,556 (1%). 18 and over 376,566 (71%), 65 and over 56,465 (11%). Median age: 29.

Committees

Banking, Finance & Urban Affairs (19th of 31 Democrats)
Financial Institutions Supervision, Regulation & Insurance; Housing & Community Development

Select Narcotics Abuse & Control (14th of 21 Democrats)

Small Business (16th of 27 Democrats)
SBA, the General Economy & Minority Enterprise Development

Joint Economic

Elections

1990 General		
Kweisi Mfume (D)	59,628	(85%)
Kenneth Kondner (R)	10,529	(15%)
1990 Primary		
Kweisi Mfume (D)	41,238	(89%)
Michael Vernon Dobson (D)	5,270	(11%)
1988 General		
Kweisi Mfume (D)	117,650	(100%)

Previous Winning Percentage: **1986** (87%)

District Vote For President

	1988	1984	1980	1976
D	123,261 (81%)	151,669 (82%)	127,824 (78%)	120,831 (77%)
R	26,360 (17%)	32,980 (18%)	27,659 (17%)	35,937 (23%)
I			6,768 (4%)	

Campaign Finance

	Receipts	Receipts from PACs	Expend-itures
1990			
Mfume (D)	$224,826	$128,000 (57%)	$205,671
1988			
Mfume (D)	$130,466	$72,250 (55%)	$110,565

Key Votes

1991	
Authorize use of force against Iraq	N
1990	
Support constitutional amendment on flag desecration	N
Pass family and medical leave bill over Bush veto	Y
Reduce SDI funding	Y
Allow abortions in overseas military facilities	Y
Approve budget summit plan for spending and taxing	N
Approve civil rights bill	Y
1989	
Halt production of B-2 stealth bomber at 13 planes	Y
Oppose capital gains tax cut	Y
Approve federal abortion funding in rape or incest cases	Y
Approve pay raise and revision of ethics rules	Y
Pass Democratic minimum wage plan over Bush veto	Y

Voting Studies

	Presidential Support		Party Unity		Conservative Coalition	
Year	**S**	**O**	**S**	**O**	**S**	**O**
1990	15	81	86	7	9	91
1989	31	66	86	5	15	83
1988	23	76	93	4	21	79
1987	13	86	93	3	9	88

Interest Group Ratings

Year	ADA	ACU	AFL-CIO	CCUS
1990	94	13	92	29
1989	90	8	100	30
1988	95	4	100	21
1987	100	0	100	7

8 Constance A. Morella (R)

Of Bethesda — Elected 1986

Born: Feb. 12, 1931, Somerville, Mass.
Education: Boston U., B.A. 1954; American U., M.A. 1967.
Occupation: Professor.
Family: Husband, Anthony C. Morella; nine children.
Religion: Roman Catholic.
Political Career: Md. House, 1979-87; Republican candidate for Md. House, 1974; sought Republican nomination for U.S. House, 1980.
Capitol Office: 1024 Longworth Bldg. 20515; 225-5341.

In Washington: Republican leaders are happier about the votes Morella wins in November than about the ones she casts in Congress. For the past three elections, she has won a suburban Washington district that Democrats had held. But in 1990 (as in 1988), Morella was the Republican least likely to support the President on House votes. Early in the 102nd Congress, she was one of only three Republicans opposing the resolution authorizing Bush to use force in the Persian Gulf.

But if Republicans are unlikely to take Morella into their inner circle, neither do they give her the cold shoulder. She is too personally pleasant to get brusque treatment, and many Republicans recognize that a more conservative member would have trouble holding the 8th, which is packed with federal bureaucrats and political activists partial to liberalism.

Inside the GOP, it helps Morella that she has largely focused her liberalism on local concerns. While many members curry favor with party bigwigs to get on "prestige" committees, Morella's lower-profile assignments suit her fine. The Post Office and Civil Service Committee handles issues of interest to the current and retired federal workers in her district; the Science Committee is important to the many research laboratories in Montgomery County.

In 1989, Morella joined most members in voting against a proposed 51 percent congressional pay raise. But she then submitted a bill to give up to 20 percent pay increases to judges and senior officials of federal agencies, whose raises were also killed by the House vote.

She has backed repeal of the Hatch Act, which restricts political activity by federal employees; President Bush vetoed a repeal measure in June 1990. Early in the 102nd Congress, Morella submitted legislation that would allow higher pay for federal workers in the high-cost Baltimore-Washington, D.C. metropolitan area.

Morella is also becoming a voice on some broader concerns, such as women's issues. She has introduced legislation on domestic violence and to address the growing incidence of AIDS among women. And Morella has promoted a ROTC-style program to help pay for the education of students who join the Peace Corps.

At Home: In 1986, Morella reawakened the 8th's proclivity for moderate-to-liberal Republicanism, which had lapsed during the four-term tenure of Democrat Michael D. Barnes. Morella linked herself to the GOP moderates — Charles McC. Mathias Jr., Gilbert Gude and Newton I. Steers Jr. — who held the district for 20 years before Barnes. (Steers had thwarted Morella's first House bid in a 1980 primary.)

Though Morella was not an activist during her eight years in the Maryland House, she was involved in environmental and social issues. The biggest factor in Morella's House victory was her personality. A vivacious English professor who quoted glibly from Shakespeare, she played up her family's immigrant heritage and her working-class upbringing.

Morella also noted that she and her husband had raised nine children (including her late sister's six), while her Democratic foe, state Sen. Stewart Bainum, was a 40-year-old bachelor. A millionaire businessman, Bainum also had a wooden campaign style that contrasted poorly with Morella's manner. He waged a costly campaign that emphasized his liberal views. But many voters saw him as trying to buy a House seat. Morella won with 53 percent.

With a district close to Washington, Morella was highly visible at home as a freshman, and she reinforced her standing with a voting record that marked her as independent-minded. None of the Democratic Party's big names challenged her in 1988. The task went to state Rep. Peter Franchot, a hard-charging liberal who accused Morella of flip-flopping on defense issues, and of hiding her GOP allegiance to appeal to Democrats. But Morella, who emphasized her independence and the importance of her committee posts to district interests, won with 63 percent. In 1990 she took an even greater share of the vote.

Maryland 8

Montgomery County

Explosive population growth over the last 25 years has turned the 8th into a compact district encompassing the more densely populated Montgomery County suburbs of Washington, D.C. Though the posh, close-in suburbs give the county one of the nation's highest per capita incomes, it also takes in numerous middle-income town-house communities and lower-income neighborhoods in Silver Spring, Takoma Park and Rockville.

A coalition of working-class voters and affluent liberals has given Democrats a stranglehold on local political power in Montgomery County. However, the 8th has a tradition of supporting moderate-to-liberal Republicans for the House. Democratic loyalties are also tenuous at the presidential level. In 1988, Michael S. Dukakis took 53 percent of the 8th District vote, and in 1984 Walter F. Mondale took 51 percent. Ronald Reagan fared well in the 8th (winning it in 1980, losing narrowly in 1984).

But many voters here do not share Reagan's anti-big-government sentiment. The federal government is the economic engine for the trade association executives, lawyers, government agency heads — and no small number of congressmen — who contribute to Montgomery County's affluent status. It also provides jobs for the thousands of bureaucrats who commute to Washington or to such local federal facilities as the National Institutes of Health in Bethesda and the National Institute of Standards and Technology in Gaithersburg.

Bethesda and Chevy Chase, with their oriental-carpet stores and gourmet shops, are at the hub of the district's upper-middle-class prosperity. Both, as well as the more upscale areas of Rockville, have sizable Jewish populations. Many of these residents abandoned less-affluent Silver Spring, where they were supplanted mainly by minority-group members.

Rockville, with 45,000 residents, is the largest incorporated city in the 8th. To the north, Gaithersburg (39,500 people) and the unincorporated areas in between have enjoyed a boom, associated with the growing high-tech corridor along Interstate 270.

Population: 528,036. White 448,865 (85%), Black 48,212 (9%), Other 22,257 (4%). Spanish origin 21,662 (4%). 18 and over 391,309 (74%), 65 and over 48,358 (9%). Median age: 32.

Committees

Post Office & Civil Service (6th of 8 Republicans)
Civil Service (ranking); Compensation & Employee Benefits

Science, Space & Technology (12th of 19 Republicans)
Environment; Technology & Competitiveness

Select Aging (14th of 27 Republicans)
Health & Long-Term Care

Elections

1990 General		
Constance A. Morella (R)	130,059	(74%)
James Walker Jr. (D)	39,343	(22%)
Sidney Altman (I)	7,485	(4%)
1990 Primary		
Constance A. Morella (R)	20,010	(87%)
Asa Beck (R)	2,990	(13%)
1988 General		
Constance A. Morella (R)	172,619	(63%)
Peter Franchot (D)	102,478	(37%)

Previous Winning Percentage: **1986** (53%)

District Vote For President

	1988	1984	1980	1976
D	150,522 (53%)	136,104 (51%)	100,363 (40%)	125,996 (52%)
R	129,919 (46%)	128,747 (49%)	116,514 (47%)	116,064 (48%)
I			31,201 (13%)	

Campaign Finance

	Receipts	Receipts from PACs	Expend-itures
1990			
Morella (R)	$542,961	$239,709 (44%)	$353,959
1988			
Morella (R)	$829,437	$305,374 (37%)	$821,574
Franchot (D)	$461,350	$190,203 (41%)	$460,847

Key Votes

1991	
Authorize use of force against Iraq	N
1990	
Support constitutional amendment on flag desecration	N
Pass family and medical leave bill over Bush veto	Y
Reduce SDI funding	Y
Allow abortions in overseas military facilities	Y
Approve budget summit plan for spending and taxing	Y
Approve civil rights bill	Y
1989	
Halt production of B-2 stealth bomber at 13 planes	Y
Oppose capital gains tax cut	N
Approve federal abortion funding in rape or incest cases	Y
Approve pay raise and revision of ethics rules	Y
Pass Democratic minimum wage plan over Bush veto	Y

Voting Studies

	Presidential Support		Party Unity		Conservative Coalition	
Year	**S**	**O**	**S**	**O**	**S**	**O**
1990	26	70	32	65	24	72
1989	41	58	18	76	34	63
1988	28	68	30	67	32	66
1987	34	65	29	66	40	60

Interest Group Ratings

Year	ADA	ACU	AFL-CIO	CCUS
1990	67	17	58	29
1989	80	21	67	80
1988	90	8	79	46
1987	60	22	50	40

Massachusetts

U.S. CONGRESS

SENATE 2 D
HOUSE 11 D

LEGISLATURE

Senate 24 D, 16 R
House 120 D, 40 R

ELECTIONS

1988 Presidential Vote

Bush	45%
Dukakis	53%

1984 Presidential Vote

Reagan	51%
Mondale	48%

1980 Presidential Vote

Reagan	42%
Carter	42%
Anderson	15%

Turnout rate in 1986	33%
Turnout rate in 1988	58%
Turnout rate in 1990	45%

(as percentage of voting age population)

POPULATION AND GROWTH

1980 population	5,737,037
1990 population (13th in the nation)	6,016,425
Percent change 1980-1990	+5%

DEMOGRAPHIC BREAKDOWN

White	90%
Black	5%
Asian or Pacific Islander	2%
(Hispanic origin)	5%
Urban	84%
Rural	16%
Born in state	72%
Foreign-born	9%

MAJOR CITIES

Boston	574,283
Worcester	169,759
Springfield	156,983
Lowell	103,439
New Bedford	99,922

AREA AND LAND USE

Area 7,825 sq. miles (45th)

Farm	12%
Forest	62%
Federally owned	2%

Gov. William F. Weld (R)
Of Cambridge — Elected 1990

Born: July 31, 1945, Smithtown, N.Y.
Education: Harvard U., B.A. 1966, J.D. 1970; attended Oxford U., England, 1967.
Occupation: Lawyer.
Religion: Episcopalian.
Political Career: GOP nominee for attorney general, 1978.
Next Election: 1994.

WORK

Occupations

White-collar	58%
Blue-collar	28%
Service workers	13%

Government Workers

Federal	62,175
State	106,876
Local	224,068

MONEY

Median family income	$ 21,166	(14th)
Tax burden per capita	$ 1,137	(7th)

EDUCATION

Spending per pupil through grade 12	$ 5,471	(5th)
Persons with college degrees	20%	(6th)

CRIME

Violent crime rate 675 per 100,000 (11th)

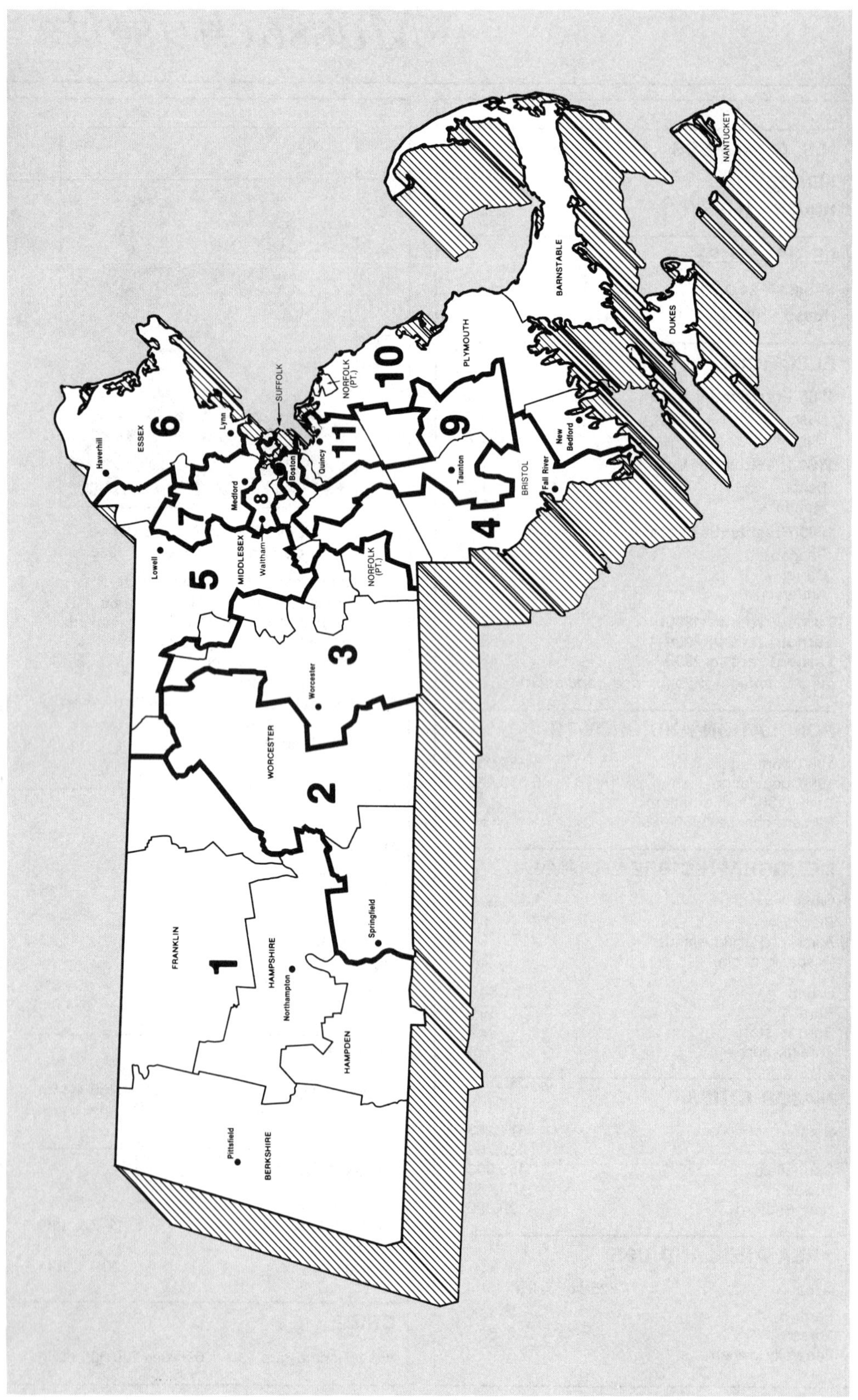
1
2
3
4
5
6
7
8
9
10
11
FRANKLIN
HAMPSHIRE
HAMPDEN
BERKSHIRE
Pittsfield
Northampton
Springfield
WORCESTER
Worcester
MIDDLESEX
Lowell
Waltham
Medford
Boston
ESSEX
Haverhill
Lynn
SUFFOLK
Quincy
NORFOLK (PT.)
NORFOLK (PT.)
PLYMOUTH
BRISTOL
Taunton
Fall River
New Bedford
BARNSTABLE
DUKES
NANTUCKET

Edward M. Kennedy (D)

Of Boston — Elected 1962

Born: Feb. 22, 1932, Boston, Mass.

Education: Harvard U., B.A. 1956; attended International Law School, The Hague, Netherlands, 1958; U. of Virginia, LL.B. 1959.

Military Service: Army, 1951-53.

Occupation: Lawyer.

Family: Divorced; three children.

Religion: Roman Catholic.

Political Career: Suffolk County assistant district attorney, 1961-62; sought Democratic nomination for president, 1980.

Capitol Office: 315 Russell Bldg. 20510; 224-4543.

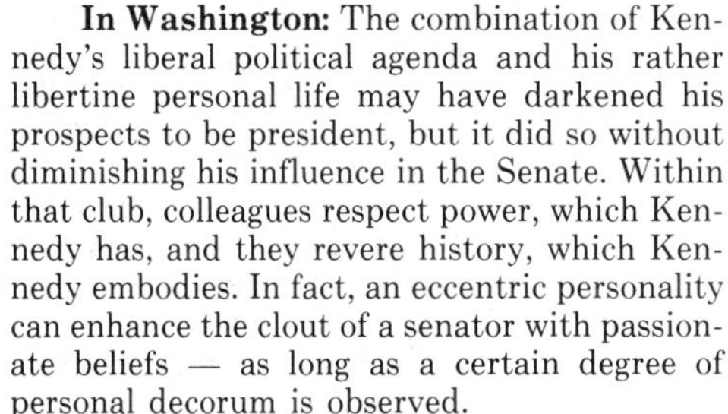

In Washington: The combination of Kennedy's liberal political agenda and his rather libertine personal life may have darkened his prospects to be president, but it did so without diminishing his influence in the Senate. Within that club, colleagues respect power, which Kennedy has, and they revere history, which Kennedy embodies. In fact, an eccentric personality can enhance the clout of a senator with passionate beliefs — as long as a certain degree of personal decorum is observed.

Staying within the bounds of decorum seems tough for Kennedy, though; his personal peccadilloes are always a threat to overshadow his legislative pursuits. Still, with nearly 30 years' Senate experience behind him and not yet 60 years of age, Kennedy has an opportunity to influence federal policy from Congress for years to come. If he does not exploit that opportunity, it will further disappoint those who had even higher hopes for him.

Kennedy's power in the Senate seemed to swell as his national ambitions waned. Since he forswore the White House in 1985, his initiatives have been taken at face value rather than as maneuvers in another national campaign. Chairman of the Labor and Human Resources Committee, with an ambitious agenda of health, education and labor issues, Kennedy presses for larger goals, but pragmatically accepts what he can get in these times of budget limits and conservative predominance.

But the legendary name that is so large a part of his influence also shines a glaring light on Kennedy's personal life. After relinquishing his national ambition, Kennedy seemed to drop his guard, but public and press fascination with his personal life have not abated. Stories about his drinking and socializing continue, and questions about his judgment resurfaced in 1991, as police investigated an alleged rape at the Kennedy compound in Palm Beach over Easter weekend.

The misfortune of proximity ensnared Kennedy in the investigation of his nephew; the senator was the host of a gathering of family and friends that weekend and had gone out with his nephew and son that night. There were intimations that Kennedy had initially dodged police who were investigating the alleged rape, but he blamed their failure to connect on simple miscommunication. The revelation most damaging to Kennedy may have been his statement to police that he had awakened his son and nephew to go drinking with him at 11 p.m.; that behavior raised anew the fundamental question of Kennedy's personal judgment.

The episode was clearly distracting Kennedy at a time when he was trying to negotiate a compromise on civil rights legislation. But operating against a backdrop of personal controversy is not new to him, nor is enduring GOP efforts to sink Democratic initiatives by labeling them as "Kennedy-style liberalism."

The label dates to the early 1980s, when the Reagan revolution had Democrats running scared. Kennedy stood almost alone articulating an opposing view of social justice and equality. Admirers praise Kennedy's steadfast liberalism during this period; it reinforced his singular stature among civil rights activists, advocates for the poor and other liberals.

Kennedy's opposition to President Ronald Reagan encouraged GOP image-makers and fundraisers to make him out as the caricature of a big-government, bleeding-heart liberal. While the label stuck, those who work with Kennedy in the Senate, especially in recent years, do not see him that way. There, his commitment to social programs is increasingly tempered by concern about the federal deficit, and an appreciation of what taxpayers will bear.

Kennedy signaled an important shift in his attitudes when he proclaimed in 1985 that "those of us who care about domestic progress must do more with less." In early 1991, as Congress began debate on reducing the federal student loan default rate, Kennedy warned,

"The American taxpayer is not going to support that program unless we get a grip on it."

Kennedy's collegial style helps him cultivate even conservatives as allies. On the Labor Committee, he and ranking Republican Orrin G. Hatch of Utah have a warm relationship. The two have worked together on numerous bills, including a comprehensive AIDS bill in the 100th Congress.

On the Judiciary Subcommittee on Immigration, which he chairs, Kennedy works closely with Wyoming Republican Alan K. Simpson, one of the more caustic Senate conservatives. After years of work, the two crafted successful compromise legislation in 1990 to limit the flow of legal immigration into the United States. Both Kennedy and Simpson were committed to providing more visas to European immigrants who may not have immediate family here.

Kennedy has achieved some of his recent successes by joining with a Republican ally, then keeping in the background so as not to spark controversy — even as he and his staff work to broker compromises to woo conservative Democrats. This was the case during debate on the 1990 civil rights bill, when he worked with Republican John C. Danforth of Missouri to fashion a bill that won the votes of all the Southern Democrats and 10 Republicans. But when President Bush vetoed the bill, Kennedy and other proponents could not offer a compelling counter to Bush's anti-quotas line; an override attempt fell one vote short.

Kennedy had more luck in the 101st Congress ushering to enactment legislation to protect the disabled from discrimination. During debate, he spoke movingly of his mentally retarded sister, Rosemary, and his son Patrick, who lost a leg to cancer.

Many of Kennedy's most significant legislative accomplishments, ironically, date to the end of the Reagan years. On a personal level, Kennedy admits a certain fondness for Reagan, but he was his political nemesis and a potent foil. In Reagan's second term, Kennedy was a key player in enacting labor legislation to give workers advance notice of plant closings and to ban most employers' use of polygraphs.

He also had a major role in the 100th Congress in steering into law two of the most important civil rights bills since the 1960s. One, the *Grove City* bill, expanded four landmark anti-bias laws that were narrowed by a 1984 Supreme Court ruling. The other strengthened the 1968 fair housing law by giving federal regulators authority to crack down on discrimination in the sale or rental of housing.

On the Judiciary Committee, Kennedy is the most consistent vote against conservative Supreme Court nominations. He was the lone panelist to oppose Bush's appointment of David H. Souter in 1990. "There is little in his record that demonstrates real solicitude for the rights of those who are the weakest and most powerless in our society," he said, later adding, "We must vote our fears, not our hopes."

But Kennedy did not seek to make Souter a cause célèbre, as he did nominee Robert H. Bork in 1987. While other Senate Democrats withheld their fire after Reagan nominated the controversial conservative, Kennedy delivered a salvo against Bork within an hour of the announcement. On the Senate floor, he blasted Bork, saying that he "stands for an extremist view of the Constitution and the role of the Supreme Court."

Though Kennedy is not a particularly active member of the Armed Services Committee, he adroitly seized the leadership of the growing nuclear freeze movement in 1983. But he could never muster a majority, and the freeze movement faded. His proposals to ban all but the smallest nuclear arms tests have lost by wide margins.

He uses his celebrity to champion the anti-apartheid movement in South Africa. His heavily publicized trip there in early 1985 helped harden public opinion against the white-minority government, setting in motion the events that led to passage of tough economic sanctions in 1986. But publicity and power do not always go together. In 1988, reacting to Pretoria's continued repression and to Reagan's laxity in enforcing the law, Kennedy sponsored a near-total trade embargo to "end, once and for all time, American complicity in and support for apartheid." But without key GOP support, the bill died.

Perhaps most painfully, his goal of national health insurance remains no closer to fulfillment today than it was 25 years ago. He still pushes the program, but no longer calls for a government-sponsored benefit. Instead, Kennedy speaks of a hybrid system requiring private employers to insure workers while government covers the poor and unemployed.

However pragmatic Kennedy has become, he has not set aside all grandiose plans; in 1991, he spoke of enacting a Social Security program for children. Proposals such as that call to mind his rousing 1980 Democratic convention speech, with its liberal affirmation that "hope lives on, the cause endures and the dream shall never die." That speech reflected Kennedy at his best. When he is psychologically ready, he can stir an audience like few others in American politics. His prepared texts have a lyricism that is indelibly linked to the Kennedy name.

Though his Oval Office prospects are faded, Kennedy has still been able to assemble a staff that is known as the most powerful — and perhaps the most arrogant — on Capitol Hill. His staff is also far larger than most — Kennedy's seniority has brought him a major committee chairmanship and three subcommittee chairs, And because Kennedy offers high salaries, which he personally supplements, his staff is also more experienced.

The combination gives him a conglomerate of creative professionals who are fiercely loyal. They screen his contacts, prepare him thoroughly, and churn out countless program initiatives. With their backing, Kennedy can march into a markup with a fistful of amendments, and even if most are dropped, he still ends up with more than his share of successes.

Kennedy started his career without any of the leadership pressures that descended on him later. He was 30 years old, his brothers were running the country, and he voted with them while looking out for his state's interests.

In time, he became an innovative and often successful legislator. Kennedy was largely responsible for creating the Teacher Corps. He helped eliminate draft deferments for college students, saying they were unfair to the poor, and he spoke for Hispanic farm workers and Alaska's Indians.

Kennedy had a particularly productive legislative period in the early 1970s, following not only the 1969 Chappaquiddick tragedy but also his most embarrassing Senate defeat, his ouster as majority whip in 1971. Kennedy had been elected whip in 1969, beating Finance Chairman Russell B. Long, who had performed erratically in the post. The vote was taken only months after New York Sen. Robert F. Kennedy's assassination, which made the youngest Kennedy the rising star.

But he was bored with the odd parliamentary jobs that make effective Senate leaders. Then that summer, his image was shattered for all time when he drove his car off a bridge at Chappaquiddick and his companion in the car, Mary Jo Kopechne, drowned. When Senate Democrats elected their leaders in 1971, they chose Robert C. Byrd of West Virginia for whip, 31-24.

As he would do a decade later upon finally shelving his national ambitions, Kennedy returned to legislating. As chairman of Labor's Health Subcommittee, he formed a productive partnership with his House counterpart, Florida Democrat Paul G. Rogers. Together they wrote legislation funding research into cancer and heart and lung diseases, family planning and doctor training. Every year brought a greater federal role in health.

Meanwhile, Kennedy was chairing Judiciary's Subcommittee on Administrative Practice and Procedure, and using it to investigate a range of subjects, from the Freedom of Information Act to the Food and Drug Administration. Critics said he used the panel for publicity, but Kennedy's hearings sometimes led to major bills, such as a 1979 revision of drug laws.

When Kennedy became chairman of Judiciary in 1979, his tenure seemed likely to last as long as he remained in the Senate. But he did not accomplish much; by fall, he was running for president, and the next year's elections brought a Republican Senate takeover.

Since 1968, people had looked to Kennedy to run for president. In the fall of 1979, apparently tempted by early polls showing him far ahead of President Jimmy Carter, Kennedy launched his campaign without offering any clear idea of why he wanted to be president. He talked of the need for stronger leadership, but so clumsily as to raise the question of whether he could provide it. Meanwhile, Carter was devoting his attention to the American hostages in Iran, in a carefully staged display of his leadership.

Only in the campaign's second half — by which time Kennedy was essentially beaten — did he present the clear liberal argument he took to the convention. After Jan. 28, when he attacked Carter's hard-line anti-Soviet policy as "Cold War II," Kennedy was a different candidate. The changes did not bring him any closer to nomination, but they kept him alive as a liberal leader. His stirring convention speech helped restore some lost luster.

Kennedy was considered a potential candidate for 1988, but late in 1985 he announced he would not seek the nomination. He acknowledged that his decision meant he probably would never occupy the White House. "The pursuit of the presidency is not my life," he said. "Public service is."

At Home: It is often said that 60 percent of Massachusetts voters love Kennedy and 40 percent hate him, and the quality of his Republican opponent can shift those percentages only marginally.

Kennedy's challenge has been to live up to the standard he set in 1964, when he ran for his first full term less than a year after his brother John's assassination. Bedridden after an airplane crash, he beat Republican Howard Whitmore Jr. by the widest margin in state history: 1,129,244 votes.

That number, rather than GOP candidate Josiah Spaulding, was the real test in 1970. There was no way Kennedy could pass it. The Chappaquiddick accident had occurred the year before, and the national skepticism over his handling of it had its effect even at home. His 62 percent showing that year established the love-hate yardstick that still holds.

Kennedy's stands for Medicaid abortions and busing in Boston seemed to pose problems in 1976, but he had a good year. He brushed aside three anti-busing and right-to-life challengers in the primary, then crushed GOP businessman Michael Robertson by a million votes.

In 1982 Kennedy met his first Republican foe able to draw attention on his own. Raymond Shamie, a wealthy inventor and engineer, spent over $1 million in a quixotic but imaginative campaign. In an effort to force Kennedy to debate him, Shamie had airplanes circle baseball games, county fairs, and crowded freeways around the country, towing banners offering a $10,000 reward to whoever could "GET TED

KENNEDY TO DEBATE RAY SHAMIE."

Kennedy fought back with his own attention-getting ploy. Confronting the "character" issue that had plagued his 1980 presidential bid, his campaign aired TV ads showing Kennedy intimates talking about his personal side — his stoicism in the face of personal tragedy and his compassion toward other people.

A month before the election, Kennedy accepted Shamie's offer, asking that the reward go to a Catholic school in Hanover, Mass. The debate gave Shamie greater recognition statewide, but did little else to help him or hurt Kennedy. The final result was 61 percent for Kennedy.

In 1988, Kennedy had a trouble-free reelection. Joe Malone, a 33-year-old former state GOP executive director, saw his bid more as a party-building endeavor than a contest with Kennedy. Rather than attack the incumbent, Malone appealed to minorities and working-class voters to take a second look at the beleaguered Bay State GOP. He made scant progress against Kennedy but established a base to run successfully for state treasurer in 1990.

Kennedy burst into politics in 1962 by winning the election to fill the remaining two years of his brother's Senate term. John F. Kennedy had arranged for family friend Benjamin A. Smith to get the seat when he became president in 1961, and Smith then stepped aside for the younger Kennedy in 1962.

Edward J. McCormack, nephew of House Speaker John W. McCormack, was not as obliging. He derided Kennedy's qualifications, noting his meager experience as an assistant district attorney in Boston, and said in a Democratic primary debate: "If your name were Edward Moore [instead of Edward Moore Kennedy], your candidacy would be a joke." Kennedy did not lose his temper and the attacks created a backlash against McCormack.

Kennedy easily won the primary, carrying every ward in Boston and winning outstate as well. In November he took 55 percent of the vote against Republican George Cabot Lodge.

Committees

Labor & Human Resources (Chairman)
Children, Families, Drugs & Alcoholism; Education, Arts & Humanities; Labor

Armed Services (4th of 11 Democrats)
Projection Forces & Regional Defense (chairman); Manpower & Personnel; Strategic Forces & Nuclear Deterrence

Judiciary (2nd of 8 Democrats)
Immigration & Refugee Affairs (chairman); Constitution; Patents, Copyrights & Trademarks

Joint Economic

Elections

1988 General

Edward M. Kennedy (D)	1,693,344	(65%)
Joseph D. Malone (R)	884,267	(34%)

Previous Winning Percentages: **1982** (61%) **1976** (69%) **1970** (62%) **1964** (74%) **1962 *** (55%)

* *Special election.*

Campaign Finance

	Receipts	Receipts from PACs	Expend-itures
1988			
Kennedy (D)	$3,304,580	$322,972 (10%)	$2,702,865
Malone (R)	$617,806	0	$587,323

Key Votes

1991

Authorize use of force against Iraq	N

1990

Oppose prohibition of certain semiautomatic weapons	N
Support constitutional amendment on flag desecration	N
Oppose requiring parental notice for minors' abortions	Y
Halt production of B-2 stealth bomber at 13 planes	Y
Approve budget that cut spending and raised revenues	Y
Pass civil rights bill over Bush veto	Y

1989

Oppose reduction of SDI funding	N
Oppose barring federal funds for "obscene" art	Y
Allow vote on capital gains tax cut	N

Voting Studies

	Presidential Support		Party Unity		Conservative Coalition	
Year	S	O	S	O	S	O
1990	25	70	89	7	14	81
1989	48	49	90	7	18	79
1988	36	55	84	4	3	89
1987	29	62	85	5	6	81
1986	28	69	79	16	24	70
1985	27	69	81	7	17	73
1984	30	58	84	7	6	91
1983	36	54	70	17	11	82
1982	29	64	83	5	2	88
1981	31	60	80	9	4	87

Interest Group Ratings

Year	ADA	ACU	AFL-CIO	CCUS
1990	100	0	89	0
1989	85	7	90	29
1988	95	0	100	27
1987	90	0	100	24
1986	80	10	77	47
1985	85	9	90	39
1984	85	5	100	24
1983	85	0	100	22
1982	75	6	96	0
1981	100	0	94	6

John Kerry (D)

Of Boston — Elected 1984

Born: Dec. 11, 1943, Denver, Colo.

Education: Yale U., B.A. 1966; Boston College, J.D. 1976.

Military Service: Navy, 1968-69.

Occupation: Lawyer.

Family: Divorced; two children.

Religion: Roman Catholic.

Political Career: Lieutenant governor, 1983-85; Democratic nominee for U.S. House, 1972.

Capitol Office: 421 Russell Bldg. 20510; 224-2742.

In Washington: Kerry no longer appears on everyone's list of senators running for president, and for his Senate career, at least, that is good news. The White House may well be his ultimate goal, but he has benefited in his colleagues' estimation by restraining the pace of his ambition.

Kerry's first term took a serious turn in its latter half. He moved away from gaudy hearings on drug running and money laundering and immersed himself in work that, while often smaller-scale, was generally more productive.

Typical was his amendment to the 1990 crime bill that doubled the funding available to help local police cope with drug-related crime. Many of his more successful moments related to the business of Massachusetts — including his support of a tunnel project for Boston Harbor and high-speed rail from Boston to New York.

Kerry also was active in such wider arenas as the Clean Air Act and campaign finance reform. Some of the amendments he offered to the former legislation were adopted, and he also submitted at least one major toughening amendment that lost only narrowly (when Majority Leader George J. Mitchell decided its adoption would endanger the overall coalition on the bill).

He also pressed for a radical restructuring of federal campaign financing that would rely on voluntary public funding for 90 percent of campaign costs. Kerry continued to push for such a formula when the issue was rejoined in the 102nd Congress.

Moreover, in the later years of his first Senate term, Kerry found himself compelled to do some heavy political lifting. He chaired his party's Senate campaign committee through a successful electoral round in 1988, even as his former boss in the Massachusetts state government, Gov. Michael S. Dukakis, faltered in his bid for the presidency.

Kerry then turned in a strong performance in his own behalf, winning a solid re-election victory in 1990. He turned back a self-financing GOP citizen-candidate despite the worst anti-incumbent sentiment to hit Massachusetts Democrats in years.

Kerry was also one of those who seemed best at handling the political dilemma posed by the January 1991 vote authorizing the use of military force in the Persian Gulf.

A veteran of both the Vietnam War and the antiwar protests of that era, Kerry voted against the resolution authorizing President Bush to use force. "There is no consensus in America for war," he said. Yet he took pains to note his overall support for confrontation with Iraq and warned the world "not to draw too sharp a line" between the parties or the branches of government on the question of Kuwait's sovereignty.

On a related subject, in the early months of the 102nd Congress, Kerry was among those urging the administration to drop demands for concessions from Hanoi and begin normalizing trade with Vietnam.

In his early Senate years, Kerry's reputation suffered somewhat from his apparent preoccupation with image. He seemed to do too many things with an eye toward how they would look.

The impression was naturally enhanced by characteristics Kerry shares with a legendary Massachusetts politician with the same initials. Like John F. Kennedy, Kerry is a product of social privilege (his middle name, Forbes, salutes his mother's blue-blood family). Like Kennedy, Kerry was decorated for his daring as a small-craft commander in the Navy and went quickly into politics in the party of the lower income classes. But Kerry's career has been more anti-establishment than Kennedy's, especially at critical junctures.

He first came to prominence as a veteran protesting the Vietnam War, and at times in his first years in the Senate he still seemed to be carrying a protester's banner. The dutiful study he devoted to complex issues such as anti-satellite weapons testing was appreciated, but his effort to address the issue with amendments on other senators' unrelated bills was not.

Kerry continued to pursue the ASAT issue in the 101st Congress. His amendment reducing funding for the kinetic-energy ASAT program from $208 million to $77 million received 45 votes on the Senate floor.

The increasing number of senators willing to support Kerry on the ASAT issue offers one measure of his maturation.

In the 100th Congress, Kerry gained some national note by taking on Panamanian strongman Manuel Antonio Noriega. As chairman of the Foreign Relations Subcommittee on Terrorism, Narcotics and International Operations, Kerry's investigators looked for ties between drug smuggling and illegal shipments of weapons to the Nicaraguan contras. Kerry suggested Noriega was being protected by the United States because of what he knew about the connection. George Bush, then vice president and the 1988 GOP presidential nominee, attacked Kerry by name.

Early in the 101st Congress, Kerry sometimes acted in concert with the Bush administration — as when he supported the certification of Mexico's cooperation on drug interdiction and voted for Bush's compromise humanitarian-aid package for the contras.

But Kerry opposed certifying the drug interdiction efforts of the Bahamas. And he released a two-volume report on drugs and foreign policy that said such objectives as military support of the contras had interfered with the war on drugs.

Later, however, when Bush decided to invade Panama and root Noriega out, Kerry voiced his support.

Kerry's views on Central America had already caused conservative groups to bait fundraising appeals with his name. Shortly after being elected, he had traveled to Managua with fellow freshman Sen. Tom Harkin of Iowa and returned saying the Sandinista regime was ready to talk about a cease-fire. Soon after, Nicaraguan President Daniel Ortega went to Moscow to ask for more Soviet aid. Many thought the two senators had allowed themselves to be used.

Worse, in the view of others in the Senate, was his early tendency to charge ahead on the floor with little apparent regard for the chances of success or the costs of defeat.

During debate on the 1985 contra-aid bill, Kerry offered an amendment to bar use of any funds for activities violating international law. Cornered, Republicans offered to accept the amendment by voice vote. But Kerry insisted on a roll call, angering Majority Leader Bob Dole, who was trying to speed action on the bill. Dole was able to block the amendment, forcing Kerry to accept a watered-down version.

Later that year, Kerry picked the immigration bill as a vehicle for an amendment that would delay tests on an anti-satellite weapon. Convinced that the amendment faced certain rejection, arms-control lobbyists implored him not to offer it. But he did offer it and it was defeated.

Since then, however, Kerry has gradually persuaded people to take him more seriously. He has taken the time to master the technical aspects of issues such as the anti-ballistic missile treaty, and has shown a willingness to compromise and work within the system.

At Home: In 1971, Kerry, a leader of Vietnam Veterans Against the War, joined with other demonstrators as they threw their medals over the White House fence. When the incident is recounted, Kerry takes pains to explain that he opposed the returning of medals as a tactic and returned none of his own (three Purple Hearts, a Silver Star and a Bronze Star). He did throw the medals of a veteran from Worcester, Mass., who could not come to Washington, and he also threw several of the ribbons he had received with his own medals.

Kerry's ambivalence about the war protests of his day may be shared by much of his generation. But it also fits the pattern of irony in Kerry's career. He has never fully divested himself of the trappings of his privileged youth or his career as a decorated naval officer. But his political rise has been notable for its anti-establishment tone.

He became a national figure in the 1971 Vietnam protests, gaining front-page coverage by asking the Senate Foreign Relations Committee, "How do you ask a man to be the last man to die for a mistake?" He tried to exploit the publicity by moving to Lowell and running in the open 5th Congressional District in 1972. Kerry won his 10-way primary, but lost in the fall to Republican Paul Cronin.

After that defeat, Kerry went to law school, and worked as assistant district attorney in Middlesex County. In 1980, he bowed out of a House campaign in a second suburban district in favor of fellow liberal Barney Frank.

In 1982, Kerry ran for lieutenant governor in a challenge to the regular Democratic establishment. With help from Ray Flynn, then a member of the Boston City Council and now the mayor, he carried Suffolk County and edged out Evelyn Murphy in the primary.

The anti-establishment theme surfaced again in 1984, in his fight with U.S. Rep. James M. Shannon for the nomination to replace retiring Sen. Paul E. Tsongas. Kerry contrasted his image as an independent liberal to Shannon's reputation as a House insider.

Shannon argued that his knowledge of Capitol Hill was an asset Kerry could not match. But Kerry called Shannon a "backroom" politician, and cast himself as an outsider who could stand up to the Reagan administration. He won 41 percent of the vote, to Shannon's 38 percent.

In the general election, Kerry faced conservative businessman Ray Shamie, who had won the GOP nomination in a stunning upset over longtime national figure Elliot Richardson. Indications that Shamie had picked up primary votes from working-class Democrats, along with Reagan's popularity in lunch-bucket territory, forced Kerry to moderate his image. He played down foreign policy, talked about economics, and muted his anti-war background.

It turned out there was little to worry about. *The Boston Globe* ran articles tying Shamie to the ultra-conservative John Birch Society, and Shamie was not helped when some of his supporters questioned Kerry's loyalty as a U.S. citizen. Kerry took Boston by better than 2-to-1 and defeated Shamie in most other cities, winning with 55 percent overall.

In 1990, Kerry sought a second term amidst a maelstrom of statewide anti-incumbent fervor. Departing Democratic Gov. Michael S. Dukakis' popularity had fallen to subterranean levels and the commonwealth's economy was sinking. Voters' enmity toward Dukakis spilled over onto the overwhelmingly Democratic state Legislature and to others on the public payroll.

Millionaire real estate developer and lawyer Jim Rappaport tried to handcuff Kerry to the Democratic structure under siege. The son of a prominent real estate magnate, Rappaport tapped the family fount to siphon a reported $4.2 million of personal money into his campaign, his first political bid.

Able to battle Kerry on an equal financial footing, Rappaport invested heavily in television advertisements lashing Kerry to Dukakis and accusing Kerry of being a tax-and-spend liberal. His most memorable ad showed a photograph of Dukakis' face slowly metamorphosing into one of Kerry's. His strategy was simple: Persuade voters to think of Dukakis' 1982 running mate as a "Dukakis clone."

But Kerry parried Rappaport's negative ads with ones of his own. His radio and TV ads ridiculed Rappaport for his business affairs in Hawaii and Vermont and accused him of earning business profits at taxpayers' expense. Kerry also ran effective ads highlighting his career. By the end, a race that polls had shown as extremely close in September widened out to a 57-43 percent victory for Kerry.

Committees

Banking, Housing & Urban Affairs (11th of 12 Democrats)
Consumer & Regulatory Affairs; Housing & Urban Affairs

Commerce, Science & Transportation (8th of 11 Democrats)
Aviation; Communications; Science, Technology & Space; National Ocean Policy Study

Foreign Relations (6th of 10 Democrats)
Terrorism, Narcotics & International Operations (chairman); East Asian & Pacific Affairs; Western Hemisphere & Peace Corps Affairs

Small Business (7th of 10 Democrats)
Urban & Minority-Owned Business Development (chairman); Innovation, Technology & Productivity; Rural Economy & Family Farming

Elections

1990 General

John Kerry (D)	1,321,712	(57%)
Jim Rappaport (R)	992,917	(43%)

Previous Winning Percentage: **1984** (55%)

Campaign Finance

	Receipts	Receipts from PACs		Expend-itures
1990				
Kerry (D)	$6,215,076	0		$6,234,887
Rappaport (R)	$5,185,061	$177,205	(3%)	$5,177,801

Key Votes

1991	
Authorize use of force against Iraq	N
1990	
Oppose prohibition of certain semiautomatic weapons	N
Support constitutional amendment on flag desecration	N
Oppose requiring parental notice for minors' abortions	Y
Halt production of B-2 stealth bomber at 13 planes	#
Approve budget that cut spending and raised revenues	N
Pass civil rights bill over Bush veto	Y
1989	
Oppose reduction of SDI funding	N
Oppose barring federal funds for "obscene" art	Y
Allow vote on capital gains tax cut	N

Voting Studies

	Presidential Support		Party Unity		Conservative Coalition	
Year	**S**	**O**	**S**	**O**	**S**	**O**
1990	25	70	85	11	5	86
1989	47	53	86	14	18	82
1988	40	55	88	4	0	92
1987	38	59	89	8	9	84
1986	22	75	85	12	16	79
1985	26	73	91	7	13	87

Interest Group Ratings

Year	ADA	ACU	AFL-CIO	CCUS
1990	94	5	89	18
1989	95	11	100	50
1988	90	0	93	36
1987	85	4	100	25
1986	90	9	93	32
1985	85	5	95	38

1 John Olver (D)

Of Amherst — Elected 1991

Born: Sept. 3, 1936, Honesdale, Pa.

Education: Rensselaer Polytechnic Institute, B.S. 1955; Tufts University, M.S., 1956; Mass. Institute of Technology, Ph.D. 1961.

Occupation: Educator; legislator.

Family: Wife, Rose Richardson; one child.

Religion: Unspecified.

Political Career: Mass. House, 1969-73; Mass. Senate, 1973-91.

The Path to Washington: When voters must replace a legendary politician, no matter how revered, they often seem to pick someone remarkably different. And so, western Massachusetts selected Olver, a lean and angular former chemistry professor, to succeed their beloved Silvio O. Conte, who died Feb. 8, 1991, in his 17th term.

Conte was a native and lifelong resident of blue-collar Pittsfield, a Catholic with immigrant parents who built his influence in Congress through people skills and an entertaining style. Olver, a native of Pennsylvania who first came to the district to join the faculty of the University of Massachusetts at Amherst, is known for his intellect. He took his college degree at age 18, his master's at 19 and, after two years of teaching, got his doctorate in chemistry from the Massachusetts Institute of Technology at 24.

Uncomfortable at times in the media glare, Olver is often awkward with reporters. On the campaign trail he has been known as less than a barnburner with crowds. But he has built a following in the liberal confines of Amherst, where his habits of handball, cross-country skiing and rock-climbing in a purple Grateful Dead T-shirt seem as fitting as Conte's cigar and Red Sox hat did in Pittsfield.

If he lacks charisma, Olver excels in preparation and organization. Throughout the primary and general campaign to succeed Conte, Olver carefully targeted the constituencies most likely to turn out and most likely to favor him.

When he outdistanced a large field in the April 30 primary, he quickly rounded up the endorsements of his rivals to go with those of labor unions, teachers, environmentalists, women's groups and supporters of abortion rights.

Olver's great commonality with Conte is his old-style liberalism. Although a Republican, Conte had one of the more Democratic voting records in either party in the House and opposed GOP presidents more often than not. Olver is expected to take that record at least one step further to the left. Despite his background in science and his governmental focus on finance, he has been known as a social and fiscal liberal.

On the night of his election, he told his cheering supporters: "Compassion still has a place in government.... It isn't all number-crunching and policy papers. People do count."

In the Massachusetts Senate Olver often received perfect voting reviews from the National Organization for Women and unfavorable ratings from the Citizens for Limited Taxation.

He has voted for gay rights, for allowing minors access to abortion, for universal health care, for banning street-corner cigarette giveaways and for an override of the famed ballot proposition that limited taxes and spending in Massachusetts state government.

He also voted against banning prison furloughs for first-degree murderers and against a proposed commendation for Marine Lt. Col. Oliver L. North during the Iran-contra scandal.

Olver was attacked for several of these stands by his opponent in the June 4 special election to succeed Conte, Steven D. Pierce, a 41-year-old former GOP leader in the state House. A lawyer from Westfield, Pierce had been the darling of the state's New Right but lost the GOP gubernatorial primary in 1990.

Pierce moved toward the center in the 1st District contest, emphasizing that his anti-abortion position made exceptions for cases of rape, incest and saving the life of the mother. He also spoke out against the Supreme Court decision barring federal funds for family planning programs that include information on abortion.

But Pierce's main strategy was to tie Olver to former Gov. Michael S. Dukakis. He called Olver, who had been Senate chairman of the Legislature's Taxation Committee, "Dr. Taxes." He said Olver was "one of the boys who stood by silent when the state went down the drain."

Massachusetts 1

West — Berkshire Hills; Pioneer Valley

Extending over parts of five counties, the 1st is the closest thing to a rural district remaining in Massachusetts. It is dominated by small manufacturing centers and placid hill towns set amid woodland. The only heavily developed patch is a string of small cities along the winding Connecticut River, running through the Pioneer Valley on Interstate 91.

While it has significant Italian, Irish, Polish and French-Canadian enclaves, the 1st as a whole is not as heavily ethnic as eastern Massachusetts. Residents of the area west of the Connecticut River often feel cut off from Boston's influence, and this is one of the few parts of New England where as many baseball fans cheer for the New York Yankees as for the Boston Red Sox. It is also an area of the state where Republicans often run well.

All of the territory's cities, primarily redbrick mill towns with industry based on textiles, electrical equipment and light manufacturing, lost residents during the 1970s and early '80s.

Holyoke's loss was somewhat greater than that in Northampton, Pittsfield and North Adams.

The one center of population growth has been Hampshire County, which includes the youth-oriented "five-college" area that is home to the University of Massachusetts and Smith, Mount Holyoke, Amherst and Hampshire colleges.

The district's largest employer, the sprawling General Electric installation in Pittsfield, produces plastics and weapons guidance systems.

The plant's reliance on cyclical military contracts and the gradual shift of GE operations to the Sun Belt keep the local economy alternating between periods of stability and decline.

The second-oldest commercial nuclear-power plant in the nation, the Yankee Atomic plant in isolated Monroe Bridge near the Vermont border, has eased the area's dependence on imported oil, but has been the focus of a local controversy over waste disposal.

Outside the cities, dairy farming remains important to the western Massachusetts economy, although the number of farms is comparatively small. Some tobacco is also grown near the Connecticut border.

Population: 522,540. White 505,906 (97%), Black 6,097 (1%), Other 2,844 (1%). Spanish origin 10,665 (2%). 18 and over 391,008 (75%), 65 and over 66,994 (13%). Median age: 31.

Olver's response was to refuse to run away from his record. He said the money his committee raised went to support social programs for education and the environment that district residents supported. He also made sure voters did not forget the "right wing ideologue" label attached to Pierce in 1990 by GOP rival William F. Weld, who went on to be elected governor.

Olver got into politics at about the point in his academic career when he might have been moving on to another university. He was first elected to the state House in the highly charged political atmosphere of 1968. Four years later, he bucked the national GOP trend by unseating an incumbent Republican state senator in a district once represented by Calvin Coolidge. In the years since he has helped Democrats claim a dominant share of local and state officers in western Massachusetts. As Conte's successor, Olver took that process the ultimate step by becoming the first Democrat to represent the 1st District in Congress since 1893.

Elections

1991 Special Election		
John Olver (D)	70,022	(50%)
Steven D. Pierce (R)	68,052	(48%)
1991 Special Primary		
John Olver (D)	17,897	(31%)
Linda J. Melconian (D)	10,534	(18%)
Christopher J. Hodgkins (D)	10,412	(18%)
Sherwood Guernsey (D)	8,285	(14%)
James G. Collins (D)	6,346	(11%)
Others (D)	4,681	(8%)

District Vote For President

	1988	1984	1980	1976
D	134,252 (58%)	110,691 (49%)	98,141 (43%)	131,832 (56%)
R	96,012 (41%)	115,204 (51%)	92,388 (40%)	94,134 (40%)
I			36,143 (16%)	

2 Richard E. Neal (D)

Of Springfield — Elected 1988

Born: Feb. 14, 1949, Worcester, Mass.
Education: American International College, B.A. 1972; U. of Hartford, M.P.A. 1976.
Occupation: Public official; college lecturer.
Family: Wife, Maureen Conway; four children.
Religion: Roman Catholic.
Political Career: Springfield City Council, 1978-84; mayor of Springfield, 1984-89.
Capitol Office: 437 Cannon Bldg. 20515; 225-5601.

In Washington: Neal spent a quiet first term, learning the ropes on the Banking Committee, building relationships with his colleagues and repeatedly returning to his district. Now that he has rebuffed a strong challenge at home, he can focus his attention on his House career, which could last quite a long time.

On Banking, Neal made friends and strove to impress colleagues with a sober approach to legislating. He took a seat on the Financial Institutions Supervision Subcommittee, which was charged with drafting legislation to bail out insolvent savings and loan institutions and restructure the industry's deposit insurance system. Neal voted to toughen capital standards for savings and loans.

Neal generally voted the Democratic line, but on several high-profile votes, he strayed from the leadership's position. An opponent of abortion, he voted against federal funding for abortions in cases of rape or incest. He also opposed the 1989 pay raise and ethics reform package, as well as the 1990 budget summit agreement. In 1990, he backed constitutional amendments to ban desecration of the flag and to require a balanced federal budget.

He did oppose President Bush's proposed cut in the capital gains tax, preferring a Democratic alternative to restore the tax deductibility of contributions to individual retirement accounts. Neal introduced a bill in the 102nd Congress to restore IRA deductibility.

Neal also advocated re-regulating the cable TV industry, sponsoring a sense of Congress resolution in 1989 and backing reregulation bills in the 101st and 102nd Congresses. In 1990, he introduced a bill aimed at creating jobs for federal prison inmates in an effort to quell disciplinary problems stemming from idleness.

At Home: Neal began his political career in 1972, as co-chairman of George McGovern's presidential campaign in western Massachusetts. After a five-year stint working as an aide to Springfield Mayor William C. Sullivan, Neal in 1977 was elected to the first of the three terms on the City Council.

In 1983, his preparations to challenge Springfield's Democratic mayor helped persuade the incumbent, Theodore E. Dimauro, to retire. Neal then won the office with a landslide margin that he matched in 1985 and 1987. With about 40 percent of the 2nd District's voters living in Springfield and its suburbs, these electoral successes gave Neal a solid base from which to run for the House. During his tenure as mayor, public criticism of Neal was rare, and usually mild; Springfield's one newspaper is very supportive of Neal.

Though Neal was perceived as the likely heir to 36-year veteran Edward P. Boland in the 2nd, his success at clearing the field of serious competition was remarkable, particularly in a state known for its abundance of ambitious pols. By keeping his retirement plans secret until April, Boland made it tougher for other potential candidates to raise money and build an organization. Boland's April announcement was no problem for Neal, though. He had been touring the district's 38 towns and cities for more than a year and had amassed a $200,000 campaign treasury before Boland stepped down. Neal won the Democratic nomination unopposed, and crushed a weak GOP foe.

Heading into 1990, one local politician was grumbling that Neal had an unfair advantage in 1988 — former Mayor Dimauro. He challenged Neal in the Democratic primary, running an angry, bitter campaign that criticized Neal's tenure as mayor and battered the freshman as a Washington insider. But any progress Dimauro made evaporated at the end of August when he admitted spreading a false rumor about one of the region's largest banks. Dimauro said federal regulators had recommended liquidating the troubled Bank of New England, causing the institution's stock to plunge.

Threatened with lawsuits and criminal prosecution and unable to verify his claim, Dimauro retracted his statement, apologized, and blamed and fired his campaign manager. But his credibility was shot. Neal pulverized Dimauro in the primary, winning all but one community. Ironically, in January 1991, federal regulators took over the Bank of New England.

Massachusetts 2

West-Central — Springfield

The 2nd takes in a long stretch of central Massachusetts Yankee villages, binding them with industrial Springfield and Chicopee at one end, and the smaller factory towns of Leominster and Fitchburg at the other. Springfield, an ethnic city and western Massachusetts' commercial center, has about 30 percent of the district's population, heavily French-Canadian, Irish and Polish, and 19 percent black. The district as a whole has the fifth-highest percentage of ethnic French residents in the country.

Springfield's largest employers are the Baystate Medical Center and the Massachusetts Mutual Life Insurance offices, but the city has a variety of manufacturing firms — including Smith & Wesson firearms — and commercial enterprises that attract shoppers from the outlying towns. The city diversified its economy after the mid-1970s' recession and survived the economic downturn of the early 1980s in comparatively good shape, although some smaller manufacturing firms are facing stiff competition from imports. Like many Massachusetts cities, however, Springfield, suffering from cutbacks in state aid, entered the '90s beset by fiscal crisis.

Chicopee, the second-largest city in the district, has begun to climb back after a gloomy decade in the 1970s. Almost a fifth of its population left when several rubber and metals plants closed and the Strategic Air Command closed its Westover Air Force Base bomber field — once the largest on the East Coast. In recent years, however, the city has begun to attract new high-technology industries. Together with Springfield, Chicopee anchors the Democratic vote in the 2nd, outweighing the conservative bent of the rest of the district.

From Springfield and Chicopee, the 2nd reaches north and east past a series of small towns to Fitchburg, near the New Hampshire border. Most of the villages along the way have kept their uncluttered, placid Yankee character, but several are sites for major area employers, such as Milton Bradley games in East Longmeadow and Digital Equipment Corp. in Westminster.

The rural area is fertile ground for Republicans. No town in the district other than Springfield and Chicopee went to Walter F. Mondale in the 1984 presidential contest, and Republican Senate candidate Ray Shamie carried a comfortable majority of the towns in the 2nd. Gov. Michael S. Dukakis could manage only 52 percent in his 1988 presidential bid.

Population: 521,949. White 479,121 (92%), Black 27,543 (5%). Spanish origin 19,408 (4%). 18 and over 377,798 (72%), 65 and over 66,787 (13%). Median age: 31.

Committees

Banking, Finance & Urban Affairs (21st of 31 Democrats)
Domestic Monetary Policy; Financial Institutions Supervision, Regulation & Insurance; Housing & Community Development; International Development, Finance, Trade & Monetary Policy

Small Business (20th of 27 Democrats)
Regulation, Business Opportunity & Energy

Elections

1990 General		
Richard E. Neal (D)	134,152	(100%)
1990 Primary		
Richard E. Neal (D)	51,486	(64%)
Theodore E. Dimauro (D)	29,466	(36%)
1988 General		
Richard E. Neal (D)	156,262	(80%)
Louis R. Godena (I)	38,446	(20%)

District Vote For President

	1988		1984		1980		1976	
D	113,877	(52%)	100,218	(46%)	100,089	(45%)	135,571	(61%)
R	102,349	(47%)	116,729	(54%)	88,677	(40%)	80,355	(36%)
I					29,764	(14%)		

Campaign Finance

	Receipts	Receipts from PACs		Expenditures
1990				
Neal (D)	$462,672	$248,878	(54%)	$534,345
1988				
Neal (D)	$352,265	$87,000	(25%)	$268,094

Key Votes

1991	
Authorize use of force against Iraq	N
1990	
Support constitutional amendment on flag desecration	Y
Pass family and medical leave bill over Bush veto	Y
Reduce SDI funding	+
Allow abortions in overseas military facilities	+
Approve budget summit plan for spending and taxing	N
Approve civil rights bill	Y
1989	
Halt production of B-2 stealth bomber at 13 planes	Y
Oppose capital gains tax cut	Y
Approve federal abortion funding in rape or incest cases	N
Approve pay raise and revision of ethics rules	N
Pass Democratic minimum wage plan over Bush veto	Y

Voting Studies

	Presidential Support		Party Unity		Conservative Coalition	
Year	**S**	**O**	**S**	**O**	**S**	**O**
1990	19	72	85	6	19	72
1989	30	64	88	6	15	83

Interest Group Ratings

Year	ADA	ACU	AFL-CIO	CCUS
1990	83	18	92	29
1989	85	11	100	30

3 Joseph D. Early (D)

Of Worcester — Elected 1974

Born: Jan. 31, 1933, Worcester, Mass.
Education: College of the Holy Cross, B.S. 1955.
Military Service: Navy, 1955-57.
Occupation: Teacher; basketball coach.
Family: Wife, Marilyn Powers; eight children.
Religion: Roman Catholic.
Political Career: Mass. House, 1963-75.
Capitol Office: 2349 Rayburn Bldg. 20515; 225-6101.

In Washington: By Massachusetts standards, Joe Early is a conservative. He is against abortion and busing and skeptical about foreign aid, like most of his blue-collar constituents. But when it comes to labor and domestic spending, Early is a New Deal Democrat, a strong defender of federal spending for education, health and social services.

A portly, rumpled cigar smoker, Early looks the part of a Massachusetts pol. But he does not really act like one. He is a private person who cares more about his issues than about House politics, and he prides himself on his independence from any Democratic faction. Early's was one Massachusetts vote that Thomas P. O'Neill Jr. could not always count on during his 10 years as House Speaker.

But despite having friends in high places and a coveted seat on the Appropriations Committee, Early has kept a remarkably low profile. He held the first Washington press conference of his House career in 1990. "Most of you don't know who I am," he said to the assembled press corps. Indeed, the *Boston Herald* story on the event included a picture of Early with a full head of black hair, something that hasn't been seen in person in a few years.

Early called the conference to express concern about the takeover of the Worcester-based Norton Co. by foreign investors. In a show of unity as rare as an Early news conference, the entire Massachusetts delegation had come together for the session. At the conclusion, an apologetic Early said to his colleagues, "I assure you we won't have another one for another 28 years."

Early rarely speaks out on the House floor, but when he does he can be passionate in support of his New Deal ideals. Shortly after the House repealed the catastrophic health insurance act in 1989, Early expressed his deep disappointment. "We allowed the most affluent of our seniors to pressure us into turning away from 20 million elders who needed these benefits most desperately," he said.

Early also stood apart from the majority of his colleagues early in the 101st Congress when he spoke out for a 51 percent pay raise that was the subject of heated debate around the country. Early lamented the potential loss of judges that would follow the rejection of a federal pay raise, and said that members had to act responsibly rather than bow to public pressure. "You have to look at the intrinsic worth of the job, and you have to show leadership," he said. "A number of years ago in the House we didn't . . . and, in the name of public opinion, sent Marines into Beirut. There were 244 Marines killed. . . . We went with public opinion and were not leaders."

It was O'Neill, then serving as majority leader, who helped Early gain his seat on the Appropriations Committee in 1975. Early devotes almost all of his energies to his work on the committee, and if he is not the most visible member, he is tenacious at lobbying for what he wants, even if it takes some dealing to get it.

On the Labor, Health and Human Services Subcommittee, Early has fought hard against spending cuts in programs ranging from medical school grants to fuel aid for the poor. As tight budgets have put pressure on domestic programs, Early has had to give ground, but he digs in with the persistence of a bulldog if the program cuts affect his district.

Perhaps his most consistent cause has been the National Institutes of Health. Colleagues on Appropriations have said that Early's guardianship is responsible for hundreds of thousands more dollars per year in the NIH budget.

On his other subcommittee, with jurisdiction over the State Department budget, Early is stingier about spending federal money. And on foreign aid issues, outside his subcommittees, he is even more skeptical. He regularly votes to cut U.S. contributions to international organizations and aid to Third World regimes both left and right.

When he was relatively new to the House, Early won a foreign relations dispute in which the odds seemed stacked badly against him. The issue was the U.S. ambassadorship to Ireland. Early favored William Shannon, a *New York Times* columnist who grew up in Worcester. Both Speaker O'Neill and Sen. Edward M.

Massachusetts 3

Central — Worcester

Close to a third of Early's constituents live in Worcester, an old industrial city that belies the faded image commonly held of 19th-century Northeastern manufacturing towns. Worcester started as a textile and wire-making center, but it now has a broadly based economy — focused on the metals and machine-tool industries — that even during the early 1980s recession enabled it to maintain an unemployment figure below the statewide average and far below the national rate.

The Norton Co., the world's largest maker of grinding wheels, is one of Worcester's leading employers. Computer companies have been attracted in recent years to Marlborough and other communities east of Worcester on Interstate 495, the outer highway surrounding Boston. Digital Equipment Co. is in Marlborough, Data General in Westborough.

Three major insurance companies are located in Worcester, as are 10 colleges. Clark University's Public Affairs Research Center has emerged as a major political science institute. Holy Cross, a Jesuit school founded in 1843 as the first Catholic college in New England, towers over the city from a scenic hillside.

To the south of Worcester is the historic Blackstone Valley, which holds a chain of old mill towns — classic company towns like Uxbridge, Dudley, Millville and Whitinsville. But the mills that once darkened the valley's air are defunct now; the area is the poorest in the district, and most of the blue-collar residents who have jobs commute to work in Worcester.

Farther north the towns are wealthier. Some of them look toward Worcester as a commercial and cultural center, while the ones farthest to the east are in the Boston orbit. Sherborn and Holliston are home to high-tech professionals who work along Route 128 or I-495, and the area is Republican; both communities went for George Bush in 1988 and GOP Senate candidate Ray Shamie in 1984. The suburbs closest to Worcester tend to be most amenable to voting Democratic; many of them split their votes in 1984, supporting Ronald Reagan but voting Democratic for the Senate.

At the northern end of the 3rd, small New England towns like Berlin and Stow are surrounded by apple orchards and woods. Voters hold to the Yankee Republicanism that has marked their voting habits for decades.

Population: 521,354. White 504,822 (97%), Black 7,685 (2%), Other 3,408 (1%). Spanish origin 10,736 (2%). 18 and over 376,641 (72%), 65 and over 61,279 (12%). Median age: 31.

Kennedy had their own candidates. But Early worked through the Commerce, Justice, State and Judiciary Appropriations Subcommittee, and President Carter eventually named Shannon to the post.

At Home: Though one would not know it to look at his rounded physique these days, Early first became known to his future constituents in the 1950s as a basketball star at Worcester's College of the Holy Cross. Early was captain of the 1954 Holy Cross team that won the National Invitational Tournament; one of his teammates, Tom Heinsohn, went on to a notable career as a player and coach for the Boston Celtics.

After a brief career as a teacher and basketball coach, Early won a seat in the Massachusetts House. He served there from 1963 to 1975, developing a reputation as a supporter of social programs and organized labor. In his final state House term, he moved up to the vice chairmanship of the Ways and Means Committee, a position that enabled him to play a key role in the passage of legislation providing a minimum income for the elderly.

Well-matched to his blue-collar constituency, Early never had much trouble persuading voters to keep him in Boston. But getting to Washington was a slightly more difficult task.

When Democrat Harold Donohue retired in 1974 after 28 less-than-illustrious years in the House, six Democrats scrambled to take his place. Two of Early's opponents had held major office and had ethnic community support. Former Worcester Mayor Paul V. Mullaney was popular among that city's Irish-Americans; Gerard D'Amico, a youthful member of the Worcester school committee, had Italian-American support. But Early's solid reputation as a Democratic regular in the state House helped him stave off the opposition. In August, he received a critical endorsement from the AFL-CIO. Though Early won the Democratic nomination with just 32 percent of the vote, he finished nearly 7 percentage points ahead of Mullaney, his nearest rival.

In the general election against Republican state Rep. David J. Lionett, Early took the role of the conservative. He opposed the state's new public campaign finance law and supported the death penalty. Lionett had developed a reputation as a liberal and reformer in the Legislature.

Running in a Democratic district in an election year dominated by the Watergate scandal, Early defeated Lionett by more than 18,500 votes. But with an independent candidate siphoning off 12 percent of the total vote, Early won with a plurality of just under 50 percent.

As it turned out, that modest score was no harbinger of long-term difficulties. By 1976, his place in the 3rd District had become entrenched. He has faced no serious opposition since. Five of his eight re-election bids have failed to draw a Republican opponent.

Committees

Appropriations (12th of 37 Democrats)
Commerce, Justice, State & Judiciary; Labor, Health & Human Services, Education & Related Agencies; Treasury, Postal Service & General Government

Elections

1990 General		
Joseph D. Early (D)	150,992	(100%)
1988 General		
Joseph D. Early (D)	191,009	(100%)

Previous Winning Percentages: **1986** (100%) **1984** (67%) **1982** (100%) **1980** (72%) **1978** (75%) **1976** (100%) **1974** (50%)

District Vote For President

	1988	1984	1980	1976
D	120,907 (49%)	97,581 (43%)	91,764 (41%)	135,116 (58%)
R	123,471 (50%)	127,551 (57%)	98,707 (44%)	91,022 (39%)
I			32,720 (15%)	

Campaign Finance

	Receipts	Receipts from PACs	Expend-itures
1990			
Early (D)	$281,707	$86,348 (31%)	$282,012
1988			
Early (D)	$222,053	$93,250 (42%)	$205,989

Key Votes

1991	
Authorize use of force against Iraq	N
1990	
Support constitutional amendment on flag desecration	N
Pass family and medical leave bill over Bush veto	Y
Reduce SDI funding	Y
Allow abortions in overseas military facilities	N
Approve budget summit plan for spending and taxing	N
Approve civil rights bill	Y
1989	
Halt production of B-2 stealth bomber at 13 planes	Y
Oppose capital gains tax cut	N
Approve federal abortion funding in rape or incest cases	N
Approve pay raise and revision of ethics rules	N
Pass Democratic minimum wage plan over Bush veto	Y

Voting Studies

	Presidential Support		Party Unity		Conservative Coalition	
Year	**S**	**O**	**S**	**O**	**S**	**O**
1990	28	67	78	14	35	56
1989	23	69	74	14	27	61
1988	21	66	85	7	11	66
1987	13	72	82	6	23	67
1986	13	80	80	6	16	78
1985	28	69	82	6	11	78
1984	23	62	72	11	12	71
1983	6	83	74	10	17	73
1982	36	52	86	5	19	70
1981	25	62	73	13	24	64

Interest Group Ratings

Year	ADA	ACU	AFL-CIO	CCUS
1990	72	19	82	36
1989	80	20	73	40
1988	85	8	100	36
1987	92	0	94	8
1986	85	14	93	20
1985	80	10	100	21
1984	75	26	73	38
1983	85	18	87	6
1982	80	6	100	17
1981	85	14	87	0

4 Barney Frank (D)

Of Newton — Elected 1980

Born: March 31, 1940, Bayonne, N.J.
Education: Harvard U., B.A. 1962, J.D. 1977.
Occupation: Lawyer.
Family: Single.
Religion: Jewish.
Political Career: Mass. House, 1973-81.
Capitol Office: 2404 Rayburn Bldg. 20515; 225-5931.

In Washington: Less than a year after he was cut down by a sex scandal and rare House reprimand, Frank was not only back on his feet, he had also reaffirmed his status as an effective legislator and leadership ally. Long a liberal spokesman on housing and social issues, he emerged as a key Democratic strategist on defense — a role enhanced by his 1991 appointment to the Budget Committee.

Frank's comeback is a testament to his perseverance, intelligence and hard work, qualities admired across the political spectrum, even by those who disagree with his views and lifestyle.

Frank began the 101st Congress as a rising star. With a quick mind and agile debating style, Frank has always grasped the substance and process of legislation as well as anyone. And his rapid-fire repartee is legend for both its wit and its sting. In the late 1980s, as he gained seniority, Frank added coalition-building to his legislative arsenal. Matching liberalism with hard-nosed pragmatism, he became a trusted emissary between the leadership and House liberals.

Frank's maturation into that role coincided with a more personal evolution. Early in his political career, he was almost defiantly unkempt, renowned for a 1976 campaign poster that boldly declared, "Neatness isn't everything." The appeal worked in his campaigns for the Legislature, but House colleagues found it quirky. In 1984, Frank changed his image with a diet and exercise regime that helped him shed 70 pounds, a new look he polished with a fresh hairstyle and fashionable wardrobe. Then in 1987, he became the first member of Congress to acknowledge voluntarily that he is gay. "I answer every other question I'm asked," he said. "I have nothing to hide, nothing to advertise."

By early 1989, Frank was everywhere, and the self-proclaimed reformer took a high profile in the sharply partisan ethics issues that were dominating congressional business. After then-Speaker Jim Wright became embroiled in a scandal involving a book deal, Frank was among three Democrats to file an ethics complaint against Wright's accuser, Georgian Newt Gingrich, for his publishing deal. In June 1989, when a GOP memo called new Speaker Thomas S. Foley an "out of the liberal closet" Democrat, and compared him to Frank and no one else, Frank vowed that he would name prominent gay Republicans if the GOP didn't "cut the crap." He said later he believed "that if we did not threaten retaliation, they would continue unilateral shelling."

Outside these partisan tiffs, Frank was at the forefront of the Government Operations Committee investigation of the scandal at the Department of Housing and Urban Development. "It seems to me quite clear that this is a case of cashing in on political influence," he chastised one witness. And he griped that the Justice Department was "failing miserably" in its efforts to root out HUD officials involved in influence peddling.

But just then, in August 1989, *The Washington Times* published a story alleging that Frank had hired a male prostitute, Steve Gobie, a felon on probation, as a sexual companion in 1985 and later made the man a household employee.

At a Boston news conference the day the story broke, Frank confirmed many of its details, but he denied that he knew Gobie was running a prostitution business out of Frank's Capitol Hill apartment. Acknowledging that he had written to the parole board on Gobie's behalf, Frank said he fired Gobie when his landlady reported suspicious activity. Later Frank said that he had invoked a congressional privilege to waive parking tickets, some of which Gobie claimed to have gotten.

Frank, the cocky, brainy reformer, found himself before the nation humbly admitting that he had done something "incredibly stupid." Attributing his misconduct to the strain of concealing his homosexuality, he called for an ethics committee investigation of the matter. Frank then went into a self-imposed exile. "I was feeling lousy," he said later, "and I had this fear that I would harm the issues I cared

Massachusetts 4

Boston Suburbs; Fall River

The 4th is a study in contrasts. It is a district that binds the genteel Boston suburbs along its northern boundary to the gritty working-class towns at its southern end. Democrats running in districtwide elections are welcomed in both places, but they need to be sure-footed campaigners, as comfortable in the faded neon-lit taverns of Fall River as they are at catered receptions in Brookline.

Fall River, with its excellent harbor and easy access to water power, was one of the first New England towns to emerge as a textile center. Its mills — which already were being called "time-darkened" in the 1930s — drew French and Portuguese workers during the boom decades before the Great Depression; today, a politician campaigning in the city still needs multilingual literature. Job losses in the needle trades have been partially offset by the growth in high-technology fields.

At the opposite end of the district, but with an even firmer Democratic bent, are Brookline and Newton. These two affluent Boston suburbs long have been a domain for white-collar professionals who like their politics liberal as long as it does not threaten their comfortable way of life. Brookline allows no on-street parking overnight, a rule designed to keep streets clean and outsiders out. In 1988, Brookline got national exposure as the home of Democratic presidential nominee Michael S. Dukakis.

The middle section of the district is more conservative territory, a string of poorer suburbs and working-class communities where social liberalism is not received with the kind of enthusiasm usually accorded it at the northern end. The largest town in this part of the district is Attleboro, whose jewelry trade is giving way to high-technology industries.

Population: 521,995. White 507,211 (97%), Black 5,000 (1%), Other 6,678 (1%). Spanish origin 7,357 (1%). 18 and over 386,245 (74%), 65 and over 66,544 (13%). Median age: 32.

about."

After 11 months of investigation, the ethics panel unanimously recommended Frank be reprimanded for improperly using his office, a decision upheld by the House in a July 1990 vote of 408-18.

Frank did not contest the finding that his actions had brought "discredit" on the House, and ethics committee Chairman Julian C. Dixon made a passionate appeal for the House to sustain the panel's decision, casting the matter as a vote of confidence in the panel itself. A GOP effort to censure Frank was turned back 141-287, and a move to expel him lost 38-390.

Throughout the unusually partisan debate, punctuated by shouting, applause and hissing, Frank sat anxiously in the House chamber, flanked by friends and allies.

But for all the tension of that day, his place as an effective legislator in the House had been long since restored. Just two months after the Gobie scandal broke, Frank had tested a return to legislative give-and-take with floor statements on legal services and reparations for World War II Japanese-American internees.

By mid-November 1989, he was back in the Democratic Party's strategic fold. Frank is credited with being the primary force in persuading Democrats to decouple the HUD reform bill from legislation to expand federal housing. He argued that Democrats needed to move quickly on a reform to avoid charges that the party's outrage about the scandal was mere grandstanding.

His work during two weeks of hasty debate on the reform bill was classic Frank: In whispers and sideline meetings, he made deals with Republicans; in public, he lobbed sarcastic grenades at them. When Banking Committee Republicans balked at an amendment dear to HUD Secretary Jack F. Kemp, Frank chided them for "being excessively harsh" on "their" secretary.

Throughout, Frank was in the driver's seat. He all but guaranteed passage of the HUD reform bill when he backed the GOP effort to bypass the full committee and bring the bill to the House under a procedure that bars amendments. In exchange, he won approval of a Democratic amendment to extend a moratorium on efforts to convert subsidized low-rent projects to upscale units. "I think it's important to have a few hostages on each side," he quipped.

The reform bill passed, and as promised, Congress passed a 1990 housing bill — just the second one in a decade. Frank helped negotiate a critical compromise ending the moratorium on owners' ability to buy out and gentrify their holdings by offering a host of incentives to continue renting to low-income people.

Frank considers his advocacy for poor people one of his primary missions in Congress. During consideration of the savings and loan bailout, he forcefully pushed language to give low-income housing groups first pick at property seized from failed thrifts. As chairman of Administrative Law Subcommittee, he is a stalwart for the Legal Services Corporation.

Frank achieved a significant long-term goal in the 101st Congress, with the rewrite of the McCarthy-era McCarran-Walter Act, which established grounds for denying visas to foreigners, including some based on political ideology or expression. Late in 1987, he won a one-year change in the law, mandating that aliens be judged by their actions rather than their beliefs. In 1990, the change was made permanent. Congress also repealed language that barred people with AIDS from entering the country.

In recent years, Frank has emerged as a liberal sparkplug on defense issues. Until his 1991 assignment to Budget he had no formal post relevant to defense, but he made himself a leading spokesman for liberals inside and outside Congress who want to reduce defense spending in favor of domestic programs.

Frank's effort to scratch the Midgetman missile in 1989 was emblematic of his resourceful legislative style. Though he opposes the rail-MX missile, Frank assumed its deployment was a foregone conclusion, and to defeat its companion missile, the Midgetman, he formed an alliance with conservative Republican Vin Weber, who backs MX but opposes Midgetman.

When their initial effort was defeated by a wide margin, Midgetman supporters who oppose MX piled restrictions on MX funding. That effort infuriated conservatives who supported Midgetman only as part of the administration's two-missile plan. When Armed Services ranking Republican Bill Dickinson offered a motion to delete Midgetman, Frank prowled the aisles signaling to his supporters to vote with the Republican. Midgetman went down by a lopsided margin that day.

Frank played a leading role in passing an ethics bill in 1988. "This is not everybody's favorite piece of legislation," he deadpanned in the midst of tense negotiations to persuade Congress to restrict its own post-government activities, as well as those of administration appointees. In the heat of the election year, the bill won widespread support in Congress, but it was vetoed by Reagan before he left office. Most of the lobbying restrictions were included in the 1989 ethics-pay raise package.

At Home: Frank is capable of shifting on a moment's notice from the language of the Harvard government department to that of old-fashioned ward politics.

He was studying for a Ph.D. in political science when he left Harvard in 1967 to help Democrat Kevin H. White win his first term as Boston's mayor. He became White's executive assistant, establishing ties to local leaders and learning the ways of Boston politics.

In 1972 he learned that the state representative in his area was retiring, and decided to try for the job. His political contacts helped him in the primary, and that November, with a large presidential-election turnout in the district among Boston University students, Frank won the seat. "I'm one of the few people in the country who can say he benefited from George McGovern's coattails," he later commented. Frank compiled an unabashedly liberal record in the legislature, scrapping frequently with its entrenched Democratic leadership.

When Democratic Rep. Robert F. Drinan left Congress in 1980, bowing to the papal prohibition against priests running for office, Frank went for his seat. He had to move into the district to run, but his record in the Legislature and high profile in national liberal Democratic circles won him endorsements from Drinan and many liberal organizations.

Frank won the primary by 5 percentage points. But instead of coasting through the general election, he nearly lost under a last-minute flurry of ads by his little-known GOP opponent attacking his liberal stands in the Legislature.

Two years later, Massachusetts had to lose one House seat in redistricting; hostile former colleagues in the Legislature paired him with GOP Rep. Margaret M. Heckler in a district that drew 70 percent of its vote from Heckler's old territory. "If you asked legislators to draw a map in which Barney Frank would never be a congressman again," he said, "this would be it."

But Frank overcame his initial hesitation. From the beginning of 1982 until Election Day, he pursued Heckler relentlessly, raising money and building steam while she largely rested on her record over eight terms in the House.

Heckler's 1981 votes for President Reagan's economic program gave Frank his issue in the 4th. Hammering at her support for Reagan, appealing to the district's elderly, blue-collar and poor residents, Frank gradually drew former Heckler backers to his side.

Taken aback by his criticism, Heckler kept a low profile most of the year and was highly defensive when she did speak out in public. Her campaign took shape only a month before the election, and consisted largely of attacks on Frank's stands in the Legislature on behalf of homosexuals and the creation of an "adult entertainment" zone in Boston.

But while Frank's 1980 Republican opponent had used that theme with some success, it made little difference in 1982. Frank won by nearly 40,000 votes, surprising even his own managers.

Heckler's departure for Reagan administration appointments as secretary of Health and Human Services and as ambassador to Ireland left district Republicans without a serious threat to Frank. After winning easily in 1984, he ran without Republican opposition in 1986.

If there was any lingering doubt about Frank's popularity in the 4th, his 1988 re-election eliminated it. After he acknowledged publicly in mid-1987 that he is homosexual, Frank prepared for the possibility that his candor about his personal life would generate a political challenge. While his Republican opponent Debra Tucker — a little-known supporter of religious broadcaster Pat Robertson's presidential campaign — tried to make an issue of it, she failed. Frank won with 70 percent.

In 1990, the GOP nominee, Attleboro accountant and lawyer John Soto, had almost no money, no name recognition and no qualms about raising questions over Frank's actions in the Gobie scandal. He said Frank had "failed miserably" to exhibit good judgment and challenged him to undergo a test for AIDS and release the results, as he had. Frank won two-thirds of the vote.

Soto was not Republicans' first choice. After failing to locate a well-known challenger, party leaders boosted Brookline neurologist Jim Nuzzo, a former White House fellow. Soto complained that the state party was unfairly taking sides in a primary, but he had the last laugh: Nuzzo withdrew from the race in June, leaving the nomination to Soto.

Committees

Banking, Finance & Urban Affairs (10th of 31 Democrats)
Financial Institutions Supervision, Regulation & Insurance; Housing & Community Development; International Development, Finance, Trade & Monetary Policy

Budget (19th of 23 Democrats)
Budget Process, Reconciliation & Enforcement; Defense, Foreign Policy & Space; Economic Policy, Projections & Revenues

Judiciary (9th of 21 Democrats)
Administrative Law & Governmental Relations (chairman); Intellectual Property & Judicial Administration

Select Aging (11th of 42 Democrats)
Health & Long-Term Care; Social Security and Women

Elections

1990 General

Barney Frank (D)	143,473	(66%)
John R. Soto (R)	75,454	(34%)

1988 General

Barney Frank (D)	169,729	(70%)
Debra R. Tucker (R)	71,661	(30%)

Previous Winning Percentages: **1986** (89%) **1984** (74%) **1982** (60%) **1980** (52%)

District Vote For President

	1988	1984	1980	1976
D	141,008 (57%)	122,389 (52%)	101,534 (43%)	130,677 (54%)
R	104,853 (42%)	113,540 (48%)	95,429 (40%)	101,713 (42%)
I			38,947 (16%)	

Campaign Finance

	Receipts	Receipts from PACs		Expend-itures
1990				
Frank (D)	$643,920	$220,517	(34%)	$718,160
Soto (R)	$32,078	$2,250	(7%)	$31,903
1988				
Frank (D)	$431,299	$141,635	(33%)	$343,097
Tucker (R)	$34,528	$1,750	(5%)	$34,368

Key Votes

1991	
Authorize use of force against Iraq	N
1990	
Support constitutional amendment on flag desecration	N
Pass family and medical leave bill over Bush veto	Y
Reduce SDI funding	Y
Allow abortions in overseas military facilities	Y
Approve budget summit plan for spending and taxing	N
Approve civil rights bill	Y
1989	
Halt production of B-2 stealth bomber at 13 planes	Y
Oppose capital gains tax cut	Y
Approve federal abortion funding in rape or incest cases	Y
Approve pay raise and revision of ethics rules	N
Pass Democratic minimum wage plan over Bush veto	Y

Voting Studies

	Presidential Support		Party Unity		Conservative Coalition	
Year	**S**	**O**	**S**	**O**	**S**	**O**
1990	19	76	90 †	5 †	11	85
1989	27	72	92	5	10	88
1988	17	79	87	8	0	97
1987	14	79	92	3	12	88
1986	18	81	91	8	12	88
1985	25	74	91	4	5	91
1984	30	66	87	7	8	88
1983	17	82	88	8	9	89
1982	34	62	81	10	15	78
1981	29	64	85	11	9	87

† Not eligible for all recorded votes.

Interest Group Ratings

Year	ADA	ACU	AFL-CIO	CCUS
1990	94	4	100	23
1989	95	7	92	30
1988	100	0	93	21
1987	100	0	94	7
1986	100	0	86	17
1985	100	10	94	23
1984	95	0	69	25
1983	95	0	100	20
1982	90	15	100	30
1981	100	7	87	11

5 Chester G. Atkins (D)

Of Concord — Elected 1984

Born: April 14, 1948, Geneva, Switzerland.
Education: Antioch College, B.A. 1970.
Occupation: Public official.
Family: Wife, Corinne Hobbs; two children.
Religion: Unitarian.
Political Career: Mass. House, 1971-73; Mass. Senate, 1973-85.
Capitol Office: 123 Cannon Bldg. 20515; 225-3411.

In Washington: At the start of the 102nd Congress, Atkins unloaded a seat on the House ethics committee and the chairmanship of the Massachusetts Democratic Party, which had become political millstones. Atkins can now concentrate on an Appropriations Committee assignment that carries more certain rewards.

His next big challenge is to navigate the potential perils of redistricting prior to the 1992 election. Massachusetts lost a House seat in reapportionment, and the remap might not be favorable to Atkins, who already has one of the slighter Democratic districts in the state.

Difficulties during the 101st Congress stalled the quiet rise of this young political veteran. Previously, Atkins had been known as a leadership loyalist, a status that helped him beat out a "star quality" colleague — Massachusetts Democrat Joseph P. Kennedy II — for a "New England seat" on Appropriations. But in his ethics committee assignment, Atkins found himself in 1989 passing judgment on House Speaker Jim Wright of Texas, who was accused of violating a variety of House rules.

Although he once chaired a Massachusetts Senate ethics committee, Atkins (like most members of the panel) was chosen for House ethics mainly because of his reputation as a dependable party insider who would apply ethics standards with restraint. However, he surprised many observers by voting against Wright on a number of charges. He even provided one of two crucial Democratic votes in support of a charge that influenced Wright's June 1989 decision to quit the speakership and the House. Although some members credited Atkins for his independence, others accused him of disloyalty.

Then, in late 1989, the committee took up the case of Massachusetts Democratic Rep. Barney Frank's relationship with a male prostitute. Atkins, citing his political alliance with home-state colleague Frank, disqualified himself from the case.

When the leadership announced plans to re-staff the ethics committee following the 101st Congress, Atkins gladly stepped down. At about the same time, he also resigned as chairman of his state's Democratic Party.

Atkins had won that post in 1977 at the age of 29, and he held it for 13 years, including his first six in Congress. During most of that tenure, Democrats in Massachusetts dominated the congressional delegation, the governorship and the state Legislature to a degree unmatched in any other state.

However, during Atkins' final two years at the helm, things fell apart for the Democrats, due to factors mainly beyond Atkins' control, such as Democratic Gov. Michael S. Dukakis' 1988 presidential defeat and a state fiscal crisis. In 1990, an anti-incumbent mood helped Republican William Weld win to succeed the retiring Dukakis, and the Democrats lost ground in the Legislature; Atkins struggled to hold his own House seat.

Fortunately for Atkins, these problems were offset by positive publicity he had received for his efforts on Appropriations to obtain funding for 5th District projects. In his campaign against a less-experienced Republican opponent in 1990, Atkins — who won an open Appropriations seat in 1988 by a 10-9 vote over Kennedy — flaunted a weighty pile of newspaper clippings about federal grants for local projects that had his fingerprints on them.

Among Atkins' efforts during the 101st Congress was gaining approval for a National Park Service study of wild and scenic river designation for the Sudbury, Assabet and Concord Rivers in his district. A member of Appropriations' Interior Subcommittee, which has funding jurisdiction over the Environmental Protection Agency, Atkins has a strong interest in clean water issues.

In May 1990, he took a swipe at President Bush, who called polluted Boston Harbor a "national disgrace" during his 1988 campaign. "Now, as holder of our highest national office, he has ignored this problem by failing to commit federal resources to the . . . cleanup effort," Atkins said. (Bush proposed Boston Harbor funds in his fiscal 1992 budget, a move cynics attributed to Republican Weld's replacement of Dukakis.)

Massachusetts 5

North — Lowell; Lawrence

Centered around two gritty mill towns where the American textile industry began in the early 19th century, the 5th has seen bad times and, lately, modest renewal. The long-running rivalry of Lowell and Lawrence springs from their different histories as textile centers: Lowell, the model "company town," was carefully watched over by paternalistic Yankee Protestants, while Lawrence's unsafe workplaces and substandard living quarters gave rise to immigrant workers' resentment of the Boston financiers who owned the community. Soon after mill workers won Lawrence's strike of 1912, textile companies began leaving for cheaper labor in the South.

Twenty years ago, both towns were in sad economic shape. Since the mid-1970s, though, Lowell has gained high-technology firms, which, if not recession-proof, at least give the city a modernized economic base. Raytheon employs over 15,000 people in the area — including the facility that produces the Patriot missile.

Massachusetts' high-tech industry boom of the 1980s dwindled as the state's economy has declined. Wang, a computer company that employed 10,000 people in the Lowell area, laid off thousands of employees by the decade's end. Lawrence has profited less from the technology boom, but in the late 1970s new light manufacturing firms began moving into its abandoned mill spaces. Both cities are solidly Democratic.

About half the district's vote is cast in Boston suburbs to the south, including well-to-do communities such as Andover, Concord, Wayland and Sudbury. All gave pluralities to Ronald Reagan in 1980 and 1984 but have strong liberal factions. Concord gave 23 percent to John B. Anderson in 1980. In the 1988 White House race, Michael S. Dukakis carried Concord and Wayland, yet lost Andover and Sudbury to George Bush. Lincoln, as affluent as any of the district's suburbs, chose Walter F. Mondale over Reagan in 1984 and Dukakis over Bush in 1988. Framingham, in the 5th's southwestern corner, blends light manufacturing and middle-class neighborhoods. It went to Carter in 1980, to Reagan in 1984, and to Dukakis in 1988.

Population: 518,313. White 494,365 (95%), Black 7,766 (2%), Other 4,944 (1%). Spanish origin 20,255 (4%). 18 and over 368,925 (71%), 65 and over 53,808 (10%). Median age: 30.

Atkins' Appropriations slot has benefited the 5th District city of Lowell. He has pushed through funding increases for the Lowell National Historical Park, a key to economic development in the once-dying industrial city. Atkins also looks after the interests of Lowell's large population of Cambodian refugees, though he does so at some political risk: There has been ethnic tension in the 5th stemming from the influx of Cambodians, many of whom are financially struggling.

Atkins also faced a rift with some members of the Cambodian community after he changed his stance on U.S. policy toward Cambodia. Atkins had supported a rebel coalition fighting the Vietnamese-backed government that took control of Cambodia in 1979. However, in 1990, Atkins became convinced that the Khmer Rouge — whose regime is blamed for killing more than a million Cambodians during the mid-1970s before being routed from power — was ascendent in the coalition. He backed a State Department move to cut off coalition funding and begin talks with Vietnam. While some of his Cambodian constituents supported this, others accused him of forsaking non-communist elements in the anti-Vietnam force.

One of the leading anti-smoking activists in the House, Atkins has attempted to block efforts by U.S. trade agencies to promote sales of American cigarettes to foreign countries. He has also proposed legislation to ban the sale of cigarettes through vending machines.

At Home: Atkins knew what he wanted early on. In 1970, at age 22, he unseated a Republican state representative. Two years later he defeated a Republican state senator in one of the most expensive legislative campaigns in the state.

As chairman of the state Senate Ethics Committee in 1977, he handled rules changes resulting from the extortion trial of two Senate leaders in a way that convinced the party of his steady hand. He was rewarded in 1979 when Senate President William Bulger named him chairman of the Ways and Means Committee.

Though Atkins had a liberal voting record, his loyalty to Bulger's budget priorities chagrined reform-minded colleagues. But Atkins also promoted real change in the state budget. When tax-slashing Proposition 2½ was passed in 1980, he insisted that state government be cut and savings passed on to municipalities.

As state party chairman, Atkins was in good position to go for Congress in 1984 when the 5th opened up. But his primary turned out to be tougher than expected. His opponent, state Sen. Philip Shea, was a former Golden Gloves boxer whose working-class roots appealed to lunch-bucket Democrats in Lowell and Lawrence. The voting broke down along cultural lines. Atkins' victories in the suburbs and the high-tech town of Framingham enabled him to hold off Shea, who won Lowell, Lawrence and Methuen. In November, Atkins faced Gregory S. Hyatt, who led the fight for Proposition 2½. Hyatt campaigned on his anti-tax record, but Atkins easily won his liberal suburban base and carried Lawrence and Lowell.

In 1986 and 1988, Massachusetts' foundering GOP offered no challenger to Atkins. But in 1990, with the state economy sinking and Democrats — starting with Dukakis — bearing the brunt of the blame, Republicans gave Atkins all he could handle. State Rep. John F. MacGovern, a little-known legislator from the small town of Harvard, challenged Atkins with the same message being employed against Democrats throughout the commonwealth. In reciting the Republican litany of all the evils of the one-party state government, MacGovern targeted Atkins, the party chairman, as the personification of the Democratic menace.

A co-founder of the controversial, conservative off-campus student newspaper, *The Dartmouth Review*, when he attended Dartmouth College, MacGovern portrayed his House race as a battle between conservatism and liberalism, dubbing Atkins a "limousine liberal." He campaigned with a shovel, to symbolize the "housecleaning" he said Massachusetts politics required.

Atkins did not shy from an ideological clash. He attacked MacGovern for his association with *The Dartmouth Review*, whose articles had come under fire as offensive to minorities, women and homosexuals. Atkins ran a radio ad noting the latest flap — a quotation by Adolf Hitler inserted as a prank against the *Review* in the edition published on Yom Kippur — and charging that MacGovern refused to "sever his ties" with the *Review*.

Coming from the least populous part of the 5th, MacGovern had a difficult task in increasing his visibility across the district. His fundraising was sluggish as well. He also had to compete with two high-profile statewide contests, the race for the open governor's seat and the Senate re-election of John Kerry.

MacGovern won about half of the district's communities and almost won Lowell, the 5th's largest city. Boosted by a large margin in Framingham, Atkins scored a 52 percent to 48 percent win.

Committee

Appropriations (31st of 37 Democrats)
Interior; Veterans Affairs, Housing & Urban Development, & Independent Agencies

Elections

1990 General		
Chester G. Atkins (D)	110,232	(52%)
John F. MacGovern (R)	101,017	(48%)
1988 General		
Chester G. Atkins (D)	181,877	(84%)
T. David Hudson (LIBERT)	34,413	(16%)

Previous Winning Percentages: **1986** (100%) **1984** (53%)

District Vote For President

	1988	1984	1980	1976
D	112,301 (47%)	97,882 (43%)	89,068 (40%)	126,779 (55%)
R	120,945 (51%)	129,819 (57%)	100,189 (44%)	96,540 (42%)
I			35,942 (16%)	

Campaign Finance

	Receipts	Receipts from PACs	Expend-itures
1990			
Atkins (D)	$843,893	0	$861,333
MacGovern (R)	$238,736	$33,082 (14%)	$236,851
1988			
Atkins (D)	$359,508	0	$344,978
Hudson (LIBERT)	$15,434	0	$15,396

Key Votes

1991	
Authorize use of force against Iraq	N
1990	
Support constitutional amendment on flag desecration	N
Pass family and medical leave bill over Bush veto	Y
Reduce SDI funding	Y
Allow abortions in overseas military facilities	Y
Approve budget summit plan for spending and taxing	N
Approve civil rights bill	Y
1989	
Halt production of B-2 stealth bomber at 13 planes	Y
Oppose capital gains tax cut	Y
Approve federal abortion funding in rape or incest cases	Y
Approve pay raise and revision of ethics rules	Y
Pass Democratic minimum wage plan over Bush veto	Y

Voting Studies

	Presidential Support		Party Unity		Conservative Coalition	
Year	**S**	**O**	**S**	**O**	**S**	**O**
1990	20	80	93	4	17	83
1989	30	67	95	3	7	93
1988	16	81	96	1	3	97
1987	11	87	93	2	14	86
1986	18	77	86	6	10	88
1985	20	79	86	4	13	82

Interest Group Ratings

Year	ADA	ACU	AFL-CIO	CCUS
1990	89	4	100	21
1989	100	0	92	30
1988	100	0	100	23
1987	96	0	94	7
1986	90	0	92	25
1985	90	5	81	33

6 Nicholas Mavroules (D)

Of Peabody — Elected 1978

Born: Nov. 1, 1929, Peabody, Mass.
Education: Graduated from Peabody H.S., 1947.
Occupation: Personnel supervisor.
Family: Wife, Mary Silva; three children.
Religion: Greek Orthodox.
Political Career: Peabody City Council, 1958-61 and 1964-65; mayor of Peabody, 1968-79; candidate for Peabody City Council, 1955; candidate for mayor of Peabody, 1961.
Capitol Office: 2334 Rayburn Bldg. 20515; 225-8020.

In Washington: Mavroules is not the most liberal member of the Armed Services Committee, and he is by no means a certain vote against Defense Department priorities. Yet the issues on which Mavroules does challenge the Pentagon tend to have a high profile, and he pursues them with a dogged persistence.

During the 1980s' military buildup under President Reagan, Mavroules began a campaign against waste and fraud in the Pentagon: Since the start of the 101st Congress, Mavroules has kept a hot light on the Bush administration's defense bureaucracy as chairman of Armed Services' Investigations Subcommittee.

In January 1991, Defense Secretary Dick Cheney canceled the development of the A-12, an advanced carrier-based bomber program plagued by huge cost overruns. That April, at a subcommittee hearing, Mavroules grilled Pentagon officials about the project's failure.

Mavroules told Capt. Lawrence G. Elberfeld, the Navy officer who had been in charge of the program, that he should have suspected that defense contractors McDonnell Douglas and General Dynamics were "low-balling" when they came in with a bid $1 billion lower than any other. He later questioned the Navy's decision to defer repayment, on grounds of economic hardship, of $1.35 billion Cheney said the contractors owed the government. "The largest previous deferral the subcommittee has been able to uncover was for $11 million," Mavroules said.

During the 1980s, Mavroules headed an Armed Services task force on military procurement and worked on efforts to streamline the defense purchasing process. In 1990, he scored a signal victory; his amendment requiring the Defense Department to turn more of its weapons purchasing responsibilities over to professional procurement specialists passed by a 413-1 vote and was attached to the fiscal 1991 defense authorization bill.

Mavroules also was a leader in the fight to limit production of the multi-warhead MX missile, which he and others viewed as a destabilizing force in the U.S.-Soviet arms race. By lending his credentials as a Democratic moderate, Mavroules helped expand an anti-MX coalition comprising mainly Democrats from the committee's liberal wing.

Mavroules entered the MX debate with the backing of arms control activists in his district and throughout the Boston area. His amendments to block MX production lost by three votes in 1984 and by six votes in 1985. But those on both sides of the issue grew weary of the protracted debate: Mavroules joined the more conservative Democratic Rep. Dave McCurdy of Oklahoma to work out a compromise under which production would be capped at 50 MX missiles. He has since joined supporters of the single-warhead Midgetman missile, billed as an alternative to the MX.

During the 1985 MX vote, Armed Services Chairman Les Aspin sided with Reagan in favor of MX production against the wishes of many members of his own party. This "betrayal" led at the end of the 99th Congress to an attempted coup against Aspin, led by conservative Democratic Rep. Marvin Leath of Texas.

When Aspin lost an initial "no confidence" vote, the low-key Mavroules unexpectedly jumped into the contest as a "liberal alternative" to Leath. But Mavroules finished well out of the running, as Aspin survived the challenge. The mildness of his campaign enabled him to mend fences quickly with Aspin.

When Mavroules comes out against a defense project, it is not a political free throw. The House district he represents has a sizable defense sector; General Electric Co. has a plant in Lynn that makes engines for the Navy's F-18 attack fighters. He first joined Armed Services not as an issues activist, but at the behest of other Massachusetts members who asked him to watch over the state's myriad defense contracting interests.

However, Mavroules has long been an advocate of cushioning the blow of defense cutbacks by providing financial assistance to affected communities and workers. He crafted

Massachusetts 6

North Shore — Lynn; Peabody

The 6th offers chronically depressed mill towns, workaday factory cities, comfortable suburbs, pockets of aristocratic wealth and scenic ocean-front villages. Its vote-heavy areas at the southern end of Essex County are strongly Democratic.

Lynn, historically a shoe-manufacturing center but now the home of a substantial General Electric Co. aircraft engine plant, is the 6th's largest city. Lynn and nearby Peabody, once the world's largest leather-processing city, are conservative Democratic territory. They supported Edward J. King in his 1978 and 1982 Democratic gubernatorial primary battles against the more liberal Michael S. Dukakis. In 1988, when Dukakis ran for president, Lynn and Peabody backed him, although George Bush gathered 48 percent of the district vote. In 1990's gubernatorial contest, Lynn gave 57 percent to John Silber, a Democrat often compared to King.

East of Peabody is Salem, which has similar Democratic roots and dependence on the electronics industry. Salem's image, however, is inextricably tied to Colonial New England's history; it hosted the famous witch trials of the 1690s and later a prosperous port from which Yankee traders set sail for the Orient and Europe.

North of Salem in Essex County, the aristocratic Yankee tradition provides GOP votes, although they have tended to be moderate-to-liberal ones. Yankee Republican William F. Weld, in his 1990 gubernatorial campaign, carried all but a handful of the county's communities.

On the northern coast, maritime interests are central to Gloucester, home of the Fisherman's Memorial landmark, and Rockport, a historic fishing village deluged with tourists and artists in the summer. Newburyport, whose 19th-century clipper ship economy gave way to light manufacturing, is the "Yankee City" singled out for study by sociologists in the 1920s. In recent years it has attracted many urban emigrants. All three went for Dukakis in 1988 but backed Weld in 1990.

Haverhill, on the New Hampshire border, saw its economic base in the shoe industry disintegrate, but in the 1980s more high-technology jobs became available, and the city's lower living costs have lured some younger professionals from Boston.

Population: 518,841. White 508,101 (98%), Black 5,084 (1%). Spanish origin 5,898 (1%). 18 and over 383,191 (74%), 65 and over 68,157 (13%). Median age: 33.

legislation based on his experiences in coordinating relief and job placement efforts during a defense downturn in Lynn.

Mavroules says that when he first proposed his "economic adjustment" concept in 1984, "I couldn't get a [committee] hearing." But by 1990, the combination of tight federal budgets and the Soviet Union's military retrenchment raised the specter of deep defense cutbacks and advanced Mavroules' idea.

Working with Democratic Reps. Sam Gejdenson of Connecticut and Mary Rose Oakar of Ohio, Mavroules proposed a $200 million program, with half the money going to reinforce existing community assistance programs in the Commerce and Defense Departments, the rest to job search and retraining grants to displaced workers. His amendment passed, 288-128.

Mavroules fended off arguments that defense workers were being given unfair advantages over those in other industries. In March 1991, Mavroules cited the success of the U.S.-led military effort against Iraq to justify his position. "As a nation, we cannot just turn our backs on the workers responsible for creating the most powerful defense industrial base in the world," he told a union meeting.

Also a member of the House Intelligence Committee, Mavroules had voted in January 1991 against the resolution authorizing President Bush to use force to end Iraq's occupation of Kuwait, stating, "400,000 American lives are too precious to jeopardize, when staying the course on economic sanctions appears so promising." But when Bush ordered attack the next week, Mavroules backed a resolution of support, saying: "It is more important than ever to stand together as one nation."

At Home: It took Mavroules a while to get settled in this seat, but since 1984, when he won 70 percent, he has won with ease.

As a traditional urban ethnic Democrat, Mavroules has little in common with the Yankee elite that populates much of his district. He learned his politics in Peabody's City Hall, where he served 16 years, first on the City Council and later as mayor.

In 1978, Mavroules sensed that Democratic Rep. Michael J. Harrington had lost his rapport with working-class Democrats. There was a feeling he had spent too much of his career on human rights in Chile rather than on unemployment in Lynn. So Mavroules entered the primary.

Harrington, however, decided to retire rather than fight. Mavroules won the Democratic nomination against a state representative from Lynn and an Essex County commissioner who had Harrington's endorsement, but little else.

That November, Mavroules faced William E. Bronson, a conservative airline pilot making a second try after holding Harrington under 55 percent in 1976. With stronger party backing, Bronson posed a real threat to Mavroules, but he wound up winning with 54 percent. Bronson wanted another chance in 1980, but he lost the GOP primary narrowly to Tom Trimarco, a moderate lawyer with Italian ethnic support.

Viewed as the strongest candidate Republicans had put up in a decade, Trimarco worked hard to tie Mavroules to the Carter administration. He held down Mavroules' margins everywhere outside the old factory towns — Peabody, Salem and Lynn — that were responsible for the Democrat's initial election. Only a 20,000-vote plurality in those three cities allowed Mavroules to win.

Trimarco tried again in 1982, assembling a better-funded and more solidly organized campaign, and gearing his pitch to the blue-collar cities that had helped Mavroules hang on in 1980. Trimarco stressed his working-class origins and tried to put some distance between himself and the Reagan administration.

But Mavroules was stronger. His work in the House against the MX missile had helped him shake his reputation as an old-fashioned party loyalist who initiated little on his own, and gave him appeal along the moderate Republican North Shore. He also used GOP economic policies effectively against Trimarco, winning back Democrats who had defected or sat out in 1980.

Committees

Armed Services (7th of 33 Democrats)
Investigations (chairman); Military Installations & Facilities

Select Intelligence (5th of 12 Democrats)
Oversight & Evaluation

Small Business (5th of 27 Democrats)
SBA, the General Economy & Minority Enterprise Development

Elections

1990 General		
Nicholas Mavroules (D)	149,284	(65%)
Edgar L. Kelley (R)	80,177	(35%)
1988 General		
Nicholas Mavroules (D)	177,643	(70%)
Paul McCarthy (R)	77,186	(30%)

Previous Winning Percentages: **1986** (100%) **1984** (70%) **1982** (58%) **1980** (51%) **1978** (54%)

District Vote For President

	1988	1984	1980	1976
D	131,246 (50%)	110,771 (45%)	94,549 (38%)	132,384 (53%)
R	124,871 (48%)	137,258 (55%)	109,933 (44%)	109,094 (44%)
I			41,896 (17%)	

Campaign Finance

	Receipts	Receipts from PACs	Expend-itures
1990			
Mavroules (D)	$289,794	$119,749 (41%)	$333,912
Kelley (R)	$20,196	$200 (1%)	$19,771
1988			
Mavroules (D)	$349,184	$107,360 (31%)	$337,199
McCarthy (R)	$62,747	$2,865 (5%)	$63,013

Key Votes

1991	
Authorize use of force against Iraq	N
1990	
Support constitutional amendment on flag desecration	N
Pass family and medical leave bill over Bush veto	Y
Reduce SDI funding	Y
Allow abortions in overseas military facilities	N
Approve budget summit plan for spending and taxing	N
Approve civil rights bill	Y
1989	
Halt production of B-2 stealth bomber at 13 planes	N
Oppose capital gains tax cut	Y
Approve federal abortion funding in rape or incest cases	N
Approve pay raise and revision of ethics rules	Y
Pass Democratic minimum wage plan over Bush veto	Y

Voting Studies

	Presidential Support		Party Unity		Conservative Coalition	
Year	S	O	S	O	S	O
1990	23	76	88	5	20	80
1989	37	60	86	8	41	59
1988	24	71	87	4	26	74
1987	21	76	86	3	28	67
1986	19	80	87	5	18	80
1985	20	76	87	6	13	87
1984	33	62	87	8	25	75
1983	21	76	87	7	18	80
1982	40	56	85	7	25	70
1981	36	63	84	14	28	72

Interest Group Ratings

Year	ADA	ACU	AFL-CIO	CCUS
1990	94	8	100	21
1989	85	11	100	40
1988	90	8	100	23
1987	76	0	100	7
1986	85	5	93	24
1985	85	10	94	27
1984	75	4	92	38
1983	85	9	100	20
1982	80	9	100	19
1981	80	7	87	16

7 Edward J. Markey (D)

Of Malden — Elected 1976

Born: July 11, 1946, Malden, Mass.
Education: Boston College, B.A. 1968, J.D. 1972.
Military Service: Army Reserve, 1968-73.
Occupation: Lawyer.
Family: Wife, Susan Blumenthal.
Religion: Roman Catholic.
Political Career: Mass. House, 1973-77.
Capitol Office: 2133 Rayburn Bldg. 20515; 225-2836.

In Washington: Markey became the toast of liberal activists during his early years in Congress, fiercely battling the nuclear-power industry and championing consumer rights. In recent Congresses, however, he has steeped himself in telecommunications and financial issues, where he is known as more of a conciliator.

The shift has left some longtime allies scratching their heads. Consumer activist Ralph Nader told *The Boston Globe* that Markey was "getting on a first-name basis with too many people in the industries he oversees, having too many dinners with them."

But Nader and other consumerists still find much to like in Markey: In 1990, the Consumer Federation of America awarded him one of its annual public service awards.

Currently in his third term as chairman of the Energy and Commerce Committee's important Subcommittee on Telecommunications and Finance, Markey oversees those industries at a time of rapidly evolving changes on Wall Street and in the banking, telephone, broadcast and entertainment industries. Meanwhile, away from the subcommittee, he remains personally committed to the two issues for which he previously was best known, arms control and nuclear power.

A witty, gregarious sort, Markey is quick with an apt one-liner or sound-bite. But he is also conversant in the mind-numbing details of the most complex issues of the day, which come before his subcommittee.

Before 1985, Markey's critics considered him less a legislator than a mouthpiece for the outside groups dedicated to his liberal causes; more conservative House colleagues in particular complained that he preferred the moral high ground to the lowly work of political compromise. But returning to the House that year after an aborted Senate campaign, Markey immediately impressed his skeptics with his willingness and ability to work out deals on legislation important to business.

First as chairman of the Energy Conservation and Power Subcommittee in the 99th Congress, and then as the Telecommunications and Finance head since the 100th, he has proven adept at building consensus. With his affability, evenhanded attention to substance and, most important, his habit of consulting with members individually on pending matters, Markey has co-opted Democrats and Republicans alike.

The business of the subcommittee since Markey's ascension has been business — corporate mergers and hostile takeovers, insider-trading abuses, banking deregulation and, after the October 1987 stock market crash, the whole question of financial markets' regulation.

The controversies pit corporate interests against one another, producing no clear answers about what, if anything, needs to be done and spelling potential stalemate for Congress. But they also lend themselves to compromise more readily than some of Markey's other concerns, such as nuclear issues.

In the flurry of legislative and executive branch activity after the 1987 stock market crash, Markey's panel in 1988 produced the only major statute — increasing civil and criminal penalties for insider trading, providing federal bounties and holding firms accountable for their employees. It was approved unanimously in the House.

Early in the 100th Congress, Markey also cosponsored legislation with full committee Chairman John D. Dingell of Michigan to curtail the most-criticized tactics of both the raiders who capture firms and the corporate managers who defend against takeovers. That effort eventually foundered, but Markey had better luck when, after the stock market crash, he turned to the question of better regulating the market he called a "giant casino."

Markey sought to strengthen the authority of the Securities and Exchange Commission, but acknowledged that legislative action would probably have to wait until the 101st Congress. When the new session got under way, he worked closely with SEC Chairman Richard C. Breeden and the Senate on several bills to strengthen the commission's oversight powers. Many of the reforms were requested by the administration. However, Markey was instrumental in getting

Massachusetts 7

Northern Suburbs — Medford; Malden

A collection of medium-sized communities on the edge of metropolitan Boston, the 7th strings together some of Massachusetts' wealthiest towns and some of its poorest. It is nearly always Democratic territory. Ronald Reagan edged Walter F. Mondale in the 7th in 1984, though very narrowly; Democratic Senate nominee John Kerry took it easily. Four years later, Massachusetts governor and Democratic presidential nominee Michael S. Dukakis won the 7th.

The same Irish and Italian families have lived for generations in towns like Melrose, Malden, Medford and Everett. All four have seen serious decline over the past generation, as their commercial centers have faded away, but the spread of high-technology and service industries has somewhat improved conditions.

Energetic urban improvement efforts have helped Malden, which is at the end of the MBTA's Orange Line and has seen a spurt of office development. The other cities have tried to copy Malden's growth, but have lagged behind.

To the south are Revere and Chelsea, which have had even more severe troubles. Once a resort community for middle- and working-class Bay Staters, Revere's beach area was devastated by a blizzard in 1978. The most significant influx there has been of Vietnamese immigrants, who are drawn by service-sector jobs in downtown Boston and affordable housing in Revere.

Chelsea is one of Massachusetts' poorest cities. Rebuilt after a fire devastated it in 1908, it saw its downtown burn to the ground again in 1973; recovery this time has been slow, although there has been development at both ends of the housing market — subsidized units as well as condominiums.

Reading, Wilmington and Billerica, in the northern part of the district, are bedroom communities filled with second- and third-generation Irish and Italian families whose roots are in Medford or Revere. Old-timers in these one-time summer resort communities have watched with alarm as the towns have been swallowed up by suburban Boston's growth.

The district's upper crust live in Winchester and Lexington. Winchester is the district's Republican enclave. Lexington, however, is not the stronghold of Yankee Republicanism it once was. It can now be depended upon to back liberal Democrats against most opponents from the more conservative side of the GOP.

Population: 523,982. White 511,209 (98%), Black 5,714 (1%), Other 4,310 (1%). Spanish origin 7,538 (1%). 18 and over 387,217 (74%), 65 and over 65,637 (13%). Median age: 32.

the measures through committee and added provisions of his own.

One of Markey's initiatives sought to empower the government to restrict so-called program trading — computer-driven transactions in which large blocks of stock are bought or sold in seconds. The program-trading provision was highly controversial, but the final bill retained the key language Markey had sought.

Markey also passed a bill to regulate the sale of so-called penny stocks, high-risk securities that are appealing to new investors because they sell for only a few dollars per share.

Markey is well placed on Telecommunications and Finance to look after the interests of Massachusetts' many high-tech firms. But he also can use the post to boost consumer causes. A persistent foe of AT&T and a supporter of competitiveness in the telecommunications industry, he had resisted calls to lift court-imposed antitrust restrictions on the business activities of AT&T's former subsidiaries, the regional Bell Telephone companies. Markey doubted the resolve of the Federal Communications Commission to protect consumers from abuses.

However, early in the 102nd Congress, sensing strong member interest and possible court action toward deregulating the so-called Baby Bells, Markey stepped forward with his own legislative solution. Markey's bill called for freeing the Baby Bells to manufacture telecommunications equipment while simultaneously strengthening protections for the companies' existing telephone ratepayers.

Markey also planned to press ahead with his proprosed cable re-regulation measure, claiming that the cable industry is overcharging customers. Cable regulation did clear the House during the 101st, but died in the Senate.

Markey did see another initiative become law in 1990: legislation to limit advertising on children's TV shows and encourage quality programming by making stations' performance a factor in their license renewal. Congress had passed a similar bill previously, only to have it pocket-vetoed by President Ronald Reagan on grounds that it violated the First Amendment.

In the 99th Congress, as both the Energy

Conservation and Power chairman and a member of the Interior Committee's Energy Subcommittee, Markey led the effort to set national energy efficiency standards for major appliances. Though Reagan vetoed it on free-market grounds, the bill was revived early in the 100th Congress with a minor change, and the president signed it into law.

Markey also successfully resolved a battle between private and public utilities over relicensing of hydropower plants. Those utilities have long competed for access to hydropower, but public utilities years ago were given a preference in the licensing process. Markey brokered a bill removing those preferences, and putting greater emphasis on environmental concerns in the licensing process. It became law in 1986.

The Energy Conservation and Power chair also gave Markey an official platform for his crusade against the nuclear-power industry. The climate for Markey's criticisms had improved, particularly in the wake of the Chernobyl nuclear accident in the Soviet Union, and Markey regularly attacked the Nuclear Regulatory Commission, the Energy Department and private companies. He blocked legislation to streamline nuclear-plant licensing and reduce public participation in licensing decisions, pointing to Chernobyl as "a glaring example of the dangers of nuclear power if public pressure for safety is stifled."

At the same time, he pushed legislation to renew and strengthen the controversial Price-Anderson Act, which set up a system for compensating victims of nuclear accidents that limited industry liability to $640 million. Markey and other critics wanted to raise the cap at least tenfold, if not lift it altogether. Faced with strong opposition on his subcommittee, Markey kept the bill alive with a 9-7 vote to send it to the full committee without recommendation.

The committee ultimately approved the higher level, along with Markey's amendment to tie liability limits to inflation, but the bill went no further. Legislation did become law in the 100th Congress, although Markey, who had moved to the Telecommunications chair, had only a supporting role.

His most visible anti-nuclear effort in the 100th Congress was a locally oriented one. He repeatedly tried and failed to pass an amendment that would bar operating licenses for the Seabrook power plant in New Hampshire and the Shoreham plant on Long Island, which were opposed, respectively, by officials in Massachusetts and New York.

In the arms control realm, Markey and a small cadre of liberal arms controllers exploited widespread unease with Reagan's arms policies. They succeeded for three years running, 1986 through 1988, in winning House approval of a ban on nuclear testing, contingent on Soviet restraint. But in all three years, the test ban was dropped under pressure from the Senate, reflecting members' desire to close ranks behind Reagan once he finally had begun arms control talks with Soviet leader Mikhail S. Gorbachev.

In 1988, however, conferees accepted an alternative Markey amendment requiring the Energy Department to devise a non-explosive method of testing the nuclear arsenal's reliability. He had lost in the House, 201-220, but at his prodding Armed Services Committee Chairman Les Aspin of Wisconsin pressed for Markey's provision in the conference.

Markey's earlier arms control efforts centered around opposition to the MX missile and support for a nuclear-weapons freeze resolution, which he first introduced in 1982. During the freeze debate in the 98th Congress, Markey scornfully referred to defense experts as "that elite group of nuclear theologians who have controlled the fate of this Earth."

He put the freeze in more blunt terms than some of its supporters would have liked, telling critics, "You want to build the MX, the Trident II and all the first-strike weapons. We don't want to build them." That rhetoric was ammunition for Reagan's side, which depicted the freeze as a generally anti-defense position. In the end a freeze bill did pass the House, but with amendments making it conditional upon mutual arms reductions by the United States and Soviet Union.

At Home: Markey has restabilized his political base after a surge of political ambition almost cost him his district in 1984.

When Democratic Sen. Paul E. Tsongas decided against running for re-election, Markey was the first Democrat to announce for his seat. His prominence on the nuclear-weapons freeze and on nuclear energy issues had earned him a following of anti-nuclear enthusiasts, and they became the core of his campaign.

But Markey's candidacy did not keep several other prominent contenders from entering the Senate contest, including fellow Rep. James M. Shannon and Lt. Gov. John Kerry. As the campaign heated up, it became clear that despite his high name recognition, Markey was at best an even bet against his chief competitors. Early in May, he decided to drop out of the Senate race and file again for re-election to his House seat.

Markey said he wanted to return to the House to continue working on nuclear arms issues. He told reporters it no longer made sense to him to "go out and scrap for another nine months in the campaign, when I had a chance to advance the freeze in the House." Skeptics pointed out that Markey seemed in danger of losing the state party endorsement to either Shannon or Kerry, who were both staking strong claims to the support of liberal activists.

Markey had to struggle just to win renomination in his district against former state Sen. Samuel Rotondi, a combative campaigner who chose to stay in the House contest, hoping the reaction to Markey's indecision would help his campaign.

"First he was going to be a senator," a Rotondi ad noted, "now he wants to be a congressman some more. It kind of makes you dizzy, doesn't it, seeing Ed Markey twirling around like that." But Markey struck back with charges that Rotondi had received campaign contributions from executives of utility companies and nuclear industries. Rotondi, he said at a debate, "has so much radioactive money in his Federal Election Commission report it glows in the dark."

Markey ended up winning the primary with 54 percent, and a routine victory in the general election. He has not had a primary opponent since.

Before 1984, Markey's only difficult congressional campaign was his first, in 1976. When the critically ill Torbert H. MacDonald announced his retirement that year after serving 21 years in the House, virtually every prominent Democratic officeholder with any political base in Boston's northern suburbs thought about trying to replace him.

It was clear that a primary with a dozen aspirants would be decided mostly by simple name identification. Markey already had quite a bit. He had received a fair amount of attention for his arguments in the Legislature with the Democratic leadership, which had once closed his office and banished him to a desk in the hall. "They can tell me where to sit," Markey boasted, "but they can't tell me where to stand."

The notoriety helped him in the primary, as did his endorsement from Michael J. Harrington, who represented the adjoining area in the Congress. Markey lost three of the four largest towns in the district to favorite sons, but won his own hometown, Malden, and six of the remaining 11. That gave him 21 percent of the vote, enough for a comfortable win.

Committees

Energy & Commerce (5th of 27 Democrats)
Telecommunications & Finance (chairman); Energy & Power

Interior & Insular Affairs (3rd of 29 Democrats)
Energy & the Environment; National Parks & Public Lands; Water, Power & Offshore Energy

Elections

1990 General

Edward J. Markey (D)	155,380	(100%)

1988 General

Edward J. Markey (D)	188,647	(100%)

Previous Winning Percentages: **1986** (100%) **1984** (71%) **1982** (78%) **1980** (100%) **1978** (85%) **1976** (77%)

District Vote For President

	1988	1984	1980	1976
D	133,241 (53%)	121,018 (49%)	103,873 (42%)	138,724 (58%)
R	114,124 (45%)	123,559 (50%)	103,704 (42%)	91,541 (38%)
I			36,344 (15%)	

Campaign Finance

	Receipts	Receipts from PACs	Expend- itures
1990			
Markey (D)	$336,209	0	$207,273
1988			
Markey (D)	$484,319	0	$134,388

Key Votes

1991	
Authorize use of force against Iraq	N
1990	
Support constitutional amendment on flag desecration	N
Pass family and medical leave bill over Bush veto	Y
Reduce SDI funding	Y
Allow abortions in overseas military facilities	Y
Approve budget summit plan for spending and taxing	N
Approve civil rights bill	Y
1989	
Halt production of B-2 stealth bomber at 13 planes	Y
Oppose capital gains tax cut	Y
Approve federal abortion funding in rape or incest cases	Y
Approve pay raise and revision of ethics rules	Y
Pass Democratic minimum wage plan over Bush veto	Y

Voting Studies

	Presidential Support		Party Unity		Conservative Coalition	
Year	**S**	**O**	**S**	**O**	**S**	**O**
1990	15	82	92	2	7	89
1989	28	71	94	1	2	93
1988	17	78	93	3	3	97
1987	13	86	94	1	5	95
1986	11	80	86	5	8	84
1985	23	76	90	4	2	98
1984	17	58	76	3	0	85
1983	21	77	91	6	8	90
1982	32	62	90	3	8	92
1981	34	66	91	8	8	88

Interest Group Ratings

Year	ADA	ACU	AFL-CIO	CCUS
1990	94	4	100	21
1989	100	0	100	40
1988	90	0	100	23
1987	96	0	100	0
1986	95	0	85	13
1985	100	10	100	29
1984	90	5	85	23
1983	90	0	94	20
1982	100	0	100	9
1981	90	0	80	5

8 Joseph P. Kennedy II (D)

Of Boston — Elected 1986

Born: Sept. 24, 1952, Boston, Mass.
Education: U. of Massachusetts, B.A. 1976.
Occupation: Energy company executive.
Family: Divorced; two children.
Religion: Roman Catholic.
Political Career: No previous office.
Capitol Office: 1208 Longworth Bldg. 20515; 225-5111.

In Washington: Brash, impolitic, impetuous, impatient, Kennedy transgressed as many of the House's unwritten rules of comportment in his first two years as a freshman is capable of doing. His reputation as grasping and headstrong was furthered at the end of his first term, when he sought to exploit his family's name and heritage to win a seat on Appropriations.

Now, with a second term behind him, Kennedy still is regarded by many as a member for whom the House is merely a stopover on his way to a bid for statewide office. But he has demonstrated that he can channel his limitless energy into legislative endeavors on the Banking Committee, where he shares with Chairman Henry B. Gonzalez an instinct for helping the poor and minorities.

At the start of his first term, Kennedy asked House leaders for a seat on Energy and Commerce, despite advice that it was a top assignment rarely given to freshmen. He lost.

When Massachusetts Democrats had a chance in late 1988 to fill an Appropriations seat, they leaned toward a young colleague likely to stay put and build clout — Chester G. Atkins. But then Kennedy, who was rumored to be mulling a 1990 bid for governor, announced his candidacy, and a fight was on.

Turning up the pressure on members already torn between loyalty to the Kennedy dynasty and empathy for Atkins or a third candidate (Bruce A. Morrison of Connecticut), the scion employed lobbying from his uncle, Sen. Edward M. Kennedy.

The senator leaned especially on the three non-voting delegates — from the District of Columbia, the Virgin Islands and Puerto Rico — who were included in the New England Democratic caucus, since his nephew did not have much support from the Bay State. The senator also pressed Barbara B. Kennelly of Connecticut, whose father had been national party chairman, thanks to President John F. Kennedy. Joe Kennedy was expected to win by a single vote, but he lost 8-9; a round of finger-pointing for the unknown defector added a final note of bitterness to the whole affair.

Having failed to secure his preferred assignments, Kennedy has pursued his agenda on Banking, particularly its Housing Subcommittee, and to some extent on the Veterans' Affairs panel. He amended Banking's 1987 housing bill to include incentives for units affordable to low-income families. Earlier, he had joined about a dozen members for a cold night on a steam grate to draw attention to the homeless. In 1988, he was active in the panel's work to encourage investment in poor communities by tightening the law against banks' "redlining," the practice of refusing to lend in low-income or minority neighborhoods.

During House consideration in 1989 of a $50 billion bill to refinance and restructure the savings and loan industry, Kennedy offered an amendment to strengthen the anti-redlining laws. The amendment sought to require public disclosure of bank and thrift evaluations under the 1977 law that prohibits redlining, and to require mortgage lenders to report data on applications by race, sex and income level. The Banking Committee had defeated his proposal, prompting him to vote against approving the bill in committee. But the House narrowly adopted it, 214-200, and most of its provisions remained on the bill signed by President Bush.

The primary sticking point on the bailout bill was whether to finance the bailout "off budget," as Bush insisted, thus shielding its cost from the federal budget deficit's tabulation, or "on budget." During committee consideration, Kennedy pressed hard for a short-term, tax-supported financing scheme. One of the reasons he voted against the bill in committee was because it did not include his financing plan.

He was no happier with the financing scheme in 1991, when Congress approved another $30 billion for the salvage of S&Ls. He and Kansas Democrat Jim Slattery sponsored a "pay-as-you-go" method for future financing requests that was intended to force spending cuts or tax increases to pay for further bailout operations and put an end to long-term borrowing. But their amendment was opposed strongly by Republicans as well as by Speaker Thomas

Massachusetts 8

Boston and Suburbs — Cambridge

Ethnic, working-class Cambridge coexists peacefully, if not always sympathetically, with the Harvard-MIT colossus that surrounds it. There is a political cohesiveness that transcends cultural differences — both communities are Democratic and liberal on economic issues.

The cultural divisions, however, are real. Outside the university precincts exists a crowded, grimy city. The proximity of trendy Harvard Square and working-class Central Square makes Cambridge no stranger to town-gown tensions. One former city councilman repeatedly suggested paving over Harvard Yard to relieve the city's parking problems.

With a straight-ticket Democratic voting history, Cambridge gave 74 percent of its vote to George McGovern in the 1972 presidential race — his majority statewide was 54 percent — and gave Walter F. Mondale 76 percent in 1984. Michael S. Dukakis carried the 8th with 66 percent in 1988 presidential voting.

Although Cambridge is the political center of the district, more votes are actually cast within the city of Boston. The inner-city neighborhoods of Allston and Brighton, historically centers for Boston's Jewish community, today have a large transient student population. Harvard Business School, Northeastern University, Harvard Medical School, Boston University and part of Boston College are within its boundaries on the Boston side of the Charles River.

Other areas of Boston included within the district are affluent Back Bay, a symbol of high-income urban gentrification; Beacon Hill, where liberal Democrats live in 18th-century homes built by Federalists; Irish working-class Charlestown; and heavily Italian East Boston.

To the west, the district includes the working-class city of Somerville and middle-class Arlington and Watertown. Suburban Belmont, the home of the John Birch Society's national headquarters, does not have much in common with Birch Society politics; 1984 Republican Senate candidate Ray Shamie, whose past links to the Birch Society won him extensive coverage during the campaign, won only 45 percent there. In 1988 Dukakis took 55 percent in Belmont.

Farther west is the medium-sized city of Waltham, which has its own town-and-gown problems. It has a blue-collar majority, largely Italian, and is also the home of Brandeis University, with an aggressively liberal student and faculty community.

Population: 521,548. White 473,975 (91%), Black 23,901 (5%), Other 15,196 (3%). Spanish origin 15,644 (3%). 18 and over 434,109 (83%), 65 and over 67,920 (13%). Median age: 29.

S. Foley. It was offered on the House floor as one of four alternative bailout options. All four lost, although the Slattery-Kennedy plan was the only one to attract a majority of Democrats. The vote was 186-237. Slattery and Kennedy said they would press their plan again later.

In the 101st Congress, the Banking Committee also worked on the most sweeping overhaul of federal housing programs since 1974. The bill included Kennedy's Community Housing Partnership program, providing $300 million in grants to cities, states and nonprofit groups to rehabilitate, acquire and build low-income housing — and to help low-income families buy homes.

On Veterans' Affairs in the 101st Congress, Kennedy sponsored legislation to make salaries for nurses employed by Veterans Administration hospitals competitive with local labor markets. The bill was signed into law in 1990. He had less success with a veterans' housing measure he sponsored with Pennsylvania Republican Tom Ridge. Their proposed $10 million authorization for the Housing and Veterans Affairs departments to help homeless veterans find affordable housing lost on an 8-17 vote.

During congressional debate in 1991 on authorizing Bush to use force in the Persian Gulf, Kennedy staked out one boundary of discussion. He offered a resolution demanding that Bush wait one year before initiating military action against Iraq.

Kennedy's activities in behalf of Catholics in Protestant Northern Ireland have earned him international repute. In a 1988 visit to Northern Ireland, the Irish Catholic Kennedy traded insults with a British soldier after his car was stopped at gunpoint. In March 1990, he co-chaired a hearing of the Congressional Human Rights Caucus on the case of the so-called "Birmingham Six," six Irish men who said they were unjustly jailed in 1975 after being convicted of bombing British pubs. The Birmingham Six were released in March 1991 after their convictions were overturned.

At Home: Once Kennedy, the eldest son of the late Sen. Robert F. Kennedy, won the 1986 Democratic nomination, there was little doubt he could hold the 8th as long as he wanted. The question then became, how long would he want it? In a December 1987 interview with *The Boston Globe,* Kennedy mused about his political future: "I mean, I know I love the job, but I don't know that it is right for me or my family ... and I am just trying to figure it out."

Throughout his first term, he bristled at suggestions he might run for governor in 1990. Soon after his landslide 1988 House re-election, that speculation intensified when Democratic Gov. Michael S. Dukakis announced he would not seek re-election. In early 1989, Kennedy declared he would not run for governor; he also announced he was separating from his wife.

Being the front-runner in his 1986 House race to replace the retiring incumbent, Speaker Thomas P. O'Neill Jr., did not spare Kennedy a tough campaign. In addition to his familial advantages, Kennedy had attained favorable press on his own as founder of the nonprofit Citizens Energy Corporation, which buys cheap oil wholesale and provides discounts on heating oil to low-income residents of New England.

But in the primary, he became the target for a large field of opponents — and some journalists, who questioned his qualifications. Voters were reminded that Kennedy struggled through high school and graduated from college through the aid of correspondence courses. Stories rehashed the 1973 accident that crippled a passenger in the Jeep Kennedy was driving.

Kennedy's opponents also derided him as an inexperienced newcomer. He was labeled as inarticulate after some stumbling campaign performances; one Boston columnist said Kennedy had "vapor lock on the brain."

But Kennedy grew more sure of himself and the issues. He espoused liberal positions on such matters as health care and education, but positioned himself as the moderate in a field of liberals, supporting the death penalty and assailing unwieldy government bureaucracies.

This centrist move provoked a liberal backlash that fueled the campaign of state Sen. George Bachrach, who became Kennedy's closest rival. But Kennedy's moderate posture appealed to blue-collar voters, including many elderly and longtime Kennedy loyalists.

Kennedy closed with a kick. He was endorsed by O'Neill, by Boston Mayor Raymond Flynn and by the Boston daily newspapers. Carrying working-class wards by huge margins while running even on Bachrach's home turf of Somerville, Kennedy won the 11-candidate primary with a majority of the vote.

In November, the enormous Democratic advantage in the 8th gave Kennedy an easy victory over Republican Clark Abt, the founder of a Cambridge social science research firm, even though Abt spent nearly $600,000. In 1988 and 1990, Kennedy handily won re-election.

Committees

Banking, Finance & Urban Affairs (17th of 31 Democrats)
Financial Institutions Supervision, Regulation & Insurance; Housing & Community Development; International Development, Finance, Trade & Monetary Policy

Select Aging (25th of 42 Democrats)
Health & Long-Term Care

Veterans' Affairs (10th of 21 Democrats)
Hospitals & Health Care; Oversight & Investigations

Elections

1990 General		
Joseph P. Kennedy II (D)	125,479	(72%)
Glenn W. Fiscus (R)	39,310	(23%)
Susan C. Davies (NA)	8,806	(5%)
1988 General		
Joseph P. Kennedy II (D)	165,745	(80%)
Glenn W. Fiscus (R)	40,316	(20%)

Previous Winning Percentage: **1986** (72%)

District Vote For President

	1988	1984	1980	1976
D	141,366 (66%)	144,320 (63%)	106,217 (51%)	134,941 (62%)
R	70,811 (33%)	83,631 (37%)	67,209 (32%)	73,957 (34%)
I			33,656 (16%)	

Campaign Finance

	Receipts	Receipts from PACs		Expend-itures
1990				
Kennedy (D)	$805,013	$108,550	(13%)	$832,815
1988				
Kennedy (D)	$1,678,216	$272,840	(16%)	$1,445,249

Key Votes

1991	
Authorize use of force against Iraq	N
1990	
Support constitutional amendment on flag desecration	N
Pass family and medical leave bill over Bush veto	Y
Reduce SDI funding	Y
Allow abortions in overseas military facilities	Y
Approve budget summit plan for spending and taxing	N
Approve civil rights bill	Y
1989	
Halt production of B-2 stealth bomber at 13 planes	Y
Oppose capital gains tax cut	Y
Approve federal abortion funding in rape or incest cases	Y
Approve pay raise and revision of ethics rules	Y
Pass Democratic minimum wage plan over Bush veto	Y

Voting Studies

	Presidential Support		Party Unity		Conservative Coalition	
Year	**S**	**O**	**S**	**O**	**S**	**O**
1990	21	73	90	4	13	80
1989	23	73	95	4	10	90
1988	18	80	95	3	3	89
1987	14	86	90	5	12	88

Interest Group Ratings

Year	ADA	ACU	AFL-CIO	CCUS
1990	89	4	92	21
1989	95	4	100	40
1988	95	4	100	21
1987	96	9	88	13

9 Joe Moakley (D)

Of Boston — Elected 1972

Born: April 27, 1927, Boston, Mass.
Education: Attended U. of Miami; Suffolk U., J.D. 1956.
Military Service: Navy, 1943-46.
Occupation: Lawyer.
Family: Wife, Evelyn Duffy.
Religion: Roman Catholic.
Political Career: Mass. House, 1953-65; Mass. Senate, 1965-69; Boston City Council, 1971-73; sought Democratic nomination for U.S. House, 1970.
Capitol Office: 221 Cannon Bldg. 20515; 225-8273.

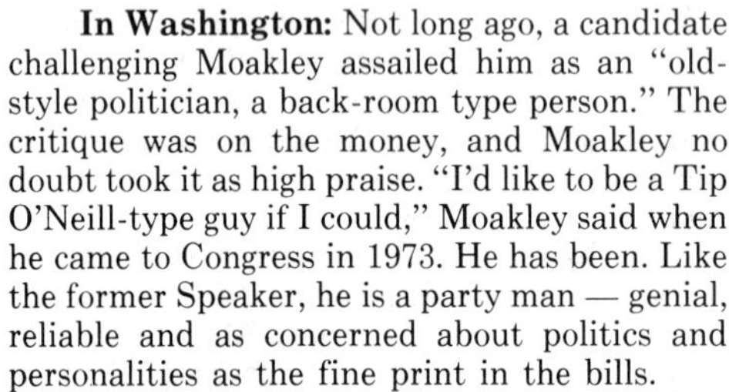

In Washington: Not long ago, a candidate challenging Moakley assailed him as an "old-style politician, a back-room type person." The critique was on the money, and Moakley no doubt took it as high praise. "I'd like to be a Tip O'Neill-type guy if I could," Moakley said when he came to Congress in 1973. He has been. Like the former Speaker, he is a party man — genial, reliable and as concerned about politics and personalities as the fine print in the bills.

These traits have served Moakley well as chairman of the Rules Committee, where process is as important as policy. Moakley ascended to the chairmanship following the May 1989 death Florida Democrat Claude Pepper. The committee is often described as the gatekeeper of the House, because it works in concert with the leadership to control the flow of legislation and set the terms of floor debate. This makes the chairman one of Congress' premier horse-traders.

Moakley's brief tenure as chairman already has set a tone different from that of his strictly partisan predecessor. Moakley's personable style — his humor helps defuse tense situations and make bitter political pills easier to swallow — has helped tame some of the more outspoken Rules Republicans, such as ranking member Gerald B. H. Solomon of New York. "The days of snarling chairmen who look through junior members are long gone," said Moakley at the end of 1990. "To survive, you have to be gracious even when you say no."

Moakley put his words to the test in early 1990, defusing a potentially ugly situation when partisan rancor threatened debate over child-care legislation. Moakley delayed committee votes by a day so Republicans could view the latest version of the measure, agreeing that they had not been given a fair chance to respond. The limits to his bipartisanship were soon clear, though; the committee rejected five GOP amendments on party-line votes the next day.

Often Moakley's work has a local angle; he has used his post to block legislation offensive to Boston's Logan Airport, and he has also looked after New England's financial institutions.

Even Moakley's forays into foreign relations hew to the dictum that all politics are local. Making the district rounds in 1983, he met some constituents working through their church with Salvadoran refugees. Since then, he has been a proponent of granting special immigration status to people immigrating illegally to the United States from the civil wars in El Salvador and Nicaragua. Such a bill passed the House in 1989 but never made it to the Senate.

When Congress passed an immigration overhaul measure in 1990, Moakley fought again for an 18-month stay-of-deportation provision for Salvadorans. The issue pitted Moakley against lead Senate negotiators, who argued against singling out one country for special treatment. But Moakley noted that he had been willing in other years to back off in the interest of whatever immigration bill was on the table. This time, he said, he was not going to budge.

Having won conferees' assent to his provision to stay deportation of Salvadorans, Moakley later helped panicky bill sponsors when they needed another rule that would allow the legislation to be put to a House vote.

For Moakley, tolerance for rights abuses perpetrated by the Salvadoran military reached a breaking point in 1990. Lawmakers from both parties agreed that the character of the issue changed substantially in November 1989, when six Jesuit priests and their two housekeepers were murdered. Eight soldiers were arrested after the execution-style slayings, and there were suspicions that high-ranking officers had prior knowledge of the murders.

Shortly after the slayings, Speaker Thomas S. Foley appointed Moakley to chair a 19-member task force, with a mandate to monitor the Salvadoran government's response to the killings. While focusing on the Jesuits' case, the Moakley task force used its report to denounce what it said were the failures of the Salvadoran judicial and military systems — both of which had been heavily subsidized by U.S. aid. In

Massachusetts 9

Boston; Southern Suburbs

While the 8th District has most of the fashionable neighborhoods of Boston, Moakley's 9th contains some of its tourist spots and most of its workaday precincts.

But more than 50 percent of the district vote is now cast outside Boston, in towns such as Stoughton, Taunton and Bridgewater. All but two of the towns outside Boston in the district went for both President Ronald Reagan and Republican Senate candidate Ray Shamie in 1984. In his 1988 presidential bid, Gov. Michael S. Dukakis carried Taunton and Stoughton but lost Bridgewater to George Bush.

The population of Boston has dipped below the 600,000 mark, and the ethnic character of the city is changing dramatically. White population dropped by 25 percent during the 1970s; in contrast, the number of blacks in Boston grew. By the 1990 census, blacks accounted for 26 percent of the city's population. Blacks and Hispanics together make up about 35 percent of the city.

The inner-city part of the 9th includes the heavily Italian North End; the trendy Waterfront area, where young professionals live; the old West End, where towering high-rises replaced a thriving ethnic community in the 1950s; the Government Center complex; and most of the downtown shopping district. Conversion of the historic Quincy Market into a glittery emporium of upscale merchandise has injected new life into the center city.

Beyond these areas are communities that have experienced serious racial tensions in the recent past. South Boston, still 99 percent white and overwhelmingly Irish, was the center of bitter opposition to school busing in the 1970s. In the 1976 Democratic presidential primary, George C. Wallace had a considerable following in this area.

In recent years, South Boston has seen substantial gentrification near Thomas Park; the condo market for yuppies has made it more difficult for low- and moderate-income families to find affordable housing.

A bit to the west, Roxbury and Mission Hill are predominantly black. Some middle-class blacks have been renovating areas of Roxbury, especially around Dudley Square, but poverty is still widespread.

Neighboring Jamaica Plain, once a predominantly white area, has become an ethnic and racial melting pot with a good number of Central American refugees. It is one of the more politically active sections of the city, with a well-organized network of community and church groups.

Outside Boston, the district is largely middle-class suburban, settled in many places by South Boston emigrants. At its southern end, it takes in towns that have long considered themselves far outside the orbit of the inner city. Taunton, an old industrial city long plagued by high unemployment, reaped some benefits from the high-technology boom of the "Massachusetts miracle" of the 1980s.

Population: 519,226. White 408,101 (79%), Black 82,873 (16%), Other 8,577 (2%). Spanish origin 26,218 (5%). 18 and over 380,987 (73%), 65 and over 63,703 (12%). Median age: 31.

general, the task force said, El Salvador's judicial system did not work. Even Republicans, while challenging some parts of the Moakley report, said most of it was fair.

During debate on a foreign aid authorization measure, lawmakers in 1990 first tackled the El Salvador aid issue. In May, the House approved a Moakley amendment calling for a 50 percent cut in military aid. "Enough is enough," Moakley said in an impassioned speech. "The time to act has come. They killed six priests in cold blood. I stood on the ground where my friends were blown away by men to whom the sanctity of human life bears no meaning — and men who will probably never be brought to justice."

For most of his years on Rules, Moakley's priorities were O'Neill's. But he also showed streaks of independence. Perhaps the most publicized — and personally painful — demonstration of Moakley's independence came early in 1984 during an ugly exchange between the Speaker and conservative "Young Turk" Republicans. O'Neill and Georgia Republican Newt Gingrich engaged in a shouting match, with the Speaker denouncing Gingrich's tactics as "the lowest thing that I have ever seen in my 32 years in Congress."

Recognizing a breach of the prohibition against personal insults on the floor, Republicans demanded that O'Neill be declared out of order. The parliamentarian concurred, and Moakley had no choice but to rule against his friend and mentor, telling O'Neill "that type of characterization should not be used in debate." It was the first time since 1797 that a Speaker had been officially rebuked for his language.

At Home: Moakley is from the same school of party politics as O'Neill, but it took a striking display of independence to elect him to Congress.

Joe Moakley, D-Mass.

Moakley was a state representative by age 25 and knew early on he would like to succeed John W. McCormack in the House. He spent 17 years in the state Legislature, where he specialized in urban affairs and environmental legislation, and waited for McCormack to retire. But when the Democratic Speaker finally stepped down in 1970, Moakley found himself overmatched in the primary against the more visible Louise Day Hicks, who had nearly been elected mayor of Boston three years earlier on an anti-busing platform. With 39 percent of the primary vote, Hicks took the nomination over Moakley and a black attorney and won in November.

Then things began to turn Moakley's way. Hicks lost a second mayoral try in 1971, straining her reputation as a political force, and the next year the district was substantially rearranged. Much of Hicks' South Boston base was removed and replaced with a suburban area where she was not as strong. Moakley, meanwhile, regained a political forum by winning a seat on Boston's City Council.

By 1972 Hicks was highly vulnerable. In the primary she was held to 37 percent; she won renomination only because five other candidates split the opposition.

Moakley was not one of the primary challengers. In the smartest political gamble of his life, he had decided to run as an independent against Hicks in the general election. Insisting he was a lifelong Democrat, he worked to stake out a position well to the incumbent's left. Hicks carried the part of Boston remaining in the district, but by only 192 votes, as Moakley cut into her vote in Irish neighborhoods and swept the black areas. He won the seat with more than 5,000 votes to spare.

Since then, only once has Moakley's re-election tally fallen below 70 percent. In 1982, Republicans drafted state Rep. Deborah R. Cochran, promising to produce her media ads. Though Cochran managed to carry several small towns in Bristol and Plymouth counties, Moakley's urban constituents gave him 74 percent of their vote. His 64 percent total was convincing enough to ward off GOP opposition in the next three elections.

In the anti-incumbent atmosphere of 1990 Massachusetts politics, Moakley, challenged only by an independent, got 71 percent.

Committee

Rules (Chairman)
Legislative Process; Rules of the House

Elections

1990 General

Joe Moakley (D)	124,534	(70%)
Robert W. Horan (I)	52,660	(30%)

1988 General

Joe Moakley (D)	160,799	(100%)

Previous Winning Percentages: **1986** (84%) **1984** (100%) **1982** (64%) **1980** (100%) **1978** (92%) **1976** (70%) **1974** (89%) **1972** (43%)

District Vote For President

	1988	1984	1980	1976
D	115,814 (54%)	110,396 (51%)	89,233 (44%)	118,663 (54%)
R	96,849 (45%)	104,268 (48%)	84,915 (42%)	91,849 (42%)
I			27,255 (13%)	

Campaign Finance

	Receipts	Receipts from PACs	Expend-itures
1990			
Moakley (D)	$512,858	$279,274 (54%)	$318,847
1988			
Moakley (D)	$385,654	$180,830 (47%)	$273,488

Key Votes

1991

Authorize use of force against Iraq	N

1990

Support constitutional amendment on flag desecration	Y
Pass family and medical leave bill over Bush veto	Y
Reduce SDI funding	Y
Allow abortions in overseas military facilities	N
Approve budget summit plan for spending and taxing	Y
Approve civil rights bill	Y

1989

Halt production of B-2 stealth bomber at 13 planes	Y
Oppose capital gains tax cut	Y
Approve federal abortion funding in rape or incest cases	N
Approve pay raise and revision of ethics rules	Y
Pass Democratic minimum wage plan over Bush veto	Y

Voting Studies

	Presidential Support		Party Unity		Conservative Coalition	
Year	S	O	S	O	S	O
1990	24	75	95	4	28	69
1989	31	65	89	4	10	83
1988	21	77	95	3	5	92
1987	19	78	91	1	12	84
1986	16	79	87	3	16	84
1985	23	65	80	4	11	85
1984	29	63	86	5	12	76
1983	22	74	89	5	11	82
1982	39	52	89	5	25	70
1981	36	47	81	8	23	63

Interest Group Ratings

Year	ADA	ACU	AFL-CIO	CCUS
1990	78	4	100	14
1989	95	4	100	44
1988	90	8	100	21
1987	84	5	100	7
1986	85	5	100	18
1985	90	5	100	23
1984	85	4	92	33
1983	80	5	94	21
1982	75	9	100	18
1981	55	7	86	6

10 Gerry E. Studds (D)

Of Cohasset — Elected 1972

Born: May 12, 1937, Mineola, N.Y.
Education: Yale U., B.A. 1959, M.A.T. 1961.
Occupation: High school teacher.
Family: Single.
Religion: Episcopalian.
Political Career: Democratic nominee for U.S. House, 1970.
Capitol Office: 237 Cannon Bldg. 20515; 225-3111.

In Washington: Not long ago, Studds' career looked to be all but over; he was censured by the House, temporarily stripped of a subcommittee chairmanship and threatened at the polls. Now he appears to have put the scandal behind him in Washington, and should have but a short wait before he is eligible to chair the Merchant Marine and Fisheries Committee. His political standing in the 10th is less certain, although he did survive a tough re-election in 1990.

Already well positioned to address a wide range of issues on Merchant Marine and on Foreign Affairs, Studds broadened his legislative territory at the start of the 102nd Congress by joining one of the most active committees in Congress, Energy and Commerce. In doing so, he passed up a chance to take the chairmanship of a Foreign Affairs subcommittee that oversees Central America, a significant area of interest for Studds. (Studds retains a temporary assignment on Foreign Affairs.)

On Energy and Commerce, Studds says he plans to "raise a little hell about why we don't have a national energy policy." He listed other top goals on his new panel as working on national health insurance and on laws to encourage recycling. He also planned to reintroduce with Chairman John D. Dingell legislation giving the Food and Drug Administation control of fish and shellfish inspection. Their attempt to clear a bill solely affecting shellfish died at the end of the 101st Congress.

In seeking and winning a seat on much-coveted Energy and Commerce, Studds demonstrated support within the Democratic Caucus; his bid was an important trial run for his expected attempt to become top man on Merchant Marine once its aging and infirm chairman, Walter B. Jones, relinquishes the chair. Also, in bypassing Foreign Affairs' Western Hemisphere chair in favor of Energy and Commerce, Studds put himself in a position to pursue closer-to-home issues.

As a rookie congressman in the mid-1970s, he decried the tendency of senior members to grow so accustomed to Washington that they lost touch with their districts. Over time, Studds has seemed to become even more oriented toward the parochial concerns of his coastal district — perhaps more than he ever imagined when he arrived in the House as a veteran of the civil rights and antiwar movements.

In part, that is because seniority has put Studds in a powerful position on Merchant Marine, which has jurisdiction over fishing, shipping and boating, ocean and coastal pollution and the Coast Guard — all matters crucial to his constituents. But his assiduous attention to their interests also is a matter of political survival; it has allowed him to survive a scandal that would have toppled many members — his 1983 House censure for sexual misconduct with a young male page.

An experience that would have reshaped the personality of a different member left Studds the same self-confident, argumentative and articulate liberal, just as tough on his opposition as before. "My sexual preference has nothing to do with my ability to do this job well or to do it badly," he said at the height of the controversy. "I'm a good or bad congressman quite apart from my sexual preference." He is still known as one of the funniest members of the House, with a piercing wit that rivals any in the chamber.

The censure briefly cost Studds his base of legislative power as chairman of Merchant Marine's Coast Guard and Navigation Subcommittee. But he got that back after he was re-elected in 1984, and, in 1987, he inherited what he calls "the premier subcommittee," the Fisheries and Wildlife panel.

For now, Fisheries and Wildlife is the most active legislative panel on Merchant Marine and the best spot for Studds to promote not only his district's interests, but also his broader environmental priorities.

On the issue of whether to open Alaska's vast Arctic National Wildlife Refuge to oil exploration, Studds has trod gingerly between environmentalists and his committee chairman. In 1988, in deference to Jones, he moved Jones'

Massachusetts 10

South Shore; Southeast; Cape Cod

While most of Massachusetts showed little population increase in the 1980s, the 10th grew by about 8 percent, as its South Shore suburbs attracted a new generation of Boston commuters and scenic Cape Cod continued its transformation from summertime retreat to year-round residence.

Some of the state's most staunchly Republican areas are in the 10th, including three of the four Massachusetts counties that Richard M. Nixon carried in 1972 — Barnstable, Nantucket and Dukes (Martha's Vineyard). Ronald Reagan's percentage in the 10th outran his statewide showing in 1984, and in 1988, two of the counties in the state carried by George Bush were in the 10th — Barnstable and Plymouth (half of which is in the district).

Lying on Buzzards Bay in Bristol County, New Bedford is the only large city in the district. It became the world's whaling center in the early 19th century and still retains its fishing orientation. The city was a pre-Civil War way station along the "Underground Railroad" that spirited runaway slaves to safety, and now it is home to a large number of illegal immigrants who live amid the city's significant legal migrant population from Portugal and the Cape Verde Islands. Strongly Democratic, New Bedford has always anchored Studds' re-election campaigns.

Plymouth County has seen a steady influx of new residents in recent years, many of them ethnic Bostonians who have resettled in its South Shore towns. Northeast Plymouth County towns such as Norwell, Hanover and Hanson, which voted for Bush in 1988, have been centers of opposition to Studds.

Cape Cod is all in Barnstable County, where every town has seen at least modest growth in recent years, and some have boomed. Overall, the county's population grew by 26 percent to 187,000 people between 1980 and 1990. Along the curve of the Cape lies the sandy National Seashore preserve, a mecca for summer tourists but a lonely winter outpost for seamen in a still vigorous fishing trade. The Cape is largely Republican, although Democrats get a good vote from Studds' home base of Provincetown, an artists' retreat and popular tourist attraction at its tip, and from the towns directly south, Truro and Wellfleet.

The 10th also includes the islands of Nantucket and Martha's Vineyard. Nantucket County provided independent presidential candidate John B. Anderson his highest nationwide showing in 1980, nearly 22 percent, and Dukes County was his third-highest territory, with 21 percent.

Population: 522,200. White 498,543 (96%), Black 7,221 (1%), Other 2,999 (1%). Spanish origin 7,761 (2%). 18 and over 377,639 (72%), 65 and over 77,422 (15%). Median age: 33.

bill to permit limited oil leasing through his subcommittee, though he himself voted against it. Studds supports the argument that whatever oil could be gained in Alaska would be unnecessary if Congress would restore auto fuel-efficiency standards to their pre-Reagan administration level. The 1989 oil spill of the *Exxon Valdez* clouded the immediate prospects for any expansion of oil exploration in Alaska.

The *Valdez* spill helped break a 15-year deadlock over increasing oil spillers' federal liability limits. Studds first introduced oil-spill liability legislation in 1975; in August 1990, President Bush signed a liability bill into law. The bill also would compensate those economically injured by accidents, enhance cleanup efforts and attempt to prevent spills. It contained another longtime Studds goal, mandating double hulls, bottoms or sides on oil vessels, though the shipping industry persuaded members to stretch out the phase-in over 25 years.

Also in the 101st Congress, Studds had an active role in enacting measures to require tuna to be labeled as to whether it was caught by methods that endanger dolphins; to double the acreage of coastal barrier islands that would be barred from federal development aid; and to bar the sale of undersized Canadian lobsters in the United States.

In his first term, Studds enjoyed perhaps his single most important success when he pushed a bill extending U.S. territorial waters to a 200-mile limit, a change the fishing industry felt was essential to fight foreign competition. Later, when President Carter proposed a new U.S.-Canadian fishing treaty, Studds opposed it because his state's fishermen thought it favored Canada. In the 101st Congress, Studds sponsored renewal of the 200-mile limit, adding a requirement that the administration seek an international ban on large-scale driftnet fishing.

In addition to the district-oriented work Studds has done on Merchant Marine over the years, he has protested what he sees as U.S.

military adventurism from his seat on the Foreign Affairs Committee.

His ability to articulate global policy, in a brashly opinionated style spiced with sarcasm and one-liners, made Studds a key player on the panel's left flank — and perhaps the least popular member among Republicans and State Department officials.

He spoke loudly against Reagan administration policies in El Salvador and Nicaragua. Studds visited El Salvador early in 1989 as the country held elections that brought to power the right-wing ARENA party, which has been linked to death-squad activities.

He said afterward he would be watching to see if the new leaders honor human rights; if not, he said he would push to cut off U.S. aid. Speaker Thomas S. Foley named him in December 1989 to a Democratic task force to review U.S. policy toward the country. When the task force discovered continued widespread abuses, and learned that an investigation into the 1989 murders of six Jesuit priests and two women had come to a halt, Studds sponsored an amendment to withhold half of the $85 million U.S. military assistance package to the country. It was approved as part of the fiscal 1991 foreign aid appropriations bill.

Though Studds has worked hard to move beyond the incident, he probably will always be best remembered outside Congress as the member censured in 1983 for having had sex with a 17-year-old male page. He publicly acknowledged his homosexuality and admitted an "error in judgment," but he never apologized. "I do not believe," he said in a prepared statement, "that a relationship which was mutual and voluntary; without coercion; [and] without any preferential treatment express or implied ... constitutes 'improper sexual conduct.'"

In contrast, GOP Rep. Daniel B. Crane of Illinois, who was cited at the same time for having sex with a teenage female page, appeared at a press conference in tears to ask for forgiveness. When the two cases came to the floor, the House voted for censure — a more severe penalty than the reprimand recommended by the ethics committee, but milder than expulsion, which several members demanded.

Censure requires that a member appear before the House to hear the reading of punishment. An emotional Crane faced his colleagues as Speaker Thomas P. O'Neill Jr. read the resolution against him. But Studds stood stoically facing O'Neill, his back to his colleagues. Crane left the chamber after the reading; Studds remained. He later issued a statement thanking his constituents for their support, adding, "All members of Congress are in need of humbling experiences from time to time."

At Home: When he first ran for Congress, many considered Studds much too liberal for a district that had consistently been in the GOP column. But Studds quickly overcame that perceived liability.

In 1984, in the midst of the scandal surrounding his censure for having sex with a male page, Studds again proved his popularity by winning with 56 percent of the vote. By 1988, he was up to 67 percent against Jon L. Bryan, an airline pilot and college professor.

But Bryan never ended his campaign, and in his rematch with Studds in 1990, the tidal wave of anti-incumbent furor in Massachusetts nearly washed Studds out of office.

Bryan made an issue of Studds' personal conduct. "I can't say Mr. Studds is an honorable person," Bryan told *The Boston Globe.* "The fact that he is the only sitting member of Congress who has been censured is surely going to be an issue."

With experience gained in his 1988 campaign, and with strong statewide GOP candidates on the ballot, Bryan was well placed to capitalize on voters' widespread disaffection with state Democrats. Studds spent about twice as much as Bryan, but Bryan carried nearly half of the 10th's cities and towns. Studds ended up with a 53 percent to 47 percent win, and Bryan vowed to run again in 1992.

The son of a Long Island architect, Studds went through a flurry of Washington jobs in the early 1960s before "retiring" to teach in an exclusive boarding school in New Hampshire.

In 1967, motivated by his opposition to the war in Vietnam, he enlisted in Eugene J. McCarthy's presidential campaign and ended up as one of the coordinators of the senator's New Hampshire primary effort. Then he moved to Massachusetts' old 12th District, sensing that incumbent Republican Hastings Keith was potentially vulnerable for 1970.

Studds won a four-way Democratic primary with a clear majority of the vote, while Keith had an ominously hard time winning renomination over moderate state senator William D. Weeks. In the general election, Studds' labor support in New Bedford and antiwar loyalists on Cape Cod brought him tantalizingly close. But Keith won back just enough of Weeks' primary vote in the fall to defeat Studds by 1,522 votes out of nearly 200,000 cast.

Over the next two years, redistricting made the district slightly more Democratic. Keith decided to retire, and Weeks was unopposed for the GOP nomination. Studds never stopped campaigning. He learned Portuguese between elections to communicate better with New Bedford's Portuguese fishing community. He began talking less about Vietnam, although he remained a "peace" candidate, and more about unemployment and President Nixon's economic programs. The outcome was even closer than in 1970 — 1,118 votes — but Studds won.

When Studds returned to the district after his censure in 1983, he embarked on a round of meetings with constituents. His traditional supporters received him warmly, while smaller groups of critics demonstrated outside. Studds waited until early 1984, after the furor subsided, to announce he would run again.

The censure brought out two primary opponents, but only one posed a threat: Plymouth County Sheriff Peter Y. Flynn, a law-and-order Democrat with close ties to the conservative wing of the party. When it became clear he was making no headway, Flynn started denouncing Studds for the incident, accusing him of "seducing a young child." The attacks backfired; Studds carried all but four of the towns in the district on primary day.

In the general election, Studds' opponent was Lewis Crampton, a former official of the Environmental Protection Agency. A boyhood friend of Studds who had once been a community organizer for the Model Cities Program, Crampton scrupulously stayed away from the censure issue except to argue that it had diminished Studds' effectiveness in the House. He cast himself as a fiscal conservative who was moderate on environmental and some foreign policy issues. Like Studds, Crampton supported a nuclear weapons freeze.

Democrats feared that Crampton's moderate approach and freedom from scandal might be enough to overcome Studds' superior organization and past popularity. But Studds was tireless in reassuring voters that his effectiveness was unimpaired, pointing to recent accomplishments on fishing and foreign policy issues. Boosted by his usual massive margins in New Bedford and the coastal communities at the southern end of the district, Studds prevailed.

Committees

Energy & Commerce (24th of 27 Democrats)
Energy & Power; Health & the Environment

Foreign Affairs (20th of 28 Democrats)
Human Rights & International Organizations; Western Hemisphere Affairs

Merchant Marine & Fisheries (2nd of 29 Democrats)
Fisheries & Wildlife Conservation & the Environment (chairman); Coast Guard & Navigation; Merchant Marine

Select Aging (37th of 42 Democrats)
Human Services

Elections

1990 General		
Gerry E. Studds (D)	137,805	(53%)
Jon L. Bryan (R)	120,217	(47%)
1988 General		
Gerry E. Studds (D)	187,178	(67%)
Jon L. Bryan (R)	93,564	(33%)

Previous Winning Percentages: **1986** (65%) **1984** (56%) **1982** (69%) **1980** (73%) **1978** (100%) **1976** (100%) **1974** (75%) **1972** (50%)

District Vote For President

	1988	1984	1980	1976
D	143,938 (51%)	116,933 (45%)	86,914 (35%)	120,609 (51%)
R	136,345 (48%)	142,887 (55%)	118,065 (48%)	110,035 (46%)
I			40,799 (16%)	

Campaign Finance

	Receipts	Receipts from PACs	Expend-itures
1990			
Studds (D)	$600,325	$221,581 (37%)	$620,387
Bryan (R)	$281,651	0	$41,129
1988			
Studds (D)	$243,095	$83,545 (34%)	$235,946
Bryan (R)	$122,953	0	$121,056

Key Votes

1991	
Authorize use of force against Iraq	N
1990	
Support constitutional amendment on flag desecration	N
Pass family and medical leave bill over Bush veto	Y
Reduce SDI funding	Y
Allow abortions in overseas military facilities	Y
Approve budget summit plan for spending and taxing	N
Approve civil rights bill	Y
1989	
Halt production of B-2 stealth bomber at 13 planes	Y
Oppose capital gains tax cut	Y
Approve federal abortion funding in rape or incest cases	Y
Approve pay raise and revision of ethics rules	Y
Pass Democratic minimum wage plan over Bush veto	Y

Voting Studies

	Presidential Support		Party Unity		Conservative Coalition	
Year	**S**	**O**	**S**	**O**	**S**	**O**
1990	18	82	95	4	4	96
1989	27	73	97	2	2	98
1988	16	77	94	4	0	97
1987	12	86	93	2	2	95
1986	16	84	93	3	6	88
1985	21	78	93	3	5	95
1984	23	66	85	5	5	83
1983	18	77	91	5	6	88
1982	32	66	92	8	10	90
1981	33	67	91	9	7	93

Interest Group Ratings

Year	ADA	ACU	AFL-CIO	CCUS
1990	100	4	100	21
1989	100	0	100	40
1988	100	0	100	21
1987	100	0	100	0
1986	95	0	86	19
1985	100	10	100	27
1984	90	0	75	29
1983	85	0	88	32
1982	95	14	95	23
1981	100	7	80	11

11 Brian Donnelly (D)

Of Dorchester — Elected 1978

Born: March 2, 1946, Dorchester, Mass.
Education: Boston U., B.S. 1970.
Occupation: High school teacher and football coach.
Family: Wife, Virginia Norton; two children.
Religion: Roman Catholic.
Political Career: Mass. House, 1973-79, assistant majority leader, 1977-79.
Capitol Office: 2229 Rayburn Bldg. 20515; 225-3215.

In Washington: After 12 years in the House, Donnelly may not be as well-known as some of his classmates, but his name is practically a household word in Ireland. A 1986 law he sponsored eased immigration restrictions on the Irish and created "Donnelly visas," allowing thousands to settle legally in the United States. (A version of Donnelly's program was reauthorized in the 1990 legal-immigration bill.)

That has made his name so well-known that an *Irish Times* columnist saw fit to quote a U.S. official deflating any notion that Donnelly would be a presidential candidate. In 1990 the *Irish Voice* newspaper and *Irish America* magazine named him Irish-American of the year.

Donnelly's involvement in immigration is not a matter of foreign affairs; it is constituent service; his district includes one of the largest populations of Irish emigrants in the country.

Proud of his roots in the Irish-American neighborhood of Dorchester — he has been known to send colleagues gift bottles of Ballygowan Irish Mineral Water — Donnelly likes to present himself as a streetwise working-class Democrat who keeps some social distance from the liberal intellectuals who make up most of the junior generation of his party.

A solid Democrat and no stranger to the liberal positions generally associated with Massachusetts lawmakers, Donnelly has a streak of blue-collar conservatism. Along with his consistent opposition to abortion, he has backed a constitutional amendment to ban physical desecration of the flag. He gets among the lowest ratings of all Massachusetts Democrats from the liberal Americans for Democratic Action. And he has voiced skepticism about the direction of his party. "We have become the party of the gays, the abortionists, the far-out feminists, you name it," he once said.

Donnelly is involved with some of the most sensitive and difficult national policy issues as a member of Ways and Means. Although he generally has good relations with Chairman Dan Rostenkowski of Illinois, Donnelly is an independent operator who can be unpredictable.

He broke with the committee and the majority of his party during the House's 1987 debate on catastrophic health insurance for Medicare beneficiaries. And when senior citizens' groups lobbied for the bill's repeal after it passed, Donnelly led the charge.

He was one of 15 Democrats to vote against the House version of the bill, after having failed in committee to redirect it from capping hospital-related costs to coverage of what many elderly consider a much greater threat to their financial well being: long-term care outside the hospital. "To call this legislation catastrophic protection is a misnomer," he said. "It was too quickly put together and costs too much for the benefits it offers."

Donnelly was prescient in warning that because the bill made the elderly bear the cost of the new benefits through higher premiums, Congress would be pressured to repeal it. Within a year after the law's enactment, the elderly were up in arms over the premiums.

Expressing exasperation at the political pounding the bill was taking, Donnelly said, "If senior citizens really want the program to go away, then fine, we'll make it go away." In 1989, he teamed with Ways and Means Democrats Marty Russo of Illinois and Barbara B. Kennelly of Connecticut — former supporters of the program — and Republicans Bill Archer of Texas and Hank Brown of Colorado, to propose an amendment to repeal it.

Under pressure from the Rules Committee, Donnelly and Archer altered their proposal to retain the 1988 law's expansions of Medicaid coverage for low-income elderly people and for pregnant women and infants. That made a repeal vote more palatable. Donnelly's repeal amendment, attached to the fiscal 1990 budget reconciliation bill, was adopted 360-66.

Donnelly's high-profile role in the catastrophic-repeal debate led him to stray temporarily out of character; he prefers anonymity to the celebrity of his better-known Bay State colleagues. On the Health Subcommittee, he tinkers with existing health policy, such as revising Medicare billing and payment rules.

In the 101st Congress, he put together a

Massachusetts 11

Part of Boston and South Shore Suburbs

A forgotten part of Massachusetts in the southern corner of Boston and the suburbs beyond, the 11th has watched as the economic development that has revitalized other communities has passed around it. The inflow of real estate capital and investment enjoyed by neighborhoods closer to downtown has yet to reach the four Boston wards of the 11th District, and the high-technology belt that surrounds the city ends just outside the district's border.

At the same time, the district has avoided much of the social dislocation that other areas of the state have undergone. Populated by blue-collar workers and their families, it remains one of the most Irish districts in the country. In the Boston part of the 11th, covering Dorchester, Hyde Park, Neponset and Mattapan, many middle-aged adults live within a few blocks of where they were born and raised. Most of the suburbanites still have family in the city neighborhoods. Boston's recent wave of yuppie gentrification has come to Dorchester.

The South Shore suburb of Quincy is the largest community in Norfolk County. It is heavily ethnic, with Irish, Italian and French-Canadian pockets. The century-old Quincy Shipyard along the Fore River was dealt a fatal blow in 1986 by General Dynamics' decision to close its operations, a move that cost thousands of jobs. The Massachusetts Water Resources Authority bought the property in 1987. President Reagan managed a 900-vote victory in the city in 1984, but generally Democrats have little to worry about in Quincy. Still, Gov. Michael S. Dukakis, his popularity on the wane, managed only 51 percent in Quincy in his 1988 presidential bid.

Brockton, with 95,000 residents, is the largest city in Plymouth County, and was long the shoemaking center of the nation. Then named North Bridgewater, it shod half the Union Army in the Civil War. But the city's footwear industry has been in decline for a generation. Reagan and George Bush carried Brockton in 1984 and 1988. Brockton voted narrowly for Democrat John Silber for governor in 1990.

Population: 525,089. White 471,482 (90%), Black 42,395 (8%), Other 3,731 (1%). Spanish origin 9,563 (2%). 18 and over 382,888 (73%), 65 and over 68,280 (13%). Median age: 31.

proposal under which Medicare's optional Part B would pay less for durable medical equipment such as wheelchairs. The fiscal 1990 reconciliation bill froze payments at 1989 levels; the fiscal 1991 bill reduced payments.

As a member of Ways and Means, Donnelly can be territorial when his district is affected. He showed a willingness to challenge Rostenkowski, a usual ally, during debate on the tax-revision bill in 1985. "I can't walk out on the floor with a bill that puts New England, or my slice of New England, at a competitive disadvantage," Donnelly said. "Everyone is saying in the back of their minds, 'If they get theirs, what do we get?' "

One of Donnelly's efforts during the tax debate was on behalf of General Dynamics' now-closed Quincy Shipyard. Rostenkowski and President Reagan proposed eliminating a deduction for funds set aside by shipowners for building commercial ships, but Donnelly pushed successfully for retaining the tax break.

The Massachusetts Water Resources Authority (MWRA), the agency in charge of the Boston Harbor cleanup, bought the property of the closed shipyard in 1987 to use as a staging area for construction of a sewage treatment plant. But after Gov. Michael S. Dukakis recommended that the agency site its headquarters in the Roxbury section of Boston, Donnelly introduced a bill to prohibit the agency from issuing tax-exempt bonds unless it sited its headquarters in Quincy. In the end, the MWRA renewed its lease at the Charlestown Navy Yard, indefinitely deferring any move.

During his years on Ways and Means, Donnelly has shown interest in regulating the use of tax-exempt revenue bonds — an interest dating back to his years as a state legislator at a time when Massachusetts was one of the largest issuers of such bonds. In the 101st Congress he introduced several bills that would have imposed restrictions on the use of tax-exempt bonds. "Tax-free bonds are not a God-given right," he told The Bond Buyer, a municipal bond trade journal, "but a gratuity from the taxpayer to do things in the public interest."

In 1989, Donnelly won passage of his bill to set up a procedure for awarding posthumous U.S. citizenship to aliens who die while on active duty with the U.S. armed forces, though it barred survivors from receiving any benefits resulting from the new status. Donnelly said his interest in the legislation dated to 1984, when he filed a private bill on behalf of a resident alien from Scotland who lived in his district and was killed in the Vietnam war.

Donnelly has matured steadily as a legislator. As a freshman, he failed to win a choice committee assignment because he did not ask then-Speaker Thomas P. O'Neill Jr. to give him one. But he made it to the Budget Committee in his second term, then left in 1985 for Ways and Means. Meanwhile, Speaker Jim Wright appointed him to the influential Steering and Policy Committee, the panel that makes committee assignments, in 1987 and again in 1989.

On the Budget Committee, Donnelly worked closely with the liberal Democratic bloc, questioning Reagan administration spending cuts. But his conservative streak showed when it came to federal entitlement programs, which he considers a huge source of waste.

At Home: Donnelly owes his House seat largely to support from James A. Burke, his Democratic predecessor, and former state Sen. Joseph Timilty, an influential Dorchester Democrat. Their endorsements in the 1978 primary identified Donnelly as the choice of party loyalists determined to keep the district away from Patrick McCarthy, a liberal maverick. McCarthy challenged Burke's renomination in 1976, and the aging incumbent wanted to make sure the young "upstart" failed on his second try.

Among the six Democrats who entered the primary to succeed Burke, Donnelly had the best base of support in the Boston part of the district. For six years, he had represented about a fifth of that section in the Legislature. He was assistant House majority leader for three years.

Donnelly's first endorsement came from Timilty, a locally popular legislator who had run for mayor three years before. When Burke added his public backing, it was over for McCarthy and the other four candidates. Donnelly carried the four Boston wards by a 6-to-1 margin and won 43 percent districtwide, to McCarthy's second-place 20 percent.

Although Donnelly has yet to reach the level of personal popularity that Burke enjoyed, his careful attention to constituents has achieved the same political results. In most re-elections, he has run unopposed.

In 1984, Donnelly toyed with running for the Senate seat being vacated by Democrat Paul E. Tsongas. But he backed off, judging that his centrist record was an obstacle in the face of what he called "the machinelike dominance of would-be party bosses" — the liberal Dukakis wing of the state Democratic Party.

Committee

Ways & Means (17th of 23 Democrats)
Health; Select Revenue Measures

Elections

1990 General		
Brian Donnelly (D)	145,480	(100%)
1988 General		
Brian Donnelly (D)	169,692	(81%)
Michael C. Gilleran (R)	40,277	(19%)

Previous Winning Percentages: **1986** (100%) **1984** (100%) **1982** (100%) **1980** (100%) **1978** (92%)

District Vote For President

	1988	1984	1980	1976
D	113,465 (51%)	107,407 (48%)	92,420 (42%)	124,179 (56%)
R	104,005 (47%)	116,490 (52%)	98,415 (44%)	90,036 (40%)
I			29,073 (13%)	

Campaign Finance

	Receipts	Receipts from PACs	Expend-itures
1990			
Donnelly (D)	$303,943	$168,850 (56%)	$104,221
1988			
Donnelly (D)	$264,323	$131,300 (50%)	$167,960
Gilleran (R)	$18,687	$500 (3%)	$18,090

Key Votes

1991	
Authorize use of force against Iraq	N
1990	
Support constitutional amendment on flag desecration	Y
Pass family and medical leave bill over Bush veto	N
Reduce SDI funding	Y
Allow abortions in overseas military facilities	N
Approve budget summit plan for spending and taxing	N
Approve civil rights bill	Y
1989	
Halt production of B-2 stealth bomber at 13 planes	N
Oppose capital gains tax cut	Y
Approve federal abortion funding in rape or incest cases	N
Approve pay raise and revision of ethics rules	Y
Pass Democratic minimum wage plan over Bush veto	Y

Voting Studies

	Presidential Support		Party Unity		Conservative Coalition	
Year	**S**	**O**	**S**	**O**	**S**	**O**
1990	26	71	82	10	35	56
1989	33	63	85	9	37	61
1988	15	69	86	8	18	66
1987	20	74	83	8	35	60
1986	18	79	86	4	18	82
1985	26	74	90	6	24	73
1984	35	56	83	7	24	71
1983	17	80	84	12	22	75
1982	38	60	84	13	33	60
1981	33	55	81	10	25	63

Interest Group Ratings

Year	ADA	ACU	AFL-CIO	CCUS
1990	61	29	83	36
1989	75	12	92	30
1988	80	8	100	23
1987	76	5	94	21
1986	75	14	93	29
1985	80	5	100	23
1984	80	8	92	27
1983	80	9	88	20
1982	80	14	95	30
1981	65	14	93	0

Michigan

U.S. CONGRESS

SENATE 2 D
HOUSE 11 D, 7 R

LEGISLATURE

Senate 18 D, 20 R
House 61 D, 49 R

ELECTIONS

1988 Presidential Vote

Bush	54%
Dukakis	46%

1984 Presidential Vote

Reagan	59%
Mondale	40%

1980 Presidential Vote

Reagan	49%
Carter	43%
Anderson	7%

Turnout rate in 1986	35%
Turnout rate in 1988	54%
Turnout rate in 1990	35%

(as percentage of voting age population)

POPULATION AND GROWTH

1980 population	9,262,078
1990 population (8th in the nation)	9,292,297
Percent change 1980-1990	0%

DEMOGRAPHIC BREAKDOWN

White	83%
Black	14%
Asian or Pacific Islander	1%
(Hispanic origin)	2%
Urban	71%
Rural	29%
Born in state	72%
Foreign-born	5%

MAJOR CITIES

Detroit	1,027,974
Grand Rapids	189,126
Warren	144,864
Flint	140,761
Lansing	127,321

AREA AND LAND USE

Area 56,954 sq. miles (22nd)

Farm	30%
Forest	50%
Federally owned	10%

Gov. John Engler (R)
Of Mt. Pleasant — Elected 1990

Born: Oct. 12, 1948, Mt. Pleasant, Mich.
Education: Michigan State U., B.S. 1971; Thomas Cooley School of Law, J.D. 1981.
Occupation: Lawyer.
Religion: Roman Catholic.
Political Career: Mich. House, 1971-79; Mich Senate, 1979-91, majority leader, 1984-91.
Next Election: 1994.

WORK

Occupations

White-collar	51%
Blue-collar	34%
Service workers	14%

Government Workers

Federal	57,761
State	163,664
Local	386,511

MONEY

Median family income	$ 22,107	(8th)
Tax burden per capita	$ 956	(18th)

EDUCATION

Spending per pupil through grade 12	$ 4,692	(14th)
Persons with college degrees	14%	(35th)

CRIME

Violent crime rate 709 per 100,000 (9th)

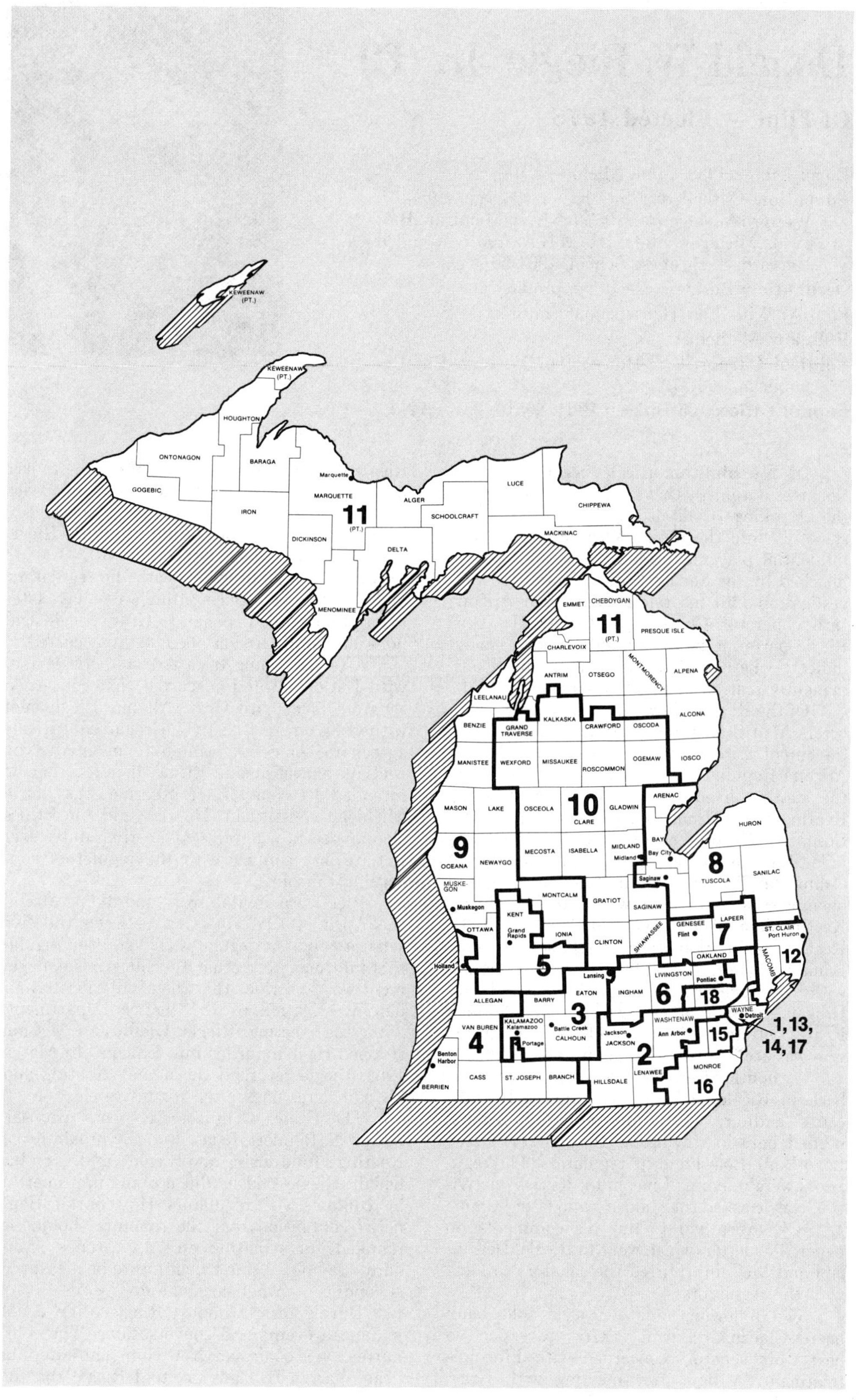
KEWEENAW (PT.)
KEWEENAW (PT.)
HOUGHTON
ONTONAGON
BARAGA
GOGEBIC
Marquette
MARQUETTE
IRON
11 (PT.)
ALGER
LUCE
CHIPPEWA
SCHOOLCRAFT
DICKINSON
DELTA
MACKINAC
MENOMINEE
EMMET
CHEBOYGAN
11 (PT.)
PRESQUE ISLE
CHARLEVOIX
ANTRIM
OTSEGO
MONTMORENCY
ALPENA
LEELANAU
KALKASKA
BENZIE
GRAND TRAVERSE
CRAWFORD
OSCODA
ALCONA
MANISTEE
WEXFORD
MISSAUKEE
ROSCOMMON
OGEMAW
IOSCO
ARENAC
MASON
LAKE
OSCEOLA
10
CLARE
GLADWIN
HURON
9
OCEANA
NEWAYGO
MECOSTA
ISABELLA
MIDLAND
Midland
BAY
Bay City
8
TUSCOLA
SANILAC
Saginaw
MUSKE-GON
Muskegon
MONTCALM
GRATIOT
SAGINAW
KENT
Grand Rapids
OTTAWA
IONIA
CLINTON
SHIAWASSEE
GENESEE
Flint
LAPEER
7
ST CLAIR
Port Huron
Holland
5
OAKLAND
MACOMB
12
Lansing
LIVINGSTON
Pontiac
ALLEGAN
BARRY
EATON
INGHAM
6
18
3
WASHTENAW
WAYNE
Detroit
VAN BUREN
KALAMAZOO
Kalamazoo
Battle Creek
CALHOUN
Jackson
JACKSON
Ann Arbor
15
1, 13, 14, 17
4
Portage
2
Benton Harbor
CASS
ST. JOSEPH
BRANCH
HILLSDALE
LENAWEE
MONROE
16
BERRIEN

Donald W. Riegle Jr. (D)

Of Flint — Elected 1976

Born: Feb. 4, 1938, Flint, Mich.

Education: Attended Flint Junior College, 1956-57; Western Michigan U., 1957-58; U. of Michigan, B.A. 1960; Michigan State U., M.B.A. 1961; attended Harvard U. Business School, 1964-66.

Occupation: Business executive; professor.

Family: Wife, Lori Hansen; four children.

Religion: Methodist.

Political Career: U.S. House, 1967-77; served as Republican, 1967-73.

Capitol Office: 105 Dirksen Bldg. 20510; 224-4822.

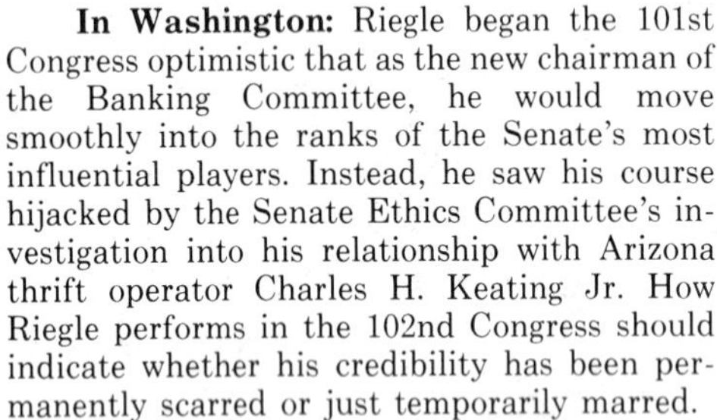

In Washington: Riegle began the 101st Congress optimistic that as the new chairman of the Banking Committee, he would move smoothly into the ranks of the Senate's most influential players. Instead, he saw his course hijacked by the Senate Ethics Committee's investigation into his relationship with Arizona thrift operator Charles H. Keating Jr. How Riegle performs in the 102nd Congress should indicate whether his credibility has been permanently scarred or just temporarily marred.

Of the Keating Five senators (Riegle, Democrats Alan Cranston of California, Dennis DeConcini of Arizona and John Glenn of Ohio, and Arizona Republican John McCain), Riegle had the shortest-lived relationship with Keating. Keating was chairman of American Continental Corp. (ACC) of Phoenix, which owned the failed Lincoln Savings and Loan Association of California: The two met in 1986 at the grand opening of an old downtown Detroit hotel that Keating had bought and renovated. In 1987, Keating, seeing that Riegle would soon become Banking chairman, sought a closer association with the senator. Keating's lobbyist, James Grogan, set up a meeting with Riegle, at which Keating offered to host a fundraiser for Riegle, who was seeking re-election. He raised $78,250.

A month after the meeting, Grogan was back in Riegle's office, accompanied by Lincoln's auditor, who explained why Lincoln needed help in staving off the Federal Home Loan Bank Board and its regulators. The regulators were pursuing Lincoln for its risky activities. Riegle asked the auditor (who later became an ACC executive) to put his comments on paper. The letter, which went to Riegle, DeConcini and McCain, spurred the senators to meet with the regulators.

The following month, Riegle told bank board Chairman Edwin J. Gray to expect to hear from senators concerned with Lincoln's treatment. A day after meeting with Gray, Riegle went to Arizona. While there, he took a helicopter tour of ACC developments with Keating and spoke to company employees. Grogan told the Ethics Committee that Riegle mentioned the idea of meeting with Gray to resolve Lincoln's problems with the regulators, and that Riegle called Keating a few days later to say that he had spoken to Gray. Riegle said none of the discussion about Gray occurred.

After returning from Arizona, Riegle met with DeConcini and suggested that concerned senators meet with Gray. All but Riegle met with Gray on April 2, 1987. Grogan said Riegle agreed to come but wanted to be invited by McCain or DeConcini; Riegle disputed that he intended to come, since Keating was not a Michigan constituent. He also told the Ethics Committee in a letter, "At no time did I ever initiate any contact with the regulators concerning Lincoln."

Riegle was invited to — and did — attend the April 9, 1987, meeting between the five senators and the regulators. There, the regulators informed them that Lincoln's mismanagement was so serious that they could face criminal investigation by the Justice Department. After the meeting, Riegle, Glenn and McCain stopped their inquiries into Lincoln. In March 1988, Riegle returned the money Keating and his associates had raised for his re-election.

The Ethics Committee's special counsel, Robert S. Bennett, focused on the proximity of Keating's fundraising and Riegle's efforts on his behalf. Riegle said he did nothing improper in his contacts with regulators. He rebutted Bennett's contention that the senators should be rebuked for violating an "appearance standard," saying, "I think what has to be measured is conduct — what does one do?"

During his testimony, Riegle often could not recall events and conversations. The committee's vice chairman, New Hampshire Republican Warren B. Rudman, told Riegle that he found his testimony "remarkably inconsistent."

In the end, the committee concluded that Riegle's conduct "gave the appearance of being improper and was certainly attended with insensitivity and poor judgment . . . [but] did not reach a level requiring institutional action" — the same verdict given DeConcini.

Contrite, Riegle called the findings "fair and constructive. . . . I certainly regret and accept responsibility for this [conflict of interest] appearance problem, even though no conflict or wrongful conduct" occurred. He added that "every senator is vulnerable" to a problem of apparent conflict of interest given the existing campaign finance system.

In 1990, Common Cause issued a study that showed Riegle having received more campaign contributions in the 1980s from the thrift industry than all but one member of Congress. He later announced that he would turn over to the Treasury all S&L-related campaign contributions he had received since 1983; he estimated that it would total about $120,000. He also vowed not to accept contributions from companies whose principal business falls under the panels he chairs, the Banking Committee or the Finance Subcommittee on Health.

With the Ethics Committee's investigation behind him, Riegle attempted to regain the course he had hoped to navigate two years earlier. He gave every indication that he would not let the Keating scandal deter him from remaining an effective player in Senate affairs.

Even in the 101st Congress, Riegle maintained a weighty agenda. With seats on the Banking, Budget, and Finance committees, Riegle is well-positioned to get into almost any domestic policy issue he chooses. But it is Banking that dominates his agenda.

In his first year as Banking chairman, he faced the problem of refinancing and restructuring the ailing S&L industry. Bad loans, poor management and a depressed oil economy had pushed hundreds of S&Ls, mostly in the Southwest, into insolvency, bankrupting the Federal Savings and Loan Insurance Corporation.

In early 1989, President Bush proposed to borrow $50 billion to sell or close insolvent S&Ls. But the focus soon turned to how the bailout would be financed. Riegle was among the most vocal critics of Bush's plan to keep the cost "off budget," thus shielding it from the federal budget deficit. He argued that off-budget financing agencies would have to pay higher interest rates than would the U.S. Treasury.

Riegle drew up a complicated alternative under which the Treasury would have issued the bailout bonds, saving as much as $4.5 billion in interest costs over 30 years. To get around the Gramm-Rudman anti-deficit law's automatic spending cuts, it would have put the entire cost of the borrowing on budget in fiscal 1989, thus unaffected by Gramm-Rudman.

The administration fiercely opposed Riegle's plan. So did nearly every Republican senator and three Banking Committee Democrats. The committee voted 11-10 to knock Riegle's financing arrangement out of the bill.

Despite losing that fight, the new Banking chairman won high marks from committee members for steering a bill quickly through the rough waters of industry infighting, with bipartisan courtesy and without being swamped.

On the Senate floor, Riegle and Florida Democrat Bob Graham tried again to win support for the alternative financing arrangement. But their bid to waive budget act constraints fell 12 votes short of the requisite 60.

However, the House, led by the Ways and Means Committee, voted in favor of an on-budget plan with a Gramm-Rudman waiver. Eventually, after two bitter House-Senate conferences — the second one required after the Senate rejected the first conference report — conferees agreed to put $20 billion on budget and keep $30 billion off.

Early in the 102nd Congress, another installment in the S&L bailout was due; this time the administration called for $30 billion to close failed thrifts. Riegle sped a bill through Banking, convincing skeptical lawmakers that the need was too urgent to permit delays.

In the 101st Congress, Riegle and House Banking Chairman Henry B. Gonzalez drafted comprehensive bills to reform the federally backed system of deposit insurance. They introduced their bills ahead of the Bush administration, which issued its sweeping bank-reform proposal in 1991. Both Riegle and Gonzalez said that the deposit-insurance system ought to be shored up before Congress addresses the broader question of giving banks new powers to help the industry grow.

At the start of the 101st Congress, the Finance Committee split its Health Subcommittee in two; Riegle became chairman of the Subcommittee on Health for Families and the Uninsured. With Labor and Human Resources Committee Chairman Edward M. Kennedy, he assembled a bipartisan, inter-committee working group between those often-competitive panels to consider health care plans for the uninsured.

Riegle emerged as a leading opponent in the 102nd Congress of Bush's efforts to secure a free-trade agreement with Mexico. "Manufacturing jobs are going to slide away," he said, noting that the average hourly wage in Mexico is 57 cents, but $10.47 in the United States.

On the Budget Committee, Riegle has been a relentless opponent of cuts in domestic spending programs. In 1985, he strongly resisted efforts to freeze cost-of-living adjustments (COLAs) for Social Security recipients. When the committee endorsed that step as part of a spending plan it approved in March 1985, Riegle denounced the Republicans who drafted it. "You didn't have the courage to run on that basis," he said, noting Reagan's 1984 campaign pledge not to tamper with Social Security.

Riegle and New York's Daniel Patrick Moynihan vowed to try to block the COLA freeze on the Senate floor, and lobbying groups for the elderly swung into high gear, denouncing Reagan for going back on his word and pressuring senators up for re-election in 1986. A preliminary vote revived the COLAs, but they were frozen in a GOP leadership budget approved 50-49 after Vice President Bush came in to break a tie.

But in the end, Riegle got his way. To the dismay of Senate GOP leaders, Reagan reversed field, abandoned the budget Bush had supported and threw in with a House-drafted budget that preserved Social Security COLAs.

Riegle's long record of devotion to the automobile industry and the United Auto Workers is well-known. Whether fighting auto-emission standards, promoting federal loan guarantees for a beleaguered Chrysler Corp. or demanding curbs on foreign car imports, Riegle has gone all out for Detroit.

A few years ago, when he was grand marshal of a parade in Traverse City, Mich., he refused to ride in the foreign car assigned to him; flustered organizers of the event hastily located a Chevrolet for the senator.

In 1977, when the Clean Air Act was up for renewal, Riegle offered the industry's principal amendment to relax standards for carbon monoxide emissions from automobiles. It succumbed a stricter substitute version, whose passage led Riegle to complain, "We just cannot mandate technology that does not exist."

In 1990, Riegle led the floor fight against a bill to raise automobile fuel-efficiency standards. "We cannot assume we are back in 1974, and there is another 1,500 pounds to wring out of a car," he said. Heavy lobbying by the auto industry and the Bush administration helped kill the bill for the 101st Congress.

Riegle was crucial in the 1979 passage of the Chrysler bailout, arranging a compromise that averted a filibuster and moving the plan through the full Senate just before the year's recess. The compromise involved more than $500 million in wage concessions on the part of Chrysler employees, in addition to federal protection for the company's future loans.

When auto industry layoffs put thousands out of work in the early 1980s, Riegle, on both Banking and Labor, fought for more federal benefits for the unemployed, usually against strong administration resistance.

At Home: Riegle's first plunge into politics was enough to give anyone visions of grandeur. He was working toward a business degree at Harvard in 1966 when his hometown Republican Party, which had been having trouble finding candidates, recruited him to run against Democratic Rep. John C. Mackie. Riegle's name had some advantage; his father was active as a Republican officeholder in Flint and surrounding Genesee County.

Ignoring the odds in his heavily Democratic district, Riegle campaigned furiously, winding up his handshaking only after the polls had closed on Election Day. Mackie, ignoring the warnings of friends, decided he would have no trouble winning and lapsed into a somnolent campaign. He woke up with an 11,000-vote deficit. Riegle quickly concluded that if he could win a Democratic House seat that easily, there was no reason to restrain his ambitions.

A freshman in the House in 1967 at age 28, he was seen as a brash and transparently ambitious young man who overstepped the bounds of protocol by announcing the timetable for his presidential aspirations — 15 years.

Although he quickly developed a maverick reputation in the House, Riegle managed to stay on good terms with his party leader, Gerald R. Ford. Even after Riegle tried to take the 1970 Michigan Senate nomination away from Lenore Romney, the choice of GOP leaders, Ford seemed to remain an ally.

The Vietnam War, however, gradually turned Riegle from maverick to full-time rebel. He was one of a small group of anti-war Republicans that backed Rep. Paul N. McCloskey Jr. of California against President Nixon during the 1972 Republican primaries. Also that year, he further ruffled feathers with the publication of "O Congress," his legislate-and-tell look at life in the Capitol.

By then he had burned his Republican bridges and was winning re-election by comfortable margins mainly because he was popular among Flint's blue-collar Democratic majority. He became a Democrat in 1973, won a fifth term the next year and began a well-financed effort to win the Senate seat vacated in 1976 by Democrat Philip A. Hart.

In the 1976 Democratic primary, he closed fast to upset the favorite, black Secretary of State Richard H. Austin. Austin was hurt by criticism of alleged irregularities in the collection of his campaign funds and by his refusal to debate his opponents. Riegle, campaigning with his usual vigor, stressed the contrast between his age (38) and Austin's (63).

Sparking a crossover primary vote by liberal Republicans and independents, Riegle won stunning victories in all of the state's Democratic strongholds except Wayne County (Detroit), which he lost by just 2,000 votes.

Riegle's primary win put him on a clear path toward a Senate victory that fall against moderate GOP Rep. Marvin Esch. Despite Esch's attempt to woo suburban Detroit Democrats by attacking busing and abortion, Riegle maintained a comfortable lead.

Then *The Detroit News* published transcripts of taped conversations between Riegle and a staff member with whom he had had an affair in 1969. Riegle acknowledged the affair, calling it a "foolish mistake." He also sought to create a sympathetic backlash in his favor, charging that Esch's campaign had been misrepresenting his policy positions. "I hold Marvin Esch personally responsible for the gutter-level tone of this campaign," Riegle declared. The defense worked, and Riegle withstood a last-minute media flurry by Esch.

In 1982, although few vestiges were left of the earlier "young man in a hurry," Riegle again had to fight off attacks on his character. His opponent, former Republican Rep. Philip E. Ruppe, latched onto a *Washington Post* article in which Republican senators were quoted to the effect that Riegle's confrontational approach cost him legitimacy.

That was Ruppe's only decent weapon against Riegle. With Michigan in the throes of a depression that many voters blamed on GOP policies, the time was anything but auspicious for a Republican. Moreover, Riegle's work on behalf of the auto industry had already preempted some traditional sources of GOP funding in Michigan, including Henry Ford II. Riegle had little trouble, winning even the Upper Peninsula, Ruppe's base, with 55 percent.

Six years later, Michigan's Republican Party was fractured by feuding caused by their complex presidential delegate-selection process. With party regulars — loyalists of George Bush — openly battling supporters of religious broadcaster Pat Robertson, the GOP scarcely had time to think about challenging Riegle. The GOP nomination fell to former Rep. Jim Dunn, an East Lansing developer who had been on the outs with the party hierarchy after a bitter and unsuccessful Senate primary bid in 1984.

While Dunn was never considered a serious threat, Riegle took no chances. His campaign produced over 20 TV commercials, including an environmental spot featuring the senator fishing with his 4-year-old daughter, and a testimonial by New Jersey Sen. Bill Bradley likening Riegle's work on the trade bill to that of an athletic star leading his team to a championship. Pumping well over $3 million into his campaign, Riegle outspent Dunn nearly 8-to-1 and won more than 60 percent of the vote.

Committees

Banking, Housing & Urban Affairs (Chairman)

Budget (4th of 12 Democrats)

Finance (8th of 11 Democrats)
Health for Families & the Uninsured (chairman); Deficits, Debt Management & International Debt; International Trade

Elections

1988 General

Donald W. Riegle Jr. (D)	2,116,865	(60%)
Jim Dunn (R)	1,348,219	(38%)

Previous Winning Percentages: **1982** (58%) **1976** (53%) **1974 *** (65%) **1972 *** (71%) **1970 *** (69%) **1968 *** (61%) **1966 *** (54%)

** House elections.*

Campaign Finance

	Receipts	Receipts from PACs		Expend-itures
1988				
Riegle (D)	$3,289,327	$1,281,641	(39%)	$3,383,849
Dunn (R)	$470,976	$8,055	(2%)	$442,693

Key Votes

1991

Authorize use of force against Iraq	N

1990

Oppose prohibition of certain semiautomatic weapons	N
Support constitutional amendment on flag desecration	N
Oppose requiring parental notice for minors' abortions	Y
Halt production of B-2 stealth bomber at 13 planes	Y
Approve budget that cut spending and raised revenues	N
Pass civil rights bill over Bush veto	Y

1989

Oppose reduction of SDI funding	N
Oppose barring federal funds for "obscene" art	Y
Allow vote on capital gains tax cut	N

Voting Studies

	Presidential Support		Party Unity		Conservative Coalition	
Year	**S**	**O**	**S**	**O**	**S**	**O**
1990	30	63	85	12	27	70
1989	45	54	93	5	13	84
1988	41	57	94	3	24	73
1987	35	64	92	6	19	78
1986	18	82	96	4	5	95
1985	24	74	87	10	22	75
1984	31	68	92	6	2	98
1983	34	64	93	4	14 †	86 †
1982	24	66	89	3	4	86
1981	34	60	88	4	7	87

† Not eligible for all recorded votes.

Interest Group Ratings

Year	ADA	ACU	AFL-CIO	CCUS
1990	83	9	78	25
1989	85	12	100	38
1988	90	4	93	36
1987	100	4	100	17
1986	95	9	93	26
1985	95	4	90	24
1984	100	5	100	28
1983	85	4	94	28
1982	80	24	92	16
1981	90	14	89	22

Carl Levin (D)

Of Detroit — Elected 1978

Born: June 28, 1934, Detroit, Mich.
Education: Swarthmore College, B.A. 1956; Harvard U., LL.B. 1959.
Occupation: Lawyer.
Family: Wife, Barbara Halpern; three children.
Religion: Jewish.
Political Career: Detroit City Council, 1970-73; president, 1974-77.
Capitol Office: 459 Russell Bldg. 20510; 224-6221.

In Washington: During his first two terms in the Senate, Levin proved himself to be intelligent, reasonable, aware of Michigan interests and liberal. By emphasizing the first three traits and playing down the fourth, he easily won re-election in 1990 to a third Senate term.

Levin showed his political seasoning throughout his campaign against GOP Rep. Bill Schuette, an aggressive, young but somewhat callow conservative.

One exchange between the two began after Levin went to the Persian Gulf region and was filmed aboard the USS *Wisconsin*, which was part of the massive U.S. military effort that followed Iraq's August 1990 invasion of Kuwait. Schuette then ran ads telling voters that Levin had once voted to keep that ship in mothballs, but Levin quickly responded by pointing to his efforts to save conventional weapons — including the endangered, Michigan-built M-1 tank — at the expense of nuclear weapons programs.

Levin also likes to take rhetorical aim at old-fashioned liberal assumptions. "We messed up those social programs," he likes to say. "Those of us who believe in them have an obligation to make them work."

But the career of this thoughtful, pragmatic Democrat reflects the elusive nature of the revisionist liberalism in which Levin and his allies seem interested. Except for some moves to rein in "unaccountable bureaucrats" through congressional veto power, it is hard to see many instances where Levin's record differs from a traditional liberal one.

This certainly applies to Levin's work on the Armed Services Committee. In January 1991, Levin voted against giving President Bush authorization to use force against Iraq.

As chairman of the Conventional Forces and Alliance Defense Subcommittee, Levin has stood out during the Reagan and Bush administrations as a constructive and well-informed debater. After President Ronald Reagan warned that the Soviets had far outstripped U.S. military capability, Levin responded with "Chart Wars" — elaborate graphics showing that the United States had the upper hand in a number of important military categories. To back up his claim, he solicited from the chairman of the Joint Chiefs of Staff the admission that "not on your life" would he trade U.S. military forces for those of the Soviet Union.

But as reasoned as Levin's arguments typically are, he has nevertheless been a consistent Pentagon critic. He complains that the Defense Department under Reagan and Bush has put too much emphasis on buying complicated new weapons systems, especially nuclear ones, while skimping on maintenance and production of conventional weaponry.

Levin waged a long battle against MX missiles and Pentagon plans to make them mobile by basing them on rail cars. In August 1989, a Levin amendment to cut MX funding nearly in half — in effect eliminating money for the rail-basing mode — was killed on a 61-39 vote. However, the brewing fiscal crisis and the lessening of U.S.-Soviet tensions brought Levin and other anti-MX members a reversal in 1990: Over the objections of the Bush administration, Congress cut funding for the MX rail system.

Unlike some Democratic arms control advocates, Levin never bought into the idea of using the single-warhead Midgetman as an alternative to the multi-warhead MX: He is a doubter of the threat of a Soviet nuclear "sneak attack" which underlies the need for a mobile missile. In early 1989, Levin called for putting a hold on both programs pending the results of the U.S.-Soviet strategic arms reduction treaty (START) talks, which he said might obviate the need for either the MX or Midgetman.

Levin is among those Armed Services members who urge budget savings through burden-sharing — getting U.S. allies to pick up more of the cost of their own defense. Citing South Korea's increasing prosperity and security from attack by North Korea, Levin called in 1989 for the United States to reduce its troop commitment to South Korea.

Levin is not always looking to cut defense programs, particularly some of the conventional weapons programs Bush has tried to cannibalize to secure continued funding for expensive, high-tech systems such as the B-2 bomber. His most passionate efforts have been in behalf of the M-1 tank, which is built on production lines in Warren, Mich., and Lima, Ohio.

Levin says that while he supports Defense Secretary Dick Cheney's plans to develop an advanced-model tank, the immediate cancellation of the M-1 would leave the United States with no "warm" tank production lines until the unspecified date when its replacement is ready.

In part through the efforts of Levin and 14th District Democratic Rep. Dennis M. Hertel, Congress threw the Warren plant a lifeline in 1990. Under the fiscal 1991 defense authorization bill, new tank production will be phased out as requested by Bush; however, the Warren plant would then be authorized to refit older-model M-1s with larger cannons and other improvements standard on newer models.

With his home state's industrial sector hard hit by foreign competition, Levin came out in 1989 against the "FS-X" deal, under which the United States and Japan would co-produce a fighter plane based on the U.S. F-16. "I am not mad at the Japanese," Levin said. "I am mad at us because we will not act to protect our own economy and our own jobs."

Off the committee, Levin's concerns about Michigan's autoworkers lead him to oppose sharp increases in automobile fuel-efficiency standards. In September 1990, advocates of boosting those standards tried to move a long-stalled bill, and seemed to have majority support in the Senate. But Levin, working with business-oriented Republican Don Nickles of Oklahoma, was able to block cloture on debate, killing the bill for the 101st Congress.

Throughout his Senate career, Levin has pursued issues that could fall into the broad category of "good government." On Armed Services, he has been a leading advocate of defense procurement reform.

During the February 1989 debate on the doomed nomination of former Sen. John G. Tower as Defense secretary, Levin seemed less concerned with allegations about Tower's personal life than with the nominee's potential conflicts of interest. Levin asked whether Tower would recuse himself from decisions on programs he had advocated as a paid lobbyist from 1986 through 1988. Tower refused to commit to doing so, and Levin opposed his confirmation.

As chairman of the Governmental Affairs Subcommittee on Oversight of Government Management, Levin crafted legislation providing job protections to whistleblowers, federal employees who expose corruption or mismanagement. The bill passed in 1988, but was unexpectedly vetoed by Reagan after Attorney General Dick Thornburgh raised objections to some provisions. However, Levin and Thornburgh (who had been reappointed by Bush) reached compromises on those details, and the bill was enacted in April 1989.

Governmental Affairs also has been the forum for Levin's most conspicuous crusade to reform the federal bureaucracy — he favors a legislative veto, which would allow Congress to revoke federal regulations of all sorts. Levin had some success here, but it was largely overturned by the Supreme Court in 1983.

More recently, Levin has questioned the growing power of the Office of Management and Budget over regulations issued by government agencies. Upset that OMB conducted its reviews behind closed doors, he forced through changes in 1986 that required OMB to disclose what regulatory changes it was demanding. Dissatisfied with what he viewed as OMB's disregard of those procedures, Levin supported an unsuccessful effort during the 101st Congress to tighten congressional oversight of OMB.

At Home: Levin has made it through two re-election campaigns waged in years not entirely favorable to his party. In 1984, Levin survived a big Reagan presidential victory in Michigan; six years later, Levin won comfortably even as the state's Democratic governor was being ousted from office.

Levin had been anticipating a tough race in 1984 and pumped up his fundraising with dire warnings that the national GOP planned to spend millions against him. The warnings worked so well that Levin outspent his Republican opponent, former astronaut Jack Lousma, who went heavily into debt in the primary and was strapped for funds in the fall campaign.

But Levin needed more than a monetary advantage as Walter F. Mondale's presidential campaign faded and it became apparent that Reagan's coattails could cause Levin real problems. So he unveiled an "October surprise." He aired a film clip of Lousma warming up a Japanese audience in 1983 by telling them about the Toyota he owned. In Michigan, where Japanese cars mean joblessness for autoworkers, Lousma's statement was a major embarrassment. Few were soothed by his plea that the Toyota belonged not to him, but to his son.

The Toyota film clip meshed well with Levin's overall campaign theme; he had billed himself as "A Proven Fighter for Michigan" and stressed his work to limit auto imports, extend unemployment benefits and help relieve the state unemployment compensation debt.

Lousma, who had flown on Skylab and space shuttle missions in the 1970s and early 1980s, was strongly supported by anti-abortion forces, anti-tax advocates and other conservative Republicans, who helped him win nomination. But he suffered from his own unfamiliarity with politics and Michigan issues. He had retired from NASA in Houston and moved to his boyhood home of Grand Rapids just before launching his campaign.

In spite of those handicaps, Lousma might have been able to ride Reagan's coattails to victory had Levin's fundraising been less vigorous and his strategy less well devised. Reagan carried Michigan with 59 percent, but Levin held on to win with 52 percent.

In 1990, Levin's political skills were again on view. With national GOP leaders sharpening their knives for him, Levin amassed a daunting campaign treasury and early on aired television ads touting his accomplishments. Only after Schuette began attacking did Levin fire back, thereby preserving his "nice guy" image.

Schuette tried to link Levin to the state's senior senator, Donald W. Riegle Jr. — then under scrutiny for his ties to the S&L crisis — by charging that both men were party to "cozy deals" in Washington. Schuette also tried to make Levin out to be soft on defense.

But Levin's past support for conventional weaponry protected him from Schuette's assault. And the Republican, who had battled perceptions of superficiality, never developed the stature he needed to get into Levin's weight class. As Democratic Gov. James J. Blanchard lost his bid for a third term, Levin won a decisive 57 percent of the vote.

Levin's older brother, Sander, now in the House, first spread the family name statewide with gubernatorial campaigns in 1970 and 1974. Carl Levin made his name in politics in the mid-1970s as president of the Detroit City Council, where he teamed with black Mayor Coleman A. Young to provide for demolition of thousands of abandoned buildings. The two strayed apart at times in the late 1970s, but this probably helped Levin in later statewide races by showing suburban voters that he was not inextricably tied to Detroit's black majority.

The big break in Levin's successful 1978 Senate challenge was a major misstep by the GOP incumbent, Robert P. Griffin. Disappointed at losing the contest for Senate Republican leader in 1977, Griffin announced that he would retire the next year and began skipping votes on the floor. He eventually changed his mind about running, but by that time had missed a third of the Senate votes over an entire year. Levin said Griffin was obviously tired of the job, and the voters agreed that the incumbent deserved a rest.

Committees

Armed Services (3rd of 11 Democrats)
Conventional Forces & Alliance Defense (chairman); Readiness, Sustainability & Support; Strategic Forces & Nuclear Deterrence

Governmental Affairs (3rd of 8 Democrats)
Oversight of Government Management (chairman); Government Information & Regulation; Permanent Subcommittee on Investigations

Small Business (4th of 10 Democrats)
Innovation, Technology & Productivity (chairman); Rural Economy & Family Farming

Elections

1990 General

Carl Levin (D)	1,471,753	(57%)
Bill Schuette (R)	1,055,695	(41%)
Susan Farquhar (WW)	32,796	(1%)

Previous Winning Percentages: **1984** (52%) **1978** (52%)

Campaign Finance

	Receipts	Receipts from PACs		Expend-itures
1990				
Levin (D)	$6,948,096	$1,392,502	(20%)	$6,930,262
Schuette (R)	$2,488,958	$735,932	(30%)	$2,417,705

Key Votes

1991	
Authorize use of force against Iraq	N
1990	
Oppose prohibition of certain semiautomatic weapons	N
Support constitutional amendment on flag desecration	N
Oppose requiring parental notice for minors' abortions	Y
Halt production of B-2 stealth bomber at 13 planes	N
Approve budget that cut spending and raised revenues	N
Pass civil rights bill over Bush veto	Y
1989	
Oppose reduction of SDI funding	N
Oppose barring federal funds for "obscene" art	Y
Allow vote on capital gains tax cut	N

Voting Studies

	Presidential Support		Party Unity		Conservative Coalition	
Year	**S**	**O**	**S**	**O**	**S**	**O**
1990	33	66	82	18	35	65
1989	50	50	80	16	39	61
1988	42	52	91	6	14	84
1987	32	67	89	8	28	69
1986	23	77	91	9	11	88
1985	25	73	89	6	25	72
1984	34	61	89	8	9	85
1983	33	66	86	12	14	82
1982	34	63	92	6	5	94
1981	35	63	92	5	6	93

Interest Group Ratings

Year	ADA	ACU	AFL-CIO	CCUS
1990	78	22	78	33
1989	80	14	100	25
1988	80	0	92	21
1987	90	4	90	17
1986	90	9	87	26
1985	85	4	90	31
1984	100	14	82	35
1983	95	8	94	16
1982	95	20	96	14
1981	100	7	100	0

1 John Conyers Jr. (D)

Of Detroit — Elected 1964

Born: May 16, 1929, Detroit, Mich.
Education: Wayne State U., B.A. 1957, LL.B. 1958.
Military Service: National Guard, 1948-52; Army, 1952-53; Army Reserve, 1953-57.
Occupation: Lawyer.
Family: Wife, Monica Ann Esters; one child.
Religion: Baptist.
Political Career: Candidate for mayor of Detroit, 1989.
Capitol Office: 2426 Rayburn Bldg. 20515; 225-5126.

In Washington: The 101st Congress began auspiciously for Conyers. Seniority had yielded him a significant committee chairmanship even as his handling of a sensitive judicial impeachment trial raised his stock among colleagues.

The 101st did prove eventful for Conyers, but generally not in the sense he might have hoped. Some of the key initiatives he pushed as Government Operations chairman ended in frustration. His effort to get out of Congress by challenging Detroit Mayor Coleman A. Young ended dismally. Even the non-political fates were harsh; Conyers suffered a head injury when his driver collided with a Capitol Hill security barrier.

Despite these difficulties, however, Conyers did move some legislation and attract a number of headlines during the 101st. And his chairmanship still guarantees a bully pulpit from which to broadcast his well-established liberal views.

During most of his quarter-century in Congress, Conyers had seemed more interested in being a rebel than in becoming a power broker. Some colleagues found his style sarcastic and abrasive, making it difficult for him to coordinate alliances needed to pass legislation. Conyers managed to alter that image in the 100th Congress, thanks to his leadership on the impeachment trial of U.S. District Judge Alcee L. Hastings.

As chairman of the Judiciary Subcommittee on Criminal Justice, Conyers was charged with investigating Hastings, who had been accused of conspiring to solicit a bribe and leaking wiretap information. The politics were particularly sticky for Conyers, a black veteran of the civil rights movement investigating a black judge who claimed the charges against him were racially motivated. Further, Hastings had been acquitted by a jury.

When Conyers began the proceedings in 1987, he indicated that he, too, saw the possibility of racial bias in the charges. But as the investigation progressed, Conyers reached what he later called the most difficult decision of his House career: that Hastings was guilty and had fabricated his court defense.

"We did not fight the civil rights struggle to replace one sort of judicial corruption with another," Conyers said, recalling the difficulties blacks had had with white judges.

The impeachment resolution easily cleared the subcommittee and full committee, and Conyers gave a floor speech on the case that brought him a standing ovation and helped to deliver a vote of 413-3.

That performance raised expectations for his tenure heading Government Operations. And in his first session as chairman, Conyers did get favorable national media coverage of several issues he pressed in committee. Among them were improprieties by defense contractor Northrop Corp. and alleged malfeasance within the Internal Revenue Service (Conyers complained of "crooks auditing crooks").

But Conyers was scuffed up on two high-profile issues that came through his committee.

The first was a set of proposals for revising the Paperwork Reduction Act. Conyers believed the Office of Management and Budget was using the paperwork law as a pretext for challenging regulations it disliked.

Working with ranking committee Republican Frank Horton of New York, Conyers threatened to restrict the administration's control of the regulatory review process. Each time they issued an ultimatum, however, they backed off when they thought they had reached an accord with the White House on the issue. Each of those deals fell through, however, as did an 11th-hour accord brokered by members of the Senate committee working on the issue.

The administration also abandoned Conyers on his bill to elevate the Environmental Protection Agency to Cabinet status. President Bush had signaled his support for the change, and Conyers gleefully predicted his bill would sail through the 101st. But the House-passed bill stalled in the Senate when the administration raised objections.

The Government Operations chairmanship has taken time away from Conyers' duties on

Michigan 1

Detroit — North Central; Highland Park

Detroit was not all that special at the turn of the century. It brewed beer and turned out carriages and stoves, and its complacent citizens took to calling it "the most beautiful city in America." But Henry Ford's first large factory in Highland Park, built in 1909, was followed by others, plants put up by Buick, R. E. Olds and the Fisher brothers. The north side of Detroit became a sea of single- and two-family houses for the workers who flocked to the assembly lines from rural Michigan, Appalachia and Eastern Europe.

The 1st, now overwhelmingly black (71 percent) and Democratic, is generally better off than its inner-city neighbor, the 13th. More of its homes are owner-occupied, and its residents are better educated. The racially mixed communities north of Seven Mile Road have a high percentage of professionals and white-collar city employees living in well-preserved prewar houses.

East of Southfield Road, the neighborhoods are poorer and more exclusively black. Both skilled and unskilled workers live in Highland Park and in the area north of the University of Detroit.

Highland Park, a city entirely surrounded by Detroit, is the home of the Chrysler Corp. Once a white-ethnic bastion, Highland Park is now over 80 percent black. Although the city retained its middle-class character through most of the 1960s and early '70s, hard times and rising unemployment have hurt its increasingly marginal neighborhoods.

The several white enclaves in the district include Poles living in the northeast corner, north of Hamtramck, and middle-class ethnics around the Southfield Freeway in the southwest. These voters tend to be older and more conservative.

Population: 514,560. White 137,827 (27%), Black 364,021 (71%), Other 3,202 (1%). Spanish origin 10,587 (2%). 18 and over 349,182 (68%), 65 and over 47,777 (9%). Median age: 28.

the Judiciary Committee. On that panel, he is probably best known for legislation he opposes: attempts to revise the federal anti-racketeering law.

The law, known as the Racketeer Influenced and Corrupt Organizations Act (RICO), was designed to combat organized crime, but had been used increasingly for civil suits against corporations with no criminal record.

Business and labor groups felt the law was being overused, but Conyers in 1986 embarked on a full-scale campaign in defense of its use. He argued that any restrictions would hinder efforts to fight white-collar crime.

Conyers first kept the RICO overhaul bill bottled up in his subcommittee and later employed other blocking tactics. Subsequent revision attempts also failed, due in part to Conyers' opposition.

Conyers is outspoken on issues pertaining to civil rights and minority concerns. During the 101st, he sponsored a crime bill amendment that would allow prisoners on death row to challenge their sentence if they could show a pattern of racial bias in death penalty sentencing.

He also made an about-face on the nomination of William Lucas, a black attorney, to head the Justice Department's civil rights division. Conyers introduced Lucas to the Senate Judiciary Committee saying Lucas was destined for "greatness." But the next day, after hearing Lucas tell the Senate he did not consider recent Supreme Court rulings a significant threat to established civil rights guarantees, Conyers withdrew that support.

Conyers has always seen a role for himself that goes beyond day-to-day legislative politics. He has spent considerable time outside Washington and his district campaigning for other black politicians. In 1988 he claimed to have spent more days campaigning for Jesse Jackson than any other black member of the House.

During hostilities in the Persian Gulf, he was one of the most outspoken in opposition to military intervention. He repeatedly deplored the disproportionate number of minorities serving in the military.

Conyers' interest in civil rights also blends in with a strong interest in jazz (he keeps a stand-up bass in his office amidst posters of various jazz artists). "Whites who have had all kinds of trouble with me have never had any trouble embracing Belafonte," he has said, referring to popular singer Harry Belafonte. He has successfully sponsored a House resolution declaring jazz "a rare and valuable national American treasure," and legislation designating May 25 — the birthday of memorable black tap artist Bill Robinson — National Tap Dance Day.

Conyers' personal life was also in the news during the 101st. In June 1990, the 61-year-old Conyers married a 25-year-old former aide who gave birth to a son one month later.

At Home: The son of an autoworker, Conyers became interested in politics while in law school and worked loyally in the party apparatus. The creation in 1964 of a second black-majority district in Detroit gave him his first opportunity. He ran for Congress on a platform of "Equality, Jobs and Peace," pledging to strengthen the United Nations and to exempt low-income families from paying federal income tax.

Among the qualifications Conyers cited for holding office were three years as a district aide to Rep. John D. Dingell and service on a panel of lawyers picked by President John F. Kennedy to look for ways of easing racial tensions in the South. Conyers won the primary by just 108 votes over Richard H. Austin, a Detroit accountant who has remained a political rival ever since.

Racial troubles in Conyers' district exploded in 1967, when rioting destroyed many blocks in the heart of the district. Conyers was booed when he stood atop a car telling rioters to return to their homes. Later his office was gutted by fire. But those episodes had no lasting political impact, nor did his initial reluctance to support Hubert H. Humphrey for the presidency in 1968.

Conyers' primary challenges have been infrequent and minor, though he has not always been on the best of terms with Mayor Young and the United Auto Workers, the major political powers in the city. In 1989, Conyers challenged Young's re-election and finished third in the September primary, ceding a runoff berth against Young to accountant Thomas Barrow. The next year, however, Conyers was unchallenged for the Democratic nomination for his House seat, and breezed to a November win.

Some Conyers partisans were worried about the 1982 redistricting process; his district had lost population, and the state had to give up one seat in the House. But Conyers' territory remained basically intact. He is unlikely to suffer from the 1991 remapping, either, as Michigan legislators will be obliged by federal court rulings to preserve the state's majority-black districts.

Committees

Government Operations (Chairman)
Legislation & National Security (chairman)

Judiciary (3rd of 21 Democrats)
Civil & Constitutional Rights; Intellectual Property & Judicial Administration; Economic & Commercial Law

Small Business (14th of 27 Democrats)
SBA, the General Economy & Minority Enterprise Development

Elections

1990 General

John Conyers Jr. (D)	76,556	(89%)
Ray Shoulders (R)	7,298	(9%)
Robert Mays (I)	1,134	(1%)
Jonathan Paul Flint (LIBERT)	764	(1%)

1988 General

John Conyers Jr. (D)	127,800	(91%)
Bill Ashe (R)	10,979	(8%)

Previous Winning Percentages:				**1986**	(89%)	**1984**	(89%)
1982	(97%)	**1980**	(95%)	**1978**	(93%)	**1976**	(92%)
1974	(91%)	**1972**	(88%)	**1970**	(88%)	**1968**	(100%)
1966	(84%)	**1964**	(84%)				

District Vote For President

	1988	1984	1980	1976
D	108,814 (90%)	144,684 (86%)	143,653 (86%)	148,065 (84%)
R	11,376 (9%)	23,737 (14%)	19,341 (12%)	27,136 (15%)
I			3,471 (2%)	

Campaign Finance

	Receipts	Receipts from PACs	Expend-itures
1990			
Conyers (D)	$300,877	$178,360 (59%)	$288,906
Shoulders (R)	$545	0	$545
1988			
Conyers (D)	$151,676	$82,614 (54%)	$124,823

Key Votes

1991	
Authorize use of force against Iraq	N
1990	
Support constitutional amendment on flag desecration	N
Pass family and medical leave bill over Bush veto	Y
Reduce SDI funding	Y
Allow abortions in overseas military facilities	Y
Approve budget summit plan for spending and taxing	Y
Approve civil rights bill	Y
1989	
Halt production of B-2 stealth bomber at 13 planes	?
Oppose capital gains tax cut	Y
Approve federal abortion funding in rape or incest cases	Y
Approve pay raise and revision of ethics rules	N
Pass Democratic minimum wage plan over Bush veto	Y

Voting Studies

	Presidential Support		Party Unity		Conservative Coalition	
Year	**S**	**O**	**S**	**O**	**S**	**O**
1990	16	81	86	3	7	85
1989	14	57	72	2	2	85
1988	13	74	83	1	3	89
1987	8	81	82	2	5	81
1986	11	73	71	4	4	78
1985	13	68	69	6	7	67
1984	21	73	88	6	5	92
1983	6	73	73	6	4	73
1982	22	60	68	8	8	75
1981	32	59	78	9	9	85

Interest Group Ratings

Year	ADA	ACU	AFL-CIO	CCUS
1990	78	0	100	15
1989	90	5	88	30
1988	90	0	100	21
1987	92	0	100	0
1986	85	0	92	9
1985	75	12	92	28
1984	95	4	85	21
1983	100	0	100	11
1982	80	6	88	6
1981	90	9	93	0

2 Carl D. Pursell (R)

Of Plymouth — Elected 1976

Born: Dec. 19, 1932, Imlay City, Mich.

Education: Eastern Michigan U., B.A. 1956, M.A. 1961.

Military Service: Army, 1957-59; Army Reserve, 1959-65.

Occupation: High school teacher; real estate salesman; owner of office supply business.

Family: Wife, Peggy Jean Brown; three children.

Religion: Christian Scientist.

Political Career: Wayne County Commission, 1969-70; Mich. Senate, 1971-77; sought Republican nomination for Mich. Senate, 1966.

Capitol Office: 1414 Longworth Bldg. 20515; 225-4401.

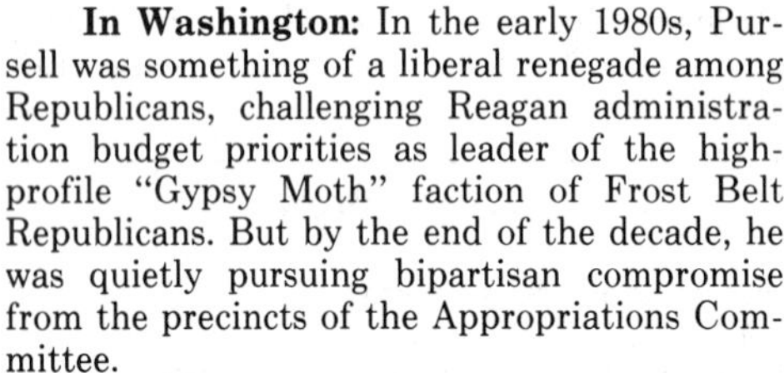

In Washington: In the early 1980s, Pursell was something of a liberal renegade among Republicans, challenging Reagan administration budget priorities as leader of the high-profile "Gypsy Moth" faction of Frost Belt Republicans. But by the end of the decade, he was quietly pursuing bipartisan compromise from the precincts of the Appropriations Committee.

Now Pursell's House career seems to be in a third stage, this one just as public as his Gypsy Moth mode, but ideologically distinct from it. In the 101st Congress, Pursell emerged as a key point man for Republicans seeking a no-new-taxes budget. Also, with the strong backing of minority whip and conservative firebrand Newt Gingrich, Pursell tried in late 1990 to topple Jerry Lewis of California from his post as chairman of the Republican Conference.

When the compromise budget summit agreement between President Bush and congressional leaders collapsed in early October 1990, Pursell (who attacked the "deluded summiteer process") and Ohioan John R. Kasich were tapped by the GOP leadership to draft an alternative proposal. Their antitax plan, which claimed to reduce the federal deficit by $417 billion over five years, gained some praise within the House Republican Conference, but Democrats blocked the package from reaching a floor vote.

Pursell initially caught his colleagues' attention during the budget wrangling — and emerged as a conservative favorite — when he became the first to voice GOP anger at White House Chief of Staff John H. Sununu, who implied that Bush would withdraw political support from Republicans who opposed the summit agreement.

One of Pursell's sidelines is coaching the GOP's baseball and basketball teams, and he says that just as a coach must have a game plan, the GOP should have a game plan for the budget process. Pursell argues that the White House and congressional Republicans should agree up front on a spending strategy, then enforce it with presidential vetoes whenever Democrats pass appropriations measures the GOP deems excessive.

Pursell, who denounces "business as usual" in Congress, took the unusual step in the 101st of removing some of his own projects from spending bills in the name of deficit reduction. Among the funding he removed was a $3 million environmental cleanup of the River Rouge in his district.

The Pursell-Lewis face-off hinged on questions of personality, generational differences and leadership styles. Announcing his challenge to Lewis, Pursell said, "I think there is a lot of sentiment out there for change." He called for more emphasis on presenting clear GOP alternatives to Democratic policy offerings, noting: "We're on the defensive all the time.... We can be major players in giving the country two major strategies, not just a piece of the Democratic agenda."

Some members never took Pursell's challenge to Lewis very seriously, treating the move as more of a nuisance than a real threat. "Their purpose was not to help Carl Pursell but rather to dump Jerry Lewis," said Lewis of those members who tried to unseat him. (Lewis and Pursell's chief backer, Gingrich, are rivals for influence in the House GOP.) Despite his aggressive effort, Pursell lost to Lewis by a decisive vote of 98-64.

Pursell did win his state's seat on the influential Committee on Committees, the panel that makes assignments for House Republicans; ironically, Lewis lost his seat on that panel the same day.

Pursell began to evolve away from his moderate-to-liberal Gypsy Moth persona after redistricting in 1982, which gave him a district that was safely Republican and markedly more conservative than the one he had held for three previous terms. A comfortable win in 1988 over

Michigan 2

Southeast — Ann Arbor; Jackson

The 2nd, which reaches south and west from the Detroit suburbs to the northern edge of the Corn Belt, is home to an uneasy mix of academics, blue-collar workers and conservative farmers.

The GOP dominates the rural townships. The small towns and farms that dot the flat land of Hillsdale, Lenawee, Jackson and Branch counties are a steady source of Republican votes. The last time any of those counties voted for a Democratic presidential candidate was in 1944.

The other block of Republican votes comes from the Detroit suburbs. About a fifth of the district's residents live in a sliver of Wayne County that begins only a mile and a half west of Detroit in the upper-middle-class neighborhoods of Livonia. Professionals and middle-level managers from the area's auto plants give northern Livonia its Republican character, although some blue-collar Democrats live in the older northeast corner of the city.

In Washtenaw County, which holds a third of the district's population, there is a clash of interests. The students and academic community at the University of Michigan in Ann Arbor give that city a bohemian image; that stands in marked contrast to the conservatism found among the vegetable farms to the south and west.

The two poles of the county — the rural west and urban east — have swung Washtenaw from Republican to Democratic in recent presidential elections; it was the only county in the nation to support George McGovern in 1972, then back Gerald R. Ford in 1976. In the 1980s, Washtenaw has gone Republican once (1984) and Democratic twice (1980 and 1988).

Besides Ann Arbor, most of the district's Democratic vote comes from Jackson, an industrial city with nearly 37,000 residents. Jackson's Democrats work in the tool-and-die and auto parts factories scattered throughout the city. Unlike Detroit's autoworkers, however, many of those living here were raised in the surrounding Republican countryside, and they sometimes reflect that background in statewide and national elections.

Population: 514,560. White 478,266 (93%), Black 24,349 (5%), Other 7,767 (2%). Spanish origin 6,677 (1%). 18 and over 375,911 (73%), 65 and over 45,010 (9%). Median age: 29.

a well-financed Democratic challenger gave Pursell even more breathing room.

But Pursell still exhibits obvious signs that he will never be any kind of right-wing ideologue. In the 101st Congress, he voted to curb spending on the strategic defense initiative, cast some pro-abortion rights votes and was one of just 34 Republicans in the House to support the civil rights bill. In the 100th Congress, he voted against the overwhelming majority of Republicans who opposed a seven-day waiting period for handgun purchases and a 60-day plant-closing notification measure.

On Appropriations, Pursell is well liked and can often bridge the gap between the GOP's conservative and moderate wings. He also has ties to the Democratic side of the aisle, joining with Michigan Democrat Bob Carr to protect home-state interests.

Pursell's position on the Appropriations subcommittee that handles education funding — where he became ranking member after the death of Silvio Conte of Massachusetts — is crucial to him, because there he can lobby for federal help for the University of Michigan, whose 36,000 students make it a dominant industry in the district.

At Home: Pursell's record has stood him well during his years representing the starkly diverse 2nd. He is liberal enough on social issues and independent enough from the national GOP to pick off some votes in the Democratic-leaning university community at Ann Arbor, yet the suburban and rural communities in his district find his overall record sufficiently conservative to suit their tastes.

When he first came to Congress, Pursell took his political cues from Marvin L. Esch, the five-term moderate Republican he succeeded when Esch ran unsuccessfully for the Senate in 1976. Pursell has knit together the different parts of his district, as did his predecessor.

Pursell won his first term in 1976 by just 344 votes, due to his strength in Wayne County, which he represented in the state Senate. He won 65 percent there, while losing the rest of the district to Democrat Edward C. Pierce, a much more liberal Ann Arbor doctor.

His first re-election was a breeze, but he slipped more than 10 percentage points in 1980 against Kathleen O'Reilly, who as director of the Consumer Federation of America had won enthusiastic liberal support in Washington. But she had trouble uniting feuding factions of local Democrats, and her campaign could not broaden its appeal beyond Ann Arbor.

Redistricting in early 1982 brought the 2nd more in line with the GOP mainstream, shoring up Pursell against the threat of a strong Democratic attack.

After winning routinely in 1982 and 1984, Pursell dropped under 60 percent again in 1986, when he faced Democrat Dean Baker, a University of Michigan graduate student. Baker based his campaign on strong opposition to Reagan's Central American policies. The appeal of that issue in Ann Arbor helped Baker carry Washtenaw County by a 350-vote margin. But Pursell swamped him elsewhere, especially in the Republican's Wayne County base, where he won 70 percent of the vote.

Pursell's 59 percent tally against the unheralded Baker inspired Democratic state Sen. Lana Pollack to launch a challenge in 1988. While her liberal record in the Legislature was considered a liability by most local observers, it helped Pollack win the backing of the auto workers' union, which had never before made a concerted effort to oust Pursell. Pollack also gained credibility when she proved to be a prolific fund-raiser; her total expenditures for the campaign exceeded $750,000.

Pollack claimed that despite Pursell's moderate image, he voted like a conservative in Washington. She got a boost when Environmental Action named him to its "Dirty Dozen" list of House members. But while Pollack had a devoted following in Ann Arbor, she ran into the usual obstacle of a Democratic nominee in the 2nd — wooing independents and moderate Republicans, especially those in rural areas whose votes are essential to victory.

Pursell took the challenge seriously. Spending more than $875,000 and airing the first television advertisements of his political career, the genial incumbent campaigned like a man on the run. His final tally of 55 percent was Pursell's lowest re-election total, but because he held his ground against such an aggressive and well-funded opponent, Pursell may have scared off challengers for a time. In 1990, he climbed back above the 60 percent mark.

Committee

Appropriations (7th of 22 Republicans)
Labor, Health & Human Services, Education & Related Agencies (ranking); Energy & Water Development

Elections

1990 General		
Carl D. Pursell (R)	95,962	(64%)
Elmer White (D)	49,678	(33%)
Paul S. Jensen (TIC)	4,119	(3%)
1988 General		
Carl D. Pursell (R)	120,070	(55%)
Lana Pollack (D)	98,290	(45%)

Previous Winning Percentages: **1986** (59%) **1984** (69%) **1982** (66%) **1980** (57%) **1978** (68%) **1976** (50%)

District Vote For President

	1988	1984	1980	1976
D	92,837 (43%)	79,684 (36%)	88,499 (37%)	90,250 (41%)
R	122,482 (56%)	142,867 (64%)	125,724 (52%)	126,141 (57%)
I			21,730 (9%)	

Campaign Finance

	Receipts	Receipts from PACs		Expend-itures
1990				
Pursell (R)	$285,808	$96,415	(34%)	$135,801
White (D)	$9,575	$4,800	(50%)	$9,573
1988				
Pursell (R)	$811,384	$264,993	(33%)	$876,779
Pollack (D)	$764,491	$238,912	(31%)	$750,493

Key Votes

1991	
Authorize use of force against Iraq	Y
1990	
Support constitutional amendment on flag desecration	Y
Pass family and medical leave bill over Bush veto	N
Reduce SDI funding	Y
Allow abortions in overseas military facilities	N
Approve budget summit plan for spending and taxing	N
Approve civil rights bill	Y
1989	
Halt production of B-2 stealth bomber at 13 planes	N
Oppose capital gains tax cut	N
Approve federal abortion funding in rape or incest cases	Y
Approve pay raise and revision of ethics rules	Y
Pass Democratic minimum wage plan over Bush veto	N

Voting Studies

	Presidential Support		Party Unity		Conservative Coalition	
Year	S	O	S	O	S	O
1990	53	38	57	30	65	19
1989	60	37	52	42	83	15
1988	47	46	62	35	79	16
1987	52	44	51	38	72	21
1986	51	46	50	46	74	22
1985	56	35	57	32	75	20
1984	50	40	53	32	63	20
1983	63	28	56	33	69	26
1982	42	42	38	40	45	37
1981	49	45	42	50	31	60

Interest Group Ratings

Year	ADA	ACU	AFL-CIO	CCUS
1990	28	57	18	92
1989	30	57	8	100
1988	45	46	62	79
1987	20	55	20	71
1986	45	55	43	76
1985	15	71	21	75
1984	45	45	36	79
1983	15	61	18	85
1982	45	21	29	71
1981	65	73	53	76

3 Howard Wolpe (D)

Of Lansing — Elected 1978

Born: Nov. 2, 1939, Los Angeles, Calif.

Education: Reed College, B.A. 1960; Massachusetts Institute of Technology, Ph.D. 1967.

Occupation: Professor of political science.

Family: Divorced; one child.

Religion: Jewish.

Political Career: Kalamazoo City Commission, 1969-72; Mich. House, 1973-77; Democratic nominee for U.S. House, 1976.

Capitol Office: 1535 Longworth Bldg. 20515; 225-5011.

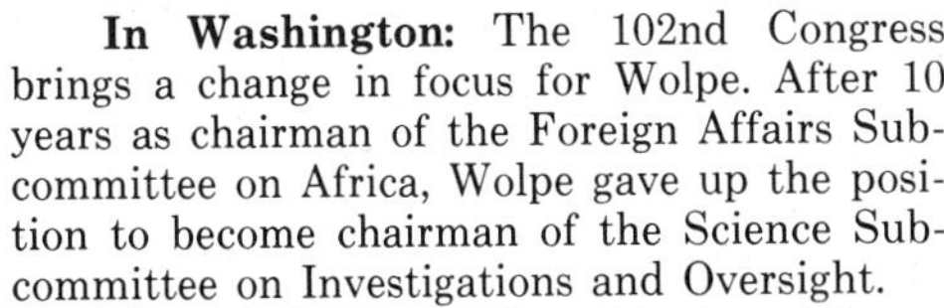

In Washington: The 102nd Congress brings a change in focus for Wolpe. After 10 years as chairman of the Foreign Affairs Subcommittee on Africa, Wolpe gave up the position to become chairman of the Science Subcommittee on Investigations and Oversight.

The switch is more of an adjustment than a metamorphosis. Wolpe was active on the Science Committee even as he pursued a lengthy agenda on Foreign Affairs; he also remained on the Africa subcommittee after passing his chairman's gavel to Democratic Rep. Mervyn M. Dymally of California in January 1991.

Wolpe leaves a legacy as chairman of that panel, a position he sought because of his background as a professor of African studies. Wolpe used the post as a bully pulpit and worked to force a range of issues onto the congressional priority list, including topics such as South Africa's apartheid system, U.S. aid priorities in Africa and famine relief.

Although heading that subcommittee provided few political benefits — and some risks — for a member from a heartland district, Wolpe said it was simply a desire for new challenges that led him to take the Science panel chair.

It is unlikely Wolpe would have relinquished the Africa chair had South African President F.W. de Klerk not made moves to reform his nation's racial separatist system in 1989 and 1990. Wolpe earlier had passed three times on Science subcommittee chairmanships.

But with changes he sought in South Africa under way, Wolpe was tempted by the oversight chairmanship vacated by New Jersey Democrat Robert A. Roe, who became chairman of the Public Works Committee. The position will allow Wolpe — a liberal activist with strong interests in the environment and in federal research priorities — to hold hearings on a variety of science-related subjects.

The superconducting super collider is certain to be a program that Wolpe watches. He has criticized the multibillion dollar atom-smasher, to be built in Texas, as having the potential to soak up much of the federal science budget. He joined other super collider critics in 1989 in an unsuccessful attempt to block funding for the project.

Also during the 101st Congress, Wolpe used his Science seat to promote a bill aimed at expanding waste reduction efforts by U.S. businesses. The measure, providing matching state grants to aid businesses in reducing hazardous waste and setting up a federal Office of Pollution Prevention under the Environmental Protection Agency, was enacted as part of a deficit-reduction law in October 1990. Wolpe also is chairman of the Democratic Caucus Task Force on the Environment and Energy.

Wolpe points to efforts such as these when 3rd District GOP foes try to convince voters that he is more concerned with foreigners than Michiganders. Wolpe also touts his co-chairmanship of the Northeast-Midwest Congressional Coalition, a caucus that works to develop economic strategies for the region.

Still, Wolpe is best known for his work on issues involving U.S.-Africa relations in general and policy toward South Africa in particular. Wolpe had established himself as a crusader against apartheid long before he set out against President Ronald Reagan's "constructive engagement" approach toward South Africa. The result of that policy, Wolpe said in 1985, was "to increase the violence, because the intransigent [white] elements have been led to believe they can engage in repression without any real cost or American response."

That June, Wolpe and Pennsylvania Democrat William H. Gray III moved a bill through the House that would have imposed immediate economic sanctions on South Africa. Although a compromise bill, negotiated by conferees from the House and the GOP-controlled Senate, was never approved by the full Senate, pressure for its passage played a role in Reagan's September 1985 issuance of an executive order incorporating some of the compromise language.

In 1986, South Africa's bombing raids into neighboring countries helped Wolpe and his allies obtain stronger sanctions. The House

Michigan 3

South Central — Lansing; Kalamazoo

Although the 3rd is anchored by the medium-sized industrial cities of Kalamazoo and Battle Creek, votes from the surrounding farmland have traditionally defined district politics as Republican.

Because the last redistricting added Democratic territory in downtown and western Lansing to the 3rd, the Republican vote is lower than it was in the 1970s, but it is still a clear majority in most elections.

In Kalamazoo, paper mills and automobile assembly plants provide the base of a powerful union presence and blue-collar Democratic vote, although Checker Motors' last car rolled off the lines there in 1982. The city also has a large academic community, with Western Michigan University, where Wolpe once taught, and Kalamazoo College.

But the pharmaceutical workers at the Upjohn Co., the corporate managers in the southern half of the city and the area's Dutch residents give Kalamazoo County a strong moderate-to-conservative Republican vote. Reagan carried the county as a whole with 64 percent in 1984, and George Bush got 54 percent there in 1988.

Battle Creek, half the size of Kalamazoo, is widely recognized by morning cereal-box readers as the source of both Kellogg's and Post breakfast cereals. Together with Ralston-Purina and several truck manufacturers, those companies provide the bulk of the city's jobs. Their unionized workers provide one of the steadiest sources of Democratic votes.

Between the major cities are large patches of rural and suburban GOP territory. White-collar suburbs such as Delta Township, west of Lansing, and Battle Creek Township, home to Kellogg executives, usually provide Republicans with overwhelming electoral margins. The small towns and rolling fields of Eaton, Kalamazoo and Calhoun counties provide strong conservative reinforcement. Only in southern Barry County, settled over the years by workers from Battle Creek and Kalamazoo, do Democrats find a welcome in the countryside.

Population: 514,560. White 456,405 (89%), Black 45,053 (9%), Other 4,691 (1%). Spanish origin 12,462 (2%). 18 and over 367,512 (71%), 65 and over 49,244 (10%). Median age: 28.

passed a Wolpe-Gray bill to impose a trade embargo on South Africa and force all U.S. companies to stop doing business there.

When the Senate approved a milder bill, Wolpe urged his House colleagues to press for a conference. But other Democrats, including Gray, concluded that a hard-line approach could scuttle the legislation. They accepted Senate Foreign Relations Chairman Richard G. Lugar's promise to support an override of Reagan's expected veto and passed the Senate bill. In the end, both chambers overrode Reagan's veto, making the sanctions law.

Wolpe got an even tougher sanctions bill through the House in 1988, this one banning almost all U.S. trade with South Africa, but it died in the Senate. By 1990, de Klerk's reforms, including the release of jailed black leader Nelson Mandela, convinced Wolpe to table further such efforts.

Wolpe praised President Bush at that time for unequivocally criticizing South Africa's white-minority government and for upholding the sanctions enacted in 1986. "It really is a very dramatic contrast to the Reagan years, and I think it's been very useful," he said.

Wolpe also has supported Bush for providing aid to leftist-run African nations, such as Mozambique, that seek closer relations with the United States. However, he criticizes Bush, as he did Reagan, for backing nations such as Kenya and Zaire, whose leaders have pro-Western sentiments but repressive domestic policies.

Like many House Democrats, Wolpe tried for years to rechannel part of the defense budget into domestic programs. As a member of the Budget Committee (1983-89), Wolpe pressed to divert funds to "programs that are most critical to our economic future — education, research and development and retraining."

In January 1991, Wolpe opposed the resolution authorizing Bush to use military force against Iraq, warning that military action would cost lives and could sap the U.S. economy.

At Home: Wolpe continues to succeed in the Republican-majority 3rd in spite of his liberal voting record. Although Wolpe often appears vulnerable — he has cleared the 60 percent mark only once in his seven House campaigns — a variety of GOP challengers have all failed to bring him down. The constituent-service skills that Wolpe first honed as a Kalamazoo city councilman and as a state legislator clearly have been crucial to his re-elections.

A narrow 1976 loser to GOP Rep. Garry Brown, Wolpe worked for Sen. Donald W. Riegle Jr. for two years while preparing for a rematch. He won it by reducing Brown's margin in the Lansing suburbs of Eaton County without losing support in Kalamazoo.

In 1984 and 1986, Wolpe survived noisy contests with conservative Jackie McGregor, a former vice chairman of the state GOP with a clear knack for controversy.

In 1984, McGregor received the endorsement of a National Rifle Association official who called Wolpe a communist sympathizer. She then got 4th District GOP Rep. Mark D. Siljander (who was defeated in 1986) to cosign a letter to ministers urging them to "send another Christian to Congress" by supporting her. After Wolpe, who is Jewish, complained, McGregor said it was he who injected religion into the campaign by enlisting six Jewish congressmen to send a letter supporting him.

Key GOP contributors disliked her style, and she fell far behind in fundraising. But aided by Reagan's strong showing in the 3rd, McGregor held Wolpe to 53 percent, which encouraged her to try again in 1986.

In the rematch, McGregor assailed Wolpe's defense record, claiming that his opposition to Reagan's military priorities cost the district defense-related jobs. The candidates also had another exchange over religion.

Many in the moderate Republican business community closed their wallets to McGregor, and Wolpe cultivated more business support than before. His efforts to block repeal of certain real-estate deductions during the 1986 tax-revision debate earned him National Association of Realtors support. Wolpe's 60 percent tally was the highest of his House electoral career.

In 1988, Wolpe slipped under 60 percent again against political newcomer Cal Allgaier, the owner of several local convenience stores. Considered a long shot, Allgaier gained legitimacy when Kellogg's corporate political action committee endorsed him. Though Wolpe is popular with the cereal company's unionized work force, Kellogg has facilities in South Africa, and management objected to his position on U.S. sanctions.

As in the past, Wolpe met his opponent in several debates, where he persuasively defended his liberal record. But Bush's strong showing in the 3rd boosted the underfunded Allgaier well over 40 percent.

Allgaier's showing encouraged Republicans to recruit a strong 1990 challenger, and they thought they had one in Brad Haskins, a young lawyer who grew up in the district. But while Haskins was a more appealing candidate than prior GOP nominees, his anti-incumbent message was not nearly enough to dislodge Wolpe.

Committees

Foreign Affairs (5th of 28 Democrats)
Africa; International Economic Policy & Trade

Science, Space & Technology (6th of 32 Democrats)
Investigations & Oversight (chairman); Energy; Environment

Elections

1990 General		
Howard Wolpe (D)	82,376	(58%)
Brad Haskins (R)	60,007	(42%)
1988 General		
Howard Wolpe (D)	112,605	(57%)
Cal Allgaier (R)	83,769	(43%)

Previous Winning Percentages: **1986** (60%) **1984** (53%) **1982** (56%) **1980** (52%) **1978** (51%)

District Vote For President

	1988		1984		1980		1976	
D	91,304	(45%)	75,445	(36%)	79,581	(37%)	77,860	(40%)
R	108,237	(54%)	130,891	(63%)	112,115	(52%)	114,346	(58%)
I					20,803	(10%)		

Campaign Finance

	Receipts	Receipts from PACs		Expend-itures
1990				
Wolpe (D)	$791,685	$414,976	(52%)	$815,244
Haskins (R)	$280,311	$56,300	(20%)	$274,106
1988				
Wolpe (D)	$576,393	$263,224	(46%)	$600,940
Allgaier (R)	$165,710	$67,000	(40%)	$164,856

Key Votes

1991	
Authorize use of force against Iraq	N
1990	
Support constitutional amendment on flag desecration	N
Pass family and medical leave bill over Bush veto	Y
Reduce SDI funding	Y
Allow abortions in overseas military facilities	Y
Approve budget summit plan for spending and taxing	N
Approve civil rights bill	Y
1989	
Halt production of B-2 stealth bomber at 13 planes	Y
Oppose capital gains tax cut	Y
Approve federal abortion funding in rape or incest cases	Y
Approve pay raise and revision of ethics rules	Y
Pass Democratic minimum wage plan over Bush veto	Y

Voting Studies

	Presidential Support		Party Unity		Conservative Coalition	
Year	**S**	**O**	**S**	**O**	**S**	**O**
1990	15	82	90	7	15	85
1989	28	70	92	4	7	90
1988	17	81	92	6	18	82
1987	14	82	91	2	12	88
1986	16	82	91	7	10	88
1985	21	76	91	6	7	93
1984	23	76	93	6	5	95
1983	16	82	93	4	11	88
1982	34	66	88	11	11	88
1981	26	72	92	8	8	91

Interest Group Ratings

Year	ADA	ACU	AFL-CIO	CCUS
1990	100	13	100	21
1989	100	4	100	40
1988	100	0	100	36
1987	92	0	94	7
1986	90	5	93	33
1985	85	10	94	20
1984	95	0	92	38
1983	95	0	94	35
1982	100	0	100	18
1981	95	0	80	11

4 Fred Upton (R)

Of St. Joseph — Elected 1986

Born: April 23, 1953, St. Joseph, Mich.
Education: U. of Michigan, B.A. 1975.
Occupation: Congressional aide; budget analyst.
Family: Wife, Amey Rulon-Miller; one child.
Religion: Protestant.
Political Career: No previous office.
Capitol Office: 1713 Longworth Bldg. 20515; 225-3761.

In Washington: A serious, detail-minded man, Upton quickly impressed colleagues with his willingness to stand and take a punch — even if it's from his own corner.

During the 1990 budget battle, he gained a degree of media attention when, at a meeting at the White House attended by President Bush, Chief of Staff John Sununu exploded after Upton calmly explained why he opposed the bipartisan package. "What are you smoking?" Sununu demanded of Upton, according to the New York Times. Upton refused to waver.

His moxie has not gone unrewarded. When Newt Gingrich became minority whip in March 1989, Upton gained a position in his whip organization. He also won a seat on the Energy and Commerce Committee in the new Congress.

Upton's early involvement in the budget debate surprised no one. The former director of legislative affairs for the Office of Management and Budget (OMB), he entered Congress fully abreast of the complexities of federal spending.

As a freshman, he joined an effort, led by Republican Tom Tauke of Iowa and Democrat Timothy J. Penny of Minnesota, to shrink the deficit with small cuts in appropriations bills. Upton offered several like floor amendments to appropriations bills, but none passed.

Upton's aptitude for management and budget matters led to his most noticed first-term victory — blocking an effort to declare a one-time federal holiday on Sept. 17, 1987, honoring the bicentennial of the U.S. Constitution. "We all realize that the Constitution is a working document," Upton said. "If this is true, does it really make sense to celebrate a working document by taking a day off work?"

Citing OMB estimates of potential $330 million in savings, Upton gained passage of an amendment that struck out the federal holiday provisions and instead proposed a "National Day of Recognition."

Upton lobbied hard — some colleagues felt too hard — for a seat on the Budget Committee as a freshman. He did not achieve that goal, ending up on the Public Works and Small Business committees.

At Home: In 1986, Upton was the only House Republican to unseat an incumbent in a primary. But his victory over GOP Rep. Mark D. Siljander was not a total shock.

Much of the local GOP establishment had long disliked Siljander, an activist in the religious right whose efforts to link religion and politics had often fed controversy. And Upton was unusually well-positioned to challenge the vulnerable incumbent.

Upton is a member of one of the district's most prominent families — his grandfather was a founder of the Whirlpool appliance company. And although he had never sought office before, Upton had a strong résumé. He spent 10 years as an aide to David A. Stockman during Stockman's tenures as 4th District House member and as President Reagan's OMB director.

Siljander had emerged on the scene in 1981, winning a special election after Stockman's move to OMB. He beat a longtime Stockman ally by mobilizing his fundamentalist backers, and he went on to establish a reputation as a conservative firebrand known to denounce the "perverted" philosophy of "secular humanists." Although his voting record was in line with the majority philosophy of the 4th, Siljander's style alienated GOP regulars. Upton decided to run when he returned to the district in 1985 after Stockman resigned his OMB post.

Upton generally avoided challenging Siljander's issue positions; instead, he hoped to convince voters that he was simply a more appealing, less confrontational conservative. He got a break late in the campaign, when Siljander committed an astounding gaffe. He taped an appeal to fundamentalist ministers, implying that the challenge to him was linked to evil forces, and calling on voters to "break the back of Satan." Upton aides claim he would have won anyway, but the tape clinched his victory.

The religious right did mount a 1990 primary challenge to Upton, in the form of conservative state Sen. Ed Fredricks. But Upton won the nomination and he continued his string of solid general election victories.

Michigan 4

Southwest — Holland; Benton Harbor-St. Joseph

Stretching 100 miles on the eastern shore of Lake Michigan and another 100 miles along the Indiana border, the L-shaped 4th is among the most Republican constituencies in the country.

It is overwhelmingly agricultural; fewer than a fifth of its residents live in its five small cities. Cass, St. Joseph and Branch counties form the northeastern edge of the Corn Belt; the conservative Democratic votes of workers in the plants and foundries of Dowagiac, Three Rivers and Coldwater barely touch the GOP majorities in these three counties.

The gentle climate produced by the lake has made fruits and berries the chief crops of the four lakeshore counties — Berrien, Van Buren, Ottawa and Allegan. Berrien, which voted for every Republican statewide candidate in 1990, has a small food-processing industry, and several wineries dot the fields around Paw Paw in Van Buren County. The shoreline is also a retirement and tourist draw. Some of Michigan's strongest Republican precincts are in Allegan and Ottawa counties.

The city of Holland, on the line between Ottawa and Allegan, is a GOP bastion. The westernmost point of the "Dutch Triangle" formed by Holland, Grand Rapids and Kalamazoo, Holland and its environs were settled by immigrants from the Netherlands in the mid-19th century. Holland's Dutch character goes beyond its name and its wooden shoe factory and Tulip Festival to a Calvinist religious style.

The major chunk of Democratic votes in the 4th comes from the Benton Harbor-St. Joseph area. Benton Harbor once offered haven to runaway slaves on the underground railroad; today it is mostly black, and fighting industrial decline. St. Joseph, once a bedroom community for Benton Harbor, now has a significant manufacturing base. The blue-collar workers in St. Joseph and towns to the south like conservative Democrats, as do retirees from industrial Illinois and Indiana who now live in shore cottages in towns such as New Buffalo.

Population: 514,560. White 468,675 (91%), Black 37,396 (7%), Other 3,934 (1%). Spanish origin 8,278 (2%). 18 and over 355,746 (69%), 65 and over 56,287 (11%). Median age: 30.

Committees

Energy & Commerce (16th of 16 Republicans)
Commerce, Consumer Protection & Competitiveness; Oversight & Investigations

Public Works & Transportation (10th of 21 Republicans)
Economic Development; Surface Transportation; Water Resources

Select Hunger (7th of 12 Republicans)
Domestic

Small Business (9th of 17 Republicans)
Environment & Employment; Procurement, Tourism & Rural Development

Elections

1990 General		
Fred Upton (R)	75,850	(58%)
JoAnne McFarland (D)	55,449	(42%)
1990 Primary		
Fred Upton (R)	29,480	(63%)
Ed Fredricks (R)	17,140	(37%)
1988 General		
Fred Upton (R)	132,270	(71%)
Norman J. Rivers (D)	54,428	(29%)

Previous Winning Percentage: 1986 (62%)

District Vote For President

	1988		1984		1980		1976	
D	72,584	(36%)	61,604	(32%)	66,585	(32%)	72,586	(37%)
R	127,631	(63%)	130,742	(68%)	126,001	(60%)	119,110	(61%)
I					13,095	(6%)		

Campaign Finance

	Receipts	Receipts from PACs		Expend-itures
1990				
Upton (R)	$445,881	$152,654	(34%)	$503,164
McFarland (D)	$82,095	$48,100	(59%)	$78,392
1988				
Upton (R)	$422,884	$117,465	(28%)	$323,829
Rivers (D)	$8,629	$4,300	(50%)	$8,577

Key Votes

1991	
Authorize use of force against Iraq	Y
1990	
Support constitutional amendment on flag desecration	Y
Pass family and medical leave bill over Bush veto	N
Reduce SDI funding	N
Allow abortions in overseas military facilities	N
Approve budget summit plan for spending and taxing	N
Approve civil rights bill	N
1989	
Halt production of B-2 stealth bomber at 13 planes	N
Oppose capital gains tax cut	N
Approve federal abortion funding in rape or incest cases	Y
Approve pay raise and revision of ethics rules	Y
Pass Democratic minimum wage plan over Bush veto	N

Voting Studies

	Presidential Support		Party Unity		Conservative Coalition	
Year	**S**	**O**	**S**	**O**	**S**	**O**
1990	61	39	89	11	85	15
1989	74	26	85	15	88	12
1988	60	40	86	14	87	13
1987	60	40	90	10	91	9

Interest Group Ratings

Year	ADA	ACU	AFL-CIO	CCUS
1990	17	71	17	93
1989	20	75	8	100
1988	30	64	50	100
1987	16	70	13	87

5 Paul B. Henry (R)

Of Grand Rapids — Elected 1984

Born: July 9, 1942, Chicago, Ill.

Education: Wheaton College, B.A. 1963; Duke U., M.A. 1968, Ph.D. 1970.

Occupation: Professor of political science.

Family: Wife, Karen Anne Borthistle; three children.

Religion: Christian Reformed.

Political Career: Mich. House, 1979-83; Mich. Senate, 1983-85.

Capitol Office: 215 Cannon Bldg. 20515; 225-3831.

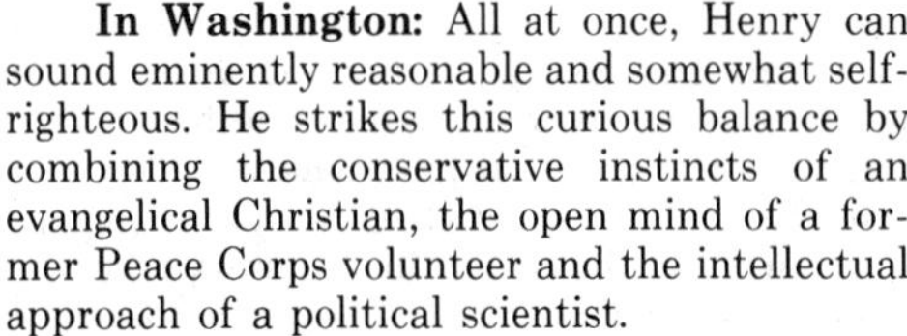

In Washington: All at once, Henry can sound eminently reasonable and somewhat self-righteous. He strikes this curious balance by combining the conservative instincts of an evangelical Christian, the open mind of a former Peace Corps volunteer and the intellectual approach of a political scientist.

This combination of traits has long made Henry a much talked-about politician. As far back as 1984, when he was seeking his first House term, syndicated columnist David Broder foresaw a career in the Senate for the gifted Republican. More recently, Henry has been widely mentioned as a challenger to Democratic Sen. Donald W. Riegle Jr. in 1994.

But for all the respect his integrity earns him personally, his independence tends to isolate rather than ingratiate him politically. Neither a political conservative nor a moderate, Henry plays a supporting role in House debates more often than a lead.

During debate in the 101st Congress over the National Endowment of Art's funding of controversial works, Henry was committed to saving the NEA and to convincing Congress that restrictions on obscenity were only fair to taxpayers. "I am your friend, I support the arts personally," he said. "But please do not blind yourself to political reality.... In order to save [the NEA] we are going to have to reform it."

His proposal would have restricted funding of projects that "deliberately denigrate" the United States or religious, racial or ethnic groups, and he called for the NEA to uphold "general standards of decency." As the debate wore on, however, Henry's attempt to find a middle ground placed him well to the right of those in the thick of the legislative fight. In a nod to his efforts, his language on "standards of decency" was included in the final measure.

Henry continues to work to advance his national bottle bill, which has been bottled up in committee for years. Modeled on Michigan's legislation, Henry's plan would ban require a 5-cent deposit on beverage containers — glass, aluminum and plastic. Cosponsors of his proposal quadrupled in the 101st Congress to 100.

In the 100th Congress, when the Education and Labor Subcommittee on Health and Safety debated legislation to require notification of workers who may be exposed to hazardous substances, Henry commended the bill's "very laudable goals," but took a lead in warning of "an avalanche" of new liability problems. A substitute he offered with GOP Rep. James M. Jeffords of Vermont to mandate stricter enforcement of existing laws was rejected on a largely party-line vote.

At Home: Though the national GOP was touting Reagan-style conservatism when Henry won the 5th in 1984, he built his political credentials in the party's moderate wing. His introduction to politics was his work an an aide to Illinois Rep. John B. Anderson in the late 1960s. He backed Anderson in Michigan's 1980 GOP presidential primary.

Henry's centrist outlook was the norm for the state GOP in the 1970s, when moderate William G. Milliken was governor. But after the GOP lost the governorship in 1982, the state party shifted right. In his initial House campaign, Henry tried to keep step while retaining his moderate image. "I'm a fiscal conservative," he said, "but not a scrooge." In the GOP primary, Henry was challenged from the right by Keary W. Sawyer, the son of retiring GOP Rep. Harold S. Sawyer.

But Henry contrasted his record in the state House, where he was assistant floor leader, and in the state Senate, where he chaired the Education and Health Committee, with his foe's lack of experience.

Sawyer had never sought public office, and was not plugged into the local party network because his father lacked close ties with the GOP establishment. Henry won the nomination decisively.

Democrat Gary J. McInerney, a lawyer and businessman, seemed to have appeal beyond his party's normal base. But the political neophyte was no match for Henry, who as a state legislator had served about half the people in the 5th. Henry's easy victories since then have fueled talk of his prospects as a statewide candidate.

Michigan 5

West Central — Grand Rapids

The 5th, Gerald R. Ford's old constituency, is centered on Grand Rapids, Michigan's second-largest city. During Ford's presidency, Grand Rapids attained an image as clean-cut, all-American, middle-class and Republican.

The high-tech and service industries in the area — aircraft instrumentation firms, a Keebler cookie distribution center and, nearby, the national headquarters of the Amway Corp. — have brought in technicians, managers and professionals whose neat houses, manicured lawns and Republican votes reinforce that picture.

But Grand Rapids' heavy industry, including furniture and auto-parts factories, gives it a sizable working-class presence. It has the largest black population in Michigan outside the Detroit-to-Bay City auto corridor, and blue-collar voters in the central and western parts of the city put it in the Democratic column in the early post-Ford House elections.

The local GOP is two-pronged. The conservative community around Calvin College and the small-business people in southeast Grand Rapids are largely descendants of the Dutch craftsmen brought in by the city's once-famous furniture industry; they are the "Dutch Wing." The executives and younger professionals to the northeast and in East Grand Rapids and Kentwood are the more cosmopolitan "Ford Wing." Henry, as a Calvin College professor with a pragmatic manner and some moderate views, unites the two factions.

Outside the city stretch miles of farm land peppered with small towns. Townships north and south of Grand Rapids have generally attracted blue-collar Democrats who moved from the west side. Conservative Dutch influence is strong in the Allegan County towns near Holland.

Population: 514,560. White 472,168 (92%), Black 31,855 (6%), Other 4,932 (1%). Spanish origin 9,750 (2%). 18 and over 359,611 (70%), 65 and over 52,190 (10%). Median age: 28.

Committees

Education & Labor (8th of 14 Republicans)
Health & Safety (ranking); Elementary, Secondary & Vocational Education; Employment Opportunities; Postsecondary Education

Science, Space & Technology (8th of 19 Republicans)
Space; Technology & Competitiveness

Select Aging (12th of 27 Republicans)
Health & Long-Term Care

Elections

1990 General		
Paul B. Henry (R)	126,308	(75%)
Thomas Trzybinski (D)	41,170	(25%)
1988 General		
Paul B. Henry (R)	166,569	(73%)
James Catchick (D)	62,868	(27%)

Previous Winning Percentages: **1986** (71%) **1984** (62%)

District Vote For President

	1988	1984	1980	1976
D	83,859 (35%)	73,849 (32%)	80,701 (35%)	66,634 (32%)
R	151,713 (64%)	158,992 (68%)	128,842 (55%)	140,552 (67%)
I			19,541 (8%)	

Campaign Finance

	Receipts	Receipts from PACs		Expend-itures
1990				
Henry (R)	$398,627	$92,880	(23%)	$241,151
1988				
Henry (R)	$387,878	$97,425	(25%)	$309,436
Catchick (D)	$53,137	$12,200	(23%)	$50,977

Key Votes

1991	
Authorize use of force against Iraq	Y
1990	
Support constitutional amendment on flag desecration	N
Pass family and medical leave bill over Bush veto	N
Reduce SDI funding	N
Allow abortions in overseas military facilities	N
Approve budget summit plan for spending and taxing	N
Approve civil rights bill	Y
1989	
Halt production of B-2 stealth bomber at 13 planes	N
Oppose capital gains tax cut	N
Approve federal abortion funding in rape or incest cases	N
Approve pay raise and revision of ethics rules	Y
Pass Democratic minimum wage plan over Bush veto	N

Voting Studies

	Presidential Support		Party Unity		Conservative Coalition	
Year	**S**	**O**	**S**	**O**	**S**	**O**
1990	58	40	75	21	70	30
1989	66	33	69	29	80	20
1988	49	48	81	17	84	11
1987	56	42	75	22	77	23
1986	43	57	67	31	66	34
1985	60	40	69	29	65	35

Interest Group Ratings

Year	ADA	ACU	AFL-CIO	CCUS
1990	33	63	9	86
1989	30	68	8	90
1988	50	52	57	93
1987	36	45	40	87
1986	40	45	43	89
1985	25	67	24	68

6 Bob Carr (D)

Of East Lansing — Elected 1974

Did not serve 1981-83.

Born: March 27, 1943, Janesville, Wis.
Education: U. of Wisconsin, B.S. 1965, J.D. 1968.
Occupation: Lawyer.
Family: Wife, Kate Smith.
Religion: Baptist.
Political Career: Democratic nominee for U.S. House, 1972; defeated for re-election, 1980.
Capitol Office: 2439 Rayburn Bldg. 20515; 225-4872.

In Washington: Carr's electoral defeat in 1980 did more than keep him out of public office for two years. It transformed his legislative personality, in ways that work both for and against him.

The humbling experience stripped Carr of the brash arrogance he displayed as a junior member in the 1970s. But along with it went Carr's taste for national policy-making. His focus these days is almost entirely on Michigan and his district, and he reveals little of the penchant for crusades and innovation that characterizes many of his class of 1974 colleagues.

As the 1990s opened, a number of Carr's classmates are assuming senior positions enabling them to effect change in the institution. But Carr seems to stand apart from many of his peers.

At the Democratic Caucus meeting at the start of the 102nd Congress, Carr recommended that committee chairmen file written explanations of the cost and purpose of official travel. The move reinforced the notion that advancement within the House is not a top priority for Carr.

At times Carr seems unusually sensitive to prevailing political winds. During the 101st Congress, he recommended stripping flag burners of their citizenship and then expediting deportation procedures for them. "Putting them in jail or giving them a fine like a common purse snatcher is not appropriate," he explained. "Raising questions about their citizenship is."

Mostly, however, Carr quietly focuses on the Appropriations Committee, where he dwells on bread-and-butter, district-oriented issues that have helped him build steadily stronger electoral margins. In 1990, he was unopposed for the first time.

Where Carr shines most is on Appropriations' Transportation Subcommittee. A pilot, he has a keen interest in the Federal Aviation Administration (FAA), and when aviation is discussed, he can speak eloquently on technically complex matters with no notes to guide him. His expertise helps him influence other members, but leaves some of them wondering why he does not also apply his intellect to other issues.

But even on Appropriations, Carr has begun to reveal a frustration with the powers that be. During the 1990 House-Senate conference on the transportation spending bill, Carr complained bitterly about Senate earmarks for research. Not only was he unhappy that none of the money went to Michigan, but also he felt that the pool of money available was so small that earmarks for specific states would hurt the overall research program. But the Senate funding proposal had been approved in a deal with the House chairman.

Similarly, in 1989, when Appropriations took up the proposed repeal of the Section 89 tax rules designed to weed out discrimination in employee benefit plans, Carr was an early supporter. He said his vote not only reflected his opposition to the tax rules, but also his objection to the way the Ways and Means Committee does business. He complained that members are practically never given the chance to amend the tax panel's work on the floor.

Carr's early opposition to Section 89 is reflective of his warming rapport with small business. In 1990, for instance, his support score from the U.S. Chamber of Commerce rose to 57 percent. He also parted from the Democratic majority on two key business issues in the 101st Congress: He voted to sustain President Bush's veto of the Family and Medical Leave Act and he supported the capital gains cut.

First elected in the Watergate landslide, Carr made an instant reputation as a rebel by calling for the resignation of House Speaker Carl Albert of Oklahoma and leading his fellow freshmen in a series of assaults on the congressional establishment. After his 1980 defeat and comeback two years later, Carr called his attack on Albert "sheer, naive stupidity."

At Home: Though Carr was a political newcomer when he first ran for the House in 1972, he performed surprisingly well against

Michigan 6

Central — Lansing; Pontiac

The 6th stretches from the state capital of Lansing about 70 miles east to the manufacturing city of Pontiac. It is not easy territory for either party; any candidate trying to win it has to stitch votes together from its disparate communities.

The 52,000 residents of Lansing who live in the district — about two-fifths of the city's population — make up a politically marginal bloc. The upper-level professionals and executives in the northwest or in the Groesbeck section along Lansing's eastern edge turn in solid GOP votes, but state employees and younger professionals south of the Grand River are more independent. Democratic votes come from Eastern European and Hispanic blue-collar neighborhoods in the northeastern and southeastern sections.

East Lansing, with a student population of more than 40,000 at Michigan State University, is an important source of Democratic votes, although the students themselves have grown less liberal in the last decade. State government workers and university faculty in the suburban communities of Meridian Township and Okemos give those areas a Democratic tilt, but the business people and company managers who also live there exert a Republican influence.

The truck farms of eastern Ingham County stretch into neighboring Livingston County. During the 1970s, Livingston was the state's second fastest-growing county, though the population has stabilized in the 1980s. One of Michigan's most conservative areas, Livingston was settled by German Protestant farmers who made it a center of German-American Bund activism in the 1930s and a GOP stronghold; Democratic sympathizers trying for local office still run as nominal Republicans.

But the farmland in eastern Livingston County has been eaten up by development spurred by white flight from Lansing, Detroit, Flint and Pontiac. Townships such as Hartland and Hamburg more than doubled in size in the 1970s, and the newcomers moderated the conservative makeup of the county.

To the east is Oakland County; its major city, Pontiac, is made up of low-income blacks, Hispanics and socially conservative Southern whites — George C. Wallace got 51 percent of the vote here in the 1972 presidential primary. Just to the west of Pontiac is Waterford Township, also with a large community of blue-collar whites. They fluctuate politically: Reagan supporters in 1980, they went back to the Democratic ticket in 1982 as the auto industry slump pushed local unemployment toward 30 percent. Oakland County went Republican in the 1988 presidential election, but Democrat Carr has carried it in his last three elections.

Population: 514,559. White 464,591 (90%), Black 36,837 (7%), Other 5,760 (1%). Spanish origin 12,600 (2%). 18 and over 360,961 (70%), 65 and over 36,341 (7%). Median age: 26.

veteran GOP Rep. Charles E. Chamberlain, taking advantage of the new 18-year-old vote in the college town of East Lansing to come within 2,500 votes. When Chamberlain retired in 1974, Carr won the election to replace him.

Carr's liberalism seemed out of place in his traditionally GOP district, but his strong constituent service helped him defeat his next two challengers. After pulling in 57 percent in 1978, Carr looked secure.

But in 1980, conservative building contractor Jim Dunn poured money into a hard-hitting campaign. A complacent Carr failed at first to see the threat; when he did, it was too late.

After losing narrowly, there was little question Carr would try again in 1982. He was helped by a Democratic remap that removed several GOP counties from the 6th and added Pontiac, a Democratic stronghold, and its blue-collar suburbs. With the district's economy devastated by recession, Carr tied Dunn to Reaganomics and won back his seat.

Dunn bypassed the 1984 House race for an unsuccessful GOP Senate primary bid. Carr prepared carefully anyway. He emphasized his work on district concerns, and collected over a half-million dollars.

His efforts paid off against Republican Tom Ritter, though not as richly as expected. Carr carried Oakland County with 57 percent and Ingham County with 53 percent. But Ritter, whose family produce business was a fixture in the 6th's eastern end, did well in Livingston County, and he held Carr to 52 percent. The slim margin emboldened Republicans.

Dunn's negative tone during his 1984 Senate primary against eventual nominee Jack Lousma angered many GOP insiders, but his image as Carr's strongest challenger forced them to shelve their reservations when Dunn decided to tackle Carr again in 1986.

From the outset, there was a bitter edge to

Dunn's effort. Republican officials claimed Carr owned an airplane, a horse and a Florida condo, but did not have a district residence because he said he could not afford homes in both Washington and Michigan.

Carr denied each charge. He claimed he did have a district residence — a rented room in a friend's East Lansing home. He also said he had sold his airplane and the Florida home, which was built for his mother; the horse, Carr said, belonged to his estranged wife.

Dunn resurrected a 14-year-old newspaper article in which Carr supported marijuana decriminalization. Carr said he had changed his opinions on many issues and noted that Dunn campaigned as a foe of abortion, but had voted for federal abortion funding in the House.

The campaign moved from bitter to bizarre in its closing days. *The Detroit News* reported that Carr's wife Susan had amended her divorce action to request an annulment, charging that Carr failed to inform her at the time of their 1980 marriage that he had "a highly contagious and incurable social disease" that "would prevent child bearing as well as adversely affecting marital relations." The information came from a caller identifying herself as a member of Susan Carr's family. Carr adamantly denied the charges, and claimed they were timed to affect the election outcome.

Despite Dunn's attacks and the last-minute hint of scandal, Carr won with surprising ease. Republicans blamed Dunn's lopsided defeat on Democratic ticket-leader James J. Blanchard's landslide gubernatorial re-election. But Carr's campaign said there was a public backlash against Dunn's negative campaigning.

In 1988, the local GOP was not up for another vigorous assault and Carr reached 60 percent against little-known stockbrocker Scott Schultz. Two years later, he faced only write-in opposition.

Committees

Appropriations (25th of 37 Democrats)
Commerce, Justice, State & Judiciary; Transportation

Select Hunger (6th of 22 Democrats)
International

Elections

1990 General		
Bob Carr (D)	97,547	(100%)
1988 General		
Bob Carr (D)	120,581	(59%)
Scott Schultz (R)	81,079	(40%)

Previous Winning Percentages: **1986** (57%) **1984** (52%) **1982** (51%) **1978** (57%) **1976** (53%) **1974** (49%)

District Vote For President

	1988	1984	1980	1976
D	89,344 (42%)	72,935 (35%)	85,927 (38%)	80,770 (39%)
R	121,258 (57%)	133,362 (64%)	114,729 (50%)	120,518 (58%)
I			23,452 (10%)	

Campaign Finance

	Receipts	Receipts from PACs		Expend-itures
1990				
Carr (D)	$397,155	$208,550	(53%)	$223,595
1988				
Carr (D)	$534,741	$277,823	(52%)	$504,217
Schultz (R)	$82,562	$7,910	(10%)	$81,586

Key Votes

1991	
Authorize use of force against Iraq	N
1990	
Support constitutional amendment on flag desecration	N
Pass family and medical leave bill over Bush veto	N
Reduce SDI funding	Y
Allow abortions in overseas military facilities	Y
Approve budget summit plan for spending and taxing	N
Approve civil rights bill	Y
1989	
Halt production of B-2 stealth bomber at 13 planes	N
Oppose capital gains tax cut	N
Approve federal abortion funding in rape or incest cases	Y
Approve pay raise and revision of ethics rules	N
Pass Democratic minimum wage plan over Bush veto	Y

Voting Studies

	Presidential Support		Party Unity		Conservative Coalition	
Year	**S**	**O**	**S**	**O**	**S**	**O**
1990	29	69	81	15	46	52
1989	30	67	80	13	37	63
1988	31	65	80	10	50	47
1987	21	74	82	11	40	56
1986	21	74	75	21	56	44
1985	29	68	81	14	38	56
1984	26	72	87	11	34	66
1983	12	83	86	10	25	72

Interest Group Ratings

Year	ADA	ACU	AFL-CIO	CCUS
1990	72	25	67	57
1989	85	25	67	50
1988	80	21	93	46
1987	88	9	100	31
1986	70	24	86	33
1985	65	15	76	50
1984	80	22	85	38
1983	85	17	88	10

7 Dale E. Kildee (D)

Of Flint — Elected 1976

Born: Sept. 16, 1929, Flint, Mich.

Education: Sacred Heart Seminary, B.A. 1952; attended U. of Peshawar, Pakistan, 1958-59; U. of Michigan, M.A. 1961.

Occupation: Teacher.

Family: Wife, Gayle Heyn; three children.

Religion: Roman Catholic.

Political Career: Mich. House, 1965-75; Mich. Senate, 1975-77.

Capitol Office: 2239 Rayburn Bldg. 20515; 225-3611.

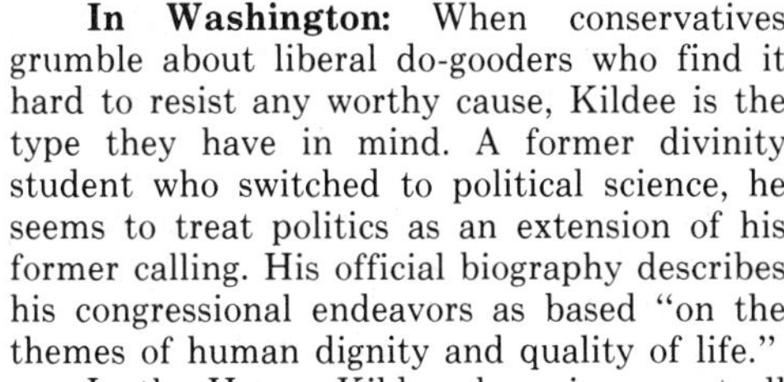

In Washington: When conservatives grumble about liberal do-gooders who find it hard to resist any worthy cause, Kildee is the type they have in mind. A former divinity student who switched to political science, he seems to treat politics as an extension of his former calling. His official biography describes his congressional endeavors as based "on the themes of human dignity and quality of life."

In the House, Kildee champions most all social programs to aid the poor, the elderly and the very young. In Michigan, he has filled out tax forms for senior citizens and helped fix their leaky roofs. A local headline in 1989 proclaimed, "Kildee to the Rescue" for his efforts to improve the food at a senior citizen center.

At the start of the 101st Congress, Kildee won a seat on the Budget Committee, where he is a consistent voice for increasing funds for social programs at the expense of the defense budget. But Kildee is no militant liberal. Though he debates with a degree of philosophical purity, he is more comfortable in coalitions than crusades.

Kildee is low-key but persistent in his efforts to increase funds for Head Start, child care and education. While he occasionally meets with success — in 1989, the committee approved his language to allow as much as $1.8 billion for a new child care package — his is a frustrating role in an era of limited resources. After a particularly tense, closed-door meeting in 1989, Kildee said, "Everyone wanted a little more for their own programs. We did a lot of shouting. I did some shouting myself."

Kildee devotes most of his energy to his work on the Education and Labor Committee, where he chaired the Human Resources Subcommittee for several years. In the 102nd Congress, he took over the Elementary, Secondary and Vocational Education Subcommittee, which is due to reauthorize the adult education program. His new forum will enhance his role in literacy programs, drop-out prevention and the school lunch, child nutrition and WIC program.

Kildee's more ambitious schemes for social welfare rarely go far, but his Act for Better Child Care Services — the ABC bill sponsored by Connecticut Democrat Christopher J. Dodd in the Senate — became a touchstone for many Democratic candidates in 1988. That helped create a political climate to pass child care legislation in the 101st Congress. Though the final bill included key portions of Kildee's original proposal, the legislation's passage was tangled in a bitter turf battle he shunned.

In the 100th Congress, the bill snagged on the issue of whether church-sponsored day care centers should receive federal funds. While the issue was again controversial in the 101st, it was eventually resolved by allowing government vouchers to be used at church-sponsored centers. In 1990, the bill nearly faltered because of a struggle between Ways and Means and Education Democrats over how to fund the proposal.

In 1989, the Education and Labor Committee approved Kildee's bill, which was co-authored by Chairman Augustus F. Hawkins. The $1.78 billion bill established minimum health and safety standards for child care facilities and provided vouchers for low- and middle-income parents and subsidies for child care providers. Kildee and Hawkins wanted to set up a new grant program funded through regular appropriations. But Ways and Means Democrats wanted to expand the existing earned income tax credit for poor families (an idea Republicans agreed with) and roll the measure into the existing Title XX Social Services entitlement program. Kildee and Hawkins objected to that plan, both because they wanted the emphasis to be on education rather than on welfare, and because they feared that funding would be restricted more than politically necessary.

The battle to resolve the issue was fought out on the budget reconciliation bill in the House and in conference with the Senate. Kildee did not play a high-profile role in the internecine strife. In the end, the bill had a scaled-down grant program, a limited entitle-

Michigan 7

East Central — Flint

This is the most Democratic district in the state outside the Detroit area. About 80 percent of the vote is cast in Flint and surrounding Genesee County, and while the out-county portions of Genesee are politically mixed, the city itself leaves no doubt about its partisan leanings. It swam against the Reagan tides both in 1980 and 1984, although the outlying GOP vote in Genesee enabled Reagan to win the overall county vote in 1984. Michael S. Dukakis got 60 percent in Genesee County in 1988.

Flint has always made its living from General Motors. Both the automaker and the United Auto Workers (UAW) were born in this city, and G.M. has been the largest employer for over 50 years. The UAW is the most potent political force in the city; if the union's endorsement no longer translates directly into rank-and-file votes, it does guarantee volunteers and financial support. Many of the white UAW members arrived in Flint from the South after World War II.

Flint has been harmed by its overwhelming reliance on the auto industry. While the well-to-do professionals have stayed put, the empty houses and broken windows of Flint's north side reflect a gloomy statistic: The city lost more than 20,000 residents in the last decade. GM's Chevrolet, Buick, AC Spark Plug and Fisher Body plants once employed over 70,000 workers here, but that number has dwindled to about 40,000. "Roger and Me," a 1989 documentary on the economic troubles facing Flint and G.M., won rave reviews but painted a dismal portrait of Flint.

Much of the area encircling Flint consists of Democratic and racially mixed blue-collar communities, particularly in Mount Morris and Genesee townships. The GOP is strongest in the southeast corner of the county around the white-collar suburbs of Atlas and Goodrich and in the wealthy developments of Grand Blanc Township.

The 7th includes nearly all of Genesee County's eastern neighbor, largely agricultural Lapeer County.

Some of suburban Flint's development has spilled over into western Lapeer, where UAW members from Flint's auto plants give the area a Democratic cast. Farther east in Lapeer, the influence of rural Republicans is strong, often strong enough to tilt the overall county vote to the GOP.

Population: 514,560. White 425,935 (83%), Black 78,880 (15%), Other 4,873 (1%). Spanish origin 8,873 (2%). 18 and over 346,868 (67%), 65 and over 40,344 (8%). Median age: 28.

ment expansion and tax credits.

Kildee had wanted Head Start funding to be included in the child care package, but when it was spun off, he took the issue and ran with it. Seizing momentum generated by the popular program's 25th anniversary, Kildee helped draft a package to improve the program and make it available to all eligible 3-, 4-and 5-year-olds for the first time. In 1990, the program served only an estimated 25 percent of eligible children. "These are the greatest advances in Head Start since the program began," he said after the House passed the bill. It was later signed into law.

In the 100th Congress, Kildee was a key negotiator on the bilingual education provision of the omnibus education bill. But the deal he helped strike to ensure passage was as much capitulation as compromise. The massive reauthorization was threatened by Republican demands to increase funding for programs using English-only methods instead of native-language instruction. Kildee and GOP Rep. Steve Bartlett of Texas sought a middle ground, but when none was found, GOP demands largely prevailed. Hispanic House members were furious. "It was not a happy compromise," Kildee said. "There would be wounds no matter what we would do. This preserved bilingual education and minimized bloodletting."

In the 99th Congress, he was chief sponsor of the Older Americans Act, which authorized programs ranging from meals-on-wheels to legal services for senior citizens. He subsequently fought for across-the-board funding increases for those programs, and advocated a new program to provide in-home care for the frail elderly. Kildee described the program as "morally more sound because it really respects their dignity — home is where they want to remain. And fiscally, it's more sound because it's much less expensive than putting them in a home."

Kildee is also a strong labor loyalist. He has maintained an average AFL-CIO rating of over 90 percent, scoring perfect 100s in the last four Congresses. His near-perfect liberal record on social issues is marred only by his opposition to federal funding of abortion.

As a freshman in 1977, Kildee launched a crusade against child pornography. Revelations in his hometown of Flint about a growing trade in obscene photos of children set off a flurry of letters to him. He drafted a bill setting heavy criminal penalties for using children in pornographic films and photographs.

Kildee believed a bill like that would be unstoppable on the House floor. But to get there, it had to go through the Judiciary Committee, where Michigan Democrat John Conyers Jr., chairman of the Criminal Justice Subcommittee, considered it a violation of First Amendment rights. Kildee rewrote the bill so it could be considered by his Education and Labor Committee. He offered it as an amendment to child-abuse legislation, and it passed. Later Conyers conceded and moved a milder bill through his panel. By 1981, child pornography penalties were law.

At Home: As a Democrat from the General Motors town of Flint, Kildee draws his political strength from the labor movement he supports in Washington.

The United Auto Workers and the AFL-CIO have deserted him only once — when he first ran for Congress in 1976. Trying to succeed five-term Rep. Donald W. Riegle Jr., who was running for the Senate, Kildee left a state Senate seat he had won only two years before. Labor, which had worked exceptionally hard to help Kildee oust a 26-year state Senate veteran in 1974, felt he should have served out his four-year term. But Kildee insisted on making his move.

Winning was relatively easy, even with division in the ranks of labor. Kildee beat a local union official with 76 percent in the Democratic primary and went on to trounce his general-election opponent. Since then, he has never won less two-thirds of the vote, and often he takes considerably more.

After giving up his plans to be a priest, Kildee spent a year studying in Pakistan, then returned to Michigan to teach Latin. By the time he arrived in the Michigan Legislature, he was a political maverick. During his brief state Senate career, he earned the animosity of some colleagues as self-appointed head of the "conscience caucus." He attacked the use of state funds for redecorating senators' offices. Kildee also pushed through a "truth in packaging" bill and an act to guarantee civil rights to the handicapped.

Committees

Budget (7th of 23 Democrats)
Economic Policy, Projections & Revenues (chairman); Human Resources

Education & Labor (6th of 25 Democrats)
Elementary, Secondary & Vocational Education (chairman); Human Resources; Labor-Management Relations; Postsecondary Education

Elections

1990 General

Dale E. Kildee (D)	90,307	(68%)
David J. Morrill (R)	41,759	(32%)

1988 General

Dale E. Kildee (D)	150,832	(76%)
Jeff Coad (R)	47,071	(24%)

Previous Winning Percentages: **1986** (80%) **1984** (93%) **1982** (75%) **1980** (93%) **1978** (77%) **1976** (70%)

District Vote For President

	1988	1984	1980	1976
D	112,101 (56%)	94,715 (46%)	98,309 (47%)	95,588 (50%)
R	88,166 (44%)	111,228 (54%)	94,845 (45%)	91,817 (48%)
I			14,107 (7%)	

Campaign Finance

	Receipts	Receipts from PACs		Expend-itures
1990				
Kildee (D)	$259,480	$187,746	(72%)	$222,531
Morrill (R)	$6,382	0		$6,382
1988				
Kildee (D)	$152,246	$103,770	(68%)	$150,594
Coad (R)	$1,310	0		$1,310

Key Votes

1991

Authorize use of force against Iraq	N

1990

Support constitutional amendment on flag desecration	N
Pass family and medical leave bill over Bush veto	Y
Reduce SDI funding	Y
Allow abortions in overseas military facilities	N
Approve budget summit plan for spending and taxing	N
Approve civil rights bill	Y

1989

Halt production of B-2 stealth bomber at 13 planes	Y
Oppose capital gains tax cut	Y
Approve federal abortion funding in rape or incest cases	N
Approve pay raise and revision of ethics rules	N
Pass Democratic minimum wage plan over Bush veto	Y

Voting Studies

	Presidential Support		Party Unity		Conservative Coalition	
Year	**S**	**O**	**S**	**O**	**S**	**O**
1990	19	81	95	5	9	91
1989	35	65	94	6	10	90
1988	17	83	95	5	11	89
1987	16	84	98	2	0	100
1986	13	87	97	2	6	94
1985	18	78	94	3	4	96
1984	26	74	94	6	7	93
1983	11	89	92	8	9	91
1982	36	64	92	8	10	90
1981	26	74	90	10	15	85

Interest Group Ratings

Year	ADA	ACU	AFL-CIO	CCUS
1990	94	4	100	21
1989	95	11	100	20
1988	95	4	100	14
1987	96	4	100	7
1986	95	0	100	17
1985	85	5	100	25
1984	95	8	100	38
1983	90	13	100	5
1982	95	9	100	23
1981	90	0	80	5

8 Bob Traxler (D)

Of Bay City — Elected 1974

Born: July 21, 1931, Kawkawlin, Mich.
Education: Michigan State U., B.A. 1952; Detroit College of Law, LL.B. 1959.
Military Service: Army, 1953-55.
Occupation: Lawyer.
Family: Divorced; three children.
Religion: Episcopalian.
Political Career: Mich. House, 1963-74.
Capitol Office: 2366 Rayburn Bldg. 20515; 225-2806.

In Washington: Traxler once was known for a boisterous sense of humor that could border on clownishness, but of late he is more likely to be heard issuing grave warnings that current federal spending priorities will ruin the country's future.

Now in his ninth term, Traxler has finally attained a position of real power in the House — he assumed the helm of an Appropriations subcommittee at the start of the 101st Congress. But facing a huge deficit and a Republican White House, he despairs of ever seeing enough invested in what he calls "the nation's physical and human infrastructure." As a result, Traxler told a group of reporters in early 1991, "I see us as a nation in decline."

Though Traxler was elected with the reform-minded Watergate class of 1974, he came to Congress with a New Deal mindset. "In my heart of hearts, I'm probably the last of the wild-ass liberals," is the way Traxler puts it. It is no wonder, then, that he chafes to find himself finally in a position to dole out federal dollars at a time when those dollars are in short supply.

Through his years in the House, Traxler has not been involved in party strategizing, preferring to stick to his Appropriations duties. But in the latter part of 1990, he began attending Democratic Caucus meetings, in part to share his frustration with seeing so much being spent on a military buildup in the Persian Gulf as his favored domestic programs were being cut. But Traxler does not seem optimistic of taking away the GOP's agenda-setting power. "I don't see the Democratic Party winning the presidency in my lifetime," he said in February 1991.

Although comments such as that could raise his visibility, Traxler has typically kept a low media profile, like most of the members on Appropriations. He mastered the ways of the committee working on subcommittees with two very able legislators, Jamie L. Whitten of Mississippi on Agriculture and Edward P. Boland of Massachusetts on Housing and Urban Development. The latter panel fell to Traxler in 1989 after Boland retired, and he remains a force on Agriculture, where he ranks second behind the 81-year-old chairman.

In the 101st Congress, his first as one of the committee's elite "College of Cardinals," Traxler proved adept at the guerrilla tactics of appropriating. He doubled the number of earmarks for specific projects in the spending bill under his jurisdiction, and then won the ensuing turf battles over the programs. And in an effort to increase the dollars at his disposal he resorted to an accounting gimmick that led to a bitter dispute with the Budget Committee.

When Traxler took over the Appropriations subpanel, the first question on colleagues' minds was: Will he back pet projects? The answer was a resounding 'yes.' "I have great sensitivity to members' requests and needs," he said. "I want to be in every way helpful in fulfilling these national needs that are specific to localities.... This is the function of Congress. This is the appropriations process."

In preparing his first bill in 1989, Traxler received some 350 requests. In that context, the 40 he earmarked seems minuscule, but it was twice the number earmarked in the previous bill. Reflecting new budget constraints, however, the dollar value of Traxler's projects fell $10 million under the previous total of $170 million. The earmarks for housing caused a lengthy and bitter contretemps between Traxler and Housing Secretary Jack F. Kemp, who briefly threatened to ignore the earmarks, and then between Traxler and the authorizing committees. But in the end, the earmarks stuck.

A budget gimmick in the same bill also helped a simmering feud between the Appropriations and Budget panels boil over. Appropriators chafed at Budget's imposition of funding ceilings that they considered unrealistic. So to add $850 million to its spending allotment, Traxler's panel shifted a payday into another fiscal year. The Budget Committee so vehemently objected to the tactic that its chairman, Leon E. Panetta of California, testified against

Michigan 8

East — Bay City; Saginaw

When singer-songwriter Paul Simon took off to look for America in the late 1960s, he began in Saginaw, taking four days to hitchhike east. In more recent, less prosperous days, entire families have been leaving Saginaw, but they have headed south looking for work.

Saginaw and Bay City are the centers of Democratic strength in the 8th, but each has been losing population — Saginaw dropped 10 percent in the 1980s — while the Republican counties of Michigan's rural Thumb were growing. The Bay City-Saginaw corridor now has less than one-third of the 8th's residents.

Along the Saginaw River from Bay City to Saginaw is a gray industrial stretch of auto plants, chemical and cement factories, tool-and-die shops and port facilities. White ethnics, blacks and Hispanics in Saginaw gave Jimmy Carter 58 percent of the city's vote in 1980 at the same time that Saginaw County as a whole went for Ronald Reagan. In 1988, Democrat Michael S. Dukakis carried the county by 3,175 votes. Bay City's politically active blue-collar Poles join with steel and chemical workers between there and Midland to anchor Democratic strength in Bay County.

While northern Bay County's generally poor farmland gave rise to a Democratic-leaning impoverished rural sector, the rich soil of the Saginaw Valley south of Saginaw produced a well-off and conservative agricultural community specializing in potatoes, dry beans and soft white winter wheat. German Lutheran influence is strong in the eastern part of the county, particularly around the well-kept town of Frankenmuth, whose prosperous burghers live in neat, brown-trimmed Bavarian-style houses.

Arenac County, north of Bay County, is a small, forested area whose proximity both to I-75 and Lake Huron has made it a popular vacation spot and home for retired autoworkers. The UAW's influence in Arenac County has put it in the Democratic column in recent contests for U.S. Senate and governor. In 1990, all four Democrats running for statewide office won Arenac.

Once heavily timbered, the vast flat reaches of Michigan's Thumb now bear sugar beets and dry beans, corn and wheat. The state's top two dairy counties are Sanilac and Huron; the latter has more than twice as many cows as people. The long Lake Huron coastline stretching around the Thumb is dotted with small fishing villages and lakeside resorts. The only heavy industry is in the huge tool-and-die plants at Sebewaing and Elkton at the western end of Huron County.

Although Traxler has made inroads in the Thumb, most of its voters remain die-hard Republicans. Sanilac County, for example, gave 62 percent of its 1990 gubernatorial vote to GOP challenger John Engler.

Population: 514,560. White 463,068 (90%), Black 37,197 (7%), Other 3,457 (1%). Spanish origin 17,488 (3%). 18 and over 350,577 (68%), 65 and over 53,116 (10%). Median age: 29.

the plan before the Rules Committee.

The panel and the full House agreed with Panetta, and the "smoke and mirrors" plan was scrapped. But Traxler took advantage of a quirk in House rules and passed his bill without paring the $850 million. And then he squelched an across-the-board cut to the bill by rushing the proceedings when he saw that the member sponsoring that cut was absent. "The gentleman was tardy," he said afterward, and then expressed sympathy. "It's a situation that could happen to anybody."

Traxler's panel funds both housing programs and space programs, and in recent years, the two have competed for scarce dollars. "I'm constantly torn between providing for those here and now who are needy, and providing for a future technological and industrial base," Traxler has said. He has resisted deep cuts proposed for NASA and for the National Science Foundation, but he also has complained that "Mega-science projects are intentionally sold to us with a low price tag, with the understanding that as the project begins to gain momentum, it gains friends within the Congress."

In May 1991, Traxler's subcommittee made headlines when it voted to eliminate funding for NASA's planned space station *Freedom*, which is projected to cost $40 billion over the next 10 years. "We simply can no longer afford huge new projects, with huge price tags, while trying to maintain services that the American people expect to be provided," Traxler said.

On Agriculture, Traxler learned at the feet of master appropriator Whitten. For Whitten, Traxler has been an important bridge to the Agriculture Committee when it comes to formulating agricultural spending plans. In particular, Traxler sees to it that "non-program" crops, such as the dry beans grown in Michigan, are protected.

Traxler also takes care to provide funds to other special projects in his district. He regularly steers funding to Michigan State University to study such things as blueberry shoestring virus and asparagus-yield decline.

At Home: Traxler came to Washington in 1974 amid as much attention as any House newcomer had received in years. He had turned his special election campaign into a referendum on President Richard M. Nixon in the midst of the unfolding Watergate scandal. Traxler called his Republican opponent, James M. Sparling, a "stand-in for Mr. Nixon," who stumped for Sparling in the district against the advice of some local GOP leaders.

With help from organized labor, the Democrat won just enough votes in the urbanized counties to offset his opponent's strength in the rural Thumb region — the area Nixon visited on his whistle-stop tour. Traxler became the first Democrat in 42 years to represent some parts of the district.

Many thought that with Nixon gone by the next election, voters in the 8th would revert to their traditional GOP habits. But Traxler's combination of populism and gregarious constituent relations gave him a firm lock on the 8th, and re-election never has been a problem.

Traxler wins by 2-to-1 and better in Saginaw and Bay City, and has even brought to his side many of the bean and sugar beet farmers in the Republican Thumb.

During 11 years representing Bay City in the Michigan House, Traxler was rated as one of the more able legislators. One of his most conspicuous crusades was for a bill to allow bingo games in churches, a successful campaign that gave him the nickname "Bingo Bob." As the chairman of the state Judiciary Committee, he helped modernize the Michigan district court system.

Committee

Appropriations (11th of 37 Democrats)
Veterans Affairs, Housing & Urban Development, & Independent Agencies (chairman); Legislative; Rural Development, Agriculture & Related Agencies

Elections

1990 General		
Bob Traxler (D)	98,903	(69%)
James White (R)	45,259	(31%)
1988 General		
Bob Traxler (D)	139,904	(72%)
Lloyd F. Buhl (R)	54,195	(28%)

Previous Winning Percentages: **1986** (73%) **1984** (64%) **1982** (91%) **1980** (61%) **1978** (67%) **1976** (59%) **1974** (55%) **1974** * (52%)

* *Special election.*

District Vote For President

	1988	1984	1980	1976
D	101,006 (49%)	80,321 (39%)	88,369 (41%)	88,638 (45%)
R	102,608 (50%)	123,682 (60%)	113,128 (52%)	107,682 (54%)
I			13,552 (6%)	

Campaign Finance

	Receipts	Receipts from PACs		Expend-itures
1990				
Traxler (D)	$295,544	$186,860	(63%)	$176,479
White (R)	$558	0		$433
1988				
Traxler (D)	$238,000	$148,987	(63%)	$128,400
Buhl (R)	$4,847	0		$2,188

Key Votes

1991	
Authorize use of force against Iraq	N
1990	
Support constitutional amendment on flag desecration	Y
Pass family and medical leave bill over Bush veto	Y
Reduce SDI funding	Y
Allow abortions in overseas military facilities	N
Approve budget summit plan for spending and taxing	Y
Approve civil rights bill	Y
1989	
Halt production of B-2 stealth bomber at 13 planes	Y
Oppose capital gains tax cut	Y
Approve federal abortion funding in rape or incest cases	N
Approve pay raise and revision of ethics rules	Y
Pass Democratic minimum wage plan over Bush veto	Y

Voting Studies

	Presidential Support		Party Unity		Conservative Coalition	
Year	S	O	S	O	S	O
1990	25	66	81	11	39	57
1989	28	63	83	10	32	63
1988	19	73	84	7	26	68
1987	23	73	86	5	28	60
1986	19	73	79	7	34	54
1985	26	74	83	5	16	71
1984	28	59	80	8	22	66
1983	6	88	82	8	24	70
1982	27	61	84	7	25	68
1981	39	57	79	14	37	56

Interest Group Ratings

Year	ADA	ACU	AFL-CIO	CCUS
1990	56	9	100	17
1989	80	12	90	33
1988	80	14	100	21
1987	80	4	94	14
1986	80	9	100	29
1985	80	5	88	27
1984	70	25	69	46
1983	90	22	100	5
1982	75	21	100	19
1981	65	20	73	17

9 Guy Vander Jagt (R)

Of Luther — Elected 1966

Born: Aug. 26, 1931, Cadillac, Mich.
Education: Hope College, A.B. 1953; Yale U., B.D. 1955; attended Bonn U., 1956; U. of Michigan, LL.B. 1960.
Occupation: Lawyer.
Family: Wife, Carol Doorn; one child.
Religion: Presbyterian.
Political Career: Mich. Senate, 1965-66.
Capitol Office: 2409 Rayburn Bldg. 20515; 225-3511.

In Washington: Vander Jagt entered the 102nd Congress fresh off a 98-66 victory over Tennessean Don Sundquist for another term as chairman of the National Republican Congressional Committee (NRCC). But Vander Jagt's re-election did not quell rumblings of discontent within the party over how the committee is run, how it spends its money and why it has not been more effective in electing Republicans to the House.

Though Vander Jagt and his allies — including Minority Whip Newt Gingrich — managed to beat back Sundquist's challenge rather comfortably, his charges of financial impropriety at the NRCC and a bloated committee infrastructure linger. Sundquist's critique focused on the gap between the money the NRCC raises and what it spends on candidates. He directed his fire at the high number of consultants on the committee's payroll, and questioned the committee's relationship with its finance director and chief fundraiser, Wyatt Stewart.

In part, Sundquist's campaign was derailed because Vander Jagt and his allies were able to cast him as a stalking horse for the White House; heavy-handed administration lobbying by White House Chief of Staff John H. Sununu during the 101st Congress had embittered House Republicans. Sundquist denied that the White House had urged him to run.

While Vander Jagt would not acknowledge that the Republican Conference (as Gingrich said) was sending him a message that there needed to be drastic changes at the NRCC, some changes did occur in the aftermath. Co-chairman Edward J. Rollins, hired amid great fanfare in January 1989 for $250,000 a year by the national party leadership, resigned, as did the executive director, R. Marc Nuttle. Heading into 1992 — a year Republicans once thought could bring them a House majority — the NRCC looked, at best, to be in a rebuilding mode.

What a difference a decade can make.

The horizons seemed limitless for Vander Jagt as the 1980s dawned. He was bathing in accolades for his stewardship of the NRCC. The NRCC's huge edge over its Democratic counterpart in fundraising and computer technology was widely noted. The committee's slogan — "Vote Republican, For a Change" — had produced big GOP House gains and reinforced Ronald Reagan's conservative presidential campaign message.

Vander Jagt boasted then that Reagan's leadership would lift the Republicans to a House majority. He even promoted himself as a leader for those surging Republicans, running an aggressive though unsuccessful campaign for minority leader in 1981.

A GOP House backslide during the 1982 recession preceded a partisan standoff in Reagan's no-coattails 1984 re-election. In the final House elections of the 1980s, Republicans suffered a three-seat loss even as George Bush swept to the presidency. In 11 special elections in the 101st Congress, Republicans won only three. The 1990 elections brought a net loss of eight seats. The total number of House Republicans who took the oath of office in January 1991 was 166 — 26 fewer than in 1981.

During the 1980s, a revived Democratic Congressional Campaign Committee made major gains in both fundraising capacity and campaign technology. By 1989, Republican grumblings about a "dead in the water" NRCC were being widely voiced, accompanied by comments that Vander Jagt's earlier reputation as a political strategist was vastly overblown.

By no means was Vander Jagt held solely responsible for the failure of the GOP to attain a House majority. Factors beyond his control — redistricting and the power of incumbency, for instance — played a large role. Some of his advocates even credited him for helping the GOP avoid the cataclysmic midterm losses (in 1982 and 1986) that had been traditional for the party in the White House.

Vander Jagt was also insulated by the personal chits he had earned in his tireless campaign-year efforts. Using his well-honed skills as an orator and fundraiser, Vander Jagt has assisted practically every Republican House

Michigan 9

West — Muskegon; Traverse City

The Republican 9th covers 150 miles of Lake Michigan shoreline, but it is dominated politically by its two southernmost lakeshore counties, Muskegon and Ottawa, which together hold more than half its residents.

Ottawa County remains the Republican anchor, even though part of it was transferred to the 4th in 1982 redistricting. Ottawa, one of just three Michigan counties to vote Republican in every presidential election since 1960, gave Ronald Reagan his highest percentages in the state in 1980 and 1984. In 1988, it voted for George Bush by better than 3 to 1, and gave 68 percent to the GOP's ill-fated Senate nominee, Jim Dunn. Many of those Republican votes were cast in conservative Dutch towns like white-collar Zeeland, by fruit and dairy farmers in the county's northern reaches, and in the fast-growing towns west of the border with Kent County (Grand Rapids).

Democrats' strongest constituency in the 9th is in and around the city of Muskegon. A community of 40,000, Muskegon first rose out of the sawdust of Michigan's lumbering era, then built up one of western Michigan's heaviest manufacturing bases, turning out auto parts, tank engines, cranes and hoists, paper, bowling equipment and office furniture.

Democratic strength is highest in the city's ethnic blue-collar neighborhoods, in the black precincts inland from the shore and in black-majority Muskegon Heights. But the party's vote in the city is generally offset by GOP margins from North Muskegon, upper-middle-class suburbs like Norton Shores and Roosevelt Park, and farm areas north of Muskegon.

The rest of the 9th District consists of sparsely populated counties whose chief industries are farming, tourism and food processing. Fremont, in Newaygo County, is international headquarters for Gerber baby foods, while Oceana County's fruits and asparagus are processed in towns such as Pentwater and Shelby. The orchards in Leelanau County are the most productive in the United States; nine of the nation's 50 leading cherry-producing counties are in the 9th. Towns all along the shore draw retirees and summertime residents, and the inland lakes and forests pull in hikers and hunters year-round.

Population: 514,560. White 481,640 (94%), Black 23,294 (5%), Other 4,416 (1%). Spanish origin 9,909 (2%). 18 and over 356,896 (69%), 65 and over 58,147 (11%). Median age: 29.

member elected since 1976.

But there was an overriding sense among Republicans following the 1988 elections that the NRCC needed reinvigoration. That led to the high-profile installation of Rollins, a former political adviser to Reagan.

Vander Jagt's congressional efforts appeared to lack focus until 1975, when he took over the NRCC chairmanship. He came on board at a time when the committee was developing the innovative campaign tools — campaign schools for budding candidates, a sophisticated year-round polling operation and commercials on prime-time network television — that were to make it a focus of political attention over the next few years.

The payoff for these efforts was not immediate. It seemed at first that Vander Jagt would spend the rest of his career living down his prediction of a Republican House gain of "76 in '76"; the party lost two seats as Democrat Jimmy Carter won the presidency. However, early restiveness over Carter's leadership enabled the Republicans to post an 11-seat gain in 1978.

Republican plaudits for the NRCC began piling up, and Vander Jagt got much of the credit. He was building the committee into a huge public-relations apparatus, one that promoted Vander Jagt's own ideas and image in a glossy magazine every month. His name was on the checks that the NRCC was donating to GOP House challengers across the country. Vander Jagt was chosen to give the keynote speech at the 1980 Republican National Convention, at which he was briefly mentioned as a vice presidential possibility.

In 1980, as Reagan swept Carter from office, the NRCC not only orchestrated a whopping 33-seat pickup, but also helped set the political agenda with an ad campaign centered on the "change" slogan. Vander Jagt still insists it was the House Republican campaign that carried Reagan, and not the other way around.

The rave reviews he received after 1980 emboldened Vander Jagt to take on Robert H. Michel of Illinois for the Republican House leadership the next year. Vander Jagt, by his own admission, was no parliamentary strategist; he had rarely appeared on the floor during the preceding four years, except to vote. He argued that the party needed an eloquent House spokesman rather than a tactician like Michel. He also said he would supply "aggressive confrontation" with the Democratic majority when it was needed.

That argument might have been stronger had Reagan not been elected president, obviating the need for a new party spokesman. Michel was forced to work hard, but he managed to hold Vander Jagt off by 16 votes.

That marked the apogee of Vander Jagt's national prominence. An economic downturn, the most serious since the Great Depression, hit prior to the 1982 elections. That year, NRCC officials agreed to the campaign theme of "Stay the Course" urged upon them by the Reagan White House. In the face of Vander Jagt's contention that Republicans would make "substantial and significant gains" despite the recession, the Democrats regained 26 House seats that November.

Reagan's 1984 don't-rock-the-boat "Morning in America" theme undercut NRCC efforts to develop a case for the sweeping change needed to upset the "permanent" House Democratic majority. Despite the imminent Reagan landslide, Vander Jagt resisted hyperbole and predicted modest GOP House gains. This time, he was right; the Republicans gained 14 seats.

By the late 1980s, House politics had faded into the background of the nation's political consciousness. Even Vander Jagt appeared to lose some interest. In 1986, a year in which the Democrats made a minor gain of five seats, Vander Jagt spent much of the campaign on a quixotic effort to repeal the constitutional amendment that barred presidents from pursuing third terms.

The NRCC's strong influence over individual Republican House campaigns also appeared to be waning. In 1988, several GOP challengers complained that the NRCC had failed to communicate effectively with them, and failed to help them raise money from political action committees (PACs) and other sources.

Considering the damage that might have ensued, the GOP did well to hold its 1990 House losses to eight. To get an agreement on the fiscal 1991 budget, Bush in 1990 had abandoned his "no new taxes" campaign pledge, robbing Republican candidates across the country of a successful defining partisan issue. Vander Jagt tried to steer a growing antipathy toward Washington to the GOP's advantage, but while anti-incumbent sentiment reduced many incumbents' margins, it ousted few. Vander Jagt himself was held to a career-low reelection tally.

Before the election, Vander Jagt had tried to revive the tax issue himself when the House debated a Democratic alternative to the fiscal 1991 deficit-reduction bill, which contained new taxes aimed at wealthier Americans. House Republicans chose Vander Jagt to close the floor debate, a signal that the focus was mostly about the approaching elections and less about substance. "For tonight, for one glittering, golden moment, House Republicans were united and had something to cheer about," he said. "We wanted it nice and simple. . . . Democrats are 'tax and spend,' we're 'no new taxes.' "

Vander Jagt's partisan labors have clearly exceeded his legislative achievements during a House career of a quarter-century. Though he has risen to the second-ranking Republican position on the high-profile Ways and Means Committee, Vander Jagt is known as neither a legislative crusader nor a craftsman. Ways and Means colleagues do credit Vander Jagt with being attentive to the committee's business, which can be challenging for him given his extensive travel schedule in behalf of GOP candidates.

The big issues that come before Ways and Means usually find other champions, though. In 1985, as the deliberations over the wide-ranging trade bill were coming to a head, Vander Jagt voluntarily gave up the ranking Republican position on the Trade Subcommittee, telling colleagues it was too time-consuming. He took a less demanding job as ranking member on the Select Revenue Measures Subcommittee.

In the 101st Congress, he joined Washington Democrat Al Swift to lead a bipartisan House task force to study the partisan-charged issue of campaign finance reform. The task force produced agreement on a range of minor issues in August 1989. But less than a year later, even those were in dispute.

Vander Jagt was generally known in his first years in the House as a moderate Republican in the tradition of his close friend George W. Romney, then Michigan's governor. Vander Jagt's early work against pollution gave him a reputation as an environmentalist. But when he assumed the NRCC chairmanship, he was moving to the right. The limited work he did on Ways and Means in the late 1970s added to the newer image, enabling him to campaign credibly against Michel in 1980 as the conservative choice.

At Home: For years, Vander Jagt has felt free to travel the country as campaign committee chairman, confident that his 9th District seat was secure. But in the 102nd Congress, he may be a bit more reluctant to roam. In November 1990, a little-known, lightly financed Democratic opponent took 45 percent of the vote against him.

Vander Jagt's scare came at the hands of Geraldine Greene, a Traverse City real estate agent who had held local office but was generally unknown in the district. She had little money and was given no chance of beating Vander Jagt. Greene herself said she began the campaign expecting little, but wanted to give voters a more liberal alternative on issues such as abortion rights and defense spending.

As the federal budget debate lurched

along, Greene profited as some voters began focusing their distaste for Congress on Vander Jagt. There was also some resentment toward the incumbent among voters who felt he spent too much time helping GOP congressmen and candidates and not enough helping constituents. The Republican's stock fell further in October, when ABC aired a program showing Vander Jagt and other members of the Ways and Means Committee frolicking on the beach during a taxpayer-paid trip to Barbados on committee business.

Vander Jagt ignored Greene for most of the race, and Congress' late adjournment kept him out of the district until the final phase of the campaign. But he rallied with an eleventh-hour surge of advertising and appearances. In the traditionally Republican 9th, that was enough.

The race marked only the second time since 1966, his first congressional win, that Vander Jagt has dipped below the 60 percent mark. The first occasion was in 1974, the year Watergate took its toll on many Republican candidates.

The son of a livestock dealer and farmer, Vander Jagt grew up on a 120-acre farm near Cadillac. He originally thought the ministry would be a good place to exercise his oratorical skills, but after earning a divinity degree he decided to be a lawyer. He paid for law school with money he made working part time at various radio stations.

After four years practicing law in Grand Rapids with Harold Sawyer, who represented the 5th District from 1977 to 1985, Vander Jagt returned to Cadillac and easily won a state Senate seat. In 1966, when 9th District Rep. Robert P. Griffin was appointed to a Senate vacancy, Vander Jagt announced for Congress and easily won the special election and the one for the full term — both held the same day. His percentage was the highest of any GOP newcomer elected that year.

Committees

Ways & Means (2nd of 13 Republicans)
Select Revenue Measures (ranking); Trade

Joint Taxation

Elections

1990 General		
Guy Vander Jagt (R)	89,078	(55%)
Geraldine Greene (D)	73,604	(45%)
1988 General		
Guy Vander Jagt (R)	149,748	(70%)
David Gawron (D)	64,843	(30%)

Previous Winning Percentages: **1986** (64%) **1984** (71%) **1982** (65%) **1980** (97%) **1978** (70%) **1976** (70%) **1974** (57%) **1972** (69%) **1970** (64%) **1968** (68%) **1966 *** (67%)

** Elected to a full term and also to fill an unexpired term in a special election held the same day.*

District Vote For President

	1988	1984	1980	1976
D	84,628 (37%)	69,708 (31%)	77,925 (33%)	78,806 (37%)
R	141,226 (62%)	156,545 (69%)	136,272 (59%)	131,374 (62%)
I			15,481 (7%)	

Campaign Finance

	Receipts	Receipts from PACs	Expend-itures
1990			
Vander Jagt (R)	$448,892	$270,171 (60%)	$452,960
Greene (D)	$22,554	$12,000 (53%)	$22,155
1988			
Vander Jagt (R)	$456,634	$238,725 (52%)	$450,801
Gawron (D)	$15,540	$8,000 (51%)	$14,948

Key Votes

1991	
Authorize use of force against Iraq	Y
1990	
Support constitutional amendment on flag desecration	Y
Pass family and medical leave bill over Bush veto	N
Reduce SDI funding	N
Allow abortions in overseas military facilities	N
Approve budget summit plan for spending and taxing	Y
Approve civil rights bill	N
1989	
Halt production of B-2 stealth bomber at 13 planes	N
Oppose capital gains tax cut	N
Approve federal abortion funding in rape or incest cases	N
Approve pay raise and revision of ethics rules	Y
Pass Democratic minimum wage plan over Bush veto	N

Voting Studies

	Presidential Support		Party Unity		Conservative Coalition	
Year	**S**	**O**	**S**	**O**	**S**	**O**
1990	66	29	73	20	91	9
1989	78	14	57	28	80	10
1988	58	36	81	9	87	5
1987	61	33	68	20	88	12
1986	62	23	76	15	76	10
1985	65	25	74	18	87	5
1984	56	30	62	19	80	3
1983	66	22	70	19	79	13
1982	53	36	62	28	77	14
1981	64	21	68 †	13 †	76	12

† Not eligible for all recorded votes.

Interest Group Ratings

Year	ADA	ACU	AFL-CIO	CCUS
1990	6	83	8	85
1989	0	91	18	90
1988	15	91	21	100
1987	0	90	13	93
1986	0	79	14	89
1985	5	79	6	89
1984	0	77	31	81
1983	5	64	6	100
1982	15	68	20	65
1981	10	93	7	100

10 Dave Camp (R)

Of Midland — Elected 1990

Born: July 9, 1953, Midland, Mich.
Education: Albion College, B.A. 1975; U. of California, San Diego, J.D. 1978.
Occupation: Congressional aide; lawyer.
Family: Single.
Religion: Roman Catholic.
Political Career: Mich. House, 1989-91.
Capitol Office: 511 Cannon Bldg. 20515; 225-3561.

The Path to Washington: GOP Rep. Bill Schuette was popular in Michigan's 10th, and his constituents probably would have been pleased to re-elect him. But when Schuette denied voters that chance by running for the Senate, they did the next-closest thing and sent Camp to Congress.

Camp and Schuette were both born in Midland in 1953 and were childhood friends and neighbors. Camp went on to study economics at Albion College in Michigan, then attended law school at the University of California at San Diego. Law degree in hand, he returned to Midland and joined a private firm. While a practicing lawyer there, he worked on several workers' compensation cases for the state attorney general's office.

Along the way, Camp, like Schuette, became active in Republican politics. In 1984, Schuette, who had also become a lawyer, made a successful run for Congress, upsetting Democratic incumbent Don Albosta. Camp followed Schuette to Washington and worked for two years as his administrative assistant. In 1986, Camp returned to Michigan to manage Schuette's re-election campaign and resume his law career.

But when the local state representative unexpectedly announced his retirement, Camp decided to run for the job. He won the 1988 race for a state House district that includes Midland and smaller communities to the north and west.

He had barely found his chair in the Legislature, however, when strategists began talking up Schuette to run against Democratic Sen. Carl Levin and, almost in the same breath, suggesting Camp as a replacement candidate for Schuette's job.

From the outset, Camp was seen as the spiritual heir to Schuette. Not only did Camp have Schuette's endorsement, but the two men seemed cut of the same political cloth. Both took a hard line against tax increases and abortion. Both sport a moderate demeanor and athletic looks. And both enjoyed strong support from the GOP establishment and executives at the Midland-based Dow Chemical Co., the district's largest employer.

Democrats put up no heavyweights for the seat, but several ambitious Republicans decided to try for the GOP nomination. The result was a heated four-way primary that included Camp, former U.S. Rep. Jim Dunn, and former state Sens. Al Cropsey and Richard J. Allen.

Camp, who ran an unexciting but polished campaign, faced a strong challenge from Cropsey, a hard-line conservative backed by many abortion foes and religious fundamentalists. But Camp prevailed on the strength of a strong margin in his Midland base.

From there, the campaign was an extended prelude to Camp's inaugural party. The GOP would have been strongly favored in any case, but Camp lucked out when Joan L. Dennison pulled an upset in the sparsely attended Democratic primary. A politically inexperienced dairy farmer whose radical platform included some of the views of Lyndon H. LaRouche Jr., Dennison failed to rally even solid Democratic support. Though Camp said he took nothing for granted, some of his operatives privately said their toughest November foe was overconfidence. Camp won with two-thirds of the vote.

The 10th is a heavily rural district and Camp, like Schuette, plans to focus on agricultural issues. During the campaign he also talked about improving district roads and bridges, and implementing a school voucher program.

Michigan loses two House seats in reapportionment, and some Democrats in Lansing had hoped to make the 10th one of the cuts. But Republican John Engler's upset over Democratic Gov. James J. Blanchard leaves the GOP in control of the state Senate and governorship. This should ease, though perhaps not eliminate, Camp's worries of being drawn out of office.

Michigan 10

North Central — Midland

The southern half of the 10th, which casts some 70 percent of the district's vote, has a smattering of small cities surrounded by farm land. Midland, with 36,000 residents, is the largest city in the 10th. Dow Chemical's international headquarters and a Dow Corning plant face each other across Midland Road, dominating the city's economy and setting the tone for its Republican politics. The counties around Midland contribute to the normal districtwide Republican success.

Dow employs about a quarter of Midland County's labor force and makes up a quarter of the city's tax base. It also endows numerous local foundations. But there has been a price. Dow was recently ranked as the third worst polluter in the state and the Tittabawassee River has shown the effects of industrial discharges.

Owosso and Alma are more traditional manufacturing cities, reliant on the auto industry and hospitable ground for Democrats. Some of the blue-collar workers here also work small farms in Shiawassee, Saginaw and Gratiot counties, giving the countryside a more Democratic flavor than is found elsewhere in rural Michigan.

Weekend skiers, hikers and snowmobilers fuel the economy of the hilly counties in the northern part of the district; retirees have arrived in force as year-round residents in this region. The elderly newcomers are mostly from Michigan's industrial southeast, and they have brought with them political and social concerns they developed as urban dwellers and union members. Their migration has forced a gradual shift in the political tone of this part of the 10th. Counties such as Clare, Gladwin and Roscommon were routinely Republican a decade ago; now no GOP candidate can afford to take them for granted.

Missaukee County has experienced some spillover development in the area near Houghton Lake, although farther west its hilly terrain is still given over to dairy cattle and bedrock conservatism. The depressed industrial city of Cadillac in Wexford County is the population center and its only traditional source of Democratic votes.

Population: 514,560. White 504,863 (98%), Black 2,668 (1%), Other 3,809 (1%). Spanish origin 6,367 (1%). 18 and over 357,369 (69%), 65 and over 52,523 (10%). Median age: 28.

Committees

Agriculture (13th of 18 Republicans)
Cotton, Rice & Sugar; Wheat, Soybeans & Feed Grains

Select Children, Youth & Families (12th of 14 Republicans)

Small Business (13th of 17 Republicans)
Regulation, Business Opportunity & Energy; SBA, the General Economy & Minority Enterprise Development

Campaign Finance

	Receipts	Receipts from PACs	Expend-itures
1990			
Camp (R)	$667,713	$175,075 (26%)	$657,229

Key Vote

1991

Authorize use of force against Iraq	Y

Elections

1990 General		
Dave Camp (R)	99,952	(65%)
Joan Louise Dennison (D)	50,923	(33%)
Charles Congdon (LIBERT)	2,496	(2%)
1990 Primary		
Dave Camp (R)	17,794	(33%)
Al Cropsey (R)	16,127	(30%)
Richard J. Allen (R)	10,197	(19%)
Jim Dunn (R)	9,898	(18%)
Joseph P. Simcox (R)	524	(1%)

District Vote For President

	1988	1984	1980	1976
D	90,052 (41%)	69,336 (32%)	81,232 (36%)	81,184 (41%)
R	126,547 (58%)	146,060 (67%)	122,741 (55%)	114,855 (58%)
I			17,180 (8%)	

11 Robert W. Davis (R)

Of Gaylord — Elected 1978

Born: July 31, 1932, Marquette, Mich.

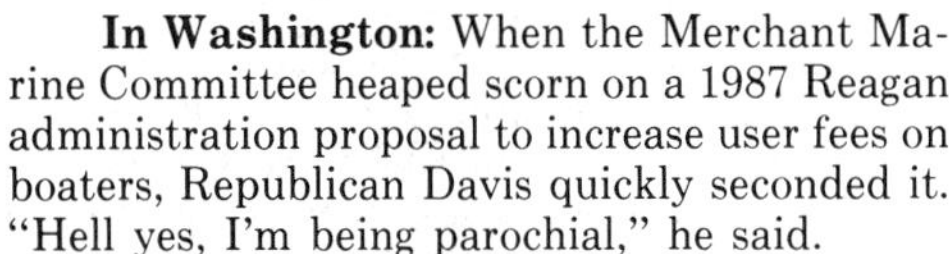

Education: Attended Northern Michigan U., 1950-52; Wayne State U. College of Mortuary Science, B.S. 1954.

Occupation: Funeral director.

Family: Separated; four children.

Religion: Episcopalian.

Political Career: St. Ignace City Council, 1964-66; Mich. House, 1967-71; Mich. Senate, 1971-79, Senate Republican leader, 1974-79.

Capitol Office: 2417 Rayburn Bldg. 20515; 225-4735.

In Washington: When the Merchant Marine Committee heaped scorn on a 1987 Reagan administration proposal to increase user fees on boaters, Republican Davis quickly seconded it. "Hell yes, I'm being parochial," he said.

That, in a nutshell, is Davis' political credo. His northern Michigan district is battling to recover from long-term decline in its resource-based economy. Davis never misses an opportunity to help out by channeling available federal dollars through his work on the Armed Services and Merchant Marine committees.

Davis' list of priorities for the 102nd Congress indicates his local focus. He cited the proposed Calumet National Historical Park, Great Lakes environmental initiatives and rural health care programs; also, his desire to promote funding for the Coast Guard (present in this lakeside district) and to preserve the 11th's Wurtsmith and K. I. Sawyer Air Force Bases.

Davis takes pride in his efforts to help local businesses lure federal contracts. "I spend a lot of time getting defense contracts for our people," he says. "I am a strong supporter of defense and I get a sympathetic ear."

Fond of congressional prerogatives, Davis is reluctant to give even a Republican administration complete say over which defense programs get funded. When Defense Secretary Dick Cheney presented President Bush's military budget in 1989, Armed Services Chairman Les Aspin of Wisconsin called it a good first effort to trim spending. The Procurement Subcommittee passed the package by a 10-9 vote, with Davis the only Republican to vote against it. Normally, Davis' approval of most defense programs makes him a useful ally to Bush. He is an advocate of the B-2 stealth bomber program. In July 1989, Davis marked the 20th anniversary of the first moon landing by comparing critics of the B-2 to skeptics of the space program, noting that the moon project had been labeled "too expensive" and "unnecessary." Davis extolled, "Well, the critics were wrong, and the critics who say we do not need a stealth bomber are wrong too."

As ranking Republican on Merchant Marine, Davis was the point man for Bush administration (and oil industry) positions on oil spill liability legislation, which raced to passage following the 1989 *Exxon Valdez* oil spill off Alaska. Although the consensus was that environmentalists won big on the bill, some complained that it was not enough. Davis was unsympathetic, stating, "On issues like this, they ask for the sun, and if they end up with the moon, they're still not satisfied."

However, Davis can sound like an environmentalist when it comes to the Great Lakes. He has called for federal action to control nonnative species of fish that have infiltrated and upset the ecological balance in the Great Lakes. In the 100th Congress, he succeeded in including the Great Lakes in legislation to control the dumping of medical waste.

Protecting district industries — such as forest products, iron and copper mining and shipbuilding — affected by foreign competition often requires Davis to distance himself from prevailing GOP sentiment on trade issues. In 1987, he voted for the Gephardt amendment mandating retaliatory tariffs, to override the president's veto of the trade bill, and to require plant-closing notification.

At Home: Davis faced some vigorous opposition in the 1980s, but with nine district offices and a three-person traveling staff, he has his territory covered so thoroughly that no challenger ever came close to beating him — even in usually Democratic areas of the Upper Peninsula (UP).

In 1988, Democrats had high hopes for their candidate, youthful state Sen. Mitch Irwin. He had a reputation as an activist legislator and could tout his efforts to help the elderly and protect the environment. Democrats felt this image would contrast favorably with Davis, who campaigned primarily on seniority and his efforts to bring defense contracts to the district.

Irwin tried to make political hay out of the

Michigan 11

Upper Peninsula; Northern Lower Peninsula

The vast, empty forests that cover the 470 miles from Ironwood on the Wisconsin border to Tawas City on Lake Huron inhabit a sparsely settled district that, despite an abundance of natural resources, offers its residents a depressed standard of living. The 11th has only one city of over 15,000, Marquette.

The 11th is contiguous only because of the Mackinac Bridge, which joins Michigan's Upper and Lower peninsulas. The UP, attached by land to Wisconsin, has roughly 60 percent of the district's residents, the bulk of its Democrats and a rough-hewn pride of place that induces occasional secessionist grumblings among its partisans. People in the western part of the UP root for the Green Bay Packers, not the Detroit Lions.

The UP's once-busy mining industry has basically collapsed. Many of the mines have closed, some are played out, and the ones still operating have been hurt by competition from foreign copper and steel. Calumet, located in the northwestern arm of the UP, once was a booming copper-mining town of 50,000. Now it is a village of just 4,000. Ten of the UP's 15 counties lost population in the early 1980s.

Lumber and wood products are still a factor in mill towns like Escanaba and Manistique, but forestry's future seems brighter in more hospitable climates elsewhere in the country.

K. I. Sawyer Air Force Base, located just south of Marquette in the west-central portion of the UP, is one of the district's largest employers.

The western UP, where the most significant population losses have occurred, traditionally has been the one Democratic stronghold of Michigan north of Saginaw. Eastern European and Scandinavian immigrants brought in to mine copper established a liberal, union-oriented tradition; their descendants and other miners, mill workers, loggers and longshoremen still dominate politics in the UP's western counties. In 1988, Michael S. Dukakis carried nine of the 23 counties wholly contained in the 11th.

The eastern UP is far more Republican and representative of the part of the district below the bridge. The only major city in the eastern part of the UP is Sault Ste. Marie, which sends grain, ores and pulpwood eastward from the port cities of Lake Superior. Thanks to the presence of the Army Corps of Engineers and the Coast Guard, much of Sault Ste. Marie's work force is on the federal payroll. Most of Chippewa County and Mackinac County are heavily dependent on tourism and farming, and lacking in the industry that creates Democratic sympathies farther west.

The migration of former city dwellers that has begun to transform the 10th District is also evident in the 11th below the bridge. Many military retirees from Wurtsmith Air Force Base in Oscada have stayed in the district, and retired autoworkers have settled in Emmet, Presque Isle and Cheboygan counties. Democrats have begun to make inroads in local elections. But the area remains mostly as it has been: The communities are conservative and spread far apart, and the emphasis is on farming and tourism, with a few small industries in such Lake Michigan tourist cities as Charlevoix and Petoskey.

Population: 514,560. White 500,721 (97%), Black 2,875 (1%), Other 9,699 (2%). Spanish origin 1,945 (0.4%). 18 and over 367,779 (72%), 65 and over 70,884 (14%). Median age: 30.

Pentagon procurement scandal, vigorously attacking Davis for accepting $25,000 in honoraria, most of it from defense contractors. But with so many defense-related jobs in the 11th, the message failed to resonate. Irwin spent over $400,000, but Davis matched that, added some $200,000 more, and took 60 percent.

That seemed to dampen Democratic hopes. Davis won in 1990 without much difficulty.

Earlier on, in 1984, Davis had beaten back another energetic challenger: Tom Stewart, a young golf professional with a varied background of volunteer activities, including work with Mother Teresa in India and for a nuclear-freeze initiative in Michigan in 1982.

Stewart raised and spent roughly $250,000, about $40,000 more than Davis, and he blamed Davis for not doing enough to help the district's chronically ailing economy. When asked if his work as a golf pro was suitable training for Congress, Stewart noted that Davis was a mortician, then added, "I think a lot more people are interested in golf than in dying."

In the end, voters preferred Davis' record to Stewart's promises. Though Reagan got only 53 percent in the 11th's presidential voting, Davis reached nearly 60 percent, carrying all but five of the district's 28 counties. In 1986, after a minor heart attack, Davis enjoyed a routine re-election.

Davis first won his House seat in 1978. He replaced GOP Rep. Philip Ruppe, who had stepped down to run for the Senate seat of supposedly retiring Republican Robert P. Griffin. When Griffin changed his mind and decided to run again for the Senate, it was too late for Ruppe to get his old seat back. He could only watch as Davis outran eight candidates for a seat Ruppe could have retained easily.

Davis had been a popular figure in the Michigan Legislature. In his first Senate term he was chosen GOP whip, and later he served as the minority leader. When he first ran for Congress, he was living on the Lower Peninsula, while a majority of the 11th's voters were from the UP. He won the GOP primary on the strength of Lower Peninsula support, then temporarily moved to the UP and stressed his boyhood roots there.

Campaigning like an incumbent, Davis contrasted his 12 years of legislative experience with the record of Democrat Keith McLeod, a savings and loan executive and political neophyte. McLeod, from the UP, narrowly won that area, but Davis did well enough there to assure a comfortable districtwide win.

In March 1989, Davis announced he was filing for divorce from his wife Marty. As divorce proceedings grew difficult and public, it was disclosed that Davis was living with a 27-year-old woman. After the two had begun dating, Davis had hired the woman for a job on the Merchant Marine Committee, though Davis said he checked with the ethics committee before doing so. Marty Davis told *The Washington Post* that she was forced to collect welfare to support herself and their child.

Davis' wife had been in the news before. In 1987, amid a congressional pay-raise controversy, she had called the members' salary "pin money." Her remarks brought a strong response from a number of Davis' constituents, but she did not back down, writing a defense of her views in *The Washington Post*.

Committees

Merchant Marine & Fisheries (Ranking)

Armed Services (5th of 22 Republicans)
Research & Development (ranking)

Elections

1990 General

Robert W. Davis (R)	94,555	(61%)
Marcia Gould (D)	59,759	(39%)

1988 General

Robert W. Davis (R)	129,085	(60%)
Mitch Irwin (D)	86,526	(40%)

Previous Winning Percentages: **1986** (63%) **1984** (59%) **1982** (61%) **1980** (66%) **1978** (55%)

District Vote For President

	1988	1984	1980	1976
D	105,251 (47%)	93,179 (46%)	99,755 (42%)	108,130 (48%)
R	116,722 (52%)	106,092 (53%)	119,100 (50%)	112,569 (50%)
I			15,498 (7%)	

Campaign Finance

	Receipts	Receipts from PACs	Expend-itures
1990			
Davis (R)	$340,079	$242,224 (71%)	$325,232
Gould (D)	$3,721	0	$4,072
1988			
Davis (R)	$582,616	$310,359 (53%)	$680,819
Irwin (D)	$417,196	$140,034 (34%)	$415,660

Key Votes

1991	
Authorize use of force against Iraq	Y
1990	
Support constitutional amendment on flag desecration	Y
Pass family and medical leave bill over Bush veto	Y
Reduce SDI funding	?
Allow abortions in overseas military facilities	N
Approve budget summit plan for spending and taxing	N
Approve civil rights bill	Y
1989	
Halt production of B-2 stealth bomber at 13 planes	N
Oppose capital gains tax cut	N
Approve federal abortion funding in rape or incest cases	N
Approve pay raise and revision of ethics rules	Y
Pass Democratic minimum wage plan over Bush veto	Y

Voting Studies

	Presidential Support		Party Unity		Conservative Coalition	
Year	S	O	S	O	S	O
1990	44	52	46	49	74	22
1989	52	30	41	47	76	15
1988	35	62	43	54	66	29
1987	49 †	48 †	34 †	57 †	72 †	21 †
1986	39	43	36	42	76	14
1985	49	49	55	41	78	18
1984	52	38	48	44	78	17
1983	52	44	53	44	73	24
1982	45	47	37	56	62	29
1981	59	36	69	26	84	12

† Not eligible for all recorded votes.

Interest Group Ratings

Year	ADA	ACU	AFL-CIO	CCUS
1990	56	43	83	29
1989	40	54	82	60
1988	60	42	100	29
1987	44	33	81	40
1986	40	60	92	57
1985	35	62	65	55
1984	35	50	42	54
1983	35	57	53	40
1982	35	52	74	40
1981	15	87	40	74

12 David E. Bonior (D)

Of Mount Clemens — Elected 1976

Born: June 6, 1945, Detroit, Mich.
Education: U. of Iowa, B.A. 1967; Chapman College, M.A. 1972.
Military Service: Air Force, 1968-72.
Occupation: Probation officer; adoption caseworker.
Family: Wife, Judy Briggs; two children.
Religion: Roman Catholic.
Political Career: Mich. House, 1973-77.
Capitol Office: 2242 Rayburn Bldg. 20515; 225-2106.

In Washington: Passionate yet introverted, Bonior has won praise from liberals for his commitment to their issues and from others for his low-key diligence and keen appreciation of the value of teamwork. His 1987 ascent to a formal leadership position certified the progress Bonior had made since his early House years, when he was a restless Vietnam-era veteran searching for a role.

Bonior exhibits traits from his two long-held passions: marathon running and basketball. He has retained the qualities of the solitary marathoner — patience, endurance and a disdain for flashiness — while evolving into a team player with a knack for parliamentary tactics. He compares the dynamics of the House to the style of the Boston Celtics, a team known for unselfishness and teamwork.

Chosen chief deputy whip by then-Speaker Jim Wright in 1987, Bonior was a bridge to liberals and Midwesterners. Despite being handpicked by Wright, Bonior had a personal following strong enough to make him a contender for promotion in the leadership scramble that followed the spring 1989 resignations of Wright and Majority Whip Tony Coelho.

In seeking to replace Coelho as whip, Bonior faced an uphill fight against William H. Gray III of Pennsylvania, who had won the No. 4 leadership job of Democratic Caucus chairman in late 1988. Bonior, by contrast, had never waged a caucuswide campaign. But Bonior ran a surprisingly strong second and retained his appointed position as chief deputy whip. In June 1991, when Gray announced plans to leave Congress later in the year, Bonior sought to succeed him as majority whip.

He has been playing on the team for some time, having been named to the Rules Committee in 1981 and appointed one of seven deputy Democratic whips in 1985. On Rules, he remains a voice for House liberals, often floor-managing high-profile legislation, such as the major oil-spill bill Congress passed in 1990.

Bonior breaks with party leaders on occasion; he is an opponent of abortion, and he voted against the 1990 budget summit agreement. But usually, Bonior is there when his party needs him; he voted with a majority of Democrats 95 percent of the time in 1990. He took the lead in the fight against proposals to amend the Constitution to ban flag desecration and he backed the controversial pay raise package enacted in late 1989.

Bonior also typified the group of liberals who were the nucleus of opposition to authorizing use of force in the Persian Gulf. Earlier, in the politically charged atmosphere created by Iraq's occupation of Kuwait, Bonior won approval of a burden-sharing amendment that became a lightning rod for festering congressional anger at Japan's modest defense efforts and its aggressive commercial policies.

Bonior's measure required Japan to pay the costs for U.S. military troops stationed in the country. An overwhelming number of members wanted to signal their unhappiness with Japan's foot-dragging in supporting the multinational effort against Iraq, and Bonior's amendment was adopted 370-53. Two days later, Japan quadrupled to $4 billion the amount it pledged to support the multilateral campaign against Iraq.

Bonior was at his most passionate in recent years when fighting military aid to the Nicaraguan contras. Beginning in 1983, he headed the Democrats' task force coordinating the party's approach to the region and he consistently fought administration military aid requests.

To ward off a persistent GOP, Bonior was instrumental in helping the Democratic leadership offer some contra aid alternative. When a non-military aid package passed in 1988, it did so with a number of liberal votes brought on board by Bonior. He played that role again in 1989, when Congress and President Bush agreed on another "humanitarian" aid package. In March 1990, Bonior cautiously praised a Bush administration aid plan, saying the proposal "seems at the outset to be reasonable."

Bonior also served as a member of a Democratic task force that traveled to Central America in early 1990 to investigate a continuing pattern of human rights violations by the

Michigan 12

Southeast — Macomb County; Port Huron

The heart of the 12th is the six-mile industrial corridor from Detroit north to Fraser, in southern Macomb County. More than 40 percent of the vote is cast there, virtually all by blue-collar ethnics.

Southern Macomb County was built on the increasing prosperity of the Poles, Italians, Belgians, Germans and Slovenes who had first settled on the east side of Detroit early in the 20th century. The neighborhoods nearer the city retain their lower-middle-class character; farther out, in Fraser and the northern parts of Roseville, Warren and St. Clair Shores, the lawns are larger and the houses more expensive.

In the inner suburbs, most of the wage earners are autoworkers and United Auto Workers members. While respect for the union and the Democratic Party continues here, blind allegiance does not. Most of these areas have lost population in the last two decades because of migration outward.

North of Fraser, townships like Clinton, Harrison and Macomb have sprouted new subdivisions in recent years. The population here remains mostly blue-collar, but middle-level managers have moved into the classier developments. Suburban Macomb County is an electoral bellwether. It was once a Democratic bastion, but Republicans have made considerable inroads among the white, middle-class ethnic residents who inhabit the state's third-largest county. In 14 of the last 15 elections for president, governor, or U.S. senator, the winner in Macomb has also been the statewide winner. In 1990, successful GOP gubernatorial challenger John Engler won 53 percent here, and Democratic Sen. Carl Levin netted 58 percent on his way to re-election. The county's black population is only one percent, and a successful GOP tactic in Macomb has been to rail against majority-black Detroit's city government. Supporters of religious broadcaster Pat Robertson have also given the local GOP an evangelical flavor.

The only sizable city in Macomb outside the immediate Detroit area is safely Democratic Mount Clemens, with 18,000 residents. The land stretching from Mount Clemens up to Port Huron at the northern end of St. Clair County is rural and primarily Republican. Only in Port Huron, the seat of St. Clair County, do concentrations of blue-collar workers live.

Population: 514,560. White 496,842 (97%), Black 11,009 (2%), Other 4,218 (1%). Spanish origin 5,842 (1%). 18 and over 362,035 (70%), 65 and over 45,200 (9%). Median age: 29.

Salvadoran military.

Part of a vocal group of House liberals urging a significant cut in aid to El Salvador, Bonior helped persuade Congress to vote to withhold half of its $85 million military assistance package. Over strenuous administration objections, Congress attached a complex set of conditions to future aid.

Some staunch supporters of Israel have objected to Bonior's record on issues important to that country, such as his vote against authorizing the president to withhold funds from the United Nations if the World Health Organization admitted the Palestine Liberation Organization. He also voted against an amendment adopted overwhelmingly in April 1990 stating that Jerusalem "is and should remain" the capital of Israel.

Bonior was instrumental in forming the Vietnam-era Veterans Congressional Caucus in 1977. He has long sought to make the Vietnam War and its veterans a topic of discussion. "No one even wants to talk about the war," he once complained. "It was a disaster."

Bonior found a new forum for his foreign policy views in the 102nd Congress, joining the Intelligence Committee.

At Home: After a decade of easily deflecting GOP charges that he is too liberal for his blue-collar district, Bonior was held to 54 percent of the vote in 1988, encouraging Republican hopes for the next cycle. But after much advance billing, the GOP's 1990 challenge to Bonior fizzled; he won re-election with two-thirds of the vote.

It is unclear whether Bonior's 1988 slippage (he had won two-thirds of the vote in 1986) was caused mostly by genuine voter displeasure, or by outside factors. In the final month of the campaign, President Reagan visited the Macomb County district twice, and George Bush once. This helped Bush carry the county handily. Macomb also was a battleground in a successful state ballot measure to ban abortion funding.

Bonior's GOP opponent was state Sen. Douglas Carl, whose northern Macomb County district takes in about 20 percent of the 12th. Two years earlier — with the help of activists associated with Pat Robertson's presidential campaign — Carl had upset an incumbent GOP legislator. He immediately began building bridges to party establishment figures and, midway through 1988, won their unanimous backing to challenge Bonior.

Short on cash, however, Carl was unable to advertise much. And because most of his complaints about Bonior's liberal record were familiar, Carl drew little media attention.

Overall, Bonior's voting record places him to the left of majority opinion in the working-class 12th, and he has occasionally shown political daring by following the Democratic line. In 1979, he opposed an anti-busing constitutional amendment, though the issue had nearly unseated his Democratic predecessor, James G. O'Hara.

Bonior's 1988 endorsement from Michigan's Right-to-Life organization helped him undercut Carl's base, but Bonior owed his victory to his hefty financial advantage and his campaign apparatus, which persuaded many voters going Republican for president to swing back and return a Democrat to the House.

In 1990, Republicans came at Bonior with businessman and developer Jim Dingeman. He tossed the too-liberal charge at Bonior again, citing the incumbent's opposition to the death penalty and his support for a congressional pay raise.

But Bonior responded with another aggressive and well-financed effort. He faulted Dingeman's business record and charged him with carpetbagging; Dingeman had lived in Colorado, and even held elective office there, as recently as 1988. By late fall, national Republican officials had stopped talking up the race, and Bonior went on to win handily.

All of Bonior's re-election campaigns have been supported by organized labor and the Macomb County Democratic organization, but he has not been on the closest of terms with either. In the crowded 1976 contest to find a successor to O'Hara, the unions were split and the Macomb Democratic Party favored Bonior's major primary opponent. Bonior narrowly won the primary and general election with an aggressive personal campaign; he went door to door handing out pine tree seedlings.

At the time, Bonior was a two-term state representative, having been elected to the Legislature only months after completing military duty; he served stateside as an Air Force cook.

Committees

Rules (5th of 9 Democrats)
Rules of the House

Select Intelligence (10th of 12 Democrats)
Legislation; Oversight & Evaluation

Elections

1990 General		
David E. Bonior (D)	98,232	(65%)
Jim Dingeman (R)	51,119	(34%)
Robert W. Roddis (LIBERT)	2,472	(2%)
1990 Primary		
David E. Bonior (D)	23,121	(86%)
Leah Joan Peltier (D)	3,890	(14%)
1988 General		
David E. Bonior (D)	108,158	(54%)
Douglas Carl (R)	91,780	(45%)

Previous Winning Percentages: **1986** (66%) **1984** (58%) **1982** (66%) **1980** (55%) **1978** (55%) **1976** (52%)

District Vote For President

	1988	1984	1980	1976
D	80,158 (39%)	70,125 (33%)	89,069 (39%)	93,854 (45%)
R	123,989 (60%)	144,403 (67%)	124,419 (54%)	109,186 (53%)
I			14,930 (6%)	

Campaign Finance

	Receipts	Receipts from PACs		Expend-itures
1990				
Bonior (D)	$1,189,127	$728,055	(61%)	$1,188,905
Dingeman (R)	$296,051	$31,156	(11%)	$295,184
1988				
Bonior (D)	$475,462	$328,317	(69%)	$434,200
Carl (R)	$154,163	$54,662	(35%)	$143,886

Key Votes

1991	
Authorize use of force against Iraq	N
1990	
Support constitutional amendment on flag desecration	N
Pass family and medical leave bill over Bush veto	Y
Reduce SDI funding	Y
Allow abortions in overseas military facilities	N
Approve budget summit plan for spending and taxing	N
Approve civil rights bill	Y
1989	
Halt production of B-2 stealth bomber at 13 planes	Y
Oppose capital gains tax cut	Y
Approve federal abortion funding in rape or incest cases	N
Approve pay raise and revision of ethics rules	Y
Pass Democratic minimum wage plan over Bush veto	Y

Voting Studies

	Presidential Support		Party Unity		Conservative Coalition	
Year	**S**	**O**	**S**	**O**	**S**	**O**
1990	18	81	95	4	6	94
1989	36	63	92	4	15	83
1988	19	80	93	2	3	92
1987	11	73	79	1	5	88
1986	16	79	90	1	6	84
1985	19	76	90	3	5	84
1984	25	69	84	4	10	83
1983	21	78	87	6	13	81
1982	26	58	85	5	12	71
1981	25	74	86	8	9	85

Interest Group Ratings

Year	ADA	ACU	AFL-CIO	CCUS
1990	94	8	100	31
1989	95	4	100	30
1988	95	4	100	21
1987	88	0	100	8
1986	95	0	100	6
1985	90	5	94	25
1984	75	5	92	33
1983	80	4	94	25
1982	70	11	100	5
1981	90	0	79	5

13 Barbara-Rose Collins (D)

Of Detroit — Elected 1990

Born: April 13, 1939, Detroit, Mich.
Education: Attended Wayne State U.
Occupation: Public official.
Family: Widowed; two children.
Religion: Shrine of the Black Madonna (a Pan-African Orthodox Christian Church).
Political Career: Detroit Public School Board, 1971-73; Mich. House, 1975-81; Detroit City Council, 1982-91; sought Democratic nomination for U.S. House, 1988.
Capitol Office: 1541 Longworth Bldg. 20515; 225-2261.

The Path to Washington: Detroit is one of the American cities most associated with the violence, poverty and decline plaguing many urban centers. So it is not surprising that Collins, the new member from the Detroit-based 13th, comes to Congress with urban decay and the underclass at the top of her agenda.

Collins had ample time to think about what she would like to do in the House. She first tried for the job in 1988, challenging Rep. George W. Crockett Jr. in the Democratic primary. Crockett held on that time, but Collins' run helped nudge him into retirement. Collins won the 1990 Democratic primary to replace him; in the heavily urban and Democratic 13th, that was tantamount to election. Her November election was a blowout.

Collins, a Detroit native, is a well-known figure in city politics. After many years as a community activist, Collins in 1970 was elected to the Detroit school board, where she served for three years. In 1975, she moved on to the state House. During her seven years in the Legislature, Collins focused on consumer and civil rights, economic development and women's issues. She sponsored bills on sex education, sexual harassment and urban enterprise zones.

Since 1982, she has served on the Detroit City Council, where she became known as an ally of Mayor Coleman A. Young. Collins carried over into her council work some of the issues she had pursued in the Legislature, including enterprise zones and other economic development matters. She also sponsored legislation calling for the city to divest its South Africa-linked investments.

Collins' 1988 run for the 13th was characteristic of her outspoken, ambitious style. At the time, most black leaders were reluctant to challenge Crockett, who built his name as a Detroit labor activist and pioneer in the civil rights movement. But Collins said she was "tired of waiting" for Crockett to retire, and the veteran congressman had angered some blacks by not endorsing 1988 presidential candidate Jesse Jackson.

Collins finished 8 percentage points behind Crockett; her strong campaign helped persuade him not to run again in 1990 and made Collins an immediate front-runner to replace him. She made her second run with the endorsement of Young. Though Young's backing can be a mixed blessing, in this case it helped set Collins apart from a crowded primary field that included several strong contenders. She was also backed by the United Auto Workers and by the Shrine of the Black Madonna, a major black church in Detroit.

With the primary behind her, Collins had little to worry about in underfunded, unknown GOP nominee Carl R. Edwards Sr.

Collins entered her new job with an ambitious agenda. She talked of plans to "save the black male," to diminish class divisions in her district and to help build a national urban planning policy. Those goals would be challenging for any freshman, and some critics said Collins, while on the Detroit City Council, did not put in the careful work to translate her rhetoric into legislative action. She does have a head start on many representatives when it comes to understanding urban problems. Collins was a teenage mother who had a baby die at 2 months. In 1990, her son Christopher was jailed for armed robbery.

Collins planned to make her voice heard on the Hill, but she claims she is also a good bridge-builder who can work with politicians from different backgrounds.

The 13th has lost population and might appear to be a possible target in redistricting, with Michigan losing two seats. But with the Voting Rights Act prohibiting dilution of minority voting strength, the 13th is likely to be preserved, along with the adjoining 1st, which has likewise lost population and is represented by a black.

Michigan 13

Downtown Detroit

After their first settlement burned to the ground in 1805, Detroiters coined the motto, "It shall rise again from the ashes." That is what the city has been trying to do since riots in 1967 desolated its inner core, leaving physical and emotional scars that have proved resistant to quick cure.

Returning to the thriving Motor City of old will require a phoenix-like recovery. Entire neighborhoods have fallen to urban blight, and nearly 15 percent of the city's population has left in the past decade. The surrounding suburbs are estranged from the city, a reflection of deteriorating race relations. In the first half of the 1980s, population in the 13th dropped by nearly 14 percent, more than any other congressional district in the country. The district suffered even greater losses in the 1970s, and reapportionment for the 1980s reduced the overwhelming black majority somewhat. But blacks remain the dominant force, and the area has been represented by a black Democrat since 1955.

Most of the district is a mix of working-class and poverty-level black neighborhoods, largely clustered south of Ford Freeway. The heart of the ghetto is east of Woodward Avenue, which bisects the city, heading northwest through successively wealthier suburbs until it reaches Pontiac.

Outside the inner-city core are moderate-income areas, black and racially mixed, such as Chandler Park and the community around Wayne State University. Working-class white ethnics live in the district's northeast end, around the Detroit City Airport.

Downtown Detroit tries to defy its surroundings. Deserted during the "Murder City" days of the early 1970s, there is more activity today, but within well-fortified glass towers. The 73-story Renaissance Center, opened in 1977, symbolizes the difficulty of revitalizing the city's commercial core; filling the Center with tenants has been a struggle.

To the southwest, the 13th includes many of Detroit's Hispanic neighborhoods, while farther south is an edge of the Arab section that has spilled over from Dearborn. Standing in sharp contrast to most of the district are Grosse Pointe Park and Grosse Pointe at its far eastern end. Once a white WASP enclave that screened out "undesirable" prospective residents, Grosse Pointe consists of upper-middle-class communities of corporate managers and professionals. They are the sole concentrated source of GOP votes in the 13th.

Population: 514,560. White 133,857 (26%), Black 365,835 (71%), Other 5,068 (1%). Spanish origin 16,073 (3%). 18 and over 360,241 (70%), 65 and over 67,365 (13%). Median age: 29.

Committees

Public Works & Transportation (34th of 36 Democrats)
Aviation; Economic Development; Water Resources

Science, Space & Technology (32nd of 32 Democrats)
Science; Technology & Competitiveness

Select Children, Youth & Families (18th of 22 Democrats)

Campaign Finance

	Receipts	Receipts from PACs	Expend-itures
1990			
Collins (D)	$335,736	$68,620 (20%)	$274,688

Key Vote

1991

Authorize use of force against Iraq	N

Elections

1990 General		
Barbara-Rose Collins (D)	54,345	(80%)
Carl R. Edwards Sr. (R)	11,203	(17%)
Joyce Ann Griffin (WW)	1,090	(2%)
Jeff J. Hampton (LIBERT)	649	(1%)
Cleve Andrew Pulley (I)	530	(1%)
1990 Primary		
Barbara-Rose Collins (D)	11,994	(34%)
Tom Barrow (D)	6,742	(19%)
Charles C. Vincent (D)	6,430	(18%)
Alberta Tinsley-Williams (D)	5,162	(15%)
Mike Patterson (D)	2,333	(7%)
Juanita Watkins (D)	1,666	(5%)
Michael Hartt (D)	472	(1%)
Henry Stallings II (D)	429	(1%)

District Vote For President

	1988	1984	1980	1976
D	83,633 (85%)	136,454 (85%)	123,194 (91%)	127,666 (80%)
R	13,673 (14%)	24,188 (15%)	8,190 (6%)	29,140 (18%)
I			2,393 (2%)	

14 Dennis M. Hertel (D)

Of Harper Woods — Elected 1980

Born: Dec. 7, 1948, Detroit, Mich.
Education: Eastern Michigan U., B.S. 1971; Wayne State U., J.D. 1974.
Occupation: Lawyer.
Family: Wife, Cynthia S. Grosscup; four children.
Religion: Roman Catholic.
Political Career: Candidate for Detroit City Council, 1973; Mich. House, 1975-81.
Capitol Office: 2442 Rayburn Bldg. 20515; 225-6276.

In Washington: Although there is a good bit of overlap, members of the Armed Services Committee can be roughly divided into two categories: those driven by a desire to influence U.S. defense policy and those mainly interested in the pork-barrel opportunities to be derived from the nation's massive military budget.

During his House career of more than a decade, Hertel has usually lined up in the former category. He has been an activist on defense procurement issues and is a liberal arms control advocate who made a particular cause of fighting the MX missile program.

Yet Hertel is recognized less these days for his broader agenda than for his efforts to save a defense project in his district. The Defense Department plans to end production of the M-1 tank as it advances a new generation of high-tech armor. But Hertel is battling to block the elimination, which could wipe out numerous jobs at tank plants in Warren, Mich. (in Hertel's 14th District) and in Lima, Ohio.

The M-1 is one of several weapons programs that have been whipsawed by tight defense budgets and by changing strategic needs in light of the Soviet Union's recent military retrenchment. The lobbying efforts to save some of these programs — such as the F-14 fighter and the Osprey hybrid helicopter/-airplane — have elicited hardball tactics and histrionics. The campaign to save Warren's M-1 production line, led by Hertel in the House and Michigan Democrat Carl Levin in the Senate, has been quieter, but dogged.

Hertel has adopted a strategy common among members fighting defense cuts in their districts: He eschews parochial arguments while insisting on the program's vital role in the nation's defense structure. Hertel points to the fact that there would be no active tank production lines in the United States between the time of the M-1 shutdown and the still-unspecified startup date for the new model of tanks.

"Defense means you're prepared to defend the country this afternoon, not five or six years from now," Hertel says. He and other M-1 allies won a partial victory in 1990. The fiscal 1991 defense authorization bill included a phase-out of new production following completion of the currently authorized 225 tanks, as requested by the Bush administration. However, it also authorized the upgrading of 3,300 older model M-1s, which would be retrofit with the larger cannons that are standard on the more advanced M-1A1 models. These upgrades would keep the M-1 production lines up and running for several years after new production is completed.

Pentagon planners, who say their tank requirements will be met under their phase-out plan, showed they were not swayed at the start of the 102nd Congress. The fiscal 1992 budget proposal presented by Defense Secretary Dick Cheney contained no money for the M-1 upgrades. However, the issue was clearly not settled at that point. The image of the M-1 — once plagued by operation and maintenance problems — was enhanced by its strong performance in the 1991 Persian Gulf War.

Hertel's advocacy of the M-1 has hardly moved him from his position in the liberal camp on the Armed Services Committee. In January 1991, he voted against the resolution authorizing President Bush to use force to end Iraq's occupation of Kuwait. He remains a resolute foe of nuclear weapons systems that he views as too expensive and militarily destabilizing.

Among these is the multi-warhead MX missile. Although a 1985 law capped MX production, Hertel continued to battle plans to develop a mobile, rail-based launching system for the weapon. As late as 1989, his effort appeared quixotic: His amendment to block funding for the program was defeated on a 168-253 vote. However, just a year later, members worried about defense program cutbacks were scavenging money from big-ticket items, and the MX rail-basing system became a consensus target: Over the objections of the Bush administration, the fiscal 1991 authorization bill barred funding for the program.

Hertel saw another of his pet ideas indirectly advanced in that bill. A provision authored by Rep. Nicholas Mavroules, D-Mass.,

Michigan 14

Detroit Suburbs — Warren

The 14th is a 15-mile corridor with an ethnic and social diversity that takes in the rumbling auto plants of Warren, the graceful old mansions of the Grosse Pointes, the kielbasa of Hamtramck and the pétanque games of Detroit's Belgian neighborhoods.

At the district's far eastern end, the mansions and estates lining Lake Shore Drive in Grosse Pointe Shores and Grosse Pointe Farms — the Ford family estate is among them — offer the kind of Republicanism associated with corporate board rooms and casual access to political power. Farther inland, in Grosse Pointe Woods and Harper Woods, are three-bedroom ranch houses and middle-level managers whose national and statewide allegiance is usually to the GOP, but who are comfortable splitting their tickets in local contests.

To the west stretches northeast Detroit, an ethnic quilt of solid working-class neighborhoods where a Democrat stumping for votes can spend his time productively at the corner bar. The auto industry attracted Poles, Germans, Italians and Belgians who settled here.

The center of Polish activity is Hamtramck, a city-within-a-city. Its neat seas of two-story frame houses, broken only by the spires of Catholic churches, were once home to 50,000 people. Most worked at the huge Dodge plant at the southern end of town.

Now down to a population of 18,000, Hamtramck is dependent these days on jobs at smaller factories.

North of Detroit the 14th takes in a small part of Oakland County and southwestern Macomb County, and these areas have nearly half the district residents. Middle-class ethnics live in East Detroit, Hazel Park and northern Warren, and lower-middle-class Appalachians reside in the shadow of steel plants and auto parts factories in southern Warren. The combination makes this area the socially conservative heart of Democratic strength in this area.

Population: 514,559. White 478,987 (93%), Black 25,311 (5%), Other 7,037 (1%). Spanish origin 4,993 (1%). 18 and over 372,422 (72%), 65 and over 58,019 (11%). Median age: 31.

calls for the creation of a professional Defense Department purchasing staff to streamline and reduce waste in the procurement process. The measure is a cousin to a proposal to create an independent "Defense Acquisition Agency," first made by Hertel in 1986 but subsequently stalled by Pentagon opposition.

Procurement issues have been of interest to Hertel since early in his House career, when he raised questions about exorbitant costs paid by the Defense Department for spare parts and other equipment. He served as chairman of a House task force on Pentagon waste and fraud during the 99th Congress.

Hertel's stature within Armed Services has suffered from his lack of success at institutional politics. In a series of contentious battles for the Armed Services chairmanship in the 99th and 100th Congresses, Hertel showed an unfortunate knack for supporting the losing candidate.

During a 1985 effort by junior Democrats to replace the aged and infirm Illinois Democrat Melvin Price as Armed Services chairman, Hertel decided to stick with the seniority system. But Price was deposed and Wisconsin Democrat Les Aspin installed to replace him.

Two years later, an unusual coalition of dissident liberal and conservative Democrats, led by Marvin Leath of Texas, sought to remove Aspin from the chair. Although Hertel did not seem eager to have Aspin back, he supported him in an initial up-or-down vote; Aspin lost. Hertel then switched loyalties, first backing Mavroules for chairman, then Charles E. Bennett of Florida. But these candidates were eliminated on early ballots. Not until the final showdown did Hertel pick right, supporting Aspin's comeback victory over Leath.

Whatever stumbles Hertel has made in Armed Services' leadership fights, he has progressed on the Merchant Marine and Fisheries Committee. He serves as chairman of the Oceanography, Great Lakes and the Outer Continental Shelf Subcommittee, which has jurisdiction over the National Oceanic and Atmospheric Administration.

Hertel's interest in oceanography stems from the proximity of the Great Lakes to his district. During the 100th Congress, he was part of a successful effort to have the Great Lakes included in a law prohibiting ocean dumping of medical wastes. He is also active in efforts to obtain funding to control the propagation of non-native species, such as the zebra mussel, that have infiltrated and threatened the ecological balance of the Great Lakes.

At Home: The three Hertel brothers have been a potent political force on the northeastern side of Detroit. Dennis Hertel spent six years in the state Legislature. His older brother is a former state senator and Wayne County commissioner, and his younger brother was elected to Dennis' state House seat in 1980. The success of the Hertel family stems from their moderate, labor-oriented politics.

Running for the seat given up by Democratic Rep. Lucien N. Nedzi in 1980, Dennis Hertel assembled a volunteer force 2,500 strong to counter the money and polish of his Republican opponent, Vic Caputo. A former television news anchorman and host of a morning talk show on Detroit's CBS affiliate, Caputo made up for his lack of political experience with oratorical polish and districtwide prominence. With help from the national GOP, he mounted a high-spending effort that relied largely on the media to push his candidacy across to voters.

Lacking the money and the flair of his opponent, Hertel concentrated on personal visits with voters, reportedly wearing out four pairs of shoes walking through the precincts. With the support of the Democratic organization, he scored a comfortable win.

Hertel went unchallenged in 1982, but in 1984, he faced John Lauve, who had drawn publicity for launching a drive to recall Gov. James J. Blanchard after he pushed through a huge tax increase. Hertel, however, was hard to label as a high-tax advocate; he pointed out that he had never voted for a tax increase during 10 years in state and federal office. Hertel won easily.

In 1986, GOP officials hoped to influence the district's Polish-American community by recruiting Polish immigrant Stanley T. Grot, a former autoworker and owner of a Hamtramck restaurant. But Hertel's popularity among Polish voters blunted Grot's efforts, which enabled the incumbent to win re-election by a margin of nearly 3-to-1.

The GOP all but ignored Hertel in 1988, nominating little-known classroom instructor Kenneth C. McNealy. The Democrat topped 60 percent for the first time in a presidential-election year, outpolling McNealy by nearly 47,000 votes in his 63-36 percent win. McNealy tried again two years later, but with no more success.

Committees

Armed Services (12th of 33 Democrats)
Investigations; Military Personnel & Compensation; Research & Development

Merchant Marine & Fisheries (8th of 29 Democrats)
Oceanography, Great Lakes & Outer Continental Shelf (chairman); Merchant Marine

Select Aging (15th of 42 Democrats)
Health & Long-Term Care

Elections

1990 General

Dennis M. Hertel (D)	78,506	(64%)
Kenneth C. McNealy (R)	40,499	(33%)
Robert Gale (TIC)	2,692	(2%)
Kenneth Morris (LIBERT)	1,721	(1%)

1988 General

Dennis M. Hertel (D)	111,612	(63%)
Kenneth McNealy (R)	64,750	(36%)

Previous Winning Percentages: **1986** (73%) **1984** (59%) **1982** (95%) **1980** (53%)

District Vote For President

	1988	1984	1980	1976
D	78,626 (43%)	77,597 (37%)	97,621 (43%)	99,782 (46%)
R	102,373 (56%)	130,491 (62%)	114,356 (50%)	114,792 (53%)
I			13,568 (6%)	

Campaign Finance

	Receipts	Receipts from PACs	Expend-itures
1990			
Hertel (D)	$306,850	$186,680 (61%)	$187,545
McNealy (R)	$1,256	0	$1,068
1988			
Hertel (D)	$251,004	$154,565 (62%)	$137,560
McNealy (R)	$3,525	0	$3,537

Key Votes

1991

Authorize use of force against Iraq	N

1990

Support constitutional amendment on flag desecration	N
Pass family and medical leave bill over Bush veto	Y
Reduce SDI funding	Y
Allow abortions in overseas military facilities	N
Approve budget summit plan for spending and taxing	N
Approve civil rights bill	Y

1989

Halt production of B-2 stealth bomber at 13 planes	Y
Oppose capital gains tax cut	Y
Approve federal abortion funding in rape or incest cases	N
Approve pay raise and revision of ethics rules	N
Pass Democratic minimum wage plan over Bush veto	Y

Voting Studies

	Presidential Support		Party Unity		Conservative Coalition	
Year	**S**	**O**	**S**	**O**	**S**	**O**
1990	18	82	93	6	7	91
1989	28	67	86	7	12	83
1988	22	78	92	6	24	76
1987	20	78	93	5	21	79
1986	14	83	90	8	10	90
1985	29	71	88	12	16	84
1984	27	71	84	13	20	75
1983	20	80	87	11	20	78
1982	32	64	80	9	21	68
1981	25	64	80	12	27	73

Interest Group Ratings

Year	ADA	ACU	AFL-CIO	CCUS
1990	94	17	100	21
1989	90	12	100	30
1988	95	4	100	21
1987	88	0	100	13
1986	85	9	93	19
1985	80	14	88	27
1984	75	17	92	44
1983	90	13	100	5
1982	75	26	100	15
1981	80	7	79	6

15 William D. Ford (D)

Of Taylor – Elected 1964

Born: Aug. 6, 1927, Detroit, Mich.

Education: Attended Nebraska State Teachers College, 1946; Wayne State U., 1947-48; U. of Denver, B.S. 1949, J.D. 1951.

Military Service: Navy, 1944-46; Air Force Reserve, 1950-58.

Occupation: Lawyer.

Family: Wife, Mary Whalen; three children.

Religion: United Church of Christ.

Political Career: Taylor Township justice of the peace, 1955-57; Melvindale city attorney, 1957-59; Taylor Township attorney, 1957-64; Mich. Senate, 1963-65.

Capitol Office: 2371 Rayburn Bldg. 20515; 225-6261.

In Washington: Raised by working-class parents — New Deal disciples who told him, "The Democratic Party cared and the Republican Party didn't" — Ford came to the House in time to champion Lyndon B. Johnson's Great Society.

For a man so steeped in party dogma, the 1980s were trying times, as Ford faced a Republican administration hostile to the idea of government as social engineer; then he watched as the hostility caught on among his constituents, the blue-collar Democrats who came to typify "Reagan Democrats."

While budget deficits will limit domestic initiatives in the 1990s, the decade promises more visibility for Ford and his causes.

The Bush administration has pledged a "kinder and gentler" approach, and Ford himself has more power, having taken over the chairmanship of the Education and Labor Committee in 1991, at the start of the 102nd Congress.

Although for years many considered Ford the de facto chairman of Education and Labor — where he spent more time than on the committee he did chair during the past decade, Post Office and Civil Service — his official designation is expected to markedly advance the panel's influence and reach. The previous chairman, Augustus F. Hawkins of California, who retired at the end of the 101st Congress at the age of 83, shared Ford's New Deal ideology, but Ford is expected to be more involved in legislative details and more aggressive in pushing the Democratic line.

Ford is known as a tenacious legislator, with one of the best institutional memories in Congress. He spent 14 years working to pass legislation to give workers 60 days' notice before a plant closed, and he is said to remember the name of every member who voted against the successful 1987 bill. Ford's keen memory, however, can be a double-edged sword, as it occasionally leads him to hold forth long after those listening are ready to move on.

Temperamentally, Ford is a crusty old-school pol, blunt, aggressive and partisan. Ford counts John D. Dingell, powerful chairman of Energy and Commerce, as a close friend. Now hunting buddies, the two first met when Ford was a justice of the peace outside Detroit and Dingell a young prosecutor there. Institutional observers are watching to see if Ford, like Dingell, will strive to expand his committee's jurisdiction.

But even without claiming any new turf, Ford is guaranteed a high profile in the 102nd Congress as his panel considers the Civil Rights Act, the Family Leave Act, striker protection legislation and the reauthorization of the Higher Education Act.

Over the years, the committee has had something of a split personality. The panel tends to function in a cooperative, bipartisan manner on education issues, while resorting to partisan fisticuffs on labor issues. While Ford quickly imposed a new ban on foreign cars parking in committee spaces at the Capitol, he says relations with the GOP are unlikely to change dramatically now that he is committee chairman. "I worked my way up from the last seat to the first one over 26 years," he explains. "It's not like bringing a movie star from California to be president."

Republicans worried about Ford's confrontational style look to his efforts on the 1990 education bill as a good-faith gesture. After months of political stalemate, Hawkins and ranking Education & Labor Republican Bill Goodling agreed to a compromise that included many of the president's proposals but focused them on disadvantaged students. Democrats balked, however, saying the bill was mere window dressing. And when they offered their own plan, Republicans walked out.

In order to offer himself as an honest

Michigan 15

Southwestern Wayne County

The Industrial Expressway heading west from Detroit is the spine of the 15th District. Lining the ribs that branch from it on its way out toward the airport are automobile and chemical plants, trucking firms and auto parts factories. In the distance squat retreating rows of suburban tract houses, home to more than a quarter of the district's voters.

Wayne County holds more than 80 percent of the population of the 15th; the rest is in Ypsilanti and its neighboring townships and a hook south of Ann Arbor around the small city of Saline. Within the territory are several Ford and General Motors plants; the automakers are the district's prime employers.

Most of the towns along the Industrial Expressway are lower-middle-class communities. Almost entirely white and originally settled by Eastern Europeans and migrants from Kentucky and Tennessee, they are Democratic, socially conservative and not particularly friendly to blacks. The politics practiced here are volatile, sometimes marked by a "throw the bums out" attitude that shortens the careers of local officeholders trying to deal with declining tax bases and poverty-stricken school systems.

Farther out in Wayne County, things are less crowded. Small farms are scattered around suburban townships inhabited by autoworkers who were prosperous enough to move beyond the central suburban ring. Canton Township is the district's only substantially Republican community, a white-collar suburb of split-level ranch houses encroaching into the surrounding farmland.

The district's largest population of blacks is in Ypsilanti, which was devastated by the early 1980s recession, and Ypsilanti Township. Many of the white autoworkers living there moved up from the South, and relations between the two communities have sometimes been tense. But together they give Democrats a grip on the area that far outweighs the small Republican margins turned in by the nearby farms.

Population: 514,560. White 476,107 (93%), Black 28,459 (6%), Other 6,777 (1%). Spanish origin 7,788 (2%). 18 and over 356,253 (69%), 65 and over 30,909 (6%). Median age: 27.

broker, Ford did not sign on to the Democrats' bill, and he and Goodling wrote the outlines of yet another plan. "You can't just spit on somebody and expect the next time you go to them they'll want to work with you," he explained.

While that bill passed the House late in 1990, conservatives blocked its consideration in the Senate. Ford has indicated that he is less than interested in resuming the debate in the 102nd.

College aid has been Ford's specialty over the years, and his priority now is the reauthorization of the Higher Education Act. He had a hand in its 1965 creation as well as numerous reauthorizations since.

In the debate over how best to help students finance an education, Ford's interest is in helping not just the poor, but also the middle class, whose support he believes is politically crucial to the programs' survival.

He complains that the current system, which emphasizes loans, is creating a class of "indentured servants," overburdened with heavy loans and sometimes unable to complete their education.

The last time out in 1985, Ford succeeded by brokering a complex bipartisan bill, packed with enough pork-barrel projects for each panel member to have a vested interest in its fate. He also had to accommodate Congressional Black Caucus members who were protective of aid for historically black colleges. "I have real difficulty," Ford said, with the idea "that a school that was created to keep blacks separate from other people in college should have money on a continuing basis." A compromise funneled funds to black colleges and to institutions with minority enrollments.

In drafting the 1978 higher education bill, he helped expand the program of Basic Education Opportunity Grants, which provides money directly to students, and broadened eligibility for guaranteed loans to all students. Two years later, the 1980 bill provided even more generous aid for students, young and old, who wanted to continue their schooling. But Reagan targeted these programs for some of his deepest cuts, and in 1981, Congress agreed to reimpose an income test for student loans. Ford spent most of the rest of the decade fending off other reductions.

Protecting trade and technical schools will be a priority for Ford in the 1991 reauthorization. His interest in the schools dates back to his youth, when Ford attended the Henry Ford Trade School. He earned 20 cents an hour and was guaranteed a job for life at the Ford Motor Co. But Ford, no relation to the auto magnate, joined the Navy and then attended college and law school on the GI Bill.

Ford maintains that students who choose to attend Harvard and study pre-Columbian art should be treated no better than students who study plumbing or computers at trade schools. "I think that when the federal government breaks away from that and decides that one kind of student is a better kind of student than another . . . then we are in effect dictating a new class system in this country," he says. "I will be no part of it."

When trade schools drew criticism in 1989 for their default rates on student loans, however, Ford joined the chorus and helped pass legislation to deny loans to schools with exceedingly high default rates. "I've worked on these student aid programs for 25 years," he said. "And I'm not about to see them destroyed by schools abusing this program."

In the 100th Congress, Ford helped strike a compromise that cleared the way for a major bill renewing all federal elementary- and secondary-school programs, and providing some modest increases for the first time in the Reagan years, by meeting the GOP halfway on bilingual education. While some Democrats balked at giving schools more flexibility to teach English, fearing a return to controversial immersion methods, Ford called for conciliation. "I see this compromise as a political compromise to get enough votes from opponents of bilingual education to keep bilingual education alive," he said.

On the civil rights bill in the 102nd Congress, Ford is among those trying to redefine the legislation as advancing women's rights. His committee included in the bill sweeteners on pay equity and other language designed to appeal to women. Ford even proposed renaming the bill "The Women's Equity in Employment and Civil Rights Act," a title that was reversed when the bill was introduced in 1991.

A former labor lawyer, Ford is a union stalwart. As with other pieces of his legislative agenda, life experience contributed to Ford's personal commitment to organized labor. His father worked at Kaiser-Frazer, and when he collapsed at the auto plant, at age 42, officials claimed that he died of a heart attack. Suspicious, Ford, then 20, began a personal investigation and learned that his father had been killed by toxic smoke inhalation. When confronted with the facts, the company offered the family just $5,000.

Passage of the 1987 plant-closing bill was the end of a long struggle for Ford. Some 14 years and many compromises after he first introduced the legislation, it became the Democrats' *cause célèbre* in the 100th Congress, the issue they hoped would prove GOP callousness to workers and win back the Reagan Democrats in the 1988 election.

The proposal was attached to a major trade bill in the House. With typical bluntness, Ford repeatedly warned his party's waverers, many from the oil states, that if his provision were challenged, he would go after the section in the trade bill repealing the windfall-profits tax on oil.

After Reagan vetoed the trade bill, citing the plant-closing language, Congress passed the bill separately by a margin that indicated a veto could not hold. Ultimately, the president allowed the plant-closing bill to become law without his signature.

As chairman of Post Office and Civil Service, Ford was best known for his role as the undertaker eager to bury any proposals that would block pay raises for lawmakers and federal employees, indulging his love for legislative sleight of hand. Ford could afford to lead the pro-pay-raise side because he has never had serious political problems at home. "I know for a fact that the vast majority of the people I represent think I'm vastly underpaid," he once boasted.

On Post Office, Ford is an advocate for the unions that represent federal employees. In 1990, Congress passed legislation supported by the union to permit the nation's 3 million federal workers to participate in political activities. But Bush vetoed the Hatch Act revision bill, and though the House voted to override by a lopsided margin, the Senate fell two votes short.

In 1978, Ford was labor's negotiator on President Jimmy Carter's civil service revision bill, expressing the unions' fears that merit incentives written into the bill would weaken job protection. Ultimately, he reached a compromise on behalf of the unions with the administration and with the bill's chief sponsor, Arizona Democrat Morris K. Udall.

The one issue that Ford has been politically cautious about over the years is busing to achieve racial balance in schools. He signed congressional petitions, held hearings and voted for measures aimed against busing. But when he balked at an effort in 1972 to pry an anti-busing constitutional amendment out of the Judiciary Committee, demonstrators marched around his Michigan office, chanting, "Sign or Resign." Ford insisted he simply did not like stripping a committee of its jurisdiction, but the groups were not appeased. In 1979 he voted for an anti-busing amendment on the floor.

At Home: An energetic Democrat, Ford has never had much trouble winning election even though his constituents are no longer the Democratic "true believers" they once were.

He put in seven years as a political apprentice in township politics on the western side of Wayne County, then went to the state Senate in 1962. It was an easy move because he had the blessing of the man who was retiring.

Taking a U.S. House seat two years later was not too much harder. The newly created

15th District had no incumbent, and most local party leaders favored Ford for the opening. His only significant primary opposition came from township politician William Faust, who later became majority leader of the state Senate. Ford defeated Faust 45-36 percent, with the rest of the vote split among three others.

Since then, Ford has carefully tended to his district. As a senior legislator on Education, he has invited city and school officials from Detroit to come to Washington for conferences on how to get money from the federal government. He has been rewarded with routine elections. In 14 campaigns, he has not fallen below 60 percent.

Ford drew more publicity than most secure incumbents in the early 1980s when he had to contend with Gerald Carlson, a "white rights" advocate who once had ties to the Ku Klux Klan and the American Nazi Party. Carlson ran against Ford as a Republican in 1980 and 1984 and as a Democrat in 1982.

Carlson's 1982 candidacy went nowhere, but in November 1984 he polled 40 percent, a result that shocked and embarrassed local Republican officials, who had disavowed him. Pressed to explain how Carlson had won the GOP nomination over a party-endorsed candidate, one Republican official, noting that Carlson took the lightly attended GOP primary with just over 5,000 votes, said, "There are that many rednecks in the district ... that many voters who believe that a little fascism would not be all bad."

Committees

Education & Labor (Chairman)
Postsecondary Education (chairman)

Elections

1990 General

William D. Ford (D)	68,742	(61%)
Burl C. Adkins (R)	41,092	(37%)
David R. Hunt (LIBERT)	2,497	(2%)

1988 General

William D. Ford (D)	104,596	(64%)
Burl C. Adkins (R)	56,963	(35%)

Previous Winning Percentages: **1986** (75%) **1984** (60%) **1982** (73%) **1980** (68%) **1978** (80%) **1976** (74%) **1974** (78%) **1972** (66%) **1970** (80%) **1968** (71%) **1966** (68%) **1964** (71%)

District Vote For President

	1988	1984	1980	1976
D	79,091 (46%)	71,126 (39%)	89,641 (43%)	95,762 (50%)
R	92,840 (54%)	112,328 (61%)	101,740 (49%)	91,237 (48%)
I			14,289 (7%)	

Campaign Finance

	Receipts	Receipts from PACs		Expend-itures
1990				
Ford (D)	$384,737	$280,598	(73%)	$354,964
Adkins (R)	$42,511	$5,200	(12%)	$42,834
1988				
Ford (D)	$335,331	$267,901	(80%)	$234,435
Adkins (R)	$8,022	0		$7,993

Key Votes

1991	
Authorize use of force against Iraq	N
1990	
Support constitutional amendment on flag desecration	N
Pass family and medical leave bill over Bush veto	Y
Reduce SDI funding	Y
Allow abortions in overseas military facilities	?
Approve budget summit plan for spending and taxing	N
Approve civil rights bill	Y
1989	
Halt production of B-2 stealth bomber at 13 planes	?
Oppose capital gains tax cut	Y
Approve federal abortion funding in rape or incest cases	Y
Approve pay raise and revision of ethics rules	Y
Pass Democratic minimum wage plan over Bush veto	Y

Voting Studies

	Presidential Support		Party Unity		Conservative Coalition	
Year	S	O	S	O	S	O
1990	12	65	67	3	9	65
1989	24	73	90	2	7	90
1988	13	80	83	2	5	89
1987	11	84	88	3	9	88
1986	18	79	84	4	12	78
1985	16	76	71	2	7	87
1984	23	65	82	5	17	75
1983	12	78	87	2	8	82
1982	30	62	90	1	8	77
1981	26	58	84	3	12	68

Interest Group Ratings

Year	ADA	ACU	AFL-CIO	CCUS
1990	78	5	100	33
1989	95	0	91	40
1988	100	0	100	23
1987	92	0	100	0
1986	80	5	93	6
1985	80	5	100	20
1984	85	0	100	38
1983	90	0	100	10
1982	85	5	100	14
1981	70	0	100	6

16 John D. Dingell (D)

Of Trenton — Elected 1955

Born: July 8, 1926, Colorado Springs, Colo.
Education: Georgetown U., B.S. 1949, J.D. 1952.
Military Service: Army, 1944-46.
Occupation: Lawyer.
Family: Wife, Deborah Insley; four children.
Religion: Roman Catholic.
Political Career: Wayne County assistant prosecutor, 1953-55.
Capitol Office: 2328 Rayburn Bldg. 20515; 225-4071.

In Washington: Dingell has always seemed to care more about accumulating power and winning legislative battles than about being perceived as a nice guy in the process.

"Occasionally, I'm going to have to do ugly things that hurt me politically," he once said. "But I was sent here to win."

In fact, Dingell does not win as often as such bravado might suggest. But he has proven that one need not always win to be perceived as powerful. On clean air and other issues, Dingell has had to yield ground, but still, anyone who challenges him knows to brace for battle against a shrewd and persistent legislative tactician.

Ironically, Dingell's most significant legislative accomplishment of late was helping pass a reauthorization of the Clean Air Act in the 101st Congress. Although he had fought the issue with environmentalists for much of the 1980s, passage of the measure in the 101st Congress was not seen as a defeat for Dingell. Instead, he was credited with holding off action far longer than most lawmakers could have, and then — when pressure for passage became irresistible — driving a decent bargain for automakers in Michigan.

As chairman of the Energy and Commerce Committee, Dingell has helped pass bills on a staggering array of subjects, from laboratory regulation to toxic waste to insider trading.

For years, he has been considered one of the House's most skillful legislators, aggressive turf-fighters and hard-nosed negotiators. His mastery of House rules and procedural minutiae is renowned, as is his maxim about the power that knowledge gives him: "If you let me write procedure and I let you write substance," he told the Rules Committee in 1982, "I'll screw you every time."

Dingell has suffered some recent setbacks that suggest that there are limits to what his blunt use of the tools of legislative power can accomplish. He has yet to succeed in writing into law the "fairness doctrine" for broadcasting, despite staking his reputation on doing so. Rival chairmen have raised their voices against his power grabs and turned back some. And Dingell began the 101st Congress with an embarrassing admission that his famed investigative staff had gone too far.

Yet without question, Dingell still has the clout and the skill to triumph in his patented fashion. Further, Dingell's power to obstruct is not to be underestimated, as demonstrated by his effectiveness at keeping new clean air legislation from the House floor until the 101st Congress. That required hand-to-hand combat with another of the House's master legislators, Democrat Henry A. Waxman of California.

Dingell felt that environmentalists were seeking to impose drastic restrictions on industry with little regard to the costs, while the poor air quality in Waxman's Los Angeles district was its own argument for greater regulation.

In 1982, Waxman blocked Dingell's effort to loosen auto emissions standards. Afterward, Dingell spent years thwarting Waxman's attempts to strengthen those standards as well as other air pollution laws. Dingell shored up his lines of defense by arranging for coal-country allies to fill Energy and Commerce openings.

Even so, the scales began to tip against Dingell late in 1987, when he lost a floor fight over how long to extend the deadline for cities to comply with air-quality standards. In the meantime, a group of nine moderate Energy and Commerce Democrats were meeting to try to find middle ground between the Waxman and Dingell positions on clean air legislation.

No clean air bill emerged from the 100th Congress, but in June 1989 President Bush broke with his predecessor to submit a new clean air bill, and in so doing he broke the legislative stalemate as well.

Dingell then took the offensive to get a bill he could live with; he sponsored Bush's legislation, but opened the Energy and Commerce markup session by introducing a 302-page substitute with ranking Republican Norman Lent of New York. It became the working draft.

Most of the trench warfare that followed occurred in Waxman's Health and Environment Subcommittee. Relying on a coalition of subcommittee Republicans and conservative

Michigan 16

Southeast Wayne County; Monroe County

The 16th was once called "the most polluted congressional district in the nation" by *The Detroit News*. Redistricting in 1982 probably cost it that honor, not because great strides had been made in cleaning its air or rivers but because the boundaries were pushed down the Lake Erie shoreline into more rural southeastern Michigan.

Still, the 16th remains an overwhelmingly industrialized district. At its northern end is Dearborn, home of the Ford Motor Co. and site of an immense Ford plant. Known simply as "the Rouge," the plant employed close to 100,000 during its heyday, but now employs about 14,000. The haze-covered stretch of communities along the Detroit River in Wayne County from River Rouge to Gibraltar is a conglomeration of steel mills, foundries, auto factories, tool-and-die shops and chemical plants that looms over a broken sea of apartments and tract homes on uniform lots.

The Wayne County portion of the district, which accounts for about two-thirds of its population, is one of the most Democratic areas in Michigan. The eastern end of Dearborn, with its dilapidated prewar housing, is home to the country's largest single community of Arab-Americans. They join other residents of Dearborn in solid support of Democratic candidates.

Similar sentiments hold among the autoworkers and steelworkers, many of them black, who fill the duplexes of River Rouge and Ecorse; the tool-and-die and foundry workers of Melvindale; the transplanted Appalachians living in postwar tract homes in Lincoln Park and Southgate; the Polish auto and chemical workers of Wyandotte; and the Eastern Europeans of Allen Park.

Republicans do well among the white-collar residents of Riverview and the company managers of Lincoln Park, many of them reaching retirement age. The shaded streets of western Dearborn and Grosse Ile border large old homes whose white-collar owners cast the most solid Republican votes in the area.

Monroe County, south of Wayne, is home to 134,000 of the 16th District's constituents. It is politically marginal territory. Local factories give the county a firm union presence, but the rural western portions are staunchly conservative. The county's Lake Erie shoreline has attracted retirees from Detroit and Toledo.

The only substantial blue-collar vote outside Wayne County comes from industrial Adrian. Democrats are well organized in the city, but they have little strength among the farmers in the rest of eastern Lenawee County.

Population: 514,560. White 491,483 (96%), Black 14,133 (3%), Other 3,631 (1%). Spanish origin 12,403 (2%). 18 and over 367,589 (71%), 65 and over 52,476 (10%). Median age: 30.

Democrats, Dingell defeated many of Waxman's attempts to adopt tougher environmental controls. Yet Waxman built some winning coalitions of his own; over Dingell's strenuous objections, he won a vote forcing automakers to equip vehicles with charcoal canisters to capture gasoline vapors.

Dingell's committee work showcased all the tools he can bring to bear on an issue. Well-versed in the technical issues underlying many of the bill's provisions, Dingell could often outargue less-informed opponents. He let committee meetings run on, even into the small hours, seemingly hoping to wear down his foes.

Dingell also had created a climate in which junior committee members, who had gained their seats on the panel with Dingell's blessing, felt a need to express their thanks on critical clean air votes. "Either you were with him, or you were in the doghouse," said one committee member. Dingell reportedly sought to exclude from the conference committee on the bill some members whom he felt had been disloyal.

But Dingell kept the bill moving through committee, surprising some who had expected him to stall. He forged several compromises with Waxman — the most significant on auto emissions — sparing members some agonizing votes and himself some uncertain outcomes.

The end result was a bill strong enough for environmentalists to support, but more favorable toward the auto industry than many would have anticipated, given the political climate. Gone, for instance, was most of the administration's ambitious proposal requiring Detroit to build cars that could run on non-gasoline fuels.

After the bill passed, Dingell told the *Detroit Free Press* that he made no apology for looking out for the auto industry in his district: "That's what I'm sent here to do."

At the outset of the 102nd Congress, Dingell was again looking out for the industry as some lawmakers began to press for mandating higher vehicle fuel economy standards.

Energy and Commerce is an octopus of a committee with jurisdiction not only over energy but also health, communications, transportation and numerous regulatory agencies.

Because of the array of issues that pass through his committee, Dingell is a force with which nearly every House member must reckon at some point. But his legislative imperialism has met with increasing resistance in recent years. In October 1987, one day after Dingell masterfully established his jurisdiction over a securities-related provision in the farm bill, the House said "no" to another Dingell power play. Capitalizing on widespread resentment of Dingell, Public Works Chairman James J. Howard of New Jersey persuaded the House to kill a provision of a Federal Trade Commission bill to transfer oversight of airline advertising from Public Works to Energy and Commerce.

"Has the Energy and Commerce Committee Ever Tried to Steal Your Jurisdiction?" read the headline of a "Dear Colleague" letter circulated by Public Works leaders. A growing number of members have been able to answer "yes."

The 101st Congress added Agriculture Chairman E. "Kika" de la Garza to that list when Dingell sought to limit a proposed fish inspection program to shellfish, and transfer regulatory authority to an agency under Energy and Commerce review. The so-called "surf and turf" fight lasted the better part of 1990. Dingell's position prevailed, but at the price of dooming the bill's passage in that Congress.

Much of Dingell's reputation for ruthlessness comes from his role as the House's most aggressive and merciless investigator. As chairman of the Energy and Commerce Subcommittee on Oversight and Investigations, Dingell zealously probes the propriety and performance of federal agencies. He can force some sluggish federal regulators into action merely by threatening to call them before his subcommittee.

His admirers say his exposés of such problems as pesticides in food and second-rate prescription drugs are a service to the public. His detractors say his oversight of executive agencies is meddlesome, intrusive and an example of congressional government run amok.

In 1983, Dingell aggressively probed problems with the "superfund" hazardous-waste cleanup program and subpoenaed Rita M. Lavelle, the director, to testify before Energy and Commerce. When she failed to appear, Dingell brought a contempt of Congress resolution before the House; it passed 413-0 and led to Lavelle's indictment.

The panel's reputation was clouded in March 1989, when Dingell aired allegations that a private investigator had impersonated a member of his subcommittee staff. The ensuing fracas raised questions about the operating procedures of Dingell's own investigative staff, and Dingell dropped the matter while expressing "regret" over some of his staff's actions.

But early in the 102nd Congress, the investigations subcommittee was again winning favorable headlines for its scrutiny of university billing practices for research grants. Its first target was Stanford University, which admitted to charging the government for "indirect" research costs such as a wedding reception for the school's president.

Dingell is known for bullying witnesses and badgering colleagues; he intimidates nearly everyone. He has assembled one of the biggest and best technical staffs on Capitol Hill. Personally, he is a complex man, stubborn and vindictive on occasion, self-confident to the point of arrogance. And yet one must wonder whether Dingell's "meanness" is at least in part simply a device for building a public reputation he believes will be helpful to his causes. He is nearly always friendly and helpful to bright young Democrats who join his committee, and his protégés are fiercely loyal. Many of the colleagues who know him best seem not only to respect him, but genuinely to like him.

Because he appreciates and encourages aggressive young talent on his committee, he is often required to protect his own power against junior Democrats, sometimes by making common cause with the Republican side.

That is how he formed a majority to ram through the committee a business-backed bill to set federal product-liability standards in 1988. He faced a near revolt among Democrats who did not want to consider the divisive issue in an election year — especially since it was clear the bill would go no further than the committee.

That stance won him scorn from consumer groups, but Dingell is more in line with their interests on some of the telecommunications issues expected to occupy the committee during the 102nd Congress. In early 1991, he gave a green light to legislators interested in placing new restrictions on the cable television industry. Speaking to the U.S. Conference of Mayors in January 1990, Dingell complained of a "rapacious" cable industry in which "customer service is an oxymoron." He also supports efforts to allow the so-called Baby Bells to expand into making telecommunications equipment.

Overall, Dingell has been a liberal national Democrat, supporting civil rights, Great Society programs and expansion of the role of the federal government. On health issues, he is often aligned with Waxman in advocating more federal support for health care.

But his liberal profile is blurred by his fealty to the auto industry. And Dingell sometimes seems to be a bundle of contradictions — especially to environmentalists who have benefited enormously from Dingell's effectiveness when he has been on their side.

For instance, in the 101st Congress, the man environmentalists dubbed "Dirty Dingell" over clean air legislation provided crucial support for a bill requiring federal agencies to comply with solid- and hazardous-waste regulations. And the Dingell who pushed measures to protect endangered species and establish a National Wildlife System infuriates liberals with his militant pro-gun views and active alliance with the National Rifle Association.

At Home: The Dingell family has represented the Detroit area in Congress since 1932. For 23 years, John D. Dingell Sr., a New Deal champion of national health insurance, served from the city's West Side. When he died suddenly in 1955, while undergoing a routine physical examination, his 29-year-old son stepped in.

John Dingell Jr. grew up on Capitol Hill — not in Detroit. It was only when he received his law degree and went to work as an assistant prosecutor that he learned the intricacies of Detroit politics. But after three years as "my father's ears and eyes," he was ready for the 1955 special election. With backing from organized labor, he trounced a dozen Democratic candidates in the primary and went on to overwhelm his 26-year-old GOP opponent.

Since then, Dingell has had to worry about re-election only once, in 1964, when part of his constituency was combined with a larger part of the district held by Democratic Rep. John Lesinski Jr., who had also succeeded his father in the House. The Dingell-Lesinski primary got national attention because it was thought to be a measure of "white backlash" over recent civil rights legislation. Dingell, whose old district was about one-third black, had voted for the 1964 Civil Rights Act. Lesinski, whose district was nearly all white, was one of four Northern Democrats who had voted against it.

The issue was not brought up in the campaign, but both sides knew it was the main reason Dingell received such strong help from labor, civil rights groups and the state Democratic Party. Dingell won with 55 percent of the vote and has not had any problems since.

Continuing a family tradition, Dingell is now said to be grooming his son, state Sen. Christopher D. Dingell, to succeed him.

Committees

Energy & Commerce (Chairman)
Oversight & Investigations (chairman)

Elections

1990 General		
John D. Dingell (D)	88,962	(67%)
Frank Beaumont (R)	42,629	(32%)
Roger Conant Pope (LIBERT)	2,019	(2%)
1988 General		
John D. Dingell (D)	132,775	(97%)
Russell W. Leone (I)	3,561	(3%)

Previous Winning Percentages:				**1986**	(78%)	**1984**	(64%)
1982	(74%)	**1980**	(70%)	**1978**	(77%)	**1976**	(76%)
1974	(78%)	**1972**	(68%)	**1970**	(79%)	**1968**	(74%)
1966	(63%)	**1964**	(73%)	**1962**	(83%)	**1960**	(79%)
1958	(79%)	**1956**	(74%)	**1955 ***	(76%)		

* *Special election.*

District Vote For President

	1988	1984	1980	1976
D	90,630 (45%)	90,525 (35%)	95,357 (44%)	114,987 (53%)
R	109,695 (54%)	164,851 (64%)	103,367 (48%)	97,607 (45%)
I			13,913 (7%)	

Campaign Finance

	Receipts	Receipts from PACs	Expend-itures
1990			
Dingell (D)	$843,579	$625,727 (74%)	$602,952
Beaumont (R)	$3,775	0	$3,774
1988			
Dingell (D)	$619,770	$459,242 (74%)	$468,180

Key Votes

1991	
Authorize use of force against Iraq	Y
1990	
Support constitutional amendment on flag desecration	N
Pass family and medical leave bill over Bush veto	Y
Reduce SDI funding	Y
Allow abortions in overseas military facilities	Y
Approve budget summit plan for spending and taxing	Y
Approve civil rights bill	Y
1989	
Halt production of B-2 stealth bomber at 13 planes	Y
Oppose capital gains tax cut	Y
Approve federal abortion funding in rape or incest cases	Y
Approve pay raise and revision of ethics rules	Y
Pass Democratic minimum wage plan over Bush veto	Y

Voting Studies

	Presidential Support		Party Unity		Conservative Coalition	
Year	**S**	**O**	**S**	**O**	**S**	**O**
1990	20	78	87	5	37	61
1989	35	62	81	7	34	61
1988	22	75	88	3	29	61
1987	16	78	88	1	16	74
1986	24	70	80	5	32	58
1985	23	71	76	5	27	64
1984	30	59	84	7	31	63
1983	23	67	84	6	16	78
1982	44	55	90	7	25	74
1981	36	55	73	11	27	55

Interest Group Ratings

Year	ADA	ACU	AFL-CIO	CCUS
1990	67	4	100	15
1989	75	8	82	20
1988	80	13	100	29
1987	92	0	100	7
1986	75	19	92	6
1985	85	14	88	25
1984	75	9	92	33
1983	90	0	100	28
1982	80	14	100	18
1981	70	15	86	21

17 Sander M. Levin (D)

Of Southfield — Elected 1982

Born: Sept. 6, 1931, Detroit, Mich.
Education: U. of Chicago, B.A. 1952; Columbia U., M.A. 1954; Harvard U., LL.B. 1957.
Occupation: Lawyer.
Family: Wife, Victoria Schlafer; four children.
Religion: Jewish.
Political Career: Mich. Senate, 1965-71; Democratic nominee for governor, 1970, 1974.
Capitol Office: 323 Cannon Bldg. 20515; 225-4961.

In Washington: For a time in 1990 the hottest book in Washington was "The Japan That Can Say No," Shintaro Ishihara's tough-talking defense of Japan's economic nationalism. While trade hawks critical of Japanese trade policies were much incensed by the book, Levin invited its author to accompany him to a Michigan factory town crippled by competition from Japanese imports. And he went a long step further, going to visit some of the people Ishihara represents in the Japanese Diet.

"We have pussyfooted around too long," Levin said at the time. "We must be willing to say to each other what we are saying to ourselves."

A believer in international cooperation and a liberal on many foreign policy questions, Levin has nonetheless been confrontational on issues such as trade that politically affect his hard-pressed working-class constituents. In other ways, as well, Levin has been something of a political hybrid. He shares the fiscal concerns of the younger Democrats elected with him in 1982, a year of recession and concern about the federal deficit. Yet, as he turns 60, he retains the orthodox liberalism of his first days in politics in the mid-1960s, and thus a zeal to address today's social needs on the scale of the Great Society.

Now in his fifth House term, he has won considerable respect as a thoughtful and judicious legislator determined to find right answers even if they are not simple answers. His standing would be even higher were it not for his penchant for discussing complex issues in all their details and abstractions, a trait that contributed to his losses in two elections for the Michigan governorship in the 1970s.

It might also have cost him a coveted seat on the Ways and Means Committee, but his dogged pursuit of the prize and his support of the panel's 1986 tax-overhaul bill overcame what qualms Chairman Dan Rostenkowski had that Levin would make himself too obtrusive on the tightly controlled panel. Also, Michigan had a geographic claim on the seat.

Joining the committee in the 100th Congress, Levin has used the assignment largely to pursue a previous interest in trade. He has been a leading proponent of legislation affecting auto parts, and in 1990 offered a bill making the "Super 301" retaliation provisions of the 1987 Trade Act mandatory against countries that exclude U.S. goods.

He also supported the controversial Gephardt "fair trade" amendment, defending it against those who called it protectionist. Responding to a negative editorial, Levin described himself as a non-isolationist and "a committed internationalist." But, he added, that "doesn't mean allowing others to run roughshod over our home market or lock us out of theirs." He also campaigned vigorously for the amendment's sponsor, Missouri Democratic Rep. Richard A. Gephardt, in the 1988 spring presidential primaries.

Levin again expressed the auto industry's concerns when Ways and Means turned to legislation implementing a U.S.-Canada trade pact phasing out tariffs between the two nations over 10 years. Several industries feared that Canada would maintain various subsidies and trade barriers to benefit its firms. At one point, Clayton Yeutter and James A. Baker III, then President Reagan's trade representative and Treasury secretary, respectively, testified before Ways and Means to ask members to focus not on individual areas but on the pact's overall benefits. Levin countered, "We don't come from nowhere, or everywhere." In the end, he voted for the bill, which became law.

But Levin has also had something substantive to say on just about every major issue the panel considered. He was among the core group of Democrats most opposed to cutting taxes on capital gains in the 101st Congress. He was also among the last defenders of the 1988 Medicare insurance against catastrophic illness. Levin continued to support the program after most of Congress had bowed to senior citizens enraged by the associated surtax. Levin had no illusions about the politics; when members made pool bets on the size of the repeal vote, Levin's guess was closest.

Michigan 17

Northwest Detroit; Southeast Oakland County

The 17th combines white-collar suburban territory with a blue-collar presence inside the Detroit city limits.

The Detroit section of the district, at the far western end of the city, includes black neighborhoods and racially mixed Brightmoor, with large numbers of Appalachian blue-collar workers. The civil servants of Rosedale Park and the police families of "Coppers' Corner" — where many of Detroit's white police officers cluster — give the city portion of the 17th a relatively conservative Democratic presence.

The largest of the suburban towns is Southfield, with a population of 76,000. It is one of two centers for corporate headquarters and professional offices in the suburbs northwest of Detroit. Its 40-story high-rises lining the Northwestern Highway house a substantial population of Jewish senior citizens, while many younger, middle-class Jewish people live in the single-family houses away from the expressway. Coupled with the black community in the southern half of Southfield, the Jewish vote helps put the city solidly behind Democratic candidates. There is also a substantial Jewish vote in neighboring Oak Park, where a significant Orthodox community has been growing more conservative politically in recent years.

Black-majority Inkster, an overwhelmingly Democratic blue-collar town, bulges out of the district's southern tip. Nearby Dearborn Heights is politically mixed; the wealthy neighborhoods north and east of Inkster lean Republican while the blue-collar workers in the bungalows north of Ford Road are more sympathetic to Democrats. The liberal young professionals in the eastern tip of Dearborn Heights reinforce the Democratic vote.

There is Republican support here in the Catholic neighborhoods that stand in the shadow of Royal Oak's Shrine of the Little Flower, where Father Charles Coughlin, the right-wing radio commentator, preached in the 1930s. Solid Republican votes also come from the ranch homes of Lathrup Village and Pleasant Ridge and the larger homes of Huntington Woods.

Population: 514,560. White 440,607 (86%), Black 65,691 (13%), Other 5,484 (1%). Spanish origin 5,653 (1%). 18 and over 382,414 (74%), 65 and over 60,307 (12%). Median age: 31.

When he first arrived on Ways and Means, Levin had his own legislation for overhauling the welfare system (co-sponsored in the 99th Congress with Democratic Sen. Daniel Patrick Moynihan of New York). It would have required states to establish work, training and education programs for recipients of Aid to Families with Dependent Children and to provide child care, transportation and other services for those trying to become self-sufficient. Levin filed his bill in early 1987, a day before the House Democratic leadership's version. In doing so, he staked out the left for the coming debate, and ultimately some of his bill's provisions were reflected in the final product.

In mid-1988, he unsuccessfully opposed a GOP motion instructing House negotiators to settle for the lower price tag on the Senate's welfare-reform package; he knew that any cost-cutting would doom his efforts to raise welfare benefits toward the poverty line. Though the bill was much reduced from the House version, it still contained provisions Levin had long sought, and he voted for it on final passage.

As a member of Ways and Means' Health Subcommittee, he worked to maintain higher payments to Northeastern and Midwestern hospitals when the panel had to reduce Medicare during a round of budget-cutting for fiscal 1988 and 1989. He also has focused on legislative efforts to address the AIDS epidemic.

Like his brother Carl in the Senate, Levin was a leader within the House minority opposing a new federal death penalty included in the 1988 antidrug package. Unable to block pre-election support for the provision, opponents could merely pick at it; Levin won adoption of his amendment barring execution of the mentally retarded. Unlike 30 fellow liberals, he voted for the drug bill on final passage despite the capital punishment provision.

While serving on the Banking, Finance and Urban Affairs Committee in his first two terms, he focused on policies for the disadvantaged and unemployed, and on Third World debt. In his first term, Levin worked with Connecticut Democrat Bruce A. Morrison to ensure that jobs funding is targeted to areas with the highest unemployment.

As a one-time international development official in the Carter administration, he has long taken an interest in economic difficulties faced by other nations, and has been critical of moves to cut funding for the World Bank agency that lends money to the poorest nations.

But Levin is also concerned about job losses in this country. In 1986, when the House reauthorized the Export-Import Bank, which makes loans to foreign countries that buy U.S. products and services, he supported an amendment to ban all loans for foreign industries whose products or commodities compete with U.S.-made items. The amendment was watered down before being passed.

At Home: Levin's 1982 election capped his unexpected return to politics after an eight-year absence from the public eye. Levin first won office in 1964, taking a state Senate seat in the heavily Jewish Oakland County suburbs north of Detroit. He served as state Democratic Party chairman in the late 1960s and was viewed as one of the party's rising stars in 1970, when he challenged incumbent Republican William G. Milliken for the governorship.

But the low-key, even-tempered manner that had made Levin a successful legislator and party leader was less useful against Milliken. In 1970 and in a 1974 rematch, Levin was unable to develop a knack for fighting Milliken's "nice-guy" image — the more Levin presented voters with detailed factual information about state government programs, the less interested they seemed. One reporter referred to the 1974 campaign as "the bland leading the bland." Levin won almost 49 percent of the vote in 1970, but four years later, he slipped under 47 percent.

After that, Levin's name left the front pages. He ran the technical assistance program for the Agency for International Development under President Jimmy Carter. But when Democratic Rep. William M. Brodhead decided not to seek re-election 12 weeks before the 1982 primary, Levin returned to the area he represented in the state Senate and announced his candidacy. Levin's name and his support from the party establishment helped him overcome five primary opponents.

Critics accused Levin of trying to regain public office on the popularity of his younger brother, Sen. Carl Levin, although Sander's statewide races had in fact helped pave the way for Carl's 1978 victory. Sander Levin won the 17th easily in November, and has not been seriously challenged since.

Committees

District of Columbia (8th of 8 Democrats)

Select Children, Youth & Families (8th of 22 Democrats)

Ways & Means (20th of 23 Democrats)
Health; Human Resources

Elections

1990 General		
Sander M. Levin (D)	92,205	(70%)
Blaine L. Lankford (R)	40,100	(30%)
1988 General		
Sander M. Levin (D)	135,493	(70%)
Dennis Flessland (R)	55,197	(29%)

Previous Winning Percentages: 1986 (76%) **1984** (100%) **1982** (67%)

District Vote For President

	1988	1984	1980	1976
D	100,638 (53%)	102,650 (46%)	104,307 (48%)	97,333 (45%)
R	87,179 (46%)	119,681 (54%)	94,266 (43%)	114,031 (53%)
I			16,950 (8%)	

Campaign Finance

	Receipts	Receipts from PACs	Expend-itures
1990			
Levin (D)	$356,280	$241,525 (68%)	$271,072
1988			
Levin (D)	$300,654	$193,430 (64%)	$233,421

Key Votes

1991	
Authorize use of force against Iraq	N
1990	
Support constitutional amendment on flag desecration	N
Pass family and medical leave bill over Bush veto	Y
Reduce SDI funding	Y
Allow abortions in overseas military facilities	Y
Approve budget summit plan for spending and taxing	Y
Approve civil rights bill	Y
1989	
Halt production of B-2 stealth bomber at 13 planes	N
Oppose capital gains tax cut	Y
Approve federal abortion funding in rape or incest cases	Y
Approve pay raise and revision of ethics rules	Y
Pass Democratic minimum wage plan over Bush veto	Y

Voting Studies

	Presidential Support		Party Unity		Conservative Coalition	
Year	S	O	S	O	S	O
1990	19	81	97	3	19	81
1989	31	69	98	2	20	80
1988	24	73	94	2	11	89
1987	19	80	97	2	19	81
1986	19	81	97	2	12	86
1985	23	78	97	3	13	87
1984	30	70	93 †	7 †	15	85
1983	28	72	94	6	19	81

† Not eligible for all recorded votes.

Interest Group Ratings

Year	ADA	ACU	AFL-CIO	CCUS
1990	89	4	100	21
1989	95	0	100	20
1988	100	0	100	31
1987	84	0	100	13
1986	85	0	100	33
1985	85	10	88	32
1984	90	5	85	25
1983	95	0	94	25

18 William S. Broomfield (R)

Of Lake Orion — Elected 1956

Born: April 28, 1922, Royal Oak, Mich.
Education: Attended Michigan State U., 1951.
Military Service: Army Air Corps, 1942.
Occupation: Insurance executive.
Family: Wife, Jane Smith Thompson; three children.
Religion: Presbyterian.
Political Career: Mich. House, 1949-55; Mich. Senate, 1955-57.
Capitol Office: 2306 Rayburn Bldg. 20515; 225-6135.

In Washington: The ranking Republican on the Foreign Affairs Committee since 1975, Broomfield is one of the most settled figures in the House. Now in his 18th term, he is tied with Minority Leader Robert H. Michel of Illinois for most seniority among House Republicans.

Like Michel, Broomfield is from the school of conservative but pragmatic Midwestern Republicans who long dominated the House GOP leadership. His name has appeared annually on foreign aid proposals drawn up by the GOP administrations of Ronald Reagan and George Bush. While more ideological Republicans dominate the charged foreign policy debates, Broomfield is more likely to be in the House chambers trying to craft passable legislation.

Broomfield works well with his Democratic counterpart, Foreign Affairs Chairman Dante B. Fascell of Florida, a moderate who leans to the right on foreign policy issues. Unlike many of the committee's activist Democrats, Broomfield says, Fascell "doesn't try to pretend he's secretary of State."

Though content with his self-defined role as a "consensus-builder," Broomfield has his career frustrations. Chief among these is Broomfield's historic status as a member of the "permanent" GOP minority in the House. He and Michel, both of the House class of 1956, share the record for the longest continuous tenure as a member of a minority party.

Broomfield also must deal with the fact that his labor on the Foreign Affairs Committee's main annual assignment — the foreign aid bill — is often wasted. Burdened by the general unpopularity of foreign assistance programs and by the many controversies over its specific provisions, the foreign aid authorization bill has rarely been enacted in recent years.

In some years, the bill has been stalled by unbridgeable disputes between House liberals and conservatives. Even when the bill gets through the House, it can falter in the Senate, where rules make it easier to attach ideologically loaded amendments, and where archconservative Republican Jesse Helms of North Carolina (the Senate Foreign Relations Committee's ranking Republican) uses his parliamentary skills to delay things.

Broomfield's efforts to craft legislation have also not been helped by the dislike both Reagan and Bush have had for foreign aid authorizations: They prefer instead to set aid levels directly through the appropriations process. Bush, like Reagan before him, frequently condemns efforts by Foreign Affairs members to "micromanage" a foreign-policy-making role the Constitution reserves mainly for the executive branch.

This posture has caused some of the rare disagreements between Broomfield and Republican adminstrations. In the aftermath of the Chinese government's June 1989 crackdown on pro-democracy demonstrators, Broomfield supported a measure to impose economic sanctions against China. When the Bush administration argued that the sanctions would impinge on presidential prerogatives, Broomfield responded that the amendment was "not an attempt to undercut" Bush's foreign policy role. "It simply recognizes that Congress has a role in stating broad policy directions," he said.

While Broomfield supported Bush's deployment of U.S. troops in response to Iraq's August 1990 occupation of Kuwait, he insisted that the president had an obligation to obtain input from Congress on his Persian Gulf policy. When Bush in November 1990 ordered a massive troop buildup, Broomfield said his "failure to consult broadly with Congress could eventually serve to undermine his policy."

However, when Bush did come to Congress the following January to ask approval of a resolution authorizing the use of force against Iraq, Broomfield was in the fold. "The president has done everything he could do to convince [Iraqi President Saddam Hussein] through diplomatic channels to leave Kuwait ...,"

Michigan 18

Oakland County

This district is the one GOP bastion in metropolitan Detroit. In the cluster of towns on both sides of Woodward Avenue, the artery running northwest from Detroit and the route along which the city's affluent first escaped to the suburbs, Republicans and golf courses abound; GOP presidential candidates prevail by more than 2-to-1.

Bloomfield Hills and Birmingham, like the Grosse Pointes, are dotted with the 1920s mansions and newer ranch houses of top-level auto executives and professionals. Bloomfield Hills was former GOP Gov. George Romney's hometown in his days as an auto executive.

To the west are the only slightly more modest shaded streets of Farmington Hills, a town of lawyers, doctors and business executives. To the east is Troy, a gathering ground for gleaming suburban business headquarters and professionals' offices; off the main roads live upper-middle-class Protestant voters.

The southwestern end of the 18th is a jumble of suburbs whose exploding populations helped make the district the second fastest-growing constituency in the state in the 1970s. Its far western end jabs into two Livingston County townships: the older blue-collar suburbs of Green Oak Township, some of its houses sporting two or three rusting cars in front, and Brighton Township, whose newer subdivisions have attracted a mix of factory workers and professionals from Ann Arbor and Detroit.

The old horse country of western Oakland County has turned decidedly blue-collar around South Lyon and in more ethnic Commerce Township. Wixom and Walled Lake house factory workers who tend toward conservatism on social issues.

The northern end of the district is less wealthy. Pontiac Township, east of Pontiac, is a melting pot into whose 25-year-old subdivisions the surrounding area's autoworkers, mid-level managers and small-business people have poured. The outlying townships in northeastern Oakland County are strongly Republican and rural, but much farmland north of Rochester has gone for development.

One of the few Democratic toeholds here is Macomb County's Shelby Township whose small, postwar brick houses hold blue-collar workers from Utica and Warren.

Population: 514,560. White 500,199 (97%), Black 4,160 (1%), Other 8,085 (2%). Spanish origin 4,792 (1%). 18 and over 360,726 (70%), 65 and over 36,119 (7%). Median age: 31.

Broomfield said. "We must give the president the power he needs to convince Saddam that he has no other alternative. . . ." This statement is more typical of Broomfield's supportive posture towards his party's presidents. He remains, above all else, a party loyalist and a faithful spear-carrier for Republican presidents.

In early 1989, Broomfield waxed effusive about Reagan, whom he praised for "the finest foreign policy record of any administration" he served under during more than 30 years in the House. "It is ironic that the candidate who was portrayed . . . as some kind of cowboy who could not understand the subtleties and complexities of international relations would in eight years restore the United States to a position of respect throughout the world," Broomfield said.

Broomfield's partisan loyalty came to the fore during the controversy over efforts in the mid-1980s to sell arms to Iran and divert the proceeds to the "contra" rebels fighting Nicaragua's Marxist government. While he criticized Reagan for allowing the Iran-contra affair to occur, Broomfield expressed concern that the congressional investigation of the covert policies would become a drawn-out forum for Democratic attacks on Reagan.

As senior Republican on Foreign Affairs, Broomfield took a seat on the joint Iran-contra panel, though the ranking position went to the more assertive Dick Cheney of Wyoming (then the House minority whip and later Bush's secretary of Defense). Broomfield was not one of the committee's dogged inquisitors, joining in mainly to ask lengthy rhetorical questions aimed at eliciting a pro-Reagan response.

In one instance, Broomfield stretched for a metaphor to sum up the need for renewed U.S. support to the contras. In May 1987, he obliquely asked contra leader Adolfo Calero, "Would you say that to the people of Nicaragua yearning for freedom the United States is now viewed more like a lighthouse whose beam is growing dimmer currently or a lighthouse temporarily encased in a fog bank of itself by indulgent self-examination?"

Although not a fire-breather in the Republican Conference, Broomfield took a tough stand after the Soviet bugging of the unfinished U.S. Embassy in Moscow was made public in early 1987: Broomfield worked to make it more difficult for U. S. S. R. diplomats to occupy their new Washington embassy, located on a high point overlooking the downtown area. He added an amendment to an intelligence funding bill, requiring the secretary of Defense to report to Congress on whether it would be consistent with national security for the Soviets to occupy that embassy.

At Home: Broomfield's longevity in Congress has little to do with his work on Foreign Affairs. It is a result of his ability to project himself to his suburban district as a pleasant, service-oriented Republican. Handling constituent requests and flooding the district with newsletters over 30-plus years have made Broomfield all but untouchable.

The few political struggles have come within his own party. But at the two critical junctures in his political career, when he seemed to be up against unfavorable odds, Broomfield managed to be on the popular side.

The first time was 1956, when he challenged a more senior state senator to succeed retiring Republican George A. Dondero, who had served in Congress from suburban Detroit since 1933. The major issue was construction of a toll road through a residential section of Oakland County. Broomfield's opponent supported it. Broomfield argued that any new highway should go through a more rural area. Most of the county's voters shared his view. He narrowly won and the road was never built.

Sixteen years later, Broomfield faced his second political crisis upon the re-alignment of Oakland County's congressional districts. Since 1964, he had been winning re-election easily in the eastern part of the county. But in 1972, this area was attached to a blue-collar section of Macomb County; Broomfield decided he would do better in western Oakland County, against the GOP incumbent there, Jack H. McDonald.

McDonald was already representing most of the new constituency, but again Broomfield had the paramount issue on his side: busing. In the House, Broomfield has been at the forefront of the opposition to federally mandated busing. Even though McDonald was just as firmly opposed to busing, Broomfield had been more vocal. He won the primary with 59 percent.

Committees

Foreign Affairs (Ranking)
Arms Control, International Security & Science (ranking)

Small Business (3rd of 17 Republicans)
Regulation, Business Opportunity & Energy

Elections

1990 General		
William S. Broomfield (R)	126,629	(66%)
Walter O. Briggs IV (D)	64,185	(34%)
1988 General		
William S. Broomfield (R)	195,579	(76%)
Gary Kohut (D)	57,643	(22%)

Previous Winning Percentages: **1986** (74%) **1984** (79%) **1982** (73%) **1980** (73%) **1978** (71%) **1976** (67%) **1974** (63%) **1972** (70%) **1970** (65%) **1968** (60%) **1966** (68%) **1964** (60%) **1962** (60%) **1960** (56%) **1958** (53%) **1956** (57%)

District Vote For President

	1988	1984	1980	1976
D	80,246 (29%)	65,252 (25%)	67,833 (28%)	76,445 (37%)
R	192,002 (71%)	190,888 (74%)	150,366 (62%)	127,570 (61%)
I			20,583 (9%)	

Campaign Finance

	Receipts	Receipts from PACs		Expend-itures
1990				
Broomfield (R)	$243,762	$56,200	(23%)	$78,205
Briggs (D)	$98,767	$25,600	(26%)	$97,203
1988				
Broomfield (R)	$235,699	$57,700	(24%)	$77,103
Kohut (D)	$9,460	$3,350	(35%)	$9,459

Key Votes

1991	
Authorize use of force against Iraq	Y
1990	
Support constitutional amendment on flag desecration	Y
Pass family and medical leave bill over Bush veto	N
Reduce SDI funding	N
Allow abortions in overseas military facilities	N
Approve budget summit plan for spending and taxing	N
Approve civil rights bill	N
1989	
Halt production of B-2 stealth bomber at 13 planes	N
Oppose capital gains tax cut	N
Approve federal abortion funding in rape or incest cases	N
Approve pay raise and revision of ethics rules	Y
Pass Democratic minimum wage plan over Bush veto	N

Voting Studies

	Presidential Support		Party Unity		Conservative Coalition	
Year	**S**	**O**	**S**	**O**	**S**	**O**
1990	72	26	76	19	80	19
1989	74	20	62	33	78	17
1988	58	35	67	20	84	11
1987	69	30	71	27	84	14
1986	70	29	69	23	72	26
1985	73	24	67	28	84	13
1984	61	31	78	17	90	10
1983	77	18	77	16	80	16
1982	65	26	72	20	82	12
1981	63	26	77	19	73	24

Interest Group Ratings

Year	ADA	ACU	AFL-CIO	CCUS
1990	17	83	17	100
1989	20	88	9	100
1988	30	84	36	92
1987	0	96	0	93
1986	5	73	7	100
1985	5	85	13	71
1984	5	71	23	80
1983	5	87	7	95
1982	10	67	16	77
1981	20	80	13	94

Minnesota

U.S. CONGRESS

SENATE 1 D, 1 R
HOUSE 6 D, 2 R

LEGISLATURE

Senate 46 D, 21 R
House 79 D, 55 R

ELECTIONS

1988 Presidential Vote	
Bush	46%
Dukakis	53%
1984 Presidential Vote	
Reagan	50%
Mondale	50%
1980 Presidential Vote	
Reagan	43%
Carter	47%
Anderson	9%
Turnout rate in 1986	45%
Turnout rate in 1988	66%
Turnout rate in 1990	55%

(as percentage of voting age population)

POPULATION AND GROWTH

1980 population	4,075,970
1990 population (20th in the nation)	4,307,000
Percent change 1980-1990	+7%

DEMOGRAPHIC BREAKDOWN

White	94%
Black	2%
Asian or Pacific Islander	2%
(Hispanic origin)	1%
Urban	67%
Rural	33%
Born in state	75%
Foreign-born	3%

MAJOR CITIES

Minneapolis	368,383
St. Paul	272,235
Bloomington	86,335
Duluth	85,493
Rochester	70,745

AREA AND LAND USE

Area	79,548 sq. miles (14th)
Farm	54%
Forest	33%
Federally owned	7%

Gov. Arne Carlson (R)
Of Shoreview — Elected 1990

Born: Sept. 24, 1934, New York, N.Y.
Education: Williams College, B.A., 1957; U. of Minnesota, 1957-58.
Military Service: Army, 1959-60.
Occupation: Computer executive.
Religion: Protestant.
Political Career: Minneapolis City Council, 1965-67; Minn. House, 1971-79; Minn. state auditor, 1979-91.
Next Election: 1994.

WORK

Occupations	
White-collar	53%
Blue-collar	27%
Service workers	14%
Government Workers	
Federal	32,323
State	81,266
Local	202,821

MONEY

Median family income	$ 21,185	(13th)
Tax burden per capita	$ 1,247	(5th)

EDUCATION

Spending per pupil through grade 12	$ 4,386	(17th)
Persons with college degrees	17%	(20th)

CRIME

Violent crime rate	288 per 100,000 (36th)

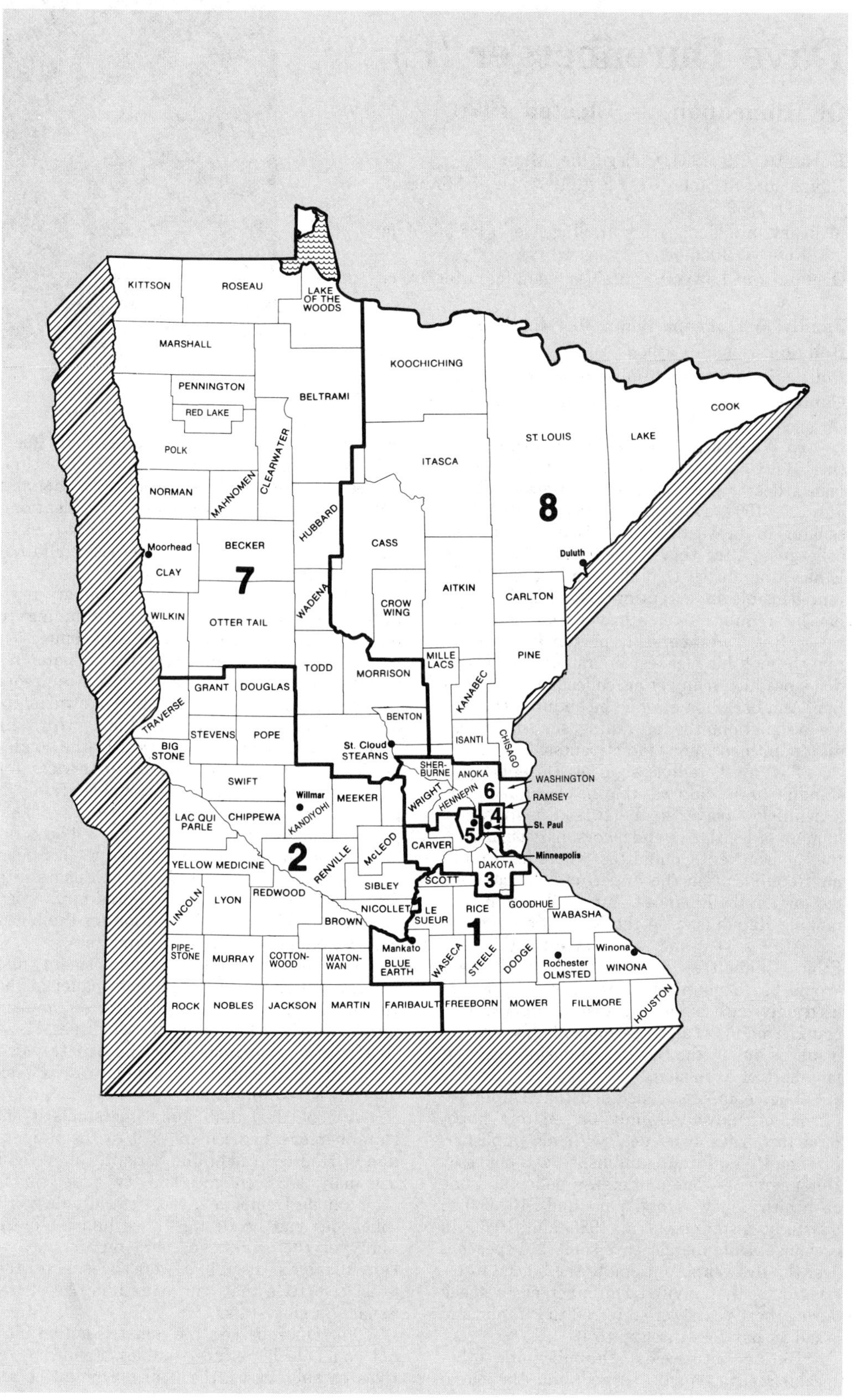
KITTSON
ROSEAU
LAKE OF THE WOODS
MARSHALL
KOOCHICHING
PENNINGTON
RED LAKE
BELTRAMI
COOK
POLK
CLEARWATER
ST. LOUIS
LAKE
ITASCA
NORMAN
MAHNOMEN
HUBBARD
8
CASS
Moorhead
BECKER
Duluth
CLAY
7
AITKIN
CARLTON
CROW WING
WADENA
WILKIN
OTTER TAIL
PINE
MILLE LACS
TODD
MORRISON
KANABEC
GRANT
DOUGLAS
TRAVERSE
BENTON
STEVENS
POPE
ISANTI
CHISAGO
BIG STONE
St. Cloud
STEARNS
SHER-BURNE
ANOKA
WASHINGTON
SWIFT
6
Willmar
MEEKER
WRIGHT
HENNEPIN
RAMSEY
KANDIYOHI
4
LAC QUI PARLE
CHIPPEWA
St. Paul
5
CARVER
McLEOD
Minneapolis
2
RENVILLE
YELLOW MEDICINE
DAKOTA
SIBLEY
SCOTT
3
LYON
REDWOOD
LINCOLN
NICOLLET
LE SUEUR
RICE
GOODHUE
WABASHA
BROWN
1
Mankato
BLUE EARTH
WASECA
STEELE
DODGE
Rochester
OLMSTED
Winona
WINONA
PIPE-STONE
MURRAY
COTTON-WOOD
WATON-WAN
ROCK
NOBLES
JACKSON
MARTIN
FARIBAULT
FREEBORN
MOWER
FILLMORE
HOUSTON

Dave Durenberger (R)

Of Minneapolis — Elected 1978

Born: Aug. 19, 1934, Collegeville, Minn.

Education: St. John's U., B.A. 1955; U. of Minnesota, J.D. 1959.

Military Service: Army Intelligence, 1955-56; Army Reserve, 1956-63.

Occupation: Lawyer; adhesives manufacturing executive.

Family: Wife, Penny Baran; four children.

Religion: Roman Catholic.

Political Career: No previous office.

Capitol Office: 154 Russell Bldg. 20510; 224-3244.

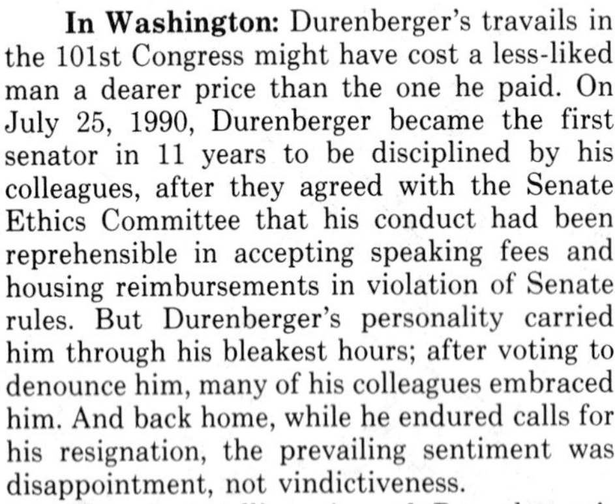

In Washington: Durenberger's travails in the 101st Congress might have cost a less-liked man a dearer price than the one he paid. On July 25, 1990, Durenberger became the first senator in 11 years to be disciplined by his colleagues, after they agreed with the Senate Ethics Committee that his conduct had been reprehensible in accepting speaking fees and housing reimbursements in violation of Senate rules. But Durenberger's personality carried him through his bleakest hours; after voting to denounce him, many of his colleagues embraced him. And back home, while he endured calls for his resignation, the prevailing sentiment was disappointment, not vindictiveness.

The most telling sign of Durenberger's standing in the club was that he continued to be a significant player in the 101st Congress in a number of legislative endeavors, particularly on the Environment Committee, where he is ranking Republican on the Superfund Subcommittee, and on the Finance Committee, where he is ranking Republican on the Medicare panel.

After a year-and-a-half investigation, the Ethics Committee decided that Durenberger should be "denounced," a term of opprobrium used only once before, against Georgia Democrat Herman E. Talmadge in 1979. "Denouncement" is one of the Senate's punishments that fall short of expulsion.

The committee concluded that Durenberger had circumvented limits on senators' honoraria through a book deal with his publisher, Piranha Press. Piranha published two books by Durenberger — one on defense policy and one on health policy — and paid him $100,000 in quarterly installments in 1985 and 1986. In exchange, Durenberger gave some 113 speeches over the two years to promote the books. Interest groups that invited Durenberger to speak during those years were referred to Piranha and asked to pay fees directly to it.

During both years, Durenberger's other speaking engagements earned him the maximum amount of honoraria senators could keep: $22,500 in 1985 and $30,000 in 1986. The committee's special counsel, Robert S. Bennett (later to lead the Keating Five investigation), said the Piranha deal was a gimmick to "sanitize" speaking fees that he otherwise could not have accepted under Senate limits.

The Ethics Committee's disciplinary resolution also cited Durenberger for failing to report expense-paid trips he took in connection with the book deal; accepting Senate reimbursement for rent paid on a Minnesota condominium in which he shared ownership; having improper communications with the blind trust that held his interest in the condominium; accepting free limousine services for personal use; and converting campaign funds to personal use when he signed over a $5,000 political donation to Piranha Press. The committee concluded that Durenberger "has been reprehensible and has brought the Senate into dishonor and disrepute." It ordered him to pay more than $120,000 in restitution for the housing reimbursements and speaking fees.

Durenberger called denouncement too harsh a penalty, but he did not challenge the verdict or the version of events presented on the Senate floor by committee Chairman Howell Heflin of Alabama. After the Senate voted 96-0 to denounce him, Durenberger rose to seek his colleagues' forgiveness.

A book deal that bore some similarity to Durenberger's had led in 1989 to the resignation of House Speaker Jim Wright. But Wright had many GOP enemies and few close friends even among Democrats. Most of Durenberger's colleagues had no desire to see him removed. Many of their floor speeches on the day of Durenberger's discipline were paeans to the legislative style that had made him one of the Senate's rising stars.

For Durenberger, the Senate's action may not conclude his ethics troubles. Following its rules on such cases, the Ethics Committee referred the matter to the Justice Department, which is looking into matters that were before the Ethics Committee.

Even before the Senate's disciplinary action, Durenberger had been working to reassert his influence over a range of domestic issues, particularly health policy. He was aiming to rebuild the reputation for thoughtful legislating that had marked his career before he entered, as he once said, his "so-called flake period." Compounding his ethics problems in the late 1980s were personal difficulties; he went through a particularly trying "mid-life crisis," about which he spoke frankly to newspapers in interviews that detailed his separation from his family and search for happiness.

With seats on the Finance and Environment committees, Durenberger has been able to exercise his legislative skills on an impressive variety of domestic policy over the years. He joined Labor and Human Resources as the 101st Congress began, which with Finance writes most of the law for health and human services legislation. He has always been one of the least ideological Republicans in the Senate, frequently abandoning the party or administration line to vote his own way.

On Environment, Durenberger has been one of a small group of Republicans who often ally with environmental groups in pushing for tighter safeguards. In the 101st Congress, he was the chief Senate sponsor of the Clean Air Act's air toxics proposal, which imposed tough new controls to reduce industrial emissions of 189 toxic substances, most of which had never been regulated by the federal government. He was a conferee on the bill.

Durenberger was wary of imposing the most stringent anti-pollution requirements for vehicles. He opposed language favored by Democrats that would have required a second round of tailpipe emission reductions in 2003. (The final bill gave the Environmental Protection Agency leeway to loosen the second-round restrictions.) To control pollution from urban buses, Durenberger supported a measure requiring them to make greater use of cleaner alternative fuels. An alternative fuels standard was adopted, but with a three-year delay.

Durenberger was chairman of the Finance Subcommittee on Health during Republican control of the Senate; he kept the ranking slot with the change in party control in 1987. At the start of the 101st Congress, the committee split the Health Subcommittee in two; Durenberger became ranking Republican on the new Medicare and Long-Term Care panel.

He was a leading sponsor of provisions in the 1983 Social Security bill that established the "prospective payment" system for Medicare, perhaps the most significant measure enacted in the 1980s to cut health-care costs. The plan, originally proposed by the Reagan administration, established the principle that Medicare would pay hospitals fixed amounts for treatment of various types of diseases — replacing the old system under which Medicare paid hospitals their costs to treat patients.

In a similar vein, Durenberger was involved in 1989 when Congress overhauled the way Medicare pays doctors. He and Medicare Subcommittee Chairman John D. Rockefeller IV co-authored the Finance Committee's proposal on physician payment reform, seeking a middle ground between two competing House proposals. Drawing qualified support from the Bush administration and the American Medical Association, their proposal phased in changes more gradually than the House plans.

The new scheme did away with a system that based payments on whatever a doctor chose to charge for a service. Under the new plan, payments are set by a national fee schedule that takes into account the time, training and skill required to perform a given service. It was signed into law as part of the fiscal 1990 budget "reconciliation" bill.

Durenberger was a strong supporter of the 1988 law that expanded Medicare to cover catastrophic health expenses for the elderly. But senior citizens' groups were angry at having to pay the entire cost of their new benefits, and in 1989, Congress repealed virtually the entire law. Durenberger joined key former backers in opposing efforts to change the law, but the momentum for repeal was irresistible.

The Senate rejected several alternatives, including one by Durenberger that would have preserved the unlimited hospital and doctor-bill coverage that constituted the program's core benefits. It had the backing of the bipartisan Senate leadership and of Health and Human Services Secretary Louis W. Sullivan. But the Bush administration was split; budget director Richard G. Darman overruled Sullivan's endorsement the same day he made it. Durenberger's amendment lost on a vote of 37-62.

In repealing the catastrophic law, Congress did preserve legislative authority for the Pepper Commission, a bipartisan body studying the problems of long-term care and access to health care for the uninsured. Durenberger was one of the 15 members of the commission and one of its three vice chairmen. The commission issued its conclusions on how to reform the health-care system in 1990, but was criticized for not prescribing how to fund its recommendations.

Durenberger's rise to the chairmanship of the Senate Intelligence Committee in 1985 brought repeated confrontations with the Reagan administration and criticism from his colleagues. He had to cope with a series of disturbing revelations about Soviet and Israeli espionage activity in the United States, a public break with the GOP administration over Nicaragua and a nasty feud with William J. Casey, the CIA director.

Then, just as Durenberger was about to

leave the chairmanship at the end of 1986, news of the Iran-contra affair broke. Within days, he was caught up in an extremely sensitive political inquiry, topped off by a heated dispute with some of his committee colleagues over whether to release the results of their investigation.

He incurred the wrath of many of his colleagues after deciding to brief President Reagan on the contents of the committee's report in December 1986. It was the second time in a year Durenberger was criticized for talking to outsiders about Intelligence Committee business. After a U.S. citizen was caught spying for Israel, Durenberger told a group of American Jews that the United States had once tried to recruit a spy in Israel; he was criticized, but not punished, by the Ethics Committee.

At Home: Durenberger's ethics case and his subsequent denunciation by the Senate dominated the first half of 1990 and was but the first in a series of incidents that soured Minnesota voters on the party establishment and on politicians in general that year.

The mood of antipathy helped elect three anti-establishment candidates running against entrenched incumbents: Democrat Collin C. Peterson, who ousted scandal-tainted GOP Rep. Arlan Stangeland; Democrat Paul Wellstone, who defeated GOP Sen. Rudy Boschwitz; and Republican Arne Carlson, who dethroned 10-year Democratic Gov. Rudy Perpich.

News of Durenberger's erratic personal behavior in the 99th Congress seemed to make him a prime target as the 1988 election cycle began. Democrats, frustrated by Durenberger's ability to present himself as a quiet and independent problem-solver in two impressive Senate campaigns, saw an opportunity to present him as an unpredictable "flake." And they had a very well-known candidate to do the job: Hubert H. "Skip" Humphrey III, son of former Vice President Hubert H. Humphrey, the revered Democrat who once held this Senate seat.

But Humphrey's campaign against Durenberger proved to be one of the most disappointing challenges in the country. Throughout his Senate bid, Humphrey, who had built his own popularity as state attorney general, struggled to meet high expectations that came with his famous name. Instead of keeping the focus on Durenberger, Humphrey was fending off unflattering comparisons between himself and his father. Often it was Humphrey's fellow Democrats who were the most critical.

Durenberger, meanwhile, carefully reinforced his old image as a thoughtful legislator. Always a personable campaigner, he spent considerable time traveling the state, holding hearings and forums on health care, rural development and the environment. And Durenberger ignored Humphrey for much of the campaign, much to the frustration of the challenger, who was consistently trailing in the polls and searching for an effective theme.

In one early exchange, Durenberger swatted down a Humphrey ad by effectively drawing the father-and-son comparison that was already plaguing the Democrat. Humphrey's ad sharply criticized Durenberger's record and noted the Ethics Committee rebuke over the Israeli spying flap; in response, Durenberger said Humphrey's "late great father would never have started a campaign this way.... Skip Humphrey should know better."

Humphrey's slow start and inability to meet high fund-raising expectations made it difficult for him to run the sort of media effort many had expected. In the fall, he started throwing some populistic punches. Humphrey accused Durenberger of having misguided priorities, that, among other things, led him to cast votes for the Nicaraguan contras and against Medicare. Humphrey also accused Durenberger of voting for a tax break for corporations that paid for a vacation he took in Puerto Rico.

But by October there was not much evidence he had done himself any good, and there was some sense Minnesota voters were tiring of negative media assaults. Durenberger, who had run ads accusing Humphrey of being soft on crime, halted his negative advertising and challenged the Democrat to do the same. After trying to get Durenberger to drop all ads for the last 10 days of the campaign, Humphrey switched to positive spots. On Election Day, he was swamped, losing 56-41 percent.

Durenberger waged his first two Senate campaigns in a period of four years. In 1978, he rode a Minnesota Republican tide to a comfortable victory. Four years later he had to buck the economic failures of national and state GOP administrations and the unlimited financial resources of his Democratic rival. Although he won by a narrower margin, his second victory was a more striking personal triumph.

Durenberger's presence in the Senate is the result of an unusual set of events. When the 1978 political year began, he was preparing a gubernatorial challenge that seemed to be going nowhere. When the year ended, he was the state's senior senator.

Durenberger had hovered on the periphery of public office for years, as chief aide to GOP Gov. Harold Levander during the late 1960s and as a well-connected Minneapolis lawyer after that. But he was politically untested, and, in spite of a yearlong campaign, he was given little chance to wrest the nomination for governor from popular U.S. Rep. Albert H. Quie.

When interim Sen. Muriel Humphrey announced that she would not run for the remaining four years of her late husband's term, Republican leaders asked Durenberger to switch contests. He was easy to persuade.

Democratic disunity aided Durenberger immensely. The party's endorsed candidate, U.S. Rep. Donald M. Fraser, was defeated in a primary by Bob Short, a blustery conservative whose campaign against environmentalists alienated much of the Democratic left. Some Democrats chose not to vote in the general election, but even more deserted to Durenberger, who had the endorsement of Americans for Democratic Action. He won a solid victory.

Durenberger's moderate views antagonized some in the GOP's conservative wing. At the 1980 state party convention, a group of conservative activists, mainly from southern Minnesota, warned him to move right if he wanted their backing for re-election in 1982. Durenberger publicly dismissed the Republicans' warning, calling it "minority party mentality."

Durenberger cleared a major hurdle in early 1981 when former Vice President Walter F. Mondale, a Minnesota senator from 1964 to 1976, announced he would not seek the office again. That made Durenberger a heavy favorite, while opening the Democratic side for Mark Dayton, liberal young heir to a department store empire. Although politically inexperienced, Dayton sank about $7 million of his fortune into a two-year Senate campaign.

Dayton made no apologies for his spending; he said that unlike Durenberger, he was not dependent on special-interest contributions, and that lavish spending was the only way he could offset the incumbent's perquisites and hefty campaign treasury.

For months Dayton saturated the media with ads that sought to tie Durenberger to Reaganomics. This expensive blitz pulled Dayton up in the polls, but Durenberger was well positioned for re-election. He contended that while an independent voice in Washington, he had the president's respect and could help moderate the administration's course. Dayton swept the economically depressed Iron Range and the Democratic Twin Cities, but little else. Durenberger's wide lead in the suburbs of Minneapolis-St. Paul and most of rural Minnesota carried him to a 53 percent victory statewide.

With some newspapers calling for his resignation following his 1990 Senate denunciation, Durenberger returned to Minnesota in June 1990 to apologize for his actions and to attend the state party convention. Despite their past coolness toward Durenberger, Republican delegates embraced the embattled senator.

Committees

Environment & Public Works (4th of 7 Republicans)
Superfund, Ocean & Water Protection (ranking); Environmental Protection; Water Resources, Transportation & Infrastructure

Finance (6th of 9 Republicans)
Medicare & Long Term Care (ranking); Health for Families & the Uninsured; Social Security & Family Policy

Labor & Human Resources (6th of 7 Republicans)
Disability Policy (ranking); Aging; Children, Families, Drugs & Alcoholism; Employment & Productivity

Special Aging (7th of 10 Republicans)

Elections

1988 General		
Dave Durenberger (R)	1,176,210	(56%)
Hubert H. "Skip" Humphrey III (D)	856,694	(41%)
1988 Primary		
Dave Durenberger (R)	112,413	(93%)
Sharon Anderson (R)	5,464	(5%)

Previous Winning Percentages: **1982** (53%) **1978 *** (61%)

* _Special election._

Campaign Finance

	Receipts	Receipts from PACs		Expend-itures
1988				
Durenberger (R)	$4,969,448	$1,499,382	(30%)	$5,410,783
Humphrey (D)	$2,483,491	$557,234	(22%)	$2,477,068

Key Votes

1991	
Authorize use of force against Iraq	Y
1990	
Oppose prohibition of certain semiautomatic weapons	Y
Support constitutional amendment on flag desecration	N
Oppose requiring parental notice for minors' abortions	N
Halt production of B-2 stealth bomber at 13 planes	N
Approve budget that cut spending and raised revenues	Y
Pass civil rights bill over Bush veto	Y
1989	
Oppose reduction of SDI funding	Y
Oppose barring federal funds for "obscene" art	Y
Allow vote on capital gains tax cut	Y

Voting Studies

	Presidential Support		Party Unity		Conservative Coalition	
Year	**S**	**O**	**S**	**O**	**S**	**O**
1990	62	35	55	40	76	19
1989	77	18	56	42	63	37
1988	57	38	43	48	32	59
1987	51	44	54	43	47	50
1986	64	33	65	32	66	34
1985	70	21	59	34	62	25
1984	71	23	68	25	70	21
1983	75	19	60	28	57	36
1982	60	28	45	41	39	48
1981	73	24	68	25	59	33

Interest Group Ratings

Year	ADA	ACU	AFL-CIO	CCUS
1990	44	45	56	25
1989	40	41	30	50
1988	60	26	77	43
1987	55	28	90	56
1986	40	43	40	58
1985	30	48	47	54
1984	50	55	25	65
1983	40	38	19	61
1982	70	25	59	28
1981	40	47	26	72

Paul Wellstone (D)

Of Northfield — Elected 1990

Born: July 21, 1944, Washington, D.C.

Education: U. of North Carolina, B.A. 1965, Ph.D. 1969.

Occupation: College professor.

Family: Wife, Sheila Ison; three children.

Religion: Jewish.

Political Career: Democratic National Committee, 1984-91; Minn. co-chairman, Jesse Jackson for President, 1988; Minn. co-chairman, Michael S. Dukakis for President, 1988; Democratic nominee for state auditor, 1982.

Capitol Office: 702 Hart Bldg. 20510; 224-5641.

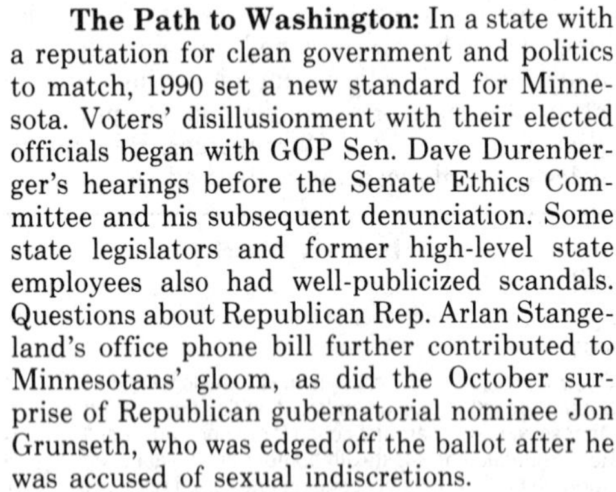

The Path to Washington: In a state with a reputation for clean government and politics to match, 1990 set a new standard for Minnesota. Voters' disillusionment with their elected officials began with GOP Sen. Dave Durenberger's hearings before the Senate Ethics Committee and his subsequent denunciation. Some state legislators and former high-level state employees also had well-publicized scandals. Questions about Republican Rep. Arlan Stangeland's office phone bill further contributed to Minnesotans' gloom, as did the October surprise of Republican gubernatorial nominee Jon Grunseth, who was edged off the ballot after he was accused of sexual indiscretions.

Touting a fresh, anti-establishment message, Wellstone found himself perfectly positioned to exploit voters' antipathy and topple a senator who as late as mid-October had been considered a safe bet for re-election.

It was an upset unrivaled since 1980, when several surprise Republican victories propelled the GOP to a 12-seat pickup and a Senate majority. In ideological terms, the switch from Boschwitz to Wellstone is as stark as any in 1980. A political science professor at Carleton College, Wellstone co-chaired Jesse Jackson's 1988 presidential campaign in Minnesota. (In his one previous try for office, he lost a statewide bid for auditor.) He favors national health insurance and abortion rights as well as farm production controls.

Boschwitz may point to the Grunseth affair as his downfall — until then he had led Wellstone by double digits in every statewide poll, but after Grunseth's problems began, the Senate race dropped into a statistical dead heat — but other factors contributed to his loss. The protracted budget debate kept the Republican in Washington until late October, a delay that had a debilitating effect on Boschwitz, a master at personal campaigning. When he did return, he had to explain why he had voted against a civil rights bill in July but voted Oct. 24 to override President Bush's veto of it. Boschwitz's effort was also damaged by the disclosure of a letter, written to his Jewish supporters on campaign stationery, saying that Wellstone "has no connection whatsoever with the Jewish community" and that his children were "brought up as non-Jews."

Wellstone's humorous television campaign caught the imagination of voters. In some of the most original advertisements of the year, Wellstone starred in a Minnesota version of Michael Moore's sardonic documentary "Roger and Me," in which Wellstone, instead of stalking General Motors Corp. Chairman Roger Smith, seeks out Boschwitz. In another ad, Wellstone races across the state speaking increasingly rapidly, explaining that he must talk fast because he does not have Boschwitz's $6 million treasury.

On Election Day, Minnesotans revolted against establishment candidates. They threw out 10-year Democratic Gov. Rudy Perpich, voting in maverick Republican Arne Carlson, who had replaced Grunseth as the party's nominee only a week earlier. (Carlson beat Wellstone in the 1982 auditor's race.) Stangeland lost his re-election bid. And Wellstone beat Boschwitz by fewer than 50,000 votes, 50-48 percent.

Wellstone continued to demonstrate that his advertised iconoclasm was no act, and in the process contravened some unwritten canons of senatorial manners. Soon after the election, he told reporters that he "despised" North Carolina Republican Sen. Jesse Helms. "I have detested him since I was 19," he said. Then he defied the tradition of having the other home-state sitting senator — Durenberger in this case — escort him to the well to be sworn in. Instead, he invited former Minnesota Democratic Sen. (and Vice President) Walter F. Mondale to do the honor.

When he arrived in Washington, he held an emotional news conference near the Vietnam Veterans Memorial. He handed Vice President Dan Quayle an audio tape of a Minnesota town meeting, challenging Quayle on the administration's policy in the Persian Gulf. "This gives you a real feeling for what people are really worried about," he said he told the vice president. Wellstone was so forceful in plying his opinions on Bush that the president asked members of the Minnesota delegation, "Who is this chickenshit?"

Wellstone became one of the Senate's most passionate opponents of the Persian Gulf War. "I could not accept the loss of life of any of our children in the Persian Gulf right now, and that tells me in my gut I do not believe it is time to go to war," he said during debate on authorizing Bush to use military force against Iraq. "I do not believe the administration has made the case to go to war. And if I apply this standard to my children, then I have to apply this standard to everyone's children. I have to apply this standard to all of God's children."

Wellstone's style has not been an instant hit with the chairman of the Energy and Natural Resources Committee, J. Bennett Johnston. As Johnston sought to speed his comprehensive energy bill through the committee, Wellstone persevered in reading his opening statement despite Johnston's admonition.

In the euphoria following the successful execution of the war, Wellstone's performance cost him support at home. A poll taken shortly after Bush called for a cease-fire showed 51 percent of Minnesotans disapproving of the way Wellstone was handling his job.

Committees

Energy & Natural Resources (11th of 11 Democrats)
Energy Regulation & Conservation; Energy Research & Development; Public Lands, National Parks & Forests

Labor & Human Resources (10th of 10 Democrats)
Children, Families, Drugs & Alcoholism; Education, Arts & Humanities; Labor

Select Indian Affairs (9th of 9 Democrats)

Small Business (10th of 10 Democrats)
Rural Economy & Family Farming; Urban & Minority-Owned Business Development

Campaign Finance

	Receipts	Receipts from PACs		Expend-itures
1990				
Wellstone (D)	$1,403,208	$294,520	(21%)	$1,340,708
Boschwitz (R)	$6,086,588	$1,211,209	(20%)	$6,221,333

Key Vote

1991

Authorize use of force against Iraq	N

Elections

1990 General		
Paul Wellstone (D)	911,999	(50%)
Rudy Boschwitz (R)	864,375	(48%)
Russell B. Bentley (GR)	29,820	(2%)
1990 Primary		
Paul Wellstone (D)	226,306	(60%)
Jim Nichols (D)	129,302	(35%)
Gene Schenk (D)	19,379	(5%)

1 Timothy J. Penny (D)

Of New Richland — Elected 1982

Born: Nov. 19, 1951, Albert Lea, Minn.
Education: Winona State U., B.A. 1974; attended U. of Minnesota, 1975.
Military Service: Naval Reserve, 1986-present.
Occupation: Sales representative.
Family: Wife, Barbara Christianson; four children.
Religion: Lutheran.
Political Career: Minn. Senate, 1977-83.
Capitol Office: 436 Cannon Bldg. 20515; 225-2472.

In Washington: As a Democrat in a Republican district, Penny is often conflicted. But the competing forces were especially complicated on the issue of using military force in the Persian Gulf; foreign interventions were unpopular in the grain-growing heartland long before Vietnam.

Penny, a member of the Veterans' Affairs Committee, agonized about his vote. He met with peace marchers and military families, with the confused and the passionate. It was no surprise to see Penny struggling with his decision; for all his wholesome looks, there has always been something of the Scandinavian brooder about him.

In the end, Penny voted to rely on sanctions and delay the use of force. He later professed to being comfortable with his choice, but added, "I'll probably have fewer doubts the next time around."

The preoccupation of Penny's career to date has been the intractability of federal fiscal problems and the unwillingness of senior members of Congress to strike out in new directions. As a budget watchdog trying to restrain the Democratic Party's inclinations toward generosity in spending, he often jousts with party leaders.

In 1987 and 1988, he opposed the Democratic position on partisan votes more often than any other Northern Democrat. In 1989 and 1990, he voted against his party's majority more often than the average Southern Democrat did, going his own way on one of every three party-line votes.

In the 100th Congress, he fought to keep a bill increasing the minimum wage from becoming laden with so many special provisions that it could not pass. He and Labor Standards Subcommittee Chairman Austin J. Murphy of Pennsylvania were the only Democrats opposed to a labor-backed move to add a fourth-year raise, to $5.05 an hour.

Penny had established an early beachhead from which to wage his war on deficits. In 1983 he became chairman of the Freshman Budget Task Force, a group of Democratic first-termers touting an across-the-board budget freeze. This effort begat the Budget Study Group, an organization that discusses deficit-reduction options and that has grown in both size and acceptance.

In 1987, Penny and Iowa Republican Tom Tauke formed the Truth-in-Budgeting Task Force, of which Penny is still a co-chairman. "The only way we can meet our deficit reduction is to cut a little more as each opportunity arises," Penny said.

Penny, Tauke and other task force members offered amendments to fiscal 1988 appropriations bills making across-the-board cuts in funding levels. They met with limited success; most of the amendments lost, many by sizable margins.

In 1988, Penny and Tauke rolled all their deficit-reduction ideas into one package and proposed their own budget resolution as an alternative to the bipartisan package agreed to at the 1987 White House-congressional budget summit. Theirs was a radical plan that called for replacing the inflation-based Social Security cost-of-living adjustments with a flat-rate COLA increase of $5 per month. The plan would have delayed income tax indexing for a year, trimmed a pay increase for federal and military employees and specified a budget deficit $22 billion below the summit-pact level.

On the floor, Penny struck an ironic tone. By voting against the resolution, he said, "you can be popular, you can say the things folks want to hear and get yourself re-elected. But . . . if you are concerned about next year's deficit being bigger than this year's deficit, you might want to reconsider and vote yes." Only 27 members did so.

Penny has also been willing to take his budget philosophy personally. Although he has four children and his wife does not have an outside income, Penny in 1987 and 1989 voted against measures that by 1991 had brought House pay to $125,000. He still keeps only about $77,500 in salary, returning the rest to the Treasury or donating it to charity.

Penny attacks his work with energy and enthusiasm, spinning out ideas and proposals.

Minnesota 1

Southeast — Rochester; Mankato

It seems odd now, but Penny represents a district that was redrawn in 1982 to be more Republican than the 1st District constituency that had been electing GOP candidates routinely for years.

Farm discontent and Penny's deficit-conscious record have combined to make this the sort of district that explains why Republicans seem stuck in a "permanent minority" in the House.

German Protestants settled southeast Minnesota just north of Iowa before the Civil War. The rolling hills that extend from the Mississippi to the great bend in the Minnesota River offer the corn, grain and hog farmers some of the state's most productive farm land. Except for Rochester and some Mississippi River towns, the population centers in the 1st are devoted to serving the surrounding farms, or, in the case of Austin, processing the primary local product — hogs.

Rochester is the state's fifth-largest city, with 71,000 people. The home not only of the Mayo Clinic but also of a large IBM facility, Rochester has much more of a white-collar orientation than the rest of the district, and its voters are more reliably Republican than many of the district's disgruntled farmers, who have strayed from their GOP traditions. When Ronald Reagan made an election-eve foray into Minnesota in his bid for a 50-state sweep in 1984, he chose Rochester for his campaign stop.

Over the years, the most consistently Democratic area in the district has been Mower County (Austin), where the meatpacking industry is heavily unionized. Since 1932 all Democratic presidential candidates except John F. Kennedy and Adlai E. Stevenson have carried the county. Michael S. Dukakis won it with more than 60 percent of the vote in 1988. In his failed 1990 re-election bid, Democratic Gov. Rudy Perpich received 55 percent in Mower.

Population: 509,460. White 503,533 (99%), Black 1,007 (0.2%), Other 3,193 (1%). Spanish origin 3,333 (1%). 18 and over 362,626 (71%), 65 and over 66,631 (13%). Median age: 29.

But erasing the deficit and overhauling farm policy, the two goals that have consumed most of his energy, are tall orders.

While Penny has contributed to the dialogue on both issues, his concrete accomplishments have been more modest than if he had pursued less sweeping issues.

On the Agriculture Committee, the assignment most crucial to Penny politically, he is part of a younger generation of lawmakers who contend that farmers are fed up with old subsidy programs and want Congress to try something different. Penny's record makes it clear he is willing to try almost *anything* different. In the 99th Congress, he endorsed two quite dissimilar farm policy overhaul proposals and introduced a third himself.

In 1985, Penny backed a Minnesota colleague's "marketing loan" proposal, which would allow farmers who take out government crop loans to pay back only as much as their crops earned at the market.

Proponents said it would allow prices to fall to natural levels, would guarantee farmers steady income and would protect the government from having to absorb huge quantities of crops, which farmers currently forfeit when they default.

The Agriculture Committee defeated the proposal 22-20, partly because it was such a radical departure from current policy. Said Penny, "We're trying to increase world competition and decrease surpluses. A lot of us thought the marketing loan might be the thing to accomplish both of those objectives.... But most of the members weren't ready."

Later, Penny endorsed a farm plan offered by Iowa Sen. Tom Harkin and Missouri Rep. Richard A. Gephardt that sought to raise crop prices by tightly restricting how much a farmer could produce. But this concept of production controls stirred widespread opposition.

In search of a politically salable alternative, Penny and Rep. Byron L. Dorgan of North Dakota came forward in 1987 with a plan to target crop subsidies to smaller farmers and close loopholes in current law that allow some large farming operations to collect huge subsidy payments. Penny said the plan would save $24 billion over five years.

Though he is a defender of his home-state dairy farmers, Penny can work with others seeking a middle ground on dairy provisions. The emergency drought-relief bill in 1988 hit a snag over a controversial provision to increase the federal government's price-support payments to dairy farmers by 50 cents per hundredweight. The provision, pushed by dairy-state members and the dairy industry, rankled many members; they felt it violated the spirit of the 1985 farm bill — which called for lowering price supports for commodities — and smacked of favoritism to just one portion of the agriculture community.

The resentment gave rise to a compromise amendment offered by Penny and Republican Rep. Steve Gunderson of Wisconsin, allowing for a 50-cent increase, but only for the three-month period when dairy farmers would be hardest hit by drought-related feed costs. The House adopted the compromise by a 246-155 vote.

At Home: The first Democrat to hold this district in nearly a century, Penny defied GOP predictions that he would be a one-term fluke.

Penny has been running for office virtually his entire adult life. In 1976, barely a year out of graduate school, he ran for the state Senate in south-central Minnesota. Treading in staunchly GOP territory, Penny visited each household in the district three times and drew 52 percent to oust a Republican incumbent.

Redistricting carved up his state Senate district and left him without a familiar place to seek re-election. So he decided to run for Congress in 1982. His chances of making it seemed minimal until a vicious quarrel developed between two GOP incumbents, Tom Hagedorn and Arlen Erdahl, who ended up running against each other after redistricting.

When Hagedorn won the GOP district convention, Penny worked to exploit lingering bitterness, calling himself a moderate in the Erdahl tradition. As the race tightened, Hagedorn unleashed a barrage of charges, including criticism that Penny had never worked in the private sector. Penny responded with ads that showed him with his young family, a contrast with the divorced Hagedorn. Penny prevailed with 51 percent of the vote.

In 1984, Republicans nominated Keith Spicer, a Rochester sales manager with close ties to southern Minnesota's fundamentalist Christian community. Spicer was articulate, but he was a novice campaigner, and he had little appeal to the district's large contingent of moderate Republicans, whom Penny had cultivated. Although President Ronald Reagan swept the 1st District, Penny carried it by nearly 35,000 votes.

GOP leaders hoped Erdahl would run in 1986, but he bowed out in late 1985, choosing a position in the national office of the Peace Corps. Republicans fielded a weak challenger then, and again in 1988. In early 1990, Republican state Rep. Dave Bishop, a popular moderate from Rochester, said he was considering challenging Penny because the Democrat was too conservative. But Bishop opted against running, and once again the GOP settled for insignificant opposition. Penny racked up his biggest House election mark: 78 percent.

Committees

Agriculture (15th of 27 Democrats)
Conservation, Credit & Rural Development; Livestock, Dairy & Poultry; Wheat, Soybeans & Feed Grains

Select Hunger (7th of 22 Democrats)
International

Veterans' Affairs (5th of 21 Democrats)
Education, Training & Employment (chairman); Compensation, Pension & Insurance

Elections

1990 General		
Timothy J. Penny (D)	156,749	(78%)
Doug Andersen (R)	43,856	(22%)
1988 General		
Timothy J. Penny (D)	161,118	(70%)
Curt Schrimpf (R)	67,709	(29%)

Previous Winning Percentages: **1986** (72%) **1984** (57%) **1982** (51%)

District Vote For President

	1988	1984	1980	1976
D	115,800 (48%)	107,763 (44%)	81,000 (36%)	115,365 (48%)
R	121,930 (51%)	134,866 (55%)	120,765 (53%)	117,325 (49%)
I			18,998 (8%)	

Campaign Finance

	Receipts	Receipts from PACs	Expend-itures
1990			
Penny (D)	$230,040	$113,050 (49%)	$197,442
1988			
Penny (D)	$284,554	$125,377 (44%)	$165,016
Schrimpf (R)	$86,090	$2,862 (3%)	$85,532

Key Votes

1991	
Authorize use of force against Iraq	N
1990	
Support constitutional amendment on flag desecration	N
Pass family and medical leave bill over Bush veto	N
Reduce SDI funding	Y
Allow abortions in overseas military facilities	N
Approve budget summit plan for spending and taxing	Y
Approve civil rights bill	Y
1989	
Halt production of B-2 stealth bomber at 13 planes	Y
Oppose capital gains tax cut	Y
Approve federal abortion funding in rape or incest cases	N
Approve pay raise and revision of ethics rules	N
Pass Democratic minimum wage plan over Bush veto	N

Voting Studies

	Presidential Support		Party Unity		Conservative Coalition	
Year	**S**	**O**	**S**	**O**	**S**	**O**
1990	34	66	66	33	56	44
1989	57	43	67	33	68	32
1988	37	63	59	41	66	34
1987	35	65	59	41	49	51
1986	34	66	61	39	48	52
1985	25	75	53	47	35	65
1984	35	65	69	31	36	64
1983	13	87	84	16	29	69

Interest Group Ratings

Year	ADA	ACU	AFL-CIO	CCUS
1990	67	25	50	43
1989	55	46	50	80
1988	60	36	71	64
1987	64	30	50	53
1986	75	18	64	50
1985	60	24	47	50
1984	75	33	38	50
1983	75	17	76	40

2 Vin Weber (R)

Of North Mankato — Elected 1980

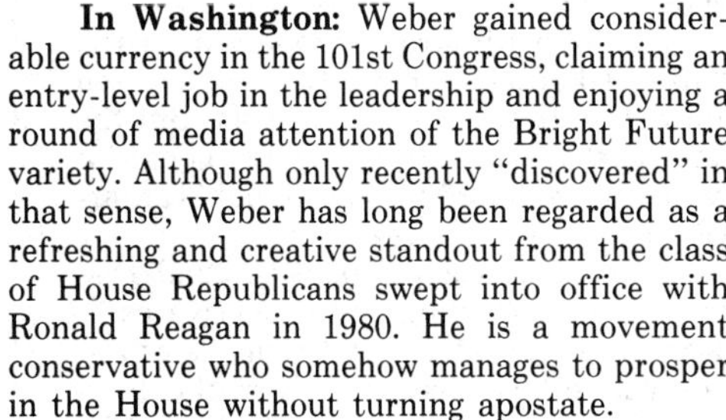

Born: July 24, 1952, Slayton, Minn.
Education: Attended U. of Minnesota, 1970-74.
Occupation: Congressional aide; publisher.
Family: Wife, Cheryl Foster; one child.
Religion: Roman Catholic.
Political Career: Republican nominee for Minn. Senate, 1976.
Capitol Office: 106 Cannon Bldg. 20515; 225-2331.

In Washington: Weber gained considerable currency in the 101st Congress, claiming an entry-level job in the leadership and enjoying a round of media attention of the Bright Future variety. Although only recently "discovered" in that sense, Weber has long been regarded as a refreshing and creative standout from the class of House Republicans swept into office with Ronald Reagan in 1980. He is a movement conservative who somehow manages to prosper in the House without turning apostate.

Members in both parties, impressed by Weber's cool demeanor and clear head, have recently taken to calling him "the new Cheney," a reference to former House GOP Whip Dick Cheney, now the secretary of Defense.

A variety of factors had delayed Weber's emergence. He represents a distant, rural district that took several terms to pacify electorally. Personally, he lacks the mediagenic qualities some of his colleagues enjoy in abundance. Politically, he is not always an easy read. Like the man he supported for president in 1988, former Rep. Jack F. Kemp, Weber starts out a bedrock conservative but veers into harder-to-categorize ideas about government and social problems.

Weber insists the GOP cannot thrive indefinitely on national security and tax cuts alone. He wants his party to achieve majority status by addressing the economic and social problems of the nation, not by insisting those problems are beyond the government's ken or control. Speaking of President Bush, Weber has said, "His agenda needs to be fleshed out a bit," making it clear he thinks that fleshing out involves more government activism than most conservatives are used to embracing.

But Weber has also been closely associated with another movement hero in the House, Newt Gingrich of Georgia. Weber was a key strategist in Gingrich's election as Republican whip in 1989. The Georgian's triumph over a more traditional Republican, Edward Madigan of Illinois, signaled the growing impatience of younger Republicans with the conciliatory politics of their senior colleagues.

The same forces had helped Weber win his own place in the lower ranks of the party hierarchy just four months earlier. In a leadership shake-up before the 101st Congress, Weber was elected secretary of the Republican Conference by a 21-vote margin over old-breed Republican Joseph M. McDade of Pennsylvania.

When Gingrich became whip, comparisons between his swaggering style and Weber's far more self-effacing manner became inevitable. Weber made his way in politics as a staffer and campaign manager and still seems more comfortable in something approximating those roles. After working hard for Gingrich's leadership bid, Weber seemed to distance himself when it had been achieved. As two prospective rivals for the GOP helm when Minority Leader Robert H. Michel of Illinois retires, Weber and Gingrich offer one of the more interesting subplots in the House of the 1990s.

The two had joined forces earlier, cofounding (with Bob Walker of Pennsylvania) the Conservative Opportunity Society that harassed Democratic House leaders in the early 1980s. Since those salad days, however, Weber has moderated his tone.

"You can't make every battle a scorched-earth battle, because this institution is going to have to confront other issues," he has said.

Weber has also been friendlier than some of his colleagues to the process that doles out federal dollars. His slot on the Appropriations Committee, won in the 100th Congress, has put him at the meat of things while freeing him from the hearing-and-markup drudgery that afflicts so many legislative panels.

Adapting to the clubby, logrolling ethos of that money-wielding committee has been a challenge, and Weber has not yet been entirely domesticated. He and other young members complain that senior GOP appropriators are often more loyal to the committee's products than to party principles. Those complaints peaked in mid-1987, when senior Republicans were joining committee Democrats to fight efforts to cut their spending recommendations.

But Weber is not above crowing about his

Minnesota 2

Southwest — Willmar

The landscape of the 2nd District is dotted for mile upon mile with silos and grain elevators, broken up occasionally by small crossroads market centers. The district's largest town, Willmar, has only about 16,000 residents. Bisected by the broad Minnesota River, the sprawling 30-county district includes some of the best farm land in the state, and some that is not so productive.

The well-to-do farmers in the south along the Iowa border enjoy bountiful harvests of corn and soybeans. Worthington, located in Nobles County, claims to be the "Turkey Capital of the World."

Many voters in the southern two tiers of counties are of German ethnic stock. Like those in the adjoining 1st District, they share a strong Republican tradition and an allegiance to the Farm Bureau, the most conservative of the state's three major farm organizations.

As one moves north along the Minnesota River, dairy farms become more common. The flat farm lands yield to a more rolling terrain broken up by lakes. Until one reaches the prairie counties north of the Minnesota River, the political flavor remains largely Republican.

Above the river, north of Renville and Yellow Medicine counties, the land is sandy and rocky and the politics unpredictable. Farmers here have to work harder to scratch out a living, and they display a frequent dissatisfaction with any party that is in power.

At the turn of the century the Scandinavian settlers in this area battled constantly with railroads, bankers and grain merchants. Disillusioned by Republicans and Democrats alike, they were ripe for third-party alternatives. The Farmer-Labor Party found early support in this region, as did presidential candidate Robert LaFollette in 1924, when his Progressive Party carried the vast majority of the counties north of the Minnesota River that are wholly contained in the district.

Today, with strong support from the National Farmers Union, Democrats often run well in this part of the district. But the vote here is generally not large enough to overcome the more heavily Republican areas to the south and east.

Running a campaign in the 2nd District is an exhausting and expensive exercise. To reach voters via television, a candidate has to buy time not only in the Twin Cities but also in Mankato and Alexandria, Minn., and in Sioux Falls, S.D. Some might prefer to run their campaigns by mail order, in the tradition of one of the district's most famous sons: R. W. Sears, who began shipping watches from Redwood in 1886 with the help of his partner, Alvah Roebuck.

Population: 509,500. White 505,241 (99%), Black 288 (0.1%), Other 2,630 (1%). Spanish origin 2,508 (1%). 18 and over 363,087 (71%), 65 and over 82,298 (16%). Median age: 32.

ability to get federal funds for his district, now that he is so close to the trough. He happily takes credit for securing funding for agriculture research projects in Minnesota, graduate fellowships and other programs overseen by his two Appropriations subcommittees, one on Agriculture and the other on Labor, Health and Human Services and Education.

That pride in parochial accomplishments is the legacy of an important stage in the political education of Weber: a brush with electoral defeat that drove him to spend more time on the day-to-day problems of his troubled farm constituents and less on after-hours speeches with the COS crowd.

He faced a tough re-election contest in 1986, when the farm economy at home was in a tailspin and his opponent was saying Weber was not doing enough to help. He added office hours in his district, and began soft-pedaling his role as partisan firebrand in the House. "You can't stand on philosophical fine points when people are hurting," he said later.

He placed plenty of distance between himself and the Reagan administration's farm policies. In early 1985, he wrote Reagan a letter protesting his veto of a farm credit bill. Later, in debate on the 1985 farm bill, Weber was one of a handful of House Republicans to defy the White House and support a "populist" proposal aimed at imposing strict production controls to drive up prices.

As a member of the House Budget Committee, Weber cast the sole GOP vote in 1986 for a Democratic-drafted budget resolution. Among the factors that inclined him favorably to that budget was that then-Chairman William H. Gray III of Pennsylvania had earned Weber's gratitude by holding a hearing on agriculture programs in his Minnesota district.

"I've responded to an ongoing disaster in my district," he said amid the 1986 farm crisis. "I've changed my behavior more than my basic philosophy. But then, it's a misconception that

I ever believed in being rigidly ideological."

Indeed, when COS was at its peak as a bomb-throwing force in the early 1980s, Weber always seemed a little miscast as its chief co-ordinator. In a group given to theatrics and grand ideas, he stood out as a pragmatist more concerned with sound strategy than with ideological debating points.

Even as Weber joined his COS colleagues in guerrilla floor tactics, he distinguished himself by reaching out more to other elements of the House GOP.

While some COS leaders remained in minor committee assignments that left them free to focus on floor confrontation, Weber got a seat on the Budget Committee in his third term, and then won his Appropriations assignment at the start of his fourth term.

At Home: First elected to the House in 1980, Weber could have won re-election in 1982 and 1984 with something less than the energetic, high-budget campaigns that he mounted. But in 1986, Weber needed to marshal all of his considerable political skills to hold office. He was faced with a double challenge in the form of a depressed agrarian economy and an aggressive Democratic opponent, who pounded away at Weber as a right-wing ideologue who did not understand the depth of the farm crisis.

While the rural 2nd has Republican proclivities, in 1986 it was mired as discouragingly in economic depression as any district in the Farm Belt. Its grain farmers, hard hit by the decline in export markets and plummeting land values, were picketing county courthouses and disrupting farm-foreclosure sales.

Weber sought to insulate himself from the agrarian discontent by distancing himself from the unpopular Reagan administration farm policy — he voted against the 1981 and 1985 farm bills, each of which cut income support to farmers. Before the 1986 election, Weber also held regular office hours in the district to listen to farmers who came to him in search of federal help. In the process, he confessed, he had become "less anti-government, maybe."

But Weber's change of heart was unimpressive to Democratic challenger Dave Johnson, who complained that if the incumbent was really concerned about struggling farmers, he would have taken a seat on the House Agriculture Committee, like Minnesota's other two rural House members.

Johnson maintained that Weber had virtually no influence on agricultural policy. As a third-generation farmer, Johnson claimed a personal understanding of farm problems that he said Weber, whose background is in newspaper publishing, lacked.

Republicans, in turn, sought to depict Johnson as a political opportunist who switched parties on the eve of his congressional bid because his hopes of winning office as a Republican were stymied. Johnson was intensely involved in local GOP politics in the early 1980s, frequently accompanying Weber around the district and even serving as a delegate to the 1984 Republican National Convention in Dallas.

Johnson defended his party switch, saying that he decided to join the Democrats because Reagan's free-market farm policy was driving prices down and undermining the district's economy.

Making his political debut, Johnson was an unknown quantity to many voters in the large, 31-county district. Despite that, he was able to win a majority of counties in the 2nd; he finished barely 6,000 votes short of Weber.

Johnson might have been able to overcome the deficit if the incumbent had not run a $1 million, state-of-the-art campaign. Weber bombarded voters with an array of appeals ranging from ads on expensive Twin Cities television to direct-mail appeals to individual commodity groups.

By 1988 it was apparent that Weber had shored up his support in the district. He had been more visible tending to district concerns, and had an achievement to tout in 1987 when he took a seat on the Appropriations Subcommittee on Agriculture. Democrats had difficulty coming up with a strong candidate, although Johnson considered another attempt, as did Gene Wenstrom, who had previously mounted three campaigns against Republican Rep. Arlan Stangeland in the 7th District.

The Democratic nomination went to Doug Peterson, a farmer and a party chairman in Lac Qui Parle County. Peterson said that he was a better fit for the predominantly rural district than was Weber, but he had considerable difficulty raising funds to get his message out. With a late start and without much help from the national party, Peterson managed just 42 percent of the vote. Weber topped that in 1990, coming within a point of his career high of 63 percent.

Lavishly financed campaigns have been a Weber hallmark. When he won the seat of retiring Democratic Rep. Richard Nolan in 1980, Weber put so much money into television ads that to many voters he seemed like an incumbent by November. He rolled to a 14,000-vote victory over former Nolan aide and Farmers Union organizer Archie Baumann.

Two years later, court-ordered redistricting placed Weber and GOP Rep. Tom Hagedorn together in the same rural southwest Minnesota constituency. Rather than challenge Weber, his fellow conservative and one-time press secretary, Hagedorn moved east into the district of GOP Rep. Arlen Erdahl. (That set off a messy game of political musical chairs that ended with both Hagedorn and Erdahl losing in separate districts in November.)

In the 2nd, a sluggish farm economy and a feisty challenger gave Democrats hope of beating Weber. But by building a large lead in the district's eastern counties formerly represented by Hagedorn, Weber offset Democrat Jim Nichols' strength in his home base along the South Dakota border to win by 20,000 votes.

Nichols' decision to become state agriculture commissioner freed Weber to take an active role in national Republican politics in 1984, highlighted by an influential stint on the national convention platform committee. With the Democrats nominating an underfunded political newcomer to oppose him that fall, his own re-election was never in doubt.

For three generations, the Webers have been a conservative voice in southwestern Minnesota, publishing a family-run weekly newspaper. But when Vin Weber first tried to make the leap from journalism to elective office, he failed, drawing only 42 percent in a 1976 campaign for the state Senate. His political career revived when he successfully managed Rudy Boschwitz' Senate campaign two years later.

Committees

Appropriations (17th of 22 Republicans)
Labor, Health & Human Services, Education & Related Agencies; Rural Development, Agriculture & Related Agencies

Elections

1990 General

Vin Weber (R)	126,367	(62%)
Jim Stone (D)	77,935	(38%)

1988 General

Vin Weber (R)	131,639	(58%)
Doug Peterson (D)	96,016	(42%)

Previous Winning Percentages: **1986** (52%) **1984** (63%) **1982** (55%) **1980** (53%)

District Vote For President

	1988	1984	1980	1976
D	112,838 (48%)	105,232 (43%)	101,134 (39%)	128,804 (53%)
R	118,769 (51%)	140,304 (57%)	135,287 (52%)	107,252 (44%)
I			17,000 (7%)	

Campaign Finance

	Receipts	Receipts from PACs		Expend-itures
1990				
Weber (R)	$613,549	$240,653	(39%)	$670,684
Stone (D)	$17,785	$825	(5%)	$17,778
1988				
Weber (R)	$728,427	$232,704	(32%)	$623,776
Peterson (D)	$154,006	$70,165	(46%)	$152,295

Key Votes

1991	
Authorize use of force against Iraq	Y
1990	
Support constitutional amendment on flag desecration	Y
Pass family and medical leave bill over Bush veto	N
Reduce SDI funding	N
Allow abortions in overseas military facilities	N
Approve budget summit plan for spending and taxing	N
Approve civil rights bill	N
1989	
Halt production of B-2 stealth bomber at 13 planes	N
Oppose capital gains tax cut	N
Approve federal abortion funding in rape or incest cases	N
Approve pay raise and revision of ethics rules	N
Pass Democratic minimum wage plan over Bush veto	N

Voting Studies

	Presidential Support		Party Unity		Conservative Coalition	
Year	**S**	**O**	**S**	**O**	**S**	**O**
1990	63	33	80	15	80	17
1989	77	22	84	14	80	17
1988	61	37	84	11	92	8
1987	62	38	86	14	84	16
1986	69	31	80	17	80	20
1985	64	33	79	12	73	18
1984	60	37	85	11	80	17
1983	63	35	79	16	72	25
1982	61	38	80	18	74	25
1981	55	41	79	20	76	24

Interest Group Ratings

Year	ADA	ACU	AFL-CIO	CCUS
1990	22	83	0	92
1989	5	89	8	100
1988	15	96	14	93
1987	20	87	19	80
1986	15	73	21	72
1985	15	85	20	76
1984	15	83	8	69
1983	15	83	6	84
1982	20	77	5	77
1981	30	100	7	74

3 Jim Ramstad (R)

Of Minnetonka — Elected 1990

Born: May 6, 1946, Jamestown, N.D.
Education: U. of Minnesota, B.A. 1968; George Washington U., J.D. 1973.
Military Service: Army Reserve, 1968-74.
Occupation: Lawyer; legislative aide.
Family: Single.
Religion: Protestant.
Political Career: Minn. Senate, 1981-91.
Capitol Office: 504 Cannon Bldg. 20515; 225-2871.

The Path to Washington: For all intents and purposes, Ramstad's 1990 race ended before it even began. Once Ramstad won the support of the 3rd District Republican convention and was spared a significant primary challenge, the trickiest part of the election was behind him.

That Ramstad will follow 20-year Rep. Bill Frenzel is no surprise. For years he made plain his desire to serve in Congress once Frenzel stepped down. He worked for Frenzel in the Minnesota and U.S. houses. He has been described more than once as a Frenzel heir apparent. When he announced that he would run for the open seat, he described Frenzel as his "role model, mentor and friend."

During the campaign, Ramstad sought to paint his election as a continuation of the Frenzel legacy. His billboards bore more than a passing resemblance to the ones Frenzel used.

Ramstad's earliest and most daunting obstacle was the 3rd District Independent-Republican convention in May. Ramstad's pro-abortion rights position placed him at odds with the anti-abortion delegates who dominate Minnesota Republican conventions. In the affluent, suburban Twin Cities 3rd, voters prefer Republicans of a moderate stripe, such as Frenzel. Although Democrats had not held the seat since Dwight D. Eisenhower was president, they saw a chance to compete if Republicans selected an anti-abortion candidate at the convention; that would likely have mired the GOP in an abortion-rights debate through the primary in mid-September.

But GOP Sen. Rudy Boschwitz, an opponent of abortion, put pragmatism over personal preference and wrote to convention delegates urging them to unify and support Ramstad. Another anti-abortion Republican, 2nd District Rep. Vin Weber, also endorsed Ramstad before the convention. Anti-abortion delegates greeted Boschwitz coolly as he worked the floor in Ramstad's behalf, but ultimately they acceded to his lobbying: After seven ballots, Ramstad defeated four other candidates to win the convention endorsement. His convention opponents vowed not to carry their challenge to a primary, and Ramstad easily defeated a minor foe in the primary.

At the outset of the fall campaign, neither Ramstad nor his Democratic opponent, investment executive Lewis DeMars, was particularly well-known in the 3rd. DeMars had served on the Minneapolis City Council from 1971 to 1980, the last six years as president. But Minneapolis is not in the 3rd, and DeMars had been out of politics for 10 years.

Most of Ramstad's Senate district lay outside the 3rd. But the district's demographics worked in Ramstad's favor. White-collar professionals in such well-off suburbs as Edina and St. Louis Park have made the 3rd reliable Republican territory. The 3rd was George Bush's best Minnesota district in 1988 (he received 54 percent of the vote while losing statewide) and Walter F. Mondale's worst in 1984. The former Minnesota senator and vice president only managed 41 percent in the district.

With the most serious impediment behind him, Ramstad lost little time demonstrating how formidable a candidate he could be. Renowned for his fundraising skills, Ramstad vaulted to the top ranks of congressional candidates in contributions raised. DeMars could not keep pace. With three weeks to go before voting, Ramstad had raised a half-million dollars more than DeMars. On Election Day, Ramstad crushed DeMars 2-to-1.

In the state Senate, Ramstad specialized in crime and drug issues. He backed mandatory prison sentences for dealing drugs and committing violent crimes, and "boot camps" for felony drug offenders. He may not conform entirely with 3rd District voters' concept of a social-issues moderate, however: He co-authored legislation against flag burning and pornography.

Minnesota 3

Southern and Western Twin Cities Suburbs

Once confined only to the inner core of Minneapolis suburbs within Hennepin County, the 3rd now ranges into five counties, extending beyond the western and southern extremities of the metropolitan area. Although the farther reaches of the district still appear largely rural, they are among the fastest-growing parts of the state and are feeling the march of suburbanization.

The heart of the district remains the upper-class suburbs just west of Minneapolis, places such as Edina, St. Louis Park and Golden Valley. Numerous golf courses service the white-collar professionals in these three suburbs alone. Many of the weekend golfers spend their weekdays working for such high-technology firms as Control Data and Honeywell, which are headquartered in the Twin Cities area. The Republican vote here and in Minnetonka, just to the west, is overwhelming. In a number of precincts, home-state presidential nominee Walter F. Mondale drew less than one-third of the vote in 1984.

Bloomington, the district's largest suburb and the state's fourth-largest city, is divided between the 3rd and 5th districts. The 3rd District part, west of Interstate 35W, contains about 70 percent of the city's 86,000 residents and is considerably more Republican than the eastern portion.

The 3rd District's quest for voters extends in three directions — everywhere but north. Carver County, on the western side, tends to be the most Republican county in the Twin Cities area. In 1988, it voted about 60 percent for George Bush for president, and it gave GOP Sen. Dave Durenberger two-thirds of its votes in his re-election bid. In 1990, Ramstad took 69 percent of the vote in Carver.

More populous but somewhat less Republican is Dakota County, which anchors the eastern side of the district. Nearly 150,000 people live in the 3rd District portion of the county in the lower reaches south of St. Paul. This area is the fastest-growing part of the district. Ramstad took 64 percent of Dakota's vote in 1990.

Population: 509,499. White 498,684 (98%), Black 3,280 (1%), Other 5,794 (1%). Spanish origin 2,932 (1%). 18 and over 352,682 (69%), 65 and over 36,066 (7%). Median age: 29.

Committees

Judiciary (13th of 13 Republicans)
Administrative Law & Governmental Relations; Crime and Criminal Justice

Select Narcotics Abuse & Control (14th of 14 Republicans)

Small Business (12th of 17 Republicans)
Exports, Tax Policy & Special Problems; SBA, the General Economy & Minority Enterprise Development

Campaign Finance

	Receipts	Receipts from PACs		Expend-itures
1990				
Ramstad (R)	$936,208	$237,745	(25%)	$935,454
DeMars (D)	$338,261	$107,925	(32%)	$337,321

Key Vote

1991

Authorize use of force against Iraq	Y

Elections

1990 General		
Jim Ramstad (R)	195,833	(67%)
Lewis DeMars (D)	96,395	(33%)
1990 Primary		
Jim Ramstad (R)	43,252	(79%)
Dave Drummond (R)	11,387	(21%)

District Vote For President

	1988		1984		1980		1976	
D	151,187	(45%)	120,859	(41%)	122,756	(41%)	105,384	(45%)
R	183,869	(54%)	174,225	(59%)	141,887	(47%)	122,673	(52%)
I					31,117	(10%)		

4 Bruce F. Vento (D)

Of St. Paul — Elected 1976

Born: Oct. 7, 1940, St. Paul, Minn.
Education: U. of Minnesota, A.A. 1961; Wisconsin State U., B.S. 1965; attended U. of Minnesota, 1965-70.
Occupation: Science teacher.
Family: Wife, Mary Jean Moore; three children.
Religion: Roman Catholic.
Political Career: Minn. House, 1971-77.
Capitol Office: 2304 Rayburn Bldg. 20515; 225-6631.

In Washington: Vento is a workhorse. He chairs the Interior Subcommittee on National Parks and Public Lands, a panel with a huge mandate and a massive workload. In the 101st Congress by his count, he shepherded 109 bills through the House and saw 92 of them enacted. He was also quite active on the Banking Committee, where he helped assemble major bills addressing the savings and loan crisis and revamping housing programs.

But even those who admire Vento's legislative diligence acknowledge that he has one problem: He talks and talks and talks. Once he gets started on an issue, he can continue long after those listening have lost the train of thought. And worse, his loquacity has been known to verge on condescension.

Were he any less conscientious a lawmaker, his verbosity might make it hard for him to build the delicate coalitions needed to pass legislation on Interior. On Banking, where alliances are drawn and redrawn, issue by issue, and where the chairman, Henry B. Gonzalez, is on amicable terms with but a few of his fellow Democrats, traditional coalition politicking does not necessarily prevail.

Before the start of the 102nd Congress, Vento attempted to become the vessel for Democrats' frustration with Gonzalez, challenging him for the chairmanship in the Democratic Caucus. But the competing personalities on Banking failed to coalesce behind Vento's coup attempt, which he launched on the very day of balloting. Nevertheless, more than a third of the caucus stood with Vento, as Gonzalez held on by a vote of 163-89.

Vento has been involved in a range of issues on the Banking Committee. In the 101st Congress, he devoted considerable time to succoring the nation's ailing savings and loan industry.

In 1989, as the Banking Committee was considering a bill to provide $50 billion to bail out insolvent S&Ls, Vento joined New York Democrat Charles E. Schumer and others to craft a compromise amendment to a Gonzalez proposal imposing stringent requirements for the amount of capital an S&L would be required to keep on its books. The Vento amendment gave S&Ls more time to meet the stricter standard, but also toughened other requirements, such as increasing the percentage of tangible capital S&Ls would be required to maintain and banning intangible, or "good will," assets after 1994. Vento's substitute was adopted 36-15.

Frank Annunzio, chairman of the Financial Institutions Subcommittee, named Vento chairman of a task force on the Resolution Trust Corporation, the government's S&L salvage agency, to oversee the implementation of the bailout. He criticized the RTC's administrative structure and advocated eliminating its oversight board.

In the 101st Congress, the Banking Committee also worked on the most sweeping overhaul of federal housing programs since 1974. Vento teamed with Pennsylvania Republican Tom Ridge to remedy the Federal Housing Administration's troubled mortgage insurance program. The Vento-Ridge plan aimed to curtail the losses in the program without shutting out families from home ownership. An administration-backed scheme would have forced buyers to pay more cash up front. Vento-Ridge did not increase the up-front costs but charged an annual 0.6 percent premium over the life of a 30-year loan.

Although Vento-Ridge attracted support from both industry and advocacy groups, Housing Secretary Jack F. Kemp opposed it. But House GOP leaders liked Vento-Ridge, as did the House, which adopted it by a vote of 418-2. Kemp's opposition helped split the cosponsors in conference, however. Ridge broke with Vento and offered a compromise costing buyers $833 up front in cash. Vento opposed it, but it prevailed.

Vento was one of the first members to urge congressional action to deal with the homeless. In 1982 he attached an amendment to a housing bill to provide $50 million to repair unused buildings to be used as temporary shelters. That bill was never considered by the full

Minnesota 4

St. Paul and Suburbs

St. Paul is a Democratic city with a German- and Irish-Catholic population and a strong labor tradition that grew up in the days when it was a major port and railroading hub. In every aspect except its Democratic loyalties, it differs from its supposed twin, Minneapolis.

The working-class neighborhoods on St. Paul's East Side are drab and solidly Democratic. The precincts here have routinely supported virtually every major statewide Democratic candidate of recent years.

West of Lexington Avenue, where the houses and the spaces between them are larger, Republicans usually do slightly better, but only occasionally do they prevail. Several colleges — Macalester, Hamline, St. Thomas and St. Catherine, and the University of Minnesota's School of Agriculture — give this area a young and culturally vibrant quality that is missing elsewhere in the 4th.

Thirty years ago, when Eugene J. McCarthy represented St. Paul in the U.S. House, nearly 90 percent of the 4th District vote came from the city. But with the growth of the suburbs and a decline in St. Paul's population from its 1960 peak of 313,000 to 272,000 in the 1980s, St. Paul makes up just half the current district.

Most of the suburban vote lies north of the city in Ramsey County. There, nearly 190,000 people in postwar suburban housing tracts vote about 10 percent less Democratic than their counterparts in St. Paul itself. While Vento never has difficulty carrying any section of St. Paul, he has sometimes struggled in several of the state legislative districts in suburban Ramsey.

South St. Paul, added to the 4th in 1982 redistricting, is known for its stockyards, which give off an aroma extending as far south into Dakota County as the district itself. This well-worn community of 20,000 is dependent on the meat factory that sits on the west bank of the Mississippi River. West St. Paul is not quite as Democratic as South St. Paul, but still supported Jimmy Carter, Walter F. Mondale and Michael S. Dukakis by convincing margins. In West St. Paul, Dukakis outpolled George Bush 60-39 percent; he carried South St. Paul by 25 percentage points, 62-37 percent.

Mendota Heights, also added in the last remap, votes Republican. Unlike the nearby areas, extensions of the working-class part of St. Paul, Mendota Heights is a new Twin Cities bedroom community.

Population: 509,532. White 476,141 (93%), Black 14,825 (3%), Other 8,694 (2%). Spanish origin 10,151 (2%). 18 and over 375,922 (74%), 65 and over 59,518 (12%). Median age: 29.

House, but Vento has since seen his efforts pay off as many other lawmakers focused on the issue. In the 100th Congress, he was the prime sponsor of the $1.3 billion McKinney homeless-aid reauthorization bill, which won widespread support. It was reauthorized in the 101st Congress.

Vento shares the philosophy of the conservationist majority on the Interior Committee, and his productivity helps them tolerate his garrulous style.

Vento's subcommittee mandate also allows him to offer colleagues tangible benefits to attract them to his side. It can approve historical sites and designate trails and rivers, national parks and wilderness land. In the 99th Congress, Vento helped guide the creation of Nevada's Great Basin National Park, the first full-scale national park added to the system outside Alaska since 1971. In the 101st Congress, he won passage of a bill transferring nearly 8,000 acres of land to the state of Minnesota for recreation and conservation.

In 1990, Vento injected himself into the turbulent debate over protecting the threatened northern spotted owl and the ancient, "old-growth" forests that are its habitat. He drew up a bill that would have protected from commercial logging 6.3 million acres of old-growth forest in Oregon, Washington and Northern California. It also would have set minimum timber sales in the region well below existing harvest levels. His subcommittee approved the bill by a vote of 19-13, but he was unable to get it through the full committee. He planned to reintroduce it in the 102nd Congress.

When a mammoth shopping mall was planned near the Manassas National Battlefield Park in Virginia, Civil War buffs found a friend in Vento. His subcommittee approved a bill to annex the proposed mall site as part of a 600-acre parcel that included the site of Gen. Robert E. Lee's headquarters during the second battle of Manassas in 1862. The House cleared the measure over White House objections. It languished in the Senate until a midnight stand by Sen. Dale Bumpers got the House language attached to the technical corrections tax bill.

At Home: Vento has the right personal and political background to represent his labor-dominated district.

The son of a Machinists' union official, he

was a union steward at a plastics plant, then worked in a brewery and on a refrigerator assembly line before becoming a junior high school teacher and state representative.

During his three terms in the Legislature he echoed the interests of the working-class residents of St. Paul's Phalen Park. A loyal team player, he won the assistant majority leader post under Speaker Martin Olav Sabo, now his Minnesota congressional colleague.

When nine-term House veteran Joseph E. Karth decided to retire in 1976, he endorsed Vento for the seat. Karth's backing and labor support gave him the party endorsement.

Still, Vento faced four foes in the Democratic primary. Two were significant: St. Paul attorney John S. Connolly, running as an even more liberal alternative to Vento, and 27-year-old state Auditor Robert W. Mattson, who twice defeated party-endorsed candidates. But Vento had too many factors working in his favor. He won a convincing primary victory with 52 percent. The November election was just as easy for Vento as it usually had been for Karth.

In 1978, Vento met an aggressive, conservative GOP challenger who held the incumbent under 60 percent. But with the same candidate and a much better-financed campaign in 1980, Republicans got no closer. Since then they have offered only token opposition. In 1986 Vento easily turned back a challenge from one of the nation's foremost perennial candidates, Harold E. Stassen, making his first bid for the House after numerous tries for other offices. In 1988 and 1990, he easily repelled challenges by Republican Ian Maitland, a professor at the University of Minnesota.

Committees

Banking, Finance & Urban Affairs (7th of 31 Democrats)
Economic Stabilization; Financial Institutions Supervision, Regulation & Insurance; Housing & Community Development

Interior & Insular Affairs (6th of 29 Democrats)
National Parks & Public Lands (chairman); Water, Power & Offshore Energy

Select Aging (10th of 42 Democrats)
Health & Long-Term Care; Housing & Consumer Interests

Elections

1990 General		
Bruce F. Vento (D)	143,353	(65%)
Ian Maitland (R)	77,639	(35%)
1988 General		
Bruce F. Vento (D)	181,227	(72%)
Ian Maitland (R)	67,073	(27%)

Previous Winning Percentages: **1986** (73%) **1984** (74%) **1982** (73%) **1980** (59%) **1978** (58%) **1976** (66%)

District Vote For President

	1988	1984	1980	1976
D	159,663 (61%)	163,312 (59%)	137,337 (53%)	148,298 (58%)
R	99,668 (38%)	113,641 (41%)	88,633 (34%)	97,026 (38%)
I			25,260 (10%)	

Campaign Finance

	Receipts	Receipts from PACs	Expend-itures
1990			
Vento (D)	$259,456	$187,095 (72%)	$265,699
Maitland (R)	$57,086	0	$57,415
1988			
Vento (D)	$268,237	$189,759 (71%)	$216,172
Maitland (R)	$36,998	0	$35,789

Key Votes

1991	
Authorize use of force against Iraq	N
1990	
Support constitutional amendment on flag desecration	N
Pass family and medical leave bill over Bush veto	Y
Reduce SDI funding	Y
Allow abortions in overseas military facilities	Y
Approve budget summit plan for spending and taxing	N
Approve civil rights bill	Y
1989	
Halt production of B-2 stealth bomber at 13 planes	Y
Oppose capital gains tax cut	Y
Approve federal abortion funding in rape or incest cases	N
Approve pay raise and revision of ethics rules	Y
Pass Democratic minimum wage plan over Bush veto	Y

Voting Studies

	Presidential Support		Party Unity		Conservative Coalition	
Year	**S**	**O**	**S**	**O**	**S**	**O**
1990	13	86	95	4	7	91
1989	30	69	92	7	12	85
1988	21	77	94	4	11	89
1987	12	85	95	2	5	88
1986	19	81	94	5	6	94
1985	21	78	95	3	4	91
1984	28	67	90	6	3	95
1983	17	82	94	4	4	96
1982	34	65	94	5	5	92
1981	29	61	86	9	9	84

Interest Group Ratings

Year	ADA	ACU	AFL-CIO	CCUS
1990	100	4	100	21
1989	100	4	83	30
1988	90	4	100	36
1987	100	0	94	8
1986	90	0	93	28
1985	95	5	100	18
1984	95	0	92	43
1983	90	0	94	20
1982	100	9	100	14
1981	90	0	80	13

5 Martin Olav Sabo (D)

Of Minneapolis — Elected 1978

Born: Feb. 28, 1938, Crosby, N.D.

Education: Augsburg College, B.A. 1959; attended U. of Minnesota, 1960.

Occupation: Public official.

Family: Wife, Sylvia Ann Lee; two children.

Religion: Lutheran.

Political Career: Minn. House, 1961-79, minority leader, 1969-73, Speaker, 1973-79.

Capitol Office: 2201 Rayburn Bldg. 20515; 225-4755.

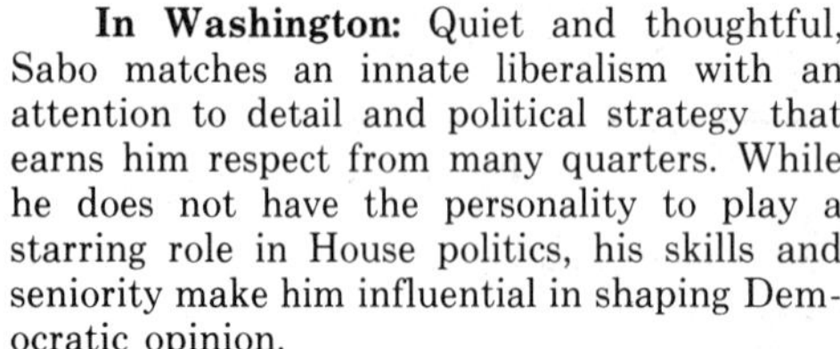

In Washington: Quiet and thoughtful, Sabo matches an innate liberalism with an attention to detail and political strategy that earns him respect from many quarters. While he does not have the personality to play a starring role in House politics, his skills and seniority make him influential in shaping Democratic opinion.

His low-key approach is well suited to the Appropriations Committee, where he has added a liberal's perspective to defense and transportation debates for more than a decade. In the 101st Congress, he began to play a broader role when he took a seat on the Budget Committee and assumed the chairmanship of the Democratic Study Group (DSG). In the 102nd, he notched upward again when he was appointed to the Intelligence panel.

This full plate of activities may help satisfy Sabo's desire for the kind of leadership role he played in the state Legislature, where he was House Speaker. Sabo once tried for a top leadership job in the U.S. House, seeking the Democratic whip post for the 100th Congress (he was already a deputy whip). But he ran an oddly laconic campaign and gave it up in mid-1986 for a seat on the Appropriations Subcommittee on Defense. "I think I know how to count," he said. "My chances of winning are remote."

The Defense Subcommittee seat was a reasonable consolation prize. Sabo has long had an interest in arms control issues, and anti-Pentagon Democrats badly wanted him on the panel. Until the Minnesotan's arrival, Oregon's Les AuCoin was the only subcommittee member with a critical attitude toward the Reagan administration's defense buildup and controversial new weapons systems.

Sabo's left-of-center perspective on those issues contributed to Speaker Thomas S. Foley's decision to name him to Intelligence in 1991. While Foley drew some GOP criticism for selecting Sabo and three other skeptics of covert operations — all of whom had voted against authorizing the use of force in the Persian Gulf in January — it was widely viewed as a move to balance the influence of new chairman Dave McCurdy, a moderate from Oklahoma.

During the 101st Congress, Sabo and other arms control advocates found more common ground with the Bush administration than they ever had with President Ronald Reagan. Working from the Bush administration's pledge not to test the anti-satellite missile (ASAT) and to observe the U.S.-Soviet agreement on nuclear testing, Sabo backed off efforts to formally extend the treaty. Instead he pushed legislation to set up methods for verifying a ban on ASAT lasers and international seismic monitoring networks.

One of the more contentious defense fights of the 101st Congress pitted Sabo and other House liberals against Armed Services Committee Chairman Les Aspin. After the House passed a defense authorization that Sabo and other Democrats said made a policy shift from redundant strategic weapons to badly needed conventional weapons, Aspin blasted the bill as "a Dukakis defense budget." Complaining that Aspin could not then defend the House bill in conference, Sabo and others prevailed on Foley to appoint special group of House conferees whose votes reflected the will of the House on key strategic arms issues.

As DSG chairman, Sabo is credited with helping make the liberal policy group a source of agitation again. The group had been a key agent for change during the late 1970s, but was less visible in the 1980s. During the protracted budget debate in late 1990, the DSG issued meaty and highly partisan reports on "tax fairness," dubbing Bush's capital gains tax cut as a sop to the rich.

At the start of the 102nd Congress, the DSG went on record for a more legislatively assertive Democratic Caucus when it helped orchestrate the ouster of two old-school Democratic chairmen. Sabo contributed to the episode with a letter to Foley raising questions about whether Banking Chairman Henry B. Gonzalez of Texas had violated caucus rules by taping a political ad for a Republican. While Gonzalez survived the flap, he was served notice that the caucus took seriously longstanding complaints about his coziness with committee

Minnesota 5

Minneapolis and Suburbs

This is one of the select number of districts in the country where candidates are not afraid to refer to themselves as liberals.

Minneapolis residents account for nearly three-fourths of the 5th's voters, and except for those on the city's southwest side, they predictably choose liberal candidates over conservatives.

Scandinavians remain the most conspicuous ethnic group; it is no coincidence that Sabo includes his middle name, Olav, on all his official papers. That name eliminates any vestiges of doubt that he is Norwegian, not Italian.

Although many of the flour mills that once lined the Mississippi River at St. Anthony's Falls have moved away, the major milling companies that settled in Minneapolis — Pillsbury and General Mills — have remained and diversified. They are among the major employers in the Twin Cities, along with the new "brain power" firms that find Minneapolis ideally suited for their needs.

Honeywell and Control Data have their worldwide headquarters in the district. The white-collar professionals who have been attracted by these "clean" industries help to give the city a clean-cut image that is reflected in the glistening towers of its downtown area.

But Minneapolis is not only parks, lakes, glass and chrome. Northwest of the downtown office towers are some poor neighborhoods, home to blacks and the city's Chippewa Indian population. East of the Mississippi are older, more traditional blue-collar areas adjoining the main campus of the University of Minnesota.

But even the presence of Fortune 500 manufacturers could not halt a late 1980s downturn in the regional economy; many high-paying, white-collar jobs were eliminated. The city's population, having peaked in 1950 at 522,000, dropped by 29 percent during the 1970s to 371,000 and continued to slide, albeit more gradually, in the 1980s.

To make up for the declining population, the last redistricting expanded the boundaries of the 5th. The southern border, which formerly coincided with the Minneapolis city limits, was extended to include Richfield and the eastern portion of Bloomington. Although the southern addition is not as Democratic as Minneapolis, the map was drawn to keep the most Republican parts of Bloomington in the 3rd District.

On the northern side of the 5th, three solidly Democratic suburbs from Anoka County were removed, and three larger communities in Hennepin County added. Again, the area added is not quite as Democratic as the rest of the district, but Robbinsdale, Brooklyn Center and Crystal all have Democratic preferences.

Population: 509,506. White 458,433 (90%), Black 29,776 (6%), Other 14,993 (3%). Spanish origin 5,544 (1%). 18 and over 401,381 (79%), 65 and over 69,437 (14%). Median age: 30.

Republicans.

On Appropriations, Sabo mixes parochial interests and national policy on spending bills through his interest in scientific research. He looks out for the major high-technology firms in his district as well as for the University of Minnesota, while advocating development of a federal policy on supercomputers. He supported amendments to the 1988 and 1989 defense appropriations bill to require the Pentagon to buy only American supercomputers.

On the the Transportation Subcommittee, Sabo plays the money-earmarking game as well as anyone in Congress. When the fiscal 1987 transportation appropriations bill was approved, it contained, among other provisions, $10 million for a "demonstration project" to improve a highway linking downtown Minneapolis and the Twin Cities' airport, and $2.8 million to build a bus transitway on the University of Minnesota campus. Sabo is a strong believer in buses; during his years on the subcommittee, he has lobbied repeatedly for more money for bus service as opposed to more expensive rail mass-transit systems.

In 1990, he offered legislation to fund a national bicycle coordinator within the Department of Transportation and to require a study of ways to promote bicycles as an alternative mode of transportation. The concept squared with his energy-efficiency policy goals and his personal reputation for physical fitness. Though a few years older than others in the Democratic "basketball caucus" — an informal and influential group that regularly competes at the House gym — he is one of their stalwarts.

In each Congress since he arrived in Washington, Sabo has offered legislation to provide access to basic health insurance for those who now lack coverage. During the early 1980s, he was furious about Reagan administration budget cuts in social programs and scornful of Democrats who he felt went too far in accommodating the conservative mood.

At Home: Sabo has never been a flashy campaigner, but he has been a significant presence in Minnesota politics virtually all his adult life.

When Democratic Rep. Donald Fraser left the House for his unsuccessful Senate try in 1978, nearly a dozen candidates began maneuvering to succeed him. But when Sabo announced he wanted the job, nearly all of them bowed out of the contest. Those who remained lost either at the endorsing convention or in Sabo's 81 percent primary victory.

One of the reasons for Sabo's strength has been his amazing combination of youth and longevity. Elected to the state Legislature at 22, he had been in the public spotlight for 18 years and served as Speaker for six years before running for Congress. He was seen by most voters as the logical liberal successor to Fraser.

Sabo's first Republican opponent, dentist Mike Till, conducted a much more visible campaign than Republicans usually wage in this heavily Democratic district. When businessman Bob Short defeated Fraser in a bitter Senate primary, Till hoped some of the animosity liberals felt toward Short would rub off on Sabo for the general election. But Sabo carefully avoided making any connection between his campaign and Short's, which was a wise move. Short received less than 24 percent in the 5th.

Sabo's winning percentage in 1978 was not quite up to what Fraser had been receiving. But by his second election, he had achieved solid support throughout the area, even in the communities of the district where he was weakest against Till.

Committees

Appropriations (17th of 37 Democrats)
Defense; District of Columbia; Transportation

Budget (10th of 23 Democrats)
Budget Process, Reconciliation & Enforcement; Economic Policy, Projections & Revenues

Select Intelligence (11th of 12 Democrats)
Legislation; Program & Budget Authorization

Elections

1990 General		
Martin Olav Sabo (D)	144,682	(73%)
Raymond C. "Buzz" Gilbertson (R)	53,720	(27%)
1988 General		
Martin Olav Sabo (D)	174,416	(72%)
Raymond C. "Buzz" Gilbertson (R)	60,646	(25%)
T. Christopher Wright (I)	6,468	(3%)

Previous Winning Percentages: **1986** (73%) **1984** (70%) **1982** (66%) **1980** (70%) **1978** (62%)

District Vote For President

	1988	1984	1980	1976
D	166,580 (65%)	162,599 (63%)	163,443 (60%)	161,266 (61%)
R	85,100 (33%)	97,062 (37%)	77,062 (28%)	94,618 (36%)
I			29,812 (11%)	

Campaign Finance

	Receipts	Receipts from PACs	Expend-itures
1990			
Sabo (D)	$355,684	$226,950 (64%)	$321,644
Gilbertson (R)	$7,950	0	$9,497
1988			
Sabo (D)	$363,965	$237,550 (65%)	$281,455
Gilbertson (R)	$21,776	$479 (2%)	$16,915

Key Votes

1991	
Authorize use of force against Iraq	N
1990	
Support constitutional amendment on flag desecration	N
Pass family and medical leave bill over Bush veto	Y
Reduce SDI funding	Y
Allow abortions in overseas military facilities	Y
Approve budget summit plan for spending and taxing	Y
Approve civil rights bill	Y
1989	
Halt production of B-2 stealth bomber at 13 planes	N
Oppose capital gains tax cut	Y
Approve federal abortion funding in rape or incest cases	Y
Approve pay raise and revision of ethics rules	Y
Pass Democratic minimum wage plan over Bush veto	Y

Voting Studies

	Presidential Support		Party Unity		Conservative Coalition	
Year	**S**	**O**	**S**	**O**	**S**	**O**
1990	19	81	95	3	15	83
1989	30	69	97	2	12	88
1988	20	80	96	2	8	92
1987	17	80	91	2	12	84
1986	20	80	95	3	12	88
1985	16	84	98	1	5	95
1984	26	70	92	4	12	80
1983	18	80	93	3	9	90
1982	35	64	92	5	10	89
1981	29	70	89	8	7	92

Interest Group Ratings

Year	ADA	ACU	AFL-CIO	CCUS
1990	94	0	100	14
1989	95	0	92	20
1988	100	0	100	21
1987	100	0	94	7
1986	95	0	93	11
1985	95	5	94	18
1984	95	4	85	31
1983	100	0	94	30
1982	100	0	95	29
1981	90	0	93	5

6 Gerry Sikorski (D)

Of Stillwater — Elected 1982

Born: April 26, 1948, Breckenridge, Minn.
Education: U. of Minnesota, B.A. 1970, J.D. 1973.
Military Service: Naval Reserve, 1984-present.
Occupation: Lawyer.
Family: Wife, Susan Erkel; one child.
Religion: Roman Catholic.
Political Career: Minn. Senate, 1977-83; Democratic nominee for U.S. House, 1978.
Capitol Office: 403 Cannon Bldg. 20515; 225-2271.

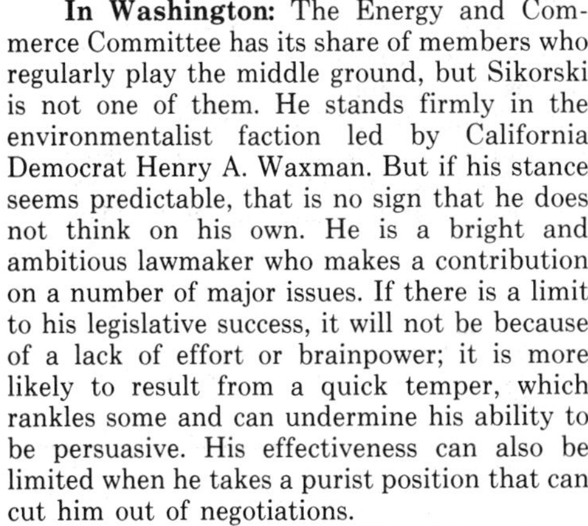

In Washington: The Energy and Commerce Committee has its share of members who regularly play the middle ground, but Sikorski is not one of them. He stands firmly in the environmentalist faction led by California Democrat Henry A. Waxman. But if his stance seems predictable, that is no sign that he does not think on his own. He is a bright and ambitious lawmaker who makes a contribution on a number of major issues. If there is a limit to his legislative success, it will not be because of a lack of effort or brainpower; it is more likely to result from a quick temper, which rankles some and can undermine his ability to be persuasive. His effectiveness can also be limited when he takes a purist position that can cut him out of negotiations.

In the 101st Congress, Sikorski sought an active role during consideration of clean air legislation. His staunchly pro-environmental stands, though, earned him the wrath of committee Chairman John D. Dingell of Michigan, who leads the more industry-oriented faction on clean air issues. A monthlong delay in naming House conferees on the measure in June 1990 was at least partly due to Dingell's unsuccessful efforts to keep Sikorski and other environmentalists off the conference panel.

Sikorski had clashed throughout the 101st Congress with Dingell over acid rain and the impact of air toxics contaminants on fish in the Great Lakes, fights that Dingell won. But Sikorski bested Dingell on a provision that extended warranty requirements for some kinds of auto emissions control equipment; the House adopted the amendment 239-180.

Sikorski started taking a leading role in promoting acid rain legislation shortly after joining the committee in 1983, and built an invaluable alliance with Waxman. Along with that, however, has come conflict with Dingell. There are those who oppose Dingell on clean air, but go out of their way to placate him on other issues. Not Sikorski.

Sikorski began his Energy and Commerce career teaming with Waxman to introduce legislation calling for a 10 million-ton acid rain control program requiring installation of expensive "scrubbers" on the dirtiest utility smokestacks. The authors sought to ease the financial burden on Midwest utility users by spreading the cost with a nationwide tax on non-nuclear power — amounting to a $2.2 billion a year subsidy. The measure was popular in the full House, but Dingell and his committee allies managed to kill it by one vote.

Sikorski met with little success in the 99th and 100th Congresses as less stringent acid rain bills never made it out of committee. When the 101st Congress began, Sikorski was optimistic about breaking the impasse. He joined with Republican Silvio Conte of Massachusetts to offer a provision calling for a 10 million-ton reduction in sulfur-dioxide emissions by 1998; the final clean air legislation contained somewhat weaker standards.

During consideration of a measure reauthorizing the Consumer Product Safety Commission, Sikorski got Congress to agree to an amendment that mandated a voluntary standard to require safety devices on garage doors that operate automatically. Sikorski said at least 68 children had been killed and 26,959 injured since the voluntary standard went into effect in 1973.

Sikorski is a force partly because he has considerable energy and the ability to master issues quickly, but sometimes he seems too energetic, and he can anger too quickly for his own good. Opponents who deal with him say the fastest route to victory is often to needle him until he loses his temper, and along with it, his ability to make a sound argument.

His temper and other personal behavior received unfavorable public attention in 1988, when *The Washington Post* ran a story detailing Sikorski's treatment of his staff. The newspaper reported that he often had staff members do personal chores, such as helping his wife's dog-breeding enterprise by bobbing the tails of puppies. It also reported that he could fly into a tirade over seemingly minor incidents, such as preparing the wrong kind of sandwich for his daughter's school lunch. Sikorski claimed that

Minnesota 6

Northern and Eastern Twin Cities Suburbs

The 6th District surrounds the Twin Cities, taking in nearly all the suburban fringe areas on the north, east and west, plus some farmland just beyond. It includes many marginally Democratic areas and a few hard-core Democratic strongholds.

Anoka County, which casts nearly 40 percent of the vote, is the strongest Democratic area of the 6th; the cornerstone of Sikorski's congressional victories, it remained loyal to Walter F. Mondale in 1984 and Michael S. Dukakis in 1988. While losing statewide in 1990, Democratic Gov. Rudy Perpich carried Anoka, albeit by less than 5,000 votes.

Anoka is a mix of new suburbs, farms and small towns. Lake Wobegon, the mythical sleepy town in Garrison Keillor's one-time weekly radio program "A Prairie Home Companion," is modeled after Keillor's boyhood home in Anoka County. But the Lake Wobegons of this part of Minnesota are quickly disappearing as the Twin Cities metropolitan area expands farther into the surrounding counties.

Changing even more rapidly are Wright and Sherburne counties, the two areas of largest growth in the state during the 1970s. Both have been friendly to such moderate Democratic candidates as Perpich (he carried both in 1990), but both went narrowly to George Bush in 1988.

More than a quarter of the vote is cast in Hennepin County, in close-in Minneapolis suburbs, and this is where most of the GOP vote lies. This part of the district includes the affluent area around Lake Minnetonka, which is among the most Republican parts of the state.

Wedged on the eastern side of the district between St. Paul and the St. Croix River is Washington County. It is home for Sikorski and about 20 percent of the district voters. In 1982, the county gave Sikorski a 218-vote margin, but it has since provided him with a more substantial edge.

Population: 509,446. White 499,670 (98%), Black 2,114 (0.4%), Other 5,877 (1%). Spanish origin 3,414 (1%). 18 and over 332,303 (65%), 65 and over 27,040 (5%). Median age: 27.

the story was "full of untruths and distortions" and in January 1990, the House ethics committee dismissed the complaints filed against him.

Like many Minnesotans, Sikorski is at odds with his party's official stance on abortion. He opposes abortion, and when Energy and Commerce marked up legislation to set product liability standards in the 100th Congress, he was concerned that new standards would make it easier for manufacturers of contraceptives and abortion-inducing drugs to sell their products.

His effort to prevent this from happening was backed not only by anti-abortion groups, but also by a group representing women injured by the Dalkon Shield intrauterine device. Sikorski's wife had been injured by the Dalkon Shield, but had previously settled her claim with the manufacturer.

In 1989, Sikorski was one of 26 House members who switched their votes on abortion language, voting to allow federal funding of abortions in cases of rape and incest. He returned firmly to the anti-abortion fold in 1990, opposing efforts to allow privately funded abortions in overseas military facilities.

While most of Sikorski's attention goes toward Energy and Commerce, he also chairs the Civil Service Subcommittee on the Post Office panel, where he has backed unsuccessful efforts to revise the Hatch Act, which bars federal workers from engaging in political activities.

At Home: Sikorski has been described as a Democratic version of Minnesota Republican Vin Weber — aggressive, smart and well financed. In his affluent suburban constituency, he needs all those attributes.

Republicans view the 6th as favorable terrain, but they have found no way to beat him. Massive redistricting in 1982 created the 6th and enabled Sikorski to unseat GOP Rep. Arlen Erdahl. In 1984, he trounced a well-financed champion of the religious right. And in each of the next three elections, Sikorski won nearly two-thirds of the total vote.

In 1990, Minnesota Vikings football player Joey Browner showed interest in challenging Sikorski. Republicans attending the 6th District convention waited to hear his decision before making an endorsement. But Browner decided against a 1990 run.

Elected to the state Senate at age 28, Sikorski quickly established a reputation for strong organizational skills and driving ambition. He was just two years into his freshman Senate term in 1978 when he took on Rep. Erdahl in the old 1st District.

That constituency spread north all the way to the border of St. Paul, but most of the vote was cast in nine farming counties. Worse for Sikorski, 1978 was a year in which the GOP took both U.S. Senate seats and the governorship out of Democratic hands.

Sikorski tried to adjust to the Republican year, campaigning for a $50 billion tax cut and stressing his opposition to legalized abortion. But the timing and the district demographics were against him. He was held to 43 percent.

Sikorski returned to the state Senate, becoming majority whip in 1980. But court-ordered redistricting in early 1982 created a new district in the Twin Cities suburbs, and Sikorski was a front-runner from the start. Although he faced opposition from some groups opposed to his stand on abortion, he needed only three ballots to seal his party's endorsement over two other state legislators.

Meanwhile, Erdahl was having a complicated year. When the remap placed his home in the solidly Democratic 4th District, Erdahl moved into the redrawn 1st, but lost the nomination to GOP Rep. Tom Hagedorn. Party leaders talked Erdahl into moving to the new 6th, where he drew criticism as a carpetbagger and needed 13 ballots to win the GOP endorsement.

Sikorski seized on the carpetbagging charge, distributing state maps charting Erdahl's tortuous path to the 6th. More important, the circumstances of 1978 were reversed. The new 6th was friendly Democratic territory, and 1982 was almost as good a year for Minnesota Democrats as 1978 had been for Republicans. Sikorski won with 51 percent.

In 1984, the GOP nominated Patrick Trueman, an articulate, energetic campaigner with fervent support from Minnesota's potent anti-abortion movement. He had been a co-founder of its legal arm, Americans United for Life.

Trueman accused Sikorski of being a part of the "Mondale tax increase team," but in a district still reasonably sympathetic to national Democrats, the charge had modest impact. Sikorski drove home his message with a late media blitz, turning what was thought to be a close race into a solid victory.

Committees

Energy & Commerce (15th of 27 Democrats)
Health & the Environment; Oversight & Investigations; Transportation & Hazardous Materials

Post Office & Civil Service (5th of 15 Democrats)
Civil Service (chairman); Postal Operations & Services

Select Children, Youth & Families (10th of 22 Democrats)

Elections

1990 General

Gerry Sikorski (D)	164,816	(65%)
Bruce D. Anderson (R)	90,138	(35%)

1988 General

Gerry Sikorski (D)	169,486	(65%)
Ray Ploetz (R)	89,209	(34%)

Previous Winning Percentages: **1986** (66%) **1984** (60%) **1982** (51%)

District Vote For President

	1988	1984	1980	1976
D	148,030 (51%)	124,587 (48%)	73,786 (46%)	85,390 (53%)
R	140,362 (48%)	136,681 (52%)	68,292 (43%)	70,450 (44%)
I			15,258 (10%)	

Campaign Finance

	Receipts	Receipts from PACs	Expend-itures
1990			
Sikorski (D)	$443,201	$335,487 (76%)	$378,087
Anderson (R)	$16,718	0	$16,219
1988			
Sikorski (D)	$547,198	$358,582 (66%)	$320,437
Ploetz (R)	$103,945	$5,568 (5%)	$100,941

Key Votes

1991	
Authorize use of force against Iraq	N
1990	
Support constitutional amendment on flag desecration	N
Pass family and medical leave bill over Bush veto	Y
Reduce SDI funding	Y
Allow abortions in overseas military facilities	N
Approve budget summit plan for spending and taxing	Y
Approve civil rights bill	Y
1989	
Halt production of B-2 stealth bomber at 13 planes	Y
Oppose capital gains tax cut	Y
Approve federal abortion funding in rape or incest cases	Y
Approve pay raise and revision of ethics rules	Y
Pass Democratic minimum wage plan over Bush veto	Y

Voting Studies

	Presidential Support		Party Unity		Conservative Coalition	
Year	**S**	**O**	**S**	**O**	**S**	**O**
1990	15	82	79	17	15	81
1989	30	70	72	28	10	90
1988	22	77	75	23	16	84
1987	12	88	82	18	14	86
1986	17	81	79	20	22	76
1985	23	78	70 †	28 †	20	78
1984	33	67	85	15	22	78
1983	16	83	89	8	13	87

† Not eligible for all recorded votes.

Interest Group Ratings

Year	ADA	ACU	AFL-CIO	CCUS
1990	89	0	100	8
1989	100	4	92	40
1988	90	12	100	36
1987	92	9	94	13
1986	85	5	100	33
1985	75	14	88	27
1984	80	13	92	44
1983	90	4	100	25

7 Collin C. Peterson (D)

Of Detroit Lakes — Elected 1990

Born: June 29, 1944, Fargo, N.D.
Education: Moorhead State U., B.A. 1966.
Military Service: Army National Guard, 1963-69.
Occupation: Accountant.
Family: Divorced; three children.
Religion: Lutheran.
Political Career: Minn. Senate, 1977-86; sought Democratic nomination for U.S. House, 1982, 1988; Democratic nominee for U.S. House, 1984, 1986.
Capitol Office: 1725 Longworth Bldg. 20515; 225-2165.

The Path to Washington: Peterson is living proof of the saying "persistence pays off." The loser on his first four tries for the 7th, Peterson won comfortably on his fifth attempt, ousting 13-year GOP Rep. Arlan Stangeland.

Peterson's victory was due in no small part to Stangeland's personal baggage. The Republican had been living on the political edge — winning five of six re-elections with less than 55 percent of the vote, including a 121-vote win over Peterson in 1986.

But Stangeland went over the edge in 1990. In January, *The St. Cloud Daily Times* reported that he had used his House credit card to charge several phone calls to or from the phone of a female Virginia lobbyist. A subsequent story revealed that he allowed a lobbyist to use his House parking space. Stangeland denied any wrongdoing, but he was never able to dispel the impression of impropriety.

Word of Stangeland's problems was enough to lure Peterson into the race, and he ran a virtually error-free campaign, uniting the district's often-divided Democratic Party and creating a more sophisticated voter targeting effort than ever before. Peterson harnessed the anti-incumbent tide that ran strongly across Minnesota — the only state in 1990 to turn out both an incumbent governor and senator.

At first glance, Peterson's occupation does not seem a natural fit for the 7th. In a sprawling, rural district where many people make their living in agriculture, he is a certified public accountant.

But Peterson was raised on a farm near Moorhead and boasted that as an accountant he had a detailed understanding of the farm economy. During a decade in the state Senate, he was a key player on taxation and natural resource matters, helping to draft Minnesota's original "superfund" toxic-waste law.

Yet many voters' first brush with Peterson came through music. A singer-guitar player, he entertained for years at social events throughout the district with his band, "Collin Peterson and the Establishment." During congressional debate on the 1985 farm bill, he traveled to Washington several times to lobby for the Democratic alternative, even recording a song in support of the legislation, called "Don't Do Nothin.' "

But not everything Peterson does has been music to the ears of district voters. He tends to follow his own internal compass, and even Democrats have been irritated from time to time by some of his actions.

In 1982, he unsuccessfully challenged Gene Wenstrom for the Democratic nomination in the 7th. Wenstrom had held Stangeland to 52 percent in two previous elections, and many Democrats felt Wenstrom deserved a third shot without having to hurdle intraparty competition.

In 1984, Wenstrom did not run, and Peterson won the nomination. But lacking money and name identification, he was trampled by Stangeland.

The farm crisis helped pull Peterson within several dozen votes of victory in 1986. But he was less than graceful in defeat; he lashed out at the Democratic Congressional Campaign Committee for failing to provide adequate support, and he refused to concede his loss without a recount. Two years later, he was beaten in the Democratic primary.

He might not have run again in 1990 had it not been for Stangeland's problems, but once he entered the race he was careful to present himself as a "new Collin Peterson," more mellow than in his past campaigns and ready to mend fences with Democratic activists he had previously offended.

At the district convention, he won the party endorsement over a field that included a female abortion rights supporter (Peterson is anti-abortion). In November, he swept to victory, carrying all but three of the 23 counties that are entirely or partially within the 7th.

Minnesota 7

Northwest — St. Cloud; Moorhead

From the prairie wheat fields along the Red River to the hills, forests and lakes in the middle of the state, this is Minnesota's most marginal district — economically as well as politically.

Farmers struggle each year to meet their high operating costs on land that does not match the quality of the soil farther south. Those living in the chilly central section try to eke out a living any way they can. A few dollars can usually be made from the sportsmen who hunt and fish in the region, and there is some money in the region's lumber business, which once was an economic mainstay but now is in decline. The snowmobile industry, a more recent economic boon to the area, was hurt by the early 1980s recession and several dry winters, and it has been slow to recover.

Politically, the district has been in the marginal category ever since popular Democrat Bob Bergland left it in 1977 to become Jimmy Carter's agriculture secretary.

St. Cloud, the seat of Stearns County with 43,000 residents, is the district's largest city. For years a major center for granite quarrying, St. Cloud attracted a diverse ethnic population that German Catholics dominated. Today the descendants of the old stonecutters share their ancestors' support of the Democratic Party on economic issues, but they often stray to the GOP when social issues, especially abortion, become paramount. Stearns County went Democratic in the 1990 House race; Peterson and GOP Rep. Arlan Stangeland both opposed abortion.

Apart from St. Cloud and Moorhead, a sister city to Fargo, N.D., about a half day's drive to the northwest, there are few population centers. But there is a significant Catholic influence in the small towns around St. Cloud, where large Catholic churches loom above the surrounding farm land — giving the area some of the feel of rural France or Germany.

Outside the orbit of St. Cloud, the towns are vintage Americana. Sauk Centre — about 40 miles northwest of St. Cloud — was the birthplace of novelist Sinclair Lewis, who used his hometown as the model for his famous work "Main Street." Street signs along the prime thoroughfare in Sauk Centre, in fact, describe it as the "Original Main Street."

The wheat-growing central sections of the district are slightly more populous than the rest, and also more Republican. Sugar beets are grown around Moorhead in the Red River Valley, which possesses some of the most fertile farm land in the district. Polk and Clay counties were number one and two in sugar beet harvesting in the U.S. between 1982 and 1987. In the rolling countryside just to the east are hundreds of lakes — ranging from small ponds to bodies of water several miles wide. The area draws hunters, fishermen and summer tourists.

Farther north, near the Canadian border, the land supports fewer people, and the vote is usually Democratic. The Red Lake and White Earth Indian reservations are in the northern part of the 7th.

Population: 509,521. White 497,050 (98%), Black 660 (0.1%), Other 10,189 (2%). Spanish origin 2,464 (1%). 18 and over 355,632 (70%), 65 and over 68,572 (14%). Median age: 28.

Committees

Agriculture (25th of 27 Democrats)
Cotton, Rice & Sugar; Livestock, Dairy & Poultry; Wheat, Soybeans & Feed Grains

Government Operations (22nd of 25 Democrats)
Government Information, Justice & Agriculture; Legislation & National Security

Campaign Finance

	Receipts	Receipts from PACs		Expend-itures
1990				
Peterson (D)	$266,773	$185,598	(70%)	$242,864
Stangeland (R)	$489,490	$298,670	(61%)	$487,224

Key Vote

1991

Authorize use of force against Iraq	N

Elections

1990 General

Collin C. Peterson (D)	107,126	(54%)
Arlan Stangeland (R)	92,876	(46%)

District Vote For President

	1988	1984	1980	1976
D	112,654 (48%)	102,205 (43%)	103,081 (42%)	140,207 (54%)
R	119,763 (51%)	135,304 (57%)	123,905 (50%)	109,051 (42%)
I			16,542 (7%)	

8 James L. Oberstar (D)

Of Chisholm — Elected 1974

Born: Sept. 10, 1934, Chisholm, Minn.

Education: College of St Thomas, B.A. 1956; College of Europe, Bruges, Belgium, M.A. 1957.

Occupation: Language teacher; congressional aide.

Family: Wife, Jo Garlick; four children.

Religion: Roman Catholic.

Political Career: Sought Democratic nomination for U.S. Senate, 1984.

Capitol Office: 2209 Rayburn Bldg. 20515; 225-6211.

In Washington: In some ways Oberstar seems miscast for the Public Works and Transportation Committee, despite his quarter-century there as staffer and member. He has the instincts of a scholar and reformer, but Public Works is a place where members like to dig first and ask questions later; policy analysts take a back seat to pork-barrelers.

At the same time, Oberstar is only part scholar. The rest of him is Minnesota Iron Range street-fighter, a self-described bohunk. He is the son of a miner and a shirt-factory worker, and an unrepentant New Deal-style Democrat with deep faith in the job-creating potential of public works and deeper faith yet in his party.

With the 101st Congress, Oberstar assumed his third subcommittee chairmanship on the panel. Having headed the Economic Development and the Investigations and Oversight subcommittees, he took charge of the one covering aviation.

Oberstar has made his career and built seniority at Public Works. Even so, not long ago he was restless enough to want to surrender it for something more. He unsuccessfully sought the Democratic Senate nomination in 1984, and returned to the House in 1985. Then he lost his bid for a seat on the Ways and Means Committee, and went back to Public Works.

Oberstar also has a seat on the Budget Committee, an assignment that helps satisfy that side of him that seeks a hand in broader policy debate beyond Public Works.

Oberstar's restlessness came to the fore again at the start of the 102nd Congress, when he joined a group of younger Public Works members in engineering the ouster of politically weak Chairman Glenn M. Anderson of California. As fourth-ranking Democrat, Oberstar was willing to run for the post, but he instead lent his support to Norman Y. Mineta, the panel's No. 3 Democrat. The coup, however, was not completed; second-ranking Robert A. Roe of New Jersey gained the chair.

Even before the late 1990 coup, Public Works had been in some turmoil. Oberstar unsuccessfully proposed at the start of the 101st Congress that subcommittee chairmen get more power over staff and budgeting decisions. He was opposed by Roe, who as chairman-in-waiting did not want to inherit a weakened position, and by other subcommittee heads who felt that under the passive Anderson they already enjoyed greater power without changing committee rules.

As a Public Works subcommittee chairman, Oberstar generally is considered fair and bipartisan by Republicans, despite his occasional partisan flashes in House debates. More conservative Democrats consider him someone they can deal with.

As chair of the Aviation Subcommittee, Oberstar in 1990 reached a compromise with House appropriators to spend some of the Airport and Airway Trust Fund on improving the nation's airports. Public Works members and the aviation industry had long contended that the White House hoarded the trust fund surplus to disguise the size of the general budget deficit. Oberstar also shed his previous opposition to President Bush's proposal of assessing airline travelers a user fee as another way to fund increased airport capacity and air traffic control improvements.

In 1989, Oberstar the pro-labor partisan quickly jumped into the controversy surrounding a strike against Eastern Airlines that was aimed at its chairman, Frank Lorenzo, a hated symbol of union-busting to organized labor nationwide. When President Bush refused to intervene, Oberstar became the Democratic leadership's point man in a strategy designed to paint the president as anti-labor. He sponsored a bill requiring Bush to set up an emergency panel to forge a settlement.

The Aviation Subcommittee approved it 21-12, and a week later it passed the House 252-167, both tallies roughly along party lines. "A vote for this legislation is a vote for the continued survival of competition in the airline industry," Oberstar told the House. But the bill died in the Senate, where Democratic leaders lacked the votes to choke a threatened GOP filibuster.

Minnesota 8

Northeast — Duluth

Based in the barren and remote northern reaches of Minnesota, the 8th District has a long Democratic tradition. Immigrants from Sweden, Finland and Eastern Europe settled here after the turn of the century to work in the iron mines scattered throughout the Mesabi and Vermillion iron ranges in the center of the district. Strongly allied with unions, the workers on the Iron Range today are unswerving in their allegiance to the Democrats.

Life on the Range, as it is called, has not been easy in recent decades. By the end of World War II the high-quality iron ore mines were largely depleted. Singer Bob Dylan, who grew up in Hibbing, bemoaned the fate of his native region in "North Country Blues." The discovery of new taconite mining technology has saved the local economy from collapse, but taconite is pulled from the earth in huge open-pit mines requiring far fewer people to operate than the old underground mines. Today, the prolonged slump of the steel industry has created additional job shortages by chain reaction.

Income from summer and winter tourism is crucial in helping the North Country survive, and Democrats here have little patience with those who want to protect the wilderness areas from recreational development.

The district's only major population center is the port city of Duluth, the state's fourth-largest city. With 85,000 people, it casts about one-fifth of the district's vote. From Duluth's steep bluffs, 800 feet above Lake Superior, one can survey the active port where much of the grain from the Plains states is shipped east. Iron ore and other raw materials for heavy industry also pass through the port, although in diminishing amounts. Duluth and surrounding St. Louis County, which extends to the Canadian border and includes most of the Iron Range population, are firmly Democratic. Though Democratic Gov. Rudy Perpich lost statewide in 1990, St. Louis County gave him 75 percent.

Population: 509,506. White 497,018 (98%), Black 1,394 (0.3%), Other 10,182 (2%). Spanish origin 1,777 (0.3%). 18 and over 360,529 (71%), 65 and over 70,002 (14%). Median age: 31.

The Eastern affair helped shape Oberstar's view that airline deregulation prompted concentration in the industry, which in turn has brought higher prices and fewer choices for passengers. Unlike Mineta, his predecessor as Aviation chairman, Oberstar favors making the Federal Aviation Administration independent of the Transportation Department. Proponents say that would free the FAA of the department's political manipulation, but others fear that a free-standing FAA would have even less clout in battles against the administration and industry.

A political scientist and amateur linguist, Oberstar can theorize at length about the proper balance for public works policy. In fact, he talks a lot, whether intensively questioning witnesses or explaining a bill. He opened one hearing in early 1989 with a long reading from the prize-winning Thornton Wilder novel, "The Bridge of San Luis Rey." He occasionally beseeches the committee to "rise above" pork-barrel thinking and seek innovative ways to address problems.

On the other hand, Oberstar has not been known to turn down a new project for northern Minnesota. He spent years learning how to use Public Works to bring Duluth and the Iron Range a share of the pie, as an aide and protégé to John Blatnik, the Minnesota Democrat who chaired Public Works until 1974, when he retired and Oberstar won his seat.

As chairman of Public Works' Economic Development Subcommittee prior to 1985, Oberstar was in a key position to help bring federal money to depressed areas like the Iron Range. With ranking Republican William F. Clinger Jr. of Pennsylvania, he worked to preserve the Economic Development Administration (EDA) against President Reagan's repeated efforts to abolish it.

Oberstar's partisan instincts tend to flash when the issue is jobs. In 1982 he helped write a jobs bill that, with changes, became law the next year. "I just never cease to be amazed," he said in 1982, "by our colleagues on the other side of the aisle who refuse to do anything to help the unemployed but complain about those who try."

He was even more critical of fellow Democrats in 1985 when the House agreed to end a supplemental compensation program for the long-term unemployed. "We cannot let our party be Reaganized," he declared, adding that Democrats must make clear "we're not backing away" from employment issues.

Oberstar also has defended protectionist efforts to promote domestic employment by limiting imports. He cites his experience as a graduate student during the formation of the European Common Market, which, as Oberstar recalls, promoted economic development by protecting domestic markets.

Oberstar owes his Budget Committee assignment to a Public Works connection — former committee member Jim Wright. When Wright became Speaker in 1987, he appointed Oberstar to the Democratic Steering and Policy Committee, the leadership panel that makes committee assignments. Oberstar was among those who spoke up for Wright during the long ethics probe that eventually forced the Speaker to resign in June 1989.

Partisan wrangling on the Budget Committee also can bring out the scrapper in Oberstar. When a panel Republican quipped in 1987 that Democrats only ask the GOP along on a double date when they do not have enough money or gas themselves, Oberstar said that where he comes from, double-dating with Republicans is unthinkable. Later, when Republicans complained about the final product, he snapped, "At moments of courage, they voted 'present.' At other times, they voted 'no.' "

In 1990, Oberstar declined to join the rebellion against the budget summit agreement between President Bush and congressional leaders of both parties. The House rejected it, later accepting a final budget reconciliation package that modified the summit agreement.

Oberstar earlier had a voice in budget and tax debates as chairman of the liberal Democratic Study Group (DSG) in the 99th Congress. He was among those urging, unsuccessfully, that the budget include a tougher minimum tax on corporations. And when Ways and Means was drafting its landmark rewrite of the tax code, Oberstar and the DSG argued that revenues raised by closing loopholes should be used for deficit reduction, not more tax cuts. "We simply cannot afford to cut taxes at this time," Oberstar said.

A couple of issues provide the only exceptions to his traditional liberalism. He opposes gun control bills and abortion. Oberstar is also against the death penalty. When the House debated a capital punishment provision that became law as part of Congress' 1988 drug bill, Oberstar supported instead an unsuccessful substitute that would have required mandatory life imprisonment for drug-related killers.

During his six-year turn on the Budget Committee, Oberstar is on leave from the Merchant Marine Committee, where he retains his place among senior members.

At Home: After his grueling 1984 Senate campaign ended disappointingly in mid-summer, Oberstar had to go back to his district and fight hard just to retain his seat.

His Senate candidacy enjoyed the support of much of the state's organized-labor movement, but he could not match the strength of his major rival, Secretary of State Joan Growe; she was the favorite of the liberal party activists who dominated the Democratic endorsement process. She got the party endorsement on the 19th ballot at the state convention in June.

The two contenders actually had agreed two ballots earlier to end the marathon and settle the issue in a primary, but Growe's supporters refused to abide by the agreement and pushed her endorsement through two ballots later.

Oberstar could have continued the fight into a September primary anyway, but decided instead to switch races and run again for his House seat. That was a sensible decision. By the time the angry convention adjourned, it was becoming clear that no Democratic nominee would have much of a chance against the popular Republican incumbent, Rudy Boschwitz.

Oberstar's shift back to the 8th District was made possible by the willingness of the Democrats' endorsed candidate there, state Sen. Ron Dicklich, to step aside. But an old nemesis, former Duluth City Councilman Thomas E. Dougherty, was unwilling to withdraw so Oberstar could return.

Four years earlier, Dougherty had run an aggressive primary challenge that caught Oberstar off guard. Portraying the incumbent as inattentive to his Iron Range constituents and their declining economic status, Dougherty netted 44 percent of the vote. He hammered away on that basic theme in 1984, using as his slogan: "Our District Is His First Choice."

But Oberstar was well prepared for the 1984 rematch. He emphasized his work to promote the local iron industry through support of temporary quotas on steel and iron ore imports. He launched one of the most extensive voter identification programs ever seen in northeast Minnesota.

The result was a Democratic primary turnout about 25 percent higher than in 1980, with Oberstar winning by nearly 2-to-1. The general election was anticlimactic, with Oberstar overwhelming his GOP challenger.

Republicans have not cost Oberstar any sleep since he inherited the 8th in 1974 from Blatnik, his employer and predecessor. But fighting within the Democratic Party has made his life far from tranquil.

For years there was a feud between the Blatnik wing of the Democratic Party and the faction headed by the three Perpich brothers, whose leader, Rudy, was governor of Minnesota.

The battle between the two sides broke into the open in 1974, and flared up again in 1980. In 1974 Blatnik tried to anoint Oberstar as his successor, but the result was an acrimonious party-endorsing convention lasting 30 ballots. Eventually Blatnik and Oberstar lost, and the party's endorsement went to state Sen. A. J. "Tony" Perpich.

Blatnik then threw all his prestige and

political power behind Oberstar in the Democratic primary, and Oberstar won by more than 20,000 votes.

Six years later, Oberstar faced a second Perpich. This time it was Tony's younger brother, George. When Rudy was elected lieutenant governor in 1970, George took his seat in the state Senate and carried on the populist Perpich crusade against the mining companies.

At the 1980 nominating convention, George tried to keep the party endorsement out of the incumbent's hands, arguing for a neutral party stand in the second Oberstar-Perpich match-up. But Oberstar won the endorsement with just one-third of a vote more than the 60 percent needed.

Perpich decided not to force a primary, but Dougherty did. Concentrating his campaign in the northern part of the district where unemployment was high, Dougherty picked up votes from Perpich supporters bent on protest. Oberstar was saved by his backing at the southern end of the district, in the Twin Cities media area.

Committees

Budget (3rd of 23 Democrats)
Human Resources (chairman); Urgent Fiscal Issues

Public Works & Transportation (4th of 36 Democrats)
Aviation (chairman); Economic Development; Investigations & Oversight; Public Buildings & Grounds; Water Resources

Elections

1990 General		
James L. Oberstar (D)	151,145	(73%)
Jerry Shuster (R)	56,068	(27%)
1988 General		
James L. Oberstar (D)	165,656	(75%)
Jerry Shuster (R)	56,630	(25%)

Previous Winning Percentages: **1986** (73%) **1984** (67%) **1982** (77%) **1980** (70%) **1978** (87%) **1976** (100%) **1974** (62%)

District Vote For President

	1988	1984	1980	1976
D	144,668 (60%)	149,807 (59%)	171,636 (54%)	185,726 (63%)
R	92,876 (39%)	100,520 (40%)	117,437 (37%)	101,000 (34%)
I			21,003 (7%)	

Campaign Finance

	Receipts	Receipts from PACs	Expend-itures
1990			
Oberstar (D)	$364,577	$248,780 (68%)	$229,262
Shuster (R)	$16,696	0	$16,681
1988			
Oberstar (D)	$281,331	$206,320 (73%)	$157,802
Shuster (R)	$7,744	0	$7,743

Key Votes

1991	
Authorize use of force against Iraq	N
1990	
Support constitutional amendment on flag desecration	N
Pass family and medical leave bill over Bush veto	Y
Reduce SDI funding	Y
Allow abortions in overseas military facilities	N
Approve budget summit plan for spending and taxing	Y
Approve civil rights bill	Y
1989	
Halt production of B-2 stealth bomber at 13 planes	Y
Oppose capital gains tax cut	Y
Approve federal abortion funding in rape or incest cases	N
Approve pay raise and revision of ethics rules	Y
Pass Democratic minimum wage plan over Bush veto	Y

Voting Studies

	Presidential Support		Party Unity		Conservative Coalition	
Year	S	O	S	O	S	O
1990	17	82	92	4	13	83
1989	35	64	88	10	10	90
1988	21	77	93	6	8	92
1987	12	87	93	3	5	95
1986	18	79	92	4	18	82
1985	16	84	91	3	7	93
1984	19	71	88	4	5	83
1983	12	84	90	6	9	89
1982	34	65	95	4	10	89
1981	33	67	89	8	16	81

Interest Group Ratings

Year	ADA	ACU	AFL-CIO	CCUS
1990	78	0	100	15
1989	95	4	83	30
1988	90	12	100	21
1987	96	4	94	7
1986	85	5	93	6
1985	95	5	100	18
1984	80	4	89	33
1983	90	9	94	15
1982	100	9	100	14
1981	85	7	87	5

Mississippi

U.S. CONGRESS

SENATE 2 R
HOUSE 4 D, 1 R

LEGISLATURE

Senate 43 D, 9 R
House 104 D, 18 R

ELECTIONS

1988 Presidential Vote

Bush	60%
Dukakis	39%

1984 Presidential Vote

Reagan	62%
Mondale	37%

1980 Presidential Vote

Reagan	49%
Carter	48%
Anderson	1%

Turnout rate in 1986	29%
Turnout rate in 1988	50%
Turnout rate in 1990	20%

(as percentage of voting age population)

POPULATION AND GROWTH

1980 population	2,520,638
1990 population (31st in the nation)	2,573,216
Percent change 1980-1990	+2%

DEMOGRAPHIC BREAKDOWN

White	64%
Black	36%
Asian or Pacific Islander	1%
(Hispanic origin)	1%
Urban	47%
Rural	53%
Born in state	79%
Foreign-born	1%

MAJOR CITIES

Jackson	196,637
Biloxi	46,319
Greenville	45,226
Hattiesburg	41,882
Meridian	41,036

AREA AND LAND USE

Area	47,233 sq. miles (31st)
Farm	41%
Forest	55%
Federally owned	6%

Gov. Ray Mabus (D)
Of Choctaw County — Elected 1987

Born: Oct. 11, 1948, Choctaw County, Miss.
Education: U. of Mississippi, B.A. 1969; Johns Hopkins U., M.A. 1970; Harvard U., J.D. 1976.
Military Service: Navy, 1970-73.
Occupation: Lawyer; tree farmer.
Religion: Methodist.
Political Career: Miss. auditor, 1984-88.
Next Election: 1991.

WORK

Occupations

White-collar	45%
Blue-collar	38%
Service workers	12%

Government Workers

Federal	24,022
State	51,894
Local	115,821

MONEY

Median family income	$ 14,591	(50th)
Tax burden per capita	$ 693	(45th)

EDUCATION

Spending per pupil through grade 12	$ 2,548	(49th)
Persons with college degrees	12%	(46th)

CRIME

Violent crime rate	311 per 100,000 (35th)

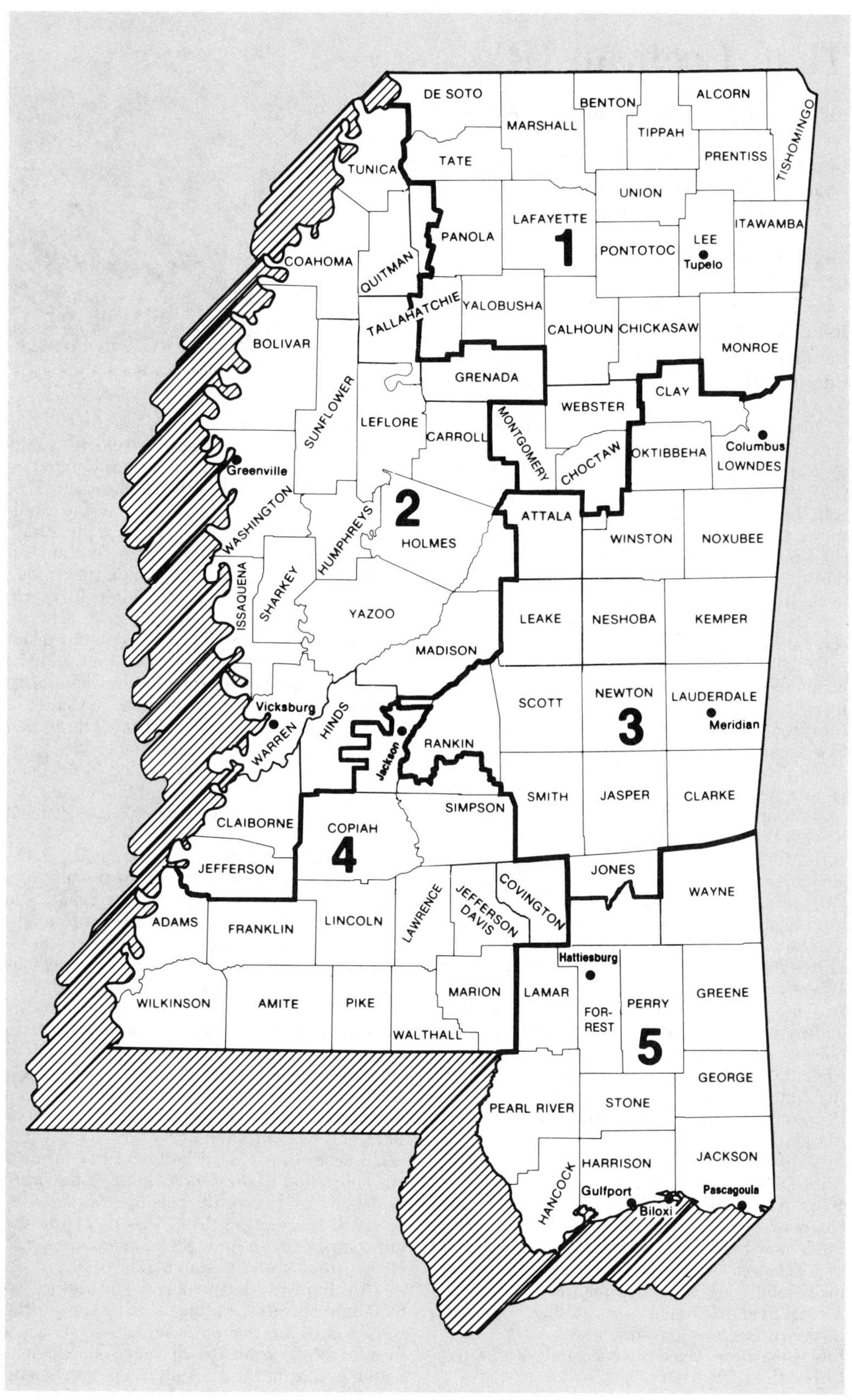

DE SOTO
MARSHALL
BENTON
TIPPAH
ALCORN
PRENTISS
TISHOMINGO
TUNICA
TATE
UNION
PANOLA
LAFAYETTE
1
PONTOTOC
LEE
Tupelo
ITAWAMBA
COAHOMA
QUITMAN
TALLAHATCHIE
YALOBUSHA
CALHOUN
CHICKASAW
MONROE
BOLIVAR
GRENADA
CLAY
WEBSTER
SUNFLOWER
LEFLORE
CARROLL
MONTGOMERY
CHOCTAW
OKTIBBEHA
Columbus
LOWNDES
Greenville
WASHINGTON
HUMPHREYS
2
HOLMES
ATTALA
WINSTON
NOXUBEE
ISSAQUENA
SHARKEY
YAZOO
LEAKE
NESHOBA
KEMPER
MADISON
SCOTT
NEWTON
LAUDERDALE
3
Meridian
Vicksburg
WARREN
HINDS
Jackson
RANKIN
SMITH
JASPER
CLARKE
SIMPSON
CLAIBORNE
COPIAH
4
JEFFERSON
JONES
COVINGTON
WAYNE
ADAMS
FRANKLIN
LINCOLN
LAWRENCE
JEFFERSON DAVIS
Hattiesburg
WILKINSON
AMITE
PIKE
MARION
WALTHALL
LAMAR
FOR-REST
PERRY
GREENE
5
GEORGE
PEARL RIVER
STONE
HARRISON
JACKSON
HANCOCK
Gulfport
Biloxi
Pascagoula

Thad Cochran (R)

Of Jackson — Elected 1978

Born: Dec. 7, 1937, Pontotoc, Miss.
Education: U. of Mississippi, B.A. 1959, J.D. 1965; Attended Trinity College (U. of Dublin, Ireland), 1963-64.
Military Service: Navy, 1959-61.
Occupation: Lawyer.
Family: Wife, Rose Clayton; two children.
Religion: Baptist.
Political Career: U.S. House, 1973-78.
Capitol Office: 326 Russell Bldg. 20510; 224-5054.

In Washington: It is no longer surprising that a Republican should serve as a U.S. senator from Mississippi. Although the state had no GOP senators for a century, it now has two. Still, heads were turned in 1990 when Cochran won a third term without so much as a token challenger — even though Democrats held the top state offices and all five of the state's seats in the House at the time.

Cochran comes close to defining the modern paradigm of a statewide political success. Although a relative moderate in a state GOP dominated by conservatives, he has established himself or made peace with every important constituency in Mississippi. That kind of home base security usually leads to power and influence in the Senate — and beyond — even if it takes a few terms for it to happen.

Cochran's Senate career did, in fact, start slowly. When he arrived in 1979 he had to outlast the impression that his presence amounted to an electoral fluke. But when the GOP seized Senate control in 1981, Cochran was ideally situated to take advantage.

Because he had preceded the bumper crop of Republicans elected with Ronald Reagan in 1980, Cochran was elevated to real status while still in his freshman term. He moved from the Judiciary Committee to Appropriations and quickly advanced to the chairmanship of its Agriculture Subcommittee. Meanwhile, on the Agriculture Committee, he moved up to chair the Subcommittee on Domestic and Foreign Marketing.

His career bogged down again, however, when Democrats restored their majority in the 100th Congress and Cochran forfeited the chairs of the two farm-related subcommittees (he is now ranking member on each panel).

Yet even now, with the Democrats seemingly solidifying their dominance, Cochran is not eclipsed. He remains a leading voice for Southern interests on farm issues, and a vital bridge between conservatives and moderates within the GOP itself.

And if Republicans regain control of the Senate in the 1990s, Cochran could reach the chairmanship of the Appropriations Committee before he is 60. The three Republicans ahead of him on Appropriations are all reasonable candidates for retirement after their current term.

Alternatively, Cochran could find himself chairman of the Agriculture Committee (where he also ranks fourth), a candidate for party leader or part of a national ticket.

Cochran has already risen to the third slot in the Senate GOP hierarchy; he won the chairmanship of the Senate Republican Conference, beating moderate incumbent John H. Chafee of Rhode Island in November 1990. Cochran had been the conference's secretary since 1984, winning re-election without opposition in 1986 and 1988. Beginning in the spring of 1990 he campaigned for Chafee's job and eventually claimed it by a single vote (22-21).

Since gaining the conference chair, Cochran has tried to make good on his promise of a sharper profile for his party in the Senate. He has pressed for blocks of floor time for Republicans to present coordinated policy speeches — rather like the "special orders" of rebellious junior Republicans on the House side.

Cochran himself is not immune to the partisan impulse. When U.S.-led military forces drove Iraqi invaders out of Kuwait, Cochran noted that "most of the Democrats in Congress voted to the left of the United Nations — that's something the voters are going to have to consider and will consider."

Cochran rarely can be found in conspicuous opposition to the White House or the party leadership and sometimes helps lead the conservative bloc on the floor — as he did on the bill that sought to limit private employers' use of polygraph tests in March 1988.

Cochran regularly opposes such efforts to dictate to business, and he usually votes for the conservative position on social issues. He took a forward position on the proposed amendment banning flag burning. And when the Senate passed civil rights legislation in 1990, Cochran voted against the bill and against an unsuccessful effort to override the veto of President Bush. In the 100th Congress he fought for confirmation of Robert H. Bork's ill-fated appointment to the Supreme Court.

But he has avoided strong identification with the conservatives — "I vote on the social issues because I have to," he once said — and he has been a supporter of funding for food stamps, rural housing and traditionally black colleges. In 1989, he supported continued federal funding for the Martin Luther King Jr. Federal Holiday Commission. (His Republican colleague in the Senate, Trent Lott, opposed the money.)

That said, Cochran is no liberal. His conservative inclinations came out most clearly on issues before the Judiciary Committee, where he served during his first two years in the Senate. As soft-spoken as he usually is, he becomes livid at the mention of language in the Voting Rights Act requiring Southern states to get Justice Department approval before making any changes in their election procedures.

"Local officials have to go to Washington, get on their knees, kiss the ring and tug their forelock to all these third-rate bureaucrats," Cochran once complained. He argues that Mississippi officials are now sensitive to the concerns of black voters. But his effort to make all states comply with the same requirements was rejected by the Senate, 16-74.

Cochran has played an important behind-the-scenes role in mediating splits within the Agriculture Committee, which is torn by conflicts among commodity interests. He works well with Richard G. Lugar of Indiana, the panel's ranking Republican, and is acknowledged as the GOP leader on Southern agricultural interests. His reasoned, gentlemanly style (he has been called "the Southern Lugar") is well suited to settling disagreements rather than inflaming them.

When the 1990 farm bill was in its final birthing phase, Cochran's knowledge of the issue and sense of timing helped strike the key deal on a new loan program for soybean producers. He generally enjoys high credibility among committee Democrats, in part because he is more supportive of the programs being authorized than many of his GOP brethren, including Lugar. That was why some among the majority were surprised when Cochran sided with Lugar on the crucial issue of subsidy levels in the 1990 bill.

Precocious in authority, Cochran was already writing key sections of major farm bills in the early 1980s. His influence was even more significant during work on the 1985 farm bill. Allied with then-Majority Leader Bob Dole, he worked to develop an overall GOP stance on farm issues out of competing regional interests.

Cochran hardly overlooked the interests of Mississippi and other Southern farmers, though, especially those raising cotton or rice. Making full use of the key tactical position they had during action on the farm bill, Cochran and a few others from the region pushed through a radically new and potentially expensive form of price support for growers of the two crops.

At Home: Each time Cochran has run for the Senate, he has made history. In 1978, he became the first Republican to win a Mississippi Senate seat in a century. Six years later, he became the first GOP candidate for any major statewide office to capture a majority of the vote since Reconstruction. In 1990, he became the first statewide Republican to go without Democratic opposition this century.

The lack of Democratic enthusiasm for challenging Cochran was understandable, considering his last outing in 1984. Facing Democrat William F. Winter, the state's popular governor from 1980-84, Cochran won by a decisive 61-39 percent.

Little had happened in the interim to encourage Democrats to believe they could beat Cochran in 1990. And by the beginning of the election year he had more than $865,000 on hand.

Cochran has always shown a considerable talent for making friends across the political spectrum. Despite his conservative House voting record, Cochran drew significant support in most of his House campaigns from blacks, who made up more than 40 percent of his 4th District. After a close first election in 1972, when the presence of a black independent allowed him a narrow victory, he drew over 70 percent of the total vote in both his 1974 and 1976 House campaigns.

In 1976 the Mississippi GOP was beset by an internal struggle between supporters of Gerald R. Ford and Ronald Reagan for the presidential nomination. Cochran sided with Ford at the national convention in Kansas City, and the delegation voted 30-0 for Ford's position in the critical rules fight that played a large role in ending Reagan's chances. Although there was considerable anger within the delegation at the time, Cochran suffered no lasting damage.

His election to the Senate in 1978 was made possible in part by another independent black campaign siphoning off votes from the Democratic nominee, ex-Columbia Mayor Maurice Dantin. Democrat James O. Eastland retired in 1978 after 36 years in the Senate and endorsed Dantin to succeed him. But a flamboyant campaign by Fayette Mayor Charles Evers, a veteran black activist, drew more attention than Cochran and Dantin combined.

In a state where Democrats must have the black vote, Evers virtually guaranteed GOP success. Drawing 45 percent statewide, Cochran finished nearly 80,000 votes ahead of Dantin.

Many Democrats regarded Cochran's election as a fluke, but he proved his vote-getting ability in 1984 against Winter. A veteran of more than three decades in state politics, Winter left the governor's chair in early 1984 as a well-respected chief executive. His administration, limited to four years by the state's one-term-and-out law, was highlighted by passage of a landmark education bill designed to improve the quality of public schools and make Mississippi attractive to new industry.

But Winter dissipated much of the good will when he accepted, then rejected, the University of Mississippi chancellorship in late 1983. By taking more than six weeks after that to decide whether to challenge Cochran, he reinforced an image of indecisiveness. Winter sought to make up ground with an increasingly aggressive campaign. He criticized Cochran as a likable but ineffective "backbencher" whose Senate approach was to "go along to get along."

But with a smooth-running, well-financed operation, Cochran gave Winter few openings. He dominated the airwaves, dismissing Winter's candidacy as Washington-inspired and stressing his own seniority and growing stature in the Senate. Cochran emphasized that he was 15 years younger than Winter and already held two chairmanships of importance to Mississippi, including that of the Appropriations Subcommittee on Agriculture. Cochran swept all but a handful of Mississippi's 82 counties, including nearly half of those with majority-black populations.

Cochran often takes a strong interest in other GOP candidates in Mississippi, but in 1988 he did not conspicuously work to defeat freshman Rep. Mike Espy, the state's first black congressman in a century. That may have just been the result of Cochran's respect for Espy's incumbency, but by not alienating black voters in the Delta district, Cochran successfully laid the groundwork for his unanimous victory in 1990.

Committees

Agriculture, Nutrition & Forestry (4th of 8 Republicans)
Domestic & Foreign Marketing & Product Promotion (ranking); Rural Development & Rural Electrification (ranking); Agricultural Production & Stabilization of Prices

Appropriations (4th of 13 Republicans)
Agriculture, Rural Development & Related Agencies (ranking); Defense; Energy & Water Development; Interior; Labor, Health & Human Services, Education

Select Indian Affairs (3rd of 7 Republicans)

Labor & Human Resources (7th of 7 Republicans)
Aging (ranking); Education, Arts & Humanities; Labor

Elections

1990 General

Thad Cochran (R)	274,244	(100%)

Previous Winning Percentages: **1984** (61%) **1978** (45%) **1976 *** (76%) **1974 *** (70%) **1972 *** (48%)

** House elections.*

Campaign Finance

	Receipts	Receipts from PACs	Expend-itures
1990			
Cochran (R)	$1,316,810	$534,450 (41%)	$567,446

Key Votes

1991

Authorize use of force against Iraq	Y
1990	
Oppose prohibition of certain semiautomatic weapons	Y
Support constitutional amendment on flag desecration	Y
Oppose requiring parental notice for minors' abortions	N
Halt production of B-2 stealth bomber at 13 planes	N
Approve budget that cut spending and raised revenues	Y
Pass civil rights bill over Bush veto	N
1989	
Oppose reduction of SDI funding	Y
Oppose barring federal funds for "obscene" art	N
Allow vote on capital gains tax cut	Y

Voting Studies

	Presidential Support		Party Unity		Conservative Coalition	
Year	**S**	**O**	**S**	**O**	**S**	**O**
1990	85	15	83	15	100	0
1989	94	6	85	14	97	0
1988	70	22	66	22	97	0
1987	68	26	78	19	97	3
1986	88	10	88	10	91	4
1985	80	14	81	14	87	5
1984	87	8	93	5	96	2
1983	71	22	69	28	77	16
1982	77	20	88	9	85	3
1981	82	9	87	11	88	7

Interest Group Ratings

Year	ADA	ACU	AFL-CIO	CCUS
1990	0	87	33	83
1989	0	78	10	75
1988	5	96	15	100
1987	20	68	40	78
1986	5	78	0	89
1985	5	74	15	81
1984	10	82	9	74
1983	20	48	18	74
1982	10	72	16	63
1981	10	53	16	94

Trent Lott (R)

Of Pascagoula — Elected 1988

Born: Oct. 9, 1941, Grenada County, Miss.
Education: U. of Mississippi, B.P.A. 1963, J.D. 1967.
Occupation: Lawyer.
Family: Wife, Patricia Elizabeth Thompson; two children.
Religion: Baptist.
Political Career: U.S. House, 1973-89.
Capitol Office: 487 Russell Bldg. 20510; 224-6253.

In Washington: When Lott moved over to the Senate in 1989, he gave up the power he had accrued as a member of the House Republican leadership, but he gained freedom to do more of what he seems to enjoy most — conservative rabble-rousing.

In the House, Lott's heart was clearly with the younger-generation conservative Republicans eager for a more confrontational stance toward the Democratic majority. But as minority whip, he was obliged to placate the more pragmatic, "Old Bull" establishment Republicans. Now unencumbered by this obligation, Lott seems liberated.

In the Senate, Lott's rhetoric can be so ideological as to place him at odds not only with Democrats but also some in his own party. He seems to want a leadership role in the Senate, but on his own terms. While his path to a formal post is blocked by fellow Mississippian Thad Cochran, who was elected GOP Conference chairman for the 102nd Congress, Lott is a key player in an informal coalition that helped Cochran and other conservatives work their way into key leadership and committee posts.

Perhaps in an effort to give Lott a more "insider" role, Minority Leader Bob Dole appointed him to the Budget Committee in 1991, and named him chairman of the panel that makes GOP committee assignments. Two years earlier, Dole put Lott on the Ethics Committee.

While these roles afford Lott the chance to influence Senate proceedings in ways beyond throwing stones, he seems keen on establishing himself as an independent-minded conservative. While congressional leaders (including Dole) and the White House labored to produce a budget-summit agreement in 1990, Lott warned, "I am not going to vote for just any package that comes out of these negotiations, especially if 50 percent of it comes out of tax increases and where the priorities are clearly not in the proper order."

Shortly before the budget summit deal went down to defeat in the House, Lott said that if the White House expected easy approval of spending cuts and tax increases, "They're smoking something."

As during his House career — when he abandoned President Ronald Reagan on his top legislative priority in 1985, the tax overhaul — Lott has not shied from criticizing President Bush when he feels the administration is insufficiently conservative. Lott voted to sustain most of Bush's vetoes in the 101st Congress, but made it plain that loyalty to the White House line sometimes pained him. "On FS-X, I thought he was wrong; on China students, I thought he was wrong; then comes the Hatch Act," Lott said of his votes to sustain presidential vetoes of bills he had earlier supported. "I don't want to embarrass [Bush], but there's a limit to where you'll bite that bullet."

Lott's sharp rhetoric, however, is most often aimed at liberals. In late 1990, he used the legal definition of treason to warn Democrats to stick with the president in the Persian Gulf crisis. "If we start allowing this to be a backing away from [administration] policy," he said, "it could be giving aid and comfort to [Iraqi President] Saddam Hussein." Discussing the suit filed by some Democrats to block offensive military action unless Congress had given prior approval, Lott said, "It's typical that would come from the loony left."

Many Democrats feared that Lott would use the Ethics Committee as a partisan grandstand during the investigation of five senators — four of them Democrats — associated with savings and loan tycoon Charles H. Keating Jr. Lott was said to be most closely allied with North Carolina Republican Jesse Helms, an Ethics panelist who backed tough sanctions on three of the senators involved (all Democrats).

But if Lott had any notion that the Keating affair could besmirch the Democratic Party, the slow pace of the investigation instead caused him to worry that the affair was damaging the reputation of the entire Senate. He complained that the questioning of witnesses had led to gratuitous assaults on the legislators and the whole notion of what constitutes constituent service. He was furious with the panel's slow progress. "I feel like I've been an accomplice to a crime," he said.

As the panel labored over the minutiae of the report language, Lott reportedly attempted to detonate the committee into action by stalking out or threatening to do so. In the end, the Ethics panel unanimously decided to scold four of the senators and further investigate the fifth. Lott said he opposed further action against the four because it would have amounted to "setting the standards after the fact."

Lott came out of the proceedings concerned about the "appearance standard" the case seemed to set. "You've got to be prepared to tell a constituent, 'If you contribute, you've got to understand, I might not be able to help you,' " he said.

Lott's concern about an overly rigid "appearance standard" could stem from the fact there there is a bit of the old pol in this young Turk. Lott airs roughly four television spots a year promoting his activities in the Senate. The advertisements are paid for from his campaign coffers, but they are produced without any media consultant's help in the taxpayer-financed Senate TV studio — a practice approved by the Ethics Committee.

In 1989, Lott took advantage of an accounting quirk that allowed him to keep almost $3,000 more in honoraria than other senators. The amount of honoraria senators may keep is based on a percentage of their congressional income. Because Lott did not receive his last House pay check until after he joined the Senate in January 1989, he ended up with a higher congressional salary.

In the House, Lott was a key GOP strategist both on the Rules Committee and as minority whip. In 1981, he became the first Deep South Republican to take the No. 2 GOP position, doing so more on the strength of his personal skills than his legislative achievements. The close contest with Pennsylvania Rep. Bud Shuster went Lott's way partly because he had made many friends and few enemies. Through his tenure as whip, the list of enemies no doubt grew, particularly among Democrats, but so did his political savvy.

Throughout the Reagan years, Lott had a tough balancing act to perform. With a president of his own party trying to set the agenda for a Democratic House, Lott had to win over Democrats while attempting to keep his own unruly troops in line. Neither job was easy.

In his first year as whip, Lott was working in a favorable climate. Reagan's big victory in 1980 made it easier to sell Reaganomics to a Democratic House. Carefully cultivating Southern Democratic members in the early months of 1981, Lott helped usher through much of Reagan's fiscal agenda.

As the number of Republican House members declined in the 1980s, Lott kept up his personal ties to moderate and conservative Democrats, and on defense issues in particular he had some success. But Lott's work got much tougher in Reagan's final years in office. Many House Republicans began distancing themselves from unpopular White House policies. Democrats who had been on the defensive in 1981 by 1987 did not need a single GOP vote to pass a budget resolution.

In Lott's last years on Rules, the Democratic leadership made increasingly effective use of the committee to limit debate on numerous measures, frustrating Lott and the GOP, outnumbered more than 2-to-1 on the panel. "The Democratic leadership is trying to turn the Rules Committee into the stranglehold on this institution that it was 30 years ago," he said in 1987.

Given the difficulty of playing a constructive role on the committee, Lott spent considerable energy looking for ways to use procedure to frustrate the Democrats. His main function was to try out partisan arguments in committee for presentation later on the House floor.

At the beginning of his House career, on Judiciary, he took part in the historic impeachment proceedings of 1973 and 1974. Lott was a staunch defender of President Richard M. Nixon, which was not a liability for him back home. Nixon was still well liked by many Gulf Coast conservatives when his political support was eroding elsewhere in the country.

At Home: The 1988 presidential election created a favorable atmosphere for Lott to wage a Senate campaign, but he also rose to the occasion. Mississippi, though conservative, is traditional Democratic territory that regularly elected Lott's predecessor, Democratic Sen. John C. Stennis, beginning in 1947. It took a strong campaign for Lott to overcome a skilled opponent, Rep. Wayne Dowdy, with a solid 54 percent of the vote.

While Dowdy depleted his financial resources to win a tough primary, Lott was free to focus on the fall election. He took the offensive with an early media blitz Dowdy could not afford to answer for much of the summer. Lott, long identified as a strong supporter of Reagan's policies, used the airwaves to stress issues that often had been turned against Republicans in the 1980s. To Democrats' dismay, he positioned himself as a champion of Social Security, student loans and public works.

To appeal to rural and blue-collar conservatives often sympathetic to Democrats, Lott stressed his background. Though he has the polished appearance of a blue-suit conservatives, Lott reminded voters that his father farmed cotton and drove a school bus. He said Dowdy, whose rumpled appearance and folksy manner belied his family's wealth, was a "millionaire, country-club type."

Dowdy faulted Lott for election-year conversions on issues, and insisted the Republican was out of step with Mississippi. His late-starting ad campaign included a spot criticizing

Lott for having a $50,000 per-year "chauffeur," George Awkward. But Lott blasted the ad, which featured a limousine cruising through the countryside, saying that Awkward was a member of the Capitol security force, funded by a bill Dowdy supported. He added that Awkward showed up for work more often than Dowdy, whose House attendance dropped dramatically during the campaign year.

By summer's end, the sophistication of Lott's effort was apparent, and Democrats were complaining that Dowdy, though a good stump candidate, had an inadequate organization. Michael S. Dukakis' almost non-existent campaign in the state did not boost party spirits.

But Democrats held out hope that Dowdy's strength might not be apparent until Election Day. Part of that optimism stemmed from his apparent appeal in the black community, which accounts for more than a third of Mississippi's population. While Dowdy was first elected as a champion of the Voting Rights Act, Lott had cast several votes that alienated black leaders, including those against renewal of that act and against the Martin Luther King Jr. holiday.

But Lott came through on Election Day. In addition to his strong showing among whites, he got a surprising 13 percent of the black vote, according to CBS News-*New York Times* exit polls. Dowdy won three of the state's five House districts, but even in his home territory his margin was narrow. Lott, meanwhile, got a giant boost from his Gulf Coast district.

Lott suffered a public relations black eye in 1989 when he helped steer the GOP nomination in a special House election to a longtime aide rather than the widow of GOP Rep. Larkin Smith, whose death in a plane crash necessitated the new election. The treatment of Smith's widow was considered by many as brusque and heavy-handed; Republicans lost the seat Lott had won and held since 1973.

Lott did not become a Republican until the eve of that first House campaign in 1972. As Democratic Rep. William M. Colmer's administrative assistant, he had remained a nominal Democrat. But when the venerable Rules chairman decided to retire in 1972 at age 82, Lott filed in the GOP primary, saying he was "tired of the Muskies and the Kennedys and the Humphreys and the whole lot.... I will fight against the ever-increasing efforts of the so-called liberals to concentrate more power in the government in Washington."

The wisdom of Lott's switch was soon confirmed. Running that fall against Democrat Ben Stone, chairman of the state Senate Banking Committee, Lott stayed on the offensive by linking Stone with the national Democratic Party. Aided by the Nixon landslide and an endorsement from Colmer, Lott carried all but two of the district's 12 counties.

Committees

Armed Services (6th of 9 Republicans)
Readiness, Sustainability & Support (ranking); Projection Forces & Regional Defense; Strategic Forces & Nuclear Deterrence

Budget (8th of 9 Republicans)

Commerce, Science & Transportation (9th of 9 Republicans)
Merchant Marine (ranking); Science, Technology & Space; Surface Transportation; National Ocean Policy Study

Select Ethics (2nd of 3 Republicans)

Elections

1988 General

Trent Lott (R)	510,380	(54%)
Wayne Dowdy (D)	436,339	(46%)

Previous Winning Percentages: **1986 *** (82%) **1984 *** (85%) **1982 *** (79%) **1980 *** (74%) **1978 *** (100%) **1976 *** (68%) **1974 *** (73%) **1972 *** (55%)

* *House elections.*

Voting Studies

Year	Presidential Support S	Presidential Support O	Party Unity S	Party Unity O	Conservative Coalition S	Conservative Coalition O
1990	76	24	82	16	97	0
1989	82	16	92	6	95	3
House Service						
1988	51	33	59	13	84	0
1987	63	24	83	8	88	5
1986	78	18	79	14	84	4
1985	73	24	82	9	89	5
1984	73	25	86	8	97	2
1983	73	22	86	7	97	1
1982	75	17	78	19	88	11
1981	84	16	90	6	95	3

Key Votes

1991	
Authorize use of force against Iraq	Y
1990	
Oppose prohibition of certain semiautomatic weapons	Y
Support constitutional amendment on flag desecration	Y
Oppose requiring parental notice for minors' abortions	N
Halt production of B-2 stealth bomber at 13 planes	N
Approve budget that cut spending and raised revenues	N
Pass civil rights bill over Bush veto	N
1989	
Oppose reduction of SDI funding	Y
Oppose barring federal funds for "obscene" art	N
Allow vote on capital gains tax cut	Y

Interest Group Ratings

Year	ADA	ACU	AFL-CIO	CCUS
1990	0	91	22	100
1989	5	96	20	88
House Service				
1988	5	95	33	82
1987	4	91	19	77
1986	5	95	23	86
1985	0	90	12	95
1984	0	96	8	80
1983	0	100	6	85
1982	5	85	5	70
1981	0	93	7	95

Campaign Finance

	Receipts	Receipts from PACs	Expenditures
1988			
Lott (R)	$3,602,481	$1,118,111 (31%)	$3,405,242
Dowdy (D)	$2,195,960	$962,719 (44%)	$2,355,957

1 Jamie L. Whitten (D)

Of Charleston — Elected 1941

Born: April 18, 1910, Cascilla, Miss.
Education: Attended U. of Mississippi, 1927-32.
Occupation: Grammar school teacher and principal; lawyer; author.
Family: Wife, Rebecca Thompson; two children.
Religion: Presbyterian.
Political Career: Miss. House, 1931-33; district attorney, 17th District, 1933-41.
Capitol Office: 2314 Rayburn Bldg. 20515; 225-4306.

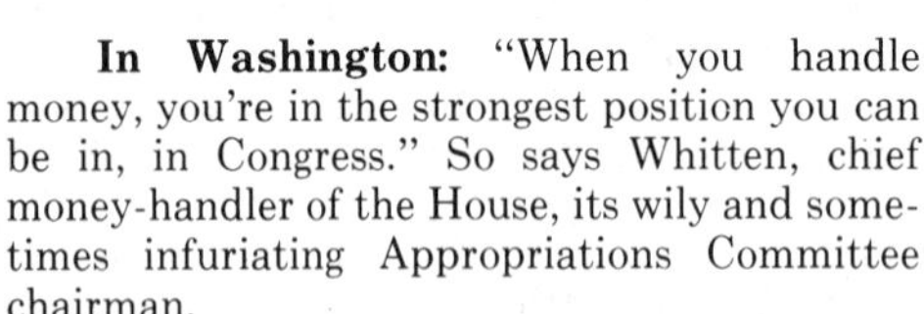

In Washington: "When you handle money, you're in the strongest position you can be in, in Congress." So says Whitten, chief money-handler of the House, its wily and sometimes infuriating Appropriations Committee chairman.

After more than a decade in the chair, Whitten has a firm grip on the seat that has signified power on Capitol Hill for a century. He is pope to what is irreverently known as the College of Cardinals — Appropriations' 13 subcommittee chairmen. And he is a cardinal himself, having led the Agriculture panel for four decades.

A one-time grammar school principal and county prosecutor, Whitten claims, "I came to Congress by accident; my ambition was to practice law." But after winning a special election the month before Pearl Harbor, he has stayed to become the dean of the House. In that role, Whitten takes pride in having sworn in the Speaker in the last eight Congresses.

Most observers figure Whitten may well be around for some time to come; if he is, all sorts of tenure records will fall. In November 1991, Whitten would hit his 50th anniversary in Congress, and two months later he would break the record for continuous service set by Carl Vinson, D-Ga. (1914-65). In August 1993, he would break the record for continuous chairmanship of Appropriations set by his predecessor George Mahon, D-Texas (1935-79).

And as long as Whitten is around, so is the spirit of the New Deal. A Depression survivor, he is a true believer in government's pump-priming potential. A shrewd trader in appropriations pork, Whitten sees his role in grander terms than that, in keeping with his theme that the nation's wealth is measured not in money but in its physical assets. He gives that lecture often, stupefying committee colleagues and exasperating senators and administration officials who may have provoked it by challenging him on some spending item.

As the deficit has tightened his spending in recent years, Whitten has added a new mantra: "Since 1945, the total of appropriations bills has been $180.8 billion below the total requested by various presidents." In his heavy Hill Country accent, Whitten made the point in 29 floor speeches during the 101st Congress, sometimes repeating it two or three times in a single speech and once at 2:45 in the morning.

Whitten is indeed a power, if not the omnipotent force of some of his predecessors. He is the last of a breed — the conservative Southern Democrats who once ruled the Hill — and like the others who survived, he had to adjust. At the committee, the cardinals have become virtually independent in their spheres.

In the House, Whitten is a vassal to Democratic leaders, and answerable to junior activists who have been empowered in the last decade to depose chairmen they deem unfit (two were deposed in late 1990).

But while the authority of the chairmanship has been checked, other forces have enhanced Appropriations' collective power. After watching helplessly as the Budget Committee set increasingly restrictive caps on discretionary spending, the tables turned in 1990. To get Whitten and his Senate counterpart, Robert C. Byrd, to sign off on the budget deal, domestic spending was allowed to rise with inflation and given an added $20 billion in budget authority. In exchange, Whitten and Byrd agreed to let the White House determine whether supplemental spending bills qualify as emergency measures exempt from spending cuts.

Since 1988, when Congress passed all 13 spending bills for the first time in a dozen years, the supplementals have superseded the omnibus "continuing resolutions" as powerful vessels for pork. Like the CRs, which were passed to keep the government in business when the regular appropriations ran out, the supplementals were usually considered on an emergency basis, receiving relatively little scrutiny and all but certain presidential approval. Within their pages, appropriators tuck a variety of items that might not pass muster on their own.

Whitten once said, according to House lore, "I've never seen a disaster that wasn't an

Mississippi 1

North — Clarksdale

Whitten's domain for nearly 50 years, the 1st District stretches from the Mississippi River east to the Alabama line, running along the northern border of the state. Not too long ago, this was the state's most reliably Democratic district. Jimmy Carter won 60 percent here in 1976, his best showing in any Mississippi district. Four years later, when he lost statewide, Carter won the area within the 1st with 55 percent.

But there is a limit to the party loyalty of the district's "yellow dog" Democrats. Presidential nominees Walter F. Mondale and Michael S. Dukakis both drew less than 40 percent of the district's vote.

Overwhelmingly rural, the 1st takes in the flat, rich farmland on the edge of the Delta region in northwestern Mississippi and the less fertile plots of the northeastern Hill Country. Although cotton was once the dominant crop in this region, 1st District farmers now also produce soybeans, rice, corn, wheat, livestock and poultry.

The one population center — Tupelo, in Lee County — is an industrial town also famous as the birthplace of Elvis Presley. About 50 miles to the west in Lafayette County is Oxford, the district's cultural center. It was the home base for William Faulkner, and is the site of the University of Mississippi (9,000 students), more popularly known as "Ole Miss."

The district's population grew by nearly 14 percent in the 1970s, before slowing to about five percent in the 1980s, with the largest boom occurring in the Memphis, Tenn., suburbs in De Soto County. De Soto's population — which swelled 50 percent in the 1970s, and another 18 percent in the first half of the 1980s — has also grown whiter. The county's white population grew by 33 percent in the 1980s, while its black population decreased by 10 percent.

As it has grown, De Soto County's politics have been leaning more toward the GOP in races for federal offices. Since 1976, the county has gone with GOP presidential candidates. Republican Trent Lott carried De Soto easily in his successful 1988 Senate race, and it was the only county carried by veteran Democratic Rep. Jamie L. Whitten's Republican challenger in 1990.

There have also been population gains in the eastern and central portions of the district, where the arrival of new industry and construction of the Tennessee-Tombigbee Waterway provided new jobs.

Population: 504,136. White 378,536 (75%), Black 124,179 (25%). Spanish origin 3,701 (1%). 18 and over 345,943 (69%), 65 and over 62,955 (13%). Median age: 29.

opportunity." Indeed, the so-called "dire emergency" spending bills designed to address such disasters came under question as the 101st Congress labored for months at a time to reach agreement on what projects to insert. The new budget deal should rein in that practice.

The appropriators' power peaked in 1986 and 1987 when Congress, divided against itself and President Ronald Reagan, both years resorted to a continuing resolution in place of all 13 appropriations bills — a single measure worth more than a half-trillion dollars. Up against criticism, Whitten would drawl that his committee had done its work; that the president and the Senate had held up the bills. That response illustrates the limits of Whitten's influence — he does not try to be a force beyond Appropriations — and the disingenuousness that so frustrates his legislative adversaries.

It also speaks of his disdain for the Senate. "I realize your rules are somewhat different," he told senators at a 1990 conference, "if you have any rules — sometimes I wonder."

The Senate got that rebuke for padding a supplemental bill with programs after Whitten had resisted. The House thus entered the conference with no pet projects and little bargaining power, except of course, Whitten's stubbornness. He dug in, and after weeks went by, the Senate finally agreed to add $100 million for House projects.

Arkansas Sen. Dale Bumpers, who is in line to chair the Agriculture Appropriations Subcommittee someday, came up short in a test of wills with Whitten in 1989. He had included $1.1 million for a home-state nonprofit dedicated to helping farmers reduce their use of fertilizers, which can cause environmental damage. After agreement was reached on every other issue in the agriculture spending bill, Whitten sat on it because he objected to Bumpers' amendment. Eventually, Byrd got Bumpers to relent by promising to look for funding elsewhere.

Whitten's public clashes with environmentalists date back to 1971, when he got jurisdiction over the Environmental Protection Agency (EPA), the Food and Drug Administration and the Federal Trade Commission, and he soon made clear how he felt about the agencies. He called environmentalists "extremists," and said, "those people at EPA have been given more money than they can possibly use."

While public support for environmental causes has blossomed, Whitten's attitudes remain fixed. In 1989, he tried to debunk the idea that farmers could reduce their use of chemicals without diminishing crop yields. "I wrote a book about it," he said, referring to "That We May Live," a book he wrote in 1962 in response to Rachel Carson's "Silent Spring."

Except for two years since 1949, his power base has been the Agriculture Subcommittee. He has fought for crop subsidies, rural electrification and soil conservation programs, and for rural home loans. His activism has fed a running turf battle with House Agriculture Committee Chairman E. "Kika" de la Garza of Texas. In 1987, de la Garza objected to a Whitten bill during House debate, snapping, "How many days of hearings did you have?" Whitten shot back: "I've been doing this for 39 years!"

At one time, his subcommittee was his virtual fiefdom. From it, as late as the 1960s, he was railing against integration and social programs and dictating crop subsidies without much challenge. But it was his views on the environment that so angered liberals that they plotted to oust him in 1975. Armed with a new rule requiring Appropriations subcommittee chairmen to be elected by the Democratic Caucus, their effort was finally defused by Appropriations Chairman Mahon, who arranged for Whitten to give up environmental and consumer issues in return for keeping the chair.

If Whitten meets increasing resistance to some of his ideas, it will not be the first time his views have not prevailed. In fact, more notable are some recent losses.

In 1986, he slipped into the continuing resolution $3.4 billion to resurrect revenue sharing, a popular program of aid to state and local governments that had been eliminated. Democrats complained angrily about Whitten's move, and the leadership-controlled Rules Committee forced him to remove the item before it would allow floor action on the resolution.

The next year, his $11 billion supplemental bill sparked a revolt. The House voted by an overwhelming 263-123 for an amendment to slash the bill by 21 percent. The result of that slap was a pact between Whitten and the leadership: If he complies with the limits of the annual budget resolution, the leaders will shield his bills from meat-ax amendments on the floor.

Such setbacks are rooted in Whitten's disdain for budget law, which he shares with other senior appropriators who opposed creation of the Budget Committee and a centralized budget process in 1974. They also opposed the 1985 Gramm-Rudman-Hollings anti-deficit law, which gave budget resolutions new teeth; in conference, Whitten did everything he could to limit the law's intrusions on Appropriations. "The budget resolution is sound, but only as a target," he said in 1987. "If the target is going to tie the hands of the Congress to meet the need, it is time we begin to look to see whether we should abolish it."

Even as Appropriations faces restrictions on its spending, it is more involved than ever in the details of programs it funds. Many programs for housing, the environment and aid to the poor — all so sensitive that Congress often cannot agree on bills reauthorizing them — have been kept alive by continuing resolutions from Whitten's committee. In the process, the panel can quietly add language altering the programs.

Through the years, various bills have allowed Whitten to pour money into Mississippi. Often he slips in provisions unnoticed, or explains them in his famous Mississippi mumble that leaves listeners more perplexed than enlightened. He is not apologetic: "Somebody told me, 'Jamie, you're the biggest pork-barreler in Congress.' I said, 'I guess I am, because pork barrel is what you do in the other fella's district, and I've helped more districts than anybody.' "

Perhaps the largest monument to Whitten's power is the Tennessee-Tombigbee waterway that cuts through his district. Completed in 1985, the project was his pet cause for two decades. To Whitten it is one of his proudest contributions; to critics, a symbol of pork-barrel excess.

Whitten inherited the chairmanship that let him build that waterway and scores of other projects over the objections of House liberals. When Mahon retired in 1979, liberals favored Edward P. Boland of Massachusetts, longtime roommate of Speaker Thomas P. O'Neill Jr. of Massachusetts, for the job. But O'Neill was on good terms with Whitten and would not breach seniority.

In turn, O'Neill and every Speaker since has had a loyal chairman. Whitten, who once voted against civil rights bills, Medicare and anti-poverty programs, now backs party goals even at the risk of political controversy back home. Once an avowed segregationist, Whitten signed the 1956 Southern Manifesto and said the Supreme Court's 1954 school-desegregation decision had started the nation "on the downhill road to integration and amalgamation and ruin." Today he represents a district that is 26 percent black, a smaller population than in the past but one that votes in significant numbers now. He is as free of racial rhetoric as the younger Southern Democrats who have joined him since the 1970s.

At Home: Whitten has accrued his seniority with barely a scent of opposition in his northern Mississippi district.

Between 1941, when he first won his House seat, and 1978, the year he inherited the Appropriations chairmanship, he faced GOP opposition only once. That challenger did not reach 20 percent of the vote. Nor has there been much opposition inside the Democratic Party; the only real threat was in 1962, when redistricting forced Whitten to battle Rep. Frank Smith for the nomination.

The son of a Tallahatchie County farmer, Whitten has spent his entire adult life in politics. He was elected to the Mississippi House at 21, and two years later was chosen district attorney. At 31 he was elected to Congress to succeed Wall Doxey, who had moved to the Senate. For the next two decades Whitten ran virtually unopposed. But in 1962, Mississippi lost one House seat in reapportionment. The state Legislature combined the northern Delta region's two districts, forcing a bitter showdown between Whitten and Smith. The two had been on opposite sides during the 1960 presidential election, when Smith backed John F. Kennedy while Whitten supported an unpledged slate of segregationist electors.

The new district's population was more than half black, but virtually none of the blacks voted. Each congressman tried to outdo the other in support of segregation. Smith was a populist, and Whitten claimed that he worked with Northern liberals and the Kennedy administration rather than trying to "preserve the Southern way of life." Smith said Whitten was more of a "prima donna" than an effective champion of Southern rights.

Building a huge lead in the counties of his old constituency, Whitten won easily with 60 percent of the vote. Smith was appointed by President Kennedy to the board of the TVA.

Mississippi's resurgent Republicans have been challenging Whitten in most recent election years, but to little avail. In 1980, while Reagan was carrying Mississippi — if not the 1st District — against Jimmy Carter, GOP challenger T. K. Moffett picked up 37 percent.

That is the closest anyone has come. In 1986, Republican Larry Cobb tried to convince voters that for all of Whitten's alleged clout, the area was being shortchanged. Cobb maintained that the Mississippi 1st ranked 391st among the 435 districts in getting federal dollars.

Cobb, a Vietnam fighter pilot, airline pilot and cattleman, covered northeast Mississippi with his placards. But lacking funds for a media campaign, Cobb mustered just 34 percent. Republican Bill Bowlin, an underfinanced farm equipment dealer, got 35 percent in 1990.

Committee

Appropriations (Chairman)
Rural Development, Agriculture & Related Agencies (chairman)

Elections

1990 General

Jamie L. Whitten (D)	43,668	(65%)
Bill Bowlin (R)	23,650	(35%)

1988 General

Jamie L. Whitten (D)	137,445	(78%)
Jim Bush (R)	38,381	(22%)

Previous Winning Percentages: **1986** (66%) **1984** (88%)

1982	(71%)	**1980**	(63%)	**1978**	(67%)	**1976**	(100%)
1974	(88%)	**1972**	(100%)	**1970**	(87%)	**1968**	(100%)
1966	(84%)	**1964**	(100%)	**1962**	(100%)	**1960**	(100%)
1958	(100%)	**1956**	(100%)	**1954**	(100%)	**1952**	(100%)
1950	(100%)	**1948**	(100%)	**1946**	(100%)	**1944**	(99%)
1942	(100%)	**1941** *	(69%)				

* *Special election.*

District Vote For President

	1988	1984	1980	1976
D	71,336 (39%)	66,789 (37%)	98,927 (54%)	92,846 (59%)
R	107,290 (59%)	111,841 (62%)	78,095 (43%)	60,313 (38%)
I			3,083 (2%)	

Campaign Finance

	Receipts	Receipts from PACs	Expend-itures
1990			
Whitten (D)	$183,612	$129,450 (71%)	$96,254
Bowlin (R)	$14,780	$250 (2%)	$14,750
1988			
Whitten (D)	$175,925	$135,400 (77%)	$58,370

Key Votes

1991	
Authorize use of force against Iraq	Y
1990	
Support constitutional amendment on flag desecration	Y
Pass family and medical leave bill over Bush veto	Y
Reduce SDI funding	N
Allow abortions in overseas military facilities	N
Approve budget summit plan for spending and taxing	N
Approve civil rights bill	Y
1989	
Halt production of B-2 stealth bomber at 13 planes	N
Oppose capital gains tax cut	N
Approve federal abortion funding in rape or incest cases	N
Approve pay raise and revision of ethics rules	Y
Pass Democratic minimum wage plan over Bush veto	N

Voting Studies

	Presidential Support		Party Unity		Conservative Coalition	
Year	**S**	**O**	**S**	**O**	**S**	**O**
1990	34	62	79	16	69	30
1989	52	47	79	19	66	34
1988	28	68	90	8	45	53
1987	33	61	82	10	70	21
1986	30	64	76	16	60	34
1985	33	68	79	13	55	35
1984	39	58	76	18	56	39
1983	30	66	71	22	63	31
1982	40	53	66	27	49	34
1981	50	49	63	36	67	31

Interest Group Ratings

Year	ADA	ACU	AFL-CIO	CCUS
1990	44	43	75	38
1989	50	42	67	70
1988	65	20	100	15
1987	68	13	88	13
1986	55	16	69	31
1985	55	26	75	20
1984	50	33	69	60
1983	60	18	88	33
1982	45	52	70	38
1981	30	20	67	22

2 Mike Espy (D)

Of Yazoo City — Elected 1986

Born: Nov. 30, 1953, Yazoo City, Miss.

Education: Howard U., B.A. 1975; Santa Clara U., J.D. 1978.

Occupation: Lawyer; businessman.

Family: Divorced; two children.

Religion: Baptist.

Political Career: Miss. assistant secretary of state, 1980-84; assistant attorney general, 1984-85.

Capitol Office: 216 Cannon Bldg. 20515; 225-5876.

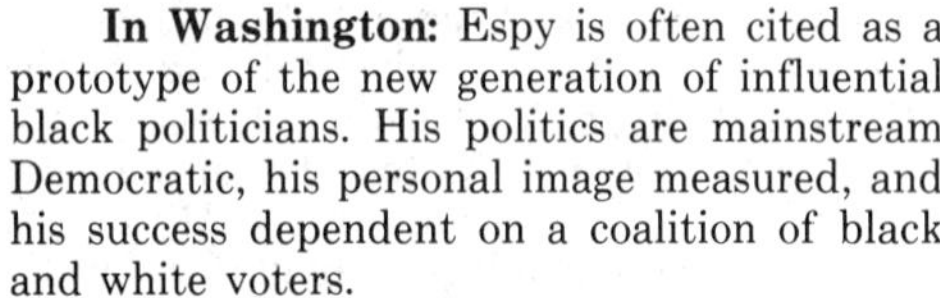

In Washington: Espy is often cited as a prototype of the new generation of influential black politicians. His politics are mainstream Democratic, his personal image measured, and his success dependent on a coalition of black and white voters.

Unlike many of his older black colleagues, Espy did not begin his political career at the bully pulpit of the church or early civil rights movement. He is the well-educated product of one of the Delta's more prominent black families, and got his start as a professional. His early political experience was essentially administrative — as an assistant secretary of state and then as the director of the attorney general's consumer protection division.

"Our successes have come in the boardrooms and courtrooms," he says of his generation of black leaders. "My development has always been in a multiracial environment."

Any political differences between Espy and older members of the Congressional Black Caucus might be attributed to their contrasting backgrounds. But there are other, perhaps more salient, factors: Espy is the only black to represent a rural district, and one of a handful to represent nearly as many white voters as black.

Espy has made himself remarkably secure in his marginal district by focusing primarily on economic development issues that transcend party label and are vital to his poor constituents, whatever their color. He calls himself "a spokesman for rural America," and in the 102nd Congress, he has a new platform as chairman of a Budget Committee Task Force on Community Development and Natural Resources.

In his first term, Espy was a player in enacting legislation to create the Lower Mississippi Delta Commission, which was given two years to develop ideas to combat poverty in Mississippi and other states in the region. "America is a chain of states, and in order to make it strong, you've got to focus on the weak links," he said. "Mississippi is a weak link."

When the commission's report was released in late 1990, Espy described it as a "call to action," but also found some recommendations too costly. "I'd like to have seen more for the money," he said of the report.

But to help enact some of the economic development programs, Espy helped form (and now chairs) the Lower Mississippi Delta Congressional Caucus, a bipartisan group representing the seven-state region. One of the caucus' first coups came with the 1990 Housing and Community Development Act, which included language sponsored by Espy and Missouri Republican Bill Emerson to increase funding for underserved counties.

The Agriculture Committee provides Espy with another forum to aid his diverse constituency. During debate on the 1990 farm bill, he quietly watched out for the 2nd District's large-scale cotton and soybean farmers as well as for those on food stamps. He offered a successful amendment to provide additional technical assistance and education for minority farm families, down from 14 percent of all farmers in 1920 to less than 1 percent today.

Promoting the catfish has been an Espy trademark. Most of the nation's catfish farming is done in Espy's district, which includes about 85,000 acres of man-made catfish farms employing 6,000 people. He helped persuade the Army to increase its catfish purchases, and delivered block grants for two new processing plants for the 2nd. His successful drive for a "National Catfish Day" also made headlines.

But his efforts to promote the whiskered delicacy placed him in a difficult situation when the workers at Delta Pride Catfish Inc. — most of them black women — went on strike shortly before the 1990 election. He avoided a Congressional Black Caucus October hearing on worker complaints about sub-poverty-level wages, saying he wanted to remain neutral to help facilitate a settlement. "My position as a member of Congress is to keep jobs in the district," he said.

Over the years, Espy had carefully cultivated support from the industry as well as its workers, and some saw politics in his reluctance to take sides. Rep. William L. Clay called him a "gigolo" at the Black Caucus hearing and

Mississippi 2

North Central — Mississippi Delta

Ever since swamp-draining technology and cheap black labor transformed the Delta into an agricultural gold mine in the years after the Civil War, the region has had a far larger population of poor rural blacks than monied white cotton growers. But throughout the decades, the white establishment managed to keep a firm grip on political power; Espy's election marked a passage into a dramatically new political order.

The largest city in the 2nd is Greenville, an old river port and cotton market and the traditional "capital" of the Mississippi Delta. This is one of the few areas in the region that has gained population in recent years. Greenville, the seat of Washington County, is the home of the *Delta Democrat*, the politically moderate newspaper published for a generation by Hodding Carter Jr.'s family. Greenville still has a reputation as one of the more racially tolerant communities in the state.

In the past generation, thousands of Delta blacks have been pushed out of work by farm mechanization and have moved on to Chicago, St. Louis and closer Sun Belt cities such as Little Rock and Memphis. Preliminary census figures showed a mass exodus from the 2nd in the 1980s — about 30,000 — mainly from the Delta's rural areas.

Many of those remaining live under Third World conditions. 53 percent of majority-black Tunica County live under the poverty line, making it the poorest county in the nation; in Humphreys County, about 29 of every 1,000 babies die before their first birthday.

The result is that the 2nd District has displaced the 1st as the Mississippi constituency kindest to statewide Democratic candidates. Eleven of the 18 Mississippi counties carried by Michael S. Dukakis in 1988 were entirely within the 2nd District.

Vicksburg, seat of Warren County, is the district's second-largest city. Its Catfish Row is considered to be the southern terminus of the Delta region. The major Republican enclave in the 2nd, Warren County gave Franklin a 5,442-vote edge in 1984, but two years later, Espy cut that advantage in half, a major factor in Franklin's downfall. By 1990, Espy was carrying Warren County handily.

Population: 503,935. White 207,501 (41%), Black 293,809 (58%), Other 2,599 (1%). Spanish origin 6,109 (1%). 18 and over 323,647 (64%), 65 and over 62,636 (12%). Median age: 26.

accused Espy of trying to cancel the hearing. Those comments eventually drew a written apology from Clay. Days later, Espy came out in support of the workers. "There will not be another Mike Espy-sponsored catfish dinner and another Mike Espy-sponsor catfish day until this thing is over," he said. The strike was settled in early December.

Despite his focus on local matters, Espy gets more national limelight than a typical junior House member: He was showcased at the 1988 Democratic National Convention, where he was asked to introduce the keynote speaker. And in early 1989 he appeared in a national magazine advertisement for the National Rifle Association. The ad shocked many Democrats, but Espy, an NRA member since 1974, viewed the ad as "a statement of my independence."

While Espy votes with a majority of Democrats more often than anyone else in Mississippi's delegation, he is not shy about going his own way when it suits his rural district. In addition to opposing gun control, Espy parts ways with most Democrats by supporting the death penalty in certain cases, and he backs prayer in schools.

Nonetheless, House Democratic leaders did everything they could to boost Espy's reelection chances early in his career. They gave him a seat on Agriculture, and made him the only Democrat in his class to win a spot on the Budget Committee, an attention-getting assignment both at home and in Washington. At the start of the 101st Congress, he was named an at-large whip. But he has not been given carte blanche. He lobbied unsuccessfully for a seat on Appropriations in the 102nd Congress.

At Home: Espy faced considerable skepticism when he challenged GOP Rep. Webb Franklin in 1986. Espy's prominent Delta family owns a chain of funeral homes, but he did not begin with a significant political base. Although roughly half the district's voters are black, there had not been evidence they would turn out in numbers sufficient to produce a congressional victory.

In 1982 and 1984, Franklin won as the House vote split essentially along racial lines; each time, black Democratic nominee Robert G. Clark, a state representative and old-line civil rights leader, fell a few thousand votes short.

But Espy effectively combined old-fashioned inspirational oratory and modern organizational techniques. He mounted a skillful turnout drive that exceeded anything the black community had put together in the past.

At the same time, Espy had some success wooing the white Democratic establishment. A well-educated young professional with a low-key, businesslike manner, Espy presented a less threatening front to ingrained white prejudices. He got the backing of several white county sheriffs and of Mississippi's secretary of state and attorney general. He won official neutrality from other white Democratic officials who had put out the word for Franklin in the past. Espy also made a direct play for the support of farmers, many of whom were suffering through hard times and were angered by some of Franklin's laissez-faire rhetoric.

On Election Day, Espy won only about 10 percent of the white vote, but that was enough in a year when white turnout was low and the Delta's black community was mobilized.

It seemed Espy could have a big fight on his hands in 1988, when the presidential election would bring out a larger white Republican vote. But Espy toiled throughout his first term to win over some of the monied establishment that had supported Franklin.

GOP nominee Jack Coleman, an attorney who had worked for a business trade association in Washington, sought to polarize the electorate. Although he touted his own ability to boost economic development, his literature told voters that Espy is "representing the interests of the Radical Left: for unions, for abortions, against jobs, against defense, against America and against Americans." When vandals attacked Espy's home during the campaign and scrawled "nigger" on the door, Coleman suggested Espy might have staged the whole thing to generate sympathy. In the end, Espy took roughly 40 percent of the ballots cast by whites, and won about two-thirds of the overall vote. In 1990, Espy easily dispatched his GOP foe.

Committees

Agriculture (21st of 27 Democrats)
Conservation, Credit & Rural Development; Cotton, Rice & Sugar; Domestic Marketing, Consumer Relations & Nutrition

Budget (6th of 23 Democrats)
Community Development & Natural Resources (chairman); Budget Process, Reconciliation & Enforcement

Select Hunger (9th of 22 Democrats)
Domestic (chairman)

Elections

1990 General		
Mike Espy (D)	59,393	(84%)
Dorothy Benford (R)	11,224	(16%)
1988 General		
Mike Espy (D)	112,401	(65%)
Jack Coleman (R)	59,827	(34%)

Previous Winning Percentage: **1986** (52%)

District Vote For President

	1988	1984	1980	1976
D	87,968 (50%)	90,653 (49%)	94,761 (57%)	77,986 (54%)
R	83,997 (48%)	93,213 (50%)	68,715 (41%)	60,798 (42%)

Campaign Finance

	Receipts	Receipts from PACs		Expend-itures
1990				
Espy (D)	$448,212	$219,225	(49%)	$365,825
1988				
Espy (D)	$880,227	$480,490	(55%)	$886,540
Coleman (R)	$226,486	$25,377	(11%)	$225,873

Key Votes

1991	
Authorize use of force against Iraq	N
1990	
Support constitutional amendment on flag desecration	N
Pass family and medical leave bill over Bush veto	Y
Reduce SDI funding	Y
Allow abortions in overseas military facilities	Y
Approve budget summit plan for spending and taxing	N
Approve civil rights bill	Y
1989	
Halt production of B-2 stealth bomber at 13 planes	Y
Oppose capital gains tax cut	Y
Approve federal abortion funding in rape or incest cases	Y
Approve pay raise and revision of ethics rules	N
Pass Democratic minimum wage plan over Bush veto	Y

Voting Studies

	Presidential Support		Party Unity		Conservative Coalition	
Year	**S**	**O**	**S**	**O**	**S**	**O**
1990	20	75	82	9	50	48
1989	35	59	80	10	34	59
1988	20	69	78	5	42	50
1987	20	73	89	4	40	58

Interest Group Ratings

Year	ADA	ACU	AFL-CIO	CCUS
1990	67	17	83	31
1989	80	16	92	40
1988	85	12	93	25
1987	84	0	88	7

3 G.V. "Sonny" Montgomery (D)

Of Meridian — Elected 1966

Born: Aug. 5, 1920, Meridian, Miss.
Education: Mississippi State U., B.S. 1943.
Military Service: Army, 1943-46; National Guard, 1946-80; active duty, 1951-52.
Occupation: Insurance executive.
Family: Single.
Religion: Episcopalian.
Political Career: Miss. Senate, 1956-66.
Capitol Office: 2184 Rayburn Bldg. 20515; 225-5031.

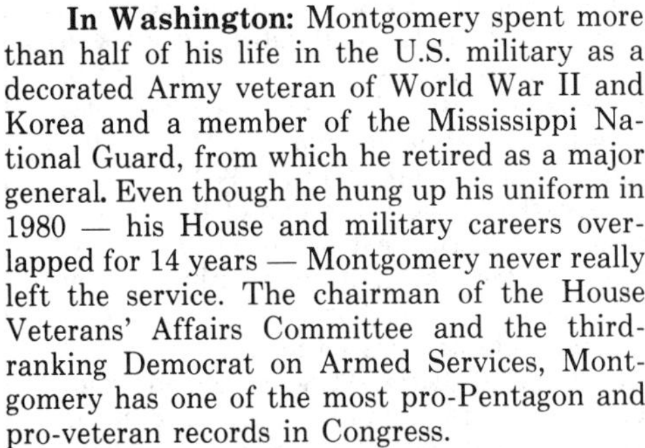

In Washington: Montgomery spent more than half of his life in the U.S. military as a decorated Army veteran of World War II and Korea and a member of the Mississippi National Guard, from which he retired as a major general. Even though he hung up his uniform in 1980 — his House and military careers overlapped for 14 years — Montgomery never really left the service. The chairman of the House Veterans' Affairs Committee and the third-ranking Democrat on Armed Services, Montgomery has one of the most pro-Pentagon and pro-veteran records in Congress.

A bachelor, Montgomery regards the men and women of the armed forces almost as family members, whose interests he oversees from his strategic committee positions. Yet as a lawmaking guardian, Montgomery is caring but stern. He will invest all of his energies to protect and expand benefits he believes veterans have coming to them; but he fights tooth and nail against program initiatives — even those with strong constituencies — that he sees as unwarranted or that might divert funds from established programs that he favors.

So strong is Montgomery's devotion to educational and training benefits for veterans that when Congress passed a major revision of these programs during the 100th Congress, it was named the Montgomery GI Bill. On the other hand, Montgomery believes that no absolute link has been established between the herbicide Agent Orange, used during the Vietnam War, and cancers suffered by Vietnam veterans. For four years, he blocked legislation providing compensation for victims of these diseases, yielding only after being outmaneuvered by benefit supporters at the start of the 102nd Congress.

Montgomery is far more often the advocate of veterans' programs — which are popular in Congress — than an opponent. One of his pet projects, the enactment of a 60-year-old proposal to convert the Veterans Administration into a Cabinet-level Department of Veterans Affairs, reached fruition during the 100th Congress. "Veterans' programs are too important to be left to mid-level decision-makers," he argued.

Following the U.S.-led military campaign to end Iraq's occupation of Kuwait in early 1991, Montgomery constructed a $1 billion House measure to provide benefits for veterans of that conflict. The provisions of this bill were not controversial, but its funding mechanism was. Under the 1990 federal budget agreement, new entitlement spending was to be offset by an across-the-board cut in other programs. However, Montgomery promoted the benefits bill as an "emergency" measure resulting from the war, which would have permitted a waiver of the "pay-as-you-go" rule.

The Bush administration, backed by the leadership of the House Budget Committee, argued that the bill mainly funded expansions of existing programs, and opposed Montgomery's funding language as a loophole that could slacken the new regimen of fiscal discipline. However, when Budget Committee Chairman Leon E. Panetta, D-Calif., tried to get the House to set up a dedicated funding source for the program, Montgomery cast the debate as a matter of patriotism and fairness to those who faced combat against Iraq. "All we're trying to do here is be fair to these Persian Gulf veterans, do the same thing we did for others who fought in different wars," Montgomery said.

Panetta's amendment to remove the bill's emergency spending designation was defeated by a 175-248 vote.

Although Panetta is himself highly regarded, he learned early into his Budget chairmanship the risks of tangling with Montgomery on veterans' issues. During committee debate in early 1989 on a budget resolution for fiscal 1990, Panetta parried attempts to raise veterans' medical benefits by $600 million over the previous year's levels. Montgomery then tapped his skills as a military commander, mobilizing veterans to lobby for more funds.

"I sent a brigade of wheelchair people to see Panetta," Montgomery said. "He saw that

Mississippi 3

South Central — Meridian

The 3rd is mostly agricultural, but it includes a burgeoning timber industry, outlying suburbs of Jackson and a major Air Force base at Columbus.

In the 1970s the district extended west into the Mississippi Delta, but redistricting for the '80s centered it in the Hill Country at the eastern end of the state. The rural hill counties are still reliably Democratic in local contests, but the 3rd's suburban and small-city vote has been tilting toward the GOP.

Lauderdale County, on the Alabama border, is the largest county wholly within the 3rd. Meridian, population 41,000, the seat of Lauderdale County, is an increasingly Republican industrial town with Lockheed and General Motors facilities. The Meridian Naval Air Station is a training center for naval pilots.

Another small city with growing Republican strength is Laurel, population 22,000. The seat of Jones County on the district's southern edge, Laurel is home to a timber-related industry fueled by its proximity to Mississippi's Piney Woods. Oil and gas drilling in southern Mississippi have spawned oil-related industries in the area, though they have struggled as oil has slumped in recent years. Court-ordered redistricting in early 1984 split the increasingly Republican county, with the northern half, including Laurel, remaining in the 3rd District and the southern half joining the 5th.

Northwest of Jones County is Smith County, the home of the National Tobacco Spitting Contest, which annually attracts curious spectators and serious expectoraters. Neighboring Rankin County is more cosmopolitan; it is home to more than 50,000 people, many of them suburbanites oriented toward the state capital of Jackson. One of the fastest-growing areas of the state, Rankin went solidly Republican in the 1987 gubernatorial contest, and it gave George Bush nearly 80 percent of its presidential votes in 1988. Like Jones County, it was split by the 1984 redistricting, with the more populous northern portion remaining in the 3rd District and the southern part joining the 4th.

To the northeast is Neshoba County, famous these days as the home of an annual county fair that is a must stop for any Mississippi politician. In national elections, even presidential candidates have been known to appear. Neshoba's county seat of Philadelphia, though, has greater notoriety. It was near Philadelphia that three civil rights workers were slain in 1964.

At the far northern end of the district is Columbus, the seat of Lowndes County. Another Republican stronghold in national elections, Columbus has a significant population of military-related residents from the North and Midwest. These voters add considerably to the Republican presence in the district. The local Air Force base offers basic training for prospective Air Force pilots. Neighboring Oktibbeha County (Starkville) is home to Mississippi State University and its 11,600 students.

Population: 505,169. White 336,707 (67%), Black 161,833 (32%), Other 5,722 (1%). Spanish origin 4,104 (1%). 18 and over 348,335 (69%), 65 and over 60,228 (12%). Median age: 28.

we weren't just whistling 'Dixie' — that there are needs out there." Eager to avoid a floor fight, Panetta and other Budget leaders agreed to add back $525 million for the veterans' programs, to be financed by a small across-the-board cut in other discretionary spending.

Montgomery also resists efforts to piggyback unrelated proposals onto priority veterans' legislation. In June 1989, a coalition of House Democrats tried to put President Bush on the spot by attaching $822 million for anti-drug law-enforcement programs to a supplemental appropriations bill providing $1.2 billion in emergency funding for veterans' hospitals. When Bush threatened a veto, Montgomery called for a "clean" bill including only the veterans' funding. A compromise figure of $75 million in anti-drug funding was eventually reached, freeing the veterans' bill for passage.

Montgomery's assertive leadership on veterans' issues gives him a command over the committee he chairs. However, some members, particularly those of the "Vietnam generation," occasionally bridle at Montgomery's efforts to set priorities for all veterans' programs.

One of these, Democrat Lane Evans of Illinois, led the fight to set up benefits for victims of Agent Orange-related diseases. A Vietnam War-era Marine veteran (he was not assigned to fight in that conflict), Evans first proposed in 1987 to provide compensation to veterans who had contracted five types of cancer linked to the dioxin-based defoliant. Montgomery opposed the measure — citing studies by the Defense Department and the Centers for Disease Control that showed no definitive evidence that the diseases were caused by Agent Orange — and supported efforts by Presidents Ronald Reagan and Bush to block the new benefits.

Montgomery insisted that his opposition was no sign of bias against Vietnam veterans. In December 1989, he said that most of the recent Veterans' Affairs Committee legislation had been targeted to that group, adding, "I've been the best friend they've had." But Vietnam veterans' organizations disagreed, stating that Montgomery was trying to protect programs for World War II and Korean War veterans at the expense of their younger counterparts; one lobbyist said that "on the issues of greatest importance to us, it seems he's always on the wrong side."

In early 1990, Veterans Affairs Secretary Edward J. Derwinski announced that compensation would be provided to Agent Orange-exposed veterans suffering from non-Hodgkin's lymphoma or soft-tissue sarcoma. Evans adopted this approach after Montgomery blocked his more sweeping measure at the subcommittee level. His amendment to codify Derwinski's rules and to mandate a National Academy of Sciences review of Agent Orange studies was attached to a bill providing a cost-of-living adjustment (COLA) for recipients of veterans' retirement and disability payments. The amendment passed the Veterans' Affairs Committee in October 1990 by a 16-14 vote, a rare defeat for Montgomery.

Although the amended bill passed the House by voice vote, Montgomery tried to get the Agent Orange provisions stripped out. He failed, but an ensuing deadlock in the Senate scuttled both the COLA and Agent Orange legislation for the 101st Congress. Montgomery tried to blame the COLA's failure on the advocates of Agent Orange benefits, and proposed a clean bill in January 1991. However, Evans persisted, proposing a combined COLA-Agent Orange bill. Montgomery then relented to a compromise under which the COLA and the Agent Orange benefits would pass separately.

Montgomery, whose courtly manner makes him a popular figure in the House, was typically gracious, praising Evans in a speech for his work on the compromise. But Montgomery also thanked several other members, most of whom had supported his efforts to block the bill.

Earlier in his career, Montgomery chaired a special committee to determine the fate of Americans listed missing in action during the Vietnam War. The panel reported in December 1976 that Vietnam held no remaining American prisoners; though widely accepted, the assertion is still disputed by groups demanding an accounting of the remaining "MIAs."

In May 1990, Montgomery led a delegation that accepted from North Korea the remains of five American servicemen lost during the Korean War. It was the first such repatriation since 1954.

It is unlikely that Montgomery will ever gain the prominence on Armed Services that he has on Veterans' Affairs. His star there was eclipsed in 1985, when Wisconsin Democrat Les Aspin jumped the seniority line as leader of the coup that deposed the aged and infirm Armed Services chairman, Melvin Price of Illinois.

The analytical Aspin is probably better suited than Montgomery to guide Armed Services through the current period of spending cutbacks. Montgomery — a member of the conservative "Old Guard" that used to dominate the committee — rarely criticizes weapons programs, and has not been a dominant force in debate over spending priorities. Instead, Montgomery continues to concentrate on issues involving the National Guard and reserve forces.

Since the military draft was abandoned in lieu of the all-volunteer armed forces, Montgomery has been a leading advocate of the "total force concept," which integrates National Guard and reserve units into the nation's fighting force. His efforts to obtain top-flight equipment for the Guard and reserves have been successful.

"Total force" received its first major test during the Persian Gulf War. Guard and reserve units were deployed to provide much of the logistical support for Operations Desert Shield/Storm, and Guard and reserve members flew air sorties against Iraq. However — to the disappointment of Montgomery and other advocates — three National Guard ground-combat brigades remained stateside for further training and never shipped out to the battle theater.

There has never been a doubt about Montgomery's pro-military stand. He first ran for Congress in 1966 pledging to "bring the boys home" from Vietnam in honor. "The time is past when we can discuss whether this is the wrong war," he said in 1967. "Our flag is committed." He visited South Vietnam several times; his exposure to Agent Orange without ill effect shaped his views on the benefits issue.

Montgomery's conservatism on defense reflects his overall philosophy. Like most Mississippi Democrats of the civil rights era, Montgomery came to Washington believing that his party had moved too far left for him to support it very often. During the Reagan presidency, Montgomery's leadership role among the Boll Weevils, a coalition of conservative Democrats who backed the president's policies, caused consternation in the Democratic Caucus: At the start of the 98th Congress, he received a less-than-resounding 179-53 vote for re-election as Veterans' Affairs chairman.

Montgomery then adopted a lower profile in the conservative coalition. However, his voting record did not change much. The only year in which he voted against Reagan's positions more than half the time was in 1988.

In 1989, Montgomery supported Bush's position on 78 percent of House votes before cooling off to 56 percent in 1990. Montgomery's ties to Bush are personal as well as political. Elected with Bush to the House class of 1966, Montgomery was a racquetball partner of the future president.

At Home: For years Montgomery has had the best of both worlds — personal popularity in Congress and bipartisan support back home. Not since 1968 has he won a primary or general election with less than 89 percent of the vote. Montgomery's 1988 GOP opponent, Columbia contractor Jimmie Ray Bourland, was so frustrated by the lack of attention to his effort that he climbed a TV tower to protest. He soon descended back into obscurity, eventually winning 11 percent of the vote.

Montgomery was a state senator and prominent National Guard officer when he first ran for the House in 1966. The 3rd District had gone Republican on a fluke in 1964, electing little-known chicken farmer Prentiss Walker, the only Republican who had filed for Congress anywhere in the state that year. Barry Goldwater carried Mississippi easily in his 1964 presidential campaign, and he propelled Walker into office. Two years later Walker ran for the Senate — he would have been beaten for re-election to the House anyway — leaving the 3rd open.

There were three other candidates for the Democratic House nomination in 1966, but Montgomery won with little difficulty. He drew 50.1 percent of the primary vote, avoiding a runoff.

His general-election campaign was easier. Describing himself as "a conservative Mississippi Democrat," Montgomery said he opposed the new, big-spending Great Society programs but favored older ones like Social Security and rural electrification. He claimed that his Republican opponent, state Rep. L. L. McAllister Jr., was against all federal programs, and he linked McAllister with the national GOP, which he called the "party of Reconstruction, Depression and 'me-too' liberalism." Montgomery won every county.

He had little trouble in 1968, drawing 85 percent of the primary vote against a black civil rights activist and 70 percent in the fall against Walker, who was trying to regain the seat. The Republican had lost his Senate race to veteran Democrat James O. Eastland by 2-to-1, and carried only one county in his comeback attempt against Montgomery.

That crushing defeat seemed to remove any remaining GOP interest in tackling Montgomery.

Committees

Veterans' Affairs (Chairman)
Hospitals & Health Care (chairman)

Armed Services (3rd of 33 Democrats)
Military Installations & Facilities; Military Personnel & Compensation

Elections

1990 General

G. V. "Sonny" Montgomery (D)	49,162	(100%)

1988 General

G. V. "Sonny" Montgomery (D)	164,651	(89%)
Jimmie Ray Bourland (R)	20,729	(11%)

Previous Winning Percentages: **1986** (100%) **1984** (100%) **1982** (93%) **1980** (100%) **1978** (92%) **1976** (94%) **1974** (100%) **1972** (100%) **1970** (100%) **1968** (70%) **1966** (65%)

District Vote For President

	1988	1984	1980	1976
D	63,886 (33%)	63,693 (33%)	81,147 (44%)	71,731 (46%)
R	124,666 (65%)	125,745 (66%)	99,130 (54%)	83,145 (53%)

Campaign Finance

	Receipts	Receipts from PACs	Expend-itures
1990			
Montgomery (D)	$112,779	$55,250 (49%)	$71,181
1988			
Montgomery (D)	$148,077	$71,650 (48%)	$116,761
Bourland (R)	$671	0	$671

Key Votes

1991	
Authorize use of force against Iraq	Y
1990	
Support constitutional amendment on flag desecration	Y
Pass family and medical leave bill over Bush veto	N
Reduce SDI funding	N
Allow abortions in overseas military facilities	N
Approve budget summit plan for spending and taxing	Y
Approve civil rights bill	N
1989	
Halt production of B-2 stealth bomber at 13 planes	N
Oppose capital gains tax cut	N
Approve federal abortion funding in rape or incest cases	N
Approve pay raise and revision of ethics rules	Y
Pass Democratic minimum wage plan over Bush veto	N

Voting Studies

	Presidential Support		Party Unity		Conservative Coalition	
Year	S	O	S	O	S	O
1990	56	44	60	37	94	6
1989	78	22	57	41	98	2
1988	45	53	64	34	89	8
1987	53	43	56	38	93	5
1986	58	42	53	45	92	8
1985	66	34	53	44	98	0
1984	59	41	34	59	97	3
1983	68	30	28	67	94	3
1982	74	23	29	66	90	5
1981	78	21	26	68	97	3

Interest Group Ratings

Year	ADA	ACU	AFL-CIO	CCUS
1990	22	63	25	71
1989	10	59	25	90
1988	25	71	57	71
1987	16	65	19	71
1986	5	86	29	76
1985	15	76	18	82
1984	0	70	31	50
1983	10	96	13	80
1982	5	91	5	73
1981	0	93	13	83

4 Mike Parker (D)

Of Brookhaven — Elected 1988

Born: Oct. 31, 1949, Laurel, Miss.
Education: William Carey College, B.A. 1970.
Occupation: Funeral director.
Family: Wife, Rosemary Prather; three children.
Religion: Presbyterian.
Political Career: No previous office.
Capitol Office: 1504 Longworth Bldg. 20515; 225-5865.

In Washington: For a man who went out of his way to run against his party's 1988 presidential nominee, Parker has fared pretty well with House leaders so far.

Parker keeps a close eye on his conservative district; he was one of only ten Southern Democrats voting against the 1990 civil rights bill. But on another vote important to Democratic leaders — approval of the tax-raising 1990 bipartisan budget compromise — Parker voted "yea"; not coincidentally, he got a seat on the Budget Committee at the start of the 102nd Congress.

Some Republicans who knew businessman Parker before his 1988 House bid had hoped he would seek the GOP nomination. He did not, but did give himself the rather laborious label of "Mike Parker mainstream Mississippi Democrat." Still, in the campaign, he tried to reassure the party faithful. "I support the broad principles of the Democratic Party," he said. "The party that gave us Social Security, Medicaid, Medicare, veterans' benefits ... gave us [Rep.] 'Sonny' Montgomery and [Sen.] John Stennis."

As a freshman, Parker took seats on Public Works and Veterans' Affairs, where partisan distinctions are less obvious and ideological sparring less prevalent than in the House as a whole. There he worked to secure funds for several highway and airport development projects. He also pushed for continued funding of the Natchez National Historical Park and for establishment of an Afro-American research center at Jackson State University.

At Home: Parker was a political novice when he began his 1988 campaign, but as a funeral home director and one-time drama student, he was no neophyte at presenting himself to the public. Parker's 55 percent showing — which came in the face of a solid George Bush victory in the 4th — was proof he possesses campaign skills beyond his political years.

An early wave of TV ads helped Parker distinguish himself from more than a dozen contenders, Democrats and Republicans, after Democratic Rep. Wayne Dowdy launched a Senate bid. Drawing on sizable personal loans, Parker touted his business background and dedication to "family" values.

In the primary, Parker ran second to Jackson attorney Brad Pigott, who had better party connections. In the runoff, Parker won endorsements from the third- and fourth-place primary finishers and stormed past Pigott.

Parker's strong runoff showing made him the November favorite against GOP nominee Thomas Collins, but in the conservative-minded 4th (which has elected GOP House members in the recent past), Parker had to run a careful general-election campaign.

Collins, who spent nearly eight years as a POW during the Vietnam War, had significant patriotic appeal — a real plus against the backdrop of a presidential campaign that focused on flag-waving issues such as the Pledge of Allegiance. And Collins' appeal to veterans was enhanced by his recent service as director of the Mississippi Veterans Farm and Home Board.

Collins tried to tie Parker to Democratic presidential nominee Michael S. Dukakis, but Parker disconnected himself with an ad that said he was not endorsing Dukakis. Parker's blunt denial of his party's national nominee temporarily infuriated some local party activists. But if it struck some as disloyal, Parker's move was not a dramatic shift in his campaign, which never had embraced the national Democratic agenda.

Parker, who comes from a Republican-leaning county in the southern half of the 4th, was actually very close to Collins on a number of national issues. Both supported the strategic defense initiative and military aid for the Nicaraguan contras. And Parker, son of a Baptist preacher, also spoke in favor of organized prayer in schools.

Stressing the need for "business principles" in Washington, Parker was successful at adding to his rural base the votes of many business-oriented Republicans in Hinds County (Jackson), home to roughly half of the district's voters. Parker won by 11 points and was virtually unopposed in 1990.

Mississippi 4

Southwest — Jackson

The 4th amply illustrates the Democratic Party's ability to retain its huge advantage in the House while falling time and time again in elections for the presidency.

Along with the Gulf Coast 5th, the Jackson-based 4th is the backbone of the GOP resurgence in Mississippi. These are the only two districts in the state in modern times to elect two Republican representatives in a row, and the 4th is the base of Thad Cochran, who in 1979 became the state's first GOP senator in over a century. Yet through the political skill of its candidates — first Wayne Dowdy and now Mike Parker — the Democratic Party has held the 4th since 1981.

With a population of nearly 200,000, Jackson is the state's capital and its largest city. A prosperous commercial and financial center that has drawn corporate migrants from the North. Jackson and its suburbs cast nearly half the 4th's vote. Jackson and surrounding Hinds County have given Republicans a strong political base to build on: Jackson is home to many of the state GOP's financial kingpins, and Hinds County has not gone Democratic in a presidential election since 1956. In the 1987 gubernatorial election, though, Democrat Ray Mabus narrowly carried Hinds.

In the 1970s, independent black candidates were a political force in the district. In 1972, 1978 and 1980, independent black challengers siphoned enough votes from Democratic House nominees to elect Republicans Cochran and Jon Hinson. But the GOP lost the 4th after a sexual scandal drove Hinson from office in April 1981.

When black voters are in the party fold, they make the district winnable for Democrats; the 4th has a black population well in excess of 40 percent. A candidate such as Parker or Dowdy who can link black and rural white votes is in a good position to prevail.

Population: 503,297. White 290,052 (58%), Black 211,376 (42%). Spanish origin 3,975 (1%). 18 and over 345,335 (69%), 65 and over 57,957 (12%). Median age: 28.

Committees

Budget (23rd of 23 Democrats)
Budget Process, Reconciliation & Enforcement; Economic Policy, Projections & Revenues

Public Works & Transportation (24th of 36 Democrats)
Aviation; Surface Transportation; Water Resources

Elections

1990 General		
Mike Parker (D)	57,137	(81%)
Jerry "Rev" Parks (R)	13,754	(19%)
1988 General		
Mike Parker (D)	110,184	(55%)
Thomas Collins (R)	88,433	(44%)

District Vote For President

	1988	1984	1980	1976
D	88,469 (43%)	85,253 (41%)	90,830 (47%)	73,611 (44%)
R	113,449 (56%)	122,466 (59%)	100,650 (52%)	90,090 (54%)

Campaign Finance

	Receipts	Receipts from PACs	Expend-itures
1990			
Parker (D)	$526,415	$286,473 (54%)	$479,651
1988			
Parker (D)	$844,541	$234,164 (28%)	$843,142
Collins (R)	$406,944	$56,311 (14%)	$394,250

Key Votes

1991	
Authorize use of force against Iraq	Y
1990	
Support constitutional amendment on flag desecration	Y
Pass family and medical leave bill over Bush veto	N
Reduce SDI funding	N
Allow abortions in overseas military facilities	N
Approve budget summit plan for spending and taxing	Y
Approve civil rights bill	N
1989	
Halt production of B-2 stealth bomber at 13 planes	N
Oppose capital gains tax cut	N
Approve federal abortion funding in rape or incest cases	N
Approve pay raise and revision of ethics rules	N
Pass Democratic minimum wage plan over Bush veto	N

Voting Studies

	Presidential Support		Party Unity		Conservative Coalition	
Year	**S**	**O**	**S**	**O**	**S**	**O**
1990	56	44	52	46	96	4
1989	71	23	47	45	93	5

Interest Group Ratings

Year	ADA	ACU	AFL-CIO	CCUS
1990	22	63	25	79
1989	20	68	27	100

5 Gene Taylor (D)

Of Bay St. Louis — Elected 1989

Born: Sept. 17, 1953, New Orleans, La.

Education: Tulane U., B.A. 1976; Attended U. of Southern Mississippi, Gulf Park, 1978-80.

Military Service: Coast Guard, 1971-84.

Occupation: Sales representative.

Family: Wife, Margaret Gordon; three children.

Religion: Roman Catholic.

Political Career: Bay St. Louis City Council, 1981-83; Miss. Senate, 1983-89; Democratic nominee for U.S. House, 1988.

Capitol Office: 1429 Longworth Bldg. 20515; 225-5772.

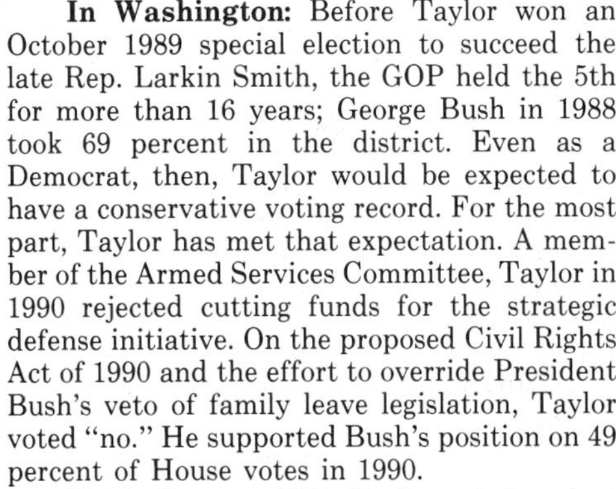

In Washington: Before Taylor won an October 1989 special election to succeed the late Rep. Larkin Smith, the GOP held the 5th for more than 16 years; George Bush in 1988 took 69 percent in the district. Even as a Democrat, then, Taylor would be expected to have a conservative voting record. For the most part, Taylor has met that expectation. A member of the Armed Services Committee, Taylor in 1990 rejected cutting funds for the strategic defense initiative. On the proposed Civil Rights Act of 1990 and the effort to override President Bush's veto of family leave legislation, Taylor voted "no." He supported Bush's position on 49 percent of House votes in 1990.

Yet in January 1991, Taylor voted against the resolution authorizing Bush to commit U.S. troops to war against Iraq. He said government often finds "the most costly way to accomplish our goals," adding, "Must that apply to the waste of young men and women as well? True conservatives know the value of conserving all of our resources, not just our money."

Taylor had sought a seat on Armed Services — and was promised one by the Democratic leadership during his 1989 campaign — in order to oversee the interests of such 5th District military facilities as Camp Shelby and the proposed Navy homeport in Pascagoula.

During his first term, Taylor cannily tapped the support of a powerful Mississippian, Appropriations Committee Chairman Jamie L. Whitten, to delay the closure of an ammunition plant in his district. "I'm a little bitty fish, but I've got some big fish helping me," he said.

On the Merchant Marine and Fisheries Committee, Taylor looks out for the interests of the shipbuilders, shrimpers and fishermen of his Gulf Coast district.

At Home: The Democratic Party was cool to Taylor in his first two campaigns for the 5th — in 1988 and the special election the following year to succeed Smith, who died in an August 1989 plane crash. But he drew a respectable 45 percent against Smith in 1988, when both were competing for the seat vacated by Senate aspirant Trent Lott. He captured 65 percent of the vote in dispatching Lott's longtime Hill aide, Tom Anderson Jr., in a 1989 special election. And he drew 81 percent against Smith's widow, Sheila, to win re-election in 1990.

A sales representative for a company that manufactured cardboard boxes, Taylor entered politics in 1981 to run for the Bay St. Louis City Council. In 1983, he won election to the state Senate. He focused on education issues, such as raises and merit pay for teachers.

In 1988, Taylor was considered the strongest candidate in the Democratic field for the open 5th, and he easily dispatched Hattiesburg District Attorney Glenn White in a runoff. But he seemed slow to organize for the fall; national party sources concluded that they could better spend their money elsewhere.

Taylor tried to make political capital out of the absence of national Democratic support. He told voters he was being snubbed by party officials for his refusal to moderate his conservative posture on issues such as aid to the Nicaraguan contras (which he backed) and federal funding for abortion (which he opposed). But Taylor had trouble raising money and was outspent by Smith by more than 3-to-1.

Taylor was heavily outspent in 1989 as well, but Anderson had an unflattering image as Lott's "anointed" successor; and Democratic state Attorney General Mike Moore, who had the backing of organized labor, Mississippi's main association of educators and Democratic Gov. Ray Mabus, struck many voters as politically overambitious; he had just been elected attorney general in 1987. In the primary, Taylor took 42 percent to Anderson's 37 percent and Moore's 21 percent. The one-on-one match-up with Anderson was a Taylor runaway.

The size of Taylor's victory was due in part to a feeling among many voters that Smith's widow should have been given the GOP nomination. She was in 1990, but it quickly became apparent her chance came a year too late.

Mississippi 5

Southeast — Gulf Coast; Hattiesburg

Mississippi's long-dormant Republican Party made its initial modern-day inroads in the 5th District, a solidly conservative region where Democrats are no longer even competitive in national elections. Ronald Reagan carried Mississippi in 1980 only because of a 30,000-vote edge in the 5th. As George Bush carried the state easily in 1988, the 5th was his strongest district. In his 1988 Senate bid, Trent Lott did not lose a county in the 5th.

Yet while the district has been a GOP beachhead, it is not impregnable, evidence Democratic Rep. Gene Taylor's special election victory in 1989 and his smashing reelection win a year later.

The political heart of the 5th is the Mississippi Gulf Coast. The coastal counties of Jackson, Hancock and Harrison cast about three-fifths of the district vote, and none gave Bush less than 67 percent in 1988. However, all three counties backed Democrat Ray Mabus for governor in 1987.

This area is home for gulf shrimpers and seafood-processing plants, as well as government and military installations. Shipbuilding is big business, especially in Pascagoula, where a Litton Industries shipyard, the leading private employer in the district, handles major Navy contracts.

The Gulf Coast area has little in common with the rest of Mississippi. Tourism is a major source of dollars; U.S. Route 90 between Bay St. Louis and Biloxi is lined with white-sand beaches and dotted with seafood restaurants.

The coastal counties have a far smaller black population than other parts of the state, and racial issues have never been an overriding preoccupation. Biloxi, the largest Gulf Coast city, with a population of 46,000, was built around its seafood industry. In the past 20 years, however, it has developed a white-collar and service-based economy tied to the military and to Litton. Nearby Gulfport is less ethnic than Biloxi and more Republican.

The tier of counties above the coast are part of the poorer Piney Woods region, where the economy is centered on wood products. The land is not particularly good for agriculture, but there is some dairy and poultry farming.

The sole population center in the northern part of the district is Hattiesburg, the seat of Forrest County. Hattiesburg is a white-collar town whose leading employer is the University of Southern Mississippi with just under 12,000 students and 670 faculty. The absence of a big blue-collar population has made it fertile GOP territory for 20 years, though Mabus was able to get 48 percent in Forrest.

Population: 504,101. White 402,394 (80%), Black 96,009 (19%), Other 3,870 (1%). Spanish origin 6,842 (1%). 18 and over 343,181 (68%), 65 and over 45,581 (9%). Median age: 27.

Committees

Armed Services (30th of 33 Democrats)
Procurement & Military Nuclear Systems; Seapower & Strategic & Critical Materials; Military Education

Merchant Marine & Fisheries (24th of 29 Democrats)
Coast Guard & Navigation; Merchant Marine; Oceanography, Great Lakes & Outer Continental Shelf

Elections

1990 General		
Gene Taylor (D)	89,926	(81%)
Sheila Smith (R)	20,588	(19%)
1989 Special Runoff		
Gene Taylor (D)	83,296	(65%)
Tom Anderson Jr. (R)	44,494	(35%)
1989 Special		
Gene Taylor (D)	51,561	(42%)
Tom Anderson Jr. (R)	45,727	(37%)
Mike Moore (D)	25,579	(21%)

District Vote For President

	1988		1984		1980		1976	
D	53,686	(29%)	45,663	(26%)	63,102	(39%)	63,802	(46%)
R	126,873	(69%)	128,148	(73%)	93,868	(58%)	71,690	(51%)
I					2,386	(2%)		

Campaign Finance

	Receipts	Receipts from PACs		Expend-itures
1990				
Taylor (D)	$316,052	$143,426	(45%)	$322,048
Smith (R)	$205,068	$10,400	(5%)	$205,067

Key Votes

1991	
Authorize use of force against Iraq	N
1990	
Support constitutional amendment on flag desecration	Y
Pass family and medical leave bill over Bush veto	N
Reduce SDI funding	N
Allow abortions in overseas military facilities	N
Approve budget summit plan for spending and taxing	N
Approve civil rights bill	N
1989	
Approve pay raise and revision of ethics rules	N

Voting Studies

	Presidential Support		Party Unity		Conservative Coalition	
Year	S	O	S	O	S	O
1990	49	51	57	43	93	7
1989	68 †	32 †	67 †	33 †	71 †	29 †

† Not eligible for all recorded votes.

Interest Group Ratings

Year	ADA	ACU	AFL-CIO	CCUS
1990	28	63	50	64
1989	-	100	100	-

Missouri

U.S. CONGRESS

SENATE 2 R
HOUSE 6 D, 3 R

LEGISLATURE

Senate 23 D, 11 R
House 98 D, 66 R

ELECTIONS

1988 Presidential Vote	
Bush	52%
Dukakis	48%
1984 Presidential Vote	
Reagan	60%
Mondale	40%
1980 Presidential Vote	
Reagan	51%
Carter	44%
Anderson	4%
Turnout rate in 1986	38%
Turnout rate in 1988	55%
Turnout rate in 1990	35%

(as percentage of voting age population)

POPULATION AND GROWTH

1980 population	4,916,686
1990 population (15th in the nation)	5,117,073
Percent change 1980-1990	+4%

DEMOGRAPHIC BREAKDOWN

White	88%
Black	11%
Asian or Pacific Islander	1%
(Hispanic origin)	1%
Urban	68%
Rural	32%
Born in state	70%
Foreign-born	2%

MAJOR CITIES

Kansas City	435,146
St. Louis	396,685
Springfield	140,494
Independence	112,301
St. Joseph	71,852

AREA AND LAND USE

Area	68,945 sq. miles (18th)
Farm	66%
Forest	28%
Federally owned	5%

Gov. John Ashcroft (R)
Of Jefferson City — Elected 1984

Born: May 9, 1942, Chicago, Ill.
Education: Yale U., B.A. 1964; U. of Chicago, J.D. 1967.
Occupation: Professor; lawyer.
Religion: Assembly of God.
Political Career: Mo. auditor, 1973-75; Mo. attorney general, 1977-85; GOP nominee for U.S. House, 1972.
Next Election: 1992.

WORK

Occupations	
White-collar	51%
Blue-collar	31%
Service workers	14%
Government Workers	
Federal	66,553
State	84,436
Local	196,587

MONEY

Median family income	$ 18,784 (31st)
Tax burden per capita	$ 667 (46th)

EDUCATION

Spending per pupil through grade 12	$ 3,786 (32nd)
Persons with college degrees	14% (39th)

CRIME

Violent crime rate	633 per 100,000 (13th)

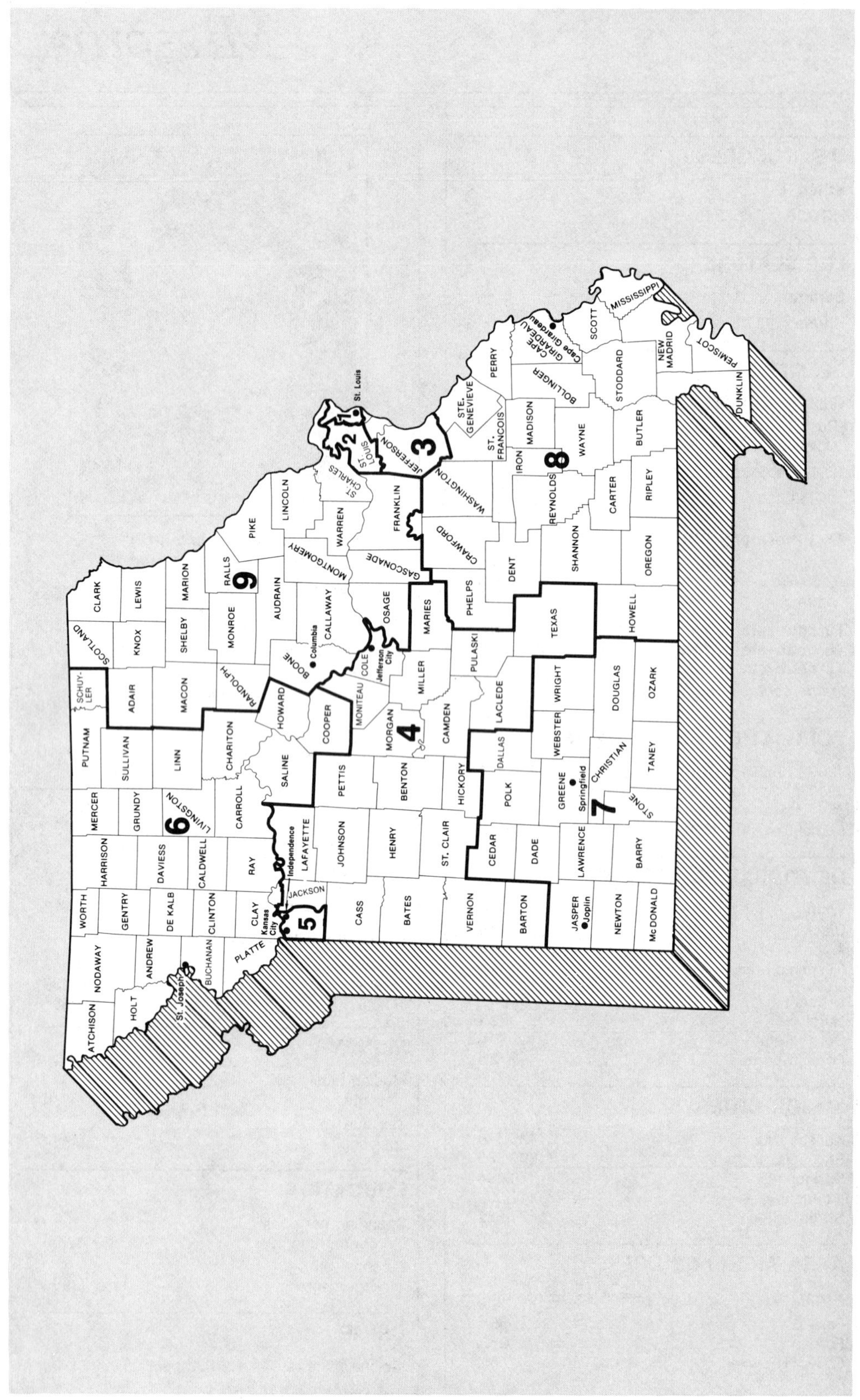
ATCHISON
NODAWAY
HOLT
ANDREW
St. Joseph
BUCHANAN
WORTH
GENTRY
DE KALB
CLINTON
PLATTE
CLAY
Kansas City
5
JACKSON
Independence
HARRISON
DAVIESS
CALDWELL
RAY
MERCER
GRUNDY
LIVINGSTON
6
CARROLL
LAFAYETTE
PUTNAM
SULLIVAN
LINN
CHARITON
SALINE
SCHUY-LER
ADAIR
MACON
RANDOLPH
HOWARD
COOPER
SCOTLAND
KNOX
SHELBY
MONROE
BOONE
Columbia
CLARK
LEWIS
MARION
RALLS
9
AUDRAIN
CALLAWAY
PIKE
LINCOLN
MONTGOMERY
WARREN
ST. CHARLES
CASS
JOHNSON
PETTIS
BATES
HENRY
BENTON
MORGAN
4
MONITEAU
COLE
Jefferson City
MILLER
OSAGE
GASCONADE
MARIES
CAMDEN
VERNON
ST. CLAIR
HICKORY
BARTON
CEDAR
DADE
POLK
DALLAS
LACLEDE
PULASKI
PHELPS
JASPER
Joplin
LAWRENCE
GREENE
Springfield
WEBSTER
WRIGHT
TEXAS
NEWTON
BARRY
McDONALD
STONE
7
CHRISTIAN
TANEY
DOUGLAS
OZARK
HOWELL
OREGON
FRANKLIN
ST. LOUIS
St. Louis
1
2
JEFFERSON
3
WASHINGTON
CRAWFORD
DENT
SHANNON
REYNOLDS
IRON
8
ST. FRANCOIS
STE. GENEVIEVE
PERRY
MADISON
WAYNE
CARTER
RIPLEY
BOLLINGER
CAPE GIRARDEAU
Cape Girardeau
BUTLER
STODDARD
SCOTT
MISSISSIPPI
NEW MADRID
PEMISCOT
DUNKLIN

John C. Danforth (R)

Of Newburg — Elected 1976

Born: Sept. 5, 1936, St. Louis, Mo.
Education: Princeton U., A.B. 1958; Yale U., B.D., LL.B. 1963.
Occupation: Lawyer; clergyman.
Family: Wife, Sally Dobson; five children.
Religion: Episcopalian.
Political Career: Mo. attorney general, 1969-77; Republican nominee for U.S. Senate, 1970.
Capitol Office: 249 Russell Bldg. 20510; 224-6154.

In Washington: Having prepared for both the priesthood and the law, Danforth continues to exhibit some of the ethos of each. At times, he seems consumed in pursuit of the greater good: famine relief, arms control, safety regulation. But he can also seem as sharp-eyed and contractual as any corporate attorney.

If Danforth has had a problem with the way others perceive him, it may be because the righteous tone of the priestly Danforth is sometimes audible in the lawyerly, as well. Danforth also has a penchant for changing his mind on issues, although this trait seems to be viewed as an outgrowth of his serious reflective nature, not as a sign that he is an indecisive flip-flopper.

Perhaps the most notable Danforth switch occurred during 1989 consideration of a constitutional amendment to ban flag burning. An original sponsor of the idea, Danforth made a high-profile shift, telling his colleagues on the floor that his support was "a mistake of the heart, but nonetheless it was a mistake."

In 1987, Danforth voted to strike a provision from the trade bill requiring employers to give employees 60 days' advance notice before plant closings. The next year, Danforth backed a separate bill requiring similar plant-closing notice. A leading foe in the mid-1980s of televising the Senate, Danforth conceded on that issue in 1989. "I was wrong. My predictions have not come true. The abuse has not occurred. The posturing I foresaw has not come into being," he said.

Despite this catalog of shifts — and the questions about his consistency that they raise — Danforth has made one of the more successful transitions from majority to minority status since the Democrats regained control in the 100th Congress. Unlike some senior Republicans who seemed eclipsed when they lost chairmanships, Danforth's effectiveness does not appear diminished. He has maintained visibility on issues such as trade, transportation and civil rights.

The main reason for Danforth's success in the Democratic-controlled chamber may have been his importance in developing the omnibus trade bill of 1988. Having previously been chairman of the Finance Subcommittee on Trade, Danforth was the ideal GOP partner for Democrat Lloyd Bentsen of Texas, the new chairman of the full committee. And Danforth delivered enough Republican support in committee and on the floor to earn his share of the credit.

Danforth's trade views had been evolving through the decade, as he sought a middle ground between the strict free-trade policy of the Reagan administration and the increasing appeal of protectionism. In the 97th Congress, he and Bentsen pressured the Japanese into voluntary agreements to restrain their car exports. In the 98th, they urged reciprocity without sanctions.

By 1985, though, Danforth was angry enough with the Japanese to call for sterner actions. Bitterly criticizing Japan's restrictive trade policies, he proposed a bill to require restraints on imports from Japan if that country did not remove barriers to the sale of American-made goods.

When the Bush administration in April 1990 decided not to cite Japan for unfair trade practices, Danforth was an immediate and outspoken critic. He called the decision "deeply disappointing" and a "serious tactical mistake ... sure to result in an extremely adverse reaction from the Congress."

In another high-profile action, Danforth in 1988 managed to amend the *Grove City* civil rights bill to make it "abortion neutral." The bill reversed the Supreme Court's *Grove City* ruling, which said an institution's federal funds could be cut off only for the activity in which the institution was guilty of racial or other discrimination. In effect, Danforth's amendment restricted some women's access to abortion services. That angered some sponsors, but it also brought in votes the bill would not otherwise have had and assured the two-thirds margin needed to survive a veto. After voting for the bill, however, Danforth opposed the successful override. He said he was convinced the president would offer a preferable successor bill.

Danforth has also pressed hard for random drug testing of transportation workers. The provision was included in the Senate-passed antidrug bill in the 100th Congress, but not in the final version that emerged from the House-Senate conference. Early in 1989, the Supreme Court ruled favorably on drug testing for safety and law-enforcement personnel. Danforth called it "the green light" for his reintroduced legislation.

In 1989, Danforth moved from the Budget Committee (which had never ranked high among his priorities) to the Select Committee on Intelligence. There he pledged himself to developing a new bipartisan consensus, a concept he had endorsed in working with the committee's chairman, Democrat David L. Boren of Oklahoma, even before joining the panel.

Danforth worked with Senate Majority Leader George J. Mitchell of Maine in 1990 to help shape a new consensus on U.S.-Cambodian policy. With Danforth's backing, Congress withdrew diplomatic support for the antigovernment coalition that included the communist Khmer Rouge and the two U.S.-backed factions; the Bush administration then announced that it would open a dialogue with Vietnam.

Overall, Danforth seems to be bouncing back from the acutely personal disappointment he seemed to have suffered in the final act of the tax-reform drama in 1986. The problem was not that Danforth opposed the conference version of the tax-revision bill. He was one of 23 senators who voted "no," and few others offered as cogent and detailed a critique as Danforth's eloquent, all-afternoon speech before the final vote on the measure.

Nor, for that matter, would many senators necessarily have resented his switch from supporter to critic. Final provisions in the bill affected Missouri interests adversely — notably, a tax accounting change harmful to McDonnell Douglas and other major defense contractors in the state.

It was the manner in which Danforth both supported and opposed the bill that proved disturbing. In both cases, he took a strongly moralistic approach in criticizing those who disagreed with his views. Some of his colleagues suspected that Danforth was using a tone of righteous indignation to cover his pique at losing out on his home-state concerns. The essence of his argument was that the measure's combination of business tax increases with personal tax cuts would foster consumption at the expense of long-term investment in the economy.

Important as he has been on Finance, Danforth's first committee responsibility has been on Commerce, Science and Transportation. As chairman of the committee in the 99th Congress, he displayed a more positive attitude toward federal regulation than had Oregon's Bob Packwood, the previous chairman. Danforth strongly opposed, for example, Packwood's efforts in 1984 to loosen federal broadcasting laws that require radio and television stations to air contrasting views.

Danforth expanded his efforts in broadcasting issues during the 101st and 102nd Congresses when the Senate considered legislation to re-regulate the cable television industry. Danforth sponsored strong re-regulation bills that included measures to open cable to more competition and to give certain rate-setting powers back to local governments. His 1991 bill also sought to strengthen Federal Communications Commission (FCC) regulations for basic cable service.

As the FCC gains enhanced authority in a number of areas in the burgeoning telecommunications industry, Danforth sees himself as a likely intermediary between the agency and the Congress; FCC Chairman Alfred C. Sikes is a longtime friend and once served under Danforth in Missouri.

Danforth's reluctance to abandon regulation was most apparent earlier on the issue of auto safety. Over the years, he had come into conflict with both the Reagan administration and the auto industry, both of which had tried to reduce federal regulation.

During the 101st and 102nd Congresses, Danforth stepped up congressional efforts to encourage the installation of air bags in passenger cars and light trucks. He sponsored a bill in 1991 to require air bags in all such vehicles by 1995; in 1990, he had pushed an amendment on fuel efficiency legislation to give credit to automakers that installed air bags in their vehicles.

Danforth has similarly involved himself in the airline industry and efforts to re-regulate it. Concerned about the continued industry shakeout — more and more carriers filing for bankruptcy — he has started to promote legislation to ensure competition. In 1990, Danforth strongly backed successful efforts to impose new airline ticket fees of up to $3 per flight to pay for facility improvements.

During consideration in 1990 of the civil rights measure, Danforth joined Massachusetts Democrat Edward M. Kennedy in offering a proposal aimed at ensuring that the bill would not lead to hiring quotas — the Bush administration's greatest objection. Danforth's compromise helped bring on another Republican and five Southern and Western Democrats in support of the measure, though the bill ultimately fell to a Bush veto.

When the Senate voted on the bill, the priestly Danforth pre-empted the lawyer as he criticized the legal minutiae that had consumed the discussion. "I am a Republican. I believe in our free enterprise system. I believe that it is very important in this country to have business that can compete and that can be successful," he said. "But in the end, as a matter of national identity, national value, clearly if we are forced to make the choice, the choice must be in favor of equal opportunity for employment." Danforth was one of just 11 Republicans in the Senate to vote to override Bush's veto.

Some of Danforth's legislative efforts reflect the humanitarian and moral ideals that led him into the ministry. Deeply concerned about world hunger, he helped win $150 million in emergency food aid for Africa after touring the drought-ravaged continent early in 1984. He also was active in pushing the Reagan administration to step up the pace of nuclear arms reduction talks with the Soviet Union. In 1990, he offered "living will" legislation to allow people in advance of a medical crisis to dictate what kind of treatment they would want.

Danforth has also been disturbed by the growing negativity of political campaigns and has pushed for revisions in their financing and conduct. In an attempt to raise the level of political dialogue, Danforth has pushed legislation to require federal candidates to appear personally in ads that refer to their opponents and to require television stations to offer free airtime for candidates to respond to direct attacks.

At Home: A former Wall Street lawyer and Ralston-Purina heir hardly seems the type to represent a state whose political hero is Harry S Truman, champion of the common folk. Moreover, Danforth's air of detachment strikes some as a sign of political vulnerability. Prior to his re-election in 1988, there was talk of his being ripe for the taking. But Danforth showed he had learned the lessons of his first re-election (which he won with just 51 percent). He raised millions of dollars early and made manifest to all his intent to fight for his job.

Partly because of Danforth's early effort, the Democrats failed to field a challenger in his weight class. Prominent Democratic Rep. Richard A. Gephardt decided to run for president and popular six-term Democratic Rep. Ike Skelton decided to stay in the House. The party's top state official, Lt. Gov. Harriett Woods, was retiring and opted to skip the race. She had given Danforth his scare in 1982, but had also lost a bruising Senate race in 1986 to former Gov. Christopher S. Bond.

So the party turned to youthful state Sen. Jay Nixon, a 32-year-old in his first legislative term. Nixon struggled to raise a quarter of the money Danforth had at his disposal. He also struggled to find an effective theme. Danforth never had to run hard. He won all 114 counties, losing only in the city of St. Louis. His share was 68 percent, and he drew over a third of a million votes more than George Bush.

Danforth's patrician pedigree was no hindrance in his early political career; he won his first election in 1968 as an outsider, a young insurgent vowing to rid the state attorney general's office of deadwood that had collected during a succession of Democratic administrations.

But in 1982, after eight years in state office and six more in Washington, Danforth struck many Missouri voters not as a reformer but as a wealthy man distant from their economic concerns. That was why he was nearly ambushed by Woods, a clever liberal Democrat who sold herself as a populist under the slogan "Give 'em hell, Harriett."

Woods' entry had initially brought little cheer to party leaders. She had gained valuable media exposure representing a liberal St. Louis County constituency, but offered a record of questionable appeal to rural and conservative voters and to business interests the Democrats needed to compete with Danforth's fundraising. Woods also supported legalized abortion and the use of busing as a tool to desegregate schools.

But Woods managed to portray herself as an average working person and hit Danforth as an aristocrat who supported cuts in health care, social services and education. As the only female Democratic candidate for the Senate in 1982, her candidacy became a priority for women's groups.

Danforth's fundraising advantage over Woods was more than 2-to-1. But his money and excellent organization were offset by Woods' most important asset: desire. Voters were impressed with her enthusiastic dawn-to-midnight campaigning, while Danforth gave the impression he was not really hungry to be re-elected. More than once, he lamented that the campaign was making it difficult for him to watch the baseball playoffs (the St. Louis Cardinals were on their way to a World Series championship).

But Danforth's strategy changed abruptly Oct. 15, when the *St. Louis Globe-Democrat's* poll showed his comfortable lead of a month earlier had vanished. The incumbent went on the attack. He called Woods a liberal and a throwback to an era of discredited Democratic tax-and-spend practices. He accused her of demagoguery for portraying the Republican Party as a menace to Social Security without offering any constructive suggestions of her own. He brought up abortion and busing, topics he had avoided earlier in the campaign.

The shift to a negative campaign had the desired effect. Some conservative Democrats took a second look at Woods and lost their enthusiasm, and complacent Republicans were jolted into realizing that a high GOP turnout would be necessary to keep the seat.

Woods won where Democrats usually do in Missouri — St. Louis, Kansas City and the majority of rural counties — but in each of those areas, her liberalism cost her just enough votes to enable Danforth to escape.

His 1982 struggle, in any event, did not sully his reputation as the founder of the modern-day Missouri GOP. Elected state attorney general in 1968 in his political debut, Danforth became the first Republican in 22 years to win statewide office.

He lured bright young lawyers to the attorney general's office — among them Bond, who served two non-consecutive terms as governor before his 1986 election to the Senate, and John Ashcroft, who has been governor since Bond left that office in 1985. Danforth also developed a reputation as a protector of consumers and the environment.

In 1970 Danforth was the GOP's only hope to dislodge Democratic Sen. Stuart Symington, who was seeking a fourth term. In an expensive campaign that introduced Missouri to modern media-oriented politics, Danforth won 48 percent of the vote. Two years later, he returned as attorney general by over 450,000 votes, and awaited his next Senate chance.

It came, as expected, when Symington retired in 1976. Democrats appeared to seize the momentum by nominating U.S. Rep. Jerry Litton, described by a state political expert as "one of the most exciting political personalities to come along in years." But Democratic enthusiasm was tragically brief. Litton died in a primary-night plane crash, and Danforth was suddenly the favorite.

The state Democratic committee chose as its replacement former Gov. Warren Hearnes, whose courthouse-style administration had been the focus of Danforth's campaign attacks in 1968. Hearnes had finished a poor second to Litton in the primary. Against Litton, Danforth would have had a difficult contest; against Hearnes, he won easily.

Committees

Commerce, Science & Transportation (Ranking)
National Ocean Policy Study

Finance (4th of 9 Republicans)
International Trade (ranking); Medicare & Long Term Care; Taxation

Select Intelligence (4th of 7 Republicans)

Elections

1988 General

John C. Danforth (R)	1,407,416	(68%)
Jay Nixon (D)	660,045	(32%)

Previous Winning Percentages: **1982** (51%) **1976** (57%)

Campaign Finance

	Receipts	Receipts from PACs		Expend-itures
1988				
Danforth (R)	$4,077,855	$1,149,207	(28%)	$3,992,995
Nixon (D)	$884,513	$241,231	(27%)	$880,160

Key Votes

1991

Authorize use of force against Iraq	Y

1990

Oppose prohibition of certain semiautomatic weapons	Y
Support constitutional amendment on flag desecration	N
Oppose requiring parental notice for minors' abortions	N
Halt production of B-2 stealth bomber at 13 planes	N
Approve budget that cut spending and raised revenues	Y
Pass civil rights bill over Bush veto	Y

1989

Oppose reduction of SDI funding	Y
Oppose barring federal funds for "obscene" art	Y
Allow vote on capital gains tax cut	Y

Voting Studies

	Presidential Support		Party Unity		Conservative Coalition	
Year	**S**	**O**	**S**	**O**	**S**	**O**
1990	74	25	71	29	81	19
1989	90	10	75	24	76	21
1988	75	23	65	28	76	22
1987	60	37	68	30	75	19
1986	80	20	77	21	82	17
1985	81	17	77	20	70	20
1984	86	13	85	15	83	17
1983	80	16	72	27	64	32
1982	71	19	72	21	76	18
1981	85	13	84	15	83	16

Interest Group Ratings

Year	ADA	ACU	AFL-CIO	CCUS
1990	39	43	44	0
1989	15	71	20	63
1988	20	72	42	71
1987	35	54	80	61
1986	30	57	33	61
1985	15	65	19	75
1984	35	68	27	63
1983	40	32	13	53
1982	40	50	23	52
1981	25	73	17	89

Christopher S. Bond (R)

Of Mexico — Elected 1986

Born: March 6, 1939, St. Louis, Mo.
Education: Princeton U., A.B. 1960; U. of Virginia, LL.B. 1963.
Occupation: Lawyer.
Family: Wife, Carolyn Reid; one child.
Religion: Presbyterian.
Political Career: Mo. assistant attorney general, 1969-70; Mo. state auditor, 1971-73; governor, 1973-77, 1981-85; Republican nominee for U.S. House, 1968; Republican nominee for governor, 1976.
Capitol Office: 293 Russell Bldg. 20510; 224-5721.

In Washington: A conservative who does not manifest strongly partisan instincts, Bond is active on a variety of issues, particularly where there is a home-state concern at stake. On the Agriculture Committee, where he spent his first four Senate years, those characteristics inspired comparisons with another well-liked conservative who has not let ideology interfere with his legislative pursuits, Thad Cochran of Mississippi. That style should also help Bond on the Appropriations Committee, his new assignment in the 102nd Congress. He joins Cochran on Appropriations' Agriculture Subcommittee.

Like other former governors, Bond had a little trouble adjusting to the Senate's competing egos. But unlike some others, he took a low-key approach to the adjustment. He willingly cut a modest figure in his first Congress, finding his way gradually, choosing his shots with care.

By the 101st Congress, he appeared to have become more accustomed to the ways of the Senate. He ran for a party leadership position before the start of the 102nd Congress, losing 26-17 to Bob Kasten of Wisconsin in a bid for Republican Conference secretary.

Having tweaked the Reagan administration in his 1986 campaign for being "too slow to respond" to the farm crisis, Bond found himself on the spot as one of four freshmen — and the only first-term Republican — on the Agriculture Committee. He also won seats on Banking, Budget and Small Business.

Bond's early bills on Agriculture tended toward the dull but doable — improving meat and fowl inspection, providing flood relief, reducing farmers' paperwork. He began stretching out in the 101st Congress, when the committee assembled the five-year reauthorization of government agriculture programs in the 1990 farm bill.

In 1989, he and South Dakota Democrat Tom Daschle sponsored legislation to create a system to ensure clean U.S. grain exports. Critics have long contended that U.S. grain exports are dirtier than foreign grain and less suitable for flour milling. The measure established a grain-quality coordinator in the Agriculture Department and created a system by which the head of the Federal Grain Inspection Service could determine future grain standards. It was approved as a separate bill by the Agriculture Committee; a version of it became law as part of the farm bill.

Bond's most active parochial interest in the farm bill was soybeans. But ranking Republican Richard G. Lugar wanted to maintain a unified party flank to combat the impulse to lard the bill with significantly higher government crop subsidies. Although Bond was considered a potential Republican vote for Democratic proposals to secure a generous new marketing loan for soybean growers, he was unwilling to buck the GOP leadership to do so. The 1990 farm bill included a marketing loan plan for soybeans, though the loan rate was far lower than that sought by members from soybean-producing states.

The pet proposal of committee Chairman Patrick J. Leahy of Vermont would have curtailed the so-called "circle of poison," in which domestically banned pesticides re-enter the United States on imported fruit and vegetables. Bond vigorously opposed Leahy's plan, arguing that the plan would export some pesticide production, costing U.S. jobs. "If these pesticides can be manufactured offshore," he said, "we will then be in a position to have no control over them." Monsanto Co., one of world's largest chemical companies, is headquartered in St. Louis.

As a member of both the Agriculture and Banking committees in the 101st Congress, Bond worked with Leahy to try to forge a compromise in a turf war between the Commodity Futures Trading Commission and the Securities and Exchange Commission. The dispute was over which commission should regulate esoteric financial instruments known as stock-index futures contracts. One Bond constituent, the Kansas City Board of Trade, is a small but active player in the futures market. The debate spilled over into the 102nd Congress.

On Banking in the 101st Congress, Bond took a keen interest in a sweeping overhaul of housing programs, even though he does not sit on the Housing Subcommittee. He helped broker a compromise by California Democrat Alan Cranston, enabling it to attract Republican votes in winning committee approval. He was later appointed to the House-Senate conference. The bill contained $5.9 million to authorize the sale of more than 200 public housing units to residents at the Carr Square Village project in St. Louis.

Bond has delved into defense policy to help workers at the St. Louis-based McDonnell-Douglas Corp., which announced in July 1990 that it would lay off 17,000 workers. During Banking Committee consideration of a bill reauthorizing the Export Administration Act, Bond and Connecticut Democrat Christopher J. Dodd sponsored an amendment to open the coffers of the Export-Import Bank to finance military sales abroad. (The Ex-Im Bank is prohibited by law and by agency regulation from financing military sales.)

Bond and Dodd contended that defense-based companies needed to find new outlets for their products and that other developed countries provide government financing to military sales. The committee adopted their amendment on a 16-5 vote, but it was dropped in conference; the bill died in the 101st Congress. When it resurfaced in the 102nd Congress, Dodd and Bond tried again, but the Senate voted to kill their amendment by a vote of 48-47.

Although Bond is generally a chamber-of-commerce conservative, his vote is not always easy to predict. Most would place him to the right of Republican John C. Danforth, the state's senior senator, but an ideologue he is not. He supported military aid to the contras, but described the decision as "a close call." On Banking, he supported measures granting faster access to deposited funds and greater disclosure of credit card terms, both of which were resisted by the financial community.

One consistent motivation for Bond is his deference to the states. This often aligns him with other former governors, including Democrats such as David L. Boren of Oklahoma, Bob Graham of Florida and Terry Sanford of North Carolina, who favor regulatory decision making by states. When the Banking Committee mulled banks' right to sell insurance, and when Agriculture debated who would distribute rural development grants, Bond spoke up for letting each state decide. When Banking took up an anti-takeover bill in 1987, Bond sided with the more moderate Republicans who preferred to empower each state to set limits on takeovers.

During Senate consideration in the 101st Congress of a bill creating child-care grant programs, Bond offered an amendment to permit states to make grants to school districts for before- and after-school programs for so-called "latch-key" children. The Senate adopted his proposal by voice vote. It became law as part of the year-end deficit-reduction bill.

In 1990, Bond and Danforth introduced a proposed constitutional amendment to reverse a 5-4 ruling by the Supreme Court that said federal courts may, in some circumstances, order a locality to increase its taxes. The court in 1989 ruled that a lower court could order a municipality, in this case Kansas City, Mo., to raise property taxes to pay for a school desegregation plan. The proposed amendment by Bond and Danforth would have prohibited a court from ordering or instructing states or municipalities to increase taxes.

At Home: Missouri is unique in having two senators who not only attended the same private out-of-state university but studied there at the same time. Like Danforth, Bond is a product of a wealthy family who attended Princeton in the 1950s and then earned a law degree from an exclusive law school. In Bond's case, the family money came from making bricks. At law school, he was class valedictorian.

Through most of Missouri's history, such well-heeled Republicans have stood little chance of statewide office. But the 1960s brought a political sea change in this border state. Danforth was elected attorney general in 1968 and has been in statewide office ever since. Bond went to work for Danforth, and just four years later, at age 33, became governor.

In 1986, Bond was one of the few Republican success stories in a Senate election year fraught with disaster for the GOP. He overcame an aggressive, well-known challenger and the rumblings of farm protest to win the seat vacated by retiring Democrat Thomas F. Eagleton. As a result, he was the only Republican to capture an open Democratic seat in 1986.

His contest with Lt. Gov. Harriett Woods was a bitter one. Bond offered himself as a budget-conscious conservative, citing his two-term gubernatorial record of avoiding major tax increases. He painted Woods as a liberal with values out of synch with most Missourians.

Woods portrayed herself as a scrappy Truman-style populist, a strategy she had used in nearly upsetting Danforth in 1982. She called Bond a passive governor, an aloof aristocrat and a likely rubber stamp for Reagan.

Woods' campaign foundered, however, when she ran a TV ad depicting a weeping farmer describing how he was foreclosed by a company on whose board Bond served. The ad provoked a firestorm of controversy, as Republicans and editorialists branded it a crass attempt to put farm troubles to political use. The ad damaged Woods' attempts to win conservative rural Democrats.

Bond, too, had past problems with members of his own party. Many conservatives remembered his support of Gerald R. Ford over Ronald Reagan at the 1976 national GOP convention, and never really considered him one of their own. But any lingering doubts they might have had about Bond were drowned out by their antipathy toward Woods. Bond lost in St. Louis and Kansas City, but buoyed by good showings in the suburbs of both cities, and in most rural areas, he won with 53 percent. He had outspent Woods by about $900,000 and campaigned despite physical pain. Early in 1987, he underwent surgery to remove bone spurs in his neck.

Bond broke into politics in 1968, seeking a seat in the U.S. House from northeastern Missouri. Although he lost, it was the year the modern GOP in Missouri was born. Richard M. Nixon carried the state and Danforth was elected attorney general. Bond took a job with Danforth and in 1970 won the office of state auditor. Two years later, he was elected the state's first GOP governor since World War II.

He had a troubled first term. Democrats in the Legislature found him aloof; Republicans chafed at his efforts to abolish patronage jobs. In 1976, he lost to Democrat Joseph P. Teasdale. But he avenged this loss in 1980, riding Reagan's popularity atop the ticket and exploiting Teasdale's image as an incompetent administrator. In his second term, Bond warmed up to the Legislature and generally won points for being more accessible.

Committees

Appropriations (12th of 13 Republicans)
District of Columbia (ranking); Agriculture, Rural Development & Related Agencies; VA, HUD and Independent Agencies; Legislative Branch

Banking, Housing & Urban Affairs (4th of 9 Republicans)
Consumer & Regulatory Affairs (ranking); International Finance & Monetary Policy

Budget (7th of 9 Republicans)

Small Business (4th of 8 Republicans)
Government Contracting & Paperwork Reduction (ranking); Rural Economy & Family Farming

Elections

1986 General		
Christopher S. Bond (R)	777,612	(53%)
Harriett Woods (D)	699,624	(47%)
1986 Primary		
Christopher S. Bond (R)	239,961	(89%)
Richard J. Gimpelson (R)	10,471	(4%)
David Andrew Brown (R)	10,407	(4%)
Joyce Padgett Lea (R)	9,022	(3%)

Campaign Finance

	Receipts	Receipts from PACs		Expenditures
1986				
Bond (R)	$5,464,030	$1,320,353	(24%)	$5,396,255
Woods (D)	$4,380,643	$761,339	(17%)	$4,377,661

Key Votes

1991	
Authorize use of force against Iraq	Y
1990	
Oppose prohibition of certain semiautomatic weapons	Y
Support constitutional amendment on flag desecration	Y
Oppose requiring parental notice for minors' abortions	N
Halt production of B-2 stealth bomber at 13 planes	N
Approve budget that cut spending and raised revenues	Y
Pass civil rights bill over Bush veto	N
1989	
Oppose reduction of SDI funding	Y
Oppose barring federal funds for "obscene" art	Y
Allow vote on capital gains tax cut	Y

Voting Studies

	Presidential Support		Party Unity		Conservative Coalition	
Year	**S**	**O**	**S**	**O**	**S**	**O**
1990	82	16	86	12	100	0
1989	86	12	85	12	89	3
1988	75	20	73	19	89	8
1987	64	23	86	11	94	0

Interest Group Ratings

Year	ADA	ACU	AFL-CIO	CCUS
1990	11	77	44	67
1989	5	85	10	100
1988	0	88	23	86
1987	10	81	25	82

1 William L. Clay (D)

Of St. Louis — Elected 1968

Born: April 30, 1931, St. Louis, Mo.
Education: St. Louis U., B.S. 1953.
Military Service: Army, 1953-55.
Occupation: Real estate broker; insurance executive.
Family: Wife, Carol Ann Johnson; three children.
Religion: Roman Catholic.
Political Career: St. Louis Board of Aldermen, 1959-64; St. Louis Democratic Committee member, 1964-67.
Capitol Office: 2470 Rayburn Bldg. 20515; 225-2406.

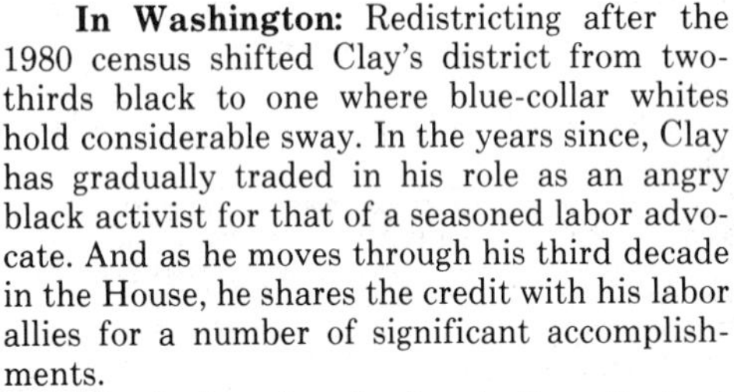

In Washington: Redistricting after the 1980 census shifted Clay's district from two-thirds black to one where blue-collar whites hold considerable sway. In the years since, Clay has gradually traded in his role as an angry black activist for that of a seasoned labor advocate. And as he moves through his third decade in the House, he shares the credit with his labor allies for a number of significant accomplishments.

Clay is the voice of unions both on the Post Office and Civil Service Committee, which he chairs, and on Education and Labor, where he served as chairman of the Labor-Management Relations Subcommittee until 1991. Most of his efforts fizzled in the early 1980s, as labor-backed initiatives met with strong opposition from the newly installed Reagan administration. But during the last three Congresses, Clay slowly chipped away at his ambitious agenda, enacting several major pieces of legislation and coming close on others.

He was the author and lead Education and Labor Committee conferee on a bill to ban so-called pension reversions. The provisions, stripped at the last minute from legislation in 1989, sought to protect employees' pension assets from employer raids of overfunded pension plans. Congress in 1990 did pass, as part of its omnibus deficit-reduction bill, provisions expected to slow the practice by sharply increasing taxation of any excess pension plan funds retained by an employer.

Protecting workers' pensions has long been a top priority for Clay. In the 99th Congress, he helped author pension law provisions that were included in the Tax Reform Act of 1986. Those provisions were expected to result in new coverage for an estimated 2 million workers, and to shorten the eligibility period (vesting period) for others to five years on the job, rather than 10 under previous law.

In the last two Congresses, Clay was a leading advocate of legislation that made other sweeping changes in the nation's pension protection law, the Employee Retirement Income Security Act (ERISA). His efforts were spurred on by the plight of workers in troubled industries that were sidestepping promised pension benefits, and by the soaring deficits of the Pension Benefit Guaranty Corporation.

As the original sponsor and floor manager of compromise legislation in 1990 reversing a Supreme Court ruling that allowed age-based discrimination in employee benefits, Clay helped steer the measure through Congress late in the session. Despite opposition from GOP lawmakers and business groups, President Bush ultimately signed the measure.

Clay was also a primary House sponsor of the plant-closing notification bill that finally won approval in 1988. Clay won committee approval of a bill much like a broader 1985 version, but the Senate was unwilling to go that far. When the measure was finally attached to the trade bill, the notice provision was scaled back from 90 days to 60 days and other controversial language dropped. Still, the measure provoked a veto from President Ronald Reagan. But when a separate notification bill then passed both chambers by lopsided margins, Reagan allowed it to become law without his signature.

Clay has been frustrated in his efforts to win approval for "family leave" legislation, which would require most employers to allow unpaid, job-protected leave to a worker upon the birth or adoption of a child, or to care for an ailing family member. The bill appeared to gain momentum in 1988, only to fall victim to end-of-the-session politicking in the Senate. It made it through both chambers in 1990 before being vetoed by President Bush.

When Clay took up the cause at the start of the 101st Congress, he explained simply, "It's not fair to ask a man or woman to choose between their job or caring for a newborn baby." He served as floor manager for the bill, but his efforts fell more than 50 votes short of overriding Bush's veto.

Another long and frustrating battle for Clay is his effort to revise the Hatch Act, which restricts political activity by government work-

Missouri 1

North St. Louis; Northeast St. Louis County

Eero Saarinen's Gateway Arch, despite its modern design, serves as a symbolic reminder of the old St. Louis — a strategically located threshold to the West luring enough steamship, railroad and manufacturing trade to make it one of the nation's leading commercial centers.

But the city's postwar story is one of retreat rather than advance. Blacks and whites alike have fled once-great St. Louis — the well-off to distant suburbia and the less affluent to neighborhoods just outside the borders. Numerous factories and businesses have closed; parts of the downtown area have declined to an extent that shocks even those visitors accustomed to inner-city blight. An ambitious program of renovating historic buildings in the city is under way, but much work remains before St. Louis' image is restored.

Reflecting the exodus from the city, the 1st District lost over one-quarter of its people during the 1970s, more than any other Missouri district. In order to survive for the 1980s, the district had to be stretched south to pick up urban territory, and west and north into the suburbs of St. Louis County. More than half of the district's residents live outside the city limits.

Although suburban communities such as University City are among the most liberal in Missouri, much of the St. Louis County territory is populated with working-class conservatives who find jobs in the auto assembly and aerospace manufacturing facilities ringing the city. In predominantly white communities such as Ferguson, Bellefontaine Neighbors and Jennings, the blue-collar voters are fiercely opposed to abortion and busing. Republicans often win here in statewide elections.

But GOP sentiments are drowned in a tide of Democratic votes from the city portion of the 1st. Most of the district's blacks — who make up 52 percent of the 1st's population — live within the city limits, north of Interstate 44. The poverty of the Near North and Near South sides contrasts with parts of the West End, where some of the city's remaining white-collar professionals live. In 1988, the 1st gave Michael S. Dukakis an overwhelming 72 percent of its presidential vote.

Although St. Louis' manufacturing economy today is overshadowed by the plants outside its limits, the 1st District is not without an industrial presence. Ralston-Purina, the cereal company to which Missouri Republican Sen. John C. Danforth is heir, is headquartered here, and a corridor of light manufacturing is located toward the city's northern end.

Population: 546,208. White 259,259 (48%), Black 281,529 (52%), Other 3,383 (1%). Spanish origin 4,923 (1%). 18 and over 393,146 (72%), 65 and over 74,588 (14%). Median age: 30.

ers. He came close to obtaining the modifications sought by federal employee unions in 1975, when Congress passed his Hatch Act bill but failed to override President Ford's veto. He has introduced legislation to reform the act in each Congress since.

During the 101st Congress, Clay came closest to achieving his goal. Both chambers in 1990 passed revision measures, but Bush vetoed the legislation. The House voted to override the veto but the Senate effort failed by two votes. Clay has cited the issue as a priority for the 102nd Congress in his new post as committee chairman.

Clay has served notice that he intends to use his new office to further his critique of the Bush administration. He has said his agenda would also include the accuracy of the 1990 census and its probable undercount of minorities as well as focusing on reform of federal employees' health insurance.

Clay also spent the early months of the 102nd Congress leading the fight for a bill that would prevent companies from hiring permanent replacements for striking workers.

An opponent of the use of military force in the Persian Gulf, Clay nonetheless recognized the need to pay "the astronomical cost of this military confrontation." He offered legislation in early 1991 to permit U. S. taxpayers to make a special contribution on their federal tax forms to finance the war effort.

Successful or not, these serious legislative endeavors have allowed Clay to move beyond his early bellicose reputation. While he still rarely pulls a punch, his comments these days are tame compared with his earlier days in the House. He once referred to President Nixon's vice president as "Zero" Agnew. Early in the Reagan administration, he often implied that racism motivated its efforts to cut the domestic budget, modify civil rights laws and avoid sanctions against the white-minority government of South Africa.

Assailing provisions of the 1986 antidrug bill that applied the death penalty to certain drug crimes, Clay called capital punishment immoral. "Not one rich person has ever gone to the gallows," Clay said. "Only poor whites and minorities are forced to walk the last mile and choose a last supper."

In 1988, his opposition to the death penalty amendment to the drug bill remained, but his rhetoric toned down. "Official violence is not the answer to unofficial violence," he said.

More recently, during consideration of the parental leave bill in 1991, Clay insisted that Bush's incredibly high popularity ratings would not deter Democrats from pushing ahead with their liberal domestic agenda. "I don't see his popularity equating into positive votes of insane positions on domestic matters," Clay said. He was also critical of the administration's proposed civil rights bill offered in 1991, denouncing it as "toothless." During an earlier period in his House career, Clay's harshest rhetoric was aimed at the House ethics committee. In 1980, when the committee recommended censure of his close friend and Postal Operations Subcommittee ally, Charles H. Wilson of California, he called the panel a "kangaroo court" that was "perverted" and "devoid of fairness, justice and equity."

He spoke equally sharply of the press, referring to reporters as "bloodthirsty scribes ... awaiting the carnage." In the 101st Congress, Clay was one of just 18 members to vote against reprimanding Democrat Barney Frank of Massachusetts for misusing his official position to help a male prostitute.

Clay himself was the source of some controversy over ethics issues in the 1970s. He was accused at one point of billing the House for trips home he did not take. His administrative assistant went to jail in 1976 for fraudulently placing a sister-in-law on the federal payroll. The Justice Department spent months scrutinizing Clay's tax returns and campaign finances. But no charges were ever filed against him. He settled the House travel account by repaying some of the money, saying there had been a bookkeeping error. When the Justice Department dropped its probe, Clay charged that it had been politically motivated.

At Home: There was both good news and bad news for Clay in the 1990 election returns. While he won a 12th term by a margin of more than 22,000 votes, his 61 percent vote share was the lowest in his congressional career and hints at future troubles. With declining population in his St. Louis base, it is almost certain that before 1992 his district will have to be drawn further into the suburbs.

Clay, though, will never be beaten because he is out of touch. For someone who has spent more than 20 years in Washington, he remains unusually active in local politics. Clay occasionally uses his congressional mailing privileges to advise constituents of his views on local matters, as he did in a 1987 letter criticizing two tax proposals backed by St. Louis Mayor Vincent C. Schoemehl Jr.

Though both measures passed, Clay had won a 1986 round against Schoemehl, when he opposed the mayor's decision to turn control of a city-run health care facility over to a private, non-profit corporation. The dispute prompted Schoemehl to field a slate of candidates to challenge Clay-backed contenders for city offices in the Democratic primary. Clay's slate swept Schoemehl's in the primary.

Clay's career has thrived on confrontation. His own campaign literature once noted that he had been "arrested, convicted of contempt of court [and] served 110 days in jail" for demonstrating at a St. Louis bank.

That incident took place years before his election to the House in 1968. But it was one of a string of such confrontations that gave him a reputation as a civil rights activist. In 1954, while going through military training at Fort McClellan in Alabama, Clay found the post swimming pool and barber shop closed to blacks, and the NCO club off limits when there were white women present. He led blacks to swim en masse in the pool, boycott haircuts and picket the club.

After returning to St. Louis, Clay became active in the NAACP and CORE. He was elected to the city's Board of Aldermen in 1959 and became an official in the politically active Pipefitters union in 1966. While keeping his identification as a civil rights militant, he moved closer over the years to the patronage politics of the local Democratic Party.

Redistricting by the Missouri Legislature in 1967 placed most of St. Louis' 257,000 blacks in the 1st District, ending years of fragmentation of the black vote. Democrat Frank M. Karsten, the 1st District representative for 22 years, decided to retire rather than seek re-election in 1968.

With the backing of most local black leaders, Clay emerged from a racially divided four-way primary with a 48 percent plurality. In the general election, he ran on a platform geared to the district's 55 percent black majority. He called for more federal money for jobs, housing, health and education, and for changes in police agencies and the court system to eliminate bias against blacks. The Republican candidate, also black, was Curtis C. Crawford, former director of the local legal aid society. Crawford suggested that Clay's talent was militant protest, not lawmaking. But the district was too strongly Democratic for Crawford to be a serious threat. Clay won 64 percent to become Missouri's first black congressman.

From 1970 through 1980, Clay encountered no strong challengers. Though Republican candidates usually held him even in the predominantly white St. Louis County portion of the district, Clay regularly coasted to re-election by taking 80 percent or more in the heavily black north part of St. Louis.

But as Clay extended his tenure in the House, the population in his district dwindled steadily. The 1st lost one-quarter of its people during the 1970s, and redistricting in 1981 gave Clay nearly 200,000 new constituents, many of them blue-collar workers in largely white sections of St. Louis County. In Clay's old district, two-thirds of the population was black; in the redrawn 1st, blacks barely formed a majority, and more whites than blacks were registered to vote.

A sizable number of Clay's new constituents fiercely objected to his support for abortion and for busing of students to integrate schools. Anti-Clay Democrats coalesced behind a white candidate, state Sen. Al Mueller, an opponent of abortion and busing. Mueller also chided the incumbent for missing roll-call votes, for wasting taxpayers' money on foreign junkets and for billing the government for hotel expenses when visiting St. Louis.

Clay ridiculed his primary opponent as a parochial haggler over trivial matters. Saying he could not afford to keep houses in Washington and St. Louis, Clay brushed off the charges about his hotel stays. Maintaining that his stands on abortion and busing were consonant with current laws and court rulings, Clay also criticized his opponent for ignoring important national problems, such as unemployment and cutbacks in federal aid to the disadvantaged.

In a year when working-class voters of both races were preoccupied with economic troubles, Clay's visible role as a quotable foe of Reaganomics was well received. He was strongly backed by organized labor.

Mueller carried the St. Louis County portion of the 1st, but Clay crushed him in the city en route to a 61 percent victory districtwide.

Committees

Post Office & Civil Service (Chairman)
Investigations (chairman)

Education & Labor (3rd of 25 Democrats)
Labor-Management Relations; Labor Standards

House Administration (7th of 15 Democrats)
Libraries & Memorials (chairman)

Elections

1990 General		
William L. Clay (D)	62,550	(61%)
Wayne G. Piotrowski (R)	40,160	(39%)
1988 General		
William L. Clay (D)	140,751	(72%)
Joseph A. Schwan (R)	53,109	(27%)

Previous Winning Percentages: **1986** (66%) **1984** (68%) **1982** (66%) **1980** (70%) **1978** (67%) **1976** (66%) **1974** (68%) **1972** (64%) **1970** (91%) **1968** (64%)

District Vote For President

	1988	1984	1980	1976
D	143,802 (72%)	140,858 (65%)	142,545 (65%)	116,330 (56%)
R	54,578 (27%)	74,447 (35%)	68,196 (31%)	82,828 (40%)
I			8,546 (4%)	

Campaign Finance

	Receipts	Receipts from PACs	Expend-itures
1990			
Clay (D)	$213,965	$182,550 (85%)	$196,909
Piotrowski (R)	$12,767	0	$12,666
1988			
Clay (D)	$204,094	$141,830 (69%)	$159,700

Key Votes

1991	
Authorize use of force against Iraq	N
1990	
Support constitutional amendment on flag desecration	N
Pass family and medical leave bill over Bush veto	Y
Reduce SDI funding	Y
Allow abortions in overseas military facilities	Y
Approve budget summit plan for spending and taxing	N
Approve civil rights bill	Y
1989	
Halt production of B-2 stealth bomber at 13 planes	Y
Oppose capital gains tax cut	Y
Approve federal abortion funding in rape or incest cases	Y
Approve pay raise and revision of ethics rules	Y
Pass Democratic minimum wage plan over Bush veto	Y

Voting Studies

	Presidential Support		Party Unity		Conservative Coalition	
Year	**S**	**O**	**S**	**O**	**S**	**O**
1990	16	80	75	12	7	89
1989	28	62	71	21	7	88
1988	12	67	68	12	0	82
1987	11	74	72	12	2	91
1986	8	78	71	11	2	74
1985	15	80	73	18	4	91
1984	19	65	83	3	2	92
1983	9	80	83	2	2	85
1982	19	43	74	5	3	67
1981	22	68	86	2	4	89

Interest Group Ratings

Year	ADA	ACU	AFL-CIO	CCUS
1990	94	4	100	31
1989	95	0	92	33
1988	90	0	100	18
1987	92	0	100	0
1986	75	0	100	15
1985	100	5	100	24
1984	95	5	100	33
1983	90	0	100	17
1982	65	13	100	29
1981	95	0	87	0

2 Joan Kelly Horn (D)

Of St. Louis — Elected 1990

Born: October 18, 1936, St. Louis, Mo.
Education: U. of Missouri-St. Louis, B.A. 1973, M.A. 1975.
Occupation: Political research and consulting firm president.
Family: Husband, E. Terrence Jones; six children.
Religion: Roman Catholic.
Political Career: No previous office.
Capitol Office: 1008 Longworth Bldg. 20515; 225-2561.

The Path to Washington: Horn, a political consultant, accomplished in 1990 what most people in her business only dream about; she won a seat for herself in Congress.

And she did it on her first try in seemingly hostile terrain. In a suburban St. Louis district that George Bush and Republican Rep. Jack Buechner each swept easily in 1988, Horn won by 54 votes. Her victory required a recount, but the fact that she won at all is surprising, because she was hardly a household name in the 2nd even at the end of the campaign.

But Horn effectively marshaled her limited resources for a late negative advertising blitz that the overconfident Buechner failed to counter. And on Election Day, she was bolstered by a strong Democratic tide in St. Louis County that not only elected her to Congress, but enabled a Democrat to win the county executive's post for the first time since 1958.

Horn's decision to run in 1990 turned out to be a fortuitous bit of timing. She had considered a House race two years earlier but deferred to a Democratic legislative veteran who was swamped by Buechner.

At first, Horn's chances of unseating Buechner in 1990 seemed little better. Early on, a St. Louis commentator described her as possessing the voice and looks of a modern-day June Cleaver, the mother on the original "Leave It to Beaver" TV show.

But Horn's life was far grittier than the stereotypical sitcom mom of the 1950s. She noted during the campaign that she knew the problems of working families well because she was once a divorced, working mother.

And Horn quickly showed she was no political innocent. She entered the campaign with a wide network of contacts from her membership on the Democratic state committee and leadership positions in the Missouri Women's Political Caucus and the Freedom of Choice Council (a local abortion rights group). She had gained other political expertise through a research and polling firm she operated with her husband, the dean of the college of arts and sciences at the University of Missouri-St. Louis. Among their clients were Democratic Rep. Richard A. Gephardt and former Democratic Rep. Robert A. Young, ousted by Buechner in 1986.

Horn's contacts enabled her to win endorsements from St. Louis Mayor Vincent Schoemehl, the Missouri state Labor Council and most of the 16 Democratic township clubs in the suburban 2nd. Her consulting experience helped her put together a classic grass-roots campaign, replete with phone banks and targeted direct-mail appeals.

An underfinanced primary foe, John M. Baine, proved only a temporary diversion. He promoted himself as an anti-abortion candidate and distributed a brochure questioning Horn's "family values." It reminded voters that she violated a town ordinance in the mid-1980s in the suburban community of Ladue by living with her husband before they were married.

Horn responded with radio ads noting that she had a husband, six children, seven grandchildren and the credentials to go to Congress. She won the primary by better than 2-to-1.

Any doubts about Horn's willingness to play hardball were eliminated in the fall campaign, when she aimed a steady stream of criticism at Buechner that depicted him as regularly abusing his congressional power. Her campaign culminated with a TV ad that began with a 1988 shot of Buechner saying service in Congress was "a public trust, not a public trough," then cut to a shot of hogs slopping in the mud while an announcer recited Buechner's financial benefit from honoraria, overseas travel, the congressional pay raise and a cable TV stock deal.

Missouri 2

Western St. Louis County

Anchored in the suburbs west and northwest of St. Louis, the 2nd holds many of the manufacturing and assembly plants that overshadow the remaining industrial activity within the city. McDonnell Douglas, Chrysler, Emerson Electric, Ford and Monsanto are among the district's major employers. But the district's manufacturing base is shrinking; McDonnell Douglas laid off 4,000 workers in 1990 and Monsanto cut 300 employees.

Employees of all these companies — and of St. Louis' Lambert International Airport also located here — lend a blue-collar flavor to the northern portion of the district. A proposed expansion of the airport, which would eliminate almost 1,000 homes in Bridgeton, has added a volatile element to local politics.

But more and more, the character of the 2nd is being defined by white-collar communities in the central part of the district — suburbs such as Ladue and Chesterfield, which are populated by affluent business and banking executives. While the blue-collar "North County" tends to be anti-abortion, a pro-abortion rights Democrat such as Joan Kelly Horn can run well in the affluent municipalities located by the city's western border. While the 2nd is heavily Catholic territory, it also takes in a significant Jewish community.

The southwestern part of the district is home to the ghost town of Times Beach. Site of one of the nation's worst environmental disasters, Times Beach residents were afflicted by health problems linked to dioxin-tainted soil.

Separate from the city of St. Louis since 1876, St. Louis County includes nearly 90 percent of the 2nd's population. The county has steadily filled up with St. Louisans taking refuge from the declining urban center.

Also included in the 2nd is a small chunk of politically marginal eastern St. Charles County. Located just across the Missouri River from St. Louis County is the city of St. Charles, a community of 42,000, which served briefly as Missouri's capital in the 19th century.

From 1951 until he ran for the Senate in 1968, GOP Rep. Thomas B. Curtis held this district. Even during the time that Democrats James Symington and Robert A. Young occupied the 2nd, it favored Republicans in most other contests. Propelled by strong showings in St. Louis County, GOP presidential candidates amassed comfortable margins districtwide in the past four elections. The GOP enjoys similar successes in statewide races, although Horn's win in 1990 was accompanied by Democratic successes in several other countywide races.

Population: 546,039. White 509,598 (93%), Black 29,094 (5%), Other 5,631 (1%). Spanish origin 4,646 (1%). 18 and over 386,511 (71%), 65 and over 46,702 (9%). Median age: 31.

Committees

Public Works & Transportation (33rd of 36 Democrats)
Aviation; Economic Development; Water Resources

Science, Space & Technology (31st of 32 Democrats)
Environment; Technology & Competitiveness

Select Children, Youth & Families (19th of 22 Democrats)

Campaign Finance

	Receipts	Receipts from PACs		Expend-itures
1990				
Horn (D)	$356,766	$160,515	(45%)	$340,390
Buechner (R)	$639,968	$259,595	(41%)	$670,758

Key Vote

1991

Authorize use of force against Iraq	N

Elections

1990 General		
Joan Kelly Horn (D)	94,378	(50%)
Jack Buechner (R)	94,324	(50%)
1990 Primary		
Joan Kelly Horn (D)	17,165	(65%)
John M. Baine (D)	7,550	(29%)
Leif O. Johnson (D)	1,485	(6%)

District Vote For President

	1988	1984	1980	1976
D	111,170 (39%)	87,719 (31%)	93,845 (37%)	97,561 (44%)
R	173,201 (61%)	190,521 (69%)	153,176 (60%)	120,324 (54%)
I			5,216 (2%)	

3 Richard A. Gephardt (D)

Of St. Louis — Elected 1976

Born: Jan. 31, 1941, St. Louis, Mo.
Education: Northwestern U., B.S. 1962; U. of Michigan, J.D. 1965.
Military Service: Air National Guard, 1965-71.
Occupation: Lawyer.
Family: Wife, Jane Ann Byrnes; three children.
Religion: Baptist.
Political Career: St. Louis Board of Aldermen, 1971-76; sought Democratic nomination for president, 1988.
Capitol Office: 1432 Longworth Bldg. 20515; 225-2671.

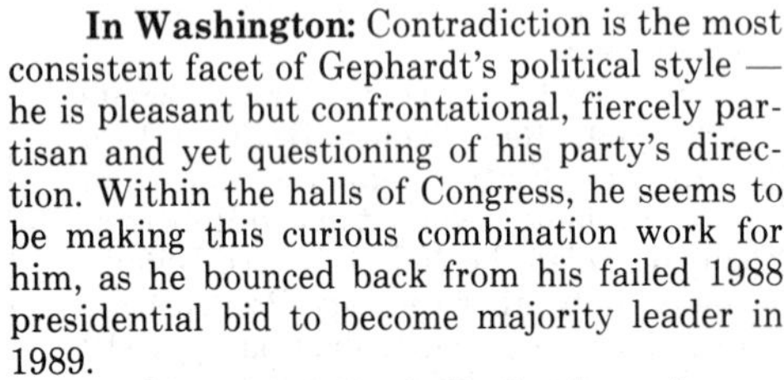

In Washington: Contradiction is the most consistent facet of Gephardt's political style — he is pleasant but confrontational, fiercely partisan and yet questioning of his party's direction. Within the halls of Congress, he seems to be making this curious combination work for him, as he bounced back from his failed 1988 presidential bid to become majority leader in 1989.

On a personal level, Gephardt projects a clean-cut image with his pressed shirts and polite Midwestern manner. He is well regarded by Democratic colleagues, who describe him as a good listener and an able negotiator. But politically, he can be blunt, aggressive and defiantly partisan; he is the one Democratic leader who has been singled out for personal criticism by President Bush, who complained of the harshness of his rhetoric.

Gephardt's political incongruities run even deeper than the stylistic ones. In 1984, he seemed to be leaning to the right: He helped found the Democratic Leadership Council (DLC), which aimed to pull the national party away from its close identification with liberal special interest groups. Critics called the DLC an elitist, establishment tool, and Gephardt, as chairman of the House Democratic Caucus, was the ultimate insider. Yet in 1988, Gephardt campaigned for president as an angry populist outsider, and won Iowa's left-leaning Democratic caucuses. Then in the 101st Congress, he was back at the insider's game. After winning election as majority leader, he became more of a partisan liberal than he was as caucus chairman in the mid-1980s.

Admirers view these contradictions as a sign of Gephardt's independence, critics a sign of opportunism. In the presidential arena, they contributed to his falter after Iowa. But his ability to catch hot issues and shift from genial negotiator to partisan provocateur well suits the dual roles of his current office.

His earnest, consensus-seeking side is suited to the housekeeping aspects of the majority leader's job — scheduling floor debate and the like. But Gephardt plays a more partisan role than did his predecessor as majority leader, Thomas S. Foley of Washington, now the Speaker. To define party themes, Gephardt institutionalized morning "message" meetings with a Kitchen Cabinet of aggressive House colleagues. Under his leadership, Democrats are matching the GOP in the use of televised one-minute floor statements.

Never was Gephardt's ability to play opposing roles so clear as during the 1990 budget debate. During the protracted debate, he managed to be a leading negotiator at the bipartisan budget summit, and then when that deal collapsed, he won praise for leading the charge for a Democratic alternative with a politically potent tax on millionaires.

When the process began the recession was focusing public concern on the deficit, and President Bush and congressional leaders from both parties agreed to seek a bipartisan solution through private summit talks. Gephardt was appointed to lead the Democratic House delegation, serving as chairman when Bush was not present. Despite Gephardt's increasingly partisan posture, he seemed a natural for the role. He has always thrived on long, thorough meetings, and he had played a major part in the conference negotiations over the Gramm-Rudman-Hollings anti-deficit law in late 1985.

During the 1990 budget summit, Gephardt kept negotiators from both parties at the table for marathon sessions over seven months. He also kept Democrats from publicly airing their many differences by giving them a chance to work things out among themselves. He behaved as if failure of the summit would tarnish his image as a leader.

After hammering out a package that included painful budget cuts and tax increases and presenting it to the public and colleagues, however, Gephardt distanced himself from the agreement. "I must tell you that I was personally deeply disappointed with the results that

Missouri 3

South St. Louis; Southeast St. Louis County and Jefferson County

Traditionally based in the blue-collar, ethnic neighborhoods of South St. Louis, the 3rd has been forced to change by the city's population decline. Like the 1st District, its companion to the north, the 3rd now reaches into the suburbs of St. Louis County and beyond to fill itself out. The city accounts for only a little more than one-third of the district vote.

What remains of St. Louis in the 3rd, however, still has a heavily ethnic cast. Italians are clustered in The Hill, where family-owned taverns, sausage shops and pasta restaurants have survived several generations. Bevo Mill and Carondelat are old-line German communities. The 3rd also includes some signs that South St. Louis is experiencing growth. Lafayette Square, at the northeastern edge of the district, was largely an urban wasteland a decade ago. But it has undergone significant development in recent years.

Once rooted firmly in the New Deal coalition, South St. Louis voters have become increasingly concerned about taxes, government spending, abortion and busing. Nonetheless, they still tend to give Democrats their votes.

Monsanto and Mallinckrodt chemical facilities and barge operations along the Mississippi River are important to the district's economy. But the most prominent enterprise in this part of the city is Anheuser-Busch, the nationally known brewery that employs some 5,000 people in its headquarters and plants located here.

Nearly 40 percent of the 3rd's population lives in suburban St. Louis County, home to more conservative voters who regularly vote for the GOP. The county has been responsible for pushing the 3rd into the GOP column in most recent national and statewide elections; George Bush carried the 3rd with 53 percent in 1988.

Some of the county voters are longtime suburbanites; close-in communities such as Gravois and Lemay are where many of them make their homes. Others grew up on St. Louis' South Side and moved out in the past decade.

The residents of politically marginal Jefferson County constitute the remaining quarter of the district's population. Jefferson has come under the umbrella of metropolitan St. Louis in recent years, and the closer-in places such as Arnold are hard to distinguish from suburban St. Louis County turf. But farther west, Jefferson still is rural. Farmers in the Hillsboro area often truck their produce to markets in downtown St. Louis.

Population: 546,102. White 533,831 (98%), Black 7,442 (1%), Other 3,260 (1%). Spanish origin 5,603 (1%). 18 and over 403,646 (74%), 65 and over 76,186 (14%). Median age: 32.

we achieved," he said not long before the House rejected the package.

It was not the first time Gephardt had backed away from a public stand. Early in his House career, he was a forceful critic of liberal Democratic thinking, but he soon found himself defending many of the traditional programs from Reagan's attack. Long a foe of abortion, Gephardt had backed away from that position during his presidential campaign. In 1989, he was on both sides of the issue — voting to ban all abortion funding on the District of Columbia spending bill and months later voting to permit abortion funding for victims of rape and incest on another bill.

On the 1990 budget deal, Gephardt's split sentiments reflected that of many of his colleagues. Leadership loyalists were willing to set aside their discomfort and support the summit package, fearing Republicans would blame the fiscal crisis on them if they did not. But none liked it. After it was rejected, Gephardt moved the House quickly toward a more partisan budget — one with a surtax on wealthy Americans. While Senate Republicans would not consider the package and the final budget resembled the summit deal, Gephardt had helped Democrats gain the rhetorical high ground.

Soon afterward, he vowed to "devote the 102nd Congress to kitchen-table economics," pushing for tax relief for the middle class and the surtax for millionaires, themes that made some wonder if Gephardt would stand by the pledge he made when he became majority leader — not to run for president in 1992.

Gephardt's success with the tax fairness slogan was long in coming. In mid-1989, Gephardt and Foley dubbed the president's capital gains tax cut a sop to the rich. But that rhetoric drew sharp criticism for its class warfare tone, which echoed from Gephardt's "it's your fight, too" presidential slogan. Shortly before the House approved the tax cut, Foley and Gephardt backed away from making it a party loyalty test, but House approval of the capital gains tax cut was viewed as a significant defeat for the new leaders.

It was during that dispute that President Bush revealed his personal pique with Gephardt. "I tell you," Bush said to a House Republican, who unbeknownst to the president had taken the White House's call at a press conference on a telephone connected to the Capitol sound studio, "I'm displeased with Gephardt, the way he made it so really kind of personal."

The capital gains debate allied Gephardt with Ways and Means Chairman Dan Rostenkowski of Illinois, who was often displeased with Gephardt during 1986 deliberations on overhauling the tax code. Though Gephardt was then a member of the tax-writing panel and the impetus for reform came from tax-simplification legislation he co-authored with Democratic Sen. Bill Bradley of New Jersey, Gephardt was busy campaigning for president as the bill was hammered out.

Over the years, however, Gephardt had been a heavy lifter on Ways and Means. He made it on to the panel in his first term with the help of his mentor, Richard Bolling, dean of the Missouri delegation and Rules Committee chairman. In 1981, he was among those who argued that the committee should present a clear alternative to President Ronald Reagan's tax plan, regardless of whether anyone thought it would win. When Rostenkowski decided to try to compete with Reagan for conservative votes, Gephardt worked to persuade Southern Democrats to vote with Rostenkowski in exchange for improved tax treatment for the oil industry. He presented the Democratic response to Reagan's televised speech on behalf of his tax plan.

Gephardt left the panel in 1989, taking an *ex officio* seat on the Budget Committee, where he had served from 1979 through 1984.

Gephardt has shown a remarkable combination of concern about long-term problems and willingness to hammer out short-term solutions, traits on display as he worked to pass the "fair trade" amendment that lifted him to national prominence. With its call for retaliation against countries that maintain large trade surpluses with the United States and have barriers to U.S. exports, Gephardt's amendment was attacked as a dangerous "protectionist" measure by the administration and congressional critics. In order to win a 218-214 vote in 1987, Gephardt scaled it back, allowing the president to ignore the provisions if he determined there would be substantial harm to the United States or the other country. House conferees on the trade bill eventually backed even further away from the idea.

When it came to debate about the U.S.-Mexico free-trade talks, Gephardt again laid out far-reaching goals of protecting American jobs and the environment, but pulled back from a confrontation he seemed unlikely to win. In May 1991, he gave the administration a go-ahead to negotiate the deal on a fast track that allows the treaty to be presented to Congress for an up-or-down vote. The price of his support on the fast-track agreement was introduction of a congressional resolution reminding the administration of his concerns.

Gephardt's stand on trade was the backbone of his presidential campaign, and coupled with scores of endorsements from House colleagues, he enjoyed more success than many initially predicted, eventually winning 170 delegates. Gephardt was the first Democrat to enter the race in February 1987, and, staking his future on Iowa, he spent more time there than any other candidate. His campaign played to a "have not" coalition of economically troubled farmers and blue-collar workers concerned with foreign competition.

While he placed first in Iowa, the media boost he expected from his win was undercut by headline-grabbing turmoil in the GOP contest, where Bush ran third. And outside the farm state, his populist appeal did not sell well. Gephardt finished second in the New Hampshire primary, but that, and a win in South Dakota, was not enough to put his name in lights as he headed into 14 Southern primaries on Super Tuesday. Short on money for advertising, Gephardt won only his home state on Super Tuesday. A subsequent third-place finish in Michigan brought his campaign to an end.

Gephardt returned to an uncertain future in the House. Many believed he would try to use the House as a platform for another national campaign, but that changed as ethics controversies undermined the careers of Speaker Jim Wright of Texas and Democratic Whip Tony Coelho of California. When his political ally Coelho announced in May 1989 that he was not making an expected race for majority leader and would resign from Congress, Gephardt became an overwhelming favorite for the post over Georgia Democrat Ed Jenkins, whom he ultimately defeated 181-76.

In the 99th Congress, he had encountered even less trouble winning the caucus chairmanship; his main opponent, David R. Obey of Wisconsin, dropped out nearly a year before the vote.

At Home: Gephardt could find himself in the ironic position of acquiring more power in Washington at the same time he is growing more vulnerable back home. Since he ran unopposed for re-election in 1984, Gephardt has seen his vote share fall from 69 percent in 1986 to 63 percent in 1988 to 57 percent in 1990 — by far his lowest share since he first won the seat in 1976.

As a leader in Congress, Gephardt has been tied by recent GOP challengers to Congress' negative image. And in 1990, Gephardt was also victimized by the nationwide anti-incumbent mood that struck particularly hard in Missouri;

six of the state's nine congressmen fell below the 60 percent mark. But Gephardt's modest showing in 1990 will force him to stay alert to his home base.

Gephardt might really have had to sweat in 1990 if state and national Republicans had been able to run their preferred candidate, St. Louis County Election Board member Stephen Doss. He was lured into the race with broad hints that he would be assured a hefty campaign treasury.

But at the same time, a number of St. Louis County Republicans were lining up behind Malcolm L. "Mack" Holekamp, a former Webster Groves City Council member. Both filed for the GOP primary and, after several weeks of finger-pointing, Doss quit the race.

At that point, the national GOP lost interest in the contest and Holekamp had trouble raising money. But he proved to be a feisty challenger, lambasting Gephardt as "a PAC rat" and the Democrats' "No. 1 Bush-whacker." At one point he reportedly dressed up as a "dark horse" to draw attention to his campaign.

Gephardt was first elected to Congress in 1976 on the strength of his reputation as a young activist on the machine-dominated St. Louis Board of Aldermen. While on the board, he had sponsored zoning laws to preserve ethnic neighborhoods, building a constituency among German-American working-class communities on the city's South Side, the core of the 3rd District electorate. He was also supportive of a constitutional amendment to restrict abortions, a position that he abandoned later in his career.

In the 1976 Democratic primary, Gephardt defeated state Sen. Donald J. Gralike, head of an electrical workers' local. Gephardt's November opponent was Republican Joseph L. Badaracco, who had served eight years as a St. Louis alderman, six of those as board president.

Badaracco stressed his reputation for honesty in city politics and tried to convince voters that Gephardt was really a rich downtown lawyer groomed for Congress by the pin-striped establishment. Gephardt promised to emulate the moderate approach of Democratic Rep. Leonor K. Sullivan, who was retiring. He won with ease, rolling up a 2-to-1 advantage in St. Louis and taking nearly 60 percent of the vote in St. Louis County.

Committees

Majority Leader

Budget (2nd of 23 Democrats)

Elections

1990 General		
Richard A. Gephardt (D)	88,950	(57%)
Malcolm L. Holekamp (R)	67,659	(43%)
1990 Primary		
Richard A. Gephardt (D)	34,919	(80%)
Nicholas F. Clement (D)	8,523	(20%)
1988 General		
Richard A. Gephardt (D)	150,205	(63%)
Mark F. "Thor" Hearne (R)	86,763	(36%)

Previous Winning Percentages: **1986** (69%) **1984** (100%) **1982** (78%) **1980** (78%) **1978** (82%) **1976** (64%)

District Vote For President

	1988	1984	1980	1976
D	111,956 (47%)	85,385 (35%)	94,314 (40%)	118,403 (50%)
R	126,310 (53%)	156,443 (65%)	127,018 (54%)	114,390 (48%)
I			10,227 (4%)	

Campaign Finance

	Receipts	Receipts from PACs		Expend-itures
1990				
Gephardt (D)	$1,647,415	$762,687	(46%)	$1,455,794
Holekamp (R)	$82,784	$4,966	(6%)	$82,077
1988				
Gephardt (D)	$513,893	$183,196	(36%)	$512,206
Hearne (R)	$209,102	$12,154	(6%)	$202,524

Key Votes

1991	
Authorize use of force against Iraq	N
1990	
Support constitutional amendment on flag desecration	N
Pass family and medical leave bill over Bush veto	Y
Reduce SDI funding	Y
Allow abortions in overseas military facilities	?
Approve budget summit plan for spending and taxing	Y
Approve civil rights bill	Y
1989	
Halt production of B-2 stealth bomber at 13 planes	N
Oppose capital gains tax cut	Y
Approve federal abortion funding in rape or incest cases	Y
Approve pay raise and revision of ethics rules	Y
Pass Democratic minimum wage plan over Bush veto	Y

Voting Studies

	Presidential Support		Party Unity		Conservative Coalition	
Year	**S**	**O**	**S**	**O**	**S**	**O**
1990	14	74	89	2	17	74
1989	33	63	95	3	22	78
1988	18	58	73	4	16	76
1987	5	22	18	0	5	21
1986	16	53	69	1	18	54
1985	26	71	84	6	31	65
1984	33	60	87	7	27	69
1983	26	70	90	6	25	69
1982	44	53	71	24	56	40
1981	54	43	64	33	69	27

Interest Group Ratings

Year	ADA	ACU	AFL-CIO	CCUS
1990	83	4	100	14
1989	90	4	100	30
1988	75	10	92	20
1987	20	0	100	0
1986	70	0	100	18
1985	60	19	88	19
1984	75	14	92	38
1983	85	9	94	25
1982	55	33	80	35
1981	45	27	73	11

4 Ike Skelton (D)

Of Lexington — Elected 1976

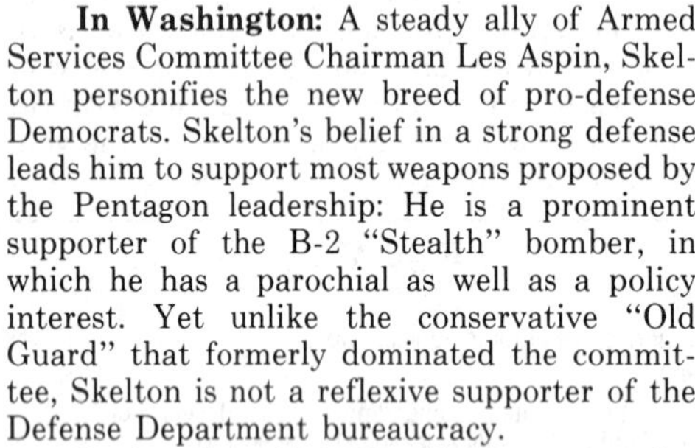

Born: Dec. 20, 1931, Lexington, Mo.

Education: Attended Wentworth Military Academy, 1949-51; U. of Edinburgh, Scotland, 1953; U. of Missouri, B.A. 1953, LL.B. 1956.

Occupation: Lawyer.

Family: Wife, Susan Anding; three children.

Religion: Christian Church.

Political Career: Lafayette County prosecuting attorney, 1957-60; special assistant attorney general, 1961-63; Lafayette County Democratic Committee chairman, 1962-66; Mo. Senate, 1971-77.

Capitol Office: 2134 Rayburn Bldg. 20515; 225-2876.

In Washington: A steady ally of Armed Services Committee Chairman Les Aspin, Skelton personifies the new breed of pro-defense Democrats. Skelton's belief in a strong defense leads him to support most weapons proposed by the Pentagon leadership: He is a prominent supporter of the B-2 "Stealth" bomber, in which he has a parochial as well as a policy interest. Yet unlike the conservative "Old Guard" that formerly dominated the committee, Skelton is not a reflexive supporter of the Defense Department bureaucracy.

During the mid-1980s, Skelton was active in efforts to reform the military command structure, providing more authority to the chairman of the Joint Chiefs of Staff and strengthening coordination between the service branches. Advocates of these reforms say they reduced interservice rivalries and provided the foundation for the near-flawless U.S. military operation against Iraq in early 1991. Skelton has since chaired an Armed Services task force studying reforms in the Defense Department's education programs for its officers corps.

The B-2 issue has given a higher-than-usual profile to the laconic Missourian. Air Force plans to build a large fleet of the radar-evading bombers have come under fire because of the project's huge price tag. Skelton, on the other hand, knows what losing the project would cost 4th District communities near Whiteman Air Force Base, slated to be home to the first B-2 bomber wing. But like most members facing defense cutbacks in favored projects, Skelton emphasizes not jobs, but the B-2's importance to the nation's defense.

"Stealth technology incorporated in the B-2 will force the Soviet defense establishment to devote more of its military resources to air defense, a much more benign activity from the United States' point of view," Skelton said in an April 1990 speech. "It is far better to have them spend on defense than offense."

Skelton was a staunch supporter of the January 1991 resolution authorizing President Bush to use force, if necessary, to end Iraq's occupation of Kuwait. "[Iraqi dictator] Saddam Hussein threatens the interests of our country and the interests of the free world," he said during debate on the resolution. During the ensuing conflict, Skelton took to the House floor several times to praise American troops, without mentioning what was widely known on Capitol Hill — that his son James, an Army lieutenant, was stationed in the war zone.

While he speaks out on these sometimes emotional defense matters, Skelton spends much of his time on the crucial but highly esoteric issues involving the Defense Department's decision-making process.

When Skelton became chairman of the Armed Services Panel on Military Education, he criticized the Defense Department for stressing management skills over military strategy since the 1960s in its professional education programs. "An M.B.A. became a prized achievement," Skelton said. "But the management emphasis hasn't reduced cost overruns, while it has reduced the quality of strategic skills."

In November 1988, the panel issued a report recommending the conversion of the National War College, based in Washington, D.C., to the National Center for Strategic Studies, which would be attended by military officers from the ranks of colonel/Navy captain to major general/rear admiral, as well as by several civilians involved in the national security sector. Reflecting Skelton's interest in coordinated joint military operations, the task force also recommended that the Armed Forces Staff College in Norfolk, Va., be made the flagship school for officers in "joint specialty" training.

The latter proposal is an extension of Skelton's efforts on the command reforms which passed in the 99th Congress. The Pentagon establishment — particularly the heads of the service branches who stood to lose turf to the chairman of the Joint Chiefs of Staff — initially

Missouri 4

West — Kansas City Suburbs; Jefferson City

Sprawling across west-central Missouri, the 4th is an amalgam of rural farm land, scenic tourist resorts and blue-collar suburban turf outside Kansas City.

Much of the area is given over to small farming. The 4th's cattle business is focused toward its southern end; corn, soybeans, pork and dairy production are important districtwide. Pockets of rural poverty — especially in parts of Texas County — contrast with the economic climate enjoyed by comfortable landowners living in Lafayette and Pettis counties at the 4th's northern end.

Tourism has supplemented the district's agriculture in recent years. Winding around Camden County's northern border is the Lake of the Ozarks, a stretch of water that draws boaters, swimmers and skiers from around the state and nurtures a growing restaurant and motel trade.

Roughly 40 miles northeast of the lake lies Jefferson City, all but a sliver of which falls within the 4th's boundaries. Missouri's capital since 1826, it has never developed into a city of much size or sophistication. State government is the largest employer.

The district reaches into the Kansas City area to pick up some 80,000 constituents, many of whom commute to work in Kansas City factories. Other population centers include Sedalia, and Warrensburg, a grain and livestock center that is home to Central Missouri State University. Between these two cities is Whiteman Air Force Base, whose Minuteman missiles make civil defense a paramount concern. The Pentagon's 1991 base closing plan received a mixed reaction in the 4th; the Richards-Gebaur Air Force Base (near Kansas City) will be shut down, but the Army's Fort Leonard Wood (Pulaski County) will gain nearly 6,000 new military and civilian jobs.

The 4th contains some solidly Democratic areas of Jackson County east of Kansas City. But votes from this region have not been sufficient to overcome the GOP margins districtwide in recent elections for state and national office.

Population: 546,637. White 524,772 (96%), Black 14,950 (3%), Other 4,383 (1%). Spanish origin 5,503 (1%). 18 and over 390,415 (71%), 65 and over 70,341 (13%). Median age: 30.

opposed the effort. But the resistance wilted when such formidable defense-oriented legislators as Sens. Sam Nunn, D-Ga., and Barry Goldwater, R-Ariz., and Rep. Bill Nichols, D-Ala., headed the charge. Although the final bill was named for Goldwater (who has since retired) and Nichols (who died in December 1988), Skelton's early contributions were crucial in bringing the process forward.

Skelton's conservative leanings helped him form a bond with Aspin, the Wisconsin Democrat whose generally pro-Pentagon attitude is viewed with suspicion by more liberal Democratic members of Armed Services. The two first found common cause during the 99th Congress, when Skelton supported efforts to oust enfeebled Armed Services Chairman Melvin Price of Illinois and replace him with Aspin. Skelton also helped out in 1987 as Aspin fought off a challenge to his chairmanship from Marvin Leath of Texas.

A childhood polio victim who went on to attend a military academy, Skelton has worked to add money to boost ROTC scholarships and to require ROTC students to complete their education.

Aside from military-related issues, Skelton's major preoccupation is looking out for the interests of rural areas, such as those that make up much of his central Missouri district. The past chairman of the Congressional Rural Caucus, Skelton argues against what he views as a bias in federal funding that favors cities over rural areas. "Rural Americans suffer from many of the same problems that are seen in our large cities. . .," Skelton said in April 1989. "Citizens in non-metropolitan areas deserve the same level of federal assistance as urban residents."

Skelton is also a strong supporter of using tourism as an economic development tool in rural areas, an idea he promotes as chairman of the Small Business Subcommittee on Procurement, Tourism and Rural Development.

At Home: Although Skelton won easy reelection in 1990, he was brushed by the anti-incumbent sentiment that swept Missouri. His vote fell to 62 percent, the lowest since redistricting threw him together with freshman Republican Rep. Wendell Bailey in 1982.

Map makers gave Skelton a head start in that race. When Bailey's old 8th District was dismembered, the largest single block of his constituents was added to Skelton's 4th. So Bailey decided that was the place to seek a second term. But for every one of his old constituents in the new district, there were nearly two of Skelton's.

Numerous political action committees and nationally known politicians came into the 4th and billed the Skelton-Bailey match as a referendum on Reaganomics in the rural heartland. The candidates responded with appropriate rhetoric: Skelton called Bailey a "rubber stamp" because he supported nearly all the president's budget and tax proposals, and Bailey countered that Skelton's mixed record of support for Reaganomics showed him to be a liberal who occasionally waffled to appease conservatives.

Bailey, known as one of Missouri's most effective Republican campaigners, was relying on the gregarious, hard-charging style he developed as a car salesman to help him pull Democrats away from the less-dynamic Skelton.

But Skelton, a small-town lawyer with a sincere, low-key style, benefited from greater familiarity with the new district's voters. Of the seven counties that had been part of Bailey's old 8th District, Bailey carried six. But Skelton had represented 13 counties, and managed to carry 12 of them. That brought him in nearly 18,000 votes ahead.

Skelton's only other tough election was in 1976, when he won the seat of retiring Democratic Rep. William Randall. As a rural state legislator with a narrow political base, Skelton did not look particularly well-positioned when the campaign began. Only two counties in his state Senate district were within the borders of the 4th District as it was then drawn. His major rivals for the Democratic nomination were state senators from the Kansas City suburbs, which cast about 40 percent of the district vote.

Skelton chose to emphasize that he was the only major candidate from the rural part of the district, and campaigned successfully for farm and small-town support. He ran third in the suburbs, but with the rural vote he won with 40 percent overall.

Independence Mayor Richard A. King was the GOP nominee. A protégé of Gov. (and now Sen.) Christopher S. Bond, King tied his campaign to the GOP ticket of Bond and Senate candidate John C. Danforth. But Skelton cited his farm background and fiscal conservatism, voting against a pay raise for state legislators as an example. And the top of the GOP ticket did not provide King much coattail pull. Danforth carried the 4th, but Bond lost it. Skelton won by 24,350 votes.

Committees

Armed Services (9th of 33 Democrats)
Military Education (chairman); Military Personnel & Compensation; Procurement & Military Nuclear Systems

Select Aging (14th of 42 Democrats)
Health & Long-Term Care; Rural Elderly

Small Business (3rd of 27 Democrats)
Procurement, Tourism & Rural Development (chairman)

Elections

1990 General		
Ike Skelton (D)	105,527	(62%)
David Eyerly (R)	65,095	(38%)
1988 General		
Ike Skelton (D)	166,480	(72%)
David Eyerly (R)	65,393	(28%)

Previous Winning Percentages: **1986** (100%) **1984** (67%) **1982** (55%) **1980** (68%) **1978** (73%) **1976** (56%)

District Vote For President

	1988	1984	1980	1976
D	95,131 (40%)	75,862 (33%)	90,030 (40%)	97,502 (48%)
R	139,390 (59%)	155,939 (67%)	125,179 (56%)	103,436 (51%)
I			6,185 (3%)	

Campaign Finance

	Receipts	Receipts from PACs		Expend-itures
1990				
Skelton (D)	$390,115	$242,050	(62%)	$306,485
Eyerly (R)	$7,115	0		$7,137
1988				
Skelton (D)	$314,323	$195,725	(62%)	$273,316

Key Votes

1991	
Authorize use of force against Iraq	Y
1990	
Support constitutional amendment on flag desecration	Y
Pass family and medical leave bill over Bush veto	N
Reduce SDI funding	N
Allow abortions in overseas military facilities	N
Approve budget summit plan for spending and taxing	Y
Approve civil rights bill	Y
1989	
Halt production of B-2 stealth bomber at 13 planes	N
Oppose capital gains tax cut	N
Approve federal abortion funding in rape or incest cases	N
Approve pay raise and revision of ethics rules	Y
Pass Democratic minimum wage plan over Bush veto	Y

Voting Studies

	Presidential Support		Party Unity		Conservative Coalition	
Year	**S**	**O**	**S**	**O**	**S**	**O**
1990	50	48	68	29	94	4
1989	59	34	62	35	85	12
1988	43	52	63	30	92	8
1987	45	48	66	24	81	19
1986	48	47	66	26	76	20
1985	44	46	66	25	85	15
1984	54	38	63	27	76	15
1983	45	50	56	37	74	22
1982	48	34	40	41	73	14
1981	58	39	45	45	91	5

Interest Group Ratings

Year	ADA	ACU	AFL-CIO	CCUS
1990	33	50	50	62
1989	35	56	58	70
1988	40	58	83	62
1987	48	38	86	40
1986	35	55	86	47
1985	40	50	63	33
1984	35	36	77	33
1983	50	57	82	30
1982	10	65	50	63
1981	25	43	67	37

5 Alan Wheat (D)

Of Kansas City — Elected 1982

Born: October 16, 1951, San Antonio, Texas.
Education: Grinnell College, B.A. 1972.
Occupation: Legislative aide; federal economist.
Family: Wife, Yolanda Townsend; one child.
Religion: Church of Christ.
Political Career: Mo. House, 1977-83.
Capitol Office: 1210 Longworth Bldg. 20515; 225-4535.

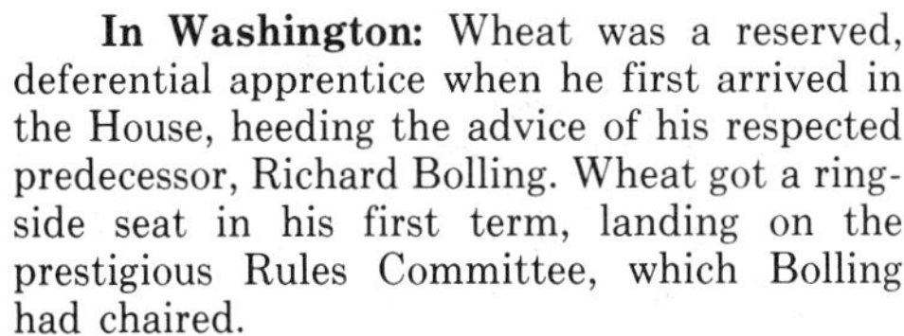

In Washington: Wheat was a reserved, deferential apprentice when he first arrived in the House, heeding the advice of his respected predecessor, Richard Bolling. Wheat got a ringside seat in his first term, landing on the prestigious Rules Committee, which Bolling had chaired.

Before long, he seemed restless to graduate into a higher-profile position: He considered a race for Democratic Caucus vice chairman in the 101st Congress, and then unsuccessfully sought a seat on the Budget Committee.

Although those moves did not pan out, Wheat has not been idle. He assumed a more prominent role in the Black Caucus Foundation, serving as its president in 1990 and 1991. In January 1990, he traveled to South Africa and later met with African National Congress leader Nelson Mandela. During debate over U.S. relations with South Africa, Wheat echoed a suggestion by Mandela, urging that sanctions continue until the United States determines that the nation's movement toward democracy is "irreversible."

And Wheat has continued to use his seat on Rules to win concessions for his urban district, including a number of multimillion-dollar flood-control projects. Other committee leaders are eager to accommodate members of Rules, given its role as traffic cop for nearly all bills.

He rarely introduces legislation of his own but instead sponsors Rules' resolutions for floor debate on issues of interest to him, such as the Civil Rights Act of 1990 and the leadership's top priority 1987 homeless-aid bill. His latter concern also helped him win a 1990 appointment to the House Select Committee on Hunger.

A trained economist and former state legislator, Wheat has the distinction of representing far more white constituents (75 percent) than any other black member. He seeks to appeal to a broad and moderate, but loyally Democratic, base. Once more of an agitator — as a Grinnell College student, Wheat led a campus protest to demand black-studies courses — in the House he personifies the House's younger generation of mainstream-oriented blacks.

At Home: Wheat's election in 1982 breached the custom that candidates of his race win only those districts dominated by liberals and minority voters. Just one-fourth of his district's residents are black and, though the white majority usually votes Democratic, most of the electorate stands to his right.

After attending Grinnell, a prestigious liberal-arts school in Iowa, Wheat worked in Kansas City for the Department of Housing and Urban Development, and was an aide to the Jackson County executive. Elected at age 25 to the state House, he served three terms and chaired its Urban Affairs Committee.

In 1982, Wheat was one of eight Democrats to enter the congressional primary following Bolling's retirement announcement. The only black candidate in the field, Wheat won nomination with 31 percent of the vote.

The bulk of Wheat's support in the primary came from 10 Kansas City wards where the black political organization, Freedom Inc., is an influential force. But he refuted those who said he was the candidate only of blacks by amassing about one-third of his primary vote in mostly white and relatively prosperous neighborhoods in southwest Kansas City.

Republicans nominated state Rep. John A. Sharp, who sought to woo moderate and conservative Democrats who found Wheat too liberal. Though Sharp did not portray the contest in racial terms, he often warned that Wheat would be a tool of Freedom Inc.

But Wheat found a unifying theme, holding up Reaganomics as a threat to working-class voters of all races. Armed with Bolling's endorsement, Wheat found support among local business people and union members alike, and he took an impressive 58 percent.

Wheat's liberal leanings and narrow margin of victory in the 1982 primary prompted some conservative white Democrats to seek an alternative candidate for 1984. But no prominent challenger came forward. Wheat has won re-election easily since then, although his 62 percent showing in 1990 was his lowest vote share since he first won the seat.

Missouri 5

Kansas City and Eastern Suburbs

Long sensitive about its reputation as an overgrown cow town, Kansas City still offers some support for that point of view — it remains a nationally prominent market for feeder cattle and hard winter wheat.

But that image obscures the diverse economy it has maintained throughout this century. Auto assembly is a major industry; metropolitan Kansas City is the nation's sixth-largest auto producer. IBM and Hallmark are crucial concerns. Hallmark is a hometown corporation and has spent millions of dollars on commercial redevelopment within the city. The company built Crown Center, which provides an array of restaurants, shops, pricey apartments and a luxury hotel. The federal government also is a large employer, with many regional branches located in the city. The metropolitan area is not particularly large, but is home for two major pro teams, the Royals in baseball and the Chiefs in football.

Though Kansas City has not suffered the massive flight of people and businesses that has crippled St. Louis, its population has declined to about 435,000 — fewer people than were living in the city 30 years ago. To compensate in the last redistricting, the 5th was extended into the suburbs of Jackson County, but Kansas City still casts about two-thirds of the vote.

The district cuts through the eastern sections of blue-collar Independence and Lee's Summit, leaving most of both towns in the 5th. Partisan allegiances are closely divided in these suburbs, but Kansas City's Democratic vote — bolstered by the black community — usually determines the political outcome districtwide. In 1988, Democratic presidential nominee Michael S. Dukakis won 60 percent of the district's vote, and it voted for Walter F. Mondale and Jimmy Carter in the elections before that.

Population: 546,882. White 407,941 (75%), Black 125,181 (23%), Other 5,901 (1%). Spanish origin 15,385 (3%). 18 and over 405,263 (74%), 65 and over 71,266 (13%). Median age: 31.

Committees

District of Columbia (5th of 8 Democrats)
Government Operations & Metropolitan Affairs (chairman); Judiciary & Education

Rules (7th of 9 Democrats)
Legislative Process

Select Children, Youth & Families (11th of 22 Democrats)

Select Hunger (18th of 22 Democrats)
International

Elections

1990 General		
Alan Wheat (D)	71,890	(62%)
Robert H. Gardner (R)	43,897	(38%)
1990 Primary		
Alan Wheat (D)	54,664	(80%)
Gus Dubbert (D)	13,620	(20%)
1988 General		
Alan Wheat (D)	149,166	(70%)
Mary Ellen Lobb (R)	60,453	(28%)

Previous Winning Percentages: **1986** (71%) **1984** (66%) **1982** (58%)

District Vote For President

	1988		1984		1980		1976	
D	129,421	(60%)	121,869	(54%)	122,645	(55%)	119,296	(57%)
R	83,888	(39%)	105,868	(46%)	89,058	(40%)	84,849	(41%)
I					10,692	(5%)		

Campaign Finance

	Receipts	Receipts from PACs		Expend-itures
1990				
Wheat (D)	$311,266	$224,435	(72%)	$245,132
1988				
Wheat (D)	$303,515	$205,500	(68%)	$240,623
Lobb (R)	$15,658	$650	(4%)	$14,636

Key Votes

1991	
Authorize use of force against Iraq	N
1990	
Support constitutional amendment on flag desecration	N
Pass family and medical leave bill over Bush veto	Y
Reduce SDI funding	Y
Allow abortions in overseas military facilities	Y
Approve budget summit plan for spending and taxing	N
Approve civil rights bill	Y
1989	
Halt production of B-2 stealth bomber at 13 planes	Y
Oppose capital gains tax cut	Y
Approve federal abortion funding in rape or incest cases	Y
Approve pay raise and revision of ethics rules	Y
Pass Democratic minimum wage plan over Bush veto	Y

Voting Studies

	Presidential Support		Party Unity		Conservative Coalition	
Year	**S**	**O**	**S**	**O**	**S**	**O**
1990	13	86	95	3	11	87
1989	27	71	80	17	7	90
1988	15	83	79	18	5	92
1987	9	91	97	2	5	95
1986	14	86	96	3	12	88
1985	15	84	97	1	5	95
1984	23	77	96	4	3	97
1983	12	87	97	3	10	90

Interest Group Ratings

Year	ADA	ACU	AFL-CIO	CCUS
1990	100	4	100	21
1989	95	0	100	40
1988	100	0	93	21
1987	100	0	100	0
1986	95	0	86	22
1985	100	0	100	14
1984	100	0	92	38
1983	95	0	100	15

6 Tom Coleman (R)

Of Kansas City — Elected 1976

Born: May 29, 1943, Kansas City, Mo.

Education: William Jewell College, B.A. 1965; New York U., M.P.A. 1966; Washington U., J.D. 1969.

Occupation: Lawyer.

Family: Wife, Marilyn Anderson; three children.

Religion: Protestant.

Political Career: Mo. assistant attorney general, 1969-72; Mo. House, 1973-77; candidate for Clay County clerk, 1970.

Capitol Office: 2468 Rayburn Bldg. 20515; 225-7041.

In Washington: A youthful looking Kansas City lawyer with a public administration degree from New York University, Coleman seems an unlikely candidate to be a senior player on rural and agricultural issues. But having come to the House at the young age of 33, he has moved up to the ranking Republican spot on the Agriculture Committee. Coleman balances his assignment there with his role as the second-ranking Republican on another committee, Education and Labor.

Coleman got national attention during the 101st Congress as ranking member of the Education and Labor Subcommittee on Postsecondary Education, where funds for the National Endowment for the Arts are authorized.

In response to the uproar over works by NEA grant recipients that many found sacrilegious or obscene, Congress in 1989 barred the NEA from funding work that could be considered obscene, sadomasochistic or homoerotic.

When the issue resurfaced in 1990 as part of the NEA's annual reauthorization, it again triggered a debate over obscenity vs. government censorship, with conservatives urging further funding restrictions, or outright abolishment of the NEA. But Coleman and fellow subcommittee Republicans Steve Gunderson of Wisconsin and Paul B. Henry of Michigan set out to forge compromise language imposing some restrictions on NEA's latitude in grant-making, but preserving the endowment.

Opposing any attempt to restrain the NEA was subcommittee Chairman Pat Williams of Montana. Williams and Coleman agreed to move the reauthorization bill — and the fight — directly to the House floor. Coleman and Gunderson proposed shifting the distribution of arts funds from the NEA to state arts agencies. If the NEA chairman found that an artist had created an obscene work, the grant would have to be stopped and the money returned.

But Coleman had to rethink his position when conservative Utah GOP Sen. Orrin G. Hatch offered a less intrusive compromise, dumping restrictions on the NEA but requiring grant recipients to return money used for projects determined by courts to be obscene. Williams and Coleman produced a compromise that followed Hatch's approach. It tightened the grant application process, making the NEA chairman more accountable. "We believe we have a middle position and the middle will hold," Coleman said. It did: The compromise was adopted by the House 382-42.

Sober and unassuming, Coleman regularly represents the middle ground on Education and Labor, where bipartisan cooperation frequently evaporates, and on the House floor, where he is not an automatic vote for the GOP line. In 1990, Coleman was one of 17 House Republicans to vote against a constitutional amendment to ban desecration of the flag.

Early in his career on Agriculture, Coleman was most visible as a caustic critic of farm programs sponsored by Democrats. That Coleman is not heard much anymore. Now he is often found defending his committee's product, regardless of authorship, against critics in both parties who consider farm subsidies wasteful.

As ranking member of the Agriculture Subcommittee on Conservation and Credit, Coleman spent much time working with genial Democratic Chairman Ed Jones, who retired after the 100th Congress. The new Conservation chairman, Glenn English of Oklahoma, differs greatly from Jones in style and temperament. But English and Coleman nevertheless teamed in the 101st Congress to promote a rural development measure that had been greeted coolly by the Reagan administration when Coleman introduced it in the 100th Congress.

Frustrated by efforts to address problems in the agricultural economy, Coleman introduced rural development legislation to target economically distressed areas. The bill aimed to overhaul the way the federal government delivers roughly $1 billion in assistance to rural areas. It appeared to be on a fast track after winning subcommittee approval, but budget problems and powerful interest groups derailed the initial attempt to send it to the House floor.

Missouri 6

Northwest — St. Joseph

A vast stretch of northwestern Missouri, the 6th covers 27 counties, although half the district's residents live in a three-county patch of urbanized territory in the 6th's southwest corner. The region has rebounded slowly from the farm crisis of the mid-1980s; erosion, drought and flooding have also taken their toll. In 1988 presidential voting, the 6th was the most competitive Missouri district: George Bush edged past Michael S. Dukakis by just 200 votes.

The "northlanders" of the Kansas City environs in Clay and Platte counties seek an identity distinct from the city's, but many of them work in its industries and businesses. Cutbacks at Kansas City International Airport, particularly by Trans World Airlines, have upset the economy.

The city of St. Joseph anchors Buchanan County, the district's third urbanized county. A booming supply depot for gold prospectors heading to California in the 1800s, St. Joseph gained a place in history as the eastern end of the Pony Express and today is a flour-milling and agribusiness center.

Typically, Clay and Platte yield GOP majorities, while Buchanan leans Democratic. All three voted Republican for president in 1980 and 1984, but Buchanan supported Democrat Harriett Woods' unsuccessful Senate bids in 1982 and 1986, Dukakis in 1988, and Coleman's Democratic foe in 1990.

The rest of the 6th is rural and generally conservative. While parts of the rolling north prairie resemble the Iowa breadbasket, the family farms that once dotted the landscape are fading; from 1980-87, eight of the 10 counties in Missouri with the largest rate of population loss were in the 6th. The sluggish economy has led business leaders in several counties to consider landfills as economic stimulants, despite local opposition.

There is evidence of a Yankee influence in Putnam, Mercer and a few other 6th District counties on or near the Iowa border, where Ohio and Iowa farmers moved long ago; for years it rivaled the Ozarks for GOP loyalty. Poor economic conditions have weakened the GOP grip in these counties, though.

Population: 546,614. White 532,071 (97%), Black 9,571 (2%), Other 2,912 (1%). Spanish origin 5,688 (1%). 18 and over 396,507 (73%), 65 and over 78,169 (14%). Median age: 32.

Months later, the full committee approved the bill, but only after deliberating eight hours and debating nearly 40 amendments.

The English-Coleman bill centralized federal efforts by pooling the existing funds and giving authority for distributing them to a new agency within the Agriculture Department — the Rural Development Administration.

That proved to be the most controversial aspect of the legislation. North Carolina Democrat Charlie Rose, whose state received a disproportionately large sum of Farmers Home Administration assistance under the existing plan, offered an amendment to remove the agriculture secretary's authority to transfer funds among the various federal loan and grant programs. The House first approved it, but a week later, English and Coleman worked out a compromise with Rose restoring some of the transfer authority. The House adopted it and the bill became law as part of the 1990 farm bill.

Coleman also has a strong interest in conservation issues. When the committee wrote the 1985 farm bill, Coleman and Jones cooperated on soil conservation provisions, one of the few elements of the legislation with wide support. The conservation section included a "sodbuster" program, which denied federal farm benefits to farmers tilling highly erodible land.

Beyond his work on the rural development issue, most of Coleman's contributions to the 1990 farm bill were again in its conservation title. Unlike in 1985, though, Coleman voted for the final farm bill package.

At Home: The electoral downdraft that caught nearly all Missouri's congressmen in 1990 almost pulled Coleman into political oblivion. Since his Democratic foe was a little-known farmer with hardly any money, the election was essentially a referendum on the incumbent. Coleman barely passed, polling only 52 percent — a modest showing that indicated after seven terms in office he has yet to secure his predominantly rural northwest Missouri district.

Few political observers saw Coleman in any political danger before the 1990 vote. Yet after the vote, few were greatly surp ised. Many of Coleman's constituents evidently felt that he was no longer greatly interested in his job. In 1986, he thought seriously about challenging former Gov. Christopher S. Bond for the GOP senatorial nomination, scuttling his plans only after it seemed that Bond had widespread support among state party leaders. After the 1988 election, Coleman was mentioned as a possible agriculture secretary in the Bush administration.

Coleman did not endear himself to elderly voters in the 6th by backing the original 1990 budget compromise, which included cuts in Medicare. He probably saved his seat by mounting an 11th-hour ad blitz that portrayed himself as a friend of senior citizens.

Coleman had faced much feistier and better-financed Democratic opposition in 1986 and 1988, when his opponent was Doug Hughes, a Vietnam veteran and farm activist. A rash of farm foreclosures had ravaged northwestern Missouri in 1986, and Hughes' pleas for higher farm price supports and mandatory production controls struck an emotional chord among some of the 6th District's struggling farmers.

Still, Hughes was unable to persuade voters to assign Coleman personal blame for the ailing farm economy. The incumbent took pains to publicize his disagreements with Reagan's agricultural policies, and made regular rounds of farm meetings, urging farmers to experiment with alternative crops and counseling them on coping with stress. Coleman emerged with a surprisingly strong 57-43 victory.

Hughes was back for a rematch in 1988. Though the appeal of the GOP presidential ticket in rural Missouri was well below what it had been in Ronald Reagan's landslides of 1980 and 1984, Coleman slightly increased his margin over Hughes. He was not, however, quite able to achieve the 60 percent threshold.

Coleman's initial election in 1976 was regarded by Democrats, at least, as something of a fluke. Morgan Maxfield, a millionaire Texan transplanted to Kansas City, had won the Democratic primary with the help of an expensive media barrage, and he was outspending Coleman 3-to-1 in the general election.

But less than a month before the voting, the *Kansas City Star* reported that Maxfield had lied about his early life, marital status and educational degrees. His campaign chairman resigned and criticized him. Coleman swept to an easy victory in a district that had not gone Republican in a quarter-century.

Committees

Agriculture (Ranking)

Education & Labor (2nd of 14 Republicans)
Postsecondary Education (ranking); Human Resources

Elections

1990 General

Tom Coleman (R)	78,956	(52%)
Bob McClure (D)	73,093	(48%)

1990 Primary

Tom Coleman (R)	27,382	(84%)
Don R. Sartain (D)	5,197	(16%)

1988 General

Tom Coleman (R)	135,883	(59%)
Doug R. Hughes (D)	93,128	(41%)

Previous Winning Percentages: **1986** (57%) **1984** (65%) **1982** (55%) **1980** (71%) **1978** (56%) **1976 *** (59%)

** Elected to a full term and to fill a vacancy at the same time.*

District Vote For President

	1988	1984	1980	1976
D	115,470 (50%)	97,920 (40%)	102,849 (42%)	119,405 (52%)
R	115,670 (50%)	145,284 (60%)	122,321 (50%)	107,314 (47%)
I			17,086 (7%)	

Campaign Finance

	Receipts	Receipts from PACs		Expenditures
1990				
Coleman (R)	$281,837	$184,870	(66%)	$315,922
McClure (D)	$19,431	0		$22,428
1988				
Coleman (R)	$305,961	$175,134	(57%)	$341,344
Hughes (D)	$199,256	$100,250	(50%)	$198,617

Key Votes

1991

Authorize use of force against Iraq	Y

1990

Support constitutional amendment on flag desecration	N
Pass family and medical leave bill over Bush veto	N
Reduce SDI funding	N
Allow abortions in overseas military facilities	N
Approve budget summit plan for spending and taxing	Y
Approve civil rights bill	N

1989

Halt production of B-2 stealth bomber at 13 planes	N
Oppose capital gains tax cut	N
Approve federal abortion funding in rape or incest cases	N
Approve pay raise and revision of ethics rules	Y
Pass Democratic minimum wage plan over Bush veto	N

Voting Studies

	Presidential Support		Party Unity		Conservative Coalition	
Year	**S**	**O**	**S**	**O**	**S**	**O**
1990	64	33	75	23	89	7
1989	67	30	70	26	78	17
1988	51	46	83	15	95	5
1987	56	40	76	19	95	5
1986	67	28	76	20	82	16
1985	56	40	76	19	89	5
1984	55	43	66	27	80	14
1983	65	33	70	27	83	13
1982	56	32	67	28	75	14
1981	70	28	74	18	85	12

Interest Group Ratings

Year	ADA	ACU	AFL-CIO	CCUS
1990	28	65	17	57
1989	5	78	25	100
1988	25	76	64	93
1987	4	62	13	87
1986	5	75	21	75
1985	10	67	29	75
1984	20	70	31	75
1983	15	73	19	74
1982	10	67	25	68
1981	0	100	21	94

7 Mel Hancock (R)

Of Springfield — Elected 1988

Born: Sept. 14, 1929, Cape Fair, Mo.
Education: Southwest Missouri State U., B.S. 1951.
Military Service: Air Force, 1951-53; Air Force Reserve, 1953-65.
Occupation: Businessman.
Family: Wife, Alma "Sug" McDaniel; three children.
Religion: Church of Christ.
Political Career: Sought Republican nomination for U.S. Senate, 1982; Republican nominee for lieutenant governor, 1984.
Capitol Office: 318 Cannon Bldg. 20515; 225-6536.

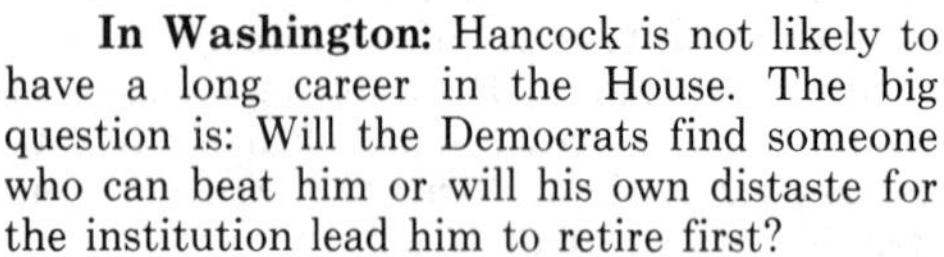

In Washington: Hancock is not likely to have a long career in the House. The big question is: Will the Democrats find someone who can beat him or will his own distaste for the institution lead him to retire first?

The author of an antitax measure that revolutionized — some say hamstrung — Missouri government beginning in 1980, Hancock seemed to have earned the good will of southwestern Missourians for life. But that kind of reverence does not always translate into respect in the House. Meanwhile, Hancock's antipathy to government remains so visceral as to suggest that his time within it will be limited.

Hancock opposes government involvement in economic affairs and endorses the privatizing of even such basic governmental activities as air traffic control. His speeches at times recall the heartland antigovernment rhetoric of a generation ago, sprinkled with references to "the road to socialism" and "the kind of system they have in Russia." Hancock has also become a sharp critic of the news media, which he accused of undermining the national morale prior to the Persian Gulf War.

He has set as his primary goal for the 102nd Congress the same goal he pursued in the 101st, the legislative repeal of the Supreme Court ruling in *Missouri v. Jenkins*. The case arose when a federal judge in Kansas City ordered the school district to raise taxes to finance court-ordered integration. Hancock's ban on "judicial taxation" had 147 cosponsors in the 101st Congress, but no hearings were held on it. A companion measure was introduced by South Carolina Republican Strom Thurmond in the Senate.

Also in the 102nd, Hancock has moved to the Banking, Finance and Urban Affairs Committee, where he hopes to push his bill creating tax-free savings accounts for parents and grandparents saving for college for their children and grandchildren.

First elected at 59, Hancock was the oldest freshman in his class. But he is less likely to be noticed for his age than for his energy, his size (he is almost a head taller than Ronald Reagan in a 1976 photo of the two) and the big, bass-baritone voice that he says "tends to carry."

At Home: Most House freshmen enjoy a "sophomore surge" when they first run for re-election, but not Hancock. He saw his vote share decline from 53 percent in 1988 to 52 percent in 1990, even though his Democratic opponent was neither as well-known nor as well financed as the one Hancock faced in 1988.

But Hancock was apparently hurt by his "Congressman No" image, especially in populous Greene County (Springfield), the most cosmopolitan part of the district. He lost that county in 1990 by more than 3,000 votes to Democrat Thomas Patrick Deaton, a Springfield lawyer. Of the other 16 counties in the historically Republican district, Hancock carried 15, but his share of the vote outside Greene County was still a modest 55 percent.

Hardly anyone expected the election to be so close. Before the campaign began, Hancock told the *St. Louis Post-Dispatch* that he would "rather be back home, hunting," and might not run for re-election. He quickly changed his mind, though, and seemed to clear his only real hurdle for re-election early in the year when former Greene County Circuit Judge Max E. Bacon, the Democrats' 1988 nominee, announced that he would not run.

When veteran GOP Rep. Gene Taylor announced that he was stepping down in 1988, competitive races ensued in both parties. Hancock won his primary by dominating the rural counties and holding off Gary Nodler, Taylor's district aide, whose base was in Joplin.

The Democrats nominated Bacon, a tough judge whose nickname was "Maximum Max" and who was best known for singing gospel duets with GOP Gov. John Ashcroft (also from Springfield). Bacon came within 500 votes in Greene County. But Hancock ran up a 6,000-vote margin in the three counties bordering Kansas and swept the 13 outlying counties.

Missouri 7

Southwest — Springfield; Joplin

Long a poor, isolated area resembling Appalachia, the scenic Ozark highlands have been discovered by tourists, retirees and new industry. But while newcomers have streamed into the 7th in the past two decades, they have not greatly altered the district's bedrock Republican character.

More than a third of the district's residents live in Springfield and surrounding Greene County, the region's industrial and commercial center. Kraft, Litton, 3M, Rockwell and Zenith are major employers. Springfield also is the home of Southwest Missouri State University, with more than 17,000 students.

The other population center in the district is Joplin, an old lead- and zinc-mining town now also engaged in manufacturing. The GOP preference was cemented in the Joplin area when President Woodrow Wilson lowered tariffs on lead and zinc and crippled the local mining industry.

Despite population growth, the rural and agricultural character of the Ozarks has not yielded completely to development and modernization. There remain many small, isolated communities, the legacy of the region's original settlers — Scotch-Irish mountaineers from eastern Tennessee, western Virginia and Kentucky who generally kept to themselves and coaxed crops from the rocky soil.

This area was Republican territory in the Civil War and has been ever since. The Ozark settlers had no use for slavery on their small, hilly farms; most were pro-Union. Today, statewide GOP candidates often take more than 60 percent of the vote in southwest Missouri. In 1984 and 1988, Republican voting was spurred by the presence of gubernatorial nominee John Ashcroft, a Springfield resident, near the top of the ticket. Despite a less-than-impressive victory statewide in 1988, George Bush took all 17 counties in the 7th District.

Population: 545,921. White 535,587 (98%), Black 4,367 (1%), Other 4,881 (1%). Spanish origin 3,392 (1%). 18 and over 399,610 (73%), 65 and over 81,401 (15%). Median age: 32.

Committees

Banking, Finance & Urban Affairs (15th of 20 Republicans)
Economic Stabilization; General Oversight; International Development, Finance, Trade & Monetary Policy

Public Works & Transportation (13th of 21 Republicans)
Aviation; Investigations & Oversight; Water Resources

Small Business (10th of 17 Republicans)
Procurement, Tourism & Rural Development; Regulation, Business Opportunity & Energy

Elections

1990 General		
Mel Hancock (R)	83,609	(52%)
Thomas Patrick Deaton (D)	76,725	(48%)
1990 Primary		
Mel Hancock (R)	75,860	(86%)
Jim Mundy (R)	8,032	(9%)
Ray Eaton (R)	4,605	(5%)
1988 General		
Mel Hancock (R)	127,939	(53%)
Max Bacon (D)	111,244	(46%)

District Vote For President

	1988	1984	1980	1976
D	92,861 (38%)	74,275 (31%)	85,364 (36%)	98,916 (47%)
R	148,460 (61%)	164,696 (69%)	141,329 (60%)	110,814 (53%)
I			6,173 (3%)	

Campaign Finance

	Receipts	Receipts from PACs	Expend-itures
1990			
Hancock (R)	$280,787	$122,782 (44%)	$182,474
Deaton (D)	$103,759	$47,445 (46%)	$103,265
1988			
Hancock (R)	$373,434	$79,913 (21%)	$338,125
Bacon (D)	$219,441	$114,460 (52%)	$215,064

Key Votes

1991	
Authorize use of force against Iraq	Y
1990	
Support constitutional amendment on flag desecration	Y
Pass family and medical leave bill over Bush veto	N
Reduce SDI funding	N
Allow abortions in overseas military facilities	N
Approve budget summit plan for spending and taxing	N
Approve civil rights bill	N
1989	
Halt production of B-2 stealth bomber at 13 planes	N
Oppose capital gains tax cut	N
Approve federal abortion funding in rape or incest cases	N
Approve pay raise and revision of ethics rules	N
Pass Democratic minimum wage plan over Bush veto	N

Voting Studies

	Presidential Support		Party Unity		Conservative Coalition	
Year	**S**	**O**	**S**	**O**	**S**	**O**
1990	80	20	98	2	94	6
1989	78	22	98	1	95	5

Interest Group Ratings

Year	ADA	ACU	AFL-CIO	CCUS
1990	11	100	0	79
1989	0	96	8	90

8 Bill Emerson (R)

Of Cape Girardeau — Elected 1980

Born: Jan. 1, 1938, Hillsboro, Mo.
Education: Westminster College, B.A. 1959; U. of Baltimore, LL.B. 1964.
Military Service: Air Force Reserve, 1964-present.
Occupation: Government relations executive; congressional aide.
Family: Wife, Jo Ann Hermann; four children.
Religion: Presbyterian.
Political Career: No previous office.
Capitol Office: 438 Cannon Bldg. 20515; 225-4404.

In Washington: Emerson has a streak of ideological conservatism that reveals itself on certain issues through his votes and rhetoric. But the hallmark of Emerson's legislative identity is pragmatism. This pragmatism often shows up on the Agriculture Committee, where he was the ranking minority member of the Nutrition Subcommittee through the 101st Congress. Beginning in the 102nd Congress, he is the ranking Republican on the Cotton, Rice and Sugar panel. He is also vice chairman of the Select Committee on Hunger.

Emerson first came to the House as a high school student in the 1950s, when he served as a page. Later, he worked as both a House and Senate staffer and as a lobbyist. He cultivates an image as a man who knows how the game is played. He likes to work with Democrats to forge compromises and move bills to passage.

The Nutrition panel can be a tough spot for a conservative striving to hold the line on the budget. To do so is sometimes to appear the scrooge. Still, Emerson seems to take a curmudgeonly pride in his ability to cast difficult votes in favor of controlling the cost of the nation's nutrition programs.

In the 99th and 100th Congresses, Emerson worked with subcommittee Chairman Leon E. Panetta of California on a food-stamp bill requiring states to set up employment and training programs for stamp recipients. In the 101st Congress, Emerson and Kansas Democrat Dan Glickman sponsored an amendment to the 1990 farm bill to toughen penalties for grocers who illegally traffic in food stamps. A modified version was included in the final bill.

Emerson is active on Agriculture outside the Nutrition Subcommittee, and in 1985 introduced the farm bill alternative endorsed by the American Farm Bureau Federation. His major crop interest is the soybean. He and Iowa Democrat Dave Nagle sponsored a package of amendments to establish a new price support program for soybean producers that would have raised substantially the loan rate for soybeans. Emerson has long advocated legislation requiring the secretary of agriculture to implement a new marketing loan program. It would allow soybean farmers to repay their price-support loans at the market price, which could be significantly lower than the loan rate. The 1990 farm bill included a marketing loan plan for soybeans, though the loan rate was far lower than that sought by members from soybean-producing states.

The more partisan and combative Emerson emerges in areas such as federal spending. Emerson, who supports a constitutional amendment to require a balanced budget, avers, "We've had enough of the budget chicanery from the liberals in Congress." He also favors constitutional amendments to allow voluntary school prayer, to ban desecration of the flag and forced busing of schoolchildren. An abortion foe, he introduced a bill in the 101st Congress to prohibit using federal funds for abortion except when the woman's life is endangered.

Emerson fought the creation of a new House Select Committee on Hunger. Still, when it was formed, Emerson accepted appointment to it. By the 101st Congress, he was the committee's vice chairman.

As a member of the committee, Emerson has been a sort of conservative watchdog, willing to challenge the assumptions of the Democratic majority. Like other conservative Republicans, he is concerned about Democrats using hunger in America as a political issue against the Republican administration. But he has taken an interest in the world famine problem, working well with Mickey Leland, who chaired the panel until his 1989 death; when Leland took the panel to observe conditions in Africa early in 1989, Emerson went along.

Emerson joined the Public Works Committee in the 101st Congress, leaving his post on the Interior Committee. Just as he had on Interior, he uses his Public Works seat as a vehicle for tending to local concerns. He secured funding for the Ste. Genevieve and Cape

Missouri 8

Southeast — Cape Girardeau

The state's most sparsely populated district, the 8th extends northwest from the Tennessee border toward central Missouri, covering more than 16,000 square miles.

In the extreme southeastern corner lies the Bootheel, a cluster of counties that looks and votes like the Old South. Predominantly a wheat-growing region until the mid-1920s, the Bootheel underwent a transformation when cotton growers and black sharecroppers, driven north by the boll weevil, settled here amid the rich Mississippi River delta land. The area grows 40 percent of the state's cash crops. Soybeans and corn have since supplanted cotton as the Bootheel's leading crops, but the Southern Democratic habits forged during cotton's heyday have persisted. While three out of the five core counties of the Bootheel voted Republican for president in 1988, they remained firmly in the Democratic column in most down-ballot races.

TV reporters with their sound trucks descended on the region in late 1990, after a prominent forecaster predicted that an earthquake would rumble across southeast Missouri and into parts of Arkansas and Tennessee on Dec. 3. Some schools closed that day and earthquake survival courses drew standing-room-only crowds. But no earthquake was reported.

Above the Bootheel along the Mississippi River, dairy production and beef cattle spark the agricultural economy. Residents of the city of Cape Girardeau work in agribusinesses and a Procter & Gamble Co. paper plant. The names of communities such as Bonne Terre and Beauvais are vestiges of the area's French heritage.

Offsetting Democratic strength in the Bootheel, Cape Girardeau and neighboring Perry counties typically give Republicans solid margins in contests for statewide offices. Toward the center of the 8th are Madison and Iron counties, traditional centers for Missouri's lead-mining industry. Farther west, the district moves into the foothills of the Ozark Mountains, some of Missouri's loveliest if poorest territory.

Population: 546,112. White 519,118 (95%), Black 24,050 (4%). Spanish origin 2,970 (1%). 18 and over 387,786 (71%), 65 and over 81,160 (15%). Median age: 31.

La Croix flood control projects in his district.

In March 1988, Emerson voluntarily began a 30-day treatment program for alcohol dependency. Remarkably, however, Emerson's adversities seemed to strengthen him. Reaction to his decision to seek treatment was almost uniformly sympathetic, a testament to his personal standing in the House. By openly seeking help, he seemed to win respect and even admiration from colleagues and constituents alike. He sailed to re-election with unexpected ease.

At Home: In North Carolina, there are "Jessecrats"; in southeast Missouri, there are "Emercrats": conservative Democrats who support members of their own party for local office but Republican Emerson for the House.

Emerson ousted an ethically tainted Democrat in 1980 and has relied on Emercrat votes to win re-election in the 8th ever since, though Democrats control virtually all the area's county courthouses and state legislative seats. Democratic challengers ran best against Emerson in 1982 and 1986, holding him to 53 percent of the vote each time.

He had to overcome the effects of recession and redistricting in 1982. Remapping moved Emerson's Jefferson County base from the district, and he relocated 80 miles to the southeast in Cape Girardeau, the 8th's largest city.

That gave Democrats an opening to label Emerson a "carpetbagger." Democratic nominee Jerry Ford, a state representative, hoped Democrats who strayed in 1980 would return to the fold in 1982. But Emerson, playing down partisan rhetoric and stressing support from several prominent Democrats and the state Farm Bureau, held on to win.

After winning easily in 1984, Emerson faced a serious 1986 challenge from Democrat Wayne Cryts. A farmer from Puxico, Cryts burst into national prominence in 1981 by leading a band of frustrated cohorts to a bankrupt grain elevator and seizing more than 30,000 bushels of soybeans.

Cryts' actions earned him widespread publicity and made him something of a folk hero to farm activists associated with the American Agriculture Movement. He used this celebrity to launch attacks on Emerson's support for the 1985 farm bill. But Cryts did not command unanimous support in the farm community; the Missouri Farm Bureau and the heads of many state and local farm commodity groups backed Emerson.

Even some farmers sympathetic to Cryts recalled that the incumbent had worked to help spring Cryts from jail following the 1981 soybean raid — and introduced legislation to revise federal bankruptcy laws to allow farmers prompt grain-removal rights.

Cryts carried 15 of the 26 counties wholly or partially contained within the 8th. But that was not enough to overcome Emerson's nearly 5,000-vote margin in Cape Girardeau County.

In 1988, Cryts was back. But the working boots and blue-denim jackets of his first campaign were gone. This time, Cryts campaigned in a suit and tie. He moved his headquarters from tiny Puxico to Cape Girardeau. He compiled a sizable campaign treasury, raising twice as much as he had in 1986.

Emerson's admission of alcohol dependency in early 1988 suggested vulnerability. Surveys said voters appreciated the way he was handling his problem, but some observers suspected damage below the waterline.

But there was a lessened sense of economic crisis among Bootheel farmers in 1988. The challenger talked more about trade, education and health care, issues that lit few fires. And as the fall wore on, the stumbling fortunes of Democratic candidates nationally and statewide cost Cryts some of his momentum as well. In the end, Emerson won 22 counties, including Stoddard, which had once been the base of Cryts' operations.

In 1990, Democrats ran a young lawyer whose main asset was his famous political name. Russ Carnahan was the son of Lt. Gov. Mel Carnahan and a grandson of the late Democratic Rep. A.S.J. Carnahan, who represented the 8th for seven terms (1945-47, 1949-61).

But he lacked the dedicated cadre of supporters that Cryts had mobilized and failed to find a cutting issue to lure back the Emercrats. Emerson carried 21 counties, including Carnahan's home base of Phelps.

The Washington bug bit Emerson early — when he was a teenage page in the 83rd and 84th Congresses — and he has not strayed far from the city since. Soon after finishing college in Missouri, he was back in Washington working on Capitol Hill.

Emerson held Hill-related jobs throughout the 1960s and 1970s, including lobbying positions with defense and energy-related companies. In 1979 he returned to Missouri to challenge 10th District Democratic Rep. Bill D. Burlison. The incumbent was hurt by charges that he had an affair with a woman, then interceded improperly on her behalf in a dispute involving her performance in a federal job. Burlison denied all charges, but many conservative Democrats deserted him. Aided also by Ronald Reagan's coattails, Emerson became the first Republican in 50 years to take the 10th.

Committees

Select Hunger (Ranking)

Agriculture (5th of 18 Republicans)
Cotton, Rice & Sugar (ranking); Domestic Marketing, Consumer Relations & Nutrition; Forests, Family Farms & Energy

Public Works & Transportation (11th of 21 Republicans)
Economic Development; Surface Transportation; Water Resources

Elections

1990 General		
Bill Emerson (R)	81,452	(57%)
Russ Carnahan (D)	60,751	(43%)
1988 General		
Bill Emerson (R)	117,601	(58%)
Wayne Cryts (D)	84,801	(42%)

Previous Winning Percentages: **1986** (53%) **1984** (65%) **1982** (53%) **1980** (55%)

District Vote For President

	1988	1984	1980	1976
D	91,369 (45%)	82,860 (39%)	94,184 (44%)	109,866 (56%)
R	111,605 (55%)	127,137 (61%)	114,559 (54%)	84,280 (43%)
I			4,107 (2%)	

Campaign Finance

	Receipts	Receipts from PACs		Expend-itures
1990				
Emerson (R)	$625,060	$326,541	(52%)	$704,447
Carnahan (D)	$250,002	$120,950	(48%)	$246,595
1988				
Emerson (R)	$850,739	$421,852	(50%)	$768,792
Cryts (D)	$662,184	$300,566	(45%)	$650,100

Key Votes

1991	
Authorize use of force against Iraq	Y
1990	
Support constitutional amendment on flag desecration	Y
Pass family and medical leave bill over Bush veto	N
Reduce SDI funding	N
Allow abortions in overseas military facilities	N
Approve budget summit plan for spending and taxing	N
Approve civil rights bill	N
1989	
Halt production of B-2 stealth bomber at 13 planes	N
Oppose capital gains tax cut	N
Approve federal abortion funding in rape or incest cases	N
Approve pay raise and revision of ethics rules	N
Pass Democratic minimum wage plan over Bush veto	N

Voting Studies

	Presidential Support		Party Unity		Conservative Coalition	
Year	**S**	**O**	**S**	**O**	**S**	**O**
1990	57	41	65	31	96	2
1989	78	21	75	22	95	2
1988	47	38	75	14	84	3
1987	60	38	86	13	95	2
1986	69	31	82	18	92	8
1985	60	36	78	17	95	2
1984	57	42	78	19	93	5
1983	70	27	85	13	90	9
1982	58	34	88	9	85	10
1981	78	22	90	10	99	1

Interest Group Ratings

Year	ADA	ACU	AFL-CIO	CCUS
1990	11	78	17	85
1989	10	93	17	100
1988	10	90	50	83
1987	4	78	25	87
1986	10	77	29	72
1985	10	80	25	81
1984	15	83	31	75
1983	5	87	12	85
1982	10	91	15	86
1981	0	100	20	89

9 Harold L. Volkmer (D)

Of Hannibal — Elected 1976

Born: April 4, 1931, Jefferson City, Mo.
Education: U. of Missouri, LL.B. 1955.
Military Service: Army, 1955-57.
Occupation: Lawyer.
Family: Wife, Shirley Ruth Braskett; three children.
Religion: Roman Catholic.
Political Career: Marion County prosecuting attorney, 1960-66; Mo. House, 1967-77.
Capitol Office: 2411 Rayburn Bldg. 20515; 225-2956.

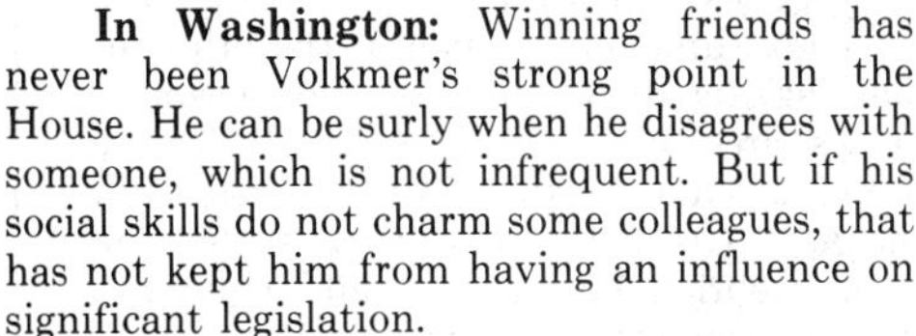

In Washington: Winning friends has never been Volkmer's strong point in the House. He can be surly when he disagrees with someone, which is not infrequent. But if his social skills do not charm some colleagues, that has not kept him from having an influence on significant legislation.

Volkmer has shown a particular aptitude for legislating on the Agriculture Committee, where he chairs the Subcommittee on Forests, Family Farms and Energy. He is an active participant in committee debates, and can be a team player who will sometimes work to whip up support for legislation produced by the committee. But Volkmer's willingness to play ball wanes when the subject turns to price supports for feed grains and dairy; he will scrap to the last for those.

During debate on the 1985 farm bill, Volkmer was an early proponent of imposing mandatory production quotas to raise prices of wheat, corn and other major crops. He pushed the proposal at the Agriculture subcommittee level, but later let others lead. The plan was struck from the bill on the House floor.

When Congress produced disaster-relief legislation for farmers in the 100th Congress, Volkmer pushed a portion of the bill that would permit farmers whose crops had been destroyed by floods to receive 92 percent of their deficiency payments without planting fields likely to be flooded again.

The 1990 farm bill was assembled amidst budget-cutting pressures, but Volkmer had little sympathy for the cost-cutters. At one point during committee consideration of the bill, he rebuked Kansas Republican Pat Roberts for suggesting that spending was out of control. "If you're afraid to give farmers out there a little increase," Volkmer said, "fine."

Volkmer championed the proposal of a national group of dairy farmer cooperatives; it called for a 50-cent increase — from $10.10 to $10.60 per 100 pounds of milk products — in the existing dairy price-support level, and it barred any decreases below $10.60 for the five-year life of the bill. Volkmer's proposal was at odds with one backed by the chairman and ranking Republican of the dairy subpanel, Charles W. Stenholm of Texas and Steve Gunderson of Wisconsin, who sought a floor of $10.10 for the sliding support scale. Still, the subcommittee adopted Volkmer's plan by voice vote.

But when the full committee considered the bill, the Stenholm-Gunderson plan prevailed. "If we can work within the budget to provide more money for farmers, I think we should be doing it, even if it means the consumer has to pay 10 cents more a gallon for milk," Volkmer argued. But the committee rejected his plan by a vote of 14-24.

Volkmer is best known for his opposition to gun-control legislation; he is the leading ally of the National Rifle Association in the House. The organization's intense lobbying has buoyed Volkmer's anti-gun-control efforts, but lobbyists don't kill bills, legislators do, and Volkmer has shown he can be effective.

In the 100th Congress he helped scuttle a portion of a drug bill requiring a seven-day waiting period for the purchase of handguns. The proposal, known as the "Brady bill," gained steam in the 102nd Congress when former President Reagan endorsed it. The House passed it in early 1991.

Volkmer's most notable achievement in this area came in 1986, when he won passage of a bill rolling back gun-control laws that had been on the books nearly 20 years.

Volkmer's crusade against gun control began soon after his arrival in the House. But for years the issue was bottled up in the Judiciary Committee by Chairman Peter W. Rodino Jr. In the 99th Congress, Volkmer did an end run on the committee, gathering 218 signatures on a petition to discharge his bill from Judiciary and bring it to the House floor.

Opponents of Volkmer's proposal, which lifted a ban on the interstate sale of rifles, shotguns and handguns, as well as easing other restrictions, called it "cop killer" legislation. But Volkmer said he was simply protecting the right to bear arms. The House adopted his pack-

Missouri 9

Northeast — Columbia

Among Missouri's earliest settlers were westward-moving Virginians and bluegrass Kentuckians who liked the rich soils in the northeastern part of the state. They planted their Southern roots here, tried to pull Missouri into the Confederacy and have voted Democratic into the modern era.

But latter-day residents of the northeastern Little Dixie area that anchors the 9th have voted Republican in recent national elections. All 22 counties wholly or partially constituting the 9th supported Ronald Reagan in 1984. In 1988, the counties split evenly between the major-party presidential contenders, but George Bush won 54 percent of the vote overall.

The moderate-to-liberal University of Missouri community in Columbia lends uncertainty to Boone County elections. Boone has gone GOP in the last four gubernatorial contests, but Democrat Harriett Woods won it narrowly in her 1986 Senate race. In 1988 Boone County voted Democratic for president and Republican for governor.

East of Boone lies Callaway County, whose residents declared it a kingdom unto itself in defiance of the Union during the Civil War. Crossing the Missouri River, the 9th includes Osage, Gasconade and Franklin counties. Gasconade's reliably GOP residents gave George Bush 72 percent in 1988, his best showing statewide.

On the banks of the Mississippi River, rests Hannibal (Marion County), hometown of author Mark Twain. Over 250,000 visitors a year travel to Hannibal to view Tom Sawyer's fence, Twain's boyhood home, and related special events like National Tom Sawyer Days.

Soybeans, corn and cattle drive the economy throughout much of the 9th's remaining territory, and related agribusinesses are found districtwide. With clay found around Mexico (Audrain County), the A. P. Green Refractory has fueled the local firebrick business — and enhanced the financial fortunes of Sen. Christopher S. Bond's family for several generations.

Population: 546,171. White 523,344 (96%), Black 18,092 (3%), Other 2,954 (1%). Spanish origin 3,543 (1%). 18 and over 391,319 (72%), 65 and over 68,313 (13%). Median age: 29.

age by a 286-136 vote. Though opponents managed to retain a ban on interstate sale of handguns, otherwise the House-passed legislation was very similar to the Senate's.

Volkmer clashed with an alliance of environmentalists and budget-cutters in 1990 over a Bush administration proposal to attempt a phaseout of "below-cost" timber sales on federal lands. Volkmer's Forests Subcommittee adopted his bill to bar the agriculture secretary from going ahead with the proposed one-year pilot program. His effort was backed by the timber industry and by members from affected states, who contended that the phaseout proposal was poorly planned and would hurt timber-dependent economies. But enough sparks flew during subcommittee debate that Volkmer pulled his bill from full committee consideration. The administration proposal won funding in the Appropriations Subcommittee on Interior but was left off the final appropriations bill.

Volkmer's strength as a legislator, and his weakness in personal relations, stems from his sheer stubbornness. He is a familiar figure in the chamber as he hunches down over a microphone, waiting as long as necessary for a chance to jump into the debate. One day several years ago, Volkmer asked California Democrat John Burton how long he planned to keep talking. If Burton talked much longer, Volkmer said, he would go back to his office. "I think I could probably get unanimous consent," Burton responded, "for the gentleman to go back to his office for the rest of the evening."

But Volkmer is not swayed by criticism of his personality. "I'm not short-tempered," he said in 1986. "Someone's got an erroneous impression. Gruff, possibly. Short shrift sometimes. Sometimes I can cut people off short."

At Home: Though it can irk colleagues in the House, Volkmer's tireless, hard-charging style has brought him consistent political success in Missouri. When told that his 1982 opponent called him "abrupt and abrasive," Volkmer replied, "Could be," and went on to take 61 percent of the vote.

A lawyer from the Mississippi River town of Hannibal, Volkmer has always been popular among rural northeast Missouri voters.

With the announcement by Democratic Rep. William L. Hungate that he would retire in 1976, Volkmer and 10 other Democrats sought to succeed him. Drawing on his reputation as an influential five-term member of the Missouri House, Volkmer sewed up a comfortable 17,000-vote margin over his closest primary competitor. Although his November opponent, GOP state Sen. J. H. Frappier, was well-known in the area near St. Louis, Volkmer held his own there and mustered enough rural support to capture 56 percent of the vote.

Volkmer faced a tougher test in 1984, squaring off with Republican Carrie Francke, a former assistant state attorney general with close ties to Sen. John C. Danforth and a Boone County (Columbia) base. Francke claimed Volkmer was insufficiently conservative and had waffled on a constitutional amendment to balance the federal budget. Danforth lent his support, and the national GOP helped her establish a healthy treasury.

Despite her advantages, however, Francke had trouble making inroads into the 9th's rural territory. Her support for the Equal Rights Amendment and for legalized abortion did not endear her to conservative Democrats. She did not enhance her image by touring the 9th's corn and cattle country in a pink van.

Francke carried Boone County, and took five more of the 22 counties included in the 9th. But Volkmer's strength in St. Charles County and the rural reaches again pulled him through.

Francke sought a rematch in 1986, but was defeated in the primary by state Sen. Ralph Uthlaut, a conservative farmer whose legislative constituency gave him a base at the 9th's southern end. Against Volkmer, Uthlaut sought to cash in on the farm crisis, touting his farming background and arguing that a gradual withdrawal of government price supports would better aid ailing agriculturists than what he termed Volkmer's "liberal, almost McGovernite" approach to farm policy.

Volkmer took the attacks in stride. He called for higher farm price supports, and argued that he was well positioned to try to help farmers from his post on the Agriculture Committee.

Bolstered further in rural Missouri by press reports of his influence in scaling back federal gun controls, Volkmer racked up a comfortable 57-43 percent victory.

In 1990, Volkmer again lost Boone County to his GOP opponent, but won virtually everywhere else to secure an eighth term in Congress.

Committees

Agriculture (10th of 27 Democrats)
Forests, Family Farms & Energy (chairman); Department Operations, Research & Foreign Agriculture; Livestock, Dairy & Poultry; Wheat, Soybeans & Feed Grains

Science, Space & Technology (5th of 32 Democrats)
Space

Select Aging (21st of 42 Democrats)
Retirement, Income & Employment; Rural Elderly

Elections

1990 General		
Harold L. Volkmer (D)	94,156	(58%)
Don Curtis (R)	69,514	(42%)
1988 General		
Harold L. Volkmer (D)	160,872	(68%)
Ken Dudley (R)	76,008	(32%)

Previous Winning Percentages: **1986** (57%) **1984** (53%) **1982** (61%) **1980** (57%) **1978** (75%) **1976** (56%)

District Vote For President

	1988	1984	1980	1976
D	110,436 (45%)	84,495 (36%)	97,269 (42%)	113,745 (50%)
R	131,829 (54%)	150,683 (64%)	126,289 (54%)	112,799 (49%)
I			8,799 (4%)	

Campaign Finance

	Receipts	Receipts from PACs	Expend-itures
1990			
Volkmer (D)	$308,533	$218,715 (71%)	$238,679
Curtis (R)	$36,020	$1,000 (3%)	$36,045
1988			
Volkmer (D)	$300,348	$218,185 (73%)	$210,841
Dudley (R)	$9,561	0	$9,565

Key Votes

1991	
Authorize use of force against Iraq	Y
1990	
Support constitutional amendment on flag desecration	Y
Pass family and medical leave bill over Bush veto	Y
Reduce SDI funding	Y
Allow abortions in overseas military facilities	N
Approve budget summit plan for spending and taxing	N
Approve civil rights bill	Y
1989	
Halt production of B-2 stealth bomber at 13 planes	N
Oppose capital gains tax cut	Y
Approve federal abortion funding in rape or incest cases	N
Approve pay raise and revision of ethics rules	Y
Pass Democratic minimum wage plan over Bush veto	Y

Voting Studies

	Presidential Support		Party Unity		Conservative Coalition	
Year	**S**	**O**	**S**	**O**	**S**	**O**
1990	35	65	73	25	81	19
1989	53	47	72	28	80	20
1988	35	60	72	23	79	13
1987	34	66	77	20	74	26
1986	33	67	79	20	60	40
1985	30	70	77	21	55	44
1984	42	56	72	27	56	44
1983	26	74	71	29	46	54
1982	35	60	66	34	55	41
1981	43	51	65	31	67	29

Interest Group Ratings

Year	ADA	ACU	AFL-CIO	CCUS
1990	39	38	75	36
1989	60	25	83	40
1988	60	35	93	50
1987	64	9	88	27
1986	45	32	79	33
1985	40	33	59	36
1984	55	25	69	44
1983	80	17	88	20
1982	45	55	65	52
1981	30	29	67	26

Montana

U.S. CONGRESS

SENATE 1 D, 1 R
HOUSE 1 D, 1 R

LEGISLATURE

Senate 29 D, 21 R
House 61 D, 39 R

ELECTIONS

1988 Presidential Vote

Bush	52%
Dukakis	46%

1984 Presidential Vote

Reagan	60%
Mondale	38%

1980 Presidential Vote

Reagan	57%
Carter	32%
Anderson	8%

Turnout rate in 1986	53%
Turnout rate in 1988	62%
Turnout rate in 1990	55%

(as percentage of voting age population)

POPULATION AND GROWTH

1980 population	786,690
1990 population (44th in the nation)	799,065
Percent change 1980-1990	+2%

DEMOGRAPHIC BREAKDOWN

White	93%
Black	0.3%
American Indian, Eskimo, or Aleut	6%
(Hispanic origin)	2%
Urban	53%
Rural	47%
Born in state	57%
Foreign-born	2%

MAJOR CITIES

Billings	81,151
Great Falls	55,097
Missoula	42,918
Butte-Silver Bow	33,941
Helena	24,569

AREA AND LAND USE

Area 145,388 sq. miles (4th)

Farm	65%
Forest	24%
Federally owned	30%

Gov. Stan Stephens (R)
Of Havre — Elected 1988

Born: Sept. 16, 1929, Calgary, Alberta, Canada.
Education: Graduated West Canada H.S., 1947.
Military Service: U.S. Army, 1951-53.
Occupation: Radio broadcaster; cable television executive.
Religion: Lutheran.
Political Career: Mont. Senate, 1969-1987, Republican floor whip, 1977, majority leader, 1979, 1981, president, 1983, minority leader, 1985.
Next Election: 1992.

WORK

Occupations

White-collar	50%
Blue-collar	26%
Service workers	15%

Government Workers

Federal	11,370
State	21,774
Local	41,922

MONEY

Median family income	$ 18,413	(32nd)
Tax burden per capita	$ 776	(36th)

EDUCATION

Spending per pupil through grade 12	$ 4,246	(20th)
Persons with college degrees	18%	(18th)

CRIME

Violent crime rate 116 per 100,000 (49th)

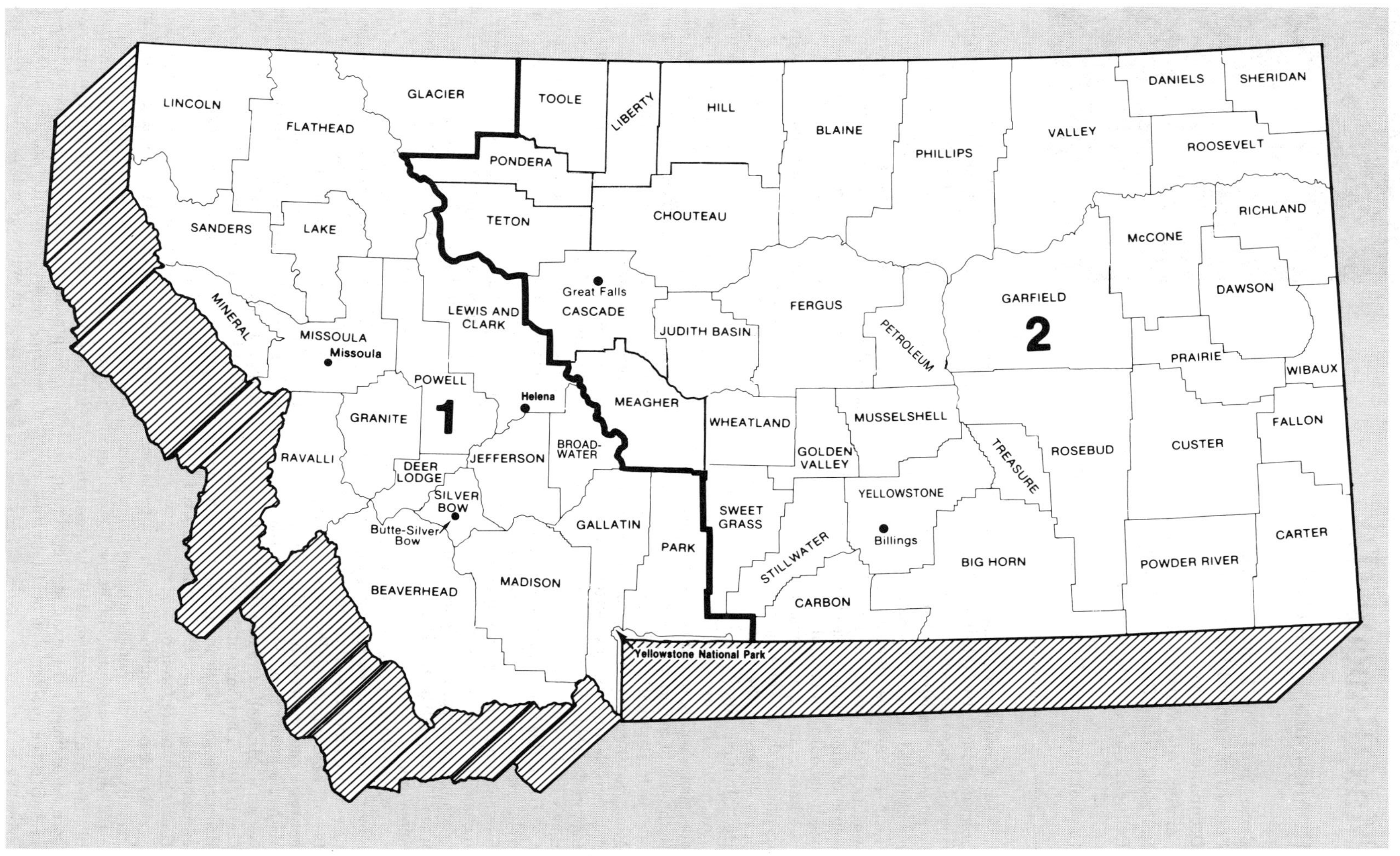
LINCOLN
FLATHEAD
GLACIER
TOOLE
LIBERTY
HILL
BLAINE
PHILLIPS
VALLEY
DANIELS
SHERIDAN
ROOSEVELT
PONDERA
TETON
CHOUTEAU
SANDERS
LAKE
RICHLAND
McCONE
DAWSON
Great Falls
CASCADE
MINERAL
LEWIS AND CLARK
FERGUS
GARFIELD
2
MISSOULA
Missoula
JUDITH BASIN
PETROLEUM
PRAIRIE
WIBAUX
POWELL
Helena
MEAGHER
GRANITE
1
WHEATLAND
MUSSELSHELL
FALLON
RAVALLI
DEER LODGE
JEFFERSON
BROAD-WATER
GOLDEN VALLEY
TREASURE
ROSEBUD
CUSTER
SILVER BOW
Butte-Silver Bow
YELLOWSTONE
GALLATIN
SWEET GRASS
PARK
Billings
STILLWATER
BIG HORN
POWDER RIVER
CARTER
BEAVERHEAD
MADISON
CARBON
Yellowstone National Park

Max Baucus (D)

Of Missoula — Elected 1978

Born: Dec. 11, 1941, Helena, Mont.
Education: Stanford U., B.A. 1964, LL.B. 1967.
Occupation: Lawyer.
Family: Wife, Wanda Minge; one child.
Religion: United Church of Christ.
Political Career: Mont. House, 1973-75; U.S. House, 1975-79.
Capitol Office: 706 Hart Bldg. 20510; 224-2651.

In Washington: Suddenly thrust into a prominent legislative role in the 101st Congress, Baucus availed himself of the opportunity to step beyond the somewhat limited confines he has occupied to lead the Senate effort on the Clean Air Act reauthorization. It was a role weightier than most he has played over the course of more than 15 years in Congress, but one he handled to critical acclaim.

Baucus has spent considerably more time tending to home-state interests than staking out positions on the controversies of the day. His "Montana First" politics and low profile on most national issues cushioned him against the effects of a voting record that sometimes strays to the left of majority opinion in Montana. His approach is evidently a hit back home: In 1990, Montana voters gave him a resounding endorsement, re-electing him by better than a 2-to-1 margin over his Republican opponent, Montana's lieutenant governor.

But if this approach has served him well in Montana, Baucus has disappointed those who foresaw him achieving greater stature in Washington. He sometimes seems lost in the background, concentrating on parochial matters or, when he does latch onto larger issues, playing a minor role.

In the 101st Congress, he was given the opportunity to redress that assessment. As the new chairman of the Environment Subcommittee on Environmental Protection, Baucus inherited a choice position at an opportune time. With the guidance of Senate Majority Leader George J. Mitchell of Maine (Baucus' predecessor in the Environmental Protection chair), Baucus steered the clean-air bill through committee, managed it on the floor and chaired the House-Senate conference.

By 1989, the combination of a sympathetic majority leader, a president who actively sought a bill, and the resolution of major House-side disputes had dislodged some of the most stubborn impediments to enacting legislation to deal with the problems of acid-rain and auto pollution.

Baucus sponsored urban smog provisions that would set new tailpipe emission standards and require auto manufacturers to implement by 1993 strict vehicle emission standards similar to California's. Baucus and Democrats on his subcommittee supported a controversial second round of reductions to go into effect in 2003 that would require a 50 percent reduction beyond first-round emission levels.

The second-round question produced a rare partisan split on the panel. Automakers and their allies argued that it would cost about $500 a car to develop new technology to meet the requirement; Democrats countered with estimates of $100 per car. "It's about the cost of a new hubcap — a nice, new hubcap — to meet [the second round]," Baucus said. The subcommittee approved it on a 7-6 vote.

Armed with Mitchell's request that the Environment Committee report a clean-air package before Thanksgiving, Baucus had a mandate to barrel the bill through. The committee met Nov. 16, 1989, to mark up the massive package. "Keep going, keep going," Baucus implored members, as the session stretched into the evening. "We have got to get done." In a single day, the committee approved the bill, on a 15-1 vote.

Baucus was a key player in the closed-door Senate-White House negotiations that produced a compromise. As Democratic floor manager of the bill, he joined the Senate leadership in fending off assaults on the bill from senators seeking to make the bill more environmentally stringent. Arguing against one amendment by a liberal Democrat, he said, "I'm much less ideological about this. I'm much more practical. I want a bill that works."

The House-Senate conference pitted Baucus against formidable House Energy and Commerce Chairman John D. Dingell. (At Baucus' request, Environment Chairman Quentin N. Burdick, who was not a visible participant, gave the Montanan the gavel.) After three months of agonizing negotiations, the gridlock broke and an agreement was reached, producing the first clean-air rewrite in 13 years.

Before the 101st Congress, Baucus had been cultivating a higher profile on a politically potent issue, and the most fashionable trade concept of the day: America's economic "competitiveness" in the world economy. In the 101st Congress, he acquired a forum to vent his views on unfair foreign trading practices — particularly by U.S. trading partners in the Pacific Rim — as chairman of the Finance Subcommittee on International Trade.

One opportunity to advance the concept of competitiveness was the omnibus trade bill of 1988, a bill bossed primarily by Lloyd Bentsen of Texas, Democratic chairman of the Finance Committee. Baucus had a seat at the table, but his most visible contributions sought to protect Montana's cattle, mining and timber industries. In the 101st Congress, he introduced bills to expand the president's power to retaliate against unfair trade. But he tempered some of his more pointed criticism after the Bush administration reached agreement with the Japanese government on allowing U.S. wood products into Japan, worth some $1 billion or more plus 10,000 to 20,000 jobs in timber-producing states such as Montana.

On the Agriculture Committee, a new assignment in the 101st Congress, Baucus aligns with the group of partisan Midwestern "prairie populist" Democrats. They battled to make the 1990 farm bill a more distinctly Democratic product. He lacks their profound knowledge of farm programs, however. Baucus did participate when the committee worked on the farm bill, working on its trade provisions, but ended up voting against the bill in committee and on the floor.

Baucus offered an amendment that would have increased so-called target prices — the guaranteed minimum prices farmers receive for their crops — by whatever percentage inflation exceeds 4.3 percent. It was rejected in committee and on the floor.

He also opposed Chairman Patrick J. Leahy's "whole-herd buyout" program, added to the 1985 farm bill, which paid milk producers to send their entire herds to slaughter to cut milk production. Cattlemen oppose the buyout because it lowers beef prices. Baucus, who represents the sixth-leading state for beef cows, offered an amendment to bar a whole-herd buyout on the 1990 bill; it was adopted 16-2.

At Home: The son of a wealthy Helena ranching family, Baucus used his good looks and personal charm to rise rapidly in Montana politics. After working in Washington as a lawyer for the Securities and Exchange Commission, he returned home to serve as coordinator of the state constitutional convention in 1972. The same year, he won his state legislative seat.

In 1974 Baucus moved up to the U.S. House, dislodging Republican Richard G. Shoup, who was trying for a third term. To gain publicity for the race, Baucus walked 631 miles across his congressional district. He managed to impress the labor-oriented Democrats who dominate the party in western Montana, and he did little to antagonize Republicans. He was a comfortable winner over Shoup in 1974 and an easy winner for re-election in 1976.

Meanwhile, he was focusing on the Senate. His hopes were temporarily frustrated in early 1978 by Democratic Gov. Thomas L. Judge, a political rival. After the death of veteran Democrat Lee Metcalf, the governor bypassed Baucus and appointed Paul Hatfield, chief justice of the Montana Supreme Court, to succeed Metcalf in the Senate.

But Baucus had already begun his 1978 Senate campaign, and he did not step aside for Hatfield. The newly appointed senator could not match Baucus' head start in organizing, and he hurt himself by voting for the Panama Canal treaties. Baucus did not oppose the treaties, but as a member of the House, he did not have to vote on the issue. He easily won the primary.

That fall, he had a hard-nosed Republican competitor in financier Larry Williams, who castigated him as too liberal. But just as Williams seemed on the verge of overtaking him, Baucus' Democratic allies released their "bombshell" — a picture of the "conservative" Williams in shaggy hair and love beads, taken before he moved from California to Montana. Baucus kept his distance from the issue, but the AFL-CIO made sure the picture was all over Montana in the weeks before the election. Baucus won a comfortable victory.

Heading into 1984, Baucus organized and raised money at a feverish pace. His preparations daunted Republican recruiting efforts: No well-known GOP figure stepped forward to take on the incumbent. Former state Rep. Chuck Cozzens won the GOP primary.

Cozzens had trouble attracting the attention he needed to be viewed as a credible challenger to Baucus. He tried to solve that problem by airing a series of radio advertisements calling Baucus a "wimp" who "talks out of both sides of his mouth." But the "wimp" portrayal backfired; many editorial writers and even some Republicans criticized Cozzens for running a mudslinging campaign. In spite of President Reagan's 60 percent showing in Montana, Baucus took 57 percent of the vote.

In 1990, national Republicans, fresh from their 1988 upset of Democratic Sen. John Melcher, hungrily eyed Baucus. Like Melcher in 1988, Baucus was seeking a third term. And like Melcher's lightly regarded GOP challenger, Conrad Burns, Baucus' opponent, Lt. Gov. Allen C. Kolstad, was not the first choice of national Republicans.

That, Baucus resolved, was where the similarities to 1988 would end. Whereas Melcher did not mobilize his re-election effort until the summer of 1988, Baucus began scouring the state in 1989. His work on the Clean Air Act and his vote for the anti-flag-burning amendment inoculated him against attacks similar to those aimed at Melcher — that he lacked clout and was too liberal. And on Melcher's albatross issue, wilderness, Baucus had avoided staking out an unnecessarily controversial position.

Baucus also forearmed himself against the type of monetary infusion from the National Republican Senatorial Committee that boosted Burns late in the 1988 campaign. Burns received nearly $200,000 in the final weeks from the NRSC, enough to fund a heavy TV ad campaign. Baucus' first TV ads aired early in 1990, and his fundraising from January 1989 through midyear 1990 topped $2 million.

A wealthy farmer-rancher from Chester in northern Liberty County, Kolstad was elected lieutenant governor on a tandem ticket with Stan Stephens in 1988 after 20 years in the Legislature. There, he concentrated on agriculture and small-business issues. In 1989 he earned some statewide publicity by chairing the Montana Centennial Commission. He was also a prominent opponent of abortion; Baucus supports abortion rights.

On entering the contest, however, Kolstad had to fight three other Republicans for the nomination. He was held under 44 percent in the June primary, while Baucus breezed past his primary opposition.

In the general election, Baucus' polished, energetic campaign style complemented his superior campaign operation. In contrast, Kolstad's effort was lackluster and ineffective. Kolstad touched off a storm of controversy in July when, in citing a disputed federal government study, he said that "the threat of global warming and acid rain are really more scare tactics."

But that focused as much attention on Kolstad's campaign as it was to receive all year. Maintaining wide leads in polls, Baucus continued to steam unchecked toward Election Day. His 68 percent showing was the best by any Montana Senate candidate since Mike Mansfield won a second term in 1958.

Committees

Agriculture, Nutrition & Forestry (9th of 10 Democrats)
Agricultural Production & Stabilization of Prices; Conservation & Forestry; Domestic & Foreign Marketing & Product Promotion

Environment & Public Works (4th of 9 Democrats)
Environmental Protection (chairman); Superfund, Ocean & Water Protection; Toxic Substances, Environmental Oversight, Research & Development

Finance (3rd of 11 Democrats)
International Trade (chairman); Medicare & Long Term Care; Taxation

Small Business (3rd of 10 Democrats)
Rural Economy & Family Farming (chairman); Innovation, Technology & Productivity

Joint Taxation

Elections

1990 General		
Max Baucus (D)	217,563	(68%)
Allen C. Kolstad (R)	93,836	(29%)
Westley F. Deitchler (LIBERT)	7,937	(2%)
1990 Primary		
Max Baucus (D)	81,687	(83%)
John B. Driscoll (D)	12,622	(13%)
"Curly" Thornton (D)	4,367	(4%)

Previous Winning Percentages: **1984** (57%) **1978** (56%) **1976 *** (66%) **1974 *** (55%)

* *House elections.*

Campaign Finance

	Receipts	Receipts from PACs	Expend-itures
1990			
Baucus (D)	$2,667,328	$1,377,663 (52%)	$2,409,262
Kolstad (R)	$748,100	$74,898 (10%)	$747,661

Key Votes

1991	
Authorize use of force against Iraq	N
1990	
Oppose prohibition of certain semiautomatic weapons	Y
Support constitutional amendment on flag desecration	Y
Oppose requiring parental notice for minors' abortions	Y
Halt production of B-2 stealth bomber at 13 planes	Y
Approve budget that cut spending and raised revenues	N
Pass civil rights bill over Bush veto	Y
1989	
Oppose reduction of SDI funding	N
Oppose barring federal funds for "obscene" art	Y
Allow vote on capital gains tax cut	N

Voting Studies

	Presidential Support		Party Unity		Conservative Coalition	
Year	**S**	**O**	**S**	**O**	**S**	**O**
1990	51	49	70	28	51	46
1989	48	48	69	27	50	47
1988	47	51	86	12	51	49
1987	33	65	86	13	44	56
1986	30	66	74	22	37	54
1985	30	68	83	15	47	52
1984	40	58	76	21	34	66
1983	38	60	77	21	45	55
1982	44	53	80	18	31	67
1981	45	50	84	14	29	66

Interest Group Ratings

Year	ADA	ACU	AFL-CIO	CCUS
1990	56	41	44	45
1989	80	19	100	43
1988	80	8	86	29
1987	75	8	80	28
1986	80	13	60	37
1985	65	9	75	37
1984	75	14	50	50
1983	75	25	71	32
1982	85	16	85	40
1981	85	13	67	39

Conrad Burns (R)

Of Billings — Elected 1988

Born: Jan. 25, 1935, Gallatin, Mo.
Education: Attended U. of Missouri, 1952-54.
Military Service: Marine Corps, 1955-57.
Occupation: Radio and television broadcaster.
Family: Wife, Phyllis Kuhlmann; two children.
Religion: Lutheran.
Political Career: Yellowstone County Commission, 1987-89.
Capitol Office: 183 Dirksen Bldg. 20510; 224-2644.

In Washington: When he arrived in the Senate, Burns was faced with a difficult political balancing act. A former rancher and farm broadcaster with little political experience, Burns sought credibility as a legislator while maintaining the crowd-pleasing cowboy image that helped him overcome Democratic Sen. John Melcher in the biggest Senate upset of 1988.

Burns plunged into his Senate work, engaging in issues as detailed as telephone industry regulation. Yet the countrified image Burns projected at a freshman orientation session — to which he wore aged cowboy boots and a leather belt with a "C" on the buckle — remains his persona to most Senate-watchers.

Burns' backroads image was reinforced by incidents during his first Congress. After a tree-planting ceremony near the Lincoln Memorial, Burns walked over to a police horse and examined its mouth to see how old the animal was; a syndicated story on the incident was carried by Burns' hometown newspaper, *The Billings Gazette*. In November 1990, Burns suffered minor wounds when a young member of his pheasant-hunting party accidentally winged him with shotgun pellets.

In philosophy and style, Burns has less in common with Democratic Senate colleague Max Baucus, a liberal with an intellectual approach, than with Republican Rep. Ron Marlenee, a rancher who shares Burns' eastern Montana base. Both Republicans exude a rugged and rambunctious conservative populism deeply rooted in the state's rural traditions, although Burns' personality is more folksy and his manner is more appealing than Marlenee's.

This image helped Burns unseat two-term Sen. Melcher, an insider he portrayed as too taken with the ways of Washington. Burns' style, which has made him a popular dinner speaker, has caught the eyes of the Eastern press. *USA Today*, one of several media outlets to run friendly profiles of Burns, reported that the tobacco-chomping newcomer had promised, "I'll never take a chew under the Capitol dome."

To his acolytes back home, Burns is an expression of themselves: natural, independent, and unbound by elitist (read: Eastern) pretensions. To his critics, Burns is feeding damaging stereotypes of Montana as a remote and unsophisticated backwater. "Thanks, Conrad, thanks for telling the world what hicks we are," the *Gazette* has written. The harshest criticism came over Burns' glib remark that "there are awful good folks" in Montana, including some who "can read and write."

But the comment, far from being an attack on his constituents, was typical of the joshing and often self-deprecating humor that made Burns popular on the campaign stump in 1988. Burns denied that his cowboy characterization would make him an ineffective spokesman for Montana interests. "I don't take myself seriously. I take my job damn serious," Burns told *The Washington Post*.

Burns sought to prove that in his work on his committee assignments. A member of the Senate Commerce Committee, Burns used his experience as a broadcaster to make a mark on telecommunications issues.

During the debate on a bill to reinstitute rate and programming regulations on the cable television industry, Burns became a leading advocate of allowing local telephone companies to offer cable television services under certain conditions. The phone companies are barred from such services under provisions of federal law.

Burns and other advocates argued that allowing telephone companies to provide TV programming over their lines would create competition for cable companies, most of which have local monopolies. They also say the phone companies need to expand in order to provide the financial base to build a nationwide fiber-optics network; fiber optics, in turn, are hailed as opening American households to an array of communications services.

However, opponents say that the "telcos," which have monopolies over local phone services, could become juggernauts that would crush cable TV companies and limit phone network access of other communications companies. The strength of this opposition during the 101st Congress deterred Burns.

From his seat on the Energy and Natural Resources Committee, Burns waded into the thorny issue of wilderness preservation. Burns, like many western conservatives, is wary of extensive wilderness protections and is sympathetic to the arguments of developers and recreationists who desire access to the lands. Baucus proposed a solution to a Montana wilderness stalemate, but Burns offered his own plan, which covered less acreage.

However, Burns stepped on some toes when he criticized a land-management agreement for Montana's Lolo and Kootenai national forests worked out by an ad hoc council of millworkers, environmentalists and others that Baucus helped set up. Burns argued in a July 1990 statement that the agreement was reached in a closed process that ignored "the legitimate interests of the many people who were left out."

But supporters of the plan accused Burns of undercutting a hard-won agreement. By year's end, Burns had softened his tone. "I think the way they've approached that problem up there has been very good," he said. "I still want to involve more people."

Burns and Baucus did find common ground on some issues. For example, their outcry over Attorney General Dick Thornburgh's attempt to close an FBI office in Butte in 1989 led to the passage of a provision barring the Justice Department from relocating, reorganizing and consolidating offices under its jurisdiction.

Although he is not on the Agriculture Committee, Burns' background enabled him to speak freely on the 1990 farm bill. Discussing the bill's cattle provisions, Burns was every bit the independent westerner. He noted in May 1990 that there was a dairy title in the bill, but none for beef cattle. "That is precisely the way that those of us involved in the beef cattle industry want it . . . ," Burns said. "To them, the stability comes from keeping the government out of the cattle business."

At Home: When he entered the 1988 Senate contest, Burns had served less than two years in his only elective office, Yellowstone County (Billings) commissioner. He had no broad expertise on national or international issues. And he seemed to be a fall-back candidate, recruited by the National Republican Senatorial Committee (NRSC) for a state party that failed to find a well-known elected official to challenge Melcher.

However, Burns actually had a much stronger political base than most observers, including Melcher, recognized. His broadcasts on the Northern Agricultural Network, which he co-founded, had given him a statewide following and far greater name recognition than any of the state legislators the GOP had tried to recruit. He also had a lifetime of experience in agriculture, a crucial economic sector in Montana.

Melcher, for his part, was a far less formidable incumbent than widely presumed. A veterinarian widely known as "Doc," Melcher had built his popularity with his own folksy charm. But he was a stumbling campaigner, and his Senate voting record, which often earned him 100 percent ratings from the Americans for Democratic Action, left him vulnerable to charges that he was to the left of the state mainstream.

The NRSC spotted this vulnerability early on, and promoted Burns, to a disbelieving political and media establishment, as their "upset special." The campaign committee poured in nearly $200,000, enough to buy plenty of TV ad-time in a state where airtime is inexpensive. Many of the ads blasted Melcher as too liberal and as ineffective in promoting Montana's agenda.

Burns' campaign planted doubt in voters' minds, and Melcher's double-digit lead in the polls slowly began to evaporate. Melcher tried to strike back by portraying Burns as a packaged candidate, bought and controlled by the national Republican political machine. He even reprised a previously successful TV ad concept, "talking" cows who derided the "greenhorn" Republican.

But not even talking cows could save Melcher from an onslaught of untimely news headlines in the last weeks of the campaign. Burns benefited from an article in the Great Falls *Tribune* detailing Melcher's interest in Philippine issues; Burns had labored to draw attention to the fact that the incumbent had visited the Philippines three times in five years. Burns also gained from the publicity attending a Billings campaign visit by Republican presidential nominee George Bush in late October.

But the event that may have clinched the win for Burns was President Reagan's veto of a wilderness bill, authored by Melcher, just days before the election. The bill, which had long been stalled in Congress, had been an albatross for Melcher, endearing him neither to development interests, who opposed wilderness legislation in general, nor environmentalists, who wanted more land protected than the bill provided. Then, when Reagan vetoed the bill, it appeared to reinforce Burns' claim that Melcher lacked the clout to get his proposals enacted.

Burns won by a fairly narrow 52-48 percent margin, but his support was well distributed across the state. In fact, he ran slightly better in the normally Democratic 1st District than in the Republican 2nd, a home base he shared with Melcher.

The NRSC intervention in the campaign

remained controversial, however. In 1989, a former Montana Republican Party official filed a federal lawsuit against the state and national GOP organizations, alleging he was fired for raising questions about financial transactions on behalf of Burns' campaign. In 1990, a Democratic state representative from Montana and the public interest group Common Cause filed complaints with the Federal Election Commission, alleging that the NRSC transferred funds to the Montana Republican Party for Burns' use that were in excess of legal limits.

Committees

Commerce, Science & Transportation (7th of 9 Republicans)
Foreign Commerce & Tourism (ranking); Communications; Surface Transportation

Energy & Natural Resources (6th of 9 Republicans)
Water & Power (ranking); Energy Research & Development; Public Lands, National Parks & Forests

Small Business (5th of 8 Republicans)
Urban & Minority-Owned Business Development (ranking); Rural Economy & Family Farming

Special Aging (9th of 10 Republicans)

Elections

1988 General		
Conrad Burns (R)	189,445	(52%)
John Melcher (D)	175,809	(48%)
1988 Primary		
Conrad Burns (R)	63,330	(85%)
Tom Faranda (R)	11,427	(15%)

Campaign Finance

	Receipts	Receipts from PACs		Expenditures
1988				
Burns (R)	$1,099,488	$315,387	(29%)	$1,076,010
Melcher (D)	$1,237,661	$812,560	(66%)	$1,338,622

Key Votes

1991	
Authorize use of force against Iraq	Y
1990	
Oppose prohibition of certain semiautomatic weapons	Y
Support constitutional amendment on flag desecration	Y
Oppose requiring parental notice for minors' abortions	N
Halt production of B-2 stealth bomber at 13 planes	N
Approve budget that cut spending and raised revenues	N
Pass civil rights bill over Bush veto	N
1989	
Oppose reduction of SDI funding	Y
Oppose barring federal funds for "obscene" art	N
Allow vote on capital gains tax cut	Y

Voting Studies

	Presidential Support		Party Unity		Conservative Coalition	
Year	**S**	**O**	**S**	**O**	**S**	**O**
1990	81	19	92	7	95	5
1989	86	12	92	7	92	5

Interest Group Ratings

Year	ADA	ACU	AFL-CIO	CCUS
1990	6	91	11	83
1989	0	85	0	88

1 Pat Williams (D)

Of Helena — Elected 1978

Born: Oct. 30, 1937, Helena, Mont.

Education: Attended U. of Montana, 1956-57; William Jewell College, 1958; U. of Denver, B.A. 1961; Western Montana College, 1962.

Military Service: Army, 1960-61; National Guard, 1962-69.

Occupation: Elementary and secondary school teacher.

Family: Wife, Carol Griffith; three children.

Religion: Roman Catholic.

Political Career: Mont. House, 1967-71; sought Democratic nomination for U.S. House, 1974.

Capitol Office: 2457 Rayburn Bldg. 20515; 225-3211.

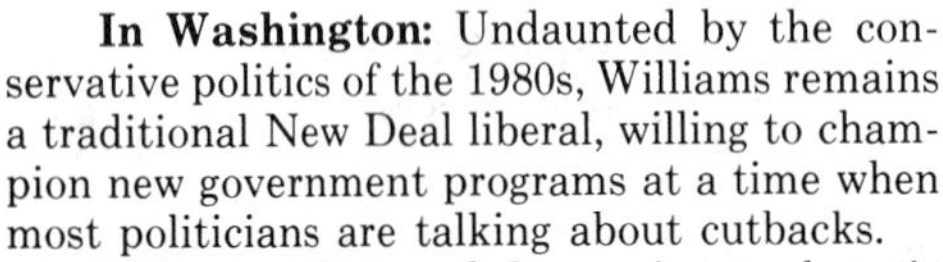

In Washington: Undaunted by the conservative politics of the 1980s, Williams remains a traditional New Deal liberal, willing to champion new government programs at a time when most politicians are talking about cutbacks.

This mentality, and the passionate rhetoric that goes with it, leads many conservatives to write him off as a relic of a bygone era. But the Montanan matches his partisanship with healthy doses of pragmatism and patience, and that has earned him some significant legislative accomplishments.

Williams' ties to organized labor first helped bring him to Congress, and he has been faithful to the union movement. He is a deputy whip designated to watch labor issues in the House, and he serves the same function from his post on the Education and Labor Committee. At the start of the 102nd Congress, he became chairman of the Labor-Management Relations Subcommittee. He opened his tenure with a confrontational hearing on parental leave legislation — a top labor priority that had been vetoed by President Bush in 1989.

In the 100th Congress, Williams was the prime mover behind successful labor-backed legislation to bar most private employers from requiring workers and job applicants to take lie-detector tests. "Thumbscrews and the rack, even if they are now electronic, should be outlawed," he said.

In the 101st Congress, Williams stepped outside his primary interests in labor and education to become a front-line player in the debate on decency standards for the National Endowment for the Arts. The issue placed him in rare alliance with Bush, who supported Williams' five-year NEA reauthorization without the restrictions sought by those who complained that the organization was funding obscene art. "A little bit of censorship is like being a little bit pregnant," Williams said.

Williams was thrust into the debate as chairman of the Postsecondary Education Subcommittee, which had jurisdiction over the NEA's authorization bill. When the subcommittee could not agree on whether or how to write language restricting the agency from funding certain types of work, it sent along Williams' bill to the full committee. When it too failed to come up with a solution and sent the bill to the full House, a major floor fight was slated.

But Williams spent weeks negotiating with key Republican activists. They eventually reached an agreement that would ban funding of obscene art, but leave it to the courts to determine whether a project has crossed that line. The amendment eventually passed the House 382-42, and formed the basis of the legislation that was eventually signed into law.

On education issues, Williams' relationship with Bush is more typical of his overall adversarial tone toward the White House. "You become the education president not with Rose Garden ceremonies but with genuine innovative solutions," he said in 1989.

A former schoolteacher, Williams took a middle course on the problem of student-loan defaults. He echoed the conservative demand to crack down on "charlatans," but said the default rate had skyrocketed in part because the loan program was intended as a supplement for middle-income students, but instead has become the principal path to college for low-income students, who often are ill-equipped to repay their loans. In the 101st Congress, he backed legislation to crack down on trade schools with exceptionally high default rates.

For three terms (through 1988), Williams served on the Budget Committee, where he reveled in the fierce partisan rivalry that prevailed early in his tenure, but in later years joined the move toward bipartisanship.

When he first joined Budget, Williams teamed with liberal members who were determined to resist Reagan administration cuts in their priority programs. "Folks believe the nation is not being well governed because the two

Montana 1

Western Mountains — Helena; Missoula

The Continental Divide meanders the length of this district, separating Montana's rugged west from its eastern plains and the labor Democrats of the 1st from the Republican ranchers of the 2nd.

The mountains of western Montana begat lumber mills and mines early in this century. While the prodigious lodes of copper, zinc and lead in Butte's "richest hill on Earth" produced some of the richest mine owners in America, they also spawned strong unions to represent those who labored in them.

Though forestry and mining have not always provided a steady living — a sharp recent decline in demand has forced many miners out of work and caused a population drain near Butte — union-inspired Democratic voting habits have been quite regular at the House level. Only one Republican has represented the 1st since 1942, and he lasted just two terms.

The Democratic loyalties are not nearly as strong in elections for higher office. Ronald Reagan won easily in 1980 and 1984, though George Bush defeated Democrat Michael S. Dukakis by a modest 50-48 percent margin. While western Montana has been a breeding ground for Democratic senators — including former Senate Majority Leader Mike Mansfield and current Sen. Max Baucus — the 1st District in 1988 turned its back on Democratic Sen. John Melcher, an eastern Montanan. Republican Conrad Burns took the 1st with 53 percent on his way to victory statewide.

Nowhere are the district's Democratic ties stronger than in heavily unionized Silver Bow County (Butte) and Deer Lodge County (Anaconda). In 1988, Dukakis took 72 percent of the vote in Silver Bow and 68 percent in Deer Lodge. In his 1990 Senate re-election, Baucus won over 80 percent of the vote in these counties against Republican Senate nominee Allen C. Kolstad.

Dukakis also carried the two counties with sizable urban centers: Missoula and Lewis and Clark (Helena). The district's largest city, Missoula, which lies at the hub of several agricultural valleys, is a lumber processing center and is home to the University of Montana. Dukakis took 54 percent of the county vote in 1988, though Reagan managed an identical margin for the GOP in 1984.

The state capital of Helena is near the eastern edge of the 1st: It got its start when gold was discovered in Last Chance Gulch during the Civil War. Dukakis edged Bush in Lewis and Clark County, though Melcher failed there.

The more rural counties provide the margin for statewide Republicans who carry the 1st. Bush carried Flathead County in the north (where tourists in Glacier National Park provide income for people in Kalispell and Whitefish) and Gallatin County in the south (site of Bozeman and Montana State University) with 57 percent. Republicans tend to be competitive in each of the district's four southernmost counties, which are geared more toward farming and cattle than toward lumber and mining. Tourism in nearby Yellowstone National Park also boosts this area's economy.

Beaverhead County, at the southwestern corner of the state, was one of two counties that Kolstad carried against Baucus in 1990.

Population: 393,298. White 376,235 (96%), Black 446 (0.1%), Other 14,535 (4%). Spanish origin 3,869 (1%). 18 and over 280,180 (71%), 65 and over 41,811 (11%). Median age: 29.

parties are Tweedledum and Tweedledee," Williams once said. "This time they're going to perceive a real difference between the president's budget and the Democratic budget."

The partisan mood began to change after the 1987 stock market crash, which prompted a budget summit to craft a deficit-reduction compromise. Williams was named to the House negotiating team, where his role was to protect low- and middle-income programs. Early in 1988, as Democrats and Republicans moved toward agreement, he reported, "We're serious about giving it the old college try."

Although Williams was appointed a deputy whip by then-Speaker Thomas P. O'Neill Jr. — who shared Williams' New Deal ideology — he was one of the few liberals to strike up a friendship with Jim Wright, a fellow boxing buff. At the start of the 101st Congress, Speaker Wright appointed him to a spot on Steering and Policy, which makes Democratic committee assignments. In 1989, when the ethics committee released the report of its investigation into Wright's financial dealings, it was widely seen as an ominous sign for Wright that Williams said, "The Speaker is in hip-deep water, and the white rapids are straight ahead.'

At Home: While districts all over the

mountain West were voting Republican in 1978, Williams posted a comfortable victory over a strong GOP opponent in the open 1st.

Williams had been active in Montana politics for a decade before coming to Congress. His political career was temporarily derailed in 1974, when he lost the Democratic House nomination to Max Baucus. But when Baucus ran for the Senate in 1978, Williams had another shot.

He entered a multicandidate primary and was blessed with strong labor backing. Williams campaigned on the need for more jobs in the western part of Montana, but also on the need to keep the district's industry clean. He won nomination with 41 percent of the vote.

Williams' Republican opponent was 29-year-old Jim Waltermire, then a Missoula County commissioner. At the time, Waltermire was not well-known outside his home county, and his pro-development views were a liability against Williams, an environmental moderate who stressed the need for protection as well as job development. Williams comfortably defeated Waltermire (who went on to become Montana's secretary of state and a 1988 candidate for governor, but died in a plane crash).

Williams has not been held below 60 percent in any election since. In 1990 — his final election in the 1st District before reapportionment reduced Montana's House representation to one seat — Williams took 61 percent against first-time Republican candidate Brad Johnson.

A former state party official and district aide for 2nd District Rep. Ron Marlenee, Johnson sought to tap voter discomfort with some of Williams' liberal positions, such as his support for the NEA and his opposition to a flag-desecration amendment. Out-of-state conservative religious organizations attacked Williams for his opposition to setting obscenity standards for NEA grants. But their efforts were futile.

In early 1991, there was speculation Williams would run for governor in 1992 rather than face a House contest against Marlenee for the state's new at-large seat. But Williams announced he would not go for governor.

Before 1978, Williams had filled a variety of positions besides serving two terms in the state Legislature. He was Montana director of Hubert H. Humphrey's presidential campaign in 1968 and chairman of the Jimmy Carter campaign in western Montana in 1976. He spent two years on Capitol Hill as an aide to Democrat John Melcher, who was then representing Montana's other district in the House and later served two Senate terms.

Committees

Education & Labor (7th of 25 Democrats)
Labor-Management Relations (chairman); Elementary, Secondary & Vocational Education; Postsecondary Education; Select Education

Interior & Insular Affairs (7th of 29 Democrats)
National Parks & Public Lands

Elections

1990 General		
Pat Williams (D)	100,409	(61%)
Brad Johnson (R)	63,837	(39%)
1988 General		
Pat Williams (D)	115,278	(61%)
Jim Fenlason (R)	74,405	(39%)

Previous Winning Percentages: **1986** (62%) **1984** (66%) **1982** (60%) **1980** (61%) **1978** (57%)

District Vote For President

	1988		1984		1980		1976	
D	91,519	(48%)	78,513	(40%)	62,332	(34%)	74,522	(46%)
R	95,054	(50%)	113,967	(58%)	101,743	(55%)	85,786	(53%)
I					15,843	(9%)		

Campaign Finance

	Receipts	Receipts from PACs		Expend-itures
1990				
Williams (D)	$458,293	$296,640	(65%)	$345,258
Johnson (R)	$86,542	$4,300	(5%)	$90,238
1988				
Williams (D)	$399,066	$185,656	(47%)	$369,486
Fenlason (R)	$106,821	$13,256	(12%)	$106,808

Key Votes

1991	
Authorize use of force against Iraq	N
1990	
Support constitutional amendment on flag desecration	N
Pass family and medical leave bill over Bush veto	Y
Reduce SDI funding	Y
Allow abortions in overseas military facilities	Y
Approve budget summit plan for spending and taxing	N
Approve civil rights bill	Y
1989	
Halt production of B-2 stealth bomber at 13 planes	N
Oppose capital gains tax cut	Y
Approve federal abortion funding in rape or incest cases	Y
Approve pay raise and revision of ethics rules	N
Pass Democratic minimum wage plan over Bush veto	Y

Voting Studies

	Presidential Support		Party Unity		Conservative Coalition	
Year	**S**	**O**	**S**	**O**	**S**	**O**
1990	24	72	77	12	20	72
1989	31	60	72	12	22	71
1988	14	77	70	5	13	79
1987	18	79	81	5	21	74
1986	12	82	76	8	18	74
1985	18	80	76	4	7	87
1984	30	65	72	14	17	75
1983	18	72	77	9	18	74
1982	35	61	81	11	16	79
1981	34	62	86	10	21	73

Interest Group Ratings

Year	ADA	ACU	AFL-CIO	CCUS
1990	89	9	82	33
1989	80	7	91	40
1988	85	0	100	15
1987	96	0	94	7
1986	85	5	92	20
1985	95	10	94	23
1984	90	13	82	33
1983	90	9	94	37
1982	85	9	100	23
1981	95	20	93	6

2 Ron Marlenee (R)

Of Scobey — Elected 1976

Born: Aug. 8, 1935, Scobey, Mont.
Education: Attended U. of Montana, 1953, 1960; Montana State U., 1960.
Occupation: Rancher.
Family: Wife, Cynthia Tiemann; three children.
Religion: Lutheran.
Political Career: No previous office.
Capitol Office: 2465 Rayburn Bldg. 20515; 225-1555.

In Washington: Like most Mountain state Republicans in the House, Marlenee brings to his work an ornery individualism rooted in resentment of federal control over his state's land. His antipathy toward government involvement in land matters defines his approach to issues on the Interior Committee; he is equally unyielding toward liberal Democrats on social and foreign policy. But on the Agriculture Committee, Marlenee discards confrontation for cooperation as he looks for allies to help him get the best deal for the farmers and ranchers of his vast district.

If he wants to continue his House career, he will have to win in a considerably vaster district: The 1990 census cost Montana a House seat, leaving the state with a single, at-large district.

Despite the focus on fiscal restraint prevailing in the 101st Congress, Marlenee showed no compunction in promoting a sharp increase in the loan rate for soybeans during consideration of the 1990 farm bill. Marlenee proposed to raise the rate from $4.50 to $6 per bushel. (The final bill set a rate of $5.02 with an assessment that would make the effective rate $4.92.) He was the only committee Republican to vote for Iowa Democrat Dave Nagle's amendment to raise U.S. commodity price-support levels above the world market price.

Marlenee also proposed authorizing payments to farmers on top of their crop subsidies as an incentive to grow soybeans or any other crop the Agriculture secretary designated. But his efforts to change policy on soybeans and wheat were dismissed by the committee.

The best example of Marlenee's ability to tame his fury and work toward a positive goal came during debate on the 1985 farm bill. Marlenee and Wheat Subcommittee Chairman Thomas S. Foley of Washington formed an alliance to push through Foley's proposals on the bill. In the crucial voting, Marlenee sided with Foley, even rebuffing Republicans' alternatives to Foley's ideas.

The alliance was logical. Foley was one of Agriculture's most conservative Democrats, an opponent of production controls, and a man whose wheat-growing district in eastern Washington bears some similarities to Marlenee's constituency in eastern Montana.

While Marlenee can cooperate on farm policy, he never seems far from combustion. He launched a one-man crusade against the one section of the 1985 farm bill that had attracted broad bipartisan support, the "sodbuster" section, aimed at cutting off crop subsidies to farmers who do not practice soil conservation. On the House floor, he referred to a proposal for a farmer referendum on production controls for wheat and feed grains as the "Hollywood-Hayden-Fonda-Willie Nelson-Harkin farm referendum."

Marlenee's deeply rooted resentment of the federal government shows up primarily on Interior, where he is in a good position to fight with environmentalists as ranking member of the National Parks and Public Lands Subcommittee. But Marlenee's inflexibility limits his role as a GOP strategist; he often seems more eager to make his own views known than to solicit others' opinions.

Sheer stubborness, however, did pay off for Marlenee in 1988, as he battled a bill designating more than 1.4 million acres of national forestland in Montana as wilderness. The bill was a compromise worked out among Montana's Senate and House Democrats, including Sen. John Melcher, who was locked in a tough re-election battle. But many environmentalists felt it added too few wilderness acres, and development advocates (including Marlenee) said it added too many. When President Ronald Reagan vetoed the bill a week before Election Day, it was a heavy blow to Melcher's prestige, and a factor in his loss to Republican Conrad Burns.

One of Marlenee's priorities on Interior is protecting cattlemen whose herds graze on federal lands. One-third of ranch families in Montana have cattle grazing on Forest Service and Bureau of Land Management land, and Marlenee has fought to prevent the government from increasing their grazing fees.

Marlenee's contempt for the central gov-

Montana 2

East

This is flat country — a land of sizzling summer heat and numbing winter cold, given over to wheat growing, cattle raising and, more recently, energy development. Covering three-quarters of the state, the 2nd tends to favor Republicans, but Democrats, especially those with a farm background, can compete here.

One such Democrat was 2nd District resident and two-term Sen. John Melcher. But in 1988, the 2nd abandoned Melcher for an eastern Montana Republican, Yellowstone County (Billings) commissioner and former farm broadcaster Conrad Burns. Melcher, who had taken 35 of the district's 37 counties in 1982, won only 10 against Burns in 1988.

The 2nd was fertile territory for Ronald Reagan, who won it with 63 percent in 1984. His successor, George Bush, had more difficulties in farm areas such as the 2nd; he won it in 1988, but with a modest 54 percent.

Roughly half the district's people live in and around the state's two largest cities, Billings and Great Falls (Cascade County). Billings is the more dependable of the two for Republicans, though Democratic Sen. Max Baucus won surrounding Yellowstone County by almost 3-to-1 in 1990.

From its beginnings as a market center for sugar beets and other farm products, Billings grew in the 1970s to become headquarters for the many energy ventures that sprouted across the plains. Yellowstone gave Bush 55 percent and Billings resident Burns 52 percent in 1988.

Great Falls is at the western edge of the 2nd. Cheap hydroelectric power drawn from the nearby falls on the Missouri River spurred its industrial development early in the century, as well as a surviving tradition of union activism. Democratic presidential nomineee Michael S. Dukakis barely lost Cascade County in 1988, and Melcher's 53 percent there was one of his better showings in the 2nd.

The district's ranching and wheat-growing counties are sparsely populated, but most of them deliver hefty GOP margins. In huge but almost vacant Garfield County in the center of the district, Bush won by nearly 3-to-1 — and that was down from Reagan's nearly 6-to-1 margin in 1984.

One of the areas transformed by energy development was Rosebud County, east of Billings, where coal discoveries caused a 64 percent population boom during the 1970s. Population growth slowed to 6 percent in the 1980s, but the political result has been to render this former GOP bastion into a Democratic-leaning area.

Population: 393,392. White 363,913 (93%), Black 1,340 (0.3%), American Indian, Eskimo and Aleut 23,940 (6%). Spanish origin 6,105 (2%). 18 and over 274,615 (70%), 65 and over 42,748 (11%). Median age: 29.

ernment touches even the host city of that government. As reports of violent drug-related crime and municipal corruption in the District of Columbia made national news in 1989, he suggested that the new slogan for the District should be: "D.C., A Work-Free Drug Place." He decried "a city out of control ... with a homicide rate so high its tourist promotion should issue every visitor a handgun."

He has been accused by home-state columnists and editorial writers of racial insensitivity. He stirred controversy by going to South Africa in 1987 to hunt Cape buffalo, but dismissed critics, saying, "We are not dealing with a banana republic." He entered the 1989 GOP state convention clutching an arrow to his chest, as if he had been shot by an Indian; he was seeking to prevent Indians from imposing taxes and recreation restrictions on non-Indians on reservations. He responded to the outcry with a guest editorial in which he wrote, "When an individual disagrees with problems and conditions on the reservation, it does not follow that he is prejudiced or racist."

At Home: Marlenee's style and opinions are not for everybody: Only twice in eight House elections has he won over 60 percent. In 1990, his last battle before Montana loses its second House district, he polled 63 percent against minor opposition.

But only once was his margin really meager — in 1986, when he took 53 percent against Democratic rancher Richard "Buck" O'Brien.

Given O'Brien's background, it was not surprising that Marlenee underestimated him. The Democrat had never sought office before; his political experience consisted of work as state party committeeman and as chairman of the Montana Aeronautics Commission. But O'Brien's background as a rancher and farmer lent weight to his complaints that the farm economy was failing because of policies favored by Marlenee and Reagan.

Seeking shelter from farm-crisis fallout,

Marlenee played up his differences with the administration's agricultural policy, and he reminded audiences that his posts on the Agriculture and Interior committees put him in a good position to address farm problems. O'Brien ran close to Marlenee in many of the 2nd's rural counties, but that was not enough to break the incumbent's grip.

Marlenee blamed the close outcome on his own complacency. O'Brien, saying he would have won had his name been better known, set out to overtake Marlenee in a 1988 rematch.

He kept his name in the news during 1987 by issuing a steady stream of press releases, and by piloting his own plane to speaking engagements across the huge district. He blamed Marlenee for continued farm problems and assailed him for visiting South Africa.

But Marlenee applied himself to his reelection. He organized early, spent around $400,000 (compared with $250,000 in 1986) and ran ads lauding his record and accusing O'Brien of being a liberal in populist's clothing.

Marlenee was bolstered by attention he got for criticizing the National Park Service's "let-burn" policy during the Yellowstone forest fires in mid-1988. Marlenee also got a boost when, as he had suggested, Reagan vetoed Melcher's wilderness bill. Marlenee carried all but three counties, winning 56 percent overall.

Marlenee started farming in 1953 with 320 acres of leased land and built a wheat and Hereford cattle operation known as "Marlenee's Big Sky Ranch." He began working with the Montana Stockgrowers, the Montana Grain Growers and the state political arm of the American Farm Bureau Federation.

These affiliations made him a familiar name in GOP circles, but his 1976 House campaign was his first bid for public office. He started early, announcing before incumbent Democrat Melcher had indicated his intention to run for the Senate. Marlenee had to work against his coming from a rural area remote from most of the district's population; his chief primary opponent, former state legislator John Cavan, came from Billings, the largest city. But Marlenee overcame Cavan, and went on to win in the fall against Democrat Tom Towe, whose family banking fortune gave him a well-financed campaign, but whose populist approach disturbed conservative Democrats.

In 1982, Democrats nominated a candidate who could compete with Marlenee outside urban areas. He was Howard Lyman, a farmer and rancher with a blunt manner and conservative views. But Lyman ran into trouble when a local newspaper disclosed that he had handed over title to his ranch and feed-lot operation to a creditor to meet $2.5 million in debts. Marlenee took 54 percent of the vote.

Committees

Agriculture (2nd of 18 Republicans)
Wheat, Soybeans & Feed Grains (ranking); Forests, Family Farms & Energy

Interior & Insular Affairs (3rd of 17 Republicans)
National Parks & Public Lands (ranking); Water, Power & Offshore Energy

Elections

1990 General		
Ron Marlenee (R)	96,449	(63%)
Don Burris (D)	56,739	(37%)
1988 General		
Ron Marlenee (R)	97,465	(56%)
Richard "Buck" O'Brien (D)	78,069	(44%)

Previous Winning Percentages: **1986** (53%) **1984** (66%) **1982** (54%) **1980** (59%) **1978** (57%) **1976** (55%)

District Vote For President

	1988		1984		1980		1976	
D	77,437	(44%)	68,229	(36%)	55,700	(31%)	74,737	(45%)
R	95,358	(54%)	118,483	(63%)	105,071	(59%)	87,917	(53%)
I					13,438	(8%)		

Campaign Finance

	Receipts	Receipts from PACs		Expend-itures
1990				
Marlenee (R)	$297,771	$140,750	(47%)	$310,981
Burris (D)	$29,822	0		$22,129
1988				
Marlenee (R)	$416,031	$171,992	(41%)	$380,928
O'Brien (D)	$396,369	$198,284	(50%)	$394,102

Key Votes

1991	
Authorize use of force against Iraq	Y
1990	
Support constitutional amendment on flag desecration	Y
Pass family and medical leave bill over Bush veto	N
Reduce SDI funding	N
Allow abortions in overseas military facilities	N
Approve budget summit plan for spending and taxing	N
Approve civil rights bill	N
1989	
Halt production of B-2 stealth bomber at 13 planes	N
Oppose capital gains tax cut	N
Approve federal abortion funding in rape or incest cases	N
Approve pay raise and revision of ethics rules	N
Pass Democratic minimum wage plan over Bush veto	N

Voting Studies

	Presidential Support		Party Unity		Conservative Coalition	
Year	S	O	S	O	S	O
1990	69	24	83	12	81	9
1989	70	21	86	4	90	7
1988	68	25	85	8	92	8
1987	69	28	82	10	88	9
1986	74	22	80	9	82	12
1985	61	26	71	16	80	11
1984	54	34	72	15	81	8
1983	63	32	71	17	80	9
1982	55	31	73	17	82	12
1981	66	24	72	21	79	12

Interest Group Ratings

Year	ADA	ACU	AFL-CIO	CCUS
1990	6	87	0	93
1989	0	96	0	100
1988	0	96	7	86
1987	8	83	19	93
1986	0	95	7	82
1985	10	95	18	71
1984	5	86	9	87
1983	0	90	13	84
1982	5	74	22	72
1981	20	93	13	79

Nebraska

U.S. CONGRESS

SENATE 2 D
HOUSE 1 D, 2 R

LEGISLATURE

49 nonpartisan senators in unicameral assembly

ELECTIONS

1988 Presidential Vote

Bush	60%
Dukakis	39%

1984 Presidential Vote

Reagan	71%
Mondale	29%

1980 Presidential Vote

Reagan	66%
Carter	26%
Anderson	7%

Turnout rate in 1986	47%
Turnout rate in 1988	57%
Turnout rate in 1990	50%

(as percentage of voting age population)

POPULATION AND GROWTH

1980 population	1,569,825
1990 population (36th in the nation)	1,578,385
Percent change 1980-1990	+1%

DEMOGRAPHIC BREAKDOWN

White	94%
Black	4%
American Indian, Eskimo, or Aleut	1%
(Hispanic origin)	2%
Urban	63%
Rural	37%
Born in state	70%
Foreign-born	2%

MAJOR CITIES

Omaha	335,795
Lincoln	191,972
Grand Island	39,386
Bellevue	30,982
Kearney	24,396

AREA AND LAND USE

Area	76,644 sq. miles (15th)
Farm	92%
Forest	1%
Federally owned	1%

Gov. Ben Nelson (D)
Of Omaha — Elected 1990

Born: May 17, 1941, McCook, Neb.
Education: U. of Nebraska, Lincoln, B.A. 1963, M.A. 1965, J.D. 1970.
Occupation: Lawyer; insurance executive.
Religion: United Methodist.
Political Career: No previous office.
Next Election: 1994.

WORK

Occupations

White-collar	49%
Blue-collar	27%
Service workers	14%

Government Workers

Federal	15,688
State	35,253
Local	83,347

MONEY

Median family income	$ 19,122	(29th)
Tax burden per capita	$ 648	(47th)

EDUCATION

Spending per pupil through grade 12	$ 3,943	(27th)
Persons with college degrees	16%	(26th)

CRIME

Violent crime rate	280 per 100,000 (37th)

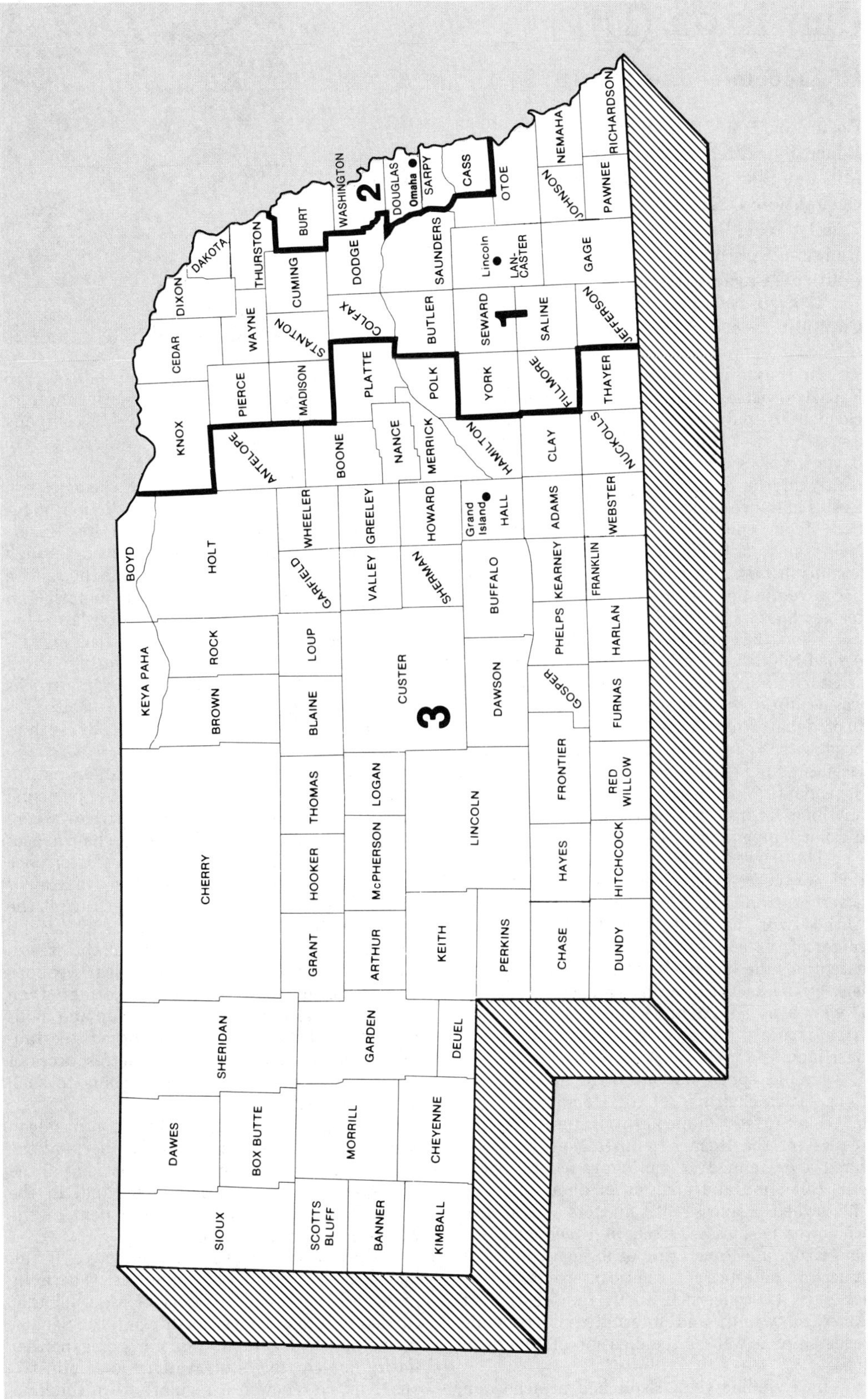

RICHARDSON
NEMAHA
PAWNEE
JOHNSON
OTOE
CASS
SARPY
Omaha
DOUGLAS
2
WASHINGTON
BURT
DODGE
SAUNDERS
Lincoln
LAN-CASTER
GAGE
JEFFERSON
SALINE
1
SEWARD
BUTLER
COLFAX
CUMING
THURSTON
DAKOTA
DIXON
WAYNE
STANTON
PLATTE
POLK
YORK
FILLMORE
THAYER
NUCKOLLS
CLAY
HAMILTON
MERRICK
NANCE
BOONE
MADISON
PIERCE
CEDAR
KNOX
ANTELOPE
WHEELER
GREELEY
HOWARD
Grand Island
HALL
ADAMS
WEBSTER
FRANKLIN
KEARNEY
BUFFALO
SHERMAN
VALLEY
GARFIELD
HOLT
BOYD
KEYA PAHA
ROCK
BROWN
LOUP
BLAINE
CUSTER
3
DAWSON
GOSPER
PHELPS
HARLAN
FURNAS
FRONTIER
RED WILLOW
HITCHCOCK
HAYES
LINCOLN
LOGAN
THOMAS
HOOKER
McPHERSON
CHERRY
GRANT
ARTHUR
KEITH
PERKINS
CHASE
DUNDY
DEUEL
GARDEN
SHERIDAN
DAWES
BOX BUTTE
MORRILL
CHEYENNE
KIMBALL
BANNER
SCOTTS BLUFF
SIOUX

Jim Exon (D)

Of Lincoln — Elected 1978

Born: Aug. 9, 1921, Geddes, S.D.
Education: Attended U. of Omaha, 1939-41.
Military Service: Army, 1941-45; Reserve, 1945-49.
Occupation: Office equipment dealer.
Family: Wife, Patricia Ann Pros; three children.
Religion: Episcopalian.
Political Career: Democratic National Committee, 1968-70; Neb. governor, 1971-79.
Capitol Office: 528 Hart Bldg. 20510; 224-4224.

In Washington: Any legislative visibility Exon had achieved in the 101st Congress was clouded by publicity surrounding a personal issue that arose in his 1990 re-election campaign. In early 1989, Exon had figured prominently in the Senate's rejection of President Bush's nominee for secretary of Defense, former Sen. John Tower. In 1990, Tower came to Nebraska to campaign against Exon and made the unsubstantiated charge that the Nebraskan had a reputation as "one of the two or three biggest boozers in the Senate."

Exon, the second-ranking Democrat on the Armed Services Committee, had been the first senator to announce his conviction that Tower was not up to the Cabinet job. In the emotional floor debate that ensued, Exon went head to head with Republicans who said Tower's colleagues would have known if he were alcohol dependent. "Just because we did not . . . see anything . . . does not necessarily mean that it did not happen," said Exon.

The Tower flap was the first broad national exposure for the big and plain-spoken ex-governor from the Plains whom friends call "J. J." Exon has not generally been at the center of the action in the Senate. With a few exceptions, he has not been a leader on major legislative issues. But even as a backbencher, he is viewed as an attentive and intelligent contributor and a mirror of public opinion in the heartland.

Exon stepped out on stage in the 101st Congress as chairman of the Commerce Committee's Surface Transportation panel. At the request of the Bush administration, he sponsored a bill aimed at improving federal agencies' collection and analysis of data from foreign-owned businesses. "It matters a great deal who owns businesses, assets and technologies," said Exon, a leading critic of foreign control of American enterprise. "American economic policy must be concerned about the creation of American wealth and international economic leadership, as well as the creation of American jobs."

In a similar vein, Exon had attached an amendment to the omnibus trade bill of 1988 granting the president discretionary power to block a foreign takeover of any U.S. company doing defense work or other work related to national security.

Exon was also the original sponsor of two measures directly under the jurisdiction of his Commerce subcommittee (though his fingerprints on each grew faint as it moved through Congress). One, designed to prevent the release of chemicals and other hazardous materials in transit across the country, beefed up laws governing the transportation of hazardous materials. The other was aimed at prohibiting "backhauling" (transporting food in the same trucks used to ship garbage or chemicals). Both bills were passed by Congress and signed by Bush in 1990.

Exon had begun assuming a larger institutional role in the late 1980s. The principal reason was his ascent on Armed Services, where in the 100th Congress he became chairman of the Strategic Forces and Nuclear Deterrence Subcommittee. Few titles bespeak the gravity of their responsibility more clearly. But at the outset of the 101st Congress, the panel faced a different sort of nuclear challenge: the waste-cleanup crisis at the nation's nuclear-weapons plants. Exon joined in the promotion of an oversight board to ensure the cleanup and modernization of the facilities and worked to establish a council in 1990 to apply the resources of the Energy and Defense departments to such environmental problems.

As a military policy-maker, Exon has been a supporter of the B-2 stealth bomber and the rail-based MX missile, a wary backer of the strategic defense initiative (SDI) and, in the 101st Congress, a converted proponent of the Midgetman mobile missile.

Previously, Exon's most effective forum had been the Budget Committee, where he preached the fiscally conservative gospel that carried him to the governorship and the Senate. He established a reputation for being neither flashy nor creative, but cautious and industrious. And he renewed it regularly with the kind of cracker-barrel skepticism Nebraskans appreciate. At the start of the 102nd Congress, when Congress was reviewing the administration's budget projections, Exon warily viewed elaborate administration charts projecting lower deficits. Said a skeptical Exon, "Never have I seen a chart going up and up and up; they always seem to be going down and down and down. But it never seems to work out that way."

During the Reagan administration, Exon's vote was something of a bellwether of conservative opinion on Reaganomics. In 1981 he supported President Reagan's tax and spending cuts, while warning of deficits to come. Two years later, as Reagan's influence on the budget process waned, Exon was siding more regularly with his party on the Budget Committee. But he kept his conservative credentials by voting for a balanced-budget constitutional amendment and opposing a congressional pay raise.

Exon also regularly returns a substantial portion of his office allowance to the Treasury.

Despite his fiscal conservatism, Exon has had nothing but scorn for the signal effort at deficit reduction in the 99th Congress — the Gramm-Rudman-Hollings balanced-budget amendment. The automatic spending reductions mandated by that 1985 law were a "ruse," he said, to enable Congress to evade the responsibility of voting on cuts in individual programs.

Exon has been a relative hard-liner on defense, though not an automatic vote for weapons requests. Toward the end of the Reagan administration, he criticized its military spending and arms policies. He joined with the liberal minority on Armed Services to oppose the White House-backed budget levels for the Pentagon, arguing that defense should not be spared reductions in a period of austerity.

In the 101st Congress, though, he concentrated on staving off threats to the B-2. An amendment in 1989 to curb production of the B-2 was rejected by 42 votes; in 1990, an amendment to kill the program was rejected by just 13 votes. By late 1990, even Exon conceded the B-2 was "in big, big trouble."

Previously a supporter of the rail-MX as a cheaper alternative to the Midgetman, Exon decided to support Bush's request for $100 million for the small missile as part of a political compromise to secure congressional funding for both weapons. Congress ultimately apportioned $680 million between the two projects but also said the country would not be able to afford both missiles as U.S. defense budgets continued to decline.

But Exon has been less certain about SDI. He accused Reagan of overselling the program and expressed concern that SDI had become "a sponge that sops up far too great a percentage of research and development funds." Still, he has sought a middle approach on SDI funding.

During debate on the defense authorization bill in 1986, he supported a level of funding below Reagan's request but above the level sought by many other Democrats. Two years later, with the Senate in Democratic hands, the debate had shifted. Deep cuts of $600 million or more were proposed for the SDI budget. In this atmosphere, Exon voted to protect the program from such cuts. Exon similarly opposed efforts on the floor in 1990 to slash funding for the program.

At Home: After his narrow (52 percent) win over a little-known challenger in 1984, Exon ranked near the top of the Republican target list for 1990. GOP Senate strategists — who recruited heavily from the House that year — failed to coax 1st District Rep. Doug Bereuter into the contest. But they did get former four-term 2nd District Rep. Hal Daub, who had been seen as promising prior to his defeat by interim Sen. David K. Karnes in the 1988 Republican Senate primary.

Daub had angered many Republicans by challenging Karnes (who eventually lost to Democrat Bob Kerrey), but his 1990 entry received strong backing from the party leadership. He drew quick attention with a January 1990 salvo in which he renounced political action committee contributions and challenged Exon to do the same. Exon refused to be drawn in.

Exon said rejecting PAC money would imply that he might be corrupted by it. He also recalled Daub dismissing a similar "no PACs" campaign by a 1984 Democratic House challenger as "a gimmick."

Exon aired an early flight of image-building TV ads, playing on his biggest strengths: his grandfatherly image and his long career of public service to Nebraska.

Daub, by contrast, had been known for his gratingly intense manner. He tried to soften his image, campaigning in a more relaxed style as "the new Hal Daub." But these efforts were undercut, and the challenge doomed, by the controversy over Tower's allegations concerning Exon's drinking.

When Daub declined to apologize for the incident, Exon said Daub's "pit bull" image had been revived. The incumbent maintained wide leads in the polls and won with 59 percent.

With his strong campaign effort, Exon lent credence to his argument that his weaker 1984 showing was attributable to his own complacency and to the coattails of President Reagan, who took 71 percent of the Nebraska vote that year. Exon's 1984 opponent, University of Nebraska Regent Nancy Hoch, surprised even her GOP supporters with her performance.

The 1984 aberration was the only close contest of Exon's political career. The owner of an office supply business in Lincoln, he broke into politics in the 1950s as a local Democratic Party coordinator. In 1964, he ran Lyndon B. Johnson's 1964 presidential campaign in Nebraska, and in 1968 he became a Democratic

National Committee member.

Although Exon had never run for office himself before 1970, he did not start small: He challenged incumbent Republican Gov. Norbert T. Tiemann. Exon benefited in that campaign from public disenchantment over newly enacted state income and sales taxes. The anti-tax backlash spurred a strong primary challenge to Tiemann, who was then swept aside by Exon.

The 1974 re-election campaign caused Exon no problems. Running on a fiscal austerity program that had produced a state government surplus that year, Exon turned back GOP state Sen. Richard D. Marvel.

His 1978 bid to move up to the Senate was nearly as easy. Republican Carl T. Curtis chose to retire after four terms, and his former aide, Donald E. Shasteen, was overmatched against Exon from the start. The ease with which Exon collected 68 percent of the vote may have set him up for the tumble his winning percentage would take in 1984.

Committees

Armed Services (2nd of 11 Democrats)
Strategic Forces & Nuclear Deterrence (chairman); Manpower & Personnel; Projection Forces & Regional Defense

Budget (5th of 12 Democrats)

Commerce, Science & Transportation (4th of 11 Democrats)
Surface Transportation (chairman); Aviation; Communications

Elections

1990 General

Jim Exon (D)	349,779	(59%)
Hal Daub (R)	243,013	(41%)

Previous Winning Percentages: **1984** (52%) **1978** (68%)

Campaign Finance

	Receipts	Receipts from PACs	Expend-itures
1990			
Exon (D)	$2,598,356	$1,503,897 (58%)	$2,349,739
Daub (R)	$1,461,846	0	$1,452,681

Key Votes

1991

Authorize use of force against Iraq	N

1990

Oppose prohibition of certain semiautomatic weapons	Y
Support constitutional amendment on flag desecration	Y
Oppose requiring parental notice for minors' abortions	N
Halt production of B-2 stealth bomber at 13 planes	N
Approve budget that cut spending and raised revenues	N
Pass civil rights bill over Bush veto	Y

1989

Oppose reduction of SDI funding	Y
Oppose barring federal funds for "obscene" art	N
Allow vote on capital gains tax cut	N

Voting Studies

	Presidential Support		Party Unity		Conservative Coalition	
Year	**S**	**O**	**S**	**O**	**S**	**O**
1990	54	42	63	34	68	30
1989	65	35	53	46	79	21
1988	65	31	66	30	86	11
1987	44	56	74	23	72	28
1986	34	64	66	31	45	53
1985	43	45	54	30	65	28
1984	58	36	51	45	68	28
1983	54	46	56	43	70	25
1982	55	40	64	33	70	26
1981	56	41	69	27	67	31

Interest Group Ratings

Year	ADA	ACU	AFL-CIO	CCUS
1990	33	61	67	55
1989	35	36	100	25
1988	35	48	71	50
1987	65	38	80	50
1986	35	48	53	32
1985	25	59	43	46
1984	55	48	36	65
1983	40	60	44	61
1982	40	74	48	55
1981	45	47	33	50

Bob Kerrey (D)

Of Lincoln — Elected 1988

Born: Aug. 27, 1943, Lincoln, Neb.
Education: U. of Nebraska, B.S. 1966.
Military Service: Navy, 1966-69.
Occupation: Restaurateur.
Family: Divorced; two children.
Religion: Congregationalist.
Political Career: Neb. governor, 1983-87.
Capitol Office: 316 Hart Bldg. 20510; 224-6551.

In Washington: In his first two years in the Senate, Kerrey impressed his colleagues with his swift acclimation in matters legislative and political. His quick mastery of the arcana of agriculture policy propelled him into a central role in negotiations on the 1990 farm bill. And by the end of the 101st Congress, he had become an articulate moral compass for the left wing of the Democratic Party on volatile partisan issues such as the Persian Gulf War and flag burning.

Kerrey has a belief in activist government that stems in part from his personal experience. He credits assistance from federal programs in helping him make the transformation from an embittered Vietnam veteran to a wealthy businessman. A glamorous ex-governor with a streak of quirkiness and a penchant for impulsive discourse, Kerrey is one of the more unusual Democrats who are considered rising stars in national party circles.

Kerrey was the only member of his class to win a seat on the Appropriations Committee for the 101st Congress. His other committee assignment, Agriculture, was promised to him by Chairman Patrick J. Leahy during his election campaign.

Although Kerrey did not enter the Senate with a detailed grounding in the intricacies of agriculture, he hired respected staff and immersed himself in government farm programs. By the time the committee turned to the 1990 farm bill, he was prepared to spearhead the activist, prairie populist wing on the panel.

On a committee characterized by bipartisan log-rolling, Kerrey was advocating partisan confrontation to craft a distinctively Democratic bill. He led the populists' charge to raise price-support loan rates to ensure farmers higher prices for their crops. They were stymied in their attempt to attract Republican support for their stand, however: On a key committee vote to strip the Agriculture secretary's authority to lower loan rates, every Republican and two senior Democrats, David Pryor of Arkansas and David L. Boren of Oklahoma, voted against it and it failed, 7-11.

Unlike some other populists, Kerrey did not summarily reject trying to craft an acceptable compromise bill (though he ended up voting against the final package). Partly because of his standing with the populists and partly because he was sympathetic to some of Leahy's environmental initiatives, Leahy picked Kerrey, the most junior Democrat on the committee, to be a Senate conferee on the farm bill. In taking Kerrey, Leahy snubbed fourth-ranking Democrat Howell Heflin of Alabama, who was not considered a loyal vote for Leahy's conservation provisions. Earlier, Kerrey had been selected to serve on a bipartisan committee task force to resolve some issues blocking the bill's progress.

Another reason Leahy may have valued Kerrey's presence in the conference was his unflinching tenacity in the face of administration opposition — particularly when it was led by Agriculture Secretary Clayton Yeutter. The feud between Kerrey and Yeutter, a Nebraska Republican, predates Kerrey's Senate service and has extended beyond farm policy, prompting some to view their conflict as a prelude to Kerrey's 1994 re-election campaign.

Soon after Yeutter was tapped in 1991 to become chairman of the Republican National Committee, he singled out Kerrey when he criticized Democrats who opposed the congressional resolution authorizing President Bush to use force in the Persian Gulf. "Americans do not share the negative and depressed viewpoints of Senator Kerrey and others," he said. Kerrey responded on the Senate floor, saying that Yeutter's comments "trivialize the deep misgivings which all Americans have about sending our sons and daughters into combat."

Kerrey's record as a war hero in Vietnam — he lost part of his right leg in combat and earned a Congressional Medal of Honor — gave him credibility, and other anti-war Democrats cover, when he launched his early opposition to the U.S. buildup of forces in the Persian Gulf in 1990. After supporting the initial dispatch of troops to Saudi Arabia, saying it was justifiable to prevent an Iraqi invasion, he became one of the most conspicuous opponents of Bush's gulf policy as it escalated toward creating an offensive force.

"I question the response that says we're going to go there and have our young people die so we can have cheap oil and cheap gasoline here at home," he said in August 1990. He chastised the administration for its record of passivity while Iraqi President Saddam Hussein amassed weapons and oppressed his citizens. "To say that anyone who had an objection to the [administration's gulf] policy was an appeaser," he said in January 1991, "was to ignore the administration's own participation in appeasement." He voted to continue applying economic sanctions to pressure Iraq's withdrawal from Kuwait.

Kerrey had opposed an earlier move to sanction Iraq. He was one of only 12 senators — most of whom were from farm states — to vote against imposing economic sanctions on Iraq as the Iraqi army was about to invade Kuwait. Some farm-state lawmakers opposed the amendment, added to the farm bill, for fear that a lucrative market might be lost. The State Department also opposed it.

Earlier, Kerrey had lent his patriotic prestige to liberals' debate when he denounced vehemently Bush's initiative to amend the Constitution to ban physical desecration of the flag. He accused Bush of trying "to divide the nation" by pushing the amendment. "I am ashamed of what he did," he said in a passionate floor speech in 1990. He concluded, "I grieve for us. I weep for America today."

While Kerrey has involved himself in debates on a wide range of prominent issues, he has also kept his eye on legislative matters. On Appropriations, he was able to secure $5 million to expand a cancer research center in Omaha affiliated with the University of Nebraska.

During debate on the 1989 bill to bail out and restructure the savings and loan industry, Kerrey offered an amendment to make more accountable the Resolution Trust Corporation, which was established in the bill to close down insolvent thrifts. But Banking Committee leaders opposed any amendments to their bill, and the Senate voted to kill Kerrey's, 66-32.

In April 1990, Kerrey visited Vietnam and Cambodia for the first time since 1969. He has advocated easing U.S. economic sanctions on Cambodia. During the conference on a 1990 supplemental foreign aid bill, Kerrey won adoption of an amendment he and California Democrat Alan Cranston sponsored to allow $5 million in aid to be spent helping children in Cambodia.

Kerrey's uninhibited readiness to take a stand drew praise from a most unlikely source in 1989. He took the floor to argue against an amendment to enable former Marine Lt. Col. Oliver L. North to receive his military pension despite his felony conviction. "Just so there can be no doubt," Kerrey told its sponsor, North Carolina Republican Jesse Helms, "in case this does not come to a vote and the senator from North Carolina wonders where I stand on this issue, I am against it."

"Let me say to my friend from Nebraska," Helms replied, "that I respect him, because he does not pussyfoot on issues. He stated his case unequivocally, and I admire him for that. It is this business of avoiding votes, avoiding taking a position, that I can't understand. I admire the senator from Nebraska for his willingness to state a position."

At Home: "Charismatic" and "enigmatic" are the two descriptors commonly applied to Kerrey during his rise in Nebraska public life. An unconventional style and disregard for the accepted rules of political behavior vaulted Kerrey into the governorship in 1982, and sent him to the Senate six years later.

Although Kerrey was known locally as a war hero and a successful restaurateur, he was a political novice when he bid against Republican Gov. Charles Thone in 1982. However, Thone had a reputation for being bland and indecisive. Employing an aggressive campaign style and a wry, self-deprecating sense of humor, Kerrey attracted publicity and scored a narrow upset.

Kerrey soon showed he was unafraid to buck political trends: He became a critic of President Reagan, who in 1984 would carry 71 percent of the Nebraska vote. Kerrey attacked Reagan's economic and farm policies and accused the president of taking an approach to foreign affairs that "drapes euphemism and simplistic slogans over the realities of war." His views on war were well-known: After accepting the Medal of Honor, he had protested the Vietnam War as immoral.

But it was Kerrey's relationship with actress Debra Winger, not his political agenda, that left the most enduring impression from his gubernatorial tenure. Kerrey, who was divorced, met Winger in 1983 while she was making a movie in Lincoln.

While Kerrey's public romance made him something of a dashing figure, it also led to criticisms that he was long on style and short on substance. Although he cut an activist image early in his term, pushing deficit-reduction and banking-law-reform measures to passage, his relationship with the unicameral Legislature soured somewhat.

Still, Kerrey was heavily favored to win a second term; his job-approval rating hung at about 70 percent. He thus sealed his reputation for unpredictability when he announced he would not run for re-election in 1986. Although some observers tied the decision to distress over the breakup of his romance with Winger, Kerrey cited business obligations and a desire to spend more time with his two children.

With both Senate seats held by Democrats, it appeared that Kerrey might have plenty of quality time before seeking higher office. However, Democratic Sen. Edward Zorinsky died suddenly in March 1987; Republican Gov. Kay A. Orr picked an obscure businessman, David K. Karnes, as an interim replacement. Knowing his political base was much stronger than Karnes', Kerrey needed no armtwisting before entering the 1988 contest for a full Senate term.

As it turned out, Kerrey received an unexpected assist from a would-be Republican rival. Four-term 2nd District GOP Rep. Hal Daub, angered that Orr had passed him over in favor of Karnes, jumped into the Republican Senate primary. Bolstered by his brief incumbency and the support of the state Republican leadership, Karnes held on to win with 55 percent of the vote. But he was bloodied, and entered the fall campaign against Kerrey as a distinct underdog.

Kerrey, who had token opposition for the Democratic nomination, had already filled the airwaves with image-building biographical ads. He was able to stick to his own script for the general election, touting his support for catastrophic health insurance, parental leave legislation and an overhaul of the welfare system. He called for a mix of spending cuts and tax increases to reduce the deficit.

Karnes, meanwhile, had spent much of his money on the primary, and was $200,000 in debt by the end of June. He also made a disastrous gaffe: In discussing improved agricultural technology, Karnes said, "We need fewer farmers at this point in time," a remark that provoked jeers from a state-fair audience. Karnes immediately retreated, saying he had misspoken, but the damage was done.

Even a flawless campaign might have fallen short of upending the popular Kerrey; one as fraught with errors as Karnes' was doomed. Kerrey won by 15 percentage points, running nearly 20 points ahead of Democratic presidential nominee Michael S. Dukakis.

Committees

Agriculture, Nutrition & Forestry (10th of 10 Democrats)
Agricultural Production & Stabilization of Prices; Agricultural Research & General Legislation; Nutrition & Investigations

Appropriations (16th of 16 Democrats)
Agriculture, Rural Development & Related Agencies; District of Columbia; VA, HUD and Independent Agencies; Treasury, Postal Service & General Government

Elections

1988 General		
Bob Kerrey (D)	378,717	(57%)
David K. Karnes (R)	278,250	(42%)
1988 Primary		
Bob Kerrey (D)	156,498	(91%)
Ken L. Michaelis (D)	14,248	(8%)

Campaign Finance

	Receipts	Receipts from PACs		Expend-itures
1988				
Kerrey (D)	$3,485,728	$799,279	(23%)	$3,461,148
Karnes (R)	$3,423,237	$883,895	(26%)	$3,411,361

Key Votes

1991	
Authorize use of force against Iraq	N
1990	
Oppose prohibition of certain semiautomatic weapons	N
Support constitutional amendment on flag desecration	N
Oppose requiring parental notice for minors' abortions	Y
Halt production of B-2 stealth bomber at 13 planes	Y
Approve budget that cut spending and raised revenues	N
Pass civil rights bill over Bush veto	Y
1989	
Oppose reduction of SDI funding	N
Oppose barring federal funds for "obscene" art	Y
Allow vote on capital gains tax cut	N

Voting Studies

	Presidential Support		Party Unity		Conservative Coalition	
Year	**S**	**O**	**S**	**O**	**S**	**O**
1990	40	60	84	16	49	51
1989	51	49	88	12	26	74

Interest Group Ratings

Year	ADA	ACU	AFL-CIO	CCUS
1990	83	13	67	25
1989	80	11	100	50

1 Doug Bereuter (R)

Of Utica — Elected 1978

Born: Oct. 6, 1939, York, Neb.

Education: U. of Nebraska, B.A. 1961; Harvard U., M.C.P. 1963, M.P.A. 1973.

Military Service: Army, 1963-65.

Occupation: Urban planner; associate professor of planning.

Family: Wife, Louise Anna Meyer; two children.

Religion: Lutheran.

Political Career: Neb. Legislature, 1975-79.

Capitol Office: 2348 Rayburn Bldg. 20515; 225-4806.

In Washington: Most House members who aspire to state party leadership or statewide office tend to gravitate to high-profile committees and headline-grabbing issues. Bereuter — who has taken a leadership role in the Nebraska GOP and has been mentioned as a potential Senate candidate — is an exception.

On the Banking and Foreign Affairs Committees, Bereuter has built a reputation as a legislative craftsman who spends much of his time on such esoteric issues as savings-and-loan capital requirements, Third World debt, cargo preference laws and international human rights.

It would seem that Bereuter's devotion to such details could entail some political risk. Most Nebraska House members over the years have focused on state economic issues: Until 1991, Bereuter's colleague to the west was 3rd District Republican Rep. Virginia Smith, who concentrated on issues affecting Nebraska's agricultural base. Also, while central Nebraska is not the isolationist bastion of old, there still exists there a suspicion of foreign entanglements, especially foreign aid programs.

Yet Bereuter's earnest efforts as a committed internationalist, combined with his attentions to 1st District issues, have brought success. He has had no serious challenge for reelection in years, and party leaders urged him to run in 1990 against Democratic Sen. Jim Exon.

Bereuter is a rare moderate Republican on the ideologically divided Foreign Affairs Committee. During the partisan warfare over such issues as aid to the Nicaraguan contras during the 1980s, Bereuter was often one of the committee's few voices urging compromise.

An example of Bereuter's willingness to take a bipartisan attitude toward foreign affairs occurred during the run-up to the February 1990 election that ended leftist rule in Nicaragua. Bereuter was a member of a delegation, headed by Jimmy Carter, that monitored the campaign. After the victory by Nicaragua's opposition forces, the Republican House member credited the former Democratic president for his efforts to guarantee an open, fair and violence-free election. "President Carter played a crucial role in all of this," Bereuter said.

Although Bereuter has sided with the Reagan and Bush administrations on most foreign policy issues, he has not shied from publicly criticizing the White House when he disagrees.

Executive branch officials have long complained that their ability to target U.S. foreign aid has been hindered by the congressional practice of "earmarking" money for specific purposes; in 1989, the House made an effort to restrict the practice. However, Bereuter backed an amendment by New Jersey Republican Christopher H. Smith to earmark $245 million for immunization and other child-health programs. While other members were "willing to give the administration the benefit of the doubt," Bereuter said, "I am not."

The ranking GOP member on Foreign Affairs' Human Rights Subcommittee, Bereuter took umbrage in early 1990 at the State Department's efforts to develop a closer relationship with Iraq. Citing the "abysmal" record of Saddam Hussein's Iraqi regime — which included the use of poison gas in 1988 against the nation's Kurdish minority — Bereuter co-sponsored a non-binding resolution with Democratic subcommittee chairman Gus Yatron of Pennsylvania condemning Iraq for a "consistent pattern" of human rights violations.

The resolution easily passed the subcommittee. However, the Bush administration, maintaining that Saddam Hussein's Iraq had "an important role to play" in Middle Eastern affairs, blocked the resolution from advancing.

U.S.-Iraqi relations were wrecked that August by Iraq's occupation of Kuwait. In January 1991, Bereuter supported President Bush's effort to obtain authorization to use force against Iraq. Bereuter, who is also a member of the Intelligence Committee, said sanctions that had been instituted against Iraq were not sufficient. "Since sanctions were enacted, private firms have been seeking ways to supply Iraq with the goods it demands," Bereuter said.

Nebraska 1

East Central — Lincoln

The state capital, Lincoln, gives the 1st District a modest urban flavor, but the city does not dominate the district the way Omaha influences the neighboring 2nd District.

Lancaster County, which includes Lincoln and its few suburbs, casts just under 40 percent of the vote. Essentially a white-collar town, Lincoln is dominated by the state government and the University of Nebraska (24,000 students).

Partisan registration in the county is nearly evenly split and Lancaster can go either way in a close statewide election. In 1988, George Bush won Lancaster over Democrat Michael S. Dukakis by 345 votes out of over 90,000 cast. Democratic Sen. Jim Exon is a powerful force in the county, his home base; he carried it with 70 percent in his 1990 re-election.

The rest of the district is made up largely of prosperous, predominantly Republican farming areas where corn is the major crop. The few small cities, such as Fremont, Norfolk and Beatrice, are market centers closely tied to farming.

The counties along the Platte River (Colfax, Dodge, Butler and Saunders) provide some Democratic votes, along with Saline County, southwest of Lincoln, and Dakota, a meatpacking area along the Missouri River and a nascent suburb of Sioux City, Iowa.

The rest of the district's 27 counties, particularly those toward the northern border, are overwhelmingly Republican.

When Nebraska redistricted for the 1980s, there was talk of moving Knox County, on the South Dakota border, from the 1st District to the 3rd. But Bereuter had been active on behalf of the Santee Indians, who have a reservation in that county. He did not want to lose it, and the Legislature accommodated him.

Population: 523,079. White 509,424 (97%), Black 4,026 (1%), Other 7,026 (1%). Spanish origin 4,795 (1%). 18 and over 383,987 (73%), 65 and over 74,959 (14%). Median age: 30.

Bereuter is not a great fan of economic sanctions, particularly those that hinder farm exports. In July 1990, as Iraq was stepping up its aggressive rhetoric, the House moved to cut off $1 billion in farm export guarantees to that nation. However, Bereuter attached an amendment allowing the Agriculture secretary to suspend credit restrictions if it is determined that they would do more harm to American farmers than to the targeted country.

One of Bereuter's persistent causes on foreign affairs has a sharp farm-state angle: He opposes cargo-preference statutes, which require certain countries receiving direct U.S. economic aid to spend a like amount on U.S. products and to ship at least half their purchases on U.S. vessels.

Although these rules are aimed at boosting U.S. shippers, Bereuter says they hurt American farmers by placing them at a disadvantage with foreign counterparts who export goods without strings attached. In 1989, he tried to attach an amendment to a foreign aid bill that would have replaced cargo-preference provisions with a resolution urging aid recipients to use U.S. ships to "the extent possible"; the amendment failed, 186-230.

Bereuter takes an interest in efforts to reduce debt owed by developing nations to U.S. banks, an issue overlapping his Foreign Affairs and Banking beats. Although he generally supported the 1989 plan by Treasury Secretary Nicholas F. Brady to reduce such debt, Bereuter was wary of proposals to force banks to grant relief. "If debt relief is mandated, then we have to be concerned about the chilling effect with respect to future lending," he said.

During the 101st Congress, the usually low-profile Banking Committee was thrust into the spotlight as it debated the savings-and-loan bailout bill. Bereuter favored tougher capital requirements on S&Ls.

A city planner by profession, Bereuter has been active in the Banking Committee's housing and urban affairs jurisdictions. With Lincoln as the 1st District's only large city, he spends much of his time making sure that smaller localities get a share of federal money. When Housing Secretary Jack F. Kemp proposed a housing bill in 1990 targeting Community Development Block Grants to low-income areas, Bereuter expressed concern worried that this would reduce money for rural areas.

Bereuter is ranking Republican on the Banking Subcommittee on Policy Research and Insurance. The position enables him to oversee issues that pertain to Nebraska's large insurance industry, and to promote the federal flood-insurance program that benefits farmers.

As on foreign policy, Bereuter agrees with Bush on most, but not all, economic issues. In September 1989, he was the only House Republican to vote against Bush's plan to reduce capital gains taxes; he said the cut would "exacerbate a growing income inequality and contribute to the federal deficit."

At Home: Bereuter rejected a media theory that he voted against the capital gains cut to get even for a personal slight. Bush had joined GOP strategists in recruiting House members to take on Democratic senators, and was displeased that Bereuter failed to consult him before announcing in June 1989 that he would not run against Exon. When Bush visited Lincoln shortly thereafter, Bereuter was not invited to sit on the stage.

The flap caused no problems for Bereuter at the polls. He won a seventh term in 1990 with 65 percent of the vote, despite Republican losses for governor and senator. Afterward, noting the failure of these conservative-oriented campaigns, Bereuter stated that he would play a leadership role in the state GOP and seek a more moderate course for the party.

Bereuter's background is unusual for a Nebraska politician. He held the state's top city-planning post under moderate GOP Gov. Norbert Tiemann from 1969-71. Then he served one four-year term in the Legislature, winning a reputation as one of the more liberal members by sponsoring a land-use planning bill that farming and ranching interests regarded as an intrusion into private-property decisions.

Bereuter used conservative rhetoric during his 1978 House campaign, but he was still seen as a moderate because of his legislative record and his Tiemann connections. That helped him attract Lincoln voters in the GOP primary, in which he defeated a conservative state senator who focused on the rural areas of the district. Bereuter prevailed only by carrying Lancaster County (Lincoln) overwhelmingly.

In November he drew united GOP support and a large independent vote against Hess Dyas, the former Democratic state chairman. His strength in Lincoln helped him to a 58 percent victory. Since then, he has never won less than 64 percent.

Committees

Banking, Finance & Urban Affairs (5th of 20 Republicans)
Policy Research & Insurance (ranking); Financial Institutions Supervision, Regulation & Insurance; Housing & Community Development; International Development, Finance, Trade & Monetary Policy

Foreign Affairs (9th of 18 Republicans)
Human Rights & International Organizations (ranking); International Economic Policy & Trade

Select Hunger (6th of 12 Republicans)
International

Select Intelligence (3rd of 7 Republicans)
Legislation; Program & Budget Authorization

Elections

1990 General

Doug Bereuter (R)	129,654	(65%)
Larry Hall (D)	70,587	(35%)

1988 General

Doug Bereuter (R)	146,231	(67%)
Corky Jones (D)	72,167	(33%)

Previous Winning Percentages: **1986** (64%) **1984** (74%) **1982** (75%) **1980** (79%) **1978** (58%)

District Vote For President

	1988	1984	1980	1976
D	96,105 (43%)	69,741 (33%)	57,724 (28%)	82,128 (41%)
R	123,621 (56%)	143,356 (67%)	129,333 (62%)	116,065 (57%)
I			17,348 (8%)	

Campaign Finance

	Receipts	Receipts from PACs	Expend-itures
1990			
Bereuter (R)	$254,654	$147,250 (58%)	$223,898
Hall (D)	$65,064	$43,400 (67%)	$65,064
1988			
Bereuter (R)	$215,704	$99,120 (46%)	$221,530
Jones (D)	$97,118	$28,940 (30%)	$96,278

Key Votes

1991	
Authorize use of force against Iraq	Y
1990	
Support constitutional amendment on flag desecration	Y
Pass family and medical leave bill over Bush veto	N
Reduce SDI funding	N
Allow abortions in overseas military facilities	N
Approve budget summit plan for spending and taxing	N
Approve civil rights bill	N
1989	
Halt production of B-2 stealth bomber at 13 planes	N
Oppose capital gains tax cut	Y
Approve federal abortion funding in rape or incest cases	N
Approve pay raise and revision of ethics rules	N
Pass Democratic minimum wage plan over Bush veto	N

Voting Studies

	Presidential Support		Party Unity		Conservative Coalition	
Year	S	O	S	O	S	O
1990	62	38	73	25	87	13
1989	69	29	58	41	80	17
1988	56 †	42 †	79 †	20 †	87 †	13 †
1987	59	41	63	35	81	19
1986	58	42	73	26	78	22
1985	58	43	74	22	78	18
1984	54	43	64	35	71	29
1983	61	37	69	26	70	29
1982	75	25	77	23	79	21
1981	68	30	75	23	79	19

† Not eligible for all recorded votes.

Interest Group Ratings

Year	ADA	ACU	AFL-CIO	CCUS
1990	17	67	0	100
1989	15	61	33	80
1988	20	76	57	93
1987	24	57	19	80
1986	15	59	21	72
1985	15	67	12	82
1984	35	54	23	63
1983	25	70	6	95
1982	26	68	20	86
1981	20	87	0	89

2 Peter Hoagland (D)

Of Omaha — Elected 1988

Born: Nov. 17, 1941, Omaha, Neb.
Education: Stanford U., A.B. 1963; Yale U., LL.B. 1968.
Military Service: Army, 1963-65.
Occupation: Lawyer.
Family: Wife, Barbara Erickson; five children.
Religion: Episcopalian.
Political Career: Neb. Legislature, 1979-87.
Capitol Office: 1710 Longworth Bldg. 20515; 225-4155.

In Washington: Hoagland gives the politically marginal 2nd representation markedly different from that of his intense and conservative predecessor, Republican Hal Daub. A soft-spoken moderate Democrat, Hoagland as a freshman backed abortion rights and a higher minimum wage and opposed a constitutional amendment banning flag desecration.

Hoagland impresses constituents and colleagues alike with his sincerity, diligence and intellect. That image helped his first re-election campaign, and made him a plausible, though unsuccessful, candidate for a spot on the Appropriations Committee in late 1990. Still, his skills should serve him well on his new committee assignments, Interior and Judiciary.

Hoagland retains a seat on the Banking Committee. As a member of its Housing Subcommittee in the 101st Congress, he participated in the first major overhaul of federal housing programs since 1974. Hoagland joined a bloc of moderate and conservative Democrats who forged compromise language to provide incentives for landlords to continue renting to low-income families. In 1989, when the committee worked on a $50 billion S&L bailout bill, Hoagland took a tough stand on stiffening capital standards for thrifts, despite heavy lobbying by a large Omaha-based savings and loan.

As a freshman and again in the 102nd Congress, Hoagland proposed scrapping a provision in the 1986 tax-overhaul law that taxed proceeds from "pickle cards" — licensed pull-tab gaming devices used in Nebraska and Minnesota to raise funds for charitable groups.

Judiciary offers Hoagland a forum to pursue his interest in drug interdiction. In 1990 he testified before the Judiciary Committee of the Nebraska Legislature on a drug bill he helped draft; it included provisions to set up military-style "boot camps" for certain drug offenders.

On Interior, Hoagland will continue his push for a bill designating parts of the Niobrara River in Nebraska and a segment of the Missouri River in Nebraska and South Dakota as part of the national wild and scenic rivers system. Democratic Sen. Jim Exon of Nebraska has been promoting similar legislation.

At Home: Due largely to the blue-collar population in Omaha, the 2nd is regarded as Nebraska's most Democratic turf. However, the district votes Republican for president, and was won four times by Republican Daub. Hoagland had tough campaigns in both 1988 and 1990.

Hoagland's opportunity came when Daub sought the GOP Senate nomination in 1988. With eight years' experience in Nebraska's Legislature, Hoagland entered the contest with a large political base. A fifth-generation Omahan, he had spent his young adulthood away from home: in college, in the Army, in law school, and in Washington, D.C., where he was a law clerk and trial lawyer. Hoagland returned to Omaha in 1973 to practice law, and he got involved in public affairs, working to push a tough ethics law through the Nebraska Legislature in 1976.

Hoagland began his own political career in 1978, winning a seat in the Legislature, where he backed initiatives on water conservation, hospital cost containment and education. He did not seek a third term in 1986, but ran in the 1988 Democratic House primary, and defeated Cece Zorinsky, the widow of Democratic Sen. Edward Zorinsky, 51 percent to 43 percent.

His Republican foe, pathologist Jerry Schenken, was little known, but had a war chest that bought instant credibility. However, Hoagland linked up with the Senate campaign of former Gov. Bob Kerrey, headed for a resounding victory over appointed GOP Sen. David K. Karnes. Hoagland won by 2,981 votes.

In 1990, Hoagland's GOP foe was lawyer Ally Milder, a conservative former aide to Iowa Sen. Charles E. Grassley. Milder stressed her opposition to abortion and called Hoagland a liberal, citing vote studies that showed him frequently opposing President Bush. Hoagland styled himself as an independent voice for the 2nd, and emphasized his efforts to reform the S&L system and fight drug-related crime. He also gained when Secretary of Veterans Affairs Edward J. Derwinski visited Omaha for Milder and created a huge flap by calling Hispanics "wetbacks." Hoagland won with 58 percent.

Nebraska 2

East — Omaha

The 2nd is dominated by the Missouri River city of Omaha, Nebraska's largest city and the seat of Douglas County, which casts four-fifths of the district's vote. Omaha's newspapers and television stations are the main sources of information not only for the 2nd, but also for many residents of southwest Iowa. Taking into account Omaha's smaller sister-city across the river — Council Bluffs, Iowa — metropolitan Omaha is home to more than 618,000 people.

Omaha is famous for the stockyards that traditionally have served the region's cattle, hog and sheep growers. Although meatpacking, dairy products and food processing are the major industries, the economy is diversified. Omaha is an insurance, medical and educational center and the headquarters of the Union Pacific Railroad.

Omaha's blue-collar electorate, heavily Irish and Slavic, resembles that of ethnic areas in other Midwestern cities, but has somewhat weaker Democratic Party ties. Omaha's 13 percent black population helps boost the Democratic vote.

In presidential elections, Douglas County is reliably, if not overwhelmingly, Republican. It has voted for the GOP White House candidate every time but once in the post-Roosevelt era. In 1988, George Bush won Douglas County with 56 percent of the vote. But in contests for other offices, Douglas often goes Democratic. In the 1990 Senate race, it gave Democrat Jim Exon 59 percent of its vote; state treasurer Dawn Rockey won 68 percent in 1990.

Although growth in Omaha's suburbs and population decline in the city made Douglas County favorable ground for GOP House candidates during most of the 1980s, Democrat Hoagland carried it narrowly in 1988 and comfortably in his 1990 re-election.

After Douglas, the largest county in the 2nd is Sarpy County, just to the south of Omaha. Located there is Offutt Air Force Base, which provides jobs for thousands of military and civilian personnel and is headquarters for the Strategic Air Command. Several military contractors are also located in Bellevue. Sarpy County has a solid GOP presence — partly due to a large number of military retirees — though Hoagland and Exon carried it in 1990. Burt, the smallest of the district's five counties, was the only one to lose population during the 1980's.

Population: 522,919. White 467,490 (89%), Black 43,681 (8%), Other 5,792 (1%). Spanish origin 10,747 (2%). 18 and over 364,998 (70%), 65 and over 50,168 (10%). Median age: 28.

Committees

Banking, Finance & Urban Affairs (20th of 31 Democrats)
Economic Stabilization; Financial Institutions Supervision, Regulation & Insurance

Interior & Insular Affairs (26th of 29 Democrats)
National Parks & Public Lands; Water, Power & Offshore Energy

Judiciary (19th of 21 Democrats)
Crime and Criminal Justice

Elections

1990 General		
Peter Hoagland (D)	111,903	(58%)
Ally Milder (R)	80,845	(42%)
1990 Primary		
Peter Hoagland (D)	49,693	(87%)
Jess M. Pritchett (D)	7,439	(13%)
1988 General		
Peter Hoagland (D)	112,174	(50%)
Jerry Schenken (R)	109,193	(49%)

District Vote For President

	1988		1984		1980		1976	
D	94,100	(42%)	70,050	(33%)	61,075	(30%)	75,218	(39%)
R	130,246	(58%)	144,478	(67%)	123,845	(61%)	114,370	(59%)
I					15,621	(8%)		

Campaign Finance

	Receipts	Receipts from PACs		Expend-itures
1990				
Hoagland (D)	$935,652	$615,587	(66%)	$929,247
Milder (R)	$632,229	$152,769	(24%)	$625,716
1988				
Hoagland (D)	$860,865	$325,900	(38%)	$858,762
Schenken (R)	$1,162,518	$179,672	(15%)	$1,158,294

Key Votes

1991	
Authorize use of force against Iraq	Y
1990	
Support constitutional amendment on flag desecration	N
Pass family and medical leave bill over Bush veto	N
Reduce SDI funding	Y
Allow abortions in overseas military facilities	Y
Approve budget summit plan for spending and taxing	N
Approve civil rights bill	Y
1989	
Halt production of B-2 stealth bomber at 13 planes	N
Oppose capital gains tax cut	Y
Approve federal abortion funding in rape or incest cases	Y
Approve pay raise and revision of ethics rules	N
Pass Democratic minimum wage plan over Bush veto	Y

Voting Studies

	Presidential Support		Party Unity		Conservative Coalition	
Year	**S**	**O**	**S**	**O**	**S**	**O**
1990	27	73	84	16	50	50
1989	35	65	86	14	49	51

Interest Group Ratings

Year	ADA	ACU	AFL-CIO	CCUS
1990	72	29	83	50
1989	70	25	92	40

3 Bill Barrett (R)

Of Lexington — Elected 1990

Born: Feb. 9, 1929, Lexington, Neb.
Education: Hastings College, B.A. 1951.
Military Service: Navy, 1951-52.
Occupation: Insurance and real estate company owner.
Family: Wife, Elsie Carlson; four children.
Religion: Presbyterian.
Political Career: Neb. Legislature, 1979-91; Speaker, 1987-91.
Capitol Office: 1607 Longworth Bldg. 20515; 225-6435.

The Path to Washington: When Barrett told voters he would follow in the footsteps of of retiring Rep. Virginia Smith, he meant he would maintain the popular incumbent's dedication to the 3rd's farm-based economy. However, Barrett's first run for the House ended up mirroring Smith's first campaign in a less positive sense: He struggled to hold the traditional Republican bastion.

When she first ran for the open 3rd, Smith won by 737 votes in the Watergate election of 1974. Barrett's 51 percent win over Democratic state Sen. Sandra K. Scofield in 1990 was unexpectedly narrow in a district in which two-thirds of the 1988 presidential vote went to George Bush.

Barrett now has the opportunity to solidify his hold on the district, as did Smith, who never faced a difficult re-election contest. Although he will next be up in a presidential election year, it seems unlikely that 1992 will be worse for Nebraska Republicans than 1990.

Barrett's House bid received no help from the top of the ticket. Embattled Republican Gov. Kay A. Orr's mediocre performance in western Nebraska sealed her defeat at the hands of Democrat Ben Nelson. In addition, Democratic Sen. Jim Exon scored a big win over his GOP challenger, former 2nd District Rep. Hal Daub.

Barrett found his greatest strength — his position as Speaker of Nebraska's Unicameral Legislature — to also be his greatest weakness in a year of anti-incumbent sentiment. While Barrett's position gave him a boost in stature over Unicameral colleague Scofield, it also enabled the Democrat to tie him to some of the more unpopular Orr policies.

Barrett tried hard to avoid such a link. He emphasized his sponsorship of the "New Horizons" program to develop a comprehensive economic development plan for Nebraska. His agenda hewed to the interests of the sprawling, heavily agricultural 3rd: farm subsidy programs, water supply, rural health care, transportation and education.

Barrett also recounted his partisan activities in hopes of evoking voters' Republican tendencies. Barrett, a small-town real estate and insurance executive, was a member of the state Republican committee for eight years and served as state GOP chairman from 1973 to 1975. He had served his south-central Nebraska legislative district since 1979.

However, Barrett lacked the loyalty of many Republican voters entering the general election. He won the GOP primary with barely 30 percent of the vote, edging out rancher Merlyn Carlson and businessman Fred Lockwood. Ominously, Barrett did worst in the Panhandle area where Scofield, a farmer and rancher, was strongest.

Scofield's farm background made it difficult for Barrett to stereotype her as a liberal. Scofield's interest in child care and her support for abortion rights (Barrett opposes abortion in most instances) appealed to Democratic partisans. But her efforts on rural issues — including her project to establish a state airline commission to preserve service to Nebraska's small cities — expanded her appeal.

Scofield also attacked Barrett's support for several controversial tax initiatives by Orr. She focused on a 1987 tax revision that unintentionally resulted in a tax increase. Barrett responded that Scofield was absent when the measure was voted on, but Scofield said her opposition to the bill was firmly established.

Scofield's aggressive campaign made her a contender, but it was not enough to put her over the top. Barrett carried 41 of the district's 62 counties, generally dominating the eastern two-thirds (although he carried populous Hall County with barely 50 percent). His margins there enabled him to overcome the strength of his opponent in the west — where she won her home base, Dawes County, with 62 percent of the vote.

Nebraska 3

Central and West — Grand Island

Covering three-quarters of the state's land area, this rural district runs from the Corn Belt at its eastern end to the wheat and ranching highlands west of the 100th meridian. One can drive for hours along some of its straight, flat roads without passing any community larger than a village. Many of the 62 counties have one market town and little else but pasture.

The 3rd is the most Republican district in the state — it gave more than 70 percent of its vote to Ronald Reagan in 1980 and 1984, and 67 percent to George Bush in 1988. Popular Democrats like Sen. Jim Exon can sometimes carry the region, but the huge GOP registration advantage is more than enough to keep most Republican candidates comfortable. In 1990, even Exon was able to carry just 34 of the district's counties.

The only city with more than 30,000 people is Grand Island, a retail center for the surrounding farmlands. Grand Island's major industries are farm implements and meatpacking. There is a small group of Southeast Asians in the city, most of whom work at the Montfort meatpacking facility.

North of Grand Island are the only counties in the district with a Democratic registration lead (Sherman, Greeley and Howard) and another, Nance, that has a slimmer Democratic registration edge. Their residents still tend to vote almost as Democratic as their Polish and Irish ancestors did generations ago.

The smaller population centers of Kearney, North Platte and Scottsbluff are strung along the Platte River west of Grand Island. West of Kearney along the Platte is Lexington, a small town of 6,600. Once a victim of the mid-1980s farm crisis, the town has been revitalized by a new $75 million meatpacking plant.

North Platte, located in the valley where the North and South Platte rivers meet, was the home of Buffalo Bill Cody; it tries to coax Omaha-to-Denver travelers into staying awhile by putting on Buffalo Bill shows and rodeos. The Union Pacific runs through North Platte and is its biggest employer. Corn and livestock are raised in the valley, with wheat fields to the west and huge cattle ranches to the north.

The Oregon and Mormon trails run through Scottsbluff, which has the only sizable Hispanic population in western Nebraska, a legacy of the migrant labor used to harvest sugar beets over a period of several decades. Great northern beans are a major crop in the farm areas surrounding Scottsbluff. With recent layoffs at the Lockwood Corp., the major employer in town is now the Regional West Medical Center, a health-management organization employing around 850 people. In 1990, unsuccessful Democratic House candidate Sandra Scofield won seven western Nebraska counties, including Scotts Bluff County.

The 3rd lost over 30,000 residents in the decade, mainly from the rural, western reaches. Most came from cattle lands just beyond the Platte River, or the western Panhandle, the state's major wheat-growing area. The 3rd was hard hit by debt crisis and drought.

Population: 523,827. White 513,467 (98%), Black 683 (0.1%), Other 3,379 (1%). Spanish origin 12,483 (2%). 18 and over 373,670 (71%), 65 and over 80,557 (15%). Median age: 31.

Committees

Agriculture (15th of 18 Republicans)
Conservation, Credit & Rural Development; Department Operations, Research & Foreign Agriculture; Wheat, Soybeans & Feed Grains

Education & Labor (11th of 14 Republicans)
Human Resources; Labor-Management Relations; Postsecondary Education

House Administration (9th of 9 Republicans)
Libraries & Memorials (ranking); Accounts

Select Children, Youth & Families (14th of 14 Republicans)

Joint Library

Campaign Finance

1990	Receipts	Receipts from PACs		Expend-itures
Barrett (R)	$644,559	$193,583	(30%)	$624,575
Scofield (D)	$457,931	$239,816	(52%)	$457,655

Key Vote

1991

Authorize use of force against Iraq — Y

Elections

1990 General		
Bill Barrett (R)	98,607	(51%)
Sandra K. Scofield (D)	94,234	(49%)
1990 Primary		
Bill Barrett (R)	25,199	(30%)
Merlyn Carlson (R)	23,097	(27%)
Fred Lockwood (R)	20,390	(24%)
Rod Johnson (R)	12,961	(15%)

District Vote For President

	1988		1984		1980		1976	
D	69,030	(32%)	47,598	(22%)	48,052	(21%)	76,346	(36%)
R	144,087	(67%)	171,000	(78%)	166,759	(72%)	129,270	(61%)
I					12,024	(5%)		

Nevada

U.S. CONGRESS

SENATE 2 D

HOUSE 1 D, 1 R

LEGISLATURE

Senate 11 D, 10 R

House 22 D, 20 R

ELECTIONS

1988 Presidential Vote

Bush	59%
Dukakis	38%

1984 Presidential Vote

Reagan	66%
Mondale	32%

1980 Presidential Vote

Reagan	63%
Carter	27%
Anderson	7%

Turnout rate in 1986	36%
Turnout rate in 1988	45%
Turnout rate in 1990	37%

(as percentage of voting age population)

POPULATION AND GROWTH

1980 population	800,493
1990 population (39th in the nation)	1,201,833
Percent change 1980-1990	+50%

DEMOGRAPHIC BREAKDOWN

White	84%
Black	7%
Asian or Pacific Islander	3%
(Hispanic origin)	10%
Urban	85%
Rural	15%
Born in state	22%
Foreign-born	7%

MAJOR CITIES

Las Vegas	258,295
Reno	133,850
Henderson	64,952
Sparks	53,367
North Las Vegas	47,707

AREA AND LAND USE

Area 109,894 sq. miles (7th)

Farm	14%
Forest	13%
Federally owned	85%

Gov. Bob Miller (D)
Of Carson City — Elected 1990

Born: March 30, 1945, Evanston, Ill.
Education: U. of Santa Clara, B.A. 1967; Loyola Law School, Los Angeles, J.D. 1971.
Military Service: Air Force Reserve, 1967-73.
Occupation: Lawyer.
Religion: Roman Catholic.
Political Career: Clark County district attorney, 1979-86; lieutenant governor, 1987-89; assumed governorship, 1989.
Next Election: 1994.

WORK

Occupations

White-collar	50%
Blue-collar	23%
Service workers	26%

Government Workers

Federal	10,338
State	18,042
Local	41,950

MONEY

Median family income	$ 21,311	(11th)
Tax burden per capita	$ 1,005	(14th)

EDUCATION

Spending per pupil through grade 12	$ 3,623	(35th)
Persons with college degrees	14%	(33rd)

CRIME

Violent crime rate	625 per 100,000	(14th)

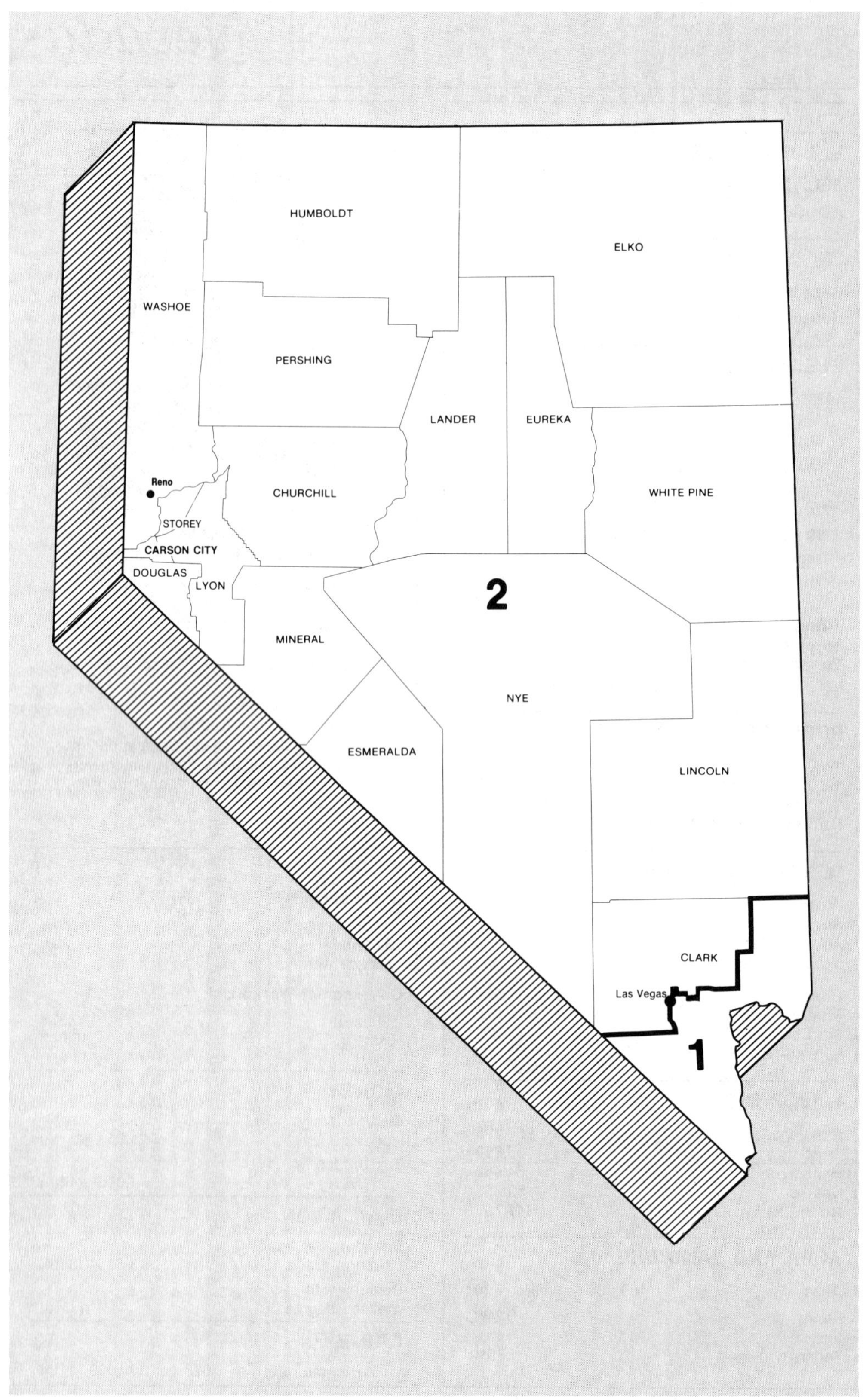
HUMBOLDT
ELKO
WASHOE
PERSHING
LANDER
EUREKA
Reno
CHURCHILL
WHITE PINE
STOREY
CARSON CITY
DOUGLAS
LYON
2
MINERAL
NYE
ESMERALDA
LINCOLN
CLARK
Las Vegas
1

Harry Reid (D)

Of Searchlight — Elected 1986

Born: Dec. 2, 1939, Searchlight, Nev.

Education: Southern Utah State College, A.S. 1959; Utah State U., B.A. 1961; George Washington U., J.D. 1964.

Occupation: Lawyer.

Family: Wife, Landra Gould; five children.

Religion: Mormon.

Political Career: Nev. Assembly, 1969-71; lieutenant governor, 1971-75; U.S. House, 1983-87; Democratic nominee for U.S. Senate, 1974; candidate for mayor of Las Vegas, 1975.

Capitol Office: 324 Hart Bldg. 20510; 224-3542.

In Washington: A man of patience and caution, Reid prefers compromise to confrontation. While he excels at the first, he, by force of circumstances, has become entangled in the latter.

Late in 1987, Sen. J. Bennett Johnston of Louisiana began trumpeting Nevada as the site of a national nuclear-waste dump. That move, incorporated into what came to be known as the "Screw Nevada" bill, has cast a spreading shadow over the state's politics.

Reid had been resisting the siting of the dump at Yucca Mountain, Nev., since 1985. At that point, others in the state's establishment were saying the dump might mean jobs. "I'm not going to go chasing jobs for jobs' sake," said Reid. The dump was not a dominant issue in Reid's election in 1986, but Johnston's moves in the Energy and Appropriations committees soon brought it to the fore.

Johnston was able to amass a coalition among members in the House and Senate who were glad to see Nevada picked and their own states off the hook. His plan was embodied in the fiscal 1988 energy and water appropriations bill, against which Reid staged a two-week filibuster on the Senate floor. Aided by Sen. Brock Adams of Washington, Reid managed to get a majority of Senate Democrats to vote for requiring the Department of Energy to consider public health and safety first in its site selection. But even so favorably worded a test vote got him only 37 votes overall. He needed 41 to stop a cloture petition to close off debate.

Johnston also won in the House-Senate conference on that year's reconciliation bill, persuading House conferees to accept the Nevada site as a virtual *fait accompli.* Since then, Reid has been reduced to a rear-guard action as the site-selection process grinds on. One lingering hope is that scientists will find something wrong with Yucca Mountain and look elsewhere. To help that possibility along, Nevada asked for $23 million in federal funds for state double-checking of DOE's site studies. The state received less than half that amount.

In the fall of 1988, the dump issue contributed to Democratic Gov. Richard H. Bryan's victory over GOP Sen. Chic Hecht. Neither Bryan nor Reid has been able to get on the Energy and Natural Resources Committee (of which Johnston is chairman). But Reid has continued to pepper the Department of Energy with his disapproval from a distance. In 1988 he gave the agency a "Globe Rotter award" after radiation leaks were discovered at its nuclear-weapons production plants.

The intensity of the dump issue is an aberration in Reid's congressional career. More typical were his efforts in diplomatically forging an agreement among feuding water users, environmentalists and Indian tribes in Nevada and California. In 1990, Reid helped steer through the Senate a bill that allocates water from the Carson and Truckee rivers and should help protect Nevada from droughts.

Reid's style is derived partly from his political personality and partly from political imperative. He does not want to earn a reputation as a liberal and so rile the significant conservative element of his constituency. But he also wants to cooperate reasonably often with the Democratic leadership in the Senate, as he had done in the House. That helps him retain good standing and perpetuate the attention paid to a swing voter.

Reid has also developed into a sensitive listening post. After voting for the Medicare expansion for catastrophic illnesses in 1988, Reid was the first to denounce its financing mechanism on the Senate floor after negative reactions began to be heard.

Taking the floor to compare the Persian Gulf crisis to the Italian fascist invasion of Ethiopia in 1935, Reid also was one of the first Democrats in the Senate to voice support for President Bush's request for authority to use force against Iraq.

His accommodating approach was demonstrated in the 101st Congress, when he joined Republican Mitch McConnell of Kentucky in proposing a bipartisan campaign-finance reform plan that would cut the cost of political advertising. "This is comparable to the Washington Redskins and the Dallas Cowboys sitting down and having dinner together on the night before the game," said Reid. Despite this effort, a House-Senate conference on campaign-finance legislation deadlocked.

Representing a state with a high percentage of senior citizens, Reid — who has been called the "Claude Pepper of Nevada," a reference to the late Florida congressman who championed causes for the elderly — wants to reimburse the so-called "notch babies," who say their Social Security benefits were cut because they were born between 1917 and 1921.

Reid has taken on a range of other issues in the "human-needs" category — help for battered women; a children's bill of rights that would aid prosecution of sexual abuse; and limiting the use of certain chemicals used on test animals to measure toxicity. Reid began pushing for additional funds to research women's diseases when three women who suffered from interstitial cystitis showed up at his office asking for help.

During the 101st Congress, Reid and Bryan overcame years of debate and opposition from the state's lone GOP member of Congress, Barbara F. Vucanovich, to carve out more than 700,000 acres of protected Nevada wilderness. The law gave the state its first wilderness area in 25 years.

In the House, Reid staked out a conservative position on a few highly publicized issues, then voted with the majority of Democrats much of the rest of the time. Reflecting the cultural values of his state and his own Mormonism, he shared Ronald Reagan's opposition to the Equal Rights Amendment (ERA) and legalized abortion. He has also supported the MX missile program. But on a wide range of other issues — the nuclear-weapons freeze, aid to the Nicaraguan contras, anti-satellite missile testing and funding for several social programs — Reid sided with the more liberal Democratic leadership.

At Home: Reid's race with Republican Jim Santini in 1986 was one of the year's most closely watched contests — not only because it seemed so evenly matched, but also because Santini's fortunes reflected on retiring Sen. Paul Laxalt and Republican National Committee Chairman Frank J. Fahrenkopf Jr., a former head of the Nevada GOP. Both were involved in recruiting Santini, a former four-term Democratic House member, to the Republican Party in 1985, and in clearing the way for him to run for the Senate.

But Santini's campaign had headaches from the start. Supporters of GOP Rep. Vucanovich only slowly warmed to Santini, since his entry derailed her Senate ambitions. And many Nevada Democrats were outraged by his candidacy. A number of them were still smoldering over Santini's primary challenge to veteran Democratic Sen. Howard W. Cannon in 1982, which they believe weakened Cannon so much that he lost his seat that fall to Hecht.

Santini sought to depict the 1986 race as "the classic conservative vs. liberal test," but he was stymied a bit by his own Democratic past. Reid responded to Santini's efforts to tag him as a big-spending "Tip O'Neill" liberal by noting that when Santini sought re-election in 1978, Fahrenkopf lambasted him as a big spender and O'Neill came into the state for a Santini fundraiser.

The heated byplay between the candidates obscured the fact that they held similar positions on many issues. Reid clearly had been more sympathetic to organized labor, but both he and Santini were opposed to abortion, the ERA and gun control. Both supported the death penalty and said they were generally supportive of Reagan's foreign policy.

Reagan helped raise money for Santini, and Laxalt campaigned extensively for him. But Reid minimized their impact by tapping the state's distrust of Washington with an "us vs. them" campaign intimating that Washington power brokers were forcing Santini onto Nevada voters.

When all the votes were counted, Reid had carried only two of the state's 16 counties. But one of them was Clark County (Las Vegas), Reid's political base and home for a majority of Nevada voters. Reid amassed a 32,000-vote lead in the county, enough to offset Santini's 18,000-vote advantage in the rest of the state.

Reid's self-made career has been part sky-rocket and part slow, hard climb. He was born into modest circumstances in remote Searchlight. He worked his way through school, including a stint as a policeman in the U.S. Capitol while attending law school in Washington. Within five years he was a successful lawyer in booming Las Vegas, well on his way toward becoming a millionaire and a freshly elected member of the state Legislature — all before he was 30.

In 1970, he ran successfully for lieutenant governor on a ticket with his former high school boxing coach, Mike O'Callaghan, who was elected governor. After one term in the No. 2 job, at the age of 34, Reid came within 625 votes of election to the U.S. Senate. It was 1974, and the Watergate scandal almost lifted Reid past the state's Republican former governor, Laxalt. But Reid's youth and even more boyish appearance did not wear well over the course of the campaign; the firm, articulate and mature Laxalt seemed to fit the part of a senator better. Seeking a quick rebound a year later, Reid lost a bid to be mayor of Las Vegas. Some thought he was through in politics.

Then, in 1977, O'Callaghan appointed him chairman of the Nevada Gaming Commission. While Reid held that job, an FBI investigation uncovered evidence of organized-crime influence in the Nevada gaming industry, and one reputed mobster accused Reid of being on the take.

Reid was cleared of charges that he intervened on behalf of organized-crime figures in cases before the Gaming Commission. When he finally left the commission in 1981, Reid was praised for weathering the earlier difficulties and staying on to help eliminate criminal elements from the gaming industry. Politically, he was alive again.

Redistricting in 1981 created a House seat for Las Vegas separate from the rest of Nevada; it would have been held by Santini, but he decided to run for the Senate in 1982 against Cannon. Reid announced his House campaign early, seeking support from friends and from business leaders he dealt with as Gaming Commission chairman. Reid was able to raise and spend more than $250,000 against inconsequential primary foes.

In November Reid faced an attractive, articulate Republican, former state Rep. Peggy Cavnar. She had run an impressive race in 1980 for the state Senate, losing narrowly in a district where Democrats normally had a clear advantage.

But her House bid was strapped for funds because she had embarrassed the Las Vegas GOP establishment by defeating its handpicked candidate in the primary. And she was unable to cast the contest in liberal-conservative terms, partly because Reid was careful not to criticize Reagan and partly because he concurred with her stands against the ERA and abortion. Reid's superior financial resources and organization resulted in a 58 percent win.

In a 1984 rematch, both Reid and Cavnar were in a stronger position to compete. Reid had the advantages of incumbency, while Cavnar had gained the backing of the GOP establishment. The new advantages offset each other, and Reid won convincingly, with just a slightly lower percentage than he took in 1982.

Committees

Appropriations (13th of 16 Democrats)
Legislative Branch (chairman); Energy & Water Development; Interior; Labor, Health & Human Services, Education; Military Construction

Environment & Public Works (6th of 9 Democrats)
Toxic Substances, Environmental Oversight, Research & Development (chairman); Nuclear Regulation; Water Resources, Transportation & Infrastructure

Select Indian Affairs (6th of 9 Democrats)

Special Aging (8th of 11 Democrats)

Elections

1986 General		
Harry Reid (D)	130,955	(50%)
Jim Santini (R)	116,606	(45%)
1986 Primary		
Harry Reid (D)	74,275	(83%)
Manny Beals (D)	7,039	(8%)

Previous Winning Percentages: **1984** * (56%) **1982** * (58%)

* *House elections.*

Campaign Finance

	Receipts	Receipts from PACs		Expend-itures
1986				
Reid (D)	$2,089,246	$817,377	(39%)	$2,055,756
Santini (R)	$2,696,285	$768,378	(28%)	$2,688,462

Key Votes

1991	
Authorize use of force against Iraq	Y
1990	
Oppose prohibition of certain semiautomatic weapons	Y
Support constitutional amendment on flag desecration	Y
Oppose requiring parental notice for minors' abortions	N
Halt production of B-2 stealth bomber at 13 planes	Y
Approve budget that cut spending and raised revenues	Y
Pass civil rights bill over Bush veto	Y
1989	
Oppose reduction of SDI funding	N
Oppose barring federal funds for "obscene" art	Y
Allow vote on capital gains tax cut	N

Voting Studies

	Presidential Support		Party Unity		Conservative Coalition	
Year	**S**	**O**	**S**	**O**	**S**	**O**
1990	44	55	79	20	32	68
1989	63	37	71	28	61	39
1988	56	40	76	20	54	46
1987	40	58	88	11	44	56
House Service						
1986	26	74	84	16	48	52
1985	44	55	87	13	40	60
1984	42	58	84	16	42	58
1983	29	67	86	13	35	65

Interest Group Ratings

Year	**ADA**	**ACU**	**AFL-CIO**	**CCUS**
1990	61	30	67	17
1989	65	21	100	38
1988	55	28	92	29
1987	80	19	90	22
House Service				
1986	60	32	93	44
1985	55	29	82	32
1984	75	17	100	38
1983	70	35	82	25

Richard H. Bryan (D)

Of Carson City — Elected 1988

Born: July 16, 1937, Washington, D.C.

Education: U. of Nevada, B.A. 1959; U. of California, Hastings College of Law, LL.B. 1963.

Military Service: Army, 1959-60.

Occupation: Lawyer.

Family: Wife, Bonnie Fairchild; three children.

Religion: Episcopalian.

Political Career: Nev. Assembly, 1969-73; Nev. Senate, 1973-79; Nev. attorney general, 1979-83; governor, 1983-89; Democratic nominee for Nev. attorney general, 1974.

Capitol Office: 364 Russell Bldg. 20510; 224-6244.

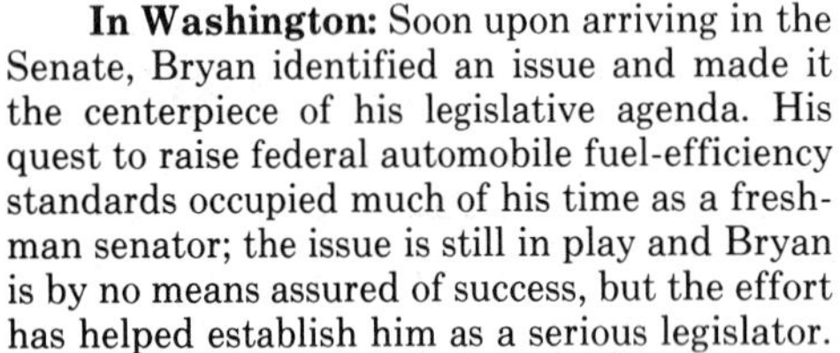

In Washington: Soon upon arriving in the Senate, Bryan identified an issue and made it the centerpiece of his legislative agenda. His quest to raise federal automobile fuel-efficiency standards occupied much of his time as a freshman senator; the issue is still in play and Bryan is by no means assured of success, but the effort has helped establish him as a serious legislator.

Heavy lobbying by the auto industry and the Bush administration stalled Bryan's attempt at the end of the 101st Congress. The Senate fell three votes short of the 60 votes needed to limit debate on a bill that would have required automakers to increase 1988 Corporate Average Fuel Economy (CAFE) levels by 20 percent by 1995 and by 40 percent by 2001. The existing standard is 27.5 miles per gallon.

The legislation got a boost after the August 1990 Iraqi invasion of Kuwait set off renewed debate over U.S. energy policy. Bryan said his bill would save 2.8 million barrels of oil per day and lead automakers to produce fleets with an average rating of 40 mpg.

But White House opposition offset any momentum Bryan gained from the Persian Gulf crisis. The administration argued that the bill was not economically sound or technically feasible. The auto industry said that Bryan's legislation would require further vehicle downsizing, raising the specter of small, unsafe cars. Bryan and other proponents of the bill disagreed, saying the technology exists or could be developed to allow cars to meet tougher requirements without downsizing.

Unlike the original fuel-economy law, which imposed a flat fleet-average standard, Bryan's bill would require percentage increases in CAFE, using the 1988 fuel-economy averages of each manufacturer's fleet as a baseline. "It requires everyone to put their shoulder to the wheel to do better," Bryan said.

Thus, Japanese companies that make smaller, more fuel-efficient cars would have to increase their fuel economy by the same percentage as U.S. companies, which concentrate more on catering to larger-car buyers.

Bryan redoubled his efforts at the start of the 102nd Congress, when prospects for moving new CAFE legislation improved amid efforts by Congress and the White House to come up with a new national energy policy. The Commerce Committee approved Bryan's CAFE bill, slightly amended from the 1990 version, in March 1991 and sent it to the full Senate for consideration once again.

Bryan arrived in the Senate with a mandate from Nevada's voters to defend his state aggressively against federal efforts to put a nuclear-waste dump there. The dump site was a salient issue for Bryan in unseating one-term GOP Sen. Chic Hecht in 1988. Hecht's failure to block the siting decision, or even to oppose it in its formative stage, lent weight to criticism that he was out of his league in the Senate.

However, Bryan was not able to tackle the issue promptly in Washington. He did not get the seat on the Energy and Natural Resources Committee he sought; it is chaired by Louisiana's J. Bennett Johnston, an engineer of the efforts to put the nuclear waste dump in Nevada. And the other two committees where Bryan might have a swing at the siting decision — Appropriations and Environment — already had a Democratic member from Nevada in Harry Reid.

Instead, Bryan landed seats on the Commerce and Banking committees, somewhat unusual assignments for a Western senator, but ones that suit the businesslike Bryan well.

On Commerce, Bryan has the chairmanship of the Consumer Subcommittee, where in the 101st Congress he oversaw the reauthorization of the Consumer Product Safety Commission, the first stand-alone reauthorization of the watchdog agency since 1981.

The bill, a long-sought victory for consumer activists, was aimed at jump-starting the commission, which for a decade had seen its budget and staff cut and its role as a consumer watchdog diminished by Reagan administration appointees. After some effort, Bryan succeeded in keeping the reauthorization measure free of product-specific provisions that had stopped earlier bills.

Bryan also sponsored legislation before the Commerce panel to strengthen the authority of the Federal Trade Commission in dealing with fraud committed in connection with telephone sales. Bryan said the legislation was needed to combat the "bad actors who are out to defraud and harass the consumer," adding that he supported legislation "carefully crafted to avoid unduly burdening the many legitimate telemarketers." The bill passed the Senate but died at the end of the 101st Congress.

Bryan so far has compiled a generally moderate record in the Senate. His annual ratings from the liberal Americans for Democratic Action have been in the mid-50s and on a number of high-profile issues — abortion, civil rights, the nomination of former Sen. John Tower as secretary of Defense — he has voted in step with most Democrats. But he is also a fiscal conservative and has gone his own way on some defense and foreign policy issues.

Bryan has backed a cut in the capital gains tax, opposed banning certain semiautomatic weapons as well as halting production of the B-2 stealth bomber, and he supported a constitutional amendment to ban flag burning. He was also one of the 10 Democratic senators to support the January 1991 resolution authorizing the president to use force in the Persian Gulf.

A lawyer and former state attorney general, Bryan was chosen to serve on the 12-member ad hoc committee that took testimony in the impeachment trial of U.S. District Judge Alcee L. Hastings in 1989. And in the aftermath of the Keating Five scandal — five senators accused of unduly assisting a wealthy contributor to their campaigns — Senate leaders in April 1991 named Bryan to a new six-member task force to decide where to draw the line of propriety in such situations.

Bryan was also a freshman member of the Democratic Senate Policy Committee and took an interest in strategy sessions for the party's campaign committee in 1990. After the 1990 elections, however, Majority Leader George J. Mitchell of Maine selected the more nationally known Charles S. Robb of Virginia over Bryan to head the Democratic Senatorial Campaign Committee for the 1992 election cycle.

At Home: Bryan ran for the Senate in the middle of his second term as governor. First elected to that job in 1982, he was re-elected in 1986 with 72 percent of the vote. Even then, it was widely assumed he would challenge Hecht in 1988.

Bryan won his reputation as a fiscal conservative when he cut hundreds of state government jobs in a budget-balancing drive in his first term. He was helped by growth in the state's revenues from gambling, which made higher burdens on the state's taxpayers largely unnecessary. In his second term, a health-cost-containment bill, successfully steered through the Legislature, was one of his major projects.

Bryan began his political career as a public defender and prosecutor in Clark County (Las Vegas), which includes slightly more than half the state's population. He had also served a decade in the state Assembly and Senate before winning his first statewide office, state attorney general, in 1978.

By the time Bryan sought the Senate, Hecht offered an irresistible target. He had been elected in 1982 in large part because the Democratic incumbent, Howard W. Cannon, was rendered vulnerable by a tough primary and by the trial of Teamsters union officials charged with trying to bribe him. Despite these circumstances, Hecht won with just 50 percent.

In the interim, Hecht had enjoyed some sunny moments, including passage of his amendment restoring the 65 mph speed limit. But he had also been battered by the nuclear-waste controversy. When Hecht finally turned against siting the dump in Nevada, the momentum in Congress for choosing the state was unstoppable. For years before, Hecht had viewed the dump as a patriotic duty and as a potential source of federal money and jobs.

Hecht also had to compensate for an unimposing personal presence and a tendency to utter malapropisms (he once said the state should not become a "a nuclear suppository"). After Bryan announced his candidacy early in 1988, he emphasized these perceptions of Hecht. At one point he referred to the state's senior senator as being "unable to find the men's room."

These tactics played into the hands of Hecht's campaign managers, who used some of their $2 million treasury for a TV blitz that defined the early stage of the campaign. The ads portrayed a humble, hard-working Hecht, devoted to helping the little guy. Bryan, by contrast, came off seeming harsh and a touch arrogant.

But Bryan righted his campaign in the summer, moving belatedly to counter Hecht's efforts on the airwaves and shifting his aim to issues. He kept up the heat on the nuclear waste dump, an issue that had helped Reid move up from the House in 1986.

Bryan's other attacks on Hecht also helped contrast the two on domestic issues: He targeted Hecht's votes to eliminate cost-of-living adjustments to Social Security recipients and against restoration of certain Medicare benefits. Bryan found support from labor groups; he backed the bill Congress passed in 1988 to give workers 60 days' notice of plant closings. Hecht opposed it. Bryan's support for contra aid, however, placed him apart from the mainstream of Democrats nationally.

With all his ammunition, and despite a resurgent lead in the summer polls, Bryan could not knock Hecht flat. The plucky incumbent had to deal with a state GOP rife with internal disputes involving new leaders associated with the presidential campaign of Pat Robertson. He was distracted when the Clark County GOP chairman impugned Bryan's marital fidelity on a radio program. Still, Hecht pressed his case, raking Bryan for leaving the governorship in midterm and for being too close to the power elements of the national Democratic Party.

The race was close to the end. At one point on election night, at least one TV network projected Hecht the winner. Bryan ran nearly 43,000 votes ahead of his party's presidential ticket, but still got just over 50 percent.

Committees

Banking, Housing & Urban Affairs (12th of 12 Democrats)
Consumer & Regulatory Affairs; Housing & Urban Affairs

Commerce, Science & Transportation (10th of 11 Democrats)
Consumer (chairman); Foreign Commerce & Tourism; Science, Technology & Space

Joint Economic

Elections

1988 General		
Richard H. Bryan (D)	175,548	(50%)
Chic Hecht (R)	161,336	(46%)
1988 Primary		
Richard H. Bryan (D)	62,278	(79%)
Patrick M. Fitzpatrick (D)	4,721	(6%)

Campaign Finance

	Receipts	Receipts from PACs		Expend-itures
1988				
Bryan (D)	$2,986,727	$802,792	(27%)	$2,957,789
Hecht (R)	$2,907,927	$977,024	(34%)	$3,007,864

Key Votes

1991	
Authorize use of force against Iraq	Y
1990	
Oppose prohibition of certain semiautomatic weapons	Y
Support constitutional amendment on flag desecration	Y
Oppose requiring parental notice for minors' abortions	Y
Halt production of B-2 stealth bomber at 13 planes	N
Approve budget that cut spending and raised revenues	Y
Pass civil rights bill over Bush veto	Y
1989	
Oppose reduction of SDI funding	Y
Oppose barring federal funds for "obscene" art	N
Allow vote on capital gains tax cut	N

Voting Studies

	Presidential Support		Party Unity		Conservative Coalition	
Year	**S**	**O**	**S**	**O**	**S**	**O**
1990	44	55	81	19	51	49
1989	59	40	75	24	58	39

Interest Group Ratings

Year	ADA	ACU	AFL-CIO	CCUS
1990	56	30	78	25
1989	55	30	100	25

1 James Bilbray (D)

Of Las Vegas — Elected 1986

Born: May 19, 1938, Las Vegas, Nev.

Education: American U., B.A. 1962; Washington College of Law, J.D. 1964.

Military Service: National Guard, 1955-63; Reserve, 1963-present.

Occupation: Lawyer.

Family: Wife, Michaelene Mercer; three children.

Religion: Roman Catholic.

Political Career: Democratic nominee for U.S. House, 1972; Nev. Senate, 1981-87.

Capitol Office: 319 Cannon Bldg. 20515; 225-5965.

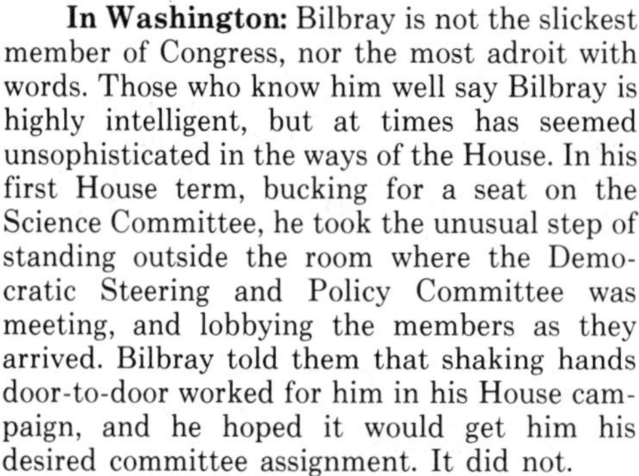

In Washington: Bilbray is not the slickest member of Congress, nor the most adroit with words. Those who know him well say Bilbray is highly intelligent, but at times has seemed unsophisticated in the ways of the House. In his first House term, bucking for a seat on the Science Committee, he took the unusual step of standing outside the room where the Democratic Steering and Policy Committee was meeting, and lobbying the members as they arrived. Bilbray told them that shaking hands door-to-door worked for him in his House campaign, and he hoped it would get him his desired committee assignment. It did not.

Bilbray then tried twice during the 100th Congress to get on the Armed Services Committee and failed. He finally got on during the 101st Congress, but only after two more junior members were chosen.

Although he has not yet established himself as a major player on broad policy questions, Bilbray has proven a fighter on issues pertaining to the Las Vegas-based 1st and to Nevada in general. Bilbray has joined the rest of the Nevada delegation in opposing a high-level nuclear waste dump at Yucca Mountain in southern Nevada. He says he will "use every legal means" to halt the development.

Bilbray has used his position to defend the honor of his hometown's pride and joy, the University of Nevada at Las Vegas basketball team. Although UNLV won the National Collegiate Athletic Association championship in 1990, its program faces NCAA penalties over its recruiting and academic practices. Bilbray has proposed a bill to guarantee due process to schools that face NCAA sanctions.

In 1990, Bilbray supported a bill providing compensation to residents of Nevada, Utah and Arizona exposed to radiation from open-air nuclear weapons testing during the 1950s. Bilbray described these "downwinders" as "no different from the veterans of World War II, Korea and Vietnam — they are veterans of the Cold War."

At Home: When Democrat Harry Reid vacated this House seat to run for the Senate in 1986, Bilbray was a logical replacement. Son of the longtime Clark County assessor, he had close personal ties to the Las Vegas hotel and casino establishments. He had chaired the Taxation Committee in the state Senate. And he was running in a district with a 3-to-2 Democratic advantage. But by Election Day, Bilbray's campaign had run into so many problems his victory over Republican state Sen. Bob Ryan turned out to be a surprise.

For example, at a meeting of the state AFL-CIO in September, Bilbray warned of the dangers of a sympathy vote for Ryan because the Republican was blind. "Voters feel sorry for a man who knocks on their door with a white cane," he said. Bilbray made a personal apology to Ryan the next day.

Meanwhile, Bilbray had to fend off questions about his personal ethics. In the Democratic primary, his principal opponent asked Bilbray why he acted as legal counsel to companies that stood to benefit from legislation he promoted in the state Senate. Bilbray denied any wrongdoing, but his narrow primary victory encouraged Ryan to keep up the line of attack.

But Bilbray survived with some hardball of his own. On election eve, he sent out an anti-Ryan mailer that pictured Sirhan Sirhan and Charles Manson on the cover and suggested that Ryan supported measures that would let killers like Sirhan and Manson out of jail. Ryan protested, but the mailer, coupled with Bilbray's superior grass-roots organization and fundraising, brought him a 10-point victory. In 1988 and 1990, Bilbray surpassed 60 percent.

Bilbray's recent successes have softened the memories of a 1972 House effort. Then, as a youthful and more liberal Democrat, he upset 10-term House veteran Walter S. Baring in the Democratic primary. But Baring and many of his supporters remained cool to Bilbray, and a virtually unknown Republican defeated him in the general election.

Nevada 1

South — Las Vegas

Las Vegas has come a long way from its days as a Mormon mission in the mid-1800s. In the 50 years since legalized gambling and the building of Boulder Dam brought a construction boom to the city, it has developed from a dusty town of fewer than 10,000 people to a neon extravaganza with 258,000 full-time residents. Clark County, including Las Vegas and its suburbs, grew by more than 60 percent in the 1980s. In the 1980s, growth in southern Nevada helped make the state the fastest-growing in the country. Today, this one corner of Nevada contains over 60 percent of the state's population. The 1st District itself takes in most of Las Vegas and the southeastern half of Clark County.

The "Strip" of casinos, nightclubs and hotels that gives Las Vegas its image is actually outside the city limits. But the Strip is the economic focal point of the area. Most of the 1st District's residents are connected in some way to the gaming, entertainment and tourism industries; whenever recessions strike, Las Vegas quickly feels the pinch, because there are fewer visitors with money to burn. The local economy is better-guarded against economic downturns, though, as California businesses fleeing gridlock and high taxes move across the border.

Most voters in the 1st are registered Democrats, but in general elections party affiliation yields more to ideology. In 1988, for instance, Clark County supported George Bush for president and Democratic Gov. Richard H. Bryan in his successful bid for the Senate. Las Vegas' large Mormon community has long been a force for conservatism; government workers employed at nearby Nellis Air Force Base and the Department of Energy's Nevada Test Range also help GOP candidates in Clark County.

But the bulk of the vote comes from the area's largely unionized service workers. This group includes a sizable black population. North Las Vegas, whose portion of the 1st is 42 percent black, and Las Vegas' West Side — its poorest area — have most of the district's 40,000 blacks.

Population: 400,636. White 338,725 (85%), Black 39,797 (10%), Other 10,447 (3%). Spanish origin 30,345 (8%). 18 and over 292,870 (73%), 65 and over 32,739 (8%). Median age: 30.

Committees

Armed Services (26th of 33 Democrats)
Military Installations & Facilities; Procurement & Military Nuclear Systems; Seapower & Strategic & Critical Materials

Select Aging (27th of 42 Democrats)
Housing & Consumer Interests

Small Business (15th of 27 Democrats)
Exports, Tax Policy & Special Problems; Procurement, Tourism & Rural Development

Elections

1990 General		
James Bilbray (D)	84,650	(61%)
Bob Dickinson (R)	47,377	(34%)
William "Bill" Moore (LIBERT)	5,825	(4%)
1990 Primary		
James Bilbray (D)	30,747	(86%)
Joshua Elliott Jr. (D)	4,883	(14%)
1988 General		
James Bilbray (D)	101,764	(64%)
Lucille Lusk (R)	53,588	(34%)

Previous Winning Percentage: **1986** (54%)

District Vote For President

	1988		1984		1980		1976	
D	67,468	(41%)	47,267	(36%)	32,778	(30%)	43,872	(51%)
R	90,671	(56%)	82,023	(63%)	64,073	(59%)	40,483	(47%)
I	4,575 *	(3%)			7,270	(7%)		

* *"None of these candidates"*

Campaign Finance

	Receipts	Receipts from PACs		Expend-itures
1990				
Bilbray (D)	$686,010	$218,056	(32%)	$705,037
Dickinson (R)	$149,863	$9,775	(7%)	$149,778
1988				
Bilbray (D)	$669,014	$300,116	(45%)	$652,199
Lusk (R)	$148,957	$19,645	(13%)	$147,891*

Key Votes

1991	
Authorize use of force against Iraq	Y
1990	
Support constitutional amendment on flag desecration	Y
Pass family and medical leave bill over Bush veto	Y
Reduce SDI funding	Y
Allow abortions in overseas military facilities	N
Approve budget summit plan for spending and taxing	Y
Approve civil rights bill	Y
1989	
Halt production of B-2 stealth bomber at 13 planes	N
Oppose capital gains tax cut	Y
Approve federal abortion funding in rape or incest cases	Y
Approve pay raise and revision of ethics rules	Y
Pass Democratic minimum wage plan over Bush veto	Y

Voting Studies

	Presidential Support		Party Unity		Conservative Coalition	
Year	**S**	**O**	**S**	**O**	**S**	**O**
1990	33	67	83	15	63	37
1989	45	53	83	17	78	22
1988	30	67	79	16	68	29
1987	34	66	79	17	67	30

Interest Group Ratings

Year	ADA	ACU	AFL-CIO	CCUS
1990	50	25	75	29
1989	55	25	75	50
1988	60	44	93	43
1987	68	26	94	33

2 Barbara F. Vucanovich (R)

Of Reno — Elected 1982

Born: June 22, 1921, Camp Dix, N.J.
Education: Attended Manhattanville College, 1938-39.
Occupation: Congressional aide; travel agency owner.
Family: Husband, George F. Vucanovich; five children.
Religion: Roman Catholic.
Political Career: No previous office.
Capitol Office: 206 Cannon Bldg. 20515; 225-6155.

In Washington: With the retirement of Nebraska's Virginia Smith at the end of the 101st Congress, Vucanovich became the most-senior Republican woman west of New Jersey. Smith's retirement also opened up a spot on the Appropriations Committee, which Vucanovich acquired at the start of the 102nd Congress.

The Appropriations seat will enable Vucanovich to pursue the parochial legislative interests of her state. Beyond her work on that panel, Vucanovich is a member of the GOP whip organization and a consistent conservative, even on so-called "women's issues," such as abortion. She vociferously opposed an amendment to the fiscal 1991 defense authorization bill that would have permitted members of the armed services and their dependents to obtain abortions in overseas hospitals if they paid the cost themselves.

Appropriations is normally an exclusive committee assignment, but Vucanovich received a waiver to continue serving on the Interior Committee as well. There, she battles attempts to grant even greater authority over Nevada's land to the federal government, which owns 85 percent of it. It has been a full-time job. The 100th Congress, for example, enacted a law to put all of the nation's high-level nuclear waste in Yucca Mountain, Nev.

Vucanovich was a bit slow to join opponents of the waste site, but once she did, she became one of their most ardent allies. From her post on Interior, she contributed to a bill sponsored by committee Chairman Morris K. Udall that would have established a special commission to study placement of a waste site.

Unfortunately for Vucanovich, the real action occurred in the Senate, where Democrat J. Bennett Johnston strong-armed passage of an amendment to the 1988 budget-reconciliation bill to accelerate the site-selection process. With no Nevadans on the House-Senate conference committee considering the bill, Johnston struck a deal to name Nevada as the dump site. Vucanovich condemned the action, but she was powerless to stop the juggernaut. The bill became law in 1987.

The 1988 defeat of GOP Sen. Chic Hecht left Vucanovich as the only Republican in the state's four-member congressional delegation. With a 3-1 advantage, Democratic Sens. Harry Reid and Richard H. Bryan and Rep. James Bilbray were able to unblock a longstanding stalemate during the 101st Congress and win enactment of legislation to designate wilderness land in Nevada. Vucanovich was among those most strongly opposed to a large designation, and her side had the upper hand for a time. Through the 99th Congress, both Nevada's senators were Republicans.

Vucanovich got embroiled in the wilderness issue in the 99th Congress, when she went head-to-head with Reid, then the state's other House member. Reid's proposal, backed by then-Gov. Bryan, was to establish wilderness areas totaling 592,000 acres, plus the first national park in Nevada, Great Basin National Park, with 174,000 acres. Vucanovich's proposal, supported by the state's two GOP senators, would have set aside only 137,000 acres.

The House passed Reid's proposal after a party-line vote rejecting Vucanovich's amendment to kill creation of the park. With then-Sens. Hecht and Paul Laxalt stifling action in the Senate, the House finally agreed to a compromise late in 1986 to create a more modest 77,000-acre Great Basin National Park.

When the wilderness issue was revisited in the 100th Congress, Interior Democrats offered a bill calling for a 731,000-acre wilderness preserve, and agreed to a few compromises. Among them: Mount Rose was designated a recreation area instead of wilderness, and certain lands on Ruby Mountain were exempted for use as a helicopter ski area. That bill died in the Senate, but it was an issue in Bryan's successful 1988 Senate race against Hecht, and, as expected, it resurfaced in the 101st Congress.

But the bill that passed the Senate and reached the House floor in 1989 dropped some of the exemptions included in the previous bill, among them the designation of Mount Rose as

Nevada 2

North — Reno and the Cow Counties

Although 25 percent of its people live in metropolitan Las Vegas, the 2nd is referred to as the "non-Las Vegas" district. It is dominated by Reno, a Republican stronghold that grew by 33 percent in the 1980s.

Gambling is an important component of the Reno (Washoe County) economy, but Reno, Sparks and Lake Tahoe take pains to differentiate themselves from Las Vegas. Though still reliant on gaming and tourism, the area's economy has diversified as a number of small manufacturers and warehouses have moved to the region.

Republicans have a registration advantage in Washoe County and nearby Douglas County and Carson City. Those three areas have awarded Republican presidential candidates significant margins in the last elections. But while GOP Sen. Chic Hecht won Douglas County in 1988, he lost Washoe on his way to a narrow statewide defeat.

About one-fourth of the district's residents are dispersed through the mostly conservative "Cow Counties," a huge expanse of mountain and desert that occupies most of the state. The Cow Counties were populist and Democratic for most of this century, but their voters are gradually turning Republican in frustration over national Democratic liberalism, especially the party's land and water policies. (Most of the land in the 2nd District is federally owned.) Cattle and sheep raising are the main economic activities here, but gold mining is mounting an impressive comeback. Small, rural towns like Elko have seen their populations double due to a modern-day gold rush that has made Nevada the leading gold-producing state.

Yucca Mountain, 100 miles northwest of Las Vegas, looms ominously over Nye County as the proposed site of a federal nuclear waste dump. Nevadans of both parties bristle at mere mention of the "Screw Nevada" bill, which stipulates that high-level radioactive waste be shipped and stored there.

Population: 399,857. White 361,620 (90%), Black 11,202 (3%), Other 17,025 (4%). Spanish origin 23,534 (6%). 18 and over 291,824 (73%), 65 and over 33,017 (8%). Median age: 30.

a recreation area. Vucanovich offered her own proposal to cut back the total wilderness acreage to 412,000 acres, but the House rejected her amendment on a 126-283 vote.

She also objected to the bill's water allocation language, arguing that it would set a precedent by pre-empting state water-rights jurisdiction. But Bilbray insisted that the language was no threat to states' rights, saying that it was a necessary response to a Reagan administration decision that there would be no water rights for wilderness areas unless Congress expressly legislated them. Vucanovich's amendment to strike the water language was rejected 118-285. The bill passed 323-75. Over her objections, President Bush signed it into law in 1989.

Vucanovich testified before the Energy and Commerce Committee and the Select Committee on Aging in the 101st Congress on mammogram screening. She introduced legislation to provide annual coverage under the Social Security Act of mammography screening for women 65 years or older.

At Home: Vucanovich's first election to the House rewarded her long involvement in Republican politics. She had worked in presidential campaigns since the Eisenhower era and had been president of several GOP women's groups. In 1962 she signed on with Laxalt, and for two decades worked behind the scenes for him as a grass-roots organizer and constituent-service specialist. Laxalt returned the favor in 1982 by actively helping her win the newly created 2nd District. His backing all but guaranteed Vucanovich the GOP nomination against five others.

Much of her campaign time was spent boosting her low name recognition. She benefited from TV ads featuring the popular Laxalt. But her grandmotherly image also helped her establish a rapport with voters. She won a solid 43 percent in the large primary field.

In the general-election campaign, Democrat Mary Gojack urged voters not to elect a Laxalt clone. A former state senator and unsuccessful challenger to Laxalt in 1980, Gojack was a stronger personal campaigner than Vucanovich. But she suffered in much of the district from her reputation as a feminist liberal closer to the politics of the East than to those of Nevada. Vucanovich played up her devout conservatism, Laxalt less, and she won 56 percent.

In 1984, she won handily. Two years later, Vucanovich drew a challenge from Reno Mayor Peter J. Sferrazza, the recent chairman of the Nevada Democratic Party. Sferrazza sought to make an issue of the proposed placement of a nuclear-waste dump in the vast desert reaches of the district, saying he had been against it while Vucanovich was trying to make up her mind. One Sferrazza TV ad featured a campaign volunteer in goggles and an iridescent painter's suit checking a Vucanovich campaign sign with a Geiger counter.

Despite Sferrazza's creativity, he was burdened with a liberal image that hurt his fund-raising. As a result, Sferrazza had to resort to campaign gimmicks — such as a six-day, 340-mile, cross-district bicycle trip along the shoulder of Interstate 80 in the dog days of August. The well-financed Vucanovich crisscrossed the district in her private plane. The results were predictable. Vucanovich took 56 percent in populous Washoe County (Reno), home base for both her and Sferrazza, and won with 58 percent overall.

In 1988, another popular mayor challenged Vucanovich. He was James Spoo, the mayor of Sparks. Spoo raised more than six times the money Sferrazza did, and he projected the kind of moderate-to-conservative image Democrats have found success with in the mountain West. The perfect symbol of this appeal arrived when Sen. Lloyd Bentsen of Texas, the Democratic nominee for vice president, came through the 2nd and campaigned with Spoo.

But presidential-year voting trends helped ensure Vucanovich's victory. George Bush won 61 percent in the 2nd, and Vucanovich was close behind with 57 percent.

In 1990, feisty state Assemblywoman Jane Wisdom moved to the district to challenge Vucanovich. She attracted some press attention by advising the incumbent "to do what she does best: Stay at home and tend to her knitting." She also compared government action to restrict abortions to anti-abortion legislation sponsored by the Nazi government.

For Wisdom, this verbal bomb-throwing was an effort to publicize her fund-free campaign. But her abortion rights, pro-labor message did not suit the conservative 2nd. Vucanovich took 59 percent, her second-highest re-election tally.

Committees

Appropriations (21st of 22 Republicans)
Legislative; Rural Development, Agriculture & Related Agencies

Interior & Insular Affairs (5th of 17 Republicans)
Mining & Natural Resources (ranking); National Parks & Public Lands

Elections

1990 General		
Barbara F. Vucanovich (R)	103,508	(59%)
Jane Wisdom (D)	59,581	(34%)
Dan Becan (LIBERT)	12,120	(7%)
1990 Primary		
Barbara F. Vucanovich (R)	42,166	(84%)
Dick Baker (R)	5,144	(10%)
Brooklyn Harris (R)	2,816	(6%)
1988 General		
Barbara F. Vucanovich (R)	105,981	(57%)
James Spoo (D)	75,163	(41%)

Previous Winning Percentages: **1986** (58%) **1984** (71%) **1982** (56%)

District Vote For President

	1988	1984	1980	1976
D	65,270 (35%)	44,388 (29%)	32,358 (24%)	46,521 (44%)
R	115,369 (61%)	106,747 (70%)	86,565 (65%)	57,957 (55%)
I	6,813 * (4%)		9,784 (7%)	

* *"None of these candidates"*

Campaign Finance

	Receipts	Receipts from PACs		Expend-itures
1990				
Vucanovich (R)	$445,465	$166,275	(37%)	$441,075
Wisdom (D)	$41,771	$22,500	(54%)	$41,287
1988				
Vucanovich (R)	$608,009	$201,719	(33%)	$614,853
Spoo (D)	$434,976	$176,950	(41%)	$430,155

Key Votes

1991	
Authorize use of force against Iraq	Y
1990	
Support constitutional amendment on flag desecration	Y
Pass family and medical leave bill over Bush veto	N
Reduce SDI funding	N
Allow abortions in overseas military facilities	N
Approve budget summit plan for spending and taxing	Y
Approve civil rights bill	N
1989	
Halt production of B-2 stealth bomber at 13 planes	N
Oppose capital gains tax cut	N
Approve federal abortion funding in rape or incest cases	N
Approve pay raise and revision of ethics rules	Y
Pass Democratic minimum wage plan over Bush veto	N

Voting Studies

	Presidential Support		Party Unity		Conservative Coalition	
Year	**S**	**O**	**S**	**O**	**S**	**O**
1990	72	23	84	8	89	2
1989	79	19	91	5	98	2
1988	68	32	92	4	92	3
1987	63	31	89	7	91	9
1986	69	24	84	12	90	10
1985	70	29	87	9	91	7
1984	64	31	83	11	90	5
1983	78	16	87	6	90	7

Interest Group Ratings

Year	ADA	ACU	AFL-CIO	CCUS
1990	6	88	8	79
1989	5	89	8	100
1988	10	92	14	77
1987	20	74	19	86
1986	0	86	7	89
1985	10	86	13	95
1984	10	96	8	75
1983	0	96	0	90

New Hampshire

U.S. CONGRESS

SENATE 2 R

HOUSE 1 D, 1 R

LEGISLATURE

Senate 11 D, 13 R

House 127 D, 268 R, 2 Independents
3 vacancies

ELECTIONS

1988 Presidential Vote	
Bush	63%
Dukakis	36%
1984 Presidential Vote	
Reagan	69%
Mondale	31%
1980 Presidential Vote	
Reagan	58%
Carter	28%
Anderson	13%
Turnout rate in 1986	32%
Turnout rate in 1988	55%
Turnout rate in 1990	34%

(as percentage of voting age population)

POPULATION AND GROWTH

1980 population	920,610
1990 population (40th in the nation)	1,109,252
Percent change 1980-1990	+21%

DEMOGRAPHIC BREAKDOWN

White	98%
Black	1%
Asian or Pacific Islander	1%
(Hispanic origin)	1%
Urban	52%
Rural	48%
Born in state	49%
Foreign-born	5%

MAJOR CITIES

Manchester	99,567
Nashua	79,662
Concord	36,006
Derry	29,603
Rochester	26,630

AREA AND LAND USE

Area	8,993 sq. miles (44th)
Farm	8%
Forest	88%
Federally owned	13%

Gov. Judd Gregg (R)
Of Greenfield — Elected 1988

Born: Feb. 14, 1947, Nashua, N.H.
Education: Columbia U., A.B. 1969; Boston U., J.D. 1972, LL.M. 1975.
Occupation: Lawyer.
Religion: Protestant.
Political Career: N.H. Governor's Executive Council, 1979-81; U.S. House, 1981-89.
Next Election: 1992.

WORK

Occupations	
White-collar	52%
Blue-collar	35%
Service workers	12%
Government Workers	
Federal	8,028
State	20,531
Local	39,864

MONEY

Median family income	$ 19,723	(25th)
Tax burden per capita	$ 435	(50th)

EDUCATION

Spending per pupil through grade 12	$ 4,457	(16th)
Persons with college degrees	18%	(13th)

CRIME

Violent crime rate	169 per 100,000	(44th)

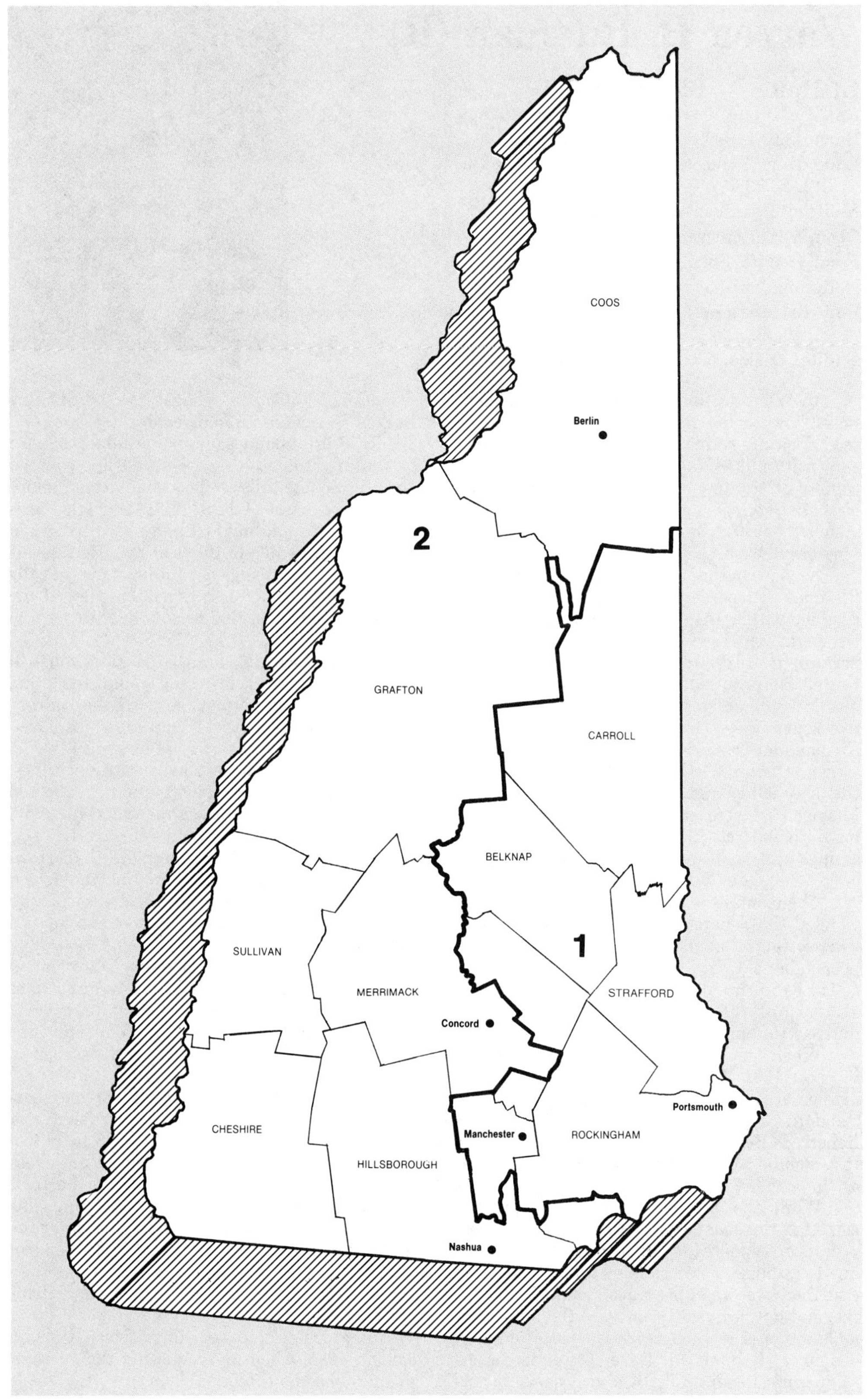
COOS
Berlin
2
GRAFTON
CARROLL
BELKNAP
SULLIVAN
1
MERRIMACK
STRAFFORD
Concord
Portsmouth
CHESHIRE
Manchester
ROCKINGHAM
HILLSBOROUGH
Nashua

Warren B. Rudman (R)

Of Hollis — Elected 1980

Born: May 18, 1930, Boston, Mass.

Education: Syracuse U., B.S. 1952; Boston College, LL.B. 1960.

Military Service: Army, 1952-54.

Occupation: Lawyer.

Family: Wife, Shirley Wahl; three children.

Religion: Jewish.

Political Career: N.H. attorney general (appointed), 1970-76.

Capitol Office: 530 Hart Bldg. 20510; 224-3324.

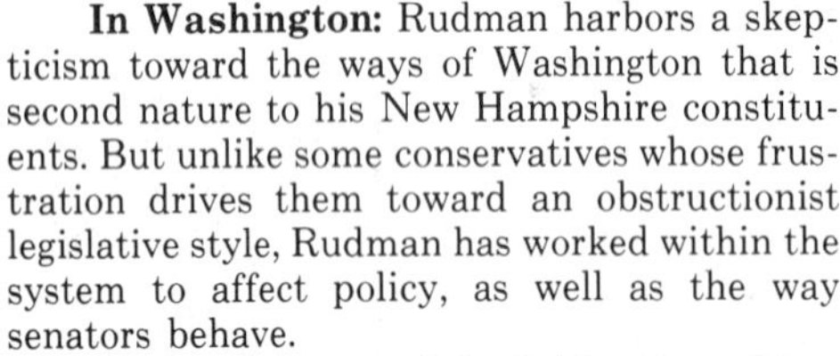

In Washington: Rudman harbors a skepticism toward the ways of Washington that is second nature to his New Hampshire constituents. But unlike some conservatives whose frustration drives them toward an obstructionist legislative style, Rudman has worked within the system to affect policy, as well as the way senators behave.

As vice chairman of the Ethics Committee, Rudman is regarded as an arbiter of proper conduct within the Senate. He and Michigan Democrat Carl Levin drew up an ethics reform package in 1989. In 1990, he and Chairman Howell Heflin of Alabama presided over hearings into the actions of the Keating Five. The five senators — Republican John McCain of Arizona and Democrats Alan Cranston of California, Dennis DeConcini of Arizona, John Glenn of Ohio and Donald W. Riegle Jr. of Michigan — were under scrutiny for intervening with federal thrift regulators in behalf of savings and loan operator Charles H. Keating Jr.

The committee found that Cranston likely violated the Senate standard against improper behavior and that the other four were guilty of poor judgment, and recommended that further action be taken only against Cranston. Editorialists across the country denounced the committee's findings as a whitewash.

When they issued the committee's findings in early 1991, Rudman and Heflin said they neither accepted nor rejected an "appearance standard" applied by committee special counsel Robert S. Bennett to the senators' actions — that members can be punished for appearing to act improperly.

While the Ethics Committee declined to condemn the senators for transgressing an appearance standard, Rudman and North Carolina Republican Jesse Helms appeared to agree that there was an appearance standard, though they did not necessarily embrace Bennett's formulation. Earlier, before the Senate voted to denounce Republican Dave Durenberger of Minnesota, for example, Rudman said his colleague had "failed his obligation of protecting both the appearance and reality of propriety."

Still, Rudman was prepared for a backlash to findings that the senators had not violated specific Senate rules. "The committee cannot act on the basis of laws, rules and standards that some people might like to see," Rudman said at the opening of the hearings. He said his view would not change even if he knew that the public would have a less charitable view of the Senate. "If that's the price, then that's the price."

On the Ethics Committee, the tart-tongued Rudman plays a bracing counterpoint to Heflin, the ambling Southern judge with the country drawl. Both are lawyers, and they displayed their personal brands of legal expertise.

They shared duties chairing the hearings; when Rudman presided, he frequently exhorted Bennett and the senators' lawyers to avoid tangents and make their points succinctly. "I do have my foot on the throttle more than Howell," Rudman said. "I'm a New Englander, and we tend to move briskly because it's cold up there. He's a Southerner. They tend to move a bit more slowly."

Earlier in the 101st Congress, Rudman and Levin produced the first big ethics rules changes since 1977. They chaired party task forces that reviewed a range of rules and laws governing ethics. They produced a package of changes tightening Senate rules governing travel, gifts and financial disclosure, and barring lobbying by senators and staff for a year after they leave the Senate. In 1988, Rudman was instrumental in devising legislation, eventually pocket-vetoed by President Ronald Reagan, to restrict post-employment lobbying. The changes were adopted as part of the pay raise and ethics reform bill approved at the end of 1989.

Yet no matter how much he excels at his craft, Rudman will probably never warm up to Washington. "I don't like this town," Rudman said in 1985, when he seemed on the verge of abandoning the capital. "I don't like the whole atmosphere. There's too much money, too much influence, too much phoniness. And I just don't like it. Period."

But he discovered that he need not like the press, embassy parties or even his colleagues in order to make a difference. Even as he threatened in 1985 to quit the Senate out of disgust with the federal deficit, Congress approved a radical new procedure aimed at balancing the budget, and thus began Rudman's second life in Washington.

The Gramm-Rudman-Hollings anti-deficit amendment that became law in the fall of 1985 was not only a personal watershed for Rudman. It was a national watershed as well, the catchbasin for a tide of anger that grew from the political system's failure to cut the deficit. The law still drives the budget process.

The achievement could not help but contribute to Rudman's considerable estimate of his own influence. He is a man of unusual intelligence and ability; a man of modesty he is not.

Neither is he a man of modest accomplishment. While he is not well liked, he is respected. The blunt and determined former attorney general has a bulldog's tenacity. He was well suited for his service in the 100th Congress as vice chairman of the select committee that investigated the Iran-contra affair. By charting a tough, independent course, he comported himself well in the eyes of most of his colleagues, save those on his right.

While many Republicans used the Iran-contra hearings to promote a conservative agenda for Central America, Rudman seemed more interested in developing facts. He hammered away at witnesses and scoffed at the notion that Lt. Col. Oliver L. North was any kind of hero. Rudman's only bias seemed to be a determination to show that Reagan was ill-served by a "whole bunch of imbeciles" around him. In the end, Rudman signed the majority report, dismissing the minority report as "pathetic." He said the 1989 conviction of North on three of 12 felony counts "reaffirms the conclusions of the committees."

Rudman is nothing if not sure of himself, and colleagues can tire of his lecturing manner, especially on his favorite topic, the law. This became obvious during the early 1989 battle over President Bush's nomination of John Tower to be secretary of Defense. Rudman became a staunch supporter of Tower, arguing there was "not one iota, one shred" of evidence to support claims that Tower was impaired by alcohol while a senator or arms control negotiator.

When Majority Leader George J. Mitchell of Maine characterized Rudman's conclusion as "opinion, pure opinion," Rudman countered: "One thing I learned in 24 years of practicing law is how to read evidence, and I know how to state it, and I know how not to misstate it."

Replied Mitchell, himself a former federal judge: "I think I know how to do that just as well as you do."

Rudman had better luck ushering through the 1990 nomination of his friend and protégé, David H. Souter, to be a Supreme Court justice.

There is little doubt that Rudman is a capable legislator. It took him only a short time to win a reputation in the Senate for hard and thoughtful work, particularly on the Appropriations Committee. If he has irritated some with his healthy sense of his own importance, he has gained the trust of the GOP leadership, as evidenced not only by the Iran-contra assignment but also by the Ethics Committee chairmanship, which he took in the 99th Congress.

At the end of the 100th Congress, he was also assigned to play an important leadership role in shaping anti-drug legislation. He and Hollings cosponsored an amendment in 1989 that would have made a 0.225 percent cut in all discretionary domestic spending and defense programs and directed the $1.8 billion saved entirely toward Bush's anti-drug plan and his anti-crime package. Their proposal rivaled — and eventually lost out to — a more expensive one proposed by Appropriations Chairman Robert C. Byrd of West Virginia and backed by Senate Democrats boosting funds for anti-drug education and treatment.

When Republicans held the Senate, Rudman served for several years as de facto chairman of Appropriations' Commerce-Justice-State Subcommittee. The actual chairman, Nevada's Paul Laxalt, was content to let Rudman handle most of the day-to-day work and manage the annual appropriations bill.

Defense of the Legal Services Corporation (LSC), which was targeted for extinction by the Reagan administration, has been one of Rudman's most visible causes on the spending panel. Rudman helped work out a compromise proposal in 1984 that pleased both friends and critics of legal aid; it extended restrictions on lobbying and political activities, while also providing recipients of legal services protection against the loss of assistance.

Rudman vigorously complained that the Reagan-appointed LSC board was defying Congress by approving regulations that conflicted with congressional desires. He amended the 1989 judiciary appropriations bill to bar the LSC board from adopting any new regulations until a new board took over. He said the members were trying to "disassemble" the corporation before Bush could appoint a new board. Between November 1989 and January 1990, Bush replaced all 11 members. Rudman praised his selections.

His work for the LSC is not the only example of Rudman's refusal to fall in line behind every conservative cause. He votes against school prayer and for abortion funding, and he has called for new taxes, especially on alcohol and tobacco, if they would pay for programs he favors, such as drug interdiction.

Rudman has been an outspoken supporter of tough federal enforcement of trade and anti-trust laws. He is also a force on the Appropriations Subcommittee on Defense. In his maiden speech in the Senate, he expressed concern over the "fascination" of Pentagon strategists with complicated, expensive, high-technology weaponry. One of his targets was the Viper, a disposable bazooka that had grown far more expensive and complicated than originally planned. After a determined assault by Rudman, the Pentagon eventually canceled its Viper contract.

At Home: Democrats would have been hard pressed to oust Rudman from the Senate in 1986 even if they had been well organized and well financed. As it turned out, they were neither. Neither of the state's best-known Democrats — former Sen. John A. Durkin nor former Rep. Norman E. D'Amours — expressed much interest in a long-shot challenge to Rudman. Only when the Democratic nomination threatened to go by default to a supporter of Lyndon H. LaRouche Jr. were party leaders able to coax Endicott Peabody, a former governor of Massachusetts (1963-65), into the race.

Peabody had moved to Hollis, N.H., several years earlier to practice law. But while he possessed a familiar name, he had not cut a wide swath in Granite State politics. In 1984, Peabody lost a race for a seat in the 400-member New Hampshire House of Representatives, and he was vulnerable to charges of being a carpetbagger.

For Peabody to have even an outside chance of winning, a conservative independent candidate — retired Navy officer Bruce Valley — needed to carve deeply into Rudman's base. That did not happen. Valley mustered only 5 percent of the vote, while Rudman swamped Peabody by a margin of nearly 2-to-1.

Rudman had come to Washington in 1980 without experience in elective politics, but with a reputation for activism that he built during six years as New Hampshire attorney general.

He overhauled the little-noticed office in the early 1970s by creating a consumer protection division, and he successfully fought the legalization of gambling in New Hampshire. That gave him the statewide recognition he used in his contest for the Senate in 1980.

Rudman's background dovetailed with one of his major campaign themes — the need for clean government. He pledged not to accept any contributions from out-of-state political action committees and recommended a two-term limit for senators.

As a former legal counsel to Gov. Walter Peterson (1969-73), Rudman was clearly viewed as a part of the New Hampshire GOP's moderate wing. But he was not anathema to conservatives. Rudman campaigned on a platform of increased defense spending and opposition to the Equal Rights Amendment.

Although the 1980 Senate race marked his debut as a candidate — the state attorney general's post was appointive — Rudman proved to be an aggressive campaigner, interspersing political argument with stories of his days as a platoon commander in Korea.

Rudman led the 11-man GOP primary with only 20 percent of the vote, but moved quickly to unite the party by installing the primary runner-up, former state Rep. (later governor, and now White House chief of staff) John H. Sununu, as his campaign manager. Former Gov. Wesley Powell, who ran third in the primary, briefly considered running in the fall election as an independent — a move that would have seriously crippled Rudman against Durkin, the Democratic incumbent. But Republican leaders, including Ronald Reagan, persuaded Powell to stay out.

Durkin tried to consolidate his position with New Hampshire's conservative electorate by attacking Soviet expansionism, but Rudman peppered Durkin's generally liberal, pro-labor voting record. Rudman criticized Durkin for representing "big labor" and not New Hampshire.

Reagan's long coattails helped sweep Rudman to victory. Although Durkin ran 70,000 votes ahead of President Jimmy Carter, he fell short of Rudman by 16,000 votes.

It was sweet revenge for Rudman. Bad blood had developed between the two politicians in 1974, when Rudman was a member of the state panel that overturned the certification of Durkin's Senate election in a virtually even contest with Republican Louis C. Wyman. (That forced a 1975 special election that Durkin won.)

Durkin returned the favor shortly afterward. When Rudman was nominated by President Gerald R. Ford to chair the Interstate Commerce Commission, Durkin worked behind the scenes to block the nomination. Rudman subsequently withdrew his name.

Committees

Select Ethics (Vice Chairman)

Appropriations (7th of 13 Republicans)
Commerce, Justice, State & Judiciary (ranking); Defense; Foreign Operations; Interior; Labor, Health & Human Services, Education

Governmental Affairs (4th of 6 Republicans)
Government Information & Regulation (ranking); Oversight of Government Management; Permanent Subcommittee on Investigations

Select Intelligence (5th of 7 Republicans)

Elections

1986 General		
Warren B. Rudman (R)	154,090	(63%)
Endicott Peabody (D)	79,225	(32%)
Bruce Valley (I)	11,423	(5%)

Previous Winning Percentage: **1980** (52%)

Campaign Finance

	Receipts	Receipts from PACs		Expend-itures
1986				
Rudman (R)	$852,877	$5,200	(1%)	$831,098
Peabody (D)	$309,968	$46,950	(15%)	$307,760
Valley (I)	$37,410	$955	(3%)	$35,322

Key Votes

1991	
Authorize use of force against Iraq	Y
1990	
Oppose prohibition of certain semiautomatic weapons	Y
Support constitutional amendment on flag desecration	N
Oppose requiring parental notice for minors' abortions	Y
Halt production of B-2 stealth bomber at 13 planes	N
Approve budget that cut spending and raised revenues	Y
Pass civil rights bill over Bush veto	N
1989	
Oppose reduction of SDI funding	Y
Oppose barring federal funds for "obscene" art	Y
Allow vote on capital gains tax cut	Y

Voting Studies

	Presidential Support		Party Unity		Conservative Coalition	
Year	**S**	**O**	**S**	**O**	**S**	**O**
1990	74	20	73	23	81	14
1989	80	19	62	38	68	32
1988	65	28	58	36	68	32
1987	71	26	79	12	88	6
1986	90	8	89	10	91	8
1985	84	14	80	17	78	20
1984	81	17	79	19	74	26
1983	85	15	82	17	80	20
1982	73	27	79	20	69	31
1981	83	14	82	16	70	25

Interest Group Ratings

Year	ADA	ACU	AFL-CIO	CCUS
1990	17	77	11	75
1989	25	70	10	75
1988	15	68	29	93
1987	25	80	30	75
1986	10	83	0	84
1985	10	68	14	86
1984	30	82	0	84
1983	25	40	18	58
1982	35	47	35	52
1981	15	53	21	94

Robert C. Smith (R)

Of Tuftonboro — Elected 1990

Born: March 30, 1941, Trenton, N.J.
Education: Trenton Junior College, A.A. 1963; Lafayette College, B.A. 1965.
Military Service: Navy, 1965-67.
Occupation: Real estate broker; high school teacher.
Family: Wife, Mary Jo Hutchinson; three children.
Religion: Roman Catholic.
Political Career: Gov. Wentworth Regional School Board (Wolfeboro, N.H.), 1978-84; U.S. House, 1985-91; sought GOP nomination for U.S. House, 1980; GOP nominee for U.S. House, 1982.
Capitol Office: 332 Hart Bldg. 20510; 224-2841.

In Washington: With his House career clearly going nowhere, Smith in 1990 sought the Senate seat being vacated by retiring Republican Sen. Gordon J. Humphrey. He won, and now brings his obstreperous conservatism — which caused him trouble in the collegial House — to the Senate, a more individualistic body that is used to seeing members with iconoclastic views.

In the Senate, Smith was able to get a seat on the Armed Services Committee, where he can team up with other conservative ideologues on defense and foreign policy issues. A Vietnam veteran, Smith has frequently called for stepped-up efforts to locate the U.S. servicemen who remain missing in Southeast Asia. He is one of those lawmakers who believes that Americans are still being held as prisoners of war in Vietnam.

Smith's voting record was one of the most conservative in the House and will probably remain so in the Senate. His annual rating from the American Conservative Union has been at least 90 percent every year he has served in Congress. And though Smith appeared to temper his anti-abortion rhetoric during his Senate campaign, he continued to vote a solid anti-abortion line on legislation during the entire 101st Congress.

Priding himself on his fiscal conservatism, Smith rails against federal spending at every turn. He took to the floor in March 1991 to lambaste what he saw as wasteful spending in a supplemental appropriations bill that had just passed the Senate. He proudly points to his consistently high ratings from groups such as the National Taxpayers Union; he was among the first members of Congress to urge President Bush in mid-1990 to reject any budget deal that included any tax increase; and he is a strong proponent of a constitutional amendment requiring a balanced budget.

In the House, Smith was a vocal opponent of congressional pay raises. When the House voted in February 1989 to block a proposed 51 percent salary hike for members of Congress, Smith was a big winner, and a big loser.

He was a winner because he helped lead the fight against a procedure that would have allowed the raise to be enacted without a House vote.

"Would I like to have a $45,000 raise? ... You're damned right I would," Smith said. "But that's not the way to get it. If we can't convince the American people we should have a raise, then we shouldn't have it."

Smith was a loser, though, because many House colleagues resented the way in which he helped provoke a public backlash against the raise. Smith is a large man physically, and rhetoric can be a blunt instrument in his hands. While others could oppose the pay raise and retain their reputations in the House as moderate insiders, Smith was derided by many of his colleagues as a hard-right iconoclast at best, and a demagogue at worst.

Smith's manner of expressing his conservatism caused him trouble in the House even before the pay-raise vote was cast. When Republicans made committee assignments for the 101st Congress, Smith's request for a seat on House Armed Services was rejected, leaving him with low-profile slots on Science and Veterans' Affairs. Smith attributed this rebuke to his activism on the pay issue, and said the "cold shoulder of the leadership of my own party hurt me the most." He gained a seat on Armed Services in November 1989 when a slot opened up in mid-term.

In light of the Keating Five incident — five senators accused of improperly intervening with federal regulators on behalf of a wealthy contributor to their campaigns — Senate leaders in April 1991 formed a six-member task force to figure out where to draw the line of propriety in such situations. Smith was named to the panel.

He had written a chapter on ethics for a 1987 book by conservative Republicans titled "House of Ill Repute." In it, Smith said, "I happen to believe that being ethical is like being pregnant — you either are or you are not!"

Smith parts company with his conservative stalwarts and joins with environmentalists on acid rain, an issue that cuts across party and ideological lines in New Hampshire, whose lakes and streams show signs of damage from the pollution problem. In the 101st Congress, Smith was elected co-chairman of the House Republican Task Force on Acid Rain, and when he joined the Senate in the 102nd Congress, he got a seat on the Environment and Public Works Committee.

Smith has also taken up an issue that has started to gain some national attention. In 1990, he teamed with California Democrat Tom Lantos to form the Congressional Friends of Animals Caucus to push legislation promoting animal rights. The caucus serves as a counterpart to Minnesota Republican Vin Weber's Animal Welfare Caucus, which is allied with biomedical researchers on the issue.

At Home: A small-town real estate agent and one-time junior high school teacher, New Hampshire's new senator has cultivated the image of a real-life "Mr. Smith Goes to Washington." But he also exhibited a good bit of political savvy in 1990 to navigate his job switch from one side of Capitol Hill to the other.

In three terms of representing New Hampshire's 1st District, Smith had forged a reputation as an ardent Congress-basher and hard-right conservative immersed in few issues beyond accounting for Vietnam MIAs.

But when Sen. Humphrey announced in early 1989 that he would not seek re-election, Smith moved quickly to assume the mantle of heir apparent. He announced his candidacy for the open seat, wrapped up the support of key Republican leaders (including John H. Sununu, White House Chief of Staff and former New Hampshire Governor) and began to project a more moderate stance on several key issues.

In the 101st Congress, as co-chairman of the GOP's acid rain task force, Smith showed an interest in environmental issues that had not previously been widely noted. And he tempered his anti-abortion position to say that he could accept legislation that allowed abortion in cases of rape or incest.

In the GOP primary, Smith's well-heeled campaign rolled up nearly two-thirds of the vote against Tom Christo, a wealthy lawyer specializing in computer law who was backed by the National Abortion Rights Action League. Smith ran just as well in the general election, crushing the comeback bid of former Democratic Sen. John A. Durkin (1975-80).

Smith was favored to win the seat, but the ease of his victory was a surprise. On paper, Durkin looked like the best candidate the Democrats could nominate. He was a proven vote-getter with a feisty, tart-tongued manner that seemed capable of skewering the affable Smith. Durkin tried to, mocking Smith as "Bumbling Bob" and the "abominable no-man." And he portrayed Smith as a conservative ideologue who would be intellectually over his head in the Senate.

But Smith was able to keep Durkin on the defensive for much of the fall, in large part by attacking aspects of his Senate record in the late 1970s. Smith accused Durkin of being a tax-and-spend liberal who supported the federal bailout of New York City but opposed the Kemp-Roth tax cut.

And he charged that Durkin was a flip-flopper to boot. During his Senate years, Durkin was strongly anti-abortion and readily accepted political action committee (PAC) money. In 1990, Durkin backed abortion rights and refused PAC donations. Heavily outspent, Durkin was in no position to compete effectively against Smith in the final days of the campaign. In Republican New Hampshire, the result was a rout.

Smith's early campaigns were far more modest, short on money, long on Rotary Club luncheons. But they gave him a chance to demonstrate his persistence.

On his first House try in 1980, Smith lost the GOP primary. On his second try, in 1982, he won the primary but lost the general election to Democratic Rep. Norman E. D'Amours (1975-85). On his third try in, 1984, when D'Amours ran for the Senate, Smith finally won the seat. In beating the highest-ranking Democrat in state government, Executive Councilor Dudley Dudley, he returned the eastern New Hampshire House seat to the GOP for the first time in a decade.

Unlike D'Amours, whose roots were in ethnic Manchester, Smith reflected small-town Yankee New Hampshire. It was there that he wrote his brief political résumé as a member and chairman of the Wolfeboro School Board. In private life, he was a civics and gym teacher at the local junior high school.

Rather than embellish his modest credentials when he ran for the House, Smith presented himself as a citizen-politician who understood New Hampshire's common-sense values. Each campaign played up the affable, down-home manner of the big, burly baseball coach and emphasized his fervent conservatism.

Smith began the 1984 campaign with a lingering debt from his earlier efforts. But with wide name identification and outspoken support from the state's largest newspaper, the conservative Manchester *Union Leader*, he easily outdistanced a crowded GOP primary field. He entered the fall campaign with momentum, running on a strong ticket headed by Reagan in an open district with GOP moorings.

Dudley, by contrast, struggled through an unexpectedly close primary race, burdened by a reputation as a liberal Democrat that Smith reinforced with references to her as "Dudley Dudley, Liberal Liberal." Smith won by a margin of about 3-to-2, sweeping not only rural portions of the 1st but also blue-collar cities such as Manchester and Rochester.

In 1986, Smith had to put down a Republican primary challenge from Executive Councilor Louis J. Georgopoulos, a Manchester haberdasher whose political post and gregarious nature gave him high name identity. He called Smith, who grew up in New Jersey and boasted close ties to national conservative groups, an "outsider," and he criticized Smith's preoccupation with tracing the whereabouts of missing Vietnam-era servicemen, contrasting it with his own work to keep nuclear waste out of the state. But Smith had perfected his "man of the people" style of campaigning and again enjoyed strong support from the *Union Leader*. Smith won by a margin of more than 3-to-1.

In the fall, he faced an aggressive challenger in former state Rep. James M. Demers, who won the Democratic primary easily after falling 1,100 votes short of nomination two years earlier. Demers offered himself as a centrist Democrat, not saddled with the liberal reputation that hurt Dudley in 1984.

Demers had legislative experience as assistant minority whip in the Democratic state House leadership; he had a French name that sounded similar to that of the district's previous Democratic incumbent; and he had been campaigning virtually non-stop since 1984.

Demers carried Democratic coastal cities such as Portsmouth, Rochester and his hometown of Dover, but won little else. In spite of his French name, he lost heavily ethnic Manchester by about 2,000 votes.

In 1988, Democratic nominee Joseph F. Keefe, a Manchester attorney, began and ended his campaign with less of a following than Demers had. Smith reached 60 percent of the vote for the first time.

Committees

Armed Services (9th of 9 Republicans)
Defense Industry & Technology; Manpower & Personnel; Strategic Forces & Nuclear Deterrence

Environment & Public Works (7th of 7 Republicans)
Superfund, Ocean & Water Protection; Water Resources, Transportation & Infrastructure

Joint Economic

Elections

1990 General		
Robert C. Smith (R)	189,630	(65%)
John A. Durkin (D)	91,262	(31%)
John Elsnau (LIBERT)	9,717	(3%)
1990 Primary		
Robert C. Smith (R)	56,215	(65%)
Tom Christo (R)	25,286	(29%)
Theo De Winter (R)	2,768	(3%)
Ewing E.J. Smith (R)	2,009	(2%)

Previous Winning Percentages: **1988 *** (60%) **1986 *** (56%) **1984 *** (59%)

** House elections.*

Campaign Finance

	Receipts	Receipts from PACs	Expend-itures
1990			
Smith (R)	$1,509,288	$663,400 (44%)	$1,420,172
Durkin (D)	$334,025	0	$319,879

Key Votes

1991	
Authorize use of force against Iraq	Y
House Service	
1990	
Support constitutional amendment on flag desecration	Y
Pass family and medical leave bill over Bush veto	N
Reduce SDI funding	N
Allow abortions in overseas military facilities	N
Approve budget summit plan for spending and taxing	N
Approve civil rights bill	N
1989	
Halt production of B-2 stealth bomber at 13 planes	N
Oppose capital gains tax cut	N
Approve federal abortion funding in rape or incest cases	N
Approve pay raise and revision of ethics rules	N
Pass Democratic minimum wage plan over Bush veto	N

Voting Studies

	Presidential Support		Party Unity		Conservative Coalition	
Year	**S**	**O**	**S**	**O**	**S**	**O**
House Service						
1990	73	27	91	8	87	13
1989	62	37	91	9	88	12
1988	73	26	97	2	95	5
1987	80	20	95	5	81	19
1986	82	18	96	4	94	6
1985	84	16	91	8	82	18

Interest Group Ratings

Year	ADA	ACU	AFL-CIO	CCUS
House Service				
1990	6	91	17	71
1989	10	96	8	100
1988	5	100	14	93
1987	4	96	13	100
1986	0	91	14	100
1985	5	90	18	95

1 Bill Zeliff (R)

Of Jackson — Elected 1990

Born: June 12, 1936, East Orange, N.J.
Education: U. of Connecticut, B.S. 1959.
Military Service: Army National Guard, 1959-64.
Occupation: Hotel owner.
Family: Wife, Sydna Taylor; three children.
Religion: Protestant.
Political Career: Sought Republican nomination for N.H. Senate, 1984.
Capitol Office: 512 Cannon Bldg. 20515; 225-5456.

The Path to Washington: Weekend vacationers have their choice of dozens of places to stay in New Hampshire's White Mountains. But at only one are they likely to be welcomed by a member of Congress. Zeliff, owner of the Christmas Farm Inn in Jackson, won the open 1st in his first House contest and only his second bid for public office.

An ally of White House Chief of Staff and former New Hampshire Gov. John H. Sununu, Zeliff emerged victorious despite a bitter primary campaign and a determined effort by a seasoned Democratic opponent in the fall. He succeeded Rep. Robert C. Smith, elected to the Senate in 1990.

Among Zeliff's strengths was his image as a successful businessman. In 1976, Zeliff gave up his job as a corporate executive, purchased the Christmas Farm Inn and moved his family north from Pennsylvania. With his wife, Zeliff converted the aging inn into a year-round resort with rooms that include whirlpool baths and other upscale comforts.

Zeliff refers to his business success often, linking it to the Yankee traditions of entrepreneurialism and frugality. His campaign slogan was "The Spirit of New Hampshire." He carried a jar of pennies, stating, "Watch the pennies and the dollars will take care of themselves."

The rapport Zeliff honed as an innkeeper helped him overcome hard feelings resulting from the GOP primary. Zeliff spent nearly $400,000; his main foes — former Reagan administration official Larry Brady and longtime state Rep. Douglas Scamman Jr. — accused him of trying to buy the election.

Zeliff also angered other contenders with his TV ads, such as one describing Brady, an executive with a Washington, D.C., public relations company with overseas clients, as a "foreign agent." After Zeliff edged Brady by 314 votes, the runner-up refused to endorse him.

But the Manchester *Union Leader*, the staunchly conservative newspaper that dominates the district's media, lined up behind Zeliff. Its editorials lauded Zeliff's fiscal conservatism, particularly his adherence to the "no new taxes" principle that is political gospel in New Hampshire.

The paper also assailed Democratic nominee Joseph F. Keefe — who challenged Smith in 1988 — as an arch-liberal.

A lawyer and a forceful campaigner, Keefe ran on an economic platform that had an overall moderate tone; he favored a presidential line-item veto and investment tax credits. However, he took a risk on the tax issue, stating that Zeliff's aversion to tax increases was unrealistic given the size of the federal deficit.

With the district in the throes of a deepening regional recession, Keefe used a populist pitch, calling for shifting more of the tax burden to the wealthy.

Yet not even hard times could stay the 1st's antitax mainstream. Zeliff skewered Keefe for saying he would have reluctantly voted for the federal budget legislation in October 1990, which included a variety of tax increases Zeliff said hit the middle class.

Zeliff's opposition to the budget deal put him at odds with Sununu, his political mentor. During his tenure as governor (1983-89), Sununu encouraged Zeliff to run for office and appointed him to Vice President George Bush's campaign steering committee for the 1988 New Hampshire presidential primary. Sununu's endorsement of Zeliff in the House primary was a key to his narrow victory.

However, Zeliff paid no penalty for breaking with Bush. He appeared with the president during his October 1990 visit to New Hampshire; Bush also taped a TV ad for Zeliff.

Zeliff's image as a party regular helped him secure the support of GOP loyalists, while his antitax stance appealed to angry conservatives. Despite polls indicating the contest was a tossup, Zeliff won by 10 percentage points.

New Hampshire 1

East — Manchester

New Hampshire's eastern district, extending from the state's 13 miles of coastline to the granite peaks of the White Mountains, is an area of rich geographical and political variation.

The district's southern tier is dominated by ethnic industrial cities, while the rugged northern territory is home to small Yankee Republican towns. While Democrat Norman E. D'Amours represented the district for a decade until 1985, Republican Robert C. Smith won three comfortable House elections in the 1st before moving up to the Senate in 1990.

The state's largest concentration of voters is in Manchester. Textile mills, attracted there in the 19th century by the hydropower of the Merrimack River, drew large numbers of immigrants, especially French Canadians. But the Depression paralyzed the region's economy. Some of the city's long-abandoned redbrick mills are finding new life as light manufacturing or retail space, but others still stand empty.

The huge Franco-American vote in Manchester is nominally Democratic, but often is influenced by the *Union Leader's* blistering editorials urging voters to abandon Democratic candidates accused of liberalism or worse. In 1990, Bill Zeliff, a Republican from the northern part of the district, narrowly carried the city over Democrat and Manchester lawyer Joseph Keefe.

Just south of Manchester is Londonderry, which during the 1980s was the fastest-growing town in the fastest-growing state in the Northeast. The town's population grew by 46 percent, to just under 20,000.

New Hampshire's major coastal town is Portsmouth, home to wealthy sea captains two centuries ago. It has been in decline most of this century, but its architectural grace and proximity to Boston recently have made it a fashionable day-trip tourist center. Although the Portsmouth Naval Shipyard is centered across the river estuary in Kittery, Maine, many shipyard workers live in New Hampshire, where they generally cast Democratic votes. The area took an economic hit in early 1991, when Pease Air Force Base in nearby Newington closed as recommended by a national commission, throwing several hundred civilian employees out of work.

A bit south of Portsmouth is the site of the Seabrook nuclear power plant, a facility that has been the subject of intense debate — especially with neighboring Massachusetts — since its construction began in 1976.

Moving north into Strafford County, the University of New Hampshire, with 11,500 students, dominates the town of Durham and leads the area in supporting liberal candidates. Further north, ski resorts dot the landscape of upper Carroll County, around Jackson and North Conway. North Conway has also attracted a strip of factory outlet shops, which some residents point to as evidence of overdevelopment. Among the most Republican counties in the nation, Carroll County has provided overwhelming margins for the GOP in every statewide race since World War II.

Population: 460,863. White 455,399 (99%), Black 2,169 (1%), Other 2,168 (1%). Spanish origin 3,028 (1%). 18 and over 332,498 (72%), 65 and over 51,279 (11%). Median age: 30.

Committees

Government Operations (13th of 15 Republicans)
Commerce, Consumer & Monetary Affairs; Human Resources & Intergovernmental Relations

Public Works & Transportation (20th of 21 Republicans)
Surface Transportation; Water Resources

District Vote For President

	1988	1984	1980	1976
D	80,604 (35%)	58,709 (30%)	53,617 (27%)	71,632 (43%)
R	145,996 (64%)	137,615 (70%)	115,356 (60%)	93,141 (56%)
I			23,122 (12%)	

Campaign Finance

	Receipts	Receipts from PACs		Expend-itures
1990				
Zeliff (R)	$807,514	$130,601	(16%)	$802,680
Keefe (D)	$378,930	$175,279	(46%)	$377,993

Key Vote

1991

Authorize use of force against Iraq	Y

Elections

1990 General		
Bill Zeliff (R)	81,684	(55%)
Joseph F. Keefe (D)	66,176	(45%)
1990 Primary		
Bill Zeliff (R)	13,266	(27%)
Larry Brady (R)	12,952	(27%)
Douglas Scamman Jr. (R)	12,678	(26%)
Dean Dexter (R)	3,637	(7%)
Bill Johnson (R)	3,069	(6%)
Chris Tremblay (R)	1,633	(3%)
Dennis C. Hogan (R)	697	(1%)
Michael R. Weddle (R)	582	(1%)

2 Dick Swett (D)

Of Bow — Elected 1990

Born: May 1, 1957, Bryn Mawr, Pa.
Education: Yale U., B.A. 1979.
Occupation: Architect.
Family: Wife, Katrina Lantos; five children.
Religion: Mormon.
Political Career: No previous office.
Capitol Office: 128 Cannon Bldg. 20515; 225-5206.

The Path to Washington: New Hampshire's long-suffering Democrats, who had been locked out of federal office since 1985, thought the 1990 open seat race in the 1st District might break the jinx. But when the returns were in, it was 2nd District nominee and political newcomer Dick Swett who had delivered a congressional seat to the party.

Swett's victory surprised local and national observers alike. The 2nd has been in GOP hands since 1915 and at first glance Swett seemed a marginal challenger. Though Swett was raised in New Hampshire, he lived in California for many years before returning in 1987. He has never held political office and has a limited background in community service.

But Swett was able to tap atypical political expertise and connections through his wife, Katrina Lantos-Swett, the daughter of California Democratic Rep. Tom Lantos. That backing helped him to exploit Republican incumbent Chuck Douglas' weaknesses, including overconfidence about his first re-election campaign.

The contest centered more on the candidates' personal qualities than on their issue papers. Douglas' conservative views were palatable to many voters in the 2nd, but his demeanor was not. Douglas' combative style had led to run-ins with advocates for the mentally ill and with the Presbyterian Synod of the Northeast, among others.

Douglas' three divorces also created unease in some voters' minds. After making some initial comments about Douglas' marital track record, Swett stopped calling attention to it directly. But he did make prominent use of his own family — which includes five children — and his campaign slogan was "Integrity for a Change."

In the closing campaign push, Swett sent out mailings featuring quoted remarks by Nancy Sununu — wife of former New Hampshire governor and White House Chief of Staff John H. Sununu — questioning Douglas' morals and values.

Douglas countered with his own attacks, casting Swett as the puppet of his liberal father-in-law and of out-of-state political action committees. But Douglas, as a freshman House member with a sharp tongue, had not stockpiled the credibility he needed to make his charges stick.

Further, Swett is not easily slipped into a liberal slot. During the campaign, he supported a balanced budget constitutional amendment and a presidential line-item veto and favored restricting abortions after the first trimester. Nor did it hurt Swett that he is a former high school football hero and college track star with all-American good looks and the model family life of a dedicated Mormon.

Swett's election probably would surprise friends and associates who have not been in touch with him lately. By his own admission, Swett for many years was more disgusted by politicians than inspired to join their ranks. He credits his politically-minded wife and his "maturing" with convincing him that public office could be a constructive avenue for service.

Still, when Swett moved back to New Hampshire in 1987, it was to develop alternative energy projects with his father, not to run for Congress. Only after he had settled in Bow and watched Douglas in action did he decide the incumbent could and should be beaten. When no other Democrat stepped forward, Swett tried it himself.

Swett was unknown to many party regulars, and he ruffled some feathers with his charges that the Democratic Party had strayed from the needs and values of its working-class base. He began the campaign without clear stands on some issues and without poise on the stump.

His victory was testimony to how much his message and delivery improved over the course of the campaign. However, Swett admitted after winning that much of his support came from anti-Douglas sentiment and that he must go on to prove himself a better alternative.

New Hampshire 2

West — Concord; Nashua

New Hampshire's scenic western district is lightly populated outside the fast-growing southern tier that borders Massachusetts.

Nashua, the largest city in the 2nd, has grown to more than 76,000 people. Spurred by the arrival of high-technology firms, Nashua feeds into the belt of electronics-oriented industry that straddles the Bay State border. Area residents tend to be well-educated, upwardly mobile refugees from "Taxachusetts." Nearby Salem has shared in the southern tier's boom.

Despite its growth, Nashua has been slow to break its longtime Democratic voting habit. George Bush did carry Nashua handily in 1988, but in the open House race that year, the city sided with its Democratic mayor, Jim Donchess. In 1990, Democratic House challenger Dick Swett carried Nashua over GOP Rep. Chuck Douglas. Salem favors Republicans most of the time.

State government workers dominate the capital city, Concord, but New Hampshire does not have a large or politically influential bureaucracy, and Concord has not grown very rapidly in the past 20 years. The city's electorate is generally liberal, but independent. It opposed Meldrim Thomson Jr., the state's belligerently conservative three-term governor of the 1970s, but the city supported Ronald Reagan and narrowly went for George Bush in 1988.

Keene, in Cheshire County, has been a wellspring of Democratic votes. The liberal politics of the town newspaper combined with votes from the Keene State College community helped Swett and unsuccessful Democratic gubernatorial candidate Joe Grandmaison carry the town in 1990.

Outside the Concord-Nashua corridor, the district is mostly rural Republican territory. Autumn in Sullivan County, where the upper Connecticut River Valley forms the border with Vermont, means an influx of tourists, attracted to the brilliant foliage and covered bridges. Coos County is New Hampshire's "North Country," an isolated woodland. The only town of any size in the North Country is Berlin, a lonely Democratic outpost in a solidly Republican area. Berlin's paper mills on the Androscoggin River attracted many Canadian immigrants; the area remains so heavily ethnic that some radio stations broadcast in French.

In 1976, Jimmy Carter carried only four communities in Coos County, but his sweep of Berlin provided him his winning county margin. No Democratic presidential candidate — not even Massachusetts Gov. Michael S. Dukakis in 1988 — has carried a county in New Hampshire since then.

Population: 459,747. White 454,700 (99%), Black 1,821 (0.4%), Other 2,113 (1%). Spanish origin 2,559 (1%). 18 and over 330,030 (72%), 65 and over 51,688 (11%). Median age: 30.

Committees

Public Works & Transportation (29th of 36 Democrats)
Aviation; Economic Development; Surface Transportation

Science, Space & Technology (29th of 32 Democrats)
Environment; Technology & Competitiveness

Select Aging (39th of 42 Democrats)
Human Services; Rural Elderly

Campaign Finance

	Receipts	Receipts from PACs		Expend-itures
1990				
Swett (D)	$470,252	$186,000	(40%)	$465,160
Douglas (R)	$575,748	$223,050	(39%)	$540,605

Key Vote

1991

Authorize use of force against Iraq	Y

Elections

1990 General

Dick Swett (D)	74,829	(53%)
Chuck Douglas (R)	67,063	(47%)

District Vote For President

	1988	1984	1980	1976
D	83,092 (37%)	61,638 (32%)	70,171 (31%)	76,003 (44%)
R	135,541 (61%)	129,435 (67%)	124,612 (55%)	92,794 (54%)
I			31,629 (14%)	

New Jersey

U.S. CONGRESS

SENATE 2 D
HOUSE 8 D, 6 R

LEGISLATURE

Senate 23 D, 17 R
House 43 D, 37 R

ELECTIONS

1988 Presidential Vote

Bush	56%
Dukakis	43%

1984 Presidential Vote

Reagan	60%
Mondale	39%

1980 Presidential Vote

Reagan	52%
Carter	39%
Anderson	8%

Turnout rate in 1986	27%
Turnout rate in 1988	52%
Turnout rate in 1990	31%

(as percentage of voting age population)

POPULATION AND GROWTH

1980 population	7,364,823
1990 population (9th in the nation)	7,730,188
Percent change 1980-1990	+5%

DEMOGRAPHIC BREAKDOWN

White	79%
Black	13%
Asian or Pacific Islander	4%
(Hispanic origin)	10%
Urban	89%
Rural	11%
Born in state	57%
Foreign-born	10%

MAJOR CITIES

Newark	275,221
Jersey City	228,537
Paterson	140,891
Elizabeth	110,002
Trenton	88,675

AREA AND LAND USE

Area 7,468 sq. miles (46th)

Farm	19%
Forest	43%
Federally owned	3%

Gov. James J. Florio (D)
Of Gloucester Township — Elected 1989

Born: Aug. 29, 1937, Brooklyn , N.Y.
Education: Trenton State College, B.A. 1962; Columbia U., 1962-63; Rutgers U., J.D. 1967.
Military Service: Navy, 1955-58; Naval Reserve, 1958-74.
Occupation: Lawyer.
Religion: Roman Catholic.
Political Career: N.J. Assembly, 1970-74; U.S. House, 1975-90; Democratic nominee for U.S. House, 1972; sought Democratic gubernatorial nomination, 1977; Democratic nominee for governor, 1981.
Next Election: 1993.

WORK

Occupations

White-collar	59%
Blue-collar	29%
Service workers	12%

Government Workers

Federal	76,975
State	123,758
Local	327,043

MONEY

Median family income	$ 22,906	(4th)
Tax burden per capita	$ 1,021	(12th)

EDUCATION

Spending per pupil through grade 12	$ 6,564	(3rd)
Persons with college degrees	18%	(12th)

CRIME

Violent crime rate 609 per 100,000 (15th)

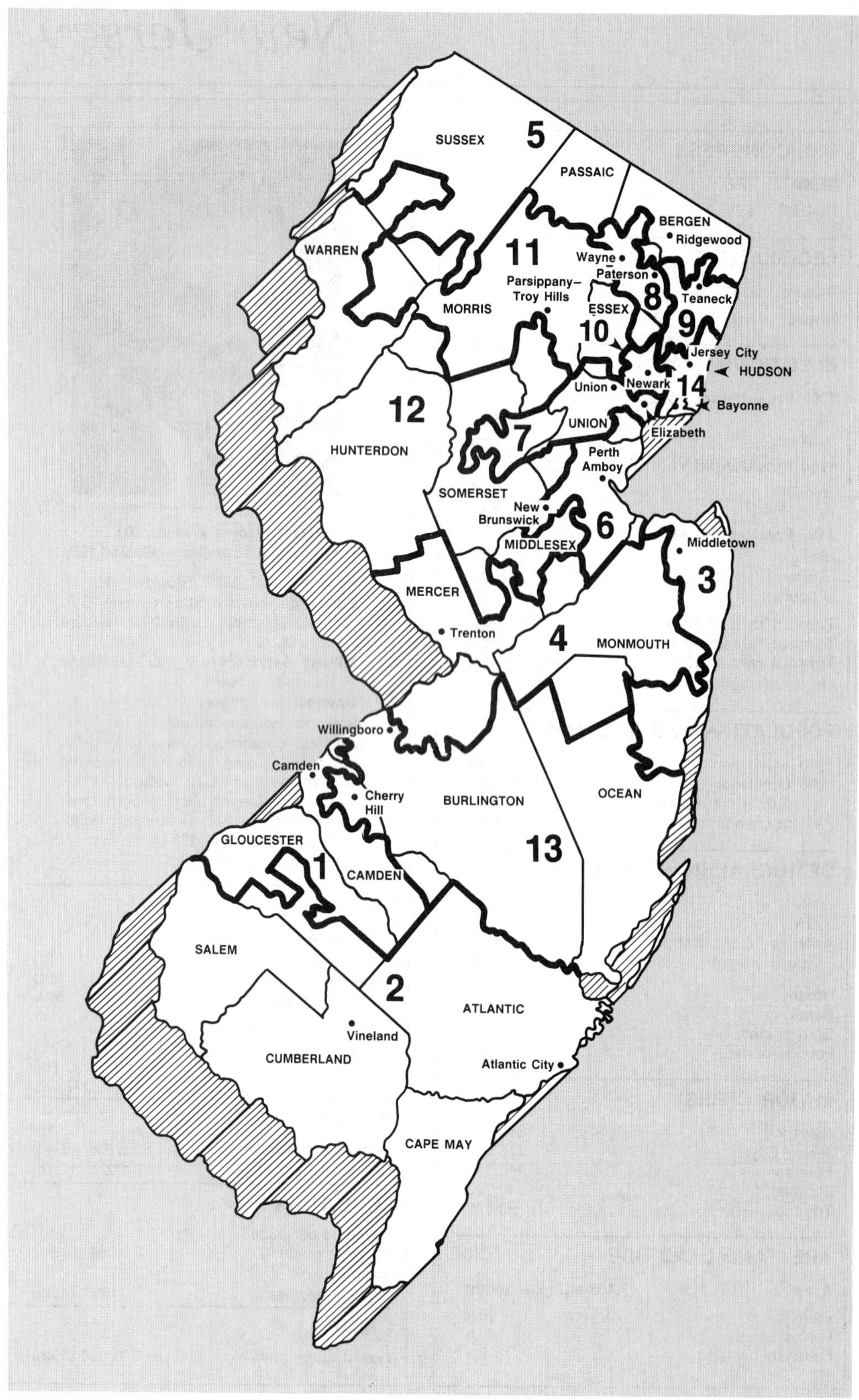
SUSSEX
5
PASSAIC
BERGEN
Ridgewood
WARREN
11
Wayne
Paterson
Parsippany–
Troy Hills
8
Teaneck
MORRIS
ESSEX
9
10
Jersey City
HUDSON
Union
Newark
14
12
Bayonne
UNION
7
Elizabeth
HUNTERDON
Perth
Amboy
SOMERSET
New
Brunswick
6
MIDDLESEX
Middletown
3
MERCER
Trenton
4
MONMOUTH
Willingboro
Camden
Cherry
Hill
BURLINGTON
OCEAN
GLOUCESTER
13
1
CAMDEN
SALEM
2
ATLANTIC
Vineland
CUMBERLAND
Atlantic City
CAPE MAY

Bill Bradley (D)

Of Denville — Elected 1978

Born: July 28, 1943, Crystal City, Mo.
Education: Princeton U., B.A. 1965; Oxford U., M.A. 1968.
Military Service: Air Force Reserve, 1967-78.
Occupation: Professional basketball player; author.
Family: Wife, Ernestine Schlant; one child.
Religion: Protestant.
Political Career: No previous office.
Capitol Office: 731 Hart Bldg. 20510; 224-3224.

In Washington: For years, Bradley has insisted to skeptical questioners that he is not interested in running for president, that he merely wishes to serve as a senator from New Jersey. After his performance in the 101st Congress and his 1990 re-election campaign, onlookers may finally believe him.

After years of viewing Bradley as a potential savior of the Democratic Party — if not the country — Congress-watchers and Democratic operatives alike have seen their hopes give way to resignation, realizing that they may have set their expectations too high. Bradley's 1990 election-night squeaker showed that New Jersey voters also no longer view him with unyielding awe.

While priding himself on his attention to hard work and seriousness of thought, Bradley remains an extremely cautious politician, loath to take the public lead on some major issues. While he was a force on tax reform in the mid-1980s, he has been noticeably reticent on a number of tax issues since; his refusal to comment on state tax policies during his campaign nearly cost him his seat. Yet he has been a maverick within the party on other issues — touting free trade and on occasion backing the Nicaraguan contras. He has also wholeheartedly pursued some causes, particularly those of women and children.

If not for his height and giraffe-like lope, it might be easy to forget that a basketball court rather than the Senate floor provided Bradley's first professional arena. During more than a decade in office, he has shown a zest for the tedious substance of policy-making, and little of the backslapping collegiality and street-smart style expected of sports figures — or successful national political figures. Bradley's Senate performance to date also raises questions whether this cerebral loner and political maverick has the style and personality that would wear well through a long national campaign.

While hard legislative work earned Bradley a place on Democrats' short list of potential presidential candidates throughout the 1980s, he has yet to emerge as an institutional leader. Though he played a major and well-documented role in the enactment of the landmark 1986 tax revision law, with each passing Congress, his greatest achievement fades further in memory.

Even supporters and admirers question the absence of a clear theme in Bradley's agenda. Democratic freshman Rep. Robert E. Andrews told a New Jersey magazine that Bradley needed to rethink and sharpen his message. "It was almost like the ghost of Dan Quayle got inside Bill Bradley," said Andrews. "I think he needs to start saying something again."

The 101st Congress started inauspiciously for Bradley. In a move seen as a sign of his ambition, Bradley considered a maneuver to seize the chairmanship of the Intelligence Committee for the 101st Congress from Oklahoma Democrat David L. Boren. But precedent was not on Bradley's side, and as chairman in the 100th Congress, Boren had generated no antagonisms. Bradley's plan was quickly aborted for lack of support.

That Bradley has failed to reach the level of influence that his boosters have wished should not detract from his contributions in the Senate. A hardliner on dealing with the Soviet Union, Bradley has stood out from many in his party in his wariness toward Mikhail S. Gorbachev's regime — and events in that nation during the early 1990s seemed to vindicate his opinions. He warned of a crackdown in the Baltic states and scolded President Bush for his muted criticism of the situation there. Bradley joined conservative Republicans in opposition to Bush's suspension of a 15-year-old ban on extending commercial credits to the Soviet Union for food purchases.

Bradley also used the 101st Congress to re-affirm free trade policies. He was one of just nine Democrats to vote against the protectionist textile trade act and one of the few Finance Committee members to praise the administration's April 1990 decision not to cite Japan for unfair trade practices.

During consideration of the 1990 farm bill, Bradley tried to cut the 18-cent sugar price support by two cents. Bradley's free-market tendencies and the large number of candymakers and soda companies in New Jersey led him to attack the program as costly, irresponsible and protectionist. His effort to cut back the price supports failed by 10 votes.

In many ways, though, Bradley's role in the remarkable legislative history of the tax law illustrates and defines this paradoxical man. On the tax bill, as throughout his public life, he went about his business without taking much notice of the customary rules of politics. His sheer determination and intellectual persistence kept the idea alive for years and, in the end, his seeming indifference to political advantage and to tactical maneuvering was crucial in pushing the bill through Congress. He succeeded where a craftier political operator might well have failed.

If there is a stereotype that celebrity politicians are more style than substance, Bradley is evidence against it. With his rumpled suits and tousled hair, he looks more like a professor than the media superstar he was at Princeton and with the New York Knicks. Considered somewhat aloof by his colleagues, he does not frequent the Senate equivalents of a locker room.

Long before President Reagan and others had adopted the idea, Bradley was urging that the accumulated layers of deductions and special-interest provisions be replaced by a simpler system based on lower tax rates. Certainly the prospects for tax restructuring did not look particularly bright to most experienced political professionals when Bradley finally presented his "Fair Tax" proposal in 1982.

Gradually, though, Bradley's perseverance began to pay off, as tax-revision proposals similar to his own surfaced. When a reform bill began moving in the House in 1985, Bradley backed up his tireless public advocacy with some private persuasion of the good-old-boy sort that is rare for him — playing basketball with House members.

Bradley's most significant contribution, though, came when the Senate Finance Committee drafted its bill the following spring. Patiently but to little avail, Bradley kept reminding his colleagues they were reducing the bill's benefits for the middle class every time they approved a costly tax advantage for corporations and the wealthy.

When committee members realized they had a package that would reduce federal revenues by some $30 billion, the bill seemed doomed. In desperation, Chairman Bob Packwood huddled with Bradley and a few others to produce a radically new proposal that looked a lot like Bradley's original plan. Enthusiasm for its low rates carried the measure through the Senate almost unscathed. Aided by Bradley, who served as a kind of intermediary between Packwood and House Ways and Means Committee Chairman Dan Rostenkowski, conferees soon produced the compromise that led to the most profound change in the tax code in a generation.

With the passage of the tax bill, Bradley turned his attention to another idea of limited appeal and great complexity — relief from the huge debt burden carried by Third World nations, particularly those in Latin America.

As chairman of Finance's International Debt Subcommittee, Bradley opposed Reagan administration policies to increase loans to developing nations, charging that debt was being piled on debt. In 1986, he proposed his own debt relief plan, calling for interest-rate reductions and selective forgiveness of loans, combined with new policies aimed at promoting economic growth within debtor nations.

Although he was basically allied with the Reagan administration on tax revision, Bradley was a forceful critic of Reagan's overall economic policies. He was the only member of Finance to vote against the 1981 tax cut, which he opposed as excessive and too generous to the wealthy. When deficits subsequently climbed, he told administration officials, "Basically what you did is give too much away."

After enactment of the tax revision law, Bradley has spent years fending off attempts to revise it. He has been an outspoken opponent of a cut in the capital gains tax, arguing that it would disproportionately benefit the wealthy. "If capital gains gets put back in the code," said Bradley, "it's a knife in the back of tax reform."

Bradley also has taken advantage of Finance's responsibility for taxes and federal health policies to become one of the leading and most innovative proponents of aid to the poor. A son of privilege who came of age in the civil rights and Great Society years, and a man grown rich thanks to his physical and intellectual gifts, Bradley exhibits a sense of social obligation to those lacking his advantages.

He has focused extensive time and energy toward children's issues; in the 101st Congress, he pushed a measure aimed at cutting infant mortality, helped pass legislation that reauthorized a program that helps pay for childhood vaccines, and got the Senate in 1990 to back an international effort to establish basic standards of protection for children.

Bradley has worked to expand Medicaid to reach more of the poor, especially mothers and infants, and to stretch Medicare to cover more home-care costs for the elderly. A strong supporter of the 1988 expansion of Medicare and catastrophic health coverage, Bradley was one of just three senators in October 1989 to vote against waiving a budget requirement and forgiving the fact that repealing the program would add billions of dollars to the budget deficit. Bradley also has long favored enlarging the earned income tax credit, a break for the working poor.

In the 101st Congress, Bradley also successfully sponsored the student "right to know" measure that makes it easier for athletes and scholars alike to gauge their prospects for obtaining a degree at any given school by entitling college students and applicants to detailed information about graduation rates.

It is not unusual for Bradley to act as a sort of Senate conscience or scold, even if it is not a role that endears him to colleagues.

During action on the 1988 welfare-overhaul bill, Bradley embarrassed lawmakers into preserving a tax credit for child care. "We are paying for welfare reform with a tax on child care," Bradley objected. "I am against punishing women for their success." He proposed instead to end the business entertainment deduction for those making more than $360,000 a year. The Senate agreed, although another financing measure was substituted in conference.

He wages other fights that, taken alone, might not cost much. But collectively, they aggravate a good many senators. Bradley espouses higher cigarette taxes and other antismoking measures, provoking tobacco-state members. During the 101st Congress, Bradley continued to push for an end to the income tax deduction that tobacco companies take for advertising expenses.

In the interests of his oil-consuming state, Bradley battles the oil industry and its allies, including Finance Chairman Lloyd Bentsen of Texas. In 1987, Bradley helped persuade the Senate to strike from the trade bill Bentsen's provision to limit oil imports, although Bentsen prevailed in a second skirmish to repeal the windfall profits tax. In general, Bradley does not have great influence on the Energy and Natural Resources Committee, where his strong pro-conservation and anti-industry sentiments often put him in a small minority on that industry-oriented panel.

On Intelligence, Bradley received special insight into Reagan administration policies against Nicaragua. Bradley stunned colleagues in 1986 by voting for a $100 million military aid package; he said he did so to keep pressure on Nicaragua's rulers to democratize. But by 1988, Bradley again opposed contra aid, citing Reagan's failure to pursue diplomatic moves. In 1989, he was one of just nine senators who voted against the compromise contra aid package, arguing that the Bush administration had failed to adequately define its policy toward the country.

At Home: Under normal circumstances, the retirement of two-term GOP Gov. Thomas H. Kean after the 1989 election would have given Bradley an undisputed position as New Jersey's most popular officeholder. Republicans were not expected to put up much of a struggle as Bradley sought re-election in 1990.

But 1990 proved to be anything but normal circumstances, and Bradley came within a whisker of seeing his political career come to a halt. His 50-47 percent victory against an unheralded opponent was one of the more startling results of election night.

Democratic Gov. James J. Florio's $2.8 billion tax increase, enacted in response to a state budget deficit, enraged Garden State voters and touched off waves of antitax protests. Democrats across the state scurried for cover as voters hunted for targets against whom to vent their fury.

With no state legislative seats on the ballot, the tallest target was the well-known two-term senator. Bradley had not voiced an opinion on the tax plan, but his Republican opponent, former state Public Utilities Commissioner Christine Todd Whitman, did everything in her power to equate a vote for her with a vote against Florio. One of her radio advertisements attacked Florio and exhorted voters to "send a message that higher taxes are just not acceptable . . . by supporting someone who's not just another politician." Her campaign also ordered bumper stickers that proclaimed: "Get Florio, Dump Bradley."

Bradley campaigned as if oblivious to the ferocious disapproval thousands of voters were expressing toward the tax package. He avoided commenting on the plan; armed with a massive fundraising advantage, he strove to avoid specifics altogether. Bradley's television ads were "warm and fuzzy," depicting the senator walking on a beach or playing basketball. In post-election interviews by *The New York Times*, voters said they were insulted by the ads, considering the economic problems confronting the state and federal governments.

Late in the campaign, when polls showed the race tightening, Bradley ran ads criticizing Whitman for backing tax increases when she was a freeholder in Somerset County.

Many voters said they did not intend to defeat Bradley, merely to send him and his fellow state Democrats a message. "I got the message! I got the message!" Bradley insisted after the election.

Bradley was already well-known in New Jersey from his basketball success with Princeton and the New York Knicks before he began his first campaign. During his 10-year pro career, Bradley was looking ahead to politics. In the off-season, he spoke at Democratic Party gatherings, worked as a reading teacher in Harlem and spent a summer doing administrative work in the federal Office of Economic Opportunity in Washington.

His interest in politics came early, nurtured by his father, a Republican banker in Crystal City, Mo., and by his days at Princeton, where he wrote his senior thesis on Harry S. Truman's 1940 Senate campaign.

Bradley considered returning to Missouri to seek office, but marriage to a New Jersey college professor and years of television exposure in the New York metropolitan area convinced him to run in the Garden State. To finance his 1978 Senate bid, he relied on some of his own wealth, then valued at nearly $1.6 million, and on fundraising events by such prominent friends as singer Paul Simon and actor Robert Redford.

With superior name recognition, Princeton and Oxford degrees and a clean-cut reputation, he scored an easy Democratic primary victory over Gov. Brendan T. Byrne's candidate, former state Treasurer Richard C. Leone.

Bradley drew as his general-election opponent Jeffrey Bell, a former campaign aide to Ronald Reagan. Bell had ousted four-term Sen. Clifford P. Case in the Republican primary, and his campaign had split the GOP badly. Without the liberal Case on the November ballot, labor and minorities felt free to go with Bradley.

Bell spoke enthusiastically of the Kemp-Roth tax-cut plan, but his campaign lacked substance outside the issue of taxes. Bradley was not much as a personal campaigner, but he made the most of his status as a fresh face in a state dominated by organization politicians. He won with 55 percent.

His first term coincided with efforts, particularly by Kean, to improve the image of a state that had been derided for years as a chemical junkyard and a playground for organized crime. Bradley, with his intellectual bearing and distance from grimy organization politics, was a model for how New Jerseyans preferred their state to be viewed.

By 1984, Bradley was poised for a landslide re-election. Once clearly uncomfortable on the stump, he worked crowds now with more ease. He had learned the nuts and bolts of politics, assembling a talented political organization and showing an impressive ability to raise funds. He had $2 million salted away before the Republicans even came up with an opponent.

The candidate they finally settled on was Mary Mochary, the mayor of Montclair, who hitched her wagon to Reagan's re-election campaign, trying to convince Reagan supporters that the Democrat would stand in the way of the president's goals. It made no difference. Bradley won close to two-thirds of the vote.

Committees

Energy & Natural Resources (4th of 11 Democrats)
Water & Power (chairman); Energy Regulation & Conservation; Public Lands, National Parks & Forests

Finance (5th of 11 Democrats)
Deficits, Debt Management & International Debt (chairman); Health for Families & the Uninsured; International Trade

Select Intelligence (4th of 8 Democrats)

Special Aging (3rd of 11 Democrats)

Elections

1990 General		
Bill Bradley (D)	977,810	(50%)
Christine Todd Whitman (R)	918,874	(47%)
John L. Kucek (POP)	19,978	(1%)
Louis M. Stefanelli (LIBERT)	13,988	(1%)
1990 Primary		
Bill Bradley (D)	197,454	(92%)
Daniel J. Seyler (D)	16,287	(8%)

Previous Winning Percentages: **1984** (64%) **1978** (55%)

Campaign Finance

	Receipts	Receipts from PACs		Expend-itures
1990				
Bradley (D)	$8,134,268	$1,062,309	(13%)	$9,563,942
Whitman (R)	$827,006	$10,782	(1%)	$801,660

Key Votes

1991	
Authorize use of force against Iraq	N
1990	
Oppose prohibition of certain semiautomatic weapons	N
Support constitutional amendment on flag desecration	N
Oppose requiring parental notice for minors' abortions	Y
Halt production of B-2 stealth bomber at 13 planes	Y
Approve budget that cut spending and raised revenues	N
Pass civil rights bill over Bush veto	Y
1989	
Oppose reduction of SDI funding	N
Oppose barring federal funds for "obscene" art	Y
Allow vote on capital gains tax cut	Y

Voting Studies

	Presidential Support		Party Unity		Conservative Coalition	
Year	**S**	**O**	**S**	**O**	**S**	**O**
1990	32	66	80	19	14	86
1989	46	51	82	14	16	74
1988	48	45	81	9	22	70
1987	32	55	81	12	38	56
1986	51	48	66	24	36	61
1985	33	59	69	23	17	73
1984	42	45	66	25	28	60
1983	42	58	82	18	23	75
1982	37	63	87	13	14	85
1981	44	48	80	10	11	77

Interest Group Ratings

Year	ADA	ACU	AFL-CIO	CCUS
1990	94	13	67	8
1989	85	15	80	25
1988	75	9	75	25
1987	80	21	100	28
1986	85	23	87	31
1985	85	9	81	28
1984	85	35	64	29
1983	85	16	82	32
1982	100	15	85	29
1981	90	7	82	13

Frank R. Lautenberg (D)

Of Secaucus — Elected 1982

Born: Jan. 23, 1924, Paterson, N.J.
Education: Columbia U., B.S. 1949.
Military Service: Army, 1942-46.
Occupation: Computer firm executive.
Family: Divorced; four children.
Religion: Jewish.
Political Career: No previous office.
Capitol Office: 506 Hart Bldg. 20510; 224-4744.

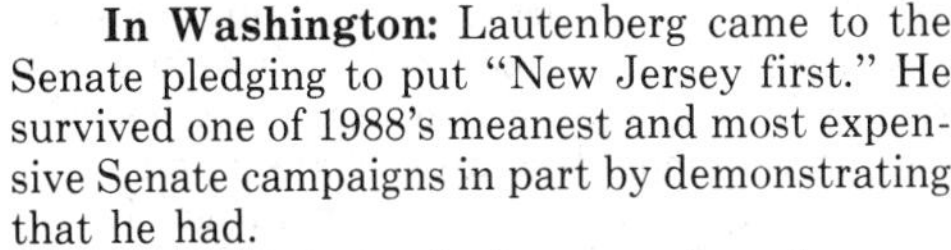

In Washington: Lautenberg came to the Senate pledging to put "New Jersey first." He survived one of 1988's meanest and most expensive Senate campaigns in part by demonstrating that he had.

In his first term, he became a key player on transportation and pollution policy, two matters of considerable concern in the Garden State. His position was enhanced when the Democrats took control of the Senate in 1987.

Yet Lautenberg's interests range far beyond the Jersey shores, and he is fortunate that his state provides a base to delve into issues of national and international scope as well. As a result, he has set up his Senate office much like a diversified business venture that explores all types of legislative activity.

But learning to make the system work should not be confused with liking it. As with many self-made men, Lautenberg has trouble coming to terms with the slow grind of legislation. For example, in 1989 Lautenberg sought to short-circuit the legislative process in a manner requiring the consent of every senator on a resolution calling for a presidential commission to investigate the explosion of Pan Am Flight 103 over Scotland, an act of terrorism that took 270 lives. He got angry when a GOP colleague raised objections.

Similar frustration has accompanied Lautenberg throughout his career as a lawmaker. The tough, hard-driving entrepreneur has elbowed his way into issues where his presence was not always welcome. Nonetheless, he generally has done so without alienating colleagues.

There have been exceptions. In 1989, Lautenberg showed he had learned to play hardball. A former two-pack-a-day smoker, he counseled tobacco farmers to go "grow soybeans or something" as he steered a smoking ban on all domestic airline flights through the Senate, besting a master obstructionist, Jesse Helms of North Carolina. When Helms and other senators supporting tobacco howled that Lautenberg had bypassed their committees by attaching the ban to an appropriations bill, Lautenberg snapped: "The committee system is safe. The flying public is not." A conference committee retained the ban for almost all flights.

Upon arriving in the Senate, Lautenberg joined the Banking and Commerce committees, but he had shed both by the 100th Congress. Lautenberg is among those who would confer Cabinet status on the Environmental Protection Agency (EPA), and in 1987 he became chairman of the Environment and Public Works subcommittee that has jurisdiction over EPA's "superfund" toxic-waste cleanup program — an issue important to New Jersey, home to dozens of toxic-waste sites bad enough to make the superfund list.

New Jersey has long resented New York City's sludge washing up on its shores. Lautenberg was instrumental in putting through a measure to eventually halt this practice. He also pressed for laws to stop ocean dumping of other garbage, including plastics that do not degrade like organic materials. Allied with environmentalists, he was deeply involved in the ultimately successful effort to reauthorize the superfund program.

Lautenberg's subcommittee broadened its scope in the 101st Congress, enhancing its reach on New Jersey matters. Ocean dumping, drinking water, groundwater and indoor pollution were added to its jurisdiction.

In 1990, Lautenberg locked horns with Daniel R. Coats of Indiana, who sought to block New Jersey's export of garbage, some of which ends up in landfills. Smelling an issue he thought Coats stirred up for campaign purposes, Lautenberg managed to remove the provision from a District of Columbia appropriations bill in conference.

Lautenberg was not as successful on 1990 clean-air legislation. He broke with Majority Leader George J. Mitchell of Maine and led a floor fight for tighter controls on toxic air pollution caused in large part by auto emissions. The Senate rejected his amendment.

Lautenberg's other subcommittee chairmanship, the Transportation Subcommittee on

Appropriations, allows him to plunge even deeper into issues of rail, air and highway safety. He has pushed for more transportation funds for densely populated, East Coast states, and has fought attempts to eliminate federal funding for Amtrak.

In the 98th Congress, Lautenberg won legislation aimed at curbing drunken driving by forcing states to raise their minimum drinking age to 21. To get the bill through the Senate, Lautenberg worked out a "stick-and-carrot" compromise — threatening states that refused to raise their drinking age with the loss of up to $500 million a year in federal highway money, while also offering them incentives to try other measures to reduce drunken driving.

In the 99th Congress, Lautenberg moved to close a loophole in the drinking-age law that would have ended the fiscal sanctions on states within two years: Some states had passed laws raising the drinking age to 21 only until 1988.

Lautenberg hounded the Reagan administration to rehire air-traffic controllers who were fired after they went on strike in 1981. Contending that the current controllers are so overworked that the Federal Aviation Administration is hard-pressed to keep the skies safe, Lautenberg tried to get the rehiring ban lifted. The Senate endorsed his proposal in 1986, but backed down when Reagan threatened to veto the transportation funding bill to which it was attached.

With his leverage increased in the 100th Congress, he continued to harass the FAA, saying it could make the system even safer with additional measures. He sought more money for air safety, including air-traffic control.

During the 101st Congress, Lautenberg got a seat on the Defense Appropriations subcommittee largely to try to save Fort Dix, a New Jersey army base slated for closing.

Lautenberg has been a fast friend of Israel and Jewish causes. Although he joined with other senators in signing a 1988 letter that expressed displeasure with Israeli Prime Minister Yitzhak Shamir for saying he rejected a negotiating formula that would trade land for peace, he nevertheless criticized the Bush administration in 1990 for attempting to pressure Israel to make concessions. During the Persian Gulf crisis, he sought stepped up aid for Arab allies who joined the coalition against Iraq.

At Home: For the New York City and Philadelphia TV stations that provide most of New Jersey's news coverage, Lautenberg's workmanlike performance on state issues has been pretty dull stuff, especially compared with the activities of senior Democratic Sen. Bill Bradley and former GOP Gov. Thomas H. Kean, both of whom have been players on the national stage in their parties. So when Lautenberg began his 1988 re-election campaign, he had a fairly low public profile.

But by the end of the contest, Lautenberg's name and deeds were widely known, and he had beaten back an aggressive challenge from Republican Pete Dawkins by 250,000 votes.

Dawkins was the national GOP's premier "résumé" candidate for Senate in 1988. His life had been an unbroken string of accomplishments — winner of the Heisman Trophy (while playing for Army in 1958), a Rhodes scholar, the Army's youngest brigadier general, a high-ranking Pentagon official, a Wall Street financial executive. He tried to mold his golden image to political advantage, describing himself as a potential national leader in the Bradley-Kean mold. He denigrated Lautenberg as "the junior senator."

But Dawkins soon found his superstar image challenged. An article in a Manhattan business magazine described him as a failure in a variety of military and business positions, who still was promoted because of the public relations value of his all-American image. It was said that he had shopped for a state in which to seek public office and settled on New Jersey, moving in just before announcing his Senate candidacy.

While Dawkins denied that assertion and dismissed the magazine story, he and his campaign were caught in several instances of résumé padding that had to be retracted. These included statements that Dawkins had played a major combat role in Vietnam, and that he had been an innovator in international finance as an executive for a Wall Street brokerage firm.

Dawkins spent $1 million-plus in the spring to get his name in front of voters, but he entered the fall trailing Lautenberg in the polls. At that point, Lautenberg went on the attack, beginning with an unusual ad showing Dawkins himself making a flowery statement about the glories of New Jersey. "Be Real, Pete" was superimposed on the film clip, conveying Lautenberg's theme that Dawkins was a carpetbagger and a phony. Another ad accused Dawkins of viewing New Jersey as a pit stop on his route to national office.

Dawkins bemoaned Lautenberg's mudslinging, but then got into a tit-for-tat war of negativism that sank to its lowest when Dawkins charged multimillionaire Lautenberg with using his Senate seat for personal profit.

Lautenberg's lead weathered the fierce exchanges, Dawkins' money dried up and the incumbent at the end switched to positive ads extolling his work for the state. In spite of George Bush's solid victory in New Jersey, Lautenberg won 54 percent of the vote.

While Lautenberg had been involved for years as a Democratic activist and fundraiser — his $90,000 contribution to George McGovern's campaign in 1972 earned him a place on President Nixon's "enemies list" — he had never sought office prior to his 1982 bid for the seat vacated by appointed GOP Sen. Nicholas F.

Brady (now Treasury secretary). After winning with a plurality in a Democratic primary, he came from behind to defeat Republican Rep. Millicent Fenwick.

Both candidates were wealthy. But while Fenwick inherited her fortune, Lautenberg, the son of an immigrant silk-mill worker, was a self-made man. The Democrat spent some $4 million of his own money to drive home that contrast. At one campaign stop, he pointed to the gap between his front teeth and said, "If my parents had money I wouldn't have this. I keep it as a badge of my roots."

Irreverent, witty and eccentric, Fenwick was frequently profiled and quoted in the national media, and was a heroine to numerous good-government causes. She started out with a sizable lead over Lautenberg.

But Lautenberg overcame Fenwick's reformist credentials and personal popularity by painting her and the GOP as insensitive to working-class people. He touted himself as an expert on creating jobs, talking about how he had turned his company, Automatic Data Processing, from a three-man business into one of the world leaders in computer services.

To erase organized labor's doubts about him, Lautenberg advocated a minimum tax on corporations and elimination of the third year of Reagan's tax cut for those earning over $40,000 per year. Labor finally went along with him against Fenwick, overlooking the absence of unions at ADP. Lautenberg said no one had tried to organize the firm.

With the endorsements of several major newspapers, the unions and such liberal forces as the National Organization for Women, Lautenberg showed Fenwick's lead was soft. He hammered on her votes for the 1981 Reagan economic package. She could not equal his media effort, as she would not dip as heavily into her wealth and refused donations from political action committees. Lautenberg rejected her request that each side limit spending to $1.6 million. He won with 51 percent of the vote.

Committees

Appropriations (10th of 16 Democrats)
Transportation (chairman); Commerce, Justice, State & Judiciary; Defense; Foreign Operations; VA, HUD and Independent Agencies;

Budget (6th of 12 Democrats)

Environment & Public Works (5th of 9 Democrats)
Superfund, Ocean & Water Protection (chairman); Environmental Protection; Water Resources, Transportation & Infrastructure

Elections

1988 General		
Frank R. Lautenberg (D)	1,599,905	(54%)
Peter M. Dawkins (R)	1,349,937	(45%)
1988 Primary		
Frank R. Lautenberg (D)	362,072	(78%)
Elnardo J. Webster (D)	51,938	(12%)
Harold J. Young (D)	41,303	(10%)

Previous Winning Percentage: **1982** (51%)

Campaign Finance

	Receipts	Receipts from PACs		Expend-itures
1988				
Lautenberg (D)	$7,087,476	$1,410,360	(20%)	$7,289,663
Dawkins (R)	$7,766,535	$855,144	(11%)	$7,616,249

Key Votes

1991	
Authorize use of force against Iraq	N
1990	
Oppose prohibition of certain semiautomatic weapons	N
Support constitutional amendment on flag desecration	N
Oppose requiring parental notice for minors' abortions	Y
Halt production of B-2 stealth bomber at 13 planes	Y
Approve budget that cut spending and raised revenues	N
Pass civil rights bill over Bush veto	Y
1989	
Oppose reduction of SDI funding	N
Oppose barring federal funds for "obscene" art	Y
Allow vote on capital gains tax cut	N

Voting Studies

	Presidential Support		Party Unity		Conservative Coalition	
Year	**S**	**O**	**S**	**O**	**S**	**O**
1990	25	75	88	12	8	92
1989	49	50	87	12	24	76
1988	42	53	92	4	0	92
1987	33	63	87	6	19	72
1986	30	69	79	15	12	86
1985	28	69	85	14	7	92
1984	35	61	85	12	6	91
1983	40	56	77	20	14	80

Interest Group Ratings

Year	ADA	ACU	AFL-CIO	CCUS
1990	100	4	78	17
1989	80	7	90	29
1988	90	0	100	17
1987	85	8	89	33
1986	85	17	100	22
1985	90	4	95	32
1984	100	0	91	24
1983	85	16	94	26

1 Robert E. Andrews (D)

Of Bellmawr — Elected 1990

Born: Aug. 4, 1957, Camden, N.J.
Education: Bucknell U., B.A. 1979; Cornell U., J.D. 1982.
Occupation: Law professor.
Family: Single.
Religion: Episcopalian.
Political Career: Camden County Board of Chosen Freeholders, 1987-90, director of board of freeholders, 1988-90.
Capitol Office: 1005 Longworth Bldg. 20515; 225-6501.

The Path to Washington: Anger toward Democratic Gov. James J. Florio among those he used to represent in Congress gave a scare to Andrews, his heir apparent.

Florio, who left the 1st in January 1990 to become governor, ignited a statewide voter revolt when he raised taxes early in his tenure as chief executive. Running to keep the vacant 1st in Democratic hands in November, Andrews had to sweat out a victory in a contest that originally figured to be a cakewalk for him. Also on Nov. 6, Andrews won the special election to fill Florio's vacant seat for the balance of the 101st Congress.

After Florio moved to Trenton, Andrews, director of the Camden County Board of Freeholders, looked like a good bet to succeed him in the 1st. A political ally of the governor, Andrews was known as a young reformer in the Florio mold. He lined up the backing of the Camden County Democratic Party organization and brushed off faint primary opposition.

His GOP opponent, businessman Daniel J. Mangini, backed into the nomination after a better-known candidate could not be found. While Mangini, a Gloucester County freeholder, directed his understaffed, underfunded effort from the back of an appliance store, Andrews was headquartered in the spacious end unit of a Somerdale shopping center. Andrews outraised Mangini by more than 10 to 1.

But the $2.8 billion increase in sales and income taxes Florio pushed through the Legislature in June leveled the playing field. Democrats at every level, alarmed at bumper stickers and signs across the state with exhortations such as "Flush Florio," attempted to distance themselves from the governor.

Mangini repeatedly referred to Andrews as "Florio's handpicked protégé," but Andrews held steady and refrained from directly repudiating Florio. The "Florio factor" did not prove powerful enough to offset Andrews' money and organization. The Democrat carried all three counties in the 1st, winning with 54 percent.

Andrews' first foray into electoral politics came in 1986, after practicing law at several area firms and teaching at Rutgers University College of Law. He was elected to the Camden County Board of Freeholders and two years later was chosen freeholder director by the board.

Although Andrews' experience is in county government, during his House campaign he spoke smoothly on local as well as federal issues. At age 33, he already has the skill of a veteran pol, moving easily among both inner-city and suburban voters — a trait he shares with Florio.

Andrews' new constituency is in many ways different from the one Florio faced when he first won the seat in 1974. The district's population has grown in the past decade, but the staunchly Democratic city of Camden has hemorrhaged both voters and jobs, with many people leaving for the greener suburban pastures of southern Camden and Gloucester counties.

The district still has a sizable Democratic voter registration advantage, but the younger, middle-class, suburban voters are independent-minded and have shown a willingness to support Republicans at the local and presidential levels.

The changing demographics of the district present different priorities for Andrews. He has stated that he will not vote for any tax increases in his first term, and, unlike Florio, who focused on an environmental and consumer agenda, Andrews is primarily concerned with economic revitalization, particularly Delaware River port development.

While some areas surrounding Camden prospered in the 1980s, many of the city's neighborhoods are in desperate straits. Camden has lost thousands of jobs in recent years and has more than 12 percent unemployment, partly due to the shutdown of the Campbell Soup Co. plant, a longtime pillar, and layoffs at the General Electric Aerospace plant.

New Jersey 1

Southwest — Camden

The 1st is an amalgam of decaying urban areas, older suburbs and a rapidly developing countryside once covered by tomato patches but now sprouting subdivisions. Many of the suburbanites have Philadelphia roots and retain their Democratic loyalties. The Philadelphians were largely responsible for the district's switch in representation in 1974, when it elected Democrat James J. Florio after choosing only Republicans for 75 years.

Democrats long have prevailed in the industrial region near the Delaware River — in Camden and the other river towns, and in the blue-collar suburbs beyond them. But in the 1980s, election outcomes here revealed a degree of blue-collar disaffection with national Democratic tickets.

The window-pierced facades, porches, arches, and ascending steps described by Camden's favorite son Walt Whitman have given way to block after block of boarded-up and burnt-out buildings. Numerous businesses and residents have fled depressed Camden; since 1960, the city has lost 40,000 residents. More than half of its high school students drop out before graduation; over 60 percent of its children live in poverty.

For a time, an economic upturn across the river in downtown Philadelphia helped stabilize the economy and population in Camden, which remains the district's hub. Hopes were raised by an ambitious plan to revitalize the Delaware River waterfront, and by the possibility of two professional sports teams relocating to Camden. But the city suffered economic setbacks in 1990 when the Campbell Soup Co. closed its factory after nearly a century in business, and GE Aerospace announced layoffs. Between the two, almost 1,800 jobs were eliminated. The Camden County government complex is also a major indigenous employer. Slightly more than half of Camden's residents are black; the rest are largely Italian and Hispanic.

Pennsauken (population 34,000) is a port city like Camden, filled with factories and oil storage yards. Pennsauken is still essentially Democratic, as are some of the older suburban communities near it on the Black Horse Pike. Italian-Americans have a strong influence.

Though Camden and its close-in environs are declining, the area south of the city — southern Camden County and Gloucester County — is faring much better. It was one of the state's fastest-growing parts in the 1980s, and its voters tend to be younger and more independent than those in the city. In southern Camden County, land that was recently farm country now sprouts rapidly developing suburbs, such as Winslow Township along Route 73. Gloucester County has a chemical industry along the waterfront and substantial agricultural interests further inland.

Population: 526,069. White 427,390 (81%), Black 78,545 (15%), Other 4,025 (1%). Spanish origin 21,405 (4%). 18 and over 370,997 (71%), 65 and over 52,874 (10%). Median age: 30.

Committees

Education & Labor (19th of 25 Democrats)
Employment Opportunities; Health & Safety; Postsecondary Education

Select Narcotics Abuse & Control (21st of 21 Democrats)

Small Business (24th of 27 Democrats)
Antitrust, Impact of Deregulation & Ecology; Regulation, Business Opportunity & Energy

Campaign Finance

	Receipts	Receipts from PACs		Expend-itures
1990				
Andrews (D)	$542,535	$236,190	(44%)	$541,960
Mangini (R)	$83,705	$23,850	(28%)	$79,662

Key Vote

1991

Authorize use of force against Iraq	N

Elections

1990 General		
Robert E. Andrews (D)	73,522	(54%)
Daniel J. Mangini (R)	57,801	(43%)
Jerry Zeldin (LIBERT)	1,599	(1%)
William Henry Harris (POP)	1,078	(1%)
Walter E. Konstanty (PH)	1,431	(1%)
1990 Special *		
Robert E. Andrews (D)	72,324	(55%)
Daniel J. Mangini (R)	58,671	(45%)
1990 Primary		
Robert E. Andrews (D)	14,589	(53%)
Linda Bowker (D)	8,290	(30%)
John A. Dramesi (D)	3,922	(14%)
Joel S. Farley (D)	908	(3%)

** On Election Day, Andrews was elected to a full term and to fill out the remainder of the term of James J. Florio, D-N.J., who resigned Jan. 16, 1990, to become governor of New Jersey.*

District Vote For President

	1988		1984		1980		1976	
D	97,534	(48%)	96,877	(45%)	87,763	(47%)	120,345	(57%)
R	107,017	(52%)	118,015	(55%)	91,587	(49%)	85,452	(41%)
I					6,663	(4%)		

2 William J. Hughes (D)

Of Ocean City — Elected 1974

Born: Oct. 17, 1932, Salem, N.J.
Education: Rutgers U., A.B. 1955, J.D. 1958.
Occupation: Lawyer.
Family: Wife, Nancy L. Gibson; four children.
Religion: Episcopalian.
Political Career: Assistant prosecutor, Cape May County, 1960-70; Ocean City solicitor, 1970-74; Democratic nominee for U.S. House, 1970.
Capitol Office: 341 Cannon Bldg. 20515; 225-6572.

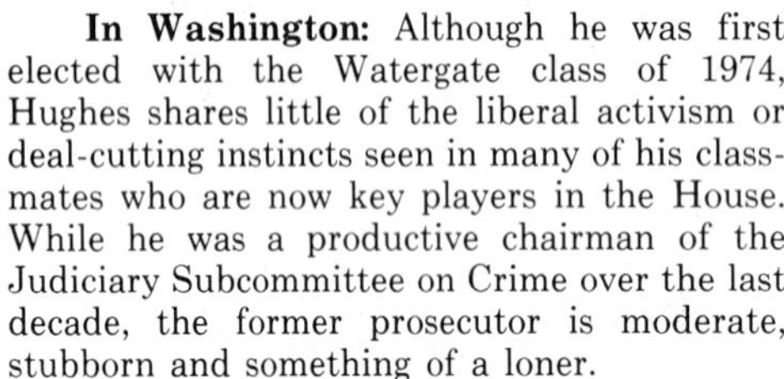

In Washington: Although he was first elected with the Watergate class of 1974, Hughes shares little of the liberal activism or deal-cutting instincts seen in many of his classmates who are now key players in the House. While he was a productive chairman of the Judiciary Subcommittee on Crime over the last decade, the former prosecutor is moderate, stubborn and something of a loner.

But Hughes is regarded as an able legislator, and at the start of the 102nd Congress he took a new chairmanship that will allow him to expand his focus, if he chooses. His new subcommittee — Intellectual Property and Judicial Administration — has jurisdiction over business concerns such as patents, copyrights and trademarks as well as responsibility for federal courts and prisons.

As chairman of the Judiciary Subcommittee on Crime from 1981-91, Hughes left his mark on the law enforcement provisions of the 1986, 1988 and 1990 drug bills, the 1984 overhaul of the federal criminal code, a stronger law against child pornography and a measure to ban "plastic" guns.

But Hughes always had trouble seizing political control of the charged debates on the issues these bills addressed. He is more conservative than the Democratic bloc on Judiciary, yet less reactionary than the full House on these emotional issues. This left him as frustrated by Judiciary liberals as by the more conservative House majority during election-year debates. "I hope we never, ever bring up a crime bill again a month before an election," he fumed in 1990.

Hughes' obstinate streak flared during a late 1989 conference on legislation to streamline the transfer from federal to state governments of proceeds from assets seized in drug investigations. The Senate wanted to repeal language in a 1988 bill that blocked the transfer, while Hughes wanted to delay the effective date of repeal. Although the Senate language had already been enacted in other legislation, Hughes nonetheless refused to budge. The conference adjourned and no further action was taken.

When he set his mind to it, however, Hughes used his place between Judiciary liberals and the more conservative House to moderate dissent. A supporter of the death penalty in certain instances, Hughes offered the "racial justice" language adopted by the House in 1990. Although his amendment diluted language wanted by liberals on Judiciary, it maintained the basic premise that there should be more precautions against racism in sentencing. The Senate and White House balked, however, and the measure was dropped in conference.

Hughes' efforts to devise acceptable habeas corpus language did not even get that far. When the bill came to the floor, the full House stripped out language Hughes helped craft that set standards for the experience of defendants' lawyers and overturned a Supreme Court decision barring inmates from using new, favorable rulings in their appeals. Hughes made a last gasp at compromise, but his amendment was rejected on a 189-239 vote.

Hughes did succeed in his efforts to improve the federal prison system and find alternatives to traditional incarceration. His 101st Congress bill provides funds to develop "boot camps" and other intermediate sanctions.

Hughes' frustrations on crime legislation have been matched by those on gun control. Though he owns hunting rifles himself, Hughes has often feuded with the National Rifle Association (NRA); his sympathies lie with law enforcement officials who favor certain restrictions on gun ownership.

Once Hughes did find common ground with the NRA, and it helped bring about a rare victory. In the 100th Congress, the NRA reluctantly joined a coalition of police groups in opposing the sale of firearms made mostly of plastic, which could not be picked up by conventional metal detectors. Hughes was instrumental in obtaining congressional passage of the bill.

In the 100th and 101st Congresses, however, NRA opposition — and Bush veto threats — blocked legislation favored by Hughes to mandate a seven-day waiting period to purchase a handgun. In the 101st Congress, those

New Jersey 2

South — Atlantic City; Vineland

Atlantic City, the 2nd District's largest population center, is actually two cities. There is the one that local officials prefer outsiders to think of: the home of glitzy gambling casinos and luxury hotels which over the past decade have revived Atlantic City's once-faded image as an adult playground-by-the-sea. To the busloads of working-class elderly hoping to win a fortune and the high-rollers who come to spend some of theirs, Atlantic City has been reborn as a year-round resort.

But those visitors who wander from the seafront hotel strip will find the other Atlantic City: a seedy, blighted town, whose predominately black population has been disappointed in the casinos' failure to deliver the pervasive prosperity promised when New Jersey legalized gambling in the 1970s. The city's population (about 38,000) fell 14 percent in the 1970s, and another 5 percent in the 1980s.

This Atlantic City contrasts sharply with the rest of the 2nd District. The story elsewhere is one of growth. The small communities outside Atlantic City, once summer towns, recently have attracted thousands of new year-round residents, many of them refugees from older, urban parts of the state. Retirement communities have sprung up inland.

The Democratic voting tendencies of Atlantic City's minority population are also not duplicated elsewhere. Though Hughes' personal popularity has made him safe — he carried every county by wide margins in 1988 — the district is far more favorable to Republicans running statewide.

In 1988, George Bush easily carried all four counties — Atlantic, Cape May, Cumberland and Salem — that are completely within the 2nd. In the closely contested Senate race, Democratic incumbent Frank R. Lautenberg held onto Atlantic County and Cumberland County, whose glass industry is based in the towns of Bridgeton, Millville and Vineland. But his GOP opponent, Pete Dawkins, took Salem and Cape May counties. Democratic Sen. Bill Bradley had trouble in his 1990 re-election, but in the 2nd carried all four counties handily.

Though Cape May is Hughes' home county, the summer-resort area is probably the most Republican in the district. From north to south, the county takes in family-oriented Ocean City, wealthy Avalon and Stone Harbor, then rowdier Wildwood, whose amusement parks were celebrated by pop singer Bobby Rydell in "Wildwood Days." The elegant Victorian homes of Cape May city are at the southern tip.

Like Cumberland, Salem County has an industrial presence in the chemical plants that line the Delaware River. But both counties are mainly agricultural.

Population: 526,070. White 435,627 (83%), Black 73,331 (14%), Other 3,825 (1%). Spanish origin 23,022 (4%). 18 and over 381,227 (72%), 65 and over 75,506 (14%). Median age: 32.

factors caused Congress to drop House-approved language that Hughes had sponsored to ban domestic as well as foreign assault rifles.

Hughes has also made a personal cause of cracking down on white-collar crime. Boosted by publicity about the Pentagon procurement scandal in mid-1988, Hughes pushed through a bill making it a federal crime to commit fraud in government contracts of $1 million or over.

During the 101st Congress, Hughes sponsored legislation to limit private damage suits under the federal anti-racketeering law known as RICO. Hughes' proposal required federal judges to throw out civil RICO suits unless they meet strict criteria, including that the triple-damages remedy in the RICO law be "appropriate because of the magnitude or significance of the injury." The Judiciary Committee approved the bill, but RICO reform stalled, partly because consumer groups said it is the most effective tool for prosecuting prominent figures in the S&L crisis. In the 102nd Congress, Hughes' new subcommittee has jurisdiction over RICO, and he is certain to revisit the matter.

When not preoccupied with Judiciary, Hughes can usually be found defending the interests of his coastal district on the Merchant Marine Committee. In the 101st Congress, Hughes contributed to the oil spill clean-up bill and won House approval for legislation requiring states to test beaches and ocean waters for pollution.

In the 100th Congress, Hughes successfully spearheaded legislation to ban after 1991 the ocean dumping of sewage sludge. For years, New York City and other cities, including some in New Jersey, had dumped their sludge off the New Jersey shore. Concern about the effect on the state's shoreline led the state Legislature to ban ocean dumping. But when beach wash-ups of ocean-dumped garbage and medical waste damaged the tourist industry in the summer of 1988, the issue became a national concern. The anti-sewage dumping legislation also included Hughes' provisions making it a crime to dispose of medical waste in U.S. coastal or navigable waters.

Blueberries thrive in the sandy soil of Hughes' coastal district, and when a series of record harvests caused a glut in the frozen blueberry market in 1990, Hughes successfully lobbied the Department of Agriculture to buy six million pounds of the berries for school menus and other nutrition programs.

At Home: Though Hughes votes a standard Democratic line on most issues, he occasionally goes against the grain. In the 100th Congress, for instance, he was the only New Jersey Democrat to oppose the retaliatory Gephardt "fair trade" amendment. Such actions, combined with his tough-on-crime image, have made him a secure and popular figure in the Republican-leaning 2nd District.

Hughes was Ocean City solicitor in 1974 when he challenged four-term GOP Rep. Charles W. Sandman Jr. He had run against Sandman once before, in 1970, coming within 6,000 votes. The second time he began in a stronger position, because Sandman had hurt himself badly with slashing attacks on President Nixon's detractors during the 1974 impeachment debate. The result was as much a judgment of Sandman as it was a triumph for Hughes; the incumbent drew only 41 percent of the vote.

Hughes worked hard to cultivate his sprawling district. His mobile van constantly toured the area, looking for people needing help. Hughes was visible on numerous local issues, helping to get military uniform contracts for the ailing garment industry in Cumberland County, pushing for higher gasoline allocations to help seashore tourism during the 1979 energy crunch and fighting against local storage of nuclear waste.

These efforts have yielded impressive electoral dividends. Hughes won his first re-election with 62 percent and has dropped into the 50s only once, in the Reagan-dominated election of 1980. Republicans did not even field an opponent in 1990.

Committees

Judiciary (5th of 21 Democrats)
Intellectual Property & Judicial Administration (chairman); Crime and Criminal Justice

Merchant Marine & Fisheries (4th of 29 Democrats)
Coast Guard & Navigation; Fisheries & Wildlife Conservation & the Environment; Oceanography, Great Lakes & Outer Continental Shelf

Select Aging (4th of 42 Democrats)
Retirement, Income & Employment (chairman)

Select Narcotics Abuse & Control (8th of 21 Democrats)

Elections

1990 General		
William J. Hughes (D)	98,734	(88%)
William A. Kanengiser (POP)	13,246	(12%)
1988 General		
William J. Hughes (D)	134,505	(66%)
Kirk W. Conover (R)	67,759	(33%)

Previous Winning Percentages: **1986** (68%) **1984** (63%) **1982** (68%) **1980** (58%) **1978** (66%) **1976** (62%) **1974** (57%)

District Vote For President

	1988	1984	1980	1976
D	89,367 (41%)	84,704 (38%)	80,965 (39%)	109,701 (52%)
R	127,327 (59%)	138,241 (62%)	107,007 (52%)	97,824 (46%)
I			15,271 (7%)	

Campaign Finance

	Receipts	Receipts from PACs	Expend-itures
1990			
Hughes (D)	$282,731	$91,270 (32%)	$211,686
1988			
Hughes (D)	$283,532	$112,150 (40%)	$235,629
Conover (R)	$45,426	$100 (0%)	$47,159

Key Votes

1991	
Authorize use of force against Iraq	Y
1990	
Support constitutional amendment on flag desecration	N
Pass family and medical leave bill over Bush veto	?
Reduce SDI funding	Y
Allow abortions in overseas military facilities	Y
Approve budget summit plan for spending and taxing	N
Approve civil rights bill	Y
1989	
Halt production of B-2 stealth bomber at 13 planes	Y
Oppose capital gains tax cut	Y
Approve federal abortion funding in rape or incest cases	Y
Approve pay raise and revision of ethics rules	Y
Pass Democratic minimum wage plan over Bush veto	Y

Voting Studies

	Presidential Support		Party Unity		Conservative Coalition	
Year	**S**	**O**	**S**	**O**	**S**	**O**
1990	26	73	79	19	39	59
1989	30	69	84	14	51	49
1988	30	68	85	15	47	50
1987	24	75	79	17	49	51
1986	28	72	78	20	32	68
1985	30	70	76	23	40	60
1984	41	58	71	24	46	47
1983	34	66	74	26	38	62
1982	43	57	80	19	40	59
1981	41	58	64	31	41	59

Interest Group Ratings

Year	ADA	ACU	AFL-CIO	CCUS
1990	78	13	91	38
1989	70	14	75	50
1988	70	16	100	43
1987	80	9	81	27
1986	75	9	79	22
1985	75	19	82	41
1984	60	25	46	40
1983	70	17	82	25
1982	80	18	90	27
1981	65	13	71	24

3 Frank Pallone Jr. (D)

Of Long Branch — Elected 1988

Born: Oct. 30, 1951, Long Branch, N.J.
Education: Middlebury College, B.A. 1973; Tufts U., M.A. 1974; Rutgers U., J.D. 1978.
Occupation: Lawyer.
Family: Single.
Religion: Roman Catholic.
Political Career: Long Branch City Council, 1982-88; N.J. Senate, 1984-88.
Capitol Office: 213 Cannon Bldg. 20515; 225-4671.

In Washington: From his posts on the Merchant Marine and Public Works committees, Pallone as a freshman looked for ways to please the voters of his coastal district. Three of his ideas made it into the 101st Congress' Water Resources Development Act, including a provision to reduce disposal of floatable and dredge material on ocean waters.

Beyond these and other efforts as a sort of "sludge sentinel" for the Jersey shore, Pallone, a narrow winner in 1988, voted a politically careful line on money matters, opposing the congressional pay raise approved in late 1989 and rejecting the budget summit agreement of October 1990 and a later Democratic spending plan, both of which included higher taxes. Despite these precautions, Pallone was nearly turned out of office in 1990 by an electorate outraged at the Democratic Party over a huge state tax increase imposed by Gov. James J. Florio.

Pallone did take one high-profile risk in the 101st, shifting from his longtime anti-abortion stance. After the Supreme Court's *Webster* decision giving states more authority to regulate abortion, Pallone said, "I have come to the conclusion that it is inappropriate for me to impose my religious beliefs on those who do not share those beliefs or whose circumstances demand that other choices be available."

At Home: Pallone was a protégé of Democratic Rep. James J. Howard, whose death during his 12th term in office left the 3rd District open. But Pallone's own state Senate record on environmental issues affecting the pollution-conscious 3rd made the difference in his campaign against a game GOP opponent, former state legislator Joseph Azzolina.

Pallone inherited his political interest from his father, an activist in local Democratic politics involved in Howard's campaigns. The younger Pallone developed friendships with the veteran incumbent and his family.

It was Howard who urged Pallone, a maritime lawyer, to run for the Long Branch City Council in 1982. Just one year later, Pallone won a state Senate seat in Monmouth County, upsetting a Republican incumbent.

Serving a shore district, Pallone sponsored laws to limit ocean dumping of garbage and sewage sludge, and he worked to set up a committee on coastal pollution that he later headed.

Pallone's legislative efforts paid electoral dividends in 1987, when he won re-election with 60 percent of the vote. The next March, Howard, chairman of the Public Works Committee, died of a heart attack. Many Democratic insiders, including Howard's widow, lined up behind Pallone, and he won the House nomination without a contest.

Though both candidates had name-recognition problems outside their home areas, Pallone enjoyed an advantage because of his work on environmental issues.

Azzolina tried to increase his visibility on the issue, releasing a 12-point plan to combat ocean pollution. He also sought to tie Pallone to Democratic presidential nominee Michael S. Dukakis, who was blasted by George Bush during a 3rd District visit for seeking permission for Massachusetts to dump sludge off the New Jersey coast.

But Pallone's activism in Trenton earned him endorsements from leading environmental groups. His strong showing in his home area — he took 73 percent in Long Branch — helped him carry the Monmouth County part of the district by nearly 14,000 votes. Azzolina won the county's largest community, his home city of Middletown Township, with a modest 53 percent. He carried generally Republican Ocean County by fewer than 3,000 votes.

In 1990, Democrats across the state fretted over what voters, angered by Florio's $2.8 billion tax increase, might wreak upon them.

Pallone's little-known Republican challenger, lawyer Paul A. Kapalko, attacked Pallone with an anti-Florio message. With his fiscally conservative voting record — he trumpeted his votes against the two major budget packages in the fall of 1990 — Pallone hoped to hold off the antitax fury. He did, but just barely, beating Kapalko by 4,258 votes.

New Jersey 3

Central Coast — Asbury Park; Long Branch

Jersey shore towns such as Long Branch and Asbury Park were places where 19th-century plutocrats, presidents and gangsters came to bathe, mingle on the boardwalks and play. Ulysses S. Grant, the Guggenheims and Diamond Jim Brady all stayed there. President James A. Garfield was brought to his summer cottage in Long Branch in 1881 after he was shot; he died there a few weeks later.

Today, this area along the coast in Monmouth County is a collection of wealthy shore communities and working-class towns. Although no longer the elitist playground it once was, the 3rd remains a popular seaside vacation spot.

The longtime Democratic hold on the 3rd belies its political competitiveness; the Monmouth County portion, which casts three-fifths of the overall vote, went solidly for George Bush in 1988; in his close 1990 race, Pallone barely carried Monmouth.

The Democratic heart of the district is in the north, in the chain of communities along the Lower New York Bay shore. The Asbury Park glorified by singer Bruce Springsteen, a local hero, is on the road to recovery with the recent renovation of the Berkeley-Carteret Hotel.

Spring Lake, locally known as the "Irish Riviera," is home to the transplanted North Jerseyites who abound in the 3rd. Predominantly Republican, a large percentage commute into New York City. Other bastions of Republicanism are in the bordering seaside communities of Deal and Rumson. Inland Monmouth shows the same mix.

Middletown Township, the 3rd's second-largest political entity, votes firmly Republican. Across the Navesink River is working-class Red Bank, hometown of jazz musician Count Basie. Democrats have their strongest inland enclave there.

Ocean County turns in a bit over a third of the vote, and is less favorable territory for Democrats than Monmouth; in 1990, Pallone lost the county by 1,026 votes. Brick Township is a middle-income suburb proving more amenable to Republicans.

Population: 526,074. White 474,254 (90%), Black 41,093 (8%), Other 4,921 (1%). Spanish origin 15,009 (3%). 18 and over 379,673 (72%), 65 and over 76,485 (15%). Median age: 33.

Committees

Merchant Marine & Fisheries (20th of 29 Democrats)
Coast Guard & Navigation; Fisheries & Wildlife Conservation & the Environment; Oceanography, Great Lakes & Outer Continental Shelf

Public Works & Transportation (22nd of 36 Democrats)
Surface Transportation; Water Resources

Select Aging (31st of 42 Democrats)
Housing & Consumer Interests; Human Services

Elections

1990 General		
Frank Pallone Jr. (D)	77,709	(49%)
Paul A. Kapalko (R)	73,451	(46%)
1990 Primary		
Frank Pallone Jr. (D)	12,544	(80%)
Pat Daly (D)	2,555	(16%)
1988 General *		
Frank Pallone Jr. (D)	117,024	(52%)
Joseph Azzolina (R)	107,479	(47%)

* *Elected to a full term and to fill a vacancy at the same time.*

District Vote For President

	1988		1984		1980		1976	
D	91,035	(37%)	79,811	(33%)	74,361	(34%)	92,176	(43%)
R	151,517	(62%)	161,447	(67%)	128,729	(58%)	117,780	(55%)
I					15,771	(7%)		

Campaign Finance

	Receipts	Receipts from PACs		Expend-itures
1990				
Pallone (D)	$632,450	$394,464	(62%)	$634,109
Kapalko (R)	$118,692	$11,050	(9%)	$115,202
1988				
Pallone (D)	$681,073	$437,739	(64%)	$680,647
Azzolina (R)	$998,854	$137,800	(14%)	$981,865

Key Votes

1991	
Authorize use of force against Iraq	Y
1990	
Support constitutional amendment on flag desecration	Y
Pass family and medical leave bill over Bush veto	Y
Reduce SDI funding	Y
Allow abortions in overseas military facilities	Y
Approve budget summit plan for spending and taxing	N
Approve civil rights bill	Y
1989	
Halt production of B-2 stealth bomber at 13 planes	Y
Oppose capital gains tax cut	Y
Approve federal abortion funding in rape or incest cases	N
Approve pay raise and revision of ethics rules	N
Pass Democratic minimum wage plan over Bush veto	Y

Voting Studies

	Presidential Support		Party Unity		Conservative Coalition	
Year	**S**	**O**	**S**	**O**	**S**	**O**
1990	29	71	79	20	54	46
1989	34	65	82	16	59	39

Interest Group Ratings

Year	ADA	ACU	AFL-CIO	CCUS
1990	61	29	83	43
1989	75	25	92	40

4 Christopher H. Smith (R)

Of Robbinsville — Elected 1980

Born: March 4, 1953, Rahway, N.J.
Education: Trenton State College, B.A. 1975.
Occupation: Sporting goods wholesaler.
Family: Wife, Marie Hahn; four children.
Religion: Roman Catholic.
Political Career: Republican nominee for U.S. House, 1978.
Capitol Office: 2440 Rayburn Bldg. 20515; 225-3765.

In Washington: Smith could well be described as the most liberal conservative Republican in the House. The GOP member from a largely urban and industrial district, Smith has one of the most pro-labor records in the House; his willingness to buck his party leadership was evident in 1990, when he supported President Bush on only 43 percent of House votes. Yet Smith is nationally recognized only for his staunch opposition to abortion, the issue on which he initially built his political base.

This combination appears to be a potent one for Smith. Regarded as a "fluke" when he upset scandal-plagued Democratic Rep. Frank Thompson Jr. in 1980, Smith has consistently won by solid margins.

Smith's fight against abortion remains at the top of his agenda. The co-chairman of the Congressional Pro-Life Caucus, he was in the thick of the debate when abortion emerged as a major issue during the 101st Congress.

When the Supreme Court in early 1989 took up *Webster v. Reproductive Health Services* — involving a Missouri law that restricted abortion and declared life as beginning at conception — Smith led a group of House signatories to a legal brief urging the Supreme Court to use the case to overturn the 1973 *Roe v. Wade* decision that legalized abortion. Smith said at the time that the nation was viewing "the incremental dismantling of *Roe*."

The court did not overturn *Roe* but did uphold the Missouri law, thus giving tacit permission for other states to pass restrictive abortion laws. Smith applauded the decision, but said he would continue to pursue federal legislation limiting abortion.

The upswing in abortion rights activism following the *Webster* decision emboldened "pro-choice" members of Congress. They moved to eliminate an amendment by Rep. Robert K. Dornan, R-Calif., to the District of Columbia appropriations bill, identical to one enacted in 1988, barring the city from using federal or local funds to pay for abortions.

Abortion rights advocates used a strategy aimed at forcing Smith and other "Dornan amendment" supporters to justify a draconian measure. They cited a House rule barring legislation on appropriations bills to eliminate tempering language — including a provision allowing funding of abortion when the life of the woman was in danger. Smith's effort to add "life of the woman" language to the provision was blocked, and the Dornan amendment went down by a 206-219 vote. However, Smith continued to work his side of the issue, with the support of Bush, whose veto of the D.C. appropriations bill forced the reinstitution of the Dornan amendment.

A similar scenario played out when abortion rights supporters tried to broaden Medicaid abortion funding, restricted to protecting the life of the woman, to include instances of rape and incest. Bush vetoed the fiscal 1990 Labor, Health and Human Services appropriations bill that included the funding extensions; Smith's hardline stance as a negotiator then contributed to the decision by Kentucky Democrat William H. Natcher, chairman of the Appropriations subcommittee that drafted the bill, to drop the new abortion language.

During debates on abortion, Smith's arguments cut to the quick of the emotion-laden issue. "The 'choice' rhetoric is hollow and shallow," Smith said in 1990. "A choice to do what? To dismember a child?"

Smith takes his anti-abortion crusade international through his work on the Foreign Affairs Committee. Since 1985, he has led successful efforts to block U.S. funding for population control programs run by the International Planned Parenthood Foundation and the United Nations population fund. Smith accuses the latter organization of supporting China's "one-child-per-couple" policy, which he says relies on forced abortions and sterilizations.

Yet Smith's "pro-life" politics are broad enough to include such issues as child health care in the Third World. In 1989, he attached an amendment to a foreign aid bill authorizing $245 million for "child survival" programs, such as immunization; in doing so, he defied Bush's express request that Congress limit its

New Jersey 4

Central — Trenton

"Trenton Makes, the World Takes" is the motto of the city that forms the core of the 4th. While many state-capital cities now boast of their post-industrial economies based on professional employment, Trenton — which produces metal products, pharmaceuticals, auto parts and electrical wiring — still emphasizes its blue-collar heritage.

Trenton is 49 percent black, and blacks have begun to advance in local political offices. But Italian-Americans, clustered in the Chambersburg section of town, have retained a large share of political power.

With just under 89,000 residents, Trenton retains its standing as the district's largest city, but just barely. While Trenton's population has dropped slightly, the suburbs of Hamilton Township have boomed; its population stands at 86,500.

Their solid base in industrial Trenton enables Democrats to carry Mercer County in most competitive statewide elections. Presidential nominee Michael S. Dukakis edged out George Bush there in 1988, and Sen. Frank R. Lautenberg carried the county by more than 30,000 votes in his contest with Republican Pete Dawkins. Sen. Bill Bradley's 5,466-vote margin in Mercer reflected his close shave statewide in 1990.

The suburban growth outside Trenton, combined with the Republican leanings in the exurban areas of Burlington, Middlesex, Monmouth and Ocean counties comprising the balance of the district, have given the 4th an overall GOP tilt in recent elections. Ronald Reagan carried the district twice; Bush won there with 56 percent of the vote.

Population: 526,080. White 442,773 (80%), Black 69,793 (13%), Other 5,627 (1%). Spanish origin 15,153 (3%). 18 and over 379,038 (72%), 65 and over 58,139 (11%). Median age: 32.

"earmarks" for specific foreign aid programs.

Smith is also an active member of the Foreign Affairs Subcommittee on Human Rights, and a member of the Commission on Security and Cooperation in Europe, better known as the Helsinki commission; Bush appointed Smith in 1989 as a congressional delegate to the United Nations, where he served on the Human Rights Committee.

Like other Foreign Affairs Republicans, Smith frequently expresses his contempt for the Soviet Union's human rights record. In August 1990, he and Virginia GOP Rep. Frank Wolf visited a Soviet labor camp, and later helped secure the release of several people he called political prisoners.

Beginning in 1985, Smith called for revocation of Romania's most-favored-nation trade status, though that communist nation was then viewed positively because of President Nicolae Ceausescu's contrary relationship with Moscow. Smith claimed vindication in late 1989, when Ceausescu's downfall revealed a regime based on repression and corruption.

But Smith can also be critical of rightist regimes he views as violators of human rights, a position that often places him in league with members across the aisle. In both the 99th and 100th Congresses, Smith was one of a handful of Foreign Affairs Republicans to support economic sanctions against the white-minority government of South Africa.

Smith does not need to worry much about ideology in his other major field of legislative endeavor: He joins in the bipartisan consensus in favor of veterans' programs as a member of the Veterans' Affairs Committee.

As ranking Republican on the Veterans' Affairs Subcommittee on Education, Training and Employment, Smith is a strong advocate of the educational programs for veterans under the GI Bill. When the job status of military personnel called up during the Persian Gulf crisis became an issue in early 1991, Smith and subcommittee Chairman Timothy Penny of Minnesota proposed a bill to bar job discrimination against veterans, active-duty personnel and those planning to join the military.

At Home: There was a widespread belief after Smith's original victory that his win was a temporary happenstance. But Smith became ensconced in the 4th with surprising ease, demolishing Democratic hopes of recapturing a district that was long theirs.

Smith's diligent constituent work and well-run campaigns were important, but the secret of his success was his unexpectedly moderate voting record. Though steadfast in the anti-abortion activism that drew him into politics, his attention to the interests of blue-collar workers and organized labor gave Smith considerable crossover appeal.

Smith had ousted 13-term Democrat Thompson in 1980 solely because of Thompson's involvement in Abscam. In 1978, as a political novice running almost exclusively on his contacts in the right-to-life movement, Smith had failed to draw even 40 percent against Thompson. On the second try, after Thompson's bribery indictment, Smith won every major town in the 4th except Trenton.

Though he defeated Thompson by a substantial margin, Smith was viewed as certain to fall victim in 1982 to Democrat Joseph P. Merlino, the former president of the New Jersey Senate. As it turned out, Merlino came across in areas outside Trenton as a gruff, horse-trading pol. After one debate, when Smith approached him to exchange pleasantries, Merlino growled, "Beat it, kid." Smith made the most of Merlino's image problem; one of his television spots simply showed a lit cigar in an ashtray.

Two years later, the Democrats tried again with a protégê of Merlino, former Mercer County Freeholder James C. Hedden. Unlike his mentor, Hedden took Smith seriously. He campaigned extensively door-to-door, accusing his opponent of being obsessed with abortion.

But Smith, who picked up new, marginally GOP areas and lost some Democratic territory in a court-ordered remap, had used his second term further to cultivate constituents. He carried Mercer County by double his 1982 margin, and ran ahead everywhere else, winning districtwide with 61 percent of the vote.

The 1986 Democratic nominee was Jeffrey Laurenti, a researcher for a New York City public-affairs foundation. Laurenti, who lost the 1984 primary to Hedden, campaigned persistently, continuing the Democratic theme that Smith was, at heart, a right-winger. But Smith played up his moderate House voting record, dismissed Laurenti as an extreme liberal, and won again with 61 percent.

The 1988 campaign underlined Smith's dominance as a political figure in his district. He defeated Betty Holland, the wife of veteran Trenton Mayor Arthur Holland, by a 2-to-1 margin. Before that re-election, Smith was endorsed by a local of the United Auto Workers, a testament to his liaison with district unions.

Two years later, he faced Democrat Mark Setaro, a Trenton lawyer. Setaro, who lost his post as a lector at his Catholic parish for his pro-abortion stand, fell to Smith 63-34 percent.

Committees

Foreign Affairs (10th of 18 Republicans)
Human Rights & International Organizations; International Operations

Select Aging (5th of 27 Republicans)
Housing & Consumer Interests (ranking); Human Services; Rural Elderly

Select Hunger (10th of 12 Republicans)
International

Veterans' Affairs (4th of 13 Republicans)
Education, Training & Employment (ranking); Hospitals & Health Care

Elections

1990 General		
Christopher H. Smith (R)	101,508	(63%)
Mark Setaro (D)	55,454	(34%)
Carl Peters (LIBERT)	2,168	(1%)
Joseph J. Notarangelo (POP)	1,219	(1%)
J.M. Carter (God We Trust)	1,029	(1%)
1988 General		
Christopher H. Smith (R)	155,283	(66%)
Betty Holland (D)	79,006	(33%)

Previous Winning Percentages: **1986** (61%) **1984** (61%) **1982** (53%) **1980** (57%)

District Vote For President

	1988	1984	1980	1976
D	110,261 (44%)	98,386 (41%)	88,317 (41%)	104,217 (50%)
R	139,123 (56%)	141,308 (59%)	105,443 (49%)	99,564 (48%)
I			17,937 (8%)	

Campaign Finance

	Receipts	Receipts from PACs	Expend-itures
1990			
Smith (R)	$280,579	$113,126 (40%)	$292,826
Setaro (D)	$55,701	$4,000 (7%)	$55,772
1988			
Smith (R)	$329,835	$124,781 (38%)	$252,823
Holland (D)	$55,145	$1,658 (3%)	$53,964

Key Votes

1991	
Authorize use of force against Iraq	Y
1990	
Support constitutional amendment on flag desecration	Y
Pass family and medical leave bill over Bush veto	N
Reduce SDI funding	N
Allow abortions in overseas military facilities	N
Approve budget summit plan for spending and taxing	N
Approve civil rights bill	N
1989	
Halt production of B-2 stealth bomber at 13 planes	N
Oppose capital gains tax cut	N
Approve federal abortion funding in rape or incest cases	N
Approve pay raise and revision of ethics rules	Y
Pass Democratic minimum wage plan over Bush veto	Y

Voting Studies

	Presidential Support		Party Unity		Conservative Coalition	
Year	**S**	**O**	**S**	**O**	**S**	**O**
1990	43	56	44	54	56	44
1989	55	44	36	61	66	34
1988	40	59	44	53	68	32
1987	38	62	39	59	77	23
1986	46	54	32	66	60	40
1985	45	55	43	53	55	44
1984	56	44	45	48	63	37
1983	50	50	44	56	60	39
1982	49	51	41	57	52	47
1981	64	36	65	35	67	33

Interest Group Ratings

Year	ADA	ACU	AFL-CIO	CCUS
1990	56	63	50	64
1989	45	43	75	70
1988	60	48	100	43
1987	52	39	81	53
1986	45	45	93	33
1985	65	52	88	41
1984	45	43	69	50
1983	40	48	53	40
1982	50	41	75	57
1981	40	87	40	79

5 Marge Roukema (R)

Of Ridgewood — Elected 1980

Born: Sept. 19, 1929, West Orange, N.J.
Education: Montclair State College, B.A. 1951.
Occupation: High school government and history teacher.
Family: Husband, Richard Roukema; two children.
Religion: Protestant.
Political Career: Ridgewood Board of Education, 1970-73; Republican nominee for U.S. House, 1978.
Capitol Office: 2244 Rayburn Bldg. 20515; 225-4465.

In Washington: Representing one of the nation's wealthier districts, Roukema tends to be conservative on many fiscal and business matters, but relatively liberal on social issues. Within the House GOP, she is too mild-mannered to be an agitator, but too liberal to be an insider. As a senior member of the Education and Labor Committee, often a venue for sharp partisan exchanges, Roukema tries to stake out territory as a compromiser. But it is a panel with little middle ground; she frequently must choose either the left or the right.

In 1991, for instance, Roukema probed Secretary of Labor Lynn Martin about President Bush's threat to veto Democratic-backed legislation giving job-protection rights to striking workers. "Is that unequivocal," Roukema asked of Bush's stand, "or do you see any area for compromise?" Concluding that there was none, Roukema joined the chorus of Republicans opposing the bill.

However, Roukema departs from the White House line on the issue with which she is most closely identified — the Family and Medical Leave Act. The 102nd marked the fourth consecutive Congress in which Roukema has been the lead Republican sponsor of legislation to require large- and medium-sized businesses to provide unpaid leave to new parents, disabled workers and those caring for a seriously ill family member.

After years fighting for the bill, which she calls a "bedrock family issue," Roukema in mid-1990 revealed a personal facet to her commitment. In 1976, when she was a graduate student, her 17-year-old son died of leukemia. When he became ill, she dropped out of school to care for him. "What would I have done if not only did I have the tragedy and trauma of caring for my child," she asks, "but also had to worry about losing a job and the roof over my head?"

In the 100th Congress, Roukema secured some compromises on the family leave bill — limiting the length of leave and the size of companies involved. But they were not enough to bring along many Republican votes. After that bill died, a similar measure was introduced with Roukema as a lead sponsor in the 101st Congress. It finally won congressional approval, but Bush vetoed it in 1990.

As the 102nd Congress opened, Roukema again sponsored the proposal, and she implored the president and Republican colleagues to support it. "This is not about working families getting rich. It's about working families getting by," she said, pointedly adding, "It's really a very modest, minimalist bill."

Alongside this and some other high-profile defections from the business line over the years, Roukema has cast scores of pro-business votes on less visible issues. In the 101st Congress, for instance, she offered a successful amendment to strike a proposal to give workers equal representation with management on trustee boards that run single-employer pension plans. Similarly, she argued that "fairness and common sense" dictated that business be given extra time to comply with the legislation to prevent age discrimination.

Also, there are a handful of issues on which Roukema stands with GOP conservatives. She noisily opposed legislation to lift a ban on permitting people with AIDS to immigrate to the United States, and during debate on the 1990 housing bill, she echoed outrage over a provision to provide $150 million in housing assistance for people with AIDS.

In 1990, Roukema unsuccessfully offered an amendment to crack down on the default rate for student loans; most members wanted the matter to be handled during reauthorization of the higher-education act in the 102nd Congress.

But on two major bills handled by Education and Labor in the 100th Congress — polygraph testing and plant-closing notification — Roukema's position ultimately prevailed. On the bill to restrict most private employers from making workers take a lie-detector test as a condition of employment, Roukema's amendments to allow polygraph tests in selected businesses were turned back. But when the bill reached the House floor, her amendment to

New Jersey 5

North and West — Ridgewood

In the early 1980s, Roukema's district was an ungainly flight of cartographic fancy dubbed "the Swan." A revised map gave her a territory still extensive, but no longer quite the affront to tidiness it once was.

The 5th runs from river to river along the New York border, from the wealthy Bergen County suburbs fronting the Hudson to the back country of the Delaware Water Gap in Sussex County.

Its political complexion is a matter of shades of Republicanism. In 1990, Roukema's winning percentages ranged from 76 percent in Bergen County to 78 percent in Sussex.

Along the Delaware in Sussex County, one finds rural values, farming and a deep-seated suspicion of government. Close to the New York border, the terrain is mountainous and even less populous, with old vacation homes scattered among small lakes. The Ramapo Mountains extend into upper Passaic County, where a back-country group long known as the "Jackson Whites" lives in cultural isolation. They are descendants of miners, a symbol of the old Ringwood ironworks that made cannonballs for the American Revolutionary War.

Although both Sussex and Passaic bid to become New Jersey's next boom area as commuters move out along Route 80, Bergen County has the district's most important single voting bloc. Two-thirds of the vote is cast there. The Bergen towns are politically well organized and Republican voters are active in helping local candidates. Bergen's reputation as New Jersey's banner Republican county comes from the large turnout its northern section produces. Still, this part of the district is more moderate than either Sussex or Passaic; a candidate cannot move too far to the right without risking a loss of support.

Affluent Upper Bergen communities such as Alpine, Tenafly and Norwood are filled with business executives who commute to New York or to the county's many corporate offices.

Population: 526,076. White 509,409 (97%), Black 4,884 (1%), Other 9,483 (2%). Spanish origin 10,082 (2%). 18 and over 377,765 (72%), 65 and over 52,981 (10%). Median age: 33.

permit certain security firms to use lie-detector tests was adopted, 210-209.

On the plant-closing bill, Roukema warned committee Democrats that their goals — to require employers to give up to six months' notice of a plant closing or layoff, and consult with employees and local officials — would encounter the same fate as in the 99th Congress. Then, a business coalition led by the U.S. Chamber of Commerce worked to kill the bill; the House rejected it by 203-208.

In the 100th Congress, Roukema offered a substitute eliminating the consultation requirement — especially troubling to business — and requiring only a 60-day notice. With Democrats dismissing her substitute as too weak, it was rejected in committee 10-22. But when plant-closing legislation reached the floor nearly a year later as part of the omnibus trade bill, the Senate had agreed to a 60-day notice period without a consultation requirement. Still, Roukema voted to strip the measure from the trade bill; she later voted for the separate plant-closing bill that became law.

Roukema also sits on the Banking Committee, and is the ranking member of the Housing Subcommittee. There she is considered a housing advocate, and is often the only Republican to side with panel Democrats. During consideration of the 1990 housing bill, she was the lone Republican to back an amendment prohibiting those buying homes through a new federal program from reaping a profit on a later sale.

At the same time, Roukema watches out for her affluent district. She opposed a housing bill provision that would have targeted more Community Development Block Grant money to anti-poverty programs; some feared it would make CDBG money harder to use in rural and better-off areas.

On about two in three floor votes, Roukema sides with the majority of House Republicans. But those on the party's right wing view her askance because of her moderate outlook on certain high-profile issues and her readiness to seek compromise on hard-fought labor-business battles. In 1989, when several moderate Northeastern Republican women were earning publicity and points with the right for endorsing conservative Newt Gingrich's candidacy for GOP whip in 1989, Roukema backed moderate Edward Madigan of Illinois.

In 1989, she took pains to distance herself from Bush's veto of federal funding of abortion in limited cases. "How could such a leader make such a harsh choice and throw the gauntlet down to Congress on an indefensible position," she asked, "namely, that we vote, yet again, to deny the poor victims of rape and incest a legal right to an abortion, a right open to all other women in our society?"

At Home: Roukema struggled to wrest a seat from a Democratic incumbent in 1980. But redistricting gave her a constituency that is content with moderate GOP representation.

The Democratic Legislature's 1981 remap paired her with fellow Republican Jim Courter, but Courter moved to the 12th. Roukema then coasted in 1982 against Democratic lawyer Fritz Cammerzell. In 1984, a second redistricting plan gave her a more compact but equally Republican district. Roukema won 71 percent.

Two years later, Roukema had to work harder in the primary than in the general election. Her GOP opponent, conservative businessman Bill Grant, accused Roukema of being too liberal, especially on defense, and voting too often against Reagan. But Roukema easily dismissed Grant's challenge. She went on to defeat a little-known Democrat by a 3-to-1 margin, a feat she repeated in 1988 and again in 1990.

Elections were much more difficult for Roukema in her original House district. The old 7th was less Republican, and she had to run twice there to unseat liberal Democrat Andrew Maguire. In 1978, her first challenge, she lost by only 8,815 votes. A former teacher returning to politics five years after leaving the Ridgewood Board of Education, she attacked Maguire for being "anti-defense."

In 1980, she focused on complaints that Maguire, a critic of big oil companies during the 1979 gasoline shortage, was anti-business. With a strong Reagan showing in northern New Jersey, she won by nearly 10,000 votes.

Committees

Banking, Finance & Urban Affairs (4th of 20 Republicans)
Housing & Community Development (ranking); Financial Institutions Supervision, Regulation & Insurance; International Development, Finance, Trade & Monetary Policy

Education & Labor (4th of 14 Republicans)
Labor-Management Relations (ranking); Elementary, Secondary & Vocational Education; Postsecondary Education

Select Hunger (2nd of 12 Republicans)
Domestic (ranking)

Elections

1990 General		
Marge Roukema (R)	118,101	(76%)
Lawrence Wayne Olsen (D)	35,010	(22%)
Mark Richards (POP)	2,998	(2%)
1988 General		
Marge Roukema (R)	175,562	(76%)
Lee Monaco (D)	54,828	(24%)

Previous Winning Percentages: **1986** (75%) **1984** (71%) **1982** (65%) **1980** (51%)

District Vote For President

	1988	1984	1980	1976
D	73,330 (33%)	75,000 (29%)	67,719 (27%)	88,261 (35%)
R	146,095 (66%)	182,030 (71%)	150,854 (61%)	163,146 (64%)
I			24,589 (10%)	

Campaign Finance

	Receipts	Receipts from PACs	Expend-itures
1990			
Roukema (R)	$446,589	$219,068 (49%)	$443,540
1988			
Roukema (R)	$406,465	$181,513 (45%)	$400,555
Monaco (D)	$28,134	$1,280 (5%)	$28,137

Key Votes

1991	
Authorize use of force against Iraq	Y
1990	
Support constitutional amendment on flag desecration	Y
Pass family and medical leave bill over Bush veto	Y
Reduce SDI funding	Y
Allow abortions in overseas military facilities	Y
Approve budget summit plan for spending and taxing	N
Approve civil rights bill	Y
1989	
Halt production of B-2 stealth bomber at 13 planes	Y
Oppose capital gains tax cut	N
Approve federal abortion funding in rape or incest cases	Y
Approve pay raise and revision of ethics rules	Y
Pass Democratic minimum wage plan over Bush veto	N

Voting Studies

	Presidential Support		Party Unity		Conservative Coalition	
Year	**S**	**O**	**S**	**O**	**S**	**O**
1990	45	45	58	32	63	24
1989	53	42	60	37	68	29
1988	42	55	68	28	79	21
1987	45	51	61	36	70	28
1986	56	43	62	26	64	36
1985	49	50	56	41	60	40
1984	51	45	57	38	56	42
1983	61	35	49	47	47	51
1982	62	34	57	39	60	37
1981	66	32	70	29	56	41

Interest Group Ratings

Year	ADA	ACU	AFL-CIO	CCUS
1990	28	59	42	58
1989	30	57	33	90
1988	40	50	79	69
1987	36	52	38	87
1986	30	36	43	78
1985	45	40	29	68
1984	45	36	15	63
1983	40	30	18	80
1982	50	41	30	68
1981	35	80	27	89

6 Bernard J. Dwyer (D)

Of Edison — Elected 1980

Born: Jan. 24, 1921, Perth Amboy, N.J.
Education: Attended Rutgers U.
Military Service: Navy, 1940-45.
Occupation: Insurance salesman and executive.
Family: Wife, Lilyan Sudzina; one child.
Religion: Roman Catholic.
Political Career: Edison Township Council, 1958-69; mayor of Edison, 1969-73; N.J. Senate, 1974-80, majority leader, 1980.
Capitol Office: 2428 Rayburn Bldg. 20515; 225-6301.

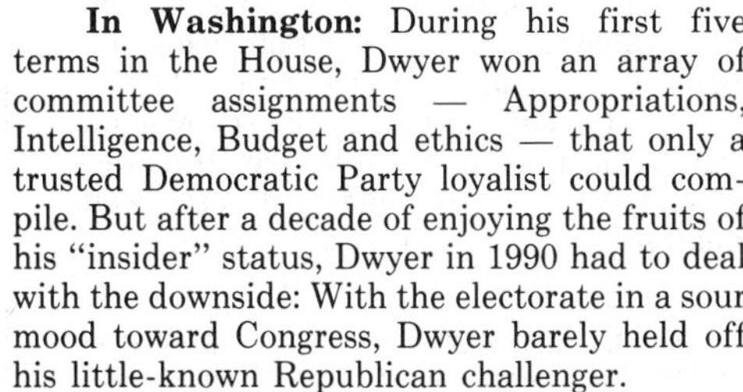

In Washington: During his first five terms in the House, Dwyer won an array of committee assignments — Appropriations, Intelligence, Budget and ethics — that only a trusted Democratic Party loyalist could compile. But after a decade of enjoying the fruits of his "insider" status, Dwyer in 1990 had to deal with the downside: With the electorate in a sour mood toward Congress, Dwyer barely held off his little-known Republican challenger.

This tough contest came at the end of the 101st Congress, a trying period for Dwyer. As a member of the ethics committee in 1989, he sat in judgment on Speaker Jim Wright and joined with one other Democrat and the committee's Republicans to approve a key charge that contributed to Wright's decision to resign. It was an ironic turn of events for Dwyer, who said then-Speaker Thomas P. O'Neill Jr. of Massachusetts appointed him to ethics in 1985 because "I have no reservations about saying 'no comment' to the press."

When Dwyer voted against Wright, some Democrats warned of retaliation. Their threats were vacant. As a member of the Appropriations Committee, Dwyer was pretty much untouchable; when he switched off the subcommittees on Commerce, Justice and State and on Labor, Health and Human Services at the start of the 102nd Congress, seniority brought Dwyer his choice.

Dwyer surprised some colleagues by opting for the Appropriations Subcommittee on Defense. His central New Jersey district has little defense-related industry; in claiming the seat, he boxed out New York Democratic Rep. Robert J. Mrazek, whose Long Island district has a large aerospace sector. But Dwyer explained that he just wanted to be part of the key debate on defense spending priorities.

The other new assignment Dwyer chose — on the Energy and Water Subcommittee — has more direct benefits for his district. New Jersey members have tried for years to secure funding for a billion-dollar drainage tunnel to divert the waters of the flood-prone Passaic River. With Dwyer and 11th District Republican Rep. Dean A. Gallo both joining up, the nine-member energy and water panel now has two members from the Passaic River Valley.

Though he has rotated off ethics and Intelligence, Dwyer remains on Budget. While widely regarded as politically astute, Dwyer is so low-key that his legislative tracks are invisible to all but his closest colleagues.

Dwyer's vote remains one of the most reliable for the Democratic leadership. During the 101st Congress, as through most of his tenure, Dwyer voted with the majority of Democrats on nearly 90 percent of House votes.

At Home: Dwyer is one of the older junior members of the House. First elected at age 59, he turned 70 in January 1991.

Dwyer was known during his tenure in the New Jersey Senate as a legislative tactician who avoided the public spotlight. In his 1980 campaign to succeed Democratic Rep. Edward J. Patten, Dwyer ran with a confidence born of solid party support, particularly in Middlesex County with its powerful Democratic organization.

Dwyer's work as a state legislator also helped him win endorsements from leading district newspapers. He defeated four other primary contenders, and won 53 percent of the general-election vote.

Dwyer had little trouble in his first reelection campaign. He slipped under 60 percent in 1984, but in the next two contests he won with greater comfort, even as he spent modestly on his campaigns (about $120,000 in 1986 and the same amount in 1988).

The relative ease of his wins in those years may have contributed to his surprise in 1990. Running on a shoestring, Republican real estate agent Paul Danielczyk nonetheless whipped up voter anger toward Congress over the federal budget mess and toward Democrats in New Jersey. (Democratic Gov. James J. Florio had pushed through a massive state tax increase in 1989.) Dwyer hung on with just 51 percent of the vote, edging Danielczyk by 5,487 votes.

New Jersey 6

Central — New Brunswick; Perth Amboy

Exxon's giant Bayway refinery, with its flaring gas and oppressive stench, is responsible for much of New Jersey's image problem. Travelers seeing the refinery from the turnpike wonder why anyone would live near it. But thousands of the 6th's voters do. They are predominantly white ethnics and Hispanics, many of them within sight and smell of the refinery complex.

The 6th extends for miles beyond the refinery and the turnpike. Covering most of industrial Middlesex County, it traditionally has favored Democrats, whose organization is one of the few strong county machines left in the state. In his 1988 re-election bid, Democratic Sen. Frank R. Lautenberg carried the 6th with 56 percent.

The 1988 county results for president indicate that those Democratic tendencies no longer apply at the top of the ticket. George Bush took Middlesex with 57 percent, nearly matching President Ronald Reagan's 59 percent four years earlier. But the more exurban sections of Middlesex are in the 4th and 12th districts; the sections in the 6th, closest to New York City, are more industrial, have more minority-group residents, and are more dependably Democratic.

Middlesex is a place where heavy things are made. The closer one gets to the Arthur Kill, separating New Jersey and Staten Island, the heavier and dirtier the industry becomes. Bleak Perth Amboy, over 40 percent Hispanic, illustrates the economic problems troubling this industrial belt. A Canadian company opened a steel plant there in 1977, but ensuing layoffs dashed hopes that it would spark a resurgence.

The presence of Rutgers University and a one-quarter black population keep New Brunswick reliably Democratic. Though parts of the city are faded, Johnson & Johnson led an effort to revitalize New Brunswick several years ago by building its new headquarters in the middle of downtown.

Population: 526,075. White 459,480 (87%), Black 44,718 (9%), Other 8,690 (2%). Spanish origin 34,643 (7%). 18 and over 394,413 (75%), 65 and over 51,841 (10%). Median age: 31.

Committees

Appropriations (23rd of 37 Democrats)
Defense; Energy & Water Development

Budget (11th of 23 Democrats)
Budget Process, Reconciliation & Enforcement; Community Development & Natural Resources

Elections

1990 General		
Bernard J. Dwyer (D)	63,696	(51%)
Paul Danielczyk (R)	58,209	(46%)
Randolph Waller (POP)	2,364	(2%)
Howard Schoen (LIBERT)	1,784	(1%)
1990 Primary		
Bernard J. Dwyer (D)	22,440	(88%)
Sebastian Del Duca (D)	2,994	(12%)
1988 General		
Bernard J. Dwyer (D)	120,125	(61%)
Peter J. Sica (R)	74,824	(38%)

Previous Winning Percentages: **1986** (69%) **1984** (56%) **1982** (68%) **1980** (53%)

District Vote For President

	1988		1984		1980		1976	
D	100,931	(47%)	94,024	(41%)	90,536	(42%)	110,702	(52%)
R	115,055	(53%)	135,654	(59%)	105,490	(49%)	97,129	(46%)
I					14,110	(7%)		

Campaign Finance

	Receipts	Receipts from PACs		Expend-itures
1990				
Dwyer (D)	$146,908	$125,747	(86%)	$147,925
Danielczyk (R)	$8,987	$800	(9%)	$8,887
1988				
Dwyer (D)	$136,330	$113,000	(83%)	$123,632
Sica (R)	$39,483	0		$38,919

Key Votes

1991	
Authorize use of force against Iraq	N
1990	
Support constitutional amendment on flag desecration	N
Pass family and medical leave bill over Bush veto	Y
Reduce SDI funding	Y
Allow abortions in overseas military facilities	Y
Approve budget summit plan for spending and taxing	N
Approve civil rights bill	Y
1989	
Halt production of B-2 stealth bomber at 13 planes	N
Oppose capital gains tax cut	Y
Approve federal abortion funding in rape or incest cases	Y
Approve pay raise and revision of ethics rules	Y
Pass Democratic minimum wage plan over Bush veto	Y

Voting Studies

	Presidential Support		Party Unity		Conservative Coalition	
Year	**S**	**O**	**S**	**O**	**S**	**O**
1990	19	73	87	5	24	69
1989	34	63	91	3	37	63
1988	21	75	92	7	32	66
1987	19	77	90	4	35	60
1986	19	80	95	3	22	78
1985	25	75	97	2	18	82
1984	37	60	91	7	24	75
1983	22	76	93	4	17	82
1982	39	57	94	5	22	78
1981	41	57	93	5	16	83

Interest Group Ratings

Year	ADA	ACU	AFL-CIO	CCUS
1990	83	9	100	31
1989	80	0	92	40
1988	85	4	100	31
1987	84	0	100	7
1986	80	9	100	22
1985	80	0	100	23
1984	75	13	92	38
1983	85	9	100	25
1982	90	0	90	27
1981	75	7	93	22

7 Matthew J. Rinaldo (R)

Of Union — Elected 1972

Born: Sept. 1, 1931, Elizabeth, N.J.
Education: Rutgers U., B.S. 1953; Seton Hall U., M.B.A. 1959; New York U., D.P.A. 1979.
Occupation: Industrial relations consultant.
Family: Single.
Religion: Roman Catholic.
Political Career: Union County Board of Freeholders, 1963-64; N.J. Senate, 1968-72.
Capitol Office: 2469 Rayburn Bldg. 20515; 225-5361.

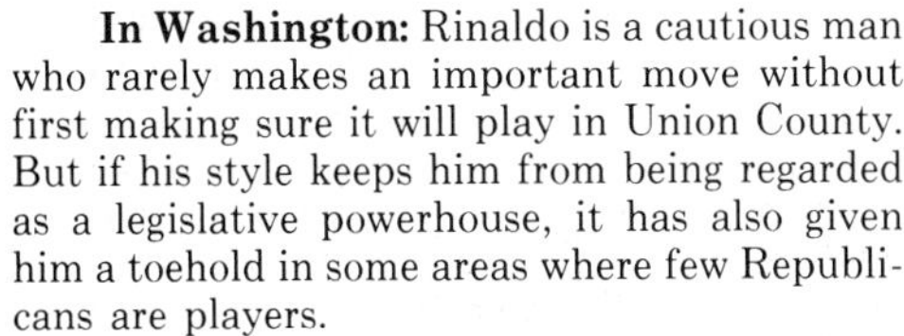

In Washington: Rinaldo is a cautious man who rarely makes an important move without first making sure it will play in Union County. But if his style keeps him from being regarded as a legislative powerhouse, it has also given him a toehold in some areas where few Republicans are players.

Rinaldo's "New Jersey first" record — more often than not requiring him to vote against a majority of GOP House members — has helped him build a strong following in his district's urban Democratic areas. And his willingness to work with Democrats has made him a relatively productive member of the Energy and Commerce Committee, where less yielding Republicans are confined to mere nay-saying.

Unlike some other moderate Republicans, Rinaldo has had scant criticism within the GOP for his renegade record. His state party has embraced moderates, and in Congress, Rinaldo's insistence that he is just "voting New Jersey" gives him cover with most GOP partisans. However, his penchant for keeping his options open sometimes frustrates colleagues looking for a commitment from him.

In the 101st Congress, Rinaldo's New Jersey-related proposals included efforts to study noise generated by the Newark and New York City airports, and to revise the 67-year-old National Butter Act, aiding a state dairy company that produced a low-fat "butter."

When he does turn to national concerns, Rinaldo has done his most significant legislating on the Commerce Subcommittee on Telecommunications and Finance, where he is ranking member. His moderate views on government regulation of the securities industry allow him to work comfortably with Chairman Edward J. Markey on most issues.

In the wake of 1980s insider-trading scandals on Wall Street, Rinaldo shared the majority view that stronger enforcement and stiffer penalties were needed to prevent abuses by those with non-public information. He was among the sponsors of legislation to put new demands on firms to police the activities of their employees. Congress enacted this concept as well as language that Rinaldo advocated to commission a special study of federal securities laws to determine what changes could be made to protect stock market investors.

During the 101st Congress, he and Markey cosponsored legislation to strengthen the authority of the Securities and Exchange Commission, including its regulation of program trading. Rinaldo noted that small investors perceived the market as rigged and "unless you're part of the inside crowd, you're better off going to Atlantic City." A weaker version of their proposal eventually became law.

Rinaldo also worked with Markey in the ongoing effort to re-regulate portions of the cable television industry, and to limit unwanted telephone and fax solicitations.

Rinaldo is far more responsive to the interests of organized labor than the average Republican. He typically earns high rankings from the AFL-CIO; in 1988 he scored a perfect 100 on the organization's legislative scorecard.

In 1989, Rinaldo backed an unsuccessful attempt to override Bush's veto of a Democratic-backed proposal to increase the minimum wage. The next year, Rinaldo voted to overturn Bush's veto of the Family and Medical Leave Act, and he supported assistance for workers who would lose their jobs due to provisions in the bill reauthorizing the Clean Air Act.

When the 100th Congress took up the omnibus trade bill, Rinaldo was one of only 29 Republicans to vote against eliminating language requiring companies to give advance notice of plant closings. He joined even fewer Republicans in backing the Gephardt "fair trade" amendment, seeking to mandate retaliatory tariffs against countries with unfair trade practices; it did not survive.

Trade issues have helped earn Rinaldo media attention at home. In 1988, he invited a top Japanese diplomat to appear on his cable TV show to discuss trade, and then spent much of the 30-minute broadcast berating the official. This prompted an angry phone call from the Japanese Embassy to Rinaldo's office, but no apology.

New Jersey 7

North and Central — Elizabeth

Anchored by blue-collar Elizabeth and Plainfield, the 7th is a district Democrats have every reason to covet. But votes from the suburbs outside those two grimy industrial cities make it difficult for Democratic candidates to win.

Elizabeth found its place on the 19th-century industrial map as a manufacturing town for Singer Sewing Machines, and it became an ethnic, working-class city. Today, it retains an ethnic diversity reinforced by an infusion of blacks and Hispanics. It casts a fifth of the district vote, and in most elections is heavily Democratic.

The petrochemical industry and heavy manufacturing make Elizabeth a dingy place famous for toxic-waste problems. The city is run by Democratic Mayor Tom Dunn, known for his willingness to deal with Rinaldo and other GOP politicians.

In the southwest corner of Union County is predominantly black Plainfield, which was the first of New Jersey's cities to explode in the summer of 1967. The city has recently mounted a major effort to rehabilitate its decaying areas.

Clustered between Elizabeth and Plainfield in northern Union County are mostly Republican, suburban towns such as Summit, Westfield and Cranford. This is an area of bedroom communities for Newark and New York. Liberal young professionals here frequently prefer Democrats for local office, but at the national level, the towns anchor the 7th's GOP vote.

For the most part, the Somerset County portion of the 7th is equally Republican. Nestled against the Watchung Mountains, affluent towns such as Watchung, Warren and Bridgewater Township give Democratic candidates scarcely a glance. The industrial boroughs to the south, however, Bound Brook and Manville, often join Elizabeth and Plainfield in voting Democratic.

Johns-Manville not only gave Manville borough its name, but also provided thousands of jobs for the Slavic immigrants who settled there. The company was forced to file for bankruptcy in 1982, though, after being hit with tens of thousands of asbestos-related lawsuits. Three years later, the Manville plant closed down.

Population: 526,076. White 449,916 (86%), Black 58,922 (11%), Other 7,084 (1%). Spanish origin 38,374 (7%). 18 and over 393,910 (75%), 65 and over 64,042 (12%). Median age: 35.

During the Telecommunications Subcommittee debate on children's television — which critics say has declined in quality and quantity in the 1980s — it was Rinaldo who found the middle ground between those seeking to mandate one hour of children's educational programming per day and those wanting a temporary suspension of antitrust laws to allow broadcasters and advertisers to consider the issue on their own. Rinaldo's compromise plan, which cleared both the House and Senate, capped advertising time during children's programs. The bill was vetoed by President Reagan, but similar legislation became law in the 101st Congress.

Rinaldo often sides with environmentalist Democrats on Energy and Commerce. He introduced his own legislation to restrict acid-rain pollution, and has pushed to have acid-rain controls and the "superfund" toxic-waste cleanup program included in the platform of the national Republican Party.

In addition to his duties on Energy and Commerce, Rinaldo serves as ranking Republican on the Select Aging Committee. He has long advocated establishing the Social Security Administration as a separate entity outside the Department of Health and Human Services, and he wants to establish a public-private partnership to provide long-term health care insurance for the elderly.

At Home: Rinaldo is a traditional big-city neighborhood politician, and that helps explain his success in Union County's blue-collar bastions such as Elizabeth. Even though the 7th was drawn to be a Democratic district in 1982, he carried it handily against an aggressive, high-spending Democrat. Rinaldo then benefited from another remap before the 1984 election, which favored the GOP.

The ever-watchful Rinaldo seldom fails to make the rounds of weddings and testimonial dinners in his district, stroking the labor leaders who have political influence. He receives quiet help from Elizabeth Mayor Tom Dunn, a sympathetic Democrat who in 1984 backed Ronald Reagan for re-election, and while the Union County GOP organization is more conservative than Rinaldo, it has always been supportive.

Because of his reputation as a Republican who attracts Democrats, Rinaldo used to be mentioned as a possible candidate for governor or senator. But Rinaldo has bypassed several chances to go for statewide office.

Rinaldo guaranteed himself a place in the hearts of the state GOP leadership in 1982. A congressional map drawn by the Democratic Legislature threw his hometown of Union into the 12th District, a much safer Republican constituency than the 7th. Rinaldo agreed to run in the 7th as a favor to two other GOP incumbents, Jim Courter and Marge Roukema. Rinaldo's decision freed the 12th for Courter, and left Roukema alone and secure in the 5th.

By that act of generosity, Rinaldo also guaranteed himself a tough re-election campaign. Adam K. Levin, former state consumer affairs director, had helped mold the new 7th with himself in mind as its congressman. The son of a multimillionaire shopping center developer, Levin had given copiously from his inherited wealth to the campaigns of Democratic legislators, and they remembered his gifts when drawing the congressional map.

Levin had made a first try in 1974 at age 25, but Rinaldo crushed him. It was clear from the beginning, however, that the second challenge was serious. The Democrat threw Rinaldo on the defensive with repeated personal attacks. Television ads lambasted Rinaldo for junketeering and accused him of being an ineffective legislator.

Far behind his challenger in campaign funds (one of the few incumbents in the country who was), Rinaldo did not run TV spots. He retaliated by taking full advantage of his incumbency, deluging the new parts of the district with franked mailings, a batch of press releases and a mobile constituent-service van.

Rinaldo also benefited in Elizabeth from the help of Dunn, who disliked Levin. The Republican's longstanding support of union-backed legislation brought him endorsements from groups normally kind to Democratic candidates, including the New Jersey AFL-CIO. In the end, Levin managed to win only the liberal Mercer County portion of the 7th. Rinaldo won with 56 percent.

Running within more favorable lines since the court-ordered second redistricting prior to his 1984 contest, Rinaldo has returned to his normal landslide margins. In the presidential years of 1984 and 1988, he won by better than 100,000 votes. His campaign treasury is well-stocked for 1992, when redistricting may again give him less-hospitable territory.

Committees

Select Aging (Ranking)
Health & Long-Term Care

Energy & Commerce (3rd of 16 Republicans)
Telecommunications & Finance (ranking); Transportation & Hazardous Materials

Elections

1990 General		
Matthew J. Rinaldo (R)	100,274	(75%)
Bruce H. Bergen (D)	31,114	(23%)
Thomas V. Sarnowski (POP)	2,929	(2%)
1988 General		
Matthew J. Rinaldo (R)	153,350	(75%)
James Hely (D)	52,189	(25%)

Previous Winning Percentages: **1986** (79%) **1984** (74%) **1982** (56%) **1980** (77%) **1978** (73%) **1976** (73%) **1974** (65%) **1972** (64%)

District Vote For President

	1988		1984		1980		1976	
D	90,584	(41%)	88,874	(37%)	82,436	(36%)	87,131	(42%)
R	132,211	(59%)	151,973	(63%)	126,362	(55%)	116,182	(56%)
I					18,650	(8%)		

Campaign Finance

	Receipts	Receipts from PACs		Expend-itures
1990				
Rinaldo (R)	$626,502	$240,920	(38%)	$405,355
1988				
Rinaldo (R)	$607,728	$271,527	(45%)	$370,387

Key Votes

1991	
Authorize use of force against Iraq	Y
1990	
Support constitutional amendment on flag desecration	Y
Pass family and medical leave bill over Bush veto	Y
Reduce SDI funding	N
Allow abortions in overseas military facilities	N
Approve budget summit plan for spending and taxing	N
Approve civil rights bill	Y
1989	
Halt production of B-2 stealth bomber at 13 planes	N
Oppose capital gains tax cut	N
Approve federal abortion funding in rape or incest cases	N
Approve pay raise and revision of ethics rules	Y
Pass Democratic minimum wage plan over Bush veto	Y

Voting Studies

	Presidential Support		Party Unity		Conservative Coalition	
Year	S	O	S	O	S	O
1990	47	51	46	51	63	37
1989	55	42	39	59	71	27
1988	48	51	44	54	71	29
1987	41	59	40	57	65	35
1986	40	58	34	63	60	40
1985	50	45	43	51	71	29
1984	50	49	42	54	54	44
1983	46	51	36	61	53	44
1982	45	49	26	71	41	58
1981	63	33	58	39	71	28

Interest Group Ratings

Year	ADA	ACU	AFL-CIO	CCUS
1990	50	46	67	54
1989	45	56	83	60
1988	45	54	100	36
1987	56	39	88	47
1986	45	55	100	28
1985	55	52	81	41
1984	45	41	92	64
1983	65	41	82	21
1982	60	36	95	38
1981	20	71	47	84

8 Robert A. Roe (D)

Of West Wayne — Elected 1969

Born: Feb. 28, 1924, Wayne, N.J.

Education: Attended Oregon State U. and Washington State U.

Military Service: Army, 1943-46.

Occupation: Construction company owner; engineer.

Family: Single.

Religion: Roman Catholic.

Political Career: Wayne Township mayor, 1956-61; Passaic County freeholder, 1959-63; sought Democratic nomination for governor, 1977, 1981.

Capitol Office: 2243 Rayburn Bldg. 20515; 225-5751.

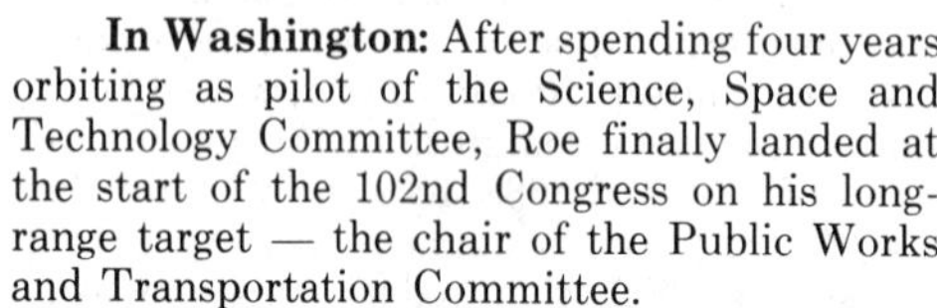

In Washington: After spending four years orbiting as pilot of the Science, Space and Technology Committee, Roe finally landed at the start of the 102nd Congress on his long-range target — the chair of the Public Works and Transportation Committee.

When Public Works Chairman Glenn M. Anderson was felled in a coup by younger committee members, Roe — the second-ranking Democrat — managed to cash in enough chits to hold off a bid by Norman Y. Mineta to buck the seniority system. "Everybody I looked at [for support], I think, either had a bridge or a highway or a railroad or something we worked with them on," said Roe.

It is that kind of horse-trading savvy that should make Roe an ideal leader for Public Works, where he will be able to give free rein to his renowned dogged attention to detail and his almost single-minded crusader's drive to, as he says, spread public works "from the sewers to the stars."

Still, Roe's performance on the Science Committee left some lingering questions. Some members criticized Roe's inability to juggle several issues at once and his preoccupation with Public Works. "I always felt he was in a holding pattern," said New York Republican Sherwood Boehlert, who serves on both the Science and Public Works panels. "He was thrust into the chairmanship of a committee in which he was not actively involved."

During Roe's tenure, the Science Committee became increasingly irrelevant in driving space policy. Roe occasionally won battles with the Appropriations Committee on isolated issues — such as allocations for the proposed National Aerospace Plane and the manned space station. But his committee's authorization bill usually arrived too late to matter in the annual appropriations process, where real decisions on NASA's budget are made.

Roe defended his leadership, blaming the committee's decline in part on the year-to-year budget process, which gives Appropriations more clout. Roe lobbied to have the space agency's biggest projects authorized on a multiyear basis, a move he felt would increase the committee's power over NASA. But he received little cooperation from his panel's counterpart in the Senate, the Commerce, Science and Transportation Committee.

Roe's insistence on changing the budget process, over the objections of Sen. Ernest F. Hollings (chairman of the Senate panel), appeared to doom a bill reauthorizing the space agency. Finally, an 11th-hour compromise on Congress' last day in 1988 authorized $11 billion for fiscal 1989 only. Roe did win a three-year, $6 billion commitment to the space station and agreement that NASA would submit a long-term plan.

On some individual Science Committee projects, Roe showed signs of being fully capable of wielding the kind of pork-barrel trading last demonstrated on Public Works by former Chairman James J. Howard, Roe's longtime ally from New Jersey. For example, when Texans thought they had Roe in their camp on funding for the superconducting super collider (SSC) in 1989, he threatened to block the project until he was dealt a $25 million grant for magnetic research fusion, most of which would take place at Princeton Universty.

Moreover, he quickly gave notice at the start of the 102nd Congress of his intent to be more aggressive than Anderson in protecting his new committee's turf. Roe managed to excise several provisions from an emergency appropriations bill for Operation Desert Storm after arguing to the Rules Committee that he had not been consulted first.

Roe's ascension to Public Works came at a crucial time; Congress in 1991 began considering a huge highway and mass transit authorization bill that would set the nation's transportation policy in the wake of completion of the Interstate highway system. Roe early on voiced suspicions of the Bush administration's proposal to wean Congress from the most expan-

New Jersey 8

North — Paterson

To Alexander Hamilton, the Great Falls of the Passaic River was an ideal location for a factory town. Then Treasury secretary, he set up the Society for Establishing Useful Manufactures in 1791 to build Paterson.

In time, the thriving "Silk City" became one of the world's leading textile producers, attracting Irish, Polish, Italian and Russian craftsmen to work the looms; Paterson was once the nation's leading silk producer. The city also played out a history of labor strife and strong unions whose influence lives on.

During the 1960s and '70s, though, Paterson tumbled into a sharp industrial decline which left a trail of unemployment and poverty, particularly among the blacks and Hispanics who now make up the majority of the city's population. Racial tensions also were palpable, particularly after the controversial 1967 case in which black boxer Rubin "Hurricane" Carter was found guilty for the murders of three white patrons in a local tavern.

During the last several years, Paterson's situation has stabilized somewhat; unemployment rates fell below double digits and population increased by 2 percent in the 1980s. Paterson still contains 25 percent of the district's electorate, and it is firmly Democratic. Passaic County suburbs such as Clifton, Totowa and West Paterson are where the white ethnics went when they fled the city. Down the Passaic River lies the city of Passaic, a smaller but equally troubled version of Paterson, whose textile jobs also have evaporated. Its public school system is more than 90 percent non-white.

To the north, the district is more Republican. Wayne Township houses the headquarters of American Cyanamid. Its white, middle-class subdivisions usually vote Republican but have made an exception for favorite-son Roe. The affluent Franklin Lakes area, which is rock-solid GOP, is the sole outpost of upper-crust Bergen County in the 8th.

The 8th also reaches into Essex County, where it picks up the politically mixed older suburbs of Montclair and Nutley. Affluent Montclair, with its mansions built as summer places by the 19th-century New York rich, blends quiet, tree-shaded streets and large frame houses with more modest homes and neighborhoods; the ethnic and class mix makes it more competitive politically than some of the other suburban territory in the 8th. With the Oranges, Montclair is a center of Essex Democrats' liberal wing.

Population: 526,087. White 415,905 (79%), Black 72,054 (14%), Other 7,900 (2%). Spanish origin 64,546 (12%). 18 and over 390,558 (74%), 65 and over 67,534 (13%). Median age: 33.

sive and expensive public works project in world history by emphasizing repair and gridlock relief rather than new projects.

In just his second year as Science chairman, Roe was the subject of speculation among Public Works Democrats who hoped he would leave the chair to head Public Works. But Roe, loyal to Anderson and House tradition, urged his junior colleagues to give the unassertive Anderson a chance. After Anderson failed to show improvement, Roe asserted his right to the job when the dethroning became imminent in late 1990.

While on Science, Roe began mastering the agencies' wish lists, and supporting most of the big-ticket items — the space station, space shuttles, overhaul of the nation's research labs and the SSC. Roe was accused by some of spreading a limited budget too thinly rather than choosing priorities. But just as with water projects, Roe took an apocalyptic view that the nation cannot afford not to invest in space.

"The greatest threat facing this nation, short of nuclear war," he once said as Water Resources chairman, "is the destruction and poisoning of our water supply."

A bachelor who has called a motel room his home during two decades in Washington, Roe works long stretches of 16-hour days. He takes an almost pedagogical approach to his panel, referring to himself as "the chairman" or "we," insisting that members and witnesses stick to defined themes, summing up testimony and dismissing what he considers errant points. But he is responsive to his members, accommodating their requests for projects at home. He jealously guards his turf, and his strategy. Roe can be counted on to resist compromise until the last minute, a tactic that has not always been a winning one.

Above all, he does not tolerate the words commonly used to describe his work. "They use the word pork barrel and they use the word boondoggle," he complained in 1987. "The boondoggle is if you do not get it in your own state."

Roe hews to his party's New Deal tradition, viewing public works as an economic boost and a force for progressive change. Pinched by deficit concerns, Roe has been able to carry on partly due to the changing nature of public works. While he chaired the Water Resources Subcommittee, the sewers and toxic-waste cleanups he espoused were popularly defensible as environmental programs against foes, including President Reagan, who cried "pork." At Science, projects fit the vogue for high technology and international competitiveness.

In his first Congress as chairman, Roe oversaw NASA's revival of the space shuttle program. In 1986, he had presided over the panel's investigation of the Challenger explosion, and cast himself as the tough customer in a company town. "Congress and NASA must begin a new era," he said, "one in which Congress must apply the same strong oversight to NASA that it does to any other government agency." He is intent on instituting multi-year budgeting for NASA.

A last-minute compromise also cleared a bill Roe favored that limited private launch firms' liability in case of major accidents. It was a victory for the fledgling rocket industry, which Roe wants to promote. But he had held the bill hostage until he was sure the industry would not try to attach a provision blocking a U.S.-China deal to launch three private U.S. satellites on Chinese rockets. Roe supported the deal on diplomatic, economic and scientific grounds. When Sen. Jesse Helms, a China foe, tried to kill the deal with an amendment to a foreign aid bill, Roe worked feverishly to scrap Helms' amendment in the House. It was rejected by an overwhelming 23-234 vote.

In the 100th Congress, Roe's committee was the source of one controversial measure that proved beyond his control. Republican Robert S. Walker amended bills for two science agencies with proposals to cut funding to departments and contractors not free of drugs in the work place. Roe could have killed the proposal outright but, accustomed to bipartisanship on his committees, he delayed debate, thinking Walker could be placated. Instead, the panel was stalemated for weeks, more bills were snagged and two rival committees demanded to review bills Walker amended. Roe redrafted the amendment to escape others' jurisdiction, but House leaders stepped in to engineer a final compromise with Walker, defusing the drug issue without threatening hundreds of federal contractors. As Water Resources chairman from 1981-87, Roe teamed with Howard to emphasize urban water systems rather than the flood control and irrigation projects that traditionally had priority when rural Southerners and Westerners ran the panel. But both men were more than willing to satisfy farm-state colleagues to build support for their own legislative goals.

Roe presided over some $50 billion in federal largess, playing a lead role in twice extending the Clean Water Act, in 1982 and 1987, and in passing a landmark water-projects bill and a "superfund" hazardous-waste cleanup bill in 1986. The hundreds of projects in those measures probably reached every district. The 1987 Clean Water Act became law over Reagan's veto because Republicans and Democrats alike had a stake in its anti-pollution projects.

Though supportive of environmentalists, Roe often collided with them owing to his advocacy of various dams and dredging projects. But in the 99th Congress, he emerged as their darling in the effort to renew superfund.

After James J. Florio, his former rival for the New Jersey governorship, failed to win the Energy and Commerce Committee's approval of a measure strong enough for environmentalists to support, Roe and Howard pushed a bill more to their liking through Public Works. Voters in New Jersey were passionate on the issue because the state had more superfund sites than any other. The two committees eventually compromised, but environmentalists got much of what they wanted.

At Home: Pork-barrel politics, by whatever name, endear Roe to his constituents, especially to the labor unions that benefit from the jobs his programs have created.

Thanks to his work, Roe's district has received a large number of new town halls, fire stations and other structures that have generated construction employment. He also has secured grants to rescue a plant and to restore Paterson's historic Great Falls area.

Passaic County was Roe's base for forays into statewide politics, but it was not enough to bring him his goal — the Democratic nomination for governor. New Jersey chooses its governors in off years, so House members can seek the Statehouse without giving up their places in Washington.

Roe tried twice. In 1977 he ran a strong primary race against incumbent Brendan T. Byrne, coming within 40,000 votes of an upset. That showing made him a front-runner in 1981, when his main competition was fellow Rep. Florio.

But Florio defeated Roe easily. Roe had refused public financing and tried to make an issue of the state's public-financing system. The strategy never caught on, and he was left underfunded. Florio, who accepted public financing and was also better on television than Roe, took the nomination by more than 150,000 votes. (Florio went on to lose to Republican Thomas H. Kean in New Jersey's closest gubernatorial election ever.)

Since that defeat, Roe has avoided statewide politics. Given his new prominence as Science chairman and dean of New Jersey's delegation, he seems content to stay in the House. In 1989, he was campaign chairman for his former rival, Florio, who won easily in his third attempt to become governor.

Roe's dominance in Passaic has never been seriously threatened. He was long known as a peacemaker for various local Democratic factions, presiding over conclaves at Paterson's Brownstone House restaurant. He also gained a foothold in Republican towns, supplementing his usual big margins in blue-collar Democratic bastions. In 1988, Roe ran without GOP opposition for the first time.

Part of the reason for Roe's appeal in the Republican suburbs may be that he is not a product of Paterson, the district's biggest town and a home of organization politics. He is from suburban Wayne Township, which swings between the two parties. Roe boasts that he knows all levels of government, having served at each — city, county, state and federal.

He won his House seat in a tight 1969 special election to replace Democrat Charles S. Joelson, who became a state judge. Since then, he has always won re-election with more than 60 percent of the vote.

In 1990, though, Florio had gone from revered to reviled after he pushed through a $2.8 billion tax increase. Roe was fortunate not to have a Republican opponent, but he still lost 23 percent of the vote to two third-party candidates.

Committees

Public Works & Transportation (Chairman)

Select Aging (36th of 42 Democrats)
Housing & Consumer Interests; Social Security and Women

Elections

1990 General		
Robert A. Roe (D)	55,212	(77%)
Stephen Sibilia (I-C)	13,239	(18%)
Bruce Eden (POP)	3,347	(5%)
1990 Primary		
Robert A. Roe (D)	11,559	(80%)
Edward S. Hochman (D)	2,955	(20%)
1988 General		
Robert A. Roe (D)	96,036	(100%)

Previous Winning Percentages: **1986** (63%) **1984** (63%) **1982** (71%) **1980** (67%) **1978** (75%) **1976** (71%) **1974** (74%) **1972** (63%) **1970** (61%) **1969 *** (49%)

** Special election.*

District Vote For President

	1988	1984	1980	1976
D	94,329 (44%)	89,625 (42%)	74,286 (40%)	89,494 (47%)
R	121,172 (56%)	121,422 (58%)	93,766 (51%)	96,428 (50%)
I			13,667 (7%)	

Campaign Finance

	Receipts	Receipts from PACs	Expend-itures
1990			
Roe (D)	$651,952	$329,910 (51%)	$558,625
1988			
Roe (D)	$490,884	$273,100 (56%)	$267,609

Key Votes

1991	
Authorize use of force against Iraq	N
1990	
Support constitutional amendment on flag desecration	Y
Pass family and medical leave bill over Bush veto	Y
Reduce SDI funding	Y
Allow abortions in overseas military facilities	N
Approve budget summit plan for spending and taxing	N
Approve civil rights bill	Y
1989	
Halt production of B-2 stealth bomber at 13 planes	N
Oppose capital gains tax cut	N
Approve federal abortion funding in rape or incest cases	?
Approve pay raise and revision of ethics rules	Y
Pass Democratic minimum wage plan over Bush veto	Y

Voting Studies

	Presidential Support		Party Unity		Conservative Coalition	
Year	**S**	**O**	**S**	**O**	**S**	**O**
1990	27	71	86	9	41	50
1989	35	48	77	11	44	44
1988	29	66	84	8	50	47
1987	22	74	83	5	49	44
1986	22	77	89	6	28	68
1985	18	76	89	6	24	73
1984	34	59	86	8	29	61
1983	24	72	87	9	26	71
1982	35	60	83	12	33	66
1981	39	39	70	16	36	51

Interest Group Ratings

Year	ADA	ACU	AFL-CIO	CCUS
1990	67	18	92	36
1989	65	25	83	44
1988	70	13	100	21
1987	80	9	93	23
1986	75	10	100	18
1985	75	11	94	29
1984	70	4	85	38
1983	80	13	100	21
1982	75	23	90	55
1981	60	8	100	17

9 Robert G. Torricelli (D)

Of Englewood — Elected 1982

Born: Aug. 26, 1951, Paterson, N.J.
Education: Rutgers U., A.B. 1974, J.D. 1977; Harvard U., M.P.A. 1980.
Occupation: Lawyer.
Family: Divorced.
Religion: Methodist.
Political Career: No previous office.
Capitol Office: 317 Cannon Bldg. 20515; 225-5061.

In Washington: Torricelli's brash self-assurance can be nettlesome, both to Republicans — who have been targets for his hard-hitting partisan rhetoric — and to Democrats, with whom Torricelli has broken ranks on some high-profile issues. Yet his aggressiveness and an intelligence that he clearly articulates have enabled Torricelli to muscle his way into a number of major policy debates.

As a member of the Foreign Affairs Committee, Torricelli has been a leading critic of the Central American policies of Presidents Bush and Reagan, particularly as they pertain to Nicaragua and El Salvador. (At the start of the 102nd Congress, Torricelli became chairman of the Foreign Affairs Subcommittee on Western Hemisphere Affairs.)

Yet on the climactic foreign policy issue of recent years — the decision to authorize Bush in January 1991 to use military force against Iraq — Torricelli firmly backed the president.

A longtime critic of the Iraqi regime of Saddam Hussein and — like most other Democratic liberals who favored authorizing force — a strong supporter of Israel, Torricelli worked with Democratic Rep. Stephen J. Solarz in crafting the resolution. He also managed much of the debate on the House floor for the pro-resolution forces.

"Give an answer that will be heard not simply throughout the world, but throughout the years; a message that every despot and dictator in every corner of the globe will hear," Torricelli said in urging the resolution's passage. "It is a new time of international law, with real international sanctions for those who violate the peace."

Torricelli takes a similarly unpredictable posture on the "inside Congress" issues in which he involves himself. In early 1989, he volunteered for the thankless task of acting as the House lawyer for Speaker Jim Wright, who was in the course of a futile effort to fend off charges of ethics violations. Although he had not previously been known as especially close to Wright, Torricelli so strongly defended the Speaker that some colleagues took umbrage.

Referring to George Mallick, a developer whose gifts to Wright were a focus of the investigation, Torricelli said that all members of Congress had old friends or associates who enjoyed their contact with power but had no interest in federal legislation. "You went to school with him, you met him somewhere, you worked with him one time," Torricelli said. "We all know George Mallick." Rep. John T. Myers of Indiana, the ranking Republican on the House ethics committee, responded angrily that the remark "impugns every member."

While his defense of Wright might have marked him as an ultimate leadership loyalist, he has since proved unafraid of challenging Wright's successor, Speaker Thomas S. Foley of Washington. During closed meetings of the House Democratic Caucus in 1990, Torricelli forcefully disagreed with Foley's priority of passing a House campaign finance reform bill that year. He also called for a rethinking of plans to reform congressional franking laws, stating that any cutback in mailings could hurt members from large metropolitan areas (like himself) who get little local television time.

Actions such as these burnish Torricelli's image as an independent thinker, but they may not do as much for his goal of becoming a major player in House Democratic politics. Although Torricelli openly campaigned for the post of chairman of the Democratic Congressional Campaign Committee in 1990, Foley instead cajoled an initially reluctant Vic Fazio of California to take the position.

Despite his occasional strayings, Torricelli is usually a dependable vote for the Democratic leadership. He voted with the majority of his party well over 80 percent of the time during the 101st Congress.

In May 1990, Torricelli claimed that Bush was aiming to raise taxes on the middle class and had been "intellectually dishonest" on the tax issue during his 1988 campaign. Republican Rep. Robert S. Walker of Pennsylvania objected; the presiding officer, Pennsylvania Democrat John P. Murtha, ruled that Torricelli's comment "transgresses proper debate" on

New Jersey 9

North — Fort Lee; Hackensack

The George Washington Bridge, connecting Manhattan's 181st Street and the New Jersey Palisades, is a fitting symbol for the 9th. Opened in 1931, the majestic span spurred the growth of Bergen County.

Today, the bridge's tired roadbed requires frequent commuter-vexing repairs. Similarly, the 9th's close-in suburbs are showing signs of age. Population has slumped slightly, as suburbanites push deep into New Jersey in search of more open spaces.

However, the southern part of Bergen regularly receives a temporary influx of outsiders, who come to attend sports events and concerts at the Meadowlands stadium complex. The jewel of the otherwise homely marshlands along the New Jersey Turnpike, the Meadowlands includes Giants Stadium, a state-of-the-art facility that drew both of New York City's National Football League teams, the Giants and the Jets, to New Jersey. To the chagrin of New Jersey boosters, though, the teams continue to identify themselves as "New York." There is also an indoor arena, named for former Democratic Gov. Brendan T. Byrne, and a horse-racing track.

The complex is surrounded by several working-class towns, where warehouses and truck depots predominate. But the Meadowlands development has had a salutary effect on the city of Secaucus. Once a pig-farming area whose odoriferous atmosphere made it a laughingstock, Secaucus is attracting hotels and other new housing. Hartz Mountain Corp., which is headquartered there, owns the upscale Harmon Cove condominiums, popular with Republican business people.

The area closest to the George Washington Bridge is Democratic and mainly liberal. Apartments in Fort Lee, Cliffside Park and Edgewater line the Hudson River Palisades and house younger professionals who work in New York City. Academics who teach at New Jersey colleges have an enclave in Leonia and also vote Democratic. Englewood, 40 percent black, votes Democratic.

To the west, out Route 4, are largely Democratic towns such as Lodi, Garfield and Lyndhurst. Hackensack is blue-collar and has a large black population, although the western part of the town is more affluent. Rutherford and East Rutherford are generally lower middle class, and conservative on social matters. Teaneck and Fair Lawn are heavily Jewish and Democratic.

Population: 526,066. White 478,193 (91%), Black 29,687 (6%), Other 12,466 (2%). Spanish origin 23,162 (4%). 18 and over 415,175 (79%), 65 and over 73,688 (14%). Median age: 36.

grounds of "personal abuse, innuendo or ridicule." Torricelli then modified his remark, stating, "I believe the president has committed intellectually inconsistent acts."

Torricelli can be similarly critical when he has a foreign policy dispute with the White House. In December 1989, he blasted the Bush administration's support of the right-wing leadership of El Salvador in its fight against leftist rebels, despite accusations of human rights violations by the government. "This administration has failed to grasp that the war in El Salvador is driven not by a remnant of Cold War tensions, and not by foreign church and relief workers, but by social, political and economic problems specific to that country," he said.

The Foreign Affairs forum also gives Torricelli occasion to tweak his partisan adversaries. When the scandal over arms sales to Iran broke in 1986, Torricelli recalled President Reagan's frequent accusation that Democrats were weak toward hostile nations, and said, "We now discover that the emperor has no clothes."

Torricelli is also active on the Science Committee; he chaired the Subcommittee on Transportation, Aviation and Materials in the 101st Congress. A member from the crowded Northeast transportation corridor, Torricelli supports development of a high-tech "magnetic levitation" train system and backs civilian use of the tilt-rotor aircraft (a combination airplane/helicopter) based on the military's V-22 Osprey. He also advocates federal support for research into new industrial technologies.

At Home: Torricelli entered politics with the same drive and intensity that have marked his career in Washington. As a teenager, he worked for the Bergen County Democratic organization. In college, he ran three successful campaigns for class president using a sound truck to attract voters. He went on to become an aide to Democratic Gov. Brendan T. Byrne.

After a brief stint as executive director of the New Jersey Democratic Party, Torricelli joined the staff of Vice President Walter F. Mondale. That connection got him the important job of running the 1980 Illinois primary for President Carter, whose lopsided victory over Sen. Edward M. Kennedy proved he did well.

In 1982, redistricting made the 9th District attractive to Democrats, so Torricelli moved there from his home in northern Bergen County and launched a campaign against GOP Rep. Harold Hollenbeck. A moderate Republican with labor support, Hollenbeck had survived three terms in his blue-collar constituency, but had never before faced strong opposition.

Hollenbeck played down his partisan affiliation, but he had backed President Reagan's economic plan in 1981, something Torricelli emphasized. The incumbent also suffered from his lackadaisical manner, staying in Washington while Torricelli campaigned door-to-door. Hollenbeck returned home during the October recess, but even his own staff sometimes did not know where to find him. Torricelli ended up winning only 12 of the district's 38 towns, but nearly all were among the larger ones; he won 53 percent of the overall vote.

Aided by a redistricting plan that gave him a somewhat more Democratic constituency, Torricelli did not meet much GOP opposition in 1984. In 1986, district Republicans hoped that a hot contest down the ballot, for Bergen County executive, would spur turnout and give county legislator Arthur F. Jones a chance against Torricelli. But the reverse occurred: Torricelli won with 69 percent of the vote. He took two-thirds of the vote in 1988.

Torricelli's big winning margins sparked speculation about his potential as a future statewide candidate, which the Democrat fueled by testing the waters for a 1989 campaign to succeed retiring GOP Gov. Thomas H. Kean. But by early 1989, his Democratic House colleague James J. Florio — the party's gubernatorial nominee and a narrow loser to Kean in 1981 — had established himself as the front-runner. Torricelli took himself out of the competition and strongly endorsed Florio — even writing a letter to other potential Florio foes, suggesting they stay out of the race to avoid a divisive primary.

In 1990, with voters furious at Florio for his $2.8 billion tax increase package, Torricelli slipped to 57 percent.

Committees

Foreign Affairs (9th of 28 Democrats)
Western Hemisphere Affairs (chairman); Asian & Pacific Affairs

Science, Space & Technology (11th of 32 Democrats)
Space; Technology & Competitiveness

Elections

1990 General		
Robert G. Toricelli (D)	82,736	(57%)
Peter J. Russo (R)	59,759	(41%)
Chester Grabowski (POP)	2,573	(2%)
1990 Primary		
Robert G. Torricelli (D)	12,734	(96%)
Robert Wesser (D)	486	(4%)
1988 General		
Robert G. Torricelli (D)	142,012	(67%)
Roger J. Lane (R)	68,363	(32%)

Previous Winning Percentages: **1986** (69%) **1984** (63%) **1982** (53%)

District Vote For President

	1988	1984	1980	1976
D	107,910 (46%)	103,831 (41%)	92,979 (38%)	119,853 (48%)
R	125,417 (54%)	150,514 (59%)	127,731 (52%)	127,785 (51%)
I			20,687 (9%)	

Campaign Finance

	Receipts	Receipts from PACs	Expend-itures
1990			
Torricelli (D)	$818,917	$236,389 (29%)	$495,219
Russo (R)	$34,591	$1,600 (5%)	$34,513
1988			
Torricelli (D)	$631,151	$177,488 (28%)	$403,059
Lane (R)	$59,127	$250 (0%)	$57,260

Key Votes

1991	
Authorize use of force against Iraq	Y
1990	
Support constitutional amendment on flag desecration	N
Pass family and medical leave bill over Bush veto	Y
Reduce SDI funding	?
Allow abortions in overseas military facilities	?
Approve budget summit plan for spending and taxing	N
Approve civil rights bill	Y
1989	
Halt production of B-2 stealth bomber at 13 planes	N
Oppose capital gains tax cut	Y
Approve federal abortion funding in rape or incest cases	Y
Approve pay raise and revision of ethics rules	Y
Pass Democratic minimum wage plan over Bush veto	Y

Voting Studies

	Presidential Support		Party Unity		Conservative Coalition	
Year	**S**	**O**	**S**	**O**	**S**	**O**
1990	20	65	83	8	35	57
1989	34	56	86	5	29	66
1988	23	71	88	6	39	58
1987	18	78	81	5	33	63
1986	19	74	85	7	20	68
1985	24	71	87	4	18	78
1984	31	61	76	17	31	66
1983	17	78	82	6	16	80

Interest Group Ratings

Year	ADA	ACU	AFL-CIO	CCUS
1990	83	10	100	31
1989	75	0	100	30
1988	85	4	100	25
1987	84	5	93	15
1986	70	9	100	13
1985	80	5	100	19
1984	70	13	69	31
1983	85	4	100	15

10 Donald M. Payne (D)

Of Newark — Elected 1988

Born: July 16, 1934, Newark, N.J.
Education: Seton Hall U., B.A. 1957.
Occupation: Community development executive.
Family: Widowed; two children.
Religion: Baptist.
Political Career: Essex County Board of Chosen Freeholders, 1972-78; Newark Municipal Council, 1982-88; sought Democratic nomination for Essex County executive, 1978; sought Democratic nomination for U.S. House, 1980, 1986.
Capitol Office: 417 Cannon Bldg. 20515; 225-3436.

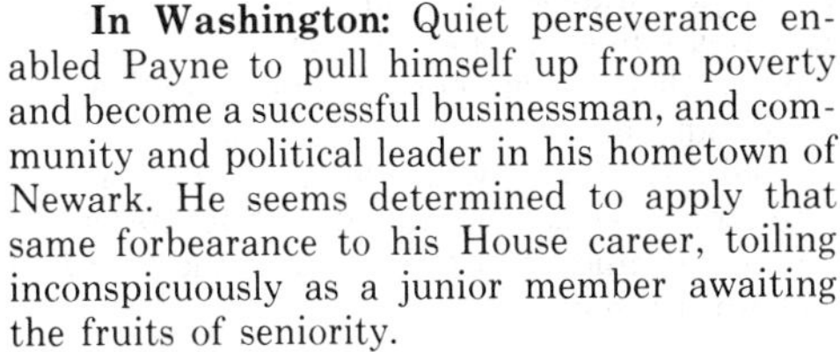

In Washington: Quiet perseverance enabled Payne to pull himself up from poverty and become a successful businessman, and community and political leader in his hometown of Newark. He seems determined to apply that same forbearance to his House career, toiling inconspicuously as a junior member awaiting the fruits of seniority.

"I would not call myself electrifying," he says of his low-key style. "But I think there is a lot of dignity in being able to achieve things without having to create rupture."

As a freshman, Payne worked around the edges of major legislation before the committees on which he served, particularly Education and Labor. A loyal Democratic vote on committee and in the full House, he vigorously supported the Family Leave Act, and backed funding for literacy programs. The only bill bearing his name enacted in the 101st Congress established July 2, 1990, as National Literacy Day, a commemorative he hopes to make permanent in the 102nd Congress.

But if a junior House member cannot move mountains in Washington, he can be a role model, and Payne takes that job seriously. In his district, blighted by poverty and drugs, Payne visits schools to encourage young people to stay in school and stay straight. He even turns his vote for a congressional pay raise into part of his appeal, telling students that his $125,000 salary is a lot more than any drug pusher makes.

In January 1991, Payne was one of several members to vote "present" on a resolution supporting President Bush and the military after the air war on Iraq had begun. Later, he was one of 42 members to sign a letter urging the president not to launch a ground offensive.

At Home: There is a good reason why it took Payne three tries to win in the majority-black, Newark-based 10th District: His path was blocked by the legendary Democratic Rep. Peter W. Rodino Jr., who held the seat for 40 years. Rodino, chairman of the Judiciary Committee, achieved national fame during the 1974 Watergate hearings, but it was Rodino's steadfast advocacy of civil rights legislation that earned him the loyalty — and votes — of many black residents in the 10th.

Insisting that the time had come for Newark-area blacks to be represented by one of their own, Payne challenged Rodino in the 1980 Democratic primary, and again in the 1986 primary. However, black good will toward Rodino, combined with his base in Newark's mainly Italian North Ward, enabled the incumbent to win easily. Payne got 23 percent of the vote in 1980 and 36 percent in 1986.

But when Rodino said the 1986 contest would be his last, local Democrats got behind Payne, a longtime party insider who had served on the Essex County Board and was in his second term on the Newark City Council.

Payne's only opposition came in the Democratic primary from City Council colleague Ralph T. Grant Jr. But Payne's advantages — party support, a sizable campaign treasury and recognition earned in his earlier campaigns — brought him the nomination in a landslide. Payne's November victory was a formality in the overwhelmingly Democratic district.

For a man so determined to become a black political pioneer, the soft-spoken Payne does not cut a dynamic figure. A high school teacher and football coach after college, he moved into business in 1963 as community affairs director for the Newark-based Prudential Insurance Co. More recently, he was vice president of a computer forms company founded by his brother.

The head of a "storefront YMCA" in inner-city Newark in the late 1950s, Payne became the first black president of the National Council of YMCAs in 1970, and later served two four-year terms as chairman of the YMCA's international committee on refugees. While participating in all these activities, the widowed Payne was raising two children and building his political career.

New Jersey 10

Newark

In 1948, Newark was a city of nearly a half-million people in which Irish and Italians competed for political power. Today, Payne serves a city with just over 275,000 residents, where blacks make up 58 percent of the population: A black has held the mayoralty since 1970 — first Kenneth Gibson, and now Sharpe James.

"Wherever America's cities are going," Gibson once said, "Newark will get there first." The city in fact presaged many of the urban problems that have spread throughout the Northeast in the past decade. Its Central Ward, devastated by riot in 1967, has not recovered in the years since.

But Newark remains the largest city in the state: The corporate headquarters of Prudential Insurance and other companies along with Newark Airport and the busy docks are economic mainstays.

Newark is an ethnic potpourri. Blacks populate the Central, West and South wards; Hispanics live in the East Ward. Nearly all of the remaining white population is found in the heavily Italian North Ward. Now only about 60 percent of the district lives in Newark; the rest live in towns such as Hillside and Irvington where, as in Newark, blue-collar whites share an uneasy coexistence with blacks.

The 10th also includes Orange and East Orange, whose stockbrokerage houses once earned it the nickname "Wall Street of New Jersey." Both now have their own problems with poverty.

Political intrigue and corruption are constant issues in Newark and its environs. Gibson's predecessor, Hugh Addonizio, was convicted in 1970 of extortion. Gibson, who defeated Addonizio for mayor that year, had his own problems with the law — a grand jury indicted him in 1981 for giving an ally an alleged "no-show" city job, even though this is common practice in New Jersey and many other states.

Gibson later was cleared, but his vaunted organization waned as the 1980s progressed, and he lost to James in the 1986 mayoral primary.

Population: 525,886. White 177,814 (34%), Black 304,047 (58%), Other 5,551 (1%). Spanish origin 71,650 (14%). 18 and over 360,309 (69%), 65 and over 52,645 (10%). Median age: 29.

Committees

Education & Labor (13th of 25 Democrats)
Labor-Management Relations; Postsecondary Education; Select Education

Foreign Affairs (26th of 28 Democrats)
Africa; International Narcotics Control

Government Operations (18th of 25 Democrats)
Human Resources & Intergovernmental Relations

Select Narcotics Abuse & Control (16th of 21 Democrats)

Elections

1990 General		
Donald M. Payne (D)	42,616	(81%)
Howard E. Berkeley (R)	9,072	(17%)
George Mehrabian (SW)	617	(1%)
1988 General		
Donald M. Payne (D)	84,681	(77%)
Michael Webb (R)	13,848	(13%)
Anthony Imperiale (I)	5,422	(5%)

District Vote For President

	1988		1984		1980		1976	
D	91,060	(78%)	110,470	(75%)	90,284	(70%)	97,465	(68%)
R	24,150	(21%)	36,554	(25%)	32,945	(26%)	42,429	(30%)
I					4,469	(4%)		

Campaign Finance

	Receipts	Receipts from PACs	Expend-itures
1990			
Payne (D)	$282,420	$185,642 (66%)	$162,612
1988			
Payne (D)	$545,049	$205,177 (38%)	$413,338

Key Votes

1991	
Authorize use of force against Iraq	N
1990	
Support constitutional amendment on flag desecration	N
Pass family and medical leave bill over Bush veto	Y
Reduce SDI funding	Y
Allow abortions in overseas military facilities	Y
Approve budget summit plan for spending and taxing	N
Approve civil rights bill	Y
1989	
Halt production of B-2 stealth bomber at 13 planes	Y
Oppose capital gains tax cut	Y
Approve federal abortion funding in rape or incest cases	Y
Approve pay raise and revision of ethics rules	Y
Pass Democratic minimum wage plan over Bush veto	Y

Voting Studies

	Presidential Support		Party Unity		Conservative Coalition	
Year	**S**	**O**	**S**	**O**	**S**	**O**
1990	16	81	92	5	9	89
1989	24	62	86	2	2	90

Interest Group Ratings

Year	ADA	ACU	AFL-CIO	CCUS
1990	89	4	100	29
1989	90	4	100	30

11 Dean A. Gallo (R)

Of Parsippany — Elected 1984

Born: Nov. 23, 1935, Hackensack, N.J.
Education: Graduated Boonton (N.J.) H.S.
Occupation: Real estate broker.
Family: Divorced; two children.
Religion: Methodist.
Political Career: Parsippany-Troy Hills Township Council, 1968-71; Morris County Board of Chosen Freeholders, 1971-75; N.J. Assembly, 1976-84, minority leader, 1982-84.
Capitol Office: 1318 Longworth Bldg. 20515; 225-5034.

In Washington: Gallo can often be seen around the House chamber, slapping backs and swapping gossip. His garrulous style can overpower, but it reinforces the deal-maker image he had in the New Jersey Assembly.

That reputation helped Gallo secure a House assignment that allows him to deal with the best of them: Appropriations. So far, Gallo has not carved out a distinct identity there, but he could break out of the pack with his new assignment to the Energy and Water Subcommittee in 1991. To get that, he gave up a seat on the Foreign Operations panel.. Gallo is likely to try to steer money to the massive Passiac River flood control project partially in his district that has languished with minor appropriations for more than a decade.

Until 1991, Gallo was most visible as the ranking member of the D.C. Appropriations Subcommittee. That put him in a tough spot in 1989, when Democrats used the D.C. funding bill to force the first House vote on abortion since the Supreme Court's *Webster* decision. Gallo took part in meetings to discuss strategy for repealing a ban on using D.C. funds to pay for abortion in cases of rape or incest. Gallo supported repealing the ban, a position at odds with the majority GOP view, and he apparently neglected to tip off his party about the strategy of the abortion-rights activists. An amendment repealing the ban won congressional approval, but prompted a presidential veto.

That episode illustrates that on some issues at least, Gallo does not excel at partisan one-upmanship. An urban Republican from the Northeast, Gallo is somewhat more loyal to the conservative GOP majority than most of his regional neighbors, but he still votes with the party less often than the average Republican.

The Northeasterner in Gallo shows most clearly on environmental issues, where he reflects the green movement that crosses party lines in New Jersey. In the 101st Congress, he won House approval for an amendment to the oil-spill liability bill that required tankers to have double hulls. Gallo's amendment was weakened in conference to impose the requirement only on newly built tankers.

In the 99th Congress, Gallo staked out a portion of the "superfund" legislation as his specialty by proposing a "community right to know" amendment, joining with Bob Wise, a West Virginia Democrat. The final bill included their language to provide federal money for local committees to gather information about dangerous substances and develop plans for dealing with any emergency that might occur.

At Home: Gallo is well connected in state GOP circles, and popular among moderates and conservatives alike. In 1981, Gallo, then the state Assembly Republican leader, joined U.S. Rep. Jim Courter as a co-chairman of Thomas H. Kean's successful gubernatorial campaign. With Kean retiring in 1989, Gallo signed on as chairman of Courter's campaign for the GOP nomination.

In 1983, the U.S. Supreme Court struck down the Democratic-drawn district map used for the 1982 elections; a new court-drawn plan gave the 11th a GOP hue, placing veteran Democratic Rep. Joseph G. Minish at a disadvantage. Gallo was seen as Minish's greatest threat. A business-oriented moderate, he had been elected minority leader of the Assembly in 1981, and represented the eastern half of heavily Republican Morris County, added to the 11th by the remap. Gallo, unopposed in the primary, got an early start against Minish.

In letters to GOP and independent voters, Gallo hammered at the incumbent, a former union official, for being anti-business and for opposing Ronald Reagan's tax and budget policies. An old-school personal campaigner, Minish reacted slowly but eventually went on the offensive, criticizing Gallo for supporting tax increases in the Legislature. But Gallo, helped by Reagan's strong showing, won easily, as he has in three re-election campaigns since.

New Jersey 11

North — Morris County

Before redistricting in 1984, the 11th had enough Democratic territory in Essex County to offset the growing strength of suburban Republicans. The new lines changed that. The bulk of the votes are now in suburban Republican villages and towns dotting the green Morris County landscape. At its eastern end, the 11th still reaches into Essex County to include West Orange and several other traditionally Democratic towns.

The largest community in the 11th is Parsippany-Troy Hills, a middle-class township in eastern Morris County; after years of fast growth, it has leveled off at about 50,000 people. Around Parsippany, towns such as Chatham and Florham Park are well-to-do bastions of moderate Republicanism.

Farther west, the district is pastoral, with newer tract developments set among woods and rolling hills. Towns here, such as Randolph and Roxbury, are viscerally Republican. So are the communities at the exurban and rural western end, where the 11th juts into Warren and Sussex counties. There is some Democratic vote from the central Morris towns of Dover and Rockaway, which are blue-collar in character, and from the hamlet of Victory Gardens, which is about 40 percent black and Hispanic.

The remnant of the district in Essex County is the only solid Democratic base. Here, close to Newark, white flight from the city determined the ethnic distribution of the suburbs. Verona was fed by the heavily Italian North Ward of Newark. West Orange is home to Jews who once lived in Newark's South Ward. Farther west are politically marginal suburbs; Livingston, hometown of former two-term GOP Gov. Thomas H. Kean, is filled with wealthy Republicans and a large Jewish community that often votes Democratic.

Population: 526,078. White 503,714 (96%), Black 9,803 (2%), Other 9,543 (2%). Spanish origin 12,145 (2%). 18 and over 381,844 (73%), 65 and over 51,245 (10%). Median age: 33.

Committees

Appropriations (20th of 22 Republicans)
District of Columbia (ranking); Energy & Water Development

Elections

1990 General		
Dean A. Gallo (R)	95,198	(65%)
Michael Gordon (D)	47,782	(33%)
Jasper Gould (POP)	3,610	(2%)
1988 General		
Dean A. Gallo (R)	154,654	(70%)
John C. Shaw (D)	64,773	(30%)

Previous Winning Percentages: **1986** (68%) **1984** (56%)

District Vote For President

	1988	1984	1980	1976
D	84,568 (35%)	78,701 (31%)	69,321 (30%)	97,922 (43%)
R	155,998 (65%)	171,632 (69%)	136,120 (59%)	136,658 (57%)
I			23,168 (10%)	

Campaign Finance

	Receipts	Receipts from PACs		Expend-itures
1990				
Gallo (R)	$652,386	$189,245	(29%)	$694,735
Gordon (D)	$106,599	$5,850	(5%)	$105,031
1988				
Gallo (R)	$531,548	$151,245	(28%)	$490,751

Key Votes

1991	
Authorize use of force against Iraq	Y
1990	
Support constitutional amendment on flag desecration	Y
Pass family and medical leave bill over Bush veto	N
Reduce SDI funding	N
Allow abortions in overseas military facilities	Y
Approve budget summit plan for spending and taxing	Y
Approve civil rights bill	N
1989	
Halt production of B-2 stealth bomber at 13 planes	N
Oppose capital gains tax cut	N
Approve federal abortion funding in rape or incest cases	Y
Approve pay raise and revision of ethics rules	Y
Pass Democratic minimum wage plan over Bush veto	N

Voting Studies

	Presidential Support		Party Unity		Conservative Coalition	
Year	**S**	**O**	**S**	**O**	**S**	**O**
1990	60	37	65	29	85	13
1989	64	34	48	50	73	27
1988	59	40	84	14	87	13
1987	55	44	71	27	88	12
1986	70	29	71	27	86	14
1985	63	38	80	19	82	18

Interest Group Ratings

Year	ADA	ACU	AFL-CIO	CCUS
1990	17	65	8	77
1989	25	61	25	100
1988	30	72	31	79
1987	32	57	44	67
1986	35	68	57	61
1985	20	81	29	68

12 Dick Zimmer (R)

Of Flemington — Elected 1990

Born: Aug. 16, 1944, Newark, N.J.
Education: Yale U., B.A. 1966, LL.B. 1969.
Occupation: Lawyer.
Family: Wife, Marfy Goodspeed; two children.
Religion: Jewish.
Political Career: Republican nominee for N.J. Assembly, 1979; N.J. Assembly, 1982-87; N.J. Senate, 1987-91.
Capitol Office: 510 Cannon Bldg. 20515; 225-5801.

The Path to Washington: In 1990's most expensive House race, Zimmer won the right to succeed Republican Rep. Jim Courter, who retired after suffering a devastating defeat for governor in 1989. Zimmer achieved a 2-to-1 victory over his Democratic opponent, millionaire businesswoman Marguerite Chandler, who spent more than $1.7 million — and got just 52,000 votes in return.

A corporate attorney for Johnson & Johnson, Zimmer has held a variety of posts in and out of government. He chaired New Jersey Common Cause from 1974 to 1977. He co-chaired Courter's 1989 campaign and was campaign counsel in all of Thomas H. Kean's gubernatorial bids — his two successful ones (in 1981 and 1985) and his failed primary run (in 1977).

Zimmer narrowly lost a 1979 campaign for the state Assembly, but two years later he prevailed; he was re-elected in 1983 and 1985. In the spring of 1987, he won a special election for the state Senate.

In the Legislature, he complemented a "good government" agenda with a resolutely conservative approach to fiscal matters. He was in the forefront of efforts to give New Jersey voters the right of initiative and referendum, and he backed campaign finance reform. He also sponsored environmental bills dealing with radon gas testing and farmland preservation.

During the GOP primary, he unveiled a plan that would, among other things, reduce a political action committee's (PAC) maximum allowable contribution to a congressional candidate from $5,000 to $2,000, raise maximum allowable individual contributions from $1,000 to $2,000, remove limits on the amount political parties may contribute to campaigns, and eliminate members' franking privileges as well as PACs controlled by members.

One of three Republicans on the Senate Appropriations Committee, Zimmer was an unswerving opponent of new taxes. But his fiscal conservatism was not bound by partisan bonds.

He attracted attention during 1989 budget action when he opposed Kean's budget as relying on erroneous revenue projections and thus being out of balance. Zimmer's pronouncements were later verified: Kean left the state with an estimated $600 million deficit.

In the Legislature, Zimmer took his commitment to ethics in government quite far: To avoid conflicts of interest with his work for Johnson & Johnson, he abstained from voting on legislation that would affect the company. (Chandler ridiculed the practice in a radio ad, chiding Zimmer for "ducking" issues.)

Courter had performed miserably in his 1989 statewide race, collecting a meager 37 percent of the vote and frittering away his political credibility by running a stumbling campaign and equivocating on his opposition to abortion. Still, his March 1990 announcement that he would not seek re-election stunned many in the 12th. Courter had been considered potentially vulnerable to a challenge from a candidate with Chandler's profile — a well-funded, abortion rights woman with ties to the area business community. But Chandler, a political neophyte, was unproven and largely unknown in the heavily Republican 12th.

With Courter out of the running, the focus fell to the GOP primary. Zimmer faced Assemblyman Rodney P. Frelinghuysen, former New York Giants player Phil McConkey and a minor fourth candidate. Frelinghuysen boasted the most famous political name in the race: His family's tradition of public service dated back to the Revolutionary War. Four Frelinghuysens had served in the U.S. Senate, and Frelinghuysen's father had served in the House from New Jersey from 1953 to 1975.

Zimmer criticized Frelinghuysen for supporting Kean's budget and had an edge among environmental activists. He also was helped by McConkey's anti-establishment campaign, which hurt the blue-blooded Frelinghuysen more than it did Zimmer.

New Jersey 12

North and Central — Morristown

On paper, the 12th is an ungainly blotch. It contains only one whole county; the pieces of the other six seem to be leftovers from map-drawing efforts in the rest of northern New Jersey.

On the ground, however, there is little that is ugly about the 12th. Large stretches of rolling countryside and wood-shaded lakes mingle with some of the state's most affluent communities. The entire prospect is especially pleasing to Republicans, who have a tight hold on most voters.

New Jersey's hunt country is in the district, in towns such as Far Hills and Peapack, nestled in northern Somerset County. Quaint Morristown and its surrounding old-line Morris County suburbs are home to commuters who work on Wall Street and elsewhere in the Manhattan business world. Farther west and south the district grows more rural, dotted with middle-class subdivisions.

However, this pastoral and remote area has undergone change in recent years, as the New York City metropolis creeps down Route 1 to Princeton and beyond. With its high-technology industry, Route 1 is becoming New Jersey's answer to Massachusetts' Route 128. Recently completed Interstate 78, from Newark into Pennsylvania, has also drawn some corporate headquarters from Manhattan to the rolling greenery of Morris and Somerset counties.

Though farming still dominates in Hunterdon and Warren counties, that far-flung corner of the state is beginning to see the first signs of corporate development as well. Hunterdon was New Jersey's third-fastest growing county in the early 1980s, its population jumping by 10 percent between 1980 and 1986. Many of these new arrivals are white-collar workers, as well as state employees.

The growth in these areas has not changed their Republican leanings. Ronald Reagan and George Bush both dominated in the 12th District. Hunterdon, the only county wholly within the 12th, gave 70 percent of its 1988 presidential vote to Bush, and 71 percent of its 1990 House vote to Zimmer.

There are a few pockets of Democratic strength, however. The portion of Middlesex County in the district includes the blue-collar towns of Piscataway and South Plainfield. Democrats also have small strongholds in Princeton, with a liberal academic segment associated with its Ivy League university; in industrial Raritan and Somerville, with their chemical and pharmaceutical works; and in Hackettstown, where there is blue-collar employment at an M&M/Mars candy factory.

Population: 526,063. White 485,399 (92%), Black 27,563 (5%), Other 9,946 (2%). Spanish origin 9,117 (2%). 18 and over 380,628 (72%), 65 and over 48,331 (9%). Median age: 32.

Committees

Government Operations (12th of 15 Republicans)
Commerce, Consumer & Monetary Affairs; Government Activities & Transportation

Science, Space & Technology (18th of 19 Republicans)
Environment; Space

Select Aging (24th of 27 Republicans)
Health & Long-Term Care

Campaign Finance

	Receipts	Receipts from PACs		Expend-itures
1990				
Zimmer (R)	$1,227,742	$204,983	(17%)	$1,224,626
Chandler (D)	$1,716,554	$51,864	(3%)	$1,707,539

Key Vote

1991

Authorize use of force against Iraq	Y

Elections

1990 General		
Dick Zimmer (R)	108,173	(64%)
Marguerite Chandler (D)	52,498	(31%)
Joan I. Bottcher (Back to Basics)	4,443	(3%)
C. Max Kortepeter (Independent Reform)	2,442	(1%)
Michael A. Notarangelo (POP)	1,408	(1%)
1990 Primary		
Dick Zimmer (R)	15,834	(38%)
Phil McConkey (R)	12,925	(31%)
Rodney P. Frelinghuysen (R)	12,257	(29%)
Joseph F. Shanahan (R)	989	(2%)

District Vote For President

	1988	1984	1980	1976
D	93,339 (36%)	84,541 (35%)	74,811 (34%)	92,672 (43%)
R	162,814 (63%)	160,027 (65%)	122,046 (55%)	117,774 (55%)
I			21,566 (10%)	

13 H. James Saxton (R)

Of Vincentown — Elected 1984

Born: Jan. 22, 1943, Nicholson, Pa.

Education: East Stroudsburg (Pa.) State College, B.A. 1965; graduate work, Temple U., 1967-68.

Occupation: Real estate broker; elementary school teacher.

Family: Separated; two children.

Religion: Methodist.

Political Career: N.J. Assembly, 1976-82; N.J. Senate, 1982-84.

Capitol Office: 324 Cannon Bldg. 20515; 225-4765.

In Washington: After two terms as an obscure backbencher, Saxton has begun to emerge from the shadows. In the 101st Congress he waged an animated campaign to stave off the partial closing of Fort Dix, and has joined other Garden State colleagues to cosponsor environmental legislation. While Saxton may not quite have made it into the spotlight, at least he has moved on stage. In the 102nd Congress, he won a seat on the Armed Services Committee, leaving behind his assignment on Banking.

Up to 1988, Saxton had amassed a voting record of high party support. He still received a post-Christmas lump of coal in 1988: The defense secretary's commission charged with drawing up recommendations for closing military bases listed the Army's Fort Dix, which lies partly in the 13th, for partial closure, threatening elimination of some 4,600 base-related jobs.

Saxton and Republican Christopher H. Smith, whose 4th District contains the other part of Fort Dix, objected to the commission's findings. On the House floor in early 1989, Saxton said the commission used incomplete information on Fort Dix; he called the base-closing plan "flawed, seriously flawed." But an effort to kill the plan failed, 43-381.

Saxton continued to press for relief, but to no avail. When he was named to Armed Services, Saxton made no promises about Fort Dix, only that he would make sure "New Jersey gets its fair share" of military money and projects. The 1991 base-closing plan recommended shutting down Fort Dix.

On the Merchant Marine Committee, Saxton tends to the ample environmental concerns of his district, with its high concentration of hazardous waste sites. He began the 102nd Congress as ranking Republican on the Oversight and Investigations Subcommittee. In 1988, after a summer riddled with reports of medical waste washing up on New Jersey beaches, Saxton and New Jersey Democrat William J. Hughes, a fellow Merchant Marine member, sponsored a bill to ban the dumping of medical waste in oceans and the Great Lakes.

Saxton advocates creating the National Institutes for the Environment to fund environmental research. He and New Jersey Democratic Sen. Bill Bradley, sponsor of a companion bill, testified before the House Science Committee in the 101st Congress in behalf of legislation to have the National Academy of Sciences study the feasibility of such an institute.

At Home: Saxton struggled to win the nomination for the seat left open by the 1984 death of GOP Rep. Edwin B. Forsythe. But after surviving a tough primary, he has had little trouble in this heavily Republican district.

A state legislator for eight years, Saxton came in with the backing of the strong GOP organization in Burlington County, which has roughly half of the 13th's people. But the 13th also includes Camden and Ocean counties, and each supplied a candidate. M. Dean Haines and his Ocean County organization gave Saxton his stiffest challenge. Assemblyman John A. Rocco of Camden County entered the primary, but his differences with his county organization resulted in the GOP endorsement of Saxton.

The lesser-known Haines concentrated his efforts on Ocean County, where turnout was traditionally high. Saxton, with his large state Senate constituency, ran ads on Philadelphia TV stations to reach voters in Camden and Burlington counties.

The strategy paid off. With Saxton and Haines winning on their home turf, the contest was decided in Camden County. Saxton's second-place showing behind Rocco there allowed him to win the primary by about 1,400 votes.

In 1990, Saxton faced aggressive young Democrat John H. Adler, a former Cherry Hill City Council member. With voters furious over Democratic Gov. James J. Florio's $2.8 billion tax package and looking for victims at the polls, the House race attracted a decade-high turnout. While 1990 may have been a dicey year for Democrats elsewhere, Adler managed to hold Saxton under 60 percent for the first time.

New Jersey 13

South and Central

The 13th runs the width of south-central New Jersey, from the Delaware River towns of western Burlington County to the oceanfront strip of Long Beach Island. There is a bit of everything: densely settled suburbs, small villages, beach resorts, patches of industrial development and the Pine Barrens wilderness.

But the diversity does little to dilute the area's Republican cast. Ocean County has long been a GOP stronghold. The portion of Burlington County in the 13th has some pockets of Democrats as well as many independent-minded voters, but the GOP usually commands their loyalty. Only Camden County is competitive, but its most Democratic areas, including the city of Camden, are in the neighboring 1st District.

The population center of Burlington County is at its western end, in Philadelphia suburbs such as Moorestown and Mount Laurel. By design, it is difficult to find apartment buildings or low-income housing in much of this area.

But the traditional residential patterns continue to prevail, and the affluent area remains firmly Republican. There is an exception, though, in Willingboro, the planned town built in the late 1950s as Levittown, which has many black voters.

Eastward toward the Pinelands, the population thins out. Agriculture is a major trade, but the region's small towns have been highly dependent through the years on McGuire Air Force Base and also on Fort Dix, which is now slated for shutdown.

The portion of Camden County in the 13th is dominated by Cherry Hill, one of New Jersey's first post-World War II suburbs. The city and its environs have many affluent GOP voters, but there are also young professionals and Jewish voters, and they are prone to vote Democratic. Former Cherry Hill City Council member John Adler, Saxton's 1990 Democratic foe, received 45 percent in Camden County.

Southern Ocean County is mostly residential. Manchester Township has huge retirement communities; along the shore are resort towns drawing summer residents from nearby states.

Population: 526,062. White 472,404 (90%), Black 40,734 (8%), Other 7,767 (2%). Spanish origin 10,372 (2%). 18 and over 377,446 (72%), 65 and over 68,455 (13%). Median age: 32.

Committees

Armed Services (20th of 22 Republicans)
Military Personnel & Compensation; Procurement & Military Nuclear Systems; Readiness

Merchant Marine & Fisheries (6th of 17 Republicans)
Oversight & Investigations (ranking); Fisheries & Wildlife Conservation & the Environment; Oceanography, Great Lakes & Outer Continental Shelf

Select Aging (7th of 27 Republicans)
Rural Elderly (ranking); Health & Long-Term Care; Human Services

Elections

1990 General		
H. James Saxton (R)	100,537	(58%)
John H. Adler (D)	68,286	(39%)
Howard Scott Pearlman (WWW)	4,178	(2%)
1990 Primary		
H. James Saxton (R)	16,719	(93%)
William Monk (R)	1,186	(7%)
1988 General		
H. James Saxton (R)	167,470	(69%)
James B. Smith (D)	73,561	(31%)

Previous Winning Percentages: **1986** (65%) **1984 *** (61%)

* *Elected to a full term and to fill a vacancy at the same time.*

District Vote For President

	1988		1984		1980		1976	
D	97,084	(38%)	86,540	(35%)	73,063	(36%)	89,933	(45%)
R	156,439	(61%)	161,435	(65%)	124,823	(61%)	105,241	(53%)
I					3,862	(2%)		

Campaign Finance

	Receipts	Receipts from PACs		Expend-itures
1990				
Saxton (R)	$628,142	$250,149	(40%)	$730,989
Adler (D)	$210,993	$56,599	(27%)	$203,147
1988				
Saxton (R)	$491,036	$195,430	(40%)	$411,620

Key Votes

1991	
Authorize use of force against Iraq	Y
1990	
Support constitutional amendment on flag desecration	Y
Pass family and medical leave bill over Bush veto	N
Reduce SDI funding	Y
Allow abortions in overseas military facilities	N
Approve budget summit plan for spending and taxing	N
Approve civil rights bill	N
1989	
Halt production of B-2 stealth bomber at 13 planes	N
Oppose capital gains tax cut	N
Approve federal abortion funding in rape or incest cases	N
Approve pay raise and revision of ethics rules	Y
Pass Democratic minimum wage plan over Bush veto	N

Voting Studies

	Presidential Support		Party Unity		Conservative Coalition	
Year	**S**	**O**	**S**	**O**	**S**	**O**
1990	57	42	68	29	78	22
1989	65	33	50	48	83	15
1988	57	42	80	19	82	16
1987	58	42	73	27	91	9
1986	64	34	67	33	78	22
1985	61	39	81	19	76	24

Interest Group Ratings

Year	ADA	ACU	AFL-CIO	CCUS
1990	33	63	17	92
1989	20	64	42	100
1988	30	72	50	79
1987	24	52	38	73
1986	30	64	57	56
1985	15	81	12	82

14 Frank J. Guarini (D)

Of Jersey City — Elected 1978

Born: Aug. 20, 1924, Jersey City, N.J.
Education: Dartmouth College, B.A. 1947; New York U., J.D. 1950, LL.M. 1955.
Military Service: Navy, 1944-46.
Occupation: Lawyer.
Family: Divorced.
Religion: Roman Catholic.
Political Career: N.J. Senate, 1966-72; sought Democratic nomination for U.S. Senate, 1970.
Capitol Office: 2458 Rayburn Bldg. 20515; 225-2765.

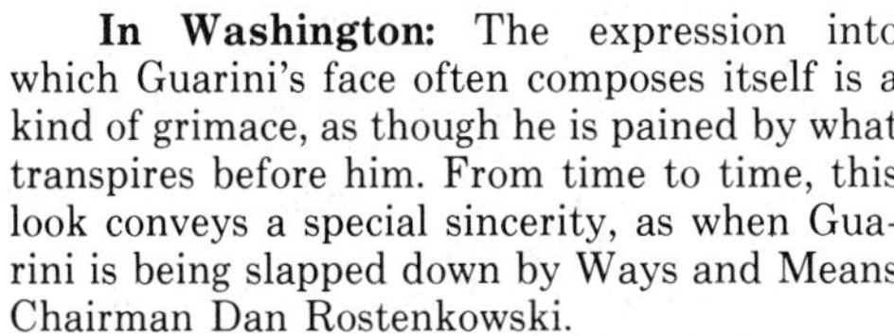

In Washington: The expression into which Guarini's face often composes itself is a kind of grimace, as though he is pained by what transpires before him. From time to time, this look conveys a special sincerity, as when Guarini is being slapped down by Ways and Means Chairman Dan Rostenkowski.

While Guarini's authentic Jersey accent and roots in Hudson County politics would seem to make him a natural ally for Rostenkowski, Guarini is an unpredictable individualist rather than a team player, and he is not part of the committee's powerful inner circle.

In one memorable instance, Guarini was so badly mauled in committee that his name became synonymous with a particular kind of ambush. It was in the 100th Congress, and Guarini was championing a proposal to expand tax breaks for education benefits. A law allowing employees to deduct up to $5,250 in tuition benefits was set to expire at the end of 1987. Guarini gathered more than 300 cosponsors for his bill to continue the current exclusion and add one for graduate students. Observing Rostenkowski's decree that any member advocating a tax break propose an offsetting revenue source, Guarini suggested that the exclusion be limited to lower-paid workers.

But when Ways and Means voted on the measure, they accepted only the revenue increase. The committee rejected Guarini's original purpose of expanding the benefit to graduate teaching assistants and ultimately capped undergraduate benefits at $1,500. The Senate eventually opted for a higher cap, which was agreed to in conference, but the spectacle of Guarini's ambush in committee remained firmly in memory.

"I raised the revenue and they stole it from me," said Guarini in 1991. "It was like the Great Train Robbery." Since then, offering a revenue proposal for a specific purpose and seeing the revenue diverted to another purpose has been known on Ways and Means as "getting Guarinied."

Unlike the gritty urban-machine Democrats the chairman prefers, Guarini is at least part Eastern establishment. When he is home, he spends some of his time in a luxury apartment overlooking Central Park in New York's Manhattan, across the river from his district. When he travels abroad on congressional business, he often returns with expensive *objets d'art*, the purchase of which is made possible by his substantial private fortune.

It was Guarini's training as a tax lawyer — coupled with some lobbying by influential home-state colleague Robert A. Roe — that helped him win a seat on Ways and Means early in his career. Guarini has fashioned an image as a spokesman for the small taxpayer.

In the 102nd Congress, Guarini is a cosponsor of legislation attempting to rescind $4.2 billion in tax breaks granted to big investors who took over failed thrifts in the late 1980s. He is also the lead House sponsor of New York Sen. Daniel Patrick Moynihan's proposed cut in the Social Security payroll tax. Assailed by some as an attack on Social Security itself (and rejected by the Senate in early 1991), the Moynihan proposal at least offers a quick way to cut taxes for wage earners. Rostenkowski's ruling clique on Ways and Means was not prepared to go with it, but Guarini was.

But Guarini also watches out for those in the upper echelon. He pushed the controversial "love boat" deduction for expenses incurred while attending a convention on a cruise ship and a 10 percent investment tax credit on the cost of any horse up to $100,000. Before coming to Congress, Guarini was attorney for the Standard Breeders and Owners Association of New Jersey. He has also been a racehorse owner himself.

This pattern disappointed committee Democrats who expected him to be a loyal ally, but it is a point of pride for Guarini. Asked about his loyalties on the committee, he once said: "You don't walk a middle ground. You walk to the left, to the right, to the middle. You always have to keep them guessing, so they need you."

Some of his rhetoric gives Guarini a kind of

New Jersey 14

North — Jersey City

Heavily ethnic and heavily Democratic, Hudson County long embodied all the color — and meanness — of urban machine politics. From 1917 to the late 1940s, the legendary political boss, Frank "I Am the Law" Hague, ruled the county by sending his opponents to jail or the hospital. Unions were equally rough in Hudson, especially along the docks, which remain central to the county's economy; the 1954 film "On the Waterfront" was set in Hoboken.

As in most urban areas, Hudson County's machine has lost much of its iron-fisted dominance in recent years. Independent-voting young professionals, driven across the river by New York City's high housing prices, have set up pockets of "gentrification" in grimy Jersey City and Hoboken. Communities of Cuban-Americans, now 8 percent of the 14th District population, are mainly staunch anti-communists who idolize Ronald Reagan. Even some of the bedrock blue-collar Democrats have become amenable to national Republican candidates because of their conservative social views.

But while Reagan and Republican Gov. Thomas H. Kean carried Hudson County in the mid-1980s, it is still, in the main, a Democratic county. In 1988, Democratic presidential candidate Michael S. Dukakis took Hudson with 54 percent of the vote. As voters across the state expressed their displeasure with Democratic Gov. James J. Florio's $2.8 billion tax package by shaving Democratic Sen. Bill Bradley's re-election margin, Hudson County voters helped keep Bradley in office, giving him a 2-to-1 margin.

Jersey City, with 228,500 residents, has nearly two-fifths of Hudson County's population. About 54 percent black and Hispanic, it has its problems with poverty, much of it concentrated in the Paulus Hook section. The city contains Liberty State Park, and local boosters are fond of pointing out that the Statue of Liberty actually stands within their city limits, not New York's. However, the statue has its back to Jersey City's rugged industrial waterfront.

Bayonne — site of huge shipping terminals — has a longstanding political rivalry with equally Democratic Jersey City. Because it is No. 2 in the county in size, Bayonne often loses out.

Union City and West New York, located in the northern part of Hudson County, house most of the burgeoning Cuban population. The Cubans, many of them professionals and merchants, have helped stabilize a deteriorating urban area; their shops now crowd Bergenline Avenue. While their conservative foreign policy views lead many of these voters to the Republican line for national office, they are more favorable to Democrats at the local level.

Population: 526,062. White 395,189 (75%), Black 68,892 (13%), Other 15,414 (3%). Spanish origin 143,203 (27%). 18 and over 388,408 (74%), 65 and over 66,005 (13%). Median age: 32.

populist appeal in his working-class district, but while he speaks out on a variety of issues on Ways and Means, his interests sometimes turn out to be wider than they are deep. He has a reputation for moving on ideas without rounding up support from other members or fully considering the implications of his proposal.

Guarini has also "walked both sides" on the free-trade street. He favored continuation of normal trading status for China when other members demanded a cessation after the Tiananmen Square massacre. In 1989 he urged quick action on the U.S.-Canada free-trade agreement, noting that Canada is New Jersey's largest trading partner.

But the following year he raised questions about a similar pact with Mexico, saying some experts had calculated the agreement would cost 400,000 U.S. jobs.

Guarini has also had sharp words for Japan. In 1990 he dismissed years of Japanese trade-deficit promises, saying, "It's just been talk," and sponsored a bill mandating retaliation against persistently unfair trade practices.

In 1987, he backed an amendment to help firms seeking to sue foreign manufacturers accused of dumping goods in the United States at prices below production costs.

Guarini is perhaps most aggressive when involved in border disputes between New Jersey and New York. In 1989, he sponsored legislation to bar New York from increasing the income-tax rates on commuters.

Guarini is a friend of labor on most issues, an old-fashioned public works Democrat who believes in federally subsidized jobs as part of the answer to economic stagnation. In the 97th and 98th Congresses he introduced legislation to create a Reconstruction Finance Corporation, similar to the Depression-era agency, to back new industrial projects that would provide jobs on a massive basis.

At Home: Guarini developed keen political instincts while navigating his way through Hudson County's Byzantine power struggles. Apart from an unsuccessful primary bid against Democratic Sen. Harrison A. Williams Jr. in 1970, Guarini, a former Hudson County Democratic chairman, has taken no false steps; he has won each of his House elections with at least 64 percent of the vote.

In 1977, Democratic Rep. Joseph A. LeFante backed the loser in a divisive Jersey City mayoral election and chose to retire after one term rather than face a challenge for renomination. Guarini, a former state senator who was on the winning side in the mayoral contest, had the seat all but handed to him.

Another shift in 1981 brought a new set of people into power in Jersey City. But Guarini by then had moved into a protective neutral posture.

After a series of easy elections, Guarini's fine-tuned political radar enabled him to head off a possible threat in 1986. A slackening of the Democratic stranglehold over Hudson County — President Reagan and GOP Gov. Thomas H. Kean carried the county in the early 1980s — emboldened district Republicans to think that Guarini could be weakened. They recruited Albio Sires, a member of the county's small but staunchly conservative Cuban-American community, to run against the incumbent.

Sires, a strong Reagan supporter who decried Guarini's opposition to aid to the Nicaraguan contras, did help Republicans solidify their Cuban base. But the inexperienced candidate, a state official and former teacher, failed to expand his appeal to the other ethnic groups that populate Hudson County.

For his part, Guarini was not about to be blindsided. After coaxing an unusually large turnout for his routine primary win, he campaigned diligently and made good use of his large campaign treasury. Guarini's nearly 3-to-1 victory margin dispelled GOP notions of his vulnerability: His 1988 win was routine, as was his 1990 re-election.

Committees

Budget (4th of 23 Democrats)
Urgent Fiscal Issues (chairman); Defense, Foreign Policy & Space

Select Narcotics Abuse & Control (6th of 21 Democrats)

Ways & Means (10th of 23 Democrats)
Trade

Elections

1990 General		
Frank J. Guarini (D)	57,581	(66%)
Fred J. Theemling Jr. (R)	25,473	(29%)
Michael Ziruolo (BAG)	1,897	(2%)
Jane E. Harris (SW)	1,355	(2%)
Donald K. Stoveken Sr. (POP)	519	(1%)
1990 Primary		
Frank J. Guarini (D)	32,637	(91%)
Gil Corby (D)	3,337	(9%)
1988 General		
Frank J. Guarini (D)	104,001	(67%)
Fred J. Theemling Jr. (R)	47,293	(31%)

Previous Winning Percentages: **1986** (71%) **1984** (66%) **1982** (74%) **1980** (64%) **1978** (64%)

District Vote For President

	1988	1984	1980	1976
D	91,042 (55%)	89,414 (47%)	87,026 (50%)	105,453 (56%)
R	73,382 (44%)	102,475 (53%)	78,796 (45%)	80,607 (43%)
I			7,465 (4%)	

Campaign Finance

	Receipts	Receipts from PACs	Expend-itures
1990			
Guarini (D)	$461,948	$299,833 (65%)	$299,807
1988			
Guarini (D)	$552,280	$213,835 (39%)	$369,578

Key Votes

1991	
Authorize use of force against Iraq	N
1990	
Support constitutional amendment on flag desecration	Y
Pass family and medical leave bill over Bush veto	Y
Reduce SDI funding	Y
Allow abortions in overseas military facilities	Y
Approve budget summit plan for spending and taxing	N
Approve civil rights bill	Y
1989	
Halt production of B-2 stealth bomber at 13 planes	N
Oppose capital gains tax cut	Y
Approve federal abortion funding in rape or incest cases	Y
Approve pay raise and revision of ethics rules	Y
Pass Democratic minimum wage plan over Bush veto	Y

Voting Studies

	Presidential Support		Party Unity		Conservative Coalition	
Year	**S**	**O**	**S**	**O**	**S**	**O**
1990	33	64	78	16	41	56
1989	34	63	90	7	49	49
1988	26	65	85	8	37	61
1987	23	76	88	6	35	65
1986	22	76	89	8	28	70
1985	21	79	93	3	15	80
1984	27	60	80	5	15	64
1983	18	76	90	4	15	80
1982	34	60	89	7	23	71
1981	33	57	85	5	16	77

Interest Group Ratings

Year	ADA	ACU	AFL-CIO	CCUS
1990	78	13	92	31
1989	85	11	92	40
1988	70	14	100	46
1987	88	0	94	20
1986	80	14	93	17
1985	85	5	94	20
1984	70	14	92	31
1983	90	9	100	21
1982	90	10	90	21
1981	85	7	93	0

New Mexico

U.S. CONGRESS

SENATE 1 D, 1 R
HOUSE 1 D, 2 R

LEGISLATURE

Senate 26 D, 16 R
House 49 D, 21 R

ELECTIONS

1988 Presidential Vote

Bush	52%
Dukakis	47%

1984 Presidential Vote

Reagan	60%
Mondale	39%

1980 Presidential Vote

Reagan	55%
Carter	37%
Anderson	7%

Turnout rate in 1986	37%
Turnout rate in 1988	47%
Turnout rate in 1990	33%

(as percentage of voting age population)

POPULATION AND GROWTH

1980 population	1,302,894
1990 population (37th in the nation)	1,515,069
Percent change 1980-1990	+16%

DEMOGRAPHIC BREAKDOWN

White	76%
Black	2%
American Indian, Eskimo, or Aleut	9%
(Hispanic origin)	38%
Urban	72%
Rural	28%
Born in state	52%
Foreign-born	4%

MAJOR CITIES

Albuquerque	384,736
Las Cruces	62,126
Santa Fe	55,859
Roswell	44,654
Farmington	33,997

AREA AND LAND USE

Area 121,335 sq. miles (5th)

Farm	61%
Forest	24%
Federally owned	33%

Gov. Bruce King (D)
Of Stanley — Elected 1990
(also served 1971-75; 1979-83)

Born: April 6, 1924, Stanley, N.M.
Education: Attended U. of New Mexico, 1943-44.
Military Service: Army, 1944-1946.
Occupation: Farmer; rancher.
Religion: Baptist.
Political Career: Santa Fe County Commission, 1954-59; N.M. House, 1959-69, Speaker, 1963-69; sought Democratic gubernatorial nomination, 1968; state Democratic chairman, 1968-69.
Next Election: 1994.

WORK

Occupations

White-collar	54%
Blue-collar	29%
Service workers	14%

Government Workers

Federal	26,685
State	50,386
Local	60,152

MONEY

Median family income	$ 16,928 (42nd)
Tax burden per capita	$ 993 (15th)

EDUCATION

Spending per pupil through grade 12	$ 3,691 (34th)
Persons with college degrees	18% (16th)

CRIME

Violent crime rate	704 per 100,000 (10th)

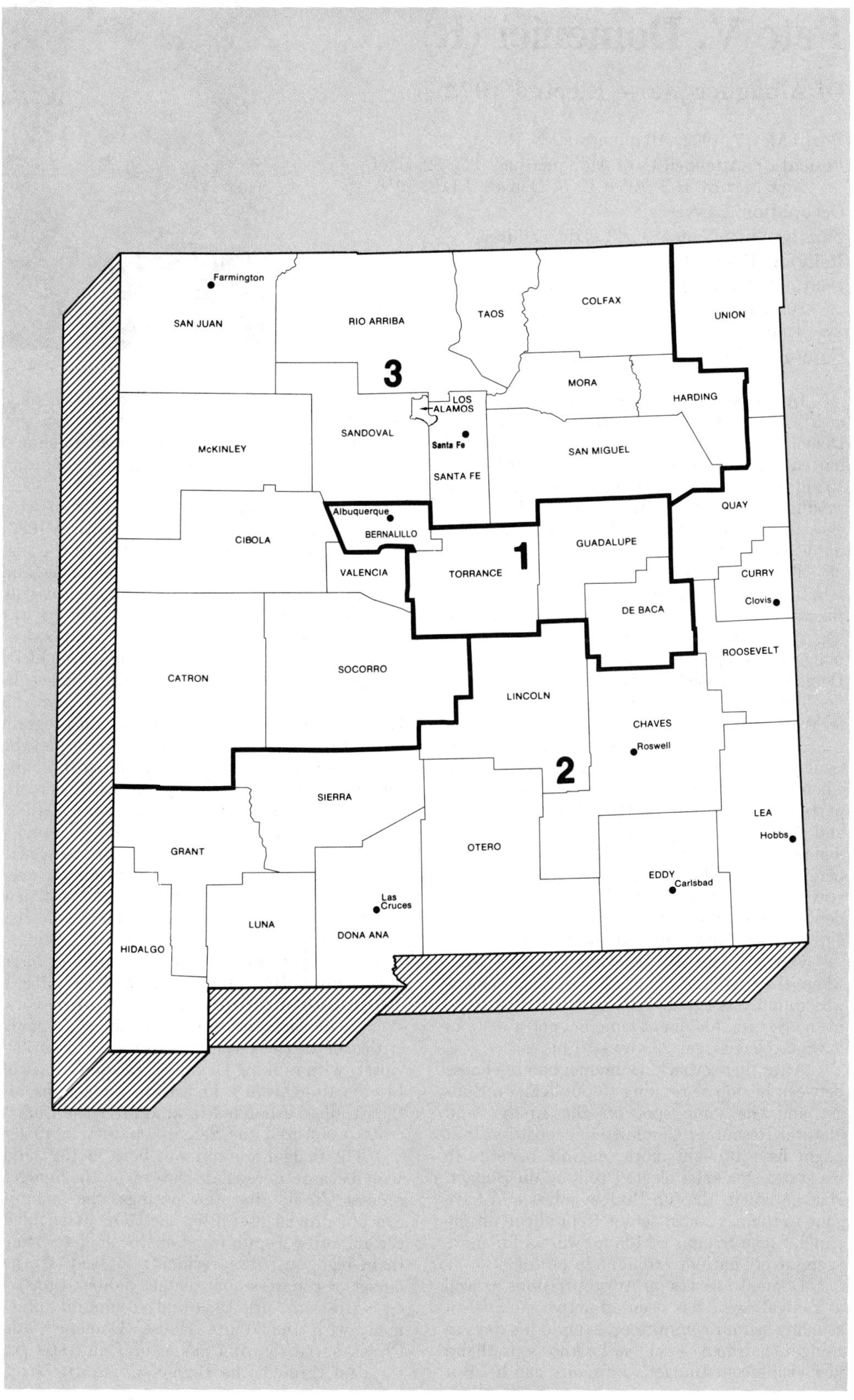
Farmington
SAN JUAN
RIO ARRIBA
TAOS
COLFAX
UNION
3
MORA
HARDING
LOS ALAMOS
SANDOVAL
Santa Fe
SANTA FE
SAN MIGUEL
McKINLEY
QUAY
Albuquerque
BERNALILLO
CIBOLA
GUADALUPE
1
TORRANCE
VALENCIA
CURRY
Clovis
DE BACA
ROOSEVELT
CATRON
SOCORRO
LINCOLN
CHAVES
Roswell
2
SIERRA
LEA
Hobbs
GRANT
OTERO
EDDY
Carlsbad
Las Cruces
LUNA
DONA ANA
HIDALGO

Pete V. Domenici (R)

Of Albuquerque — Elected 1972

Born: May 7, 1932, Albuquerque, N.M.

Education: Attended U. of Albuquerque, 1950-52; U. of New Mexico, B.S. 1954; U. of Denver, LL.B. 1958.

Occupation: Lawyer.

Family: Wife, Nancy Burk; eight children.

Religion: Roman Catholic.

Political Career: Albuquerque City Commission, 1966-70, chairman and ex-officio mayor, 1967-70; Republican nominee for governor, 1970.

Capitol Office: 434 Dirksen Bldg. 20510; 224-6621.

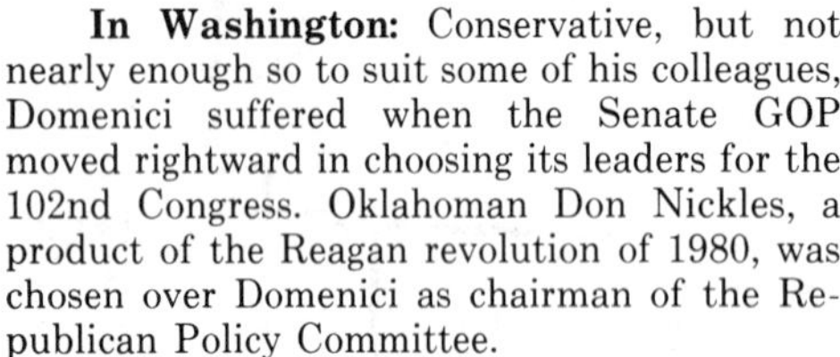

In Washington: Conservative, but not nearly enough so to suit some of his colleagues, Domenici suffered when the Senate GOP moved rightward in choosing its leaders for the 102nd Congress. Oklahoman Don Nickles, a product of the Reagan revolution of 1980, was chosen over Domenici as chairman of the Republican Policy Committee.

That disappointment, Domenici's second rebuff in a bid for leadership, demonstrated the thanklessness of the fiscal issues on which he has spent his Senate career. As a dedicated budget-and-appropriations man in lean times, Domenici has come to embody the challenge of the budget deficit and the frustration Congress feels about it.

The defeatism that surrounds the deficit issue was especially thick in November 1990, when the leadership election was held. The party had lost ground in the midterm elections and was generally perceived to be losing the momentum of the previous decade. Some of the blame descended on the drawn-out budget process of that summer and fall, which left President Bush's no-new-taxes pledge broken and embarrassed both him and the Congress.

Outright rebellion had flared in the House, where the first version of the budget agreement was roundly rejected. But frustration festered in the Senate, too, and Domenici got a taste of it when Nickles got 23 votes to his 20.

After that setback, Domenici had to choose between his job as ranking Republican on Budget and the same spot on the Energy and Natural Resources Committee, a position that might have brought more tangible benefits to his state. Domenici elected to stay on Budget. Had he left it, the top Budget job would have gone to the next most senior Republican on the panel, Steve Symms of Idaho, who is far more aggressively anti-government in outlook.

Domenici serves on Appropriations as well as Budget — he has been an active member of as many as four committees, even in his days as Budget chairman — and so he knows firsthand how evanescent Budget's influence can be. But he believes the committee has a role to play, even under the post-1990 "pay as you go" system. He still thinks Budget leaders should pass a resolution and function as "good enforcers."

Domenici chaired the Budget Committee in all six of the years (from 1981 through 1986) Republicans controlled the Senate. In the historic session of 1981, he led the committee and the full Senate in approving the spending cuts President Ronald Reagan wanted. But he was more interested in balancing the federal budget than in providing the fiscal stimulus sought by "supply side" conservatives (Reagan budget director David A. Stockman called him "a Hooverite"). He feared the full tax-cut program of the Reagan administration would deepen the deficit, and he later worked with Finance Chairman Bob Dole and Majority Leader Howard H. Baker Jr. to pass the $98 billion tax bill of 1982.

Domenici's budget odyssey proved equally difficult in 1985, and even more dramatic. He had to cope not only with a deadlock over spending priorities, but with a dominant new ally in Dole, who had succeeded Baker as leader and threatened to overshadow the Budget chairman. The two worked for months to forge a consensus GOP plan and then to force a compromise budget to passage by a single vote.

By his last year in the chair he was openly critical of the Reagan administration and worked closely with ranking Democrat Lawton Chiles of Florida to achieve a bipartisan budget resolution. Chiles responded in kind after the Democrats recaptured the Senate majority in 1986.

The budget summit was born in 1987 and soon became a regular feature of the budget process. In its first few outings, the summit concept proved useful for the GOP. It enabled the minority Republicans on the Hill to bring their big gun, the president, to bear at the outset of congressional budget deliberations.

After an April 1989 budget summit agreement with the White House, Domenici and Chiles' successor, Jim Sasser of Tennessee, got the deal through the Budget Committee on a vote of 16-7. But few, if any, really difficult decisions were attempted on the way to meeting the deficit-reduction target for fiscal 1990. The real pain of a tax vs. cut decision was postponed until deliberations for fiscal 1991.

By the 1990 renewal of the dance, a summit was no longer a last resort so much as a prior assumption of the process (beginning this time in May and lasting four-and-a-half months). Members in both parties who were not part of the summit felt excluded and therefore unbound by its result. The summit deal collapsed and was replaced by an unlovely, hurried compromise built around the pay-as-you-go concept.

In the first months of this new regimen, Domenici signaled Sasser that he would be happy to work on a bipartisan, compromise budget. But a relatively minor disagreement called their prior working trust into question.

Domenici thought the two had agreed late in 1990 on a 60-vote "firewall" protecting the surplus in the Social Security trust fund. Domenici wanted such a hurdle because he knew pressures were building to cut the Social Security payroll tax (and diminish the surplus). But the following spring, Domenici learned that the actual resolution passed the previous year permitted a simple-majority vote for a payroll tax cut such as the one proposed by Democrat Daniel Patrick Moynihan of New York.

Piqued at Sasser and feeling betrayed, Domenici tried to reconstruct his firewall in committee, but failed. In the longer run, however, he prevailed: Moynihan mustered only 38 votes on the floor in a preliminary test of strength and withdrew his tax cut from further consideration on the Senate floor.

At times during the 1980s, the budget struggle seemed to push Domenici to the brink of despair. "I think we're getting very close to abandoning the notion of ever truly balancing the budget," he said in 1986.

But if this duty-driven man was able to make only modest progress in curbing the deficit, he demonstrated a sincere commitment to goals that many of his colleagues seemed satisfied to pursue with nothing more than rhetoric. Along the way, though, Domenici became less a leader than a manager, a technician focused more on getting *something* passed than on enacting his own conservative views.

As Budget chairman, Domenici worked hard to build unity on his committee, heeding colleagues' wishes on everything from meeting times to spending priorities. He avoided using high-pressure tactics to persuade senators to do things they did not want to do.

But Domenici's earnest temperament sometimes produced irritated outbursts that worked against his consensus-building efforts. He is an intense presence, smoking heavily in committee rooms where he may be the only one smoking. He is a sensitive man who appears genuinely distressed when a colleague is angry at him. He does not suffer criticism lightly, and frequently bristles at reporters and others who question his actions.

Domenici's record as chairman loomed over his bid to become majority leader at the start of the 99th Congress. His fellow Republicans saw him as hard-working and intelligent, but without the flair for firm direction that an eventual majority saw in Dole. Domenici was eliminated on the second ballot.

Before the Republican takeover of the Senate in 1981 imposed the Budget chair on Domenici, he had been a legislative dabbler, stubborn and intense about promoting a variety of issues but not widely identified with any. Much of his hardest work was oriented to New Mexico.

Added to the Appropriations Committee in the 98th Congress, Domenici has been a voice for spending restraint — as one would expect — and for the traditional Western concerns of water, power and rangeland agriculture. But he has also been a strong, often impassioned advocate of spending on science and research. Some of his concern stems from the role of Los Alamos' laboratories in New Mexico. But he has also warned that a diminished commitment to pure science, including the National Science Foundation's programs, will diminish the nation's future.

Freed by the Democratic Senate takeover from the constant siege of budget business in the 100th Congress, Domenici could devote more time to other interests. One was the drug bill of 1988, where he supported expedited procedures and tougher penalties for drug users, who could face civil fines of up to $10,000. But he shied away from some of the more onerous details of the House plan. "Ours is better than the House provision because it is constitutional," he said at one juncture.

Like many Western senators, Domenici took a close interest in the free-trade pact with Canada, especially in a feature he persuaded the administration to include. It contained the substance of his long-sought bailout for the U.S. uranium industry, including a federal commitment to buy $750 million of U.S. uranium. The bailout also committed the government and the industry to a billion-dollar cleanup of uranium tailings — the radioactive residue produced when uranium ore is mined.

Domenici and other Westerners wanted the deal stuck to the Canadian agreement because that country is a major source of the uranium now used in the United States. But the maneuver aroused the opposition of the Senate Finance Committee and three House committees and was dropped from the administration's final package of legislation implementing the trade pact. Later, the bailout was attached to other energy legislation and passed overwhelmingly by the Senate. But it was not given consideration in the House.

It was the renewal of an old crusade for Domenici. He held up passage of a Nuclear Regulatory Commission bill in the 97th Congress until he could get the Senate to agree to suspend proposed NRC regulations requiring the cleanup of uranium tailings. The industry considered the proposed regulations burdensome. Domenici proposed instead that the Environmental Protection Agency issue health standards; based on those standards, the NRC would issue new regulations, which would have to take costs into consideration. His proposal became law.

On the same measure, Domenici won a limit on uranium imports, despite opposition from the Reagan administration. Domenici's proposal required that at least 80 percent of the uranium used by utilities be produced in the United States. In addition, his plan required a two-year moratorium on new contracts for uranium imports if imports rose above 37.5 percent of U.S. consumption.

Domenici was an active member of the Environment Committee for several years. In the 99th Congress, he helped hammer out the compromise in the toxic-waste "superfund" cleanup bill regarding settlement terms for private entities responsible for cleanup costs. He was a vocal proponent of the industry point of view on reauthorization of the Clean Air Act, urging relaxation of some pollution standards.

At Home: Seeking a first term in 1972, Domenici had the advantage of speaking Spanish in a state that was 37 percent Hispanic. He also had a Hispanic-sounding surname, even though he was born Pietro Vichi Domenici, the son of an immigrant Italian grocer. He drew more votes in Hispanic northern New Mexico than Republicans normally do.

Domenici's background was in municipal government. After law school, he had made his first political foray by winning a seat on the Albuquerque City Commission, and later became chairman, the equivalent of mayor. As a city official, he prided himself on neighborhood meetings he held to hear residents' complaints.

Counting on his Bernalillo County (Albuquerque) base, which cast a third of the vote in the state, Domenici ran for governor in 1970. He captured the Republican nomination in a six-way race with slightly less than 50 percent of the vote. Domenici was seen as a moderate in that campaign. His closest primary rival was Stephen C. Helbing, the GOP floor leader in the state House, who advocated a crackdown on student demonstrators.

In the fall, Bernalillo County did not come through for Domenici the way he had hoped. He carried it by only 8,909 votes, not enough for him to win statewide against Democrat Bruce King, the state House Speaker. King had the party registration advantage and was better known statewide. Domenici tried to raise doubts about King by criticizing his lack of administrative experience, but with little success.

Undeterred, Domenici came back in 1972, this time running for the Senate seat being vacated by Democrat Clinton P. Anderson. His Democratic opponent was former state Rep. Jack Daniels, who had also run for governor in 1970 but lost to King in the Democratic primary.

Daniels, a wealthy banker, differed little from Domenici on the issues. But Domenici pointed out that Daniels had stood on the same platform as Sen. George McGovern that year and pledged to back him as the Democratic presidential nominee. While Daniels had repudiated McGovern's call for reduced defense spending, the association hurt him. Domenici won with 54 percent of the vote.

Domenici's percentage dropped slightly in 1978. The Democratic candidate, state Attorney General (and later one-term governor) Toney Anaya, was Hispanic. Domenici had taken most of the heavily Hispanic counties in 1972, but six years later he lost most of them. In addition, his 1972 plurality of 31,240 votes in Bernalillo shrank to 6,766 in 1978.

Fortunately for Domenici, Anaya did not have a united Democratic Party behind him. As chief state prosecutor, he had secured indictments against several important party figures, arousing resentment among regulars and prompting many of them not to vote.

With a massive campaign treasury and his new national role as chairman of the Budget Committee, Domenici's re-election in 1984 was never much in doubt. He all but locked up the victory when no prominent Democrats chose to challenge him.

Domenici's eventual opponent, liberal state Rep. Judith A. Pratt, attempted to tie him to Reagan budget cuts that she said had hurt the state, but in a Republican year she could not begin to make a dent in Domenici's lead. The incumbent won a third term with more than 70 percent of the vote.

In 1990, Domenici's continued popularity with voters was reaffirmed when he trounced Democratic state Sen. Tom R. Benavides, a legislative maverick who once introduced a bill to legalize ostrich and camel racing in the state and tried to create a new county near Albuquerque to be named "Benavides County."

Committees

Budget (Ranking)

Appropriations (9th of 13 Republicans)
Treasury, Postal Service & General Government (ranking); Defense; Energy & Water Development; Interior; Transportation

Banking, Housing & Urban Affairs (7th of 9 Republicans)

Energy & Natural Resources (3rd of 9 Republicans)
Energy Research & Development (ranking); Energy Regulation & Conservation; Public Lands, National Parks & Forests

Select Indian Affairs (5th of 7 Republicans)

Elections

1990 General

Pete V. Domenici (R)	296,712	(73%)
Tom R. Benavides (D)	110,033	(27%)

Previous Winning Percentages: **1984** (72%) **1978** (53%) **1972** (54%)

Campaign Finance

	Receipts	Receipts from PACs		Expend-itures
1990				
Domenici (R)	$2,110,973	$773,374	(37%)	$1,925,057
Benavides (D)	$38,643	$13,250	(34%)	$38,510

Key Votes

1991

Authorize use of force against Iraq	Y

1990

Oppose prohibition of certain semiautomatic weapons	Y
Support constitutional amendment on flag desecration	Y
Oppose requiring parental notice for minors' abortions	?
Halt production of B-2 stealth bomber at 13 planes	N
Approve budget that cut spending and raised revenues	Y
Pass civil rights bill over Bush veto	Y

1989

Oppose reduction of SDI funding	Y
Oppose barring federal funds for "obscene" art	Y
Allow vote on capital gains tax cut	Y

Voting Studies

	Presidential Support		Party Unity		Conservative Coalition	
Year	**S**	**O**	**S**	**O**	**S**	**O**
1990	67	29	69	24	84	8
1989	90	7	74	23	76	24
1988	76	19	77	19	97	0
1987	69	31	78	20	88	13
1986	88	12	89	10	95	5
1985	82	15	90	6	88	8
1984	88	8	86	14	91	9
1983	74	18	72	14	75	9
1982	85	15	90	9	97	3
1981	84	13	86	8	94	4

Interest Group Ratings

Year	ADA	ACU	AFL-CIO	CCUS
1990	22	50	56	67
1989	10	88	11	88
1988	15	72	46	79
1987	20	65	30	78
1986	5	83	13	79
1985	5	82	10	83
1984	25	77	36	63
1983	15	44	19	35
1982	15	55	19	80
1981	15	64	11	94

Jeff Bingaman (D)

Of Santa Fe — Elected 1982

Born: Oct. 3, 1943, El Paso, Texas.
Education: Harvard U., B.A. 1965; Stanford U., LL.B. 1968.
Military Service: Army Reserve, 1968-74.
Occupation: Lawyer.
Family: Wife, Anne Kovacovich; one child.
Religion: Methodist.
Political Career: N.M. attorney general, 1979-83.
Capitol Office: 524 Hart Bldg. 20510; 224-5521.

In Washington: Bingaman is a detail man, a relative rarity in a body whose members frequently are more comfortable expounding on the state of the world than examining esoteric issues. Although he is rarely seen on the network news shows, or even on C-SPAN, Bingaman has quietly made a name for himself with his efforts on the defense, energy, education and government operations issues in which he specializes.

The serious-minded Bingaman is not one for the colorful quip. Once or twice a week, he abandons his Senate office for a quiet corner of the Supreme Court library down the street. He had a similarly secluded cubbyhole in Santa Fe when he was New Mexico attorney general — a place where he could retreat to think.

This studious style has served him well on the Armed Services Committee, where his mastery of military research and management issues impresses defense specialists. He chairs the Defense Industry and Technology Subcommittee, giving him a voice in the debate over the impact of post-Cold War spending cutbacks on the "defense industrial base."

Liberal by instinct, Bingaman is a rather reliable ally for the conservative committee Chairman Sam Nunn, D-Ga., widely regarded as the guiding force in Senate defense policy.

Bingaman's deliberate approach led him in January 1991 to oppose the resolution authorizing President Bush to use military force to end Iraq's occupation of Kuwait. Bingaman favored instead a resolution, proposed by Senate Majority Leader George J. Mitchell and advanced by Nunn, to continue an economic blockade to pressure Iraq to withdraw from Kuwait.

"I am not convinced that offensive military action is the correct course to accomplish that goal at this time," Bingaman said. "In fact, I have come to believe the exact opposite. That is, that a rush to action would be imprudent, it would be unwise, and it would involve unnecessary costs, chief among them the unnecessary loss of human life." In calling on the president to continue the embargo, Bingaman said, "Time is on our side if we have the patience to use it; it is not on Saddam Hussein's side."

He also rejected the argument that Congress was micromanaging the Persian Gulf policy by debating the resolutions just before the Jan. 15 deadline for Iraq's withdrawal from Kuwait, which had been set by the United Nations at Bush's request. At the end of Bingaman's speech, Pennsylvania Republican Arlen Specter implied that the debate was a forum for Democrats "second-guessing the president." Bingaman responded that "the Congress is doing what it is required under our Constitution to do today, and that is meeting to debate whether we should go to war. . . ."

During the 101st Congress, Bingaman made his mark in the debate over the strategic defense initiative (SDI). Like Nunn, Bingaman opposes the Reagan/Bush vision of a space-based "shield" of anti-ballistic missile (ABM) weapons as infeasible under current technology and as violative of the 1972 ABM treaty between the United States and Soviet Union. But Bingaman is not opposed to SDI research: He wants to see priorities reordered in favor of ground-based anti-missile systems that have near-term possibilities.

In August 1990, Bingaman joined with Alabama Democrat Richard C. Shelby on an amendment to the fiscal 1991 defense authorization bill diverting money from "brilliant pebbles," a system of small interceptor missiles that was the current favorite of those advocating rapid deployment of a space-based SDI. The funds would be applied to research on ground-based systems and on exotic space-based technologies that would not be deployable for years. The Senate adopted the measure by a 54-44 vote.

Hoping for a comeback, SDI advocates tried in early 1991 to ride the success of Patriot anti-ballistic missiles at shooting down Iraq's Scuds during the Persian Gulf War. However, Bingaman warned against what he viewed as pro-SDI hype: "The public should not be mesmerized by the [Patriots'] great success against

Iraqi missiles ... into believing that the SDI program should receive blanket support...."

Bingaman, whose home state includes the Los Alamos National Laboratory, is a proponent of efforts to reduce such facilities' dependence on weapons research. As the 101st Congress worked to shape a plan to clean up toxic waste sites and other hazards at the nation's defense installations, Bingaman fell in behind a proposal by Nunn that was heavy on environmental research, some of which would be performed by the Department of Energy labs.

After a long effort, Bingaman in 1990 pushed through a measure that would allow the Defense and Energy departments to raise the pay of certain engineers and scientists nearer to private-sector levels. To accomplish this goal, he had to overcome the opposition of Democrat John Glenn of Ohio, the chairman of the Senate Governmental Affairs Committee (of which Bingaman was then a member).

Glenn initially argued that such a differential pay scale would sow "the seeds of the destruction of the civil service system." Bingaman argued that the need to retain technicians was critical.

During debate on the fiscal 1990 defense authorization bill, Bingaman's motion to table Glenn's proposal to kill the proposed 50 percent pay increase for senior scientists and engineers passed 69-31. But the provisions were stripped out in conference, forcing Bingaman to reintroduce them the next year.

This time, he found Glenn to be more flexible. In fact, it was Glenn who proposed the somewhat broader pay-related amendments to the fiscal 1991 defense authorization bill that became law. Those provisions would allow up to 800 people holding critical jobs in all federal agencies to be paid as much as the most senior executive branch officials, and allow federal laboratories to try out flexible pay scales for scientists and engineers.

Bingaman is also a supporter of defense-related research into such items as high-definition television and computer chips, which can have spin-off benefits for the civilian economy. "Dual-use technologies provide the underpinnings for both our national security and competitiveness in the long run," he says.

Another of Bingaman's persistent causes — one that could only engage a devotee of government process — is the reform of the Paperwork Reduction Act of 1980. Under that law, the Office of Management and Budget (OMB) is authorized to review all proposed federal regulations in order to ensure that they do not create burdensome paperwork requirements for agencies or the public. However, Bingaman and others have criticized OMB over the past decade for using this role to weaken regulations not in the conservative mold of the Reagan and Bush administrations.

In 1990, Bingaman tried to push through a measure that would have set a 60-day deadline for OMB reviews and required a detailed explanation for substantial changes in the regulations. The Bush administration strongly opposed the bill, arguing that it was an intrusion on executive branch prerogatives, and calling instead for an informal agreement between the White House and Congress on OMB review procedures. The result was a stalemate that killed the bill during the 101st Congress.

In May 1990, Bingaman left Governmental Affairs to fill a vacancy on the Labor and Human Resources Committee. But he did not lose interest in governmental issues. In April 1991, Bingaman was named to a Senate task force formed in the aftermath of the Keating Five controversy to develop standards for "constituent service."

As a member of the Energy and Natural Resources Committee and chairman of the Mineral Resources Subcommittee, Bingaman follows national energy policy. Like his GOP counterpart, senior Sen. Pete V. Domenici, Bingaman guards the interests of New Mexico's coal, natural gas and uranium industries.

At Home: When he launched his 1982 Senate campaign, Bingaman was in his third year as New Mexico's attorney general, little-known outside the legal and political communities, but politically unscarred. Lucky or shrewd, he stayed that way through his successful primary campaign against former Democratic Gov. Jerry Apodaca and then against GOP Sen. Harrison Schmitt.

In the primary, the ex-governor was hamstrung by reports that he had ties to underworld figures. Bingaman did not directly mention Apodaca's problems, but he gave voters a not-so-subtle reminder with his slogan — "a senator we can proudly call our own."

Bingaman was endorsed by the state AFL-CIO, then narrowly won the support of the party convention. In the primary, he swept to nomination by a margin of nearly 3-to-2.

Incumbent Schmitt, a former Apollo astronaut, lacked Apodaca's political scars. But he appeared more interested in pet subjects such as 21st-century technology than in the state's struggling economy. Bingaman lambasted Schmitt for supporting supply-side economics, sharp increases in defense spending and cuts in Social Security payments. With statewide unemployment at 10 percent, Schmitt's ties to President Reagan were a campaign liability.

Schmitt also ran poorly researched advertisements that accused Attorney General Bingaman of condoning the release of a convicted murderer and failing to prosecute the instigators of a deadly prison riot. The charges backfired when the head of the state Supreme Court and an archbishop of the Catholic Church in New Mexico defended Bingaman. Labor backing, a voter-targeting program by the Democratic National Committee and a heavy Hispanic turnout for gubernatorial candidate Anaya all helped Bingaman. He also owed a literal debt of thanks to his wife, a successful Santa Fe lawyer. She and Bingaman lent his campaign more than $600,000, enabling it to compete with Schmitt's. Bingaman took 54 percent of the vote.

Long before 1988, national GOP operatives were portraying Bingaman as one of their top targets in the nation. His low-profile manner had left him with a fairly fuzzy image after one term in the Senate, and the GOP to define it, claiming that Bingaman lacked stature and had achieved little in Congress.

But the GOP line lost credibility when the party chose a nominee with stature problems of his own, and who could be less compelling on the stump even than Bingaman.

GOP state Sen. Bill Valentine tried to put Bingaman on the defensive but he had trouble whipping up enthusiasm, or money, for his campaign. There was also no significant animosity toward Bingaman for Valentine to capitalize on. And with cash to run waves of advertising that began early in the year, Bingaman was able to raise his profile and publicize his efforts in the Senate. On Election Day, Valentine got less than 40 percent of the vote.

Bingaman grew up in the isolated New Mexico mining town of Silver City, the son of a professor and nephew of John Bingaman, a confidant of Democratic Sen. Clinton Anderson. At Stanford Law School, Bingaman worked for Robert F. Kennedy's 1968 presidential campaign. Returning to New Mexico, he served as counsel to the 1969 state constitutional convention. Although the new constitution was defeated at the polls, Bingaman drew notice. In 1972 he became a partner in the law firm of former Democratic Gov. Jack M. Campbell.

Bingaman ran for attorney general six years later. During the primary against another Santa Fe lawyer, Richard C. Bosson, Bingaman emphasized his concept of the office as a public law firm. Criticizing Bingaman's lucrative private practice, Bosson contended that he was the true populist. But Bingaman drew the support of much of the legal community and won nomination handily. When his Republican opponent withdrew, Bingaman was guaranteed election.

Committees

Armed Services (5th of 11 Democrats)
Defense Industry & Technology (chairman); Readiness, Sustainability & Support; Strategic Forces & Nuclear Deterrence

Energy & Natural Resources (5th of 11 Democrats)
Mineral Resources Development & Production (chairman); Energy Research & Development; Public Lands, National Parks & Forests

Labor & Human Resources (9th of 10 Democrats)
Children, Families, Drugs & Alcoholism; Education, Arts & Humanities; Employment & Productivity

Joint Economic

Elections

1988 General		
Jeff Bingaman (D)	321,983	(63%)
Bill Valentine (R)	186,579	(37%)

Previous Winning Percentage: **1982** (54%)

Campaign Finance

	Receipts	Receipts from PACs		Expenditures
1988				
Bingaman (D)	$3,176,793	$1,100,451	(35%)	$3,164,973
Valentine (R)	$661,825	$91,363	(14%)	$659,624

Key Votes

1991	
Authorize use of force against Iraq	N
1990	
Oppose prohibition of certain semiautomatic weapons	Y
Support constitutional amendment on flag desecration	N
Oppose requiring parental notice for minors' abortions	Y
Halt production of B-2 stealth bomber at 13 planes	N
Approve budget that cut spending and raised revenues	Y
Pass civil rights bill over Bush veto	Y
1989	
Oppose reduction of SDI funding	Y
Oppose barring federal funds for "obscene" art	Y
Allow vote on capital gains tax cut	N

Voting Studies

	Presidential Support		Party Unity		Conservative Coalition	
Year	**S**	**O**	**S**	**O**	**S**	**O**
1990	35	54	76	18	32	57
1989	54	46	84	16	34	66
1988	52	47	71	22	68	30
1987	32	60	74	21	53	38
1986	41	58	70	29	41	59
1985	33	66	75	24	37	60
1984	40	56	79	19	28	72
1983	45	54	81	15	25	73

Interest Group Ratings

Year	ADA	ACU	AFL-CIO	CCUS
1990	67	19	56	17
1989	65	15	90	38
1988	70	20	77	43
1987	65	13	90	40
1986	65	35	73	26
1985	70	13	81	34
1984	100	9	91	42
1983	90	4	94	42

1 Steven H. Schiff (R)

Of Albuquerque — Elected 1988

Born: March 18, 1947, Chicago, Ill.
Education: U. of Illinois, Chicago Circle, B.A. 1968; U. of New Mexico, J.D. 1972.
Military Service: N.M. Air National Guard, 1969-present.
Occupation: Lawyer.
Family: Wife, Marcia Lewis; two children.
Religion: Jewish.
Political Career: Bernalillo County district attorney, 1981-89; candidate for district judge, 1978.
Capitol Office: 1427 Longworth Bldg. 20515; 225-6316.

In Washington: A former high-profile prosecutor, Schiff has become a task-oriented House back-bencher satisfied with patiently learning the legislative ropes while serving the needs of his district. His success is due largely to his doggedly methodical — some might say bland — personality, and his lawyerly approach to issues. A moderate Republican who supports a balanced budget and a line-item veto, he also strikes out on his own; in 1990, he voted only 55 percent of the time with President Bush.

When, for example, the controversial bill to ban physical desecration of the flag came to a vote in the 101st Congress, Schiff was one of only 43 House members voting against it. He said he felt the language of the bill did not pass constitutional muster.

At the start of the 102nd Congress, Schiff was rewarded with a seat on the Judiciary Committee, where as chairman of the Republican Task Force on Crime he will likely pursue his favorite subjects — issues concerning the legal and criminal justice systems.

He has called for regulation of private jails housing federal prisoners and has encouraged state legislatures to adopt uniform treatment of juveniles, including the right to prosecute as adults individuals age 15 or older who commit certain violent crimes. He successfully included in the 1990 crime bill a provision barring convicted criminals from escaping court-ordered restitution by declaring bankruptcy.

A lieutenant colonel in the New Mexico Air National Guard, Schiff was called for active service during the Persian Gulf crisis; he did not go overseas, but volunteered to serve three days drafting wills and performing other legal aid for reservists. Schiff, whose wife is in the Army Reserve, opposed bills introduced during the war that would have exempted some military parents with dependent children from combat service. Schiff argued such risks are accepted when one joins a volunteer army.

At Home: Schiff won his 1988 House election on a pledge to deliver constituent service, a rather modest agenda for a Republican who toppled two family dynasties to win in a politically competitive district. But constituent service had been the hallmark of his GOP predecessor, Manuel Lujan Jr.

When Lujan announced his plans to leave the House after 20 years (he was later named Bush's interior secretary), a dozen candidates jockeyed to succeed him, including his brother, former state GOP Chairman Edward Lujan, and Democrat Tom Udall, the son of former Interior Secretary Stewart Udall and nephew of Arizona Rep. Morris K. Udall.

Schiff had been contemplating a Senate bid, but quickly shifted his sights to the open House seat. In eight years as popular district attorney in Bernalillo County, Schiff had become a familiar face in the media; he directed the prosecution of numerous high-profile criminal cases. Outspent in the House primary by nearly 2-to-1, Schiff came under fire for his willingness to plea-bargain. But the charge did not stick, because Schiff's image as a law-and-order figure was well-known to voters.

In Democrat Udall, an attorney and environmental activist, Schiff faced a well-funded and well-organized foe whose name had helped him win a 10-way primary. While Schiff boasted that his office had won the most death-penalty cases in state history, he was again accused of letting criminals off easy. He also was accused of lacking legislative experience.

In 1990, Democrat nominee Secretary of State Rebecca Vigil-Giron was sent reeling by revelations that she had exaggerated her academic record, had once defaulted on a student loan and had witnessed her roommate forge a signature on her 1986 ballot petition. Schiff coasted to a 70 percent victory.

New Mexico 1

Central — Albuquerque

Originally a health resort and trade center, Albuquerque had fewer than 40,000 residents in 1940. Its postwar emergence as a Republican stronghold was fueled by the development of a prosperous military-aerospace industry. By 1960 the population topped 200,000; now it is almost twice that.

During the past two decades a diversified economy has sustained the boom. The city's population grew 36 percent in the 1970s and another 16 percent in the 1980s, enhancing Albuquerque's position as New Mexico's commercial hub and major population center. Including the Bernalillo County suburbs, the Albuquerque area is home for one-quarter of New Mexico's 1.5 million residents.

Electronics firms provided the impetus for Albuquerque's latest round of population growth. Young engineers and scientists, attracted by jobs, and retirees, attracted by the weather, have helped in recent years to preserve the county's Republican tilt. Albuquerque and surrounding Bernalillo County have voted Republican in all but one presidential election since 1952. But Albuquerque is not as militantly conservative as some of the other Sun Belt population centers. Though it was strong territory for George Bush in 1988, at the same time it went Democratic for U.S. Senate.

The county's large minority population provides a good Democratic base vote. Hispanics comprise 37 percent of the county's population. In addition, the newest generation of white-collar migrants exhibits some liberal tendencies. Independent John B. Anderson drew 10 percent of the county vote in his 1980 presidential bid, well above his statewide mark of 6 percent.

Three sparsely populated counties east of Albuquerque are also included in the 1st. Together, the three — De Baca, Guadalupe and Torrance counties — hold only 3 percent of the district's population. Ranching is the mainstay of the economy in De Baca and Guadalupe counties.

Population: 434,141. White 345,939 (80%), Black 9,816 (2%), Other 14,937 (3%). Spanish origin 162,171 (37%). 18 and over 307,647 (71%), 65 and over 35,961 (8%). Median age: 28.

Committees

Government Operations (7th of 15 Republicans)
Government Information, Justice & Agriculture; Legislation & National Security

Judiciary (12th of 13 Republicans)
Administrative Law & Governmental Relations; Crime and Criminal Justice

Science, Space & Technology (14th of 19 Republicans)
Energy; Science

Elections

1990 General		
Steven H. Schiff (R)	97,375	(70%)
Rebecca Vigil-Giron (D)	41,306	(30%)
1988 General		
Steven H. Schiff (R)	89,985	(51%)
Tom Udall (D)	84,138	(47%)

District Vote For President

	1988	1984	1980	1976
D	81,687 (45%)	70,395 (39%)	57,566 (35%)	67,451 (45%)
R	96,586 (54%)	108,766 (60%)	87,583 (54%)	79,679 (54%)
I			15,291 (9%)	

Campaign Finance

	Receipts	Receipts from PACs		Expend-itures
1990				
Schiff (R)	$554,465	$223,203	(40%)	$538,273
Vigil-Giron (D)	$127,218	$34,732	(27%)	$123,215
1988				
Schiff (R)	$563,429	$158,911	(28%)	$559,134
Udall (D)	$580,819	$226,631	(39%)	$576,677

Key Votes

1991	
Authorize use of force against Iraq	Y
1990	
Support constitutional amendment on flag desecration	Y
Pass family and medical leave bill over Bush veto	N
Reduce SDI funding	N
Allow abortions in overseas military facilities	Y
Approve budget summit plan for spending and taxing	Y
Approve civil rights bill	Y
1989	
Halt production of B-2 stealth bomber at 13 planes	N
Oppose capital gains tax cut	N
Approve federal abortion funding in rape or incest cases	N
Approve pay raise and revision of ethics rules	N
Pass Democratic minimum wage plan over Bush veto	N

Voting Studies

	Presidential Support		Party Unity		Conservative Coalition	
Year	S	O	S	O	S	O
1990	55	44	56	41	78	22
1989	69	30	63	37	78	22

Interest Group Ratings

Year	ADA	ACU	AFL-CIO	CCUS
1990	22	58	17	71
1989	15	86	25	90

2 Joe Skeen (R)

Of Picacho — Elected 1980

Born: June 30, 1927, Roswell, N.M.
Education: Texas A&M U., B.S. 1950.
Military Service: Navy, 1945-46; Air Force Reserve, 1949-52.
Occupation: Sheep rancher; soil and water engineer; flying service operator.
Family: Wife, Mary Jones; two children.
Religion: Roman Catholic.
Political Career: N.M. Senate, 1961-71, minority leader, 1965-71; GOP state chairman, 1962-65; GOP nominee for lieutenant governor, 1970; GOP nominee for governor, 1974, 1978.
Capitol Office: 2447 Rayburn Bldg. 20515; 225-2365.

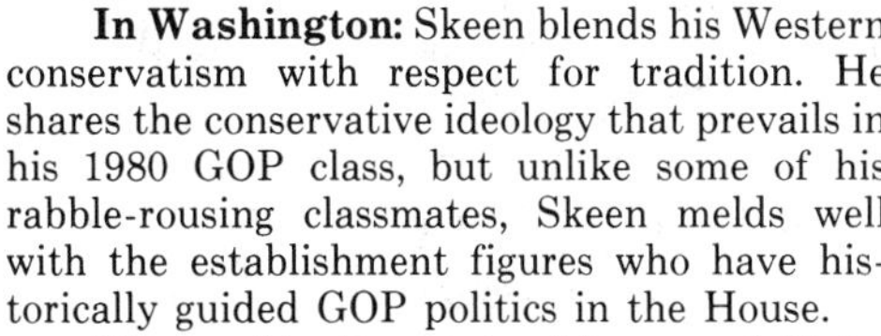

In Washington: Skeen blends his Western conservatism with respect for tradition. He shares the conservative ideology that prevails in his 1980 GOP class, but unlike some of his rabble-rousing classmates, Skeen melds well with the establishment figures who have historically guided GOP politics in the House.

The combination makes him a good fit for the Appropriations Committee, where his best-known legislative cause is a perennial effort with Indiana Democrat Andrew Jacobs Jr. to reduce the allowances and pensions for former presidents. The usual routine is for Jacobs to propose a draconian cut, and then for Skeen to offer a more modest reduction that is often adopted by the House.

At the start of the 102nd Congress, Skeen won a seat on the Appropriations Agriculture Subcommittee, which puts him in a choice position to watch out for his district's cattle and sheep ranchers. A former rancher himself, Skeen is a staunch opponent of increasing fees charged for use of federal grazing land.

Like his committee colleagues, Skeen looks for ways to bring home federal dollars. In the 101st Congress, he helped win $36 million to bring a stealth fighter wing to Holloman Air Force Base in the 2nd. In his first term on Appropriations, he attached an amendment to the omnibus drug bill providing $350,000 for the Los Alamos National Laboratory's research on a low-level radar detection system that could aid in catching drug smugglers.

Skeen is one of the few House members willing to entertain the idea of locating a nuclear-waste site in his district. The Waste Isolation Pilot Project (WIPP) is proposed for the salt beds below ground near the 2nd District city of Carlsbad. The controversial plan would make Carlsbad the first permanent facility to store defense-generated low-level waste.

Skeen was not able to enact legislation to pave the way for opening WIPP in either the 100th or the 101st Congress. But along with the rest of the New Mexico delegation, he opposes the administration-supported effort to do so through rulemaking because it does not go far enough toward meeting the health and safety concerns of area residents.

At Home: After narrowly losing two carefully planned bids for governor, Skeen won a House seat without even being on the ballot. He is one of the few write-in candidates ever elected to the House.

Skeen's unusual victory came after Democratic Rep. Harold E. Runnels, who was unopposed for re-election, died on Aug. 5, 1980. Runnels' death set off three months of complex maneuvering, with Skeen and Runnels' widow, Dorothy, mounting unsuccessful court challenges to win a spot on the ballot against the substitute Democratic nominee, David King.

Skeen and Mrs. Runnels pursued separate write-in campaigns, aided by negative publicity that hit King. A former state finance commissioner, King moved to the district only after Harold Runnels' death, and there were complaints that his choice was arranged by his uncle, Democratic Gov. Bruce King.

Skeen based his campaign on the contention that no one should be appointed to Congress. His write-ins totaled 38 percent of the vote, enough to win the three-way contest. He has had little trouble since then.

Before his election in 1980, Skeen showed more interest in the New Mexico governor's mansion than he did in a U.S. House seat. In 1974 and 1978, he was the Republican candidate for governor, offering an aggressive conservative campaign that emphasized his support for right-to-work legislation. He lost each time by less than 3,800 votes, but was a substantial winner in the counties that now make up his district. Skeen was mentioned as a possible 1990 gubernatorial candidate, but in March 1989, he said he wanted to stay in the House.

New Mexico 2

South and East — Las Cruces; Roswell

Southern New Mexico was once firmly Democratic, but traditional party ties have eroded there. During the 1970s, the area developed a strong habit of voting Republican in statewide contests, as ranchers and other Southern-style Democrats came to resent their party's national program.

The centerpiece of the 2nd District is "Little Texas," the southeastern corner of New Mexico. Settled by Texans early in the 20th century, the region is economically, culturally and politically similar to the adjoining Texas plains. Most of the land here is devoted to grazing cattle or sheep. But oil and military projects have reshaped voting habits in a Republican direction.

Nearly half the vote in the 14-county district is concentrated in four counties of "Little Texas." The oil- and gas-producing centers of Chaves County and Lea County are bastions of conservatism. Equally conservative Curry County is the site of a large Air Force base.

Near Carlsbad in Eddy County are the nation's most productive potash mines, and the area's unionized miners occasionally give Democrats enough votes to carry the county. George Bush won it in 1988, but it has twice supported Democratic Sen. Jeff Bingaman.

To the west are Otero and Dona Ana counties, which account for nearly one-third of the district population. Otero County favors the GOP. Dona Ana, which contains Las Cruces, has a Hispanic majority, giving the Democrats a substantial base, but Republicans generally carry it. Parts of Dona Ana, Otero and Sierra counties hold the sprawling White Sands Missile Range.

The district's lone Democratic strongholds are in the Mexican Highlands, along the Arizona border, where copper and lead mines have attracted union labor. But they have less than 10 percent of the vote.

Population: 436,261. White 359,531 (82%), Black 12,144 (3%), Other 6,438 (2%). Spanish origin 146,474 (34%). 18 and over 297,158 (68%), 65 and over 45,900 (11%). Median age: 28.

Committees

Appropriations (14th of 22 Republicans)
Rural Development, Agriculture & Related Agencies (ranking); Interior

Elections

1990 General		
Joe Skeen (R)	80,677	(100%)
1988 General		
Joe Skeen (R)	100,324	(100%)

Previous Winning Percentages: **1986** (63%) **1984** (74%) **1982** (58%) **1980** * (38%)

* *Write-in candidate.*

District Vote For President

	1988		1984		1980		1976	
D	67,307	(41%)	53,600	(33%)	50,472	(35%)	60,392	(46%)
R	96,142	(58%)	108,723	(66%)	86,337	(60%)	68,581	(53%)
I					4,843	(3%)		

Campaign Finance

	Receipts	Receipts from PACs	Expend-itures
1990			
Skeen (R)	$197,830	$109,210 (55%)	$80,737
1988			
Skeen (R)	$143,944	$87,050 (60%)	$67,727

Key Votes

1991	
Authorize use of force against Iraq	Y
1990	
Support constitutional amendment on flag desecration	Y
Pass family and medical leave bill over Bush veto	N
Reduce SDI funding	N
Allow abortions in overseas military facilities	N
Approve budget summit plan for spending and taxing	Y
Approve civil rights bill	N
1989	
Halt production of B-2 stealth bomber at 13 planes	N
Oppose capital gains tax cut	N
Approve federal abortion funding in rape or incest cases	N
Approve pay raise and revision of ethics rules	N
Pass Democratic minimum wage plan over Bush veto	N

Voting Studies

	Presidential Support		Party Unity		Conservative Coalition	
Year	S	O	S	O	S	O
1990	68	32	63	35	91	9
1989	86	14	70	29	100	0
1988	56	43	80	19	89	11
1987	63	34	76	24	93	7
1986	68	30	79	20	94	6
1985	68	31	81	17	93	4
1984	62	38	84	15	93	7
1983	82	17	89	8	94	4
1982	82	16	90	10	100	0
1981	75	24	83	15	96	4

Interest Group Ratings

Year	ADA	ACU	AFL-CIO	CCUS
1990	6	71	8	79
1989	0	96	0	90
1988	5	100	29	93
1987	12	83	25	80
1986	10	82	7	67
1985	0	76	6	86
1984	15	75	15	69
1983	5	91	0	90
1982	5	82	5	82
1981	0	100	20	89

3 Bill Richardson (D)

Of Santa Fe — Elected 1982

Born: Nov. 15, 1947, Pasadena, Calif.
Education: Tufts U., B.A. 1970, M.A. 1971.
Occupation: Business consultant.
Family: Wife, Barbara Flavin.
Religion: Roman Catholic.
Political Career: N.M. Democratic Party executive director, 1978-80; Democratic nominee for U.S. House, 1980.
Capitol Office: 332 Cannon Bldg. 20515; 225-6190.

In Washington: A quick tour of some of Richardson's legislative concerns would span the globe: nuclear waste issues and American Indian affairs in New Mexico, tobacco policy and pollution control nationally, arms control talks in Vienna, and Cambodian rebels in Southeast Asia.

While that sort of trip might take many legislators a decade, those were Richardson's stopovers in the 101st Congress alone. He delves into an array of issues with uncommon energy, and in many cases gets results.

Yet with such a bulging portfolio, it is no surprise that some papers occasionally slip to the ground. Richardson's voracious legislative appetite, coupled with his oft-stated desire to hold statewide office someday, naturally leads some colleagues to wonder whether he is motivated primarily by policymaking or by political ambition.

In the 100th Congress, colleagues' eyebrows raised when Richardson did not show for the first day of Energy and Commerce's work on a product-liability bill for which he was chief sponsor. Richardson has said a family illness necessitated that absence, but he was missing at other times throughout the deliberations, and colleagues came to identify the bill with its other, more active proponents.

Richardson has heard the criticisms that he can get overcommitted. "The rap is that I'm spread too thin," Richardson told a reporter from the *Albuquerque Journal* in 1990. "And there's another rap. That I seek publicity." But Richardson believes many are unaware of how much he has achieved. "For all the criticism I might get, I have done more than most," Richardson told the paper. "That's not because of ambition, that's because I want to do things. I mean look at my schedule compared to most members of Congress."

Richardson is in a better position than most to do things; he sits on the powerful Energy and Commerce Committee, and also is a member of the Interior, Intelligence and Select Aging panels.

Meanwhile, he has assumed a prominent role in Democratic Party affairs, particularly as a national spokesman for fellow Hispanics. He keeps a very high profile in New Mexico, where he is expected to seek statewide office someday.

Widely identified as a liberal Democrat on most issues, Richardson has generally been regarded as a centrist, business-oriented vote on Energy and Commerce. Both there and at Interior, he is usually a voice for the oil, gas and uranium industries of the Southwest.

But during negotiations on the Clean Air Act during the 101st Congress, Richardson drew fierce attacks from oil lobbyists when he pushed a plan to promote non-gasoline car fuels. Richardson's proposal, offered first as an amendment in an Energy and Commerce subcommittee, would have required the use of special, cleaner-burning gasolines in the nation's most polluted cities.

Opposed by Energy and Commerce Chairman John D. Dingell, the proposal was narrowly defeated in subcommittee and again in full committee, 22-21. But the Senate had approved similar provisions in its clean air bill, and the committee later agreed to a compromise that included parts of Richardson's amendment.

On Interior, Richardson has been a critic of administration plans to operate a nuclear waste repository in underground salt beds near Carlsbad, New Mexico; he has expressed skepticism that safety issues are being fully addressed. In 1989, Richardson also persuaded the House to temporarily block the Los Alamos National Laboratory from burning radioactive waste until the state could approve safety regulations.

Although he bears an Anglo name, Richardson's mother was Mexican, and he has been a leader on Hispanic issues. At the end of his first term, he was chosen to chair the Hispanic Caucus, but he later stepped down, saying he wanted to spend more time on state issues. His decision came at a time of controversy over his support for an immigration bill that a majority of the caucus opposed.

The bill combined legalization of many illegal aliens with new sanctions against employers of undocumented workers. Most His-

New Mexico 3

North and West — Farmington; Santa Fe

With three-fifths of its voters either Hispanic or Indian, the 3rd is decidedly more liberal and more Democratic than either of the state's other constituencies.

The population is divided between the Hispanic counties of northern New Mexico and the energy-rich Indian lands along the Arizona border. The Hispanic north is the more loyally Democratic. It contains eight of the 10 New Mexico counties carried by Michael S. Dukakis in 1988.

The centerpiece of the region is Santa Fe, the third-largest city in the state, and a pleasant mix of Spanish and Indian cultures has attracted a steady influx of young Anglos. The rest of the Hispanic north is primarily mountainous, semi-arid grazing land that supports some subsistence farming. Unemployment has been high in the area; the Mora County jobless rate was well above 30 percent for much of the last decade.

An economic oasis is the Anglo community of Los Alamos, where the atomic bomb was developed during World War II. One of the most prosperous counties in the country, its voters are well educated, scientifically inclined and largely Republican. But there is a strong moderate streak in some of those Republicans; John B. Anderson's presidential bid drew 15 percent in Los Alamos County in 1980.

The Indian country divides more closely at the polls. The Indians, most of them Navaho, usually vote Democratic. But they turn out in small numbers and occasionally bolt to the Republicans.

The largest county in the region is San Juan, where a conservative Anglo population settled around Farmington (population 34,000) to tap the vast supply of oil, gas and coal in the Four Corners area. San Juan went solidly for George Bush in 1988.

Driving south from San Juan on U.S. 666 — known locally as the Devil's Highway — motorists reach Gallup, ignominiously referred to as the "Drunk Driving Capital of the World." Located just south of the vast Navajo Indian Reservation, this portion of McKinley County is infamous for the frequency of its motor vehicle fatalities.

Population: 432,492. White 272,117 (63%), Black 2,060 (1%), American Indian, Eskimo and Aleut 90,403 (21%). Spanish origin 168,577 (39%). 18 and over 280,182 (65%), 65 and over 34,045 (8%). Median age: 26.

panic members objected that the sanctions would lead to discrimination against anyone who looked or sounded foreign. Richardson had voted against immigration reform himself in 1984, but by 1986 he concluded that a bill was inevitable and voted for the bill that became law, calling it "the last gasp for legalization to take place in a humane way."

He had second thoughts in 1990, when a report by the General Accounting Office showed that the penalties in the immigration law had led to discrimination against workers who look foreign. Richardson introduced a resolution designed to trigger fast-track consideration of repealing the sanctions.

Richardson also pays particular attention to the needs of American Indians, a significant presence in his district. His proposals addressing alcohol and drug abuse among Indians as well as their health, education and job training needs have made it into various pieces of legislation.

In the 101st Congress, the House approved Richardson's bill to revitalize the anemic National Health Service Corps, a federal program to channel health professionals to doctor-poor rural areas, inner cities and Indian reservations.

Richardson's background is in foreign policy, and in 1987 he joined the Intelligence Committee. On that panel, he has been wary of covert aid programs, and late in the 101st Congress, he won House approval of an amendment to unshroud U.S. aid to non-communist Cambodian rebels. Richardson's amendment set a timetable for the administration to transform its covert aid to the resistance into open assistance upon reaching a peace settlement among warring Cambodian factions.

With the Bush administration aggressively pursuing a free trade pact with Mexico at the outset of the 102nd Congress, Richardson was part of a task force lobbying colleagues to grant the administration's request for an extension of "fast-track" negotiating authority. The fast-track procedures bar lawmakers from amending trade agreements submitted for approval.

Richardson himself needed little convincing; he had been offering U.S.-Mexico free trade bills for years and had successfully pushed for House hearings on the matter.

At Home: Richardson, who has made no secret of his hankering to hold statewide office, gave serious thought to joining the open-seat governor's race in 1990. But he opted to stay put, and had no trouble winning another House term against Republican Phil T. Archuletta, the owner of a highway sign-crafting company.

A former staff member of the Senate Foreign Relations Committee, Richardson made his entry into politics in 1978, when he moved to New Mexico to become executive director of the Democratic State Committee. Within months he was planning a 1980 congressional campaign against GOP Rep. Manuel Lujan Jr. He was criticized as a carpetbagger, but he responded that his ethnic heritage — he was raised in Mexico City by a Mexican mother and an American father — made heavily Hispanic New Mexico a logical home.

By coming within 5,200 votes of the seemingly entrenched Lujan, Richardson became a star in his state party overnight. When the northern New Mexico 3rd District was created the next year, he was the early favorite to win.

His campaign survived some serious problems. He had to retract a statement in his literature that he had been a "top" foreign policy adviser to Sen. Hubert H. Humphrey. Questions about a $100,000 campaign loan produced a probe by the Federal Election Commission. Although he was eventually cleared of any wrongdoing, the probe did bring him negative publicity.

Richardson countered the bad press by campaigning dawn to dusk through the small towns and pueblos, reaching the Hispanic and Indian voters who together cast a majority of the ballots. With his 1980 organization still in place and a substantial campaign treasury, Richardson won the four-way primary with 36 percent of the vote. In the most loyally Democratic House constituency in the state, his win was tantamount to election.

Richardson has not had any problems since then, although at least one of his campaigns attracted attention. In 1986, he was challenged for re-election by former GOP Gov. David F. Cargo, a whimsical man who was seeking a political comeback 15 years after leaving office, following a long absence from the state.

Cargo managed to land some blows. When Richardson accepted an honorarium for touring a southwest Virginia coal mine, Cargo branded him "Peso Bill" — a move that generated home-state pressure and eventually helped encourage Richardson to donate the money to charity. Unfortunately for Cargo, his organization and vote-getting abilities did not match his capacity for one-liners. Richardson, capitalizing on publicity for his work on a bill to grant a national historic designation to the Santa Fe Trail, blew Cargo away with over 70 percent of the vote.

Richardson almost passed up politics for a career in baseball. Following his boyhood in Mexico City, he moved to the United States to attend school. At age 18, he was drafted by the Kansas City (now Oakland) Athletics. But an elbow injury ended his sports career.

After graduating from Tufts University, Richardson moved to Washington and found work in the State Department's congressional relations office. He subsequently worked for three years as a Senate Foreign Relations Committee staffer before moving to New Mexico.

Committees

Energy & Commerce (13th of 27 Democrats)
Health & the Environment; Telecommunications & Finance; Transportation & Hazardous Materials

Interior & Insular Affairs (13th of 29 Democrats)
Energy & the Environment; National Parks & Public Lands

Select Aging (20th of 42 Democrats)
Health & Long-Term Care; Human Services; Rural Elderly

Select Intelligence (6th of 12 Democrats)
Oversight & Evaluation; Program & Budget Authorization

Elections

1990 General		
Bill Richardson (D)	104,225	(74%)
Phil T. Archuletta (R)	35,751	(26%)
1988 General		
Bill Richardson (D)	124,938	(73%)
Cecilia M. Salazar (R)	45,954	(27%)

Previous Winning Percentages: **1986** (71%) **1984** (61%) **1982** (65%)

District Vote For President

	1988		1984		1980		1976	
D	95,503	(54%)	77,774	(46%)	59,788	(40%)	73,305	(53%)
R	77,613	(44%)	89,612	(53%)	76,859	(52%)	63,159	(46%)
I					9,325	(6%)		

Campaign Finance

	Receipts	Receipts from PACs		Expend-itures
1990				
Richardson (D)	$531,096	$346,707	(65%)	$420,907
Archuletta (R)	$19,557	$5,500	(28%)	$20,902
1988				
Richardson (D)	$456,787	$297,898	(65%)	$267,633
Salazar (R)	$41,848	$2,750	(7%)	$41,669

Key Votes

1991	
Authorize use of force against Iraq	N
1990	
Support constitutional amendment on flag desecration	Y
Pass family and medical leave bill over Bush veto	Y
Reduce SDI funding	N
Allow abortions in overseas military facilities	?
Approve budget summit plan for spending and taxing	Y
Approve civil rights bill	Y
1989	
Halt production of B-2 stealth bomber at 13 planes	N
Oppose capital gains tax cut	Y
Approve federal abortion funding in rape or incest cases	Y
Approve pay raise and revision of ethics rules	N
Pass Democratic minimum wage plan over Bush veto	Y

Voting Studies

	Presidential Support		Party Unity		Conservative Coalition	
Year	**S**	**O**	**S**	**O**	**S**	**O**
1990	29	69	84	10	54	44
1989	37	58	86	11	54	46
1988	28	66	83	12	55	34
1987	26	71	88	9	58	42
1986	24	76	90	9	52	44
1985	25	71	89	6	33	65
1984	31	66	89	9	19	80
1983	16	82	87	9	29	71

Interest Group Ratings

Year	ADA	ACU	AFL-CIO	CCUS
1990	61	26	92	21
1989	70	21	92	44
1988	75	21	93	42
1987	80	9	88	29
1986	75	18	100	41
1985	70	14	76	32
1984	85	17	100	43
1983	95	13	88	20

New York

U.S. CONGRESS

SENATE 1 D, 1 R
HOUSE 21 D, 13 R

LEGISLATURE

Senate 26 D, 35 R
House 95 D, 55 R

ELECTIONS

1988 Presidential Vote

Bush	48%
Dukakis	52%

1984 Presidential Vote

Reagan	54%
Mondale	46%

1980 Presidential Vote

Reagan	47%
Carter	44%
Anderson	8%

Turnout rate in 1986	29%
Turnout rate in 1988	48%
Turnout rate in 1990	27%

(as percentage of voting age population)

POPULATION AND GROWTH

1980 population	17,558,072
1990 population (2nd in the nation)	17,990,455
Percent change 1980-1990	+3%

DEMOGRAPHIC BREAKDOWN

White	74%
Black	16%
Asian or Pacific Islander	4%
(Hispanic origin)	12%
Urban	85%
Rural	15%
Born in state	69%
Foreign-born	14%

MAJOR CITIES

New York	7,322,564
Buffalo	328,123
Rochester	231,636
Yonkers	188,082
Syracuse	163,860

AREA AND LAND USE

Area 47,377 sq. miles (30th)

Farm	30%
Forest	62%
Federally owned	5%

Gov. Mario M. Cuomo (D)
Of Holliswood — Elected 1982

Born: June 15, 1932, Queens, N.Y.
Education: St. John's U., B.A. 1953, LL.B. 1956.
Occupation: Lawyer.
Religion: Roman Catholic.
Political Career: N.Y. secretary of state, 1975-79; lieutenant governor, 1979-83; sought Democratic nomination for lieutenant governor, 1974; sought Democratic nomination for New York City mayor, 1977; Liberal Party nominee for New York City mayor, 1977.
Next Election: 1994.

WORK

Occupations

White-collar	59%
Blue-collar	26%
Service workers	14%

Government Workers

Federal	158,969
State	302,575
Local	957,060

MONEY

Median family income	$ 20,180	(19th)
Tax burden per capita	$ 1,164	(6th)

EDUCATION

Spending per pupil through grade 12	$ 7,151	(2nd)
Persons with college degrees	18%	(14th)

CRIME

Violent crime rate 1,131 per 100,000 (1st)

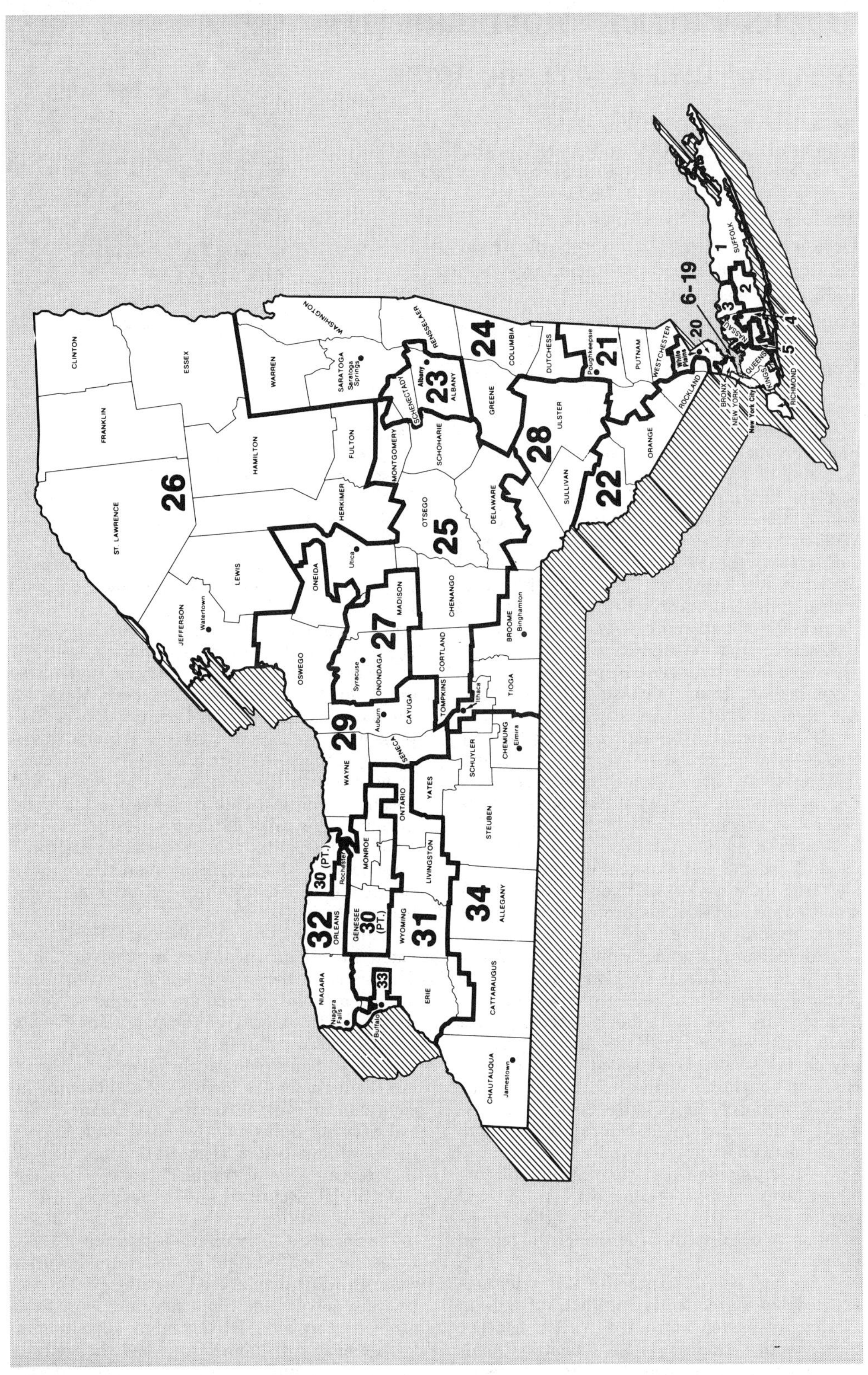
CLINTON
FRANKLIN
ESSEX
ST. LAWRENCE
26
HAMILTON
WARREN
WASHINGTON
SARATOGA
Saratoga Springs
FULTON
HERKIMER
LEWIS
JEFFERSON
Watertown
ONEIDA
Utica
MONTGOMERY
SCHENECTADY
Albany
23
ALBANY
RENSSELAER
24
COLUMBIA
GREENE
SCHOHARIE
OTSEGO
25
DELAWARE
28
ULSTER
SULLIVAN
22
ORANGE
DUTCHESS
Poughkeepsie
21
PUTNAM
WESTCHESTER
White Plains
ROCKLAND
20
6-19
BRONX
NEW YORK
New York City
QUEENS
KINGS
RICHMOND
NASSAU
SUFFOLK
1
2
3
4
5
OSWEGO
MADISON
27
ONONDAGA
Syracuse
CHENANGO
BROOME
Binghamton
CORTLAND
TIOGA
TOMPKINS
Ithaca
CAYUGA
Auburn
29
WAYNE
SENECA
YATES
SCHUYLER
CHEMUNG
Elmira
ONTARIO
STEUBEN
30 (PT.)
Rochester
MONROE
LIVINGSTON
32
ORLEANS
GENESEE
30 (PT.)
WYOMING
31
34
ALLEGANY
NIAGARA
Niagara Falls
33
Buffalo
ERIE
CATTARAUGUS
CHAUTAUQUA
Jamestown

Daniel Patrick Moynihan (D)

Of Pindars Corners — Elected 1976

Born: March 16, 1927, Tulsa, Okla.
Education: Attended City College, N.Y., 1943; Tufts U., B.N.S. 1946, B.A. 1948; Fletcher School of Law and Diplomacy, M.A. 1949, Ph.D. 1961.
Military Service: Navy, 1944-47.
Occupation: Professor of government; writer.
Family: Wife, Elizabeth Brennan; three children.
Religion: Roman Catholic.
Political Career: Sought Democratic nomination for N.Y. City Council president, 1965.
Capitol Office: 464 Russell Bldg. 20510; 224-4451.

In Washington: In a public career spanning three decades, Moynihan has been hailed as a prophet and denounced as a racist, run with the backing of the Liberal Party of New York and been designated "man of the year" by William F. Buckley's *National Review* magazine. When the height of fashion required prefixing ideologies as "neo-," both camps pinned him. But mostly he has been Daniel Patrick Moynihan, and clearly it is the title of U.S. senator that he enjoys most.

Moynihan is sui generis in today's Senate, a genuine intellectual of considerable scholarly, not to mention legislative, accomplishment. At certain moments, listening to him is both an education and a treat, as when he interrupts routine debate with a scholarly discourse on the role of the London School of Economics, or the decline of private charity in Europe, or discusses an algebraic formula for determining national income and explains in comprehensible terms how it works. When he focuses his attention on an issue, his pronouncements are invariably provocative.

Moynihan disrupted economic politics in both parties in the 101st Congress when he proposed to cut Social Security taxes and stop building surpluses in the Social Security trust funds. He said the 1990 rate increase in the payroll tax should be repealed and refunded. His plan sought to restore the initial pay-as-you-go approach to funding Social Security, under which it operated before 1983, and to make the tax plan progressive by giving a cut to lower- and middle-class workers and placing higher taxes on upper-income workers. He said surpluses in the trust funds allowed the administration to disguise the true size of the federal budget deficit.

In a city where the promise of new ideas is extolled but infrequently fulfilled, officials in Washington were confronted with a concept that upended traditional alignments. Prominent conservatives endorsed it. President Bush called it a "charade," warning against "messing around" with Social Security. Democratic congressional leaders approached it warily. It dominated fiscal debate for the first several weeks of 1990 and loomed over budget discussions throughout the year.

Few Democrats joined Moynihan initially. House Ways and Means Committee Chairman Dan Rostenkowski called the idea irresponsible; Senate Finance Committee Chairman Lloyd Bentsen expressed deep misgivings as well.

But the Democratic National Committee endorsed it, as did New York Gov. Mario M. Cuomo. Ways and Means Democrats, over Rostenkowski's objections, gave it a symbolic approval, voting to include it in the panel's recommendations to the Budget Committee. And it became a political club Democrats could wield during budget talks: If the president pressed for a cut in the capital gains tax, Democrats could counter with the Moynihan plan. Republican congressional leaders lined up their members behind Bush.

For two days in October, the Senate debated Moynihan's plan but decided to kill it. The vote, however, was on a parliamentary motion and did not require senators to go on record on the merits of the plan. The Senate voted it down again in 1991.

Moynihan's plan caught many by surprise, not the least for the identity of its author. The chairman or ranking senator on Finance's Social Security Subcommittee since 1981, he was the most outspoken Democratic opponent of the Reagan administration's proposals to cut back Social Security in 1981, and was instrumental in working out the compromise that led to the Social Security reform legislation of 1983. In leading the 1981 fight against Social Security changes, Moynihan argued that the system was basically solvent and could meet any short-term problems through relatively minor adjustments. By the next year, however, he had changed his mind. Working with Finance Committee Chairman Bob Dole, he developed the last-minute agreement that allowed the National Commission on Social Security Reform to issue a set of recommendations for saving the system with a combination of tax increases and benefit restraints.

Few seem happier than Moynihan with life as a senator. The body appreciates high oratory but forgives the merely partisan. Moynihan can deliver both. Impressed colleagues do not always appreciate his manner, though; his digressions can cross the border to pomposity and appear as self-aggrandizement wrapped in disheveled, professorial tweed.

Moynihan has been a player on the world stage, and he prefers to act much as he speaks, on the grand scale. But he can frustrate by refusing to engage in the mundane that others must attend to. Long one of the nation's foremost authorities on work and family in the welfare state, he was challenged as never before in the 100th Congress to make social policy of social science, as momentum built to try for the third time in 20 years to overhaul the nation's welfare system.

He rose to the occasion as the chief Senate sponsor of welfare legislation. He did homework and legwork along with brain work writing an entitlement program designed to move welfare recipients into the work force. It was in many ways vindication, but one he would have preferred not to have collected, for experience had come to support his theory that black families in urban ghettoes would break up even if the nation as a whole prospered.

The restructured welfare program replaced the Aid to Families with Dependent Children. It aims first to hold families together, and then, if they break apart, to move welfare recipients, mostly mothers, from the dole into the work force. Moynihan's ideas about poverty and the black family structure, which caused him to be denounced as a racist 25 years ago, came to be seen by many as farsighted and the key to the restructuring of the welfare system.

He was back in 1989 fuming at the Department of Human Services, which he said lacked the ability and commitment to carry out the overhaul mandated in the bill. "HHS has become simply a Department of Health," he said, angry at the Bush administration for its tardiness in nominating someone to the office charged with carrying out the new law.

On many other domestic issues, though, Moynihan has been less intent on rethinking fundamental questions than on lining up emotionally with liberal Democrats in support of preserving the New Deal and Great Society. His ringing declarations of support for traditional Democratic Party ideas strike some colleagues as cynical political rhetoric, since they remember him as a critic of those ideas.

But Moynihan has made the transition back from neo-conservative to bread-and-butter liberal with great success in New York, and without terrible cost in the Senate. In his choice of a committee assignment at the very start, Moynihan made clear his intention to bring home the goods to New York. At first he eschewed the Foreign Relations Committee, a natural post given his service as United Nations ambassador. He took aim at the Finance Committee, on which no New Yorker had sat for half a century.

Foreign policy questions no longer preoccupy Moynihan the way they did when, as U.N. ambassador, he was a staunch anti-communist and the scourge of radical Third World regimes. In the Senate, Moynihan has figured prominently as an arms-control supporter and backer-turned-critic of aid for the Nicaraguan contras. His was a lonely voice on Finance arguing to deny normal trading status to China in the 101st Congress following the Chinese government's massacre of pro-democracy demonstrators and subsequent repression.

Moynihan stirred up considerable controversy in 1989 with his proposal to bar any administration from trying to provide aid indirectly to a foreign country or group that is prohibited by law from receiving direct U.S. aid — as the Reagan administration was accused of doing in the Iran-contra affair. The Senate attached his amendment to the fiscal 1990 State Department authorization and included a modified version on a foreign-aid appropriations bill, prompting Bush to veto both bills.

Known at the United Nations for his outspoken defense of Israel, Moynihan has been equally militant in the Senate. He sponsored a resolution, unanimously adopted by the Senate, threatening to pull the United States out of the United Nations if Israel was expelled. He also has been a leading advocate of the controversial proposal to move the U.S. Embassy in Israel from Tel Aviv to Jerusalem.

He opposed authorizing Bush to use force to oust Iraq from Kuwait when the Senate debated the question in January 1991, denouncing Kuwait's prior behavior. "I remember Kuwait at the United Nations as a particularly poisonous enemy of the United States," he said. "One can be an antagonist of the United States in a way that leaves room for further discussions afterwards. But the Kuwaitis were singularly nasty. Their anti-Semitism was at the level of the personally loathsome."

Moynihan argued for continuing economic sanctions to weaken Iraq. "Why could we not just stay with that policy?" he asked. "I suggest it was because it was too new to us. Suddenly, from a situation where the world was defending a small country that had been attacked by a larger neighbor, we switched to a situation where the United States had engaged a major Islamic country in a countdown to Armageddon."

Moynihan has long maintained that New York is shortchanged in the distribution of federal funds for a variety of programs. One area in which he has fought to correct that imbalance is water policy, a subject he has been involved in both as ranking Democrat and now chairman on the Environment Subcommittee on Water Resources and Transportation.

At Home: The professorial Moynihan may not have the populist appeal of his earthier colleague, Republican Sen. Alfonse M. D'Amato. But Moynihan's election results powerfully attest to his political popularity. After unseating GOP Sen. James Buckley in 1976, Moynihan won his first re-election in 1982 with 65 percent of the vote. In 1988, he defeated Republican attorney Robert R. McMillan with 67 percent — breaking his own state record for Senate vote percentage and setting a national record with his margin (2.2 million votes).

At the outset of the 1988 campaign, a Moynihan landslide was no given: Possible Republican opponents included U.S. Attorney Rudolph W. Giuliani, the high-profile prosecutor of organized crime figures and corrupt Wall Street financiers, and Rep. Jack F. Kemp, then a candidate for the GOP presidential nomination. Moynihan prepared as if for the fight of his life, raising money early and running TV ads in January. He even took the unusual step of denying a persistent but unsubstantiated rumor that he had a problem with alcohol.

His concerns turned out to be unfounded. Giuliani became embroiled in a public feud with D'Amato over his possible successor as U.S. attorney and decided to stay on as prosecutor (he went on to lose narrowly for New York City mayor in 1989). Kemp was courted after ending his White House bid, but also declined.

New York Republicans then resorted to McMillan. The longtime GOP activist had many friends inside the state party, but was virtually unknown to the voting public. He had run one previous race, a losing campaign for New York City Council in 1964.

McMillan campaigned hard, driving across the state in his personal car, caustically criticizing Moynihan. Running as a "compassionate conservative," McMillan described Moynihan's support for a federal grant for a homosexual "safe sex" program as a vote for "safe sodomy." He portrayed Moynihan as aloof and lazy, with poor management skills that resulted in high turnover on his Senate staff.

But few New Yorkers heard McMillan's attacks. Republican financial backers wrote off the race as a loss; McMillan raised a meager half-million dollars, enough to buy one week of one ad in the expensive New York TV market. Meanwhile, Moynihan was flooding the airwaves with ads lauding his accomplishments, including his September victory on welfare reform. He swept the state, losing just a single rural county in upstate New York.

The landslide was a crowning moment in Moynihan's rise from Manhattan's ethnic, blue-collar precincts to the heights of academia and government. Moynihan's father, a hard-drinking journalist, walked out on the family when the senator was 6; his mother ran a saloon near Times Square. Moynihan walked into the entrance exam for City College with a longshoreman's loading hook in his back pocket.

After establishing himself as an academic — he taught his personal combination of economics, sociology and urban studies at Harvard and at the Joint Center for Urban Studies — Moynihan turned to government service in the 1960s. He worked in the Labor Department in the Kennedy and Johnson administrations, and as an urban affairs expert for Nixon.

In the latter role, Moynihan was the architect of the ill-fated Nixon "family assistance" welfare proposal, whose history he detailed in a book. He also caused himself great trouble when he counseled "benign neglect" toward minorities. The dispute caused by this advice revived accusations that Moynihan's scholarship was highbrow racism, an issue that first surfaced in 1965, when his book "Beyond the Melting Pot" attributed social problems among blacks to unstable family structure. Though Moynihan insisted he had been misunderstood, his social views created a gulf between him and some minority-group leaders that had to be bridged after he entered elective politics.

But the positive press Moynihan earned in his other roles in GOP administrations — as ambassador to India and to the United Nations under Presidents Nixon and Ford — set him on the road to political success. In his last year in New Delhi, Moynihan drew attention for his articles criticizing a lack of firmness in U.S. foreign policy, especially toward the Third World. His reputation made him a logical choice in 1975 for the U.N. post, whose most recent appointees, including future President George Bush, had been inconspicuous.

Moynihan's service at the United Nations clearly helped his political prospects in New York, although he denied any connection. His staunch defense of Israel earned him support among New York's sizable Jewish constituency, and his televised militance at the United Nations in 1975 allowed him to begin the 1976 campaign as a celebrity, rather than just an articulate Harvard professor. "He spoke up for America," one campaign advertisement said. "He'd speak up for New York."

Given his previous work for GOP presidents and his neo-conservative profile, Moynihan would have had difficulty running in a Democratic primary against a single liberal candidate in 1976. But he found himself challenged not only by Rep. Bella Abzug, the flamboyant feminist leader, but also by two other well-known figures of the Democratic left: former U.S. Attorney General Ramsey Clark and New York City Council President Paul O'Dwyer. Moynihan's chief political sponsor, Erie County

Democratic Chairman Joseph Crangle, kept the liberal vote split by pushing the state Democratic convention to guarantee ballot spots for all three liberal candidates.

Abzug depicted Moynihan as a Buckley in Democratic clothing and emerged as his main rival. But Clark and O'Dwyer took a combined 19 percent, enough to sink her. Moynihan came in first with 36 percent, 10,000 votes up on Abzug.

Buckley had won the seat six years earlier as the Conservative Party candidate, taking advantage of a three-way contest involving liberal Republican incumbent Charles Goodell and liberal Democratic challenger Richard L. Ottinger. He had no such advantage in 1976.

Moynihan started with a strong lead over Buckley in the polls, and he neither said nor did anything in the fall to fracture his tenuous party harmony. He spent much of his time in Massachusetts, teaching at Harvard to protect his tenure. When he did speak out, he called Buckley a right-wing extremist out of step with the state's politics — citing Buckley's initial opposition in 1975 to federal loan guarantees for New York City. He sailed to victory over Buckley by a half-million votes.

For the first few years of his Senate career, it seemed likely he would be challenged from the left in seeking renomination in 1982. But by the time of the primary, his belligerent and unexpected defense of traditional Democratic policies had had its effect. New York's Democratic left was pacified, and the National Conservative Political Action Committee helped Moynihan by airing TV ads calling him "the most liberal United States senator." Even the Liberal Party, which had been upset by his support of tuition tax credits for non-public schools, backed Moynihan in 1982.

Former U.S. Rep. Bruce F. Caputo wanted the GOP nomination, and he might have made an attractive candidate. But he was forced to withdraw following a disclosure that he had misstated his military background: Caputo claimed he had served as an Army lieutenant. No other major Republican felt a campaign was worth waging. Conservative state Assemblywoman Florence Sullivan won the nomination; she carried only 16 rural counties in November.

Committees

Environment & Public Works (2nd of 9 Democrats)
Water Resources, Transportation & Infrastructure (chairman); Environmental Protection; Nuclear Regulation;

Finance (2nd of 11 Democrats)
Social Security & Family Policy (chairman); International Trade; Private Retirement Plans & Oversight of the Internal Revenue Service

Foreign Relations (9th of 10 Democrats)
African Affairs; Near Eastern & South Asian Affairs; Terrorism, Narcotics & International Operations

Rules & Administration (7th of 9 Democrats)

Joint Library

Joint Taxation

Elections

1988 General

Daniel Patrick Moynihan (D)	4,048,649	(67%)
Robert R. McMillan (R)	1,875,784	(31%)

Previous Winning Percentages: **1982** (65%) **1976** (54%)

Campaign Finance

	Receipts	Receipts from PACs		Expend-itures
1988				
Moynihan (D)	$4,350,271	$892,773	(21%)	$4,809,810
McMillan (R)	$536,445	$33,495	(6%)	$528,989

Key Votes

1991	
Authorize use of force against Iraq	N
1990	
Oppose prohibition of certain semiautomatic weapons	N
Support constitutional amendment on flag desecration	N
Oppose requiring parental notice for minors' abortions	Y
Halt production of B-2 stealth bomber at 13 planes	Y
Approve budget that cut spending and raised revenues	Y
Pass civil rights bill over Bush veto	Y
1989	
Oppose reduction of SDI funding	N
Oppose barring federal funds for "obscene" art	Y
Allow vote on capital gains tax cut	N

Voting Studies

	Presidential Support		Party Unity		Conservative Coalition	
Year	**S**	**O**	**S**	**O**	**S**	**O**
1990	31	69	89	9	11	89
1989	52	45	90	7	24	71
1988	48	47	91	6	27	70
1987	37	60	93	5	19	78
1986	40	59	72	25	36	63
1985	33	65	81	13	27	67
1984	36	53	68	25	21	66
1983	46	51	74	21	16	80
1982	28	71	86	11	14	84
1981	41	47	71	14	8	87

Interest Group Ratings

Year	ADA	ACU	AFL-CIO	CCUS
1990	94	4	78	17
1989	75	4	100	38
1988	90	8	93	31
1987	95	0	100	31
1986	85	13	67	39
1985	90	4	100	33
1984	85	18	80	39
1983	80	8	82	26
1982	95	22	96	22
1981	75	13	94	33

Alfonse M. D'Amato (R)

Of Island Park — Elected 1980

Born: Aug. 1, 1937, Brooklyn, N.Y.
Education: Syracuse U., B.S. 1959, J.D. 1961.
Occupation: Lawyer.
Family: Wife, Penny Collenburg; four children.
Religion: Roman Catholic.
Political Career: Nassau County public administrator, 1965-68; receiver of taxes, town of Hempstead, 1969-71; Hempstead town supervisor, 1971-77; Nassau County Board of Supervisors, 1971-80, presiding supervisor, 1977-81.
Capitol Office: 520 Hart Bldg. 20510; 224-6542.

In Washington: D'Amato was a town and county supervisor in the years leading up to his long-shot 1980 Senate bid. He brought to Congress a tried and true formula for success in local politics — catering to his constituents' every need — and applied it to one of the largest constituencies imaginable: New York's 18 million people.

D'Amato ran on the right in his 1980 Senate campaign and voiced strong support for Ronald Reagan. But he quickly established himself as a senator who would fight for every dime he could get for New York, especially for the transportation and housing programs crucial to his heavily urbanized state. On the Appropriations Committee, he has pursued federal aid in a brazen and persistent manner, earning the nickname "Senator Pothole."

During D'Amato's first term, his hustling for the home folks made him enormously popular. Winner by a narrow plurality in 1980, he decisively won re-election in 1986. Thus, it is ironic that as D'Amato nears a 1992 campaign, it is his image as a senatorial ward heeler that most greatly threatens his career.

As the scandal involving influence-peddling in the Department of Housing and Urban Development (HUD) unfolded in July 1989, *The New York Times* published allegations that D'Amato had developed a too-cozy relationship with HUD's New York regional office (which included New Jersey and Puerto Rico as well); the article said he used his contacts there to steer federal housing money to his campaign contributors and other associates, including members of his family.

At an October 1989 hearing on a bill to revamp the nation's housing programs — which D'Amato, ranking Republican on the Banking Subcommittee on Housing, played a key role in crafting — he answered the allegations. Saying that trying to bring federal dollars home "is our job, and I certainly make no apologies for that," D'Amato denied any wrongdoing.

"I went to bat for every single thing that had merit . . . ," he said. "I've done it for my constituents, and the attempts to make it look like it's for my contributors, that's totally wrong." But the timing was unfortunate for D'Amato: His words echoed the defense of the "Keating Five" senators, who said they had aided savings and loan scandal figure Charles H. Keating Jr. only as a constituent.

That November, the Senate Ethics Committee, acting on a complaint from D'Amato's 1986 Democratic Senate foe, Mark Green, decided to investigate the accusations. The case dragged on into the 102nd Congress; the Ethics Committee, which had been tied up with the Keating Five case, was still considering whether to pursue charges against D'Amato.

In April 1991, the CBS News program "60 Minutes" broadcast a scathing recitation of D'Amato's problems, dating back to his ties to Nassau County Republican boss Joseph Margiotta. Reporter Mike Wallace said that during a phone conversation D'Amato agreed to appear only in an unedited interview, then unleashed a stream of obscenities and hung up.

The incident highlighted D'Amato's hot-and-cold relationship with the media. The same D'Amato who avoids the cameras when his ethics are questioned has used them to his political advantage throughout his career.

Many New Yorkers have the enduring image of D'Amato — a crusader in the federal war against illegal drugs and advocate of the death penalty for drug "kingpins" — dressed in battle fatigues and participating in a filmed undercover cocaine sting in 1986. In 1990, D'Amato showed his support for independence in the Soviet Baltic states by trying to enter Lithuania without a Soviet visa.

There is more to D'Amato than his ethics problems, his parochial pursuits and his knack for publicity. He may not have the biggest legislative portfolio in the Senate, but he has made his mark.

For more than three years leading up to its enactment in November 1990, D'Amato worked with Housing Subcommittee Chairman Alan Cranston, D-Calif., to craft an omnibus housing bill. As the administration's point man during the conference on the bill, D'Amato secured many priorities sought by President Bush and HUD Secretary Jack F. Kemp. These included a new program to help residents of low-income housing purchase their homes.

D'Amato also took the lead in shoring up the Federal Housing Administration's troubled mortgage insurance program. Warning of a potential disaster on the scale of the savings-and-loan crisis, D'Amato pushed through provisions raising the down payment required of home buyers with FHA-backed mortgages and adding an annual premium to buyers' mortgages.

D'Amato is also likely to play a major role in a reauthorization of federal transportation programs during the 102nd Congress. The ranking Republican on the Appropriations Subcommittee on Transportation, he is a leading Senate proponent of mass transit. This issue caused some of D'Amato's strongest conflicts with the Reagan administration. When Reagan proposed huge cuts in transit funding in 1982, D'Amato said, "There's no way I'm going to be a good ol' boy and roll along with the team."

D'Amato is also on the Appropriations Subcommittee on Foreign Operations, where he voices the international interests of the dozens of ethnic communities residing in New York. His strong support of Israel reflects that of his large Jewish constituency.

A hardline anticommunist and a human rights supporter, D'Amato generally has backed Reagan and Bush foreign policies. When he disagrees, it is usually because he favors a tougher line than the White House has taken.

For example, D'Amato responded in April 1990 to Iraqi dictator Saddam Hussein's threats toward Israel by proposing trade sanctions against Iraq. His efforts were stalled by the Bush administration, which viewed Saddam as a key player in Middle East politics, and by farm-state senators, who feared a cutoff of agricultural exports. However, with Iraqi troops massing on the border of Kuwait that July, D'Amato won passage of his measure, by an 83-12 vote, as an amendment to the 1990 farm bill.

Days after its passage, Iraqi troops invaded and occupied Kuwait. While he bemoaned the State Department's past "mollycoddling" of Saddam, D'Amato gave solid support to Bush's deployment of troops to stem Iraqi aggression. Saying the crisis was a matter of "vital, bottom-line, live-or-die, long-term national interests," D'Amato voted for the January 1991 resolution authorizing Bush to use military force against Iraq.

D'Amato also takes a hawkish tone on Appropriations' Defense Subcommittee. But his parochial interests are also involved. D'Amato has recently had to battle budget cuts affecting New York defense contractors; since 1989, he has fought Pentagon plans to cancel the F-14 fighter plane, built on Long Island by Grumman Corp.

In October 1986, D'Amato held up consideration of a must-pass omnibus appropriations bill in an attempt to block an amendment to halt production of the T-46 trainer airplane, built by the Fairchild Republic Co. on Long Island. "To this product, to this company, this is life or death.... I'm not going to sit by and allow that company to be closed," he said.

At noon that Oct. 17, there was still no compromise and no catchall spending bill, so non-essential federal functions were shut down. Later that day, D'Amato won a temporary reprieve for his plane. In the end, the program was canceled.

At Home: Democrats tried to dismiss D'Amato as a fluke after his narrow 1980 win, but they had to eat their words in 1986. D'Amato's home-state orientation and his straight talk — delivered with his distinctive "LongIsland" accent — quickly made him a popular figure. D'Amato swept aside Green, a consumer activist, with 57 percent of the vote to win a second term.

However, D'Amato did not have long to enjoy the accolades. Allegations of unethical behavior sent D'Amato's approval ratings plummeting. But even if he has not fully recovered his standing by November 1992, D'Amato is unlikely to duck a fight. He beat all odds in getting to the Senate in the first place.

D'Amato's ties to the Nassau County GOP, an old-fashioned political organization, have long been controversial. Just a year after D'Amato was elected to the Senate, his mentor, Nassau County Republican chairman Margiotta, was convicted of fraud and extortion.

But the Margiotta machine was also D'Amato's springboard. He was just out of law school when a friend of his politically connected father got him a job in the Island Park town attorney's office. After serving in various local offices, he was elected presiding supervisor of Hempstead Township in 1977.

Had he stayed on this path, D'Amato might have become county executive and possibly Margiotta's successor. Instead, he made an audacious move by running for the Senate in 1980 as a conservative challenger to Sen. Jacob K. Javits, a liberal Republican.

D'Amato aggressively sought nomination from the Conservative and Right-to-Life parties, neither of which liked Javits. After he won these lines, Margiotta broke with tradition and agreed to back him against Javits.

D'Amato's campaign struck at Javits, then 76, as too old, too ill — he had a progressive motor neuron disease — and too liberal. Javits stressed his years of service and aired endorsements from Gerald R. Ford and Sen. Barry Goldwater. But D'Amato was armed with ample funding and many volunteers. He won the primary, sweeping New York City's suburbs and edging Javits in the city and upstate.

Javits remained in the general election on

the Liberal Party line, but his presence was more of a hindrance to the Democratic nominee, Rep. Elizabeth Holtzman.

Holtzman went after D'Amato, bringing up alleged illicit practices of the Nassau GOP. D'Amato denied involvement in anything unlawful (later he was the subject of three separate investigations, all of which absolved him of any wrongdoing), and called Holtzman "an absolute witch" for attacking him. D'Amato took just 45 percent of the vote, but that was one percentage point better than Holtzman.

D'Amato's aggressive attention to New York interests won him widespread praise, even from Democrats such as New York City Mayor Edward I. Koch. Better-known Democrats took a pass at challenging him in 1986, so the nomination went to Green, a former associate of consumer crusader Ralph Nader. Again, the Democratic nominee questioned D'Amato's ethics — particularly his activities as then-chairman of the Banking Subcommittee on Securities (a *Wall Street Journal* article said D'Amato had received generous campaign contributions from Wall Street firms he had aided legislatively), and about D'Amato's ties to the Nassau GOP. But the accusations rolled off his back, and he won easily.

With his new-found clout, D'Amato worked to establish conservative dominion in the state GOP, but several of his efforts as a power broker backfired. His avid support of Kansas Sen. Bob Dole's 1988 White House bid irritated the Bush supporters who would dominate the state's delegate-selection process.

Also in 1988, D'Amato tried to recruit popular U.S. Attorney Rudolph W. Giuliani to challenge Democratic Sen. Daniel Patrick Moynihan. But Giuliani demanded the right to nominate his successor as U.S. attorney, a prerogative that was D'Amato's as the state's leading GOP official. D'Amato and Giuliani feuded, and Giuliani passed up the Senate bid.

When Guiliani quit his federal post to run for mayor of New York City in 1989, D'Amato supported the primary candidacy of Ronald Lauder, a former U.S. ambassador to Austria and son of cosmetics magnate Estee Lauder. But Lauder spent over $12 million and got just 33 percent of the vote. Guiliani went on to lose narrowly to Democrat David Dinkins.

D'Amato did score one intraparty victory in early 1991. His longtime aide William Powers was elected chairman of the state GOP.

Committees

Appropriations (6th of 13 Republicans)
Transportation (ranking); Defense; Foreign Operations; VA, HUD and Independent Agencies; Treasury, Postal Service & General Government

Banking, Housing & Urban Affairs (2nd of 9 Republicans)
Housing & Urban Affairs (ranking); Consumer & Regulatory Affairs; Securities

Select Intelligence (3rd of 7 Republicans)

Elections

1986 General		
Alfonse M. D'Amato (R)	2,378,197	(57%)
Mark Green (D)	1,723,216	(41%)

Previous Winning Percentage: **1980** (45%)

Campaign Finance

	Receipts	Receipts from PACs	Expend-itures
1986			
D'Amato (R)	$6,523,394	$855,518 (13%)	$8,104,587
Green (D)	$1,640,154	0	$1,635,676

Key Votes

1991	
Authorize use of force against Iraq	Y
1990	
Oppose prohibition of certain semiautomatic weapons	N
Support constitutional amendment on flag desecration	Y
Oppose requiring parental notice for minors' abortions	N
Halt production of B-2 stealth bomber at 13 planes	N
Approve budget that cut spending and raised revenues	N
Pass civil rights bill over Bush veto	N
1989	
Oppose reduction of SDI funding	Y
Oppose barring federal funds for "obscene" art	Y
Allow vote on capital gains tax cut	Y

Voting Studies

	Presidential Support		Party Unity		Conservative Coalition	
Year	**S**	**O**	**S**	**O**	**S**	**O**
1990	68	31	68	32	65	32
1989	67	32	52	46	66	32
1988	68	30	70	28	84	16
1987	58	38	65	33	69	28
1986	77	23	66	32	66	30
1985	71	28	69	28	88	8
1984	68	25	67	25	72	19
1983	67	28	67	30	70	27
1982	71	26	76	22	78	17
1981	82	14	81	13	78	17

Interest Group Ratings

Year	ADA	ACU	AFL-CIO	CCUS
1990	28	70	44	67
1989	35	48	70	63
1988	15	80	57	64
1987	30	56	70	44
1986	35	70	53	56
1985	20	70	62	62
1984	25	85	36	78
1983	20	44	33	63
1982	15	50	46	47
1981	10	64	22	94

1 George J. Hochbrueckner (D)

Of Coram — Elected 1986

Born: Sept. 20, 1938, Queens, N.Y.

Education: Attended State U. of New York, 1959-60; Hofstra U., 1960-61; Pierce College, 1961-62; California State U., Northridge, 1962-63.

Military Service: Navy, 1956-59.

Occupation: Engineer.

Family: Wife, Carol Ann Joan Seifert; four children.

Religion: Roman Catholic.

Political Career: N.Y. Assembly, 1975-85; Democratic nominee for U.S. House, 1984.

Capitol Office: 124 Cannon Bldg. 20515; 225-3826.

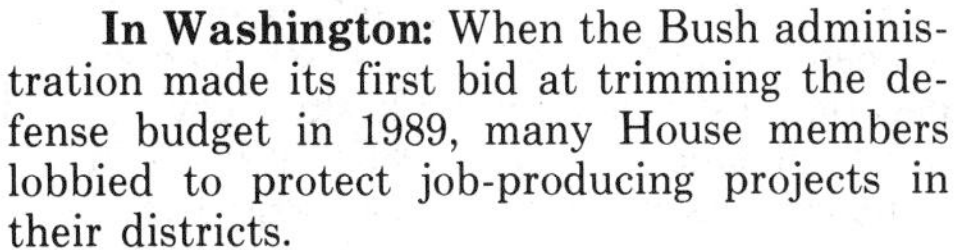

In Washington: When the Bush administration made its first bid at trimming the defense budget in 1989, many House members lobbied to protect job-producing projects in their districts.

Hochbrueckner, in arguing to save the F-14D fighter plane, had a special edge. A member of the Armed Services Committee, Hochbrueckner not only supported the Long Island-built jet — he helped design it.

An engineer before entering politics, Hochbrueckner worked on some of the F-14's electronic systems for Grumman, a defense contractor headquartered on Long Island. Years later, he would join other members of the Long Island delegation in a rescue mission, lavishing his colleagues with explanations of the plane's technical specifications.

Defense Secretary Dick Cheney's determination to cancel the program eventually won the day: The fiscal 1990 defense authorization law capped F-14D production.

However, the persistence of Hochbrueckner and his colleagues won Grumman one concession; 18 new F-14Ds were authorized to be built prior to shutdown of the production lines.

The F-14 "Tomcat" had appeared an unlikely victim of austerity efforts. The fighter had performed well since its introduction in 1970 and had avoided the production problems that plagued many other defense systems. The plane also had an aura of glamour from its featured role in the 1986 movie "Top Gun."

However, the Navy was developing a high-tech Advanced Tactical Fighter (ATF) to replace the F-14, and Cheney was determined to expedite the process. As the battle over the program intensified, it took on symbolic importance for the Bush administration as a test of Congress' willingness to cut popular weapons systems.

Thanks in part to Hochbrueckner's intricate knowledge of the aircraft, its supporters were able to play down jobs-related arguments. Handing out models of the plane to Armed Services colleagues at one point, Hochbrueckner praised its military prowess.

But Hochbrueckner also warned that a cancellation would ruin the F-14's manufacturer and damage the nation's "defense-industrial base." "You are putting Grumman out of business," he railed, noting that McDonnell Douglas would be the only builder of Navy aircraft if Grumman went under. Hochbrueckner cautioned that if ATF fell behind schedule and the Navy needed new planes to fill the void, "Grumman won't be there."

Hochbrueckner and his associates won in the House, amending the fiscal 1990 defense authorization bill to include 12 new F-14Ds. However, the Senate went along with Cheney. A member of the conference committee on the bill, Hochbrueckner held out against the cut. But in the end, his side accepted a compromise providing funding for 18 F-14Ds in exchange for a promise from Grumman that the production lines would then be decommissioned.

When Cheney in January 1991 canceled development of the A-12, an advanced Navy attack plane that had been plagued by cost overruns, Hochbrueckner suggested the F-14, modified for air-to-ground combat, as a replacement. But Cheney's fiscal 1992 budget proposal went the other way: Cheney proposed to cancel the planned conversion by Grumman of older F-14s into the more advanced F-14Ds.

Although Hochbrueckner's doggedness earned him reams of positive publicity back home, it antagonized some colleagues. His engineer's devotion to detail also left some cold. However, these aspects of Hochbrueckner's persona have also led him to pursue some of the more esoteric House issues. He has worked to obtain funding for research on X-ray lithography, a process that may produce smaller, faster computer chips; much of the research is being performed at Long Island's Brookhaven Na-

New York 1

Long Island — Eastern Suffolk County

There has been a full generation of population growth in eastern Suffolk County, the potato fields giving way to housing developments and the commercial fishing fleets yielding the waters to pleasure boats.

The demographic changes in the district have not affected its voting habits, however. The 1st is nearly always reliably Republican turf. Prior to Hochbrueckner's 1986 election, the area within the boundaries of the 1st had voted Democratic in a race for federal office only once since 1976; it has gone Republican for president in every contest since 1964.

Republicans come in three varieties here: longtime residents who fish and farm; landed gentry living on inherited wealth; and middle-income ethnics moving farther and farther from New York City. The fishermen generally work out of Montauk, while the remaining farmers are found mostly around Southold. The rich live in Sag Harbor and Shelter Island. Shirley, Mastic and the Moriches host large numbers of ethnic newcomers.

The district's Republican tendencies have been bolstered over the years by its dependence on defense manufacturing: Grumman maintains major facilities here. Thus, the 1st — which enjoyed the fruits of the Reagan administration's defense buildup in the early 1980s — finds itself vulnerable to defense cuts resulting from President Bush's agreement with Congress to spread the pain of deficit-related budget reductions. Already reeling from the Navy's 1988 decision to cancel its A-6 bomber project, Grumman has been rocked since 1989 by the Bush administration's efforts to cancel production of the Long Island-built F-14 fighter.

One project initially touted as a technological plus for the district is literally a non-starter. The Shoreham nuclear plant — controversial because of cost overruns and safety concerns — sits completed but unopened on the North Shore. After years of negotiations, the New York state government announced in early 1989 that it would purchase the plant from the Long Island Lighting Co. and close it permanently. But Energy Secretary James D. Watkins warned he would intervene to block any effort to mothball the plant permanently.

Population: 516,407. White 486,111 (94%), Black 20,253 (4%), Other 5,453 (1%). Spanish origin 18,408 (4%). 18 and over 350,987 (68%), 65 and over 55,046 (11%). Median age: 30.

tional Laboratory. He also is an activist on environmental restoration at the nation's nuclear production facilities, attempting to boost clean-up funding beyond Pentagon requests.

Another of Hochbrueckner's main causes is promoting garbage composting to relieve pressure on overflowing landfills. He calls himself "the compost man of Congress." Parts of his "Composting Research Act," calling for a Department of Agriculture study on the subject, were attached to the 1990 farm bill.

Hochbrueckner is also engaged in other pursuits with local bearing. He has called for stepped-up federal research on Lyme disease, a major health problem in the 1st. He supported legislation in the 100th Congress to phase out sludge dumping off New York and other coastal areas. A member of the Merchant Marine Committee, he obtained funding to dredge Shinnecock Inlet, a Long Island waterway that had become treacherous for mariners.

Hochbrueckner, a Navy veteran, voted in January 1991 against authorizing President Bush to use force to end Iraq's occupation of Kuwait. After the war broke out, Hochbrueckner — who had a temporary assignment to the Veterans' Affairs Committee in the 101st Congress — proposed a bill providing veterans' benefits to members of the merchant marine who serve in a combat zone.

His interest in defense issues and local projects helps Hochbrueckner fend off charges by Republicans that he is far too liberal for his GOP-leaning district. During 1990, Hochbrueckner voted against Bush's position on House legislation 77 percent of the time.

At Home: Hochbrueckner struggled to gain a hold on the 1st, which has a strong Republican tilt in presidential contests. He took 51 percent of the vote when the seat was open in 1986 to succeed GOP Rep. William Carney (who had defeated Hochbrueckner in 1984). Against an underfunded GOP challenger in 1988, Hochbrueckner got caught in a Republican tide and again took 51 percent.

But just as Hochbrueckner found himself near the top of the Republican target list, he became the beneficiary of one of the biggest GOP recruiting foul-ups of 1990. District Republicans went through three prospects before settling on a political unknown, who entered after the candidate filing deadline. Hochbrueckner's winning percentage soared.

Early in 1990, Republicans had touted conservative state Rep. John Behan. A Vietnam veteran who lost both legs to war wounds but recovered to become a success in business and politics, Behan was viewed by Hochbrueckner as a threat. In a fundraising letter, he described Behan as a demogogue and a "demon I will have to exorcise."

But after attending a National Republican Congressional Committee meeting, Behan announced he would not run, blaming a "lack of real support" by GOP officials.

Next up for the GOP was former New York Stock Exchange Chairman James J. Needham, whose business ties gave him fundraising potential. But Needham dropped out, citing a strain on his health.

Then came Suffolk County Supervisor Fred Thiele, who did not get an endorsement from the state Conservative Party and dropped out. Retired Army Col. Francis W. Creighton, who was not well-known in GOP circles, then impressed party officials with his articulate views. He got the nomination.

Creighton, an eastern Long Island native who spent most of his 27-year military career elsewhere, tried gamely to show how his background melded with interests of the district's defense industry. He also highlighted issues, such as the death penalty, on which he was more conservative than Hochbrueckner. But Hochbrueckner had already geared up for a more formidable foe. His ads stressed his efforts to save the F-14, increase spending on Lyme disease research and protect the regional coastline. He won with 56 percent.

It was Hochbrueckner's opposition to the controversial Shoreham nuclear power plant project in eastern Long Island that first built his political reputation. From his seat in the state Assembly, which he held from 1975 to 1985, Hochbrueckner became one of the leading critics who viewed Shoreham as located dangerously in a densely populated area.

In 1984, Hochbrueckner challenged Carney, a Shoreham supporter, and came within about 12,000 votes of winning. Carney's vulnerability on the nuclear issue loomed large in his decision not to run in 1986.

Republicans replaced him with county legislator Gregory J. Blass. Blass was also a Shoreham opponent, but Hochbrueckner stood out as the candidate who had opposed Shoreham earlier and louder. With a Conservative candidate draining votes from Blass, Hochbreuckner won by nine points.

In 1988, the Republicans turned to county legislator Edward Romaine, another Shoreham foe. Romaine appealed to his GOP base by calling the incumbent a liberal, but profiled himself as a moderate on environmental, education and other domestic issues. Hochbrueckner was well-financed, with a big chunk of defense PAC money, but Romaine got a boost from Bush in the 1st. Hochbrueckner's margin slipped to two points, a red flag that prompted him to organize early for 1990.

Committees

Armed Services (22nd of 33 Democrats)
Military Personnel & Compensation; Research & Development; Seapower & Strategic & Critical Materials

Merchant Marine & Fisheries (17th of 29 Democrats)
Coast Guard & Navigation; Fisheries & Wildlife Conservation & the Environment

Select Narcotics Abuse & Control (19th of 21 Democrats)

Elections

1990 General		
George J. Hochbrueckner (D)	75,211	(56%)
Francis W. Creighton (R)	46,380	(35%)
Clayton Baldwin Jr. (C)	6,883	(5%)
Peter J. O'Hara (RTL)	5,111	(4%)
1988 General		
George J. Hochbrueckner (D)	105,624	(51%)
Edward P. Romaine (R)	102,327	(49%)

Previous Winning Percentage: 1986 (51%)

District Vote For President

	1988		1984		1980		1976	
D	85,652	(39%)	70,592	(34%)	61,687	(33%)	85,138	(46%)
R	131,180	(60%)	137,855	(66%)	105,748	(57%)	100,390	(54%)
I					15,180	(8%)		

Campaign Finance

	Receipts	Receipts from PACs		Expend-itures
1990				
Hochbrueckner (D)	$655,297	$398,062	(61%)	$638,635
Creighton (R)	$45,545	$550	(1%)	$45,544
1988				
Hochbrueckner (D)	$738,139	$417,961	(57%)	$734,621
Romaine (R)	$218,458	$42,950	(20%)	$217,971

Key Votes

1991	
Authorize use of force against Iraq	N
1990	
Support constitutional amendment on flag desecration	Y
Pass family and medical leave bill over Bush veto	Y
Reduce SDI funding	Y
Allow abortions in overseas military facilities	N
Approve budget summit plan for spending and taxing	N
Approve civil rights bill	Y
1989	
Halt production of B-2 stealth bomber at 13 planes	N
Oppose capital gains tax cut	Y
Approve federal abortion funding in rape or incest cases	Y
Approve pay raise and revision of ethics rules	N
Pass Democratic minimum wage plan over Bush veto	Y

Voting Studies

	Presidential Support		Party Unity		Conservative Coalition	
Year	**S**	**O**	**S**	**O**	**S**	**O**
1990	23	77	94	6	22	78
1989	33	64	92	5	32	68
1988	22	78	89	10	37	63
1987	18	81	87	5	19	81

Interest Group Ratings

Year	ADA	ACU	AFL-CIO	CCUS
1990	89	13	100	21
1989	85	7	100	30
1988	80	12	93	36
1987	92	4	93	27

2 Thomas J. Downey (D)

Of Amityville — Elected 1974

Born: Jan. 28, 1949, S. Ozone Park, N.Y.
Education: Cornell U., B.S. 1970; Attended St. John's U., 1973-74; American U., J.D. 1978.
Occupation: Personnel manager.
Family: Wife, D. Chris Milanos; two children.
Religion: Methodist.
Political Career: Suffolk County Legislature, 1972-75.
Capitol Office: 2232 Rayburn Bldg. 20515; 225-3335.

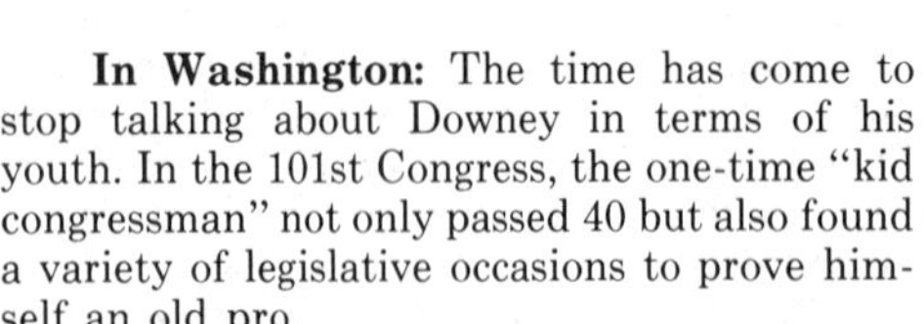

In Washington: The time has come to stop talking about Downey in terms of his youth. In the 101st Congress, the one-time "kid congressman" not only passed 40 but also found a variety of legislative occasions to prove himself an old pro.

Salient among these was his drive to shape the child-care legislation finally passed in 1990. Through months of negotiation, Downey refused to yield to Education and Labor Chairman Augustus F. Hawkins of California, a veteran not only twice as senior but literally twice as old. Downey argued for expanding the earned-income tax credit for poor families rather than increasing the dependent-care tax credit. In the end, the EITC was expanded by $12.4 billion over five years.

In 1990, Downey also risked antagonizing an equally venerable and considerably more dangerous colleague, Ways and Means Chairman Dan Rostenkowski of Illinois, the man to whom he owed his seat on that committee. Downey ventured into the deep waters of tax policy when he persuaded his Subcommittee on Human Resources to double the period of extended federal jobless pay from 13 weeks to 26 weeks in hard times. Financing such boosted coverage would mean billions in extra payroll levies — a big-time "backdoor" tax increase.

The proposal cleared the subcommittee, where Downey is acting chairman (a position he has held since Chairman Harold E. Ford of Tennessee had to step down after a federal indictment in 1987). But Downey's plan did not receive attention from the full committee. As the recession deepened in 1991, Downey revived the idea and said he thought he had the chairman's ear. The urgency was even greater for Downey as reduced defense spending threatened jobs at Grumman Aerospace Corp., the single largest employer in his district.

The presence of Grumman, along with the district's 61 percent majority for George Bush in 1988, made it interesting to watch Downey decide his vote on the Persian Gulf force-authorizing resolution in January 1991. He voted with most Democrats in favoring an extended use of sanctions over immediate force. But when the battle had been won, he was quick to see the political lesson for his party.

"The hardest thing for people on the left to understand is that there are people with whom you cannot reason, and Saddam Hussein may have been one of them," he said.

Now in his ninth term, Downey retains some of the wise-guy reputation of his first, occasionally alienating opponents and even would-be allies with sarcasm and intellectual arrogance that detracts from his recognized debating skills.

However, he is respected in both parties as a serious legislator who holds his own in highly technical arguments, whether the subject is welfare, the tax code or arms control. He is an organizer and a leader, from the bipartisan basketball games in the House gym to the caucus of his fellow House liberals that waged a sustained and partly successful assault on President Ronald Reagan's arms buildup.

In the late 1980s, Downey came to focus most of his attention on Ways and Means and less on the defense and foreign policy issues that had been his primary concerns while he sat on the Armed Services Committee.

By the 100th Congress, he was ready to advance his reputation (and probably his aging process also) with a dogged, politically harrowing and ultimately successful effort to overhaul the welfare system. Unexpectedly thrust into a lead role early in 1987, he spent the next 18 months shepherding that complex, controversial legislation into law. It was a characteristic performance throughout, with Downey at times brash and bitingly partisan, and yet also patient and conciliatory enough with foes and waverers to overcome some missteps and see the cause to completion.

Through the long and contentious welfare debate, Downey was a tenacious advocate, expressing confidence that a bill would pass, telling doubters, "You've got Beltway fever." Yet he did not underestimate the difficulty. "Welfare reform is very hard to do," he said before House passage, "because it is so subject to mythologies and prejudices and racism."

New York 2

Long Island — Western Suffolk County

The 2nd is filled with technicians and executives who work for the defense contractors and other aerospace companies that constitute the district's dominant industry. Fairchild Republic operates a huge aircraft plant in Farmingdale, and spinoff companies abound along the Route 110 industrial corridor. Grumman Aerospace Corp. and Unisys Corp. (formerly Sperry Systems) also operate plants here.

But defense is not the 2nd District's only major industry. As with the 1st, the 2nd's proximity to the water has spawned an important local vacation economy. Many residents have boat slips on the Great South Bay. Each Saturday morning during warm weather, the ferry is full from Bay Shore to Ocean Beach on Fire Island. Cars are banned on Fire Island, where summer people run errands with toy wagons in tow. Bay Shore hosts a commercial fishing industry.

Although Democrat Downey has represented the 2nd for more than a decade and a half, the district generally votes Republican in statewide contests.

The heavy Republican vote comes from such well-to-do towns as Babylon Village and Sayville, located on Long Island's South Shore. Italian-American Copiague is a bastion of blue-collar Republican voting. North Babylon and Deer Park have high Republican enrollments, although Downey has made inroads there. Another of the district's swing areas is blue-collar Lindenhurst, once a German community.

Pockets of Democratic strength exist in Dix Hills and in North Amityville, which contains a population of low-income blacks whose ancestors moved to Long Island to work as servants in the mansions of South Amityville.

Population: 515,595. White 457,700 (89%), Black 44,364 (9%), Other 4,125 (1%). Spanish origin 34,579 (7%). 18 and over 351,055 (68%), 65 and over 40,282 (8%). Median age: 29.

The bill aimed to help welfare recipients get off the dole and into jobs, while improving benefits for those, especially single mothers, who depend on assistance. He moved it through Ways and Means on a party-line vote, and fueled some of the partisanship himself. Referring to GOP objections about his bill's proposed cost and expanded benefits, he said, "There's just a very different view of how we treat the poor and how to encourage people to get off welfare. [Republicans] want to reduce benefits. We want to give them training and education."

Next, Downey monitored the work of three other committees with minor parts in the process, and engineered the compromises necessary to fashion a package for the House floor. Getting there, however, was a rocky road.

In late October 1987, he persuaded House leaders to roll the welfare bill into a pending deficit-reduction package of spending cuts and minor tax increases; he hoped the budget-cutting vehicle would carry his bill through the Senate and past Reagan's desk. But it created a politically explosive mix — higher welfare spending and higher taxes — and the tactic backfired. Many Democrats joined Republicans in opposition, forcing the welfare bill to be stripped off. On several occasions, floor debate on the stand-alone bill was postponed as Democrats balked, conservatives offered their own version and everyone worried about the economy after the October stock market crash.

A fellow Democrat suggested Downey himself could be part of the problem: "Tom is usually so convinced that he is right that he doesn't have a lot of sympathy for people who hold opposing views," said Ways and Means liberal Don J. Pease of Ohio.

But Downey countered, "I understand that successful politics is the art of compromise." Amid the delays, he tried to show patience toward reluctant Democrats, and credited Republicans for the bill's premise — putting welfare recipients to work. "We have to give the conservatives their due," he said. "They always emphasized the importance of work."

Finally the bill came to the floor in mid-December, and was approved 230-194. But the key vote had come earlier on the rule opening debate, which allowed just two amendments: a GOP substitute sure to fail, and a leadership amendment cutting $500 million from the bill's five-year cost as a gesture to conservatives. With Democratic whips frantically rounding up votes, the rule narrowly passed, 213-206.

After the Senate passed its bill in 1988, a sometimes rancorous conference met over the summer to reconcile the House's $7.1 billion plan and the Senate's $2.8 billion version. Meanwhile, twice the House voted for nonbinding GOP resolutions endorsing the Senate's price tag. Finally, the two sides settled on a $3.34 billion deal including the workfare provision sought by conservatives — "the price of passing a welfare bill," Downey told complaining liberals. For liberals, there were guarantees of medical and child care for parents moving from the welfare rolls to jobs.

Downey had clashed with Rostenkowski not long after joining the committee when the chairman proposed to limit the deduction for state and local taxes. The outcry in New York and other high-tax states was considerable. "People are telling me, 'No compromise,' " Downey said. "That's going to be my position. It's a matter of political survival."

Becoming a self-described "guerrilla warrior," he made deals with oil- and timber-state members to protect certain deductions, and cast some early votes against Rostenkowski in committee to send a signal. Faced with such intense opposition from Downey and others, and realizing the provision had become a major stumbling block, Rostenkowski had little choice but to retain the state and local tax deduction. Downey in turn supported the chairman's tax bill.

Whatever Downey's responsibilities at Ways and Means, it seems unlikely he will ever drop his involvement with defense policy. He was part of a small liberal minority on Armed Services, at a time when hawkish conservatives still were firmly in control. But in early 1985, after he had left for Ways and Means, Downey was one of the colonels who helped oust enfeebled Chairman Melvin Price of Illinois and install Les Aspin of Wisconsin in his place. Two years later, though disappointed himself with Aspin's support of the MX missile and contra aid, Downey helped defend Aspin against a near-successful coup by a coalition of disaffected liberals and vengeful conservatives. He said he advised Aspin to commit to "no more MXs, and a change of heart on contras."

Since leaving Armed Services, he has continued to seek institutional posts from which to pursue his goals.

He made use of his temporary stint on the Budget Committee, chairing its Defense Task Force in the 99th Congress and thus leading the House fight for a lower defense budget in conferences with the Senate. His term on Budget ended with that Congress, in 1986, but by then he had begun convening weekly meetings of arms control activists in his office. They came to play a major role during Reagan's second term in slowing the president's ambitious arms buildup.

From 1985 on, it became routine for the House to slash Reagan's defense budget, specifically his requests for the strategic defense initiative (SDI); to mandate compliance with past arms control treaties; and, for three of the four years, to ban most nuclear arms tests. Though the provisions were either dropped or modified in conference with the Senate, they served to push compromises to the left and to pressure Reagan to negotiate arms cuts with the Soviets. Ironically, Reagan's doing so diminished support for the arms controllers' efforts, as members became reluctant to undermine the president during his talks with Soviet leader Mikhail S. Gorbachev.

The activists' biggest victory was in 1985, when Congress capped the number of MX missiles. Downey and his allies had the support of House Democratic leaders to try to kill the missile and they came within a handful of votes of victory, losing to Reagan's all-out lobbying blitz. Even so, the loss set the stage for the ultimate compromise limiting the number of the multi-warhead missiles to 50.

With the arrival of a new administration in 1989, Downey was one of 20 Democrats, including Aspin, who wrote President Bush petitioning him to respect that cap in the interest of political consensus, and also to support the smaller, single-warhead Midgetman missile. Bush wants more MXs, and on a mobile rail system instead of the current underground silos, thus renewing debate over the weapon.

In the 100th Congress, Downey traveled with Democrats Jim Moody of Wisconsin and Bob Carr of Michigan deep inside the Soviet Union, where they videotaped the controversial Krasnoyarsk radar project, and determined for House leaders that it was of little military significance. That contradicted the administration, which considered the radar a dangerous breach of U.S.-Soviet accords against anti-ballistic missile systems, proof of Soviet duplicity and reason to proceed with SDI. A Pentagon official charged that Downey's mission had been used for a Soviet "propaganda coup." And during the 100th Congress, the Soviets actually admitted the facility had been intended for use in an anti-ballistic system and agreed to begin dismantling it.

At Home: Although his re-election was hardly threatened, 1990 was not the easiest year for Downey. Already faced with a general anti-Washington and anti-tax sentiment that affected most Long Island incumbents, Downey had to deal with reaction following ABC-TV's October exposé of his holiday junket to the Caribbean with other Ways and Means members and a bevy of lobbyists. The program featured the lawmakers, who were returning from a trade-related tour, frolicking on a beach.

Despite some bruising publicity, Downey managed to win handily, defeating Republican John W. Bugler by 20 percentage points. But Downey's 56 percent showing was his lowest since 1984, a year in which the Democrat was running against a Reagan landslide in his district.

Downey was elected in 1974, a few weeks after Richard M. Nixon had resigned as president in the Watergate scandal. At age 25, Downey was the youngest of the "Watergate babies." But he already had a reputation for precocity. In 1971, as a 22-year-old college student, he was elected to the Suffolk County Legislature. In his three years there, he sponsored legislation to regulate sewer construction, restrict smoking in public places and impose rent control on trailer courts.

He won his congressional seat by unseating GOP Rep. James R. Grover. Grover's winning margins had been so large he was thought to be invulnerable, an opinion he shared. Even Downey's strong showing in a debate did little to shake GOP confidence. But Downey won by nearly 5,000 votes.

Once Downey took office, he practiced all the new techniques of constituent service while adding some wrinkles of his own. He stayed in his office in the evening telephoning voters personally and held teas for them on Sundays.

His methods worked. Republicans thought they had a winner in 1976 when they nominated Peter F. Cohalan, a popular town supervisor from Islip who later became Suffolk County executive. But Downey dispatched him with surprising ease, and followed with three routine re-election victories.

In the last two presidential election years, district Republicans tried to imitate Downey's own youthful rise by nominating extremely fresh faces to challenge him. The tactic failed.

In 1984, 28-year-old Paul Aniboli, a former Suffolk County prosecutor, attacked Downey's political style and philosophy, branding the incumbent a "radical liberal," "dangerous," and "a wimp." Despite Aniboli's support from national conservative groups, Downey won 55 percent.

After Downey took 64 percent in 1986, Suffolk Republicans in 1988 nominated a 28-year-old attorney, Joseph Cardino Jr. But Downey again coasted to victory, taking 62 percent.

Committees

Select Aging (2nd of 42 Democrats)
Human Services (chairman); Health & Long-Term Care

Ways & Means (9th of 23 Democrats)
Human Resources (acting chairman); Trade

Elections

1990 General		
Thomas J. Downey (D)	56,722	(56%)
John W. Bugler (R, RTL)	36,859	(36%)
Dominic A. Curcio (C)	8,150	(8%)
1988 General		
Thomas J. Downey (D)	107,646	(62%)
Joseph Cardino Jr. (R)	66,972	(38%)

Previous Winning Percentages: **1986** (64%) **1984** (55%) **1982** (64%) **1980** (56%) **1978** (55%) **1976** (57%) **1974** (49%)

District Vote For President

	1988	1984	1980	1976
D	70,283 (38%)	62,326 (34%)	61,484 (34%)	78,810 (45%)
R	111,927 (61%)	123,453 (66%)	106,088 (58%)	94,673 (54%)
I			12,226 (7%)	

Campaign Finance

	Receipts	Receipts from PACs		Expend-itures
1990				
Downey (D)	$612,878	$330,762	(54%)	$635,392
1988				
Downey (D)	$790,000	$333,761	(42%)	$564,732
Cardino (R)	$52,912	0		$35,057

Key Votes

1991	
Authorize use of force against Iraq	N
1990	
Support constitutional amendment on flag desecration	N
Pass family and medical leave bill over Bush veto	Y
Reduce SDI funding	Y
Allow abortions in overseas military facilities	Y
Approve budget summit plan for spending and taxing	N
Approve civil rights bill	Y
1989	
Halt production of B-2 stealth bomber at 13 planes	Y
Oppose capital gains tax cut	Y
Approve federal abortion funding in rape or incest cases	Y
Approve pay raise and revision of ethics rules	Y
Pass Democratic minimum wage plan over Bush veto	Y

Voting Studies

	Presidential Support		Party Unity		Conservative Coalition	
Year	**S**	**O**	**S**	**O**	**S**	**O**
1990	19	81	93	4	6	94
1989	28	72	96	1	7	93
1988	23	77	93	4	8	92
1987	21	78	93	3	12	86
1986	18	81	91	4	16	80
1985	21	75	91	4	9	87
1984	29	67	92	4	5	93
1983	26	71	90	4	10	84
1982	38	58	92	4	11	88
1981	29	63	84	7	12	81

Interest Group Ratings

Year	ADA	ACU	AFL-CIO	CCUS
1990	100	8	92	21
1989	95	0	100	10
1988	100	0	86	36
1987	92	9	87	20
1986	95	5	79	17
1985	85	5	94	26
1984	95	4	77	31
1983	85	5	82	37
1982	100	0	95	18
1981	80	0	85	11

3 Robert J. Mrazek (D)

Of Centerport — Elected 1982

Born: Nov. 6, 1945, Newport, R.I.
Education: Cornell U., B.A. 1967.
Military Service: Navy, 1967-68.
Occupation: Congressional aide.
Family: Wife, Catherine Susan Gurick; two children.
Religion: Methodist.
Political Career: Suffolk County Legislature, 1976-83; sought Democratic nomination for U.S. House, 1972; Democratic nominee for N.Y. Senate, 1978.
Capitol Office: 306 Cannon Bldg. 20515; 225-5956.

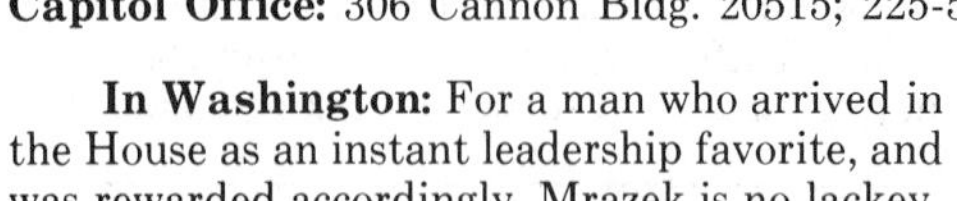

In Washington: For a man who arrived in the House as an instant leadership favorite, and was rewarded accordingly, Mrazek is no lackey.

He is not disloyal; with liberal instincts, Mrazek is among the most reliable supporters of the party line, though he hails from a Republican-minded district. But the same independence and political passion that prompt Mrazek to vote in ways that could be troublesome back home also make him unafraid to buck the Democratic hierarchy. Fortunately for his cause, Mrazek operates with enough fairness, savvy and good humor to remain popular.

In the early months of the 102nd Congress, Mrazek began actively talking about a 1992 Senate bid against GOP incumbent Alfonse M. D'Amato. About the same time, he shifted subcommittees on Appropriations, dropping off the Foreign Operations and Transportation panels and taking a seat on the subcommittee that oversees three Cabinet departments — Labor, Health and Human Services and Education. That may afford Mrazek more publicity beyond the 3rd, although he had hoped for a plum seat on the Defense Subcommittee. A more senior Democrat, Bernard J. Dwyer of New Jersey, got the Defense vacancy.

Mrazek got onto the Appropriations Committee as a freshman, because then-Speaker Thomas P. O'Neill Jr. was grateful Mrazek had ousted Rep. John LeBoutillier, an iconoclastic Republican who had spent much of his single term harassing O'Neill. But Mrazek has never been shy about pressing his case on Appropriations, even if it means going against one of the panel's powerful subcommittee chairmen. And unlike most Appropriations insiders, who concentrate their legislative efforts there, Mrazek has interests that take him far from the committee — and far from Long Island.

That is not to say that he is inattentive to parochial concerns. He has worked actively to save the F-14 fighter plane, built on Long Island by Grumman, where Mrazek's father worked for more than 30 years. When Appropriations considered a supplemental spending bill to pay for the Persian Gulf War in early 1991, Mrazek offered a successful amendment to require previously authorized production of 12 more of the carrier-based planes, which flew thousands of missions in the gulf. Over Pentagon objections, Mrazek won a 37-12 vote. Administration efforts to kill the F-14 continue.

Mrazek also used his seat on the Transportation Subcommittee to steer funds to his suburban region to help relieve its crowded highways and improve its mass transit. He is a leading supporter of research on the magnetic levitation train (maglev), and in 1990, helped secure $12 million in seed money for it.

But Mrazek is best known for his involvement in an eclectic range of national policy issues, large and small. He prides himself on being a preservationist — cultural, historical and environmental. On these issues, his style is to fight for all he can get, then strike a bargain to keep the package afloat.

Working largely through the Interior Committee, of which he is not a member, Mrazek led environmentalists' fight to preserve the Tongass National Forest in Alaska. In the 101st Congress, he won House passage of legislation to impose tough restrictions on logging in the nation's largest national forest. His bill also eliminated federal contracts with two large pulp mills, a provision he argued would restore economic fairness to an industry dominated by mills with "incredible sweetheart" deals. "We're giving them those trees for the price of a cheeseburger," he said.

The House passed similar Mrazek-sponsored legislation in the previous Congress that died in the Senate. In the 101st, the Senate passed a much weaker bill than the House version. The final bill preserved more than 1 million acres in the Tongass, but merely ordered that the pulp mill contracts be renegotiated.

In the 100th Congress, Mrazek opposed the colorization of classic black-and-white films, arguing that the old movies are artworks deserving of protection. But many Appropriations colleagues did not share Mrazek's passion.

New York 3

Long Island — Parts of Nassau and Suffolk Counties

When the 3rd was created before the 1982 election, it was almost evenly split between Long Island's two giant suburban counties. Over the decade, Nassau County developed somewhat more weight in the district than Suffolk County: In the 1990 House race, Nassau cast 55 percent of the district vote.

Defense remains the crucial industry. The district hosts the Hazeltine works in Huntington and the Unisys operation in Lake Success. Many of the residents who are not involved in defense commute to jobs in New York City.

The Nassau portion of the district is a partisan patchwork. Northern Oyster Bay houses Republican corporate executives in such prosperous communities as Bayville and Muttontown. Largely Jewish Roslyn turns in a heavy Democratic vote. North Hempstead communities such as Manhasset and New Hyde Park lean to the GOP.

F. Scott Fitzgerald set "The Great Gatsby" on Long Island's North Shore. While affluent people still live in Gatsby's estate country, some of the mansions have been turned into museums. A small garment industry is attracting Hispanic residents to Glen Cove. The Hispanics there vote Democratic, cutting into the GOP vote.

The Suffolk portion of the district displays a more uniformly Republican cast, although Democrats have made inroads in local offices. Huntington is home to many Irish and Italian Republicans. Smithtown, another ethnic area, lies to the east. Huntington and Smithtown, settled earlier than much of burgeoning Suffolk County, have grown minimally in recent years.

Population: 516,610. White 491,113 (95%), Black 14,344 (3%), Other 7,846 (2%). Spanish origin 13,902 (3%). 18 and over 378,027 (73%), 65 and over 53,356 (10%). Median age: 34.

Mrazek's proposal pitted Hollywood artists against industry financiers, including some top Democratic Party contributors. But he found a key ally in Sidney R. Yates, the equally independent chairman of Appropriations' Interior Subcommittee, which has jurisdiction over the arts. Yates included an anti-colorization proposal in his subcommittee's annual spending bill. But threatened with a point of order that would kill his proposal on the floor, Mrazek accepted a weak compromise. The substitute that became law set up a national film preservation board to identify U.S. film classics and see that they are labeled to disclose any alteration.

In 1988, Mrazek cosponsored a successful bill expanding Virginia's Manassas National Battlefield Park to prevent a shopping mall from being built there. A Civil War buff, Mrazek asked foes of the purchase, "What is the price of our national historical heritage?"

Mrazek is the only Czech-American in the House, and when Czechoslovakia's communist government was overthrown in 1989, Mrazek traveled to Prague to visit newly elected President Vaclav Havel. Later, after Havel delivered a spellbinding speech to Congress, Mrazek approached him to express his admiration for his words, reminiscent of those he had heard about Czechoslovakian democracy from his grandfather. But, as Mrazek wrote in an opinion column for *The Washington Post*, when Havel asked him to speak some Czech, Mrazek could come out only with, "Please pass the bread and butter" before Havel was gone. "I'm sure he thinks Czechoslovakia is well-represented in the U.S. Congress," wrote Mrazek.

A Vietnam-era Navy veteran, Mrazek in 1987 sponsored a law expediting immigration of Amerasians to the United States; in 1989, he sponsored a successful amendment to boost the money to resettle them here. He has been a leader in the fight to reduce funding for the proposed strategic defense initiative. And as a representative for a large Jewish constituency, he supports Israel in foreign aid debates.

A devoted free-trader, Mrazek was one of only two Democrats to oppose the 1988 trade bill, which was a leadership priority, and he cast the only Democratic vote in support of President Reagan's veto of the measure.

Well-known as outspoken, Mrazek still shocked colleagues in early 1989 when he gave *The New York Times* one of the earliest and bluntest on-the-record assessments from a Democrat on Speaker Jim Wright's ethics problems. "There is a recognition by virtually all of the people I would consider professional politicians that he will not survive," Mrazek said.

At Home: Mrazek's ability to win — often with a substantial vote cushion — in a suburban Long Island district has encouraged him to consider a bid against D'Amato in 1992.

Mrazek has never won by a landslide in the 3rd, which has a Republican bent (Bush carried it with 59 percent in 1988). But he has fended off a series of aggressive challengers branding him as a far-out liberal.

Mrazek has been in government his entire adult life. After a stint in the Navy, where he lost partial sight in one eye during a training exercise, he worked for Sen. Vance Hartke, D-Ind. After one failed campaign for the House nomination in 1972, he won a seat in the Suffolk County Legislature in 1975.

Mrazek developed a reputation as a reform-minded official with a special interest in environmental issues. He brought together the feuding Democratic minority in the Legislature and became the group's leader in 1979.

Mrazek revived his House ambitions in 1982. The campaign focused more on the Republican's personality than his ideological differences with Mrazek. LeBoutillier's abrasive outspokenness had offended both parties: He had described GOP Sen. Charles H. Percy of Illinois as "a wimp," and O'Neill as "big, fat and out of control."

Mrazek convinced voters that the incumbent's "obnoxious behavior" rendered him ineffective. Meanwhile, an overconfident LeBoutillier spent much of the campaign in Massachusetts, heading an independent effort to defeat O'Neill. The Speaker won with 75 percent and LeBoutillier lost by 10,000 votes.

The 1984 GOP hope was retired investment banker Robert Quinn. A millionaire, Quinn filled the airwaves with radio ads. Mrazek attacked Quinn as naive and shallow on issues, and for not voting since 1980. Mrazek barely won with 51 percent.

In 1986, Republicans put up an organization insider, Joseph Guarino. He said Mrazek was inattentive to local concerns, but that charge did not stick. Mrazek — who had received regular publicity for his efforts to get funding for public transit and toxic-waste cleanup — jumped to 56 percent. Republican despair of unseating Mrazek was evident in 1988. Bank executive Robert Previdi got meager party support, and Mrazek won 57 percent.

However, Previdi was back again in 1990, with more solid backing, and with an anti-Washington and anti-tax mood on Long Island boosting him. He called Mrazek a "super duper liberal," highlighting his vote against the flag-burning constitutional amendment.

Mrazek fought back, telling Long Islanders that "Mr. Previdi has never been involved in one issue to improve the quality of life of people here." Mrazek won by 53-43 percent.

Committee

Appropriations (26th of 37 Democrats)
Labor, Health & Human Services, Education & Related Agencies; Legislative

Elections

1990 General		
Robert J. Mrazek (D)	73,029	(53%)
Robert Previdi (R)	59,089	(43%)
Francis A. Dreger (RTL)	4,915	(4%)
1988 General		
Robert J. Mrazek (D)	128,336	(57%)
Robert Previdi (R)	91,122	(41%)

Previous Winning Percentages: **1986** (56%) **1984** (51%) **1982** (52%)

District Vote For President

	1988	1984	1980	1976
D	94,975 (40%)	87,643 (36%)	82,250 (34%)	128,327 (47%)
R	142,108 (59%)	159,039 (64%)	132,779 (55%)	146,614 (53%)
I			20,457 (9%)	

Campaign Finance

	Receipts	Receipts from PACs		Expend-itures
1990				
Mrazek (D)	$602,613	$193,185	(32%)	$458,759
Previdi (R)	$186,877	$14,900	(8%)	$184,513
1988				
Mrazek (D)	$447,902	$176,931	(40%)	$364,087
Previdi (R)	$93,063	$3,480	(4%)	$90,892

Key Votes

1991	
Authorize use of force against Iraq	N
1990	
Support constitutional amendment on flag desecration	N
Pass family and medical leave bill over Bush veto	Y
Reduce SDI funding	Y
Allow abortions in overseas military facilities	Y
Approve budget summit plan for spending and taxing	N
Approve civil rights bill	Y
1989	
Halt production of B-2 stealth bomber at 13 planes	Y
Oppose capital gains tax cut	N
Approve federal abortion funding in rape or incest cases	Y
Approve pay raise and revision of ethics rules	Y
Pass Democratic minimum wage plan over Bush veto	Y

Voting Studies

	Presidential Support		Party Unity		Conservative Coalition	
Year	**S**	**O**	**S**	**O**	**S**	**O**
1990	16	81	92	2	4	91
1989	31	65	91	2	17	80
1988	19	75	91	4	13	84
1987	16	81	91	4	7	93
1986	17	77	86	8	16	80
1985	24	70	87	7	16	80
1984	28	68	88	7	17	83
1983	23	73	85	11	27	73

Interest Group Ratings

Year	ADA	ACU	AFL-CIO	CCUS
1990	100	9	100	29
1989	80	8	82	40
1988	95	4	79	31
1987	96	9	88	13
1986	80	5	85	31
1985	90	19	81	43
1984	80	0	92	33
1983	85	22	88	25

4 Norman F. Lent (R)

Of East Rockaway — Elected 1970

Born: March 23, 1931, Oceanside, N.Y.
Education: Hofstra U., B.A. 1952; Cornell U., J.D. 1957.
Military Service: Navy, 1952-54.
Occupation: Lawyer.
Family: Wife, Barbara Morris; three children.
Religion: Methodist.
Political Career: N.Y. Senate, 1963-71.
Capitol Office: 2408 Rayburn Bldg. 20515; 225-7896.

In Washington: A product of the Nassau County Republican machine, Lent seems to enjoy making deals and getting things done. He is not the most eloquent member of the Energy and Commerce Committee, but he has forged good personal relationships with Republicans and Democrats, and that has helped make him an effective ranking member of the panel.

Lent filled a vacancy in the committee's No. 1 GOP spot in the midst of the 99th Congress, and the move required some adjustment. He had spent much of his career tending to his Long Island district, not acting as the spokesman for his side of the aisle.

But Lent's adjustment to the top spot has generally gone well, with the New Yorker comfortably brokering debates among members of the committee and with GOP administrations. By the time new clean air legislation finally moved in the 101st Congress, Lent was positioned to be a major player in the negotiations.

Although he did not always see eye to eye with the Bush administration, Lent served as the White House point man in much of the deliberations. Often, though, Lent seemed most closely aligned with Energy and Commerce Chairman John D. Dingell. He and Lent built a bipartisan consensus on many controversial issues, often splitting the difference between environmentalists and the administration's more industry-friendly approach.

On the contentious issue of mandating vehicles that run on alternative fuels, however, Lent was among those seeking to weaken a White House proposal. The administration plan would have required automakers to build a million clean-fuel vehicles for use in the nation's smoggiest cities, including the New York City area. Together with Dingell, Lent successfully advocated a less stringent alternative.

Lent is also likely to be a player if there is action on major energy legislation during the 102nd Congress. As the Persian Gulf crisis highlighted U.S. dependence on imported oil, Lent stepped forward late in the 101st Congress with a sweeping energy bill. Although it included tax incentives for oil and gas producers and other measures unpopular with environmentalists, the package also contained substantive measures to promote conservation.

Lent praised President Bush for submitting an energy package early in the 102nd. But he and other House Republicans later put in their own energy bill, saying the administration bill did not do enough to promote conservation.

But if Lent has become his party's spokesman on many energy and environmental issues, there is one area where some members are not comfortable tipping their hand to him: telephone issues. His wife works for Nynex, the New York-based offspring of AT&T.

Lent initially campaigned for the House as a challenger to "dangerous leftists," but he has turned out not to be a partisan ideologue. He is, however, a man who knows what he wants. Lent brings a bluntness to negotiation that one might expect from the product of a political machine. Some feel his high-pressure style is better suited to salesmanship than to statesmanship, but when he is through negotiating, he usually has gotten much of what he wanted.

Lent's strong will is occasionally a little surprising. At one point in the 100th Congress he fought with a vengeance to defeat an amendment designed to prevent startup of the Shoreham Nuclear Plant on Long Island, and another in New Hampshire.

During the debate, Lent attacked fellow New Yorker George J. Hochbrueckner, whose successful House campaign centered on opposition to Shoreham. "Many of us in this room were elected here on the basis of running against something," Lent said, "but after we get here awhile we calm down a little bit and we try to become statesmen." The amendment failed.

But Lent and Hochbrueckner, along with the rest of the Long Island delegation, joined forces in the 101st to save the F-14 fighter plane, manufactured by the Long Island-based Grumman Corp. and on the Defense Department's to-be-discontinued list. The plane was featured in the movie "Top Gun," and part of the lobbying effort involved distributing videocassettes of the movie to Armed Services

New York 4

Long Island — Southeastern Nassau County

In 1947, row after row of inexpensive Cape Cod homes began sprouting on what had been Long Island farm land, and Levittown was under way. Today, the last farm land has long since been developed, and Levittown and the surrounding middle-income suburbs of the 4th have the settled, comfortable look of established suburbia. They also generally vote Republican.

The 4th is an overwhelmingly white, middle-class area. The aerospace and electronics industries are major employers in the district; the Grumman Corp. maintains its headquarters in Bethpage, and many residents of the 4th cross district lines to work in defense plants in the neighboring 2nd. As elsewhere in Nassau, the railroad platforms are filled each morning with commuters clutching their early editions of *Newsday*, the Long Island daily.

While thousands of the 4th's constituents may stream into New York City on weekdays, thousands of citydwellers head for the district on summer weekends — in particular to Jones Beach, a state park on the Atlantic Ocean.

The district is ethnically diverse. Massapequa attracted a combination of Jewish and Italian homeowners following World War II, leading wags to refer to it as "Matzo-Pizza." Massapequa today is largely Italian and increasingly Republican. Plainview, toward the district's northern end, is a middle-income Jewish suburb.

The 4th includes all of Levittown except the western area. Its share of the community shows Republican leanings but occasionally supports Democrats in statewide elections.

Closer to the water, identification with the Republican Party is stronger. Alfonse M. D'Amato, the one-time GOP municipal official and twice-elected U.S. senator, comes from this section of the 4th. The now-faded older suburbs here that boomed in the postwar years — Baldwin, Oceanside and Freeport, a commercial fishing center — are Irish and Italian strongholds. Bellmore, Merrick and Seaford have a more prosperous look and equally firm GOP ties. The same can be said for the half of Long Beach Island in the 4th.

Population: 516,641. White 489,145 (95%), Black 19,186 (4%), Other 4,695 (1%). Spanish origin 15,428 (3%). 18 and over 376,675 (73%), 65 and over 42,004 (8%). Median age: 33.

Committee members. "We feel it tells the story of the F-14," Lent said. "It may be a little hokey, but we think it's called for."

The delegation won a temporary reprieve for F-14 production, but did not reverse the administration's plans to stop building the jet.

Like other Republicans representing districts troubled by hazardous chemicals, Lent was actively involved in crafting "superfund" legislation to clean up toxic-waste sites.

Lent was ranking Republican on the Commerce, Transportation and Tourism Subcommittee during the period it was chaired by New Jersey Democrat James J. Florio. He went along with Florio in pushing the original superfund bill, toward the end of President Jimmy Carter's administration.

But in the fights over superfund reauthorization in the 98th and 99th Congresses, the two were on opposite sides. Both wanted to see the fund increased, but Lent sought to give the Environmental Protection Agency (EPA) more leeway in administering the program than did most environmentalists. He feared Florio's anti-EPA position would jeopardize passage of any superfund bill. Once a compromise version passed the 99th Congress, however, Lent backed its passage despite continued White House objections.

Lent's cooperative relations with Dingell predate the Clean Air deliberations. In the 100th Congress he was among the leaders of an effort to set a national standard for product liability.

Along with Dingell, Florio and New Mexico Democrat Bill Richardson, Lent helped produce a scheme to replace conflicting state laws used by courts to determine whether a person injured by a defective product recovers damages from a manufacturer. The bill, opposed by consumer groups and plaintiffs' lawyers because it might make it tougher for victims to receive damages, passed the committee 30-12, but later died.

Lent is also in the top ranks on the Merchant Marine and Fisheries Committee. There he has supported ocean pollution control and coastal management legislation important to Long Island's numerous wetlands, inlets, estuaries and beaches.

In the 100th Congress, he was involved in the debate on legislation banning the dumping of sewage sludge in the ocean. New Jersey, whose beaches bear the brunt of ocean pollution, had fought with New York, a major dumper, over the issue for years. Lent complained in committee that the measure, which imposed fees and penalties on municipalities failing to halt dumping by the early 1990s, was designed to "beat up" on New York.

But with Congress seemingly determined to pass some dumping bill, Lent eventually took some credit for helping to hammer out a compromise. It set a deadline in 1991 for dumping to end, and set a schedule of fees and penalties that would initially go into a trust fund, which could be spent for the development of waste-disposal alternatives.

Representing a district with a large Jewish population, and frequently confronting Jewish re-election challengers, Lent has been a prolific author of resolutions and speeches supporting the rights of Jews in the Soviet Union and is a fervent supporter of Israel.

At Home: Lent rose through the ranks of the Nassau County Republican organization, during the heyday of organization chief Joseph Margiotta. He started as an associate police justice in East Rockaway, then was elected to the state Senate in 1962.

Operating in 1970 under a court order to draw a new House redistricting plan, state Republicans redrew the lines of the southernmost Nassau County district to the disadvantage of its one-term Democratic incumbent, Allard K. Lowenstein. Lent then ran as the organization's choice to oust Lowenstein.

A well-known liberal activist, Lowenstein restarted the grass-roots organization that was his political trademark. But he could not withstand a campaign offensive by Lent's allies, who called Lowenstein a dupe of radical leftists, and urged the district to "give up Lowenstein for Lent." Though the incumbent's backers tried to portray the slogan as a slap at Jews, Lent won.

He has had a relatively easy time since then, winning with at least 60 percent since 1976, and topping out with 70 percent in 1988 against Democrat Francis T. Goban, a waste-management executive.

Although Lent, like other Long Island incumbents, lost a few percentage points in 1990 to a general anti-incumbent and anti-tax mood, he defeated Goban again with 61 percent.

Committees

Energy & Commerce (Ranking)
Oversight & Investigations

Merchant Marine & Fisheries (3rd of 17 Republicans)
Merchant Marine (ranking)

Elections

1990 General

Norman F. Lent (R)	79,304	(61%)
Francis T. Goban (D)	41,308	(32%)
John J. Dunkle (RTL)	6,706	(5%)
Ben-Zion J. Heyman (L)	2,343	(2%)

1988 General

Norman F. Lent (R)	151,038	(70%)
Francis T. Goban (D)	59,479	(28%)

Previous Winning Percentages: **1986** (65%) **1984** (69%) **1982** (60%) **1980** (67%) **1978** (66%) **1976** (56%) **1974** (54%) **1972** (62%) **1970** (51%)

District Vote For President

	1988	1984	1980	1976
D	93,960 (41%)	88,949 (36%)	70,189 (34%)	99,242 (48%)
R	134,425 (58%)	155,948 (64%)	117,359 (57%)	107,420 (52%)
I			15,434 (8%)	

Campaign Finance

	Receipts	Receipts from PACs	Expend-itures
1990			
Lent (R)	$596,305	$406,820 (68%)	$398,706
1988			
Lent (R)	$589,323	$358,299 (61%)	$436,310
Goban (D)	$5,427	$3,500 (64%)	$4,715

Key Votes

1991

Authorize use of force against Iraq	Y

1990

Support constitutional amendment on flag desecration	Y
Pass family and medical leave bill over Bush veto	N
Reduce SDI funding	N
Allow abortions in overseas military facilities	N
Approve budget summit plan for spending and taxing	Y
Approve civil rights bill	N

1989

Halt production of B-2 stealth bomber at 13 planes	N
Oppose capital gains tax cut	N
Approve federal abortion funding in rape or incest cases	N
Approve pay raise and revision of ethics rules	Y
Pass Democratic minimum wage plan over Bush veto	N

Voting Studies

	Presidential Support		Party Unity		Conservative Coalition	
Year	S	O	S	O	S	O
1990	67	28	60	33	78	19
1989	76	21	56	40	83	15
1988	48	42	61	33	76	13
1987	58	35	54	36	77	21
1986	61	33	65	27	72	18
1985	65	33	72	25	89	9
1984	55	35	65	24	80	14
1983	68	24	65	29	78	19
1982	66	27	60	32	71	27
1981	68	30	75	23	80	17

Interest Group Ratings

Year	ADA	ACU	AFL-CIO	CCUS
1990	17	63	9	77
1989	10	70	33	90
1988	25	68	62	69
1987	12	59	33	79
1986	20	64	46	64
1985	10	75	31	57
1984	10	70	38	79
1983	10	76	19	80
1982	35	50	50	65
1981	10	93	13	95

5 Raymond J. McGrath (R)

Of Valley Stream — Elected 1980

Born: March 27, 1942, Valley Stream, N.Y.
Education: State U. of New York, Brockport, B.S. 1963; New York U., M.A. 1968.
Occupation: Physical education teacher.
Family: Wife, Sheryl Peterson; two children, one stepchild.
Religion: Roman Catholic.
Political Career: N.Y. Assembly, 1977-81.
Capitol Office: 205 Cannon Bldg. 20515; 225-5516.

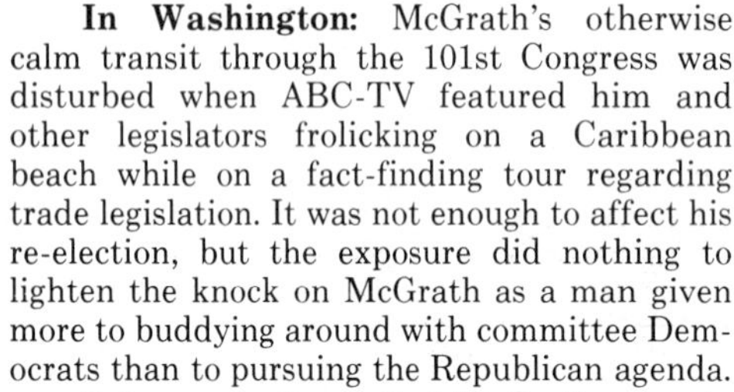

In Washington: McGrath's otherwise calm transit through the 101st Congress was disturbed when ABC-TV featured him and other legislators frolicking on a Caribbean beach while on a fact-finding tour regarding trade legislation. It was not enough to affect his re-election, but the exposure did nothing to lighten the knock on McGrath as a man given more to buddying around with committee Democrats than to pursuing the Republican agenda.

It is easy to forget that McGrath came to Congress with the firebrand class of 1980. Some of his classmates struggled to reconcile Reaganism with constituency needs; McGrath just chose the latter. Yet he was popular enough with New York colleagues (few of whom are ideologues) to win a much-sought-after seat on Ways and Means he assumed in the 99th Congress.

If after a decade in Congress McGrath is known largely for his good looks, his district-first approach and his friendship with Dan Rostenkowski, D-Ill., it is hard to see how any of these have done his Long Island district harm. His willingness to deal with powerful Ways and Means Chairman Rostenkowski should come as little surprise. Both men were products of political machines and both are given more to skillfully winning political fights than to taking part in ideological debates.

McGrath seems content at his cruising speed, emphasizing achievable victories such as securing $900,000 to dredge his district's Jones Inlet. When he goes to the mat, he is probably opposing higher taxes, higher fees at Long Island airports or the practice of blacking out cable TV coverage of local sports teams.

The biography his office distributes cites his "amiable manner," his "close personal friendships with congressional leaders on both sides" and his "ability to work with all factions." But McGrath's relationship with Rostenkowski, in particular, has spawned criticism from some GOP colleagues that his deal-making is a sellout.

In recent sessions, McGrath has voted with the Democrats on plant-closing notification and on "double-breasting," the practice of opening subsidiary companies to escape union labor contracts. In the 101st, he strayed from the party fold (along with Rep. Bill Gradison, R-Ohio) in voting to put the cost of the S&L bailout on budget. And he voted (with Gradison and Nancy L. Johnson, R-Conn.) to support the Democrats' child-care package.

McGrath was back with the GOP program on the proposed cut in capital gains tax rates. But McGrath is more generally suspected of apostasy because GOP colleagues suspect his ties to Democrats help him come out ahead in day-to-day committee dealings rarely noticed in roll calls and records.

Shortly after joining Ways and Means in 1985, McGrath made it clear that he put parochialism above partisanship. During debate on the 1986 tax code overhaul, McGrath focused his attention on saving the deductibility of state and local taxes. It is an issue that has stayed with him. He attributed his vote against the 1990 budget-summit agreement to its limits on state income-tax deductions.

Back in 1985, both the administration and Rostenkowski wanted to eliminate the deduction; that proposal caused a widespread uproar, especially in New York, a high-tax state that would have been hit particularly hard by the change.

McGrath and many others stood adamant against Rostenkowski over the deduction. After the chairman gave in to their demands, McGrath repaid the favor by supporting Rostenkowski's bill. His support was important because Rostenkowski was struggling to get Republicans signed on to his proposal so he could bill it as a bipartisan measure.

McGrath's support for Rostenkowski helped him get favorable consideration for "transition rules" beneficial to projects in his district, including a tax break on bonds to build a waste-disposal plant.

Responding to Republican criticism at one point, he said, "I'm an old-fashioned guy. When you make a deal, you stick with it."

When Ways and Means Democrats staged an impromptu champagne celebration in the wee hours of the morning after voting to approve the legislation, McGrath, who has a repu-

New York 5

Long Island — Southwestern Nassau County

The horse races here are at Belmont Park, not at the polls. Politics in the home district of former GOP boss Joseph Margiotta has been under control for more than two decades. Republicans have held the 5th since its creation in 1962 — thanks in large part to the effective GOP machine Margiotta built.

The organization has undergone change in the last few years. Margiotta was convicted in 1981 on federal mail fraud and extortion charges, and was forced to give up his post as chairman of the Nassau GOP organization. His successor, Joseph N. Mondello, was initially viewed as a Margiotta puppet but has been consolidating his own power base. The party apparatus, organized down to the block level in some places, remains perhaps the most potent political machine in the country.

But while the local GOP lock boosts Republican presidential candidates, they tend to win by somewhat less spectacular margins than farther out on Long Island. George Bush won the 5th with 56 percent of the vote, his lowest percentage of any Long Island district. The same was true for President Reagan in 1984, though he took 60 percent of the 5th District vote.

The village of Hempstead is the seat of enormous Hempstead Township, most of whose roughly 750,000 residents vote in the 5th District. Hempstead Township is Margiotta's original political base. Hempstead Village hosts Hofstra University and a mixture of light industries.

Republican totals are padded by the vote from such towns as Elmont and Valley Stream, McGrath's hometown. Residents here are primarily Irish and Italian homeowners a generation removed from Brooklyn or Queens.

Predominantly black North Freeport and the sizable black communities in Roosevelt and Hempstead Village contribute to the district's Democratic vote. Other Democratic pockets are Long Beach, a run-down seaside resort given over to senior citizen residential hotels, and the wealthy "Five Towns" area in Nassau's southwestern corner. These communities — Woodmere, Cedarhurst, Inwood, Lawrence and Hewlett — have the district's largest concentration of Jews. Jewish voters make up about 30 percent of the 5th's population.

Population: 516,712. White 442,946 (86%), Black 63,361 (12%), Other 5,130 (1%). Spanish origin 18,818 (4%). 18 and over 386,288 (75%), 65 and over 62,806 (12%). Median age: 34.

tation for enjoying Washington's social scene, joined them.

At Home: Despite his cozy relationship with Democratic powerhouse Rostenkowski, McGrath reportedly has expressed weariness with House existence. In February 1990, the Long Island newspaper *Newsday* reported that McGrath not only was contemplating retirement but might resign before the end of the 101st Congress. The paper said McGrath was considering a career as a lobbyist, a job that could earn him much more than his congressional salary.

If McGrath hoped to dwell on his decision, the retirement rumors forced his hand. Although he had until the July candidate filing deadline to make up his mind, McGrath announced just days after publication of the *Newsday* story that he would run for a sixth House term.

That fall, McGrath faced one of his most aggressive Democratic challengers, 33-year-old Mark S. Epstein. A former lawyer for the Environmental Defense Fund, Epstein hit McGrath hard on the issues of abortion and gun control. He said the incumbent would support the jailing of women who had abortions and implied that he opposed all forms of gun control. McGrath fired back that the Democrat had grossly distorted his positions, noting his support for the Brady bill, which called for a waiting period before gun purchases, and for allowing abortion in the case of rape, incest or threat to the woman's life.

Although he was affected somewhat by an anti-incumbent mood among Long Island voters, McGrath was bolstered by his district's Republican tendencies and by his big fundraising advantage. Even health problems — he collapsed in his House office in late October and was hospitalized with a blood clot on his lung — did not seriously hinder McGrath. He won with 55 percent of the vote, down somewhat from his usual tally but still 14 percentage points ahead of Epstein.

McGrath made it to Congress as the hand-picked candidate of Joseph Margiotta, then the head of the Nassau County Republican machine. There was an opening in the 5th District in 1980 because of the retirement of GOP Rep. John W. Wydler, who had served 18 years in the House.

McGrath had been a loyal Margiotta organization man in the Legislature, working primarily on issues of local interest to suburban Nassau County. He labored to end a state toll on a local parkway and to require the state to pay for school busing it ordered in a Nassau County town. He helped win state approval for local hospital expansion.

McGrath had no opposition in the 1980 primary. In November, his strong party base helped him defeat Democrat Karen Burstein, a former member of the state Public Service Commission. She waged a spirited campaign, but foundered in the face of the local Republican machine, the conservative trend in 1980 and the effectiveness of McGrath's campaign.

By 1982, many of McGrath's constituents had gained from President Reagan's defense spending proposals, since higher defense spending meant work for Grumman and other Long Island contractors. Still, voter doubts about Reagan's economic policies (1982 was a recession year) and the presence of another respectable Democratic candidate — Arnold Miller, a former Carter White House aide — kept McGrath under 60 percent.

In 1984, McGrath faced Michael D'Innocenzo, a Uniondale history professor who accused the Republican of "putting public relations above the public good." McGrath dispatched him with 62 percent.

McGrath was the subject of some unusual publicity in 1986 — the result of an unorthodox investigation into his private life conducted by his Democratic opponent.

The Democrat, Valley Stream attorney Michael Sullivan, hired female undercover investigators — equipped with hidden tape recorders — to record conversations McGrath had in a Capitol Hill restaurant. Sullivan claimed that on one segment of the tapes, whose poor sound quality made conversation difficult to discern, McGrath was instructing fellow Republican Rep. George C. Wortley of New York on how to get around campaign contribution limits with the help of a prominent Syracuse businessman.

Sullivan was roundly criticized for his actions by other New York Democrats and by the local media. McGrath denied any wrongdoing, launched a counteroffensive blasting his opponent for "Watergate dirty tricks" and looked on as Sullivan's campaign essentially collapsed. McGrath won going away. He had no difficulty in 1988; with 65 percent of the vote, he easily outran George Bush in the 5th.

Committee

Ways & Means (7th of 13 Republicans)
Health; Trade

Elections

1990 General

Raymond J. McGrath (R)	71,948	(55%)
Mark S. Epstein (D)	53,920	(41%)
Edward K. Kitt (RTL)	6,000	(5%)

1988 General

Raymond J. McGrath (R)	134,881	(65%)
William G. Kelly (D)	68,930	(33%)

Previous Winning Percentages: **1986** (65%) **1984** (62%) **1982** (58%) **1980** (58%)

District Vote For President

	1988	1984	1980	1976
D	97,609 (44%)	95,566 (39%)	76,701 (36%)	111,254 (48%)
R	124,622 (56%)	146,086 (60%)	117,106 (55%)	118,897 (52%)
I			14,561 (7%)	

Campaign Finance

	Receipts	Receipts from PACs	Expend-itures
1990			
McGrath (R)	$537,366	$225,358 (42%)	$618,882
Epstein (D)	$292,463	$11,350 (4%)	$291,412
1988			
McGrath (R)	$502,509	$251,324 (50%)	$337,792
Kelly (D)	$37,167	$4,200 (11%)	$35,627

Key Votes

1991	
Authorize use of force against Iraq	Y
1990	
Support constitutional amendment on flag desecration	Y
Pass family and medical leave bill over Bush veto	Y
Reduce SDI funding	N
Allow abortions in overseas military facilities	N
Approve budget summit plan for spending and taxing	N
Approve civil rights bill	N
1989	
Halt production of B-2 stealth bomber at 13 planes	N
Oppose capital gains tax cut	N
Approve federal abortion funding in rape or incest cases	N
Approve pay raise and revision of ethics rules	Y
Pass Democratic minimum wage plan over Bush veto	N

Voting Studies

	Presidential Support		Party Unity		Conservative Coalition	
Year	**S**	**O**	**S**	**O**	**S**	**O**
1990	49	46	56	37	54	39
1989	60	36	59	37	71	27
1988	46	42	62	20	74	18
1987	54	42	61	28	77	19
1986	60	37	61	31	70	26
1985	64	33	62	25	75	20
1984	49	34	60	26	73	17
1983	60	35	69	25	79	20
1982	61	34	66	31	66	29
1981	64	34	78	20	75	23

Interest Group Ratings

Year	ADA	ACU	AFL-CIO	CCUS
1990	50	52	75	36
1989	30	59	50	70
1988	25	55	83	82
1987	28	59	44	64
1986	20	55	43	69
1985	20	71	41	52
1984	20	74	30	64
1983	15	83	18	60
1982	35	68	50	73
1981	15	93	7	89

6 Floyd H. Flake (D)

Of Queens — Elected 1986

Born: Jan. 30, 1945, Los Angeles, Calif.
Education: Wilberforce U., B.A. 1967; attended Payne Theological Seminary, 1968-70; Northeastern U., 1974-75; St. John's U., 1982-85.
Occupation: Minister.
Family: Wife, M. Elaine McCollins; four children.
Religion: African Methodist Episcopal.
Political Career: No previous office.
Capitol Office: 1034 Longworth Bldg. 20515; 225-3461.

In Washington: A handsome and elegantly dressed minister who speaks in the captivating cadences of the black church, Flake has inspired comparisons with another black clergyman elected to Congress from New York — the late Rep. Adam Clayton Powell Jr.

For a time, the parallel with Powell, who faced legal and ethical problems during much of his House career, seemed to be getting uncomfortably close.

In August 1990, Flake was indicted on 17 counts of evading taxes and diverting $141,000, including federal housing funds, from his church. His wife, Margarett, faced similar charges. But in April 1991, the government's case was dismissed after a federal judge barred prosecutors from presenting what one called "the heart" of the case to the jury.

The Allen African Methodist Episcopal Church in Queens, of which Flake has been pastor for 15 years, is one of the city's oldest churches, with one of its largest black congregations. Prosecutors accused the Flakes of embezzling funds from a senior citizens' housing project run by the church and failing to report the income on their tax returns. They alleged that Flake siphoned off $75,000 in transportation funds from the Allen Senior Citizens Apartments and used $66,000 in other church funds to subsidize a lavish lifestyle. If convicted, Flake would have faced a maximum of 87 years in prison and nearly $4 million in fines. Flake denied the charges and said he had cooperated with the investigation.

During the trial, Flake's top aide testified that Flake may have inadvertently underreported outside income on his House financial disclosure forms. And though the Flakes denied evading taxes, their lawyers repeatedly emphasized that the couple would discuss their returns with the Internal Revenue Service. The U.S. attorney prosecuting the case said he expected the IRS to "go after" the Flakes for unpaid taxes.

Flake said the case "probably had something to do with politics. There also could be some racism in it."

Flake is a contemporary of the new generation of black House members who view their role less in racial terms than do some more senior Congressional Black Caucus members. Democrats Alan Wheat of Missouri, Mike Espy of Mississippi and Kweisi Mfume of Maryland exemplify this new generation; they try to effect change by working through the power structure, rather than by agitating primarily from the outside.

But in style and ideology, Flake does not fit quite so readily with the new generation, as he can be more vociferous and controversial. His failure in a bid for the Budget Committee in the 101st Congress may have been caused as much by the impression Flake made on his colleagues as a freshman as by their knowledge of a difficulty Flake had with a woman in his district.

With the federal case over, Flake is hoping that the distractions that have enveloped his brief career are behind him and he can settle into a player's role in House affairs.

On the Banking Committee, Flake sits on the Housing Subcommittee, which gives him a role in shaping housing programs for lower-income people. In the 101st Congress, he battled to ensure that more low-income families benefited from a $300 million rental-housing production program. The program, authored by New York Democrat Charles E. Schumer, was included in a bill overhauling the nation's federal housing programs. It established a revolving loan fund to provide advances to developers, nonprofit groups and public housing agencies to construct or rehabilitate affordable rental housing.

Republicans called it "a scandal waiting to happen" and tried to kill it. Flake, too, was troubled. He proposed increasing the percentage of low- and lower-income families who would live in the rental projects from 15 percent to 35 percent. "We ought to be doing the most for the people who need the most," he said. His amendment was rejected by the Housing Sub-

New York 6

Southern Queens — Ozone Park; Jamaica

In some respects, this southern Queens constituency has not changed much since it was settled by New York's burgeoning Catholic middle class more than a generation ago. Civil servants, teachers and small-business people abound, occupying block upon block of single-family brick homes.

But if the presence of a solid middle class has remained a constant, its composition has changed dramatically. Many of the Irish and Italian families that initially settled here have left; today, most of the middle-class population is black. Blacks are most prevalent in quiet, tree-lined communities such as Springfield Gardens and St. Alban's. In Jamaica, though, the black community is poorer, and urban problems of drugs and crime are more rife.

There is a diverse mixture across Jamaica Bay in the Rockaways, whose beaches attract myriad New Yorkers in the summertime. Far Rockaway has many elderly Jews. Neponsit is home to wealthy Jews and WASPs.

South of Jamaica lies Ozone Park, a white working-class area populated by Italians and Jews. Nearby Howard Beach has a similar makeup but a rougher reputation, due to a notorious racial incident in 1986, in which a group of white youths chased a black man onto a highway, where he was struck by a car and killed .

There have been other instances of racial strife here. White parents in Rosedale staged demonstrations in 1981 over a court order to transfer their children to a mostly black school. White flight from the 6th has taken its toll on the local economy. But the district's demographic changes have only reinforced its Democratic cast. The 6th supported Michael S. Dukakis for president in 1988, and Walter F. Mondale in 1984.

Population: 516,312. White 227,798 (44%), Black 259,693 (50%), Other 7,691 (1%). Spanish origin 48,653 (9%). 18 and over 368,500 (71%), 65 and over 61,547 (12%). Median age: 32.

committee by voice vote.

But Flake's reservations threatened the program; committee Chairman Henry B. Gonzalez of Texas worried that some Democrats might join Republicans in opposing it if Flake did so. Flake met with Schumer and agreed to return to the fold in exchange for a promise to modify the program so that either 40 percent of a building's tenants would be low-income or 20 percent would be lower income. That proposal, offered by Flake, was adopted by the committee

Flake joined Texas Republican Steve Bartlett in adding another amendment to the housing bill. Their proposal enabled the Department of Housing and Urban Development to buy properties for affordable housing from the Resolution Trust Corporation, which had taken them over from failed savings and loans.

In the 100th Congress, Flake attached an amendment to the omnibus housing authorization bill to provide for timely repair of major equipment systems in public-housing facilities.

When the Banking Committee worked on legislation in 1989 to bail out and restructure the savings and loan industry, Flake stood with the S&Ls in offering an amendment to allow thrifts that carried on their books "supervisory good will" — a form of phantom capital — to count it toward their required amount of capital. Even though the proposal had previously been debated and withdrawn, Flake offered it again. When debate clearly showed it would fail, he withdrew it. On the floor, Flake voted for the unsuccessful goodwill amendment sponsored by Illinois Republican Henry J. Hyde.

From his spot on the Small Business Committee, Flake has worked on legislation overhauling the minority set-aside program for federal contracts.

At Home: Flake's political tenure has been brief, but stormy. He narrowly lost a special House election in 1986, then came back later that year to unseat the man who had beaten him. In 1988, Flake brushed aside allegations of sexual impropriety. But just as he appeared to be settling into security, the federal charges of embezzlement came down against him.

Flake's indictment had no effect at the polls in 1990. Many of Flake's supporters in the 6th District's black community rallied to him: Some implied that the charges against Flake were part of a conspiracy against black leaders. Flake defeated a nearly invisible Republican with 72 percent of the vote.

Flake has a diverse background in corporate marketing and in education. He was an administrator at Lincoln University and Boston University.

But it was his long tenure as pastor of the Allen African Methodist Episcopal (AME) Church, that gave Flake a base for a political career. Flake's sponsorship of the church's 300-unit senior-citizens' home — later to become controversial — helped make him a popular figure.

Black leaders had targeted the 6th after 1982 redistricting gave it a black majority. But the opportunity to cash in on that demographic edge did not occur until 1986, following the death of Democratic Rep. Joseph P. Addabbo.

The special election that June occurred at a time of chaos within the white-run Queens Democratic machine, brought on by a corruption scandal and the suicide of county Democratic leader Donald M. Manes. Black state Assemblyman Alton R. Waldon Jr. had support from surviving fragments of the Democratic organization, enabling him to edge out Flake.

Flake, who did not appear on absentee ballots because of a filing technicality, appealed the results in court. He lost that battle, but the case helped Flake rally backers who believed the election was stolen by a corrupt Queens machine.

That sentiment gave Flake momentum going into the September primary to choose a nominee for a full term in the 100th Congress. Fusing his support in the black church with elements of black organized labor, Flake defeated Waldon and two other black primary candidates.

By 1988, Flake drew no significant opposition. His only difficulty was of a personal nature. In May, Thelma M. Singleton-Scott, a former aide to Flake at his Queens church, appeared before a conference of AME churches to accuse Flake of harassing her to quit after she broke off a sexual affair with him. Flake denied the accusations; a church panel rejected the woman's claim.

Committees

Banking, Finance & Urban Affairs (18th of 31 Democrats)
Financial Institutions Supervision, Regulation & Insurance; General Oversight; Housing & Community Development; International Development, Finance, Trade & Monetary Policy

Select Hunger (10th of 22 Democrats)
Domestic

Small Business (17th of 27 Democrats)
Regulation, Business Opportunity & Energy

Elections

1990 General

Floyd H. Flake (D)	44,306	(73%)
William Sampol (R)	13,224	(22%)
John Cronin (RTL)	3,111	(5%)

1988 General

Floyd H. Flake (D)	94,506	(86%)
Robert L. Brandofino (C)	15,547	(14%)

Previous Winning Percentage: **1986** (68%)

District Vote For President

	1988	1984	1980	1976
D	100,131 (71%)	111,658 (70%)	89,495 (58%)	115,346 (69%)
R	39,160 (28%)	47,665 (30%)	55,064 (36%)	50,369 (30%)
I			7,737 (5%)	

Campaign Finance

	Receipts	Receipts from PACs	Expend-itures
1990			
Flake (D)	$240,869	$122,440 (51%)	$205,031
1988			
Flake (D)	$344,391	$150,681 (44%)	$370,236
Brandofino (C)	$3,139	0	$3,071

Key Votes

1991

Authorize use of force against Iraq	N

1990

Support constitutional amendment on flag desecration	N
Pass family and medical leave bill over Bush veto	?
Reduce SDI funding	Y
Allow abortions in overseas military facilities	Y
Approve budget summit plan for spending and taxing	N
Approve civil rights bill	Y

1989

Halt production of B-2 stealth bomber at 13 planes	Y
Oppose capital gains tax cut	Y
Approve federal abortion funding in rape or incest cases	Y
Approve pay raise and revision of ethics rules	Y
Pass Democratic minimum wage plan over Bush veto	Y

Voting Studies

	Presidential Support		Party Unity		Conservative Coalition	
Year	S	O	S	O	S	O
1990	14	81	85	5	9	80
1989	27	67	85	4	7	93
1988	14	74	82	3	5	82
1987	13	75	79	2	12	70

Interest Group Ratings

Year	ADA	ACU	AFL-CIO	CCUS
1990	89	4	91	38
1989	95	4	100	30
1988	95	0	100	30
1987	92	0	100	0

7 Gary L. Ackerman (D)

Of Queens — Elected 1983

Born: Nov. 19, 1942, Brooklyn, N.Y.
Education: Queens College, B.A. 1965.
Occupation: Teacher; publisher and editor; advertising executive.
Family: Wife, Rita Gail Tewel; three children.
Religion: Jewish.
Political Career: N.Y. Senate, 1979-83; sought Democratic nomination for N.Y. City Council at large, 1977.
Capitol Office: 238 Cannon Bldg. 20515; 225-2601.

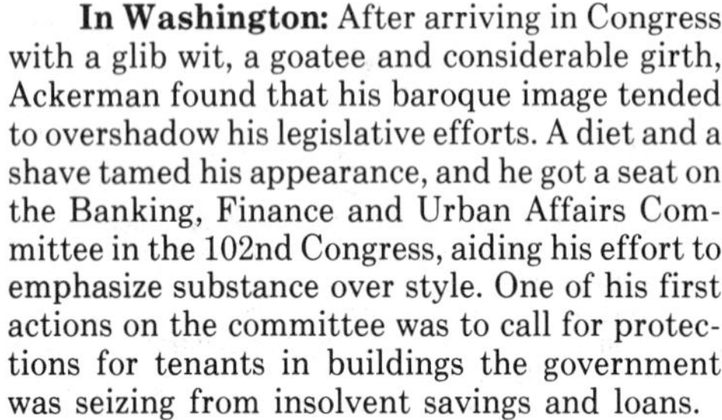

In Washington: After arriving in Congress with a glib wit, a goatee and considerable girth, Ackerman found that his baroque image tended to overshadow his legislative efforts. A diet and a shave tamed his appearance, and he got a seat on the Banking, Finance and Urban Affairs Committee in the 102nd Congress, aiding his effort to emphasize substance over style. One of his first actions on the committee was to call for protections for tenants in buildings the government was seizing from insolvent savings and loans.

Prior to the 102nd, Ackerman was known for his work on the Foreign Affairs Committee. His district has a large Jewish population, and Ackerman has pursued their concerns for Israel. In 1988, he rejected a letter sent to the Israeli government by 30 senators, which called on Israel to soften its resistance to Palestinian demands. "We're not talking about a banana republic," Ackerman said of Israel. Like many pro-Israel legislators, Ackerman was an early supporter of U.S. involvement, and the eventual war, in the Persian Gulf.

Ackerman's interest in human rights often centers on the oppression he sees Jews facing, including the emigration rights of Soviet Jewish "refuseniks"and Ethiopian Jews.

But Jewish issues are just one Ackerman interest; he has been a solid contributor on Foreign Affairs' Human Rights panel (which he dropped in the 102nd) and on the Select Hunger Committee. As a member of the Hunger Committee, Ackerman staged a campaign in 1985 for Ethiopian famine relief that raised nearly $200,000 from New York City schoolchildren. His "Children to Children" crusade became the subject of an ABC television documentary.

On Post Office and Civil Service, Ackerman first gained note for opposing proposals for widespread drug testing of federal workers. Ackerman chairs the Subcommittee on Compensation and Employee Benefits, and in the 101st Congress he helped win passage of a federal pay raise plan to help close the gap between public- and private-sector salaries. Ackerman continues to chair the subcommittee in the 102nd, and he also joins the ethics committee.

But if Ackerman has worked hard for respect, he is still capable of burlesque. After U.S. forces began their bombing campaign against Iraq in January 1991, Ackerman read a jubilant poem on the House floor that began, "Slam, bam, thanks Saddam," and concluded, "Now take the loss, reverse the course, because it ain't going to get no better."

On the House floor in 1990, Ackerman displayed swimming trunks, pantyhose and other paraphernalia emblazoned with a flag motif to convey the impracticality of a constitutional ban on flag desecration.

And Ackerman still has not lost his zeal for his native New York cuisine: Decrying the lack of a decent deli sandwich in Washington, he stages an annual fundraiser for which he ships down corned beef, pastrami and other delicacies from a restaurant in his district.

At Home: When veteran Democratic Rep. Benjamin S. Rosenthal died in early 1983, Ackerman did not lead the list of likely successors. He had been a frequent antagonist of the Queens Democratic organization. But with a hard-charging campaign style and his own organization, Ackerman forced Democrats to take him seriously. His prospects improved when a popular state legislator dropped from the race. Ackerman then convinced Democratic leaders he could shield the party from an independent campaign being waged by wealthy pollster Douglas Schoen.

Schoen did eclipse the GOP nominee as Ackerman's toughest foe. But Ackerman won the special election with 50 percent of the vote. Since then, he has won easily. He gained a full term in 1984 with 69 percent and ran unopposed in 1988 and 1990.

A former social studies teacher, Ackerman started in politics in 1977, when, as publisher of a weekly Queens newspaper, he editorialized against a machine Democratic incumbent in a City Council race. He unsuccessfully challenged the incumbent as an independent, then won an open state Senate seat in 1978.

New York 7

Central Queens — Hollis; Kew Gardens

The 7th District travels from semi-suburban neighborhoods near the Nassau County border to apartment towers in the heart of Queens. Mostly white and largely Jewish, the district is solidly Democratic. It gave 60 percent of its presidential vote to Democrat Michael S. Dukakis in 1988, and has voted overwhelmingly for Queens Democrat Mario M. Cuomo for governor.

Besides its territory in eastern Queens, the 7th extends south to take in East Elmhurst, Kew Gardens and part of Jamaica, which contributes much of its black population. Another concentration of minorities is in Corona's massive Lefrak City complex. Middle-income whites have been leaving the 20-building development off the Long Island Expressway, and blacks and Hispanics have been replacing them.

Rego Park, developed in the 1920s, typifies the middle-class Jewish portion of the district that formed the support base of the late Democratic Rep. Benjamin S. Rosenthal. A community of six-story apartment buildings and tightly spaced brick houses, Rego Park has turned more conservative on social issues, but most of its residents remain loyal Democrats.

The most significant Republican enclave in the 7th is near the Queens-Nassau line in tree-shaded Bellerose and Queens Village. The suburban-oriented homeowners there, most of Irish and Italian background, regularly flout their Democratic registration and vote for GOP candidates in state and national elections.

Like much of the rest of Queens, the 7th is almost exclusively bedroom communities, with no major industrial activity. Hospitals such as the Long Island Jewish Hillside Medical Center in New Hyde Park are its largest employers.

Population: 516,544. White 377,844 (73%), Black 61,190 (12%), Asian and Pacific Islander 35,365 (7%). Spanish origin 101,893 (20%). 18 and over 407,309 (79%), 65 and over 81,051 (16%). Median age: 35.

Committees

Banking, Finance & Urban Affairs (31st of 31 Democrats)
General Oversight

Foreign Affairs (14th of 28 Democrats)
International Narcotics Control (co-chairman); Arms Control, International Security & Science; Asian & Pacific Affairs; Europe & the Middle East

Post Office & Civil Service (7th of 15 Democrats)
Compensation & Employee Benefits (chairman)

Select Hunger (8th of 22 Democrats)
Domestic

Standards of Official Conduct (3rd of 7 Democrats)

Elections

1990 General		
Gary L. Ackerman (D)	51,091	(100%)
1988 General		
Gary L. Ackerman (D)	93,120	(100%)

Previous Winning Percentages: **1986** (77%) **1984** (69%) **1983 *** (50%)

* *Special election.*

District Vote For President

	1988	1984	1980	1976
D	87,703 (60%)	89,940 (52%)	75,859 (49%)	110,300 (63%)
R	57,244 (39%)	81,401 (47%)	68,309 (44%)	65,412 (37%)
I			9,734 (6%)	

Campaign Finance

	Receipts	Receipts from PACs	Expend-itures
1990			
Ackerman (D)	$305,414	$186,537 (61%)	$272,549
1988			
Ackerman (D)	$280,467	$196,120 (70%)	$142,041

Key Votes

1991	
Authorize use of force against Iraq	Y
1990	
Support constitutional amendment on flag desecration	N
Pass family and medical leave bill over Bush veto	Y
Reduce SDI funding	Y
Allow abortions in overseas military facilities	Y
Approve budget summit plan for spending and taxing	Y
Approve civil rights bill	Y
1989	
Halt production of B-2 stealth bomber at 13 planes	Y
Oppose capital gains tax cut	Y
Approve federal abortion funding in rape or incest cases	Y
Approve pay raise and revision of ethics rules	Y
Pass Democratic minimum wage plan over Bush veto	Y

Voting Studies

	Presidential Support		Party Unity		Conservative Coalition	
Year	**S**	**O**	**S**	**O**	**S**	**O**
1990	14	79	92	2	7	85
1989	27	66	92	1	10	83
1988	15	74	93	0	3	87
1987	19	74	93	2	7	86
1986	12	79	91	0	4	82
1985	20	74	87	3	4	95
1984	22	66	85	5	5	86
1983	20 †	79 †	91 †	4 †	12 †	87 †

† *Not eligible for all recorded votes.*

Interest Group Ratings

Year	ADA	ACU	AFL-CIO	CCUS
1990	94	0	100	15
1989	90	0	100	40
1988	95	0	100	23
1987	96	0	100	14
1986	85	0	100	13
1985	100	10	100	20
1984	95	9	92	36
1983	85	0	100	22

8 James H. Scheuer (D)

Of Douglaston — Elected 1964

Did not serve 1973-75.

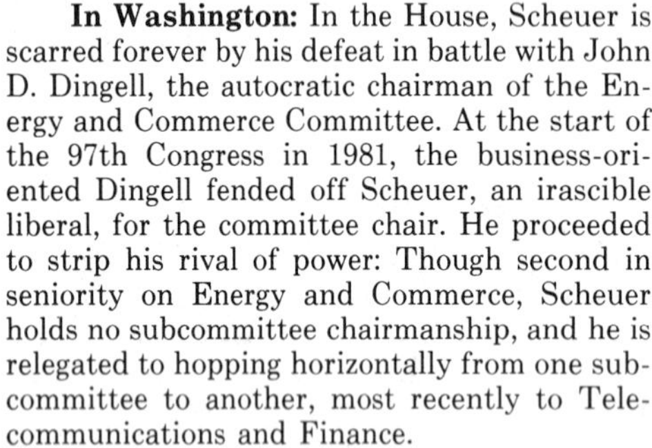

Born: Feb. 6, 1920, New York, N.Y.

Education: Swarthmore College, A.B. 1942; Harvard U., M.A. 1943; Columbia U., LL.B. 1948.

Military Service: Army, 1943-45.

Occupation: Lawyer; economist.

Family: Wife, Emily Malino; four children.

Religion: Jewish.

Political Career: Sought Democratic nomination for mayor of New York City, 1969; defeated for renomination for U.S. House, 1972.

Capitol Office: 2221 Rayburn Bldg. 20515; 225-5471.

In Washington: In the House, Scheuer is scarred forever by his defeat in battle with John D. Dingell, the autocratic chairman of the Energy and Commerce Committee. At the start of the 97th Congress in 1981, the business-oriented Dingell fended off Scheuer, an irascible liberal, for the committee chair. He proceeded to strip his rival of power: Though second in seniority on Energy and Commerce, Scheuer holds no subcommittee chairmanship, and he is relegated to hopping horizontally from one subcommittee to another, most recently to Telecommunications and Finance.

Scheuer — who electorally has endured some extreme permutations of redistricting — has shown a good deal of resilience. On consumer and environmental issues, the ornery survivor remains a crusader, often acting as a front man for California Democrat Henry A. Waxman, the committee's leading liberal and chairman of the Health and the Environment Subcommittee, who prefers to play the inside game.

Scheuer has also found a niche on the Science, Space and Technology Committee, where he is the second-ranking Democrat and the chairman of the lower-profile Environment Subcommittee. It is there where Scheuer finds a forum for voicing issues he might have otherwise championed on Energy and Commerce — such as renewable fuels, energy conservation, indoor air pollution and the preservation of biological diversity.

Scheuer's trademark, though, remains the gruff and belligerent manner that hindered him in his fights with Dingell. No one ever accused Dingell of disarming opponents with charm, but he expertly charted the deal-cutting route to institutional power. Scheuer, on the other hand, was the angry activist, firing off bromides against injustices done to consumers and the environment. While Scheuer was making caustic statements, Dingell was making political allies.

The chairmanship battle grew out of an animosity that developed between the two men over several years. Dingell's main legislative role on Energy and Commerce had been to protect the automakers based in or near his Detroit-area district; Scheuer was a leading proponent of requiring air bags in cars, an idea Dingell vehemently opposed. Dingell also was irked by Scheuer's persistent calls for stringent anti-pollution standards under the Clean Air Act, and his defense — while serving in the 1970s as chairman of the Energy and Commerce Subcommittee on Consumer Protection — of the Federal Trade Commission, which had become an irritant to many members by seeking to regulate business activity.

For years, the two rarely spoke to each other. And after Dingell defeated Scheuer to take over the full committee in 1981, he "decided" Energy and Commerce had too many subcommittees. There was little doubt which one had to go: Scheuer's cherished Consumer Protection panel.

The deed was done over the furious objections of Scheuer, who said he was being punished for his air bag crusade. But the 14-7 vote stripping him of his subcommittee also reflected his standing among colleagues. The abrasive Scheuer had not impressed many with his abilities as chairman, and had not made up for that in personal terms.

In the years since, Scheuer has continued in his role as an outspoken activist. But his limited legislative clout is illustrated by the history of the legislation to ban smoking on passenger-airline flights. For years, Scheuer had submitted anti-smoking proposals that went nowhere. But in the 100th Congress, Illinois Democrat Richard J. Durbin, a fast-rising junior member of Appropriations, took up the cause, built a constituency for it, and pushed to passage a smoking ban on flights of two hours or less, which was subsequently extended to most flights of less than six hours.

The blow of his 1981 chairmanship defeat

New York 8

Northern Queens; Eastern Bronx; Western Nassau County

The 8th is a masterpiece of redistricting art. It starts in the east Bronx, leaps across the East River into Queens, then pushes out of New York City into the Nassau County suburbs.

Northeast Queens, a middle- to upper-middle-class residential area, makes up the heart of the district: Large homes front Little Neck Bay and Long Island Sound. However, Flushing, a Dutch settlement as early as 1645, has more closely packed housing and a more urban feel; its downtown area is a historic district. Flushing was the site of world's fairs in 1939 and 1964 and today contains both Shea Stadium and La Guardia Airport.

In all, the Queens portion of the district has about two-thirds of the population. Roughly 8 percent of the district's residents live across the city line in Nassau County; the Bronx contributes the remainder, a little more than 20 percent.

The Nassau portion of the 8th takes in more than 10,000 constituents in suburban Great Neck, an affluent, largely Jewish community. Jutting into Long Island Sound, Great Neck is the site of the U.S. Merchant Marine Academy at Kings Point.

On the other side of Flushing Bay, in the Bronx, the 8th reaches north from the East River almost up to the Bronx Zoo. Jews, many of them elderly, dominate the quiet neighborhoods of Parkchester, Van Ness and Pelham Parkway. Scheuer represented some of this territory in his original constituency in the 1960s.

South of the Cross Bronx Expressway, the 8th has its main concentration of blacks and Hispanics in Soundview. Their votes help affirm the 8th's Democratic nature, but their political ties tend toward the western end of the Bronx, outside the district.

The 8th is strongly if not monolithically Democratic. Walter F. Mondale won it narrowly in 1984, but Michael S. Dukakis did better four years later.

Population: 516,165. White 407,294 (79%), Black 51,618 (10%), Asian and Pacific Islander 25,547 (5%). Spanish origin 71,542 (14%). 18 and over 402,776 (78%), 65 and over 81,916 (16%). Median age: 36.

was cushioned somewhat by the fact that his Science subcommittee has jurisdiction over the Environmental Protection Agency (EPA). Scheuer went to war with the Reagan administration over what he viewed as its efforts to eviscerate the EPA's regulatory functions, and rushed to the forefront of the investigation into misconduct at that agency in 1982.

It was Scheuer who charged that former EPA official Rita M. Lavelle might have perjured herself in denying that she sought the dismissal of an employee who criticized management of hazardous-waste programs. That charge was one of several that led to Lavelle's dismissal in early 1983; she was later convicted and sentenced to time in federal prison.

Scheuer also charged that EPA kept a "hit list" on which staff scientists and scientific advisers were rated for political acceptability during the Reagan transition.

In the 100th Congress, Scheuer promoted his proposal to create an executive branch advisory board on issues affecting biotechnology, the field in which scientists perform genetics research into improved strains of agricultural plants and animals, and cures for diseases such as cancer and AIDS. Scheuer's bill was approved by the Science Committee in August 1988, despite the Reagan administration's opinion that it would create an unnecessary layer of bureaucracy. But the bill was blocked in Energy and Commerce by Dingell.

When Scheuer first came to Congress in 1965, he was a strong advocate of President Lyndon B. Johnson's "War on Poverty." He remains supportive of those programs that have survived the years and has sought a national health care plan. He describes Head Start, the preschool program for children of low-income families, as "the jewel in the crown of the poverty program . . . and it has had an unblemished record of success."

At Home: If many House colleagues have had an irritable relationship with Scheuer, so have New York Democratic officials been put off by his thorny political personality. As New York's stagnating population has put a redistricting squeeze on its House delegation, Scheuer has received precious little aid from his party's state legislators.

Yet Scheuer has exhibited unique survival skills. Buffeted about by a series of remaps, Scheuer has challenged three incumbent members of his own party for renomination and beaten two of them. He has run in five different districts and won in four. Even if the jerry-built 8th District is dismantled before 1992, Scheuer's track record shows that he is no sure bet to retire.

The son of a wealthy real estate man, Scheuer had a successful career himself in home-building and construction. He entered politics in 1964 as part of the reform wave that swept over the Bronx that year, defeating Rep. James Healey, a Democrat allied with the traditional party organization.

Scheuer mounted a disastrous campaign for mayor of New York City in 1969, finishing last in a field of five candidates despite an expenditure of $550,000.

In 1970, when a new Hispanic district was created in the South Bronx, much of it from Scheuer's territory, he moved into a neighboring district and defeated Rep. Jacob Gilbert, another Democratic organization loyalist, for renomination. Two years later, the Bronx lost a district and Scheuer was thrown in with Democratic Rep. Jonathan B. Bingham. This time he lost and had to retire, albeit briefly, from the House.

Another opportunity opened for Scheuer in Brooklyn's 11th District, when Democratic Rep. Frank J. Brasco got into legal trouble and retired in 1974. After Scheuer won a primary over the candidate backed by the Brooklyn organization, his electoral career quieted down for the balance of the decade. The organization did not challenge him, and he did not bother the organization.

This peaceful arrangement served Scheuer well in 1982, when the Legislature merged his district with that of Queens Democrat Joseph P. Addabbo. Scheuer moved one more time, to the new 8th, and the Queens Democratic leadership accepted him. Scheuer has not had any trouble since then, running in 1988 without Republican opposition.

In 1990, he appeared likely to face a primary challenge from Democratic state Sen. Leonard Stavisky, a longtime Queens rival. But three weeks after launching his challenge, Stavisky dropped out.

Committees

Energy & Commerce (2nd of 27 Democrats)
Energy & Power; Health & the Environment; Telecommunications & Finance

Science, Space & Technology (2nd of 32 Democrats)
Environment (chairman); Space

Select Narcotics Abuse & Control (4th of 21 Democrats)

Joint Economic

Elections

1990 General		
James H. Scheuer (D)	56,396	(72%)
Gustave Reifenkugel (R)	21,646	(28%)
1988 General		
James H. Scheuer (D)	100,240	(100%)

Previous Winning Percentages:				**1986**	(90%)	**1984**	(63%)
1982	(90%)	**1980**	(74%)	**1978**	(79%)	**1976**	(74%)
1974	(72%)	**1970**	(72%)	**1968**	(83%)	**1966**	(84%)
1964	(84%)						

District Vote For President

	1988	1984	1980	1976
D	100,779 (58%)	99,844 (52%)	71,229 (45%)	105,219 (59%)
R	69,751 (41%)	91,933 (48%)	73,444 (47%)	72,954 (41%)
I			10,091 (6%)	

Campaign Finance

	Receipts	Receipts from PACs	Expend-itures
1990			
Scheuer (D)	$403,345	$94,800 (24%)	$397,799
1988			
Scheuer (D)	$77,854	$55,600 (71%)	$98,919

Key Votes

1991	
Authorize use of force against Iraq	N
1990	
Support constitutional amendment on flag desecration	N
Pass family and medical leave bill over Bush veto	Y
Reduce SDI funding	Y
Allow abortions in overseas military facilities	Y
Approve budget summit plan for spending and taxing	Y
Approve civil rights bill	Y
1989	
Halt production of B-2 stealth bomber at 13 planes	Y
Oppose capital gains tax cut	Y
Approve federal abortion funding in rape or incest cases	Y
Approve pay raise and revision of ethics rules	Y
Pass Democratic minimum wage plan over Bush veto	Y

Voting Studies

	Presidential Support		Party Unity		Conservative Coalition	
Year	**S**	**O**	**S**	**O**	**S**	**O**
1990	16	81	93	3	6	91
1989	30	59	89	2	7	90
1988	21	70	82	8	13	74
1987	15	78	81	4	14	77
1986	18	79	88	5	8	92
1985	19	73	90	3	7	91
1984	32	64	84	8	15	80
1983	21	77	92	5	10	90
1982	35	60	91	6	14	82
1981	32	61	92	5	13	83

Interest Group Ratings

Year	ADA	ACU	AFL-CIO	CCUS
1990	89	0	100	14
1989	85	0	100	44
1988	85	5	86	46
1987	84	5	79	9
1986	95	0	100	18
1985	90	0	100	23
1984	90	4	67	21
1983	85	0	100	20
1982	95	0	95	14
1981	90	0	93	11

9 Thomas J. Manton (D)

Of Queens — Elected 1984

Born: Nov. 3, 1932, New York, N.Y.
Education: St. John's U., B.B.A. 1958, LL.B. 1962.
Military Service: Marine Corps, 1951-53.
Occupation: Lawyer.
Family: Wife, Diane Mason Schley; four children.
Religion: Roman Catholic.
Political Career: N.Y. City Council, 1970-84; sought Democratic nomination for U.S. House, 1972, 1978.
Capitol Office: 331 Cannon Bldg. 20515; 225-3965.

In Washington: Manton brought from Queens to Congress a keen understanding of political machinations. As chairman of the Democratic organization in Queens, he has been deeply involved in complex parochial politics; in Washington, he has worked to find the centers of power and gravitated toward them.

After currying favor with the party leadership, Manton was able to secure a seat at the start of the 102nd Congress on House Administration, which oversees internal House matters such as committee budgets. He also got a seat on the Democratic Steering and Policy Committee, which makes committee assignments.

In the 101st Congress, Manton had won a place on Energy and Commerce, a committee of considerable reputation and legislative reach. He had tried for the panel two years earlier, but failed to win the backing of the New York delegation. He then laid careful groundwork, playing an active role on the Democratic Congressional Campaign Committee, serving as a regional co-chairman and raising money for party candidates. He was also careful to court committee Chairman John D. Dingell of Michigan, who worked hard to add members to his panel who would not undermine his efforts to block tough clean air legislation.

During consideration of such legislation in 1990, Manton returned the favor. Despite the urgings of New York lobbyists, Manton joined Dingell in successfully opposing an amendment to require cleaner car fuels. "We're here in a political climate of give and take, with amendments we may need some help on," Manton said. "People don't need to fracture my arm to get my attention."

A former policeman, Manton also touts his sponsorship of federal disability pay to law enforcement officials disabled in the line of duty, passed as part of omnibus anti-crime legislation in 1990.

At Home: During his first successful House campaign in 1984, Manton was overshadowed by his predecessor, Democrat Geraldine A. Ferraro. When Ferraro accepted Walter F. Mondale's invitation to be his vice presidential running-mate, Manton stepped in and won a House seat for which he had twice been defeated, once by Ferraro.

Manton has since obtained prominence in his own right, taking over as Queens Democratic chairman and stabilizing a party organization that had been wracked by scandal and suicide.

In 1972, as a junior member of the New York City Council, Manton unsuccessfully challenged longtime Democratic Rep. James J. Delaney in the primary. He tried again when Delaney retired in 1978; Ferraro defeated him decisively.

But when Mondale tapped Ferraro in 1984, Manton became a front-runner in the primary to replace her. His 14 years on the council gave Manton an edge in name recognition that enabled him to overcome a state assemblyman, a prominent lawyer and a Queens election official. Stressing his Irish-Catholic working-class roots, Manton eked out a narrow primary win.

In November, Manton faced Serphin R. Maltese, then-executive director of New York's Conservative Party. The district had a nearly 3-1 Democratic registration edge, and Maltese's positions on labor and rent control issues antagonized some key interest groups. He staged a vigorous campaign, though, and surprised many observers by holding Manton to 53 percent of the vote.

But Manton firmed up his grip on the 9th in 1986, racking up 69 percent against Queens attorney Salvatore Calise.

Meanwhile, Manton devoted much of his political effort to his position as Queens Democratic chairman. Manton won the post in October 1986, after pledging to improve the image of the party organization. He succeeded an interim replacement to Donald Manes, the Queens borough president and longtime party chairman who committed suicide earlier that year following his implication in a city corruption scandal.

Manton has won without difficulty in his last two contests. He ran unopposed in 1988, and took 64 percent — 40 points better than his GOP rival — in 1990.

New York 9

Western Queens — Astoria; Jackson Heights

Queens' melting-pot 9th encompasses old factories, drug-ridden slums, world-class tennis courts and the home of Archie Bunker, of TV's "All in the Family" fame. Bunker's opinions on race, drugs and modern morality are often expressed in the row houses of Astoria and Ridgewood. The neighborhood shown in the program was on Astoria's Steinway Street.

Though the 9th votes consistently Democratic for the House, it has shown GOP tendencies in presidential elections. It gave Ronald Reagan a majority in 1984 even with 9th District Rep. Geraldine A. Ferraro as the Democratic vice presidential nominee. In 1988, a boost from the large community of his fellow Greek-Americans in Astoria helped Michael S. Dukakis carry the 9th, but George Bush still got 48 percent districtwide. Many of the Greeks moved in during the 1960s, when their country was under military rule. Some of the city's best gyros can be bought on Ditmars Boulevard.

Aging industrial loft buildings are clustered in Long Island City and Sunnyside. Former occupants, mostly light manufacturers, have moved to suburban facilities. But Long Island City has taken on a new identity as yuppies restore its old living quarters, and Citicorp recently built Queens' biggest office skyscraper. These events are applauded by city economic development officials, but not always by the area's blue-collar bedrock.

Generally liberal Democratic politics prevail in Forest Hills, where affluent Jews and WASPs live in elegant Tudor-style homes. In the early 1970s Forest Hills in a display of conservatism, objected to the construction of public housing within its borders.

Until the 1970s, Jackson Heights was mostly white and middle class. Then low-income minorities moved in, many from South America, and some neighborhoods deteriorated. Among the white residents, Jews and Italians predominate, many of them elderly. There is a large Irish-American population, including numerous illegal aliens.

Population: 516,143. White 433,944 (84%), Black 18,962 (4%), Asian and Pacific Islander 28,615 (6%). Spanish origin 85,780 (17%). 18 and over 407,420 (79%), 65 and over 87,148 (17%). Median age: 37.

Committees

Energy & Commerce (21st of 27 Democrats)
Commerce, Consumer Protection & Competitiveness; Telecommunications & Finance; Transportation & Hazardous Materials

House Administration (11th of 15 Democrats)
Accounts; Personnel & Police

Merchant Marine & Fisheries (15th of 29 Democrats)
Coast Guard & Navigation; Fisheries & Wildlife Conservation & the Environment

Select Aging (23rd of 42 Democrats)
Housing & Consumer Interests; Retirement, Income & Employment; Social Security and Women

Joint Library

Elections

1990 General		
Thomas J. Manton (D)	35,177	(64%)
Ann Pfoser Darby (R)	13,330	(24%)
Thomas V. Ognibene (C)	6,137	(11%)
1988 General		
Thomas J. Manton (D)	72,851	(100%)

Previous Winning Percentages: **1986** (69%) **1984** (53%)

District Vote For President

	1988		1984		1980		1976	
D	70,764	(51%)	64,860	(42%)	57,779	(40%)	82,228	(51%)
R	66,203	(48%)	87,573	(57%)	76,761	(53%)	76,869	(49%)
I					7,849	(5%)		

Campaign Finance

	Receipts	Receipts from PACs		Expend-itures
1990				
Manton (D)	$620,609	$452,323	(73%)	$316,301
1988				
Manton (D)	$424,381	$263,545	(62%)	$256,832

Key Votes

1991	
Authorize use of force against Iraq	N
1990	
Support constitutional amendment on flag desecration	Y
Pass family and medical leave bill over Bush veto	Y
Reduce SDI funding	Y
Allow abortions in overseas military facilities	N
Approve budget summit plan for spending and taxing	Y
Approve civil rights bill	Y
1989	
Halt production of B-2 stealth bomber at 13 planes	N
Oppose capital gains tax cut	Y
Approve federal abortion funding in rape or incest cases	N
Approve pay raise and revision of ethics rules	Y
Pass Democratic minimum wage plan over Bush veto	Y

Voting Studies

	Presidential Support		Party Unity		Conservative Coalition	
Year	**S**	**O**	**S**	**O**	**S**	**O**
1990	26	72	89	6	35	61
1989	38	53	82	12	41	56
1988	24	67	89	6	32	63
1987	19	78	92	2	23	77
1986	18	77	88	3	30	60
1985	23	71	88	5	24	69

Interest Group Ratings

Year	ADA	ACU	AFL-CIO	CCUS
1990	67	9	100	21
1989	70	4	100	40
1988	60	18	100	23
1987	80	4	100	7
1986	75	9	100	29
1985	70	10	81	27

10 Charles E. Schumer (D)

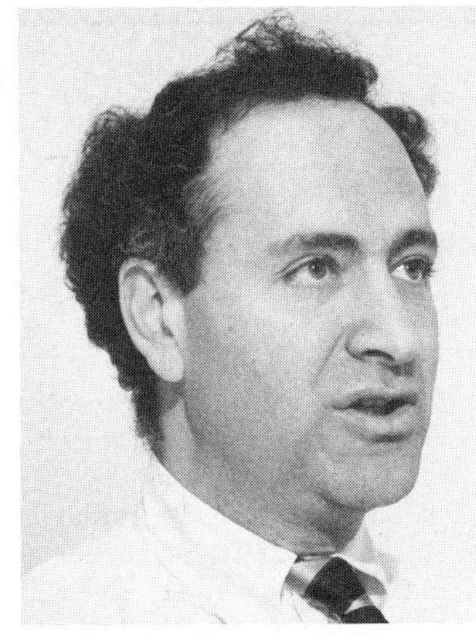

Of Brooklyn — Elected 1980

Born: Nov. 23, 1950, Brooklyn, N.Y.
Education: Harvard U., B.A. 1971, J.D. 1974.
Occupation: Lawyer.
Family: Wife, Iris Weinshall; two children.
Religion: Jewish.
Political Career: N.Y. Assembly, 1975-81.
Capitol Office: 2412 Rayburn Bldg. 20515; 225-6616.

In Washington: Schumer has all the traits to make him a most unpopular fellow: He is hot-headed and camera-craving, and he has an ego as big as his agenda. But for all that, colleagues accord him the respect reserved for a select group of notably effective legislators.

Schumer is the rare legislator who thrives not only in the public eye, but also in the back-rooms that are the incubators of legislative accomplishment. He is shrewd and tough, sees the big picture but attends to detail, and can make necessary compromises. Indeed, he did more before the age of 40 than many legislators manage in a career. A keen mind and an abundance of energy have enabled him, in just six terms, to put his imprint on housing, trade, immigration, farm and banking policy.

Most New York City liberals tend to be suspect in Democratic leadership circles, but Schumer has made his way in the House as a leadership insider. He has benefited from sharing a house on Capitol Hill with Democrats Marty Russo of Illinois and George Miller and Leon E. Panetta of California, well-placed members who have helped channel Schumer and smooth his abrasiveness.

When he needs to build support for a key legislative proposal, he can also call on allies in the Wall Street business community or on the editorial board of *The New York Times.* He makes skillful use of the media, publishing countless opinion pieces in national newspapers and appearing so often on TV news talk shows that it is sometimes hard to tell whether he is a guest or a host.

At the start the 102nd Congress, Schumer became chairman of the Judiciary Subcommittee on Crime, after it was merged with his old subcommittee on Criminal Justice. While some wonder how the hyperactive Schumer will endure the hours of painstaking testimony the panel hears from a myriad of interest groups concerned about crime and drugs, many Democrats are hopeful that Schumer's skill with the spin and substance of nettlesome issues will take their party off the defensive on crime.

With scandals to investigate and reforms to write, the 101st Congress was tailor-made for Schumer. He was at the forefront of high profile investigations of the savings-and-loan industry and the Department of Housing and Urban Development. And then he was a key player in the legislative cleanup of both.

Schumer will long be known for his skillful navigation of the savings and loan bailout bill. He managed to be the Bush administration's biggest helper and hindrance, and if his willingness to cut deals frustrated allies and adversaries alike, it also enabled the House to pass the legislation by a wide bipartisan margin.

A senior Democrat on the Banking, Judiciary and Budget committees, Schumer was uniquely well-placed to seize control of the debate. Then when the bill was drafted, he became a pivotal expert witness as the Rules Committee deliberated how to send it to the floor.

Schumer's fingerprints are on virtually every one of the 732 pages of the House thrift bill. Both in committee and on the floor, he championed the tough capital standards sought by the administration and ultimately adopted by Congress. He succeeded in his own efforts to increase civil and criminal penalties for banking law violations. And he made the rhetorical case for adding the cost of the bailout directly to the budget, in direct opposition to the administration.

Ultimately, Schumer lost only one issue where he put up a fight. He unsuccessfully opposed the sale of so-called bank investment certificates that compete directly with investments offered by insurance companies, except they carry deposit insurance. The result is that deposits can greatly exceed the $100,000 federal insurance limit, but are nonetheless insured. While Schumer predicted that it was an issue that would force Congress to reopen the bill in the future, he knew where the votes were and let his plan die on a voice vote.

Schumer was also in top form during the widely publicized 1989 Banking Committee investigation of influence peddling at HUD. When former Interior Secretary James Watt

New York 10

Central and Southern Brooklyn — Flatbush

The 10th is a loose descendant of the heavily Jewish Flatbush-based district that sent Democrat Emanuel Celler to Congress for 50 years before his primary loss to Elizabeth Holtzman in 1972. The old district changed dramatically in the 1970s, with Jews moving out and blacks coming to constitute a majority.

But the 1982 remap essentially restored the district's earlier ethnic complexion. Map makers shifted black areas in the district's northern half to the two Brooklyn districts designed for black representation.

More than 80 percent of the people in the 10th are white. Jews predominate, although Italians are a significant presence.

The 10th retains its Democratic cast, though the party's victory margins have fluctuated considerably in recent presidential elections. After winning 68 percent of the district's vote in 1976, Jimmy Carter slipped to just 50 percent four years later. Walter F. Mondale barely kept the district Democratic in 1984, but Michael S. Dukakis won the 10th with a more comfortable 57 percent in 1988.

The chief tensions here are between the "reform" and "regular" wings of the Democratic Party. Holtzman's win over Celler in 1972 was a victory for the reform faction. Schumer is considered a reformer, but he has maintained friendly relations with some regulars in the Brooklyn Democratic Party organization.

Flatbush is an amalgam of apartment buildings and single-family homes, such as the one on Marlboro Road where portions of the motion picture "Sophie's Choice" were filmed. The yeshivas and bagel bakeries along Ocean Parkway testify to the area's ethnic character.

Blue-collar Canarsie and Sheepshead Bay contain a mixture of Italians and Jews. Many residents work in small factories, turning out plastics and electrical parts. A different breed of Democrat inhabits Park Slope, where the town houses are elegant and the politics liberal. Park Slope has become increasingly attractive for young professionals with jobs in Manhattan.

Population: 516,471. White 455,541 (88%), Black 26,732 (5%), Other 14,145 (3%). Spanish origin 45,481 (9%). 18 and over 401,703 (78%), 65 and over 86,395 (17%). Median age: 36.

testified about his $420,000 consulting fee, a disgusted Schumer asked, "Was it moral what you did? .... Were you lured by the crumbs of subsidies? Were you? Everyone else in this room sees the hypocrisy of what you've done."

An aide to Schumer discovered one of the most damning pieces of evidence in the investigation — a report from a government ethics review team that concluded that "HUD's ethics program is one of the most ill-managed this team has ever seen." Ever savvy, Schumer held on to the document until a key hearing, when he ambushed a former HUD ethics lawyer.

While Schumer was among those who argued to move a HUD reform bill "arm in arm" with a housing bill, he was persuaded to shift tactics and move the reform package quickly. He was an architect of much of that bill and went on to author housing bill provisions to build new rental property.

Schumer's savvy helped him get around administration opposition to his rental package. Though he had cut a deal with HUD Secretary Jack F. Kemp that would result in passage of both the rental program and the home-ownership program that was a top White House priority, Schumer took no chances. He ensured that the vote on his package came first. If Schumer's rental program had been gutted, he would have moved to strike the ownership package. Few doubted that he would succeed, and his language was adjusted on the margins in conference.

Schumer was a key negotiator on the 1990 legal immigration reform bill, supporting an increase in the number of job-related visas and creation of a category of "diversity" visas for individuals from countries that under the current system are all but shut out. He entered that debate with considerable credibility from the 99th Congress, when his work helped lead to passage of landmark new U.S. immigration laws.

The legislation was at least five years in the making, and Schumer did not become a major player until the 98th Congress. By then, much of the groundwork had been laid. But Schumer stepped in to play a critical role in resolving a farm labor controversy that was the last major obstacle to enactment in 1986. After seemingly interminable negotiations with California Democrats, Schumer brokered a compromise that would give growers the supply of foreign labor they were demanding to help pick perishable crops. That concession was linked to a new program to protect foreign workers against exploitation.

Schumer stuck with the issue even after a

Republican-led revolt blocked the immigration bill from coming to the floor in late 1986 — largely because Democratic leaders insisted on barring amendments to the delicately crafted farm worker provisions. Although some lawmakers then left the immigration bill for dead, Schumer helped revive it with negotiations that put the bill back on the road to enactment.

While Schumer rotated off the Budget Committee at the start of the 102nd Congress and took a seat on Interior, he helped establish an aggressive faction of liberals on Budget (including housemates Russo and Miller) that became a force to be reckoned with. Schumer's particular concern on the panel was making sure that defense and farm programs suffered the same spending cuts as the social programs that benefit cities.

For a city slicker, Schumer has earned a reputation as a knowledgeable and articulate critic of arcane farm law. During consideration of the 1990 farm bill, Schumer and conservative Texas Republican Dick Armey led a coalition of urban liberals and free-market conservatives who waged war on waste and inequity in federal farm programs. Their efforts were greeted with fanfare from the media and fear from some farm-state members. While their more ambitious cutback legislation failed, 159-263, their efforts did lead Agriculture Committee to exercise spending restraint in drafting the farm bill.

In the 99th and 100th Congresses, Schumer took the lead on legislation providing new consumer protection for credit card users. He became so closely associated with the credit card issue, one trade paper said, that mail addressed to "Credit Cards, Washington, D.C." was delivered to his office.

Schumer originally pushed a bill to impose a cap on credit card interest rates, but it did not get out of subcommittee in the 99th Congress. In the 100th Congress, though, Schumer managed to get his fallback position through; he won passage of a measure that forces banks to disclose more fully the terms under which a credit card is used.

Another issue on which Schumer will continue to play a role is bank deregulation. Arguing on the side of the New York securities industry — and against the major banks — Schumer has opposed the entry of banks into such fields as securities and insurance.

Schumer tries to speak up for New York banking interests when he can. He has pushed for a form of nationwide branch banking — a development the major Wall Street banking institutions want. With congressmen from other regions trying to keep the powerful New York banks out by allowing interstate banking only within regions, Schumer has declared his opposition to any such measures unless they are a prelude to nationwide banking.

At Home: Never seriously challenged at the polls, Schumer nonetheless will have some anxiety as he awaits the results of redistricting prior to 1992. New York is losing three seats, with at least one certain to come from New York City. Since the city's minority-group House members are likely to be protected under the Voting Rights Act, other members of the city's House delegation may be squeezed.

Schumer is well-prepared for any eventuality, though. Like his Democratic colleague (and former boss) Stephen J. Solarz of the neighboring 13th District, he has amassed a sizable campaign treasury, in case his district is greatly changed or merged with that of another House member.

The situation is similar to one that occurred in the early days of Schumer's House career. Elected in 1980, Schumer had to worry about being thrown in with the more senior Solarz. But the situation was easily resolved. Schumer was given a comfortable district; Solarz's district was merged with that of scandal-plagued Democratic Rep. Frederick W. Richmond, who then retired.

Schumer came to the House as the successor to Democratic Rep. Elizabeth Holtzman, who was engaged in what would be an unsuccessful Senate campaign. A liberal who had Holtzman's endorsement, Schumer was a three-term member of the state Assembly. He previously had served as an Assembly aide to Solarz.

To win his House seat, Schumer had to beat two more conservative candidates in the Democratic primary. Theodore Silverman attracted Orthodox Jewish support with his stand in favor of the death penalty; Susan Alter criticized Schumer for not fighting hard enough against pornography. But Schumer had the best organization, and he won centrist support and an endorsement from Mayor Edward I. Koch. He took almost 60 percent of the vote, and sailed through the general election.

After clearing the redistricting hurdle in 1982, Schumer won 72 percent in 1984. Even that landslide figure would turn out to be his career low.

His strength at home and rising prominence in Washington have led some to speculate on Schumer's potential as a statewide candidate. Should Schumer entertain an opportunity to run for higher office at a future date, though, he may find himself handicapped by the lack of coverage that local television stations give to individual House members in the crowded New York City media market. Comparing New York members with those from broader geographical areas who dominate their media markets, Schumer says, "Local television is a far less important part of our lives."

Schumer adds that New York-area members are lucky to get on local TV twice a year. But unlike most of his metropolitan colleagues, Schumer has made up some of the media deficit by availing himself of frequent opportunities to appear on national television.

Committees

Banking, Finance & Urban Affairs (9th of 31 Democrats)
Financial Institutions Supervision, Regulation & Insurance; Housing & Community Development

Interior & Insular Affairs (24th of 29 Democrats)
Energy & the Environment

Judiciary (10th of 21 Democrats)
Crime and Criminal Justice (chairman); Intellectual Property & Judicial Administration; International Law, Immigration & Refugees

Elections

1990 General

Charles E. Schumer (D)	61,468	(80%)
Patrick J. Kinsella (R)	14,963	(20%)

1988 General

Charles E. Schumer (D)	107,056	(78%)
George S. Popielarski (R)	24,313	(18%)

Previous Winning Percentages: **1986** (93%) **1984** (72%) **1982** (79%) **1980** (78%)

District Vote For President

	1988	1984	1980	1976
D	88,439 (57%)	90,540 (51%)	64,034 (50%)	105,965 (68%)
R	65,354 (42%)	85,358 (48%)	56,294 (44%)	49,084 (32%)
I			6,588 (5%)	

Campaign Finance

	Receipts	Receipts from PACs		Expend-itures
1990				
Schumer (D)	$819,952	$163,612	(20%)	$93,863
1988				
Schumer (D)	$437,574	$137,325	(31%)	$87,129

Key Votes

1991

Authorize use of force against Iraq	N

1990

Support constitutional amendment on flag desecration	N
Pass family and medical leave bill over Bush veto	Y
Reduce SDI funding	Y
Allow abortions in overseas military facilities	Y
Approve budget summit plan for spending and taxing	N
Approve civil rights bill	Y

1989

Halt production of B-2 stealth bomber at 13 planes	Y
Oppose capital gains tax cut	Y
Approve federal abortion funding in rape or incest cases	Y
Approve pay raise and revision of ethics rules	Y
Pass Democratic minimum wage plan over Bush veto	Y

Voting Studies

	Presidential Support		Party Unity		Conservative Coalition	
Year	**S**	**O**	**S**	**O**	**S**	**O**
1990	19	78	89	6	6	89
1989	26	70	91	2	10	88
1988	20	77	90	5	5	92
1987	18	76	88	4	9	86
1986	17	78	88	5	14	82
1985	28	64	84	7	7	84
1984	29	68	87	6	3	93
1983	23	73	89	5	13	84
1982	29	64	91	4	7	92
1981	30	67	83	11	12	83

Interest Group Ratings

Year	ADA	ACU	AFL-CIO	CCUS
1990	94	4	92	21
1989	95	0	100	30
1988	100	4	86	36
1987	88	9	81	21
1986	85	5	86	29
1985	90	14	93	32
1984	90	4	83	33
1983	85	0	100	25
1982	95	0	100	16
1981	100	0	93	6

11 Edolphus Towns (D)

Of Brooklyn — Elected 1982

Born: July 21, 1934, Chadbourn, N.C.
Education: North Carolina A&T U., B.S. 1956; Adelphi U., M.S.W. 1973.
Military Service: Army, 1956-58.
Occupation: Professor; hospital administrator.
Family: Wife, Gwendolyn Forbes; two children.
Religion: Independent Baptist.
Political Career: Deputy Brooklyn borough president (appointed), 1976-82.
Capitol Office: 1726 Longworth Bldg. 20515; 225-5936.

In Washington: Towns has progressed in politics more because of whom he has aligned himself with than because of what he has done. His ties to New York's regular organization Democrats gave him a solid base to build on in Brooklyn; in Washington, Towns usually sticks close to his party leaders.

However, Towns entered the 102nd Congress well-positioned to play a more assertive role should he desire to; he held a seat on the powerful Energy and Commerce panel, and took over as chairman of the Congressional Black Caucus.

While Towns' unobtrusive party loyalty has been matched by a low-profile legislative agenda, he did get considerable attention for his cosponsorship of the Student-Athlete Right-to-Know Act. During the NCAA basketball tournament in early 1989, Towns joined for the second consecutive Congress with Rep. Tom McMillen and Sen. Bill Bradley, both former college basketball stars, to offer legislation requiring colleges to provide information about the graduation rates of their scholarship athletes.

As athletics has become a big business for many colleges, sports reporters have focused attention on schools that seem more concerned about drawing paying customers to games than about making sure athletes meet graduation requirements.

"If we can have reporting as to the on-time arrivals of airlines, surely we can let student-athletes know whether they are likely to receive a useful college degree if they sign a letter of intent at 'X' University," Towns said in reintroducing the bill, which passed during the 101st.

Towns won a mid-session vacancy on Energy and Commerce after gaining backing from Chairman John D. Dingell and the Congressional Black Caucus. His agenda there appears focused on the needs of his multi-racial, urban district.

During the 101st Congress, for example, he persuaded the committee to reauthorize federal community and migrant health centers that serve rural and inner city areas.

But Towns appears reluctant to cross the leadership, even in the name of district interests. During deliberations over the Clean Air Act, Dingell opposed a committee amendment requiring the use of cleaner car fuels. Towns voted against the measure although it had support from New York lobbyists.

At Home: Towns is as liberal as his predecessor in this district, but the similarities end there. A black social worker, Towns succeeded a white millionaire, Democrat Frederick W. Richmond, who resigned from the House in 1982 and later was convicted of income-tax evasion and marijuana possession.

If Richmond's downfall opened the door for Towns, redistricting provided his red carpet into the House. Although New York's Legislature wanted to make the 11th a largely Hispanic district, black Democrats in Brooklyn objected to the plan, and the Justice Department ultimately threw it out. The final version, creating a constituency almost evenly split between blacks and Hispanics, was much more congenial to Towns.

In the turbulent world of Brooklyn politics, Towns benefited from a lack of enemies. He had the support not only of his own party, then headed by Meade H. Esposito, but of the "reform" faction led by black power broker and then-state Assemblyman Al Vann, plus many of the borough's Hispanic officeholders.

No established politician challenged Towns for the Democratic nomination, but two businessmen with Spanish surnames ran and split the Hispanic vote. Towns won the nomination with barely 50 percent of the vote, assuring his election in the heavily Democratic 11th.

Towns had to work to win renomination in 1984. Rafael Esparra, a former adviser to New York City Mayor Edward I. Koch, was his lone opponent.

Esparra pushed to unify the Hispanic vote by arguing that Towns had focused on black issues at Hispanics' expense. Towns won anyway with 65 percent. He has had no difficulty since; in 1990, he had no Republican opponent.

New York 11

Northern Brooklyn — Bedford-Stuyvesant

The desires of both Hispanics and blacks for greater representation came into conflict in New York City in the early 1980s. To satisfy the city's large Hispanic community, which wanted a second House seat to go with the 18th, state legislators created an 11th District that stretched from Brooklyn to the Lower East Side and East Harlem in Manhattan. But Brooklyn blacks said the remap diluted their voting strength, and the Justice Department agreed. State mapmakers removed the Manhattan portion, yielding an 11th nearly half black, almost 40 percent Hispanic and overwhelmingly Democratic.

Bedford-Stuyvesant is the district's oldest black community. Once a fashionable white area, large parts of "Bed-Stuy" now resemble the devastated South Bronx. But some efforts have been made to rejuvenate the area. In the late 1960s Sen. Robert F. Kennedy helped establish a shopping mall and office complex, and International Business Machines opened a typewriter assembly plant. Still, the 11th has little industry of major importance.

East New York has enjoyed little revitalization. Until the 1960s, this was an Italian and Jewish neighborhood. But as low-income blacks and Hispanics moved there from Bedford-Stuyvesant seeking better housing, whites fled. A small section of overwhelmingly black Brownsville, long one of the most blighted areas anywhere in the nation, also is in the 11th.

Roughly 40 percent of the 11th was culled from the old 14th, which was a north Brooklyn mix of minorities and upper-middle-class white professionals. But the 11th excludes the latter group; the white population, about 30 percent of the district's total, is largely Italian and working-class, settled in old neighborhoods just outside Williamsburg and Greenpoint.

Population: 516,554. White 151,797 (29%), Black 244,060 (47%), Other 6,763 (1%). Spanish origin 196,603 (38%). 18 and over 331,181 (64%), 65 and over 38,165 (7%). Median age: 26.

Committees

Energy & Commerce (22nd of 27 Democrats)
Commerce, Consumer Protection & Competitiveness; Energy & Power; Health & the Environment

Government Operations (13th of 25 Democrats)
Environment, Energy & Natural Resources; Government Information, Justice & Agriculture

Select Narcotics Abuse & Control (12th of 21 Democrats)

Elections

1990 General

Edolphus Towns (D)	36,286	(93%)
Ernest Johnson (C)	1,676	(4%)
Lorraine Stevens (NA)	1,094	(3%)

1988 General

Edolphus Towns (D)	73,755	(89%)
Riaz B. Hussain (R)	7,418	(9%)

Previous Winning Percentages: **1986** (89%) **1984** (85%) **1982** (84%)

District Vote For President

	1988	1984	1980	1976
D	85,212 (81%)	94,083 (78%)	71,142 (70%)	88,151 (76%)
R	18,421 (18%)	25,285 (21%)	25,844 (25%)	27,437 (24%)
I			3,664 (4%)	

Campaign Finance

	Receipts	Receipts from PACs	Expend-itures
1990			
Towns (D)	$335,807	$186,250 (55%)	$282,933
1988			
Towns (D)	$327,722	$129,291 (39%)	$278,709
Hussain (R)	$253,860	$2,000 (1%)	$265,034

Key Votes

1991	
Authorize use of force against Iraq	N
1990	
Support constitutional amendment on flag desecration	N
Pass family and medical leave bill over Bush veto	Y
Reduce SDI funding	Y
Allow abortions in overseas military facilities	Y
Approve budget summit plan for spending and taxing	N
Approve civil rights bill	Y
1989	
Halt production of B-2 stealth bomber at 13 planes	Y
Oppose capital gains tax cut	Y
Approve federal abortion funding in rape or incest cases	Y
Approve pay raise and revision of ethics rules	Y
Pass Democratic minimum wage plan over Bush veto	Y

Voting Studies

	Presidential Support		Party Unity		Conservative Coalition	
Year	**S**	**O**	**S**	**O**	**S**	**O**
1990	11	82	88	4	6	93
1989	19	67	83	1	0	95
1988	13	71	76	2	0	76
1987	14	77	80	1	2	86
1986	14	77	81	4	8	86
1985	11	75	81	3	2	87
1984	18	69	78	4	3	86
1983	12	87	90	2	7	89

Interest Group Ratings

Year	ADA	ACU	AFL-CIO	CCUS
1990	94	4	100	31
1989	90	0	100	33
1988	90	0	100	33
1987	92	0	100	0
1986	95	0	100	15
1985	95	5	93	15
1984	85	5	100	36
1983	95	0	100	25

12 Major R. Owens (D)

Of Brooklyn — Elected 1982

Born: June 28, 1936, Memphis, Tenn.
Education: Morehouse College, B.A. 1956; Atlanta U., M.S. 1957.
Occupation: Librarian.
Family: Wife, Maria Cuprill; three children, two stepchildren.
Religion: Baptist.
Political Career: N.Y. Senate, 1975-83.
Capitol Office: 114 Cannon Bldg. 20515; 225-6231.

In Washington: Owens is reserved and sometimes gruff, but he is a diligent legislator capable of impassioned oratory in defense of causes important to his poor, mostly black, district. He has even turned to the rhythm and rhyme of rap music to express his convictions. During the 1990 budget summit talks between the White House and congressional leaders, he wrote in the *Congressional Record*: "At the big white D.C. mansion/There's a meeting of the mob/And the question on the table/Is which beggars will they rob."

Owens says he likes rap for the same reasons it has mass appeal. "Rap is a way that angry young men are getting things off their chest," he says. "So it seemed a good way to get some things off my chest."

Owens has been angry on the floor before. When the House approved the 1989 minimum wage bill with a subminimum wage, Owens said that the latter would create a class of "peons or serfs or simply slave workers."

While many of Owens' ambitious goals have stalled in recent years, he has made a name as an advocate for the disabled on the Education and Labor Committee. After he failed to win support of a 5 percent set aside in the Vocational Education Act for handicapped students, the 1990 enactment of the Americans with Disabilities Act achieved many of his goals. The bill authorized programs to help preschoolers, train teachers and develop technologies to help the disabled.

Owens guided the bill to passage as chairman of the Education and Labor Subcommittee on Select Education, making productive use of the panel's somewhat narrow scope. In the 101st Congress, he cleared the way for the federal volunteer agency ACTION to be reauthorized and for wide ranging reforms in the VISTA program. Congress also approved Owens' relatively modest proposals for programs assisting abused and disabled children.

The only trained librarian in Congress, Owens regularly emphasizes the importance of libraries. He also works to protect funding for historically black colleges and aid for poor students. Sometimes Owens draws on his library background for non-book issues. During one committee session, he suggested that a variation of the Dewey Decimal System be used on child-welfare program information.

At Home: Owens co-founded the black "reform" faction of the Brooklyn Democratic Party, and his 1982 primary victory over an organization stalwart testified to the movement's progress. Owens was a community organizer in 1964, setting up the Brownsville Community Council, which brought government programs to this devastated area. Under Mayor John V. Lindsay, he headed the city's Community Development Agency. In his first bid for elective office (in 1974), Owens led a slate seeking to oust machine-backed incumbents. He won a state Senate seat, and his allies wrested several posts from party regulars.

When Owens set his sights on the House in 1982, he faced a tough opponent, state Sen. Vander Beatty, who as deputy Democratic leader in the state Senate had built a patronage empire in the Brooklyn black community.

But Owens capitalized on Beatty's unsavory connections. A longtime Beatty ally, former City Councilman Samuel Wright, was convicted of extortion and conspiracy in 1978. Owens emphasized his own reputation for honesty and his scandal-free tenure as community development chief. Endorsed by *The Amsterdam News*, an important force in the black community, Owens won that election by a narrow margin.

Beatty challenged the result, accusing Owens' forces of forging signatures on voter-registration cards. Although an acting state Supreme Court judge in Brooklyn ordered a second vote, Owens ultimately triumphed in the New York Court of Appeals, which canceled the rerun and cleared his path to Congress.

Since then, Owens has faced only one foe of note. In the 1986 primary, he met Congress of Racial Equality Chairman Roy Innis, who had drawn attention with his brashly conservative stands against crime. Owens romped to victory.

Owens' son Geoffrey is also in the public eye — as an actor on TV's "The Cosby Show."

New York 12

Central Brooklyn — Crown Heights

The 12th is the most solid minority district in New York City. It is 80 percent black, only 13 percent white, and thoroughly Democratic.

The district would have have had an even higher black population had the Justice Department not complained in 1982 that it was being packed with blacks to keep them out of the neighboring 11th, designed initially by the Legislature for Hispanic representation.

Mapmakers substantially reshaped the 12th at the behest of the Justice Department, moving chunks of Bedford-Stuyvesant and other black neighborhoods into the 11th and pushing the 12th south.

The courts have been the crucible of Brooklyn's black congressional representation. Pressured by the Supreme Court, the Legislature in 1968 made the 12th the city's second black-majority district; the first was the traditional one in Harlem.

Urban blight and poverty characterize most of the 12th, as they do the 11th. In Brownsville, economic survival is the overriding concern. Large public housing projects and a sizable welfare clientele are basic parts of the district.

Most of the district's white vote comes from the northern part of Flatbush, a longstanding middle-class Jewish community in which Brooklyn College is located.

Crown Heights, just north of Flatbush, once was predominantly Jewish. Now it is largely black and Hispanic, although tightly knit communities of orthodox Jews remain. While some of Crown Heights' neighborhoods are declining, others still maintain a middle-class stability. Ebbets Field, home of the Brooklyn Dodgers, was in Crown Heights. After the Dodgers left for Los Angeles in 1958, an apartment complex replaced the ballpark.

Population: 516,983. White 66,870 (13%), Black 413,909 (80%), Other 8,454 (2%). Spanish origin 52,403 (10%). 18 and over 348,549 (67%), 65 and over 37,671 (7%). Median age: 28.

Committees

Education & Labor (9th of 25 Democrats)
Select Education (chairman); Elementary, Secondary & Vocational Education; Labor-Management Relations; Labor Standards

Government Operations (12th of 25 Democrats)
Government Activities & Transportation

Elections

1990 General		
Major R. Owens (D)	40,570	(95%)
Joseph Caesar (C)	1,159	(3%)
Mamie Moore (NA)	1,021	(2%)
1988 General		
Major R. Owens (D)	74,304	(93%)
Owen Augustin (R)	5,582	(7%)

Previous Winning Percentages: **1986** (92%) **1984** (91%) **1982** (91%)

District Vote For President

	1988	1984	1980	1976
D	91,590 (87%)	91,492 (86%)	68,133 (60%)	99,093 (73%)
R	12,449 (12%)	14,978 (14%)	39,400 (35%)	36,579 (27%)
I			5,181 (5%)	

Campaign Finance

	Receipts	Receipts from PACs	Expend-itures
1990			
Owens (D)	$161,086	$111,525 (69%)	$172,498
1988			
Owens (D)	$154,022	$125,085 (81%)	$193,618
Augustin (R)	$7,507	0	$7,099

Key Votes

1991	
Authorize use of force against Iraq	N
1990	
Support constitutional amendment on flag desecration	N
Pass family and medical leave bill over Bush veto	Y
Reduce SDI funding	Y
Allow abortions in overseas military facilities	Y
Approve budget summit plan for spending and taxing	N
Approve civil rights bill	Y
1989	
Halt production of B-2 stealth bomber at 13 planes	Y
Oppose capital gains tax cut	Y
Approve federal abortion funding in rape or incest cases	Y
Approve pay raise and revision of ethics rules	Y
Pass Democratic minimum wage plan over Bush veto	Y

Voting Studies

	Presidential Support		Party Unity		Conservative Coalition	
Year	S	O	S	O	S	O
1990	12	80	86	3	2	93
1989	21	70	91	1	2	93
1988	13	73	79	3	3	79
1987	9	85	88	3	7	88
1986	11	83	89	2	6	90
1985	16	76	86	1	4	82
1984	18	78	90	4	3	93
1983	12	77	79	2	6	78

Interest Group Ratings

Year	ADA	ACU	AFL-CIO	CCUS
1990	94	4	100	29
1989	100	4	100	20
1988	95	0	100	15
1987	100	0	100	0
1986	95	0	93	20
1985	95	0	100	14
1984	90	5	100	44
1983	85	0	100	26

13 Stephen J. Solarz (D)

Of Brooklyn — Elected 1974

Born: Sept. 12, 1940, New York, N.Y.

Education: Brandeis U., A.B. 1962; Columbia U., M.A. 1967.

Occupation: Public official.

Family: Wife, Nina Koldin; two children.

Religion: Jewish.

Political Career: N.Y. Assembly, 1969-75; sought Democratic nomination for Brooklyn borough president, 1973.

Capitol Office: 1536 Longworth Bldg. 20515; 225-2361.

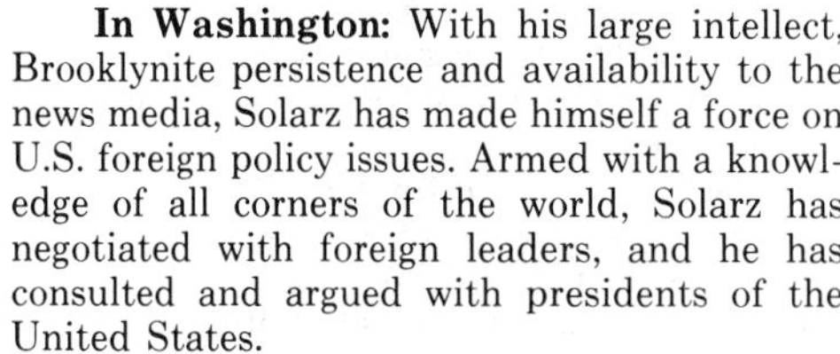

In Washington: With his large intellect, Brooklynite persistence and availability to the news media, Solarz has made himself a force on U.S. foreign policy issues. Armed with a knowledge of all corners of the world, Solarz has negotiated with foreign leaders, and he has consulted and argued with presidents of the United States.

As chairman of the Foreign Affairs Subcommittee on Asian and Pacific Affairs, he has raised the profile of nations and problems that are remote to most Americans. A strong ally of Israel, Solarz has been a frequent visitor to the nations of the Middle East.

Solarz admits he would like to be secretary of State in some future Democratic administration, and that might be the only job that would put him closer to the fulcrum of history than he was in January 1991. Once an activist against the Vietnam War, Solarz joined with House Minority Leader Robert H. Michel of Illinois to sponsor the resolution that authorized President Bush to use force to end Iraq's occupation of Kuwait.

Usually calm and collected, Solarz made an emotional and unusually introspective speech on the House floor in favor of the resolution. He opened by addressing the irony of his situation. "It was almost 25 years ago that I got my start in politics as the campaign manager for one of the first anti-war candidates for Congress in the country," said Solarz, referring to the unsuccessful 1966 Democratic House primary challenge by Brooklyn Democrat Mel Dubin.

However, Solarz said, the aggressive Iraqi regime of Saddam Hussein — with its million-man army, stockpiles of chemical weapons and developing nuclear potential — was too dangerous to ignore. "Driven by a megalomaniacal lust for power, [Saddam] is determined to dominate the entire Middle East, and if he is not stopped now, we will have to stop him later under circumstances where he will be much more difficult and much more dangerous to contain," Solarz said.

Like Bush, Solarz had insisted throughout the Persian Gulf crisis that war was a last resort. However, he also set goals — stiffer even than those stated by Bush — that seemed likely to be achieved only through the use of force. Shortly after Iraqi troops invaded Kuwait in August 1990, Solarz questioned the effectiveness of the economic embargo the United States and allied nations had instituted against Iraq: Any outcome short of the removal of Saddam, Solarz said, would be a "Pyrrhic victory." He went on to co-found a bipartisan and cross-ideological coalition, the Committee for Peace and Security in the Gulf, which called for the dismantling of Iraq's war machine.

There were those, including many Democrats who had come up through the ranks of the liberal movement with Solarz, who questioned his motives. Some implied that Solarz, who is Jewish and has a large Jewish constituency, had suddenly become a hawk when the security of Israel was at stake. In a newspaper interview, Solarz called that "a complete and total canard," adding, "I haven't been urged by the organized Jewish community or Israel."

Other cynics noted that Solarz, who had just passed age 50, had spent the 1960s in graduate school and in anti-war politics, but was ready to send another generation off to battle. But Solarz's defenders noted that this was no overnight conversion: In recent years, he had become an advocate of a position — more associated with the Democratic Leadership Conference than with the Americans for Democratic Action — that judicious use of American might can be a force for good in the world. He has been described as a pre-Vietnam War, John F. Kennedy-style internationalist.

For example, as Asian and Pacific Affairs chairman, Solarz is the leading House advocate of providing U.S. military and economic aid to non-communist insurgents fighting the Vietnam-installed government of Cambodia. First securing a token $5 million humanitarian aid program for these factions in the mid-1980s, Solarz in the 101st Congress sponsored a successful provision to send $20 million to the

New York 13

Western and Southern Brooklyn — Bensonhurst; Brooklyn Heights

The elongated 13th reaches north from Brooklyn's Atlantic beaches to the East River waterfront. It is overwhelmingly white, and has one of the largest percentages of Jewish residents in the country. Redistricting in 1982 extended the 13th's boundaries to include Williamsburg, center of Hasidic Jewish life in America.

The 13th is usually Democratic territory, even in national Republican years. In each of the last three presidential elections, the district went Democratic.

The heart of the district is in middle-class Bensonhurst. Jewish delicatessens and Italian open-air markets signal its ethnic makeup. The Jews generally live in the apartment buildings in Bensonhurst, while Italians inhabit its row houses. Bensonhurst has been wracked by racial tension since a 1989 incident in which a black youth, who had gone to the community to shop for a used car, was murdered by a gang of whites. While many residents voiced regret over the murder, others responded to marches through Bensonhurst by black activists with anger and even violence: During a January 1991 march, controversial black organizer Al Sharpton suffered a knife wound.

Brighton Beach, south of Bensonhurst, has become a magnet for Soviet Jewish immigrants. Russian is spoken routinely on its business streets, and its restaurants bear such names as "Café Odessa."

Coney Island is the best-known section of the district. At one time New Yorkers of all races and incomes flocked to Coney's beaches, thrill rides and hot dog stands. Now this fun center attracts mostly low-income minorities; the beaches and amusements are run-down. Puerto Ricans, blacks and elderly Jews live in uneasy coexistence.

The 13th also takes in the Brooklyn Navy Yard, an old federal facility now owned by the city. Although some ships are still repaired there, light-manufacturing firms occupy most of the yard. A Norwegian community, descended from merchant seamen, lives on in otherwise Hispanic Sunset Park.

Brooklyn Heights, where expensive co-ops and town houses abound, displays an upper-class liberalism. Celebrities abound there, lured by the elegant brownstones and the spectacular views of the Lower Manhattan skyline.

Farther north up the East River is the nation's largest concentration of Hasidic Jews. The Hasidim in Williamsburg form an insular community not often involved in politics. However, the fundamentalist religious beliefs and austere lifestyles of this community, combined with its tense relations with neighboring minority communities, has made some Hasidic Jews friendly to conservative candidates; Ronald Reagan's ethnic outreach operation made some successful inroads.

Synagogues give way to Catholic parishes in Greenpoint, which lies to the north. Poles and Italians inhabit Greenpoint's neatly kept row houses.

Population: 516,512. White 424,123 (82%), Black 37,376 (7%), Other 11,155 (2%). Spanish origin 82,554 (16%). 18 and over 387,947 (75%), 65 and over 85,695 (17%). Median age: 34.

rebels.

However, the program was by that time embroiled in controversy. The Khmer Rouge, which had run a notoriously murderous regime out of Phnom Penh from 1975 to 1979, was also fighting to oust the existing government. Its forces were supposedly separate, if not in conflict, with the non-communist groups; the U.S. aid program specifically stated that no money was to be used by the Khmer Rouge. But critics argued that all the guerrilla forces, including the Khmer Rouge, were part of an informal alliance.

Solarz, who said there was no credible evidence that the Khmer Rouge received any U.S. money, stuck by the program, and at the same time opened a window on his Realpolitik approach to foreign policy. "Sometimes, in order to achieve a morally desirable objective, it becomes necessary to engage in what on the surface may look like morally questionable behavior," he said in April 1991. However, the Bush administration bowed to criticism that month and suspended aid to the non-communist forces.

Solarz is not a universal supporter of gunboat diplomacy. He opposed President Ronald Reagan's policy of supporting the contras fighting the then-Marxist government of Nicaragua. As a member of the Intelligence Committee, he also sought without success to place strict conditions on U.S. aid to UNITA, an insurgent group battling the Soviet-backed government of Angola.

Even in his interventionist mode, Solarz can be sharply critical of Republican administrations. He turned quickly from Bush supporter to critic in the ambiguous aftermath of the Persian Gulf War.

Despite the quick and total rout of Iraqi forces in February 1991, Saddam remained in power; Solarz argued that Bush was basking in the glow of victory and was preoccupied with extracting American troops from the region, and should have continued to press for Saddam's downfall. He called for U.S. sponsorship of a United Nations resolution barring a permanent cease-fire until Saddam and his Baathist Party had given up control of Iraq.

Solarz has also scorned Bush's mild reaction to the Chinese government's repression of a pro-democracy movement. Bush's May 1991 decision to continue most-favored-nation trade status for China he said "sends a signal that we really do have a double standard when it comes to human rights — one for the Soviet Union, Cuba, Vietnam . . . and another for China."

Solarz's pro-active role on foreign policy has had an impact. Solarz received publicity for his role in the 1986 downfall of Philippine President Ferdinand E. Marcos: Solarz did his best to force change despite Reagan's contention that the only available alternative to Marcos was communism. An avid supporter of Marcos' successor, Corazon Aquino, Solarz in 1987 joined several colleagues in proposing what came to be known as the multilateral assistance initiative, a "mini-Marshall Plan" to rebuild the Philippine economy.

Concerned about Pakistan's efforts to develop a nuclear weapons program, Solarz has also succeeded in placing conditions on U.S. aid to that country. In doing so, Solarz has overridden opposition from Republican administrations and congressional opponents who want to reward Pakistan for its longtime assistance to anti-communist guerrillas in Afghanistan.

There are those, particularly in the Asian communities of the United States, who view Solarz as a mighty political figure. Solarz's advocacy of human rights and financial assistance to their native countries has spurred Asian-Americans to fill Solarz's campaign coffers, making him a fundraising juggernaut.

However, Solarz does have his critics. In the view of some administration officials — who always are wary of congressional "micromanagement" of foreign policy — Solarz acts as though he already is secretary of State. Even some Democrats, who have been on the wrong end of a stinging Solarz retort, see in him an unattractive intellectual arrogance.

During the April 1991 Cambodia debate, Solarz called for continued aid until a peace plan, drawn up by members of the U.N. Security Council, could be put in place. But Democratic Rep. Chester G. Atkins of Massachusetts, whose district includes many Cambodian refugees who escaped Khmer Rouge repression, called for an aid cutoff. "Have you read the [U.N.] proposal?" Solarz questioned Atkins in an accusatory tone. "Are you familiar with it?"

Although he has never had political difficulties back home, Solarz takes some flak about his focus on foreign affairs. According to *New York* magazine, he conceded the point during an early 1991 visit to a Jewish center in his district. "I may not have much influence in Brooklyn, but they think I'm very important in Mongolia," he said.

Solarz has sought to mitigate potential local problems by taking a seat on the Merchant Marine and Fisheries Committee, which has an impact on the economy of the Brooklyn waterfront. He also, during the 101st Congress, proposed a most locally oriented piece of legislation: The bill resulted from a trademark infringement lawsuit by the Los Angeles Dodgers baseball team against the "Brooklyn Dodgers" bar in that New York City borough.

Solarz — reflecting the undying rancor of Brooklyn residents over the departure of their beloved "Bums" to the West Coast in 1957 — proposed to prohibit a sports organization from claiming as a trademark the name of a team that includes a locality from which it had moved.

At Home: Solarz's Democratic base in the 13th District, his ties to the large Jewish community there and his prodigious fundraising skills have been an unbeatable combination. Solarz typically wins by margins of 3-to-1 or better; only once in nine House contests has he slipped below 70 percent of the vote.

With his hawkish stance during the Persian Gulf crisis, Solarz had moved far from his political roots in the 1960s' movement against the Vietnam War. A native Brooklynite, Solarz joined the ranks of reform Democrats when he returned home from Brandeis and Columbia universities. In 1966 he managed Dubin's antiwar primary campaign against longtime 13th District Democratic Rep. Abraham Multer. Dubin lost that contest by fewer than 1,000 votes.

Two years later, Solarz struck out on his own and won a seat in the state Assembly. In 1973 Solarz made what seemed to be a quixotic campaign as a reform candidate for Brooklyn borough president. But he did relatively well in the Democratic primary, running only 11 percentage points behind the winner, Sebastian Leone. Solarz carried the 13th District in the boroughwide primary.

That same year, the indictment of Democrat Rep. Bertram L. Podell created the opportunity for Solarz to run for Congress. Although Podell faced charges of conspiracy, bribery, perjury and conflict of interest, he insisted on seeking renomination in 1974. The party organization backed him, but Solarz staged a strong primary challenge and won.

Since then, Solarz has faced no serious contests. His biggest problem was caused not by an opposing candidate, but by redistricting. In 1982 Brooklyn had to give up one of its districts, and Solarz faced the prospect of seeing the 13th merged with a neighboring constituency. So he amassed nearly $700,000, gathering donations from around the country.

The money went largely unspent. The Legislature paired Solarz with Democratic Rep. Fred Richmond, who had pleaded guilty to income-tax evasion and other federal charges. Richmond first decided to run in another district, then resigned.

Committees

Foreign Affairs (4th of 28 Democrats)
Asian & Pacific Affairs (chairman); Africa; Western Hemisphere Affairs

Merchant Marine & Fisheries (19th of 29 Democrats)
Fisheries & Wildlife Conservation & the Environment; Merchant Marine

Select Intelligence (7th of 12 Democrats)
Legislation; Program & Budget Authorization

Joint Economic

Elections

1990 General

Stephen J. Solarz (D)	47,446	(80%)
Edwin Ramos (R)	11,557	(20%)

1988 General

Stephen J. Solarz (D)	81,305	(75%)
Anthony M. Curci (R)	27,536	(25%)

Previous Winning Percentages: **1986** (82%) **1984** (66%) **1982** (81%) **1980** (79%) **1978** (81%) **1976** (84%) **1974** (82%)

District Vote For President

	1988	1984	1980	1976
D	71,418 (54%)	74,815 (52%)	65,323 (50%)	101,302 (65%)
R	60,376 (45%)	69,193 (48%)	55,585 (43%)	52,759 (34%)
I			6,547 (5%)	

Campaign Finance

	Receipts	Receipts from PACs		Expend-itures
1990				
Solarz (D)	$1,218,914	$57,674	(5%)	$517,794
1988				
Solarz (D)	$910,663	$60,605	(7%)	$564,882

Key Votes

1991

Authorize use of force against Iraq	Y

1990

Support constitutional amendment on flag desecration	N
Pass family and medical leave bill over Bush veto	Y
Reduce SDI funding	Y
Allow abortions in overseas military facilities	Y
Approve budget summit plan for spending and taxing	Y
Approve civil rights bill	Y

1989

Halt production of B-2 stealth bomber at 13 planes	N
Oppose capital gains tax cut	Y
Approve federal abortion funding in rape or incest cases	Y
Approve pay raise and revision of ethics rules	Y
Pass Democratic minimum wage plan over Bush veto	Y

Voting Studies

	Presidential Support		Party Unity		Conservative Coalition	
Year	S	O	S	O	S	O
1990	22	75	89	5	15	76
1989	37	63	92	4	20	78
1988	24	73	88	5	11	82
1987	19	76	91	3	14	86
1986	18	76	89	5	16	80
1985	24	69	89	4	11	87
1984	35	59	85	6	15	78
1983	24	55	76	5	16	72
1982	38	58	94	4	11	86
1981	36	58	82 †	6 †	13	77

† Not eligible for all recorded votes.

Interest Group Ratings

Year	ADA	ACU	AFL-CIO	CCUS
1990	89	0	92	21
1989	85	0	92	40
1988	95	4	93	33
1987	88	0	94	8
1986	90	5	86	20
1985	90	14	94	20
1984	85	4	69	33
1983	90	0	100	24
1982	95	0	95	10
1981	90	0	80	6

14 Susan Molinari (R)

Of Staten Island — Elected 1990

Born: March 27, 1958, Staten Island, N.Y.
Education: State U. of New York, Albany, B.A. 1980, M.A. 1982.
Occupation: Political aide.
Family: Separated.
Religion: Roman Catholic.
Political Career: N.Y. City Council, 1985-90.
Capitol Office: 315 Cannon Bldg. 20515; 225-3371.

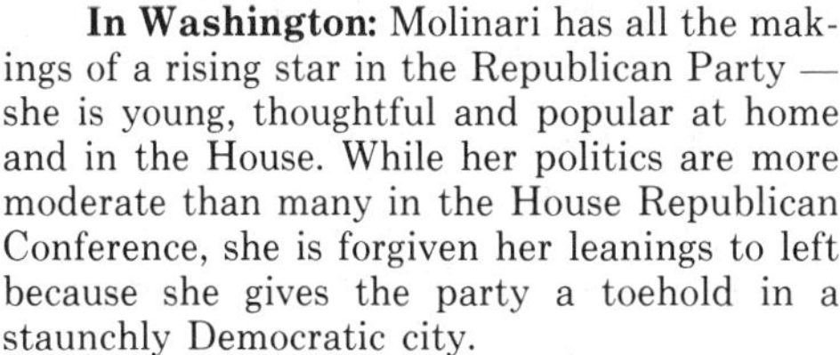

In Washington: Molinari has all the makings of a rising star in the Republican Party — she is young, thoughtful and popular at home and in the House. While her politics are more moderate than many in the House Republican Conference, she is forgiven her leanings to left because she gives the party a toehold in a staunchly Democratic city.

While Molinari was a week short of turning 32 when she won a House special election, she quickly proved her weight as a legislator in 1990 when she succeeded in striking an amendment to the defense authorization bill that would have closed down the Navy homeport being built in her Staten Island district. Arguing that the facility had been unfairly singled out, Molinari lined up fellow Republicans and trumped the opposition of most of New York City's delegation, noting that Democratic Gov. Mario M. Cuomo backed the homeport. But her energy and efforts may not be enough in the face of persistent pressures to trim defense spending; in 1991, a Pentagon base-closing list included the Staten Island homeport.

Molinari's father, Guy V. Molinari, gave up the 14th District in January 1990 after he was elected Staten Island borough president. His daughter quickly emerged as the frontrunner to succeed him, in part because her political profile as a New York City Council member was much like her father's in the House. She balances her anti-crime, anti-tax conservatism with an environmentalist streak. The biggest issue difference between the two is on abortion; the younger Molinari supports abortion rights.

Once elected, Molinari took a seat on the Public Works Committee, where her father sat, and also a seat on Education and Labor.

Although many sons have succeeded their fathers in the House, Molinari is only the second woman ever to do so. Illinois Republican Winnifred Mason Huck was elected in 1922 to replace her late father, William Mason, who died in midterm, but she served only that partial term.

At Home: Guy Molinari's victory for Staten Island borough president forced a special election in a House district where Democrats once were competitive. But there was little doubt that the major effect of the 14th District transition would be a change in the House nameplates to read "Ms. Molinari" rather than "Mr. Molinari."

Susan Molinari entered the House contest with huge advantages over any potential Democratic candidate. Her father blazed a path for her in the 14th, winning strongly both in his Staten Island base and in the Brooklyn part of the district. In winning two terms on the New York City Council, Molinari had established herself as a popular officeholder.

After stints with the Republican Governors' Association and the Republican National Committee, Molinari ran for the council in 1985 and won. Her status on the council was singular: She was the only Republican in the city's legislative body. Although she earned the title of minority leader by default, Molinari gained entree to the council's decision-making process and *ex officio* status on major committees.

Several well-known Democrats nonetheless expressed interest in the March 1990 special election, but Democratic leaders put their muscle behind lawyer and party insider Robert Gigante. While he secured the nomination, Gigante's campaign never got off the ground. From the outset, he trailed far behind Molinari in name identification and he lacked the financial resources to build recognition.

Hoping to make up the difference with a splash in the press, Gigante wound up splattering himself. In an early campaign forum, Gigante described himself as more typical of the average district voter by noting that he and his wife had four children while Molinari, who was recently married, had none. The political reporter for the *Staten Island Advance* then criticized the Democrat for trying to make family size a qualification for office.

Molinari won easily, taking 59 percent to Gigante's 35 percent. She won a first full term in 1990 over Democratic lawyer Anthony J. Pocchia by a similar margin.

New York 14

Staten Island; Southwest Brooklyn

Staten Island's physical isolation ended with the 1964 opening of the Verrazano-Narrows Bridge (the longest suspension bridge in the world), connecting it with Brooklyn. But the island remains in many ways a place apart from the rest of New York City.

Despite a major population influx in the decade following the bridge's opening, Staten Island remains the most suburban and least-populated of New York City's five boroughs. But Staten Island's landfills and its location in the soiled waters of New York harbor make residents not only more environment-conscious than most other New Yorkers, but also sensitive to an image of the island as a city dumping ground. When the Supreme Court in 1989 ruled New York City's Board of Estimate unconstitutional — thus reducing the borough's clout in shaping city policies — talk of secession from the city stepped up. A referendum was passed in 1990 approving the formation of a commission to study the consequences of independence.

As a suburban area with a large, upwardly mobile, conservative ethnic population, Staten Island also deviates from the liberal Democratic dominance in the rest of the city. Though the more popular statewide Democrats, such as Sen. Daniel Patrick Moynihan and Gov. Mario M. Cuomo, have done as well there as elsewhere, Republican presidential candidates win easily: George Bush took 62 percent of the vote there in 1988.

The Irish and the Italians are the most visible ethnic groups on Staten Island. The few minority-group residents (about 10 percent of the total) cluster in low-income housing in such northern shore communities as Stapleton (the site of the Navy homeport, whose future is in doubt) and Port Richmond. Generally, incomes are higher south of the Staten Island Expressway. Many registered Republicans reside in the large homes of Todt Hill and Emerson Hill. The South Shore and Tottenville areas are middle-income.

Although Staten Island provides nearly 75 percent of the district's vote, its population is too small to constitute an entire district on its own. Linked with liberal Lower Manhattan during the 1970s, the island is now joined with Brooklyn's more conservative Bay Ridge.

With its row houses and brownstones, Bay Ridge displays a more urban character than Staten Island. Overwhelmingly white and largely Italian, this is the community John Travolta danced and swaggered his way through in "Saturday Night Fever." There are few minorities.

Population: 516,537. White 464,689 (90%), Black 26,351 (5%), Other 12,722 (2%). Spanish origin 33,961 (7%). 18 and over 379,638 (74%), 65 and over 66,743 (13%). Median age: 33.

Committees

Education & Labor (10th of 14 Republicans)
Elementary, Secondary & Vocational Education; Employment Opportunities; Postsecondary Education

Public Works & Transportation (15th of 21 Republicans)
Aviation; Investigations & Oversight; Water Resources

Elections

1990 General		
Susan Molinari (R)	58,616	(60%)
Anthony J. Pocchia (D)	34,625	(35%)
Christine Sacchi (RTL)	4,370	(4%)
1990 Special		
Susan Molinari (R)	29,336	(58%)
Robert Gigante (D)	17,302	(34%)
Barbara S. Bollaert (RTL)	2,649	(5%)
Carl F. Grillo (L)	427	(1%)

District Vote For President

	1988	1984	1980	1976
D	75,069 (42%)	61,933 (34%)	55,789 (36%)	72,736 (47%)
R	99,788 (56%)	118,437 (66%)	87,135 (56%)	81,884 (53%)
I			9,286 (6%)	

Campaign Finance

	Receipts	Receipts from PACs	Expend-itures
1990			
Molinari (R)	$157,229	$71,788 (46%)	$141,216
Pocchia (D)	$35,054	$1,080 (3%)	$35,052

Key Votes

1991	
Authorize use of force against Iraq	Y
1990	
Support constitutional amendment on flag desecration	Y
Pass family and medical leave bill over Bush veto	Y
Reduce SDI funding	N
Allow abortions in overseas military facilities	Y
Approve budget summit plan for spending and taxing	Y
Approve civil rights bill	N

Voting Studies

	Presidential Support		Party Unity		Conservative Coalition	
Year	**S**	**O**	**S**	**O**	**S**	**O**
1990	56 †	44 †	70 †	28 †	79 †	19 †

† Not eligible for all recorded votes.

Interest Group Ratings

Year	ADA	ACU	AFL-CIO	CCUS
1990	31	57	40	57

15 Bill Green (R)

Of Manhattan — Elected 1978

Born: Oct. 16, 1929, New York, N.Y.
Education: Harvard U., B.A. 1950, J.D. 1953.
Military Service: Army, 1953-55.
Occupation: State government lawyer; federal housing official.
Family: Wife, Patricia Freiberg; two children.
Religion: Jewish.
Political Career: N.Y. Assembly, 1965-68; sought Republican nomination for U.S. House, 1968.
Capitol Office: 2301 Rayburn Bldg. 20515; 225-2436.

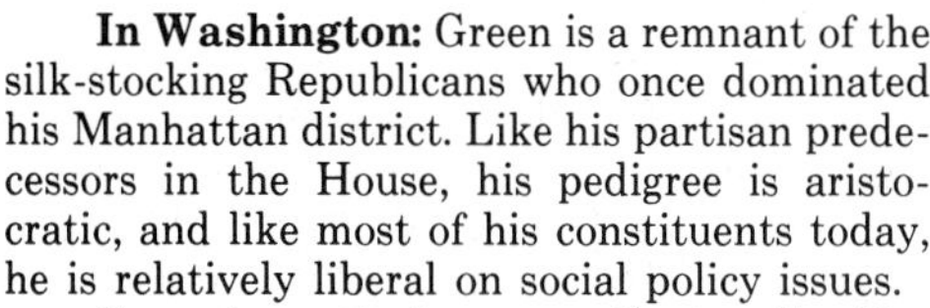

In Washington: Green is a remnant of the silk-stocking Republicans who once dominated his Manhattan district. Like his partisan predecessors in the House, his pedigree is aristocratic, and like most of his constituents today, he is relatively liberal on social policy issues.

Green is routinely among the top five Republicans voting in opposition to a majority of his party colleagues, but then he holds a district swept by Walter F. Mondale in 1984 and Michael S. Dukakis in 1988. While some Republicans feel Green is more liberal than even his constituents demand, most find his renegade record an acceptable trade-off for possession of a House seat that should not be theirs.

Green has tested the tolerance for his dissident views in recent years, emerging as a leading spokesman for moderate Republicans. In the 101st Congress, his abortion rights advocacy provoked a heated public confrontation with Republican orthodoxy.

Prior to the Supreme Court's 1989 *Webster* ruling giving states more authority in setting abortion policy, abortion foes rode high in Congress. *Webster* galvanized congressional abortion-rights supporters, and Green became their leading GOP strategist. He played a high-profile role in efforts to permit federal and D.C. government funding of abortion in cases of rape and incest. In late 1989, when the abortion issue looked as if it could be a hot item in the coming campaign year, Green pointedly warned that President Bush's anti-abortion stand "would leave him and us in an indefensible position."

On Appropriations, Green is ranking Republican on the VA, HUD and Independent Agencies Subcommittee. In recent years, the panel has been the scene of an increasingly tense tug of war between funding for the National Aeronautics and Space Administration and funding for other domestic social programs. Green, a former Department of Housing and Urban Development (HUD) administrator, consistently comes down on the side of housing and urban programs, and is perhaps the most outspoken critic of NASA's space policy. When President Bush announced his 1990 plan to send men to Mars, Green said, "The question is, what for?"

Green is also the rare Republican to speak out for AIDS victims' rights, and in favor of significant funding for research on the disease. He describes himself as "a longtime supporter of the rights of gay men and lesbian women."

In the 100th Congress, Green was one of just a few Republicans to cosponsor California Democrat Henry A. Waxman's AIDS legislation, which sought to ensure confidentiality of test records and to protect those who test positive for the virus from discrimination. In the 101st Congress, he was the only member to voice objections when funding was struck for a Public Health Service national study of sexual behavior. Public health officials said they needed updated information to make reliable predictions about the spread of AIDS, but Congress refused to approve funding.

Green has been active in environmental issues throughout his career. During deliberations on the Clean Air Act in 1990, he co-authored a successful amendment to lengthen the federally required warranty period for key pollution control components in motor vehicles.

Green also occasionally joins with liberals on foreign policy and defense issues. Over Reagan administration objections, he and Democrat Les AuCoin of Oregon sponsored a successful amendment to the 1987 supplemental appropriations bill to bar all but the smallest nuclear weapons tests, provided the Soviet Union observes a similar moratorium.

In the early 1980s, Green was among the "Gypsy Moth" moderate Republicans who sought to protect Medicaid, mass transit and social programs from the budget-cutting axe. Green and other like-minded Republicans withheld their votes on key appropriations bills in 1981 until mass transit and low-income energy assistance funding was preserved.

In 1988, he unsuccessfully implored the GOP platform-drafting committee to include the Equal Rights Amendment (ERA) and to

New York 15

Manhattan — East Side

The combination of a soaring cost of living in its affluent neighborhoods and urban collapse in its poorer areas has cost Manhattan most of its middle-class population. Former residents of modest means complain that the island at the heart of New York City has become a province of "the very rich and the very poor."

The chasm between those at the ends of the economic spectrum is glaring in the 15th, mainly located on Manhattan's East Side. From the midtown business center to the exclusive shops and expensive apartments of the Upper East Side, the district smacks of wealth. The 15th contains most of the elements — the office towers, the fine restaurants and hotels, the cultural attractions — that make New York the nation's most vibrant city. But the 15th also takes in the meaner streets of the Lower East Side, a heavily Hispanic area plagued by poverty, unemployment, drugs and crime.

Despite the economic gulf between them, the rich and the poor share a common thread politically. The 15th is a liberal-voting place. Low-income minority voters show the expected Democratic tendencies, but so do the affluent; this is, after all, where the phrase "limousine liberal" was born. Michael S. Dukakis' 66 percent here was crucial to his state win; Walter F. Mondale's 61 percent in 1984 was one of his highest percentages anywhere. A liberal Republican voting record has been the key to Green's survival.

This political trend is fairly recent. In the 1930s, the "Silk Stocking District" on Manhattan's East Side was a bastion of aristocratic Republicans who disdained the New Deal. But by 1980, Republican presence in the East Side area making up the 15th had dwindled to less than 20 percent of the district's registered voters. Signs of the area's changing political climate were evident as early as 1968, when Edward I. Koch, now New York City's mayor, became the first Democrat to represent the East Side district.

Many district residents work in the corporate headquarters that loom over midtown Manhattan, threatening to block the sun entirely from some of its streets. One of those buildings is Trump Tower, a mixed office-and-residential skyscraper named for its controversial developer, billionaire Donald Trump, whose brash entrepreneurship symbolized the go-go growth of the 1980s, and whose current attempts to keep his overextended empire solvent bespeak the cooled-down business climate of the 1990s.

In addition to the Lower East Side, the 15th takes in Chinatown and Little Italy.

Population: 516,409. White 399,014 (77%), Black 27,086 (5%), Asian and Pacific Islander 51,886 (10%). Spanish origin 75,144 (15%). 18 and over 444,395 (86%), 65 and over 78,336 (15%). Median age: 37.

soften the anti-abortion language. In a subsequent column in *The Washington Post*, Green rooted his rebellion in GOP tradition. "In 1919, it was a Republican Congress that proposed the 19th Amendment giving women the vote," he wrote. "It was the Republican Party that, in 1940, placed the ERA in its platform, four years before the Democrats."

At Home: With a liberal posture that assured voter support and personal wealth — he is a supermarket heir — to fuel his campaigns, Green has deflected all challenges in his otherwise Democratic district. However, he must now warily await the outcome of redistricting prior to the 1992 elections. New York is to lose three seats, with at least one to come from within New York City.

Yet Green's history of strength at the polls may deter state Democrats from trying to redistrict him out of business. During the early part of Green's House career, local Democrats persisted in believing that Green could be ousted from a district that otherwise had become inhospitable to Republicans.

But he applied a *coup de grâce* to Democratic hopes in 1984 by crushing then-Manhattan Borough President Andrew Stein.

Although Stein, the son of a wealthy real-estate developer, spent $1.8 million to Green's $1.1 million (the combined total was a House campaign-spending record at the time), Green won 56 percent of the vote. Green had to overcome an atypical problem that year: While scores of House Democrats were struggling to escape the effects of President Reagan's coattail power, Green faced a strong pro-Mondale tide.

He also had to contend with Stein, a tough young political veteran. Stein hired consultant David Garth to produce TV ads condemning Green for supporting Reagan budget cuts that Stein said had hurt New York City.

Green at first responded by accusing Stein of absenteeism in his earlier New York Assembly career. But he abandoned that approach midway through the fall campaign, opting to return to his normal low-key methods.

Wary of the effects of his party label, Green took pains to remind voters that he was on the November ballot on both the GOP and Independent lines. Democratic crossover votes helped him to a comfortable victory, even as Mondale won the 15th with 61 percent.

Green's 1986 opponent, magazine publisher George Hirsch, echoed Stein's complaint that the incumbent was too supportive of Reagan's economic program. But Green quietly emphasized his significant differences with the administration en route to a 58 percent tally.

After Green scored a personal best in 1988 with 61 percent of the vote, Democrats had trouble finding a 1990 challenger; the party had no candidate as the July filing deadline passed. Democratic officials filled the slot by appointing Liberal Party candidate Frances L. Reiter as their nominee. But Green again had no difficulty, winning with 58 percent.

Green began his public career as a housing and urban finance specialist. He was chief counsel to the New York Legislative Committee on Housing and Urban Development from 1961 to 1964. He then spent four years in the state Assembly before moving to HUD in 1970.

When Green burst into congressional politics in a February 1978 special election, his career became entangled with two of New York City's most colorful Democrats. To succeed Rep. Edward I. Koch — who resigned after his 1977 election as New York City mayor — Green had to upset well-known liberal activist and former Rep. Bella S. Abzug.

Abzug, who had represented Manhattan's West Side in the House, moved to the East Side for a comeback after losing bids for Senate and mayor. But Abzug's advantage over Green in name recognition was offset by criticisms that she was brash, confrontational and overridingly ambitious.

Green won partly because of an anti-Abzug vote, and partly because he spent a large sum of money on the campaign. Although he was little known to the average voter when he began, he spent heavily on radio and television commercials, mass mailings and bus ads that boosted his visibility, enabling him to edge out Abzug.

Committee

Appropriations (10th of 22 Republicans)
Veterans Affairs, Housing & Urban Development, & Independent Agencies (ranking); Foreign Operations, Export Financing & Related Programs

Elections

1990 General		
Bill Green (R)	52,919	(59%)
Frances L. Reiter (D)	33,464	(37%)
Michael T. Berns (C)	3,654	(4%)
1988 General		
Bill Green (R)	107,599	(61%)
Peter G. Doukas (D)	64,425	(37%)

Previous Winning Percentages: **1986** (58%) **1984** (56%) **1982** (54%) **1980** (57%) **1978** (53%) **1978** * (51%)

* *Special election.*

District Vote For President

	1988	1984	1980	1976
D	130,661 (66%)	122,204 (61%)	94,130 (52%)	118,721 (65%)
R	65,654 (33%)	77,223 (39%)	64,562 (36%)	62,931 (34%)
I			19,429 (11%)	

Campaign Finance

	Receipts	Receipts from PACs	Expend-itures
1990			
Green (R)	$705,383	$162,996 (23%)	$458,486
Reiter (D)	$21,005	$3,000 (14%)	$19,403
1988			
Green (R)	$656,289	$154,233 (24%)	$602,942
Doukas (D)	$171,965	$24,700 (14%)	$171,838

Key Votes

1991	
Authorize use of force against Iraq	Y
1990	
Support constitutional amendment on flag desecration	N
Pass family and medical leave bill over Bush veto	Y
Reduce SDI funding	Y
Allow abortions in overseas military facilities	Y
Approve budget summit plan for spending and taxing	Y
Approve civil rights bill	Y
1989	
Halt production of B-2 stealth bomber at 13 planes	Y
Oppose capital gains tax cut	N
Approve federal abortion funding in rape or incest cases	Y
Approve pay raise and revision of ethics rules	Y
Pass Democratic minimum wage plan over Bush veto	N

Voting Studies

	Presidential Support		Party Unity		Conservative Coalition	
Year	**S**	**O**	**S**	**O**	**S**	**O**
1990	41	58	37	60	41	56
1989	57 †	37 †	28 †	68 †	46	54
1988	37	63	38	59	29	66
1987	37 †	61 †	28 †	65 †	62 †	38 †
1986	38	62	26	73	36	64
1985	35	61	34	62	33	67
1984	42	56	29	69	29	69
1983	48	50	33	64	35	64
1982	51	42	32	60	30	67
1981	55	39	39	58	35	63

† Not eligible for all recorded votes.

Interest Group Ratings

Year	ADA	ACU	AFL-CIO	CCUS
1990	61	13	42	36
1989	50	39	20	90
1988	75	25	50	64
1987	56	13	50	47
1986	70	18	64	39
1985	60	35	65	57
1984	70	25	62	69
1983	50	22	35	55
1982	70	14	60	52
1981	70	60	40	72

16 Charles B. Rangel (D)

Of Manhattan — Elected 1970

Born: June 11, 1930, New York, N.Y.
Education: New York U., B.S. 1957; St. John's U., LL.B. 1960.
Military Service: Army, 1948-52.
Occupation: Lawyer.
Family: Wife, Alma Carter; two children.
Religion: Roman Catholic.
Political Career: N.Y. Assembly, 1967-71; sought Democratic nomination for N.Y. City Council president, 1969.
Capitol Office: 2252 Rayburn Bldg. 20515; 225-4365.

In Washington: For nearly two decades, as Rangel moved up the House Democratic ladder and aimed for a leadership rung, he was known for his pragmatic skill at backroom negotiation. His taste for cigars and hearty laughter helped make him part of the club.

But times have changed. Defeated in his bid for majority whip in 1987, Rangel has watched with increasing frustration as a new generation of Democrats moves up. Chastened by a decade under popular Republican presidents, these Democrats do not share Rangel's unalloyed liberalism or intense partisanship.

During the 101st Congress, Rangel sounded as annoyed by his own party as he was by the White House. A senior member of the Ways and Means Committee, Rangel is routinely rebuffed when he suggests raising taxes to pay for human services. "I got kicked by the chairman of the Democratic National Committee for mentioning the 'T' word," Rangel said in 1990. "No one wants any damn taxes. You have really got to be good to tell somebody why it's in their interest to take home less pay. And we don't have that in either party."

Now the fourth most senior Democrat on Ways and Means, Rangel had a rapport with Chairman Dan Rostenkowski that helped him win a prized place on the conference committee wrestling with tax code overhaul in the 99th Congress. But more recently, he has griped at being shut out. During budget talks in the 101st Congress, Rangel routinely peppered his comments with sarcastic asides about not being invited to the summit.

After criticizing the new House leadership for its hesitancy in challenging President Bush's proposed capital gains tax head-on, Rangel was elated when the new Democratic leadership took up the cause. After Speaker Thomas S. Foley spoke to Ways and Means Democrats, Rangel said, "Foley was eloquent. He was good.... Goddamn, we're going to the mat. I'm ready."

While his politics have not changed, this sharp confrontational tone is new. Once regarded as the least ideological of the senior black members of Congress — the one most likely to choose modest but tangible help for his constituents over the opportunity to express outrage — Rangel has warmed to the idea of positioning the Congressional Black Caucus as a counterbalance to those who would pull the Democratic Party to the right. "We are the conscience of the Congress," Rangel says. "We protect the truest traditions of the Democratic Party."

One cause for which Rangel is eager to raise taxes is an anti-drug campaign. Chairman of the Select Committee on Narcotics since 1983, he was among the first members of Congress to focus his attention on the impact of drugs on society — a problem he has seen up close in his Harlem-based district. But if he can take some satisfaction in the widespread attention the issue receives these days, he sounds increasingly frustrated by the anti-drug legislation approved in recent years, with its focus on the death penalty for various criminals. Rangel said the 1990 bill showed "a lust for blood."

Early in the Bush administration, Rangel praised the president as "willing to meet us halfway" with his anti-drug proposal. But that relationship deteriorated quickly as Rangel and Bush's first drug policy director, William J. Bennett, fell into partisan fisticuffs. Bennett once called Rangel a "gas bag." The congressman responded, "I feel more sorrow for him than anything else."

As the 102nd Congress opened, Rangel was critical of the administration's rush toward a free-trade agreement with Mexico, which he said "would make it more difficult to keep contraband from entering the United States."

Rangel's leadership bid faltered in part because of the easygoing style that had made him a popular House member. While Rangel relied on seniority and the argument that electing a whip from New York would bring regional balance to the leadership, his opponent in the

New York 16

Manhattan — Harlem

A territory once divided among four districts, Harlem today forms the core of just one. With its mainly minority population, that district, the 16th, is bedrock Democratic. Republican presidential candidates can count on little more than 15 percent of the vote here.

Home to wealthy whites in the 19th century, Harlem was transformed after World War I, as Southern blacks drawn by the prospect of jobs flocked to its low-rent housing units. Musicians such as Cab Calloway and Duke Ellington and writers such as James Baldwin and Ralph Ellison made it the center of American black cultural life; the parents of Ronald H. Brown, the current Democratic National Committee chairman, managed a thriving hotel near the famed Apollo Theater.

But Harlem lost this flashy veneer years ago. Modern-day Harlem is plagued by crime, drug problems, deteriorating housing and a lack of job opportunities. Its central business district along 125th Street is seedy. Polo Ground Towers and other low-income projects house many of the residents. Sugar Hill, once the home of black professionals, declined as many prosperous blacks gravitated to less troubled regions of the metropolitan area.

East Harlem, Italian until midcentury, boasts the largest population of Puerto Ricans outside Puerto Rico. Beneath the elevated railroad tracks on Park Avenue lies La Marqueta, a diverse open retail market.

West of Harlem, across Morningside Park, is Columbia University, where a major student revolt in 1968 was sparked by the school's plans to build a gymnasium despite the objections of many of the school's low-income black neighbors. Today Columbia is more aloof from the black community.

The 16th's Hispanic areas at the northern end of Manhattan lie east of Broadway in the Washington Heights and Inwood sections. Many of the residents come from South America.

While signs of Harlem's poverty are ubiquitous, there are also signs of change. Young white professionals have refurbished brownstones in areas such as the Mount Morris Park Historic District, and some middle-class blacks have begun to move back in. The Apollo Theater, long dormant, is open, though struggling financially.

Population: 516,405. White 126,438 (25%), Black 250,555 (49%), Other 8,539 (2%). Spanish origin 195,920 (38%). 18 and over 381,724 (74%), 65 and over 66,773 (13%). Median age: 32.

whip's race, Tony Coelho of California, worked virtually non-stop to win the election, building on his success as chairman of the Democratic Congressional Campaign Committee.

Any chance Rangel might have had to catch up was undercut by the impression that in seeking a job that demands strong buttonholing skills, Rangel simply was not courting support as vigorously as Coelho. Rangel made a final tactical error, when he traveled to Asia with a congressional delegation not long before the vote. In the end, the race was not even close. Coelho got 167 votes to Rangel's 78.

At the same time, Rangel lost his closest leadership ally with the retirement of Speaker Thomas P. O'Neill Jr. in 1986. Had O'Neill still been around, Rangel almost certainly would have been chosen chief deputy whip as he wanted, but that did not happen.

On the heels of his loss, Rangel mounted a last-minute bid to reassert his seniority on Ways and Means and recapture the Health Subcommittee chairmanship, which he had held in 1979-81. But there was an incumbent in the post, Pete Stark of California, who lobbied hard to keep the job. His work paid off; committee Democrats voted 17-4 to retain Stark, leaving Rangel to continue as chairman of the less important Select Revenue Measures Subcommittee.

Early in 1989, Rangel accompanied a state task force on a raid of New York City pharmacists who improperly billed Medicaid and doctors who over-prescribed amphetamines and barbiturates. Rangel called them "bums."

Rangel also has played an active role in House debates on South Africa. A strong advocate of tougher sanctions against the apartheid regime, Rangel authored a far-reaching provision enacted as part of the 1987 budget reconciliation to end foreign tax credits for income derived from South African holdings.

At Home: Rangel's 1970 primary victory over flamboyant Democratic Rep. Adam Clayton Powell was big news. But his contests since have been utterly routine. As the leading black official in a district that includes the black and Hispanic precincts of Harlem, Democrat Rangel has received the Republican endorsement as well in each of his general election campaigns.

Charles B. Rangel, D-N.Y.

A high school dropout, Rangel joined the Army and fought in the Korean War. He then returned to Manhattan and entered college in his mid-20s. He got his law degree in 1960, and the next year was appointed assistant U.S. attorney for the Southern District of New York.

In 1966 Rangel won a seat in the New York Assembly. Three years later, he made a quixotic bid for citywide office by running for City Council president in the Democratic primary on a ticket headed by U.S. Rep. James H. Scheuer. Rangel ran last in a field of six but received publicity in black areas as the only citywide black candidate.

Rangel bounced back the next year, applying the coup de grace to Powell's fading political career. The veteran Democrat had been "excluded" from the 90th Congress on charges that he had misused committee funds for parties and travel to the Caribbean. The Supreme Court ruled the exclusion unconstitutional, and Powell was seen as a martyr by constituents. But when he took a seat in the 91st Congress and then spent most of the following year out of the country, that view changed.

Rangel had the backing of a coalition of younger black politicians who were tired of Powell's behavior and wanted someone who would work harder for blacks and for New York: He portrayed Powell as an absentee representative and promised to work full time for his constituents. Although the anti-Powell vote was split four ways, Rangel's coalition of younger blacks and liberal whites prevailed.

The primary win established Rangel as the dominant political figure in his district and gave him influence in New York City politics. He was a frequent critic of longtime Mayor Edward I. Koch, who had an often-adversarial relationship with the city's minorities.

With his strong base in the black community and the potentially broad appeal of his anti-crime and anti-drug stands, Rangel was mentioned as a possible challenger to Koch in 1989. At first he did not discourage speculation, but he eventually endorsed Manhattan Borough President David Dinkins, who went on to become the city's first black mayor.

Committees

Select Narcotics Abuse & Control (Chairman)

Ways & Means (4th of 23 Democrats)
Select Revenue Measures (chairman); Oversight

Elections

1990 General

Charles B. Rangel (D)	55,882	(97%)

1988 General

Charles B. Rangel (D)	107,620	(97%)

Previous Winning Percentages: **1986** (96%) **1984** (97%) **1982** (98%) **1980** (96%) **1978** (96%) **1976** (97%) **1974** (97%) **1972** (96%) **1970** (87%)

District Vote For President

	1988	1984	1980	1976
D	113,324 (86%)	122,516 (83%)	108,892 (75%)	129,187 (82%)
R	16,996 (13%)	23,346 (16%)	24,017 (17%)	26,088 (17%)
I			9,471 (7%)	

Campaign Finance

	Receipts	Receipts from PACs	Expend-itures
1990			
Rangel (D)	$541,762	$353,900 (65%)	$601,550
1988			
Rangel (D)	$583,012	$358,875 (62%)	$479,427

Key Votes

1991	
Authorize use of force against Iraq	N
1990	
Support constitutional amendment on flag desecration	?
Pass family and medical leave bill over Bush veto	Y
Reduce SDI funding	Y
Allow abortions in overseas military facilities	Y
Approve budget summit plan for spending and taxing	N
Approve civil rights bill	Y
1989	
Halt production of B-2 stealth bomber at 13 planes	Y
Oppose capital gains tax cut	Y
Approve federal abortion funding in rape or incest cases	Y
Approve pay raise and revision of ethics rules	Y
Pass Democratic minimum wage plan over Bush veto	Y

Voting Studies

	Presidential Support		Party Unity		Conservative Coalition	
Year	S	O	S	O	S	O
1990	13	81	85	3	6	87
1989	27	59	86	2	0	93
1988	14	71	80	2	5	87
1987	9	76	85	2	2	79
1986	17	73	89	2	4	92
1985	16	75	89	1	7	91
1984	23	67	84	4	8	85
1983	20	71	88	4	9	87
1982	31	69	87	5	10	88
1981	33	63	83	6	4	92

Interest Group Ratings

Year	ADA	ACU	AFL-CIO	CCUS
1990	89	4	100	29
1989	85	0	100	11
1988	85	0	100	31
1987	88	0	100	0
1986	100	0	93	11
1985	90	0	100	10
1984	90	0	92	27
1983	100	0	94	20
1982	100	0	95	19
1981	95	0	93	6

17 Ted Weiss (D)

Of Manhattan — Elected 1976

Born: Sept. 17, 1927, Hungary.
Education: Syracuse U., B.A. 1951, LL.B. 1952.
Military Service: Army, 1946-47.
Occupation: Lawyer.
Family: Wife, Sonya Hoover; two children.
Religion: Jewish.
Political Career: N.Y. City Council, 1962-77; sought Democratic nomination for U.S. House, 1966, 1968.
Capitol Office: 2467 Rayburn Bldg. 20515; 225-5635.

In Washington: A political thesaurus could easily list Weiss' name as a synonym for "liberal." Whether the issue is military weaponry, gay and lesbian rights or Central America policy, Weiss continues to speak for left-wing interests of the sort that have given the national Democratic Party image problems in recent presidential campaigns.

As the Persian Gulf War heightened hawkish talk early in the 102nd Congress, for example, Weiss urged restraint. When conservatives sharpened their teeth on federal arts funding for controversial artists, Weiss stood by the grants. He even campaigned, successfully, to lead the Congressional Arts Caucus.

But if Weiss' views are often predictable, he is nonetheless regarded as a capable legislator who stops short of being doctrinaire.

On domestic policy, Weiss' primary personal soapbox is his chairmanship of the Government Operations Subcommittee on Human Resources and Intergovernmental Relations. Although not a high-profile committee, it has wide berth to oversee several federal departments and gives Weiss an outlet for crusading on health-care issues.

Weiss has spotlighted what he views as weaknesses in federal health-care funding and regulation. He has also established himself as a watchdog of the Food and Drug Administration (FDA), which, among its other functions, approves and regulates marketing of new therapeutic drugs.

Weiss has a particular interest in combating AIDS: His district on the West Side of Manhattan has large homosexual and minority populations, which have been hard hit by the disease. Weiss has frequently taken the federal bureaucracy to task over what he describes as its slow response to the spread of AIDS.

During the 100th Congress, Weiss called for an expedited process for testing experimental drugs used to contain the deadly disease, and for more money for AIDS research. He regarded the beefed-up research effort as far preferable to the administration's 1987 plan to release unapproved experimental drugs for use by the critically ill. To Weiss, the rule had more to do with the Reagan administration's urge to deregulate business — in this case, the drug industry — than its desire to respond to the AIDS problem.

Weiss has continued to seek greater federal assistance on AIDS issues. One of his proposals would eliminate a customary two-year waiting period for some AIDS patients to receive Medicare coverage. Reintroducing this measure in the 102nd Congress, Weiss noted that many AIDS victims would not outlive a two-year wait.

Though gentlemanly in person and well-liked by most colleagues, Weiss can confront witnesses with accusatory tones. When a federal health official told Weiss' subcommittee that his agency had not estimated the number of workers needed to treat children with AIDS, Weiss responded angrily: "The problem I have with all of you is that all we get back when we ask for action are words. If the Public Health Service does nothing else, the least it can do is project what the needs will be. Is that too much to ask?"

Weiss has also taken up the cause of Vietnam veterans suffering from cancers that some believe were caused by exposure to the chemical Agent Orange during the war.

In July 1989, Weiss accused the White House and the Centers for Disease Control of deliberately botching a study of Agent Orange and cancer to discredit the purported link. Lawmakers, meanwhile, battled over whether to extend certain veterans' benefits to soldiers exposed to Agent Orange. In the closing days of the 101st Congress, Veterans' Affairs Committee Chairman G. V. "Sonny" Montgomery tried to pass a benefits bill that excluded these veterans.

But Weiss objected and blocked a floor vote on the bill. Vietnam veterans' groups praised Weiss' move, and went on to win the disputed Agent Orange compensation early in the 102nd.

As on Government Operations, Weiss on

New York 17

West Side Manhattan — Part of the Bronx

The West Side is a citadel of unalloyed liberalism. Some of the most active members of its aging Jewish community have lifelong roots in left-wing politics, and the more than one-quarter of the district that is black or Hispanic reinforces that tradition. Despite their national difficulties in recent years, Democratic presidential candidates regularly take over 70 percent of the 17th District vote.

Much of the West Side has been upgraded from the slum conditions prevalent a generation ago. In recent years, its roomy apartments have attracted those tired of the more cramped conditions closer to the East River. The elderly Jewish people who line its park benches observe a passing parade that includes chic young professionals as well as street people.

Other West Side neighborhoods never deteriorated at all. Central Park West still contains some of the most graceful apartment buildings in the city. The century-old Dakota is popular among celebrities; former Beatle John Lennon resided there until his 1980 assassination at its front door.

Many more unknown performers and artists live in the district, waiting tables and hoping for a break. Although the Broadway theaters and most of the city's cultural institutions are in the 15th District, the 17th includes the Lincoln Center for the Performing Arts. Above the Upper West Side, the district threads along the Hudson and includes the parts of Inwood and Washington Heights west of Broadway. Many elderly Jews live here, and many Puerto Ricans as well. The 17th extends north and east to take in the Bronx community of Williamsbridge, a middle-class black section.

The district also covers Greenwich Village and the Wall Street area to the south. The Village's bohemian culture has not been much diluted by the upper-income people who have moved in and made it fashionable during the past two decades. The Village was once an Italian political stronghold. Today, homosexuals are a more important political faction, though gay-rights activism, on the upswing until the mid-1980s, has been overshadowed by the priority of dealing with the AIDS crisis.

Rapid growth during the 1980s has turned lofts in the former industrial districts of Soho and Tribeca into residences for artists and upscale Manhattanites. Few people live around Wall Street, though that is changing with the development of Battery Park City, a large residential-office complex on landfill in the Hudson.

Population: 516,239. White 377,091 (73%), Black 81,675 (16%), Other 17,676 (3%). Spanish origin 80,203 (16%). 18 and over 442,060 (86%), 65 and over 79,933 (15%). Median age: 35.

Foreign Affairs has found plenty to dislike in White House policy.

Although Weiss supported the initial deployment of U.S. troops to the Persian Gulf following the Iraqi invasion of Kuwait, he went on to urge economic sanctions over military force. In late 1990, he joined a group of legislators who sued to assert Congress' constitutional prerogative to declare war. Weiss voted against the January 1991 resolution authorizing Bush to use force against Iraq and, once the air campaign got under way, signed a letter opposing further escalation. When the war was over and Congress voted 410-8 to praise Bush's leadership, Weiss voted "present."

Weiss' antipathy to military conflict had already been well established. He opposed the 1989 U.S. invasion of Panama. And when President Ronald Reagan sent U.S. troops to occupy the Caribbean island nation of Grenada in 1983, Weiss and seven other liberal members called for his impeachment. Weiss was also persistent in his scathing rejection of aid to the Nicaraguan contras.

Weiss is a strong proponent of international accountability on human rights, frequently seeking sanctions or condemnations against governments seen as oppressive.

Weiss is part of a cadre of arms control advocates who say the extreme accuracy of the submarine-based Trident II missile — it is designed to score direct hits on Soviet ballistic missile silos — could provoke the Soviets to launch a first strike in a crisis. However, this is a minority position in the House; Weiss' 1989 amendment to ban deployment of the missile on the original nine Trident submarines was defeated by an 83-341 vote.

Another of Weiss' pet ideas is his proposed Defense Economic Adjustment Act. The bill would create a Cabinet-level Defense Economic Adjustment Council to draw up plans for converting military facilities and defense plants to civilian uses. Conservatives deride the measure as part of a typical liberal effort to eliminate defense programs and convert military funding to domestic purposes. But Weiss, who reintroduced the measure in the 102nd Congress, insists that "in a new era of superpower relations and zero or negative growth in defense budgets, economic conversion has become a virtual necessity."

Weiss was named to a temporary spot on the Banking Committee for the 102nd Congress.

At Home: Weiss has never been as flamboyant as his predecessor, Bella S. Abzug, a liberal Democratic activist and a national feminist leader. But in pursuing liberal political goals, Weiss has been no less determined.

A long-term survivor of the Byzantine Democratic politics of Manhattan's West Side, Weiss lost three competitive primaries before making it to the House on his fourth try. Once in, however, Weiss has never been touched.

Weiss was a 38-year-old city councilman when he ran as a peace candidate against machine-backed Rep. Leonard Farbstein in the 1966 Democratic primary. Weiss appeared to have fallen 151 votes short that June, but he got another chance in a special primary in September after the state Supreme Court found 1,153 invalid ballots and ordered a new election. He lost the rerun, however, by more than 1,000 votes, and when he tried again in 1968, the organization brought Farbstein a 3,000-vote victory.

After that, it was eight years before Weiss saw an opening. When Farbstein finally lost in 1970, it was to Abzug, and only when she ran for the Senate in 1976 did Weiss re-enter the picture. By then, his dues were more than paid. In an unusual show of unity for West Side politics, he won nomination without opposition. When Abzug lost her Senate primary, some party figures suggested that Weiss accept a judgeship and let her reclaim the district. But after 10 years of waiting, he was not about to withdraw.

Weiss cruised to victory that November, riding the district's overwhelming Democratic tide. He has had no trouble since, winning with 80 percent of the vote or better each time out.

Weiss' 1990 GOP challenger was more visible than most of his opponents, but no more successful. William W. Koeppel, a young lawyer from a wealthy family, raised well over $400,000 for his campaign. But as an unknown Republican whose home in the Atlantic Beach section of Queens was nowhere near the 17th District, Koeppel had little chance of making a dent: He took just 15 percent of the vote.

Committees

Banking, Finance & Urban Affairs (29th of 31 Democrats)
Consumer Affairs & Coinage

Foreign Affairs (13th of 28 Democrats)
Human Rights & International Organizations; International Operations; Western Hemisphere Affairs

Government Operations (5th of 25 Democrats)
Human Resources & Intergovernmental Relations (chairman)

Select Children, Youth & Families (5th of 22 Democrats)

Elections

1990 General		
Ted Weiss (D)	79,161	(80%)
William W. Koeppel (R)	15,219	(15%)
Mark Goret (C)	2,928	(3%)
John Patterson (NA)	1,087	(1%)
1988 General		
Ted Weiss (D)	157,339	(84%)
Myrna C. Albert (R)	29,156	(16%)

Previous Winning Percentages: **1986** (86%) **1984** (82%) **1982** (85%) **1980** (82%) **1978** (85%) **1976** (83%)

District Vote For President

	1988		1984		1980		1976	
D	168,115	(78%)	165,064	(74%)	104,832	(62%)	131,226	(72%)
R	44,841	(21%)	55,903	(25%)	47,241	(28%)	48,786	(27%)
I					12,630	(8%)		

Campaign Finance

	Receipts	Receipts from PACs		Expend-itures
1990				
Weiss (D)	$144,408	$72,800	(50%)	$112,722
Koeppel (R)	$432,534	$1,745	(0%)	$431,513
1988				
Weiss (D)	$171,815	$64,890	(38%)	$170,567
Albert (R)	$3,685	0		$2,851

Key Votes

1991	
Authorize use of force against Iraq	N
1990	
Support constitutional amendment on flag desecration	N
Pass family and medical leave bill over Bush veto	Y
Reduce SDI funding	Y
Allow abortions in overseas military facilities	Y
Approve budget summit plan for spending and taxing	N
Approve civil rights bill	Y
1989	
Halt production of B-2 stealth bomber at 13 planes	Y
Oppose capital gains tax cut	Y
Approve federal abortion funding in rape or incest cases	Y
Approve pay raise and revision of ethics rules	Y
Pass Democratic minimum wage plan over Bush veto	Y

Voting Studies

	Presidential Support		Party Unity		Conservative Coalition	
Year	**S**	**O**	**S**	**O**	**S**	**O**
1990	14	85	92	6	0	100
1989	28	70	92	4	2	98
1988	15	72	80	5	5	84
1987	13	85	88	4	0	95
1986	12	79	81	4	4	76
1985	23	76	93	3	5	95
1984	21	74	88	7	2	93
1983	15	78	87	6	9	87
1982	18	56	74	4	7	79
1981	36	64	89	10	4	96

Interest Group Ratings

Year	ADA	ACU	AFL-CIO	CCUS
1990	100	4	100	29
1989	95	0	91	30
1988	75	0	100	21
1987	92	0	100	14
1986	95	0	79	25
1985	100	5	100	18
1984	100	8	77	31
1983	100	0	100	20
1982	90	0	95	24
1981	100	0	87	5

18 Jose E. Serrano (D)

Of the Bronx — Elected 1990

Born: Oct. 24, 1943, Mayaguez, Puerto Rico.

Education: Graduated from Dodge Vocational H.S., 1961.

Military Service: Army Medical Corps, 1964-66.

Occupation: Public official.

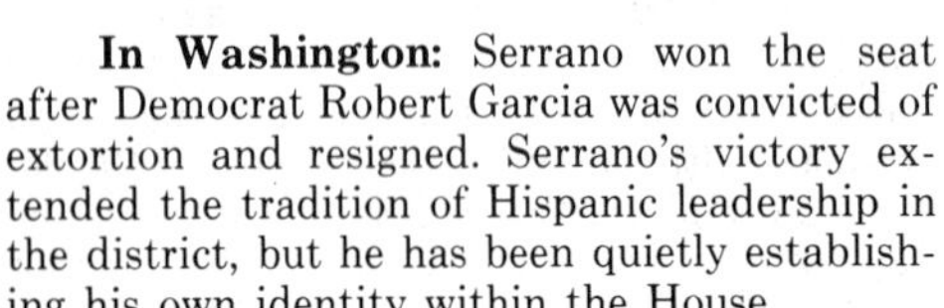

Family: Wife, Mary Staucet; three children, two stepchildren.

Religion: Roman Catholic.

Political Career: N.Y. Assembly, 1975-90; sought Democratic nomination for Bronx borough president, 1985.

Capitol Office: 1107 Longworth Bldg. 20515; 225-4361.

In Washington: Serrano won the seat after Democrat Robert Garcia was convicted of extortion and resigned. Serrano's victory extended the tradition of Hispanic leadership in the district, but he has been quietly establishing his own identity within the House.

Building on his experience in the state Legislature, Serrano got a seat on the Education and Labor Committee. Through his position there he saw one of his bills enacted during his first year in the House. Congress passed a measure designed to prevent students from dropping out of school by requiring school districts to create plans to reduce dropout rates.

Representing a district that is approximately half Hispanic, Serrano demonstrated a great deal of interest in his native Puerto Rico. During consideration of a measure to set up a plebiscite for the island's residents to let them decide their status, Serrano sought to attach a provision allowing mainland Puerto Ricans to vote in the referendum, which lost out when both political parties in Puerto Rico objected. After passing the House, the plebiscite measure died in the Senate during the 101st Congress.

When the 102nd Congress considered a new civil rights bill, Serrano took up the Hispanic cause. Amid reports that the Equal Employment Opportunity Commission was not responding adequately to assist Hispanic workers, Serrano successfully pushed the Education and Labor Committee to adopt an amendment authorizing a new public information and outreach program at the commission.

At Home: Although Serrano's state Assembly career had made him a fixture in New York Hispanic politics, his avenues for advancement looked narrow before 1989. Garcia, first elected in 1978, seemed unlikely to leave his House seat soon.

However, legal problems ruined Garcia's career. He was convicted in October 1989 of extortion in a case involving Wedtech Corp., a Bronx company whose efforts to obtain defense contracts included bribes that wrecked several political reputations. After Garcia resigned from the House in January 1990, a March election was set to fill his unexpired term.

Although Serrano expressed chagrin at the reason for his opportunity — he was a longtime supporter of Garcia — he moved quickly to stake a claim on the seat. Running in a district plagued by unemployment and crime, Serrano could tout an up-from-poverty success story.

Arriving in New York City from Puerto Rico at age 7 and reared in a housing project, Serrano graduated from a vocational high school. After serving in the Army, Serrano worked for a New York City bank. He also took a position with a community school board in the Bronx that helped him develop a core group of political allies.

In 1974, those contacts helped him win a state Assembly seat. By 1983, he was chairman of the Assembly Education Committee. The position helped Serrano win increases in school aid for New York City and push through bills aimed at his minority constituents, including a bilingual education program and a project to reduce the dropout rate in the city.

Serrano twice failed to become Bronx borough president, but in 1985, he nearly upset incumbent Democrat Stanley Simon in a primary. Two years later, Serrano's bid for party appointment as an interim replacement for Simon — who was indicted and convicted in the Wedtech case — was rejected after he referred to the Bronx as "a fetid sinkhole of corruption."

Serrano breezed to the Democratic House nomination in 1990 despite some dissent from black activists incensed at allusions to the almost half-black 18th as a "Puerto Rican" seat.

Bronx Republican officials, who seldom contested Democratic dominance in the 18th, probed that rift by running black businessman Simeon Golar. But Serrano ran away with 92 percent of the vote, and he won a full term with 93 percent in November 1990.

New York 18

South Bronx

The acres of abandoned and vandalized buildings in the South Bronx have made it the nation's symbol of contemporary urban decay. In the most blighted sections, Mott Haven and Melrose, one can sometimes walk for blocks meeting no one but the occasional stray dog.

A quick glance at Census Bureau statistics draws the rough parameters of the region's plight. The 18th has a lower per capita income than any other district in the country, and more people live below the poverty line here than anywhere else.

For more than a dozen years, presidential candidates have made a point of pledging to help the South Bronx, but little has happened to reverse or even contain its decline. Community self-help organizations exercise some political power, but this is limited because of the low voting participation among the Puerto Ricans and other Hispanics who live here.

The scene of a mass exodus during the 1970s, the South Bronx district by 1980 had seen its official census population shrink to less than half its 1970 count. Then-Democratic Rep. Robert Garcia argued this was because many of its "undocumented" residents, fearing deportation or the authorities in general, avoided the census-takers. The South Bronx was flooded then by illegal aliens from Latin America and the Caribbean. In recent years, there has been a substantial influx of legal newcomers from Cuba, classified as refugees.

In any case, the district had to double in size in the last redistricting to meet population requirements. Maintaining the ethnic makeup was not difficult — map makers were able to shift substantial numbers of Hispanics from adjoining constituencies. When redrawn in the early 1980s, the district was 51 percent Hispanic.

The additions to the district gave it slightly more middle-class territory. Fordham Heights has a considerable Italian population remaining, and Jews still live in East Tremont.

The prevalence of low-income, minority-group residents gives the Democrats an unassailable edge in the 18th. Democratic presidential nominees Michael S. Dukakis in 1988 and Walter F. Mondale in 1984 topped 80 percent there.

Population: 517,278. White 126,174 (24%), Black 226,213 (44%), Other 6,089 (1%). Spanish origin 265,768 (51%). 18 and over 327,637 (63%), 65 and over 35,026 (7%). Median age: 25.

Committees

Education & Labor (17th of 25 Democrats)
Labor-Management Relations; Postsecondary Education; Select Education

Small Business (23rd of 27 Democrats)
Antitrust, Impact of Deregulation & Ecology; SBA, the General Economy & Minority Enterprise Development

Elections

1990 General		
Jose E. Serrano (D)	38,024	(93%)
Joseph Chiavaro (R)	1,189	(3%)
Mary Rivera (NA)	866	(2%)
Anna Johnson (C)	717	(2%)
1990 Primary		
Jose E. Serrano (D)	17,983	(89%)
Ismael Betancourt (D)	2,468	(11%)
1990 Special		
Jose E. Serrano (D)	26,928	(92%)
Simeon Golar (R)	2,079	(7%)

District Vote For President

	1988	1984	1980	1976
D	92,069 (86%)	94,474 (81%)	79,399 (73%)	104,520 (79%)
R	13,051 (12%)	22,290 (19%)	24,351 (22%)	27,059 (21%)
I			3,572 (3%)	

Campaign Finance

	Receipts	Receipts from PACs	Expend-itures
1990			
Serrano (D)	$111,390	$74,550 (67%)	$132,359

Key Votes

1991	
Authorize use of force against Iraq	N
1990	
Support constitutional amendment on flag desecration	N
Pass family and medical leave bill over Bush veto	Y
Reduce SDI funding	Y
Allow abortions in overseas military facilities	Y
Approve budget summit plan for spending and taxing	Y
Approve civil rights bill	Y

Voting Studies

	Presidential Support		Party Unity		Conservative Coalition	
Year	**S**	**O**	**S**	**O**	**S**	**O**
1990	17 †	77 †	93 †	2 †	6 †	90 †

† Not eligible for all recorded votes.

Interest Group Ratings

Year	ADA	ACU	AFL-CIO	CCUS
1990	88	0	100	14

19 Eliot L. Engel (D)

Of the Bronx — Elected 1988

Born: Feb. 18, 1947, Bronx, N.Y.

Education: Hunter-Lehman College, B.A. 1969; Lehman College, M.A. 1973; New York Law School, J.D. 1987.

Occupation: Public official; teacher; guidance counselor.

Family: Wife, Patricia Ennis; two children.

Religion: Jewish.

Political Career: Bronx Democratic District leader, 1975-77; N.Y. Assembly, 1977-88.

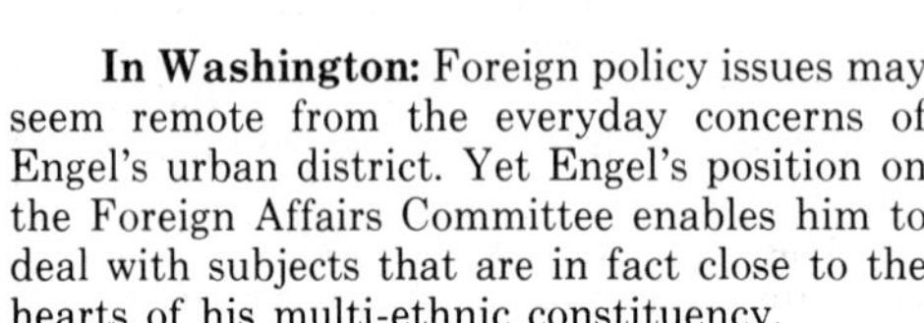

Capitol Office: 1213 Longworth Bldg. 20515; 225-2464.

In Washington: Foreign policy issues may seem remote from the everyday concerns of Engel's urban district. Yet Engel's position on the Foreign Affairs Committee enables him to deal with subjects that are in fact close to the hearts of his multi-ethnic constituency.

Engel's Bronx base includes a large Jewish population with a strong interest in U.S.-Israeli affairs. In early 1990, President Bush appeared to call Israel's hold on all of Jerusalem into question by opposing new Jewish settlements in "East Jerusalem." Engel led a House protest, sponsoring a resolution stating that Jerusalem "is and should remain" the capital of Israel.

Engel condemned efforts by Saddam Hussein to link Iraq's occupation of Kuwait to the Palestinian issue. He said: "Saddam Hussein did not invade Kuwait to help the Palestinians. He invaded Kuwait because he is a ruthless, evil dictator and aggressor." Engel voted for the resolution authorizing President Bush to use force against Iraq in January 1991.

When he moved from the state Assembly to the House, Engel gained many Irish- and Italian-American constituents. Like his predecessor, Democratic Rep. Mario Biaggi, Engel thus became an advocate for the Catholic minority in Northern Ireland. He also annually submits the resolution naming October as "Italian-American Heritage and Culture Month."

Engel's overall liberal leanings place him in the Democratic Caucus mainstream. However, his vote against a House pay raise just after his arrival in 1989 had partisan repercussions for Engel. The defeat of the pay raise also sank an increase for other federal workers, a fact remembered by Post Office and Civil Service Committee Chairman William L. Clay of Missouri, who blocked Engel's bid for his committee at the start of the 102nd Congress.

At Home: During his political career, Engel has not been known as a legislative risk-taker. But a big political gamble placed Engel in the House: He gave up his state Assembly seat in 1988 for a primary challenge to 10-term Rep. Biaggi. Although Biaggi was then facing federal trial on charges of bribery and extortion in the Wedtech case — and had been convicted for accepting illegal gratuities in a separate 1987 case — he remained highly popular in the 19th. When he defiantly announced he would seek re-election in 1988, most Democratic officials demurred.

Biaggi was convicted in August and resigned the seat he had held for nearly 20 years. Engel then easily won the primary and general elections to claim the seat. Similarly, in 1977, the public school guidance counselor had won a special election to succeed an assemblyman who had resigned after a bribery conviction.

A low-key figure in the Assembly, Engel held positions that would serve him well in his House race. He chaired a committee on drug and alcohol abuse and a subcommittee that handled moderate-income housing issues.

In the 1988 primary, with active opposition only from former Democratic state Rep. Vincent Marchiselli, Engel's biggest obstacle was the specter of Biaggi. Because Biaggi resigned after the candidate-withdrawal deadline, he remained on the Democratic primary ballot and on the GOP line in the general election as well (Republicans had ceded the district to Biaggi throughout his career).

Despite speculation that there would be a "tribute" turnout for Biaggi, Engel took nearly 50 percent of the primary vote; Marchiselli and Biaggi split the rest. In the general election, Engel received 56 percent; Biaggi had 27 percent.

There was an echo of that campaign early in 1990. *The Village Voice*, a New York weekly, wrote that a state wiretap had picked up Engel asking Louis Moscatiello — a union official with suspected ties to organized crime — for campaign help "on the sly." Engel insisted that he contacted Moscatiello only because of his union position, and that the "on the sly" remark referred to the fact that most labor officials were still backing Biaggi when the call was made. Engel easily defeated GOP political novice William J. Gouldman in 1990.

New York 19

South Yonkers; East and Central Bronx

Stretching from the eastern extremes of the Bronx to the Westchester County city of Yonkers, the 19th is a collection of ethnic neighborhoods, most of them with strong community ties and conservative social values.

The district has three arms that reach out for blue-collar Democrats. One goes south to Throgs Neck, a community of Italian- and Irish-Americans that lends its name to a bridge connecting the Bronx with Queens. Another extends west to Belmont, home to Italians and Hispanics. The third runs north to take in much of Yonkers, which in appearance, ethnicity and economic status is closer to the Bronx than to the rest of suburban Westchester.

Included in the district is Co-op City, a huge high-rise project in the East Bronx which is Engel's political base. Its 35 buildings house more than 35,000 residents, many of whom are Jewish; blacks and Hispanics have also moved into Co-op City in large numbers recently.

Minority-group residents make up more than one-third of Yonkers' total, and are generally concentrated together. The urban southwest is mainly black, while the more suburban east side is mainly white. In 1986, U.S. District Court Judge Leonard B. Sand decided this was not an accident. He ruled the city had located low-income housing so as to isolate minorities, and ordered the city immediately to construct 200 units of low-income housing in mostly white neighborhoods in East and North Yonkers.

The order spurred a backlash, mainly from blue-collar ethnics who had moved to Yonkers in the "white flight" from New York City. After five years of discord, and more than $10 million in attorneys' fees, construction contracts were finally signed in early 1991. The housing order continues to be an incendiary community issue, however, as anti-housing activists have vowed to press on.

Population: 516,498. White 399,252 (77%), Black 67,720 (13%), Other 8,218 (2%). Spanish origin 81,422 (16%). 18 and over 398,578 (77%), 65 and over 90,103 (17%). Median age: 36.

Committees

Foreign Affairs (19th of 28 Democrats)
Europe & the Middle East; Human Rights & International Organizations; International Economic Policy & Trade; Western Hemisphere Affairs

Select Hunger (16th of 22 Democrats)
Domestic

Small Business (22nd of 27 Democrats)
Regulation, Business Opportunity & Energy

Elections

1990 General		
Eliot L. Engel (D)	45,758	(61%)
William J. Gouldman (R)	17,135	(23%)
Kevin Brawley (C, RTL)	11,868	(16%)
1990 Primary		
Eliot L. Engel (D)	12,521	(72%)
Dominick A. Fusco (D)	4,928	(28%)
1988 General		
Eliot L. Engel (D)	77,158	(56%)
Mario Biaggi (R)	37,454	(27%)
Martin J. O'Grady (RTL)	11,271	(8%)
Robert Blumetti (C)	11,182	(8%)

District Vote For President

	1988	1984	1980	1976
D	84,084 (55%)	86,353 (48%)	64,980 (51%)	86,329 (60%)
R	67,775 (45%)	93,165 (52%)	54,709 (43%)	55,862 (39%)
I			5,859 (5%)	

Campaign Finance

	Receipts	Receipts from PACs	Expend-itures
1990			
Engel (D)	$399,619	$324,173 (81%)	$389,698
1988			
Engel (D)	$187,088	$99,600 (53%)	$183,145
Biaggi (R)	$152,548	$36,950 (24%)	$468,631

Key Votes

1991	
Authorize use of force against Iraq	Y
1990	
Support constitutional amendment on flag desecration	N
Pass family and medical leave bill over Bush veto	Y
Reduce SDI funding	Y
Allow abortions in overseas military facilities	Y
Approve budget summit plan for spending and taxing	N
Approve civil rights bill	Y
1989	
Halt production of B-2 stealth bomber at 13 planes	Y
Oppose capital gains tax cut	Y
Approve federal abortion funding in rape or incest cases	Y
Approve pay raise and revision of ethics rules	N
Pass Democratic minimum wage plan over Bush veto	Y

Voting Studies

	Presidential Support		Party Unity		Conservative Coalition	
Year	S	O	S	O	S	O
1990	18	75	83	2	13	80
1989	30	65	92	1	10	80

Interest Group Ratings

Year	ADA	ACU	AFL-CIO	CCUS
1990	100	9	100	21
1989	95	4	100	33

20 Nita M. Lowey (D)

Of Harrison — Elected 1988

Born: July 5, 1937, The Bronx, N.Y.
Education: Mount Holyoke College, B.A. 1959.
Occupation: Public official.
Family: Husband, Stephen Lowey; three children.
Religion: Jewish.
Political Career: N.Y. assistant secretary of state, 1985-87.
Capitol Office: 1313 Longworth Bldg. 20515; 225-6506.

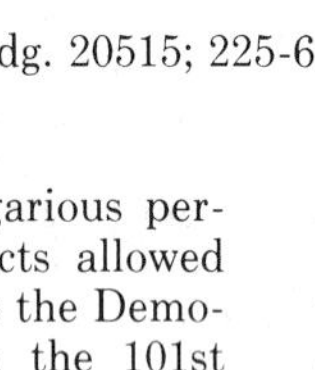

In Washington: Lowey's gregarious personality and quick political instincts allowed her to seize legislative opportunities the Democratic leadership sent her way in the 101st Congress. The opportunities were a thank you for Lowey's 1988 ouster of a GOP incumbent, and they helped her to an easy 1990 re-election.

As a freshman she got a seat on the Education and Labor Committee, a good fit for her interests, and she is a reliable liberal vote there. Looking out for the interests of working mothers and poor families, Lowey pushed an amendment to encourage public-private partnerships in developing new child-care facilities. She also sponsored an amendment to double the authorized funding to $10 million for the Nutrition Education and Training program, which provides nutritional information to students, teachers and other school personnel.

With support from committee staff, Lowey shepherded an antidrug bill through the legislative mill in 1990. The bill authorized funding for drug education and counseling services for students, and after it won committee approval, the leadership gave her a go-ahead to bring it to the House under an expedited rule. But the rule allowed a slim one-third vote of those present to derail the measure, and shortly before her bill was up, Lowey learned that the GOP intended to block its passage because of an unrelated amendment tacked on by another member. With floor time scarce as Congress wound down, Lowey pragmatically severed the amendment and won unanimous approval for her bill.

On the Merchant Marine and Fisheries Committee, Lowey advocated measures to clean up Long Island Sound. She backed legislation to create the Long Island Sound Conservancy office within the Environmental Protection Agency.

Overall, Lowey was a reliable leadership vote in the 101st Congress, voting with a majority of Democrats 94 percent of the time.

At Home: When Lowey announced her challenge to GOP Rep. Joseph J. DioGuardi in 1988, it was her first try for elective office. But she was a longtime Democratic activist, and her outgoing personality, political contacts and fundraising skills made her a strong candidate.

While raising her family in Queens, Lowey was active in civic organizations. A neighborly act in 1974 first led Lowey into the political arena: She opened her home for a coffee klatch with a Queens lawyer running in a primary for lieutenant governor. That attorney, Mario M. Cuomo, lost in the primary, but remembered Lowey's help. When he was appointed by then-Democratic Gov. Hugh Carey as New York secretary of state, he hired Lowey to work in his department's antipoverty division. She rose to become top assistant to Secretary of State Gail S. Shaffer in 1985.

Lowey by then had moved to the Westchester County suburb of Rye. Her work with local organizations earned her friends and helped her build a political base.

Lowey survived a September 1988 House primary against Hamilton Fish III, publisher of *The Nation* magazine and son of a House member, and businessman Dennis Mehiel, winning by 8 percentage points. Lowey then entered the November campaign with a solid Democratic base and a personal grass-roots network featuring strong support from abortion-rights advocates. She emphasized such issues as housing, drug abuse and Long Island Sound pollution to give herself mainstream appeal.

She also raised $1.3 million, a huge treasury for a challenger. Although DioGuardi outspent her, his fundraising prowess also turned into his downfall. A newspaper reported in October that a New Rochelle auto dealer had funnelled $57,000 in corporate contributions to DioGuardi's campaign through his employees. DioGuardi denied any knowledge of the alleged pass-through scheme, but the revelations put him on the defensive; Lowey won narrowly.

Lowey's busy agenda on local issues and her frequent "town meetings" earned her positive media coverage. Republicans tried to recruit flamboyant lawyer Barry Slotnick, who had defended "subway gunman" Bernhard Goetz; but he decided not to run, and Lowey breezed to victory over a Republican political novice.

New York 20

Central and Southern Westchester County

The elitist Westchester County that John Cheever wrote about still exists, replete with fieldstone patios, gin-and-tonics and Republican loyalties. But the county has always been more varied than that picture implies. Westchester's politics are determined at least as much by liberal Jewish suburbanites and more conservative middle-class Italian neighborhoods as by WASP enclaves.

The overall suburban profile of the 20th tends to give Republicans a slight edge in presidential voting and in competitive statewide contests. George Bush edged Michael S. Dukakis in the district in 1988.

There are several communities in today's Westchester where mansions, with estate-like grounds, still outnumber the split-levels. Bronxville had a 1985 per capita income of over $34,000; Larchmont and Rye nudged $30,000. These places have traditionally been Republican bastions, and for the most part, they remain so. One exception is Scarsdale, whose large Jewish population provides a liberal counterbalance to its upper-class Republicanism.

Though these towns have much of the 20th District's wealth, they are modest in size. Much of the district's population is in the more densely populated and economically mixed cities.

White Plains (population 49,000) is the county seat and its political nexus. The city, which had turned seedy by the 1960s, was revived by urban renewal and is now a thriving corporate and retail center. It has a mix of upper-middle-class suburbanites and lower-income residents.

The district then travels down crowded Central Avenue (N.Y. 100) to Yonkers, and takes in a chunk made up mainly of middle-class Jewish and Italian-American communities. In between, there are such comfortable suburbs as Hartsdale and Edgemont.

East of Yonkers are the two largest cities wholly within the 20th. New Rochelle (67,300), once a resort town on the Long Island Sound, now has a more working-class feel and a growing minority population. These demographics are even more prevalent in Mount Vernon (67,200), which has much more in common with the neighboring Bronx than the rest of Westchester. Blacks have gained an edge over the largely Italian white population; Mount Vernon currently has a black mayor.

Population: 516,507. White 416,373 (81%), Black 80,822 (16%), Other 9,703 (2%). Spanish origin 28,907 (6%). 18 and over 388,570 (75%), 65 and over 69,213 (13%). Median age: 35.

Committees

Education & Labor (14th of 25 Democrats)
Elementary, Secondary & Vocational Education; Human Resources; Postsecondary Education

Merchant Marine & Fisheries (22nd of 29 Democrats)
Coast Guard & Navigation; Fisheries & Wildlife Conservation & the Environment

Select Narcotics Abuse & Control (15th of 21 Democrats)

Elections

1990 General		
Nita M. Lowey (D)	82,203	(63%)
Glenn D. Bellitto (R)	35,575	(27%)
John M. Schafer (C, RTL)	13,030	(10%)
1988 General		
Nita M. Lowey (D)	102,235	(50%)
Joseph J. DioGuardi (R)	96,465	(47%)

District Vote For President

	1988		1984		1980		1976	
D	94,237	(48%)	99,756	(43%)	65,774	(37%)	89,956	(47%)
R	102,392	(52%)	129,323	(56%)	92,933	(52%)	102,539	(53%)
I					15,010	(9%)		

Campaign Finance

	Receipts	Receipts from PACs		Expend-itures
1990				
Lowey (D)	$1,223,045	$448,797	(37%)	$911,766
Bellitto (R)	$15,505	0		$15,356
1988				
Lowey (D)	$1,338,147	$164,175	(12%)	$1,309,873
DioGuardi (R)	$1,553,890	$374,079	(24%)	$1,567,129

Key Votes

1991	
Authorize use of force against Iraq	N
1990	
Support constitutional amendment on flag desecration	N
Pass family and medical leave bill over Bush veto	Y
Reduce SDI funding	Y
Allow abortions in overseas military facilities	Y
Approve budget summit plan for spending and taxing	N
Approve civil rights bill	Y
1989	
Halt production of B-2 stealth bomber at 13 planes	Y
Oppose capital gains tax cut	Y
Approve federal abortion funding in rape or incest cases	Y
Approve pay raise and revision of ethics rules	N
Pass Democratic minimum wage plan over Bush veto	Y

Voting Studies

	Presidential Support		Party Unity		Conservative Coalition	
Year	S	O	S	O	S	O
1990	14	83	94	4	15	81
1989	28	70	94	3	15	85

Interest Group Ratings

Year	ADA	ACU	AFL-CIO	CCUS
1990	100	4	100	21
1989	95	7	100	40

21 Hamilton Fish Jr. (R)

Of Millbrook — Elected 1968

Born: June 3, 1926, Washington, D.C.
Education: Harvard U., A.B. 1949; New York U., LL.B. 1957.
Military Service: Naval Reserve, 1944-46.
Occupation: Lawyer.
Family: Wife, Mary Ann Knauss; four children.
Religion: Episcopalian.
Political Career: Republican nominee for U.S. House, 1966.
Capitol Office: 2269 Rayburn Bldg. 20515; 225-5441.

In Washington: When Fish joined the Judiciary Committee as a House freshman in 1969, he aligned with the numerous moderate Republicans on the panel who supported civil rights and other liberal social causes. Today, Fish is alone at the top, the committee's senior Republican and its sole defender of the old GOP traditions.

Having weathered this sea change during the Reagan era, Fish might have hoped for more comity with President Bush, a fellow patrician who served in the House with Fish. But the dignified New Yorker voted with Bush in the 101st Congress only slightly more often than he had voted with Reagan, and Fish was at odds with the Bush administration on several key issues before the Judiciary Committee.

Though he does not often agree with the aggressively conservative GOP bloc on Judiciary, Fish maintains their trust largely on the strength of his good word and decency. They appreciate his willingness to free the committee staff to pursue the party line on key issues, rather than his own view.

Since the late 1980s, when the conservative social agenda stalled in Congress and other issues began moving to the fore, Fish has played an important role in legislative bargaining. Democrats have long looked to him to give their proposals at least a veneer of bipartisanship, and to influence the votes of the two dozen or so Republicans ideologically compatible with Fish.

In mid-1990, after seven months of marathon negotiations, Fish helped craft a compromise package that cleared the way for approval of legislation to extend civil rights protections to the disabled. He brought together the chairman and ranking member of the subcommittee working on the bill — California Democrat Don Edwards and Wisconsin Republican F. James Sensenbrenner Jr. — as well as representatives of small businesses and the disabled to craft a deal on the Americans with Disabilities Act.

The package they negotiated included six amendments, three sought by each group. Some of the changes were clarifications: Business interests wanted to ensure that actions against "anticipatory discrimination" extended only to situations where a building was about to be erected. Other changes were seemingly innocuous: The disabled wanted a guarantee that professional licensing examinations be held in accessible locations. But the package helped cement the deal. Congress overwhelmingly approved the ADA and it was signed into law.

Fish's pivotal role was plainly evident in the 100th Congress' debate on amending the Fair Housing Act, which had been at a partisan impasse for nearly a decade. Despite widespread agreement that the Department of Housing and Urban Development (HUD) needed more authority to enforce the law, no consensus could be reached on how to achieve that goal. In 1988, the Judiciary Committee approved a bill, with Fish's support, to set up a new system of administrative law judges to hear cases of alleged discrimination. But debate over whether this would subject a defendant to fines without benefit of a jury trial was so contentious that the bill appeared doomed.

Fish, however, initiated negotiations between civil rights advocates and Democrats on the left, and Realtors and the Reagan administration on the right. After more than six weeks of talks, the two sides agreed to allow either HUD or the alleged discriminator to opt for a full jury trial. This breakthrough ensured House passage; the bill was signed into law soon afterward.

Prior to taking over the senior GOP position on the full committee in 1983, Fish held the ranking post on the Immigration Subcommittee. His expertise in immigration dates to the 1950s, when he was a foreign service officer stationed in Dublin, Ireland. During the major immigration debates of the 1980s, he was not a primary GOP strategist, but he lent assistance without upstaging the lead sponsors.

This was again the case during 1990 consideration of revising the law governing legal immigration, an issue that had been deadlocked for more than 20 years. Fish brought together GOP Sen. Alan K. Simpson, who wanted a

New York 21

Hudson Valley — Poughkeepsie

As a Depression-era House member, Hamilton Fish Sr. was a furious opponent of the New Deal. He used to infuriate Franklin D. Roosevelt all the more because he was FDR's congressman — the Roosevelt family home at Hyde Park was part of the Fish constituency.

The 1980s redistricting severed that link with history by removing Hyde Park from the 21st. But the district has changed very little in partisan terms. Most of the communities that returned the elder Fish to Washington are as solidly Republican as they were 50 years ago. The only real difference is in ideology. The current constituency is far closer to the moderate politics of the current Rep. Fish than to those of his conservative father (who died in 1991).

The 21st starts in the New York suburbs of upper Westchester County, where moderate GOP politics gets a good response from "Rockefeller Republicans" in Bedford and other comfortable towns. To the north, the subdivisions of Putnam County are also wellsprings of GOP votes; Putnam gave 66 percent of its vote to George Bush in 1988.

The still-rural northern parts of Putnam give way to similar terrain in Dutchess County, a Republican territory stretching from the Hudson River to the Connecticut border that is dotted with country mansions.

Poughkeepsie, with 30,000 residents, is the district's best-known city. An important river port and conduit for Dutchess County farm products in the late 18th and early 19th centuries, Poughkeepsie today relies more heavily on electronics equipment and agricultural machinery. The Dutchess County seat is a blend of ethnic Democrats and academics from Vassar College.

Dutchess County also includes Beacon, whose population has rebounded modestly in recent years after a long-term decline caused by the loss of its hat industry. Directly across the Hudson, in Orange County, is the struggling city of Newburgh, which has also suffered a long-term industrial decline. More picturesque is the campus of the U.S. Military Academy at West Point, located on a series of hills overlooking the Hudson.

Environmental concerns animate the politics of this district on the fringe of a vast New York metropolitan region. The Hudson River gentry united in the early 1970s to stop a planned hydropower project at Storm King. And controversy plagues the nuclear power complex at Indian Point on the Hudson. Often shut down due to technical problems, the plant sits atop a geological fault line 35 miles from New York City.

Population: 516,778. White 471,247 (91%), Black 34,028 (7%), Other 5,336 (1%). Spanish origin 15,971 (3%). 18 and over 365,060 (71%), 65 and over 53,214 (10%). Median age: 31.

ceiling on overall immigration, and House members, who defended previous law that placed no cap on the number of immigrants who were joining family members who were U.S. citizens. The bill, which was approved in the waning hours of the 101st Congress, sets a limit of 675,000 immigrants a year beginning in 1994, and it established a formula for admission of family members, giving preference to spouses, parents and children.

Striking a deal on the highly controversial 1990 Civil Rights Act might have been an impossible feat, and Fish was not visible in efforts to negotiate an agreement between the bill's advocates, who said it was needed to protect women and minorities, and its detractors, who said it would lead to hiring quotas. Fish was one of just two Republicans to support the bill in committee, and one of just 34 Republicans to back it on the floor, but — perhaps mindful of the fierce resistance to the measure among GOP conservatives — his support was not very high-profile. The bill died after the Senate fell one vote short of overriding Bush's veto. If the partisan bickering cools on the politically charged measure, Fish might find a mediator's role.

In the 100th Congress, he was among those credited with engineering an approval vote and subsequent veto override of the *Grove City* bill, which reversed the Supreme Court ruling narrowing the enforcement scope of four key civil rights laws.

Fish finds common ground with his conservative GOP colleagues on issues involving Justice Department operations, as well as on matters of copyright and antitrust law. Fish is ranking Republican on Judiciary's Economic and Commercial Law Subcommittee; in the 101st Congress, he was among the critics of "vertical" price-fixing legislation, which consumer groups said was needed to prohibit manufacturers from setting a minimum retail price. Fish termed the bill too broad and said a manufacturer could be sued even if it had good reason to end a supply agreement. No compromise could be worked out, and the bill died.

Against the grain of recent Republican

orthodoxy, Fish has long been a firm supporter of the Equal Rights Amendment. But when Democrats tried to bring the ERA to the floor in 1983 under a fast-track procedure barring amendments and providing less than an hour of debate, Fish balked. He denounced the move as a political gimmick designed to frustrate legitimate discussion, and he voted against it. That defection was a key setback for ERA advocates; the measure failed by six votes.

At Home: Fish came to the House with one of the most impressive pedigrees in politics. His great-grandfather Hamilton Fish was governor of New York, U.S. senator and secretary of state. His grandfather Hamilton Fish was a U.S. representative. And his father, also Hamilton Fish, spent 24 years in the House arguing for American business and against President Franklin D. Roosevelt's New Deal.

The current Rep. Fish had long been engaged in civic activities on his ancestral turf of Dutchess County when an opportunity came to run for the House in 1966. Historically Republican, the district had gone Democratic in 1964, and the GOP was eager to retake it.

Fish engaged in a highly publicized "patrician primary" against Alexander Aldrich, cousin of Gov. Nelson A. Rockefeller. Fish won, but was beaten in November by the Democratic incumbent, Joseph Y. Resnick.

In 1968 Resnick ran for the Senate. Fish won his primary against a then-little-known lawyer, G. Gordon Liddy. Fish then won the seat, and has held it comfortably; he has not slipped below 70 percent of the vote since 1974.

In 1988, Fish's son, Hamilton Fish III, tried to extend the family's political reach by running for the 20th District in southern Westchester County. However, the youngest Fish was of a far more liberal bent — he had been publisher of *The Nation*, a liberal opinion journal — and entered the Democratic primary, aiming for GOP Rep. Joseph J. DioGuardi.

Rep. Fish greeted his son's decision with equanimity, stating that he was supportive of his personal goals even though he could not campaign for him as a member of the opposition party. But Fish's father, at age 100, denounced his grandson for his "leftist" views and his betrayal of the family's Republican roots. The family was spared a deepening of the quarrel, though; young Fish finished second in the primary to Nita M. Lowey, who went on to upset DioGuardi.

Committees

Judiciary (Ranking)
Economic & Commercial Law (ranking); Intellectual Property & Judicial Administration;

Joint Economic

Elections

1990 General		
Hamilton Fish Jr. (R)	99,866	(71%)
Richard L. Barbuto (D)	34,128	(24%)
Richard S. Curtin II (RTL)	5,925	(4%)
1988 General		
Hamilton Fish Jr. (R)	150,443	(75%)
Lawrence W. Grunberger (D)	47,294	(23%)

Previous Winning Percentages:				**1986**	(77%)	**1984**	(78%)
1982	(75%)	**1980**	(81%)	**1978**	(78%)	**1976**	(71%)
1974	(65%)	**1972**	(72%)	**1970**	(71%)	**1968**	(48%)

District Vote For President

	1988	1984	1980	1976
D	83,635 (38%)	71,014 (32%)	60,495 (31%)	80,741 (42%)
R	136,078 (62%)	150,345 (68%)	115,598 (59%)	110,434 (57%)
I			17,012 (9%)	

Campaign Finance

	Receipts	Receipts from PACs	Expend-itures
1990			
Fish (R)	$348,209	$204,990 (59%)	$411,614
Barbuto (D)	$935	0	$729
1988			
Fish (R)	$357,841	$196,388 (55%)	$277,680

Key Votes

1991	
Authorize use of force against Iraq	Y
1990	
Support constitutional amendment on flag desecration	Y
Pass family and medical leave bill over Bush veto	Y
Reduce SDI funding	N
Allow abortions in overseas military facilities	N
Approve budget summit plan for spending and taxing	Y
Approve civil rights bill	Y
1989	
Halt production of B-2 stealth bomber at 13 planes	N
Oppose capital gains tax cut	N
Approve federal abortion funding in rape or incest cases	N
Approve pay raise and revision of ethics rules	Y
Pass Democratic minimum wage plan over Bush veto	N

Voting Studies

	Presidential Support		Party Unity		Conservative Coalition	
Year	S	O	S	O	S	O
1990	42	51	44	47	56	41
1989	65	33	37	57	63	34
1988	37	59	37	59	58	42
1987	45	54	40	56	72	28
1986	40	56	33	60	56	38
1985	45	46	42	45	44	44
1984	50	43	38	51	53	37
1983	54	37	45	47	55	40
1982	45	44	41	51	49	44
1981	57	38	48	46	40	56

Interest Group Ratings

Year	ADA	ACU	AFL-CIO	CCUS
1990	56	32	50	43
1989	45	41	42	70
1988	60	32	86	71
1987	44	35	44	53
1986	45	32	57	44
1985	35	40	80	55
1984	40	23	42	69
1983	20	43	29	74
1982	45	43	55	33
1981	50	57	27	78

22 Benjamin A. Gilman (R)

Of Middletown — Elected 1972

Born: Dec. 6, 1922, Poughkeepsie, N.Y.
Education: U. of Pennsylvania, B.S. 1946; New York Law School, LL.B. 1950.
Military Service: Army, 1943-45.
Occupation: Lawyer.
Family: Wife, Rita Gail Kelhoffer; three children, two stepchildren.
Religion: Jewish.
Political Career: N.Y. Assembly, 1967-73.
Capitol Office: 2185 Rayburn Bldg. 20515; 225-3776.

In Washington: Gilman has a wide range of legislative interests and tries to involve himself in all of them. His position as a senior member on two standing committees (Foreign Affairs and Post Office and Civil Service) and two select committees (Narcotics Abuse and Hunger) has enabled Gilman to register his views on foreign aid, U.S.-Israeli relations, terrorism, drugs, famine relief, census overcounts and sundry other issues.

Though his efforts to cover this vast territory generate a succession of foreign fact-finding trips, news conferences and press releases, Gilman is regarded as much more of a plugger than a policy leader. He rarely rises to speak in debate; when he does, he usually reads at ponderous length from a prepared text.

During his nearly two-decade tenure in the House, Gilman has established a record clearly to the left of most of his Republican colleagues. His moderate voting record helps explain why he is not a major party spokesman on issues. His annual ratings from the liberal Americans for Democratic Action have been at least 55 percent every year since 1987. He has not voted with a majority of his party on more than 40 percent of recorded votes since 1985 and he backed President Bush only 33 percent of the time in 1990. That support score was the fourth lowest for any GOP member that year.

Gilman supports abortion rights. He also bucked the president and his party during the 101st Congress on the controversial civil rights bill and on bills raising the minimum wage and requiring businesses to provide employees with family leave.

Gilman has been active on the Select Committee on Narcotics Abuse and Control, even after leaving his post as ranking Republican at the start of the 101st Congress. Higher-profile House members may have dominated the scene during the highly charged debates on the 1986 and 1988 omnibus drug bills. But Gilman points out that, as an original proponent of the panel's creation in the mid-1970s, he had a role in the early efforts to crack down on illegal drugs, well before it became a hot political issue.

In 1989, Gilman sponsored an amendment to the foreign aid bill promoting the creation of an anti-narcotics "strike force" in the Western Hemisphere. In March 1990, when the administration certified that all but four major drug-producing nations had "cooperated fully" with U.S. anti-narcotics efforts, Gilman was among those in the forefront of protest. "This whole process has been a whitewash," he complained.

On Foreign Affairs — Gilman's major assignment — his moderate, bipartisan approach excludes him from the ideological combat that engages the committee's most recognized figures. While his interest in international relations may not have waned during the 101st Congress, his activity seems to have; some of his campaign literature did not even mention foreign affairs.

In 1989, Gilman did oppose an automatic five-year extension of trade benefits to Hungary. He wanted the president to retain the flexibility offered by the Jackson-Vanik amendment that bars trade benefits to East bloc nations that restrict emigration, a favorite Gilman issue.

Despite his more moderate politics, which set him apart from many House Republicans, Gilman, as a tenured member, is not without influence. During the 100th Congress, he was named as ranking Republican on a special task force empaneled to review the U.S. foreign assistance program, criticized for years as unwieldy and inefficient. A task force report, issued in February 1989, became the basis for debate in the 101st Congress on the proposed revamping of the foreign aid system.

Gilman agreed with most of the report's conclusions, but expressed reservations about a proposal to end completely the practice of congressional "earmarking" of aid to nations of strategic importance. Though he said the practice — which is criticized for limiting presidential flexibility in targeting foreign aid — should be restricted, he stressed the need to maintain earmarks for Greece, Egypt and Israel "to make

New York 22

Lower Hudson Valley

Starting in a patch of graceful old Westchester County suburbs, the 22nd crosses the Hudson River and moves west through the outer suburbia of Rockland and Orange counties to the Catskill Mountain resorts in lower Sullivan County. A Democratic registration advantage benefits the more popular Democratic statewide officials, including Sen. Daniel Patrick Moynihan and Gov. Mario M. Cuomo. But the suburban/exurban district goes Republican for president and backed GOP Sen. Alfonse M. D'Amato in 1986; it has been most hospitable territory for Gilman.

The Westchester section of the district, a place of tree-lined streets, contains white-collar New York City commuters and ethnic blue-collar families who fled the city and try to avoid its concerns. These suburbs — Hastings, Irvington, Tarrytown — have been densely populated for decades. There is a solid Jewish element here.

Rockland and Orange used to be bucolic, but that changed substantially during the big growth years of the 1970s. Rockland's numerous New York City commuters and a large blue-collar work force help make the county an electoral battleground. But in Orange, where there is still some farming done, GOP tendencies are stronger.

Jewish retirees help keep Democrats competitive in Sullivan County. Along Route 17 in the southern part of the county is the lower end of the Catskill Borscht Belt, which contains the Concord Hotel and other noted resorts.

Population: 516,625. White 464,735 (90%), Black 35,226 (7%), Other 9,216 (2%). Spanish origin 20,961 (4%). 18 and over 363,184 (70%), 65 and over 52,470 (10%). Median age: 32.

clear our unequivocal support for the security of those countries."

That Israel is on Gilman's priority list is no surprise. As ranking Republican on the Foreign Affairs Subcommittee on Europe and the Middle East, Gilman is a staunch supporter of aid to Israel, and an opponent of weapons sales that might threaten that nation. He spoke out against the sale of Stinger anti-aircraft missiles to Saudi Arabia in 1986.

During hearings in February 1991 on administration policies in the Persian Gulf, Gilman led the questioning of Secretary of State James A. Baker III on linkage of Iraq's withdrawal from Kuwait to settlement of the Israel-Palestinian issue. A testy Baker reassured Gilman that the administration firmly opposed any such linkage.

Gilman also uses his Foreign Affairs position to advance his interest in human rights, especially the cause of Jewish "refuseniks" who have been frustrated in their effort to emigrate from the Soviet Union. In 1986, Gilman was involved in American efforts to obtain the freedom of jailed Soviet dissident Anatoly Shcharansky. The New York Republican flew to East Berlin and met with East German lawyer Wolfgang Vogel, who later took part in negotiations that led to Shcharansky's release.

At Home: Gilman easily fended off the most unusual comeback attempt of 1990. His Democratic opponent was 85-year-old former Rep. John G. Dow, whom Gilman had unseated in 1972 with a plurality of the vote.

But the contest was a mild attempt at a "last hurrah" for Dow, who had not run for the House since his unsuccessful 1974 rematch with Gilman. The now-tenured Republican won in 1990 with 69 percent, a tally that conformed with his recent showings for re-election.

Gilman earned his initial contest with Dow by quietly working his way through the ranks of appointive and elective office. Shortly after receiving his law degree, he was appointed a deputy assistant attorney general of New York, and in two years he became an assistant attorney general. Later, he served as attorney for New York state's Temporary Commission on the Courts and as counsel to the Assembly's Committee on Local Finance.

Following reapportionment of the state Legislature in the mid-1960s, Gilman won a newly created Assembly seat from Orange County. After three terms in the Assembly, he decided to challenge Dow for the House.

Viewed as a moderate, Gilman had to defeat conservative builder Yale Rapkin for the Republican nomination. Strong support from his home base of Orange County allowed him to beat Rapkin, who was from Rockland County.

Although Dow was the incumbent, Gilman had demographics on his side in the general election. Dow carried a normally Republican district in the 1964 Johnson landslide, and redistricting in 1972 had made the district even more Republican. Gilman won comfortably even though Rapkin siphoned off 13 percent as the Conservative Party candidate.

His re-elections went smoothly for a decade, until his district was combined with that of Democratic Rep. Peter A. Peyser in 1982. In what legislative map makers of both parties billed as a "fair fight," Peyser had the party-registration advantage and Gilman the edge in familiar territory. Territory won out.

It was a far angrier campaign than Gilman had been used to. Peyser went after the Republican, criticizing him for opposing a nuclear-weapons freeze and for backing military aid to El Salvador. Unions, which had backed Gilman before, now sided with Peyser.

Gilman put aside his soft-spoken ways and attacked Peyser, who once had been a Republican House colleague of Gilman's before switching parties, as an "ultra-liberal Democratic congressman" and the "candidate of Teddy Kennedy and Tip O'Neill."

Gilman's close ties to his geographically dominant Rockland-Orange base paid off: He carried those two counties solidly. Gilman was almost able to carry a normally Democratic, heavily Jewish portion of Sullivan County that had been placed in the district for the first time. Peyser took the Westchester County portion, his home base, but it was not enough.

Having survived the test posed by redistricting, Gilman in 1984 reverted to his practice of winning easily, taking over two-thirds of the vote against Democratic attorney Bruce Levine. He repeated that feat in both 1986 and 1988 against Democrat Eleanor F. Burlingham, an elderly environmental activist.

Committees

Post Office & Civil Service (Ranking)
Investigations

Foreign Affairs (2nd of 18 Republicans)
Europe & the Middle East (ranking); International Narcotics Control (ranking); International Operations

Select Hunger (4th of 12 Republicans)
International

Select Narcotics Abuse & Control (2nd of 14 Republicans)

Elections

1990 General

Benjamin A. Gilman (R)	95,495	(69%)
John G. Dow (D)	37,034	(26%)
Margaret M. Beirne (RTL)	6,656	(5%)

1988 General

Benjamin A. Gilman (R)	144,227	(71%)
Eleanor F. Burlingham (D)	54,312	(27%)

Previous Winning Percentages: **1986** (70%) **1984** (69%) **1982** (53%) **1980** (74%) **1978** (62%) **1976** (65%) **1974** (54%) **1972** (48%)

District Vote For President

	1988	1984	1980	1976
D	97,516 (43%)	88,142 (40%)	91,403 (34%)	123,237 (46%)
R	129,595 (57%)	132,044 (60%)	147,407 (55%)	142,770 (53%)
I			22,397 (8%)	

Campaign Finance

	Receipts	Receipts from PACs		Expend-itures
1990				
Gilman (R)	$445,481	$195,968	(44%)	$497,635
Dow (D)	$4,038	0		$3,473
1988				
Gilman (R)	$428,176	$166,797	(39%)	$411,056
Burlingham (D)	$10,342	0		$10,427

Key Votes

1991

Authorize use of force against Iraq	Y

1990

Support constitutional amendment on flag desecration	Y
Pass family and medical leave bill over Bush veto	Y
Reduce SDI funding	N
Allow abortions in overseas military facilities	Y
Approve budget summit plan for spending and taxing	N
Approve civil rights bill	Y

1989

Halt production of B-2 stealth bomber at 13 planes	N
Oppose capital gains tax cut	N
Approve federal abortion funding in rape or incest cases	Y
Approve pay raise and revision of ethics rules	Y
Pass Democratic minimum wage plan over Bush veto	Y

Voting Studies

	Presidential Support		Party Unity		Conservative Coalition	
Year	**S**	**O**	**S**	**O**	**S**	**O**
1990	33	66	35	63	52	48
1989	44	55	29	69	44	56
1988	41	54	39	58	55	42
1987	38	61	33	60	58	42
1986	43	53	31	67	66	30
1985	44	55	43	53	60	38
1984	45	55	43	57	58	42
1983	57	43	42	56	61	38
1982	53	42	41	56	45	52
1981	51	29	42	48	48	51

Interest Group Ratings

Year	ADA	ACU	AFL-CIO	CCUS
1990	61	29	83	14
1989	55	43	92	60
1988	55	42	93	50
1987	68	26	88	21
1986	40	55	92	28
1985	45	43	82	27
1984	40	33	62	44
1983	45	57	65	45
1982	50	38	75	36
1981	45	66	43	72

23 Michael R. McNulty (D)

Of Green Island — Elected 1988

Born: Sept. 16, 1947, Troy, N.Y.
Education: College of the Holy Cross, A.B. 1969.
Occupation: Public official.
Family: Wife, Nancy Ann Lazzaro; four children.
Religion: Roman Catholic.
Political Career: Green Island supervisor, 1970-77; Democratic nominee for N.Y. Assembly, 1976; mayor of Green Island, 1977-83; N.Y. Assembly, 1983-89.
Capitol Office: 414 Cannon Bldg 20515; 225-5076.

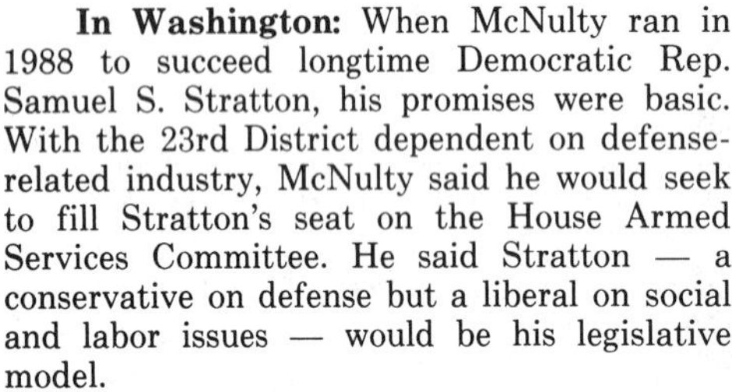

In Washington: When McNulty ran in 1988 to succeed longtime Democratic Rep. Samuel S. Stratton, his promises were basic. With the 23rd District dependent on defense-related industry, McNulty said he would seek to fill Stratton's seat on the House Armed Services Committee. He said Stratton — a conservative on defense but a liberal on social and labor issues — would be his legislative model.

McNulty has been true to his word. As a freshman, he obtained a seat on Armed Services. His overall record is about as liberal as that of the average House Democrat from New York. In 1989, he received a perfect rating on an AFL-CIO scorecard; in 1990, he voted against President Bush's position on 72 percent of House votes.

But McNulty tends to be more supportive of Defense Department priorities than many Democratic colleagues. He voted in 1989 against capping production of the B-2 "Stealth" bomber and in 1990 against a deep slash in funding for the strategic defense initiative.

There is a sharp personality contrast between the former and current member from the 23rd District. In his heyday, Stratton (who died in September 1990) was one of the more combative members of Congress. McNulty is a seasoned political insider — he served as one of two Democratic whips for his freshman class — but his style is more reflective.

This trait was evident during the January 1991 debate on whether to commit U.S. troops to war against Iraq. Stating that the ongoing economic embargo might eventually end Iraq's occupation of Kuwait, McNulty voted for the Democratic leadership's resolution calling for continued sanctions rather than war. However, when that measure was defeated, McNulty voted for the resolution authorizing Bush to use military force against Iraq. McNulty said defeat of both measures would send a signal of weakness to Iraqi President Saddam Hussein; he was one of only three Democrats who voted for both.

At Home: McNulty said in 1988 that serving in Congress had been a lifelong goal. But he did not expect to have the chance that year, since Stratton had filed for re-election.

When New York's candidate filing deadline passed, McNulty had already re-upped to run for a fourth term in the New York Assembly. However, Stratton, a 30-year House member who had been in ill health, suddenly announced his retirement. Democratic leaders in the 23rd met within hours of the announcement and selected McNulty to replace Stratton on the ballot.

Although McNulty's opportunity to run for the House was unanticipated, his easy wins in 1988 and in 1990 were predictable.

Deeply rooted in Albany County politics, McNulty's family is virtually dynastic in its home base of Green Island. His grandfather was elected town tax collector in 1914, and went on to serve as town supervisor, county board chairman and county sheriff. McNulty's father was supervisor for eight years, mayor for 16 years and county sheriff for six.

McNulty joined his elders in 1969, winning a seat on the town board at age 22. While in this post, he waged his only unsuccessful campaign, a 1976 challenge to a Republican assemblyman. He recouped the next year by winning a contest for Green Island mayor, then won an Assembly seat in 1982.

In his 1988 House campaign, while taking typically Democratic stands on domestic issues, McNulty said he had no major differences with Stratton on defense. McNulty's opponent, Peter Bakal, was a local GOP party official who said he was closer to Stratton on defense but called for tougher government action on acid rain. McNulty, with endorsements from Stratton and environmentalist groups, won with 62 percent.

In 1990, McNulty was one of the few New York House Democrats to be endorsed by the Conservative Party. He defeated GOP public relations consultant Margaret Buhrmaster with 64 percent.

New York 23

Hudson and Mohawk Valleys — Albany; Schenectady

State bureaucrats, blue-collar workers and a strong party organization give Democrats a big edge in Albany County, site of New York state's capital city. The vote there, combined with the Democratic leanings of industrial workers elsewhere in the district, make the 23rd a pleasant place for Democrats up and down the ticket.

Michael S. Dukakis easily carried the district with 57 percent of the vote in 1988; Democratic Sen. Daniel Patrick Moynihan did even better. Despite his delayed start brought about by veteran Rep. Samuel S. Stratton's late retirement announcement, McNulty swept all four district counties.

McNulty's base is in Albany County, where his family members have held political office for over 70 years. Though he comes from the village of Green Island (population 2,500), the former state assemblyman is well-known in Albany, the district's dominant city with 101,000 residents.

Albany's most familiar location is the mammoth state office complex named for longtime GOP Gov. (and later Vice President) Nelson A. Rockefeller (the expensive project was derided as Rockefeller's monument to himself). Democratic candidates mostly dominate Albany County, which has about three-fifths of the 23rd District vote. Dukakis took 59 percent there in 1988, and McNulty 65 percent. Moynihan won 74 percent in his landslide Senate win.

The 23rd reaches across the Hudson River into Rensselaer County and includes the aging industrial city of Troy (population 54,000). Also the site of Rensselaer Polytechnic Institute, Troy votes Democratic. McNulty carried the Rensselaer section of the 23rd by nearly 2-to-1.

From the Albany-Troy area, the district heads north and west along the Mohawk River, picking up another industrial city, Schenectady, along the way. That city maintains its history as a company town: Thousands of its residents work for General Electric, assembling turbines, generators and other products. Democrats again hold the edge in Schenectady, though a GOP tradition among the city's Italian-Americans tempers Democratic margins somewhat. Dukakis took Schenectady County with 52 percent; McNulty won 56 percent.

The district also takes in a small piece of Montgomery County, and the city of Amsterdam (21,000). Rocked by the Mohawk Carpet plant closing in the early 1960s, Amsterdam today is sustained by smaller-scale industry.

Population: 516,943. White 482,010 (93%), Black 27,101 (5%), Other 4,688 (1%). Spanish origin 6,432 (1%). 18 and over 389,983 (75%), 65 and over 73,332 (14%). Median age: 32.

Committees

Armed Services (28th of 33 Democrats)
Investigations; Procurement & Military Nuclear Systems; Military Education

Post Office & Civil Service (12th of 15 Democrats)
Census & Population; Investigations; Postal Personnel & Modernization

Select Hunger (14th of 22 Democrats)
International

Elections

1990 General		
Michael R. McNulty (D)	117,239	(64%)
Margaret B. Buhrmaster (R)	65,760	(36%)
1988 General		
Michael R. McNulty (D)	145,040	(62%)
Peter M. Bakal (R)	89,858	(38%)

District Vote For President

	1988		1984		1980		1976	
D	140,440	(57%)	120,950	(47%)	120,535	(48%)	121,113	(47%)
R	106,755	(43%)	135,744	(53%)	98,824	(40%)	133,750	(52%)
I					24,591	(10%)		

Campaign Finance

	Receipts	Receipts from PACs		Expend-itures
1990				
McNulty (D)	$240,736	$149,179	(62%)	$149,204
Buhrmaster (R)	$23,300	$250	(1%)	$23,299
1988				
McNulty (D)	$314,940	$141,975	(45%)	$306,072
Bakal (R)	$167,450	$8,625	(5%)	$174,790

Key Votes

1991	
Authorize use of force against Iraq	Y
1990	
Support constitutional amendment on flag desecration	Y
Pass family and medical leave bill over Bush veto	Y
Reduce SDI funding	N
Allow abortions in overseas military facilities	N
Approve budget summit plan for spending and taxing	Y
Approve civil rights bill	Y
1989	
Halt production of B-2 stealth bomber at 13 planes	N
Oppose capital gains tax cut	Y
Approve federal abortion funding in rape or incest cases	Y
Approve pay raise and revision of ethics rules	Y
Pass Democratic minimum wage plan over Bush veto	Y

Voting Studies

	Presidential Support		Party Unity		Conservative Coalition	
Year	S	O	S	O	S	O
1990	27	72	92	7	35	65
1989	42	57	83	14	56	44

Interest Group Ratings

Year	ADA	ACU	AFL-CIO	CCUS
1990	78	21	92	21
1989	75	25	100	40

24 Gerald B.H. Solomon (R)

Of Glens Falls — Elected 1978

Born: Aug. 14, 1930, Okeechobee, Fla.
Education: Attended Siena College, 1949-50; St. Lawrence U., 1952-53.
Military Service: Marine Corps, 1951-52.
Occupation: Insurance executive.
Family: Wife, Freda Parker; five children.
Religion: Presbyterian.
Political Career: Queensbury town supervisor, 1968-72; N.Y. Assembly, 1973-79.
Capitol Office: 2265 Rayburn Bldg. 20515; 225-5614.

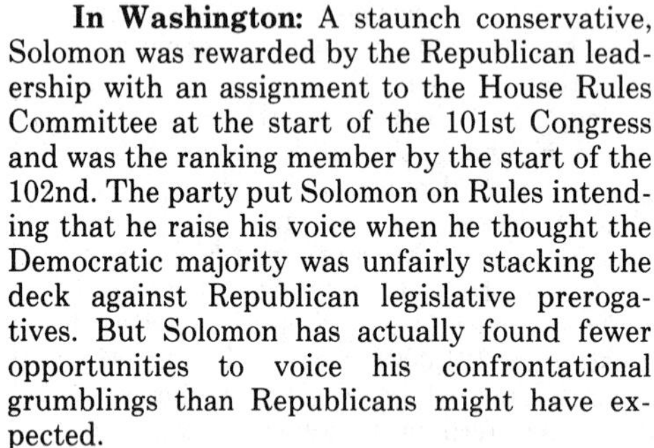

In Washington: A staunch conservative, Solomon was rewarded by the Republican leadership with an assignment to the House Rules Committee at the start of the 101st Congress and was the ranking member by the start of the 102nd. The party put Solomon on Rules intending that he raise his voice when he thought the Democratic majority was unfairly stacking the deck against Republican legislative prerogatives. But Solomon has actually found fewer opportunities to voice his confrontational grumblings than Republicans might have expected.

The partisan and divisive world of Speaker Jim Wright of Texas and Rules Committee Chairman Claude Pepper of Florida has been replaced by the more conciliatory reign of Thomas S. Foley of Washington and Joe Moakley of Massachusetts. "I will say that we have a much more cordial working relationship with the new Speaker and Rules Committee chairman," said Solomon at the end of 1990. "But that has not yet translated into greater procedural fairness." The changes have forced the combative Solomon to assume a more cooperative tone at times.

Still upset with some procedures on Rules — he said in October 1990 that the powerful panel "can literally break the law legally, and we do it all the time" — Solomon has not shied from criticizing the Democratic majority. But in the 102nd Congress, he started to push for substantive reform of the legislative process. Solomon proposed creation of a bipartisan commission to study and revise the structure and operation of the congressional process.

Solomon's move onto Rules did not come without a cost: He had to give up his seats on the Foreign Affairs Committee, a forum for his anticommunist rhetoric and fierce denunciation of liberal views that often irritated those across the aisle, and Veterans' Affairs, where the strait-laced ex-Marine was one of the most stalwart defenders of veterans' benefit programs and where he showed himself willing and able to work with the equally pro-vet Democrats who inhabited the committee.

During foreign policy debates especially, Solomon remains a vocal participant. In January 1991, the day after President Bush launched the ground offensive against Iraq, the outspoken Solomon took to the House floor to issue his ringing endorsement of the president's actions and to call once again for a constitutional amendment to ban flag burning. "What we cannot be proud of," Solomon told his colleagues, "is the unshaven, shaggy-haired, drug culture, poor excuses for Americans, wearing their tiny round wire-rim glasses, a protester's symbol of the blame-America-first crowd, out in front of the White House burning the American flag."

In the 101st Congress, Solomon continued to be active on a number of foreign policy fronts. He was in the forefront of congressional efforts to deny favorable trade status to China as punishment for its crackdown on pro-democracy demonstrators in June 1989. Solomon said Congress should act "to send a message to the angry old men who are hiding out in the so-called Great Hall of the People" in Beijing. Despite House passage of a Solomon measure, the Senate never acted.

Critical of U.S. technology getting into the hands of certain foreign governments, Solomon in 1989 opposed the joint development with Japan of the new FS-X fighter plane and warned in 1991 against selling Patriot missile and other technology to the Soviet Union.

During his tenure on the Foreign Affairs Committee, Solomon regularly excoriated committee Democrats for being too hard on American allies and too soft on anti-American regimes and insurgent movements. One of the staunchest supporters of the Nicaraguan contras, Solomon charged during one of the debates on cutting off U.S. aid to the contras that the committee was "about to sell the United States down the drain and is aiding and abetting the spread of communism in Central America."

A December 1986 appearance by Marine

New York 24

Upper Hudson Valley — Saratoga Springs

Anchored in the developing suburbia of the Albany-Schenectady-Troy area, the 24th is one of the most consistently Republican districts in the state.

GOP presidential candidates win easily here: In 1984, President Ronald Reagan took 69 percent of the 24th District vote, defeating Democrat Walter F. Mondale by nearly 90,000 votes. George Bush could not match Reagan's numbers in 1988, but still carried the district with 59 percent even as Democrat Michael S. Dukakis won the state. Democratic Sen. Daniel Patrick Moynihan's landslide 1982 and 1988 re-elections against weak Republican opponents marked the only times the 24th has strayed from the GOP column in contests for federal office since 1976.

Growth in the tri-cities area's suburbs made the 24th one of only six New York districts that registered a population increase during the 1970s. Such suburban towns as Greenbush, Half Moon and Clifton Park reliably give comfortable margins to GOP candidates.

Democrats running in the district used to find consolation in the city of Troy, a community of 54,000, packed with blue-collar residents involved in its heavy industry. But 1982 redistricting moved Troy to the neighboring 23rd. Pockets of blue-collar Democratic voting remain in Glens Falls (Warren County), Hudson (Columbia County), and Rensselaer.

The 24th dips south to take in the upper part of Dutchess County, where the landed gentry maintained their estates. Hyde Park, the home of President Franklin D. Roosevelt, overlooks the Hudson River in Dutchess County.

Despite the suburban growth, agricultural pursuits still occupy much of the 24th. Dairy farming is a mainstay of the local economy. Columbia County, in the district's southern arm, specializes in horse breeding. The Catskill Mountains of Greene County and the Adirondacks of Warren County are year-round resort areas. Lake George, in the district's northern end, is popular for boating and fishing.

But Saratoga Springs attracts the most notice from the outside world. Located about 30 miles north of Albany up Interstate 87, the old town is widely known for its mineral spas, elegant architecture and beautiful race track. The resort also has developed into a regional winter-sports center, with speed skating, cross-country skiing and snowshoe competitions luring crowds of sports fans.

Population: 515,614. White 504,100 (98%), Black 7,664 (2%). Spanish origin 4,313 (1%). 18 and over 364,047 (71%), 65 and over 62,425 (12%). Median age: 31.

Lt. Col. Oliver L. North before the Foreign Affairs Committee during early House deliberations on the Iran-contra affair provided a revealing glimpse of Solomon. Some members criticized North, who at the time was invoking his Fifth Amendment rights to avoid answering committee questions. But Solomon, whose 24th District includes North's hometown, heaped praised on his fellow Marine and ideological soul mate. "You are truly a great American, Colonel, and we back home deeply admire and respect your past history and what you've done for your country," Solomon said.

Solomon is as clearly opposed to leftist-oriented insurgent groups as he is supportive of groups like the contras. During 1988 debate on a bill to toughen sanctions against South Africa, Solomon attached an amendment barring the African National Congress, an anti-apartheid group, or the South West Africa People's Organization, based in neighboring Namibia, from administering any part of a $4 million refugee-assistance program. The overall bill, opposed by Solomon, passed the House, but died in the Senate.

Another passion on clear display during the 101st Congress was Solomon's antidrug fervor. Throughout 1989 and 1990, he authored successful amendments requiring random drug testing of employees in the CIA, the Coast Guard, at NASA and within the Washington Metro system. He also got Congress to accept a provision reducing federal highway funds to states that do not suspend the driver's licenses of those convicted of drug offenses, and another making students convicted of drug possession ineligible for financial aid.

In the 102nd Congress, Solomon has proposed legislation to make permanent the Select Committee on Narcotics Abuse and Control and has said he will continue to attach drug-testing provisions to appropriations measures.

Solomon left the Veterans' Affairs panel just after his signal achievement and his most notable show of bipartisan cooperation — the elevation of the Veterans Administration to Cabinet-level status. Solomon signed on in 1987 with Texas Democrat Jack Brooks, then the chairman of the Government Operations Committee, and worked for the measure's passage. The enactment of the bill was cinched when President Ronald Reagan climbed aboard in November 1987.

In the 101st Congress, Solomon continued his work with a number of veterans' organizations, unsuccessfully pushing for a flag-burning amendment.

A corollary of Solomon's respect for veterans is his disdain for those who shirk military duty. Since 1982, Solomon has successfully sponsored amendments barring men who avoid their draft-registration requirements from receiving federal student aid, job training funds and contracted defense work.

At Home: Running as an outspoken conservative in a solidly conservative district, Solomon was an easy winner in 1978 over Democratic Rep. Ned Pattison, one of the Watergate winners of 1974. Unlike Pattison's upset win four years earlier — when he became the first Democrat to represent the district in the 20th century — Solomon's victory was not a surprise.

Although Pattison had managed to hold his seat in 1976, he was burdened in his 1978 campaign against Solomon by his own candid interview in *Playboy* magazine, in which he admitted that he had smoked marijuana. Conservatives referred to him derisively as "Pot-tison."

Solomon had been a popular state legislator who regularly won his Assembly seat by wide margins. His Assembly constituency lay entirely within the old 29th District, so he had a good base from which to launch a congressional bid.

Solomon was able to reconstruct the Republican-Conservative coalition that had split apart in 1976. The two parties had run separate candidates in 1976, enabling Pattison to capture a second term with less than a majority of the vote. But Solomon was backed by both parties, pretty much guaranteeing him victory. He has had no serious electoral trouble since then.

Co-founder of an insurance and investment firm, Solomon got his start in politics in 1968, winning election as Queensbury town supervisor. He held that post — and served simultaneously as a member of the Warren County Legislature — until 1972, when he won a seat in the New York Assembly. He served there until his 1978 election to Congress.

Committee

Rules (Ranking)
Rules of the House

Elections

1990 General		
Gerald B. H. Solomon (R)	121,206	(68%)
Bob Lawrence (D)	56,671	(32%)
1988 General		
Gerald B. H. Solomon (R)	162,962	(72%)
Fred Baye (D)	62,177	(28%)

Previous Winning Percentages: **1986** (70%) **1984** (73%) **1982** (74%) **1980** (67%) **1978** (54%)

District Vote For President

	1988	1984	1980	1976
D	98,968 (41%)	72,837 (31%)	79,593 (35%)	85,243 (39%)
R	142,159 (59%)	162,234 (69%)	121,819 (54%)	134,171 (61%)
I			19,885 (9%)	

Campaign Finance

	Receipts	Receipts from PACs	Expend-itures
1990			
Solomon (R)	$255,758	$147,715 (58%)	$240,615
Lawrence (D)	$98,649	$32,340 (33%)	$95,100
1988			
Solomon (R)	$210,592	$79,150 (38%)	$212,652
Baye (D)	$15,957	$80 (1%)	$15,936

Key Votes

1991	
Authorize use of force against Iraq	Y
1990	
Support constitutional amendment on flag desecration	Y
Pass family and medical leave bill over Bush veto	Y
Reduce SDI funding	N
Allow abortions in overseas military facilities	N
Approve budget summit plan for spending and taxing	N
Approve civil rights bill	N
1989	
Halt production of B-2 stealth bomber at 13 planes	N
Oppose capital gains tax cut	N
Approve federal abortion funding in rape or incest cases	N
Approve pay raise and revision of ethics rules	Y
Pass Democratic minimum wage plan over Bush veto	Y

Voting Studies

	Presidential Support		Party Unity		Conservative Coalition	
Year	**S**	**O**	**S**	**O**	**S**	**O**
1990	67	32	84	13	87	13
1989	67	33	86	13	90	10
1988	65	32	90	9	95	5
1987	69	29	92	5	88	7
1986	79	16	84	10	92	4
1985	70	20	86	5	82	13
1984	64	34	85	10	83	14
1983	76	21	92	5	94	4
1982	60	26	85	9	78	10
1981	70	24	92	5	93	4

Interest Group Ratings

Year	ADA	ACU	AFL-CIO	CCUS
1990	22	83	36	64
1989	15	79	33	80
1988	15	88	57	86
1987	4	91	20	86
1986	0	81	21	83
1985	15	84	25	86
1984	5	79	31	81
1983	5	96	6	80
1982	5	90	22	76
1981	5	100	7	89

25 Sherwood Boehlert (R)

Of New Hartford — Elected 1982

Born: Sept. 28, 1936, Utica, N.Y.
Education: Utica College, A.B. 1961.
Military Service: Army, 1956-58.
Occupation: Congressional aide; public relations manager.
Family: Wife, Marianne Willey; four children.
Religion: Roman Catholic.
Political Career: Oneida County executive, 1979-82; sought GOP nomination for U.S. House, 1972.
Capitol Office: 1127 Longworth Bldg. 20515; 225-3665.

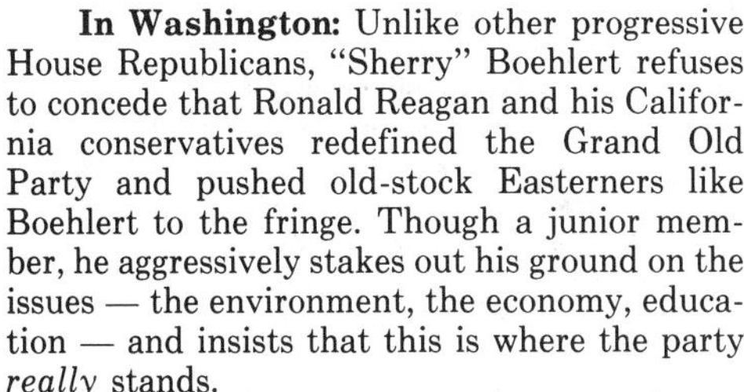

In Washington: Unlike other progressive House Republicans, "Sherry" Boehlert refuses to concede that Ronald Reagan and his California conservatives redefined the Grand Old Party and pushed old-stock Easterners like Boehlert to the fringe. Though a junior member, he aggressively stakes out his ground on the issues — the environment, the economy, education — and insists that this is where the party *really* stands.

With George Bush, a man of similar political heritage, taking over the White House in 1989, Boehlert expected to have a new opportunity to help demonstrate that the Reagan years were an aberration. To some degree, Boehlert is a happier man today; he finds Bush's rhetoric on issues such as the environment and education much more pleasing than Reagan's. But Boehlert still has major disagreements with the Bush administration, which remains largely driven by conservative principles popularized by Reagan.

During the 101st Congress, Boehlert voted for the Democrats' plan to raise the minimum wage, he voted to override Bush's veto of family leave legislation, and he was one of just 34 Republicans to back a major civil rights bill. On the October 1990 budget summit agreement — an issue in which Bush invested more personal capital — Boehlert stood behind the president, backing the measure as it went down to defeat.

During the Reagan years, Boehlert ran into a good deal of bad luck in angling for a seat on a prestige House committee; he tried to win appointment to Ways and Means or Appropriations, but was passed over for members more loyal to the party line.

Other Republicans had scored higher in opposition to Reagan or to the party line, but unlike Boehlert, they tended to be senior members who arrived in a past era, or junior members who were excused because they came from Democratic-leaning districts. As a representative of solid GOP territory, Boehlert gets cut little slack by party leaders in Washington, who see no particular political necessity behind his independent voting habits. In Reagan's second term, he opposed the president up to 60 percent of the time.

During the first two years of the Bush administration, Boehlert had surprisingly similar scores. He backed Bush just 51 percent of the time in 1989 and only 40 percent of the time in 1990. He voted with a majority of his party on fewer than 50 percent of House votes in both those years.

In a somewhat surprising move for a moderate, Boehlert backed conservative champion Newt Gingrich in his successful bid for House GOP whip early in the 101st Congress. Siding with Gingrich might position Boehlert more favorably in some future round of committee openings, but for now, he remains a member on two second-line panels, Public Works and Science. Both committees operate in the kind of bipartisan fashion that allows an affable and articulate activist such as Boehlert to thrive.

He is also involved in issues off his committees. He has been a leader in the fight against acid rain, reflecting not only his parochial concern for the acidic Adirondack lakes, but also his general worry about his party's image. "A lot of people have the traditional belief that Republicans don't give a damn about the environment," he said in 1989. "Well, a lot of people are wrong."

Saying that "George Bush is a welcomed change" from his predecessor on environmental issues, Boehlert cited 1990 passage of clean air legislation as the major accomplishment of the 101st Congress. "We're disproving the theory widely held in many quarters that nothing is happening in Washington these days," he boasted, just after the comprehensive measure cleared Congress. Boehlert also supports legislation to elevate the Environmental Protection Agency to Cabinet status; the bill has attracted the qualified support of the administration.

On Public Works' Aviation Subcommittee, he has been a voice for airline consumer and safety bills. On Science, he has opposed the proposed superconducting super collider (SSC) — an atom-smasher that could be the largest public works project in U.S. history — not on

New York 25

Central — Rome; Utica

The 25th is a Republican patchwork stitched together from several old New York districts that stretched across the central portion of the state. The boundaries reach from the outskirts of Ithaca on the west to the suburbs of Albany on the east, and the district juts north to include part of Oneida County, in the Mohawk Valley.

Oneida County casts a bit over 40 percent of the district's vote. Democrats normally hold their ground in Utica (population 70,000) and Rome (42,000), aging industrial cities undergoing a steady population decline. But outside this Mohawk Valley corridor, Oneida has a reliable Republican majority. George Bush carried the county (part of which is in the 29th District) with 54 percent of the vote in 1988; it last went Democratic for president in 1964.

The rural Republican vote dominant in the rest of the district reinforces that GOP trend. Otsego County also gave Bush 54 percent; he ran even stronger in Chenango and Cortland counties, 59 percent in each.

Otsego, by a slight margin over the others, provides the second-largest number of votes in the district. The college town of Oneonta, home of Hartwick College and a State University of New York campus, has 14,000 residents. But Cooperstown, on Otsego Lake, is far better known. Though the village of 2,300 contributes little vote, it draws much of central New York's tourist trade: It is the site of the Baseball Hall of Fame, as well as a museum dedicated to native son James Fenimore Cooper, author of "The Last of the Mohicans."

During the 1970s, sleepy Schoharie County on the eastern edge of the 25th saw a burst of suburban growth. An influx of suburbanites from the Albany-Schenectady area sent county population soaring 20 percent, to nearly 30,000. This turned out to be just a spurt, though; population remained level through the early 1980s.

Population: 516,201. White 501,968 (97%), Black 9,457 (2%), Other 2,612 (1%). Spanish origin 4,511 (1%). 18 and over 374,606 (73%), 65 and over 68,669 (13%). Median age: 31.

the merits but due to the cost.

Boehlert spoke out loudly during the 101st Congress against excessive spending on the super collider and unsuccessfully sought in committee to delay funding for the project. Calling for spending limits and imploring the project's staunchest backers to practice moderation, Boehlert said, "The SSC will not cure cancer, will not solve the problem of male pattern baldness and will not guarantee a World Series victory for the Chicago Cubs."

He also joined critics of NASA in voicing doubts about the agency's whopping budget. "We've given them a blank check in the past, and I don't think we're going to sign that blank check in the future," Boehlert said. "NASA is trying to do too much too soon."

Insisting that expensive projects such as the super collider and the space station could no longer be the norm, Boehlert warned his colleagues that such federal spending would have to be corralled. "This is going to be the Congress where priorities are really going to have some meaning," Boehlert said at the start of the 102nd. "We'd like to be all things for all people, but those days are history."

As senior Republican on the Science, Research and Technology Subcommittee, Boehlert sponsored a bill in 1990 that put added pressure on hotels and motels to install sprinklers and smoke detectors by steering federal business from those that lacked the fire safety equipment. While the bill ultimately passed with broad support from the hotel-motel industry, fire safety officials and others, it endured a long and obstacle-ridden path of negotiation and compromise to get there.

When the Science Committee organized under new chairman George E. Brown Jr. for the 102nd Congress, Boehlert took the ranking spot on the Investigations and Oversight Subcommittee.

At Home: During Boehlert's early years in the House, his moderate voting record vexed some of the more conservative Republican elements in the 25th. In 1986, they put forward music professor Robert S. Barstow, who was also the Conservative Party candidate, to challenge Boehlert in the GOP primary.

But Boehlert won renomination by a 2-to-1 margin, and his subsequent victory that November with nearly 70 percent of the vote appeared to settle the issue for Republicans and Democrats alike. He was unopposed for reelection in 1988, and faced only a Liberal Party candidate in 1990, when he won with 84 percent of the vote.

This security was hard-won for Boehlert, a longtime congressional aide whose House ambitions were deferred for a decade after an initial defeat in 1972. That year, Boehlert had hoped to succeed his boss, retiring GOP Rep. Alexander Pirnie, but lost to Donald J. Mitchell in a Republican primary.

Boehlert swallowed his disappointment and went to work for Mitchell. In 1977, he left Washington to run Mitchell's Utica office, which put him in the right place when the Oneida County executive position opened up. He held that job from 1979 to 1982.

By 1982, Mitchell was ready to retire. Boehlert was driving along an Interstate highway in Oneida County when he heard the news. He pulled into a rest stop, called a radio station and announced his candidacy.

As county executive he had earned high marks from labor unions, and was one of only two New York state Republicans to win the state AFL-CIO's endorsement in the 1982 elections. Lining up Republican support in each of the 25th's nine counties, he won the primary comfortably.

In November, Boehlert had a huge organizational and financial advantage over his Democratic foe, dairy farmer Anita Maxwell, who had lost badly to Mitchell in 1976. Maxwell attacked Boehlert for overseeing a county budget deficit that forced consideration of a sales tax for the first time. But Boehlert brushed aside the criticism, and made no issue of the fact that Maxwell's residence was outside the district. He won with 56 percent.

Committees

Public Works & Transportation (6th of 21 Republicans)
Aviation; Economic Development; Surface Transportation

Science, Space & Technology (3rd of 19 Republicans)
Investigations & Oversight (ranking); Science

Select Aging (6th of 27 Republicans)
Retirement, Income & Employment (ranking)

Elections

1990 General		
Sherwood Boehlert (R)	91,348	(84%)
William L. Griffen (L)	17,481	(16%)
1988 General		
Sherwood Boehlert (R)	130,122	(100%)

Previous Winning Percentages: **1986** (69%) **1984** (73%) **1982** (56%)

District Vote For President

	1988	1984	1980	1976
D	94,654 (45%)	79,242 (37%)	79,689 (39%)	87,132 (42%)
R	114,280 (54%)	136,248 (63%)	105,701 (51%)	120,009 (58%)
I			17,027 (8%)	

Campaign Finance

	Receipts	Receipts from PACs	Expend-itures
1990			
Boehlert (R)	$303,746	$130,950 (43%)	$272,533
Griffen (L)	$12,882	0	$10,577
1988			
Boehlert (R)	$235,512	$90,173 (38%)	$145,883

Key Votes

1991	
Authorize use of force against Iraq	Y
1990	
Support constitutional amendment on flag desecration	Y
Pass family and medical leave bill over Bush veto	Y
Reduce SDI funding	N
Allow abortions in overseas military facilities	Y
Approve budget summit plan for spending and taxing	Y
Approve civil rights bill	Y
1989	
Halt production of B-2 stealth bomber at 13 planes	N
Oppose capital gains tax cut	N
Approve federal abortion funding in rape or incest cases	Y
Approve pay raise and revision of ethics rules	Y
Pass Democratic minimum wage plan over Bush veto	Y

Voting Studies

	Presidential Support		Party Unity		Conservative Coalition	
Year	**S**	**O**	**S**	**O**	**S**	**O**
1990	40	60	47	52	61	39
1989	51	47	46	51	44	56
1988	37	59	58	40	58	37
1987	37	60	46	49	65	35
1986	46	54	53	45	66	32
1985	41	59	54	44	56	44
1984	58	39	38	59	61	37
1983	52	43	34	61	49	47

Interest Group Ratings

Year	ADA	ACU	AFL-CIO	CCUS
1990	61	33	50	50
1989	65	43	75	70
1988	65	24	86	64
1987	60	9	69	67
1986	50	41	93	56
1985	45	52	65	57
1984	65	25	62	47
1983	45	30	47	55

26 David O'B. Martin (R)

Of Canton — Elected 1980

Born: April 26, 1944, St. Lawrence County, N.Y.
Education: U. of Notre Dame, B.B.A. 1966; Albany Law School, J.D. 1973.
Military Service: Marine Corps, 1966-70.
Occupation: Lawyer.
Family: Wife, DeeAnn Hedlund; three children.
Religion: Roman Catholic.
Political Career: St. Lawrence County Legislature, 1974-77; N.Y. Assembly, 1977-81.
Capitol Office: 442 Cannon Bldg. 20515; 225-4611.

In Washington: A Phantom jet aviator during the Vietnam War, Martin still lives by the Marine Corps motto *semper fidelis*. From his post on the Armed Services Committee, he faithfully defends the Marine Corps position in budget debates and keeps his eye trained on finding ways for his economically struggling district to benefit from Pentagon spending.

In the 102nd Congress, Martin will have a chance to broaden his scope beyond defense policy and contract procurement: He is a new member of the Intelligence Committee.

Now in his sixth term, Martin is approaching the GOP's upper tier on Armed Services, and he is regarded as one of the party's steady and solid contributors on the panel. But he is his own man: In 1989, he was one of just three Republicans to oppose Defense Secretary Cheney's plan to cancel the Marine Corps' Osprey aircraft and the Navy's F-14D fighter — a cut endorsed by Democratic Chairman Les Aspin . "Talk to experts: the people flying them," Martin urged. The committee ultimately restored some funding for both programs.

The following year, Martin worked with the administration, offering an amendment to restore funding to relocate a Air Force fighter wing to a proposed new base in Crotone, Italy.

Committee Democrats who wanted NATO to pick up a larger share of the facility's cost defeated one Martin amendment on a party-line vote. He tried again when the 1991 Defense Authorization came before the full House, but it too was rejected on a largely partisan vote.

Martin's most determined congressional effort involved convincing the Army to locate a new light infantry division at Fort Drum, in the 26th District city of Watertown. He launched a personal lobbying campaign to land the prize in the fall of 1984, and it paid off early the next year, when the Department of the Army announced activation of the 10th Mountain Division at Fort Drum. As the ranking GOP member of the Military Installations Subcommittee, he helped secure $1.3 billion to construct new facilities for some 25,000 soldiers, family members and civilian employees now on the base.

On the Readiness Subcommittee, Martin places high priority on his work on the Morale, Welfare and Recreation panel, where he focuses on improving the quality of life of military personnel.

Also active on veterans' issues, Martin was involved in the negotiations over constructing the Vietnam Veterans Memorial, dedicated in Washington, D.C., in 1982. He was one of several members selected to represent the House during a ceremony to inter the remains of the Unknown Soldier of the war in Vietnam.

The St. Lawrence Seaway, headquartered in the 26th District, also is a Martin concern. During the 97th Congress, he argued strongly on behalf of a measure aimed at keeping down costs for its users. In the mid-1980s, Martin worked with Michigan Rep. David E. Bonior to block efforts to allow winter navigation of the seaway. They successfully argued that extending the navigation season into the frozen winter months could lead to nautical disasters and environmental damage.

At Home: Martin's quiet conservatism has made him a political force in New York's mainly rural North Country. He has never received less than 71 percent of the vote for reelection; in 1986 and 1990, he ran unopposed.

After returning from Vietnam and graduating from law school, Martin entered politics in 1973 at the county level. In 1976 he moved on to the state Assembly. A party regular, Martin had the support of six of the district's seven county GOP chairmen in his 1980 bid for the nomination to succeed retiring eight-term Republican Rep. Robert C. McEwen.

Martin defeated a well-known Democrat for the House seat — former New York Lt. Gov. Mary Anne Krupsak. Krupsak moved into the 26th District to run, but could not break the hold the Republican organization has there. Martin won handily and has had no trouble since.

New York 26

North — Plattsburgh; Watertown

Democrats competing for the 26th must feel a little fatalistic about their task. Residents of this sparsely populated region have not deserted the GOP column in a single House election in this century. Among presidential candidates, President Reagan won 67 percent here in 1984; George Bush took 55 percent in 1988.

Bounded by Canada to the north and the Adirondacks to the east, the 26th is the state's largest House district. While the district is dotted with such small cities as Watertown, Massena and Plattsburgh, its best-known location is the village of Lake Placid, which hosted the 1932 and 1980 Winter Olympics.

Though the district contains some of the most economically depressed regions in the state outside New York City — location and terrain make it difficult to attract large-scale industry — the rural 26th is solidly Republican.

The 26th's landmark economic event of the 1980s — the basing of an Army light infantry division at huge Fort Drum near Watertown — has given the district an even more conservative tilt. The Army undertook a $1.3 billion expansion of Fort Drum during the decade. The 10,000 soldiers stationed here support 14,000 dependents. But the Strategic Air Command base in Plattsburgh (Clinton County), with an impact of about $178 million on the county economy, is slated for job cuts under the military base-closure plan enacted in 1989.

The St. Lawrence Seaway helps the North Country's economy. Billions of dollars' worth of minerals and manufactured goods move through its locks yearly.

In the 26th's rural counties, Yankee dairy farmers maintain their Republican heritage. Leavening the district's conservative bent is an environmental consciousness brought on by the threat acid rain poses to fish in the Adirondack lakes.

Population: 516,196. White 506,428 (98%), Black 3,665 (1%), Other 4,564 (1%). Spanish origin 3,439 (1%). 18 and over 364,170 (71%), 65 and over 62,928 (12%). Median age: 29.

Committees

Armed Services (7th of 22 Republicans)
Military Installations & Facilities (ranking); Procurement & Military Nuclear Systems

Select Intelligence (6th of 7 Republicans)
Program & Budget Authorization

Elections

1990 General		
David O'B. Martin (R)	97,340	(100%)
1988 General		
David O'B. Martin (R)	131,043	(75%)
Donald R. Ravenscroft (D)	43,585	(25%)

Previous Winning Percentages: **1986** (100%) **1984** (71%) **1982** (72%) **1980** (64%)

District Vote For President

	1988		1984		1980		1976	
D	87,213	(44%)	67,605	(33%)	79,352	(43%)	62,609	(36%)
R	109,749	(55%)	140,016	(67%)	91,909	(49%)	103,830	(59%)
I					13,212	(7%)		

Campaign Finance

	Receipts	Receipts from PACs		Expend-itures
1990				
Martin (R)	$74,891	$52,050	(70%)	$59,112
1988				
Martin (R)	$133,256	$84,316	(63%)	$120,423
Ravenscroft (D)	$11,348	0		$10,635

Key Votes

1991	
Authorize use of force against Iraq	Y
1990	
Support constitutional amendment on flag desecration	Y
Pass family and medical leave bill over Bush veto	Y
Reduce SDI funding	N
Allow abortions in overseas military facilities	N
Approve budget summit plan for spending and taxing	Y
Approve civil rights bill	N
1989	
Halt production of B-2 stealth bomber at 13 planes	N
Oppose capital gains tax cut	N
Approve federal abortion funding in rape or incest cases	N
Approve pay raise and revision of ethics rules	Y
Pass Democratic minimum wage plan over Bush veto	N

Voting Studies

	Presidential Support		Party Unity		Conservative Coalition	
Year	**S**	**O**	**S**	**O**	**S**	**O**
1990	60	39	72	22	85	13
1989	71 †	22 †	70 †	26 †	95 †	3 †
1988	45	47	66	28	84	8
1987	54 †	39 †	61 †	30 †	86 †	12 †
1986	53	41	56 †	34 †	86	8
1985	59	40	66	26	75	18
1984	54	38	58	28	81	10
1983	73	23	72	18	88	11
1982	62	27	77	19	88	7
1981	63	25	80	8	75	7

† Not eligible for all recorded votes.

Interest Group Ratings

Year	ADA	ACU	AFL-CIO	CCUS
1990	28	63	33	64
1989	5	81	17	89
1988	25	68	64	79
1987	20	64	38	57
1986	15	74	42	79
1985	15	71	47	71
1984	20	57	23	85
1983	0	83	18	75
1982	15	67	22	65
1981	5	100	13	88

27 James T. Walsh (R)

Of Syracuse — Elected 1988

Born: June 19, 1947, Syracuse, N.Y.
Education: Saint Bonaventure U., B.A. 1970.
Occupation: Marketing executive; social worker.
Family: Wife, DeDe Ryan; three children.
Religion: Roman Catholic.
Political Career: Syracuse Common Council, 1979-89, president, 1985-89; sought Republican nomination for Onondaga County executive, 1987.
Capitol Office: 1238 Longworth Bldg. 20515; 225-3701.

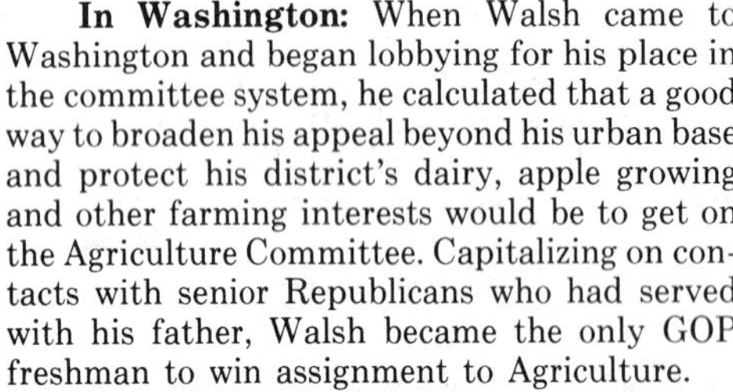

In Washington: When Walsh came to Washington and began lobbying for his place in the committee system, he calculated that a good way to broaden his appeal beyond his urban base and protect his district's dairy, apple growing and other farming interests would be to get on the Agriculture Committee. Capitalizing on contacts with senior Republicans who had served with his father, Walsh became the only GOP freshman to win assignment to Agriculture.

As the panel deliberated on the 1990 farm bill, Walsh showed a knack for gauging when his input would be helpful, and when he would be best-served by listening to his elders. On the House floor, he offered an amendment that combined his dairy interests with his concern for a balanced budget. The aim of Walsh's proposal was to reduce federal payouts to dairy farmers while providing them with the income security derived from operating in a tighter market, one without surpluses. Walsh's amendment was adopted by the House, but was dropped in a House-Senate conference.

However, Walsh was successful in his proposal to establish a clearinghouse for national data on farm safety, which he said would facilitate lower insurance rates for farmers.

On the House Administration Committee, Walsh drew on his background as a Nynex telephone executive in pushing for implementation of a new telephone system that established dedicated lines for members to transfer information electronically between Washington and their districts.

Walsh takes his share of conservative stands — he opposes abortion and supports a constitutional ban on flag desecration, for instance — but he can diverge from the party line on issues affecting Syracuse's large blue-collar population. In 1989, he voted to override President Bush's veto of a Democratic-backed bill increasing the minimum wage. Overall, Walsh votes with the majority of his party a little more than half the time.

At Home: The retirement of a House incumbent is often a source of worry for his party's strategists. But Republican officials were hardly unhappy in 1988 when Walsh, a young veteran of local politics, supplanted retiring Rep. George C. Wortley on the GOP line.

A Reaganite widely viewed as too conservative for the 27th, Wortley looked likely to face a 1988 rematch with Democrat Rosemary S. Pooler, whom he barely defeated in 1986. But his replacement by Walsh dramatically changed the campaign's chemistry.

An advocate of urban programs and a former Peace Corps volunteer, Walsh had a centrist profile consistent with the electorate in the 27th. But his background as a Nynex executive reassured Syracuse's mainly Republican business community.

Unlike Wortley, a suburban newspaper publisher, Walsh also had a strong political heritage in Syracuse. His father, William F. Walsh, was a former House member (1973-79) who had also served as mayor. The younger Walsh served 11 years on the Syracuse City Council, the last two as its president. In 1987, he lost a GOP primary for Onondaga County executive by a razor-thin margin.

Walsh's strong base in Syracuse cut off Pooler's main avenue for success. Democrats must do well in the city in order to compete in the 27th. Pooler — a former state public service commissioner and outspoken consumer advocate — did so in her 1986 near-upset.

Walsh made his pitch to conservatives by describing Pooler as an extreme liberal and an adversary of business. But he also appealed to moderate voters, defending the federal Urban Development Action Grants program and claiming credit for obtaining a state "economic development zone" for Syracuse.

As Walsh praised the Reagan-Bush administration for a decline in local unemployment during the 1980s, Pooler said the statistics masked an attrition of blue-collar jobs. Voters voters apparently favored Walsh's optimistic view. He took 57 percent of the vote.

Democrats put little effort into the 1990 campaign against Walsh. Against their challenger, 30-year-old political consultant Peggy L. Murray, Walsh won with 63 percent.

New York 27

Central — Syracuse

Despite its industrial heritage and large blue-collar population, Syracuse was for years a solid Republican bastion. The electorate's GOP leanings, spurred by the typical upstate antipathy toward Democratic New York City, were reinforced by a ward-based Republican organization that mirrored the Democratic machines in other Northern cities.

However, Syracuse Democrats saw their party's themes on jobs programs and trade protection gain popularity in recent years, as the disappearance of jobs in the chemical, steel and other industries sent the city's population tumbling. Democrats have now controlled the mayor's office for two decades.

Republicans continue to dominate, however, in the Onondaga County suburbs and outlying rural areas, enabling GOP candidates for the House and for president to win the 27th District as a whole. Walsh, boosted by his personal strength within Syracuse, has swept Onondaga and Madison counties in his two House elections; George Bush also won both in 1988.

In the 1970s, Syracuse was divided between two congressional districts. But with the city's population declining, the Legislature in 1982 reunited the city in one constituency. Once the nation's leading supplier of salt, Syracuse still has a base in heavy industry and electronics. But the clear skies over the once-sooty downtown area symbolize a conversion to a service economy.

Syracuse has a diverse ethnicity. Italians, blacks, Poles, Jews, Lithuanians and Irish traditionally have had their own well-defined neighborhoods, although gentrification of sections such as Tipperary Hill, the old Irish enclave, has blurred distinctions. The eastern part of town, the site of Syracuse University (16,000 students), is white-collar and Republican.

Places such as Baldwinsville and Skaneateles set the Republican tone in the Onondaga County suburbs. Democrats do better in industrial Salina, which was named during salt's 19th-century heyday.

The remaining 10 percent of the vote comes from solid Republican, bucolic Madison County, all but a sliver of which lies within the 27th. The only hint of a Democratic vote is in Hamilton, home of Colgate University.

Population: 516,364. White 476,544 (92%), Black 30,457 (6%), Other 6,324 (1%). Spanish origin 5,000 (1%). 18 and over 372,785 (72%), 65 and over 55,655 (11%). Median age: 29.

Committees

Agriculture (12th of 18 Republicans)
Department Operations, Research & Foreign Agriculture; Livestock, Dairy & Poultry

House Administration (6th of 9 Republicans)
Office Systems (ranking); Elections; Campaign Finance Reform

Select Children, Youth & Families (6th of 14 Republicans)

Elections

1990 General		
James T. Walsh (R)	95,220	(63%)
Peggy L. Murray (D)	52,438	(35%)
1988 General		
James T. Walsh (R)	124,928	(57%)
Rosemary S. Pooler (D)	90,854	(42%)

District Vote For President

	1988	1984	1980	1976
D	103,274 (47%)	88,234 (39%)	78,189 (37%)	83,172 (39%)
R	116,123 (53%)	135,976 (60%)	107,128 (51%)	128,045 (60%)
I			20,213 (10%)	

Campaign Finance

	Receipts	Receipts from PACs	Expend-itures
1990			
Walsh (R)	$365,536	$140,186 (38%)	$340,553
Murray (D)	$11,934	$2,200 (18%)	$11,779
1988			
Walsh (R)	$610,935	$202,620 (33%)	$594,965
Pooler (D)	$643,565	$313,269 (49%)	$647,959

Key Votes

1991	
Authorize use of force against Iraq	Y
1990	
Support constitutional amendment on flag desecration	Y
Pass family and medical leave bill over Bush veto	N
Reduce SDI funding	N
Allow abortions in overseas military facilities	N
Approve budget summit plan for spending and taxing	N
Approve civil rights bill	Y
1989	
Halt production of B-2 stealth bomber at 13 planes	N
Oppose capital gains tax cut	N
Approve federal abortion funding in rape or incest cases	N
Approve pay raise and revision of ethics rules	Y
Pass Democratic minimum wage plan over Bush veto	Y

Voting Studies

	Presidential Support		Party Unity		Conservative Coalition	
Year	S	O	S	O	S	O
1990	44	54	54	41	74	24
1989	69	30	57	42	85	12

Interest Group Ratings

Year	ADA	ACU	AFL-CIO	CCUS
1990	44	58	33	62
1989	35	64	33	80

28 Matthew F. McHugh (D)

Of Ithaca — Elected 1974

Born: Dec. 6, 1938, Philadelphia, Pa.

Education: Mount St. Mary's College, B.S. 1960; Villanova U., J.D. 1963.

Occupation: Lawyer.

Family: Wife, Eileen Alanna Higgins; three children.

Religion: Roman Catholic.

Political Career: Tompkins County district attorney, 1969-72.

Capitol Office: 2335 Rayburn Bldg. 20515; 225-6335.

In Washington: McHugh is one of those rare members of whom colleagues like to say, he doesn't have an enemy in the House. He has capitalized on that popularity to carve out an influential role for himself, becoming in effect politically bilingual: His first language is that of a dedicated liberal, but McHugh also can speak as a trusted pragmatist to those of different ideological tongues.

He is quiet, courteous and respected on both sides of the aisle for his intellectual and personal integrity. An unflappable negotiator, he often is singled out to be the Appropriations Committee's emissary when the panel needs to settle jurisdictional or procedural tiffs with other committees or with Republicans.

The reservoir of good will he enjoys has not brought McHugh a formal leadership post, a personal goal of his. But he is a valued leadership ally. When the 1990 budget-summit agreement was on the table, Democratic leaders recruited McHugh to help count votes, hoping his support would give the agreement credibility among skeptical liberals. But McHugh is more pragmatic and loyal than many liberals, who were skeptical of the leadership promise that important details could change when the actual spending cuts and tax increases were enacted. Opposition from the Democratic left and the GOP right doomed the summit agreement.

As a reward for his labors, McHugh serves on the Democratic Steering and Policy Committee, a prestige party panel that makes committee assignments for Democratic members. His 1991 assignment to the ethics panel is another sign of leadership respect for his judgment and institutional loyalty.

During the scandal-marred 101st Congress, McHugh peripherally dealt with ethics questions. He was one of roughly a dozen influential Democrats who met during the investigation of Speaker Jim Wright to develop a damage control strategy. Later in 1989, he was one of three Democrats to call for an investigation of Illinois Rep. Gus Savage, who was implicated by news accounts in a sexual harassment dispute.

A former district attorney who proudly notes that he is also a member of his local chapter of the American Civil Liberties Union, McHugh in early 1991 echoed the cautious approach for which the ethics committee is noted: "We have to be careful not to go on witch hunts just because the political climate is negative."

McHugh is best known, however, as a central figure on foreign policy questions. A member of the Appropriations Subcommittee on Foreign Operations, he was also a member of the Intelligence panel from 1984 through 1990.

An articulate advocate for a strong congressional role in foreign policy, McHugh has supported economic and humanitarian foreign aid over military assistance to allies and opposed military intervention in Central America. These larger issues place him shoulder to shoulder with his close friend David R. Obey of Wisconsin, chairman of the Foreign Operations Subcommittee. But on the details of legislating, McHugh is neither as partisan nor as aggressive as Obey, and as a result, he often plays the role of mediator.

McHugh shares fellow Democrats' willingness to use the power of the purse to challenge administration policies, but he also warns against pushing too far. On Foreign Operations, he often describes Democratic efforts as "the best we could get." As chairman of the Intelligence Subcommittee on Legislation in 1990, McHugh helped draft language to strengthen the reporting requirements for covert activities, but he also repeatedly warned members not to tamper with the bill because of the president's veto threat.

McHugh is philosophical about the limits of congressional reach in foreign policy. "The president has much more of an opportunity to take the initiative on foreign policy than Congress," he says. "We react more than we can initiate."

As fiscal pressures have made it more difficult to sell foreign aid expenditures to the American public, McHugh called on the administration to do its part to rally support in 1990.

New York 28

Southern Tier — Binghamton; Ithaca

The elongated 28th reaches from high above Cayuga's waters to high above those of the Hudson. Made up mainly of small cities and rural areas, the district maintains a Republican lean. But pockets of industry and academia have helped Democrat McHugh become a fixture; popular statewide Democrats such as Sen. Daniel Patrick Moynihan and Gov. Mario M. Cuomo also win easily here.

Broome County, which includes the "Triple Cities" of Binghamton, Johnson City and Endicott, provides nearly 45 percent of the district vote. Binghamton — by far the 28th's largest city with 53,000 residents — is industrial but politically marginal. This is the area in which Thomas J. Watson located his first IBM plant, and it still reflects some of the corporate paternalism the Watson family practiced for generations.

Conservative working-class voters, many of them Italian, can join with white-collar technicians and professionals to form a potent bloc for the GOP. Binghamton was represented for years by state Senate Majority Leader Warren Anderson, a Republican who retired in 1989. However, Democrats win here on occasion: Michael S. Dukakis edged out George Bush in Broome County in 1988 by a little over 500 votes.

The northwest corner of the 28th takes in a portion of Tompkins County, McHugh's political base and site of Cornell University and Ithaca College. Cornell dominates the picturesque city of Ithaca economically and politically. The Ivy League school, sitting on a hill overlooking Lake Cayuga, keeps the city Democratic and relatively liberal.

The heavily Jewish parts of Sullivan County, well-known for Grossinger's and other Catskill resort hotels, also lean to the Democrats.

Ulster County, at the district's eastern end, generally provides a powerful Republican counterbalance. The county, which contributes the district's second-largest bloc of votes, went 57 percent for Bush in 1988. There are, however, some Democratic votes in Kingston, a textile city of 24,000 people.

The best-known site in Ulster County is an open field in the village of Bethel. It was here that the famous rock festival, named after the nearby artists' colony in Woodstock, was held in 1969.

Population: 516,402. White 492,630 (95%), Black 14,330 (3%), Other 5,070 (1%). Spanish origin 9,240 (2%). 18 and over 382,338 (74%), 65 and over 63,575 (12%). Median age: 30.

"There's a feeling in the country that foreign aid is not well spent," he said. "We need to explain, and the president especially needs to explain, what it is we are doing with these foreign aid dollars and why they are important."

McHugh is also an ardent supporter of the 1973 War Powers Resolution, which requires presidents to consult Congress when U.S. forces are committed to hostile areas. Opposed by every administration since its enactment, the law has become a lightning rod for the two branches' longstanding debate over their shared constitutional powers to declare and fight wars. "I really believe that the War Powers act is not just Congress stamping its feet, but that it makes long-term sense," McHugh says. He maintains that presidential policies backed by Congress rest on more secure political footing.

Early in 1991, McHugh was among those urging Democratic leaders to accept President Bush's challenge for a quick up-or-down vote on the use of force in the Persian Gulf. If members failed to act, he said, "a lot of people would say that Congress hasn't done its job — again." McHugh was among the majority of Democrats who opposed the use of force, favoring continued economic sanctions.

During the Reagan years, he lamented the limitations of the Intelligence Committee when it was divulged that the administration secretly had sold arms to Iran and that proceeds had gone to the contras, all at a time when U.S. military aid to the rebels was banned. "If you have an administration that is determined to violate the law," he said, "it's difficult to do oversight."

A longtime supporter of Israel whose office walls are lined with plaques from the United Jewish Appeal and other pro-Israel groups, McHugh in recent years has stepped out of the crowd to voice gentle criticism of Israel. He publicly protested when it was discovered that American Jonathan Jay Pollard had spied on the United States for Israel. Then, in early 1989, he urged Israeli leaders to reverse stance and negotiate directly with the Palestine Liberation Organization. Representing a significant number of Jews, McHugh acknowledged the political risk of his statement, but added that even Israel's supporters "don't have to accept every policy position the Israeli government takes."

A member of the Select Committee on Children, McHugh advocates international nutrition and preventive health programs to decrease infant mortality. He pursues these issues domestically as a member of the Appropriations Subcommittee on Agriculture, where he is a reliable vote for efforts to increase funding for nutrition assistance programs, particularly the WIC program, designed to aid pregnant women, infants and young children.

Beyond McHugh's personal reserve lies a reservoir of ambition. To get on Appropriations in 1978, he had to win the support of his state's New York City-dominated Democratic delegation for a seat that had belonged to Manhattan's former representative (and later mayor), Edward I. Koch. But McHugh campaigned assiduously and defeated a candidate from the city, James H. Scheuer, 14-11, drawing several city votes. New York Democrats backed McHugh again in late 1985, choosing him over Samuel S. Stratton and Gary L. Ackerman for the Steering and Policy Committee.

He was less successful in 1980, when he tried to become chairman of the House Democratic Caucus. The other candidates, Gillis W. Long of Louisiana and Charlie Rose of North Carolina, were both Southerners, and McHugh saw an opening for a Northern liberal. But he started late, and in challenging Long, he was up against one of the most popular members. McHugh finished a distant third, with 41 votes, to 146 for Long and 53 for Rose. He considered trying again for the caucus post when the 101st Congress was getting organized, but was dissuaded by the thought of a long campaign and by the early lead of William H. Gray III of Pennsylvania.

In the meantime, however, McHugh did serve in his first leadership position, as chairman of the Democratic Study Group (DSG), the organization of liberal and moderate Democrats, during the 98th Congress. He won unopposed in late 1982. Under his leadership in 1984, the DSG offered an alternative budget to the House Budget Committee's product. It would have reduced the federal deficit by about $260 billion in three years, chiefly by freezing defense spending at the inflation rate and increasing taxes substantially. The draft's appeal beyond liberal Democrats was limited, but it still drew 132 votes on the floor.

In early 1987, McHugh played a bit of uncharacteristic hardball in helping Armed Services Committee Chairman Les Aspin of Wisconsin withstand a near-successful coup by popular conservative Marvin Leath of Texas. Aspin's base among liberals had eroded badly due to his support for the MX missile and contra aid, but McHugh joined with Don Edwards of California for a liberal counterattack. The two men circulated a letter documenting Leath's conservative voting record in detail, and concluding that the Texan "has made a career of voting against his party." It broke Leath's momentum, and Aspin was re-elected on a third ballot.

At Home: Given his strong popularity at the polls, only those with long political memories recall that McHugh's 1974 victory made him the first Democrat to represent the Binghamton area in this century. He succeeded a popular retiring Republican, Howard W. Robison, whose moderate tradition McHugh promised to carry on. He was helped in that stance by the hard-line conservative campaign of his Republican opponent, Binghamton Mayor Alfred Libous.

McHugh's security in the former Republican bastion was launched by a series of campaigns against flawed Republican challengers. In 1978 and 1980, businessman Neil Tyler Wallace demonstrated an abrasive personality that cost him votes.

In 1982 lawyer David F. Crowley seemed a bright and formidable challenger until he committed a series of gaffes that doomed his candidacy. For instance, in an attempt to show how military spending could be cut, Crowley suggested that the military's LAMPS III helicopter be scrapped. It turned out that a plant in the 28th District made parts for the aircraft. McHugh won comfortably.

That track record did not dim Republicans' optimism about their chances against McHugh in 1984. Their candidate, former Cornell University administrator Constance E. Cook, had built up her name recognition as a member of the New York state Assembly for a decade until her retirement in 1976. Cook also benefited from a special interest the national GOP took in female congressional candidates that year.

Unlike Crowley, Cook avoided making any glaring errors. But the 65-year-old Republican still had formidable problems in trying to blaze a comeback trail. When she expressed reservations about the Reagan administration's cuts in social welfare programs and scored McHugh for opposing federal funding for abortions, her stands did not sit well with many of the district's conservatives. Further, Cook negotiated a campaign spending limit with McHugh that wound up impairing her ability to spread her name outside of her Ithaca base.

Cook got a boost in mid-September, when President Ronald Reagan spoke in the district on her behalf. But even that did not help her generate sufficient momentum. McHugh, who openly attacked Reagan's economic policies and embraced Walter F. Mondale's call for a tax increase, took 57 percent of the vote.

McHugh has faced absolutely no strain since. After he won by a 2-to-1 margin in 1986, district Republicans put up no opposition in

1988. In 1990, McHugh faced a Republican challenger, lawyer Seymour Krieger, but won with a solid 65 percent.

Before running for Congress, McHugh served as district attorney of Tompkins County, at the far western edge of the sprawling district. In that office, he was popular with the Cornell University community in Ithaca. He organized a local drug treatment facility and demanded peaceful handling of student protests.

Committees

Appropriations (15th of 37 Democrats)
Foreign Operations, Export Financing & Related Programs; Rural Development, Agriculture & Related Agencies

Select Children, Youth & Families (4th of 22 Democrats)

Standards of Official Conduct (2nd of 7 Democrats)

Elections

1990 General		
Matthew F. McHugh (D)	97,815	(65%)
Seymour Krieger (R)	53,077	(35%)
1988 General		
Matthew F. McHugh (D)	141,976	(93%)
Mary C. Dixon (RTL)	10,395	(7%)

Previous Winning Percentages: **1986** (68%) **1984** (57%) **1982** (56%) **1980** (55%) **1978** (56%) **1976** (67%) **1974** (53%)

District Vote For President

	1988	1984	1980	1976
D	108,157 (48%)	94,304 (39%)	83,039 (38%)	110,702 (48%)
R	118,542 (52%)	147,818 (61%)	108,287 (49%)	121,263 (52%)
I			24,117 (11%)	

Campaign Finance

	Receipts	Receipts from PACs		Expend-itures
1990				
McHugh (D)	$227,716	$121,815	(53%)	$200,047
Krieger (R)	$24,293	0		$23,766
1988				
McHugh (D)	$276,595	$129,633	(47%)	$172,905

Key Votes

1991	
Authorize use of force against Iraq	N
1990	
Support constitutional amendment on flag desecration	N
Pass family and medical leave bill over Bush veto	Y
Reduce SDI funding	Y
Allow abortions in overseas military facilities	Y
Approve budget summit plan for spending and taxing	Y
Approve civil rights bill	Y
1989	
Halt production of B-2 stealth bomber at 13 planes	N
Oppose capital gains tax cut	Y
Approve federal abortion funding in rape or incest cases	N
Approve pay raise and revision of ethics rules	Y
Pass Democratic minimum wage plan over Bush veto	Y

Voting Studies

	Presidential Support		Party Unity		Conservative Coalition	
Year	**S**	**O**	**S**	**O**	**S**	**O**
1990	23	77	92	7	26	74
1989	35	64	92	5	27	71
1988	25	70	91	7	21	76
1987	18	78	93	3	14	86
1986	23	76	91	6	18	82
1985	25	73	92	4	11	87
1984	35	62	89	9	24	75
1983	24	76	92	5	12	87
1982	39	53	89	8	19	81
1981	32	68	89	11	19	80

Interest Group Ratings

Year	ADA	ACU	AFL-CIO	CCUS
1990	89	4	92	14
1989	85	0	92	30
1988	95	4	92	46
1987	92	9	88	13
1986	80	9	71	17
1985	85	10	94	18
1984	75	21	38	19
1983	90	9	88	30
1982	100	10	95	23
1981	95	0	73	11

29 Frank Horton (R)

Of Penfield — Elected 1962

Born: Dec. 12, 1919, Cuero, Texas.

Education: Louisiana State U., B.A. 1941; Cornell U., LL.B. 1947.

Military Service: Army, 1941-45.

Occupation: Lawyer.

Family: Wife, Nancy Richmond; two children, two stepchildren.

Religion: Presbyterian.

Political Career: Rochester City Council, 1955-61.

Capitol Office: 2108 Rayburn Bldg. 20515; 225-4916.

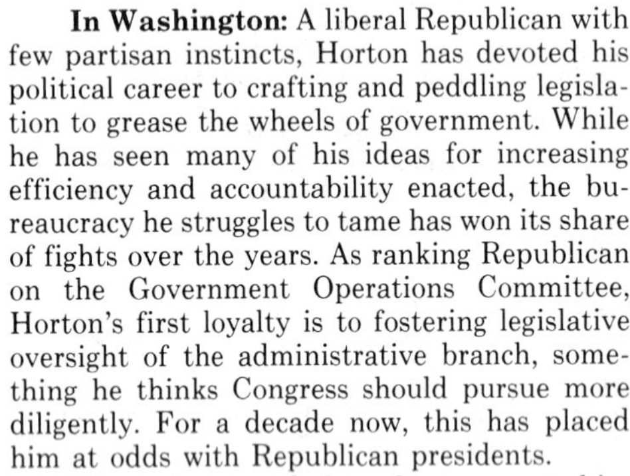

In Washington: A liberal Republican with few partisan instincts, Horton has devoted his political career to crafting and peddling legislation to grease the wheels of government. While he has seen many of his ideas for increasing efficiency and accountability enacted, the bureaucracy he struggles to tame has won its share of fights over the years. As ranking Republican on the Government Operations Committee, Horton's first loyalty is to fostering legislative oversight of the administrative branch, something he thinks Congress should pursue more diligently. For a decade now, this has placed him at odds with Republican presidents.

His voting record alone, however, sets him apart from most Republicans. In seven of Ronald Reagan's eight years in office, Horton voted against a majority of his GOP colleagues on House votes far more often than he voted with them; only in 1981 did his support of Reagan's legislative positions reach 50 percent. George Bush did not fare much better; Horton voted against Bush's stated view half of the time in 1989 and 65 percent of the time in 1990.

Horton's opposition may be consistent, but he is no rabble-rouser. The mild-mannered Republican sometimes uses confrontational rhetoric in press releases to his politically marginal Rochester district, but it is rarely heard in Congress. Some GOP conservatives gripe that he is more liberal than his district demands, but overall, Horton's kindly nature protects him from harsh criticism by the GOP right.

In the 101st Congress, Horton refought two old battles, one on the Whistle Blower Protection Act and the other over the reauthorization of the Paperwork Reduction Act. He won the former, and vows a rematch on the latter.

Horton and Democrat Patricia Schroeder introduced the whistleblower bill in 1987. It was designed to protect federal workers who expose waste and fraud. Congress had proceeded on the assumption that Reagan supported the bill; many members were taken aback by his veto of it. Reagan said he feared workers could "manipulate the process to their advantage," to which Horton responded with uncharacteristic harshness. He called Reagan's veto a "reprehensible act" that was "orchestrated after adjournment of Congress to prevent an override." In 1989, Horton and Schroeder reintroduced the bill, and although the initial veto had come at the urging of Reagan-appointed Attorney General Dick Thornburgh — who continued in office under Bush — negotiations progressed swiftly, and the bill was approved in April 1989.

The 1980 Paperwork Reduction Act is one of Horton's proudest achievements, and the struggle to reauthorize the measure in 1990 was one of his most frustrating endeavors.

Early in the process, Horton helped Government Operations Chairman John Conyers Jr. broker a deal with Richard G. Darman, director of the Office of Management and Budget. Conyers had introduced legislation that sought to curtail severely the power of OMB to review regulations. Horton and the administration opposed the bill. Conyers and Horton worked out a side agreement with Darman whereby Congress would simply reauthorize the old law and OMB would internally adopt some of Conyers' changes. The White House, however, balked, and Darman denied making the agreement. By fall, Conyers, Horton and the White House had worked out another informal agreement, but Senate Democrats were not convinced that the administration would hold up its end of the bargain without a legislative mandate, and the bill died.

The setback, however, may not appear insurmountable to veteran Horton, who has worked on this issue for many years. In 1975, he first steered legislation through Congress to set up a paperwork study commission, and headed the inquiry himself. After two years, 36 reports and 770 recommendations, the commission issued its findings. Citing a "profusion of inconsistent and often conflicting laws, policies and practices," the commission recommended that government policy-makers, including Congress, consider paperwork costs when writing and implementing laws. It suggested consolidating federal forms, writing regulations in understand-

New York 29

West — Part of Rochester

The House representation of divided Rochester is something of a paradox. The working-class and minority neighborhoods of east Rochester, which generally lean Democratic, are represented by 29th District Republican Horton. But the more affluent west Rochester communities, which were thought at the time of the last redistricting to reinforce the neighboring 30th District's GOP tilt, have since 1986 favored Democratic Rep. Louise M. Slaughter.

The inclusion of the more Democratic parts of Rochester in Horton's district does not faze him, since he has one of the most liberal records among House Republicans. In 1990, Rochester and the eastern Monroe County suburbs — which provide about two-fifths of the 29th District vote — only gave the Democratic nominee 26 percent.

The 29th includes the black and Puerto Rican neighborhoods in northeast Rochester, contrasting with the generally suburban and rural character of the rest of the district. Some Eastman Kodak plants, which anchor the city's industrial base, are in this section.

The district also takes in the affluent Republicans who live along East Avenue, which leads out to the suburbs. The suburbs contain a Xerox facility and other high-tech plants that employ engineers who maintain Republican voting habits.

The remainder of the 29th is rural Republican country that stretches from the Lake Ontario shoreline to the fruit orchards of central New York. Oswego County, which contains a State University of New York campus at Oswego, provides the district's second-largest bloc of votes; the county gave George Bush 58 percent in 1988.

Cayuga and Seneca counties, at the heart of the scenic Finger Lakes area, are tourist magnets. These mainly rural counties are generally Republican, but not overwhelmingly so; Cayuga in particular has some Democratic votes in the working-class city of Auburn (population 31,000).

The 29th contains a slice of Oneida County, but not the most populous part; Utica and Rome are in the neighboring 25th District. Some 29th District residents are military personnel who work at Griffiss Air Force Base, also in the 25th.

Population: 515,404. White 483,123 (94%), Black 23,683 (5%), Other 3,933 (1%). Spanish origin 7,774 (2%). 18 and over 365,972 (71%), 65 and over 59,666 (12%). Median age: 30.

able English and creating a new Cabinet agency, a Department of Administration. Horton was able to write some of these recommendations into the 1980 Paperwork Reduction Act. The law set up a central bureau in the Office of Management and Budget to identify unnecessary paperwork.

Horton's other major committee assignment is Post Office and Civil Service, where he is a leading advocate of removing the U.S. Postal Service from the federal budget and thereby insulating it from future budget cuts.

Horton has worked hard over the years to place "inspectors general" in various federal agencies to root out waste. In 1988, he worked on successful legislation to create new inspector general offices in five federal departments and agencies. Four years earlier, he supported moves to add the position to the Treasury and Justice departments. Horton claims these offices, which exist in 18 other federal agencies, have saved more than $120 billion. He first succeeded in securing the appointment of an inspector general to the Pentagon in the 97th Congress, a difficult feat considering fears that classified information might be released.

In his earlier years on Government Operations, Horton was the only Republican to enthusiastically support creation of the Department of Education, and one of just a few to support establishing the Department of Energy. In both cases, he avoided philosophical debates, saying he simply wanted to make government more efficient. During the 100th Congress' consideration of legislation to elevate the Veterans Administration to the Cabinet, Horton was part of the GOP majority that backed the proposal. He said high-level representation was needed to ensure that commitments are carried out.

In 1990, Horton and Conyers co-authored a bill to elevate the Environmental Protection Agency to Cabinet status. The concept had Bush's support, but he objected to provisions that also would have given the new Department of the Environment added clout.

Horton, the dean of the New York delegation, has such a low-key style that few regard him as a dealmaker. But as New York's spokesman on the Republican committee assignment panel, he pulls off some impressive moves, despite his lack of party fealty. The opening of the 99th Congress was one of his best moments. In a year when there were few vacancies on major committees, he managed to get one home-state colleague on Ways and Means and another on Energy and Commerce.

At Home: Although Horton has a low national profile for such a long-tenured member, he is a most familiar figure in upstate New York. His re-election has never been in doubt.

While thousands were leaving upstate New York for the Sun Belt after World War II, Horton — born in Texas and educated in Louisiana — headed north, graduated from Cornell Law School, and settled in Rochester to practice law.

Had he remained in Texas in the 1950s, he would have found it difficult to get far in politics as a Republican. In Rochester, he fit right in. Elected to the Rochester City Council in 1955 to fill an unexpired term, Horton was re-elected in 1957 for a four-year term. During his time on the council he was chairman of its Public Utilities and Special Services Committee. He served until 1961, when he became a casualty of a political sweep by the Democrats. It was the first time the GOP had lost control of the city government in 25 years.

Meanwhile, he had become involved in minor-league baseball. He was president of the Rochester Redwings and executive vice president of the International League from 1959-60.

In 1962 a Rochester-area congressional seat opened up with the illness and retirement of GOP Rep. Jessica Weis, who had been a power in the national Republican Party as New York committeewoman for 20 years. Horton was the consensus choice of the Republican leaders in the district, and became the GOP nominee without a primary. Horton's comfortable win that November set the pattern for his career. A series of redistrictings has taken away some of his Rochester base, but his Democratic opposition has been minimal.

Horton has regularly received two-thirds of the vote or better. His 63 percent tally in 1990 was actually his lowest since 1964, but 12 percent of the vote went to minor-party candidates more conservative than Horton: He defeated Democrat Alton F. Eber by nearly 40 points. In 1976 Horton was arrested for speeding and drunken driving. He pleaded guilty, accepted a punishment of a few days in jail, and weathered the incident without political damage.

Committees

Government Operations (Ranking)
Legislation & National Security (ranking)

Post Office & Civil Service (2nd of 8 Republicans)
Postal Operations & Services (ranking); Human Resources

Elections

1990 General		
Frank Horton (R)	89,105	(63%)
Alton F. Eber (D)	34,835	(25%)
Peter DeMauro (C)	12,599	(9%)
Donald M. Peters (RTL)	4,878	(3%)
1988 General		
Frank Horton (R)	132,608	(69%)
James R. Vogel (D)	51,243	(27%)

Previous Winning Percentages: **1986** (71%) **1984** (70%) **1982** (66%) **1980** (73%) **1978** (87%) **1976** (66%) **1974** (68%) **1972** (72%) **1970** (71%) **1968** (70%) **1966** (67%) **1964** (56%) **1962** (59%)

District Vote For President

	1988	1984	1980	1976
D	99,636 (46%)	82,066 (37%)	83,709 (40%)	77,962 (42%)
R	113,988 (53%)	140,599 (63%)	101,446 (49%)	108,699 (58%)
I			18,552 (9%)	

Campaign Finance

	Receipts	Receipts from PACs		Expend-itures
1990				
Horton (R)	$207,092	$160,040	(77%)	$186,967
1988				
Horton (R)	$163,751	$126,560	(77%)	$130,597
Vogel (D)	$7,478	0		$4,514

Key Votes

1991	
Authorize use of force against Iraq	Y
1990	
Support constitutional amendment on flag desecration	Y
Pass family and medical leave bill over Bush veto	Y
Reduce SDI funding	Y
Allow abortions in overseas military facilities	Y
Approve budget summit plan for spending and taxing	Y
Approve civil rights bill	Y
1989	
Halt production of B-2 stealth bomber at 13 planes	Y
Oppose capital gains tax cut	N
Approve federal abortion funding in rape or incest cases	Y
Approve pay raise and revision of ethics rules	Y
Pass Democratic minimum wage plan over Bush veto	Y

Voting Studies

	Presidential Support		Party Unity		Conservative Coalition	
Year	**S**	**O**	**S**	**O**	**S**	**O**
1990	32	65	27	66	56	39
1989	50	49	25	70	49	46
1988	30	58	28	62	55	34
1987	35	59	27	64	74	26
1986	27	67	18	74	48	40
1985	31	68	25	66	51	36
1984	48	45	35	59	68	32
1983	39	56	32	61	43	47
1982	39	47	39	50	55	36
1981	50	34	45	37	37	44

Interest Group Ratings

Year	ADA	ACU	AFL-CIO	CCUS
1990	61	25	83	36
1989	70	29	92	56
1988	65	22	92	50
1987	52	10	69	43
1986	75	10	100	31
1985	50	30	82	35
1984	60	21	69	56
1983	40	32	44	53
1982	50	18	65	35
1981	35	69	53	82

30 Louise M. Slaughter (D)

Of Fairport — Elected 1986

Born: Aug. 14, 1929, Harlan County, Ky.
Education: U. of Kentucky, B.S. 1951, M.S. 1953.
Occupation: Market researcher.
Family: Husband, Robert Slaughter; three children.
Religion: Episcopalian.
Political Career: Monroe County legislator, 1975-79; N.Y. Assembly, 1983-87.
Capitol Office: 1424 Longworth Bldg. 20515; 225-3615.

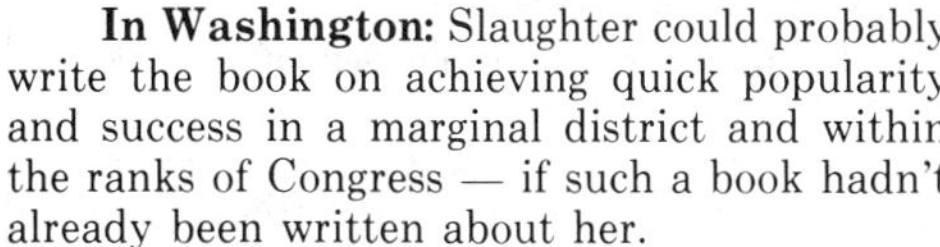

In Washington: Slaughter could probably write the book on achieving quick popularity and success in a marginal district and within the ranks of Congress — if such a book hadn't already been written about her.

Two local political science professors chose the district as a case study for a book on congressional campaigns. The book, published in June 1989, analyzed Slaughter's election to Congress and the reasons for her success.

Slaughter has proven she could go far in the House on the force of her personality alone. But her ability to win and hold a normally Republican district and her record as a liberal Democratic loyalist have continually ingratiated Slaughter with the party leadership.

When House Democrats caucused to organize for the 101st Congress, Slaughter was asked to make nominating speeches for four members of the leadership, including Speaker Thomas S. Foley, then majority leader. Having friends in such high places was of great benefit to Slaughter, who was awarded a high-profile Rules Committee seat early in her second term.

Into her third term, Slaughter was named to the Budget Committee — the lone New York Democrat on the panel — and chair of the Democratic Caucus' Committee on Study, Organization and Review, making her the only woman to hold a top party position in the House. In one of the few defections from her mentors, Slaughter in October 1990 voted against the budget summit agreement, bowing to the conservative nature of her district. Party leaders apparently did not hold it against her as her 1991 committee appointments made clear.

Though slower to achieve concrete legislative goals, Slaughter successfully attached an amendment to a 1990 homeless-assistance measure to reduce barriers preventing homeless children from attending school by providing incentive grants to states.

She also sought to have the president appoint a special envoy to negotiate the release of U.S. hostages still held abroad: Longtime hostage Terry Anderson, allegedly held in Lebanon, is a resident of her district.

At Home: Slaughter's charm, grass-roots organization and fundraising were major factors in her 1986 upset of conservative GOP Rep. Fred J. Eckert and her easy re-elections.

With her liberal views and Southern accent (she moved north from Kentucky in the 1950s), Slaughter has been a rather singular figure in western New York politics since the mid-1970s. She entered public life as a Monroe County legislator and as an assistant to Mario M. Cuomo, then New York's secretary of state.

In 1982, Slaughter upset a GOP state assemblyman. Slaughter's arguments with the state's private power companies earned her support from liberals and labor activists and gave her a base for her 1986 challenge to Eckert.

Although Eckert, a former state legislator, had won the seat in 1984, he was far more conservative than his predecessor, veteran GOP Rep. Barber B. Conable Jr. Backed by Democratic PACs that had targeted Eckert for defeat, Slaughter led him in fundraising with nearly $600,000. She ran TV ads depicting Eckert as a right-wing obstructionist, including one featuring an Eckert imitator slapping the word "NO" on legislation with a huge rubber stamp. Parrying Eckert's efforts to portray her as an ultraliberal, Slaughter won with 51 percent of the vote.

While she quickly solidified her growing popularity, Slaughter's continued fundraising success made her a strong front-runner in 1988.

Her Republican opponent, 33-year-old Monroe County legislator John D. Bouchard, ran a two-pronged campaign, patterning himself after Conable while portraying Slaughter as a puppet of organized labor. But his campaign never jelled; Slaughter won with 57 percent.

District Republicans justifiably held out little hope for unseating Slaughter in 1990, placing their chips instead on the changes redistricting would bring to the district lines after the election.

Slaughter breezed to a third term, defeating Republican lawyer John M. Regan Jr. with 59 percent.

New York 30

West — Part of Rochester; Batavia

Over the years, the Rochester-area districts — including the present 30th — were Republican strongholds. The region's corporate giants — the Eastman Kodak Co. and the Xerox Corp. — spawned a large white-collar managerial class that leaned Republican. The generally moderate GOP leadership seldom antagonized the blue-collar population enough to benefit Democratic candidates. Add in the traditional upstate animosity to Democratic New York City, and the 30th contained the ingredients for Republican dominance.

However, in 1984, conservative hard-liner Fred J. Eckert succeeded Republican Barber B. Conable Jr., a popular centrist. Two years later, voter qualms about Eckert opened the door for Slaughter, who quickly secured the seat for her party.

Voter attitudes shifted quickly after Slaughter took the seat. In 1986, Slaughter had narrowly won on the strength of the urban and suburban vote in west Rochester and its Monroe County environs; Eckert held on in the more rural areas spread across four counties. By 1990, Slaughter was not only winning big in metro Rochester, but also carried the outlying counties.

There is some irony in the recent Democratic upsurge: The redistricting of the early 1980s seemingly made the district more Republican. Rochester was split, and the district's political tone was set by the GOP-minded suburbs along Lake Ontario, such as Greece and Parma. Their normal GOP tendencies were fortified by the addition of Irondequoit, also on Lake Ontario, and Perinton, Pittsford and Mendon, Monroe County suburbs southeast of Rochester, which are largely bedroom communities for middle-management employees of Kodak, Xerox and other firms.

Outside Rochester and its immediate environs, the district is mainly dairy and vegetable farmland that is more reliable for Republicans. But Genesee County harbors industrial Batavia. Through the county flows the Genesee River, one of the few in the United States that flows northward.

Population: 516,819. White 481,183 (93%), Black 25,075 (5%), Other 4,741 (1%). Spanish origin 9,174 (2%). 18 and over 371,098 (72%), 65 and over 54,869 (11%). Median age: 30.

Committees

Budget (21st of 23 Democrats)
Defense, Foreign Policy & Space; Urgent Fiscal Issues

Rules (9th of 9 Democrats)
Rules of the House

Select Aging (26th of 42 Democrats)
Health & Long-Term Care; Human Services; Social Security and Women

Elections

1990 General		
Louise M. Slaughter (D)	97,280	(59%)
John M. Regan Jr. (R)	67,534	(41%)
1988 General		
Louise M. Slaughter (D)	128,364	(57%)
John D. Bouchard (R)	89,126	(39%)

Previous Winning Percentage: **1986** (51%)

District Vote For President

	1988	1984	1980	1976
D	106,373 (45%)	86,561 (37%)	107,324 (45%)	113,013 (44%)
R	127,468 (54%)	146,976 (63%)	106,460 (44%)	143,933 (56%)
I			21,123 (9%)	

Campaign Finance

	Receipts	Receipts from PACs	Expend-itures
1990			
Slaughter (D)	$446,664	$282,817 (63%)	$322,216
Regan (R)	$24,863	0	$24,712
1988			
Slaughter (D)	$882,554	$444,422 (50%)	$953,577
Bouchard (R)	$319,621	$78,448 (25%)	$310,704

Key Votes

1991	
Authorize use of force against Iraq	N
1990	
Support constitutional amendment on flag desecration	Y
Pass family and medical leave bill over Bush veto	N
Reduce SDI funding	N
Allow abortions in overseas military facilities	Y
Approve budget summit plan for spending and taxing	N
Approve civil rights bill	Y
1989	
Halt production of B-2 stealth bomber at 13 planes	Y
Oppose capital gains tax cut	Y
Approve federal abortion funding in rape or incest cases	Y
Approve pay raise and revision of ethics rules	Y
Pass Democratic minimum wage plan over Bush veto	Y

Voting Studies

	Presidential Support		Party Unity		Conservative Coalition	
Year	**S**	**O**	**S**	**O**	**S**	**O**
1990	16	84	94	5	11	89
1989	27	71	93	4	20	80
1988	23	73	92	8	37	61
1987	17	78	83	9	35	60

Interest Group Ratings

Year	ADA	ACU	AFL-CIO	CCUS
1990	94	17	92	29
1989	95	4	100	40
1988	85	8	100	43
1987	76	10	87	29

31 Bill Paxon (R)

Of Amherst — Elected 1988

Born: April 29, 1954, Buffalo, N.Y.
Education: Canisius College, B.A. 1977.
Occupation: Public official.
Family: Single.
Religion: Roman Catholic.
Political Career: Erie County Legislature, 1978-82; N.Y. Assembly, 1983-89.
Capitol Office: 1314 Longworth Bldg. 20515; 225-5265.

In Washington: Paxon's voting record is consistently conservative, and his first-term loyalty (he sided with his party 93 percent of the time in 1990 House votes) helped win him a place in the party structure under Whip Newt Gingrich; in the 102nd Congress, Paxon became one of three assistant deputy whips.

The House successor to Jack F. Kemp, now Housing and Urban Development secretary, Paxon sits on the Banking, Finance and Urban Affairs Committee and has pursued Kemp's enterprise zone initiative. Intended to encourage investment and create jobs in economically depressed areas, the zones provide financial incentives to investors, primarily in the form of tax moratoriums. Paxon cites the state-level success of such zones in pushing for federal use of the concept.

In late 1990, Paxon sought a seat on the high-profile Energy and Commerce Committee, but the seat went to another young GOP conservative, Fred Upton of Michigan. Upton had a one-term seniority edge, and Paxon's bid was also hampered by speculation that he might be the odd man out in western New York when new district lines are drawn for 1992. The state lost three House seats in reapportionment.

But Paxon is doing all he can to keep a seat in Congress. He notes that the suburban Buffalo 31st was the only area district to grow in the 1980s, and he has aggressively raised funds for New York's state Senate Republican Campaign Committee, hoping legislators will protect him in the remap.

At Home: When Kemp stepped aside to run for president in 1988, Paxon was touted as his heir apparent. In December 1987, Kemp described Paxon, a like-minded conservative, as "our next congressman."

Paxon's election was not so predetermined: He weathered a vigorous challenge from Democratic Erie County Clerk David Swarts. In the end, Paxon's decade-long career in office and the district's GOP tilt tipped the scales; Paxon won with 53 percent of the vote.

Although Paxon was 34 years old when elected, he was already a political veteran. The son of an Erie County family court judge, Paxon worked while in college as a state Assembly aide and as an assistant to then-Erie County Executive Edward Regan (the current state comptroller). At age 23, he became the youngest-ever member of the Erie County Legislature.

Paxon was twice re-elected to county office by huge margins, then easily won an open Assembly seat in 1982.

He cut a conservative profile in Albany, promoting efforts to cut state welfare costs and often opposing efforts to expand state regulation. Paxon also gained the ranking position on the Assembly corrections committee; his district included the Attica state prison.

Since Paxon's district encompassed the Erie County suburbs that form the population core of the 31st District, Republicans were confident of his prospects to succeed Kemp.

But Democrats countered with Swarts, who had honed his campaign skills in a futile 1983 challenge to a Republican Erie County executive and in a successful 1986 county clerk bid. He denounced Paxon as an ideologue with a reflexive opposition to business regulation. Paxon called Swarts an "off-the-scale" liberal.

The race was close in Erie County, where Paxon prevailed with just 51 percent of the vote. But he had more breathing room elsewhere, including rural Wyoming County, where he won nearly 70 percent.

Despite Paxon's rather narrow margin, Swarts skipped a rematch in 1990, and Democratic recruiters had a hard time finding a candidate. Part of their problem stemmed from expectations that the oddly shaped 31st would be dismembered in redistricting.

Their eventual nominee, lawyer Kevin P. Gaughan, tried to tie Paxon to the savings and loan scandal, noting his receipt of campaign contributions from banking industry sources just before voting on the 1989 S&L bailout bill. But Paxon brushed off the criticism, and national Democratic officials, who targeted the 31st in 1988, paid it little notice in 1990. Paxon won 56 percent.

New York 31

West — Buffalo Suburbs; Canandaigua

During the years leading up to long-time 31st District Republican Rep. Jack F. Kemp's presidential bid, it was often said that he would have unusual Republican appeal to industrial workers because he was from a Buffalo district. But in reality, Kemp always represented the Erie County suburbs, not the heavily unionized and Democratic city of Buffalo. The redistricting of the early 1980s moved the district to the east, making it even more likely that a 31st District voter would be a banker, not a blue-collar worker.

Still, there are a few working-class towns, such as West Seneca and Hamburg, in the Erie County part of the district, making it a place where Democrats can compete; the three Democratic candidates for statewide office carried the Erie portion of the 31st in 1990, and Paxon carried it only narrowly over his Democratic opponent in his 1988 House bid. But the Republican nature of the more rural counties of the 31st make it, as a whole, a fairly comfortable place for Paxon and other Republican candidates.

Losing Erie County, though, can go a long way toward holding down a Republican's victory margin; 75 percent of the district vote is cast there. It includes Amherst, site of the State University of New York at Buffalo campus and, with about 110,000 residents, easily the district's largest city. The 31st's slice of Erie County also takes in Orchard Park, a small town most notable as the site of Rich Stadium, home of the Buffalo Bills football team on which Kemp once starred.

To the south, the 31st takes in a small, working-class strip of Cattaraugus County. The district then ranges east, absorbing all of rural Wyoming County. This is the most solidly Republican turf in the district. Paxon won the county with almost 70 percent in 1990; George Bush took 64 percent of the vote in the 1988 presidential race.

Completing the eastern flank of the district are large portions of Livingston and Ontario counties. In Ontario County, the 31st takes in a portion of the scenic Finger Lakes region. Republicans have the registration advantage over Democrats in both counties.

Population: 516,271. White 501,526 (97%), Black 6,545 (1%), Other 6,386 (1%). Spanish origin 3,943 (1%). 18 and over 369,104 (72%), 65 and over 56,281 (11%). Median age: 31.

Committees

Banking, Finance & Urban Affairs (12th of 20 Republicans)
Economic Stabilization; Financial Institutions Supervision, Regulation & Insurance; Housing & Community Development

Select Narcotics Abuse & Control (10th of 14 Republicans)

Veterans' Affairs (10th of 13 Republicans)
Housing & Memorial Affairs; Oversight & Investigations

Elections

1990 General		
Bill Paxon (R)	90,237	(57%)
Kevin P. Gaughan (D)	69,328	(43%)
1988 General		
Bill Paxon (R)	117,710	(53%)
David J. Swarts (D)	102,777	(47%)

District Vote For President

	1988	1984	1980	1976
D	101,948 (44%)	88,266 (38%)	89,161 (40%)	94,307 (43%)
R	130,099 (56%)	145,871 (62%)	112,088 (50%)	123,578 (56%)
I			17,605 (8%)	

Campaign Finance

	Receipts	Receipts from PACs		Expend-itures
1990				
Paxon (R)	$692,799	$239,020	(35%)	$506,934
Gaughan (D)	$101,182	$51,492	(51%)	$100,353
1988				
Paxon (R)	$702,136	$242,558	(35%)	$702,038
Swarts (D)	$457,504	$233,314	(51%)	$457,262

Key Votes

1991	
Authorize use of force against Iraq	Y
1990	
Support constitutional amendment on flag desecration	Y
Pass family and medical leave bill over Bush veto	N
Reduce SDI funding	N
Allow abortions in overseas military facilities	N
Approve budget summit plan for spending and taxing	N
Approve civil rights bill	N
1989	
Halt production of B-2 stealth bomber at 13 planes	N
Oppose capital gains tax cut	N
Approve federal abortion funding in rape or incest cases	N
Approve pay raise and revision of ethics rules	N
Pass Democratic minimum wage plan over Bush veto	N

Voting Studies

	Presidential Support		Party Unity		Conservative Coalition	
Year	S	O	S	O	S	O
1990	69	30	93	5	94	6
1989	73	26	89	9	90	10

Interest Group Ratings

Year	ADA	ACU	AFL-CIO	CCUS
1990	6	88	8	86
1989	0	93	8	100

32 John J. LaFalce (D)

Of Tonawanda — Elected 1974

Born: Oct. 6, 1939, Buffalo, N.Y.
Education: Canisius College, B.S. 1961; Villanova U., J.D. 1964.
Military Service: Army, 1965-67.
Occupation: Lawyer.
Family: Wife, Patricia Fisher; one child.
Religion: Roman Catholic.
Political Career: N.Y. Senate, 1971-73; N.Y. Assembly, 1973-75.
Capitol Office: 2367 Rayburn Bldg. 20515; 225-3231.

In Washington: Those who work with LaFalce regard him as one of the smartest members of the House. The chairman of the Small Business Committee, LaFalce has labored to change the panel's backwater image and give it a role in the setting of tax and regulatory policy. On Banking, LaFalce is actively involved in debate on such detailed issues as the savings-and-loan bailout.

However, even endorsements of LaFalce's acumen tend to be qualified: His abrasive public manner and his intellectual certitude can be off-putting. An observer once said that LaFalce "has an innate ability to rub people the wrong way." And in his zeal for pursuing a broad range of legislative interests, LaFalce has run over some big feet, both in and out of Congress.

There is no doubt that LaFalce has expanded the reach of the Small Business Committee. Early in 1989, LaFalce conceded that "99 out of 100" issues that he gets involved in are outside the committee's jurisdiction, adding, "I can either say we'll tend to our knitting or we can become the aggressive ombudsman of the small-business community."

To do this, he has had to encroach on the turf of some of the most powerful House members. His biggest victory came in 1989 at the expense of Ways and Means Committee Chairman Dan Rostenkowski, D-Ill.

At issue was the repeal of Section 89 of the 1986 Tax Reform Act. The goal of this provision — to eliminate disparities in employee health programs that provided greater benefits to higher-paid workers — was widely accepted. But the measure required a complicated series of tests to prove non-discrimination that business groups decried as burdensome to employers.

With the provision due to take effect a year later, LaFalce proposed in January 1989 to repeal Section 89. Rostenkowski, who helped craft the section, at first resisted. But members were getting their ears singed by small-business constituents, and LaFalce lined up a cosponsors' list that included more than half the House.

"I didn't sit down and talk until I had 218 cosponsors," he said. Rostenkowski backed down, introducing a bill easing the testing requirements and making it easier for employers to meet anti-discrimination guidelines.

LaFalce pledged to work with Rostenkowski. However, he discovered that the issue had taken on a life of its own. House members of both parties pressed on for outright repeal. Some Republicans jumped on the issue to reinforce the GOP's image as the party of business and deregulation.

LaFalce appeared somewhat melancholy in September 1989 when the House passed a Section 89 repeal bill by a 390-36 vote. Referring to his belated outreach to the rolled-over Rostenkowski, LaFalce told a colleague, "I wanted a Ways and Means victory."

This would not be the only time during the 101st Congress that LaFalce, as a small-business advocate, would break some china in the Democratic pantry. Well into deliberations on the proposed Civil Rights Act of 1990, LaFalce intervened with a substitute proposal that became a rallying point for House Republicans and provoked the wrath of some on his own side of the aisle.

The Democratic leadership had made an election-year priority of the bill, which aimed at reversing court decisions limiting the right to sue and recover compensatory damages for claims of job discrimination. However, LaFalce took seriously President Bush's threat to veto the measure as a "quotas" bill, and produced a plan that addressed some of the small-business community's objections. LaFalce's bill would have established an easier test for employers to prove they had not discriminated and set a lower cap on damages that could be claimed.

However, LaFalce did not pick up on two political realities: House Democrats had adopted a hard-line strategy to put Bush on the spot on civil rights issues, and House Republicans were floundering for a counter to the main bill. When LaFalce was blocked from offering

New York 32

West — Niagara Falls; Part of Rochester

The 32nd, which stretches the way from the west side of Rochester to the north side of Buffalo, provides one of the more even partisan balances in New York state. It has gone for Republican Sen. Alfonse M. D'Amato; but it has also been dominated by Democratic Sen. Daniel Patrick Moynihan and Gov. Mario M. Cuomo. In presidential races, it tends to be close; in 1988, Democrat Michael S. Dukakis carried the 32nd with 51 percent.

Veteran Democratic House member LaFalce, who has close ties to northwestern New York's sizable Italian-American community, typically wins comfortably in the 32nd. Italian neighborhoods dominate north Buffalo; significant numbers of Italians also live in the Rochester portion of the district, which also is home to many blacks and young professionals. Rochester hosts much of the district's industry: Bausch & Lomb and Eastman Kodak both maintain their corporate headquarters here.

But while the elongated district grabs off chunks of western New York's largest cities, the biggest share of the vote — over 40 percent — comes from Niagara County. Western Niagara County has the Democratic mill cities of North Tonawanda, Lockport and Niagara Falls.

Niagara Falls is, of course, renowned for its natural beauty. But the city of 64,000 developed a sinister ecological reputation a decade ago, when the local chemical industry was held responsible for contaminating the groundwater in the Love Canal residential neighborhood. Twelve years after the area was evacuated in 1978, plans were made to resettle it under the name "Black Creek Village." Despite opposition from environmental groups that claim the area is still highly contaminated, over 200 families applied for the new housing.

The more rural areas of eastern Niagara County, where fruit trees abound, provide a Republican balance to the blue-collar cities. Dukakis carried the county with 51 percent of the vote. Neighboring Orleans County, which is heavily farmed, is mainly Republican; George Bush took 60 percent there.

Population: 516,387. White 465,285 (90%), Black 43,511 (8%), Other 4,717 (1%). Spanish origin 5,937 (1%). 18 and over 375,165 (73%), 65 and over 60,874 (12%). Median age: 31.

his bill as a Democratic alternative, Minority Leader Robert H. Michel, R-Ill., put his name on it and promoted it as a GOP plan. With the Democratic leadership whipping against it, the alternative failed by a 188-238 vote.

LaFalce gained the Small Business helm in 1987, following the retirement of the previous chairman, Parren Mitchell of Maryland. With his hard-charging style, LaFalce presented a sharp contrast to the low-key Mitchell, a black Democrat who expended much of his effort on minority contracting set-aside programs.

When he took the Small Business position, LaFalce gave up his chairmanship of the Banking Subcommittee on Economic Stabilization. LaFalce had attempted to use that position to shape the diverse proposals for a "national industrial policy" into legislation, but had limited practical success. Republicans, led by President Ronald Reagan, opposed industrial policy as "micromanagement" of the economy and an attempt by the federal government to pick the economy's "winners and losers."

Although he no longer chairs a Banking panel, LaFalce remains one of the committee's more active members. Disapproving of many provisions in the savings-and-loan bailout bill in 1989, LaFalce typically tried to blaze his own path.

During debate in the Subcommittee on Financial Institutions, a LaFalce amendment, requiring states with large numbers of failed S&Ls to pick up part of the tab, was defeated by voice vote. He objected to the off-budget financing mechanism in the bill; but his amendment to place the bailout "on-budget" was ruled non-germane by Banking Chairman Henry B. Gonzalez, D-Texas, who said it was a tax-writing issue under Ways and Means jurisdiction. Gonzalez and LaFalce, both headstrong and prickly House veterans, have a cat-and-dog relationship on Banking.

LaFalce's aggressiveness extends to issues outside his committee assignments. LaFalce, who is among the House Democrats most opposed to abortion, warned in 1989 that the Democratic leadership's advocacy of abortion rights could create a lasting rift between the party and working-class voters. "We're just inviting people to vote against us," LaFalce said. "It's suicide within our party. We're alienating the ethnics and the Catholics that have built the party."

Yet LaFalce risked the wrath of his large Roman Catholic constituency in June 1990 when he criticized the head of the archdiocese of New York. Cardinal John J. O'Connor had said that Catholic politicians might face excommunication if they supported abortion rights. Remarking that such comments might energize the pro-abortion rights cause, LaFalce said, "He has no political smarts.... The cardinal and his cause would be better off if he kept his mouth shut."

LaFalce's pro-small business attitude and his anti-abortion position might indicate that he is a conservative Democrat. However, on most issues, he votes with his Democratic colleagues. LaFalce voted against Bush's position on House legislation more than two-thirds of the time during the 101st Congress.

At Home: His aggressive manner, an ethnic link to many of his constituents and the Democratic lean in the 32nd District enabled LaFalce to dominate his first eight House contests. However, in 1990, he unexpectedly slipped to 55 percent of the vote, 5 percentage points under his previous career low.

LaFalce was never actually threatened with defeat. His Republican opponent, communications executive Michael T. Waring, received only 31 percent, while Conservative Party candidate Kenneth J. Kowalski drew off 14 percent.

LaFalce blamed his slippage on complacency and his absence from the district during the long session of the 101st Congress. However, there also was evidence of dissatisfaction in LaFalce's conservative, blue-collar base, which likely stemmed from a general unhappiness with Congress.

LaFalce, a lawyer in his hometown of Buffalo, burst onto the political scene in 1970 with an upset victory for the state Senate. Determined to pre-empt his political career, Republicans in the Legislature redrew the Senate district in 1972 to make his re-election hopeless.

But LaFalce outfoxed his adversaries: He moved down a rung and ran for a seat in the state Assembly. When he won that, he secured a reputation as one of the strongest Democratic candidates western New York had seen in years.

In the Legislature, LaFalce concentrated on procedural reform. He was a critic of Gov. Nelson A. Rockefeller and capitalized in his campaigns on deep-seated resentments against downstater Rockefeller among upstaters.

In 1974, when GOP Rep. Henry P. Smith retired, LaFalce campaigned in a semi-suburban district that had not been won by a Democrat in 62 years. He carried 60 percent of the vote, then proceeded to win with even greater margins until his 1990 dropoff.

Committees

Small Business (Chairman)
SBA, the General Economy & Minority Enterprise Development (chairman)

Banking, Finance & Urban Affairs (5th of 31 Democrats)
Economic Stabilization; Financial Institutions Supervision, Regulation & Insurance; Housing & Community Development; International Development, Finance, Trade & Monetary Policy

Elections

1990 General		
John J. LaFalce (D)	68,367	(55%)
Michael T. Waring (R)	39,053	(31%)
Kenneth J. Kowalski (C)	16,853	(14%)
1988 General		
John J. LaFalce (D)	133,917	(73%)
Emil K. Everett (R)	50,229	(27%)

Previous Winning Percentages: **1986** (91%) **1984** (69%) **1982** (91%) **1980** (72%) **1978** (74%) **1976** (67%) **1974** (60%)

District Vote For President

	1988	1984	1980	1976
D	104,507 (51%)	98,894 (45%)	89,401 (46%)	95,793 (46%)
R	98,419 (48%)	119,656 (55%)	87,703 (45%)	111,359 (54%)
I			15,345 (8%)	

Campaign Finance

	Receipts	Receipts from PACs	Expend-itures
1990			
LaFalce (D)	$339,919	$196,675 (58%)	$145,079
Kowalski (C)	$273	0	$231
1988			
LaFalce (D)	$241,784	$141,022 (58%)	$133,738
Everett (R)	$13,703	0	$13,702

Key Votes

1991	
Authorize use of force against Iraq	N
1990	
Support constitutional amendment on flag desecration	N
Pass family and medical leave bill over Bush veto	N
Reduce SDI funding	Y
Allow abortions in overseas military facilities	N
Approve budget summit plan for spending and taxing	Y
Approve civil rights bill	Y
1989	
Halt production of B-2 stealth bomber at 13 planes	Y
Oppose capital gains tax cut	Y
Approve federal abortion funding in rape or incest cases	N
Approve pay raise and revision of ethics rules	Y
Pass Democratic minimum wage plan over Bush veto	Y

Voting Studies

	Presidential Support		Party Unity		Conservative Coalition	
Year	S	O	S	O	S	O
1990	30	67	80	14	35	61
1989	34	59	81	15	41	51
1988	24	70	85	11	32	61
1987	20	77	83	9	26	74
1986	19	76	80	11	20	64
1985	30	66	77	15	22	73
1984	35	56	78	13	25	68
1983	30	67	84	12	19	75
1982	38	57	80	10	21	73
1981	36	61	78 †	15 †	27	68

† Not eligible for all recorded votes.

Interest Group Ratings

Year	ADA	ACU	AFL-CIO	CCUS
1990	72	21	67	46
1989	90	12	83	50
1988	80	8	93	38
1987	88	5	87	14
1986	85	10	83	25
1985	70	14	94	38
1984	80	24	83	43
1983	80	9	94	35
1982	85	5	94	24
1981	70	7	87	17

33 Henry J. Nowak (D)

Of Buffalo — Elected 1974

Born: Feb. 21, 1935, Buffalo, N.Y.
Education: Canisius College, B.B.A. 1957; State U. of New York at Buffalo, J.D. 1961.
Military Service: Army, 1957-62.
Occupation: Lawyer.
Family: Wife, Rose Santa Lucia; two children.
Religion: Roman Catholic.
Political Career: Erie County comptroller, 1966-74.
Capitol Office: 2240 Rayburn Bldg. 20515; 225-3306.

In Washington: Nowak plays politics in the House the way he learned to in the Erie County Democratic organization: He tends to those who elect him, listens to his party leaders and leaves lofty oratory to members who yearn for recognition beyond their constituencies.

Elected in a class of activist Democrats with wide-ranging agendas, Nowak stands out as one who has kept his politics local. Fortunately for him, he is a senior member of a committee where good personal relations are the key to getting things done. Nearly everybody on Public Works is there to bring federal money to his district, and Nowak's reluctance to make speeches has never been a disadvantage in securing federal funds.

The Buffalo News has described him as "Buffalo's foremost ambassador to Washington in winning federal aid for vital community projects"; it estimated that the city and surrounding area has received 15 percent of all sewer project funds allocated to cities in the Great Lakes region. Nowak gauges that he has snagged several hundred million federal dollars for public works projects, ranging from the Buffalo Light Rail Transit Project to a swimming pool at Cazenovia Park.

In the 100th Congress, Nowak gained the chairmanship of the Public Works Subcommittee on Water Resources, which Robert A. Roe of New Jersey gave up after his signal achievement, passage of the 1986 Water Resources Act (after a 10-year struggle). Before that, Nowak had played no leadership role on the subcommittee, but characteristically made sure his district got its share of funds. Even though his profile was not much higher as subcommittee chairman, he kept the projects flowing home.

The 1986 water resources law authorized several Buffalo-area projects, including $9 million for a Gateway Bridge across the Buffalo River, $3.5 million for improvements in the Buffalo port area, and $1.54 million for Cazenovia Creek flood control. The act also provided for the federal government to fund 50 percent of the operation and maintenance costs of the New York State Barge Canal.

In 1988, the Water Resources Subcommittee produced another water-projects bill, putting the regular cycle of biennial authorizations back on track. The 1988 bill authorized a $2 million repair — with the federal government paying half — at a Buffalo small-boat harbor.

As subcommittee chairman, he has been an advocate of controlling the pesty zebra mussel, revitalizing the Great Lakes fishing industry and getting the U.S. Army Corps of Engineers more involved in the cleanup of toxic sediments.

In the 99th Congress, Nowak served as chairman of the Public Works Subcommittee on Economic Development. In 1985, he tried to protect the Economic Development Administration from Reagan administration's cutbacks. His bill, authorizing the EDA for three years, passed the House easily, and though the Senate took no action, the EDA survived.

At Home: Practically invisible to the rest of the nation, Nowak's dedication to his home base makes him invincible in Buffalo. In nine House general elections, Nowak has never received less than three-quarters of the vote.

Nowak made his way in politics as a party loyalist allied with Buffalo Democratic leader Joseph Crangle. After serving for a year as an assistant district attorney, Nowak was plucked from obscurity by Crangle in 1965 and, at the age of 30, made the Democratic nominee for Erie County comptroller. His Polish name and background as a basketball star at Canisius College made him a good choice, and a strong Democratic showing in the county that year boosted him to victory.

He was re-elected twice, in 1969 and 1973, and became the heir apparent to Democratic Rep. Thaddeus J. Dulski, chairman of the House Post Office Committee. When Dulski decided to retire in 1974, he delayed his announcement until four days before the filing deadline so nobody could mount a serious campaign against Nowak. His 75 percent that November would be the lowest total of his House career.

New York 33

West — Buffalo

Decades of Rust Belt decline had a corrosive effect on Buffalo's morale and national image. Though still one of the nation's 50 largest cities with just over 328,000 people, Buffalo lost over 20 percent of its population in the 1970s, and another 8 percent in the the 1980s. The grimy and economically flagging city, like Philadelphia and Cleveland before it, became the butt of derogatory jokes.

But the city that television personality Johnny Carson once referred to as a good place to view the end of the world is slowly resurrecting itself from the ranks of the economically dead.

The U.S.-Canada free-trade agreement is beginning to pay dividends for Buffalo-area businesses, and unemployment rates, as high as 15 percent in the early 1980s, dropped to under 5 percent by the summer of 1989. A sparkling new 19,000-seat ballpark has replaced venerable War Memorial Stadium — where the baseball movie "The Natural" was filmed: record-breaking crowds at the AAA-level minor league games there abet the city's efforts to obtain a major league baseball team.

Blue-collar Poles are the predominant ethnic group in the city and throughout the district. They are concentrated in single-family frame houses on the eastern side of Buffalo and in the town of Lackawanna, just to the south. Lackawanna suffered from the closing of a Bethlehem Steel plant in 1983 — it once accounted for close to two-thirds of the city's tax base — though it maintains some steel-finishing facilities.

Though Democratic loyalties have slipped in many ethnic blue-collar cities, they remain strong in Buffalo. Michael S. Dukakis, who carried the state, won the 33rd District with 66 percent of the vote. Democratic strength here is bolstered by a black community that amounts to 30 percent of Buffalo's population.

Population: 516,392. White 406,449 (79%), Black 98,074 (19%), Other 4,334 (1%). Spanish origin 11,024 (2%). 18 and over 383,256 (74%), 65 and over 69,957 (14%). Median age: 31.

Committees

Public Works & Transportation (5th of 36 Democrats)
Water Resources (chairman); Aviation; Economic Development; Public Buildings & Grounds;

Science, Space & Technology (16th of 32 Democrats)
Environment

Elections

1990 General

Henry J. Nowak (D)	84,905	(78%)
Thomas K. Kepfer (R)	18,181	(17%)
Louis P. Corrigan Jr. (C)	6,460	(6%)

1990 Primary

Henry J. Nowak (D)	28,117	(87%)
Louis P. Corrigan (D)	2,934	(9%)
John A. Basar Jr. (D)	1,336	(4%)

1988 General

Henry J. Nowak (D)	139,604	(100%)

Previous Winning Percentages: **1986** (85%) **1984** (78%) **1982** (84%) **1980** (83%) **1978** (79%) **1976** (78%) **1974** (75%)

District Vote For President

	1988		1984		1980		1976	
D	130,124	(66%)	138,667	(63%)	126,145	(63%)	127,760	(57%)
R	65,217	(33%)	82,638	(37%)	60,282	(30%)	94,722	(42%)
I					11,125	(6%)		

Campaign Finance

	Receipts	Receipts from PACs		Expend-itures
1990				
Nowak (D)	$150,832	$98,908	(66%)	$93,158
1988				
Nowak (D)	$122,306	$91,225	(75%)	$94,042

Key Votes

1991	
Authorize use of force against Iraq	N
1990	
Support constitutional amendment on flag desecration	N
Pass family and medical leave bill over Bush veto	Y
Reduce SDI funding	Y
Allow abortions in overseas military facilities	N
Approve budget summit plan for spending and taxing	N
Approve civil rights bill	Y
1989	
Halt production of B-2 stealth bomber at 13 planes	N
Oppose capital gains tax cut	Y
Approve federal abortion funding in rape or incest cases	N
Approve pay raise and revision of ethics rules	Y
Pass Democratic minimum wage plan over Bush veto	Y

Voting Studies

	Presidential Support		Party Unity		Conservative Coalition	
Year	**S**	**O**	**S**	**O**	**S**	**O**
1990	17	82	90	7	31	67
1989	37	60	85	12	34	66
1988	25	70	93	4	16	74
1987	19	78	89	5	30	67
1986	18	82	92	5	16	82
1985	23	76	89	4	11	89
1984	32	64	88	7	19	76
1983	23	74	91	6	12	85
1982	34	65	90	8	14	86
1981	38	61	87	10	17	77

Interest Group Ratings

Year	ADA	ACU	AFL-CIO	CCUS
1990	89	4	100	31
1989	80	15	83	40
1988	90	12	100	36
1987	76	4	100	7
1986	95	5	100	28
1985	80	10	100	27
1984	85	17	92	40
1983	85	17	94	30
1982	100	5	100	23
1981	75	0	67	17

34 Amo Houghton (R)

Of Corning — Elected 1986

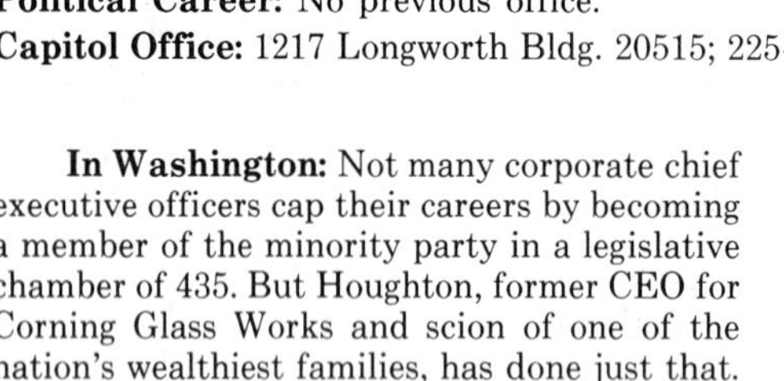

Born: Aug. 7, 1926, Corning, N.Y.
Education: Harvard U., A.B. 1950, M.B.A. 1952.
Military Service: Marine Corps, 1945-46.
Occupation: Glassworks company executive.
Family: Wife, Priscilla Dewey; four children.
Religion: Episcopalian.
Political Career: No previous office.
Capitol Office: 1217 Longworth Bldg. 20515; 225-3161.

In Washington: Not many corporate chief executive officers cap their careers by becoming a member of the minority party in a legislative chamber of 435. But Houghton, former CEO for Corning Glass Works and scion of one of the nation's wealthiest families, has done just that. At age 64, he does not plan a long stay in Washington, but while here, he has a missionary's enthusiasm for making a contribution.

Congress, however, has shown a resistance to being converted to Houghton's view that government's fiscal affairs should be run like those of a corporation. Houghton's business acumen helped him get a seat on the Budget Committee as a freshman. While he has participated actively in the panel's business, he has gained no special influence on the committee, where Republicans often are shut out by Democrats who view the budget as a partisan statement more than an economic blueprint. For a man used to giving orders, though, Houghton has shown little frustration. He is affable, with a sense of humor he can turn on himself.

Houghton has been able to do some things for his district. Late in the 101st Congress, he worked to resolve a looming conflict between the Seneca Indian Nation and the federal government over the renegotiation of federal leases of Indian lands.

The dispute centered on the 1991 expiration of 99-year leases of Seneca lands — negotiated on terms very unfavorable to the Senecas — upon which the town of Salamanca was built. With the leases due to expire, Houghton successfully helped craft a deal under which the federal and state governments paid the Indian nation $60 million and the Senecas renewed the land leases on terms acceptable to the governments.

Not surprisingly for a Northeastern Republican, Houghton stands to the left of the House GOP line on a number of issues. He was one of only 17 Republicans opposing a constitutional amendment to ban flag desecration. He opposes a balanced-budget amendment, saying that it is "legal fancy footwork" and that it is Congress' responsibility to control spending.

As a member of the Foreign Affairs Committee, Houghton has made trips to the Soviet Union and Nicaragua. But unlike colleagues who travel abroad on military aircraft, Houghton pays for all such travel himself.

Houghton opposed military aid for the Nicaraguan contras, preferring another way to make an impact in Central America: In the 100th Congress, he worked to put together private funding for a scholarship program to bring Nicaraguan students to colleges and universities in western New York. "Many times when congressmen go down there . . . they come back and have a press conference and that's all. Here is a way of saying 'we want to help' in a human way," Houghton said of his plan.

At Home: The Houghton family tradition can be summed up in these words: Corning Glass and public office. Houghton followed his forebears into the executive suite of Steuben County's Corning Glass Works Co., serving 19 years as chief executive officer. Then, at age 60, he entered the public sector, as had his father and grandfather.

Houghton's political opportunity came in 1986, after Democratic Rep. Stan Lundine was tapped by Gov. Mario M. Cuomo to run for lieutenant governor. Houghton was popular in his hometown, where Corning Glass is the major employer: The company helped finance restoration after a flood devastated the city in 1972. While he had never been particularly active in local Republican affairs, he had little trouble securing the GOP nomination.

Seeking across-the-board appeal, Houghton pointed to his experience at creating jobs. The Democratic nominee, Cattaraugus County District Attorney Larry Himelein, portrayed Houghton as an elitist, and his case was boosted by a satirical profile of Houghton in *The Wall Street Journal.* It focused on Houghton's posh campaign style: He traveled either in a plush motor home stocked with liquor, cigars and homemade cookies or in his private plane. But Houghton ably deflected criticism, and a 3-1 margin in Steuben County propelled him to 60 percent overall.

New York 34

Southern Tier — Jamestown; Elmira

The long and narrow 34th stretches across the bottom of New York state — the Southern Tier — all the way from Lake Erie on the west to Elmira in the east. Though Democrat Stan Lundine, now lieutenant governor, held the House seat for a decade, he was an exception; these hilly, rural counties favor the GOP.

In 1988, George Bush took Chautauqua County, the district's largest, with 55 percent of the vote, and won 2-to-1 in both Steuben County, the district's second-largest, and in more rural Alleghany County.

Steuben County contains Houghton's home base of Corning, one of America's better-known company towns. Corning Glass produces utilitarian dishes and cookware; its Steuben Glass Works makes more costly decorative crystal pieces. Long a rather seedy industrial town, Corning (population 13,000) suffered severe flood damage from Hurricane Agnes in 1972. Corning Glass financed its rehabilitation, including a new City Hall and an "old town" style downtown area that is now a tourist attraction. The northern part of Steuben County is overtaken by wine vineyards. The state's most widely known wines, Taylor and Great Western, are produced there.

On the western edge of the 34th is Chautauqua County. It contains Chautauqua Lake, a popular tourist spot first developed in 1876 as a center for religious training.

Chautauqua also contains much of the 34th's Democratic vote. The city of Jamestown there is the district's largest (35,000 people); Lundine was its mayor before moving to Congress. Jamestown's Democratic industrial workers are a counterbalance to the GOP dairy farmers elsewhere in the county.

In Chemung County, at the 34th's eastern end, Republican farmers are arrayed against the blue-collar Democrats of Elmira, a city of 34,000. Like Corning, Elmira suffered severe hurricane damage, but it did not bounce back as well.

Population: 516,154. White 502,383 (97%), Black 7,720 (2%), Other 3,564 (1%). Spanish origin 4,212 (1%). 18 and over 368,422 (71%), 65 and over 67,643 (13%). Median age: 31.

Committees

Budget (6th of 14 Republicans)
Budget Process, Reconciliation & Enforcement; Economic Policy, Projections & Revenues

Foreign Affairs (16th of 18 Republicans)
Africa; International Economic Policy & Trade

Select Aging (19th of 27 Republicans)
Social Security and Women (ranking); Retirement, Income & Employment

Elections

1990 General		
Amo Houghton (R)	89,831	(70%)
Joseph P. Leahey (D)	37,421	(29%)
Nevin K. Eklund (L)	1,807	(1%)
1988 General		
Amo Houghton (R)	131,078	(96%)
Ian Kelly Woodward (L)	4,797	(4%)

Previous Winning Percentage: **1986** (60%)

District Vote For President

	1988	1984	1980	1976
D	78,930 (40%)	67,870 (32%)	71,056 (37%)	83,721 (42%)
R	118,087 (60%)	142,401 (68%)	104,050 (54%)	116,622 (58%)
I			15,091 (8%)	

Campaign Finance

	Receipts	Receipts from PACs	Expend-itures
1990			
Houghton (R)	$333,962	$102,000 (31%)	$178,401
Leahey (D)	$6,483	0	$6,462
1988			
Houghton (R)	$501,195	$129,950 (26%)	$362,990

Key Votes

1991	
Authorize use of force against Iraq	Y
1990	
Support constitutional amendment on flag desecration	N
Pass family and medical leave bill over Bush veto	N
Reduce SDI funding	N
Allow abortions in overseas military facilities	Y
Approve budget summit plan for spending and taxing	Y
Approve civil rights bill	Y
1989	
Halt production of B-2 stealth bomber at 13 planes	N
Oppose capital gains tax cut	N
Approve federal abortion funding in rape or incest cases	Y
Approve pay raise and revision of ethics rules	Y
Pass Democratic minimum wage plan over Bush veto	N

Voting Studies

	Presidential Support		Party Unity		Conservative Coalition	
Year	**S**	**O**	**S**	**O**	**S**	**O**
1990	57	39	58	36	72	22
1989	65	26	45	46	71	20
1988	52	45	61	32	92	8
1987	63	35	62	33	84	14

Interest Group Ratings

Year	ADA	ACU	AFL-CIO	CCUS
1990	33	43	25	54
1989	20	65	10	90
1988	45	56	57	100
1987	28	39	38	80

North Carolina

U.S. CONGRESS

SENATE 1 D, 1 R
HOUSE 7 D, 4 R

LEGISLATURE

Senate 36 D, 14 R
House 82 D, 37 R, 1 Independent

ELECTIONS

1988 Presidential Vote

Bush	58%
Dukakis	42%

1984 Presidential Vote

Reagan	62%
Mondale	38%

1980 Presidential Vote

Reagan	49%
Carter	47%
Anderson	3%

Turnout rate in 1986	33%
Turnout rate in 1988	43%
Turnout rate in 1990	40%

(as percentage of voting age population)

POPULATION AND GROWTH

1980 population	5,881,766
1990 population (10th in the nation)	6,628,637
Percent change 1980-1990	+13%

DEMOGRAPHIC BREAKDOWN

White	76%
Black	22%
American Indian, Eskimo, or Aleut	1%
(Hispanic origin)	1%
Urban	48%
Rural	52%
Born in state	76%
Foreign-born	1%

MAJOR CITIES

Charlotte	395,934
Raleigh	207,951
Greensboro	183,521
Winston-Salem	143,485
Durham	136,611

AREA AND LAND USE

Area 48,844 sq. miles (29th)

Farm	33%
Forest	61%
Federally owned	7%

Gov. James G. Martin (R)
Of Lake Norman — Elected 1984

Born: Dec. 11, 1935, Savannah, Ga.
Education: Davidson College, B.S. 1957; Princeton U., Ph.D. 1960.
Occupation: Professor.
Religion: Presbyterian.
Political Career: U.S. House, 1973-85.
Next Election: 1992.

WORK

Occupations

White-collar	45%
Blue-collar	41%
Service workers	11%

Government Workers

Federal	46,353
State	120,350
Local	280,081

MONEY

Median family income	$ 16,792	(43rd)
Tax burden per capita	$ 831	(26th)

EDUCATION

Spending per pupil through grade 12	$ 3,368	(40th)
Persons with college degrees	13%	(43rd)

CRIME

Violent crime rate 546 per 100,000 (20th)

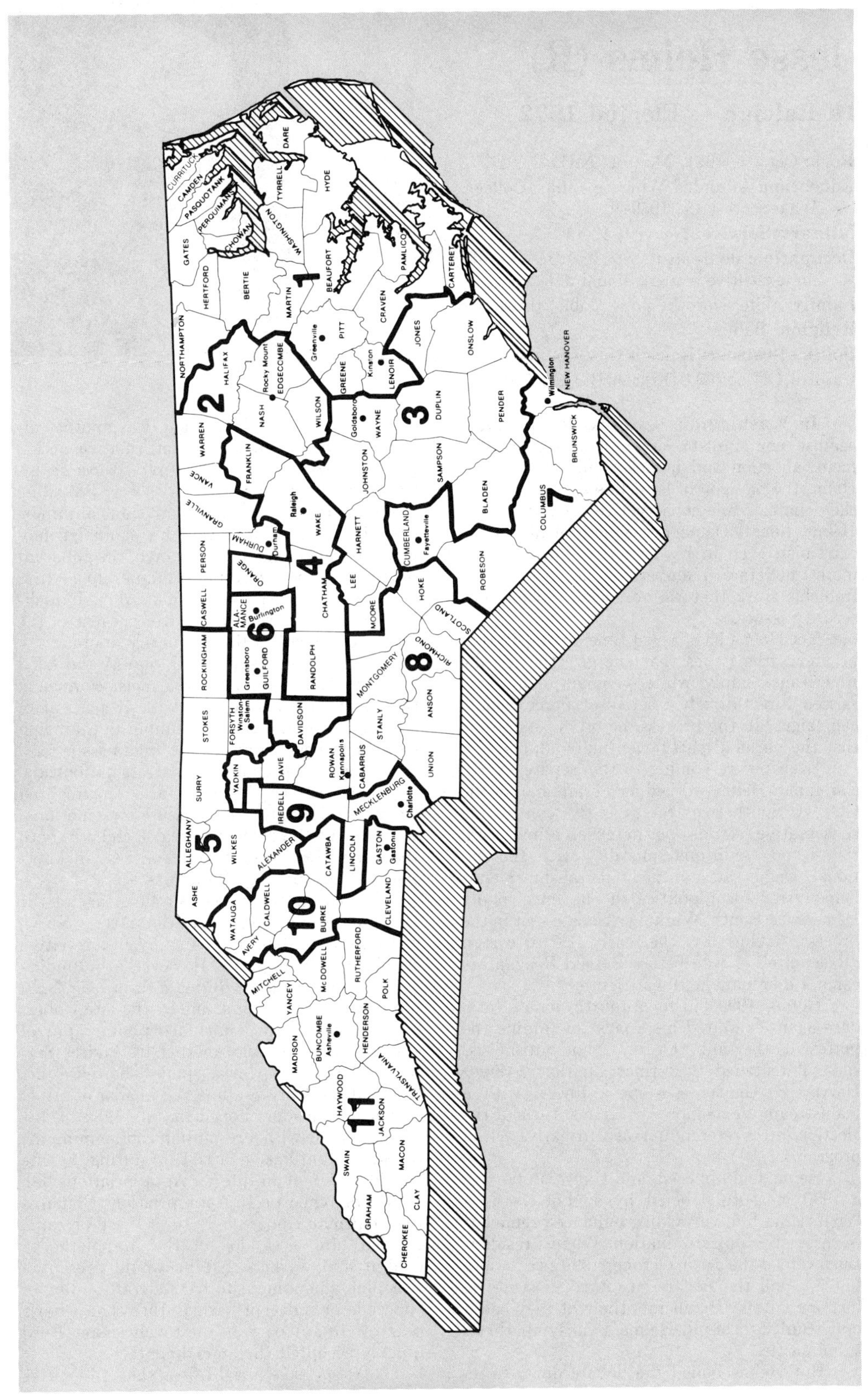
CURRITUCK
CAMDEN
PASQUOTANK
PERQUIMANS
CHOWAN
GATES
HERTFORD
NORTHAMPTON
BERTIE
DARE
TYRRELL
WASHINGTON
HYDE
MARTIN
BEAUFORT
1
PAMLICO
CARTERET
CRAVEN
PITT
Greenville
HALIFAX
2
NASH
Rocky Mount
EDGECOMBE
WILSON
GREENE
Kinston
LENOIR
JONES
ONSLOW
Goldsboro
WAYNE
3
DUPLIN
PENDER
Wilmington
NEW HANOVER
WARREN
VANCE
FRANKLIN
JOHNSTON
SAMPSON
BRUNSWICK
GRANVILLE
Raleigh
WAKE
BLADEN
COLUMBUS
7
PERSON
DURHAM
Durham
HARNETT
CUMBERLAND
Fayetteville
ROBESON
ORANGE
4
CASWELL
ALA-MANCE
Burlington
6
CHATHAM
LEE
MOORE
HOKE
SCOTLAND
ROCKINGHAM
Greensboro
GUILFORD
RANDOLPH
MONTGOMERY
8
RICHMOND
STOKES
FORSYTH
Winston Salem
DAVIDSON
STANLY
ANSON
SURRY
YADKIN
DAVIE
ROWAN
Kannapolis
CABARRUS
UNION
IREDELL
9
MECKLENBURG
Charlotte
ALLEGHANY
5
WILKES
ALEXANDER
CATAWBA
LINCOLN
GASTON
Gastonia
ASHE
WATAUGA
CALDWELL
10
BURKE
CLEVELAND
AVERY
MITCHELL
YANCEY
McDOWELL
RUTHERFORD
POLK
MADISON
BUNCOMBE
Asheville
HENDERSON
TRANSYLVANIA
HAYWOOD
11
JACKSON
SWAIN
MACON
GRAHAM
CLAY
CHEROKEE

Jesse Helms (R)

Of Raleigh — Elected 1972

Born: Oct. 18, 1921, Monroe, N.C.

Education: Attended Wingate Junior College, 1938-39; Wake Forest U., 1939-40.

Military Service: Navy, 1942-45.

Occupation: Journalist; broadcasting executive; banking executive; congressional aide.

Family: Wife, Dorothy Jane Coble; three children.

Religion: Baptist.

Political Career: Raleigh City Council, 1957-61.

Capitol Office: 403 Dirksen Bldg. 20510; 224-6342.

In Washington: Two decades of tirades against communism, liberalism, big government, abortion and homosexuality have made Helms the paragon of hard-line conservatism in the Senate. While conservative activists lionize Helms, liberal Democrats villainize him as an extremist; even in his own Republican Party, more moderate members sometimes shrink from his stark rhetoric on social and national security issues.

Yet Helms has proved time and again that he knows the issues that energize the Middle American, mainly white yeomanry that has carried him through a series of fierce Senate campaigns. In the process, he often sets a tone that the national party eventually adopts.

Even before coming to the Senate, North Carolinian Helms worked as a craftsman of the GOP's "Southern strategy." By contrasting conservative stands on defense, crime, civil rights and traditional morality with the national Democrats' alleged liberalism, Helms helped transform politics in the once-solidly Democratic South. Winning a Senate seat in the process, Helms by the early 1970s was a "Reaganite" — well before Ronald Reagan became a dominant national figure.

Helms' 1990 bid for a fourth Senate term once again exhibited his knack for finding the hottest of the rank-and-file's "hot button" issues. Threatened by former Charlotte Mayor Harvey B. Gantt — a black liberal with a mainstream demeanor — Helms turned the election into a referendum on affirmative action programs.

Helms had opposed, and Gantt supported, a 1990 measure, labeled by supporters as a "civil rights bill," providing enhanced remedies in cases of job discrimination. When President Bush vetoed the act in October 1990 as a "quota bill" — and the Senate sustained his veto by just one vote — Democrats thought they had a opportunity to brand Helms as unsympathetic to minorities.

But Helms boiled the debate down to its essence. At issue, Helms said, was another effort by liberals to expand affirmative action programs that he — and many of those in his white, working-class base — saw as providing unfair preferences to members of racial minorities. In a TV ad that gave his campaign momentum, the hand of a white man, the apparent recipient of a job rejection, crumples up a letter; a voiceover implies that the man, though qualified for the job, was passed over because of the employer's need to fill a minority quota.

Gantt denied supporting quotas and tried to brand Helms as running a racist campaign. But Helms went on to win with 53 percent of the vote. Soon thereafter, Republican campaign strategists began touting the quota issue as a viable one to use against Democrats nationwide.

The 101st Congress also highlighted Helms' skill for elevating obscure but emotional issues to the top of the political agenda. In both 1989 and 1990, Helms tied Congress in knots over federal funding of the arts.

Helms had long been an adversary of the National Endowment for the Arts (NEA), which he viewed as dominated by elitists with a zeal for the avant-garde. However, arts funding became a wedge issue during a furor over NEA funding of two exhibits: one by the late Robert Mapplethorpe, which included photographs of gay sex practices, and another by Andres Serrano, whose "Piss Christ" photo showed a picture of Jesus Christ submerged in a jar of urine.

Senate leaders hoped in July 1989 to dismiss the issue with a resolution condemning the funding of offensive art. But during Senate consideration of an Interior Appropriations bill, Helms marched up to Appropriations Committee Chairman Robert C. Byrd of West Virginia, handed him a catalog of the Mapplethorpe exhibit and warned that he would present a sweeping amendment to bar federal funding of "obscene or indecent" art. Rather than expose senators to a debate on the touchy issue, Byrd quickly accepted the amendment.

"Artists have a right, it is said, to express

their feelings as they wish; only a philistine would suggest otherwise," Helms said. "Fair enough, but no artist has a pre-emptive claim on the tax dollars of the American people."

House-Senate conferees eventually crafted a milder provision barring use of NEA and National Endowment for the Humanities money to fund works that "may be considered" obscene or that do not have "serious literary, artistic, political or scientific value." The measure was not strong enough for Helms, because it left the judgments of artistic merit to the NEA and NEH.

Helms promised to revive the fight the next year, but was blocked by an unexpected adversary: Utah Republican Orrin G. Hatch, usually a conservative ally of Helms but also a supporter of arts funding. While Helms again sought stricter limits, Hatch pushed through a bill that would not set standards for NEA funding.

The Hatch bill called for arts organizations or artists to refund federal money if an NEA-funded art work was deemed by a court as obscene or in violation of child pornography laws. But Helms, who tried unsuccessfully to restore a funding ban with an amendment, was defiant in defeat. "I say to the arts community and all homosexuals upset about this amendment: What is past is prologue," he warned. "You ain't seen nothing yet."

During the 1970s and 1980s, Helms helped set the New Right's social agenda. He remains one of the Senate's fiercest opponents of abortion and one of its strongest supporters of school prayer. He has made a crusade of limiting access to telephone "dial-a-porn" services.

Homosexuality has also become a defining issue in Helms' social agenda. In February 1990, he was one of four senators to vote against a bill requiring the Justice Department to collect and publish data on hate crimes, because it included "sexual orientation" as one of its criteria. Helms said Congress was being "hoodwinked" to pass "the flagship of the homosexual and lesbian legislative agenda."

Helms, who says that the crisis caused by AIDS is overstated, has tried without success to shift money for AIDS research to efforts against other diseases. He also tried, but failed, to amend the 1990 Americans with Disabilities Act to allow restaurant owners to remove people with AIDS from food-handling jobs.

These efforts underline one of the most notable aspects of Helms' long Senate career: With his unyieldingly ideological posture, Helms has had relatively little success at winning enactment of the legislation into which he puts so much furious effort.

But winning is not the point for Helms. "You got to understand how I operate," he once told a reporter. "Somebody said, 'Jesse, why do you so often advance things or take positions that you know you don't have any chance to win?' And my answer to that is, I do it on principle." His propensity to cast the solo "no" led the *The News and Observer* of Raleigh, N.C., his ardent foe, to dub him "Senator No." Helms relishes the title.

Helms has always had greater success at blocking legislation than at getting it passed. He is a master of Senate arcanery; together with his mulelike stubbornness, it is a formidable combination. He can often be found on the Senate floor, using his parliamentary skills to tie up legislative action.

His handling of the intermediate-range nuclear forces (INF) treaty in 1988 was vintage Helms. He opened the hearings by handing out a 180-page catalog of his complaints with a treaty he called an "invitation to cheat." His daily objections prompted treaty proponents to launch what was dubbed the "Helms Watch," to keep tabs on him and answer his objections.

Helms' hatred of communism and suspicion of the Soviet Union are the major attributes of his work as ranking Republican on the Foreign Relations Committee. For Helms, the committee is more of a forum for his anti-communist crusades than a place to craft passable legislation.

To many members of Congress and to the Bush administration, the Cold War appeared to end with the fall of the Berlin Wall in late 1989. But Helms — who had thrived on President Reagan's "evil empire" rhetoric of the early 1980s — warned against a too-rapid rapprochement with the Soviet Union.

In 1990, Helms tried to block expanded U.S. trade benefits to the Soviet Union, citing the plight of the Baltic States as a reason. In March 1990, he tried to attach an amendment to the Clean Air Act, calling for U.S. recognition of Lithuania's independence; it was defeated, 36-59.

Throughout the 1980s, the threat of communism in Central America — in the form of the Sandinista government of Nicaragua and the leftist insurgency against El Salvador's rightist government — fueled Helms' efforts on Foreign Relations. By 1989, Bush and Congress exhibited a willingness to emphasize diplomatic over military efforts in the region: Helms resisted the change in direction.

After long negotiations between administration officials and congressional leaders, Congress in April 1989 weighed shifting from support of the Nicaraguan contras to a policy of backing free elections. Helms instead proposed allowing the contras to receive $50 million in military aid at an "appropriate" time if the election process faltered. But his amendment was tabled on a 73-25 vote.

Helms was skeptical throughout about the election process, fearing that it would leave the Sandinistas in power, but still give contra-aid opponents the excuse to end U.S. involvement in that country. He said the United States was merely legitimizing a fraudulent election that was "controlled and contrived by the Sandinistas." Even after opposition candidate Violetta Chamorro defeated Sandinista leader Daniel Ortega the next February, Helms was unenthused; her coalition included too many leftist groups to earn Helms' trust.

Sensing a communist threat in any insurgency against a pro-Western government, Helms has found himself under attack over the years for supporting right-wing regimes accused of human rights abuses. He opposed U.S. sanctions against South Africa and supported the governments of Augusto Pinochet of Chile and Ferdinand Marcos of the Philippines.

Helms had an opportunity to take over as Foreign Relations chairman in 1985 (when Republicans held the Senate majority); however, he had made a promise during a 1984 campaign to stay as Agriculture chairman and oversee the interests of North Carolina's tobacco growers in the 1985 farm bill.

With that pledge met, Helms in 1987 sought the top GOP spot on Foreign Relations (even though the Republicans had receded into the minority). Helms had to step over Indiana Republican Richard G. Lugar, who had been serving as chairman. Citing his seniority and contrasting his hard line approach to Lugar's pragmatism, Helms won the post on a 24-17 vote.

However, Helms' efforts, here as elsewhere, have not been proactive. His invariable opposition to provisions in committee legislation has contributed to the committee's failure to pass foreign aid authorization bills in most recent years.

Helms relishes his contrarian role. In May 1989, committee Chairman Claiborne Pell of Rhode Island suggested tying a bill authorizing State Department operations, which routinely passed, to the foreign aid bill. But Helms had no interest in giving foreign aid a fast track. "If you have foreign aid on the State bill, down she goes like the *Titanic*," he said.

However, Foreign Relations' poor record at moving its major annual legislative responsibility has taken its toll on its image and that of the unassertive Pell. In early 1991, Foreign Relations Democrats gave new powers to its subcommittees at Pell's expense. Helms, who viewed the move as a threat to his committee power as well, opposed it and pledged not to spend any of the money that had been allotted to beef up subcommittee staffs.

Whatever his legislative legacy on Foreign Relations, Helms is surely more visible there than in his past position as Agriculture chairman. He virtually abdicated control of the committee during his first four years as chairman, allowing a coalition of Republicans, led by then-Majority Leader Bob Dole of Kansas, to take the lead on farm legislation.

One of the little noticed aspects of Helms' highly public career was his long tenure on the Senate Ethics Committee. A member since 1979, Helms gained most notice in this position just before he stepped down in February 1991.

Helms was one of the six committee members who sat in judgment of the five senators who were accused of ethics violations relating to their association with thrift scandal figure Charles H. Keating Jr. Helms took one of the tougher stands, favoring Senate punishment for at least three of the senators. But when the committee decided to refer only the case of California Democrat Alan Cranston for full Senate action — recommending lighter reprimands for the others — Helms denied that he and his colleagues had gone soft. "I don't think you would think that you had been dealt with lightly if your peers had judged you as these men have been judged," he said.

At Home: The smoke from Helms' monumental 1984 re-election battle had scarcely lifted before another defense loomed. But the toll on purse and psyche that the bitter 1984 campaign exacted served to dissuade "heavyweight" Democrats from challenging Helms in 1990.

When his bid for re-election to a third Senate term began taking shape two years before the 1984 balloting, Helms' future influence in state politics was very much in doubt. His vaunted political organization, the National Congressional Club, had suffered severe setbacks in 1982, losing every one of the five congressional contests it had targeted in the state.

Further, Helms was being plagued by negative publicity. His 1982 vote for raising the cigarette tax had drawn fire from North Carolina's crucial tobacco constituency. He was widely vilified for his unsuccessful efforts to block creation of a federal holiday for the Rev. Dr. Martin Luther King Jr. Pollsters tracking the battle between Helms and Democratic Gov. James B. Hunt Jr. found Helms significantly behind through most of 1983.

But Helms battled back, drawing on financial support from conservatives across the country to invest $16.5 million in the race, shattering the record for the most money spent by a Senate candidate in U.S. history. His ads assaulting Hunt and the national Democratic Party not only bolstered his own campaign, they created a climate in which other North Carolina Republicans could prosper. When the dust settled on election night, the GOP had captured the governorship and three new House seats.

In many ways, it was an unusually static Senate campaign. The national media dutifully detailed each tortuous twist and turn, from Hunt's charge that Helms was a supporter of right-wing death squads in El Salvador, to the incumbent's complaint that Hunt had misused state airplanes. But most North Carolinians seemed little affected by the long and vituperative debate. Faced with a choice between a leading apostle of the New Right and an activist Democratic governor, most knew relatively early on how they would vote. Only 4 percentage points separated the two contenders in polls taken in May 1984; in late October, it was still considered a dead heat.

Hunt focused his campaign on his record as governor, tirelessly sounding his commitment to improved education and arguing he was experienced in bringing the state jobs. He cast Helms as a right-wing radical, too extreme in his views to serve the state's interests effectively.

Helms embraced President Reagan wholeheartedly, using taped telephone messages in which Reagan endorsed him. Helms also sought to link Hunt to Democratic presidential candidate Walter F. Mondale and his national party. That charge left Hunt hamstrung, as he sought to distance himself from Mondale's proposal for a tax increase without repudiating his party's presidential nominee.

In the end, Hunt won strong support from the extensive network of teachers, unions, party regulars and other activists he had built up during 10 years in state government. He carried the rural northeast, traditional Democratic territory that both men had taken in previous campaigns. Hunt also carried most of the state's major urban areas, thanks in part to the overwhelming allegiance of black voters.

But Hunt's eastern margins were not as decisive as he had hoped, and his black support helped produce a conservative white backlash that benefited Helms. Further aided by Reagan's top-of-the-ticket strength and a strong turnout from newly registered fundamentalists, Helms built his victory in the small towns and crossroads communities of the central and western Piedmont. He finished with a 52 percent to 48 percent edge.

Any Helms re-election effort is bound to attract national attention. But Helms' 1990 campaign against Gantt was guaranteed saturation national coverage.

Despite Gantt's obvious vulnerabilities — his liberal positions, his lack of statewide recognition and his race (Gantt was the first black ever to win a major party's statewide nomination in North Carolina) — he also could point to certain advantages that might boost his effort against Helms.

Where Hunt had struggled against Helms' ads to retain his political identity as a moderate, Gantt expended little effort fending off charges that he was liberal. Gantt opposed capital punishment and a capital gains tax cut, supported a woman's right to choose an abortion, and favored increased spending on education, the environment and health care.

Anticommunism, the perennial red-meat issue for Helms, had fallen in relevance in 1990. Gantt also did not have to contend with Republican presidential coattails. A national abortion rights group ran ads attacking Helms for his staunch opposition to abortion.

Gantt also wielded one unpredictable and powerful weapon: enthusiasm. His primary and runoff wins had galvanized a coalition of traditional Helms opponents, students and young professionals.

As always, Helms depended on media ads to get his message out. He refused to debate Gantt and shunned reporters. His campaign's policy required reporters seeking answers from the senator to submit written questions to the campaign fax machine. Helms regularly denounced the state's major newspapers, which he said were biased against him.

On television, Gantt and Helms pounded away at each other in negative ads, each trying to paint the other as extreme. Helms' ads compared his "North Carolina values" with Gantt's "extreme liberal values." Another ad accused Gantt of supporting abortion for sex selection and in the final weeks of pregnancy. One of Helms' radio ads warned that "the gay and lesbian political groups" have come to North Carolina "to elect Harvey Gantt." Helms saved the crusher — the "quotas" ad — for the end.

Gantt's 47 percent showing was only four-tenths of a percentage point off Hunt's 1984 posting. Gantt had secured the Democratic nomination by running up huge margins in the state's most populous county, Mecklenburg (Charlotte), and in the central Piedmont counties. But in November, he carried Mecklenburg by fewer than 30,000 votes. As had Hunt, Gantt won several of the rural northeastern counties. Gantt received 53 percent in the 10 counties with the most registered voters; in those same counties, Hunt received 50 percent. But the margins were not wide enough for Gantt to overcome Helms' strength in the state's less populous counties.

For most of his adult life, Helms was a Democrat himself, even while he delivered conservative editorials for 12 years over WRAL-TV in Raleigh. He left the Democratic Party in 1970 and two years later ran for the Senate.

He was an underdog in that campaign against U.S. Rep. Nick Galifianakis, who had convincingly defeated aging Sen. B. Everett Jordan in the Democratic primary. Press accounts regularly described Helms as a "right-winger," but that label was far less dangerous to him than the liberal McGovern-Shriver presidential ticket was to Galifianakis.

Helms played down his rhetoric and shifted to a pro-Nixon tone. "President Nixon Needs Jesse Helms," the advertisements read, although Helms was far to the right of Nixon on most issues. A year earlier he had called Nixon's trip to China "appeasement" of the communists. In a Republican sweep, Nixon won nearly

70 percent of the state's presidential vote. Helms defeated Galifianakis with 54 percent of the vote, and the GOP won the governorship for the first time since 1896.

Six years later, a host of Democrats sought to prove Helms' win a coattail fluke. The early favorite for the nomination was Luther H. Hodges Jr., a moderate banker with a well-financed campaign but a "stuffed shirt" image. Another Democrat, state Insurance Commissioner John Ingram, pledged to fight for the common man against insurance companies, banks and other monied interests he accused both Helms and Hodges of defending. Ingram was underfinanced and disorganized, but he forced Hodges into a runoff and won.

Ingram appeared to pose a threat to Helms. His populist themes had some appeal for rural and working-class conservatives who had supported Helms in 1972. But Helms had a reputation and an organization. Many of his constituents were proud that in a single Senate term he had become an articulate and nationally known defender of the right, one who had been promoted as a vice presidential choice by more than 800 national convention delegates in 1976. Helms' Congressional Club had been powerful enough to engineer Ronald Reagan's victory in the 1976 North Carolina primary.

Helms also had plenty of money. As direct-mail solicitations brought contributions from across the nation, Ingram derided the incumbent as "the six million dollar man." Helms eventually collected about $7.5 million, more than any Senate candidate in U.S. history up to that time, and won with 55 percent.

Committees

Foreign Relations (Ranking)
African Affairs; Western Hemisphere & Peace Corps Affairs

Agriculture, Nutrition & Forestry (3rd of 8 Republicans)
Agricultural Production & Stabilization of Prices (ranking); Conservation & Forestry; Domestic & Foreign Marketing & Product Promotion; Nutrition & Investigations

Rules & Administration (3rd of 7 Republicans)

Elections

1990 General		
Jesse Helms (R)	1,088,331	(53%)
Harvey B. Gantt (D)	981,573	(47%)
1990 Primary		
Jesse Helms (R)	157,345	(84%)
L.C. Nixon (R)	15,355	(8%)
George Wimbish (R)	13,895	(7%)

Previous Winning Percentages: **1984** (52%) **1978** (55%) **1972** (54%)

Campaign Finance

	Receipts	Receipts from PACs		Expend-itures
1990				
Helms (R)	$13,306,640	$835,104	(6%)	$13,355,336
Gantt (D)	$7,859,877	$695,852	(9%)	$7,811,520

Key Votes

1991	
Authorize use of force against Iraq	Y
1990	
Oppose prohibition of certain semiautomatic weapons	Y
Support constitutional amendment on flag desecration	Y
Oppose requiring parental notice for minors' abortions	N
Halt production of B-2 stealth bomber at 13 planes	N
Approve budget that cut spending and raised revenues	N
Pass civil rights bill over Bush veto	N
1989	
Oppose reduction of SDI funding	Y
Oppose barring federal funds for "obscene" art	N
Allow vote on capital gains tax cut	Y

Voting Studies

	Presidential Support		Party Unity		Conservative Coalition	
Year	**S**	**O**	**S**	**O**	**S**	**O**
1990	68	32	88	11	84	14
1989	71	28	86	11	87	11
1988	60	26	72	12	81	5
1987	77	22	94	5	94	3
1986	90	10	95	5	95	5
1985	79	21	94	6	97	3
1984	86	10	90	8	100	0
1983	56	41	77	20	95	2
1982	75	25	87	13	99	1
1981	84	16	88	11	94	6

Interest Group Ratings

Year	ADA	ACU	AFL-CIO	CCUS
1990	6	100	22	92
1989	5	100	20	75
1988	5	100	23	75
1987	10	100	20	89
1986	0	100	0	95
1985	0	100	5	93
1984	0	100	0	89
1983	0	100	0	89
1982	0	100	8	95
1981	0	100	5	100

Terry Sanford (D)

Of Durham — Elected 1986

Born: Aug. 20, 1917, Laurinburg, N.C.

Education: Attended Presbyterian Junior College; U. of North Carolina, A.B. 1939, J.D. 1946.

Military Service: Army parachute infantry, 1942-46; N.C. National Guard, 1948-60.

Occupation: University president; lawyer; FBI agent.

Family: Wife, Margaret Rose Knight; two children.

Religion: Methodist.

Political Career: N.C. Senate, 1953-55; governor, 1961-65; sought Democratic nomination for president, 1972, 1976.

Capitol Office: 716 Hart Bldg. 20510; 224-3154.

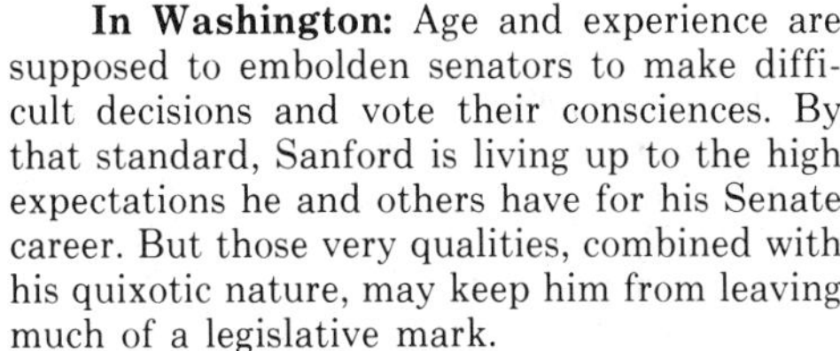

In Washington: Age and experience are supposed to embolden senators to make difficult decisions and vote their consciences. By that standard, Sanford is living up to the high expectations he and others have for his Senate career. But those very qualities, combined with his quixotic nature, may keep him from leaving much of a legislative mark.

The amiable former governor and two-time presidential candidate is well-liked and respected by fellow Democrats and party leaders, who appreciate his loyalty. And he has earned a share of national recognition for a variety of memorable stands — ranging from his opposition to Supreme Court nominee Robert H. Bork to his opposition to the Persian Gulf War.

But Sanford lacks the seniority or legislative focus that would enhance his influence. He speaks out on controversial legislation more often than he shapes it. His stature assures a hearing for his sometimes-ponderous reform proposals — such as changing the budget process and altering the Democratic presidential nominating process. But he plays a limited role in effecting policy change.

Sanford took a high profile against the war in the Persian Gulf when he wrote an August 1990 opinion piece for *The New York Times,* cautioning, "The Bush administration is playing into Mr. Hussein's desperate effort to depict his naked aggression as a confrontation between Iraq and the 'imperialist' United States." Later, shortly before the Senate voted to authorize the use of force, Sanford said, "It has always been easier to settle an argument with a gun.... to go to war now is not only unacceptable impatience, but, I suggest, a lack of real courage."

But unlike the last time Sanford positioned himself at center stage of a national political disagreement — during the Bork nomination — his warnings failed to sway many of his colleagues or constituents.

The Bork nomination was an entirely different story. Sanford's reputation for moderation led Democrats to choose him to respond to Reagan's October 1988 speech castigating the campaign against Bork's nomination. In defending the Senate's right to dissent, Sanford said, "We are tired of having our integrity impugned. We are tired of having our sincerity questioned. We are tired of having our intelligence insulted." His speech won high marks for laying down the proper political covering fire for foes of Bork, especially Southern ones.

On Foreign Relations, Sanford sought entry into one of the most controversial arenas, Central American policy, from his places on the Western Hemisphere Subcommittee and the Central American Observer Group. He considers the region's prime problem to be economic. He created an international commission, operating under the auspices of North Carolina's Duke University, to develop a long-range economic development strategy for the region.

Though Sanford tries to find a middle ground on most Central American issues, he is nonetheless at loggerheads with North Carolina's GOP senior senator Jesse Helms over U.S. policy in the region. When Foreign Relations Democrats in 1989 tried to cap military aid to El Salvador at $85 million ($12 million less than the Bush administration requested), Helms offered an amendment to lift the cap. Sanford held a deciding vote. He warned Democrats that he opposed the limit, but would favor stronger conditions on human rights. To win his support, the committee approved a $90 million cap, over Helms' strenuous objections.

Sanford's effort to mediate differences on Central America was evident in his first year in the Senate. He arrived as a leading advocate of U.S. backing for the Central American peace proposal of Oscar Arias, then president of Costa Rica. But in March 1987, Sanford voted to release $40 million in military aid for the Nicaraguan contras to honor a campaign pledge "not to pull the rug out from under the president's contra aid program too abruptly." Subsequently, he worked for non-military aid only.

When it comes to trade and parochial matters, Sanford does find common ground with Helms. During consideration of the 1990 trade bill, the two joined forces to win Senate approval of an amendment to lower the tariff for imported ranitidine hydrochloride, an ingredient in an ulcer drug manufactured in North Carolina. Despite objections from the Pennsylvania delegation (representing a pharmaceutical competitor), the North Carolinians were able to call in chits from across the political spectrum and won a 68-30 vote. The House, however, passed no such provision, and after a lengthy delay in the House-Senate conference, it was dropped in exchange for a House promise to hold hearings on the matter.

When it comes to tariffs on textile and footwear imports, however, Sanford is all for them. Sanford helped persuade the Senate to kill an amendment that would have halved the tariff on athletic shoes, a cut he said would harm struggling domestic manufacturers, including Converse in Lumberton, N.C.

Throughout much of 1990, Sanford was distracted by his work on the Ethics Committee, which conducted a 14-month investigation of the "Keating Five" case. From the outset, Sanford seemed the most sympathetic to the five senators being investigated for their involvement with savings and loan executive Charles Keating. "If indeed there is an appearance of wrongdoing when in fact no wrongdoing is found," he said, "the problem is not that of the individual but, rather, of the institution."

When the counsel who was pressing for charges against three of the five senators questioned him, Sanford retorted, "I'll lay my standard down and judge these people by it. And I dare say my standards will be broadly accepted — by at least 99 senators." Within the ethics panel, Sanford was said to favor the most lenient treatment for the five senators, while Helms favored the harshest. The panel came around to Sanford's view, ordering further investigation of just one senator. In 1991, he took over as Ethics Committee chairman.

Sanford's views on the Keating case separated him from "good-government" liberals who wanted stiff penalties for the senators. But his position was consistent with his past tendency to give the benefit of the doubt to those under ethics scrutiny. In 1989, Sanford was one of just 26 senators (most of them liberals) to vote against the impeachment of U.S. District Judge Alcee L. Hastings. He was one of just seven senators (five of whom were conservative Republicans) voting not to impeach U.S. District Judge Walter L. Nixon Jr.

Although Sanford voted against John Tower's nomination as Defense secretary in 1989, he has broken with his party to support two controversial Bush administration nominations. In 1990, he was one of just two Banking Committee Democrats to support the nomination of T. Timothy Ryan to be the nation's top savings and loan regulator, and he was one of three Foreign Relations Democrats to support the nomination of Donald P. Gregg as ambassador to South Korea.

On the Banking Committee, Sanford seeks to protect insurance operations within his state's important banking industry. He also pushed legislation to clamp down on corporate takeovers. This became a hot political issue in North Carolina after several major corporations in the state underwent restructurings following merger-and-acquisition activity.

During the 101st Congress, Sanford went a long way toward shedding the unflattering nickname "Turnaround Terry" that he picked up shortly after arriving in the Senate. He earned the sobriquet because of a highly publicized series of votes he cast in April 1987 that culminated in the override of President Reagan's veto of an $88 billion highway bill.

Sanford had been the only Democrat to vote against the legislation's conference report, arguing it did not adequately provide for North Carolina. He told a number of public officials in Washington and at home that, accordingly, he would support the president's veto.

When the override vote came, Sanford stood for a full five minutes in the well of the Senate, looking agonized as his arm was twisted from all sides. He first voted "present" to buy time, but when Republicans questioned the quality of his word, he switched his vote to "no," backing the president. Four hours later, after parliamentary maneuvering enabled the Democrats to schedule another vote, Sanford announced he would vote "yes" to override.

At Home: Despite a four-decade track record in Democratic politics — and the distinction of having been named one of America's 10 best governors of the century by a Harvard University study — Sanford had to struggle to win the confidence of his own party's hierarchy when he ran for the Senate in 1986.

North Carolina Democratic leaders searching for a candidate in late 1985 and early 1986 were not focusing on Sanford's accolades. What they saw was a 68-year-old man who had not won an election in 25 years.

As a result, party leaders resisted when Sanford first offered to run for the seat being vacated by retiring GOP Sen. John P. East. Only after failing to recruit a top-flight alternative did they champion Sanford's bid. But Sanford surprised many of his critics with a strong Democratic primary showing. With ads stressing moderate-to-conservative stands on issues and portraying his involvement in a wilderness adventure program (to overcome the age question), Sanford coasted past a weak field.

Republicans, meanwhile, staged a more significant primary battle — one from which Sanford would ultimately benefit. Rep. James

T. Broyhill, a moderate, chamber-of-commerce style Republican, faced David Funderburk, a political scientist and former U.S. ambassador to Romania backed by hard-right conservatives loyal to Sen. Helms' political organization, the National Congressional Club. Broyhill won his primary easily, and shortly afterward was appointed to fill out the remaining months left in the term of East, who committed suicide in June. But Broyhill never came to terms with the GOP right, enabling Sanford to capitalize on North Carolina's natural Democratic majority.

Broyhill's efforts to paint Sanford as a tax-loving liberal in league with the Kennedys (Sanford was one of the first Southern gubernatorial candidates to embrace John F. Kennedy's 1960 presidential campaign) met with only a lukewarm response. Sanford won narrowly.

Election to the Senate capped Sanford's long and distinguished career. Born, raised and educated in North Carolina, he served two years as an FBI agent before joining the Army. He was a paratrooper in World War II, and earned a Purple Heart and a Bronze Star.

He won election to the state Senate in 1952, and organized former Democratic Gov. W. Kerr Scott's successful Senate bid two years later. He made his own statewide move in 1960, winning election as governor. He was known for his moderate stance on race relations and his decision to levy a food tax to help fund an ambitious education program.

Barred by law from seeking re-election, Sanford returned to law practice. He considered challenging Democratic Sen. Sam B. Ervin in 1966; in 1970, he became president of Duke University, a position he held for 15 years.

He served as chairman of Hubert H. Humphrey's national presidential campaign in 1968. Four years later, Sanford was ready to test the national waters himself. In his bid for the presidency, he counted heavily on a strong showing in his home state's presidential preference primary to propel him to greater heights. But George C. Wallace handed him an embarrassing defeat in his own back yard.

Sanford announced for the presidency again in 1976, but withdrew after he discovered insufficient support to compete nationwide. In 1985, he unsuccessfully sought the chairmanship of the Democratic National Committee.

Committees

Select Ethics (Chairman)

Banking, Housing & Urban Affairs (7th of 12 Democrats)
International Finance & Monetary Policy; Securities

Budget (8th of 12 Democrats)

Foreign Relations (8th of 10 Democrats)
Near Eastern & South Asian Affairs (chairman); African Affairs; Western Hemisphere & Peace Corps Affairs

Special Aging (11th of 11 Democrats)

Elections

1986 General		
Terry Sanford (D)	823,662	(52%)
James T. Broyhill (R)	767,668	(48%)
1986 Primary		
Terry Sanford (D)	409,394	(60%)
John Ingram (D)	111,557	(16%)
Fountain Odom (D)	49,689	(7%)
William Irwin Belk (D)	33,821	(5%)
Theodore Kinney (D)	27,228	(4%)
Others (D)	47,798	(7%)

Campaign Finance

	Receipts	Receipts from PACs		Expend-itures
1986				
Sanford (D)	$4,181,701	$571,787	(14%)	$4,168,509
Broyhill (R)	$5,182,187	$1,367,212	(26%)	$5,168,244

Key Votes

1991	
Authorize use of force against Iraq	N
1990	
Oppose prohibition of certain semiautomatic weapons	Y
Support constitutional amendment on flag desecration	N
Oppose requiring parental notice for minors' abortions	Y
Halt production of B-2 stealth bomber at 13 planes	X
Approve budget that cut spending and raised revenues	N
Pass civil rights bill over Bush veto	Y
1989	
Oppose reduction of SDI funding	N
Oppose barring federal funds for "obscene" art	Y
Allow vote on capital gains tax cut	N

Voting Studies

	Presidential Support		Party Unity		Conservative Coalition	
Year	**S**	**O**	**S**	**O**	**S**	**O**
1990	41	54	81	16	43	49
1989	56	40	85	14	55	42
1988	41	52	89	4	24	68
1987	32	56	85	9	41	50

Interest Group Ratings

Year	ADA	ACU	AFL-CIO	CCUS
1990	67	17	67	25
1989	65	19	100	50
1988	90	4	85	43
1987	85	8	90	28

1 Walter B. Jones (D)

Of Farmville — Elected 1966

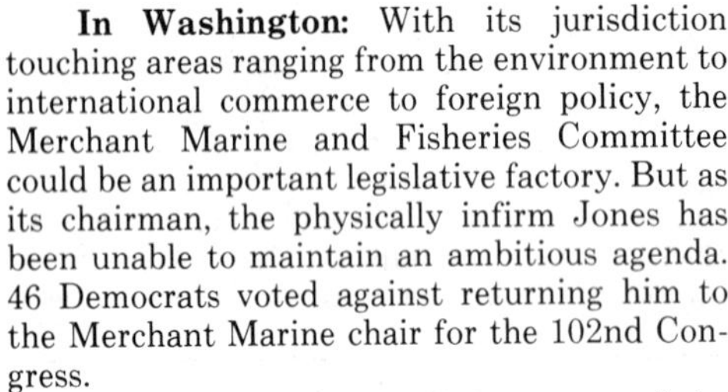

Born: Aug. 19, 1913, Fayetteville, N.C.
Education: North Carolina State U., B.S. 1934.
Occupation: Office supply company owner.
Family: Wife, Elizabeth Fisher; two children.
Religion: Baptist.
Political Career: Farmville Commission, 1948; mayor of Farmville, 1949-53; N.C. House, 1955-59; N.C. Senate, 1965-66; sought Democratic nomination for U.S. House, 1960.
Capitol Office: 241 Cannon Bldg. 20515; 225-3101.

In Washington: With its jurisdiction touching areas ranging from the environment to international commerce to foreign policy, the Merchant Marine and Fisheries Committee could be an important legislative factory. But as its chairman, the physically infirm Jones has been unable to maintain an ambitious agenda. 46 Democrats voted against returning him to the Merchant Marine chair for the 102nd Congress.

The frail Jones, now 78, gets some of the blame for the committee's diminished standing in House politics. "He retired years ago and didn't tell anyone about it," complained one Democrat. But many members expect second-ranking Democrat Gerry E. Studds of Massachusetts to ascend to the chair and steer the committee on a new, aggressive course.

When Jones manages a Merchant Marine bill on the House floor these days, it is hard to recall that almost a decade ago, when he first took over the scandal-plagued committee, he was regarded as something of a fresh breeze. Now, Jones, who has diabetes, often appears in a wheelchair because of a circulatory problem. On the floor, he stands shakily at the lectern, reading verbatim from a looseleaf script, turning its pages slowly, rarely lifting his head.

Still, if Jones has failed to chart an ambitious course for his committee, he at least has tried to change its reputation as a den of unsavory ethical behavior. Jones is a stark contrast to the panel's three previous chairmen, two of whom were indicted for criminal links to maritime industry figures. In 1987, after Mario Biaggi's indictment cost him the Merchant Marine Subcommittee chairmanship, Jones, with a calming presence and trustworthy reputation, assumed the post.

When Jones took over the full committee in 1981, he cleared out some deadwood in the staff and dismissed several aides to his predecessor, New Yorker John M. Murphy, who was caught up in the Abscam scandal. He has tried to run the committee in a more open and collegial manner. Maritime industry lobbyists, who still contribute generously to committee members, concede there have been fewer backroom deals during Jones' tenure.

But Jones has not been assertive enough to translate these changes into legislative accomplishments, even on his top priority, helping the ailing merchant marine industry. It is swamped by international competition and split by dissension among unions, shipbuilders and ship operators. But the committee's recommendations to assist the industry have been roundly criticized as unaffordable responses to special-interest pleading. The last notable merchant marine initiative by the committee dates back to the 98th Congress.

On other matters, the sheer scope of the committee's jurisdiction allows Jones to play a minor role on a variety of major bills. In 1988, his committee had a hand in crafting the drug bill, and the omnibus trade bill includes Jones-backed language to increase the volume of U.S. imports and exports carried by U.S. ships.

Environmental matters have consumed a good bit of the committee's time recently. In the 101st Congress, the committee issued a bill increasing oil spillers' federal liability limits. The bill, which Studds first introduced in 1975, also sought to compensate those economically injured by accidents, enhance cleanup efforts and attempt to prevent spills by mandating double hulls on oil vessels. The 1989 *Exxon Valdez* oil spill in Alaska cleared the way for the bill's enactment after 15 years in the works. President Bush signed it into law in 1990.

During the House-Senate conference, Jones added a provision placing a one-year moratorium on gas and oil drilling off North Carolina. Jones has lobbied heavily to stop oil exploration in the Outer Banks; Mobil Corp. owns a lease, and the Appropriations Subcommittee on Interior has not been receptive to Jones' calls to stop drilling. However, a move to kill the spill bill — by Interior Appropriations' ranking Republican, Ralph Regula — failed on the House floor.

In the 100th Congress, Jones was a prime

North Carolina 1

Northeast — Greenville; Kinston

The 1st begins at the ocean, passes through fishing ports and coastal swamps, and ends in flat fields of soybeans, corn, peanuts and tobacco.

This long has been the poorest and most agricultural region in North Carolina. Through much of the post-World War II era, out-migration was heavy; young people, especially blacks, fled the farms for urban areas. During the last two decades, however, there has been a population upturn in the district, thanks mainly to rapid growth in resort areas along the Atlantic coast.

On the Outer Banks, a thin strand of sand between the Atlantic and the Albemarle and Pamlico sounds, the flood of people into communities such as Nags Head, Hatteras and Kill Devil Hills increased the population of Dare County by 70 percent in the 1980s. Carteret, the most populous of the 1st District's coastal counties, grew by 28 percent.

Farther inland, the growth of population and economic opportunity has been more modest. Industries process tobacco and make paper and clothing; machinery and chemical factories are moving in, but harvests from the farm land still pay most of the bills. In Northampton and Hertford counties, where blacks are a majority, the problem of out-migration persists.

In the southern half of the district are the small cities of Greenville (Pitt County), Kinston (Lenoir County) and New Bern (Craven County). The counties of Pitt, Lenoir and Craven joined Dare, Carteret and Beaufort counties in supporting Ronald Reagan in 1980 and 1984 and George Bush in 1988, indicating that the district's urbanized areas and increasingly affluent coastal counties are fertile ground for the GOP. In 1990, black Democratic Senate nominee Harvey B. Gantt carried 10 counties in the 1st against GOP Sen. Jesse Helms, including Pitt and Dare.

Voters in the 15 rural counties usually stay in the Democratic column in local elections. The Democratic habits of conservative rural whites here go back to the Civil War. Many of the rural counties did cross party lines for Reagan in 1984 and Bush in 1988, but in races for statewide office, their traditions shine through. Only one of the 15 counties defected to the GOP in the 1984 Senate race, and GOP Gov. James G. Martin carried only one in his successful 1988 re-election bid. Helms carried the 1st in 1990 with 52 percent.

Population: 536,219. White 343,468 (64%), Black 189,088 (35%). Spanish origin 5,236 (1%). 18 and over 382,422 (71%), 65 and over 58,247 (11%). Median age: 29.

sponsor of legislation to allow oil drilling in the Arctic National Wildlife Refuge (ANWR). Merchant Marine swiftly approved his measure, defeating all amendments the chairman did not like. But the bill was widely criticized by environmentalists, and the legislation stalled in the Interior Committee. The *Valdez* spill doomed the bill in the 101st Congress, but the Persian Gulf War revived interest in domestic energy exploration. Jones introduced a bill in the 102nd Congress similar to his prior effort.

Jones credited the *Valdez* spill with his success in overturning a 1984 Supreme Court decision in *Secretary of the Interior v. California* that weakened states' ability to block oil and gas drilling off their shores. His proposal intended to give states more power to block leases by rewriting a provision in the Coastal Zone Management Act to cover drilling in the outer continental shelf. It was attached to the fiscal 1991 budget "reconciliation" bill as part of the reauthorization of the act.

Prior to taking over Merchant Marine, Jones scarcely showed up at committee hearings, and when he did, he was so passive that many thought he might yield the chairmanship voluntarily if it ever fell to him. By 1981, when it became vacant, a case of gout had reduced Jones' walk to a shuffle (and has since confined him to a wheelchair for long periods). But he surprised colleagues with a methodical campaign for the chairmanship. His effort and the sway of seniority won him the prize.

Earlier in his career, Jones chaired the Agriculture Subcommittee on Tobacco. There he focused on maintaining federal price supports for his district's most important crop.

At Home: The late Herbert Bonner, whose longtime Merchant Marine chairmanship gave Jones an issue in his campaign for the job, would have had a much shorter tenure if Jones had had his way in the first place.

In 1960, five years after Bonner took over the committee, Jones challenged him for renomination. But Bonner won with 58 percent of the vote, and Jones had to wait until after the chairman's death in 1965 to make it to Washington, defeating John P. East, who went on to serve six years in the U.S. Senate before committing suicide in 1986. Jones won 60 percent against East in the special election in February 1966 and defeated him again in November by a similar margin. He has had little trouble in general elections since then.

In the 1984 Democratic primary, though, Jones faced his first credible challenger since his initial election. His opponent was state Rep. John B. Gillam III, a 37-year-old peanut farmer who staked his challenge to the 70-year-old incumbent on a call for generational change.

Gillam raised questions about Jones' effectiveness, and claimed the incumbent had confused the 1st's priorities by abandoning the chairmanship of the Tobacco Subcommittee to take over Merchant Marine. "It's time for a change," Gillam argued. "We need to look at our old problems in a new way."

Jones' physical appearance did not help him against such complaints. He often appeared drawn and tired in public, and his foot ailment made it difficult for him to walk.

But Jones battled back by playing up his seniority and citing his role in obtaining funds for a construction project at a heavily used North Carolina coastal inlet, popular with the local fishing industry.

Jones also had plenty of chits to call in. In addition to his loyal following among local party leaders and teachers' groups, Jones picked up support from farmers and others in the tobacco trade who remembered his single-minded defense of that crop during his tenure as Tobacco Subcommittee chairman.

Gillam carried his home base of Bertie County as well as Hertford County, Bertie's neighbor to the north. But the rest of the district was Jones country. He clinched renomination with a resounding 61 percent, and cruised to an easy November victory.

A number of Democrats are anxiously awaiting word of whether Jones will retire after the 102nd Congress. One potential candidate bears a familiar name: state Rep. Walter B. Jones Jr.

Committees

Merchant Marine & Fisheries (Chairman)
Merchant Marine (chairman)

Agriculture (2nd of 27 Democrats)
Cotton, Rice & Sugar; Peanuts & Tobacco

Elections

1990 General

Walter B. Jones (D)	105,832	(65%)
Howard D. Moye (R)	57,526	(35%)

1988 General

Walter B. Jones (D)	118,027	(65%)
Howard D. Moye (R)	63,013	(35%)

Previous Winning Percentages: **1986** (70%) **1984** (67%) **1982** (81%) **1980** (100%) **1978** (80%) **1976** (76%) **1974** (78%) **1972** (69%) **1970** (70%) **1968** (66%) **1966** (61%) **1966** * (60%)

* *Special election.*

District Vote For President

	1988	1984	1980	1976
D	83,301 (46%)	82,194 (43%)	84,207 (52%)	82,605 (61%)
R	97,424 (54%)	109,441 (57%)	72,815 (45%)	53,042 (39%)
I			3,337 (2%)	

Campaign Finance

	Receipts	Receipts from PACs	Expend-itures
1990			
Jones (D)	$127,710	$72,100 (56%)	$111,622
Moye (R)	$20,570	$250 (1%)	$20,463
1988			
Jones (D)	$141,476	$96,550 (68%)	$82,147
Moye (R)	$16,758	0	$16,758

Key Votes

1991	
Authorize use of force against Iraq	Y
1990	
Support constitutional amendment on flag desecration	Y
Pass family and medical leave bill over Bush veto	N
Reduce SDI funding	Y
Allow abortions in overseas military facilities	Y
Approve budget summit plan for spending and taxing	N
Approve civil rights bill	Y
1989	
Halt production of B-2 stealth bomber at 13 planes	Y
Oppose capital gains tax cut	Y
Approve federal abortion funding in rape or incest cases	?
Approve pay raise and revision of ethics rules	Y
Pass Democratic minimum wage plan over Bush veto	Y

Voting Studies

	Presidential Support		Party Unity		Conservative Coalition	
Year	S	O	S	O	S	O
1990	28	66	80	12	57	41
1989	36	51	78	11	34	54
1988	19	72	83	6	37	47
1987	15	57	76	5	28	33
1986	27	62	76	11	56	30
1985	20	74	76	7	38	49
1984	30	50	70	12	49	41
1983	38	57	70	19	62	29
1982	39	44	65	22	56	32
1981	37	30	47	20	40	15

Interest Group Ratings

Year	ADA	ACU	AFL-CIO	CCUS
1990	50	39	82	54
1989	70	26	75	60
1988	80	13	75	46
1987	56	0	87	21
1986	55	22	77	40
1985	70	5	71	25
1984	55	19	75	43
1983	60	25	67	42
1982	40	47	61	65
1981	25	21	82	36

2 Tim Valentine (D)

Of Nashville — Elected 1982

Born: March 15, 1926, Nash County, N.C.
Education: The Citadel, A.B. 1948; U. of North Carolina, LL.B. 1952.
Military Service: Army Air Force, 1944-46.
Occupation: Lawyer.
Family: Wife, Barbara Reynolds; four children, three stepchildren.
Religion: Baptist.
Political Career: N.C. House, 1955-61; N.C. Democratic Party chairman, 1966-68.
Capitol Office: 1510 Longworth Bldg. 20515; 225-4531.

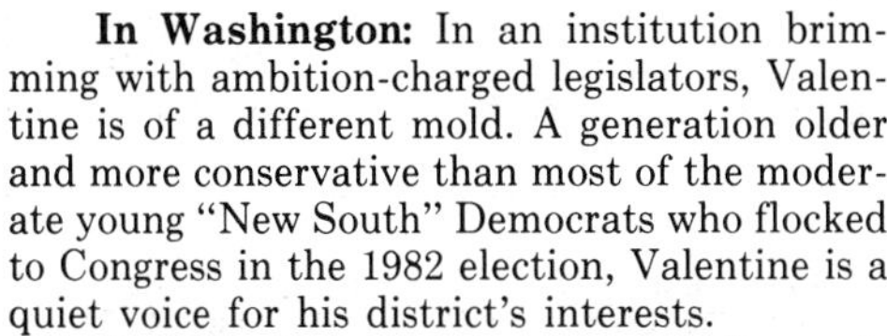

In Washington: In an institution brimming with ambition-charged legislators, Valentine is of a different mold. A generation older and more conservative than most of the moderate young "New South" Democrats who flocked to Congress in the 1982 election, Valentine is a quiet voice for his district's interests.

Chairing the new Technology and Competitiveness Subcommittee, Valentine speaks for the scientific community in the Research Triangle (Durham County, one corner of the Triangle, is in the 2nd). In 1988, he introduced a bill to create a national board to coordinate semiconductor research and development.

Amending the Constitution twice became an issue for Valentine in 1990. An original signer of the proposed amendment to ban flag desecration, Valentine at the last minute "heard the voice of his own conscience" and voted against the measure.

Valentine, however, had no qualms about constitutional tinkering to require the exclusion of illegal aliens for purposes of determining population for reapportionment. The issue was important for North Carolina's bid to gain a 13th congressional seat.

A defender of rural interests in his district, Valentine gravitated to the bloc of Southerners who swap old-time stories in the back of the House chamber. On most issues, his votes follow in the tradition of L. H. Fountain, the 30-year veteran he replaced in 1983. Although Valentine often sides with the conservative coalition of Republicans and Southern Democrats, he is no party turncoat; in recent Congresses, he has voted with a majority of House Democrats at least two-thirds of the time.

Valentine handled a difficult assignment in the 101st Congress by waging the tobacco industry's fight against a smoking ban on airline flights. Fearful of a renewed assault by anti-smoking advocates, Valentine opted to accept a two-year extension of a ban on flights of two hours or less. The strategy failed, however, as a permanent ban on most domestic flights eventually became law.

At Home: Capturing and holding the 2nd involved Valentine in racially divisive campaigns. Boundary changes in the 2nd wrought by 1982 redistricting go a long way toward explaining the tensions. Fountain's old small-town and rural constituency was merged with urban Durham County, home to a large and politically assertive black community. The resulting district provided blacks their best shot at winning a House seat in the state.

To win nomination in the 2nd in 1982, Valentine had to overcome H. M. "Mickey" Michaux Jr., a black former U.S. attorney and state legislator from Durham County. Valentine finished second to Michaux in the primary, but won the runoff by casting himself as a conservative and Michaux as a labor lackey who would raise taxes and cut defense. Lingering black dissatisfaction was evident in a general election write-in campaign waged for Michaux, but Valentine won comfortably.

Two years later, black state Rep. Kenneth B. Spaulding challenged Valentine in the Democratic primary. Determined to avoid being labeled a liberal, Spaulding portrayed himself as a fiscal conservative. That helped him cut his losses among white voters, and the Rev. Jesse Jackson helped Spaulding stoke black voters' passions. But Jackson's activity also sparked a backlash among rural whites, benefiting Valentine. The incumbent's rural strength helped him clinch renomination with 52 percent.

The son of a state Supreme Court justice, Valentine was elected to the Legislature in 1954 at age 28. He served three terms, then left to spend more time practicing law. In 1965 he became the legislative liaison for Democratic Gov. Dan K. Moore. Valentine returned to his Nash County home when Moore's term ended, devoting his time to the chamber of commerce and the Baptist Church. After an auto accident that killed his wife in August 1981, a desire to put that tragedy behind him persuaded Valentine to run for Congress.

North Carolina 2

North Central — Durham; Rocky Mount

The 2nd is an uneasy marriage of different kinds of voters who happen to share the same party label.

In one corner of the district are the urban Democrats in Durham, where blacks, labor unions and white liberals are a political force. Elsewhere, the 2nd is predominantly rural, and conservative white Democrats are uncomfortable with blacks gaining political power. The 2nd has the largest minority population of any North Carolina district. Two counties are majority-black, and several have black populations over 40 percent.

Durham's best-known industry is the one that for a century has given the city its strong aroma — cigarette manufacturing. In addition to the gritty, working-class Durham of tobacco factories and textile mills, there is the ivory tower academic world of Duke University.

Durham's blacks traditionally have played a prominent role in commerce and politics. Today, 46 percent of the city's people are black, and their influence made possible the strong showings by black Democratic House contenders in the 1982 and 1984 primaries. Running against GOP Sen. Jesse Helms in 1990, black Democratic Senate nominee Harvey B. Gantt received 64 percent in Durham.

Tobacco is equally important in the rural, eastern part of the 2nd District, but it is grown there, not processed in factories. Cotton and peanuts also are important crops. The area's two cities, Rocky Mount and Wilson, are marketing centers for the farms — Wilson has the world's largest flue-cured tobacco warehouse. They also make pharmaceuticals, tires and textiles.

Population: 536,210. White 316,200 (59%), Black 214,899 (40%), Other 4,016 (1%). Spanish origin 4,571 (1%). 18 and over 382,220 (71%), 65 and over 58,389 (11%). Median age: 30.

Committees

Public Works & Transportation (12th of 36 Democrats)
Aviation; Surface Transportation

Science, Space & Technology (10th of 32 Democrats)
Technology & Competitiveness (chairman); Science

Elections

1990 General		
Tim Valentine (D)	130,979	(75%)
Hal C. Sharpe (R)	44,263	(25%)
1988 General		
Tim Valentine (D)	128,832	(100%)

Previous Winning Percentages: **1986** (75%) **1984** (68%) **1982** (54%)

District Vote For President

	1988	1984	1980	1976
D	93,727 (50%)	92,146 (47%)	80,350 (53%)	77,733 (57%)
R	92,745 (49%)	103,780 (53%)	65,911 (43%)	57,761 (42%)
I			4,402 (3%)	

Campaign Finance

	Receipts	Receipts from PACs	Expend-itures
1990			
Valentine (D)	$261,712	$159,202 (61%)	$286,351
Sharpe (R)	$58,015	$1,400 (2%)	$56,842
1988			
Valentine (D)	$78,527	$58,650 (75%)	$84,671

Key Votes

1991	
Authorize use of force against Iraq	Y
1990	
Support constitutional amendment on flag desecration	N
Pass family and medical leave bill over Bush veto	N
Reduce SDI funding	Y
Allow abortions in overseas military facilities	Y
Approve budget summit plan for spending and taxing	Y
Approve civil rights bill	Y
1989	
Halt production of B-2 stealth bomber at 13 planes	N
Oppose capital gains tax cut	Y
Approve federal abortion funding in rape or incest cases	Y
Approve pay raise and revision of ethics rules	Y
Pass Democratic minimum wage plan over Bush veto	N

Voting Studies

	Presidential Support		Party Unity		Conservative Coalition	
Year	S	O	S	O	S	O
1990	42	58	66	30	89	11
1989	52	47	69	29	73	27
1988	40	58	70	25	95	5
1987	40	55	67	30	88	9
1986	41	57	67	31	90	8
1985	46	52	71	25	84	13
1984	43	44	51	38	86	7
1983	44	56	54	42	90	8

Interest Group Ratings

Year	ADA	ACU	AFL-CIO	CCUS
1990	33	42	42	43
1989	30	39	33	70
1988	45	48	71	62
1987	44	29	50	60
1986	30	55	43	65
1985	35	48	35	59
1984	20	55	46	38
1983	40	57	35	60

3 H. Martin Lancaster (D)

Of Goldsboro — Elected 1986

Born: March 24, 1943, Wayne County, N.C.
Education: U. of North Carolina, A.B. 1965, J.D. 1967.
Military Service: Navy, 1967-70; Naval Reserve, 1970-present.
Occupation: Lawyer.
Family: Wife, Alice Matheny; two children.
Religion: Presbyterian.
Political Career: N.C. House, 1979-87.
Capitol Office: 1417 Longworth Bldg. 20515; 225-3415.

In Washington: Although Lancaster comes from conservative East Carolina tobacco country, he is not bashful about voting with his party's leadership. But he is much more than just a reliable vote; he is an astute politician, well-connected around his home state and bent on getting connected in Washington.

In the 101st Congress, Lancaster passed such leadership litmus tests as voting for the 1989 congressional pay raise and ethics reform package, for the controversial fiscal 1991 budget summit agreement and for a Democratic plan to kill a cut in the capital gains tax. Also, on two key abortion votes in the 101st, Lancaster voted with the abortion-rights side.

Lancaster's committee assignments put him in a good position to look after his district, whose economy is tied to agriculture and military bases. On Armed Services he follows some broad issues; when he sought work from committee Chairman Les Aspin, Aspin appointed him to chair a task force on chemical weapons. Lancaster was an observer to the international negotiations on banning chemical weapons.

Lancaster also has a closer-to-home concern on Armed Services: Twenty percent of the entire Marine Corps is located at the corps' training center at Camp Lejeune, in the coastal 3rd District city of Jacksonville. Lancaster's hometown, Goldsboro, is home to the Seymour Johnson Air Force Base. In January 1991, Lancaster voted to give President Bush the authority to use force against Iraq.

On Agriculture, Lancaster watches out for other important economic interests, including North Carolina tobacco, peanut and corn growers. He has introduced legislation to mandate degradable plastics for consumer products — to help the environment, he says, and also for growers of corn, used to make plastics degradable.

At Home: When Lancaster announced in 1985 that he was leaving the state Legislature to devote more time to his family and law practice, he did not expect to be back campaigning within six months. But Rep. Charles Whitley's surprise retirement announcement caused him to reassess.

Lancaster had left his mark in the state House on a range of issues, from licensing for medical practitioners to the creation of grass-roots arts programs. The high point of his legislative career occurred when Democratic Gov. James B. Hunt Jr. asked him to shepherd through the House a controversial measure to toughen the state's drunken-driving laws.

As soon as he announced his candidacy for Whitley's seat in Congress, Lancaster became the Democratic primary favorite. He moved quickly to shore up his one potential weakness — a perception by some that he had associated with the more liberal bloc of Democrats in the state House. Lancaster devoted much of his campaign to courting business leaders and establishing conservative credentials.

The only one of his opponents who could hope to match Lancaster's support was Lewis Renn, Whitley's top aide in Washington. But while Renn had access to a quiet network of Whitley backers scattered throughout the district, he had no broad-based name recognition, and he never managed to achieve very much.

Lancaster was able to take most of the black vote, which comprises a significant proportion of the total in the Democratic primary. He benefited from a high turnout in Wayne County prompted by a liquor-by-the-drink referendum on the ballot there. While each of the candidates won his home county, Lancaster finished either first or second in the remaining seven counties. Renn was eligible for a runoff, but finished so far behind Lancaster in the primary that he chose to pass up the opportunity.

The well-financed Lancaster then had little trouble defeating GOP state Rep. Gerald Hurst in this Democratic district. Lancaster had no opposition in 1988.

In 1990, the third-place finisher in the Republican primary, a 100-year-old ophthalmologist, drew more attention than the nominee. With GOP Sen. Jesse Helms winning the 3rd comfortably, Lancaster captured 60 percent of the vote.

North Carolina 3

Southeast Central — Goldsboro

The 3rd's flat, sandy countryside is broken up by small market towns serving the tobacco fields that make this district the nation's No. 1 producer of flue-cured tobacco. Goldsboro (Wayne County), the largest city in the 3rd, has a thriving tobacco market; textiles are also key. Cotton has begun to make a comeback as a major crop, but it lags behind the leaf. There also is a military component to Goldsboro's economy: the Seymour Johnson Air Force Base, just south of the city.

Recent elections suggest the divided sympathies of the 3rd, where Democrats have traditionally dominated, but GOP candidates are having more success. The areas within the 3rd supported Jimmy Carter in 1976 and 1980, and the district went comfortably for Democrat Terry Sanford in his 1986 Senate contest. But the 3rd has given GOP Sen. Jesse Helms solid margins in his four elections, and it backed GOP Gov. James G. Martin in 1988.

The district's three most populous counties — Wayne, Onslow and Johnston — together cast about 45 percent of the vote. Though Democrats still number more registered voters in these counties, GOP candidates often win them in national and statewide elections. Reagan carried all three in 1980 and 1984, as did George Bush and Gov. Martin in 1988.

In addition to tobacco and cotton, soybeans and sweet potatoes grow here, and the district's farmers raise poultry and hogs. Duplin County produces more turkeys than any other in the state. Onslow, one of the district's two Atlantic coast counties, draws many visitors, but most are not seaside tourists; they are the "few good men" being whipped into shape at the Camp Lejeune Marine Corps training center near Jacksonville.

Population: 535,906. White 380,813 (71%), Black 146,519 (27%), Other 5,042 (1%). Spanish origin 8,326 (2%). 18 and over 379,853 (71%), 65 and over 48,581 (9%). Median age: 27.

Committees

Armed Services (24th of 33 Democrats)
Military Personnel & Compensation; Readiness

Small Business (18th of 27 Democrats)
Exports, Tax Policy & Special Problems; Procurement, Tourism & Rural Development; Regulation, Business Opportunity & Energy

Elections

1990 General		
H. Martin Lancaster (D)	83,930	(59%)
Don Davis (R)	57,605	(41%)
1988 General		
H. Martin Lancaster (D)	95,323	(100%)

Previous Winning Percentage: **1986** (64%)

District Vote For President

	1988	1984	1980	1976
D	62,638 (42%)	62,777 (39%)	71,695 (51%)	71,701 (59%)
R	85,233 (58%)	98,610 (61%)	65,996 (47%)	50,107 (41%)
I			2,042 (2%)	

Campaign Finance

	Receipts	Receipts from PACs		Expend-itures
1990				
Lancaster (D)	$421,283	$204,450	(49%)	$499,436
Davis (R)	$88,138	$500	(1%)	$84,160
1988				
Lancaster (D)	$195,992	$132,249	(67%)	$98,956

Key Votes

1991	
Authorize use of force against Iraq	Y
1990	
Support constitutional amendment on flag desecration	Y
Pass family and medical leave bill over Bush veto	N
Reduce SDI funding	N
Allow abortions in overseas military facilities	Y
Approve budget summit plan for spending and taxing	Y
Approve civil rights bill	Y
1989	
Halt production of B-2 stealth bomber at 13 planes	N
Oppose capital gains tax cut	Y
Approve federal abortion funding in rape or incest cases	Y
Approve pay raise and revision of ethics rules	Y
Pass Democratic minimum wage plan over Bush veto	N

Voting Studies

	Presidential Support		Party Unity		Conservative Coalition	
Year	**S**	**O**	**S**	**O**	**S**	**O**
1990	38	61	76	22	83	17
1989	45	52	73	23	78	22
1988	38	62	78	19	84	16
1987	37	62	71	25	86	12

Interest Group Ratings

Year	ADA	ACU	AFL-CIO	CCUS
1990	39	50	50	43
1989	40	30	42	80
1988	60	40	71	64
1987	60	17	75	40

4 David Price (D)

Of Chapel Hill — Elected 1986

Born: Aug. 17, 1940, Johnson City, Tenn.

Education: Attended Mars Hill College, 1958-59; U. of North Carolina, B.A. 1961; Yale U., B.D. 1964, Ph.D. 1969.

Occupation: Professor of political science and public policy.

Family: Wife, Lisa Kanwit; two children.

Religion: American Baptist.

Political Career: N.C. Democratic Party chairman, 1983-84.

Capitol Office: 1406 Longworth Bldg. 20515; 225-1784.

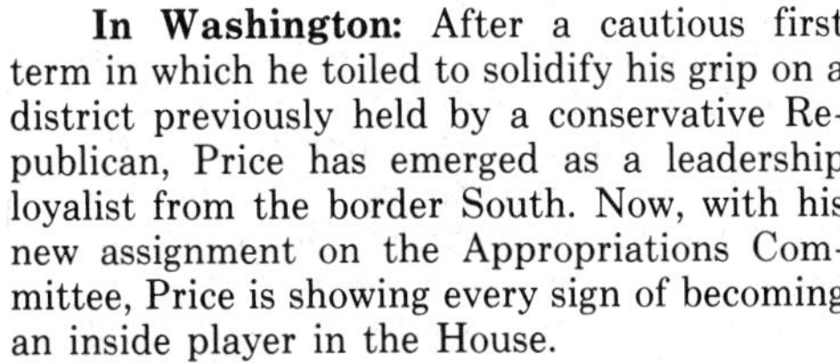

In Washington: After a cautious first term in which he toiled to solidify his grip on a district previously held by a conservative Republican, Price has emerged as a leadership loyalist from the border South. Now, with his new assignment on the Appropriations Committee, Price is showing every sign of becoming an inside player in the House.

A political science professor and former state party chairman who was staff director of the Democratic Party's post-1980 presidential rules commission, Price quickly caught the eye of the House leadership. His first term was somewhat shaky, as he reversed positions on a gun-control amendment he had cosponsored shortly before the 1988 election and broke party ranks over House recitation of the Pledge of Allegiance.

But in the 101st Congress, Price's voting record reflected the confidence he placed in his political organization following a comfortable re-election win. He voted against a constitutional amendment to ban physical desecration of the flag and opposed cutting the tax on capital gains. He also backed federal funding for abortion, mandatory family and medical leave, the 1990 budget "summit" agreement and the 1989 congressional pay raise package that revised Congress' ethics rules.

Price made an impressive legislative debut on the Banking Committee with his bill requiring banks to disclose fully the terms of home-equity loans. He touted the bill, which was signed into law in 1988, in his re-election campaign, appealing to the sizable white-collar suburbanite population in his district.

In the 101st Congress, Price pursued his goal to make housing more affordable as the committee worked on the first major overhaul of federal housing programs since 1974. Price added language expanding a federally backed "reverse mortgage" program that allows senior citizens to draw cash equity from their homes. He also won inclusion of a program allowing state and local governments to help lower-income families buying their first homes by providing low-interest "soft-second mortgages." Repayment on the government-guaranteed loans would be deferred for five years.

Price and Delaware Democrat Thomas R. Carper led a bloc of conservative and moderate Democrats in sealing a compromise on a provision, sponsored by Texas Republican Steve Bartlett, to offer new incentives and requirements to persuade owners of federally subsidized housing to continue renting to low-income families. The Democratic bloc backed Bartlett's proposal during committee consideration. Carper and Price then negotiated a compromise, which they offered on the House floor. It was adopted 400-12.

Price authored legislation in the 101st Congress giving the Federal Deposit Insurance Corporation authority to limit "golden parachutes" given to executives, officers or shareholders of federally insured depository institutions. His proposal was signed into law as part of the omnibus 1990 crime bill.

On the Science, Space and Technology Committee, Price introduced legislation to establish a grant program to improve science and mathematics teaching in schools. Portions of his bill became law at the end of the 101st Congress as part of a mathematics-science scholarship bill. Price also introduced legislation in the 101st and 102nd Congresses to restore income tax deductibility for student loans and scholarships.

In 1987, Price added his name to a growing list of cosponsors of a bill establishing a waiting period for the purchase of handguns. When the issue came to the floor in 1988, Price found himself confronted with the dilemma of bucking the powerful National Rifle Association just weeks before the election, or voting against a proposal he had cosponsored. He decided on the latter course, sparking an outcry from gun-control advocates.

A week earlier, in what was widely perceived as another issue testing Democrats' po-

North Carolina 4

Central — Raleigh; Chapel Hill

Universities are not only cultural centers in this part of the state — they are major sources of jobs. Home to 14 post-secondary schools, the 4th comprises two corners of the Research Triangle area — Wake County (Raleigh) and Orange County (Chapel Hill). Chapel Hill hosts the University of North Carolina, and North Carolina State is in Raleigh. Drawing upon them, and employing thousands of white-collar professionals, is a collection of laboratories and research facilities run by private firms and government agencies. Additional white-collar jobs are available in government agencies in Raleigh, North Carolina's capital.

The outlying parts of Wake County are more traditional rural Deep South territory. Wake, which casts a little more than 60 percent of the 4th's vote, has usually split its tickets in recent years. In 1988, Wake went Republican in both the presidential and gubernatorial contests, but voted for Democrat Price in the House race. In 1990, Wake backed black Democratic nominee Harvey B. Gantt in his race against GOP Sen. Jesse Helms, giving Gantt 56 percent.

Orange County, home to about 15 percent of the district's voters, has a more Democratic bent, thanks in large part to the university community of Chapel Hill. In 1988 and 1990, Orange County gave Price 72 percent in his House contest. Gantt received 71 percent in Orange.

South of Orange lies Chatham County, largely rural territory dotted with textile plants, tobacco fields and dairy farms. Chatham's agrarian complexion is changing somewhat, however, as growth from Chapel Hill spills over into its northern end.

Chatham County is solidly Democratic in most state and local elections, and in 1988, Michael S. Dukakis managed to carry it in presidential voting. But Helms took 50 percent against Gantt.

Randolph, just south of the Greensboro-High Point metropolis, is the most populous county in the state to give the GOP a numerical advantage. Price has lost Randolph decisively in each House race. At the district's eastern end lies rural Franklin County, dominated by tobacco and farming: It clings to its Democratic traditions in most statewide and local races but only gave Gantt 46 percent in 1990.

Population: 533,580. White 421,508 (79%), Black 105,942 (20%), Other 4,270 (1%). Spanish origin 4,152 (1%). 18 and over 395,635 (74%), 65 and over 44,974 (8%). Median age: 29.

litical nerve, Price was one of only seven Democrats supporting a GOP effort to require recitation of the Pledge of Allegiance at the start of each day's House proceedings.

At Home: Price laid the groundwork for his move from academia to electioneering with a long career as a party activist at the state and national level. In 1986, he beat GOP Rep. Bill Cobey by 12 points — the largest victory margin of any House challenger that year.

While teaching political science at Duke, Price spent nearly two years as state party chairman, winning generally high marks for his performance. He also made invaluable contacts with local party leaders in the district, and used them to build an early financial and organizational edge over three primary rivals.

In the primary, Price, a somewhat stiff and awkward campaigner, fell short of the 50 percent needed to avoid a runoff. But his strongest opponent declined to force a runoff.

Cobey, who had won the traditionally Democratic 4th in 1984, was considered vulnerable from the outset. His affable nature and constituent-service operation helped him win over some voters who disagreed with his conservative ideology, but he was operating with little margin for error. And he committed a serious one in mid-September.

Cobey mailed out a campaign letter addressed to "Dear Christian Friend," in which he said he was "an ambassador for Christ" who needed the support of fundamentalists "so our voice will not be silenced and then replaced by someone who is not willing to take a strong stand for the principles outlined in the word of God." Injecting religion in the campaign might have been a questionable tactic against any candidate, but it seemed particularly inappropriate against Price, an active Southern Baptist who taught Sunday school and has a divinity degree. The letter aided Price's contention that Cobey was "isolated ... from mainstream thinking in both parties."

Price, who had criticized Cobey throughout the year for opposing such diverse proposals as African famine relief and the Clean Water Act, zeroed in with late TV ads hitting Cobey for casting votes against Social Security and emergency farm credit legislation in 1985.

In 1988, Price faced Republican Tom Fetzer, a former operative for GOP Sen. Jesse Helms' political organization, the National Congressional Club. The Club's past campaign tactics and attention to social issues had put off Democrats and even some Republicans, but the organization's resources helped make Fetzer a threat. Price, however, was on guard to deflect charges that he was too liberal for the 4th; his work on the home-equity legislation aimed straight at affluent suburbanites who might be tempted to vote Republican. In the end, Price improved on his 1986 showing.

In 1990, Price stared down another well-financed Republican challenge. Raleigh businessman John H. Carrington had run two close statewide campaigns in the 1980s, financing them largely out of his own pocket. A political loner, he depended on television commercials and shunned public appearances in those races.

Carrington ran radio ads throughout the spring and summer attacking Congress; in September he began his TV campaign with ads criticizing Price for accepting money from banking and savings and loan interests while he sits on the Banking Committee. "Should Congress Have a Price?" his ads queried. But voters were not swayed: Price posted a 58 percent win.

Committees

Appropriations (36th of 37 Democrats)
Rural Development, Agriculture & Related Agencies; Transportation

Elections

1990 General		
David Price (D)	139,396	(58%)
John Carrington (R)	100,661	(42%)
1990 Primary		
David Price (D)	51,122	(91%)
Robert B. Coats Sr. (D)	2,482	(4%)
Paul E. Moore (D)	2,377	(4%)
1988 General		
David Price (D)	131,896	(58%)
Tom Fetzer (R)	95,482	(42%)

Previous Winning Percentage: **1986** (56%)

District Vote For President

	1988	1984	1980	1976
D	105,357 (44%)	90,622 (40%)	86,907 (47%)	84,276 (53%)
R	132,495 (55%)	137,174 (60%)	87,832 (47%)	74,839 (47%)
I			9,967 (5%)	

Campaign Finance

	Receipts	Receipts from PACs	Expend-itures
1990			
Price (D)	$771,624	$385,210 (50%)	$793,291
Carrington (R)	$893,349	0	$890,838
1988			
Price (D)	$1,031,004	$489,658 (47%)	$1,006,641
Fetzer (R)	$759,367	$85,051 (11%)	$759,164

Key Votes

1991	
Authorize use of force against Iraq	N
1990	
Support constitutional amendment on flag desecration	N
Pass family and medical leave bill over Bush veto	Y
Reduce SDI funding	Y
Allow abortions in overseas military facilities	Y
Approve budget summit plan for spending and taxing	Y
Approve civil rights bill	Y
1989	
Halt production of B-2 stealth bomber at 13 planes	Y
Oppose capital gains tax cut	Y
Approve federal abortion funding in rape or incest cases	Y
Approve pay raise and revision of ethics rules	Y
Pass Democratic minimum wage plan over Bush veto	Y

Voting Studies

	Presidential Support		Party Unity		Conservative Coalition	
Year	**S**	**O**	**S**	**O**	**S**	**O**
1990	24	75	92	8	48	52
1989	34	66	90	9	56	44
1988	28	68	83	14	71	24
1987	29	69	84	13	72	28

Interest Group Ratings

Year	ADA	ACU	AFL-CIO	CCUS
1990	61	21	75	29
1989	75	14	83	60
1988	75	24	93	62
1987	80	9	81	33

5 Stephen L. Neal (D)

Of Winston-Salem — Elected 1974

Born: Nov. 7, 1934, Winston-Salem, N.C.
Education: Attended U. of California, Santa Barbara, 1954-56; U. of Hawaii, A.B. 1963.
Occupation: Publisher; mortgage banker.
Family: Wife, Rachel Landis Miller; two children.
Religion: Presbyterian.
Political Career: No previous office.
Capitol Office: 2463 Rayburn Bldg. 20515; 225-2071.

In Washington: Neal's politically cautious style and the seniority that has put him within sight of the Banking Committee chairmanship have combined to help him survive repeated Republican challenges in a district that leans toward more clear-cut conservatism.

He has fostered ties to the state's business community, especially the financial institutions that have become Southern powerhouses under deregulation. With Neal a Banking subcommittee chairman, and third among 31 Democrats in line for the full committee chair, local business leaders have shied from opposing him, even when one of their own is the GOP nominee, as was the case in 1988.

Reserved yet personable, Neal fits in well politically with other North Carolina Democrats, a group of moderates who are the most reliable supporters of House Democratic leaders among Southerners. Meanwhile, he keeps enough distance from the national party's more controversial stands to survive at home.

Still, the full-time effort at electoral survival — he has garnered 60 percent only once in nine elections — seems to have detracted from Neal's profile in Banking, and in the House in general. He is a low-key chairman who is more given to compromise than confrontation.

In the 100th Congress, however, Neal did play a leading role in the controversial effort to save the Federal Savings and Loan Insurance Corporation (FSLIC) from insolvency. He sponsored an S&L industry-backed proposal to raise $5 billion over two years for the FSLIC from higher industry fees. The Reagan administration wanted $15 billion over five years. Foes said the FSLIC could not effectively absorb that much money, but many experts maintained that it would take much more than $15 billion to shut down the many bankrupt S&Ls.

Neal's proposal had a formidable supporter in Speaker Jim Wright, who personally lobbied the committee for the $5 billion plan. A day after a Banking subcommittee approved the administration-backed proposal, Democratic vote switches in the full committee reversed the outcome. Neal's amendment passed, 25-24.

Then Wright and Chairman Fernand J. St Germain switched after weeks of negative press coverage of Wright's role. The two men endorsed the $15 billion option. But as Neal said later, Wright "wasn't very active" in pushing it, while the S&L lobby fought it. By 153-258, the House defeated the $15 billion plan when St Germain proposed it, and adopted Neal's $5 billion package. In the end, $10.8 billion was authorized, and Neal had little hand in the outcome. It was negotiated between then-Treasury Secretary James A. Baker III and the House and Senate Banking Committee heads to avert Reagan's veto.

By 1989, the huge-scale woes of the S&L industry were indisputable. Neal backed legislation to provide $50 billion to salvage the industry and enact strict standards for the percentage of capital thrifts must maintain. On a key House vote on whether to allow thrifts with "supervisory good will" — a type of "phantom" capital — to continue to count it to meet the new standards, Neal bucked the industry and voted against the amendment.

In early 1991, when Congress authorized another $30 billion for the bailout, Neal voted against all but one bailout option — a Democrat-sponsored plan to finance it on a pay-as-you-go basis.

Neal is chairman of the Subcommittee on Domestic Monetary Policy, which oversees the Federal Reserve Board and its regulation of the money supply. It is a good place for a monetarist like Neal, who believes with conservative Milton Friedman that national economic health depends on a modest and steady growth in the money supply, rather than any combination of federal tax and spending policies.

In the 101st Congress, Neal introduced legislation to have Congress order the Fed to try to bring inflation down to zero. His proposal would have set a five-year goal for the Fed of reducing inflation to zero or to a level where it no longer affects economic decision-making. In an appearance before Neal's subcommittee, Fed Chairman Alan Greenspan endorsed the plan. The Bush administration opposed it, however,

North Carolina 5

Northwest — Winston-Salem

The heart of the 5th is Winston-Salem, an old-time tobacco town whose links to the leaf were established over a century ago. The first factory opened in Winston-Salem in 1872; three years later R. J. Reynolds constructed his first processing plant. The city remains a tobacco-processing center, although it produces textiles and communications equipment as well. The population of Winston-Salem is almost 40 percent black. The city and surrounding Forsyth County cast almost half the district's overall vote.

In national elections, Forsyth has a Republican tilt that has been building for more than a decade. The county gave Democratic presidential nominee Jimmy Carter the barest of margins in 1976, crossed party lines to go narrowly for Ronald Reagan in 1980, and then went comfortably Republican in the 1984 and 1988 White House contests. Its allegiances are divided in elections closer to home. Democratic Gov. James B. Hunt Jr. narrowly carried Forsyth in his 1984 bid against GOP Sen. Jesse Helms, but Helms received 52 percent in 1990 against black Democratic nominee Harvey B. Gantt.

Republicans traditionally have been strong in several of the hill counties in the western reaches of the district, between the Blue Ridge and Appalachian mountains. Early settlers of this area set up small farms with dairy cows, poultry, apple trees and tobacco, and developed strong antagonism toward the flatland tobacco planters, who were wealthier, politically powerful and Democratic.

Wilkes County has been strong for the GOP. In 1990, Neal won Wilkes by 331 votes over his little-known opponent, but Helms ran up 58 percent against Gantt.

Hosiery is the critical branch of the textile industry in the outlying areas of the 5th. Mount Airy, a town of some 7,000 people near the Virginia border, hosts several plants involved in the manufacture of stockings, men's briefs and infants' nightwear.

Population: 535,212. White 445,932 (83%), Black 86,748 (16%). Spanish origin 3,667 (1%). 18 and over 388,006 (63%), 65 and over 58,381 (11%). Median age: 31.

criticizing it as an effort by Congress to "micromanage" the Fed. It did not make it out of the subcommittee.

Certainly, Domestic Monetary Policy is less of a burden than Neal's previous job, as chairman of the International Finance Subcommittee. That panel is charged with recommending funding for the U.S. contributions to the International Monetary Fund (IMF) and the Export-Import Bank. At times of suspicion about foreign assistance, bills for these international lenders have provoked conservatives

Opponents of legislation for the IMF, source of aid to dozens of Third World nations, in 1983 offered more than 60 amendments, and several passed over Neal's objections. As he predicted, they were killed in conference with the Senate, largely because Reagan was among the backers of IMF funding.

Still, Neal took considerable heat, on the House floor and off, for his role. Conservative Republicans who disagreed with Reagan's stand launched ad campaigns in the districts of many Democrats, including Neal, charging that lawmakers had given aid to communist countries.

Meanwhile, the Ex-Im Bank seemed to gain political strength as members came to see it as a way to protect American jobs by stimulating exports. Neal's job was to fend off Reagan's proposed cuts. In the 99th Congress, the administration recommended that the Ex-Im Bank subsidize interest rates on private banks' loans rather than make direct loans itself to foreign buyers of U.S. goods. But with record trade deficits, the plan found a cool reception on Capitol Hill, since it was perceived as an attempt to kill the bank entirely. "If ever we needed the Ex-Im Bank," Neal said at one point, "we need it now."

His subcommittee rejected Reagan's plan 18-1. It passed a bill reauthorizing the bank, although the measure finally approved by Congress in 1986 did include an experimental program of subsidies for private banks. The bill also included a $300 million "war chest" for grants and low-interest loans to boost exports, an idea backed by Neal and the administration.

Although it has caused him some problems at home, Neal has voted with the Democratic leadership more often than not. For example, he consistently opposed Reagan's policy of military aid to the Nicaraguan contras. Despite a $40,000 offer for campaign help from the National Conservative Political Action Committee, Neal voted against the Reagan-backed tax cut in 1981. He complained to the Justice Department that the offer was a bribe, but officials concluded it "did not go beyond the bounds of traditionally acceptable lobbying."

In the 101st Congress, he voted against a

proposed constitutional amendment to ban physical desecration of the flag. He also voted against giving Bush authority to use force against Iraq, instead backing continued economic sanctions.

During House floor consideration in 1990 of a comprehensive civil rights bill, Neal and Texas Democrat Michael A. Andrews offered a compromise amendment designed to answer the administration's objection that the legislation would impose racial hiring quotas. The Andrews-Neal amendment stated that nothing in the bill "shall be construed to require an employer to adopt hiring or promotion quotas on the basis of race, color, religion, sex or national origin." It also said that a mere statistical imbalance in an employer's shop on account of race, color, religion, sex or national origin cannot establish that a boss discriminates. The amendment was adopted by a vote of 397-24, but the bill died after the Senate failed by a single vote to override Bush's veto.

Neal also is a member of the Government Operations Committee, where he has proposed a bill to raise the Environmental Protection Agency to Cabinet level, in an effort to boost its visibility and clout.

Other of his efforts are more closely linked to the interests of his district, perched geographically and politically between the Republican-leaning Appalachian foothills and the traditionally Democratic Piedmont. Besides banking, Neal promotes two more troubled industries, tobacco and textiles.

He opposes the increasing number of measures to raise cigarette taxes and limit smoking; in 1986, he dubbed bills to restrict smoking in federal buildings the "Smokers Segregation and Persecution Acts." In the past three Congresses, he has joined fellow Southerners in a feisty but unsuccessful fight to limit textile imports. All three trade bills were vetoed.

At Home: A Watergate-spawned Democrat in a district with a demonstrated affection for the GOP, Neal always expects tough elections, and is always prepared for them. But the wave of Republicanism that has swept through the state in recent presidential elections has tested even his best-laid plans.

His opponent in 1980 was state Sen. Anne Bagnal, an energetic Republican who stressed her strong opposition to abortion and the Equal Rights Amendment and criticized Neal's support for President Carter. Although Neal voted with Carter no more often than the average House Democrat, he enthusiastically touted the president and invited him to appear in the district during the campaign.

Reagan carried the 5th over Carter by nearly 15,000 votes, laying down coattails for Bagnal that helped her hold Neal to 51 percent, the worst showing he had made since his initial election to the House in 1974.

Neal rebounded in 1982, winning handily over Bagnal in a good Democratic year in North Carolina. But by 1984, he was in trouble again. Reagan's position at the top of the ticket helped spark an outbreak of straight-ticket GOP voting in North Carolina.

The GOP nominee was broadcast executive Stuart Epperson, a political neophyte who entered the race only shortly before the filing deadline. Epperson's appeal was hampered not only by low visibility but also by his quixotic style. Early on, he sought to attract attention to his candidacy by walking the district with a lantern, asking voters if they had seen Neal.

A graduate of fundamentalist Bob Jones University, Epperson began by stressing his conservative stance on school prayer. But local GOP leaders convinced him that an economic emphasis would give him broader appeal. He spent the later stages of the campaign criticizing Neal's support for U.S. involvement in the IMF, arguing that such a stance would encourage foreign competition and thus hurt local textile markets.

Neal defended his record and dismissed Epperson as an amateur dependent for support upon Reagan's coattails. "He has no record of accomplishment, service or understanding," the incumbent said. Still, he needed all his political strength to hold on to his seat. Bolstered by the campaigns of Reagan, GOP gubernatorial candidate James G. Martin and Sen. Jesse Helms, Epperson took five of the district's eight counties and came within 3,232 votes of an upset.

Epperson returned for a rematch in 1986, and proved more polished than in his first outing. He also offered a more focused message. Hoping to capitalize on discontent over the slumping textile industry, Epperson spent most of the campaign railing against Neal for supporting IMF loans that the Republican claimed were used to help build textile plants in foreign countries — and thus cost the 5th District jobs. He also touted his efforts to encourage radio stations across the country to donate free air time to a buy-American clothing campaign dubbed "Crafted With Pride."

Neal sought to discredit his opposition by arguing that the only people who saw sinister implications in the IMF were Epperson and fringe political figure Lyndon H. LaRouche Jr. But he also was careful to address Epperson's charges, denying that IMF money had been used to finance any foreign textile plants.

In the end, Epperson could not match the momentum of his 1984 campaign. Without the benefit of the top-of-the-ticket presence of a Reagan or a Helms, the Republican managed to carry only two counties — rural Alexander and Wilkes — as Neal posted a 54 percent tally.

Neal again had cause for concern in 1988. Michael S. Dukakis was not expected to run well in North Carolina, and the GOP offered a different style of candidate in Lyons Gray, a wealthy and well-known business-oriented establishment Republican.

Gray, owner of an industrial roofing company, was a member of a very prominent family in Winston-Salem, and he had had some political exposure as well. Gray lost to Epperson in the 1986 Republican House primary.

Unlike previous GOP nominees, Gray did not try to paint Neal as a dangerous liberal. In fact, his ads said Neal was not a bad representative. But the ads continued, "Not bad isn't good enough." He criticized Neal as an ineffective member overly attentive to big banks.

But Neal, experienced at tough campaigns, quickly put Gray on the defensive. He got an opening in late summer when Gray returned a questionnaire to the AFL-CIO stating his opposition to legislation limiting textile imports. That position is not palatable to most in North Carolina, and Gray quickly insisted it was a staff error. But the incident and a few other missteps shifted the focus from Neal.

In the end, Neal did almost as well as he had in 1986, taking 53 percent of the vote. Gray carried three counties, leaving five, including sizable Forsyth (Winston-Salem), to Neal.

Two years later, Republicans failed to offer a well-funded challenger, and Neal soared to his second-best election margin.

Neal had been one of the nation's most surprising winners in 1974, defeating four-term Rep. Wilmer D. Mizell, one of the most popular Republicans in the state. Mizell, a former National League pitcher, flirted with the idea of running for the Senate in 1974, finally deciding to keep what he and everyone else considered a safe House seat.

But it was not a good year to be a Republican in North Carolina. Neal, a publisher of several suburban newspapers, linked Mizell to the Nixon administration and the state's economic troubles and took 52 percent.

Two years later, Mizell came back for a rematch, arguing that Neal was a liberal who had sold his property in Winston-Salem and "gone Washington." Neal's cautious legislative record helped belie that charge, and a strong Democratic ticket helped him win with 54 percent of the vote.

Committees

Banking, Finance & Urban Affairs (3rd of 31 Democrats)
Domestic Monetary Policy (chairman); Financial Institutions Supervision, Regulation & Insurance; Housing & Community Development; International Development, Finance, Trade & Monetary Policy

Government Operations (7th of 25 Democrats)
Legislation & National Security

Elections

1990 General		
Stephen L. Neal (D)	113,814	(59%)
Ken Bell (R)	78,747	(41%)
1988 General		
Stephen L. Neal (D)	110,516	(53%)
Lyons Gray (R)	99,540	(47%)

Previous Winning Percentages: **1986** (54%) **1984** (51%) **1982** (60%) **1980** (51%) **1978** (54%) **1976** (54%) **1974** (52%)

District Vote For President

	1988	1984	1980	1976
D	81,340 (40%)	76,012 (36%)	84,718 (45%)	92,851 (52%)
R	123,725 (60%)	136,330 (64%)	99,410 (52%)	84,578 (48%)
I			4,431 (2%)	

Campaign Finance

	Receipts	Receipts from PACs		Expend-itures
1990				
Neal (D)	$671,884	$398,879	(59%)	$647,331
Bell (R)	$178,200	$2,550	(1%)	$174,574
1988				
Neal (D)	$715,578	$411,180	(57%)	$756,115
Gray (R)	$717,953	$52,887	(7%)	$718,015

Key Votes

1991	
Authorize use of force against Iraq	N
1990	
Support constitutional amendment on flag desecration	N
Pass family and medical leave bill over Bush veto	N
Reduce SDI funding	Y
Allow abortions in overseas military facilities	Y
Approve budget summit plan for spending and taxing	N
Approve civil rights bill	Y
1989	
Halt production of B-2 stealth bomber at 13 planes	N
Oppose capital gains tax cut	Y
Approve federal abortion funding in rape or incest cases	Y
Approve pay raise and revision of ethics rules	N
Pass Democratic minimum wage plan over Bush veto	Y

Voting Studies

	Presidential Support		Party Unity		Conservative Coalition	
Year	**S**	**O**	**S**	**O**	**S**	**O**
1990	36	59	66	25	74	24
1989	29	65	74	16	59	41
1988	24	68	76	12	55	24
1987	32	67	73	21	74	26
1986	28	71	75	18	54	40
1985	36	64	72	17	60	33
1984	39	51	65	22	51	36
1983	38	50	64	20	55	33
1982	42	44	48	32	59	25
1981	42	55	66	27	64	29

Interest Group Ratings

Year	ADA	ACU	AFL-CIO	CCUS
1990	50	32	55	43
1989	65	19	67	60
1988	70	21	92	50
1987	68	5	60	60
1986	65	29	71	50
1985	50	33	53	48
1984	65	32	42	31
1983	60	32	73	59
1982	25	50	60	50
1981	55	20	73	17

6 Howard Coble (R)

Of Greensboro — Elected 1984

Born: March 18, 1931, Greensboro, N.C.

Education: Attended Appalachian State U., 1949-50; Guilford College, 1950-52, 1957-58, A.B. 1958; U. of North Carolina, J.D. 1962.

Military Career: Coast Guard, 1952-56; Coast Guard Reserve, 1960-81.

Occupation: Lawyer; insurance agent.

Family: Single.

Religion: Presbyterian.

Political Career: N.C. House, 1969, 1979-83; secretary, N.C. Department of Revenue, 1973-76; Republican nominee for N.C. treasurer, 1976.

Capitol Office: 430 Cannon Bldg. 20515; 225-3065.

In Washington: Coble shares many of the conservative views of the new generation of Southern Republicans, but it is more than his 60 years that sets him apart from those aggressive younger members. A backslapping, amiable pol with a penchant for cigars, Coble seems to have more in common with the old-time courthouse crowd. He usually skirts partisan confrontation and has not had a high profile in national policy debates.

When Coble's views do get wider notice, it is for his occasional nipping at the ankles of the House for its pay, pensions and perks. He was part of the chorus of criticism against the congressional pay raise in 1989, and was among the first to call for term limits. In February 1989, Coble introduced legislation to limit House members to three four-year terms. He points out that his plan would also keep a lid on congressional pensions. "A lot of [House members] are fat, a lot are soft, and a lot are sitting around waiting for their pensions," he said.

Coble's objections to the pension program date to his first term. In 1985, he introduced legislation to reduce retirement pay for House members, a move that some colleagues regarded as rank demagoguery. His news conference to announce the bill played to a nearly empty room. One of his aides, asked about the empty chairs, said they represented all the cosponsors the bill had attracted. Coble concluded it would be futile to re-introduce the measure, but he keeps up the criticism, recently calling the system, which he eschews, "a taxpayer rip-off."

In another swipe at congressional practices, in 1990 he cosponsored a bill to put strict limits on congressional travel, after the airing of a critical TV news report about a Ways and Means Committee trip to Barbados.

Coble's anti-institutional bent does put him on common ground with some of the younger Republicans, and he was an early supporter of Newt Gingrich's bid for minority whip early in the 101st Congress. Once elected, Gingrich named Coble an assistant regional whip.

Coble also is vocal when the subject is textiles. More than 30,000 of his constituents work in the textile industry, and he has consistently demanded protectionist relief for textile companies. "The only place free trade exists is in an economics textbook," he says. President Reagan vetoed textile protection measures in 1985 and 1988, and President Bush vetoed a bill to limit textile imports in 1990. A former vice chairman of the Textile Caucus, Coble took some solace in the fact that Congress came closer to overriding Bush's veto than it had either of Reagan's.

Searching for ways to boost local industry, Coble is an ardent foe of a government policy that gives preferential treatment to the federal prison system in awarding furniture contracts. In 1990, the Judiciary Committee, on which he serves, considered legislation to reform the Federal Prison Industries program. The bill did not pass, but the Commerce, State and Justice appropriations bill mandated an outside review of the program.

Coble prides himself on being a fiscal conservative, but he is ready enough to play the federal spending game when the 6th District benefits. Federal sewer and construction grants he announced in 1988 did not hurt his re-election bid, nor did the nearly $500,000 grant to upgrade the security system at the Piedmont Triad International Airport in 1990.

One of the few amendments enacted into law bearing Coble's name was a 1986 measure increasing the penalties and fines for interfering with satellite transmissions.

At Home: Coble started 1984 thinking about running for governor. He had gained some statewide name recognition among Republicans, not only in the Legislature but also

North Carolina 6

Central — Greensboro; High Point

Greensboro, the third-largest city in North Carolina, and surrounding Guilford County are comfortably middle class. The economy blends manufacturing and service industry. Burlington Industries and Cone Mills, two textile giants, employ thousands, in both headquarters operations and mills, as does AT&T Federal Systems, a key defense contractor. The city also has two major state universities and a large insurer.

The managerial personnel in Greensboro industries have given Guilford County an appreciable GOP vote, but one that is far from monolithic. Guilford backed President Reagan's 1984 bid for re-election — and Democrats in contests for the U.S. Senate and House. In 1990, Guilford gave Coble 64 percent, and Democratic Senate nominee Harvey B. Gantt 53 percent against GOP Sen. Jesse Helms. In September 1990, Guilford voting officials reported two out of every three new registrants that month were Democrats.

South of Greensboro is High Point, which refers to itself as the "furniture capital of the world." Visitors are directed to a building in the center of town that resembles a giant chest of drawers. Nearby Thomasville, in Davidson County, also a furniture-producing center, boasts a giant chair.

East of Greensboro, the 6th takes in Alamance County whose agricultural and textile base has been steadily supplemented by branch manufacturing, including a plant where Honda builds lawnmowers.

While Democrats enjoy a registration advantage in Alamance County, that jurisdiction gave Reagan comfortable margins in both 1980 and 1984, and George Bush carried it easily in 1988. Helms won 62 percent in Alamance in 1990.

In the district's southwest corner is Davidson County, another traditional furniture- and textile-producing area. Davidson has a substantial population of Republicans.

Population: 529,635. White 415,746 (79%), Black 109,806 (21%), Other 3,106 (1%). Spanish origin 3,607 (1%). 18 and over 386,301 (73%), 65 and over 54,361 (10%). Median age: 31.

as an assistant U.S. attorney, and as secretary of the Department of Revenue under GOP Gov. James E. Holshouser Jr. in the mid-1970s. But he bypassed a statewide bid to challenge freshman Democrat Robin Britt in the 6th.

Despite his reputation, it took all of Coble's efforts just to make himself the Republican nominee. Former state Sen. Walter C. Cockerham, a millionaire construction company owner, already had been stumping the district and courting Republican votes for several months before Coble entered the race.

The primary caused a split between local GOP moderates and the party's more militant conservative faction. Coble's roots were on the moderate side, as evidenced by his close ties to Holshouser, archenemy of the conservative wing. Cockerham devoted much of his time trying to outflank his opponent on the right, branding Coble a "liberal lawyer" and casting himself as a "consistent conservative" in the mold of North Carolina's GOP Sens. Jesse Helms and John P. East.

Although Helms himself did not make an endorsement, Cockerham had the support of the Helms-affiliated National Congressional Club, a group Coble had publicly criticized.

But Coble found a theme that enabled him to capture ample conservative support of his own. He played up his reputation for fiscal stinginess in monitoring the state budget, earned following his return to the North Carolina House in 1979. Armed with the support of most local GOP leaders, Coble pulled through by a scant 164 votes.

Coble continued to stress his fiscal conservatism against Britt, whom he sought to paint as an extravagant liberal. Coble criticized the incumbent for having gone against Reagan on two of every three votes cast in 1983, and accused Britt of voting to spend money to pay people to operate automatic elevators on Capitol Hill.

Britt did everything he could to fight the liberal label. He ran TV ads reminding voters that he was one of 24 House Democratic freshmen who joined Republicans to derail briefly a stopgap spending measure as a sign of their distaste for deficits in 1983. Reaching into Coble's record, Britt accused him of voting in the Legislature for state funding for abortion, then opposing federal funding as a congressional candidate.

But it was not enough to win him a second term. Although Britt's careful cultivation of the Greensboro business community helped him carry Guilford County, he failed to run up sufficient margins to compensate for Coble's strength in the 6th's outlying territory. Tapping into the flow of conservative Democrats who crossed party lines for Reagan, Coble finished with a 2,662-vote edge.

But Coble could not rest long on his laurels. Britt returned home to Greensboro following his defeat and began plotting his comeback. The 1986 results would be even closer than those of 1984; only 79 votes separated the winner and the loser on Election Day.

Britt's 1986 campaign targeted workers in the slumping textile industry, which he contended was suffering from Coble's inability to persuade his House GOP colleagues to override Reagan's veto of the 1985 textile bill.

Coble countered that he had more influence with the Reagan administration than any freshman Democrat could have. Coble also took pains to emphasize his fiscally conservative credentials at every turn, frequently reminding audiences that he was a strong supporter of the Gramm-Rudman budget-cutting measure.

Coble's strategy helped inoculate him from charges leveled by Britt and the national Democratic Party, whose leaders had targeted the 6th in part because of the troubled textile industry. But the Republican had very few votes to spare. Britt again carried Guilford County, and also eked out a narrow margin in more rural Alamance County. Only by establishing a 555-vote edge in Davidson County — which is especially dependent on textiles — did Coble secure victory. Britt spent the early months of 1987 appealing the election results, but his challenge proved unsuccessful.

When Britt opted not to run again in 1988, Democrats turned to Tom Gilmore, a well-known and well-funded former state legislator. But while Gilmore had a zest for campaigning, his campaign itself had little zest. He continued with some of Britt's attacks on the textile issue, and criticized Coble's record on the environment, calling attention to the incumbent's presence on Environmental Action's "Dirty Dozen" list. But Coble had personally endeared himself to many in the 6th, and could point to his success at delivering for the district after two terms. With national trends going his way, Coble won 62 percent of the vote and two years later, 67 percent.

Committees

Judiciary (7th of 13 Republicans)
Civil & Constitutional Rights; Intellectual Property & Judicial Administration

Merchant Marine & Fisheries (8th of 17 Republicans)
Coast Guard & Navigation; Fisheries & Wildlife Conservation & the Environment

Select Narcotics Abuse & Control (12th of 14 Republicans)

Elections

1990 General		
Howard Coble (R)	125,392	(67%)
Helen R. Allegrone (D)	62,913	(33%)
1988 General		
Howard Coble (R)	116,534	(62%)
Tom Gilmore (D)	70,008	(38%)

Previous Winning Percentages: 1986 (50%) **1984** (51%)

District Vote For President

	1988	1984	1980	1976
D	76,208 (39%)	68,726 (35%)	74,137 (42%)	82,056 (51%)
R	118,565 (61%)	129,630 (65%)	94,162 (54%)	76,934 (48%)
I			5,458 (3%)	

Campaign Finance

	Receipts	Receipts from PACs		Expend-itures
1990				
Coble (R)	$572,043	$223,860	(39%)	$572,846
Allegrone (D)	$35,188	$9,500	(27%)	$33,135
1988				
Coble (R)	$736,254	$282,524	(38%)	$738,088
Gilmore (D)	$586,449	$258,082	(44%)	$583,013

Key Votes

1991	
Authorize use of force against Iraq	Y
1990	
Support constitutional amendment on flag desecration	Y
Pass family and medical leave bill over Bush veto	N
Reduce SDI funding	Y
Allow abortions in overseas military facilities	N
Approve budget summit plan for spending and taxing	N
Approve civil rights bill	N
1989	
Halt production of B-2 stealth bomber at 13 planes	N
Oppose capital gains tax cut	N
Approve federal abortion funding in rape or incest cases	N
Approve pay raise and revision of ethics rules	N
Pass Democratic minimum wage plan over Bush veto	N

Voting Studies

	Presidential Support		Party Unity		Conservative Coalition	
Year	**S**	**O**	**S**	**O**	**S**	**O**
1990	68	32	92	7	93	7
1989	81	17	94	6	98	2
1988	61	39	90	10	92	8
1987	70	30	92	7	95	5
1986	68	31	84	14	92	8
1985	69	30	87	9	91	9

Interest Group Ratings

Year	ADA	ACU	AFL-CIO	CCUS
1990	6	83	8	93
1989	10	82	8	100
1988	10	92	21	93
1987	4	87	6	100
1986	10	81	36	89
1985	0	81	12	91

7 Charlie Rose (D)

Of Fayetteville — Elected 1972

Born: Aug. 10, 1939, Fayetteville, N.C.
Education: Davidson College, B.A. 1961; U. of North Carolina, J.D. 1964.
Occupation: Lawyer.
Family: Wife, Joan Teague; three children.
Religion: Presbyterian.
Political Career: Chief district court prosecutor, 1967-71; sought Democratic nomination for U.S. House, 1970.
Capitol Office: 2230 Rayburn Bldg. 20515; 225-2731.

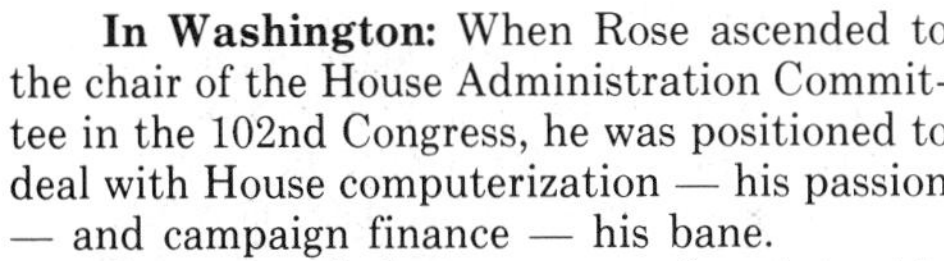

In Washington: When Rose ascended to the chair of the House Administration Committee in the 102nd Congress, he was positioned to deal with House computerization — his passion — and campaign finance — his bane.

Once regarded as a comer for statewide office or for a party leadership position in the House, Rose recently has been seen as biding his time until seniority gives him the chairmanship of the Agriculture Committee, where he is fourth-ranking Democrat and staunch defender of tobacco and peanuts interests.

But in 1991, Rose gave up his chairmanship of the Tobacco and Peanuts subcommittee and took the helm at House Administration when the Democratic Caucus voted to oust aging Frank Annunzio of Illinois from the chair of that committee. In his new job, Rose oversees internal House matters such as committee budgets, and he will be spending more time on what had been a side interest for him — nudging Congress into the technological age.

Rose is considered the resident expert on computers and Congress' technological capacity. His office is an electronic village, loaded with expensive equipment that allows him to chart legislation at a glance and hold staff meetings where computer terminals do all the talking.

The House's computer system when Rose arrived in 1973 was a primitive one used mainly for payrolls and retrieving information on the status of bills. Rose quickly joined House Administration and got himself appointed to lead a new task force on computers. By lobbying carefully for funds with the leadership, Rose gradually created an ambitious House information bureaucracy. The new technology has given members not only better legislative data, but also the computerized mailing lists that have brought incumbents political success courting constituents and contributions in recent years.

While computerizing the institution, Rose was also putting it on television for the first time. He was instrumental in setting up the system that currently broadcasts floor proceedings, implementing a 20-year-old idea that no one had been able to sell politically. He helped conquer Speaker Thomas P. O'Neill Jr.'s suspicion by keeping control of the cameras away from commercial networks and by proposing a limited closed-circuit experiment that paved the way for public gavel-to-gavel TV coverage beginning in 1979.

Yet the biggest issue facing Rose on House Administration will be campaign finance, which was initially dealt with by an ad hoc subcommittee. Rose's position on campaign-finance reform was somewhat of a mystery when he took over as chairman in the 102nd; but he was not seen as likely to stonewall legislation, because of intense leadership interest in the issue and because of questions regarding his own past ethical practices.

In 1987, Rose was forced to defend himself against a complaint that he improperly converted nearly $64,000 in campaign contributions for his own use and also used campaign funds as collateral for a $75,000 personal loan.

Rose maintained that the $64,000 was repayment for loans he and his father had made to his first campaign. He did not deny he used campaign funds as collateral for the $75,000 personal loan, but said that since he had no legal authority to do that, the transaction was invalid and no House rules had been violated.

The House ethics committee found no evidence that the $64,000 had been considered a loan, and said the collateral-and-loan arrangement was a clear use of campaign funds for personal benefit. In early 1988, the committee issued a formal "letter of reproval" for breaking House rules. Noting that Rose had repaid the funds (although after the inquiry began), the panel recommended no formal sanctions. Rose apologized for "inadvertent human errors."

In May 1989 the Justice Department filed a civil lawsuit against Rose for failing to report the loans on his financial-disclosure forms. Rose accused the administration of political retaliation and released a letter from the ethics panel saying that he did not have to amend his disclosure forms. The panel objected that his

North Carolina 7

Southeast — Fayetteville; Wilmington

Nearly half the people in the 7th live in Fayetteville and surrounding Cumberland County, a part of south central North Carolina that has a heavy military cast. In addition to the 43,000 troops stationed here between Fort Bragg and Pope Air Force Base, thousands of other jobs are dependent on these facilities. So when 74 percent of these troops were deployed for the Persian Gulf War, the county took the equivalent of an economic Scud missile. Unemployment claims rose 34 percent, sales tax revenues dropped dramatically, and mobile home sales were cut in half. The governor declared the county an economic emergency area.

Politically, the county has a Democratic flavor in local and statewide campaigns. It went for Democrat James B. Hunt Jr. in his unsuccessful 1984 challenge to GOP Sen. Jesse Helms and for Harvey B. Gantt in his 1990 bid against Helms. Cumberland has also voted Democratic in the last two gubernatorial races, both won statewide by Republican James G. Martin. Cumberland's presidential vote has drifted toward the GOP in recent years, though. Ronald Reagan won Cumberland handily in 1984, and George Bush carried the county in 1988.

Outside Fayetteville, the only other major city in the 7th is Wilmington (New Hanover County). The restoration of Wilmington's historic waterfront district has brought tourism and some white-collar prosperity into this old port and fishing center. Republican sentiment is strong; New Hanover County gave a majority to Reagan in 1980, the only county in the 7th District to do so. It voted Republican in the 1988 gubernatorial and presidential contests. Helms carried New Hanover by 400 votes over Gantt.

Of North Carolina's 80,000 American Indians, over 50 percent live in Robeson County, a heavily Democratic area where there are some tensions between the white, black and Indian populations. Robeson County is about the same size as New Hanover County and more than compensates for GOP majorities on the coast. Robeson gave Gantt 61 percent.

Population: 539,055. White 340,271 (63%), Black 147,378 (27%), American Indian, Eskimo and Aleut 40,737 (8%), Other 4,641 (1%). Spanish origin 11,897 (2%). 18 and over 371,808 (69%), 65 and over 40,425 (8%). Median age: 26.

suit — which has sat dormant — violated the separation of powers doctrine.

On Agriculture, Rose has often found himself fending off attacks on government support for farmers. When California Republican Dana Rohrabacher suggested in 1990 that the need for small farmers might be obviated by more efficient corporate agribusiness, Rose damned such talk as "heresy." During the 101st Congress, he offered an amendment to the 1990 farm bill that would have required grocery stores to tell consumers how little of their food bill actually filtered down to farmers. And he blocked a plan that would have given the Agriculture secretary wide discretion to transfer funds marked for rural water and sewer projects to efforts to attract new businesses.

As chairman of the Tobacco and Peanuts Subcommittee, Rose spent the 1980s besieged by anti-smoking forces. Despite his efforts, there were some losses, both for the tobacco industry in general and for the growers he champions in the internecine tug of war with cigarette manufacturers.

Rose had his biggest successes in 1981, the first year he led the subcommittee. President Reagan proposed eliminating federal allotments for peanut farmers, and tobacco was being attacked by a coalition of consumer advocates and urban fiscal conservatives.

As chief strategist and spokesman, Rose came up with an ingenious argument. He told fellow Democrats that the entire North Carolina Democratic delegation might be wiped out at the polls in 1982 if the tobacco subsidy program died on the House floor. By the time of the vote, Speaker O'Neill sounded as loyal to tobacco as any Tarheel, and the anti-tobacco onslaught was defeated by almost 50 votes on the floor. Even so, Rose was forced to accept an amendment to the program requiring growers to pay the costs of storing surplus tobacco purchased by the government.

Rose had some struggles to maintain peanut allotments — rules allowing only specified farmers to market peanuts commercially — against the Reagan and Bush administrations' arguments for more competition. As eventually rewritten, the peanut program did not restrict additional farmers from entering the market, but guaranteed higher price supports to those who had been in it before the change.

In 1982, Rose — aiming to defuse criticism of the tobacco program — won enactment of a measure that made changes in the program so it would run at no net cost to taxpayers, except for administrative expenses.

In the 99th Congress, Rose had additional frustrations coping with growing tension between tobacco farmers and tobacco companies, which were importing more and more foreign tobacco. He found himself sparring not only with tobacco opponents, but also with GOP Sen. Jesse Helms, a longtime home-state rival.

In the Senate, Helms pushed a tobacco plan that sold government-held tobacco surpluses to cigarette makers at a discount and gave them a role in determining future supplies; in exchange, they picked up part of the cost of the program. Rose, who had been purposefully excluded from discussions that led up to Helms' plan, said the approach, omitting limits on tobacco imports, favored manufacturers over farmers, who accepted lower price supports.

In the House, Rose promoted his own tobacco plan, which involved setting aside 2 cents of a 16-cent federal excise tax on cigarettes to pay for tobacco supports. A modified version was attached to a House reconciliation measure on Ways and Means. But Helms prevailed in conference and Rose reluctantly supported Helms' plan; it conceded to a permanent extension of the 16-cents-per-pack excise tax in exchange for the discount buyout of surplus tobacco and changes in price supports.

In the 101st Congress, Rose and Helms again locked horns over language offered by Rose and eventually retained in the 1990 farm bill that required cigarette companies to track their use of foreign-grown tobacco.

At various times, Rose has worked to fend off requirements for new and tougher warning labels on cigarette packages. He succeeded in 1981, but by 1984, after months of negotiations — and in hopes of staving off even tougher restrictions — major tobacco companies dropped their opposition and the warning labels were approved in Energy and Commerce by a vote of 22-0. Afterward, asked if he was pleased with the vote, Rose replied wearily, "No, I'm just glad it's over."

In 1987, Rose and other tobacco legislators were powerless to prevent a ban on smoking for short domestic air flights. The proposal arose on the House floor as an amendment to an appropriation bill and sailed to enactment.

Rose's interest in the cutting edge of technology combined with home-district farm politics in 1988 on the question of whether patents could be granted for genetically altered animals. Controversy was set off began when the U.S. Patent Office granted Harvard University a patent for mice genetically engineered to be more useful in cancer experiments.

Rose introduced a bill to impose a two-year moratorium on such patents, which farmers feared would eventually increase the cost of raising animals. Rose's bill was rejected in a Judiciary subcommittee as interest in technological advances overcame fears of genetic experimentation. On the floor, a compromise was worked out that exempted farmers from royalty payments, and Rose supported the final bill.

In the 101st Congress, Rose and Texas Democrat Charles W. Stenholm clashed over bills aimed at protecting farms and research labs from "animal rights" activists. Stenholm introduced a bill that would have made it a federal crime to trespass or commit other illegal acts against such facilities. Rose, who made clear his disdain for Stenholm's bill, introduced a bill prohibiting fines when the illegal act uncovered documented violations of federal animal-care rules. No legislation passed.

At the beginning of the 102nd Congress, Rose was reportedly wavering between retaining his chairmanship of the Tobacco Subcommittee and moving to a new subcommittee, Department Operations. Stenholm wanted the Department Operations chair, but he and Rose could not agree on how to run the panel, which could claim jurisdiction over animal research. Rose took the Department Operations chair.

Rose saw his flirtation with being a part of the House Democratic leadership dashed in 1980 when he ran for chairman of the Democratic Caucus. He was defeated 146-53 by another moderate Southerner, Gillis W. Long of Louisiana, who had all of Rose's personal popularity and fewer controversial alliances.

At Home: Unwilling to wait for Rep. Alton Lennon's long-promised retirement, Rose went after him in a 1970 primary and came so close that Lennon finally did retire two years later.

To run in 1970, Rose had to take a leave from his work as chief prosecutor in the 12th Judicial District (Cumberland and Hoke counties). Before he took that job, he had been an aide to Gov. Terry Sanford (1961-65), and he was supported by many of the moderate Democrats who found Sanford appealing. Running a well-financed, well-organized campaign that called attention to Lennon's 64 years, Rose received a respectable 43 percent of the vote.

Early in 1971, Rose began producing a monthly television program outlining the history of each county in the district. He said the shows were not political, but made it clear he would try again for Congress in 1972. In December, Lennon announced his retirement.

State Sen. Hector McGeachy and Fayetteville lawyer Doran Berry joined Rose in the 1972 Democratic primary. Few issues separated them; Rose was better known because of his earlier campaign and because his father and grandfather had served in the Legislature.

Rose polled 49 percent in the initial primary, far ahead of McGeachy's 26 percent. Still, McGeachy demanded a runoff, and Rose won it with 56 percent. The general election was no problem. Rose got 60 percent even as Richard M. Nixon carried the 7th overwhelmingly.

In 1974, McGeachy was back again, challenging Rose in the primary with a campaign that courted the black vote. But Rose had used a mobile office during his first term to keep in touch with rural constituents, and he developed close ties with the district's business community. Rose won renomination with 61 percent, and that was his last significant primary challenge. Rose was unopposed in November 1974.

Some Republicans thought Rose's personal life might hamper him in the 1982 election. Shortly after receiving an uncontested divorce from his wife, Rose was married in September 1982 to a staffer on his Tobacco and Peanuts Subcommittee. Voters, however, were apparently not bothered by the divorce and quick remarriage — Rose got 71 percent of the vote.

Rose was mentioned as a possible candidate for governor in 1984, when incumbent Democrat James B. Hunt Jr. left office. But he decided to stay in the House. Battling a Republican tide that diminished the Democrats' ranks in the congressional delegation from nine members to six, he was re-elected with 59 percent.

Rose also suffered a scare in 1986. He appeared headed for routine re-election when a political bomb dropped on him in mid-September. Press reports that Rose had borrowed money from his campaign committee raised questions about the propriety of his actions — and gave a much-needed burst of momentum to GOP challenger Thomas J. Harrelson.

But if voters were concerned about Rose's propriety, they did not show it. Although Harrelson, a Southport businessman, former state House member and former state Environmental Management official, amassed more money than any Rose challenger in memory, he managed only 36 percent of the vote districtwide.

The ethics issue kept Republicans talking about Rose for part of the next election cycle, but that was about all they did. Rose was re-elected overwhelmingly.

Committees

House Administration (Chairman)

Joint Printing (Chairman)

Joint Library (Vice Chairman)

Agriculture (4th of 27 Democrats)
Department Operations, Research & Foreign Agriculture (chairman); Cotton, Rice & Sugar; Livestock, Dairy & Poultry; Peanuts & Tobacco; Wheat, Soybeans & Feed Grains

Elections

1990 General		
Charlie Rose (D)	94,946	(66%)
Robert C. Anderson (R)	49,681	(34%)
1988 General		
Charlie Rose (D)	102,392	(67%)
George G. Thompson (R)	49,855	(33%)

Previous Winning Percentages: **1986** (64%) **1984** (59%) **1982** (71%) **1980** (69%) **1978** (70%) **1976** (81%) **1974** (100%) **1972** (60%)

District Vote For President

	1988	1984	1980	1976
D	73,231 (48%)	65,964 (43%)	70,334 (54%)	78,021 (66%)
R	77,438 (51%)	87,143 (57%)	57,184 (44%)	39,640 (34%)
I			3,119 (2%)	

Campaign Finance

	Receipts	Receipts from PACs	Expend-itures
1990			
Rose (D)	$328,232	$196,654 (60%)	$153,315
Anderson (R)	$24,449	0	$21,131
1988			
Rose (D)	$293,187	$177,500 (61%)	$185,039

Key Votes

1991	
Authorize use of force against Iraq	N
1990	
Support constitutional amendment on flag desecration	N
Pass family and medical leave bill over Bush veto	Y
Reduce SDI funding	Y
Allow abortions in overseas military facilities	Y
Approve budget summit plan for spending and taxing	Y
Approve civil rights bill	?
1989	
Halt production of B-2 stealth bomber at 13 planes	N
Oppose capital gains tax cut	Y
Approve federal abortion funding in rape or incest cases	Y
Approve pay raise and revision of ethics rules	N
Pass Democratic minimum wage plan over Bush veto	Y

Voting Studies

	Presidential Support		Party Unity		Conservative Coalition	
Year	**S**	**O**	**S**	**O**	**S**	**O**
1990	19	75	88	7	48	44
1989	36	58	85	10	37	61
1988	19	65	77	7	47	26
1987	30	61	79	10	72	19
1986	29	64	78	12	54	42
1985	28	70	84	10	53	42
1984	35	50	77	13	47	39
1983	26	61	74	12	42	42
1982	32	49	63	19	60	32
1981	49	43	54	22	63	25

Interest Group Ratings

Year	ADA	ACU	AFL-CIO	CCUS
1990	61	21	75	23
1989	80	15	83	50
1988	60	11	100	25
1987	76	5	75	43
1986	55	37	67	44
1985	60	17	56	25
1984	60	14	67	42
1983	75	10	75	31
1982	40	35	58	47
1981	50	23	85	29

8 W.G. "Bill" Hefner (D)

Of Concord — Elected 1974

Born: April 11, 1930, Elora, Tenn.
Education: High school graduate.
Occupation: Broadcasting executive.
Family: Wife, Nancy Hill; two children.
Religion: Baptist.
Political Career: No previous office.
Capitol Office: 2161 Rayburn Bldg. 20515; 225-3715.

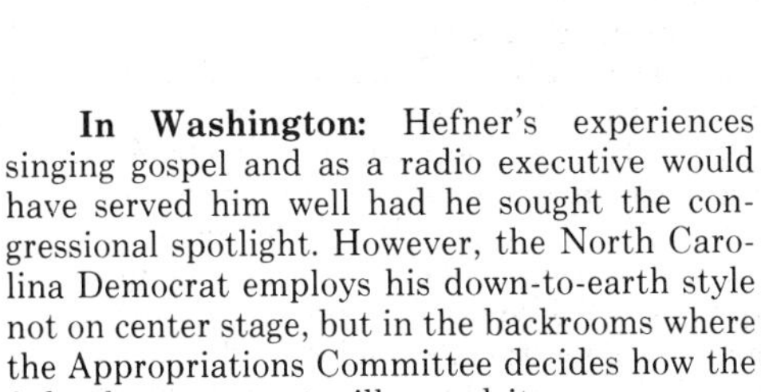

In Washington: Hefner's experiences singing gospel and as a radio executive would have served him well had he sought the congressional spotlight. However, the North Carolina Democrat employs his down-to-earth style not on center stage, but in the backrooms where the Appropriations Committee decides how the federal government will spend its money.

Despite his low public profile, Hefner wields the influence that comes with having a hand on the purse strings: The chairman of the Subcommittee on Military Construction, Hefner is a member of the Appropriations Committee's "College of Cardinals." Hefner, who also is on the Appropriations Defense Subcommittee, is positioned to play a role in the ongoing effort to scale back post-Cold War military spending.

Hefner did make one bid for a House leadership position, when he ran for majority whip at the start of the 100th Congress. A moderate Southern Democrat, Hefner had sometimes acted during the Reagan administration as a liaison between the Democratic leadership and members of the party's conservative wing: As a member of the House Budget Committee from 1981 to 1987, Hefner advised the leaders on what conservative Democrats would and would not accept on the House floor.

Yet Hefner seemed uncomfortable asking colleagues for support. Tony Coelho of California ended up winning the Democratic Caucus ballot with 167 votes to 78 for Charles B. Rangel of New York; Hefner carried 15 votes.

However, changing fiscal and defense contingencies combined to place Hefner — in his role as House overseer of military construction spending — in a role of increasing importance.

During the defense boom years under President Reagan, the question faced by Hefner's subcommittee was how to divvy up the pot of military construction dollars; few brick-and-mortar programs went wanting. But the budget-driven effort to trim spending and the new realities forged by the decline of Soviet might and the Persian Gulf War have forced the subcommittee to make more concrete decisions based on a developing global defense strategy.

Early in the 101st Congress, a plan for full or partial closure of 91 military facilities, developed by a bipartisan commission, was enacted over cries of members from affected districts, who said the criteria for closing many bases were faulty. Some critics tried to use the appropriations process to block funding for the base phaseouts. However, Hefner stated his support for the closure plan, and pledged to block any rear-guard action. "The [full] committee can do whatever it wants, but I don't see it in this subcommittee," Hefner said in March 1989. A bill providing funding for the full list of base closings was enacted later that year.

But Hefner casts a wary eye on Defense Department projects overseas. In 1990, Pentagon officials pressed to fund a new NATO airbase in Crotone, Italy, on the alliance's southern flank. Hefner — an advocate of military "burden-sharing" by U.S. allies — said that the decline of communism in Eastern Europe and the weakening of the Soviet Union's position had made the base a luxury. The Appropriations Committee later reported a bill withholding money for the base that was enacted despite a veto threat by President Bush.

Like all Appropriations members, Hefner makes sure his position benefits his constituents, as with the recent funding of a geriatic unit at the VA Medical Center in Salisbury.

Hefner, who had close calls at the polls in 1984 and 1988, can be outspoken on some conservative "cause" issues. In 1990, he supported the constitutional amendment to ban flag desecration and voted against overriding Bush's veto of "family leave" legislation.

But in 1989, he voted to raise the pay of House members while tightening ethics restrictions. The next year, he voted not to censure Democratic Rep. Barney Frank of Massachusetts over Frank's past relationship with a male prostitute; Hefner cited the bipartisan ethics committee's support for the lighter punishment of reprimand.

Hefner looks out for the cause of a local constituency, textile workers. A member of the Congressional Textile Caucus, Hefner voted in

North Carolina 8

South Central — Kannapolis; Salisbury

Politics in the 8th are delineated by geography. The mountain counties in the northern part of the district and the textile towns in the center lean Republican. The farm counties farther south vote for Democrats.

Yadkin and Davie counties anchor the GOP base at the 8th's northern end. They make their party preference clear in nearly every election, supporting GOP statewide candidates even when they are non-contenders; Yadkin and Davie went Republican for governor in 1980, when the nominee got only 37 percent statewide. Yadkin is one of the district's major tobacco-growing counties; Davie residents are more oriented toward dairy products and grains. In his 1990 re-election against Democrat Harvey B. Gantt, GOP Sen. Jesse Helms received 70 percent in Davie. Yadkin was one of three counties Hefner lost in 1990.

The Democratic stronghold in the district is Hoke County, a rural area where the 44 percent black population combines with a significant American Indian minority to deliver an overwhelming Democratic vote. Hoke is often joined in the Democratic column by nearby Scotland, Richmond and Anson counties. Gantt carried all four handily.

North of Hoke is the part of Moore County in the 8th, which takes in affluent resort communities such as Pinehurst and Whispering Pines.

Moore County used to share Hoke's Democratic proclivities, but a steady stream of retirees has transformed it into a Republican bastion.

In the center of the district, small cities and towns such as Kannapolis, Salisbury and Concord manufacture textiles and textile machinery. Founded by Cannon Mills, the textile manufacturer, Kannapolis — the district's largest population center — remained an unincorporated company town for years; the company paid for the police and fire departments, and owned many of the city's houses. But in 1984, the city voted to become an incorporated community, two years after Cannon Mills was bought out.

Population: 535,526. White 420,470 (79%), Black 107,482 (20%), Other 6,871 (1%). Spanish origin 3,730 (1%). 18 and over 381,299 (71%), 65 and over 62,412 (12%). Median age: 31.

October 1990 for an unsuccessful attempt to override Bush's veto of a bill restricting textile imports. After supporting Bush's position on 41 percent of House votes in 1989 — a healthy score for a Democrat — Hefner backed the president 33 percent of the time in 1990.

At Home: Through the years, Hefner has been able to neutralize much of the natural GOP sentiment that pervades the 8th District. But in the last two presidential election years, he was almost dragged under.

In 1984, Hefner's GOP opponent was Harris D. Blake, a hardware store owner and former member of the Moore County Board of Education who had challenged him two years earlier. In their first meeting, Blake won 42 percent by arguing that Hefner had not voted the interests of the local textile industry. Hefner cast himself as committed to protecting voters from the budget knife of the GOP.

Blake began his second campaign early and took pains to showcase his support for Reagan, whose popularity increased with improvement in the economy. Blake hit Hefner hard for having opposed the administration's 1981 tax and budget cuts. But the challenger also repeated his complaint that Hefner's vote to grant most-favored-nation status to China aided Chinese textiles in competition with those produced at home. Hefner then met with local textile executives and production workers to discuss legislation affecting the industry.

Blake benefited from Reagan's presence at the top of the ticket, and from the financial support of Helms' National Congressional Club; he carried a five-county area in the northern and central parts of the district. Hefner clung to his base among the traditionally Democratic counties at the district's southern end, eking out 51 percent of the vote overall.

Two years later, Hefner climbed back up to 58 percent, but 1988 brought more trouble for him. The GOP touted its challenger, 38-year-old attorney Ted Blanton, but most Democrats did not take his effort too seriously, and even some Republicans said the race was a long shot. But Blanton, who had worked as an aide for three U.S. senators, used Washington ties to generate attention for his campaign. A number of prominent Republicans visited the district on his behalf, including Assistant Secretary of State Elliot Abrams and former Transportation Secretary Elizabeth H. Dole, who was raised in this part of North Carolina. And Blanton aggressively attacked Hefner as a big spender on the Appropriations Committee.

Blanton put himself in a position to ride a wave of GOP presidential votes, and that wave came crashing in on Election Day. The challenger took 49 percent overall, running particularly well in the northern and central parts of the district and carrying seven counties. Hefner again survived because of his strong base in the Democratic counties in the south; he won five counties.

With great fanfare from national Republicans, Blanton was back for seconds in 1990. But Hefner was ready for him. The incumbent campaigned hard over the summer, returning to the district each weekend.

Despite the heavy buildup from the GOP, Blanton did not excel at fundraising. His campaign's prestige did not soar when media reports noted that he had spent $11,660 for "living expenses" from February to June 1990, using campaign funds for such personal expenses as his home mortgage and babysitting.

Blanton counted on a torrent of anti-incumbent sentiment to wash Hefner out of office. (He wielded a broom to symbolize his desire to sweep out the Democrat.) He criticized Hefner for voting for a congressional pay raise and for failing to support expulsion or censure of Rep. Frank.

But a more attentive Hefner, armed with a superior campaign operation, rebuffed the Republican, winning all but three counties in his 55-45 percent victory.

Running for his first term in Congress in 1974 against the backdrop of Watergate, Hefner pledged to revive "Christian morality" in government and laced his political speeches with renditions of his favorite hymns. That might have been seen as an incautious church-state mixture in some places, but not in the Bible Belt 8th. As a promoter and singer of gospel music in the Carolinas and Virginia, he had made many local and statewide TV appearances. With his excellent name recognition, he gradually won back thousands of conservative Democrats who had drifted toward GOP Rep. Earl B. Ruth. Hefner's blend of inspiration, entertainment and politicking helped him soundly defeat Ruth.

Committee

Appropriations (20th of 37 Democrats)
Military Construction (chairman); Defense

Elections

1990 General

W.G. "Bill" Hefner (D)	98,700	(55%)
Ted Blanton (R)	80,852	(45%)

1990 Primary

W.G. "Bill" Hefner (D)	50,832	(81%)
Helen A. Garrels (D)	12,111	(19%)

1988 General

W.G. "Bill" Hefner (D)	99,214	(51%)
Ted Blanton (R)	93,463	(49%)

Previous Winning Percentages: **1986** (58%) **1984** (51%) **1982** (57%) **1980** (59%) **1978** (59%) **1976** (66%) **1974** (57%)

District Vote For President

	1988	1984	1980	1976
D	73,080 (38%)	64,505 (35%)	76,466 (46%)	86,180 (55%)
R	118,357 (62%)	121,459 (65%)	86,672 (52%)	68,522 (44%)
I			3,519 (2%)	

Campaign Finance

	Receipts	Receipts from PACs		Expend-itures
1990				
Hefner (D)	$660,311	$445,293	(67%)	$656,383
Blanton (R)	$306,813	$34,074	(11%)	$300,893
1988				
Hefner (D)	$432,432	$272,625	(63%)	$581,888
Blanton (R)	$243,901	$21,280	(9%)	$242,782

Key Votes

1991

Authorize use of force against Iraq	N

1990

Support constitutional amendment on flag desecration	Y
Pass family and medical leave bill over Bush veto	N
Reduce SDI funding	Y
Allow abortions in overseas military facilities	Y
Approve budget summit plan for spending and taxing	N
Approve civil rights bill	Y

1989

Halt production of B-2 stealth bomber at 13 planes	N
Oppose capital gains tax cut	Y
Approve federal abortion funding in rape or incest cases	Y
Approve pay raise and revision of ethics rules	Y
Pass Democratic minimum wage plan over Bush veto	Y

Voting Studies

	Presidential Support		Party Unity		Conservative Coalition	
Year	S	O	S	O	S	O
1990	33	67	79	19	89	11
1989	41	55	75	19	78	10
1988	29	61	76	15	68	16
1987	33	65	81	15	84	16
1986	30	67	80	13	64	26
1985	35	49	63	12	60	7
1984	48	45	64	25	80	17
1983	40	54	66	21	72	22
1982	47	48	57 †	39 †	87 †	10 †
1981	53	41	57	33	76	23

† Not eligible for all recorded votes.

Interest Group Ratings

Year	ADA	ACU	AFL-CIO	CCUS
1990	44	38	58	50
1989	65	26	75	50
1988	65	25	92	50
1987	64	4	75	40
1986	50	36	57	40
1985	25	46	53	37
1984	40	33	54	47
1983	45	27	75	56
1982	20	67	50	64
1981	35	33	79	31

9 Alex McMillan (R)

Of Charlotte — Elected 1984

Born: May 9, 1932, Charlotte, N.C.
Education: U. of North Carolina, B.A. 1954; U. of Virginia, M.B.A. 1958.
Military Service: Army Intelligence, 1954-56.
Occupation: Food store executive.
Family: Wife, Caroline Houston; two children.
Religion: Presbyterian.
Political Career: Mecklenburg County Commission, 1972-74.
Capitol Office: 401 Cannon Bldg. 20515; 225-1976.

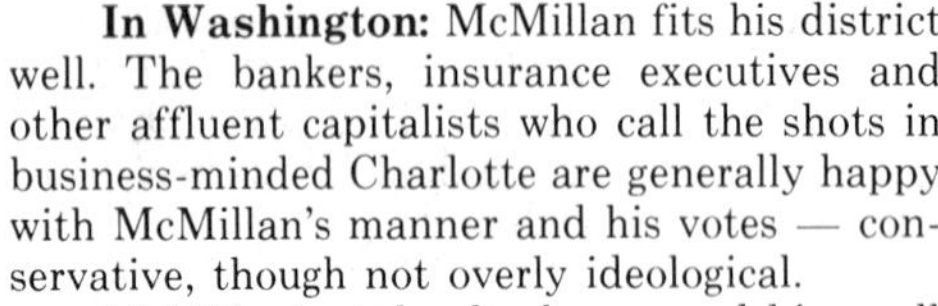

In Washington: McMillan fits his district well. The bankers, insurance executives and other affluent capitalists who call the shots in business-minded Charlotte are generally happy with McMillan's manner and his votes — conservative, though not overly ideological.

McMillan's style also has served him well in Washington: He is becoming a key ally of the House GOP leadership, and he fits the pragmatic Republicanism favored by Minority Leader Robert H. Michel of Illinois.

During the budget debate of 1990, McMillan supported the bipartisan budget summit agreement backed by congressional leaders and the president. McMillan lobbied his colleagues to support it — even though it included gasoline and cigarette tax increases. The package was defeated, but McMillan's effort helped his standing inside the party. At the outset of the 102nd Congress, Michel rewarded McMillan with a spot on the Budget Committee.

McMillan's other base is the Energy and Commerce Committee, where North Carolina Republicans once had an influential voice in ranking Republican James T. Broyhill. (He was appointed to the Senate in 1986.) McMillan made Energy and Commerce on his second try, at the start of the 101st Congress, after first lobbying for a place on Ways and Means. Earlier, McMillan sat on the Banking Committee, another key panel for North Carolina, whose financial institutions are playing an ever-widening role in regional and national banking.

In keeping with his business background, McMillan is loath to impose mandates on employers. In 1989 he supported President Bush's veto of a bill raising the minimum wage to $4.55. Also in the 101st Congress, McMillan voted against family leave and civil rights legislation that employers claimed would unduly burden them.

While sensitive to the problems of the underprivileged, McMillan is even more mindful of the weaknesses of government in trying to help. When Democrats brought a housing bill to the floor in 1986, McMillan was among those Republicans seeking to scale back the construction of new public housing units and focus on repairing existing ones. But he opposed some of more drastic GOP efforts to slash the amount of money in the bill. In subsequent years, McMillan has advocated enabling public housing tenants to purchase their own homes.

McMillan also revealed a more moderate streak during 1988 debate on the omnibus drug bill. He was one of five Southern Republicans voting to retain a seven-day waiting period for handgun purchases. Though he had received over $10,000 in campaign contributions from the National Rifle Association since first running for Congress, he voted against the NRA position. McMillan did so again in May 1991, when the House approved the waiting period.

In recognition of the important role the textile industry plays in his region, McMillan argued against the president's veto of a textile protection bill in the 99th Congress; two days after the House failed to override the veto, he introduced a bill of his own calling for the licensing of imported textiles. During the 101st Congress, McMillan again defied a presidential veto to back textile import quotas. The override effort failed by 10 votes.

McMillan has taken a general interest in reducing the federal deficit. He has been part of a bipartisan group of fiscal conservatives that has tried — with limited success — to trim the deficit by making across-the-board spending cuts on appropriations bills. McMillan believes that if spending is merely restrained, not cut, revenues will grow on their own and eliminate the deficit.

At Home: McMillan may have a more patrician demeanor than James G. Martin and Charles Raper Jonas, the previous two GOP incumbents in his district. But his fiscal conservatism and his emphasis on economics over social issues put him in the Martin-Jonas mold.

In securing his 1984 victory, McMillan drew heavily on a local GOP network established a generation ago by Jonas and cultivated by Martin, whose bid for governor opened the

North Carolina 9

West Central — Charlotte

Charlotte is the largest city of the two Carolinas. Its role as the supply, service and distribution center for the North and South Carolina Piedmont area gives it a diversified economy not directly dependent on the textile-and-tobacco base traditional in the region. Large construction and trucking firms are based here, and insurance concerns abound. North Carolina's major banks have built office towers that give the city an impressive skyline. There is also a new indoor coliseum, home of the Hornets, the recently arrived pro basketball franchise.

Many of Charlotte's bankers, lawyers and insurance executives make their homes in the affluent southeastern part of the city; it is here that the old-line GOP establishment has its base. The Democratic vote is strongest in the northwestern section, where the bulk of Charlotte's black population lives. The city elected its first black mayor, Harvey B. Gantt, in 1983; his successor, white Republican Sue Myrick, is the city's first female mayor.

A blend of white-collar economic conservatism, working-class Democratic allegiances and a 26 percent black population makes for close elections in Mecklenburg County. Mecklenburg voted for Ronald Reagan in 1980 and 1984, but sided with Democratic candidates for the Senate in those years. In 1990, Gantt, the Democratic nominee against GOP Sen. Jesse Helms, captured 58 percent of the vote.

Mecklenburg contains three-quarters of the district's population. The rest is split among three counties to the north of Charlotte — Iredell, Lincoln and Yadkin. In the 1980s, Iredell and Lincoln have seen an influx of residents moving into comfortable new homes along the shores of sprawling Lake Norman. The completion of Interstate 77 in the late 1970s brought the lake within reasonable daily commuting distance of downtown Charlotte.

Most of Iredell is still rural territory; apples and cattle are important to the economy. The county also has developed some light industry, such as electronics companies and manufacturing plants.

Iredell split its tickets in 1980, voting Republican for president and the Senate while giving Democratic Gov. James B. Hunt Jr. an easy margin in his re-election bid. But the county abandoned even Hunt in 1984, backing Helms against the Democrat in an outbreak of straight-ticket GOP voting. Lincoln County also voted a straight GOP line in 1984. Republicans carried both Iredell and Lincoln in 1988 voting for president and governor, and Helms posted strong showings in both counties in 1990.

Voters in Yadkin County, about one-fourth of which is in the 9th, are oriented more toward nearby Winston-Salem than to Charlotte. Longtime solid GOP territory, Yadkin was one of just 13 North Carolina counties to back Republican Barry Goldwater for president in 1964.

Population: 536,325. White 404,831 (75%), Black 125,148 (23%), Other 4,566 (1%). Spanish origin 4,835 (1%). 18 and over 385,849 (72%), 65 and over 48,307 (9%). Median age: 30.

9th. That network, anchored in wealthy southeastern Charlotte, helped McMillan get past a strong Democratic foe by a scant 321 votes.

Although he had last served in public office in 1974, McMillan was widely regarded as a top GOP prospect. A Democrat-turned-Republican, he won his one previous election in 1972, capturing the Mecklenburg County (Charlotte) Commission seat left vacant by Martin, who ran successfully that year for the House. McMillan retired from his post after one term, citing a desire to focus on his business career.

He moved up in the ranks in the retail food industry to become president of Harris-Teeter Super Markets Inc., a local chain. He made a name for himself in civic affairs, promoting a performing arts complex downtown and helping establish an authority to raise money for a public television station. McMillan also kept his hand in local GOP activities.

When Martin announced his gubernatorial candidacy in 1983, McMillan began actively seeking the seat. His support among the local GOP establishment and Charlotte business community made him appear a prohibitive favorite to become the party nominee. But he encountered a formidable primary obstacle in Carl "Buddy" Horn, who served for two years in the Civil Rights Division of the Reagan Justice Department and who had the endorsement of Sen. Jesse Helms' National Congressional Club. Horn's impassioned support for school prayer and a constitutional amendment to ban abortion rallied fundamentalist Christians, and contrasted markedly with McMillan's more moderate politics and more reserved style.

With early spring polls showing Horn ahead, McMillan went on the offensive, running television ads branding the 32-year-old Horn a "rookie," and reminding Republicans that Horn had voted for Democrat George McGovern for president in 1972. The result was a 58-42 percent primary win for McMillan.

McMillan had an even tougher time in the fall. His opponent was D. G. Martin, a lawyer and political neophyte who proved capable of attracting support not only in Democratic areas but also in southeastern Charlotte's wealthy white communities. Although unrelated to the departing incumbent, Democrat Martin had the added advantage of bearing a familiar name.

McMillan invoked his experience as a retailer to legitimize his call for a freeze on federal spending. He criticized Martin for his willingness to raise taxes to deal with the deficit, and for supporting homosexual rights.

Martin won Mecklenburg County, which dominates the district, but thanks to a financial advantage and top-of-the-ticket GOP strength, McMillan took enough margins in three outlying counties to overcome his Mecklenburg loss.

Martin tried again in 1986. He kept up his visibility between elections by writing a column in a weekly newspaper distributed free throughout Mecklenburg County, and by making regular appearances on a local cable television show. But Martin had trouble finding issues to use against the incumbent. He tried casting McMillan as a prisoner of special interests, pointing to the political action committee contributions McMillan had accepted (and Martin refused). But that failed to stir voters.

McMillan, practicing his quiet brand of chamber of commerce conservatism and returning home regularly, left little to chance. His used his position on Banking to court some of the businessmen behind Martin in 1984.

Martin deployed an army of volunteers on Election Day, and he again got a narrow lead in Mecklenburg. But McMillan's well-funded advertising blitz helped him stay close in the Charlotte area, and he overcame the deficit in the outlying counties to win with 51 percent.

With those first two tough campaigns under his belt, Martin moved on to easy victories in 1988 and 1990.

Committees

Budget (2nd of 14 Republicans)

Energy & Commerce (13th of 16 Republicans)
Commerce, Consumer Protection & Competitiveness (ranking); Health & the Environment

Elections

1990 General		
Alex McMillan (R)	131,936	(62%)
David P. McKnight (D)	80,802	(38%)
1988 General		
Alex McMillan (R)	139,014	(66%)
Mark Sholander (D)	71,802	(34%)

Previous Winning Percentages: **1986** (51%) **1984** (50%)

District Vote For President

	1988	1984	1980	1976
D	89,307 (39%)	81,750 (35%)	87,144 (46%)	86,436 (52%)
R	140,731 (61%)	150,223 (65%)	93,258 (49%)	80,603 (48%)
I			7,496 (4%)	

Campaign Finance

	Receipts	Receipts from PACs		Expend-itures
1990				
McMillan (R)	$399,007	$278,085	(70%)	$385,183
1988				
McMillan (R)	$515,294	$214,455	(42%)	$445,852
Sholander (D)	$34,124	$6,000	(18%)	$32,949

Key Votes

1991	
Authorize use of force against Iraq	Y
1990	
Support constitutional amendment on flag desecration	Y
Pass family and medical leave bill over Bush veto	N
Reduce SDI funding	N
Allow abortions in overseas military facilities	N
Approve budget summit plan for spending and taxing	Y
Approve civil rights bill	N
1989	
Halt production of B-2 stealth bomber at 13 planes	N
Oppose capital gains tax cut	N
Approve federal abortion funding in rape or incest cases	N
Approve pay raise and revision of ethics rules	Y
Pass Democratic minimum wage plan over Bush veto	N

Voting Studies

	Presidential Support		Party Unity		Conservative Coalition	
Year	**S**	**O**	**S**	**O**	**S**	**O**
1990	66	33	79	19	85	13
1989	80	17	78	20	98	0
1988	61	38	79	19	89	11
1987	64	36	83	16	98	2
1986	66	32	69	28	94	6
1985	79	20	81	15	98	2

Interest Group Ratings

Year	ADA	ACU	AFL-CIO	CCUS
1990	11	67	17	79
1989	0	74	8	100
1988	15	88	21	100
1987	4	83	6	100
1986	10	82	36	100
1985	5	81	6	91

10 Cass Ballenger (R)

Of Hickory — Elected 1986

Born: Dec. 6, 1926, Hickory, N.C.

Education: Attended U. of North Carolina, 1944-45; Amherst College, B.A. 1948.

Military Service: Navy Air Corps, 1944-45.

Occupation: President of plastics packaging company.

Family: Wife, Donna Davis; three children.

Religion: Episcopalian.

Political Career: Catawba County Board of Commissioners, 1966-74, chairman, 1970-74; N.C. House, 1975-77; N.C. Senate, 1977-87.

Capitol Office: 328 Cannon Bldg. 20515; 225-2576.

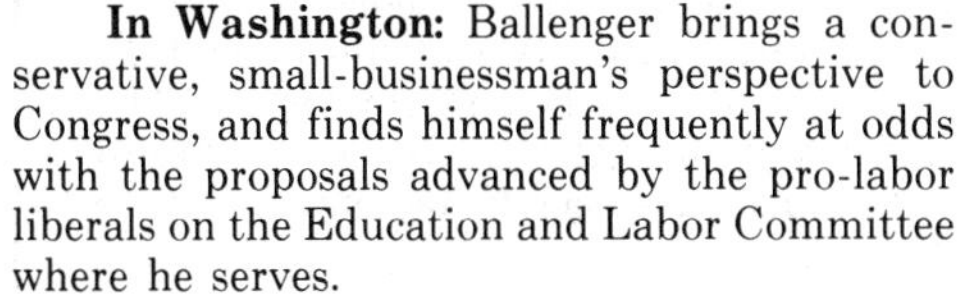

In Washington: Ballenger brings a conservative, small-businessman's perspective to Congress, and finds himself frequently at odds with the proposals advanced by the pro-labor liberals on the Education and Labor Committee where he serves.

Ballenger has fought efforts to raise the minimum wage, arguing that it would hurt small businesses by increasing labor costs. He has opposed committee bills requiring businesses to provide unpaid parental leave, and one requiring employers to notify employees before they could close a plant.

The health of the textile industry is a special Ballenger concern. His district leads the nation in textile workers, and as a member of the House Textile Caucus, in 1990 he helped gain a three-year extension of a suspension of duties on some imported textile machines.

Ballenger is a loyal party man, but he can stray from the conservative fold. Although he supported President Reagan's anti-abortion stance, he was one of 27 House members who changed position in 1989 by voting with the abortion-rights side on an appropriations bill. Ballenger said he was persuaded to change his mind by his wife and three daughters.

In the years when Congress hotly debated U.S. support for the Nicaraguan contras, Ballenger took a personal interest the region; he and his wife had performed volunteer work in Guatemala in the 1970s. In October 1987, they went to Nicaragua to help resume operation of Radio Catolica, the voice of the Catholic Church. Shortly after Radio Catolica resumed broadcasting, the Sandinista government renewed its censorship of the station. Incensed, Ballenger took the House floor to denounce the government, and called those sympathetic to it "witless peaceniks."

In the heat of the 1990 campaign season, Ballenger drew fire from Beryl Anthony of Arkansas, then chairman of the Democratic Congressional Campaign Committee. Anthony accused Ballenger of "one of the lowest forms of dirty tricks I have ever encountered" when a Ballenger aide staged a Capitol Hill photo aimed at helping the GOP challenger to North Carolina Democrat Bill Hefner. The photo purported to show a stack of Hefner newsletters, when, in fact, the aide had placed one Hefner newsletter on top of another member's stack.

At Home: The 10th was open in 1986 because its veteran incumbent, Republican James T. Broyhill, was campaigning for the Senate. Both Ballenger and George S. Robinson, his chief GOP rival, promised to emulate Broyhill.

Ballenger was a state senator who had founded a plastics company and built it into a 250-employee business. He reminded audiences that he had been on the state advisory budget commission under two GOP governors, and once served on a White House panel on economic affairs. Robinson, a pro-business state representative from Broyhill's hometown of Lenoir, was president of a lumber company.

Robinson's backers pointed out that their candidate, who at age 40 was roughly 20 years younger than Ballenger, would be able to build seniority in the way Broyhill had. But Ballenger enhanced his link with Broyhill by endorsing him in his Senate primary fight, then chastising Robinson for not doing the same. (Robinson subsequently did.)

Ballenger also accused Robinson of having ties to the National Congressional Club, Sen. Jesse Helms' political organization that was backing Broyhill's primary foe. The claim irked some Robinson supporters all the way through November. Robinson had no official links to the Club, and did have ties to Broyhill: He started his political career as his campaign driver.

Ballenger, a former Catawba County commissioner, had a strong base in the district's second-largest county, and he ran harder than Robinson in Gastonia, the largest population center. In November, Ballenger won a comfortable 57 percent against Democrat Lester D. Roark, the former mayor of Shelby.

North Carolina 10

West — Gastonia; Hickory

The 10th starts at the Tennessee line in Watauga and Avery counties, popular Appalachian mountain retreats, and runs south to industrial Gaston County on the border with South Carolina. Within those boundaries lies some of the best Republican territory in the state.

The 10th gave Ronald Reagan and George Bush their strongest showings anywhere in North Carolina in the 1980s, and the district voted solidly for its longtime representative, James T. Broyhill, in his 1986 bid to win a full Senate term.

Some Democrats have found footholds here in the past. Democrat James B. Hunt Jr. won 61 percent in the 10th in his victorious 1976 race for the governorship; four years later, Hunt carried the district again. But he failed to carry any county in the 10th in his 1984 Senate race against Republican Jesse Helms.

Gastonia, the seat of Gaston County, is home to some 55,000 and the district's largest city by far; it is one of the leading textile-manufacturing centers in the South. But the city has diversified and machinery, electronics and plastics are also part of the economy. Surrounding Gaston County contains some choice farmland.

A triangle of cities in the central part of the district — Hickory, Morganton and Lenoir — make furniture and textiles. Morganton also hosts a psychiatric hospital.

Avery and Watauga counties, in the northwest corner of the 10th, typically vote Republican. The economic fortunes of both counties are increasingly tied to the patronage of skiers and the influx of newcomers who own vacation homes in the mountains. Watauga County also is home to Appalachian State University (enrollment 11,000), in Boone, which helps explain why in 1990, Watauga County gave a narrow majority to Helms' black Democratic opponent, Harvey B. Gantt.

Population: 532,954. White 474,151 (89%), Black 56,556 (11%). Spanish origin 2,886 (1%). 18 and over 379,876 (71%), 65 and over 53,367 (10%). Median age: 30.

Committees

Education & Labor (9th of 14 Republicans)
Health & Safety; Labor-Management Relations; Select Education

Public Works & Transportation (9th of 21 Republicans)
Aviation; Economic Development; Water Resources

Elections

1990 General		
Cass Ballenger (R)	106,400	(62%)
Daniel R. Green Jr. (D)	65,710	(38%)
1990 Primary		
Cass Ballenger (R)	17,052	(87%)
Cherie K. Berry (R)	2,508	(13%)
1988 General		
Cass Ballenger (R)	112,554	(61%)
Jack L. Rhyne (D)	71,865	(39%)

Previous Winning Percentage: **1986** (57%)

District Vote For President

	1988	1984	1980	1976
D	63,531 (34%)	59,780 (30%)	71,693 (42%)	87,054 (54%)
R	120,337 (65%)	136,129 (69%)	93,520 (55%)	74,185 (46%)
I			3,775 (2%)	

Campaign Finance

	Receipts	Receipts from PACs	Expend-itures
1990			
Ballenger (R)	$297,417	$183,749 (62%)	$302,006
Green (D)	$39,178	$11,800 (30%)	$37,846
1988			
Ballenger (R)	$322,903	$153,375 (47%)	$302,215
Rhyne (D)	$44,508	$500 (1%)	$44,329

Key Votes

1991	
Authorize use of force against Iraq	Y
1990	
Support constitutional amendment on flag desecration	Y
Pass family and medical leave bill over Bush veto	N
Reduce SDI funding	N
Allow abortions in overseas military facilities	N
Approve budget summit plan for spending and taxing	N
Approve civil rights bill	N
1989	
Halt production of B-2 stealth bomber at 13 planes	N
Oppose capital gains tax cut	N
Approve federal abortion funding in rape or incest cases	Y
Approve pay raise and revision of ethics rules	Y
Pass Democratic minimum wage plan over Bush veto	N

Voting Studies

	Presidential Support		Party Unity		Conservative Coalition	
Year	**S**	**O**	**S**	**O**	**S**	**O**
1990	73	26	90	6	91	6
1989	79	20	93	5	95	5
1988	63	35	94	5	95	5
1987	71	27	91	7	98	2

Interest Group Ratings

Year	ADA	ACU	AFL-CIO	CCUS
1990	6	83	8	86
1989	10	96	9	100
1988	10	92	14	100
1987	8	82	19	93

11 Charles H. Taylor (R)

Of Brevard — Elected 1990

Born: Jan. 23, 1941, Brevard, N.C.
Education: Wake Forest U., B.A. 1963, J.D. 1966.
Occupation: Tree farmer; banker.
Family: Wife, Elizabeth Owen; three children.
Religion: Baptist.
Political Career: N.C. House, 1967-73, minority leader, 1969-71; N.C. Senate, 1973-75, minority leader, 1973-75; Republican nominee for U.S. House, 1988.
Capitol Office: 516 Cannon Bldg. 20515; 225-6401.

The Path to Washington: Many members commute to their districts every weekend to keep in touch with the voters, but Taylor might feel pressured to return home every night. For Taylor represents unquestionably the most competitive district in the nation, the Asheville-based 11th. This volatile constituency has changed between Democratic and Republican hands five times in the past decade, with Democratic Rep. James McClure Clarke getting knocked out of the seat on two separate occasions. Every contest since 1980 has been decided by fewer than 5,000 votes.

Taylor's 1990 upset of Clarke, though not a huge surprise, was notable in that it came in a non-presidential year. Taylor's best opportunity appeared to be in 1988, as George Bush polled 59 percent in the 11th; despite the coattails, Taylor fell 1,500 votes short of Clarke. Some saw that Clarke victory as a sign that an incumbent had finally planted roots in the district.

But Taylor, a wealthy tree farmer and banking executive, decided to take another shot in 1990, and easily dispatched four other primary contenders. While Clarke's campaign staff bragged that the former state House and Senate minority leader had blown his best chance in 1988, Taylor was busy assembling a more professional campaign than he had two years earlier. Gone were the amateurish commercials and micromanagement, replaced by slick ads and seasoned staff.

Taylor also softened some of his rough edges. His attacks on the low-key and grandfatherly Clarke in 1988 grated on some voters, so in the rematch Taylor ran commercials aimed at toning down his image. Presenting him as a folksy family man in shirt sleeves, Taylor's ads also addressed concerns voters had about his pro-development attitude by picturing him planting trees.

Many of the campaign themes of 1988 were rehashed, with Taylor portraying Clarke as an out-of-touch liberal and Clarke characterizing Taylor as a shady businessman. Both camps tried to take advantage of the savings and loan debacle, but neither Taylor nor Clarke could establish a clear advantage on that issue.

As the race tightened, Taylor capitalized on the rising anti-Congress sentiment. Clarke tried to inoculate himself with ads distancing himself from the institution, but to no avail. Trapped in Washington during October budget negotiations, Clarke — a talented one-on-one campaigner — lost precious time on the hustings in this large and mountainous district; he was forced to rely more heavily on television commercials.

Taylor took 11 of the 17 counties in the 11th, winning by 2,673 votes. He defeated Clarke soundly in Republican Henderson County and won the five counties at the western tip of the district, but lost Transylvania County, his home base.

Taylor is unlikely to garner the environmental accolades that Clarke did. He criticized Clarke's bill designating 90 percent of the Great Smoky Mountains National Park as a federal wilderness area, and he is noted for his pro-development orientation.

In 1988, Taylor complained that Clarke had not done enough to prevent the Environmental Protection Agency from imposing restrictions on a local paper mill blamed for polluting the Pigeon River.

In 1992, it will be Taylor's turn to test this volatile district as an incumbent. The 11th lacks a dominant industry, and interest groups do not have a strong toehold. While it has a sizable Republican constituency that has expanded with the influx of Republican-leaning retirees, the district maintains a Democratic registration edge.

And with North Carolina gaining a House seat in reapportionment, the Democratic-held Legislature may tinker with the 11th to Taylor's disadvantage.

North Carolina 11

West — Asheville

Democrats lead comfortably in registration here, but Republicans have been a potent minority in the mountains of western North Carolina since the Civil War.

In recent years, a wave of affluent retirees moving into picturesque Henderson and Polk counties has added to traditional GOP strength. About 20 percent of the population in Polk County is 65 or older, the largest concentration of senior citizens in western North Carolina.

With help from these newcomers and from national trends favorable to the GOP, Bill Hendon was able to win the 11th in 1980 (the first win for the GOP here since 1928), and in 1984. Henderson and Polk counties backed Ronald Reagan and Sen. Jesse Helms in 1984, and both went Republican in 1988 presidential and gubernatorial voting. Democratic Rep. James McClure Clarke held down his losses in the two counties in 1988, helping secure his narrow re-election over GOP challenger Charles H. Taylor. But in the 1990 Clarke-Taylor rematch, Taylor ousted Clarke from office.

The 11th's sole urban center is Asheville, a resort town, home of author Thomas Wolfe and a regional market center whose relatively small population of 60,000 belies its commercial importance. Along with surrounding Buncombe County, Asheville casts almost 30 percent of the district vote. Asheville also serves as a hub for the Southern Appalachian and Cherokee arts and crafts produced in the region.

Democrats usually enjoy an edge in local Buncombe County contests. But in statewide and national races, the county's partisan preferences are mixed. Buncombe went Republican for president in 1988 — as in five of the last six presidential elections — even as it supported Democrat Clarke for the House. Clarke carried Buncombe again in 1990, but by a smaller margin. Buncombe went for Democratic Senate nominee Harvey B. Gantt over GOP Sen. Jesse Helms in 1990, but by only 269 votes.

Industrial activity in the counties surrounding Asheville focuses on paper, pulp and textiles. In Democratic Haywood County, a Canton paper mill has been the focus of an intense debate between North Carolina and Tennessee over pollution of the Pigeon River. Though much of the terrain is steep and rocky, there is cultivation of tobacco, corn, potatoes and oats. Some Democratic labor strength can be found in the factory towns strewn through the valleys, and Democrats have an edge in traditional courthouse-level organizations.

The federal government has jurisdiction over significant scenic areas in the 11th District, including the Nantahala and Pisgah national forests, the Great Smoky Mountains National Park and the Cherokee Indian Reservation, that draw tourist dollars.

Population: 531,144. White 494,117 (93%), Black 29,291 (6%), Other 7,042 (1%). Spanish origin 3,710 (1%). 18 and over 390,762 (74%), 65 and over 75,737 (14%). Median age: 33.

Committees

Interior & Insular Affairs (14th of 17 Republicans)
Energy & the Environment; National Parks & Public Lands; Water, Power & Offshore Energy

Public Works & Transportation (18th of 21 Republicans)
Surface Transportation; Water Resources

Select Aging (22nd of 27 Republicans)
Housing & Consumer Interests; Retirement, Income & Employment; Rural Elderly

Campaign Finance

	Receipts	Receipts from PACs		Expend-itures
1990				
Taylor (R)	$523,580	$111,689	(21%)	$523,867
Clarke (D)	$486,131	$278,941	(57%)	$499,869

Key Vote

1991

Authorize use of force against Iraq	Y

Elections

1990 General		
Charles H. Taylor (R)	101,991	(51%)
James McClure Clarke (D)	99,318	(49%)
1990 Primary		
Charles H. Taylor (R)	16,381	(56%)
Herschel "Scotty" Morgan (R)	6,089	(21%)
Lanier M. Cansler (R)	4,158	(14%)
Richard Bridges (R)	1,630	(6%)
James T. Harper (R)	945	(3%)

District Vote For President

	1988	1984	1980	1976
D	87,755 (40%)	79,098 (37%)	87,984 (46%)	98,452 (54%)
R	128,469 (59%)	135,030 (63%)	98,258 (51%)	81,747 (45%)
I			5,254 (3%)	

North Dakota

U.S. CONGRESS

SENATE 2 D
HOUSE 1 D

LEGISLATURE

Senate 27 D, 26 R
House 48 D, 58 R

ELECTIONS

1988 Presidential Vote	
Bush	56%
Dukakis	43%
1984 Presidential Vote	
Reagan	65%
Mondale	34%
1980 Presidential Vote	
Reagan	64%
Carter	26%
Anderson	8%
Turnout rate in 1986	58%
Turnout rate in 1988	62%
Turnout rate in 1990	49%

(as percentage of voting age population)

POPULATION AND GROWTH

1980 population	652,717
1990 population (47th in the nation)	638,800
Percent change 1980-1990	−2%

DEMOGRAPHIC BREAKDOWN

White	95%
Black	1%
American Indian, Eskimo, or Aleut	4%
(Hispanic origin)	1%
Urban	49%
Rural	51%
Born in state	73%
Foreign-born	2%

MAJOR CITIES

Fargo	74,111
Grand Forks	49,425
Bismarck	49,256
Minot	34,544
Dickinson	16,097

AREA AND LAND USE

Area 69,300 sq. miles (17th)

Farm	91%
Forest	1%
Federally owned	4%

Gov. George Sinner (D)
Of Casselton — Elected 1984

Born: May 29, 1928, Casselton, N.D.
Education: St. John's U., B.A. 1950.
Military Service: Air Force, 1951-52.
Occupation: Sugar beet farmer; businessman.
Religion: Roman Catholic.
Political Career: N.D. Senate, 1963-67; N.D. House, 1983-85; Democratic nominee for U.S. House, 1964.
Next Election: 1992.

WORK

Occupations	
White-collar	46%
Blue-collar	24%
Service workers	15%
Government Workers	
Federal	8,059
State	20,279
Local	33,654

MONEY

Median family income	$ 18,023	(34th)
Tax burden per capita	$ 1,011	(13th)

EDUCATION

Spending per pupil through grade 12	$ 3,519	(37th)
Persons with college degrees	15%	(31st)

CRIME

Violent crime rate	63 per 100,000	(50th)

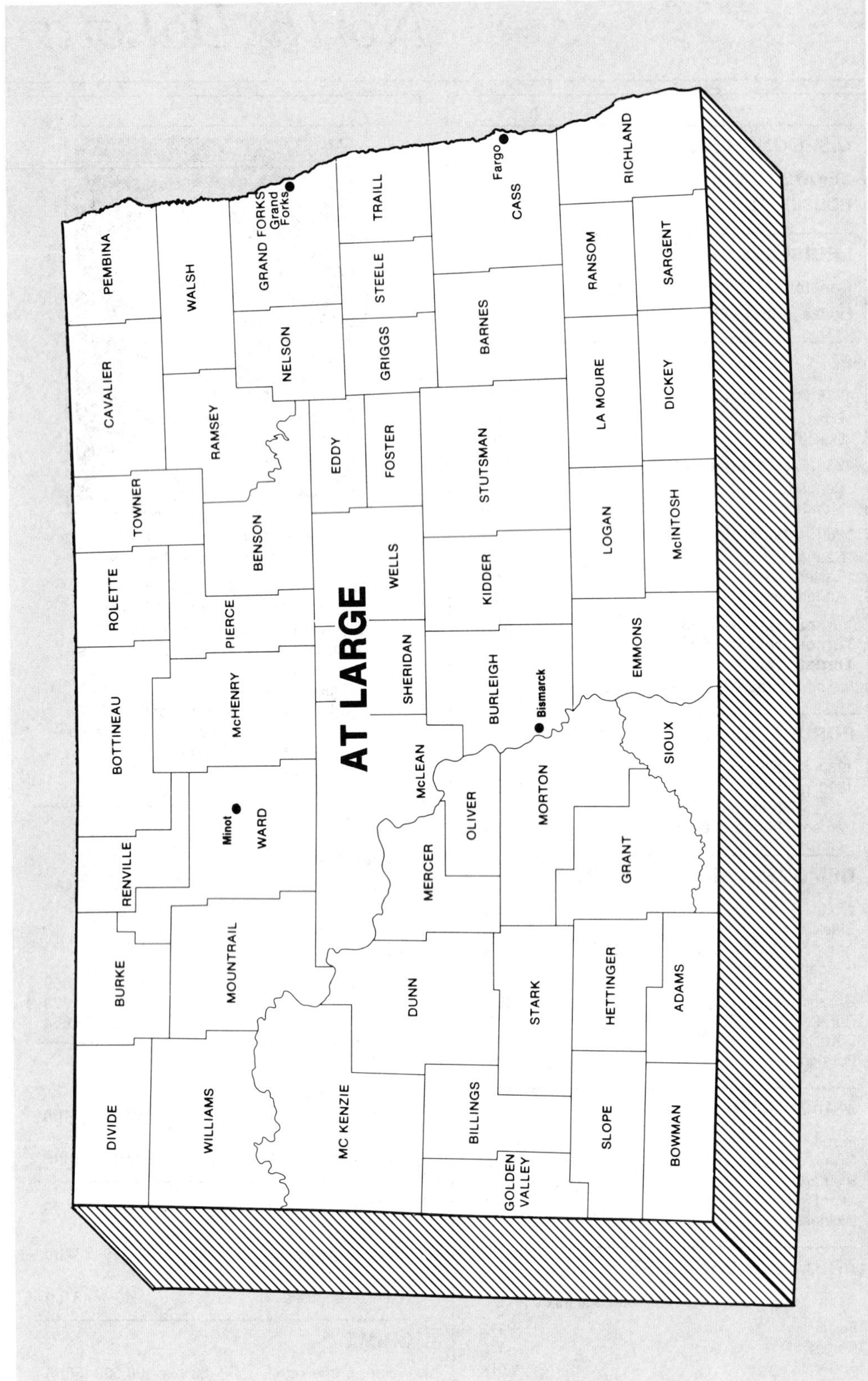
AT LARGE
PEMBINA
WALSH
GRAND FORKS
Grand Forks
TRAILL
CASS
Fargo
RICHLAND
CAVALIER
RAMSEY
NELSON
STEELE
GRIGGS
BARNES
RANSOM
SARGENT
TOWNER
ROLETTE
BENSON
EDDY
FOSTER
STUTSMAN
LA MOURE
DICKEY
PIERCE
WELLS
KIDDER
LOGAN
McINTOSH
BOTTINEAU
McHENRY
SHERIDAN
BURLEIGH
Bismarck
EMMONS
RENVILLE
WARD
Minot
McLEAN
OLIVER
MORTON
SIOUX
GRANT
MERCER
BURKE
MOUNTRAIL
DUNN
STARK
HETTINGER
ADAMS
DIVIDE
WILLIAMS
MC KENZIE
BILLINGS
GOLDEN VALLEY
SLOPE
BOWMAN

Quentin N. Burdick (D)

Of Fargo — Elected 1960

Born: June 19, 1908, Munich, N.D.

Education: U. of Minnesota, B.A. 1931, LL.B. 1932.

Occupation: Lawyer.

Family: Wife, Jocelyn Birch Peterson; four children, two stepchildren.

Religion: United Church of Christ.

Political Career: U.S. House, 1959-60; candidate for Cass County state's attorney, 1934, 1940; Republican candidate for N.D. Senate, 1938; Republican nominee for lieutenant governor, 1942; Democratic nominee for governor, 1946, and U.S. Senate, 1956.

Capitol Office: 511 Hart Bldg. 20510; 224-2551.

In Washington: For two years leading up to the 1988 election, Burdick broke character and endeavored to show North Dakota voters that he was an important and influential player who shaped legislation of consequence. Like an ambitious freshman, he worked the press, announced a lengthy agenda and otherwise sought to demonstrate clout. In Burdick's case, it was the politics of necessity. Then 79, he was preparing for a reelection battle in which his health would be the key issue. His counter: a show of Washington muscle to the folks back home. But on Capitol Hill, Burdick's staff did the heavy lifting.

After his re-election in 1988, Burdick reverted to his well-worn role of ducking the heavy responsibility of running a major committee — his subcommittee chairmen ran Burdick's Environment and Public Works Committee — while picking plums to send back to his state from his seat on the Appropriations Committee.

Burdick's presence in the Senate is rarely detected outside the pages of committee reports. He has concentrated on constituent service and protecting the interests of his home state. "I just want to be a good North Dakota senator," he has said. "I try to represent the people of my state and hope their interests coincide with the national interest." His capacity for home-state boosterism was enhanced in the 100th Congress, when he got the chairmanship of the Appropriations subcommittee that doles out money for agriculture and rural development. "I will get everything North Dakota is entitled to now," he proclaimed.

One of the things Burdick thought North Dakota deserved was a $500,000 appropriation to assist companies working to restore the Strasburg, N.D., birthplace of band leader Lawrence Welk. The money eased through when the Agriculture appropriations bill passed in October 1990, but in an election year in which Congress' low esteem produced outpourings of anti-congressional antipathy, a half-million dollars to commemorate a living band leader provoked accusations of pork-barrel politicking.

That was unusual for Burdick — to be near the center of a public debate. More frequently, he quietly wins funding for North Dakota projects, his notice limited to the home-state media: According to a Southern Illinois University study, Burdick was one of only three senators never to appear on the nightly network news in 1987 and 1988.

Burdick views as his major accomplishment in Congress the 1965 authorization of the Garrison Diversion project in North Dakota, a giant public works program now under fire as unaffordable. There have been votes to delete funding for the project or to scale it back. But Burdick defends his monument from his Senate Appropriations post; in 1990, he obtained $35 million for the project. In 1990, Burdick's literature listed such appropriations victories as $25.4 million for a dam for Minot and $16 million for agricultural research and rural development projects at North Dakota universities.

During more than a quarter-century in the Senate, Burdick had never chaired any committee of any consequence until 1987. Self-effacing, good-natured and never one to seek the power or pressure of leadership, it was more Burdick's fault than the system's. He shifted repeatedly from one panel to another, serving at various times on the Interior, Labor, Judiciary, Post Office, Public Works, Appropriations and Environment committees. He voluntarily gave up his membership on several committees just as he was being asked to assume some responsibility for managing them.

But the Democrats regained control of the Senate in 1987, and with his own seat on the line in 1988 Burdick was in no position to turn down the chairmanship of the Environment and Public Works Committee. With an aide never far from his ear, Burdick ran the committee in a somnambulent style, as if following a script. Republican Robert T. Stafford of Vermont coached him on the technical points of amendments and motions. The committee's floor work often fell to the majority leader or subcommittee chairmen.

Wyoming Republican Alan K. Simpson, the minority whip, stumping during the 1988 campaign for Burdick's Republican opponent, scoffed at Burdick's claim of clout and noted that senior Democrats had divvied up the committee's responsibilities in Burdick's absence, presenting it to him as a *fait accompli*. "They just took a piece and left your senator with nothing to do but to call the committee to order," Simpson said. Burdick called Simpson's account "purely political."

But Simpson's description fairly aptly described Burdick's role on Environment in the 101st Congress, as the committee worked on the first rewrite of the Clean Air Act in 13 years. Burdick played little visible role, while Montana Democrat Max Baucus, chairman of the Environmental Protection Subcommittee, took charge on the committee. When the bill went to a House-Senate conference, Burdick acceded to Baucus' wish and let the Montanan head the conferees.

Burdick also has shown an interest in postal issues. Before 1987, the one committee he seemed to want to chair was Post Office and Civil Service; he was in line to head it in 1977, but the Senate decided that year to fold it into the Governmental Affairs Committee as part of a major overhaul of the Senate's committee structure. Piqued by this development, Burdick cast the sole dissenting vote in the Senate on the reform plan.

The North Dakota Democrat has been a fairly consistent liberal throughout his congressional career. He was a staunch supporter of the Kennedy and Johnson administrations, an early critic of the Vietnam War and a strong backer of all major civil rights legislation. He was, however, one of the first Northern Democrats to criticize busing for racial balance and to support anti-busing legislation.

Burdick has long been one of the more absent-minded senators; usually this causes him no particular trouble. In 1983, though, he inserted in the *Congressional Record* not only a statement on the issue of truck-weight regulations, but private instructions he had received on the subject from a lobbyist. Burdick's floor speech that day includes the words, "Greyhound Bus Co. would like you to insert the attached floor statement in today's *Congressional Record*."

At Home: Burdick's ascent to a committee chairmanship came at a very good time — when he appeared to be facing his most serious electoral challenge in more than 20 years. In the end he used his new position in Washington, and a sophisticated campaign in the state, to win overwhelming approval for another term.

Many North Dakotans assumed Burdick would retire and make way for popular Democratic Rep. Byron L. Dorgan. When Burdick made it clear he wanted another term, a primary bloodbath seemed possible. A number of Democrats suggested privately and publicly that Burdick should step aside, and many expected Dorgan to run for the Senate regardless.

But Burdick demonstrated his resolve with his decision to distribute press releases and newspaper clips citing his new importance, and with his decision to take out early media advertising. He touted his new position in Washington and encouraged Dorgan to stay in the House. Seeing that he might have a tough fight on his hands, Dorgan announced late in 1987 that he would not challenge Burdick.

Dorgan's decision was a major boost for Burdick, but it did not signal the end of his vulnerability. In the fall he faced Earl Strinden, the GOP leader in the state House, who repeatedly questioned Burdick's ability to serve in the Senate another six years.

Burdick worked to dispel doubts about his age, at one point mailing "The Walking Workout, A Guide to Fitness Walking," a pamphlet describing how he keeps in good condition and how others can as well. The subject moved to the headlines a few months before the election, when Burdick underwent surgery to have an 18-inch section of his large intestine removed.

Republicans were also frustrated by Burdick's careful campaign, which seemed to keep him either in Washington or in scripted appearances before friendly audiences. The GOP did not get the boost it expected when the incumbent finally participated in a candidate debate. Burdick's performance was strong enough to dispel charges that he was incompetent.

Burdick had more than a sophisticated campaign and committee chairmanship going for him. In a state that takes its political history and traditions seriously, his family name has been appearing on North Dakota ballots for most of the 20th century. Quentin's father, Usher Burdick, served as a state legislator, lieutenant governor and U.S. House member. From 1938 to 1956, Quentin ran unsuccessfully for a string of offices — state senator, lieutenant governor, governor and U.S. senator.

Like his father, Burdick started out as a Republican. In his early races, he also ran under the banner of the old populist Non-Partisan League. But in 1946, when he tried for governor, he shifted to the Democratic label.

Burdick finally won office in 1958, taking a seat in Congress. In 1960, upon the death of the state's senior GOP senator, William Langer, he upset Republican Gov. John E. Davis in a special election for the unexpired Senate term. The contest turned on farm issues. Burdick owed his narrow victory to his attacks on the unpopular farm policies of the Eisenhower administration.

In 1964, when he ran for a full term, it was Burdick's turn to be on the defensive. Republican businessman Thomas Kleppe, later a House member and U.S. Interior secretary, decried falling farm prices under the Kennedy administration. But Burdick countered by linking Kleppe to GOP presidential nominee Barry Goldwater, who advocated scrapping some farm subsidies altogether.

In a 1970 rematch, Burdick criticized the Nixon administration for refusing to back increased price supports, and he benefited from resentment over Kleppe's attempts to link him with "radical liberal" Democrats. He won easily that year and even more easily in 1976, when the GOP essentially gave up and nominated a little-known state legislator.

Republicans tried harder in 1982, but the results were no more satisfying. Burdick's opponent was Gene Knorr, a Washington lobbyist, former U.S. Treasury official and member of President Reagan's transition team.

Knorr crisscrossed the state by private plane and van, telling voters that Burdick was simply too liberal for them. Burdick's age and low profile in the Senate seemed to make him a perfect candidate for an upset at the hands of the younger, more energetic Knorr.

Burdick pegged his re-election effort only partly to criticism of GOP economic policies. He also made an issue of Knorr's extended absence from the state. Burdick aired commercials noting that at the time Knorr was nominated in North Dakota, he was still registered to vote in Virginia.

It had been widely assumed that Burdick will step down in 1994, at the age of 86, but late in 1990 North Dakota Democrats were shocked to hear Burdick assert his intention to run for re-election, health permitting. Burdick's frequent memory lapses and health problems — he has been hospitalized several times since 1988 — led many state observers to dismiss the statement. But North Dakotans have shown no qualms about sending popular yet physically infirm congressmen back to Washington. In 1958, Sen. Langer carried every county in the state despite being too ill to return to the state to campaign. He died less than a year after being re-elected in 1958.

Committees

Environment & Public Works (Chairman)

Appropriations (5th of 16 Democrats)
Agriculture, Rural Development & Related Agencies (chairman); Energy & Water Development; Interior; Labor, Health & Human Services, Education

Select Indian Affairs (3rd of 9 Democrats)

Special Aging (4th of 11 Democrats)

Elections

1988 General

Quentin N. Burdick (D)	171,899	(59%)
Earl Strinden (R)	112,937	(39%)

Previous Winning Percentages: **1982** (63%) **1976** (62%) **1970** (61%) **1964** (58%) **1960** † (50%) **1958** * (50%)

† Special Senate election.
** House election.*

Campaign Finance

	Receipts	Receipts from PACs		Expenditures
1988				
Burdick (D)	$1,755,318	$1,059,524	(60%)	$2,026,617
Strinden (R)	$908,607	$254,518	(28%)	$906,807

Key Votes

1991

Authorize use of force against Iraq	N
1990	•
Oppose prohibition of certain semiautomatic weapons	N
Support constitutional amendment on flag desecration	Y
Oppose requiring parental notice for minors' abortions	Y
Halt production of B-2 stealth bomber at 13 planes	Y
Approve budget that cut spending and raised revenues	Y
Pass civil rights bill over Bush veto	Y
1989	
Oppose reduction of SDI funding	N
Oppose barring federal funds for "obscene" art	Y
Allow vote on capital gains tax cut	N

Voting Studies

	Presidential Support		Party Unity		Conservative Coalition	
Year	**S**	**O**	**S**	**O**	**S**	**O**
1990	27	73	86	14	32	68
1989	51	48	90	10	29	71
1988	43	52	88	10	41	59
1987	33	64	88	10	25	75
1986	18	81	87	13	20	80
1985	25	73	87	10	30	70
1984	31	56	78	11	26	57
1983	46	54	85	14	36	59
1982	50	50	81	17	48	51
1981	52	46	81	17	41	58

Interest Group Ratings

Year	ADA	ACU	AFL-CIO	CCUS
1990	89	9	78	17
1989	85	11	100	38
1988	85	16	100	29
1987	95	8	100	24
1986	100	4	93	21
1985	85	9	86	21
1984	100	0	91	33
1983	75	12	82	32
1982	70	25	88	50
1981	75	13	74	44

Kent Conrad (D)

Of Bismarck — Elected 1986

Born: March 12, 1948, Bismarck, N.D.
Education: Stanford U., B.A. 1971; George Washington U., M.B.A. 1975.
Occupation: Management and personnel director.
Family: Wife, Lucy Calautti; two children.
Religion: Unitarian.
Political Career: N.D. tax commissioner, 1981-87; candidate for N.D. auditor, 1976.
Capitol Office: 724 Hart Bldg. 20510; 224-2043.

In Washington: North Dakota has long been fertile soil for populists willing to till its natural distrust of powerful outsiders — Eastern bankers, railroad magnates and flour-mill barons. When hard times sweep across the prairie, these attitudes harden, to the benefit of politicians like Conrad. He built his reputation as a tax commissioner willing to take on big business. He spent his first four years in the Senate carrying water for his farmers.

No mere windmill tilter, Conrad earned the sobriquet "Chainsaw" back home because, he once said, "When you are going after big timber you have to use strong tactics." Yet his manner does not suggest a giant-killer: Fresh-faced, earnest, and conservative in style and dress, Conrad looks as if he would fit better with an assembly of junior executives than a crowd of angry farmers. During his first month in office, he shared an elevator with a senator's wife who informed him it was for senators only, and then challenged his claim to the title.

Whether or not Conrad looks his part, he has certainly played it, holding fast by his causes. From the 1990 farm bill to "emergency" supplemental appropriations bills, he has agitated to get the best deal for his farmers.

Conrad was the least experienced of the 11 Democrats in the Senate class of 1986, all of the 10 others former governors or House members. He has taken traditional steps to close this gap — developing expertise in a limited number of areas by doing his homework. This was perhaps even more essential for Conrad than most, for farm policy is one of Capitol Hill's most complex issue areas, politically and substantively.

Seats on the Agriculture and Budget committees position Conrad strategically for defending agriculture as farm programs run headlong into pressures for deficit reduction.

On Agriculture, he is part of a clique of junior populist Democrats who advocate greater government subsidies for their farmers. Led by Conrad and Nebraskan Bob Kerrey, the prairie populists sought a more partisan slant to the 1990 farm bill.

Having been elected with the help of farmers disgruntled about policies included in the 1985 farm bill, Conrad was hardly receptive to suggestions that the 1990 farm bill continue the 1985 bill's trend of lowering federal support levels. "The agriculture sector has been pushed to the limit," he said. Continuing the decline in target prices for commodities "is not a policy that is going to do anything but threaten the health of rural America."

Conrad's unflagging persistence in pursuit of his causes — and his preference for long impassioned speeches — can wear on his colleagues. While his hard work and thorough preparation are readily acknowledged, he is also criticized for a tendency toward stridency. Unlike Kerrey, who voted for the farm bill when it first passed the Senate, Conrad voted against Senate passage as well as the House-Senate conference agreement.

At one especially contentious backroom session, supporters of a compromise on the farm bill's section revamping federal wetlands protections virtually dared Conrad to break the deal. Conrad favored extensive loosening of a federal law, known as "swampbuster," that bars draining swamps and marshes for farming.

Conrad has attempted to board a number of money bills in his search for vehicles to aid drought-stricken farmers in North Dakota. In 1990, he offered an amendment to a midyear aid bill (ostensibly for Panama and Nicaragua) that would have allowed farmers in drought areas to avoid repaying crop subsidies that were paid but later reduced when the droughts of 1988 and 1989 raised market prices. Senators voted 52-43 to kill it, but Conrad waged a last-ditch effort to add it to the bill. As the Senate was preparing to clear the bill late in the evening, Conrad offered his amendment again. Frustrated colleagues, however, convinced him that most senators were in bed and in no mood to vote on it again, and he conceded defeat.

In early 1987, during floor action on drought relief for winter-wheat farmers, Conrad bucked Agriculture Committee Chairman Patrick J. Leahy of Vermont — who wanted no amendments on the bill — and managed to amend it to gain treatment for sunflower growers equal to that of soybean producers; the two crops compete in the cooking-oil market. Conrad also pressed the Farmers Home Administration to write down overdue loans instead of foreclosing on them.

His other passion is the budget deficit, which he would attack with measures as harsh as a spending freeze, Social Security excepted. He voted against Treasury Secretary Nicholas F. Brady's confirmation after Brady expressed the belief that the nation's economy could simply grow out of the deficit. He founded the bipartisan Deficit Reduction Caucus in 1988, which has grown to 40 members.

Conrad offered a plan in 1990 to reduce the budget deficit by $56.5 billion, in part through $19.5 billion in new revenues and an $11.1 billion "tax compliance program." The Budget Committee rejected his proposal by a 7-16 vote, but Chairman Jim Sasser of Tennessee, in order to win the vote of Virginia Democrat Charles S. Robb, included the tax compliance program in the committee's budget resolution.

When a deficit-reduction package finally made it to the Senate floor late in the 101st Congress, Conrad and Montana Democrat Max Baucus tried to increase taxes on the rich. Their amendment would have imposed a 10 percent surtax on the wealthy while paring back the proposed gasoline tax increase and proposed Medicare and farm program cuts. It was defeated, however, on a procedural vote, 32-67.

In 1992, Conrad could find himself scrambling to explain away a pledge he made upon coming to Washington: He promised voters he would not seek re-election unless real interest rates fell and the trade and budget deficits came under control (he even specified an 80 percent cut in each). Not surprisingly, he has since backed off the pledge, joking that he wrote it under the influence of a 104-degree fever and saying he might run again even if his goals are not met.

One way Conrad has sought to entwine his desires to shift more funds to domestic programs and to bring the budget into shape is through cutting U.S. troops stationed overseas, requiring allies to assume a greater burden for their defense. During consideration of the 1989 defense appropriations bill, he offered an amendment to return 30,000 troops stationed in Europe and transfer from the Pentagon's budget to education programs the $1 billion that he said would be saved. "We are paying for their defense umbrella even though we have to borrow the money from them to do it," he said. His amendment was rejected 23-76.

In 1990, he pressed on with an amendment to cut U.S. Army and Air Force personnel stationed in Europe by 80,000 — 30,000 more than called for in the pending defense authorization bill. The Senate voted to kill it, 59-40. But when he offered it two months later to the defense appropriations bill, it lost by only four votes, 46-50. "There is the beginning of a very clear change of opinion in this country," he said. "It is time to send a clear and unmistakable message to our allies that they must take on a greater share of this common defense burden." The Senate later adopted his amendment reducing the number of U.S. military personnel stationed in Japan by 10,000 per year, except for those whose costs are paid in full by Japan.

Conrad also serves on the Energy Committee, where he has found additional ways to look out for North Dakota. In the 101st Congress, he agreed to support a natural gas price decontrol bill only after he was assured of language to promote the continued fiscal health of a coal-gasification plant in his state.

Conrad has shown himself a party loyalist in his early going. But he is given more to discussion of policy than politics, and his populism, though no passing fancy, is tempered with pragmatism. "Hard ideological positions carry a danger," he says. "Hiding behind rhetorical barriers doesn't get things done."

At Home: The troubles besetting North Dakota's farms and small towns gave Conrad a clear opening in 1986 against Republican Sen. Mark Andrews, and his skillful use of the issue propelled him into contention against the favored incumbent. On Election Day, Conrad carried only one of the state's four major population centers; his victory was built in the countryside.

Conrad succeeded Democratic Rep. Byron L. Dorgan as tax commissioner and he won widespread popularity by vigorously auditing out-of-state corporations. He also fought an ongoing battle with the Burlington Northern Railroad Co., challenging its abandonment of rail lines used by farmers within the state.

Conrad's chief Senate campaign issue was the Reagan administration's farm policy, which was wildly unpopular in a state where farms and small-town banks were failing and where rural families were breaking apart as their members headed to the cities to find work. The election, Conrad insisted, was a referendum on Republican farm and economic policies; if voters wanted to send a message to Washington, he told them, he would be the messenger.

He went on the attack early, trying to tie Andrews to the administration's programs. Though the Republican had by and large opposed Reagan agricultural policies, he had voted for the 1985 farm bill, which many farmers believed hurt them. Storming around the state with Dorgan, Conrad relentlessly pressed the point, bringing up Andrews' vote whenever the opportunity arose.

He also set out to undermine Andrews' credibility. When the senator aired a commercial claiming that the price of wheat had risen after the Senate passed an export amendment he had sponsored, Conrad pointed out that the price rise was only a brief interruption in a long-term decline.

Andrews responded in kind. He challenged Conrad's claim to have cut his departmental budget as tax commissioner, and pointed out that Conrad had been endorsed in a *Village Voice* article — a sure sign that he was too liberal for North Dakota.

But the debate between the two may have been secondary to the deeper factors working in Conrad's favor. In addition to the farm situation, there was a growing perception that Andrews had lost touch with his base.

Part of the way into the campaign, Andrews was stung by press stories revealing that a close friend of his had hired private detectives to investigate first Dorgan and then Conrad. Democrats jumped on the matter, trying to tie Andrews directly to the incident; Andrews denied any involvement, but the publicity hurt him all the same.

Possibly as troubling to voters was a multimillion-dollar lawsuit that Andrews and his wife Mary had pursued against family physicians after Mary Andrews was crippled by meningitis. Though early in the case there had been widespread sympathy for the incumbent and his wife, by the time of the election there was evidence that voters had grown uncomfortable with the sight of a wealthy senator demanding large sums of money from family doctors in a state where, as one North Dakota journalist wrote, "not even clergy are more highly thought of."

Andrews was further hurt by the delay in ending Congress' 1986 session. As Conrad's attacks found their mark, Republicans worried that Andrews' continued presence in Washington would only underline the Democrats' contention that he had grown distant from the state's concerns. By the time Andrews did return home, Conrad had taken a slight lead in the polls, and Andrews had to try to make up lost ground. He never succeeded.

Committees

Agriculture, Nutrition & Forestry (6th of 10 Democrats)
Agricultural Credit (chairman); Agricultural Production & Stabilization of Prices; Domestic & Foreign Marketing & Product Promotion

Budget (11th of 12 Democrats)

Energy & Natural Resources (7th of 11 Democrats)
Mineral Resources Development & Production; Public Lands, National Parks & Forests; Water & Power

Select Indian Affairs (5th of 9 Democrats)

Elections

1986 General

Kent Conrad (D)	143,932	(50%)
Mark Andrews (R)	141,797	(49%)

Campaign Finance

	Receipts	Receipts from PACs		Expend-itures
1986				
Conrad (D)	$993,040	$453,440	(46%)	$908,374
Andrews (R)	$2,063,395	$1,019,595	(49%)	$2,270,557

Key Votes

1991	
Authorize use of force against Iraq	N
1990	
Oppose prohibition of certain semiautomatic weapons	N
Support constitutional amendment on flag desecration	Y
Oppose requiring parental notice for minors' abortions	N
Halt production of B-2 stealth bomber at 13 planes	Y
Approve budget that cut spending and raised revenues	N
Pass civil rights bill over Bush veto	Y
1989	
Oppose reduction of SDI funding	N
Oppose barring federal funds for "obscene" art	N
Allow vote on capital gains tax cut	N

Voting Studies

	Presidential Support		Party Unity		Conservative Coalition	
Year	**S**	**O**	**S**	**O**	**S**	**O**
1990	34	66	75	24	38	62
1989	55	45	70	30	42	58
1988	48	50	78	20	35	65
1987	37	63	82	17	47	53

Interest Group Ratings

Year	ADA	ACU	AFL-CIO	CCUS
1990	67	30	56	42
1989	70	29	90	50
1988	80	24	93	29
1987	85	8	90	39

AL Byron L. Dorgan (D)

Of Bismarck — Elected 1980

Born: May 14, 1942, Regent, N.D.
Education: U. of North Dakota, B.S. 1965; U. of Denver, M.B.A. 1966.
Occupation: Public official.
Family: Wife, Kimberly Olson; four children.
Religion: Lutheran.
Political Career: N.D. tax commissioner, 1969-80; Democratic nominee for U.S. House, 1974.
Capitol Office: 203 Cannon Bldg. 20515; 225-2611.

In Washington: Dorgan is regarded in the Capitol and in North Dakota as the state's senator-in-waiting. He has twice weighed challenges to incumbents and decided to stay put, but he makes no secret of his wish to succeed octogenarian Democratic Sen. Quentin N. Burdick when the time comes.

So widely assumed is this succession that North Dakota's other senator, Democrat Kent Conrad, found it hard to compete for a seat on the Senate Finance Committee in 1990. North Dakota could not expect to have two seats on Finance, and influential Democrats were said to be holding one for Dorgan.

In the meantime, the Dorgan viewpoint has become a familiar feature of House debates on economic policy. An aggressive partisan on taxes and trade, he has generally and often bitterly opposed the administrations of Presidents Bush and Reagan. In the 101st Congress, when much of the rhetorical exchange had to do with big financial institutions and taxes on the wealthy, Dorgan was in his glory.

"Those who make millions can well afford to pay more in taxes than two-wage-earner families with four children struggling to make ends meet on $25,000 a year," he said.

In recent years he has gleefully taken aim at leveraged buyouts as the epitome of run-amok capitalism: "buying $100,000 houses with a $60-dollar downpayment." In the 101st, Dorgan proposed strict limits on tax deductions that businesses take for interest paid on buyout-related debt. He also helped organize a group of more than 50 members interested in buyout legislation.

Dorgan was a leader among Ways and Means Democrats opposing any cut in the capital gains tax — President Bush's "top tax policy priority" in the 101st Congress. When it was clear that some form of cut would win committee approval, Dorgan tried to limit its benefits for taxpayers making more than $100,000 a year and eliminate them altogether for those making more than $200,000.

In the same Congress, Dorgan attached an amendment to the House-passed bailout bill for the savings and loan industry that banned thrifts from investing in junk bonds. He tried to repeal a law that lets big utilities accumulate capital investment dollars in the guise of tax-payment reserves. He co-sponsored a bill giving the president far more direct influence over decisions of the Federal Reserve Board. He also co-sponsored legislation to eliminate the Social Security trust fund's surplus when calculating the federal deficit, and he co-sponsored a bill rolling back the 1990 increase in Social Security payroll taxes. He also sponsored legislation phasing out the urban-rural differential in Medicare payments made to hospitals.

Dorgan is a contemporary echo of the prairie populism that swept North Dakota in the early 1900s. His rhetorical targets are big banks, railroads and grasping corporations. His talk dwells on the struggles of common folk against distant forces over which they have no control. "People feel powerless," he has said, "and they feel powerless because they're preyed upon by bigger interests."

But Dorgan's legislative style has little in common with the crude bluster of predecessors like William L. Langer, the North Dakotan who once pounded on a Senate lectern so hard that it broke. Dorgan rarely shouts or waves his arms, even when denouncing a David Rockefeller or a Paul Volcker. But he denounces them nonetheless.

Dorgan's populism smacks at times of old-fashioned isolationism when he turns his attention to trade. He is chairman of the House Hunger Committee's International Task Force, a job that tries to match U.S. surplus with need around the world. And he certainly understands the need for foreign markets for his state's vast production of wheat. Yet he seems more exercised in his defense of every farm and business against the hazards of international competition.

He voted against the free trade pact with Canada, arguing that it failed to guarantee access for U.S. wheat. In 1991 he was an early critic of the proposed free-trade agreement with Mexico, offering legislation to deny special

North Dakota — At Large

North Dakota's centennial anniversary festivities in 1989 masked a troubling uncertainty denizens have about the state's future. One of only four states to lose population in the 1980s, North Dakota is the only state with fewer people now than in 1930. As farmland values dropped during the 1980s, small farms began disappearing from the map. In 1989, the state itself disappeared from the map in a manner of speaking: Rand McNally did not include North Dakota in its new photographic world atlas. Some locals ascribed the omission to a conspiracy against the state by outsiders.

Much of North Dakota's population exodus has occurred from the western portion of the state. Too dry for a good wheat crop, the west produces livestock, and it developed an energy industry that was hard hit in the 1980's by the slide in oil prices. As oil production diminished, population moved east; the state's largest city, Fargo (population 74,000) grew by 21 percent in the 1980s, while the other major Red River Valley city, Grand Forks (population 49,000), posted a moderate gain. The combination of large medical facilities, the two major state universities and normally prosperous farmers makes eastern North Dakota Republican in most elections.

While North Dakota now has a strong two-party system, its political character has largely been molded by a third force, the agrarian populist movement. The original vehicle for populism, the Non-Partisan League, has not been a major factor for a generation, but agrarian populism continues to shape the state's politics.

The 1980s were tough for the state GOP. In 1981, Republicans vastly outnumbered Democrats in the state Legislature; there were only 10 Democrats in the 50-member state Senate. But in 1986, Democrats won control of the state Senate for the first time in history, and maintained that hold through 1990. Republicans continue to hold a majority in the state House, but the governorship, the House seat and the two Senate seats are all in Democratic hands.

In recent years, the Democratic Party has come to be viewed by many farmers as the inheritor of the old Non-Partisan League populism. Agrarian discontent — directed toward Minnesota business interests and East Coast bankers — is palpable in the western reaches of the state.

The migration from the rural areas to the cities has chipped away at the cities' traditional Republican orientation. This is particularly noticeable in the capital of Bismarck, in the south-central part of the state. In the many small towns, Republican strength persists, although even there the GOP has lost steam because farm problems are affecting Main Street businesses.

Although the politics of North Dakota have traditionally been the politics of wheat, the state's farm community is more diverse than its political rhetoric would imply. The Red River, which marks the state's eastern border with Minnesota, flows through the state's most prosperous agricultural area, a rich growing region that produces sugar beets and potatoes.

The stagnant coal industry in the southwestern corner of the state received a boost when the Great Plains coal gasification plant in Beulah reopened in 1989. Constructed with grand expectations of transforming huge amounts of coal to natural gas, the plant was considered a failure until private interests bought it from the federal government in 1988 and turned a profit one year later.

Population: 652,717. White 625,557 (96%), Black 2,568 (0.4%), Other 22,137 (3%). Spanish origin 3,902 (1%). 18 and over 461,726 (71%), 65 and over 80,445 (12%). Median age: 28.

"fast track" consideration of any such pact in Congress.

In the 101st Congress he also joined with other members questioning the tax payments of foreign, primarily Japanese corporations.

"A nation up to its neck in debts should look to [taxing] deadbeats before it starts raising taxes on honest folks," he said.

On another occasion, explaining the U.S. trade deficit with Japan, he said: "While they open their arms to our sailors and soldiers they close their markets to our telephones and TVs."

Dorgan's 11 years as state tax commissioner provided him with expertise and credibility that help make him a force on Ways and Means. He spends a great deal of time working on schemes to guarantee that the earnings of large corporations are taxed. In the 99th Congress, he was a strong supporter of efforts on Ways and Means to revise the tax code, which he called "a feedlot for the rich, and a straitjacket for the rest."

Dorgan knows how to craft an amendment and round up the support he needs for its passage. During work on the tax bill in 1985, he pushed through an amendment to help farm co-ops by retaining a tax exemption for credit unions. That, in effect, gave them an advantage over competing savings and loans.

On other issues, however, Dorgan argued that achieving an overhaul of the tax code was more important than protecting parochial interests. He opposed some agriculture tax subsidies, such as accelerated write-offs for new hog barns, though some North Dakotans wanted them. "Doing tax reform is like administering medicine," Dorgan said. "They don't like the taste, but they will like the result."

Dorgan also generated some national press in 1990 by opposing the MX missile program, which would have brought $70 million and 350 jobs to Grand Forks, N.D.

Overall, however, Dorgan has put home-state interests first. He astutely voted against the 1985 farm bill; while criticized for not revealing his position until passage was assured, Dorgan avoided the fate that befell GOP Sen. Mark A. Andrews — whose vote for the bill helped cost him his job in the next election.

On a smaller scale, Dorgan bore the brunt of ridicule early in 1991 for defending a $500,000 appropriation for a German-Russian interpretive center at the North Dakota birthplace of bandleader Lawrence Welk. Derided as ordinary pork-barreling, the project was lauded by Dorgan as a boost to a part of North Dakota devastated by drought.

Dorgan's populism has made him a skeptic about foreign aid, as well. When the Reagan administration proposed an $8.4 billion increase in the U.S. donation to the International Monetary Fund in 1983, Dorgan joined with colleagues on both the right and the left to delay its passage. He said the money went to help large banks that had made bad loans to the Third World.

"If we could dye those dollar bills purple, within a month after the IMF got the money, the bankers on Wall Street would have deep purple pockets," he said.

He has been a longtime foe of an unfettered Federal Reserve Board and the high interest rates he says it has caused. In 1981 he introduced a bill he called "The Paul Volcker Retirement Act," which would have let Congress remove the Fed chairman with a 60 percent vote of both chambers. "With a central bank like the Federal Reserve Board," he wrote in a 1983 article on farm problems, "who needs soil erosion, grasshoppers or drought?"

One of Dorgan's biggest legislative concerns is the Garrison Diversion water project, an article of faith for most elected officials in North Dakota. The immense project was promised to the state in 1944, but funding for construction has been a perennial controversy. In early 1986, a compromise was worked out scaling back the project.

At Home: In 1985, some polls suggested Dorgan could easily defeat GOP Sen. Andrews. When Dorgan demurred, Conrad, his one-time protégé and successor as state tax commissioner, ran and won.

Heading into the 1988 election, Dorgan got plenty of encouragement from polls and fellow Democrats to run for the Senate seat occupied by Burdick, who was nearing 80 years old. Dorgan backers hoped to pressure the veteran senator into retiring, but it soon became clear there was no budging him. At the end of 1987 Dorgan said he would seek another House term; Burdick went on to win re-election easily.

Dorgan had been stiff-armed by Burdick in similar fashion in 1982, with Burdick dismissing retirement rumors and winning re-election. In 1989 Burdick said he would not rule out seeking yet another term in 1994, by which time he would be 85.

Dorgan's stands are rooted partly in the populism of the state's old Non-Partisan League and partly in the small-town values with which he was raised. His father was active in the Democratic-leaning Farmers' Union in Regent, N.D., where Dorgan grew up and where, he likes to say, he graduated in the top five in his high school class — of nine.

Dorgan was working in the state tax department in 1969 when he caught the eye of Democratic Gov. William Guy; when the incumbent tax commissioner died in 1969, Dorgan, then 27 years old, was appointed to the post.

As tax commissioner, Dorgan spoke out on local issues such as property tax revision and on global ones such as military spending. He sued out-of-state corporations to force them to pay taxes, sending auditors to ensure that the firms were accurately reporting financial information. The voters loved it.

Dorgan made it clear he had political ambitions by taking on then-Rep. Andrews in 1974. It was an all-uphill battle, but Dorgan held Andrews to 56 percent, the only time the Republican had fallen below 60 percent since 1964.

In 1980, GOP Sen. Milton R. Young retired and Andrews was nominated to succeed him. Dorgan ran for Andrews' House seat. Although he was the favorite from the start, Dorgan still sought to temper his liberal reputation by supporting an anti-abortion constitutional amendment and decrying government waste. That was a successful combination; the state went overwhelmingly for Ronald Reagan, but Dorgan won with a comfortable 57 percent.

Considered by many observers to be the state's most popular politician, Dorgan won in 1990 by a margin most politicians would envy. Despite a sluggish farm economy, he carried all 53 counties and garnered 65 percent of the vote. Yet it was the first time Dorgan's share of the vote had dipped below 70 percent since 1980.

The GOP nominee, wealthy businessman Ed Schafer, criticized Dorgan's big campaign fund and his reliance on out-of-state PAC money; that cut a slice — albeit a very small one — off the incumbent's constituency of rural residents and farmers.

Committees

Select Hunger (5th of 22 Democrats)
International (chairman)

Ways & Means (15th of 23 Democrats)
Select Revenue Measures; Trade

Elections

1990 General		
Byron L. Dorgan (D)	152,530	(65%)
Ed Schafer (R)	81,443	(35%)
1990 Primary		
Byron L. Dorgan (D)	60,359	(93%)
Gerald W. Kopp (D)	4,244	(7%)
1988 General		
Byron L. Dorgan (D)	212,583	(71%)
Steve Sydness (R)	84,475	(28%)

Previous Winning Percentages: **1986** (76%) **1984** (79%) **1982** (72%) **1980** (57%)

District Vote For President

	1988	1984	1980	1976
D	127,739 (43%)	104,429 (34%)	79,189 (26%)	136,078 (46%)
R	166,559 (56%)	200,336 (65%)	193,695 (64%)	153,470 (52%)
I			23,640 (8%)	

Campaign Finance

	Receipts	Receipts from PACs	Expend-itures
1990			
Dorgan (D)	$598,971	$449,050 (75%)	$504,800
Schafer (R)	$285,042	0	$284,855
1988			
Dorgan (D)	$687,234	$462,346 (67%)	$747,594
Sydness (R)	$261,883	$7,605 (3%)	$260,727

Key Votes

1991	
Authorize use of force against Iraq	N
1990	
Support constitutional amendment on flag desecration	N
Pass family and medical leave bill over Bush veto	Y
Reduce SDI funding	Y
Allow abortions in overseas military facilities	N
Approve budget summit plan for spending and taxing	N
Approve civil rights bill	Y
1989	
Halt production of B-2 stealth bomber at 13 planes	N
Oppose capital gains tax cut	Y
Approve federal abortion funding in rape or incest cases	Y
Approve pay raise and revision of ethics rules	N
Pass Democratic minimum wage plan over Bush veto	Y

Voting Studies

	Presidential Support		Party Unity		Conservative Coalition	
Year	**S**	**O**	**S**	**O**	**S**	**O**
1990	17	82	82	16	35	61
1989	24	74	83	14	37	61
1988	28	70	81	16	47	53
1987	13	83	83	12	30	70
1986	26	73	82	15	44	56
1985	23	78	83	15	22	78
1984	33	61	75	22	31	68
1983	18	77	77	18	33	60
1982	36	62	81	17	33	64
1981	37	55	80	18	37	53

Interest Group Ratings

Year	ADA	ACU	AFL-CIO	CCUS
1990	72	21	73	43
1989	85	21	75	30
1988	75	17	93	38
1987	92	0	81	14
1986	70	27	71	29
1985	65	10	76	27
1984	75	22	46	33
1983	80	32	67	45
1982	85	5	90	32
1981	65	20	73	16

Ohio

U.S. CONGRESS

SENATE 2 D
HOUSE 11 D, 10 R

LEGISLATURE

Senate 12 D, 21 R
House 61 D, 38 R

ELECTIONS

1988 Presidential Vote

Bush	55%
Dukakis	44%

1984 Presidential Vote

Reagan	59%
Mondale	40%

1980 Presidential Vote

Reagan	52%
Carter	41%
Anderson	6%

Turnout rate in 1986	39%
Turnout rate in 1988	55%
Turnout rate in 1990	42%

(as percentage of voting age population)

POPULATION AND GROWTH

1980 population	10,797,630
1990 population (7th in the nation)	10,847,115
Percent change 1980-1990	+1%

DEMOGRAPHIC BREAKDOWN

White	88%
Black	11%
Asian or Pacific Islander	1%
(Hispanic origin)	1%
Urban	73%
Rural	27%
Born in state	73%
Foreign-born	3%

MAJOR CITIES

Columbus	632,910
Cleveland	505,616
Cincinnati	364,040
Toledo	332,943
Akron	223,019

AREA AND LAND USE

Area 41,004 sq. miles (35th)

Farm	59%
Forest	28%
Federally owned	1%

Gov. George V. Voinovich (R)
Of Cleveland — Elected 1990

Born: July 15, 1936, Cleveland, Ohio.
Education: Ohio U., B.A. 1958; Ohio State College of Law, J.D. 1961.
Occupation: Lawyer.
Religion: Roman Catholic.
Political Career: Ohio House, 1967-71; Cuyahoga County auditor, 1971-76; Cuyahoga County commissioner, 1977-78; lieutenant governor, 1979; Mayor of Cleveland, 1979-90; GOP nominee for U.S. Senate, 1988.
Next Election: 1994.

WORK

Occupations

White-collar	50%
Blue-collar	35%
Service workers	13%

Government Workers

Federal	92,993
State	170,008
Local	440,605

MONEY

Median family income	$ 20,909	(16th)
Tax burden per capita	$ 805	(29th)

EDUCATION

Spending per pupil through grade 12	$ 3,998	(26th)
Persons with college degrees	14%	(40th)

CRIME

Violent crime rate	469 per 100,000 (28th)

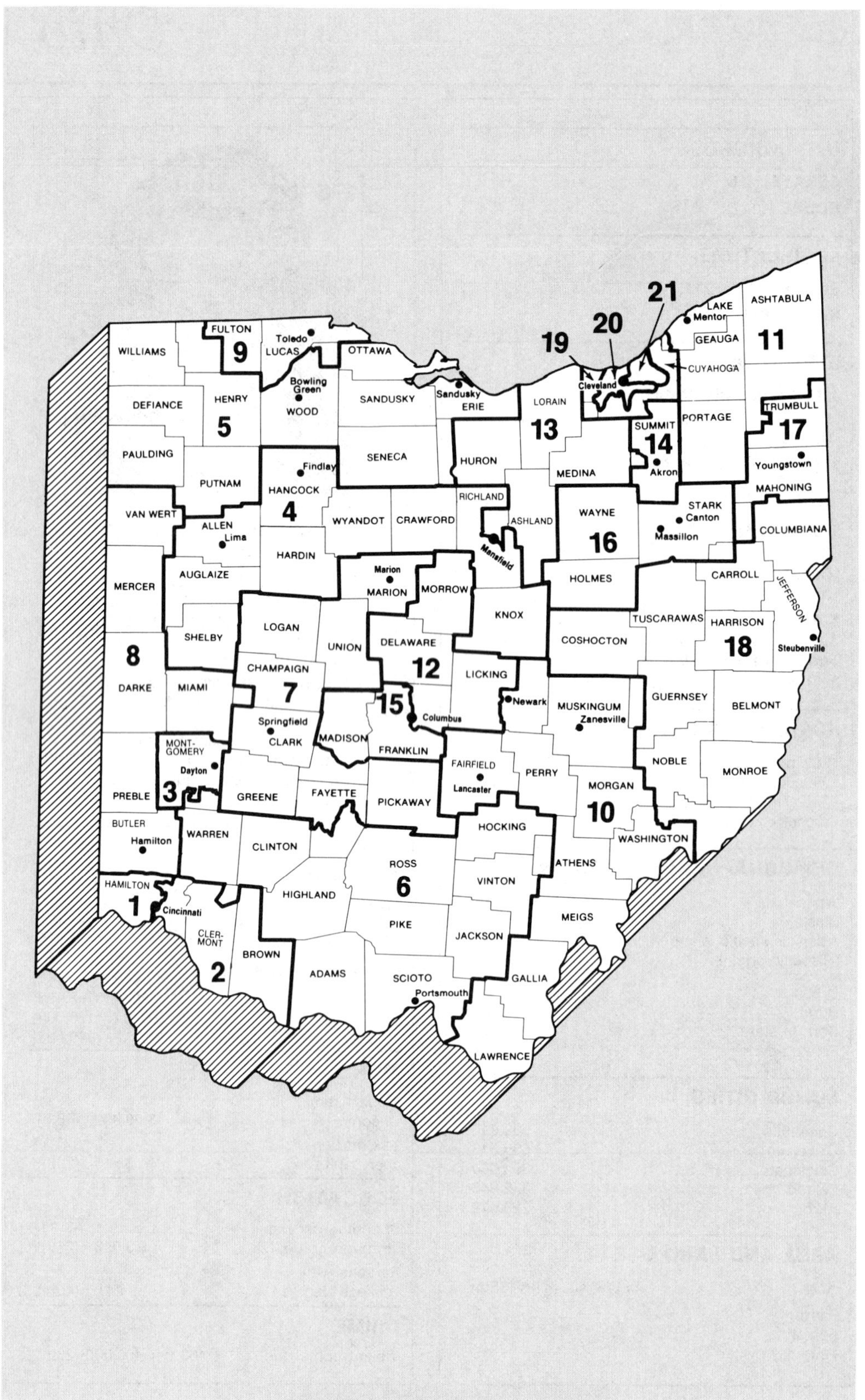
FULTON
9
Toledo
LUCAS
WILLIAMS
OTTAWA
Bowling Green
WOOD
DEFIANCE
HENRY
5
SANDUSKY
Sandusky
ERIE
PAULDING
PUTNAM
SENECA
HANCOCK
Findlay
4
VAN WERT
ALLEN
Lima
WYANDOT
CRAWFORD
HARDIN
MERCER
AUGLAIZE
SHELBY
LOGAN
UNION
Marion
MARION
MORROW
DELAWARE
12
8
DARKE
MIAMI
CHAMPAIGN
7
Springfield
CLARK
MADISON
15
Columbus
FRANKLIN
MONT-GOMERY
Dayton
PREBLE
3
GREENE
FAYETTE
PICKAWAY
BUTLER
Hamilton
WARREN
CLINTON
HAMILTON
1
Cincinnati
CLER-MONT
2
BROWN
HIGHLAND
ADAMS
ROSS
6
PIKE
SCIOTO
Portsmouth
19
20
21
Cleveland
LAKE
Mentor
ASHTABULA
GEAUGA
11
CUYAHOGA
LORAIN
13
HURON
MEDINA
SUMMIT
14
Akron
PORTAGE
TRUMBULL
17
Youngstown
MAHONING
RICHLAND
Mansfield
ASHLAND
WAYNE
16
STARK
Canton
Massillon
COLUMBIANA
HOLMES
CARROLL
JEFFERSON
KNOX
COSHOCTON
TUSCARAWAS
HARRISON
18
Steubenville
LICKING
Newark
MUSKINGUM
Zanesville
GUERNSEY
BELMONT
FAIRFIELD
Lancaster
PERRY
NOBLE
MONROE
MORGAN
10
HOCKING
WASHINGTON
VINTON
ATHENS
JACKSON
MEIGS
GALLIA
LAWRENCE

John Glenn (D)

Of Columbus — Elected 1974

Born: July 18, 1921, Cambridge, Ohio.
Education: Muskingum College, B.S. 1962.
Military Service: Marine Corps, 1942-65.
Occupation: Astronaut; soft drink company executive.
Family: Wife, Anna Margaret Castor; two children.
Religion: Presbyterian.
Political Career: Sought Democratic nomination for U.S. Senate, 1970; sought Democratic nomination for president, 1984.
Capitol Office: 503 Hart Bldg. 20510; 224-3353.

In Washington: During a televised interview a few blocks from the Capitol in October 1989, a man approached Glenn and punched him in the jaw. Glenn's chin — as well as his pride — were not seriously injured. But little could Glenn have suspected that the incident would actually be one of his less painful moments in the 101st Congress.

Respected as an American icon throughout his prominent public life, Glenn has tried to live by the words he issued even after his dismal 1984 bid for the presidency: "You keep climbing." But Glenn's entanglement in the Keating Five scandal has made his climb a steeper one. The Senate Ethics Committee's investigation into his dealings with savings and loan operator Charles H. Keating Jr. concluded that Glenn had not done anything improper or illegal, but the episode took some luster off Glenn's public image.

Glenn was caught up early in the investigation of possible wrongdoing by five lawmakers suspected of doing favors for a wealthy campaign contributor. The Keating case first came to the attention of the Senate when Ohio Republicans filed a complaint in September 1989. Of the five senators (the others were Democrats Alan Cranston of California, Donald W. Riegle Jr. of Michigan and Dennis DeConcini of Arizona, and Republican John McCain of Arizona), Glenn may have been Keating's oldest friend in the Senate. They had both personal and political connections. The two met in 1970, when Glenn first ran for the Senate.

After Keating left Ohio for Phoenix to set up American Continental Corp., he recruited several former Glenn aides. Jim Grogan, Keating's lobbyist, had worked as an intern on Glenn's staff in Washington and Ohio; his wife had run Glenn's Cincinnati office for a time.

Glenn and Keating dined together, sometimes with their wives. Keating marshaled more than $230,000 in contributions for Glenn's campaigns and political action committee. All the money was contributed by February 1986.

Prompted by home-state thrift interests, Glenn took an interest in the Federal Home Loan Bank Board's direct investment rule in 1984 and 1985. Glenn also heard from Keating on the issue.

Glenn, meanwhile, had come to dislike bank board Chairman Edwin J. Gray in 1985 during the Ohio savings and loan crisis. He blamed Gray for not moving fast enough to avert the crisis. So, when Grogan and Keating began seeking Glenn's help with Lincoln in 1987 — and the idea of a meeting with Gray came up — Glenn was happy to be a party.

He came to the April 1987 meeting determined to get to the bottom of things. Later, Glenn said he did not recall DeConcini offering a deal on behalf of Lincoln, a charge Gray made and DeConcini denied. But Glenn also refused to call Gray a liar. He said he did not recall much at all of what was said.

But he was interested enough to go to a follow-up meeting a week later with the bank board regulators. There, Glenn raised some of Lincoln's complaints. "To be blunt, you should charge them or get off their backs," Glenn said. "I'm not trying to get anyone off. If there is wrongdoing, I'm on your side."

Taking a low-key approach as he made his case before the Ethics Committee in January 1991, Glenn said he did nothing inappropriate by attending the two meetings with federal regulators. His case was buttressed by special counsel Robert S. Bennett, who had declared on the opening day of the hearings that Glenn had done nothing wrong.

Glenn emphasized that he ended virtually all contacts with Keating after the second meeting, at which regulators informed the senators that criminal charges might be filed. "I came to the conclusion that Lincoln was in deep trouble," Glenn said.

His only action after that time was to set up a lunch meeting in January 1988 between Keating and then-House Speaker Jim Wright of Texas. In the summer of 1987, Glenn testified, he turned down Keating's offer to raise campaign contributions because of Keating's battles with the regulators.

The Ethics Committee concluded that Glenn had "exercised poor judgment" in arranging the luncheon meeting some eight months after Glenn learned of the possible criminal referral. But, the committee added, the evidence indicated that Glenn's participation did not go beyond serving as host and his actions "did not reach the level requiring institutional action against him."

In response to the findings, Glenn said the "committee was very clear on the subject of my innocence." He added: "I've said it before, and now the Senate Ethics Committee has said it again: John Glenn does not peddle influence, period." Those were words few observers would ever have thought Glenn would need to utter.

A centrist Democrat with a technocrat's temperament, Glenn remains well suited to the nuts-and-bolts matters on the docket of the Governmental Affairs Committee, which he chairs. His passion for detail mixes well with the committee's mission to study the government's entrails.

Glenn is the polar opposite of the typically ambitious legislator; he has spent most of his career focusing on a handful of issues. Indeed, colleagues who admire Glenn's character and dedication wonder if he might have accomplished more had he not always been so narrowly focused. To a great extent, Glenn's career has been restricted because that is the way his mind works. He does not take readily to new concepts or easily shift his tactics. Once he gets an idea into his head, he sticks to it tenaciously.

It is a style well suited to a pressing item on Glenn's agenda: cleaning up the nation's nuclear-weapons plants. Ohio has one of the Department of Energy's (DOE) dirtiest facilities, a uranium fuel-processing plant near Cincinnati. Revelations about seepage of radioactive and hazardous waste at DOE's Feed Material Production Center made headlines and helped fuel support for legislation in the 101st Congress that would have allowed states to levy fines against federal facilities that failed to comply with hazardous and solid waste laws. The bills moved ahead in the House and Senate, but fell short of final passage.

Glenn, the master of General Accounting Office detail, does not transfer well into macro politics. This was evident in his 1984 presidential campaign. Advertised for months as the main competitor to Walter F. Mondale for the Democratic nomination, he proved poor at public speaking, made weak showings in a succession of primaries and caucuses and quickly dropped out of the race.

Glenn has been no more exciting on the Senate floor than he was in his presidential campaign. His tendency to read speeches in full — even when no one is listening — can drive his colleagues off the floor.

Just when Glenn seemed resigned to ending his political career as chairman of the Governmental Affairs Committee, Massachusetts' Democratic Gov. Michael S. Dukakis began to hint strongly in 1988 that he might make Glenn his running mate. Instead, Dukakis chose Lloyd Bentsen, whom he hoped could put Texas in the Democratic column for president. Ever the good sport, Glenn introduced Bentsen at the convention in what, ironically, was perhaps his best-ever national speech — one that generated more audience response than Bentsen's.

On Governmental Affairs, Glenn has been increasingly active. He played a key role in the passage of legislation to create the Cabinet-level Department of Veterans Affairs. But he unsuccessfully advocated new agencies — created from components of the Commerce Department and the Office of the U.S. Trade Representative — to enhance U.S. competitiveness in trade and industrial policy. In 1990 and 1991, he sponsored legislation to elevate the Environmental Protection Agency to Cabinet-level status.

As U.S. troops began to fight in the Persian Gulf in January 1991, Senate Majority Leader George J. Mitchell appointed Glenn chairman of a Democratic task force to review legislative proposals for aiding military families. In March, Congress cleared a package of new benefits — including a broad range of tax, health, pay and other benefits for returning troops — for veterans and military personnel.

Glenn led the effort in the 101st Congress to amend the Hatch Act, which prohibits the nation's 3 million federal employees from taking part in partisan politics. Glenn's committee approved the measure in July 1989 and Congress cleared the bill in 1990, only to see President Bush veto it.

Glenn said the Hatch Act was outdated and that its hundreds of unclear rules intimidated federal workers from any political participation. "We must balance the need to protect the integrity of the civil servants with our duty to protect the constitutional right of all citizens who participate in the nation's political processes," Glenn said. The Senate fell two votes short of overriding Bush's veto.

Glenn has also been promoting legislation in the 102nd Congress to repeal the honoraria ban on federal employees, which prohibits them from accepting writing or speaking fees.

Aiming to close the gap between federal and private-sector salaries, Glenn sponsored a sweeping overhaul of the federal pay system in 1990. The new plan provides federal workers with raises equal to the average annual salary increases in the private sector.

Glenn is the acknowledged expert in Congress on the nuclear non-proliferation issue, urging foreign nations not to use materials or technology to build nuclear weapons.

Glenn's anti-proliferation efforts brought

him into frequent conflict with the Reagan administration. Throughout the 1980s, Glenn fought President Ronald Reagan over efforts to send military aid to India and Pakistan, to sell nuclear-power materials to China and to offer U.S. nuclear fuels to the Japanese.

Since the start of the 99th Congress, Glenn has served on Armed Services. Over most of his career, Glenn has tilted to the hawkish side on national security matters. "No one has ever accused me of being soft on the Soviets," he says. But his overall record is that of a centrist who does not hesitate to oppose weapons systems. In 1982, Glenn offered a floor amendment to stop development of the MX missile. A longtime supporter of the B-2 stealth bomber — Glenn was a test pilot before he gained fame as an astronaut — he announced in August 1990 that the plane had gotten so expensive that he could no longer back its development.

Glenn also has reservations about the use of force abroad when it becomes, in his mind, overly adventurist — as in U.S. efforts to protect Kuwaiti tankers in 1987 or to liberate Kuwait from Iraqi occupation in 1991. And in 1989, when Kentucky Republican Mitch McConnell proposed allowing federal law enforcement agents to shoot down planes suspected of drug-trafficking, Glenn called the proposal "ludicrous." The proposal, although initially adopted, ultimately was rejected after Glenn took the Senate floor to complain of the "piranha-like feeding frenzy" every time the word "drugs" is mentioned in Congress.

Glenn also has used his position on Armed Services to defend abortion rights. He coauthored a controversial 1990 amendment to permit overseas military hospitals to perform abortions. The proposal was supported by most senators, but did not have enough support to end a filibuster or overturn a veto, and it was eventually withdrawn.

At Home: Although Glenn drew no punishment in the Keating Five investigation, the whiff of scandal did weaken his popularity in Ohio and spur talk that he might face a serious challenge — or even decide not to seek a fourth term — in 1992.

Political vulnerability has been a stranger to Glenn for many years. After he won his Senate seat in 1974 with 65 percent of the vote, he has twice been easily re-elected.

However, Glenn did have difficulty getting to the Senate in the first place. His career in Congress was delayed for a decade, first by an injury and then by an unexpected defeat.

Glenn had achieved national hero status in 1962, when he became the first American to orbit the Earth. Still basking in the glow of his space exploits — which had brought him into close contact with the Kennedys — Glenn decided to run for office in 1964 as a Democrat.

Glenn returned to Ohio to challenge 74-year-old Sen. Stephen M. Young in the 1964 Democratic primary. But he did not get very far: A bathroom fall injured his inner ear, and he had to drop out of the primary.

Glenn's political ambitions then temporarily subsided. Instead of attending party functions, he plunged into business. Glenn served on the boards of Royal Crown Cola and the Questor Corp., oversaw four Holiday Inn franchises he partly owned, lectured and filmed television documentaries.

In 1970, with Young retiring, Glenn decided to run for the seat, competing for the Democratic nomination against Howard M. Metzenbaum, then a millionaire businessman and labor lawyer. Initially a strong favorite, Glenn found that his frequent absences from Ohio over the preceding six years had hurt him politically, giving him the image of an outsider among state Democrats. Although not well-known then to the public, Metzenbaum had the support of the party establishment and a superb, well-financed campaign organization.

Glenn, whose celebrity status was bringing out large crowds, was overconfident. Meanwhile, Metzenbaum erased his anonymity through saturation television advertising. On primary day, Glenn carried 75 of the state's 88 counties but was badly beaten in the urban areas. He lost the nomination by 13,442 votes.

Metzenbaum was beaten in the general election by Republican Robert A. Taft Jr. Three years later, however, he made it to the Senate as an appointee, chosen by Democratic Gov. John J. Gilligan to fill a vacancy. Metzenbaum immediately began campaigning for a full term in his own right, and Glenn — who made up for his previous mistake by becoming a regular on the political circuit — decided to challenge him for the nomination.

The Metzenbaum appointment outraged Glenn and gave him an issue during their rematch in the 1974 primary. Glenn rejected Gilligan's offer to be his running mate as lieutenant governor and denounced the governor as a "boss" who practiced "machine politics."

The underdog Glenn of 1974 proved to be much tougher than the favored Glenn of 1970. This time, he did much better in Metzenbaum's base of Cuyahoga County (Cleveland) and maintained his customary strength in rural areas. Glenn was thus able to even the score with Metzenbaum, winning the primary by 91,000 votes. In the fall, Glenn crushed a weak Republican opponent, Cleveland Mayor Ralph J. Perk, whose campaign was disorganized and underfinanced.

Six years later, Glenn had only nominal opposition for a second term. His win, with 69 percent of the vote, marked him as a 1984 presidential contender. His bid for the Democratic nomination fell flat, though. Despite his and his image as a hero and as a moderate alternative to Mondale, Glenn was never able to spark widespread interest in his campaign.

Glenn bounced back with another strong Senate campaign in 1986. He had worked hard to mend fences with Ohio voters in the wake of his failed White House bid, making dozens of appearances across the state to boost other Democrats and his own political stock.

His GOP foe, Rep. Thomas N. Kindness, was aggressive and relatively well-financed. He pounded away at what he saw as Glenn's main weakness — a lingering multimillion-dollar debt from his presidential campaign.

Glenn was saddled with a debt that included $1.9 million worth of loans from four Ohio banks. (Glenn did not reach an agreement with the Federal Election Commission on paying off the debt until 1987.) Kindness maintained that Glenn received preferential treatment from the banks that the average Ohioan would not get.

But Kindness was unable to wound Glenn. Not well-known outside his conservative southwest Ohio district, he lacked the money to mount a statewide media blitz that might have shaken the incumbent's image. Kindness lost in a landslide, although he did have the consolation of carrying nearly a dozen counties. Neither of Glenn's previous GOP challengers had carried more than one.

Since their battles in the 1970s, Glenn has come to terms with Metzenbaum, who in 1976 was elected to the Senate in his own right and is now in his third term. While much has been made of the long rivalry between the two, Glenn helped ensure Metzenbaum's re-election during a heated 1988 contest with then-Cleveland Mayor George Voinovich.

Many expected Glenn to give his Senate colleague just token support, but Glenn piloted Metzenbaum around the state the day he formally announced he was seeking re-election. And late in the campaign, after Voinovich accused Metzenbaum of being soft on child pornography, Glenn appeared in a hard-hitting TV ad and accused the Republican of "the lowest gutter politics." While Metzenbaum was already on his way to victory, the Glenn ad was credited with boosting him to a comfortable 57 percent of the vote.

Committees

Governmental Affairs (Chairman)
Permanent Subcommittee on Investigations

Armed Services (7th of 11 Democrats)
Manpower & Personnel (chairman); Conventional Forces & Alliance Defense; Strategic Forces & Nuclear Deterrence

Special Aging (2nd of 11 Democrats)

Select Intelligence (8th of 8 Democrats)

Elections

1986 General		
John Glenn (D)	1,949,208	(62%)
Thomas N. Kindness (R)	1,171,893	(38%)
1986 Primary		
John Glenn (D)	678,171	(88%)
Don Scott (D)	96,309	(12%)

Previous Winning Percentages: 1980 (69%) **1974** (65%)

Campaign Finance

	Receipts	Receipts from PACs		Expend-itures
1986				
Glenn (D)	$2,088,191	$637,186	(31%)	$1,319,026
Kindness (R)	$664,227	$172,648	(26%)	$657,908

Key Votes

1991	
Authorize use of force against Iraq	N
1990	
Oppose prohibition of certain semiautomatic weapons	N
Support constitutional amendment on flag desecration	N
Oppose requiring parental notice for minors' abortions	Y
Halt production of B-2 stealth bomber at 13 planes	Y
Approve budget that cut spending and raised revenues	Y
Pass civil rights bill over Bush veto	Y
1989	
Oppose reduction of SDI funding	N
Oppose barring federal funds for "obscene" art	Y
Allow vote on capital gains tax cut	N

Voting Studies

	Presidential Support		Party Unity		Conservative Coalition	
Year	**S**	**O**	**S**	**O**	**S**	**O**
1990	39	61	79	21	41	59
1989	59	38	82	16	50	47
1988	53	45	86	11	27	73
1987	38	60	82	12	28	66
1986	42	52	74	23	29	70
1985	42	56	79	18	42	57
1984	39	43	55	25	28	51
1983	39	35	57	12	20	52
1982	35	45	67	17	26	51
1981	53	42	74	21	34	66

Interest Group Ratings

Year	ADA	ACU	AFL-CIO	CCUS
1990	89	9	67	25
1989	65	26	100	38
1988	80	9	79	31
1987	80	12	100	18
1986	65	30	87	44
1985	75	27	86	34
1984	65	5	67	38
1983	65	16	93	31
1982	70	28	87	55
1981	80	7	68	44

Howard M. Metzenbaum (D)

Of Lyndhurst — Elected 1976

Also served Jan. 4, 1974-Dec. 23, 1974 (appointed).

Born: June 4, 1917, Lyndhurst, Ohio.
Education: Ohio State U., B.A. 1939, LL.B. 1941.
Occupation: Lawyer; newspaper publisher; parking lot executive.
Family: Wife, Shirley Turoff; four children.
Religion: Jewish.
Political Career: Ohio House, 1943-47; Ohio Senate, 1947-51; Democratic nominee for U.S. Senate, 1974.
Capitol Office: 140 Russell Bldg. 20510; 224-2315.

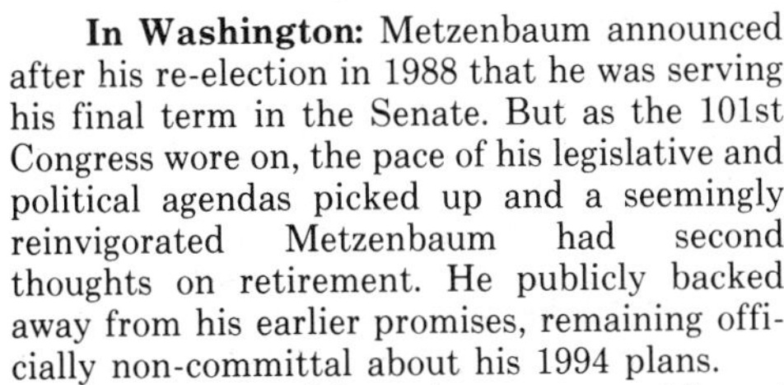

In Washington: Metzenbaum announced after his re-election in 1988 that he was serving his final term in the Senate. But as the 101st Congress wore on, the pace of his legislative and political agendas picked up and a seemingly reinvigorated Metzenbaum had second thoughts on retirement. He publicly backed away from his earlier promises, remaining officially non-committal about his 1994 plans.

In May 1990, Metzenbaum gave up his seat on the Energy and Natural Resources Committee — including a subcommittee gavel — to join Environment and Public Works. A consistent critic of the oil and gas industry, Metzenbaum had little success with his crusades on the Energy Committee, where he was one of just a few consumer- and environment-oriented members. In 1989, he vigorously opposed the successful efforts to decontrol natural gas prices — a defeat that may have helped lead to his leaving the panel.

The switch to Environment gave him the chance to swap clout for a panel he likes better. Metzenbaum remains a very visible chairman of two subcommittees — one on Labor and Human Resources and one on Judiciary.

Meanwhile, upset by what he saw as a large number of fellow Democrats becoming "shadow Republicans," Metzenbaum in 1990 used $50,000 in leftover 1988 campaign funds to found the Center for Democratic Values (CDV), a left-of-center organization aimed at promoting traditional liberalism. In a slap at the growing number of moderate- and conservative-leaning Democrats — such as those active in the Democratic Leadership Council — the CDV's manifesto declared that the country "does not need two Republican parties."

His productive debut as head of his subcommittees in the 100th Congress, when Democrats regained Senate control, and his continued activity through the 101st Congress, dispelled questions about whether Metzenbaum had the skills of a coalition-builder and bill-passer; in the previous decade, he had derived his powers from being the Senate's leading liberal obstructionist and bill-killer.

On Judiciary, where he leads the Antitrust Subcommittee, Metzenbaum helped enact antitrust bills, a measure protecting workers' insurance benefits at bankrupt companies, a ban on plastic guns and the first penalties aimed at fraud by major contractors. A strong proponent of gun control, Metzenbaum was the chamber's point man on the Brady bill, which aimed to establish a seven-day waiting period for people wanting to purchase handguns.

Metzenbaum has used his Judiciary Subcommittee most recently for oversight hearings on how the government is restructuring the thrift industry. He is a stern critic of the Resolution Trust Corporation (RTC), which manages and disposes of assets from thrifts that have failed since January 1989.

Republicans have accused Metzenbaum of using his hearings for political purposes. His response: "I am trying to get the government to do what it should be doing. A senator has to jump up and down and make enough noise to get the bureaucrats to work."

A February 1991 hearing implicating a GOP gubernatorial candidate in Arizona led Minority Leader Bob Dole of Kansas to charge that Metzenbaum had abused his Senate power. The flap arose from a hearing on losses stemming from the insolvency of Southwest Savings and Loan Association in Phoenix. The subcommittee had investigated a tip that the RTC failed to investigate the possible liability of Southwest's directors and officers for the losses.

The subcommittee also looked at the business dealings of a former director, J. Fife Symington, who at the time of the hearing was in a tight race for governor of Arizona. In a Senate floor speech, Dole accused Metzenbaum of trying to tilt the Arizona race with a "sneak attack" on Symington. Despite the hearing and the controversy, Symington won his election. Republicans, however, continued to criticize Metzenbaum, demanding that he investigate failed S&Ls with ties to Democrats as well.

Metzenbaum has also used the subcommit

tee to push legislation to ensure that retailers could take legal action against vertical price fixing, which occurs when a manufacturer conspires with a retailer to force a rival dealer to charge at least a certain price for the manufacturer's goods.

Demonstrating his legislative horse-trading skills, Metzenbaum got the bill through committee in 1990 when he persuaded Arizona Democrat Dennis DeConcini, who opposed the measure, to vote for it if it meant the difference between committee approval and rejection. Earlier, Metzenbaum had dropped efforts to block committee consideration of a DeConcini bill overhauling RICO, the federal anti-racketeering law.

In an effort to get a floor vote on his bill in the 101st Congress, Metzenbaum held up a major judgeships bill until the last day of Congress. He finally relented after winning a promise from Senate Judiciary leaders that the vertical price fixing measure would be sent to the floor early in 1991. The Senate finally passed the bill in May 1991.

Active on a wide range of Judiciary issues, Metzenbaum worked with Massachusetts Democrat Edward M. Kennedy on a major civil rights bill in 1990 and 1991. Metzenbaum sparked a controversy when he criticized opponents of the measure by saying, "We do not agree and are not going to yield to the David Dukes of America" — a reference to the controversial Louisiana state representative and former Ku Klux Klan leader. The remark upset Republicans, who repudiated Metzenbaum's charge of racism.

As Labor Subcommittee chairman, Metzenbaum had a lead role in battling for a law mandating advance notice to workers of plant closings, a top Democratic priority in 1988. He also used his place on Labor in 1990 to help produce compromise legislation reversing a 1989 Supreme Court ruling that allowed age-based discrimination in employee benefits. Democratic-backed bills moved out of committee in both chambers in early 1990, but continued to draw opposition from GOP lawmakers, the Bush administration and business groups that feared the legislation would restrict early-retirement incentive plans — an important method of trimming personnel costs.

Late in the session, however, Metzenbaum and Republican Orrin G. Hatch of Utah put together a complex compromise aimed at neutralizing employers' opposition by exempting most early-retirement incentive plans. Both chambers overwhelmingly approved the measure.

Metzenbaum helped enact measures improving the system of nutrition labeling of food products, increasing certain penalities for child labor law violations, and restricting employers' ability to terminate pension plans. His bill to amend the Orphan Drug Act — which granted marketing monopolies and other incentives to companies that developed drugs to treat diseases afflicting a small fraction of the public — was vetoed by Bush at the end of 1990. The measure sought to allow marketing rights to be shared for certain drugs.

Though Metzenbaum's role has changed now that seniority has given him official leadership positions, he has not abandoned the confrontational, independent style that had previously forced his influence upon the Senate. He remains the self-appointed scourge of "special interest" legislation on behalf of consumers and the Treasury.

He often defies Senate traditions of quiet, mutual back-scratching, publicly exposing the tax breaks and special provisions that colleagues bury deep within big bills, and opposing federal spending for some members' local projects that typically would get a rubber stamp of approval. He is a master of Senate rules, and most effective at employing them at the end of each congressional session, when time is short and members are eager to leave town. Just his threat of a filibuster has killed many bills.

In 1977, his first full year in the Senate, Metzenbaum and South Dakota Democrat James Abourezk filibustered for two weeks against a bill to lift price controls on natural gas. When debate on the bill was formally cut off, the two resorted to a new technique: filibuster by amendment. Armed with some 500 amendments, the two men sought roll call votes on each one, temporarily sending the Senate into round-the-clock sessions.

All this has not made Metzenbaum the Senate's most popular member. But like many self-made men, he has a skin grown thick over a long, successful life. Well past 70 now, peer approval is not a big thing to him.

In keeping with his fighting spirit, Metzenbaum remains the Democrats' point man in the Senate on controversial nominations. He opposed the 1991 nomination of former Florida Gov. Bob Martinez to serve as drug czar and raised questions about some of the financial dealings of former Tennessee Gov. Lamar Alexander when he was nominated to be Education secretary. During the Reagan administration, Metzenbaum led the unsuccessful charge against Edwin Meese III to be attorney general and was in the forefront of the effort to reject Supreme Court nominee Robert H. Bork.

Also a member of the Intelligence Committee, Metzenbaum received some negative publicity from a trip he took to the Middle East in April 1990, when he and four other senators met with Iraqi President Saddam Hussein — less than four months before Iraq's Aug. 2 invasion of Kuwait. A transcript of the meeting released by the Iraqis after their invasion quoted Metzenbaum as telling Saddam: "I am now aware that you are a strong and intelligent man and that you want peace."

The transcript made all five senators seem clueless about the destructive intentions of the Iraqi dictator. But at a news conference after the session, Metzenbaum called the meeting with Saddam "the least gratifying or satisfying" of the trip and criticized the Iraqi strongman for having "somewhat of a war psychosis."

At Home: An early and overwhelming success in business, Metzenbaum had to struggle through years of trial and failure in Ohio politics to reach the Senate. But the experience made him a wily, independent politician, adept at gut-level tactics, fundraising and quasi-populist oratory. These traits may not lend much to Senate comity, but they enabled the veteran Democrat to dismiss a well-funded Republican challenger in 1988.

That year, national GOP officials were high on Cleveland Mayor George Voinovich, who was popular in the state's most Democratic territory and had solid business backing. But as the GOP ballyhooed its strategy — Voinovich could win in Republican-dominated southern and western Ohio and cut into the Democratic base in Cleveland's Cuyahoga County — Metzenbaum took control of the debate.

Brandishing the national GOP game plan, he convinced even those Democrats with reservations about his style that anyone with such determined Republican enemies must be worth re-electing. With the party united, he raised enough early money to ensure a campaign treasury sufficient for any need.

Metzenbaum also met every challenge with a sledgehammer. When a national GOP document labeling him a communist sympathizer was leaked to the press in July 1987, Democrats (and some Republicans) took to the Senate floor within hours to defend Metzenbaum and condemn such campaign tactics. Voinovich's repudiation of the document was lost in the well-orchestrated fury.

That episode established the pace and intensity of the campaign. Voinovich sought to portray the Democrat as a cranky liberal gadfly, while Metzenbaum took care to behave in a senatorial fashion. As the Republican struggled to make himself known downstate, Metzenbaum championed his efforts to help the elderly and his leadership on the plant-closing notification bill. And while Voinovich ultimately raised almost as much money as Metzenbaum, the Democrat had enough cash on hand to run almost non-stop TV advertising from midsummer through Election Day.

In late September, Voinovich ran tough TV ads portraying Metzenbaum as soft on child pornography. The Democrat countered with a testimonial TV ad by fellow Ohio Sen. John Glenn condemning Voinovich's "gutter politics." Coming from Glenn — who had twice clashed with Metzenbaum in bitter Senate primaries — the ad hit home. Editorialists characterized Voinovich's ad as a desperation tactic. Metzenbaum won Cuyahoga County by 2-to-1 and showed surprising strength downstate. He won a decisive 57 percent overall.

(Despite his failure against Metzenbaum, Voinovich's potential as a statewide candidate was not necessarily overstated; he came back to easily defeat Democrat Anthony J. Celebrezze Jr. for Ohio's governorship in 1990.)

Even before Metzenbaum suggested he might not seek a fourth term, he was promoting his son-in-law, Joel Hyatt, as a future Democratic leader. The founder of Hyatt Legal Services, the younger man frequently appeared at campaign events with Metzenbaum and is said to harbor his own ambitions for elective office.

Glenn's role in Metzenbaum's win seemed to put an end to years of talk about the cool relationship between the two. They first clashed in the 1970 primary to succeed Democratic Sen. Stephen M. Young, who was retiring. At the time Glenn was a national hero and a household name, and Metzenbaum was an obscure figure even in much of Cleveland.

Metzenbaum had worked his way through college selling magazines and Fuller brushes, but soon struck it rich in business, winning franchises for the operation of parking lots at airports.

For a while, Metzenbaum pursued business and politics simultaneously. In 1942, the year after he graduated from law school, he bucked the Cuyahoga County Democratic organization and won a race for the state House. Later, he moved up to the state Senate. His major achievement in the Legislature came in 1949, when he won passage of a bill regulating consumer credit.

Metzenbaum left public office in 1951 to run his parking lots and practice law. His record as a labor lawyer was to help him build a political base in the 1970s.

Over the years, Metzenbaum served as a board member and financial angel for such groups as Karamu, a black cultural institution in Cleveland, and the National Council on Hunger and Malnutrition. He fought to integrate a number of exclusive Cleveland clubs.

Before he sought to go to Washington himself, Metzenbaum worked for other Democrats in Ohio and nationally. He was campaign manager for Young in his 1958 and 1964 Senate bids, he backed both John and Robert Kennedy for president, and supported George McGovern for the White House in 1972.

In the 1970 primary, the aggressive millionaire put Glenn on the defensive by arguing that money should be diverted from the space program to domestic concerns. Glenn had to play down his astronaut days. To counter Glenn's celebrity, Metzenbaum aired TV ads presenting himself as an independent-minded businessman driven to run for office by the declining state of government.

Metzenbaum, with years of party work

behind him, had the endorsement of most party leaders. He built a superior campaign organization and won the nomination by 13,442 votes.

That fall, Metzenbaum faced another famous name, Robert A. Taft Jr., son of Ohio's most dominant political figure of modern times. Taft won narrowly, taking a hard line against campus protesters and labeling the Democrat "an ultra-liberal."

Three years later, Metzenbaum found himself occupying the office he could not win in 1970. GOP Sen. William B. Saxbe resigned to become President Richard M. Nixon's attorney general. Democratic Gov. John J. Gilligan, looking for support from organized labor, named Metzenbaum to the vacancy, giving him a full year in the Senate before Saxbe's term was to expire.

But incumbency was no advantage in his 1974 rematch loss to Glenn. Metzenbaum's wealth backfired on him in ways he had managed to avoid in 1970. Under pressure from Glenn, he made public his tax returns — thus uncovering the politically damaging fact that he had paid no federal taxes in 1969. Metzenbaum also revealed that he had deposited $110,000 with the Internal Revenue Service to cover a back-tax claim, an action that did not imply any wrongdoing but was politically touchy in the Watergate climate.

So Metzenbaum had to run as a challenger again in 1976 to realize his ambitions for a full Senate term. This time in the Democratic primary he had advantages in money, name recognition and party support, and the wealth and tax issues were behind him. He easily took the nomination from Rep. James V. Stanton.

In the fall, Metzenbaum launched a new attack on Taft's effectiveness. He claimed he had accomplished more in one year in the Senate than Taft had in six, and focused on the energy issue, blaming much of America's economic problem on the oil companies. He campaigned in alliance with Jimmy Carter, taking advantage of Carter's spring and summer popularity in Ohio. By November, his winning margin was 117,000 votes — more than 10 times as great as Carter's margin in Ohio.

Metzenbaum's 1982 re-election was never close. The decline in the auto and steel industries severely affected Ohio, creating a favorable forum for Metzenbaum's feisty brand of economic populism. After the sudden death in April of the front-running GOP challenger, Rep. John M. Ashbrook, Republican leaders backed state Sen. Paul E. Pfeifer. Viewed as more of a mainstream Republican than Ashbrook, he lacked name identification and money. Metzenbaum coasted to victory with 57 percent of the vote.

Committees

Environment & Public Works (9th of 9 Democrats)
Environmental Protection; Superfund, Ocean & Water Protection; Water Resources, Transportation & Infrastructure

Judiciary (3rd of 8 Democrats)
Antitrust, Monopolies & Business Rights (chairman); Constitution; Courts & Administrative Practice

Labor & Human Resources (3rd of 10 Democrats)
Labor (chairman); Aging; Education, Arts & Humanities; Disability Policy

Select Intelligence (7th of 8 Democrats)

Elections

1988 General		
Howard M. Metzenbaum (D)	2,480,038	(57%)
George Voinovich (R)	1,872,716	(43%)
1988 Primary		
Howard M. Metzenbaum (D)	1,070,934	(84%)
Ralph A. Applegate (D)	210,508	(16%)

Previous Winning Percentages: **1982** (57%) **1976** (50%)

Campaign Finance

	Receipts	Receipts from PACs		Expend-itures
1988				
Metzenbaum (D)	$7,312,533	$1,028,183	(14%)	$8,547,545
Voinovich (R)	$7,828,764	$1,326,627	(17%)	$8,236,432

Key Votes

1991	
Authorize use of force against Iraq	N
1990	
Oppose prohibition of certain semiautomatic weapons	N
Support constitutional amendment on flag desecration	N
Oppose requiring parental notice for minors' abortions	?
Halt production of B-2 stealth bomber at 13 planes	Y
Approve budget that cut spending and raised revenues	N
Pass civil rights bill over Bush veto	Y
1989	
Oppose reduction of SDI funding	N
Oppose barring federal funds for "obscene" art	Y
Allow vote on capital gains tax cut	N

Voting Studies

	Presidential Support		Party Unity		Conservative Coalition	
Year	**S**	**O**	**S**	**O**	**S**	**O**
1990	27	68	85	10	8	89
1989	39	59	92	7	8	89
1988	36	55	87	6	24	68
1987	32	65	88	9	3	91
1986	24	76	86	13	5	93
1985	26	72	87	10	17	83
1984	26	69	79	16	4	91
1983	36	60	80	19	11	86
1982	32	64	88	5	4	85
1981	30	59	82	5	7	81

Interest Group Ratings

Year	ADA	ACU	AFL-CIO	CCUS
1990	78	10	89	8
1989	95	7	100	25
1988	80	4	100	15
1987	100	4	100	22
1986	100	4	93	21
1985	100	0	100	29
1984	100	5	91	22
1983	100	12	100	11
1982	100	28	92	11
1981	85	0	94	7

1 Charles Luken (D)

Of Cincinnati — Elected 1990

Born: July 18, 1951, Cincinnati, Ohio.
Education: U. of Notre Dame, B.A. 1973; U. of Cincinnati, J.D. 1976.
Occupation: Lawyer.
Family: Wife, Marcia Spaeth; three children.
Religion: Roman Catholic.
Political Career: Cincinnati City Council, 1981-90; mayor of Cincinnati, 1985-90.
Capitol Office: 1632 Longworth House Office Building 20515; 225-2216.

The Path to Washington: Luken's narrow victory over Republican J. Kenneth Blackwell extended his family's hold, and that of the Democratic Party, on the 1st District. Luken, a three-term mayor of Cincinnati, succeeded his father, Thomas A. Luken, who served the 1st for seven consecutive terms. He also kept the Democratic label on a district that votes heavily Republican in presidential elections.

Thomas Luken's surprise January 1990 announcement that he would not seek re-election initially made his son a solid favorite for the 1st. Like his father, Charles Luken had a conservative image, enabling him to appeal not only to blue-collar ethnics in Cincinnati but also to GOP-leaning voters in the suburbs that make up most of the district. During his House campaign, Luken took some credit for the city's fiscal solvency and for its low crime rate compared with that of other large cities.

Luken also was viewed as more personable than his rough-edged father, known as one of the toughest bosses on Capitol Hill. Luken presented himself with a more polished manner, leavened by a wry sense of humor.

However, his indomitable position was endangered by the entry of Blackwell, a former Cincinnati mayor who enjoyed strong popularity during nearly 12 years on the City Council. Blackwell was reluctant to leave his position as a top assistant to Housing and Urban Development Secretary Jack F. Kemp, for which he gave up his council seat in 1989. But a full-court recruiting effort, which included President Bush, coaxed Blackwell into running for the House.

The contest became a priority for Republican officials who hoped to claim a district in which Bush had received 63 percent of the vote in 1988. Blackwell, a black conservative, also had a shot at becoming the first black Republican elected to the House since 1932. (Gary Franks, the GOP winner in Connecticut's 5th District, ended up with that honor.)

Luken and Blackwell had been friendly rivals. When the City Council chose the mayor in 1985, Blackwell voted for Luken, who supported Blackwell as the council's Finance Committee chairman. In 1987, the city converted to a system by which the mayor would be the candidate getting the most votes in the open-ballot election for the nine City Council seats; Luken edged Blackwell for the post.

Their past alliances made it difficult for Blackwell to portray himself as a more stalwart conservative than Luken. He tried to loosen Luken's ties with Cincinnati's business community, pointing to issues on which Luken favored organized labor's position. Although both candidates opposed abortion, Blackwell touted his endorsement from the Ohio Right-to-Life Committee. However, Luken's role in a bipartisan council coalition shielded him from the liberal label.

At the same time, Luken portrayed Blackwell as too hard-line on such issues as the environment. He called Blackwell an opportunist who campaigned for Jimmy Carter against Ronald Reagan in 1980, then switched to the Republicans after Reagan won.

Down the stretch, Blackwell accused Thomas Luken, chairman of an Energy and Commerce subcommittee, of intimidating business political action committees into giving to his son's campaign. Charles Luken responded that Blackwell had brought Bush, Vice President Dan Quayle and Cabinet officials into the district, "then whines ... about my dad helping me."

Luken ended up with 51 percent of the vote. He ran up 57 percent in the Cincinnati part of the district. Although Blackwell won more than 40 percent of the district's black vote, his support of Bush's veto of a civil rights bill may have kept him from cutting further into that key Democratic bloc. Blackwell edged Luken in the suburbs with 52 percent, not enough to overcome Luken's urban margin.

Ohio 1

Hamilton County — Western Cincinnati and Suburbs

Nestled snugly in the southwestern corner of the state, the 1st stretches westward from the skyscrapers of downtown Cincinnati to the rolling farmland along the Indiana border. GOP domination in the suburbs north and west of the city made the district a Republican bastion during the 1970s. But the black population within Cincinnati helped former Democratic Rep. Thomas A. Luken build a majority here.

The western half of Cincinnati casts nearly 40 percent of the district's vote. Most of the other voters live in middle-class suburbs nearby.

Democrats can count on heavy support from a few solidly black wards in Cincinnati, but the dominant political bloc is made up of German Catholics who have defined the city's cautious, conservative personality for more than 100 years.

Once clustered in the West Side section of the city known as "Over-the-Rhine," the German-Americans gradually moved to suburbs like Cheviot and Green Township.

As a fairly conservative Catholic Democrat, Charles Luken was able to retain the support of this crucial bloc when he ran in 1990 to succeed his father, who retired. But in state and national contests, the German Catholics often join with the area's sizable number of Appalachian whites — drawn from the rural hills to work in Cincinnati's industries — in voting Republican.

Cincinnati's diverse economy prevented it from suffering the degree of hardship that hit other industrial cities in the state in the early 1980s' recession. A major Ohio River port and a regional center of commerce, the city is headquarters for the giant Procter & Gamble Co. and Cincinnati Milacron, a world leader in the production of machine tools.

The 1980s defense buildup boosted the revenues of numerous area defense contractors, the largest being General Electric Co. Like several other major Cincinnati employers, G.E. is located in the 2nd District, but it provides jobs for blue-collar workers in the western section of the city.

Population: 514,190. White 426,908 (83%), Black 82,897 (16%), Other 3,133 (1%). Spanish origin 3,106 (1%). 18 and over 364,014 (71%), 65 and over 57,362 (11%). Median age: 29.

Committees

Banking, Finance & Urban Affairs (22nd of 31 Democrats)
Economic Stabilization; Financial Institutions Supervision, Regulation & Insurance; Policy Research & Insurance

Government Operations (24th of 25 Democrats)
Employment & Housing; Environment, Energy & Natural Resources

Elections

1990 General

Charles Luken (D)	83,932	(51%)
J. Kenneth Blackwell (R)	80,362	(49%)

District Vote For President

	1988	1984	1980	1976
D	76,661 (37%)	79,193 (35%)	72,697 (36%)	74,367 (38%)
R	131,747 (63%)	146,217 (65%)	116,565 (58%)	115,736 (60%)
I			9,583 (5%)	

Campaign Finance

	Receipts	Receipts from PACs		Expenditures
1990				
Luken (D)	$680,789	$369,725	(54%)	$651,544
Blackwell (R)	$671,848	$183,490	(27%)	$670,640

Key Vote

1991

Authorize use of force against Iraq	Y

2 Bill Gradison (R)

Of Cincinnati — Elected 1974

Born: Dec. 28, 1928, Cincinnati, Ohio.

Education: Yale U., B.A. 1948; Harvard U., M.B.A. 1951, D.C.S. 1954.

Occupation: Investment broker; federal official.

Family: Wife, Heather Jane Stirton; nine children.

Religion: Jewish.

Political Career: Cincinnati City Council, 1961-74; mayor of Cincinnati, 1971.

Capitol Office: 1125 Longworth Bldg. 20515; 225-3164.

In Washington: Few members of either party in either chamber of Congress seem as free of political cant and catechism as Gradison. But every freedom has its price, and Gradison has had occasion to pay for his.

President Bush, a Yale classmate of Gradison, considered naming him to the post of Health and Human Services secretary. But Gradison did not get the job, in part perhaps because he is insufficiently orthodox in his opposition to abortion to be acceptable to the party's right wing.

Similar objections were heard at the end of the 101st Congress, when Bill Frenzel of Minnesota retired and vacated the top GOP slot on Budget — presumably for No. 2 man Gradison to inherit. Those who found Gradison too unreliable on economic issues were unhappy at the thought of promoting him.

Gradison, after all, had disputed the supply-siders who said growth alone would eliminate budget deficits. He had even engaged the supply-side hero, Rep. Jack F. Kemp (1971-89), in a public exchange of letters on the subject in 1985, exposing deep divisions within the party. In 1987, Gradison had chimed in with Democrats who said the Gramm-Rudman deficit-reduction target could not be reached without deep defense cuts or a recessionary dose of taxes and program cuts.

But in bidding to move up to ranking on Budget for the 102nd Congress, Gradison had a powerful ally in the institutional customs of the House. Gradison had been the No. 2 Republican on Budget since the beginning of the 101st Congress, when House GOP leaders ratified his stature on economic matters by naming him the party representative to the committee. His detractors simply did not have the muscle to deny the ranking member's job to the man in line to have it.

Now installed, Gradison has proven far from a pushover for Democratic Chairman Leon E. Panetta. In April 1991, he led GOP criticism of the Democrats' budget in committee, portraying it as a hypocritical makeover of Bush's own proposals. In May, when the Democratic spending plan came to the floor, Gradison was front and center, jousting with the Rules Committee and contending that Republicans had been denied their say in the fiscal 1992 budget process.

In the early 102nd, at least, Gradison's performance in the politically sensitive budget role has had a partisan edge that suggests he is answering his intraparty critics. He has patiently consulted with other committee Republicans, many of them well to his right ideologically, to develop a unified strategy.

Gradison is better known for his intellect than for his horse-trading skills. Yet he is the kind of problem-solving pragmatist who would rather make a deal than a speech. One of his party's most thoughtful legislators, Gradison wants not only to bring some intellectual coherence to conservative economic ideas, but also to put them into action.

Observing Gradison's earnest attempt to put the cost of the savings and loan bailout on budget (thus saving some of the immense cost of issuing bonds over 30 years), a Democratic colleague from Ways and Means called the Ohioan "the epitome of someone who tries to call the shots as straight as he can."

In the process of trying to do that, he has earned respect that translates into significant influence over tax, budget and health policy. But as such a player, he has had to share not only in the achievements but also in the bitter disappointments of recent sessions.

In the 101st Congress, Gradison watched a triumph turn to dust. The catastrophic health insurance program for Medicare beneficiaries, achieved in the previous session largely because of Gradison's labors and skills, was repealed in 1989 because many of the affected elderly protested the surtax they had to pay for the coverage.

When the program had passed, Gradison was praised not only for his years of effort in its behalf but also for his remarkable working relationship with liberal California Democrat Pete Stark, chairman of Ways and Means' Health Subcommittee. When public support

Ohio 2

Hamilton County — Eastern Cincinnati and Suburbs

The 2nd is a district of political extremes. It includes the most Democratic part of Cincinnati and the most Republican suburbs around it. With the bulk of the voters outside the city, Republican candidates usually win.

The eastern half of Cincinnati houses about one-third of the district's residents. Blacks make up just under 40 percent of the total population of Cincinnati, and most live in Avondale and Walnut Hill, within the boundaries of the 2nd.

At the bottom of Walnut Hill, in the flat Ohio River basin, is downtown Cincinnati. The wharves for old stern-wheelers like the *Delta Queen*, the headquarters of Procter & Gamble and the Taft Museum are mainstays. But the area has undergone a face lift. Construction of Riverfront Stadium and Coliseum in the early 1970s symbolized a downtown renewal project designed to lure suburban dollars back to the city.

Cincinnati's wealthy Republican establishment — including the Taft family — has exercised a great deal of influence over the years. But that influence is now concentrated more in the suburbs than in the city. Unlike suburban Cleveland, suburban Cincinnati is solidly in Republican hands.

The Cincinnati area has less heavy industry than the urban centers of northeastern Ohio. But manufacturing plants dot the Mill Creek Valley, which extends north from downtown into the suburbs. While the valley weaves back and forth between the 1st and 2nd districts, the 2nd includes a large Procter & Gamble plant at St. Bernard and a General Electric plant at Evendale.

In the last redistricting, the 2nd moved eastward, beyond the Cincinnati suburbs and into the rural Ohio River Valley. More than 140,000 of Gradison's constituents are now in fast-growing Clermont County, which grew 35 percent in the 1970s, and another 9 percent in the 1980s. As Clermont moves closer to the Cincinnati metropolitan orbit, it is increasingly Republican.

Population: 514,168. White 425,752 (83%), Black 84,316 (16%), Other 2,972 (1%). Spanish origin 3,092 (1%). 18 and over 370,100 (72%), 65 and over 59,533 (12%). Median age: 30.

began to unravel, Gradison found himself fighting a desperate rear guard action throughout 1989.

"This is an honest disagreement about whether the benefits are worth the cost," said Gradison.

As other defenders of the program became embittered, Gradison preserved a certain dry humor. "It's reached the point in my town where I don't refer to this as the 'Gradison-Stark' bill anymore," he said. "I refer to it as the 'Stark bill.' "

While other backers of the plan fell away, Gradison fought to the last to salvage as much as possible. He saw a corrective bill out of subcommittee that won approval from Ways and Means (where even Chairman Dan Rostenkowski had felt the sting of retirees' ire).

But on the floor it was another matter, as the program's defenders were overwhelmed by members' eagerness to dismiss the pain. The vote was 360-66 to repeal the program outright. While some members said it was time to go back to the drawing board, Gradison saw a darker portent in wiping the slate clean. "I think the slate's going to remain clean for some time to come," he said.

Life got no easier in 1990, as Gradison found himself confronting the issue of how $40 billion or more could be cut from Medicare, as ordered by the compromise budget resolution of October. Gradison was among the handful of Republicans who stuck with President Bush in voting for that month's first, ill-fated budget summit agreement, despite his displeasure at the summit process. Gradison said the summits of the 1980s had left Ways and Means Republicans feeling "left out, unloved and unappreciated."

On Ways and Means, Gradison is among the Republicans most likely to work with committee Democrats. He enjoys a good relationship with Rostenkowski, a fellow Midwesterner who, like Gradison, has the taste for getting the job done that is the hallmark of urban machine politics.

Gradison has also been one of Ways and Means' most influential Republicans on tax policy. When the committee overhauled the Internal Revenue Code in the 99th Congress, Gradison was as committed as anyone to the idea of tax reform. He neither denounced the Democrats' control of the tax bill nor scrambled behind the scenes for breaks for parochial interests, as many of his colleagues did. Instead, he stuck to broad concepts, arguing that it was a rare opportunity for a major overhaul, even if most voters were not very interested in the issue.

Gradison decided that in order to make

productive changes, it would be necessary to challenge some traditional GOP bastions of support, and he was willing to do so. He endorsed repeal of investment tax credits, for instance, despite their allure for heavy industries, including many in Ohio.

In previous Congresses, Gradison's major effort at Ways and Means was for indexing the federal tax system — gradually adjusting tax rates to inflation so that people would not be forced into higher brackets. He won a stunning victory when indexing was included in the Republican substitute to the 1981 tax bill, which the House approved. The administration initially wanted to leave indexing out of the bill; Gradison was largely responsible for persuading them to put it back.

In 1983, with key Democrats seeking to repeal the indexing provisions in order to increase long-term revenues, Gradison won a seat on the Budget Committee to defend the concept. It survived, and the principle, by now firmly entrenched, was included in the 1986 tax code overhaul bill.

Early in the 100th Congress, Gradison struck out in a different direction from other Budget Committee Republicans, agreeing with Democratic leaders that it was probably necessary to revise upward the $108 billion deficit target set for fiscal 1988 by the Gramm-Rudman-Hollings deficit-reduction law. He said the only way to reach the $108 billion target might be to make major cuts in defense spending or generate a recession. Gradison had been an important player in the 1985 House-Senate conference that hammered together the Gramm-Rudman concept of annual deficit ceilings. But his 1987 assessment was not particularly popular with most of his GOP colleagues on the Budget Committee, who wanted to be able to charge Democrats with willful failure to meet the target.

A few months later, Gradison joined other Republicans on the Budget Committee in refusing to participate with Democrats in the panel's budget markup sessions. The GOP bloc insisted the Democrats were operating with faulty economic assumptions and were not providing specific enough information about how much they wanted to spend in individual categories.

Gradison has complained about rosy economic assumptions in the past, and he has turned out to be right. In 1986, the deficit turned out to be almost $50 billion higher than the projected $172 billion because of slower growth.

In another effort to make congressional budget-drafting a more accurate reflection of economic reality, Gradison has long championed the idea of revamping the way credit programs are handled in the federal budget, in order to convey more accurately the cost of the subsidies involved.

On Social Security, another crucial Ways and Means issue, Gradison was an early and vocal critic of interfund borrowing, the practice of financing the system by transferring money from other trust funds. He withheld his signature from a conference report on a Social Security bill in 1981 until the conferees agreed to put a one-year deadline on interfund borrowing. In 1983 he opposed the Social Security rescue plan in subcommittee because of an interfund borrowing provision, but voted for the plan in full committee, and on the House floor.

Gradison has generally supported a free-trade position. He reluctantly voted for the omnibus trade bill that emerged from Ways and Means in 1987, but when it was amended to include strict limits on imports into the United States, he ended up opposing it on the House floor.

Beyond the economic realm, Gradison has generally taken a moderate stand on social issues. This may have hurt him in 1979, when he tried to become chairman of the Republican Research Committee, a middle-level leadership position. He split the "moderate" vote with Pennsylvania's Lawrence Coughlin, allowing conservative Trent Lott of Mississippi to win easily and position himself to become party whip two years later. In the 100th Congress, Gradison was named chairman of the House Wednesday Group, a caucus of moderate Republicans.

Gradison is one of several GOP members of Congress whose wives received appointments in the Reagan administration. Heather Gradison, a former railway company employee, became a commissioner on the Interstate Commerce Commission in 1982, and was named its chairman in 1985. After tangling with Democrats on the Senate Commerce, Science and Transportation Committee, she announced in 1989 that she would not seek reappointment and left the commission.

At Home: Staying in Congress has been much easier for Gradison than getting there in the first place.

A member of Cincinnati's City Council for 14 years and a close friend of the Taft family, Gradison first ran for the House in a 1974 special election. As an investment broker, he had been actively involved in the redevelopment of downtown Cincinnati. He ran a moderate, urban-oriented campaign, trying to keep his distance from the beleaguered Nixon administration. But Watergate was the central issue, and it resulted in a 4,000-vote victory for Gradison's Democratic City Council colleague, Thomas A. Luken.

The two men opposed each other again in the general election that fall. By then President Richard M. Nixon was out of office, and Gradison had worked to win back some of the votes he had lost earlier for refusing to support a constitutional ban on abortion. A larger Republican turnout and a switch of independents back to the GOP side resulted in a 2,600-vote victory for Gradison.

Two years later Luken recognized Gradison's popularity and decided to run in the other Cincinnati-based district, rather than compete with him a third time. The former rivals turned into longtime colleagues. Both Gradison and Luken established themselves and proceeded to win re-election easily over the years.

Although Thomas Luken did not seek re-election in 1990, his son, Charles Luken, now shares the Cincinnati House delegation with Gradison. The pitched open-seat battle between Charles Luken, then mayor of Cincinnati, and Republican J. Kenneth Blackwell, a former mayor, overshadowed Gradison's more routine re-election bid that year.

After winning consistently with about 70 percent of the vote during the 1980s, Gradison's role in the federal budget debate and in the catastrophic care hassle may have cost him a few votes in 1990. However, he still held off Democrat Tyrone K. Yates, a black lawyer, taking 64 percent of the vote.

Committees

Budget (Ranking)

Ways & Means (5th of 13 Republicans)
Health (ranking)

Elections

1990 General

Bill Gradison (R)	103,817	(64%)
Tyrone K. Yates (D)	57,345	(36%)

1988 General

Bill Gradison (R)	153,162	(72%)
Chuck R. Stidham (D)	58,637	(28%)

Previous Winning Percentages: **1986** (71%) **1984** (69%) **1982** (63%) **1980** (75%) **1978** (65%) **1976** (65%) **1974** (51%)

District Vote For President

	1988	1984	1980	1976
D	83,471 (37%)	75,603 (35%)	67,068 (36%)	99,150 (40%)
R	138,729 (62%)	141,544 (65%)	108,486 (58%)	108,668 (58%)
I			8,790 (5%)	

Campaign Finance

	Receipts	Receipts from PACs	Expend-itures
1990			
Gradison (R)	$202,259	0	$124,331
Yates (D)	$5,546	$1,200 (22%)	$5,350
1988			
Gradison (R)	$197,743	0	$125,682
Stidham (D)	$13,962	$9,700 (69%)	$13,961

Key Votes

1991	
Authorize use of force against Iraq	Y
1990	
Support constitutional amendment on flag desecration	Y
Pass family and medical leave bill over Bush veto	N
Reduce SDI funding	N
Allow abortions in overseas military facilities	N
Approve budget summit plan for spending and taxing	Y
Approve civil rights bill	N
1989	
Halt production of B-2 stealth bomber at 13 planes	N
Oppose capital gains tax cut	N
Approve federal abortion funding in rape or incest cases	N
Approve pay raise and revision of ethics rules	Y
Pass Democratic minimum wage plan over Bush veto	N

Voting Studies

	Presidential Support		Party Unity		Conservative Coalition	
Year	S	O	S	O	S	O
1990	76	24	74	24	81	15
1989	67	28	51	46	78	20
1988	61	34	62	33	66	24
1987	63	32	65	29	77	14
1986	61	34	59	38	60	34
1985	65	30	63	31	75	22
1984	65	32	68	30	69	31
1983	72	27	72	23	73	26
1982	75	22	76	20	81	18
1981	68	29	67	27	64	33

Interest Group Ratings

Year	ADA	ACU	AFL-CIO	CCUS
1990	11	75	0	86
1989	15	68	8	80
1988	35	62	21	83
1987	20	65	6	100
1986	15	59	7	94
1985	20	60	8	85
1984	35	48	0	71
1983	30	74	6	90
1982	20	73	15	73
1981	35	80	7	89

3 Tony P. Hall (D)

Of Dayton — Elected 1978

Born: Jan. 16, 1942, Dayton, Ohio.
Education: Denison U., A.B. 1964.
Occupation: Real estate salesman.
Family: Wife, Janet Dick; two children.
Religion: Christian.
Political Career: Ohio House, 1969-73; Ohio Senate, 1973-79; Democratic nominee for Ohio secretary of state, 1974.
Capitol Office: 2162 Rayburn Bldg. 20515; 225-6465.

In Washington: More than a decade in Congress has done little to dampen the sincerity and enthusiasm that Hall brings to his personal crusades against hunger and for human rights. Once a college football star and later a Peace Corps volunteer, he is a dedicated legislator whose agenda flows from his own deeply held religious beliefs. And in his new role as chairman of the Hunger Task Force, Hall has an influential vantage point from which to press these concerns.

Hall, who had chaired the Hunger group's international task force, took over the full committee following the death of Texas Rep. Mickey Leland in 1989. Although Hall has a quieter manner than did Leland, he has worked energetically on hunger issues and seen some of his work pay off.

Domestically, Hall's efforts were most visible in congressional deliberations over the federal government's nutrition program for women, infants and children, known as WIC. In 1990, rising food prices had forced many states to overspend their budgets for the program, potentially forcing them to cut out thousands of eligible people. After first conducting a survey to gauge the extent of the problem, Hall sponsored legislation to let states borrow against their 1991 WIC budgets to avoid kicking people out of the program. "We must not force innocent children to pay the price for inflation," Hall said. "If we fail to act now, we will consign these children to months of inadequate nutrition."

The emergency authorization sped through Congress in late June. Early in the 102nd Congress, Hall introduced broad anti-hunger legislation that included a large funding increase for the WIC program.

Even before assuming the chairmanship, Hall had shown a knack for drawing attention to hunger issues. He and other House members once organized a media-savvy gourmet luncheon serving only food that had been culled from Capitol Hill trash cans.

Consistent with this effort is Hall's promotion of gleaning programs, which gather the produce left behind after commercial harvests. In 1987, Hall helped initiate a gleaning program in his Dayton district that delivered almost 21 tons of fresh fruit and vegetables to area food banks in its first year.

Hall has turned a similar determination toward hunger abroad, be it on high-profile causes such as Ethiopian famine or more technical ones, such as satellite programs that will gather information about threats to the ecosystem and world agriculture.

During the 102nd, Hall argued that U.S. food aid had become politicized; he was among a group of legislators who fought to redirect food assistance toward the neediest countries.

Hall once advocated legislation to freeze all U.S. military aid to foreign countries, while increasing food distribution. He has also pushed efforts to increase funding for immunization and basic health-care programs.

"Development assistance is the most important thing we can do," he said. "Just shoving food at the problem is not going to solve it."

Besides international development programs, Hall has also been an advocate for human rights abroad. In the 99th Congress, Hall saw his longtime fight against U.S. support for the Marcos regime in the Philippines blossom into a full-fledged movement. As early as 1979, Hall had urged cutting off aid to Marcos. Even after the 1983 assassination of leading Philippine dissident Benigno S. Aquino Jr., Congress ignored Hall's pleas to stop aid.

In 1985, however, Hall finally succeeded with an amendment calling into question further military aid to the Philippines unless the Marcos regime made sufficient political, economic and military reforms. A few months later, Marcos was in exile and Aquino's widow, Corazon, became the Philippines' president.

Hall has earned respect for his pursuit of issues that otherwise might get lost in the legislative shuffle, but he is a very unlikely member of the Rules Committee. He won a seat there in his second term, though Hall has never been inclined toward the stratagems and backroom maneuvering that characterize most of

Ohio 3

Southwest — Dayton

With a large blue-collar work force and a population 40 percent black, Dayton is a Democratic island in a sea of rural western Ohio Republicanism. Most of Dayton's suburbs yield GOP majorities, but the urban vote has managed to keep the 3rd District Democratic in most elections. Jimmy Carter carried the 3rd in both 1976 and 1980, and before 1990, no GOP candidate for governor or the U.S. Senate had won here in more than a decade. Still, Ronald Reagan and George Bush had little trouble taking the district in 1984 and 1988.

The Dayton area claims to be the birthplace of aviation, the refrigerator, the cash register and the electrical automobile starter. Much of the high-skill industry in the region is a legacy of these local inventions. The city is the headquarters of the NCR Corp. (formerly National Cash Register Co.). General Motors Corp. is a major employer with several plants in the district. The Wright-Patterson Air Force Base northeast of the city is one of the nation's largest military installations.

In the early 1970s, the Dayton area was the most affluent part of Ohio outside the Cleveland suburbs. But in recent years, there have been severe economic problems. GM's large Frigidaire division, Firestone Tire and Rubber and the McCall Publishing Co. have all left. NCR Corp. remains, but the work force has diminished drastically. Without jobs, many people have left the area. Dayton's population declined 16 percent in the 1970s and another 6 percent in the 1980s, to 182,000, its lowest level in a half-century.

South of Dayton are the staunchly Republican white-collar suburbs of Kettering and Oakwood. Together they cast about 15 percent of the district vote, compared with Dayton's 40 percent. The fast-growing townships north of the city are largely blue-collar suburban. This is a swing-voting area.

Population: 514,173. White 415,053 (81%), Black 94,065 (18%), Other 3,193 (1%). Spanish origin 3,737 (1%). 18 and over 370,952 (72%), 65 and over 52,874 (10%). Median age: 30.

the committee's work. If he is a less active member of Rules, however, he is well liked by committee colleagues, and generally regarded as a team player by his fellow Democrats.

Hall comes alive on Rules primarily on issues affecting his district. During the 101st Congress, he used his leverage on Rules to safeguard money for the nuclear weapons plant at Miamisburg.

His influence on the committee was also credited with helping Hall win projects for the Wright-Patterson Air Force Base in his district.

In the 100th Congress, Hall was also an active participant in committee deliberations on "dial-a-porn." The Senate attached language to the 1988 omnibus education bill to ban the sexually explicit services, but conferees, citing constitutional questions, scaled back the ban and restricted access instead. When the bill arrived at the House Rules Committee, however, Hall was one of two Democrats to buck the leadership and block consideration until a floor vote on an outright ban was secured.

While Hall's international principles often link him to House liberals — he was among those who voted to continue sanctions against Iraq rather than authorize force — he splits company with them on certain social issues.

Closer to home, Hall advocates teaching ethics in American schools. In both the 100th and 101st Congresses, he introduced legislation to establish a commission to identify what values should be taught and how. "Our nation is in the grips of a moral recession," he wrote in a statement for the *Congressional Record.* "We are raising a generation of children who cannot distinguish between right and wrong. They are not prepared to make tough choices when there are gray areas, or when values seem to conflict."

On the issue where values seem to conflict more dramatically than on any other — abortion — Hall stands on the anti-abortion side. In 1988, he was one of 90 Democrats who joined with 126 Republicans in a 216-166 House vote in favor of allowing federal funding of abortions only when the mother's life would be endangered by the pregnancy — not in cases of rape or incest.

But in 1990 Hall was among those voting against a constitutional amendment banning flag desecration.

Hall received unusual press attention in late 1986 when his brother Sam was arrested in Nicaragua for trespassing on a military installation. Sam Hall claimed to be gathering intelligence for a private American group aiding the contras, but was soon released by the Nicaraguan government, which expressed doubts about his mental stability. Tony Hall said he was unaware of his brother's activities.

At Home: Hall was the clear choice of organized labor and the Montgomery County Democratic Party when liberal GOP Rep. Charles W. Whalen decided to retire in 1978.

Once a small-college football all-star at Denison University, Hall had represented Dayton in the Ohio Legislature for nearly a decade. He had access to ample campaign funds through his father, who ran a lucrative real-estate business and served as the city's mayor for five years.

Four years before his congressional bid, Hall had gained attention as the Democratic nominee for secretary of state against Republican stalwart Ted W. Brown, who had held that post for 24 years. Hall chastised Brown for not reporting campaign contributions from a chicken dinner fundraising event, brandishing a rubber chicken during one appearance. He lost but came closer to defeating Brown than anyone had in 16 years; the campaign placed him in a good position to run for Congress.

To reach Washington, Hall had to defeat Republican Dudley P. Kircher, a former chamber of commerce official who was considerably more conservative than Whalen. Hall emphasized his legislative experience and attacked Kircher as the "voice of big business." Strong support from organized labor helped Hall offset Kircher's $130,000 spending edge. The Democrat took 70 percent of the vote in Dayton, allowing him to win narrowly districtwide.

Redistricting gave Hall a safer seat in 1982. Republicans did not field a candidate that year or in 1984.

In the two ensuing elections, Hall faced Ron Crutcher, a black Republican. Crutcher received some attention from the national media, but Hall trounced him both times, taking 74 percent in 1986 and 77 percent in 1988. This experience again deterred the district GOP, which in 1990 gave Hall a free ride for the third time in a decade.

Committees

Select Hunger (Chairman)

Rules (6th of 9 Democrats)
Rules of the House

Elections

1990 General		
Tony P. Hall (D)	116,797	(100%)
1988 General		
Tony P. Hall (D)	141,953	(77%)
Ron Crutcher (R)	42,664	(23%)

Previous Winning Percentages: **1986** (74%) **1984** (100%) **1982** (88%) **1980** (57%) **1978** (54%)

District Vote For President

	1988	1984	1980	1976
D	83,142 (45%)	87,950 (43%)	93,420 (51%)	99,150 (53%)
R	98,495 (54%)	115,330 (56%)	78,220 (42%)	85,208 (45%)
I			10,953 (6%)	

Campaign Finance

	Receipts	Receipts from PACs		Expend-itures
1990				
Hall (D)	$173,805	$130,592	(75%)	$133,861
1988				
Hall (D)	$216,111	$140,160	(65%)	$182,889
Crutcher (R)	$48,661	$1,750	(4%)	$46,403

Key Votes

1991	
Authorize use of force against Iraq	N
1990	
Support constitutional amendment on flag desecration	N
Pass family and medical leave bill over Bush veto	Y
Reduce SDI funding	Y
Allow abortions in overseas military facilities	N
Approve budget summit plan for spending and taxing	Y
Approve civil rights bill	Y
1989	
Halt production of B-2 stealth bomber at 13 planes	N
Oppose capital gains tax cut	Y
Approve federal abortion funding in rape or incest cases	N
Approve pay raise and revision of ethics rules	Y
Pass Democratic minimum wage plan over Bush veto	Y

Voting Studies

	Presidential Support		Party Unity		Conservative Coalition	
Year	**S**	**O**	**S**	**O**	**S**	**O**
1990	22	72	78	12	28	63
1989	31	62	77	13	34	56
1988	24	66	79	8	37	50
1987	23	68	72	11	40	49
1986	14	83	78	13	20	74
1985	29	68	81	12	33	56
1984	27	63	72	15	25	63
1983	21	74	75	17	26	72
1982	36	57	73	14	30	60
1981	47	46	69	24	51	44

Interest Group Ratings

Year	ADA	ACU	AFL-CIO	CCUS
1990	72	8	100	8
1989	80	7	83	56
1988	75	17	93	23
1987	72	9	73	29
1986	65	9	64	44
1985	65	11	88	41
1984	70	22	77	38
1983	85	13	94	10
1982	70	17	76	30
1981	45	33	62	44

4 Michael G. Oxley (R)

Of Findlay — Elected 1981

Born: Feb. 11, 1944, Findlay, Ohio.
Education: Miami U. (Ohio), B.A. 1966; Ohio State U., J.D. 1969.
Occupation: FBI agent; lawyer.
Family: Wife, Patricia Pluguez; one child.
Religion: Lutheran.
Political Career: Ohio House, 1973-81.
Capitol Office: 2448 Rayburn Bldg. 20515; 225-2676.

In Washington: Oxley is an affable man with a ready smile and handshake. But he also likes to compete, and the competitive energy he does not work off on the golf course or in the House gym, he invests in blunt talk and partisan sparring on the issues of the day.

Oxley was characteristically unsentimental about his support for the 1990 budget summit agreement that included new taxes. "Trying to sell this agreement is like putting earrings on a pig," Oxley admitted, saying he preferred a no-new-taxes, spending-freeze budget. But Oxley backed the White House-sanctioned package, calling it the best compromise likely to emerge from the Democrat-controlled Congress.

On Energy and Commerce, Oxley's normally easygoing nature can make him appear to be open to cooperation with the majority — especially with Chairman John D. Dingell, who shares his aversion to strict acid rain controls.

A member of the conference committee on the 1990 clean-air bill, Oxley fought an uphill battle to include protections for Ohio utilities and industries that would be affected by the law. Oxley successfully pushed for allowing utilities exceeding sulfur dioxide reduction goals to auction their "credits" to other utilities; he supported the compromise package as an acceptable, if imperfect, reality.

But Oxley can also be a Republican partisan on Energy and Commerce, playing the advocate as often as the negotiator. He has opposed Democratic efforts to reinstate the "fairness doctrine" regulation on the broadcasting industry; it was repealed administratively in 1987. President Ronald Reagan vetoed a reinstatement bill passed in the 100th Congress, but Democratic leaders revived the issue in 1989, when many members felt the media were giving them an unfair rap over a proposed pay raise. Oxley also criticized the media, complaining, "We had disc jockeys whose total IQ probably doesn't reach the top number on the FM dial, who earn twice as much as a member of Congress, working up the electorate ... giving them false information." But on the vote to reinstate the fairness regulation, he did not budge from his earlier opposition.

Oxley lost a House floor vote to strip the fairness doctrine provision from the 1989 budget reconciliation bill, but the measure was eventually dropped from the budget package.

During the 101st Congress, Oxley also spoke against administration plans to mothball the Lima tank factory in his district. Congress kept money for the plant in the budget.

A former FBI agent and a member of the Select Committee on Narcotics Abuse and Control, Oxley urged in the 100th Congress that the national drug director be in the Cabinet, saying, "I want a stud in there fighting the war on drugs, someone with real clout." He successfully offered a measure making it easier to set up "sting" operations against money-launderers.

At Home: After a tough special election contest in 1981, Oxley has faced no difficulty holding his House seat. But the general voter dissatisfaction with Congress in 1990 cost several Ohio House members a few points off their normal victory margins. Oxley was one of them; after running unopposed in 1988, Oxley defeated Democrat Thomas E. Burkhart, a bus factory worker, with 62 percent.

When GOP Rep. Tennyson Guyer died in April 1981, Oxley, a four-term state House member, was an early favorite in the special election to succeed him. But Oxley faced stiff primary competition. Running in the early days of Reagan's presidency, the Republican candidates tried to out-Reagan one another. Robert J. Huffman, a Reagan backer in the 1976 presidential race, branded Oxley a latecomer because he had supported George Bush for president in 1980. Oxley won narrowly.

Oxley then had to survive an unusually tough Democratic foe to win the seat. State Rep. Dale Locker, a farmer and chairman of the state House Agriculture and Natural Resources Committee, had appeal in the mainly rural district. Oxley spent $275,000 on a media blitz in order to eke out a 341-vote victory.

Locker weighed a rematch in 1982, but backed off when the state Legislature fashioned new district boundaries to Oxley's advantage.

Ohio 4

West Central — Lima; Findlay

The 4th arches ominously in west-central Ohio like a giant set of jaws about to devour Columbus. But the strange shape is no accident. The 4th includes some of the most Republican counties in the state, placed within its borders to help Oxley. Not one of the nine counties in the 4th has supported a Democratic presidential candidate since 1944. Two of the three largest — Allen (Lima) and Hancock (Findlay) — have backed the GOP national ticket since the Roosevelt-Landon contest of 1936. Allen was the largest county east of the Mississippi carried by Barry Goldwater in 1964.

Dominated by farms and small towns, the 4th is standard Corn Belt GOP territory. The fertile soil supports large farms that raise livestock, soybeans, corn and wheat. Industry is widely scattered and attracts local craftsmen rather than poor migrants.

Lima (population 45,500) and Findlay (36,000) both emerged as small manufacturing centers at the end of the 19th century when oil and gas were found nearby. Lima was one of the original refinery centers for Standard Oil, then owned by John D. Rockefeller. Although the petroleum boom passed long ago, Findlay, as headquarters of Marathon Oil, is the most prosperous part — and the most Republican — of the 4th.

Close ties to the automobile industry caused economic hardships in Lima and Mansfield (Richland County) during the 1982 recession, but the picture has brightened some since then. Lima's Ford engine plant and Mansfield's Fisher body plant are not working at pre-recession capacity, but smaller auto-related companies have taken up some of the slack. Still, Richland County was hampered by ten percent unemployment in early 1991. In 1982, General Dynamics located in Lima and became the town's largest single employer.

Population: 514,172. White 492,852 (96%), Black 17,622 (3%). Spanish origin 4,244 (1%). 18 and over 360,450 (70%), 65 and over 58,720 (11%). Median age: 30.

Committees

Energy & Commerce (8th of 16 Republicans)
Commerce, Consumer Protection & Competitiveness; Energy & Power; Telecommunications & Finance

Select Narcotics Abuse & Control (3rd of 14 Republicans)

Elections

1990 General		
Michael G. Oxley (R)	103,897	(62%)
Thomas E. Burkhart (D)	64,467	(38%)
1988 General		
Michael G. Oxley (R)	160,099	(100%)

Previous Winning Percentages: **1986** (75%) **1984** (78%) **1982** (65%) **1981** * (50%)

* *Special election.*

District Vote For President

	1988		1984		1980		1976	
D	65,992	(32%)	55,078	(26%)	64,890	(32%)	76,257	(40%)
R	140,667	(68%)	158,577	(74%)	128,382	(63%)	108,916	(57%)
I					9,585	(5%)		

Campaign Finance

	Receipts	Receipts from PACs		Expend-itures
1990				
Oxley (R)	$298,581	$200,333	(67%)	$330,272
Burkhart (D)	$19,103	$12,000	(63%)	$19,102
1988				
Oxley (R)	$251,619	$170,850	(68%)	$207,157

Key Votes

1991	
Authorize use of force against Iraq	Y
1990	
Support constitutional amendment on flag desecration	Y
Pass family and medical leave bill over Bush veto	N
Reduce SDI funding	N
Allow abortions in overseas military facilities	N
Approve budget summit plan for spending and taxing	Y
Approve civil rights bill	N
1989	
Halt production of B-2 stealth bomber at 13 planes	N
Oppose capital gains tax cut	N
Approve federal abortion funding in rape or incest cases	N
Approve pay raise and revision of ethics rules	Y
Pass Democratic minimum wage plan over Bush veto	N

Voting Studies

	Presidential Support		Party Unity		Conservative Coalition	
Year	S	O	S	O	S	O
1990	73	27	82	14	94	2
1989	80	19	86	11	93	7
1988	68	31	81	9	92	5
1987	67	26	80	12	98	2
1986	80	16	85	8	86	14
1985	75	24	88	6	96	4
1984	67	26	86	8	93	5
1983	85	12	87	10	83	16
1982	77	17	81	13	90	10
1981	67 †	29 †	85 †	13 †	88 †	12 †

† *Not eligible for all recorded votes.*

Interest Group Ratings

Year	ADA	ACU	AFL-CIO	CCUS
1990	0	79	17	93
1989	5	93	8	100
1988	20	88	14	100
1987	4	95	0	100
1986	0	95	7	100
1985	10	86	0	91
1984	5	75	0	64
1983	10	91	0	95
1982	10	90	15	82
1981	0	83	20	92

5 Paul E. Gillmor (R)

Of Port Clinton — Elected 1988

Born: Feb. 1, 1939, Tiffin, Ohio.

Education: Ohio Wesleyan U., B.A. 1961; U. of Michigan, J.D. 1964.

Military Service: Air Force, 1965-66.

Occupation: Lawyer.

Family: Wife, Karen Lako; two children.

Religion: Protestant.

Political Career: Ohio Senate, 1967-89, minority leader, 1978-80, 1983-84; president, 1981-82, 1985-88; sought Republican nomination for governor, 1986.

Capitol Office: 1203 Longworth Bldg. 20515; 225-6405.

In Washington: Gillmor stands apart from many of the restless GOP conservatives elected to Congress these days. While they are feisty and intent on shaking things up, Gillmor brought to Congress an appreciation of the legislative process, nurtured during his two-decade tenure in the state Legislature.

House Republican leaders recognized and rewarded Gillmor's institutional bent; he was the only freshman named to a bipartisan task force set up at the start of the 101st Congress to review ethics standards and members' pay. Gillmor is his own man, though; he ended up opposing the ethics reform/pay raise legislation approved by Congress in November 1989, citing his opposition to the large salary increase.

But in the main, Gillmor seems more pragmatic than confrontational. In October 1990, he supported the bipartisan budget summit agreement, reviled by GOP conservatives for its tax-increase provisions. Of the 15 GOP House members first elected in 1988, Gillmor was one of just three to vote for the package.

Gillmor sits on Banking (where he has supported funding for the S&L bailout) and on House Administration, a panel that deals with the internal business of the House. There and as a member of a GOP task force on franking privileges, Gillmor supported a measure requiring each representative to disclose the amount spent on franked mailings and giving each member an individual mailing budget.

At Home: A state legislator who comes to Congress is uniformly regarded as having received a promotion. Gillmor, however, had to sacrifice a good bit of power when he left Columbus for Washington. As president of the Ohio Senate for six of his last eight years there, Gillmor was the highest-ranking Republican in state government.

When he decided to seek the House seat of retiring GOP Rep. Delbert L. Latta, Gillmor knew well that his biggest challenge would be in the primary. As Senate president in the early 1980s, Gillmor had a say over the redistricting plan that made the 5th a GOP stronghold.

The 1988 GOP primary was a bruising one, however. The 30-year incumbent wanted to hand the seat to his son, 32-year-old lawyer Robert E. Latta. The resulting face off turned bitter and personal; Gillmor won narrowly.

During Gillmor's 22 years in the state Senate, he represented more than two-thirds of Latta's House territory, and the two men competed for dominance of the local political scene. When Gillmor announced he would run for the House, Rep. Latta briefly threatened to drop his retirement plans and seek re-election.

The younger Latta campaigned aggressively, aided by his father's ready-made organization. However, Gillmor towered over the newcomer in personal recognition. Gillmor not only had his own solid political base in most of the 5th, but also was known throughout the district from his 1986 bid for the GOP gubernatorial nomination. (Although he lost statewide, he carried the 5th in that primary.)

Gillmor ran a media-oriented campaign, highlighting his legislative experience. He stressed his fiscal conservatism — pointing to two tax-cut bills he authored and 11 balanced budgets he supported. He also cited his successes as the Senate Republican leader: He was known as an accessible, consensus-oriented leader able to move legislation despite the GOP's narrow Senate majority.

Those credentials boosted Gillmor to victory, but just barely. He won by 27 votes — the smallest margin in any 1988 House contest.

In the general election, though, the district's Republican tendencies kicked in for Gillmor. His foe was wealthy Democratic attorney Thomas Murray, who had gotten just 35 percent against Del Latta in 1986.

Although Murray spent nearly $850,000, mainly on TV ads, Gillmor topped 60 percent. By 1990, Gillmor was solidly established in the 5th.

Ohio 5

Northwest — Bowling Green; Sandusky

The 5th looks like a big bow tie, with Wood County (Bowling Green) as the knot.

This solidly Republican district is a mixture of good, flat farmland and small towns. The Lake Erie port of Sandusky (population 30,000) is the largest community. Bowling Green (population 28,000), home of Bowling Green State University and its 18,000 students, is the district's second most-populous city.

The western counties are almost exclusively devoted to agriculture. Packing plants operated by Heinz and Campbell attest to the quality of the region's tomatoes. But the Mexican-American farm workers who live in migrant camps during harvest season have added an ethnic element to the otherwise homogeneous region. The 5th has the greatest concentration of Hispanics in Ohio.

Changes in district lines over the past three decades have gradually brought in more territory on the east, including Erie County, with more than 77,000 residents. Located midway between Cleveland and Toledo, it has long been a major recreation area. Sandusky, the county seat, is a fishing market and coal port. In the surrounding countryside, fruit orchards and vineyards abound. German immigrants established wineries in Sandusky a century ago that are still a key feature of the local economy. The sizable blue-collar element occasionally pushes Erie County into the Democratic column. But with just 15 percent of the district vote, Erie is but a ripple in the large Republican pond.

Wood County, which sprawls from the outskirts of Toledo deep into the Ohio Corn Belt, accounts for one-sixth of the district's voters. The county is consistently Republican, although the Bowling Green university community provides some base for moderate-to-liberal contenders. Independent John B. Anderson drew 10 percent of the Wood County vote for president in 1980, his best county showing in Ohio.

Population: 514,173. White 493,503 (96%), Black 10,318 (2%). Spanish origin 16,537 (3%). 18 and over 358,616 (70%), 65 and over 53,806 (10%). Median age: 28.

Committees

Banking, Finance & Urban Affairs (11th of 20 Republicans)
Financial Institutions Supervision, Regulation & Insurance; Housing & Community Development; International Development, Finance, Trade & Monetary Policy

House Administration (5th of 9 Republicans)
Accounts (ranking); Elections

Select Narcotics Abuse & Control (13th of 14 Republicans)

Elections

1990 General		
Paul E. Gillmor (R)	113,615	(68%)
P. Scott Mange (D)	41,693	(25%)
John E. Jackson (I)	10,612	(6%)
1988 General		
Paul E. Gillmor (R)	123,838	(61%)
Tom Murray (D)	80,292	(39%)

District Vote For President

	1988	1984	1980	1976
D	80,083 (38%)	69,036 (32%)	66,593 (33%)	83,017 (44%)
R	128,731 (61%)	145,926 (67%)	116,836 (58%)	102,353 (54%)
I			13,995 (7%)	

Campaign Finance

	Receipts	Receipts from PACs	Expend-itures
1990			
Gillmor (R)	$325,743	$230,425 (71%)	$254,688
Mange (D)	$250	0	$248
1988			
Gillmor (R)	$833,178	$319,120 (38%)	$860,603
Murray (D)	$719,754	$21,700 (3%)	$850,819

Key Votes

1991	
Authorize use of force against Iraq	Y
1990	
Support constitutional amendment on flag desecration	Y
Pass family and medical leave bill over Bush veto	Y
Reduce SDI funding	N
Allow abortions in overseas military facilities	N
Approve budget summit plan for spending and taxing	Y
Approve civil rights bill	N
1989	
Halt production of B-2 stealth bomber at 13 planes	N
Oppose capital gains tax cut	N
Approve federal abortion funding in rape or incest cases	N
Approve pay raise and revision of ethics rules	N
Pass Democratic minimum wage plan over Bush veto	N

Voting Studies

	Presidential Support		Party Unity		Conservative Coalition	
Year	**S**	**O**	**S**	**O**	**S**	**O**
1990	69	29	66	32	91	9
1989	77	22	65	32	90	10

Interest Group Ratings

Year	ADA	ACU	AFL-CIO	CCUS
1990	11	74	17	57
1989	0	93	0	100

6 Bob McEwen (R)

Of Hillsboro — Elected 1980

Born: Jan. 12, 1950, Hillsboro, Ohio.
Education: U. of Miami (Fla.), B.B.A. 1972.
Occupation: Real estate developer.
Family: Wife, Elizabeth Boebinger; four children.
Religion: Protestant.
Political Career: Ohio House, 1975-81.
Capitol Office: 2431 Rayburn Bldg. 20515; 225-5705.

In Washington: In the waning hours of any legislative day, after the floor has emptied and "special order" speeches are under way, you may see McEwen playing the trusty sidekick Sancho Panza to Bob Dornan of California, both tilting at the latest liberal windmill.

McEwen embodies the type of confrontational conservative who has gained increasing influence in House Republican ranks; in the 102nd Congress, he was tapped by the leadership to sit on the Rules Committee.

Honing a reputation as a man who thinks about politics nearly every waking minute, McEwen added to that image at the start of the 100th Congress by feeding the Washington press corps a stream of publicity about his plans to run for the Senate in 1988. Although McEwen did enter the race, he halted his campaign after two months.

When McEwen legislates, he nearly always manages to produce something of tangible benefit to his district and the broader political constituency he is courting. Before moving to Rules, he used his assignments on the Public Works and Veterans' Affairs committees to funnel government money back to Ohio.

McEwen headed for Public Works as soon as he got to Washington in 1981, and began practicing the skills he had learned as a congressional aide. He has never let his opposition to the federal deficit and taxes stand in the way; at a time of budget cutbacks, McEwen employed his congenial personality to lobby successfully for funding of favorite projects such as bridges, dams, flood walls and navigation locks. The Ohio River forms the southern boundary of the 6th.

In foreign affairs, McEwen echoes Dornan in calling for a strong U.S. military. He supported the Persian Gulf War and sought to lift the ban against political assassinations so Iraqi President Saddam Hussein could be targeted. But he criticized the Bush administration for not attacking Iraqi helicopters that harassed Kurdish refugees rafter the cease-fire.

At Home: McEwen's mix of conservative rhetoric and pork-barrel politics have made him invincible in the 6th. The southern Ohio district, though conservative, is amenable to almost any plan that will help it fight economic decline.

McEwen has carried on the devotion to public works projects that characterized his mentor and House predecessor, Republican William H. Harsha. After starting a career in real-estate development, McEwen won a state House seat at age 24. He would later direct two of Harsha's House campaigns.

When Harsha retired in 1980, McEwen became the likely successor. Harsha remained publicly neutral in the eight-candidate GOP primary, but McEwen was the choice of the local Republican establishment. In the Ohio House, he had gained visibility by working to get the state to dredge a flood-prone creek in his district. He also advocated abolishing the Ohio lottery. On primary day, McEwen swept 10 of the district's 12 counties. McEwen enjoyed Harsha's backing in the general election and presented himself as the incumbent's protégé. He pushed past Democrat Ted Strickland, a minister with a Ph.D. in psychology and counseling, with 55 percent of the vote.

Coasting to re-election in his next three campaigns, McEwen had time to contemplate a statewide race. After months of promoting his plans to challenge Democratic Sen. Howard M. Metzenbaum, McEwen announced in October 1987. But he had a hard time gaining a foothold against fellow Republican George Voinovich, who as mayor of Cleveland was better known.

While McEwen gathered considerable conservative backing — including an endorsement from Texas Sen. Phil Gramm — he ran into money troubles. Voinovich, by contrast, had strong financial backing from GOP business interests. McEwen backed out, saying party unity was vital to winning the Senate seat.

Voinovich lost badly to Metzenbaum, but rebounded to win the open governorship in 1990. Meanwhile, McEwen stayed in his House seat, winning easily in his next two contests and reviving talk about his statewide future.

After his 1990 win, McEwen did not head off speculation that he might run in 1992 for the Senate seat held by Democrat John Glenn.

Ohio 6

South Central — Portsmouth; Chillicothe

The 6th is a mixture of suburbia and Appalachia. Republican majorities in the Cincinnati and Dayton suburbs and the countryside nearby enable the GOP to win most elections. But when the Democrats run well in Appalachia, as they occasionally do, the outcome can be close.

Nearly one-third of the voters in the 6th live in a suburban sector between Cincinnati and Dayton, part of which was gained in the last redistricting. The territory, which lies north of Interstate 71, the major Cincinnati-to-Columbus artery, is Republican. It grew rapidly in the 1970s as the result of commercial development, and managed to hold its own even through the 1982 recession.

Immediately east is rural Republican country. Clinton and Highland counties and the southern portion of Fayette County lie on the outer fringe of the Corn Belt.

Farther east the land is poorer and GOP strength begins to diminish. When entering Adams County, one is in Appalachia. Adams, Pike and Vinton counties are among the poorest counties in Ohio.

Nearly one-half the land area of this Appalachian portion of the district is enclosed in the Wayne National Forest. What little industry exists is concentrated in Portsmouth (22,000) and Chillicothe (23,000).

While steel and bricks have been linchpins of Portsmouth's economy throughout the century, the largest employer in the district is the nearby uranium-enrichment facility owned by the Atomic Energy Commission and operated by Goodyear. In Chillicothe, 44 miles due north of Portsmouth, nearby forests support a large paper plant.

Population: 514,173. White 501,021 (97%), Black 10,506 (2%). Spanish origin 2,524 (1%). 18 and over 359,077 (70%), 65 and over 55,960 (11%). Median age: 30.

Committees

Rules (4th of 4 Republicans)
Legislative Process

Select Children, Youth & Families (8th of 14 Republicans)

Elections

1990 General		
Bob McEwen (R)	117,220	(71%)
Ray Mitchell (D)	47,415	(29%)
1988 General		
Bob McEwen (R)	152,235	(74%)
Gordon R. Roberts (D)	52,635	(26%)

Previous Winning Percentages: **1986** (70%) **1984** (74%) **1982** (59%) **1980** (55%)

District Vote For President

	1988	1984	1980	1976
D	72,552 (35%)	65,222 (31%)	74,614 (38%)	89,145 (48%)
R	134,828 (64%)	140,525 (68%)	110,714 (57%)	93,080 (50%)
I			7,502 (4%)	

Campaign Finance

	Receipts	Receipts from PACs	Expend-itures
1990			
McEwen (R)	$292,650	$144,630 (49%)	$196,934
Mitchell (D)	$16,745	0	$11,171
1988			
McEwen (R)	$787,103	$147,066 (19%)	$884,754
Roberts (D)	$43,532	$22,450 (52%)	$43,485

Key Votes

1991	
Authorize use of force against Iraq	Y
1990	
Support constitutional amendment on flag desecration	Y
Pass family and medical leave bill over Bush veto	N
Reduce SDI funding	N
Allow abortions in overseas military facilities	N
Approve budget summit plan for spending and taxing	N
Approve civil rights bill	N
1989	
Halt production of B-2 stealth bomber at 13 planes	N
Oppose capital gains tax cut	N
Approve federal abortion funding in rape or incest cases	N
Approve pay raise and revision of ethics rules	Y
Pass Democratic minimum wage plan over Bush veto	N

Voting Studies

	Presidential Support		Party Unity		Conservative Coalition	
Year	**S**	**O**	**S**	**O**	**S**	**O**
1990	69	29	77	16	94	2
1989	72	21	67	24	90	7
1988	65	29	73	21	92	3
1987	60	28	68	16	81	7
1986	67	22	63	26	84	4
1985	69	26	79	13	87	11
1984	60	29	81	9	88	5
1983	72	28	82	13	87	9
1982	58	34	77	18	77	18
1981	76	24	90	8	91	7

Interest Group Ratings

Year	ADA	ACU	AFL-CIO	CCUS
1990	6	100	8	93
1989	5	93	17	100
1988	5	96	14	100
1987	4	86	8	90
1986	5	86	31	79
1985	15	85	6	79
1984	5	80	15	71
1983	15	87	12	85
1982	30	85	30	86
1981	0	100	20	89

7 David L. Hobson (R)

Of Springfield — Elected 1990

Born: Oct. 17, 1936, Cincinnati, Ohio.
Education: Ohio Wesleyan U., B.A. 1958; Ohio State U., J.D. 1963.
Occupation: Financial corporation executive.
Family: Wife, Carolyn Alexander; three children.
Religion: Methodist.
Political Career: Ohio Senate, 1982-91.
Capitol Office: 1338 Longworth Bldg. 20515; 225-4324.

The Path to Washington: In English vernacular, the term "Hobson's choice" has come to represent a no-win situation. But in 1990, David Hobson's choice was definitely a winning one.

When Republican Rep. Mike DeWine embarked on what would be a successful bid for lieutenant governor, Hobson ran for the House and upheld his reputation as DeWine's heir apparent. Hobson, who was serving as state Senate president pro tem at the time, took 62 percent of the vote to defeat Democrat Jack Schira.

Hobson's election marked the second time he followed DeWine's footsteps. He was appointed in December 1982 to the state Senate seat DeWine gave up to run for the House. (DeWine quit the Senate early so his seat could be filled by outgoing Republican Gov. James A. Rhodes rather than incoming Democratic Gov. Richard F. Celeste.)

Elected in 1984, Hobson was chosen by his Republican colleagues as Senate majority whip two years later. In November 1988, the same month he won re-election, Hobson moved up to president pro tem, the Senate's second-ranking position. Hobson also had a lengthy list of legislative successes. Many of the bills he sponsored were in the area of health care, including measures dealing with AIDS, aging and mental health that earned him widespread praise in the state and district media.

This interest in health issues did not stem from Hobson's personal experience. He entered politics as a businessman who served as chairman of financial corporations and on the boards of a bank, an oil company and a restaurant company. Some of Hobson's early legislative efforts were business-related: A member of a committee that probed the collapse of an Ohio savings and loan, he sponsored a bill to protect depositors and reform state S&L supervision.

However, Hobson was appointed early in his career to the Senate Health Committee and became engrossed in health-care issues. He led an investigation into the scandal-plagued state Department of Mental Retardation that brought the ouster of the agency's director, and he sponsored reform legislation that provided more local control over mental-health care provision. He also drew up a measure to provide respite care for sufferers of Alzheimer's disease. He was generally supportive of abortion rights, a position that contrasted with DeWine's strong anti-abortion stance.

Hobson also authored a comprehensive bill for the detection and treatment of AIDS. The bill encouraged AIDS testing by ensuring confidentiality, instituted state regulation of long-term facilities for AIDS patients and provided protection from discrimination for victims of the disease. Staving off conservative critics who portrayed the proposal as a gay rights bill, Hobson pushed it through the Republican-controlled Senate by a 22-8 vote.

His record on health issues and his sizable voter base — he already represented more than half of the 7th District in the state Senate — made Hobson the strong favorite in the House contest.

Schira, a retired Air Force colonel who took 26 percent in a 1988 challenge to DeWine, was a determined but poorly funded candidate who borrowed against his home and credit cards to finance his campaign. Schira showed a knack for publicity: During the campaign, he founded Operation Support, which organized mailings of letters to U.S. soldiers stationed in the Persian Gulf. Schira also attacked Hobson's contributions from oil- and tobacco-related political action committees, portraying him as a corporate tool.

However, Schira's charges had little effect on the outcome. Hobson dominated his home turf, winning 64 percent in Clark County, 66 percent in Greene County and 70 percent in Fayette County. His margins were more modest in the northern part of the 7th, but he carried all of the district's counties.

Ohio 7

West Central — Springfield; Marion

Situated between Columbus and Dayton, the 7th is bisected by U.S. Route 40. North of the highway are four solidly Republican counties casting one-third of the district vote. Combining agriculture and small industry, they have been GOP strongholds for generations. Champaign, Logan and Union counties backed Alfred M. Landon for president in 1936. Marion County was President Warren G. Harding's home.

Marion claims to be the birthplace of the steam shovel, but it has been mired in economic troubles, partly because the demand for large power shovels has decreased. In 1982, unemployment in Marion County was so high that Democratic Gov. Richard F. Celeste nearly carried it, even though GOP gubernatorial nominee Clarence J. Brown Jr. was the area's congressman. Democrats have a slight lead in voter registration.

The economic picture is rosier in neighboring Union County. Just northwest of Columbus, it is an attractive site for industries seeking open land and low taxes. Honda located its first American auto plant in the western part of the county and runs a motorcycle plant nearby. Honda has planned a $27 million expansion to these existing facilities near Marysville. Union and adjacent Logan counties are both solidly Republican.

South of Route 40, the people are concentrated in Clark County (Springfield) and Greene County, which extends into Dayton's eastern suburbs. Greene has a working-class mixture of blacks and Southern whites. Wright-Patterson Air Force Base is responsible for a substantial amount of military-related employment.

Springfield's site along Route 40, the old National Road, enabled it to develop into the area's leading population center. The city's economy suffered substantially in the early 1980s but got a boost in 1983 when International Harvester consolidated its truck-making in Springfield.

Population: 514,170. White 482,499 (94%), Black 27,488 (5%), Other 2,800 (1&). Spanish origin 3,092 (1%). 18 and over 362,126 (70%), 65 and over 51,300 (10%). Median age: 30.

Committees

Government Operations (14th of 15 Republicans)
Environment, Energy & Natural Resources; Human Resources & Intergovernmental Relations

Public Works & Transportation (16th of 21 Republicans)
Aviation; Investigations & Oversight; Surface Transportation

Select Aging (21st of 27 Republicans)
Health & Long-Term Care

Standards of Official Conduct (7th of 7 Republicans)

Elections

1990 General		
David L. Hobson (R)	97,123	(62%)
Jack Schira (D)	59,349	(38%)
1990 Primary		
David L. Hobson (R)	28,530	(79%)
Todd Gordon (R)	7,516	(21%)

District Vote For President

	1988	1984	1980	1976
D	70,238 (35%)	62,580 (31%)	71,020 (36%)	82,201 (44%)
R	126,632 (64%)	136,042 (68%)	105,772 (54%)	98,272 (53%)
I			10,369 (5%)	

Campaign Finance

	Receipts	Receipts from PACs	Expend-itures
1990			
Hobson (R)	$389,738	$202,427 (52%)	$389,136
Schira (D)	$89,592	$32,200 (36%)	$89,019

Key Vote

1991	
Authorize use of force against Iraq	Y

8 John A. Boehner (R)

Of West Chester — Elected 1990

Born: Nov. 17, 1949, Cincinnati, Ohio.
Education: Xavier U., B.S. 1977.
Military Service: Navy, 1969.
Occupation: Plastics and packaging sales company president.
Family: Wife, Debbie Gunlack; two children.
Religion: Roman Catholic.
Political Career: Ohio House, 1985-91.
Capitol Office: 1020 Longworth Bldg. 20515; 225-6205.

The Path to Washington: In the reliably Republican 8th, the GOP primary surprise in 1990 was not that embattled Rep. Donald E. "Buz" Lukens was ousted but that Boehner emerged victorious. A state representative and local businessman, Boehner was barely a blip on the radar screen at the beginning of the campaign, but he steadily climbed until upsetting former Republican Rep. Thomas N. Kindness in the May primary.

Despite being re-elected in 1988 with 76 percent of the vote, Lukens was doomed after his May 1989 conviction on a misdemeanor charge stemming from a sexual liaison with a 16-year-old girl.

Though Lukens insisted he would be vindicated, all seven county Republican leaders demanded that Lukens either resign or at least not seek re-election. Lukens held on through the primary but was forced to resign the seat after a second allegation of sexual misconduct in October.

Kindness started out as the heavy favorite, with polls showing him leading Boehner by more than 60 percentage points. Boehner made up for a lack of name recognition by running a smart and aggressive primary campaign.

Boehner aimed his attacks at the former six-term representative, while Kindness focused his sights on the wounded incumbent.

Ignoring Lukens, Boehner chipped away Kindness' lead by questioning his ethics. He tapped a deep vein of voter resentment by listing Kindness' votes against limits on honoraria and for congressional pay raises. He framed Kindness as a shady lobbyist who abandoned the district after losing a 1986 Senate challenge to Democratic Sen. John Glenn (Kindness remained in Washington as a partner in a consulting firm).

Drawing on his contacts in the business community, Boehner used his financial resources to keep the heat on Kindness. He outspent Kindness more than 5 to 1, pummeling him with extensive media coverage.

The campaign tone became progressively harsher, as Kindness responded to the barrage of negative ads by describing Boehner as "an immature yuppie." But Boehner stuck to his theme and suggested that Kindness might have conflicts of interest on issues involving his former clients.

The general election was not nearly as close or nasty, with Boehner sweeping every county against the Democratic nominee, former Hamilton Mayor Gregory V. Jolivette.

Though Lukens had ceased to be an issue, he threw a monkey wrench into the race late in the fall campaign. His October resignation triggered a series of cumbersome electoral problems. Upon Lukens' resignation, the governor signed an order requiring a special election to fill the remainder of the unexpired term. Expecting the special race to be settled by Boehner and Jolivette, the district needed only to print a special election ballot coinciding with the general election ballot on Nov. 6.

But several unknown candidates unexpectedly filed, necessitating an Election Day primary and a general election two weeks later. State and local officials from both parties protested the costs involved, and the order was rescinded. The seat remained vacant for the remainder of the 101st Congress.

The tradition of a conservative representing the 8th carries on with Boehner, although he was not regarded as an ideologue during his three-term tenure in the state House.

As former president of a company that markets plastics, Boehner brings a business-oriented outlook to Congress.

He has expressed opposition to government interference in labor-management matters, to government-mandated employee health benefits and to universal health insurance. He also has ruled out supporting tax increases.

Ohio 8

Southwest — Middletown; Hamilton

Butler County is the anchor of this southern Ohio district that has changed shape several times in recent redistrictings but always remained solidly Republican.

Butler contains two medium-sized manufacturing centers along the Great Miami River — Hamilton (population 65,000) and Middletown (population 46,000). Steel, paper, automobile bodies, machine tools and a variety of other metal products are made in the two cities.

But both cities havc lost population in recent years. Most of Butler County's 271,000 residents live not in Hamilton or Middletown but in suburban communities and small towns such as Oxford, the home of Miami University (16,000 students).

Population expansion in Butler County's suburban territory, just north of the Cincinnati beltway, has made the county one of the state's fastest-growing, and the new arrivals have escalated a rightward trend in the local GOP.

In recent years the county has elected some of the most conservative Republican legislators in the state. Ronald Reagan carried Butler in 1980 with 62 percent of the vote, and increased that to 73 percent in 1984. In 1988, George Bush carried Butler with 67 percent of the vote, well above his statewide average of 55 percent.

Half the residents of the 8th live outside Butler County in a string of fertile Corn Belt counties running north along the Indiana border. The land is flat and the roads are straight. Once a motorist leaves the Miami Valley in northern Butler, he can drive north through the district along Route 127 without more than an occasional slight turn of the steering wheel.

Corn and soybeans are major cash crops in the rural counties. Poultry and livestock also are moneymakers. In recent years, Darke and Mercer counties have been the leading Ohio counties in farm income.

Mercer was settled by German Catholics and is the only county in the 8th with much of a Democratic heritage; Democrats have a slight voter-registration lead in Darke County.

But Mercer likes its Democrats conservative. It has not backed the party's presidential candidate since 1968.

Population: 514,171. White 496,757 (97%), Black 14,280 (3%). Spanish origin 3,057 (1%). 18 and over 361,343 (70%), 65 and over 52,071 (10%). Median age: 29.

Committees

Agriculture (17th of 18 Republicans)
Conservation, Credit & Rural Development; Cotton, Rice & Sugar; Department Operations, Research & Foreign Agriculture; Livestock, Dairy & Poultry

Education & Labor (12th of 14 Republicans)
Elementary, Secondary & Vocational Education; Health & Safety; Labor-Management Relations

Small Business (16th of 17 Republicans)
Exports, Tax Policy & Special Problems

Campaign Finance

	Receipts	Receipts from PACs		Expend-itures
1990				
Boehner (R)	$737,441	$219,526	(30%)	$732,765
Jolivette (D)	$115,495	$48,825	(42%)	$114,852

Key Vote

1991

Authorize use of force against Iraq	Y

Elections

1990 General		
John A. Boehner (R)	99,955	(61%)
Gregory V. Jolivette (D)	63,584	(39%)
1990 Primary		
John A. Boehner (R)	25,071	(49%)
Thomas N. Kindness (R)	16,360	(32%)
Donald E. "Buz" Lukens (R)	8,686	(17%)
Mort W. Meier (R)	719	(1%)

District Vote For President

	1988	1984	1980	1976
D	65,826 (31%)	55,507 (27%)	67,442 (34%)	76,480 (42%)
R	147,196 (69%)	151,869 (73%)	119,158 (60%)	102,855 (56%)
I			10,727 (5%)	

9 Marcy Kaptur (D)

Of Toledo — Elected 1982

Born: June 17, 1946, Toledo, Ohio.
Education: U. of Wisconsin, B.A. 1968; U. of Michigan, M.U.P. 1974.
Occupation: Urban planner; White House staff member.
Family: Single.
Religion: Roman Catholic.
Political Career: No previous office.
Capitol Office: 1228 Longworth Bldg. 20515; 225-4146.

In Washington: After several years of striving, Kaptur now has a seat on the coveted Appropriations Committee. But the jury is still out on whether she will turn out to be a deal-broker and legislative heavy lifter the Democratic leadership can depend on. For now, she is known mostly for her personable manner and her moral outrage over issues of concern to her Rust Belt constituency.

Kaptur arrived in Congress without elective-office experience, and she sought to compensate for that by hitching her fortunes to those of Texan Jim Wright, then the majority leader. Soon after he became Speaker in 1987, Wright rewarded Kaptur's loyalty with an appointment to the panel that makes Democrats' committee assignments. In 1989, he backed her successful bid for the Budget Committee. He also named her vice chairman of the leadership task force on trade. But when Wright had to relinquish the speakership in June 1989, Kaptur failed in her first solo try for a leadership spot: She ran third in a bid for Democratic Caucus vice chairman.

Her next reach for a higher rung came in mid-1990, when there was a vacancy on Appropriations. Kaptur had tried for the panel before, but this time, playing the gender and geography cards, she succeeded. Kaptur noted that the committee had just one Democratic woman, Lindy Boggs of Louisiana, who was retiring at the end of the 101st Congress; she also stirred up other Rust Belt members to quash a move by Californians for a sixth Appropriations seat. Kaptur finally won the post after four ballots.

To join Appropriations, she had to leave the Banking Committee, where she vented her blue-collar constituents' frustration with the S&L bailout. She offered unsuccessful amendments to shift more of the bailout burden to Sunbelt states where most of the failures occurred, and to limit the extent of foreign investment in the bond offering to finance the bailout. Her amendment to require that bonds be available to small investors was adopted.

First swept into office by voter anger over the 1982 recession, Kaptur remains an ardent spokesman for industrial Toledo, which is heavily dependent on the automobile industry. Republican free-traders set her blood to boiling. Kaptur backed the Democratic trade bill that was three years in the making, and, in 1987, strongly supported the Gephardt "fair trade" amendment. She added her own amendment, calling on U.S. trade negotiators to oppose most-favored-nation status for countries not maintaining open markets.

The 1989 ethics legislation included language Kaptur backed to restrict former government officials from working on behalf of foreign interests for one year. Kaptur is now pushing to extend the prohibition to four years.

At Home: Kaptur's victory over GOP Rep. Ed Weber was one of the Democrats' surprise 1982 successes. Although a poised and aggressive candidate, she had to overcome a late start and a poorly financed, under-organized campaign with little help from the national party.

Kaptur cited Weber's support for Reagan's economic policies during a recession as evidence of insensitivity to Toledo's plight. Weber never shifted in his public backing for Reagan's program; that was his undoing in a region with double-digit unemployment.

Overconfident, he failed to exploit one vulnerability in Kaptur's record. Although she was a Toledo native, Kaptur had spent many years away, most recently as the assistant director of urban affairs for President Jimmy Carter. But with Weber ignoring the issue, neither Kaptur's absence nor her Carter connection proved to be any problem.

In 1984, Republicans nominated Frank Venner, a longtime TV newscaster. Although he had no previous political experience, Venner was a familar figure to a generation of Toledo voters. But he had trouble translating his avuncular, non-ideological TV image into a partisan campaign. He had plenty of campaign money, but neither a strong grass-roots organization nor a potent local issue to use against Kaptur. Fortified by support from labor and the district's large ethnic population, Kaptur won 55 percent. That was her last close race.

Ohio 9

Northwest — Toledo

Traditionally, Toledo has been a city whose fortunes rose and fell with the health of the automobile industry, but by the end of the 1980s, it was Wall Street, not Detroit, that undermined Toledo's economy.

The city climbed back from the depths of the recession in 1982 by mid-decade, and there was some cause for optimism. An American Motors Jeep plant and a General Motors transmission factory were operating at full capacity; unemployment in Toledo slipped below 10 percent in 1986. But then a wave of corporate takeovers and restructurings by out-of-town interests weakened such major Toledo glass producers as Libbey-Owens-Ford, Owens-Illinois and Owens-Corning Fiberglas.

Two-thirds of the vote in the 9th is cast in Toledo, a Democratic outpost in rural Republican northwestern Ohio. Democrats outnumber Republicans in surrounding Lucas County by more than 2-to-1. But the absence of a large black population keeps Democratic majorities in Toledo lower than those in Dayton or Cleveland. Jimmy Carter carried the city in 1980, but with only 49 percent. President Reagan took it in 1984, but four years later it swung back to Democrat Michael S. Dukakis.

Toledo is an ethnic city. There are major concentrations of Germans, Irish, Poles and Hungarians. While traditionally Democratic, most blue-collar ethnics here now vote Republican at least occasionally.

To the east of the city are blue-collar, traditionally Democratic suburbs. Republicans are concentrated in the more affluent suburbs west of Toledo, where Ottawa Hills has one of the highest per capita incomes of any community in Ohio.

The eastern edge of Fulton County was included in the 9th in 1982 redistricting. Fulton is one of the most Republican counties in Ohio, but the portion that joined the 9th is in the orbit of Toledo and includes most of the county's best Democratic precincts.

Population: 514,174. White 438,504 (85%), Black 64,148 (13%), Other 3,454 (1%). Spanish origin 13,253 (3%). 18 and over 364,640 (71%), 65 and over 58,484 (11%). Median age: 29.

Committee

Appropriations (33rd of 37 Democrats)
Rural Development, Agriculture & Related Agencies; Veterans Affairs, Housing & Urban Development, & Independent Agencies

Elections

1990 General		
Marcy Kaptur (D)	117,681	(78%)
Jerry D. Lammers (R)	33,791	(22%)
1988 General		
Marcy Kaptur (D)	157,557	(81%)
Al Hawkins (R)	36,183	(19%)

Previous Winning Percentages: **1986** (78%) **1984** (55%) **1982** (58%)

District Vote For President

	1988		1984		1980		1976	
D	107,960	(53%)	103,846	(48%)	91,749	(44%)	112,084	(56%)
R	92,563	(46%)	109,766	(51%)	97,119	(46%)	83,584	(42%)
I					17,998	(9%)		

Campaign Finance

	Receipts	Receipts from PACs		Expend-itures
1990				
Kaptur (D)	$227,820	$114,830	(50%)	$211,524
Lammers (R)	$200	0		$200
1988				
Kaptur (D)	$277,724	$201,740	(73%)	$244,030
Hawkins (R)	$47,946	0		$47,945

Key Votes

1991	
Authorize use of force against Iraq	N
1990	
Support constitutional amendment on flag desecration	N
Pass family and medical leave bill over Bush veto	?
Reduce SDI funding	Y
Allow abortions in overseas military facilities	N
Approve budget summit plan for spending and taxing	Y
Approve civil rights bill	Y
1989	
Halt production of B-2 stealth bomber at 13 planes	Y
Oppose capital gains tax cut	Y
Approve federal abortion funding in rape or incest cases	N
Approve pay raise and revision of ethics rules	N
Pass Democratic minimum wage plan over Bush veto	Y

Voting Studies

	Presidential Support		Party Unity		Conservative Coalition	
Year	S	O	S	O	S	O
1990	23	76	86	8	41	56
1989	33	64	86	9	29	71
1988	21	70	86	8	45	50
1987	19	75	82	6	30	60
1986	17	77	84	4	24	68
1985	26	70	84	9	27	69
1984	26	63	79	12	20	73
1983	12	85	85	10	15	82

Interest Group Ratings

Year	ADA	ACU	AFL-CIO	CCUS
1990	72	8	100	15
1989	75	11	82	44
1988	75	13	100	43
1987	80	0	94	21
1986	75	5	93	33
1985	60	14	88	41
1984	75	22	83	33
1983	90	4	94	20

10 Clarence E. Miller (R)

Of Lancaster — Elected 1966

Born: Nov. 1, 1917, Lancaster, Ohio.
Education: Graduated from Lancaster H.S., 1935.
Occupation: Electrical engineer.
Family: Widowed; two children.
Religion: Methodist.
Political Career: Lancaster City Council, 1957-63; mayor of Lancaster, 1963-65.
Capitol Office: 2308 Rayburn Bldg. 20515; 225-5131.

In Washington: Back in the 1970s, year after year, on bill after bill, "Five Percent Clarence" Miller took the floor to propose that appropriations be reduced by 5 percent across the board, or, failing that, 2 percent. But as his ideas have gained legitimacy in these deficit-conscious times, Miller himself has been fading. It has been years since a Miller-authored budget-cut amendment has come up for a recorded vote in the full House.

During the war in the Persian Gulf, Miller did receive a bit of national attention as the only member of Congress to have a grandson fighting in the Persian Gulf War.

Despite his status as the panel's third most senior Republican, and a courtly manner that suits the comity of the Appropriations Committee, he is not a strong force there. In 1985, he gave up his ranking position on the Treasury-Postal Service Subcommittee for a spot on the Defense Subcommittee, where he ranks third in seniority. Miller was passed over for a largely symbolic post in 1989, when Ohio Republicans chose Chalmers P. Wylie as their delegation chairman. The two are equal in seniority, and Miller created some bitterness in the normally cohesive group with his campaign for the post it was clear he could not win.

On the Appropriations Defense Subcommittee during the 101st Congress, Miller rarely engaged in debate on restructuring the U.S. military to meet new budget demands. Instead, he urged cutting the Pentagon's recruiting budget. In his first term, Miller was already standing up to endorse a 5 percent cut proposed by fellow Ohioan Frank T. Bow, then senior GOP member on Appropriations. After Bow retired in 1973, Miller carried on the idea.

His first victory came in 1977, when the House cut foreign aid spending by 5 percent. The next year he successfully offered an amendment to cut labor, education and welfare spending by a modest 2 percent. But on foreign aid, his ambitious 8 percent cut lost by 15 votes. Then his 2 percent nick in agriculture spending died after serious lobbying by House leaders.

In the next few years, Miller seemed to be on a losing streak; the only Miller amendments that passed were in the 2 percent range. But the enormous deficits of the early 1980s and the difficulty of reducing them any other way rehabilitated the Miller method, even as he moved into the background. By 1985, automatic or across-the-board budget reductions were being institutionalized as part of the Gramm-Rudman-Hollings deficit-reduction bill.

At Home: Despite Miller's low profile in Congress, he is firmly entrenched in his southeast Ohio district. Miller, like most Ohio House incumbents, was affected in 1990 by voter grumpiness: Facing a fourth consecutive contest against Democratic auto salesman John M. Buchanan, Miller slipped by 9 percentage points from his 1988 showing. Yet he defeated Buchanan with 63 percent of the vote.

Miller's only tough House contest was his first. Running in 1966 against Democratic Rep. Walter H. Moeller, Miller won with 52 percent of the vote.

Miller, who emerged from local politics in Lancaster to run for the House, benefited greatly from the coattails of then-Republican Gov. James A. Rhodes. A district native, Rhodes — en route to a second term as governor — carried the 10th by 34,000 votes; Miller won his House seat by 4,401 votes.

Since then, Miller has kept in touch with the voters mostly through newsletters and ceremonial visits to county fairs and other gatherings. The 10th's population is widely dispersed, making it difficult for challengers to campaign or even to make their names known districtwide. With the district's GOP tilt added in, Miller has had a virtual lock on re-election.

In some early House campaigns, Miller was challenged by professors from Ohio University at Athens. Only one drew even a third of the vote against him. A countrified ex-mayor with a correspondence degree in engineering, Miller simply fit the constituency better than his academia-based opponents. Such recent opponents as an accountant, a hotel manager and an engineer — before Buchanan became the semi-permanent Democratic candidate — also lost.

Ohio 10

Southeast — Lancaster; Zanesville

Nearly as large as Connecticut, the 10th is a part of Appalachia grafted onto a Midwestern state. Redistricting in 1982 enlarged the industrial blue-collar base, but the 10th has not lost its traditional Republican character. It was the only district in the state not to elect a Democrat to the House during the New Deal years.

During the 1960s, much of this area stagnated economically and lost population. In the 1970s, this changed, in part due to increased interest in coal mining. But the picture clouded in the 1980s with the downturn in the coal and petrochemical industries.

Licking County is a pocket of prosperity; the Newark-Granville-Heath metropolitan area is a growing center for manufacturing and research, with Owens-Corning and Diebold as major employers. Dow Chemical and the Newark Air Force station have large civilian research facilities in the 10th.

Fairfield County has seen more growth in recent years than almost any part of the 10th, as bedroom communities blossomed along Route 33, a four-lane highway connecting Lancaster with the thriving city of Columbus, 30 miles northwest.

Athens County has a number of government employers, including Ohio University, with over 16,000 students; that cushions it somewhat from adverse economic conditions. Athens and Perry counties make up the Democratic-leaning part of the district. Athens was one of just two Ohio counties to support George McGovern for president in 1972; in 1988, Michael S. Dukakis carried it with 52 percent. The Democratic influence is counterbalanced by neighboring Morgan and Meigs counties, where the GOP has a better than 2-to-1 registration advantage. Many of the poorer voters in other counties along the Ohio River still call themselves Democrats — a remnant of Civil War days — but their conservative outlook leads them toward GOP candidates in most elections.

Population: 514,173. White 499,615 (97%), Black 10,925 (2%). Spanish origin 2,519 (1%). 18 and over 362,509 (71%), 65 and over 57,433 (11%). Median age: 30.

Committees

Appropriations (3rd of 22 Republicans)
Defense

Elections

1990 General		
Clarence E. Miller (R)	106,009	(63%)
John M. Buchanan (D)	61,656	(37%)
1988 General		
Clarence E. Miller (R)	143,673	(72%)
John M. Buchanan (D)	56,893	(28%)

Previous Winning Percentages: **1986** (70%) **1984** (73%) **1982** (63%) **1980** (74%) **1978** (74%) **1976** (69%) **1974** (70%) **1972** (73%) **1970** (67%) **1968** (69%) **1966** (52%)

District Vote For President

	1988		1984		1980		1976	
D	79,268	(38%)	67,532	(33%)	75,455	(39%)	85,428	(47%)
R	125,373	(61%)	136,089	(66%)	108,319	(55%)	92,932	(51%)
I					8,550	(4%)		

Campaign Finance

	Receipts	Receipts from PACs		Expend-itures
1990				
Miller (R)	$99,589	$71,250	(72%)	$75,367
1988				
Miller (R)	$129,695	$99,436	(77%)	$99,247
Buchanan (D)	$9,231	0		$9,429

Key Votes

1991	
Authorize use of force against Iraq	Y
1990	
Support constitutional amendment on flag desecration	Y
Pass family and medical leave bill over Bush veto	N
Reduce SDI funding	?
Allow abortions in overseas military facilities	N
Approve budget summit plan for spending and taxing	Y
Approve civil rights bill	N
1989	
Halt production of B-2 stealth bomber at 13 planes	N
Oppose capital gains tax cut	N
Approve federal abortion funding in rape or incest cases	N
Approve pay raise and revision of ethics rules	N
Pass Democratic minimum wage plan over Bush veto	N

Voting Studies

	Presidential Support		Party Unity		Conservative Coalition	
Year	**S**	**O**	**S**	**O**	**S**	**O**
1990	68	29	87	10	89	9
1989	76	20	85	13	100	0
1988	62	38	85	13	95	5
1987	60	28	77	15	86	0
1986	77	22	83	14	86	14
1985	70	24	79	11	85	7
1984	60	38	84	16	83	17
1983	68	29	80	18	73	25
1982	70	30	80	18	78	22
1981	72	28	86	14	91	9

Interest Group Ratings

Year	ADA	ACU	AFL-CIO	CCUS
1990	0	91	25	71
1989	0	100	17	100
1988	15	92	43	93
1987	8	100	13	71
1986	5	86	14	78
1985	0	89	0	85
1984	5	71	8	75
1983	15	91	6	74
1982	5	96	25	64
1981	5	100	20	84

11 Dennis E. Eckart (D)

Of Mentor — Elected 1980

Born: April 6, 1950, Cleveland, Ohio.
Education: Xavier U., B.S. 1971; Cleveland State U., J.D. 1974.
Occupation: Lawyer.
Family: Wife, Sandra Pestotnik; one child.
Religion: Roman Catholic.
Political Career: Lake County assistant prosecutor, 1974; Ohio House, 1975-81.
Capitol Office: 1111 Longworth Bldg.20515; 225-6331.

In Washington: In early October of 1990, when the House leadership went about the difficult task of selling a bipartisan budget package with tax increases, they tapped Eckart to help rally votes on the floor. But as it became clear that Republicans were not going to deliver their share of votes, Eckart jumped ship. He told the Cleveland *Plain Dealer* afterwards, "The more the fine print was read, the more troublesome the bill became for Democrats, myself included."

The budget vote exemplifies Eckart's ambiguous status in the House; although dubbed a rising star throughout much of his congressional tenure, he does not display the loyalty that typically precedes advancement. In the 101st Congress, Eckart also broke with the leadership to vote against a congressional pay raise and for a constitutional amendment banning flag desecration. To cast the flag vote, Eckart had to leave the Washington, D.C., hospital where he was being treated for kidney stones.

Instead, Eckart seems most concerned with cementing his hold on the suburban Cleveland district he has held since 1980. First elected at age 30, he quickly drew attention on Capitol Hill as a politician who melded reform-minded liberalism with old-school politicking. He won a whip's post in his freshman term, and a seat on Energy and Commerce the next.

Eckart has prospered on the committee, where he is known as one of Chairman John D. Dingell's favorites. The two have a strong personal relationship, bolstered by time spent pursuing the chairman's favorite sport, hunting. It is an unusual but legislatively useful interest for a native of the streets of Cleveland.

On Energy and Commerce, Eckart's home-state concerns often coincide with the interests of Dingell's Detroit-area voters. Eckart does not always vote with Dingell, however. His standing also reflects colleagues' respect for his ability to master the details of highly technical issues that come before the committee. Those issues have often forced Eckart to make difficult choices between his seeming environmental leanings and the needs of his industry-dependent district.

Ohio power plants emit more of the pollutants said to cause acid rain than any other state, making Eckart resist stringent measures aimed at their elimination. In 1984, he cast the decisive vote on the Health Subcommittee that doomed acid-rain legislation that year.

But Eckart played a more constructive role in the subsequent debates over clean air legislation. In the 100th Congress, he was a member of the committee's moderate "group of nine" that tried to negotiate a compromise acceptable to industry and environmentalists.

As the major clean air reauthorization bill wound its way through the 101st, Eckart fought for protections for Ohio utilities, such as pollution credits that could be bought and sold among utilities to help them comply with new emissions standards. But he also pushed for strong measures to combat urban smog, and to get a bill passed that session.

During the 101st, Eckart sponsored a bill requiring the federal government to comply with its own solid and hazardous waste rules at federal facilities. And when the 100th Congress debated nuclear-accident insurance legislation, Eckart was a leader in the environmental-consumer faction. He teamed up with Energy and Commerce liberals Gerry Sikorski of Minnesota and Edward J. Markey of Massachusetts to try to increase safety incentives, victims' compensation and industry accountability. It was not a popular cause with Dingell, nor a success in the committee, but it did gratify neighbors of the Perry nuclear plant in Eckart's district.

Eckart's pro-nuclear critics said he was trying to gut the law, originally drafted in 1957 to help encourage civilian nuclear power by limiting risks that might discourage investors. But Eckart, rarely at a loss for a pithy quote, countered that it was time to "take the training wheels off" the industry. He called the bill a "K-Mart blue-light special for the nuclear-power industry," and a "raw deal for the taxpayers."

By contrast, in the previous Congress, Eckart was at odds with committee environmentalists over the "superfund" hazardous-waste cleanup program. While Eckart, too, wanted to

Ohio 11

Northeast — Cleveland Suburbs

The small industrial cities of northeast Ohio have shared in Cleveland's economic problems, but not in its emerging solutions. Reliant on the steel, chemical and automobile industries for jobs, the blue-collar communities of the 11th District are among the most depressed parts of the state.

Ashtabula County, on Lake Erie, casts about a fifth of the vote. Employment there has recovered only modestly since the early 1980s recession, when the jobless rate hit 20 percent. The steel and chemical plants situated along Lake Erie have been severely hurt by foreign competition, and it is hard to find signs of revival. Ashtabula is reliably Democratic in most elections; only a strong GOP county organization keeps the party's candidates close.

Southwest of Ashtabula is equally Democratic Portage County, sandwiched between Youngstown on the east and Akron on the west. Ravenna and Kent are in the middle of the county.

As migration from Cleveland moved eastward between 1950 and 1970, the population of Lake and Geauga counties more than doubled. The rapid growth has slowed, but the suburbs continue to creep farther east, obliterating the truck gardens and vineyards along Lake Erie.

Lake County's Republican farmers and suburbanites are canceled out politically by ethnic Democrats who have settled in the western part of the county.

Settled by Yankee Protestants, Geauga County is GOP country. Successful GOP gubernatorial nominee George V. Voinovich took 70 percent here in 1990. However, the county usually does not offset the Democratic vote elsewhere; it casts only about 15 percent of the district vote.

Population: 514,173. White 499,454 (97%), Black 10,438 (2%), Other 2,800 (1%). Spanish origin 3,224 (1%). 18 and over 355,787 (69%), 65 and over 43,049 (8%). Median age: 29.

enlarge the fund, the bill's sponsor, James J. Florio of New Jersey, pushed for stricter cleanup standards. Eckart complained that Florio's bill would never win bipartisan support and belonged "in a time capsule" rather than in a practical legislative debate. The Ohioan won a bruising committee fight, but the full House restored much of what Florio wanted.

In that episode, Eckart was credited for his grasp of the issue, but he lost points when he lashed out at environmental groups that claimed his proposals would benefit polluters. He complained of "character besmirchment" by a "few shrill extremists" with an "insatiable appetite" for more concessions.

While the Clean Air Act took up much of Eckart's time during the 101st Congress, some of his other causes included efforts to restrict spending on the superconducting super collider project in Texas, and to authorize Secret Service agents to investigate wrongdoing at savings and loans.

Eckart also dabbles in national politics. Since 1987, he has been a regional chairman of the Democratic Congressional Campaign Committee, and in 1988, he was an early supporter of Michael S. Dukakis' campaign. Eckart played the role of Dan Quayle during Sen. Lloyd Bentsen's vice presidential debate preparations.

At Home: Eckart's rather rapid move into a position of influence in the House was no shock to those who had watched his quick rise in the Ohio Legislature. First elected to the state House at age 25, Eckart became known as a consumer affairs specialist who pushed through a bill giving state-subsidized tax credits to the elderly for their energy bills.

Eckart was in line to become chairman of the state House Judiciary Committee in 1980, but decided instead to run for the seat of retiring Democratic Rep. Charles A. Vanik. Eckart's principal primary rival was maverick state Sen. J. Timothy McCormack, who accused him of being "a classic go-along person."

Eckart had the benefit of a good organization and the support of the popular Vanik: McCormack had antagonized Vanik loyalists by jumping into the contest before the incumbent — who loathed fundraising — had decided whether to retire. Eckart won the primary by nearly 12,000 votes; he went on to defeat Republican Joseph Nahra, a former probate judge, with 55 percent.

Eckart then had to skillfully navigate the shoals of redistricting, taking over a brand-new — but favorable — constituency. The Ohio Legislature, redrawing the congressional district map to adjust for the loss of two House seats, gutted Eckart's old 22nd District in Cleveland's eastern suburbs, leaving Eckart with a complicated series of options.

He planned at first to follow most of his constituents into the reshaped 19th District, taking a chance on a primary campaign against the more conservative Democratic Rep. Ronald M. Mottl. But when GOP Rep. J. William Stanton announced he was retiring, the 11th became more attractive to Eckart, although it contained barely 15 percent of his former constituents. The young Democrat moved from Euclid to the 11th District community of Concord Township, near Madison, where he grew up.

Eckart portrayed himself as the incumbent, papering the district with franked mail, blaming President Reagan's economic policy for the troubles of northeast Ohio and talking about his rising stature in Congress. With his superior organization, campaign treasury and talent for attracting media attention, Eckart swept past two rivals in the Democratic primary and won easily in the fall.

After two lopsided victories, Eckart felt secure in 1988 and began dedicating considerable time to the Dukakis campaign. But his GOP foe, social worker Margaret Mueller, began making enough noise to draw Eckart back home by late fall.

Eckart had defeated Mueller decisively in a 1986 campaign that received little attention. But in 1988, Mueller came on strong with a vituperative campaign that surprised the Democrat. She poured $500,000 of her own money into the campaign, and ran TV ads that criticized Eckart as soft on crime and drugs.

Mueller outspent Eckart until late in the campaign, when he fired back. Saying she had "earned a gold medal for sleaze," Eckart ran TV ads that featured a chicken scampering back and forth across a street — symbolizing Mueller changing positions. Eckart also issued a mailing that included a photo of Mueller and the caption, "Good Girls Shouldn't Lie."

On Election Day, Eckart's percentage dropped 10 points from 1986, but he still surpassed 60 percent of the vote. The victory established Eckart's security. With no other well-known Republican willing to take Eckart on in 1990, Mueller again volunteered, but lacked her former zeal and willingness to spend her own money. While most Ohio House incumbents lost several percentage points to the electorate's general displeasure with Congress, Eckart bounced back to 66 percent.

Committees

Energy & Commerce (12th of 27 Democrats)
Oversight & Investigations; Telecommunications & Finance; Transportation & Hazardous Materials

Small Business (8th of 27 Democrats)
Antitrust, Impact of Deregulation & Ecology (chairman)

Elections

1990 General

Dennis E. Eckart (D)	111,923	(66%)
Margaret Mueller (R)	58,372	(34%)

1988 General

Dennis E. Eckart (D)	124,600	(61%)
Margaret Mueller (R)	78,028	(39%)

Previous Winning Percentages: **1986** (72%) **1984** (67%) **1982** (61%) **1980** (55%)

District Vote For President

	1988	1984	1980	1976
D	93,486 (44%)	84,171 (40%)	66,054 (37%)	89,687 (50%)
R	115,947 (55%)	125,163 (59%)	93,307 (53%)	84,438 (47%)
I			14,025 (8%)	

Campaign Finance

	Receipts	Receipts from PACs	Expend-itures
1990			
Eckart (D)	$510,699	$371,536 (73%)	$453,883
Mueller (R)	$66,674	0	$72,686
1988			
Eckart (D)	$569,638	$382,928 (67%)	$561,070
Mueller (R)	$1,006,371	0	$860,766

Key Votes

1991	
Authorize use of force against Iraq	N
1990	
Support constitutional amendment on flag desecration	Y
Pass family and medical leave bill over Bush veto	Y
Reduce SDI funding	Y
Allow abortions in overseas military facilities	Y
Approve budget summit plan for spending and taxing	N
Approve civil rights bill	Y
1989	
Halt production of B-2 stealth bomber at 13 planes	Y
Oppose capital gains tax cut	Y
Approve federal abortion funding in rape or incest cases	Y
Approve pay raise and revision of ethics rules	N
Pass Democratic minimum wage plan over Bush veto	Y

Voting Studies

	Presidential Support		Party Unity		Conservative Coalition	
Year	**S**	**O**	**S**	**O**	**S**	**O**
1990	20	79	83	15	46	52
1989	31	69	87	12	44	56
1988	21	78	88	12	37	63
1987	19	80	87	11	42	58
1986	21	78	87	13	40	60
1985	24	76	88	10	35	65
1984	31	67	81	16	27	71
1983	18	82	84	14	26	74
1982	31	64	87	10	21	78
1981	33	63	82	17	25	68

Interest Group Ratings

Year	ADA	ACU	AFL-CIO	CCUS
1990	56	29	92	29
1989	90	18	83	40
1988	90	8	100	29
1987	88	4	94	29
1986	65	14	86	22
1985	70	19	76	36
1984	75	17	77	25
1983	90	9	94	20
1982	70	36	95	23
1981	80	15	87	11

12 John R. Kasich (R)

Of Westerville — Elected 1982

Born: May 13, 1952, McKees Rocks, Pa.
Education: Ohio State U., B.A. 1974.
Occupation: Legislative aide.
Family: Divorced.
Religion: Roman Catholic.
Political Career: Ohio Senate, 1979-83.
Capitol Office: 1133 Longworth Bldg. 20515; 225-5355.

In Washington: Perpetually in motion, Kasich is a whirlwind of restless energy. While some of that energy fuels a drive for self-promotion that nettles colleagues, Kasich is gaining credit for his efforts to apply conservative fiscal principles across the federal budget.

Like most Republicans, Kasich — who is in his second term on the Budget Committee — has argued for domestic spending restraints. But Kasich differs from most young conservative firebrands in his willingness to take on defense spending programs as well.

He does so from a position of increasing seniority on the Armed Services Committee. It was from there that Kasich launched his most audacious budget-cutting effort: the elimination of the B-2 bomber.

Planned as the high-tech replacement for the aging fleet of B-52 bombers, the bat-winged stealth aircraft was touted by the Reagan and Bush administrations for its radar-evading capabilities. However, even advocates of the B-2 program were rocked early in 1989 by reports that the cost of each bomber had risen to over $600 million, raising the total price of the planned fleet to more than $70 billion.

Kasich, expressing concern that the B-2 would soak up too much of the defense budget, stepped out front with a small group of GOP conservatives who called themselves "cheap hawks." He also struck an unusual alliance with California Rep. Ronald V. Dellums, an arms control advocate and one of the most liberal House Democrats, in an effort to scrap the B-2.

Kasich provided a strategic justification for the cutback. He said that with the development of highly accurate air-launched cruise missiles that elude enemy air defenses, the need for a manned bomber to do the same thing had greatly diminished. However, his main case against the B-2 was budgetary. "We don't have the money to pay for this," he said.

The campaign to kill the B-2 fell short in 1989. A Kasich amendment to the defense authorization bill, which would have limited B-2 production to the 13 planes then being built, was defeated by 144-279.

However, the subsequent fall of communism in Eastern Europe and the warming of U.S.-Soviet relations boosted Kasich's cause. Kasich, along with Dellums and other allies, lobbied to line up commitments; by July 1990, it appeared that a new stealth-axing measure would carry in the House. At that point, Armed Services Chairman Les Aspin got on board, ensuring its inclusion in the fiscal 1991 House defense authorization bill.

The Senate, however, passed a bill that included funding for the Defense Department request of two B-2s to add to the 15 already authorized. With powerful Senate Armed Services Committee Chairman Sam Nunn holding the line, a House-Senate conference settled on $2.35 billion for the B-2 program.

The ambiguous language of the conference report led to conflicting interpretations of the health of stealth. Nunn insisted that nothing in the law precluded the production of additional planes. However, Kasich said the sense of Congress was that the additional funds were to be used only on the already authorized bombers, and promised to continue his efforts in the 102nd Congress to apply the *coup de grâce* to the B-2.

Kasich has also taken on the Pentagon's "black budget" of secret weapons programs whose classified nature makes them difficult for Congress to monitor. His efforts obtained credibility in January 1991, when Defense Secretary Dick Cheney canceled the A-12, an advanced, carrier-based "black budget" bomber plagued by hidden cost overruns.

Kasich's zeal for Pentagon efficiency dates to his early days in the House. As a freshman, he teamed with veteran Alabama Democrat Bill Nichols of Alabama to lead a House inquiry into the high price the Pentagon was paying to get spare parts for weaponry.

Kasich takes pride in the maverick status he has earned with his defense budget-watching. "Some people have remarked that my efforts as a conservative Republican to eliminate waste in the Pentagon is a classic man-bites-dog story," he says.

Ohio 12

Northeast Columbus and Suburbs

Columbus has not suffered from the kind of economic collapse that has afflicted most of Ohio's industrial cities in the past few years. It is primarily a white-collar town, one whose diverse industrial base is bolstered by the state government complex, a major banking center and numerous scientific research firms.

No longer is Columbus recognized only for the Ohio State University football team; an economic renaissance in the early 1990s led a slew of national publications to list the city as one of the most progressive and prosperous.

Nearly three-quarters of the 12th District vote is cast in Columbus and its Franklin County suburbs. Democrats must do very well in the city to have a chance districtwide.

Blacks make up 23 percent of Columbus' population but are split evenly between the 12th and 15th districts, reducing Democratic prospects in both.

As one moves east from the state Capitol building along Broad Street, the black Democratic vote goes down and the Republican vote goes up.

About three miles east of the Capitol is affluent Bexley, an independent community of 13,000 surrounded by the city.

While normally Republican, Bexley has a large Jewish population and sometimes votes for strong Democratic candidates. Two miles farther east is Whitehall, another independent town. Site of the Defense Construction Supply Center, it has a large blue-collar base with frequent ticket-splitting.

Farther out are newer suburbs. Some of these, such as Reynoldsburg and Gahanna, are predominantly blue-collar. Residents are employed at large plants such as McDonnell Douglas and AT&T.

The rest of the 12th is rural and Republican, with a smattering of light industry. The half of Licking County in the district often gives Kasich a 3-to-1 margin, and Delaware and Morrow counties are equally favorable to Republican candidates.

Population: 514,173. White 430,939 (84%), Black 77,731 (15%), Other 3,233 (1%). Spanish origin 3,534 (1%). 18 and over 366,117 (71%), 65 and over 42,505 (8%). Median age: 29.

However, Kasich's defense belt-tightening efforts do not indicate any shifting from his ideological moorings. On most defense issues, he is on the right flank of Armed Services, with such new-breed Republicans as Duncan Hunter of California and Jon Kyl of Arizona.

A staunch advocate of the strategic defense initiative (SDI), Kasich takes particular umbrage at efforts by other members to shift funds from that program to their own pet defense projects.

In 1988, Kasich asked his committee colleagues if they had adopted any "parochial add-ons" to the defense authorization bill that could be jettisoned. When Aspin jokingly rejoined that "all of the add-ons here are essential to the national defense," Kasich did not seem to see the humor. "That's what I thought," he shot back.

Kasich himself can wax sarcastic about liberal Democrats who advocate deep military cutbacks, but go to the mat to save defense "pork" for their districts. As New York Democrat Thomas J. Downey battled the elimination of the F-14 fighter plane in the 101th Congress, Kasich took to calling him "Jimmy Dean," after a brand of pork sausage.

It is not unusual for Kasich's defense rhetoric to take on a partisan cast. In 1987, he cautioned Democrats against slashing President Reagan's defense spending request, warning that voters might retaliate at the ballot box. "You put those [cutbacks] together and that is not where the American people are at," Kasich said.

Kasich's drive for overall fiscal stringency informs his work on the Budget Committee. He has taken to offering his own budget alternatives in recent years.

In 1989, Kasich proposed a federal budget freeze, which would have held all discretionary spending at fiscal 1989 levels while cutting Medicare by $2.7 billion. The bill was swamped by a 30-393 vote. Kasich's 1990 proposal went somewhat further, freezing all domestic and defense spending levels, slicing Medicare by $3.2 billion and providing $13 billion in increased revenues. This bill did better, but still went down by 106-305.

Although both his budget bills lost badly, Kasich gained a place at the budget-crafting table. When the budget summit deal between President Bush and congressional leaders collapsed in early October 1990, Kasich was tapped by the GOP leadership along with Michigan Republican Rep. Carl Pursell to draft an alternative. Their proposal, which claimed to reduce the federal deficit by $417 billion over five years without tax increases, gained some praise in the House Republican Conference, but

Democrats blocked it from reaching a floor vote.

Along with his sweeping attempts to realign the budget, Kasich often takes a "micro" approach. For instance, an authorization bill passed by the House in April 1989 contained a Kasich amendment requiring the State Department and United States Information Agency to use private collection agencies to handle their delinquent debts. The bill also contained another anti-waste provision authored by Kasich: It limited the number of officials at a U.S. embassy entitled to "extraordinarily" spacious housing for purposes of official entertainment.

At Home: When Kasich won a House seat in 1982, his district stood out as a political oddity. In 1980, a Republican year nationally, district voters turned out a GOP incumbent for Democrat Bob Shamansky. In 1982, a recession year marked by Democratic House gains, Kasich unseated Shamansky.

However, Kasich moved with ease to reestablish a Republican pattern in the 12th. He won his first re-election with 70 percent, and has not fallen below that mark since.

Republican officials had targeted the 12th in 1982. They considered Shamansky's 1980 victory a fluke, due more to the complacency of GOP Rep. Samuel Devine than to any change in the district's traditional Republican leanings.

Although Shamansky had the advantage of incumbency, Kasich was well-positioned for his challenge. A redistricting plan, passed by the Legislature in which Kasich served, added a rural, predominantly Republican area to the 12th while removing some heavily black wards on the east side of Columbus.

Although Shamansky carried Franklin County (Columbus), his margin was not enough to overcome Kasich's lead in the rural counties. Kasich won with 51 percent of the vote.

An energetic grass-roots campaigner, Kasich entered electoral politics by upsetting a veteran Democratic state senator in 1978. He visited every household in his district several times during that campaign.

Committees

Armed Services (8th of 22 Republicans)
Readiness (ranking); Procurement & Military Nuclear Systems

Budget (8th of 14 Republicans)
Human Resources (ranking); Defense, Foreign Policy & Space Economic Policy, Projections & Revenues

Elections

1990 General

John R. Kasich (R)	130,495	(72%)
Mike Gelpi (D)	50,784	(28%)

1988 General

John R. Kasich (R)	154,727	(79%)
Mark P. Brown (D)	41,178	(21%)

Previous Winning Percentages: **1986** (73%) **1984** (70%) **1982** (51%)

District Vote For President

	1988	1984	1980	1976
D	83,561 (38%)	72,607 (33%)	79,143 (39%)	79,422 (42%)
R	133,563 (61%)	144,741 (65%)	110,235 (54%)	105,399 (56%)
I			10,361 (5%)	

Campaign Finance

	Receipts	Receipts from PACs		Expenditures
1990				
Kasich (R)	$328,624	$128,715	(39%)	$278,977
Gelpi (D)	$42,854	$5,463	(13%)	$47,815
1988				
Kasich (R)	$370,579	$130,686	(35%)	$351,517

Key Votes

1991

Authorize use of force against Iraq	Y

1990

Support constitutional amendment on flag desecration	Y
Pass family and medical leave bill over Bush veto	N
Reduce SDI funding	N
Allow abortions in overseas military facilities	N
Approve budget summit plan for spending and taxing	N
Approve civil rights bill	N

1989

Halt production of B-2 stealth bomber at 13 planes	Y
Oppose capital gains tax cut	N
Approve federal abortion funding in rape or incest cases	N
Approve pay raise and revision of ethics rules	N
Pass Democratic minimum wage plan over Bush veto	N

Voting Studies

	Presidential Support		Party Unity		Conservative Coalition	
Year	**S**	**O**	**S**	**O**	**S**	**O**
1990	69	30	78	19	94	6
1989	70	29	68	30	90	10
1988	61	38	76	20	100	0
1987	68	31	74	21	93	5
1986	70	29	75	22	88	12
1985	74	26	90	7	98	2
1984	61	38	82	17	92	8
1983	77	23	90	10	87	13

Interest Group Ratings

Year	ADA	ACU	AFL-CIO	CCUS
1990	11	92	17	86
1989	20	100	9	90
1988	15	92	29	93
1987	8	78	0	93
1986	10	82	29	89
1985	5	90	12	86
1984	5	67	23	75
1983	10	91	6	85

13 Don J. Pease (D)

Of Oberlin — Elected 1976

Born: Sept. 26, 1931, Toledo, Ohio.
Education: Ohio U., B.S. 1953, M.A. 1955; attended U. of Durham, England, 1954-55.
Military Service: Army, 1955-57.
Occupation: Newspaper editor.
Family: Wife, Jeanne Wendt; one child.
Religion: Methodist.
Political Career: Oberlin City Council, 1962-64; Ohio Senate, 1965-67 and 1975-77; Ohio House, 1969-75; defeated for re-election to Ohio Senate, 1966.
Capitol Office: 2410 Rayburn Bldg. 20515; 225-3401.

In Washington: Late in his 14th year in Congress, Pease started appearing in news headlines far beyond the small-town precincts of Ohio where he was once a newspaper editor. His plan for extracting more tax dollars from the affluent became his party's rallying point in budget-summit negotiations with President Bush. And his conditional approach to renewing trade relations with China, worked out in cooperation with the White House, provided a compromise solution to another stalemate. For a season, "the Pease plan" became a common phrase in the Capitol.

Through most of his first seven terms, however, the soft-spoken Pease has been something of an enigma on the Ways and Means Committee. He approaches politics as an ethical pursuit and legislation as an intellectual exercise.

His success is largely predicated on an unlikely alliance with Chairman Dan Rostenkowski, the veteran product of Chicago machine politics. Loyalty is the first word in any relationship with the chairman, and Pease abides by it. He also has a personable nature and a shared interest with Rostenkowski in taking care of blue-collar workers. All this has helped Pease have a hand in most major bills that have passed through Ways and Means in recent years. At the beginning of the 102nd Congress, Pease moved into one of three seats on the Budget Committee reserved for Ways and Means members.

When the budget summit between congressional leaders and the Bush administration foundered on tax policy in the fall of 1990, Pease refined a plan he had been pushing for months and, with Rostenkowski's help, sold it to both sides. The Pease plan cuts back itemized deductions by 3 percent of the amount by which a taxpayer's income exceeds $100,000.

In the same autumn, the House passed legislation requiring the president to find that China was making "significant progress" toward human-rights goals before renewing China's "most favored nation" trade status. The plan specified the freeing of political prisoners and easing of media restrictions.

By working with Pease, the Bush administration headed off more severe restrictions on Chinese trade pushed by other members in both parties. But the House took so long to finish the bill that the 101st Congress ended before the Senate could act.

The China question was back in 1991, alongside a hot new wrangle over a proposed free-trade agreement with Mexico. As in the Chinese case, Pease found himself torn between promoting world economic growth through free trade and protecting jobs in his economically troubled industrial district.

"A lot of workers will simply lose their jobs as whole factories are shipped down to Mexico," he said as the free-trade debate gained steam. On substance, Pease had leaned toward the protectionist side of the debate as a member of the Trade Subcommittee and the 1987 conference committee on the omnibus trade bill. But even then, he argued for compromise and a cooling in the rhetorical war.

The 1987 bill included a handful of Pease-inspired amendments, including a proposal that combined his labor interest with an interest in human rights abroad — an interest he had pursued on the Foreign Affairs Committee earlier in his career.

Arguing that American workers cannot compete with imports produced by exploited workers in foreign countries, Pease successfully pushed for language on international labor standards. Closer to home, Pease argued that the federal government's fiscal policies, particularly the budget deficit, are a major cause of the nation's trade deficit. He authored a successful trade amendment requiring "trade impact statements" in the president's and the Congress' budgets. With these, legislators can "take into account the impact of the budget on our

Ohio 13

North — Lorain

Lying squarely in the midst of industrial northern Ohio, the 13th has all the problems of a declining Frost Belt economy. Heavily dependent on the automobile and steel industries, populous Lorain County approached Depression-era conditions in the early 1980s.

The most serious trouble spot is the once-booming port city of Lorain. But while the local economy there has been battered, the old New Deal coalition is alive and well. Blue-collar ethnics, blacks and Hispanics in Lorain combine with those in nearby Elyria and academics in the college town of Oberlin to produce Democratic majorities. Walter F. Mondale and Pease each won the city of Lorain with 80 percent in 1984, although President Ronald Reagan carried Lorain County. Four years later, even the countywide vote was Democratic; Michael S. Dukakis eked out a 51 percent victory there.

As one of the traditional immigration centers on the Great Lakes, the city of Lorain has an ethnic diversity that matches the West Side of Cleveland. Fifty-six different ethnic groups have been counted within its borders. Today, Hispanics alone comprise 17 percent of Lorain's population, a far higher share than in any city in Ohio.

About 10 miles due south of Lorain is Oberlin, which roughly divides urban, Catholic Democrats in the northern part of the district from rural, Protestant Republicans in the southern part. Founded in 1833, Oberlin College was the first coeducational institution of higher learning in the country and among the first to admit black students. The Yankees who founded Oberlin and other towns in this part of Ohio took strong anti-slavery stands in the 19th century, and their descendants (such as Pease) have continued to show an affinity for social reforms and causes of various kinds, including civil rights and the anti-war movement.

South and west is rural Republican territory. Some farms in this area raise grains and livestock, but the emphasis is on dairy products, fruits and vegetables. Democrats can normally count on support in Richland County, especially from the industrial city of Mansfield. But Ashland County usually rewards statewide Republican candidates with 60 percent or more of the vote.

Population: 514,176. White 477,543 (93%), Black 26,559 (5%). Spanish origin 14,618 (3%). 18 and over 350,858 (68%), 65 and over 44,544 (9%). Median age: 28.

trade accounts and international competitiveness while they draft the budget," he said, "not after it has been passed and the damage is done."

Pease also was active in the 1988 debate on the welfare reform bill. He co-authored successful language with Henry A. Waxman of California to require states to provide coverage to families that move off public assistance for six months, and then to extend certain coverage for an additional 18 months if the family's income does not exceed 185 percent of the federal poverty level.

As a former journalist, Pease has long supported "sunshine" open government rules, but he is also an experienced legislator. "I hate to say it, but members are more willing to make tough decisions on controversial bills in closed meetings," he once said. "In a closed meeting, you can come out and say, 'I fought like a tiger for you in there, but I lost.' "

During the many closed conference markups on the 1986 tax overhaul, Pease was a reliable source for reporters. But when Rostenkowski instructed members to stop leaking news, Pease complied. Given that he had been handpicked by Rostenkowski for the conference committee (over eight more senior members), that was an astute move. Pease had waited a long time for a chance to overhaul the tax system, and he was not going to deal himself out of the process just to help his former colleagues in the media. Pease supported the final House bill for its lower rates on the poor and the middle class and its cuts in subsidies for corporations and the wealthy.

At Home: Ohio voters had a generally grumpy attitude toward Washington in 1990. While none of the state's House incumbents was seriously threatened, most fell several points below their normal performances.

Pease suffered one of the sharpest dropoffs of all. After defeating a weak Republican opponent with 70 percent of the vote in 1988, Pease slipped by 13 points in 1990.

Ironically, the usually low-profile Pease was penalized for his emergence in a public role during the budget debate. Although his efforts conformed with the Democratic intent of shifting more of the tax burden to the wealthy, he was attacked by local critics for crafting a tax increase. He also took some heat for voting in favor of the congressional pay raise and for voting against the flag-burning amendment.

Pease also had to deal with a Republican challenger who was no patsy. William D. Nielsen, a well-financed business executive, had given Pease a sporting race as the GOP nominee in 1986, losing 63-37 percent. In 1990, he took Pease down to 57 percent, a career low. Pease nonetheless was able to win with a rather substantial cushion, an outcome attributable to his deep political roots in the 13th District.

Pease had some trouble getting his political career off the ground. After one term in the state Senate, he lost re-election in 1966. He switched to the Ohio House, spent three terms there, then made it back to the state Senate by defeating a GOP incumbent in 1974.

During his legislative career, Pease was a close ally of Ohio's teachers. The state teachers' union joined with other labor organizations in backing Pease's 1976 successful bid to replace retiring Republican Rep. Charles A. Mosher. Despite their partisan differences, the incumbent and his Democratic successor were longtime friends: Pease had succeeded Mosher as editor of the *Oberlin News-Tribune*.

Pease won the 1976 election by about 2-to-1, a margin he matched against middling Republican competition in most of his re-election campaigns. However, he appeared to have a more serious challenge on his hands in his first matchup with Nielsen in 1986.

Nielsen blanketed the district with billboards, direct-mail appeals and postcards in an aggressive campaign that sought to discredit Pease as a big-spending liberal who had not looked out for the area's troubled manufacturing interests.

But Pease proved to be less vulnerable than Nielsen hoped. The low-key incumbent had a place in the Washington spotlight during the summer of 1986 as a House conferee on the tax-revision bill. That time, Pease's position on Ways and Means earned him favorable publicity back home, and helped him build the largest campaign treasury to that point of his career.

Pease defeated Nielsen in every county in the district, then had a 1988 breather before having to gear up for another Nielsen onslaught in 1990.

Committees

Budget (16th of 23 Democrats)
Defense, Foreign Policy & Space; Economic Policy, Projections & Revenues; Urgent Fiscal Issues

Ways & Means (12th of 23 Democrats)
Trade

Elections

1990 General		
Don J. Pease (D)	93,431	(57%)
William D. Nielsen (R)	60,925	(37%)
John Michael Ryan (I)	10,506	(6%)
1988 General		
Don J. Pease (D)	137,074	(70%)
Dwight Brown (R)	59,287	(30%)

Previous Winning Percentages: **1986** (63%) **1984** (66%) **1982** (61%) **1980** (64%) **1978** (65%) **1976** (66%)

District Vote For President

	1988	1984	1980	1976
D	93,620 (46%)	84,403 (40%)	67,998 (37%)	86,395 (51%)
R	109,701 (54%)	121,317 (58%)	98,859 (53%)	77,579 (46%)
I			12,439 (7%)	

Campaign Finance

	Receipts	Receipts from PACs	Expend-itures
1990			
Pease (D)	$311,899	$184,728 (59%)	$348,032
Nielsen (R)	$125,580	0	$124,483
1988			
Pease (D)	$292,904	$189,677 (65%)	$157,632
Brown (R)	$16,681	0	$16,682

Key Votes

1991	
Authorize use of force against Iraq	N
1990	
Support constitutional amendment on flag desecration	N
Pass family and medical leave bill over Bush veto	Y
Reduce SDI funding	Y
Allow abortions in overseas military facilities	Y
Approve budget summit plan for spending and taxing	Y
Approve civil rights bill	Y
1989	
Halt production of B-2 stealth bomber at 13 planes	Y
Oppose capital gains tax cut	Y
Approve federal abortion funding in rape or incest cases	Y
Approve pay raise and revision of ethics rules	Y
Pass Democratic minimum wage plan over Bush veto	Y

Voting Studies

	Presidential Support		Party Unity		Conservative Coalition	
Year	**S**	**O**	**S**	**O**	**S**	**O**
1990	30	69	87	10	19	81
1989	30	66	86	11	27	71
1988	29	69	88	9	24	71
1987	25	74	90	8	30	65
1986	26	74	92	8	32	68
1985	28	71	93	7	20	80
1984	40	59	85	15	22	78
1983	20	80	91	9	18	82
1982	38	61	87	11	16	81
1981	32	64	83	9	16	77

Interest Group Ratings

Year	ADA	ACU	AFL-CIO	CCUS
1990	89	4	92	21
1989	90	0	91	10
1988	90	8	86	50
1987	88	0	88	7
1986	75	18	79	17
1985	70	14	82	38
1984	80	8	62	25
1983	90	4	88	35
1982	90	5	100	23
1981	95	0	93	6

14 Tom Sawyer (D)

Of Akron — Elected 1986

Born: Aug. 15, 1945, Akron, Ohio.
Education: U. of Akron, B.A. 1968, M.A. 1970.
Occupation: Teacher.
Family: Wife, Joyce Handler; one child.
Religion: Presbyterian.
Political Career: Ohio House, 1977-83; mayor of Akron, 1984-86.
Capitol Office: 1518 Longworth Bldg. 20515; 225-5231.

In Washington: Sawyer is more introverted than many politicians, but he stood out from the crowd in 1989, when he began chairing a subcommittee — a rare responsibility for a second-term member. His subcommittee on the census oversees an area very important to House members — the count dictates the apportionment of House districts for the 1990s — and Sawyer has been cautious in handling his responsibilities.

The accuracy of the 1990 census came under fire even before the counting officially began. Of greatest concern was the potential undercount of minorities, and the Census Bureau's thinking about whether or not to adjust the count to compensate for those missed. Many members — especially those from urban areas — insisted early on that a statistical adjustment to the census would be essential. Opponents of an adjustment said the census had always been a head count and should not be turned into a statistical estimate.

Throughout 1989 and early 1990, Sawyer was deliberative in his statements on the undercount issue, perhaps mindful that he was one of the few lawmakers who actually had to deal with the Bureau on the issue. By May 1990, however, even Sawyer was sounding more like an advocate for adjustment, and in March 1991 he pointed out that the undercount of blacks in the 1990 census was likely to be higher than in 1980.

"You get the standard question: 'If we could go to the moon, why can't we count the nation?' " said Sawyer. "It just seems to me if we had tried to go the moon using the kind of celestial navigation that Columbus crossed the Atlantic with, we wouldn't have gotten there.... We are still using celestial navigation to count the nation."

Debate over an adjustment persisted through the spring of 1991, with all involved awaiting a scheduled July 15 decision on the matter by the Commerce Department (of which the Census Bureau is a part).

In 1990, Sawyer attempted to pre-empt some potential problems in the count by helping enact legislation enabling the Census Bureau to hire a sufficient number of temporary employees to conduct the enumeration. In the 102nd Congress, Sawyer has focused his efforts on reforming the process to assist and improve future counts. He has pushed for early, comprehensive planning for the 2000 census and the commitment of adequate resources for that effort.

Sawyer's ascent to the chairmanship of the subcommittee was equal parts skillful politicking and good timing. At the start of the 101st Congress, there were two Post Office subcommittee chairs open, and every other Democratic committee member already headed a panel at Post Office or elsewhere. Sawyer gathered enough support to make it onto the full committee, and then competed with another new member, Pennsylvania Democrat Paul E. Kanjorski, for the Census chairmanship.

One key to Sawyer's winning the subcommittee chair was his stand on the counting procedure for the 1990 census. He, along with most House Democratic leaders, wanted to continue the policy of counting undocumented aliens. Kanjorski opposed counting illegal aliens. Sawyer had also proven himself loyal to the leadership on a range of issues; he voted with a majority of House Democrats more than 90 percent of the time during all four of his years in Congress.

Sawyer, a former teacher who chaired the Education Committee in the Ohio House, also serves on the Education and Labor Committee. Despite his experience in the field, he seemed unusually modest about making a mark quickly on educational policy. "You've got to be patient," he said in 1987. "You get into a position where you're trusted by sufficient numbers of others in those areas where you hope to make a difference."

By the 101st Congress, Sawyer had gained enough confidence and influence to attempt to make his mark. He pushed a measure aimed at eliminating adult illiteracy by providing $1.25 million to set up a national center, state resource centers and work force literacy dem-

Ohio 14

Northeast — Akron

The 14th District is in a part of Ohio built out of rubber — tires in particular. Within the district's confines are the corporate headquarters of the Goodyear, Goodrich, Firestone and General Tire companies. The 14th became one of the most Democratic districts in the state on the strength of votes from the blue-collar workers who kept the rubber factories humming.

But the economy of the district is changing. While the major rubber companies are still important employers, the jobs with a future are white-collar, not blue-collar. The last quarter-century has seen a steady transfer of manufacturing from the old, high-wage factories in Akron to new plants in low-wage areas of the Sun Belt. Many Akron residents have left: Its 1990 population of 223,000 was less than it was a half-century earlier. Many downtown storefronts are vacant, and the streets can be eerily quiet, especially at night.

Sawyer and other Akron leaders have fought to forge a new high-tech future for the city, and they have had enough success that Akron's unemployment rate has been lower in recent years than in some other industrial centers in northern Ohio.

In the boom years of the rubber industry before World War II, Akron was a mecca for job-seeking Appalachians. The annual West Virginia Day was one of the city's most popular events, and it was said that more West Virginians lived in Akron than in Charleston.

These days, the Appalachian descendants combine with blacks, ethnics and the academic community at the University of Akron to keep the city reliably Democratic. North of Akron, suburbs and farm land in northern Summit County provide Republican votes. Usually, they are too few to overcome the Democratic advantage in Akron and swing the 14th to the GOP. Both Jimmy Carter in 1980 and Michael S. Dukakis in 1988 won Akron by a wide enough margin to carry Summit County narrowly.

Population: 514,172. White 453,372 (88%), Black 56,277 (11%), Other 2,885 (1%). Spanish origin 2,692 (1%). 18 and over 373,433 (73%), 65 and over 57,938 (11%). Median age: 31.

onstration programs. The measure was eventually incorporated into an omnibus education measure that stalled shortly before Congress adjourned in October 1990. Congress returned to the issue in early 1991.

In July 1990, the House overwhelmingly passed a Sawyer-sponsored measure to authorize $250 million for programs aimed at improving the quality of science and mathematics education in the United States. Congress cleared the measure in October, but only after reducing the spending levels in the bill significantly.

Cognizant of the industrial interests in his district, Sawyer joined a number of midwestern colleagues in securing $250 million for workers who are displaced because of implementation of the Clean Air Act.

Sawyer received a temporary, two-year assignment to the Foreign Affairs Committee at the start of the 102nd Congress. He had served in 1990 as a member of a congressional task force to assist the parliaments of the new Eastern Europe democracies in Czechoslovakia, Poland and Hungary.

At Home: Like most of Ohio's House delegation, Sawyer saw his victory margin in 1990 sliced by a general anti-Washington mood among voters. Although he still defeated Republican Jean E. Bender, a state Board of Education member, with relative ease, his tally was 15 points lower than in 1988.

Sawyer first won the seat in 1986 after surviving a primary battle between the new Akron and the old Akron. On one side was Sawyer, the young mayor of Akron and an apostle of high technology; on the other was state Sen. Oliver Ocasek — a 60-year-old, Humphrey-style, pro-labor war horse.

Ocasek might have been an ideal House candidate in the days when Akron was the "rubber capital of the world." But as the rubber industry and many of its blue-collar jobs fled to the Sun Belt, the influence of organized labor here diminished.

Sawyer, on the other hand, came from a white-collar background. The son of a prominent Akron businessman, he was a high school teacher before he won a seat in the Ohio House. His election to the Akron mayoralty in 1983 ended nearly 20 years of GOP rule.

When Sawyer announced his House bid, some Akron residents were upset: He had promised to serve at least one full four-year term as mayor, but was running for higher office after only three years. However, Sawyer received a key boost when retiring Democratic Rep. John F. Seiberling endorsed his candidacy.

Sawyer proved to be the consummate media-age politician. While Ocasek was garrulous and emotional and boasted ties to old-time labor leaders, Sawyer was reserved, methodical and adept at the task of nuts-and-bolts organization. He emerged from the primary with a comfortable 49-39 percent victory.

Sawyer then had to get past the Republicans' most prominent local officeholder, Summit County Prosecutor Lynn Slaby. Although he ran a well-funded campaign in which he emphasized his blue-collar roots, Slaby could not get an angle on Sawyer. When Slaby called his foe a tax-and-spend liberal, Sawyer noted that Akron had not raised taxes during his mayoralty. He won 54 percent, then soared to 75 percent against a lesser-known candidate in 1988.

Sawyer had a tougher time in 1990. First, Slaby jumped on Sawyer's vote for a House pay raise and threatened a rematch. He backed off, but threw his support to William Fink, an insurance man with local GOP backing.

However, Fink never made it to the main event, losing narrowly to the low-key Bender in the primary. Yet Sawyer — who saw 27 percent of the Democratic primary vote go to a little-known opponent — remained shadowed by the pay raise issue and the simple fact that he was the incumbent. Although Bender never achieved much visibility, Sawyer won with a comfortable but not overwhelming 60 percent.

Committees

Education & Labor (12th of 25 Democrats)
Elementary, Secondary & Vocational Education; Labor-Management Relations; Postsecondary Education

Foreign Affairs (25th of 28 Democrats)
Arms Control, International Security & Science

Post Office & Civil Service (9th of 15 Democrats)
Census & Population (chairman)

Elections

1990 General		
Tom Sawyer (D)	97,875	(60%)
Jean E. Bender (R)	66,460	(40%)
1990 Primary		
Tom Sawyer (D)	34,343	(73%)
Lillian Ryan (D)	12,454	(27%)
1988 General		
Tom Sawyer (D)	148,951	(75%)
Loretta A. Lang (R)	50,356	(25%)

Previous Winning Percentage: **1986** (54%)

District Vote For President

	1988	1984	1980	1976
D	110,669 (52%)	107,405 (49%)	100,313 (48%)	121,174 (59%)
R	98,478 (47%)	112,288 (51%)	89,588 (43%)	78,215 (38%)
I			14,578 (7%)	

Campaign Finance

	Receipts	Receipts from PACs	Expend-itures
1990			
Sawyer (D)	$262,812	$187,195 (71%)	$264,793
Bender (R)	$2,003	0	$3,021
1988			
Sawyer (D)	$447,420	$314,754 (70%)	$419,005
Lang (R)	$13,816	0	$13,815

Key Votes

1991	
Authorize use of force against Iraq	N
1990	
Support constitutional amendment on flag desecration	N
Pass family and medical leave bill over Bush veto	Y
Reduce SDI funding	Y
Allow abortions in overseas military facilities	Y
Approve budget summit plan for spending and taxing	Y
Approve civil rights bill	Y
1989	
Halt production of B-2 stealth bomber at 13 planes	Y
Oppose capital gains tax cut	Y
Approve federal abortion funding in rape or incest cases	Y
Approve pay raise and revision of ethics rules	Y
Pass Democratic minimum wage plan over Bush veto	Y

Voting Studies

	Presidential Support		Party Unity		Conservative Coalition	
Year	**S**	**O**	**S**	**O**	**S**	**O**
1990	21	79	92	8	30	70
1989	33	67	97	2	22	78
1988	24	75	94	5	18	82
1987	21	79	93	4	30	70

Interest Group Ratings

Year	ADA	ACU	AFL-CIO	CCUS
1990	89	0	92	14
1989	95	0	100	40
1988	95	4	93	36
1987	88	0	88	20

15 Chalmers P. Wylie (R)

Of Columbus — Elected 1966

Born: Nov. 23, 1920, Norwich, Ohio.
Education: Attended Otterbein College, 1939-40; Ohio State U., 1941-43; Harvard U., J.D. 1948.
Military Service: Army, 1942-45; Army Reserve, 1945-53; National Guard, 1958-78.
Occupation: Lawyer.
Family: Wife, Marjorie Siebold; two children.
Religion: Methodist.
Political Career: Columbus city attorney, 1954-57; Ohio House, 1961-67; candidate for Ohio attorney general, 1956.
Capitol Office: 2310 Rayburn Bldg. 20515; 225-2015.

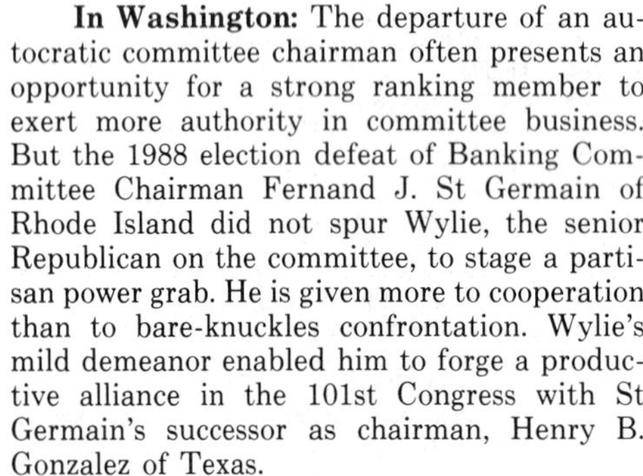

In Washington: The departure of an autocratic committee chairman often presents an opportunity for a strong ranking member to exert more authority in committee business. But the 1988 election defeat of Banking Committee Chairman Fernand J. St Germain of Rhode Island did not spur Wylie, the senior Republican on the committee, to stage a partisan power grab. He is given more to cooperation than to bare-knuckles confrontation. Wylie's mild demeanor enabled him to forge a productive alliance in the 101st Congress with St Germain's successor as chairman, Henry B. Gonzalez of Texas.

Wylie was well prepared for dealing with the new chairman — a sensitive undertaking given Gonzalez's propensity for pugnacity. Wylie serves on Gonzalez's Housing Subcommittee, where he has steadily pushed for less costly housing bills than those sought by the chairman. And while Gonzalez has been known to combust at Republican administration witnesses, he and Wylie have coexisted at a considerably more comfortable temperature, allowing Wylie to be a more active participant in committee business.

Indeed, Gonzalez's coordination with Wylie has become a source of irritation for some committee Democrats, who complain that the chairman confides more in Wylie than in his own party's members. Democrats' frustration boiled over at the Democratic Caucus' organizational meeting before the start of the 102nd Congress. Gonzalez faced allegations that he had recorded a campaign endorsement of Wylie. Although Gonzalez explained that his comments were not intended as an endorsement and, in fact, were never aired, he did have to weather a challenge to his chairmanship.

Wylie's position involves him in a wide range of banking issues, and his name appears on most of the major pieces of legislation handled by the committee. During the Reagan years, he usually was willing to speak for the administration's point of view. But some of the Republicans under Wylie on Banking have a more activist bent; second-ranking Republican Jim Leach of Iowa is often seen as one who may assume greater prominence as a voice for those younger Republicans.

Working in tandem with Gonzalez in the 101st Congress, however, Wylie was at the heart of the committee's work. In 1989, the two reworked a Bush administration bill aimed at bailing out the faltering savings and loan industry and dramatically overhauling thrift industry regulation.

The most significant issue of contention in the three-year, $50 billion bill was whether the money borrowed should be counted as part of the federal budget. By borrowing "on budget," congressional Democrats and some Republicans argued the government could save as much as $20 billion by marketing the bailout bonds at a lower interest rate. But President Bush and his advisers favored keeping the money "off budget" so as not to balloon an already bulging budget deficit.

During conference deliberations, Wylie proposed putting half the cost on budget and half off. His proposal was further revised by Democratic Sen. Alan Cranston of California. The conference ended up agreeing to a version of the Wylie-Cranston proposal, putting the $50 billion on budget and exempting the resulting three-year increase in red ink from the Gramm-Rudman anti-deficit law.

But Bush raised a last-minute veto threat after the conference reached agreement, and a second conference had to renegotiate the financing plan. Wylie criticized the White House for the veto threat, saying, "It was bad timing, and it showed bad political judgment on someone's part." Wylie said he would have preferred that Bush simply accept the conference agreement. After bitter wrangling between conferees and administration officials, members agreed to put $20 billion on budget and $30 billion off.

Ohio 15

Central — Western Columbus and Suburbs

Of the two districts that divide Columbus, the 15th traditionally has been the more Republican. Although it includes most of the academic community at Ohio State University, the Democratic vote there is offset by the solid Republican areas in northern Columbus and the rock-ribbed GOP suburbs west of the Olentangy and Scioto rivers. In Upper Arlington and similar affluent suburbs, it is not unusual for Republican presidential candidates to draw well over two-thirds of the vote.

Apart from the large university vote — Ohio State has 54,000 students — the major pocket of Democratic strength in the district is on the near west side of Columbus. Sandwiched between the Scioto River and the Ohio State Hospital for the Insane are neighborhoods of lower-income Appalachian whites.

The 15th includes some portions of the heavily black East Side of Columbus and blue-collar communities in the southeast portion of Franklin County, which swell the Democratic vote a bit. But these are low-turnout areas.

In 1982 redistricting, the 15th gave up the heart of downtown Columbus, with the state Capitol and the offices of Ohio's major banking and commercial institutions. But with three-quarters of the land area of Franklin County, the district still contains most of the region's expanding service base, which includes three large high-technology research centers.

Columbus is no tourist attraction. Swarms of visitors descend on the city only at Ohio State Fair time in August and on the half-dozen Saturdays in the fall when the Buckeyes are playing football at home. But the area has gained a reputation as a good place to raise a family. During the 1970s, it was the only major urban center in Ohio to gain population, and in the 1980s recession years, the suffering of service-oriented Columbus did not compare to that felt in many other Ohio cities.

Population: 514,176. White 449,644 (87%), Black 56,641 (11%), Other 5,066 (1%). Spanish origin 3,767 (1%). 18 and over 377,458 (73%), 65 and over 46,640 (9%). Median age: 28.

In 1990, Wylie helped get Gonzalez's pet housing initiative airborne when, during a February ride aboard Air Force One, he lobbied Bush to meet with him and Gonzalez about the bill. The meeting took place a week later, with Housing and Urban Development Secretary Jack F. Kemp in attendance. Wylie said, "I am determined to see that [Gonzalez] gets a housing bill," adding that the chairman had been good to committee Republicans.

The bill, the first major overhaul of federal housing programs since 1974, authorized some $57 billion over two years to continue existing housing programs and to create a number of new ones in an effort to increase the nation's stock of affordable housing and to help public housing tenants become homeowners. While Wylie served as a conduit between the administration and the committee, his alliance with Gonzalez thoroughout the process was a key factor in bringing the housing bill to fruition. Wylie and Gonzalez teamed to offer compromise "leadership" amendments to settle differences on some sections of the bill and to repel an assault on the bill's funding levels by conservatives. Bush signed it into law in November.

Also in the 101st Congress, Wylie sponsored legislation setting new penalties for bank fraud and giving prosecutors more muscle against savings and loan wrongdoing. Some of Wylie's proposals became law as part of the 1990 anticrime package.

Although Wylie generally shared St Germain's suspicions of extended banking deregulation, he has supported efforts to remove the longstanding ban on interstate banking. In 1991, the Bush administration unveiled a long-awaited bank reform plan. The plan proposed removing barriers to interstate banking while putting stiff limits on deposit insurance coverage. Gonzalez and Wylie introduced separate, comprehensive measures on deposit insurance early in the 102nd Congress.

At Home: Wylie has steered clear of controversy throughout his political career, and has prospered for more than 30 years. Well liked by GOP voters and the Columbus business community, he has consistently won by large margins.

However, even the bland and affable Wylie could not totally escape the voters' angry anti-Washington mood in 1990. Running against little-known Democrat Thomas V. Erney, a 26-year-old college counselor, Wylie was held to 59 percent of the vote — his lowest general election percentage in 13 House campaigns.

Wylie had topped that figure even in 1986, when Ohio Democrats made one of their rare efforts to target him. Their candidate, David L. Jackson, was a political neophyte, but he had won high marks as state health director in the administration of Democratic Gov. Richard F. Celeste.

Jackson pounded away at Wylie for a wide range of "sins" — from flip-flopping on aid to the Nicaraguan contras to being a captive of "rich and powerful" interests in Washington. But Wylie, who had not needed to campaign seriously in years, responded to the challenge. He returned regularly to Columbus, where he had a weekly radio show; ran ads that detailed the federal funding he had procured for central Ohio projects; and even formed a group called "Physicians for Wylie" to counter Jackson's appeal in the medical community.

Meanwhile, Jackson, who was a prominent Cleveland-area neurologist before joining the Celeste administration, faced criticism that he was a carpetbagger. With Wylie fitting "his district like a comfortable old shoe" (as one newspaper said), the Democrat made no headway: Wylie took 64 percent.

Wylie's political rise to that point had been steady and rather uneventful. After graduating from law school in 1948, Wylie entered public life as assistant state attorney general, became city attorney, then moved to the state Legislature. He was careful not to offend potential political allies, and always made sure of his support before stepping up.

In 1964 Wylie had the good fortune to be on the legislative committee that redrew congressional district lines for the 1966 elections. The plan that emerged included a new district in Columbus that had no incumbent but included most of Wylie's legislative district. With the blessing of the county Republican chairman, Wylie ran and was easily elected.

Wylie never had trouble winning re-election, soaring to a career-high 75 percent in 1988. While he won with a reasonable cushion two years later, the amorphous voter dissent toward Congress contributed to a 16 percentage-point decline for Wylie.

Committees

Banking, Finance & Urban Affairs (Ranking)
Financial Institutions Supervision, Regulation & Insurance (ranking); Consumer Affairs & Coinage; Housing & Community Development

Veterans' Affairs (3rd of 13 Republicans)
Compensation, Pension & Insurance; Education, Training & Employment

Joint Economic

Elections

1990 General

Chalmers P. Wylie (R)	99,251	(59%)
Thomas V. Erney (D)	68,510	(41%)

1990 Primary

Chalmers P. Wylie (R)	31,798	(78%)
Clifford Arnebeck (R)	8,863	(22%)

1988 General

Chalmers P. Wylie (R)	146,854	(75%)
Mark S. Froehlich (D)	49,441	(25%)

Previous Winning Percentages: **1986** (64%) **1984** (72%) **1982** (66%) **1980** (73%) **1978** (71%) **1976** (66%) **1974** (62%) **1972** (66%) **1970** (71%) **1968** (73%) **1966** (60%)

District Vote For President

	1988	1984	1980	1976
D	75,999 (37%)	68,366 (32%)	82,909 (36%)	79,511 (41%)
R	126,613 (62%)	139,407 (66%)	128,975 (56%)	107,607 (56%)
I			13,908 (6%)	

Campaign Finance

	Receipts	Receipts from PACs	Expend-itures
1990			
Wylie (R)	$227,878	$167,153 (73%)	$242,592
Erney (D)	$16,000	$4,500 (28%)	$15,977
1988			
Wylie (R)	$231,063	$158,415 (69%)	$211,963
Froehlich (D)	$9,910	$7,000 (71%)	$6,682

Key Votes

1991

Authorize use of force against Iraq	Y

1990

Support constitutional amendment on flag desecration	Y
Pass family and medical leave bill over Bush veto	N
Reduce SDI funding	N
Allow abortions in overseas military facilities	N
Approve budget summit plan for spending and taxing	Y
Approve civil rights bill	N

1989

Halt production of B-2 stealth bomber at 13 planes	N
Oppose capital gains tax cut	N
Approve federal abortion funding in rape or incest cases	N
Approve pay raise and revision of ethics rules	N
Pass Democratic minimum wage plan over Bush veto	N

Voting Studies

	Presidential Support		Party Unity		Conservative Coalition	
Year	S	O	S	O	S	O
1990	69	25	69	22	80	9
1989	83	12	68	29	88	5
1988	54	37	61	30	84	3
1987	66	30	65	24	84	7
1986	63	31	58	36	76	22
1985	68	31	61	32	85	9
1984	53	42	65	24	92	5
1983	79	17	73	20	72	20
1982	56	35	63	29	60	26
1981	64	29	68	22	79	20

Interest Group Ratings

Year	ADA	ACU	AFL-CIO	CCUS
1990	11	74	8	71
1989	0	93	0	90
1988	30	80	36	92
1987	4	73	0	100
1986	15	64	31	71
1985	10	76	29	73
1984	20	52	23	67
1983	5	67	13	89
1982	15	65	30	73
1981	20	86	15	94

16 Ralph Regula (R)

Of Navarre — Elected 1972

Born: Dec. 3, 1924, Beach City, Ohio.
Education: Mount Union College, B.A. 1948; William McKinley School of Law, LL.B. 1952.
Military Service: Navy, 1944-46.
Occupation: Lawyer.
Family: Wife, Mary Rogusky; three children.
Religion: Episcopalian.
Political Career: Ohio House, 1965-67; Ohio Senate, 1967-73.
Capitol Office: 2207 Rayburn Bldg. 20515; 225-3876.

In Washington: Regula is well suited to the collegial atmosphere of the Appropriations Committee, where he has served for nearly two decades. A serious man, he is an entrenched establishment Republican who generally works well with Democrats. This has made him a key player on the committee — he is the ranking GOP member of the Interior Subcommittee — but his moderate politics and conciliatory disposition can rankle more confrontational right-of-center Republicans.

Californian Dana Rohrabacher was one such Republican who found his way impeded by Regula in the 101st Congress. In 1989, conservatives, responding to protests that the National Endowment for the Arts had supported blasphemous and pornographic projects, sought to restrict the NEA's funding discretion.

Rohrabacher planned to offer a motion to instruct conferees on the Interior appropriations bill to support North Carolina GOP Sen. Jesse Helms' amendment to restrict art funding. But Regula blocked Rohrabacher by offering a less controversial motion backing Senate restrictions on lobbying. Conferees subsequently watered down Helms' language.

That earned Regula, the former chairman of a national prayer breakfast group, the enmity of a conservative religious lobbying group. An article in the group's journal with Rohrabacher's byline said Regula's maneuver was tantamount to continuing tax support for pornography. Regula protested that he opposed funding obscene projects but that Helms' amendment was too broad.

On environmental concerns, Regula is viewed as more sympathetic than many Republicans. In the Reagan years, he had a hand in crafting legislation to fund the nation's parks, forests and energy conservation programs; the White House often deemed the funding in these bills excessive, and threatened vetoes.

When it comes to energy development, however, Regula sharply disagrees with many Appropriations Democrats. He ardently believes that the United States should aggressively tap its domestic energy resources. While this position places him firmly in his party's pro-development mainstream, Regula has criticized the administration and Congress for failing to develop a comprehensive energy policy — a lapse he says could lead to a return of gasoline lines in the 1990s.

Regula fervently supports oil drilling on the Outer Continental Shelf of the United States. He generally gets along well with Interior Subcommittee Chairman Sidney R. Yates, but the two clash annually over this issue, with Yates usually winning. In the 100th Congress, the full Appropriations Committee rebuffed Regula's challenges to the one-year extension of moratoriums on drilling in the Gulf of Mexico off the Florida coast and in Georges Bank off the Massachusetts coast.

In 1989, the Interior Subcommittee renewed the one-year moratoriums and added some new bans on drilling and exploration, including one on previously sold leases in Bristol Bay, Alaska. Regula offered an amendment to block the Bristol Bay ban, but it lost in subcommittee on a 3-5 show of hands and in full committee by 22-29. In 1990, Regula attempted to stop a ban on oil and gas drilling off North Carolina. He lost when the House voted 281-82 to ratify the drilling ban.

Iraq's 1990 invasion of Kuwait bolstered Regula's argument for greater domestic oil exploration. "It illustrates what I've been saying for eight years," he said, "which is we need an orderly development of our own resources to avoid Middle East blackmail."

But even at the outset of the Persian Gulf crisis in August 1990, Regula predicted there would be no popular move to reorder energy priorities. "Prices will stabilize, and we will once again go back to sleep," he said.

Regula tends to stray from the party line more often than the average Republican. His independence came at an unusual cost in 1990 after he told an administration lobbyist he was

Ohio 16

Northeast — Canton

Although it has undergone a variety of changes over the years, the 16th District is still centered on Stark County and the city of Canton, just as it was when William McKinley represented it a century ago.

While it is a working-class city like Akron and Youngstown and often votes Democratic in local elections, Canton does not share in the solidly Democratic tradition of the rest of northeastern Ohio. That is partly a result of the conservative mentality brought to the community by the family-run Timken Co. — a large steel and roller-bearing firm that is the district's largest employer.

With sizable black and ethnic populations, Canton proper goes Democratic on occasion. But the suburbs in surrounding Stark County are solidly Republican. Since 1920, the only Democratic presidential candidates to carry the county — which accounts for nearly three-quarters of the district's population — have been Franklin D. Roosevelt and Lyndon B. Johnson.

Besides Timken, Canton is the national headquarters of the Hoover Co., the vacuum-cleaner manufacturer, and Diebold Inc., a producer of bank safes and office equipment. But it is more famous as the home of the Pro Football Hall of Fame and for the front porch from which McKinley ran his 1896 presidential campaign. The slain president is buried in a park on the west end of Canton in a large memorial that roughly resembles the Taj Mahal. The Hall of Fame is at the other end of the park.

The portion of the 16th outside Stark County is mostly rural and Republican. Wooster, the Wayne County seat, claims to be the site of America's first Christmas tree. Rubbermaid has its corporate headquarters there. Nearby Orrville is the seat of the Smucker family, which markets jams and peanut butter.

The 16th was extended south in 1982 by redistricting to annex Holmes County from the old 17th District. Many of Holmes' 30,000 residents are Amish, and motorists driving through the county have to be careful not to plow into the back of a horse-drawn buggy. Houses without electricity are common in the county, and the income level is the lowest in the state outside the Appalachian portion of the 6th District. Although leather and noodle factories have brought new employment to the agricultural area, most business is conducted in small Amish family-owned shops that sell buggies and other necessities.

Population: 514,171. White 485,489 (94%), Black 25,465 (5%). Spanish origin 4,047 (1%). 18 and over 363,139 (71%), 65 and over 55,348 (11%). Median age: 30.

inclined not to support the fiscal 1991 budget-summit agreement. Shortly before Regula was to take his wife and four constituents to see a play from the president's box at the Kennedy Center for the Performing Arts, the White House called to say the box was no longer available.

Regula also serves on the Appropriations Subcommittee on Commerce, Justice and State, where he gently pushes his minority views. In the 100th Congress, the subcommittee approved his language to cut $3 million from $41.6 million that had been allocated for the Organization of American States (OAS). He said he "had a hard time trying to figure out what the OAS does outside of giving receptions." In the 101st Congress, the House adopted his amendment requiring all U.S. dealings with the OAS to be overseen by the Bureau of Inter-American Affairs. Authority over OAS matters had been divided between that bureau and the Office of International Organizations.

Regula also has a firm grasp of the subcommittee's arcanum, which he has used to protect the State Department budget. He worked to get agencies with personnel stationed at U.S. embassies — such as the CIA and the Marines — to fund the administrative costs of maintaining their forces, which had been entirely borne by the State Department. He now hopes to get his cost-sharing plan extended to include security and capital costs.

As a member of the District of Columbia Subcommittee, Regula intervened in 1990 in the continuing debate over voting rights for District residents. He introduced a bill to annex the District back into Maryland, an idea also espoused by Maryland Democratic Gov. William Donald Schaefer. The Rev. Jesse Jackson denounced the proposal, saying it was akin to creating a South African-style segregated black "homeland." The bill went nowhere.

Representing an industrial district, Regula has taken a number of stands to please union organizers back home. In the 100th Congress, he was one of just 17 Republicans to support the Gephardt amendment to the trade bill. The measure would have mandated retaliatory tariffs against countries with unfair trade practices, but was so controversial most of its provisions were eventually dropped from the bill.

Though he backed an unsuccessful effort to strike language requiring plant-closing notification from the trade bill, Regula voted to override the president's veto of the measure. In 1990, Regula voted to override President Bush's veto of a textile trade bill.

One of Regula's minor but consistent crusades is for federal recognition of President William McKinley, his hometown's most famous native. A graduate of the McKinley School of Law, Regula observes the former president's January birthday by giving red carnations to his colleagues; he once got the Interior Subcommittee to adopt an amendment prohibiting the renaming of Mount McKinley in Alaska.

At Home: Regula has been a political force in northeast Ohio since winning a House seat in 1972. Between 1978 and 1988 — a period of economic difficulty for the industrial areas of his district — Regula dipped below 70 percent of the vote only once.

But in 1990, Regula could not avoid a general anti-incumbent mood that affected most House incumbents in Ohio; nor could he totally escape voter wrath over his vote for a congressional pay raise. Running against Democrat Warner D. Mendenhall, an underfinanced college professor, Regula won with 59 percent.

Although Regula still had a comfortable cushion of 30,000 votes, his vote percentage was 20 points off from 1988. It was his lowest tally in any of his nine re-election campaigns.

Regula came to the House after eight years in the state Legislature, where he specialized in writing conservation bills. His state Senate constituency included a large part of Stark County, the heart of the 16th, and when GOP Rep. Frank T. Bow retired in 1972 after 22 years in Congress, Regula won Bow's endorsement.

Redistricting that year removed part of Democratic Mahoning County from the district, making it more Republican. Regula defeated Democrat Virgil Musser, who was Bow's last opponent, with 57 percent of the vote.

By 1974 — a poor Republican year nationally — Regula was up to 66 percent. Democrats then quit making serious efforts against Regula. He hit 79 percent in 1980, a peak he matched in 1988 before his unusual 1990 dropoff.

Committees

Appropriations (6th of 22 Republicans)
Interior (ranking); Commerce, Justice, State & Judiciary; District of Columbia

Select Aging (3rd of 27 Republicans)
Health & Long-Term Care (ranking)

Elections

1990 General		
Ralph Regula (R)	101,097	(59%)
Warner D. Mendenhall (D)	70,516	(41%)
1988 General		
Ralph Regula (R)	158,824	(79%)
Melvin J. Gravely (D)	43,356	(21%)

Previous Winning Percentages: **1986** (76%) **1984** (72%) **1982** (66%) **1980** (79%) **1978** (78%) **1976** (67%) **1974** (66%) **1972** (57%)

District Vote For President

	1988		1984		1980		1976	
D	87,090	(42%)	79,525	(38%)	74,357	(37%)	87,184	(47%)
R	116,518	(57%)	130,136	(62%)	112,060	(56%)	94,013	(51%)
I					10,825	(5%)		

Campaign Finance

	Receipts	Receipts from PACs		Expend-itures
1990				
Regula (R)	$110,331	0		$156,205
Mendenhall (D)	$68,042	$10,750	(16%)	$68,021
1988				
Regula (R)	$108,672	0		$94,492

Key Votes

1991	
Authorize use of force against Iraq	Y
1990	
Support constitutional amendment on flag desecration	Y
Pass family and medical leave bill over Bush veto	N
Reduce SDI funding	N
Allow abortions in overseas military facilities	N
Approve budget summit plan for spending and taxing	N
Approve civil rights bill	Y
1989	
Halt production of B-2 stealth bomber at 13 planes	N
Oppose capital gains tax cut	N
Approve federal abortion funding in rape or incest cases	N
Approve pay raise and revision of ethics rules	Y
Pass Democratic minimum wage plan over Bush veto	N

Voting Studies

	Presidential Support		Party Unity		Conservative Coalition	
Year	S	O	S	O	S	O
1990	56	44	75	24	81	19
1989	70	30	60	40	93	7
1988	56	43	67	30	87	13
1987	52	48	56	43	81	19
1986	56	44	56	43	80	20
1985	60	40	57	42	82	18
1984	58	41	63	35	78	19
1983	66	32	68	31	80	20
1982	64	35	65	34	75	23
1981	72	28	75	25	79	21

Interest Group Ratings

Year	ADA	ACU	AFL-CIO	CCUS
1990	17	63	42	71
1989	20	54	25	100
1988	30	76	64	93
1987	28	52	38	67
1986	15	45	71	61
1985	25	52	35	59
1984	35	33	46	75
1983	25	61	35	75
1982	25	59	35	59
1981	15	87	27	89

17 James A. Traficant Jr. (D)

Of Poland — Elected 1984

Born: May 8, 1941, Youngstown, Ohio.
Education: U. of Pittsburgh, B.S. 1963; Youngstown State U., M.S. 1973, M.S. 1976.
Occupation: County drug program director; sheriff.
Family: Wife, Patricia Choppa; two children.
Religion: Roman Catholic.
Political Career: Mahoning County sheriff, 1981-85.
Capitol Office: 312 Cannon Bldg. 20515; 225-5261.

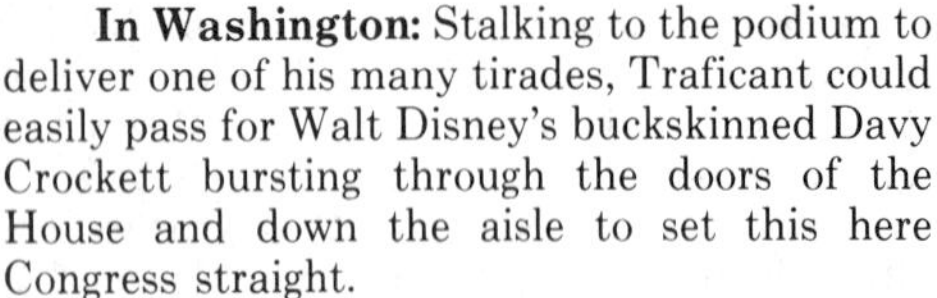

In Washington: Stalking to the podium to deliver one of his many tirades, Traficant could easily pass for Walt Disney's buckskinned Davy Crockett bursting through the doors of the House and down the aisle to set this here Congress straight.

Though no Fess Parker in looks, Traficant serves for angry blue-collar workers of the Rust Belt the same gadfly role Crockett served for the Tennessee homesteaders who felt abandoned by Washington. He does so in a forceful and often crude way that sets him far apart from most other House members.

With his fist pounding and his hair askew, Traficant shouts the frustrations of factory workers whose jobs in heavy industry have disappeared. His approach is usually bombastic and often vulgar: He is probably the only House member for whom the phrase "shit or get off the pot" is common coin in public discourse. Even he himself admits on rare occasions that he goes too far. In 1990, he apologized and tried to strike from the record a floor attack against members, whom he called "wimps, prostitutes and sellouts" after they declined to adopt several of his amendments to cut defense spending.

But if there is a madness to Traficant's manner, it certainly is not without its method. His tough talk about industrial decline and foreign competition resonates in the working-class wards of Youngstown and the other aging mill towns of his district. His "raging populist" image has made him a local folk hero, enabling him to thrive even in the face of questions about his personal ethics.

Nor is Traficant's rage unfocused. He has channeled his desire to bolster U.S. industry into a series of legislative amendments, and has had some success in getting them enacted. The core of his effort is "Buy American" legislation aimed at gaining preference for American-made products in federal contracting. The idea is not new, but early versions of it were often "buy only American" proposals; Congress rejected them as too extreme. Traficant hit on a formula he has attached to a number of spending bills requiring an agency to give preference to a bid from an American company if its finished product is made domestically, the "domestic content" is at least half American parts, and the bid is within 6 percent of the lowest foreign bid.

To Traficant, unfair foreign competition is the source of America's industrial slide, and he is unapologetic about his support for tough trade sanctions. During the Persian Gulf crisis, he singled out Japan for what he said was a lukewarm response to the allied call for help. "While we are protecting their oil, the Japanese are selling hot dogs in Yosemite," said Traficant.

In 1987, Traficant won approval of a $30 million program to provide counseling for persons faced with mortgage foreclosure because of circumstances beyond their control, such as job layoffs. The measure harked back to the incident that first made him a local legend: In 1982, during his tenure as Mahoning County (Youngstown) sheriff, Traficant went to jail for three days rather than serve several laid-off factory workers with foreclosure orders.

That act helped give Traficant such a loyal following that he has survived legal problems to which other politicians would have succumbed. In 1987, a federal Tax Court ruled that Traficant had accepted $108,000 in bribes from organized-crime figures while serving as sheriff, and held him liable for back taxes, interest and civil penalties. But Traficant — who was acquitted in 1983 on federal criminal charges involving the same allegations — brushed off questions of corruption and portrayed himself as a victim of the Internal Revenue Service (IRS). Traficant appealed the ruling all the way to the U.S. Supreme Court, adding that he would go over to the IRS and "punch their lights out."

He was even more pugnacious in early 1987, when Miami Beach industrialist Victor Posner took Sharon Steel, the nation's 12th largest steel producer and a major local employer, into bankruptcy. "I think Posner now has to think of someone other than himself," Traficant said. "And if he doesn't, I'm going to go to Florida and assault him.... If he rips off

Ohio 17

Northeast — Youngstown; Warren

Once called America's "Little Ruhr" as a symbol of its industrial productivity, the Youngstown-Warren area now is a symbol of the nation's industrial decline. Many of the giant steel furnaces that once lighted the eastern Ohio sky are dark for good. Most of the workers who have not retired or left the area are scrounging for other jobs.

Located on the state's eastern border with Pennsylvania, the region was long a steel center serving both Cleveland and Pittsburgh. Only a decade ago the large steel plants in the Mahoning River Valley employed more than 50,000 workers. Now the work force is a fraction of that.

The 17th has begun to diversify its economy, but the process is slow and painful. Youngstown (population 96,000) lost 17 percent of its population in the last decade, and for those who stayed, an unemployment rate upwards of 20 percent has not been uncommon. In the 1980s, the city was one of only five to drop from the ranks of those with 100,000 or more people.

With its remaining blue-collar base, the 17th is one of Ohio's solidly Democratic areas in most elections. About 56 percent of the voters live in Mahoning County (Youngstown); 42 percent reside in Trumbull County (Warren). Mahoning and Trumbull were among the 10 Ohio counties that voted for Jimmy Carter in 1980. In 1984 they divided slightly: Walter F. Mondale ran up nearly 60 percent in Mahoning, but Reagan held him to 55 percent in Trumbull. Both were in the Democratic column in 1988.

Most Democratic candidates build comfortable majorities in the string of declining ethnic communities along the Mahoning River. Italians dominate in Niles and Lowellville. Eastern Europeans and Greeks are the most important groups in Campbell. In the two largest cities — Youngstown and Warren — blacks are part of the demographic mixture.

As one moves south, beyond the industrial Mahoning Valley, the GOP vote increases. Homes in these suburbs are too dear for most blue-collar workers. Boardman Township, due south of Youngstown, one of the most affluent parts of Mahoning County, is a typical swing area.

Population: 514,172. White 453,689 (88%), Black 55,177 (11%). Spanish origin 6,694 (1%). 18 and over 372,108 (72%), 65 and over 59,249 (12%). Median age: 32.

the last industrial facility in the Shenango Valley ... someone should grab him by the throat and stretch him ...."

Traficant's empathy for the underdog led him to champion the causes of two individuals — Arthur Rudolph and John Demjanjuk — accused of being former Nazi war criminals and deported to Israel for trial. Jewish groups accused Traficant of making anti-Semitic remarks during public appearances on behalf of the men.

Even with his mercurial nature and his sense for the dramatic, Traficant startled his colleagues by announcing plans to run in the 1988 Democratic presidential primaries (while seeking House re-election) in order to promote the interests of the Rust Belt. Traficant made the ballot only in a handful of House districts in Ohio and Pennsylvania. Still, he topped 30,000 votes in the Ohio primary (just over 2 percent of the total) and earned a delegate to the Democratic National Convention.

At Home: The 1990 campaign in Ohio was marked by voter disgust toward Washington over the chaotic federal budget debate. Most Ohio House incumbents saw their normal victory margins shrink by several points. The iconoclastic Traficant was an exception, though. After nearly six years as the angry man of the House, he could finally claim he was a trendsetter. Already a landslide winner in his previous two elections, Traficant scored a career-high 78 percent in 1990.

Traficant has always been most comfortable operating outside political convention. While serving as Mahoning County sheriff in the early 1980s, he became a political hero by successfully defending himself against the bribery charges that could have sent him to prison.

A former football star at the University of Pittsburgh, Traficant ran an anti-drug-abuse program in Mahoning County before being elected sheriff in 1980. He quickly became a hero to the district's hard-hit factory workers. But within two years, he had alienated virtually every government official in the area, claiming that most were controlled by organized crime.

Those allegations took on an ironic cast, when Traficant himself was indicted for bribery. It seemed certain that he would be convicted: The FBI had tape recordings of Traficant accepting $163,000 from underworld figures.

Yet Traficant, despite a lack of legal training, elected to defend himself in court, and put on a tour de force against some of the federal government's best lawyers. Traficant said he took the money only to get evidence against the mobsters, and managed to convince the jury. After a seven-week trial, he was acquitted, touching off an ecstatic celebration by his fans in Youngstown and generating national media attention, including a front-page profile in *The Wall Street Journal.*

Traficant's soaring popularity spurred him to challenge GOP Rep. Lyle Williams in 1984. A genial ex-barber with a knack for reaching the working-class majority, Williams had defied expectations by capturing the usually Democratic district in 1978. He managed to win re-election twice, holding the seat even during the 1982 recession, when decaying industrial towns in the 17th were hit hard.

But running against Traficant was a different matter. Although he was underfinanced and had to overcome the hostility of Democratic leaders with whom he had previously butted heads — one official sought to get him committed to a mental institution — he had broad popular support. Traficant drew large crowds with his attacks on banks, big business and the IRS. He advocated limits on imported steel, a commission to monitor IRS abuses and the death penalty for illegal-drug sellers.

Saying, "I fight with dignity," Williams warned that Traficant would embarrass the district. But the 17th's continuing high unemployment became an insurmountable problem for an incumbent who had promised to bring more jobs: Traficant won with 53 percent.

Traficant's unexpected victory hardly mollified district Democratic leaders. Rather than line up behind him in 1986, they threw their support in the primary to Austintown Township Trustee Michael R. Antonoff. But he proved incapable of derailing Traficant. Largely ignoring his challenger, Traficant relied on his personal popularity and support from organized labor to win renomination by nearly 4-to-1.

That win established Traficant as an indomitable local figure. He won with 72 percent in 1986. After his brief flare of a presidential campaign in 1988, Traficant refocused on the 17th and won re-election with 77 percent. When Williams, who had hinted at a comeback attempt, deferred in 1990, Traficant ran up his personal best over Republican Robert R. DeJulio Jr., a 28-year-old contractor.

Committees

Public Works & Transportation (15th of 36 Democrats)
Aviation; Economic Development; Surface Transportation

Science, Space & Technology (15th of 32 Democrats)
Energy; Space

Select Narcotics Abuse & Control (13th of 21 Democrats)

Elections

1990 General		
James A. Traficant Jr. (D)	133,207	(78%)
Robert R. DeJulio Jr. (R)	38,199	(22%)
1990 Primary		
James A. Traficant Jr. (D)	78,470	(92%)
Leonard A. Viselli (D)	3,466	(4%)
Michael J. Metaxas (D)	3,436	(4%)
1988 General		
James A. Traficant Jr. (D)	162,526	(77%)
Frederick W. Lenz (R)	47,929	(23%)

Previous Winning Percentages: **1986** (72%) **1984** (53%)

District Vote For President

	1988	1984	1980	1976
D	131,232 (62%)	129,520 (57%)	132,461 (62%)	126,759 (60%)
R	80,437 (38%)	95,528 (42%)	64,375 (30%)	80,635 (38%)
I			15,367 (7%)	

Campaign Finance

	Receipts	Receipts from PACs	Expend-itures
1990			
Traficant (D)	$99,644	$54,930 (55%)	$79,064
DeJulio (R)	$1,125	0	$1,700
1988			
Traficant (D)	$100,063	$54,500 (54%)	$96,003
Lenz (R)	$2,406	0	$2,391

Key Votes

1991	
Authorize use of force against Iraq	N
1990	
Support constitutional amendment on flag desecration	Y
Pass family and medical leave bill over Bush veto	Y
Reduce SDI funding	Y
Allow abortions in overseas military facilities	Y
Approve budget summit plan for spending and taxing	N
Approve civil rights bill	Y
1989	
Halt production of B-2 stealth bomber at 13 planes	Y
Oppose capital gains tax cut	Y
Approve federal abortion funding in rape or incest cases	Y
Approve pay raise and revision of ethics rules	N
Pass Democratic minimum wage plan over Bush veto	Y

Voting Studies

	Presidential Support		Party Unity		Conservative Coalition	
Year	S	O	S	O	S	O
1990	19	81	86	14	37	63
1989	29	71	83	17	37	63
1988	17	83	89	10	37	63
1987	17	82	89	7	28	72
1986	10	90	87	13	24	76
1985	13	85	87	7	11	89

Interest Group Ratings

Year	ADA	ACU	AFL-CIO	CCUS
1990	72	13	92	29
1989	90	25	100	40
1988	95	8	100	21
1987	88	5	100	0
1986	95	9	100	28
1985	95	0	100	27

18 Douglas Applegate (D)

Of Steubenville — Elected 1976

Born: March 27, 1928, Steubenville, Ohio.
Education: Graduated from Steubenville H.S., 1947.
Occupation: Real estate broker.
Family: Wife, Betty Engstrom; two children.
Religion: Presbyterian.
Political Career: Ohio House, 1961-69; Ohio Senate, 1969-77.
Capitol Office: 2183 Rayburn Bldg. 20515; 225-6265.

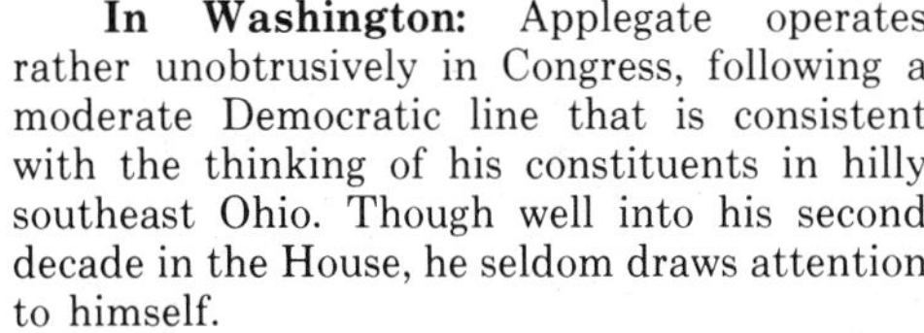

In Washington: Applegate operates rather unobtrusively in Congress, following a moderate Democratic line that is consistent with the thinking of his constituents in hilly southeast Ohio. Though well into his second decade in the House, he seldom draws attention to himself.

There are a couple of policy areas on which Applegate will raise his voice. One is veterans' benefits, an issue on which Applegate has a major say as chairman of the Veterans' Affairs Subcommittee on Compensation, Pension and Insurance.

A strong supporter of efforts during the 100th Congress to establish the Veterans Administration as a Cabinet post, Applegate generally mans the barricades against efforts to reduce veterans' benefits. In 1985, he proposed a cost-of-living adjustment (COLA) to recipients of veterans' retirement benefits that was a middle ground between a higher House-passed increase and a lower Senate figure; the Senate prevailed.

Applegate is not inflexible about budget savings, however. In 1988, he supported a more moderate COLA increase proposed by the Reagan administration. And in the 101st Congress, he pushed for a probe of how the VA manages its home loans and medical programs after an internal auditor found that the department may have known about more than $50 million in benefit overpayments.

The other issue that drives Applegate is economic hardship in his district, where manufacturers have been wounded by foreign competition. Applegate has emblazoned his House stationery with the slogan "Buy American! Save American Jobs!" In early 1989, Applegate called on the Customs Service to investigate a "blatantly outrageous" solicitation by a Taiwanese flag-maker, who enticed American companies to save on labor costs by having their U.S. flags made by his company, then switching the labels from "Made in Taiwan" to "Made in the U.S.A." after delivery.

In the 101st Congress, Applegate advocated a centralized computer data bank to track hazardous waste shipments across the country. The proposal is a priority for firefighters, who must respond to highway accidents involving vehicles carrying chemicals without adequate information about the chemicals involved.

At Home: Although the 18th District's Democratic loyalties have weakened in presidential contests, Applegate has been unaffected. He has received at least 74 percent of the vote in each election since 1978; twice during that time, he has run unopposed.

When he first ran for the House in 1976, Applegate's bland manner helped distance him from the scandal that felled his predecessor, Democrat Wayne Hays. Chairman of the House Administration Committee, Hays quit his campaign for a 15th term that year following allegations that he had kept a woman, Elizabeth Ray, on his payroll solely to provide him with sex.

Though Hays' downfall was unexpected, Applegate was prepared to step in. During his career in the state Legislature, Applegate had quietly planned for a campaign when Hays retired. When Hays renounced his nomination just three months before the election, party leaders turned to Applegate, who represented about half the district in the state Senate.

He had little trouble defeating the GOP candidate and William Crabbe, the Democratic mayor of Steubenville who earlier had launched an independent campaign aimed at Hays.

By the time other Democrats could get a shot at Applegate, he already had a firm hold. He took 82 percent of the primary vote in 1978.

With his low profile in Washington, Applegate seems an unlikely presidential candidate. Yet he briefly was one in 1988. Democratic Rep. James A. Traficant Jr. from the neighboring 17th District entered the Ohio presidential primary as a favorite-son candidate. Applegate followed suit, and wound up winning a delegate to the Democratic National Convention.

Like Traficant, Applegate said his main goal was to draw attention to the plight of the region's Rust Belt cities. But he was also trying to blunt the publicity edge held by Traficant: There was talk that the two could get thrown into a single district in 1990s redistricting.

Ohio 18

East — Steubenville

Coal and steel gave the 18th its polluted air, its dirty rivers, its economic livelihood and its Democratic vote.

Cramped along the steep banks of the Ohio River, Steubenville — the district's largest city (population 22,000) — long had some of the nation's foulest air pollution. But jobs in the smoke-belching plants along a 50-mile stretch of the Ohio take priority over clean air, a fact successful politicians quickly learn.

Locals boast there was not an air pollution alert in Steubenville in the 1980s. But the clearing skies are not a good sign for the local economy. For years the unemployment rate in Steubenville and surrounding Jefferson County has been in or near double digits.

West of Jefferson is economically depressed Harrison County. The closing in 1985 of a pottery plant that employed about 1,000 people pushed up the already high unemployment rate there. The same dismal conditions exist in East Liverpool, located about five miles from where the West Virginia, Ohio, and Pennsylvania borders meet. This Columbiana County town of 16,000 has lost more than 10,000 jobs in the steel and pottery industries over the last quarter-century.

South of Jefferson, Belmont and Monroe counties the steelworking and coal-mining Democrats of the district show strong party allegiance, though they tend to shy away from liberals. This part of Ohio resembles West Virginia and eastern Kentucky. Some cattle are raised, but the hilly terrain makes farming generally unprofitable. Under the hills, however, there are extensive coal deposits.

About half the voters in the 18th live within a few miles of the industrialized Ohio River Valley. As one moves west, the district becomes less Democratic, and the tractors of Republican farmers replace the giant shovels of Democratic coal miners.

Population: 514,173. White 501,793 (98%), Black 10,250 (2%). Spanish origin 1,924 (0.4%). 18 and over 367,705 (72%), 65 and over 66,832 (13%). Median age: 32.

Committees

Public Works & Transportation (7th of 36 Democrats)
Economic Development; Surface Transportation; Water Resources

Veterans' Affairs (3rd of 21 Democrats)
Compensation, Pension & Insurance (chairman); Hospitals & Health Care

Elections

1990 General		
Douglas Applegate (D)	120,782	(74%)
John A. Hales (R)	41,823	(26%)
1990 Primary		
Douglas Applegate (D)	64,104	(88%)
Donald K. Dickey (D)	8,973	(12%)
1988 General		
Douglas Applegate (D)	151,306	(77%)
William C. Abraham (R)	46,130	(23%)

Previous Winning Percentages: **1986** (100%) **1984** (76%) **1982** (100%) **1980** (76%) **1978** (60%) **1976** (63%)

District Vote For President

	1988		1984		1980		1976	
D	102,997	(52%)	98,096	(46%)	84,479	(44%)	112,109	(54%)
R	93,955	(47%)	114,896	(54%)	97,509	(50%)	92,379	(44%)
I					9,619	(5%)		

Campaign Finance

	Receipts	Receipts from PACs		Expend-itures
1990				
Applegate (D)	$125,772	$78,205	(62%)	$94,754
1988				
Applegate (D)	$120,435	$66,751	(55%)	$86,061
Abraham (R)	$7,233	$760	(11%)	$7,095

Key Votes

1991	
Authorize use of force against Iraq	N
1990	
Support constitutional amendment on flag desecration	Y
Pass family and medical leave bill over Bush veto	Y
Reduce SDI funding	Y
Allow abortions in overseas military facilities	N
Approve budget summit plan for spending and taxing	N
Approve civil rights bill	Y
1989	
Halt production of B-2 stealth bomber at 13 planes	Y
Oppose capital gains tax cut	Y
Approve federal abortion funding in rape or incest cases	Y
Approve pay raise and revision of ethics rules	N
Pass Democratic minimum wage plan over Bush veto	Y

Voting Studies

	Presidential Support		Party Unity		Conservative Coalition	
Year	S	O	S	O	S	O
1990	30	69	73	24	52	46
1989	45	52	67	29	63	34
1988	28	65	71	24	63	29
1987	31	68	73	23	60	40
1986	24	74	75	20	50	50
1985	29	69	63	23	45	51
1984	39	60	65	32	54	44
1983	27	72	69	27	48	49
1982	39	57	64	31	56	41
1981	45	53	45	50	72	25

Interest Group Ratings

Year	ADA	ACU	AFL-CIO	CCUS
1990	50	33	92	36
1989	70	33	83	50
1988	70	24	100	29
1987	64	13	75	27
1986	65	23	93	35
1985	55	19	59	50
1984	50	33	69	44
1983	70	30	88	35
1982	45	46	84	41
1981	35	27	60	21

19 Edward F. Feighan (D)

Of Lakewood — Elected 1982

Born: Oct. 22, 1947, Lakewood, Ohio.

Education: Attended Borromeo College of Ohio, 1965-66; Loyola U., New Orleans, B.A. 1969; Cleveland-Marshall College of Law, J.D. 1978.

Occupation: Lawyer.

Family: Wife, Nadine Hopwood; four children.

Religion: Roman Catholic.

Political Career: Ohio House, 1973-79; Cuyahoga County Commission, 1979-83; candidate for mayor of Cleveland, 1977.

Capitol Office: 1124 Longworth Bldg. 20515; 225-5731.

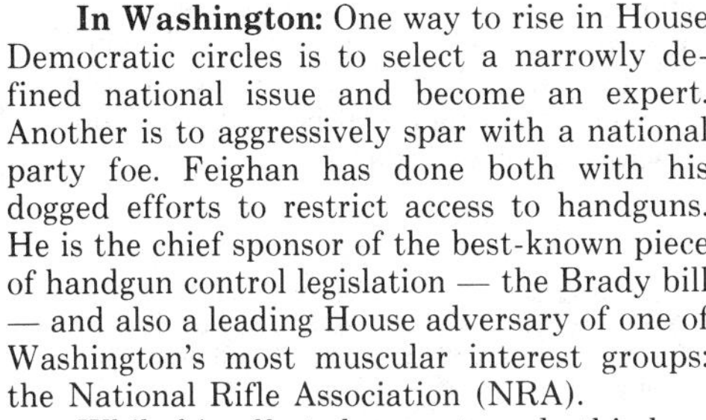

In Washington: One way to rise in House Democratic circles is to select a narrowly defined national issue and become an expert. Another is to aggressively spar with a national party foe. Feighan has done both with his dogged efforts to restrict access to handguns. He is the chief sponsor of the best-known piece of handgun control legislation — the Brady bill — and also a leading House adversary of one of Washington's most muscular interest groups: the National Rifle Association (NRA).

While his efforts have not made this low-key and bookish-looking Ohioan a top-flight Democratic insider, they did earn him an important legislative victory in May 1991: House passage of Feighan's bill mandating a national seven-day waiting period for handgun purchases. The bill is named for James S. Brady, the former press secretary to Ronald Reagan, who was seriously wounded in the 1981 assassination attempt on the president, and for his wife, Sarah, now a leading gun-control activist.

The victory came at an opportune time for Feighan, who has yet to secure a subcommittee chair after nearly a decade in the House. Going into the 102nd Congress, he was next in line to take a subcommittee on Judiciary, but the panel reduced its total of subcommittees by one, and the only vacancy — the Immigration Subcommittee chair — went to Romano L. Mazzoli, who is senior to Feighan and had been ousted from the job in 1989.

Feighan thought about moving on to another political arena early in the 101st Congress. Concerned that his suburban Cleveland 19th would be adversely affected by redistricting before the 1992 election, he set up a committee to look into a 1990 gubernatorial bid. But he dropped the idea when it became apparent that Attorney General Anthony Celebrezze had the party hierarchy behind him. Instead, to protect his turf, Feighan raised and contributed a total of $55,000 for Democratic candidates to the Legislature in 1990.

Feighan should get a boost from publicity following House passage of the Brady bill. His success followed years of frustration as Feighan made little headway winning support for the seven-day waiting period to allow law-enforcement officials to identify those potential buyers, especially convicted felons, prohibited from owning guns.

In a 1987 piece in *The New York Times*, Feighan wrote, "Who would argue against legislation that could keep criminals and crazies from buying a handgun? . . . Not surprisingly, the National Rifle Association is preparing to fight such legislation with all the high-powered political ammunition it can muster."

In the 101st Congress, there was a revival of public interest in gun-control measures, spurred by a proliferation of rapid-fire weapons, an onslaught of drug-related murders, and such incidents as the January 1989 schoolyard massacre in Stockton, Calif. But for the third consecutive time, Feighan watched the waiting period, though favored in most public opinion polls, die at the end of the Congress.

The Judiciary Committee had twice approved the measure, but it had never been approved by the full House. In 1988, Feighan attached his language to the omnibus crime bill, but when it got to the floor, opponents replaced it with an amendment that required the Justice Department to develop a system to enable gun dealers to identify immediately a felon trying to buy a firearm.

A similar proposal (the Staggers amendment) was offered during debate on the Brady bill in 1991, but Feighan had on hand a 1989 letter from the Justice Department that said such a system would take several years to develop. Coupled with an endorsement from Reagan, Feighan scored a 239-186 win.

Until the Brady bill's success in the House, gun-control advocates focused on stopping the rollback of gun laws that occurred in the early 1980s. In the 99th Congress, Feighan tried to push a 15-day waiting period, but an opposing House faction marshaled its forces to deal gun-

Ohio 19

Cleveland Suburbs

The 19th is the "ring around the county" district — a "U-shaped" monstrosity that merges the bulk of Cleveland's two former suburban districts into one. Critics complain that the quickest way from one end of the district to the other is by boat across Lake Erie.

A drive around the "U" takes one through a string of politically diverse suburbs — some dominated by ethnic Democrats, others by white-collar Republicans. There are, however, some common threads. Nearly all these communities are monolithically white and socially conservative.

Along the lake are wealthy GOP towns such as Bay Village and Rocky River. Inland, Democratic bowling alleys replace Republican golf clubs as social centers.

Children and grandchildren of European immigrants have moved out of Cleveland to inner suburbs like Parma, due south of the city. In recent years they have moved again. Parma's population declined in the 1970s and '80s, as residents left their ranch homes of the 1950s for the open spaces of outer suburbs such as Strongsville. But even with the population loss, Parma (population 88,000) is still the eighth-largest city in Ohio and the largest city in the 19th. Nearby steel mills and automobile plants give this section of the district a strong union presence.

Much of the Cleveland financial elite lives in outlying suburbs along Cuyahoga County's eastern boundary, such as Hunting Valley and Chagrin Falls Township. This is solid Republican territory.

Moving north toward the lake, one reenters the world of ethnic politics. The blue-collar workers of Polish and Slovenian descent who fled the city for suburbs such as Euclid and Mayfield have retained their Democratic allegiance, although with a conservative bent nowadays.

Population: 514,174. White 499,960 (97%), Black 7,918 (2%), Other 4,785 (1%). Spanish origin 2,946 (1%). 18 and over 386,888 (75%), 65 and over 66,615 (13%). Median age: 35.

control advocates an embarrassing setback. The pro-gun members pushed through an NRA-backed alternative that not only eliminated many of the gun-control proposals, but even weakened some provisions of the landmark 1968 gun-control law.

Besides provoking the NRA, Feighan's gun-control efforts pose other political risks. The issue has usually been seen as a liberal stance, and the 19th is packed with socially conservative, blue-collar ethnics. However, Feighan has gained some political cover from police organizations that support gun limits. In the 101st Congress, he bolstered his ties to such groups by offering legislation to require federal standards for bullet-resistant vests.

Feighan appeals to his more conservative constituents with a tough anti-drug stand. Chairman of the House Task Force on International Narcotics Control, Feighan also uses his position on the Foreign Affairs Committee to push for tougher economic pressures against nations that are the source of illegal drug exports to the United States.

His other major role on Foreign Affairs has been as a human rights activist, which also has a local impact: A member of the "Helsinki commission," he has aided several Jewish and Lithuanian families in the Cleveland area in obtaining emigration rights for their relatives in the Soviet Union.

At Home: Feighan unseated a member of his own party to win his House seat in 1982, then had to fend off a pair of vigorous Republican challenges to hold it. By 1988, however, he had established himself in the 19th.

A veteran of state and county office with longstanding family ties to the Cuyahoga County Democratic organization, Feighan was relatively well-known when he took on Democratic Rep. Ronald M. Mottl in the 1982 primary. However, he had to overcome the conservative Mottl's popularity among his base of working-class and ethnic voters, and had to make himself known throughout the newly — and oddly — reshaped 19th.

Feighan found a winning issue, though: He played up Mottl's support for President Reagan's 1981 tax and spending cuts, which had infuriated the local Democratic establishment. Feighan lined up the offended party loyalists and upset Mottl by 1,113 votes.

The general election was relatively routine for Feighan. Fairview Park Mayor Richard G. Anter, the GOP nominee, never connected with Mottl's constituency. Feighan carried not only the district's affluent areas but also the blue-collar communities, taking 59 percent.

With Reagan en route to a landslide reelection in 1984, Republicans thought they had a good chance of activating the conservative Mottl vote with former Cuyahoga County Auditor Matthew J. Hatchadorian.

An experienced and aggressive campaigner, Hatchadorian charged that Feighan was too oriented to the inner city. He faulted Feighan for not supporting Reagan on economic and defense issues and said his own moderate Republicanism better suited suburban needs.

Feighan refused to back down, but he did make some efforts to reassure centrist voters, stressing his support for a balanced budget and his work against illegal drugs. In the closing days of the campaign, he unleashed some harsh TV ads, blunting the challenger's momentum: Feighan won with 55 percent of the vote.

His 1986 challenger was state Sen. Gary C. Suhadolnik, who in many respects was a GOP version of Mottl. Young and personable, Suhadolnik lived in the ethnic suburbs south of Cleveland that were Mottl's political base. He was a leader in the 1983 drive to roll back a state income-tax increase and was a high-profile opponent of abortion.

Suhadolnik pounded away at Feighan as a liberal globe-trotter, more concerned with human rights in South Korea than with struggling industrial workers in Cleveland. Feighan countered by pointing to his formation of the Cuyahoga Partnership Project, which mobilized Cleveland-area congressmen to develop ways to assist the local business community.

The incumbent's ace card was his experience in tough campaigns and a willingness to use hardball tactics. On separate occasions he accused Suhadolnik of distributing anti-Semitic campaign literature and of playing to "racial fears." Again, Feighan won 55 percent.

With three costly and futile efforts behind them, Republicans finally gave Feighan a pass in 1988. Rather than enjoy the quiet, he decided to clean up some unfinished business from the 1986 campaign. In 1988, he filed charges with the Federal Election Commission against three people he said were involved in distributing anti-Semitic literature in 1986. This led to accusations and finger-pointing within the GOP and headlines for the Democrat.

Feighan, like most other Ohio incumbents, lost several percentage points to the prevalent anti-Washington mood in 1990. However, he still won almost two-thirds of the vote.

Committees

Foreign Affairs (12th of 28 Democrats)
International Narcotics Control (chairman); Africa; Europe & the Middle East; International Economic Policy & Trade

Judiciary (11th of 21 Democrats)
Crime and Criminal Justice; Economic & Commercial Law

Elections

1990 General		
Edward F. Feighan (D)	132,951	(65%)
Susan M. Lawko (R)	72,315	(35%)
1990 Primary		
Edward F. Feighan (D)	65,771	(85%)
Bruce L. Edwards (D)	11,813	(15%)
1988 General		
Edward F. Feighan (D)	168,065	(70%)
Noel F. Roberts (R)	70,359	(29%)

Previous Winning Percentages: 1986 (55%) **1984** (55%) **1982** (59%)

District Vote For President

	1988	1984	1980	1976
D	114,751 (45%)	94,595 (41%)	81,481 (36%)	90,411 (42%)
R	139,652 (55%)	137,021 (59%)	124,246 (56%)	120,799 (56%)
I			16,943 (8%)	

Campaign Finance

	Receipts	Receipts from PACs		Expend-itures
1990				
Feighan (D)	$323,072	$217,618	(67%)	$229,857
Lawko (R)	$7,863	0		$9,508
1988				
Feighan (D)	$391,199	$205,414	(53%)	$226,086
Roberts (R)	$522	$95	(18%)	$522

Key Votes

1991	
Authorize use of force against Iraq	N
1990	
Support constitutional amendment on flag desecration	N
Pass family and medical leave bill over Bush veto	Y
Reduce SDI funding	?
Allow abortions in overseas military facilities	?
Approve budget summit plan for spending and taxing	N
Approve civil rights bill	Y
1989	
Halt production of B-2 stealth bomber at 13 planes	Y
Oppose capital gains tax cut	Y
Approve federal abortion funding in rape or incest cases	Y
Approve pay raise and revision of ethics rules	N
Pass Democratic minimum wage plan over Bush veto	Y

Voting Studies

	Presidential Support		Party Unity		Conservative Coalition	
Year	**S**	**O**	**S**	**O**	**S**	**O**
1990	18	71	86	5	17	78
1989	31	66	89	3	17	71
1988	17	80	86	4	18	79
1987	16	81	88	6	35	63
1986	17	81	90	5	14	86
1985	29	71	88	9	24	76
1984	26	71	81	17	17	81
1983	20	78	86	11	22	75

Interest Group Ratings

Year	ADA	ACU	AFL-CIO	CCUS
1990	94	9	100	29
1989	90	4	100	40
1988	95	0	100	38
1987	92	0	100	29
1986	95	0	100	33
1985	70	10	82	32
1984	85	13	77	31
1983	90	4	94	20

20 Mary Rose Oakar (D)

Of Cleveland — Elected 1976

Born: March 5, 1940, Cleveland, Ohio.
Education: Ursuline College, B.A. 1962; John Carroll U., M.A. 1966.
Occupation: High school English and speech teacher.
Family: Single.
Religion: Roman Catholic.
Political Career: Cleveland City Council, 1973-77.
Capitol Office: 2231 Rayburn Bldg. 20515; 225-5871.

In Washington: A favorite among colleagues on the Banking Committee and within the Democratic Caucus, Oakar holds a number of positions of prominence in the House, chairing subcommittees on Banking and House Administration and a task force on the Select Aging Committee. She is involved in many small ways in a number of issues and makes some headway on her causes, even if she has not established a reputation as a legislator with a grand vision.

Oakar is now the sixth-ranking Democrat on Banking and is one of the most popular of those members who sit on the committee's top tier. Though she participated in crafting Banking's most important legislation in the 101st Congress, such as restructuring the savings and loan industry and overhauling federal housing programs, she was not a central player.

Oakar is also the fourth-ranking Democrat on the Post Office and Civil Service Committee, where she pursues her most enduring interest, protecting federal employees. During consideration of the 1989 S&L bailout bill, Oakar was given the responsibility of bridging the Banking and Post Office committees to satisfy each panel's interests on personnel matters in the bill and avoid having to refer it to Post Office. Oakar authored an amendment to give thrift regulatory agencies greater flexibility in paying outside bank examiners. It was adopted by voice vote.

In the 101st Congress, Oakar sponsored a bill to increase pay for unscheduled overtime for federal employees. The bill, aimed at compensating FBI agents and other federal law officers, became law in 1989.

Oakar and Majority Leader Richard A. Gephardt of Missouri teamed in 1990 to promote a package designed to help workers and communities adjust to the loss of defense contracts. Their plan was added to the fiscal 1991 defense authorization bill.

As chairman of the Banking Subcommittee on Economic Stabilization through the 101st Congress, Oakar was in a good position to look out for economic development issues important to Cleveland and the industrial Midwest. She did fail, however, in an effort to have jurisdiction over the Export-Import Bank moved to her panel in the 101st Congress. Blocked from doing so by freshman Rep. Jim McDermott of Washington at an early organizational meeting, Oakar became very upset. Unable to alter jurisdictions, Oakar switched subcommittee chairs: In the 102nd Congress, she is chairman of the Subcommittee on International Development.

Oakar misses few opportunities to promote Cleveland. She conditioned her support for the 1979 Chrysler Corp. loan guarantee on assurances that Chrysler would not relocate any plants in the South. The appropriations bill for housing programs often contains funds earmarked for Oakar.

She is also a booster of space programs, in part because some of the funds trickle to the National Aeronautics and Space Administration's Lewis Research Center in Cleveland. Oakar and others in the Ohio delegation are big fans of the planned space station *Freedom*; Lewis is responsible for overseeing production of the station's power system.

Oakar's loyalty to space programs placed her in the unusual position of opposing an amendment to shift $714 million from NASA to domestic programs, including housing. Oakar told the sponsor, New York Democrat Charles E. Schumer, "This would be gutting the future of our country, and I have to oppose it."

On House Administration, Oakar chairs the Subcommittee on Personnel and Police, where she has pushed to give House employees some benefits already enjoyed by other federal employees. In the 101st Congress she began touting an amendment to the Family and Medical Leave Act giving House employees the same family leave as other federal workers.

The daughter of Maronite Catholics, Oakar has taken a passionate interest in the plight of war-torn Lebanon. The House approved her amendments to foreign aid bills in the 101st Congress earmarking $7.5 million in development assistance to Lebanon.

Oakar invests much energy and feeling into

Ohio 20

Cleveland — Central, West Suburbs

The line between the 20th and 21st districts generally divides Cleveland's white and black populations. The 20th is the white district, containing the state's largest concentration of ethnic voters. Poles, Czechs, Italians and Germans are the largest groups, but there are dozens of other ethnic communities represented by at least a restaurant or two on the West Side.

The city's steel industry fueled the ethnic influx around the turn of the century, with immigrants settling near the West Side mills. Steel, automobile and aluminum plants combine with smaller businesses to make up the employment base today.

But many of the younger people who work there have bought homes in the suburbs. The West Side district suffered a 19 percent population loss in the 1970s, a rate of decline exceeded in Ohio only by the neighboring 21st. A large proportion of those who remain on the West Side are elderly.

As a result of this population loss, almost half the electorate now lies outside the Cleveland city limits. With Berea, Middleburg Heights and part of Strongsville joining the 20th, the district now pushes past the Ohio Turnpike, about 12 miles from downtown Cleveland. It is still a heavily ethnic district, however, and solidly Democratic.

The downtown area remains totally within the 20th. The city's economic problems of the 1970s, notably its near-bankruptcy under then-Mayor Dennis Kucinich, made it a national symbol of urban decay. But Cleveland today is stronger than many industrial cities of the Frost Belt, mainly because it is making the successful transition to a service economy. To offset auto and steel slumps, a consortium comprised of the city's largest companies has mapped out a long-term, diversified plan for growth — a number of small, high-tech firms have already been attracted. Condominiums are being constructed near the new $200 million Standard Oil of Ohio (Sohio) headquarters, and old dry-goods warehouses are being converted to homes — the first downtown housing to go up in a generation. To help keep suburbanites in the city after dark, several art deco theaters have been restored, and Cleveland's Lake Erie waterfront is receiving a facelift. Even the Cuyahoga River — which was once so polluted that it caught fire — has been cleaned up.

Population: 514,164. White 486,329 (95%), Black 12,918 (3%), Other 5,254 (1%). Spanish origin 16,217 (3%). 18 and over 383,041 (75%), 65 and over 66,146 (13%). Median age: 32.

legislating. She received training at the Royal Academy of Dramatic Arts in London, and she still seems to be on stage sometimes as she speaks of the plight of women, the elderly, or her beleaguered hometown.

At the end of the 101st Congress, Oakar went on a crusade to provide Medicare coverage for mammograms to detect breast cancer. Oakar had promoted the benefit in the 1988 catastrophic coverage law, but Congress repealed that law in 1989. But Democratic budget negotiators were unable to persuade Republicans to accept the program. "When I found out they left it out, I just lost it," Oakar said. She complained loudly and repeatedly on the House floor, pursuing it during Democratic Caucus and whip meetings. "It was just day after day of badgering," she said. "Finally, [Ways and Means Chairman Dan] Rostenkowski said to me, 'OK, Mary Rose, you've convinced me.' " The funding was tucked into the final version of the 1990 budget-reconciliation bill.

Early in her career, Oakar joined the Democratic whip organization and showed party leaders a capacity for hard work on routine leadership tasks. She joined House Administration in 1983 to protect leadership interests. When Geraldine A. Ferraro of New York left the House to run for vice president in 1984, Oakar took her place as secretary (later changed to vice chairman) of the Democratic Caucus.

But in 1988, Oakar failed in her bid for the caucus chair, losing to then-Budget Committee Chairman William H. Gray III of Pennsylvania, the most prominent black member of the House. She got 80 votes, while Gray won with 146 votes. Oklahoman Mike Synar ran third with 33 votes.

In early 1987, the Cleveland *Plain Dealer* disclosed questionable dealings between Oakar and two aides. In one case, Oakar was found to have kept a former aide and housemate on salary for two years after the woman had moved to New York City; in another, Oakar had given a $10,000 salary increase to an aide the same month she and Oakar bought a house together. The House ethics committee conducted an investigation and found she had broken House rules and federal laws that require a staffer to work in a member's district or Washington office. The committee did not recommend any punishment, and Oakar repaid the money.

At Home: Oakar's efforts to help Cleveland may not always bring her legislative success, but they have helped her win elections with ease.

Oakar has used her communicating ability to make her achievements well known to constituents. During the four years she represented a largely Irish and Puerto Rican ward on Cleveland's City Council, she got considerable media attention for her plan to make "creative use" of vacant lots and for working to outlaw the sale of airplane glue to minors.

In 1976, when Democratic Rep. James V. Stanton left the district for an unsuccessful run at the Senate, Oakar and 11 others entered the Democratic primary. Oakar's campaign focused on the fact that she was the only woman running and, among the major candidates, the only one without a law degree. Although she did not mention it as much, she was also the only one who had been a telephone operator or a high school English and speech teacher.

The power blocs in Cleveland divided their support among Oakar and three other candidates. Oakar's most significant endorsements were from a United Auto Workers local and from the Fire Fighters Union.

After the 1980 census Oakar became concerned about the effect of redistricting on her political future. She suggested enlarging the size of the House — "There's nothing magic about 435 members," she said — to protect urban representation. She also offered a job to the daughter of the Speaker of Ohio's House, which would draw the new districts.

The Legislature made sure Ohio's only female House member would have a safe district, drawing the lines so she retained virtually all her old constituents and gained new Democrats.

Oakar demonstrated her home-base strength in 1988. The previous year, the ethics committee inquiry into her payroll practices received prominent coverage in the local media, but not for a moment was Oakar's re-election threatened.

Colorful and controversial former Cleveland Mayor Dennis J. Kucinich entered the 1988 Democratic primary. He ran an underfunded and quiet — by Kucinich standards — campaign, scarcely mentioning the ethics issue. Oakar, meanwhile, stumped the district in her usual fashion. She won the primary by a 3-to-1 margin, and had no trouble in November.

Committees

Banking, Finance & Urban Affairs (6th of 31 Democrats)
International Development, Finance, Trade & Monetary Policy (chairman); Economic Stabilization; Housing & Community Development

House Administration (6th of 15 Democrats)
Personnel & Police (chairman); Accounts

Post Office & Civil Service (4th of 15 Democrats)
Compensation & Employee Benefits (vice chairman)

Select Aging (6th of 42 Democrats)
Social Security and Women (chairman); Health & Long-Term Care; Retirement, Income & Employment

Elections

1990 General		
Mary Rose Oakar (D)	109,390	(73%)
Bill Smith (R)	39,749	(27%)
1990 Primary		
Mary Rose Oakar (D)	65,890	(80%)
David Perry (D)	16,892	(20%)
1988 General		
Mary Rose Oakar (D)	146,715	(83%)
Michael Sajna (R)	30,944	(17%)

Previous Winning Percentages: **1986** (85%) **1984** (100%) **1982** (86%) **1980** (100%) **1978** (100%) **1976** (81%)

District Vote For President

	1988		1984		1980		1976	
D	103,933	(57%)	95,297	(51%)	80,701	(55%)	99,119	(61%)
R	77,551	(42%)	88,691	(48%)	57,398	(39%)	59,483	(36%)
I					8,934	(6%)		

Campaign Finance

	Receipts	Receipts from PACs		Expend-itures
1990				
Oakar (D)	$337,442	$283,859	(84%)	$284,053
1988				
Oakar (D)	$691,256	$392,918	(57%)	$783,180

Key Votes

1991	
Authorize use of force against Iraq	N
1990	
Support constitutional amendment on flag desecration	N
Pass family and medical leave bill over Bush veto	Y
Reduce SDI funding	Y
Allow abortions in overseas military facilities	N
Approve budget summit plan for spending and taxing	N
Approve civil rights bill	Y
1989	
Halt production of B-2 stealth bomber at 13 planes	Y
Oppose capital gains tax cut	Y
Approve federal abortion funding in rape or incest cases	N
Approve pay raise and revision of ethics rules	Y
Pass Democratic minimum wage plan over Bush veto	Y

Voting Studies

	Presidential Support		Party Unity		Conservative Coalition	
Year	S	O	S	O	S	O
1990	17	80	87	6	15	85
1989	33	60	91	5	12	85
1988	19	65	88	5	8	63
1987	17	77	87	4	19	74
1986	16	80	92	2	8	88
1985	18	79	94	3	11	89
1984	25	73	94	5	8	90
1983	26	73	86	13	22	75
1982	31	61	83	11	22	70
1981	34	59	80	11	23	65

Interest Group Ratings

Year	ADA	ACU	AFL-CIO	CCUS
1990	83	4	92	23
1989	90	0	92	40
1988	90	8	100	17
1987	96	5	100	0
1986	95	5	93	12
1985	80	5	94	23
1984	95	4	83	31
1983	80	4	100	20
1982	70	21	100	33
1981	55	7	93	0

21 Louis Stokes (D)

Of Warrensville Heights — Elected 1968

Born: Feb. 23, 1925, Cleveland, Ohio.
Education: Western Reserve U., 1946-48; Cleveland-Marshall College of Law, J.D. 1953.
Military Service: Army, 1943-46.
Occupation: Lawyer.
Family: Wife, Jeannette Francis; four children.
Religion: African Methodist Episcopal.
Political Career: No previous office.
Capitol Office: 2365 Rayburn Bldg. 20515; 225-7032.

In Washington: With two decades in the House behind him, Stokes has had something of a two-track career. He is a senior Democrat on the Appropriations Committee, where he works quietly on minority issues and urban policy. But he is best known as the man to whom the Democratic leadership turns when it has a touchy assignment, especially if the matter of ethics is involved.

In 1991, with Congress searching to define its ethical standards in the wake of several financial and personal scandals involving members during the 101st Congress, Stokes was asked for the second time in a decade to chair the ethics committee.

During his years in the House, Stokes generally has favored milder forms of punishment for members under ethics scrutiny. "My whole career has been one of fighting for the underdog. I'm sure that's reflected in my votes," he said in 1991. "But I think that even more than that, my record for being fair is what makes people respect me."

Stokes' first turn in the ethics chair was from 1981 to 1985. He took the job at the request of then-Speaker Thomas P. O'Neill Jr. of Massachusetts. In calling on Stokes, O'Neill took the chair from Florida's Charles E. Bennett, a man with a rigid code of personal ethics O'Neill found too unyielding. Bennett had presided over hearings into the Abscam bribery scandal, and under him the ethics committee issued recommendations that led to a series of House disciplinary actions, including the first-ever expulsion of a member.

With the case of the last Abscam figure, valued leadership lieutenant John P. Murtha of Pennsylvania, pending before the committee, O'Neill replaced Bennett with Stokes, a committee member who had been a voice for the accused. The committee ultimately recommended no action against Murtha, provoking its counsel to resign.

Stokes' flexibility was illustrated in 1983, when the committee brought charges against two members, Democrat Gerry E. Studds of Massachusetts and Republican Daniel B. Crane of Illinois, for engaging in sex with teenage House pages. The committee recommended a reprimand (the lowest level of punishment) in both cases; Stokes called it a stern decision, because, he said, "the member must live with this condemnation forever."

But there was an outcry from many members that the punishment was too weak, and the House increased the penalties to censure.

While they reversed his position, Stokes' House colleagues praised his leadership on a committee assigned to the onerous job of casting judgment on fellow House members. Republican leader Robert H. Michel of Illinois called the ethics chairmanship "the most distasteful job in the House," and when Stokes finished his final remarks on the Studds-Crane cases, he received a standing ovation.

Outside of ethics, Stokes served in the late 1960s on the House Committee on Un-American Activities, a panel he worked to abolish. He was tapped during the late 1970s to chair the committee investigating the assassinations of President John F. Kennedy and the Rev. Dr. Martin Luther King Jr., and between 1983 and 1989, he served on the Intelligence Committee. His rise to the chairmanship of that panel during the 100th Congress also earned Stokes a seat on the special committee probing the Reagan administration's secret arms sales to Iran and the diversion of profits from those sales to the Nicaraguan contras.

A strong critic of the administration's actions in the Iran-contra affair, Stokes gained the spotlight with his dogged questioning of committee witnesses. He stood out when he expressed doubts about the truthfulness of Rear Adm. John M. Poindexter, the former national security adviser who said he had authorized the contra-aid scheme without ever involving President Reagan.

Stokes also lectured then-Marine Lt. Col. Oliver L. North, whose dramatic professions of patriotic duty had earned him a national constituency. North — who wore his medal-bedecked uniform to the hearings — criticized Congress for failing to back Reagan's contra aid

Ohio 21

Cleveland — East; Cleveland Heights

One of the axioms of Ohio politics is that to win statewide, a Democratic candidate must build a 100,000-vote edge in Cuyahoga County. Most of that lead has to be built in the 21st, which is anchored in Cleveland's heavily black East Side.

The district includes poor inner-city areas as well as middle-class territory farther from the downtown area. Devastated by the riots of the 1960s, inner-city neighborhoods Hough and Glenville still bear the scars of poverty but can claim some new residential and commercial development. Farther east toward the lake are the middle-class, white ethnic neighborhoods of Collinwood, inhabited by Italians, and St. Clare, dominated by Poles, Yugoslavs and other Eastern Europeans.

The 21st is 62 percent black and heavily Democratic. During the last decade, it has been the most Democratic district in the state. In 11 East Side wards in 1980, Jimmy Carter outpolled Ronald Reagan by margins of at least 20-to-1. In 1984, 10 of these wards gave Walter F. Mondale a 14-1 margin over Reagan. In 1988, Michael S. Dukakis carried eight of these wards by 14-to-1 or better over George Bush.

The 21st's major suburbs are Cleveland Heights, Shaker Heights and the western half of University Heights. With a large proportion of Jews and young professionals, these are among Ohio's most liberal communities. North of Shaker Heights is Cleveland Heights, many of whose integrated neighborhoods are a short walk from University Circle, home of Case Western Reserve University and Cleveland's cultural hub.

From the circle area, commuters drive along historic Euclid Avenue to their jobs downtown. While the avenue now bears the marks of poverty, it was known as "Millionaires' Row" at the turn of the century. Few of the old mansions are left today. The one belonging to John D. Rockefeller, founder of Standard Oil, was razed to make way for a gas station.

Population: 514,169. White 186,814 (36%), Black 320,809 (62%), Other 3,314 (1%). Spanish origin 5,059 (1%). 18 and over 372,949 (73%), 65 and over 63,051 (12%). Median age: 31.

policy. But Stokes, who served in the Army during World War II, reminded North that many Americans, including military veterans, opposed aid to the contras. "I hope . . . that you will never forget that others, too, love America just as much as you do and that others, too, will die for America, just as quick as you will," Stokes told North.

During his tenure on Intelligence Stokes successfully advocated legislation to create a scholarship program to increase the role of minorities in the intelligence-gathering field.

Though Stokes came to Congress in an era of black activism — he was first elected the year King was assassinated — he has not been known for stridency in his advocacy of minority causes. "I think most blacks are still willing to work within the system," he has said.

However, Stokes fumed during the Reagan administration over what he viewed as the president's antipathy toward minority interests, and occasionally his anger boiled over. "Ronald Reagan has made racism respectable," he complained.

Much of Stokes' legislative activity is informed by the black experience. In making his point to North about respecting even those laws he opposed, Stokes reminisced about being a black soldier in the segregated Army of World War II. "I wore [the uniform] as proudly as you do, even though our government required black and white soldiers in the same Army to live, sleep, eat and travel separate and apart, while fighting and dying for our country," Stokes said.

On the Veterans Affairs-Housing and Urban Development Subcommittee at Appropriations, Stokes is a consistent spokesman for minority concerns, supporting funds for black colleges and housing programs and backing affirmative action in the work place. In recent years, Stokes has pushed a variety of amendments in Appropriations that illustrate his priorities. One added $140 million for Pell grants for college tuition, another restored $100 million for grants to elementary schools in poor communities. A third added $25 million in operating subsidies for public housing programs.

At Home: Stokes is feeling some pressure from a new generation of black leaders emerging in Cleveland, symbolized by the 1989 election of Michael White as mayor. But the Stokes family is still a dominant force in city politics, as it has been for more than two decades. Louis Stokes' younger brother, Carl, grabbed the spotlight in the mid-1960s when he first ran for mayor of Cleveland. Carl temporarily left politics after two terms as mayor (1967-71), but he re-emerged in 1983 to be elected to the Cleveland Municipal Court, and was re-elected in 1987.

Louis Stokes' first victory was won as much in court as on Cleveland's East Side. Representing a black Republican, he charged in a 1967 suit that the Ohio Legislature had gerrymandered the state's congressional districts, dividing the minority vote and preventing the election of a black candidate. Stokes won an appeal before the U.S. Supreme Court, forcing the lines to be redrawn.

In remapping, Rep. Charles A. Vanik, a white Democrat, wound up with a 21st District that was about 60 percent black. Vanik then decided to run in an adjacent district that contained much of his former, heavily ethnic constituency.

Stokes had plenty of company in the 1968 contest for the open 21st: 13 other candidates filed to run in the Democratic primary. The outcome was little in doubt, though. Aided by his brother in City Hall and by his reputation as a civil rights lawyer, Stokes won with 41 percent of the primary vote. That November, he became the first black congressman from Ohio by defeating Charles P. Lucas — the Republican he had represented in court the previous year.

Republicans have offered no resistance against Stokes in recent years. Engineer Franklin H. Roski has been Stokes' GOP opponent in the last three elections: Stokes' 80 percent in 1990 was his lowest showing.

Committees

Standards of Official Conduct (Chairman)

Appropriations (7th of 37 Democrats)
District of Columbia; Labor, Health & Human Services, Education & Related Agencies; Veterans Affairs, Housing & Urban Development, & Independent Agencies

Elections

1990 General

Louis Stokes (D)	103,338	(80%)
Franklin H. Roski (R)	25,906	(20%)

1988 General

Louis Stokes (D)	148,388	(86%)
Franklin H. Roski (R)	24,804	(14%)

Previous Winning Percentages: **1986** (82%) **1984** (82%) **1982** (86%) **1980** (88%) **1978** (86%) **1976** (84%) **1974** (82%) **1972** (81%) **1970** (78%) **1968** (75%)

District Vote For President

	1988	1984	1980	1976
D	144,023 (80%)	159,536 (78%)	154,021 (61%)	159,656 (66%)
R	33,866 (19%)	41,967 (21%)	81,587 (32%)	75,311 (31%)
I			16,092 (6%)	

Campaign Finance

	Receipts	Receipts from PACs	Expend-itures
1990			
Stokes (D)	$250,022	$137,575 (55%)	$198,984
1988			
Stokes (D)	$241,646	$147,800 (61%)	$173,534

Key Votes

1991

Authorize use of force against Iraq	N

1990

Support constitutional amendment on flag desecration	N
Pass family and medical leave bill over Bush veto	Y
Reduce SDI funding	Y
Allow abortions in overseas military facilities	Y
Approve budget summit plan for spending and taxing	N
Approve civil rights bill	Y

1989

Halt production of B-2 stealth bomber at 13 planes	Y
Oppose capital gains tax cut	Y
Approve federal abortion funding in rape or incest cases	Y
Approve pay raise and revision of ethics rules	Y
Pass Democratic minimum wage plan over Bush veto	Y

Voting Studies

	Presidential Support		Party Unity		Conservative Coalition	
Year	S	O	S	O	S	O
1990	14	81	88	5	7	89
1989	28	70	90	1	7	80
1988	16	59	81	1	0	66
1987	13	77	91	1	9	77
1986	11	82	87	2	2	80
1985	15	83	93	1	5	93
1984	22	68	88	3	0	93
1983	11	80	86	3	6	85
1982	27	65	91	4	10	86
1981	29	66	93	4	5	91

Interest Group Ratings

Year	ADA	ACU	AFL-CIO	CCUS
1990	100	4	100	29
1989	95	0	91	33
1988	70	0	100	25
1987	88	0	100	7
1986	100	0	93	12
1985	95	0	100	24
1984	95	0	85	33
1983	80	0	94	18
1982	85	10	100	24
1981	90	0	93	11

Oklahoma

U.S. CONGRESS

SENATE 1 D, 1 R

HOUSE 4 D, 2 R

LEGISLATURE

Senate 37 D, 11 R

House 69 D, 32 R

ELECTIONS

1988 Presidential Vote	
Bush	58%
Dukakis	41%
1984 Presidential Vote	
Reagan	69%
Mondale	31%
1980 Presidential Vote	
Reagan	61%
Carter	35%
Anderson	3%
Turnout rate in 1986	30%
Turnout rate in 1988	49%
Turnout rate in 1990	37%

(as percentage of voting age population)

POPULATION AND GROWTH

1980 population	3,025,290
1990 population (28th in the nation)	3,145,585
Percent change 1980-1990	+4%

DEMOGRAPHIC BREAKDOWN

White	82%
Black	7%
American Indian, Eskimo, or Aleut	8%
(Hispanic origin)	3%
Urban	67%
Rural	33%
Born in state	63%
Foreign-born	2%

MAJOR CITIES

Oklahoma City	444,719
Tulsa	367,302
Lawton	80,561
Norman	80,071
Broken Arrow	58,043

AREA AND LAND USE

Area	68,655 sq. miles (19th)
Farm	74%
Forest	17%
Federally owned	2%

Gov. David Walters (D)
Of Oklahoma City — Elected 1990

Born: Nov. 20, 1951, Canute, Okla.
Education: U. of Oklahoma, B.S. 1973; Harvard U., M.B.A. 1977.
Occupation: Real estate executive.
Religion: Roman Catholic.
Political Career: Democratic nominee for governor, 1986.
Next Election: 1994.

WORK

Occupations	
White-collar	51%
Blue-collar	33%
Service workers	13%
Government Workers	
Federal	47,395
State	76,003
Local	125,951

MONEY

Median family income	$ 17,688	(35th)
Tax burden per capita	$ 903	(20th)

EDUCATION

Spending per pupil through grade 12	$ 3,093	(43rd)
Persons with college degrees	15%	(28th)

CRIME

Violent crime rate	492 per 100,000	(24th)

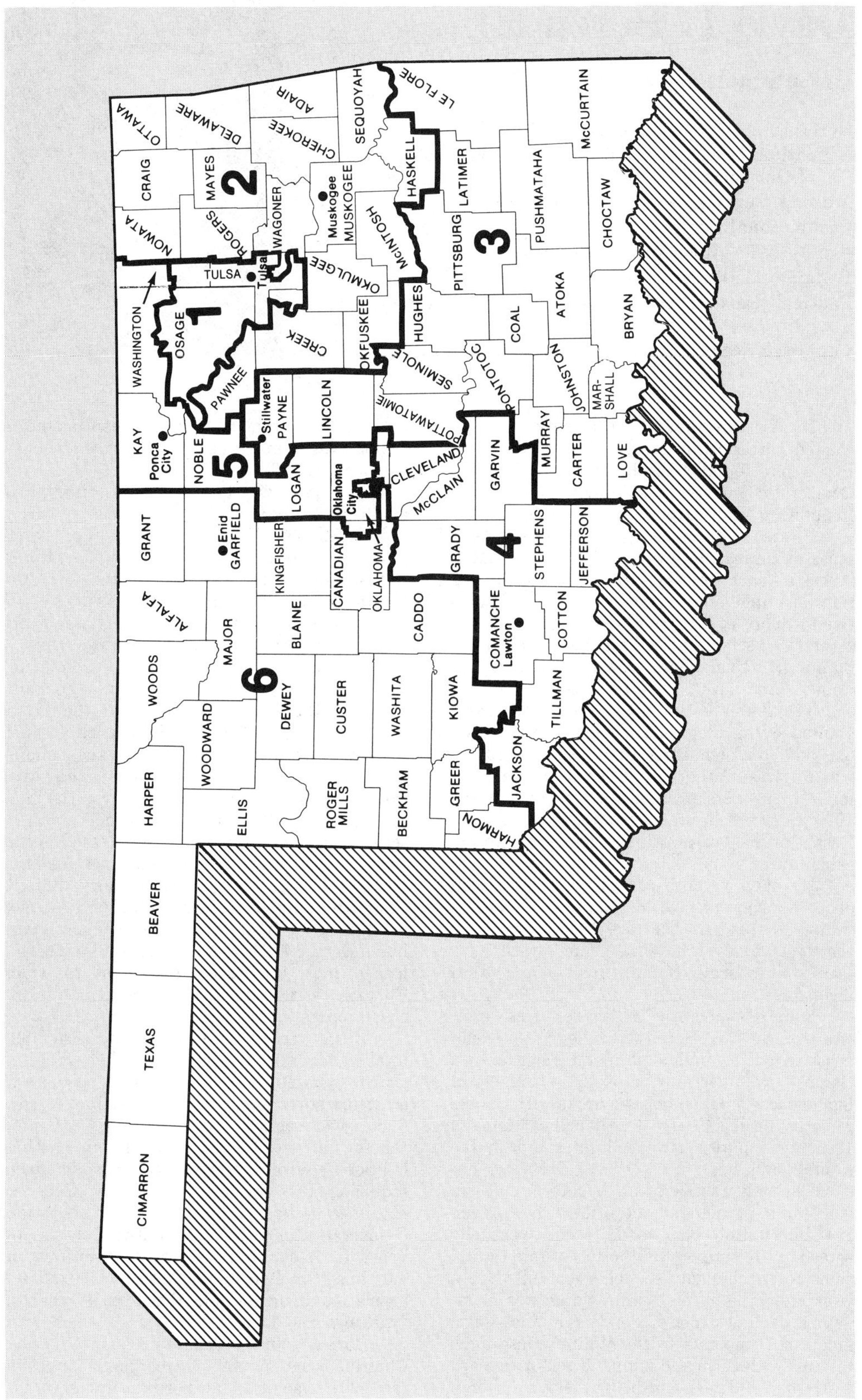
OTTAWA
DELAWARE
ADAIR
SEQUOYAH
LE FLORE
McCURTAIN
CRAIG
MAYES
2
CHEROKEE
HASKELL
LATIMER
PUSHMATAHA
CHOCTAW
NOWATA
ROGERS
WAGONER
Muskogee
MUSKOGEE
McINTOSH
PITTSBURG
3
TULSA
Tulsa
OKMULGEE
WASHINGTON
OSAGE
1
CREEK
OKFUSKEE
HUGHES
COAL
ATOKA
BRYAN
PAWNEE
SEMINOLE
PONTOTOC
JOHNSTON
MAR-
SHALL
KAY
Ponca
City
NOBLE
Stillwater
PAYNE
LINCOLN
POTTAWATOMIE
MURRAY
CARTER
LOVE
5
LOGAN
Oklahoma
City
CLEVELAND
McCLAIN
GARVIN
GRANT
Enid
GARFIELD
KINGFISHER
CANADIAN
OKLAHOMA
GRADY
4
STEPHENS
JEFFERSON
ALFALFA
MAJOR
BLAINE
CADDO
COMANCHE
Lawton
COTTON
WOODS
6
DEWEY
CUSTER
WASHITA
KIOWA
TILLMAN
WOODWARD
HARPER
ELLIS
ROGER
MILLS
BECKHAM
GREER
JACKSON
HARMON
BEAVER
TEXAS
CIMARRON

David L. Boren (D)

Of Seminole — Elected 1978

Born: April 21, 1941, Washington, D.C.
Education: Yale U., B.A. 1963; Oxford U., M.A. 1965; U. of Oklahoma, J.D. 1968.
Military Service: National Guard, 1968-75.
Occupation: Lawyer.
Family: Wife, Molly Wanda Shi; two children.
Religion: Methodist.
Political Career: Okla. House, 1967-75; governor, 1975-79.
Capitol Office: 453 Russell Bldg. 20510; 224-4721.

In Washington: A centrist who has eschewed partisanship during his Senate tenure, Boren has found himself at odds with the Democratic leadership as often as with the Republican White House.

Blessed with a sharp mind and a keen sense of timing, Boren — like President Bush — has a knack for staying close to the shifting tides of public opinion without appearing captive to them. In fact, Boren resembles Bush in several respects; both call oil-rich states home, both went to Yale, both grew up around politicians — and both like to be liked.

Yet Boren is not about to be taken for granted by his Republican friends, nor locked out by fellow Democrats. In January of 1991 he voted against authorizing Bush to use military force in the Persian Gulf, but throughout the 101st Congress he was a leading proponent of Bush's prime tax priority: cutting the capital gains tax.

He plays to both camps by being candid about his conservative inclinations. He is also willing to run with the rare Democratic issue that suits him. "I have to make myself be a team player," says Boren. "It's not a natural inclination."

Some Democratic colleagues who grow weary of watching Boren shift allegiances would insist that is an understatement. For example, Boren — who has long enjoyed the support of big business in Oklahoma — broke with Senate Majority Leader George J. Mitchell of Maine in 1989 to support Bush's call for a cut in the capital gains tax.

The only Democrat on Senate Finance to vote for a permanent cut offered by Oregon Republican Bob Packwood, Boren eventually agreed not to support GOP efforts to tie capital gains to the budget reconciliation bill. But a week later, the never-bashful Boren was trumpeting the "Packwood-Boren" cut and leading a group of Democrats to the White House for a meeting with Bush and budget director Richard G. Darman. "That's not being disloyal," Boren said. "I think that it's helping keep people in the party who might otherwise get disillusioned with the party."

Yet just when Democratic grumblings might begin to erupt, Boren can weigh in with a well-timed partisan counterpunch. For example, during his apostasy on capital gains, Boren was one of the first to voice outrage over the White House's handling of the failed 1989 attempt by members of the Panamanian military to oust Gen. Manuel Antonio Noriega.

As chairman of the Intelligence Committee since 1987, Boren had nurtured quiet cooperation with the White House. But on the day of the failed coup, Boren spontaneously headed straight from the briefing room to the cameras to criticize Bush's staff for bungling the situation. Although Boren was willing to let the issue subside, the White House was not; national security adviser Brent Scowcroft lashed out at what he said was congressional micromanagement of foreign policy. Subsequently, Boren's committee and its House counterpart — now led by his even more aggressive fellow Oklahoma Democrat Dave McCurdy — have become locked in a duel over the extent to which Congress should have a hand in monitoring covert operations.

Bush unexpectedly vetoed a fiscal 1991 intelligence authorization bill that required Congress be notified of requests by agencies to a foreign government or private citizen to conduct covert actions on behalf of the United States. The veto was a slap to Boren, who had led Senate efforts to excise legislative language requiring the president to notify Congress within 48 hours of initiating a covert operation. Democrats thought the administration was on board for a compromise requiring notification only in a "timely fashion," but Bush balked at a legislative report defining that term as meaning "within a few days."

Boren joined Senate Armed Services Chairman Sam Nunn of Georgia in opposing the 1991 resolution authorizing Bush to use force against Iraq. But Boren quickly shifted gears after the firing commenced, chastising those Democrats who balked at a concurrent resolution supporting Bush. "This is not the time to micromanage," he said. "This is time for Congress to play a supporting role."

Even as Boren was seeking bipartisanship in foreign affairs, Republicans greeted his continuing efforts to overhaul the campaign finance system with deep partisan suspicion.

After acrimonious debates that spanned several Congresses, the Senate in the 101st passed a bill along the lines proposed by Boren, only to have it die in conference. The Democratic measure would have created voluntary spending limits on a state-by-state basis, with participating candidates receiving incentives such as vouchers for reduced broadcast and postage costs. It would also have eliminated political action committees. Boren reintroduced his bill in the 102nd Congress.

"Good government" issues have always worked well for Boren, who as a candidate for governor in 1974 campaigned with a broom close to hand, promising to sweep Oklahoma City clean. With then-Majority Leader Robert C. Byrd as his chief ally, he pushed the Senate repeatedly to overhaul the system of financing congressional elections, meeting fierce Republican resistance. Byrd allowed the issue to return time and again to the Senate floor in the 100th Congress, producing eight cloture votes, a record for a single issue.

Boren's crusade for limits on political action committees and on campaign spending has attracted widespread attention and made him something of a hero for those who worry about the effects of the current campaign finance system on American politics. He refuses contributions from PACs, though he does accept a substantial share of his own campaign funding from wealthy individual oil producers; he has consistently sought to protect federal support for the oil and gas industry.

Boren's assault on PACs began in earnest in 1985. The explosive growth of PAC funding over the previous decade, he said, was perverting the political system and sapping Congress' ability to make independent judgments. "You begin to ask yourself whether we're going to have any grass-roots democracy left," he worried.

Boren pushed his bill relentlessly, even when there were only a handful of other senators who agreed with him. After an initial skirmish in 1985 — when an overwhelming majority voted to avoid having to make a decision on the issue — the bill reached an important moment shortly before the 1986 elections. A strong majority actually voted for Boren's plan, 69-30, but this was deceptive. Amendments that drew Republican votes made House passage politically impossible. In 1987 and 1988, Boren and Byrd were unable to muster the 60 votes needed to shut debate, despite reworking the bill several times.

Cynics see Boren's commitment as a reflection not only of his beliefs but of his own campaign fundraising situation. Boren can afford to reject PAC money because the independent oil producers and royalty holders so important to Oklahoma's economy generally do not operate through PACs, preferring to give money to candidates on their own.

Meanwhile, Boren has been one of the most effective supporters of the oil and gas industries, working on matters such as the 1988 repeal of the windfall-profits tax on oil. Boren is well suited for this role because he knows how to fight for Oklahoma interests without alienating his party's Northern majority in the Senate. He is a hard man to dislike, even for those who disagree with him.

Boren does not look on first glance to be a power broker or even a politician. Oklahoma political cartoonists used to draw him as the Pillsbury Doughboy. But he knows the system and how to operate within it. "The appearance of having influence develops rapidly," Boren once said, "and so can the appearance of not having influence." From his first days in the Senate, when he got Finance Committee Chairman Russell B. Long to find him a seat on the tax-writing panel, he has developed that influence to benefit his state's oilmen.

When the Democrats took control of the Senate in 1987, Boren was seventh in seniority on the Intelligence Committee and best known for his involvement with domestic issues, particularly those associated with Oklahoma's oil and farm interests. Because every Democrat that ranked above him on Intelligence chaired another standing committee, however, Boren became chairman of one of the three committees most often associated with foreign policy.

He stepped into the pages of an international thriller. The intelligence community was reeling from spy scandals. The Iran-contra affair had deepened the legislative branch's mistrust of executive branch covert activities. And President Reagan was determined to negotiate an arms deal before leaving office.

Boren became a frequent guest on television news shows as an important bipartisan and centrist voice on foreign policy. A conservative Democrat, he is an internationalist who does not mind letting Uncle Sam wield a big stick. His support for contra aid gave him entree at the White House, and he cultivated the role of bridge-builder between Senate Democrats, Republicans and the president on that issue and others.

He also has taken an active role in shaping the United States' relationship with South Africa. He hosted congressional receptions for both African National Congress leader Nelson Mandela and South African president F. W. deKlerk during their 1990 visits to Washington.

At Boren's behest, the Intelligence Committee adopted new rules designed to plug the leaks of sensitive information from within the committee. Frustrated by what he views as inadequate briefings by intelligence analysts, he has also sought to streamline the bureacracy of the Central Intelligence Agency and shift its espionage focus from Cold War ideological threats to broader economic and cultural factors.

Boren's visibility rose as a result of his membership on the select committee named to investigate the Iran-contra affair during the 100th Congress, but his work left no clear impression. He concentrated on the CIA's role and used the perch to advance his views on bipartisanship. At one point, he criticized the committee lawyers for their questions. Still, when his turns came, he was given more to speechmaking than asking detailed questions.

Throughout the 1986 debate that produced major tax reform, Boren had little to say about the general philosophy of tax revision, or about most of the issues contained in the legislation. But he played a key role in developing a coalition for it on Finance, providing oil-state support for the bill's attacks on many business tax breaks in exchange for preservation of the depletion allowance and other tax support for the oil and gas industries.

Boren also wants to help oil producers by protecting them from foreign competition. He is a prominent supporter of legislation to impose a fee on imported oil.

Boren was unable to muster majority Democratic support for one of his favorite economic solutions — a constitutional amendment to balance the budget. But he did play an important role in the balanced-budget law that Congress passed in 1985. Boren referred to the measure as the "Gramm-Rudman-Hollings-Boren" amendment.

Boren stood out after the 1980 elections as a leading Democratic proponent of cooperation with the new Reagan administration and the GOP leadership in the Senate.

By 1985, a new, more militant Boren had emerged, most visibly as a spokesman for farmers suffering from the devastated agricultural economy. In tandem with Nebraska Democrat Jim Exon, Boren led Farm Belt Democrats into a confrontation with the Reagan administration and the Senate leadership over emergency help for debt-ridden farmers.

As chairman of the Agriculture Committee's Farm Credit Subcommittee, Boren played a major role in the $4 billion bailout and overhaul of the Farm Credit System. In early 1987, he announced his intention to move quickly. "We're not going to play ring around the rosy around here," he said, adding, "This train is going to move." But it took most of the year for the subcommittee and then the full committee to produce a bill. A major reason was that Boren pushed hard to produce a consensus, requiring dozens and dozens of hours of markups.

A strong critic of the increasing use of the filibuster in the Senate, Boren nevertheless used that and other dilatory tactics to pressure Senate leaders to act on farm credit aid. He and his allies for a time blocked approval of the nomination of Edwin Meese III as attorney general, giving new Majority Leader Bob Dole his first test of strength and leading the White House to denounce the strategy as "blackmail." Eventually, Congress cleared legislation to provide farmers with extra loan money to finance spring plantings. But Reagan vetoed the measure.

Boren's most original contribution to the farm policy debate was a plan he developed in 1985 with Minnesota Republican Rudy Boschwitz. The two Agriculture Committee members proposed that the federal government move toward abolishing the whole system of price supports for farmers. To help ease the transition to a free-market economy, they suggested providing farmers with direct income support for a period of time. The proposal was rejected as an amendment to the 1985 farm bill, but has continued to attract attention. It was included in modified form in the administration's fiscal 1988 budget, although Boren considered that language inadequate and opposed it.

Boren has become increasingly outspoken in criticism of the Senate's procedures, which he sees as leading the institution into paralysis and decline. He believes individual senators have too much power to frustrate the majority.

To solve those problems, Boren has proposed setting up an Emergency Joint Committee for Congressional Reform. He argues that such a committee should consider major changes in Senate rules, especially those that allow senators to propose amendments unrelated to the bill being considered on the floor. "To preserve Congress," Boren has said, "we must reform it."

At Home: Boren advanced very quickly in politics by knowing how to promote the right issue at the right time.

Few Oklahoma Democrats took him seriously in 1974, when, as a four-term state legislator, he decided to run for governor. A Rhodes scholar and political science professor, he had been neither influential nor popular among insiders in the Oklahoma House. But he had a reputation as a reformer, which he exploited at a time of scandal not only in Washington but in Oklahoma City, where Democratic Gov. David Hall was under investigation on corruption charges that later sent him to prison.

Boren campaigned with a broom, promising to sweep out corruption in the state capital, supporting financial disclosure and open government. He edged into a spot in the primary runoff and won big in November.

As governor, Boren changed focus, drawing national attention as a spokesman for his state's oil producers. When he chose to run for the Senate in 1978, he was in a perfect position to seek votes and campaign support as an oil industry loyalist, and he was the favorite throughout the year. He led a seven-man primary field and went on to defeat former U.S. Rep. Ed Edmondson in a runoff.

The primary took a bizarre turn when, after a minor candidate accused the governor of being a homosexual, Boren swore on a Bible that it was not true. The accuser was discredited, and Boren suffered no lasting damage.

Boren's gubernatorial record brought him far more business support than most Democrats can expect in Oklahoma, and he had no trouble against his 1978 Republican opponent.

By 1984, Boren's stock had soared so high that state Republican leaders seemed reluctant even to talk about their chances against him. When no Republicans of stature challenged him for re-election, they shifted attention toward their 1986 chances of capturing the governorship.

Will E. Crozier, a former state Transportation Department worker who became the eventual Republican nominee, voiced concern that Boren had moved too far left on some issues. Boren blew him away, carrying every county in the state in amassing 76 percent of the vote.

In 1990, Republicans so feared Boren's political organization could damage their shot at the open governor's seat that they tried to persuade their only candidate, Stephen Jones, a lawyer and former party official, to withdraw. But Jones remained in the race, unable to stomach his party's giving Boren a free ride.

Boren demolished Jones, carrying every county in the state and posting the highest re-election mark — 83 percent — of any Senate candidate in 1990 who had an opponent on the ballot. Democrat David Walters was elected governor by a wide margin.

Committees

Select Intelligence (Chairman)

Agriculture, Nutrition & Forestry (3rd of 10 Democrats)
Domestic & Foreign Marketing & Product Promotion (chairman); Agricultural Credit; Agricultural Production & Stabilization of Prices

Finance (4th of 11 Democrats)
Taxation (chairman); Energy & Agricultural Taxation; International Trade

Elections

1990 General		
David L. Boren (D)	735,684	(83%)
Stephen Jones (R)	148,814	(17%)
1990 Primary		
David L. Boren (D)	445,969	(84%)
Virginia Jenner (D)	47,909	(9%)
Manuel Ybarra (D)	25,169	(5%)

Previous Winning Percentages: **1984** (76%) **1978** (66%)

Campaign Finance

	Receipts	Receipts from PACs	Expend-itures
1990			
Boren (D)	$1,253,344	0	$1,372,014
Jones (R)	$140,911	0	$140,912

Key Votes

1991	
Authorize use of force against Iraq	N
1990	
Oppose prohibition of certain semiautomatic weapons	N
Support constitutional amendment on flag desecration	N
Oppose requiring parental notice for minors' abortions	N
Halt production of B-2 stealth bomber at 13 planes	N
Approve budget that cut spending and raised revenues	Y
Pass civil rights bill over Bush veto	Y
1989	
Oppose reduction of SDI funding	Y
Oppose barring federal funds for "obscene" art	Y
Allow vote on capital gains tax cut	Y

Voting Studies

	Presidential Support		Party Unity		Conservative Coalition	
Year	S	O	S	O	S	O
1990	58	39	58	34	76	22
1989	77	20	51	46	71	24
1988	63	31	59	30	81	11
1987	46	46	60	32	91	3
1986	67	30	42	54	92	4
1985	47	45	52	39	75	18
1984	62	29	41	53	91	0
1983	41	56	60	35	73	25
1982	60	38	52	42	87	10
1981	60	35	54	40	86	10

Interest Group Ratings

Year	ADA	ACU	AFL-CIO	CCUS
1990	56	23	63	55
1989	30	63	50	100
1988	25	48	62	58
1987	35	63	56	50
1986	40	65	27	65
1985	45	55	47	54
1984	35	71	30	79
1983	55	54	53	56
1982	45	84	50	65
1981	30	60	32	71

Don Nickles (R)

Of Ponca City — Elected 1980

Born: Dec. 6, 1948, Ponca City, Okla.
Education: Oklahoma State U., B.B.A. 1971.
Military Service: Army National Guard, 1970-76.
Occupation: Machine company executive.
Family: Wife, Linda Lou Morrison; four children.
Religion: Roman Catholic.
Political Career: Okla. Senate, 1979-81.
Capitol Office: 713 Hart Bldg. 20510; 224-5754.

In Washington: With his youthful vigor and staunchly conservative views, Nickles has been touted by the Republican right as a rising star since his long-shot victory in 1980. Now with over a decade in the Senate, Nickles has started to make that prediction more tangible.

At the start of the 102nd Congress, Nickles was elected to the Senate GOP leadership as chairman of the Republican Policy Committee. His election was part of a move by younger Senate conservatives to increase their role in setting the party's legislative agenda: He defeated the more senior and more moderate Sen. Pete V. Domenici of New Mexico by a 23-20 vote in the Republican Conference.

Nickles had previously served during the 1990 election cycle as chairman of the National Republican Senatorial Committee (NRSC). His win for the policy post showed that Nickles paid no penalty — at least among his fellow conservatives — for the Republicans' net loss of a seat in the 1990 Senate elections.

Early in that campaign year, Nickles was credited by many of his partisan allies for helping recruit a savvy group of Republican House members — Lynn Martin of Illinois, Patricia Saiki of Hawaii, Claudine Schneider of Rhode Island, Tom Tauke of Iowa, Bill Schuette of Michigan and former Rep. Hal Daub of Nebraska — to run against targeted Democratic incumbents. However, this crop of challengers was uprooted, mainly for reasons beyond Nickles' control.

A wave of anti-Washington sentiment among the electorate made 1990 the wrong year for a slate of "insider" challengers. Moreover, the efforts of these candidates to uphold antitax positions against their more liberal opponents were undercut by President Bush's decision to draw back on his "no new taxes" pledge.

With his move to the Republican policy post, Nickles escapes the vagaries of electoral politics for a more certain role as an ideological spokesman. He will also be able to give fuller attention to prestige committee assignments — Appropriations and Budget — that he obtained at the start of the 101st Congress.

Nickles leaves little doubt about where he fits on the political spectrum. He is a solidly conservative Republican, who supported Bush on over 80 percent of Senate votes during the 101st Congress. He is an advocate of cutting the federal budget and barring tax increases, while maintaining hefty spending levels for the military. Part of the "New Right" movement when he was first elected, Nickles remains a leading Senate opponent of abortion.

A former business executive, Nickles stands out as a supporter of business interests. In 1990, he was one of only three senators who received ratings of 100 percent from the U.S. Chamber of Commerce.

One of Nickles' persistent causes is to temper the provisions of the Davis-Bacon Act, which requires contractors on federal construction projects to pay "prevailing wage" rates. In September 1989, he proposed to allow builders of federally subsidized homes or shelters to hire poor tenants and homeless people at lower wage rates; his amendment was tabled, 58-42.

Nickles came closer but failed to ease the environmental enforcement provisions of the Clean Air Act revisions in 1990. An amendment by Nickles and Democrat Howell Heflin of Alabama to that effect was defeated on a 47-50 vote.

Nickles has joined with the senators from Michigan to battle sharp increases in automobile fuel efficiency standards. During debate on the Clean Air Act, he and Michigan Democrat Carl Levin led the fight against strict limits on carbon dioxide emissions, which they said would result in a "backdoor" increase in fuel efficiency requirements.

When Iraq's invasion of Kuwait in August 1990 set off concerns about U.S. dependency on Middle East oil, advocates of higher fuel efficiency standards resumed their efforts; a bill proposed that September by Democratic Sen. Richard H. Bryan and Washington Republican Slade Gorton appeared to have majority support. But Nickles helped block a cloture vote to cut off debate. Supporters of the bill gave in, but reintroduced it in the 102nd Congress.

Like most members from the "energy belt," Nickles backs most priorities of the oil, gas and nuclear power industries. In 1989, Nickles — the ranking Republican on the Senate Energy and Natural Resources subcommittee on regulation and conservation — co-authored a bill to abolish price controls on natural gas. That bill was subsumed in legislation that went out under the name of Energy Committee Chairman J. Bennett Johnston of Louisiana.

Nickles favors boosting the economies of oil-reliant states like Oklahoma by providing incentives for domestic oil exploration and placing a fee on imported oil. At the beginning of the 102nd Congress, he gained the position of ranking Republican on the Appropriations Interior Subcommittee, which may give him somewhat more influence on such issues.

Still a relatively junior member of the minority party, Nickles has not had a big impact on the federal budget process. Instead, he has found a variety of means for chipping away at the margins.

In 1989, the Appropriations Committee passed an amendment increasing the maximum size of a Federal Housing Administration-insured mortgage from $101,250 to $150,000 in areas with high housing costs. But Nickles, who said the measure would put the federal government at too great a financial risk, fought it on the Senate floor, using populist rhetoric as his weapon.

"Why should we ask Joe Lunchbucket, who is working hard making $7 an hour in a machine shop, to guarantee somebody's $200,000 home?" he said. His proposal to limit the mortgage cap increase to $124,875 was enacted.

During his time as ranking Republican on the Appropriations Legislative Branch Subcommittee, Nickles tried without much success to strictly limit taxpayer-funded mailings by members of Congress. He did work to push through certain reforms of Senate "franking" practices in 1990, including bans on the use of campaign and personal funds for mass mailings and the transfer of mail funds between senators. He also proposed a 5 percent across-the-board cut in legislative branch funding; House-Senate conferees accepted a 2 percent cut.

In his budget-cutting zeal, Nickles sometimes steps on some big toes. During the 1990 budget debate, Nickles proposed an amendment to limit fiscal 1991 spending to the previous year's levels. The amendment failed, and Nickles incurred the wrath of Appropriations Committee Chairman Robert C. Byrd.

The wily West Virginian allowed a $975,000 earmark for a levee in Tulsa, requested by Nickles, but not without a lecture on how the money might not have been available if Nickles' amendment had passed. Byrd later eliminated funding favored by Nickles to resume Amtrak service to Oklahoma.

Although his legislative education is continuing, Nickles does show an aptitude for moving out front on populist issues. He picked up on the rising anger over the 1988 catastrophic health care law, which required Medicare recipients to pay for the benefits themselves through premium increases and an income tax surcharge. During deliberations on a minimum-wage increase bill in March 1989, Nickles proposed an amendment calling for the Senate to reconsider the law's financing mechanisms; it passed on a 97-2 vote. The law was revoked that year.

Nickles would later translate public anger toward Jordan — which had sided with Iraq against the United States during the Persian Gulf War — into financial terms. In March 1991, Nickles attached an amendment to a supplemental appropriations bill to cut $57 million in U.S. aid to Jordan. However, the Bush administration objected that the amendment could impede efforts to achieve an overall Middle East peace plan. The restrictions were then weakened to allow Bush to resume aid if he viewed it as in the national interest.

At Home: When the 1986 campaign began, Nickles was regarded as one of the most vulnerable Republicans facing re-election. He had been aided in 1980 by President Ronald Reagan's coattails. And unlike his first contest, in which he defeated former Oklahoma City District Attorney Andy Coats, this one presented him with a formidable Democratic opponent: 1st District Rep. James R. Jones.

Nickles' re-election contest was thus expected to be pivotal in the partisan battle for control of the Senate. But while the Democrats did achieve a Senate majority, the Oklahoma contest did not contribute to it. Convincing voters that Jones was a liberal, Nickles won handily, with 55 percent of the vote.

Jones assailed Nickles for lacking leadership skills needed in a state hard-hit by the energy and farm recessions. He decried the soaring federal deficits and blamed Republican policies for Oklahoma's economic problems. But his campaign was slow in starting; he did not declare his Senate candidacy until May.

The first sign that Jones had problems came in the August Democratic Senate primary. His opponent, George Gentry, a farmer and supporter of political extremist Lyndon H. LaRouche Jr., did not run an active campaign, but still received one of every three votes.

Shortly after the primary, Nickles began his media campaign. Though some of his efforts aimed to reinforce his conservative, clean-cut image, the core of Nickles' campaign was a series of ads portraying Jones as a liberal and accusing him of persistently voting for congressional pay raises.

Jones did not respond immediately to Nickles. Instead, he ran a homespun spot about his working-class childhood in Muskogee during the Great Depression. Another ad showed the balding Jones holding a hair dryer and stating that he would not have to waste much of his valuable time using it.

Finally, with polls indicating that the liberal label was sticking, Jones attempted to refute Nickles' claims. He cited House vote studies that placed him as a Democratic moderate, and quoted Washington sources who said Nickles was distorting Jones' record. But Jones' delayed reaction to Nickles' attacks placed him on the defensive during the crucial late weeks of the campaign.

Six years earlier, Nickles had risen from the state Legislature to become the Senate's youngest member. The journey took place almost overnight. Although he had been active in Republican politics for several years, Nickles waited until 1978 to run for public office, winning election to the state Senate. His first-term status there did not deter him from entering the 1980 Republican primary to replace retiring GOP Sen. Henry Bellmon.

Nickles' calls for a return to traditional family values drew a favorable response from Oklahoma's large evangelical community. Boosted by organizational support from fundamentalist Christian groups, Nickles startled political observers by topping a five-man field in the GOP primary, then winning the runoff by a nearly 2-to-1 margin.

The general election pitted Nickles against Coats, whose role in the prosecution of a famous Oklahoma City murder case made his name a household word in central Oklahoma. But Coats was on the defensive much of the time, seeking to convince voters that he was not a closet liberal, as Nickles alleged. Nickles also charged that the Senate was overrun with lawyers and that Coats would add to the surplus.

Nickles' organization mounted successful voter registration drives to shore up Republican strength and helped spread his conservative themes to sympathetic Democrats. Aided by Reagan's strong showing in the state, Nickles won with 54 percent of the vote.

Committees

Appropriations (10th of 13 Republicans)
VA, HUD and Independent Agencies; Interior (ranking); Agriculture, Rural Development & Related Agencies; Energy & Water Development; Foreign Operations

Budget (5th of 9 Republicans)

Energy & Natural Resources (5th of 9 Republicans)
Energy Regulation & Conservation (ranking); Energy Research & Development; Mineral Resources Development & Production

Select Indian Affairs (7th of 7 Republicans)

Elections

1986 General		
Don Nickles (R)	493,436	(55%)
James R. Jones (D)	400,230	(45%)

Previous Winning Percentage: **1980** (54%)

Campaign Finance

	Receipts	Receipts from PACs		Expend-itures
1986				
Nickles (R)	$2,955,708	$886,841	(30%)	$3,252,964
Jones (D)	$2,529,160	$994,491	(39%)	$2,564,983

Key Votes

1991	
Authorize use of force against Iraq	Y
1990	
Oppose prohibition of certain semiautomatic weapons	Y
Support constitutional amendment on flag desecration	Y
Oppose requiring parental notice for minors' abortions	N
Halt production of B-2 stealth bomber at 13 planes	N
Approve budget that cut spending and raised revenues	N
Pass civil rights bill over Bush veto	N
1989	
Oppose reduction of SDI funding	Y
Oppose barring federal funds for "obscene" art	N
Allow vote on capital gains tax cut	Y

Voting Studies

	Presidential Support		Party Unity		Conservative Coalition	
Year	**S**	**O**	**S**	**O**	**S**	**O**
1990	83	16	91	7	89	11
1989	86	11	96	4	97	3
1988	80	20	92	6	100	0
1987	73	22	91	6	91	9
1986	86	14	82	18	99	1
1985	82	18	79	20	87	12
1984	83	14	85	13	96	2
1983	66	34	83	16	91	5
1982	81	19	85	15	95	5
1981	85	13	87	11	89	10

Interest Group Ratings

Year	ADA	ACU	AFL-CIO	CCUS
1990	0	96	11	100
1989	0	96	0	88
1988	0	92	7	86
1987	5	100	10	94
1986	0	91	0	79
1985	0	87	0	90
1984	0	91	0	95
1983	10	96	7	78
1982	10	100	4	75
1981	5	100	5	94

1 James M. Inhofe (R)

Of Tulsa — Elected 1986

Born: Nov. 17, 1934, Des Moines, Iowa.
Education: U. of Tulsa, B.A. 1959.
Military Service: Army, 1954-56.
Occupation: Real estate developer; insurance company executive.
Family: Wife, Kay Kirkpatrick; four children.
Religion: Presbyterian.
Political Career: Okla. House, 1967-69; Okla. Senate, 1969-77; mayor of Tulsa, 1978-84; defeated for reelection, 1984; Republican nominee for governor, 1974; Republican nominee for U.S. House, 1976.
Capitol Office: 408 Cannon Bldg. 20515; 225-2211.

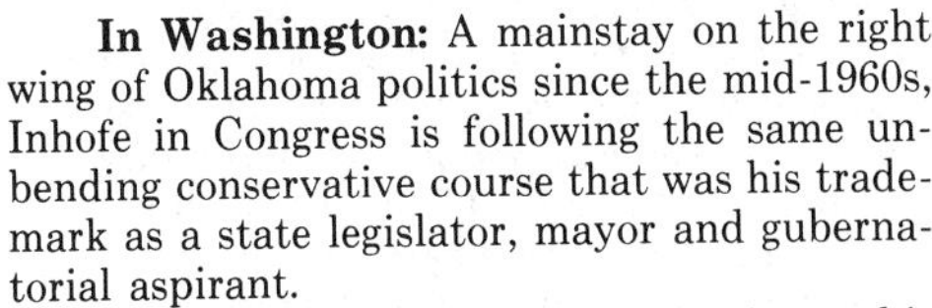

In Washington: A mainstay on the right wing of Oklahoma politics since the mid-1960s, Inhofe in Congress is following the same unbending conservative course that was his trademark as a state legislator, mayor and gubernatorial aspirant.

The unique thing about Inhofe is not his voting record; there are plenty of down-the-line conservatives like him in the House Republican Conference. What is unusual about Inhofe is his affinity for unbridled personal criticism of House members with whom he does not agree.

Few members, for example, would publicly opine that there are "a bunch" of communists in Congress, as Inhofe told a town meeting in 1987. "It is not five or 10," he said. "It is a very serious problem." He named Michigan Democrat George W. Crockett Jr. as a House member who "has been a member of the Communist Party and has been sympathizing with all of them." (Crockett, who retired in 1991, said he was never in the Communist Party.)

"You have to wonder whose side they [House members] are on sometimes," Inhofe said in 1988. He has also said that Massachusetts Democrat Barney Frank tells his constituents "the reason to keep him in office is that he is a practicing homosexual."

Inhofe's ferreting does not stop in Washington. During a 1989 drug enforcement conference in Ecuador, he was outraged upon discovering a mural in the Parliament building depicting a skull wearing a Nazi helmet emblazoned with the letters "CIA." Inhofe sought to withhold 40 percent of Ecuador's aid unless the mural was altered.

Inhofe says his priorities in Congress are promoting business development in Tulsa and looking for ways to help Oklahoma's energy and agricultural sectors. He can cite some successes: He was involved, for instance, in persuading State Farm Insurance to locate its regional headquarters in Tulsa.

A free-market advocate, Inhofe in 1989 nevertheless sought to protect his district — whose largest employer is American Airlines — by calling for a federal slowdown of leveraged buyouts, including a bid to buy the airlines by New York developer Donald J. Trump.

But Inhofe is probably best-known for his belief that liberalism is a threat to "family values" and for his strong anti-communist views. He says that both the Soviet Union and China remain "committed ... to world communist domination."

A member of the Select Committee on Narcotics Abuse and Control, Inhofe has sought increased federal funds for community-based drug education. He has also called for a mandatory death penalty for airline terrorists.

Although he demonstrated early on in his career that he was not reticent about publicly confronting opponents, Inhofe does not see himself as unschooled in the customs of House comity. In a 1987 interview with the *Tulsa World*, Inhofe said: "I know how coalitions are built. If you ask anyone in the freshman delegation who they have most communication with, who they feel most comfortable talking about issues with, who they seek advice from, I suspect you'd probably find that I was on the top of that list."

At Home: Inhofe was one of the comeback stories of 1986. Two years after being unseated as Tulsa's mayor, he won election to Congress in a district that Tulsa dominates. But that is the sort of up-and-down career Inhofe has had over a quarter-century in politics. Few officeholders have endured as many setbacks as he has and still remained viable as candidates.

Inhofe won his first elective contest, for a seat in the state House, in 1966. After one term, he moved up to the state Senate, where he opposed the Equal Rights Amendment and sponsored a resolution calling for a constitutional amendment to balance the federal budget. He was an early supporter of Ronald Reagan for president.

Inhofe also established a reputation for

Oklahoma 1

Tulsa; Parts of Osage, Creek and Washington Counties

In its white-collar Republican leanings and its antagonism to rural Democratic power, Tulsa was a forerunner of other Sun Belt cities now catching up with it. Tulsa County has gone Republican in all but two presidential elections since 1920. The city makes up more than two-thirds of the district's population.

Once a post office along the trail of the Pony Express, Tulsa was transformed by the discovery of oil in a nearby field in 1906 — and oil has sparked Tulsa's economic development throughout most of this century. Tulsa today calls itself "The Oil Capital of the World," a label justified by the myriad petroleum companies that maintain their corporate headquarters there. Chief executives and senior engineers regularly gather to discuss business and politics in downtown Tulsa's Petroleum Club.

Tulsa's economy has diversified considerably in recent years. With the opening of the Arkansas River Navigation System in 1971, Tulsa became a deep-water port accessible to the Gulf of Mexico. The city also maintains a thriving aeronautics industry; McDonnell Douglas and Rockwell International are among its leading companies, and American Airlines has moved its national headquarters for flight reservations to Tulsa as well. Tulsa also has a major tourist attraction in Oral Roberts University (4,500 students), which anchors a large fundamentalist community. Visitors flock from around the country to view the "City of Faith," the huge medical complex that offers itself as a nexus of science and prayer.

Tulsa's fundamentalists are concentrated in the city's eastern part; affluent business executives populate the southeast, and the central section is a mixture of blue-collar whites and young professionals. North Tulsa hosts a sizable black community that provides Democrats with their best turf.

Southeast of Tulsa, the 1st takes in most of Broken Arrow, home to many Tulsa workers who commute via the Broken Arrow Expressway. It also contains parts of Osage and Creek counties, which include some growing Tulsa suburbs. In Osage, which has most of the district's land area, cattle ranching supplements the oil and gas trade. Rounding out the northeast side, the 1st District covers southern Washington County.

Population: 503,739. White 423,755 (84%), Black 47,433 (9%), American Indian, Eskimo and Aleut 25,146 (5%), Other 2,976 (1%). Spanish origin 7,894 (2%). 18 and over 365,006 (73%), 65 and over 52,774 (11%). Median age: 30.

being outspoken. In 1972, he said Sen. George S. McGovern should "be hanged with Jane Fonda" after the Democratic presidential nominee implied U.S. soldiers were guilty of atrocities in Vietnam. "There are no gray areas in my views," Inhofe has said.

Democratic efforts to portray Inhofe as an extremist contributed to his first defeats. As the GOP nominee for governor in 1974, he suffered a humiliating loss at the hands of then-state Rep. David L. Boren, attracting barely one-third of the vote. Two years later, Inhofe left the state Senate to challenge Democratic Rep. James R. Jones; he lost by almost 9 percentage points.

But Tulsa's conservative communities, including important energy interests and many religious fundamentalists, remained supportive of Inhofe. He built on this base for his first comeback, winning the Tulsa mayoralty in 1978.

As mayor, Inhofe was strongly opposed to federal budget expansion and frequently avoided seeking the kinds of urban assistance from Washington that other cities depended on. While most big-city mayors decried President Reagan's domestic budget cuts, Inhofe defended them.

Having served three terms, Inhofe was a strong favorite for re-election in 1984. But a heavy black turnout in north Tulsa helped Democrat Terry Young win a stunning upset. After the loss, Inhofe said, "I will never run for any office in Oklahoma City or Washington."

Two years later, the 1st District came open with Jones' decision to run for the Senate. Inhofe did not leap into the congressional opportunity; energy company executive D. W. "Bill" Calvert announced early, and lined up many of Inhofe's campaign financiers. Besides, Inhofe had personal financial problems, stemming from the failure of some of his investments in Oklahoma's oil-based recession.

After struggling with the decision for months, Inhofe finally announced his candidacy in May, describing himself as "a little bit on the hard right." He quickly activated his grass-roots network, and with a significant name-recognition advantage over Calvert, he easily won nomination.

Although Jones had kept the 1st Democratic for seven terms, Democrats failed to recruit a well-known candidate to succeed him. Their nominee, law professor Gary Allison, ran a vigorous campaign, but Inhofe blasted him for supporting legalized abortion and opposing aid to the Nicaraguan contras. Allison accused Inhofe of playing on religion when he brought in TV evangelist Pat Robertson for a fundraiser. Outspent more than 3-to-1, Allison managed to keep Inhofe's winning tally down to 55 percent.

Inhofe weathered a turbulent 1988. He stirred considerable local publicity by suing his brother over the sale of stock in the family insurance business; his brother countersued. Also, Inhofe's district chief of staff quit, castigating Inhofe for not providing enough staff for adequate constituent service. Inhofe dismissed the incident as office politics.

Fortunately for Inhofe, Democrats offered a candidate with no name recognition and little political experience — 33-year-old Kurt Glassco, who was an assistant district attorney in Tulsa before becoming legal counsel to Democratic Gov. George Nigh. He was more moderate than Inhofe's 1986 foe: Glassco supported some contra aid and favored research on the strategic defense initiative.

Inhofe again had a substantial financial advantage; he outspent Glassco nearly 2-to-1. In spite of that, the incumbent was re-elected with only 53 percent of the vote — a margin that raised eyebrows in Oklahoma and Washington, especially since George Bush won the 1st comfortably.

Glassco tried again in 1990. With greater name recognition and more success in fundraising, he hoped to benefit from the absence of a presidential race on the ticket. Glassco also expected to catch some Democratic coattails: Democratic Sen. Boren always scored well in Tulsa. And the governor's race had focused attention on Tulsa, where support for a controversial education and tax plan was high. Democrat David Walters backed the plan, while his Republican opponent had advocated repealing it.

As expected, Boren and Walters carried Tulsa by large margins. But Glassco, who captured 46 percent in Tulsa County in 1988, fell to 44 percent in 1990. His switched position on abortion rights — in 1988 he opposed abortion, but in 1990, challenged by an abortion rights supporter in the primary, he renounced his opposition — may have cost him votes in the city that is home to Oral Roberts University.

His lawsuits behind him, Inhofe posted his highest tally in three House elections.

Committees

Merchant Marine & Fisheries (11th of 17 Republicans)
Coast Guard & Navigation; Merchant Marine

Public Works & Transportation (8th of 21 Republicans)
Aviation; Economic Development; Public Buildings & Grounds

Select Narcotics Abuse & Control (7th of 14 Republicans)

Elections

1990 General		
James M. Inhofe (R)	75,618	(56%)
Kurt Glassco (D)	59,521	(44%)
1988 General		
James M. Inhofe (R)	103,458	(53%)
Kurt Glassco (D)	93,101	(47%)

Previous Winning Percentage: 1986 (55%)

District Vote For President

	1988	1984	1980	1976
D	76,540 (39%)	65,241 (29%)	54,809 (31%)	64,514 (38%)
R	120,950 (61%)	158,304 (71%)	114,517 (64%)	101,276 (60%)
I			7,216 (4%)	

Campaign Finance

	Receipts	Receipts from PACs		Expend-itures
1990				
Inhofe (R)	$609,786	$306,071	(50%)	$612,116
Glassco (D)	$411,069	$194,950	(47%)	$406,280
1988				
Inhofe (R)	$482,552	$263,222	(55%)	$484,585
Glassco (D)	$255,822	$112,700	(44%)	$256,220

Key Votes

1991	
Authorize use of force against Iraq	Y
1990	
Support constitutional amendment on flag desecration	Y
Pass family and medical leave bill over Bush veto	N
Reduce SDI funding	N
Allow abortions in overseas military facilities	N
Approve budget summit plan for spending and taxing	N
Approve civil rights bill	N
1989	
Halt production of B-2 stealth bomber at 13 planes	N
Oppose capital gains tax cut	N
Approve federal abortion funding in rape or incest cases	N
Approve pay raise and revision of ethics rules	N
Pass Democratic minimum wage plan over Bush veto	N

Voting Studies

	Presidential Support		Party Unity		Conservative Coalition	
Year	**S**	**O**	**S**	**O**	**S**	**O**
1990	69	31	92	6	96	4
1989	72	24	93	5	95	5
1988	64	34	88	6	95	3
1987	73	23	91	2	95	5

Interest Group Ratings

Year	ADA	ACU	AFL-CIO	CCUS
1990	11	88	0	77
1989	5	96	17	100
1988	10	92	38	92
1987	4	100	0	100

2 Mike Synar (D)

Of Muskogee — Elected 1978

Born: Oct. 17, 1950, Vinita, Okla.
Education: U. of Oklahoma, B.B.A. 1972, LL.B. 1977; Northwestern U., M.S. 1973; attended U. of Edinburgh, Scotland, 1974.
Occupation: Rancher; real estate broker; lawyer.
Family: Single.
Religion: Episcopalian.
Political Career: No previous office.
Capitol Office: 2441 Rayburn Bldg. 20515; 225-2701.

In Washington: Still boyish and appealing in his seventh term, Synar has for several years stood just outside the inner circle of House leaders. He seems suspended there, anxiously waiting like a younger brother at the edge of the big kids' game.

Just before the 101st Congress, Synar made a bid for the chairmanship of the Democratic Caucus, but won just 33 votes. That put him a poor third to Mary Rose Oakar (80 votes) and the winner, William H. Gray III (146).

Synar, who took the unusual step of making a speech on his own behalf before the caucus vote, presented himself as the activist with the most legislative experience. But he had gotten into the race much later than his opponents and had less experience in conducting an institutionwide campaign. Synar's showy nature was also not what some members wanted in a caucus chairman.

He seemed to get the message. When the June 1989 resignations of Speaker Jim Wright and Majority Whip Tony Coelho opened up a succession of leadership jobs, Synar let the opportunity pass.

His occasional brashness, coupled with the sheer wattage of his personality, probably would alienate more of his colleagues if it were not for one thing: He seems genuinely concerned about making what he sees as good public policy, and he has a knack for doing it. There is a macho quality to his style and an affection for winning attention, but at the core, he is a serious pursuer of issues. And he pursues a far broader range of issues than most.

In the summer of 1989, for example, he cosponsored an amendment with Armed Services Chairman Les Aspin restricting procurement funds for the B-2 stealth bomber. Later in the same Congress, he joined with Wisconsin Democrat David R. Obey to propose severe restrictions on political action committees and greater reliance on public financing of campaigns. Their efforts were unsuccessful, but Synar was back on the issue early in 1991, this time working with Kansas Democrat Dan Glickman on a bill restricting both PAC money and individual contributions. Their bill would allow public financing for those who agreed to spending limits.

Synar undertook the campaign-finance crusade in the belief the public's opinion of Congress had reached a dangerously low ebb. He opposed the pay raise passed during the 101st Congress and has warned members to take seriously the term limits on legislators passed in states such as Oklahoma. "The term limit was a wake up call for improving democracy," he said in 1990.

While it is sometimes difficult to find a member's fingerprints on legislation, Synar, with an enthusiasm for jumping into major issues, leaves the trail of a child who has dipped his hands in an inkwell. He is among the most active members on the Energy and Commerce Committee, and also contributes to Judiciary and Government Operations, where he chairs the Environment, Energy and Natural Resources Subcommittee.

Synar has used this matrix of committee posts to project himself into an array of disputes from pesticides and grazing rights to oil drilling in wildlife preserves and regulating the Food and Drug Administration. He freely involves himself in politically difficult issues, and freely reminds others that he does so. "If you don't like fighting fires, don't be a fireman ... and if you don't like voting, don't be a congressman," he said while working on product liability legislation that split business and consumer groups and made some members queasy.

Business groups had long sought federal legislation to pre-empt sometimes conflicting state liability standards (which are used by courts to determine when manufacturers should be held accountable for damages caused by their products). But consumer groups and trial lawyers feared that new legislation would make it more difficult for consumers to claim damages. Energy and Commerce Chairman John D. Dingell wanted Synar to alter a plan then before the panel to make it more palatable to consumer leaders and moderate Democrats.

Synar did produce changes that many Democrats considered more favorable to con-

Oklahoma 2

Northeast — Tulsa; Muskogee

This northeastern Oklahoma territory has had some good fortune. Sheltered somewhat by the low-lying Ozark Mountains, it was spared the worst of the Dust Bowl winds that ravaged much of the state during the 1930s and 1940s. Equally important, it has attracted numerous state and federal water projects over the years — projects that have bolstered agriculture, drawn vacationers and prompted some local chambers of commerce to bill the area as "Green Country."

The growing tourism industry is crowding the area's traditional enterprises, cattle ranching and the oil and gas business. Recent oil and gas activity has been confined largely to recovery from older wells.

With a 27 percent population increase, the 2nd was Oklahoma's fastest-growing district during the 1970s. Much of the growth occurred in the eastern Tulsa suburbs in Rogers and Wagoner counties, home to a substantial number of GOP voters. Muskogee, with 38,000 people the largest city wholly contained in the 2nd, dredges sand from the Arkansas River beds for use in its glass industry; it is Democratic.

The largest Indian population in Oklahoma is concentrated within the 2nd's boundaries, in the area settled by the Five Civilized Tribes in the 19th century. The Cherokee Nation has its headquarters in Tahlequah, the seat of Cherokee County, and members of other tribes are scattered through surrounding counties.

Although the 2nd has had a suburban Tulsa component for some time, 1982 redistricting moved the district into the city limits for the first time. The southeastern Tulsa portion of the 2nd is a GOP haven populated by middle-rung and top-level executives from the city's corporate offices. It often votes for Synar's little-known Republican opponents.

The 2nd as a whole retains a basically Democratic cast. Only Haskell County supported Walter F. Mondale for president in 1984, but in 1988, Michael S. Dukakis fared considerably better, carrying 10 counties in the 2nd and winning 47 percent of the districtwide vote. Mostly the district has voted Democratic in other recent statewide and local elections.

Population: 505,149. White 420,537 (83%), Black 22,965 (5%), American Indian, Eskimo and Aleut 58,472 (12%). Spanish origin 4,528 (1%). 18 and over 353,938 (70%), 65 and over 67,761 (13%). Median age: 32.

sumers than the original bill, but many still complained it was worse than existing law. The panel voted to pass it, but acrimony was dulled by the fact that few expected the legislation to become law. It did not.

Synar's belief that members should have the courage of their convictions has led him to take some risks and win some glory. He took a heavily publicized gamble in the 99th Congress. While most members rushed to embrace the Gramm-Rudman-Hollings deficit-reduction plan, which was portrayed as a test of congressional will to cut the budget, Synar led the charge against it, splitting with the rest of the Oklahoma delegation on final passage and launching the legal challenge that succeeded in having the pivotal section of the new law declared unconstitutional.

In early 1986 a three-judge federal panel ruled that the automatic cuts violated the separation of powers by giving executive power to the comptroller general. Synar's final victory came a few months later when the Supreme Court upheld that ruling in a 7-2 decision.

The best evidence that Synar means what he says about legislating in the national interest is the tenuous connection between many of his crusades and his own political interests in Oklahoma. One of his goals is to pass legislation that would ban all tobacco company advertising and promotions. He sees that as a step that could lead to a tobacco-free society. His bill has prompted attacks from advertisers and tobacco companies, and also from the American Civil Liberties Union, which says it would violate the constitutional right to free speech.

Along the way, he co-founded in 1987 the Rural Health Care Coalition. Initially dismissed by some as a publicity vehicle, the group has had some tangible achievements, including passage of a measure giving rural hospitals Medicare inflation increases that are larger than those going to urban centers.

At Home: A clean-cut son of a prominent ranching family, Synar jumped into a House campaign in 1978, just one year after returning home from school to practice law.

Although he was inexperienced at politics, he was the right sort of challenger to Democratic Rep. Ted Risenhoover, who had become controversial because of a divorce and a reputation as a playboy. The incumbent spent much of the primary trying to refute charges that he slept in a heart-shaped water bed in his Washington apartment. Compared with Risenhoover, Synar appeared fresh, polished and seemly, and he won an 8,000-vote upset.

Synar was helped by his name. His father and five uncles have long been prominent in the Muskogee area. In 1971, they were selected the "Outstanding Family" in the United States by the All-American Family Institute.

After his 1978 election, Synar set up an intensive constituent-service operation. He announced that a majority of his staff members would remain in Oklahoma. These steps helped protect him in 1980 when GOP nominee Gary Richardson attacked him for having a liberal record; Synar held on with 54 percent of the vote. That was the last time anyone held Synar below 60 percent in a general election.

Conservative Democrats who feel Synar maintains too high a profile on national issues and is too liberal had a chance to gripe in the 1988 Democratic primary, in which state Sen. Frank Shurden challenged Synar from the right. But Synar got 70 percent of the primary vote and won easily in November.

Two years later, conservative Democrats lined up behind Jack Ross, a businessman, lawyer and rancher who criticized Synar for what he described as the incumbent's antipathy toward business. He accused Synar of voting with the "Eastern liberal establishment." Synar, in turn, labeled Ross "the special-interest candidate" for accepting political action committee contributions from the oil, banking, savings and loan, and tobacco industries.

Ross hammered at Synar in TV ads and appearances for voting against the flag-desecration constitutional amendment. One of his last TV ads, however, brought down the wrath of the state party. In mock-surveillance-film footage, a man dressed in shirt-sleeves and suspenders — Synar's characteristic garb — was depicted stepping out of a car and accepting a briefcase in a surreptitious manner as the announcer criticized him for accepting a contribution from the owner of a troubled thrift. The Democratic chairman scolded Ross for crossing the line. Synar held on for a 56-44 percent victory and won easily again in November.

Committees

Energy & Commerce (8th of 27 Democrats)
Energy & Power; Health & the Environment; Telecommunications & Finance

Government Operations (6th of 25 Democrats)
Environment, Energy & Natural Resources (chairman)

Judiciary (6th of 21 Democrats)
Economic & Commercial Law; Intellectual Property & Judicial Administration

Select Hunger (20th of 22 Democrats)
Domestic

Elections

1990 General		
Mike Synar (D)	90,820	(61%)
Terry M. Gorham (R)	57,331	(39%)
1990 Primary		
Mike Synar (D)	63,584	(56%)
Jack Ross (D)	50,255	(44%)
1988 General		
Mike Synar (D)	136,009	(65%)
Ira Phillips (R)	73,659	(35%)

Previous Winning Percentages: **1986** (73%) **1984** (74%) **1982** (73%) **1980** (54%) **1978** (55%)

District Vote For President

	1988	1984	1980	1976
D	97,030 (47%)	77,923 (36%)	82,689 (42%)	99,467 (54%)
R	110,189 (53%)	139,721 (64%)	108,520 (55%)	82,469 (45%)
I			4,654 (2%)	

Campaign Finance

	Receipts	Receipts from PACs	Expend-itures
1990			
Synar (D)	$622,454	0	$631,839
Gorham (R)	$63,271	$6,625 (10%)	$62,793
1988			
Synar (D)	$310,865	0	$358,705
Phillips (R)	$84,777	$5,447 (6%)	$81,634

Key Votes

1991	
Authorize use of force against Iraq	N
1990	
Support constitutional amendment on flag desecration	N
Pass family and medical leave bill over Bush veto	Y
Reduce SDI funding	Y
Allow abortions in overseas military facilities	Y
Approve budget summit plan for spending and taxing	N
Approve civil rights bill	Y
1989	
Halt production of B-2 stealth bomber at 13 planes	N
Oppose capital gains tax cut	Y
Approve federal abortion funding in rape or incest cases	Y
Approve pay raise and revision of ethics rules	Y
Pass Democratic minimum wage plan over Bush veto	Y

Voting Studies

	Presidential Support		Party Unity		Conservative Coalition	
Year	S	O	S	O	S	O
1990	17	82	93	4	13	85
1989	28	71	92	6	24	76
1988	26	73	93	5	13	87
1987	21	76	90	7	23	74
1986	24	71	83	11	24	70
1985	25	75	88	10	33	65
1984	44	51	80	13	36	53
1983	33	66	85	12	43	55
1982	43	55	79	17	44	52
1981	37	61	90	10	27	72

Interest Group Ratings

Year	ADA	ACU	AFL-CIO	CCUS
1990	94	8	91	21
1989	85	4	67	40
1988	100	0	86	38
1987	84	13	75	13
1986	70	15	57	22
1985	75	14	53	36
1984	80	17	38	31
1983	75	17	71	50
1982	55	26	70	50
1981	80	13	73	16

3 Bill Brewster (D)

Of Marietta — Elected 1990

Born: Nov. 8, 1941, Ardmore, Okla.
Education: Southwestern Oklahoma State U., B.S. 1964.
Military Service: Army Reserve, 1966-71.
Occupation: Pharmacist; rancher; real estate company owner.
Family: Wife, Suzie Nelson; one child.
Religion: Baptist.
Political Career: Okla. House, 1983-91.
Capitol Office: 1407 Longworth Bldg. 20515; 225-4565.

The Path to Washington: Brewster is only the third person to represent the 3rd in the past 44 years. Voters in "Little Dixie" — the poor, southeastern region of the state — are accustomed to having their House members around for a while. Carl Albert held the 3rd from 1947 to 1977, the last six as Speaker. Wes Watkins was in the House for 14 years.

First elected to the state House in 1982, Brewster, from Marietta (Love County), represented two counties and part of a third in the southwestern corner of the 3rd.

In the Legislature, Brewster specialized in business and energy issues. He touts his sponsorship of legislation to provide financing for industrial and manufacturing initiatives, and legislation to give tax incentives to companies promoting tourism in Oklahoma.

Brewster sponsored bills to promote tire recycling and to assess a 1-cent-per-gallon fuel tax to pay for cleaning up and enforcing regulations on leaking underground storage tanks.

He also supported legislation to require insurance companies to provide coverage for mammograms for women older than 45. He is a former chairman of the South/West Energy Council.

Brewster's House campaign began tragically, but by the time the Democratic primary balloting was over, he had bested the scion of a political legend to secure his party's nomination, making his election a virtual lock.

Anticipating Watkins' long-rumored departure to run for governor, Brewster began assembling a campaign organization in the summer of 1989. In six months, he had a preliminary organization in all 20 counties in the district. With Watkins still reticent about his election plans, Brewster kicked off his campaign in January.

But the day Brewster officially launched his campaign, two of his children died in a plane crash on their way home from the districtwide campaign swing. Three weeks later, on the floor of the state House, Brewster affirmed his intention to continue his run for Congress.

Following Brewster into the House contest was the namesake of an Oklahoma political legend. Lt. Gov. Robert S. Kerr III is the grandson of the late Robert S. Kerr, the powerful Democratic senator (1949-63) and governor responsible for bringing many federal irrigation projects to Oklahoma.

Kerr began with near-universal name recognition. His grandfather is revered in the area; the Kerr home, in the 3rd District town of Poteau, is a museum.

But the lieutenant governor's own ties to the district were more tenuous. Born and raised in Oklahoma City, Kerr made his career in various public- and private-sector jobs in the state capital.

He bought a home in the district only after he switched his sights from the governor's race to the House bid.

Brewster worked hard to compete with the Kerr name. He had assembled a formidable organization and was able to keep pace with Kerr in fundraising. Brewster chided Kerr for his recent move to the district.

The 3rd District is not conducive to electronic media campaigns: The largest city has fewer than 40,000 people. Brewster and Kerr attacked the daunting geography of the sprawling district by waging an old-fashioned, town-by-town canvass for votes.

Television helped Brewster bolster his message that Kerr was a carpetbagger, but the rudiments of his successful effort lay in his ground-level campaign. Despite the presence of two other minor candidates on the ballot, Brewster managed to win a majority — 51 percent — of the vote in the primary, averting a runoff with Kerr, who received 41 percent.

In November, Brewster crushed his GOP opponent, who had lost to Watkins three times. Brewster kept intact the 3rd's unblemished heritage: Since Oklahoma became a state in 1907, the 3rd has never elected a Republican to the House.

Oklahoma 3

Southeast — "Little Dixie"

The most reliably Democratic district in Oklahoma, the sprawling southeastern 3rd has not elected a Republican to the House in the 84 years since statehood. The area was settled largely from Texas and Arkansas, and most of its voters are conservative. But the "Little Dixie" region in which the 3rd is based has largely missed out on the oil discoveries that brought wealth — and burgeoning Republicanism — to central and western Oklahoma.

Wracked by rural depression in the 1920s, this region is the least prosperous area of Oklahoma today. The cotton crop that once dominated the local economy has been superseded by livestock production, but the region lacks the expansive ranches that are more common to the west. The Ouachita Mountain pines help fuel the timber trade in the district's southeastern corner; the Weyerhaeuser Co. has a plant in McCurtain County. The relatively small amount of oil exploration here, currently focused on the district's eastern side, picked up as Standard Oil of Ohio began drilling on lands leased from Weyerhaeuser.

The area's poor agricultural base was one reason for the steady exodus of its population between 1920 and 1970; many counties here lost roughly half their people during that time. But the 3rd — which encompasses 19 whole counties and part of another — reversed the trend between 1970 and 1980, showing a 20 percent population increase.

In the two presidential elections when Ronald Reagan was on the Republican ballot, the 3rd broke loose of its Democratic moorings. Before that, though, the district gave Jimmy Carter a big victory in his 1976 White House bid. And in 1988, Democrat Michael S. Dukakis carried 14 counties in the 3rd, falling only 459 votes short of winning the district outright against George Bush. In elections for other offices, most voters in the 3rd harbor little sympathy for the GOP.

A two-county appendage (Payne and Lincoln counties) at the district's northern end has some GOP presence, but not enough to offset the rest of the 3rd's Democratic tendencies. Stillwater (Payne County) is home to 20,000 students at Oklahoma State University.

Population: 504,268. White 438,897 (87%), Black 22,133 (4%), American Indian, Eskimo and Aleut 38,321 (8%). Spanish origin 5,341 (1%). 18 and over 365,865 (73%), 65 and over 77,856 (15%). Median age: 31.

Committees

Public Works & Transportation (30th of 36 Democrats)
Investigations & Oversight; Surface Transportation; Water Resources

Veterans' Affairs (18th of 21 Democrats)
Hospitals & Health Care; Housing & Memorial Affairs

Elections

1990 General		
Bill Brewster (D)	107,641	(80%)
Patrick K. Miller (R)	26,261	(20%)
1990 Primary		
Bill Brewster (D)	67,069	(51%)
Robert S. Kerr III (D)	54,471	(41%)
Will Robison (D)	8,141	(6%)
Eugene Poling (D)	2,173	(2%)

District Vote For President

	1988	1984	1980	1976
D	94,164 (50%)	75,671 (38%)	86,781 (46%)	110,972 (60%)
R	94,623 (50%)	124,798 (62%)	95,640 (51%)	71,260 (39%)
I			4,884 (3%)	

Campaign Finance

	Receipts	Receipts from PACs	Expend-itures
1990			
Brewster (D)	$448,824	$179,466 (40%)	$446,766

Key Vote

1991

Authorize use of force against Iraq	Y

4 Dave McCurdy (D)

Of Norman — Elected 1980

Born: March 30, 1950, Canadian, Texas.

Education: U. of Oklahoma, B.A. 1972, J.D. 1975; attended U. of Edinburgh, Scotland, 1977-78.

Military Service: Air Force Reserve, 1969-72, 1985-present.

Occupation: Lawyer.

Family: Wife, Pamela Plumb; three children.

Religion: Lutheran.

Political Career: Okla. assistant attorney general, 1975-77.

Capitol Office: 2344 Rayburn Bldg. 20515; 225-6165.

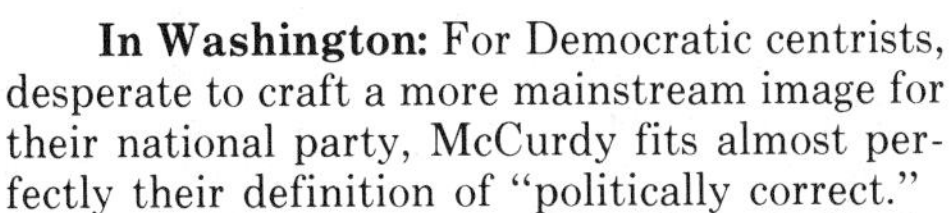

In Washington: For Democratic centrists, desperate to craft a more mainstream image for their national party, McCurdy fits almost perfectly their definition of "politically correct."

This Oklahoman is no "Old Guard" Southern Democrat: Through most of his House career, he has voted against the positions of Republican presidents more often than he has supported them. Yet his strong pro-defense views, as voiced on the Armed Services Committee and now as chairman of the House Select Intelligence Committee, give McCurdy a right-of-center cast, at least within the Democratic Caucus.

As a leader in the Democratic Leadership Conference (DLC), a group made up mainly of moderate-to-conservative Democrats, McCurdy co-chaired a panel that issued a report in 1989 calling for a U.S. foreign policy that "rejects the neo-isolationism and ambivalence about U.S. leadership that often characterizes our party's left." During the 1990-91 Persian Gulf crisis, McCurdy supported President Bush's hard-line approach to ending Iraq's occupation of Kuwait.

Like many members, McCurdy visited in late 1990 with U.S. troops deployed in Operation Desert Shield (which later became Desert Storm). But unlike others, he went not as a member of a touring delegation, but as a member of the Air Force Reserve, which enabled him to get a more inside view of the military operations there.

The scenes of McCurdy in uniform burnished a public image that was already positive. With his square-jawed good looks and a soft-spoken manner — offset at times by his pointed rhetoric — McCurdy has long been regarded as a man on the rise. When his support for the U.S. war effort against Iraq was vindicated by a quick military victory, McCurdy even earned some mention as a potential prospect for the national political stage.

Such talk would appear to be presumptuous, at best. While he is easily identified by Washington political insiders, McCurdy is virtually unknown outside Oklahoma. In his early 40s, he certainly has time to gain more seasoning and more visibility in the House, where he assumed the Intelligence chair in the 102nd Congress and can hold it for four years.

But it is plausible to speculate about McCurdy's prospects for higher office, because in addition to earning a reputation as a skillful legislator and a tough adversary, McCurdy has also shown himself to be a man of driving ambition who can be headstrong and even caustic toward his foes.

A number of McCurdy's colleagues were displeased with his maneuvers to obtain the Intelligence chairmanship. McCurdy did not attain the position during an earlier (1983-87) stint on the committee. But in 1989, he persuaded then-Speaker Jim Wright not only to reappoint him to the panel, but to place him second in seniority to then-Chairman Anthony C. Beilenson of California.

Preferring Beilenson's liberal slant and peeved by McCurdy's guile, some Democrats urged Speaker Thomas S. Foley to seek a waiver of the committee's three-term limit for Beilenson at the start of the 102nd Congress. Although Foley declined and named McCurdy chairman, the appointment to Intelligence of such liberals as Ronald V. Dellums of California and David E. Bonior of Michigan was widely seen as an effort by Foley to counterbalance the right-leaning McCurdy.

McCurdy may have assuaged some Democratic doubters when he immediately established a confrontational approach to the Bush administration's intelligence structure. "We are not going to be a shrinking violet," McCurdy pronounced in a February 1991 interview with *The Washington Post*. "I intend to stand up to Judge [William H.] Webster." (Then the director of the Central Intelligence Agency, Webster resigned in May 1991.)

McCurdy had a history of dispute with Webster. In 1989, McCurdy, then chairman of

Oklahoma 4

Southwest — Part of Oklahoma City

This slice of southwestern Oklahoma maintains a military presence that no politician can afford to forget for very long. In addition to Altus Air Force Base and the Army's Fort Sill, near the Texas border, the district stretches northeast to take in Tinker Air Force Base, just east of Oklahoma City. With a combined civilian and military staff averaging 24,000, Tinker is Oklahoma's largest single-site employer. Fort Sill, the site of the Army's principal artillery training school, employs nearly as many.

Despite the military orientation, Democratic candidates usually carry the 4th. Sen. David L. Boren polled 72 percent of its vote — his best showing statewide — in his 1978 Senate bid, and carried every county in the 4th in 1984 and 1990. Democrat David Walters won every county in the 4th in his successful 1990 campaign for governor.

But Ronald Reagan took the district easily twice, and in 1980 his coattails helped Republican Senate nominee Don Nickles win it by a narrow margin. George Bush comfortably won the district in 1988. The GOP is strongest at the northern end of the 4th, in the Oklahoma City suburbs of Moore and Midwest City.

McCurdy's district is still largely agricultural — it ranks fifth in the nation in cotton production — but it has become increasingly dependent on the energy industry. In the 1970s, Oklahoma's energy boom brought new oil and gas businesses to many of the district's southwestern counties. But declining demand has weakened the economy considerably since.

With 81,000 people, Lawton (Comanche County) is the 4th's largest city and a commercial center of southwest Oklahoma. The Goodyear tire and rubber plant nearby is the third-largest factory in the state.

The city of Norman is home to the University of Oklahoma (22,000 students) and the district's most liberal voters. The economy here is stronger than in most of the other counties; the university and such government-sponsored research programs as the National Severe Storm Laboratory are attracting high-technology industries.

Population: 505,869. White 441,346 (87%), Black 31,953 (6%), Other 20,859 (4%). Spanish origin 16,368 (3%). 18 and over 356,658 (71%), 65 and over 47,534 (9%). Median age: 27.

the Intelligence Oversight Subcommittee, requested more information than provided by the CIA on actions by its inspector general, who investigates allegations of wrongdoing in the agency. When Webster rejected the request on grounds that it intruded on executive branch authority, McCurdy pushed through an amendment requiring that inspector general's reports be made available to Congress.

Yet McCurdy's Intelligence Committee disputes with the Reagan and Bush administrations have tended to be over procedure, not policy. Over the years, McCurdy has backed covert actions to support insurgents fighting leftist governments in such nations as Nicaragua, Afghanistan and Angola.

In 1985, he gained attention for the "McCurdy compromise," a measure that contained $100 million for the Nicaraguan contras but would have required a second, later vote to release the funds. However, President Reagan pushed through his own plan calling for $100 million with no strings attached.

In 1989, McCurdy favored U.S. aid, channeled through the National Endowment for Democracy, to the Nicaraguan political opposition challenging the Marxist Sandinista government in elections the next February. He also exhibited a disdain for liberal hard-liners, denouncing "Sandinista supporters" who tried to bar funding for the opposition. "The leadership should not be beholden to the left on this," he said.

McCurdy often speaks along the same lines on the Armed Services Committee, where he takes on liberal "slashers and burners" who have advocated deep cuts in defense spending to provide funds for domestic programs. He is a powerful advocate for the U.S. Army (Fort Sill is in his House district); his efforts in 1990 helped cinch production of the LH helicopter, an Army priority. However, he is not a certain vote for the Pentagon. In 1985, he brokered the compromise that capped MX missile production. That same year, McCurdy's skepticism of the defense bureaucracy led him to play a key role in ousting aged Armed Services Chairman Melvin Price, an uncritical Pentagon ally.

McCurdy helped engineer the election of Wisconsin Democrat Les Aspin to replace Price. He remains one of the most influential members of the group of centrist Democrats who form "Aspin's team."

On both the Armed Services and Science committees, McCurdy pursues a pet project: the National Aerospace Plane, a high-tech aircraft that would be designed to achieve low-earth orbit. Formerly a subcommittee chairman, McCurdy gave up his subcommittee assignments on Science when he gained the Intelligence chair in the 102nd Congress.

Despite his stinging criticisms of Democratic liberals on defense and foreign policy, McCurdy is often with them on domestic issues. In 1990, he voted to override Bush's veto of a family leave bill, and voted against a constitutional amendment to ban flag burning.

Liberals were not thrilled with a bill proposed in 1989 by McCurdy and Democratic Sen. Sam Nunn, which would have tied most student aid programs to performance of civilian or military "national service." But McCurdy and Nunn, despite the rejection of their approach, were credited with giving visibility to the national service issue.

At Home: A former assistant attorney general with a law practice in Norman, McCurdy had not been active in politics when he began his 1980 campaign. But what McCurdy lacked in political experience he made up for in hustle. With help from several key backers of retiring Democratic Rep. Tom Steed, he built his own organization. That network and his appeal as a "fresh face" enabled McCurdy to get within 5,000 votes of veteran state Rep. James B. Townsend in the primary, and overtake him in the runoff.

The general-election race was just as tight. Republicans nominated Howard Rutledge, a retired Navy captain and former prisoner of war in Vietnam whose calls for strengthening defense capability endeared him to the district's sizable community of military employees and retirees. But McCurdy held on, winning enough support for his conservative economic themes to prevail by 2,906 votes.

Rutledge returned in 1982, asking conservative Democrats to cross party lines. Rutledge commercials painted McCurdy as a profligate liberal, but McCurdy carried all 12 counties in the 4th, amassing 65 percent of the vote. He won just as easily in 1984, a good GOP year.

Though urged to make a 1986 Senate bid, McCurdy deferred to 1st District Rep. James R. Jones, the state's senior House Democrat. Jones lost to GOP Sen. Don Nickles while McCurdy enjoyed a routine, overwhelming victory.

Committees

Select Intelligence (Chairman)
Program & Budget Authorization (chairman)

Armed Services (10th of 33 Democrats)
Military Installations & Facilities; Research & Development

Science, Space & Technology (8th of 32 Democrats)

Elections

1990 General

Dave McCurdy (D)	100,879	(74%)
Howard Bell (R)	36,232	(26%)

1988 General

Dave McCurdy (D) Unopposed

Previous Winning Percentages: **1986** (76%) **1984** (64%) **1982** (65%) **1980** (51%)

District Vote For President

	1988	1984	1980	1976
D	74,914 (41%)	57,118 (30%)	58,544 (36%)	82,330 (54%)
R	105,870 (58%)	131,690 (69%)	95,129 (59%)	67,060 (44%)
I			6,778 (4%)	

Campaign Finance

	Receipts	Receipts from PACs		Expend-itures
1990				
McCurdy (D)	$342,376	$149,775	(44%)	$357,531
Bell (R)	$3,905	0		$2,923
1988				
McCurdy (D)	$273,015	$142,272	(52%)	$251,956

Key Votes

1991

Authorize use of force against Iraq	Y
1990	
Support constitutional amendment on flag desecration	N
Pass family and medical leave bill over Bush veto	Y
Reduce SDI funding	Y
Allow abortions in overseas military facilities	Y
Approve budget summit plan for spending and taxing	Y
Approve civil rights bill	Y
1989	
Halt production of B-2 stealth bomber at 13 planes	N
Oppose capital gains tax cut	Y
Approve federal abortion funding in rape or incest cases	Y
Approve pay raise and revision of ethics rules	Y
Pass Democratic minimum wage plan over Bush veto	N

Voting Studies

	Presidential Support		Party Unity		Conservative Coalition	
Year	**S**	**O**	**S**	**O**	**S**	**O**
1990	44	56	73	25	78	17
1989	55	44	69	25	73	24
1988	33	58	73	22	79	13
1987	36	57	74	20	70	21
1986	31	62	70	21	72	24
1985	44	56	68	27	85	15
1984	46	45	56	29	71	12
1983	41	51	55	37	79	13
1982	58	36	48	43	79	19
1981	57	42	55	43	88	12

Interest Group Ratings

Year	ADA	ACU	AFL-CIO	CCUS
1990	56	33	58	14
1989	35	40	50	89
1988	60	30	71	64
1987	44	27	36	40
1986	35	38	42	80
1985	30	52	35	64
1984	35	30	33	33
1983	50	50	53	47
1982	25	67	28	62
1981	35	40	60	37

5 Mickey Edwards (R)

Of Oklahoma City — Elected 1976

Born: July 12, 1937, Cleveland, Ohio.

Education: U. of Oklahoma, B.S. 1958; Oklahoma City U., J.D. 1969.

Occupation: Lawyer; journalist.

Family: Separated; three children.

Religion: Episcopalian.

Political Career: Republican nominee for U.S. House, 1974.

Capitol Office: 2330 Rayburn Bldg. 20515; 225-2132.

In Washington: There are few more complex figures in Congress than Edwards. A former president of the American Conservative Union, Edwards views himself as one of the preeminent thinkers of the Republican right; yet he eschews some conservative policy totems, including a presidential line-item veto on appropriations bills.

Edwards can be tenaciously partisan: He is chairman of the Republican Policy Committee and the former head of the Republican Research Committee. But he also is known as a political bridge-builder, particularly on the Appropriations Committee, where he works with Democrats to produce legislative results.

Even Edwards' personal life is paradoxical. Generally mild-mannered, Edwards is well-liked by most colleagues. Yet he can be demanding and intense, traits that apparently contributed to the ending of his fourth marriage in 1990.

After his marital separation in late 1990, Edwards' wife published a story about the breakup in *Washingtonian* magazine. But Lisa Edwards had no "kiss-and-tell" story. Hers was a plaint about the difficulties of her 10 years as the wife of a congressman: long hours alone, the sacrifice of her singing career (she was a former Miss Oklahoma), the demands of socializing with constituents.

The article even included a political endorsement of sorts. Lisa Edwards said she did not end the marriage until after the 1990 election, which Mickey Edwards "fortunately" won. "I say that because he is an honest, hard-working congressman who gives his constituents so much that the emotional part of his life gets short-changed," she added.

There is no question that Edwards applies plentiful energy to his work. Much of his effort is given over to his role as ranking Republican on Appropriations' Foreign Operations Subcommittee, which decides how U.S. aid to other nations will be spent.

The Foreign Operations chairman, David Obey of Wisconsin, stands out on the collegial Appropriations Committee with his hard-nosed attitude and his strongly ideological (liberal) bearings: He differs from Edwards in both style and philosophy. Yet their differences are tempered by a shared view of foreign aid. Both are rather skeptical of foreign aid programs, and both have the political sense of the programs' unpopularity among the electorate.

In late 1990, President Bush sought to cancel Egypt's $7 billion military debt to the United States; he meant to reward Egypt for its support of military moves to counter Iraq's invasion of Kuwait. Edwards, noting that the proposal came just after passage of an unpopular deficit-reduction package, argued that it was hard to justify "when we have just made a substantial increase in the taxes on the American people." The measure passed anyway.

Edwards at times has played a partisan role on the subcommittee. During deliberations on a foreign aid appropriations bill in July 1989, Edwards and Obey negotiated a fine-tuned bill that included compromises on a number of contentious issues. But Obey, who disliked much of what he had accepted, told a subcommittee meeting that GOP members had to pledge to support the bill on the House floor.

Several GOP members objected and the meeting devolved into a shouting match. "You're not going to tell members they can't offer amendments," Edwards argued. Obey, noted for his temper, soon cut the meeting short. However, within a week, a second compromise was reached and the bill moved through the subcommittee.

Another partisan role for Edwards, one he held from the mid-1980s on, was as a Republican point man on U.S. relations with Nicaragua. As the ranking Republican on the Appropriations Military Construction Subcommittee in the 99th Congress, Edwards was a leader in the fight for President Reagan's $100 million package to aid the contras fighting Nicaragua's then-Marxist government.

Shortly after taking office in 1989, Bush reached an agreement with the congressional leadership to redirect U.S. policy from support for the contras to an effort to institute demo-

Oklahoma 5

North Central — Part of Oklahoma City; Bartlesville

Stretching 175 miles from the affluent northern reaches of Oklahoma City at one end to the historic oil town of Bartlesville on the other, the 5th gathers in GOP-minded voters all along the way.

Registered Democrats actually outnumber Republicans in most of the district's counties, but Democratic candidates have trouble winning their votes.

Oklahoma City accounts for nearly half of the 5th's population. The district takes in the northern portion of the city and the well-to-do suburbs of Nichols Hills and The Village. Some of Oklahoma City's wealthiest oil executives make their homes here. This area also includes the corporate headquarters of Kerr-McGee, one of Oklahoma's two big native-born petroleum companies.

Since the discovery of a large oil pool underneath Oklahoma City in the 1930s, much of the economy has revolved about the oil industry. The capital also has important meatpacking, trucking and aviation industries. Along with state government, the military has a significant presence, with Tinker Air Force Base located on the outskirts of the city.

For decades Oklahoma County was a Democratic center, balancing Tulsa's Republicanism. Between 1920 and 1948, the county supported a Republican presidential nominee only once — Herbert Hoover in 1928. But the county has gradually switched its allegiance in the postwar years and now is almost as reliable in its national GOP voting habits as its rival to the northeast. Since 1952, only Lyndon B. Johnson has carried it for the Democrats in a presidential election.

Oil has been of paramount importance to the local economy of Bartlesville (Washington County) since 1897, when production began on a well found here. A town of 34,000 people, Bartlesville is the home of Phillips Petroleum. Across Osage County from Bartlesville lies Ponca City, which hosts a Conoco refinery.

Population: 502,974. White 446,198 (89%), Black 30,826 (6%), Other 19,133 (4%). Spanish origin 9,915 (2%). 18 and over 367,630 (73%), 65 and over 60,357 (12%). Median age: 31.

cratic processes in Nicaragua. Edwards expressed concern: When he voted for the bill, he said his goal was "to keep the contras alive." But as the campaign for the February 1990 election (which ended leftist rule) got under way, Edwards supported the new policy. "The field of battle has changed from bullets to ballots," Edwards said.

Edwards can be more sharply partisan on issues other than foreign aid. Just as negotiations were beginning on a deficit-reduction bill in July 1990, Edwards blasted Democrats whom he said had not proposed spending cuts, but had "merely pouted and whined and stamped their feet and demanded the right to increase taxes on the American people."

Yet Edwards can be hard on the administration when he believes the House is being ignored. During the October 1990 budget impasse, Bush consulted closely with Senate Republicans. When budget director Richard G. Darman came to the Capitol to meet with House GOP leaders, Edwards took his shot. "Hi, I'm Mickey Edwards," he greeted Darman. "Pleased to meet you."

Edwards is an institutionalist, holding fast to what he sees as the constitutional responsibilities of Congress — especially in the appropriations process. Edwards says it is up to Congress to set the nation's spending priorities, which is why he opposes a line-item veto.

This philosophy separates Edwards from many of his conservative colleagues, who have expressed their frustrations with Democratic control of Congress by trying to invest more power in an executive branch that has been dominated in recent years by Republicans.

"Political conservatism, at its root, is a philosophy of diffusion [of power]," he says. He also says those favoring expanded presidential power are ignoring the long-term implications. "How will Republicans react when a Democrat becomes president and says, 'Let me have the line-item veto?' "

Edwards also disagrees with House Republican activists, including Minority Whip Newt Gingrich of Georgia, who say the advantages of incumbency have created a "permanent Congress" that perpetuates Democratic rule. In an opinion article published by *The New York Times* in January 1990, Edwards provided statistics showing that the membership of Congress changes frequently, even as incumbents enjoy a high re-election rate. "We must correct the abuses of power, legislative failures and other inadequacies," Edwards wrote. "But we must do so without undermining the existence of the institution. . . ."

Edwards' institutional interests have engaged him in the issue of campaign finance reform. He took a higher profile on that at the start of the 102nd Congress, when he got a seat on the House Administration Committee.

At Home: After a career in journalism, public relations and teaching, Edwards challenged Democratic Rep. John Jarman for Oklahoma City's House seat in 1974 and came within 3,402 votes of winning. That achievement in a national Democratic year made Edwards the logical choice for 1976. Jarman switched to the Republican Party himself in 1975, but did not run again.

Edwards had been unopposed for the 1974 GOP nomination. But in 1976, with the seat open and the Republican chances obviously good, he received a primary challenge from former state Attorney General G. T. Blankenship. It was a close race, but Edwards' non-stop campaign won him the nomination.

Edwards also had a harder time in November than had been expected, with stiff competition from Democrat Tom Dunlap, a young hospital administrator and son of the popular state chancellor of higher education. Edwards won by just 3,899 votes, but quickly set about establishing himself. He has had no trouble winning since then.

In addition to developing close ties with Oklahoma City's blue-collar workers, Edwards has pursued black support more effectively than other area Republicans. In 1979 he asked the U.S. Justice Department to investigate Ku Klux Klan activity in Oklahoma and complained about "foot-dragging" when there was no prompt response.

Redistricting made the 5th's boundaries more awkward in 1981, stretching the district north to the Kansas border, thus obligating candidates to advertise in the Oklahoma City, Tulsa and Wichita, Kan., markets. But this has posed no problem for Edwards; the current 5th is more Republican than the old one.

Before running for Congress, Edwards was a reporter and editor for *The Oklahoma City Times*, director of public relations for an advertising agency and editor of *Private Practice* magazine, writing editorials in defense of private medicine. He was the author of "Hazardous to Your Health," a treatise against national health insurance.

Committees

Appropriations (8th of 22 Republicans)
Foreign Operations, Export Financing & Related Programs (ranking); Military Construction

Education & Labor (14th of 14 Republicans)
Elementary, Secondary & Vocational Education; Labor-Management Relations

House Administration (7th of 9 Republicans)
Procurement & Printing (ranking); Campaign Finance Reform

Elections

1990 General		
Mickey Edwards (R)	114,608	(70%)
Bryce Baggett (D)	50,086	(30%)
1988 General		
Mickey Edwards (R)	139,182	(72%)
Terry J. Montgomery (D)	53,668	(28%)

Previous Winning Percentages: **1986** (71%) **1984** (76%) **1982** (67%) **1980** (68%) **1978** (80%) **1976** (50%)

District Vote For President

	1988	1984	1980	1976
D	68,503 (32%)	50,701 (23%)	55,490 (25%)	87,988 (42%)
R	145,413 (67%)	170,703 (76%)	150,272 (69%)	117,924 (56%)
I			8,774 (4%)	

Campaign Finance

	Receipts	Receipts from PACs	Expend-itures
1990			
Edwards (R)	$326,283	$147,525 (45%)	$373,414
Baggett (D)	$6,395	$2,200 (34%)	$6,277
1988			
Edwards (R)	$362,570	$122,430 (34%)	$341,250
Montgomery (D)	$460	0	$302

Key Votes

1991	
Authorize use of force against Iraq	Y
1990	
Support constitutional amendment on flag desecration	Y
Pass family and medical leave bill over Bush veto	N
Reduce SDI funding	N
Allow abortions in overseas military facilities	N
Approve budget summit plan for spending and taxing	N
Approve civil rights bill	N
1989	
Halt production of B-2 stealth bomber at 13 planes	N
Oppose capital gains tax cut	N
Approve federal abortion funding in rape or incest cases	N
Approve pay raise and revision of ethics rules	Y
Pass Democratic minimum wage plan over Bush veto	N

Voting Studies

	Presidential Support		Party Unity		Conservative Coalition	
Year	**S**	**O**	**S**	**O**	**S**	**O**
1990	69	25	79	10	87	4
1989	81	9	72	18	90	7
1988	59	39	84	9	95	5
1987	64	30	82	8	84	9
1986	71	23	72	20	82	10
1985	71	25	79	10	91	5
1984	58	36	78	15	80	12
1983	68	27	79 †	14 †	90	7
1982	68	23	78	13	81	12
1981	75	24	84	15	88	11

† Not eligible for all recorded votes.

Interest Group Ratings

Year	ADA	ACU	AFL-CIO	CCUS
1990	6	92	0	79
1989	0	85	18	100
1988	10	92	36	93
1987	12	90	7	100
1986	5	85	14	81
1985	5	90	0	85
1984	10	96	23	88
1983	10	95	6	83
1982	5	100	0	81
1981	5	100	7	79

6 Glenn English (D)

Of Cordell — Elected 1974

Born: Nov. 30, 1940, Cordell, Okla.
Education: Southwestern State College, B.A. 1964.
Military Service: Army Reserve, 1965-71.
Occupation: Petroleum landman.
Family: Wife, Jan Pangle; two children.
Religion: Methodist.
Political Career: No previous office.
Capitol Office: 2206 Rayburn Bldg. 20515; 225-5565.

In Washington: Starting the 101st Congress as the new chairman of the Agriculture Subcommittee on Conservation, Credit and Rural Development, English introduced a more combative style of leadership than the panel had seen under its previous chairman, mild-mannered Tennessean Ed Jones (who retired at the end of the 100th Congress.)

But English's more forceful manner did not hinder him from working with the subcommittee's ranking Republican, Tom Coleman of Missouri, and the panel moved some significant pieces of legislation in English's first term with the gavel.

The Conservation and Credit chairmanship ensured English a central role in the federal investigation of fraud in the commodity futures trading markets. In the 101st Congress, his subcommittee produced a bill to strengthen government regulation of the commodity futures industry. The measure, added to a bill reauthorizing the Commodity Futures Trading Commission, would have forced futures exchanges to become more aggressive in rooting out illegal and unfair trading practices. The bill sailed through the House but died in the Senate, snagged on a dispute over what regulatory agency would have jurisdiction over certain stock-index future contracts.

After his subcommittee conducted 14 hearings in Washington and in five states, English joined Coleman on an initiative the Republican had offered in the 100th Congress designed to promote rural economic development. But it took some astute negotiating with a canny foe before English could win committee and House approval.

The English-Coleman bill sought to pool roughly $1 billion in existing rural-development loan and grant programs and create a new agency within the Agriculture Department, the Rural Development Administration, to distribute the funds. It also decentralized the funding process by giving state-appointed boards in five pilot states authority to allocate their share of the funds among projects they deem worthy.

The bill easily won subcommittee approval, but budget problems and opposition from powerful interest groups derailed the initial attempt to send it to the House floor. After a three-month delay, the full Agriculture Committee approved the bill, but only after an eight-hour markup that dealt with nearly 40 amendments.

In committee and on the floor, North Carolina Democrat Charlie Rose was the chief obstacle to the English-Coleman bill. His state received a disproportionately large sum of Farmers Home Administration assistance under the existing system; shifting authority for distributing funds would likely end that advantage. English told the committee: "This legislation would make it much more likely that money would go into your home state, not into North Carolina." To assuage members who supported the existing system and to ward off Rose, English offered a compromise that increased the authorization for water and sewer grants and kept $34 million annually for water and sewer grants out of the rural development pool. The amendment was adopted 25-18.

But on the floor, Rose offered an amendment to remove the agriculture secretary's authority to transfer funds among the various federal loan and grant programs. The House first approved it, but English and Coleman worked out a compromise with Rose restoring some of the transfer authority. The House adopted it and the bill became law as part of the 1990 farm bill.

English's subcommittee was responsible for the conservation title of the 1990 farm bill, which necessitated negotiating an accord between environmentalists and farm groups. Under the terms of the deal, the two factions vowed to support three areas of the controversial section of the bill: the "swampbuster" program, which denies government subsidies to farmers who drain and plant wetlands; an incentive program to pay farmers to reduce water pollution; and a program to pay farmers to retire 2.5 million acres of wetlands from production. "Many felt that the gap could not be bridged," English said. "It took a lot of meet

Oklahoma 6

West and Panhandle; Part of Oklahoma City

The 6th unites rural western Oklahoma and downtown Oklahoma City, an odd combination that creates a constituency with little common politics or sense of identity.

Just over a quarter of the district's population lives in Oklahoma City, the site of the most famous symbols of the state's oil wealth: working wells on the grounds of the state Capitol and the lawn of the governor's residence. Though the wells on the governor's lawn are out of operation, several on the Capitol grounds continue to be productive.

The now-slumping petroleum industry has been a major force in the local economy since the discovery of a large oil pool beneath the city in the 1930s. The capital also has important meatpacking, trucking and aviation industries.

A Democratic center for decades, Oklahoma City as a whole has begun to shift its allegiance to national Republican candidates in recent years. The 6th's portion of the city has some residual Democratic strength, however; it includes most of Oklahoma City's 71,000 blacks, who bring the black share of the 6th's population to almost 15 percent.

Beyond Oklahoma City, the 6th sweeps west 300 miles across the dusty plains to the New Mexico border. Part of the Dust Bowl, western Oklahoma was devastated by droughts and soil erosion in the 1930s and '40s. It made great strides toward prosperity in the two postwar decades, becoming a region of massive wheat farms and cattle ranches. But it began to slip again in the farm credit crisis of the 1980s. Though the state registered a slight increase in population from 1980 to 1990, most counties in the 6th lost residents; Ellis County lost almost 20 percent of its population.

Western Oklahoma is traditionally the state's most conservative region. Residents of this area share a general aversion to most governmental activity other than military expenditures and agricultural subsidies. Democrats such as Sen. David L. Boren have enjoyed strong support here, but the 6th has given healthy margins to recent GOP presidential candidates. In 1988, George Bush won the 6th by 17 percentage points. Texas and Beaver counties, in the Panhandle, were the only two counties in the state won by 1990 Republican gubernatorial nominee Bill Price.

Population: 503,291. White 427,058 (85%), Black 49,364 (10%), Other 19,173 (4%). Spanish origin 13,373 (3%). 18 and over 361,309 (72%), 65 and over 69,844 (14%). Median age: 31.

ings, ... table-pounding and hand-wringing."

Through the years, English has been an unceasing advocate of high price-support levels for wheat and other Oklahoma commodities. During work on the farm bill in the 99th Congress, English failed in his attempts to raise or maintain the existing price supports for wheat. He favored a plan to allow farmers to vote for mandatory production controls as a way to raise prices. Frustrated in those efforts, English voted against the entire farm bill, arguing that it would drive down market prices and increase surpluses.

English got an opportunity in the 100th Congress to help disaster-affected wheat growers. His 1987 bill, signed into law that spring, authorized payments to certain winter wheat producers — mainly in Oklahoma, Kansas and Missouri — who could not plant their 1987 crop due to heavy floods.

But instead of giving outright disaster-relief payments, the bill created a separate one-time program that essentially paid farmers not to plant. English's bill gave 92 percent of expected income subsidies to wheat farmers who were unable to plant their crops — and who agreed not to plant another crop in 1987. The so-called "0/92" plan was endorsed by Reagan administration officials as a test case of their "decoupling" strategy, which aimed to eliminate overproduction by encouraging farmers to plant only as much of a crop as they believe will sell on the open market. The 0/92 plan was reauthorized as part of the 1990 farm bill.

On Government Operations, English used his subcommittee chairmanship on Government Information, Justice and Agriculture to crusade for personal privacy and against Reagan administration attempts to soften the Freedom of Information Act (FOIA).

In the 99th and 100th Congresses, he made drug enforcement a top priority of his subcommittee, using his chairmanship to help write sweeping antidrug bills. He pushed successfully to get the military to lend aircraft and radar to the Customs Service to intercept smugglers. When drugs suddenly became a prominent national issue shortly before the 1986 elections, members racing to familiarize themselves with the subject looked to English. Five of the 12 committees reporting legislation for an omnibus antidrug package based their recommendations at least in part on proposals by English.

There was a particular legislative plum for Oklahomans in the 99th Congress' drug package: a $20 million National Command and Control Center in Oklahoma City, intended to be the hub for law enforcement, intelligence and planning in the war on drugs.

When the 100th Congress began work on another antidrug bill, English was one of the authors of the original package, along with Sens. Alfonse M. D'Amato of New York and Dennis DeConcini of Arizona. English questioned the Reagan administration's commitment to the war on drugs, issuing a report through his subcommittee in 1987 criticizing an administration oversight board for inactivity.

At Home: English started his career as a petroleum landman — someone who arranges oil and gas leases. But politics soon attracted him. In the 1960s he went to California to be chief assistant to the Democrats in the California Legislature, at a time when dictatorial Assembly Speaker Jesse Unruh held sway. English then returned to Oklahoma and served as executive director of the Oklahoma Democratic Party from 1969 to 1973.

In 1974 English entered the Democratic primary in the 6th District, held for the previous three terms by Republican John Newbold Happy Camp, a genial and innocuous small-town banker. English was forced into a runoff against insurance agent David Hutchens, but defeated him by 9,435 votes.

In November, English conducted a town-to-town campaign, contrasting his youth and energy with the barely visible effort conducted by Camp. He beat Camp by 9 percentage points.

English's closest election — and it was not very close — came in 1984. He faced Enid attorney Craig Dodd, who spent most of the campaign trying to get the incumbent to agree to debate. Ronald Reagan's overwhelming victory in the 6th aided Dodd, but English still won almost 60 percent of the vote.

Committees

Agriculture (5th of 27 Democrats)
Conservation, Credit & Rural Development (chairman); Peanuts & Tobacco; Wheat, Soybeans & Feed Grains

Government Operations (3rd of 25 Democrats)
Government Activities & Transportation; Legislation & National Security

Elections

1990 General		
Glenn English (D)	110,100	(80%)
Robert Burns (R)	27,540	(20%)
1988 General		
Glenn English (D)	122,887	(73%)
Mike Brown (R)	45,239	(27%)

Previous Winning Percentages: **1986** (100%) **1984** (59%) **1982** (75%) **1980** (65%) **1978** (74%) **1976** (71%) **1974** (53%)

District Vote For President

	1988	1984	1980	1976
D	72,272 (41%)	58,426 (30%)	60,622 (32%)	83,601 (46%)
R	101,322 (58%)	136,314 (69%)	120,834 (64%)	97,052 (53%)
I			5,221 (3%)	

Campaign Finance

	Receipts	Receipts from PACs		Expend-itures
1990				
English (D)	$238,141	$146,050	(61%)	$157,414
1988				
English (D)	$385,373	$183,408	(48%)	$306,600
Brown (R)	$86,210	$3,190	(4%)	$86,209

Key Votes

1991	
Authorize use of force against Iraq	N
1990	
Support constitutional amendment on flag desecration	Y
Pass family and medical leave bill over Bush veto	Y
Reduce SDI funding	N
Allow abortions in overseas military facilities	N
Approve budget summit plan for spending and taxing	N
Approve civil rights bill	Y
1989	
Halt production of B-2 stealth bomber at 13 planes	N
Oppose capital gains tax cut	N
Approve federal abortion funding in rape or incest cases	N
Approve pay raise and revision of ethics rules	N
Pass Democratic minimum wage plan over Bush veto	N

Voting Studies

	Presidential Support		Party Unity		Conservative Coalition	
Year	**S**	**O**	**S**	**O**	**S**	**O**
1990	47	53	60	38	93	7
1989	64	35	60	39	95	5
1988	47	52	65	33	95	5
1987	52	48	62	35	81	16
1986	43	51	63	34	82	18
1985	58	43	53	44	95	4
1984	52	44	43	50	75	12
1983	46	51	53	46	85	15
1982	65	35	43	57	82	16
1981	55	43	54	46	80	20

Interest Group Ratings

Year	ADA	ACU	AFL-CIO	CCUS
1990	50	54	58	64
1989	25	68	33	100
1988	40	60	64	71
1987	44	39	38	73
1986	35	48	50	61
1985	15	76	24	82
1984	15	78	23	63
1983	45	61	47	60
1982	20	64	30	77
1981	25	47	47	53

Oregon

U.S. CONGRESS

SENATE 2 R

HOUSE 4 D, 1 R

LEGISLATURE

Senate 20 D, 10 R

House 28 D, 32 R

ELECTIONS

1988 Presidential Vote

Bush	47%
Dukakis	51%

1984 Presidential Vote

Reagan	56%
Mondale	44%

1980 Presidential Vote

Reagan	48%
Carter	39%
Anderson	10%

Turnout rate in 1986	51%
Turnout rate in 1988	59%
Turnout rate in 1990	50%

(as percentage of voting age population)

POPULATION AND GROWTH

1980 population	2,633,105
1990 population (29th in the nation)	2,842,321
Percent change 1980-1990	+8%

DEMOGRAPHIC BREAKDOWN

White	93%
Black	2%
Asian or Pacific Islander	2%
(Hispanic origin)	4%
Urban	68%
Rural	32%
Born in state	44%
Foreign-born	4%

MAJOR CITIES

Portland	437,319
Eugene	112,669
Salem	107,786
Gresham	68,235
Beaverton	53,310

AREA AND LAND USE

Area 96,184 sq. miles (10th)

Farm	29%
Forest	46%
Federally owned	49%

Gov. Barbara Roberts (D)
Of Salem — Elected 1990

Born: Dec. 21, 1936, Corvallis, Ore.
Education: Attended Portland State U., 1961-64.
Occupation: Political consultant.
Religion: Unspecified.
Political Career: Ore. House, 1981-85, majority leader, 1983-84; Ore. secretary of state, 1985-91.
Next Election: 1994.

WORK

Occupations

White-collar	53%
Blue-collar	29%
Service workers	14%

Government Workers

Federal	28,922
State	60,142
Local	121,028

MONEY

Median family income	$ 20,027	(21st)
Tax burden per capita	$ 738	(39th)

EDUCATION

Spending per pupil through grade 12	$ 4,789	(12th)
Persons with college degrees	18%	(15th)

CRIME

Violent crime rate 519 per 100,000 (21st)

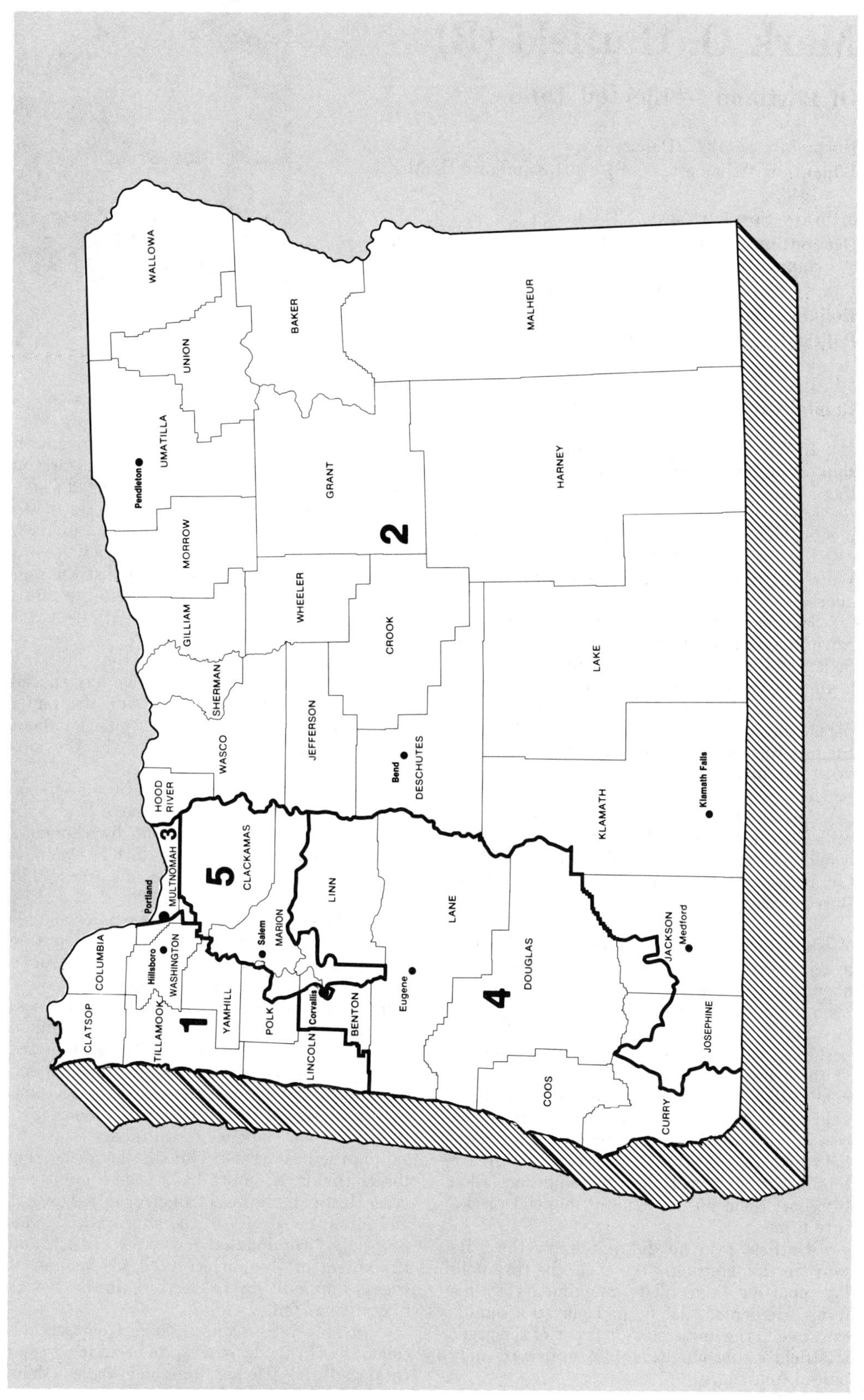

WALLOWA
UNION
BAKER
MALHEUR
UMATILLA
Pendleton
GRANT
HARNEY
MORROW
2
WHEELER
GILLIAM
CROOK
LAKE
SHERMAN
JEFFERSON
WASCO
DESCHUTES
Bend
HOOD RIVER
Klamath Falls
KLAMATH
3
MULTNOMAH
Portland
5
CLACKAMAS
LINN
LANE
MARION
Salem
COLUMBIA
Hillsboro
WASHINGTON
DOUGLAS
JACKSON
Medford
Eugene
4
CLATSOP
TILLAMOOK
1
YAMHILL
POLK
Corvallis
BENTON
LINCOLN
JOSEPHINE
COOS
CURRY

Mark O. Hatfield (R)

Of Portland — Elected 1966

Born: July 12, 1922, Dallas, Ore.

Education: Willamette U., B.A. 1943; Stanford U., M.A. 1948.

Military Service: Navy, 1943-46.

Occupation: Professor of political science; college administrator.

Family: Wife, Antoinette Kuzmanich; four children.

Religion: Baptist.

Political Career: Ore. House, 1951-55; Ore. Senate, 1955-57; Ore. secretary of state, 1957-59; governor, 1959-67.

Capitol Office: 711 Hart Bldg. 20510; 224-3753.

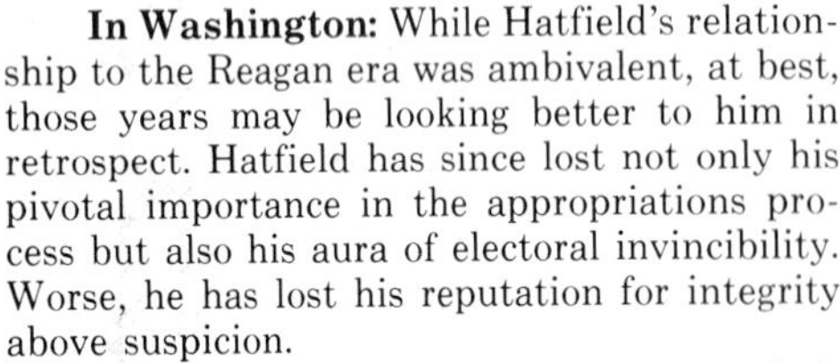

In Washington: While Hatfield's relationship to the Reagan era was ambivalent, at best, those years may be looking better to him in retrospect. Hatfield has since lost not only his pivotal importance in the appropriations process but also his aura of electoral invincibility. Worse, he has lost his reputation for integrity above suspicion.

Hatfield gave up the Appropriations chair when the Democrats regained control of the Senate in the 100th Congress. But he remained a kind of co-chairman de facto for two years under the aged and ailing chairman, John Stennis of Mississippi. That changed in 1989, when Stennis was succeeded by Robert C. Byrd of West Virginia, who had his own plans for the panel.

In 1990, Hatfield eased into a low-gear run for a fifth term, reasonably sure the Democrats would once again fail to field a tough competitor. He was wrong, and only an eleventh-hour flurry of campaigning saved him.

But Hatfield had no sooner returned to Washington than he was confronted with damaging revelations about his family finances and about personal benefactors who stood to benefit from his political friendship.

Perhaps the most incriminating of these pertained to James Holderman, the president of the University of South Carolina. Holderman's office granted a full scholarship to Hatfield's son at about the same time the school was winning a $16.3 million federal grant. Hatfield had also received four artworks worth a total of $9,265 from Holderman and had failed to report them on his Senate financial disclosure forms.

Hatfield said he did not know the gifts were worth more than $100 each, the threshold for reporting, and filed amendments to his forms. He denied that he had played a significant role in the university's pursuit of the grant (Hatfield's subcommittee had approved only partial funding).

In March 1991, *The Portland Oregonian* reported that the president of the Oregon Health Sciences University had arranged a special admissions policy that allowed Hatfield's daughter to attend the medical school in 1989. Two of the nine members of the admissions committee resigned in protest against the policy, which was not public and which the president directed be applied to Hatfield's daughter and three other applicants.

"I specifically recall telling the university that I did not want her to receive any special consideration," Hatfield said. But the paper noted that Hatfield helped the school get about $91 million in federal grants in the previous decade.

Since coming to the Senate in 1967, Hatfield and his wife, Antoinette, have been subjected to several investigations by the news media and three by the Senate Ethics Committee. But none had evoked the uneasiness that surrounded the new episodes.

In the best-known case, the senator and his wife were criticized for $55,000 in real estate and interior decorating fees she received from a Greek businessman who solicited — and got — help from the senator in a major business venture. Hatfield tried to advance a $15 billion trans-Africa oil pipeline project being promoted by the entrepreneur, Basil Tsakos. Hatfield and his wife said that she had earned the $55,000.

In 1984 the Ethics Committee decided it lacked enough evidence for a full-scale investigation; the next year it issued a report clearing the Hatfields. A month before the committee's vote, Hatfield admitted "an error in judgment" and an "insensitivity to the appearance of impropriety." He donated $55,000 to charity, and the voters of Oregon accepted his version of events implicitly by re-electing him by a wide margin that fall.

In May 1991, Congressional Quarterly detailed the Hatfields' real estate investments and cataloged the friends who had loaned them more than $680,000 over the years on favorable terms. Much of the debt had been forgiven outright.

It did not appear that Hatfield had ever done anything for these longstanding friends that did not mesh with his own well-known political convictions. But at the very least, his records indicated he had repeatedly veered close to the line of impropriety in his dealings with those who might benefit from decisions made in his committee.

Hatfield has occasionally acknowledged lapses over the years, but the Holderman scrape jarred him, friends say. He has announced new ethics rules for his office: no more speaking fees and no more gifts from anyone except family and close friends with no stake in the business of his office. And he has appointed an aide to be his office's ethical watchdog.

When the GOP controlled the Senate from 1981 to 1987, Hatfield held the storied position of Appropriations chairman. Proud as he was of the job, it forced upon him responsibility for a rightward march he himself did not wholly support.

President Reagan's military buildup violated Hatfield's personal philosophy, which is deeply averse to weaponry and war. The tax cuts, he believed, were regressive. The spending cuts, he often said, went too far.

As chairman, Hatfield sometimes seemed little more than an overworked "traffic cop" sorting through the conflicting demands of autonomous subcommittee chairmen. Much of his work consisted of shepherding annual continuing resolutions — massive "emergency" funding bills — through an unruly Senate.

That was an arduous undertaking that required endless hours at the end of each session. Yet it yielded only a modest amount of control over spending decisions for Hatfield or his committee.

Moreover, Reagan and his congressional allies pressed repeatedly for procedural changes of which Hatfield disapproved. These included a balanced budget amendment to the Constitution and a presidential license to veto individual items in appropriations bills ("line-item veto"). Given his steadfast opposition to both, Hatfield was often cast as an apostate within his own party.

With the return of the Democratic majority in 1987, Hatfield was in some respects liberated. As ranking minority member on Appropriations, he could practice his unorthodox combination of moral indignation and pork-barrel politics without the burdens or restraints of the chairmanship. Yet at times, Hatfield seemed disengaged, as if finding the supporting role unexciting.

Few senators have achieved Hatfield's popularity while clinging so tenaciously to views outside the mainstream. He is a near-pacifist on defense issues and an automatic vote against any military spending bill. When war loomed in the Persian Gulf in 1991, Hatfield was the only senator to oppose not only the authorization of military action (a course chosen by only one other GOP senator) but also the extension of sanctions offered as an alternative by the Democratic leadership. Both options were too bellicose for Hatfield, whose floor statement said,"They do not offer us the alternative of peace."

"If we want to avoid war we ought to say so, right here and now. Instead of playing this dangerous game ... we ought to bring our troops home once and for all." In March, he even cast the lone opposing vote when the Senate approved a package of benefits for Persian Gulf veterans by a tally of 97-1.

Hatfield is nearly as lonely in his outspoken contention that U.S. policy in the Middle East tilts too far toward Israel. He moralizes about the importance of human rights as an emphasis in U.S. foreign policy.

In the 100th Congress, Hatfield pressed legislation to grant foreign aid, in the form of disaster relief, to the communist government of Vietnam (he had been elected as an opponent of U.S. involvement in the Vietnam War a generation earlier). He was also willing to stand against the drug bill at the end of the 1988 session because it contained a death penalty.

"It is not responsible for this body to have an eye-for-eye mentality," he said. Hatfield introduced multiple amendments before casting one of just three votes in the Senate against the politically popular bill.

Hatfield renewed his efforts against the death penalty in June 1990, proposing to amend the Senate's anticrime package by changing every death sentence in the bill to life in prison without possibility of release. His amendment received only 25 votes.

Despite all this, Hatfield has functioned well in the world of Appropriations, which carries a long tradition of collegiality and accommodation. The reason is that he has always been careful to place personal friendship above ideological combat. While outsiders sometimes listen to Hatfield's speeches and decide he must be sanctimonious, senators find him amiable and unpretentious. He is good at making friends with people whose opinions he would never endorse.

A classic case was his relationship with the hawkish Stennis, who retired from the Senate in 1989. Starting with a mutual interest in waterways and public power, the two men formed a close friendship that survived numerous jousts on defense issues. After Stennis was shot by a burglar in 1973, Hatfield rushed to the hospital and, without identifying himself, took command of a telephone switchboard jammed with calls.

While some other liberal Republicans were stripped of party influence for straying from the dominant conservative ideology, Hatfield avoided a great deal of criticism despite holding views that even many Democrats would find too radical.

It cannot happen very often, for example, that a chairman castigates members of the opposition party for failing to provide strong enough criticism of his own party's president. But it happened in 1986, when Hatfield essentially wrote off the GOP as a source of resistance to the strategic defense initiative (SDI) and other aspects of President Reagan's defense buildup. "Face up to the facts," he told the Democrats during debate on that year's continuing resolution. "There are only a handful of Republicans ... who will challenge this madness. You are the loyal opposition. Take a stand."

Even while he was denouncing Reagan, Hatfield was working behind the scenes to find a compromise with the president's views on spending. In the first year of the Reagan administration, Hatfield's voting did drift slightly toward the right. He went along with the outlines of Reaganomics — budget and tax cuts — and while he continued to vote against new weapons systems, he did not try to use his chairmanship to sabotage the military buildup.

But by 1982, the loosening of Reagan's grip on Congress made it easier for Hatfield to reassert his independent streak. He signed on as co-leader of the nuclear weapons freeze campaign and championed more spending for job-creation programs.

For the next two years, Hatfield was part of a small group of moderate Republicans who tried to make their own mark on the budget. They relied on a mixture of confrontation and negotiations with the administration to produce budgets that cut defense spending requests and moderated the assault on social spending.

By the 99th Congress, Hatfield had adopted a more unyielding stance, particularly when the administration tried to change the budget and appropriations process itself. He led the 1985 filibuster that killed Reagan's request for line-item veto authority.

Even so, Hatfield concluded that accommodations with the administration sometimes were necessary if critical funding bills were to be approved. He often urged his colleagues not to approve amendments to spending bills that might incite a presidential veto.

Despite the many frustrations, being chairman of Appropriations was not without its compensations. The position allowed Hatfield to practice the lessons of constituent service he learned at the knee of Warren G. Magnuson of Washington, a Pacific Northwest cohort and longtime Appropriations powerhouse. The ports along the Oregon coast and the funding for federal lands have profited handsomely.

Hatfield once explained that he would like to cut the federal budget substantially, but since that was impossible he was determined to steer as much of it as possible to his home state. He has never been bashful about doing that.

Hatfield has bent his effort to such thorny Northwestern perennials as the balancing of nature and livelihood. While he has attempted to mediate the long-running debate over saving the rare northern spotted owl, he has taken a more conventional stance with respect to the salmon and attendant concern for river levels. "Every man woman and child in the region has a direct relationship in this by the fact of where they get their power."

Hatfield is the only member of Congress who has been able to get a bill to the floor instituting a national policy of nickel deposits on bottles and cans. All other suggestions of this kind since 1970 have died in committee (Hatfield's died on the floor, 26-60).

Over the years, his Appropriations assignment has brought him not only political benefits at home (jurisdiction over public forests and range lands, hydroelectric power and harbors) but also leverage in Congress. As a member of Appropriations, he quickly became adept at the senatorial art of quid pro quo.

Most of Hatfield's efforts on Appropriations are quiet, however; he is best-known to the public for his sallies on foreign policy and defense issues.

In recent years, he has spoken for Palestinian refugees and advocated limits on military aid to Israel. He has led the opposition to the MX missile and SDI, pressed for human rights concessions from authoritarian foreign regimes, and filibustered against reinstatement of the draft.

He was equally unyielding in opposition to Reagan's policies in Central America. Early in 1984, he led the Appropriations Committee in rejecting an administration attempt to add military aid for the Nicaraguan contras to a home heating assistance bill.

While serving on Appropriations, Hatfield has remained on the Energy and Natural Resources Committee. He was one of the most active Senate opponents of the nuclear breeder reactor. His feeling was partially explained by the fact that, as a young naval officer, he was a member of the first American military team to enter Hiroshima, one month after the atom bomb demolished the city.

Hatfield's politics are shaped by a born-again religious conviction. Not to be confused with the fundamentalism of the evangelical right, Hatfield's religious views emphasize help for the poor and separation of church and state.

An opponent of abortion, Hatfield also opposes a constitutional amendment to permit prayer in the public schools. But he does believe that student religious organizations should have access to public educational facilities.

Though he does not flaunt his faith in Senate debate, Hatfield courts a religious constituency with speeches and newsletters. He participates regularly in Capitol prayer meetings and has written three books for religious publishing houses describing the tribulations of a Christian in politics.

Over the years he has developed many bills to encourage neighborhood-based social programs, and he often tells churches that if each of them would take charge of a few poor families, the government welfare burden could be virtually eliminated.

At Home: In 40 years in Oregon politics, Hatfield has never lost an election. But in 1990, his broad-based coalition built largely on peace and pork suffered widespread defections.

Hatfield did not look like he had serious political problems when he launched his bid for a fifth Senate term. With well-known Democrats such as Reps. Ron Wyden and Les AuCoin staying out of the race, the nomination went virtually by default to a political newcomer, Harry Lonsdale.

But as the founder of a high-tech research firm, Lonsdale was able to pump roughly $800,000 into his campaign. And he benefited from an array of issues on which Hatfield was at odds with vocal and well-organized interest groups.

Since the Vietnam War, Hatfield had drawn widespread support from the left as a near-pacifist on defense issues. But other parts of his voting record were in the spotlight in 1990. His anti-abortion stance drew opposition from the National Abortion Rights Action League and the National Organization for Women. His sympathy for the timber industry in its battle with environmentalists over the future of old-growth forests and the northern spotted owl drew opposition from such "green" groups as the League of Conservation Voters.

Hatfield also found his integrity sharply questioned by Lonsdale, who voiced concern about the incumbent's ready acceptance of honoraria and political action committee (PAC) money. Lonsdale boasted that he was accepting no PAC contributions.

By late September it was clear that Hatfield was vulnerable to what the media began to describe as an "Oregon surprise." A summertime lead of 36 percentage points in *The Oregonian*'s poll was sliced to just 6 percentage points.

But to Hatfield's advantage, he had time to respond. And faced with the prospect of defeat, he responded aggressively, dropping his traditional low-budget, "speak no evil" style of campaigning in favor of an attack strategy. His ads trumpeted allegations that Lonsdale's company had engaged in improper toxic waste disposal and chided the challenger for defending in writing during the mid-1980s the activities of religious cult leader Bhagwan Shree Rajneesh, who had set up a commune in Oregon.

Lonsdale's momentum stalled, and Hatfield won re-election with 54 percent of the vote. The Democrat narrowly carried Multnomah County (Portland) but Hatfield more than offset that with a strong showing in the Portland suburbs and populous Willamette Valley. Altogether, Hatfield carried 31 of Oregon's 36 counties.

A major factor in Hatfield's victory was the reservoir of good will that he had built up over four decades in Oregon politics. It has enabled him to attract support across partisan and ideological lines.

Earlier in his career, Hatfield won the gratitude of liberals with his opposition to loyalty oaths for teachers; their support was reinforced by his opposition to the Vietnam War.

Organized labor, when it has not been able to back him against a Democratic competitor, usually has remained neutral. Hatfield sometimes likes to play up his labor connections; his father, a blacksmith, belonged to the railroad brotherhood.

A political science professor and university dean, Hatfield acquired Republicanism from his mother, who had been raised in the staunchly GOP territory of East Tennessee. In 1958, as secretary of state in Oregon, he blended an effective campaign style with youthful good looks to unseat Democratic Gov. Robert D. Holmes.

As governor, Hatfield ran an administration that kept state spending down and did not raise taxes. He launched an aggressive "Sell Oregon" drive that helped spur exports. And in 1962 he withstood a strong re-election challenge from Democrat Robert Y. Thornton, the state attorney general, who was unable to mobilize the labor support he needed to defeat a popular governor.

Constitutionally forbidden to run for a third term as governor in 1966, Hatfield took aim at the Senate seat being vacated by Democrat Maurine Neuberger.

In that race, the central issue was the Vietnam War, which Hatfield opposed and his Democratic rival, Rep. Robert B. Duncan, favored. As Duncan saw it, the conflict concerned whether "Americans will die in the buffalo grass of Vietnam or the rye grass of Oregon."

Hatfield had been the lone dissenting vote on a National Governors' Conference resolution supporting the war. Afterward, in his Senate campaign, he put up billboards with the word "Courage" in large letters. He blamed the war for the state's lagging lumber industry, reasoning that the conflict had brought a downturn in home construction. Fearful of being painted as unpatriotic, however, Hatfield criticized the "inexcusable excesses of some antiwar demonstrations." Hatfield defeated Duncan, but with a slim 52 percent majority.

Running for re-election six years later, however, he did better against an even more militant Vietnam dove, former Sen. Wayne Morse, who was seeking a comeback as the

Democratic nominee. Despite Hatfield's antiwar activities, the Nixon White House cooperated with his re-election that year, and this helped defuse conservative resentment that had built up toward him in Oregon. Morse had difficulty finding an issue to use against Hatfield; in 1966, Morse had announced that he would vote for Hatfield over Duncan because of the war issue.

Hatfield won re-election with 54 percent of the vote; more comfortable victories followed in 1978 and 1984.

Committees

Appropriations (Ranking)
Energy & Water Development (ranking); Commerce, Justice, State & Judiciary; Foreign Operations; Labor, Health & Human Services, Education; Transportation

Energy & Natural Resources (2nd of 9 Republicans)
Energy Regulation & Conservation; Public Lands, National Parks & Forests; Water & Power

Rules & Administration (2nd of 7 Republicans)

Joint Library

Joint Printing

Elections

1990 General

Mark O. Hatfield (R)	590,095	(54%)
Harry Lonsdale (D)	507,743	(46%)

1990 Primary

Mark O. Hatfield (R)	220,449	(78%)
Randy Prince (R)	59,970	(21%)

Previous Winning Percentages: 1984 (67%) **1978** (62%) **1972** (54%) **1966** (52%)

Campaign Finance

	Receipts	Receipts from PACs	Expend-itures
1990			
Hatfield (R)	$2,200,139	$969,720 (44%)	$2,357,058
Lonsdale (D)	$1,496,111	0	$1,479,099

Key Votes

1991

Authorize use of force against Iraq	N

1990

Oppose prohibition of certain semiautomatic weapons	N
Support constitutional amendment on flag desecration	Y
Oppose requiring parental notice for minors' abortions	?
Halt production of B-2 stealth bomber at 13 planes	#
Approve budget that cut spending and raised revenues	N
Pass civil rights bill over Bush veto	Y

1989

Oppose reduction of SDI funding	N
Oppose barring federal funds for "obscene" art	Y
Allow vote on capital gains tax cut	Y

Voting Studies

	Presidential Support		Party Unity		Conservative Coalition	
Year	**S**	**O**	**S**	**O**	**S**	**O**
1990	38	51	31	58	32	59
1989	69	30	39	58	34	66
1988	55	38	39	51	30	70
1987	41	46	47	48	41	56
1986	42	57	54	43	50	47
1985	45	40	49	35	32	42
1984	43	45	48	48	45	51
1983	64	29	56	33	45	45
1982	61	29	57	27	45	45
1981	76	19	71	26	58	39

Interest Group Ratings

Year	ADA	ACU	AFL-CIO	CCUS
1990	78	35	67	22
1989	80	21	50	63
1988	70	30	62	57
1987	65	28	60	61
1986	75	30	47	39
1985	45	18	39	70
1984	75	24	40	72
1983	60	13	29	50
1982	60	30	47	50
1981	55	29	22	88

Bob Packwood (R)

Of Portland — Elected 1968

Born: Sept. 11, 1932, Portland, Ore.
Education: Willamette U., B.A. 1954; New York U., LL.B. 1957.
Occupation: Lawyer.
Family: Divorced; two children.
Religion: Unitarian.
Political Career: Ore. House, 1963-69.
Capitol Office: 259 Russell Bldg. 20510; 224-5244.

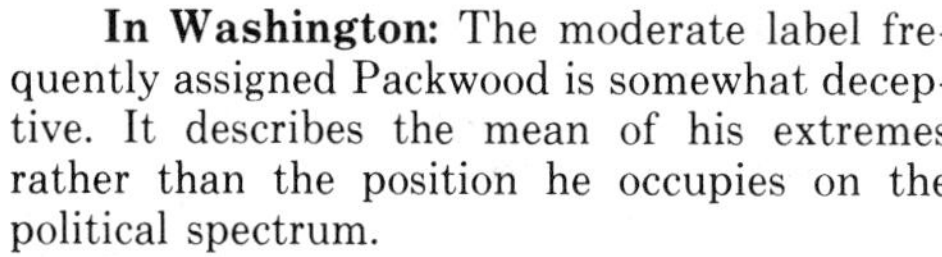

In Washington: The moderate label frequently assigned Packwood is somewhat deceptive. It describes the mean of his extremes rather than the position he occupies on the political spectrum.

In a sense, his tendency to appear at one end of the spectrum or the other bespeaks the exuberant, anti-establishment traditions of his state. In the often offbeat climate of Oregonian politics, Packwood has threaded his way through contested primaries and third-party challenges to nearly 30 years of unbroken electoral success.

Blunt and independent, Packwood has been a crusader for abortion rights, Israel and free enterprise. And for the better part of two decades he has taken stances contrary to his party and president.

In 1990, he voted to override President Bush's veto of civil rights legislation and sided with the Republicans on just over half the issues that split the chamber on party lines.

Nonetheless, Packwood has proved willing to serve in harness in his role as the top Republican on the Finance Committee. He has been more than willing to carry the White House water on the issue Bush called his top tax priority: In 1989 and again in 1990, Packwood as ranking Republican on Finance served as point man in pursuit of a lower tax rate on capital gains.

Many found this an ironic, if not cynical, reversal for Packwood. The elimination of the differential rate for capital gains, paired with a lower tax rate for income overall, was a centerpiece of the tax overhaul of 1986 — the single most memorable achievement of Packwood's career. Packwood himself allowed in 1989 that lowering the capital gains rate again would renew the pressure for higher overall rates.

But one of the industries most sensitive to capital gains taxes is timber, one of Oregon's economic roots. Moreover, Packwood's turnabout on the issue was as much a continuation of his earlier performance as a contradiction of it.

Packwood's role in the tax overhaul legislation of the 99th Congress was one of the great riddles of recent congressional history. It may never be possible to unravel its tangle of sincere conversion and opportunism, of tactical weakness and strategic insight.

Packwood took the Finance chair when Bob Dole of Kansas became majority leader in 1985. It was widely assumed that his chairmanship would follow a predictable course. As he said soon after taking over the committee in 1985, "I kind of like the present tax code."

He believed the tax code should not only produce revenue, but also enable government to enact a social and economic agenda.

So Packwood found himself in an uneasy position in 1985 when Reagan proposed eliminating most tax subsidies in order to reduce rates for individual taxpayers. Packwood backed away from his wholesale defense of the existing tax code, but made clear there were two points on which he was immovable: the tax-free status of employee fringe benefits, such as employer-paid health insurance, and the favorable tax treatment granted to the timber industry. He insisted that those be kept.

Packwood opened committee work on the overhaul with a "reform" proposal that reflected his longtime interests. His bill would have retained many existing tax breaks for business and recovered the cost of reducing individual rates by removing the deduction for state and local taxes and increasing excise taxes on tobacco, liquor and gasoline.

The Finance markup quickly threatened to become a fiasco. Members kept voting to add new breaks, rejecting efforts to cut back. Within a few weeks, the panel had written legislation adding an estimated $30 billion to the federal deficit. "There are some things that make us look foolish," Packwood said plaintively of an amendment, "and there are some things that *really* make us look foolish."

Packwood faced genuine embarrassment, if not ridicule; one national magazine was calling him "Senator Hackwood." Desperate, he canceled further markups. It was then, over a long liquid lunch with an aide at a Capitol Hill bar, that the Oregon Republican had his key insight. Concluding that his current approach was hopeless, he settled on a drastic tack: Set the top individual tax rate at 25 percent and eliminate virtually all deductions to pay for it. He described it as nothing less than the end of engineering social and economic change through the tax code.

The plan proved too radical — it lacked even a mortgage-interest deduction — but it broke the deadlock. Working with a small core group of allies, Packwood developed a modified plan with a 27 percent top rate that sailed through the committee and even managed to clear the Senate without major amendments.

His role in conference with the House was more controversial. Unable to resolve key differences on the bill, conferees asked Packwood and House Ways and Means Chairman Dan Rostenkowski to work out things in private. They did, but in a way that left a number of Senate Republicans upset at the loss of tax incentives for business. Still, by the end of the year the bill was law, and a good portion of the credit was due to Packwood.

Although Packwood turned 180 degrees — to the point of saying publicly that the tax code should be used to fund the government, not engineer change — he nonetheless left the impression that his true feelings remained masked. Many of the closest observers of the process remained convinced that Packwood fought for tax reform less because he believed in it than because there was no politically safe way to avoid it.

Many expected Packwood to return to business as usual in the 100th Congress. But Democratic success in the 1986 Senate elections deprived him of the chair. And it was trade, not taxation, that defined his work as ranking member. With industries that export natural resources and import components, Oregon is especially sensitive to trade matters. So it is not surprising that Packwood is one of the Senate's most active free-traders. He played a major role in opposing quotas to restrict textile and shoe imports, and he worked for the U.S.-Canada free-trade accord and for a similar pact with Mexico.

His vote for omnibus trade legislation, enacted over a presidential veto in 1988, was crucial. He voted for it only after protecting Israel's interests by specifically exempting its trade agreement with the United States from any damage, and after mitigating the harshest sanctions in the bill for trading partners.

Packwood's most publicized moment in the 100th Congress stemmed from his opposition to campaign-finance legislation pushed by the Democratic leadership. Republicans were dodging quorum calls as a tactic for stalling debate. Packwood had retreated into his office, where he had bolted one door and blocked another with a heavy chair. On orders from the majority leader, the sergeant-at-arms of the Senate arrested Packwood to force his attendance at a quorum call, a tactic not used in the Senate since 1942. Packwood forced the sergeant's deputies to carry him into the chamber. During the fracas he reinjured a broken finger, which he proudly displayed at a press conference the next day.

Packwood seems to pride himself in a sore-thumb sort of prominence. In 1982 he startled the capital by publicly accusing Reagan of alienating blacks, Jews, women and blue-collar workers. He was not only a senior GOP senator; he was chairman of the National Republican Senatorial Committee. Campaign officials do not usually talk that way.

Packwood, however, does. In the Reagan era, he managed to vote with the president almost as often as the average Senate Republican and still become one of the administration's most visible antagonists.

When Reagan promised in 1981 to sell advanced radar aircraft to Saudi Arabia, Packwood, long a devout supporter of Israel, served as the inside orchestrator in a fierce (if unsuccessful) campaign to prevent Senate approval of the deal. Three years later, Packwood was so successful in organizing Senate opposition to the proposed sale of Stinger anti-aircraft missiles to Jordan that Reagan dropped the idea. In the 100th Congress, he led the Senate opposition to the sale of 1,600 Maverick antitank missles to Saudi Arabia.

Meanwhile, Packwood was reinforcing his reputation as the Senate's foremost advocate of legalized abortion. He helped filibuster to death a 1982 anti-abortion bill that had Reagan's blessing, and led the opposition to a related constitutional amendment that fell well short of the required two-thirds Senate majority in 1983. "More and more," he complained, "my party is certain that it knows what's morally good for you and me."

Packwood got into an equally sharp confrontation with his more conservative colleagues in 1984, this time over a bill to reverse the Supreme Court's *Grove City* ruling limiting the effect of sex-discrimination and other civil rights laws. Working with Massachusetts Democrat Edward M. Kennedy, Packwood led a bipartisan coalition seeking to ensure that educational institutions receiving any federal aid would have to comply with antibias laws.

Packwood's reputation as a maverick arrived with him in 1969, when at 36 he was the youngest senator. He was fresh from a stunning upset of veteran Democrat Wayne Morse, and he was heralded by *Newsweek* as one of the "bright new stars" of the Senate. He promptly demonstrated his independent-mindedness by helping Democrats defeat two of President Richard M. Nixon's Supreme Court nominees and by a series of speeches chiding the Senate as irresponsible, especially in its practice of awarding chairmanships purely by seniority.

Scattershot interests, youthful impatience and a perennially high staff turnover later contributed to an impression that Packwood had not settled into a legislative niche. But in the 96th Congress, when the Commerce Committee began cutting back federal regulation, his political skills were instrumental in passing a controversial and complex trucking-deregulation bill over Teamsters' opposition.

Republican control of the Senate elevated Packwood to the Commerce chairmanship, and the deregulating continued. "There's no reason why we should be controlling capitalistic acts by consenting adults," Packwood said.

At Home: The success of his tax-reform efforts, his huge campaign treasury and some chaos on the Democratic side helped Packwood win re-election easily in 1986. It was a first for Packwood, whose Senate career had been shadowed by a cloud of vulnerability.

Burdened by conservative animosity to his stand on abortion and by his image as a slick political operator, Packwood won less-than-robust margins against modest Democratic opposition in 1974 and 1980. He even faced an unexpectedly strong primary challenge from a young fundamentalist minister in 1986. But a convergence of fortuitous events enabled Packwood to glide comfortably through that year's general election.

Campaigning, organizing and fundraising are in Packwood's blood. His great-grandfather was a member of the 1857 Oregon constitutional convention and held a variety of political appointments; his father was a business lobbyist before the state Legislature.

As an undergraduate at Willamette University, Packwood studied political science under Mark O. Hatfield, his Senate colleague since 1969. That experience may have colored their future relationship, which was for a long time the cordial but cool cooperation of an established senior statesman and an ambitious rival for public recognition.

As a young politician, Packwood had a reputation for outspokenness and boat-rocking. In 1962, he startled the party establishment by announcing that Sig Unander, that year's GOP Senate nominee against Morse, stood no chance of winning. But no matter how critical Packwood has been of the GOP, he has always seen himself as a force for revitalizing it.

The Morse whom Packwood encountered in 1968 was a weaker political figure than the one who beat Unander. Morse had narrowly survived a rough primary with former Rep. Robert Duncan, whereas Packwood had negligible party opposition.

Packwood was to the right of Morse on several issues, including the most salient issue of the day, the Vietnam War. While Packwood was critical of the South Vietnamese government, he castigated Morse for voting to cut off funds for the war.

But ideology was not the focal point of the campaign. The main issue was Morse himself. Packwood labeled Morse as ineffective, saying that the state had been harmed by the Democrat's contentious style. Other senators were reluctant to help Morse get federal projects for Oregon, he charged. Morse was 68 years old in 1968; he was feisty and vigorous, but Packwood still managed to win support on the issue of youth vs. age. Starting out far behind but building a splendid campaign organization, Packwood edged Morse by 3,293 votes out of nearly 815,000 cast.

The 1974 contest began as a rematch between Packwood and Morse. But Morse died suddenly in midsummer, and the Democrats replaced him with state Sen. Betty Roberts, who had just lost the 1974 gubernatorial primary. Roberts benefited from statewide name recognition and a good campaign organization, but she also had a large debt from her bid for governor. Packwood worked hard to insulate himself from Watergate in the year of Nixon's resignation. He was sharply critical of the departed president and objected to the pardon he received from President Gerald R. Ford. Packwood's 55 percent of the vote was respectable in a terrible Republican year.

In 1980, abortion rights advocate Packwood found himself targeted by anti-abortion groups. There was talk of a $200,000 "right to life" drive to unseat him in the primary. The immediate effect of this rumor was to mobilize support for Packwood in the women's movement. In the primary, two conservative Republican opponents, Brenda Jose and Rosalie Huss, spent most of their time fighting each other. Packwood won renomination handily.

In the general election, Packwood's campaign finances became a central issue. Democrat Ted Kulongoski, a state senator, charged that Packwood was trying to buy the election and was also profiting handsomely from speaking engagement fees. Labor had trouble making up its mind, with the state AFL-CIO backing Kulongoski against the wishes of its executive council, which recommended no endorsement. Packwood drew the support of the building trades unions in Portland.

With a nearly 8-to-1 financial advantage and a strong Republican tide building nationwide, Packwood was an overwhelming favorite. He won, but Kulongoski and one minor candidate held him to 52 percent of the vote.

Packwood responded to his mediocre 1980 finish by embarking on a nationwide fundraising effort for 1986. His direct-mail strategy targeted feminists, pro-Israel voters and other activists who supported his policy stands. Adding in a healthy dose of business-related PAC money, Packwood raised over $6 million before the campaign year began.

Though his opponents attempted to make

an issue of his fundraising efforts, describing him as a tool of "special interest" campaign contributors, Packwood's tax-reform efforts in 1986 helped blunt these claims. Packwood responded to his critics by noting that the historic bill eliminated numerous tax benefits enjoyed by business interests that had earlier given to his campaign.

Packwood returned to Oregon and blitzed the airwaves with a media campaign that his primary opponent, Joe Lutz, a Portland preacher and anti-abortion activist, could not match. But while Packwood prevailed, his below-60 percent tally again suggested vulnerability.

The Democratic primary winner, 4th District Rep. James Weaver, was an aggressive populist and a caustic critic of Packwood's support of Reagan defense policies and his alleged ties to special interests. But a campaign-finance problem cut Weaver's effort short. In August, he was called to testify before the House ethics committee concerning his investment and loss of $89,000 in funds from earlier House campaigns. Though he denied any wrongdoing — saying he invested the money to enhance his campaign treasury and not for personal gain — he unexpectedly announced on the eve of his testimony that he was withdrawing from the Senate race.

Scrambling to choose a replacement for Weaver, state Democrats settled on state Rep. Rick Bauman, who earlier in the year had finished last in the three-man Senate primary. Though Bauman, a personable liberal, was respected by his state House colleagues, he lacked name recognition and money. The last obstacle to Packwood's re-election disappeared when Lutz decided not to run as a write-in candidate. Packwood coasted to victory.

Committees

Finance (Ranking)
International Trade; Medicare & Long Term Care; Taxation

Commerce, Science & Transportation (2nd of 9 Republicans)
Communications (ranking); Foreign Commerce & Tourism; National Ocean Policy Study; Surface Transportation

Joint Taxation

Elections

1986 General		
Bob Packwood (R)	656,317	(63%)
Rick Bauman (D)	375,735	(36%)
1986 Primary		
Bob Packwood (R)	171,985	(58%)
Joe P. Lutz Sr. (R)	126,315	(42%)

Previous Winning Percentages: **1980** (52%) **1974** (55%) **1968** (50%)

Campaign Finance

	Receipts	Receipts from PACs		Expend-itures
1988				
Packwood (R)	$6,725,027	$974,367	(14%)	$6,523,492
Bauman (D)	$63,394	$16,260	(26%)	$64,139

Key Votes

1991	
Authorize use of force against Iraq	Y
1990	
Oppose prohibition of certain semiautomatic weapons	N
Support constitutional amendment on flag desecration	N
Oppose requiring parental notice for minors' abortions	Y
Halt production of B-2 stealth bomber at 13 planes	Y
Approve budget that cut spending and raised revenues	Y
Pass civil rights bill over Bush veto	Y
1989	
Oppose reduction of SDI funding	Y
Oppose barring federal funds for "obscene" art	Y
Allow vote on capital gains tax cut	Y

Voting Studies

	Presidential Support		Party Unity		Conservative Coalition	
Year	**S**	**O**	**S**	**O**	**S**	**O**
1990	56	41	45	53	51	46
1989	79	18	55	43	79	18
1988	58	40	41	56	54	46
1987	53	45	56	40	38	50
1986	49	45	58	36	63	30
1985	72	25	67	26	63	28
1984	65	27	58	36	62	32
1983	66	24	56	35	50	41
1982	75	24	67	32	59	40
1981	86	13	80	16	71	25

Interest Group Ratings

Year	ADA	ACU	AFL-CIO	CCUS
1990	72	35	44	42
1989	30	61	60	57
1988	55	40	64	57
1987	60	31	80	61
1986	60	33	40	58
1985	35	40	43	66
1984	60	33	40	56
1983	30	30	31	47
1982	55	30	58	52
1981	35	47	21	94

1 Les AuCoin (D)

Of Portland — Elected 1974

Born: Oct. 21, 1942, Portland, Ore.
Education: Pacific U., B.A. 1969.
Military Service: Army, 1961-64.
Occupation: Public relations executive; journalist.
Family: Wife, Susan Swearingen; two children.
Religion: Protestant.
Political Career: Ore. House, 1971-75, majority leader, 1973-75.
Capitol Office: 2159 Rayburn Bldg. 20515; 225-0855.

In Washington: The 101st Congress was something of a coming-out party for AuCoin. After 16 years in Congress, he had finally achieved the electoral security at home and seniority in the House to take a place as a leading strategist on liberal Democratic causes.

That done, however, AuCoin said he wanted more: In May 1991, he announced a Senate bid for the seat now occupied by Republican Bob Packwood.

In describing his strategy to root out federal restrictions on access to abortion, AuCoin shed light on his own gradual ascent. "You seldom achieve quantum leaps in politics," he said. "You have to chip away in increments."

In recent years, AuCoin also has shed an image of haughtiness conveyed by his starched collars and his passionately held views, which can border on the sanctimonious in debate with foes.

But as ever, AuCoin relishes floor fights. He approaches them with single-minded intensity and typically is prepared, articulate and sharply partisan.

AuCoin earns good marks from the House Democratic leadership by coming through on tough votes. Unlike many liberals, AuCoin voted for the budget summit agreement in 1990. A year earlier, he stuck with the leadership in opposing a capital gains tax cut despite special language included to curry favor with his home-state timber industry.

The full force of AuCoin's skills and partisanship were on display in the opening rounds of the abortion debate in the 101st Congress. A longtime supporter of abortion rights, AuCoin became the lead strategist in efforts to roll back federal restrictions on abortion funding in the wake of the Supreme Court's 1989 *Webster* decision. But granting state governments more authority to restrict access to abortion, the court energized the abortion-rights movement. In countless skull sessions in his office, AuCoin worked to ensure that House abortion-rights backers were ready to capitalize on the momentum.

The first opportunity came in the summer of 1989, when the District of Columbia spending bill came to the House floor. In past years, abortion foes had struck language to permit D.C. to spend locally raised money on abortions by assuring members that an exception to protect the life of a woman would be added in conference. AuCoin, a member of the D.C. Appropriations Subcommittee, helped change the dynamic of the vote by hewing to a technical reading of the anti-abortion language. By making the D.C. vote one against abortion with no exceptions, AuCoin helped defeat anti-abortion forces for the first time in nine years.

President Bush vetoed the D.C. bill, which would have permitted city funding of abortion in cases of rape and incest, as well as a later bill permitting similar federal funding. Though AuCoin never had the votes for an override, he taunted, "I say let him [veto the bill]. If he wants to bring injury to himself and his backers in Congress, there's no better way."

When the GOP tried to water down the anti-abortion language by permitting federal funding in cases of "promptly reported" rape and incest, AuCoin was instrumental in getting abortion-rights advocates to drop the matter rather than permit a vote. "We'll be damned if we're going to give them a vote on an unworkably narrow reporting period and then let them pretend they're protecting rape and incest victims," he said.

While AuCoin's abortion rights stand was consistent with the view of most of his suburban constituents, controversy over the northern spotted owl put him between friends in the environmental community and workers in the timber industry vital to his state. Over the years on the Interior Appropriations Subcommittee, AuCoin has been seen as an environmentalist, but a politically sensitive one. He has lobbied for additional wilderness designations in Oregon but supports the forest industry's moves for multi-use management of non-wilderness areas.

The spotted owl dispute involved how much "old growth" forest should be preserved to provide habitat for the threatened owls, and

Oregon 1

Western Portland and Suburbs

Decisions shaping Oregon and the entire Northwest are made by the banks, businesses and law firms of downtown Portland. Many of the important decision makers live in AuCoin's district, in the fashionable West Hills area of the city or the suburbs beyond the western city limits.

Much of this affluent professional community identifies with the Republican Party, but Democrats such as AuCoin have considerable strength there, and independent voters wield decisive influence. In 1980, independent presidential candidate John B. Anderson won nearly 14 percent in western Multnomah County, leaving Jimmy Carter and Ronald Reagan virtually tied.

As one moves farther west into Washington County, GOP strength increases. Republicans outnumbered Democrats in the county in 1980 for the first time, reflecting the enormous demographic changes of the preceding decade, in which population grew 55 percent. The county grew another 27 percent in the 1980s. Bedroom communities such as Beaverton, Tigard and Hillsboro, once modest in size, have blossomed into economic satellites of Portland, with electronics and computer firms such as Mentor Graphics, Intel and Tektronix providing more than 15,000 high-tech jobs.

The strongest Democratic areas of the district are along the Columbia River and Pacific coast in the fishing and logging counties of Columbia, Clatsop, Tillamook and Lincoln. Columbia has voted for every Democratic presidential candidate since 1932; Clatsop went for Adlai E. Stevenson in 1956 and has stayed Democratic since. Even Walter F. Mondale managed to carry the county in 1984 — by three votes. Michael S. Dukakis carried it more comfortably in 1988.

Some areas of the district were particularly hard hit by the poor economic conditions in the early 1980s. Astoria (Clatsop County), plagued by 20 percent unemployment in 1982, found economic salvation by improving its harbor facilities to handle large shipments of coal from Western states to new markets in Japan, South Korea and Taiwan. Sharply curbed logging activities in the Siuslaw National Forest pushed the jobless rate in Tillamook County above 20 percent in the early 1980s, though the jobless rate now has dipped below 10 percent.

Tourism props up the local economy in some coastal areas.

Population: 526,840. White 503,854 (96%), Black 2,717 (1%), Other 11,900 (2%). Spanish origin 11,485 (2%). 18 and over 387,395 (74%), 65 and over 59,440 (11%). Median age: 31.

whether time limits should be imposed on resolving court challenges to federal policies that have disrupted timber sales. Working with Oregon GOP Sen. Mark O. Hatfield and Washington Democratic Rep. Norm Dicks, AuCoin helped win passage of a 1989 compromise that temporarily freed timber sales from court-ordered bans, in return for lower limits on timber harvests and additional protection for wildlife habitats.

In June 1990, the owl was officially placed on the threatened species list, requiring the government to prepare a plan to protect it. Three months later, the temporary compromise expired. However, Congress could only agree on another short-term solution — reducing the amount of timber harvested in the ancient forests to its lowest level in 30 years. The issue will be revisited in the 102nd Congress.

On the issue of gun control, the middle ground is even more elusive. For eight terms, AuCoin received a 100 percent rating from the National Rifle Association, but in early 1991, he said that would change. In an opinion piece in *The Washington Post,* AuCoin called the NRA's approval an "ideological straightjacket," and said he would support a seven-day waiting period for handgun purchases.

Over the years, AuCoin's chief outpost has been the Defense Appropriations Subcommittee, where his technological mindset distinguishes him from other more reflexive arms control advocates and Pentagon critics. When AuCoin criticizes a weapon system, something he does often, he applies a technical understanding of the system's capability and its strategic value. He has also developed an understanding with subcommittee Chairman John P. Murtha that often allows him to bring his proposals to the floor without a preliminary skirmish in subcommittee, which is more sympathetic to the Pentagon than is the whole House.

In the 101st Congress, AuCoin emerged as a leading critic of the strategic defense initiative (SDI). When a partisan breakdown occurred on the 1989 supplemental appropriation bill, AuCoin readied his "Star Wars for Drug Wars" measure, which sought to shift money out of SDI into anti-drug programs.

In a complicated parliamentary maneuver, the leadership allowed AuCoin to bring up the proposal as a freestanding measure during debate on the supplemental, with no chance for amendment.

While Republicans railed against the maneuver — which would have allowed the bumper sticker bill to be tacked on to the must-pass supplemental — AuCoin argued that the drug crisis was America's real enemy. Beyond the partisan procedural dispute, the substance of AuCoin's proposal was expected to meet with disapproval from conservative Southern Democrats. But AuCoin lost by just eight votes, a sign of weakening support for SDI.

In 1990, Murtha appointed AuCoin and Louisiana Republican Robert L. Livingston to examine SDI. They traveled to the many research labs working on the massive missile defense project, and returned with a recommendation to create a "red-team" of technical experts charged with trying to anticipate enemy countermoves that could thwart the system. The concept was included in the 1991 defense authorization, and when the appropriation bill came up, AuCoin sponsored a successful amendment to make the red-team bureaucratically independent of the SDI development organization.

During the 1980s, AuCoin pushed wary Democratic leaders to confront the Reagan administration on arms issues. Repeated floor victories — including a restriction on testing of anti-satellite weapons (ASAT) and a rejection of President Reagan's plan to renew production of chemical weapons — and public-opinion polls finally convinced leaders that strong arms control policies would not hurt them at election time. Pragmatists such as Armed Services Chairman Les Aspin of Wisconsin were swept along in the tide.

Although he has at times been at odds with Aspin, AuCoin shares his technological approach. He was among those who supported Aspin's 1985 bid for the chairmanship, and was among those who criticized his continued support for the MX missile just weeks later. AuCoin, however, hesitated when others tried to unseat Aspin as chairman at the start of the 100th Congress. After detailed conversations with the Wisconsin Democrat, AuCoin ended up endorsing him in a seconding speech that praised his leadership and intelligence. In the 101st Congress, AuCoin nudged Aspin to remain open to liberal input.

When AuCoin joined the Defense Subcommittee in 1983, he said he wanted to combat rampant "pork-barreling" in defense contracts. But he has not been above using his post for home-state interests. He has been able, for instance, to force some changes in Navy procedures to help Oregon shipyards get business.

Oregon's interests are also behind AuCoin's work against restrictions on imports; he believes other countries would retaliate and bar the lumber, wheat, electronic instruments and other high-technology products Oregon exports. AuCoin is mindful of a predecessor whose name has become synonymous with ill-advised protectionism. "There once was another congressman from the 1st District of Oregon named Hawley. He joined a fellow named Smoot," says AuCoin. "I'm not going to be a part of causing history to repeat itself." He was one of only six Democrats to vote against the omnibus trade protection bill that passed the House in 1987.

At Home: After spending most of the 1980s as a top GOP target, AuCoin got a chance to breathe easy at decade's end. Redistricting and well-financed opponents forced him to struggle for victory in 1982 and in the following two elections; but as the decade came to a close the GOP barely made an effort.

AuCoin in 1974 became the first Democrat to represent the 1st, but he had little problem deflecting GOP claims that he was too liberal for his constituency in his early re-election efforts. That changed after 1980, when a number of Republican voters were remapped into the district. His modest victory margins in 1982 and 1984 spurred GOP claims that the district had become permanently "marginal" and would eventually be theirs. It was not until 1986 that AuCoin burst the GOP's bubble of optimism by scoring a surprisingly one-sided victory over Tony Meeker, the well-regarded state Senate minority leader.

In both 1982 and 1984, AuCoin's challenger was Bill Moshofsky, a former executive with the forest products firm of Georgia-Pacific and former board member of the Business-Industry Political Action Committee.

The first time, Moshofsky was running in a recession year tough on Republicans nationally. He told voters that Oregon's economic problems were not the fault of Reagan policies, but of environmental regulations that diverted capital to compliance and away from job creation. This pitch impressed some in the district's lumber and wood-products industries, but the fishing and logging counties, wary of the former corporate executive, stayed with AuCoin, albeit by smaller margins.

Moshofsky came into his second bid with a better organization and an improved campaign style. Between contests he had managed to keep his name in the news through the Coalition for Responsible Spending, an organization he formed to lobby for tighter state budgets.

But the second time around, AuCoin was better prepared. He canvassed the district a year before the election, outspent Moshofsky, and also stepped up his overtures to the high-tech business community, strengthening his position in populous Washington County, west of Portland. AuCoin actually won by a slightly smaller margin than in 1982, but considering the strong Reagan tide, AuCoin's 53 percent tally was quite an achievement.

Moshofsky moved on to the state GOP chairmanship, but Republicans had high hopes for Meeker in 1986. The state senator had the political base Moshofsky lacked, and he stressed his legislative record, emphasizing juvenile justice and child pornography.

Meeker also approached moderate Republicans and independents by talking about his support for the state ban on no-return bottles, and for efforts to protect women from employment discrimination. But Meeker's appeal to these vital voters was limited by his sponsorship of an anti-abortion initiative on the general-election ballot.

AuCoin's aggressive fundraising gave him one of the largest House campaign treasuries in the nation — more than $950,000. Meeker's fundraising was more than respectable, but he trailed AuCoin by $450,000. The disparity enabled AuCoin to dominate the media, and he won with 62 percent.

A journalist by training, AuCoin had drifted into public-relations work by 1968, when the Vietnam War lured him into politics. He campaigned for Sen. Eugene J. McCarthy, who won Oregon's Democratic presidential primary.

Two years later AuCoin won a seat in the Legislature from Washington County. By 1974, when Republican Wendell Wyatt decided to retire from Congress after five terms, AuCoin had risen to House majority leader. He was an obvious choice for the Democratic nomination from the 1st District. With that support and a forceful primary campaign criticizing the Nixon administration, AuCoin had little trouble defeating four lesser-known foes.

His Republican opponent, the former director of the state Department of Environmental Quality, was equally articulate and had Wyatt's strong endorsement. But labor and education groups helped give AuCoin a better organization than the GOP could muster. AuCoin stressed his legislative record, and the pension reform, energy policy and tax relief measures that came out of committees he chaired. He carried every county.

Committees

Appropriations (21st of 37 Democrats)
Defense; District of Columbia; Interior

Select Hunger (17th of 22 Democrats)
Domestic

Elections

1990 General		
Les AuCoin (D)	150,292	(63%)
Earl Molander (R)	72,382	(30%)
Rick Livingston (I)	15,585	(7%)
1988 General		
Les AuCoin (D)	179,915	(70%)
Earl Molander (R)	78,626	(30%)

Previous Winning Percentages: **1986** (62%) **1984** (53%) **1982** (54%) **1980** (66%) **1978** (63%) **1976** (59%) **1974** (56%)

District Vote For President

	1988	1984	1980	1976
D	137,972 (51%)	112,950 (42%)	96,633 (38%)	92,985 (44%)
R	126,763 (47%)	148,057 (55%)	119,438 (47%)	112,179 (53%)
I			28,388 (11%)	

Campaign Finance

	Receipts	Receipts from PACs	Expend-itures
1990			
AuCoin (D)	$599,295	$308,748 (52%)	$445,342
Molander (R)	$2,163	$139 (6%)	$2,024
Livingston (I)	$32,309	0	$32,309
1988			
AuCoin (D)	$724,149	$340,550 (47%)	$542,224
Molander (R)	$9,825	$100 (1%)	$11,741

Key Votes

1991	
Authorize use of force against Iraq	N
1990	
Support constitutional amendment on flag desecration	N
Pass family and medical leave bill over Bush veto	Y
Reduce SDI funding	?
Allow abortions in overseas military facilities	?
Approve budget summit plan for spending and taxing	Y
Approve civil rights bill	Y
1989	
Halt production of B-2 stealth bomber at 13 planes	N
Oppose capital gains tax cut	Y
Approve federal abortion funding in rape or incest cases	Y
Approve pay raise and revision of ethics rules	Y
Pass Democratic minimum wage plan over Bush veto	Y

Voting Studies

	Presidential Support		Party Unity		Conservative Coalition	
Year	**S**	**O**	**S**	**O**	**S**	**O**
1990	20	66	81	5	13	76
1989	26	69	84	8	20	76
1988	22	68	81	8	21	76
1987	21	77	82	9	19	81
1986	29	67	82	11	36	64
1985	24	69	71	19	31	64
1984	29	68	72	18	22	71
1983	20	76	75	16	19	75
1982	30	61	76	7	15	71
1981	29	55	67	11	15	67

Interest Group Ratings

Year	ADA	ACU	AFL-CIO	CCUS
1990	78	0	82	21
1989	85	8	100	30
1988	95	8	86	43
1987	88	14	81	20
1986	90	9	86	33
1985	65	29	71	64
1984	90	8	77	50
1983	70	18	69	50
1982	85	26	94	26
1981	70	15	79	13

2 Bob Smith (R)

Of Burns — Elected 1982

Born: June 16, 1931, Portland, Ore.
Education: Willamette U., B.A. 1953.
Occupation: Cattle rancher.
Family: Wife, Kaye Tomlinson; three children.
Religion: Presbyterian.
Political Career: Ore. House, 1961-73, Speaker, 1969-73; Ore. Senate, 1973-82, minority leader, 1977-82.
Capitol Office: 118 Cannon Bldg. 20515; 225-6730.

In Washington: Having shown his capacity to make a mark on agriculture policy, Smith broadened his interests by joining the Interior Committee in 1989, after winning party permission to serve on both panels.

Smith believes government should give free enterprise wide latitude. This antipathy toward federal involvement defines Smith's role on Interior, where he balances his concern for the outdoors with his attention to Oregon's vital timber industry.

The biggest recent threat to timber jobs in the Northwest has been the movement to restrict logging in ancient "old-growth" forests to protect the threatened northern spotted owl. Environmentalists, seeking to ban logging in the old-growth forests that are the owls' habitat, won court-ordered bans on logging in broad areas in Oregon and Washington.

In 1989, House and Senate members from those states negotiated a bipartisan compromise plan that lifted the bans but reduced the level of timber sales in 1989 and 1990. The proposal also strengthened language protecting old-growth forests and the spotted owl and made it harder for environmentalists to challenge timber sales.

Smith, who had introduced a bill to allow timber sales during a five-year period of study of the owl's status, denounced the compromise as appeasement to "radical environmentalists," blaming Oregon's two chief contributors on the agreement, GOP Sen. Mark O. Hatfield and Democratic Rep. Les AuCoin. "I call this the Neville Chamberlain Act of 1989," he said. He argued that the agreement tacitly acknowledged that the owl belonged on a threatened or endangered species list before its official listing. "The spotted owl is endangered by congressional fiat, not by science and not by fact."

AuCoin accused Smith of grandstanding, saying he was "sitting on the porch . . . throwing a snowball" at his compromise. The House agreed by voice vote to the plan; it became law as part of the fiscal 1990 Interior appropriations bill. In 1990, the Fish and Wildlife Service listed the owl as a threatened species.

Smith fits right in on the GOP side of the Interior Committee, where most of his party colleagues share his "Sagebrush Rebellion" antagonism toward federal government encroachment. When he joined the committee, all but two of its 14 Republicans were from states west of the Missouri River.

Shortly into his first year on the panel, Smith triggered a GOP walkout during committee consideration of a bill to set up a $1 billion-a-year trust fund to buy land for parks, wildlife preserves, forests and historic sites. Smith offered an amendment stipulating that money from the trust fund could not be used to buy land unless the seller were willing. Smith said the intent was to protect private lands from federal condemnation.

Tempers rose as Democrats rejected GOP arguments for the amendment. Smith warned that Western members were "very sensitive" about the question of condemnation. "I guarantee you," he said, "if you want an East-West fight . . . this is an East-West fight." The amendment was rejected by 14-24, and the Republicans got up and left. The bill never advanced beyond the committee, however.

On another matter, though, Smith worked with Minnesota Democrat Bruce F. Vento, chairman of the National Parks and Public Lands Subcommittee, to win passage of Smith's bill to create a 56,000-acre national volcanic monument at Newberry Crater in the Deschutes National Forest. A local committee that included environmentalists, hunters, geothermal energy interests, timber interests and the federal government helped Smith forge an agreement on the designation. The bill, which included an exchange of geothermal leases with an energy company, was signed into law in 1990.

During the wilderness lands debate in the 98th Congress, Smith was dismissed by a coalition of environmentalists who felt differently about government's role when he argued his free-enterprise perspective.

Smith seemed astonished the House would approve 1.1 million acres of new wilderness — most of it in his district — though he and most

Oregon 2

East and Southwest — Bend; Medford

There are more jackrabbits than voters here, so any candidate has to focus on a few widely scattered population centers.

In the southwest, Jackson County (Medford) and Josephine County (Grants Pass) together cast one-third of the district vote. Both counties prefer Republicans; in the 1990 gubernatorial contest, GOP nominee Dave Frohnmayer comfortably carried Jackson and Josephine while losing statewide. Josephine grew about 17 percent in the 1980s.

Medford is surrounded by pear, peach and apple orchards of the fruit-growing Rogue River Valley. Lumbering is the main work in Grants Pass, although visitors to the nearby Siskiyou National Forest also contribute to the economy. The only other sizable town in southwest Oregon is Klamath Falls, 75 miles east of Medford. Though the lush forests become drier and thinner on the way east to Klamath Falls, lumbering is still important there. Crater Lake National Park, in the northwestern corner of Klamath County, is a major tourist lure.

Population in Deschutes County has soared since 1970, as nearby skiing areas lured people to build summer homes and vacation condominiums; the county's population center is Bend, in the west central part of the 2nd.

In 1986, Democratic gubernatorial candidate Neil Goldschmidt referred to Bend as "the middle of nowhere"; in the ensuing four years, Deschutes County grew faster than any other in the state.

Many of the newcomers are young and liberal; they helped Democratic House candidate Larryann Willis run well in Deschutes County in 1982 and 1984. GOP Sen. Mark O. Hatfield managed to carry the county narrowly in 1990, even though Democratic challenger Harry Lonsdale lived in Bend where he operated a high-tech research firm. Wasco County (The Dalles) is the population center in the district's northwest corner. It usually votes Republican, although Michael S. Dukakis won it in 1988.

Most of eastern Oregon is a sparsely populated plateau dusted with sagebrush and dry grasses. In the northern part, most people live along or near the irrigated Columbia River Valley, where wheat ripens on steep golden hillsides. The largest town is Pendleton (Umatilla County). Like most counties here, Umatilla is solidly Republican.

Population: 526,968. White 502,232 (95%), Black 1,082 (0.2%), Other 12,784 (2%). Spanish origin 17,934 (3%). 18 and over 374,066 (71%), 65 and over 64,403 (12%). Median age: 31.

of his constituents opposed it. He warned of the adverse economic impact of taking national forest lands out of commercial timber production, and expressed exasperation with the federal appeals process that enables environmentalists to delay timberland sales.

In 1988, Smith was the only Oregon member to oppose a landmark river-protection bill for his state. His objections were not eased until the House tacked on a section authorizing construction of Oregon's Umatilla Basin water project. In the 101st Congress, he steadfastly opposed a move by Oregon Democrat Peter A. DeFazio to add a portion of the upper Klamath River to the federal Wild and Scenic Rivers system. The measure would have blocked construction of a hydroelectric plant in Smith's district. Smith lobbied House members, showering them with "Dear Colleague" letters. He succeeded: The bill did not make it to the floor before the end of the session.

At the end of the 101st Congress, Smith fought an amendment on the House floor that would have gradually imposed a 500 percent increase in fees on ranchers who graze their cattle on public lands. A rancher himself, Smith characterized the amendment, sponsored by Oklahoma Democrat Mike Synar, as an attack by environmentalists whose real aim was to drive livestock operators and other industries that rely on public lands out of business.

"Eliminate the livestock," Smith said. "Eliminate the timber industry with the spotted owl. Eliminate the sheep industry in this country. Let us vote for the Synar amendment and eliminate all of us." Despite Western members' entreaties, the House adopted the amendment by a wide margin as part of the fiscal 1991 Interior appropriations bill. Conferees, however, stripped it from the final bill.

A veteran legislative leader in Oregon who was already past age 50 when he came to Congress, Smith started his House career knowing he would never be the power in Washington that he was in Salem. But he soon began looking to escape the status of middle-aged minority backbencher.

The route he found was his relationship with Edward Madigan of Illinois, the shrewd senior Republican on the Agriculture Committee who became secretary of Agriculture in 1991. As the panel began writing the 1985 farm bill, Smith offered Madigan strategy ideas — and Madigan realized there was a good deal to be learned from a man with 25 years of legislative experience. Eventually, Smith joined Madigan at agriculture conferences with Bob Dole, the Senate's key farm-policy voice.

Smith has earned respect from his committee colleagues for his grasp of the cost of programs as well as for his political skills. He tends to the wheat growers and cattlemen of his sprawling district, advocating ways to reduce foreign barriers to U.S. exports. Early in the 102nd Congress, Smith took over the ranking position on Agriculture's Subcommittee on Conservation, Credit and Rural Development.

Founder and co-chairman of the House beef caucus, Smith often serves as a liaison with Western cattle producers. During work on the 1985 farm bill he was upset with a proposal to reduce dairy surpluses by slaughtering dairy cows and adding them to the beef supply. Fearing the plan would drive down meat prices, Smith pushed for language requiring the government to buy surplus meat for schools and for the military. In 1989, Smith advocated legislation to direct U.S. military commissaries in Europe to sell fresh U.S. beef. (Far East commissaries already sold U.S. beef.)

On the last night of the session, Smith went to lobby for the measure in the Senate, where Iowa Democrat Tom Harkin had added the language as an amendment to the defense authorization bill. It was signed into law as part of another bill.

At Home: Redistricting in 1981 gave Smith an opening to move to Congress. When GOP Rep. Denny Smith chose to run in the newly created 5th, eastern Oregon's rural, sprawling, conservative 2nd was left without an incumbent.

Stressing his legislative experience as Republican leader of the state Senate and Speaker of the Oregon House, Smith easily won his primary. The surprise Democratic primary winner was Larryann Willis, a rancher and Democratic National Committee member.

Trusting in opinion polls that showed him leading, Smith stayed clear of Willis. She tried to provoke Smith; when he refused to debate, she challenged him to a steer-roping contest, but he refused that, too.

Accustomed to easy campaigns in his safe legislative district, Smith had some difficulty adjusting to a hotly contested election. His organization was embarrassed when a poorly planned fundraiser featuring Bob Hope drew a sparse crowd and actually lost money.

But Smith reassured rural voters with his opposition to designating more wilderness in Oregon, and he convinced others that Willis was a liberal because she advocated deferring the third phase of the Reagan income-tax cut. Smith took 56 percent, beat Willis in a 1984 rematch and has won handily since then.

Committees

Agriculture (9th of 18 Republicans)
Conservation, Credit & Rural Development (ranking); Forests, Family Farms & Energy; Livestock, Dairy & Poultry; Wheat, Soybeans & Feed Grains

Interior & Insular Affairs (9th of 17 Republicans)
National Parks & Public Lands; Water, Power & Offshore Energy

Select Hunger (5th of 12 Republicans)
International (ranking)

Elections

1990 General		
Bob Smith (R)	127,998	(68%)
Jim Smiley (D)	60,131	(32%)
1990 Primary		
Bob Smith (R)	51,951	(88%)
Dane Coefer (R)	7,250	(12%)
1988 General		
Bob Smith (R)	125,366	(63%)
Larry Tuttle (D)	74,700	(37%)

Previous Winning Percentages: **1986** (60%) **1984** (57%) **1982** (56%)

District Vote For President

	1988		1984		1980		1976	
D	98,318	(43%)	85,796	(35%)	59,546	(32%)	87,938	(46%)
R	122,996	(54%)	155,524	(63%)	108,856	(58%)	96,543	(50%)
I					12,765	(7%)		

Campaign Finance

	Receipts	Receipts from PACs		Expend-itures
1990				
Smith (R)	$374,114	$148,953	(40%)	$284,700
1988				
Smith (R)	$381,363	$153,366	(40%)	$340,643
Tuttle (D)	$207,190	$94,600	(46%)	$208,513

Key Votes

1991	
Authorize use of force against Iraq	Y
1990	
Support constitutional amendment on flag desecration	Y
Pass family and medical leave bill over Bush veto	N
Reduce SDI funding	N
Allow abortions in overseas military facilities	N
Approve budget summit plan for spending and taxing	N
Approve civil rights bill	N
1989	
Halt production of B-2 stealth bomber at 13 planes	N
Oppose capital gains tax cut	N
Approve federal abortion funding in rape or incest cases	N
Approve pay raise and revision of ethics rules	N
Pass Democratic minimum wage plan over Bush veto	N

Voting Studies

	Presidential Support		Party Unity		Conservative Coalition	
Year	**S**	**O**	**S**	**O**	**S**	**O**
1990	66	34	91	9	96	4
1989	79	21	89	9	88	12
1988	66	33	91	8	92	8
1987	57	40	77	15	84	14
1986	66	31	82	13	86	12
1985	63	33	82	14	84	11
1984	53	38	70	20	83	14
1983	71	21	74	8	90	7

Interest Group Ratings

Year	ADA	ACU	AFL-CIO	CCUS
1990	6	88	8	93
1989	10	79	17	100
1988	5	92	21	86
1987	24	64	19	86
1986	5	82	14	100
1985	20	75	12	90
1984	10	71	8	75
1983	0	85	12	82

3 Ron Wyden (D)

Of Portland — Elected 1980

Born: May 3, 1949, Wichita, Kan.
Education: Stanford U., B.A. 1971; U. of Oregon, J.D. 1974.
Occupation: Public interest lawyer.
Family: Wife, Laurie Oseran; two children.
Religion: Jewish.
Political Career: No previous office.
Capitol Office: 2452 Rayburn Bldg. 20515; 225-4811.

In Washington: A committed liberal, Wyden arrived in Washington in 1981, the start of an era of federal retrenchment. But while blockbuster liberal solutions to pressing social problems are passé these days, Wyden has found a way to act on his belief in an activist federal government: His strategy is to identify definable, sometimes obscure, evils, then attack them with a barrage of hearings, press releases and amendments.

He is tireless and imaginative, and by couching his arguments in language that makes him sound more a pragmatist than a crusader, Wyden has been able to pass laws in several areas, including health care, the environment and crime. He succeeds incrementally, advancing modest legislation with obvious political appeal.

Wyden markets his endeavors aggressively. He is accessible to the media, understands its deadlines and caters to its love of the quotable line. Critics say he is too eager for headlines and — considering his safe Democratic district — too shy about tackling tough issues, choosing instead ones that play well in the press.

Although many had expected him to challenge GOP Sen. Mark O. Hatfield in 1990, Wyden opted to stay put, saying his seat on Energy and Commerce would better enable him to pursue his interests in policy issues such as health insurance, energy and the environment.

Wyden did go on to score some victories on those fronts during the 101st Congress, most notably in the field of medical insurance.

Working with Sen. Thomas A. Daschle of South Dakota, Wyden pushed through stringent federal controls on so-called Medigap insurance, private policies designed to cover services not included by Medicare. Wyden argued that the elderly are often railroaded into buying overpriced or duplicative coverage, and his legislation forced greater standardization of the supplemental policies to combat such abuses.

The medigap bill passed as part of the omnibus budget bill of fall 1990, as did another Wyden initiative on drug purchasing for state Medicaid programs. That law requires drug companies to sell to Medicaid at the same discounts they offer their best private customers. "The fact is the nation's health care program for the poor is being taken to the cleaners," Wyden complained. "When it comes to Medicaid, the government has handed a blank check to the drug companies and said, 'You fill in the numbers.' "

The near-limitless jurisdiction of the Energy and Commerce Committee suits Wyden well, and his close ties to Chairman John D. Dingell have allowed him to play a role in some high-profile issues. As ranking Democrat on Dingell's Investigations Subcommittee in past Congresses, Wyden participated in hearings on the Pentagon procurement scandal as well as those on Wall Street's insider trading scandal.

However, the less-noticed Small Business Committee gives perhaps the best snapshot of Wyden's legislative style. In 1987, he assumed the chairmanship of a new Small Business Subcommittee on Regulation, Business Opportunity and Energy. With limited legislative authority and a small staff, the panel could well have escaped notice under a less ambitious chairman. But Wyden pledged "to use it as a very aggressive tool," and that he does.

Under Wyden, the panel created news with hearings on fertility clinics and cosmetics labeling. Building on that foundation, the committee went on to tackle plastic surgery and diet treatments. In the fall of 1989, Wyden appeared on the "Geraldo" program to discuss the potential hazards of cosmetic surgery.

The subcommittee has found occasion to probe the issues of medical waste, child care and computer crime, as well as giving Wyden a forum for airing Northwest concerns. In 1988, his hearings on Canadian plywood tariffs led to a written assurance from the Reagan administration that the federal government would fight this trade barrier.

As legislators wrestled with the AIDS dilemma in the 100th Congress, Wyden's subcommittee held hearings exposing quality control problems in labs testing for the deadly disease. This prompted Dingell to bring the is-

Oregon 3

Eastern Portland and Suburbs

Sitting along the Willamette River, Oregon's largest city (population 437,000) is considered a pleasant, livable place. As the only major metropolitan area between San Francisco and Seattle, Portland has attracted large banks, law firms, headquarters of giant lumber firms and an important shipping trade.

Socially and politically, Portland is two cities. East of the Willamette River, in the 3rd, live most of Portland's working-class people; the area west of the river, in the 1st, is generally more affluent and elegant. Democrats take comfortable margins in the 3rd, thanks to blacks in the Albina section, blue-collar whites in the North End and the East Side's many elderly residents.

The 3rd has nearly 90 percent of the population of Multnomah County, which includes Portland and some suburbs. In 1984, Walter F. Mondale carried Multnomah as a whole by nearly 24,000 votes — by far his best showing in the state. He did even better within the 3rd District portion of the county. Michael S. Dukakis took Multnomah by more than 60,000 votes in 1988.

As one moves farther east from the Willamette, light manufacturing districts give way to comfortable middle-income neighborhoods such as Parkrose, with a blend of business and professional people.

Over the last decade there has been growth in the east side suburbs, a few of which are as sumptuous as the in-town residential areas west of the Willamette. The largest of the suburban cities in the 3rd District is Gresham, which tripled in size during the 1970s and grew in the 1980s to a population of 68,000. Troutdale, to the north, is smaller than Gresham but also fast growing, having expanded by more than 20 percent in the first half of the 1980s.

Beyond suburbia, there are a few farms along the Columbia River, the 3rd's northern boundary, but Mount Hood National Forest occupies most of the county's eastern part.

Population: 526,715. White 471,726 (90%), Black 28,858 (6%), Other 17,563 (3%). Spanish origin 10,458 (2%). 18 and over 394,345 (75%), 65 and over 68,230 (13%). Median age: 31.

sue before his Investigations Subcommittee. As the debate expanded to problems at unregulated physician-run labs conducting Pap tests for cervical cancer — recommended annually for all women — the hearings gained widespread publicity and became a springboard for successful legislation offered by Dingell and Wyden to crack down on the labs.

The two do not always agree like this, but Wyden gives the chairman as many votes as he can. As Wyden tells it, when he first joined Energy and Commerce in 1981, he went straight to Dingell to tell him he could not support his efforts to weaken the Clean Air Act, but would try to help whenever he could. This candor formed the basis of a productive relationship.

At the same time, Wyden is often in philosophical agreement with Dingell rival Henry A. Waxman of California, the powerful chairman of the Health Subcommittee, where Wyden has a seat.

Their relationship dates back to the 1982 Clean Air debate, when Wyden became a key figure in an alliance of liberals opposed to a Dingell-backed effort to relax pollution controls. The environmentalist faction scored a major victory with Wyden's amendment to keep tight controls in areas that met air quality standards.

While Dingell postponed further action that time, the committee did at last rewrite the Clean Air Act during the 101st Congress. Wyden was not a pivotal figure in the reauthorization, but he pushed to protect national parks and wilderness areas from nearby polluters and to provide technical assistance to help small businesses required to comply with the clean-air legislation.

Lately, Wyden has taken on a high profile role in the abortion debate: During the 101st Congress, he sought to reverse the administration's ban on abortion counseling at federally-funded family planning clinics. Wyden renewed the fight in the 102nd, decrying the administration's attempts at "full-scale medical censorship."

Wyden first won his House seat as the candidate of environmentalists and the elderly, and many of his efforts in the House are directly linked to the interests of those groups. But if he should ever run for the Senate, he would need to appeal to a more conservative statewide constituency, and his annual record typically contains a few conspicuous votes that would play well with this broader voting bloc.

In 1988, Wyden voted for a controversial amendment to the drug bill that imposed the death penalty for certain drug-related crimes.

Earlier in his career, concern about the vulnerability of older people to crime prompted

Wyden to sponsor a "career criminal" bill allowing the federal government to prosecute certain repeat offenders and punish them with a mandatory 15-year sentence. The 98th Congress approved Wyden's bill, and in 1986, its scope was expanded to include drug traffickers.

At Home: The main imponderable about Wyden is if and when he will mount a bid for higher office. He has passed twice on a Senate challenge that could have pitted him against Republican Bob Packwood in 1986 or Mark O. Hatfield in 1990.

Instead, Wyden seems content to bide his time. "What's wrong with being a senator at 50?" his father and informal adviser, Peter Wyden, has been quoted as saying.

Electorally secure in his staunchly Democratic district, Wyden has not had a tough race since he first won the seat in 1980. Then, he already had a high profile in Portland as executive director of the state's Gray Panthers, an organization promoting senior citizens' interests.

In his primary challenge to incumbent Democrat Robert Duncan, Wyden relied on a sizable volunteer force made up of senior citizens, environmentalists and other young urban liberals like himself. He charged that Duncan's record on mass transit, housing and heating cost issues revealed insufficient sensitivity to urban needs in the 1980s.

Duncan, a more traditional labor Democrat, had loyal supporters in the district's working-class neighborhoods. But Wyden cut into that voting bloc by winning some union endorsements that had routinely gone to Duncan in earlier elections.

While Wyden campaigned full time for several months, Duncan tended to his work in Washington and mostly ignored his opponent. Wyden took 60 percent of the vote to win the primary comfortably. He won an even larger vote share in November and has continued in that pattern ever since.

Committees

Energy & Commerce (10th of 27 Democrats)
Health & the Environment; Oversight & Investigations; Telecommunications & Finance

Select Aging (13th of 42 Democrats)
Health & Long-Term Care

Small Business (7th of 27 Democrats)
Regulation, Business Opportunity & Energy (chairman)

Elections

1990 General		
Ron Wyden (D)	169,731	(81%)
Philip E. Mooney (R)	40,216	(19%)
1990 Primary		
Ron Wyden (D)	63,178	(93%)
Sam Kahl Jr. (D)	4,908	(7%)
1988 General		
Ron Wyden (D)	190,684	(99%)

Previous Winning Percentages: **1986** (86%) **1984** (72%) **1982** (78%) **1980** (72%)

District Vote For President

	1988	1984	1980	1976
D	143,542 (60%)	127,701 (54%)	110,009 (47%)	119,325 (53%)
R	89,744 (38%)	111,211 (46%)	93,356 (40%)	98,753 (44%)
I			23,697 (10%)	

Campaign Finance

	Receipts	Receipts from PACs	Expend- itures
1990			
Wyden (D)	$708,598	$341,242 (48%)	$693,855
Mooney (R)	$5,739	0	$4,436
1988			
Wyden (D)	$596,224	$316,772 (53%)	$287,996

Key Votes

1991	
Authorize use of force against Iraq	N
1990	
Support constitutional amendment on flag desecration	N
Pass family and medical leave bill over Bush veto	Y
Reduce SDI funding	Y
Allow abortions in overseas military facilities	Y
Approve budget summit plan for spending and taxing	N
Approve civil rights bill	Y
1989	
Halt production of B-2 stealth bomber at 13 planes	N
Oppose capital gains tax cut	N
Approve federal abortion funding in rape or incest cases	Y
Approve pay raise and revision of ethics rules	N
Pass Democratic minimum wage plan over Bush veto	Y

Voting Studies

	Presidential Support		Party Unity		Conservative Coalition	
Year	**S**	**O**	**S**	**O**	**S**	**O**
1990	24	76	94	6	22	78
1989	27	69	91	7	20	80
1988	29	70	87	13	34	66
1987	18	79	89	8	23	77
1986	23	76	89	11	38	62
1985	26	74	84	14	36	64
1984	25	75	88	12	20	80
1983	13	85	91	8	15	84
1982	30	69	92	7	8	90
1981	26	68	83	10	12	85

Interest Group Ratings

Year	ADA	ACU	AFL-CIO	CCUS
1990	89	4	92	29
1989	80	18	82	50
1988	90	16	86	43
1987	84	9	81	14
1986	80	14	79	28
1985	60	29	71	59
1984	95	8	62	31
1983	90	9	82	35
1982	95	18	95	18
1981	100	13	87	6

4 Peter A. DeFazio (D)

Of Springfield — Elected 1986

Born: May 27, 1947, Needham, Mass.
Education: Tufts U., B.A. 1969; attended U. of Oregon, 1969-71, M.S. 1977.
Military Service: Air Force, 1967-71.
Occupation: Congressional aide.
Family: Wife, Myrnie L. Daut.
Religion: Roman Catholic.
Political Career: Lane County Commission, 1982-86.
Capitol Office: 1233 Longworth Bldg. 20515; 225-6416.

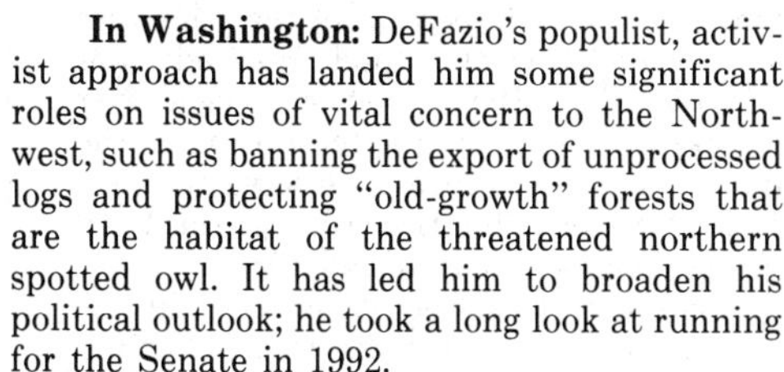

In Washington: DeFazio's populist, activist approach has landed him some significant roles on issues of vital concern to the Northwest, such as banning the export of unprocessed logs and protecting "old-growth" forests that are the habitat of the threatened northern spotted owl. It has led him to broaden his political outlook; he took a long look at running for the Senate in 1992.

Like fellow Oregon Democrats Les AuCoin and Ron Wyden, DeFazio is a legislative activist, and he has found opportunity to act serving on the Public Works and Interior committees. Thanks in part to his background as a congressional staffer, he is one of the more knowledgeable members on timber and energy issues. Also, he was actively involved in a successful effort to expand the Wild and Scenic Rivers Act to protect 1,400 miles of Oregon's rivers.

In the spotted owl debate, the most roiling Northwest issue in the 101st Congress, DeFazio trod gingerly. His district has more old-growth forest than any other; the listing of the owl as a threatened species by the Fish and Wildlife Service would curtail logging in its habitat. DeFazio introduced a compromise bill calling for alternatives to mitigate the listing's impact. The bill had five Northwestern cosponsors but did not advance beyond subcommittee level.

In the 101st Congress, DeFazio redoubled his efforts for a bill to allow states to ban the export of unprocessed, or "raw," logs from state lands to foreign processing mills — intended to save jobs in Oregon mills. The bill was opposed by the major timber companies and did not move in the 100th Congress.

In 1989, after initially signaling that it opposed a ban on raw log exports, the Bush administration, heavily lobbied by Oregon GOP Sen. Mark Hatfield, reversed itself. Oregon's other senator, Republican Bob Packwood, attached a permanent ban on raw log exports from federal lands to a bill revising customs and trade law, but did not attempt to extend the amendment to timber taken from state land.

The Public Works Committee, normally a lair for bipartisan logrolling, served DeFazio as a forum for other verbal assaults on the Bush administration in the 101st Congress. He greeted the administration's 1990 transportation policy initiative with derision. "This is a Twinkie transportation policy. Airy and light with nothing but fluff at the core. I sincerely hope it will have a shorter shelf life."

DeFazio took an active interest in the airline industry's financial woes. He introduced a bill to limit the leveraged-buyout acquisitions of airlines. The House, reacting to takeovers by Frank Lorenzo and Donald J. Trump, overwhelmingly approved a similar bill, but it languished in the Senate, threatened with a veto.

He also pushed for a bill to force the Bush administration to intervene in the management dispute between Eastern Airlines and its unions. Bush, he said, "did nothing" to avert Eastern's bankruptcy.

During House floor consideration of the five-year farm programs reauthorization in 1990, DeFazio added one of the few significant amendments to the bill. It replaced a hodgepodge of state laws with a national standard governing what foods may be labeled organic. Agriculture Committee Democrat Charles W. Stenholm of Texas offered an alternative amendment giving the Agriculture Department authority for setting standards. But DeFazio said that approach was a ploy to kill the organic standard by lawmakers who saw it as a threat to traditional, chemical-intensive agriculture. DeFazio's amendment was adopted, 234-187.

DeFazio's independent populism can rankle some colleagues, and his tendency not to take all his cues from the Democratic leadership may help explain why his ambitions to win a seat on the Budget Committee have been thwarted. Although he votes a large majority of the time with his party, on some votes dear to the leadership, he is prone to go his own way.

In the 100th Congress he was one of 48 Democrats to vote against a deficit-reduction package calling for a $12 billion tax increase.

"I think the bill's a turkey," he said. "It was presented as a test of faith in leadership. I am a strong supporter of leadership in the

Oregon 4

Southwest — Eugene

The 4th starts at the Pacific, crosses the Coastal Range and ends at the Cascade Range, taking in all or part of nine counties in southwestern Oregon. Lane County, with Oregon's second-largest city, Eugene, casts more than half the vote.

Home to the University of Oregon (enrollment 18,000), Eugene in the 1960s and 1970s was a mecca for the back-to-nature counterculture. Many of the students stayed on after graduation. As they moved into workaday society, they learned how to influence local politics; they usually elect liberal Democrats.

Often matched against this environmentalist faction are the people whose paychecks come from the large segment of Eugene's economy linked to timber processing. For many millworkers and managers in the lumber industry, jobs and growth are more important than environmental preservation. Industrial employment has been unsteady in Eugene and timber-dominated Springfield, its suburb. Downturns in housing construction bring layoffs and plant shutdowns, and even in good times, increasing mechanization in the mills means they will never employ as many people as in the past.

As concern over the long-term economic health of the Eugene area has grown, there has been more cooperation between environmentalists and development advocates in Lane County. But there is still a good measure of the conflict that has produced some strongly competitive races in Lane County over the years. Richard M. Nixon carried Lane in 1968 and 1972, but Jimmy Carter won it in 1976; Ronald Reagan was the victor in 1980, but it went for Walter F. Mondale in 1984 and for Michael S. Dukakis in 1988. Republican Mark O. Hatfield won it in his 1990 Senate race. In House contests, Democrats usually prevail. DeFazio won 59 percent of the Lane County vote in his first House bid in 1986, and more than 70 percent in his 1988 re-election.

Two counties south of Lane together make up about 30 percent of the 4th's vote — Douglas County (Roseburg) and Coos County (Coos Bay). Douglas, given over mostly to farming and sheep raising, is the district's most significant conservative area. It was the base for Bruce Long, the GOP House nominee in 1984 and 1986.

Coastal Coos County suffered in the 1980s, as dozens of mills went idle and unemployment reached as high as 20 percent. The current economic downturn has further hobbled the county's timber industry. Also, the traditional salmon fishermen have been losing ground to corporate aquaculture facilities that produce higher yields. Coos County narrowly backed Reagan in 1984 and Hatfield in 1990, but gave DeFazio 58 percent in 1986, and went for Dukakis in 1988.

Population: 526,462. White 509,012 (97%), Black 1,932 (0.4%), Other 10,055 (2%). Spanish origin 9,972 (2%). 18 and over 378,675 (72%), 65 and over 56,042 (11%). Median age: 30.

House, but they made a mistake on this bill."

In the 101st Congress, he opposed the 1989 pay raise and ethics rules revision as well as the 1990 budget summit plan.

DeFazio shares with many of his Northwestern constituents a skepticism toward international adventurism, voting against foreign aid and questioning U.S. military missions. As a freshman, he opposed President Reagan's efforts to provide naval escorts to Kuwaiti oil tankers in the Persian Gulf. "It's like Lebanon all over again," DeFazio said. "The president is putting American lives and prestige on the line without any clearly defined goals or objectives."

DeFazio was among the most active in pushing for a showdown with Reagan over the War Powers Resolution, which requires congressional approval for the continued deployment of U.S. forces when hostilities are under way. While the Reagan administration questioned the constitutionality of the law and maintained that U.S. forces were not in hostilities, DeFazio introduced legislation to declare that the resolution had been triggered. After the courts dismissed a lawsuit intended to force the president to initiate War Powers procedures, DeFazio proposed tightening the law.

DeFazio continued his efforts in the 101st Congress, as the United States intensified its involvement in the Persian Gulf. As Congress neared adjournment in 1990, DeFazio won a last-minute insertion in the resolution of adjournment authorizing congressional leaders to summon Congress back into session if they believed it was in the public interest — after circulating a letter and receiving support from more than 50 colleagues.

At Home: DeFazio's strength and his weakness as a House candidate were the same — his identification with Jim Weaver, his predecessor in the 4th. In the end, the Weaver connection was more help than hindrance.

DeFazio portrayed himself as heir to Weaver's populist appeal, but kept apart from Weaver's personal quarrels and financial entanglements.

DeFazio first went to work for Weaver in 1977, fresh from a graduate program in gerontology at the University of Oregon. He handled senior citizens' issues in Weaver's Eugene office, spent two years in Washington as his legislative aide, then returned to Eugene as Weaver's constituent services director. After that, DeFazio won election to the Lane County (Eugene) commission in 1982.

As an elected official, DeFazio proved to be less abrasive than Weaver but equally aggressive. He sued to nullify contracts between Oregon utilities and the Washington Public Power Supply System, whose failed nuclear projects had resulted in utility rate increases. He also led the fight against a 1983 proposal for a Eugene city income tax.

When Weaver announced he would not seek re-election in 1986, DeFazio stepped in. He had ties to environmentalists and liberals in Eugene's university community, a residence in the timber-oriented suburb of Springfield, and name familiarity throughout Lane County. DeFazio had primary opposition from state Sen. Bill Bradbury, popular in the coastal areas, and state Sen. Margie Hendriksen, who had labor and feminist support. But DeFazio edged Bradbury by just under 1,000 votes; Hendriksen finished a close third.

Republicans nominated Bruce Long, who took 42 percent against Weaver in 1984. Long sought to cultivate the many voters Weaver had alienated over the years; time and again, he described DeFazio as "Jim Weaver Jr." Allegations Weaver had used campaign funds to play the commodities market made DeFazio's ties to the incumbent seem even more undesirable.

But DeFazio had no connection with Weaver's financial troubles, and he deflected the "clone" criticisms by insisting that he was an independent thinker who had picked up valuable experience in Weaver's office. DeFazio called Long a dogmatic conservative lacking in sympathy for district voters.

Long was better financed than in 1984, but his media efforts could not undo DeFazio's Lane County base and strong organization. DeFazio carried Lane by almost 18,000 votes, won with similar ease in Coos County and held down Long's margin in Douglas County. In 1988 and 1990, DeFazio won re-election with ease.

Committees

Interior & Insular Affairs (21st of 29 Democrats)
Mining & Natural Resources; National Parks & Public Lands; Water, Power & Offshore Energy

Public Works & Transportation (17th of 36 Democrats)
Aviation; Surface Transportation

Select Aging (33rd of 42 Democrats)
Human Services; Retirement, Income & Employment; Rural Elderly

Elections

1990 General

Peter A. DeFazio (D)	162,494	(86%)
Tonie Nathan (LIBERT)	26,432	(14%)

1988 General

Peter A. DeFazio (D)	108,483	(72%)
Jim Howard (R)	42,220	(28%)

Previous Winning Percentage: **1986** (54%)

District Vote For President

	1988	1984	1980	1976
D	120,021 (54%)	109,587 (46%)	107,296 (38%)	102,060 (52%)
R	99,106 (44%)	126,453 (53%)	138,645 (49%)	88,526 (45%)
I			23,305 (8%)	

Campaign Finance

	Receipts	Receipts from PACs		Expend-itures
1990				
DeFazio (D)	$257,547	$172,635	(67%)	$217,527
Nathan (LIBERT)	$3,341	0		$3,343
1988				
DeFazio (D)	$330,899	$235,589	(71%)	$283,068
Howard (R)	$60,048	$5,250	(9%)	$58,563

Key Votes

1991	
Authorize use of force against Iraq	N
1990	
Support constitutional amendment on flag desecration	N
Pass family and medical leave bill over Bush veto	Y
Reduce SDI funding	Y
Allow abortions in overseas military facilities	Y
Approve budget summit plan for spending and taxing	N
Approve civil rights bill	Y
1989	
Halt production of B-2 stealth bomber at 13 planes	Y
Oppose capital gains tax cut	Y
Approve federal abortion funding in rape or incest cases	Y
Approve pay raise and revision of ethics rules	N
Pass Democratic minimum wage plan over Bush veto	Y

Voting Studies

	Presidential Support		Party Unity		Conservative Coalition	
Year	S	O	S	O	S	O
1990	19	75	86	8	19	80
1989	23	73	89	6	2	98
1988	20	71	86	10	24	61
1987	12	87	87	10	19	81

Interest Group Ratings

Year	ADA	ACU	AFL-CIO	CCUS
1990	83	14	83	36
1989	95	7	92	40
1988	80	13	86	25
1987	100	4	93	20

5 Mike Kopetski (D)

Of Keizer — Elected 1990

Born: Oct. 27, 1949, Pendleton, Ore.
Education: American U., B.A. 1971; Lewis and Clark College, J.D. 1978.
Occupation: Advertising executive.
Family: Wife, Linda Zuckerman; one child.
Religion: Not specified.
Political Career: Ore. House, 1985-89; sought Democratic nomination for U.S. House, 1982; Democratic nominee for U.S. House, 1988.
Capitol Office: 1520 Longworth Bldg. 20515; 225-5711.

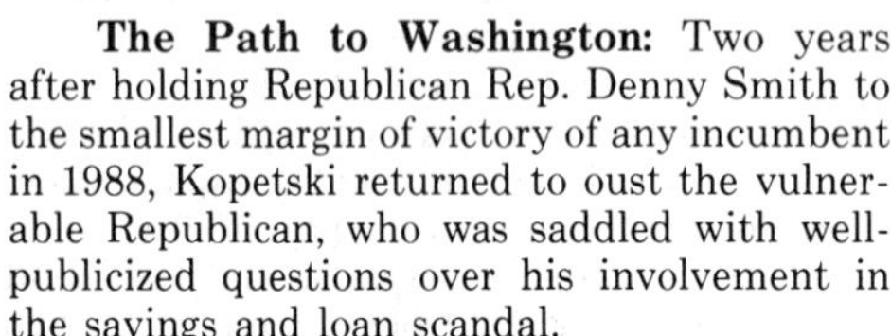

The Path to Washington: Two years after holding Republican Rep. Denny Smith to the smallest margin of victory of any incumbent in 1988, Kopetski returned to oust the vulnerable Republican, who was saddled with well-publicized questions over his involvement in the savings and loan scandal.

As in 1988, Smith tried to convince 5th District voters that Kopetski was too liberal. He portrayed the Democrat as sympathetic to radical environmentalists who oppose logging. But Kopetski shifted the campaign debate away from a polarizing, left vs. right struggle over timber onto issue turf on which Smith was more vulnerable.

Adopting a moderate position on the contentious timber question and criticizing Smith's voting record on issues relating to the environment, women, education and senior citizens, Kopetski argued that it was the incumbent who was outside the district's mainstream.

Smith's opposition to abortion cost him votes among moderate Republicans newly focused on the issue because of the Supreme Court's 1989 decision in *Webster v. Reproductive Health Services.* Two anti-abortion questions on state ballots heightened voters' attention to the issue.

Kopetski's 707-vote loss to the heavily favored Smith had been one of the surprises of Election Day 1988. With limited resources, Kopetski built a crack organization and effectively disseminated his message with free media. Smith seemed to take his race for granted; he spent much of his time outside the 5th promoting his "anticrime" ballot initiative.

Kopetski called Smith a hypocrite for touting his crime-fighting initiative in Oregon but voting against crime-fighting legislation in the House. He also capitalized on Smith's proposal to freeze Social Security cost-of-living adjustments. Although he lacked the money for a TV ad campaign, Kopetski was aided by an independent cable TV ad campaign financed by a wealthy Oregon family unhappy with Smith's conservatism.

Late in the 1988 campaign, Smith started to worry and began running TV ads criticizing Kopetski as a tax-and-spend liberal. That last-minute offensive may have made the difference. The anticrime initiative passed overwhelmingly, but Smith did not pull ahead of Kopetski until absentee ballots were counted. After the voting, Smith was one of the few Republican candidates anywhere to blame his showing on Michael S. Dukakis' coattails. The Democrat narrowly lost the 5th District's presidential vote.

Smith could not lay the blame for his 1990 loss on a presidential candidate, however. Rather, his S&L entanglements, combined with a negative ad that backfired, helped bring his House career to a close. Kopetski returned with another strong organizational effort, but Smith's added woes enabled Kopetski to market his second campaign as more than a recycled bid.

In his campaign literature, Kopetski detailed "five ways Denny Smith personally contributed to the $500 billion savings and loan crisis." Smith was the director of a Salem S&L for 10 years, had business dealings with another Oregon thrift and lobbied in behalf of a third. All three failed. In September, the Democratic Congressional Campaign Committee filed a complaint with the House ethics committee charging Smith with using his office for personal gain by lobbying state regulators for civil immunity for himself as director of the failed S&L. A former investigator for the Senate Watergate Committee, Kopetski was able to cast himself as an upright alternative to Smith.

When Smith ran a hard-hitting radio ad in August, it was Kopetski who benefited. The ad, featuring the sounds of Adolf Hitler speaking to a frenzied crowd, accused Kopetski of insufficiently supporting President Bush's Persian Gulf policy. An announcer intoned, "Mike, appeasement is wrong." Local media lambasted Smith for running the "Hitler ad."

Oregon 5

Willamette Valley — Salem; Corvallis

Created in 1981 from parts of three other districts, the 5th contains no entire county, covering instead parts of five counties that lie on either side of the Willamette River south of Portland.

With its mix of blue-collar and white-collar workers, logging towns and affluent suburbs, farming areas and college towns, the 5th reflects much of the state's diversity. Politically, most of it is GOP territory, but the Republicans tend to be moderate, especially on social questions.

Marion County, nearly all of which is in the 5th, casts about 40 percent of the vote and is usually a good Republican base; GOP Rep. Denny Smith's paltry 1,500-vote margin there in 1988 set the tone for his near-loss districtwide to Democrat Mike Kopetski. In their rematch two years later, Kopetski won Marion by more than 3,500 votes. Marion includes Salem, which contains just under 108,000 people. The third-largest city in the state, Salem's population grew by 21 percent in the 1980s.

Salem is Oregon's capital, so many residents are on the state payroll; the city is also a market town for the Willamette Valley's abundant agricultural produce.

Clackamas County has about as much clout in the 5th as Marion does, casting just over 35 percent of the district's vote. The county's population has grown with the expansion of Portland's suburbs into the northwest section of the county. Democrats have a considerable edge over Republicans among registered voters in Clackamas, but some who label themselves Democrats frequently cross party lines. Republican Smith carried the county easily in 1984 and 1986, but got only 52 percent there in 1988, and lost the county by more than 13,000 votes in 1990. Conservatism is strong in affluent white-collar suburbs such as Lake Oswego, which is partially in the district, and in blue-collar towns such as Oregon City and West Linn.

The 5th contains only a small corner of Benton County, but that includes the city of Corvallis, the district's only major city outside Salem. The home of Oregon State University's 16,000 students and numerous political activists, Corvallis is the most liberal area in the district. Benton County stubbornly went against Smith, giving Kopetski roughly 60 percent of its vote in both 1988 and 1990.

The district also includes the western portion of Linn County, which is dominated by Albany, a conservative blue-collar logging and metal-producing town. It was the only county in the district to favor Smith in 1990 House voting. Because of its dependence on those cyclical industries, Linn has been one of the more economically depressed counties in the state.

Population: 526,120. White 503,786 (96%), Black 2,471 (1%), Other 9,787 (2%). Spanish origin 15,998 (3%). 18 and over 375,567 (71%), 65 and over 55,221 (10%). Median age: 29.

Committees

Agriculture (27th of 27 Democrats)
Department Operations, Research & Foreign Agriculture; Forests, Family Farms & Energy

Judiciary (20th of 21 Democrats)
Civil & Constitutional Rights; International Law, Immigration & Refugees

Science, Space & Technology (30th of 32 Democrats)
Environment; Science

Campaign Finance

	Receipts	Receipts from PACs		Expend-itures
1990				
Kopetski (D)	$851,729	$399,283	(47%)	$843,297
Smith (R)	$841,077	$386,986	(46%)	$884,828

Key Vote

1991

Authorize use of force against Iraq — N

Elections

1990 General

Mike Kopetski (D)	124,610	(55%)
Denny Smith (R)	101,650	(45%)

District Vote For President

	1988	1984	1980	1976
D	116,353 (48%)	100,445 (41%)	83,406 (37%)	88,099 (46%)
R	121,517 (50%)	144,455 (59%)	110,749 (49%)	96,119 (50%)
I			24,234 (11%)	

Pennsylvania

U.S. CONGRESS

SENATE 1 D, 1 R
HOUSE 11 D, 12 R

LEGISLATURE

Senate 24 D, 26 R
House 107 D, 96 R

ELECTIONS

1988 Presidential Vote	
Bush	51%
Dukakis	48%
1984 Presidential Vote	
Reagan	53%
Mondale	46%
1980 Presidential Vote	
Reagan	50%
Carter	43%
Anderson	6%
Turnout rate in 1986	37%
Turnout rate in 1988	50%
Turnout rate in 1990	31%

(as percentage of voting age population)

POPULATION AND GROWTH

1980 population	11,863,895
1990 population (5th in the nation)	11,881,643
Percent change 1980-1990	0%

DEMOGRAPHIC BREAKDOWN

White	89%
Black	9%
Asian or Pacific Islander	1%
(Hispanic origin)	2%
Urban	69%
Rural	31%
Born in state	82%
Foreign-born	3%

MAJOR CITIES

Philadelphia	1,585,577
Pittsburgh	369,879
Erie	108,718
Allentown	105,090
Scranton	81,805

AREA AND LAND USE

Area	44,888 sq. miles (32nd)
Farm	29%
Forest	59%
Federally owned	2%

Gov. Robert P. Casey (D)
Of Scranton — Elected 1986

Born: Jan. 9, 1932, Jackson Heights, N.Y.
Education: College of the Holy Cross, B.A. 1953; George Washington U., LL.B. 1956.
Occupation: Lawyer.
Religion: Roman Catholic.
Political Career: Pa. Senate, 1963-67; Pa. auditor general, 1969-77; sought Democratic nomination for governor in 1966, 1970 and 1978.
Next Election: 1994.

WORK

Occupations	
White-collar	50%
Blue-collar	36%
Service workers	13%
Government Workers	
Federal	135,591
State	145,185
Local	401,773

MONEY

Median family income	$ 19,995	(24th)
Tax burden per capita	$ 857	(24th)

EDUCATION

Spending per pupil through grade 12	$ 4,989	(11th)
Persons with college degrees	14%	(41st)

CRIME

Violent crime rate	379 per 100,000 (31st)

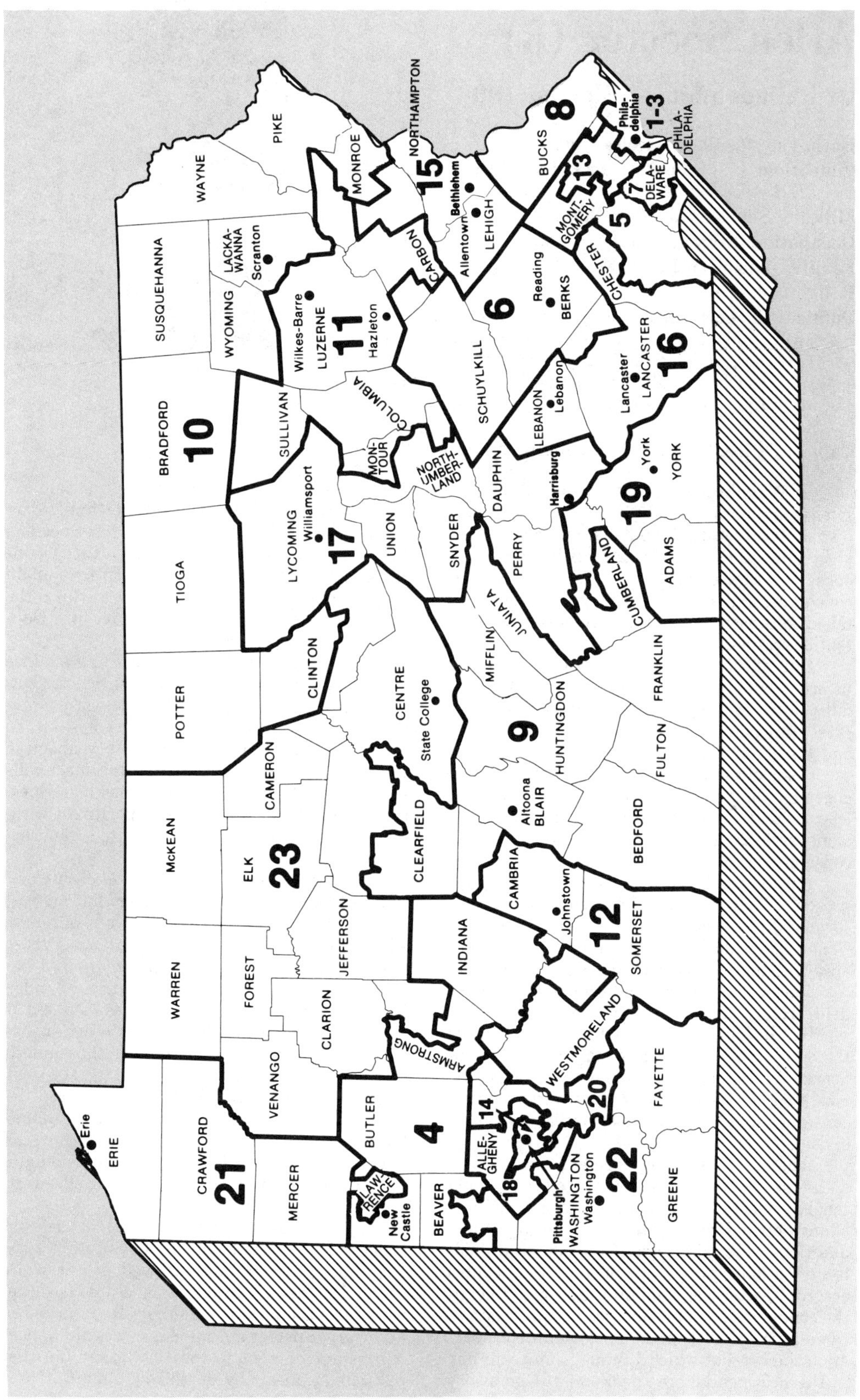
ERIE
Erie
CRAWFORD
21
MERCER
LAW-RENCE
New Castle
BEAVER
BUTLER
4
VENANGO
WARREN
FOREST
CLARION
ARMSTRONG
JEFFERSON
ELK
23
McKEAN
CAMERON
POTTER
CLEARFIELD
INDIANA
ALLE-GHENY
14
18
Pittsburgh
WASHINGTON
Washington
22
GREENE
FAYETTE
20
WESTMORELAND
CAMBRIA
Johnstown
12
SOMERSET
BEDFORD
BLAIR
Altoona
HUNTINGDON
9
FULTON
FRANKLIN
MIFFLIN
JUNIATA
CENTRE
State College
CLINTON
TIOGA
LYCOMING
Williamsport
17
UNION
SNYDER
PERRY
CUMBERLAND
ADAMS
YORK
York
19
Harrisburg
DAUPHIN
NORTH-UMBER-LAND
MON-TOUR
COLUMBIA
SULLIVAN
BRADFORD
10
SUSQUEHANNA
WYOMING
LACKA-WANNA
Scranton
LUZERNE
Wilkes-Barre
Hazleton
11
WAYNE
PIKE
MONROE
CARBON
NORTHAMPTON
15
Bethlehem
Allentown
LEHIGH
SCHUYLKILL
6
Reading
BERKS
LEBANON
Lebanon
LANCASTER
Lancaster
16
CHESTER
5
MONT-GOMERY
13
BUCKS
8
DELA-WARE
7
Phila-delphia
1-3
PHILA-DELPHIA

Arlen Specter (R)

Of Philadelphia — Elected 1980

Born: Feb. 12, 1930, Wichita, Kan.
Education: U. of Pennsylvania, B.A. 1951; Yale U., LL.B. 1956.
Military Service: Air Force, 1951-53.
Occupation: Lawyer; professor of law.
Family: Wife, Joan Levy; two children.
Religion: Jewish.
Political Career: Philadelphia district attorney, 1966-74; Republican nominee for mayor of Philadelphia, 1967; defeated for re-election as district attorney, 1973; sought Republican nomination for U.S. Senate, 1976; sought Republican nomination for governor, 1978.
Capitol Office: 303 Hart Bldg. 20510; 224-4254.

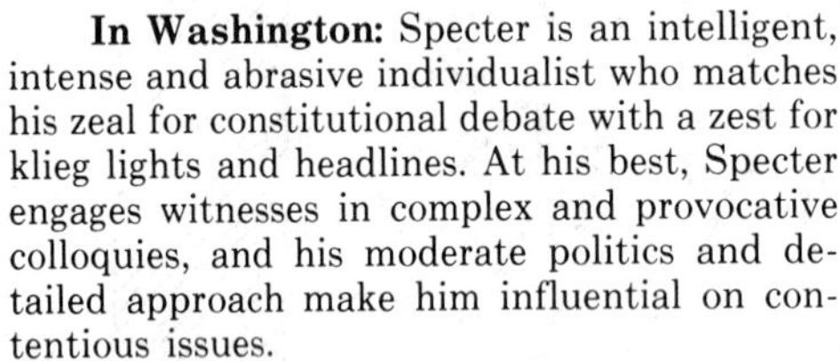

In Washington: Specter is an intelligent, intense and abrasive individualist who matches his zeal for constitutional debate with a zest for klieg lights and headlines. At his best, Specter engages witnesses in complex and provocative colloquies, and his moderate politics and detailed approach make him influential on contentious issues.

But at his worst, Specter plays Hamlet before a bored and frustrated Judiciary Committee. His questioning of witnesses can unravel into ponderous and esoteric statements, and his commitment to weighing all the facts can obstruct action. A loner, Specter does not engender the fellowship that might incline colleagues to tolerate his digressions. His go-it-alone style is even more nettlesome on the collegial Appropriations Committee.

Specter makes no apologies for his approach. "They can't say I'm dumb or crooked, so what do they say?" he once asked a reporter. "That I'm calculating or ambitious? I have always thought those were good qualities."

Politically, Specter is similarly independent. He is among the top half-dozen GOP senators in opposing President Bush, and near the bottom in voting with a majority of Republicans. While he is considered the Democrats' most frequent ally among Judiciary Republicans, he stands with conservatives in most divisive crime debates.

The one constant is Specter's love of legal discourse. Widely considered a constitutional scholar, Specter hustles to the floor to be part of any debate involving the Constitution. When questions were raised about the constitutionality of certain provisions of the 1989 contra accord, Specter was soon on the scene. "I heard the comments . . . and thought it appropriate to come to the floor to raise for general consideration some issues which I brought up yesterday in the hearings before the Foreign Operations Subcommittee on Appropriations," he said.

Even the rare whiff of Specter humor can involve the Constitution. In mid-1989, Specter's wife, a member of the Philadelphia City Council, asked whether it was all right to complain about the miserable conditions on a trip to the Amazon. "That's guaranteed under the Constitution," he quipped.

Often one of the last senators to announce his vote on controversial matters, Specter saw his image shift from thoughtful toward tentative as a result of a series of votes on an amendment to ban certain assault weapons in 1989. First, when the Constitution Subcommittee was deadlocked on the weapons ban, Specter cast the lone vote against reporting it without recommendation; he wanted another hearing.

Months later, when the full Judiciary Committee took up the issue, Specter did not participate. He "took a walk," in insiders' parlance. Although he was one of just two swing votes, Specter said he was not prepared to vote because he was at the impeachment trial of Judge Alcee L. Hastings. But the trial was in recess at the time, and the subcommittee's other swing-vote senator managed to vote on the amendment even though he too served on the Hastings trial panel. Specter's failure to vote allowed the ban to pass by a one-vote margin; a tie would have killed it. When the amendment to the crime bill was brought before the full Senate, Specter voted with a majority of Republicans to kill it.

Opposition to gun control and a tough-on-crime stance are tailor-made for Specter's rural Republican constituents as well as for white ethnic Democratic voters in the cities. Together with Strom Thurmond, ranking Republican on Judiciary, Specter authored a successful habeas corpus amendment to the 1990 crime bill that restricted appeals by death row inmates. He is also a leading supporter of the death penalty for major drug distributors, terrorists and those guilty of espionage and treason.

On the Judiciary Committee, Specter is often allied with liberal Democrats on social policy. He has opposed legislative efforts to curb abortion and busing and was a crucial defector from the GOP in several highly publicized votes on presidential appointees opposed by civil rights groups.

Nomination hearings are Specter's forte. While many tire of the tedious review of court decisions, lengthy background checks and meticulous questioning to grasp a nominee's philosophy, protracted debate suits Specter.

Perhaps his finest hours in the Senate occurred in 1987 during consideration of Robert H. Bork's nomination to the Supreme Court. During the Judiciary hearings, Specter was one of Bork's most persistent and aggressive interrogators. Intent on pinning down Bork's judicial philosophy, he engaged Bork in intellectual combat, arguing with him on what he believed the court has said and how it differed from Bork's interpretation.

Specter was lobbied by the White House, deluged with mail and prominently featured in news stories. But as the contentious and partisan debate dragged on through the summer and fall, Specter drew criticism for fence-sitting. Finally, just days before the committee vote, he announced "with great reluctance" that he would vote against Bork.

As if to make amends for that high-profile rift with Reagan, Specter bent over backwards for President Bush's nominees in the 101st Congress. Featured on news talk shows, he was a leading supporter of John Tower's unsuccessful bid to be secretary of Defense. Specter also backed Bush's unsuccessful nomination of William Lucas to the top civil rights post at Justice. Lucas, who is black, drew criticism for his lack of legal experience, and Specter was among his toughest inquisitors. But Specter — one of just 11 Senate Republicans to vote to override Bush's veto of the civil rights bill — voted to confirm Lucas.

"It is much more important for Mr. Lucas to sense injustice in his stomach," he explained, "than to master legal technicalities in his head."

The nomination of David H. Souter to the Supreme Court was never destined to be the pitched battle the Bork nomination was, but Specter's relatively low profile surprised many. In committee questioning of Souter, Specter prowled the same territory as other senators on civil rights, testing new ground only on Souter's view of the Establishment Clause — a constitutional standard prohibiting state sponsorship of religion that a Pennsylvania case had recently posed to the court.

Specter's approach to all issues is detailed and analytical. After he voted against impeaching Hastings, Specter released a 76-page statement explaining his decision. Asked by Congressional Quarterly to describe his accomplishments in the 101st Congress and goals for the 102nd, Specter provided a thick notebook, with seven sections and 77 subsections.

Specter's argumentative style makes him difficult to work for, and some on the Appropriations Committee consider him difficult to work with.

His weak rapport with colleagues contributed to an embarrassing snub in 1990 when Democratic Sen. Frank R. Lautenberg bluntly denied a request by Specter to address transportation appropriations conferees. Specter had wanted to talk about a House provision that would have cut Pennsylvania's highway budget by 25 percent if the state failed to dedicate funding to mass transit.

Not being a conferee, Specter had no right to speak, according to Lautenberg. "I know of no precedent for a senator objecting to a unanimous consent request to speak before a committee," Specter fumed outside the meeting. Finally, teaming up with fellow Pennsylvanian John Heinz, Specter blocked consideration of the bill, and hours before Congress adjourned, the amendment was effectively nullified.

Occasionally, Specter will beat the partisan drum, as if to remind his GOP colleagues that he is still one of them. As a member of the Intelligence Committee, Specter has argued in favor of a broad interpretation of the anti-ballistic missile treaty — a position shared by conservative advocates of the strategic defense initiative (SDI).

But Specter has been a less ready ally on the MX missile. Originally opposed to the MX, he grew more sympathetic to the weapon as a bargaining chip for arms control negotiations. But shortly before a crucial 1985 vote, his change of mind was stalled when White House aides hinted that Republicans who opposed Reagan on key issues would be denied White House help in campaign fundraising in 1986.

Outraged by the apparent threat, Specter finally backed the missile, after publicly vowing not to accept any campaign help from the president. In the years since then, Specter has opposed efforts to substantially reduce funding for the program.

Representing a state with more registered Democrats than Republicans, Specter routinely calls attention to the plight of struggling Rust Belt cities, and for a Republican, he earns good marks from labor unions. Specter has pressed for legislation aimed at giving U.S. firms more protection from subsidized imports and goods "dumped" below cost in this country by foreign producers.

The Foreign Operations Subcommittee

gives Specter a platform for his ardent support for Israel. In late 1990, Specter criticized an administration proposal to sell advanced weapons to Saudi Arabia. He also condemned the administration's "rush to judgment" when it backed a U.N. resolution criticizing Israel for the killing of 21 Palestinians at Temple Mount.

At Home: Democrats began the 1986 campaign hopeful that they could defeat Specter and end their 24-year drought in Pennsylvania Senate elections. They ended the year buried under the third-largest Senate election landslide in the state in the last half-century.

Specter won with money, high name recognition and the type of moderate Republican image that has enabled GOP candidates to monopolize recent Keystone State Senate elections. A weak campaign by his Democratic rival, Rep. Bob Edgar, boosted Specter.

A liberal from the Philadelphia suburbs, Edgar seemed miscast for a statewide race in heavily blue-collar and ethnic Pennsylvania. But from his first House victory in 1974 to his narrow win in the Democratic Senate primary, he was able to combine an ardent grass-roots organization with a thoughtful and non-threatening persona to defeat a string of opponents who underestimated him.

Specter did not make that mistake. He easily outspent Edgar and he claimed to have visited each of Pennsylvania's 67 counties at least four times during his term.

Edgar sought to portray Specter as a flip-flopper who claimed to be independent but actually supported the Reagan administration on key issues.

But with superior financing, Specter projected his political moderation and dominated the airwaves with skillfully crafted, locally targeted ads that illustrated how he had steered federal money into the state from his Appropriations Committee post.

Specter blunted Edgar virtually everywhere. He won 61 counties, including all of rural central Pennsylvania, Allegheny County (the centerpiece of western Pennsylvania) and Delaware County (Edgar's base in the Philadelphia suburbs).

For Specter, the impressive victory added luster to a political career that seemed to be on the verge of expiring just six years earlier. When he started his 1980 Senate campaign, Specter looked like a fading politician making a last-gasp try. Once the bright young star of Pennsylvania GOP politics, he had lost much of his appeal following defeats for mayor of Philadelphia in 1967 and for re-election as the city's district attorney in 1973. When he lost two more statewide primaries, in 1976 and 1978, it appeared that his triumphs were behind him.

But he decided to make one more try when Republican Richard S. Schweiker announced he would not seek re-election in 1980.

Although Specter's past campaigns had given him greater statewide exposure than any other GOP candidate, he was thought to be laden with too much baggage even to win the nomination over Bud Haabestad, the state GOP chairman.

But Haabestad was not popular among organization Republians. He had been picked as state chairman by GOP Gov. Dick Thornburgh (later to become U.S. Attorney General), who had abolished much of the traditional GOP patronage system in the state. It had been Haabestad's task to bear Thornburgh's bad tidings to Republican workers. This issue allowed Specter to win the primary.

In the general election, Specter had the good fortune of running against a Democrat who was also a two-time statewide loser — former Pittsburgh Mayor Pete Flaherty. Immensely popular in the western part of the state, Flaherty had suffered in the past from a tendency to run his statewide campaigns on his own, disdaining modern organization and financing. In 1980, determined not to make the same mistake, he put more effort into building a statewide network.

It was not enough. Thornburgh and Sen. Heinz agreed to support Specter after the primary, and with their help, he made inroads on Flaherty's territory in western Pennsylvania. At the same time, Flaherty could not overcome the longstanding suspicion of him in the Philadelphia area. Specter carried Philadelphia by 12,000 votes and won immense margins in the Philadelphia suburbs, enough to offset Flaherty's showing in the west.

Specter's roots in Philadelphia politics reach back to the early 1960s, when he was an assistant district attorney making a name for himself among Democrats as a hard-working young reformer. After a stint with the Warren commission, where he was chief author of the theory that a single bullet hit both President Kennedy and Texas Gov. John B. Connally, he returned to conduct an investigation of Philadelphia's judicial system for the state attorney general.

In 1965, he released a report calling the system a "cesspool" of corruption. The same year he challenged his former boss, James Crumlish, for district attorney. When Crumlish was renominated by the Democrats, Specter ran as a Republican and won.

Two years later, Specter took on Mayor James Tate directly. The Democratic Party had been split by feuds between machine regulars and reformers, and the mayor seemed in no shape to fight off a concerted GOP challenge. Specter and his "clean government" campaign were expected to romp.

They did not. Tate, rejected by the organization, nonetheless won the Democratic nomination easily. Then, as riots were breaking out in other cities, he and his new police chief,

Frank Rizzo, clamped a "limited emergency" on the city to prevent disturbances. Specter could not stop Tate from riding voters' gratitude to a narrow victory.

By 1973, as he completed his second term in the district attorney's office, Specter was considered the favorite candidate in state GOP circles to wrest the governorship from the Democrats the following year. But the speculation ended abruptly when he lost his campaign for a third term as district attorney that fall.

Specter announced he was going into private law practice, and for the first time in over a decade, his name left the front pages. It did not take long to resurface. In 1976 he entered the GOP primary to replace retiring Sen. Hugh Scott. The front-runner in the contest was then-Rep. Heinz, whose tremendous financial resources gave him a clear edge. But Heinz had been hurt by disclosures that he had received illegal contributions from the Gulf Oil Co., an issue Specter kept alive throughout the campaign. At the end of a bitter contest that kept relations between the two delicate for years, Heinz scraped past Specter.

In 1978, with Democrat Milton Shapp retiring as governor, Specter tried for that office. Though he rounded up strong financial and organizational backing in Philadelphia and its suburbs, he split the area's vote with two other candidates. The winner was Thornburgh — a former assistant attorney general in the Ford administration and the only candidate from western Pennsylvania.

Thornburgh and Specter came close to having another primary battle in 1986, this time for Specter's Senate seat. Conservative Republicans unhappy with what they perceived as Specter's lukewarm support for President Reagan encouraged Thornburgh, then the state's popular outgoing governor, to challenge Specter. Thornburgh weighed the idea, but announced in December 1985 that he would not run.

Committees

Veterans' Affairs (Ranking)

Appropriations (8th of 13 Republicans)
Labor, Health & Human Services, Education & Related Agencies (ranking); Agriculture, Rural Development & Related Agencies; Defense; Energy & Water Development; Foreign Operations

Judiciary (5th of 6 Republicans)
Constitution (ranking); Antitrust, Monopolies & Business Rights

Elections

1986 General		
Arlen Specter (R)	1,906,537	(56%)
Bob Edgar (D)	1,448,219	(43%)
1986 Primary		
Arlen Specter (R)	434,623	(76%)
Richard A. Stokes (R)	135,673	(24%)

Previous Winning Percentage: 1980 (51%)

Campaign Finance

	Receipts	Receipts from PACs		Expend-itures
1986				
Specter (R)	$5,450,763	$1,256,626	(23%)	$5,993,230
Edgar (D)	$3,905,186	$793,871	(20%)	$3,872,779

Key Votes

1991	
Authorize use of force against Iraq	Y
1990	
Oppose prohibition of certain semiautomatic weapons	Y
Support constitutional amendment on flag desecration	Y
Oppose requiring parental notice for minors' abortions	Y
Halt production of B-2 stealth bomber at 13 planes	N
Approve budget that cut spending and raised revenues	N
Pass civil rights bill over Bush veto	Y
1989	
Oppose reduction of SDI funding	N
Oppose barring federal funds for "obscene" art	Y
Allow vote on capital gains tax cut	Y

Voting Studies

	Presidential Support		Party Unity		Conservative Coalition	
Year	**S**	**O**	**S**	**O**	**S**	**O**
1990	58	42	53	46	59	41
1989	66	34	55	45	71	29
1988	63	35	48	49	59	35
1987	40	60	46	53	41	59
1986	31	65	27	68	29	64
1985	61	34	51	43	58	37
1984	65	35	67	32	55	45
1983	59	41	46	54	45	55
1982	55	44	50	49	40	59
1981	77	22	64	34	51	47

Interest Group Ratings

Year	ADA	ACU	AFL-CIO	CCUS
1990	39	48	89	50
1989	40	57	50	75
1988	60	33	83	62
1987	80	15	90	47
1986	75	33	87	44
1985	55	36	71	55
1984	50	36	45	68
1983	80	16	76	37
1982	70	26	56	35
1981	50	40	58	72

Harris Wofford (D)

Of Bryn Mawr — Appointed 1991

Born: April 9, 1926, New York, N.Y.
Education: U. of Chicago, B.A. 1948; Yale U., LL.B. 1954; Howard U., J.D. 1954.
Military: Army Air Force, 1944-45.
Occupation: Lawyer; educator.
Family: Wife, Clare Lindgren; three children.
Religion: Roman Catholic.
Political Career: Pa. Democratic Party chairman, 1986.
Capitol Office: 277 Russell Bldg. 20510; 224-6324.

The Path to Washington: Wofford has owed his position in the public eye to two Irish Catholic Democrats — former President John F. Kennedy and Pennsylvania Gov. Robert P. Casey. It was Kennedy who first brought Wofford onto the national scene as a liaison to the black community in the 1960 presidential campaign, and as special assistant for civil rights during his administration.

It was Casey who returned Wofford to the national stage May 8, 1991, by appointing him to fill the vacancy created by the death of GOP Sen. John Heinz, who was killed April 4 in a midair collision of his private plane with a helicopter.

With Casey's backing, Wofford was nominated by the Democratic state committee to be the party's candidate in the Nov. 5, 1991, special election to fill the last three years of Heinz's term. The GOP was expected to nominate Attorney General Dick Thornburgh in August.

But election plans were disrupted in June when a federal district judge ruled unconstitutional Pennsylvania's law allowing state parties to pick nominees without holding primaries. The state and the two parties appealed the ruling. Thornburgh said he would stay on as attorney general if the special election could not be held.

Wofford is Pennsylvania's first Democratic senator since Joseph S. Clark was driven from office in 1968. But holding the seat will not be easy. Wofford is not widely known across Pennsylvania, has never run for public office and faces the daunting task of trying to win in a state in which Democrats have lost nine straight Senate elections.

It was as a child during the New Deal that Wofford began to identify with the Democrats. He recounts that as a 10-year-old during the 1936 presidential campaign, he walked to school for months rather than ride in the family car, which bore a bumper sticker supporting the GOP candidate, Alfred M. Landon.

Wofford also showed an early interest in civil liberties. He and his wife visited India and then wrote a book titled "India Afire" (1951), about the work of Mohandas K. Gandhi. While speaking on Gandhi and his method of non-violent protest, Wofford gained the ear and trust of the Rev. Dr. Martin Luther King Jr.

In 1954, Wofford was one of the first white students to earn a law degree at predominantly black Howard University in Washington. He subsequently taught law at Howard and the University of Notre Dame and served on the staff of the U.S. Commission on Civil Rights before being hired by Kennedy to be an adviser in his 1960 presidential campaign.

In the final days of the campaign, Wofford became a footnote to history by advising Kennedy to call Coretta Scott King and express his concern for her husband's safety in a Georgia jail, where King had been imprisoned for violating probation on a minor driving violation. The call is credited with solidifying crucial support for Kennedy in the black community. After the election, Wofford served in the White House as Kennedy's point man on civil rights before helping R. Sargent Shriver launch the Peace Corps.

With the passing of the New Frontier, Wofford opened a new phase of his life in academia that brought him to Pennsylvania. He was a university president, first at a small college in New York, then starting in 1970, at Bryn Mawr College. In 1978, Wofford left Bryn Mawr to join a Philadelphia law firm.

He soon reconnected with Casey, whom he had met in the 1950s when both were young lawyers at a Washington law firm. When Casey was mounting his first successful gubernatorial campaign in 1986, he tapped Wofford to head the Democratic state committee. The following year, he brought Wofford into his Cabinet as secretary of Labor and Industry.

Wofford was considering a 1992 challenge to GOP Sen. Arlen Specter when Heinz's Senate seat came open. But he was not Casey's first choice for the vacancy. Chrysler Corp. Chairman Lee A. Iacocca was offered the appointment but turned it down, and several other Democrats Casey was reportedly considering withdrew their names. Yet Wofford did not seem to mind that he was not Casey's top pick. He labeled the governor's overture to Iacocca "a bold move that had my support and, luckily, he said no."

1 Thomas M. Foglietta (D)

Of Philadelphia — Elected 1980

Born: Dec. 3, 1928, Philadelphia, Pa.
Education: St. Joseph's College, B.A. 1949; Temple U., J.D. 1952.
Occupation: Lawyer.
Family: Single.
Religion: Roman Catholic.
Political Career: Philadelphia City Council, 1955-75; Republican nominee for mayor of Philadelphia, 1975.
Capitol Office: 231 Cannon Bldg. 20515; 225-4731.

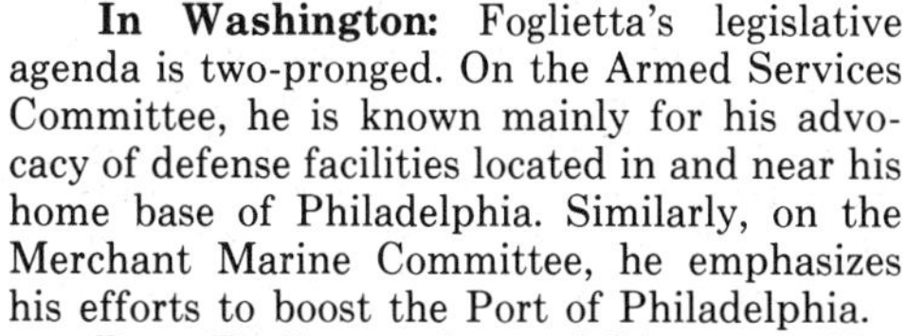

In Washington: Foglietta's legislative agenda is two-pronged. On the Armed Services Committee, he is known mainly for his advocacy of defense facilities located in and near his home base of Philadelphia. Similarly, on the Merchant Marine Committee, he emphasizes his efforts to boost the Port of Philadelphia.

But Foglietta also exhibits a wider worldview. He is one of the leading House advocates of international human rights, with a particular interest in what he sees as the suppression of dissent by the government of South Korea. Foglietta can now pursue these interests from the Foreign Affairs Committee, where he gained a seat at the start of the 102nd Congress.

As the Armed Services Committee debates post-Cold War defense strategy and the effects of the U.S.-led war against Iraq, Foglietta keeps a close eye on what it all means for Philadelphia. In his district is the Philadelphia Naval Shipyard (PNSY), an aging facility on the Pentagon's list of military bases slated for closing, which he has labored to keep operating.

During the 100th Congress, Foglietta lobbied hard to keep PNSY off the list of military bases to be recommended for closure by a presidential commission. He marshaled a coalition of legislators from Pennsylvania, New Jersey and Delaware to defend the facility, where battleships and aircraft carriers are maintained.

In November 1988, Foglietta released a long report intended "to demonstrate . . . that the Philadelphia Navy Yard is the Navy's most efficient and most productive shipyard." The report noted that PNSY is the only facility fully equipped to refit conventional carriers.

The commission spared the shipyard from cutbacks when it reported to President Reagan the following month. However, the commission did recommend the shutdown of the Philadelphia Naval Hospital in the southern part of the 1st District; Foglietta responded by calling for a replacement hospital to be built nearby.

Then, in February 1990, President Bush's Defense Secretary Dick Cheney included PNSY on his "hit list" for a second round of base closings. Foglietta howled, noting that most of the closures would affect bases in Democratic-held House districts. But in early 1991, another presidentially appointed commission also recommended closing PNSY.

While the future of the shipyard is in question, Foglietta worked during the 101st Congress to assure that it will have a productive present. He lobbied for funding to refit the carrier *USS Kennedy* at PNSY. The project — aided by Pennsylvanians John P. Murtha and Joseph M. McDade, the chairman and ranking Republican on Appropriations' Defense Subcommittee — got $405 million in funding.

On the "big picture" defense issues, Foglietta tends to be less enamored of the military. In the 99th Congress, he suggested that Congress set up a nonpartisan board of scientists and other experts to determine the technical feasibility of the strategic defense initiative.

In January 1991, Foglietta voted against the House resolution authorizing Bush to use military force to dislodge Iraq from Kuwait. A month after war broke out, he joined 41 House colleagues in urging Bush not to escalate the conflict.

Foglietta also waxes passionate on human rights issues, particularly the restoration of full democratic procedures in South Korea. He and several other Americans attracted international publicity in 1985 when they were roughed up by government police at the Seoul airport while accompanying exiled opposition leader Kim Dae Jung on his re-entry into South Korea. In July 1990, Foglietta wrote an op-ed piece for the *Los Angeles Times* that called South Korea's tentative moves towards reunification with North Korea "a smokescreen to hide [South Korea's] human-rights violations and to abolish direct election of the president."

But the man who is still known to his south Philly constituents as "Tommy" turns his glance back homeward on Merchant Marine, where he works to obtain funding for dredging and port construction in the Philadelphia area.

Pennsylvania 1

South and Central Philadelphia

William Penn's statue atop Philadelphia's City Hall looks out on a city of distinct ethnic neighborhoods, each with the clannishness and occasional suspicion of outsiders more commonly associated with small towns. The diversity is most apparent in the 1st, which takes in the wealthy liberals of Center City, the Italians of South Philadelphia, the Irish and Poles of the "river wards" and the blacks along North Broad Street. While Ronald Reagan did well among the white ethnics in 1980 and 1984, he did not carry the 1st either time. In 1988, the district went comfortably for Democrat Michael S. Dukakis.

Blue-collar South Philadelphia holds most of the city's piers and the Philadelphia Navy Yard, as well as its huge sports complex — the Spectrum and Veterans and JFK stadiums. Italians are the dominant group here, and though most of them now vote Democratic in local elections, the Republican Party is the party of tradition: A generation ago, most Italian-Americans in Philadelphia sided with the GOP because the Irish controlled the Democratic Party. The law-and-order appeal of former Mayor Frank Rizzo, who grew up here and walked its streets as a patrolman, is strong among the dock and factory workers.

The one ward west of the Schuylkill River included in the 1st has most of the liberal academic community of Drexel University and the University of Pennsylvania. Other centers of liberal Democratic activity are Society Hill and Olde City, the sites of many of the city's historic landmarks and now affluent restoration areas. The gentrification of nearby Queen Village and Fairmount is displacing ethnic whites who esteem Rizzo-style politics with young professionals who disdain it.

Running north from Center City, the Frankford El railway binds together the river wards, a grimy part of town where factories and warehouses sit cheek-by-jowl with row houses. The white ethnic voters here are as Democratic as those in South Philly at the local level, and somewhat more likely to support Democrats for federal offices. But they are conservatives; they matched South Philly in backing Rizzo.

Blacks make up about one-third of the 1st. They are clustered in the rundown neighborhoods extending into North Philadelphia on either side of North Broad Street. The academic enclave of Temple University sits along Broad Street as well.

Population: 515,145. White 310,738 (60%), Black 164,862 (32%), Other 10,310 (2%). Spanish origin 50,440 (10%). 18 and over 374,046 (73%), 65 and over 65,470 (13%). Median age: 29.

He is a founder of the Delaware River Strike Force and the Delaware River Port Caucus.

Foglietta also helped push through a $654,000 appropriation to repair the roof of Independence Hall and to upgrade its deteriorating grounds.

At Home: Foglietta's outward-looking interests caused him some political difficulty early in his House career. He was challenged in the 1984 and 1986 primaries by Jimmy Tayoun, who, in the state House and then the Philadelphia City Council, became famous for tending to the personal needs of his constituents. One Tayoun campaign leaflet noted that he "keeps faith with the Bill Barrett tradition of personal evening service." Barrett, who represented the 1st for 29 years following World War II, was a bit player in Washington, but was very popular in Philadelphia because he returned there every night to hold evening office hours.

In addition to their differing attitudes toward a congressman's role, there were other contrasts between Foglietta and Tayoun in the 1984 primary: Foglietta drew strong support from the district's black voters and from young, liberal professionals in the affluent Center City area. Tayoun's most faithful backers were old-line, working-class whites, including many Irish and Poles in the "river wards" along the Delaware River. Tayoun won the endorsement of a majority of the 1st's Democratic ward leaders.

The crucial votes were in the Italian community of South Philadelphia. Tayoun voiced more conservative views than Foglietta on social issues and hoped Italians would feel they had more in common with him than with Foglietta. But Foglietta's roots in the Italian community are deep. His father was a Republican city councilman, and Foglietta followed in those footsteps, serving on the City Council for two decades. With Italian ethnic loyalty prevailing in South Philadelphia and the Rev. Jesse Jackson's presidential candidacy pulling out a large primary vote in the district's black wards, Foglietta won renomination.

When Tayoun ran again in 1986, he sought — in part, at least — to oust the incumbent by making the rematch a referendum on Philadelphia's controversial black Mayor W. Wilson Goode. The mayor — a prominent Foglietta supporter in 1984 — saw his popularity sink in the wake of the city's disastrous 1985 ouster of the MOVE cult and a deterioration in the delivery of basic city services.

Tayoun's effort to link the two politicians failed, though, as Foglietta kept Goode at a distance. And in the rematch, the incumbent had much more money than Tayoun and broader support from Democratic ward leaders. The result was a much more substantial victory. Foglietta's tally — a tenuous 52 percent in 1984 — jumped to 60 percent, and he expanded his base from liberals, blacks and Italians to include some non-Italian ethnics. Foglietta has had little electoral trouble since then.

Foglietta got his seat in Congress in 1980 by shedding his lifelong GOP label and fighting his way through a complicated political situation. He ran in November as an independent, normally a guarantee of failure. But Democratic incumbent Michael "Ozzie" Myers, indicted in the Abscam bribery scandal, had won renomination, leaving anti-Myers Democrats without a candidate in the general election. Foglietta became that candidate. When Myers was convicted on bribery charges and expelled from the House Oct. 2, Foglietta gained the strength he needed to win. Once elected, he acknowledged his political debt by voting with Democrats to organize the 97th Congress.

To gain a second term as a Democrat in 1982, Foglietta survived a tough primary that pitted him not only against another incumbent but also against the organization of former Mayor Frank Rizzo, still a powerful figure in the 1st. As a Republican, Foglietta had unsuccessfully challenged Rizzo for mayor in 1975.

The 1982 redistricting had paired Foglietta with U.S. Rep. Joseph F. Smith, a machine Democrat and Rizzo loyalist. Rizzo's support helped make Smith competitive in South Philadelphia. But it also brought out a large vote for Foglietta from blacks and Center City liberals antagonistic toward Rizzo.

Committees

Armed Services (11th of 33 Democrats)
Military Installations & Facilities; Research & Development; Seapower & Strategic & Critical Materials

Foreign Affairs (23rd of 28 Democrats)
Arms Control, International Security & Science; Asian & Pacific Affairs

Merchant Marine & Fisheries (7th of 29 Democrats)

Select Hunger (12th of 22 Democrats)
International

Elections

1990 General		
Thomas M. Foglietta (D)	73,423	(79%)
James Love Jackson (R)	19,018	(21%)
1990 Primary		
Thomas M. Foglietta (D)	28,394	(83%)
Willis W. Berry Jr. (D)	5,977	(17%)
1988 General		
Thomas M. Foglietta (D)	128,076	(76%)
William J. O'Brien (R)	39,749	(24%)

Previous Winning Percentages: **1986** (75%) **1984** (75%) **1982** (72%) **1980** (38%)

District Vote For President

	1988	1984	1980	1976
D	105,706 (64%)	140,157 (65%)	117,737 (61%)	137,596 (66%)
R	57,788 (35%)	75,202 (35%)	60,347 (31%)	67,057 (32%)
I			11,420 (6%)	

Campaign Finance

	Receipts	Receipts from PACs		Expend-itures
1990				
Foglietta (D)	$465,317	$226,918	(49%)	$234,057
Jackson (R)	$9,230	$1,000	(11%)	$5,969
1988				
Foglietta (D)	$337,467	$172,700	(51%)	$238,277
O'Brien (R)	$4,182	0		$1,643

Key Votes

1991	
Authorize use of force against Iraq	N
1990	
Support constitutional amendment on flag desecration	N
Pass family and medical leave bill over Bush veto	Y
Reduce SDI funding	Y
Allow abortions in overseas military facilities	N
Approve budget summit plan for spending and taxing	Y
Approve civil rights bill	Y
1989	
Halt production of B-2 stealth bomber at 13 planes	Y
Oppose capital gains tax cut	Y
Approve federal abortion funding in rape or incest cases	?
Approve pay raise and revision of ethics rules	Y
Pass Democratic minimum wage plan over Bush veto	Y

Voting Studies

	Presidential Support		Party Unity		Conservative Coalition	
Year	**S**	**O**	**S**	**O**	**S**	**O**
1990	24	76	92	5	17	80
1989	28	63	91	2	15	83
1988	16	70	83	4	8	79
1987	16	77	81	2	21	72
1986	16	68	79	5	10	82
1985	20	75	90	4	13	80
1984	22	57	80	2	7	83
1983	24	68	87	4	11	85
1982	32	56	81	5	18	77
1981	25	58	80	8	13	73

Interest Group Ratings

Year	ADA	ACU	AFL-CIO	CCUS
1990	78	4	100	14
1989	95	0	100	40
1988	90	4	92	42
1987	84	0	93	8
1986	90	5	100	14
1985	90	5	94	14
1984	95	0	100	50
1983	90	4	100	20
1982	85	5	100	20
1981	90	0	87	11

2 William H. Gray III (D)

Of Philadelphia — Elected 1978

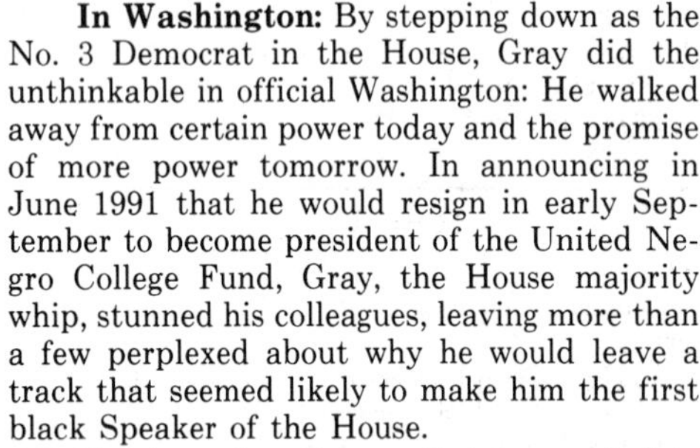

Born: Aug. 20, 1941, Baton Rouge, La.
Education: Franklin and Marshall College, B.A. 1963; Drew Theological Seminary, M.Div. 1966; Princeton Theological Seminary, Th.M. 1970.
Occupation: Minister.
Family: Wife, Andrea Dash; three children.
Religion: Baptist.
Political Career: Sought Democratic nomination for U.S. House, 1976.
Capitol Office: 2454 Rayburn Bldg. 20515; 225-4001.

In Washington: By stepping down as the No. 3 Democrat in the House, Gray did the unthinkable in official Washington: He walked away from certain power today and the promise of more power tomorrow. In announcing in June 1991 that he would resign in early September to become president of the United Negro College Fund, Gray, the House majority whip, stunned his colleagues, leaving more than a few perplexed about why he would leave a track that seemed likely to make him the first black Speaker of the House.

Gray's explanation — that he wanted to follow his parents' footsteps into higher education — did not fit the mold on Capitol Hill. But in interviews following his announcement, he reiterated that theme. "I come from a family where my father was president of two historically black colleges," he said. "My mother was dean of students at a black college, and my sister teaches now at a black college. So that's really my roots."

On ABC-TV's "Good Morning America," he said, "I'm giving up political power to have a very big impact on the education of black young people throughout this decade.... And to me, that's very important." As president of the fund, Gray will take charge of a campaign to raise $250 million.

Coming two years to the month after Speaker Jim Wright and Whip Tony Coelho resigned amid scandal, Gray's announcement triggered considerable speculation about unstated motives for leaving a secure seat and a obvious route up the leadership ladder. The House was rife with alternative theories: that he was weary of answering questions raised by a federal investigation into his finances; that financial pressures demanded he earn a higher income; that he was ill-suited temperamentally to the whip's job; or that his political ambitions might be better served by a turn in the private sector.

Gray has never been at a loss for words, but his words rarely reveal much about his plans. Behind his supreme self-confidence is a large supply of reticence and caution; during his tenure as chairman of the Budget Committee, he was often reluctant even to show his hand to other Democrats.

Gray was characteristically clandestine about his plans to resign. Talk of his leaving began circulating widely in late May, but until the week of his announcement, his staff denied that there was any substance to the speculation, confirming only that Gray had been first approached about the job in 1990.

Fair or not, once he became majority whip in 1989 following Coelho's sudden resignation, Gray was bound to face comparisons with his assertive and partisan predecessor. In his first 18 months on the job, Gray won some praise for his nuts-and-bolts whip operation. But he relinquished the role of high-profile partisan spokesman once played by Coelho — and even by Gray himself.

His altered style may have been an attempt to demonstrate diligence over flashiness in his new post. His lower profile may also be attributed to the hints of ethics problems raised by Justice Department investigations.

Just as he was about to ascend to the whip's post, the Justice Department confirmed in late May 1989 that it was examining allegations of payroll padding on Gray's staff. Attorney General Dick Thornburgh said Gray himself was not a target of the probe, and Gray's comfortable margin over his two rivals in the whip election suggested that his stock was still strong. In July, a report in *The Washington Post* raised questions about free housing provided to Gray and his mother by the church where he and his father and grandfather had preached. The Justice Department was still looking into Gray's finances in 1990 as part of an investigation that his attorney said centered on a former employee.

During the 1980s, Gray evolved into one of the nation's leading black politicians, winning the favor of Democratic leaders eager to showcase prominent blacks. As chairman of the House Budget Committee and of the Demo-

Pennsylvania 2

North and West Philadelphia

Generally speaking, the 2nd is black, poor and Democratic. Whites are just one-fifth of the population, and one in every three residents lives below the poverty line. Democrats Jimmy Carter in 1980, Walter F. Mondale in 1984, and Michael S. Dukakis in 1988 all scored huge wins here, while losing statewide.

But there are wide variations in income and neighborhood character. The 2nd includes the poorest, most blighted areas of black North Philadelphia, but also takes in many well-kept working-class black sections of West Philly. The far northern reaches of the 2nd are quasi-suburban, blending into affluent Montgomery County. At the southern end is Center City's Rittenhouse Square area, filled with condo-dwelling yuppies and with banks, insurance companies and other white-collar employers.

North Philly has more of a reputation as a crime zone than West Philly, so it is ironic that one of the city's worst disasters occurred in West Philadelphia — the May 1985 police battle against the cult group MOVE that killed 11 and destroyed five dozen houses in a black neighborhood at the western edge of the 2nd.

Cutting a wide green swath through the central part of the district is vast Fairmount Park, which flanks the Schuylkill River and contains the city's famous art museum, zoo and "boathouse row." Adjoining the park in the northwest part of the 2nd is Germantown. Once home to Philadelphia's upper crust, it and nearby Mount Airy now are racially mixed and mostly middle class.

The whites in the Rittenhouse Square area are not a large part of the district vote, but they are influential. Along with nearby Society Hill in the 1st District, the Rittenhouse area is the center for the reform movement in Philadelphia politics. As an activist legislator, Gray is popular among the liberal, socially conscious Rittenhouse voters.

Population: 517,215. White 94,623 (18%), Black 413,852 (80%), Other 4,137 (1%). Spanish origin 6,229 (1%). 18 and over 378,182 (73%), 65 and over 68,596 (13%). Median age: 31.

cratic Caucus, he was often found before TV cameras.

In one of the House's toughest assignments, the Budget Committee chairmanship, he showed uncommon skills as a coalition-builder and party spokesman. When that four-year stint expired at the end of 1988, colleagues promoted him to chairman of the House Democratic Caucus and, just months later, to the suddenly vacated No. 3 job of House majority whip.

From mid-1987, when Gray first announced his candidacy to succeed Caucus Chairman Richard A. Gephardt, he was the front-runner in a contest still more than a year away. He seasoned his political claim to the post with money, giving more than $136,000 to House Democrats. The final tally in December 1988 was 146 votes for Gray, 80 for Caucus Vice Chairman Mary Rose Oakar of Ohio and 33 for Mike Synar of Oklahoma. The next June, when Coelho resigned rather than face an ethics investigation, Gray was the immediate favorite to replace him. He took 134 votes on the first ballot — four more than the majority he needed — to 97 votes for David E. Bonior of Michigan and 30 for Beryl Anthony Jr. of Arkansas.

Gray approached the job differently from Coelho, who ran the whip's organization with a determination bordering on religious fervor. Gray did not spend as much time socializing on the House floor as Coelho, who savored regular personal contact with his colleagues and employed it in his whip strategy.

Coelho was also the consummate partisan. Gray, too, has launched assaults on Republican administrations. But that more public aspect of Gray dissipated in the 101st Congress, as Gephardt, the new majority leader, adopted the role of partisan spokesman. In the wake of Gray's 1991 resignation announcement, one Democrat observed, "I know he has not enjoyed being whip. He's not a nuts-and-bolts guy. He enjoys politics in the sense that he can move people, but the whip's job is more mechanical."

Gray was conspicuous during the crafting of the fiscal 1991 budget agreement. He was one of the 20 negotiators from Congress and the executive branch at the budget summit, held in seclusion at Andrews Air Force Base. The agreement that the summit issued, however, was untenable, as liberals and conservative Republicans deserted it.

From the time he arrived in Congress just a dozen years ago as a first-time officeholder in a class full of seasoned pros, Gray jumped knowingly into House politics by aligning with those outside his natural base of urban liberals and the Congressional Black Caucus. In particular, fellow Pennsylvanian John P. Murtha, a power broker with a small-town, white ethnic constituency, helped Gray win choice seats on Budget and on Steering and Policy as a freshman. Two years later, Gray landed a coveted place on the Appropriations Committee.

By late 1984, overcoming concern that a black liberal could not be a serious budget-cutter, Gray had put together a diverse regional and ideological coalition to win the Budget chairmanship. The coalition mirrored the unity he would help bring to the once-fractured party over the next four years, as Democrats finally assaulted President Ronald Reagan's fiscal policies.

The testament to Gray's success is the combined Democratic vote for the four budget resolutions he shepherded through the House in Reagan's second term — 919-77. That means hardly more defections over four years than the party suffered in most single years in Reagan's first term. A clever consensus builder, Gray treated the budget process as a political puzzle, not an economic problem; he saw the budget for what it is: a political statement rather than a blueprint for fiscal governance.

He let members debate issues for hours, exasperating them but ultimately forcing them into commitments. Meeting perhaps the hardest test of all, he got along better than his predecessors with the territorial chairmen of the authorizing committees and Appropriations, who do not conceal their disdain for Budget and the spending limitations it seeks to impose.

That is not to suggest Gray did not make enemies. His natural allies among Budget and Black Caucus liberals groused throughout the 100th Congress that in his drive to cut deals with conservatives, Gray left liberals' interests — and some of his promises to them — on the cutting room floor. Several would later support his rivals for Democratic Caucus chairman. But Gray retained the trust of Southern Boll Weevils such as Texan Charles W. Stenholm, who helped him end the Democratic desertions of the early Reagan years. In a speech to the Caucus supporting Gray's election as its chairman, Stenholm praised the big-city Easterner for showing "West Texas tractor-seat common sense."

At Appropriations, Gray has fought hard for Africa aid programs. He ceased being active on that panel after becoming Budget chairman and then a leadership official, but Gray worked through his staff and allies on Appropriations to attend to hometown interests, such as mass transit and housing.

Gray sparked a ferocious intrastate scuffle in 1990 by adding language to the transportation appropriations bill to cut Pennsylvania's federal highway funds by 25 percent — about \$144 million — unless the state agreed to adopt a dedicated funding source for the state's mass transit systems. The provision, added during the House-Senate conference on the bill, was aimed at forcing Pennsylvania to fund SEPTA, the mass transit authority that serves metropolitan Philadelphia, as well as the state's 37 other mass transit authorities.

Pennsylvania's two GOP senators, Arlen Specter and John Heinz, vigorously protested the provision — Specter called it blackmail of rural Pennsylvanians — and their opposition held up Senate passage of the bill. The three lawmakers met with Senate Appropriations leaders and agreed to delay the threatened cut for a year.

Gray's behind-the-scenes acumen was on prominent display in his 1984 campaign for the Budget chairmanship. Most Democrats concentrated on the rivalry between James R. Jones of Oklahoma, who had been Budget chairman for four years, and Leon E. Panetta of California, who wanted the job. To be eligible for the chairmanship, both needed a change of the rule limiting service on Budget.

Gray sidestepped the Jones-Panetta argument, simply asking members to vote for him if the rule was not changed. In the end, Speaker Thomas P. O'Neill Jr. of Massachusetts opposed the change and the Democratic Caucus went along. When Martin Frost of Texas launched a last-minute bid for chairman, he found Gray had the votes sewn up.

O'Neill also aided Gray by naming to Budget three fiscally conservative Democrats who served as able links to party moderates and conservatives; Gray could thus be confident of selling his proposals to the entire Democratic House if he had his panel's support. In 1985, the fiscal conservatives failed to sway the committee, but they promised to support Gray's budget in return for a chance to offer their own on the floor. Theirs lost badly; Gray won all but 15 Democrats and even got 24 Republican votes. The next year, Congress and the White House agreed to reach the deficit target mandated by the Gramm-Rudman anti-deficit law largely by accounting gimmicks rather than taxes or spending cuts.

After Democrats regained control of the Senate in 1987, Gray took the lead on that year's budget. In committee Democrats' private talks, he first had to smooth over the growing tension between conservatives concerned about defense cuts and liberals unwilling to endure more domestic program cuts. Republicans, meanwhile, decided not to participate at all, even helping vote down Reagan's budget, 27-394. Gray's budget passed the House without a single GOP vote.

But that year and the next, Gray's fellow Democrats in the Senate would prove the bigger obstacle. In the 1987 conference, Gray negotiated privately with Senate Budget Committee Chairman Lawton Chiles of Florida, whose demands reflected his desire to assuage both conservative Democrats and some Republicans, given Senate Democrats' small majority. It was at this time that Gray's former liberal allies began muttering that he was giving too much away. Still the impasse persisted, until unfavorable publicity spurred congressional leaders to compel an agreement.

Gray's final year as Budget chairman in 1988 was eased by the fact that, in late 1987, Reagan and congressional leaders reached a modest, two-year budget agreement. Yet relations between House and Senate Democrats deteriorated, in a clash that was less one of substance than of egos and institutional rivalries. In conference, Gray and Chiles exchanged insults and charges of bad faith. But they had been rendered less relevant as the House and Senate Appropriations committees began work without a final budget resolution.

In his first term, as a member of Foreign Affairs, Gray won establishment of a new African development program, an unusual achievement for a freshman.

At Home: The church, a dominant institution in black North Philadelphia, was Gray's springboard to a political career. Like his father and grandfather before him, Gray is the chief minister of the 4,000-member Bright Hope Baptist Church. Two Sundays every month, he returns home to preach there. On election days, his parishioners are out working for him.

This church support was vital to him in 1978, when he ousted 73-year-old Robert N. C. Nix Jr., whom Gray dubbed "the phantom," charging that he made only infrequent visits to the district.

Nix had the allegiance of ward leaders and organized labor, and had held off Gray by 339 votes in the 1976 Democratic primary. But Gray trounced him in 1978. Gray got endorsements from such national black figures as Atlanta Mayor Maynard Jackson and Coretta Scott King. He also won the backing of the white Philadelphia business community.

A few old-guard Nix allies still view Gray with suspicion, but his main political troubles have come from young militants who say he is too close to the white power structure.

One faction made an attempt to dump him in 1982. The challenge came from Milton Street, a tough-talking black state senator. Street had switched his party allegiance from Democratic to Republican in 1980 as part of a deal that brought the GOP control of the state Senate.

Street tried to find a black to challenge Gray in the Democratic primary, and when none emerged he decided to become a candidate himself in the general election. The Republican filing deadline had passed, however, so he had to go on the November ballot as an independent.

The result, though, was not even close. Gray drew more than three-fourths of the vote, securing his hold on the district.

Committees

Majority Whip *

Appropriations (22nd of 37 Democrats)
Foreign Operations, Export Financing & Related Programs; Transportation

District of Columbia (3rd of 8 Democrats)
Fiscal Affairs & Health; Government Operations & Metropolitan Affairs

House Administration (13th of 15 Democrats)
Elections; Procurement & Printing; Campaign Finance Reform

** Gray announced June 20, 1991, that he would resign from the House in early September 1991 to become president of the United Negro College Fund. He planned to remain as whip until his departure.*

Elections

1990 General

William H. Gray III (D)	94,584	(92%)
Donald Bakove (R)	8,118	(8%)

1988 General

William H. Gray III (D)	184,322	(94%)
Richard L. Harsch (R)	12,365	(6%)

Previous Winning Percentages: **1986** (98%) **1984** (91%) **1982** (76%) **1980** (96%) **1978** (82%)

District Vote For President

	1988		1984		1980		1976	
D	189,477	(91%)	211,740	(89%)	179,978	(86%)	171,872	(82%)
R	17,125	(8%)	24,613	(10%)	19,058	(9%)	32,849	(16%)
I					7,335	(4%)		

Campaign Finance

	Receipts	Receipts from PACs	Expend-itures
1990			
Gray (D)	$725,717	$516,953 (71%)	$814,125
Bakove (R)	$135	0	$506
1988			
Gray (D)	$656,859	$377,752 (58%)	$660,456

Key Votes

1991	
Authorize use of force against Iraq	N
1990	
Support constitutional amendment on flag desecration	N
Pass family and medical leave bill over Bush veto	Y
Reduce SDI funding	Y
Allow abortions in overseas military facilities	Y
Approve budget summit plan for spending and taxing	Y
Approve civil rights bill	Y
1989	
Halt production of B-2 stealth bomber at 13 planes	Y
Oppose capital gains tax cut	Y
Approve federal abortion funding in rape or incest cases	Y
Approve pay raise and revision of ethics rules	Y
Pass Democratic minimum wage plan over Bush veto	Y

Voting Studies

	Presidential Support		Party Unity		Conservative Coalition	
Year	S	O	S	O	S	O
1990	16	76	90	2	11	81
1989	30	63	88	3	15	78
1988	14	70	78	2	11	74
1987	14	78	85	1	12	74
1986	13	77	88	1	8	82
1985	15	78	82	3	13	73
1984	19	73	90	3	7	86
1983	11	78	93	1	2	93
1982	21	65	80	5	8	84
1981	29	59	87	2	4	88

Interest Group Ratings

Year	ADA	ACU	AFL-CIO	CCUS
1990	94	0	92	14
1989	95	4	100	30
1988	95	0	100	31
1987	92	0	100	0
1986	80	5	92	33
1985	95	0	93	15
1984	90	0	92	38
1983	85	0	100	21
1982	85	11	100	26
1981	90	0	93	6

3 Robert A. Borski (D)

Of Philadelphia — Elected 1982

Born: Oct. 20, 1948, Philadelphia, Pa.
Education: U. of Baltimore, B.A. 1971.
Occupation: Stockbroker.
Family: Wife, Karen Lloyd; three children.
Religion: Roman Catholic.
Political Career: Pa. House, 1977-83.
Capitol Office: 407 Cannon Bldg. 20515; 225-8251.

In Washington: Borski came to Congress after three terms as a backbencher in the Pennsylvania Legislature, and nothing in his record over four House terms has suggested much change in that low-key style of representation.

But beginning with the 102nd Congress, he will at least get the chance to prove otherwise, as he takes over the chairmanship of the Public Works Investigations and Oversight Subcommittee.

In a House where many crave a role in national and international policy-making, Borski views the world through the lens of his district; after the Persian Gulf War, he called upon President Bush to mount a similar assault upon unemployment. Although he has not been a power on either the Public Works or Merchant Marine panel, he effectively monitors activity affecting Philadelphia's port and strives to prevent federal cutbacks in his district. With the help of Philadelphia colleague William H. Gray III, who sits on the Appropriations Transportation Subcommittee, Borski has co-authored proposals for mass-transit projects, including one to reconstruct a local elevated railway line.

Borski rarely speaks on the floor or attracts publicity outside Philadelphia; he is not well-known to many of his colleagues. But he is a reliable vote for his party leadership on most key issues, except abortion.

In the 101st Congress, Borski helped pass legislation that restricted "backhauling" — the practice of permitting trucks to carry food in one direction and garbage and toxic chemicals on the way back.

Borski, first elected with the help of Irish-Americans (who make up roughly one-third of his district's population), unintentionally ruffled some British feathers as a freshman when, on a trip to Northern Ireland, he met with leaders of Sinn Fein, the political wing of the Irish Republican Army, which militantly opposes British rule.

At Home: Borski may not cut a high profile in Washington, but his concentration on local issues and his assiduous courtship of constituents so far has given him a firm grip on a once-Republican seat.

Overwhelmingly white and middle class, the 3rd was the only Philadelphia district to support George Bush in 1988 and is the only one to elect a GOP congressman in the last three decades. But by playing the role of the old-time urban congressman, Borski has rebuffed GOP challenges.

Borski launched himself toward Congress by managing another candidate's campaign — the losing 1981 special election effort of Democratic City Chairman David Glancey in the old 3rd District. Borski emerged from the effort with greater visibility and a determination to run for Congress himself. In 1982, when redistricting grafted his state legislative base in the blue-collar "river ward" of Bridesburg onto GOP Rep. Charles Dougherty's territory in Philadelphia's semi-suburban Northeast, Borski made his move.

More experienced Democrats stayed out, convinced Dougherty was too strong. Despite the recession, several unions sided with the more dynamic and articulate Dougherty. But concerns about reductions in Social Security helped Borski, and Dougherty's disdain for the Irish Republican Army hurt him. With economic discontent strong in blue-collar Philadelphia, the clean-cut Borski seemed a good vehicle for protesting hard times. He won by 2,664 votes.

After Borski won easily in 1984, Dougherty tried a comeback in 1986, only to lose the GOP primary to former state Sen. Robert A. Rovner. But Rovner was dogged by controversy: He had lost his Senate seat in 1974 after being indicted for extortion and income-tax evasion. Although acquitted, he drew criticism after that for hosting bus trips to Atlantic City for Bucks County district judges. Rovner tried to tie Borski to Philadelphia's controversial black mayor, W. Wilson Goode, but Borski kept the focus on his steadiness and accessibility, and won by over 40,000 votes. In 1988, Borski reached 63 percent. But in 1990 he slipped slightly to 60 percent of the vote. Republican Joseph Marc McColgan, a young former Navy officer, might have run closer if he had been able to find money for a late advertising campaign.

Pennsylvania 3

Northeast Philadelphia

In a city of deep-rooted neighborhoods, Philadelphia's 3rd District is somewhat of an anomaly. With the exception of the "river wards" — the Polish and Irish communities that front the Delaware River — most of the 3rd is made up of people who have migrated there in the past generation from other parts of the city. This is particularly true in the Great Northeast (so named because of its geographic expanse). In much of this area, the surroundings are more suburban than urban. In the 1950s, there were still some farms here.

Much of the migration from the inner city came about after the growth of the black population in North and West Philadelphia. This accounts, in part, for the overwhelmingly white population of the 3rd. Concern about crime inspires conservative social attitudes in the neat little houses along the tree-lined streets of this area. Former Mayor Frank Rizzo's tough law-and-order image made him a hero here.

The Great Northeast has a large Jewish population, concentrated west of Roosevelt Boulevard. Farther east, Irish and other Catholic ethnics predominate.

The 3rd is the only Philadelphia district where Republicans have a chance to be competitive. Ronald Reagan won it against Jimmy Carter in 1980, taking all except two wards. And even though 1982 redistricting added some Democratic river wards, Reagan won the 3rd again in 1984, as did George Bush in 1988. The areas added in the remap were Frankford and Bridesburg, both of which have been hit hard by factory layoffs.

On the presidential level, the best ward for Republicans is the 66th, a favorite residence of police officers and firefighters. Prevailing opinion is different in Oak Lane and West Oak Lane, two sections that line the border with suburban Montgomery County. Here, young professional whites and middle-class blacks prefer a more liberal brand of politics.

Population: 516,154. White 470,248 (91%), Black 39,120 (8%), Other 4,128 (1%). Spanish origin 5,683 (1%). 18 and over 391,605 (76%), 65 and over 80,592 (16%). Median age: 35.

Committees

Merchant Marine & Fisheries (10th of 29 Democrats)
Merchant Marine; Oversight & Investigations

Public Works & Transportation (10th of 36 Democrats)
Investigations & Oversight (chairman); Public Buildings & Grounds; Water Resources

Select Aging (16th of 42 Democrats)
Health & Long-Term Care

Elections

1990 General		
Robert A. Borski (D)	89,908	(60%)
Joseph Marc McColgan (R)	59,901	(40%)
1988 General		
Robert A. Borski (D)	135,590	(63%)
Mark Matthews (R)	78,909	(37%)

Previous Winning Percentages: **1986** (62%) **1984** (64%) **1982** (50%)

District Vote For President

	1988		1984		1980		1976	
D	105,791	(47%)	116,330	(46%)	100,811	(41%)	148,687	(56%)
R	115,404	(52%)	136,340	(54%)	124,484	(50%)	110,829	(42%)
I					19,789	(8%)		

Campaign Finance

	Receipts	Receipts from PACs		Expend-itures
1990				
Borski (D)	$325,222	$152,800	(47%)	$277,011
McColgan (R)	$74,723	$1,000	(1%)	$74,417
1988				
Borski (D)	$337,723	$189,654	(56%)	$250,480
Matthews (R)	$23,071	0		$23,101

Key Votes

1991	
Authorize use of force against Iraq	Y
1990	
Support constitutional amendment on flag desecration	N
Pass family and medical leave bill over Bush veto	Y
Reduce SDI funding	Y
Allow abortions in overseas military facilities	N
Approve budget summit plan for spending and taxing	N
Approve civil rights bill	Y
1989	
Halt production of B-2 stealth bomber at 13 planes	N
Oppose capital gains tax cut	Y
Approve federal abortion funding in rape or incest cases	N
Approve pay raise and revision of ethics rules	Y
Pass Democratic minimum wage plan over Bush veto	Y

Voting Studies

	Presidential Support		Party Unity		Conservative Coalition	
Year	**S**	**O**	**S**	**O**	**S**	**O**
1990	27	71	90	7	33	67
1989	41	59	87	10	41	59
1988	26	73	92	6	24	74
1987	19	81	91	3	26	72
1986	20	77	93	6	24	76
1985	24	74	94	4	20	78
1984	30	68	93	6	17	81
1983	21	73	91	6	16	83

Interest Group Ratings

Year	ADA	ACU	AFL-CIO	CCUS
1990	83	8	100	21
1989	75	7	92	50
1988	80	12	100	23
1987	80	5	100	13
1986	75	10	100	33
1985	80	5	88	23
1984	75	8	100	38
1983	85	4	100	20

4 Joe Kolter (D)

Of New Brighton — Elected 1982

Born: Sept. 3, 1926, McDonald, Ohio.
Education: Geneva College, B.S. and B.A. 1950.
Military Service: Air Force, 1945-46.
Occupation: Accountant.
Family: Wife, Dorothy Gray; four children.
Religion: Roman Catholic.
Political Career: New Brighton City Council, 1962-66; Pa. House, 1968-83; sought Democratic nomination for U.S. House, 1974.
Capitol Office: 212 Cannon Bldg. 20515; 225-2565.

In Washington: Kolter is the kind of member who measures the breadth of his political success by the width of the highways in his district.

During the 101st Congress he coaxed Norman Mineta, D-Calif., a subcommittee chairman on Public Works, to his district to plead for funds to build a new expressway. On a day-long tour of country roads (during which Mineta nodded off), Kolter told a *Wall Street Journal* reporter that he envied his neighboring colleague, GOP Rep. Bud Shuster, whose name is immortalized on a throughway. "All he has are four-lane highways over there," Kolter told the *Journal.*

Kolter, who ascended to the chair of the Economic Development subcommittee of Public Works in the 102nd Congress, has concentrated on committee work and voicing the concerns of industrial workers in his economically distressed district. Although he has managed to obtain some federal money — such as a $4 million appropriation in 1990 for a truck bypass — he has run into obstacles, including Mineta, who chaired the Aviation Subcommittee in the 100th Congress before taking over the Surface Transportation Subcommittee.

Kolter took the unusual step of inviting committee colleagues to contribute projects to an amendment he planned to offer to the 1987 airport-reauthorization bill. This flouted Mineta's opposition to naming specific programs.

One member labeled Kolter's $200 million proposal the "pork amendment of 1987." But Democrat Douglas H. Bosco defended Kolter, saying the only reason to be on Public Works is "to bring home projects.... [It is] certainly not for intellectual stimulation." The amendment was defeated 9-18.

An early 1987 dabble in foreign affairs brought Kolter both success and some embarrassment. Following revelations that proceeds from U.S. arms sales to Iran had been diverted to the Nicaraguan contras, Kolter proposed in January 1987 that additional contra aid be withheld until all previous aid was accounted for. A modified version of this proposal passed the House in March, but it died in the Senate.

Kolter stirred up trouble for himself, however, with a TV appearance on C-SPAN during which he referred to the U.S.-backed contra forces as "communists" and portrayed UNO, an umbrella contra organization, as an individual rather than a group.

Kolter's staff later said he meant to call the contras "totalitarian" instead of "communist," and blamed his errors on the fact that he was a last-minute replacement on the show and had misread his notes.

At Home: It is hard to tell what to make of Kolter's 56 percent vote share in 1990 — his lowest ever. It could have been the product of an anti-incumbent tide that washed away Democratic Rep. Doug Walgren in the neighboring 18th, or it could have been the response of an electorate that has begun to view Kolter as an anachronistic practitioner of pork barrel politics in an age of budgetary limits.

At the least, Kolter's showing should put him on guard. His underfinanced Republican opponent, a college chemistry professor, was the same candidate that Kolter crushed in 1988 with 70 percent of the vote.

Kolter's recent campaigns have drawn little attention outside his western Pennsylvania district, in contrast to his 1982 challenge to GOP Rep. Eugene V. Atkinson, a Democrat who had switched parties the previous year.

The race drew national attention. Democrats targeted Atkinson to discourage further conversions to the GOP; saving Atkinson was a priority for the national Republican Party.

Kolter was far outspent and could muster the money to run his single TV ad only the week before the election. Still, his 3-to-2 victory was no surprise, given the towering jobless rate in the 4th. Kolter, who boasted an almost perfect labor record in the Legislature, called Atkinson a traitor to working people, and the Republican's rejoinder — that Reaganomics would benefit the district in the long run — was not well received.

Pennsylvania 4

West — New Castle

In the last round of redistricting, the GOP-controlled Pennsylvania Legislature tried to make the 4th more Republican, to help its newly converted GOP incumbent hold on in the 1982 election. But Democrat Joe Kolter recaptured the district that year and has held it since, though his lukewarm 1990 56 percent tally indicated that Republicans still matter here.

Steel-producing Beaver County is firmly Democratic, though its clout in the 4th was reduced some by the 1982 remap; Beaver casts less than one-third of the district's vote, a slightly larger share than neighboring Butler County, which is considerably more Republican.

The northern portion of Beaver is in the 4th, along with Aliquippa and a few other towns in the county. Union influence remains strong in northern Beaver County. Though Republicans often pick up votes from the farms outside Beaver Falls, Democrat Michael S. Dukakis carried the county by nearly 2-to-1 in 1988.

Lawrence County (New Castle), frustrated by steel-plant closings in nearby Youngstown, Ohio, flirted with Ronald Reagan in 1980, almost giving him a majority. But that did not last; Walter F. Mondale won Lawrence in 1984, Dukakis carried it in 1988, and it has voted Democratic in the last three gubernatorial elections.

Butler County, however, voted Republican for president in 1980, 1984 and 1988, as well as in both the Senate and gubernatorial elections in 1986. Armstrong County, a swing area, went for Dukakis in 1988. Kittanning, a commercial center, is the party's best town in Armstrong.

At the eastern end of the 4th is Indiana County, which last went Democratic for president in 1964. Actor Jimmy Stewart grew up in the small town of Indiana; a local airport is named for him. The county is a mixture of coal mines and farms, and its rural vote is dominant. One small slice of Westmoreland County also is part of the 4th. It is the Ligonier Valley, where the Pittsburgh elite maintain summer homes.

Population: 515,572. White 499,971 (97%), Black 13,506 (3%). Spanish origin 1,876 (0.4%). 18 and over 375,245 (73%), 65 and over 62,104 (12%). Median age: 31.

Committees

House Administration (9th of 15 Democrats)
Libraries & Memorials; Personnel & Police

Public Works & Transportation (11th of 36 Democrats)
Aviation; Economic Development (chairman); Public Buildings & Grounds; Water Resources

Joint Library

Elections

1990 General		
Joe Kolter (D)	74,114	(56%)
Gordon R. Johnston (R)	58,469	(44%)
1990 Primary		
Joe Kolter (D)	31,955	(83%)
Frank M. Clark (D)	6,613	(17%)
1988 General		
Joe Kolter (D)	124,041	(70%)
Gordon R. Johnston (R)	52,402	(29%)

Previous Winning Percentages: **1986** (60%) **1984** (57%) **1982** (60%)

District Vote For President

	1988		1984		1980		1976	
D	97,696	(54%)	106,267	(52%)	82,901	(45%)	92,937	(50%)
R	80,911	(45%)	98,148	(48%)	87,644	(48%)	87,987	(48%)
I					10,289	(6%)		

Campaign Finance

	Receipts	Receipts from PACs		Expend-itures
1990				
Kolter (D)	$199,605	$162,520	(81%)	$132,920
Johnston (R)	$8,870	0		$8,837
1988				
Kolter (D)	$175,980	$146,606	(83%)	$90,710

Key Votes

1991	
Authorize use of force against Iraq	N
1990	
Support constitutional amendment on flag desecration	Y
Pass family and medical leave bill over Bush veto	Y
Reduce SDI funding	Y
Allow abortions in overseas military facilities	N
Approve budget summit plan for spending and taxing	N
Approve civil rights bill	Y
1989	
Halt production of B-2 stealth bomber at 13 planes	N
Oppose capital gains tax cut	Y
Approve federal abortion funding in rape or incest cases	N
Approve pay raise and revision of ethics rules	N
Pass Democratic minimum wage plan over Bush veto	Y

Voting Studies

	Presidential Support		Party Unity		Conservative Coalition	
Year	**S**	**O**	**S**	**O**	**S**	**O**
1990	24	69	83	13	52	44
1989	45	48	73	17	54	39
1988	26	63	78	11	45	37
1987	32	61	78	10	53	44
1986	26	72	83	15	54	44
1985	28	69	80	12	38	60
1984	29	65	80	14	27	64
1983	13	67	77	12	30	62

Interest Group Ratings

Year	ADA	ACU	AFL-CIO	CCUS
1990	44	30	92	36
1989	65	28	100	40
1988	60	22	100	17
1987	68	5	100	36
1986	70	14	100	33
1985	65	10	69	23
1984	65	23	92	38
1983	80	14	100	10

Pennsylvania - 5th District

5 Dick Schulze (R)

Of Tredyffrin — Elected 1974

Born: Aug. 7, 1929, Philadelphia, Pa.

Education: Attended U. of Houston, 1949-50; Villanova U., 1952; Temple U., 1968.

Military Service: Army, 1951-53.

Occupation: Household-appliance dealer.

Family: Widowed; four children.

Religion: Presbyterian.

Political Career: Tredyffrin Township Republican Committee, 1960-67; Chester County Registrar of Wills and Clerk of Orphans Court, 1967-69; Pa. House, 1969-75.

Capitol Office: 2267 Rayburn Bldg. 20515; 225-5761.

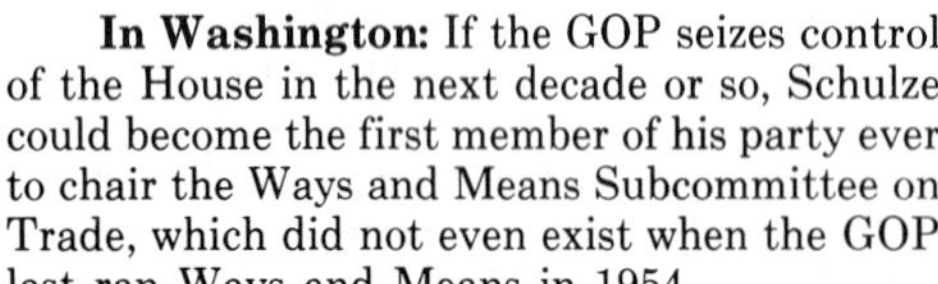

In Washington: If the GOP seizes control of the House in the next decade or so, Schulze could become the first member of his party ever to chair the Ways and Means Subcommittee on Trade, which did not even exist when the GOP last ran Ways and Means in 1954.

Schulze is now the third-ranking Republican on the trade panel, and one of the two men ahead of him might well celebrate a GOP takeover by becoming chairman of the full committee (where Schulze ranks fourth). Were Schulze to get hold of the trade gavel, he would have a chance to avenge more than a decade of frustration on the issue of utmost importance to him.

Schulze, an appliance dealer from a once-proud manufacturing center, has never fully adjusted to his party's historic shift from protectionism to free trade. Instead, he advocates a "fair trade" policy of retaliation (or at least threatened retaliation) against countries with barriers to U.S. goods. This has allied him with many Democrats from Rust Belt states and placed him at odds with White House orthodoxy under Presidents Reagan and Bush.

In 1990, Schulze signaled his disaffection by sponsoring a bill reclaiming the authority to conduct trade relations. Congress has legally ceded that power to the president since 1934. "Do I really mean we should take it all back? Of course not," he said. "But every now and then I want to remind them."

Schulze's highest post within the Ways and Means power structure is the ranking Republican slot on the Oversight Subcommittee. But even there, he is likely to talk trade. In 1990, he used that perch to decry foreign firms that do business in the United States without paying "their fair share of the tax load."

Still, Schulze's sharpest clash with the Bush administration has been over trade with China. Schulze fought doggedly against renewal of full trading status (known as "most favored nation" or MFN status) for the Beijing regime after the bloody 1989 suppression of dissidents in Tiananmen Square. "I want the outrage that is ringing throughout the world to ring through the halls of Congress," he cried.

Schulze had been opposed to MFN for China since it was conditionally granted in 1980, complaining that Chinese exports were a "brutal incursion" into the domestic market that not only hurt American producers, but posed potential health hazards for American consumers. He has been exercised in particular about the dumping of Chinese mushrooms on a domestic market otherwise supplied, in large part, by Pennsylvanians. In introducing his American Mushroom Week bill in both 1989 and 1990, and in adding mushroom promotion language to the 1990 farm bill, Schulze noted that his own district is the nation's top mushroom producer.

Schulze promotes the industries of his state in general, and he does so just as single-mindedly as his predecessors did in the salad days of the Pennsylvania Manufacturers Association. In the 101st Congress, he cosponsored an extension of the international agreement restraining foreign steelmakers' exports to the United States.

Schulze's anger over the U.S. trade deficit has not been limited to the White House. He has scolded his colleagues for failing to recognize the severity of the trade-imbalance problem. As Congress worked on omnibus trade legislation in the 100th Congress, Schulze more than once expressed his "disappointment ... that it took a $170 billion trade deficit to finally remove our rose-tinted glasses."

During the debate on the 1986 trade bill, Schulze was the only Republican member of the Ways and Means Committee to vote for the controversial Gephardt amendment. That language — offered by Ways and Means member Rep. Richard A. Gephardt, D-Mo. — threatened action, such as the imposition of tariffs or quotas, to reduce large trade surpluses some countries have with the United States.

Pennsylvania 5

Western Philadelphia Suburbs — Chester

Mushrooms, horses and tract houses all grow well in the outer suburbs of Philadelphia. Despite some islands of Democratic industrial territory, this is Republican turf. About half the district's population lives in Chester County, which is the most strongly Republican of the four suburban Philadelphia counties. In 1988, Bush won 67 percent of the vote in Chester, while he tallied 60 percent in Bucks, Delaware and Montgomery counties.

Farmers around the self-designated Mushroom Capital of the World in Kennett Square keep the southern part of Chester County solid for the GOP. Nearby, the Brandywine Creek meanders through estate country, where the du Ponts and other Republican millionaires maintain their mansions.

A housing boom, however, has turned northern Chester County's coloration from rural Republican to suburban Republican. Exton, once a tiny farm town, received a giant shopping mall in the 1970s. Farther north, the 5th covers rural northern Montgomery County — most of whose Mennonite farmers have been voting Republican as a matter of habit for generations.

During the 1970s, the district had Democratic enclaves in Phoenixville and Pottstown. In 1980s redistricting, these were joined by another small mill town, Coatesville. But a more significant infusion of Democrats comes from the city of Chester, a run-down part of Delaware County with struggling industries. Democrats in Chester and the other industrial towns in the 5th are consigned to a small minority in the district's electorate.

Population: 515,528. White 449,987 (87%), Black 57,488 (11%), Other 3,666 (1%). Spanish origin 8,294 (2%). 18 and over 370,556 (72%), 65 and over 50,556 (10%). Median age: 31.

Schulze altered his course in the 1987 trade debate, and joined most of his Republican colleagues in voting against a similar amendment offered by Gephardt. Unlike most Republicans, however, Schulze voted for the entire bill even though it contained the Gephardt amendment.

Schulze supported other trade measures opposed by the administration. "We're viewed around the world as being Mr. Nice Guy," he said at one point. "We talk tough, but we don't usually deliver." Schulze reserves some of his harshest words on trade for Japan, railing against its "grossly unfair barriers." "It defies common sense," he said in 1987, "how Japan can criticize the protectionist provisions in our trade bill while maintaining some of the most stringent import barriers in the world."

But if Schulze found himself swimming against the GOP tide on trade in the 101st, he did share in two notably successful challenges to the will of Ways and Means Chairman Dan Rostenkowski. The first was the 1989 repeal of the surtax by which seniors' catastrophic health care insurance was to have been financed. The second, less final victory, was the committee's passage of a reduction in the capital gains tax rate in September of 1989. Although approved by the House, the cut was killed in the Senate.

The vehicle for tax-law changes in 1988 was the sweeping "technical corrections" bill, ostensibly passed to fix typographical errors in the 99th Congress' tax bill, but adding a variety of new provisions. Schulze was a sponsor of the "Taxpayer Bill of Rights" that was attached to the technical corrections bill. He also attached a measure to continue an exemption from the Social Security self-employment tax for Amish, Hutterites and Mennonites, who are conscientiously opposed to public insurance.

His contribution to 99th Congress tax reform efforts had a similarly local flavor, with such things as tax breaks for the tuxedo business in Pennsylvania. But also Schulze was bitterly opposed to the bill being written largely by the committee's Democrats and seemed more concerned with sinking it than trying to improve it. He did suggest his own idea, a "business alternative minimum tax" on business receipts, which would have provided revenues for the retention of investment incentives. But this was not seriously considered.

His one departure from predictability in the tax bill debate left most colleagues puzzled. He offered an amendment in committee to bar the Internal Revenue Service from granting tax-exempt status to religious organizations that promote "satanism" or "witchcraft." That proposal, which was also pushed by Republican Jesse Helms in the Senate, was not among the priorities of most committee members.

At Home: A spate of unflattering publicity helped hold Schulze to 57 percent of the vote in 1990, his lowest congressional vote share ever.

The *Philadelphia Inquirer* wrote several pieces about Schulze during the campaign. Probably the most critical was a mid-October article that implied that Schulze had used his position on the Ways and Means Committee to seek tariff relief or tax-law changes for a number of trade organizations and manufacturers, many of which provided him with campaign money, honoraria or free trips.

Schulze denied any wrongdoing, responding to the charges with a written statement in mid-October that referred to "Philadelphia gutter-type political tactics." The charges, he wrote, were based on "twisting facts to create the appearance of impropriety." That, however, did not stop Schulze's Democratic opponent from saying that the incumbent was "for lease."

Adding to the combustible nature of the campaign was the independent candidacy of Lewis du Pont Smith, a follower of Lyndon H. LaRouche Jr. Smith's wealthy family had gone to court several years earlier to have him declared legally incompetent after he had contributed or lent several hundred thousand dollars to a LaRouche organization. Smith spent much of 1990 back in court trying to get access to money to run his campaign.

Normally, Schulze's campaigns have not been so colorful. He came up through the ranks of Chester County politics, taking on such chores as chairmanship of Nixon Day festivities in 1968 and serving as county registrar of wills. In November 1968, he was elected to the state Legislature.

As a dependable party man, he got his chance to run for Congress in 1974 when GOP Rep. John H. Ware III announced his retirement. Schulze got organization backing, but faced a rough primary against four opponents.

Schulze's top competitor was Robin West, a wealthy young former aide in the Nixon White House. West had a host of volunteers and favorable publicity from a laudatory column about him in *Time* magazine. Using his family money, he outspent Schulze, whom he blasted as "the machine candidate." But Schulze, reminding voters that "I don't drive a Ferrari," easily outdistanced the field.

In 1986, Schulze faced an energetic challenger in Tim Ringgold, a West Point graduate and former Army captain. Ringgold mocked the incumbent as "the invisible congressman" and drew some good reviews; the *Inquirer* endorsed him, saying it preferred "vigor over seniority." But Schulze took two-thirds of the vote.

Committees

Interior & Insular Affairs (12th of 17 Republicans)
National Parks & Public Lands; Water, Power & Offshore Energy

Ways & Means (4th of 13 Republicans)
Oversight (ranking); Social Security; Trade

Elections

1990 General		
Dick Schulze (R)	75,097	(57%)
Samuel C. Stretton (D)	50,597	(38%)
Lewis Dupont Smith (ASI)	5,795	(4%)
1988 General		
Dick Schulze (R)	153,453	(78%)
Donald A. Hadley (D)	42,758	(22%)

Previous Winning Percentages: **1986** (66%) **1984** (73%) **1982** (67%) **1980** (75%) **1978** (75%) **1976** (60%) **1974** (60%)

District Vote For President

	1988	1984	1980	1976
D	70,744 (35%)	66,501 (33%)	57,836 (32%)	73,374 (42%)
R	132,933 (65%)	134,327 (67%)	106,938 (58%)	100,620 (57%)
I			15,678 (9%)	

Campaign Finance

	Receipts	Receipts from PACs		Expend-itures
1990				
Schulze (R)	$578,161	$370,759	(64%)	$672,705
Stretton (D)	$26,717	$3,000	(11%)	$26,396
1988				
Schulze (R)	$428,745	$258,420	(60%)	$444,205

Key Votes

1991	
Authorize use of force against Iraq	Y
1990	
Support constitutional amendment on flag desecration	Y
Pass family and medical leave bill over Bush veto	N
Reduce SDI funding	N
Allow abortions in overseas military facilities	N
Approve budget summit plan for spending and taxing	N
Approve civil rights bill	Y
1989	
Halt production of B-2 stealth bomber at 13 planes	Y
Oppose capital gains tax cut	N
Approve federal abortion funding in rape or incest cases	N
Approve pay raise and revision of ethics rules	Y
Pass Democratic minimum wage plan over Bush veto	N

Voting Studies

	Presidential Support		Party Unity		Conservative Coalition	
Year	S	O	S	O	S	O
1990	61	37	67	23	74	13
1989	69	30	64	33	85	15
1988	55	40	63	30	84	13
1987	65	28	62	26	84	16
1986	58	37	60	29	60	14
1985	64	33	68	23	82	15
1984	62	27	68	21	85	10
1983	72	23	75	11	83	8
1982	57	31	63	15	73	11
1981	70	14	87	6	93	4

Interest Group Ratings

Year	ADA	ACU	AFL-CIO	CCUS
1990	17	71	27	86
1989	20	71	25	90
1988	30	76	46	92
1987	4	77	25	85
1986	15	58	46	81
1985	10	71	29	82
1984	5	60	25	69
1983	10	77	0	80
1982	15	56	31	81
1981	10	100	13	94

6 Gus Yatron (D)

Of Reading — Elected 1968

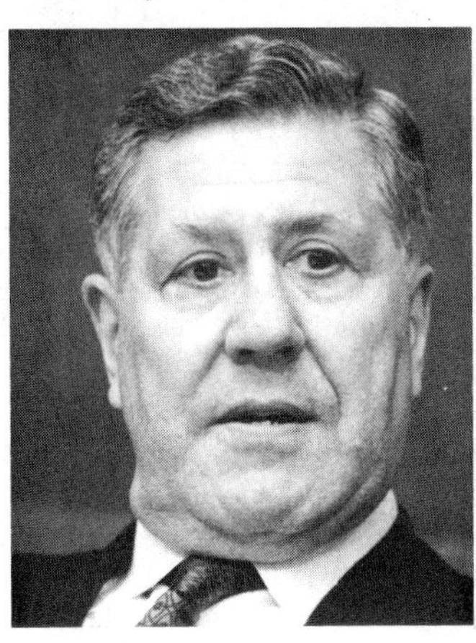

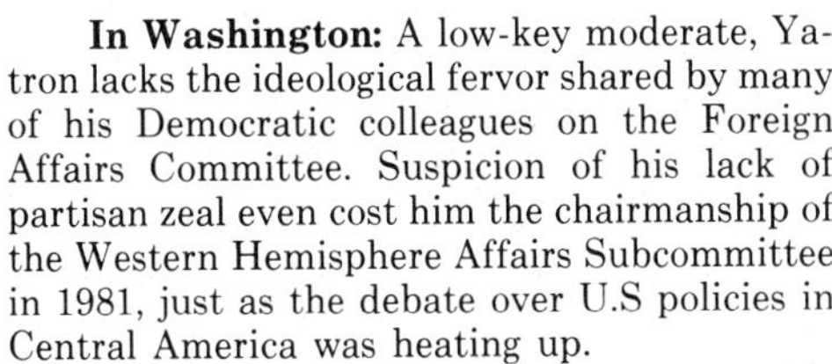

Born: Oct. 16, 1927, Reading, Pa.
Education: Attended Kutztown State U., 1950.
Occupation: Ice cream manufacturer; professional boxer.
Family: Wife, Millie Menzies; two children.
Religion: Greek Orthodox.
Political Career: Reading School Board, 1955-57; Pa. House, 1957-61; Pa. Senate, 1961-69.
Capitol Office: 2205 Rayburn Bldg. 20515; 225-5546.

In Washington: A low-key moderate, Yatron lacks the ideological fervor shared by many of his Democratic colleagues on the Foreign Affairs Committee. Suspicion of his lack of partisan zeal even cost him the chairmanship of the Western Hemisphere Affairs Subcommittee in 1981, just as the debate over U.S policies in Central America was heating up.

Yet Yatron has recouped much of his standing in his latest role as chairman of the Foreign Affairs Subcommittee on Human Rights and International Organizations. The non-ideological approach that contributed to that earlier setback is more appreciated at Human Rights, where he challenges U.S. friends and adversaries alike.

Though he is the third-most senior Democrat on Foreign Affairs, Yatron is not usually in the thick of crafting major committee legislation. But with his subcommittee chairmanship Yatron has staked out a role as a leading House advocate of placing human rights concerns at the center of U.S. foreign policy-making.

Yatron has frequently criticized President Bush — as he did President Ronald Reagan before him — for practicing a pragmatic, Realpolitik-style foreign policy that pays insufficient heed to human rights concerns. In February 1990, he called for "a policy which places America's commitment to human rights and democratic institutions above offending ruthless regimes, with which the administration is currently seeking to curry favor."

One such regime Yatron criticized during the 101st Congress was that of Saddam Hussein in Iraq. Yatron had supported efforts to institute trade sanctions after Saddam's military attacked members of Iraq's Kurdish minority with poison gas in 1988. When an embargo failed to clear the 100th Congress, Yatron pursued a non-binding resolution condemning Iraq for a "consistent pattern of gross [human rights] violations" and calling on the Bush administration to confront Saddam about these concerns.

Interest in the measure, introduced in April 1990, was fueled by Saddam's increasingly belligerent tone. But the Bush administration opposed the resolution, citing the need to avoid a disruption in the nation's strategic relationship with Iraq.

Iraq "is an important country, with an important role to play in the region," said State Department official Edward Gnehm at a Human Rights Subcommittee hearing. "We hope this role will be a constructive one." Although the resolution passed Yatron's subcommittee, it went no further.

Yatron, a consistent supporter of trade sanctions as a tool of U.S. foreign policy, favored continuation of the international trade embargo that was later enforced against Iraq following the invasion of Kuwait, and voted in January 1991 against authorizing Bush to use military force against Iraq.

Yatron also played a role in debate over U.S. policy toward China following the Tiananmen Square massacre of pro-democracy protesters in June 1989. Yatron and many other House members argued for strict sanctions, including a revocation of most-favored-nation trade status, against China. However, the Bush administration, fearing a rupture of the United States' fragile ties with the world's most populous nation, held out successfully for limited sanctions.

Yatron's efforts are not always at cross-purposes with the White House. In May 1989, he sponsored a Bush-supported resolution barring U.S. funding for any international agency or organization that admitted the Palestine Liberation Organization (PLO) as a full-fledged member state. The measure was aimed specifically at the World Health Organization, which had made moves to endorse PLO membership.

Because of his opposition to Iraq, his skepticism of the PLO and his support for the emigration of Soviet Jews, Yatron is generally seen as a friend to Israel. However, Yatron has steered his panel into some politically choppy waters by holding hearings on alleged Israeli abuses of Palestinian Arabs during unrest in the occupied West Bank. While Yatron assured advocates of Israel in 1988 that U.S. support for

Pennsylvania 6

Southeast — Reading

Politics here have changed a bit since the area's two most famous authors wrote novels about their birthplaces.

John Updike's "Rabbit Run" explores the ethnic, working-class life of his home, Berks County (Reading). In Updike's Reading (which he calls Brewer), life has a Democratic flavor. John O'Hara's "Appointment in Samarra" focuses on the wealthy families that rule the fictionalized version of his native Schuylkill County (Pottsville). In Pottsville, which O'Hara calls Gibbsville, Republicans are in charge.

Though the old political patterns are still visible, changing economic conditions have made voting behavior less predictable in both Berks and Schuylkill counties.

Reading, once known for its railroad and heavy industry, now is famous for its discount outlet stores, which lure busloads of bargain hunters from far away. The growth of the outlets and attendant development of a diversified light industrial base around Reading have helped Berks County fare better economically than some other once-mighty industrial centers in Pennsylvania. The power of the local unions has faded somewhat, and with it the Democratic habits of the voters.

In 1982, when GOP Gov. Dick Thornburgh's re-election bid was jeopardized by recession, Berks voted for Thornburgh. In 1988, George Bush won 62 percent of the Berks vote, aided by strong support from Reading's suburbs and surrounding farming country. Yatron won Berks County only narrowly in his 1990 re-election.

At first blush, it seems odd that the GOP should have been the traditional power in Schuylkill County; it is a coal-laden area, and Democrats usually fare well among coal miners. But the Eastern Europeans who toiled in the anthracite pits earlier this century had a reason to be Republican: The O'Hara characters who owned the mines made that a condition of employment.

There is still considerable loyalty to the GOP in Schuylkill, but the decline of employment in the mines has brought hard times to many in the county, and Democrats can enjoy some success here. In 1986, Schuylkill went narrowly Democratic for governor; in 1988, Michael S. Dukakis won 43 percent of the vote, better than his showing in Berks, but well below his statewide average. In 1990, Yatron's ability to carry the county decisively boosted him past an aggressive GOP challenger.

Population: 515,952. White 500,032 (97%), Black 8,055 (2%). Spanish origin 9,653 (2%). 18 and over 384,537 (75%), 65 and over 76,603 (15%). Median age: 34.

that nation had not weakened, he warned that the beating of Palestinians was "unacceptable by any standard."

Although these controversial issues attract some attention to Yatron's subcommittee, he also has used the panel as a forum to explore international environmental concerns, and his subcommittee's nuts-and-bolts work revolves around its International Organizations jurisdiction — most prominently the U.S. relationship with the United Nations.

Although many conservatives long viewed the United Nations as dominated by the Soviet Union and anti-American Third World nations, Yatron remained supportive of the institution and fought Reagan administration efforts to withhold U.S. funding for it. Yatron may now find more allies for his pro-U.N. point of view, given its role in organizing international opposition to the Iraqi occupation of Kuwait.

Outside his subcommittee, Yatron is actively involved in issues affecting U.S. relations with Greece. Along with Maine Republican Olympia J. Snowe, a Foreign Affairs member and a fellow Greek-American, Yatron has worked to advance the interests of Greece, and has persistently lobbied for increased American pressure on Turkey — a U.S. ally but Greece's traditional enemy — to withdraw its forces from the portion of the island nation of Cyprus it has occupied since 1974.

Aside from an occasional intervention on human rights issues, Yatron has not been a key player on Central American issues since his ouster as Western Hemisphere Subcommittee chairman. The leaders of the revolt said then that their move was spurred by Yatron's perceived lack of interest in the issues over which he had jurisdiction.

Despite several trips to Latin American nations, he played little role in the argument over the two most controversial Western Hemisphere issues faced by Congress in the late 1970s — the Panama Canal treaties and aid to the newly installed Sandinista government of Nicaragua. Yatron called the 10-9 vote against him in 1981 a "political power play" on the part of the committee's liberals, but expressed no bitterness over the outcome.

While Yatron's interest in human rights

and other foreign policy issues occupies much of his House effort, he hardly ignores the particular interests of his industrial eastern Pennsylvania district. Yatron has maintained strong ties to labor unions, supporting trade legislation to shield U.S. metal-producing and textile industries — among the major employers in his district — from foreign competition.

At Home: Yatron may not be smooth and articulate, but he projects a down-to-earth manner that goes over well in a town where people eat pizza at private key clubs. He has a prodigious memory for names and faces, and like many members from areas close to Washington, he returns home on weekends.

Yet Yatron's old-fashioned formula for success showed signs of fraying in 1990. Tied up for much of the fall by Congress' budget wrangling, he found himself exposed to the assaults of a hard-charging GOP challenger, John F. Hicks, who belittled Yatron as an underachiever who had served more than two decades in Congress without attaining a committee chairmanship.

Yatron won. But never effectively rebutting the charges, he saw his vote share drop to 57 percent; it was his worst showing since he first won the seat in 1968.

Yatron used his celebrity in the Reading area to get his start in politics. He was a locally famous boxer and with his father ran a family ice cream-making business.

Yatron started on the school board before eventually moving to the state Legislature. When Democrat George M. Rhodes decided to retire in 1968, he anointed Yatron as his successor and served as his campaign chairman.

Yatron won that first House election with just 51 percent; he had some problems in Schuylkill County (Pottsville), where Republicans dominated the electorate and he was not well known. Since then, Yatron has devoted a great deal of time to Schuylkill, where his office specializes in solving black-lung claim problems. That attentiveness paid off in 1990. By beating Hicks more than 2-to-1 in Schuylkill, Yatron offset a virtual dead heat in Berks and posted his solid, if not spectacular, re-election.

Committees

Foreign Affairs (3rd of 28 Democrats)
Human Rights & International Organizations (chairman); International Narcotics Control

Post Office & Civil Service (3rd of 15 Democrats)
Human Resources; Postal Personnel & Modernization

Elections

1990 General		
Gus Yatron (D)	74,394	(57%)
John F. Hicks (R)	56,093	(43%)
1988 General		
Gus Yatron (D)	114,119	(63%)
James R. Erwin (R)	65,278	(36%)

Previous Winning Percentages: **1986** (69%) **1984** (100%) **1982** (72%) **1980** (67%) **1978** (74%) **1976** (74%) **1974** (75%) **1972** (65%) **1970** (65%) **1968** (51%)

District Vote For President

	1988	1984	1980	1976
D	70,916 (38%)	68,281 (36%)	66,156 (36%)	91,016 (49%)
R	112,040 (61%)	121,264 (64%)	104,703 (56%)	93,417 (50%)
I			12,557 (7%)	

Campaign Finance

	Receipts	Receipts from PACs		Expend-itures
1990				
Yatron (D)	$204,114	$127,955	(63%)	$191,152
Hicks (R)	$72,084	$1,618	(2%)	$71,317
1988				
Yatron (D)	$145,914	$109,700	(75%)	$121,435
Erwin (R)	$12,016	$330	(3%)	$12,002

Key Votes

1991	
Authorize use of force against Iraq	N
1990	
Support constitutional amendment on flag desecration	Y
Pass family and medical leave bill over Bush veto	Y
Reduce SDI funding	Y
Allow abortions in overseas military facilities	N
Approve budget summit plan for spending and taxing	N
Approve civil rights bill	Y
1989	
Halt production of B-2 stealth bomber at 13 planes	Y
Oppose capital gains tax cut	?
Approve federal abortion funding in rape or incest cases	?
Approve pay raise and revision of ethics rules	N
Pass Democratic minimum wage plan over Bush veto	Y

Voting Studies

	Presidential Support		Party Unity		Conservative Coalition	
Year	**S**	**O**	**S**	**O**	**S**	**O**
1990	34	66	73	26	65	35
1989	27	47	56	15	39	32
1988	32	66	75	23	76	24
1987	23	73	87	9	44	49
1986	22	76	80	15	48	44
1985	44	54	80	17	49	51
1984	41	53	70	25	58	37
1983	28	70	78	18	42	57
1982	40	56	71	23	52	44
1981	49	50	58	39	72	25

Interest Group Ratings

Year	ADA	ACU	AFL-CIO	CCUS
1990	44	33	92	36
1989	45	24	100	25
1988	65	24	100	36
1987	84	13	100	33
1986	65	27	100	38
1985	50	33	69	36
1984	50	35	92	38
1983	60	27	94	26
1982	60	33	85	41
1981	40	47	73	28

Pennsylvania - 7th District

7 Curt Weldon (R)

Of Aston — Elected 1986

Born: July 22, 1947, Marcus Hook, Pa.
Education: West Chester State U., B.A. 1969.
Occupation: Teacher; consultant.
Family: Wife, Mary Gallagher; five children.
Religion: Protestant.
Political Career: Mayor of Marcus Hook, 1977-82; Delaware County Council, 1981-86; Republican nominee for U.S. House, 1984.
Capitol Office: 316 Cannon Bldg. 20515; 225-2011.

In Washington: While plenty of members aim to to set the world on fire when they come to Congress, Weldon makes a splash by trying to stamp fires out. A founder of the Fire Services Caucus — the largest in Congress — he aggressively promotes fire safety. If there's smoke, count on Weldon to be there.

During the 1990 debate over a constitutional amendment to ban flag burning, Weldon led a squad of GOP House members who cased Capitol Hill brandishing fire extinguishers in search of demonstrators who might set Old Glory afire. In 1988, the former volunteer fireman fought a blaze in the office of then-Speaker Jim Wright.

In a more conventional legislative pursuit during the 101st Congress, Weldon helped save firefighting equipment from the Clean Air Act's phaseout of chlorofluorocarbons and worked on the 1990 Hotel-Motel Fire Safety Act.

On Armed Services, Weldon is typically a Pentagon ally. In 1987, Weldon was named the "most effective freshman" by the conservative American Security Council. That year, his amendment stating that the Soviets had violated the 1972 anti-ballistic missile treaty by building a radar facility in Siberia passed 418-0.

In one high-profile break with the Pentagon, Weldon helped lead the successful fight against Defense Secretary Dick Cheney's proposal to cancel the V-22 Osprey aircraft in 1989. Weldon was one of three committee Republicans to buck Cheney on the tilt-rotor Osprey, which is partially built in his district.

Those who know only Weldon's conservative bent on defense might be surprised by his record on floor votes, which marks him as one of the more moderate House Republicans. Elected from an urban-suburban amalgam in and near Philadelphia, Weldon sided with President Reagan less than half the time in the last two years of his term, and has backed President Bush only slightly more often.

During 1990 debate on the Family and Medical Leave Act, Weldon co-authored the compromise that offered enough protection to small businesses to win the support of some centrist Republicans and Democrats. Congress approved the bill, but Bush vetoed it.

At Home: Weldon's first victory in the GOP-leaning 7th ended 12 years of Democratic control. The man frustrating Republicans was Bob Edgar, who lost a Senate bid in 1986. Weldon was the unanimous choice of local Republicans to succeed Edgar. The son of a factory worker and the youngest of nine children, Weldon is a former volunteer fireman, teacher and mayor of his hometown, Marcus Hook — a good fit for the 7th's conservative mix of blue- and white-collars.

Weldon rose to prominence as the architect of Marcus Hook's revival. A small working-class city at the 7th's southern end, it was gripped by economic decline and gang warfare when Weldon became GOP mayor in 1977. Ordering a series of tough police raids, he smashed the Pagan motorcycle gang and ended its illicit drug trafficking.

Weldon's accomplishments caught the eye of the powerful Delaware County GOP, and in 1981, with machine backing, Weldon won a County Council seat. He was elected chairman by popular ballot in early 1984. Styling himself a proponent of economic development, Weldon encouraged county government to lure new businesses to the Delaware River waterfront.

In 1984, Weldon ran against Edgar, taking on a task that had thwarted five Republicans before him. Weldon lost by only 412 votes, and his near-miss made him the favorite when Edgar's Senate race opened up the 7th.

Weldon has won easy victories since then, although in 1990 he was criticized by his Democratic foe for his role in a Delaware County economic development agency he founded and chaired. According to a June 1989 audit by the Department of Housing and Urban Development, the agency misspent at least $1.6 million in federal funds. Weldon said that he had a largely absentee role in the agency's management, and that a disgruntled former agency employee was trying to make him appear guilty of a cover-up. Voters seemed to accept Weldon's explanation; he won by nearly 2 to 1.

Pennsylvania 7

Southwest Philadelphia Suburbs

Scores of working-class towns dot this suburban Philadelphia district — comprised of most of Delaware County and a slice of Philadelphia — but in elections from the township level to the presidency, most voters pull the Republican lever.

From the 1920s to the mid-1970s, local politics were ruled by the "War Board," a secretive group officially called the Delaware County Republican Board of Supervisors. The current GOP organization is a looser confederation, but has retained unanimous control of the County Council and every County seat in the state Legislature. Republicans outnumber Democrats in the county by almost 3-1.

Marple, Newtown and Rose Valley are typical Delaware County bastions of well-off Republicanism. Springfield, the county's commercial hub, often finds itself a locus of GOP campaign activity, with candidates swarming the shopping centers every Saturday. In adjacent Swarthmore, the academic influence of Swarthmore College makes Democrats competitive in a nominally business executives' town.

Of the 7th's suburban turf, the Main Line community of Radnor, an old-money township where Sun Oil and TV Guide have their headquarters, weighs in as the wealthiest. Conservative state Rep. Steve Freind, a nationally recognized anti-abortion spokesman, is based in Havertown, and draws heavy support from Catholic voters.

Closer to Philadelphia, one comes to older, ethnic suburbs such as Upper Darby, Yeadon and Colwyn. But here the demographics do not translate automatically into Democratic votes.

The Delaware River marshes by Tinicum were formerly infamous as a dumping ground for organized crime-related murder victims, but new office buildings and hotels near Philadelphia's International Airport have spruced up the area's image.

The 7th's southwest Philadelphia tip melds Irish, Italians and blacks in a workaday setting along with Interstate 95, numerous factories and modest row houses. It gives Democrats solid majorities.

Population: 515,766. White 478,934 (93%), Black 30,578 (6%), Other 4,751 (1%). Spanish origin 3,269 (1%). 18 and over 387,309 (75%), 65 and over 68,570 (13%). Median age: 33.

Committees

Armed Services (13th of 22 Republicans)
Procurement & Military Nuclear Systems; Seapower & Strategic & Critical Materials

Merchant Marine & Fisheries (9th of 17 Republicans)
Fisheries & Wildlife Conservation & the Environment; Oceanography, Great Lakes & Outer Continental Shelf

Select Children, Youth & Families (4th of 14 Republicans)

Elections

1990 General		
Curt Weldon (R)	105,868	(65%)
John Innelli (D)	56,292	(35%)
1988 General		
Curt Weldon (R)	155,387	(68%)
David Landau (D)	73,745	(32%)

Previous Winning Percentage: **1986** (61%)

District Vote For President

	1988		1984		1980		1976	
D	93,469	(40%)	93,850	(38%)	84,935	(35%)	112,341	(43%)
R	141,028	(60%)	155,166	(62%)	136,488	(56%)	141,436	(55%)
I					20,255	(8%)		

Campaign Finance

	Receipts	Receipts from PACs		Expend-itures
1990				
Weldon (R)	$504,744	$207,805	(41%)	$480,165
Innelli (D)	$109,966	$6,400	(6%)	$109,618
1988				
Weldon (R)	$564,109	$215,617	(38%)	$507,360
Landau (D)	$211,213	$27,175	(13%)	$206,591

Key Votes

1991	
Authorize use of force against Iraq	Y
1990	
Support constitutional amendment on flag desecration	Y
Pass family and medical leave bill over Bush veto	Y
Reduce SDI funding	N
Allow abortions in overseas military facilities	N
Approve budget summit plan for spending and taxing	N
Approve civil rights bill	N
1989	
Halt production of B-2 stealth bomber at 13 planes	N
Oppose capital gains tax cut	N
Approve federal abortion funding in rape or incest cases	N
Approve pay raise and revision of ethics rules	Y
Pass Democratic minimum wage plan over Bush veto	?

Voting Studies

	Presidential Support		Party Unity		Conservative Coalition	
Year	**S**	**O**	**S**	**O**	**S**	**O**
1990	50	44	67	29	80	15
1989	65	33	56	39	85	12
1988	45	49	66	25	84	16
1987	52	41	69	27	79	16

Interest Group Ratings

Year	ADA	ACU	AFL-CIO	CCUS
1990	33	54	42	69
1989	35	62	60	89
1988	30	59	77	71
1987	40	55	40	73

8 Peter H. Kostmayer (D)

Of Solebury — Elected 1976
Did not serve 1981-83.

Born: Sept. 27, 1946, New York, N.Y.
Education: Columbia U., B.A. 1971.
Occupation: Public relations consultant.
Family: Separated.
Religion: Episcopalian.
Political Career: No previous office.
Capitol Office: 2436 Rayburn Bldg. 20515; 225-4276.

In Washington: After some shakiness attaining a grip on his tony suburban district, Kostmayer has posted three consecutive reelection wins of more than 10 percentage points. His security at home mirrors his comfort in the House, where he is a loyal vote for the Democratic leadership. His strong party standing enabled him to garner a seat on the Energy and Commerce Committee in the 102nd Congress despite the opposition of its powerful chairman, John D. Dingell.

First elected — and still, by some, remembered — as a hard-liner on ethics, Kostmayer was once known primarily for his crusade against the free mailing of wall calendars to constituents. But that Kostmayer did not survive the election of 1980. Defeated then for reelection, Kostmayer came back two years later determined to change. He wanted to be a House insider, trusted by the Democratic leadership for his work behind the scenes and his disavowal of freelance headline-grabbing. He loyally took on routine party leadership chores he never would have touched in the old days.

In the 101st Congress, he staked out high-profile positions in opposition to a proposed constitutional amendment to ban flag desecration and to restrictions on National Endowment for the Arts grants. The NEA had drawn conservatives' ire for funding projects many members found sacrilegious or obscene. During 1989 consideration of the Interior appropriations bill, Kostmayer criticized attempts to impair the NEA's grantmaking discretion.

"Artists should be accountable only to themselves and their work. Artists in America should not be accountable, even to the American people," he said. "When we ask art and artist to be accountable to the public, we appeal to a kind of public common denominator."

Kostmayer is on the Interior Committee, familiar ground for him because it was his major assignment in his first two terms. In the 101st Congress, it became more of a focus as it provided him with his first chairmanship: the Subcommittee on General Oversight and Investigations. In 1990, Kostmayer's panel probed the conduct of President Bush's nominee to take over the nation's nuclear-bomb system. The subcommittee issued a report that stopped just short of accusing Victor Stello Jr. of lying to Congress over his actions in an investigation of the Nuclear Regulatory Commission's second-ranking criminal investigator. It gave ammunition to Senate opponents of Stello's nomination to be the Energy Department's assistant secretary for defense programs. With opposition mounting, Stello asked Bush to withdraw his nomination.

Kostmayer still has his abrasive side, but he is more careful about displaying it. He has a professional background in public relations, and it shows in his masterful handling of constituency groups at home.

As a member of the Foreign Affairs Committee, he has been known for baiting and challenging administration witnesses, and he is no favorite among the Republican members of the committee. In the 101st Congress, he backed human-rights restrictions on aid to El Salvador.

Population control has been a Kostmayer priority as a member of Foreign Affairs, and on that subject he has fought repeatedly with Republican administrations. Kostmayer wants the United States to increase funding for international agencies that promote family planning in developing nations, but many conservatives object to those expenditures because some of the money is used for abortions.

Kostmayer can reveal an impolitic strain at times. At the Democratic National Convention in 1988, he offered this description of the party's presidential-election strategy to a Congressional Quarterly reporter: "Just shut up, gays, women, environmentalists. Just shut up. You'll get everything you want after the election. But just for the meantime, shut up so that we can win." The quote was later used in the keynote address to the Republican National Convention by New Jersey Gov. Thomas H. Kean.

At Home: By bringing together working-class Democrats from lower Bucks County and independent-minded yuppies from upper

Pennsylvania 8

Northern Philadelphia Suburbs; Bucks County

Known for its winding country lanes and 18th-century stone farmhouses, Bucks County's rural charm helped lure 62,000 new residents in the 1980s, more than any other Pennsylvania county.

As the county's image of genteel country living suggests, the Republicans have a comfortable registration edge in the 8th, which includes all of Bucks and a small piece of wealthy and very Republican Montgomery County. But most GOP candidates have to show some moderate inclinations to win.

The new suburban voters have an independent streak, and combined with blue-collar workers in Lower Bucks, they can make Democrats competitive here, as Kostmayer has proven.

Lower Bucks tends to be Democratic. Far from the bucolic vistas commonly associated with the rest of the county, lower Bucks offers factories, commercial strips, tract developments and the Keystone Racetrack. Levittown's tightly spaced homes built after World War II attracted thousands of ethnic Democrats moving from inner-city Philadelphia. Lower Bucks has had economic problems in the 1980s, most acutely in Fairless Hills, where there have been layoffs and fluctuations in the remaining work force at the USX Corp. (formerly U.S. Steel) Fairless Works.

The farther north one goes, the more Republican Bucks becomes. But Democrats can hold their own in the county's midsection; they win their share of local elections in communities such as Warminster and Doylestown. Democrats do especially well in and around New Hope, a quaint river town famous for its antique shops and artists' colony. Writer James Michener is one Bucks artist (and liberal Democrat) living near New Hope.

Upper Bucks, with its landed gentry and farmers, usually stays with the Republicans. Towns such as Upper Black Eddy harbor business executives who commute to Manhattan and, when home, vote for Republican candidates.

Population: 516,902. White 497,154 (96%), Black 12,471 (2%), Other 4,508 (1%). Spanish origin 5,923 (1%). 18 and over 364,239 (70%), 65 and over 42,528 (8%). Median age: 30.

Bucks, Kostmayer is the only Democrat to succeed in this district in a half-century. His coalition is sometimes shaky: in eight elections starting with 1976, he has lost once and been held to no more than 51 percent three times.

Over the last decade, frustrated Republicans have been unable to find a candidate who could defeat Kostmayer. He ousted a GOP incumbent and beat back two challenges from a Vietnam War hero, one from a veteran state legislator and one from a young female veteran of the Reagan administration.

The woman, Audrie Zettick Schaller, challenged Kostmayer in 1990 after more prominent Bucks County GOP officeholders decided to sit out the race. Schaller had never run for public office before but she was feisty. "I'm ready for this guy," she wrote in a letter to prominent Pennsylvania Republicans, "and he knows it."

Early events broke her way. She threw Kostmayer on the defensive by proposing that both sides abide by a $400,000 spending limit. Even though he had made a point of challenging some of his earlier opponents to a voluntary spending cap, he balked now, citing the candidates' inability to control either independent expenditures or the "soft money" spent by political parties. Local newspapers ran editorials critical of the incumbent; one appeared in March entitled "Kostmayer's Hypocrisy."

But little went well for Schaller after that. The campaign finance controversy quickly faded and Kostmayer built up a huge treasury that Schaller could not match. In September, she fired her campaign manager, who subsequently held a news conference to discount her chances of winning. In November, Kostmayer was re-elected by a comfortable margin.

Kostmayer launched his first congressional campaign in 1976 as a long shot even in the Democratic primary, challenging an organization-backed opponent for the seat being vacated by retiring GOP Rep. Edward G. Biester. But Kostmayer, who was regional coordinator for George McGovern's presidential campaign in 1972, had enough support from independents and liberals outside the party apparatus for the nomination. A divisive GOP primary that year had lingering effects that helped Kostmayer win in November. A weak 1978 challenger tipped him a solid re-election margin.

In 1980, however, Republican nominee James K. Coyne criticized Kostmayer as a big spender and, with the help of Reagan's strong showing in the 8th, reclaimed the seat. Kostmayer became a public relations consultant, but immediately began planning for a rematch. He hit on the idea of using campaign volunteers to keep up his constituent service. Coyne was flabbergasted when Kostmayer aides helped local flood victims with lodgings and food.

Although Coyne had deserted Reagan on several important votes, in his 1982 rematch with Kostmayer he refused to back away from his 1981 support for Reaganomics. That did not go over well in Lower Bucks, where unemployment had made many blue-collar workers regret the GOP votes they cast in 1980. Kostmayer reclaimed the seat in a heavy turnout.

In 1984 Republican leaders drafted David Christian, a highly decorated veteran of the Vietnam War. Christian was not as articulate as Coyne, and except for supporting a nuclear freeze, he mainly recited the GOP platform. Yet despite Christian's weaknesses as a candidate and the incumbent's sizable spending advantage, a strong showing by Reagan helped hold Kostmayer's margin under 4,000 votes.

In 1986, Christian shifted strategy and decided to stress his own roots. He recited his military record and upbringing in a blue-collar, Catholic family in Lower Bucks. But Kostmayer kept Christian on the defensive by focusing on one aspect of the challenger's past — his management of a veterans' center. Kostmayer accused Christian of misrepresenting the cost of the center to a state official. "If the state of Pennsylvania doesn't trust David Christian, why should we?" intoned one Kostmayer ad.

Christian protested his innocence, accusing Kostmayer of "pure, unmitigated mudslinging." But he was unable to redirect the focus of the campaign. Kostmayer expanded his margin of victory to more than 15,000 votes.

In 1988, the GOP shifted tactics again. Coyne wanted a rematch, but he was knocked off the ballot on a filing technicality, clearing the way for former state Sen. Ed Howard, who had a reputation as a liberal maverick on social and environmental issues. His political profile seemed a good fit for the district but Howard proved to be a disappointing campaigner. He also had to spend time defending his attendance record in the state Senate, an issue Kostmayer exploited effectively. Kostmayer ended up winning by nearly 35,000 votes, his first comfortable presidential-year election.

Committees

Energy & Commerce (25th of 27 Democrats)
Commerce, Consumer Protection & Competitiveness; Health & the Environment

Foreign Affairs (22nd of 28 Democrats)
Western Hemisphere Affairs

Interior & Insular Affairs (11th of 29 Democrats)
Energy & the Environment (chairman); General Oversight & California Desert Lands

Select Hunger (4th of 22 Democrats)
International

Elections

1990 General

Peter H. Kostmayer (D)	85,015	(57%)
Audrie Zettick Schaller (R)	65,100	(43%)

1988 General

Peter H. Kostmayer (D)	128,153	(57%)
Ed Howard (R)	93,648	(42%)

Previous Winning Percentages: **1986** (55%) **1984** (51%) **1982** (50%) **1978** (61%) **1976** (50%)

District Vote For President

	1988	1984	1980	1976
D	88,334 (38%)	79,185 (36%)	60,414 (32%)	81,782 (47%)
R	139,248 (60%)	142,258 (64%)	105,284 (56%)	90,142 (51%)
I			18,630 (10%)	

Campaign Finance

	Receipts	Receipts from PACs		Expend-itures
1990				
Kostmayer (D)	$759,657	$295,528	(39%)	$826,742
Schaller (R)	$146,322	$15,300	(10%)	$142,957
1988				
Kostmayer (D)	$1,148,619	$418,821	(36%)	$1,127,812
Howard (R)	$506,241	$49,900	(10%)	$507,682

Key Votes

1991	
Authorize use of force against Iraq	N
1990	
Support constitutional amendment on flag desecration	N
Pass family and medical leave bill over Bush veto	Y
Reduce SDI funding	Y
Allow abortions in overseas military facilities	Y
Approve budget summit plan for spending and taxing	Y
Approve civil rights bill	Y
1989	
Halt production of B-2 stealth bomber at 13 planes	Y
Oppose capital gains tax cut	Y
Approve federal abortion funding in rape or incest cases	Y
Approve pay raise and revision of ethics rules	N
Pass Democratic minimum wage plan over Bush veto	Y

Voting Studies

	Presidential Support		Party Unity		Conservative Coalition	
Year	**S**	**O**	**S**	**O**	**S**	**O**
1990	20	80	89	8	13	85
1989	26	72	94	4	15	85
1988	21	76	89	5	16	82
1987	13	87	92	2	7	93
1986	17	81	87	9	24	74
1985	29	70	90	8	20	80
1984	35	63	83	13	20	80
1983	16	77	86	5	8	84

Interest Group Ratings

Year	ADA	ACU	AFL-CIO	CCUS
1990	89	0	100	14
1989	90	7	92	50
1988	85	4	100	31
1987	96	0	100	7
1986	90	5	100	39
1985	90	19	76	36
1984	85	4	85	31
1983	90	0	100	25

9 Bud Shuster (R)

Of Everett — Elected 1972

Born: Jan. 23, 1932, Glassport, Pa.
Education: U. of Pittsburgh, B.S. 1954; Duquesne U., M.B.A. 1960; American U., Ph.D. 1967.
Military Service: Army, 1954-56.
Occupation: Computer industry executive.
Family: Wife, Patricia Rommel; five children.
Religion: United Church of Christ.
Political Career: No previous office.
Capitol Office: 2188 Rayburn Bldg. 20515; 225-2431.

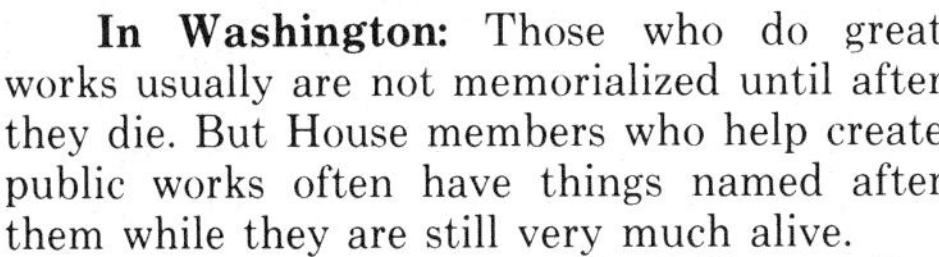

In Washington: Those who do great works usually are not memorialized until after they die. But House members who help create public works often have things named after them while they are still very much alive.

Take, for example, the Bud Shuster By-Way. Funding for this brief stretch of four-lane highway, running parallel to the Pennsylvania Turnpike through the town of Everett, was obtained by Shuster, who is now in his prime as the second-ranking Republican on the House Public Works and Transportation Committee and the senior GOP member on the Surface Transportation Subcommittee. Everett also happens to be Shuster's hometown.

Yet Shuster's interests are not confined to Pennsylvania asphalt. In the 102nd Congress, as the new ranking Republican on the Intelligence Committee, he took up the cause of requiring members and staff of the committee to take an oath of secrecy in dealing with U.S. intelligence information. That effort by Shuster, opposed by Democrats, signaled that the committee's Republicans would be more confrontational toward its liberal majority.

Still, Shuster has been best known as a prototype of the "Public Works Republican." His overall voting record is quite conservative. In only one year — 1982 — did Shuster's votes in support of Ronald Reagan's and George Bush's positions on House legislation drop below 60 percent. This support was not only on defense and foreign policy, but also on many of Reagan's efforts to cut or limit the growth of domestic spending.

However, public works funding, or "infrastructure investment" as it has come to be known, is the one area inviolate to Shuster and like-minded committee members. Projects derided by some administration and congressional figures as "pork barrel" are typically defended by public works advocates as not only worthy, but critical, federal investments in the nation's future economic viability.

When the Reagan administration attacked congressional proposals for highway "demonstration projects" as wasteful, Shuster was enraged. "It's a congressional prerogative," he said. "We find it absolutely repugnant that an administration can say that it's all right for a faceless bureaucrat to decide where money should be spent, but it's wrong for a congressman to identify crucial, needed projects."

It was on a measure loaded with such demonstration projects — the $88 billion highway bill enacted in the 100th Congress — that Shuster had one of his most notable breaks with Reagan. Working closely, as he had on previous road-funding bills, with then-Public Works Chairman James J. Howard of New Jersey, Shuster helped craft the legislation; when Reagan vetoed the bill, Shuster strongly supported its override. He played a similar role on the Clean Water Act amendments enacted in 1987 over Reagan's veto.

Each of these pieces of legislation contained projects that Shuster had promoted as necessary to economic development and recovery of Pennsylvania's 9th District, a rugged, rural stretch dotted with struggling blue-collar towns like Altoona.

Projects Shuster has pushed recently include a $90 million upgrade for Route 220 from Altoona to Tyrone; a Franklin County exit off Interstate 81; a $5.5 million Route 36 bypass around the town of Loysburg; and $3.2 million for a bus-testing facility in Altoona.

Shuster, whose district's industrial areas have an interest in trade protection, also uses his ranking position to promote "Buy American" provisions in public works bills. One "domestic content" provision sponsored by Shuster in the 1987 highway bill increased the minimum amount of American-made parts in transit vehicles from 50 to 60 percent.

Shuster does engage himself in Public Works legislation that is outside the brick-and-mortar (or asphalt-and-concrete) funding arena. When a decline in the efficiency of passenger airline service became a widely reported subject in 1987, Shuster and other members of the Public Works Aviation Subcommittee called for action.

Describing what he called a "disgraceful

Pennsylvania 9

South Central — Altoona

To Pennsylvania Turnpike travelers, this district, which crosses the Allegheny Mountains, is a series of tunnels, long climbs and sharp descents. To Republicans, it is a predictable source of votes.

This central Pennsylvania region long has been a passageway to the West and, other than farming, transportation has been its central focus. Before the coming of the railroad, trade and travel had to take the long way around the mountains, ducking south. The city of Altoona, in Blair County, prospered as a rail center.

With the decline of the rail system, a new travel-related culture sprung up along the turnpike, the nation's first superhighway, which opened in 1940. Its epitome is Breezewood, the celebrated "Town of Motels" — by night, a garish glow of neon signs amid the mysterious mountain darkness.

For the most part, the 9th is a series of small villages scattered among the mountains. It has little industry; its farmers raise cattle for beef and milk. The isolation and agricultural character of the area have bred a strong strain of conservatism. Local Republicans there like to boast that much of the area within the 9th District has gone Republican since 1860.

Altoona, which lost 10 percent of its population in the 1970s and another 10 percent in the 1980s, used to be a Democratic stronghold. Developed by the Pennsylvania Railroad, it has the giant Samuel Rea Railroad Shops nearby; just to the west of it, the tracks form the famous Horseshoe Curve, an engineering marvel. But many of the railroad workers who voted Democratic lost their jobs and left. Nowadays, Republicans win Blair; George Bush carried it with 62 percent of the vote.

Population: 515,430. White 508,728 (99%), Black 4,727 (1%). Spanish origin 1,841 (0.4%). 18 and over 368,331 (71%), 65 and over 64,934 (13%). Median age: 31.

deterioration in service," Shuster attached an amendment to an aviation bill during committee markup that dealt with one of the most common and infuriating air passenger grievances: lost luggage. The provision would have required an airline that could not produce a passenger's missing baggage within two hours of arrival to provide the passenger with a one-way standby ticket between the same two cities. A bag missing for more than 24 hours would have cost the airline a round-trip standby ticket.

A series of hot aviation issues, from efficiency to air terrorism to the effects of the 1989 Eastern Airlines strike, preoccupied the committee during the 101st Congress. There had been something of a lull on Public Works since the passage of the major highway and water bills, and the March 1988 death of Shuster's close Democratic ally, committee Chairman Howard.

But the committee erupted in controversy at the start of the 102nd Congress when a group of younger Democratic members ousted Howard's successor, Glenn M. Anderson of California. Anderson lacked the horse-trading skills necessary for Public Works, and the new chairman, Robert A. Roe of New Jersey, should prove closer to Shuster, both in geography and in style.

The changing of the guard came at a critical time; Public Works was about to take up a major highway reauthorization bill that will shape the future of the Interstate highway system. From this perch, Shuster will likely continue his opposition to increases in the gas tax and will champion formulas for divvying up federal money that give a greater share to urbanized, East Coast states with large populations and heavier traffic.

Shuster's comfort with his Democratic colleagues on Public Works once sharply contrasted with his highly partisan behavior outside the committee. During his early years in the House, Shuster angled for a GOP leadership position, and tried to earn his stripes by blasting the Democrats from the House floor.

Shuster was president of his 1972 Republican House class; six years later, he outcampaigned front-runner Bill Frenzel of Minnesota for the chairmanship of the Republican Policy Committee. In that position, he gained a reputation as a partisan "hatchet man," firing a verbal barrage at the Democratic majority nearly every day on the floor, launching a brief filibuster to protest changes in the schedule, and bringing a toy duck on the floor to complain about a "lame-duck" session.

However, Shuster's one big thrust at a leadership position, minority whip, was thwarted by Trent Lott of Mississippi in 1981. Starting as a distinct underdog, Shuster campaigned with his typical intensity and closed the gap. But Lott held on to win by a 96-90 vote of the House Republican Conference.

At Home: While Shuster has some detractors in local political circles, even in the GOP organization of the 9th's most populous county, Blair (Altoona), he remains untouchable at the polls. Not since 1984 has he had primary or general election opposition.

In 1984, he had an interesting, though unsuccessful, Democratic challenger in 62-year-old Nancy Kulp, who played Miss Jane Hathaway on "The Beverly Hillbillies" television comedy. Retired from show business and living on a Pennsylvania farm, she accused Shuster of voting down the line with Reagan and ignoring the needs of farmers, veterans and elderly constituents.

Shuster counterattacked vigorously. Among his salvos was a radio commercial featuring the leading actor from the series, Buddy Ebsen. In the ad Ebsen said that he had "dropped her a note to say, 'Hey, Nancy, I love you dearly but you're too liberal for me — I've got to go with Bud Shuster." Voters agreed; Shuster won re-election with two-thirds of the vote.

Before entering politics, Shuster had a successful business career with the Radio Corporation of America and as an independent electronics entrepreneur. When GOP Rep. J. Irving Whalley announced his retirement in 1972, Shuster embarked on a self-generated campaign and won the Republican primary over state Sen. D. Elmer Hawbaker. Hawbaker was backed by the party committees of Bedford and Blair counties.

Committees

Select Intelligence (Ranking)
Program & Budget Authorization (ranking); Oversight & Evaluation

Public Works & Transportation (2nd of 21 Republicans)
Surface Transportation (ranking); Aviation; Investigations & Oversight

Elections

1990 General		
Bud Shuster (R)	106,632	(100%)
1988 General		
Bud Shuster (R)	158,702	(100%)

Previous Winning Percentages: **1986** (100%) **1984** (67%) **1982** (65%) **1980** (100%) **1978** (75%) **1976** (100%) **1974** (57%) **1972** (62%)

District Vote For President

	1988	1984	1980	1976
D	63,899 (37%)	59,047 (33%)	59,422 (35%)	71,159 (42%)
R	104,396 (61%)	118,500 (67%)	101,766 (60%)	94,421 (56%)
I			7,245 (4%)	

Campaign Finance

	Receipts	Receipts from PACs	Expend-itures
1990			
Shuster (R)	$417,658	$181,469 (43%)	$429,942
1988			
Shuster (R)	$402,210	$153,665 (38%)	$332,647

Key Votes

1991	
Authorize use of force against Iraq	Y
1990	
Support constitutional amendment on flag desecration	Y
Pass family and medical leave bill over Bush veto	N
Reduce SDI funding	N
Allow abortions in overseas military facilities	N
Approve budget summit plan for spending and taxing	N
Approve civil rights bill	N
1989	
Halt production of B-2 stealth bomber at 13 planes	N
Oppose capital gains tax cut	N
Approve federal abortion funding in rape or incest cases	N
Approve pay raise and revision of ethics rules	N
Pass Democratic minimum wage plan over Bush veto	N

Voting Studies

	Presidential Support		Party Unity		Conservative Coalition	
Year	**S**	**O**	**S**	**O**	**S**	**O**
1990	63	36	78	19	85	9
1989	76	23	74	26	100	0
1988	68	27	75	21	89	5
1987	66	31	74	23	88	12
1986	77	22	85	11	90	8
1985	66	34	86	10	87	11
1984	63	37	83	15	90	8
1983	71	21	85	5	90	8
1982	56	23	60	13	60	18
1981	76	22	89	11	99	1

Interest Group Ratings

Year	ADA	ACU	AFL-CIO	CCUS
1990	11	96	9	92
1989	10	89	17	100
1988	5	100	14	100
1987	20	70	47	80
1986	5	90	29	94
1985	10	81	24	86
1984	0	83	31	56
1983	0	91	0	85
1982	20	80	29	93
1981	0	100	20	89

10 Joseph M. McDade (R)

Of Scranton — Elected 1962

Born: Sept. 29, 1931, Scranton, Pa.
Education: U. of Notre Dame, B.A. 1953; U. of Pennsylvania, LL.B. 1956.
Occupation: Lawyer.
Family: Wife, Sarah Scripture; five children.
Religion: Roman Catholic.
Political Career: No previous office.
Capitol Office: 2370 Rayburn Bldg. 20515; 225-3731.

In Washington: Early in 1991, McDade ascended to one of the pivotal positions in the Congress as ranking Republican on the House Appropriations Committee. The job confers significant influence over spending in virtually every function of the federal establishment. McDade's predecessor in the job, the late Silvio O. Conte of Massachusetts, had been one of the most powerful and familiar figures in Congress. But McDade has found it difficult to inherit much more than Conte's title to date, largely because of a bribery investigation back home in Pennsylvania.

Since 1988, the Federal Bureau of Investigation and a federal grand jury have been trying to determine whether the congressman violated bribery or election laws in accepting more than $45,000 in campaign contributions and speaking fees from officials of a now-bankrupt defense firm, United Chem-Con Corp. of Lancaster, Pa.

Reports of the matter first surfaced in *The Wall Street Journal*, which reported the firm won $54 million in defense contracts with McDade's help. At that time, McDade said he helped the minority-owned business obtain Navy contracts in order to help bring jobs to his economically troubled district. He would not comment further. In November 1990, a former top aide to McDade pleaded guilty to charges under federal bribery laws and was said to be cooperating with prosecutors. McDade had spent about $148,000 in campaign funds on legal fees by the end of 1990.

"I have been patient to let the process work," said McDade in February 1991. "I look forward to its speedy termination and to the end of false speculation."

Popular with his colleagues and skilled at the inside give-and-take of the Appropriations Committee, McDade was already in his fourth term as the ranking member of the Defense Subcommittee when the 102nd Congress began. In channeling the immense sums within that jurisdiction, he had enjoyed special inside leverage thanks to his pairing with the subcommittee chairman — his longtime Pennsylvania colleague John P. Murtha.

The two worked together to bring Pennsylvania a $963 million modernization contract for an aircraft carrier in 1990. McDade was also able to secure $13 million in 1990 for a train museum in his district.

Snaring such prizes for the folks back home led some Republicans to criticize Conte, but McDade's harder line on defense issues may serve to insulate his position from similar attacks. Conte had emphasized the social-domestic side of Appropriations business, but McDade signaled a new emphasis by pressing for more Republican seats on the Defense and Interior subcommittees after assuming the ranking member's office.

Spurring economic development at home has been at the heart of McDade's political career, and his committee assignments have positioned him well to pursue that goal. In addition to his place on Defense Appropriations, he was the top Republican on the Small Business Committee (until he took over as ranking member on Appropriations). The confluence of these two assignments had given him influence with two important sources of federal contracts: the Pentagon and the Small Business Administration. McDade's savvy in using his positions on behalf of his constituents made him secure in an otherwise politically marginal district.

Even after stories began appearing regarding the investigation into his finances, McDade's standing at home remained high. Asked in 1989 why the Democrats did not mount more of an effort against McDade, a top local Democratic official said, "If Joe McDade were indicted and convicted it would still be tough for us to beat him."

McDade has not been quite so impervious on Capitol Hill. Shortly after the *Journal* story appeared, McDade was dealt a setback in the House: He lost a bid to become GOP Conference secretary. For such a senior member to seek such a modest leadership post was unusual, but McDade said he decided to run after

Pennsylvania 10

Northeast — Scranton

The city of Scranton dominated the politics of northeastern Pennsylvania in the early part of the century, but as the coal-and-railroad town has declined in population, Scranton and Lackawanna County have had to speak with a quieter political voice.

Generally, they have been a small Democratic voice within an increasingly Republican 10th District. In 1988, Lackawanna gave Democrat Michael S. Dukakis 52 percent while the district went comfortably for George Bush.

Lackawanna County still has half the district's people, despite the prolonged slump in anthracite mining that has led to declines in employment and population. The county's Democratic majority casts its vote in Scranton and in such blue-collar towns as Moosic and Old Forge. The Republicans cluster in affluent suburbs such as Clarks Summit and Dalton (home of former Gov. William W. Scranton). Ethnically, the scramble for political office in this polyglot county has been between the Italians and the Irish.

In contrast to Scranton's shrinkage (its population dropped 14 percent in the 1970s and just over 7 percent in the '80s), there has been spectacular population growth in some of the outlying counties of the 10th. Pike, a Pocono Mountain county east of Scranton, contains many vacation cottages and is home to business executives who commute to New York. Pike's population boomed by 54 percent in the 1970s and another 53 percent in the '80s. Republican Monroe County, to the south of Pike, also is home to Pocono resorts such as Buck Hill Falls and Camelback.

West of Scranton are sparsely populated rural counties along the New York border such as Potter and Tioga, which are made up of woods, dairy farms and Republicans.

Population: 515,442. White 510,782 (99%), Black 2,262 (0.4%). Spanish origin 2,214 (0.4%). 18 and over 376,348 (73%), 65 and over 75,215 (15%). Median age: 33.

Northeastern Republicans met and concluded they needed a regional representative in the leadership. Another factor that made the move curious is that McDade's politics do not fit the usual pattern for a party leader. Over the course of his career, he has voted against a majority of House Republicans more often than he has voted with them. He has, however, managed to do so without personally alienating party colleagues. He tends to break from the GOP line on labor votes, rather than on the more ideologically divisive social-policy issues.

McDade's strategy for the leadership contest was to call in chits he had collected in years of service on Appropriations. But his timing was off. His strategy served to emphasize his place in the "Old Bull" politics-as-usual wing of the House GOP. This was not what many restive House Republicans wanted in their new leaders. Conservative activist Vin Weber of Minnesota was elected instead.

When McDade first took over the ranking spot on Defense Appropriations — after the retirement of Alabama's Jack Edwards in 1985 — many GOP conservatives feared McDade would not be as reliable a party loyalist as his predecessor. McDade had expressed skepticism about spending massive sums on the military, given pressing domestic needs. Shortly before taking over the job, McDade cautioned, "The deficit demands that the defense budget be part of the [spending] reduction process."

But McDade proved to be a dependable foot soldier for Republican views on the panel, though he tended to couch his support for the Reagan administration defense buildup in his own terms. In 1985, he submitted a joint resolution containing President Ronald Reagan's request for the production of 21 additional MX missiles. But unlike conservatives who said the weapon was needed to counter the Soviet threat, McDade talked of the missile system's supposed benefits for arms control. The resolution passed by a 217-210 vote.

McDade's previous role on Appropriations — ranking member on the Interior Subcommittee — did not require such partisan diligence on his part. For nearly a decade, he and Chairman Sidney R. Yates of Illinois were one of the more successful legislative teams in the House. Rarely did their bills generate much floor opposition on either side of the aisle, even when they exceeded administration budget requests.

At Home: McDade has endeared himself to constituents of both parties with his efforts to promote economic development — vital in his depressed coal-producing region. In 1988, he won a typical landslide re-election; in 1990, he had no opposition at all.

McDade's Republican label appeals to voters in the outlying, rural portions of the 10th, and his pro-labor voting record pleases the blue-collar Democrats in Lackawanna County (Scranton), the district's focal point. Unions regularly back McDade, and local Democratic organizations stopped endorsing candidates to run against him long ago. As an Irish Catholic, he has unusual appeal for a Republican among the county's large ethnic population.

A lawyer and former municipal solicitor in his home city, McDade succeeded Republican William W. Scranton, after whose ancestors the city is named. Scranton had served one House term before being elected governor.

Handpicked by Scranton for the 1962 House nomination, McDade won an unspectacular election victory. In the face of Lyndon B. Johnson's presidential landslide in 1964, his winning margin was narrower yet. By 1966, however, he had enlisted the support of organized labor, and his vote tally has not dipped below 60 percent since.

Committees

Appropriations (Ranking)
Defense (ranking); Interior

Small Business (2nd of 17 Republicans)
SBA, the General Economy & Minority Enterprise Development

Elections

1990 General

Joseph M. McDade (R)	113,490	(100%)

1988 General

Joseph M. McDade (R)	140,096	(73%)
Robert C. Cordaro (D)	51,179	(27%)

Previous Winning Percentages: **1986** (75%) **1984** (77%) **1982** (68%) **1980** (77%) **1978** (77%) **1976** (63%) **1974** (65%) **1972** (74%) **1970** (65%) **1968** (67%) **1966** (67%) **1964** (51%) **1962** (53%)

District Vote For President

	1988	1984	1980	1976
D	80,514 (41%)	75,727 (38%)	79,276 (39%)	101,832 (48%)
R	112,001 (58%)	123,130 (61%)	110,645 (54%)	105,197 (50%)
I			10,128 (5%)	

Campaign Finance

	Receipts	Receipts from PACs	Expend-itures
1990			
McDade (R)	$383,030	$236,778 (62%)	$373,388
1988			
McDade (R)	$442,808	$271,620 (61%)	$430,322
Cordaro (D)	$69,674	0	$66,299

Key Votes

1991

Authorize use of force against Iraq	Y

1990

Support constitutional amendment on flag desecration	Y
Pass family and medical leave bill over Bush veto	Y
Reduce SDI funding	?
Allow abortions in overseas military facilities	?
Approve budget summit plan for spending and taxing	Y
Approve civil rights bill	N

1989

Halt production of B-2 stealth bomber at 13 planes	N
Oppose capital gains tax cut	N
Approve federal abortion funding in rape or incest cases	N
Approve pay raise and revision of ethics rules	Y
Pass Democratic minimum wage plan over Bush veto	Y

Voting Studies

	Presidential Support		Party Unity		Conservative Coalition	
Year	**S**	**O**	**S**	**O**	**S**	**O**
1990	47	41	43	40	65	20
1989	66	29	47	44	80	12
1988	44	51	61	33	71	24
1987	45	47	34	53	72	19
1986	49	42	31	58	66	24
1985	59	38	44	47	67	29
1984	57	35	41	48	63	25
1983	57	30	44	43	60	31
1982	40	45	36	55	53	41
1981	62	30	55	34	63	25

Interest Group Ratings

Year	ADA	ACU	AFL-CIO	CCUS
1990	33	57	58	46
1989	35	46	67	80
1988	40	54	86	50
1987	40	37	71	36
1986	45	63	93	35
1985	20	57	75	38
1984	30	41	77	56
1983	30	52	60	60
1982	60	33	75	32
1981	25	93	47	78

11 Paul E. Kanjorski (D)

Of Nanticoke — Elected 1984

Born: April 2, 1937, Nanticoke, Pa.

Education: Attended Temple U., 1957-62; Dickinson School of Law, 1962-65.

Military Service: Army, 1960-61.

Occupation: Lawyer.

Family: Wife, Nancy Hickerson; one child.

Religion: Roman Catholic.

Political Career: Sought Democratic nomination for U.S. House, special election, 1980, regular primary, 1980.

Capitol Office: 424 Cannon Bldg. 20515; 225-6511.

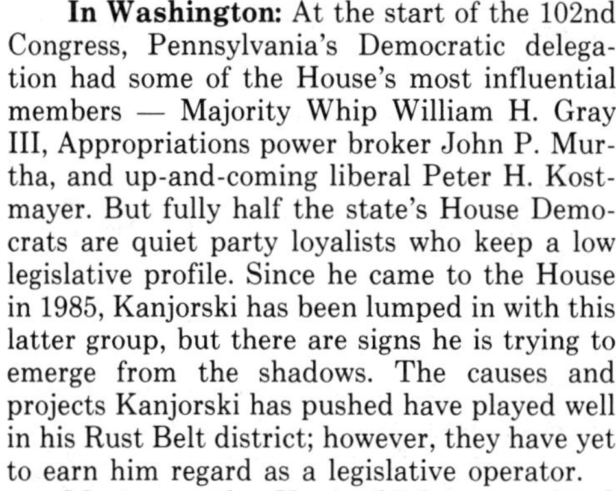

In Washington: At the start of the 102nd Congress, Pennsylvania's Democratic delegation had some of the House's most influential members — Majority Whip William H. Gray III, Appropriations power broker John P. Murtha, and up-and-coming liberal Peter H. Kostmayer. But fully half the state's House Democrats are quiet party loyalists who keep a low legislative profile. Since he came to the House in 1985, Kanjorski has been lumped in with this latter group, but there are signs he is trying to emerge from the shadows. The causes and projects Kanjorski has pushed have played well in his Rust Belt district; however, they have yet to earn him regard as a legislative operator.

Most recently, Kanjorski has excoriated Texas financiers and officials for their disproportionately high number of failed savings and loan institutions, and for the cost to the U.S. taxpayer of bailing them out. He also has blasted the oil companies for profiteering.

During the 101st Congress and into the 102nd, Kanjorski stepped up his activities on the Banking Committee. His pet project there has been trying to win approval of a "burden-sharing" amendment, which would require states (such as Texas) with large numbers of failed thrifts to pay part of the bailout costs of their state-chartered S&Ls if they want these institutions to remain eligible for federal deposit insurance. Opponents of Kanjorski's measure say the costs of the S&L bailout should be spread equally among taxpayers in all states.

Kanjorski's attempt to pass his burden-sharing plan failed in early 1991 when it threatened to derail legislation to provide crucially needed funds for continued operation of the Resolution Trust Corporation; his similar efforts had been repeatedly blocked during consideration of the original thrift salvage bill in 1989.

Kanjorski stood out in July 1989, when he was one of just four House members to vote against an anti-bank fraud bill. He complained that members had not had enough time to study or debate the bill.

Another Kanjorski initiative is reimposing the windfall profits tax whenever the price of oil rises above a certain level. He proposed directing the windfall revenue to help finance the thrift bailout. His tax proposal, floated at a September 1989 hearing of the House Ways and Means Committee, raised the hackles of Texas members on that panel. In response to Iraq's invasion of Kuwait in 1990 and attendant concerns about a run-up in oil prices, Kanjorski began to push anew for the tax.

At the start of the 102nd Congress, Kanjorski sought a higher-profile platform for espousing his ideas — a seat on the Budget Committee. But he fell short by one vote.

Kanjorski's 1989 election to the Post Office and Civil Service Committee — and his subsequent bid for the Census Subcommittee chairmanship — demonstrated both the extent and the limit of the influence of his Pennsylvania colleague, Murtha.

At the start of the 101st Congress, Murtha backed Kanjorski for an opening on Post Office. After two ballots, Kanjorski won. Once on the panel, Kanjorski sought the Census Subcommittee chair; every Post Office Democrat chaired a panel either on Post Office or another committee. In that job, he would be utile to Murtha in his fight to keep illegal aliens from being counted in the 1990 census. Members from Pennsylvania and other states slated to lose congressional seats had filed a lawsuit to stop the Census Bureau from including illegal aliens.

But the Democratic leadership supported Ohioan Tom Sawyer — who opposed changing census counts of aliens — for the Census chair, and Sawyer won easily. Kanjorski got the chairmanship of the Human Resources Subcommittee instead.

Representing a district that had rejected three incumbents in four years, Kanjorski spent much of his first term worrying about how sensitive floor votes might affect his popularity

Pennsylvania 11

Northeast — Wilkes-Barre

Nowadays, being the hard-coal center of the world is a dubious honor. The energy crises of the 1970s spurred a modest comeback for anthracite, but mining this coal is very expensive, and no boom is on the horizon. In a town like Wilkes-Barre, unemployment and black lung disease are constant concerns of a legislator's life.

In most years, this is Democratic territory. But Democratic candidates have found some of their fellow partisans to be fickle. The area within the 11th went for Jimmy Carter in 1976, then turned against him four years later. In 1988, George Bush was a winner there.

Luzerne County, with two-thirds of the district's population, anchors the district. It is a rich ethnic stew of Eastern Europeans, Italians, Irish and Welsh. The surnames of Wilkes-Barre's many nationalities adorn mailboxes outside white frame homes that betray the town's New England roots.

Wilkes-Barre and Pittston are the county's Democratic vote centers. Another good town for the Democrats is Hazleton, in the southern part of Luzerne County. Republicans predominate in more affluent Kingston and Dallas and in the town of Forty-Fort.

The district also includes a Democratic coal-mining section of Northumberland County and the rural Republican turf of northwestern Monroe County. The Monroe section holds the Tobyhanna Army Depot and resorts such as Mount Pocono.

Rounding out the district are two politically marginal counties that mix farming, mining and light industry (Columbia and Montour), as does part of a third (Carbon). Bosky Sullivan County tilts Republican.

Population: 515,729. White 510,659 (99%), Black 2,914 (1%). Spanish origin 2,165 (0.4%). 18 and over 388,822 (75%), 65 and over 83,140 (16%). Median age: 35.

at home. An easy win over a well-financed opponent in 1986, and uncontested races in 1988 and 1990, are testimony that his legislative agenda, if not a big winner in Washington, has at least helped him build his political popularity in the 11th District.

At Home: Kanjorski owes his presence in the House largely to an intestinal parasite and a sunny beach. Those are peculiar agents of change, but the 11th is a district with peculiar politics. In one five-year span (1980-85), five different people represented it.

The outcome of Kanjorski's 1984 primary challenge to incumbent Democrat Frank Harrison might have been different but for the discovery that water supplies in parts of the 11th were contaminated with the giardiasis parasite. In January, as people boiled their water to make it drinkable, Harrison flew off for his second congressional excursion to Central America.

Kanjorski pounced on Harrison with a largely self-financed blitz of clever ads portraying him as an aloof globe-trotter. One ad showed a picture of a sunny Costa Rican beach and noted Harrison's visit there, then switched to a shot of a tea kettle on a stove and concluded, "It's enough to make you boil."

Harrison tried to ignore Kanjorski and campaigned on a vague, uninspiring "help me continue" line, stressing his experience in Washington. That pitch failed to excite voters, and Kanjorski leaped from long shot to victor.

Kanjorski was rated the favorite over Republican Robert P. Hudock. But Hudock stirred some life into the race by accusing Kanjorski of charging excessive fees for his private legal work on behalf of local communities seeking federal grants. Hudock also accused Kanjorski of taking payment from citizens and businesses seeking relief money from Washington after Hurricane Agnes hit the area in 1972.

Kanjorski responded that his firm charged competitive fees, and he said he had helped bring over $50 million in federal aid to the 11th. He noted that during his 18 years of practicing law, he had often provided free legal services, including working without pay as Nanticoke's assistant city solicitor for 14 years.

Kanjorski also cast aspersions on Hudock's fitness to represent the district, noting that Hudock had been living and practicing law in the Virginia suburbs of Washington, D.C. A local reporter who visited Hudock's Pennsylvania office said it seemed little used, and calls to that office were forwarded automatically to Hudock's Virginia office.

An opponent of abortion and gun control and an advocate of prayer in schools and tuition tax credits, Kanjorski was viewed by most voters as reflecting their values, not those of the national Democratic Party. So even though Walter F. Mondale lost the district to Ronald Reagan, Kanjorski won with 58 percent of the vote.

In his 1986 re-election bid, Kanjorski was

not as much the focus as was his extraordinary GOP challenger, Marc L. Holtzman, who waged one of the country's most novel — and, in the end, most spectacularly unsuccessful — campaigns. In a district that is aging, heavily Catholic and struggling economically, Holtzman was 26 years old, Jewish and wealthy. He counted on White House connections and a treasury well in excess of $1 million to make him competitive.

Kanjorski pointed to things he had already done — such as obtaining federal funds to refurbish the Wilkes-Barre Public Square. And he noted his ties to House leaders through his position on the Steering and Policy Committee.

Holtzman boasted of what he could do if given a chance. Son of the owner of Jewelcor, a Wilkes-Barre-based national catalog sales company, Holtzman had parlayed his role as executive director of Reagan's 1980 Pennsylvania campaign into contacts with conservative leaders across the country. He said his contacts would help him bring new industry to the 11th. But voters did not buy Holtzman's pitch. He drew a lower share of the vote than any GOP House candidate in the 11th District in a decade — spending approximately $29 per vote in the process.

That victory and Kanjorski's re-election without opposition in 1988 and 1990 have brought stability to a district that once was a turnstile.

The door began revolving in 1980, after powerful 31-year veteran Daniel J. Flood was forced to resign from the 11th for soliciting illegal campaign contributions. The local Democratic Party fell into squabbling: The Democrat who replaced Flood in an April 1980 special election, Raphael E. Musto, lost to Republican James L. Nelligan that November. Because of the recession, Nelligan lost to Harrison in 1982. In the 1984 Democratic primary, Harrison lost to Kanjorski.

Kanjorski's 1984 campaign was his third try for Congress. In the 1980 special election to replace Flood, Kanjorski finished fourth, trailing Musto, Nelligan and Harrison; shortly afterward, he sought the Democratic nomination for a full two-year term and finished third, behind Musto and Harrison.

Committees

Banking, Finance & Urban Affairs (15th of 31 Democrats)
Economic Stabilization; Financial Institutions Supervision, Regulation & Insurance; Housing & Community Development; Policy Research & Insurance

Post Office & Civil Service (10th of 15 Democrats)
Human Resources (chairman)

Elections

1990 General		
Paul E. Kanjorski (D)	88,219	(100%)
1988 General		
Paul E. Kanjorski (D)	120,706	(100%)

Previous Winning Percentages: **1986** (71%) **1984** (59%)

District Vote For President

	1988	1984	1980	1976
D	84,902 (47%)	84,587 (43%)	86,508 (43%)	109,718 (54%)
R	94,100 (52%)	108,063 (56%)	102,980 (51%)	92,193 (45%)
I			8,283 (4%)	

Campaign Finance

	Receipts	Receipts from PACs	Expend-itures
1990			
Kanjorski (D)	$308,351	$224,185 (73%)	$405,637
1988			
Kanjorski (D)	$539,603	$286,370 (53%)	$420,305

Key Votes

1991	
Authorize use of force against Iraq	N
1990	
Support constitutional amendment on flag desecration	Y
Pass family and medical leave bill over Bush veto	Y
Reduce SDI funding	Y
Allow abortions in overseas military facilities	N
Approve budget summit plan for spending and taxing	N
Approve civil rights bill	Y
1989	
Halt production of B-2 stealth bomber at 13 planes	Y
Oppose capital gains tax cut	Y
Approve federal abortion funding in rape or incest cases	N
Approve pay raise and revision of ethics rules	Y
Pass Democratic minimum wage plan over Bush veto	Y

Voting Studies

	Presidential Support		Party Unity		Conservative Coalition	
Year	**S**	**O**	**S**	**O**	**S**	**O**
1990	25	74	87	13	44	54
1989	36	63	85	14	44	56
1988	32	68	88	12	50	50
1987	26	74	88	11	56	44
1986	22	78	83	14	54	46
1985	33	63	80	17	47	53

Interest Group Ratings

Year	ADA	ACU	AFL-CIO	CCUS
1990	67	21	92	21
1989	80	14	92	40
1988	70	20	100	36
1987	80	4	94	13
1986	65	32	93	28
1985	55	19	76	32

12 John P. Murtha (D)

Of Johnstown — Elected 1974

Born: June 17, 1932, New Martinsville, W.Va.
Education: U. of Pittsburgh, B.A. 1962.
Military Service: Marine Corps, 1952-55, 1966-67.
Occupation: Car wash operator.
Family: Wife, Joyce Bell; three children.
Religion: Roman Catholic.
Political Career: Pa. House, 1969-74.
Capitol Office: 2423 Rayburn Bldg. 20515; 225-2065.

In Washington: As public dissatisfaction with Congress has grown in recent years, voters have developed a paradoxical attitude about the legislative process: They love the deal, but loathe the dealmakers. This was borne out by the dilemma that Murtha, a consummate congressional horse-trader, faced in 1990.

As a longtime member of the Appropriations Committee, Murtha had channeled millions of federal dollars into roads, bridges, research facilities and economic development programs back home; no one in Pennsylvania's 12th District called for sending that money back. But when an aggressive young challenger, taking advantage of an anti-incumbent mood, portrayed Murtha as a sleazy political operator in the 1990 Democratic primary, the incumbent received just 51 percent of the vote.

The close call was a blow to a member who once campaigned as "John P. Murtha — the 'P' Is for Power." It came just as Murtha was settling in to the chairmanship of the Appropriations Subcommittee on Defense, which he gained at the start of the 101st Congress.

Legislatively, that position fit Murtha like a glove: A decorated Marine combat veteran who led troops during the Vietnam War, he is one of the most conservative, pro-defense House Democrats. But his rise to that position also enabled his primary challenger, Kenneth B. Burkley, to portray Murtha as more interested in national issues than in the economic problems of the largely blue-collar district.

Murtha argued otherwise, running down a long list of district programs he helped fund in the 12th. He also asked voters' forbearance about the extra time he would have to spend in Washington dealing with his responsibilities as subcommittee chairman. "I just thought people would understand that," Murtha later said during a district visit. "I got the message; they don't understand it, and we're out here working."

Murtha moved quickly to reinforce his local position. Though congenial to his colleagues, Murtha over the years had been rather inaccessible to the news media. But after his narrow escape, Murtha for the first time hired a press secretary and embarked on a series of "community days" around his district.

When he visited Latrobe, Pa., in February 1991, Murtha did not highlight his management of the $269 billion defense spending bill in 1990. Instead, he talked up his success at obtaining a waiver from a federal alcoholic-beverage labeling law for that city's Rolling Rock brewery, which had a large inventory of recyclable, preprinted bottles.

Murtha's ability to get a detail like that enshrined in law is an example of his skill at the legislative process. Moving noiselessly in a House dominated by media-conscious political free-lancers, Murtha built his formidable political reputation the old-fashioned way: He wields influence in the back rooms of Congress, not before the television cameras.

Murtha almost never gives a speech on the House floor, but he spends many afternoons there, and is one of the few members who will rarely leave to answer a reporter's question. When he is not plotting strategy with a leadership lieutenant, he is talking politics with his allies in his corner — the "Pennsylvania corner" — of the House chamber.

Murtha uses his clout to bolster the institutional roles of friends in his home-state delegation. One of the beneficiaries has been Philadelphia Democrat William H. Gray III. In 1985, Murtha helped engineer Gray's election as Budget Committee chairman. Murtha's support also played a key role in Gray's victories for chairman of the House Democratic Caucus, then for majority whip in 1989 to succeed California Rep. Tony Coelho, who had resigned.

One of the few remaining power brokers who can dependably deliver a bloc of voters for the House Democratic leadership, Murtha has influence over a group of Democrats, not just from Pennsylvania, but from blue-collar districts in surrounding states as well. Under Murtha's aegis, for example, Alan B. Mollohan of West Virginia got on Appropriations in 1986.

An affiliation with Murtha can have legislative benefits as well. In 1990, Murtha and

Pennsylvania 12

Southwest — Johnstown

The chronically unlucky industrial city of Johnstown, the biggest city in the 12th, exemplifies the hard times felt throughout this blue-collar district. A flood, the third in the past century — though not as serious as the first two — overwhelmed Johnstown in 1977 and left 80 dead. The early 1980s recession devastated the city's coal and steel industries, skyrocketing unemployment rates to 27 percent. The economic expansion later in the decade did little to help the area.

Spread over the foothills of the Allegheny Mountains, Johnstown's Cambria County and neighboring Westmoreland County are similar in demographics and voting habits, and both are plagued by high unemployment. Their ethnic industrial towns, many of them 95-98 percent white, sit in the hollows between the hills, often dependent on one local industry. Westmoreland County was dealt a crushing economic blow when New Stanton's Volkswagen assembly plant closed in 1988, but the Sony Corp. of America served as deus ex machina, agreeing to move into the facility two years later. The plant, expected to open in 1992, will provide 1,000 jobs.

Though Greensburg, Westmoreland's county seat, has no major military installation, it was perhaps the American town most tragically touched by the Persian Gulf War. Eleven reservists of the 14th Quartermaster Detachment, based in Greensburg, were killed by an Iraqi Scud missile attack one week after arriving in Saudi Arabia.

In the past four presidential elections, both Cambria and Westmoreland have gone Democratic. Jimmy Carter won them narrowly in 1980, as some Democrats deserted to Ronald Reagan, hoping he could cure the economic doldrums. In 1984, Walter F. Mondale improved on Carter's showing as voters registered their unhappiness with Reagan's economic policies, including his unwillingness to impose mandatory steel import quotas. And in 1988, Michael S. Dukakis posted comfortable victories in both counties. While Cambria and Westmoreland counties have a more than 2-to-1 Democratic registration advantage, Somerset County has a slight GOP voter edge. George Bush carried it in 1988.

Population: 515,915. White 507,805 (98%), Black 5,918 (1%). Spanish origin 1,965 (0.4%). 18 and over 374,878 (73%), 65 and over 64,054 (12%). Median age: 32.

Pennsylvanian Joseph M. McDade, the ranking Republican on the Defense Subcommittee, secured $963 million in the fiscal 1991 defense appropriations bill to refit the aircraft carrier *John F. Kennedy* at the Philadelphia Naval Shipyard, in the House district of Democrat Thomas M. Foglietta; House-Senate conferees whittled the figure to $401 million. (In March 1991, McDade became ranking Republican on the full Appropriations Committee, succeeding the late Silvio O. Conte of Massachusetts.)

But even as he keeps an eye on Keystone State interests, Murtha's subcommittee chairmanship gives him a greater opportunity than he has ever had to shape defense policy. Murtha has never left any doubt about where he stands on military issues: He is a Democratic hawk. Murtha steadfastly supported President Bush's Persian Gulf policy, from the initial defensive deployment following Iraq's August 1990 invasion of Kuwait to the decision to wage war against Iraq in January 1991.

Murtha's stance appeared driven at times by his empathy, born of personal experience, with the soldiers in the field. During his floor speech favoring a resolution authorizing Bush to use force, Murtha berated those who called for a go-slow policy. "If you sit here in an air-conditioned office and you say, 'Let our soldiers sit there in the sand,' you do not know what it's like," Murtha said. "You put your hand on metal and you get a third-degree burn. It is so hot they have to train at nighttime and sleep in the daytime."

Murtha made clear early in his chairmanship that the interests of military personnel came first with him, before weapons systems and other defense programs. "In order to accomplish the needed [budget] reductions and adequately fund today's quality-of-life and procurement needs ... some [weapons] programs must be terminated," said an August 1989 Appropriations Committee report that clearly reflected Murtha's views.

Murtha's role on defense policy is somewhat circumscribed. The congressional defense agenda is greatly determined by the Armed Services authorizing committees and their influential chairmen, Sen. Sam Nunn of Georgia and Rep. Les Aspin of Wisconsin.

But Murtha has never needed an assigned role to have his say. During the 1980s, he was a leading Democratic supporter of President Ronald Reagan's Central America policies, backing U.S. aid to the contras fighting the then-Marxist government of Nicaragua and to the El Salvador government, which was battling a leftist insurgency.

In recent years, though, Murtha has softened his position. Disturbed by continued allegations of human rights abuses by the El Salvador military, including the murders of six Jesuit priests in 1989, Murtha and Massachusetts Democrat Joe Moakley sponsored an amendment, which became law in 1990, withholding half of authorized U.S. aid to El Salvador.

Murtha's rather conservative views on defense and foreign policy are balanced by his liberal, typically Democratic views on most domestic issues. He is a particular advocate of organized labor — he regularly receives 100 percent ratings from the AFL-CIO — and gives special attention to issues relating to the coal miners and steelworkers of his district. A leader in the Congressional Steel Caucus, he urged Bush in 1989 to renew expiring voluntary restraint agreements on steel imports into the United States.

While Murtha has succeeded at the seniority route to congressional influence, his hopes for a formal leadership role were crushed in 1980 by a brush with scandal. Murtha was a tangential figure in what was known as the "Abscam affair."

Murtha was on a leadership track during the 1970s, handling such thankless jobs as serving on the ethics committee and managing congressional pay raise legislation. A special favorite of former Speaker Thomas P. O'Neill Jr. of Massachusetts, Murtha seemed likely to become majority whip in 1981. But in February 1980, Murtha was reported to be one of the targets of the FBI undercover agents who posed as Arab sheiks and offered members of Congress $50,000 to help them get into the United States.

Videotapes of the FBI sessions clearly show that Murtha turned down the money. "I'm not interested," he said at one point. "I'm sorry." He explained that he was on the House ethics committee and told the "sheiks" that "if you get into heat with politicians, there's no amount of money that can help."

The tapes do, however, show Murtha discussing money for Reps. Frank Thompson Jr., D-N.J., and John M. Murphy, D-N.Y., who were later convicted on charges related to the sting. "Let me make it very clear, the other two guys expect to be taken care of," Murtha said at one point.

Murtha said he participated in the meeting only to seek investments by the Arabs in coal mining operations, banks and other businesses in his district. "I broke no law," he explained later. "I took no money. I was pursuing a policy of trying to attract industry to the district." The ethics committee in July 1981 cleared Murtha of wrongdoing. However, the damage to Murtha's leadership ambitions had already been done.

At Home: The talk of a nationwide anti-incumbent tide during the 1990 campaign was largely spawned by Murtha's unexpectedly close Democratic primary victory. When word filtered down from the hills of southwest Pennsylvania the night of May 15 that Murtha had survived with just 51 percent of the vote, much of the national political community acted stunned. If the seemingly invincible Murtha could be threatened, many thought, so, too, could scores of other House incumbents across the country.

Murtha's opponent, Greensburg lawyer Burkley, essentially made the contest a referendum on Murtha's use of congressional power. Murtha, he argued, might be an influential member of Congress, but he was using his clout to secure his own financial well-being rather than helping his economically struggling constituency in the coal and steel country of western Pennsylvania.

The challenger's campaign was both feisty and irreverent. He mocked the value of Murtha's incumbency by appearing at abandoned factories and vacant storefronts in the 12th with a cardboard likeness of the incumbent. He offered a $1,000 reward to anyone who could get Murtha to debate him, an offer that was prominently featured on posters bearing the incumbent's likeness.

And Burkley capped his low-budget campaign with a mailing to 40,000 Democratic households in the district titled "John P. Murtha's Wheel of Fortune." It was graphically designed with drawings that resembled the spinning wheel and the block letter board of the TV game show.

Spelled out in large letters were the words "Pay Raises," "Junkets" and "Money Laundering," a reference to personal items that Burkley said had been bought by Murtha's campaign committee. The thrust of the mailing was summed up in bold letters under a gaudy drawing of a gaming wheel: "With every spin ... Murtha continues to line his pockets — and you pay for the fabulous prizes."

If Murtha had ignored the attacks, he probably would have lost. But tapping defense contractors and lobbyists, heavy industry and unions, Murtha was able to respond with a massive blitz that accused Burkley of lies and distortion, while pointing to a variety of economic development projects within the district that Murtha had helped make possible.

Prominent political figures, business leaders and celebrities — including Gov. Robert P. Casey, former House Speaker O'Neill, Chrysler Corp. Chairman Lee A. Iacocca and actor E. G. Marshall — made ads attesting to Murtha's honesty, integrity and effectiveness in Congress. And Murtha billboards dotted roadsides across the district reading: "Experience ... Makes It Happen."

Some Murtha advisers feared that his saturation advertising ran the risk of overkill, but it probably staved off an upset. Burkley carried his home base, populous Westmoreland County on the outskirts of Pittsburgh, but Murtha won elsewhere to attain a 4,775-vote victory. Against a less aggressive Republican opponent, Murtha's re-election that fall was anti-climactic.

Murtha has not been involved in many close races. When longtime Republican Rep. John P. Saylor died in 1973, the Cambria County (Johnstown) Democratic organization seized its chance to recapture a nominally Democratic district. They found an attractive candidate in Murtha, a personable state legislator who had won a Bronze Star and two Purple Hearts as a Marine in Vietnam.

Murtha won narrowly over Harry M. Fox, a former Saylor aide, in a 1974 special election focused on the Republican Party's Watergate problems. He handily dispatched Fox the following November and won easily for the next decade and a half.

That included 1980, when Abscam had become public. Murtha's opponent tried to make the bribery scandal an issue, but he did not succeed. Murtha's plurality was down, but he still drew 59 percent of the vote.

In 1982, Pennsylvania's Republican-controlled Legislature combined Murtha's district with that of fellow-Democrat Don Bailey. The primary paired two excellent campaigners and close friends with similar pro-labor views.

The merged district contained about the same number of former constituents of each candidate, making it a battle between two organizations: Murtha had one in his home base, Cambria County, and Bailey had one in his native Westmoreland County. Bailey refused suggestions that he bring up Abscam or a second Murtha liability — his sponsorship of House members' tax breaks and pay increases.

While both Democrats worked hard, Murtha fielded a superior get-out-the-vote operation. In addition, Murtha convinced voters that he could better help the economically depressed steel district through his greater seniority and influence with the House leadership. Murtha won by a comfortable 52-38 percent margin.

Committees

Appropriations (10th of 37 Democrats)
Defense (chairman); Interior; Legislative

Elections

1990 General

John P. Murtha (D)	80,686	(62%)
Willeam Choby (R)	50,007	(38%)

1990 Primary

John P. Murtha (D)	29,369	(51%)
Kenneth B. Burkley (D)	24,594	(43%)
John K. Shrader (D)	3,679	(6%)

1988 General

John P. Murtha (D)	133,081	(100%)

Previous Winning Percentages: **1986** (67%) **1984** (69%) **1982** (61%) **1980** (59%) **1978** (69%) **1976** (68%) **1974** (58%) **1974 *** (50%)

** Special election.*

District Vote For President

	1988	1984	1980	1976
D	96,040 (52%)	98,636 (49%)	87,100 (46%)	94,428 (51%)
R	85,953 (47%)	101,854 (51%)	94,584 (49%)	88,982 (48%)
I			7,535 (4%)	

Campaign Finance

	Receipts	Receipts from PACs	Expend-itures
1990			
Murtha (D)	$878,887	$496,920 (57%)	$1,097,107
Choby (R)	$6,454	0	$5,951
1988			
Murtha (D)	$447,087	$310,815 (70%)	$401,945

Key Votes

1991

Authorize use of force against Iraq	Y

1990

Support constitutional amendment on flag desecration	Y
Pass family and medical leave bill over Bush veto	Y
Reduce SDI funding	Y
Allow abortions in overseas military facilities	N
Approve budget summit plan for spending and taxing	Y
Approve civil rights bill	Y

1989

Halt production of B-2 stealth bomber at 13 planes	N
Oppose capital gains tax cut	Y
Approve federal abortion funding in rape or incest cases	N
Approve pay raise and revision of ethics rules	Y
Pass Democratic minimum wage plan over Bush veto	Y

Voting Studies

	Presidential Support		Party Unity		Conservative Coalition	
Year	**S**	**O**	**S**	**O**	**S**	**O**
1990	33	64	85	13	61	39
1989	51	47	77	17	61	37
1988	35	60	79	16	58	39
1987	43	55	82	12	70	30
1986	42	56	76	15	68	28
1985	52	46	77	20	75	22
1984	52	43	77	18	63	34
1983	54	40	74	22	58	38
1982	53	39	68	21	64	30
1981	45	50	70	27	64	33

Interest Group Ratings

Year	ADA	ACU	AFL-CIO	CCUS
1990	56	22	100	21
1989	45	27	100	30
1988	55	46	100	29
1987	60	26	100	13
1986	40	52	93	25
1985	45	50	82	14
1984	40	27	69	38
1983	55	35	88	16
1982	45	37	90	33
1981	45	13	80	22

13 Lawrence Coughlin (R)

Of Plymouth Meeting — Elected 1968

Born: April 11, 1929, Wilkes-Barre, Pa.
Education: Yale U., A.B. 1950; Harvard U., M.B.A. 1954; Temple U., LL.B. 1958.
Military Service: Marine Corps Reserve, 1948-58, active duty, 1951-52.
Occupation: Lawyer.
Family: Wife, Susan MacGregor; four children.
Religion: Episcopalian.
Political Career: Pa. House, 1965-67; Pa. Senate, 1967-69.
Capitol Office: 2309 Rayburn Bldg. 20515; 225-6111.

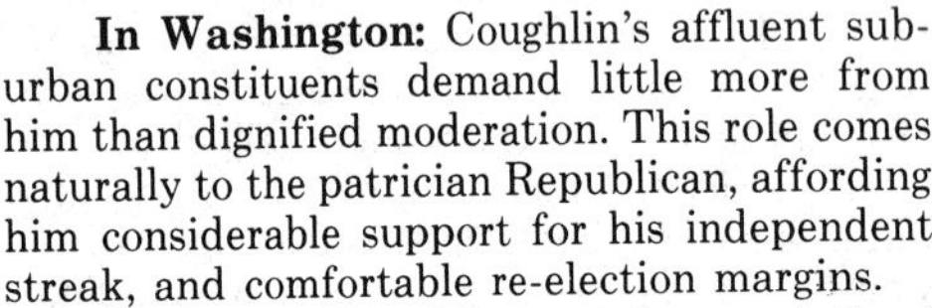

In Washington: Coughlin's affluent suburban constituents demand little more from him than dignified moderation. This role comes naturally to the patrician Republican, affording him considerable support for his independent streak, and comfortable re-election margins.

As ranking Republican on Appropriations' Transportation Subcommittee, Coughlin's legislative interests lie chiefly in protecting urban programs vital to Philadelphia, the city where the bankers and lawyers of his Main Line district spend their workdays.

His support for these programs, however, often places him at odds with the Republican administration. During the Reagan years, he regularly endorsed Democratic efforts to restore funds for mass transit, housing subsidies and other programs. In the Bush era, Coughlin sided with Democrats who opposed administration efforts to limit congressional prerogative in funding special projects. "I do not think that the repository of all wisdom is in the executive branch," he said on more than one occasion.

He also breaks with the administration on many social policy issues. He was one of fewer than 40 House Republicans to vote for the 1990 civil rights bill and to override the president's veto of the Family and Medical Leave Act.

But Coughlin mostly keeps a low profile on his dissent. In 1989, when many suburban Republicans were calling on President Bush to reverse his opposition to federal and D.C. government funding of abortion in cases of rape and incest, Coughlin simply cast quiet votes toward that end. Moreover, he favored activism over moderation in early 1989, when he supported Georgian Newt Gingrich's bid for GOP whip.

And like his constituents, when it comes to broader GOP economic policy, Coughlin can be a loyal foot soldier. On every key budget vote in the 101st Congress, Coughlin backed Bush. He joined the vast majority of House Republicans in unsuccessful 1989 efforts to protect the capital gains tax cut and to expand earned income tax credits for child care. He also voted with a minority of Republicans for the 1990 budget summit agreement Bush wanted.

Increasingly, drugs are the most pressing urban problem facing Congress, and at the start of the 101st Congress, Coughlin became the ranking Republican on the Select Committee on Narcotics. While not a high profile player on the charged issue, Coughlin voiced the GOP credo that lavish spending is not the answer. When Senate Democrats called for higher funding of treatment and education programs in 1990, Coughlin urged study of existing programs. "We've poured money at the problem," he said. "We need to see how the various initiatives we've already taken are working."

That attitude may have pleasantly surprised more conservative GOP colleagues who have grown accustomed to Coughlin's greater openness toward federal spending on the Appropriations Committee. He is a strong advocate of continued federal funding for Amtrak and urban mass transit.

When Housing Secretary Jack F. Kemp berated Congress for protecting 40 pet projects in 1989, Coughlin joined Democrats who maintained Congress had every right to fund the projects — including two, worth $3.5 million, in his district. In 1990, when conservatives tried to pare special projects from a supplemental appropriations bill, Coughlin voted against them three out of four times. He voted only to strike $1 million from the rural areas program.

But if Coughlin is willing to defend sums for small projects important to colleagues, he is also known to fight the big ones. In the mid-1980s, he helped kill two costly government projects — Westway, a 4.2-mile highway and land development project on Manhattan's West Side, and the Clinch River breeder reactor in Tennessee. He described them as "wasteful, environmentally questionable boondoggles."

Similarly, Coughlin revealed a skepticism about water-project funding in 1987, when Appropriations Chairman Jamie L. Whitten tried to insert language into a supplemental appropriations bill to nullify a cost-sharing agreement requiring local beneficiaries of fed-

Pennsylvania 13

Northwest Philadelphia Suburbs — The Main Line

In the last century, the Pennsylvania Railroad developed the rolling countryside along its main line west of Philadelphia. Among the greenery grew the mansions of the city's aristocracy.

The Main Line, which Coughlin calls home, anchors the state's most affluent district. The posh estates in Bryn Mawr, Gladwyne and the other towns around them turn in a solid GOP vote, with a moderate bent similar to the one Coughlin practices.

Beyond the Main Line, north of the Schuylkill River, old towns like Ambler and Plymouth Meeting add to the big Republican advantage. The far-north end of the district is devoted to farming and occupied by country estates.

Most of the Democrats in the 13th gather by the river. Lined up along the Schuylkill are old mill towns like Conshohocken and Norristown and two blue-collar sections of Philadelphia, Manayunk and Roxborough.

The state's 1982 redistricting added a Democratic section of the city — Overbrook — and Philadelphia's wealthiest area, Chestnut Hill, which is nominally Republican but shows an occasional weakness for liberal Democrats. The GOP's districtwide majority among registered voters, however, is still solid.

Population: 514,346. White 472,333 (92%), Black 33,165 (6%), Other 6,941 (1%). Spanish origin 4,156 (1%). 18 and over 392,167 (76%), 65 and over 73,644 (14%). Median age: 35.

eral water projects to contribute more to their development. When Coughlin warned that he would challenge it, Whitten elected to drop the one-sentence amendment.

Coughlin made a crusade of his opposition to the anti-satellite weapon (ASAT). He waged an unsuccessful fight against funding ASAT development in 1983. Two years later, he and California Democrat George E. Brown Jr. offered an amendment banning for one year ASAT tests against objects in space, as long as the Soviet Union maintained its existing test moratorium. The measure was approved each year from 1985 through 1987.

In 1988, however, Coughlin and Brown went for the kill — a permanent ban on the current ASAT weapon so long as the Russians did not test their own ASAT — and they misfired. The amendment went down 197-205. After the vote, they speculated that the word "permanent" had made members skittish.

With warmer U.S.-Soviet relations, and an adminstration pledge not to test the weapon, the issue was not on the front burner in the 101st Congress. In mid-1989, the House passed a resolution urging U.S.-Soviet talks on eliminating antisatellite weapons systems.

In his private time, Coughlin is a well-known sailor. When two Pennsylvanians were on the crew of the *Stars and Stripes* at the 1987 America's Cup championship, he took to the floor of the House to detail their challenge. He waxed eloquent upon their victory. "Yachting's crown jewel was retrieved in the glittering, sun-splashed Indian Ocean off Freemantle, Australia," he said.

At Home: Coughlin looks every bit the Main Line gentleman he is. His bow tie, upper-class accent and prestigious education are the correct trappings for the representative from the state's most affluent district.

Coughlin comes from a prosperous family in upstate Wilkes-Barre. He served in the Marines, then moved to Philadelphia for a business and legal career. A charter member of a group of young professionals that took control of the Montgomery County GOP, he worked to elect Republican William W. Scranton governor in 1962, won election to the Legislature in 1964 and four years later was running for Congress for the seat of GOP Rep. Richard S. Schweiker, who advanced to the Senate.

In most years, Coughlin enjoys effortless re-election. He has faced aggressive opposition only twice, in 1984 and 1986, from Democrat Joe Hoeffel, who left the state House to try for Congress.

In 1984, Hoeffel attacked Coughlin as "a nice guy in a bow tie with a mediocre record and little political courage." The Democrat entered that campaign with experience running in GOP territory; for eight years, he had represented a Montgomery County state House district in which more than 60 percent of the registered voters were Republicans. He charged that Coughlin did not deserve his reputation as a moderate because he had gone along with Reagan in votes on key economic and defense issues.

Hoeffel hoped that years of electoral security had lured Coughlin into complacency, but the incumbent responded with a fair amount of aggressiveness, at one point even calling Hoeffel a "wimp" on defense issues. Coughlin said his Appropriations Committee seniority enabled him to wangle extra money for SEPTA, the Philadelphia area's regional transit system. He noted his work against the anti-satellite weapon as a sign he supported arms control.

Hoeffel managed to get 44 percent of the vote, enough to encourage him to try again in 1986. In the second campaign, he pursued largely the same themes, mocking the incumbent for spending his career "floating downstream, making no waves." But he met an even more determined Coughlin. The incumbent hired his first full-time press secretary, opened a district office in the Philadelphia portion of the 13th, and accelerated his fundraising.

Coughlin also stepped up his attacks on Hoeffel; one radio ad ridiculed the Democrat as a state legislator "who will tax and spend at every bend, doesn't give a dime about crime, awards himself a big pay raise and then walks off the job for days." Another time, Coughlin referred to Hoeffel as a "pious phony." The Democrat slipped to 41 percent of the vote.

In 1988 and 1990, Democrats subsided into their customary somnolence in the 13th, running an underfinanced former high school vice principal against Coughlin. But the anti-incumbent mood that pulled down the vote percentages of a number of veteran Pennsylvania House incumbents in 1990 also weighed down Coughlin. After winning with 67 percent in 1988, his vote share dropped 7 percentage points against the same candidate two years later.

Committees

Select Narcotics Abuse & Control (Ranking)

Appropriations (4th of 22 Republicans)
Transportation (ranking); Veterans Affairs, Housing & Urban Development, & Independent Agencies

Elections

1990 General

Lawrence Coughlin (R)	89,577	(60%)
Bernard Tomkin (D)	58,967	(40%)

1988 General

Lawrence Coughlin (R)	152,191	(67%)
Bernard Tomkin (D)	76,424	(33%)

Previous Winning Percentages:				**1986**	(59%)	**1984**	(56%)
1982	(64%)	**1980**	(70%)	**1978**	(71%)	**1976**	(63%)
1974	(62%)	**1972**	(67%)	**1970**	(58%)	**1968**	(62%)

District Vote For President

	1988	1984	1980	1976
D	101,847 (43%)	97,696 (40%)	83,825 (34%)	109,064 (43%)
R	134,835 (56%)	146,699 (60%)	134,628 (55%)	139,707 (55%)
I			23,544 (10%)	

Campaign Finance

	Receipts	Receipts from PACs		Expend-itures
1990				
Coughlin (R)	$373,205	$163,969	(44%)	$235,766
Tomkin (D)	$39,199	$5,850	(15%)	$39,173
1988				
Coughlin (R)	$396,262	$150,851	(38%)	$225,412
Tompkin (D)	$62,721	$6,200	(10%)	$60,672

Key Votes

1991	
Authorize use of force against Iraq	Y
1990	
Support constitutional amendment on flag desecration	Y
Pass family and medical leave bill over Bush veto	Y
Reduce SDI funding	Y
Allow abortions in overseas military facilities	Y
Approve budget summit plan for spending and taxing	Y
Approve civil rights bill	Y
1989	
Halt production of B-2 stealth bomber at 13 planes	N
Oppose capital gains tax cut	N
Approve federal abortion funding in rape or incest cases	Y
Approve pay raise and revision of ethics rules	Y
Pass Democratic minimum wage plan over Bush veto	N

Voting Studies

	Presidential Support		Party Unity		Conservative Coalition	
Year	**S**	**O**	**S**	**O**	**S**	**O**
1990	58	36	68	28	76	22
1989	69	28	67	29	88	12
1988	49	47	70	25	87	8
1987	51	46	56	37	67	28
1986	48	49	51	46	58	40
1985	50	49	63	33	55	45
1984	50	44	49	44	53	46
1983	57	41	56	42	52	45
1982	65	34	65	34	56	42
1981	66	32	62	34	59	39

Interest Group Ratings

Year	ADA	ACU	AFL-CIO	CCUS
1990	33	35	17	64
1989	30	57	17	90
1988	50	48	64	79
1987	36	52	38	60
1986	45	41	71	61
1985	50	43	59	57
1984	40	39	38	50
1983	40	45	12	90
1982	45	55	40	59
1981	35	67	33	89

14 William J. Coyne (D)

Of Pittsburgh — Elected 1980

Born: Aug. 24, 1936, Pittsburgh, Pa.
Education: Robert Morris College, B.S. 1965.
Military Service: Army, 1955-57.
Occupation: Accountant.
Family: Single.
Religion: Roman Catholic.
Political Career: Pa. House, 1971-73; Pittsburgh City Council, 1974-81; sought Democratic nomination for Pa. Senate, 1972.
Capitol Office: 2455 Rayburn Bldg. 20515; 225-2301.

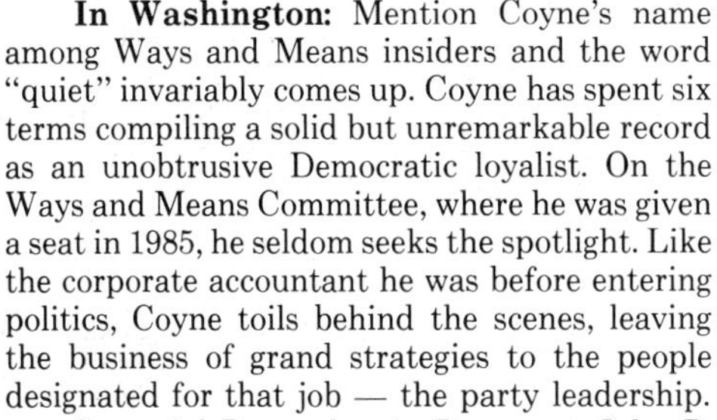

In Washington: Mention Coyne's name among Ways and Means insiders and the word "quiet" invariably comes up. Coyne has spent six terms compiling a solid but unremarkable record as an unobtrusive Democratic loyalist. On the Ways and Means Committee, where he was given a seat in 1985, he seldom seeks the spotlight. Like the corporate accountant he was before entering politics, Coyne toils behind the scenes, leaving the business of grand strategies to the people designated for that job — the party leadership.

Powerful Pennsylvania Democrat John P. Murtha is chiefly responsible for Coyne having a place on Ways and Means. Coyne did little campaigning on his own, but Murtha made it clear that Coyne was his choice to give the Pennsylvania steel industry some representation on the influential tax-writing panel. Coyne had four competitors for one remaining seat, including Michael A. Andrews, a Texan favored by then-Majority Leader Jim Wright. But after some complicated horse-trading that produced an alliance between Murtha and Ways and Means Chairman Dan Rostenkowski, Coyne won by one vote. (Andrews later joined the committee when another seat came open.)

Coyne went on to become a strong supporter of tax revision on Ways and Means in the 99th Congress, but he was not noticeably involved in crafting the legislation. Quiet during much of the debate in committee, Coyne spoke out mainly on the subject of industrial development bonds, which are important to Pittsburgh and to the Democratic city government of which he is a loyal ally.

Asked to cite accomplishments, Coyne will likely mention his work in the 101st Congress that helped establish demonstration projects for home dialysis, or a change he fostered in Medicare reimbursement rates.

As a member of the Banking Committee in his first two terms, Coyne argued for Pittsburgh's business and financial interests, supporting extension of Clean Air Act compliance dates for the steel industry, backing the Export-Import Bank and supporting money to keep the International Monetary Fund solvent.

One of Coyne's chief concerns has been the plight of urban areas in economic decline. In 1988, he introduced a bill to revive the federal revenue-sharing program and target money to local governments whose communities are suffering high unemployment.

In the 100th and 101st Congresses, he sponsored legislation to require the Bureau of Labor Statistics to collect and report data on so-called discouraged workers. Coyne says that the unemployment rate "understates the problem of joblessness in the United States" because it does not include workers who stop looking for work because they no longer believe they can find a job. Neither of Coyne's proposals has emerged from committee.

Coyne also proposed his own version of the "enterprise zone" concept. He felt the plan advanced during the Reagan administration, offering tax incentives to promote development, would be useful only to big businesses. To help cash-starved small and medium-sized businesses get started, Coyne suggested giving them direct aid through existing programs such as community development block grants.

At Home: Coyne's political career has never forced him to stray very far from his inner-city Pittsburgh roots. He still lives in the house where he was born. Before coming to Congress, he was active in Pittsburgh politics for a decade, working loyally with the city Democratic organization.

Coyne was elected to the state House in 1970 but lost a state Senate bid in 1972. In 1973, he was elected to the City Council, where he served as city chairman of the Pittsburgh Democratic Party.

When the 14th opened up in 1980 with the retirement of longtime Democratic Rep. William S. Moorhead, Coyne had the connections to claim it. The city Democratic organization helped him easily defeat Rep. Moorhead's son in the primary. He went on to an easy victory over the Republican nominee that fall and has not slipped below 70 percent of the vote since then.

Pennsylvania 14

Pittsburgh

Downtown Pittsburgh has lost its pollution and griminess over the past generation; the "Golden Triangle" at the heart of its business district has been transformed from a train yard into a cluster of office towers, pedestrian plazas and parks. Some local boosters seeking a more cosmopolitan image for Pittsburgh have taken to calling it "the San Francisco of the East," noting the city's hills, funicular railways, ethnic neighborhoods, busy port and large corporate community, which includes Westinghouse, Rockwell, Heinz, Mellon and USAir.

Business and government leaders have made some headway in propelling Pittsburgh beyond its blue-collar "Steeltown" past toward a new economic identity. Along the Monongahela River where steelworks once stood, a high-technology center is being developed, and other projects are under way that will modernize the Pittsburgh airport and promote the city as a center for research in fields such as computers and robotics.

Economic diversification and creeping cosmopolitanism have had little impact on voting habits in the 14th, which encompasses the entire city: In the city, Democrats enjoy about a 5-to-1 advantage over Republicans among registered voters.

The south side of Pittsburgh gives the city its image as a workingman's "shot-and-beer" town; it is packed with ethnic neighborhoods that revolve around local taverns and Catholic parishes.

In the district's other residential neighborhoods farther north, blacks and ethnics coexist with affluent, Jewish Squirrel Hill and the Oakland academic-medical complex, which includes Carnegie-Mellon University, the University of Pittsburgh and Children's Hospital. Republicans have some strength in the better-off areas, but Democrats still dominate.

Population: 516,629. White 398,072 (77%), Black 112,514 (22%), Other 3,413 (1%). Spanish origin 3,642 (1%). 18 and over 405,532 (78%), 65 and over 82,858 (16%). Median age: 33.

Committee

Ways & Means (18th of 23 Democrats)
Health; Select Revenue Measures

Elections

1990 General

William J. Coyne (D)	77,636	(72%)
Richard Edward Caligiuri (R)	30,497	(28%)

1988 General

William J. Coyne (D)	135,181	(79%)
Richard Edward Caligiuri (R)	36,719	(21%)

Previous Winning Percentages: **1986** (90%) **1984** (77%) **1982** (75%) **1980** (69%)

District Vote For President

	1988		1984		1980		1976	
D	140,594	(72%)	157,422	(68%)	123,121	(58%)	132,719	(59%)
R	51,387	(26%)	69,442	(30%)	70,994	(33%)	86,985	(39%)
I					13,337	(6%)		

Campaign Finance

	Receipts	Receipts from PACs		Expend-itures
1990				
Coyne (D)	$156,692	$141,600	(90%)	$130,904
1988				
Coyne (D)	$168,698	$156,075	(93%)	$80,730

Key Votes

1991

Authorize use of force against Iraq	N

1990

Support constitutional amendment on flag desecration	N
Pass family and medical leave bill over Bush veto	Y
Reduce SDI funding	Y
Allow abortions in overseas military facilities	Y
Approve budget summit plan for spending and taxing	N
Approve civil rights bill	Y

1989

Halt production of B-2 stealth bomber at 13 planes	Y
Oppose capital gains tax cut	Y
Approve federal abortion funding in rape or incest cases	Y
Approve pay raise and revision of ethics rules	Y
Pass Democratic minimum wage plan over Bush veto	Y

Voting Studies

Year	Presidential Support S	Presidential Support O	Party Unity S	Party Unity O	Conservative Coalition S	Conservative Coalition O
1990	17	81	93	2	7	91
1989	30	70	96	0	15	83
1988	19	76	92	3	11	79
1987	14	86	93	3	19	81
1986	17	81	95	3	6	94
1985	19	79	94	2	9	89
1984	30	68	91	6	17	78
1983	26	67	91	4	12	85
1982	42	57	91	7	26	74
1981	38	62	89	10	16	84

Interest Group Ratings

Year	ADA	ACU	AFL-CIO	CCUS
1990	100	4	100	29
1989	100	4	100	10
1988	95	0	100	31
1987	96	0	100	7
1986	100	0	100	22
1985	95	0	100	19
1984	85	5	85	33
1983	90	4	100	20
1982	90	5	95	27
1981	95	0	87	16

15 Don Ritter (R)

Of Coopersburg — Elected 1978

Born: Oct. 21, 1940, New York, N.Y.
Education: Lehigh U., B.S. 1961; Massachusetts Institute of Technology, M.S. 1963, Sc.D. 1966.
Occupation: Engineering consultant; professor.
Family: Wife, Edith Duerksen; two children.
Religion: Unitarian.
Political Career: No previous office.
Capitol Office: 2202 Rayburn Bldg. 20515; 225-6411.

In Washington: Ritter is a scientist, and he wants you to know it. A former metallurgy professor, he serves on two committees — Energy and Commerce, and Science, Space and Technology — where his expertise is applicable, if not always appreciated. Ritter is prone to holding forth on technical subjects, with prefatory reminders that his scientific background gives him special insight. As one observer of Ritter's work noted wryly, "Knowledge can sometimes be more effective when disguised."

An intense and energetic man, Ritter can show impatience with members from lay backgrounds who plunge into complex technical issues. He has made a name for himself as an opponent of scientific pork — or "quark barrel," as he calls it. He has been a leading House foe of the superconducting super collider (SSC). From the outset, Ritter claimed the project amounted to little more than a "triumph of good politics over good science."

In 1987, Ritter unsuccessfully sought to amend the SSC authorizing legislation to delay almost all spending on the project until after the site was selected. In November 1988, when Texas was chosen for the SSC, some non-Texans who had been ardent SSC supporters cried "politics." Ritter seemed to take great pleasure in this: He said, "I knew this would happen." Congress approved construction funding for the SSC in 1989, but debate over the project's scope and cost continues.

By contrast, Ritter is a vocal supporter of a federal role in developing domestic high-definition television (HDTV), a science the Japanese have pioneered. He is a leading member of the HDTV caucus, which maintains that the semiconductor chip at the heart of HDTV has crucial implications for the future of the American electronics industry. "Digital video must take precedence over dish towels," said Ritter.

He openly disagreed with the Bush administration's opposition to activist technology strategies and instead called for increased seed money for the Advanced Technology Program aimed at commercializing high-tech advances — a stance that some free-market conservatives criticized as reeking of "industrial policy."

Ritter's concern for high-tech competitiveness is not surprising; Allentown has a large AT&T facility that manufactures electronic circuitry. But there is another side to Ritter's desire to keep pace with the Japanese, one that reflects the frustrations of the blue-collar workers — particularly steelworkers — in the factories that make up the older industrial foundation of the Lehigh Valley economy.

When Energy and Commerce held a 1989 hearing on allowing an American aerospace company help Japan develop a new fighter plane, the FS-X, Ritter joined the opposition. While some complained that Japan would exploit American technology, Ritter also said that purchase of a U.S.-made jet "would have gone a long way toward demonstrating Japan's sincerity about reducing its $55 billion trade surplus."

A proponent of nuclear energy, Ritter in 1989 locked horns with New York Gov. Mario M. Cuomo in an unsuccessful attempt to prevent the shutdown of the Long Island-based Shoreham nuclear power plant. Ritter sought to bar the Nuclear Regulatory Commission from spending funds to approve transfer of ownership of the plant to the state — a move Cuomo attacked as an infringement on his state's regulatory responsibilities.

Though his overall record is conservative, Ritter frequently strays from the GOP line on labor issues. In the 100th Congress, he was one of just 17 Republicans to favor mandatory retaliation against countries with unfair trade practices, and one of just a handful of Republicans to vote against eliminating a plant-closing notification proposal. Ritter also voted to override Reagan's veto of the trade bill.

In 1987, Ritter joined several House colleagues on the Capitol lawn to sledgehammer Toshiba products. They were protesting the company's selling of restricted high-technology products to the Soviet Union, a country Ritter frequently decries.

A senior GOP member of the Helsinki commission, Ritter matches his sharp eye with rough rhetoric when he reviews Soviet policies.

Pennsylvania 15

East — Allentown; Bethlehem

The heavy industry, strong unions and large ethnic population (including a sizable Jewish community) of the Lehigh Valley bespeak Democratic sentiments. But disaffection with Democratic candidates, both local and national, has lured voters in the valley to the GOP in recent years. Jimmy Carter carried the area within the 15th in 1976, but Ronald Reagan and George Bush won it in the 1980s.

Lehigh County (Allentown) has the largest population and is politically competitive. Allentown had a Republican mayor until 1981, and in 1988 Lehigh County gave Bush 56 percent. Although singer Billy Joel chose Allentown in 1982 to represent the plight of the newly unemployed, the recession did not hit the city quite as hard as some other places because of its diversified economy. Even after Mack Trucks pulled out in 1987 — moving their main plant to South Carolina — the city's thriving small companies helped brace the economy.

The showpiece of the "new" Allentown economy is a huge AT&T facility that produces some of the world's most advanced electronic circuitry. Some local factories depend on the high-quality craftsmanship of Pennsylvania Dutch workers, who are attractive to the corporations because they are conservative and resist unionization.

Pennsylvania's fourth-largest city, with a population of more than 105,000, Allentown has an unspectacular downtown, but some neat and pleasant residential sections that are a legacy of its Pennsylvania Dutch founders. The prosperous West End is Republican, with blue-collar Democrats spread through the rest of the town.

Neighboring Northampton County has a grittier ambience, due to the presence of heavier industry there. The smokestacks of Bethlehem Steel dominate the Bethlehem landscape, and the massive corporation dominates the city, providing its tax base and financing urban-renewal projects. Nearby Easton produces chemicals and paper products.

The Allentown-Bethlehem-Easton corridor is becoming a refuge for New York commuters looking for affordable housing. The portions of Lehigh and Northampton counties outside the corridor are steady sources of Republican votes. Many of the farmers are of Pennsylvania Dutch heritage.

Population: 515,259. White 497,609 (97%), Black 8,189 (2%), Other 2,936 (1%). Spanish origin 14,193 (3%). 18 and over 385,814 (75%), 65 and over 65,768 (13%). Median age: 33.

In a May 1989 opinion column in *The Washington Post,* he detailed the Soviet Union's new legal code and condemned the recent reforms, saying that while they are being protrayed as efforts to defend democracy, in fact the reforms are "clearly designed to intimidate would-be critics, dissidents or nationalists into accepting *glasnost* on the state's terms — or else."

Ritter's scientific background and his constituents' concerns also coalesced on clean-air legislation. When the measure was first debated in the 97th Congress, Ritter used his familiarity with the chemical effects of air pollutants to try to shoot down arguments for tougher standards that would have further burdened industry. When clean air legislation was moving toward passage in the 101st Congress, Ritter supported a proposal to provide job-loss relief for workers displaced by the new law, a position at odds with the Bush administration.

At Home: It was Ritter's extraordinary energy, rather than his political program, that brought him victory in 1978 over Democratic Rep. Fred Rooney, chairman of the Commerce Subcommittee on Transportation. Rooney never really made enemies at home; he simply grew less and less visible. By 1978 he was sending telegrams to gatherings he once had attended personally. Ritter courted Democrats who wondered where Rooney was, and it paid off with a 53 percent victory.

Since then, Ritter has been both a salesman for his philosophy and a spokesman for his district's needs. In an area where steel and other old industries are struggling, he talks fervently about government giving private enterprise free rein so it can generate a new industrial revolution based on high technology.

But Ritter balances his interest in high technology with responsiveness to immediate economic problems. In 1984, his advocacy of import quotas for steel won him valuable publicity at home. Though Reagan did not impose the mandatory quotas sought by Ritter and others, steelworkers in the 15th ended up convinced that Ritter had gone to bat for them.

Local Democratic leaders seem at a loss to find the right kind of candidate to challenge Ritter. He has won re-election by comfortable, though by no means overwhelming, margins.

The recession brought heavy unemployment to the Lehigh Valley in 1982, but Democrats failed to field a seasoned candidate. They put up Richard J. Orloski, whose lone government experience was as a state deputy attorney general. Four GOP incumbents in Pennsylvania lost that year, but not Ritter.

The 1984 Democratic nominee was not the type one would expect to find seeking office in a working-class district. Jane Wells-Schooley came out of the feminist movement, serving as vice president of the National Organization for Women until 1982. A number of her positions were controversial; she backed legalized abortion as well as a nuclear-weapons freeze. She tried to focus voters' attention on economic issues, but the dialogue often strayed onto other topics. With most voters regarding her views as too exotic, Ritter won easily.

In 1986, Ritter's challenger was Joe Simonetta, a former commander of a NATO missile team in Greece, who focused on the need to slow down the nuclear arms race. Ritter was breezing to re-election when he jolted voters with an unexpected issue — his past drug use. The incumbent had initially brought up the topic of drug abuse when he announced that he and his staff would take drug tests. Ritter's admission that he had smoked marijuana a decade or so earlier came only after Simonetta questioned him about past drug use.

While the issue provided Simonetta with an opening he did not previously have, it did not derail Ritter. He won 57 percent of the vote.

In 1988, Democrats made a more concerted effort. Ed Reibman, an attorney active in the local party, won the Democratic nomination on the strength of his strong labor backing and his name, which is familiar because his mother is a well-known state senator from the area (she also was the party's nominee against Ritter in 1980). Reibman chastised Ritter's attendance record and acceptance of honoraria, and criticized his votes on seniors' issues. But outspent nearly 2-to-1, Reibman was no match for Ritter. The Republican portrayed himself as a hard worker, airing TV ads showing him on an airplane, coming home "like clockwork" to the district.

Orloski got a second shot at Ritter in 1990. The Democrat charged him with keeping a "secret" campaign account, and spent much of the campaign pressing Ritter to disclose details of its contents and use. Voters were not aroused; they gave Ritter 61 percent of the vote, his highest tally ever.

Committees

Energy & Commerce (5th of 16 Republicans)
Transportation & Hazardous Materials (ranking); Telecommunications & Finance

Science, Space & Technology (5th of 19 Republicans)
Environment (ranking); Technology & Competitiveness

Elections

1990 General

Don Ritter (R)	77,178	(61%)
Richard J. Orloski (D)	50,233	(39%)

1988 General

Don Ritter (R)	106,951	(57%)
Ed Reibman (D)	79,127	(43%)

Previous Winning Percentages: **1986** (57%) **1984** (58%) **1982** (58%) **1980** (60%) **1978** (53%)

District Vote For President

	1988	1984	1980	1976
D	84,618 (44%)	81,072 (42%)	68,570 (39%)	91,229 (52%)
R	103,784 (55%)	110,142 (57%)	89,260 (50%)	81,662 (46%)
I			16,201 (9%)	

Campaign Finance

	Receipts	Receipts from PACs	Expend-itures
1990			
Ritter (R)	$560,729	$275,106 (49%)	$577,790
Orloski (D)	$103,249	$2,500 (2%)	$102,312
1988			
Ritter (R)	$759,713	$293,454 (39%)	$752,332
Reibman (D)	$359,820	$97,650 (27%)	$355,016

Key Votes

1991	
Authorize use of force against Iraq	Y
1990	
Support constitutional amendment on flag desecration	Y
Pass family and medical leave bill over Bush veto	N
Reduce SDI funding	N
Allow abortions in overseas military facilities	N
Approve budget summit plan for spending and taxing	N
Approve civil rights bill	N
1989	
Halt production of B-2 stealth bomber at 13 planes	N
Oppose capital gains tax cut	N
Approve federal abortion funding in rape or incest cases	N
Approve pay raise and revision of ethics rules	N
Pass Democratic minimum wage plan over Bush veto	N

Voting Studies

	Presidential Support		Party Unity		Conservative Coalition	
Year	S	O	S	O	S	O
1990	66	32	73	22	78	19
1989	69	30	70	24	90	10
1988	57	39	66	26	84	11
1987	63	33	68	25	81	19
1986	70	29	65	29	88	10
1985	75	23	71	22	76	20
1984	56	42	74	21	73	20
1983	76	22	81	16	82	16
1982	73	26	83	16	78	21
1981	71	24	82	17	76	19

Interest Group Ratings

Year	ADA	ACU	AFL-CIO	CCUS
1990	6	83	25	79
1989	10	100	17	100
1988	10	84	62	77
1987	20	64	38	73
1986	10	90	57	94
1985	10	86	38	82
1984	15	52	50	63
1983	10	86	29	79
1982	20	82	30	76
1981	10	100	21	84

16 Robert S. Walker (R)

Of East Petersburg — Elected 1976

Born: Dec. 23, 1942, Bradford, Pa.
Education: Millersville U., B.S. 1964; U. of Delaware, M.A. 1968.
Military Service: Pa. National Guard, 1967-73.
Occupation: High school teacher; congressional aide.
Family: Wife, Sue Albertson.
Religion: Presbyterian.
Political Career: No previous office.
Capitol Office: 2369 Rayburn Bldg. 20515; 225-2411.

In Washington: For Walker, winning appointment as chief deputy whip in March 1989 vindicated the confrontational tactics he and his allies in the Conservative Opportunity Society (COS) had urged upon a House GOP leadership they viewed as too accepting of minority status.

When the COS first became a force a few years back, its leader, Newt Gingrich, got most of the credit as the spinner of ideas. Walker was seen simply as the group's blunt instrument — strident, repetitious and obstructionist, the quintessential legislative outsider.

But when Gingrich was elected GOP whip a few weeks into the 101st Congress, he brought Walker into the leadership to help him. Asked afterward whether, like many rebels-turned-insiders, he would become more accommodating to his adversaries, Walker gave no quarter.

"I don't see much evidence that Republicans won great victories when they were not confrontational but passive instead," Walker said. "In 34 years, we were not able to get a majority; there's no victory there."

For the most part, Walker has kept his pledge. Colleagues have taken him somewhat more seriously because his tactics carry leadership sanction, and he takes great pains to publicize how many of his amendments become law to downplay his gadfly label. But he has managed to continue his dissents while carrying out his body-counting and arm-twisting duties.

A self-proclaimed crusader against pork-barrel spending, Walker drew comment in 1990. Rep. Bob Traxler, D-Mich., chairman of an Appropriations subcommittee, and others discovered that Rep. Lawrence Coughlin, R-Pa., was carrying the ball for Walker on a request to forgive indebtedness on an urban renewal project in the 16th. "Whose district is that?" called out one mischievious member during the hearing. Walker said that it did not constitute "pork" because it required no new money.

Walker, Gingrich and others first gained prominence by using C-SPAN — the cable TV system that carries live broadcasts of House proceedings — to sell their conservative message nationwide. In 1984, Walker was giving a "special order" speech (at the end of the legislative day) two days after he and Gingrich used a special order to excoriate Democrats for past foreign policy statements. Speaker Thomas P. O'Neill Jr. secretly ordered the TV cameras to pull back and pan the House. For the first time, viewers saw that the chamber was virtually empty. As Gingrich grilled O'Neill for his unannounced move, the Speaker got so angry that his language overstepped the bounds of House custom. He was officially rebuked.

While the COS members were often referred to as the Republicans' "bomb throwers," their weapons actually were more like flash grenades, causing a lot of heat and smoke, but little injury to their targets. The firebrands crafted and passed few substantive pieces of legislation, and the Democrats expanded their House majority in the 1986 and 1988 elections. The heyday of the COS seemed over.

In fact, the COS leadership had spent less time on the House floor railing to an empty chamber than currying favor with a cadre of mainly young, moderate Republican colleagues frustrated with their "permanent" minority status. Their eventual support clinched Gingrich's victory for whip over a traditional GOP insider, Edward Madigan of Illinois; one of those moderates, Steve Gunderson of Wisconsin, shares the title of chief deputy whip with Walker.

In the 100th Congress, Walker and his allies also demonstrated a capacity to hone their legislative efforts, and even to compromise, to bring a sweeping proposal to fruition. After much wrangling, Walker's "drug-free work place" measure was enacted as part of an omnibus anti-drug abuse bill; it allows the federal government to end funding to contractors who fail to make a "good-faith" effort to keep illegal drug use out of their work sites.

Walker's initial version was a draconian concept — allowing a cutoff of federal contracts to a company if an employee was found in possession of a single marijuana cigarette. Democrats treated it as a joke — an example, they said, of COS extremism. When Walker, then

Pennsylvania 16

Southeast — Lancaster

Viewers of the popular movie "Witness" may have an image of the 16th District as one of horse-drawn buggies on country lanes and black-clad "plain people" tending crops. But the 16th grew by 15 percent during the 1970s, faster than any district in the state. The district's largest county — Lancaster — grew by 16 percent during the 1980s, as 60,000 new residents arrived.

One factor helping fuel the growth is the favorable business climate. Companies looking to start new plants are drawn by the strong work ethic of its labor force, a trait of the Pennsylvania Dutch who settled this area and still are an important influence.

The newcomers to the 16th do not wear black as the Amish farmers do, but they share one common outlook — they are conservative Republicans.

Lancaster County does have Democratic pockets in the city of Lancaster, where electrical appliances and other household items are made, and in the Susquehanna River town of Columbia, which has a glass plant. But it is the scenic farm country — with its oddly named hamlets, such as Bird-in-Hand and Intercourse — that sets the tone for the district. And it is a conservative tone indeed. Reportedly when Democratic incumbent Robert P. Casey beat gaffe-prone Republican Barbara Hafer in the 1990 gubernatorial race, it was the first time that Lancaster County had not voted for a Republican for governor since 1826.

Three percent of Lancaster County's population is Amish. Some of the sects cling closer to the old ways than others. They range from the Old Order Amish, who in effect live in the mid-19th century, to the "black-bumper Mennonites," who drive cars but paint the chrome bumpers black. The excellent farm land is devoted largely to dairying, although tobacco has a niche in the agricultural economy.

The district also encompasses all of Lebanon County, which like Lancaster County, is steadfastly Republican; in 1988, both counties voted overwhelmingly for George Bush.

Population: 514,585. White 494,052 (96%), Black 10,641 (2%), Other 3,290 (1%). Spanish origin 11,175 (2%). 18 and over 369,823 (72%), 65 and over 59,793 (12%). Median age: 31.

the ranking Republican of the Science Subcommittee on Space (and now ranking on the full committee), first submitted his bill in April 1988, committee Democrat Dave McCurdy of Oklahoma laughed out loud.

But Walker laughed last. In his finest confrontational manner, he threatened the bill's opponents with a soft-on-drugs label. In an election year, with drug crime a major issue, Walker's ploy persuaded many Democrats.

Walker attached his proposal to several Science authorization bills, then used his skill at House floor tactics to attach it to a series of appropriations bills. A Democratic leadership party task force drew up an alternative that softened the edges of the drug-free work place concept: Contractors would be penalized only for a track record of drug violations, rather than a single instance, and the president could waive the requirement if necessary for the national interest.

Walker at first dismissed the compromise as a "drugs-in-the-work-place amendment." But by the time the Government Operations Committee attached the revised plan to the omnibus drug bill — virtually guaranteeing its adoption — Walker was on board, despite the provision's far less stringent wording. Later, Walker vowed to require Congress to enforce the law in its own work sites.

Even with this success, though, it is doubtful that many colleagues outside his circle of allies were waiting with warm congratulations for Walker. He has raised too many hackles and rubbed too many raw nerves to be very popular.

His performance in trying to slow the rush to adjournment at the end of the 100th Congress was vintage Walker. The Democratic leadership was trying to push through a long list of bills, most on relatively minor matters, under "suspension of the rules," which limits debate but requires a two-thirds majority for passage. Walker, stating that he wanted to make a partisan point about the Democrats' rush to pass insignificant legislation while failing to act on such important bills as the Clean Air Act, demanded roll-call votes on each measure.

As a result, a record 40 roll-call votes were held on Oct. 4, 1988, requiring members who were trying to wrap up their year's work to spend their day on the floor, casting votes on less-than-urgent issues. When Walker finally relented, stating he would not request roll calls on all bills the next day, Democrat Leon E. Panetta of California said, "If Walker had continued to do it, his life would have been in jeopardy." The rancor was not limited to Democrats. "It's an asinine series of votes," said Illinois Republican Henry J. Hyde.

Just before his roll-call frenzy, Walker had

blocked a unanimous-consent request that would have brought to the floor an emergency proposal to extend an expiring program that helped AIDS patients buy life-prolonging drugs. This forced bill supporters to gain Rules Committee approval for floor consideration. In the 101st, he attempted to embarrass House Democrats with several amendments to trim the Agriculture Department's budget, including one that would have cut a mere $19.90. That one failed by 175-214.

Walker also stirred the pot with a 1990 resolution creating a task force study of what he said were abuses by members in revising their floor remarks in the *Congressional Record.* Although many members privately wished to retain the ability to amend their speeches, Walker threatened to bring the rule change to a floor vote, putting members on record.

Some find it ironic that Walker plays a more traditional, turf-conscious role as a Republican leader on the Science Committee. He strongly supports the National Aeronautics and Space Administration and other federally funded research agencies.

At Home: Walker's confrontational Republican politics have played well not only among the new arrivals in burgeoning Lancaster County but also among his Pennsylvania Dutch constituents. Conservatism sells well here, and Walker is a born salesman. To publicize his campaign against food stamp abuse, he went to work in a grocery store. When he targeted the Department of Energy, he made a list of questionable-sounding grants — for such things as a solar hot dog cooker — then cited in Johnny Carson's "Tonight" show.

After a short stint working as a teacher, Walker signed on as an aide to his representative, Republican Edwin D. Eshleman, and eventually became his administrative assistant. When Eshleman decided to step down in 1976, he backed his young protégé in an 11-way primary fight for the seat.

Walker stressed his Washington experience and, with the help of Eshleman's endorsement and the top ballot position, eked out a victory with 20 percent of the vote. That turned out to be his only big hurdle. Given Lancaster's strong Republican sentiments, he has fallen below 70 percent of the vote only once since his initial election — in 1990.

Committee

Science, Space & Technology (Ranking)

Elections

1990 General		
Robert S. Walker (R)	85,596	(66%)
Ernest Eric Guyll (D)	43,849	(34%)
1988 General		
Robert S. Walker (R)	136,944	(74%)
Ernest Eric Guyll (D)	48,169	(26%)

Previous Winning Percentages: **1986** (75%) **1984** (78%) **1982** (71%) **1980** (77%) **1978** (77%) **1976** (62%)

District Vote For President

	1988		1984		1980		1976	
D	57,122	(30%)	47,806	(26%)	45,062	(26%)	55,703	(36%)
R	132,130	(70%)	137,560	(74%)	115,623	(66%)	97,132	(63%)
I					11,416	(7%)		

Campaign Finance

	Receipts	Receipts from PACs		Expend-itures
1990				
Walker (R)	$96,737	$43,810	(45%)	$98,284
1988				
Walker (R)	$106,318	$44,375	(42%)	$91,950

Key Votes

1991	
Authorize use of force against Iraq	Y
1990	
Support constitutional amendment on flag desecration	Y
Pass family and medical leave bill over Bush veto	N
Reduce SDI funding	N
Allow abortions in overseas military facilities	N
Approve budget summit plan for spending and taxing	N
Approve civil rights bill	N
1989	
Halt production of B-2 stealth bomber at 13 planes	N
Oppose capital gains tax cut	N
Approve federal abortion funding in rape or incest cases	N
Approve pay raise and revision of ethics rules	N
Pass Democratic minimum wage plan over Bush veto	N

Voting Studies

	Presidential Support		Party Unity		Conservative Coalition	
Year	**S**	**O**	**S**	**O**	**S**	**O**
1990	85	15	95	4	85	15
1989	79	21	98	2	93	7
1988	78	22	95	3	95	5
1987	83	17	97	3	91	9
1986	82	17	96	4	94	6
1985	80	20	93	5	85	15
1984	66	30	92	6	88	12
1983	80	20	94	6	81	19
1982	68	32	92	8	84	16
1981	72	18	84	12	80	15

Interest Group Ratings

Year	ADA	ACU	AFL-CIO	CCUS
1990	11	96	8	71
1989	10	93	0	100
1988	5	100	7	93
1987	4	96	0	87
1986	0	86	14	94
1985	15	86	12	91
1984	10	83	8	60
1983	20	96	6	80
1982	15	96	20	82
1981	10	100	27	89

17 George W. Gekas (R)

Of Harrisburg — Elected 1982

Born: April 14, 1930, Harrisburg, Pa.

Education: Dickinson College, B.A. 1952; Dickinson School of Law, LL.B. 1958, J.D. 1958.

Military Service: Army, 1953-55.

Occupation: Lawyer.

Family: Wife, Evangeline Charas.

Religion: Greek Orthodox.

Political Career: Pa. House, 1967-75; Pa. Senate, 1977-83.

Capitol Office: 1519 Longworth Bldg. 20515; 225-4315.

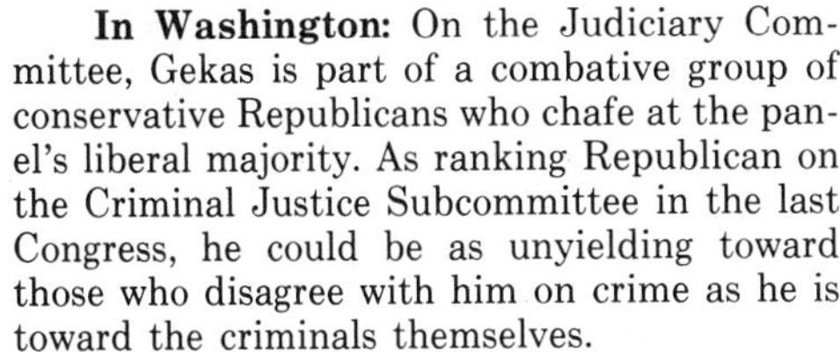

In Washington: On the Judiciary Committee, Gekas is part of a combative group of conservative Republicans who chafe at the panel's liberal majority. As ranking Republican on the Criminal Justice Subcommittee in the last Congress, he could be as unyielding toward those who disagree with him on crime as he is toward the criminals themselves.

A member of the Crime Subcommittee, Gekas is Congress' leading proponent of capital punishment. He is always on the lookout to attach death-penalty language to bills passing through Judiciary. It is hard to imagine the relevance of the issue in his assignment to the Intelligence panel in 1991, but if there's a link, count on Gekas to find it.

After years of trying, Gekas exploited election year concern about the drug epidemic in 1988 to secure his first death penalty victory. As work began on the 100th Congress drug bill, Gekas vowed to use "every parliamentary maneuver known to mankind" to ensure enactment of a death-penalty bill. His amendment, providing the death penalty for individuals convicted of drug-related murders, was adopted 299-111. The language was retained in the final bill, making it the first federal death penalty since 1972, when the Supreme Court struck down all existing death penalty statutes.

In the 101st Congress, Gekas came close to a more sweeping victory. For the first time, the House Judiciary Committee went along with a death sentence for 10 crimes. With the 1990 election less than a month away, the House voted 271-159 to approve a Gekas' amendment to expand the death penalty to 20 additional crimes, including the murder of a federal official.

Although the Senate bill included similar provisions, conferees could not agree on language on death row inmate appeals, and the entire package was dropped. Gekas was so annoyed that he alone voted against the final package, which was adopted 313-1.

In the 99th Congress, he almost single-handedly sidetracked the $1.7 billion drug bill over the death penalty. During House debate, he offered an amendment authorizing the death penalty for certain drug-related crimes. "There can be no ultimate war on drugs," he said, "if we do not cast our ultimate weapon." When the Senate bill came over without Gekas language, he won a vote to send it back. But the Senate instead split the bill, allowing passage of a compromise without his amendment.

With Three Mile Island nuclear power plant in his district, Gekas cosponsored legislation with Charles Schumer of New York in the 101st Congress to make those responsible for environmental disasters face criminal penalties. The subcommittee approved the bill, but Schumer and Gekas could not reach agreement over how much leeway to give investigators.

At Home: A member of Harrisburg's small but influential Greek community, Gekas took the traditional path to political success in central Pennsylvania. He went to a local college and law school, became an assistant district attorney, then moved on to the state Capitol.

Gekas fashioned his state legislative career around the same hard-line stand against crime. He managed capital-punishment legislation, chaired the state Senate Judiciary Committee, and wrote a tough mandatory-sentencing bill.

Gekas encountered remarkably few obstacles on his path to Congress in 1982. He launched his campaign after Democratic Rep. Allen Ertel announced for governor and after the GOP-controlled Legislature approved new district lines favoring election of a Republican.

In the primary, Gekas was endorsed by the GOP in Dauphin County (Harrisburg), and won nomination handily over a candidate backed by the Lycoming County GOP. Gekas rolled over his November opponent, Dauphin County Commissioner Larry J. Hochendoner, who had lost to Gekas in a 1976 state Senate contest. With a 3-to-1 spending advantage, Gekas ran media ads almost daily: showing him at an eatery waiting on tables and serving pizza. In 1988 and 1990 the Democrats did not field a candidate against him.

Pennsylvania 17

Central — Harrisburg; Williamsport

This elongated district, which follows the Susquehanna River, amply displays the GOP affinities of central Pennsylvania. Democrats held it three terms (until 1982), but that was an aberration. Now back in GOP hands, the 17th seems likely to stay there.

Dauphin County (Harrisburg) has almost half the people in the 17th. About a two-hour drive to the north, Lycoming County (Williamsport) is second, with slightly more than a fourth of the population.

The large state government complex and manufacturing sector in Harrisburg provide enough Democratic votes to make the party competitive for local and state offices. The state capital, a victim of white flight to the suburbs, is just over 50 percent black, enhancing Democratic strength there.

In 1982, Dauphin County went Democratic for governor (the nominee was the 17th's departing incumbent), but in 1986, the county voted Republican in both the gubernatorial and Senate contests. George Bush carried it in the 1988 presidential contest.

The presence of the state government prevents life around Harrisburg from being as placid as it is elsewhere in central Pennsylvania. More serious than the constant political flare-ups was the 1979 accident at the nearby Three Mile Island nuclear plant.

Upriver from Harrisburg, the hills and farms turn out large Republican majorities. Snyder and Union were among the four counties in the state to go for Barry Goldwater in 1964. Democrats can be found in coal-mining Northumberland County and in Williamsport, which manufactures aircraft engines, publishes *Grit* magazine and hosts the Little League World Series.

Population: 515,900. White 476,806 (92%), Black 34,261 (7%), Other 2,399 (1%). Spanish origin 4,637 (1%). 18 and over 376,440 (73%), 65 and over 63,411 (12%). Median age: 31.

Committees

Judiciary (6th of 13 Republicans)
Administrative Law & Governmental Relations (ranking); Crime and Criminal Justice

Select Intelligence (7th of 7 Republicans)
Legislation (ranking)

Elections

1990 General		
George W. Gekas (R)	110,317	(100%)
1988 General		
George W. Gekas (R)	166,289	(100%)

Previous Winning Percentages: **1986** (74%) **1984** (73%) **1982** (58%)

District Vote For President

	1988	1984	1980	1976
D	64,516 (36%)	61,212 (33%)	58,724 (32%)	75,275 (40%)
R	112,949 (63%)	123,660 (66%)	110,417 (61%)	108,300 (58%)
I			11,412 (6%)	

Campaign Finance

	Receipts	Receipts from PACs	Expend-itures
1990			
Gekas (R)	$128,438	$53,410 (42%)	$93,331
1988			
Gekas (R)	$95,878	$46,750 (49%)	$97,611

Key Votes

1991	
Authorize use of force against Iraq	Y
1990	
Support constitutional amendment on flag desecration	Y
Pass family and medical leave bill over Bush veto	N
Reduce SDI funding	?
Allow abortions in overseas military facilities	N
Approve budget summit plan for spending and taxing	Y
Approve civil rights bill	N
1989	
Halt production of B-2 stealth bomber at 13 planes	N
Oppose capital gains tax cut	N
Approve federal abortion funding in rape or incest cases	N
Approve pay raise and revision of ethics rules	N
Pass Democratic minimum wage plan over Bush veto	N

Voting Studies

	Presidential Support		Party Unity		Conservative Coalition	
Year	S	O	S	O	S	O
1990	81	19	92	7	94	6
1989	69	29	92	6	88	12
1988	72	27	93	5	97	3
1987	70	29	90	10	84	16
1986	76	23	83	16	92	8
1985	73	28	85	15	87	13
1984	62	35	81	17	88	12
1983	79	20	82	17	76	22

Interest Group Ratings

Year	ADA	ACU	AFL-CIO	CCUS
1990	0	91	17	86
1989	15	96	0	100
1988	10	92	21	93
1987	8	83	13	87
1986	10	73	36	83
1985	15	76	29	73
1984	20	67	15	75
1983	20	70	6	95

18 Rick Santorum (R)

Of Mount Lebanon — Elected 1990

Born: May 10, 1958, Winchester, Va.
Education: Pennsylvania State U., B.A. 1980; U. of Pittsburgh, M.B.A. 1981; Dickinson School of Law, J.D. 1986.
Occupation: Lawyer; legislative aide.
Family: Wife, Karen Garver.
Religion: Roman Catholic.
Political Career: No previous office.
Capitol Office: 1708 Longworth Bldg. 20515; 225-2135.

The Path to Washington: Santorum is a prime example of how the Republican Party could take over the House in spite of itself. Although his campaign was virtually ignored by the national Republican Party, Santorum combined shoe leather, an extensive volunteer network, an aggressive manner and an overconfident foe to score one of the biggest upsets of 1990.

When he launched his challenge in early 1990, no one gave the energetic young Santorum much chance of unseating seven-term Rep. Doug Walgren. Walgren had survived seemingly more difficult challenges in 1982, when redistricting made the suburban Pittsburgh district politically marginal, and in 1986, when a wealthy GOP businessman spent nearly $1 million against him. Santorum was neither rich nor a household name in the 18th.

The son of an Italian immigrant, he was born in Winchester, Va., where his father worked at a veterans' hospital. His family moved several times when Santorum was young, and he spent much of his childhood in western Pennsylvania.

While attending Penn State University, he was smitten by the political bug. After working in the 1976 Senate campaign of John Heinz and the 1978 House campaign of William F. Clinger Jr., Santorum was elected state chairman of the College Republicans.

He used his political contacts to get on the staff of GOP state Sen. J. Doyle Corman. For several years Santorum served in Harrisburg as Corman's point man on the Senate Transportation and Local Government committees, while working toward a law degree at Dickinson College.

After graduating, Santorum moved to Pittsburgh in 1986 to join the law firm of Kirkpatrick and Lockhart, which numbered Attorney General (and former Pennsylvania Gov.) Dick Thornburgh among its former employees. Santorum also dabbled in local GOP politics as legal counsel for the Allegheny County Young Republicans and as GOP committeeman in suburban Mount Lebanon. When Santorum began floating the idea in 1989 of challenging Walgren, he encountered no GOP opposition. But he did not receive much encouragement either. Some Republican leaders said he should wait until after redistricting. The National Republican Congressional Committee barely acknowledged his candidacy, limiting its involvement to giving him occasional telephone advice.

But Santorum made up for the lack of outside help and absence of a big campaign treasury — he raised barely $250,000 — by running a textbook grass-roots campaign. Taking a leave of absence from his law firm in March, he boasted of personally visiting 25,000 households and of piecing together a volunteer organization featuring anti-abortion activists and Young Republicans that reportedly numbered 2,000 workers.

Santorum drew free media attention with a flurry of press releases and news conferences that accented his calls for repeal of the congressional pay raise, institution of the line-item veto and a limit on political action committee contributions.

His thrusts, though, gradually grew more personal and more telling.

He accused Walgren of voting for seven different pay raises during his career and complained that the incumbent no longer resided in the district (one Santorum ad pictured Walgren's home in the affluent northern Virginia suburb of McLean).

Walgren was slow to respond, and when he did, he lacked much fire. In their first debate in late October, Santorum crisply depicted Walgren as a career Washington insider who had lost touch with his district. Walgren gave long rebuttals that frequently had to be cut off by the moderator.

Walgren did mount a media offensive near the end of the campaign that criticized Santorum as a carpetbagger to the Pittsburgh area. But the ads, which featured a photo of Santorum, unwittingly underscored the competitiveness of his challenge.

Pennsylvania 18

Pittsburgh Suburbs

The 18th is a suburban doughnut surrounding Pittsburgh, with a bite taken out of the eastern part of the ring. The Democratic Party has a significantly smaller registration advantage in the 18th than it once did, because the last round of redistricting cut out western Pittsburgh and some Democratic suburbs. The 18th now can be counted on to vote solidly GOP in presidential elections, but its affluent, highly educated electorate — second in the state in income and schooling only to the suburban Philadelphia 13th — knows how to split tickets, as former Democratic Rep. Doug Walgren's success in the 1980s showed.

The Democrat usually ran well in such prosperous Republican suburbs as Mount Lebanon (his home) and Sewickley. Still wealthier Fox Chapel, where zoning in some areas requires a minimum three acres for building a residence, generally opposed him. The blue-collar boroughs of Etna and Blawnox are located next to Fox Chapel.

Republican Rick Santorum carved out his upset win over Walgren in 1990 with the help of a strong performance in the fast-growing North Hills area, where a number of executives in Pittsburgh's burgeoning high-tech industry are moving. This upper part of Allegheny County contains Pine, Richland, McCandless and other newly developing towns that lean Republican.

West of the Monongahela River are several communities where Democrats have a slight registration lead — Jefferson, Bethel Park, and South Park. The West Hills suburbs clustered around the Greater Pittsburgh Airport — North Fayette, Findlay, Moon and Robinson — also include a fair number of Democrats, mostly airport-related union workers. North of the Ohio River are more well-off suburbs on the order of Sewickley.

South of the Allegheny River are Penn Hills, a sprawling and diverse township that is marginally Democratic, and the middle-class suburbs of Forest Hills and Braddock Hills. Santorum made significant inroads here in 1990.

Population: 516,050. White 499,453 (97%), Black 12,110 (2%), Other 3,487 (1%). Spanish origin 2,359 (1%). 18 and over 382,408 (74%), 65 and over 59,090 (11%). Median age: 34.

Committees

Budget (14th of 14 Republicans)
Community Development & Natural Resources; Economic Policy, Projections & Revenues

Select Children, Youth & Families (11th of 14 Republicans)

Veterans' Affairs (13th of 13 Republicans)
Education, Training & Employment

Campaign Finance

	Receipts	Receipts from PACs		Expend-itures
1990				
Santorum (R)	$257,786	$27,660	(11%)	$251,496
Walgren (D)	$601,897	$423,415	(70%)	$717,124

Key Vote

1991

Authorize use of force against Iraq	Y

Elections

1990 General

Rick Santorum (R)	85,697	(51%)
Doug Walgren (D)	80,880	(49%)

District Vote For President

	1988	1984	1980	1976
D	106,636 (46%)	103,883 (42%)	83,343 (35%)	92,265 (39%)
R	123,482 (53%)	144,352 (58%)	131,462 (56%)	141,049 (59%)
I			15,849 (7%)	

19 Bill Goodling (R)

Of Jacobus — Elected 1974

Born: Dec. 5, 1927, Loganville, Pa.

Education: U. of Maryland, B.S. 1953; Western Maryland College, M.Ed. 1956; Attended Pennsylvania State U., 1960-62.

Military Service: Army, 1946-48.

Occupation: Public school superintendent.

Family: Wife, Hilda Wright; two children.

Religion: Methodist.

Political Career: Dallastown School Board president, 1964-67.

Capitol Office: 2263 Rayburn Bldg. 20515; 225-5836.

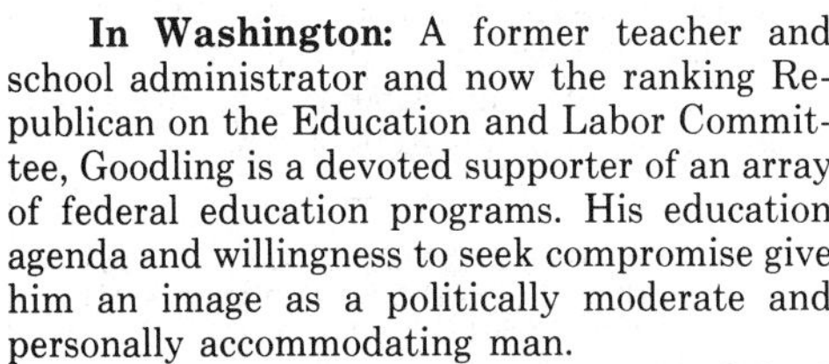

In Washington: A former teacher and school administrator and now the ranking Republican on the Education and Labor Committee, Goodling is a devoted supporter of an array of federal education programs. His education agenda and willingness to seek compromise give him an image as a politically moderate and personally accommodating man.

But that is not a complete picture. School aid aside, Goodling is a chamber of commerce Republican who sticks with his conservative colleagues on nearly every labor issue that comes before the committee. And when his hackles are up, he is a ready partisan combatant. When Democrats tried to roll a child-care bill through the committee in 1989, he led a Republican boycott; when they ignored the president's education proposals in 1990, he helped stage a GOP walkout.

Conservatives hope Goodling will bring those combative partisan traits with him as he rejoins the Foreign Affairs Committee after a six-year stint on the Budget Committee. During his earlier tenure on Foreign Affairs, Goodling was a reliable conservative vote.

Goodling may be a Bush loyalist on foreign policy, but in his chief bailiwick of Education and Labor, Goodling had some disappointing dealings with the administration in the 101st Congress. After taking the lead as the administration's spokesman on education funding and increasing the minimum wage, he wound up fighting the president from the left on the former, and from the right on the latter.

Early in the 101st, Goodling set aside his reservations about the limited scope of Bush's education program and introduced the legislation to create $400 million in new school programs. He then spent most of 1989 dogging committee Chairman Augustus F. Hawkins of California to give the bill a hearing. Hawkins went along after Goodling agreed to withhold money for new programs until more was set aside to fund Chapter 1 — a federal block grant for schools with high populations of disadvantaged children — and to focus the president's initiative on those schools.

Committee Democrats, however, balked. Calling the president's proposal too skimpy, they introduced their own $3.7 billion program. When discussion of the GOP proposal was cut off, Goodling balked. "Nothing will happen unless we do our usual bipartisan bit when it comes to writing education legislation," he said as he led a group of Republicans out of the committee room. Two years earlier, Goodling had worked closely with Hawkins to mold the education reauthorization bill. The result was a compromise that protected programs dear to committee Democrats while restraining funding to levels acceptable to President Ronald Reagan and his allies on the committee.

In 1990, Goodling eventually became so frustrated with the partisanship that he canceled a spring trip he and his wife had planned to take with the Hawkinses to visit preschools in France, Italy and Denmark.

By summer, the No. 2 Education and Labor Democrat, William D. Ford of Michigan, approached Goodling, and the two quickly worked out a $680 million compromise, which was approved 315-59 in July 1990.

But by that time, administration interest had waned, and the bill languished in the Senate. When the White House renewed its interest as the election neared, Goodling made a last-minute push that got a new compromise package through the House in late October. But conservatives blocked action in the Senate. Goodling intimated afterward that he felt abused by the administration.

The long ordeal did, however, yield a cooperative rapport between Goodling and Ford, who became Education and Labor chairman upon Hawkins' retirement in 1991. In spite of that, the two are likely to have their share of run-ins: Ford's style is more combative than Hawkins' was, and he is a staunch advocate of organized labor.

The 1989 debate on the minimum wage

Pennsylvania 19

South Central — York

This placid farm country has seen little to upset it since 1863, when Robert E. Lee's army met defeat at Gettysburg. Democrats do about as well in many of these counties as Lee did. The 19th used to change hands between the parties occasionally, but it has been solidly Republican since 1974.

The biggest concentration of Democrats lies in the industrial city of York (population 42,000), where turbines, hosiery and barbells are manufactured. The remaining portion of York County has an even split in terms of partisan registration.

Hanover, where cans, shoes and potato chips are made, is a Democratic enclave. The rest of York County is rural Republican — with a smattering of Pennsylvania Dutch influence to deepen the conservatism. Only 4 of the county's 72 boroughs and townships supported Robert P. Casey in his successful 1986 gubernatorial run.

In fruit-growing Adams County, Republicans hold sway from Gettysburg — the largest town, with 7,000 people — to the farming villages farther north. The Democrats, in the minority, are concentrated in the southeastern part of Adams. Many of them work in Hanover.

Republicans have the upper hand as well in the part of Cumberland County in the 19th, which includes the western suburbs of Harrisburg, Pennsylvania's capital; the city itself lies across the Susquehanna River in the 17th District. State employees and blue-collar workers who spend their days in Harrisburg live in Lemoyne and New Cumberland on the West Shore. Affluent West Shore Republicans reside in Camp Hill. Moving west from the West Shore area, the Cumberland County terrain becomes more rural and Republican.

Population: 516,605. White 499,717 (97%), Black 11,905 (2%), Other 2,879 (1%). Spanish origin 4,051 (1%). 18 and over 376,801 (73%), 65 and over 59,117 (11%). Median age: 32.

revealed Goodling's most conservative, probusiness instincts. With Democrats pushing a $4.65 minimum, and Bush backing a $4.25 minimum with a six-month training wage, moderate Pennsylvania Republican Tom Ridge, working with a pair of Democrats, stepped in with a compromise plan to raise the wage to $4.55, with a two-month subminimum. While the Ridge plan passed the House, Goodling criticized it as subverting Bush's hard-line stand. When asked if Ridge had any Republican friends left, he fired back, "On our side of the aisle, he would have none."

Months after Bush vetoed the Ridge plan, administration officials and labor leaders negotiated a deal that called for a $4.25 minimum wage, and a limited 3-month training wage for teenagers.

But the process left congressional Republicans out of the loop, and the deal went too far for many of them, including Goodling, who made no secret of his frustration with the administration. "I don't care who the administration is, who the leadership is in the House and Senate; once you go beyond your authorizing committee, you're going to get burned," he said. Goodling withheld his support for the bill until the last minute.

When it comes to child-nutrition programs, Goodling switches sides and fights conservative efforts to lower funding. In the 100th Congress, he supported legislation to simplify the application process for school lunches and, on the Budget Committee, he authored an amendment to protect funding. His fight to defend nutrition programs dates back to the earliest days of the Reagan administration. When budget director David A. Stockman said that budget cuts in 1981 had not hurt needy children, Goodling labeled the claim "sheer hogwash."

Yet in pursuing the nutrition issue, Goodling guards himself from being perceived as a crusading liberal. He works closely with food producers and suppliers, for whom nutrition is a business as well as a humanitarian issue. The business support provides a conservative element to Goodling's coalition.

As a member of the Budget Committee, Goodling played a partisan, if limited, role. During the Reagan administration, he often expressed his frustration with the refusal of the committee's Democratic majority to allow Republicans to play a substantive role in responding to the president's annual budget proposals and crafting the yearly congressional budget resolutions.

But Goodling did show he would come to the defense of his Budget Committee colleagues when they got embroiled in turf fights with their Senate counterparts. When Senate Budget Committee Chairman Lawton Chiles of Florida and ranking Republican Pete V. Domenici of New Mexico angrily attempted to assert Senate primacy in the 1988 budget process, Goodling described them as "two mean, bitter old people" who had "a terrible attitude."

At Home: Goodling has made the 19th more securely Republican in his House tenure than his father, who won six times between 1960 and 1972, was ever able to do. George A. Goodling lived with the possibility of defeat each election year and actually lost once, in 1964; his son has won over 70 percent eight consecutive times — even in 1982, when the GOP was in serious trouble all over the state.

They are two different men. The elder Goodling was an indifferent speaker who disdained public appearances. His son is much more outgoing and remains highly visible. Close to the local GOP organizations and active on community issues, Goodling benefits from the proximity of his southern Pennsylvania district, a direct two-hour drive north from Washington.

Until his first run for Congress in 1974, the younger Goodling was a high school principal and had held just one elective office — on the Dallastown School Board. He was the surprise winner in a seven-way congressional primary, outdistancing the favored John W. Eden, who had once challenged Goodling's father. Waging his first general-election campaign in the Watergate year of 1974, the younger Goodling won by barely 5,000 votes.

Goodling did draw a primary challenge in 1990 from a septuagenarian former state representative, Francis Worley, who had served in the Pennsylvania Legislature for more than two decades and aspired to be a voice in Congress for senior citizens. But Goodling swept to renomination by a margin of 7-to-1.

Committees

Education & Labor (Ranking)
Elementary, Secondary & Vocational Education (ranking); Postsecondary Education

Foreign Affairs (4th of 18 Republicans)
Europe & the Middle East

Elections

1990 General		
Bill Goodling (R)	96,336	(100%)
1990 Primary		
Bill Goodling (R)	33,139	(88%)
Francis Worley (R)	4,689	(12%)
1988 General		
Bill Goodling (R)	145,381	(77%)
Paul E. Ritchey (D)	42,819	(23%)

Previous Winning Percentages: **1986** (73%) **1984** (76%) **1982** (71%) **1980** (76%) **1978** (79%) **1976** (71%) **1974** (51%)

District Vote For President

	1988	1984	1980	1976
D	65,536 (34%)	57,956 (30%)	56,017 (31%)	67,964 (39%)
R	127,824 (66%)	131,202 (69%)	108,392 (61%)	101,854 (59%)
I			11,384 (6%)	

Campaign Finance

	Receipts	Receipts from PACs	Expend-itures
1990			
Goodling (R)	$41,011	0	$40,698
1988			
Goodling (R)	$54,123	0	$57,091
Ritchey (D)	$5,304	0	$5,303

Key Votes

1991	
Authorize use of force against Iraq	Y
1990	
Support constitutional amendment on flag desecration	Y
Pass family and medical leave bill over Bush veto	N
Reduce SDI funding	N
Allow abortions in overseas military facilities	N
Approve budget summit plan for spending and taxing	Y
Approve civil rights bill	N
1989	
Halt production of B-2 stealth bomber at 13 planes	N
Oppose capital gains tax cut	N
Approve federal abortion funding in rape or incest cases	N
Approve pay raise and revision of ethics rules	N
Pass Democratic minimum wage plan over Bush veto	N

Voting Studies

	Presidential Support		Party Unity		Conservative Coalition	
Year	**S**	**O**	**S**	**O**	**S**	**O**
1990	54	39	71	20	72	17
1989	65	29	76	17	83	7
1988	50	47	77	19	84	13
1987	57	39	72	24	79	21
1986	60	37	69	28	76	24
1985	61	38	74	19	69	24
1984	50	44	66	28	71	29
1983	54	40	71	26	61	38
1982	61	36	74	24	66	30
1981	59	36	74	17	65	21

Interest Group Ratings

Year	ADA	ACU	AFL-CIO	CCUS
1990	22	68	27	64
1989	25	68	17	90
1988	30	63	50	93
1987	28	48	19	80
1986	25	55	43	88
1985	25	57	18	77
1984	35	48	31	63
1983	35	61	24	65
1982	25	62	25	64
1981	30	93	20	74

20 Joseph M. Gaydos (D)

Of McKeesport — Elected 1968

Born: July 3, 1926, Braddock, Pa.
Education: Attended Duquesne U., 1945-47; U. of Notre Dame, LL.B. 1951.
Military Service: Naval Reserve, 1944-46.
Occupation: Lawyer.
Family: Wife, Alice Gray; five children.
Religion: Roman Catholic.
Political Career: Pa. Senate, 1967-68.
Capitol Office: 2186 Rayburn Bldg. 20515; 225-4631.

In Washington: Gaydos, like his ailing steel-town district, is part of a vanishing breed in American politics: He comes from one of the few remaining bastions of old-school ethnic politics and industrial union power. As if to underscore this reality, the Democratic Caucus before the start of the 102nd Congress passed over Gaydos for a committee chairmanship that by seniority should have been his.

In late 1990, an uprising by restless post-Watergate-era Democrats ousted two committee chairmen, including Illinois' Frank Annunzio, head of the House Administration Committee. Gaydos had waited patiently for Annunzio, 10 years his senior, to retire and hand the gavel to him.

But after younger Democrats, frustrated by Annunzio's plodding style, narrowly rejected him in a caucus vote, Gaydos never had a chance. The Annunzio ouster was led by North Carolinian Charlie Rose, 13 years and two terms Gaydos' junior. Rose was the driving force behind modernizing the House computer system, and his expertise in that area was one of the reasons Gaydos was passed over.

It was a jolting outcome for Gaydos, who has always observed the traditions of respect for seniority and loyalty to party — the means of ascent in the House of yesteryear. As a member of the ethics panel investigating alleged wrongdoing by Speaker Jim Wright in 1989, the burly Gaydos was one of just two members voting to exonerate Wright on every charge. Gaydos was appointed to the ethics committee by Wright in 1987, and that year declined to support publicly the panel's recommendation to reprimand Pennsylvania Democrat Austin J. Murphy, although the committee reported the recommendation without dissent. Gaydos voted "present" when the House adopted the resolution of reprimand 324-68.

It came as no surprise to knowledgeable observers that Gaydos supported Wright with very little public comment. "He's from a different era," said one GOP colleague.

Gaydos chairs the Education and Labor Subcommittee on Health and Safety, which stands guard over the Occupational Safety and Health Administration (OSHA), an agency reviled from its inception by small businesses that find its regulations onerous. During the Reagan era, Gaydos viewed his job primarily as a defensive one: fighting efforts to reduce OSHA's scope. But he sometimes had to defend himself against demands from his labor allies that he move aggressively to make OSHA stronger, rather than just protecting the status quo.

As anti-regulation zeal began to wane toward the end of the Reagan administration, Gaydos did take advantage of the new climate and in 1987 shepherded through the House the first important OSHA bill in years. The House passed legislation that required notification of workers who might be exposed to hazardous chemicals or materials on the job.

Along the way, Gaydos accepted changes designed to win some business support. But other business groups remained implacably opposed, saying that risk notification would cause them financial and legal hardship. Those forces prevailed in the Senate, where the bill died at the end of the 100th Congress. The issue was not pressed in the 101st Congress.

Gaydos' subcommittee has not been an aggressive instigator of investigations, but in early 1991, after media reports publicized excessive coal dust in many mines, Gaydos said his panel would look into whether mining companies were violating health standards. Also in the 102nd Congress, the subcommittee is slated to reauthorize OSHA, and Gaydos has pledged a vigorous review of construction safety and repetitive motion injuries.

The United Steelworkers of America is the dominant political influence in Gaydos' district; when he is not focusing on occupational safety issues, he is usually speaking out on other union interests, primarily pension rights and protection against imports. Gaydos considers his work in drafting the 1974 Employee Retirement Income Security Act (ERISA) "the shining jewel" of his career.

Gaydos serves as executive committee chairman of the Steel Caucus, the House group

Pennsylvania 20

Pittsburgh Suburbs — McKeesport

Its banks lined by old steel mills, its waters crowded with barges, the Monongahela River forms the spine of this blue-collar district.

The "Mon Valley" city of Clairton was the setting for the movie "The Deer Hunter," in which young Slavic steelworkers went off to the Vietnam War. The film depicted the ethnic celebrations and bluff male camaraderie that also animate the political life of the 20th. The wise politician here cultivates the Sons of Italy, the Polish Falcons, the Greek Catholic Union, the American Croatian Club and countless other ethnic societies. Although blacks make up a substantial portion of some towns — Clairton is one-quarter black — they are not concentrated enough to be a major political force.

Organized labor is crucial to local politics and has been for a long time. The Steelworkers' locals in the Mon Valley are some of the union's most militant in demanding that the domestic steel industry not be allowed to wither away. Thousands who used to work in the Mon Valley's steel mills now have no prospect for comparable employment because corporate officials have closed the mills for good, declaring that local wage costs are too high, the old mills too inefficient and foreign steel too cheap to make continued operation economically feasible.

It was in the 20th that steel union officials and some church leaders in unemployment-riddled communities stirred a furor in the mid-1980s by staging protests at churches in affluent communities where corporate executives worship. The protesters demanded that local investors put money into revitalizing steel in the Mon Valley.

Pittsburgh's effort to move to a service-oriented economy holds no hope for the typical unemployed steelworker in the 20th, who has no desire to take low-paying service work and no training to handle the high-tech jobs available in the skyscrapers downtown.

Not surprisingly, the 20th is firmly Democratic. Jimmy Carter carried it in both his presidential races, and the district's view of the White House occupant in 1984 was best described by a local steelworkers official, who said, "In this area, if Ronald Reagan bought a cemetery, people would quit dying." In 1988, George Bush barely got above one-third of the vote in the 20th.

Population: 516,028. White 484,336 (94%), Black 28,639 (6%). Spanish origin 2,560 (1%). 18 and over 390,171 (76%), 65 and over 71,817 (14%). Median age: 35.

seeking restrictions on steel imports into the United States. His statements on trade issues can have a strident, even caustic tone. In 1982 he introduced legislation that would have allowed the president unilaterally to impose new duties on nations that do not practice "reciprocity" in trade. "People are tired of New Testament trade based on meekness and turning the other cheek," Gaydos said. "They are ready for some Old Testament justice."

During the Reagan presidency, Gaydos sometimes would aim his anger at the administration's efforts to negotiate voluntary import restrictions with foreign countries. "I know President Reagan likes to speak of the free market; unfortunately, there is no such thing . . . ," Gaydos said. "Someone has to pay, and unfortunately, with our open doors and unrestrictive trade system, we are the ones who are paying . . . in the form of lost companies, lost jobs, lost manufacturing capability."

Gaydos also takes pride in his work on education issues. Having earned his law degree on the G.I. Bill, he is a staunch supporter of federal programs to make higher education available to working-class families.

On House Administration, Gaydos held on to the chairmanship of the Accounts Subcommittee, which oversees most House committee budgets. That means some of the House's most powerful chairmen rely on Gaydos' good will to keep their own fiefdoms well-staffed. Although Gaydos seems to relish that role, he has not built it into an institutional power base, in part because it is not easy to throw money around these days.

At Home: Gaydos' roots in organized labor and his stalwart defense of the steel industry have been the basis of his career in Pittsburgh. Gaydos' father was a factory worker, and when he himself was a student, he held factory jobs and belonged to three unions (the Glass Workers, the Steelworkers and the United Auto Workers). He later served as a United Mine Workers attorney. In the 1968 Democratic primary, Gaydos used his background to counter the formal labor support claimed by his chief opponent, a Steelworkers' local president.

A first-term state legislator at the time, Gaydos had been tapped by the Allegheny

County Democratic organization to replace U.S. Rep. Elmer Holland, whom it considered too old at 74. Holland agreed to retire, then died before his term ended. Since his initial primary, which he won handily, Gaydos has had a virtual free ride. He has slipped below 70 percent only twice.

In 1986 and 1988, Gaydos faced no Republican opposition. Competition, though, picked up a little in 1990 when he drew both primary and general election foes. In the primary, his challenger was veteran state Rep. Emil Mrkonic, who complained that Gaydos had not done enough to stem the economic decline in the "Mon Valley" or to respond to appeals for assistance from distressed constituents. Mrkonic, though, hedged his bets by simultaneously running for renomination to the state House.

In the fall, Gaydos was opposed by a Republican investment counselor. He beat back both low-budget challenges by margins of roughly 2-to-1.

Committees

Education & Labor (2nd of 25 Democrats)
Health & Safety (chairman); Postsecondary Education

House Administration (3rd of 15 Democrats)
Accounts (chairman); Procurement & Printing

Elections

1990 General		
Joseph M. Gaydos (D)	82,080	(66%)
Robert C. Lee (R)	43,054	(34%)
1990 Primary		
Joseph M. Gaydos (D)	42,910	(66%)
Emil Mrkonic (D)	21,831	(34%)
1988 General		
Joseph M. Gaydos (D)	137,472	(98%)
Richard W. Wilson (POP)	2,144	(2%)

Previous Winning Percentages: **1986** (99%) **1984** (76%) **1982** (76%) **1980** (73%) **1978** (72%) **1976** (75%) **1974** (82%) **1972** (62%) **1970** (77%) **1968 *** (70%)

** Elected to a full term and to fill an unexpired term at the same time.*

District Vote For President

	1988	1984	1980	1976
D	125,880 (65%)	136,992 (62%)	111,625 (54%)	126,788 (58%)
R	67,120 (34%)	83,148 (37%)	81,023 (39%)	86,535 (40%)
I			10,643 (5%)	

Campaign Finance

	Receipts	Receipts from PACs	Expend-itures
1990			
Gaydos (D)	$191,541	$158,250 (83%)	$158,677
Lee (R)	$2,055	$125 (6%)	$1,086
1988			
Gaydos (D)	$184,634	$143,850 (78%)	$137,023

Key Votes

1991	
Authorize use of force against Iraq	N
1990	
Support constitutional amendment on flag desecration	Y
Pass family and medical leave bill over Bush veto	Y
Reduce SDI funding	Y
Allow abortions in overseas military facilities	N
Approve budget summit plan for spending and taxing	N
Approve civil rights bill	Y
1989	
Halt production of B-2 stealth bomber at 13 planes	N
Oppose capital gains tax cut	Y
Approve federal abortion funding in rape or incest cases	N
Approve pay raise and revision of ethics rules	Y
Pass Democratic minimum wage plan over Bush veto	Y

Voting Studies

	Presidential Support		Party Unity		Conservative Coalition	
Year	**S**	**O**	**S**	**O**	**S**	**O**
1990	32	65	78	17	59	41
1989	42	56	73	20	61	34
1988	26	66	80	13	63	29
1987	31	67	80	11	63	35
1986	33	59	73	17	62	26
1985	28	65	78	14	47	44
1984	37	60	77	18	47	53
1983	40	59	76	17	35	58
1982	38	61	77	17	42	55
1981	43	45	65	25	61	29

Interest Group Ratings

Year	ADA	ACU	AFL-CIO	CCUS
1990	50	33	83	50
1989	55	26	100	40
1988	65	24	100	25
1987	64	9	94	27
1986	55	44	100	31
1985	70	15	71	32
1984	45	39	92	38
1983	60	35	94	32
1982	55	41	95	19
1981	40	21	85	12

21 Tom Ridge (R)

Of Erie — Elected 1982

Born: Aug. 26, 1945, Munhall, Pa.
Education: Harvard U., B.A. 1967; Dickinson School of Law, J.D. 1972.
Military Service: Army, 1968-70.
Occupation: Lawyer.
Family: Wife, Michele Moore; two children.
Religion: Roman Catholic.
Political Career: No previous office.
Capitol Office: 1714 Longworth Bldg. 20515; 225-5406.

In Washington: An affable lawyer with a Harvard degree and a chamber-of-commerce appearance, Ridge engages in a range of legislative interests, from minimum wage to national defense. Within the House Republican Conference, he casts frequent left-of-center votes but keeps his image just this side of "maverick."

Republican leaders realize Ridge needs some room to maneuver, since only a moderate could hold the 21st for the GOP. It is a mainly blue-collar corner of northwest Pennsylvania, centered on industrial Erie. Ridge's working-class background — like many Erie men of his generation, he enlisted in the Army and served in Vietnam — and his pro-labor voting record have made him popular at home.

Ridge's proficiency at forging cross-party alliances also has made him a likely future candidate for statewide office. He considered competing in the 1991 special Senate race and had already begun preparing for a 1994 gubernatorial bid. (He turned down a chance to run statewide in 1990.)

In seeking another forum, Ridge may be evincing some restiveness over the partisan scrapping of Congress. Following the Persian Gulf War, he lamented to *The Washington Post* that because of President Bush's success, "there may be a tendency not to be bipartisan but to polarize in an election cycle.... I loathe, but anticipate, that possibility."

There are times when Ridge breaks with the GOP leadership in a rather public manner, leaving his more conservative colleagues exasperated. His split with Bush on the minimum wage in early 1989 was one such incident.

Democrats on the Education and Labor Committee sought to boost the minimum wage well above the existing rate of $3.35 an hour, to $4.65, without the subminimum "training wage" Bush wanted for new employees; Bush proposed raising the minimum to $4.25, with a six-month training wage, and he threatened to veto anything else. Ridge joined two Democrats to propose a compromise raising the wage to $4.55 an hour, with a two-month training wage for new hires with minimal work experience. While the compromise bill passed 248-171, only 19 of the "ayes" were Republicans. As he promised, Bush vetoed the bill; Ridge was one of 20 Republicans to vote for the failed override.

The minimum-wage battle was not the first time Ridge had broken ranks on a priority issue for the GOP leadership. He was the only House Republican to make a floor speech in 1987 favoring the tough trade-sanctions amendment proposed by Missouri Democrat Richard A. Gephardt. Positions such as that make Ridge one of organized labor's favorite Republicans. But rather than shun him for disloyalty, GOP officials tend to showcase Ridge's appeal to unions. Since 1988, he has chaired the Republican National Committee's Labor Council.

Ridge has made some ventures into defense policy. A skeptic of the strategic defense initiative (SDI), he has teamed with Charles E. Bennett, a Florida Democrat and arms control liberal, in yearly attempts to cut SDI. In May 1987, House Armed Services had already reduced President Reagan's SDI request from $5.7 billion to $3.8 billion. Bennett and Ridge attached an amendment on the House floor to spend $3.1 billion. It was adopted, 219-199, with 20 GOP votes that Ridge rounded up.

In the 101st Congress, Bennett and Ridge again sponsored amendments to cut SDI funding. In 1989, by 248-175, the House adopted their amendment to spend $3.1 billion on SDI's research program instead of the $4.9 billion Bush requested. In 1990, their amendment to slice SDI to $2.3 billion was adopted 225-189.

In the 101st Congress, Ridge joined the Post Office and Civil Service Committee and got the ranking GOP slot on its Census and Population Subcommittee. Previously, he and 42 other plaintiffs had filed suit in federal court to block the inclusion of illegal aliens in the U.S. census. Ridge said such an inclusion, which he described as inherently inaccurate, penalized areas (like his home) that get few immigrants.

Ridge and his allies appeared to make progress on this issue in 1988, when Indiana Republican Dan Burton attached an amendment barring an illegal-alien count to a bill

Pennsylvania 21

Northwest — Erie

Muscled out by Buffalo to the north and Cleveland to the south, the city of Erie never developed into a Great Lakes metropolis on par with its neighbors. But it is the dominant influence in the 21st. Erie Democrats still hold a wide advantage in voter registration, but changes in the city's ethnic groups are reshaping district politics.

Until the last decade or so, the Italians on Erie's West Side and the Poles on the East Side both were blue-collar communities, tied to assembly-line jobs at General Electric and in heavy industries such as paper, metals and chemicals. But then a trend toward greater mobility among Italians began gaining steam. More Italians than Poles took white-collar jobs, and more of them moved to the suburbs, where their Democratic traditions weakened. By and large, Poles remained in the city and retained their strong Democratic allegiance.

When a Pole defeated an Italian for the 1982 Democratic House nomination, many disappointed Italians supported Ridge in November, helping him win. The results of recent presidential contests reveal what a swing-voting area Erie County has become. Jimmy Carter carried it narrowly in 1976, Ronald Reagan eked out victories here in 1980 and 1984, then Michael S. Dukakis won with 58 percent in 1988.

South of Erie in the center of the 21st is Crawford County, kept Republican by dairy farmers and retirees around Conneaut Lake. In Titusville, to the east, Edwin L. Drake drilled the first oil well in 1859.

Below Crawford is Mercer County, where the steel industry in the Shenango Valley has set a Democratic tone. As thoroughly unionized as Erie, the mill towns of Sharon, Wheatland and Sharpsville outvote eastern Mercer's rural Republicans. Mercer was one of just two Pennsylvania counties to support Reagan in 1980 and then switch to Mondale in 1984, mostly because people felt Reagan had not done enough to save the steel industry. Despite the Democratic trend at the top of the ticket in Mercer, Republican Ridge carried the county by almost 2-to-1 in 1984. Again in 1988, Mercer went Democratic for president, but backed Ridge for the House.

Population: 516,645. White 494,271 (96%), Black 18,997 (4%). Spanish origin 2,836 (1%). 18 and over 370,614 (72%), 65 and over 60,943 (12%). Median age: 30.

aimed at correcting the supposed census undercount of minorities. However, the bill's Democratic sponsors let it die in the Post Office Committee rather than send it to the floor with the illegal-alien provision included. Then, in May 1989, a U.S. district judge threw out Ridge's lawsuit on procedural grounds.

Ridge tried again when the Commerce money bill for fiscal 1990 was on the floor. He won a procedural vote to offer his amendment, which lost subsequently. He could claim one victory: At Congress' prodding, the Commerce Department, reversing itself, agreed to count military personnel stationed overseas.

In 1990, Ridge amended a fast-moving proposal allowing members of the armed services serving in the Persian Gulf free letters home, taking the funds from appropriations for congressional franked mailings. The House agreed 227-142, but Senate dropped it.

Ridge has been on the Banking Subcommittee on Housing since his freshman term. In the 101st Congress, the panel spawned the first major overhaul of federal housing programs since 1974. Ridge organized the GOP opposition to a Democratic-sponsored program to spur production of rental housing. But Democrats pitted the rental-housing program against the administration's HOPE program, which would help public housing tenants buy their buildings. Ridge agreed not to put up a fight, and Democrats promised to keep HOPE.

Ridge joined with Minnesota Democrat Bruce F. Vento to propose a way to stem the losses in the Federal Housing Administration's mortgage insurance program without shutting out families from home ownership. A scheme backed by the administration would have forced buyers to pay more cash up front. The Vento-Ridge plan did not increase the up-front costs but charged an annual 0.6 percent premium over the life of the 30-year loan.

Housing Secretary Jack F. Kemp said he would resign if it appeared in the final bill. Nevertheless, the GOP leadership backed Vento-Ridge and the House adopted it, 418-2. In conference, though, Ridge offered a compromise that would cost buyers $833 up front in cash. Vento opposed it, but conferees approved the compromise.

During consideration of the 1989 bill to bail out and restructure the savings and loan industry, Ridge allied himself with S&L interests, pressing to allow thrifts that carry on their books "supervisory good will" — a form of phantom capital — to count it toward their capital requirements. The bill's general rule prohibited counting good will as tangible capital. Ridge's amendment to grant case-by-case exceptions to the rule lost 23-28 in committee.

With the departure of four more-senior Banking Committee members, Ridge began the 102nd Congress as the ranking Republican on the Economic Stabilization Subcommittee.

Ridge — who has a hearing problem that worsened during his service in Vietnam — also serves on the Veterans' Affairs Committee, where he generally works within the panel's consensus in favor of veterans' benefits.

At Home: Blue-collar voters in many parts of the country returned to their Democratic roots in 1982, but not the ones in northwestern Pennsylvania. They elected Ridge over a labor-oriented Democrat in a district that had been expected to return to Democratic control with GOP Rep. Marc L. Marks' retirement.

Ridge capitalized on a good organization and exhaustive personal effort to defeat Democratic state Sen. Buzz Andrezeski by 729 votes. He was aided by Democratic disunity and by his departure from the Reagan line of cutting social programs and boosting military spending.

Ridge's start in local politics came as chief of George Bush's Erie County 1980 presidential campaign. He won the GOP House nomination after other prominent Republicans decided that Democrats would handily recapture the 21st, which they had held before Marks' 1976 victory.

At first, Ridge had trouble raising money from local business interests, which had written off the race. But Ridge impressed national GOP leaders and key Washington business groups, who sent him the money he needed.

Andrezeski, banking on his labor support, campaigned less vigorously than Ridge, who worked the Italian-dominated West Side of Erie, where the Polish-American Andrezeski was unpopular because he had defeated an Italian in the primary. Ridge lost Erie by 8,000 votes; suburban and rural support elected him. Since then, Ridge has worked hard to entrench himself. In 1990 he had no opposition.

Committees

Banking, Finance & Urban Affairs (6th of 20 Republicans)
Economic Stabilization (ranking); Financial Institutions Supervision, Regulation & Insurance; Housing & Community Development

Post Office & Civil Service (7th of 8 Republicans)
Census & Population (ranking); Civil Service

Veterans' Affairs (7th of 13 Republicans)
Education, Training & Employment; Hospitals & Health Care

Elections

1990 General		
Tom Ridge (R)	92,732	(100%)
1988 General		
Tom Ridge (R)	141,832	(79%)
George R.H. Elder (D)	38,288	(21%)

Previous Winning Percentages: **1986** (81%) **1984** (65%) **1982** (50%)

District Vote For President

	1988	1984	1980	1976
D	94,345 (50%)	92,936 (47%)	81,616 (43%)	100,021 (51%)
R	91,544 (49%)	105,501 (53%)	92,732 (49%)	92,089 (47%)
I			12,121 (6%)	

Campaign Finance

	Receipts	Receipts from PACs		Expend-itures
1990				
Ridge (R)	$454,349	$246,265	(54%)	$361,712
1988				
Ridge (R)	$419,770	$211,711	(50%)	$370,619

Key Votes

1991	
Authorize use of force against Iraq	Y
1990	
Support constitutional amendment on flag desecration	Y
Pass family and medical leave bill over Bush veto	N
Reduce SDI funding	Y
Allow abortions in overseas military facilities	Y
Approve budget summit plan for spending and taxing	Y
Approve civil rights bill	N
1989	
Halt production of B-2 stealth bomber at 13 planes	Y
Oppose capital gains tax cut	N
Approve federal abortion funding in rape or incest cases	Y
Approve pay raise and revision of ethics rules	N
Pass Democratic minimum wage plan over Bush veto	Y

Voting Studies

	Presidential Support		Party Unity		Conservative Coalition	
Year	**S**	**O**	**S**	**O**	**S**	**O**
1990	49	51	68	27	70	28
1989	56	43	69	27	76	24
1988	40	56	66	28	74	26
1987	40	56	59	34	56	42
1986	47	53	59	37	68	32
1985	44	54	60	35	58	36
1984	42	50	45	49	53	44
1983	51	46	56	40	66	31

Interest Group Ratings

Year	ADA	ACU	AFL-CIO	CCUS
1990	22	58	33	57
1989	45	57	67	80
1988	50	36	86	71
1987	48	19	60	64
1986	35	41	64	61
1985	30	48	47	73
1984	50	36	38	60
1983	35	39	47	80

22 Austin J. Murphy (D)

Of Monongahela — Elected 1976

Born: June 17, 1927, Speers, Pa.

Education: Duquesne U., B.A. 1949; U. of Pittsburgh, LL.B. 1952, J.D. 1972.

Military Service: Marine Corps, 1944-46; Marine Corps Reserve, 1948-50.

Occupation: Lawyer.

Family: Wife, Eileen Ramona McNamara; six children.

Religion: Roman Catholic.

Political Career: Washington County assistant district attorney, 1953-59; Pa. House, 1959-71; Pa. Senate, 1971-77.

Capitol Office: 2210 Rayburn Bldg. 20515; 225-4665.

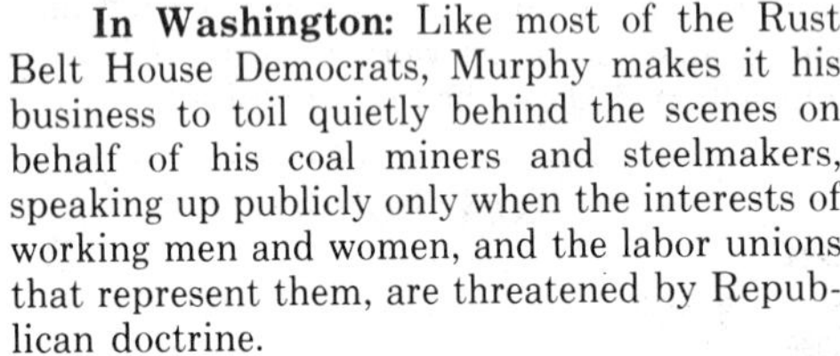

In Washington: Like most of the Rust Belt House Democrats, Murphy makes it his business to toil quietly behind the scenes on behalf of his coal miners and steelmakers, speaking up publicly only when the interests of working men and women, and the labor unions that represent them, are threatened by Republican doctrine.

Murphy likely would have spent his entire career in that mold had he not been thrust into the limelight by an ethics scandal that resulted in a rare House reprimand in 1987. In the years since then, the Monongahela Democrat has resumed his low profile, but he seems to have lost a step in House politics. In the 101st and the 102nd Congresses, he was blocked from taking a new subcommittee assignment, and after being a leading sponsor of minimum-wage legislation in two Congresses, he was not part of the final negotiating team on the bill that increased the wage.

When 324 of Murphy's colleagues voted in December 1987 to reprimand him for misconduct, he could have been excused for feeling a victim of bad timing. His punishment came as GOP activists were complaining that alleged improprieties by senior Democrats — including Speaker Jim Wright of Texas — were being ignored.

The House ethics committee had voted 11-0 to assess Murphy its mildest punishment — a reprimand — for diverting government resources to his former law firm, for allowing another member to vote for him on the House floor, and for keeping a "ghost employee" on his payroll.

Murphy and a few others said the ethics committee was singling him out for punishment to quiet criticism that the panel was lax. But some who denounced the committee did not exactly heap praise on the six-term Pennsylvanian. Georgia Republican Newt Gingrich blasted the ethics panel, saying, "You do not have the courage at this moment to raise the charges against those with power, but just before Christmas you found a member without power. It is sort of shameful." (Gingrich still voted to reprimand Murphy.)

While struggling with his ethics case in the 100th Congress, Murphy also saw his efforts to raise the minimum wage fail. But he came back ready to fight in 1989, when the landscape shifted somewhat. Unlike Ronald Reagan, President Bush expressed a willingness to consider a minimum-wage bill — but only if it did not raise the wage above $4.25 an hour, and only if it included a six-month subminimum "training wage." The subminimum wage was anathema to many Democrats and their organized-labor allies in 1988, but with the live prospect of an increase in the wage — which had been at $3.35 an hour since 1981 — they showed signs of flexibility on the issue in 1989.

Murphy forged a compromise in March 1989. Murphy, Arkansan Tommy F. Robinson and Pennsylvanian Tom Ridge hastily hammered out a bipartisan package after sponsors realized that the measure reported by Education and Labor — hiking the wage to $4.65 an hour and barring a training wage — would fail. The Murphy-Ridge-Robinson substitute, adopted by 240-179, lowered the increase to $4.55 an hour and created a two-month training wage, equal to 85 percent of the minimum, for first-time workers.

But Bush would not budge. After he vetoed the bill, Democratic leaders and union officials stepped in to negotiate a new bill with the White House, leaving Murphy and fellow Pennsylvanian Bill Goodling, ranking Republican on Education and Labor, out of the loop. Murphy complained that the result was too weak — it permitted a six-month training wage for teenagers and met Bush's $4.25 ceiling. But it was approved by a lopsided margin.

The result was a disappointment to Murphy, who had drawn some criticism in the past for his willingness to compromise. In the 100th

Pennsylvania 22

Southwest — Washington

This coal-rich corner of the state has fed the blast furnaces of the Steel Belt for most of this century, in boom times and bad. Tales of cave-ins, strikes and cutthroat politics still embroider the talk of the miners as they down schooners of beer in the taverns that nestle among the stark hills. The United Mine Workers is an important force, and it has a rough history. UMW President W. A. "Tony" Boyle was convicted here in the 1969 murder of union rival Joseph A. "Jock" Yablonski. The area's legacy of violence dates back to the Whiskey Rebellion in 1791.

The 22nd is thoroughly Democratic: Jimmy Carter won it in both 1976 and 1980; Walter F. Mondale scored in the high 50s or better in every county of the 22nd in 1984; and Michael S. Dukakis carried the district handily in 1988. In the last redistricting, industrial and Democratic southern Beaver County joined the district. That Beaver County territory includes such Ohio River factory towns as Midland and the aptly named Industry, as well as Shippingport, site of the first commercial atomic reactor.

Washington, Murphy's home county, has almost half the 22nd's population and dominates the district. It has a little coal mining, but its economy depends on heavy industry. Charleroi and other Monongahela River towns make steel, glass and industrial equipment.

The city of Washington, home of the county's old factory-owning families, often goes against the grain and votes Republican — as does Peters Township, a white-collar bedroom community for Pittsburgh commuters on the Allegheny County line. But these votes regularly are drowned by the Democratic tide.

Coal is the mainstay of Fayette and Greene counties. Fayette has been mined much longer than less-populous Greene; many of Fayette's deep mines are played out and strip mining has begun.

These two counties display an even firmer Democratic allegiance than Washington County. In the 1976 Senate contest, which was a regional clash between Pittsburgher John Heinz, the Republican, and Philadelphian William Green, the Democrat, Washington joined the rest of western Pennsylvania in supporting Heinz. But Fayette and Greene cast aside geographical considerations and voted for the Democrat.

Population: 515,122. White 495,229 (96%), Black 17,910 (4%). Spanish origin 2,779 (1%). 18 and over 378,475 (73%), 65 and over 69,425 (13%). Median age: 33.

Congress, he questioned whether an increase as large as that sought by committee Democrats could clear Congress, and he backed a move to strip from the bill a controversial, labor-backed "indexing" provision that would have guaranteed future annual increases without congressional action. But the full committee weighted the bill with a fourth installment to boost the wage to $5.05 per hour in 1992. Sponsors could not round up enough votes in either the House or Senate, and the bill died.

Murphy chairs the Education and Labor Subcommittee on Labor Standards, but in recent years he has shown some interest in moving up. At the start of the 102nd Congress, Murphy was the senior Democrat with an eye on the chair of the Labor Management Relations Subcommittee, but he never entered the formal bidding for the post, as it became clear that Montana's Pat Williams had the vote sewn up. Similarly, Murphy struck out when he tried to claim the Interior Subcommittee on Oversight for his own at the start of the 101st Congress. Fellow Pennsylvanian Peter H. Kostmayer had long since locked up his support; Murphy withdrew his bid.

Murphy looks out for coal interests on the Interior Committee, where he regularly sides with pro-development forces against environmentalists. He is generally a pro-industry vote on nuclear-power issues.

At Home: The life of a politician in coal country can be a little like the life of a miner — rough. Murphy, proud of his Marine Corps past, displays a relish for combat that suits the 22nd. In 1973 he got into a fight with motorcycle gang members who were harassing him. In 1979, after Iranians seized American hostages, Murphy declared his willingness to rejoin the Marines and attack Tehran.

Murphy might have come to blows with his 1984 GOP foe but for the fact that the adversary was a woman, Nancy Pryor. Her campaign rhetoric was unusually inflammatory; at one point she said Murphy and the national Democratic Party "endorsed and approved of humans having sex with dogs, sex with sheep, sex with chickens, to name only a few."

Murphy ran ads calling Pryor a liar, and filed a defamation suit against her in a local court. In the final weeks of the campaign, Murphy was guarded by U.S. Capitol police because of threatening calls he had received. The election itself was nowhere near as interesting as the campaign; Murphy won by a 4-to-1 margin.

In 1988, following his reprimand by the House, Murphy was ready for a fight, but no heavyweight challengers appeared.

But in 1990, he faced an aggressive primary challenge from William A. Nicolella, a candy company owner, who accused Murphy of leading a double life — with a wife and family back in the district and a woman friend and teenage son born out of wedlock in the Washington, D.C., suburbs.

The story had appeared in print before, but several days before the primary, Nicolella supplied Pittsburgh TV stations and The Associated Press with footage purportedly taken around Murphy's Northern Virginia home that Nicolella said proved his accusation.

Murphy responded in two statements, accusing Nicolella of making "venomous" and "slanderous" attacks. "I have never abandoned my responsibility to any of my children," Murphy said.

While he won with 70 percent of the primary vote, the implication of tainted ethics apparently had a lingering impact. Murphy's 63 percent vote share in the fall against a little-known GOP challenger was his lowest percentage since he first won the seat in 1976.

Then, he had to navigate his way through a 12-way primary field for the seat vacated by Democrat Thomas E. Morgan, chairman of the House Foreign Affairs Committee. Morgan had his own candidate, but with almost two decades as a state legislator under his belt, Murphy prevailed with 29 percent of the vote.

That fall Republicans offered a solid candidate, state Rep. Roger Fischer, but Murphy took 55 percent. The GOP has not made a serious effort in the strongly Democratic 22nd since then.

Committees

Education & Labor (5th of 25 Democrats)
Labor Standards (chairman); Health & Safety; Labor-Management Relations

Foreign Affairs (21st of 28 Democrats)
International Economic Policy & Trade

Interior & Insular Affairs (4th of 29 Democrats)
Energy & the Environment; National Parks & Public Lands

Elections

1990 General		
Austin J. Murphy (D)	78,375	(63%)
Suzanne Hayden (R)	45,509	(37%)
1990 Primary		
Austin J. Murphy (D)	48,455	(70%)
William A. Nicolella (D)	20,713	(30%)
1988 General		
Austin J. Murphy (D)	123,428	(72%)
William Hodgkiss (R)	47,039	(28%)

Previous Winning Percentages: **1986** (100%) **1984** (79%) **1982** (79%) **1980** (70%) **1978** (72%) **1976** (55%)

District Vote For President

	1988	1984	1980	1976
D	115,045 (65%)	121,832 (61%)	97,195 (53%)	113,800 (60%)
R	61,988 (35%)	76,002 (38%)	77,892 (42%)	72,769 (38%)
I			7,429 (4%)	

Campaign Finance

	Receipts	Receipts from PACs		Expend-itures
1990				
Murphy (D)	$199,802	$139,310	(70%)	$191,739
Hayden (R)	$3,260	$50	(2%)	$3,258
1988				
Murphy (D)	$173,164	$128,218	(74%)	$183,335
Hodgkiss (R)	$4,780	$175	(4%)	$4,676

Key Votes

1991	
Authorize use of force against Iraq	N
1990	
Support constitutional amendment on flag desecration	Y
Pass family and medical leave bill over Bush veto	Y
Reduce SDI funding	Y
Allow abortions in overseas military facilities	N
Approve budget summit plan for spending and taxing	N
Approve civil rights bill	Y
1989	
Halt production of B-2 stealth bomber at 13 planes	N
Oppose capital gains tax cut	Y
Approve federal abortion funding in rape or incest cases	N
Approve pay raise and revision of ethics rules	N
Pass Democratic minimum wage plan over Bush veto	Y

Voting Studies

	Presidential Support		Party Unity		Conservative Coalition	
Year	**S**	**O**	**S**	**O**	**S**	**O**
1990	29	69	61	33	44	54
1989	34	62	49	45	41	56
1988	28	59	50	36	47	42
1987	21	69	68	20	56	40
1986	21	77	75	19	50	42
1985	36	63	78	20	49	49
1984	35	63	65	28	46	51
1983	22	77	78	18	38	57
1982	35	57	71	19	41	49
1981	38	53	58	30	52	40

Interest Group Ratings

Year	ADA	ACU	AFL-CIO	CCUS
1990	50	33	83	69
1989	75	30	92	50
1988	60	24	100	33
1987	60	5	81	15
1986	70	19	93	33
1985	60	19	76	36
1984	55	42	77	47
1983	80	17	94	25
1982	55	33	89	25
1981	55	20	85	29

23 William F. Clinger (R)

Of Warren — Elected 1978

Born: April 4, 1929, Warren, Pa.
Education: Johns Hopkins U., B.A. 1951; U. of Virginia, LL.B. 1965.
Military Service: Navy, 1951-55.
Occupation: Lawyer.
Family: Wife, Julia Whitla; four children.
Religion: Presbyterian.
Political Career: No previous office.
Capitol Office: 2160 Rayburn Bldg. 20515; 225-5121.

In Washington: Clinger was one of the Republican moderates who set aside ideological trepidations and voted to elect conservative firebrand Newt Gingrich of Georgia as GOP minority whip in March 1989. A low-key establishment type on Public Works, Clinger seemed to be just the sort of "Old Bull" Republican who would back the whip candidacy of GOP regular Edward Madigan of Illinois.

But in supporting Gingrich, Clinger showed a willingness to play insider politics. Clinger stood to gain legislative influence with a Gingrich victory: The Georgian promised to take a leave of absence from Public Works if he won, opening his ranking GOP position on the high-profile Aviation Subcommittee for Clinger, who was next in seniority.

Clinger's new post on the Aviation panel quickly afforded him heightened visibility: air terrorism, airport overcrowding, the effects of deregulation on the airline industry and the impact of the 1989 Eastern Airlines strike were all headline topics when he took the ranking spot early in the 101st Congress.

Responding to the bombing of Pan Am Flight 103 over Lockerbie, Scotland, in 1988, the aviation panel in 1989 drafted an airport security bill designed to thwart terrorist attacks. It authorized $270 million for bomb detection devices and other security measures, prompting objections from the Bush administration, which felt the airlines should pay for the detection equipment. Clinger offered a compromise to have the government split the costs with the airlines, but he lost in subcommittee.

Clinger overlooked an administration veto threat to support the security measure on the House floor, where it passed by a wide margin.

In 1990, Clinger helped pass a law, also prompted by the Pan Am crash, which established an intelligence director for airline safety within the Department of Transportation and prohibited the selective notification of passengers about terrorist threats.

Clinger also supported a bill to give the Transportation secretary authority to review leveraged buyouts in the airline industry before they become final, and to block them if they would lead to certain conditions, such as giving a foreign buyer controlling interest in the airline.

Clinger's most visible effort in the 101st Congress concerned not aviation, but a more earthbound subject: trash.

A reporter in Clinger's Pennsylvania district alerted him to the practice of "backhauling," whereby truckers use the same vehicle to haul garbage in one direction and food in another. Clinger sponsored two hearings to investigate the matter, and in October 1989 introduced a bill to ban backhauling that poses a health threat. The House adopted most of Clinger's provisions as part of a compromise package on the issue, and a backhauling bill became law in late 1990. "We don't eat food out of garbage cans, and we shouldn't be expected to eat food out of garbage trucks," Clinger said in the House debate.

Clinger, an attorney, came to Congress with a public works background — he was general counsel to the federal Economic Development Administration (EDA) under President Gerald R. Ford — and he has dedicated his House career to the field.

Though some critics deride the committee as a funnel for "pork barrel" spending, Clinger is a steadfast supporter of public works projects and a critic of "shortsighted" people who scorn them as wasteful. "Congressional efforts to cut back on spending have the unfortunate effect of discouraging public and private investment in our infrastructure . . . ," Clinger said in 1988.

Early in the 100th Congress, Clinger crossed swords with a Pennsylvania Republican colleague — conservative activist and Gingrich ally Robert S. Walker — over public works funding. Clinger took the House floor to defend an $88 billion highway bill — which included a road-improvement project in his district — stating, "Every project that is funded under this demonstration area is a vitally needed project." Walker disagreed, saying the bill contained "page after page after page after page after page after page of pork."

Pennsylvania 23

Northwest, Central — State College

Except when Penn State University's football team plays at home or Punxsutawney Phil, the groundhog, looks for his shadow, this remote part of the state attracts little attention. One Pennsylvania politician, opposed to building an Interstate highway through it, once declared that "all they have up there is a bunch of bears."

Aside from the Penn State academic complex in State College, coal patches and small manufacturing towns, the 23rd has a rural character. It is also one of the most Republican areas of the state, although the GOP advantage is not so daunting that Democrats cannot be competitive, as the close races between Clinger and Democrat Bill Wachob proved.

Centre County, which includes State College, is the biggest population center, casting nearly one-fourth of the district's vote. The county as a whole usually goes Republican, but Democratic votes in State College introduce an element of uncertainty. Wachob, who worked hard to generate support in the university community, bucked a strong tide for President Ronald Reagan to win Centre County by a narrow margin in 1984. But it shifted back to Clinger two years later.

A sleepy college town 25 years ago, State College has grown to form the nucleus of an emerging metropolitan area. The university has spawned a small high-tech industrial complex outside town that attracts Republican-voting engineers. Many have settled in quaint villages around State College, such as Pine Grove Mills, Pleasant Gap, Lemont and Boalsburg, which claims to be the birthplace of Memorial Day. Local boosters call the whole area "Happy Valley," a label credible enough to attract a growing convention and resort trade.

Centre County is a prosperous oasis in a region that otherwise could be considered part of rural Appalachia. Mountainous and heavily forested, most of the land is better-suited for hunting and fishing than for farming. Schools have traditionally closed on the first day of hunting season.

The strongest Democratic county in the 23rd is Elk County, a paper-mill center and producer of the wood that goes into "Louisville Slugger" baseball bats. Elk, Wachob's home base, is one of two counties that backed him in 1984 and 1986. But Republican Arlen Specter carried it in the 1986 Senate race, as did George Bush in 1988 presidential voting.

There are pockets of Democratic strength in other coal-mining and industrial areas of Armstrong, Clinton, and Clearfield counties. In 1988, Democrat Michael S. Dukakis won Armstrong and Clinton.

The district's northern and western counties — sparsely populated Warren, Venango, McKean and Forest — habitually vote Republican. This part of the district produces motor oil, continuing a small industry descended from the mid-19th-century Drake Well in Titusville, in the 21st.

Population: 515,976. White 509,781 (99%), Black 2,726 (0.5%), Other 2,453 (0.5%). Spanish origin 2,030 (0.4%). 18 and over 378,256 (73%), 65 and over 62,705 (12%). Median age: 30.

Clinger also serves as ranking Republican on the Government Operations Subcommittee on Environment, Energy and Natural Resources, where he has taken a strong interest in environmental issues. In 1989, he took credit for a proposal, sent to Congress by President Bush, that allows U.S. exports of hazardous wastes only to nations with the capacity to handle them in an environmentally safe manner.

Clinger is one of the more moderate Republicans in the House; in 1988, he voted against President Ronald Reagan's legislative position as often as he voted with him. But Clinger has voted more frequently with Bush, and supported the controversial budget-summit package in October 1990.

While decrying some elements of the package, such as the increase in the federal gasoline tax, Clinger exhorted his colleagues to approve the deal reached between congressional leaders and the administration. "Failure to pass this budget will deeply embarrass our president while making ourselves irrelevant as the ship of state founders," he said.

At Home: After winning two bruising re-elections in 1984 and 1986, Clinger seems to have restored his secure position in this mountainous Pennsylvania district.

Clinger contributed to his earlier electoral woes by getting a bit too comfortable. After he returned the 23rd District to GOP control in 1978, he won two easy re-elections. Then in 1984, he seemed to relax against Democrat Bill Wachob, who controlled the campaign debate and pounded away at the wealthy incumbent, contending that the district needed a more active congressman who would fight for programs to create more jobs.

Without Reagan's coattails, Clinger might have been defeated in 1984. As it was, he lost five of the district's 12 counties, including the most populous, Centre County (State College).

In their 1986 rematch, Clinger was far more aggressive. Pointing to his foe's record as a state legislator, he said Wachob was a "very liberal Democrat" with views "out of sync" with the traditionally Republican district. And Clinger maintained he was much more effective than Wachob painted him, pointing to a number of projects he had won for the 23rd.

Wachob was supported by an array of teachers, environmentalists and consumer activists. But Clinger effectively portrayed himself as a hard-working, moderate Republican, and he had the money to make his case. He swept 10 counties, including Centre, and pushed his share of the vote up to 55 percent.

After an easy re-election in 1988, Clinger slipped a bit to 59 percent in 1990 against a little-known Democrat whose campaign was designed to tap anti-Congress sentiment.

The son of a businessman in Warren County, at the district's northwest corner, Clinger worked in advertising for a mail-order house, then became a lawyer. Following his work in the Economic Development Administration, he came home to challenge Democratic Rep. Joseph Ammerman, who had ousted the district's aging GOP incumbent, Albert Johnson, in 1976.

Ammerman had compiled a liberal voting record as a freshman, which might have been enough of a liability for a Democrat in a traditionally Republican district. But in late August 1978, Ammerman broke his hip in an automobile accident and was hospitalized for six weeks, losing valuable campaign time.

Clinger cited his Washington experience to illustrate his campaign theme that many federal programs did not work and needed revamping. While his win over Ammerman was not spectacular, it discouraged any strong opposition until 1984.

Committees

Government Operations (2nd of 15 Republicans)
Environment, Energy & Natural Resources (ranking)

Public Works & Transportation (3rd of 21 Republicans)
Aviation (ranking); Surface Transportation; Water Resources

Select Narcotics Abuse & Control (11th of 14 Republicans)

Elections

1990 General		
William F. Clinger (R)	78,189	(59%)
Daniel J. Shannon (D)	53,465	(41%)
1988 General		
William F. Clinger (R)	105,575	(62%)
Howard Shakespeare (D)	63,476	(37%)

Previous Winning Percentages: **1986** (55%) **1984** (52%) **1982** (65%) **1980** (74%) **1978** (54%)

District Vote For President

	1988	1984	1980	1976
D	73,714 (43%)	69,325 (37%)	65,367 (38%)	77,107 (45%)
R	97,493 (56%)	117,316 (63%)	94,528 (55%)	92,392 (53%)
I			10,868 (6%)	

Campaign Finance

	Receipts	Receipts from PACs		Expend-itures
1990				
Clinger (R)	$349,208	$190,302	(54%)	$338,431
Shannon (D)	$6,764	0		$6,765
1988				
Clinger (R)	$405,537	$189,036	(47%)	$336,675
Shakespeare (D)	$108,104	0		$106,463

Key Votes

1991	
Authorize use of force against Iraq	Y
1990	
Support constitutional amendment on flag desecration	N
Pass family and medical leave bill over Bush veto	N
Reduce SDI funding	N
Allow abortions in overseas military facilities	N
Approve budget summit plan for spending and taxing	Y
Approve civil rights bill	N
1989	
Halt production of B-2 stealth bomber at 13 planes	N
Oppose capital gains tax cut	N
Approve federal abortion funding in rape or incest cases	N
Approve pay raise and revision of ethics rules	N
Pass Democratic minimum wage plan over Bush veto	N

Voting Studies

	Presidential Support		Party Unity		Conservative Coalition	
Year	**S**	**O**	**S**	**O**	**S**	**O**
1990	66	32	65	29	89	9
1989	78	22	66	32	90	10
1988	47	47	67	28	76	24
1987	54	42	59	38	74	23
1986	52	47	48	49	84	14
1985	50	48	54	38	65	31
1984	56	42	54	42	64	34
1983	61	39	62 †	37 †	66	34
1982	65	35	61	38	77	23
1981	63	37	69	31	72	28

† Not eligible for all recorded votes.

Interest Group Ratings

Year	ADA	ACU	AFL-CIO	CCUS
1990	28	55	18	77
1989	20	64	17	100
1988	25	63	62	86
1987	24	43	50	73
1986	50	45	86	44
1985	35	48	59	57
1984	40	54	38	67
1983	15	52	18	95
1982	25	36	20	64
1981	30	73	20	89

Rhode Island

U.S. CONGRESS

SENATE 1 D, 1 R
HOUSE 1 D, 1 R

LEGISLATURE

Senate 45 D, 5 R
House 88 D, 12 R

ELECTIONS

1988 Presidential Vote

Bush	44%
Dukakis	56%

1984 Presidential Vote

Reagan	52%
Mondale	48%

1980 Presidential Vote

Reagan	37%
Carter	48%
Anderson	14%

Turnout rate in 1986	41%
Turnout rate in 1988	53%
Turnout rate in 1990	45%

(as percentage of voting age population)

POPULATION AND GROWTH

1980 population	947,154
1990 population (43rd in the nation)	1,003,464
Percent change 1980-1990	+6%

DEMOGRAPHIC BREAKDOWN

White	91%
Black	4%
Asian or Pacific Islander	2%
(Hispanic origin)	5%
Urban	87%
Rural	13%
Born in state	68%
Foreign-born	9%

MAJOR CITIES

Providence	160,728
Warwick	85,427
Cranston	76,060
Pawtucket	72,644
East Providence	50,380

AREA AND LAND USE

Area 1,055 sq. miles (50th)

Farm	9%
Forest	60%
Federally owned	1%

Gov. Bruce Sundlun (D)
Of Providence — Elected 1990

Born: Jan. 19, 1920, Providence, R.I.
Education: Williams College, B.A. 1946; Harvard U., LL.B. 1949.
Military Service: Army, 1942-45; Air Force Reserve, 1945-80.
Occupation: Lawyer; corporate executive.
Religion: Jewish.
Political Career: Democratic nominee for governor, 1986, 1988.
Next Election: 1994.

WORK

Occupations

White-collar	50%
Blue-collar	36%
Service workers	14%

Government Workers

Federal	10,511
State	24,106
Local	30,510

MONEY

Median family income	$ 16,978	(41st)
Tax burden per capita	$ 816	(27th)

EDUCATION

Spending per pupil through grade 12	$ 5,329	(6th)
Persons with college degrees	15%	(27th)

CRIME

Violent crime rate 378 per 100,000 (32nd)

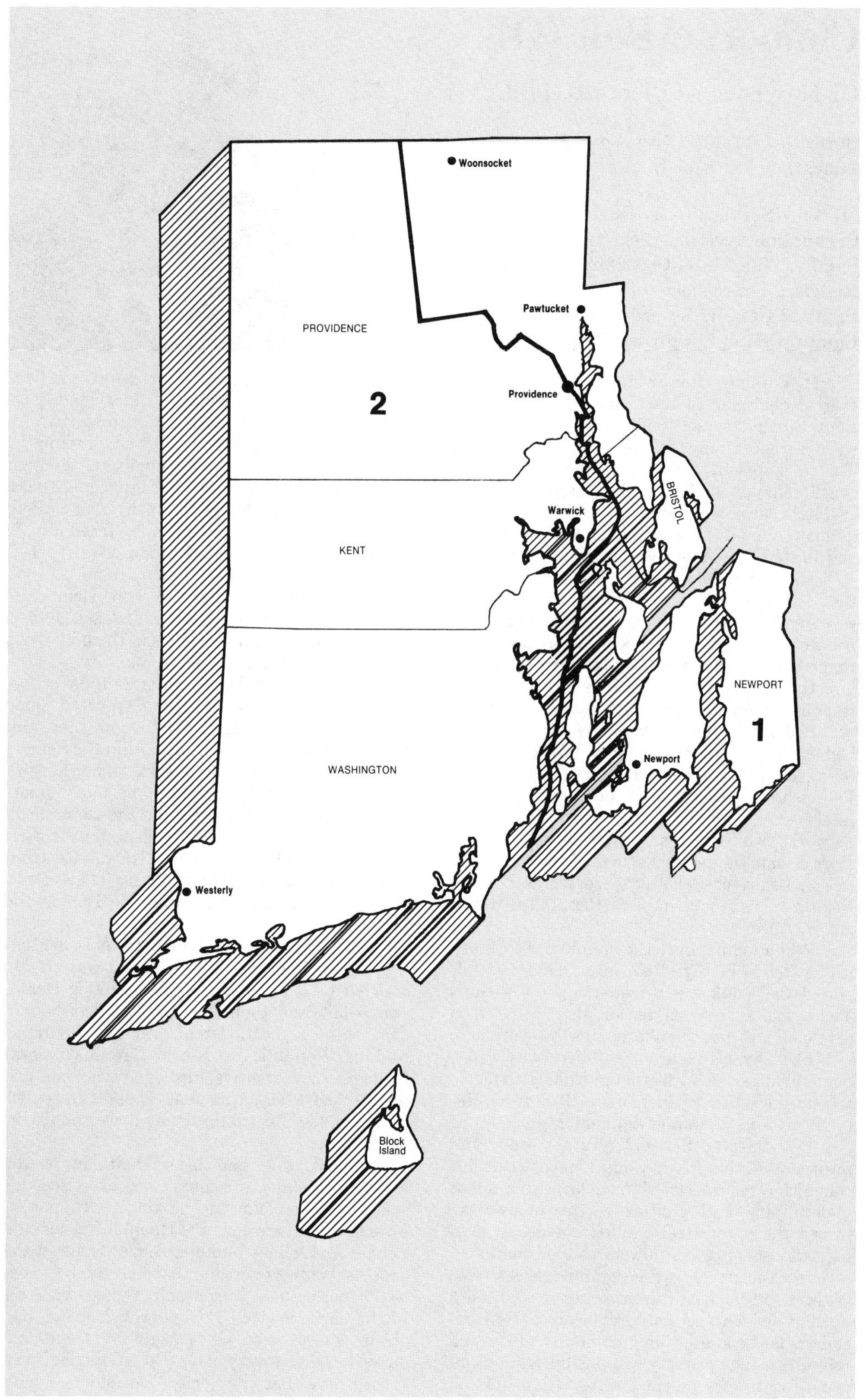
Woonsocket
Pawtucket
PROVIDENCE
Providence
2
BRISTOL
Warwick
KENT
NEWPORT
1
Newport
WASHINGTON
Westerly
Block Island

Claiborne Pell (D)

Of Newport — Elected 1960

Born: Nov. 22, 1918, New York, N.Y.
Education: Princeton U., A.B. 1940; Columbia U., A.M. 1946.
Military Service: Coast Guard, 1941-45.
Occupation: Investment executive.
Family: Wife, Nuala O'Donnell; four children.
Religion: Episcopalian.
Political Career: No previous office.
Capitol Office: 335 Russell Bldg. 20510; 224-4642.

In Washington: From the time Pell took over as chairman of the Senate Foreign Relations Committee in 1987, he has been stuck with a reputation for ineffective leadership. Tied in knots by contentious partisan battles over foreign policy issues, the committee under Pell has routinely failed to act on one or both of its main annual responsibilities: the foreign aid and State Department authorization bills.

Many times during his first four years in the position, Pell was unable even to establish a working quorum for committee meetings. The Senate's foreign assistance priorities were shaped not by his authorizing committee, but directly by the Appropriations subcommittee responsible for foreign aid.

Pell's perceived lack of assertiveness was highlighted during the Persian Gulf crisis that followed Iraq's August 1990 invasion of Kuwait. Pell, who projects poorly on television, was rarely called upon for interviews by the national networks, which instead opted for such loquacious Senate figures as Vermont Democrat Patrick J. Leahy or Pell's predecessor as Foreign Relations chairman, Indiana Republican Richard G. Lugar.

While itching over the committee's diminishing status, Foreign Relations Democrats tolerated Pell's lukewarm leadership for a time. There was a personal reason for this: Pell, a gentleman of patrician breeding, is genuinely well-liked by his colleagues. There was also a political angle: Pell was thought likely to face a tough re-election challenge in 1990 from Republican Rep. Claudine Schneider.

Pell defeated Schneider rather easily and returned for his sixth Senate term. But his committee fellows, freed from concerns about undermining Pell politically, then moved to restart the committee's stalled engines by taking away some of his powers as chairman.

In January 1991, the committee was reorganized so that its subcommittees would mark up bills (which was not previously permitted) and would be staffed independently of the full committee. The primary responsibility for managing future foreign aid authorization bills on the Senate floor was transferred to committee Democrat Paul S. Sarbanes of Maryland.

There was a "more in sorrow than in anger" air about the move. Sen. Joseph R. Biden Jr. of Delaware, who chairs the Foreign Relations Subcommittee on European Affairs, said he submitted his realignment plan to Pell, who accepted and publicly announced it. "It was not a challenge," said Biden. "We reached an accommodation with the chairman."

But others saw otherwise. "The Democrats are about to divide up his domain," said Lugar, who chaired Foreign Relations in the mid-1980s when the GOP had a Senate majority.

Pell has often been compared unfavorably as chairman with Lugar, who enforced some discipline on the centrifugal committee and restored some of its standing within the Senate. However, these comparisons are somewhat unfair. As chairman, Lugar played his most important role in mediating between the Republican administration of Ronald Reagan and the Senate, occasionally convincing Reagan to avoid defeat by accepting compromise. That role is not open to a chairman from the Democratic Party.

Also, when he attempted to move legislation through the committee, Lugar was greatly assisted by a most cooperative ranking Democrat: Claiborne Pell. Instead, Pell has had to deal with a far different kind of figure as ranking Republican: North Carolina's Jesse Helms, a conservative ideologue who has frequently used his parliamentary skills to scuttle foreign policy legislation that does not fit his worldview.

Helms, who had been chairman of the Senate Agriculture Committee, exercised his seniority to reclaim the ranking GOP spot on Foreign Relations after the Republicans lost the Senate in 1986 — bumping Lugar aside in the process. While conceding that Pell can be somewhat ineffectual, Lugar empathized with his plight early in 1991. "Claiborne has not had strong views as to what ought to occur, and Jesse has been very adept at stymieing even those views that [Pell] has," he said.

Pell also has an institutional problem that overrides even his difficult relationship with Helms: the antipathy of recent Republican administrations to the foreign aid authorization process. Presidents Ronald Reagan and George Bush have both viewed the congressional authorizers mainly as kibitzers who tread on executive branch prerogatives.

Bush provided an example of this attitude in 1990, when he vetoed a bill mandating sanctions against countries and companies that help nations obtain chemical weapons technology. Boosted in late 1990 by concerns about Iraq's stockpiles of chemical weapons, sanctions legislation cosponsored by Pell and Helms passed Congress as part of a bill reauthorizing the Export Administration Act. However, Bush pocket-vetoed the bill that November, stating that the sanctions "unduly interfere with the president's responsibility for carrying out foreign policy."

The chemical weapons bill — reintroduced in the 102nd Congress — featured rare teamwork between Pell, a liberal arms control advocate, and the archconservative Helms. In 1988, they sought to punish Iraq for its government's use of poison gas against its Kurdish minority. The bill easily passed the Senate and was attached to a larger piece of legislation. But Helms unintentionally sunk the Iraqi sanctions when his objections to unrelated provisions of the overall bill resulted in a stalemate.

Pell's chief foreign policy aide Peter W. Galbraith has established himself as a liaison to the Iraqi Kurds. The senator's interest in this ethnic group was manifest following the U.S.-led military victory over Iraq. Pell — who voted against the January 1991 resolution authorizing Bush to use force — was among the senators who raised an alarm about the president's slow response to the plight of the Kurds, who had revolted after the war and faced bloody retaliation by the troops of Iraqi President Saddam Hussein.

One of the ironies of Pell's image as a weak chairman is that he is rather an activist as a legislator. He submits dozens of bills each Congress. One of his main foreign policy causes — the ratification of a pair of nuclear test-ban treaties signed in the early 1970s — was kept alive in large part through his persistence, and reached fruition in 1990.

Pell also has had a far-reaching impact on education issues. The chairman of the Labor and Human Resources Subcommittee on Education, Pell is one of the few active members to have a major federal program — the "Pell Grants" — named after him.

In 1972, Pell pushed through legislation establishing Basic Educational Opportunity Grants (BEOGs) for low- and middle-income college students. The program marked a basic shift in policy, because it provided aid directly to students, instead of channeling it through the institutions, as earlier programs had done. The BEOG program was renamed "Pell Grants" in 1980.

Since then, Pell has fought Reagan and Bush administration efforts to cut or sharply reorient federal student-aid programs. In April 1991, Bush proposed an education bill that would hold the line on overall Pell Grant spending while raising the maximum grant from $2,400 to $3,700 — thus potentially cutting 400,000 students from the program. Pell argued that Bush "is moving in precisely the wrong direction," adding, "We need larger Pell grants for more students, not larger grants for fewer students."

In January 1989, two conservative Democrats, Sen. Sam Nunn of Georgia and Rep. Dave McCurdy of Oklahoma, proposed making nearly all federal aid for postsecondary students contingent on recipients' commitment to perform civilian or military "national service." Pell opposed the tie-in with student aid, saying, "What we need today is not a replacement for our need-based programs, but a supplement to help those programs meet more of the costs of a college education." He said the Nunn-McCurdy proposal would place most of the national service burden on students from low-income families, an idea he called "cruel."

Pell offered his own proposal to provide student aid in exchange for two years of voluntary service. His plan was included in a modest national service bill that passed the Senate in October 1990.

Pell pulls no punches about his advocacy role on education issues. In April 1989, he urged the higher education community to be more aggressive in the political process. "In this area, where the threat of cuts has been so ominous, you would expect to see a proliferation of political action committees; you do not," Pell said. "The cost of such inactivity can be enormous."

At Home: Pell's predecessor in the Senate was Theodore Green, who first arrived in the chamber when past retirement age and served into his 90s. Incredible as that seems, Pell the Newport blueblood is well on his way toward matching Green's record for Senate longevity. Far from resenting his privileged background, Pell's blue-collar constituents have handed him landslide victories five out of six times. Only Republican John H. Chafee, now his Senate colleague, was able to hold him under 60 percent of the vote.

Pell's pro-labor record has kept him in the good graces of the unions, always a potent force in Rhode Island. And while he does not have much personal rapport with the state's ethnic voters, he can talk to them: He speaks Portuguese, Italian and French.

Pell's career not only survived but prospered in the generally Republican election years of 1972, 1978 and 1984. So it should not have surprised anyone when he flourished in the more favorable climate of 1990, when Rhode Island Democrats were recapturing both the governorship and the 2nd District House seat. Some had thought Pell, at 72, a better candidate for retirement than re-election — especially after the GOP recruited five-term House veteran Schneider to challenge him.

Doubts about Pell's fitness multiplied when, in an August debate, he could not remember any bills he had sponsored strictly for Rhode Island. His memory, he said pleasantly, "is not as good as it should be."

The senator gave pause once again in the autumn when an aide asserted there were secret messages in Persian Gulf speeches by U.S. officials. The aide said a code word ("Simone") was audible when tapes of the speeches were played backwards. "It sounds wacky [but] there may be some merit to it," said Pell, who reported this research in a letter to the secretary of Defense.

But Rhode Islanders had long since grown accustomed to Pell's eccentricities, including his professed belief in parapsychology. Despite his begoggled and half-doddering manner, Pell once again managed not only to rise to electoral challenge but to crush it.

Campaigning actively and emphasizing local economic concerns, he dispelled doubts about his age, health and sensitivity to the homefolk. Criticism of his performance as Senate Foreign Relations chairman, so common in Washington, did little damage in Rhode Island. It may even have allowed Pell, the consummate inside player, some insulation against the anti-insider mood of the day.

Schneider, meanwhile, never found a suitable key for her anti-incumbent pitch. Loath to assail Pell personally, she often sounded as though she thought the only thing wrong with him was his party label (scarcely a disqualification in a Democratic state). When she shifted to more ideological grounds of attack, the similarities between her voting record and Pell's undercut her effectiveness. While voters continued to show high regard for her personally, she was unable to sell her "time for a change" theme and Pell rang up more than 61 percent of the vote.

Pell's father, Herbert, briefly represented Manhattan's Silk Stocking District in the House and served as a foreign envoy for Franklin D. Roosevelt. Claiborne Pell was born in New York and spent summers in the exclusive Rhode Island resort of Newport, where the Pells had been going for five generations. The family moved there permanently when he was 9.

After graduating from Princeton in 1940, Pell went to Europe to try to help concentration camp inmates. The Nazis arrested him several times. He was a Coast Guard officer during World War II and spent several years in the foreign service. He later became an investment banker and publisher and served as registration chairman for the Democratic National Committee.

Pell decided to run himself in 1960 and stunned the political community by overwhelming two former governors to win the Democratic nomination for the Senate. In the fall, Pell was helped to victory by his close ties to Democratic presidential nominee John F. Kennedy, a fellow New Englander highly popular in Rhode Island.

Running for a second term in 1966, Pell had an equally easy time with his GOP opponent — a retired Women's Army Corps officer named Ruth M. Briggs, who insisted upon being called "Colonel." She sought to make an issue of Pell's dovish line on the Vietnam War and to portray him as a wealthy dilettante ("the prize entertainer of the Kennedys"). She failed to draw even a third of the vote.

Chafee, in 1972, gave Pell his toughest race. He tried to weigh Pell down with his fellow anti-war Democrat Sen. George McGovern of South Dakota, the Democrats' presidential nominee.

But Pell deflected the tactic by repudiating McGovern's call for cutting the defense budget. Ultimately, the moderate Chafee had the same trouble Schneider would have 18 years later defining a compelling reason to retire Pell.

Things were back to normal for Pell in 1978, when he buried Republican James G. Reynolds, a little-known bakery executive who complained that Pell was more interested in the arts than in saving jobs for Rhode Island. In 1984, the GOP tried to recruit Schneider but had to settle for Barbara Leonard, the president of a screw manufacturing company. The widow of a longtime GOP fundraiser, Leonard herself was a political novice; Pell was re-elected with 73 percent of the vote.

Committees

Foreign Relations (Chairman)
International Economic Policy, Trade, Oceans & Environment; Terrorism, Narcotics & International Operations

Labor & Human Resources (2nd of 10 Democrats)
Education, Arts & Humanities (chairman); Aging; Children, Families, Drugs & Alcoholism

Rules & Administration (2nd of 9 Democrats)

Joint Library (Chairman)

Elections

1990 General

Claiborne Pell (D)	225,105	(62%)
Claudine Schneider (R)	138,947	(38%)

Previous Winning Percentages: **1984** (73%) **1978** (75%) **1972** (54%) **1966** (68%) **1960** (69%)

Campaign Finance

	Receipts	Receipts from PACs		Expend-itures
1990				
Pell (D)	$2,138,199	$885,678	(41%)	$2,350,128
Schneider (R)	$1,989,616	$688,865	(35%)	$2,056,923

Key Votes

1991

Authorize use of force against Iraq	N

1990

Oppose prohibition of certain semiautomatic weapons	N
Support constitutional amendment on flag desecration	N
Oppose requiring parental notice for minors' abortions	Y
Halt production of B-2 stealth bomber at 13 planes	Y
Approve budget that cut spending and raised revenues	N
Pass civil rights bill over Bush veto	Y

1989

Oppose reduction of SDI funding	N
Oppose barring federal funds for "obscene" art	Y
Allow vote on capital gains tax cut	#

Voting Studies

	Presidential Support		Party Unity		Conservative Coalition	
Year	**S**	**O**	**S**	**O**	**S**	**O**
1990	25	72	86	9	11	81
1989	49	48	85	11	18	76
1988	43	51	89	6	8	92
1987	32	67	92	7	19	81
1986	30	67	75	20	16	80
1985	29	67	82	14	7	92
1984	31	66	82	14	15	81
1983	41	48	81	15	14	82
1982	36	59	75	19	17	78
1981	42	52	82	14	10	82

Interest Group Ratings

Year	ADA	ACU	AFL-CIO	CCUS
1990	94	19	78	18
1989	85	4	80	43
1988	100	0	100	36
1987	90	0	90	28
1986	80	17	67	42
1985	95	9	95	29
1984	100	5	100	22
1983	90	0	94	26
1982	95	0	92	37
1981	95	0	95	17

John H. Chafee (R)

Of Warwick — Elected 1976

Born: Oct. 22, 1922, Providence, R.I.
Education: Yale U., B.A. 1947; Harvard U., LL.B. 1950.
Military Service: Marine Corps, 1942-45, 1951-52.
Occupation: Lawyer.
Family: Wife, Virginia Coates; five children.
Religion: Episcopalian.
Political Career: R.I. House, 1957-63, minority leader, 1959-63; governor, 1963-69; defeated for re-election as governor, 1968; U.S. secretary of the Navy, 1969-72; Republican nominee for U.S. Senate, 1972.
Capitol Office: 567 Dirksen Bldg. 20510; 224-2921.

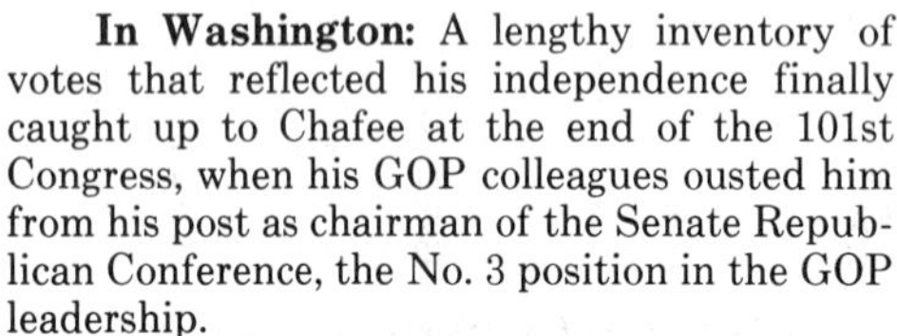

In Washington: A lengthy inventory of votes that reflected his independence finally caught up to Chafee at the end of the 101st Congress, when his GOP colleagues ousted him from his post as chairman of the Senate Republican Conference, the No. 3 position in the GOP leadership.

Chafee, a political moderate, had managed to defeat two prior challengers from the right, relying on his personal popularity to sway the more conservative GOP Conference. But in 1990, he met his equal in popularity, Thad Cochran of Mississippi. Even though Cochran did not run an overtly ideological campaign, he benefited from conservatives exasperated by Chafee's work with Democrats to produce a clean air bill and by his vote to override President Bush's veto of civil rights legislation. Even so, Cochran won by a single vote, 22-21.

Chafee's election as conference chairman in 1984 was in part a victory for a coalition of moderate senators from the Northeast and Midwest. But his 28-25 win over Jake Garn of Utah also was a product of the Rhode Islander's personal popularity. The same could be said of his 1988 re-election as conference chairman, which was challenged by Frank Murkowski of Alaska. Murkowski said Chafee had opposed the administration too often to be in leadership. But Chafee prevailed by a vote of 28-17.

Chafee now serves in a Senate far less driven by or beholden to the New Right politics that had dominated President Reagan's tenure. President Bush's politics seem closer to Chafee's own brand of Republicanism. In fact, the two New England-bred Episcopalians studied at Yale at the same time.

But Chafee's 1990 defeat was a reminder that the conservative flank of the party can still dominate its affairs. Chafee may have been able to vote against school prayer and the flag-desecration and balanced-budget amendments without generating animosity, but with Cochran as an attractive alternative it was no longer necessary for his more conservative colleagues to countenance such apostasy from the third-ranking party leader.

As ranking Republican on the Environment and Public Works Committee, Chafee played a vital role in the 101st Congress on the reauthorization of the Clean Air Act.

Chafee approached the clean air rewrite with a position on acid rain tough enough that he joined with environmental groups, and a few other senators, to condemn Sen. George J. Mitchell of Maine's proposed compromise on Clean Air Act amendments at the end of the 1988 session. Chafee was a key participant in drafting the bill's smog-reduction program, the largest title in the bill. In the Environmental Protection Subcommittee, where he is also ranking Republican, Chafee split with Democrats on how to reduce automobile tailpipe emissions. Democrats, led by Environmental Protection Chairman Max Baucus, leaned toward tough restrictions on emissions through two rounds of reductions. Chafee and the Republicans favored easing up on tailpipes and putting more emphasis on a program mandating the production and sale of alternative fuels and clean-fueled cars in the nation's nine smoggiest cities. Baucus called Chafee's proposal to require carmakers to sell clean-fueled vehicles "a pretty iffy proposition."

When Baucus refused to slow the accelerated markup process to consider the GOP proposal, Chafee led a rare partisan rebellion on the panel. He and the five other subcommittee Republicans voted against the bill's motor vehicle provisions. They were approved on a 7-6 vote. However, Chafee's proposal was included as part of the Senate-White House compromise on the bill.

Chafee also added a controversial amendment that would end by the year 2000 the use of chlorofluorocarbons (CFCs) and other chemicals blamed for destroying the ozone layer in the upper atmosphere. Under the bill, the chemicals are required to be phased out sooner than called for in an international agreement on CFCs signed by the United States.

The Environment Committee is a good spot in which Chafee can help his state and protect the nature and wildlife that have long occupied his interest. In 1988 he helped shepherd through a five-year reauthorization of the 1973 Endangered Species Act, working with Western Republicans to allay their concerns. He was the Republican co-author of a bill banning the dumping of sludge in the Atlantic Ocean. Chafee introduced a bill in the 101st Congress to expand waste reduction and recycling activities as a complement to legislation reauthorizing the Resource Conservation and Recovery Act (RCRA). But no legislation emerged in the 101st Congress, making the RCRA rewrite a top environmental priority of the 102nd Congress.

Chafee is part of the balanced-budget tradition that never felt comfortable with Reagan's reliance on "supply-side economics" and the deficits that strategy tolerated. This orientation almost caused him to oppose the 1986 tax reform drive. On the Finance Committee, he was one of the most vocal advocates of a deficit-reducing tax increase, despite Reagan's adamant opposition.

But when Finance Chairman Bob Packwood introduced a revenue-neutral tax overhaul bill, Chafee adopted the idea and became one of the core group of lawmakers who saw the tax bill through to passage in 1986.

More recently on Finance, Chafee has been closely associated with tax credits for child care expenses, an idea he continued to push with the Bush administration's support in the 101st Congress as the ranking Republican on one of Finance's two health subcommittees. The child-care legislation Bush signed into law in 1990 approved $18.3 billion in tax credits to help low- and moderate-income families cope with child-care costs.

On economic issues, Chafee's chief cause is international trade. He believes in free trade, but like most members is concerned about U.S. products' access to overseas markets. "If [the Japanese] are outsaving us and building a better mousetrap, that's fine," he said at International Trade Subcommittee hearings in 1989. "But what do we say to the refusal of U.S. goods when they're clearly superior?"

At Home: Chafee's affable personality and moderate record have carried him through more than three decades of politics in Rhode Island, winning most of the time and recovering from defeat.

His toughness showed in 1988, when he faced a telegenic and talented campaigner, Lt. Gov. Richard A. Licht. The 40-year-old nephew of the man who had ousted Chafee from the governorship in 1968, Licht organized early to assure himself the nomination and the united support of his party. Before being elected statewide, Licht had built a solid record as a legislator on issues of wide voter appeal such as child care and protection of open spaces.

Licht's early fundraising was impressive enough to draw national media attention. He was the only 1988 challenger to begin the year having raised more money than the incumbent. But when Chafee got busy, he was able to turn some of Licht's assets against him. He seized on Licht's campaign treasury to portray himself as the fiscal underdog in the race. And when Licht returned a controversial $250 contribution from Tom Hayden, a leftish California legislator (married at that time to actress Jane Fonda), Chafee said the Democrat must lack "backbone" if he caved in to pressure "over a measly $250." Such counterthrusts helped Chafee overcome Licht's appeal to youth and his charges that Chafee had larded the 1986 tax reform bill with special breaks for friends.

As expected, Democratic presidential nominee Michael S. Dukakis carried Rhode Island more easily than he did his home state of Massachusetts. But Licht badly lagged the top of his party ticket; Chafee won with a comfortable 55 percent of the vote.

Chafee's survival had been a closer question in 1982, when Democratic challenger Julius C. Michaelson came within 8,200 votes of victory simply by emphasizing that Chafee belonged to the party of Ronald Reagan and that Reagan was no friend of Rhode Island. Michaelson, a liberal former state attorney general, said Chafee had been a "very essential" supporter of the Reagan program.

It was not a bad Democratic strategy. Not only did Reagan fail to carry Rhode Island in 1980, but he drew a smaller share of the vote (37 percent) than he did in any other state.

Chafee fought off Michaelson by reasserting his value to Rhode Island. He boasted of his role in negotiations that persuaded the General Dynamics Electric Boat division to keep its large shipyard in the state.

The position Chafee held on the Finance Committee and his efforts to ease the burden on American businesses abroad helped him build a campaign treasury twice the size of Michaelson's. The challenger, general counsel to the state AFL-CIO, depended heavily on union support.

Michaelson carried Democratic Providence and the industrial Blackstone Valley by nearly 20,000 votes, a margin that Chafee barely offset by sweeping the rest of the state.

The close result was not unusual for Chafee. When he ran for governor in 1962, after serving as state House minority leader, he won by 398 votes over Democrat John A. Notte Jr. The incumbent had damaged himself by advocating a state income tax — the same issue that was to cause Chafee trouble six years later.

As a three-term governor in the 1960s,

Chafee pushed for an increase in Rhode Island's social and welfare spending, calling it "a state version of the Great Society." He won re-election easily in 1964 and in 1966.

In 1968, however, running against Democrat Frank Licht, he got caught on the wrong side of a dispute over state taxes. Chafee insisted an income tax was necessary to prevent a boost in the sales tax. Licht disagreed, and upset Chafee by 7,808 votes.

After his defeat, Chafee was appointed Navy secretary in the Nixon administration. That seemed likely to help the 1972 Senate campaign he was planning against Democratic Sen. Claiborne Pell. When he left the Pentagon to begin the campaign, he looked strong.

But it did not turn out that way. Though Pell has always been accused of aloofness, he knew what to do that year, running superb television advertising and speaking a collection of European languages to voters in the ethnic neighborhoods of Providence and the mill towns. And the old tax issue was still a partial liability for Chafee. Even the rare Republican presidential victory in the state that fall did not help him. Pell won 54 percent of the vote.

That might have been the end of Chafee's political career, had Democrats not managed to do everything but throw the state's other Senate seat at him in 1976 by fighting with each other all year.

Gov. Philip W. Noel was the front-runner for the 1976 Democratic nomination, but he crippled himself by making comments in a wire service interview that sounded like racial slurs. He had to resign as the party's national platform chairman, and he went on to lose the Senate primary by 100 votes to Cadillac dealer Richard P. Lorber, who spent lavishly of his own money and accused Noel not only of racial insensitivity but of bossism.

Noel then refused to back Lorber in the general election, allowing Chafee to resurrect his old coalition of the early 1960s — Republicans, independents and dissident Democrats. Lorber tried to paint the well-to-do Chafee as an elitist, but the charge did not stick. Chafee won every town in the state except one.

Committees

Environment & Public Works (Ranking)
Environmental Protection (ranking); Water Resources, Transportation & Infrastructure

Finance (5th of 9 Republicans)
Health for Families & the Uninsured (ranking); International Trade; Medicare & Long Term Care

Select Intelligence (7th of 7 Republicans)

Elections

1988 General

John H. Chafee (R)	217,273	(55%)
Richard A. Licht (D)	180,717	(45%)

Previous Winning Percentages: **1982** (51%) **1976** (58%)

Campaign Finance

	Receipts	Receipts from PACs		Expend-itures
1988				
Chafee (R)	$2,455,215	$1,045,319	(43%)	$2,841,985
Licht (D)	$2,838,216	$655,752	(23%)	$2,735,917

Key Votes

1991

Authorize use of force against Iraq	Y

1990

Oppose prohibition of certain semiautomatic weapons	N
Support constitutional amendment on flag desecration	N
Oppose requiring parental notice for minors' abortions	Y
Halt production of B-2 stealth bomber at 13 planes	N
Approve budget that cut spending and raised revenues	Y
Pass civil rights bill over Bush veto	Y

1989

Oppose reduction of SDI funding	N
Oppose barring federal funds for "obscene" art	Y
Allow vote on capital gains tax cut	Y

Voting Studies

	Presidential Support		Party Unity		Conservative Coalition	
Year	**S**	**O**	**S**	**O**	**S**	**O**
1990	58	41	58	36	65	30
1989	81	19	57	43	71	29
1988	45	49	34	63	22	76
1987	50	47	46	54	31	69
1986	67	31	64	34	62	37
1985	72	26	68	30	52	47
1984	71	26	66	28	60	36
1983	80	18	67	33	45	50
1982	54	45	47	50	30	69
1981	75	23	68	29	50	47

Interest Group Ratings

Year	ADA	ACU	AFL-CIO	CCUS
1990	50	43	11	55
1989	35	39	30	75
1988	90	4	86	36
1987	80	16	60	56
1986	60	35	33	63
1985	35	39	24	76
1984	60	58	18	56
1983	60	35	29	42
1982	80	14	50	43
1981	45	38	47	61

1 Ronald K. Machtley (R)

Of Portsmouth — Elected 1988

Born: July 13, 1948, Johnstown, Pa.
Education: U.S. Naval Academy, B.S. 1970; Suffolk U., J.D. 1978.
Military Service: Navy, 1970-75; Naval Reserve, 1975-present.
Occupation: Lawyer.
Family: Wife, Kati Croft; two children.
Religion: Presbyterian.
Political Career: No previous office.
Capitol Office: 132 Cannon Bldg. 20515; 225-4911.

In Washington: Perhaps the most important challenge Machtley faced in his first House term was avoiding two damaging political " 'f' words" — "frivolous" and "fluke." Machtley was, after all, the candidate who began his longshot 1988 House campaign accompanied by a pig he named "Les Pork." He won the seat mainly because the incumbent, 14-term Democrat and Banking Committee Chairman Fernand J. St Germain, was shadowed by scandal.

Yet Machtley proved skillful at building an image of substance. The collegial lawyer was elected as vice president of his freshman class. He also gained a seat on the Armed Services Committee, a key position for a member whose coastal district has a large Navy presence. These factors helped him win rather easily for a second term, no small feat in the heavily Democratic 1st District.

A Naval Academy graduate, a former Navy officer and a member of the reserve, Machtley shows a preference on Armed Services to that military branch. During the 101st Congress, he helped obtain $13 million to build a research facility at the Naval Underwater Systems Command center at Newport, R.I., and the same amount for Navy housing in his district. He opposes Bush administration efforts to eliminate funding for the Osprey, a hybrid airplane-helicopter sought by the Marines.

Machtley voiced support for the January 1991 resolution authorizing President Bush to use military force to end Iraq's occupation of Kuwait. Earlier, though, he joined more than two dozen House members in signing a letter telling Bush that he needed such a congressional authorization before committing U.S. troops to war.

Machtley, who came to Congress at a time of defense spending retrenchment, has also shown he is not averse to trimming the Pentagon budget. He favors closing out the B-2 stealth bomber program and has voted for cuts in spending on the strategic defense initiative.

These votes fit in with his overall record as one of the House's more liberal Republicans, a standing that is probably necessary for him to win in the 1st. In 1990, he voted against President Bush's position 62 percent of the time, the seventh-highest figure among House Republicans. A member of the Select Committee on Children, Youth and Families, Machtley voted in favor of the unsuccessful effort to override Bush's 1990 veto of a "family leave" bill. He is also a supporter of abortion rights.

Machtley's ability to work with Democrats was exhibited by his work with Democratic Rep. Edward J. Markey to re-establish the New England Energy Caucus, which aims to reduce that region's dependence on foreign oil. He and Markey also joined up to pass an amendment to the fiscal 1991 defense authorization bill that requires stronger energy conservation measures at U.S. military facilities.

Machtley, like most freshmen, originated little legislation of his own, but he pushed through one measure of cosmic proportions. In June 1990, Machtley proposed deleting a program to "search for extraterrestrial intelligence" from the fiscal 1991 appropriations bill funding space research.

"Does any congressperson think he or she can explain to their constituents how important it is to spend $6.1 million to find out if E.T. really exists?" he said. "And then that we're going to raise taxes to pay for it?" The House passed Machtley's amendment by voice vote.

At Home: Machtley's victory was probably the most surprising and most important upset of the 1988 federal elections. It was surprising because Machtley had begun the year as a slightly buffoonish also-ran in a primary many saw as a choice between sacrificial lambs. It was important because Machtley's eventual victim was 28-year veteran Democrat St Germain, the autocratic Banking Committee chairman and a symbol of dubious ethics in Congress.

In a year when the GOP was unable to field challengers to many key Democrats in the House, taking St Germain's scalp was significant consolation. When Machtley was introduced to the other Republican House freshmen after the election, he reportedly received a round of applause.

St Germain had been targeted by the National Republican Congressional Committee in

Rhode Island 1

East — Part of Providence; Pawtucket

Stretching around scenic Narragansett Bay from the Atlantic Ocean toward the industrial Blackstone River Valley, the 1st offers pristine coastal preserves but also some of the most densely crowded small cities in the nation.

Fishing, shipping and naval operations dominate the coast. The larger towns around the bay tend to vote Democratic; some of the smaller seacoast villages have pockets of wealthy residential areas and tend to favor the GOP. Newport and Tiverton have backed the Democratic nominee in three of the last four presidential elections, voting Republican only in 1984.

The 1st also includes part of the Democratic stronghold of Providence, along with its smaller suburbs. Within the capital city, the 1st includes all of the heavily Italian Fourth Ward and most of the Italian Fifth Ward, both generally Democratic in statewide contests. The WASP-dominated East Side, where liberal voters around the campus of Brown University offset some of the upper-income conservatives, also has communities of newcomers from Portugal and the Cape Verde Islands.

To the north, the 1st includes the industrial corridor in the Blackstone Valley, including the gritty redbrick factory towns of Woonsocket, Central Falls and Pawtucket. Now home to some 250 manufacturing plants, Pawtucket was the site of the first factory in the nation. The valley's economy includes metalworking and jewelry firms among much light manufacturing.

The Blackstone Valley is the backbone of Democratic majorities in the state. George McGovern won all three of its major cities in 1972, although Woonsocket broke with Pawtucket and Central Falls by voting for Reagan in 1984. But in 1988, all three went Democratic again.

Population: 474,429. White 452,230 (95%), Black 11,727 (3%), Other 3,657 (1%). Spanish origin: 9,357 (2%). 18 and over 357,096 (75%), 65 and over 66,675 (14%). Median age: 32.

1986 and had been opposed that year by John A. Holmes Jr., the articulate former chairman of the Rhode Island GOP. Holmes went after St Germain with hammer and tong, but the incumbent filled the airwaves with ads emphasizing his Woonsocket roots and many works on behalf of consumers. St Germain won with 58 percent.

In 1988, it seemed the worst of St Germain's legal entanglements might be over. Readers of *The Wall Street Journal* were well versed in St Germain's dealings with lobbyists for the savings and loan industry, for which his committee wrote regulatory legislation. But the Justice Department had declined to indict him, and the House ethics committee seemed unlikely to deal harshly with him.

Holmes was back in the chase to challenge St Germain again, but few gave him much chance of improving on his 1986 showing. The district seemed already to have passed its own judgment on its son. And the larger turnout of a presidential year was expected to help the Democrat.

Machtley, meanwhile, had burst on the local political scene with a gimmick that seemed sure to overshadow his message — a piglet he named "Lester T. Pork." What we need in Congress, the candidate said, is Ron Machtley and Les Pork. Machtley also organized such conventional stunts as a jog across the district. But he seemed destined to retire from politics remembered only as "the guy with the pig."

Then a series of unforeseen events changed the situation. First, Holmes vacated the primary field by inexplicably failing to file his nomination papers on time. Blame fell on a campaign aide, but some muttered that Holmes had simply lost his stomach for another beating. In any event, the nomination was Machtley's by default.

Second, St Germain received a scare in the Democratic primary in September. Scott Wolf, a young but seasoned campaign worker and pollster, collected 45 percent of the primary vote. It was St Germain's worst showing in a primary since he was elected. Suddenly, it became respectable to say St Germain was beatable. And as the fall wore on, quite a few political observers began saying it.

Machtley, having gotten the electorate's attention, knew how to communicate the seriousness of his intentions. He dropped the pig (donating its valuable weight to charity). He produced campaign literature emphasizing his acceptability as an alternative to St Germain, touting his commitment to such nonpartisan subjects as health care, housing, education and clean water.

Machtley had been trained as an engineer at the Naval Academy and served five years on active duty. He had then put himself through law school in Boston while working full time. He had built up a practice and performed community service for such causes as the YMCA and the local hospital. He was an elder in his Presbyterian church.

True, he lacked the roots of most local politicians and had never run for office. But he was a Republican attorney with his own firm in Newport. He had decided to enter the race as a kind of idealistic statement, yet he seemed to have an idea of what it would take to win.

When his campaign took hold he was still strapped for cash. But he received considerable "free media" coverage, thanks in part to the novelty of a close November race. He hounded St Germain into a debate that Machtley later called the turning point. He was able to establish that investigations of St Germain that had yet to yield an indictment or censure did not constitute total exoneration. And he highlighted the fresh news that the Justice Department had passed along its collection of evidence to the House ethics panel for further review. As the campaign became a true contest, St Germain fought back with the hardy perennial issue of Social Security. But this did not stem the tide.

In reaching almost 56 percent, Machtley ran well in his strongholds (60 percent in Newport, for example) while holding St Germain even in his. And he also managed 57 percent in normally Democratic North Providence.

In 1990, Machtley had to defend his newly won territory against Wolf, the Democrat who had softened up St. Germain for him in 1988. For a time, it appeared Wolf would have the magic again. Rhode Island's economy has been among the most severely damaged in the downturn that struck the region in the late 1980s. And Wolf thought he had found just the right issue in attacking Machtley as an anachronism from the Reagan era — conservative in economics and obsessed with the military.

Whatever its worth might have been early on, that approach was badly devalued when the Iraqi invasion of Kuwait grabbed the nation's attention in August. Wolf, moreover, had not been able to climb into the big leagues financially. So he found it difficult to force his way into the voters' consciousness in a year with hotly contested campaigns for senator, governor and mayor. Machtley, by contrast, had established himself with his heroics of 1988 and needed relatively little further introduction. He won with slightly more than 55 percent, nearly equaling his percentage showing from two years earlier.

Committees

Armed Services (19th of 22 Republicans)
Military Education (ranking); Military Installations & Facilities; Readiness; Seapower & Strategic & Critical Materials

Government Operations (11th of 15 Republicans)
Commerce, Consumer & Monetary Affairs; Government Information, Justice & Agriculture

Select Children, Youth & Families (7th of 14 Republicans)

Small Business (11th of 17 Republicans)
Procurement, Tourism & Rural Development

Elections

1990 General		
Ronald K. Machtley (R)	89,963	(55%)
Scott Wolf (D)	73,131	(45%)
1988 General		
Ronald K. Machtley (R)	105,506	(56%)
Fernand J. St Germain (D)	84,141	(44%)

District Vote For President

	1988	1984	1980	1976
D	112,131 (57%)	99,348 (49%)	98,522 (48%)	116,362 (57%)
R	82,789 (42%)	101,566 (50%)	74,354 (37%)	86,772 (43%)
I			29,351 (14%)	

Campaign Finance

	Receipts	Receipts from PACs		Expend-itures
1990				
Machtley (R)	$857,775	$333,189	(39%)	$879,464
Wolf (D)	$369,300	$104,646	(28%)	$370,118
1988				
Machtley (R)	$417,449	$81,524	(20%)	$385,402
St. Germain (D)	$668,963	$362,556	(54%)	$801,289

Key Votes

1991	
Authorize use of force against Iraq	Y
1990	
Support constitutional amendment on flag desecration	Y
Pass family and medical leave bill over Bush veto	Y
Reduce SDI funding	Y
Allow abortions in overseas military facilities	Y
Approve budget summit plan for spending and taxing	N
Approve civil rights bill	Y
1989	
Halt production of B-2 stealth bomber at 13 planes	Y
Oppose capital gains tax cut	N
Approve federal abortion funding in rape or incest cases	Y
Approve pay raise and revision of ethics rules	N
Pass Democratic minimum wage plan over Bush veto	Y

Voting Studies

	Presidential Support		Party Unity		Conservative Coalition	
Year	**S**	**O**	**S**	**O**	**S**	**O**
1990	38	62	50	48	50	48
1989	49	50	60	38	61	39

Interest Group Ratings

Year	ADA	ACU	AFL-CIO	CCUS
1990	61	25	50	64
1989	55	46	50	70

2 John F. Reed (D)

Of Cranston — Elected 1990

Born: Nov. 12, 1949, Providence, R.I.
Education: U.S. Military Academy, West Point, B.S. 1971; Harvard U., M.P.P. 1973, J.D. 1982.
Military Service: Army, 1967-69.
Occupation: Lawyer.
Family: Single.
Religion: Roman Catholic.
Political Career: R.I. Senate, 1985-91.
Capitol Office: 1229 Longworth Bldg. 20515; 225-2735.

The Path to Washington: "Jack" Reed began the 1990 election season a minor player in a drama of state politics featuring hot races for governor and senator. But before the year was out, his was the star to watch in his party's statewide future.

A reserved man given to precision in speech as well as action, Reed suggests an engineer (his field at West Point), a sophisticated bureaucrat (he has a degree from the John F. Kennedy School of Government at Harvard) or a corporate attorney (his law degree is from Harvard as well). Add his height to the cool style and the Harvard diplomas and you know why some Rhode Islanders are reminded of Michael S. Dukakis.

Reed would rather downplay that image, and he readily uses his stature and marital status for humor: He told a TV interviewer who asked about Supreme Court nominee David H. Souter that any short bachelor from Harvard ought to be on the Supreme Court.

But Reed is far more often serious, and in a season of recession and war talk, this demeanor had appeal.

By reclaiming one of the state's two House seats for his party, Reed not only broke into the big time but positioned himself to succeed one of Rhode Island's senators or its newly elected Democratic governor (the three's average age is 70). The same timeliness should serve him well in the 102nd Congress. In an hour of international confrontation, he has his military background. In an era of debate over economic and tax policy, he has his legislative history as an advocate of greater tax equity and protection of blue-collar interests.

Reed's life has been a mix of the common man and the elite opportunity. His father was a school custodian and his mother a factory worker in South Providence. At his Catholic prep school he was an over-achieving, 124-pound defensive back who graduated second in his class by three-tenths of a point (he recalls the margin). He won his West Point appointment from Democratic Sen. John O. Pastore in 1967 and, when commissioned, volunteered for Vietnam. The Army sent him to Harvard to learn administration instead. He later commanded a company of the 82nd Airborne, which did not see combat during his service, and taught at West Point.

At 29, Reed decided the Army would not be his home for life and was admitted to Harvard Law School. He studied corporate law, spent a year with a firm in Washington and then went home to get involved in politics. He took a job with Rhode Island's biggest corporate law firm and a year later was elected to the state Senate.

The road up from there was not clearly marked. Republican Rep. Claudine Schneider had ensconced herself in Congress with an ingenious blend of environmental activism, liberal social views and Republican economics. But when she ran for the Senate in 1990, Reed joined an active field of Democratic hopefuls and easily outdistanced both a deep-pockets businessman and the district's former congressman, Edward P. Beard (1975-81).

Still, Reed entered the fall campaign an underdog to Republican Trudy Coxe, a near-perfect Schneider successor who had run the state's best-known environmental organization. He attacked her for owning stocks in oil companies while preaching for pristine waterways. He ripped her for supporting a capital-gains tax cut as a sequel to tax cuts for the rich in the 1980s. He leavened his message by talking up his own work on issues such as tax credits for day care and children's mental health programs.

As concerns about war in the Persian Gulf region mounted and national Democrats gained ground pillorying Republicans as the party of the rich, Reed found himself ideally situated on both fronts.

In the end, his message of both roots and upward mobility brought traditional Democratic neighborhoods home and enabled him to win a surprisingly comfortable victory.

Rhode Island 2

West — Western Providence; Warwick

With about two-thirds of the city of Providence and its vote-heavy southern suburbs, the 2nd is largely a metropolitan district. But the area's geographical diversity — including coastal wildlife refuges, inland Yankee towns and rolling upstate hillsides — belies the urban bleakness a traveler sees from the swath of Amtrak rails through downtown Providence.

The capital, a Democratic stronghold whose population has slid from the 1970s to about 157,000, has the largest concentration of votes in the district. The 2nd includes the Providence business district, where pedestrian shopping areas have had some success at reviving the downtown; South Providence, once a mixed Irish and Jewish middle-class neighborhood that is increasingly black; Federal Hill and Silver Lake, where Italian-Americans predominate; and Elmwood, a traditional ethnic enclave now experiencing an influx of young white professionals.

Providence remains a reliable source of Democratic votes. Although Walter F. Mondale lost the state in 1984, he carried Providence by a margin of nearly 2-to-1.

Cranston and Warwick, the capital's largest suburbs, often split their tickets. Michael S. Dukakis won both in 1988, but Republican Sen. John H. Chafee has run well in these towns. Reed won Cranston easily in 1990, and also defeated Republican nominee Trudy Coxe in Warwick. To the west, Coxe carried Scituate.

Washington County, with coastal cities and maritime commerce as well as the inland marshes known as the "Great Swamp," was swept by Ronald Reagan in 1984. However, in 1988, Michael S. Dukakis won five of Washington's nine towns and carried the county.

A submarine plant is located on the site of the sprawling old Navy installation at Quonset Point, where the mid-1970s phase-out of an air station and construction battalion forced the local economy to diversify.

Westerly is an old shipping center that blends light manufacturing with its fishing trade, although many residents work at the Electric Boat facility in Groton, Conn. Westerly is more frequently found in the Democratic column than most other towns on Rhode Island's western border, many of them old Yankee enclaves.

Population: 472,725. White 444,462 (94%), Black 15,857 (3%), Other 4,544 (1%). Spanish origin 10,350 (2%). 18 and over 347,207 (73%), 65 and over 60,247 (13%). Median age: 31.

Committees

Education & Labor (21st of 25 Democrats)
Elementary, Secondary & Vocational Education; Postsecondary Education

Judiciary (21st of 21 Democrats)
Administrative Law & Governmental Relations

Merchant Marine & Fisheries (27th of 29 Democrats)
Coast Guard & Navigation; Fisheries & Wildlife Conservation & the Environment

Campaign Finance

	Receipts	Receipts from PACs		Expend-itures
1990				
Reed (D)	$902,877	$302,216	(33%)	$897,224
Coxe (R)	$577,919	$121,238	(21%)	$571,643

Key Vote

1991

Authorize use of force against Iraq	N

Elections

1990 General		
John F. Reed (D)	108,818	(59%)
Trudy Coxe (R)	74,953	(41%)
1990 Primary		
John F. Reed (D)	36,315	(49%)
Edward P. Beard (D)	20,308	(27%)
Charles H. Gifford III (D)	10,861	(15%)
Rodney D. Driver (D)	6,613	(9%)

District Vote For President

	1988	1984	1980	1976
D	111,698 (54%)	97,758 (47%)	98,573 (47%)	110,037 (54%)
R	94,370 (46%)	110,514 (53%)	80,123 (38%)	93,991 (46%)
I			30,015 (14%)	

South Carolina

U.S. CONGRESS

SENATE 1 D, 1 R

HOUSE 4 D, 2 R

LEGISLATURE

Senate 35 D, 11 R

House 76 D, 42 R, 1 Independent, 5 vacancies

ELECTIONS

1988 Presidential Vote	
Bush	62%
Dukakis	38%
1984 Presidential Vote	
Reagan	64%
Mondale	36%
1980 Presidential Vote	
Reagan	49%
Carter	48%
Anderson	2%
Turnout rate in 1986	29%
Turnout rate in 1988	39%
Turnout rate in 1990	26%

(as percentage of voting age population)

POPULATION AND GROWTH

1980 population	3,121,820
1990 population (25th in the nation)	3,486,703
Percent change 1980-1990	+12%

DEMOGRAPHIC BREAKDOWN

White	69%
Black	30%
Asian or Pacific Islander	1%
(Hispanic origin)	1%
Urban	54%
Rural	46%
Born in state	73%
Foreign-born	2%

MAJOR CITIES

Columbia	98,052
Charleston	80,414
North Charleston	70,218
Greenville	58,282
Spartanburg	43,467

AREA AND LAND USE

Area 30,204 sq. miles (40th)

Farm	29%
Forest	64%
Federally owned	6%

Gov. Carroll A. Campbell Jr. (R)
Of Greenville — Elected 1986

Born: July 24, 1940, Greenville, S.C.
Education: Attended U. of South Carolina, 1958 and 1970; American U., M.A. 1985.
Occupation: Real estate broker; farmer.
Religion: Episcopalian.
Political Career: S.C. House, 1971-75; S.C. Senate, 1977-79; U.S. House, 1979-87; GOP nominee for lieutenant governor, 1974.
Next Election: 1994.

WORK

Occupations	
White-collar	45%
Blue-collar	41%
Service workers	12%
Government Workers	
Federal	33,066
State	85,455
Local	125,962

MONEY

Median family income	$ 16,978 (41st)
Tax burden per capita	$ 816 (27th)

EDUCATION

Spending per pupil through grade 12	$ 3,408 (39th)
Persons with college degrees	13% (42nd)

CRIME

Violent crime rate	814 per 100,000 (6th)

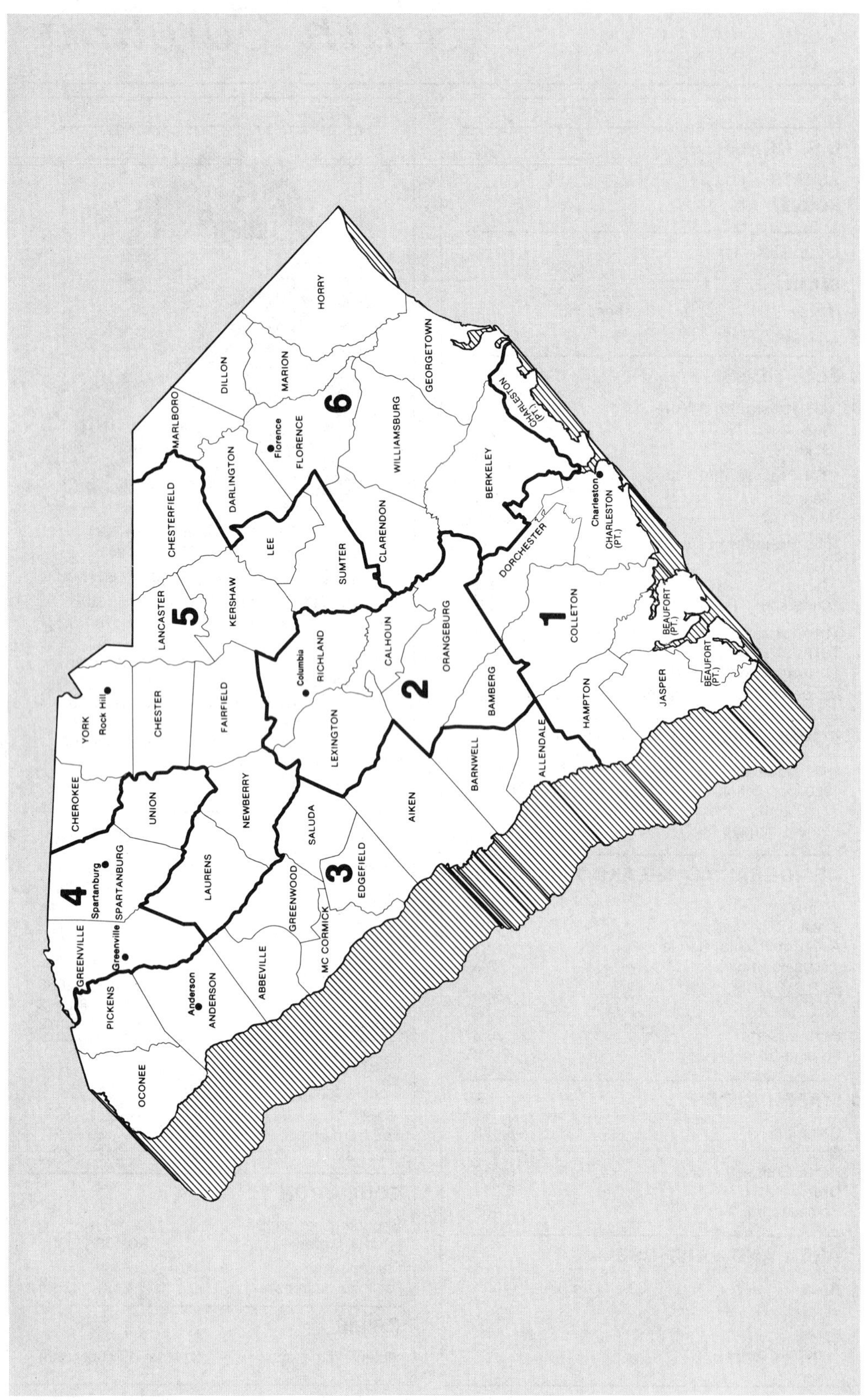
1
2
3
4
5
6
OCONEE
PICKENS
ANDERSON
Anderson
GREENVILLE
Greenville
SPARTANBURG
Spartanburg
CHEROKEE
UNION
LAURENS
ABBEVILLE
GREENWOOD
MC CORMICK
EDGEFIELD
SALUDA
NEWBERRY
YORK
Rock Hill
CHESTER
FAIRFIELD
LANCASTER
KERSHAW
CHESTERFIELD
LEXINGTON
RICHLAND
Columbia
AIKEN
BARNWELL
ALLENDALE
HAMPTON
JASPER
BEAUFORT (PT.)
COLLETON
BAMBERG
ORANGEBURG
CALHOUN
SUMTER
LEE
DARLINGTON
MARLBORO
DILLON
MARION
HORRY
FLORENCE
Florence
CLARENDON
WILLIAMSBURG
GEORGETOWN
BERKELEY
DORCHESTER
CHARLESTON (PT.)
Charleston

Strom Thurmond (R)

Of Aiken — Elected 1954

Did not serve April-November 1956.

Born: Dec. 5, 1902, Edgefield, S.C.
Education: Clemson College, B.S. 1923.
Military Service: Army, 1942-46; Army Reserve, 1924-60.
Occupation: Lawyer; teacher; coach; education administrator.
Family: Separated; four children.
Religion: Baptist.
Political Career: Edgefield Superintendent of Education, 1929-33; S.C. Senate, 1933-38; governor, 1947-51; States' Rights nominee for president, 1948; sought Democratic nomination for U.S. Senate, 1950.
Capitol Office: 217 Russell Bldg. 20510; 224-5972.

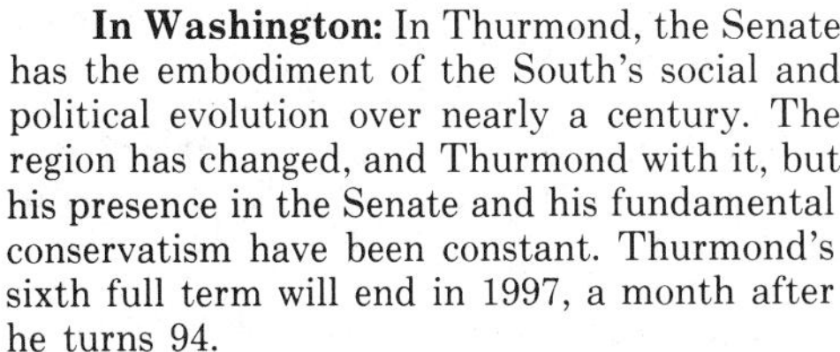

In Washington: In Thurmond, the Senate has the embodiment of the South's social and political evolution over nearly a century. The region has changed, and Thurmond with it, but his presence in the Senate and his fundamental conservatism have been constant. Thurmond's sixth full term will end in 1997, a month after he turns 94.

Thurmond is the only man in modern Senate history to have seen life in the chamber from all perspectives: he has served in the minority and majority as a Republican, in the majority as a Democrat, and even, for a few days in late 1954, as a minority Democrat. Thurmond served as chairman of the Judiciary Committee from 1981 through 1987, when he settled comfortably back into the ranking spot there as Democrats retook the Senate.

None of these changes, however, has eroded Thurmond's conservatism, which today sounds less strident as a younger generation of brash Republicans have ascended.

Time has also failed to alter the combination of Southern courtesy and hard-nosed political deal-making that he has perfected. These personal qualities enable Thurmond to work well with liberal committee chairmen Edward M. Kennedy, on Labor and Human Resources, and Joseph R. Biden Jr., who, though he took the Judiciary gavel from Thurmond in 1987, still refers to him as "Mr. Chairman."

This respect, rooted in Thurmond's experience, is a key to his success. He was long out of college before most senators were born. And none question whether Thurmond's grasp of political nuance remains firm, though he has slowed a bit in recent years and his hearing is failing. His 1991 separation from his wife, who is half his age, may deny him the imagery of a younger man, but when he threatens a filibuster, colleagues know that Thurmond, a physical fitness enthusiast, still has the stamina to make good.

In recent years, Thurmond has been conspicuously passive on civil rights legislation. While he has opposed nearly every civil rights bill to pass through the Judiciary Committee, he has allowed others to take the lead. The new, somewhat mellowed Thurmond seems to believe that dignity and courtesy are more important than winning at any cost.

Even when he chaired Judiciary in 1982, he made no move to block the Voting Rights Act extension. And on rare occasion Thurmond even lent his support to civil rights legislation. In 1983, he helped produce the compromise that preserved the U.S. Civil Rights Commission. He also voted to create a public holiday honoring the Rev. Dr. Martin Luther King Jr.

All of this is a far cry from the Thurmond of the 1950s and 1960s, who was the master of obstructionist tactics against civil rights legislation and irritated even some Southerners with his intransigence. In 1957, segregationist senators led by Georgia's Richard Russell were willing to let a weak civil rights measure pass, largely to boost the national standing of their Southern colleague and presidential aspirant, Majority Leader Lyndon B. Johnson of Texas. Thurmond alone insisted on protesting. His 24-hour, 18-minute filibuster set a record for one man.

In a legendary episode in 1964, the year Thurmond switched parties, he wrestled Democrat Ralph Yarborough of Texas to the floor outside the committee room to prevent a quorum for action on civil rights legislation. The South Carolinian won the wrestling match, but Yarborough was able to complete the quorum after the chairman rescued him.

But if Thurmond has set aside blocking civil rights legislation as his primary mission, he has chosen a new venue that liberals say is tinged with racial overtones: He is a leading Senate proponent of the death penalty.

In 1984, Thurmond sparked the first Senate debate on the issue in a decade when he offered legislation to re-establish the federal death penalty. Thurmond asserted that convicted murderers were not people but "more like animals," and "when you have individuals in society more like animals than humans, they have to be dealt with in the most severe manner." The Senate passed the bill, but it died in the House. A similar measure got no further than committee approval in 1986. Finally, in 1988, a narrower measure became law as part of an antidrugs package; it applies to drug traffickers who murder and to those who kill policemen during a drug crime.

In the 101st Congress, he introduced sweeping anti-crime legislation that would have permitted the death penalty for 30 federal crimes, allowed the sentence for those as young as 16 and for mentally retarded people, except those unable to tell right from wrong. His legislation also sought to limit the appeals process for those on death row.

As part of a unanimous-consent agreement to stop Republican members from offering death penalty amendments to unrelated legislation, Biden, who also supports the death penalty, agreed to hold hearings on Thurmond's bill.

When the panel took up the bill, Thurmond could not stop Democrats, led by Kennedy, from adding a "racial justice" provision that Thurmond called a "killer amendment." The amendment would have required prosecutors to prove by "clear and convincing" evidence that racial disparities in sentencing are not the result of discrimination. "Race should play no role whatsoever," Thurmond said. "But this would allow vicious killers to get off by talking about the race of a defendant."

When the matter got to the full Senate in mid-1990, however, Thurmond prevailed. The Kennedy language was struck by a 58-38 margin. But little agreement could be reached with the House, and the final bill was stripped of its most controversial provisions, including the death penalty.

Although Thurmond has had his differences with the National Rifle Association, he has sided with the organization in recent years. He opposed a 1990 amendment to the crime bill to ban nine semiautomatic assault-style weapons. And in 1991, as support grew for legislation mandating a seven-day waiting period for handgun purchases, Thurmond continued to say simply that he preferred a point of sale background check.

Supporters of gun control were encouraged in the 100th Congress, when Thurmond teamed up with Ohio Democrat Howard M. Metzenbaum to cosponsor a successful bill that banned the manufacture, import and sale of "plastic" guns that evade security detectors. He said then, "I think the time has come to stand with the law-enforcement people."

A major share of Thurmond's energies in recent years has been devoted to defending administration nominees to the federal bench and the Justice Department. He is skilled at crafting leading questions that highlight a nominee's credentials and give the individual a chance to explain less controversial judicial principles.

Thurmond stood with Bush in 1991 as the panel rejected the nomination of Kenneth L. Ryskamp to a federal appeals court, and in 1989, he was a leading defender of William Lucas to head the Civil Rights Division of the Justice Department. As it became apparent that Democrats who questioned Lucas' credentials were going to reject his nomination, Thurmond said,"He's a minority yes. Minorities are entitled to a chance. Years ago they didn't have a chance. I know down South they didn't, and up North either. I say let's confirm this man and show the world that we are fair."

In 1987, Thurmond was equally powerless to save Ronald Reagan from an embarrassing chapter of his presidency — the six-month, three-nominee effort to fill a Supreme Court vacancy. Much of that time, the Senate was torn over Reagan's first choice, Robert H. Bork, who was rejected as too ideologically conservative. After defending Bork, Thurmond refrained from immediately endorsing Reagan's next choice, Douglas H. Ginsburg — fortunately so, since the nominee withdrew after acknowledging he had smoked marijuana years before. Finally, Anthony M. Kennedy was approved easily.

In the 100th Congress, Thurmond helped win approval of legislation to close the "revolving door" between government and lobbying. His effort to bar top executive branch employees from lobbying after they leave government was a reaction to the case of a former Commerce Department official who allegedly disclosed to foreign clients the U.S. strategy in world negotiations on textile-import limits. As a senator from a textile-manufacturing state, Thurmond was outraged.

In the 99th Congress, Thurmond's bill got no further than committee approval. But in the 100th Congress, the effort took momentum from the lobbying controversy surrounding former Reagan aide Michael K. Deaver. As part of a compromise with the House, the bill included the first lobbying controls on former members of Congress. Reagan pocket-vetoed the bill, but a similar measure was enacted in 1989.

Given his senior role on Judiciary, Thurmond is less active on Labor and Human Resources and on Armed Services, where he has served as a pro-Pentagon member since he first came to the Senate.

On his committees and off, Thurmond looks out for South Carolina; constituent service is one reason he has survived changing times. He makes sure his state receives a flow of federal largess — even if he votes against the programs that provide the money. And as the Voting Rights Act has made blacks an important political force, they have been conspicuous among the beneficiaries of Thurmond's work. "I'm not a racist," he insists, "and I've done everything I could to help the people of both races throughout my lifetime." In 1971 he became the first Southern senator to hire a black professional staffer; he later sponsored the South's first black federal judge.

Thurmond has been active in seeking to protect the textile industry against growing foreign competition, defying Reagan's free-trade philosophy. "Free trade will destroy America," Thurmond once said.

Now approaching his 10th decade, Thurmond often seems like an envoy from another era, from the turn-of-the-century rural South. During one committee hearing, he graciously greeted a panel of women who had come to testify. "These are the prettiest witnesses we have had in a long time," Thurmond said. "I imagine you are all married. If not, you could be if you wanted to be."

Thurmond also has a fondness for ceremony not found in many younger politicians. He relished his role as president pro tempore, which he forfeited to Mississippi's John C. Stennis when Democrats regained control of the Senate, and greatly regretted losing the honor of presiding over the Senate's opening each day.

An episode illustrating Thurmond's love of ritual, as well as his relative vigor, occurred during a 1987 ceremony in Philadelphia to commemorate the bicentennial of the compromise that created the bicameral Congress. An aged and befuddled Stennis was presiding over the Senate's program and mistakenly called on Thurmond to speak. Thurmond, just a year younger than the Stennis, responded with senatorial savoir-faire. Though he had not expected to be called on, he arose and said, "I do not know of any senator who is not ready to respond at any time with any sentiment," then delivered a lucid extemporaneous address on the Constitution — with his characteristic states' rights bent.

His courtly manner was apparent in his running of Judiciary. He took care that all members had a chance to speak, insisting on silence so they could be heard. Civil rights groups and liberal Democrats always found him polite and fair.

Still, Thurmond is willing to play rough. Indeed, he agreed in 1977 to take the top GOP seat on Judiciary as part of the Senate Republican leadership's effort to keep the chair away from Sen. Charles McC. Mathias Jr. of Maryland, the Republican liberal who ranked next to Thurmond on the panel. In doing so, however, Thurmond had to give up the same post on the Armed Services Committee, where until then he had devoted most of his attention.

During his six years as Judiciary chairman, Thurmond racked up a creditable list of legislative successes, although he made little progress in pushing his conservative-backed constitutional amendments.

Thurmond's major achievement was a revision of the federal criminal code. Previously, in the 96th Congress, he had forged an alliance with then-Chairman Kennedy, but the legislation never became law. Then in 1982, Thurmond brought another criminal code bill to the floor; confronted with a potential blizzard of controversial amendments from conservatives, he offered a stripped-down measure that cleared Congress, only to be vetoed by Reagan.

Finally, in 1984, major components of the legislation were tacked onto the year-end appropriations bill, including a change in the exclusionary rule permitting use of illegally obtained evidence in federal trials if police officers could show they acted in the belief their conduct was legal.

During his years as chairman, Thurmond also delivered for the president when it came to judicial nominees. Despite the partisan warfare prompted by some nominations, notably of William H. Rehnquist to be chief justice of the United States and of Daniel A. Manion to be a federal district judge, only one of nearly 300 judicial nominees was defeated while Thurmond was chairman through 1986.

At Home: Thurmond has punctuated his long political career with turns and reversals, and always he has managed to carry his constituents with him.

They supported him in 1948 when, as governor, he bolted the Democratic Party to run as the States' Rights candidate for president. In 1964 he announced that he was joining the GOP because the Democrats were "leading the evolution of our nation to a socialistic dictatorship." And despite the state's historic partisan leanings, he easily won re-election two years later.

Since the mid-1960s, black voting strength has grown in South Carolina, and Thurmond has adjusted again, although his efforts to help black communities have never brought much of the black vote; his long record of opposing civil rights is not that easily forgotten.

For most white South Carolinians, Thurmond's feistiness and physical vigor remain appealing. As a 75-year-old in 1978 competing with a man barely half his age, Thurmond traveled the state with his wife and four young children in a camper called "Strom Trek," passing out family recipes, riding parade elephants and sliding down firehouse poles.

Thurmond learned politics from one of his father's friends, Democratic Sen. Benjamin

"Pitchfork Ben" Tillman. Early in his career Thurmond was a populist, representing poor white farmers from the upcountry against the Tidewater establishment. In 1946, after returning from World War II service in Europe, Thurmond was elected governor. He was in his second year in office when the Democratic National Convention decided to adopt a strong civil rights plank, and Thurmond offered himself as a regional candidate for president on the States' Rights Democratic ticket. He carried South Carolina, Alabama, Mississippi and Louisiana.

Thurmond made a first try for the Senate in 1950, but lost the Democratic primary to incumbent Olin D. Johnston. Four years later, however, he won — the first and so far the only senator to be elected as a write-in candidate. Sen. Burnet R. Maybank had died and the 31-member State Democratic Committee froze Thurmond out by choosing state Sen. Edgar A. Brown. Thurmond focused his campaign on whether "31 men" or the voters should make the decision. His write-in campaign defeated Brown by nearly 60,000 votes.

True to a 1954 promise, Thurmond resigned in 1956 and ran for re-election without the benefit of incumbency. No one filed against him — a happy circumstance that repeated itself in 1960, when it was time to run for a full six-year term. In 1966 and 1972 he decimated Democrats Bradley Morrah and Eugene N. Ziegler, respectively.

In 1978 Thurmond encountered a stiff re-election challenge from Charles "Pug" Ravenel, who had won the Democratic primary for governor four years before, but was ruled ineligible for failure to meet residency requirements.

A media-oriented "New South" politician, Ravenel tried to remind blacks of the senator's segregationist past. But Ravenel suffered from a carpetbagger's image. He had left the state to be an investment banker in New York, returning only shortly before his 1974 gubernatorial bid. Thurmond won 56 percent.

The 1984 campaign was no problem for Thurmond. No Democrat of any consequence wanted to challenge him; one of those mentioned as a contender, former U.S. Rep. Kenneth Holland, ended up leading a Democrats-for-Thurmond organization. For a few days in the summer, it appeared that Jesse Jackson might try an independent campaign, but Jackson quickly reconsidered, and the obscure Democratic nominee, minister Melvin Purvis, failed to reach even a third of the vote. Thurmond's 1990 re-election was another runaway.

Committees

Judiciary (Ranking)
Antitrust, Monopolies & Business Rights (ranking); Courts & Administrative Practice

Armed Services (2nd of 9 Republicans)
Strategic Forces & Nuclear Deterrence (ranking); Conventional Forces & Alliance Defense; Readiness, Sustainability & Support

Labor & Human Resources (5th of 7 Republicans)
Employment & Productivity (ranking); Children, Families, Drugs & Alcoholism; Education, Arts & Humanities; Labor

Veterans' Affairs (4th of 5 Republicans)

Elections

1990 General

Strom Thurmond (R)	482,032	(64%)
Bob Cunningham (D)	244,112	(33%)
William H. Griffin (LIBERT)	13,805	(2%)
Marion C. Metts (AM)	10,317	(1%)

Previous Winning Percentages: **1984** (67%) **1978** (56%) **1972** (63%) **1966** (62%) **1960** † (100%) **1956** † (100%) **1954** † * (63%)

** Thurmond was elected as a write-in candidate in 1954. He resigned April 4, 1956, and was elected to fill the vacancy caused by his own resignation in a 1956 special election.*

† Thurmond was elected as a Democrat in 1954-60.

Campaign Finance

1990	Receipts	Receipts from PACs		Expend-itures
Thurmond (R)	$2,077,112	$562,695	(27%)	$1,916,702
Cunningham (D)	$6,379	0		$6,232

Key Votes

1991	
Authorize use of force against Iraq	Y
1990	
Oppose prohibition of certain semiautomatic weapons	Y
Support constitutional amendment on flag desecration	Y
Oppose requiring parental notice for minors' abortions	N
Halt production of B-2 stealth bomber at 13 planes	N
Approve budget that cut spending and raised revenues	Y
Pass civil rights bill over Bush veto	N
1989	
Oppose reduction of SDI funding	Y
Oppose barring federal funds for "obscene" art	N
Allow vote on capital gains tax cut	Y

Voting Studies

	Presidential Support		Party Unity		Conservative Coalition	
Year	**S**	**O**	**S**	**O**	**S**	**O**
1990	78	22	89	10	100	0
1989	90	10	98	2	100	0
1988	82	15	80	15	89	0
1987	69	28	88	9	84	16
1986	89	10	91	8	97	0
1985	87	13	92	7	97	3
1984	87	10	95	5	98	0
1983	86	12	92	6	93	7
1982	89	9	92	5	86	4
1981	90	7	91	6	100	0

Interest Group Ratings

Year	ADA	ACU	AFL-CIO	CCUS
1990	6	83	33	75
1989	5	96	0	88
1988	0	92	21	93
1987	15	96	30	71
1986	5	91	0	78
1985	0	91	14	97
1984	0	100	9	84
1983	5	70	6	79
1982	5	75	12	86
1981	0	93	5	100

Ernest F. Hollings (D)

Of Charleston — Elected 1966

Born: Jan. 1, 1922, Charleston, S.C.

Education: The Citadel, B.A. 1942; U. of South Carolina, LL.B. 1947.

Military Service: Army, 1942-45.

Occupation: Lawyer.

Family: Wife, Rita "Peatsy" Liddy; four children.

Religion: Lutheran.

Political Career: S.C. House, 1949-55; lieutenant governor, 1955-59; governor, 1959-63; sought Democratic nomination for U.S. Senate, 1962; sought Democratic nomination for president, 1984.

Capitol Office: 125 Russell Bldg. 20510; 224-6121.

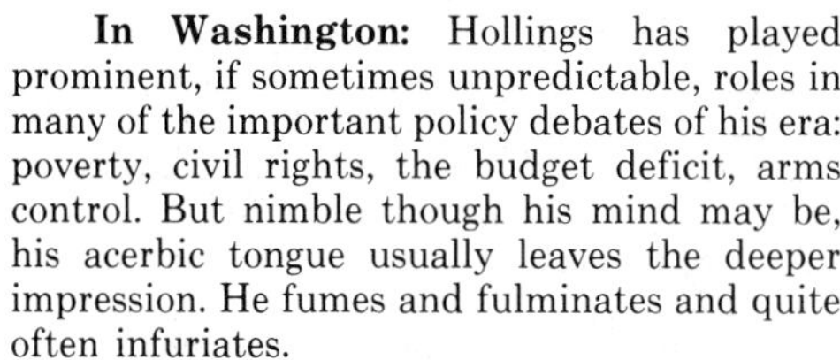

In Washington: Hollings has played prominent, if sometimes unpredictable, roles in many of the important policy debates of his era: poverty, civil rights, the budget deficit, arms control. But nimble though his mind may be, his acerbic tongue usually leaves the deeper impression. He fumes and fulminates and quite often infuriates.

A stubborn, independent cuss, Hollings often leaps mouth first into controversies. He angered GOP colleagues during the fight over John Tower's 1989 nomination to become secretary of Defense, describing Tower as "Mr. Alcohol Abuser." While appearing on ABC News' "This Week With David Brinkley" in September 1990, he snapped back when news correspondent Sam Donaldson asked Hollings where he bought his suit: "I bought it in the same place right down the street where — if you want to personalize this thing — where you got that wig, Sam," Hollings said.

It is this image of Hollings as impolitic, even mean-spirited, that can isolate him from his colleagues and divert attention from the work he does as Commerce Committee chairman, and from a legislative record lengthy with triumph.

Handsome, graceful and impeccably tailored, Hollings is an impressive presence in committee and on the Senate floor. He speaks in a rich, booming Tidewater patois and has a colorful command of the language. He dismissed the 1983 invasion of Grenada as an "an attack on a golf course." He pronounced U.S. aid to El Salvador, under one regime, as "delivery of lettuce by way of a rabbit."

But his loquaciousness knows no boundaries, and he tends toward bombast; some wonder whether his mind and his mouth simply move too quickly for discretion to keep pace, or whether he just does not care that his judgments fall harshly.

During a 1981 debate on his effort to stop the Justice Department from trying to block voluntary school prayer, he described Ohio Democrat Howard M. Metzenbaum as "the senator from B'nai B'rith." "I am the senator from Ohio," responded Metzenbaum, who is Jewish. "I was not throwing off on his religion," Hollings apologized. "I said it only in fun."

The two sides of Hollings' character were apparent during his 1984 presidential campaign. The effort failed early in the year, dragged down in part by several comments he made that enraged various ethnic groups.

At the same time, though, Hollings displayed an integrity that his rivals could not achieve. While many of his competitors were traveling from one interest group to another, pledging their loyalty, Hollings was delivering the same unpleasant message to everyone, exhorting the need to exercise old-fashioned self-restraint to solve the nation's fiscal woes.

Although he sometimes depicts himself as a lonely voice crying out against fiscal weakness, Hollings has scored some major budget victories, chief among them the radical 1985 budget-balancing plan usually referred to as Gramm-Rudman. Although his name often does not get tacked on when the Gramm-Rudman-Hollings anti-deficit law is mentioned, he can lay claim to sharing authorship of the proposal.

Despite his significant role in its passage, Hollings has since disavowed the law. "After four years of a shotgun marriage called Gramm-Rudman-Hollings," he wrote in a *New York Times* op-ed in 1990, "I'm filing for divorce on grounds of infidelity and irreconcilable differences." He labeled the 1990 budget "a spectacular jambalaya of tricks and dodges" and called the process "a sham."

"This thing was intended as a sword," he lamented about the law, "and it's being used as a shield."

Despite his new budget "marital" status, Hollings continues to father legislation to pare the deficit. He consistently pushes for deeper budget cuts than others propose.

In April 1989, Hollings offered a plan — voted down in committee — to combine program cuts and tax hikes to cut the deficit significantly. He wanted to eliminate the income tax "bubble" that favors the wealthy, delay tax-bracket indexing and add a $10-per-barrel fee on oil imports. He proposed imposition in 1992 of a 5 percent value-added tax (VAT), which is a consumption levy on each stage of a product's manufacture and distribution. That would raise $52.1 billion in 1992 alone.

The VAT proposal was an orphan on delivery, swiftly disowned by leaders of both parties. Republicans opposed nearly any tax increase and Democrats, such as Majority Leader George J. Mitchell of Maine, dismissed the tax as regressive.

Hollings also has focused on pushing his plan for a budget that would freeze spending, except for Social Security, Medicare and other entitlements with cost of living increases. It was slow going at first; the plan received only 12 votes when he first proposed it in 1982. In 1983 it attracted four more votes. With the massive budget deficit looming large in 1984, though, Hollings and two other senators put forth a three-year budget-freeze package that attracted 38 votes. He garnered 18 votes, though, in a 1989 version.

Hollings continued his harsh budget talk throughout 1990 and into 1991. In May 1990, he opposed an effort to exclude savings and loan bailout funds from deficit calculation, calling the attempt "a shenanigan that is part and parcel of the larger budget fraud." He voted against the 1990 budget-summit agreement, insisting that such summits "aren't the cure, they're the cancer."

Hollings gave up his ranking spot on Budget in 1983 to take the same position on Commerce, Science and Transportation, and he assumed the chairmanship of that panel when Democrats took control of the Senate at the start of the 100th Congress. Because he is also chairman of the Appropriations Subcommittee on Commerce, he can control both authorization and spending legislation for programs.

Home-state concerns were foremost with Hollings in the 100th and 101st Congresses, when he joined with South Carolina colleague, Republican Strom Thurmond, in an attempt to curb textile imports. The crush of foreign competition has severely pinched the state's textile industry. The two managed to steer the quota legislation to passage in 1985, 1988 and 1990, three times overcoming entrenched opposition and three times watching it later die by veto. Said a disgruntled Hollings, "We are at war, an international trade war, in which the American government shamefully has not yet begun to fight."

It was during consideration of the textile bill that it was revealed that Hollings, while backing measures to limit imports of clothing, buys custom-made suits from a Korean tailor. It was this mini-controversy that led to Hollings' televised confrontation with Donaldson.

A former trial lawyer who retains close ties to the profession, Hollings takes a harsh view of measures that would impose federal limits on a manufacturer's responsibility for harm caused by its products. He blocked the Product Liability Act in 1986 with a filibuster and helped stall it again in the 101st Congress.

Hoping to capitalize on fears that the United States is losing its competitive hold abroad, Hollings has tried to get the Senate to act to loosen court restrictions on the seven regional telephone companies formed after the breakup of the American Telephone and Telegraph Co. (AT&T) in 1984. The Commerce Committee approved a bill in 1990 to let the so-called Baby Bells make telephone equipment and enter joint manufacturing ventures, as long as they were not with other Baby Bells. The bill, however, never reached the Senate floor. In 1991, Hollings continued the efforts with the panel approving the measure overwhelmingly in March.

Despite his position as Commerce chairman and his desire to protect his tobacco-producing constituency, Hollings was unable to quash legislation in 1989 enacting a ban on smoking on virtually all airline flights within the United States.

No issue proved more difficult for Hollings during the 100th Congress than regulation of television broadcasting. He hews strongly to the principle that a broadcasting license is a privilege, and the use of public airwaves comes with strings attached. He called the Reagan-appointed Federal Communications Commission (FCC) a "runaway animal" and broadcasters the "most greedy group I've ever met in my 40 years of public service."

When the FCC appeared ready in the summer of 1987 to repeal the Fairness Doctrine, he issued a pre-emptive strike. Working with House Energy and Commerce Chairman John D. Dingell of Michigan, he gained passage of legislation to codify the doctrine, only to see President Ronald Reagan veto it. Lacking the votes to override, the two pulled budget levers and nearly succeeded in gaining passage by attaching the measure to crucial spending legislation.

Hollings played a high-profile role during consideration of the U.S.-Mexico trade pact in 1991. He opposed the Bush administration's request for an extension of "fast track" trade-negotiating authority. The fast-track procedures bar lawmakers from amending trade agreements submitted for approval. The administration considered the authority essential for negotiating a free-trade agreement with Mexico and continuing talks in Geneva on the

General Agreement on Tariffs and Trade.

In opposing the procedure, Hollings said, "Fast track operates like a gun to our heads — no amendments, no reservations." In 1990, 37 colleagues supported Hollings when he sought to revoke the authority; he had a little more difficulty attracting backers in 1991.

Hollings also helped shape antidrug legislation in the 101st Congress, co-authoring an amendment in 1989 that would have made a 0.225 percent cut in all discretionary domestic spending and defense programs and directed the $1.8 billion saved entirely toward Bush's antidrug and anticrime packages. Their proposal eventually lost out to a more costly one proposed by Appropriations Chairman Robert C. Byrd of West Virginia and backed by Senate Democrats boosting funds for antidrug education and treatment.

Hollings has long had a reputation as a hawk, despite his attempts to freeze military spending as part of a deficit-reduction package. Although he opposed the MX missile and the B-1 bomber, he has generally backed spending increases for weapons. He is not afraid, though, to cross swords with the Senate's leading conservative Democrat on defense issues, Sam Nunn of Georgia. He trod boldly onto the Armed Services chairman's turf in 1987 by challenging Nunn's reinterpretation of the antiballistic missile treaty, perhaps the key issue underlying testing of strategic defense initiative weapons.

Joining Nunn, however, Hollings opposed the resolution in January 1991 authorizing the president to use force in the Persian Gulf. Hollings was the only member of the South Carolina delegation to oppose the resolution, a fact that Republican Party officials said they would try to exploit when Hollings faces reelection in 1992.

Hollings' long-held suspicion of the Soviet Union has led him to play a central role in the debate over the fate of the bugged U.S. Embassy in Moscow. When U.S. officials revealed early in 1987 that Soviet operatives had placed listening devices throughout the unfinished embassy, Hollings joined those insisting that the building could not be used and should be torn down.

A stalemate developed, however, between those who emphasized the embassy's security and others who focused on the cost of razing and rebuilding the embassy. The need for fiscal austerity forced the Bush administration in March 1991 to back a less expensive plan, under which new secure floors would be built on top of the bugged building. Hollings vowed to continue to oppose that option from his Appropriations subcommittee perch.

Hollings has threaded his way carefully through civil rights issues during his long career. As governor, he insisted on the integration of Clemson University and campaigned to elect John F. Kennedy president. But Hollings voted against some major civil rights legislation as a junior senator. He has consistently supported the 1965 Voting Rights Act and its extensions and he backed the 1990 civil rights bill that fell to a veto by President Bush.

Damage caused by Hurricane Hugo in 1989 turned Hollings' attention back home. The Senate adopted an amendment to a defense spending bill to allow the Pentagon to transfer funds among its budget accounts to repair the damage to military facilities. According to Hollings, fixing two South Carolina bases alone could cost $75 million.

At Home: Hollings built his political career in South Carolina at a time of emotional argument about racial issues. He succeeded in combining old-time rhetoric with a tangible record of moderation.

As a candidate in the late 1950s, he firmly espoused states' rights and condemned school integration. In his inaugural speech as governor in 1959, Hollings criticized President Dwight D. Eisenhower for commanding a "marching army, this time not against Berlin, but against Little Rock." But as chief executive of the state, he quietly integrated the public schools.

In fact, despite grumblings about his rhetoric, blacks provided Hollings' margin of victory in 1966, when he won his Senate seat against a more conservative Republican opponent. Since then, he never has faced a credible candidate to his left, and blacks have generally supported him.

During the Depression, the Hollings family's paper business went bankrupt, so an uncle had to borrow money to send him to The Citadel, where he received an Army commission. After World War II, Hollings returned for law school, a legal career and eventually politics.

As a young state legislator, he attracted notice with his plan to solve the problem of inferior black schools without integration. He said a special sales tax should be imposed to upgrade the black schools.

Hollings twice won unanimous election to the state House speakership and in 1954 moved up to lieutenant governor. In 1958, Democratic Gov. George B. Timmerman was ineligible to succeed himself. Hollings won a heated three-way race for the nomination, defeating Donald S. Russell, former University of South Carolina president and a protégé of ex-Gov. James F. Byrnes. The primary turned on political alliances and geography. Hollings' base lay in Tidewater and Russell's in Piedmont.

As governor, Hollings worked hard to strengthen his state's educational system, establishing a commission on higher education. In 1960 his campaigning for Kennedy helped him carry South Carolina for president.

Barred from seeking a second gubernatorial term in 1962, he challenged Democratic Sen. Olin D. Johnston. Portraying himself as "a young man on the go," Hollings attacked Johnston's endorsement by the state AFL-CIO and charged that "foreign labor bosses" were seeking to control the state. Hollings failed to draw much more than one-third of the vote.

The senator died in 1965, however, and Donald Russell — by then governor — had himself appointed to the seat. That provided the issue for Hollings' comeback in 1966. He ousted Russell in the special primary to finish Johnston's term.

The 1966 election year was not an ordinary one in South Carolina. The national Democratic Party was unpopular, and GOP state Sen. Marshall Parker seized on Hollings' connections to it in an effort to defeat him. He nearly made it, but Hollings matched his conservative rhetoric and survived by 11,758 votes.

Running for a full term two years later, Hollings had little trouble turning back Parker. He rolled over weak opponents in 1974 and 1980, but in 1985, Republicans tried to stir up talk that Hollings was dispirited over his failed White House bid and bored with the Senate. The incumbent discredited the rumor early on by stumping all over the state and raising a hefty campaign treasury. Well-known Republicans ducked, leaving the nomination to a little-known former U.S. attorney. He was crushed in the race.

One of the most striking endorsements of the 1988 presidential campaign came from Hollings: In June, he declared he would support the Rev. Jesse Jackson at the Atlanta convention. In 1984, when Hollings' White House bid collapsed early and Jackson went on to dominate the state's Democratic caucuses, Hollings had more than a few unkind words for Jackson, at one point calling his "rainbow coalition" a "blackbow" coalition.

But in 1988, Jackson ran even better in the state's Democratic caucuses. Perhaps with an eye on maintaining a line of communication to black voters — a must-win bloc for any Democrat running statewide — Hollings went along with a majority of the convention delegation in supporting Jackson, who is a native of Greenville, S.C.

Committees

Commerce, Science & Transportation (Chairman)
National Ocean Policy Study (chairman); Communications; Foreign Commerce & Tourism; Surface Transportation

Appropriations (3rd of 16 Democrats)
Commerce, Justice, State & Judiciary (chairman); Defense; Energy & Water Development; Interior; Labor, Health & Human Services, Education

Budget (2nd of 12 Democrats)

Select Intelligence (3rd of 8 Democrats)

Elections

1986 General

Ernest F. Hollings (D)	465,500	(63%)
Henry D. McMaster (R)	262,886	(36%)

Previous Winning Percentages: **1980** (70%) **1974** (70%) **1968** (62%) **1966** * (51%)

* *Special election.*

Campaign Finance

	Receipts	Receipts from PACs		Expend-itures
1988				
Hollings (D)	$2,395,632	$950,882	(40%)	$2,233,843
McMaster (R)	$584,834	$49,722	(9%)	$584,288

Key Votes

1991

Authorize use of force against Iraq	N

1990

Oppose prohibition of certain semiautomatic weapons	Y
Support constitutional amendment on flag desecration	Y
Oppose requiring parental notice for minors' abortions	Y
Halt production of B-2 stealth bomber at 13 planes	Y
Approve budget that cut spending and raised revenues	N
Pass civil rights bill over Bush veto	Y

1989

Oppose reduction of SDI funding	Y
Oppose barring federal funds for "obscene" art	N
Allow vote on capital gains tax cut	N

Voting Studies

	Presidential Support		Party Unity		Conservative Coalition	
Year	**S**	**O**	**S**	**O**	**S**	**O**
1990	52	48	73	27	57	43
1989	67	33	61	39	71	29
1988	49	49	71	25	81	14
1987	47	53	58	42	88	13
1986	70	30	54	46	74	26
1985	52	48	59	41	75	25
1984	32	44	59	22	49	26
1983	8	35	49	8	23	20
1982	44	45	73	20	55	36
1981	54	38	58	35	67	30

Interest Group Ratings

Year	ADA	ACU	AFL-CIO	CCUS
1990	50	48	67	42
1989	45	50	80	63
1988	55	48	86	29
1987	40	62	80	17
1986	35	52	73	32
1985	45	52	62	55
1984	60	38	89	40
1983	70	12	90	36
1982	55	50	74	53
1981	55	14	58	35

1 Arthur Ravenel Jr. (R)

Of Mount Pleasant — Elected 1986

Born: March 29, 1927, St. Andrews Parish, S.C.
Education: College of Charleston, B.A. 1950.
Military Service: Marine Corps, 1945-46.
Occupation: Businessman.
Family: Wife, Jean Rickenbaker; six children, four stepchildren.
Religion: French Huguenot.
Political Career: S.C. House, 1953-59; S.C. Senate, 1981-87.
Capitol Office: 508 Cannon Bldg. 20515; 225-3176.

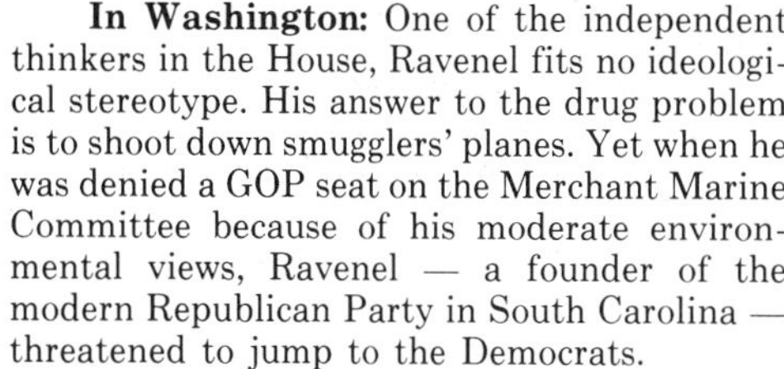

In Washington: One of the independent thinkers in the House, Ravenel fits no ideological stereotype. His answer to the drug problem is to shoot down smugglers' planes. Yet when he was denied a GOP seat on the Merchant Marine Committee because of his moderate environmental views, Ravenel — a founder of the modern Republican Party in South Carolina — threatened to jump to the Democrats.

Quick action by a fellow South Carolinian, then-ascendant Republican National Committee Chairman Lee Atwater, got Ravenel his seat in November 1989 and kept him in the party. Atwater persuaded Alaska Rep. Don Young, the No. 2 Republican on Merchant Marine and ranking member of the Fisheries Subcommittee, to lift his objection to Ravenel, who had not pledged support for Young's plan to open the Arctic National Wildlife Refuge to oil drilling.

The incident exhibited Ravenel's tendency to chart his own course. In the 101st Congress, he backed the Bush administration on just over half of the House votes — less often than any other Southern Republican. During the 1990 budget summit between Bush administration officials and congressional leaders, Ravenel railed against the exclusion of most House members' input. In a floor speech he asked: "Are we in charge as we were sent here to be or have we become a house of political eunuchs?"

On the Armed Services Committee, Ravenel watches over the many Charleston-area military facilities. He generally supports Pentagon priorities. In the 101st Congress he voted against funding cuts for the strategic defense initiative but supported a cap on production of the B-2 stealth bomber.

Ravenel unveiled his "shootdown" strategy when discussing the military role in drug interdiction. When the military identifies a plane or ship as unquestionably smuggling drugs, he said in his 1988 campaign, "I think those drug planes should be shot down and I think the ships bringing the drugs in should be sunk . . . [and] any survivors machine-gunned in the water."

At Home: In South Carolina they call Ravenel "Daddy Rabbit," a nickname that reflects both his colorful personal style and his pioneering role in establishing the Republican Party in the Charleston area.

Entering politics in the 1950s as a Democrat, he represented Charleston in the state House for three terms. He switched to the GOP in 1960 and for the next two decades worked to expand the local party, all the while making a fortune in home building, real estate and cattle raising. In 1980, he unseated a Democratic state senator. Four years later, when reapportionment placed him in another district, he defeated another incumbent Democrat.

Ravenel's personality has enabled him to establish a rapport with blacks and blue-collar workers rarely supportive of conservative GOP businessmen. In the Legislature, his interests included protection of the coastal environment and programs for the mentally retarded.

In 1986, when GOP Rep. Thomas F. Hartnett left the 1st to run for lieutenant governor, Ravenel easily secured the Republican nomination, while Democrats endured a bruising contest eventually won by Jimmy Stuckey, former chairman of the Charleston County Council.

The nominees agreed on most national issues: They supported the Reagan military buildup and opposed any tax increase. Both promised to bring federal funds to the district's military facilities. Their most substantive clashes were on aid to the Nicaraguan contras, which Ravenel favored, and increased federal support for education, which Ravenel opposed.

Ravenel put Stuckey on the defensive by reviving a charge that first surfaced in the Democratic primary — that Stuckey as a private attorney had defended drug traffickers.

On Election Day, Ravenel won 52 percent, trailing Stuckey in three rural counties, but carrying the city of Charleston, the GOP suburbs in Dorchester and lower Berkeley counties, and the Hilton Head resort area in Beaufort County. In 1988 and 1990 he won re-election with ease.

South Carolina 1

South — Charleston

Henry James, describing the city's listlessness at the turn of the century, disparaged Charleston as "effeminate." No more. While James might still recognize the carefully preserved older streets and quaint houses, the symbol of contemporary Charleston is the defense industry and the enormous postwar growth it has brought this area.

The Charleston Naval Shipyard, Charleston Air Force Base, Parris Island Marine Corps Base and numerous other military facilities place an estimated one-third of the district's payroll in the hands of the Defense Department and draw in military contractors and related businesses.

Neither growth nor destruction has shaken the city from its Old South moorings. Even Hurricane Hugo's fury in 1989 — causing billions in damage — could not disturb Charleston's gentility; within one year of the storm, much of the damaged historic district was restored to exacting standards.

Most of the people moving into the area have settled in areas around Charleston. Many of the working-class voters in North Charleston are the type of people who grew up as Southern Democrats but have abandoned the party in droves in recent years. Their growing habit of supporting the GOP supplements the automatic Republican votes that are cast by the residents of more affluent Charleston suburbs. In Charleston itself and in the poorer rural counties inland, the Democratic presence remains strong. The city, just over 40 percent black, still has a Democratic mayor, and blacks in the precincts north of Calhoun Street vote Democratic overwhelmingly. But the white population, which is beginning to encroach on formerly black areas, tends to vote Republican in national elections.

A crucial addition to the GOP column in the 1st is Beaufort County, on the coast south of Charleston. The development of the Hilton Head Island resort has brought thousands of well-off residents to a county that was rural and Democratic.

Population: 520,338. White 343,616 (66%), Black 168,058 (32%), Other 5,714 (1%). Spanish origin 8,618 (2%). 18 and over 362,866 (70%), 65 and over 38,887 (7%). Median age: 26.

Committees

Armed Services (15th of 22 Republicans)
Military Installations & Facilities; Military Personnel & Compensation

Merchant Marine & Fisheries (13th of 17 Republicans)
Fisheries & Wildlife Conservation & the Environment; Merchant Marine

Elections

1990 General		
Arthur Ravenel Jr. (R)	80,839	(65%)
Eugene Platt (D)	42,555	(34%)
1990 Primary		
Arthur Ravenel Jr. (R)	19,688	(90%)
Benjamin Hunt Jr. (R)	2,282	(10%)
1988 General		
Arthur Ravenel Jr. (R)	101,572	(64%)
Wheeler Tillman (D)	57,691	(36%)

Previous Winning Percentage: **1986** (52%)

District Vote For President

	1988	1984	1980	1976
D	62,437 (38%)	58,199 (35%)	65,690 (44%)	65,254 (53%)
R	99,698 (61%)	105,655 (64%)	78,592 (53%)	56,449 (46%)
I			3,146 (2%)	

Campaign Finance

	Receipts	Receipts from PACs	Expend-itures
1990			
Ravenel (R)	$221,611	$113,350 (51%)	$99,261
Platt (D)	$13,924	0	$14,040
1988			
Ravenel (R)	$273,828	$141,080 (52%)	$118,702
Tillman (D)	$82,118	$5,250 (6%)	$82,035

Key Votes

1991	
Authorize use of force against Iraq	Y
1990	
Support constitutional amendment on flag desecration	Y
Pass family and medical leave bill over Bush veto	Y
Reduce SDI funding	N
Allow abortions in overseas military facilities	N
Approve budget summit plan for spending and taxing	N
Approve civil rights bill	N
1989	
Halt production of B-2 stealth bomber at 13 planes	Y
Oppose capital gains tax cut	N
Approve federal abortion funding in rape or incest cases	Y
Approve pay raise and revision of ethics rules	N
Pass Democratic minimum wage plan over Bush veto	N

Voting Studies

	Presidential Support		Party Unity		Conservative Coalition	
Year	S	O	S	O	S	O
1990	54	46	59	39	83	17
1989	64	33	50	45	80	15
1988	49	48	55	44	95	5
1987	58	42	61	35	88	12

Interest Group Ratings

Year	ADA	ACU	AFL-CIO	CCUS
1990	28	63	25	57
1989	25	70	25	100
1988	25	76	64	86
1987	20	61	31	87

2 Floyd D. Spence (R)

Of Lexington — Elected 1970

Born: April 9, 1928, Columbia, S.C.
Education: U. of South Carolina, A.B. 1952, J.D. 1956.
Military Service: Navy, 1952-54; Naval Reserve, 1948-88.
Occupation: Lawyer.
Family: Wife, Deborah Williams; four children.
Religion: Lutheran.
Political Career: S.C. House, 1957-63; S.C. Senate, 1967-71, minority leader, 1967-71; GOP nominee for U.S. House, 1962.
Capitol Office: 2405 Rayburn Bldg. 20515; 225-2452.

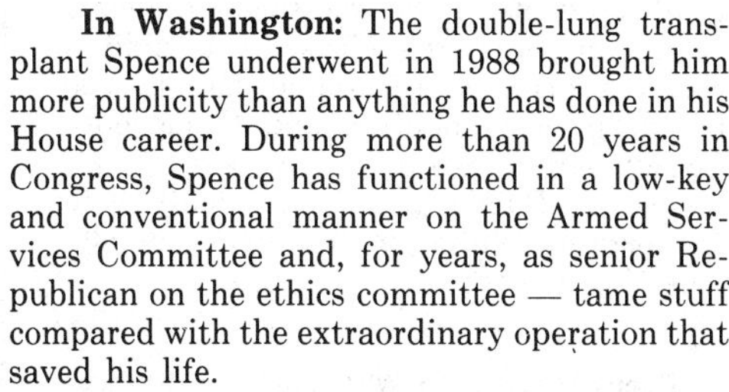

In Washington: The double-lung transplant Spence underwent in 1988 brought him more publicity than anything he has done in his House career. During more than 20 years in Congress, Spence has functioned in a low-key and conventional manner on the Armed Services Committee and, for years, as senior Republican on the ethics committee — tame stuff compared with the extraordinary operation that saved his life.

Once a star college athlete, Spence suffered from an obstructive lung disease that left him so breathless he could barely speak; he required a wheelchair and a portable oxygen supply. But in May 1988, doctors in Jackson, Miss., replaced Spence's damaged lungs with those of a young man who had been killed in a motorcycle accident. Although the double-transplant procedure was risky (only about a dozen had been performed in this country), Spence recovered well enough to seek and win a 10th House term that year in a tough campaign that was dominated by questions about his health.

The operation returned the color to Spence's pallorous appearance. "It's just like a new life," he told the Columbia, S.C., *State* in a 1989 interview. "It's more than I could have hoped for." One of the few new federal initiatives the conservative Spence has signed his name to is a proposal to include information with each 1992 income tax refund check encouraging Americans to sign organ donor cards.

The operation restored Spence's health, but it has not changed his view of his role as a congressman: He remains the antithesis of an activist member. "There are already too many regulations, too many laws, too much government, too many interferences in the personal lives of people," he told the Columbia newspaper in 1990. Limited government has ever been Spence's credo: In 1973, he proposed the first House resolution for a constitutional amendment mandating a balanced federal budget.

It is not that Spence lacks a role to play: He is the second-ranking Republican on Armed Services. But over his career, Spence has simply been too much a down-the-line Pentagon supporter to play an influential role in debates over U.S. defense policy and priorities. Although his ranking position on the Seapower Subcommittee makes him somewhat more of an advocate for Navy programs, Spence has hardly been known to speak out publicly against individual defense programs.

Defense issues have always been Spence's chief legislative interest. He arrived in the House in 1971 determined to serve on Armed Services, largely to look after the military installations scattered over South Carolina by the committee's longtime chairman, Democrat L. Mendel Rivers of Charleston. These include the military installation in Spence's district, Fort Jackson, a large Army basic training center.

A supporter of the military buildup inspired by President Reagan during the 1980s, Spence now warns against a rush to cut defense spending. "The funds spent in providing for our military were moneys well-spent . . . ," Spence said in a March 1991 speech after U.S. armed forces ended Iraq's occupation of Kuwait. "If we wish our America to remain as the vanguard of freedom, let us not now foolishly sacrifice these strides by disassembling the structure which has brought us to this great success."

At the start of the 102nd Congress, Spence got a seat on the Veterans' Affairs Committee. But he did not return to the ethics committee, on which he had served for 15 years before being forced by his health problems to step down in 1988.

Spence took a seat on ethics as a favor to then-Minority Leader Gerald R. Ford, who told him it was a prestigious committee that rarely met and would look good on his record. Instead, the committee ended up handling one difficult assignment after another, including the Korean influence-buying scandals, the Abscam bribery affair and the punishment of two members for sexual misconduct with teenage congressional pages. Spence retired from the committee just

South Carolina 2

Central — Columbia

The 2nd is a politically polarized district. Suburban Republicans in Lexington County and neighboring Richland County, which has Columbia, the capital, at its western edge, dominate the constituency. The votes from these areas exceed the margins given Democrats in the city of Columbia and in the three largely rural, black-majority counties in the southern portion of the district.

The greater Columbia area of Richland and Lexington counties enjoyed a strong economic surge in the 1980s. Lexington's new inhabitants are a mix of retirees, white-collar workers who left increasingly black Columbia, and employees of the glass, cement and synthetic-fiber companies that have moved to the county in recent years.

Whatever brought them there, Lexington County residents are overwhelmingly white and Republican. Republican Rep. Spence has won roughly 70 percent of Lexington's vote in his last two hotly contested campaigns. George Bush took it with 78 percent in 1988.

Neighboring Richland County has more political and racial diversity. The county has the largest black population in the state, most of it concentrated in Columbia, which is 44 percent black. State employees and the 27,000 students and faculty at the University of South Carolina join with blacks to give much of the city a politically liberal hue and strong Democratic presence. Diluting this influence is the suburban Republican vote, which includes ballots cast by military personnel and retirees settled around Fort Jackson.

The southern portion of the 2nd has its political and geographic center at Orangeburg, where South Carolina State College (4,100 students) is the traditional academic center for the state's blacks. The middle-class black community around the college is potent in local politics, and Orangeburg County and its two rural neighbors — Calhoun and Bamberg — consistently vote Democratic. Whites in the area generally vote Republican.

Population: 522,688. White 335,548 (64%), Black 181,061 (35%), Other 3,897 (1%). Spanish origin 6,623 (1%). 18 and over 372,290 (71%), 65 and over 41,898 (8%). Median age: 27.

as it embarked on its most difficult assignment: the investigation of House Speaker Jim Wright, which resulted in Wright's resignation in 1989.

At Home: A series of Democratic challengers has described Spence as a do-nothing congressman, citing the exceptionally low number of bills he has produced in his career. But Spence has a ready response. "I don't know that my people necessarily like hot dogs, and you see a lot of hot dogs around here [in the House]," Spence said in his 1990 interview with the *State*. "They'll introduce a bill at the drop of a hat; that's not my style." So far, Spence's perception of his constituency has proved sage.

It is usually to a challenger's advantage to campaign against an incumbent of infirm health. But in 1988, Democrats never could get a handle on the health issue against Spence, even though his illness, transplant surgery and recovery limited his campaigning.

Democrats got off to a bad start in the spring, when a national party operative working in South Carolina was quoted as saying of Spence, "If he's out there [campaigning] in a wheelchair, maybe the voters will decide we have to do something else." In the fall, Democratic challenger Jim Leventis had to campaign in the context of flattering media attention of the recovering Spence as a medical marvel who had won a reprieve from death.

Leventis was a strong, well-financed contender. A 50-year-old attorney and banker, he boasted personal or professional contacts with many in the business and political elite of Columbia, the 2nd's largest city. He vigorously campaigned door-to-door, and tried to draw Spence into face-to-face exchanges.

But the incumbent refused to oblige, campaigning in his usual low-key manner, turning up the heat just a little at the end by telling voters, "If you like Dukakis, you'll love Leventis." The Democratic presidential nominee lost the 2nd by 20 percentage points; in crucial Lexington County, suburban home of Columbia's professional class, Spence amassed 68 percent of the vote, overcoming Leventis' modest margins in Richland County (Columbia) and majority-black Orangeburg County. Overall, Spence took 53 percent.

Dispirited by the loss, Democrats in 1990 did not offer a candidate against Spence.

After his star athlete days at the University of South Carolina and then practice as a lawyer, Spence won a state House seat as a Democrat. But he quit the party in 1962, complaining it was too liberal, and began campaigning for Congress as a Republican.

Stressing his opposition to the "socialistic" Kennedy administration, Spence was a consensus choice for the 1962 GOP nomination in the open 2nd. But he narrowly lost to a conservative Democrat, state Sen. Albert W. Watson.

Watson himself switched parties in 1965, and in 1970 ran for governor as a Republican. Spence tried again for Congress, stressing his opposition to the busing decisions of the U.S. Supreme Court. He defeated Democrat Heyward McDonald by 6,088 votes.

In 1974 he took 56 percent against Matthew Perry, the first black to be nominated for Congress by South Carolina Democrats. Another black Democrat, Ken Mosely, challenged Spence in 1982 and 1984, getting around 40 percent each time. In 1986, state Democratic Party Executive Director Fred Zeigler filed against Spence at the last moment to prevent the nomination from going to a machine shop owner who was suspected of having ties to Lyndon H. LaRouche Jr., Zeigler ended up laying a foundation for Leventis' challenge.

Zeigler was late starting and outspent, but not bashful. He issued a steady barrage of attacks on Spence, portraying him as either too tired or too bored to represent the district vigorously. A 39-year-old former University of South Carolina football star, Zeigler accused Spence of dodging him in order to "avoid a side-by-side, live comparison." He said Spence had taken too many taxpayer-financed foreign junkets and had not done enough to help South Carolina's import-pinched textile industry.

Spence did his best to ignore Zeigler's taunts, saying he would not respond to an "obvious campaign tactic of engaging in untrue allegations." Spence got a 70 percent showing out of suburban Lexington County. Zeigler attracted some support among Columbia's young professionals, and their votes added to the 2nd's traditional Democratic base brought him up to 46 percent districtwide.

Committees

Armed Services (2nd of 22 Republicans)
Seapower & Strategic & Critical Materials (ranking); Military Installations & Facilities

Select Aging (13th of 27 Republicans)
Human Services; Retirement, Income & Employment

Veterans' Affairs (11th of 13 Republicans)
Compensation, Pension & Insurance

Elections

1990 General		
Floyd D. Spence (R)	90,054	(89%)
Gebhard Sommer (LIBERT)	11,101	(11%)
1988 General		
Floyd D. Spence (R)	94,960	(53%)
Jim Leventis (D)	83,978	(47%)

Previous Winning Percentages: **1986** (54%) **1984** (62%) **1982** (59%) **1980** (56%) **1978** (57%) **1976** (58%) **1974** (56%) **1972** (100%) **1970** (53%)

District Vote For President

	1988	1984	1980	1976
D	67,446 (39%)	61,368 (36%)	52,255 (43%)	70,231 (51%)
R	103,577 (59%)	105,337 (62%)	66,522 (54%)	66,194 (48%)
I			2,261 (2%)	

Campaign Finance

	Receipts	Receipts from PACs		Expend-itures
1990				
Spence (R)	$188,988	$106,533	(56%)	$130,173
1988				
Spence (R)	$363,171	$191,268	(53%)	$369,698
Leventis (D)	$389,570	$65,200	(17%)	$378,469

Key Votes

1991	
Authorize use of force against Iraq	Y
1990	
Support constitutional amendment on flag desecration	Y
Pass family and medical leave bill over Bush veto	N
Reduce SDI funding	N
Allow abortions in overseas military facilities	N
Approve budget summit plan for spending and taxing	N
Approve civil rights bill	N
1989	
Halt production of B-2 stealth bomber at 13 planes	N
Oppose capital gains tax cut	N
Approve federal abortion funding in rape or incest cases	N
Approve pay raise and revision of ethics rules	N
Pass Democratic minimum wage plan over Bush veto	N

Voting Studies

	Presidential Support		Party Unity		Conservative Coalition	
Year	**S**	**O**	**S**	**O**	**S**	**O**
1990	62	36	75	24	94	4
1989	72	24	69	29	98	0
1988	37	21	37	14	47	3
1987	61	32	68	20	91	7
1986	69	30	75	23	94	2
1985	61	39	84	13	93	7
1984	59	36	84	13	88	8
1983	74	26	87	10	97	2
1982	74	26	84	15	93	5
1981	74	26	92	8	96	4

Interest Group Ratings

Year	ADA	ACU	AFL-CIO	CCUS
1990	17	79	17	71
1989	10	93	25	100
1988	10	85	50	71
1987	4	73	20	93
1986	10	77	43	76
1985	0	81	12	95
1984	5	83	8	63
1983	0	100	6	80
1982	0	91	5	86
1981	0	100	13	89

3 Butler Derrick (D)

Of Edgefield — Elected 1974

Born: Sept. 30, 1936, Springfield, Mass.
Education: Attended U. of South Carolina, 1954-58; U. of Georgia, LL.B. 1965.
Occupation: Lawyer.
Family: Wife, Beverly Grantham; two children, two stepchildren.
Religion: Episcopalian.
Political Career: S.C. House, 1969-75.
Capitol Office: 201 Cannon Bldg. 20515; 225-5301.

In Washington: Derrick is one of the most impressive Southern legislators in the House, a product of the Democratic class of 1974 who now sits just one place down from the chairmanship of the powerful Rules Committee.

But while this moderate, pro-business Democrat is in an enviable position to deliver for his South Carolina district, he now has to worry about whether his conservative-minded constituency will deliver for him. Derrick's challenge is to be an effective inside player in the House Democratic Caucus while representing a state increasingly enamored of the GOP.

As he struggles to keep his political footing at home — he has been held under 60 percent in three of his last four elections — Derrick has also begun to gain wider recognition for his legislative talents. When Rules Chairman Claude Pepper died in May 1989, Joe Moakley of Massachusetts took over the committee, and Derrick became its No. 2 Democrat. He is nearly a decade younger than Moakley, and could chair the panel one day — if voters in the 3rd keep returning him to Washington. Democratic leaders look to him as a key link to the South when it comes to coalition building, although they know political realities sometimes require Derrick to go his own way.

For a man of the media age, Derrick has a quiet operating style, more prone to hammer out a compromise in a corner of the House chamber than to give a speech center stage. His behind-the-scenes pursuits enable him to get much more done in a given Congress than he gets, or takes, credit for. But that is not to say that Derrick shuns high-profile issues. He has been at the center of activity on some issues of national and local concern.

As chairman of Rules' Subcommittee on the Legislative Process, Derrick has engaged President Bush over the issue of the pocket veto. Bush contended that he could exercise a pocket veto — that is, disapprove a bill by merely withholding his signature — whenever Congress adjourned for more than three days. Derrick insisted, with the backing of a federal appeals court, that a president could pocket-veto a bill only after the final adjournment.

In pushing legislation during the 101st Congress to codify his position, Derrick said, "We're not trying to make a confrontation. All we're trying to do is codify what the courts have said over the last 20 years." Rules and Judiciary approved the legislation in 1990, but it stalled before reaching the House floor or the Senate.

In the 100th Congress, Derrick was chairman of the Congressional Textile Caucus, and he took the lead in pushing a major bill to aid the domestic industry, much of which is located in the South. The effort was a popular one at home and among many in Congress. Opponents called the bill protectionism that could not be accommodated under existing trade agreements; they also said the industry was on sounder economic footing than it had been in the previous Congress.

The House passed the textile bill in 1987 by a substantial margin, but one smaller than the failed veto-override vote in the previous Congress. It was little surprise in 1988 that Derrick and his allies fell 11 votes short of overriding the president's veto. Some of the shortfall was probably due to the passage of an omnibus trade bill, which gave many members an outlet for their frustration on the issue. Derrick, who is now a deputy whip, played an important role in delivering votes for that bill.

In 1990, both chambers, again by wide majorities, passed a textile quota bill that would have limited textile and apparel import growth and permanently frozen imports of most shoes at 1989 levels. The House, however, fell 10 votes short of overriding Bush's veto.

Derrick is also closely tied to nuclear issues, which have a major impact on his district, home to the Department of Energy's nuclear reactors at Savannah River. Along with other South Carolina officials, Derrick has worked to persuade DOE to build a new reactor for tritium production in the 3rd. In 1988 DOE recommended South Carolina as its preferred site for a new plant, and in May 1991, the Armed Services Committee adopted a non-binding provision urging DOE to put the reactor there. "Obviously I want the thing to go to the Savannah River site: It's in my district; there are a lot

South Carolina 3

West — Anderson; Aiken

The 3rd stretches in a band one and two counties wide from the Blue Ridge Mountains in the north to rural Allendale County, only 60 miles from the Atlantic coast beaches. It is a traditionally Democratic-dominated rural and small-town territory where newcomers arriving in a few urbanized areas are measurably enhancing Republican strength.

In the three largest counties of the 3rd — Anderson, Aiken and Pickens — George Bush won a combined 71 percent of the presidential vote in 1988. A more telling sign of changing times — since Democrats still hold most of the local offices throughout the 3rd — is that in 1986, Republican gubernatorial nominee Carroll A. Campbell Jr. managed to carry the 3rd as part of his narrow statewide victory.

Anderson is a traditional textile county that has made a successful transition to diversified manufacturing (more than 140 different industries); its hospital complex is one of the Piedmont's major medical centers, with nearly 600 beds and about 200 doctors.

Pickens County is the site of Clemson University, a mainstay of the economy with nearly 16,000 students and 1,000 faculty. The town of Clemson has a conservative bloc among some faculty and students; spillover growth from Greenville, in the neighboring 4th District, also has increased the GOP base.

The strongest Republican area of the 3rd is Aiken County, GOP Sen. Strom Thurmond's political base. A traditional winter resting place for wealthy Northerners, Aiken was once called "the polo capital of the South." Its county seat of Aiken boasts a public library built by the du Pont family. The bulk of the county's GOP support comes from white-collar suburbs clustered east of Augusta, Ga., and from the executives working at or retired from the Savannah River nuclear complex, which straddles Aiken and Barnwell counties.

There are pockets of GOP votes in other counties, but most of the rural voters consider themselves Democrats except for presidential election purposes. A good share of the farming population remains poor, with the sharecroppers of black-majority Abbeville and McCormick counties in particular scratching meager livings from the soil. Those two counties were the only in the district carried by Michael S. Dukakis in 1988.

Population: 519,280. White 399,161 (77%), Black 117,985 (23%). Spanish origin 3,836 (1%). 18 and over 366,318 (71%), 65 and over 54,173 (10%). Median age: 30.

of jobs; the citizens want it," said Derrick.

Although he casts his share of routine votes with the conservative coalition of Republicans and Southern Democrats, Derrick usually comes through when his party needs him. In 1990 he voted with his party 81 percent of the time, more than the average Southern Democrat. He was the only South Carolina House member supporting a $600 million cut in funding for the strategic defense initiative in 1990, and he also voted against the president's request for military aid to the contras in 1988 and non-military aid in 1989. In April 1991, Derrick also announced that he would support the Brady bill — imposing a seven-day waiting period for handgun purchases — contrary to his record of opposing gun control.

But when Democrats were trying to make a major issue of Republican opposition to plant-closing notification legislation in 1988, Derrick was one of 16 House Democrats who voted against the measure — a reflection of his close ties to his district's business establishment. Derrick voted to sustain Bush's veto of a Democratic plan to boost the minimum wage in 1989, and of a measure requiring businesses to provide family and medical leave to their employees. And, along with the state's entire House delegation, he voted to authorize the use of force in the Persian Gulf in 1991.

Derrick is also careful to distance himself from the overall image of his national party, whose presidential candidates have been poison in South Carolina. In 1989 he cosponsored a measure banning the importation of American flags manufactured outside the country, and he later backed a constitutional amendment to prohibit flag burning.

At Home: In November 1988, the Dukakis-Bentsen presidential ticket got just one-third of the vote in the 3rd, making Derrick's GOP foe, surgeon Henry S. Jordan, a bigger obstacle than expected. Derrick finished with 54 percent of the vote, enticing the national GOP to make a priority of his district in 1990.

Initially the GOP looked as if it had a credible challenger for 1990 in real estate broker Ray Haskett. But a slow-starting campaign earned Haskett negative publicity that dried up his contributions; he ended up spending less than $75,000. Derrick's campaign was awash in money; he spent over $900,000, about two-thirds of it given to him by political action committees. Yet that huge financial advantage earned him an underwhelming 58 percent — a sure sign that the baseline Republican vote in the traditionally Democratic 3rd is substantial.

But so far, Derrick's cushion of support has been enough to carry him through even tough presidential-election years. At the start of 1988, he looked to be in good shape. In 1984, he had won comfortably despite a Reagan landslide in the 3rd and opposition from an aggressive young Republican real estate developer.

Establishment Republicans, pessimistic about their prospects against Derrick in 1988, let a newer wing of the local GOP — evangelical conservatives — take a turn against the incumbent. Jordan, who had been active in Pat Robertson's presidential campaign, had built some name recognition in a failed 1986 bid for the GOP Senate nomination. But he had to spend much of 1988 just trying to prove he had a broader agenda than the social-issues activism associated with Robertson's movement.

Still, on Election Day, Jordan ran well in the areas of the 3rd that are the fastest-growing. He carried Aiken County and stayed close in Anderson and Pickens counties; Derrick ran strongest in the district's more rural areas.

It was a tough fight for a man who had an unusually smooth initial path to Congress, and subsequently uneventful re-elections. The 3rd was up for grabs in 1974 when veteran Democrat W. J. Bryan Dorn retired, and Derrick won it like an incumbent breezing to re-election.

He had been a state representative since 1969 and was a member of the influential Ways and Means Committee of the South Carolina House. He professed fiscal conservatism, right-to-work views and hard-line support for national defense. He also identified himself publicly as a racial moderate, nominating the first black to a South Carolina school board.

Derrick won the Democratic primary with 65 percent of the vote. In November, he carried all but one county in defeating former state Sen. Marshall J. Parker, twice an unsuccessful GOP Senate candidate, with 62 percent. He won 60 percent in a 1980 rematch with Parker and prevailed with similar ease until 1988.

Committees

Rules (2nd of 9 Democrats)
Legislative Process (chairman)

Select Aging (9th of 42 Democrats)
Rural Elderly (chairman); Health & Long-Term Care; Social Security and Women

Elections

1990 General

Butler Derrick (D)	72,561	(58%)
Ray Haskett (R)	52,419	(42%)

1988 General

Butler Derrick (D)	89,071	(54%)
Henry S. Jordan (R)	75,571	(46%)

Previous Winning Percentages: **1986** (68%) **1984** (58%) **1982** (90%) **1980** (60%) **1978** (82%) **1976** (100%) **1974** (62%)

District Vote For President

	1988	1984	1980	1976
D	54,507 (33%)	49,116 (32%)	89,433 (51%)	79,979 (60%)
R	108,043 (66%)	102,301 (67%)	82,493 (47%)	53,342 (40%)
I			2,681 (2%)	

Campaign Finance

	Receipts	Receipts from PACs	Expend-itures
1990			
Derrick (D)	$848,063	$542,789 (64%)	$907,904
Haskett (R)	$74,939	0	$74,264
1988			
Derrick (D)	$579,468	$370,841 (64%)	$641,429
Jordan (R)	$354,589	$45,511 (13%)	$354,575

Key Votes

1991	
Authorize use of force against Iraq	Y
1990	
Support constitutional amendment on flag desecration	Y
Pass family and medical leave bill over Bush veto	N
Reduce SDI funding	Y
Allow abortions in overseas military facilities	Y
Approve budget summit plan for spending and taxing	Y
Approve civil rights bill	Y
1989	
Halt production of B-2 stealth bomber at 13 planes	N
Oppose capital gains tax cut	N
Approve federal abortion funding in rape or incest cases	Y
Approve pay raise and revision of ethics rules	N
Pass Democratic minimum wage plan over Bush veto	N

Voting Studies

	Presidential Support		Party Unity		Conservative Coalition	
Year	**S**	**O**	**S**	**O**	**S**	**O**
1990	31	68	81	17	70	28
1989	43	55	79	19	73	24
1988	33	60	76	18	66	21
1987	28	68	83	15	56	42
1986	28	68	81	13	52	48
1985	29	69	74	17	60	35
1984	39	54	73	25	61	39
1983	35	57	72	16	42	49
1982	36	52	70	22	56	41
1981	50	45	62	30	55	35

Interest Group Ratings

Year	ADA	ACU	AFL-CIO	CCUS
1990	44	33	58	62
1989	35	43	50	80
1988	70	36	71	54
1987	72	17	75	40
1986	55	26	57	44
1985	60	10	53	36
1984	50	35	15	47
1983	75	23	69	53
1982	50	46	55	52
1981	60	40	53	37

4 Liz J. Patterson (D)

Of Spartanburg — Elected 1986

Born: Nov. 18, 1939, Columbia, S.C.

Education: Columbia College, B.A. 1961; attended U. of South Carolina, 1961-62.

Occupation: Legislative aide; Peace Corps recruiting officer; Head Start official.

Family: Husband, Dwight F. Patterson Jr.; three children.

Religion: Methodist.

Political Career: Spartanburg County Council, 1975-76; S.C. Senate, 1979-87.

Capitol Office: 1641 Longworth Bldg. 20515; 225-6030.

In Washington: Through a combination of strategic, visible votes in Washington and a highly personal homestyle with her constituents, Patterson has managed to win three elections in a district that by rights should be represented by a Republican.

On partisan matters that come to a vote on the House floor, Patterson tends to break with her party more often than the average Southern Democrat. She is a cautious conservative who casts business-oriented votes on high-profile issues. In the 101st Congress, she voted against a Democratic-pushed bill increasing the mininum wage to $4.55 an hour, supporting instead the White House-backed increase to $4.25. She opposed legislation to require employers to give family and medical leave and favored cutting the capital gains tax.

Patterson was one of 12 Democrats who voted to censure Massachusetts Rep. Barney Frank for misusing his official position to help a male prostitute — a penalty harsher than the ethics committee's recommendation of a reprimand. She also was among the numerous members to propose a constitutional amendment to ban physical desecration of the flag.

Patterson traces her fiscal conservatism to her days on the South Carolina Senate Finance Committee. Upon arriving in the House in 1987, she joined a bipartisan group led by Minnesota Democrat Timothy J. Penny and Iowa Republican Tom Tauke dedicated to reducing the federal budget deficit with across-the-board spending-cut amendments to appropriations bills.

In the 101st Congress, Patterson served as chairman of the Conservative Democratic Forum's task force on budget reform, where she devised a budget reform proposal that she first introduced in 1989. The bill prescribed instituting a biennial federal budget, removing Social Security trust fund receipts from calculations of the size of the deficit, eliminating catchall spending bills and giving the president greater power to rescind spending in appropriations bills.

During Banking Committee consideration of a major overhaul of federal housing programs in the 101st Congress, Patterson joined a bloc of moderate and conservative Democrats who forged a compromise on a provision aimed at offering new incentives and requirements to persuade owners of federally subsidized housing to continue renting to low-income families. The compromise was adopted by the House overwhelmingly.

On the Veterans' Affairs Committee in the 101st, Patterson offered an amendment to a bill revising various VA programs. The Education Subcommittee adopted her proposal, which would have ensured that veterans in vocational education programs receive the same credits as veterans in degree programs, if they take the same courses. The bill died in the Senate.

Patterson tried to win a seat on the powerful Energy and Commerce Committee at the start of the 102nd Congress, but more senior Democrats took the available openings.

At Home: Patterson is the daughter of a populist, the late U.S. Sen. Olin D. Johnston, and he would have been proud of the way she first won and has since held her seat in Congress.

Running against a well-financed Republican favorite in 1986, Patterson tied him in knots by portraying him as a tool of corporations and the Greenville country club elite. In 1988, she faced a smooth, well-funded establishment GOP challenger, but her warm, down-to-earth style won out over his cooler approach — even as George Bush rolled up a 2-to-1 margin in the 4th. In 1990, she topped 60 percent of the vote, even as the former occupant of the 4th, Republican Carroll A. Campbell Jr., scored an overwhelming gubernatorial re-election victory.

Patterson's three victories make this district one of the Democratic Party's biggest success stories in Southern congressional politics. For eight years, the 4th was solidly Republican, held by Campbell until he left it in 1986

South Carolina 4

Northwest — Greenville; Spartanburg

The nucleus of the 4th is Greenville County, the most populous and most industrialized county in the state and a showpiece of the New South. The city of Greenville developed as a center of the textile industry after the Civil War, and it still bustles with mills, clothing manufacturers and textile machinery producers. Reflecting a broader trend, the number of local textile jobs has declined in recent years, but unemployment remains low because work is available in the newer industries that business and government leaders have lured to the area.

Since 1960, the city's non-unionized labor force and low wage rate have combined with a favorable tax structure and warm climate to draw investment from the Frost Belt and overseas. Union Carbide, General Electric and Michelin are among the major employers.

Greenville County has a history of conservatism dating to its Tory leanings during the Revolution, and it was one of the first areas in the state to take to Republicanism after World War II. But its tendency to follow the GOP line in national elections masks a more fragmented political life.

The county's Republican Party is an uneasy alliance between mainstream partisans among the corporate business community and an intensely conservative wing made up of evangelical Christians and of fundamentalists who take their cues from Dr. Bob Jones III, president of Greenville-based Bob Jones University (4,100 students). The internal GOP rivalry between these two wings has played a part in Patterson winning the 4th for the Democrats three times. In state and national elections, though, local Republicans vote in concert; George Bush won 71 percent of the Greenville County vote in 1988.

Conservative Democrats are in the majority in Greenville County's outlying parts — the mountainous north and the agricultural southern end. There also is liberal Democratic strength within the city among blacks, organized teachers and textile workers. Patterson mobilizes all those Democratic constituencies.

Greenville's development has spilled over into Spartanburg County, bringing new industries and political change. But older textile mills and huge peach orchards dominate the area; the street signs in downtown Spartanburg have peaches painted on them.

Rank-and-file textile workers and farm laborers give Spartanburg firmer Democratic loyalties than Greenville. In her close 1986 and 1988 House races, Patterson carried 60 percent of the vote in Spartanburg County, her home base. She has won even more comfortably in rural, sparsely populated Union County, which rounds out the three-county district.

Population: 520,525. White 416,709 (80%), Black 100,769 (19%). Spanish origin 4,065 (1%). 18 and over 373,015 (72%), 65 and over 52,400 (10%). Median age: 30.

and won election as governor.

Patterson was still a teenager when she started working in Olin Johnston's campaigns, and she continued right up through the last of his four elections to the Senate, in 1962. During the 1970s, she held several posts in the Spartanburg County Democratic Party and served briefly on the Spartanburg County Council. She was elected to the state Senate in 1978.

The Republican's House nominee in 1986, Greenville Mayor William D. Workman III, was initially thought to have the advantage over Patterson, given Campbell's string of easy victories in the 4th District.

But Patterson had little trouble deflecting Workman's attempts to brand her as a big-spending liberal. Campaigning on the slogan "I'm one of us," she aired television advertisements that portrayed her as a homemaker steeped in old-fashioned family values. Her down-home style appealed to rank-and-file voters, many of whom saw Workman as something of a stuffed shirt. If they needed further prodding, Patterson gave it to them, seizing on a portrayal of the Republican as an instrument of Greenville "fat cats."

Although Patterson was a more deft campaigner than Workman, she probably could not have overcome the 4th's conservative bent had the local Republican Party been unified. But it was not.

Campbell's departure had provoked competition between two factions of the district GOP that he had held together — the business-oriented mainstream element and the sizable group of religious fundamentalists and evangelicals, many of them with ties to Bob Jones University in Greenville. Workman was unable to heal the rift by Election Day. Patterson's skillful exploiting of Workman's weaknesses also aroused the antipathy that many rural voters have for Greenville, the district's largest city. Rural votes were crucial to her becoming the first candidate from outside Greenville to win this seat since 1918.

Patterson's 1988 opponent was Knox White, a Greenville city councilman and former congressional aide to Campbell. Even though he beat the same evangelical-backed primary candidate Workman had two years earlier, White stayed on fairly good terms with the religious community.

White targeted the sizable bloc of Republicans in the city and county of Greenville who were contemplating splitting their ballots to vote for George Bush for president and Patterson for Congress. On the stump and in his advertising, he constantly linked his campaign with Bush's, and frequently referred to positions held by "my opponent and Michael Dukakis."

But Patterson had built up a considerable reservoir of good will in her first term. White tried hard to tarnish her image as an independent-thinking, conservative Democrat and portray her as out of the mainstream of the district's social conservatism.

But in the end, more voters preferred the comforting familiarity of Patterson's retail politics to White's rally for conservatism. She stayed close to White in his Greenville County base, then rolled up a 12,000-vote victory margin in her Spartanburg County base and padded her advantage by taking two-thirds of the vote in rural Union County. Overall, Patterson took 52 percent of the vote, a slim but decisive victory against the backdrop of Bush's sweep in the 4th.

After striking out twice with candidates from the GOP establishment, Republicans in 1990 offered a nominee from the Bob Jones wing of the party, state Rep. Terry Haskins. Several Bush Cabinet members and Vice President Dan Quayle campaigned for Haskins, but he was hampered by a late start and by Patterson's backing from business groups. He failed to reach 40 percent of the vote.

Committees

Banking, Finance & Urban Affairs (16th of 31 Democrats)
Economic Stabilization; Financial Institutions Supervision, Regulation & Insurance; Housing & Community Development

Select Hunger (11th of 22 Democrats)
Domestic

Veterans' Affairs (11th of 21 Democrats)
Education, Training & Employment; Hospitals & Health Care

Elections

1990 General		
Liz J. Patterson (D)	81,927	(61%)
Terry E. Haskins (R)	51,338	(38%)
1988 General		
Liz J. Patterson (D)	90,234	(52%)
Knox White (R)	82,793	(48%)

Previous Winning Percentage: **1986** (51%)

District Vote For President

	1988	1984	1980	1976
D	54,572 (32%)	48,691 (30%)	65,654 (44%)	70,211 (52%)
R	114,191 (67%)	114,650 (70%)	80,298 (54%)	63,018 (47%)
I			2,634 (2%)	

Campaign Finance

	Receipts	Receipts from PACs		Expend-itures
1990				
Patterson (D)	$485,371	$303,354	(62%)	$485,095
Haskins (R)	$144,496	$11,700	(8%)	$144,353
1988				
Patterson (D)	$1,119,822	$412,855	(37%)	$1,143,351
White (R)	$631,287	$86,318	(14%)	$630,913

Key Votes

1991	
Authorize use of force against Iraq	Y
1990	
Support constitutional amendment on flag desecration	Y
Pass family and medical leave bill over Bush veto	N
Reduce SDI funding	N
Allow abortions in overseas military facilities	Y
Approve budget summit plan for spending and taxing	N
Approve civil rights bill	Y
1989	
Halt production of B-2 stealth bomber at 13 planes	N
Oppose capital gains tax cut	N
Approve federal abortion funding in rape or incest cases	Y
Approve pay raise and revision of ethics rules	N
Pass Democratic minimum wage plan over Bush veto	N

Voting Studies

	Presidential Support		Party Unity		Conservative Coalition	
Year	**S**	**O**	**S**	**O**	**S**	**O**
1990	37	62	66	33	81	19
1989	55	45	64	35	100	0
1988	37	63	69	29	82	18
1987	36	64	71	25	77	23

Interest Group Ratings

Year	ADA	ACU	AFL-CIO	CCUS
1990	44	54	50	64
1989	40	68	42	90
1988	45	48	71	57
1987	68	26	63	60

5 John M. Spratt Jr. (D)

Of York — Elected 1982

Born: Nov. 1, 1942, Charlotte, N.C.
Education: Davidson College, A.B. 1964; Oxford U., M.A. 1966; Yale U., LL.B. 1969.
Military Service: Army, 1969-71.
Occupation: Lawyer; insurance executive.
Family: Wife, Jane Stacy; three children.
Religion: Presbyterian.
Political Career: No previous office.
Capitol Office: 1533 Longworth Bldg. 20515; 225-5501.

In Washington: There are members of the House Armed Services Committee with greater oratorical flair than Spratt. But when committee Chairman Les Aspin has an assignment requiring brainpower, tenacity and a skill for intellectual argument, he knows he can trust the job to Spratt.

It is qualities such as these that have made the South Carolina Democrat — an attorney with degrees from Davidson, Oxford and Yale — one of the most influential members of the committee that shapes House defense policy. He is one of Aspin's closest allies and advisers.

Since the start of the 101st Congress, Spratt has served as chairman of an Armed Services task force studying the difficult-to-solve safety and waste-disposal problems at the nation's nuclear-weapons-production plants. His amendment to add $300 million to cleanup efforts passed easily in 1989 as an amendment to a House defense authorization bill.

Earlier, Spratt served as Aspin's appointee to chair a committee task force on the strategic defense initiative (SDI). In 1988, Spratt — then in just his third House term — was chief House negotiator on SDI issues during a House-Senate conference on the fiscal 1989 defense authorization bill.

Spratt, like other members of Aspin's inner circle, tends to be more "pro-defense" than many of his House Democratic colleagues. For example, Spratt supported the January 1991 resolution authorizing President Bush to use military force against Iraq.

However, Spratt and others in this group of Democratic centrists keep a skeptical eye on Defense Department policies, and are quite apart from the Pentagon-allied conservative Democrats — the "Old Guard" — who long held sway on Armed Services. "Our role is to be defense advocates, but not Department of Defense advocates," Spratt has said.

This viewpoint was evident during Spratt's performance in the key House debates on SDI strategy during the 100th Congress. In early 1987, Spratt led the fight for amendments that were aimed at blocking President Ronald Reagan's efforts to reinterpret the 1972 U.S.-Soviet anti-ballistic missile (ABM) treaty in a manner that would allow space-based testing of SDI.

During 1988 debate on the defense authorization bill, Reagan argued for accelerated research on "space-based interceptors" (SBIs), small, heat-seeking missiles borne by satellites that would attack Soviet nuclear missiles shortly after launch. The supporters of this approach (later referred to as "brilliant pebbles") called for its deployment as "phase one" of SDI by the early 1990s.

But Spratt and Senate Armed Services Committee Chairman Sam Nunn of Georgia led the fight against SBIs, describing them as a ploy of SDI backers eager to show a "quick return" on investment in SDI research and thus build support for the entire SDI program. They also said SBIs would violate the 1972 ABM treaty and would divert research dollars from more promising anti-missile technologies. Their proposal called for a more modest ground-based system, which would be less expensive and would fall within the bounds of the 1972 treaty.

Spratt did get the House to approve two amendments codifying his position; a House-Senate conference maintained the provisions. However, Reagan vetoed the bill, pointing to the SBI amendments as among its objectionable features; they were removed after weeks of partisan wrangling.

Spratt's reputation for defense expertise led to his being tapped for advice by 1988 Democratic presidential candidate Michael S. Dukakis. That September, Spratt was one of the Democratic moderates who met with Dukakis at his Massachusetts home. But their efforts to insulate Dukakis from the "soft-on-defense" label were of limited effect.

The reflective Spratt rarely makes a rash move. But he proved in 1989 that even savvy legislators can make a tactical misstep.

Both Spratt and Aspin favored production of the single-warhead Midgetman intercontinental ballistic missile over the multi-warhead, rail-based MX, which they viewed as a destabilizing element in the arms race. How-

South Carolina 5

North Central — Rock Hill

Touching on four distinct regions of South Carolina, the 5th extends from the hills of Cherokee County south to the Lowcountry around Sumter. To command a districtwide media presence, a candidate has to buy time in four cities outside the district — Greenville, Columbia, Florence and Charlotte, N.C.

This geographic diversity makes it difficult to pigeonhole the district's personality, but many of the residents are dependent on the textile industry for their livelihood. Most of the counties in the central section of the district have at least one town whose name ends in "Mills," with millworkers forming the base of the electorate. The district's southern and eastern counties remain primarily agricultural. Chesterfield and tiny Lee County grow soybeans, corn, cotton and melons.

In nearly all these counties, most voters prefer Democrats for local and state offices. Nine of the district's 11 counties voted Democratic in the close 1986 gubernatorial contest, which was won by Republican Carroll A. Campbell Jr. Even Michael S. Dukakis got 40 percent of the 5th's presidential vote in 1988, his second-best district showing in the state.

The most populous and dynamic area of the district is at its northern tip, around the city of Rock Hill (York County), a onetime textile town that has become an exurban appendage of Charlotte, N.C., a half-hour's commute up Interstate 77. While Rock Hill's days as a textile town are fading from memory as more of its residents find work in the Charlotte area's white-collar businesses, York County still has a well-organized Democratic Party that just managed (by 110 votes) to win the county in the 1986 governor's race. But two years later, York went 65 percent for George Bush.

Democrats still dominate in rural western York County; the more affluent and Republican voters are in the suburbanized east. Also in the east, around the town of Fort Mill, is a contingent of fervently religious conservative Republicans who were drawn by the Heritage, U.S.A., recreation complex and religious retreat built by televangelists Jim and Tammy Bakker. The park was shut down after Jim Bakker's teleministry and financial empire collapsed in 1989, but a California televangelist purchased the property a year later and planned to reopen the resort in summer 1991.

The 5th's other GOP pockets are in Sumter and Kershaw counties. Shaw Air Force Base in Sumter has been a major source of federal dollars and conservative votes. In Kershaw, the Du Pont executives and other wealthy business people in Camden back Republican candidates.

Population: 519,716. White 347,770 (67%), Black 168,599 (32%), Other 2,561 (1%). Spanish origin 4,563 (1%). 18 and over 357,907 (69%), 65 and over 51,693 (10%). Median age: 29.

ever, during House deliberations on the fiscal 1990 defense authorization bill, Aspin worked out a compromise under which both the MX and the Midgetman would be funded.

Spratt, in a rare conflict with Aspin, nonetheless pushed ahead with his efforts to cut the MX; he scored an initial success when the House, by a 224-197 vote, passed his amendment cutting the program nearly in half. However, the move infuriated many conservatives, who said they had backed the Midgetman only as part of a package to sustain the MX. Joining in an unusual coalition with liberal arms control advocates, the MX supporters helped pass an amendment killing the Midgetman (an action that proved temporary).

During the 101st Congress, Spratt tried to expand his legislative influence by gaining a seat on the Budget Committee. His bid for one of six open Democratic seats in January 1989 fell short in the Democratic Steering and Policy Committee. However, a Budget vacancy occurred in 1990, and Spratt was picked for it.

To take the Budget position, Spratt went on leave from the Government Operations Committee, where he exercised parochial instincts that are mainly absent from his Armed Services work. As a member of the Subcommittee on Commerce, Consumer and Monetary Affairs, he tried to bring attention to the impact of foreign competition on the domestic textile industry, which has numerous outposts in the 5th District; he has supported a series of bills to restrict textile imports, which have passed Congress but have been vetoed by the Reagan and Bush administrations.

At Home: With three academic degrees and a background as a lawyer and bank president, Spratt is not the obvious representative for a district where many of the Democratic votes come from poor textile towns and dusty farms. But after emerging from a field of four

Democratic hopefuls in 1982, Spratt has had no electoral trouble at all. He won that November with 68 percent, and then it was six years before the GOP even fielded a candidate against him. He was Bob Carley, a political science professor, and he lost by more than 2-to-1, even as George Bush carried the district handily.

In his first campaign, Spratt worked hard to turn his elitist credentials into an asset. "People are glad to see a candidate with these qualifications," he said. "That's my come-on." If his style on the stump remained a bit scholarly, no one seemed to mind.

When Democratic Rep. Ken Holland announced his retirement just before the filing deadline, Spratt jumped for the Democratic nomination, as did former Holland aide John Winburn and state Rep. Ernie Nunnery.

Winburn had Holland's contacts and Nunnery had a base in Chester County, but Spratt's banking interests and his law practice gave him strong connections in political and business circles. Many Democratic leaders quietly backed him.

And when Winburn called Spratt "a millionaire banker, lawyer and hobby farmer" who could not relate to ordinary people, Spratt persuasively argued that his work with small-town clients and depositors had given him an understanding of their circumstances. "I wouldn't have kept my job if I couldn't relate to those people," he said. Spratt finished first in the primary with 38 percent of the vote, then took 55 percent in a runoff against Winburn.

In November, Republican John Wilkerson, a longtime friend and legal client of Spratt, accused the Democrat of being too liberal for the district. But Spratt appealed to the district's partisan loyalties, and had a clear organizational edge. When he visited county courthouses, rural areas and factories, he often had a locally popular political figure close at hand. One source described Wilkerson's core supporters as "the country club boys — the fellows who put ice in their whiskey."

Unable to rely on a county-by-county apparatus, Wilkerson turned to using negative ads implying that Spratt had tried to buy votes in a previous campaign for Democratic gubernatorial nominee Charles Ravenel in 1974. The commercials galvanized Spratt supporters and sealed Wilkerson's fate.

Committees

Armed Services (16th of 33 Democrats)
Investigations; Procurement & Military Nuclear Systems

Budget (15th of 23 Democrats)
Budget Process, Reconciliation & Enforcement; Defense, Foreign Policy & Space; Urgent Fiscal Issues

Elections

1990 General		
John M. Spratt Jr. (D)	91,775	(100%)
1988 General		
John M. Spratt Jr. (D)	107,959	(70%)
Robert K. Carley (R)	46,622	(30%)

Previous Winning Percentages: **1986** (100%) **1984** (92%) **1982** (68%)

District Vote For President

	1988	1984	1980	1976
D	61,398 (40%)	58,350 (38%)	74,745 (53%)	80,255 (59%)
R	91,385 (60%)	94,269 (62%)	63,496 (45%)	54,153 (40%)

Campaign Finance

	Receipts	Receipts from PACs		Expend-itures
1990				
Spratt (D)	$110,158	$84,950	(77%)	$173,157
1988				
Spratt (D)	$203,552	$140,970	(69%)	$105,620
Carley (R)	$8,225	0		$8,449

Key Votes

1991	
Authorize use of force against Iraq	Y
1990	
Support constitutional amendment on flag desecration	N
Pass family and medical leave bill over Bush veto	N
Reduce SDI funding	N
Allow abortions in overseas military facilities	Y
Approve budget summit plan for spending and taxing	Y
Approve civil rights bill	Y
1989	
Halt production of B-2 stealth bomber at 13 planes	N
Oppose capital gains tax cut	Y
Approve federal abortion funding in rape or incest cases	Y
Approve pay raise and revision of ethics rules	N
Pass Democratic minimum wage plan over Bush veto	N

Voting Studies

	Presidential Support		Party Unity		Conservative Coalition	
Year	**S**	**O**	**S**	**O**	**S**	**O**
1990	29	69	86	14	72	28
1989	49	51	83	16	68	32
1988	33	63	78	19	82	18
1987	31	66	80	16	81	12
1986	28	71	84	13	54	46
1985	41	58	79	17	73	27
1984	41	58	77	22	56	44
1983	37	61	74	20	60	40

Interest Group Ratings

Year	ADA	ACU	AFL-CIO	CCUS
1990	56	33	67	36
1989	65	29	67	80
1988	55	29	79	57
1987	72	9	69	47
1986	60	33	64	59
1985	35	38	38	57
1984	70	21	38	31
1983	65	14	75	50

6 Robin Tallon (D)

Of Florence — Elected 1982

Born: Aug. 8, 1946, Hemingway, S.C.
Education: Attended U. of South Carolina, 1964-65.
Occupation: Clothing store owner.
Family: Wife, Amelia Louise Johns; three children.
Religion: Methodist.
Political Career: S.C. House, 1981-83.
Capitol Office: 432 Cannon Bldg. 20515; 225-3315.

In Washington: Tallon has a three-pronged constituency to satisfy, and he does it in an unassuming, non-confrontational style. The Pee Dee district is home to rural, traditionally Democratic whites, a good many depending on tobacco for their livelihood; to rural, economically disadvantaged blacks with a stake in preserving and expanding government social services; and to a growing number of affluent and conservative coastal residents in Myrtle Beach and along the Grand Strand.

Each group exerts pressure on Tallon, often in different directions, but he satisfies all the people at least some of the time. His 1989 voting record was fairly typical: He backed President Bush on 56 percent of House floor votes and got favorable ratings of 58 from the AFL-CIO and 80 from the Chamber of Commerce. He stood with his party leadership on two tough votes in 1990, opposing a constitutional amendment to ban flag desecration and backing the budget summit agreement.

Tallon is the only South Carolinian on the Agriculture Committee; he tends to his tobacco growers from a seat on the Peanuts and Tobacco Subcommittee. The 6th grows more leaf than any other district in the state, and Tallon vigorously defends the crop. For the most part, he has followed the lead on tobacco issues set forth by his Democratic neighbor, North Carolina's Charlie Rose, who chaired the Tobacco Subcommittee through the 101st Congress. In the 102nd Congress, Tallon became chairman of the Domestic Marketing, Consumer Relations and Nutrition Subcommittee, the panel that oversees food stamps and other government nutrition programs for the poor.

Tallon's Merchant Marine assignment gives him a voice in matters affecting the 6th's booming coastal population, centered on Myrtle Beach. In 1989, he worked to speed emergency aid to the 6th after Hurricane Hugo, which devastated areas on the South Carolina coast.

Tallon departed from his usual legislative agenda in 1989 to seek an investigation of a 1985 plane crash in Newfoundland that killed 248 U.S. soldiers returning from a Middle East peacekeeping mission. (A family from his district lost a son in the crash.) His drive led to a two-day hearing by the Judiciary Subcommittee on Crime, which concluded that the government had neglected to investigate the possibility of terrorism as a cause.

At Home: The owner of a chain of men's clothing stores that carries his name, Tallon was elected to Congress with only brief officeholding experience. His first real brush with politics came in 1979, when he attended the White House Conference on Small Business. He returned from it determined to enter politics as a spokesman for small business. In 1980 he easily won an open state House seat.

Tallon soon started aiming for GOP Rep. John L. Napier, who had defeated flamboyant Democratic Rep. John W. Jenrette Jr. in 1980, after his conviction in the Abscam bribery case. When a potentially strong Democratic competitor for 1982 got into a bribery scandal himself, Tallon became the choice of party leaders and past backers of Jenrette. He led in first-round primary voting and won the runoff handily.

Napier, only the second Republican in this century to win the 6th, nevertheless was favored. Tobacco farmers supported him, and he had more money than Tallon. Tallon focused on personal canvassing, especially among the district's 41 percent black population. He worked with church leaders to generate black support, built an extensive get-out-the-vote apparatus, and with a sluggish economy making things tough on Napier among white Democrats, Tallon won.

Tallon's low legislative profile as a freshman led to speculation he would be weak in 1984. But Napier skipped a rematch, and Tallon smashed party activist Mary Demetrious in the primary. The GOP line went to state Rep. Lois Eargle, a former Democrat. She tried to ride the Ronald Reagan-Strom Thurmond ticket, but failed.

Early in 1986 and again in 1988, rumors circulated that Jenrette might seek his old seat. He did not, and his 1989 shoplifting conviction in suburban Washington, D.C., removed him from political speculation.

South Carolina 6

East — Florence

Agriculture has traditionally dominated this district, with tobacco the crucial product. Horry County, in the eastern corner of the state, has one of the richest tobacco crops in the country. Broadleaf from Horry's fields is stored in warehouses and bid on at auctions in such towns as Darlington, Marion and Mullins.

But in recent years, industry and tourism have begun to diversify the economy. Industrial parks have cropped up across the 6th as counties work more aggressively to attract manufacturers.

Democrats still dominate the rural parts of the 6th. In 1988, this district was the best in the state for Massachusetts' Michael S. Dukakis; he took 44 percent of its presidential vote, in large part due to the poverty in counties such as Williamsburg and Marion.

Blacks make up more than 40 percent of the 6th's population, the largest proportion in any of South Carolina's districts. Williamsburg, Marion and Clarendon counties have black majorities, and blacks there are better-organized than in most of the South.

Coastal Horry County is one of the country's fastest-growing areas (42 percent in the 1980s), drawing visitors to the surf, hotels, golf courses and honky-tonk amusements of Myrtle Beach. In 1989, Hurricane Hugo caused serious damage to some areas along the coast and just inland, but affluent retirees continue to stream into Horry, building GOP strength in the county. The Air Force base at Myrtle Beach has been slated for closure by the Pentagon, eliminating some 4,000 military and civilians jobs.

Although small factories are scattered throughout the 6th, Florence is the district's industrial center. A railhead since the Civil War, it has drawn new plants and industries in recent years, accompanied by an influx of managerial people and GOP votes.

Population: 519,273. White 304,420 (59%), Black 212,151 (41%). Spanish origin 5,721 (1%). 18 and over 347,458 (67%), 65 and over 48,277 (9%). Median age: 28.

Committees

Agriculture (12th of 27 Democrats)
Domestic Marketing, Consumer Relations & Nutrition (chairman); Cotton, Rice & Sugar; Department Operations, Research & Foreign Agriculture

Merchant Marine & Fisheries (12th of 29 Democrats)
Fisheries & Wildlife Conservation & the Environment; Merchant Marine

Elections

1990 General		
Robin Tallon (D)	94,121	(100%)
1988 General		
Robin Tallon (D)	120,719	(76%)
Robert Cunningham Sr. (R)	37,958	(24%)

Previous Winning Percentages: **1986** (76%) **1984** (60%) **1982** (53%)

District Vote For President

	1988	1984	1980	1976
D	69,938 (44%)	68,572 (42%)	79,783 (53%)	84,895 (61%)
R	88,766 (56%)	92,605 (57%)	69,806 (46%)	52,984 (38%)

Campaign Finance

	Receipts	Receipts from PACs	Expend-itures
1990			
Tallon (D)	$231,293	$145,550 (63%)	$95,350
1988			
Tallon (D)	$381,464	$203,958 (53%)	$243,559
Cunningham (R)	$10,759	$100 (1%)	$10,604

Key Votes

1991	
Authorize use of force against Iraq	Y
1990	
Support constitutional amendment on flag desecration	N
Pass family and medical leave bill over Bush veto	N
Reduce SDI funding	N
Allow abortions in overseas military facilities	N
Approve budget summit plan for spending and taxing	Y
Approve civil rights bill	Y
1989	
Halt production of B-2 stealth bomber at 13 planes	Y
Oppose capital gains tax cut	N
Approve federal abortion funding in rape or incest cases	N
Approve pay raise and revision of ethics rules	N
Pass Democratic minimum wage plan over Bush veto	Y

Voting Studies

	Presidential Support		Party Unity		Conservative Coalition	
Year	**S**	**O**	**S**	**O**	**S**	**O**
1990	43	57	67	31	85	11
1989	56	41	61	37	88	12
1988	42	56	63	33	82	11
1987	42	56	68	29	81	16
1986	40	56	59	31	86	8
1985	41	56	69	25	84	16
1984	40	54	65	31	63	32
1983	32	66	79	20	55	43

Interest Group Ratings

Year	ADA	ACU	AFL-CIO	CCUS
1990	50	42	58	43
1989	50	46	58	80
1988	40	60	79	62
1987	44	39	81	60
1986	40	57	71	44
1985	45	48	53	50
1984	40	46	50	40
1983	75	33	76	33

South Dakota

U.S. CONGRESS

SENATE 1 D, 1 R

HOUSE 1 D

LEGISLATURE

Senate 17 D, 18 R

House 24 D, 46 R

ELECTIONS

1988 Presidential Vote	
Bush	53%
Dukakis	47%
1984 Presidential Vote	
Reagan	63%
Mondale	37%
1980 Presidential Vote	
Reagan	61%
Carter	32%
Anderson	7%
Turnout rate in 1986	57%
Turnout rate in 1988	62%
Turnout rate in 1990	50%

(as percentage of voting age population)

POPULATION AND GROWTH

1980 population	690,768
1990 population (45th in the nation)	696,004
Percent change 1980-1990	+1%

DEMOGRAPHIC BREAKDOWN

White	92%
Black	1%
American Indian, Eskimo, or Aleut	7%
(Hispanic origin)	1%
Urban	46%
Rural	54%
Born in state	71%
Foreign-born	1%

MAJOR CITIES

Sioux Falls	100,814
Rapid City	54,523
Aberdeen	24,927
Watertown	17,592
Brookings	16,270

AREA AND LAND USE

Area 75,952 sq. miles (16th)

Farm	90%
Forest	3%
Federally owned	6%

Gov. George S. Mickelson (R)
Of Brookings — Elected 1986

Born: Jan. 31, 1941, Mobridge, S.D.
Education: U. of South Dakota, B.S. 1963, J.D. 1965.
Military Service: Army, 1965-69.
Occupation: Lawyer.
Religion: Methodist.
Political Career: Brookings County state's attorney, 1970-74; S.D. House, 1975-81, Speaker 1978-79.
Next Election: 1994.

WORK

Occupations	
White-collar	45%
Blue-collar	24%
Service workers	15%
Government Workers	
Federal	9,205
State	16,524
Local	34,076

MONEY

Median family income	$ 15,993	(48th)
Tax burden per capita	$ 502	(49th)

EDUCATION

Spending per pupil through grade 12	$ 3,249	(41st)
Persons with college degrees	14%	(36th)

CRIME

Violent crime rate	136 per 100,000	(47th)

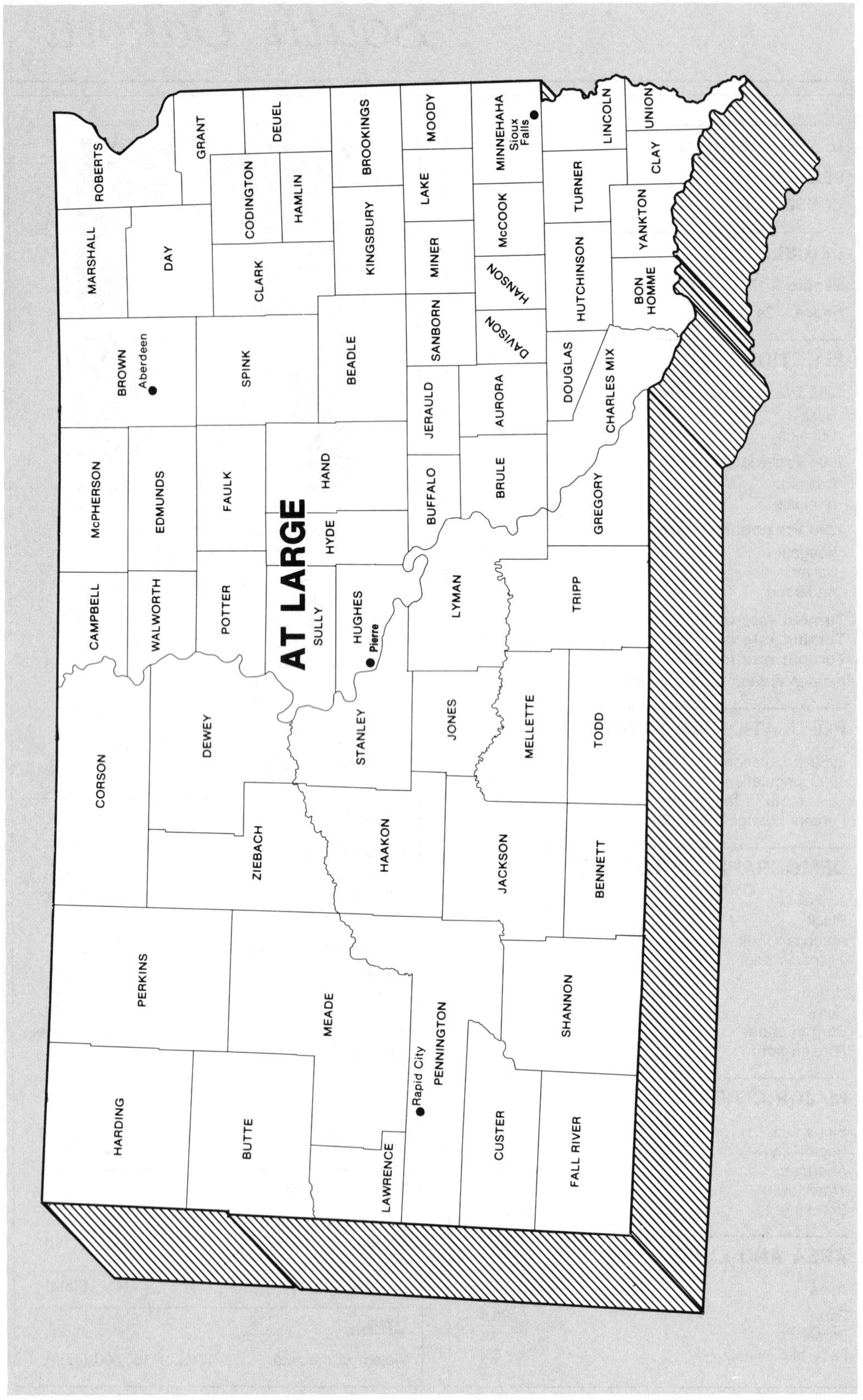
AT LARGE
ROBERTS
GRANT
DEUEL
BROOKINGS
MOODY
MINNEHAHA
Sioux Falls
LINCOLN
UNION
CLAY
CODINGTON
HAMLIN
LAKE
TURNER
McCOOK
YANKTON
MARSHALL
DAY
CLARK
KINGSBURY
MINER
HUTCHINSON
HANSON
BON HOMME
BROWN
Aberdeen
SPINK
BEADLE
SANBORN
DAVISON
DOUGLAS
CHARLES MIX
JERAULD
AURORA
McPHERSON
EDMUNDS
FAULK
HAND
BUFFALO
BRULE
GREGORY
HYDE
CAMPBELL
WALWORTH
POTTER
SULLY
HUGHES
Pierre
LYMAN
TRIPP
DEWEY
STANLEY
JONES
MELLETTE
TODD
CORSON
ZIEBACH
HAAKON
JACKSON
BENNETT
PERKINS
MEADE
PENNINGTON
Rapid City
SHANNON
HARDING
BUTTE
LAWRENCE
CUSTER
FALL RIVER

Larry Pressler (R)

Of Humboldt — Elected 1978

Born: March 29, 1942, Humboldt, S.D.
Education: U. of South Dakota, B.A. 1964; attended Oxford U., 1965; Harvard U., M.A. 1971, J.D. 1971.
Military Service: Army, 1966-68.
Occupation: Lawyer.
Family: Wife, Harriet Dent; one child.
Religion: Roman Catholic.
Political Career: U.S. House, 1975-79.
Capitol Office: 133 Hart Bldg. 20510; 224-5842.

In Washington: As the 100th Congress opened, Pressler took a seat on the Environment and Public Works Committee, just in time to tuck several million dollars' worth of South Dakota projects into highway and water pollution measures later vetoed by President Ronald Reagan. Pressler's override vote helped ensure road work at the Mount Rushmore National Memorial and erosion control along the Missouri River, which cuts through South Dakota.

Mission accomplished, Pressler traded Environment for the Banking Committee as the 101st Congress began. That panel has jurisdiction over coinage, and Pressler helped gain passage of a law to mint a coin commemorating the 50th anniversary of Mount Rushmore, with proceeds going for park improvements and to reduce the federal deficit. At the end of the 101st, Pressler left Banking.

Some might see this sort of committee hopping as parochial opportunism. But Pressler has always made plain his "South Dakota first" orientation. "I do err on the side of looking out for my state," he says.

Indeed, Pressler seems loath to stray far from the sentiments expressed in the office mail pouch. He watches the mail log like a hawk, and is as eager to discuss his constituent service (a response to every letter within 48 hours) as his stands on national issues. This approach makes Pressler very popular at home, but within the Senate it has left him short of attaining the rank of statesman.

During his 1990 campaign, Pressler was the target of a controversial public display of criticism from Democrat Wendell H. Ford of Kentucky, who serves with him on the Commerce, Science and Transportation Committee. Ford came to South Dakota to campaign in behalf of Pressler's opponent, Ted Muenster. Ford's view of Pressler, as reported in *The Washington Post*: "He doesn't work. He doesn't mingle. He doesn't prepare for anything."

Ford is hardly an unbiased observer of Pressler's work, but the South Dakota Republican has been stung before by suggestions that he cares only about publicity and winning elections, and he has worked hard to counter such criticism. After a dozen years in the Senate, he can claim involvement in debates on such important matters as nuclear arms control and U.S. policy toward South Africa.

But from time to time, Pressler acts in a manner that does not help him build an image as a serious legislator. One such episode was in early 1989, when Pressler seemed to cast himself as Hamlet for the nightly news during the drama of John Tower's nomination to be secretary of defense.

Pressler's was one of the few uncertain Republican votes on Tower. But while his colleague Nancy Landon Kassebaum of Kansas kept her counsel, Pressler deliberated publicly whether to confirm or not to confirm. In the days just before the vote, he was a favorite subject of media interviewers, and he seemed unable or unwilling to avoid sharing each step in his soul-searching.

Pressler said he had serious questions about Tower's ability to reform procurement practices and mismanagement at the Pentagon. Of particular concern to Pressler were the faulty electronics in the 34 B-1 bombers at Ellsworth Air Force Base, located near Rapid City, S.D. Before the vote, Pressler received specific assurances from the White House that the B-1s would be fixed. In the end, he voted for Tower.

As a rule, Pressler is sensitive to the ripple effect that legislation may have on what he sees as the oft-forgotten rural voter. For example, he sought a probe of whether prescription drug pricing is weighted against less-populated areas. He also opposed loosening restrictions on regional Bell telephone companies until one — U.S. West Inc. — revealed whether a $10 million settlement with the Justice Department for violating terms of the AT&T breakup would be passed on to ratepayers.

One of his legislative high points was a

1980 amendment to bar the use of federal funds to enforce the Carter administration's grain embargo against the Soviet Union. The amendment, opposed by Carter, passed the Senate but was dropped in conference.

Nonetheless, it was a signal of growing farm discontent with the embargo, and it contributed to the change of attitude that led the Reagan administration to cancel the embargo early the next year. This greatly enhanced Pressler's standing with South Dakota farmers.

Pressler's home-state focus often earns him scorn in the state's largest newspaper, the *Argus Leader* in Sioux Falls. Nonetheless, it plays well in towns such as Yankton, where after the local college shut down, Pressler combed the federal bureaucracy until he could find an agency willing to use its campus. The Bureau of Prisons complied, making plans for a minimum-security prison on the site.

The state's second largest industry is tourism, so it was not surprising that Pressler's first act as the newly installed chairman of the Commerce Subcommittee on Business, Trade and Tourism in 1981 was to move on a tourism promotion bill that had passed the Senate in the previous Congress but was vetoed by President Jimmy Carter. By the end of January, Pressler had pushed it through the Senate again, taking the Reagan administration by surprise and earning its opposition to the independent agency he proposed. Congress eventually cleared a tourism promotion bill, creating an office within the Commerce Department rather than the independent agency Pressler wanted.

Sensing an opening for the South Dakota School of Mines and Technology, Pressler has worked for several years to develop policy and authorize a program of continental drilling to explore the Earth's crust. He has also used his seat on the Commerce Committee to take on other constituent crusades. He has protected a federal satellite data center in his state and advocated for short-line railroads crucial to the farm economy.

For all the credit these activities earn Pressler at home, in Washington he still is prone to come across as unpredictable. In the early 1989 confirmation hearings of Secretary of State James A. Baker III, Pressler asked him about the Middle East and European trade before zeroing in on the diplomatic status of San Marino, a tiny mountain republic in eastern Italy. Though Baker conceded ignorance, the snickers in the audience did not stem from the secretary's geopolitical naiveté.

During an early 1987 hearing on the Nicaraguan contras, Pressler asked whether the contra forces would begin carrying out acts of terrorism. When an administration spokesman demurred, insisting that the contras would hit only military targets, Pressler responded, "I'm not saying that acts of terrorism are all necessarily bad."

Pressler might not have to be working so hard to burnish his reputation had he not launched his Senate career with a brief and implausible campaign for president in 1980. He argued the advantage of his youth (he was 37) and talked about the need to promote rural America. He withdrew after 105 days in which he raised little money, was left out of a key debate in Iowa and failed to carry on long enough to reach the voting in Iowa or New Hampshire. When he returned to the chamber early in 1980, he had a reputation for being a little flaky.

But the presidential campaign did lead to his most priceless national attention. Late in 1979, FBI agents posing as Arab sheiks invited him to a Georgetown house to offer him a bribe, knowing that he badly needed money for his presidential effort. Pressler refused to have anything to do with the offer, and stormed out of the meeting. It briefly made him a minor hero. "I turned down an illegal contribution," he said afterward. "Where have we come to if that's considered heroic?"

On the Foreign Relations Committee, Pressler over the years has exhibited a strong streak of independence. He is a swing vote who often joins with the Democrats.

He backed mild economic sanctions against South Africa in 1985, but when a harsher sanctions bill was proposed in 1986, Pressler opposed it. After a visit to South Africa, Pressler said he felt that the government there was moving toward reform, and that harsher sanctions would only hurt those they were intended to help.

Through the years, Pressler has been a consistent opponent of congressional pay raises and any mechanism that grants them without an up-or-down vote.

At Home: For years, Democrats regarded Pressler as though he were a boxer with a glass jaw. In spite of his unbeaten record in congressional races, they were confident that an aggressive, well-financed opponent cold beat him.

Democrats felt they had such a candidate in 1990 in Ted Muenster, a veteran political insider who had been a business executive, college vice president and chief of staff to Democratic Gov. Richard F. Kneip. Muenster boasted close ties to the state's business community and was on good terms with elements of the state GOP establishment unhappy with Pressler's frequent flights of independence. (In 1989 floor votes, Pressler had the highest presidential opposition score of any GOP senator.)

Muenster pounded away at the theme that Pressler was no longer the fresh-faced "farm boy from Humboldt" that South Dakota voters had first elected more than a decade earlier, but a professional politician who had lost touch with his home state in the pursuit of an upscale lifestyle in Washington. Yet in a year when anti-Congress sentiment ran high, Pressler's reputation for parochialism and independence worked to his advantage. His nearly yearlong media campaign reminded voters that he voted "South Dakota first."

To win, Muenster needed to carry his home base of Minnehaha County (Sioux Falls) and carve deeply into Pressler's rural base. But Muenster did neither. Pressler narrowly won populous Minnehaha, and his years of carefully cultivating the farm vote paid off with a sweep of 52 of South Dakota's 66 counties. Still, Pressler's tally against Muenster and a minor independent candidate was 52 percent, a lower percentage than in any of his previous House or Senate elections.

From the beginning of his political career, Pressler has offered South Dakota a political persona hard to resist: the good-natured, unassuming farm boy who succeeded early in life on sheer talent. His Rhodes scholarship and his Harvard master's degree combined perfectly with his roots on the Humboldt farm, still his official residence.

Those attributes were more than enough to give Pressler his 1974 victory over Democratic Rep. Frank Denholm. Pressler campaigned as a moderate Republican, noting his membership in Common Cause and criticizing South Dakota's Oahe irrigation project on environmental grounds. He took 55 percent. In 1976, he easily won a second term.

Democratic Sen. James Abourezk chose to retire in 1978, and Pressler began the campaign year as the odds-on favorite to succeed him. That never changed, even though Democrats had a competent challenger in former Rapid City Mayor Don Barnett. Pressler had built enormous good will through his faithful attendance at events all over the state (he still drives his 1928 John Deere "D" tractor in small-town parades), and through gestures such as donating a House pay increase to charity.

In 1984, Democrats offered George Cunningham, a longtime aide to former South Dakota Sen. George McGovern. Probably the nation's most colorful Senate loser that year, Cunningham denounced Pressler as a "flash-dancing, Fred Astaire type . . . who deals more with public relations than with public policy." But Cunningham admitted early in the year that his polling numbers were "in the toilet," and that is where they stayed. Pressler won 74 percent of the vote.

Committees

Commerce, Science & Transportation (3rd of 9 Republicans)
Science, Technology & Space (ranking); Communications; Surface Transportation; National Ocean Policy Study

Foreign Relations (4th of 8 Republicans)
European Affairs (ranking); Near Eastern & South Asian Affairs

Small Business (2nd of 8 Republicans)
Export Expansion (ranking); Rural Economy & Family Farming

Special Aging (2nd of 10 Republicans)

Elections

1990 General

Larry Pressler (R)	135,682	(52%)
Ted Muenster (D)	116,727	(45%)
Dean Sinclair (I)	6,567	(3%)

Previous Winning Percentages: **1984** (74%) **1978** (67%) **1976 *** (80%) **1974 *** (55%)

** House elections.*

Campaign Finance

	Receipts	Receipts from PACs		Expend-itures
1990				
Pressler (R)	$1,982,702	$861,339	(43%)	$1,664,341
Muenster (D)	$1,335,356	$492,661	(37%)	$1,323,770

Key Votes

1991

Authorize use of force against Iraq	Y

1990

Oppose prohibition of certain semiautomatic weapons	Y
Support constitutional amendment on flag desecration	Y
Oppose requiring parental notice for minors' abortions	N
Halt production of B-2 stealth bomber at 13 planes	Y
Approve budget that cut spending and raised revenues	N
Pass civil rights bill over Bush veto	N

1989

Oppose reduction of SDI funding	N
Oppose barring federal funds for "obscene" art	N
Allow vote on capital gains tax cut	Y

Voting Studies

	Presidential Support		Party Unity		Conservative Coalition	
Year	S	O	S	O	S	O
1990	58	39	74	22	49	46
1989	59	41	75	25	61	39
1988	73	25	88	10	97	3
1987	63	37	75	20	81	13
1986	77	20	72	25	82	16
1985	74	25	72	24	78	15
1984	61	39	50	44	72	23
1983	59	31	64	31	80	16
1982	70	24	67	20	77	13
1981	61	24	58	32	63	27

Interest Group Ratings

Year	ADA	ACU	AFL-CIO	CCUS
1990	22	83	0	83
1989	35	75	40	63
1988	0	96	29	79
1987	25	81	50	82
1986	10	86	33	68
1985	10	74	20	71
1984	45	45	55	71
1983	20	57	33	50
1982	10	67	35	70
1981	30	43	41	67

Tom Daschle (D)

Of Aberdeen — Elected 1986

Born: Dec. 9, 1947, Aberdeen, S.D.
Education: South Dakota State U., B.A. 1969.
Military Service: Air Force, 1969-72.
Occupation: Congressional aide.
Family: Wife, Linda Hall; three children.
Religion: Roman Catholic.
Political Career: U.S. House, 1979-87.
Capitol Office: 317 Hart Bldg. 20510; 224-2321.

In Washington: In a less agreeable politician, Daschle's ambition and rapid rise in Senate politics might provoke jealousy from colleagues. But the South Dakotan's engaging, almost deferential personality and his recognized ability to work within the system make him a favorite of senators above and below him on the seniority ladder.

No one expected Daschle, an activist House veteran and former Senate aide, to settle for a backbencher's role in the upper chamber. And Daschle almost invited trouble when he came over from the House with revolutionary rhetoric about changing the Senate's slow, tradition-bound ways: "Simply to come here and work in a museum is not my idea of a modern legislative process," he said.

But Daschle impressed senior members with his readiness to seek their counsel, and the veterans also were pleased with the internal reforms that Daschle and other young newcomers helped put in place, including steps to make the Senate's schedule more predictable.

Daschle seeks to build the relationships that grease legislative wheels — frequenting a senators-only lunchroom, for example, to pick up intelligence. He resists the go-it-alone style typical of the Senate, even objecting that it, unlike the House, assigns floor seating: "Camaraderie develops when you can move around," he has said. "The chemistry of intermixing — the collegiality — is very important to the way the House gets its work done."

He has shown a genius for choosing for the right mentors. Months before his election, he became the first Democrat in what would be the large and savvy 1986 class to endorse Robert C. Byrd's re-election as majority leader; Byrd in turn engineered Daschle's seating on the prestigious Finance Committee. When Byrd stepped aside in 1988, Daschle emerged as point man for the ultimate winner of a three-way succession race, George J. Mitchell; Mitchell then named Daschle co-chairman of the Democratic Policy Committee, a post previously held exclusively by the party leader.

Despite his popularity, Daschle does not yet have the seniority to be a first-string player in shaping major legislation. As co-chairman of the Policy Committee, Daschle has dusted off the organization and helped draft detailed policy papers — after due consultation with others, notably the proud committee chairmen.

So far in the Senate, Daschle has concentrated on the causes that dominated his House work — agriculture and veterans. On both the Finance and Agriculture committees, he has been able to help South Dakota's farmers.

During consideration of the 1990 farm bill, Daschle was a member of the "prairie populist" Senate faction that wanted to raise federal price support levels over those in the 1985 bill. This put them at odds not only with Republicans demanding further cuts, but also with many Democrats, including Agriculture Chairman Patrick J. Leahy, whose objective in the bill was to hold support levels steady.

While Daschle was at times passionate in his pleas for family farmers, he also revealed a pragmatic streak not evident in some of the fervent populists. "I think we have to assume that if we go to [higher price supports], we are going to face major opposition in the Congress," he said as Democrats fought among themselves over funding levels.

Daschle, along with Nebraska's Bob Kerrey, Iowan Tom Harkin and the other populists, wanted to drive a wedge between farmers and President Bush, as Democrats had done with the Reagan administration, enabling many of the party's 1986 candidates to run against the 1985 farm bill. But senior Democrats feared increased spending would derail the bill, and on vote after vote, the prairie populists lost to a coalition of senior Democrats, led by Leahy, and a united GOP. Daschle was among those voting against the final package. "For a lot of us," he explained, "there's just too much at stake to just go along and be a good guy."

Daschle uses his seat on Finance to help farmers in a variety of ways, and his clout should be enhanced now that he is chairman of the Energy and Agricultural Taxation Subcommittee. In the 101st Congress, Finance approved a tax break Daschle authored for corn-based ethanol fuels. (He also watches out for the ethanol industry as chairman of Agriculture's Subcommittee on Research.) In the 100th Congress, he helped repeal new taxes on farmers' diesel fuel and heifers, and added amendments to the trade bill that would encourage U.S. agricultural exports and threaten retaliation against foreign farm-import barriers.

Co-chairman of Vietnam-era Veterans in Congress, Daschle got a slot on the Veterans Affairs Committee at the start of the 102nd Congress. As a senator, he persisted in a campaign he began in the House to compensate Vietnam veterans for illnesses believed caused by exposure to the defoliant Agent Orange.

In the 100th Congress, he won Senate passage of legislation to compensate victims of two types of cancer related to Agent Orange, and to secure independent scientific research on the matter. Though the bill died in the House, Daschle moved quickly in 1991 to link the legislation to the swell of public support for the military brought on by the Persian Gulf conflict. Congress finally approved Agent Orange compensation legislation in early 1991.

Despite his charm and disarming candor, Daschle was a controversial figure in his earlier years at the House Agriculture Committee. Many of his proposals there went beyond anything likely to become law. They tended to put members of both parties in a spot, skeptical of the sums he wanted for farm subsidies but reluctant to oppose them. Daschle figured the more ambitious the plan, the better farmers would fare in the final compromise. But some Republicans condemned his projects, such as a 1981 farm crisis bill, as political demagoguery.

Generally, however, Daschle was a leadership favorite. He was close to Ways and Means Chairman Dan Rostenkowski, and was an effective insider on Steering and Policy, which makes Democratic committee assignments.

Early in 1985, Daschle's shrewd moves were the foundation for his successful Senate bid the next year. He won national attention as chief sponsor of a multibillion-dollar effort to advance credit to struggling farmers. Reagan vetoed the bill, but Daschle had reinforced his image as a defender of agriculture while his rival, GOP Sen. James Abdnor, had to struggle against being linked to administration stinginess.

A few months later, Daschle voted against the comprehensive farm bill, criticizing its price-support levels. Abdnor voted for the bill, giving Daschle a campaign issue.

At Home: When Daschle first began planning his Senate campaign, he was considered one of the Democrats' surest bets in 1986. The farm economy was on the ropes, and Abdnor had a reputation as bumbling and ineffective.

But Abdnor exceeded expectations, and Daschle needed all the organization and persistence he could muster to eke out a victory.

Abdnor faced a primary challenge from bombastic GOP Gov. William J. Janklow, who hammered at his support for Reagan farm policies and his inability to get things done. But Abdnor's consultants moved aggressively to inoculate the senator against charges of ineffectiveness, starting an extensive TV ad campaign in late 1985. Abdnor, whose amiable and low-key nature had endeared him to voters for nearly three decades, scored a strong primary victory.

Daschle then faced the challenge of framing the November contest as a referendum on Abdnor's politics, not his personality. The challenger showed considerable skill at controlling the campaign debate, and Abdnor handed him an issue shortly after the primary, when he stumbled at a forum by suggesting that farmers might have to "sell below cost" in order to become competitive.

In a long-running TV ad, Daschle showed Abdnor giving his faltering "below cost" explanation, and then he made his own forceful argument for a fair price for farmers. Abdnor said his remarks were misinterpreted, but his explanation did not erase the original flub.

The contest tightened considerably in the fall, however, with two visits by President Reagan and a bevy of personal attacks on Daschle over the airwaves. In his ads, Abdnor linked Daschle with actress and former anti-war activist Jane Fonda, who had been pictured with Daschle at a fund-raiser. Abdnor hoped to tie Daschle not only to Fonda's liberal reputation, but also to her efforts, in her health books, to discourage the consumption of red meat. Promoting vegetarianism in meat-producing South Dakota is a political felony.

Despite the Fonda connection and a concerted effort by media consultant Roger Ailes to convince the electorate that Abdnor was quietly effective, Daschle prevailed with his contention that Abdnor was instead effectively quiet. Daschle's massive effort to turn out the farm vote, along with his late October charge that Abdnor had voted to cut Social Security, gave him a narrow victory.

Daschle won his House seat originally on sheer energy. In a year, he and his first wife rang more than 40,000 doorbells as they campaigned to win the 1978 Democratic primary over Frank Denholm, the former representative favored to win, and then defeat Republican nominee Leo Thorsness.

The 1st District was open in 1978 with incumbent Larry Pressler running for the Senate. Early on, it seemed likely to go for Thorsness, a former prisoner of war in Vietnam who had drawn 47 percent of vote in a 1974 challenge to Democratic Sen. George McGovern.

But Daschle's non-stop campaign brought him even with Thorsness, and a few weeks before the election, Daschle looked like a winner. Then, however, Republicans began hitting Daschle on his opposition to an anti-abortion amendment and his promise to vote against right-to-work laws. The contest got close again; only a final canvass a week after Election Day gave Daschle a 139-vote win.

Daschle had become familiar with politics and legislation while working for Sen. James Abourezk as a legislative assistant. He moved back to South Dakota in late 1976 to become field director for Abourezk and to prepare his 1978 House campaign.

It took all of Daschle's ingenuity and public relations skill to win re-election in 1982, when reapportionment merged South Dakota's two districts and he met the state's other House incumbent, Republican Clint Roberts.

The contest matched not only the state's two parties, but also its two regions. Daschle represented the Corn Belt territory of eastern South Dakota; Roberts spoke for the western ranching counties. The Republican's homespun conservative style reflected western South Dakota's traditional resentment against a liberal Washington establishment.

Roberts tried to pin the Eastern label on Daschle, noting that while he had been running a ranch, Daschle had been on a government payroll most of his adult life. But Daschle told voters that what the state needed in Congress was not a farmer, but someone who knew how to write farm bills. Daschle had been traveling throughout the state for two years in preparation for the match; he was ahead in name recognition even in some of Roberts' areas. But Roberts' ample funding and his anti-establishment campaign brought him close. He took virtually every county in his old district, but Daschle got 59 percent in his eastern territory, for 52 percent overall.

In 1984, Daschle bucked the statewide GOP trend with a comfortable 57 percent re-election victory over Republican Dale Bell.

Committees

Agriculture, Nutrition & Forestry (8th of 10 Democrats)
Agricultural Research & General Legislation (chairman); Agricultural Credit; Rural Development & Rural Electrification

Finance (10th of 11 Democrats)
Energy & Agricultural Taxation (chairman); International Trade; Medicare & Long Term Care

Select Indian Affairs (4th of 9 Democrats)

Veterans' Affairs (7th of 7 Democrats)

Elections

1986 General		
Tom Daschle (D)	152,657	(52%)
James Abdnor (R)	143,173	(48%)

Previous Winning Percentages: **1984** * (57%) **1982** * (52%) **1980** * (66%) **1978** * (50%)

* *House elections.*

Campaign Finance

	Receipts	Receipts from PACs		Expend-itures
1986				
Daschle (D)	$3,515,482	$1,153,906	(33%)	$3,485,870
Abdnor (R)	$3,306,567	$1,076,326	(33%)	$3,291,101

Key Votes

1991	
Authorize use of force against Iraq	N
1990	
Oppose prohibition of certain semiautomatic weapons	N
Support constitutional amendment on flag desecration	N
Oppose requiring parental notice for minors' abortions	Y
Halt production of B-2 stealth bomber at 13 planes	Y
Approve budget that cut spending and raised revenues	Y
Pass civil rights bill over Bush veto	Y
1989	
Oppose reduction of SDI funding	N
Oppose barring federal funds for "obscene" art	Y
Allow vote on capital gains tax cut	N

Voting Studies

	Presidential Support		Party Unity		Conservative Coalition	
Year	**S**	**O**	**S**	**O**	**S**	**O**
1990	31	66	87	12	41	59
1989	49	51	90	9	24	76
1988	44	52	91	6	30	70
1987	37	62	88	12	44	53
House Service						
1986	20	80	84	15	44	56
1985	16	71	83	9	33	55
1984	32	60	67	17	41	53
1983	16	76	75	12	42	51
1982	31	62	80	14	34	56
1981	42	57	77	17	37	60

Interest Group Ratings

Year	ADA	ACU	AFL-CIO	CCUS
1990	83	9	56	33
1989	80	7	90	50
1988	85	13	93	36
1987	85	8	89	33
House Service				
1986	80	18	64	22
1985	70	16	60	38
1984	70	17	46	50
1983	75	17	71	42
1982	80	40	89	35
1981	70	20	71	22

AL Tim Johnson (D)

Of Vermillion — Elected 1986

Born: Dec. 28, 1946, Canton, S.D.
Education: U. of South Dakota, B.A. 1969, M.A. 1970, J.D. 1975.
Occupation: Lawyer.
Family: Wife, Barbara Brooks; three children.
Religion: Lutheran.
Political Career: S.D. House, 1979-83; S.D. Senate, 1983-87.
Capitol Office: 428 Cannon Bldg. 20515; 225-2801.

In Washington: A tenacious advocate for his state's farm commodities, Johnson leaves little doubt about what he seeks when he addresses the Agriculture Committee: He wants more. But his quiet and thoughtful style has allowed him to pursue his interests without generating undue contention.

In the 101st Congress, much of the committee's time was devoted to the 1990 farm bill, a five-year reauthorization of farm programs. Johnson suggested a program to set a loan level for oilseeds, such as sunflower, canola and safflower, that would make growing them as financially attractive as growing wheat, the most common crop in oilseed regions. The Wheat, Soybeans and Feed Grains Subcommittee adopted his amendment to support the price of sunflowers and other oilseeds at 10.5 cents per pound. The price dropped to 8.5 cents by the time the bill was passed, however.

Johnson also pressed for higher price-support levels for dairy products. Lawmakers decided to place a floor under the previously sliding scale of subsidies, assuring dairy farmers of a base rate of $10.10 per hundred pounds of milk product. But others sought a higher level. An amendment to raise the rate to $10.60 fell on a 14-24 vote. Johnson proposed raising the rate by $3 to $13.10; his amendment lost 13-28.

Johnson is also concerned with oats, a crop South Dakota leads the nation in harvesting. In 1987, he added his Oats Promotion Act to the budget reconciliation bill. The measure allowed more oats to be planted in 1988-90, exempting the crop from acreage limitation requirements.

Johnson won a spot on the Interior Committee in 1989, following the resignation of Majority Whip Tony Coelho. He intends to use his post to work on Indian issues as well as to seek authority for water projects.

Johnson worked with South Dakota's senators, Democrat Tom Daschle and Republican Larry Pressler, in 1988 to pass a bill authorizing a $100 million drinking-water project for south-central South Dakota. The Mni Wiconi project was needed, Johnson said, because the water in the area contained unsafe levels of chemicals, minerals and other impurities. The fiscal 1990 energy and water appropriations bill contained the first installment of funding for the project.

In the 101st Congress, Johnson won enactment of a bill to mint gold, silver and ordinary coins to commemorate the 50th anniversary of the Mount Rushmore National Memorial. President Bush also signed his bill to exchange some 12,000 acres of Black Hills forest land in South Dakota owned by a California mining company with U.S. Forest land in Colorado.

During House debate on the 1988 omnibus drug bill, Johnson won approval for his amendment concerning drunken driving. His proposal provided grants to states to implement an anti-drunken-driving enforcement program, but only if the state requires immediate suspension of the driver's license of anyone found driving while drunk.

At Home: A knack for organization and an instinct for knowing how to deal with an opponent who was his own worst enemy propelled Johnson to a resounding first-term victory in 1986. During a political year dominated by militant farm protest on the Dakota plains, Johnson managed to succeed without being a farmer or sounding militant about any subject under discussion.

Johnson's campaign came a long way in a short time. A little-known state senator from the extreme southeast corner of the state, he had not even been the early favorite in his own party to capture the seat left open by Daschle's Senate candidacy.

To win the Democratic nomination, Johnson had to defeat a folksy state senator with longstanding farm credentials; state Sen. Jim Burg had received national publicity when he led a delegation of state legislators on a farm protest mission to Washington in 1985.

The cerebral Johnson, who was one of only two attorneys in the state Senate, sometimes seemed to be arguing a case when he was socializing with voters. But a strong organization and a sophisticated direct-mail effort lifted him to a narrow primary victory.

The Republican nominee, Dale Bell, began

South Dakota — At Large

The Missouri River running north to south through the center of South Dakota divides not only the geography and economy of the state, but also its political predilections.

The flat, rich farmland east of the river holds two-thirds of the state's population and nourishes an agricultural economy based on corn. Voters in the east tend to support Democrats. "West River" is rolling, arid grassland suited for grazing and ranching. Most voters there are staunch Republicans.

The primacy of corn is symbolized by the Corn Palace in Mitchell, an auditorium whose exterior is festooned with mosaics made from colored corn cobs. Corn feeds cattle and hogs, and it provides the largest share of agricultural income in the state.

Not far from Mitchell is the focal point of eastern South Dakota and the state's largest metropolis, Sioux Falls. The city grew 24 percent in the 1980s, to 101,000, as it made the transition from meatpacking town to regional commercial hub. Today, it is a service center whose banks, insurance companies and farm implement dealers are all tied closely to the agricultural economy.

Efforts to diversify the state's economy have succeeded in attracting banking credit card operations and light manufacturing to eastern towns such as Watertown and Brookings. Automotive parts and plastics plants have crossed the border from Minnesota, attracted by South Dakota's comparatively low taxes and regulatory costs.

On the western side of the Missouri, the towns are fewer. The land, used for grazing, gradually turns from green to brown. The relatively sedate farms of the east are contrasted with the cowboy and rodeo country of the west. Much of the majestic, high plains scenery from the 1990 Academy Award-winning film "Dances With Wolves" was shot here. Near the western border of the state is South Dakota's second-largest city, Rapid City, with a population over 54,000. Originally a market for surrounding ranchers and farmers, it grew rapidly in the 1970s and has now settled into a prosperity matched only by Sioux Falls. Tourism has been an important factor in the growth: The Badlands, the Black Hills and Mount Rushmore are nearby. Legalized gambling has rejuvenated the town of Deadwood, creating a gold rush 115 years after the precious metal was discovered in a nearby stream. Adding to population growth near Rapid City are retirees who come to live in the Black Hills.

The west-central and southwestern parts of the state are home to many Indians who have returned to the reservations from jobs that disappeared in the Midwestern industrial centers. Of the six counties west of the Missouri won by Democrat Tom Daschle in his close 1986 Senate contest, five were on reservations.

Disenchantment with the Reagan administration's farm policy hindered George Bush's 1988 presidential bid, both in the GOP primary and in November against Democratic nominee Michael S. Dukakis. Bush won the state over Dukakis with 53 percent, well below Ronald Reagan's 60 percent-plus showings in 1980 and 1984.

Population: 690,768. White 639,669 (93%), Black 2,144 (0.3%), American Indian, Eskimo and Aleut 44,968 (7%). Spanish origin 4,023 (1%). 18 and over 485,162 (70%), 65 and over 91,019 (13%). Median age: 29.

with widespread name recognition stemming from two previous statewide campaigns. But Bell's belligerent ideological conservatism and the contentious nature of his earlier campaigns left him with negative ratings that amounted to a political consultant's nightmare. In a state ripe with resentment of Reagan administration farm policies, 1986 was not a good year for a Republican candidate already burdened with political baggage.

Johnson's strategy was to avoid controversy and make himself the vehicle for Bell's critics in both parties; he presented himself simply as a moderate and experienced alternative to Bell. In the Legislature, Johnson had maintained friendly relations with both sides and worked well with GOP Gov. William J. Janklow. His approach won him backing from the state's major banking interests and the Realtors' association.

Bell tried labeling Johnson a George McGovern liberal and a captive of special interests. At the same time, Bell, whose strength had always been among "movement conservatives," tried to distance himself from Reagan farm policies, developing an opposition-style theme of "Send them a message." The voters sent Bell a message instead, giving Johnson victories in 53 of the state's 66 counties and nearly 60 percent of the overall vote.

In 1988, the state's leading Republicans assessed their chances of unseating Johnson and chose to skip the race. Janklow and former GOP Sen. James Abdnor declined to challenge Johnson, leaving state Treasurer David Volk to lead the GOP charge. Despite having won statewide elections since 1972, Volk was relatively little known by voters, since the treasurer's job is not a high-visibility one.

Unlike in 1986, the GOP united behind their candidate in 1988; prominent Republicans such as Janklow, Abdnor and Gov. George S. Mickelson held fundraisers for Volk and pledged their support.

Unfortunately for Volk, Johnson's cautious first-term record gave the Republican no compelling ammunition. For that reason, much of Volk's campaign dwelt on a single issue — campaign finance. Volk spent his time criticizing Johnson's acceptance of political action committee money (Volk refused to take PAC contributions).

The PAC attack failed to impress voters. Johnson carried every county in the state on the way to a 72 percent victory, keeping alive a 90-year streak: South Dakota voters have not unseated a freshman House member in a general election since 1898.

Johnson's victory — the biggest statewide winning margin for a Democrat and the second-largest for any candidate in state history — sparked talk that he might run for higher office.

Johnson, though, decided not to take that leap in 1990. In the fall of 1989, he announced that he would not challenge Pressler's Senate re-election the following year. Johnson's 1990 House re-election campaign was anticlimactic. He won two-thirds of the vote against a Republican opponent who proposed reducing House membership to 300 as a budget-cutting move.

Committees

Agriculture (19th of 27 Democrats)
Conservation, Credit & Rural Development; Livestock, Dairy & Poultry; Wheat, Soybeans & Feed Grains

Interior & Insular Affairs (23rd of 29 Democrats)
National Parks & Public Lands; Water, Power & Offshore Energy

Select Children, Youth & Families (17th of 22 Democrats)

Elections

1990 General		
Tim Johnson (D)	173,814	(68%)
Don Frankenfeld (R)	83,484	(32%)
1988 General		
Tim Johnson (D)	223,759	(72%)
David Volk (R)	88,157	(28%)

Previous Winning Percentage: **1986** (59%)

District Vote For President

	1988	1984	1980	1976
D	145,560 (47%)	200,267 (63%)	103,855 (32%)	147,068 (49%)
R	165,415 (53%)	116,113 (37%)	198,343 (61%)	151,505 (50%)
I			21,431 (7%)	

Campaign Finance

	Receipts	Receipts from PACs		Expend-itures
1990				
Johnson (D)	$516,816	$251,800	(49%)	$463,625
Frankenfeld (R)	$215,087	$6,608	(3%)	$211,617
1988				
Johnson (D)	$676,225	$329,446	(49%)	$632,105
Volk (R)	$200,733	0		$199,420

Key Votes

1991	
Authorize use of force against Iraq	N
1990	
Support constitutional amendment on flag desecration	Y
Pass family and medical leave bill over Bush veto	Y
Reduce SDI funding	Y
Allow abortions in overseas military facilities	Y
Approve budget summit plan for spending and taxing	N
Approve civil rights bill	Y
1989	
Halt production of B-2 stealth bomber at 13 planes	Y
Oppose capital gains tax cut	Y
Approve federal abortion funding in rape or incest cases	Y
Approve pay raise and revision of ethics rules	N
Pass Democratic minimum wage plan over Bush veto	Y

Voting Studies

	Presidential Support		Party Unity		Conservative Coalition	
Year	**S**	**O**	**S**	**O**	**S**	**O**
1990	25	75	82	17	54	46
1989	34	66	83	17	41	59
1988	25	75	77	22	66	34
1987	26	74	84	14	56	44

Interest Group Ratings

Year	ADA	ACU	AFL-CIO	CCUS
1990	67	25	83	36
1989	85	21	83	40
1988	70	28	93	36
1987	80	13	81	27

Tennessee

U.S. CONGRESS

SENATE 2 D
HOUSE 6 D, 3 R

LEGISLATURE

Senate 19 D, 14 R
House 57 D, 42 R

ELECTIONS

1988 Presidential Vote

Bush	58%
Dukakis	42%

1984 Presidential Vote

Reagan	58%
Mondale	42%

1980 Presidential Vote

Reagan	49%
Carter	48%
Anderson	2%

Turnout rate in 1986	31%
Turnout rate in 1988	45%
Turnout rate in 1990	19%

(as percentage of voting age population)

POPULATION AND GROWTH

1980 population	4,591,120
1990 population (17th in the nation)	4,877,185
Percent change 1980-1990	+6%

DEMOGRAPHIC BREAKDOWN

White	83%
Black	16%
Asian or Pacific Islander	1%
(Hispanic origin)	1%
Urban	60%
Rural	40%
Born in state	72%
Foreign-born	1%

MAJOR CITIES

Memphis	610,337
Nashville-Davidson	510,784
Knoxville	165,121
Chattanooga	152,466
Clarksville	75,494

AREA AND LAND USE

Area 41,155 sq. miles (34th)

Farm	47%
Forest	50%
Federally owned	7%

Gov. Ned McWherter (D)
Of Dresden — Elected 1986

Born: Oct. 15, 1930, Palmersville, Tenn.
Education: Graduated Dresden H.S., 1948.
Military Service: Army National Guard, 1948-69.
Occupation: Farmer; businessman.
Religion: Methodist.
Political Career: Tenn. House, 1969-87, Speaker, 1973-87.
Next Election: 1994.

WORK

Occupations

White-collar	48%
Blue-collar	38%
Service workers	12%

Government Workers

Federal	56,773
State	87,528
Local	187,938

MONEY

Median family income	$ 16,564	(44th)
Tax burden per capita	$ 630	(48th)

EDUCATION

Spending per pupil through grade 12	$ 3,068	(44th)
Persons with college degrees	13%	(44th)

CRIME

Violent crime rate	549 per 100,000 (19th)

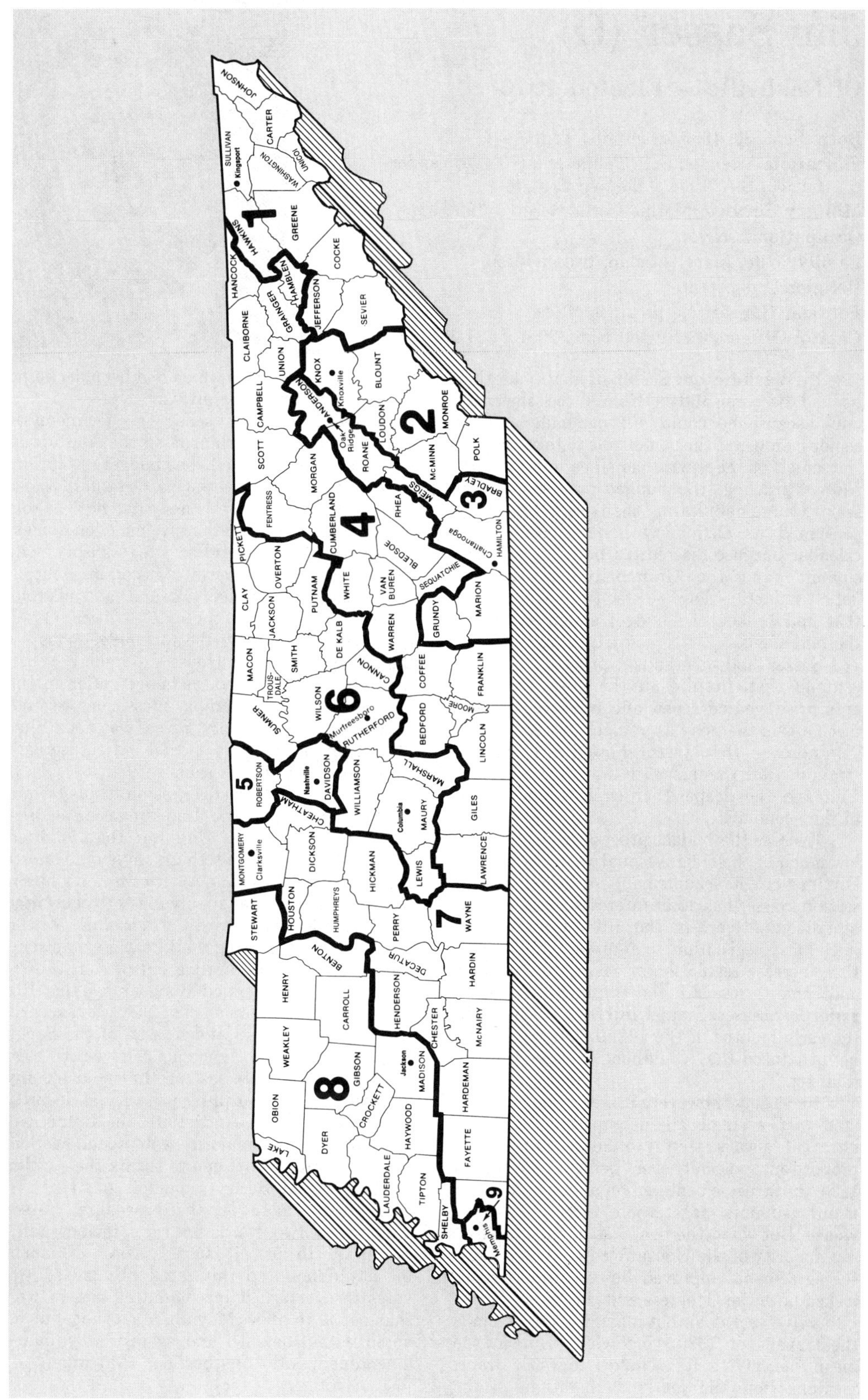
JOHNSON
CARTER
SULLIVAN
Kingsport
WASHINGTON
UNICOI
1
HAWKINS
GREENE
HANCOCK
HAMBLEN
COCKE
GRAINGER
JEFFERSON
SEVIER
CLAIBORNE
UNION
KNOX
Knoxville
BLOUNT
ANDERSON
Oak Ridge
CAMPBELL
LOUDON
2
MONROE
SCOTT
ROANE
McMINN
POLK
MORGAN
MEIGS
BRADLEY
3
FENTRESS
CUMBERLAND
RHEA
4
PICKETT
BLEDSOE
Chattanooga
HAMILTON
OVERTON
CLAY
JACKSON
PUTNAM
WHITE
VAN BUREN
SEQUATCHIE
GRUNDY
MARION
MACON
SMITH
DE KALB
WARREN
TROUS-DALE
CANNON
COFFEE
FRANKLIN
SUMNER
WILSON
6
Murfreesboro
RUTHERFORD
MOORE
BEDFORD
LINCOLN
5
ROBERTSON
Nashville
DAVIDSON
WILLIAMSON
MARSHALL
CHEATHAM
Columbia
MAURY
GILES
MONTGOMERY
Clarksville
DICKSON
HICKMAN
LEWIS
LAWRENCE
STEWART
HOUSTON
HUMPHREYS
PERRY
7
WAYNE
BENTON
DECATUR
HARDIN
HENRY
CARROLL
HENDERSON
CHESTER
McNAIRY
WEAKLEY
GIBSON
Jackson
MADISON
HARDEMAN
8
OBION
CROCKETT
HAYWOOD
FAYETTE
LAKE
DYER
LAUDERDALE
TIPTON
SHELBY
9
Memphis

Jim Sasser (D)

Of Nashville — Elected 1976

Born: Sept. 30, 1936, Memphis, Tenn.
Education: Attended U. of Tennessee, 1954-55; Vanderbilt U., B.A. 1958, J.D. 1961.
Military Service: Marine Corps Reserve, 1957-63.
Occupation: Lawyer.
Family: Wife, Mary Gorman; two children.
Religion: Protestant.
Political Career: No previous office.
Capitol Office: 363 Russell Bldg. 20510; 224-3344.

In Washington: Sasser used to joke that he had become Budget Committee chairman only because he could not persuade a more senior member of the committee to take the job. But much of the mirth has since left the jest. Always grueling, the budget process in 1990 seemed more debilitating than ever. It not only consumed its customary lion's share of the calendar but also discredited both the "budget summit" and the Gramm-Rudman-Hollings deficit-reduction law — the two mechanisms that had broken the budget stalemates since the mid-1980s.

Sasser and his budget-process confrères contend that, despite all the grief, the 1990 enterprise created a new and improved budget mechanism: the "pay as you go" system. While yet unproven, that system showed early signs of strain in 1991 thanks to the war in the Persian Gulf and the deeper-than-expected downturn in the economy.

Even as the budget process seems to swallow much of the congressional year, it obscures anything else its leaders happen to do in a given session. Sasser has other interests and serves on other committees. In the 101st Congress, he introduced legislation to improve child nutrition, increase regulation of savings institutions and enhance research and training for treating geriatric diseases. Similar interests beckoned in the early months of the 102nd Congress, when he introduced the "Childhood Hunger Prevention Act."

Inevitably, however, Sasser is now associated with a single all-encompassing problem, one that always seems to be reaching crisis proportions without ever being resolved. In 1990, the struggle centered on a four-and-a-half month summit negotiation with the White House. But when the deal was done, a bipartisan majority of the House rejected it. A successor agreement, approved before adjournment, locked both the Congress and the White House into a five-year deal that may, if it works, make the travails of 1990 worthwhile. But in the meantime, giving it a chance to work drains meaning from the yearly deliberations of the budget committees — which had been declining in perceived firepower anyway.

No one on Budget senses this decline more keenly than Sasser, who sits on the Appropriations Committee as well. The budget resolution, he admits, is "hardly the battleground it has been in past years." Yet, Sasser defends the role of Budget. "The allocations we make on domestic discretionary spending are advisory," he says, "but they have a way of becoming policy."

Although personally genial and likable, Sasser is regarded as the most political of the four men who occupy the top budget jobs for the two parties in the House and Senate. When the White House made a budget offer in the spring of 1990, for example, most congressional leaders were conciliatory. Sasser was not. "Simply putting a new suit on that old corpse isn't going to revive it," he said.

Sasser's sharper edge was on display again in the months between Iraq's invasion of Kuwait and the Persian Gulf war that followed early in 1991. "I don't think we should mortgage the future of young Americans and generations unborn in a war simply to try to guarantee ourselves a lower price for gasoline at the pump," he said, fearing that the war would send the budget deficit spiraling out of control.

Sasser also rankled Budget's ranking Republican Pete V. Domenici of New Mexico early in 1991 over the emotional issue of the Social Security trust fund. Domenici believed the 1990 deal had set 60 votes as the threshold for any vote affecting the surplus in the Social Security trust fund. But in April 1991, the Democrats wanted a simple majority vote to allow Sen. Daniel Patrick Moynihan to shrink the surplus (with a Social Security payroll tax cut). In committee debate on the procedure, Sasser pointed to two words in the previous fall's resolution to permit such a vote. Domenici bitterly denounced this tactic but lacked the votes to overturn it in committee. Sasser won that battle to allow Moynihan his shot, but he voted with Domenici and against Moynihan's amendment later on the floor (Moynihan got just 38 votes).

There is a paradox in Sasser assuming the point-man's job in budgetary debates. As chairman of a committee closely divided between the parties, he must be far more accommodating of Republicans than House Budget Chairman Leon E. Panetta, who has enough Democratic votes to prevail more easily at the committee level.

All the same, if Sasser is not free to play the budget game on politics alone, he has found himself well-suited for presenting a budget message with a Democratic spin. Thus when he recounts the details of the deal for fiscal 1991, he readily stresses the new tax rate for those earning more than $175,000 per annum and the tightening of allowed deductions on incomes greater than $125,000.

Sasser has also discovered within himself a capacity for hardball that befits a chairman, even if it does not win friends. In the spring of 1991 he insisted on observing a previous agreement to shrink the Budget Committee by one Democrat and one Republican, even though that meant dumping the high-profile Democrat Charles S. Robb of Virginia, a member of the committee for two years. Robb accused Sasser of punishing him for his conservatism and independence on committee votes. Sasser denied any such motivation and asked a reluctant Democratic Senate leadership to back him up. Robb's seat on the committee was deleted.

Sasser had spent more than a decade in the Senate without a major focus before becoming the reluctant heir to the Budget job at the start of the 101st Congress.

While he is now responsible for the broad fiscal outlines and policy implications of a $1.45 trillion federal budget, previously he had picked at its million-dollar footnotes and line items to ferret out waste and fraud. He once boasted of saving $2 million a year by barring federal funds for watering indoor plants.

In his first dozen years on Budget, Sasser had rarely been a major participant in its deliberations, and in the mid-1980s he told a reporter he wanted off. Sasser remained, but even so, he did not seem eager to claim the top seat when Chairman Lawton Chiles announced his impending retirement in 1988. Sasser was third in line, but the more senior Democrats — Ernest F. Hollings and J. Bennett Johnston — already were committee chairmen.

Sasser did not distinguish himself in his debut, helping to draft the fiscal 1990 budget in 1989. But neither did anyone else. President Bush was intent on setting a more conciliatory tone than existed throughout President Ronald Reagan's tenure, and Congress proved willing to accept bipartisanship over serious deficit reduction.

For nine weeks the two sides talked. Panetta moved aggressively, confident House Democrats would back him; Sasser was more cautious, reflecting both his nature and relative inexperience. By April the negotiators had a compromise budget that met the law's $100 billion deficit target, thanks mainly to accounting gimmicks, rosy economic assumptions and unspecified taxes.

Though the pact drew many scoffs, lawmakers were in no mood to fight. With rare speed and bipartisanship, Sasser and Panetta squired the compromise through both houses and a conference by mid-May. "This is the best we can do at this particular time in our history," Sasser told the Senate.

Once Sasser agreed to head Budget, he allowed that the job "offers a significant opportunity to affect some of the major issues of the day." Until then, Sasser had gravitated to the minutiae of policy. He came to Congress at a time when federal waste and fraud were emerging as potent political issues, but he had a difficult time moving beyond them to address complex national problems.

He persuaded the General Accounting Office to install a toll-free hot line for citizens to report government fraud, and claimed to have saved $500 million by attacking federal employees' travel costs. But lacking the flair for self-promotion of other such crusaders, Sasser remained one of the lesser-known, least visible senators.

Sasser had begun assuming a broader role in foreign policy debates. He spoke out against Reagan's policies in Central America aimed at Nicaragua, and tried to develop a consensus Democratic stand on contra aid that would put the party on record in support of a diplomatic solution without seeming to overlook Nicaragua's anti-democratic actions. But even on that issue, Sasser's involvement sprang from his line-by-line approach to policy-making.

In the 98th Congress, while others debated overall U.S. strategy in Central America, Sasser was studying federal spending for construction of military facilities in Honduras, Nicaragua's neighbor. As ranking Democrat — and chairman since 1987 — of the Appropriations Subcommittee on Military Construction, he concluded the Reagan administration was preparing for potential armed intervention in the region. Landing strips and facilities for temporary use in training exercises actually were intended to be permanent, Sasser argued. But he had mixed success in attacking the spending in Honduras.

When Reagan made a televised pitch for contra aid in 1986, Democratic leaders picked Sasser to give the party's response. That year, Sasser offered his own proposal tying aid to renewed negotiations; if Nicaragua's rulers refused to negotiate, military aid would be released to the rebels. But that satisfied neither those who favored immediate aid nor those who wanted none at all. Sasser's amendment was rejected by a 2-to-1 margin.

He later adopted a more critical approach.

"We're going precisely down the path that this country traveled in Vietnam," he said in August. He did better with a proposal to kill the entire program, losing 54-46.

In the 100th Congress, Sasser had a high-profile role on another issue, after a 1987 Iraqi attack on a U.S. frigate in the Persian Gulf drew critical attention to the Reagan policy of providing Navy escorts for Kuwaiti tankers there. Sasser was part of a Democratic leadership team that reviewed military plans for the escort policy. Also, then-Majority Leader Robert C. Byrd named Sasser one of three senators to go to the Middle East to investigate. Upon his return from the region, Sasser said Reagan should either get Kuwait to withdraw its request for protection or enlist allies' help. "We should not sail in the gulf's troubled waters alone," he said.

Such policy ventures have been real departures from Sasser's past concentration on government economy. When he chaired Appropriations' Legislative Branch Subcommittee, Sasser fought efforts to increase congressional and executive branch pay, and to suspend the limit on senators' outside income — to the occasional irritation of other senators.

Sasser came to the Senate as a loyal supporter of Jimmy Carter. He cooled, however, when the administration opposed some Tennessee federal projects, such as the Tellico Dam that was held up on environmental grounds. Pressed to vote with Carter to transfer the Panama Canal, Sasser did, but not without complaint.

Though Sasser has maintained a liberal-to-moderate record, votes on such issues as the Persian Gulf, the Panama Canal and social controversies do not come easy to a man from a conservative Southern state. One with potentially serious political consequences occurred in 1982, a Sasser re-election year, when he cast the tie-breaking procedural vote to kill Jesse Helms' amendment aimed at restricting abortions. But he consistently supported Helms' bid to restore voluntary prayer in public schools by stripping federal courts of jurisdiction over the issue.

At Home: Sasser's 1976 Senate campaign in behalf of "a government that reflects our decency" bore a pronounced and deliberate similarity to Carter's call for "a government as good as its people." When Carter won the Tennessee presidential primary that year with 78 percent of the vote, Sasser joked that he wanted not only to cling to Carter's coattails, but to get inside the coat.

It was a successful strategy. In November, Carter won Tennessee by nearly 200,000 votes, helping Sasser to a comfortable victory over GOP Sen. William E. Brock III, who a year earlier was considered safe for re-election.

Sasser had used his three-year chairmanship of the state Democratic Party to lay a base of support. His chief Democratic rival was liberal Nashville businessman John J. Hooker, whose unsuccessful tries for the governorship in 1966 and 1970 had given him wide name recognition but a loser's image. Sasser was endorsed by several minority and labor groups who saw him as a fresh face and a possible winner. With support from most of the party leadership, he defeated Hooker convincingly.

Brock displayed the same organizing skill that later was to make him a successful national GOP chairman. But his background as a candy heir, his upper-crust image and his quiet personal style contrasted unfavorably with Sasser's down-to-earth manner and ready humor.

Sasser portrayed Brock as a country-club Republican, a special-interest senator representing banks and insurance companies. It was a perfect issue in a state always susceptible to populist rhetoric, and doubly so with Carter reinforcing Sasser's themes.

Since Sasser compiled a generally non-controversial record and avoided political blunders during his first term, he was well positioned for re-election in 1982. Some conservative Republicans thought Sasser's support was soft, and on that supposition GOP Rep. Robin L. Beard gave up a safe House district to try for the Senate.

Beard failed utterly in searching for a theme that would induce voters to desert Sasser. At first, Beard called Sasser a free-spending "Kennedy liberal." In his ads he unveiled a small plastic mouse, dubbed "flipping Jimmy," meant to convince voters that Sasser had shifted from left to center as his re-election neared. In the end, Beard was stressing abortion and school prayer in an attempt to mobilize religious fundamentalists and others with strong feelings on social issues.

Sasser occasionally sparred with Beard, but mostly he stressed his work to improve government accounting practices and reduce bureaucratic costs. He was able to stay on the offensive by blaming economic hard times on Reaganomics. Beard had to contend with Tennesseans' lukewarm feelings for Reagan — Carter nearly carried the state in 1980 — and with an unemployment rate that was above the national average throughout 1982.

Sasser buried Beard in Middle and West Tennessee, and even carried traditionally Republican East Tennessee; no Democrat had done that since the GOP began seriously contesting statewide elections in the mid-1960s.

Sasser's 1982 showing was still on many minds six years later. GOP leaders again insisted Sasser's support was soft, but they failed to recruit a proven vote-getter, such as former GOP Gov. Lamar Alexander.

Their nominee was little-known Kingsport attorney Bill Andersen, a candidate who spent much of his considerable energy introducing himself to members of his own party.

Andersen criticized Sasser as a man lacking the stature of the state's other leading politicians, including junior Democratic Sen. Al Gore and Alexander. But Andersen had trouble raising money and was not really in a position to talk about stature. Again Sasser romped, taking all but one county in Republican East Tennessee.

Committees

Budget (Chairman)

Appropriations (7th of 16 Democrats)
Military Construction (chairman); Commerce, Justice, State & Judiciary; Defense; Energy & Water Development; Transportation

Banking, Housing & Urban Affairs (6th of 12 Democrats)
Housing & Urban Affairs; Securities

Governmental Affairs (4th of 8 Democrats)
General Services, Federalism & the District of Columbia (chairman); Federal Services, Post Office & Civil Service; Permanent Subcommittee on Investigations

Elections

1988 General		
Jim Sasser (D)	1,020,061	(65%)
Bill Andersen (R)	541,033	(35%)

Previous Winning Percentages: **1982** (62%) **1976** (53%)

Campaign Finance

	Receipts	Receipts from PACs		Expend-itures
1988				
Sasser (D)	$3,218,986	$1,379,817	(43%)	$3,069,615
Andersen (R)	$612,421	$26,925	(4%)	$613,704

Key Votes

1991	
Authorize use of force against Iraq	N
1990	
Oppose prohibition of certain semiautomatic weapons	N
Support constitutional amendment on flag desecration	N
Oppose requiring parental notice for minors' abortions	Y
Halt production of B-2 stealth bomber at 13 planes	Y
Approve budget that cut spending and raised revenues	Y
Pass civil rights bill over Bush veto	Y
1989	
Oppose reduction of SDI funding	N
Oppose barring federal funds for "obscene" art	Y
Allow vote on capital gains tax cut	N

Voting Studies

	Presidential Support		Party Unity		Conservative Coalition	
Year	**S**	**O**	**S**	**O**	**S**	**O**
1990	33	67	90	9	41	59
1989	55	43	89	7	29	68
1988	41	56	87	11	38	59
1987	35	65	94	6	38	63
1986	24	76	87	13	37	63
1985	33	67	87	13	52	48
1984	34	58	88	8	30	62
1983	39	58	85	11	35 †	65 †
1982	42	55	72	25	62	36
1981	57	40	72	17	57	29

† Not eligible for all recorded votes.

Interest Group Ratings

Year	ADA	ACU	AFL-CIO	CCUS
1990	72	9	78	17
1989	85	8	100	57
1988	75	9	86	43
1987	80	12	90	28
1986	70	17	87	32
1985	60	26	86	38
1984	90	18	91	37
1983	75	16	93	32
1982	55	47	84	50
1981	45	31	59	67

Al Gore (D)

Of Carthage — Elected 1984

Born: March 31, 1948, Washington, D.C.

Education: Harvard U., A.B. 1969; attended Vanderbilt School of Religion, 1972; Vanderbilt U. Law School, 1974-76.

Military Service: Army, 1969-71.

Occupation: Journalist; home builder.

Family: Wife, Mary Elizabeth "Tipper" Aitcheson; four children.

Religion: Baptist.

Political Career: U.S. House, 1977-85; sought Democratic nomination for president, 1988.

Capitol Office: 393 Russell Bldg. 20510; 224-4944.

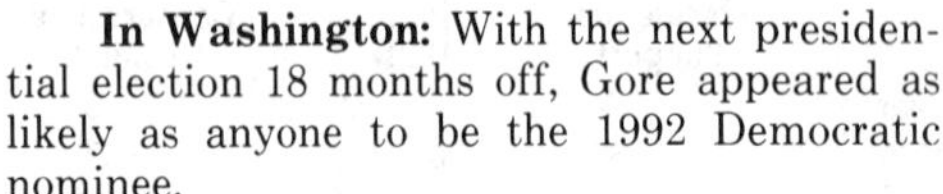

In Washington: With the next presidential election 18 months off, Gore appeared as likely as anyone to be the 1992 Democratic nominee.

His assets were abundant, his positioning enviable and his liabilities largely correctable. The drawbacks were that running poorly in 1992 might give him a loser's image, and running at all could cost him his chance for substantive legislative achievements in the 102nd Congress.

In any event, Gore's easy election to a second term in 1990 merely reaffirmed the general supposition in Washington that his political goals lay beyond the Senate.

Thanks in part to his roots in a political family, Gore has about him a dynast's air of effortlessness. He was first elected to the Senate with more than 60 percent of the vote, even in the teeth of Ronald Reagan's 49-state landslide in 1984. And almost as soon as he had settled into the Senate, Gore was out to take the White House keys when Reagan left the place.

Like other youthful senators before him, such as John F. Kennedy and Gary Hart, he had observed the number of potential rivals for the presidency and decided to get a jump on them by taking an early turn at bat. He has been willing to pay the price and take the risks that come with this beat-the-crowd strategy.

In the 1988 cycle, presidential hopeful Gore was not yet 40, still a freshman and not nearly as well funded as he had hoped to be. Yet he managed to demonstrate appeal in his native South and among party moderates. And he stepped decisively out from the shadow of his father, Albert Gore Sr., a former three-term senator.

The peak moment for Gore's 1988 bid came on Super Tuesday, March 8, when 14 Southern states held primaries. He got a bigger percentage share of the aggregate vote in those states than any other Democrat. His delegate take was almost as big as the Rev. Jesse Jackson's. Gore also prevailed in two Western states that held caucuses that day.

But Gore had to share the media splash with Jackson, with Massachusetts Gov. Michael S. Dukakis (who won Texas and Florida) and, most of all, with Vice President George Bush — who all but claimed the GOP nomination with a Southern sweep.

Gore's problem thereafter was finding a breakthrough state above the Mason-Dixon line. After flopping in Illinois, Michigan and then Wisconsin, he shoved his last chips onto New York. He struck a desperate bargain with New York City Mayor Edward I. Koch, who made himself an issue with intemperate remarks about Jews and Jackson. The city went narrowly for Jackson, Dukakis won nearly everywhere else and Gore got just 10 percent. Two days later, he suspended his campaign.

Still, Gore established himself as a player for 1992 and beyond. No other Southerner can now plot a path to the White House without dealing first with him, and the youthful claimant has given ample sign that he intends to hold his place.

Gore raised eyebrows when he broke with his party to authorize the use of military force against Iraq in January 1991. But before the vote, he unburdened himself of a lengthy explanatory floor speech — a virtual seminar in his thinking on the subject. "There are no perfect choices," he said.

If that vote convinced many that Gore was running in 1992, the impression got stronger when he later went out of his way to defend the contrary votes of his colleagues. The Republicans, he said, "seem determined to load their big guns with cheap shots." This effort may have done as much to boost his stock within the party as his vote had helped him with the electorate.

That sort of rough balance is visible in Gore's voting on other issues. His votes on national security matters position him at his party's rightward edge, but his overall pattern is decidedly liberal — particularly for a Southerner.

On those occasions in 1990 when most Southern Democratic senators voted with the Republicans, Gore sided with the Northern Democrats three times out of five. Gore also led Southern Democrats in voting against the White House, doing so on 62 percent of those votes on which the president's position was clear.

Even his party-unity score (measuring his tendency to vote with a majority of his party against a majority of the other) was 93 percent — unusually high for a moderate and one of the highest in general among Democrats in the Senate.

The relatively small and inexperienced field of presidential contenders expected in 1992 (assuming a re-election bid by President Bush) could also be a plus for Gore, a stolid speaker better at drawing a crowd than exciting one. A strong effort in a losing cause might install Gore as the early front runner for the open-presidency race of 1996, particularly if he runs well in the high-growth states of the Sun Belt.

Bright and personable, Gore seems comfortable with himself and with the political trajectory he has chosen. He also wants to continue being a legislator, however, and he returned from his first presidential foray with a flurry of activity to underscore that desire.

He shifted from the chairmanship of the Consumer Subcommittee on Commerce, Science and Technology to the chairmanship of the Subcommittee on Science, Technology and Space. This allows him ample opportunity to explore the futuristic issues that have long captivated him — and on which he would like to build a political movement.

Some of these issues have been technological, such as his advocacy of national supercomputer networking. But his leading theme has more often been environmental protection. Gore was principal sponsor of the resolution creating Earth Day 1990 and was chairman of the Environmental and Energy Study Conference in the 101st Congress.

In the 102nd Congress, Gore opened another issue front, this one aimed at appealing to middle-class pocketbooks. He joined Democratic Rep. Thomas J. Downey of New York in proposing higher income tax rates for households with more than $110,000 in taxable income. Their proposal also included a surtax of 11 percent on adjusted gross incomes greater than $250,000. The revenue from such changes would be used to fund fatter tax breaks for middle-class families with children.

Gore spent most of his pre-congressional career as a reporter, and he brought the skills and interests of a journalist with him to the House in 1977. Few there could match his ability to seize an issue, uncover a pattern of abuses, draw attention in the media and propose a solution.

But since his presidential campaign and change of subcommittee chairs, Gore is less the muckraker than the fact-gathering inspector general. He has traveled to the Antarctic to study the hole in the ozone layer and to Brazil to study the deforestation that may be affecting the global climate. He proposed a new system for warning people of earthquakes. He called for all wrapping materials to be biodegradable. He proposed a bill called the National High Performance Computer Technology Act of 1989 and called on all nations to phase out the use of chlorofluorocarbons (which harm the ozone layer) before 2000.

In 1990, Gore was among those pressing for tighter regulation of the cable industry, stressing that the telecommunications of the day were only a glimpse of what would soon be possible.

Such emphasis on the future has prompted some to comment that the future Gore cares most about is his own. But beyond the grandstanding, he has long seemed genuinely interested in adapting the present to the demands of the future. In his early years in the House, for example, Gore led the campaign for televising its floor proceedings. When that campaign succeeded, he delivered the chamber's first televised speech in March 1979. Carrying this cause to the Senate, he urged his new neighbors to emulate the House — renewing the fight long pressed by retired GOP leader Howard H. Baker Jr., the Republican who had preceded him in the Senate.

Gore also has continued to pursue his defense policy interests on the Armed Services Committee, where he serves on three subcommittees but is not yet senior enough to chair one. Gore joined Armed Services in 1987; years before, as a House member in 1980, Gore first became interested in the issue of strategic arms when he was disturbed to find that an audience of Tennessee teenagers nearly all expected a nuclear war in their lifetime.

In the early 1980s, as Reagan pushed hard for deployment of 100 MX missiles in existing silos, MX critics in the House seemed within striking distance of scotching the president's plan entirely. Gore feared this would enable Reagan to brand Democrats as soft on defense and then withdraw from arms negotiations with the Soviets. Gore and a few other Democrats supported limited MX production in return for a promise from the administration of flexibility at the strategic arms talks in Geneva and a commitment to the alternative "Midgetman," a single-warhead missile.

Moving to the Senate early in 1985, Gore and fellow Democrats Sam Nunn, David L. Boren and Robert C. Byrd helped produce an agreement with the administration holding MX deployment to 50 missiles. The White House was not thrilled with that compromise, but by then its attention was shifting to another item on the nuclear arms agenda — the strategic defense initiative.

In 1989, Gore initially seemed enthusiastic about President Bush's nomination of former Sen. John Tower as secretary of Defense. He called Tower's performance as an arms negotiator in Geneva "exemplary in every respect" (Gore had been on the Senate's team of observers). But as the nomination soured and Nunn turned against Tower, so did Gore.

Gore drew attention in the 99th Congress, when, at the initiative of his wife, "Tipper," he focused congressional attention on rock music lyrics that the Gores felt glorify casual sex, violence and satanic worship. The Senate Commerce Committee held hearings on the subject in 1985, drawing in singing stars to comment on a proposal to put warning labels on music products so parents could monitor what their children were hearing.

At Home: Despite his globe-trotting and his bursting ambition, Gore retains a certain political magic at home. It stems in part from residual support for his father, who entered the House before World War II and served in the Senate of the 1950s and 1960s.

Americans have always been ambivalent about political aristocracy. While they abhor the idea of inherited position, they have voted for political dynasties in both parties, in every era, in every region and at all levels of government.

Yet the younger Gore must be said to have also earned his voter loyalty for himself, partly with a religious devotion to small-town open meetings during his congressional career. Gore clearly has a knack for getting along with ordinary Tennesseans, even if he did grow up as a son of senatorial privilege in Washington, D.C., attending exclusive private schools.

Gore's 1984 Senate election bore the mark of inevitability from the moment Baker announced his retirement in 1982. In many past statewide campaigns, Democrats had cut themselves to ribbons in primary competition, paving the way for Republican victory in November. But Gore, with his immense popularity in Middle Tennessee and a name that needed no introduction anywhere in the state, had the Democratic field to himself. It was the Republicans, struggling to hold the seat, who were divided over the nomination.

While they squabbled, Gore campaigned. Starting early in 1983, he worked the grass roots, lining up rural Democratic courthouse networks and urban party organizations.

The eventual winner of the GOP nomination was state Sen. Victor H. Ashe, a wealthy, Yale-educated lawyer from Knoxville whose acerbic manner and habit of needling colleagues in the Legislature had turned off even some Republicans. Ashe toned his manner down in the primary, won an early endorsement from the National Republican Senatorial Committee and easily won nomination. But that endorsement angered New Right activist Ed McAteer, who withdrew from the primary and mounted an independent November campaign, foreclosing any hopes Ashe might have had.

Gore campaigned in the fall as if he were the incumbent. He pointed to his work in the House on such issues as nutritional standards for baby formula, toxic-waste cleanup and arms control, all of which played well to most audiences.

Ashe seemed outmaneuvered at every turn. When he called a press conference to accuse Gore of speaking out against busing but voting for it, Gore ignored him, responding instead by announcing that Reagan had just signed three of his bills — creating a national organ donor program, requiring stronger warning labels on cigarette packages and strengthening penalties against repeat criminal offenders. The election was a rout, with Gore even winning Ashe's home base, heavily Republican Knox County.

Republicans gave Gore a second term without a struggle in 1990. Against Knoxville antitax economist William R. Hawkins, a political unknown, Gore won with 68 percent, carrying every county in the state.

Gore's family name did not scare away competition in 1976, when he launched his first campaign for the House. Eight other Democrats entered the contest to succeed retiring Democrat Joe L. Evins. They soon found, however, that they were opposing not only a family tradition but a born campaigner.

Gore's themes had a populist flavor. He called for higher taxation of the rich and tighter strip-mine laws, and criticized "private power trusts" who wanted to dismantle the Tennessee Valley Authority. He favored cuts in defense spending and said the government should create more public jobs.

Gore's chief rival in the crowded field was state House Majority Leader Stanley Rogers. He tried to make an issue of Gore's wealth (net worth $273,000 at the time) and claimed that Gore's father was tied to energy monopolies. By stressing his legislative experience, Rogers hoped to cast Gore as a political amateur.

But Rogers' political base was in the southern part of the district, and several other candidates from that area drew votes from him. Gore, who was not seriously challenged in his Smith County base in the district's northern section, finished just ahead of Rogers. House re-elections were no problem for Gore. Only once — in 1980 — was he held below 90 percent.

Committees

Armed Services (8th of 11 Democrats)
Defense Industry & Technology; Projection Forces & Regional Defense; Strategic Forces & Nuclear Deterrence

Commerce, Science & Transportation (5th of 11 Democrats)
Science, Technology & Space (chairman); Communications; Consumer; Surface Transportation; National Ocean Policy Study

Rules & Administration (6th of 9 Democrats)

Joint Economic

Joint Printing

Elections

1990 General

Al Gore (D)	530,898	(68%)
William R. Hawkins (R)	233,703	(30%)
Bill Jacox (I)	11,191	(1%)
Charles Gordon Vick (I)	8,021	(1%)

Previous Winning Percentages: **1984** (61%) **1982** * (100%) **1980** * (79%) **1978** * (100%) **1976** * (94%)

* *House elections.*

Campaign Finance

	Receipts	Receipts from PACs		Expend-itures
1990				
Gore (D)	$2,241,915	$931,438	(42%)	$1,630,919
Hawkins (R)	$8,395	0		$6,571

Key Votes

1991

Authorize use of force against Iraq	Y
1990	
Oppose prohibition of certain semiautomatic weapons	N
Support constitutional amendment on flag desecration	N
Oppose requiring parental notice for minors' abortions	Y
Halt production of B-2 stealth bomber at 13 planes	N
Approve budget that cut spending and raised revenues	Y
Pass civil rights bill over Bush veto	Y
1989	
Oppose reduction of SDI funding	Y
Oppose barring federal funds for "obscene" art	Y
Allow vote on capital gains tax cut	N

Voting Studies

	Presidential Support		Party Unity		Conservative Coalition	
Year	**S**	**O**	**S**	**O**	**S**	**O**
1990	38	62	93	7	41	59
1989	56	30	68	18	58	37
1988	33	30	57	4	11	35
1987	10	41	49	2	9	25
1986	29	71	83	17	33	67
1985	34	66	86	14	50	50
House Service						
1984	46	45	69	22	56	34
1983	29	61	77	13	39	58
1982	45	52	89	11	47	53
1981	39	59	80	17	47	53

Interest Group Ratings

Year	ADA	ACU	AFL-CIO	CCUS
1990	78	9	89	17
1989	55	19	88	60
1988	60	9	83	45
1987	60	6	100	10
1986	70	9	87	32
1985	65	17	86	41
House Service				
1984	65	22	62	31
1983	70	20	88	28
1982	70	29	90	18
1981	70	13	93	11

1 James H. Quillen (R)

Of Kingsport — Elected 1962

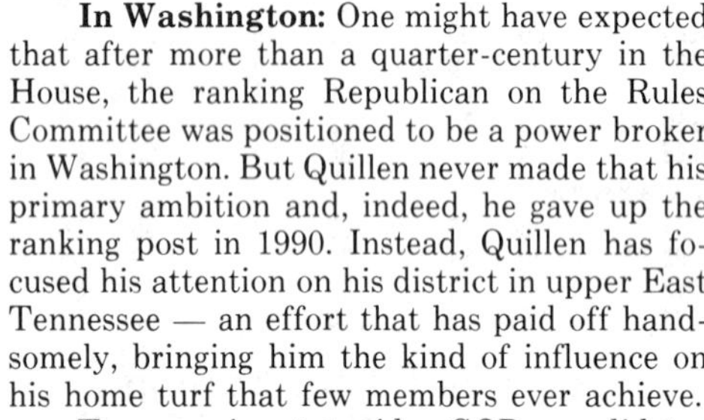

Born: Jan. 11, 1916, near Gate City, Va.
Education: Graduated from Dobyns-Bennett High School, 1934.
Military Service: Navy, 1942-46.
Occupation: Newspaper publisher; real estate and insurance salesman; banker.
Family: Wife, Cecile Cox.
Religion: Methodist.
Political Career: Tenn. House, 1955-63.
Capitol Office: 102 Cannon Bldg. 20515; 225-6356.

In Washington: One might have expected that after more than a quarter-century in the House, the ranking Republican on the Rules Committee was positioned to be a power broker in Washington. But Quillen never made that his primary ambition and, indeed, he gave up the ranking post in 1990. Instead, Quillen has focused his attention on his district in upper East Tennessee — an effort that has paid off handsomely, bringing him the kind of influence on his home turf that few members ever achieve.

Tennessee's statewide GOP candidates would like to assume they have a solid base in Quillen's traditionally Republican territory, but as some have learned, a key element to success in the region is winning over Quillen himself.

When former GOP Gov. Winfield Dunn tried to return to the governorship in 1986, his strategists worried that Quillen's network might not mobilize for Dunn because of an old feud between the two men. That is exactly what happened: Dunn's showing in the normally heavily Republican 1st was a factor in his statewide loss to Democrat Ned McWherter.

In 1988, when the GOP was trying to put the best face on its long-shot hopes of upsetting Democratic Sen. Jim Sasser, Quillen's public praise for the senior senator helped render the challenge pointless. Sasser's opponent, Kingsport attorney Bill Andersen, originally had shown some interest in taking Quillen's spot in the House, and Quillen had been miffed by that apparent attempt to nudge him out.

Quillen will be nearly 77 when the 102nd Congress ends, and he has often been rumored to be weighing retirement. But given Andersen's experience in 1988, it seems unlikely any Republican will start jockeying to succeed Quillen until it is very clear he is ready to go.

If Quillen is careful about lending his personal support to candidates in Tennessee, he is even more careful about sharing his massive campaign treasury with GOP candidates around the country. That has frustrated a number of House Republicans, who expect such a senior member to play a party-building role. But Quillen is a self-made man with a dim view of handouts, and he has learned to work with the Democratic majority to get what he wants for his district. It is not in Quillen's interest to give money to conservative candidates who aim to topple the Democratic power structure with which Quillen has reached accommodation.

Rules can be a place for partisan strategizing and legislative intrigue, but Quillen is not the person for it. He would rather look after his constituents. The importance of his seniority on Rules would seem to have increased in the 101st Congress, when newcomers filled the three GOP committee slots under him. But those newcomers, not Quillen, typically took the lead in voicing the GOP position on rules matters that reached the floor.

Quillen announced in December 1990 that, because of his wife's ill health, he would step down as ranking Republican on Rules. Though he apparently relinquished the post voluntarily, there was no groundswell in the GOP Conference asking Quillen to reconsider his decision. His willingness to work with the Democrats from his senior perch often irked the more-partisan younger generation of House Republicans, who favor the more aggressive and confrontational style epitomized by Minority Whip Newt Gingrich of Georgia.

Quillen did speak out at times, challenging Democratic procedures or policies. In 1987, when the House was voting for $725 million in new aid for the homeless, Quillen was concerned that the money would promote the problem, not redress it. "I don't want the Congress to create more homelessness on our streets," he said. "Instead of solving the problem, we would make it entirely more complicated."

When Congress considered legislation in 1989 to bail out and restructure the savings and loan industry, Quillen allied himself with S&L interests, pressing to allow thrifts that carry on their books "supervisory good will" — a form of phantom capital — to count it toward their capital requirements.

The future treatment of good will became

Tennessee 1

Northeast — Tri-cities

The Tennessee Valley Authority has freed this district and much of East Tennessee from the pervasive rural poverty of an earlier era. Isolated highland towns, tobacco patches and livestock clearings were once the 1st District norm, but in the past generation small cities have grown up around industries drawn to the area by the availability of TVA power.

But industry has not changed the district's GOP voting habits. The 10 counties that make up the 1st gave George Bush 68 percent in 1988 only a slight drop from Ronald Reagan's 1984 showing in the district. The 1st is not blindly Republican, however. It will pick Democrats in noncompetitive statewide contests, supporting Senate Democrats Jim Sasser and Al Gore in their runaway re-elections in 1988 and 1990, respectively.

Some 45 percent of the people in the 1st live in Sullivan and Washington counties, which encompass northeast Tennessee's Tri-cities — Johnson City, Kingsport and Bristol. These cities' diverse industries produce an array of items, including textiles, paper, chemicals, electronics and medical equipment.

Because of its industrial work force, the Tri-cities area has a respectable Democratic vote. In 1976 Jimmy Carter took Sullivan and Quillen carried it by only 543 votes; 12 years later, Sasser got his best margins in the district in Sullivan and Washington. But those voters have little use for Democrats of a liberal stripe, such as Michael S. Dukakis.

Even when Democrats do well in the Tri-cities, for the most part they are swamped districtwide. More than half the people in the 1st District still live in rural and small-town counties where the impact of TVA has not shaken natives from their instinctive suspicion of big government. These counties regularly elect GOP candidates by wide margins.

The rural areas raise tobacco, poultry and livestock. Zinc and limestone are mined, and some people commute to factory jobs in Knoxville or the Tri-cities.

At the southern end of the 1st, Sevier County feeds on tourist dollars. It is the gateway to the Great Smoky Mountains National Park, which draws about 10 million visitors yearly. At the park's edge is Gatlinburg, a town of only 3,500 people whose motels sleep tens of thousands. Nearby is Pigeon Forge, which has an even larger extravaganza of tourist offerings, including Dollywood, a huge family amusement area launched recently by country music star Dolly Parton, a Sevier County native.

Population: 512,702. White 500,873 (98%), Black 9,938 (2%). Spanish origin 2,636 (1%). 18 and over 371,177 (72%), 65 and over 57,367 (11%). Median age: 32.

the most charged issue during the thrift debate, cast largely as a question of treating thrifts in keeping with past practices vs. protecting taxpayers already being asked to bail out the ailing industry. For those such as Quillen who wanted to be lenient toward thrifts carrying large amounts of good will, the issue was one of fairness, and survival for a number of S&Ls. "A Deal Is a Deal," read a button often sported by Quillen. Their efforts, however, ultimately proved unsuccessful.

But over the years, Quillen has been most conspicuous when Tennessee is directly involved in an issue. An emergency appropriations bill came to Rules in 1985 packed with controversial water projects — including one worth $5 million in Quillen's district. The committee sent the bill to the floor with a rule that left a number of water projects vulnerable to procedural objections — but the projects backed by Quillen and some other Rules members were protected.

At times, the Tennessean's questions to witnesses before Rules are notable for comic relief, as when he told a committee chairman that a piece of legislation appeared to be "putting the carrot before the cart."

He once broke up a hearing at Rules by putting a goldfish in his water pitcher. The hearing was on a measure softening the Endangered Species Act, which was threatening to block construction of the $119 million Tellico Dam in Tennessee because it would destroy the habitat of a small fish, the snail darter.

Quillen was a booster of the dam. He said he wanted to see how long it would take people to notice the fish in his pitcher, hoping to demonstrate the insignificance of the even-smaller darter.

In 1978 Quillen used his committee position to force an unsuccessful floor vote on a provision to repeal the earned-income limit imposed on members of Congress the previous year. A new ethics code limited outside earned income to 15 percent of salary ($8,625 at that time). Quillen, who was a board member or president of five companies, was making considerably more than that annually in outside earned income and vigorously opposed the limit. House Democratic leaders in 1981 quietly succeeded in raising the outside earned-income limit to 30 percent of salary.

At Home: To make it to Congress in 1962, Quillen had to weather the quarrels of a Republican Party cast into disarray by the passing of a political dynasty. GOP Rep. B. Carroll Reece, a former party national chairman, dominated 1st District politics for 40 years until his death in 1961. Reece's widow served out his term, then gave her blessing to Quillen, a four-term state representative.

Quillen called himself a staunch conservative who opposed "wasteful spending overseas to buy friendship when friendship cannot be bought." Though he got only 29 percent of the vote, that topped the five-candidate GOP primary field and gave him the nomination.

The 1st had not elected a Democrat since 1878, yet Quillen was held to 54 percent in the general election. His low total was blamed partly on GOP disunity after the hard-fought primary and partly on a higher-than-usual Democratic turnout. A longstanding patronage arrangement between Reece and local Democrats had collapsed when Reece died.

Once in office, Quillen quickly learned the skills of entrenchment. A prodigious letter-writer, he sent notes of congratulation and condolence and numerous franked mailings. And he made the rounds to county courthouses during his frequent trips home.

By 1964, GOP factional fights had dissipated, and Quillen easily won re-election. Since then, Quillen occasionally has encountered Democratic foes who complain he is little more than a "pen pal" who opposes education, health and welfare measures his rural constituents need. But none of the foes has made significant headway. In 1990, he was unopposed.

The most tangible monument to Quillen's work is the Quillen-Dishner College of Medicine at East Tennessee State University in Johnson City. The congressman spent years promoting it, and it is named for him and a generous donor. Dunn's opposition to this school led to the feud between him and Quillen.

Committee

Rules (2nd of 4 Republicans)
Legislative Process (ranking)

Elections

1990 General		
James H. Quillen (R)	47,796	(100%)
1988 General		
James H. Quillen (R)	119,526	(80%)
Sidney S. Smith (D)	29,469	(20%)

Previous Winning Percentages:				**1986**	(69%)	**1984**	(100%)
1982	(74%)	**1980**	(86%)	**1978**	(65%)	**1976**	(58%)
1974	(64%)	**1972**	(79%)	**1970**	(68%)	**1968**	(85%)
1966	(87%)	**1964**	(72%)	**1962**	(54%)		

District Vote For President

	1988		1984		1980		1976	
D	54,455	(31%)	51,916	(28%)	62,841	(36%)	72,867	(45%)
R	117,511	(68%)	129,514	(71%)	105,474	(61%)	85,130	(53%)
I					4,623	(3%)		

Campaign Finance

	Receipts	Receipts from PACs		Expend-itures
1990				
Quillen (R)	$596,536	$360,350	(60%)	$263,291
1988				
Quillen (R)	$617,030	$413,800	(67%)	$227,503

Key Votes

1991	
Authorize use of force against Iraq	Y
1990	
Support constitutional amendment on flag desecration	Y
Pass family and medical leave bill over Bush veto	N
Reduce SDI funding	N
Allow abortions in overseas military facilities	N
Approve budget summit plan for spending and taxing	Y
Approve civil rights bill	N
1989	
Halt production of B-2 stealth bomber at 13 planes	N
Oppose capital gains tax cut	N
Approve federal abortion funding in rape or incest cases	N
Approve pay raise and revision of ethics rules	Y
Pass Democratic minimum wage plan over Bush veto	N

Voting Studies

	Presidential Support		Party Unity		Conservative Coalition	
Year	**S**	**O**	**S**	**O**	**S**	**O**
1990	65	29	60	31	85	7
1989	71	21	60	35	85	5
1988	48	41	59	31	82	5
1987	55	38	55	33	86	5
1986	62	33	49	40	82	8
1985	68	29	56	35	80	11
1984	69	20	60	27	81	12
1983	79	16	70	21	85	10
1982	69	29	68	26	88	11
1981	63	17	70	14	67	3

Interest Group Ratings

Year	ADA	ACU	AFL-CIO	CCUS
1990	6	83	25	92
1989	15	85	25	100
1988	15	91	36	100
1987	12	76	31	64
1986	20	77	38	60
1985	15	81	18	67
1984	20	67	42	82
1983	0	83	6	95
1982	10	76	15	76
1981	5	92	21	100

2 John J. "Jimmy" Duncan Jr. (R)

Of Knoxville — Elected 1988

Born: July 21, 1947, Lebanon, Tenn.
Education: U. of Tennessee, B.S. 1969; George Washington U., J.D. 1973.
Military Service: Army National Guard, 1970-87.
Occupation: Lawyer; judge.
Family: Wife, Lynn Hawkins; four children.
Religion: Presbyterian.
Political Career: Knox County criminal court judge, 1981-88.
Capitol Office: 115 Cannon Bldg. 20515; 225-5435.

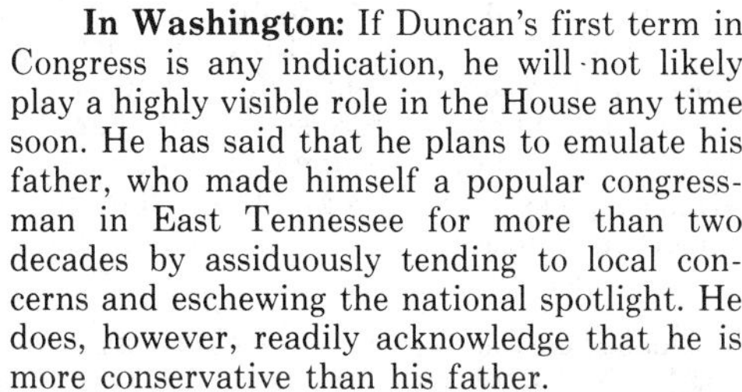

In Washington: If Duncan's first term in Congress is any indication, he will not likely play a highly visible role in the House any time soon. He has said that he plans to emulate his father, who made himself a popular congressman in East Tennessee for more than two decades by assiduously tending to local concerns and eschewing the national spotlight. He does, however, readily acknowledge that he is more conservative than his father.

Duncan spent his freshman term on Interior and Public Works, adding a few projects for his district to authorization bills as they went through his committees. He was able to get $1 million into the fiscal 1990 interior appropriations bill for the first resurfacing in 25 years of the Foothills Parkway in the Great Smoky Mountains National Park. In the 102nd Congress, he joined the Banking Committee.

The Persian Gulf War gave Duncan a couple of moments of national attention in 1990. President Bush signed into law his resolution to declare a national day of prayer for U.S. troops and citizens in the Middle East and their families.

And Duncan scored a publicity coup with his effort to send videotapes of college football games to U.S. troops.

At Home: After eight years as a criminal court judge in Knox County, the main population center in the 2nd District, Duncan had a reputation and résumé to be a strong candidate in his own right when his ill father decided not to seek another term (the elder Duncan died shortly after making his retirement announcement). But there was little doubt that Duncan, who appeared on the ballot as John J. Duncan Jr., campaigned primarily as his father's son, both in style and substance.

Duncan's strategy proved successful in the end, but it gave Democrats an opening to make a competitive challenge in this Republican bastion.

While Duncan waged the sort of old-style door-to-door, barbecue-to-barbecue campaign for which his father was known, Democrat Dudley Taylor waged a hard-hitting media campaign the likes of which had not been seen in this district.

As Duncan put together a loose-knit organization run mainly by family and friends, Taylor, who stepped down from his post as state revenue commissioner in order to run, began putting together a strong effort. He had the assistance of influential state Democrats, including his former boss, Democratic Gov. Ned McWherter. Little known to most voters at the outset, Taylor quickly raised his profile by aggressively courting the free press and making use of paid media.

Taylor hammered away at Duncan for running on his father's reputation. And the charges got some attention. Duncan's refusal to debate Taylor even once gave the Democrat an opportunity to score debating points throughout the campaign, as did the Republican's decision to hold only infrequent press conferences.

Duncan also chose to ignore a wave of more negative attacks that came at him. One of Taylor's advertisements played up links between Duncan and financier C. H. Butcher Jr. and a major banking scandal. Federal regulators had sued Duncan and other principals of a failed savings and loan, saying they engaged in a conspiracy in which control of the thrift was given to Butcher in exchange for elimination of debts Duncan's brother owed to Butcher's banks. Taylor also tried to portray Duncan as being soft on crime.

Local Republicans prodded Duncan into taking out ads rebutting Taylor's "vicious and false allegations." He easily won the general election and special election to fill out the remainder of his father's term. Taylor toyed with running again in 1990, but chose not to. Duncan had no Democratic opposition.

Tennessee 2

East — Knoxville

Since Civil War days, the 2nd has voted Republican in most elections. More than 60 percent of Duncan's constituents are Knox Countians; with 165,000 residents, Knoxville is Tennessee's third-largest city. It is headquarters for the Tennessee Valley Authority and home of the University of Tennessee's main campus. The city grew up on textiles, tobacco marketing and meat-packing, but now has a broader economic base including boats, mobile homes and electronics, and a publishing company of emerging national prominence, Whittle Communications.

In addition, Knoxville is a regional retail and entertainment center: The hordes that throng to UT football and basketball games enrich merchants, innkeepers and restaurateurs for miles around.

Knoxville underwent a massive overhaul for the 1982 World's Fair, staged on a 70-acre site downtown. The fair stimulated long-needed highway improvements and drew more visitors than expected, but its afterglow dimmed in the 1983 collapse of the financial empire of brothers Jake and C. H. Butcher, who were leading fair promoters. Their banks boomed in the 1970s and early 1980s, but sound management yielded to overexpansion.

Federal employees who work for TVA are often Democratic, but the labor vote in private industry is mixed: Union members are typically Democratic, but many blue-collar workers are conservative, shun unions and vote Republican. The university also has a conservative orientation, and the outlying sections of Knox County are strongly Republican. In recent years, popular Democrats Jim Sasser, Al Gore and Ned McWherter have won Knox, but George Bush took well over 60 percent in the county in 1988.

Blount County, south of Knoxville, has 15 percent of the 2nd's residents, and gave two-thirds of its vote to Bush in 1988. Located there are the sprawling plants of Alcoa Aluminum, a fixture since 1913. Farther south, toward Georgia, Democratic strength picks up a bit in McMinn, Monroe and Polk counties.

Population: 510,197. White 472,529 (93%), Black 33,945 (7%), Spanish origin 2,971 (1%). 18 and over 375,709 (74%), 65 and over 58,457 (11%). Median age: 31.

Committees

Banking, Finance & Urban Affairs (13th of 20 Republicans)
Domestic Monetary Policy; Financial Institutions Supervision, Regulation & Insurance; International Development, Finance, Trade & Monetary Policy

Interior & Insular Affairs (11th of 17 Republicans)
General Oversight & California Desert Lands; National Parks & Public Lands

Public Works & Transportation (12th of 21 Republicans)
Aviation; Investigations & Oversight; Public Buildings & Grounds

Select Aging (16th of 27 Republicans)
Housing & Consumer Interests; Human Services

Elections

1990 General		
John J. "Jimmy" Duncan Jr. (R)	62,797	(81%)
Peter Hebert (I)	15,127	(19%)
1988 General †		
John J. "Jimmy" Duncan Jr. (R)	99,631	(56%)
Dudley W. Taylor (D)	77,540	(44%)

† Elected to a full term and to fill a vacancy at the same time.

District Vote For President

	1988		1984		1980		1976	
D	65,552	(36%)	67,339	(35%)	71,287	(38%)	85,485	(49%)
R	117,355	(64%)	123,657	(64%)	106,979	(58%)	88,130	(50%)
I					6,026	(3%)		

Campaign Finance

	Receipts	Receipts from PACs		Expend-itures
1990				
Duncan (R)	$325,691	$165,501	(51%)	$200,935
1988				
Duncan (R)	$448,530	$161,675	(36%)	$435,567
Taylor (D)	$396,303	$101,500	(26%)	$381,980

Key Votes

1991	
Authorize use of force against Iraq	Y
1990	
Support constitutional amendment on flag desecration	Y
Pass family and medical leave bill over Bush veto	N
Reduce SDI funding	N
Allow abortions in overseas military facilities	N
Approve budget summit plan for spending and taxing	N
Approve civil rights bill	N
1989	
Halt production of B-2 stealth bomber at 13 planes	N
Oppose capital gains tax cut	N
Approve federal abortion funding in rape or incest cases	N
Approve pay raise and revision of ethics rules	N
Pass Democratic minimum wage plan over Bush veto	N

Voting Studies

	Presidential Support		Party Unity		Conservative Coalition	
Year	S	O	S	O	S	O
1990	74	26	87	13	87	13
1989	64	35	73	27	95	5

Interest Group Ratings

Year	ADA	ACU	AFL-CIO	CCUS
1990	11	88	25	79
1989	20	75	33	90

3 Marilyn Lloyd (D)

Of Chattanooga — Elected 1974

Born: Jan. 3, 1929, Fort Smith, Ark.
Education: Attended Shorter College, 1959-63.
Occupation: Radio station owner and manager.
Family: Husband, Bob Fowler; four children.
Religion: Church of Christ.
Political Career: No previous office.
Capitol Office: 2266 Rayburn Bldg. 20515; 225-3271.

In Washington: Throughout her House career, Lloyd has been identified closely, if not solely, with issues relating to the nuclear facilities at Oak Ridge, Tenn. Lloyd uses her positions on the Armed Services and Science committees mainly to oversee the interests of the nuclear-research and weapons-production complex, located in the northern part of her elongated House district.

However, Lloyd — who has faced several competitive re-election contests — has made an effort in recent years to draw attention to her activities on behalf of interests that apply to other, more populous areas of the 3rd, including her hometown of Chattanooga.

With a constituency that includes a number of textile workers, Lloyd served during the 101st Congress as chairman of the Congressional Textile Caucus. During that period, she was the chief House sponsor of a bill limiting textile imports; although a version of the bill passed both houses in 1990, President Bush vetoed it.

A member of the Select Committee on Aging since its inception in 1975, Lloyd became chairman of its Housing and Consumer Interests Subcommittee in 1990. That year, she sponsored a bill to expand availability of reverse mortgages, which provide elderly homeowners with annuities based on their home equity.

Yet much of Lloyd's work continues to revolve around Oak Ridge. She guards its interests as chairman of the Science Subcommittee on Energy and as a member of the Armed Services Subcommittee on Procurement. This devotion plays well at home, but it has earned Lloyd a reputation among Armed Services colleagues as a parochialist.

Lloyd not only labors to gain authorization of Oak Ridge programs but also monitors the appropriations measure that funds them. When the House Appropriations Subcommittee on Energy and Water passed its fiscal 1991 budget, Lloyd noted that "the bill includes funding for many projects at the Department of Energy's Oak Ridge Reservation." On the Science Committee, Lloyd is involved in oversight of the environmental cleanup effort at nuclear facilities such as Oak Ridge.

Also on that committee, Lloyd backs research that could lead to "energy independence through a balanced national energy policy." While she supports efforts on solar energy and conservation, nuclear power plays a big part in her formula. For years, she fought to preserve the Clinch River nuclear breeder reactor located in her district; however, the expensive project was scrapped in 1983.

In December 1990, Democratic Rep. Robert A. Roe of New Jersey left the Science Committee chairmanship to claim the top spot at Public Works. Although she was the fourth-ranking Democrat on Science, Lloyd bid against second-ranking George E. Brown Jr. of California to succeed Roe. She cited her long experience on Science, adding, "I would be honored by the opportunity to serve as the first woman committee chair." Brown won by a 166-33 vote in the Democratic Caucus.

Aside from her Oak Ridge focus on Armed Services, Lloyd is in the dwindling group of the committee's "Old Guard" conservative Democrats. On social service and economic development issues, however, Lloyd's views are more typical of the majority of House Democrats. She is a vocal backer of such development agencies as the Appalachian Regional Commission, and is a past chairman of the Tennessee Valley Authority Caucus.

At Home: Early in 1988 it seemed certain Lloyd would not be in the 101st Congress. Following tough re-elections in 1984 and 1986, she said in 1987 she would not run again.

But after several months, she surprised those vying to succeed her by announcing that she would run after all. Her change of heart caused a number of local Democrats to put their ambitions on hold, but it was a great relief to state Democratic officials; concerned about losing the seat, they had urged Lloyd to reconsider.

Two top GOP contenders dropped out once Lloyd got back in. But one, Harold Coker, stayed on and made Lloyd work for another

Tennessee 3

Southeast — Chattanooga; Oak Ridge

Although the 3rd usually votes Republican in national elections, Lloyd has proven that it can accept a conservative, locally oriented Democrat who backs nuclear power. This stance is a must for any legislator representing this area. With nuclear facilities both in Oak Ridge and near Chattanooga, thousands of jobs are tied to atomic energy.

A legislator from here must also pay attention to the coal industry. Anderson County is the largest coal-producing county in the state, and Grundy and Marion counties also have coal activity.

The population center of the 3rd is Chattanooga, a heavily industrialized city producing iron, steel and textiles. Chattanooga and surrounding Hamilton County hold more than half of the 3rd's residents. There has been some racial tension between Chattanooga's working-class whites, many of whom come from rural backgrounds, and blacks, who make up about one-third of the population — a high percentage by East Tennessee standards. But there has also been an ambitious private-public effort in Chattanooga to build and refurbish homes for low-income residents.

Hamilton County has voted Republican in all but one presidential contest since 1952. That was in 1968, when George C. Wallace finished first and Republican Richard M. Nixon second. George Bush carried Hamilton with more than 60 percent in 1988. At the same time, Democratic Sen. Jim Sasser won about 55 percent, a far lower percentage than he received statewide. Lloyd ran even in Hamilton in 1984, then won it narrowly in 1986 and more comfortably in her strong 1988 election. In 1990, it was the source of her troubles: She carried Hamilton by a narrow 46-44 percent over her little-known GOP opponent.

In many past elections, the district's most Democratic counties have been Anderson and Roane, where the major city is Oak Ridge. Lloyd runs extremely well there. But the presidential political loyalties of the government workers and scientific intelligentsia at Oak Ridge have shifted somewhat as the GOP has taken the leading role in promoting nuclear energy. In 1976, Jimmy Carter won 56 percent in both Anderson and Roane counties, but in 1980 he averaged only 38 percent. Reagan drew over 60 percent in Anderson and Roane in 1984, and as did Bush four years later.

Oak Ridge has had to make some adjustments during the 1980s. The government cut back on funding for some projects, such as a gaseous diffusion plant, causing concern about job losses. But Oak Ridge's work force is attractive to private industry, which has picked up some of the slack. The end of the decade has witnessed the arrival of some new medium-sized firms involved in the nuclear industry (including nuclear-waste cleanup), data systems research and other scientific endeavors.

Population: 516,692. White 449,455 (87%), Black 63,870 (12%), Other 2,418 (1%). Spanish origin 3,701 (1%). 18 and over 370,457 (72%), 65 and over 55,994 (11%). Median age: 31.

term.

In 1984, Lloyd had failed to pay attention to an aggressive but little-known foe and nearly lost; two years later, she had a tough campaign against a political neophyte who was initially not considered a serious threat. Coker, unlike those before him, began with a political base and name recognition stemming from his service on the county commission in Hamilton County, home to roughly half the 3rd's voters. He also owned a chain of tire stores that bore his name.

Coker launched a variety of attacks, saying Lloyd had not paid enough attention to the TVA, which had recently laid off workers, and that her 1982 move from the Public Works Committee to Armed Services had boosted her campaign treasury and honoraria totals more than it boosted the district.

But Lloyd, who had obviously learned the dangers of complacency in earlier years, was quick to defend herself and strike back at Coker. She was first to issue the challenge for a debate, and she criticized Coker for refusing to release his business' tax returns. Her conservative voting record, scrupulous attention to constituents and vigorous campaigning sank Coker. She posted her best showing in three elections, 57 percent.

Lloyd's strong performance in a presidential election year led many to believe she would have an easier time in 1990, when two popular Democrats, Gov. Ned McWherter and Sen. Al Gore, were running. But their popularity so overwhelmed the GOP that neither drew a credible foe.

As a result, Tennessee ended up with the lowest voter turnout rate in the nation on Election Day 1990. In the 3rd, fewer than half as many people voted in the 1990 House election as had voted in 1988. That was a prime reason why Lloyd managed only 53 percent against her little-known challenger, Republican Grady Rhoden. Two independents shared 8 percent of the vote as well.

Rhoden, who spent almost no money, attacked Lloyd for accepting political action committee money and received a modest amount of publicity. But the anemic turnout was not enough to put him over the top.

Lloyd's initial victory in 1974 was a surprise. The Democratic nomination had gone to her husband Mort, a well-known Chattanooga newsman. But when he died in a plane crash, the 3rd's county chairmen met and chose his widow as the nominee. She had owned and operated a radio station with her husband, but was a political novice and seemed to have little chance against two-term GOP Rep. Lamar Baker.

But Lloyd turned out to be surprisingly aggressive, and she found a winning combination of issues in the Watergate year: opposition to busing, more rights for women and criticism of President Ford's pardon of former President Nixon. She unseated Baker with 51 percent.

In her first term, Lloyd built a following with question-and-answer town hall meetings and covered-dish suppers. Baker tried a comeback in 1976, but lost by more than 2-to-1. After the 1978 election, Lloyd appeared on voters' ballots as Marilyn Lloyd Bouquard, a result of her marriage to Chattanooga engineer Joseph P. Bouquard. But they divorced in 1983 and she became Marilyn Lloyd once again.

In 1984 she faced John Davis, a political consultant. Davis got off to a slow start financially, but as the campaign wore on, he proved adept at winning media coverage. Combining a pro-business message with a moderate background more appealing to middle-of-the-road voters who had been turned off by Lloyd's earlier, more conservative opponents, Davis won 48 percent of the vote.

Davis was expected back for a rematch in 1986, but he was upset in the primary by Chattanooga attorney Jim Golden, a political outsider with a strong base in the 3rd's evangelical community. Handsome and articulate, Golden broadened his appeal beyond evangelicals by emphasizing economic issues.

But establishment Republicans remained wary of Golden's background. Their resistance, combined with Lloyd's renewed attention to her campaign machinery, brought her 54 percent.

Committees

Armed Services (13th of 33 Democrats)
Military Personnel & Compensation; Procurement & Military Nuclear Systems

Science, Space & Technology (3rd of 32 Democrats)
Energy (chairman)

Select Aging (5th of 42 Democrats)
Housing & Consumer Interests (chairman); Social Security and Women

Elections

1990 General

Marilyn Lloyd (D)	49,662	(53%)
Grady L. Rhoden (R)	36,855	(39%)
Peter T. Melcher (I)	5,598	(6%)
George E. Googe (I)	1,546	(2%)

1990 Primary

Marilyn Lloyd (D)	36,607	(86%)
David Ray Stacy (D)	5,973	(14%)

1988 General

Marilyn Lloyd (D)	108,264	(57%)
Harold L. Coker (R)	80,372	(43%)

Previous Winning Percentages: **1986** (54%) **1984** (52%) **1982** (62%) **1980** (61%) **1978** (89%) **1976** (68%) **1974** (51%)

District Vote For President

	1988		1984		1980		1976	
D	70,874	(37%)	72,122	(37%)	74,677	(41%)	85,514	(51%)
R	117,220	(62%)	121,921	(63%)	101,094	(56%)	79,510	(48%)
I					4,202	(2%)		

Campaign Finance

	Receipts	Receipts from PACs		Expend-itures
1990				
Lloyd (D)	$415,056	$233,750	(56%)	$234,107
Rhoden (R)	$1,415	0		$1,414
1988				
Lloyd (D)	$621,520	$320,387	(52%)	$618,173
Coker (R)	$628,222	$28,331	(5%)	$626,945

Key Votes

1991

Authorize use of force against Iraq	Y

1990

Support constitutional amendment on flag desecration	Y
Pass family and medical leave bill over Bush veto	N
Reduce SDI funding	N
Allow abortions in overseas military facilities	N
Approve budget summit plan for spending and taxing	Y
Approve civil rights bill	Y

1989

Halt production of B-2 stealth bomber at 13 planes	N
Oppose capital gains tax cut	N
Approve federal abortion funding in rape or incest cases	N
Approve pay raise and revision of ethics rules	Y
Pass Democratic minimum wage plan over Bush veto	Y

Voting Studies

	Presidential Support		Party Unity		Conservative Coalition	
Year	**S**	**O**	**S**	**O**	**S**	**O**
1990	43	56	71	25	94	6
1989	56	38	61	34	90	5
1988	47	51	59	37	89	3
1987	40	49	54	27	81	9
1986	53	44	39	55	92	6
1985	52	45	56	39	82	16
1984	52	42	48	47	90	10
1983	54	41	41	50	90	7
1982	47	47	56	38	73	22
1981	57	36	55	41	83	12

Interest Group Ratings

Year	ADA	ACU	AFL-CIO	CCUS
1990	44	46	58	50
1989	35	52	73	78
1988	50	54	100	46
1987	28	32	62	42
1986	20	62	50	53
1985	35	48	75	45
1984	35	67	50	50
1983	25	78	47	55
1982	25	55	60	52
1981	30	53	67	37

4 Jim Cooper (D)

Of Shelbyville — Elected 1982

Born: June 19, 1954, Shelbyville, Tenn.
Education: U. of NorthZCarolina, B.A. 1975; Oxford U., B.A. 1977, M.A 1977; Harvard U., J.D. 1980.
Occupation: Lawyer.
Family: Wife, Martha Hays; two children.
Religion: Episcopalian.
Political Career: No previous office.
Capitol Office: 125 Cannon Bldg. 20515; 225-6831.

In Washington: Cooper is a bright and thoughtful legislator who also understands the behind-the-scenes mechanisms of Congress. Those talents have impressed colleagues and enabled him to translate a fair number of his ideas into law.

But if Cooper understands political realities, he does not necessarily like them; he sometimes appears frustrated by the pace and parochialism of the legislative process, and his reflective, critical tone occasionally strikes some as preachy. In the 101st Congress, after an Energy and Commerce subcommittee approved a cable re-regulation bill Cooper considered too weak, he remarked, "The great credit for this legislation has to go to the very powerful cable lobby."

Urbane and soft-spoken, Cooper seems the antithesis of the backslapping Southern pol. Yet he is adept at building social relationships in the House. For a number of younger members, sweaty games of basketball in the House gym are a primary networking tool. But Cooper decided that the way to get to know some of his more senior colleagues was to meet them on their own ground, so he took up playing golf.

The contacts he made on the links with leadership figures helped him win a seat on Energy and Commerce at the start of the 100th Congress. He outpolled all other hopefuls and had a crucial ally in Chairman John D. Dingell of Michigan, who helped Cooper and two other members from coal-producing states get on the committee. Dingell for years had worked to head off controls on acid rain, which is said to be caused by coal-burning heavy industry.

In his first term on Energy and Commerce, Cooper threw himself into one of the toughest issues before the committee — the effort to write clean-air legislation to deal with urban smog and acid rain. Renewal of the Clean Air Act had been a political migraine for several years before Cooper got to the committee, because of a standoff between an environmentalist faction, led by California Democrat Henry A. Waxman, and a more industry-oriented faction, led by Dingell.

In an effort to break the deadlock, Cooper teamed with the so-called "group of nine," a caucus of moderate-to-conservative committee Democrats determined to find the acceptable middle ground that had eluded Dingell and Waxman.

Cooper was a diligent player in all aspects of the group's behind-closed-doors effort, even though some of the issues being discussed, such as urban smog, were of little concern to his rural Tennessee constituency. The group's efforts helped lay the groundwork for much of the clean-air debate in the 101st Congress. And Cooper's contributions earned him credibility with other members, perhaps making them more receptive to his views in the coal/acid rain debate, where he has a more direct interest.

On that issue, Cooper tried to sell a compromise plan that set timetables and standards for reduction of emissions from utilities that are the primary cause of acid rain. To pay for that reduction, Cooper proposed a tax on utilities based on how cleanly they burned coal. His plan also allowed utilities to choose the means of meeting the reduction requirements.

Cooper eventually saw elements of his proposal — such as the provision giving utilities flexibility in meeting the standards — written into the 1990 Clean Air Act. And during the intense negotiations leading up to the bill's passage, Cooper helped defeat an effort to require that all utilities share in the cost of cleaning up the worst polluters, many of them in the Midwest.

But for all of Cooper's hard work and acknowledged expertise on elements of the clean-air legislation, he was conspicuously absent from the list of House conferees chosen by Dingell to work out differences with the Senate. Once perceived as perhaps too closely allied to Dingell, Cooper during the clean-air deliberations had apparently shown too much independence for the chairman's taste.

Earlier, Cooper also had clashed with Dingell over legislation affecting the banking industry. Cooper seems to be one of the committee's strongest supporters of legislation granting banks powers to engage in new lines of business.

Tennessee 4

Northeast and South Central

The unwieldy 4th sprawls across eastern and Middle Tennessee for nearly 300 miles. One end of it is not far from Mississippi; the other touches the Virginia border. About the only thing these 23 counties have in common is their rural nature.

People here form their political opinions by talking with neighbors in feed stores and roadside cafés and in small-town shops that surround the courthouse squares. There is only one daily newspaper in the district, and while television is available from several cities outside the district, no station pays much attention to the rural counties. The district's largest city is Morristown (Hamblen County), with about 20,000 people.

The roots of political preference in this part of Tennessee go back many generations. In the mountainous northern counties, the GOP has been the dominant party since the Civil War. Even in Cooper's sweeping 1982 victory, the north's Hancock County went Republican. In 1990, though, Hancock voted overwhelmingly for Democratic Gov. Ned McWherter, Sen. Al Gore and Rep. Cooper.

Tobacco grows in the valleys of the northern counties, and beef and dairy cattle graze on hillsides too steep for plowing. Coal long has been an economic staple, but underground activity has mostly given way to surface mining.

As one drives south through the 4th, the terrain levels out and an Appalachian twang gives way to a Southern drawl. Rural Democratic populism has prevailed in the district's southern counties since secession. In Bedford County, Cooper's home and one of the most heavily Democratic counties in the 4th, cotton has been supplanted by soybeans and corn. Sour mash whiskey is made by the Jack Daniel Distillery in Lynchburg (Moore County) and consumed to excess at the annual Tennessee Walking Horse Celebration in Shelbyville (Bedford County).

Population: 510,732. White 489,861 (96%), Black 19,148 (4%). Spanish origin 3,448 (1%). 18 and over 359,160 (70%), 65 and over 61,644 (12%). Median age: 31.

In 1988, when Dingell offered a bill with sharper limits on some activities by banks than were included in a Banking Committee bill, Cooper complained it was "a giant step backward."

Cooper's independent, plain-speaking streak was evident even before he got onto Energy and Commerce. In the 99th Congress, he was so dissatisfied with life on the Banking Committee that he publicly criticized autocratic panel Chairman Fernand J. St Germain of Rhode Island. Others were saying privately that Banking was adrift because St Germain was preoccupied with an ethics investigation and a tough re-election campaign, but it caused a stir when the normally cautious Cooper aired his frustrations in public.

Although his work on the clean-air reauthorization was time-consuming, Cooper still found room in his schedule during the 101st Congress to push successfully several consumer-oriented bills.

One dealt with perceived abuses in the long-distance phone business. Maintaining that consumers often are unwittingly trapped into paying exorbitant long-distance rates from phones in airports, hotel lobbies and other public facilities, Cooper wrote legislation mandating that long-distance carriers identify themselves at the outset of a call, and requiring carriers to disclose their rates and in some cases justify them to the Federal Communications Commission.

Another Cooper bill established specific standards foods must meet before they can be labeled "light" or "lean." Manufacturers had been free to stamp products with the "lite" label even when they contained as many calories or fat as the standard version.

Cooper also has some parochial interests. The walking horse industry brings in a reported $37 million annually to Cooper's district, so he was agitated when the Agriculture Department, in response to a lawsuit, banned use of the padded horseshoes and bracelet-like chains that enhance the horses' famous high step.

The American Horse Protection Association, which brought the suit, argued that the devices hurt the horses. But Cooper and other members of the Tennessee delegation worked to find a compromise with Agriculture Department officials that would keep the walking-horse industry in business.

Cooper can look beyond the parochial position, however, even on issues involving his district. There are a number of tobacco farmers in the 4th, and Cooper has surprised colleagues in Washington with his criticism of cigarette smoking. During the 101st Congress, he backed continuing a smoking ban on domestic airline flights.

Cooper says, "I'm not anti-tobacco, I'm anti-cancer," and points out that he is "anxious to keep [his constituents] alive as long as possible."

At Home: Though he is a Rhodes scholar who spent his formative years at prestigious schools far from Tennessee, Cooper has an easy rapport with his overwhelmingly rural constituency. He can demonstrate his intelligence without talking down to people, and his middle Tennessee accent survived Groton, Chapel Hill, Oxford and Harvard. Cooper's three-syllable hometown comes out of his mouth as "Shelbvul," just as residents pronounce it.

Most voters in the 4th are as comfortable with Cooper's background as one front-porch philosopher, who, told in 1982 that Cooper was a Rhodes scholar, said, "That's good to hear. It's about time somebody did something about the roads around here."

Several prominent Democrats considered running in the newly created 4th in 1982, but none entered; they were dissuaded by Cooper's full-time campaigning and his family's financial resources. None could match the pedigree that gave Cooper "star quality." His father, Prentice Cooper, was Tennessee's governor from 1939-45, and many older people in the 4th remember voting for or hearing about Prentice.

After an easy primary he faced Republican Cissy Baker, the 26-year-old daughter of Senate Majority Leader Howard H. Baker Jr.

The general election, pitting two scions of famous political families, drew media from across the nation. This free coverage helped Cooper offset Baker's money advantage; she spent just over $1 million.

Cooper was rated the front-runner because of the district's Democratic leanings and because Baker had struggled in the primary, winning 55 percent against two weak opponents. But few expected Cooper to win as lopsidedly as he did, carrying all but one of 23 counties. Cooper benefited greatly from concern over unemployment, always a chronic problem here and particularly severe in 1982.

Committees

Budget (20th of 23 Democrats)
Defense, Foreign Policy & Space; Human Resources; Urgent Fiscal Issues

Energy & Commerce (18th of 27 Democrats)
Commerce, Consumer Protection & Competitiveness; Energy & Power; Telecommunications & Finance

Elections

1990 General

Jim Cooper (D)	52,101	(67%)
Claiborne "Clay" Sanders (R)	22,890	(30%)
Gene M. Bullington (I)	2,281	(3%)

1988 General

Jim Cooper (D)	94,129	(100%)

Previous Winning Percentages: **1986** (100%) **1984** (75%) **1982** (66%)

District Vote For President

	1988	1984	1980	1976
D	66,656 (42%)	69,685 (42%)	80,216 (48%)	92,374 (60%)
R	91,186 (57%)	95,172 (57%)	81,664 (49%)	59,365 (39%)
I			2,566 (2%)	

Campaign Finance

	Receipts	Receipts from PACs	Expend-itures
1990			
Cooper (D)	$183,494	$107,400 (59%)	$56,922
Sanders (R)	$16,497	0	$12,588
1988			
Cooper (D)	$292,770	$244,977 (84%)	$234,375

Key Votes

1991	
Authorize use of force against Iraq	Y
1990	
Support constitutional amendment on flag desecration	N
Pass family and medical leave bill over Bush veto	N
Reduce SDI funding	Y
Allow abortions in overseas military facilities	Y
Approve budget summit plan for spending and taxing	Y
Approve civil rights bill	Y
1989	
Halt production of B-2 stealth bomber at 13 planes	N
Oppose capital gains tax cut	Y
Approve federal abortion funding in rape or incest cases	Y
Approve pay raise and revision of ethics rules	Y
Pass Democratic minimum wage plan over Bush veto	N

Voting Studies

	Presidential Support		Party Unity		Conservative Coalition	
Year	S	O	S	O	S	O
1990	37 †	62 †	74	25	62 †	34 †
1989	48	50	78	18	66	32
1988	34	65	84	15	66	32
1987	25	66	77	14	53	35
1986	31	68	80	14	52	40
1985	43	55	85	13	40	60
1984	42	52	74	20	49	51
1983	32	59	69	24	56	35

† Not eligible for all recorded votes.

Interest Group Ratings

Year	ADA	ACU	AFL-CIO	CCUS
1990	56	29	67	64
1989	60	21	58	60
1988	70	28	79	69
1987	68	9	73	43
1986	70	14	64	53
1985	55	24	71	45
1984	80	26	67	53
1983	45	43	59	50

5 Bob Clement (D)

Of Nashville — Elected 1988

Born: Sept. 23, 1943, Nashville, Tenn.

Education: U. of Tennessee, B.S. 1967; Memphis State U., M.B.A. 1968.

Military Service: Army, 1969-71; Tenn. Army National Guard, 1971-present.

Occupation: Former college president; marketing, management, and real estate executive.

Family: Wife, Mary Carson; four children.

Religion: Methodist.

Political Career: Tenn. Public Service Commission, 1973-79; sought Democratic nomination for governor, 1978; Democratic nominee for U.S. House, 1982.

Capitol Office: 325 Cannon Bldg. 20515; 225-4311.

In Washington: Nearly 20 years ago, Clement was a fast-rising star in Tennessee Democratic politics. Son of a three-term governor, he was elected statewide at age 29 to an office often used as a stepping-stone to higher posts. But once a fiery populist with a driving personal ambition, in the House he is quieter and a loyal party man.

The senior member of the class of 1988 — he won a January 1988 special election — Clement became class representative on the Democratic Steering and Policy Committee, which makes committee assignments. The old ambition flickered in 1990 when he made a bid for a seat on the Appropriations Committee.

A junior member of the Public Works Committee, Clement has sided with his party more often than the average Southern Democrat. He voted against President Reagan's request for $36 million in military and nonmilitary aid for the Nicaraguan contras, and was one of only 20 Southern Democrats to reject killing a seven-day waiting period for purchasing handguns.

Clement has pushed for standardization of nuclear plants to provide what he says would be a safe fuel alternative to oil, and he gained passage of a law providing federal reimbursement for local efforts to abate airport noise. He also has introduced legislation to stiffen penalties for persons convicted of selling drugs at truck stops or rest areas on federal highways.

At Home: With his resounding triumph in the 1988 House special election, Clement resurrected a moribund political career. By winning the race to succeed Democratic Rep. Bill Boner, who became Nashville's mayor, Clement set aside bitter memories from two previous defeats — including a 1982 House bid he was favored to win — and stepped out of the shadow cast by his father, the late Frank G. Clement, who was Tennessee's governor for three terms in the 1950s and 1960s.

In 1972, Bob Clement became a political "boy wonder" by winning East Tennessee's seat on the state Public Service Commission (PSC). Then 29, he was the youngest candidate ever elected statewide in Tennessee. In six years on the PSC, Clement built up the already formidable visibility of the Clement name. But when he sought nomination for governor in 1978, he lost to wealthy businessman Jake Butcher.

In 1979, President Jimmy Carter appointed Clement to the Tennessee Valley Authority board, where, as he had on the PSC, he drew headlines for trying to hold down utility rates. In 1982, Clement sought the open 7th District, a Democratic-leaning constituency running from his family's traditional base west of Nashville all the way to Memphis. But the lesser-known GOP nominee, Memphis businessman Don Sundquist, won thanks to a huge Republican vote from Memphis' suburbs.

Clement recused himself from politics and became president of Cumberland College. Its location — in Lebanon, east of Nashville — helped Clement remain visible in the capital.

After Boner won the 1987 mayor's race, the special Democratic primary for the 5th boiled down to Clement, relying on a heavy vote from working-class whites who were Boner's base, and wealthy businessman Phil Bredesen, who had narrowly lost the mayoralty to Boner and ran a media-heavy House campaign aimed at more affluent Democrats and GOP-leaning voters. Clement won by 40-to-36 percent.

In the Democratic 5th, home of such House members as Andrew Jackson and Sam Houston, Republican Terry Holcomb stumbled. He raised over $300,000, but ran out of money without airing a TV ad. Clement won easily, and has not faced a GOP foe since.

Tennessee 5

Nashville

More than 90 percent of the 5th District vote comes from Nashville and surrounding Davidson County, where Democrats normally prevail. George Bush managed to carry the county (and the district) in 1988, but that did not spark any wave of straight-ticket voting; Democratic Sen. Jim Sasser won Davidson overwhelmingly.

Country music may be Nashville's most famous industry, but state government is its leading employer. Davidson County is home to 17 colleges and universities, and its factories manufacture aircraft parts, glass, clothing and tires. Also, it is headquarters for several publishers of religious materials.

As governor from 1979-87, Republican Lamar Alexander successfully touted Tennessee's work force and business climate, particularly to Japanese investors. Nissan built a huge plant south of Nashville, and other Japanese companies have followed, many locating around the city. In addition, General Motors chose a site near Nashville for its massive new Saturn facility. Economic forecasters predict that many other jobs will spin off from these major investments, so the personality of the electorate could be in for some big changes.

But for now, the Democratic inclinations of government workers, the academic communities and labor unions uphold Nashville's traditional position as the focal point of Middle Tennessee Democratic populism. That brand of politics took hold in Nashville early in this century as a reaction to the conservative Democratic machine in Memphis that controlled Tennessee politics until after World War II.

Nashville's population is 23 percent black, a relatively low figure for a large Southern city. Nashville politics has not polarized along racial lines to the degree seen in Memphis and Chattanooga, where blacks make up a higher percentage of the population and whites have drifted from Democratic loyalties. Most white voters here are still Democrats.

Population: 514,832. White 398,418 (77%), Black 111,329 (22%), Other 2,932 (1%). Spanish origin 3,961 (1%). 18 and over 384,057 (75%), 65 and over 57,539 (11%). Median age: 30.

Committees

Merchant Marine & Fisheries (18th of 29 Democrats)
Coast Guard & Navigation; Oceanography, Great Lakes & Outer Continental Shelf

Public Works & Transportation (19th of 36 Democrats)
Aviation; Surface Transportation; Water Resources

Elections

1990 General		
Bob Clement (D)	55,607	(72%)
Tom Stone (I)	13,577	(18%)
Al Borgman (I)	5,383	(7%)
Maurice C. Kuttab (I)	2,192	(3%)
1988 General		
Bob Clement (D)	155,068	(100%)

Previous Winning Percentages: **1988 *** (62%)

** Special election.*

District Vote For President

	1988	1984	1980	1976
D	95,154 (47%)	95,254 (48%)	111,122 (60%)	106,554 (62%)
R	104,313 (52%)	103,600 (52%)	69,332 (37%)	63,167 (37%)
I			4,961 (3%)	

Campaign Finance

	Receipts	Receipts from PACs	Expend-itures
1990			
Clement (D)	$424,581	$272,825 (64%)	$298,005
1988			
Clement (D)	$1,267,477	$360,500 (28%)	$1,230,310

Key Votes

1991	
Authorize use of force against Iraq	Y
1990	
Support constitutional amendment on flag desecration	Y
Pass family and medical leave bill over Bush veto	Y
Reduce SDI funding	Y
Allow abortions in overseas military facilities	Y
Approve budget summit plan for spending and taxing	Y
Approve civil rights bill	Y
1989	
Halt production of B-2 stealth bomber at 13 planes	Y
Oppose capital gains tax cut	Y
Approve federal abortion funding in rape or incest cases	N
Approve pay raise and revision of ethics rules	N
Pass Democratic minimum wage plan over Bush veto	Y

Voting Studies

	Presidential Support		Party Unity		Conservative Coalition	
Year	**S**	**O**	**S**	**O**	**S**	**O**
1990	25	74	85	14	59	41
1989	42	52	74	22	66	32
1988	31	66	79	14	63	32

Interest Group Ratings

Year	ADA	ACU	AFL-CIO	CCUS
1990	44	29	83	29
1989	60	19	64	50
1988	75	20	93	36

6 Bart Gordon (D)

Of Murfreesboro — Elected 1984

Born: Jan. 24, 1949, Murfreesboro, Tenn.
Education: Middle Tennessee State U., B.S. 1971; U. of Tennessee, J.D. 1973.
Occupation: Lawyer.
Family: Single.
Religion: Methodist.
Political Career: Tenn. Democratic Party chairman, 1981-83.
Capitol Office: 103 Cannon Bldg. 20515; 225-4231.

In Washington: Best known as the premier Jim Wright protégé from the class of 1984, few junior House members had more cause than Gordon to fret over the fall of the former Speaker. But with his mentor out of the picture and with a possible run for governor tempting him in 1994, Gordon set out to establish a more independent legislative record.

The amiable Tennessean, well-liked and recognized as a steady performer on the Rules Committee, used the 101st Congress to emerge from Wright's shadow and stake out his own reputation.

Gordon received a small burst of media attention in March 1991 when he went undercover for NBC News posing as a prospective vocational education student in order to expose waste in student loan programs. Gordon had offered legislation to bar schools with high student loan default rates from receiving Pell Grant funds.

During 1990 debate on the Family and Medical Leave Act, Gordon joined with Pennsylvania Republican Curt Weldon to co-author a compromise — a watered down version of the original committee measure — that offered enough protection to small businesses to win the support of some centrist Democrats and Republicans. Congress approved the bill, but President Bush vetoed it.

Gordon let his interests look abroad in 1990. He initiated an effort early in the year to arrange donations of $40,000 worth of computer equipment to help Czechoslovakia prepare for its elections and was later appointed to a task force to help the new Eastern Europe democracies with technological assistance.

A reliable party loyalist even after Wright's departure, Gordon rarely disappoints the leadership. In both 1989 and 1990, he voted with the majority of his party more than 90 percent of the time on the floor.

When the House debated the conflict in the Persian Gulf, however, Gordon bucked convention. He joined just two other colleagues in the chamber in voting for the continued use of sanctions and then, after the resolution failed, voting to "close ranks" with the president and support the authorization of force.

At Home: Gordon was still in college when he worked on the unsuccessful 1968 House campaign of a state representative from his hometown. Sixteen years later, the Senate candidacy of Democratic Rep. Al Gore enabled Gordon to wage his own campaign.

Gordon built his political credentials within the state party structure. Fresh out of law school, he won a seat on the state Democratic Executive Committee, and in 1979 he parlayed his contacts into a position as the party's executive director. Two years later, he won the party chairmanship. In that position he computerized the party mailing list and set up a direct-mail program — experience that proved crucial to his House campaign.

Gordon's chief rivals in the 1984 House contest were state Rep. Lincoln Davis, who represented a cluster of counties in the Upper Cumberland region of the 6th, and Bryant Millsaps, the state House chief clerk, who shared Gordon's home base of Murfreesboro.

Gordon set himself apart from his primary opponents with his sophisticated phone bank and direct-mail operation. In the final weeks, while Millsaps focused on television advertising and Davis on pulling out his Upper Cumberland vote, Gordon's forces repeatedly wrote and telephoned undecided voters. Gordon won the six-way contest with 28 percent of the vote.

During the campaign, Gordon had to deal with the potentially explosive issue of a paternity suit that had been brought against him and was later dismissed. Gordon denied fathering the child, and none of his primary opponents raised the issue. But his GOP opponent, Williamson County construction executive Joe Simkins, accused him of a "cover-up," after the *Nashville Banner* alleged that Gordon had paid the woman to drop the suit.

Simkins, whose brother was publisher of the *Banner*, set a "countdown deadline" for Gordon to explain the settlement. Gordon simply ignored the challenge, as did most voters. He won all but two counties on Election Day.

Tennessee 6

North Central — Murfreesboro

This slice of Middle Tennessee spills out of the hills along the Kentucky border and runs through the lawns of suburban Nashville into the farm country beyond. It has always been Democratic, with old courthouse networks controlling politics and people living at an unhurried pace. But with the expansion of the suburbs and the introduction of two gargantuan vehicle-assembly plants, much is changing.

Republicans have made significant inroads in the metropolitan Nashville part of the 6th. These areas, filling with commuters, have no link to the rural and small-town Democratic traditions of the past. Williamson County, south of Nashville, gave George Bush more than 72 percent of the vote in 1988. In 1984 Williamson went against Gordon.

Outside Williamson, industrial expansion in once-sleepy towns is increasing the 6th's blue-collar work force. For now at least, the labor vote seems inclined to stay Democratic. In Smyrna, southeast of Nashville in Rutherford County, Japan's Nissan Motor Co. makes cars and light trucks at a facility that is the largest Japanese investment in the United States, employing some 3,000 people.

The largest single industrial investment in U.S. history, General Motors' multibillion-dollar Saturn automobile facility, is located in the tiny Maury County hamlet of Spring Hill. The fields and front porches of this two stop-light town were featured in a nationwide $100 million GM ad campaign extolling the virtues of the Saturn.

By comparison, the "Upper Cumberland" region in the eastern side of the 6th is lagging economically. Farming is in a slump, and the textile trades that hold many of the small towns together are worse.

Population: 511,805. White 471,838 (92%), Black 37,301 (7%). Spanish origin 3,377 (1%). 18 and over 362,322 (71%), 65 and over 55,363 (11%). Median age: 30.

Committees

Rules (8th of 9 Democrats)
Legislative Process

Select Aging (22nd of 42 Democrats)
Housing & Consumer Interests

Elections

1990 General		
Bart Gordon (D)	60,538	(67%)
Gregory Cochran (R)	26,424	(29%)
Ken Brown (I)	3,793	(4%)
1988 General		
Bart Gordon (D)	123,652	(76%)
Wallace Embry (R)	38,033	(24%)

Previous Winning Percentages: **1986** (77%) **1984** (63%)

District Vote For President

	1988	1984	1980	1976
D	72,992 (39%)	75,667 (41%)	92,485 (55%)	93,751 (64%)
R	111,548 (60%)	108,626 (59%)	72,526 (43%)	49,892 (34%)
I			3,209 (2%)	

Campaign Finance

	Receipts	Receipts from PACs	Expend-itures
1990			
Gordon (D)	$620,052	$355,275 (57%)	$367,090
Cochran (R)	$11,400	0	$8,996
1988			
Gordon (D)	$587,878	$256,095 (44%)	$454,346
Embry (R)	$12,635	$500 (4%)	$12,635

Key Votes

1991	
Authorize use of force against Iraq	Y
1990	
Support constitutional amendment on flag desecration	N
Pass family and medical leave bill over Bush veto	Y
Reduce SDI funding	Y
Allow abortions in overseas military facilities	Y
Approve budget summit plan for spending and taxing	Y
Approve civil rights bill	Y
1989	
Halt production of B-2 stealth bomber at 13 planes	N
Oppose capital gains tax cut	Y
Approve federal abortion funding in rape or incest cases	Y
Approve pay raise and revision of ethics rules	Y
Pass Democratic minimum wage plan over Bush veto	Y

Voting Studies

	Presidential Support		Party Unity		Conservative Coalition	
Year	**S**	**O**	**S**	**O**	**S**	**O**
1990	25	73	93	6	46	52
1989	35	64	91	7	59	39
1988	23	73	84	8	53	45
1987	27	69	82	10	63	37
1986	27	72	83	12	56	40
1985	33	66	79	13	42	56

Interest Group Ratings

Year	ADA	ACU	AFL-CIO	CCUS
1990	67	13	92	21
1989	75	11	92	50
1988	80	12	93	36
1987	64	0	87	29
1986	75	9	86	39
1985	55	20	63	45

7 Don Sundquist (R)

Of Memphis — Elected 1982

Born: March 15, 1936, Moline, Ill.
Education: Augustana College (Ill.), B.A. 1957.
Military Service: Navy, 1957-59.
Occupation: Owner of printing, advertising and marketing firm.
Family: Wife, Martha Swanson; three children.
Religion: Lutheran.
Political Career: No previous office.
Capitol Office: 230 Cannon Bldg. 20515; 225-2811.

In Washington: Sundquist ended the 101st Congress in atypical fashion; he overreached himself by seeking a party leadership post still occupied by a senior member unwilling to give it up. The post was the chairmanship of the House GOP campaign committee, held since the 1970s by Guy Vander Jagt of Michigan, the No. 2 Republican on the Ways and Means Committee. Sundquist is usually known as a first-rate vote counter. But when the votes for the campaign chair were counted on Dec. 3, 1990, Vander Jagt had won 98-66.

The outcome had not seemed so predetermined when Sundquist declared his intentions, and the Tennessean may have thought an active candidacy would prompt Vander Jagt to step down. After all, the party had lost seats in four of the past five elections and many House Republicans were grumbling about the committee's contribution.

But Sundquist may have gone too far in aggressively criticizing the committee's operations, especially the financial end involving its chief financial officer and staff fundraiser. Airing such issues in public made some of Sundquist's colleagues more than a little uncomfortable.

Sundquist's bid also suffered from circumstances beyond his control. When he announced in the fall of 1990, many conservative House Republicans were in a boil about the budget deal cut by President Bush and the congressional leadership — especially Bush's abandoning his "no new taxes" pledge. Sundquist, an ally of Bush since the early 1970s, was perceived as the president's man. Vander Jagt was seen as the defender of the campaign committee's co-chairman, Edward J. Rollins, who had offended the White House in 1990 by telling GOP candidates to distance themselves from the president's tax and budget positions.

The failed leadership move seemed uncharacteristic of Sundquist, whose career has been remarkable in its sure-footed and consistent success. An advertising executive by profession, he made it to the House in 1983 after years of loyal party work that won him the confidence of influential Republicans in West Tennessee. In Washington, he has shown his political acumen by quietly working his way into the hearts and minds of his colleagues and party leaders. The payoff in the 101st Congress was a coveted seat on the Ways and Means Committee.

Though Sundquist has been involved in issues strategizing for the GOP, the Ways and Means assignment came to him mostly because of his political sensibilities, not any particular legislative achievement. He has worked hard to get to know his colleagues, and more than a few of them seek his political advice before a difficult vote. In the 99th Congress, he was named regional whip for Southern and border states. Two years later, he was rewarded with a seat on the Budget Committee.

When he was national chairman of the Young Republicans in the 1970s, Sundquist became acquainted with Bush, then the chairman of the Republican National Committee. Sundquist supported Bush's first presidential bid, in the 1980 cycle. And in the 1988 presidential contest, he was a chief House organizer for Bush's primary- and general-election campaigns.

Sundquist's personal style is not confrontational, and he is a strong believer in party-building. In the House he wants Republicans to do more to see that the federal government does less. He is the archetypal New South conservative businessman — a man who bemoans bureaucratic inefficiencies and believes that many things the federal government does can be done better by local government or the private sector.

As part of his push for governmental efficiency, Sundquist has called for a revival of federal revenue sharing, as a replacement for a variety of economic-development programs. He has complained that grant formulas developed in years past discriminate against rural areas — such as those in his district — and that administrative costs are excessive and unnecessary. Localities are better suited to make spending decisions, he maintains.

Sundquist is not dead-set against federal

Tennessee 7

West Central — Clarksville; Part of Shelby County

If the East Side of Memphis and its adjoining suburbs were not included in this district, Democrats would win it routinely. Most of the 7th is farmland and small towns with names like Dull, Needmore, Spot and Only. A few manufacturing plants are sprinkled through the countryside.

But the Memphis portion of the district, within Shelby County, is home to a coterie of staunchly Republican voters. Much of this area has a nouveau riche feel, with showy homes, shopping malls and office parks that draw commerce away from center-city Memphis. Voter turnout is high, and Republican margins are phenomenal. When Democratic Sen. Jim Sasser won an overwhelming statewide victory in 1988, he barely managed a majority in this part of Shelby.

Although a couple of counties have sizable black populations, most of the voters in the non-Shelby portion of the 7th are white, conservative-populist and traditionally Democratic. Five counties in this area have not voted for a Republican in a major statewide contest since 1974.

Outside Shelby, there is only one city, Clarksville (Montgomery County), near the Kentucky border. Once a marketing center for fire-cured tobacco, today it depends on its factory payroll and the military population at Fort Campbell. Though Sundquist carried Montgomery County in his easy 1986 re-election, it went solidly Democratic in the governor's contest.

There is one pocket of rural Republican strength — a handful of counties along the Highland Rim, in the hilly south-central part of the district. There the terrain and voting behavior resemble Republican East Tennessee. Many farmers in the area opposed secession and have been loyal to the GOP ever since.

Population: 503,611. White 438,768 (87%), Black 60,217 (12%), Other 3,000 (1%). Spanish origin 5,224 (1%). 18 and over 351,201 (70%), 65 and over 46,053 (9%). Median age: 29.

spending, however. Until the 101st Congress he served on the Public Works and Transportation Committee, where colleagues noted with grudging admiration how many Memphis projects found their way into legislation. On Public Works, Sundquist targeted his crusade for efficiency at the Tennessee Valley Authority, which he views as a bloated bureaucracy. He has supported cost-cutting measures put into effect by Republican-appointed TVA officials in recent years.

The Ways and Means assignment gives Sundquist an opportunity to involve himself in a variety of issues. He has already shown interest in trade legislation, serving for several years as chairman of the House Republican Task Force on Trade and Competitiveness. Sundquist has constituents employed in shoe factories, and in the 99th Congress he pushed for footwear-protection provisions in a bill limiting textile imports. While he voted to override a presidential veto of the bill in 1986, he did not support such a move when a textile bill came up in the 100th Congress because he felt the shoe industry's situation had already improved.

Sundquist is usually found in the president's corner, even when the political price looks steep. When the Ways and Means Subcommittee on Human Resources approved an ambitious increase in spending for children's programs in June, 1990, Sundquist expressed the administration's disapproval and, calling himself the "skunk at a garden party," cast the lone nay vote.

When Ways and Means marked up a tax package in July 1989 and the Bush administration registered just one objection to it (excise tax increases on pipe tobacco and snuff), Sundquist was the man offering another source of revenue so the offending provision could be struck.

At Home: A winner of four easy re-elections in a House district that stretches from Memphis to Nashville, Sundquist is now being mentioned as a possible solution to the Tennessee GOP's dearth of appealing talent for statewide office.

That is remarkable progress for a man who had little public profile just 10 years ago, when he launched his first bid for Congress. That race was an impressive debut: He parlayed expertise gained in 12 years of GOP trenchwork into an upset over the scion of a well-known Tennessee political family.

Sundquist began his campaign in late 1981, when GOP Rep. Robin Beard was preparing his Senate bid. Many of the Republican activists Sundquist contacted knew him from his stints as Shelby County (Memphis) party chairman and his work for Beard, former Gov. Winfield Dunn, and former Sens. William E. Brock III and Howard H. Baker Jr.

The district's GOP establishment and crucial business leaders supported Sundquist, keeping other Republicans out of the primary. That sent Sundquist into a tough November contest with Bob Clement, a rural populist and son of the late Gov. Frank G. Clement (Bob Clement was later elected to the House from the 5th District).

The outcome hinged on the "Shelby factor." About 40 percent of the 7th's voters live in eastern Shelby County, a heavily Republican area containing affluent residential sections of Memphis and its suburbs. The 7th's other 15 counties are predominantly rural, and most of the voters there are conservative Democrats. In 1982, unemployment was high in all the rural counties, making them even less receptive to entreaties from a well-off suburban GOP businessman.

To compensate for his problems outside the Memphis area, Sundquist concentrated on mobilizing Shelby County's GOP suburbanites, who found little to like in Clement's political message, an arm-waving populism he inherited from his father.

Sundquist took three-fourths of the Shelby vote, exceeding his most optimistic projections. The combined vote in the district's other 15 counties went 65-35 percent for Clement, but that was not enough to offset the Democrat's dismal showing in Shelby.

For a while, it looked as if Sundquist might face a 1984 battle with former state Rep. Harold Byrd, who had lost to Clement in the 1982 Democratic primary, but that challenge never materialized, nor has any other of significance. The general anti-incumbent mood of 1990 touched Sundquist; re-elected with 80 percent of the vote in 1988, he mustered 62 percent against the same Democratic nominee in 1990.

Committee

Ways & Means (10th of 13 Republicans)
Oversight; Select Revenue Measures

Elections

1990 General		
Don Sundquist (R)	66,141	(62%)
Ken Bloodworth (D)	40,516	(38%)
1988 General		
Don Sundquist (R)	142,025	(80%)
Ken Bloodworth (D)	35,237	(20%)

Previous Winning Percentages: **1986** (72%) **1984** (100%) **1982** (51%)

District Vote For President

	1988	1984	1980	1976
D	67,200 (33%)	67,173 (34%)	73,984 (41%)	74,622 (51%)
R	138,246 (67%)	130,862 (66%)	100,694 (56%)	69,443 (48%)
I			3,789 (2%)	

Campaign Finance

	Receipts	Receipts from PACs	Expend-itures
1990			
Sundquist (R)	$648,472	$351,985 (54%)	$451,944
1988			
Sundquist (R)	$393,171	$182,103 (46%)	$307,656
Bloodworth (D)	$1,130	0	$1,110

Key Votes

1991	
Authorize use of force against Iraq	Y
1990	
Support constitutional amendment on flag desecration	Y
Pass family and medical leave bill over Bush veto	N
Reduce SDI funding	N
Allow abortions in overseas military facilities	N
Approve budget summit plan for spending and taxing	Y
Approve civil rights bill	N
1989	
Halt production of B-2 stealth bomber at 13 planes	N
Oppose capital gains tax cut	N
Approve federal abortion funding in rape or incest cases	N
Approve pay raise and revision of ethics rules	Y
Pass Democratic minimum wage plan over Bush veto	N

Voting Studies

	Presidential Support		Party Unity		Conservative Coalition	
Year	**S**	**O**	**S**	**O**	**S**	**O**
1990	74	25	90	9	94	2
1989	80	17	86	10	98	0
1988	64	28	86	5	89	5
1987	60	34	86	10	91	9
1986	74	24	86	13	92	6
1985	75	23	87	10	91	7
1984	73	26	76	20	90	7
1983	70	29	83	14	91	6

Interest Group Ratings

Year	ADA	ACU	AFL-CIO	CCUS
1990	6	79	8	86
1989	5	78	17	90
1988	10	96	17	100
1987	8	82	25	80
1986	5	82	14	72
1985	15	81	18	91
1984	5	79	17	69
1983	0	87	18	74

8 John Tanner (D)

Of Union City — Elected 1988

Born: Sept. 22, 1944, Halls, Tenn.
Education: U. of Tennessee, B.S. 1966, J.D. 1968.
Military Service: Navy, 1968-72; Tenn. Army National Guard, 1974-present.
Occupation: Lawyer; banker.
Family: Wife, Betty Ann Portis; two children.
Religion: Disciples of Christ.
Political Career: Tenn. House, 1977-89.
Capitol Office: 1232 Longworth Bldg. 20515; 225-4714.

In Washington: Tanner would have been comfortable in the House of old, where junior members were seen more than heard. While Tanner as a freshman took a seat on the House Armed Services Committee and was regarded by senior colleagues as having serious potential, he maintained a very low profile.

The Armed Services post enabled Tanner to oversee funding for several military facilities that are in the 8th District.

Generally viewed as a "pro-defense" Democrat — he voted for the resolution authorizing President Bush to use military force against Iraq — he is not an automatic vote for Pentagon priorities.

"The strategic weapons systems, such as the strategic defense initiative ... the B-2 stealth bomber, and the MX mobile missile rail system may not be necessary in this changing environment... funding for these weapons programs may have to be reduced," Tanner said in a 1991 report to his constituents.

Tanner also is on the Science Committee. Then a member of the subcommittee dealing with environmental research, Tanner earned a place in 1990 on the conference committee that crafted the final version of the Clean Air Act.

In 1989, Tanner was elected as an officer of the House Sportsman's Caucus, which was formed, he said, "to educate our colleagues" about the commitment of sportsmen to conservation, wildlife management and other issues related to the outdoors.

In the wake of the October 1989 earthquake that hit San Francisco, Tanner advocated more funding for seismological research and enhanced availability of earthquake insurance for homeowners.

His district is in the potential earthquake zone near the New Madrid Fault.

At Home: The retirement of longtime Democratic Rep. Ed Jones after nearly two decades of service brought the rare prospect of a competitive election in the 8th. But Tanner came out of the blocks practically before the contest could begin. A longtime ally of the incumbent — Tanner's grandfather was a friend of Jones — Tanner had already laid the groundwork for a campaign. He quickly assembled an enviable organization and financial base, boosted by his connections to Jones and to Gov. Ned McWherter, whose home base is in the 8th. Tanner, a 12-year veteran of the Legislature, had been in the state House when McWherter was Speaker.

Tanner also had some natural appeal to business interests: In Union City he was a member of a local law firm and senior vice president of a local savings and loan association; in the state House he served as chairman of the Commerce Committee.

But Tanner, who went to the University of Tennessee on a basketball scholarship, appeals to more than just the buttoned-down set. His relaxed, "good ol' boy" style helped him win over rural voters, who hold considerable sway in the 8th.

During the primary season, Tanner traveled the district on a 230-stop listening tour, mixing easily with voters at country stores and other local gathering spots. He made a similar tour for the general election.

The five-way Democratic primary included Jackson Mayor Bob Conger and former Democratic Gov. Ray Blanton, whose gubernatorial term was so scandal-plagued it eventually landed him in prison. But none of the Democrats made a dent in Tanner's armor. On primary day, he garnered 66 percent of the vote.

The GOP nominee, Jackson attorney Ed Bryant, had organized the district for Pat Robertson's presidential campaign. Bryant tried to convince voters that Tanner would be controlled by a liberal national Democratic Party leadership in Washington.

"Bull," said Tanner. "Ed Jones has been his own man and John Tanner will be his own man."

Tanner's support for the death penalty and the presidential line-item veto, together with his opposition to national health insurance proposals made it difficult for anyone to portray him as a liberal. He won with more than 60 percent.

Tennessee 8

West — Jackson; Part of Shelby County

This is a region of soybeans, corn, wheat and cotton. It has neither grown nor changed very much in recent years; 13 rural counties account for two-thirds of the vote, and are nearly always Democratic. Jimmy Carter took all but one of them in 1980; even Walter F. Mondale and Michael S. Dukakis — hardly the type of candidates to engender much enthusiasm in rural West Tennessee — each managed to carry five counties in the 8th when they ran for president.

The fact that politics in this part of Tennessee has not changed much through the years enables some of its elected officials to acquire enough seniority to gain considerable influence. Rep. Ed Jones, who retired in 1989, is one example; another is Ned McWherter, a native of the 8th District town of Dresden who served seven terms as Speaker of the state House before winning the governorship in 1986.

The 8th includes the Frayser area of Memphis and a significant part of northern Shelby County, where suburbia and GOP dominance give way to farms and Democratic leanings. The Memphis Naval Air Station is in north Shelby, near the town of Millington. About 20 percent of the people in the 8th live in Shelby County; that figure was higher in the 1970s, but to keep the 8th securely Democratic, the last round of redistricting excised 75,000 mostly Republican voters in suburban Memphis from the district.

Madison County (Jackson) has another 15 percent of the vote. Republicans are gaining ground there, thanks in part to an influx of managerial personnel to Jackson's increasingly diversified industries, a Procter & Gamble Co. facility that makes Pringles potato chips, Porter Cable (formerly a Rockwell hand tool factory), and Allied Astermarket, once a Bendix auto parts plant.

The surrounding farm counties look to Jackson, the district's largest city, as a source of retail goods and services. Republican statewide candidates can usually hold their own in Madison County; McWherter carried it only narrowly in his 1986 gubernatorial victory, and George Bush won it with nearly 60 percent in 1988.

Population: 504,957. White 400,579 (79%), Black 101,042 (20%). Spanish origin 4,595 (1%). 18 and over 358,805 (71%), 65 and over 65,163 (13%). Median age: 30.

Committees

Armed Services (27th of 33 Democrats)
Investigations; Procurement & Military Nuclear Systems

Science, Space & Technology (22nd of 32 Democrats)
Investigations & Oversight; Space; Technology & Competitiveness

Elections

1990 General		
John Tanner (D)	62,241	(100%)
1988 General		
John Tanner (D)	94,571	(62%)
Ed Bryant (R)	56,893	(38%)

District Vote For President

	1988	1984	1980	1976
D	69,420 (43%)	74,732 (43%)	87,477 (51%)	92,833 (60%)
R	89,899 (56%)	98,966 (57%)	80,238 (47%)	59,608 (39%)

Campaign Finance

	Receipts	Receipts from PACs		Expend-itures
1990				
Tanner (D)	$314,094	$135,500	(43%)	$153,941
1988				
Tanner (D)	$931,539	$283,961	(30%)	$863,425
Bryant (R)	$106,318	$3,800	(4%)	$106,028

Key Votes

1991	
Authorize use of force against Iraq	Y
1990	
Support constitutional amendment on flag desecration	N
Pass family and medical leave bill over Bush veto	N
Reduce SDI funding	Y
Allow abortions in overseas military facilities	Y
Approve budget summit plan for spending and taxing	Y
Approve civil rights bill	Y
1989	
Halt production of B-2 stealth bomber at 13 planes	N
Oppose capital gains tax cut	N
Approve federal abortion funding in rape or incest cases	Y
Approve pay raise and revision of ethics rules	N
Pass Democratic minimum wage plan over Bush veto	Y

Voting Studies

	Presidential Support		Party Unity		Conservative Coalition	
Year	**S**	**O**	**S**	**O**	**S**	**O**
1990	31	67	73	21	85	9
1989	47†	51†	75†	21†	90	10

† Not eligible for all recorded votes.

Interest Group Ratings

Year	ADA	ACU	AFL-CIO	CCUS
1990	44	29	58	54
1989	40	44	67	70

9 Harold E. Ford (D)

Of Memphis — Elected 1974

Born: May 20, 1945, Memphis, Tenn.
Education: Tennessee State U., B.S. 1967; John Gupton Mortuary, L.F.D., L.E.D. 1969; Howard U., M.B.A. 1982.
Occupation: Mortician.
Family: Wife, Dorothy Bowles; three children.
Religion: Baptist.
Political Career: Tenn. House, 1971-75.
Capitol Office: 2305 Rayburn Bldg. 20515; 225-3265.

In Washington: Ford spent the first months of the 102nd Congress much as he had spent all the 101st, waiting for some resolution of the bank, mail and tax-fraud charges pending against him back in Memphis. Temporarily deposed as chairman of the Ways and Means Subcommittee on Human Resources (under caucus rules regarding criminal indictments), he has receded from sight on other committee business as well.

In its April 1987 indictment, a federal grand jury in Knoxville charged that Ford had traded his influence for more than $1 million in bank loans arranged by Tennessee financiers Jake and C. H. Butcher Jr. According to the government's case, these loans were never to be repaid and were, in fact, bribes.

The charges followed a three-year investigation in Memphis but were filed in Knoxville, where the Butchers were based and where federal prosecutors may have thought they could more easily obtain a conviction. Ford's attorneys won a change of venue back to Memphis, where he continues to enjoy tremendous political popularity and influence. He was tried in federal court there in 1990, but the jury, dividing largely along racial lines, could not reach a verdict and was dismissed on April 27. Undeterred, federal prosecutors refused to drop the charges.

The court has since attempted to find jurors untainted by the years of publicity surrounding the case. At one point, a judge ordered jurors to be brought by bus from Jackson, Tenn., a mostly white town 90 miles from Memphis. Ford's attorneys filed an appeal claiming the judge's action was an effort to stack the jury.

In the meantime, the House ethics committee has not acted on the charges against Ford; the panel typically takes no action involving individuals who are facing trial until court proceedings run their course.

Ford was re-elected to his subcommittee chairmanship in the 101st Congress, but under Democratic Caucus rules he cannot serve in that post until his legal problems are resolved. Thomas J. Downey of New York became acting subcommittee chairman, a role he maintained under the same arrangement in the 102nd.

Ford's legal problems began just as he had attained a position of real influence as leader of the panel rewriting national welfare policy. When discussions of overhauling the welfare system picked up steam in early 1987, Ford, as the relevant subcommittee chairman (it was then called the Subcommittee on Public Assistance and Unemployment Compensation), had the support of the House Democratic leadership for his bill. Although he soon had to cut the measure's cost in half, he moved it through his subcommittee in March 1987. He was indicted the following month.

Ford brings a minority-rights perspective to discussions of welfare policy, complementing the viewpoint of his Senate counterpart, New York's Daniel Patrick Moynihan, who is chairman of the Social Security and Family Policy Subcommittee. Ford did not wait for Moynihan to act before launching his own welfare-overhaul bill, which expanded benefits but required states to make work, education or training mandatory for welfare recipients.

In the opening rounds of the welfare debate, Ford insisted that any bill would have to focus on expanding benefits as well as moving recipients off the welfare rolls whenever possible. The centerpiece of his bill was a program aimed at training welfare recipients so they can move into the work force. Under the plan, welfare mothers with children over age 3 could be required to participate in work or training activities. Major portions of Ford's program were incorporated into the final welfare package that became law in 1988.

One of Ford's more controversial goals was to require states to make two-parent households eligible for support if the principal wage earner is unemployed; under existing law, about half the states help only if one parent is gone. For years, the Congressional Black Caucus has complained that this system encourages the breakup of poor families. Unless the federal government mandates change, Ford said, "some

Tennessee 9

Memphis

Thanks to the one-party allegiance of blacks, who make up well over half the population of the 9th, Ford's district has been reliably Democratic in good years and bad. Jimmy Carter won 63 percent of the vote there in 1980, considerably more than in any other Tennessee district; Walter F. Mondale and Michael S. Dukakis also did similarly well. Democrat Al Gore drew 70 percent in the 9th in his successful 1984 Senate campaign; Democratic Sen. Jim Sasser won even bigger in 1988.

But the fact that this district has had black representation for a dozen years should not obscure the significance of the white electorate. Though blacks are a majority of the population, blacks and whites are about even among registered voters. Because of "white flight" from inner-city Memphis in the 1970s, 1982 redistricting added about 80,000 people to the 9th, many of them white working-class people — the same ones who had fled downtown a few years earlier. It is a political challenge keeping both blacks and whites happy, because in Memphis, elections as well as neighborhoods often polarize along racial lines.

The Memphis economy is a mixture of old and new. Cotton marketing and processing of cottonseed into oil continue, as they have for more than a century and a half. But now the emphasis has shifted to employers that deliver goods, people and services. Memphis is headquarters for the air fleet of Federal Express and for the Holiday Inn empire, and the Memphis airport has become a major hub for the mid-South. Memphis has long been the stop of significance on the Mississippi River between St. Louis and New Orleans, and after years in the doldrums, the city seems to be recapturing a sense of itself as a regional capital. Its media look as much to northern Mississippi and to eastern Arkansas as they do to Nashville and the rest of Tennessee.

For years, Memphis seemed uninterested in preserving its character and traditions. But that has changed as well. The historic Peabody Hotel, whose lobby used to be described as the northern outpost of the Mississippi Delta, reopened in 1981, complete with the ducks that ride the elevator down from their rooftop pool to swim in the lobby fountain. Nearby Beale Street, where W. C. Handy and other jazz composers flourished early in this century, is emerging from blight to play host to a new generation of clubs and restaurants. And an entertainment complex on an island in the Mississippi draws attention to the city's river heritage.

Population: 505,592. White 213,131 (42%), Black 289,152 (57%). Spanish origin 4,164 (1%). 18 and over 359,672 (71%), 65 and over 60,008 (12%). Median age: 28.

of the Southern states will never adopt it."

Ford came close to getting a similar change made twice in 1986, but both times he lost in showdowns with the administration. In 1988, the House-Senate conference snagged over the requirement. White House officials had reluctantly supported adding the language to the Senate version of the bill, but only in concert with a "workfare" provision requiring one parent in such households to perform at least 16 hours of unpaid work each week. House conferees strongly opposed the workfare requirement.

After three months of wrangling, key House, Senate and White House negotiators held a two-and-a-half-hour meeting and emerged with a compromise containing both changes. President Ronald Reagan signed the final package into law.

Ford took over the Public Assistance Subcommittee in 1981, and through the decade he got generally good marks for his handling of the panel. He was an especially effective ally of labor unions. In past Congresses, Ford fought hard to get the federal government to help jobless workers who had exhausted state unemployment benefits. A 10-week supplemental benefits program was enacted as part of tax legislation in 1982.

At Home: Politicians slapped with indictments often fall prey to electoral trouble, but Ford has a strong base to support him. His is the dominant political family in the Memphis black community. His brother John, a former city councilman, serves in the state Senate; his brother James is on the City Council. Shortly after Rep. Ford was indicted, he arrived to a cheering crowd at the Memphis airport and claimed that the federal prosecutor "wants to destroy the black political power in Tennessee." Ford's faithful supporters helped him win another House term easily in 1988.

They also helped him quash his most serious primary challenger in 1990. State Rep. Pam Gaia, a 16-year legislator, waged a campaign offering "honesty and integrity." But with a huge funding advantage and continued support in Memphis' black community, Ford collected 69 percent; Gaia, who is white, managed only 27 percent. In November against typically weak GOP opposition, though, Ford was held to 58 percent, his lowest-ever re-election tally.

The Ford organization is extensive, reaching down to the block level in many neighborhoods. In addition to mobilizing that network on their own behalf, the Ford brothers often endorse candidates in Democratic primaries for local and statewide offices.

Harold Ford began his political career in 1970, winning election to the Tennessee House at age 25. In his first term, he was majority whip and chaired a committee that investigated the rates and practices of utilities in the state.

Redistricting in 1972 increased the black population in the Memphis congressional district to 48 percent. That caused trouble for Republican Rep. Dan H. Kuykendall.

Kuykendall had won three House elections with increasing ease by taking virtually all the votes of the district's whites. But in 1972, running within the new borders for the first time, he was held to 55 percent by a black Democrat who made little attempt to attract white support.

Ford challenged Kuykendall in 1974. After winning a six-way Democratic primary, Ford ran a broader and more active campaign than did the 1972 Democratic nominee. Ford reached out to white voters, stressing economic issues and promising to listen to whites as well as blacks if he were elected.

Reaping political benefit from Kuykendall's longstanding association with Richard M. Nixon, who resigned the presidency that year, Ford edged past the incumbent by 744 votes, becoming Tennessee's first black congressman.

Before the 1976 election, a court-ordered readjustment of district lines removed 12,000 white suburban voters from Ford's district and put them in the adjoining 6th. The readjustment gave Ford a black majority, and in the next three elections he won handily.

Although 1981 redistricting reduced the share of blacks in the district's voting population to just above 50 percent, Ford won easily in the 1982 primary and general election.

Committees

Select Aging (3rd of 42 Democrats)
Housing & Consumer Interests; Retirement, Income & Employment; Social Security and Women

Ways & Means (7th of 23 Democrats)
Human Resources; Oversight

Elections

1990 General		
Harold E. Ford (D)	48,629	(58%)
Aaron C. Davis (R)	25,730	(31%)
Thomas M. Davidson (I)	7,249	(9%)
Isaac Richmond (I)	2,032	(2%)
1990 Primary		
Harold E. Ford (D)	55,247	(69%)
Pam Gaia (D)	21,689	(27%)
Mark Flanagan (D)	2,862	(4%)
1988 General		
Harold E. Ford (D)	126,280	(82%)
Isaac Richmond (I)	28,522	(18%)

Previous Winning Percentages: **1986** (83%) **1984** (72%) **1982** (72%) **1980** (100%) **1978** (70%) **1976** (61%) **1974** (50%)

District Vote For President

	1988	1984	1980	1976
D	117,491 (66%)	137,826 (64%)	128,962 (63%)	121,879 (60%)
R	59,955 (34%)	77,894 (36%)	69,760 (34%)	79,724 (39%)
I			4,278 (2%)	

Campaign Finance

	Receipts	Receipts from PACs	Expend-itures
1990			
Ford (D)	$283,087	$169,925 (60%)	$284,282
1988			
Ford (D)	$298,096	$211,500 (71%)	$364,330

Key Votes

1991	
Authorize use of force against Iraq	N
1990	
Support constitutional amendment on flag desecration	N
Pass family and medical leave bill over Bush veto	Y
Reduce SDI funding	Y
Allow abortions in overseas military facilities	Y
Approve budget summit plan for spending and taxing	N
Approve civil rights bill	Y
1989	
Halt production of B-2 stealth bomber at 13 planes	Y
Oppose capital gains tax cut	Y
Approve federal abortion funding in rape or incest cases	Y
Approve pay raise and revision of ethics rules	Y
Pass Democratic minimum wage plan over Bush veto	Y

Voting Studies

	Presidential Support		Party Unity		Conservative Coalition	
Year	**S**	**O**	**S**	**O**	**S**	**O**
1990	8	53	62	3	6	67
1989	21	64	85	0	2	80
1988	12	57	61	2	5	66
1987	9	48	63	1	9	40
1986	16	73	71	4	12	70
1985	18	78	87	2	7	85
1984	29	57	81	4	15	76
1983	20	65	78	3	10	74
1982	27	56	81	6	19	64
1981	34	59	89	4	9	85

Interest Group Ratings

Year	ADA	ACU	AFL-CIO	CCUS
1990	89	5	100	27
1989	80	0	100	10
1988	85	0	100	36
1987	68	0	93	0
1986	100	0	91	8
1985	90	0	94	14
1984	80	0	83	31
1983	75	0	93	35
1982	80	0	100	30
1981	85	0	100	11

Texas

U.S. CONGRESS

SENATE 1 D, 1 R
HOUSE 19 D, 8 R

LEGISLATURE

Senate 23 D, 8 R
House 94 D, 56 R

ELECTIONS

1988 Presidential Vote

Bush	56%
Dukakis	43%

1984 Presidential Vote

Reagan	64%
Mondale	36%

1980 Presidential Vote

Reagan	55%
Carter	41%
Anderson	3%

Turnout rate in 1986	25%
Turnout rate in 1988	44%
Turnout rate in 1990	27%

(as percentage of voting age population)

POPULATION AND GROWTH

1980 population	14,229,191
1990 population (3rd in the nation)	16,986,510
Percent change 1980-1990	+19%

DEMOGRAPHIC BREAKDOWN

White	75%
Black	12%
Asian or Pacific Islander	2%
(Hispanic origin)	26%
Urban	80%
Rural	20%
Born in state	68%
Foreign-born	6%

MAJOR CITIES

Houston	1,630,553
Dallas	1,006,877
San Antonio	935,933
El Paso	515,342
Austin	465,622

AREA AND LAND USE

Area 262,017 sq. miles (2nd)

Farm	78%
Forest	8%
Federally owned	2%

Gov. Ann W. Richards (D)
Of Austin — Elected 1990

Born: Sept. 1, 1933, Waco, Texas.
Education: Baylor U., B.A. 1954.
Occupation: Teacher.
Religion: Methodist.
Political Career: Travis County commissioner, 1977-82; Texas state treasurer, 1983-91.
Next Election: 1994.

WORK

Occupations

White-collar	53%
Blue-collar	32%
Service workers	12%

Government Workers

Federal	175,607
State	248,363
Local	742,655

MONEY

Median family income	$ 19,618	(27th)
Tax burden per capita	$ 705	(43rd)

EDUCATION

Spending per pupil through grade 12	$ 3,608	(36th)
Persons with college degrees	17%	(23rd)

CRIME

Violent crime rate 659 per 100,000 (12th)

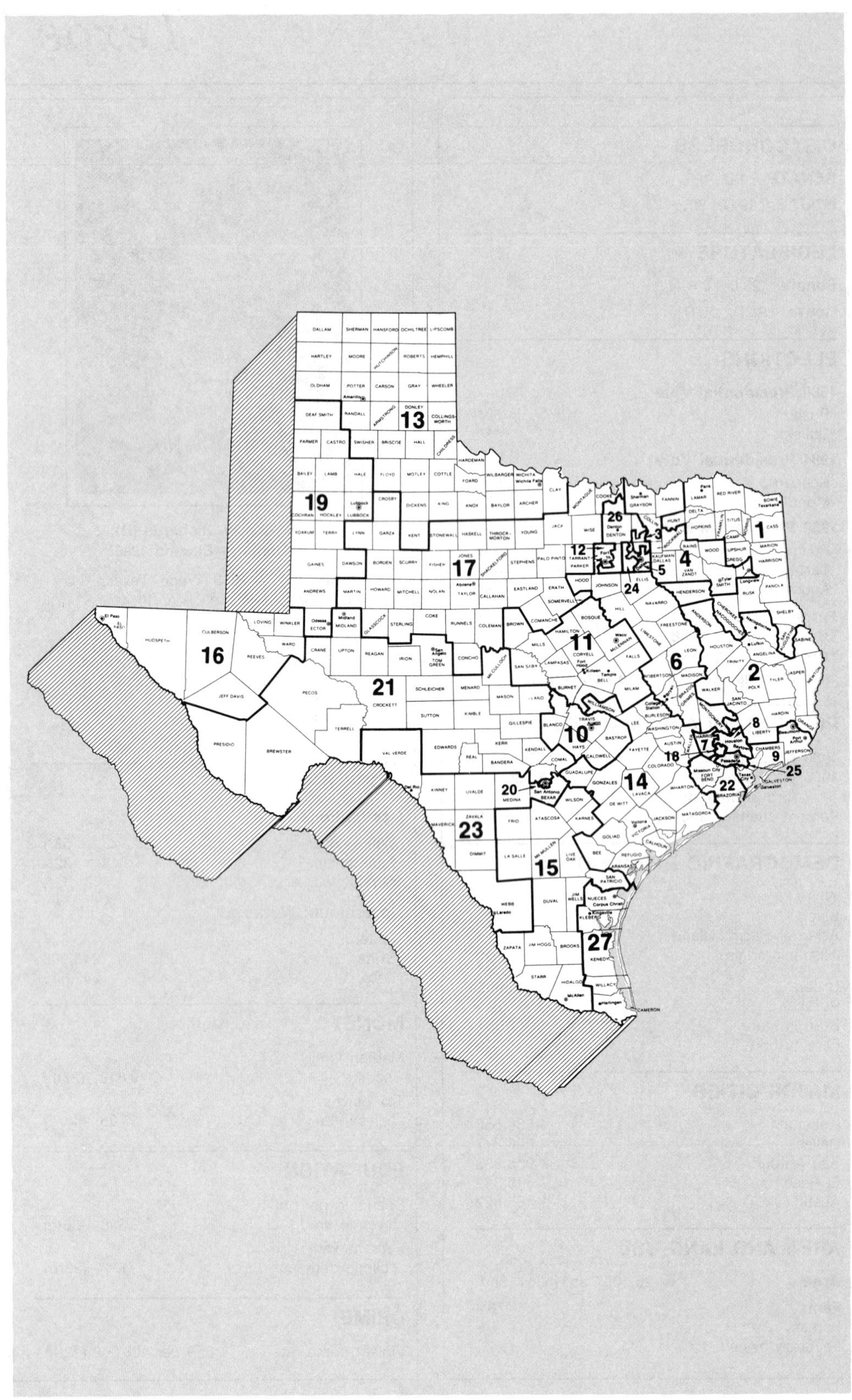

1
2
4
5
6
7
8
9
10
11
12
13
14
15
16
17
18
19
20
21
22
23
24
25
26
27

Lloyd Bentsen (D)

Of Houston — Elected 1970

Born: Feb. 11, 1921, Mission, Texas.
Education: U. of Texas, LL.B. 1942.
Military Service: Army Air Corps, 1942-45; Air Force Reserve, 1950-59.
Occupation: Lawyer; financial executive.
Family: Wife, Beryl Ann "B. A." Longino; three children.
Religion: Presbyterian.
Political Career: Hidalgo County judge, 1947-48; U.S. House, 1948-55; sought Democratic nomination for president, 1976; Democratic nominee for vice president, 1988.
Capitol Office: 703 Hart Bldg. 20510; 224-5922.

In Washington: Bentsen enjoyed a political renaissance in the late 1980s, when for several years the Democratic Party suddenly seemed to need him on every front at once. As political wiseman, legislator, major committee chairman and, ultimately, half of the national ticket, Bentsen in his late 60s seemed to personify the late-bloomer.

Since then, however, his momentum has stalled. His power-base committee, Senate Finance, has not revisited the heights it reached in the 100th Congress. And Bentsen himself — no longer as pivotal legislatively and without an apparent political objective — has receded in the national imagination.

As the vice presidential nominee in 1988, Bentsen was on a ticket that carried only 10 states, Texas not among them. But after a long and nasty presidential season, he seemed to many the least besmirched and most enhanced of all the personalities that had paraded across the stage. He could also take solace in having won re-election to the Senate that same fall by his most generous margin ever.

When he was chosen in 1989 to deliver the Senate Democrats' televised response to President George Bush's first State of the Union address, it was an acknowledgment that the silver-haired Texan had become one of the party's foremost symbols and spokesmen.

But in the rest of the 101st Congress, Bentsen's biggest accomplishment may have been helping Majority Leader George J. Mitchell scuttle a cut in the capital gains tax (a cut Bentsen himself had endorsed for many years). On his own, Bentsen's achievements have run to significant but smaller-scale items such as expanded Medicaid coverage for children and improved tax credits for working families with children.

Early in the 102nd Congress, Bentsen gave priority to health insurance and other issues of social welfare, especially as they affected children. But he gained as much notice for spiking yet another proposed tax cut: the lower Social Security payroll tax espoused by his Democratic colleague, Daniel Patrick Moynihan. While admitting the cut could put hundreds of dollars back into working people's hands, Bentsen said it would be irresponsible to leave the Social Security trust fund vulnerable to recession.

Meanwhile, Bentsen's own favorite tax idea, a revival of tax-deferred individual retirement accounts for all taxpayers, was becalmed. In 1991, Bentsen went so far as to wed his own IRA plan with a rival approach authored by GOP Sen. William V. Roth Jr. The new bill attracted a majority of the Senate as cosponsors. But it was hard to take it seriously because it included no means for recouping its five-year, $25 billion revenue loss, as required under current congressional budgeting rules.

Those same rules were also taking a lot of the fun out of life on Finance, where tax breaks now had to be paired with revenue-restoring tax increases. The committee's much defended right to oversee U.S. trade relations has proven problematic as well. Bush's trade officials have consulted regularly but kept a step or two ahead of their would-be overseers.

Bentsen still turns up on lists of prospective nominees for president in 1992. But he is less often discussed as a threat to win. He is, rather, suggested as a caretaker candidate, a conservative "firewall" insulating down-ballot Democrats in the South from damage if Bush wins re-election by a decisive margin.

It is far from clear that Bentsen would even want the nomination, especially in "firewall" terms. One sign of weak interest was his decision in 1990 to rejoin the exclusive men's clubs from which he had resigned when he was the party's vice presidential nominee.

Bentsen is a proud man who conducts his business with a sense of reserve that bespeaks another era. When he first came to Congress in the

1940s, he had extraordinary mentors in Speaker Sam Rayburn and Sen. Lyndon B. Johnson, both his fellow Texans and poker partners. But the House felt slow-moving and dull to the former bomber pilot, so he left politics and amassed a personal fortune as a Houston insurance executive. In 1970 he came storming back as a conservative Democrat to win the first of four Senate races.

By the mid-1980s, however, Bentsen's long career seemed to have led to nothing more than the ranking minority seat on Senate Environment. His one foray into presidential politics had collapsed early in 1976, and when he was courted for the vice presidency in 1984 it seemed largely for show. Even his standing in Texas seemed to have peaked. But a series of events reversed the direction of Bentsen's career and led on to new heights.

First, the Democrats recaptured control of the Senate in the 1986 elections. Sen. Russell B. Long of Louisiana, the longtime Democratic dean on Finance, had retired, and Bentsen took his place. The Finance seat proved warm immediately, as a procession of major bills moved through the committee in the 100th Congress. Bentsen handled them all with aplomb.

But a successful season in the Finance chair was the least of Bentsen's contributions to the presidential ticket. He and Dukakis were satirized as "the odd couple," but Bentsen's credentials gave Dixie a reason to consider voting for Dukakis. Most of all, Bentsen gave the ticket a shot at Texas' 29 electoral votes. No Democrat has been elected president without carrying Texas since Texas became a state.

Bentsen performed well throughout the campaign, but he was only able to distract the spotlight from Dukakis on the night of the vice presidential debate. In that encounter, Bentsen withered Bush's running mate, Sen. Dan Quayle of Indiana, with a line — "Senator, you're no Jack Kennedy" — that instantly became part of the political parlance.

Returning to the helm of Finance, Bentsen found the highlights of the previous Congress difficult to duplicate. The committee's first challenge was to produce $5.3 billion in new revenues required by the fiscal 1990 budget agreement between the White House and congressional leaders. Bush wanted a cut in the capital gains tax, which he said would spark enough asset sales to produce more revenue (even at lower rates).

Although Bentsen had been friendly to such notions before, he pronounced the case weak in 1989. When the House included a capital-gains tax cut in its budget package that October, Bentsen refused to follow suit in committee. He leaned on every lever available to keep Democrats behind him on Finance, where GOP efforts to force the capital issues to the floor failed on a tie vote. That gave Majority Leader George J. Mitchell the upper hand procedurally when the budget came before the Senate, and advocates of the cut could not muster 60 votes to break Mitchell's grip.

But apart from that defensive victory, Bentsen found the administration a tough competitor on other matters before his committee. Chief among these was the monitoring of the omnibus trade bill of 1988. The bill expressed fresh resolve to force reciprocity with trading partners. The first list of "unfair traders" had to be prepared early in 1989. Those on it would face a round of bilateral talks that would have to produce a lowering of barriers or otherwise compensate the United States for lost exports. If unsatisfied, the U.S. trade representative would be able to impose new tariffs, quotas or other sanctions.

In 1989, the administration targeted Japan, Brazil and India. Brazil was soon dropped, and so was Japan after the administration completed a separate set of talks with Tokyo under a rubric (the "structural impediments initiative") wholly separate from the 1988 trade law. Bentsen repeatedly expressed displeasure with this but found little he could do about it.

Bentsen had been in the vanguard of tough trade sentiment in 1985, joining with key House Democrats to sponsor a bill threatening a 25 percent surcharge on imports from Japan and other key trading partners. When support for that idea faded, he helped develop a Senate Democratic trade proposal strengthening the procedures for setting trade policy.

On the other hand, Bentsen's work in the 100th Congress included passage of the U.S.-Canada free-trade agreement. And in the 102nd, he favored similar arrangements to include Mexico in a North American free trade area. Bentsen also supported the president's request for two years in which to negotiate trade treaties (including Mexican free trade and the new round of agreements under the General Agreement on Tariffs and Trade) and submit them for fast-track approval — a virtual seal against amendments.

Besides trade, Finance in the 100th had taken part in a major reform of the welfare system, emphasizing education and jobs for welfare recipients, and produced a Taxpayer Bill of Rights authored by Democratic Sen. David Pryor of Arkansas. The committee also expanded Medicare to give catastrophic-illness protection to all older or disabled citizens.

The catastrophic health insurance bill began to produce an outcry early in 1989, as more affluent senior citizens began to notice the supplemental premium they were paying for the coverage. Bentsen was among the first to support reducing the premium, but he was disappointed when Congress retreated all the way to total repeal.

Bentsen may strike some observers as resembling a senior corporate executive more than a politician. Though not dour or cheerless, he strikes many as aloof and rather formal. He seems happiest working within a structured environment similar to that of a corporation, with written memos and clear lines of authority.

One would not pick him out of a crowd as a Texan, or a man who has spent nearly 30 years in public office.

He is a Texan, though, and that fact shone through in March 1989 when he cast one of just three Democratic votes in favor of John G. Tower's nomination as secretary of Defense. Tower had been Bentsen's colleague in the Senate for 14 years, and Bentsen said the FBI reports about Tower's personal behavior did not describe the man he knew.

Bentsen has devoted much of his Senate career to promoting U.S. business. He had laid out a long-term business agenda over a decade ago, in his 1976 presidential campaign. Running on a platform of economic revival through tax cuts and reductions in the capital gains tax, he put together a campaign operation that functioned like an efficient medium-sized company. But he attracted little support and disappeared from the campaign before much of the country had even begun to pay attention. Within five years, though, the basics of his proposals had become law, albeit under a GOP president.

Such close ties to business can have their downside, especially for a leader of the Democratic Party. Some liberals in Washington like to watch Bentsen for signs he is carrying his business loyalties too far. Sometimes he makes their job easy. Soon after taking over the Finance chairmanship, Bentsen informed lobbyists in the capital that they could purchase the right to have breakfast with him once a month for $10,000. Stung by the publicity and criticism this idea received, Bentsen soon pulled the plug on what he called "a doozy" of a mistake.

During the landmark overhaul of the tax code in 1986, Bentsen fought alongside Oklahoma Democrat David L. Boren to preserve benefits for the oil and gas industry. He had less success in protecting real estate investors from a crackdown on "passive loss" tax shelters.

When he took the Finance chair, Bentsen moved off the Environment and Public Works Committee, where he had been a low-key ranking member interested mainly in public works.

At Home: Bentsen began the 1988 election cycle as one of the Senate's best bets for re-election. Even without the $10,000 breakfast club, the Finance chairmanship had made Bentsen the leading collector of political action committee money in Congress. He was without visible political weaknesses other than his age, an issue Bentsen neatly dismissed by noting how active his father still was at 94.

Some Republicans preferred to leave Bentsen unchallenged for re-election in 1988, lest he mobilize his considerable resources in Texas and help other Democrats. But the National Republican Senatorial Committee was loath to have Bentsen distributing his treasury to colleagues' campaigns, so it encouraged a challenge by Rep. Beau Boulter, a two-term conservative from Amarillo. But Boulter allocated little money to the primary and ran second to Wes Gilbreath, a Houston multimillionaire who spent a fortune on TV ads. Boulter dispatched Gilbreath in the runoff, but never mounted much momentum thereafter.

Boulter produced entertaining campaign literature satirizing the $10,000 breakfast incident. And he tried hard to make Bentsen's dual candidacy the issue. But Texans did not seem offended by the so-called "LBJ Law," passed in 1960 to allow Lyndon B. Johnson to run simultaneously for re-election and for vice president. At least, they had no problem applying it to Bentsen, who won more than two-thirds of the counties on his way to a victory margin of more than a million votes.

Historically, Bentsen is part of the Texas Democratic establishment that included Johnson and John B. Connally, but his route into it was unique.

The Bentsen family has been among the conservative gentry of the lower Rio Grande Valley for most of this century. The senator's father, Lloyd Sr., was known as "Big Lloyd" around their hometown of McAllen, where he became a millionaire landowner and gave his son a boost into local politics. (Lloyd Sr. died in an auto accident in early 1989.)

Returning from World War II, Bentsen was elected judge in Hidalgo County at age 25. In 1948, taking advantage of family money and connections among the small group of Anglo Democrats that controlled politics in his heavily Hispanic South Texas district, he became the youngest member of the U.S. House.

As a representative, Bentsen pleased Texas conservatives with his hard-line anti-communism. He represented a one-party district and was politically secure; after his first primary, he faced no opposition at all.

But in 1954, Bentsen retired from Congress at age 33 and became president of Lincoln Consolidated, a holding company. By the time Bentsen was ready for politics again in 1970, he was a millionaire. Bentsen ran on the Democratic right in 1970 as a primary challenger to veteran Sen. Ralph Yarborough, an East Texas populist who had long been an enemy of party conservatives.

Bentsen ran against both Yarborough and the national Democratic Party. When Democratic Sens. Edmund S. Muskie of Maine and Harold Hughes of Iowa came to Texas for Yarborough, Bentsen labeled them "ultraliberal" outsiders. He ran ads linking Yarborough to violent antiwar protests and said the senator's vote against Supreme Court nominee G. Harrold Carswell showed he was anti-Southern.

After the primary, Bentsen moved to the center against GOP nominee George Bush, then a Houston representative. The Bush-Bentsen campaign, a battle between a Houston insurance millionaire and a Houston oil millionaire, was gentle by comparison with the primary.

There was little to argue about.

In the end, that helped Bentsen. He continued to promote the conservative image he had fostered in the spring, but recruited Yarborough supporters and campaigned against President Nixon's economic policies. Texas was still unquestionably a Democratic state in 1970 and, given a choice between two conservatives, a majority of voters preferred the Democrat.

In his first term, Bentsen sought to moderate his image, looking toward a presidential campaign in 1976. This angered his more conservative 1970 supporters and brought a primary challenge in 1976 from Phil Gramm, then teaching economics at Texas A&M.

Gramm accused Bentsen of abandoning his conservative heritage in a vain bid for national office. Bentsen retained the loyalty of the party establishment and beat Gramm by more than 2-to-1, but the challenger drew over 400,000 votes (Gramm later won election to the House, switched to the GOP and then moved up to the Senate in the 1984 election).

In seeking the Democratic presidential nomination in 1976, Bentsen called himself a "Harry Truman Democrat" and hoped to do well in an early Southern primary. But Southern voters also had Jimmy Carter and George C. Wallace to choose from, and Bentsen got just six delegates in his own home state.

Turning to the defense of his Senate seat that year, Bentsen found GOP Rep. Alan Steelman accusing him of being the captive of special interests. But Steelman had neither a firm base in his own party nor a funding base to compete with Bentsen's.

In 1982 Bentsen had an even easier time with GOP Rep. James M. Collins' crusade against "Liberal Lloyd." Bentsen's 1.8 million votes led a statewide ticket that captured the governorship, retained all its U.S. House seats and won all three newly created districts.

Committees

Finance (Chairman)
International Trade; Medicare & Long Term Care; Taxation

Joint Taxation (Vice Chairman)

Commerce, Science & Transportation (7th of 11 Democrats)
Aviation; Communications; Merchant Marine; Science, Technology & Space; National Ocean Policy Study

Joint Economic

Elections

1988 General		
Lloyd Bentsen (D)	3,149,806	(59%)
Beau Boulter (R)	2,129,228	(40%)
1988 Primary		
Lloyd Bentsen (D)	1,365,736	(85%)
Joe Sullivan (D)	244,805	(15%)

Previous Winning Percentages: **1982** (59%) **1976** (57%) **1970** (54%) **1952** * (100%) **1950** * (100%) **1948** † (100%)

* *House elections.*

† *Elected to a full House term and to fill a vacancy at the same time.*

Campaign Finance

	Receipts	Receipts from PACs		Expend-itures
1988				
Bentsen (D)	$8,280,013	$2,438,041	(29%)	$8,829,361
Boulter (R)	$1,377,357	$95,021	(7%)	$1,353,345

Key Votes

1991	
Authorize use of force against Iraq	N
1990	
Oppose prohibition of certain semiautomatic weapons	N
Support constitutional amendment on flag desecration	Y
Oppose requiring parental notice for minors' abortions	N
Halt production of B-2 stealth bomber at 13 planes	N
Approve budget that cut spending and raised revenues	Y
Pass civil rights bill over Bush veto	Y
1989	
Oppose reduction of SDI funding	N
Oppose barring federal funds for "obscene" art	?
Allow vote on capital gains tax cut	N

Voting Studies

	Presidential Support		Party Unity		Conservative Coalition	
Year	**S**	**O**	**S**	**O**	**S**	**O**
1990	52	47	75	23	89	11
1989	69	28	71	26	79	21
1988	61	27	55	20	78	11
1987	44	50	78	19	69	31
1986	60	37	46	50	87	9
1985	50	46	54	40	75	23
1984	52	34	46	28	53	17
1983	51	45	63	31	64	34
1982	61	33	54	41	88	10
1981	70	24	55	42	83	11

Interest Group Ratings

Year	ADA	ACU	AFL-CIO	CCUS
1990	44	32	78	25
1989	45	36	90	57
1988	40	42	89	25
1987	60	31	80	44
1986	45	50	33	68
1985	35	62	53	46
1984	55	25	67	46
1983	40	25	71	53
1982	40	74	75	70
1981	25	53	39	71

Phil Gramm (R)

Of College Station — Elected 1984

Born: July 8, 1942, Fort Benning, Ga.
Education: U. of Georgia, B.B.A. 1964, Ph.D. 1967.
Occupation: Professor of economics.
Family: Wife, Wendy Lee; two children.
Religion: Episcopalian.
Political Career: Sought Democratic nomination for U.S. Senate, 1976; U.S. House, 1979-85.
Capitol Office: 370 Russell Bldg. 20510; 224-2934.

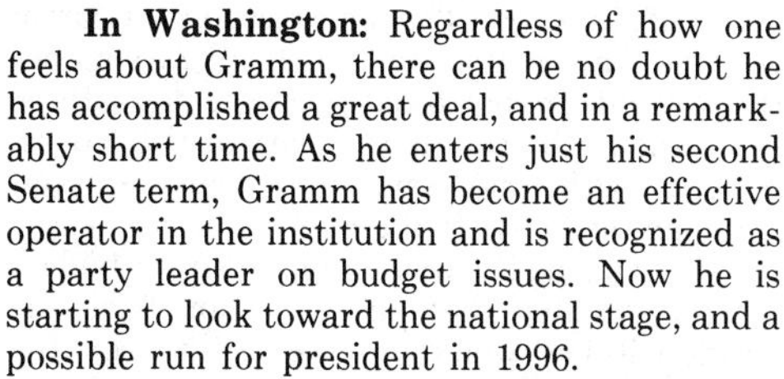

In Washington: Regardless of how one feels about Gramm, there can be no doubt he has accomplished a great deal, and in a remarkably short time. As he enters just his second Senate term, Gramm has become an effective operator in the institution and is recognized as a party leader on budget issues. Now he is starting to look toward the national stage, and a possible run for president in 1996.

It is easy to find people in Washington — his fellow Republicans as well as members of his former party — whose views of Gramm range from disdain to loathing. His critics call him arrogant, transparently ambitious, demagogic and deceitful. If popularity were the barometer of Senate success, he would be a failure.

But in less than a decade, Gramm combined politically powerful ideas, shrewd timing and boundless tenacity to enact two landmark laws that shaped budget debates for the 1980s and beyond. No recent member has had so great an impact in so short a time.

In 1981, as a second-term Democratic House member, he devised the Gramm-Latta package embodying President Reagan's priority-reordering program of social spending cuts, a defense buildup and tax reductions. In 1985, as a first-year GOP senator who had been kept off the Budget Committee, he was the driving force behind the Gramm-Rudman-Hollings law, a radical overhaul of the budget process imposing a mandated timetable for balancing the books. By 1990, he had made his way onto the Budget and Appropriations panels and onto the GOP budget summit team — signs that he and his party elders have finally come to terms with each other.

While the legislative Gramm has been achieving standing, the political Gramm also has been gaining influence. Fresh off his landslide re-election, Gramm in late 1990 earned a new perch from which to gain attention, as his Senate colleagues elected him chairman of the National Republican Senatorial Committee (NRSC). Gramm quickly installed his own people in key posts and shuffled the committee's organization.

Gramm created a political stir in March 1991 when, in a discussion of Republican political strategy, he identified the debate and vote over the war in the Persian Gulf as a GOP focal point. Gramm, an outspoken backer of President Bush on the war, said that opposition to the war by most Democrats would be a major 1992 election issue for Republicans. "They are going to pay for that vote," Gramm said of Democrats, because it was "exactly in the pattern of Jimmy Carter, Walter Mondale and Michael Dukakis. It says to the nation once again that Democrats cannot be trusted to define the destiny of America."

After years of electoral observers and political pundits mentioning Gramm as a prospective candidate for the presidency, the Texan finally confirmed the prospects in May 1991. Gramm announced he was raising funds for the 1996 election cycle and said that the funds "could be used for the presidency."

An ardent champion of free-market economics, Gramm wants to do more than tinker around the edges of the welfare state. He is out to shrink the whole concept of American government on behalf of the middle-class "people who do the work, pay the taxes and pull the wagon." For a man given to homespun, self-deprecating humor, Gramm is not modest about his own role in that revolution. "I want to make sure we've changed government forever," he says. "If I don't do it, it may not get done."

His lightning campaign for Gramm-Rudman-Hollings clearly illustrated the keys to Gramm's success. He pressed the issue with energy and a single-minded intensity that was as unstoppable as it was alienating to many of his colleagues. "You don't have to worry about stepping on people's toes," he observes. "They're going to step out of your way." Even more important, perhaps, was Gramm's sense of timing; he is an opportunist, and an effective one.

In 1981, Gramm had capitalized on Reagan's honeymoon; by 1985, Gramm saw that lawmakers and the public were ready for radical steps, despairing over spiraling deficits and

Congress' inability to control them through conventional means. The only way to force Congress to make the necessary decisions to eliminate the deficit was to install a process that threatened a worse alternative — indiscriminate, across-the-board spending cuts.

Gramm-Rudman-Hollings set a goal of a balanced budget by 1991, later pushed back to 1993. It mandated specific deficit targets each year and automatic spending cuts if Congress and the president could not agree on a budget that met the targets.

With the deficit persisting, Gramm has seen his handiwork come under increasing criticism. In 1989, South Carolina Democrat Ernest F. Hollings divorced himself from the law bearing his name, and others faulted the law for leading to accounting gimmickry rather than true deficit reduction.

Even Gramm said, "We haven't done as good a job as I had hoped for." But, he added, "it is very important not to let the little, fuzzy cheating around the edges obscure the fact that the objective is a good one."

In mid-1989, Gramm talked of offering "Gramm-Rudman 3," which called for a balanced budget by fiscal 1993 and then — after removing the Social Security trust fund surplus from budget calculations — a balanced budget by fiscal 1999. The proposal went nowhere.

Gramm was a member of the congressional budget summit team that met throughout 1990 to craft a deficit-reduction plan, and he surprised some observers by not emerging as a conservative flame thrower in the mold of House Minority Whip Newt Gingrich of Georgia, who called the summit talks "baloney."

In early October, a Gingrich-led revolt in the House helped defeat the package of tax increases and spending cuts that the White House and congressional leaders had put together. Ultimately, a five-year budget deal passed that included new mechanisms aimed at producing a balanced budget. Gramm voted against that plan, although President Bush said its reforms "extended" and "strengthened" the Gramm-Rudman-Hollings law and its enforcement mechanisms.

In landing a seat on the Budget Committee for the 101st Congress, Gramm fulfilled a goal he had had since winning election to the Senate in 1984. The fact that it took him four years to achieve it is a measure of the institutional response to his brash independence. He gave up his seat on the Armed Services Committee, where he had been a supporter of Reagan's military buildup.

Gramm does not view all federal spending as suspect, especially if it occurs in his Lone Star State. He has promoted funding the multibillion-dollar, atom-smashing superconducting super collider (SSC) being built in Texas. But Gramm can draw the line on parochialism: He has consistently opposed an oil-import fee, despite its benefits for his home state.

Gramm remains on the Banking Committee, a voice for deregulation. During the 100th Congress, amid trouble in the stock and commodity markets, Gramm counseled against government intervention (his wife, Wendy Lee, is chairman of the Commodity Futures Trading Commission). He was one of only two senators to vote against a banking deregulation bill, objecting that it did not go far enough. In the 101st Congress, Gramm successfully opposed efforts that would have significantly weakened the CFTC's authority over futures trading.

Gramm was in the middle of debate in 1989 over financing the sweeping overhaul of laws governing savings and loan institutions, aimed at cleaning up a $100 billion-plus mess in the thrift industry. The major issue for Gramm was the financing of the costly plan: whether the $50 billion borrowed over the next three years should be counted as part of the federal budget, with an exemption from Gramm-Rudman, or kept off the books.

Gramm had vowed to block an on-budget scheme, arguing that an exemption from the antideficit law would unnecessarily open the door to future exemptions. A compromise was finally approved that put two-fifths of the spending "on budget" in fiscal 1989 — a move that did not require a Gramm-Rudman exemption because the budget year was nearly over — and put the remainder of the S&L bailout cost "off budget" in fiscal 1990-91.

As the 101st Congress moved toward enacting a major overhaul of federal housing programs at the end of 1990, Gramm posed a major hurdle. He offered a "killer" amendment that snarled the proceedings for more than four hours on the day of passage.

Gramm would have allocated the $3 billion in housing block grant funds to states by population, rather than through the existing formula. Gramm complained that the existing formula — with its heavy emphasis on older housing — was designed to favor the Northeast, ignoring areas such as Texas that had inadequate new housing.

New York would have lost $95 million in 1991 under Gramm's plan; Texas would have gained $22 million. New York Republican Alfonse M. D'Amato complained bitterly that Gramm was thinking solely of parochial interests and countered that taxpayers in the Northeast were bearing the cost of the savings and loan bailout even though thrift collapses were concentrated in Texas.

The Gramm amendment was killed, 65-35, although the Senate did go on to agree to instruct the Department of Housing and Urban Development to study the formula used to distribute block grant funds.

Gramm occasionally looks beyond fiscal matters to pursue his cause on social issues such as abortion, drugs and crime. In 1990, he pushed for mandatory minimum sentencing on antidrug legislation and unsuccessfully fought to remove language from an anticrime measure that banned a number of semi-automatic assault-style weapons.

"The sad, cold reality is that felons who are smuggling drugs into the country will smuggle in guns," Gramm said. After voting down Gramm's gun ban plan, the Senate overwhelmingly passed his proposal for stricter penalties.

During Senate debate in April 1990 on a supplemental appropriation bill, abortion opponent Gramm appended language authorizing the death penalty for drug-related murders in the nation's capital to an amendment permitting the District of Columbia to use local tax money for abortions.

Gramm's complicated maneuvering on the Senate floor confounded abortion rights supporters, who could not figure out how to decouple the issues. Gramm denied that his intent was to kill the abortion funding provision, but that was the result nonetheless; both amendments were dropped in the end.

Initially at least, some top Senate Republicans were cool toward Gramm because of his stormy career in the House as a Democrat. Almost as soon as he got to the House in 1979, he had begun fighting with top Democrats.

When he campaigned for a seat on the Budget Committee at the start of his second term in 1981, Democratic House leaders sought and received Gramm's written assurance that he would loyally support the party's budget. Just months later, he did the opposite — and in a spectacular way, secretly collaborating with Republicans on Reagan's budget, while sitting in on Budget Democrats' caucuses and reporting back to the White House. The alleged spy was barred from Democrats' meetings. He then helped engineer Reagan's budget victory on the House floor by lining up conservative Democrats to vote with the GOP.

Democrats felt betrayed, and at the start of the next Congress, Gramm was evicted from Budget. But he was prepared for that eventuality, and had even hired a GOP pollster for some soundings about a party switch. Charging that he had been punished "for practicing in Washington what I preach at home," Gramm left the party, resigned his House seat and won re-election to it as a Republican in 1983. He rejoined Budget, adapting easily to the role of GOP partisan.

At Home: Whatever the effects of Gramm's 1983 party switch in Washington, the move bolstered his political career back home. His comfortable victory in the 1983 special House election set the stage for his stunning 1984 Senate triumph. In 1990, his first Senate re-election bid was never a worry.

The Democrats' hopes in 1983 rested on forcing Gramm into a runoff. But Gramm won the special election outright, tapping a massive treasury and a superior organization to take 51 percent. His victory gave the 6th District to the GOP for the first time in Texas history.

In building that victory, Gramm invested heavily in media markets encompassing Dallas, Houston and Fort Worth — giving him exposure that proved invaluable in his subsequent Senate campaign. When GOP Sen. John Tower announced he would retire at the end of the 98th Congress, Gramm was already a familiar figure in the state's populous parts.

Bolstered by his superior name recognition, Gramm took a commanding lead for the Republican Senate nomination, and he never looked back. Largely ignoring his intraparty foes, he spent the spring of 1984 canvassing areas not normally hospitable to the GOP.

The Democrats, meanwhile, were conducting a tortuous nominating campaign. State Sen. Lloyd Doggett, a hard-charging liberal, struggled to finish a close second in the grueling primary, then squeezed past conservative U.S. Rep. Kent Hance in a runoff that further polarized the party and drained Doggett's resources.

When Doggett finally emerged for the general-election campaign, Gramm had him fixed firmly in his sights. The Republican launched an aggressive statewide media campaign questioning Doggett's commitment to traditional family values. One ad observed that Doggett had accepted a contribution from a gay group that raised part of the money at an all-male striptease show. Doggett later returned the funds, but the ad kept him on the defensive.

In response, Doggett tried to cast Gramm as a right-wing extremist too radical to represent Texas. He accused Gramm of attempting to cut Social Security and of calling for the eventual elimination of federal education aid.

The Doggett counteroffensive was inadequate. The Democrat ran well among blacks and Hispanics, carried South Texas and his home base of Travis County (Austin). But Gramm made impressive inroads into conservative, rural East and West Texas — territory that would ordinarily go Democratic. Aided by a 3-to-1 spending advantage and fallout from President Reagan's strong campaign, Gramm racked up 59 percent of the vote.

Heading into 1990, Gramm's high profile in Washington discouraged Democrats with statewide stature from challenging him. The Democrat who finally emerged to make the race was State Sen. Hugh Parmer, who won his party's nomination in March over one minor foe.

Parmer assailed the incumbent for "Gramm-standing" — claiming credit for federal largess in Texas that he had nothing to do with, or had even opposed at one point. The Democrat also tried to link Gramm to anger over the savings and loan crisis, citing Gramm's campaign contributions from thrift-related sources. But Parmer was never able to build up his name or shake his underdog image; he spent

$1.7 million on the race, compared to almost $10 million for Gramm. Gramm largely ignored Parmer and spent much of his time campaigning for Republican House candidates. He won a second term with 60 percent of the vote.

Before he ran for Congress in 1976, Gramm's life was centered around the academic community at Texas A&M, where he taught economics. He wrote extensively on economics and energy and established a consulting firm that did contract research for government and private industry in the United States, Canada and Australia.

Gramm was barely known statewide when he challenged incumbent Lloyd Bentsen in the 1976 Democratic Senate primary. Claiming that Bentsen had moved to the left to mount his ill-fated 1976 presidential campaign, he presented himself as a conservative alternative. Underfinanced, he drew only 29 percent of the vote.

Two years later, with better name recognition and financial support, Gramm sought the Democratic nomination to succeed Rep. Olin E. Teague, challenging a Fort Worth television weatherman.

Gramm survived an expensive primary and runoff by building a campaign treasury of nearly a half-million dollars. In the general election, his national New Right support preempted a successful Republican challenge.

In 1982, Gramm faced a spirited primary challenge from a candidate cheered on by the national Democratic establishment — Jack Teague, son of Gramm's House predecessor. Teague called Gramm a turncoat who had abandoned his party's traditional concern for the disadvantaged and average-income people.

But Gramm cast the election as a referendum on whether he was fulfilling his promises to carry the district's fiscal conservatism to Washington, and he won the primary with 62 percent of the vote. Republicans, who had fielded a candidate in case Gramm lost, showed no interest after his renomination.

Committees

Appropriations (11th of 13 Republicans)
Labor, Health & Human Services, Education; Military Construction (ranking); Commerce, Justice, State & Judiciary; VA, HUD and Independent Agencies

Banking, Housing & Urban Affairs (3rd of 9 Republicans)
International Finance & Monetary Policy (ranking); Consumer & Regulatory Affairs; Housing & Urban Affairs; Securities

Budget (6th of 9 Republicans)

Elections

1990 General

Phil Gramm (R)	2,302,357	(60%)
Hugh Parmer (D)	1,429,986	(37%)
Gary Johnson (LIBERT)	89,089	(2%)

Previous Winning Percentages: **1984** (59%) **1983 †** (55%) **1982 *** (95%) **1980 *** (71%) **1978 *** (65%)

** House elections.*
† Special House election.

Campaign Finance

	Receipts	Receipts from PACs		Expend-itures
1990				
Gramm (R)	$11,626,377	$1,426,839	(12%)	$9,799,104
Parmer (D)	$1,674,600	$263,762	(16%)	$1,677,087

Key Votes

1991

Authorize use of force against Iraq	Y

1990

Oppose prohibition of certain semiautomatic weapons	Y
Support constitutional amendment on flag desecration	Y
Oppose requiring parental notice for minors' abortions	N
Halt production of B-2 stealth bomber at 13 planes	N
Approve budget that cut spending and raised revenues	N
Pass civil rights bill over Bush veto	N

1989

Oppose reduction of SDI funding	Y
Oppose barring federal funds for "obscene" art	N
Allow vote on capital gains tax cut	Y

Voting Studies

	Presidential Support		Party Unity		Conservative Coalition	
Year	**S**	**O**	**S**	**O**	**S**	**O**
1990	78	14	88	8	100	0
1989	86	12	91	6	82	16
1988	78	15	85	4	92	3
1987	87	9	92	5	84	13
1986	99	1	95	4	97	1
1985	87	13	95	5	88	12
House Service						
1984	37	27	58	5	69	8
1983	73	16	79 †	1 †	93	0
1982	84	14	10	87	89	10
1981	75	22	20	77	99	0

† Not eligible for all recorded votes. Gramm resigned from the House Jan. 5, 1983. He had been elected as a Democrat and cast his first three votes of 1983 as a member of that party. His party unity support score as a Democrat was 33 percent; opposition was 67 percent. Gramm was re-elected Feb. 12, 1983, as a Republican and sworn in Feb. 22. The scores for party unity reflect his votes as a Republican.

Interest Group Ratings

Year	ADA	ACU	AFL-CIO	CCUS
1990	0	91	22	92
1989	0	96	0	88
1988	0	95	0	92
1987	5	100	10	89
1986	0	100	0	89
1985	0	95	0	86
House Service				
1984	10	64	22	78
1983	0	100	0	88
1982	10	91	10	73
1981	0	93	13	89

1 Jim Chapman (D)

Of Sulphur Springs — Elected 1985

Born: March 8, 1945, Washington, D.C.
Education: U. of Texas, B.B.A. 1968; Southern Methodist U., J.D. 1970.
Occupation: Lawyer.
Family: Wife, Betty Brice; two children.
Religion: Methodist.
Political Career: District attorney, 8th Judicial District of Texas, 1977-85; sought Democratic nomination for Texas Senate, 1984.
Capitol Office: 236 Cannon Bldg. 20515; 225-3035.

In Washington: Chapman is evidence that while Jim Wright may be gone from the House, his handiwork is still evident. Wright helped Chapman win a 1985 special election and saw to it that he got an Appropriations seat at the start of the 101st Congress.

Now on his own, Chapman's mission is to protect a huge government project dear to the heart of Texas: the superconducting super collider, a massive atom smasher with a price tag in excess of $11 billion. On the SSC, Wright must be rather proud of Chapman's efforts. While funding was reduced below the goal set by the White House and Chapman, Congress nonetheless appropriated nearly $500 million for it in the 101st Congress. Chapman's efforts led Texas Republican Rep. Joe L. Barton to compare him to Sam Houston and other Texas heroes. "I'd vote for him," said the Republican of Chapman.

Chapman also used his post on the Energy and Water Subcommittee to secure $31 million for a recreation facility at the federal water project at Cooper Lake in his district. While a 1956 law requires local cost sharing on such projects, Chapman got around that stumbling block by noting that the project had been authorized in 1955 but held up in court for three decades.

When Republican Silvio O. Conte tried to scotch the funding, Chapman replied, "I am surprised and disappointed that the gentleman from Massachusetts would tear down the dreams of Texas of the past 35 years."

Chapman also authored the controversial "food-handlers" amendment to the Americans with Disabilities Act. The amendment would have allowed the transfer of workers with diseases that are not transmissible through food but are wrongly perceived to be so by much of the public. The House approved the language, and the Senate instructed its conferees to adopt it. But the conferees refused to do so. When the bill came up for final passage, support for the amendment grew tepid, and Chapman could not muster the votes to restore it.

Chapman's 1989 appointment to Appropriations added fuel to resentment of Texans profiteering under Wright, but he earned the Speaker's gratitude in late 1987, when he saved him from defeat on a controversial budget bill that contained new taxes. Chapman's post-last-minute vote change gave Wright a 206-205 victory.

At Home: In his 1985 special election, Chapman was at the center of a battle the parties saw as crucial to their future in the South.

Republican Sen. Phil Gramm had helped engineer a federal judgeship for Democratic Rep. Sam B. Hall Jr., then helped recruit rancher and engineer Edd Hargett, a former Texas A&M football star, as the Republican candidate to replace Hall. The national GOP threw its weight behind Hargett, seeing a chance for the party to make inroads in traditional Democratic territory.

Chapman was one of six Democrats competing on the same ballot with Hargett. He managed 30 percent of the vote and forced a runoff with Hargett, who took 42 percent.

In the runoff, Chapman presented himself as a traditional conservative Democrat and questioned Hargett's credentials to serve in Congress. He got his biggest boost, however, when local newspapers reported the Republican saying, "I don't know what trade policies have to do with bringing jobs to East Texas." Chapman pounced, pointing to layoffs at a local steel plant. Hargett could not overcome the trade issue. With support from courthouse Democrats, labor and trial lawyers, Chapman narrowly won the runoff.

National GOP leaders claimed that the party had shown real strength in the South by coming so close, but they dropped the issue in 1986, and Chapman won a full term unopposed. The 1988 GOP nominee, farmer-broadcaster Horace McQueen, drew 38 percent, but Republicans had higher hopes for their 1990 pick, Hamp Hodges. Hodges, a businessman and decorated Vietnam veteran, fared no better, though.

Texas 1

Northeast — Texarkana

The 1st District is a collection of farm plots, small towns and county crossroads; to find a big city, one has to travel beyond its boundaries. Texarkana (Bowie County) and Marshall (Harrison County) are the largest population centers (with 32,000 and 24,000 people, respectively). But together, Bowie and Harrison counties account for less than a quarter of the district's population.

Texarkana is the twin city of its namesake across the state line in Arkansas. Although the two are administratively separate, their development has been intertwined. Texarkana is an important regional trading center; it also hosts the Red River Army Depot, a largely civilian facility that services Army vehicles.

Marshall, once the home of an important timber trade, is still known for its scenery and myriad trees, but light industries related to East Texas' oil and natural gas wells are more important to the economy now. Defense also contributes to the manufacturing base: The Longhorn Army Ammunitions plant produces rocket fuel and is involved in destroying Pershing missiles covered under the intermediate-range nuclear-force (INF) treaty.

Much of the district's territory not devoted to oil and gas is given to cattle-ranching and the production of dairy goods. Hopkins County, in the western part of the 1st, is one of Texas' largest dairy producers. San Augustine County, at the district's southern end, is an important part of the 1st's lumber industry.

Some of the 1st's key economic underpinnings have been suffering through much of the 1980s — timber because of Canadian imports, cattle-raising due to Mexican competition, and steelmaking, also because of foreign competition. The sagging fortunes of Lone Star Steel, which has filed for bankruptcy, have done severe damage to the economy in Morris and Upshur counties, near the center of the district.

Population: 527,016. White 417,347 (79%), Black 103,249 (20%). Spanish origin 8,378 (2%). 18 and over 376,964 (72%), 65 and over 85,485 (16%). Median age: 33.

Committee

Appropriations (32nd of 37 Democrats)
Energy & Water Development; Veterans Affairs, Housing & Urban Development, & Independent Agencies

Elections

1990 General		
Jim Chapman (D)	89,241	(61%)
Hamp Hodges (R)	56,954	(39%)
1988 General		
Jim Chapman (D)	122,566	(62%)
Horace McQueen (R)	74,357	(38%)

Previous Winning Percentages: **1986** (100%) **1985 *** (51%)

* *Special election runoff.*

District Vote For President

	1988	1984	1980	1976
D	96,668 (47%)	84,954 (41%)	90,448 (50%)	95,599 (59%)
R	107,456 (53%)	120,350 (58%)	89,581 (49%)	65,538 (41%)

Campaign Finance

	Receipts	Receipts from PACs		Expend-itures
1990				
Chapman (D)	$533,989	$296,839	(56%)	$463,377
Hodges (R)	$420,961	$2,328	(1%)	$408,677
1988				
Chapman (D)	$587,159	$270,430	(46%)	$551,611
McQueen (R)	$94,842	$7,514	(8%)	$94,477

Key Votes

1991	
Authorize use of force against Iraq	Y
1990	
Support constitutional amendment on flag desecration	Y
Pass family and medical leave bill over Bush veto	Y
Reduce SDI funding	Y
Allow abortions in overseas military facilities	Y
Approve budget summit plan for spending and taxing	Y
Approve civil rights bill	Y
1989	
Halt production of B-2 stealth bomber at 13 planes	N
Oppose capital gains tax cut	Y
Approve federal abortion funding in rape or incest cases	Y
Approve pay raise and revision of ethics rules	N
Pass Democratic minimum wage plan over Bush veto	N

Voting Studies

	Presidential Support		Party Unity		Conservative Coalition	
Year	**S**	**O**	**S**	**O**	**S**	**O**
1990	34	62	71	19	78	19
1989	49	47	70	22	85	12
1988	36	61	70	23	87	3
1987	39	60	71	22	88	9
1986	37	61	69	24	86	10
1985	42†	56†	59†	32†	94†	0†

† *Not eligible for all recorded votes.*

Interest Group Ratings

Year	ADA	ACU	AFL-CIO	CCUS
1990	33	27	83	43
1989	50	39	50	60
1988	50	52	71	64
1987	48	9	63	47
1986	40	38	69	50
1985	-	71	20	92

2 Charles Wilson (D)

Of Lufkin — Elected 1972

Born: June 1, 1933, Trinity, Texas.
Education: Attended Sam Houston State U., 1950-51; U. of Texas, 1951-52; U.S. Naval Academy, B.S. 1956.
Military Service: Navy, 1956-60.
Occupation: Lumberyard manager.
Family: Divorced.
Religion: Methodist.
Political Career: Texas House, 1961-67; Texas Senate, 1967-73.
Capitol Office: 2256 Rayburn Bldg. 20515; 225-2401.

In Washington: Wilson revels in his reputation as a swashbuckler, keeping a high profile as he cavalierly courts political and physical danger. While this style has gotten him into a few embarrassing scrapes, his exploits enhance his reputation as man who lives by his own rules. That has earned him friendship and respect and grudging admiration from some unlikely quarters.

Loyalty to beleaguered Speaker Jim Wright in 1989 seemed politically foolhardy to many, but Wilson welcomed the chance to take a hit for close friend. The East Texas Democrat argued forcefully and publicly against the ethics charges that eventually toppled Wright, and was among the last of the Speaker's colleagues to give up hope for his political survival.

Wilson took chances with his physical safety as he crusaded for the anticommunist rebels battling Soviet forces in Afghanistan. A member of the House Appropriations Subcommittee on Foreign Operations, he twice visited rebel forces inside Afghanistan, and made more than a dozen trips to Pakistan.

Wilson has also faced some less salutary dangers. His taste for high living earned him unwanted attention from the Justice Department, which in 1983 investigated, but did not charge, Wilson during a probe into Capitol Hill drug use. Wilson firmly denied the allegations. That same year, Wilson was fined for colliding with a car on a Washington, D.C., bridge, then leaving the scene of the accident; the car he was driving carried his official House license plates.

Wilson even saw one of his Afghanistan adventures tarnished, when it was revealed that he had exacted revenge on the Defense Intelligence Agency (DIA) for denying his then-girlfriend a seat on a U.S. government plane in Pakistan in February 1986. The story came to light nearly two years later, when Wilson slipped a provision into a 1987 year-end omnibus spending bill that cut six planes from the DIA fleet.

While any of this might have brought down a member with a less solid base at home or in the House, none of it has slowed, or humbled, Wilson. In nearly two decades in the House, "good-time Charlie" has also earned a reputation as one of the chamber's better lobbyists and vote traders. He struts across the House floor with a cocky gait — which, ironically, is less a mannerism than the result of his chronic back problems — and has a quick, wide grin and a handshake ready for whoever is handy. But there is usually a serious purpose lurking behind his roguish friendliness.

For much of the last decade, Wilson's most serious purpose was the maintenance of U.S. support for the Mujahedeen rebels in Afghanistan. Wilson adopted the cause after the Soviet invasion of that central Asian nation in 1979, and persisted in the face of considerable congressional doubt that the loosely organized Afghan guerrillas could survive a military onslaught from the Soviet Red Army. His congressional efforts and trips to the front — where he purchased Red Army belt buckles that had been plucked off corpses — prompted CBS' "60 Minutes" to profile him as a savior of the rebel cause.

In promoting the "Muj," as he called the rebels, Wilson's rhetoric about the Soviet occupiers was pure Cold War. During the 99th Congress, he told a closed meeting of the Appropriations Subcommittee on Defense that he wanted to help the rebels in Afghanistan because "it's the only place in the world where we are killing Russians."

But in 1989, after the Soviets completed the withdrawal of their 100,000-plus army from Afghanistan and conceded the invasion had been a mistake, Wilson took to the House floor to commend the Soviet leadership. The following year, he made his first trip to the Soviet Union, and came away a "fan of *perestroika*." But Wilson cautioned, "I'm not here to proclaim the end of the Evil Empire."

As President Bush prepared to battle Iraq, Wilson was a ready ally. In late 1990, the

Texas 2

East — Lufkin; Orange

Traditionally poor, isolated and dependent on timber, the East Texas piney woods 2nd took on a new look in the 1970s with the growth of the oil industry. But oil has proven to be a fickle economic generator. The downturn in oil prices brought hard times to many here for much of the 1980s.

Lufkin, the district's largest city, once boasted some 275 sawmills, testimony to the importance of the local lumber industry. Now, a key employer is Lufkin Industries, which manufactures trailers, shell casings and other metal products. Factories making oil and gas drilling equipment also are prominent.

Orange, located to the southwest, used to draw its revenues from timber, cattle and rice. Today, it is the domain of petrochemical facilities that have been forced to lay off workers. Goodyear, Gulf Oil and Du Pont all maintain plants along Orange's major industrial corridor, known locally as "Chemical Row." The closing of a major shipyard pushed Orange's unemployment to 20 percent in 1987. Defense contract work has helped the city rebound somewhat; current unemployment is about 12 percent. Orange remains the district's only significant concentration of union members.

Independent oil outfits that have sprung up throughout the district in recent years have altered the 2nd's landscape. But the district has not entirely lost its Deep South woodland feel. Four national forests are located in the district; along the fringes, there are places resembling Louisiana's bayous.

Like all of East Texas, the 2nd is conservative territory with strong ties to Dixie. The 2nd's Deep South character was evident in 1968, when it was the only district in the state to back George C. Wallace. Its character is further evident in the slow progress blacks have made in local elections. Although they comprise 15 percent of the district's population, blacks are seldom a significant political force.

Bolstered by a residual populist streak in the rural counties, Jimmy Carter received a favorable reception in the 2nd in 1976; he took nearly 60 percent of the district vote. Even in 1980, when Carter lost the state by a decisive margin, he carried the 2nd.

But in 1984, the national Democratic Party's liberal tilt alienated even some of the most staunchly Democratic voters. Of the 16 counties wholly or partially in the 2nd, only two voted for Walter F. Mondale. In 1988, Michael S. Dukakis — running with Texan Lloyd Bentsen — brought the 2nd back into the Democratic column, although by a margin of just 355 votes over George Bush.

Population: 526,772. White 433,363 (82%), Black 81,820 (16%), Other 2,862 (1%). Spanish origin 16,906 (3%). 18 and over 372,792 (71%), 65 and over 62,165 (12%). Median age: 30.

administration was pushing a debt relief package for Egypt in exchange for its support in the alliance against Iraq. Though many Southern Democrats shied away from supporting any debt relief during economic hard times, Wilson gave the president a key vote during a late-night conference committee meeting. "Egypt is the glue that holds the Arabs together [in Operation Desert Shield]," he said.

When Wilson was appointed to the Intelligence panel in 1987, his conservatism prompted complaints from liberal Democrats who feared Wilson, the party's self-appointed "head hawk," would too often side with Republicans. In the 102nd Congress, however, his conservatism helped the leadership quell GOP complaints that the panel was being unfairly stacked with liberals. Now in his last term on Intelligence, Wilson is second-ranking Democrat behind Chairman Dave McCurdy of Oklahoma.

Wilson's affiliation with the Afghan cause contributed to his stance as one of the strongest House supporters of Pakistan, an Afghanistan neighbor and the conduit of much of the U.S. aid to the Mujahedeen. In 1987, and again in 1990, he parried efforts by liberal arms control advocates to condition U.S. aid to Pakistan on that nation's willingness to suspend efforts to develop a nuclear-weapons capability and to sign the nuclear non-proliferation treaty.

Wilson said that supporters of the aid conditions were being "very selective in moral application," and pointed out that Israel, the leading recipient of U.S. foreign aid, was widely believed to have developed a nuclear arsenal. "Are we going to cut off aid to Israel?" Wilson said. "Of course we're not."

A graduate of the U.S. Naval Academy, Wilson has also lived up to his reputation as a pro-defense conservative. From his seat on Appropriations' Defense Subcommittee, he has supported weapons systems, such as the MX missile and the B-2 stealth bomber, that have been controversial within the Democratic Caucus. In 1990, he was one of a handful of Democrats to side with President Bush and oppose further cuts in the strategic defense initiative.

In 1985, Wilson provided a blunt warning on defense issues to his party's liberal wing. "If the perception persists in this country that the Democratic Party is the party of isolation and ... weakness on defense," he said, "we are flat through in the South and West, and we can forget about winning presidential elections."

But while his hawkish views mesh well with those of his conservative constituency, Wilson's popularity at home is staked more on his attention to local issues. In particular, he has been known throughout his career as the most persistent House defender of independent oil interests. He found a chance to mix his interest in Foreign Affairs and home-state business in 1989, when he traveled to Iraq to push the Arab state to buy oil drilling equipment from Lufkin Industries.

In the 1970s, when the rising prices associated with the "energy crisis" had provoked a public reaction against the big oil companies, Wilson struck a populist pose popular in rural Texas, and exploited this anger to the benefit of the smaller independents. At one point, he warned that without federal efforts to protect the independents, "The petroleum industry of the United States will be controlled by the eight men who head the eight major oil companies in the United States."

The rest of Wilson's legislative record on domestic policy is pure East Texas populism. Even with his conservative record on foreign policy and defense issues, Wilson still has managed to vote with a majority of fellow Democrats more than 60 percent of the time since the mid-1980s. In the 101st Congress, he voted for the 1990 budget summit agreement, and with a majority of Democrats for the civil rights bill and for federal funding of abortion in cases of rape and incest. "There is something simply obscene in the people of this upper-middle-class body denying to poor young girls a privilege that we would give to our own daughters, sisters or nieces in a heartbeat," he said.

With his position on Appropriations, Wilson also has been able to obtain funding for the types of projects that earn constituent gratitude. In 1991, constituents saw his hand in the opening of a Veterans Administration Outpatient Clinic in Lufkin, his home town, and the ground breaking for the $2.5 million Big Thicket Visitors Center in Kountze.

At Home: Wilson managed through most of his years in the House to combine his active legislative career with the pursuit of pleasure. He has never seemed embarrassed about being labeled a playboy or a smiling Texas rogue; he seems to enjoy it. "I love what I'm doing," he once told a reporter. "Why should I go around looking like a constipated hound dog? I'm having the time of my life."

In the late 1970s, Wilson was a partner in a downtown Washington discotheque. With his monogrammed cowboy boots and wide-brimmed Western hat, he was a recognized man-about-town, and he always seemed to be escorting a beautiful actress, model or socialite. The divorced Wilson's steadies included a woman whose picture had appeared on the cover of *Playboy*. His 1986 traveling companion, Annelise Ilschenko, was a lobbyist and the 1975 winner of the Miss World USA contest.

At one point, Wilson's high-life routine almost wore thin on 2nd District voters. He found himself in political trouble in 1984, a year after his car accident and the federal drug probe in which his name was mentioned. The controversy surrounding these events encouraged primary challenges from four contenders who would never have taken on the popular incumbent in an ordinary year. The candidate best positioned to take advantage of Wilson's troubles was Nacogdoches bank executive Jerry K. Johnson, who was making his first bid for public office. A farm-bred Baptist church deacon and Sunday school teacher, Johnson projected a clean-cut image that contrasted with Wilson's flamboyance.

Like all of Wilson's primary opponents, Johnson avoided overt mention of the drug issue. But he was not shy about painting the incumbent as a man whose taste for glamour had superseded his interest in the concerns of the district. "Unlike the incumbent, I won't go into the Washington real estate and nightclub business and forget where I come from or who I'm working for," Johnson said.

But Wilson was well prepared for the fight. Tapping his close ties to defense contractors and the independent oil industry, he amassed a substantial treasury, using some of his money to run TV ads that showed him talking with laid-off blue-collar workers and trumpeting his support for "domestic content" legislation. He also deployed phone banks for the first time in his political career.

Wilson sought to defuse controversy over the Justice investigation by attacking the department, vehemently denying allegations against him and accusing the Justice Department of prolonging its investigation solely because he was a member of Congress. He told constituents that he was "set up" by an embittered former business partner who had embezzled money from him.

If the investigation hurt Wilson among the district's Democrats, the damage was limited. Johnson, the only challenger to clear 10 percent on primary day, carried his home base of Nacogdoches County. But the rest of the district stayed with Wilson. Squelching speculation that he might be forced into a runoff, Wilson captured 55 percent of the districtwide primary vote, and won handily in November.

The next two elections were easy for Wilson, but 1990 presented more of a challenge. Given

Wilson's reputation as a ladies' man, there were some chuckles when Republicans settled on Donna Peterson as their 1990 nominee ("Charlie would rather date his opponent than beat her," joked one Democratic activist). Peterson, a 30-year-old West Point graduate and captain in the Army Reserve, campaigned energetically and hoped to benefit from her spot on the ballot below popular U.S. Sen. Phil Gramm and Republican gubernatorial nominee Clayton Williams. She did hold Wilson to 56 percent, his lowest-ever congressional general election tally, but was never a serious upset threat.

Liberal Democrats in Washington who are dismayed by the conservative aspects of Wilson's record might be surprised to learn that in 1960, when most Texas Democrats were backing Lyndon B. Johnson for the Democratic presidential nomination, Wilson was for John F. Kennedy. In the Texas Legislature, Wilson was commonly identified as "the liberal from Lufkin"; he crusaded against high utility rates, fought for Medicaid and tax exemptions for the elderly and sponsored bills to remove a ceiling on welfare spending. His career advanced with the help of Arthur Temple, a maverick lumber millionaire who treated Wilson as a protégé and helped with campaign financing.

During his successful congressional race in 1972, Wilson softened his liberalism somewhat, opposing school busing and gun control. But he still drew the support of blacks and labor and easily defeated the wife of Rep. John Dowdy in the Democratic primary. Dowdy's husband had been sentenced to prison earlier in the year for bribery, conspiracy and perjury.

Committees

Appropriations (13th of 37 Democrats)
Defense; Foreign Operations, Export Financing & Related Programs; Military Construction

Select Intelligence (2nd of 12 Democrats)
Oversight & Evaluation (chairman)

Elections

1990 General		
Charles Wilson (D)	76,974	(56%)
Donna Peterson (R)	61,555	(44%)
1988 General		
Charles Wilson (D)	145,614	(88%)
Gary W. Nelson (LIBERT)	20,475	(12%)

Previous Winning Percentages: **1986** (66%) **1984** (59%) **1982** (94%) **1980** (69%) **1978** (70%) **1976** (95%) **1974** (100%) **1972** (74%)

District Vote For President

	1988	1984	1980	1976
D	99,075 (50%)	81,989 (42%)	86,056 (50%)	85,850 (59%)
R	98,720 (50%)	114,915 (58%)	81,093 (48%)	59,163 (41%)

Campaign Finance

	Receipts	Receipts from PACs		Expend-itures
1990				
Wilson (D)	$663,504	$439,517	(66%)	$740,342
Peterson (R)	$125,013	$8,000	(6%)	$124,884
1988				
Wilson (D)	$338,839	$254,350	(75%)	$309,355

Key Votes

1991	
Authorize use of force against Iraq	Y
1990	
Support constitutional amendment on flag desecration	Y
Pass family and medical leave bill over Bush veto	Y
Reduce SDI funding	N
Allow abortions in overseas military facilities	Y
Approve budget summit plan for spending and taxing	Y
Approve civil rights bill	Y
1989	
Halt production of B-2 stealth bomber at 13 planes	N
Oppose capital gains tax cut	N
Approve federal abortion funding in rape or incest cases	Y
Approve pay raise and revision of ethics rules	Y
Pass Democratic minimum wage plan over Bush veto	Y

Voting Studies

	Presidential Support		Party Unity		Conservative Coalition	
Year	**S**	**O**	**S**	**O**	**S**	**O**
1990	35	50	64	18	61	26
1989	47	38	61	20	51	39
1988	36	43	61	20	53	34
1987	39	54	66	17	65	26
1986	38	50	61	18	72	12
1985	40	43	63	15	60	22
1984	36	32	44	21	59	15
1983	45	37	53	28	66	13
1982	47	30	51	30	63	15
1981	57	34	54	36	68	24

Interest Group Ratings

Year	ADA	ACU	AFL-CIO	CCUS
1990	44	40	83	17
1989	45	50	82	40
1988	35	55	82	46
1987	56	43	93	8
1986	35	50	92	27
1985	40	55	75	44
1984	35	26	73	38
1983	45	48	75	50
1982	25	47	47	56
1981	20	50	50	58

3 Sam Johnson (R)

Of Dallas — Elected 1991

Born: Oct. 11, 1930, San Antonio, Texas.
Education: Southern Methodist U., B.B.A. 1951; George Washington U., M.S.I.A. 1974.
Military Service: Air Force, 1951-79.
Occupation: Home builder.
Family: Wife, Shirley Melton; three children.
Religion: Methodist.
Political Career: Texas House, 1985-91.
Capitol Office: 1223 Longworth Bldg. 20515; 225-4201

The Path to Washington: A late-starting but fast-rising star in the Texas state House, former fighter-pilot Johnson had his career path altered in March 1991 when Republican Rep. Steve Bartlett (1983-91) resigned to run for mayor of Dallas.

Johnson was one of a dozen candidates to succeed Bartlett in the initial voting May 4, finishing second to Tom Pauken, a former Reagan administration official who had twice lost close races in another congressional district. In the runoff May 18, Johnson eclipsed Pauken with 53 percent of the vote.

It is not unusual for members of Congress to have crossed paths somewhere before coming to the Capitol. But Johnson met the first of his future colleagues in a North Vietnamese prison camp, where a fellow prisoner was John McCain, later to become a Republican senator from Arizona.

Johnson was shot down over North Vietnam in 1966 and held prisoner for seven years, half that time in solitary confinement. While a POW, he lost partial use of his right arm.

Johnson's career as a highly decorated Air Force officer spanned nearly 30 years. Besides tours as a fighter pilot over both Korea and Vietnam, he flew with the Thunderbirds — the Air Force's precision flying demonstration team — and directed the Air Force's "Top Gun" fighter pilot school.

But it was during his imprisonment in North Vietnam that he began planning a future in politics. In a radio ad run during the campaign this year, Johnson told of vowing that when he was free he would never be content just to gripe about government again.

Considering his dramatic past, Johnson is surprisingly unassuming in person. His demeanor generally has proved to be an asset for him in politics, although some have criticized him for being understated to the point of lethargy.

Johnson's political debut came in 1984, when at age 54 he won a seat in the Texas House representing the GOP suburbs of Collin County. His military heroics had provided him an entree, but it was his skill at coalition-building that helped him advance. As a member of the House Corrections Committee, Johnson fashioned a reputation as a law-and-order conservative, promoting criminal justice legislation that included expanding the rights of crime victims and increasing the number of prison beds.

Johnson soon became chairman of the Policy Committee of the House Republican Caucus. While making friends in Austin, he was broadening his contacts in the Dallas area by serving as co-chairman of George Bush's North Texas campaign in 1988 and as chairman of Bartlett's re-election campaigns in 1988 and 1990.

When Bartlett decided to resign, Johnson was well-positioned to succeed him. Not only did he have a strong base in the Collin County portion of the district (he lives in a part of Dallas that reaches into Collin County), but he had the backing of three-fourths of his GOP colleagues in the Texas House, the GOP chairmen in both counties in the district (Collin and Dallas), businessman T. Boone Pickens and former Dallas Cowboys quarterback Roger Staubach.

The first round of voting went to Pauken, a former head of ACTION (the federal volunteer agency), who had 27 percent of the vote to Johnson's 20 percent. But Johnson roared past Pauken in the runoff, buoyed by endorsements from the candidates who had finished third, fourth and sixth in the May 4 vote. Johnson also did well in his base, fast-growing Collin County.

Collin County precincts cast just one-fifth of the runoff ballots, but Johnson, who represents much of the county in the Texas House, swept it with 75 percent of the vote.

In populous Dallas County, where the rest of the ballots were cast, Johnson did just well enough. His respectable 47 percent far exceeded the 10 percent he had received on May 4.

Democrats had all but conceded the seat to the GOP from the start. The 3rd includes high-status neighborhoods in Dallas and fast-grow-

Texas 3

North Dallas; Northern Suburbs

The 3rd is nestled snugly among the affluent neighborhoods and suburbs of North Dallas. The median housing value here is by far the highest in the area and second in the state only to the Houston-based 7th District. Many of Dallas' top corporate executives live here, commuting to work downtown.

But the 3rd also has a sizable business community of its own. High-rise offices and shopping malls have sprung up along the Dallas North Tollway leading into the suburbs, but Texas' economic malaise in recent years has put a damper on growth. Suburban Richardson and Carrollton are populated by young people who arrived during the boom years to take jobs with electronics manufacturers, research firms and corporate branch offices.

Among the wealthiest North Dallas communities are Highland Park and University Park, traditional enclaves of the city's business establishment. University Park hosts Southern Methodist University, a private school with an enrollment of about 9,000 students. Methodist-affiliated SMU has always had an upper-crust air about it — at football games, students have been known to hold up signs that say, "Our maids went to UT" (the University of Texas).

The GOP is firmly in control throughout the 3rd. In 1988, George Bush won three-quarters of the district's presidential ballots, just a shade below his showing in the 7th District, which Bush represented in the House in the late 1960s. Even GOP Senate candidate Beau Boulter — who lost decisively statewide to Lloyd Bentsen in 1988 — won 55 percent of the vote in the 3rd.

In 1983 redistricting, the 3rd picked up most of the city of Plano, in Collin County. Plano blends in well with the rest of the district; it consists largely of young, upwardly mobile professionals who vote Republican. Like nearby Garland, which grew by 30 percent in the 1980s, Plano is expanding rapidly; it grew by 78 percent in the last decade. About half of Garland (pop. 181,000) is in the 3rd.

Population: 527,023. White 493,748 (94%), Black 17,239 (3%), Other 8,229 (2%). Spanish origin 17,724 (3%). 18 and over 389,627 (74%), 65 and over 37,406 (7%). Median age: 30.

ing suburbs to the north where Republican candidates regularly roll up three-fourths or more of the vote. The lone Democrat in the original field in May ran seventh.

Pauken went on the offensive in the runoff, accusing Johnson of backing a controversial school financing plan that would redistribute funds from more affluent school districts in Texas to poorer ones.

Johnson argued that he had favored a procedural move to send the measure to committee for revisions but had opposed it once it came back to the floor of the Texas House.

Meanwhile, Johnson spotlighted his military record. He ran a television spot that featured footage of President Bush lauding Johnson at a ceremony at a Vietnam veterans memorial in the Dallas area. And on the day before the runoff, a fellow Vietnam pilot, freshman GOP Rep. Randy "Duke" Cunningham of California, came to the Texas 3rd to campaign in Johnson's behalf.

District Vote For President

	1988	1984	1980	1976
D	72,884 (25%)	52,426 (18%)	43,897 (20%)	43,033 (24%)
R	215,154 (75%)	235,644 (82%)	163,106 (75%)	135,688 (75%)
I			7,509 (4%)	

4 Ralph M. Hall (D)

Of Rockwall — Elected 1980

Born: May 3, 1923, Rockwall County, Texas.

Education: Attended Texas Christian U., 1943, U. of Texas, 1946-47; Southern Methodist U., LL.B. 1951.

Military Service: Navy, 1942-45.

Occupation: Lawyer; businessman.

Family: Wife, Mary Ellen Murphy; three children.

Religion: Methodist.

Political Career: Rockwall County judge, 1950-62; Texas Senate, 1963-73; sought Democratic nomination for lieutenant governor, 1972.

Capitol Office: 2236 Rayburn Bldg. 20515; 225-6673.

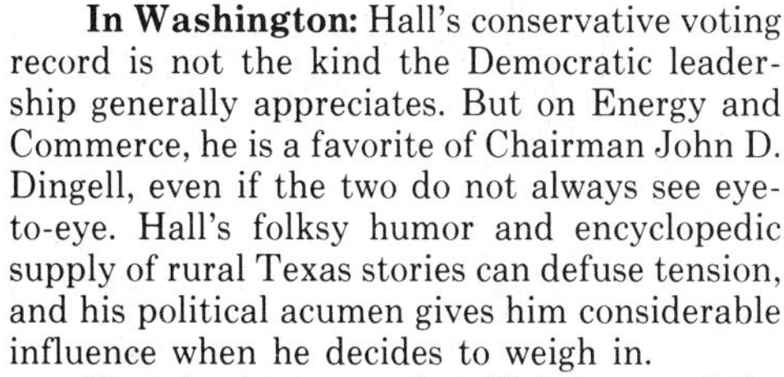

In Washington: Hall's conservative voting record is not the kind the Democratic leadership generally appreciates. But on Energy and Commerce, he is a favorite of Chairman John D. Dingell, even if the two do not always see eye-to-eye. Hall's folksy humor and encyclopedic supply of rural Texas stories can defuse tension, and his political acumen gives him considerable influence when he decides to weigh in.

That is not to say that Hall is one of the committee's more active members. But when issues important to the energy industry come up, Hall makes his presence felt.

During the intense deliberations over the 1990 Clean Air Act, for example, Hall and fellow Texan Jack Fields, a Republican, at one stage weakened proposed mandates for auto companies to build vehicles that run on alternative fuels. Their amendment increased the percentage of gasoline that could be included in a "clean fuel" mix of gasoline and methanol, and it put reformulated gasoline on the list of "clean alternative fuels." It also stripped a proposed requirement that automakers sell 1 million clean-fuel vehicles a year by 1997.

Hall and other supporters said the amendment would create a level playing field for alternative fuels other than methanol, but critics saw it as a major victory for the auto and oil industries.

Hall's energy concerns also show up in his longtime advocacy of natural gas decontrol. After years of bitter stalemate, Energy and Commerce passed a decontrol bill by voice vote in early 1989. "I wouldn't be more surprised to see my old dog Red sharing his food with the cats," he said of the unanimity, "or the mockingbird not flying down to peck at the squirrels."

As a Texan and Science committee member, Hall has been keenly interested in the superconducting super collider project. Hall wants to encourage foreign investors to buy into the project, and during the 101st Congress he persuaded the Science Committee to remove a $7.5 million overall cap that he said could restrict such investment.

More often than not, Hall is at odds with his party. In August 1990, he was one of only two Democrats voting to expel Massachusetts Rep. Barney Frank on ethics charges, and in 1985 he voted "present" rather than support Thomas P. O'Neill Jr. for Speaker. After the latter, he seemed untroubled that the leadership might retaliate by removing him from Energy and Commerce. "I wouldn't blame them if they did," he said cheerfully. "I do what I have to do, and they do what they have to do."

At Home: An early starter in politics, Hall was elected judge in his home county while still in law school. After 12 years, he moved up to the state Senate and spent a decade there, rising to become president pro tem.

In 1972 Hall entered statewide politics, running for lieutenant governor on a conservative platform. But he finished fourth in the Democratic primary, retired from politics and concentrated on business.

When 4th District Democrat Ray Roberts announced his retirement in 1980, Hall re-entered politics. His primary foe was Jerdy Gary, son of a former Oklahoma governor. Hall contrasted his Texas upbringing with Gary's Oklahoma roots, and won nomination with 57 percent. Because of Ronald Reagan's popularity among the 4th's voters, Hall's contest with Republican John H. Wright was closer than expected. Though Wright, a Tyler business manager, was well-known only in the eastern part of the district, Reagan's showing helped Wright pull 48 percent. But Republicans have not mounted a comparable challenge since.

One way Hall heads off opposition is to make his feelings about national Democratic politics perfectly clear; chosen as an uncommitted delegate to the Democratic convention in 1984, he opted not to go, saying he "didn't want to elbow some gay guy out of the way to get to a committee meeting."

Texas 4

Northeast — Tyler; Longview

The 4th is a descendant of the northeast Texas constituency that sent Sam Rayburn to Congress for 48 years; it covers much of the old, rural Rayburn territory. But the Speaker might not recognize the district. Fannin and Grayson counties remain oriented toward livestock, grain and peanuts, though Grayson is slowly breaking away from its agricultural roots as it becomes absorbed into the Dallas orbit. Sherman, the Grayson County seat, is an old cotton-processing town now turning out meat products, castings, metal pipe and electronics.

The counties in the center of the 4th are caught up in the sprawl of metropolitan Dallas. Population doubled in both Collin and Rockwall counties during the 1970s; Rockwall doubled again in the 1980s. Many people living here commute to Dallas; others work in the E-Systems facility in Greenville, which develops and modifies aircraft for military and civilian use.

At the eastern end of the 4th, where cotton was dominant a generation ago, are two cities serving as supply and distribution hubs for the East Texas oil fields — Tyler (Smith County) and Longview (Gregg County). The oil industry's downturn took its toll in the 1980s, putting a halt to the rapid growth it experienced during the '80s; the regional oil economy remained stagnant through the early 1990s. Tyler, the self-proclaimed "Rose Capital of the U.S.," is boosted by a rose industry that supplies more than one-third of the nation's rose bushes.

Democrats have won the 4th narrowly in most recent statewide contests, but the GOP continues to make strides. Ronald Reagan's strong showing in Gregg and Smith counties helped him carry the 4th in 1980, and four years later, he swept nearly 70 percent of the vote in the 4th. George Bush could not match that in 1988, but he still carried the district with ease. In 1990, Gregg and Smith counties voted Republican for governor.

Population: 526,991. White 442,913 (84%), Black 73,672 (14%), Other 2,993 (1%). Spanish origin 14,035 (3%). 18 and over 377,899 (72%), 65 and over 74,813 (14%). Median age: 32.

Committees

Energy & Commerce (11th of 27 Democrats)
Health & the Environment; Telecommunications & Finance

Science, Space & Technology (7th of 32 Democrats)
Space (chairman); Energy; Environment

Elections

1990 General		
Ralph M. Hall (D)	108,300	(100%)
1988 General		
Ralph M. Hall (D)	139,379	(66%)
Randy Sutton (R)	67,337	(32%)

Previous Winning Percentages: **1986** (72%) **1984** (58%) **1982** (74%) **1980** (52%)

District Vote For President

	1988		1984		1980		1976	
D	82,095	(39%)	65,599	(31%)	73,547	(41%)	79,514	(52%)
R	129,164	(61%)	147,991	(69%)	103,771	(58%)	74,225	(48%)

Campaign Finance

	Receipts	Receipts from PACs		Expend-itures
1990				
Hall (D)	$261,431	$202,850	(78%)	$209,902
1988				
Hall (D)	$350,284	$242,743	(69%)	$316,846
Sutton (R)	$66,711	$1,386	(2%)	$65,068

Key Votes

1991	
Authorize use of force against Iraq	Y
1990	
Support constitutional amendment on flag desecration	?
Pass family and medical leave bill over Bush veto	N
Reduce SDI funding	N
Allow abortions in overseas military facilities	N
Approve budget summit plan for spending and taxing	Y
Approve civil rights bill	N
1989	
Halt production of B-2 stealth bomber at 13 planes	N
Oppose capital gains tax cut	N
Approve federal abortion funding in rape or incest cases	N
Approve pay raise and revision of ethics rules	N
Pass Democratic minimum wage plan over Bush veto	N

Voting Studies

	Presidential Support		Party Unity		Conservative Coalition	
Year	**S**	**O**	**S**	**O**	**S**	**O**
1990	51	38	39	41	78	7
1989	69	29	39	58	93	5
1988	58	41	47	53	92	8
1987	52	45	44	52	88	9
1986	56	40	38	59	88	10
1985	58	39	45	46	84	5
1984	49	50	44	54	81	17
1983	48	49	38	57	83	11
1982	58	42	40	60	81	19
1981	61	34	40	54	80	15

Interest Group Ratings

Year	ADA	ACU	AFL-CIO	CCUS
1990	6	71	20	77
1989	5	89	8	80
1988	15	92	43	86
1987	24	70	44	73
1986	10	80	33	80
1985	15	70	31	67
1984	15	67	46	44
1983	35	62	56	61
1982	5	73	30	64
1981	5	79	27	74

5 John Bryant (D)

Of Dallas — Elected 1982

Born: February 22, 1947, Lake Jackson, Texas.
Education: Southern Methodist U., B.A. 1969, J.D. 1972.
Occupation: Lawyer.
Family: Wife, Janet Elizabeth Watts; three children.
Religion: Methodist.
Political Career: Texas House, 1974-83.
Capitol Office: 208 Cannon Bldg.20515; 225-2231.

In Washington: After announcing in 1989 that he would leave the House to run for state attorney general, Bryant reversed field and opted to continue his congressional career.

His abilities are well-regarded by his colleagues, and he was characteristically active during the 101st Congress. But all Texans in the House lost some influence with the mid-1989 departure of Jim Wright as Speaker, and at times Bryant seemed particularly ill at ease with the leadership style of Wright's successor, Thomas S. Foley of Washington.

First elected in 1982, Bryant was quick to impress. He won a place on the Energy and Commerce Committee in his first term, and in the 101st Congress, Bryant took a seat on Budget, with help from Wright.

Bryant's views seem to put him closer to the national Democratic Party than are many other Texans; only one other member of the state's delegation voted against President Bush more often in 1990. But his positions are generally more populist than liberal.

One of Bryant's most publicized crusades in the 100th and 101st Congresses was for a measure requiring new disclosures of foreign ownership of U.S. companies' assets in cases where a U.S. business is more than 5 percent foreign-owned, and more extensive ownership disclosure where the foreign stake is 25 percent or more. The measure cleared Energy and Commerce 21-20, and became one of the more contentious legislative trade issues. The bill came under strong attack on the floor by opponents who feared it would reduce foreign investment needed to counteract the inflationary effects of the federal deficit. But Bryant said he had altered the plan to meet objections from the securities industry and others who would have to comply with it.

Bryant defeated an attempt to weaken his proposal 190-230, but he faced strong opposition in a House-Senate conference. Under threat of a presidential veto, his provisions were dropped from the omnibus trade bill.

That did not end the fight, however, because Bryant pushed the bill separately on the House floor, winning 250-170. It never made it past the Senate, but Bryant tried again in the 101st Congress. This time, however, legislators and administration officials coalesced behind an alternative backed by Sen. Jim Exon of Nebraska and Rep. Philip R. Sharp of Indiana. That bill, which eventually became law, seeks to better refine and analyze existing data on foreign investment rather than collect and disclose new information, as Bryant advocated.

Bryant had better luck with his efforts to improve the quality of children's television. After bluntly telling a convention of broadcasters in Texas that he considered children's TV to be in sorry shape, Bryant during the 100th Congress worked with Democratic Rep. Terry L. Bruce of Illinois on a bill to protect children from exploitation by commercial broadcasters. Bryant wanted to limit the amount of advertising allowed on children's TV and require one hour per day of educational programming for children. A compromise including advertising limits and the consideration of educational programming during license renewal passed that Congress, but was later vetoed.

In the 101st Congress, however, Bryant saw the bill become law, without the president's signature. The law limits advertising on children's programming to a maximum of 12 minutes per hour, and ties licensing renewal to overall programming standards for children.

Bryant is also a player on the Judiciary Committee, where he has been active on immigration issues of concern to Texas. During the immigration reform debates of the 101st Congress, Bryant was one of only a few Democrats to vocally oppose raising immigration ceilings, arguing that resources were inadequate to accommodate more newcomers. But Bryant did back measures to allow the family members of illegal aliens legalized under previous "amnesty" provisions to remain in this country.

On gun control, Bryant in 1988 was one of just four Texas House members opposing the wishes of the National Rifle Association to back a seven-day waiting period for handgun purchases. Bryant had some cover: a hunter himself, he had

Texas 5

Downtown Dallas; Eastern and Southern Suburbs

Few American cities have as controversial a reputation as Dallas. Following the assassination of President Kennedy there in 1963, the city suffered from an image of frontier violence and extremism that was hard to shake. Just as that perception was fading, the television series "Dallas" came along to popularize the image of a metropolis ruled by an oligarchy of oil interests obsessed with money and power.

When Dallas was in the national spotlight during the 1984 Republican National Convention, local boosters were eager for the city to come across as a sophisticated, cosmopolitan place. It succeeded to some degree; visitors were impressed by such amenities as the stunning art museum and the fine restaurants. But many Northerners looking for characteristics that fit their definition of a city did not find them in Dallas. Reflecting on the antiseptic quality of the steel-and-concrete downtown and its rather vacant sidewalks, one joked that "anything that smacks of 'funky' here gets torn down and replaced with a high-rise."

Nonetheless, Dallas and the 5th have some diversity. Just northwest of downtown lies Oaklawn, a fashionable enclave of young professionals with a sizable gay community. East Dallas is a mix of lower-middle- and upper-middle-class residential neighborhoods and more transient young workers. The bulk of the district's black population — which stands at 20 percent — lives in the economically depressed southern part of the city. South Dallas has a sizable Hispanic community.

But while more than 60 percent of the district vote is cast within Dallas, the decisive political areas are blue-collar suburbs such as Mesquite, Sunnyvale, Seagoville and Balch Springs. These are not reliably Democratic areas: In 1980 and 1984, they voted for Ronald Reagan. But in 1988, their support enabled Michael S. Dukakis to win the district by 458 votes.

In suburbs farther south and west, the working-class voters have an affinity for Democrats, though they prefer candidates in the moderate-to-conservative mold. This area includes Hutchins, Wilmer and Lancaster, three towns transferred to the 5th in 1982 redistricting.

Population: 526,633. White 377,294 (72%), Black 103,339 (20%), Other 6,862 (1%). Spanish origin 64,455 (12%). 18 and over 374,926 (71%), 65 and over 45,962 (9%). Median age: 28.

the support of the Dallas police chief.

Underneath Bryant's low-key nature and hound dog eyes lies a strong-willed populist with driving political ambition. At times, he makes his points with a zeal that critics think borders on demagoguery. When Reagan's Energy Secretary John S. Herrington came before the Energy and Power Subcommittee in 1987 after issuing a report on the oil industry, Bryant, frustrated by the lack of recommendations for aiding the industry, attacked him mercilessly. "I'd like to see an energy secretary that only had one arm," Bryant said, "so he couldn't keep saying 'on the other hand.' " The remark caused Herrington to bristle.

Whatever Herrington's view, Bryant's comment probably played well in Texas. And he does more than just speak up for the oil industry. While he has quarreled with various elements of the business community over the years, he has worked with home-state business interests when he can. In the 99th Congress, Bryant led a fight to repeal provisions of the Fuel Use Act of 1978, which prohibited the use of oil and natural gas as boiler fuels for new utility and industrial plants. A repeal measure, strongly desired by the troubled oil industry, passed the House, but did not become law in the 99th. The act was repealed in 1987.

Bryant does not shy away from a fight, even with Energy and Commerce Chairman John D. Dingell. A former trial lawyer, Bryant went against Dingell in the 100th Congress when the committee debated legislation to establish a federal product liability standard. Businesses have long pushed for legislation to preempt state laws used by courts to determine the compensation that manufacturers must pay for damages resulting from use of their products. But business has been opposed by trial lawyers and consumer groups, who fear a change would infringe on victims' rights.

Bryant was in the latter group, and he offered one successful amendment in committee to make it clear that a manufacturer could be held liable for certain damages. He failed with an amendment that effectively would have allowed states to continue to determine liability for design flaws. But the liability bill, which cleared committee, never cleared the House.

At Home: Bryant's announced plans to run in 1990 for attorney general generated a flutter of hope among Republicans of taking the 5th. But once Bryant re-entered the House race, he had little difficulty winning.

The tortuous course of Texas redistricting

worked to Bryant's advantage in 1982, first throwing the 5th open and then virtually guaranteeing a Democratic victory. The Legislature initially altered the Dallas-based 5th to tilt it Republican, and that persuaded incumbent Democrat Jim Mattox to run for attorney general. A three-judge federal panel restored its Democratic boundaries early in 1982, but by then Mattox was committed to his statewide campaign. Bryant was left as the front-runner in a constituency considerably better for Democrats than Mattox's had been.

The real test for Bryant was the Democratic primary, in which his chief foe was former Dallas Mayor Pro Tem Bill Blackburn. Although Blackburn had good funding and name recognition, his political ties were to downtown Dallas and its business community, and these were no asset in the blue-collar 5th. The result was surprisingly one-sided, with Bryant taking 66 percent. He had no trouble in November, and the GOP did not field a candidate in 1984.

Republicans did show some interest in Bryant in 1986. But when a popular Republican politician opted not to run, local GOP leaders ended up fielding an energetic, if inexperienced, candidate. Oil and gas lobbyist Tom Carter never had sought public office before, although he had been active in area party affairs. He branded Bryant a menace to entrepreneurs.

But Bryant had established allies in the Dallas business community, including some normally Republican captains of the energy industry; others were wary of working too hard against an influential junior member of Energy and Commerce. Although Carter managed a strong showing in suburban boom communities such as Garland and Mesquite — part of the district's natural GOP base — he faltered in the 5th's more politically competitive territory. Bryant won with almost 60 percent, and in 1988 pushed his victory share back above 60 percent.

In 1990, GOP nominee Jerry Rucker tried to wound Bryant with anti-incumbent artillery such as the congressional pay raise and national S&L crisis. But despite a political base from five years on the Dallas City Council, Rucker could not drag Bryant below 60 percent.

In the Texas House, Bryant made a name for himself in a battle over taxation of farm land, leading the faction opposing tax advantages for speculators and farming corporations. He was also largely responsible for molding the infant House Study Group into a research body for moderates and liberals — much like the Democratic Study Group of the U.S. House.

By the end of his second term in the Legislature, Bryant had become the leader of a group of liberal Democrats who found themselves frequently at odds with House Speaker Billy Clayton. In 1980, Bryant unsuccessfully challenged Clayton for the Speaker's chair.

Committees

Budget (14th of 23 Democrats)
Defense, Foreign Policy & Space; Human Resources

Energy & Commerce (16th of 27 Democrats)
Health & the Environment; Oversight & Investigations; Telecommunications & Finance

Judiciary (15th of 21 Democrats)
Crime and Criminal Justice; Economic & Commercial Law; International Law, Immigration & Refugees

Elections

1990 General		
John Bryant (D)	65,228	(60%)
Jerry Rucker (R)	41,307	(38%)
Kenneth Ashby (LIBERT)	2,939	(3%)
1988 General		
John Bryant (D)	95,376	(61%)
Lon Williams (R)	59,877	(38%)

Previous Winning Percentages: **1986** (59%) **1984** (100%) **1982** (65%)

District Vote For President

	1988	1984	1980	1976
D	80,713 (50%)	68,926 (41%)	70,128 (45%)	57,813 (48%)
R	80,255 (50%)	100,261 (59%)	80,636 (51%)	60,885 (51%)
I			4,190 (3%)	

Campaign Finance

	Receipts	Receipts from PACs	Expend-itures
1990			
Bryant (D)	$936,755	$458,721 (49%)	$1,034,446
Rucker (R)	$453,796	$45,875 (10%)	$453,165
1988			
Bryant (D)	$889,511	$393,057 (44%)	$646,218
Williams (R)	$180,629	$24,676 (14%)	$179,201

Key Votes

1991	
Authorize use of force against Iraq	N
1990	
Support constitutional amendment on flag desecration	N
Pass family and medical leave bill over Bush veto	Y
Reduce SDI funding	Y
Allow abortions in overseas military facilities	Y
Approve budget summit plan for spending and taxing	N
Approve civil rights bill	Y
1989	
Halt production of B-2 stealth bomber at 13 planes	N
Oppose capital gains tax cut	Y
Approve federal abortion funding in rape or incest cases	?
Approve pay raise and revision of ethics rules	Y
Pass Democratic minimum wage plan over Bush veto	Y

Voting Studies

	Presidential Support		Party Unity		Conservative Coalition	
Year	**S**	**O**	**S**	**O**	**S**	**O**
1990	13	84	89	9	33	67
1989	24	43	70	5	24	44
1988	19	74	87	7	42	55
1987	25	71	88	5	49	44
1986	18	80	84	12	54	46
1985	23	78	89	8	31	67
1984	22	62	74	6	17	64
1983	24	76	84	10	36	60

Interest Group Ratings

Year	ADA	ACU	AFL-CIO	CCUS
1990	83	17	92	29
1989	75	12	91	30
1988	85	9	100	27
1987	80	4	100	14
1986	65	23	93	44
1985	55	10	88	41
1984	75	0	92	38
1983	80	13	94	20

6 Joe L. Barton (R)

Of Ennis — Elected 1984

Born: Sept. 15, 1949, Waco, Texas.
Education: Texas A&M U., B.S. 1972; Purdue U., M.S. 1973.
Occupation: Engineering consultant.
Family: Wife, Janet Sue Winslow; three children.
Religion: Methodist.
Political Career: No previous office.
Capitol Office: 1225 Longworth Bldg. 20515; 225-2002.

In Washington: Colleagues view Barton as a bright and hardworking member with the potential to help shape debate on national issues. Thus far, however, he is best known for his work on behalf of the 6th District — none of it more determined than his efforts to help the district get and keep the federal superconducting super collider project.

Few states celebrate money and immensity more than Texas, so the delegation was understandably gleeful over being selected to host the mammoth $8 billion-plus federal atom-smasher. Barton, however, enjoys the added pleasure of seeing the project go up on his own turf, in the 6th District city of Waxahachie.

After lobbying hard for the project, Barton and other delegation members were rewarded by the government's 1988 decision to build the atom-smasher in Texas. But the fight did not end there, and during the 101st Congress the project continued to come under fire from members who considered it an overpriced boondoggle.

Beginning in January 1989, Barton worked closely with fellow Texas Rep. Jim Chapman, a Democrat on the Appropriations Committee, to steer the super collider project through the appropriations process. Congress approved $200 million for the project by mid-year, but the assaults continued. The following year, when critics suggested Texas might not come through with its $1 billion contribution for the super collider, Barton moved to defuse the potential controversy by quickly agreeing to the notion of making Texas formalize its financial pledge.

However, Barton and others lost a fight to guarantee that Texas would get its money back should the project be scrapped before fall 1995.

With foes continuing to rail against the super collider at the outset of the 102nd Congress, Barton positioned himself to keep an even closer eye on its progress by taking a seat on the House Science Committee.

Barton's slot on Energy and Commerce enables him to tend to various district interests, particularly the oil and gas industries. Although he was not a pivotal figure in debate over the 1990 Clean Air Act, Barton was an active voice for Texas interests and he successfully pushed an amendment requiring some cities to use portable pollution detection devices. With debate over energy policy heating up at the outset of the the 102nd Congress, Barton made it clear he would like to see more production incentives for domestic oil and gas companies.

While Barton's interest in energy is predictable, he surprised some during his first term on Energy and Commerce with his dogged and methodical work on consumer-protection legislation. More than many conservatives, Barton has shown an interest in a strong Consumer Product Safety Commission, and in the 100th Congress he pushed a safety issue of his own. An engineer, Barton became concerned about the design of three-wheel all-terrain vehicles (ATVs) after an accident killed an 11-year-old in his district; he got involved in an effort to take ATVs out of circulation. Hounded by controversy about the safety of their product, ATV manufacturers had agreed to halt new sales, but Barton advocated a bill requiring those manufacturers to pay a refund to owners of the estimated 1.5 million ATVs still in use.

In committee, Barton managed to overcome opposition from ATV dealers and the four Japanese ATV manufacturers, who argued that the machines were not inherently unsafe, just misused. But Barton could not get his measure to the House floor.

Outside his committee work, Barton is known as a more combative Republican partisan. He had barely taken office in 1985 when he became enraged by the refusal of Democratic leaders to seat the Republican claimant in a disputed Indiana election. His frustration drove him to some oddly belligerent tactics — such as organizing a demonstration outside a Fort Worth committee room in which then-Majority Leader Jim Wright was about to speak. Even some of Barton's GOP colleagues thought that approach was a little extreme. And in the 100th Congress, Barton nominated aggressive conser-

Texas 6

Suburban Dallas-Fort Worth and Houston; Bryan

The 6th District is a long, narrow column of counties that begins near Dallas-Fort Worth and runs southeast to the suburbs of Houston, more than 200 miles away.

In the days of Olin E. "Tiger" Teague, who represented the area from 1946 to 1978, politics in the 6th was dominated by rural conservative Democrats. But changes in the district's demographics and 1983 redistricting helped make it more hospitable for the GOP.

Republicanism is growing fastest in the areas closest to Dallas-Fort Worth and Houston, as GOP-minded white-collar workers flood the suburbs located here.

The 6th contains the two counties that grew faster than any others in Texas during the 1970s. In the northwest corner, spillover from Fort Worth nearly tripled the population of Hood County. Far to the south, Montgomery County grew 160 percent, with affluent professionals commuting to jobs in Houston. Montgomery continued to grow in the 1980s, posting a 43 percent gain.

Hood County and two others in the Dallas-Fort Worth sphere — Johnson and Ellis — have helped boost GOP presidential vote totals in the 1980s, turning away from their 1976 preference for Jimmy Carter. All three counties voted for George Bush in 1988. Montgomery County gave Democrat-turned-Republican Rep. Phil Gramm 69 percent of the vote in the 1983 special election held as a mandate on his party switch. And in 1988, Montgomery voted narrowly for GOP Rep. Beau Boulter in his Senate race against Lloyd Bentsen.

Republican strength in the 6th is further enhanced by Brazos County, the urban exception in the district's mostly rural middle region. Located in Brazos are Bryan and College Station, home of Texas A&M University, which has almost 37,000 students. In 1984, Brazos voted overwhelmingly for Reagan and Gramm, a former Texas A&M faculty member, and Bush won the county in 1988.

Ellis County, in the northern portion of the district, was selected as the site for the much-heralded, $8 billion federal superconducting super collider. Even in the 6th's traditionally Democratic rural counties, GOP candidates are now running well in state and national contests.

Population: 526,765. White 450,732 (86%), Black 57,255 (11%), Other 3,311 (1%). Spanish origin 30,591 (6%). 18 and over 379,330 (72%), 65 and over 65,759 (12%). Median age: 29.

vative GOP Rep. William E. Dannemeyer for his long-shot bid to become Republican Conference chairman. In a three-way race, Dannemeyer ran a poor third.

In the 101st Congress, Barton was selected as a deputy GOP whip. He typically votes a strong conservative line. During the 101st, for example, he was among a group that forced a floor vote on a constitutional amendment to balance the federal budget.

However, his voting record does yield some surprises. In 1990, for instance, he was the only Texas Republican to support the civil rights bill that was later vetoed by President Bush.

At Home: Barton's 1984 victory was sweet for the Texas GOP. Until 1983, when Democratic Rep. Phil Gramm resigned the seat, switched parties and was re-elected as a Republican, the GOP had never won in the 6th. Barton, who held the seat upon Gramm's move to the Senate, represents an important wedge in Texas Republicans' drive for statewide respectability. However, Barton and the GOP could face an additional challenge in 1992, when redistricting may considerably alter the look of the 6th.

An engineering consultant for Atlantic Richfield Co., Barton had never run for office before, and entered the race as the clear underdog. After primary balloting failed to produce a majority for any candidate, a runoff was held between Barton and Max Hoyt, a former energy-company lobbyist. Although the results of the runoff initially gave Hoyt an 18-vote victory, a recount reversed the outcome, and Barton was certified the winner by just 10 votes. The three losing candidates refused to support Barton in the general election.

Behind the bitterness were accusations that Barton had misrepresented his experience as a White House fellow, and that he had suggested he had Gramm's support, when in fact Gramm was neutral in the primary competition. Barton dismissed the criticisms as semantic and political, but did adjust the wording of some disputed claims.

In the general election, Barton faced Dan Kubiak, a former state representative and rancher with a folksy Texas twang and easygoing style. Although Kubiak's political reputation had suffered somewhat from two defeats, he was a familiar figure after 12 years in the state House, where he served as chairman of the Education Committee.

Barton managed to counter those assets by sticking close to coattails provided by Reagan and Gramm, and by claiming national-issues experience as a White House fellow. He called himself a "committed conservative," while portraying Kubiak as a "convenient conservative." Barton accused Kubiak of supporting Walter F. Mondale's proposals to raise taxes, and hammered away at his sizable contributions from the AFL-CIO.

Barton also made shrewd use of his ties to his alma mater, Texas A&M University in College Station, where he had graduated in engineering. That base of support, coupled with the Reagan-Gramm electoral tide and the solid GOP vote in the suburbs of Houston and Fort Worth, were too much for Kubiak to overcome.

Area Democrats were not prepared to concede the 6th, however; they mounted an aggressive challenge to Barton in 1986 behind Fort Worth attorney Preston M. "Pete" Geren.

Geren (who was subsequently elected to fill the vacancy in the 12th created by House Speaker Jim Wright's 1989 resignation) had an ample personal fortune, the enthusiastic support of state and national party leaders and close ties to popular Democratic Sen. Lloyd Bentsen, having spent two years as director of Bentsen's Texas offices. Geren claimed Barton had taken conservatism to extremes, placing ideology over the needs of his constituency.

Barton had plenty of weapons to use in his defense. He pointed to meetings he convened to coach local entrepreneurs on how to secure federal contracts, and claimed credit for helping to free offshore oil and gas royalties that had been entangled in state and federal bureaucracy.

Geren performed well for a first-time candidate, but could not overcome Barton's support in the GOP-minded urban and suburban neighborhoods of Tarrant and Montgomery counties. A divided Democratic primary field in 1988 helped Barton capture more than two-thirds of the November vote, a showing he repeated two years later.

Committees

Energy & Commerce (11th of 16 Republicans)
Commerce, Consumer Protection & Competitiveness; Energy & Power; Telecommunications & Finance

Science, Space & Technology (17th of 19 Republicans)
Energy

Elections

1990 General		
Joe L. Barton (R)	125,049	(66%)
John E. Welch (D)	62,344	(33%)
1988 General		
Joe L. Barton (R)	164,692	(68%)
N.P. "Pat" Kendrick (D)	78,786	(32%)

Previous Winning Percentages: **1986** (56%) **1984** (57%)

District Vote For President

	1988	1984	1980	1976
D	88,308 (38%)	69,508 (30%)	72,477 (42%)	78,207 (52%)
R	141,337 (62%)	158,310 (69%)	95,171 (55%)	70,113 (47%)
I			3,566 (2%)	

Campaign Finance

	Receipts	Receipts from PACs	Expend-itures
1990			
Barton (R)	$770,957	$253,403 (33%)	$458,346
Welch (D)	$6,285	0	$6,568
1988			
Barton (R)	$750,559	$288,083 (38%)	$654,260
Kendrick (D)	$29,851	0	$17,414

Key Votes

1991	
Authorize use of force against Iraq	Y
1990	
Support constitutional amendment on flag desecration	Y
Pass family and medical leave bill over Bush veto	N
Reduce SDI funding	N
Allow abortions in overseas military facilities	N
Approve budget summit plan for spending and taxing	N
Approve civil rights bill	Y
1989	
Halt production of B-2 stealth bomber at 13 planes	Y
Oppose capital gains tax cut	N
Approve federal abortion funding in rape or incest cases	N
Approve pay raise and revision of ethics rules	Y
Pass Democratic minimum wage plan over Bush veto	N

Voting Studies

	Presidential Support		Party Unity		Conservative Coalition	
Year	**S**	**O**	**S**	**O**	**S**	**O**
1990	68	29	86	7	94	2
1989	67	27	88	8	95	5
1988	70	18	89	4	82	0
1987	77	21	90	5	88	7
1986	76	22	93	4	92	4
1985	85	15	94	3	91	5

Interest Group Ratings

Year	ADA	ACU	AFL-CIO	CCUS
1990	6	87	0	77
1989	10	89	8	90
1988	5	96	0	100
1987	4	100	6	93
1986	0	95	7	94
1985	5	100	0	95

7 Bill Archer (R)

Of Houston — Elected 1970

Born: March 22, 1928, Houston, Texas.

Education: Attended Rice U., 1945-46; U. of Texas, B.B.A. 1949, LL.B. 1951.

Military Service: Air Force, 1951-53.

Occupation: Lawyer; feed company executive.

Family: Wife, Sharon Sawyer; five children, two stepchildren.

Religion: Roman Catholic.

Political Career: Hunters Creek Village Council, 1955-62; Texas House, 1967-71, served as a Democrat, 1967-69.

Capitol Office: 1236 Longworth Bldg. 20515; 225-2571.

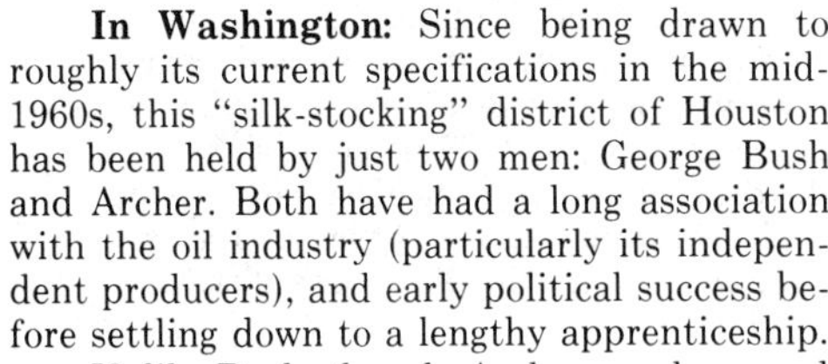

In Washington: Since being drawn to roughly its current specifications in the mid-1960s, this "silk-stocking" district of Houston has been held by just two men: George Bush and Archer. Both have had a long association with the oil industry (particularly its independent producers), and early political success before settling down to a lengthy apprenticeship.

Unlike Bush, though, Archer was born and raised in Houston. He did not start out by getting "into oil" but into law and agribusiness. Discharged from the Air Force in 1953, he won his first local office in 1955. A Roman Catholic, he entered politics a Democrat and did not switch parties until he was already in the state Legislature.

After moving on to Congress in 1970 (the year Bush lost the U.S. Senate race to Lloyd Bentsen), Archer proved himself a Republican's Republican, and he showed himself to be mindful of the commodity that is his district's lifeblood. Ascending through the ranks of the Ways and Means Committee's minority over the years, he became known as a spokesman for oil and an opponent of taxes. He helped lead the revolt against President Reagan's tax reform in the House in 1985, arguing that its lower personal tax rates were won at too great a cost in new business taxes (including on oil).

He was also an early objector to the escalating rates of payroll taxes used to finance ever-greater levels of increase for benefits under Social Security.

But with Archer's sudden rise to the top GOP slot on the Ways and Means Committee in mid-1988, he surprised observers with his flexibility and potential for effective leadership in one of the trickiest Republican posts on the Hill. When his senior colleague John J. Duncan of Tennessee announced his retirement and then died in June 1988, Archer traded his independence for consultation with senior colleagues and cooperation with key members from the majority as well.

After years of voting conservative principle rather than compromise, Archer was a surprise convert to the budget deal Bush negotiated with House and Senate leaders in 1990. The deal included taxes, but Archer stood with his president and with Ways and Means Chairman Dan Rostenkowski of Illinois in voting for the doomed package on Oct. 4.

The new Archer dovetailed well with the old on a familiar issue: capital gains. In the spring of 1989, Archer joined with Ways and Means Democrat Ed Jenkins of Georgia in introducing a capital gains tax cut that eventually passed the committee (over Rostenkowski's opposition) and triumphed on the floor of the House. Only a procedural maneuver in the Senate kept that cut from enactment.

Even as early as the summer of 1988, Archer had shown a commitment to leading while getting along. He checked staff shifts with other members and set to work on the committee's major product, a "technical corrections" tax bill. While designed chiefly to fix glitches in the tax overhaul as passed, the bill also extended important tax credits and included plums for individual companies.

Rostenkowski had let it be known that grandstanding opponents would be cut out of the locker-room action on issues important to their districts, and Archer did not bother to see if the chairman would carry through with that threat. The Republican voted for the bill on the floor and in conference, while working to hone some features he deplored. He joined with Rostenkowski to pare the House bill from $7.5 billion to $4.5 billion when the Senate insisted it would go no higher than $2.5 billion; the total ended up close to $4 billion.

Archer, however, has hardly become a Rostenkowski crony. In the 101st Congress he led a crusade that led to the repeal of one of the chairman's proudest projects of the previous year, the program to protect the elderly against catastrophic health costs. Archer and his allies had heard the outcry from the senior citizens who were having to pay up to $800 for the first

Texas 7

Western Houston and Suburbs

As Houston has grown into America's fourth-largest city and the commercial center of the Southwest, the 7th has grown dense with the homes of the prosperous corporate community. More than 400,000 people moved into the district during the 1970s, giving the 7th an 86 percent growth rate — higher than any other district in the state.

The 1980s have been a different story, however, as a downturn in the oil economy dried up jobs and left many new office buildings and apartment complexes empty.

The 7th runs west from the northwest part of Houston to the Harris County line. It has the highest property values in Texas. In River Oaks, where much of the oil elite has lived for years, imitation Spanish villas stand proudly next to imitation Tudor mansions and imitation French chateaux.

Although most of Houston's myriad corporate headquarters lie beyond the 7th's boundaries to the east, the district has its own mini-downtowns at the numerous freeway interchanges. Office buildings line the east-west Katy Freeway, and small oil-related companies are scattered throughout the district.

Once-rural areas surrounding Houston have seen rapid development in recent years, as the city's environs have spread farther and farther from its heart. Apartment complexes are burgeoning in residential communities such as Spring Branch. F/M Road 1960, part of the Texas roads system originally set up as a farm-to-market route, is a multi-lane artery today.

Along with the 3rd District in Dallas, the 7th gives Republicans their highest margins in the state. In 1976, Gerald R. Ford swept the presidential vote in the district by nearly 3-to-1. Ronald Reagan improved on that in 1980, scoring his best Texas showing with 78 percent of the vote. He did even better in 1984, and George Bush's best showing in Texas in 1988 also came in the 7th, his old House district.

Population: 527,083. White 482,555 (92%), Black 16,615 (3%), Other 15,149 (3%). Spanish origin 37,320 (7%). 18 and over 375,483 (71%), 65 and over 24,749 (5%). Median age: 29.

year of the program. When Rostenkowski sent a "fix-it" bill to the floor in September of 1989, Archer and Rep. Brian Donnelly, D-Mass., persuaded the House Rules Committee to permit a vote on near-total repeal (which eventually prevailed by a ratio of more than 5 to 1).

In past years, the focus of Archer's work has been taxation of the oil industry, the subject of endless argument at Ways and Means. His expertise on the industry is unquestioned, as is his willingness to explain its workings to colleagues. But for most of the 1980s, when the committee sat down to write an oil tax bill, Archer often faced a Democratic majority less keen on the intricacies of tertiary recovery than satisfying current political concerns.

When the so-called windfall-profits tax returned to the House floor after conference in 1980, it was Archer who offered the basic Republican proposal to exempt independents producing fewer than 1,000 barrels per day. It drew nearly all Republicans and most Southern Democrats, failing on a close 207-185 vote.

Archer's other area of expertise is Social Security, and here again he has served long enough to see some of his ideas become the prevalent view. While Congress has not yet agreed to separate the Social Security Administration from the Department of Health and Human Services, it has at long last moved to separate the Social Security trust funds with their bulging surpluses from calculations toward balancing the rest of the federal budget.

Earlier, as a member of President Reagan's National Commission on Social Security Reform, Archer argued that the Social Security system should be made solvent by reducing the growth of benefits, not by increasing the payroll tax rate for the younger people paying in.

In 1983, when the bipartisan group issued its report recommending a combination of modest benefit reductions and significant tax increases, Archer cast one of the dissenting votes in a 12-3 decision. "Any package that closes the gap with only $40 billion of restraint in cash outflow and $125 billion in new taxes," he said, "is not in the best interests of the country in the long term." The package later was amended in Archer's direction on the House floor, with the retirement age increased gradually to 67 to save money. Archer did not consider that to be enough of an improvement, however, and he voted against the legislation.

Such ironic moments have not been uncommon in Archer's career. When he was vigorously opposing the tax reform package of the 99th Congress, he found himself arrayed not only against the Democratic House majority, but also against the president and his own GOP House leaders.

Archer was adamant that the bill worked out in conference would hurt business and the economy. But his objections were not echoed by those who supported the conference report. That left Archer, second in seniority, to lead the GOP fight against the bill on the floor.

"What's fair about a tax bill that will allow deductions for interest on a second home but not on a first car?" Archer asked during debate on the conference report. But he talked more about economics than about fairness, and dismissed projections by some economists that tax revision, though economically disruptive in the short run, would have a positive impact in the long run. "There will be no long term under this bill," Archer said. "It is not going to last 10 years. So the short term is what we must consider."

Archer managed to win 160 votes for a motion to kill the tax bill by sending it back to conference. But 268 members voted against him, including the Republican leader, Illinois Rep. Robert H. Michel.

In 1982 and 1983 Archer forged to the right of President Reagan on budget and tax issues, saying that Reagan had given in too easily to defenders of federal domestic spending. But his proposals to freeze federal spending and block revenue increases fell short on the floor.

At Home: Unlike his predecessor in this House district, New England-born George Bush, Archer is a native Houstonian. Born and raised in the city, he attended both Rice University and the University of Texas before launching his political career in 1955 as a member of the Hunters Creek Village Council.

Archer made his mark as a conservative Democrat, winning a seat in the Texas Legislature in 1966. But in 1968 he switched parties and won re-election as a Republican. Since the territory of his state legislative district closely coincided with the 7th District, Archer was the early favorite for the House seat two years later when Bush ran for the U.S. Senate.

He easily won the GOP primary, and went on to defeat a young law partner of John B. Connally in November. He has had no electoral problems since then.

Committees

Ways & Means (Ranking)

Joint Taxation

Elections

1990 General		
Bill Archer (R)	114,254	(100%)
1988 General		
Bill Archer (R)	185,203	(79%)
Dianne Richards (D)	48,824	(21%)

Previous Winning Percentages: **1986** (87%) **1984** (87%) **1982** (85%) **1980** (82%) **1978** (85%) **1976** (100%) **1974** (79%) **1972** (82%) **1970** (65%)

District Vote For President

	1988	1984	1980	1976
D	53,380 (25%)	40,307 (18%)	34,478 (18%)	51,398 (28%)
R	163,767 (75%)	187,935 (82%)	147,638 (78%)	131,831 (71%)
I			5,193 (3%)	

Campaign Finance

	Receipts	Receipts from PACs	Expend-itures
1990			
Archer (R)	$241,863	0	$200,871
1988			
Archer (R)	$269,695	0	$180,255
Richards (D)	$10,650	$1,250 (12%)	$11,090

Key Votes

1991	
Authorize use of force against Iraq	Y
1990	
Support constitutional amendment on flag desecration	Y
Pass family and medical leave bill over Bush veto	N
Reduce SDI funding	N
Allow abortions in overseas military facilities	N
Approve budget summit plan for spending and taxing	Y
Approve civil rights bill	N
1989	
Halt production of B-2 stealth bomber at 13 planes	N
Oppose capital gains tax cut	N
Approve federal abortion funding in rape or incest cases	N
Approve pay raise and revision of ethics rules	Y
Pass Democratic minimum wage plan over Bush veto	N

Voting Studies

	Presidential Support		Party Unity		Conservative Coalition	
Year	**S**	**O**	**S**	**O**	**S**	**O**
1990	84	15	86	13	98	2
1989	81	16	75	22	98	2
1988	79	18	80	19	92	3
1987	82	18	84	13	91	7
1986	82	17	81	15	98	2
1985	88	11	80	15	87	7
1984	70	30	94	6	88	12
1983	77	22	92 †	5 †	96	4
1982	82	18	90	8	89	10
1981	67	30	93	5	92	7

† Not eligible for all recorded votes.

Interest Group Ratings

Year	ADA	ACU	AFL-CIO	CCUS
1990	0	88	8	86
1989	0	88	0	90
1988	0	100	0	100
1987	0	95	0	100
1986	0	95	0	94
1985	5	100	0	100
1984	0	100	15	94
1983	5	100	0	85
1982	0	100	0	86
1981	5	100	0	89

8 Jack Fields (R)

Of Humble — Elected 1980

Born: Feb. 3, 1952, Humble, Texas.
Education: Baylor U., B.A. 1974, J.D. 1977.
Occupation: Lawyer; cemetery executive.
Family: Wife, Lynn Hughes; one child, one stepchild.
Religion: Baptist.
Political Career: No previous office.
Capitol Office: 108 Cannon Bldg. 20515; 225-4901.

In Washington: Elected in 1980 at age 28, with no political experience but much conservative zeal, Fields was one of the "Reagan robots" in his early House years. But of late, he has been involved in some substantive legislative issues on the Energy and Commerce Committee, where he speaks up for Texas interests, particularly Houston's oil and gas industry.

In the 101st Congress, Fields was most visible in working the Texas angle during deliberations over the 1990 Clean Air Act. Fields assisted in maneuvering to gain subcommittee approval of a controversial amendment in October 1989, full committee approval the following March, and final conference agreement in October 1990 of a slightly modified version.

Fields joined fellow Texan Ralph M. Hall, a Democrat, to weaken President Bush's proposed mandates for auto companies to build "clean cars" — vehicles that run on alternative fuels. Their amendment increased the percentage of gasoline that could be included in a "clean fuel" mix of gasoline and methanol, and it put reformulated gasoline on the list of "clean alternative fuels." It also stripped a proposed requirement that automakers sell 1 million clean-fuel vehicles a year by 1997.

Fields said the amendment would "level the playing field" for alternative fuels other than methanol, but critics portrayed it as gutting a key portion of the administration's clean-air legislation and saw it as a major victory for the auto and oil industries.

Joining other oil-state members and the business interests they represented, Fields led the criticism of Bush for his June 1990 decision to ban offshore oil drilling for huge areas around the country. "He made a terrible mistake for all the wrong reasons," said Fields. "As a former oilman, President Bush should have known better."

Fields also serves on the Merchant Marine Committee and pushed legislation to provide new veterans benefits to about 2,000 elderly merchant mariners. His measure went through subcommittee and shortly before Congress adjourned late in 1990, Fields attached the bill to must-pass deficit-reduction legislation.

When a number of similarly extraneous measures were removed from the bill as non-deficit-reducing, Fields added to his proposal a $100 application fee to be imposed on mariners seeking benefits. But the Budget Committee said it ultimately would cost the government $3 million over five years, so it was stripped out.

At Home: A fifth-generation Houstonian, Fields won two terms as president of the Baylor student body. After law school, he joined the family cemetery business as a vice president.

A novice at public office when he announced his 1980 candidacy against Democratic Rep. Bob Eckhardt, Fields showed unusual aptitude for a newcomer; he drew the interest of New Right activists, national Republicans and corporate contributors, all eager to defeat Eckhardt, the most liberal member of the Texas delegation and a staunch anti-corporate populist. Potentially strong GOP primary opponents were scared off by Fields' prodigious organizing.

Eckhardt had been losing ground in his changing constituency; in 1978 and 1980, he was challenged in the primary by conservative Democrats who won more than 40 percent. Labor and consumer groups worked hard for him in 1980, but many blue-collar workers abandoned their Democratic voting habits to support Fields and Ronald Reagan. The challenger unseated Eckhardt by under 5,000 votes.

Redistricting strengthened Fields' position for 1982, and he did not draw top-drawer Democratic opposition. But he won less than 60 percent, and Democrats waged a more vigorous campaign two years later. Their 1984 nominee, former congressional aide Don Buford, argued that a Fields mailing to the district announcing town hall meetings had violated rules governing use of the congressional frank.

But early in October, the House ethics committee cleared Fields of any abuse of the frank. Fields cast Buford as a "suitcase politician" — referring to the Democrat's relatively recent arrival in the district. Bolstered by the district's big Reagan vote, he took 65 percent, and has coasted since.

Texas 8

Houston Suburbs; Eastern Harris County

The 8th is part of metropolitan Houston's suburban sprawl, populated by the thousands of middle-income and upper-middle-income families that have moved into the outer reaches of Harris County in recent years.

Growth here has bolstered the fortunes of the GOP. Republicans thrive in affluent communities such as Humble, Fields' home base, and Kingwood, located toward the district's northeastern end. Outside of these communities, however, support for Republican candidates is not always certain. Fields runs stronger in the 8th than most Republicans at any level.

The 8th is not as monolithically white-collar and Republican as the 7th, its neighbor to the west. Although the 8th lost many of its petrochemical plants in the last redistricting, a large number of the plants' blue-collar employees maintain their homes in an area stretching west along the Houston Ship Channel from Baytown to the 610 Loop.

Blue-collar Baytown is the site of a huge Exxon refinery as well as other chemical- and petroleum-related businesses.

The 8th also has a significant population in minority areas on Houston's perimeter; 30 percent of the people in the 8th are either black or Hispanic. Lakewood, in the southwestern part of the district, has a sizable minority population, as do nearby North Forest and Aldine.

Population: 527,531. White 396,727 (75%), Black 88,299 (17%), Other 7,310 (1%). Spanish origin 66,032 (13%). 18 and over 347,798 (66%), 65 and over 24,703 (5%). Median age: 26.

Committees

Energy & Commerce (7th of 16 Republicans)
Health & the Environment; Telecommunications & Finance; Transportation & Hazardous Materials

Merchant Marine & Fisheries (4th of 17 Republicans)
Coast Guard & Navigation (ranking); Merchant Marine

Elections

1990 General		
Jack Fields (R)	60,603	(100%)
1988 General		
Jack Fields (R)	90,503	(100%)

Previous Winning Percentages: **1986** (68%) **1984** (65%) **1982** (57%) **1980** (52%)

District Vote For President

	1988	1984	1980	1976
D	67,332 (47%)	66,720 (40%)	64,072 (41%)	70,107 (59%)
R	74,907 (53%)	98,706 (60%)	89,301 (57%)	47,856 (40%)
I			3,445 (2%)	

Campaign Finance

	Receipts	Receipts from PACs	Expend-itures
1990			
Fields (R)	$385,273	$269,275 (70%)	$420,288
1988			
Fields (R)	$510,950	$271,825 (53%)	$483,544

Key Votes

1991	
Authorize use of force against Iraq	Y
1990	
Support constitutional amendment on flag desecration	Y
Pass family and medical leave bill over Bush veto	N
Reduce SDI funding	N
Allow abortions in overseas military facilities	N
Approve budget summit plan for spending and taxing	N
Approve civil rights bill	N
1989	
Halt production of B-2 stealth bomber at 13 planes	N
Oppose capital gains tax cut	N
Approve federal abortion funding in rape or incest cases	N
Approve pay raise and revision of ethics rules	N
Pass Democratic minimum wage plan over Bush veto	N

Voting Studies

	Presidential Support		Party Unity		Conservative Coalition	
Year	**S**	**O**	**S**	**O**	**S**	**O**
1990	79	19	92	3	100	0
1989	78	20	88	6	95	5
1988	70	23	92	1	84	3
1987	73	25	94	2	95	5
1986	79	20	95	4	98	2
1985	74	21	89	4	91	9
1984	58	37	84	12	80	15
1983	83	17	91	6	92	4
1982	84	14	89	9	92	8
1981	76	18	88	8	96	1

Interest Group Ratings

Year	ADA	ACU	AFL-CIO	CCUS
1990	6	88	8	93
1989	0	96	8	100
1988	0	100	0	100
1987	4	86	13	93
1986	0	95	0	94
1985	10	90	6	91
1984	5	88	23	81
1983	5	96	6	80
1982	5	100	0	86
1981	0	100	7	95

9 Jack Brooks (D)

Of Beaumont — Elected 1952

Born: Dec. 18, 1922, Crowley, La.
Education: Attended Lamar Junior College, 1939-41; U. of Texas, B.J. 1943, J.D. 1949.
Military Service: Marine Corps, 1942-45; Marine Corps Reserve, 1945-72.
Occupation: Lawyer.
Family: Wife, Charlotte Collins; three children.
Religion: Methodist.
Political Career: Texas House, 1947-51.
Capitol Office: 2449 Rayburn Bldg. 20515; 225-6565.

In Washington: The numerous activist liberal Democrats on the Judiciary Committee — many of them from the East or West Coast — seem an unlikely posse for crusty Texan Brooks. He is attuned to business concerns, opposes gun control and is not personally cozy with civil rights and women's organizations.

But Judiciary had foundered in the last few years it was chaired by veteran Peter W. Rodino Jr. of New Jersey, who retired in 1989. With Brooks taking over at the top, Judiciary has perhaps the most partisan Democrat in the House as its leader — a man who considers the G in GOP an expletive. Brooks may not share the world view of some of the aggressive liberals under him, but like them, he relishes beating Republicans.

Brooks is an irascible junkyard dog of a legislator, considered by many the meanest, most foul-mouthed character they have ever encountered. His scrappiness during 14 years as chairman of the Government Operations Committee turned that backwater panel into an aggressive investigatory arm that touched a number of federal agencies.

But events conspired to get Brooks off to a slow start at the Judiciary helm in the 101st Congress. Not only was he learning to work with the committee's liberals, but also he was preoccupied in the early months of 1989 by the plight of his close friend and ally Jim Wright, who was in a losing battle to save his speakership.

Having arrived in the House in 1953 as a slightly awed 30-year-old protégé of the legendary Speaker Sam Rayburn of Texas, Brooks was one of Wright's most important allies. Although in 1976 he had backed Californian Phillip Burton over Wright in the majority leadership race that Wright won by a single vote, the two were like-minded, strong-willed Texans. Born four days apart, they had both suffered Depression-era hardship, served together in the state House and entered Congress two years apart. As Wright's career sank under the weight of ethics controversies, Brooks to the end was the most combative and outspoken among the Speaker's notably few public defenders.

Then, after Wright resigned and the House began settling down to business, Brooks in October 1989 was sidelined with acute pancreatitis. The next year Brooks had to worry about a significant re-election challenge. He put down the GOP hopeful, and by the beginning of 1991 seemed back in fighting form. He opened the 102nd Congress with rapid Judiciary passage of a vertical price fixing bill — a high priority of his — and a civil rights bill he sponsored that quickly drew a presidential veto threat.

Despite the distractions before him in the 101st Congress, Brooks did manage to win over Judiciary liberals who had been skeptical about how he would perform as chairman. A key test for them was his handling of a proposed constitutional amendment to ban flag desecration. Brooks was a lead sponsor of a 1989 statute to ban such behavior, and after the Supreme Court struck down the statute, he supported a constitutional amendment.

But Brooks helped liberals who opposed the amendment by quickly sending it to the House floor over protests from Republicans, who said they needed more time to persuade members to support it. The amendment was rejected. Brooks' defense to GOP complaints that he had pulled a rush job was, "If I delayed, [the Republicans] would be jumping all over me."

The GOP had accused Brooks of stalling a number of bills, including anticrime legislation, of which Brooks is no big fan. "We have got almost as many crime bills passed as they have crimes committed," he griped in 1990.

He eventually relented, however, and helped move through an election-year crime bill. While it included new death penalty language Brooks supported over liberals' objections, the bill also carried tough new habeas corpus standards for convicting capital case defendants and keeping them on death row — language that was staunchly opposed by conservatives.

When the bill got to conference, the Senate balked at the House habeas corpus language,

Texas 9

Southeast — Beaumont; Galveston

The 9th District's industrial climate is symbolized by its three largest cities: Beaumont and Port Arthur, near the Louisiana border in Jefferson County, and Galveston, farther south along the Gulf of Mexico in Galveston County.

The discovery of oil in the Spindletop Oil Field in January 1901 triggered Beaumont's modern industrial development. Within a month of the find, the town's population tripled; now every major petroleum company except Shell Oil Co. has a processing plant in the region.

Republicans enjoy support in Beaumont's western end, home of middle-management refinery employees and some of the district's oldest oil families.

Port Arthur serves as a shipping center for the district's oil and petrochemical products. The city of Galveston, located on Pelican Island, is also a major port of entry. Looking out to sea from Galveston Bay, the horizon is dotted with offshore oil rigs. Local merchants have made a business of servicing area offshore facilities, shipping out food and laundry to the laborers, who often work a 12-day-on, 12-day-off schedule. Texas City, in Galveston County, is a major petrochemical center.

There are other economic mainstays tied to the 9th's coastal setting. Commercial fishing operations harvest shrimp and a number of finfish. The beaches of Galveston County are a big tourist lure.

The district also hosts a community of people who earn their living in high technology. Reaching into southeastern Harris County, the 9th contains part of Clear Lake City, home to an enclave of Republican engineers who work at the Johnson Space Center.

The 9th is one of the most ethnically diverse regions in the state. Nearly 30 percent of its residents are either black or Hispanic, and a significant portion of the blue-collar work force is of German, Czech or Polish descent. Port Arthur hosts a Cajun community, and Kemah, a Galveston County town, has a growing population of Southeast Asians.

One of organized labor's few Texas strongholds, the 9th generally votes Democratic. Jimmy Carter won the district in 1976 and 1980, and after a brief fling with Ronald Reagan in 1984, voters went back to the Democratic side in 1988, giving the Michael S. Dukakis-Lloyd Bentsen ticket 54 percent of the vote.

Population: 526,443. White 390,211 (74%), Black 112,560 (21%), Other 8,694 (2%). Spanish origin 40,073 (8%). 18 and over 370,362 (70%), 65 and over 48,638 (9%). Median age: 29.

and Brooks would not sign off on the Senate's restrictions on the sale of automatic weapons (though he had not tried to block gun control bills in his committee). His recommendation to pass a bill stripped of these controversial provisions was adopted.

His image as an irascible, tough-talking Texan, a man of strong loyalties and fierce independence, is one Brooks has carefully nurtured; once when *The Washington Post* ran a photograph of Brooks with a snarling expression, he proudly showed it all around.

One of the House's most unrelenting inquisitors, Brooks got considerable national exposure during investigations of scandals involving two Republican presidents. He was an early critic of what he perceived as President Richard M. Nixon's abuses of office, and his subcommittee investigated federal spending on Nixon's private homes. When Watergate broke, Brooks was a ready prosecutor during Judiciary's impeachment proceedings. "He didn't even need to hear the evidence," an aide said later. "He was ready to impeach."

Thirteen years later, Wright named Brooks to the Iran-contra investigation committee and, to no one's surprise, the cigar-chomping Brooks was the most vocally partisan critic of the Reagan administration's failures. Talking to reporters, Brooks called both former national security adviser John M. Poindexter and former State Department official Elliott Abrams "a lying son of a bitch." Reflecting Government Operations' interests, Brooks charged that Poindexter broke the law protecting presidential records by shredding a key Reagan document.

Brooks was in the minority in opposing limited immunity for Lt. Col. Oliver L. North, calling it "a rotten precedent" since government officials should be accountable for their acts. He felt his stand was validated in 1990 when a court set aside North's conviction on the grounds that his congressional testimony under grant of immunity could have tainted his criminal trial.

Before the hearings, Brooks had called Poindexter before a Government Operations subcommittee to testify about an administration policy restricting release of sensitive information in its computers. But Poindexter refused to answer questions about even that limited subject; his lawyer said Brooks' panel probably would stray into the Iran-contra affair, and that it was conducting "a public spectacle."

"I want you to understand that your testimony is not a matter of right. It is a matter of indulgence of the subcommittee, and you're kind of crowding it," Brooks told the lawyer. When he tried to respond, Brooks snapped, "I think I've heard enough from you."

That hearing illustrated Brooks' ability to inject Government Operations — traditionally limited to the minutiae of federal spending — at least to the edges of major national debates, and to bedevil GOP administrations.

Republicans are not the only ones who have to be on guard against Brooks; any rival is wise to be wary. In 1987, Brooks got the House's voice-vote approval for an amendment adding $2.8 million for the Texas Accelerator Center to an appropriations bill. The victory went largely unnoticed. Later that day, lawmakers from California and Illinois, states competing with Texas to be the site of the multibillion-dollar superconducting super collider project, figured Brooks might have won some advantage for his state. "Not knowing exactly what Jack has in mind, we worry," said one. After midnight, Brooks took the floor to claim his amendment merely paid for ongoing engineering work. His colleagues were not buying. They voted 97-288 to strip it.

Brooks was frustrated for years in his battle against revenue sharing, the popular program funneling funds to state and local governments. It was finally phased out in 1985 because of budget pressures, though in 1986 Brooks had to help squelch a strong push to revive it. Brooks also opposed the 1985 Gramm-Rudman-Hollings anti-deficit law. Both revenue sharing and Gramm-Rudman violated his basic belief in government accountability — revenue sharing because Brooks feels the government unit that raises money should spend it, and Gramm-Rudman because he believes Congress and the president should not cede their responsibilities to some automatic budget-cutting procedure.

When Brooks first arrived in Washington, the youngest Democrat in the class of 1952, he went straight to Speaker Rayburn. He had worked hard against the Democrats-for-Eisenhower movement that swept Texas in 1952, and his party loyalty impressed the equally partisan Speaker. More than three decades later, when some Texas Democrats suggested the state's GOP House members might join the traditional Wednesday delegation luncheons, Brooks — the delegation chairman — thundered against it. The two parties could meet any time, he said, But the lunches were sacred — Rayburn himself had banned Republicans.

In his early House years, Brooks voted like most other Texas congressmen — in favor of the oil industry and against many of the early civil rights bills. He did refuse to sign the segregationist "Southern Manifesto" in 1956. But when his friend and fellow Texan Lyndon B. Johnson became president, Brooks moved significantly to the left. In 1964, he was one of only 11 Southern Democrats to support that year's Civil Rights Act. He voted for every subsequent civil rights bill, and for all of LBJ's Great Society legislation.

At Home: "I'm just like old man Rayburn," Brooks likes to say. "Just a Democrat, no prefix or suffix." That simple label has kept Brooks in business for almost 40 years, although critics have always portrayed him as too liberal for his Gulf Coast district.

Brooks' illness in 1989 whetted GOP appetites for a retirement that might give them a shot at the 9th. But after Brooks recovered, he moved comfortably past a credible Republican challenger.

Brooks' strong support from the district's sizable union and minority populations has enabled him to withstand several conservative challenges.

The most discomfiting of these came from within Brooks' own party in the 1980 primary. Lightly regarded Wilbur L. "Bubba" Pate, a politically inexperienced bus terminal manager, challenged Brooks from the right and nearly forced him into a runoff.

In addition to faulting Brooks as philosophically out of step with the 9th, Pate said the incumbent had amassed a personal fortune while serving most of his adult life in Congress, and noted that Brooks had earned more than $50,000 in salary and director fees from Texas banks.

Brooks won just over 50 percent in the primary (to 43 percent for Pate), avoiding a runoff only because heavily unionized Galveston gave him a hefty majority. In November, Jimmy Carter nearly lost the 9th to Ronald Reagan, but Brooks was spared trouble because the GOP offered no House candidate.

Pate tried again in the 1982 Democratic primary, and was joined by three other right-of-Brooks Democrats who believed the incumbent's 1980 stumble portended a fall. But 1980 had stirred Brooks' fighting instincts. By assuming a higher profile in the district, Brooks countered sentiment that he had grown distant from local concerns. He reminded voters of the federal plums he had brought to the 9th during his long career, including money for improvement of local port facilities and for research at area universities.

Most important, the conservative mood that swept over Texas' blue-collar workers in 1980 had evaporated by 1982; Brooks was on the offensive, criticizing Reaganomics as dangerous to working-class citizens. Brooks won renomination with 53 percent against the divided conservative field.

Republicans were hopeful about their chances in 1984, predicting that President Ronald Reagan's presence at the top of the ticket could encourage widespread defections to the GOP ticket by conservative Democrats. Reagan did carry the 9th with 52 percent of the vote, but Brooks, stressing his seniority and attacking Reaganomics as a cause of the high unemployment still plaguing parts of the district, turned back Galveston attorney Jim Mahan with 59 percent of the vote.

Brooks had no trouble in the next two elections, but his hospitalization in 1989 piqued GOP interest in the 9th. Republicans nominated Maury Meyers, a popular former four-term mayor of Beaumont. Trying to profit from voters' anti-incumbent mood in 1990, Meyers portrayed Brooks as an entrenched Washingtonian, and he advocated congressional term limits. But Brooks rebounded from his illness and reminded voters again that his seniority brought clout in Congress and federal money to the district. Brooks' traditional electoral allies held firm, and he won his 20th term with 58 percent of the vote.

A child of the Depression, Brooks was born across the state border in Crowley, La., but moved with his family to Beaumont at age 5. He worked his way through the University of Texas, served in the Marine Corps in World War II and won a seat in the state House in 1946. During his four years there, Brooks earned a law degree at the University of Texas.

Promoting himself as a lawyer and small farmer, Brooks ran for Congress in 1952, when Democratic Rep. Jesse M. Combs retired. He won, surviving a 12-way primary and a runoff.

At first, Brooks' district stretched north from his home base of Jefferson County into the rural woodland of eastern Texas. But in the mid-1960s the district was changed significantly. Though Jefferson County remained, the rest of Brooks' district was redrawn to stretch southwestward along the Gulf Coast to Galveston. Subsequent remappings have followed that configuration.

Committees

Judiciary (Chairman)
Economic & Commercial Law (chairman)

Select Narcotics Abuse & Control (2nd of 21 Democrats)

Elections

1990 General		
Jack Brooks (D)	79,786	(58%)
Maury Meyers (R)	58,399	(42%)
1990 Primary		
Jack Brooks (D)	44,781	(72%)
Jack Brookshire (D)	17,268	(28%)
1988 General		
Jack Brooks (D)	137,270	(100%)

Previous Winning Percentages:				**1986**	(62%)	**1984**	(59%)
1982	(68%)	**1980**	(100%)	**1978**	(63%)	**1976**	(100%)
1974	(62%)	**1972**	(66%)	**1970**	(65%)	**1968**	(61%)
1966	(100%)	**1964**	(63%)	**1962**	(69%)	**1960**	(70%)
1958	(100%)	**1956**	(100%)	**1954**	(100%)	**1952**	(79%)

District Vote For President

	1988	1984	1980	1976
D	104,909 (54%)	99,585 (48%)	84,259 (49%)	97,831 (58%)
R	90,891 (46%)	108,937 (52%)	81,669 (47%)	68,490 (41%)
I			4,494 (3%)	

Campaign Finance

	Receipts	Receipts from PACs		Expend-itures
1990				
Brooks (D)	$775,167	$459,444	(59%)	$885,090
Meyers (R)	$462,656	$21,900	(5%)	$447,974
1988				
Brooks (D)	$424,773	$276,562	(65%)	$226,581

Key Votes

1991	
Authorize use of force against Iraq	Y
1990	
Support constitutional amendment on flag desecration	Y
Pass family and medical leave bill over Bush veto	Y
Reduce SDI funding	Y
Allow abortions in overseas military facilities	Y
Approve budget summit plan for spending and taxing	N
Approve civil rights bill	Y
1989	
Halt production of B-2 stealth bomber at 13 planes	Y
Oppose capital gains tax cut	N
Approve federal abortion funding in rape or incest cases	Y
Approve pay raise and revision of ethics rules	?
Pass Democratic minimum wage plan over Bush veto	Y

Voting Studies

	Presidential Support		Party Unity		Conservative Coalition	
Year	**S**	**O**	**S**	**O**	**S**	**O**
1990	18	71	87	5	39	52
1989	16 †	49 †	69 †	3 †	25 †	52 †
1988	24	70	82	5	26	61
1987	20	75	87	5	40	60
1986	21	69	76	7	50	34
1985	24	74	87	5	35	56
1984	30	58	77	14	46	46
1983	32	63	81	14	47	51
1982	44	44	70	16	55	38
1981	42	33	55	23	57	35

† Not eligible for all recorded votes.

Interest Group Ratings

Year	ADA	ACU	AFL-CIO	CCUS
1990	61	17	100	23
1989	65	17	73	40
1988	75	9	100	23
1987	88	0	94	13
1986	70	9	100	33
1985	70	11	94	28
1984	55	11	77	43
1983	75	17	76	32
1982	50	20	74	40
1981	45	21	64	33

10 J.J. Pickle (D)

Of Austin — Elected 1963

Born: Oct. 11, 1913, Roscoe, Texas.
Education: U. of Texas, B.A. 1938.
Military Service: Navy, 1942-45.
Occupation: Public relations and advertising executive.
Family: Wife, Beryl Bolton McCarroll; three children.
Religion: Methodist.
Political Career: No previous office.
Capitol Office: 242 Cannon Bldg. 20515; 225-4865.

In Washington: Pickle is late in his eighth decade and nearing the 30-year mark in his House career, yet he finds himself two rungs removed from the chairmanship of Ways and Means, waiting for two men to retire who are younger than himself. He remains a legend in Austin, enjoying big re-election margins, but retirement can no longer be far from his mind.

Add to the complex personal calculus of that decision one simple financial fact: If he returns for the 103rd Congress, Pickle will lose the chance to convert about $182,000 in campaign funds to personal use. Such conversions, legal for members who were in office before 1980, will be banned if not completed by the end of the 102nd Congress.

But the betting is no better than even that Pickle will retire. And if either Ways and Means Chairman Dan Rostenkowski of Illinois or No. 2 committee Democrat Sam M. Gibbons of Florida should cash in, Pickle probably will not.

Pickle's Texas hill country drawl is an instant reminder of Lyndon B. Johnson, who represented the same congressional district for a decade. And Pickle's legislative career suggests its own echoes of Johnson, for whom he campaigned as a young man and whose name he nearly always pronounces in reverent tones.

More recently, Pickle has been associated with another Texas power, former Speaker Jim Wright. A week before Wright's resignation in the late spring of 1989, Pickle was appearing in debates on national TV to defend the Speaker against ethics charges and to say he should not resign.

Like both Wright and LBJ, Pickle is a man of rural populist roots who has also been able to hobnob with the haves and accommodate the corporate pillars of Texas politics. But he seems more comfortable with his role of small-business protector and specialist in the problems of the Social Security system. Whatever the issue, he is dogged and often successful in getting what he wants.

After more than a quarter-century in the House, Pickle has risen to the No. 3 spot on the Ways and Means Committee, where he has been involved in a variety of major issues, including Social Security, trade and revision of the tax code. During the 101st Congress he defended the chairman's position on pension anti-discrimination rules unpopular with business, and he did what he could to rescue the ill-fated catastrophic-illness extension of Medicare. Given the often rocky relations between Rostenkowski and Gibbons, Pickle has at times functioned as Rostenkowski's senior ally.

But he also displayed his independence from both Rostenkowski and the larger House leadership by joining an effort to cut the tax on capital gains (profits from the appreciation of assets). Pickle held firm against the chairman, committee Democrats and the caucus leadership.

While never viewed as beholden to the chairman, Pickle has shown deference to the chairmanship. In the 99th Congress, despite deep reservations about the tax overhaul, Pickle went along with it. He objected to the big shift of tax burden to business and to the shaving of tax breaks for the oil and gas industry. But in the end he voted for Rostenkowski's bill and was rewarded with a seat on the House-Senate conference committee.

Nevertheless, Pickle set his own course in the capital gains episode of 1989. In the spring, six Democrats organized by Ed Jenkins of Georgia declared themselves for the cut before Rostenkowski had established his opposition to it. When all 13 Ways and Means Republicans joined in, Jenkins could wield a working majority of the committee.

Pickle's presence among the rebels surprised many, not only because of his presumed fealty but because his constituency is among the most liberal in Texas. But Pickle's district, based in the state capital, has come to rely increasingly on high-tech firms attracted by the University of Texas. He has become a leading advocate of the tax credit for businesses with big research and development costs; and extending that credit in 1989 meant finding the dollars to pay for it. A capital gains cut offered at least a short-term shot of revenue as long-

Texas 10

Central — Austin

Though the 10th takes in five counties and most of a sixth, the state capital of Austin and surrounding Travis County dominate its political life. Eighty percent of the district's vote is cast there.

With a large state government work force and a huge academic community affiliated with the University of Texas (48,000 students), Austin traditionally has been one of Texas' most liberal cities.

In 1986, Travis County gave Democrat Mark White 56 percent in his unsuccessful gubernatorial re-election bid. In 1988, support for Michael S. Dukakis in the county helped the Democratic presidential nominee to a 54 percent showing districtwide. More presidential votes were cast in the 10th — nearly 290,000 — than in any other Texas district in 1988, a clear sign of the area's brisk population growth since the last redistricting.

The Austin economy has diversified beyond reliance on state government and the university. Electronics and computer companies have come to the area in recent years, luring upwardly mobile middle-class employees. In 1983, Austin won a bidding war against 56 other cities for the right to host the headquarters of Microelectronics & Computer Technology Corp., a widely publicized research consortium. In 1988, the city won a similar competition to host Semitech, a research and applied technology organization.

The influx of other such firms helped boost Travis County's population by 42 percent in the 1970s, and by 37 percent in the 1980s, both times producing the fastest growth rate among the state's six largest urban counties.

But by the late 1980s, expansion was not the story in Austin. Savings and loan institutions played a major role in fueling the city's growth, and trouble in the state and national S&L industry made money for business development hard to come by. The commercial real-estate market also went soft.

Though the city's economy registered slight gains in the early 1990s, the slowdown in development is welcomed by some in Austin; anti-growth forces had for years condemned random, unplanned growth for causing traffic congestion, water problems and overtaxed city services. They see the slowdown as an opportunity to keep Austin from being "Houstonized."

Beyond the Travis County borders, the 10th extends south and west into largely rural Democratic territory. Blanco County has attracted Republican retirees, but, with a small population, it has a limited electoral impact.

Population: 527,181. White 414,934 (79%), Black 54,566 (10%), Other 5,932 (1%). Spanish origin 97,295 (19%). 18 and over 390,909 (74%), 65 and over 45,569 (9%). Median age: 27.

frozen assets were converted, with the added potential of helping smaller, high-risk enterprises attract capital.

The capital gains cut won committee approval that fall and was passed by the full House. It was the nadir of the 101st Congress for the House Democratic leadership, which had opposed the cut as a giveaway for the rich. The cut was dropped from the annual deficit-reduction package, however, when it failed to win approval in the Senate.

In the 100th Congress, Pickle had some of the same priorities as the committee worked on technical corrections to the tax bill. He had over 270 members sign onto his plan to extend further the research and development tax credit for business and a basic research credit for universities.

"Vigorous research and development is the key to achieving the technological advances that will create and improve on products we can sell here and abroad," he argued. The expiring provisions were all modified to some degree because of revenue concerns, but Pickle took some satisfaction from seeing them extended. Yet another extension was granted in 1990.

As chairman of Ways and Means' Oversight Subcommittee, Pickle exercises a broad mandate. In the 101st Congress, he went after investors who had reaped big profits by moving money to Puerto Rico in the wake of the 1986 tax bill, but who had not lived up to the bill's quid pro quo of local investment in the island's development. The subcommittee's work also led to passage of legislation overhauling the Internal Revenue Service's system of tax penalties. He also looked into the operation of such government-sponsored enterprises as the Federal National Mortgage Association (Fannie Mae) and the organ created to close insolvent thrift institutions (the Resolution Trust Corporation).

But the biggest splash was made by the subcommittee's hearings regarding tax avoidance by the U.S. subsidiaries of huge foreign corporations, most of them Japanese. Pickle held forth before the many cameras gathered for that event, and noted that the companies in question "have been operating in the United States for years and have never sent a check to Uncle Sam for one thin dime."

In the 100th Congress, issues the subcommittee investigated included tax breaks for televangelists and lobbying and election-related activity by tax-exempt public charities. Early in the 101st Congress, Pickle was among those expressing concern about debt-laden corporate takeovers. He warned that companies heavily burdened by debt would have trouble surviving a recession, and could end up dragging down others.

"When the crash comes, everyone is going to turn to Congress and ask, 'Why didn't you do something to protect us against this?' " he said.

Whatever work he does on Oversight, Pickle will have difficulty matching an earlier achievement as head of the Social Security Subcommittee in the 98th Congress.

As chairman of that subcommittee, he was convinced that the way to save the Social Security system was to raise the retirement age. Democratic leaders, including Speaker Thomas P. O'Neill Jr. of Massachusetts and senior citizens' spokesman Claude Pepper of Florida, wanted to solve long-term financing problems with eventual increases in the payroll tax. Few expected Pickle would prevail on the floor, but he did, in what was the most impressive and significant victory of his career.

Through months of argument over what to do about Social Security, Pickle and Pepper were the spokesmen for two diametrically opposite points of view. When the Florida Democrat said he could not support an increase in the retirement age or any other benefit change, Pickle replied, "There are other possibilities we have to consider. I can take just as intractable a position as you."

In March 1983, Ways and Means approved a compromise package of tax increases and modest benefit cuts, with the understanding that Pickle and Pepper would offer their respective alternatives on the floor.

In the end, the House voted 228-202 for Pickle's plan, with support from most Republicans and a majority of Ways and Means.

Pickle's approach later became law, and he gave up his Social Security chairmanship, explaining that his main task had been accomplished.

Pickle's victory represented the culmination of a long personal struggle to put the system on a sound financial footing. In 1981, recognizing the imminent crisis, he offered a massive reform proposal, only to see it shoved aside because of partisan wrangling.

Partly in response to Pickle's proposal, President Ronald Reagan proposed massive benefit cuts in May of that year. That brought a storm of protest from Democrats, and the administration eventually backed down. Pickle was left alone to defend a proposal that both parties had decided was politically too costly.

Reagan then appointed a bipartisan commission to come up with a long-term solution to the problem. The agreement formed the basis of the plan eventually passed by Ways and Means, but it left unsolved an anticipated deficit after the turn of the century. Pickle's retirement-age proposal was designed to address that deficit.

Much of Pickle's earlier House career consisted of balancing his own New Deal instincts and LBJ's national goals against his constituents' increasing ambivalence toward liberal programs. He arrived in the House in December 1963 — less than a month after Johnson's accession — and in his first two years backed both the Civil Rights Act of 1964 and the Voting Rights Act of 1965. "I caught hell in my district," he noted later. He then opposed civil rights legislation in 1966 and 1968, both times on grounds that its open housing provisions were too strong. In the years after the Johnson administration, he, like most Texas Democrats, has gradually moved closer to the voting patterns of Democrats from other Southern states.

At Home: Pickle belongs to a dwindling generation of Texas politicians who were political protégés of LBJ. He solidified his grip on his central Texas district during the Johnson White House years, and it looks safe for him as long as he runs. But if he retires before the next redistricting takes effect (he would turn 79 the month before the 1992 elections), the 10th may well be reshaped.

Pickle was a campaign manager and a congressional aide to Johnson before World War II and an adviser in LBJ's 1948 Senate campaign. But he did not seek office himself until 1963, when he resigned from the Texas Employment Commission to run in a special election. A vacancy had been created when Democratic Rep. Homer Thornberry retired to accept a federal judgeship.

Long before Pickle made his political debut, however, he had become controversial in Texas politics. He had gained the disfavor of liberal Democrats in 1954, when he worked for the re-election of Gov. Allan Shivers against the liberal favorite, Ralph Yarborough.

Liberals supported their own candidate in the 1963 House race. But Pickle's ties to political and business interests, and the pickle-shaped campaign pins and recipe books he handed out, helped Pickle run narrowly ahead of the three-man field in the first round of voting in early November. But he fell short of the majority required and was expected to have problems winning the December runoff election against a conservative Republican opponent.

That changed with the Nov. 22 assassination of President John F. Kennedy. Pickle's House race became the first test of voter support for the district's most famous citizen, President Johnson. In a surge of party harmony, Pickle won easily.

During the height of the Johnson presidency, Pickle had no primary or GOP opposition. In 1968 he had an aggressive Republican challenger, Ray Gabler, who accused him of profiting from land condemnation for a federally aided reservoir project. Pickle denied any breach of ethics but was held to 62 percent.

Pickle had no other serious challenge until 1980, when the Reagan tide in Texas and voter dissatisfaction with a court-ordered busing plan in Austin held him to 59 percent. Pickle had been reluctant to support a constitutional amendment to ban busing, although he did vote for one on the House floor in 1979.

As in earlier races, Pickle ran better in the rural areas than in populous Austin. But he was still able to carry every county, and did not face another Republican opponent until 1986. In that year, the GOP was initially optimistic about the prospects of nominee and former Austin Mayor Carole Rylander. A lifelong Democrat, Rylander switched parties to challenge Pickle. Though Rylander was well-known and campaigned energetically, Pickle rose to the challenge.

Aided by early fundraising, laser-printed direct-mail technology and the first professional campaign manager he had hired in a half-dozen years, Pickle amassed a stunning 72 percent.

That showing deterred a GOP challenge two years later, however, in 1990 Republican nominee David Beilharz waged an aggressive campaign against the incumbent. Beilharz tried to stir up anti-incumbent fervor against Pickle, but Pickle largely ignored his opponent and to good effect; Pickle took almost two-thirds of the vote.

Committees

Ways & Means (3rd of 23 Democrats)
Oversight (chairman); Social Security

Joint Taxation

Elections

1990 General

J.J. Pickle (D)	152,784	(65%)
David Beilharz (R)	73,766	(31%)
Jeff Davis (LIBERT)	8,905	(4%)

1990 Primary

J.J. Pickle (D)	84,020	(89%)
Robin Mills (D)	6,116	(6%)
John Longsworth (D)	4,689	(5%)

1988 General

J.J. Pickle (D)	232,213	(93%)
Vincent J. May (LIBERT)	16,281	(7%)

Previous Winning Percentages: **1986** (72%) **1984** (100%) **1982** (90%) **1980** (59%) **1978** (76%) **1976** (77%) **1974** (80%) **1972** (91%) **1970** (100%) **1968** (62%) **1966** (74%) **1964** (76%) **1963** * (63%)

* *Special election.*

District Vote For President

	1988	1984	1980	1976
D	155,270 (54%)	111,685 (42%)	91,779 (47%)	97,200 (53%)
R	131,918 (46%)	154,300 (58%)	89,926 (46%)	83,817 (46%)
I			10,823 (6%)	

Campaign Finance

	Receipts	Receipts from PACs	Expend-itures
1990			
Pickle (D)	$491,649	$247,900 (50%)	$562,967
Beilharz (R)	$261,543	0	$261,528
1988			
Pickle (D)	$172,746	$46,463 (27%)	$172,921

Key Votes

1991	
Authorize use of force against Iraq	N
1990	
Support constitutional amendment on flag desecration	N
Pass family and medical leave bill over Bush veto	N
Reduce SDI funding	N
Allow abortions in overseas military facilities	Y
Approve budget summit plan for spending and taxing	Y
Approve civil rights bill	Y
1989	
Halt production of B-2 stealth bomber at 13 planes	N
Oppose capital gains tax cut	N
Approve federal abortion funding in rape or incest cases	Y
Approve pay raise and revision of ethics rules	Y
Pass Democratic minimum wage plan over Bush veto	Y

Voting Studies

	Presidential Support		Party Unity		Conservative Coalition	
Year	S	O	S	O	S	O
1990	33	66	81	17	67	33
1989	47	52	82	15	66	32
1988	32	60	80	12	53	42
1987	34	62	82	16	77	23
1986	39	57	63	25	80	18
1985	40	59	82	15	64	29
1984	47	47	70	22	69	27
1983	44	49	68	25	72	21
1982	53	43	57	36	74	19
1981	61	36	58	39	75	24

Interest Group Ratings

Year	ADA	ACU	AFL-CIO	CCUS
1990	61	25	33	50
1989	50	33	67	30
1988	80	16	100	38
1987	60	22	63	43
1986	40	38	43	44
1985	50	38	65	43
1984	65	25	62	40
1983	60	30	56	40
1982	30	43	42	58
1981	40	20	60	58

11 Chet Edwards (D)

Of Waco — Elected 1990

Born: Nov. 24, 1951, Corpus Christi, Texas.
Education: Texas A&M U., B.A. 1974; Harvard U., M.B.A. 1981.
Occupation: Radio station owner.
Family: Single.
Religion: Methodist.
Political Career: Texas Senate, 1983-91; sought Democratic nomination for U.S. House, 1978.
Capitol Office: 425 Cannon Bldg. 20515; 225-6105.

The Path to Washington: In what was arguably the year of the outsider candidate, Edwards won election as a player with a reserved seat at the congressional poker game.

Not that Edwards, an energetic state senator, had an automatic lock on the 11th. The planned retirement of Democratic Rep. Marvin Leath, whose conservative views put him in agreement with the GOP almost as often as with his own party, touched off a fierce contest for the seat.

But Edwards prevailed on the strength of political experience and contacts he claimed would make him better able to serve district voters.

Edwards' political career dates to the mid-1970s. After graduating magna cum laude from Texas A&M in 1974, Edwards spent the next three years as an aide to Rep. Olin E. "Tiger" Teague, a Texas Democrat who served in Congress for more than 30 years.

When Teague decided to retire, he encouraged Edwards to try for his seat. But Edwards narrowly missed making the Democratic primary runoff, closely trailing the eventual winner, Phil Gramm, who later switched to the GOP and was elected to the Senate.

Edwards then took time out from politics to pick up an M.B.A. at Harvard University. Back in Texas, he tried his hand at business and thought he was done with politics.

But he soon made a successful bid for state Senate and became, at age 31, the state's youngest senator. Youth did not cow Edwards in the Senate, where he sponsored dozens of bills, including measures to make Texas part of the Super Tuesday primary, to attract the superconducting super collider project, and to reform workers' compensation laws.

Edwards' energy and ambition did not go unnoticed, and it was no large surprise when he began campaigning for lieutenant governor in 1989. But once Leath announced he was stepping down, Edwards moved his residence into the 11th and set his sights on the House race.

Democrats gave him the nomination without a primary fight, but Republicans went all-out for the district. State Rep. Hugh D. Shine, the GOP nominee, labeled Edwards an out-of-touch carpetbagger. He also attacked Edwards for attending a banquet sponsored by a gay rights group, claiming Edwards pandered for gay support when running for lieutenant governor but wanted to distance them from his campaign in the conservative 11th.

Edwards countered with a radio ad in which a Baptist minister assured voters that Edwards did not support homosexuality.

At times, it was as though Edwards was campaigning against two men: Shine, and Edwards' old rival, Gramm. Gramm had been Edwards' teacher at Texas A&M, but the student and teacher fell out during their fierce 1978 competition for Teague's seat. Gramm poured it on in 1990, campaigning for Shine repeatedly in the district and appearing in one of his campaign commercials.

But Edwards battled back with powerful endorsements and political pledges. The 11th is home to Fort Hood as well as to several large veterans' facilities, and voters took notice of Edwards' chit, secured from House Speaker Thomas S. Foley, for Leath's seat on the Armed Services Committee.

Veterans' Affairs Committee Chairman G. V. "Sonny" Montgomery visited the district and also promised to try to get Edwards on his committee. When committee assignments were handed out for the 102nd Congress, Edwards got seats on both Armed Services and Veterans' Affairs.

Edwards says he had planned to dip his toe into politics before settling into a business career. But he admits his taste of politics, just out of college, proved more or less addictive. Edwards describes Teague as a mentor and almost a father figure, but he is not likely to exhibit the same fiery personality that won Teague his nickname. Though Edwards insists he is equally determined, his style is more soft-spoken.

Texas 11

Central — Waco

Most voters here are like former Rep. Marvin Leath — Democratic in name, but more loyal to a philosophy than a party label. When the Democratic nominee meets local conservative standards, he can carry the 11th. But if the Democrat is tainted with liberalism, the electorate here can cross over about as easily as Leath did on the House floor.

The areas most prone to flirt with Republicanism are the district's urbanized counties — McLennan County (Waco) and Bell County (Killeen and Temple). In 1976, Jimmy Carter carried both counties comfortably, but since then, they have voted Republican for president.

Waco, with slightly more than 103,000 people, is sometimes called the "Baptist Rome." It is the home of the largest Baptist-affiliated university in the world, Baylor University (enrollment 11,700). Waco's economy has ridden through recessionary times fairly well because of university-related employment and the city's diversified manufacturing base — products range from candy bars to military aircraft.

Southwest of Waco, in Bell County, are Temple and Killeen; during the 1970s, the two matured from oversized towns into small cities pushing toward 50,000 in population. Killeen is now approaching 60,000. The federal government's contribution to the Bell County economy is immense because Fort Hood, the second-largest Army base in the country, is located there. The base covers 339 square miles in Bell and Coryell counties and has a combined military and civilian staff of about 70,000 people. There are three Veterans Affairs medical centers within the 11th, more than in any other district.

The Defense Department's proposed downsizing of Fort Hood figures to have a big negative impact on the local economy; businesses may have glimpsed the future as troop deployments to the Persian Gulf in late 1990 and early 1991 brought business activity to a crawl.

Traditional conservative Democrats hold sway in most of the district's 11 rural counties, where 40 percent of the vote is cast. The rural counties backed George Bush in the 1988 presidential contest, but they usually show their Democratic roots in elections closer to home.

At the eastern end of the 11th, the fertile Blackland Prairie soil grows feed grains, cotton, hay and other crops. Livestock-raising — beef cattle, sheep and hogs — is a major income-producer, especially in the hillier western sections of the district.

Population: 527,382. White 417,065 (79%), Black 74,581 (14%), Other 7,001 (1%). Spanish origin 49,181 (9%). 18 and over 381,013 (72%), 65 and over 65,385 (12%). Median age: 28.

Committees

Armed Services (33rd of 33 Democrats)
Military Installations & Facilities; Research & Development; Military Education

Veterans' Affairs (16th of 21 Democrats)
Compensation, Pension & Insurance; Hospitals & Health Care

Campaign Finance

	Receipts	Receipts from PACs		Expend-itures
1990				
Edwards (D)	$672,399	$345,480	(51%)	$668,936
Shine (R)	$878,663	$133,667	(15%)	$842,226

Key Vote

1991

Authorize use of force against Iraq	Y

Elections

1990 General

Chet Edwards (D)	73,810	(53%)
Hugh D. Shine (R)	64,269	(47%)

District Vote For President

	1988	1984	1980	1976
D	75,684 (42%)	59,647 (34%)	71,042 (45%)	83,552 (56%)
R	105,713 (58%)	117,058 (66%)	84,251 (53%)	63,788 (43%)
I			2,872 (2%)	

12 Pete Geren (D)

Of Fort Worth — Elected 1989

Born: Jan. 29, 1952, Fort Worth, Texas.

Education: Attended Georgia Institute of Technology, 1970-73; U. of Texas, B.A. 1974, J.D. 1978.

Occupation: Lawyer.

Family: Wife, Rebecca Ray; one child.

Religion: Baptist.

Political Career: Democratic nominee for U.S. House, 6th District, 1986.

Capitol Office: 1730 Longworth Bldg. 20515; 225-5071.

In Washington: Geren has a tough act to follow in a district long accustomed to having its needs seen to by his powerful predecessor, House Speaker Jim Wright. Perhaps to symbolize his eagerness to hit the ground running, Geren showed up at his swearing-in ceremony carrying two bills ready for the hopper.

A wealthy lawyer holding his first public office, Geren contrasts sharply with Wright, who ended his 34-year congressional career by resigning on May 31, 1989, rather than continue to fight allegations that he had violated House gift and income rules. The soft-spoken Geren has none of Wright's theatrical manner and biting oratory that so grated on Republicans such as Georgia's Newt Gingrich, who filed a formal complaint against Wright with the ethics committee.

And while Geren says he still calls Wright occasionally for advice, he has shown little of the former Speaker's populist streak or partisan edge. During Geren's short tenure, he has voted as often against the Democratic leadership as with it, reflecting his concern about securing a constituency that supported Wright because of his influence, not his ideology.

In his first term, Geren took the conservative side on a variety of issues: He supported amending the Constitution to ban flag desecration, he favored cutting the capital gains tax, he opposed family and medical leave and also the pay raise/ethics reform package. According to the Dallas *Morning News*, Geren's staff submitted a petition asking him to change his position on the flag amendment. He declined.

During his special-election campaign, comments by Geren — such his criticism of Democrats' treatment of former Supreme Court nominee Robert H. Bork — caused party regulars to wonder if he was overly conservative, or just not politically astute. At times he has also seemed indecisive: He said he was personally opposed to abortion and advocated "reasonable restrictions" on abortion in the latter stages of pregnancy, but said he supported the landmark *Roe v. Wade* abortion-rights ruling.

Geren is a member of the Public Works and Transportation Committee, where Wright started his career. On that panel and in general, Geren concentrates on local matters. He has spoken out against a plan by Defense Secretary Dick Cheney to cut the V-22 Osprey aircraft from the defense budget. Production of the Osprey was expected to be an economic boost for Fort Worth's Tarrant County.

At Home: Despite the ethical problems that plagued Wright in Washington in the late 1980s, many voters in the 12th remained fiercely loyal to the man who had represented them in Congress since 1955. Even after he resigned, Wright had considerable influence in determining his successor.

Wright and other Democratic insiders coalesced behind the well-heeled Geren, who had worked for Sen. Lloyd Bentsen and been active in several Democratic campaigns. GOP heavyweights, meanwhile, lined up behind Bob Lanier, a physician and TV personality who had never sought public office.

Lanier ran first in the Aug. 19 special election, but fell well below the 50 percent-plus needed to avoid a runoff. A sizable chunk of Democratic votes went to Jim Lane, another Fort Worth lawyer with backing from more liberal segments of the party, such as labor and abortion-rights groups. But Geren outpolled Lane to advance to a runoff with Lanier.

Because of the district's long history of sending a Democrat to Congress, Geren was initially favored in the runoff. But his conservatism put off some Democrats, and his stiff campaign style reinforced his upper-crust image. Lanier, who was well-known to voters from appearances in a TV medical program, tried to tar Geren with the carpetbagger label; he reminded voters that Geren in 1986 had run unsuccessfully in the neighboring 6th District.

It took campaign appearances by Wright, Bentsen and others in the Texas Democratic delegation to spur Geren down the homestretch. He won the September runoff, but with only 51 percent of the vote. Geren looked more solid a year later. Running for his first full term, he beat his GOP opponent handily.

Texas 12

Fort Worth; Northwest Tarrant County

Less than half the size of neighboring Dallas, Fort Worth projects a blue-collar and Western roughneck image that contrasts with its more sophisticated neighbor. But that image of the city — which comprises nearly 60 percent of the 12th's population — is not entirely accurate. Celebrations such as the Southwestern Exposition Fat Stock Show and Rodeo may recall Fort Worth's heyday as a cattle marketing center, but since World War II the city has been a major manufacturer of military and aerospace equipment, and electronics is increasingly prominent. General Dynamics and Bell Helicopter, just beyond the 12th's eastern boundary, are among the area's leading employers. The cancellation of the A-12 stealth attack plane in early 1991 sent shock waves through the local economy, as General Dynamics was forced to lay off 3,500 workers in Fort Worth.

As many middle- and upper-income Fort Worth residents have fled the city, once-rural territory in surrounding Tarrant County has sprouted shopping malls and suburbs. Old residential neighborhoods on the city's Near South Side are now largely black; the Near North Side hosts a sizable Hispanic community.

Efforts have been made to upgrade urban Fort Worth. Once a haven for outlaws, gamblers, and other shady entrepreneurs, the downtown area now hosts four museums in its "cultural district." Sundance Square is a renovated, two-block area of restaurants, shops, galleries, and redbrick streets. The affluent western and southwestern sections of the city and its suburbs give the 12th a Republican vote of some significance. The northeastern Mid-Cities corridor between Fort Worth and Dallas is a pocket of affluent, GOP-minded voters.

In non-presidential contests, the combined forces of labor, liberals, low-income whites and minorities generally hoist Democrats to victory here.

Population: 527,715. White 400,376 (76%), Black 90,980 (17%), Other 4,695 (1%). Spanish origin 54,851 (10%). 18 and over 374,842 (71%), 65 and over 53,052 (10%). Median age: 29.

Committees

Public Works & Transportation (26th of 36 Democrats)
Aviation; Surface Transportation

Science, Space & Technology (24th of 32 Democrats)
Investigations & Oversight; Space

Veterans' Affairs (20th of 21 Democrats)
Education, Training & Employment

Elections

1990 General		
Pete Geren (D)	98,026	(71%)
Mike McGinn (R)	39,438	(29%)
1989 Special Runoff		
Pete Geren (D)	40,210	(51%)
Bob Lanier (R)	38,590	(49%)
1989 Special		
Bob Lanier (R)	21,978	(39%)
Pete Geren (D)	17,751	(32%)
Jim Lane (D)	12,308	(22%)
Others	3,673	(7%)

District Vote For President

	1988	1984	1980	1976
D	66,906 (47%)	69,159 (41%)	77,202 (48%)	74,846 (53%)
R	75,808 (53%)	97,951 (59%)	79,254 (49%)	63,612 (45%)
I			3,272 (2%)	

Campaign Finance

	Receipts	Receipts from PACs	Expend-itures
1990			
Geren (D)	$497,798	$257,509 (52%)	$495,937
McGinn (R)	$23,255	0	$22,695

Key Votes

1991	
Authorize use of force against Iraq	Y
1990	
Support constitutional amendment on flag desecration	Y
Pass family and medical leave bill over Bush veto	N
Reduce SDI funding	N
Allow abortions in overseas military facilities	Y
Approve budget summit plan for spending and taxing	N
Approve civil rights bill	Y
1989	
Oppose capital gains tax cut	N
Approve federal abortion funding in rape or incest cases	Y
Approve pay raise and revision of ethics rules	N

Voting Studies

	Presidential Support		Party Unity		Conservative Coalition	
Year	S	O	S	O	S	O
1990	44	56	69	30	91	9
1989	51†	49†	74†	24†	94†	6†

† Not eligible for all recorded votes.

Interest Group Ratings

Year	ADA	ACU	AFL-CIO	CCUS
1990	39	46	50	79
1989	-	78	60	83

13 Bill Sarpalius (D)

Of Amarillo — Elected 1988

Born: Jan. 10, 1948, Los Angeles, Calif.

Education: Clarendon Junior College, A.S. 1970; Texas Tech U., B.A. 1972; West Texas State U., M.A. 1978.

Occupation: Agriculture consultant; public school teacher.

Family: Divorced; one child.

Religion: Methodist.

Political Career: Texas Senate, 1981-89.

Capitol Office: 126 Cannon Bldg. 20515; 225-3706.

In Washington: So far in his young House career, Sarpalius has shown himself to be a conservative Democrat almost as likely to vote with President Bush as with his own party.

Both sides of his political personality were evident in the debate during 1990 and 1991 on civil rights legislation. In the 101st Congress, Sarpalius opposed the civil rights bill; but in the 102nd Congress, he switched to support the 1991 version of the measure. He was the only House member who made such a switch.

On some other high-profile controversies, Sarpalius has been more consistently conservative. He opposes abortion and was one of only two House Democrats — the other was fellow Texan Ralph M. Hall — voting in 1990 to expel Massachusetts Rep. Barney Frank from the House for misusing his official position to help a male prostitute — a penalty much harsher than the ethics committee's recommendation of a reprimand.

Sarpalius captured the 13th from the GOP in 1988, and party leaders rewarded him with a seat on the Agriculture Committee. There, during debate on the 1990 farm bill, he joined with liberal Iowa Democrat Dave Nagle in attempting to raise crop price-support levels, and he sought other benefits for the agricultural interests in his district.

Sarpalius made an unsuccessful bid to get a seat on Energy and Commerce for the 102nd Congress. Texas already was well represented on the panel, with four members of the delegation sitting on the committee.

At Home: Betting against Sarpalius' political fortunes has proved a losing proposition. He was a long shot when he first ran for office in 1980 but upset a Republican state senator in a conservative district. Because his election to Congress swung the 13th from Republican to Democratic hands, he was a top GOP target for 1990. But Sarpalius turned a supposedly close race into a strong win.

Even one term in Congress would have seemed a long shot for Sarpalius during his childhood. Sarpalius, who had polio as a child, was abandoned by his father at age 10. Two years later, his mother, an alcoholic, put Sarpalius and his two younger brothers in Cal Farley's Boys Ranch, a home for wayward boys outside Amarillo. In his last year of high school there, Sarpalius became Texas president of the Future Farmers of America.

Sarpalius went on to college, taught agriculture technology at Boys Ranch and earned a master's degree in agriculture. He joined a private agribusiness concern and then won state Senate elections in 1980 and 1984.

Though Sarpalius was not considered a legislative heavyweight in Austin, he was popular at home and was a logical contender for Congress in 1988 when Republican Rep. Beau Boulter left the 13th to run unsuccessfully for the Senate.

But shortly after announcing his candidacy, Sarpalius saw his image tarnished by a late-night incident at an Amarillo club in January 1988. The recently divorced Sarpalius had gone to celebrate his birthday at the club, but he wound up with his jaw broken as a result of a fight that he said was a setup. A blood-alcohol test Sarpalius requested revealed that he had not been drinking; subsequent investigations indicated that his assailant was paid by the bar owner to attack him.

But Sarpalius' sophisticated campaign and his wide name recognition enabled him to win a majority in a three-way primary and go on to defeat Republican nominee Larry Milner. Milner, a former chamber of commerce director and utility lobbyist, was financially competitive but lacked a rural following and could not match Sarpalius' connections across the district, much of which he had represented in the state Senate.

In 1990, the GOP recruited Dick Waterfield, a state representative with strong ties to the district's farming and ranching communities. But Waterfield's challenge began to founder when GOP Gov. William P. Clements Jr. claimed Sarpalius had told him he only lived at the Boys Ranch because his parents worked there. Ranch staff dismissed Clements' version, and the incident helped resurrect sympathy for Sarpalius' past hardships. He won 56 percent.

Texas 13

The Panhandle — Amarillo; Wichita Falls

The 13th is one of the more competitive two-party districts in Texas. Republicans generally rule in the Panhandle, and Democrats typically hold sway in the Red River Valley to the south. But the voters are uniformly conservative. Of the 37 counties in the 13th, 34 voted for Ronald Reagan in 1984, and 31 went for George Bush in 1988.

Because of its scant rainfall, most of this region traditionally was used only for cattle grazing. But discovery of underground water supplies in the 1940s sparked cultivation of wheat, cotton and sorghum grains on huge, highly mechanized farms. The agricultural revolution has been extensive enough to concern public officials about the condition of the Ogallala aquifer, which is slowly receding. Investigation has begun into alternative hydro-generation projects.

In the farm-boom years of the 1970s, some of the wheat farmers and cattle ranchers in the 13th went heavily into debt to finance expansion — a strategy that clobbered them when interest rates rose and prices dropped.

Amarillo (Potter and Randall counties) is a city of nearly 158,000 that serves as the focal point of the Panhandle's farmlands. Its factories pack meat, mill flour and handle oil and natural gas drilled locally. Like the rural areas surrounding it, Amarillo is Republican. Potter County gave GOP Senate candidate — and 13th District incumbent — Beau Boulter a slight advantage in his 1988 Senate challenge to Lloyd Bentsen. It also gave George Bush 62 percent in the presidential contest. Randall County is more solidly Republican territory. Boulter got 61 percent in Randall, and Bush cleared 75 percent. In 1990, Potter gave unsuccessful GOP gubernatorial nominee Clayton Williams 52 percent; Randall gave Williams 62 percent.

More than 200 miles to the southeast is Wichita Falls (Wichita County), a predominantly Democratic area. In 1990, Wichita voted Democratic in the contest for the House and governor, but gave GOP Sen. Phil Gramm 60 percent in his re-election.

Wichita Falls has a large industrial sector that makes fiberglass products, wearing apparel and mechanical parts. North of the city is Sheppard Air Force Base, one of the Air Force's largest training facilities and headquarters to the NATO Jet Training Center.

Population: 526,840. White 470,444 (89%), Black 27,091 (5%), Other 5,948 (1%). Spanish origin 46,875 (9%). 18 and over 376,878 (72%), 65 and over 66,383 (13%). Median age: 30.

Committees

Agriculture (22nd of 27 Democrats)
Conservation, Credit & Rural Development; Department Operations, Research & Foreign Agriculture; Livestock, Dairy & Poultry; Wheat, Soybeans & Feed Grains

Select Children, Youth & Families (16th of 22 Democrats)

Small Business (19th of 27 Democrats)
Antitrust, Impact of Deregulation & Ecology

Elections

1990 General		
Bill Sarpalius (D)	81,815	(56%)
Dick Waterfield (R)	63,045	(44%)
1988 General		
Bill Sarpalius (D)	98,345	(52%)
Larry S. Milner (R)	89,107	(48%)

District Vote For President

	1988		1984		1980		1976	
D	68,739	(36%)	50,436	(25%)	68,648	(36%)	90,518	(50%)
R	121,121	(64%)	152,448	(75%)	117,716	(62%)	90,173	(50%)
I					3,076	(2%)		

Campaign Finance

	Receipts	Receipts from PACs		Expend-itures
1990				
Sarpalius (D)	$685,539	$387,684	(57%)	$667,930
Waterfield (R)	$684,141	$68,725	(10%)	$679,117
1988				
Sarpalius (D)	$387,092	$233,950	(60%)	$384,738
Milner (R)	$483,932	$143,422	(30%)	$476,220

Key Votes

1991	
Authorize use of force against Iraq	Y
1990	
Support constitutional amendment on flag desecration	Y
Pass family and medical leave bill over Bush veto	N
Reduce SDI funding	N
Allow abortions in overseas military facilities	N
Approve budget summit plan for spending and taxing	N
Approve civil rights bill	N
1989	
Halt production of B-2 stealth bomber at 13 planes	N
Oppose capital gains tax cut	Y
Approve federal abortion funding in rape or incest cases	N
Approve pay raise and revision of ethics rules	N
Pass Democratic minimum wage plan over Bush veto	N

Voting Studies

	Presidential Support		Party Unity		Conservative Coalition	
Year	S	O	S	O	S	O
1990	48	48	58	38	94	4
1989	60	38	60	38	85	12

Interest Group Ratings

Year	ADA	ACU	AFL-CIO	CCUS
1990	28	74	45	92
1989	40	64	42	80

14 Greg Laughlin (D)

Of West Columbia — Elected 1988

Born: Jan. 21, 1942, Bay City, Texas.

Education: Texas A&M U., B.A. 1964; U. of Texas, LL.B. 1967.

Military Service: Army, 1967-70; Army Reserve, 1964-67; Army Reserve, 1970-present.

Occupation: Lawyer.

Family: Wife, Ginger Jones; two children.

Religion: Methodist.

Political Career: Democratic nominee for U.S. House, 1986.

Capitol Office: 218 Cannon Bldg. 20515; 225-2831.

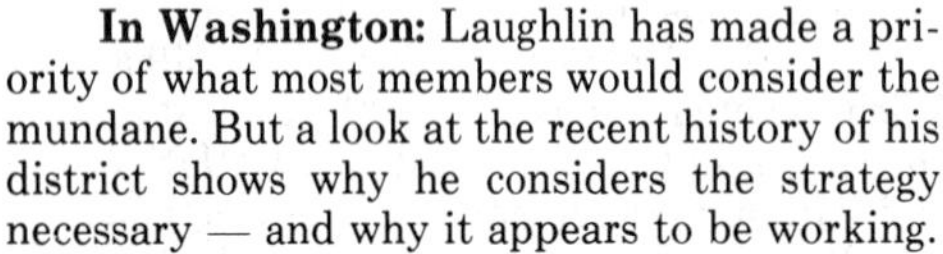

In Washington: Laughlin has made a priority of what most members would consider the mundane. But a look at the recent history of his district shows why he considers the strategy necessary — and why it appears to be working.

Touting his constituent service, Laughlin boasts of handling new cases as well as hundreds left over by his predecessor. He also proudly points out that, consistent with his fiscal conservatism, his office is listed in the bottom quarter of congressional office expenditures among the Texas delegation. Such achievements may not seem lofty, but they are critical for Laughlin, who in 1988 ousted a GOP incumbent dogged by reports of office mismanagement and constituent neglect. Laughlin combines his scrupulous attention to the 14th with a typical Tory conservatism that fits the district's majority.

Laughlin's military background has helped foster an interest in veterans issues and, combined with his assignment on the Public Works Committee, has enabled him to secure funding for district projects. During his first term, he helped deliver funding for a veterans' clinic in Victoria.

Serving on the Merchant Marine Committee, Laughlin has started taking an interest in issues such as wetlands classification. In 1990 the Congressional Sunbelt Caucus named Laughlin co-chairman of its Gulf of Mexico Task Force. Despite his stated concerns for environmental protection, during the 1990 campaign Laughlin faced the wrath of environmentalists who labeled him a member of the "blackened beach bunch" for failing to support oil spill legislation.

While Laughlin has voted a conservative line, he did face criticism back home for his votes to fund the National Endowment for the Arts (NEA). Laughlin defended his record, noting that he voted to cut $45,000 from the NEA budget — the amount it gave to the most controversial exhibits. But Laughlin said he was upset that the NEA went on to fund other projects he considered improper and said he would oppose future funding for the agency.

At Home: Laughlin was a lawyer who had never run for political office when he made his first try for the 14th in 1986. He challenged Mac Sweeney, a young former White House aide who had beaten a Democratic incumbent two years earlier. Outspent and little-known, Laughlin nevertheless drew 48 percent of the vote.

Laughlin was back in 1988, first turning aside a Democratic rival in the March primary, then raising more than $600,000 — enough to put him on competitive footing financially.

Just as important, Laughlin went beyond his prior attacks on Sweeney's office problems. Laughlin presented himself as a conservative Democrat in the old school, a man who had prosecuted criminals and who still served as a lieutenant colonel in the Army Reserve.

Sweeney distributed campaign literature portraying Laughlin, who had handled personal injury cases, as an ambulance chaser. But the ad, which included a heavy-handed appeal to Hispanics, drew charges of racism and complaints from lawyers' groups.

Sweeney also suffered from having the second-worst voting attendance record among Texas' 27 House members in 1988, and from reports of inattentiveness to constituents. Laughlin captured the seat with 53 percent of the vote.

In 1990, Laughlin was challenged by Joe Dial, a cattleman and first-time candidate. Dial played his rancher's hat against Laughlin's trial lawyer background and kept Laughlin on the defensive over votes to fund the NEA, characterizing them as support for obscene art.

But the incumbent could point to plenty of conservative votes to offset the liberal label. And with the onset of problems in the Persian Gulf, Laughlin benefited from his military background. He improved on his 1988 showing.

Laughlin grew up in a small town in Brazoria County, between Houston and the Gulf of Mexico. He went away to college and law school, then served as an intelligence officer in the Army. He worked in Houston, first as an assistant district attorney then in private practice, before moving back into the 14th.

Texas 14

Southeast; Gulf Coast

The 14th sprawls from suburban Austin to the Gulf Coast, but its core is small-town East Texas, where social life revolves around a few local cafés, and the barbershop is still a vital conduit for community news.

Victoria, with 55,000 people, is the district's only sizable city. Once dominated by its cattle and cotton trade, Victoria today has an economy driven by petrochemicals, oil-field equipment and steel products.

The areas within the 14th that rely on oil production, primarily in the north, are stagnating because of the decline in the oil industry. However, the refining sector of the industry is booming, with an influx of petrochemical concerns to the coastal counties. The prevailing political climate is conservative, but not necessarily Republican. On the state level, there is considerable support for Democrats. But in races for federal office, the district's conservatism places it more often in the Republican column. In 1990, Laughlin lost Victoria County by over 1,600 votes. In the presidential race, the county gave George Bush 62 percent of its vote.

North of Victoria, Jackson and Wharton counties anchor a major southeast Texas rice belt.

At the district's northern end, the demise of the oil industry has created a new emphasis on agriculture, with grain sorghums among the leading crops. Cattle ranching also plays an important role in the area's economy. Along the coast, in the southern end of the district, aquaculture — farming fish in ponds for commercial use — is a growing industry.

Minorities make up about one-third of the 14th's population. Most of the Hispanics are grouped in the district's southwestern counties; blacks are concentrated in the northeastern part of the district. The district also has more people of German ancestry than any other in the state.

Population: 526,920. White 421,921 (80%), Black 60,531 (12%), Other 3,131 (1%). Spanish origin 105,659 (20%). 18 and over 368,619 (70%), 65 and over 70,506 (13%). Median age: 30.

Committees

Merchant Marine & Fisheries (21st of 29 Democrats)
Coast Guard & Navigation; Fisheries & Wildlife Conservation & the Environment

Public Works & Transportation (25th of 36 Democrats)
Aviation; Investigations & Oversight; Surface Transportation

Elections

1990 General		
Greg Laughlin (D)	89,251	(54%)
Joe Dial (R)	75,098	(46%)
1988 General		
Greg Laughlin (D)	111,395	(53%)
Mac Sweeney (R)	96,042	(46%)

District Vote For President

	1988	1984	1980	1976
D	89,840 (43%)	66,718 (32%)	67,989 (41%)	71,983 (53%)
R	121,148 (57%)	138,615 (67%)	95,107 (57%)	64,145 (47%)
I			2,928 (2%)	

Campaign Finance

	Receipts	Receipts from PACs		Expend-itures
1990				
Laughlin (D)	$829,150	$433,314	(52%)	$851,294
Dial (R)	$479,218	$41,621	(9%)	$450,095
1988				
Laughlin (D)	$623,491	$240,699	(39%)	$600,114
Sweeney (R)	$637,167	$240,154	(38%)	$645,988

Key Votes

1991	
Authorize use of force against Iraq	Y
1990	
Support constitutional amendment on flag desecration	Y
Pass family and medical leave bill over Bush veto	N
Reduce SDI funding	Y
Allow abortions in overseas military facilities	N
Approve budget summit plan for spending and taxing	N
Approve civil rights bill	Y
1989	
Halt production of B-2 stealth bomber at 13 planes	N
Oppose capital gains tax cut	N
Approve federal abortion funding in rape or incest cases	N
Approve pay raise and revision of ethics rules	N
Pass Democratic minimum wage plan over Bush veto	?

Voting Studies

	Presidential Support		Party Unity		Conservative Coalition	
Year	S	O	S	O	S	O
1990	47	48	58	33	85	7
1989	63	30	59	36	95	5

Interest Group Ratings

Year	ADA	ACU	AFL-CIO	CCUS
1990	28	59	36	83
1989	20	56	44	67

15 E. "Kika" de la Garza (D)

Of Mission — Elected 1964

Born: Sept. 22, 1927, Mercedes, Texas.
Education: St. Mary's U. (San Antonio), LL.B. 1952.
Military Service: Navy, 1945-46; Army, 1950-52.
Occupation: Lawyer.
Family: Wife, Lucille Alamia; three children.
Religion: Roman Catholic.
Political Career: Texas House, 1953-65.
Capitol Office: 1401 Longworth Bldg. 20515; 225-2531.

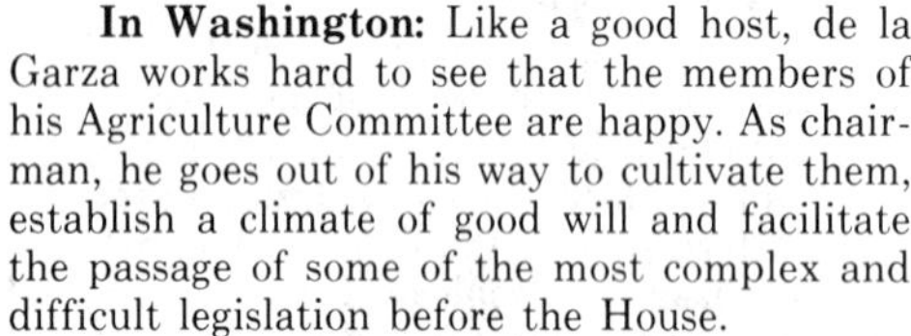

In Washington: Like a good host, de la Garza works hard to see that the members of his Agriculture Committee are happy. As chairman, he goes out of his way to cultivate them, establish a climate of good will and facilitate the passage of some of the most complex and difficult legislation before the House.

De la Garza frequently travels to the districts of junior colleagues to help with their campaigns, and steers political action funds their way. When the time comes to pick members of a conference committee on a bill, he tries to include at least one freshman. His press releases routinely credit the accomplishments of other members of the panel, including Republicans, many of whom play a major role on what is one of the least partisan committees in the institution.

After spending most of the 1980s perfecting his role as chairman, de la Garza has a good sense of how to pass cumbersome legislation. When Congress began work on the 1985 and 1990 farm reauthorizations, he made it clear he was opposed to the Republican administrations' calls for drastic cuts in agricultural spending. But he sees himself as the coordinator of the massive farm bill, rather than the craftsman of its individual parts. Stressing his role as facilitator, he gives his Agriculture subcommittees considerable freedom to draw up the various sections of the legislation.

In the deficit-conscious climate that has prevailed since the 1980s, de la Garza must worry about attacks on farm spending from urban and suburban members. De la Garza, a master political strategist, is acutely aware of the tenuous support for farm programs and is keenly sensitive to charges that they are wasteful giveaways. In overseeing the drafting of the 1990 farm bill, he succeeded in striking a balance between populists who sought to increase farm benefits, and others seeking to cut subsidies.

During House action on the 1990 farm bill, a bipartisan urban-suburban coalition led an especially concerted effort to bar subsidies to farmers who earn more than $100,000. The assault was led by Texas Republican Dick Armey and New York Democrat Charles E. Schumer.

The means-test concept had appeal in a year marked by tortuous budget negotiations, but de la Garza and the farm bloc were able to defeat the Armey-Schumer amendment, helped in part by the perception that Armey and Schumer were "anti-farmer" and that their plan, backed by the Bush administration, aimed merely to cut the budget rather than help smaller farmers. "This amendment is a meat-ax approach," de la Garza said. "Can members imagine a shoeshine boy from Mission, Texas, being accused of protecting the rich and the greedy? Ridiculous." The amendment was rejected 159-263, but the means-testing concept resurfaced in President Bush's fiscal 1992 budget.

De la Garza, who represents sugar cane growers in his South Texas district, and Louisiana Democrat Jerry Huckaby, chairman of the sugar subcommittee, worked hard to round up Democratic votes to defeat an amendment sponsored by New York Democrat Thomas J. Downey and Ohio Republican Bill Gradison. The amendment would have made a 2-cents-per-pound cut in the 18-cents-per-pound sugar price support. De la Garza forged a coalition of pro-labor, pro-environmental and pro-farm Democrats to repel the cut.

His summation was uniquely de la Garza: "So the bottom line is, it is jobs in the United States of America, farmers in the United States of America. Vote 'no' on the Downey amendment. It is jobs U.S.A., jobs U.S.A., jobs U.S.A.! [You] cannot cut it anymore. You cannot hide it anymore. It is jobs, jobs, jobs in the U.S.A.! Vote 'no' on the amendment." It was rejected 150-271.

Unlike his Senate counterpart, Vermont Democrat Patrick J. Leahy, de la Garza has little interest in enacting restrictions on farmers' use of chemicals and promoting organic farming — a position shared by most Agricul-

Texas 15

South — McAllen

The 15th is the most heavily Hispanic district in Texas (more than 70 percent of the population), and one of the most faithfully Democratic non-inner city constituencies in the South. In 1988 presidential voting, the 15th was Michael S. Dukakis' best district in Texas outside the all-urban 18th (Houston) and 20th (San Antonio). The Democratic nominee won 63 percent in the 15th.

The economic boom that transformed much of the Southwest in the 1970s and early '80s touched the Rio Grande Valley, significantly boosting the population in the district's three southernmost counties. But the growth has not brought economic stability.

The 15th District's economy was buffeted by a series of shocks in the early 1980s from which it is only now beginning to rebound. The border economy, quite dependent on retail sales, was crippled by the devaluation of the Mexican peso in the early 1980s; Mexicans who flocked across the border to shop in McAllen and other towns in the 15th could no longer afford the goods offered there, and numerous businesses closed.

Even the agriculture industry, the valley's traditional economic base, has suffered in recent years. Traditionally immune to freezes, the area usually enjoys a year-round growing season that produces an abundance of grapefruit and other citrus, vegetables, cotton and grain. But many Valley growers have moved to Mexico in recent years, hoping to escape labor problems, cumbersome regulations, and the damaging freezes that hit in the mid to late 1980s.

Lately, though, the economic outlook has been brightening. Retail sales have rebounded, as have McAllen businesses which tailored their marketing campaigns to appeal as much to American consumers as to Mexican ones.

There has been a resurgence of jobs on both sides of the border with the blossoming of "maquiladoras," or twin plants. Under this system, Mexican assembly plants receive parts and assemble them into finished products using low-cost labor. The products then are transferred to facilities just across the border in the United States that handle distribution.

Tourism remains a reliable revenue producer, with visitors drawn by the sun and the chance to shop and sightsee in Mexico.

North of the valley, beef cattle and other livestock roam the ranches, and feed grains grow well there. When oil and gas prices are strong, their extraction augments the local agrarian economy.

Hidalgo County, home to some 384,000 people, is the district's largest population center. Located on the Texas-Mexico border, it is anchored by McAllen, a major port of entry into Mexico and an important foreign trade center. The county grew by over 35 percent in the 1980s.

Outside of Hidalgo, the most populous county is San Patricio, with just under 59,000 people. San Patricio is closely linked economically to the port city of Corpus Christi, which lies just across the bay in the 27th District.

Republicans have made inroads in San Patricio, and in the rural counties located at the district's northern end. But farther south, Hidalgo County is solidly Democratic, as are such heavily Hispanic rural counties as Duval, Brooks and Jim Hogg.

Population: 527,203. White 450,853 (86%), Black 2,486 (1%). Spanish origin 378,195 (72%). 18 and over 329,023 (62%), 65 and over 52,916 (10%). Median age: 25.

ture Committee members. "Somehow it has gotten out of hand, [the idea] that organic is good for you," he said. "All this organics is going to be very, very expensive." Although he accepted a House amendment that would have greatly restricted the export of chemicals considered too dangerous for use in the United States (and which can return to this country on imported food), he opposed it in the House-Senate conference. The restrictions on the so-called "circle of poison" was Leahy's pet program, and he battled doggedly with de la Garza to keep it on the bill. In the end, Leahy withdrew it, resolving to reintroduce it in the 102nd Congress.

Early in the 102nd Congress, de la Garza proposed a bill, cosponsored by a majority of the committee, for a uniform pesticide standard nationwide.

As was the case in 1985, de la Garza's efforts in 1990 did not produce a farm bill that clearly bore his imprint, but they did produce a bill that passed the House, and by a lopsided vote, in contrast to the two-vote margin by which the farm bill had cleared Congress in 1981.

De la Garza's approach has enabled him to keep the unwieldy farm bill together. In 1985, it also helped him maintain an effective working arrangement with his predecessor as chairman, Thomas S. Foley of Washington, despite tensions that had existed between the two in previous Congresses. When he first took the chairmanship, de la Garza had been reluctant to consult Foley on much of the committee's business. But in the 99th Congress he deferred willingly to Foley on wheat and feed grains, a major portion of the bill.

That is not to say that everything goes smoothly in committee. During work on a bill to save the financially ailing Farm Credit System in 1987, there was an unusual amount of partisan bickering. Unable to work out a compromise with leading members of the committee, de la Garza, under pressure from the House leadership and system banks to move a bill, introduced his own legislation weighted toward Texas banks. The bill prompted ranking Republican Edward Madigan of Illinois, widely known as a cooperative legislator, to resort to obstructionist tactics.

But from that point, a measure began to take shape as de la Garza pursued his normal democratic approach to legislating. He tends to control his committee by not controlling it too much; to put the wrangling to rest on the farm credit bill, de la Garza set up committee task forces to hammer out compromises on the most contentious issues. Under de la Garza's watch, the panel produced a sweeping reorganization of the Farm Credit System, which passed 41-2.

"No one is entirely happy," he said. "But then no one's saying it's a no-good communist bill. It's somewhere in the middle, which is what good legislation should be."

De la Garza's cooperative style is a benefit within his committee, but he is forced into a more confrontational role when waging turf fights with other panels. During work on a supplemental appropriations bill in 1987, Appropriations Chairman Jamie L. Whitten of Mississippi included $10 million for Agriculture Department studies on mandatory production controls. De la Garza complained that the policy was unrealistic and the maneuver an encroachment on his jurisdiction.

"How many days of hearings did you have?" he demanded. Whitten shot back, "I've been doing this for 39 years!" After some discussion, de la Garza agreed not to move against the studies, and an effort by a third party to do so failed by a wide margin.

De la Garza is a man capable of considerable personal charm, an amateur linguist and gourmet cook who converses with foreign dignitaries in their own languages. But he is a proud man, a descendant of Spanish land-grantees who came to South Texas in the 18th century, and he has sometimes displayed an arrogance that made personal relations difficult.

In his earlier years on the Agriculture Committee, de la Garza was known to ridicule the idiosyncrasies of colleagues in a manner that was meant to be funny but was often taken as an insult. Outside the committee, his voting record sometimes frustrated liberal Democrats who found him reluctant to identify with liberal Hispanics of less impressive background. Both these tendencies were factors in his unexpectedly narrow 110-92 election to the Agriculture chairmanship in 1981.

"The thing about all this Chicano and Mexican-American and so forth," he once told a reporter, "is that the Spanish-speaking are members of the white race. Period. Finis."

On Agriculture, he has always paid close attention to the crops of South Texas — sugar and cotton — and to the area's water problems. During his first decade in the House, he worked hardest to obtain a federal sugar allotment for his growers and a project to control the level of salt in the Rio Grande on the Mexican border. Salt in the river's water was making it difficult to irrigate the district's farms.

As he moved toward a senior position on Agriculture, de la Garza continued to be a spokesman for sugar growers. In 1977, when major farm legislation became law, he successfully amended it to set up a sugar price support program similar to the ones for other crops. The next year, arguing that the newly enacted price supports had not been sufficient to keep the industry prosperous, he sponsored a bill to return to a system of strict quotas and fees that would limit the amount of foreign sugar entering the United States. A plan similar to this was later implemented.

De la Garza supports his South Texas growers in their demand for an ample supply of farm workers to help harvest perishable crops. When the House debated immigration policy in 1984, he argued for an Agriculture Committee amendment that established a new "guest worker" program for foreign labor. Agribusiness interests from all over the country backed that effort; Hispanics opposed it. De la Garza was the only member of the Congressional Hispanic Caucus who voted for the amendment, which passed the House. But de la Garza disagreed with other parts of the immigration package and voted against it in 1984 and in 1986. It finally became law in the 99th Congress.

Outside his committee, de la Garza votes a moderate Democratic line, supporting labor-backed initiatives such as requiring employers to give workers unpaid family leave and increasing the minimum wage. But he also opposes abortion and backed a constitutional amendment to ban desecration of the flag. In 1990, he voted for a constitutional amendment to require a balanced federal budget.

In early 1991, de la Garza — whose son, a Navy doctor, was working in the Persian Gulf — voted to continue economic sanctions and diplomatic efforts to pressure Iraq to withdraw from Kuwait. But when that resolution was rejected, he voted to authorize Bush to use military force against Iraq.

At Home: The election of de la Garza in 1964 was a milestone of sorts for South Texas Hispanics, who had always been the dominant population group in the 15th District but had never elected one of their own.

It was not, however, a political revolution. The new congressman was backed by the same "Anglo" business interests that had sent Democrats Lloyd Bentsen and Joe Kilgore to Congress in the 1950s. In six terms in the Texas Legislature, de la Garza had maintained a conservative voting record and had opposed passage of a state civil rights bill.

With Kilgore's retirement in 1964, the Democratic primary ended in a runoff between de la Garza and state Rep. Lindsey Rodriguez, an ardent supporter of the Johnson administration and the liberal 1964 Democratic platform. De la Garza featured a photograph of Johnson in his campaign literature, but hedged in his commitment to the platform or the Democratic administration.

Rodriguez had the support of PASO (Political Association of Spanish-speaking Organizations), which had succeeded in electing Hispanic slates in several Texas localities. He accused de la Garza, as a descendant of Spanish land-grantees, of being aloof from the problems that faced the large mass of poor Hispanics in the district. De la Garza, he complained, was no more than a puppet for the wealthy "Anglo" business establishment.

While de la Garza's business supporters were controversial, they did provide him a campaign budget that dwarfed Rodriguez's, and gave him the courthouse machine backing that traditionally has won elections here. De la Garza coasted to victory by a margin of nearly 2-to-1. That fall he won the seat over nominal GOP opposition by an even wider margin.

Since the 15th is one of Texas' Democratic strongholds, de la Garza has had no trouble in general elections. In his 13 re-elections since 1964, the GOP has offered opposition only four times, and in each instance de la Garza drew at least 65 percent of the vote. Only two times has he had primary opposition, and on both occasions he won handily.

Committee

Agriculture (Chairman)

Elections

1990 General		
E. "Kika" de la Garza (D)	72,461	(100%)
1988 General		
E. "Kika" de la Garza (D)	93,672	(94%)
Gloria Joyce Hendrix (LIBERT)	6,133	(6%)

Previous Winning Percentages: **1986** (100%) **1984** (100%) **1982** (96%) **1980** (70%) **1978** (66%) **1976** (74%) **1974** (100%) **1972** (100%) **1970** (76%) **1968** (100%) **1966** (100%) **1964** (69%)

District Vote For President

	1988		1984		1980		1976	
D	109,732	(63%)	89,836	(54%)	79,071	(56%)	84,143	(67%)
R	64,204	(37%)	77,440	(46%)	58,582	(42%)	40,776	(33%)

Campaign Finance

	Receipts	Receipts from PACs		Expend-itures
1990				
de la Garza (D)	$86,524	$58,675	(68%)	$121,145
1988				
de la Garza (D)	$263,843	$127,452	(48%)	$219,469

Key Votes

1991	
Authorize use of force against Iraq	Y
1990	
Support constitutional amendment on flag desecration	Y
Pass family and medical leave bill over Bush veto	Y
Reduce SDI funding	Y
Allow abortions in overseas military facilities	N
Approve budget summit plan for spending and taxing	Y
Approve civil rights bill	Y
1989	
Halt production of B-2 stealth bomber at 13 planes	N
Oppose capital gains tax cut	Y
Approve federal abortion funding in rape or incest cases	N
Approve pay raise and revision of ethics rules	Y
Pass Democratic minimum wage plan over Bush veto	Y

Voting Studies

	Presidential Support		Party Unity		Conservative Coalition	
Year	**S**	**O**	**S**	**O**	**S**	**O**
1990	24	73	84	10	56	43
1989	43	50	74	15	49	44
1988	21	57	73	6	32	37
1987	33	59	76	14	65	21
1986	27	64	72	16	64	32
1985	34	59	75	14	60	36
1984	44	46	66	21	59	25
1983	41	50	70	17	61	27
1982	49	32	67	25	67	19
1981	57	39	62	31	68	27

Interest Group Ratings

Year	ADA	ACU	AFL-CIO	CCUS
1990	61	23	83	15
1989	50	21	73	56
1988	50	20	73	50
1987	60	5	73	27
1986	55	27	85	39
1985	60	24	76	20
1984	40	43	85	53
1983	50	24	75	42
1982	25	60	61	42
1981	45	40	80	32

16 Ronald D. Coleman (D)

Of El Paso — Elected 1982

Born: Nov. 29, 1941, El Paso, Texas.
Education: U. of Texas, El Paso, B.A. 1963; U. of Texas, Austin, J.D. 1967; Attended U. of Kent, England, 1981.
Military Service: Army, 1967-69.
Occupation: Lawyer.
Family: Wife, Amy Crandus; three children.
Religion: Presbyterian.
Political Career: Texas House, 1973-83.
Capitol Office: 440 Cannon Bldg. 20515; 225-4831.

In Washington: A hint of partisan arrogance about Coleman, together with his swaggering walk, prompts comparisons with his senior Texas colleague Jack Brooks. While Coleman's wit contrasts with Brooks' ornery temperament, he does have some of the same legislative skills, and an instinct for making his way in House politics.

In his previous political life, Coleman was one of the Texas Legislature's most effective members, though an outsider there as the guerrilla leader of a progressive "Gang of Four" (with current House colleague John Bryant) that defied the entrenched conservative leadership.

In Washington, Coleman is squarely in the Democratic mainstream, and a valued lieutenant to Democratic leaders. Initially, he benefited from the patronage of Brooks and then-Majority Leader Jim Wright, but Coleman has steadily established himself as a player in his own right.

Since his second term Coleman has had a seat on the coveted Appropriations Committee, where his savvy and good-humored collegiality allow him to thrive. Since his first term, he has been an at-large whip; as such, he has proven to be good at intelligence-gathering, adept at working the floor and politically gutsy, sticking by the leadership on issues that do not always play so well in conservative West Texas.

For the most part, Coleman has concentrated on parochial matters while cementing his political foundations. The only Anglo to represent a majority-Hispanic congressional district, Coleman pays close attention to his constituents' needs. He uses his seat on Appropriations' Military Construction Subcommittee to channel funds to El Paso's Fort Bliss Army base.

Early in the 101st Congress, apparently feeling politically secure after his opposition-free 1988 election, Coleman signaled that he intends to broaden his horizons beyond West Texas. To the surprise of Appropriations colleagues, he left the Treasury, Postal Service and General Government Subcommittee to join the one for Foreign Operations.

Coleman is a champion of improved relations with Mexico. As one of the few "debt hawks" in Congress who follow the issue of Third World debt closely, Coleman is a forceful spokesman for U.S. efforts to reduce the debt burden of Mexico as a means of averting economic and political upheaval there. In 1989, when Treasury Secretary Nicholas F. Brady offered his plan to reduce Third World debt, Coleman criticized the plan's limits. "In the case of Mexico, it does not go far enough in terms of requiring shareholders in the major, private U.S. banks to bear the brunt of the consequences of extravagant and obsessive lending in the past," he said.

His position won support in the House, which passed a Coleman resolution urging the president to pressure U.S. commercial banks to negotiate a reduction of Mexico's $100 million debt. He called the negotiations "a foreign policy concern as important as any other in the United States today — our interest in an economically and politically sound Mexico."

In the 102nd Congress, Coleman is likely to be a key player in legislation involving the free trade agreement now under consideration between the United States and Mexico. As chairman of the Congressional Border Caucus, the West Texas native sponsored legislation in the 100th Congress to ease the provisions of a 1984 law that limited Mexican truckers' access to U.S. border markets.

He is an enthusiast for the economic reforms under way in Mexico. In 1989 the House passed a Coleman amendment to the foreign aid authorization commending Mexico for the reforms.

But he is also an advocate of organized labor and is concerned about the wage disparity between the United States and Mexico. A free trade agreement could shift more jobs across the border, which is apt to concern Coleman.

Coleman is also a leader, often a lonely one, in addressing the unique problems along the U.S.-Mexico border. In 1988, his bid for aid to the "colonias" — squalid border communities

Texas 16

West — El Paso

Although the 16th covers much of far West Texas, eight of every 10 votes in the district are cast in El Paso and the surrounding county of the same name. The 1990 census showed growing El Paso to be Texas' fourth-largest city; today, its population stands just over one-half million.

El Paso and its sister city across the Rio Grande, Ciudad Juarez, constitute the largest urban concentration on the Mexican-American border. They also share and coordinate some governmental services; thousands legally cross the border every day to work and shop. Juarez has an estimated one million residents.

A key commercial center since the mid-1800s, El Paso has a diversified base of businesses, many of which interact with companies across the border. For instance, there are a number of "twin plant" textile ventures, in which cloth is manufactured on the U.S. side, sent to Mexico (where wages are lower) for assembly into clothing, then sent back to the American side for sale. Copper and oil refining, electronics and food processing plants, and the federal government all provide jobs. The military presence is formidable. The U.S. Army's Fort Bliss is located in El Paso, and many district residents work across the New Mexico state line at the White Sands Missile Range.

The 16th voted Republican for president in 1980 and 1984, but changed course in 1988 and gave the Democratic ticket of Michael S. Dukakis and Texan Lloyd Bentsen 52 percent of its vote. There are a good many Republican votes cast here these days in statewide and local elections, but in most such contests the 16th's traditional conservative Democratic outlook still prevails.

Hispanics make up 60 percent of the population in the 16th and are an important segment of the electorate, although their voter turnout rate is not proportionate to their presence in the population.

Population: 527,401. White 317,443 (60%), Black 19,226 (4%), Other 5,738 (1%). Spanish origin 317,592 (60%). 18 and over 341,560 (65%), 65 and over 35,953 (7%). Median age: 25.

lacking basic utilities — reflected both his interest and his legislative technique. When his bill for comprehensive assistance seemed likely to die in at least one of four committees that claimed jurisdiction over its parts, Coleman took the housing portion that the Banking Committee had approved and reintroduced it as a separate bill; with Speaker Wright's help, he took the measure to the House and won unanimous approval in the 100th Congress' last days. Time ran out in the Senate, however.

In the 101st Congress, Coleman narrowed his sights and helped win authorization for an extension of the American Canal in El Paso. The project will salvage between 12,000 and 22,000 acre-feet of water annually, eliminate health and safety hazards and create construction jobs. He also won a waiver in the Clean Air Act for border cities, such as El Paso, that do not meet federal air quality standards due largely to pollution created across the border.

At Home: In 1988 and 1990, Coleman enjoyed the ultimate luxury, as Republicans allowed him to win without opposition. Those effortless victories must have sweetened the satisfaction he first felt in 1982, when his victory in the 16th gainsaid Democrats who had long proclaimed him too liberal to win a congressional election in West Texas. That year, without downplaying the pro-labor populism he had practiced in Austin, Coleman moved with surprising ease through a five-way Democratic primary, a runoff and a general election that Republicans felt sure they could win.

Democratic Rep. Richard C. White's retirement announcement in October 1981 was a surprise in El Paso, but Coleman reacted quickly. He mobilized his base among labor and teachers, and by early 1982 he had as sophisticated a campaign apparatus as the district had seen. Still, while that support was sufficient to allow Coleman to lead in the first round, doubts remained that it would be enough against his runoff opponent, popular El Paso County Judge T. Udell Moore Jr., who drew on White's conservative following and business ties.

The runoff was a test of strength between business and labor. A few years before, when Mexican-American clothing workers struck El Paso's Farah Manufacturing Co., Coleman was their attorney. Moore made it clear at the time that, if it came to a tie-breaking vote on the county commission, he would vote to deny them food stamps. The Hispanic vote decided the runoff; with support from the barrios of South El Paso, Coleman won with nearly 55 percent.

For the general-election campaign, the National Republican Congressional Committee designed a candidacy from scratch for El Paso Councilman Pat Haggerty, an ex-seminarian and former Democrat. With the national GOP's promise of the maximum financial help, Haggerty joined the party and aimed to take thousands of White's conservative Democratic supporters with him.

Despite a relatively liberal background, Haggerty campaigned as a Ronald Reagan Republican, denouncing Coleman as a "labor liberal" and charging that the city had become too dependent on federal help. The strategy probably would have worked in 1980, when Reagan swamped Jimmy Carter in El Paso, but in 1982, conservative Democrats seemed more concerned about the local economy. White swallowed his differences and supported the Democratic nominee, while Coleman continued to enjoy active support in the Hispanic community. He scored a 54-44 percent victory.

Republicans had good reason to suspect they might be able to topple Coleman in 1984. Unlike 1982, Sen. Lloyd Bentsen, a magnet for Democratic votes, was not on the ticket, while President Reagan, who would pull in GOP and conservative votes statewide, was. Moreover, GOP leaders felt they had a savvy nominee in Jack Hammond, a former bank executive and Republican activist from El Paso. Recognizing that Coleman's 1982 victory rested on his ability to hold conservative Democrats while picking up most of the Hispanic vote, Hammond chipped away at both pillars of support.

He stressed his business credentials and voiced a pro-Reagan, anti-tax line, but also pointed to his past work with the League of United Latin American Citizens. But Coleman survived it all, both bases intact. He called himself an independent-minded lawmaker, played up his efforts to bolster the local economy, and in the end won with 57 percent while Reagan swept all eight counties within the 16th.

The GOP threw Coleman a curve in 1986, challenging him with retired Mexican-American accountant Roy Gillia. Party leaders figured that Gillia and Roy R. Barrera Jr., the GOP nominee for attorney general, together could produce a Hispanic Republican turnout capable of toppling Coleman. It was not to be. The 16th's Hispanic community showed almost no interest in voting Republican, and Coleman walked away with two-thirds of the vote.

Committee

Appropriations (28th of 37 Democrats)
Foreign Operations, Export Financing & Related Programs; Military Construction

Elections

1990 General

Ronald D. Coleman (D)	62,455	(96%)
William Burgett (Write-in)	2,854	(4%)

1988 General

Ronald D. Coleman (D)	104,514	(100%)

Previous Winning Percentages: **1986** (66%) **1984** (57%) **1982** (54%)

District Vote For President

	1988	1984	1980	1976
D	69,550 (52%)	57,337 (43%)	45,471 (40%)	52,104 (51%)
R	63,062 (48%)	75,906 (57%)	61,651 (54%)	49,117 (48%)
I			5,255 (5%)	

Campaign Finance

	Receipts	Receipts from PACs	Expend-itures
1990			
Coleman (D)	$279,452	$162,285 (58%)	$286,407
1988			
Coleman (D)	$322,822	$175,670 (54%)	$317,444

Key Votes

1991

Authorize use of force against Iraq	N

1990

Support constitutional amendment on flag desecration	N
Pass family and medical leave bill over Bush veto	Y
Reduce SDI funding	N
Allow abortions in overseas military facilities	Y
Approve budget summit plan for spending and taxing	Y
Approve civil rights bill	Y

1989

Halt production of B-2 stealth bomber at 13 planes	N
Oppose capital gains tax cut	Y
Approve federal abortion funding in rape or incest cases	Y
Approve pay raise and revision of ethics rules	N
Pass Democratic minimum wage plan over Bush veto	Y

Voting Studies

	Presidential Support		Party Unity		Conservative Coalition	
Year	S	O	S	O	S	O
1990	20	76	90	7	44	52
1989	35	62	90	6	34	63
1988	27	69	89	6	37	58
1987	30	68	92	6	51	49
1986	29	69	81	16	64	36
1985	31	68	89	9	51	47
1984	42	55	76	21	61	37
1983	37	61	81	16	48	49

Interest Group Ratings

Year	ADA	ACU	AFL-CIO	CCUS
1990	67	17	83	23
1989	75	18	91	22
1988	80	17	93	29
1987	84	4	100	13
1986	70	35	86	56
1985	60	19	71	33
1984	65	35	92	38
1983	75	4	88	40

17 Charles W. Stenholm (D)

Of Stamford — Elected 1978

Born: Oct. 26, 1938, Stamford, Texas.
Education: Attended Tarleton State Junior College, 1957-59; Texas Tech U., B.S. 1961, M.S. 1962.
Occupation: Cotton grower.
Family: Wife, Cynthia Ann Watson; three children.
Religion: Lutheran.
Political Career: No previous office.
Capitol Office: 1226 Longworth Bldg. 20515; 225-6605.

In Washington: Although the House Democratic Caucus has an unmistakable list to the left, Stenholm is proof that a conservative can make a difference in the Democratic Party. Now that he is on the Budget Committee, a new assignment in the 102nd Congress, he will have another forum in which to articulate his austere attitude toward government spending.

Stenholm tried to legislate his fiscal principles in the 101st Congress by sponsoring a constitutional amendment to balance the budget. The amendment would have required the president to submit a balanced budget to Congress. Spending could not exceed estimated revenues without a three-fifths vote of Congress, nor could the national debt be increased without a three-fifths vote. Stenholm said the amendment was the only way to give Congress budget backbone. "Courage and guts," he said. "We do not have it and we have not shown it. We need some help and an extra tool."

The Democratic leadership denounced the amendment and drew up a balanced-budget statute as an alternative. But some previously reliable Democrats jumped ship during the amendment debate to back Stenholm's plan. The vote on the constitutional amendment was 279-150 — just seven votes short of the two-thirds majority required to send it to the states for ratification. The statutory alternative passed, but the Senate did not consider it.

Stenholm's concerns about the federal deficit have led him to push another unorthodox measure, one not very popular with most members: To cut back "pork-barreling," Stenholm has suggested a "truth-in-legislation" plan. It would require bill reports to single out provisions with 10 or fewer beneficiaries, identify the author and those who would benefit.

Another member pursuing such endeavors might risk being dismissed as a conservative gadfly. But Stenholm commands respect as a man of principle and substance, and his relationship with Democratic leaders remains cordial because he will sometimes help them on sticky votes. Stenholm's flexibility helps explain why the House leadership team that took over in mid-1989 named him a deputy whip.

When some conservative Democrats got behind President Bush's proposed cut in the capital gains tax in 1989, Stenholm agreed to lobby Southern Democrats for Speaker Thomas S. Foley. The unlikely duo of Stenholm and Illinois Democrat Marty Russo led the leadership task force against the cut, which was promoted by Georgia Democrat Ed Jenkins and Texas Republican Bill Archer. A move to kill the tax cut failed 190-239, but Senate opposition kept the cut from becoming law.

In 1989, conservative Texas Republican Dick Armey attempted to cut the appropriation for the National Endowment for the Arts by 10 percent, in response to publicity over two projects by NEA grant recipients that had been denounced as blasphemous and obscene. Interior Appropriations Subcommittee Chairman Sidney R. Yates enlisted Stenholm to offer a compromise substitute amendment, cutting NEA funding by only the amount of the two controversial grants — $45,000. The House adopted the Stenholm language, 361-65. Armey commented admiringly that it was "very good strategy to come in and 'Boll Weevil' me."

Stenholm also helped give cover to some Democrats when he added his name to the list of opponents of a constitutional amendment to ban physical desecration of the flag.

Stenholm reserves much of his energy for the Agriculture Committee, where he is respected for his mastery of highly technical legislative matters. "There is nothing that comes out of the ground that Charlie Stenholm doesn't know about," remarked one colleague.

On the committee, Stenholm's reputation for independence leads to solicitations for his support from all sides when an issue is debated. When Stenholm himself is attempting to round up support for an idea, Republicans tend to look favorably upon it, with an eye to winning him over on another issue later.

As chairman of the Livestock, Dairy and Poultry Subcommittee, Stenholm was responsible for the dairy title in the 1990 farm bill. He and ranking subcommittee Republican Steve

Texas 17

West Central — Abilene

The 17th stretches across more than 300 miles of rolling West Texas prairie. Its life revolves around cattle, cotton, oil and gas. It is predominantly Democratic territory, with a conservative tilt, partly due to fundamentalist Christian influence.

In 1990, unsuccessful GOP gubernatorial nominee Clayton Williams took 26 of the 35 counties in the district, but Stenholm felt no pressure: The GOP has offered a congressional candidate in the 17th only twice in the past quarter-century.

Republicans do best in Taylor County (Abilene) almost in the middle of the 17th, which casts about one-fifth of the vote. Abilene sprang to life when the railroad came through in 1881 and cattlemen started driving herds there for shipment. Today the city has nearly 107,000 people, but it still retains its cowhand flavor; during the 1988 presidential campaign, reporters were surprised to find Sen. Lloyd Bentsen had changed out of his customary business attire and into western garb before appearing at an Abilene campaign event.

The early 1980s oil downturn brought considerable unemployment to the city, though the situation stabilized after many of the workers who followed the boom to Abilene heeded local bumper stickers that read, "Welcome to Texas. Now Go Home."

The city processes cottonseed, meats and dairy products; it makes aircraft parts, trailers and electronic items. Another dependable employer is Dyess Air Force Base.

Other than Taylor, only six counties in the 17th have more than 20,000 people. Five of them are at the far eastern edge of the district, either in or near the metropolitan sphere of Fort Worth. Republicans are gaining strength here in the east — Williams got 56 percent in Parker County in 1990.

Settlement is generally sparse among the oil and gas wells, range land and cotton fields in the western half of the 17th.

Population: 526,913. White 470,931 (89%), Black 16,940 (3%), Other 3,194 (1%). Spanish origin 59,274 (11%). 18 and over 380,499 (72%), 65 and over 82,648 (16%). Median age: 32.

Gunderson of Wisconsin produced a plan that set a floor, at $10.10 per 100 pounds of milk products, under the previously sliding scale of government price supports for milk. Stenholm and Gunderson fended off attempts to raise the support floor, and rejected administration calls to cut subsidy levels.

Stenholm has generally preferred helping farmers cut back production rather than increasing direct subsidies. The 1990 farm bill contained a concept Stenholm and Kansas Republican Pat Roberts had long favored to reduce government subsidies. Known as "triple base," the plan reduced by 15 percent the amount of cropland eligible for government income-support payments. Farmers participating in crop programs could grow anything else (except fruits and vegetables) on that 15 percent of land normally used for subsidized crops.

Stenholm is a leading opponent of efforts to restrict farmers' use of chemical pesticides. His position is more common on Agriculture, however, than in the full House. During floor consideration of the farm bill, Oregon Democrat Peter A. DeFazio offered an amendment establishing a national standard governing what foods may be labeled organic. Stenholm proposed giving the Agriculture Department authority for setting organic standards. But DeFazio maintained that that approach was a ploy to kill the organic standard. The House adopted DeFazio's amendment 234-187.

Off the Agriculture Committee, Stenholm played a dominant role in debate on a bill increasing federal aid for child care. Stenholm and Florida Republican E. Clay Shaw Jr. offered a less ambitious, less costly alternative to the competing Democratic plans and Republican substitute. It lost on two occasions in the House, each time taking 195 votes, but it attracted Bush administration support and worried Democratic sponsors. The final version approved by the House-Senate conference had a price tag closer to Stenholm's plan and contained several similar provisions.

Prior to 1981, Stenholm had no record of leadership experience, but he emerged as the head of a Boll Weevil group that used its leverage to get conservative Democrats prime committee assignments, and to help shape and pass the 1981 Reagan economic program.

The group, which evolved into the Conservative Democratic Forum (CDF), became less strategically crucial after the 1982 elections, when Democrats added 26 seats to their majority, giving Speaker Thomas P. O'Neill Jr. enough loyalist votes to work his will. The CDF, however, still meets, and now has more than 50 regular members, according to Stenholm.

Despite his criticisms of the Democratic Party, Stenholm has made it clear he does not plan to leave it. "I'm a Democrat, period," he said in 1986. "Philosophically, I am what I am, and that's a conservative Democrat. I believe that philosophy, tempered with the liberal and moderate viewpoints, is best for the country."

But Stenholm was not prepared to accept a socialist into his party's fold. When Vermont independent Bernard Sanders, a self-described socialist, sought admission into the Democratic Caucus after he was elected to the House in 1990, Stenholm circulated among CDF members a letter opposing Sanders' admission. Sanders subsequently agreed not to apply.

At Home: Stenholm is a third-generation West Texan, descended from Swedish immigrants who settled near Stamford, where he was born. Agriculture has been the focus of his life and the basis of his political career.

He moved into politics in 1966, when the U.S. Agriculture Department made a ruling unfavorable to the cotton-growing plains section of Texas. As executive vice president of the Rolling Plains Cotton Growers Association, he visited Washington to lobby against the ruling, and had partial success in changing it.

In 1977, President Jimmy Carter appointed Stenholm to a panel advising the U.S. Agricultural and Conservation Service. He resigned that post to run for the House in 1978, when veteran Democrat Omar Burleson retired.

Stenholm had a much smaller campaign treasury than his major rival for the Democratic nomination, wealthy Abilene lawyer and businessman A. L. "Dusty" Rhodes. But as a farmer and former member of the state Democratic executive committee, Stenholm had extensive agricultural and party ties. Although Rhodes spent over $600,000, Stenholm outran the crowded primary field and defeated Rhodes by 2-to-1 in a runoff. An easy winner in the fall, he has not faced a major-party foe since then.

Committees

Agriculture (9th of 27 Democrats)
Livestock, Dairy & Poultry (chairman); Conservation, Credit & Rural Development; Cotton, Rice & Sugar; Department Operations, Research & Foreign Agriculture; Peanuts & Tobacco

Budget (17th of 23 Democrats)
Budget Process, Reconciliation & Enforcement; Community Development & Natural Resources

Elections

1990 General		
Charles W. Stenholm (D)	104,100	(100%)
1988 General		
Charles W. Stenholm (D)	149,064	(100%)

Previous Winning Percentages: **1986** (100%) **1984** (100%) **1982** (97%) **1980** (100%) **1978** (68%)

District Vote For President

	1988	1984	1980	1976
D	84,899 (42%)	65,480 (32%)	79,143 (46%)	99,077 (57%)
R	117,349 (58%)	140,748 (68%)	87,449 (51%)	73,789 (43%)
I			2,988 (2%)	

Campaign Finance

	Receipts	Receipts from PACs	Expend-itures
1990			
Stenholm (D)	$254,175	$98,075 (39%)	$311,378
1988			
Stenholm (D)	$289,551	$111,716 (39%)	$342,766

Key Votes

1991	
Authorize use of force against Iraq	Y
1990	
Support constitutional amendment on flag desecration	N
Pass family and medical leave bill over Bush veto	N
Reduce SDI funding	N
Allow abortions in overseas military facilities	N
Approve budget summit plan for spending and taxing	Y
Approve civil rights bill	N
1989	
Halt production of B-2 stealth bomber at 13 planes	N
Oppose capital gains tax cut	Y
Approve federal abortion funding in rape or incest cases	N
Approve pay raise and revision of ethics rules	Y
Pass Democratic minimum wage plan over Bush veto	N

Voting Studies

	Presidential Support		Party Unity		Conservative Coalition	
Year	**S**	**O**	**S**	**O**	**S**	**O**
1990	56	44	52	47	91	9
1989	71	28	54	45	85	10
1988	57	39	45	50	87	8
1987	64	34	39	57	93	2
1986	66	34	32	67	88	12
1985	66	31	35	64	96	2
1984	58	37	23	70	85	8
1983	63	35	21	77	92	7
1982	74	26	17	78	93	4
1981	75	24	28	67	91	5

Interest Group Ratings

Year	ADA	ACU	AFL-CIO	CCUS
1990	22	67	25	71
1989	25	61	17	80
1988	20	78	46	77
1987	12	74	25	80
1986	5	81	21	78
1985	20	90	24	86
1984	10	79	15	56
1983	15	91	13	85
1982	5	91	5	86
1981	0	93	20	84

18 Craig Washington (D)

Of Houston — Elected 1989

Born: Oct. 12, 1941, Longview, Texas.

Education: Prairie View A&M U., B.S. 1966; Texas Southern U., J.D. 1969.

Occupation: Lawyer.

Family: Separated; five children.

Religion: Baptist.

Political Career: Texas House, 1973-83; Texas Senate, 1983-90.

Capitol Office: 1711 Longworth Bldg. 20515; 225-3816.

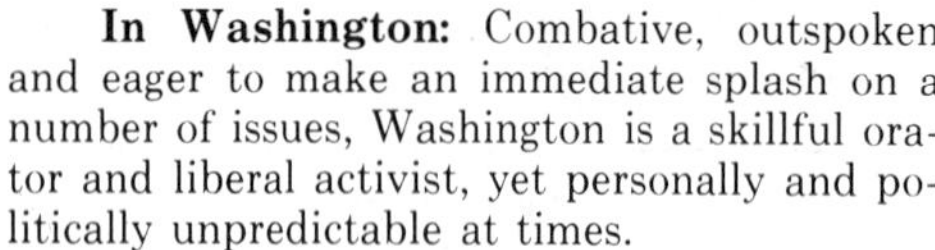

In Washington: Combative, outspoken and eager to make an immediate splash on a number of issues, Washington is a skillful orator and liberal activist, yet personally and politically unpredictable at times.

In some ways exemplary of the most liberal faction of the House, he was one of just six members to oppose a resolution backing the president and supporting U.S. troops in the Persian Gulf after the war started in January 1991. But his mercurial side occasionally sets him apart from his natural allies. "I am opposed to raising taxes of any kind," he said in mid-1990.

As a member of the Judiciary Committee, Washington tried to have his say on many of 1990's prominent issues, including crime, flag burning and discrimination against the disabled. But it was on the civil rights bill (ultimately vetoed by President Bush) where Washington gained the most attention.

When House negotiators compromised on some amendments in pursuit of administration support, Washington balked. Calling the amended version a "hollow shell of a civil rights bill," Washington was the only Democratic conferee who voted against the changes.

Later, in a floor speech, Washington took a tack contrary to congressional etiquette and unlikely to endear him to colleagues: He asked Southern voters to oust Democrats who opposed the civil rights bill. "Vote against these Democrats," he said. "Send them a message."

Possessed of a fiery personality and temperament — he once got into a fight in the Texas Legislature — Washington was involved in another contretemps on the floor in October 1990. Illinois Republican Henry J. Hyde, angry over a sarcastic floor statement by liberal Barney Frank of Massachusetts, made a sardonic quip about Frank's homosexuality. Washington jumped to Frank's defense, nearly engaging in fisticuffs with several Republicans present.

Washington began his congressional service under an unusual ethical cloud. Days before being sworn in, he was sentenced by two Texas judges to brief prison terms for contempt of court on charges stemming from his handling of two legal cases. He managed to settle the issue without serving any jail time.

At Home: Washington is the third in a string of outspoken, liberal, black Democrats who have represented the 18th.

Barbara C. Jordan held the seat for three terms in the 1970s, before retiring. Civil rights and anti-hunger activist Mickey Leland succeeded Jordan in 1978, and held the seat easily until his August 1989 death in a plane crash in Africa.

Washington had been a close ally of Leland since 1972, when they were among a group of black politicians running for the state Legislature. After Leland's death, many of the late congressman's supporters rallied behind Washington in the 11-way race to fill the vacant seat.

Washington had plenty of his own credentials and contacts to bolster his campaign. A Houston lawyer and state senator, he was known as a stirring orator willing to tackle tough battles and serve as a "conscience" in the chamber. He took first place in the November special election, but his 41 percent tally was not enough to avoid a runoff with City Council member and fellow Democrat Anthony Hall.

In the December runoff, Hall found support among members of the Houston business community who had been itching for a more conservative representative. Hall touted himself as an effective legislator, suggesting by comparison that Washington took on losing causes and paid too little attention to detail.

But Washington effectively presented some of his "losing causes" in a positive light, saying he was not afraid to champion individual rights on controversial issues such as flag burning (Washington had filibustered against a measure to amend the Texas Constitution to ban flag burning). During the campaign, he refused Hall's challenge to take a drug test. Washington got a boost when Leland's widow endorsed him. He beat Hall with almost 57 percent of the vote and ran unchallenged to win his first full term in 1990.

Texas 18

Central Houston

The 18th District is at the core of sprawling Houston, a city whose economy has seen incredible boom, debilitating bust and modest recovery over the past two decades. But whether times are good, bad or in between, this minority-dominated area has struggled.

In the 1970s, the district actually lost population in spite of greater Houston's phenomenal oil-fed growth. When the oil market plummeted in the early 1980s, the vacant office towers in the 18th became the symbol of the city's grossly overbuilt commercial real-estate sector.

Now, as many in the Houston area begin to get back on their feet and look to rebuild the economy on high technology and other modern-age ventures requiring skilled workers, the undereducated residents of the 18th fight the despair of continuing economic frustration.

After redistricting following the 1980 census, the 18th was the only Texas district in which whites were not a majority of the population. At the start of the decade, it was about 40 percent white, and, with nearly half of Houston's black population, over 40 percent black.

Since then, there has been considerable movement of whites to outlying suburbs in Harris and Fort Bend counties. Within the city, the Hispanic community has expanded rapidly in the Denver Harbor area. There is also a growing Asian population along the fringes of central Houston.

The 18th does have some residents at the upper end of the economic spectrum. River Oaks, partially contained within the district, is home to some of the district's most affluent — and most conservative — constituents. The Heights area is predominantly middle-income and blue-collar.

This ethnic and economic blend generally produces the largest Democratic margins in the state. In 1988, Michael S. Dukakis won 77 percent in the 18th, his best showing in any Texas district. Although blacks, whites and Hispanics are roughly equal in numbers in the district, the 18th has sent a black Democrat to Congress since its creation in 1971.

Population: 527,393. White 216,421 (41%), Black 215,230 (41%), Other 7,343 (1%). Spanish origin 164,616 (31%). 18 and over 366,424 (70%), 65 and over 50,691 (10%). Median age: 27.

Committees

Education & Labor (16th of 25 Democrats)
Elementary, Secondary & Vocational Education; Labor-Management Relations; Postsecondary Education

Judiciary (18th of 21 Democrats)
Civil & Constitutional Rights; Crime and Criminal Justice

Select Narcotics Abuse & Control (20th of 21 Democrats)

Elections

1990 General		
Craig Washington (D)	54,477	(100%)
1989 Special Runoff		
Craig Washington (D)	24,140	(57%)
Anthony Hall (D)	18,484	(43%)
1989 Special		
Craig Washington (D)	27,367	(41%)
Anthony Hall (D)	22,797	(34%)
Ron Wilson (D)	4,948	(7%)
Al Edwards (D)	3,095	(5%)
Beverly A. Spencer (R)	2,123	(3%)
Shirley Fobbs (D)	1,315	(2%)
Timothy John Hattenbach (D)	1,267	(2%)
Manse R. Sharp Jr. (D)	1,079	(2%)
Byron J. Johnson (D)	1,058	(2%)
Gary Johnson (LIBERT)	829	(1%)
Lee Arthur Demas Jr. (D)	342	(1%)

District Vote For President

	1988		1984		1980		1976	
D	81,611	(77%)	99,232	(73%)	79,143	(69%)	91,624	(71%)
R	24,291	(23%)	35,601	(26%)	31,836	(28%)	36,665	(28%)
I					2,988	(3%)		

Campaign Finance

	Receipts	Receipts from PACs		Expend-itures
1990				
Washington (D)	$144,647	$87,250	(60%)	$157,053

Key Votes

1991	
Authorize use of force against Iraq	N
1990	
Support constitutional amendment on flag desecration	N
Pass family and medical leave bill over Bush veto	?
Reduce SDI funding	Y
Allow abortions in overseas military facilities	Y
Approve budget summit plan for spending and taxing	N
Approve civil rights bill	Y

Voting Studies

	Presidential Support		Party Unity		Conservative Coalition	
Year	**S**	**O**	**S**	**O**	**S**	**O**
1990	12	81	73	4	7	80

Interest Group Ratings

Year	ADA	ACU	AFL-CIO	CCUS
1990	94	5	100	31

19 Larry Combest (R)

Of Lubbock — Elected 1984

Born: March 20, 1945, Memphis, Texas.
Education: West Texas State U., B.B.A. 1969.
Occupation: Farmer; congressional aide; electronics wholesaler.
Family: Wife, Sharon McCurry; two children.
Religion: Methodist.
Political Career: Hale County Republican Party chairman, 1970-71.
Capitol Office: 1527 Longworth Bldg. 20515; 225-4005.

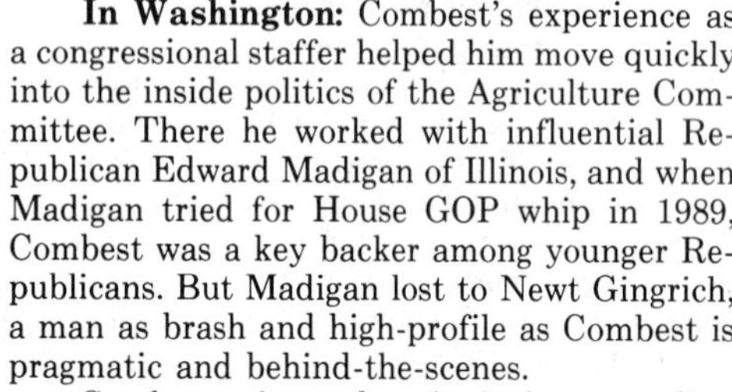

In Washington: Combest's experience as a congressional staffer helped him move quickly into the inside politics of the Agriculture Committee. There he worked with influential Republican Edward Madigan of Illinois, and when Madigan tried for House GOP whip in 1989, Combest was a key backer among younger Republicans. But Madigan lost to Newt Gingrich, a man as brash and high-profile as Combest is pragmatic and behind-the-scenes.

Combest refocused on Agriculture, tending to the interests of West Texas' cotton and feed grain producers. He has the knowledge, desire and electoral security to become a legislator with impact; though Gingrich and his combative allies draw more attention, there will be plenty of opportunities for legislative deal-making, and that is Combest's forte.

In 1985 and 1990, Combest was quietly attentive as the Agriculture Committee wrote the five-year farm bill. On farm subsidies, he generally supported the frugal views of the GOP administrations — and many conservative West Texas producers — but his fiscal austerity faded some on cotton, the 19th's key crop. He worked well with Charles W. Stenholm, the influential Agriculture Democrat who represents the adjoining 17th. During committee work on the 1988 drought-relief bill, Combest got an amendment passed to compensate cotton producers with hail-damaged crops.

Many "Old Bull" GOP insiders share Combest's pragmatic attitude toward legislative bargaining. Their influence helped him get an additional committee assignment in 1989 — Intelligence. In the 101st Congress, Combest argued against large cuts in the intelligence budget, warning that Soviet intelligence activities had not subsided.

As that stand suggests, Combest furrows a steady conservative line outside agriculture. In 1990, he was one of four House members to vote 100 percent of the time with the "conservative coalition" of Republicans and Southern Democrats. During the year, Combest was one of two Texas Republicans to vote consistently to cut funding for the superconducting super collider, an $8 billion atom smasher to be built in Texas.

Combest has been outspoken in his crusade against the Legal Services Corporation, the federal program of legal services to the poor. The business establishment in Combest's district has attacked the Texas Rural Legal Aid office for organizing unions, promoting strikes, and representing illegal aliens.

As a protégé and longtime employee of the late Sen. John Tower, Combest probably was horrified to see his account of Tower's past drinking featured in a 1989 front-page story in *The Washington Post*. The story said Combest told Armed Services Committee Sens. Sam Nunn and John W. Warner that Tower, President Bush's nominee for defense secretary, drank as much as a full bottle of Scotch two to three times a week in the 1970s. Combest later said it was Tower and a group of friends who drank a full bottle in an evening. Tower's nomination was rejected.

At Home: After a stint with the U.S. Agricultural Stabilization Service, Combest went to work for Tower in 1971 as a specialist in agricultural affairs. He later became director of Tower's Texas offices, and served as treasurer for his 1978 re-election campaign. Combest then returned to West Texas to sell electronic equipment, remaining active in GOP affairs. When Democratic Rep. Kent Hance announced for the Senate in 1984, Combest jumped for the 19th. It had not elected a Republican in its 50-year history, but voted regularly for GOP state and national candidates and was ripe to switch.

Combest was forced into a runoff by a hard-right conservative, but with support from many old-line GOP leaders, he won the runoff easily. In November, Combest met Don Richards, a former Hance aide. Both stressed their farm roots and conservatism. Combest portrayed Richards as part of a too-liberal party. Richards spurned the national Democratic line on tax increases and gay rights, and cast himself as a conservative in Hance's mold. Combest carried the most populous counties — Ector and Lubbock — to overcome Richards' rural strength. He has won easily since.

Texas 19

Northwest — Lubbock; Odessa

The stubborn, slow-talking farmers and ranchers of the West Texas plains do not change their minds easily about candidates or political parties. They sent George Mahon to the House in 1934, and kept him there for 44 years. They maintained their Democratic voting habits in Texas long after the national party had moved far beyond their generic distrust of government.

But change finally has come. The 19th has given GOP presidential candidates big margins since 1976. And Combest has brought the partisan change down to the House level.

Lubbock County casts 40 percent of the overall vote and now turns in regular GOP majorities for statewide and national office. Irrigation has enabled the agricultural region around Lubbock to replace East Texas as the state's predominant cotton-growing area. Four of the nation's top 10 counties for cotton are in the 19th. Lubbock, a city of about 186,000, calls itself the world's largest cottonseed processing center. Texas Tech U. and Reese Air Force Base are important employers.

More than 100 miles south of Lubbock is Odessa, with almost 100,000 residents. It primarily refines petroleum and provides equipment and supplies to surrounding oil fields, and has been among the Texas cities hardest-hit by the oil industry slump. Unemployment reached nearly 20 percent in 1986 and has dropped only because many have left to work elsewhere. Odessa and surrounding Ector County are the blue-collar stronghold of the Midland-Odessa population center, but the area is firmly Republican.

Sparsely populated farming and ranching counties fill out the 19th. Though rural residents prefer conservative Democrats, even those voters have been tilting to the GOP.

Population: 527,805. White 432,867 (82%), Black 28,361 (5%), Other 4,072 (1%). Spanish origin 131,919 (25%). 18 and over 360,942 (68%), 65 and over 45,903 (9%). Median age: 26.

Committees

Agriculture (10th of 18 Republicans)
Conservation, Credit & Rural Development; Cotton, Rice & Sugar; Peanuts & Tobacco

District of Columbia (2nd of 4 Republicans)
Government Operations & Metropolitan Affairs (ranking); Fiscal Affairs & Health

Select Intelligence (2nd of 7 Republicans)
Oversight & Evaluation (ranking)

Small Business (6th of 17 Republicans)
Exports, Tax Policy & Special Problems (ranking)

Elections

1990 General		
Larry Combest (R)	83,795	(100%)
1988 General		
Larry Combest (R)	113,068	(68%)
Gerald McCathern (D)	53,932	(32%)

Previous Winning Percentages: **1986** (62%) **1984** (58%)

District Vote For President

	1988	1984	1980	1976
D	54,551 (33%)	44,562 (25%)	46,373 (29%)	67,123 (44%)
R	110,148 (67%)	133,422 (75%)	108,936 (68%)	85,190 (56%)
I			3,154 (2%)	

Campaign Finance

	Receipts	Receipts from PACs	Expend-itures
1990			
Combest (R)	$197,121	$85,976 (44%)	$111,838
1988			
Combest (R)	$272,401	$119,800 (44%)	$244,821
McCathern (D)	$44,173	0	$44,082

Key Votes

1991	
Authorize use of force against Iraq	Y
1990	
Support constitutional amendment on flag desecration	Y
Pass family and medical leave bill over Bush veto	N
Reduce SDI funding	N
Allow abortions in overseas military facilities	N
Approve budget summit plan for spending and taxing	Y
Approve civil rights bill	N
1989	
Halt production of B-2 stealth bomber at 13 planes	N
Oppose capital gains tax cut	N
Approve federal abortion funding in rape or incest cases	N
Approve pay raise and revision of ethics rules	N
Pass Democratic minimum wage plan over Bush veto	N

Voting Studies

	Presidential Support		Party Unity		Conservative Coalition	
Year	**S**	**O**	**S**	**O**	**S**	**O**
1990	78	22	82	16	100	0
1989	85	15	73	27	95	5
1988	68	29	75	23	97	0
1987	64	25	75	19	86	7
1986	78	22	82	18	100	0
1985	75	25	89	11	96	4

Interest Group Ratings

Year	ADA	ACU	AFL-CIO	CCUS
1990	0	96	8	79
1989	0	96	0	90
1988	0	92	21	93
1987	0	89	13	93
1986	5	91	21	94
1985	5	100	0	91

20 Henry B. Gonzalez (D)

Of San Antonio — Elected 1961

Born: May 3, 1916, San Antonio, Texas.

Education: San Antonio Junior College, graduated 1937; attended U. of Texas, 1937-39; St. Mary's U. (San Antonio), LL.B. 1943.

Occupation: Social services professional; teacher; translator.

Family: Wife, Bertha Cuellar; eight children.

Religion: Roman Catholic.

Political Career: San Antonio City Council, 1953-56, San Antonio mayor pro tem, 1955-56; Texas Senate, 1957-61; sought Democratic nomination for governor, 1958; candidate for U.S. Senate, special election, 1961.

Capitol Office: 2413 Rayburn Bldg. 20515; 225-3236.

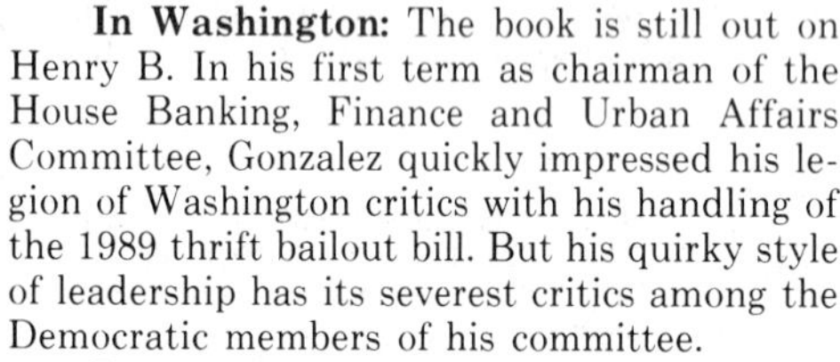

In Washington: The book is still out on Henry B. In his first term as chairman of the House Banking, Finance and Urban Affairs Committee, Gonzalez quickly impressed his legion of Washington critics with his handling of the 1989 thrift bailout bill. But his quirky style of leadership has its severest critics among the Democratic members of his committee.

Few members of Congress have had a reputation on Capitol Hill so contrary to their image back home as Gonzalez, long revered in San Antonio while all but dismissed in the House as a flake. His first term as chairman began narrowing the gulf between his critics' view of him and that held by his constituents.

Nothing, however, is likely to quell the discontent among his committee rivals. Among them are several ambitious younger liberal Democrats who are in philosophical agreement with Gonzalez, but who believe they could run the committee more firmly and effectively.

His egalitarian leadership style is a radical departure from that of his autocratic predecessor, the tyrannical Fernand J. St Germain of Rhode Island, and Gonzalez has satisfied some subcommittee chairmen by allowing them wider berth in their respective fiefdoms.

But Gonzalez also has drawn Democratic criticism for being too close to ranking Republican Chalmers P. Wylie of Ohio, and for discussing strategy more with him than with fellow Democrats.

Frustration with Gonzalez's rapport with Wylie erupted over allegations that he had recorded an endorsement of Wylie for his 1990 campaign. Before his re-election as chairman in late 1990, Gonzalez had to explain to the Democratic Caucus that his comments were not intended to be a campaign endorsement and were never aired. On the day of the balloting, the No. 7 Democrat on Banking, Bruce F. Vento, announced that he was challenging Gonzalez. The last-minute effort drew more than a third of the caucus, losing by a 163-89 vote.

Gonzalez has been a fighter from the beginning of his career, whether pressing lonely crusades of principle or personal quarrels. He is a passionate populist, and a sincere if long-winded one. He twice called for President Ronald Reagan's impeachment (after the 1983 Grenada invasion and in 1987 amid the Iran-contra scandal), and early in the 102nd Congress he introduced two resolutions to impeach President Bush for conducting the Persian Gulf War.

But he can be stubborn and short-tempered, and prone to eruptions of anger that over the years helped earn him the reputation in Washington as a high-strung eccentric.

As a consequence, it seemed Gonzalez might never inherit Banking's top chair if the panel's junior Democrats could prevent it. One reason they had never tried to oust St Germain was the fact that other senior Democrats, led by No. 2 Gonzalez, were no more desirable substitutes.

But in 1988, when St Germain lost re-election, Speaker Jim Wright of Texas and other Democratic leaders quashed any talk of a movement to block Gonzalez.

For a man attended by low expectations, Gonzalez assumed power at a time of great demands on Banking policy-makers. In addition to the longstanding pressures for banking deregulation and housing initiatives, a crisis in the savings and loan industry threatened to bankrupt the Federal Savings and Loan Insurance Corporation (FSLIC) and ignite a nationwide panic.

Gonzalez steered through the committee the Bush administration's complex bill tightening S&L regulation and restocking the insurance fund through higher S&L premiums and a taxpayer bailout. For both the liberal crusader and the Republican administration, the alliance

Texas 20

Central San Antonio

With a population of almost 936,000, San Antonio is Texas' third-largest city and the 10th-largest in the country. In 1981, it became the first major American city to elect a Mexican-American mayor, Henry Cisneros, who served until 1989.

The 20th District as a whole is 62 percent Hispanic, with the Mexican-American majority concentrated on San Antonio's West Side, one of the poorest areas anywhere in Texas. Blacks, who comprise 9 percent of the district, are most numerous across town on the East Side. Northwestern San Antonio is predominantly white, and hosts a mix of business and military people and upper-middle-class professionals. There is an academic community associated with the University of Texas at San Antonio, located across the line in the 21st District.

Despite San Antonio's Hispanic majority and background — it was founded in the early 18th century by the Spanish — its economy has been controlled by Anglos since its early days as a cattle center. Today, federal payrolls are the key economic component. There are more than a half-dozen major military installations in or near San Antonio, including five Air Force bases. Kelly Air Force Base alone employs more than 22,000 people; Fort Sam Houston, a national center for Army medical care and research, employs more than 15,000.

Because of San Antonio's historic past (the Alamo is downtown) and its stint as host for the 1968 HemisFair, the city is an active center for tourism and conventions (the convention center is named for Rep. Gonzalez). Among the sites toured by visitors is the Paseo del Rio, with its myriad small shops, bars and restaurants lining the San Antonio River on its winding course through town.

The district's politics remain solidly Democratic. In 1984, Ronald Reagan won 41 percent of the presidential vote in the 20th, a high-water GOP showing. Michael S. Dukakis' 1988 tally was a more typical Democratic performance; he won 68 percent, his second-best score in all of Texas' districts.

Population: 526,333. White 397,577 (76%), Black 46,167 (9%), Other 4,146 (1%). Spanish origin 324,910 (62%). 18 and over 358,798 (68%), 65 and over 55,129 (10%). Median age: 26.

was an unusual one. But the White House came to rely heavily on Gonzalez as GOP lawmakers defected under intense lobbying by an industry long favored by the committee.

It was Gonzalez's early performance during the committee's work on the S&L bill that began to rehabilitate his reputation.

Like most on the committee, Gonzalez traditionally had been an S&L industry supporter. But in late 1988, he signaled a heightened skepticism. "The Congress has given thrifts everything they have asked for the last two decades, and look where we are."

When Bush's $50 billion bailout bill first was taken up in the Subcommittee on Financial Institutions Supervision, Regulation and Insurance, chaired by Gonzalez's rival, Frank Annunzio of Illinois, Gonzalez quietly bided his time while Annunzio helped weaken the measure with industry amendments. After one especially controversial vote, to roll back stiffer capital requirements for S&Ls, Gonzalez objected, "This is back to the old way of doing things. I won't be a party to it."

He came out charging in the full committee. The panel approved a modified version of Gonzalez's amendment restoring the capital requirement. Also, it adopted a second amendment on which Gonzalez had staked his prestige, this one requiring the federal S&L board to help subsidize low-cost mortgages.

The mortgage-subsidy amendment drew heavy opposition from the thrift industry, and its support split on partisan lines. By a vote of 206-208, it survived a vote to knock it out of the bill; only four Republicans voted to retain it.

The House-Senate conference was an early demonstration of the new chairman's negotiating style. St Germain had excelled at the backroom deal. Gonzalez, with his undisguised distaste for horse-trading, could not have been more different. "There's no such thing as cutting deals on our side, as I see it," he said.

But to get a bill out of conference with a House-backed financing plan that placed the cost of the bailout on the federal budget, he had to give up a provision that would have prevented Federal Home Loan Bank Board Chairman M. Danny Wall from becoming director of the new Office of Thrift Supervision (OTS) without being subjected to Senate confirmation. Gonzalez in particular had been critical of Wall for underestimating the magnitude of the S&L crisis and for giving purchasers of failed thrifts overly favorable deals. That concession helped unblock the conference.

However, a last-minute veto threat by Bush over the on-budget financing forced a second conference. A fierce battle between conferees and administration officials produced a compromise in which $20 billion was put on budget and $30 billion off. House Democrats were angry at Gonzalez for his willingness to accept the compromise; Gonzalez argued that Democrats should be pleased with housing and consumer provisions in the bill. The conference report was adopted, but only 82 of 217 Democrats supported it.

As estimates of the bailout's cost soared, Gonzalez pummeled Treasury Secretary Nicholas F. Brady for not appearing in person in late 1990 to defend his request for an additional $40 billion. Gonzalez refused to mark up a bill; when he did, it was killed by Annunzio's last-minute objection. A $30 billion bailout bill passed early in the 102nd Congress.

When he became chairman, Gonzalez kept the Housing Subcommittee he has chaired since 1981 because that panel reflects his top priority. Gonzalez is the House's most ardent advocate of increased federal housing aid.

As Housing chairman, Gonzalez was a harsh critic of Reagan's efforts to dismantle many housing programs. But not until the end of his administration was Congress able to enact a free-standing housing authorization. Not only were Congress and the president split, but so also Congress was divided until 1987 between House Democrats and Senate Republicans. However, at times Gonzalez displayed an impracticality that exacerbated the stalemate.

The 101st Congress passed the first major overhaul of federal housing programs in more than 15 years. Gonzalez favored big increases for existing programs rather than creating a lot of new ones. He did have one major new idea, a National Housing Trust to subsidize first-time mortgages for low- and middle-class home buyers. Wylie helped get the process moving, lobbying Bush to meet with him and Gonzalez about enacting housing legislation.

The bill passed in 1990 authorized $57.4 billion over two years to continue existing programs and create new ones. It included $771.5 million over two years for Gonzalez's housing trust. However, Bush's fiscal 1992 budget allocated no money for the trust.

Gonzalez might not have been the earliest to recognize the decay in the S&L industry, but in the 101st Congress he became Congress' most aggressive inquisitor, holding extensive hearings in 1989 on the case of Lincoln Savings and Loan of California, a $5.7 billion thrift whose failure could cost taxpayers $2 billion. The S&L, which had been owned by Charles H. Keating Jr., was at the center of the Keating Five scandal, in which five senators who received campaign contributions from Keating were under scrutiny for intervening with federal regulators in Lincoln's behalf. After regulators testified that Wall had interfered in their efforts to rein in the high-flying thrift, Gonzalez called on Wall to step aside as OTS chairman. Under the Democrats' constant pressure and with scant White House support, Wall resigned in December 1989.

The Lincoln hearings displayed the essential Gonzalez, a populist bulldog tenaciously pursuing his agenda regardless of whose flower bed is uprooted. In this case, the discontent was almost exclusively among members of his own party. Senior and junior committee members complained that they were not consulted over the procedure. Gonzalez appeared only to have confided in Wylie.

Through the Reagan years, Gonzalez directed much of his wrath at Housing Secretary Samuel R. Pierce Jr. In 1982, he called Pierce, who is black, "Step'n Fetchit." Days later at a subcommittee hearing, Pierce lashed back at Gonzalez for his "vile, abusive and racist language." He told a HUD audience Gonzalez was "ready for the funny farm." Gonzalez, in turn, said Pierce "has kept his job despite malfeasance and misfeasance and because he is the only black member of the Cabinet."

In 1989, with Pierce out of office, Gonzalez was feeling vindicated as his subcommittee began investigating allegations that HUD had routinely awarded housing contracts to administration cronies. "It is indeed ironic that a program the Reagan administration had sought to terminate for six years was misused to feather the financial nest of ... administration favorites," he said.

Gonzalez engaged in another well-publicized feud in 1977 during his brief chairmanship of the House Assassinations Committee — a panel he had suggested to investigate the murders of President John F. Kennedy and the Rev. Dr. Martin Luther King Jr. Within weeks, Gonzalez had fired the panel's prosecutor for allegedly misusing committee funds. With the committee in an uproar, Gonzalez, too, quit a week later, saying the investigation could never succeed because "vast and powerful forces, including the country's most sophisticated crime element, won't stand for it."

Gonzalez's reputation also suffered from his quarrels that have not been merely verbal. In 1963, he threatened to "pistol whip" and then struck a House Republican who claimed Gonzalez's "left-wing voting record" served the socialist-communist cause. Twenty-three years later in a San Antonio restaurant, Gonzalez struck a man who had called him a communist; prosecutors later dropped misdemeanor charges.

Gonzalez's passion usually finds more constructive outlets. A longtime civil rights advocate in Texas, he arrived on the House floor for his 1962 swearing-in ceremony already carrying a bill to repeal the poll tax. He also began a drive for a world's fair in San Antonio, and finally HemisFair was held there in 1968.

At Home: Gonzalez does not campaign in

San Antonio as a voice for Hispanics. "I have never sought public office on an ethnic basis," he says, "and I never will.... I have never palmed myself off as some sort of ethnic leader." But he is a hero to many in his city's Mexican-American neighborhoods, and their votes have helped give him the impregnable House seat he holds today.

Since his original victory in a 1961 special election, Gonzalez has had no electoral problems of any sort. But it was different in the beginning for Gonzalez, the son of Mexican immigrants, who began climbing the local political ladder after World War II. He ran for office while helping his father, the managing editor of a Spanish-language newspaper, operate a translation service.

Gonzalez made it to the state Senate in 1956, and quickly drew attention by filibustering against Democratic Gov. Price Daniel's bill to allow the state to close schools threatened by disturbances surrounding integration.

In 1958 Gonzalez ran as the liberal alternative to Daniel in the Democratic gubernatorial primary. He was beaten by a margin of more than 3-to-1, but the defeat only encouraged his ambition. Three years later, he sought the Senate seat vacated by Lyndon B. Johnson. While Gonzalez carried his home base, Bexar County, his statewide appeal as a candidate with a Hispanic name was limited. He ran sixth with 9 percent of the vote.

But he soon had another chance. Later in 1961, Democrat Paul Kilday resigned from the House to accept a judgeship, and Gonzalez became the consensus Democratic candidate for the seat.

The special election was a clear liberal-conservative choice. Gonzalez was warmly endorsed by the Kennedy administration. Republican John Goode, a former GOP county chairman, had the active assistance of Arizona Sen. Barry Goldwater and Texas' newly elected GOP senator, John Tower. With strong support in Hispanic areas, Gonzalez won with 55 percent. He became the first person of Mexican-American extraction to be elected to the House from Texas.

Committees

Banking, Finance & Urban Affairs (Chairman)
Housing & Community Development (chairman); Consumer Affairs & Coinage; Domestic Monetary Policy; General Oversight; Policy Research & Insurance

Elections

1990 General		
Henry B. Gonzalez (D)	56,318	(100%)
1988 General		
Henry B. Gonzalez (D)	94,527	(71%)
Lee Trevino (R)	36,801	(28%)

Previous Winning Percentages:				**1986**	(100%)	**1984**	(100%)
1982	(92%)	**1980**	(82%)	**1978**	(100%)	**1976**	(100%)
1974	(100%)	**1972**	(97%)	**1970**	(100%)	**1968**	(82%)
1966	(87%)	**1964**	(65%)	**1962**	(100%)	**1961** *	(55%)

* *Special election.*

District Vote For President

	1988	1984	1980	1976
D	92,584 (68%)	82,253 (58%)	82,513 (64%)	84,087 (67%)
R	44,444 (32%)	59,014 (47%)	43,427 (33%)	39,739 (32%)
I			3,373 (3%)	

Campaign Finance

	Receipts	Receipts from PACs	Expend-itures
1990			
Gonzalez (D)	$141,688	$80,800 (57%)	$112,901
1988			
Gonzalez (D)	$225,721	$100,387 (44%)	$228,907
Trevino (R)	$58,325	$13,330 (23%)	$58,217

Key Votes

1991	
Authorize use of force against Iraq	N
1990	
Support constitutional amendment on flag desecration	N
Pass family and medical leave bill over Bush veto	Y
Reduce SDI funding	Y
Allow abortions in overseas military facilities	Y
Approve budget summit plan for spending and taxing	N
Approve civil rights bill	Y
1989	
Halt production of B-2 stealth bomber at 13 planes	N
Oppose capital gains tax cut	Y
Approve federal abortion funding in rape or incest cases	Y
Approve pay raise and revision of ethics rules	Y
Pass Democratic minimum wage plan over Bush veto	Y

Voting Studies

	Presidential Support		Party Unity		Conservative Coalition	
Year	**S**	**O**	**S**	**O**	**S**	**O**
1990	15	85	93	7	22	78
1989	38	62	93	6	20	80
1988	16	82	96	3	13	84
1987	15	85	93	6	21	77
1986	17	82	90	7	10	88
1985	21	74	94	3	15	78
1984	26	72	89	10	20	75
1983	11	88	88	10	31	63
1982	45	53	84	14	34	60
1981	34	64	81	15	31	63

Interest Group Ratings

Year	ADA	ACU	AFL-CIO	CCUS
1990	100	4	100	21
1989	80	0	92	30
1988	100	0	100	15
1987	96	9	88	7
1986	100	0	93	17
1985	85	0	88	14
1984	95	13	100	38
1983	90	17	88	10
1982	60	27	80	27
1981	70	7	93	0

21 Lamar Smith (R)

Of San Antonio — Elected 1986

Born: Nov. 19, 1947, San Antonio, Texas.
Education: Yale U., B.A. 1969; Southern Methodist U., J.D. 1975.
Occupation: Lawyer; rancher.
Family: Widowed; two children.
Religion: Christian Scientist.
Political Career: Bexar County Republican Party chairman, 1978-81; Texas House, 1981-82; Bexar County Commission, 1983-85.
Capitol Office: 422 Cannon Bldg. 20515; 225-4236.

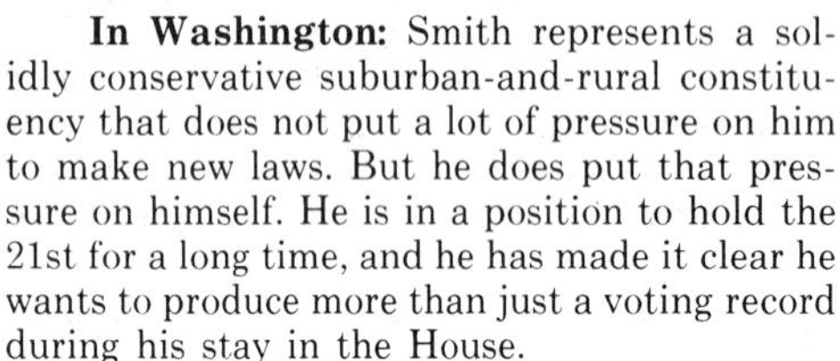

In Washington: Smith represents a solidly conservative suburban-and-rural constituency that does not put a lot of pressure on him to make new laws. But he does put that pressure on himself. He is in a position to hold the 21st for a long time, and he has made it clear he wants to produce more than just a voting record during his stay in the House.

Like many Texans, Smith has an interest in immigration, and he was in a better position than most to look into such issues as ranking Republican on the Immigration Subcommittee in the 101st Congress. Smith is concerned that higher immigration would increase joblessness, reduce wages and increase crime. "If you favor increasing immigration," he said, "you have to take responsibility for the consequences."

When the House passed its immigration measure in 1990 it rejected a number of Smith amendments. Smith sought to limit total immigration to 630,000 a year, the limit set in the Senate bill and favored by the White House. Another Smith amendment that was rejected would have ordered increased federal funds to states to pay for the education and health costs for newly legalized aliens.

Smith did support a number of provisions ultimately included in the legislation, such as streamlining the deportation process for criminal aliens; granting immigration officials greater arrest authority; and adding 20 new judges to speed deportation hearings.

Smith came to Washington in 1987 also voicing concerns about ethical standards in Congress. In particular, he wanted to restrict the lobbying activities of former members of Congress — the so-called revolving-door problem — and he cosponsored legislation with Democratic Rep. Barney Frank of Massachusetts to bring that about. The bill cleared Congress, but was later killed by President Reagan. A similar bill slowing the revolving door was ultimately enacted as part of the pay-and-ethics package cleared at the end of 1989.

Smith takes pride in having passed a bill of his own in his first term, and while it was not a major deed, it did signal his desire to move legislation. The bill authorized the Park Service to accept the donation of a 67,000-acre ranch next to Texas' Big Bend National Park.

At Home: If Smith's Yale background and polished manner are not the first things you would expect from a West Texas pol, he has made them work for him. When the 21st was open in 1986, he aggressively courted rural voters; his two re-elections have been non-events.

Smith spent a year in the Texas House and two years on the Bexar County Commission, representing San Antonio suburbs. In 1985, when GOP Rep. Tom Loeffler announced plans to leave the 21st for a gubernatorial campaign, Smith announced his candidacy immediately.

Smith was the moderate in the GOP House runoff against Van Archer, a San Antonio city councilman. Smith finished first by a modest margin in the initial GOP primary and took 53 percent of the runoff vote against Archer.

In the primary and runoff, Smith had to overcome questions about his support of legal abortion (Archer opposed it) and his affiliation with Christian Science. Critics said his religion would prevent him from voting for medical care appropriations — a problem in a district where a medical equipment company is the largest private employer.

But Smith dealt successfully with these problems, and benefited from contacts he made in three years as Bexar County Republican chairman. He had the active support of U.S. Sen. Phil Gramm, for whom he had organized Bexar County in the 1984 campaign.

His Democratic opponent was former state Sen. Pete Snelson, whose political base in Midland, at the western end of the district, positioned him to play to lingering rural perceptions of Smith as an elitist, big-city lawyer.

But Snelson was plagued by debt from previous campaigns. Smith cast himself as fiscally more conservative and signed a no-tax-increase pledge. He won San Antonio and Midland, overcoming Snelson's rural support.

Texas 21

San Antonio Suburbs; San Angelo; Midland

Spanning 26 whole counties and part of another, the 21st extends from the suburbs of San Antonio 500 miles west across Texas ranch land to the Mexican border. Republicans are not the majority party by registration, but strong GOP candidates run well nearly everywhere in the district.

More than a quarter of the vote is cast in Bexar County, much of that in a predominantly white-collar portion of northern San Antonio that is the 21st's largest population center. These strongly Republican, upper-income suburbanites are the sort of people who gave Lamar Smith his start in local politics.

Across the district from San Antonio lies another Republican redoubt — Midland County. The city of Midland is the white-collar administrative center for the vast oil fields of the Permian Basin in West Texas; scores of oil companies maintain offices here. Despite the oil industry's woes, Midland County's faith in the GOP has not wavered; it gave Republican Rep. Beau Boulter 63 percent of Midland's vote in his 1988 Senate challenge to Lloyd Bentsen.

Slightly larger and somewhat less Republican than Midland is San Angelo (Tom Green County), also in the northern part of the 21st. The city bills itself as "the sheep and wool capital" of the nation and is a center for cattle, goat and sheep raising and wool processing.

There are few other population centers; the dry range land of the rural counties is best suited to grazing and oil drilling. Unlike most other rural parts of the old Confederacy, this area has a long tradition of supporting Republicans that stems from the anti-slavery Germans who settled it in the mid-1800s.

Hispanics are nearly 25 percent of the district's population. Most favor Democrats, but their turnout rate is low.

Population: 526,846. White 469,790 (89%), Black 15,213 (3%), Other 4,132 (1%). Spanish origin 100,455 (19%). 18 and over 381,130 (72%), 65 and over 63,596 (12%). Median age: 31.

Committees

Judiciary (9th of 13 Republicans)
Economic & Commercial Law; International Law, Immigration & Refugees

Science, Space & Technology (11th of 19 Republicans)
Energy; Space

Select Children, Youth & Families (5th of 14 Republicans)

Elections

1990 General		
Lamar Smith (R)	144,570	(75%)
Kirby J. Roberts (D)	48,585	(25%)
1988 General		
Lamar Smith (R)	203,989	(93%)
James A. Robinson (LIBERT)	14,801	(7%)

Previous Winning Percentages: **1986** (61%)

District Vote For President

	1988	1984	1980	1976
D	78,971 (29%)	56,785 (22%)	53,079 (28%)	60,148 (37%)
R	192,335 (71%)	200,152 (78%)	131,809 (69%)	99,127 (62%)
I			4,644 (2%)	

Campaign Finance

	Receipts	Receipts from PACs	Expend-itures
1990			
Smith (R)	$679,487	$130,230 (19%)	$399,059
Roberts (D)	$15,763	$43 (0%)	$15,732
1988			
Smith (R)	$567,737	$97,832 (17%)	$418,989

Key Votes

1991	
Authorize use of force against Iraq	Y
1990	
Support constitutional amendment on flag desecration	Y
Pass family and medical leave bill over Bush veto	Y
Reduce SDI funding	N
Allow abortions in overseas military facilities	N
Approve budget summit plan for spending and taxing	N
Approve civil rights bill	N
1989	
Halt production of B-2 stealth bomber at 13 planes	N
Oppose capital gains tax cut	N
Approve federal abortion funding in rape or incest cases	N
Approve pay raise and revision of ethics rules	Y
Pass Democratic minimum wage plan over Bush veto	N

Voting Studies

	Presidential Support		Party Unity		Conservative Coalition	
Year	**S**	**O**	**S**	**O**	**S**	**O**
1990	68	31	82	13	91	6
1989	80	14	85	8	95	2
1988	66	32	91	7	97	0
1987	74	25	81	14	95	2

Interest Group Ratings

Year	ADA	ACU	AFL-CIO	CCUS
1990	11	83	25	86
1989	0	93	0	100
1988	5	100	23	92
1987	0	96	6	93

22 Tom DeLay (R)

Of Sugar Land — Elected 1984

Born: April 8, 1947, Laredo, Texas.
Education: Attended Baylor U., 1965-67; U. of Houston, B.S. 1970.
Occupation: Pest control company owner.
Family: Wife, Christine Ann Furrh; one child.
Religion: Baptist.
Political Career: Texas House, 1979-85.
Capitol Office: 308 Cannon Bldg. 20515; 225-5951.

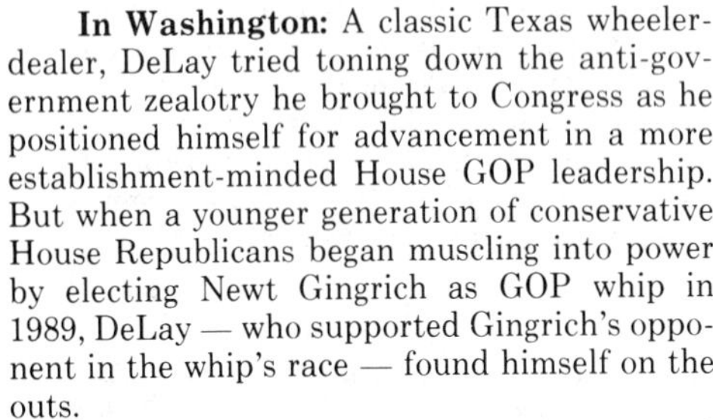

In Washington: A classic Texas wheeler-dealer, DeLay tried toning down the anti-government zealotry he brought to Congress as he positioned himself for advancement in a more establishment-minded House GOP leadership. But when a younger generation of conservative House Republicans began muscling into power by electing Newt Gingrich as GOP whip in 1989, DeLay — who supported Gingrich's opponent in the whip's race — found himself on the outs.

DeLay went to work bridging the gap, and by the start of the 102nd Congress, it was clear he had succeeded. He won the chairmanship of the House Republican Study Committee, a conservative policy group previously headed by Californian Robert K. Dornan. Though the job is not officially within the GOP leadership hierarchy, winning it must have come as a relief for DeLay, whose sights have been trained on a leadership post almost from the day he arrived in Congress.

In his first term, DeLay lined up the votes he needed to win a seat on the GOP panel that determines committee assignments, and passed the word to a competing colleague that the contest was over. In his second term, he was named an assistant regional whip, and he impressed many Republicans with his political instincts and vote-counting skills. He earned a deputy whip slot at the start of the 101st Congress. But then, DeLay decided to become chief lieutenant for Illinois' Edward Madigan in his 1989 campaign against Gingrich for the vacant post of whip.

DeLay's conservatism, age and status as a Southerner might have made him a natural ally of Gingrich. But Madigan was the favorite of the establishment leaders DeLay had courted since his freshman term, and the chances were good that if Madigan moved up, so would DeLay. When Madigan lost, Gingrich put his allies at the top of the whip structure, costing DeLay his deputy whip's job. (DeLay still had a plum committee assignment — Appropriations — that he won in 1987.)

DeLay's return to the more confrontational wing of the House GOP became plain as the debate on the 1990 budget evolved. When President Bush seemed to waver on whether he would accept a tax increase, DeLay expressed confidence that it was not so. "My president, who I believed when he said no more taxes . . . is not going to raise taxes," DeLay said. Weeks later, DeLay joined the uprising led by Gingrich and voted against the budget summit agreement worked out between top congressional leaders and the president.

By early 1991, DeLay was publicly criticizing President Bush's call for a study of how to enact a capital gains tax cut. "We usually do studies around here to keep things from coming to the floor," he said after the president's State of the Union address. "If this one lasts longer than 30 days, then we all know why they did it."

Throughout his House tenure, DeLay has been known for his impassioned opposition to government regulation, a conviction he developed when he was in the pest control business in Texas. He has issued detailed position papers calling for new deregulation of trucking, airlines, railroads, energy companies and banks, relaxation of environmental, health and safety laws, and scaling back of antitrust provisions. Declaring regulation anticompetitive, DeLay founded a grass-roots organization to fight "red tape."

He and his antiregulatory allies scored an important victory in 1989, winning repeal of tax rules designed to weed out discrimination in employee-benefit plans known as Section 89. Small businesses had launched a major lobbying campaign against the rules, which they said were overly burdensome. When their campaign got nowhere with the Ways and Means Committee, DeLay offered a repeal amendment during the Appropriations Committee's consideration of the usually non-controversial Treasury-Postal Service spending bill.

The temporary repeal was initially turned back on a 24-24 vote, but with the help of several late arrivals, a second vote gave DeLay a 29-26 victory. The action was a major blow to Ways and Means Chairman Dan Rostenkowski,

Texas 22

Southwest Houston and Suburbs; Fort Bend and Brazoria Counties

The 22nd District is a testament to suburban Houston's phenomenal growth over the past two decades. During the 1970s, the district was focused within the city, and the area DeLay now represents was a sparsely populated corner of it. Today that same territory has enough people to be a constituency itself, and DeLay represents more people outside the city limits than within them.

The 22nd's communities are highly transient and bound together by few ties of tradition. What unites them is a universally conservative outlook and a GOP preference.

The part of Houston that remains in the district is largely affluent and white-collar; it casts roughly 40 percent of the vote. Some of the district's most affluent homes lie at its northern border, near the exclusive Galleria shopping mall.

Houston's sprawl has engulfed established residential towns such as Bellaire and West University Place, once considered outlying suburbs, and they are included in the 22nd. Farther out, it also includes Missouri City, a burgeoning community divided between Harris and Fort Bend counties.

Moving south, the district encompasses all of Fort Bend County. Parts of the county are still rural and small-town in character and have little to do with Houston; here rice, cotton and oil spark the local economy, along with some cattle ranching. But high-priced residential subdivisions are becoming the norm. The influx of Houston professionals more than doubled Fort Bend's population in the 1970s, and nearly doubled it again in the 1980s.

Fort Bend County occasionally backs a moderate Democrat running statewide, but it has not gone Democratic for president since 1964. In 1988, the county voted for Lloyd Bentsen for Senate and George Bush for president.

The 22nd also takes in northeast Brazoria County, where towns such as Alvin have a conservative, blue-collar Democratic bent.

Population: 526,602. White 427,161 (81%), Black 50,585 (10%), Other 15,203 (3%). Spanish origin 71,439 (14%). 18 and over 381,492 (72%), 65 and over 29,577 (6%). Median age: 28.

who elected not to resist further. The DeLay amendment became law, and two months later a permanent repeal was enacted.

DeLay's pro-business predilection was on display again during debate on the 1990 parental leave bill. "This bill is not going to be the doom of our economy," he said. "But it is another nail in the coffin of competitiveness and productivity."

In the 99th Congress, he was among those who blocked consideration by the full House of a parental leave bill. He also worked furiously to defeat legislation to provide workers with 60 days' notice before a plant is closed.

When it comes to bringing money home to Texas, however, DeLay will often set aside his limited-government views. In 1990 he opposed two of three attempts to cut funding for the superconducting super collider (SSC), which is being built in Texas. He voted only for a two percent cut in SSC funding. DeLay's official biography boasts of numerous Texas projects he has helped fund: $700,000 for Houston's "Operation Siege," an antidrug program; $1 million for an antidrug research program at Texas A&M; $13 million for an airport in his hometown; $11 million for Freeport Harbor; and nearly $1 million for a new Army National Guard Armory.

On the Appropriations Subcommittee on Transportation, DeLay generally advocates allowing the private sector to supply mass transit services, but he also works to bring Houston what he considers its "fair return" on tax payments. However, in the 1990 House-Senate conference on the transportation spending bill, DeLay raised eyebrows by lobbying to lower the Senate appropriation for Houston from $38 million to $30 million. An amazed New Jersey Sen. Frank Lautenberg, chairman of the Senate subcommittee, remarked, "This is a novel experience," and okayed DeLay's request. DeLay said Houston was not spending previously appropriated money fast enough and added, "We don't want to appear greedy."

At Home: When Republican Rep. Ron Paul announced his candidacy for the Senate in 1984, DeLay quickly became the front-runner to fill the 22nd District seat. A six-year veteran of the Texas House, DeLay had already represented parts of the 22nd's constituency, and his efforts to scale back the size of government during his days in the Legislature stood him in good stead in a district whose residents demand an adherence to conservative orthodoxy.

But DeLay did not capture the GOP nomination easily. The 11th-hour entrance of J. C. Helms, a wealthy real-estate developer from Bellaire, gave DeLay a serious scare. Helms had had some success in the neighboring 25th two years earlier, finishing first in the GOP primary but failing to convert on his momentum in the runoff. His alliance with hard-right conservatives in the Harris County (Houston) Republican Party further heightened the impression that he might manage to force a runoff with DeLay.

Helms sought to outflank DeLay on the right, casting himself as the natural philosophical heir to the libertarian Paul. DeLay offered a more mainstream conservative approach. He cited his experience as owner of a pest control company to demonstrate knowledge of small business, and called for a balanced budget.

Helms created a stir late in the campaign by running radio ads accusing DeLay of being late in paying payroll taxes from his business — a charge DeLay acknowledged while reminding Helms that the taxes were eventually paid. Visiting up to 60 homes a day, DeLay held his own in Harris County and won easily in his home base of Fort Bend. He clinched the GOP nomination with 54 percent. Since then, his elections have been a breeze.

Committee

Appropriations (18th of 22 Republicans)
District of Columbia; Military Construction; Transportation

Elections

1990 General		
Tom DeLay (R)	93,425	(71%)
Bruce Director (D)	37,721	(29%)
1988 General		
Tom DeLay (R)	125,733	(67%)
Wayne Walker (D)	58,471	(31%)

Previous Winning Percentages: 1986 (72%) **1984** (65%)

District Vote For President

	1988	1984	1980	1976
D	68,391 (38%)	55,587 (30%)	48,188 (30%)	50,146 (37%)
R	112,088 (62%)	128,971 (70%)	104,147 (65%)	83,150 (62%)
I			5,927 (4%)	

Campaign Finance

	Receipts	Receipts from PACs	Expend-itures
1990			
DeLay (R)	$324,134	$168,475 (52%)	$297,153
1988			
DeLay (R)	$364,837	$171,650 (47%)	$361,255
Walker (D)	$112,649	$1,500 (1%)	$109,004

Key Votes

1991	
Authorize use of force against Iraq	Y
1990	
Support constitutional amendment on flag desecration	Y
Pass family and medical leave bill over Bush veto	N
Reduce SDI funding	N
Allow abortions in overseas military facilities	N
Approve budget summit plan for spending and taxing	N
Approve civil rights bill	N
1989	
Halt production of B-2 stealth bomber at 13 planes	N
Oppose capital gains tax cut	N
Approve federal abortion funding in rape or incest cases	N
Approve pay raise and revision of ethics rules	Y
Pass Democratic minimum wage plan over Bush veto	N

Voting Studies

	Presidential Support		Party Unity		Conservative Coalition	
Year	**S**	**O**	**S**	**O**	**S**	**O**
1990	83	16	91	5	98	2
1989	79	19	87	8	90	5
1988	78	18	88	7	97	0
1987	78	19	91	5	100	0
1986	83	14	91	4	100	0
1985	85	13	87	7	96	4

Interest Group Ratings

Year	ADA	ACU	AFL-CIO	CCUS
1990	6	92	8	93
1989	0	96	0	80
1988	0	100	0	92
1987	0	100	0	93
1986	0	100	7	94
1985	5	100	0	95

23 Albert G. Bustamante (D)

Of San Antonio — Elected 1984

Born: April 8, 1935, Asherton, Texas.
Education: Sul Ross State College, B.A. 1961.
Military Service: Army, 1954-56.
Occupation: Teacher; Congressional aide.
Family: Wife, Rebecca Pounders; three children.
Religion: Roman Catholic.
Political Career: Bexar County Commission, 1972-78; Bexar County judge, 1978-83.
Capitol Office: 1116 Longworth Bldg. 20515; 225-4511.

In Washington: Bustamante's generally liberal orientation surfaces occasionally during debates on U.S. defense and foreign policies. A member of the House Armed Services Committee, Bustamante opposed the January 1991 resolution authorizing President Bush to use military force against Iraq. Unlike most members from the nation's southern rim, Bustamante had a skeptical view of U.S. aid to the Nicaraguan contra forces in the late 1980s, and twice voted against it.

However, the San Antonio-based 23rd District Bustamante represents has a large military sector with five bases and a population of military retirees. He is thus constrained from an activist role in high-profile defense policy debates, and devotes much of his effort to defending his local military interests.

Bustamante is active on issues affecting soldiers and their families in the 23rd. He has prodded the Defense Department to increase subsidies, or "impact aid," for school districts attached to the Lackland, Fort Sam Houston and Randolph bases.

Although Bustamante voted against the war resolution, he gave his backing to Bush shortly after that: "It's now time to unite behind the president's decision and commit ourselves to providing our troops with every available resource...," Bustamante said. He also proposed legislation to delay cutbacks in the military personnel health care program and in the military inpatient mental health program until the end of the Persian Gulf conflict.

Though not asserting himself in weapons systems debates, Bustamante has seized on some esoteric issues. On both Armed Services and Government Operations, he is on subcommittees dealing with military nuclear materials; he spoke out on environmental and safety problems in U.S. nuclear production plants early in 1988, months before the problems showed up in headlines. Citing safety concerns, Bustamante worked to delay funding for the proposed Special Isotope Separation project in Idaho — later put on hold.

While stressing defense, Bustamante hardly ignores issues pertaining to his fellow Hispanics. A former migrant farm worker and a member of the House Select Committee on Hunger, Bustamante has tried to increase nutrition funding for the Hispanics who make up well over half of his constituency. He has focused attention on the south Texas "colonias," temporary rural slums where Hispanic immigrants live in primitive conditions.

A party loyalist, Bustamante organized the House Hispanic Caucus in April 1989 to send a telegram of support to embattled House Speaker Jim Wright of Texas. However, he remained close to the new leadership after Wright resigned. In December 1990, Bustamante was named to the House Democratic Steering and Policy Committee.

At Home: Bustamante's election, assured when he ousted veteran Democratic Rep. Abraham Kazen Jr. in a 1984 primary, was another step in southwest Texas Hispanics' drive to wrest key offices from "Anglo" control.

Bustamante grew up as a migrant laborer, picking fruit and grain crops. Kazen, of Lebanese descent, came from a family associated with the Anglo establishment that has long dominated many of Texas' border towns.

Bustamante tried to paint Kazen as inaccessible and ineffective; Kazen stressed his seniority and influence. But Bustamante clearly needed to rally Hispanics. "Help me on Cinco de Mayo [May 5, a Mexican national holiday as well as Texas' primary date] to declare our independence from an old political family who has controlled the destiny of this area," he told a predominantly Mexican-American audience.

Bustamante got an impressive 59 percent of the primary vote in the 23rd, where 1983 redistricting changes had boosted the Mexican-American population to some 56 percent. Once past the primary, he was home free. He has faced GOP opposition only twice and won soundly each time.

Texas 23

Southwest — San Antonio Suburbs; Laredo

A diverse patch of southwestern Texas, the 23rd stretches from the white-collar suburbs of San Antonio in Bexar County to the rural, overwhelmingly Hispanic terrain near the Mexican border.

That mixture generally yields Democratic victories. But the 23rd has been competitive in recent statewide races. In 1988 presidential balloting, five of the nine counties in the 23rd went Republican.

The San Antonio-area portion of the 23rd includes communities such as Windcrest, a haven for military retirees with a conservative bias. This area also boasts five military installations, including Brooks and Randolph Air Force bases, which are crucial economic and political forces. The suburbs of San Antonio roll west to the fringes of Medina County.

But the last redistricting removed 35,000 GOP-minded residents of northern Bexar County and added Val Verde County, a majority Hispanic area on the Mexican border. That change pushed the 23rd's Hispanic population to 56 percent.

Val Verde and the other Hispanic counties help ensure the district's Democratic cast. Webb County, where nine out of every 10 residents are Hispanic, gave Democrat Lloyd Bentsen 85 percent in his 1988 Senate re-election and gave the Democratic presidential ticket 70 percent.

Webb County's Laredo, with 123,000 people, is the population center in the southern part of the 23rd. A gateway for trade and tourism with Mexico, about half of all cross-border truck traffic and much of the commercial rail traffic occurs between Laredo and its sister city across the border, Nuevo Laredo. The cities call themselves "Los dos Laredos." Surrounding Laredo are vegetable-growing farmlands irrigated with water from the Rio Grande. Cattle ranching, and oil and gas exploration are in the dry areas north and east.

Population: 526,746. White 440,544 (84%), Black 21,633 (4%), Other 4,814 (1%). Spanish origin 296,148 (56%). 18 and over 332,851 (63%), 65 and over 36,920 (7%). Median age: 25.

Committees

Armed Services (20th of 33 Democrats)
Military Personnel & Compensation; Procurement & Military Nuclear Systems; Readiness

Government Operations (16th of 25 Democrats)
Commerce, Consumer & Monetary Affairs; Environment, Energy & Natural Resources

Select Hunger (13th of 22 Democrats)
Domestic

Elections

1990 General		
Albert G. Bustamante (D)	71,052	(63%)
Jerry Gonzales (R)	40,856	(37%)
1988 General		
Albert G. Bustamante (D)	116,423	(65%)
Jerry Gonzales (R)	60,559	(34%)

Previous Winning Percentages: **1986** (91%) **1984** (100%)

District Vote For President

	1988	1984	1980	1976
D	93,074 (50%)	66,148 (41%)	54,983 (48%)	52,708 (59%)
R	94,826 (50%)	95,732 (59%)	55,483 (49%)	36,020 (40%)
I			2,504 (2%)	

Campaign Finance

	Receipts	Receipts from PACs	Expend-itures
1990			
Bustamante (D)	$370,750	$192,725 (52%)	$236,046
Gonzales (R)	$22,559	$500 (2%)	$22,428
1988			
Bustamante (D)	$280,485	$155,786 (56%)	$187,302
Gonzales (R)	$6,573	0	$6,365

Key Votes

1991	
Authorize use of force against Iraq	N
1990	
Support constitutional amendment on flag desecration	Y
Pass family and medical leave bill over Bush veto	Y
Reduce SDI funding	Y
Allow abortions in overseas military facilities	?
Approve budget summit plan for spending and taxing	Y
Approve civil rights bill	Y
1989	
Halt production of B-2 stealth bomber at 13 planes	N
Oppose capital gains tax cut	Y
Approve federal abortion funding in rape or incest cases	Y
Approve pay raise and revision of ethics rules	Y
Pass Democratic minimum wage plan over Bush veto	Y

Voting Studies

	Presidential Support		Party Unity		Conservative Coalition	
Year	S	O	S	O	S	O
1990	25	69	85	7	39	48
1989	40	56	86	7	41	54
1988	25	66	88	4	45	47
1987	29	67	84	7	67	26
1986	32	63	82	9	58	30
1985	34	64	85	10	51	44

Interest Group Ratings

Year	ADA	ACU	AFL-CIO	CCUS
1990	50	17	92	36
1989	80	4	100	30
1988	70	8	100	21
1987	76	0	93	14
1986	50	33	100	20
1985	65	19	88	24

24 Martin Frost (D)

Of Dallas — Elected 1978

Born: Jan. 1, 1942, Glendale, Calif.
Education: U. of Missouri, B.A., B.J. 1964; Georgetown U., J.D. 1970.
Military Service: Army Reserve, 1966-72.
Occupation: Lawyer.
Family: Wife, Valerie Hall; three children.
Religion: Jewish.
Political Career: Sought Democratic nomination for U.S. House, 1974.
Capitol Office: 2459 Rayburn Bldg. 20515; 225-3605.

In Washington: A tumultuous 101st Congress saw Frost lose his mentor and face the prospect of losing much of his congressional district. Former Speaker Jim Wright, once Frost's Fort Worth neighbor and ally, was forced from office in 1989 amid allegations of ethical improprieties. Census results and Texas redistricting prospects then threatened to weaken Frost's re-election prospects. The Legislature may well draw upon the black and Hispanic voters who constitute almost half the 24th District population in creating a new, minority-dominated district in Dallas.

It is the redistricting process that seems likely to dominate Frost's time and activity during the 102nd Congress. "I think there should be a minority district and I am assuming that there will be one," said Frost in 1989.

Frost is also a proponent of efforts to get the Commerce Department to adjust the 1990 census to redress a possible undercounting of minorities. Frost was dissatisfied with initial guidelines established by the department, which he said weighed against an adjustment. Explaining why the administration proposed the guidelines, Frost said, "Clearly, an adjustment would benefit Democrats, and it would be harmful to Republicans." The department later said it would decide by July 15, 1991, whether to use its authority to adjust the census tally to correct for undercounting.

Ensuring himself a role in redistricting politics in Texas and throughout the country, Frost was appointed in December 1990 by Speaker Thomas S. Foley to head IMPAC 2000, a Democratic group aimed at helping the party benefit from redistricting.

As part of his efforts to help the Democrats in redistricting, Frost managed to go a bit too far. He heads a Democratic Caucus panel that offered a proposal in December 1990 that would have allowed members of Congress to accept unlimited contributions to pay legal costs of redistricting. But House Democrats ditched the idea after it met with harsh criticism that it looked like a slush fund for incumbents.

Frost played many angles to make his way in the House, but the one he played the most was his close association with Wright. When Frost came to Congress in 1979, Wright was in the early years of his tenure as majority leader. When Wright became Speaker in the 100th Congress, it was almost a dream come true for Frost. But he enjoyed the Speaker's ear for just two short years before Wright's forced departure.

A shrewd institutional player, Frost still holds seats on Rules and House Administration, where he can have an impact in his own right. And party leaders can still count on Frost despite Wright's absence; Frost backed the Democratic majority more than 90 percent of the time in 1990. A desire by the Democratic Caucus to be done with the Wright era, however, may have factored into Frost's failure in June 1989 to win the post of caucus vice chairman, one of several leadership jobs that came open in the wake of Wright's departure. Frost ran second in the four-way race, but finished far behind Californian Vic Fazio.

Foley continued to reward Frost for his party service and loyalty, naming him in April 1990 to head a task force to help the new Eastern Europe democracies. The task force visited Czechoslovakia, Poland and Hungary and set up a program of technological assistance for the newly formed parliaments of those countries.

Like most members of Texas' delegation, Frost also spent part of his time helping make the case that his home state should be chosen for the multibillion-dollar superconducting super collider. Toward the end of the 100th Congress, the Department of Energy chose Texas for the giant atom-smasher. In the 101st Congress, Frost continued his efforts in behalf of the super collider, engineering a last-minute deal that helped avert defeat for the project. The House in June 1989 resoundingly rejected an effort to eliminate construction funds for the project.

In the 100th Congress, one of his efforts

Texas 24

South Dallas and Western Suburbs

The 24th contains the largest concentration of black and Hispanic voters anywhere in the Dallas area.

The black population — comprising about one-third of the district total — is mostly at the eastern end of the 24th, south of the Trinity River in Dallas. Hispanics, who account for roughly 15 percent, are more numerous in the central part of the district. The suburbs on the western edge of the 24th, such as Irving and Grand Prairie, are mostly white.

Predominantly blue-collar Grand Prairie hosts two subsidiaries of the LTV Corp., the aerospace giant in Chapter 11 bankruptcy proceedings. While the parent company's fate has yet to be determined, Grand Prairie's two plants — one makes aircraft products and the other produces missiles and electronics — are on solid footing. However, much depends on the status of the B-2 bomber. Some of the district's most affluent — and most Republican — residents make their homes in northern Irving. The home field of football's Dallas Cowboys — Texas Stadium — is here, benefiting the community.

Both suburbs contain many factory workers and laborers in the construction trades. Another important employer is the sprawling Dallas-Fort Worth Airport, part of which is located in the district's northwestern corner.

The 1983 round of redistricting made minor adjustments in the 24th's boundaries. Map makers removed the district's share of Arlington, uniting it with the rest of the city in the neighboring 26th. In turn, a section of southwest Dallas County was brought into Frost's constituency from the 6th. This added territory includes communities such as DeSoto and Cedar Hill, areas with a substantial blue-collar presence that are caught up in southwest Dallas' urban sprawl.

The heavy minority influence helps make the southwestern Dallas portions of the district predictably Democratic; Grand Prairie and Irving also favor Democrats most of the time. Many of the district's white precincts gave George Bush solid majorities in 1988, but typically, these precincts tend to divide about evenly between the parties in statewide contests. In 1988, Michael S. Dukakis won the 24th with 53 percent, getting a boost from the minority-dominated areas of Dallas.

Population: 527,267. White 309,349 (59%), Black 167,099 (32%), Other 6,164 (1%). Spanish origin 69,340 (13%). 18 and over 352,993 (67%), 65 and over 36,962 (7%). Median age: 27.

was to try to protect low-income housing in the 24th. Working with fellow Texan Mickey Leland, he offered a successful amendment to the HUD appropriations bill barring use of agency funds to demolish 2,600 units of public housing in West Dallas and 1,000 in Houston.

In 1988 Frost also worked on legislation to prevent LTV, a major corporation in his district, from terminating health and life insurance for retirees after filing for bankruptcy under Chapter 11. The bill required companies to go before a bankruptcy court hearing before altering such benefits. Frost also helped coordinate Texas efforts on the controversial B-2 stealth bomber; major subcontract work on the B-2 is being done by LTV.

Frost's soft voice and shy smile suggest a self-effacing personality. But he is a man of calculating ambition and no small amount of self-esteem. Even some who admire his political instincts consider him at times too strong-willed, and wanting in finesse.

As ingratiating as he was with Wright, Frost has crossed swords with some other powerful members. Frost's efforts to defend industrial development bonds held up progress on tax bills in the early 1980s; the moves did not do much to endear him to Ways and Means Chairman Dan Rostenkowski.

In 1983, Frost took advantage of his place on Rules to win one of that panel's two allotted seats on Budget; the next year he was at the center of a complicated debate over the House Budget chairmanship. Frost entered the contest, saying he was "someone from the center of the party who can unite all factions within the House." But it soon was evident that William H. Gray III of Pennsylvania already had united all the factions he needed; Frost withdrew, admitting that "the votes simply are not there."

At Home: Frost got to Congress in 1978 by defeating incumbent Dale Milford in a primary, something he had failed to do four years earlier. Milford, a former television weatherman, won the seat in 1972. But Frost was encouraged to mount a challenge in 1974 after redistricting pared away conservative suburban areas while adding black sections of Dallas much less favorable to the incumbent.

Frost complained that Milford was too

supportive of the Nixon administration. But the incumbent withstood the challenge to win the 1974 Democratic primary with 58 percent of the vote. Frost bypassed a rematch in 1976 to run Jimmy Carter's campaign in north Texas.

But two years later, he tried again, reviving complaints that Milford was too conservative. Moving beyond personal door-to-door campaigning, Frost built an effective precinct organization. He also got the support of the state AFL-CIO and two of the largest newspapers in the Dallas-Fort Worth area. Drawing 55 percent, he beat Milford.

Frost's Republican rival that November tried to turn the tables, claiming that Frost was a tool of organized labor and too liberal for the district. The Democrat trailed in returns from Tarrant County, but offset the deficit in his home base of Dallas County to win 54 percent.

For a moment in 1982, it seemed Frost might be in some political trouble. The Legislature had redrawn his district to be 64 percent black and Hispanic, and professor Lucy Patterson, the first black woman elected to the Dallas City Council, planned a primary challenge to him, hoping minority voters would unite behind her.

Frost reacted quickly. He gathered early endorsements from many leaders in the black and Hispanic communities. And then, the district's boundaries were changed again before the Democratic primary. A three-judge federal panel undid the Legislature's work, making the 24th a white-majority district with a combined black and Hispanic population just under 50 percent.

Under the court-drawn lines, there were not enough minority voters in the 24th to sustain Patterson's primary challenge. She ultimately switched parties and ran as a Republican. Frost swamped her, taking more than 70 percent of the vote.

That experience bolstered Frost's confidence for 1984. He spent much of his time early in the year organizing the Texas presidential primary campaign of Colorado Democratic Sen. Gary Hart, then signed on as a state coordinator for Walter F. Mondale after Hart was beaten. Frost won re-election with 59 percent while the district was going to President Reagan. In 1986, he reached 67 percent; in the next two elections, the Republicans left him alone entirely.

Committees

House Administration (10th of 15 Democrats)
Elections; Libraries & Memorials; Office Systems; Campaign Finance Reform

Rules (4th of 9 Democrats)
Legislative Process

Elections

1990 General		
Martin Frost (D)	86,297	(100%)
1988 General		
Martin Frost (D)	135,794	(93%)
Leo Sadovy (LIBERT)	10,841	(7%)

Previous Winning Percentages: **1986** (67%) **1984** (59%) **1982** (73%) **1980** (61%) **1978** (54%)

District Vote For President

	1988	1984	1980	1976
D	97,339 (53%)	85,078 (47%)	74,070 (50%)	73,589 (56%)
R	87,596 (47%)	96,596 (53%)	70,634 (47%)	56,237 (43%)
I			2,843 (2%)	

Campaign Finance

	Receipts	Receipts from PACs	Expend-itures
1990			
Frost (D)	$679,688	$411,405 (61%)	$597,310
1988			
Frost (D)	$590,973	$298,373 (50%)	$438,949

Key Votes

1991	
Authorize use of force against Iraq	Y
1990	
Support constitutional amendment on flag desecration	N
Pass family and medical leave bill over Bush veto	Y
Reduce SDI funding	Y
Allow abortions in overseas military facilities	Y
Approve budget summit plan for spending and taxing	Y
Approve civil rights bill	Y
1989	
Halt production of B-2 stealth bomber at 13 planes	N
Oppose capital gains tax cut	Y
Approve federal abortion funding in rape or incest cases	Y
Approve pay raise and revision of ethics rules	Y
Pass Democratic minimum wage plan over Bush veto	Y

Voting Studies

	Presidential Support		Party Unity		Conservative Coalition	
Year	**S**	**O**	**S**	**O**	**S**	**O**
1990	22	77	91	5	43	57
1989	38	58	86	8	39	61
1988	21	66	84	5	37	42
1987	31	67	83	9	60	30
1986	23	66	74	11	52	38
1985	26	69	83	9	47	47
1984	33	48	63	14	42	47
1983	34	59	79	13	48	47
1982	34	58	82	12	40	59
1981	34	38	70	17	52	41

Interest Group Ratings

Year	ADA	ACU	AFL-CIO	CCUS
1990	67	8	100	14
1989	75	4	82	40
1988	70	9	92	23
1987	88	0	93	29
1986	45	26	73	43
1985	55	24	82	35
1984	65	25	100	36
1983	75	22	82	20
1982	70	10	85	23
1981	50	14	77	24

25 Michael A. Andrews (D)

Of Houston — Elected 1982

Born: Feb. 7, 1944, Houston, Texas.
Education: U. of Texas, B.A. 1967; Southern Methodist U., J.D. 1970.
Occupation: Lawyer.
Family: Wife, Ann Bowman; two children.
Religion: Episcopalian.
Political Career: Democratic nominee for U.S. House, 1980.
Capitol Office: 303 Cannon Bldg. 20515; 225-7508.

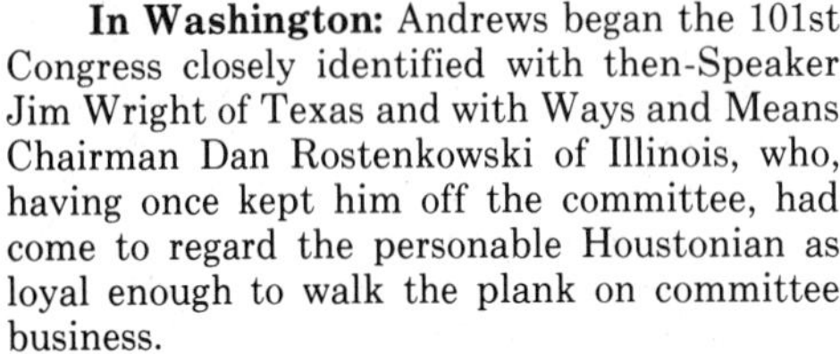

In Washington: Andrews began the 101st Congress closely identified with then-Speaker Jim Wright of Texas and with Ways and Means Chairman Dan Rostenkowski of Illinois, who, having once kept him off the committee, had come to regard the personable Houstonian as loyal enough to walk the plank on committee business.

One could scarcely hope for more powerful mentors. But within months, Wright became the first Speaker ever to resign under an ethics cloud. And Andrews found himself part of an intraparty rebellion against Rostenkowski on the biggest tax issue of the year: capital gains.

Andrews had promised to back Democratic colleague Ed Jenkins of Georgia on a bill reducing the rate on certain kinds of income from appreciating assets. That legislation was highly popular among Andrews' financial supporters back home, and for a time Rostenkowski had not clearly signaled his opposition.

When the chairman did weigh in against the cut, Andrews felt he could not renege. Standing with Jenkins, Andrews and four other Democrats enabled the committee's Republicans to report a deep cut in capital gains taxation to the floor in September of 1989, where it passed. The measure later died in the Senate, but Andrews was marked as part of the Gang of Six who "rolled Rosty."

Long regarded as an ambitious man with the looks and the yen to run for statewide office, Andrews has had to watch a few opportunities pass by. He might have run for the Senate if Texas Democrat Lloyd Bentsen had been elected vice president in 1988. He might have seen a new path had Democrat Ann W. Richards not been elected governor in 1990.

For the time being, Andrews has had to content himself with the tasks at hand, using his committee assignment to build his political treasury and seeking opportunities to raise his profile back home. He voted with most of the rest of the Texas Democrats in supporting the use of force in the Persian Gulf.

Andrews had some trouble getting his seat on Ways and Means, but once aboard he was eager to prove himself worthy by taking on two decidedly unattractive and politically risky assignments. He circumvented Southern opposition to a welfare bill and rounded up votes to defeat seniors' superhero Claude Pepper's crusade on behalf of long-term home health care.

The first mission came in late 1987, a year after Andrews made it onto Ways and Means. The committee was having trouble with its welfare-overhaul initiative. Southerners rebelled at Rostenkowski's attempt to wrap the welfare bill into a broad-ranging budget-reconciliation measure. They feared that a bill including both welfare and taxes would be fodder for vicious television ads by election opponents, and they joined Republicans in a vote that kept the welfare bill off the floor.

For seven weeks, Democratic leaders tried to find a way to bring the bill up on its own. They were determined not to allow the bill to be rewritten piecemeal on the floor, and were also intent on sidetracking an alternative welfare bill developed by conservative Democrats Charles W. Stenholm of Texas and Thomas R. Carper of Delaware that would have cost less than half the $6.2 billion version pushed by Ways and Means.

To the rescue came Andrews, with an amendment that would slice $500 million from the committee bill in ways that would ease the burden on states and limit welfare expansion. It mollified just enough Democrats. A rule allowing Andrews a floor vote (but denying Stenholm and Carper an opportunity) squeaked by, 213-206. It got no Republican votes, but 15 Southern Democrats switched their votes from the previous confrontation. Andrews' amendment was approved overwhelmingly and the welfare measure passed with a margin of 36 votes.

The next year, Rostenkowski appointed Andrews head of a task force to defeat Florida Democrat Pepper's initiative to provide long-term care at home to disabled and elderly people. Rostenkowski was furious that Pepper had used his Rules Committee chairmanship to bypass Ways and Means over the proposal to pay for the program by raising the Medicare tax

Texas 25

South Houston and Southeast Suburbs

The 25th contains all of Harris County south of the Houston Ship Channel, a waterway lined with heavy industry. The cities of Pasadena and Deer Park are filled with blue-collar workers employed at numerous local petrochemical facilities.

These working-class people are nearly all nominal Democrats, but they are not always automatic partisan voters. Ronald Reagan's conservative themes played well enough among blue-collar workers for him to carry the 25th narrowly in 1980 and 1984. He was also boosted by support from the more affluent parts of Pasadena, Deer Park and South Houston. But in 1988, George Bush could not quite match Reagan's appeal, and the district tipped Democratic for president.

Farther west in the district is a concentration of minority voters. Sunnyside, a predominantly black community, is one of Houston's most impoverished areas. The Brentwood neighborhood hosts a large number of middle-class black professionals. This part of the district is also home to the Houston Astrodome, Rice University and a large concentration of Jewish voters in Meyerland.

Blacks and Hispanics make up 39 percent of the district's population; among all the Houston-area districts, only central Houston's 18th has a higher minority percentage. The minority vote helps push the 25th into the Democratic column in most non-presidential contests.

Living in the southeastern corner of the 25th are many employees of NASA's Manned Spacecraft Center, which is across the district boundary in the 9th. But the district's largest single employer is the Texas Medical Center. Described as the largest medical complex in the world, it includes schools, research facilities and hospitals. The center's extensive facilities bring to nearly 30 the number of hospitals located within the 25th.

Population: 526,801. White 352,345 (67%), Black 131,660 (25%), Other 8,703 (2%). Spanish origin 72,400 (14%). 18 and over 366,175 (70%), 65 and over 31,561 (6%). Median age: 27.

some $28 billion over five years. Senior citizens deluged the Capitol with bags of green peppers to symbolize their support for the measure; Andrews said he felt "like cannon fodder" mobilizing opposition. In the end, however, enough members gulped at the cost to keep the bill off the floor by a vote of 169-243.

These tasks marked quite a turnaround in Rostenkowski's view of Andrews. In 1985, Wright, then Majority Leader and eager to place another Texan on Ways and Means, had sponsored Andrews for a place there. But Rostenkowski had his own candidate, Pennsylvania's William J. Coyne, and he maintained that Coyne was more of a party loyalist than Andrews, who had shown a tendency in his first term to pay more attention to the wishes of the Houston business community than to Democratic leaders. Coyne got the job.

Wright maintained his commitment to Andrews, however, and there was little question that the incoming Speaker would get his man on Ways and Means before very long. When a committee vacancy developed in mid-1986, Andrews applied for it, and nobody ran against him.

Passing his loyalty tests has not required Andrews to abandon his Houston interests. On Ways and Means, he helped win a change in 1988 in a provision of the 1986 tax-overhaul bill that would have increased tax collections on diesel fuel. Also, he joined with other oil-state members to overcome Rostenkowski's reluctance to repeal the windfall profits tax on oil as part of the 1988 omnibus trade bill.

In his previous assignment on Science and Technology, Andrews had been a protector of the Johnson Space Center, located in Houston. In 1986, he helped to ferret out and block a plan by NASA to move key work on the space station project from Houston to the space center in Huntsville, Ala. NASA's plan imperiled nearly 2,000 potential jobs as well as $1.5 billion in lost revenue for Houston, already wracked by depressed oil prices.

As chairman of the Congressional Sunbelt Caucus in the 100th Congress, Andrews pushed the group into a newly confrontational stance toward its more established regional rival, the Northeast-Midwest Congressional Coalition.

At Home: Andrews is a political consultant's dream. Handsome and articulate, he was born and educated in Texas and worked as an assistant district attorney in Houston before joining a private law firm. But he did not come by his House seat easily.

Andrews' quest for Congress began in the 1980 Democratic primary in the old 22nd District, held by GOP Rep. Ron Paul. Former Democratic Rep. Bob Gammage, seeking to reclaim the seat he had lost to Paul in 1978, was viewed as stale by Democratic financiers. That helped Andrews, who ran a close second in the primary and beat Gammage in the runoff.

If there had been no presidential contest, Andrews probably would have won in 1980. He impressed businessmen with his claim to fiscal conservatism, and won labor unionists who preferred him to a libertarian ideologue like Paul. But Ronald Reagan's strong showing in the 22nd gave Paul a narrow 51 percent victory.

In 1981, however, redistricting created a golden opportunity for Andrews — the new 25th was carved from four existing districts in the Houston area, the largest portion coming from Paul's 22nd. It was drawn to be a reliable Democratic district. Andrews, the front-runner from the start, found himself in a runoff with state District Judge John Ray Harrison.

Harrison, whose base was among blue-collar whites in Pasadena, argued that Andrews had shifted to the left to appeal to the district's sizable minority population. Andrews did make an appeal for black votes, appearing arm in arm in ads with Democratic Rep. Mickey Leland, the black liberal from central Houston. Harrison passed out copies of the ad in white areas.

But Andrews took 58 percent in the runoff, winning near-unanimous support from minorities and affluent white voters, although faring less well among poorer whites. He won the general election with surprising ease over Mike Faubion, an aggressive Republican who tried to duplicate Reagan's working-class appeal. Andrews has since been re-elected without a difficult test. In 1988, he crushed his GOP challenger by better than 2-to-1, and two years later faced no Republican opposition.

Committee

Ways & Means (19th of 23 Democrats)
Human Resources; Select Revenue Measures

Elections

1990 General		
Michael A. Andrews (D)	67,427	(100%)
1988 General		
Michael A. Andrews (D)	113,499	(71%)
George H. Loeffler (R)	44,043	(28%)

Previous Winning Percentages: **1986** (100%) **1984** (64%) **1982** (60%)

District Vote For President

	1988	1984	1980	1976
D	76,165 (53%)	82,485 (48%)	68,689 (47%)	76,849 (52%)
R	66,767 (47%)	88,412 (52%)	72,831 (49%)	68,959 (47%)
I			4,603 (3%)	

Campaign Finance

	Receipts	Receipts from PACs	Expend-itures
1990			
Andrews (D)	$539,864	$344,883 (64%)	$294,340
1988			
Andrews (D)	$638,035	$403,635 (63%)	$318,970

Key Votes

1991	
Authorize use of force against Iraq	Y
1990	
Support constitutional amendment on flag desecration	Y
Pass family and medical leave bill over Bush veto	Y
Reduce SDI funding	Y
Allow abortions in overseas military facilities	Y
Approve budget summit plan for spending and taxing	Y
Approve civil rights bill	Y
1989	
Halt production of B-2 stealth bomber at 13 planes	N
Oppose capital gains tax cut	N
Approve federal abortion funding in rape or incest cases	Y
Approve pay raise and revision of ethics rules	Y
Pass Democratic minimum wage plan over Bush veto	Y

Voting Studies

	Presidential Support		Party Unity		Conservative Coalition	
Year	**S**	**O**	**S**	**O**	**S**	**O**
1990	32	68	79	20	69	31
1989	45	51	78	21	83	17
1988	37	62	75	21	87	11
1987	39	60	75	23	81	19
1986	37	61	72	24	96	4
1985	39	59	77	21	84	16
1984	48	50	64	33	81	17
1983	45	54	61	37	78	21

Interest Group Ratings

Year	ADA	ACU	AFL-CIO	CCUS
1990	56	25	75	29
1989	35	48	45	50
1988	75	29	86	62
1987	68	0	69	47
1986	50	45	64	61
1985	30	57	50	71
1984	45	29	69	38
1983	60	36	59	65

26 Dick Armey (R)

Of Copper Canyon — Elected 1984

Born: July 7, 1940, Cando, N.D.
Education: Jamestown College, B.A. 1963; U. of North Dakota, M.A. 1964; U. of Oklahoma, Ph.D. 1969.
Occupation: Economist.
Family: Wife, Susan D. Byrd; five children.
Religion: Presbyterian.
Political Career: No previous office.
Capitol Office: 130 Cannon Bldg. 20515; 225-7772.

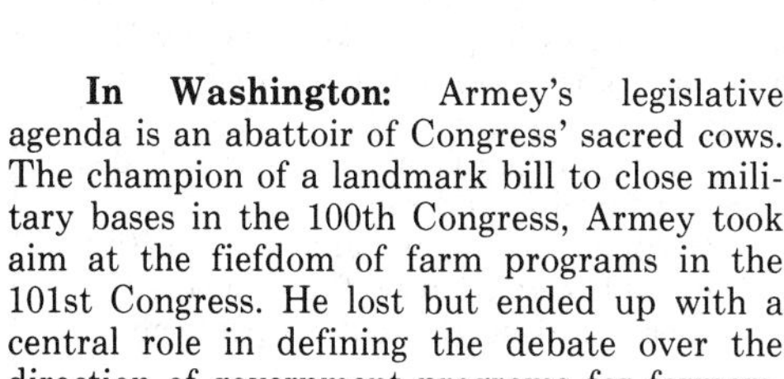

In Washington: Armey's legislative agenda is an abattoir of Congress' sacred cows. The champion of a landmark bill to close military bases in the 100th Congress, Armey took aim at the fiefdom of farm programs in the 101st Congress. He lost but ended up with a central role in defining the debate over the direction of government programs for farmers.

Passage of the base-closing measure altered this conservative Texan's reputation as a legislator. As a freshman in the 99th Congress, he sometimes seemed more interested in lecturing on free-market economics than in building consensus. But by channeling his energies into the base-closing bill and lobbying colleagues one by one to support it, Armey proved he could listen and persuade, not just lecture.

Seeking support from both Democrats and Republicans was a departure from the confrontational approach Armey used as a freshman, when he was a self-described "budget commando" arguing — mostly unsuccessfully — for federal spending reductions. But a June 1988 comment to *The Wall Street Journal* illustrated the evolution in his legislative style. Armey said he had "risked being labeled a bomb-thrower, a loose cannon," and added, "You can be so ideologically hidebound you can cut yourself out of the process."

While Armey clearly values being a part of the process, he has little tempered his free-market conservatism. When President Bush retracted his "no new taxes" pledge to help forge an agreement on the fiscal 1991 budget, Armey sponsored a resolution at a July 1990 Republican Conference meeting opposing new taxes. It carried by a 2-to-1 margin in a secret vote and presaged the later mutiny of House Republicans led by GOP Whip Newt Gingrich against the 1990 budget summit agreement.

As in the base-closing debate, Armey was peculiarly situated to launch his assault on farm programs. He was a junior member of the minority party crusading on the turf of a powerful committee — in this case, Agriculture — to which he did not belong. But he entered the debate only after immersing himself in the arcane jargon and labyrinthine network of government farm programs.

His opening strike was an article in the winter 1990 issue of the Heritage Foundation's publication *Policy Review*, titled "Moscow on the Mississippi: America's Soviet-Style Farm Policy." "Even as *perestroika* comes to the communist world," Armey began, "our own federal farm programs remain as American monuments to the folly of central planning."

Armey joined with New York Democrat Charles E. Schumer to form the Coalition for a Common Sense Farm Policy, an amalgam of free-market conservative Republicans and liberal, largely urban Democrats.

Armey's message was conservative: "The free market works and central planning does not," he wrote. But the appeal was also populist. Armey and Schumer's prime vehicle was a floor amendment to the farm bill to bar farmers earning more than $100,000 a year from collecting subsidies. "There is no reason we should be subsidizing individuals who earn more than three times the average annual income of an American family of four," Armey said.

The coalition's tactics put farm-state lawmakers on the defensive, but in the end, the Armey-Schumer amendment was rejected 159-263. Still, in his fiscal 1992 budget, Bush adopted the concept of means-testing farm subsidies, proposing to scale back benefits for individuals with high non-farm earnings.

In his fight to close obsolete military bases, Armey also lost his first battle. To insulate base-closing decisions from politics, he proposed giving all base-closing responsibility to an independent commission that would review military needs and develop a list of unnecessary bases. His bill also waived many restrictions that had tied up base closings for over a decade.

In 1987, Armey sought to attach his proposal to the fiscal 1988 defense authorization bill. Though he had lobbied only briefly, the measure fell just short, 192-199. In 1988, Armey tried again; after parliamentary wrangling, he offered a proposal with this concession: Congress would be allowed to kill the base-closing

Texas 26

Fort Worth Suburbs — Arlington; Denton

Much of this territory was open country 20 years ago, but the area has been transformed by a massive population influx. Although the northern part of the 26th is still predominantly rural, more than half the district's land has been engulfed by suburban spread.

About 55 percent of the vote comes from the Fort Worth environs in Tarrant County, although Fort Worth itself is not in the district. Living in the Tarrant suburbs south of the city are doctors, lawyers and other upper-middle-class professionals with a hard-core conservative outlook. Southeastern Tarrant towns such as Mansfield appeal to white-collar city workers seeking a more rural setting still close enough to allow them to commute to work.

Arlington, the district's largest population center, sits astride the "mid-cities" corridor between Dallas and Fort Worth, and that location has fueled its phenomenal growth. After growing 78 percent in the 1970s and more than 63 percent in the '80s, Arlington now has 262,000 people.

Arlington contains a wide array of industries, and tourism and the hotel/motel business are critical to the local economy. The city hosts "Six Flags Over Texas," a giant amusement park, and baseball's Texas Rangers. Boosted by its white-collar population, Republicans generally carry the 26th in election contests.

North of Tarrant lies Denton County, wholly contained within the 26th. Once a rural Democratic bastion, Denton's booming growth has helped make it solidly Republican. There are some residual Democratic votes in older sections of the city of Denton and in the northern areas still devoted to farming and ranching.

Portions of politically conservative Collin and Cooke counties flank the district to the east and north sides, respectively.

Population: 526,598. White 485,990 (92%), Black 19,335 (4%), Other 7,996 (2%). Spanish origin 26,041 (5%). 18 and over 372,244 (71%), 65 and over 32,184 (6%). Median age: 28.

plan, but only if both chambers passed a resolution disapproving the entire list. The amendment passed 223-186, and became law.

At year's end, the blue-ribbon panel released a list of targeted bases that was somewhat more modest than expected. Estimated savings were less than $700 million a year, rather than the originally touted $2 billion-plus. But that modesty ensured the plan's success: Only a few dozen members' districts were affected. The disapproval resolution went down 43-381, in effect ratifying the base-closure list.

Armey has clearly made an impact during his relatively short tenure in Congress, but his brashness has its costs. Perhaps in part because of his high-profile opposition to the administration's budget proposals in 1990 — conservatives outside the July GOP Conference meeting reportedly gave out buttons that said "Read Armey's Lips" — Armey failed to get a seat on the Rules Committee at the start of the 102nd Congress, when the panel had two vacancies.

Armey got a seat on the Budget Committee at the start of his second term in 1987, and showed a willingness to work with ideological opposites. In 1988, he joined liberal California Democrat Barbara Boxer on an amendment to that year's budget resolution, adding $220 million for Coast Guard drug-interdiction efforts; then-committee Chairman William H. Gray III kidded that their alliance was "historic."

On the Education and Labor Committee, where the Democratic majority has a very strong liberal bent, Armey finds it harder to eschew partisanship. He is a staunch opponent of labor-oriented measures that would increase costs or regulatory mandates for business.

He has aggressively opposed legislation requiring businesses to provide unpaid "family leave" to workers caring for a newborn child or ill family member, maintaining that because only affluent workers could afford unpaid leave, more work would fall to lower-paid employees. Armey called the family leave idea "yuppie welfare . . . a perverse redistribution of income."

In 1989, Armey revisited one of his earliest issue battles when he sought to cut funds for the National Endowment for the Arts. As a freshman in 1985, Armey circulated "dirty" poetry by NEA grant recipients to garner support for freezing NEA funding. In the 101st Congress, he tried to cut NEA's appropriation by 10 percent after an uproar over photographs many members found sacrilegious or obscene.

But Interior Appropriations Subcommittee Chairman Sidney R. Yates outmaneuvered Armey, enlisting conservative Texas Democrat Charles W. Stenholm, who offered an amendment to cut NEA funding by only the amount of two highly controversial grants. The House adopted Stenholm's language, 361-65. Armey complimented Yates for his tactics. "It was very good strategy to come in and 'Boll Weevil' me."

In the 101st Congress, Armey played musical chairs with his committee assignments. He temporarily left Education and Labor, then joined Government Operations, where, following the August 1989 death of Larkin Smith of Mississippi, he became ranking Republican on the Human Resources Subcommittee.

In the 102nd Congress, Armey rejoined Education and Labor, left Government Operations, added the Banking Committee to his assignments and also became ranking House Republican on the Joint Economic Committee.

At Home: Armey cites a belief in the free enterprise system as the genesis of his political career. He was popular on the Dallas-area conservative lecture circuit, praising the philosophy of economist George Gilder and extolling "the miracle of the market." But beyond volunteering for Jim Bradshaw, the GOP nominee in the 26th in 1982, Armey had no previous political experience when he challenged freshman Democratic Rep. Tom Vandergriff in 1984.

Although the district had been voting routinely Republican for most major offices, Vandergriff began with a solid base in Arlington, the Tarrant County city where he had been mayor for a quarter-century before narrowly winning the 1982 House election.

Armey said some things that stirred negative publicity. Following a meeting with editors of the *Fort Worth Star-Telegram*, he was quoted as saying he favored a gradual phaseout of the Social Security system. Then Armey said he was "embarrassed" to have been a professor, calling some college classes "pure junk," citing black studies courses as an example.

But Armey prevailed by stressing his conservative economic notions, allying himself firmly with President Reagan and branding Vandergriff a lackey for House Speaker Thomas P. O'Neill Jr. Taking advantage of an unusual outbreak of straight-ticket GOP voting, Armey emerged with a 51-49 percent win.

In his three re-elections, Armey has won better than two-thirds of the vote.

Committees

Banking, Finance & Urban Affairs (18th of 20 Republicans)
Consumer Affairs & Coinage; Economic Stabilization; Housing & Community Development

Budget (5th of 14 Republicans)
Urgent Fiscal Issues (ranking); Budget Process, Reconciliation & Enforcement

Education & Labor (6th of 14 Republicans)
Labor-Management Relations; Labor Standards; Postsecondary Education

Joint Economic

Elections

1990 General

Dick Armey (R)	147,856	(70%)
John Wayne Caton (D)	62,158	(30%)

1988 General

Dick Armey (R)	194,944	(69%)
Jo Ann Reyes (D)	86,490	(31%)

Previous Winning Percentages: 1986 (68%) **1984** (51%)

District Vote For President

	1988	1984	1980	1976
D	78,818 (31%)	54,062 (23%)	50,731 (32%)	51,362 (42%)
R	174,262 (69%)	182,192 (77%)	102,758 (64%)	69,342 (57%)
I			5,618 (4%)	

Campaign Finance

	Receipts	Receipts from PACs		Expend-itures
1990				
Armey (R)	$441,625	$162,306	(37%)	$198,305
Caton (D)	$15,135	$13,600	(90%)	$14,303
1988				
Armey (R)	$419,632	$150,800	(36%)	$314,903
Reyes (D)	$201,183	$44,800	(22%)	$189,780

Key Votes

1991	
Authorize use of force against Iraq	Y
1990	
Support constitutional amendment on flag desecration	Y
Pass family and medical leave bill over Bush veto	N
Reduce SDI funding	N
Allow abortions in overseas military facilities	N
Approve budget summit plan for spending and taxing	N
Approve civil rights bill	N
1989	
Halt production of B-2 stealth bomber at 13 planes	N
Oppose capital gains tax cut	N
Approve federal abortion funding in rape or incest cases	N
Approve pay raise and revision of ethics rules	N
Pass Democratic minimum wage plan over Bush veto	N

Voting Studies

	Presidential Support		Party Unity		Conservative Coalition	
Year	S	O	S	O	S	O
1990	81	18	95	4	94	6
1989	76	24	94	2	90	5
1988	82	15	94	3	92	8
1987	81	17	95	2	98	2
1986	82	17	97	2	100	0
1985	88	11	94	4	93	5

Interest Group Ratings

Year	ADA	ACU	AFL-CIO	CCUS
1990	6	96	8	93
1989	0	96	0	90
1988	0	100	0	100
1987	0	96	0	100
1986	0	100	7	100
1985	15	95	0	95

27 Solomon P. Ortiz (D)

Of Corpus Christi — Elected 1982

Born: June 3, 1937, Robstown, Texas.

Education: Attended Institute of Applied Science, 1962; attended Del Mar College, 1965-67; National Sheriff's Training Institute, 1977.

Military Service: Army, 1960-62.

Occupation: Law enforcement official.

Family: Divorced; two children.

Religion: Methodist.

Political Career: Nueces County constable, 1965-68; Nueces County Commission, 1969-76; Nueces County sheriff, 1977-82.

Capitol Office: 1524 Longworth Bldg. 20515; 225-7742.

In Washington: While other members of the Armed Services Committee debate the "big picture" defense strategy issues, Ortiz is content to act as a sentry for the military facilities in south Texas. He looks out for the two naval air stations and the port at Corpus Christi in the 27th District, and works to preserve the endangered Navy homeport project at Ingleside in the neighboring 15th District.

Ortiz's main legislative interest is also close to home: He follows issues relating to the immigration of people from Mexico and elsewhere in Latin America. In early 1989, he was a leader in efforts to make the federal government manage an influx of Central American immigrants.

Mainly from Nicaragua and El Salvador, thousands of newcomers had crossed the Rio Grande into south Texas seeking political asylum. A federal court order restricted the refugees to the Brownsville area, and encampments of immigrants sprouted up, overtaxing local governments.

Ortiz's initial reaction to the newcomers was sympathetic. But when local officials warned that they could not cope with the influx, Ortiz said the federal government should slow the flow. Noting that most of the newcomers had come for economic reasons, Ortiz said, "That doesn't mean they qualify for political asylum.... We have to draw the line somewhere." His concern about maintaining order reflects his background as a former county sheriff. In general, he follows a less liberal line than other Hispanic House members. In 1989, Ortiz supported President Bush on 50 percent of House votes, before tailing off to 30 percent in 1990.

In any case, Ortiz's agenda is driven by the local economy, not ideology. He is a leading advocate of rolling back regulations ordering gulf shrimp fishermen to install "turtle excluder devices."

Ortiz sides with shrimpers in his district who say the cumbersome devices, which keep sea turtles from getting entangled in fishing nets, could sharply reduce their shrimp yields. "The dedicated and hard-working men and women who own and operate shrimp fishing vessels are being threatened by federal regulations which may cause many of these people to lose their businesses," Ortiz said in April 1989.

At Home: Since his 1964 election as constable, Ortiz has been a groundbreaker for Hispanics in south Texas politics, holding a succession of offices before closed to Mexican-Americans. He was chosen Nueces County's first Hispanic commissioner in 1968, its first Hispanic sheriff in 1976.

Redistricting in 1982 gave Ortiz the opening he needed to get to Congress. As adjusted by a three-judge federal panel, the 27th is good territory for a Mexican-American Democrat; its Hispanic population exceeds 60 percent.

Four of the five candidates who filed for the Democratic nomination in 1982 were Hispanic. Although Jorge Rangel was the favorite in the Washington business-money community, Ortiz had the loyal backing of the poorer Hispanics in Corpus Christi who had sustained his long political career. That gave him a first-place primary finish and a spot in the June runoff.

Ortiz's runoff foe was the one non-Hispanic, Joseph Salem, a Corpus Christi jeweler and former state representative. Salem had strong labor ties, but many of the oil and other business interests who had backed Rangel turned to Ortiz, leery that Salem was too liberal.

The decisive runoff votes were cast in Brownsville. Although Salem had some initial appeal to the Hispanic majority there, Ortiz scored a coup by gaining the support of state Pardon and Parole Chairman Ruben M. Torres, who had been Brownsville's choice in the first round of primary voting. With Torres' support, Ortiz won about 60 percent of the Cameron County (Brownsville) runoff vote, allowing him to draw 52 percent districtwide. That was Ortiz's last competitive contest. In the last three elections, the GOP has not challenged him.

Texas 27

Gulf Coast — Corpus Christi; Brownsville

The 27th looks tidy and compact: Four whole counties and the bulk of a fifth are lined up along the Gulf Coast in far southern Texas. The region's two largest cities — Brownsville and Corpus Christi — are placed symmetrically at either end.

But when the boundaries of the 27th were set for the 1980s, there were grumblings in Brownsville, a Mexican-border city in the Rio Grande Valley always somewhat separate from Corpus Christi, its much larger competitor for tourists and seaport trade. Since about 55 percent of the district's population lives in the Corpus Christi area, some Brownsvillians worry that their interests may be overshadowed.

Among Texas ports, Corpus Christi is second only to Houston in tonnage handled yearly. The city has large petrochemical and aluminum plants and seafood-processing facilities. Manufacturers of clothing and oil-drilling equipment are also important employers. Tourists are drawn to Corpus Christi for its mild climate and direct access to the Padre Island National Seashore.

By comparison, Brownsville offers more of a south-of-the-border flavor. Corpus Christi's Nueces County is just over half Hispanic, but in Brownsville and Cameron County, more than 80 percent of the residents are Hispanic. Export-import trade with Mexico is vital to the Brownsville economy, and the bounteous harvests of the Rio Grande Valley keep many workers employed processing fruits and vegetables. The city's location makes illegal immigration a big problem, and cross-border trafficking in illegal drugs has increased, partly because of stepped-up enforcement in Florida.

Nueces and Cameron often behave similarly at the polls, as in the 1982, 1986, and 1990 gubernatorial results. Both counties backed Democrat Mark White in 1982 and 1986, and Ann W. Richards in 1990. Democrats generally win districtwide; the Democratic presidential ticket of Michael S. Dukakis and Lloyd Bentsen carried the 27th comfortably in 1988.

Population: 526,988. White 417,540 (79%), Black 14,443 (3%), Other 3,252 (1%). Spanish origin 324,120 (62%). 18 and over 341,512 (65%), 65 and over 46,546 (9%). Median age: 26.

Committees

Armed Services (18th of 33 Democrats)
Military Installations & Facilities; Readiness; Seapower & Strategic & Critical Materials

Merchant Marine & Fisheries (13th of 29 Democrats)
Fisheries & Wildlife Conservation & the Environment; Merchant Marine

Select Narcotics Abuse & Control (10th of 21 Democrats)

Elections

1990 General		
Solomon P. Ortiz (D)	62,822	(100%)
1988 General		
Solomon P. Ortiz (D)	105,085	(100%)

Previous Winning Percentages: **1986** (100%) **1984** (64%) **1982** (64%)

District Vote For President

	1988		1984		1980		1976	
D	79,302	(55%)	76,717	(48%)	72,902	(51%)	86,991	(61%)
R	65,419	(45%)	83,587	(52%)	69,306	(47%)	54,623	(38%)
I					3,117	(2%)		

Campaign Finance

	Receipts	Receipts from PACs		Expend-itures
1990				
Ortiz (D)	$235,873	$100,790	(43%)	$140,756
1988				
Oritz (D)	$198,217	$100,383	(51%)	$142,651

Key Votes

1991	
Authorize use of force against Iraq	Y
1990	
Support constitutional amendment on flag desecration	Y
Pass family and medical leave bill over Bush veto	Y
Reduce SDI funding	Y
Allow abortions in overseas military facilities	N
Approve budget summit plan for spending and taxing	Y
Approve civil rights bill	Y
1989	
Halt production of B-2 stealth bomber at 13 planes	N
Oppose capital gains tax cut	N
Approve federal abortion funding in rape or incest cases	Y
Approve pay raise and revision of ethics rules	Y
Pass Democratic minimum wage plan over Bush veto	Y

Voting Studies

	Presidential Support		Party Unity		Conservative Coalition	
Year	**S**	**O**	**S**	**O**	**S**	**O**
1990	30	69	86	13	52	46
1989	50	47	77	18	61	34
1988	29	61	78	10	53	34
1987	37	55	79	12	81	16
1986	36	59	78	14	70	22
1985	36	61	76	14	64	33
1984	41	51	77	17	53	41
1983	44	52	75	21	66	29

Interest Group Ratings

Year	ADA	ACU	AFL-CIO	CCUS
1990	56	21	83	43
1989	60	29	73	50
1988	55	26	100	29
1987	56	17	80	33
1986	45	40	85	29
1985	60	33	88	16
1984	60	29	92	44
1983	65	32	82	32

Utah

U.S. CONGRESS

SENATE 2 R
HOUSE 2 D, 1 R

LEGISLATURE

Senate 10 D, 19 R
House 31 D, 44 R

ELECTIONS

1988 Presidential Vote	
Bush	66%
Dukakis	32%
1984 Presidential Vote	
Reagan	75%
Mondale	25%
1980 Presidential Vote	
Reagan	73%
Carter	21%
Anderson	5%
Turnout rate in 1986	41%
Turnout rate in 1988	60%
Turnout rate in 1990	41%

(as percentage of voting age population)

POPULATION AND GROWTH

1980 population	1,461,037
1990 population (35th in the nation)	1,722,850
Percent change 1980-1990	+18%

DEMOGRAPHIC BREAKDOWN

White	94%
Black	1%
Asian or Pacific Islander	2%
(Hispanic origin)	5%
Urban	84%
Rural	16%
Born in state	66%
Foreign-born	4%

MAJOR CITIES

Salt Lake City	159,936
West Valley City	86,976
Provo	86,835
Sandy	75,058
Orem	67,561

AREA AND LAND USE

Area	82,073 sq. miles (12th)
Farm	19%
Forest	31%
Federally owned	64%

Gov. Norman H. Bangerter (R)
Of West Valley City — Elected 1984

Born: Jan. 4, 1933, Granger, Utah.
Education: Attended Brigham Young U., 1951-55; U. of Utah, 1956-57.
Military Service: Army, 1951-53.
Occupation: Building contractor.
Religion: Mormon.
Political Career: Utah House, 1975-85, assistant majority whip, 1977-79, majority leader, 1979-81, Speaker, 1981-85.
Next Election: 1992.

WORK

Occupations	
White-collar	54%
Blue-collar	31%
Service workers	12%
Government Workers	
Federal	36,965
State	40,601
Local	65,046

MONEY

Median family income	$ 20,024	(22nd)
Tax burden per capita	$ 805	(30th)

EDUCATION

Spending per pupil through grade 12	$ 2,454	(50th)
Persons with college degrees	20%	(7th)

CRIME

Violent crime rate	259 per 100,000	(40th)

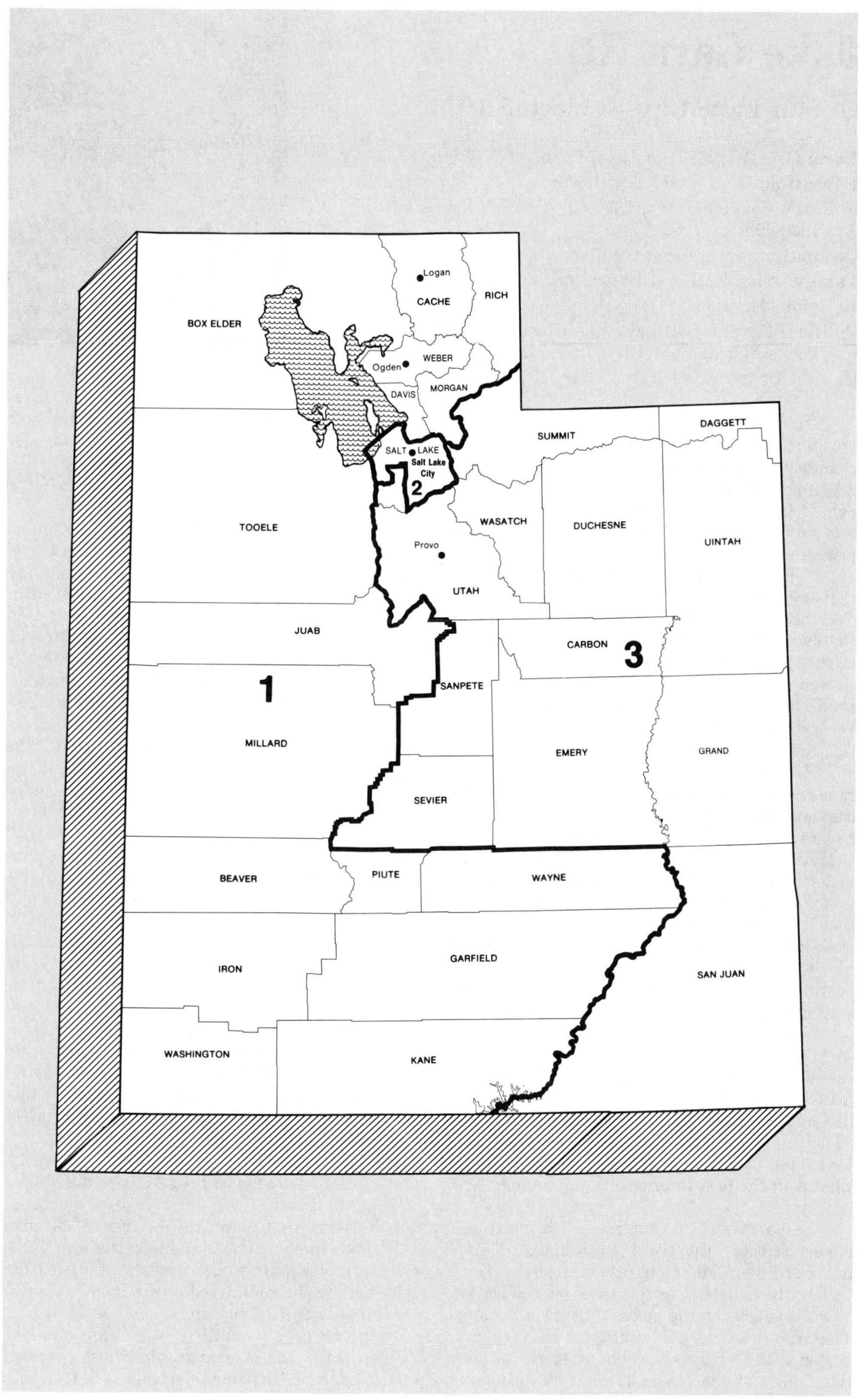

Logan
CACHE
RICH
BOX ELDER
Ogden
WEBER
MORGAN
DAVIS
SUMMIT
DAGGETT
SALT LAKE
Salt Lake City
2
TOOELE
WASATCH
DUCHESNE
UINTAH
Provo
UTAH
JUAB
CARBON
3
1
SANPETE
MILLARD
EMERY
GRAND
SEVIER
BEAVER
PIUTE
WAYNE
IRON
GARFIELD
SAN JUAN
WASHINGTON
KANE

Jake Garn (R)

Of Salt Lake City — Elected 1974

Born: Oct. 12, 1932, Richfield, Utah.
Education: U. of Utah, B.S. 1955.
Military Service: Navy, 1956-60; Air National Guard, 1960-69.
Occupation: Insurance executive.
Family: Wife, Kathleen Brewerton; seven children.
Religion: Mormon.
Political Career: Salt Lake City Commission, 1968-72; mayor of Salt Lake City, 1972-74.
Capitol Office: 505 Dirksen Bldg. 20510; 224-5444.

In Washington: Many a senator has grown frustrated with the manner in which the chamber invites obstruction and delay. Garn gets angry. If, as George Washington said, the Senate is the saucer where legislative passions are cooled, at times it seems that Garn would just as soon smash it against the nearest wall.

"The Founding Fathers did not intend that we stay in session from January until December every year," he told the Senate in October 1990. "I think they expected that we might live and work with the people who elected us to represent them.... But no, we reside inside the Capital Beltway all year long. We lost touch with reality. There is no reality in this town."

His distaste for life and work in the nation's capital is scarcely veiled: He boils over at lobbyists and colleagues alike. He sought a third Senate term in 1986 largely because of pleas from GOP leaders concerned with keeping the Senate majority. But no one could persuade Garn to re-up for a fourth tour: In May 1991, he announced that he would not seek re-election in 1992, enabling him to escape the place that provoked him to remark at a 1987 Banking Committee hearing: "Frankly, ladies and gentlemen, I'm getting sick of all of you, just really sick."

Garn's attitude might take a newcomer by surprise, for one on one, he is an affable, easygoing man. But he came to Washington disliking the federal government, and the years in Congress have not mellowed him one iota. "The Capitol Dome has become a clouded bell jar under which we are incapable of viewing what is in the best interests of our country," he has said.

Late in the 101st Congress, with the House having rejected the fiscal 1991 budget "summit" agreement and Congress in disarray, Garn took to the Senate floor to blister his colleagues. "This is getting to the point of being ridiculous. The American people ought to be very disgusted with Congress.... The rhetoric on both this floor and the House floor is so disgusting the American people ought to rise up and toss every incumbent out until we start doing our work.... We should close the place down. We are not doing anything. This senator has had a belly full of it, to put it bluntly."

As a first-termer in the 1970s, Garn joined other conservatives in battles against the Equal Rights Amendment, the SALT II treaty and the Panama Canal treaties. He led an eleventh-hour filibuster against the Clean Air Act in 1976, killing the bill as time ran out. But he found little to enjoy when he moved into the Senate majority following the 1980 elections. His record as chairman of Banking was a series of personal vexations and legislative defeats that sometimes seemed to drive him to the brink of abandoning the Senate in disgust.

It is easy to imagine Garn completing a career of distinction as a military officer, business executive or local government official, all of which he has been in the past. But he seems ill-suited temperamentally to the legislative life; he lacks tolerance for the compromises and slow pace of work in Congress.

Garn's acerbic public personality can alienate those with whom he needs to work. "I am angry," he admitted during one budget debate, appearing in the chamber unexpectedly but holding the floor for nearly an hour, waving his arms and pacing up and down the aisle. "I am angry at this body. I am angry at Congress — I do not care which party, Republican or Democrat — because there are weak-kneed, gutless politicians on both sides."

The frustration Garn has faced as a legislator can be best seen in his efforts to deregulate the banking industry. For six years as chairman of the Banking Committee, he tried and failed to move major deregulation legislation. Even when he was able to get what he wanted from the Senate, he foundered on irreconcilable differences with leading House members.

Some of his conflicts were philosophical. When Garn was chairman, his House counterpart, Banking Chairman Fernand J. St Germain of Rhode Island, had a basic disagreement over the need for regulation of the banking industry. It is hard to see how Garn could ever have moved his proposals further deregulating the industry past St Germain's adamant opposition.

Faced with the conflicting ambitions of a variety of financial interest groups, Garn alternatively denounced them for their greed and implored them to settle their differences before asking him to move any legislation.

The ranking Republican on the Banking Committee, now that Democrats control the Senate, Garn has devoted much attention to rescuing the foundering savings and loan industry. He considered the bailout bills passed in the 100th Congress inadequate, and was proven correct when President Bush sought $50 billion in bailout money in 1989. He also formed an early negative impression of notorious thrift operator Charles H. Keating Jr. when he was approached by him. Garn did not like his attitude and, after 1981, he would have nothing to do with him.

House-Senate negotiations on the 1989 bailout bill snagged on a provision in the Senate bill allowing M. Danny Wall, chairman of the Federal Home Loan Bank Board, to become director of the new Office of Thrift Supervision without being subjected to Senate confirmation. Many House members objected to giving the new job to Wall, a longtime friend of Garn and staff director of the Banking Committee during Garn's six years as chairman. They said Wall had understated the severity of the S&L crisis and gave purchasers of failed thrifts unnecessarily favorable deals. The House conferees relented, but House Banking Committee members, led by Chairman Henry B. Gonzalez, continued their barrage on Wall in hearings on the S&L crisis. Later that year, Wall resigned from his post at OTS. Garn attacked the administration for "not having the guts" to protect Wall.

Garn is the ranking Republican on the Appropriations Subcommittee on VA, HUD and Independent Agencies, where he is a cheerleader for NASA and the space program. The Thiokol Corp. manufactures part of the space shuttles in Ogden. Garn battles for funds with Chairman Barbara A. Mikulski, who prefers housing programs to space exploration. He uses his valued position on the money committee to bring home funds for military construction, water and public land projects.

Focusing solely on Garn's legislative abilities, however, omits notice of the personal qualities he exhibited in three experiences that are certain to be highlighted in any retrospective of Garn's Senate career.

In April 1985, Garn became the first incumbent member of Congress to travel in space when he completed an orbital mission aboard the space shuttle *Discovery*. He pressed for the test ride as chairman of the Appropriations subcommittee with jurisdiction over NASA's budget — part of his continuing effort to kick the tires of federal spending, or at least enjoy the toys that come with the job. (He once piloted a protoype B-1 bomber and drove a tank.) He threw himself into training for the *Discovery* mission, and came back transformed by the experience of seeing the Earth from space. "I'd stay up there forever if I could," he said.

Those exhilarating memories turned to grief when the space shuttle *Challenger* exploded the following year. Garn knew most of the seven crew members who died, and he made a moving statement on the Senate floor on the afternoon of the tragedy. "It's difficult to lose so many friends all at once," he said in a voice choked with emotion.

The courage Garn had shown on his space flight was overshadowed, however, by his personal sacrifice later that year. He underwent a major operation to donate one of his kidneys to his diabetic daughter.

At Home: Garn's longstanding war with things governmental is the basis of his political success. His attitude toward bureaucracy and his affable campaign style brought him a narrow Senate victory in 1974, a bad GOP year, and lifted him to landslide re-election victories in 1980 and 1986.

The son of Utah's first state director of aeronautics, Garn abandoned his career as a Navy pilot after the Korean War. From flying anti-submarine patrols in the Sea of Japan, he moved to the quiet life of an insurance agent in Salt Lake City.

Before long, however, he ran afoul of the municipal government. As a Utah Air National Guard officer, he had a tough time negotiating a lease at the city airport. At one juncture, a city commissioner snapped at him: "If you don't like the way the city is run, why don't you run for election?"

He did that in 1967, winning a term on the City Commission, where he oversaw the sewer and water systems. By 1972 he was mayor. Both were non-partisan posts.

During his tenure as mayor, Garn launched Salt Lake's downtown "beautification" project, which involved adding trees and fountains and widening streets. Although controversial at the time among local business people, who claimed all the construction work was driving off customers, the final result was widely praised.

But Garn gained the most notice as mayor for his strident denunciations of the federal regulations he felt were weakening local government. He often referred to Washington's "dictatorship" and "police-state tactics."

Garn's record as mayor benefited him immeasurably in his 1974 Senate campaign against Democratic Rep. Wayne Owens. Garn projected a much more mature image than the 37-year-old Owens, who looked considerably younger than his age. Owens also was a bit liberal for many Utah voters.

Initially, Garn was far behind Owens in the polls. But on Election Day, he broke even with the Democrat in Salt Lake County and won the mainly Republican rural areas. He defeated Owens by 25,000 votes statewide.

In 1980 Garn triumphed by the greatest percentage any Senate candidate has drawn in Utah history. The hapless loser was Dan Berman, a wealthy lawyer and former executive director of the state Democratic Party.

Berman lashed out at Garn as the puppet of special interests, noting that Garn, then ranking Republican on the Banking Committee, had received thousands of dollars in honoraria from the banking industry. Garn dismissed the attacks with good humor, stressing his conservative record and conducting his customary door-knocking campaign.

In 1986, no prominent Democrat stepped forward to challenge Garn, and the party leadership made little effort to find someone. In a low-turnout Democratic primary, a virtual unknown by the name of Craig Oliver beat Terry Williams, the lone black in the state Senate.

Oliver pounded away at Garn for violating his own stated aversion to congressional careerism, and complained that the incumbent's staunch support of NASA "smells of a political payoff." A loser in previous races for the state Legislature and mayor of Murray, Oliver made no headway against Garn. As in 1980, Garn drew more than 70 percent of the vote.

Committees

Banking, Housing & Urban Affairs (Ranking)

Appropriations (3rd of 13 Republicans)
VA, HUD and Independent Agencies (ranking); Defense; Energy & Water Development; Interior; Military Construction

Energy & Natural Resources (9th of 9 Republicans)
Energy Research & Development; Mineral Resources Development & Production; Public Lands, National Parks & Forests

Rules & Administration (6th of 7 Republicans)

Elections

1986 General

Jake Garn (R)	314,608	(72%)
Craig Oliver (D)	115,523	(27%)

Previous Winning Percentages: **1980** (74%) **1974** (50%)

Campaign Finance

	Receipts	Receipts from PACs	Expend-itures
1986			
Garn (R)	$1,014,148	$576,114 (57%)	$741,645
Oliver (D)	$24,508	0	$24,508

Key Votes

1991

Authorize use of force against Iraq	Y

1990

Oppose prohibition of certain semiautomatic weapons	Y
Support constitutional amendment on flag desecration	Y
Oppose requiring parental notice for minors' abortions	N
Halt production of B-2 stealth bomber at 13 planes	N
Approve budget that cut spending and raised revenues	Y
Pass civil rights bill over Bush veto	N

1989

Oppose reduction of SDI funding	Y
Oppose barring federal funds for "obscene" art	N
Allow vote on capital gains tax cut	Y

Voting Studies

	Presidential Support		Party Unity		Conservative Coalition	
Year	**S**	**O**	**S**	**O**	**S**	**O**
1990	73	24	88	6	86	3
1989	86	11	97	2	95	3
1988	77	14	88	3	73	0
1987	69	21	89	7	91	3
1986	80	5	73	4	75	3
1985	73	11	83	7	72	13
1984	83	14	95	5	98	2
1983	72	28	91	6	100	0
1982	83	16	93	7	93	6
1981	88	9	92	4	89	6

Interest Group Ratings

Year	ADA	ACU	AFL-CIO	CCUS
1990	6	95	33	92
1989	5	96	0	88
1988	0	96	7	92
1987	5	96	10	94
1986	0	94	7	100
1985	0	100	21	96
1984	0	100	0	95
1983	5	84	12	95
1982	5	75	4	67
1981	0	93	11	94

Orrin G. Hatch (R)

Of Salt Lake City — Elected 1976

Born: March 22, 1934, Pittsburgh, Pa.
Education: Brigham Young U., B.S. 1959; U. of Pittsburgh, J.D. 1962.
Occupation: Lawyer.
Family: Wife, Elaine Hansen; six children.
Religion: Mormon.
Political Career: No previous office.
Capitol Office: 135 Russell Bldg. 20510; 224-5251.

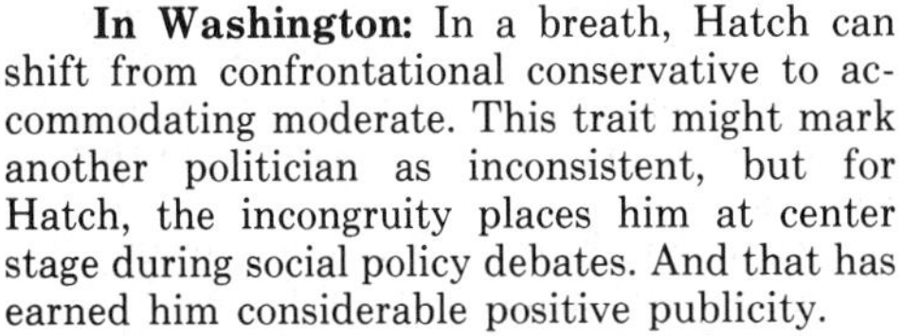

In Washington: In a breath, Hatch can shift from confrontational conservative to accommodating moderate. This trait might mark another politician as inconsistent, but for Hatch, the incongruity places him at center stage during social policy debates. And that has earned him considerable positive publicity.

The confrontational Hatch advances a New Right agenda on legal and constitutional issues from his seat on the Judiciary Committee. He is essentially the same conservative militant who came to the Senate in 1977 with a virtual declaration of war on the liberal Washington establishment and its "soft-headed inheritors of wealth." No one is more zealous in excoriating Democrats for partisan opposition to conservative judicial nominations.

The accommodating Hatch can be found on the Labor and Human Resources Committee. Now the ranking Republican, after serving as chairman during the six years of GOP Senate control, Hatch reaches out to his ideological opposites there, finding common ground with a man many conservatives love to hate, Massachusetts Democrat Edward M. Kennedy. Faced with the choice of making major concessions or passing no legislation, Hatch will opt for compromise at the expense of ideological purity.

No matter which role he is playing, Hatch is a formidable foe with a style suited to the setting. The public Hatch is ever articulate and unruffled, while in backroom negotiation, he is not a man to mince his words. In both settings, however, Hatch has a tendency to talk a bit longer than most want to listen. His monologues sustain the "Borin' Orrin" moniker he earned in 1978 for his long, slow, monotone filibuster of a labor law revision bill.

Hatch's influence is based in part on his unusual access to partisans on all sides of social policy debate. Democrats consider him a conservative they can talk to. Conservatives consider him one of them, though they also gripe that Hatch can be too eager to please those on his left.

The promise and pitfalls inherent in Hatch's role were evident during debate on the 1990 Civil Rights Bill. After articulating conservative criticism and rallying opposition, the accommodating Hatch was drawn into a bargain that might have broken the logjam had it not so outraged his allies that Hatch pulled back.

Though Hatch likes to say he is "second to none" in his support for civil rights, he was a leading foe of civil rights forces throughout the 1980s. In their first head-on clash, Hatch won a 1980 victory on Judiciary in blocking legislation to strengthen federal enforcement of open-housing laws. A decade later, he emerged as the most vocal Senate critic of the 1990 bill long before it was clear where the White House would stand.

As Hatch laid out the case against the quotas he said the bill necessitated, he also sharply criticized White House attempts to find a compromise. "They keep trying to pacify Kennedy," he complained.

Then, when a few key Republicans and southern Democrats signed off on an agreement negotiated by Kennedy and Missouri Republican John C. Danforth, Hatch squashed talk of a breakthrough. "The right of employers to hire the most qualified employees ought to be maintained," he argued.

As the end of the session approached, however, Hatch intervened to craft new language easing employers' burden of proof in defending business practices that disproportionately hurt women and minorities. Senate conservatives were dismayed by Hatch's move, particularly since the White House by then had taken up the quotas cudgel. When Bush reiterated his veto threat, Hatch quickly withdrew his support. He went on lead the successful fight to sustain the president's veto, and as the 102nd Congress opened, he was reiterating his harsh anti-quotas rhetoric.

When it came to the 101st Congress' child-care bill, however, Hatch brokered a deal and stuck by it. With support from a 35-member women's advisory group in Utah, Hatch was one of the earliest Senate supporters of a federal role in child care. "Let us get with the real world and let us try to solve these problems," he said.

Like most Republicans, Hatch opposed the original Act for Better Child Care (ABC) bill proposed in the 100th Congress. But he worked with the lead Senate sponsor, Connecticut Democrat Christopher J. Dodd, to strike a compromise. At Hatch's insistence, the 1989 version gave states a larger role in setting federal health and safety standards and more flexibility in implementing them. While the new ABC bill also included a modest child-care tax-credit proposal, it relied primarily on federal subsidies to states, rather than the tax credits to parents sought by Bush.

"I have been personally likened to Karl Marx, Benedict Arnold and even Brutus," Hatch said.

As Republicans drafted their alternative bill, they jokingly refused to let Hatch see it, and he wound up being one of three Republicans to oppose it. And as the GOP criticized the ABC bill, Hatch became incensed. "I have never seen an issue where the conservative side of the equation has distorted a bill more than this bill," he said. "I am personally offended by it."

That was perhaps as far afield as Hatch has wandered from his conservative base. In drafting legislation to protect older workers and the handicapped from discrimination, Hatch worked with Democratic sponsors to make the bills more acceptable to Republicans, but he also carried his fights to the Senate floor. On the Americans with Disabilities Act, Hatch authored an unsuccessful amendment to create a refundable tax credit for small businesses to offset the costs of the bill. Despite the failure of that plan, Hatch, the GOP floor manager, was emotional in support for the final bill. He broke down briefly as he spoke of the courage of his late brother-in-law who had battled polio.

During the debate on ADA, Hatch also revealed a longstanding sensitivity to those with AIDS. Conservatives were supporting language that would have permitted workers with a communicable disease to be transferred out of food-handling jobs even if the disease could not be transmitted through food. "Let us not use somebody's feelings, fears or misconceptions," Hatch said. "Let us use science."

He offered a successful amendment that called for the development of a list of diseases that can be transferred by food handling. Similarly, Hatch has been a key supporter of AIDS research and education legislation, and in 1990, he played a role in keeping groups helping children with AIDS from splitting their lobbying efforts from less-popular groups representing other AIDS victims.

In 1987 and again in 1990, Hatch chastised Sen. Jesse Helms for his opposition to AIDS legislation. "Should we just let the disease run rampant because we do not agree with the morals of certain people?" Hatch said in 1990. "I do not condone homosexual activity, but that does not have a thing to do with this bill."

Hatch and Helms, however, sing from the same hymnal when it comes to defending controversial conservative judicial appointees. During Judiciary Committee confirmation hearings, Hatch is a master of the carefully constructed question that casts a nominee's credentials or positions in the best possible light. Conversely, he can use his lawyer's skills to bore in on an opposing witness.

While Bush's appointments have not caused the fireworks of the Reagan era, Hatch remains a fierce ally. As Bush's nomination of William Lucas to head the Civil Rights Division of the Justice Department headed toward defeat, Hatch defended Lucas' credentials and waded into an awkward debate over racism. "As county executive, he headed a county that was larger in population than 20 states," he said. "What more does a black man or a white man or anyone else have to do? We have to give these people an opportunity, after what they've been through."

Hatch fought to the bitter end for the 1987 Supreme Court nominations of Robert H. Bork and Douglas H. Ginsburg, and then ended up bitter himself about the administration's handling of the nominations. After Bork was beaten, Ginsburg was forced to withdraw once it became known he had smoked marijuana while a law professor. Hatch said the administration aides who approved Ginsburg should resign.

Hatch is said to have an interest in a Supreme Court seat someday, although he has been kept off recent lists of candidates because of the constitutional prohibition against any lawmaker assuming an office that had its pay increased during the period the lawmaker was elected. Hatch's conservative critics say his interest in an appointment contributes to his efforts in the Senate to listen to both sides and to work with liberals.

In the 100th Congress, Hatch was appointed to the select Senate committee investigating the Iran-contra affair, where he was one of President Ronald Reagan's fiercest defenders. In the hearings, he would often answer his own rapid-fire inquiries before a witness could jump in, or invite witnesses to tout the administration's policy toward Central America. He acknowledged that some key administration decisions were flawed, but he also asserted that it was critical for members to understand the "really worthy foreign policy objectives" underlying the initiative with Iran and the support for contras fighting a pro-Soviet regime.

Prior to 1980, Hatch wore just one hat in the Senate: that of conservative ideologue. In 1979, when he ran for the chairmanship of the Senate GOP campaign committee, Hatch thought he had rounded up the support to win. But John Heinz of Pennsylvania beat him. Some senators said afterward that Hatch's reputation as a strident conservative had cost him votes.

That perception began to change as Hatch took over the Labor Committee in 1981. Even under GOP rule, the committee had a moderate-to-liberal majority, with Democrats and several Republicans combining to frustrate any strict conservative initiatives. "The chairman can't just snap his fingers and expect things to happen," Hatch said.

The course pursued by Hatch as chairman was a relatively successful one — at least in terms of the volume of legislation, particularly in the area of health policy, that became law. But his eagerness to compromise left some of his fellow Republicans wondering whether he had abandoned his principles in an unseemly rush to get something enacted.

Early in the Reagan administration, the president proposed ending many existing programs and replacing them with "block grants" to the states, at a lower level of funding. But there was no majority for that approach. Hatch sought a compromise that could win a committee majority without losing administration support. Ultimately, he agreed to a compromise turning some programs into block grants, but leaving many intact.

Hatch won committee approval for a few relatively minor bills fighting labor corruption. But more controversial proposals, such as establishment of a subminimum wage for young people, went nowhere.

As chairman of the Constitution Subcommittee at Judiciary while Republicans controlled the Senate, Hatch presided over the panel during one of the greatest rushes to amend the Constitution in the nation's history. He became repeatedly enmeshed in controversies over conservative-backed constitutional amendments, many of them proposed by him. He made only intermittent progress in moving the proposals, however, and on occasion found himself at odds with his conservative allies over strategy for getting them through Congress.

On abortion, for instance, Hatch argued that only a constitutional amendment would be sufficient to overturn the Supreme Court's decision permitting abortion — a crucial difference with groups wanting simply to ban abortion by statute and avoid the constitutional process. Moreover, Hatch's amendment in effect turned the issue over to the states, allowing them to make their own decision, while some anti-abortion groups sought a national prohibition. Despite his efforts, the amendment was defeated in 1983.

At Home: While Hatch has grown wise in the ways of Washington, he was a political neophyte when he launched his first Senate campaign in 1976. It was as pure an example of anti-Washington politics as had been seen in recent years.

Hatch's lack of government experience at any level almost certainly helped him. In his private legal practice, he had represented clients fighting federal regulations.

Hatch was recruited for a Senate race against incumbent Democrat Frank E. Moss by conservative leader Ernest Wilkerson, who had challenged Moss in 1964. Hatch's competitor for the GOP nomination was Jack W. Carlson, who had a long résumé in the federal government punctuated by service as assistant secretary of the interior. Carlson, who was seen as the front-runner, underscored his Washington experience.

That was the wrong record for Utah in 1976. Hatch, sensing that the state was fed up with federal rules, took the opposite approach. The party convention gave him nearly half the vote, and the day before the primary balloting, Hatch reinforced his conservative credentials by running newspaper ads trumpeting an endorsement from Reagan. He won by almost 2-to-1.

The primary gave Hatch a publicity bonus that helped him catch up to Moss, who faced no party competitors. Moss, seen as a liberal by Utah standards, had helped himself at home by investigating Medicaid abuses and fighting to ban cigarette ads from television. He stressed his seniority and the tangible benefits it had brought the state. But Hatch argued successfully that the real issue was limiting government and taxes, and that he would be more likely to do that than Moss.

Bidding for a second term in 1982, Hatch came under strong challenge for being rigid both in his conservative views and his personal style.

Ted Wilson, his affable Democratic opponent, was a well-known figure throughout the state, having served two terms as mayor of Salt Lake City. He carefully began building his challenge to Hatch a year in advance.

Wilson was not the only one with designs on the incumbent. After Hatch blocked the labor law revision in 1978, AFL-CIO President George Meany had vowed, "We'll defeat you no matter what it takes." But unions are not the most useful allies in conservative Utah. Being a labor target almost certainly did Hatch more good than harm.

Meanwhile, he worked hard to meet complaints about his demeanor. Funding a television campaign with a treasury nearly three times the size of his opponent's, Hatch ran ads that showed him playing with children and dogs.

Wilson, hoping to maintain his early momentum, spent much of the campaign sifting through various strategies searching for a way to undo the incumbent. He branded Hatch's politics as extremist, indicted his style as "strident and contentious," accused him of caring more about national conservative causes than about Utah, and, finally, criticized the Reagan economic philosophy that Hatch vowed he would continue to fight for if re-elected.

The latter approach probably did not help.

Utah gave Reagan 73 percent in 1980 — his best showing in the country — and the president's popularity remained high there in late 1982. Buoyed by two Reagan visits to the state during the campaign, Hatch won a solid 58 percent of the vote.

In 1988, Democrats had trouble finding an opponent for Hatch. Popular former Gov. Scott M. Matheson was probably the only Democrat with a chance of beating the incumbent, and he announced in 1987 that he would not run. Almost by default the Democratic nomination went to Brian Moss, a businessman and son of the former senator whom Hatch had ousted.

Moss boasted of his family's roots in Utah and took up the complaint that the Pittsburgh-born Hatch was pursuing a national conservative agenda rather than focusing on ways to retool Utah's struggling economy. But Moss had little going for him besides his famous name; he was outspent by a margin of nearly 25-to-1.

As in 1982, Hatch spent much of his money on media advertising that highlighted his caring side. Ads focused on his negotiating role in keeping open the Geneva Steel plant in Orem, and on his legislative proposal to provide home-based health-care services for the elderly and handicapped. As it turned out, the only campaign problem Hatch encountered was self-inflicted. Speaking in Republican southern Utah in early September, he launched into an assault on the Democratic Party, labeling it "the party of homosexuals ... the party of abortion ... the party that has basically, I think, denigrated a lot of the values that have made this country the greatest country in the world." Hatch's remarks drew national attention. But the underfunded Moss was not in position to take advantage, and Hatch coasted to victory with 67 percent of the vote.

Committees

Labor & Human Resources (Ranking)
Children, Families, Drugs & Alcoholism; Education, Arts & Humanities; Disability Policy; Labor

Foreign Relations (8th of 8 Republicans)
Near Eastern & South Asian Affairs (ranking); Terrorism, Narcotics & International Operations; Western Hemisphere & Peace Corps Affairs

Judiciary (2nd of 6 Republicans)
Patents, Copyrights & Trademarks (ranking); Antitrust, Monopolies & Business Rights; Constitution

Elections

1988 General

Orrin G. Hatch (R)	430,089	(67%)
Brian H. Moss (D)	203,364	(32%)

Previous Winning Percentages: **1982** (58%) **1976** (54%)

Campaign Finance

	Receipts	Receipts from PACs		Expend-itures
1988				
Hatch (R)	$4,138,756	$1,173,764	(28%)	$4,005,182
Moss (D)	$153,159	$71,800	(47%)	$153,475

Key Votes

1991

Authorize use of force against Iraq	Y
1990	
Oppose prohibition of certain semiautomatic weapons	Y
Support constitutional amendment on flag desecration	Y
Oppose requiring parental notice for minors' abortions	N
Halt production of B-2 stealth bomber at 13 planes	N
Approve budget that cut spending and raised revenues	Y
Pass civil rights bill over Bush veto	N
1989	
Oppose reduction of SDI funding	Y
Oppose barring federal funds for "obscene" art	N
Allow vote on capital gains tax cut	Y

Voting Studies

	Presidential Support		Party Unity		Conservative Coalition	
Year	**S**	**O**	**S**	**O**	**S**	**O**
1990	77	22	89	11	97	3
1989	81	18	85	15	97	3
1988	78	17	82	16	100	0
1987	71	24	88	8	91	6
1986	92	8	92	8	95	5
1985	82	16	85	12	85	15
1984	78	19	91	9	98	2
1983	72	28	90	9	93	7
1982	79	13	80	12	90	6
1981	87	11	89	8	91	7

Interest Group Ratings

Year	ADA	ACU	AFL-CIO	CCUS
1990	11	87	33	92
1989	5	93	10	88
1988	5	96	36	86
1987	5	92	11	100
1986	5	96	13	95
1985	10	91	19	86
1984	10	95	18	83
1983	0	80	6	100
1982	5	79	5	70
1981	0	93	11	100

1 James V. Hansen (R)

Of Farmington — Elected 1980

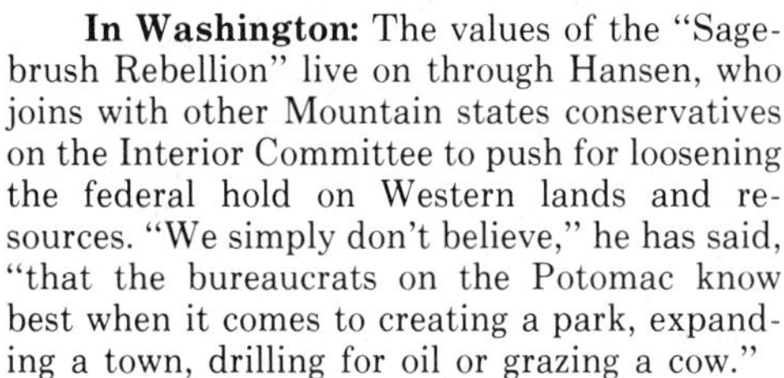

Born: Aug. 14, 1932, Salt Lake City, Utah.
Education: U. of Utah, B.S. 1960.
Military Service: Navy, 1952-54.
Occupation: Insurance executive; land developer.
Family: Wife, Ann Burgoyne; five children.
Religion: Mormon.
Political Career: Farmington City Council, 1968-72; Utah House, 1973-81, Speaker, 1979-81.
Capitol Office: 2421 Rayburn Bldg. 20515; 225-0453.

In Washington: The values of the "Sagebrush Rebellion" live on through Hansen, who joins with other Mountain states conservatives on the Interior Committee to push for loosening the federal hold on Western lands and resources. "We simply don't believe," he has said, "that the bureaucrats on the Potomac know best when it comes to creating a park, expanding a town, drilling for oil or grazing a cow."

Hansen has not disguised his interest in seeking statewide office in 1992; his dilemma is not whether to run, but which office to seek. GOP Gov. Norman H. Bangerter chose not to seek re-election. And senior Republican Sen. Jake Garn announced in May 1991 that he would not run for a fourth term in 1992.

The No. 4 Republican on the Interior Committee, Hansen began the 102nd Congress as ranking member of the Water and Power Subcommittee, leaving the ranking spot on the Energy and the Environment panel. On Interior, Hansen clashes with an in-state rival, Democrat Wayne Owens — particularly on the contentious wilderness issue.

As with many Western states, Utah has been embroiled in a lengthy debate over how much of its land should be set aside as wilderness. A sizable segment of Mountain states opinion regards wilderness legislation with deep suspicion. Yet Hansen was willing to play a mediator's role in drawing Utah wilderness boundaries during the 98th Congress.

In the latest battle, Owens and Hansen dueled in the 101st Congress to settle a dispute over 1.9 million acres identified by the Bureau of Land Management as potential wilderness. Owens' bill would set aside about 5.5 million acres; Hansen's would reserve 1.4 million acres. The debate spilled into the 102nd Congress.

In 1989, Hansen tried something bold to rid the delegation of Owens: He offered a plan to draw Owens' core constituency in Salt Lake City out of his district, and suggested that the Utah Legislature redistrict immediately rather than wait for the 1990 census figures.

In the 101st Congress, Hansen introduced an amendment during House consideration of a disability discrimination bill to permit access for wheelchair-users to designated wilderness areas; it was adopted by voice vote.

Hansen began the 102nd Congress as the new ranking Republican of the House ethics committee, where he has been known to buck the panel's wishes. In 1984, he voted against its recommendation to reprimand Idaho Republican George Hansen. In 1990, he was one of two panel Republicans to vote for harsher punishment than that recommended for Massachusetts Democrat Barney Frank, found to have misused his official position to help a male prostitute. Hansen voted to censure Frank; the committee had recommended a reprimand.

Hansen took a seat on Armed Services in the 100th Congress. There, he looks out for Hill Air Force Base, which is Utah's largest employer. In 1989, Hansen called for Congress to approve the recommendations of an independent commission on closing unneeded military bases, even though Fort Douglas, in Salt Lake City, was among those targeted for closure. Fort Douglas is in Owens' 2nd District.

At Home: Hansen's political fortunes have been closely linked to two individuals — Ronald Reagan and former Democratic Rep. Gunn McKay. Hansen ousted McKay to win the seat in 1980 and beat back his challenges in 1986 and 1988 to hold it. In the first two races, Hansen capitalized on the fact that the 1st was one of the nation's strongest Reagan districts.

Hansen needed the element of surprise to unseat McKay in 1980. Accustomed to being vulnerable and still winning, McKay was slow in preparing for the campaign.

It was a costly mistake. Hansen was Speaker of the Utah House and had already logged nearly two decades in state and local politics. In the Utah Legislature, he had developed a reputation as a pragmatic conservative adept at conciliation.

While Hansen's own proposals combined fiscal conservatism with opposition to gun control, the Equal Rights Amendment and abortion, he cast McKay as a member of the national Democratic leadership responsible for

Utah 1

Ogden and Rural Utah

The railroad center of Ogden and surrounding Weber County comprise the district's Democratic core. It was at Promontory, just north of Ogden, that the golden spike was driven in 1869, creating the nation's first transcontinental rail link. The Church of Jesus Christ of Latter-day Saints (Mormon Church) is an important influence in Weber County, as everywhere in Utah, but the railroads brought a higher number of non-Mormons than in other parts of the state.

Weber County gave Democrat Kenley Brunsdale 55 percent over Hansen in 1990, and was the only one Hansen lost in 1988. The county has a large population of blue-collar workers and union members, a legacy of the railroad era. It also has a sizable number of federal employees who work at Hill Air Force Base and nearby defense installations. Hill, the state's largest employer, prospered under the Reagan administration's defense buildup.

But there were difficult periods. Roughly 13,000 workers faced the threat of a 12-day furlough from their base jobs early in 1988. Hansen worked with other congressmen to block the furloughs, and since then, Hill Air Force Base has been awarded a lucrative C-130 maintenance contract.

Rapidly developing Davis County sits in the corridor between Ogden and Salt Lake City. It is a fast-growing county in which Republicans have a decided edge. In recent years, some of Ogden's population has shifted south to work in Salt Lake City and to live in Davis' bedroom communities. For years, Davis trailed Weber County in population, but in 1980, Davis' population finally surpassed Weber's, and by 1990 it had over 30,000 more residents.

Davis' northern part, around Clearfield and Sunset, follows the lead of adjacent Weber and sometimes votes Democratic. In southern Davis, towns such as Bountiful are part of suburban Salt Lake City and go Republican. Hansen carried Davis by only 2,390 votes in 1990, a major reason why he only received 52 percent districtwide.

The remainder of the district has an almost uniformly Republican coloration — anchored by Cache County (Logan) — the home of Utah State University — in the northeast corner and verdant Washington County in the southwest corner. The population of Washington County has nearly tripled since 1970 as retirees and the wintering wealthy find its semitropical climate attractive. But it is no population center; it has barely a fifth the population of Davis.

Population: 487,833. White 462,032 (95%), Black 4,888 (1%), Other 9,026 (2%). Spanish origin 19,430 (4%). 18 and over 303,406 (62%), 65 and over 38,009 (8%). Median age: 24.

economic troubles and a weakened defense.

But Hansen probably would not have won without Reagan's coattails. Drawing out GOP voters, Reagan polled more than three-quarters of the vote in the 1st, helping Hansen offset McKay's strength in the Ogden area and enabling the GOP challenger to register a narrow 52-48 percent victory. Against less formidable opposition, Hansen pushed his tally to 63 percent in 1982 and to 71 percent in 1984.

In 1986, McKay was ready for a rematch. But he was hampered by a late start and a district map that was substantially different from when he last ran in 1980. Then, the 1st had extended from northern Utah down the eastern side of the state. In 1986, the 1st covered the western half.

Despite Reagan's absence from the ballot, Hansen still sought to tap the president's popularity by framing the election as a referendum on the administration. He ran separate TV ads that featured Reagan and Utah Sen. Jake Garn. "Do we change direction?" Hansen asked, citing the economic successes and conservative tenor of the Reagan years.

In a district where only one out of every six voters was a Democrat, McKay did not dare take on Reagan. But he had no qualms about criticizing Hansen, whom he dismissed as a rubber stamp for the national GOP and an inadequate spokesman for the district's troubled mining, manufacturing and agricultural interests. McKay pointed to his earlier congressional career as a model of effectiveness and claimed that as a member of the House majority, he could get more done than Hansen could.

McKay's comeback bid fell just short. While the Democrat ran narrowly ahead in the populous northern part of the district that he had represented before, Hansen carried southwest Utah for another 52-48 percent victory. The close result encouraged McKay to try again in 1988. Both candidates trotted out similar campaign themes, but their tactics changed.

Certain that he had lost narrowly because he had started late, McKay began early to organize and raise money; he also made several visits to the southwest corner of the state.

Certain that his skimpy margin of victory in 1986 was due to a passive campaign, Hansen promised to challenge McKay more aggressively as a liberal in conservative's clothing.

With George Bush running almost as strongly as Reagan had atop the Republican ticket, Hansen was finally able to beat his old rival easily. He swept 15 of the district's 16 counties, taking 60 percent of the overall vote.

Hansen was expected to have an even easier time two years later, when political neophyte Kenley Brunsdale, who was chief aide to 2nd District Rep. Owens, waged a low-budget bid against him.

Hansen, who was already rumored to be angling for a statewide race in 1992, was expected to have little difficulty dispatching Brunsdale. Republicans delightedly predicted that Brunsdale's association with Owens would doom his candidacy. Owens, they said, was reviled in the 1st for his wilderness proposal. A Hansen fundraising letter derided Brunsdale as "an absolute clone" of Owens.

Brunsdale ran an aggressive, persistent campaign. Early on, he demonstrated his congressional experience while tweaking the incumbent by proposing a series of "bills" to address specific legislative interests in the district, such as his proposal to block construction of a controversial gas pipeline.

Hansen did not debate Brunsdale until five days before Election Day. In the final weeks, Brunsdale stood alongside busy roads at rush hour with large signs reading: "Congress Needs a Change," "Not a $30,000 Pay Raise," and "Honk and Wave." He aired TV ads in the last three days.

While the shock of Election Day was Democrat Bill Orton's triumph in the 3rd, Brunsdale's 44 percent against Hansen raised many eyebrows as well. Along with a third-party candidate, he held Hansen to 52 percent of the vote. Pre-election polls detected no more than one-third of voters supporting the Democrat. Brunsdale won Democratic Weber County (Ogden) handily, but his 45 percent showing in traditionally Republican Davis County, the most populous in the district, was particularly impressive. Brunsdale immediately began plans for a 1992 run.

Committees

Standards of Official Conduct (Ranking)

Armed Services (12th of 22 Republicans)
Military Installations & Facilities; Research & Development

Interior & Insular Affairs (4th of 17 Republicans)
Water, Power & Offshore Energy (ranking); National Parks & Public Lands

Elections

1990 General

James V. Hansen (R)	82,746	(52%)
Kenley Brunsdale (D)	69,491	(44%)
Reva Marx Wadsworth (AM)	6,429	(4%)

1988 General

James V. Hansen (R)	130,893	(60%)
Gunn McKay (D)	87,976	(40%)

Previous Winning Percentages: **1986** (52%) **1984** (71%) **1982** (63%) **1980** (52%)

District Vote For President

	1988	1984	1980	1976
D	60,188 (27%)	47,259 (22%)	39,968 (19%)	65,603 (35%)
R	162,713 (72%)	170,660 (78%)	158,837 (76%)	117,288 (62%)
I			7,723 (4%)	

Campaign Finance

	Receipts	Receipts from PACs		Expend-itures
1990				
Hansen (R)	$271,159	$180,750	(67%)	$237,357
Brunsdale (D)	$133,729	$66,850	(50%)	$133,084
1988				
Hansen (R)	$411,486	$258,859	(63%)	$426,902
McKay (D)	$392,478	$264,850	(67%)	$391,928

Key Votes

1991

Authorize use of force against Iraq	Y

1990

Support constitutional amendment on flag desecration	Y
Pass family and medical leave bill over Bush veto	N
Reduce SDI funding	N
Allow abortions in overseas military facilities	N
Approve budget summit plan for spending and taxing	Y
Approve civil rights bill	N

1989

Halt production of B-2 stealth bomber at 13 planes	N
Oppose capital gains tax cut	N
Approve federal abortion funding in rape or incest cases	N
Approve pay raise and revision of ethics rules	N
Pass Democratic minimum wage plan over Bush veto	N

Voting Studies

	Presidential Support		Party Unity		Conservative Coalition	
Year	S	O	S	O	S	O
1990	83	15	85	10	93	4
1989	80	17	89	7	95	2
1988	66	22	78	8	84	0
1987	73	23	86	8	91	9
1986	79	16	80	8	84	8
1985	81	15	85	9	96	2
1984	74	16	88	5	85	5
1983	77	13	83	3	89	2
1982	77	12	77	8	85	5
1981	71	16	80	4	83	4

Interest Group Ratings

Year	ADA	ACU	AFL-CIO	CCUS
1990	0	92	0	79
1989	0	100	8	100
1988	0	100	0	100
1987	4	95	0	100
1986	0	91	0	93
1985	5	95	0	86
1984	0	88	15	81
1983	0	100	0	89
1982	0	100	6	81
1981	0	100	8	94

2 Wayne Owens (D)

Of Salt Lake City — Elected 1986

Also served 1973-75.

Born: May 2, 1937, Panguitch, Utah.
Education: Attended U. of Utah, 1958-61, J.D. 1964.
Occupation: Lawyer.
Family: Wife, Marlene Wessel; five children.
Religion: Mormon.
Political Career: Democratic nominee for U.S. Senate, 1974; Democratic nominee for governor, 1984.
Capitol Office: 1728 Longworth Bldg. 20515; 225-3011.

In Washington: Owens is a marked man in Utah politics. The only Democrat to win congressional elections in the 1980s in one of the most conservative states in the country, Owens regularly casts votes that seem breathtakingly risky, but his election margins only continue to mount.

Republicans' best strategy for dislodging him may be eviscerating his district. Owens said that because of his vote early in the 102nd Congress against authorizing President Bush to use force in the Persian Gulf, "the Speaker of the [Utah] House has already threatened to reapportion me out of my seat."

Of course, Owens is getting accustomed to GOP line-drawing threats. In 1989, his 1st District neighbor, Republican James V. Hansen, offered a plan to draw Owens' core constituency out of his district — and suggested that the Utah Legislature redistrict immediately, rather than wait for the 1990 census figures.

House Democrats celebrated Owens' 1986 election, but the leadership balked when Owens spread the word that his victory would be rewarded with a seat on Energy and Commerce. No such promise had been made, it seemed, and Owens' talk of it did not go over well with Chairman John D. Dingell. Owens settled for seats on Interior and Foreign Affairs, and he has continued to fall short in his bids for a spot on Energy and Commerce.

But if his hard-charging style can seem impolitic at times, it has enabled him to sell his conservative constituents on a voting record that is quite loyal to the Democratic line. Owens voted with a majority of Democrats more than 80 percent of the time in the 101st Congress. That makes it easy for the Democratic leadership to forgive Owens' occasional stray votes. One came in 1989, when Owens was one of just 20 non-Southern Democrats to vote against a Democratic amendment to kill President Bush's proposed cut in the capital gains tax.

On Foreign Affairs, Owens is particularly interested in the Middle East, but his urgings that Israel open direct negotiations with the Palestine Liberation Organization (PLO) have provoked controversy. After meeting with PLO Chairman Yasir Arafat in early 1989, Owens' observation that Arafat was "committed to no violence" met with uncharitable skepticism from many in Congress.

In the 101st Congress, he was the House sponsor of a joint resolution calling for Antarctica to be closed to commercial development.

Owens' other area of legislative interest is on Interior, where he riles his home-state GOP colleagues by lobbying for a wilderness set-aside of about 5.5 million acres in Utah, compared with the 1.4 million acres proposed by Utah's Republican governor.

In 1990, Owens saw his "downwinders" bill signed into law. It created a $100 million trust fund to compensate those exposed to fallout from the Nevada above-ground nuclear weapons tests in the 1950s and 1960s, as well as those workers who mined uranium for nuclear weapons manufacture from 1947 to 1971.

At Home: Owens' 1986 House victory marked a political redemption not only for him but also for the Utah Democratic Party, which had not scored a congressional win since 1978. In a way, Owens was an unlikely person to end the drought. Although articulate and well-versed on issues, he has constantly faced charges that he is a liberal in one of the most conservative states in the country.

After a stint as aide to Utah's Democratic Sen. Frank E. Moss, Owens worked as Rocky Mountain states coordinator for Robert F. Kennedy's 1968 presidential campaign. When Edward M. Kennedy was Senate majority whip, Owens was his administrative assistant, and when Owens ran for the House in 1972, Kennedy came to Utah to campaign for him.

Owens bristles at GOP charges that he is still to the left of Utah's mainstream. Early in the 1986 campaign, Owens undertook an "inoculation" strategy, pointing to his votes during his first stint in Congress to cut President Richard M. Nixon's budget by $14 billion.

Utah 2

Salt Lake City

There is no mistaking the influence of the Mormon Church in Salt Lake City; Temple Square dominates downtown, relegating the city's two other major institutions located nearby — the seat of state government and the University of Utah — to secondary status on a tour guide's agenda. But even though Mormonism and Republicanism go hand in hand in Utah, the city that is the spiritual capital of the Church of Jesus Christ of Latter-day Saints has enough Democratic blue-collar workers and liberal yuppies to tilt the 2nd Democratic in many elections, as Owens' recent victories have demonstrated.

The portion of Salt Lake County in the 2nd, which includes all of the city proper, favored Democrat Scott M. Matheson in his 1976 and 1980 gubernatorial victories. And countywide returns in 1988 showed Democratic gubernatorial hopeful Ted Wilson (a one-time Salt Lake City mayor) an easy winner.

When Owens left the 2nd in 1974 for his first statewide bid, Democrat Allan T. Howe replaced him. But Howe lost two years later after being convicted of soliciting sex from a policewoman posing as a prostitute. The 2nd may be more tolerant than Utah's other districts, but it has its limits.

Salt Lake City's working-class West Side, traditional home for many copper miners, generally goes Democratic, as does the central-city section. In the northern hills, called The Avenues, professionals in their 20s and 30s sometimes vote Democratic as well. But in the wealthy Wasatch foothills section, called the East Bench, Republicans usually dominate. More 2nd District voters actually live in the Salt Lake suburbs than in the city itself. Voters in such suburban communities as Cottonwood and Murray habitually side with the GOP.

In addition to its role as a center for religion, government and education, Salt Lake City — located about a third of the way between Denver and the West Coast — is a funnel for goods and people. Its airport has become a busy hub for Portland, San Francisco and Los Angeles flights, and Interstate highways heading to each of those cities fan out from the Salt Lake City area. High-technology firms such as Sperry and Litton manufacture items ranging from missiles to communications equipment, and ski slopes east of the city help generate tourism.

Population: 487,475. White 458,410 (94%), Black 3,555 (1%), Other 10,405 (2%). Spanish origin 24,004 (5%). 18 and over 325,863 (67%), 65 and over 43,307 (9%). Median age: 26.

Utah Republicans responded with an ad that featured a man breaking into peals of laughter when he heard Owens described as a fiscal conservative. But the GOP had no aggressive candidate to drive home the point.

Their nominee, Salt Lake County Commissioner Tom Shimizu, did have some advantages over retiring GOP Rep. David S. Monson, who was weighed down by questionable business relationships and lackluster appeal to voters. But Shimizu did not have the aggressiveness needed to discredit Owens' comeback campaign. Except for one brief flurry when he uncharacteristically referred to Owens as "a crybaby and a boob," Shimizu spent his time seeking to tie himself to President Ronald Reagan.

Owens emphasized the need for Utah to have Democratic representation in the Democratic-controlled House. He made inroads in Utah's normally Republican business community, built a $700,000 campaign treasury and won with 55 percent of the vote.

In 1988, Republicans nominated a younger, more aggressive candidate than they did in 1986, picking Richard Snelgrove, the chairman of the Salt Lake County GOP and the manager of his family's large ice cream company.

Snelgrove derided Owens as "Washington Wayne" and highlighted a variety of issues, from taxes to the Pledge of Allegiance, on which he claimed a more conservative position than the incumbent. He contended that Owens was being bankrolled in large part by organized labor.

But Owens proved just as adept at deflecting Snelgrove's charges as he had Shimizu's. Owens continued to draw money from the Salt Lake City business community by wooing small-business men with his opposition to Democratic proposals for an increase in the minimum wage and mandatory parental leave. For good measure, Owens trumpeted his support of a balanced-budget constitutional amendment and a variation of the line-item veto. On Election Day, Owens improved on his 1986 showing, taking 57 percent of the vote.

Owens' next election brought the promise of a heavyweight clash. Former Republican Rep. Dan Marriott, who represented the 2nd from 1977 to 1985, sought to reclaim his seat. He began the campaign year as the prohibitive favorite to win the GOP nomination over Genevieve Atwood, a former state representative who served as state geologist for eight years.

Marriott came within a handful of votes at the 2nd District GOP convention of winning the nomination. But Atwood excelled at assembling a grass-roots organization of delegates who were attracted by her more moderate positions on the environment and military spending. She amassed enough support to force Marriott into a September primary.

The energy that propelled Atwood through the convention never flagged in the primary, while Marriott's campaign never lived up to expectations. His fundraising was sluggish, and several of his comments backfired, particularly his statement that he sanctioned U.S. use of nuclear weapons against Iraq. Atwood ran up a 17-percentage-point primary win.

Awaiting Atwood with a campaign treasury several times hers was Owens, who had been running TV ads throughout the year. Atwood may have been able to outmaneuver Marriott, but against Owens, a polished and skillful political veteran, she was overmatched.

Some Republicans may have had trouble backing a non-Mormon woman who derailed the staunchly conservative Marriott. Owens' 58 percent was his best House election showing.

When Owens made his first congressional race back in 1972, he walked more than 1,000 miles across the district, which then covered almost the entire western half of Utah. He presented himself as a fresh face who would vote unconditionally to end the Vietnam War. In a less conservative era of Utah politics, he ousted GOP Rep. Sherman P. Lloyd.

Owens likely could have won re-election in 1974, but he sought the Senate seat of retiring Republican Wallace F. Bennett. Early polls showed Owens ahead of GOP nominee Jake Garn. Garn, however, projected a more mature image than Owens, who looked considerably younger than his age. Owens lost to Garn, 50-44 percent.

That was the closest Owens came to winning higher office. Seeking the governorship in the more conservative climate of 1984, he was beaten by Republican Norman H. Bangerter by 12 percentage points.

Committees

Foreign Affairs (16th of 28 Democrats)
Europe & the Middle East; Human Rights & International Organizations

Interior & Insular Affairs (18th of 29 Democrats)
Energy & the Environment; National Parks & Public Lands; Water, Power & Offshore Energy

Select Aging (35th of 42 Democrats)
Health & Long-Term Care; Social Security and Women

Select Intelligence (12th of 12 Democrats)
Legislation; Program & Budget Authorization

Elections

1990 General		
Wayne Owens (D)	85,167	(58%)
Genevieve Atwood (R)	58,869	(40%)
Lawrence Topham (I)	3,424	(2%)
1988 General		
Wayne Owens (D)	112,129	(57%)
Richard Snelgrove (R)	80,212	(41%)

Previous Winning Percentages: **1986** (55%) **1972** (55%)

District Vote For President

	1988	1984	1980	1976
D	86,241 (40%)	64,712 (31%)	48,612 (23%)	72,856 (36%)
R	125,619 (58%)	144,966 (68%)	137,579 (66%)	125,057 (61%)
I			17,580 (8%)	

Campaign Finance

	Receipts	Receipts from PACs		Expenditures
1990				
Owens (D)	$1,014,489	$541,232	(53%)	$1,088,929
Atwood (R)	$505,299	$85,596	(17%)	$490,726
1988				
Owens (D)	$736,198	$455,310	(62%)	$676,472
Snelgrove (R)	$278,426	$60,544	(22%)	$289,305

Key Votes

1991	
Authorize use of force against Iraq	N
1990	
Support constitutional amendment on flag desecration	N
Pass family and medical leave bill over Bush veto	Y
Reduce SDI funding	Y
Allow abortions in overseas military facilities	Y
Approve budget summit plan for spending and taxing	Y
Approve civil rights bill	Y
1989	
Halt production of B-2 stealth bomber at 13 planes	Y
Oppose capital gains tax cut	N
Approve federal abortion funding in rape or incest cases	Y
Approve pay raise and revision of ethics rules	Y
Pass Democratic minimum wage plan over Bush veto	Y

Voting Studies

	Presidential Support		Party Unity		Conservative Coalition	
Year	S	O	S	O	S	O
1990	21	74	84 †	10 †	30	69
1989	27	63	86	4	20	80
1988	22	72	84	12	47	50
1987	21	69	83	7	26	56

† Not eligible for all recorded votes.

Interest Group Ratings

Year	ADA	ACU	AFL-CIO	CCUS
1990	72	13	75	23
1989	70	11	73	30
1988	75	16	93	36
1987	76	0	93	31

3 Bill Orton (D)

Of Provo — Elected 1990

Born: Sept. 22, 1949, North Ogden, Utah.
Education: Brigham Young U., B.S. 1973, J.D. 1979.
Occupation: Lawyer.
Family: Single.
Religion: Mormon.
Political Career: No previous office.
Capitol Office: 1723 Longworth Bldg. 20515; 225-7751.

The Path to Washington: Of all the districts to change party hands in 1990, Utah's 3rd was the most stunning. Home to some of the nation's most impregnable Republican territory, the 3rd had never given a Democratic House nominee more than one-third of the vote in its four-election existence.

Orton achieved the seemingly impossible, not only carrying the 3rd but winning resoundingly over his Republican foe, former state Sen. Karl Snow.

Orton, a tax lawyer who worked for the Internal Revenue Service for 10 years, was given no chance of success when he entered the contest to succeed retiring GOP Rep. Howard C. Nielson.

The Democrat was a political unknown seeking public office for the first time in a district often billed as the most Republican in the nation. But an ideological holy war tore the GOP asunder, leaving Snow a bloodied nominee who was unable to rely on united support in his party ranks.

Snow, a moderate by Utah standards, brawled with conservative think-tank chairman John L. Harmer in the GOP primary and captured 66 percent of the vote.

Harmer sought to paint Snow as a liberal, but he had to spend much of his time fending off questions about his personal finances.

In November, exit polls suggested that many former Harmer supporters turned their backs on Snow and voted for Orton.

Two other clouds gloomed Snow's horizon. He was dogged by negative publicity lingering from the primary concerning his ownership of certain stocks and his business association with a convicted felon.

Fragments of the story continued to filter out in the last weeks of the campaign. A former Harmer campaign aide, writing in a Brigham Young University (BYU) off-campus newspaper, raised questions about Snow's honesty in addressing the questions.

Snow was also damaged by an advertisement placed by his own campaign in a Provo newspaper on the Sunday before Election Day.

The ad, which asserted that "values do matter" in urging readers to "vote Republican," featured a photograph of Snow with his wife and children. The caption read: "Snow and his family." To its right was a photograph of Orton's face and the caption: "Orton and his family." Orton is not married.

Republicans and Democrats agreed that the ad largely backfired on Snow.

A former Reagan administration official who had joined the Snow campaign as the honorary chairman took responsibility for the ad.

But Orton did not manage to register a landslide victory through disaffected voters alone. Throughout the campaign, he promoted himself as a conservative Democrat acceptable to his fellow Mormons, who usually prefer the GOP.

He supports a constitutional amendment to balance the budget and a presidential line-item veto. He opposes abortion and advocates a downsized federal government.

Nielson helped Snow in the primary, endorsing his longtime friend over Harmer. But he was unable to transfer his popularity to Snow a second time in the November contest with Orton.

Even Nielson's enthusiasm appeared to wane: At a late October news conference that was hastily assembled to shore up Snow's dwindling support, Nielson reaffirmed his backing but said that Snow had used "poor judgment" in his stock-market dealings.

On Election Day, Orton's triumph was sweeping and unequivocal. He won all but two of the district's 13 counties. In Salt Lake County, Orton received 61 percent of the vote.

Most startling were the results from Utah County (Provo), the district's most populous and the home of BYU. Ronald Reagan carried Utah County with 83 percent in 1984; Orton won it 55 percent to 37 percent in 1990.

Utah 3

Provo and Rural Utah

Provo and surrounding Utah County are home to the most intense Mormon community in the state. That is in large part because Provo is the location of Brigham Young University, founded in 1875 to prepare Mormon youth for teaching and religious proselytizing.

Because of the religious connection, Provo (Utah County) is a college town like few others in the country. BYU's sprawling modern campus (with more than 27,000 students and 1,600 faculty) is the focal point of the city's life, and the school's consistently successful sports teams provide an extra element of social cohesion. The Mormon influence makes Utah County one of the nation's most impregnable Republican strongholds, which is why Democrat Bill Orton's 1990 victory in the 3rd was so earthshaking.

In the district's presidential contests, GOP margins are awesome. Ronald Reagan drew 83 percent of the county's vote in 1984; George Bush carried it with an only slightly more modest 77 percent in 1988. But against damaged Republican nominee Karl Snow, Orton drew 55 percent in Utah County.

The northern section of the county contains Lehi and American Fork — towns whose blue-collar workers have been employed at the Geneva steelworks plant, closed by USX Corp. in 1987 but subsequently reopened under independent management. Even in these communities, however, Mormon values are crucial and Democrats can rarely count on a heavy vote to help them.

Democrats are stronger in the southwest part of Salt Lake County. Although voters there differ little from those elsewhere in the district when it comes to national elections, Orton won a solid 61 percent of the Salt Lake County vote in 1990. Many of the people there, living in towns such as South Jordan and West Valley City, have worked in the Kennecott copper pit in Kearns. Kennecott severely cut back its Utah operations in 1985 due to losses tied to depressed copper prices. But the pit has since been sold to a British Petroleum subsidiary, and it is operating again with modernized facilities and a work force exceeding 2,000 at both the pit in Kearns and the refinery in Magna.

The rest of the district is rural and sparsely populated. Much of it is mountains and desert. Cattle ranching and mining are the leading industries, and the GOP is by far the dominant political party.

Cinematic legends — including John Wayne — have plied their trade in epic Western movies filmed in the canyons and desert near the town of Moab, in Grand County. To the south, many Native Americans live in San Juan County, often in near-Third World conditions. In the southeast corner of San Juan County is the only point in the United States common to four state boundaries — those of Arizona, Colorado, New Mexico and Utah.

Population: 485,729. White 462,108 (95%), Black 782 (0.2%), Other 14,901 (3%). Spanish origin 16,868 (4%). 18 and over 291,663 (60%), 65 and over 27,904 (6%). Median age: 22.

Committees

Banking, Finance & Urban Affairs (25th of 31 Democrats)
Financial Institutions Supervision, Regulation & Insurance; Housing & Community Development; International Development, Finance, Trade & Monetary Policy

Foreign Affairs (27th of 28 Democrats)
International Economic Policy & Trade

Small Business (27th of 27 Democrats)
Exports, Tax Policy & Special Problems

Campaign Finance

	Receipts	Receipts from PACs		Expend-itures
1990				
Orton (D)	$86,601	$32,000	(37%)	$88,234
Snow (R)	$291,945	$108,090	(37%)	$290,439

Key Vote

1991

Authorize use of force against Iraq — Y

Elections

1990 General

Bill Orton (D)	79,163	(58%)
Karl Snow (R)	49,452	(36%)
Robert Smith (AM)	6,542	(5%)

District Vote For President

	1988	1984	1980	1976
D	60,127 (30%)	43,398 (22%)	35,686 (19%)	43,651 (30%)
R	140,110 (69%)	153,479 (77%)	143,271 (77%)	95,563 (65%)
I			4,981 (3%)	

Vermont

U.S. CONGRESS

SENATE 1 D, 1 R
HOUSE 1 Independent

LEGISLATURE

Senate 15 D, 15 R
House 73 D, 75 R, 2 Independents

ELECTIONS

1988 Presidential Vote	
Bush	51%
Dukakis	48%
1984 Presidential Vote	
Reagan	58%
Mondale	41%
1980 Presidential Vote	
Reagan	44%
Carter	38%
Anderson	15%
Turnout rate in 1986	47%
Turnout rate in 1988	59%
Turnout rate in 1990	49%

(as percentage of voting age population)

POPULATION AND GROWTH

1980 population	511,456
1990 population (48th in the nation)	562,758
Percent change 1980-1990	+10%

DEMOGRAPHIC BREAKDOWN

White	99%
Black	0.3%
Asian or Pacific Islander	1%
(Hispanic origin)	1%
Urban	34%
Rural	66%
Born in state	62%
Foreign-born	4%

MAJOR CITIES

Burlington	39,127
Rutland	18,230
South Burlington	12,809
Barre	9,482
Essex Junction	8,396

AREA AND LAND USE

Area	9,273 sq. miles (43rd)
Farm	27%
Forest	76%
Federally owned	5%

Gov. Richard A. Snelling (R)
Of Shelburne — Elected 1990
(also served 1977-83)

Born: Feb. 18, 1927, Allentown, Pa.
Education: Harvard U., A.B. 1948.
Military Service: Army, 1944-46.
Occupation: Industrial executive.
Religion: Unitarian.
Political Career: Vt. House, 1959-61, 1973-77, majority leader, 1975-77; GOP nominee for governor, 1966; GOP nominee for U.S. Senate, 1986.
Next Election: 1992.

WORK

Occupations	
White-collar	51%
Blue-collar	31%
Service workers	13%
Government Workers	
Federal	5,087
State	14,679
Local	20,659

MONEY

Median family income	$ 17,205	(40th)
Tax burden per capita	$ 857	(25th)

EDUCATION

Spending per pupil through grade 12	$ 5,207	(7th)
Persons with college degrees	19%	(10th)

CRIME

Violent crime rate	133 per 100,000 (48th)

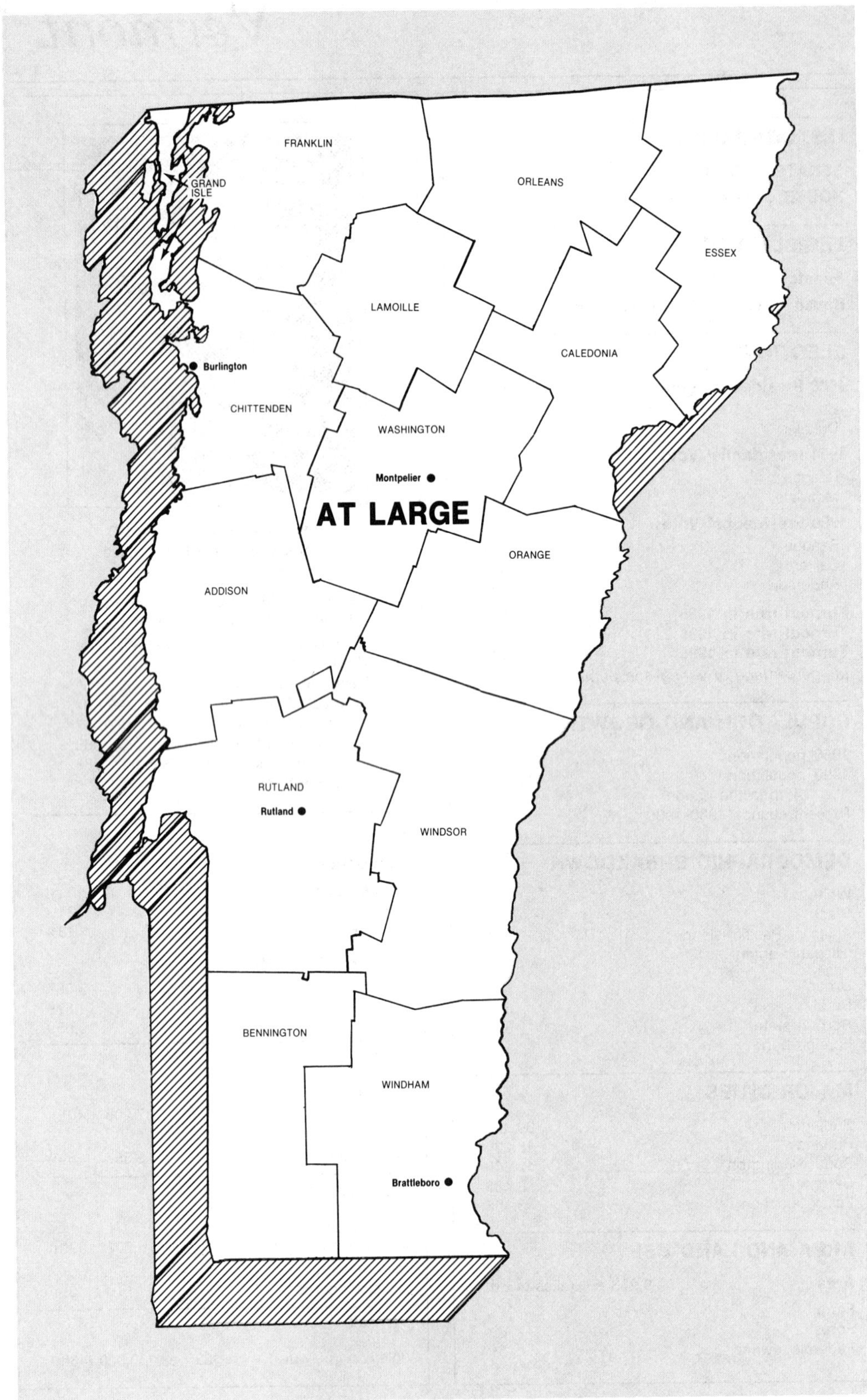
FRANKLIN
GRAND ISLE
ORLEANS
ESSEX
LAMOILLE
CALEDONIA
Burlington
CHITTENDEN
WASHINGTON
Montpelier
AT LARGE
ORANGE
ADDISON
RUTLAND
Rutland
WINDSOR
BENNINGTON
WINDHAM
Brattleboro

Patrick J. Leahy (D)

Of Middlesex — Elected 1974

Born: March 31, 1940, Montpelier, Vt.
Education: St. Michael's College, B.A. 1961; Georgetown U., J.D. 1964.
Occupation: Lawyer.
Family: Wife, Marcelle Pomerleau; three children.
Religion: Roman Catholic.
Political Career: Chittenden County state's attorney, 1967-75.
Capitol Office: 433 Russell Bldg. 20510; 224-4242.

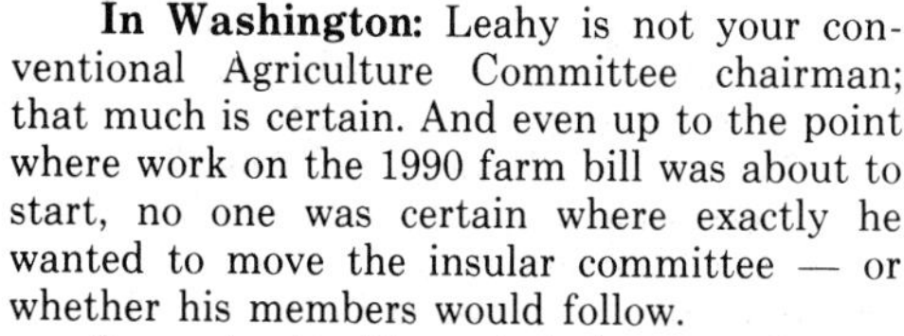

In Washington: Leahy is not your conventional Agriculture Committee chairman; that much is certain. And even up to the point where work on the 1990 farm bill was about to start, no one was certain where exactly he wanted to move the insular committee — or whether his members would follow.

In contrast with past chairmen and most current members, Leahy shows relatively little interest in the multibillion-dollar programs subsidizing America's major farm commodities. He is neither opponent nor reformer. He simply has other priorities within Agriculture's bailiwick, and they happen to be the issues that most past chairmen treated as secondary interests, or not at all — the environment, rural development and nutrition programs.

He is a big defender of dairy programs important to Vermont and, working alongside senators from the various farm belts, Leahy likes to drop lines about his own rural roots. But no one would mistake Leahy for a rustic; he is more like a gentleman farmer, or like the liberal-leaning hobby farmers who have moved to his bucolic state in recent years to escape big-city anxieties, helping transform Vermont from a Republican state to a Democratic one.

Until he became chairman in 1987, Leahy did not devote much attention to farm policy; foreign policy was his main pursuit. He chairs the Appropriations Subcommittee on Foreign Operations and is the former vice chairman of the Intelligence Committee.

After his heady work with covert actions and foreign policy, it was expected that Leahy might find Agriculture a bit boring; in that regard, he resembled the committee's senior Republican, Richard G. Lugar, who had been a celebrated Foreign Relations Committee chairman when Republicans controlled the Senate.

Farm-state members warily considered the New England liberal who was known to poke fun at farm programs and who vowed when he took over the chairmanship to put a stop to "business as usual" on the panel, where logrolling is a tradition. As work on the five-year reauthorization of agriculture programs was about to begin, members worried that the chairman would not protect government subsidies for their commodities.

"No commodity has to worry that I'm going to sell them offshore [*sic*]," Leahy said in 1989. "But neither am I wedded to a particular commodity. I'm able to sit there and say, 'Look guys, I get nothing out of this.' "

More than anything else, however, farm-state members and commodity group lobbyists worried about Leahy's environmental agenda. Long a proponent of tougher pesticide regulations, he helped engineer passage of a limited compromise in 1988 after years of stalemate.

Leahy did press for strict new pesticide regulations, and farm programs did take a $13.6 billion cut in the final farm bill. Nevertheless, Leahy received generally good grades from some who had been skeptics for his performance in negotiating the farm bill. He dexterously balanced the concerns of all interested parties on the committee — traditional farm-state senators looking out for their commodities' fair share, Republicans seeking to hold the line on spending, and an aggressive group of "prairie populist" Democrats agitating for considerably higher prices. Leahy was able to keep Republicans on board and produce a farm bill with less of the partisan recriminations that had accompanied the 1985 bill.

Earlier in the 101st Congress, Leahy had shown some ability to protect his turf. During 1989 deliberations over a drought-relief bill, he ably parried an attempt by Minority Leader Bob Dole, an Agriculture Committee veteran and the central player on the 1985 farm bill, to reassert control over the panel. And Leahy spearheaded the successful opposition to a controversial Bush administration nominee for a top environmental post at the Agriculture Department.

Leahy is a congenial chairman; no one complained that he failed to give him a fair hearing. He has forged a close working relationship with Lugar, who, like Leahy, has more interest in environmental protection than many committee members. Together, Leahy and Lugar brokered a compromise on a section of the bill that bars draining swamps and marshes for farming. The final farm bill was touted by Leahy and farm-state lawmakers as the most environmentally conscious ever.

But Leahy was well out in front of the committee's consensus with his amendment to bar the export of pesticides that cannot be used domestically and may not be present as residue on food sold in the United States.

His proposal aimed to curtail what was dubbed the "circle of poison," in which domestically banned pesticides re-enter the United States on imported fruit and vegetables. "Because [the Food and Drug Administration] waves through virtually all imported food without inspection, these chemicals often end up on America's dinner table," Leahy said.

Committee Republicans and the Bush administration opposed the pesticide export measure, as did House conferees, led by Agriculture Committee Chairman E. "Kika" de la Garza of Texas. Lugar offered an amendment to loosen the restrictions, straining his relations with Leahy, who said adopting the amendment would be "a triumph of special interests over the public interest." With no settlement in sight, Leahy withdrew the "circle of poison" provision; he reintroduced it in the 102nd Congress.

Assembling the farm bill while Washington was in an intense budget-cutting mood, Leahy worked hard trying to keep his Democratic members in tow. A group of populist Midwesterners, led by Bob Kerrey of Nebraska and Tom Daschle of South Dakota, sought an election-year fight with Republicans over increasing farm subsidies. Leahy appointed a bipartisan task force to resolve differences on the bill, but after three weeks of negotiations, the talks broke off, with the populists threatening to fight in public for their position.

But the populists could not muster enough support for their position in committee; Lugar helped Leahy by keeping Republicans from breaking ranks on key committee votes. Although the populists caused some embarrassing moments for Leahy, compelling him to delay markups as he caucused behind closed doors to reach a consensus among Democrats, they conceded under pressure from senior Democrats. On the floor, the populists found no more support for raising target prices. The conference agreement froze price- and income-support levels (the estimated $13.6 billion in cuts were made in the budget "reconciliation" bill). The populists voted against the final package.

Earlier in the decade, Leahy was best known at Agriculture for his work on dairy programs and for his attacks on President Reagan's farm policies. He helped draft the part of the 1985 farm bill that created the "whole herd buy-out" program, which paid milk producers to send their entire herds to slaughter so milk production would be cut — and with it the government's purchases of dairy surpluses.

As he took over Agriculture, Leahy had to make a premature exit from a post he had parlayed into prominence on foreign affairs — vice chairman of the Intelligence Committee — after he admitted leaking information to a reporter. With the 101st Congress, Leahy assumed a new role that has restored some of his foreign policy influence: chairman of Appropriations' Foreign Operations Subcommittee.

Leahy's early departure from Intelligence, months before his eight-year stint was to expire, was a public embarrassment, and it also reinforced some colleagues' private view of him as a spotlight seeker. That view partly explains Leahy's late 1988 loss when he tried to become secretary of the Senate Democratic Conference; also important was the fact that the winner, moderate David Pryor of Arkansas, offered regional and ideological balance to a liberal leadership circle lacking a Southerner.

The object of Leahy's leak was not classified information, but a draft Intelligence Committee report about the just-revealed Iran-contra affair. It was compiled in the last days of GOP control of the panel, and Democrats voted not to release the report when they took over for the 100th Congress. The Reagan administration, meanwhile, claimed the report cleared the president. Leahy, in a statement, said he let a reporter see the document "to show that it was being held up because there were major gaps and other problems with it, and not because of a desire to embarrass the president."

Leahy served on the committee at a time of intense controversy over intelligence issues, including a string of spy scandals and covert actions in Central America, all of which made the articulate, witty and outspoken administration critic highly sought after by the media.

He visited Central America in 1983, hinting afterward that the administration was illegally trying to overthrow the Nicaraguan regime. Leahy found few allies until the 1984 revelation of the CIA's role in the mining of Nicaraguan harbors. By year's end, Congress voted to cut off contra aid; thereafter, Leahy pressed for information about any administration or CIA role in circumventing the ban. In September 1985, national security adviser Robert C. McFarlane assured Leahy and Republican Intelligence Chairman Dave Durenberger of Minnesota that no one in the White House was violating the ban — a line the Iran-contra hearings proved false. Congress resumed open military aid in 1986; Leahy's amendment to bar the CIA from involvement was killed 57-42.

In the 101st Congress, Leahy shifted his focus to El Salvador. Leahy was far less sympathetic to administration requests for aid to that country than his predecessor in the Foreign Operations chair, Hawaiian Daniel K. Inouye. In committee, Leahy in 1989 won approval of an amendment placing detailed restrictions on military aid to El Salvador. But on the floor, the Senate voted 68-32 to remove the language. Later that year, Leahy tried again, losing 58-39.

The November 1989 murder of six priests at a Roman Catholic university in San Salvador — allegedly by Salvadoran military personnel — altered Congress' mood on restricting aid. In 1990, Leahy and Connecticut Democrat Christopher J. Dodd offered an amendment requiring an immediate 50 percent cut in the $85 million in military aid provided annually to El Salvador. The Senate adopted it 74-25. The Bush administration opposed the measure but could not make a credible veto threat because the bill contained a coveted debt-relief provision for Egypt.

Leahy balked initially at the administration's request to forgive approximately $7 billion in military debt owed by Egypt. But Bush convinced senators that the fate of Egyptian President Hosni Mubarak might depend on debt relief. Leahy ardently defended the administration's request in conference, where he clashed with his House counterpart, Wisconsin Democrat David R. Obey, who adamantly opposed it. The compromise jelled only after some verbal brawling between the chairmen, and several closed-door caucuses.

On Appropriations' Defense Subcommittee, Leahy is a leading critic of the controversial B-2 stealth bomber. His amendment in 1989 to cut off production at 13 bombers was rejected 29-71. In 1990, his amendment to kill the program outright after completing six planes under construction was rejected 43-56, after failing 15-14 in committee. He later tried to halt the program at 15 planes, but lost, 44-50.

As the troop buildup proceeded in the Persian Gulf following Iraq's invasion of Kuwait, Leahy suggested to Bush that the gulf effort be funded on a "pay-as-you-go" basis by implementing a war tax. Like most Democrats, he voted not to authorize Bush to use force against Iraq.

At the Judiciary Committee, Leahy is chairman of the Technology Subcommittee. In the 100th Congress, he helped win ratification after more than a century of the Berne Convention, which set minimum international copyright standards for artists' works.

Leahy was a conspicuous foe of moves in 1989 and 1990 to amend the Constitution to ban physical desecration of the flag. He supported a statutory ban on flag desecration that became law in 1989, but the Supreme Court ruled it unconstitutional.

In the 101st Congress, Leahy, a longtime opponent of gun-control measures, supported a bill outlawing certain semiautomatic assault weapons. He was castigated by the National Rifle Association, but he defended his action. "I'm as anti-gun control as anyone, but there are areas where the legitimate rights of gun owners have to step back." The Judiciary Committee approved the measure by a vote of 7-6, but ultimately it was stripped from the 1990 anticrime bill.

In 1987, he helped defeat conservative Supreme Court nominee Robert H. Bork, in the process coining the much-repeated phrase "confirmation conversion" to suggest that Bork had moderated his views to win approval.

At Home: Leahy's overwhelming 1986 victory over former GOP Gov. Richard A. Snelling in 1986 firmly established him as the dominant Democratic figure in Vermont. This status guarantees Leahy almost constant visibility in the state media and gives him a leg up on his 1992 re-election campaign.

However, being a partisan leader can have its down side, as Leahy learned in 1990. Leahy faced a quandary over whether to endorse little-known college professor Dolores Sandoval, the hapless Democratic nominee for Vermont's at-large House seat.

Sandoval won the nomination by default after former Burlington Mayor Bernard Sanders, an independent socialist, announced plans for a rematch with freshman GOP Rep. Peter Smith. Sanders had blown past the Democratic candidate in his near-upset of Smith in 1988, and no leading Democrat wanted to risk a similar fate.

Many members of the party's liberal wing abandoned Sandoval and endorsed Sanders. Leahy indicated that he would opt as usual to endorse the Democratic ticket, but Sandoval gave him an out by making a series of controversial statements: She called for decriminalization of drugs, opposed the initial U.S. military response to Iraq's invasion of Kuwait and called for a cutoff of aid to Israel if that nation did not negotiate with the Palestinians. Declaring his opposition to these views, Leahy withheld an endorsement. Sanders went on to defeat Smith; Sandoval got 3 percent of the vote.

That Leahy would loom large over Vermont politics was not at all clear even after his first two Senate victories. Running in 1974 in what had long been a Yankee Republican bastion, Leahy scored a breakthrough for Democrats by winning an open Senate seat with barely 50 percent of the vote. But he had to weather an unexpectedly tough race to hold the seat in 1980, winning by a similarly slim margin.

When he first won office more than two decades ago, Leahy was in the vanguard of Democratic gains in Vermont. At 26, he was elected Chittenden County state's attorney in 1967. He revamped the office and headed a national task force of district attorneys probing the 1973-74 energy crisis.

In 1974, Leahy ran for the Senate seat being vacated by Republican George D. Aiken. Leahy was just 34, presenting a contrast with the 82-year-old political institution he hoped to replace. But he was already balding and graying, and looked older than he was.

Leahy was an underdog against GOP Rep. Richard W. Mallary. But Mallary proved a rather awkward campaigner, and Watergate made Vermont more receptive to a Democrat, enabling Leahy to win narrowly.

Leahy survived in 1980 by emphasizing his roots in the state rather than his ties to the Democratic Party. Campaigning against the national GOP tide, he fought off New York-born challenger Stewart Ledbetter with the slogan: "Pat Leahy: Of Vermont, For Vermont."

It took all of Leahy's ingenuity to overcome Ledbetter, a former state banking and insurance commissioner. Using money from national GOP groups, Ledbetter argued that Leahy was a free-spending liberal who was weak on defense. Reagan's coattails almost elected him.

Although polls throughout Leahy's second term showed his popularity rising in Vermont, GOP officials looked forward to taking him on in 1986. His narrow re-election had pegged him as the most vulnerable Democratic incumbent up that year — a status that was reinforced when Snelling, who had retired in 1985 after four terms as governor, agreed to tackle Leahy.

Leahy, however, was well prepared and well financed, and the "battle of the titans" never developed. Having been criticized for the low profile of his first term, Leahy had made certain that his constituents knew about his activities through press releases and newsletters. As the senior Democrat on Intelligence, he was often on national TV. Leahy also built a strong organizational edge.

Meanwhile, Snelling had spent much of 1985 on an Atlantic sailing excursion. But a late start was not Snelling's only problem. He was bucking Vermont's pro-incumbent tradition. This bias helped Leahy to large leads in early polls, which in turn hurt Snelling's fund raising.

Snelling's biggest handicap was the lack of political distance between himself and Leahy. Snelling, a moderate, held similar positions to Leahy on many issues. His efforts to run as a Reaganite rang false; as governor, he had been a sharp critic of Reagan's budget priorities. In desperation, Snelling resorted to attacking Leahy's attendance record and labeling him one of the Senate's "biggest spenders." Leahy won in a landslide, with 63 percent of the vote.

Committees

Agriculture, Nutrition & Forestry (Chairman)

Appropriations (6th of 16 Democrats)
Defense; Foreign Operations (chairman); VA, HUD and Independent Agencies; Interior

Judiciary (5th of 8 Democrats)
Technology & the Law (chairman); Patents, Copyrights & Trademarks

Elections

1986 General		
Patrick J. Leahy (D)	124,123	(63%)
Richard A. Snelling (R)	67,798	(35%)

Previous Winning Percentages: **1980** (50%) **1974** (50%)

Campaign Finance

	Receipts	Receipts from PACs		Expend-itures
1986				
Leahy (D)	$1,919,740	$822,931	(43%)	$1,705,099
Snelling (R)	$1,495,491	$258,377	(17%)	$1,502,304

Key Votes

1991	
Authorize use of force against Iraq	N
1990	
Oppose prohibition of certain semiautomatic weapons	N
Support constitutional amendment on flag desecration	N
Oppose requiring parental notice for minors' abortions	Y
Halt production of B-2 stealth bomber at 13 planes	Y
Approve budget that cut spending and raised revenues	Y
Pass civil rights bill over Bush veto	Y
1989	
Oppose reduction of SDI funding	N
Oppose barring federal funds for "obscene" art	Y
Allow vote on capital gains tax cut	N

Voting Studies

	Presidential Support		Party Unity		Conservative Coalition	
Year	**S**	**O**	**S**	**O**	**S**	**O**
1990	32	68	98	7	22	78
1989	47	53	96	4	8	92
1988	34	58	93	5	8	92
1987	33	62	85	9	9	84
1986	24	70	83	11	21	75
1985	29	68	83	16	27	73
1984	30	62	85	11	15	77
1983	41	58	89	10	18	82
1982	37	62	91	9	12	88
1981	34	60	76	8	4	84

Interest Group Ratings

Year	ADA	ACU	AFL-CIO	CCUS
1990	94	4	56	17
1989	100	0	100	38
1988	100	0	86	36
1987	90	4	89	31
1986	85	9	87	29
1985	70	13	86	41
1984	95	10	91	35
1983	85	4	88	32
1982	90	20	92	45
1981	95	0	89	6

James M. Jeffords (R)

Of Shrewsbury — Elected 1988

Born: May 11, 1934, Rutland, Vt.
Education: Yale U., B.S.I.A. 1956; Harvard U., LL.B. 1962.
Military Service: Navy, 1956-59; Naval Reserve, 1959-present.
Occupation: Lawyer.
Family: Wife, Elizabeth Daley; two children.
Religion: Congregationalist.
Political Career: Vt. Senate, 1967-69; Vt. attorney general, 1969-73; sought Republican nomination for governor, 1972; U.S. House, 1975-89.
Capitol Office: 530 Dirksen Bldg. 20510; 224-5141.

In Washington: At times during his 14-year House career, Jeffords was best described by the word "maverick." His moderate-to-liberal leanings and his independence from party discipline were symbolized in 1987, when he was the only Republican to support a controversial budget-reconciliation measure that passed by one vote.

If Jeffords did not stand out so definitively during the 101st Congress — his first since graduating to the Senate — it was not because he had changed his philosophy or style. Rather, he had been elected in 1988 to a body in which individualism is better accepted and party unity less honored than in the House. Jeffords became part of the Senate's bloc of influential Republican moderates, and was seldom left standing alone when he bolted the party line, particularly on such domestic issues as education, child care and workers' benefits that are his fortes.

The fact that George Bush came into the presidency with less of an ideological mission than Ronald Reagan may have helped Jeffords appear as more of a GOP loyalist. In only one year of Reagan's tenure did Jeffords support the president's positions on legislation more often than he opposed them. However, he backed Bush on 68 percent of Senate votes in 1989 and on 51 percent in 1990.

On the most dramatic vote of his Senate tenure, in January 1991, Jeffords supported the resolution authorizing Bush to use force to end Iraq's occupation of Kuwait. In doing so, Jeffords crossed an anti-war constituency that is a potent force in Vermont politics.

Yet among his party's members, Jeffords remains singularly outspoken when he disagrees with presidential positions, especially on those issues that come before him as a member of the Senate Labor and Human Resources Committee. In April 1991, Jeffords questioned the intentions of Bush administration officials after they pressured business executives to break off negotiations with civil rights activists on a job-discrimination bill. "The president has assured me very sincerely that he wants a civil rights bill," Jeffords said. "But it's getting harder and harder for me to live with that [assertion]."

A similar bill — aimed at reversing several Supreme Court decisions that limited affirmative action and providing substantial monetary relief in some cases of job discrimination — was the subject of heated debate in 1990. Jeffords joined with moderate Republicans John C. Danforth of Missouri and Arlen Specter of Pennsylvania to broker a compromise between Democrats who described the bill as a successor to the landmark civil rights acts of the 1960s and Republicans (including Bush) who portrayed it as a "jobs quota" bill.

However, with the 1990 elections looming, Jeffords conceded that the issue had taken on a partisan dimension that went beyond the debate over the legislation's provisions. "No matter what we do to modify the language of the bill to address their specific concerns, it will never be enough for some of my [Republican] colleagues and the administration," said Jeffords, who voted in October 1990 for the narrowly defeated effort to override Bush's veto of the bill.

Also during the 101st Congress, Jeffords voted with committee Democrats and against the position taken by Bush and the majority of his Republican colleagues on a number of contentious issues. These included a Democratic-backed minimum wage increase, federal aid for child-care, assistance to family-planning organizations that provide abortion counseling, and mandated unpaid leave to enable workers to care for newborn infants and ill relatives.

A supporter of "family leave" since his House days, Jeffords crossed back over to that chamber in June 1990 to participate in a news conference by bill supporters. "The [bill] is a declaration of independence for the American family, and perhaps [Bush] should keep this bill and sign it on the 4th of July . . . ," Jeffords said. "Politicians talk a lot about 'motherhood' issues, but we finally have one, a chance to really put one into law." The bill was vetoed but was reintroduced in the 102nd Congress.

Although he had numerous policy disagreements with the Bush administration, Jeffords' most serious rift came over a matter of "senatorial prerogative." Jeffords submitted the name of Fred I. Parker, a Burlington lawyer and Jeffords' deputy during his tenure as Vermont attorney general, as his choice for a vacant seat on the U.S. district court in Vermont. But administration officials, seeking to reassert an executive branch role in the judicial nomination process, voiced unspecified objections to Parker and asked Jeffords in late 1989 for additional options.

Jeffords not only balked, but placed a "hold" that prevented Senate approval of judicial nominees from Alabama and Arkansas. This angered Democratic Sen. Howell Heflin of Alabama, whose home-state choice was being held up. "It hurts me to have to do this, but I hope that my distinguished colleague, who I know is a judge, recognizes the prerogative of the Senate is extremely important," Jeffords responded. He eventually acceded to White House demands for new names, but won out in the end: Parker got his judgeship.

Aside from his Labor Committee assignment, freshman Jeffords obtained a seat on the Environment and Public Works Committee. This is something of an essential position for him, given the presence of a large environmentalist community in Vermont and the widespread voter interest in maintaining the state's pastoral heritage in the face of recent growth pressures.

Jeffords was supportive during the 101st Congress of efforts to rewrite the Clean Air Act. He was unhappy, however, about a provision to set up regional, semi-autonomous commissions to oversee smog-reduction efforts. Expressing concern that Vermont, which had no areas exceeding federal air pollution standards, would be forced to pay for the cleanup of heavily polluted areas in its region, Jeffords attached an amendment subjecting regional commission decisions to approval by the federal Environmental Protection Agency.

Jeffords also took a seat on the Veterans' Affairs Committee, where early on, his support for increased federal spending on health care and other programs aiding veterans was evident. In January 1989, committee Chairman Alan Cranston of California wrote to Bush asking for increased funding for veterans' programs; 38 other senators signed on, but only two, including Jeffords, were Republicans.

Although proud of his image as an independent thinker, Jeffords is sensitive to being labeled a "gadfly." Rejecting the implication that he had simply been a nuisance to fellow Republicans, Jeffords in 1988 produced a legislative résumé of his House years that ran over 100 pages. Among his highlighted achievements was his role in crafting legislation that in 1982 replaced the expiring Comprehensive Employment and Training Act (CETA) with the Job Training Partnership Act.

However, Jeffords at least once did face a backlash from more conservative Republicans. After the 1982 election, Jeffords was in line to be ranking minority member on Agriculture. But the panel's conservative Republicans persuaded Edward Madigan of Illinois, who was on leave of absence from the committee but had more seniority than Jeffords, to return and become the ranking Republican.

Jeffords brushed off the setback and remained an advocate for Vermont's agricultural interests, especially its dairy industry. He did not get a seat on the Senate Agriculture Committee, but his presence there would be redundant: The state's farmers are amply protected by Democratic Sen. Patrick J. Leahy, the committee's chairman and Vermont's senior senator.

At Home: While Jeffords' behavior places him to the left of many of his Republican colleagues, he has never been out of the mainstream in Vermont. He is cut from the same cloth as previous moderates the state has sent to the Senate, including George D. Aiken, Winston L. Prouty and Jeffords' predecessor, Robert T. Stafford.

Jeffords is also well-suited to politics in modern-day Vermont. The traditional bastion of Yankee Republicanism has moved sharply to the left over the last two decades, with the arrival of thousands of liberal urbanites seeking the state's greener pastures. With Democrats gaining viability in the state, only moderate Republicans like Jeffords have had a chance to win statewide.

Jeffords has in fact faced stronger opposition from conservatives in his own party than he has in general elections. In the 1988 Senate primary, Jeffords received 61 percent of the vote against a conservative neophyte, Michael Griffes. Jeffords then breezed to victory over a Democrat, former U.S. Attorney William Gray, with 68 percent of the vote.

Jeffords' only political defeat came early in his career, in a Republican primary. Jeffords served in the state Senate before becoming Vermont's attorney general in 1969. After two terms there, he ran for governor. But the state GOP hierarchy viewed him as too liberal; he narrowly lost the primary to conservative Luther Hackett.

Jeffords bounced back in 1974, winning a three-way primary for Vermont's open House seat. He went on to defeat Burlington's Democratic Mayor Francis Cain with 53 percent of the vote. Jeffords quickly became indomitable in his House seat. In six re-election contests, he never received less than 65 percent of the vote. In 1986, his last House election, he ran without Democratic opposition.

During his House tenure, Jeffords was often mentioned as a possible candidate for higher office. In 1982, he was regarded as a likely Republican successor to GOP Gov. Richard A. Snelling, who was thought to be retiring; conservatives who distrusted Jeffords persuaded Snelling to run for another two-year term.

But as 1988 approached and Stafford's retirement became imminent, Jeffords gained regard as his heir apparent. No Democratic officeholder came forward to contest him, and the honor fell without opposition to Gray, who had never before sought elective office.

Before getting to Gray, Jeffords had to contend with Griffes, a 35-year-old Navy veteran who returned to Vermont from a job with the Washington, D.C., office of Grumman Corp., a defense contractor. Griffes ran an ideological campaign, describing Jeffords as "not a Republican."

But Jeffords responded by pointing out Griffes' lack of Vermont roots: His family moved to the state when he was 17, and he had spent most years since out of state. Citing Griffes' residence in the Arlington suburbs of Washington, D.C., Jeffords said the contest was between a "Vermont Republican" and a "Virginia Republican." He won easily.

Jeffords then entered the general election contest an overwhelming favorite, and was never threatened. Gray's main thrust was to make a connection between a contribution Jeffords received from the Teamsters union's PAC and his opposition to federal efforts to take over the corruption-plagued union. But Jeffords quashed the issue, denying any connection between his fundraising and his House voting behavior; he said his position on the Teamsters' takeover was based solely on his opposition to federal intervention in union operations. The Election Day result showed that the issue did Jeffords no serious harm.

Committees

Environment & Public Works (6th of 7 Republicans)
Environmental Protection; Toxic Substances, Environmental Oversight, Research & Development; Water Resources, Transportation & Infrastructure

Labor & Human Resources (3rd of 7 Republicans)
Labor (ranking); Children, Families, Drugs & Alcoholism; Education, Arts & Humanities; Disability Policy

Special Aging (5th of 10 Republicans)

Veterans' Affairs (5th of 5 Republicans)

Elections

1988 General		
James M. Jeffords (R)	163,183	(68%)
William Gray (D)	71,460	(30%)
1988 Primary		
James M. Jeffords (R)	30,555	(61%)
Mike Griffes (R)	19,593	(39%)

Previous Winning Percentages: **1986 *** (89%) **1984 *** (65%) **1982 *** (69%) **1980 *** (79%) **1978 *** (75%) **1976 *** (67%) **1974 *** (53%)

** House elections.*

Campaign Finance

	Receipts	Receipts from PACs		Expend-itures
1988				
Jeffords (R)	$976,451	$650,393	(67%)	$876,877
Gray (D)	$551,423	$109,950	(20%)	$549,908

Key Votes

1991	
Authorize use of force against Iraq	Y
1990	
Oppose prohibition of certain semiautomatic weapons	N
Support constitutional amendment on flag desecration	N
Oppose requiring parental notice for minors' abortions	Y
Halt production of B-2 stealth bomber at 13 planes	X
Approve budget that cut spending and raised revenues	Y
Pass civil rights bill over Bush veto	Y
1989	
Oppose reduction of SDI funding	?
Oppose barring federal funds for "obscene" art	?
Allow vote on capital gains tax cut	Y

Voting Studies

	Presidential Support		Party Unity		Conservative Coalition	
Year	**S**	**O**	**S**	**O**	**S**	**O**
1990	51	46	36	61	49	46
1989	68	26	40	53	58	34
1988	26	64	29	61	45	47
1987	25	71	32	60	47	51
1986	41	58	29	69	44	56
1985	30	56	37	53	33	55
1984	47	42	31	52	32	49
1983	41	51	31	60	27	67
1982	44	47	35	58	38	55
1981	41	55	35 †	55 †	24	68

† Not eligible for all recorded votes.

Interest Group Ratings

Year	ADA	ACU	AFL-CIO	CCUS
1990	72	26	44	25
1989	40	44	40	71
1988	70	21	92	54
1987	68	26	50	67
1986	60	14	71	56
1985	55	16	65	59
1984	60	29	18	50
1983	65	27	50	55
1982	65	10	45	53
1981	60	57	40	53

AL Bernard Sanders (I)

Of Burlington — Elected 1990

Born: Sept. 8, 1941, Brooklyn, N.Y.
Education: U. of Chicago, B.A. 1964.
Occupation: College lecturer; free-lance writer.
Family: Wife, Jane O'Meara Driscoll; one child.
Religion: Jewish.
Political Career: Mayor of Burlington. 1981-89; independent candidate for U.S. Senate, 1972, 1974; independent candidate for governor, 1972, 1976, 1986; independent candidate for U.S. House, 1988.
Capitol Office: 509 Cannon Bldg. 20515; 225-4115.

The Path to Washington: With his victory over freshman Republican Rep. Peter Smith, Sanders became the first self-described socialist in the House since Victor L. Berger of Wisconsin (1911-13, 1923-29), and he is the first truly independent House member since Henry F. Reams of Ohio (1951-55).

His win culminated a 20-year effort that moved him from the fringe to the vortex of Vermont politics.

The Brooklyn-raised son of Jewish immigrants from Poland, Sanders joined in leftist politics in college and became a supporter of democratic socialist systems such as that of Sweden. He denies affiliation with Marxism.

In 1968, Sanders joined a wave of liberals who abandoned urban life for bucolic Vermont. Many of the transplants joined the then-small state Democratic Party and, over time, helped convert it into a force capable of winning statewide elections. However, Sanders viewed both major parties as dominated by corporate interests and accused them of ignoring the needs of the poor, the elderly and working Americans. He helped found Vermont's Liberty Union Party.

Sanders' confrontational style brought him attention, but his first political ventures earned him a reputation as a gadfly. In four bids for state office in the 1970s, Sanders never topped 6 percent of the vote.

Yet Sanders was building a grass-roots base in Burlington. In 1981, he ran for mayor and unseated the Democratic incumbent by 10 votes.

Written off as a fluke, Sanders won three more terms by increasing margins. He pursued populist goals, but also presided over the revitalization of Burlington's downtown.

In 1986, Sanders took 15 percent of the vote for governor as an independent, and he was seen as a spoiler when he ran in 1988 for the open at-large House seat. But Sanders lost to Smith by 4 percentage points and nearly doubled the vote of Democrat Paul N. Poirier. Retiring as mayor in 1989, Sanders considered running for governor before deciding to challenge Smith to a rematch. With no prominent figure wanting to risk Poirier's fate, the Democratic nomination was left to little-known academic Dolores Sandoval.

Smith had a House record as a moderate Republican who opposed President Bush on such issues as the minimum wage and civil rights legislation. He had support among Vermont environmentalists and earned praise with his call for a special prosecutor in the savings and loan investigation.

But Sanders stayed even in the polls. His economic message was reinforced by the federal budget debate, in which leading Democrats called for taxing the wealthy. On some issues, though, he moderated his tone: He supported the initial U.S. military response to Iraq's invasion of Kuwait (although he would oppose the decision to go to war in 1991). The campaign broke sharply for Sanders in the final weeks. Smith favored the budget plan backed by Bush in early October; Sanders blasted its Medicare cutbacks and middle-class tax increases. Smith also criticized Bush on several issues; that swayed few liberals and alienated conservatives, some of whom were already angry over Smith's 1989 vote to ban certain automatic weapons.

Smith then ran TV ads attacking Sanders; one used an old quote out of context to imply that Sanders admires Fidel Castro. Vermont media blasted Smith's negativism, with the *Rutland Herald* calling him "Spiro Smith." Sanders won with 56 percent.

Fighting Smith's claims during the campaign that he would be ineffective, Sanders promised to enlist in the Democratic Caucus. But conservative Democrats opposed Sanders' admission, and even some liberals thought a socialist member would be bad for the party's image. Sanders reached a compromise with House Speaker Thomas S. Foley, under which he would not apply to the Democratic Caucus but would be granted committee assignments.

Vermont — At Large

Some things about Vermont remain immutable. The least-populous state in the Northeast and third smallest in the nation, its scenic beauty remains largely unsullied. However, a growth spurt of more than 35 percent since 1960 has driven Vermont's population to 563,000. This growth has had outsized impacts on the demographics and politics of the state.

Much of the population increase was caused by young urbanites who left behind the hassles of the Boston-New York megalopolis, but brought their liberal politics with them. These émigrés pulled the state to the left while the rest of the nation appeared to be moving right.

This trend shattered Vermont's reputation as the sturdiest bastion of Yankee Republicanism. Democratic Sen. Patrick J. Leahy is now in his third term. Democrat Madeleine M. Kunin served three terms as governor from 1985 to 1991.

An even stronger signal of the state's shift to the left was the 1990 House election of independent former Burlington Mayor Bernard Sanders, a self-described socialist. Sanders succeeded at portraying freshman GOP Rep. Peter Smith — himself a liberal Republican — as a tool of a big business-dominated establishment.

The swing has also reinforced the dominance of moderate-to-liberal leaders in the state Republican Party. Moderate Republican Rep. James M. Jeffords won in 1988 to succeed like-minded Republican Robert T. Stafford in the Senate. The stronghold of the state's liberal movement is in Burlington. While his populist message fueled his rise, Sanders as mayor was not hurt by the fact that he shepherded the state's largest city through a period of unprecedented prosperity.

Although its manufacturing heritage has faded, Burlington (population 39,000) thrived through the late 1980s, thanks in great part to the growth of its electronics industry and the success of its downtown retail mall. Unemployment slipped under 2 percent in 1988. However, the outlook for the early 1990s is not as rosy. Manufacturing, construction, and even high-tech industries have cut back, and hard economic times in neighboring states translate into lost tourist dollars throughout Vermont.

Burlington and surrounding Chittenden County cast one-quarter of the state's vote; winning there is vital to statewide Democratic candidates. Even in the more-centrist suburbs, fear about suburban sprawl works to the benefit of Democrats (and environmentally conscious Republicans).

Other small urban centers, such as Rutland and the state capital of Montpelier, used to tilt Republican, but they are now more Democratic. There have been some Democratic inroads in Bennington, Brattleboro and other southern Vermont towns, but there is more loyalty there to the GOP.

At the village level and in most rural areas, Yankee Vermonters still mainly vote Republican, keeping GOP candidates competitive. But Franklin and Grand Isle counties, in northwest Vermont, have a large French Canadian population that gives them a Democratic complexion.

Population: 511,456. White 506,736 (99%), Black 1,135 (0.2%), Other 2,339 (1%). Spanish origin 3,304 (1%). 18 and over 366,138 (72%), 65 and over 58,166 (11%). Median age: 29.

Committees

Banking, Finance & Urban Affairs
Consumer Affairs & Coinage; Housing & Community Development; International Development, Finance, Trade & Monetary Policy

Government Operations
Government Information, Justice & Agriculture; Human Resources & Intergovernmental Relations

Campaign Finance

1990	Receipts	Receipts from PACs		Expend-itures
Sanders (I)	$571,556	$72,250	(13%)	$569,772
Smith (R)	$682,870	$299,954	(44%)	$688,907
Sandoval (D)	$13,830	$300	(2%)	$12,850

Key Vote

1991

Authorize use of force against Iraq	N

Elections

1990 General

Bernard Sanders (I)	117,522	(56%)
Peter Smith (R)	82,938	(40%)
Dolores Sandoval (D)	6,315	(3%)
Peter Diamondstone (Liberty Union)	1,965	(1%)

District Vote For President

	1988		1984		1980		1976	
D	115,755	(48%)	95,730	(41%)	81,952	(38%)	80,954	(43%)
R	124,331	(51%)	135,865	(58%)	94,628	(44%)	102,085	(54%)
I					31,761	(15%)		

Virginia

U.S. CONGRESS

SENATE 1 D, 1 R
HOUSE 6 D, 4 R

LEGISLATURE

Senate 30 D, 10 R
House 59 D, 39 R, 2 Independents

ELECTIONS

1988 Presidential Vote	
Bush	60%
Dukakis	39%
1984 Presidential Vote	
Reagan	62%
Mondale	37%
1980 Presidential Vote	
Reagan	53%
Carter	40%
Anderson	5%
Turnout rate in 1986	24%
Turnout rate in 1988	48%
Turnout rate in 1990	26%

(as percentage of voting age population)

POPULATION AND GROWTH

1980 population	5,346,818
1990 population (12th in the nation)	6,187,358
Percent change 1980-1990	+16%

DEMOGRAPHIC BREAKDOWN

White	77%
Black	19%
Asian or Pacific Islander	3%
(Hispanic origin)	3%
Urban	66%
Rural	34%
Born in state	60%
Foreign-born	3%

MAJOR CITIES

Virginia Beach	393,069
Norfolk	261,229
Richmond	203,056
Newport News	170,045
Chesapeake	151,976

AREA AND LAND USE

Area	39,704 sq. miles (36th)
Farm	37%
Forest	63%
Federally owned	10%

Gov. L. Douglas Wilder (D)
Of Richmond — Elected 1989

Born: Jan. 31, 1931, Richmond, Va.
Education: Virginia Union U., B.S. 1951; Howard U., J.D. 1959.
Military Service: Army, 1952-53.
Occupation: Lawyer.
Religion: Baptist.
Political Career: Va. Senate, 1969-85; lieutenant governor, 1985-89.
Next Election: 1993.

WORK

Occupations	
White-collar	55%
Blue-collar	31%
Service workers	12%
Government Workers	
Federal	159,554
State	138,384
Local	237,782

MONEY

Median family income	$ 20,018	(23rd)
Tax burden per capita	$ 783	(34th)

EDUCATION

Spending per pupil through grade 12	$ 4,149	(22nd)
Persons with college degrees	19%	(9th)

CRIME

Violent crime rate	313 per 100,000 (34th)

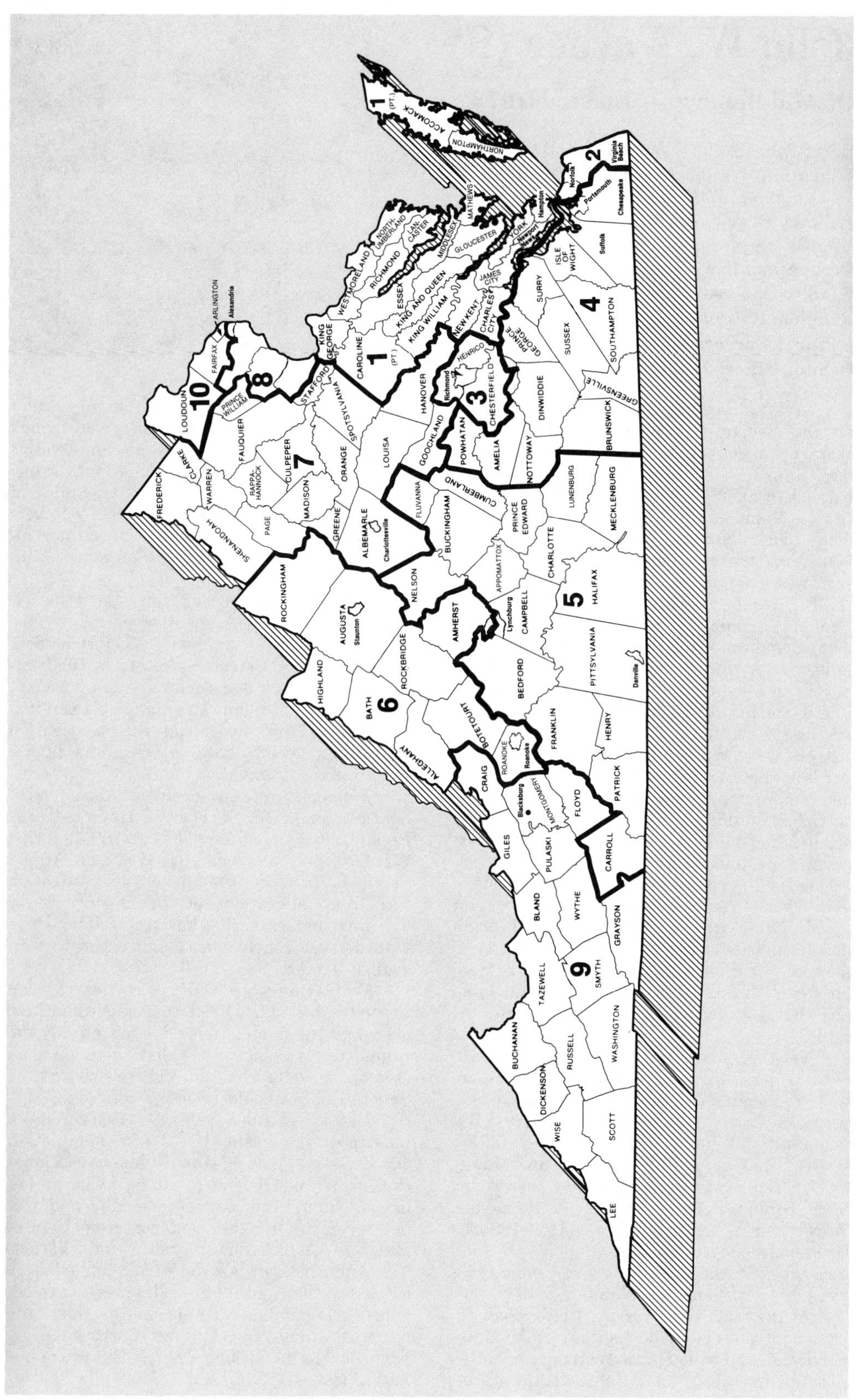
1
ACCOMACK
(PT.)
NORTHAMPTON
2
Virginia Beach
Norfolk
Portsmouth
Chesapeake
Hampton
Newport News
Suffolk
ISLE OF WIGHT
4
SOUTHAMPTON
SUSSEX
SURRY
PRINCE GEORGE
DINWIDDIE
GREENSVILLE
BRUNSWICK
3
Richmond
HENRICO
CHESTERFIELD
CHARLES CITY
JAMES CITY
YORK
NEW KENT
GLOUCESTER
MATHEWS
MIDDLESEX
LANCASTER
NORTHUMBERLAND
RICHMOND
WESTMORELAND
ESSEX
KING AND QUEEN
KING WILLIAM
KING GEORGE
CAROLINE
(PT.)
HANOVER
ARLINGTON
Alexandria
FAIRFAX
10
LOUDOUN
8
PRINCE WILLIAM
STAFFORD
SPOTSYLVANIA
FAUQUIER
CULPEPER
7
RAPPAHANNOCK
CLARKE
WARREN
FREDERICK
SHENANDOAH
PAGE
MADISON
ORANGE
LOUISA
GOOCHLAND
POWHATAN
AMELIA
NOTTOWAY
LUNENBURG
MECKLENBURG
CUMBERLAND
FLUVANNA
GREENE
ALBEMARLE
Charlottesville
BUCKINGHAM
PRINCE EDWARD
CHARLOTTE
APPOMATTOX
NELSON
ROCKINGHAM
AUGUSTA
Staunton
AMHERST
Lynchburg
CAMPBELL
5
HALIFAX
PITTSYLVANIA
Danville
BEDFORD
ROCKBRIDGE
HIGHLAND
BATH
6
ALLEGHANY
BOTETOURT
ROANOKE
Roanoke
FRANKLIN
HENRY
PATRICK
CRAIG
Blacksburg
MONTGOMERY
FLOYD
CARROLL
GILES
PULASKI
BLAND
WYTHE
GRAYSON
9
SMYTH
TAZEWELL
BUCHANAN
RUSSELL
WASHINGTON
DICKENSON
WISE
SCOTT
LEE

John W. Warner (R)

Of Middleburg — Elected 1978

Born: Feb. 18, 1927, Washington, D.C.
Education: Washington and Lee U., B.S. 1949; U. of Virginia, LL.B. 1953.
Military Service: Navy, 1944-46; Marine Corps, 1950-52.
Occupation: Lawyer; farmer.
Family: Divorced; three children.
Religion: Episcopalian.
Political Career: No previous office.
Capitol Office: 225 Russell Bldg. 20510; 224-2023.

In Washington: As ranking Republican on the Senate Armed Services Committee, Warner works cooperatively — sometimes almost in sync — with his Democratic counterpart, Chairman Sam Nunn of Georgia. Warner's ties to Nunn are strengthened by the chairman's generally conservative views on defense issues; together they have worked to protect such weapons systems as the MX missile and the B-2 bomber, which have been favored by Republican administrations and opposed by many members of the Senate's Democratic majority.

Even when they disagree on certain issues, such as the future of a space-based anti-ballistic missile system under the strategic defense initiative (SDI), Warner typically eschews harsh partisan rhetoric. Although Warner sponsored, and Nunn strongly opposed, the resolution authorizing President Bush to use military force against Iraq in January 1991, the genteel Virginian took time to praise his Democratic colleague for the conduct of the crucial debate.

"I wish to acknowledge my deep respect for ... Mr. Nunn, who consulted with me throughout this debate in a spirit of bipartisanship and fairness," Warner said in a speech on the Senate floor. "It is a relationship that I value and one that I know will continue long into the future."

Yet that relationship does not come without a political price for Warner. Both men are well-grounded in defense issues (Warner, a lawyer, is a former secretary of the Navy). But Nunn, with his intellectual approach to military strategy and his ability as chairman to sway crucial Democratic votes, is clearly the driving force behind Senate defense policy-making. Warner, on the other hand, is widely seen as a spokesman for administration policy — and sometimes for the Armed Services Committee's viewpoint, as shaped by Nunn.

At the same time, Warner's bipartisan approach inflames more ideologically oriented Republicans, who believe that Warner is too often rolled by the cagey Nunn. Bob Dole, the aggressive and highly partisan Senate minority leader from Kansas, has in recent years given Armed Services seats to such hard-line conservative members as Trent Lott of Mississippi, Daniel R. Coats of Indiana and Robert C. Smith of New Hampshire; some committee-watchers view this as an attempt by Dole to counterbalance Warner's willingness to compromise with Nunn.

Warner's rapport with some partisan colleagues may be permanently scarred by his handling of Bush's nomination of former Sen. John Tower for Defense secretary in 1989. Although Warner was a friend and supporter of Tower, several Republican senators blamed him for allowing Nunn to drag out the investigation of Tower's personal life that resulted in the defeat of the nomination.

A man of intense loyalties, Warner tried hard to uphold Bush's choice of Tower, a Texas Republican who had served as chairman during Warner's first four years (1981-85) on Armed Services. But as the panel's investigation turned up allegations of womanizing, heavy drinking and extensive business relationships with defense contractors, Nunn began to turn against Tower.

Warner, in what GOP critics viewed as an unforgiveable sin, agreed to delay committee action on the nomination. "There's no way the committee is going to say that we're going to stop on this date," he said. "There's no way the Senate can or should impose a total lid."

Despite Warner's efforts to negotiate a bipartisan agreement, the Tower nomination was defeated on an 11-9 party-line vote. Nonetheless, Warner defended Nunn, saying he believed Nunn liked Tower personally and was not trying to run the Pentagon from Capitol Hill. "It's not a power grab," said Warner. "That much I can tell you." Dole immediately countered that some of his colleagues disagreed. When the nomination went to the floor, the administration's forces were spearheaded by Dole, not the anguishing Warner. But the nomination lost, 47-53.

Tower remained embittered toward Warner. "Nunn was so determined to avoid being accused of partisanship that he continued to seduce John Warner to his cause . . . ," Tower wrote in a memoir published just before his death in an April 1991 plane crash. "One observer said [Tower's supporters on Armed Services] were so angry at what they considered Warner's dereliction of duty as the ranking Republican that in a figurative sense they threw him at the wall, picked him up, and threw him back at the wall again."

Early in the 102nd Congress, Nunn was on the defensive over his uncharacteristically dovish stance on the Persian Gulf War. Warner, in turn, adopted a more adversarial tone than usual. But their debate on SDI only served to underscore Nunn's dominant role on military matters.

SDI has been the issue on which Warner and Nunn have most consistently parted. Warner supports the vision portrayed by the Reagan and Bush administrations of a space-based network of rockets designed to destroy enemy missiles shortly after launch. But Nunn argues this plan is technologically flawed and in violation of the U.S.-Soviet anti-ballistic missile treaty of 1972; he favors a more easily realized system of ground-based missile interceptors.

Playing off the well-publicized use of Patriot missiles to destroy Iraqi Scud rockets during the Persian Gulf War, Warner in February 1991 tried to push through an amendment to a supplemental appropriations bill that would have increased spending on a space-based system. But Nunn threatened to counter with his own proposal oriented to his ground-based approach, which he said "would have prevailed substantially." Warner then withdrew his amendment.

If Warner is somewhat overshadowed by Nunn, he has at least moved beyond the skepticism that greeted his Senate arrival in 1978. He was then best known for his marriage (since ended) to actress Elizabeth Taylor. With his carefully coiffed hair, impeccable tailoring, sonorous voice and purposeful stride, Warner reminded some of an actor portraying a senator.

However, Warner emerged in the 1980s as a well-informed spokesman for the military buildup pressed by President Ronald Reagan. Along with his Armed Services position, Warner gained a seat during the 100th Congress on the Senate Intelligence Committee.

Warner shows a more moderate side on some domestic issues. A member of the Environment and Public Works Committee, Warner spoke in favor of the Clean Air Act revisions enacted in 1990. Although he backed Bush on more than 80 percent of Senate votes during the 101st Congress, his support for Reagan slumped as low as 60 percent in 1987.

That year, Warner also showed a flash of political independence, when he came out against Reagan's nomination of Robert H. Bork to the Supreme Court. Warner was the most surprising of the six Republican "no" votes, and he left some Virginia supporters in shock.

Although he would be up for re-election in 1990, Warner denied that his vote was a play for support from Virginia's blacks and white moderates. He said he had found Bork lacking "that record of compassion, of sensitivity . . . to enable him to sit on the highest court in the land."

At Home: After two terms, some senators will be secure, some will be in trouble and some will look shaky only in the presence of a specific challenger. Warner fell in the third category. His party standing was sure. Despite his vote against Bork and his ambivalence in the Tower affair, Republicans knew they had nowhere else to go. Warner's one worry heading into 1990 appeared to be outgoing Democratic Gov. Gerald L. Baliles. When Baliles declared in late 1989 that he would not challenge Warner, the Republican's bid for re-election was cinched.

In the ensuing months, the state Democratic Party heeded the advice of its newly elected governor, L. Douglas Wilder, that offering no candidate was preferable to fielding a poor one. Democrats' remaining efforts were devoted to ensuring that Nancy B. Spannaus, a supporter of fringe political figure Lyndon H. LaRouche Jr., did not appear on the ballot as a Democrat. They succeeded: Spannaus appeared as an independent. She was Warner's only opposition; he won a third term with a career-high 80 percent.

Such longevity seemed improbable in 1978, when Warner's political career looked to be stalled. His campaign for the Senate had impressed Virginia Republicans at the state GOP convention in June, but the nomination went to Richard Obenshain.

Then the state's politics and Warner's future were reordered by an airplane accident. Obenshain's light plane crashed Aug. 2 and he was killed instantly. Virginia Republicans needed a nominee, and Warner, the runner-up in June, was the obvious choice.

He had courted the convention delegates with a lavish campaign costing nearly $500,000, and attracted enough votes to force six ballots before being defeated. He had also been a good loser and backed Obenshain afterward.

Warner brought to the fall campaign the same assets he had in June: personal wealth and a statewide reputation, achieved not only as Navy secretary under Richard M. Nixon and chief bicentennial planner under President Gerald R. Ford, but as Elizabeth Taylor's husband.

He also had liabilities. Despite his Virginia education, he was looked upon as an outsider who arrived late on the state's political scene. Some voters also saw him as a socialite and fortune hunter. Before he married Taylor, he was married to heiress Catherine Mellon and received a reported $7 million from her in their divorce settlement.

But Warner's celebrity wife turned out to be a help to him. Taylor's presence on the campaign trail guaranteed large crowds, and when she proved willing to voice her enthusiasm for conservative causes, Virginia Republicans cheered her on.

The Democratic nominee, former state Attorney General Andrew Miller, was seeking to recover from a defeat in the 1977 gubernatorial primary by the state's best-known liberal Democrat, Henry E. Howell. In 1978 Miller campaigned for the Senate as a fiscal conservative, but Warner tied him to the Democratic Party of Howell, and Miller never managed to extricate himself. Warner won by fewer than 5,000 votes in the closest Senate election in Virginia history.

Six years later, Warner was in a totally different type of contest, winning re-election by more than 805,000 votes in a race that was a mismatch from the beginning.

Gov. Charles S. Robb led the search for a suitable Democratic challenger, but Warner helped to discourage the effort by raising more than $1 million by the end of 1983. After a host of better-known Democrats turned down the nomination, it went by default to former state Rep. Edythe C. Harrison, who had lost her previous race for the state Legislature.

Harrison peppered Warner with a variety of charges, including conflict of interest for investing in defense stocks while serving on the Armed Services Committee. She also made barbed personal attacks. Referring to Warner's celebrated marriages, she declared: "Women took him up, and a woman is going to bring him down."

But even leading Democrats doubted that the woman would be Harrison. A longtime ally of the liberal Howell, she was given lukewarm support by much of her own party.

With money, incumbency, strong ticket mates and a grip on Virginia's conservative political mainstream, Warner swept all but two of the state's 95 counties and all 41 independent cities. According to NBC News exit polls, he also captured nearly one-quarter of the black vote, more than twice the share won in Virginia by Reagan.

Committees

Armed Services (Ranking)

Environment & Public Works (5th of 7 Republicans)
Toxic Substances, Environmental Oversight, Research & Development (ranking); Environmental Protection; Water Resources, Transportation & Infrastructure

Select Intelligence (2nd of 7 Republicans)

Rules & Administration (4th of 7 Republicans)

Elections

1990 General		
John W. Warner (R)	876,782	(81%)
Nancy B. Spannaus (I)	196,755	(18%)

Previous Winning Percentages: **1984** (70%) **1978** (50%)

Campaign Finance

	Receipts	Receipts from PACs		Expend-itures
1990				
Warner (R)	$1,750,032	$621,899	(36%)	$1,151,605

Key Votes

1991	
Authorize use of force against Iraq	Y
1990	
Oppose prohibition of certain semiautomatic weapons	N
Support constitutional amendment on flag desecration	Y
Oppose requiring parental notice for minors' abortions	N
Halt production of B-2 stealth bomber at 13 planes	N
Approve budget that cut spending and raised revenues	Y
Pass civil rights bill over Bush veto	N
1989	
Oppose reduction of SDI funding	Y
Oppose barring federal funds for "obscene" art	Y
Allow vote on capital gains tax cut	Y

Voting Studies

	Presidential Support		Party Unity		Conservative Coalition	
Year	**S**	**O**	**S**	**O**	**S**	**O**
1990	78	22	69	31	97	3
1989	86	13	81	19	89	11
1988	74	23	71	26	95	3
1987	60	36	75	16	88	9
1986	87	13	86	13	87	12
1985	82	18	82	18	92	8
1984	86	13	87	12	91	6
1983	82	16	84	14	89	11
1982	83	17	87	13	96	2
1981	87	13	88	8	97	2

Interest Group Ratings

Year	ADA	ACU	AFL-CIO	CCUS
1990	28	70	56	75
1989	5	89	10	88
1988	5	87	36	86
1987	25	60	50	94
1986	5	73	7	79
1985	5	74	19	79
1984	10	90	0	89
1983	20	56	18	53
1982	5	86	19	81
1981	5	74	5	100

Charles S. Robb (D)

Of McLean — Elected 1988

Born: June 26, 1939, Phoenix, Ariz.

Education: Attended Cornell U., 1957-58; U. of Wisconsin, B.B.A. 1961; U. of Virginia, J.D. 1973.

Military Service: Marine Corps, 1961-70, Reserve, 1970-present.

Occupation: Lawyer.

Family: Wife, Lynda Bird Johnson; three children.

Religion: Episcopalian.

Political Career: Lieutenant governor, 1978-82; governor, 1982-86.

Capitol Office: 493 Russell Bldg. 20510; 224-4024.

In Washington: Robb has had some difficulties making the transition from Virginia chief executive and state party kingmaker to being one of 100 in Congress' upper chamber. But in his early Senate years, any problems in this regard were overshadowed by Robb's national prominence and his promise as a possible contender for the presidency.

All that changed, however, in early 1991, when a series of scandals and unflattering allegations tarnished the handsome ex-Marine's clean-cut image, raised questions about his electoral future, and called attention to the shakiness of his political base in the Senate.

Robb is one of the Senate's more conservative Democrats, and he has worn his contrarian views as a badge of honor. He is a self-described hawk on defense and a conservative on budget matters. Earnest and almost broodingly serious in his efforts since the mid-1980s to pull the national Democratic Party to the political center, Robb appeared confident that his differences with the Democratic establishment would be an asset in any national campaign.

But balancing such dissent and ambition in the Senate requires a degree of finesse Robb has not mastered. The blunt rhetoric he uses to convey his independence from party orthodoxy can strike colleagues as impolitic. Partly because of this, Robb found few public defenders in early 1991, when he was buffeted by allegations of drug use, philandering and possession of an illegally recorded tape of a phone conversation involving his political rival, Virginia Gov. L. Douglas Wilder. Invitations for Robb to campaign for Senate colleagues went on hold, undermining his usefulness as chairman of the Democratic Senatorial Campaign Committee (DSCC).

Robb was thrown badly off balance by the storm of negative publicity. "I have never claimed to be a rocket scientist, a visionary or a great musician," he said at one point. "My reputation for truthfulness and veracity is what has sustained me."

Frustration with Robb among Senate Democrats had emerged even before the questions about his personal conduct became front-page news: At the start of the 102nd Congress, he was dumped from the Budget Committee. The official story was that leaders from both parties wanted to shrink the panel. Robb was the lowest-ranking Democrat, and thus had to go. But Robb rebutted the party line, saying that the committee chairman, Tennessee Democrat Jim Sasser, told him, "If you had voted with me and provided the support I needed, I would've been more willing to go to bat for you." Robb tactlessly minimized his concern about the episode, noting that he did not mind leaving the panel since it "had almost been emasculated" by the 1990 budget agreement.

Just as that story broke in March, Robb angered other fellow Democrats when he appeared on NBC's "Meet the Press" as chairman of the DSCC and called the political impact of Democrats' voting against the Persian Gulf War "catastrophic or devastating," while emphasizing that he himself supported the war.

These transgressions might have receded from memory were it not for the series of questions about his personal conduct that followed. Robb's troubles on this front began when he learned that NBC News was about to air a report on allegations that he had an affair with a beauty queen. He offered a tortured advance commentary that was far more memorable than the broadcast, which, when it aired, was widely criticized for its lack of depth and substantiation.

The damage, however, was done. Robb's denial that he had an affair with the woman, Tai Collins, paled when he added that he had shared a bottle of wine with her and then allowed her to give him a massage in his hotel room. Admitting "peccadilloes," Robb said, "I am not immune to the laws of chemistry, or maybe physics, to the extent that opposites attract." He added that he had never "loved anyone emotionally or physically" other than his wife.

The broadcast also rekindled rumors that first surfaced during his Senate campaign that as governor Robb had attended beachfront parties with friends who were under investigation by various law enforcement agencies on suspicion of cocaine trafficking. Robb has consistently denied that he ever used drugs and said he has no knowledge of drug use by others at the parties.

In 1991, Robb's top aides hinted that Wilder was to blame for rekindling the rumors. The two men have squabbled publicly since 1985, when Wilder suggested that Robb was taking too much credit for his becoming the state's first black lieutenant governor. Robb responded by releasing two scathing letters that accused Wilder of disloyalty.

The feud stirred national interest because both men have higher political ambitions, both represent the moderate wing of the party, and both have some glamour — Wilder, as one of his party's most prominent black officials, and Robb, as son-in-law of former President Lyndon B. Johnson.

But the spat escalated into a bad soap opera in June 1991 when Wilder alleged that someone had been taping his phone conversations and passing the information on to Robb. The senator then acknowledged that his office possessed for over two years an illegally recorded tape of a conversation between Wilder and a supporter. Robb said the tape recently had been destroyed.

This prompted a GOP activist to contend that one of Robb's top aides had threatened him with the contents of another taped phone conversation — a tape that supposedly indicated the GOP activist knew that a private detective had been hired by another Republican to investigate Robb's social life. The GOP activist said he was told that unless he leaked this information to the press, Robb's office would involve him in a lawsuit about the matter.

This disclosure prompted federal and state law enforcement officials to launch an investigation of the tapings; Robb reacted by placing three top aides on administrative leave. Robb and Wilder met publicly in June and professed no hard feelings, but at midyear the tapes story was still percolating in the media, damaging not only Robb but also Wilder, who told reporters he had known about a state police investigation of Robb's personal activities.

With all this as a distracting backdrop, Robb returned in the 102nd Congress to his assignment on the Commerce Committee, where he kept a low profile during his first two years. He has been more prominent on the Foreign Relations Committee, where he is a key swing vote, and on confirmation votes of presidential appointees in the full Senate, where he often is a pivotal backer of the administration.

In early 1989, President Bush came under fire for appointing campaign contributors to ambassadorial posts, and Democrats made the key test vote the appointment of Florida real estate magnate Joseph Zappala to be ambassador to Spain. Although Robb said he was troubled by the "lack of depth" in Zappala's background, he was the only panel Democrat to vote to confirm Zappala.

One of the rare times Robb broke with Bush on an appointment was on the nomination of former Sen. John Tower to be secretary of Defense. Among the last to declare his intentions, Robb eventually delivered an exegesis on the arguments pro and con before siding with the majority, led by Sen. Sam Nunn of Georgia, the man Robb has for years pushed for national leadership. Noting first "a very substantial deference" to the president's wishes, he concluded, "I must cast my vote with my longtime friend."

But come 1991, Nunn's opposition to giving Bush authority to use force against Iraq had little influence on Robb. While Nunn worked to rally Democrats in support of continuing economic sanctions against Iraq, Robb worked with the administration to win Democratic votes for the resolution authorizing force.

In the 101st Congress, when the administration needed an ally in its efforts to provide aid to the Cambodian guerrillas, Robb offered an amendment to do just that. Democrats, including Appropriations Chairman Robert C. Byrd, complained that Robb's amendment gave Bush a "blank check," but Robb countered that it did "nothing more than give the non-communists a fighting chance." His position prevailed on a 59-39 vote.

Robb's willingness to work with the administration briefly threatened an important home-state project: a Northern Virginia commuter line. Through his role on the Commerce Committee, Robb won congressional approval of a liability waiver for Conrail, which owns a key section of track.

When Bush threatened a veto over other matters, Robb suggested that Congress simply delete provisions opposed by the president. His idea drew a rebuke from House Energy and Commerce Committee Chairman John D. Dingell, who reminded Robb that Democratic sponsors were standing by the whole bill. Dingell's message was clear, and Robb became a leading supporter of the veto override. When that failed, Congress did what Robb initially said they would do. His amendment was included in the stripped-down bill.

Robb thrust himself onto the national stage as a force for moderation in the Democratic Party in the years between his tenure as governor and his election to the Senate. In 1985, he campaigned for a mainstream chairman of the Democratic National Committee. He helped found the Democratic Leadership Council, a largely Southern group of officeholders dedicated to moving the party to the center. And he encouraged Southern states to hold their presidential primaries on a single date. He helped sell this Super Tuesday concept as a means to increase Southern leverage, and conservative influence, in the selection of the party's nominee.

At Home: Few politicians have found the road to the Senate as smoothly paved as Robb did. So popular was Robb after his governorship that he was all but conceded the Senate seat even before he announced for it. The mere belief that he would run was widely believed to have influenced Republican Paul S. Trible Jr.'s decision not to seek re-election in 1988.

It is difficult to overstate the importance of Robb's political career to Democrats in Virginia. The collapse of the old Harry Byrd organization in the 1960s brought an era of Republican dominance at the statewide level. Party-switching was common. Before Robb, the state had elected three GOP governors in succession.

But then came Robb, a decorated Vietnam War hero and former White House guard whose wife was the daughter of President Johnson. Robb had left the Marines and gone to law school. After practicing law for four years, he was elected lieutenant governor. Four years later, Robb won the governorship.

In Richmond, Robb carefully built a reputation for fiscal conservatism with a human face. He appointed minorities and women to judgeships and other state posts. But such moves were made with a kind of square-jawed respectability. Robb seemed immune to the taint of liberalism.

State law barred a successive term, but Robb's popularity was talismanic enough in 1985 to help elect a slate of other Democrats — including the first black (Wilder) and also the first woman elected statewide in Virginia history.

Although Virginia had not elected a Democrat to the Senate since 1966, polls in 1987 showed Robb running ahead of Trible. When Trible stepped aside, the Virginia GOP had no clear replacement — and the prospect of facing Robb attracted no one of note.

Robb raised $1 million almost effortlessly while the Republicans scrambled through a long list of celebrity prospects. In the end, they chose a candidate who seemed more of a political novelty than a serious contender: Maurice A. Dawkins.

A black Baptist minister, Dawkins had been a civil rights activist and a Washington lobbyist, and he was also a spellbinding speaker. But his bid was erratic from the start, running into controversy over details of his personal business. The state party took over management of the campaign, and soon Dawkins was adapting the stories about Robb's Virginia Beach friends for use on the stump.

Robb tried to ignore the matter, then dismissed it out of hand. Although the issue was not affecting the polls, Robb's campaign clearly wanted to bury it. The candidate volunteered for a drug test, which proved negative, and, before joint appearances, Robb confronted Dawkins about GOP use of the issue. Dawkins publicly accepted Robb's account of the facts, but the issue was clearly his only weapon. The final result was unmercifully lopsided.

Committees

Commerce, Science & Transportation (11th of 11 Democrats)
Consumer; Science, Technology & Space; Surface Transportation; National Ocean Policy Study

Foreign Relations (10th of 10 Democrats)
East Asian & Pacific Affairs; Near Eastern & South Asian Affairs; Western Hemisphere & Peace Corps Affairs

Election

1988 General

Charles S. Robb (D)	1,474,086	(71%)
Maurice A. Dawkins (R)	593,652	(29%)

Campaign Finance

	Receipts	Receipts from PACs		Expend-itures
1988				
Robb (D)	$3,198,630	$914,763	(29%)	$2,881,666
Dawkins (R)	$283,095	$23,148	(8%)	$282,229

Key Votes

1991

Authorize use of force against Iraq	Y
1990	
Oppose prohibition of certain semiautomatic weapons	N
Support constitutional amendment on flag desecration	N
Oppose requiring parental notice for minors' abortions	Y
Halt production of B-2 stealth bomber at 13 planes	N
Approve budget that cut spending and raised revenues	Y
Pass civil rights bill over Bush veto	Y
1989	
Oppose reduction of SDI funding	Y
Oppose barring federal funds for "obscene" art	Y
Allow vote on capital gains tax cut	N

Voting Studies

	Presidential Support		Party Unity		Conservative Coalition	
Year	**S**	**O**	**S**	**O**	**S**	**O**
1990	55	45	73	27	76	24
1989	73	27	69	31	82	18

Interest Group Ratings

Year	ADA	ACU	AFL-CIO	CCUS
1990	61	22	56	33
1989	45	36	80	63

1 Herbert H. Bateman (R)

Of Newport News — Elected 1982

Born: Aug. 7, 1928, Elizabeth City, N.C.
Education: College of William and Mary, B.A. 1949; Georgetown U., J.D. 1956.
Military Service: Air Force, 1951-53.
Occupation: Lawyer.
Family: Wife, Laura Yacobi; two children.
Religion: Protestant.
Political Career: Va. Senate, 1968-82; sought Republican nomination for U.S. House, 1976; sought Republican nomination for lieutenant governor, 1981.
Capitol Office: 1030 Longworth Bldg. 20515; 225-4261.

In Washington: A conservative Republican and an Air Force veteran, Bateman brings a pro-defense proclivity to his role on the Armed Services Committee. Such a viewpoint is a political necessity in the 1st, a Tidewater Virginia district with a strong military orientation. While Bateman generally keeps a low profile, he is front and center when his district's defense interests are being debated.

Bateman — whose district includes the huge Newport News Shipbuilding and Drydock Co. — backed the Reagan administration's plans for a 600-ship Navy. Although that goal has been downsized given new fiscal and strategic realities, Bateman works for a stream of defense projects for his district's contractors.

With the support of the Bush administration, Bateman shepherds the program to build a new U.S. aircraft carrier beginning in 1996. This project would keep the lines humming at Newport News Shipbuilding — the nation's only carrier manufacturer — through 2004.

The company is already at work on two new carriers. The 1987 effort to maintain authorization for these ships demonstrated Bateman's advocacy of naval projects.

The defense boom of the 1980s having peaked, the carrier issue was an early round in the debate over defense priorities. Opponents of the carriers argued that the amounts targeted for the project — $644 million in fiscal 1988 and $797 million in 1989 — were too high.

However, Bateman said the carriers would be needed to replace two aging conventional carriers that are to be decommissioned in the 1990s. "Why cripple our conventional capability and readiness into the 21st century?" Bateman asked. He also stressed the economic benefits of the carrier program, stating, "This is the most critical vote of this session for our faltering shipbuilding and steel industries."

As it turned out, Bateman was preaching to the converted. The House defeated two separate cutback amendments by wide margins.

A longtime state senator before coming to Washington, Bateman is acknowledged as a master of legislative detail. He exhibited this skill during a 1988 debate on a bill establishing a commission to draw up a list of military bases that should be closed to save money.

During the Armed Services markup, Bateman attached an amendment to the bill that would have ordered the commission to consider the environmental restoration and historic preservation costs of closing a base and covered a number of facilities around the country, including Fort Monroe, an ancient Army training base in Bateman's district. Built as an artillery base just after the War of 1812, the fort contains refuse — ranging from toxic waste to unexploded Confederate shells — that would be expensive to dispose of if the base were closed.

Although he took some gentle chiding from colleagues — Republican Constance A. Morella said Fort Monroe would produce more revenue for local communities if it was converted to a "theme park" — Bateman was resolute. In response to a critical editorial in *The New York Times,* Bateman called the fort "a well-functioning, well-located headquarters for the Army's Training and Doctrine Command."

The final bill enacted in October 1988 omitted Bateman's preservation clause, and it had different language on environmental costs. But ultimately, Fort Monroe was exempted from the commission's closure list. A provision in the base-closing law required that the costs for a base shutdown be offset by budget savings within six years; Pentagon officials suggested it could take 25 years to offset the costs of disposing of Fort Monroe's troublesome wastes.

Bateman has a broader agenda than sheer parochialism on Armed Services, serving as ranking Republican on the Military Personnel and Compensation Subcommittee and as a member of the Defense Policy Panel. Still, Bateman does have a notable knack for finding the local angle. In June 1987, he questioned President Reagan's decision to safeguard Kuwaiti oil tankers — then caught up in the Iran-

Virginia 1

East — Newport News; Hampton

Although Republicans have won the 1st in eight consecutive House elections, Bateman's close shave in 1990 makes it risky to say that this Tidewater constituency has completely cast off its traditional Democratic moorings. As that election showed, it is not yet automatic for the GOP; because of its black and working-class populations, it can still be a swing district. In the 1989 gubernatorial election, black Democratic Lt. Gov. L. Douglas Wilder carried the 1st with 51 percent.

Half the people in the 1st live in two cities at the district's southern end — Hampton and Newport News, both ports of the Hampton Roads harbor. Both are about one-third black, and both economies are tied to extensive military and shipbuilding facilities that Bateman has worked hard in Congress to promote; the Newport News Shipbuilding and Drydock Co. alone employs about 28,000 people and is the largest private employer in the state. In 1990, Bateman's Democratic opponent, Andy Fox, won 57 percent in Hampton and 48 percent in Newport News.

The balance of the district's population is scattered among rural inland counties and along the Chesapeake Bay. Colonial Virginia and its plantation economy were centered in this area; fishing, oystering, crabbing and the growing of corn, soybeans and wheat are important today. So is tourism. Along the southern flank of the district are some of Colonial Virginia's leading tourist attractions — Williamsburg, Jamestown and Yorktown. The basically conservative rural territory is where the GOP first began making significant inroads into the district's traditional Democratic strength.

Population: 535,092. White 358,702 (67%), Black 167,559 (31%), Other 6,072 (1%). Spanish origin 6,920 (1%). 18 and over 384,328 (72%), 65 and over 53,578 (10%). Median age: 30.

Iraq War — by re-flagging them and providing them with U.S. Navy escorts. However, Bateman was more concerned by the action's effect on the domestic merchant marine industry than foreign policy issues.

"There are nearly 40 U.S. tankers now laid up, and there is some concern that those vessels should have been given first right of refusal on routes which are to be protected by American naval vessels," said Bateman, a member of the Merchant Marine Committee. He said Kuwaiti ships should have been held to American safety standards, with those falling short to be upgraded "whenever feasible in U.S. shipyards."

Though not known as an environmental crusader, Bateman is protective of the Chesapeake Bay, which separates the two parts of his district. In the 100th Congress, he led a successful fight to restrict use of a tin-based pesticide, used to keep barnacles off ships, that had been found to be toxic to fish and crustaceans.

At Home: Every other election year, Bateman's vote totals dip. The 1st used to be safe haven for Democrats, but in presidential years this military-dependent district now votes solidly Republican. So when the White House is on the ballot, Bateman can relax a little, but midterm elections can be quite interesting.

Thus, in 1990, protracted budget negotiations, a late congressional adjournment and President Bush's reneging on his "no new taxes" pledge all contributed to an anti-incumbent mood in the electorate. Bateman struggled to defeat a 29-year-old political newcomer, Andy Fox. Fox had been a TV reporter for Norfolk's NBC affiliate.

Fox did not raise much money, but he attracted an enthusiastic squad of volunteer workers. In the final days, polls showed Bateman in a dangerously close race. Bush's late-campaign strategy of denouncing Iraqi leader Saddam Hussein may have shifted the attention of voters and helped save Bateman, who escaped by just 2,806 votes.

Bateman has been near the center of Newport News' civic and political life since he set up his legal practice three decades ago. He ran for the state Senate in 1967 as a Democrat and won. He was re-elected three times, twice as a Democrat and once as a Republican.

But until 1982, Bateman was blunted in his tries for higher office; his strong support from Virginia's conservative political establishment was neutralized by a poor sense of timing.

In early 1976, he switched parties with an eye on the Tidewater House seat of retiring Democratic Rep. Thomas N. Downing. But a hard-working young county prosecutor named Paul S. Trible Jr. had the GOP nomination locked up. In 1981 he was encouraged by GOP leaders to run for lieutenant governor. But he was challenged aggressively by a religious fundamentalist and a young state legislator and he finished second at the GOP state convention.

The two rebuffs, coupled with his narrow state Senate re-election in 1979, seemed to turn Bateman cautious on competing strenuously for higher office. When GOP officials sought a

House successor for Trible, who was running for the Senate in 1982, Bateman bluntly told them: "I'm a candidate, if I'm the nominee." Bateman easily won the district convention.

His Democratic opponent was John McGlennon, a political science professor at William and Mary who stepped in after the original nominee withdrew. The switch probably doomed Democratic hopes, but it also seemed to make Bateman somewhat overconfident. He waged a haphazard campaign that brought him victory with a tepid 54 percent.

That result encouraged McGlennon to try again in 1984. Starting earlier this time, the Democrat called Bateman a lazy legislator and used a TV commercial that showed the incumbent apparently asleep at a conference table. But with Reagan and GOP Sen. John W. Warner both carrying the 1st by more than 50,000 votes, Bateman took nearly 60 percent.

Democrats figured they still had a good chance to beat Bateman in 1986, when he would not have popular top-of-the-ticket help from Trible or Reagan. But a challenger was slow to emerge. State Sen. Robert C. Scott finally entered, bidding to become the state's first black member of Congress since the late 19th century. A Harvard-educated lawyer, he had demonstrated biracial appeal in Bateman's home base of Newport News, representing a Senate district roughly two-thirds white.

But the incumbent gave Scott few openings to exploit. Scott tried to pound away at Bateman as a captive of Tidewater business interests. But he was playing "catch-up" throughout: Bateman ran TV ads in the spring, and stressed his success at bringing jobs to the district, highlighted by Defense Secretary Caspar W. Weinberger's election-eve appearance with Bateman at the Newport News Shipbuilding and Drydock Co. to help dedicate a nuclear-powered aircraft carrier.

Scott ran virtually even with Bateman in the urban Tidewater, even carrying the city of Hampton. But Bateman rolled up 60 percent in the rural portion of the 1st to win a third term. In 1988, Bateman soared to 73 percent, his highest tally by more than a dozen points.

Committees

Armed Services (9th of 22 Republicans)
Military Personnel & Compensation (ranking); Seapower & Strategic & Critical Materials

Merchant Marine & Fisheries (5th of 17 Republicans)
Oceanography, Great Lakes & Outer Continental Shelf (ranking); Coast Guard & Navigation; Merchant Marine

Elections

1990 General		
Herbert H. Bateman (R)	72,000	(51%)
Andy Fox (D)	69,194	(49%)
1988 General		
Herbert H. Bateman (R)	135,937	(73%)
James S. Ellenson (D)	49,614	(27%)

Previous Winning Percentages: **1986** (56%) **1984** (59%) **1982** (54%)

District Vote For President

	1988	1984	1980	1976
D	83,291 (38%)	79,051 (37%)	80,434 (45%)	83,549 (51%)
R	131,341 (60%)	132,393 (62%)	90,093 (50%)	77,249 (47%)
I			7,440 (4%)	

Campaign Finance

	Receipts	Receipts from PACs		Expend-itures
1990				
Bateman (R)	$526,099	$218,750	(42%)	$549,818
Fox (D)	$106,176	$33,474	(32%)	$102,092
1988				
Bateman (R)	$293,109	$162,640	(55%)	$284,702
Ellenson (D)	$40,393	0		$40,392

Key Votes

1991	
Authorize use of force against Iraq	Y
1990	
Support constitutional amendment on flag desecration	Y
Pass family and medical leave bill over Bush veto	N
Reduce SDI funding	N
Allow abortions in overseas military facilities	N
Approve budget summit plan for spending and taxing	Y
Approve civil rights bill	N
1989	
Halt production of B-2 stealth bomber at 13 planes	N
Oppose capital gains tax cut	N
Approve federal abortion funding in rape or incest cases	N
Approve pay raise and revision of ethics rules	Y
Pass Democratic minimum wage plan over Bush veto	N

Voting Studies

	Presidential Support		Party Unity		Conservative Coalition	
Year	S	O	S	O	S	O
1990	69	31	63	33	96	4
1989	74	21	61	31	90	2
1988	64	35	68	29	92	5
1987	64 †	34 †	63 †	34 †	91 †	9 †
1986	69	29	64	35	88	12
1985	69	31	67	30	89	11
1984	71	27	71	26	90	3
1983	87	10	81	17	85	13

† Not eligible for all recorded votes.

Interest Group Ratings

Year	ADA	ACU	AFL-CIO	CCUS
1990	6	83	0	79
1989	0	81	17	100
1988	20	84	14	85
1987	12	74	25	79
1986	0	68	7	78
1985	10	71	6	77
1984	0	76	8	64
1983	0	91	0	100

2 Owen B. Pickett (D)

Of Virginia Beach — Elected 1986

Born: Aug. 31, 1930, Richmond, Va.

Education: Virginia Polytechnic Institute and State U., B.S. 1952; U. of Richmond, LL.B. 1955.

Occupation: Lawyer; accountant.

Family: Wife, Sybil Catherine Kelly; three children.

Religion: Baptist.

Political Career: Va. House, 1973-87; Va. Democratic Party chairman, 1980-82; withdrew from campaign for Democratic nomination for U.S. Senate, 1982.

Capitol Office: 1204 Longworth Bldg. 20515; 225-4215.

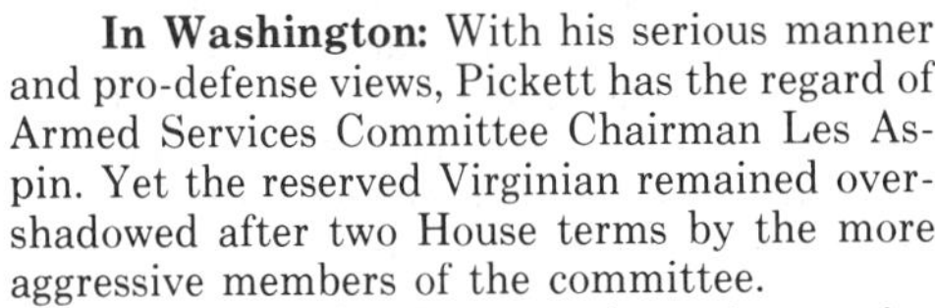

In Washington: With his serious manner and pro-defense views, Pickett has the regard of Armed Services Committee Chairman Les Aspin. Yet the reserved Virginian remained overshadowed after two House terms by the more aggressive members of the committee.

An Armed Services seat is an imperative for Pickett, whose district includes the Norfolk Naval Base and five other major military facilities. But when he came to Congress in 1987, Tidewater Virginia already had two members — Democrat Norman Sisisky and Republican Herbert H. Bateman — on the committee; Pickett finished fourth in a contest for three open seats. Nonetheless, then-Speaker Jim Wright cut a deal with the Republican leadership to expand the committee's size, creating a spot for Pickett.

On major defense issues, Pickett has generally supported Pentagon priorities. During the 101st Congress, he voted against capping production of the B-2 "Stealth" bomber and slashing funds for the strategic defense initiative.

With the Defense Department facing an era of budget limitations, though, Pickett contributed some of his own ideas. In 1990, he pushed through an amendment putting a hold on shipment of new military hardware to Western Europe, pending completion of U.S. conventional-force reduction negotiations with the Soviet Union.

Like other House members with established naval facilities in their districts, Pickett opposes a plan to disperse the U.S. Navy fleet to several "strategic homeports." He says cancelling the project would "save hundreds of millions of dollars ... without reducing America's military strength."

Pickett has also taken on some esoteric military-related issues. He is an advocate of easing access to U.S. citizenship for foreign residents, including some Filipinos, who enlist or have served in the United States Armed Forces. His bill failed in the 101st Congress, but he reintroduced it in the 102nd. He also gained a new position, a seat on the Veterans' Affairs Committee, from which to pursue such matters.

At Home: By the time he won the congressional seat vacated by retiring Republican G. William Whitehurst in 1986, Pickett had already served as chairman of the state party, launched, then abandoned a Senate bid, headed a Democratic presidential campaign in Virginia and served long enough in the state House of Delegates to be a senior member of the Appropriations Committee.

Neither an orator nor a gregarious backslapper, the wealthy Virginia Beach lawyer-accountant prefers to work studiously behind the scenes. But when state Democrats had important decisions to make, Pickett was nearly always in on them. He played a major role, for example, in fashioning the state's budget and retirement system. In 1980, he was chosen Democratic state chairman.

Pickett chaired the party through Charles S. Robb's successful gubernatorial campaign in 1981 and tried the waters as a Senate candidate in 1982, dropping out before the primary.

Two years later, Pickett chaired Walter F. Mondale's presidential campaign in Virginia. That placed him at odds with some of his old allies among party moderates but built bridges to Norfolk, which is one-third black and heavily unionized — the Democratic core of the 2nd. Pickett's personal roots in more Republican Virginia Beach helped him cut his losses there.

Pickett's GOP opponent in 1986, state Sen. A. J. "Joe" Canada, was generally regarded as the more appealing campaigner. But Canada was jolted early in the campaign by newspaper stories detailing his involvement with a bankrupt Virginia Beach mortgage company and business deals he had made with a Richmond stockbroker who had been accused of embezzlement. While no one linked Canada to criminal wrongdoing, Pickett said Canada's poor judgment was a legitimate issue.

Canada narrowly carried Virginia Beach, but Pickett won by nearly 2-to-1 in Norfolk. In 1988, Pickett surpassed 60 percent, and in 1990 the Republicans did not even field a candidate.

Virginia 2

Norfolk; Virginia Beach

The 2nd is composed of adjacent coastal cities: the fast-growing residential and resort municipality of Virginia Beach and the unionized port city of Norfolk, which has been striving to polish its image.

The two cities present a stark political contrast. For years, Norfolk has been one of the few bastions of liberalism within Virginia. It is the home of former Lt. Gov. Henry Howell, an outspoken populist, and Edythe C. Harrison, the party's unsuccessful candidate for senator in 1984. Norfolk, which is more than one-third black, gave Harrison 47 percent of its vote (she won only 30 percent statewide), and it went for Michael S. Dukakis for president in 1988. Black Democratic Lt. Gov. L. Douglas Wilder won 66 percent in Norfolk in his successful 1989 gubernatorial election.

Virginia Beach, on the other hand, is one of the state's prime strongholds of conservatism. It is home to the religious broadcasting empire of Pat Robertson, who sought the GOP presidential nomination in 1988. Like the southern portion of the 1st District, the 2nd is heavily dependent on the massive concentration of naval installations, shipbuilders and shipping firms in the Hampton Roads harbor area, which ranks first in export tonnage among the nation's Atlantic ports and is the biggest coal shipper in the world.

Recently, Norfolk has been cultivating a more cosmopolitan image. The builder of Baltimore's Inner Harbor area renovated Norfolk's waterfront, creating an area of offices and shops called "Waterside."

An influx of military families, business people and retirees during recent years has changed Virginia Beach's earlier identity as a summer tourist center. The city's retail and service trade has boomed, and its population reached 393,000 residents in the 1990 census, supplanting Norfolk as Virginia's largest city.

Population: 529,178. White 389,088 (74%), Black 120,278 (23%), Other 15,237 (3%). Spanish origin 11,234 (2%). 18 and over 383,036 (72%), 65 and over 36,388 (7%). Median age: 26.

Committees

Armed Services (23rd of 33 Democrats)
Military Personnel & Compensation; Readiness; Seapower & Strategic & Critical Materials; Military Education

Merchant Marine & Fisheries (16th of 29 Democrats)
Coast Guard & Navigation; Merchant Marine

Veterans' Affairs (19th of 21 Democrats)
Housing & Memorial Affairs

Elections

1990 General		
Owen B. Pickett (D)	55,179	(75%)
Harry G. Broskie (I)	15,915	(22%)
1988 General		
Owen B. Pickett (D)	106,666	(61%)
Jerry R. Curry (R)	62,564	(36%)

Previous Winning Percentage: **1986** (49%)

District Vote For President

	1988	1984	1980	1976
D	71,558 (40%)	63,616 (37%)	60,013 (41%)	65,119 (49%)
R	107,019 (60%)	108,931 (63%)	75,443 (52%)	62,692 (47%)
I			8,163 (6%)	

Campaign Finance

	Receipts	Receipts from PACs	Expend-itures
1990			
Pickett (D)	$240,133	$135,500 (56%)	$82,828
1988			
Pickett (D)	$437,439	$215,810 (49%)	$414,011
Curry (R)	$194,004	$15,406 (8%)	$189,391

Key Votes

1991	
Authorize use of force against Iraq	Y
1990	
Support constitutional amendment on flag desecration	Y
Pass family and medical leave bill over Bush veto	N
Reduce SDI funding	N
Allow abortions in overseas military facilities	Y
Approve budget summit plan for spending and taxing	N
Approve civil rights bill	Y
1989	
Halt production of B-2 stealth bomber at 13 planes	N
Oppose capital gains tax cut	N
Approve federal abortion funding in rape or incest cases	Y
Approve pay raise and revision of ethics rules	N
Pass Democratic minimum wage plan over Bush veto	Y

Voting Studies

	Presidential Support		Party Unity		Conservative Coalition	
Year	S	O	S	O	S	O
1990	47	52	72	27	78	22
1989	52 †	47 †	72 †	26 †	83	15
1988	34	65	80	16	82	16
1987	39	61	78	19	70	30

† Not eligible for all recorded votes.

Interest Group Ratings

Year	ADA	ACU	AFL-CIO	CCUS
1990	50	42	75	64
1989	45	37	42	80
1988	50	40	86	50
1987	72	22	81	40

3 Thomas J. Bliley Jr. (R)

Of Richmond — Elected 1980

Born: Jan. 28, 1932, Chesterfield County, Va.
Education: Georgetown U., B.A. 1952.
Military Service: Navy, 1952-55.
Occupation: Funeral director.
Family: Wife, Mary Virginia Kelley; two children.
Religion: Roman Catholic.
Political Career: Richmond City Council, 1968-77, mayor, 1970-77.
Capitol Office: 2241 Rayburn Bldg. 20515; 225-2815.

In Washington: A cordial and good-humored former mayor, Bliley has built relationships with members of the Energy and Commerce Committee that have helped make him one of the more active Republican players on a panel dominated by activist Democrats.

As ranking Republican on the Subcommittee on Oversight and Investigations, Bliley has had an opportunity to share at least some of the limelight with subcommittee (and full committee) Chairman John D. Dingell, D-Mich., including the 1989-90 probe into approval and testing of generic drugs.

Also in the 101st Congress, Bliley was a pivotal player in resolving legal conflicts over so-called "orphan drugs," which treat diseases so rare that there may not be enough of a market to support their development. The government has granted special exclusivity rights to developers of such drugs, leading to hard feelings when successful "orphans" reap huge profits for their makers. Bliley's compromise was to allow a fairer share of the new market for competitors that develop the same drug simultaneously.

But if he is usually regarded as an open-minded person to work with, Bliley can at times be an unyielding spokesman for the conservative point of view. Also, his defense of the increasingly unpopular tobacco industry — a parochial imperative for Richmond's congressman — has put him on the losing end of several battles in recent years.

As a former mayor of Richmond, Bliley has had a long association with his district's conservative business interests. Prominent among them is cigarette manufacturer Philip Morris. Bliley tries to involve himself in a variety of legislative areas, but much of his time has been spent challenging bills hostile to the cigarette industry. Though he seems sometimes to embrace the role as much with resignation as with enthusiasm, Bliley is identified as the tobacco industry's sentry on the Health Subcommittee at Energy and Commerce.

In 1990, for example, he managed to beat back an amendment barring the sale of any tobacco products to persons "who appeared" to be under 25. But he was not able to stop the subcommittee from approving a ban on the marketing of lookalike products such as bubblegum cigarettes and chewing tobacco.

Relentless anti-smoking campaigns by vocal lobby groups have helped create the impression that the tobacco lobby is fighting a losing battle in Congress. Already barred from advertising on the airwaves, the industry now is fending off demands that it be banned from advertising altogether. Bliley's search for friends for tobacco is becoming more taxing. "The circle is getting smaller and smaller all the time," he said in 1985.

That year, Bliley tried to block an initiative by Health Subcommittee Chairman Henry A. Waxman aimed at snuff and chewing tobacco. Waxman wanted to require health warnings on labels and in ads for these products, and he sought to mandate a label design that drew attention to the warning. Bliley temporarily managed to block this, but the producers, facing the prospect of conflicting labeling requirements in several states, soon consented to federal regulation. Waxman also prevailed in an effort to ban radio and TV advertising of chewing tobacco and snuff.

In the 100th Congress, the tobacco industry's biggest loss came when Congress banned smoking on certain domestic airline flights. The battle was fought outside Energy and Commerce, but Bliley spoke against the legislation, saying it would cause administrative problems for airlines and airports and could be a fire hazard by causing surreptitious smoking on airplanes. "The bottom line," he said, "is that there is no significant scientific evidence to support the assertion that environmental tobacco smoke is harmful to non-smokers." The airline tobacco ban was broadened to include nearly all domestic flights.

While defending tobacco is a necessary focus for Bliley, in the 100th Congress he won much more attention for taking the offensive to ban so-called "dial-a-porn" services. In the teleporn fight in 1988, Bliley joined with con-

Virginia 3

Richmond and Suburbs

The 3rd District has two distinct parts: the black-majority, traditionally Democratic city of Richmond, and the surrounding suburbs in Chesterfield and Henrico counties, which are overwhelmingly white and predominantly Republican.

Because the population has grown in the suburbs and shrunk in the city — Richmond lost just over 7 percent in the last decade — the 3rd in recent years has emerged as a GOP stronghold. With redistricting in 1981, Bliley saw his constituency become even more of a Republican bastion.

Although Richmond is probably best known as the capital of the Confederacy, the city's black majority has made it one of the most loyally Democratic population centers in the South. It has backed the Democratic presidential ticket in five of the last six elections. In 1989, black Democratic Lt. Gov. L. Douglas Wilder carried Richmond by 2-to-1 over his white Republican foe, J. Marshall Coleman.

But in the 3rd, Richmond is outvoted by Chesterfield and Henrico, which have never given the Democratic presidential nominee more than one-third of the vote in the same period.

The political split between Richmond and its suburbs was obvious in 1988. George Bush took 69 percent in Henrico County and 83 percent in the Chesterfield County portion of the 3rd. Michael S. Dukakis carried Richmond with 56 percent. In 1989, Coleman ran up wide margins in both counties against Wilder and won the 3rd with 52 percent.

The third-largest city in the state, Richmond has long been the center of Virginia government and commerce. From wood-paneled corporate offices along the Main Street corridor, Richmond's business elite exercises considerable influence over politics in the district and in the state.

The city was also one of the South's early manufacturing centers, concentrating on tobacco processing. Richmond still boasts the country's largest cigarette plant, but manufacturing has diversified into chemicals, textiles, paper and processed foods, and downtown redevelopment has freshened the center city's once-gray image.

Population: 533,668. White 376,664 (71%), Black 150,852 (28%), Other 4,554 (1%). Spanish origin 4,560 (1%). 18 and over 394,810 (74%), 65 and over 54,731 (10%). Median age: 30.

servative GOP Sen. Jesse Helms to change the Communications Act of 1934 in order to prohibit the use of the telephone for "any obscene or indecent communication for commercial purposes," whether directly or by recording. In June 1989, however, the Supreme Court ruled the ban unconstitutional, saying that, if the government wanted to ban indecent (as opposed to obscene) expression to protect minors, it would have to do so with detailed regulations rather than with a wholesale ban.

Bliley is conversant with a variety of health issues, especially preventive medicine. Arguing that increased federal spending for maternity and pediatric care could prevent more expensive medical problems later in life, Bliley joined with liberals on Energy and Commerce in 1983 to back a Child Health Assurance Program, designed to expand Medicaid coverage for mothers and children. He wrote a successful amendment permitting states to make pregnant teenagers eligible for Medicaid regardless of parents' income.

Though he is a fierce critic of abortion, his strong feelings on the issue lead him down a different path from that of many conservatives. He wants to do more than discourage abortion: He wants to encourage federal spending for infant health care. "In order to be fair," he says, "we are under some moral obligation to take care of the living."

Other Bliley pursuits are more in the vein of traditional conservatism. In 1985, he sought to block federal funding for family planning clinics located in or near facilities that perform abortions. The next year, he introduced a bill to prohibit the inclusion of abortion-related expenses as deductible medical care.

The sizable black population in the 3rd District has also shaped Bliley positions. He praised some of President Reagan's budget in 1987, but also said the cuts in education were "simply not acceptable." "The most disturbing cut," he said, "and one that strongly impacts the Richmond area, is that aid to historically black colleges would be cut by two-thirds. This proposal is clearly out of the question."

Bliley's attitude toward South Africa also differed from that of some conservatives. In 1985 and 1986, he went against President Reagan and voted to impose sanctions on South Africa.

At Home: A pleasant, soft-spoken Richmond mortician, Bliley was coaxed into politics in 1968 by civic leaders who sought him out to run for City Council. He left city government in

1977 after nearly a decade of service — including a stint as mayor — to devote more time to his funeral home. But he enthusiastically reentered politics shortly after Democrat David E. Satterfield announced his retirement from Congress in 1980.

A Democrat himself when in Richmond government, Bliley announced his conversion to the GOP only when he launched his House campaign in 1980. Critics said the switch was motivated by the district's GOP voting pattern; Bliley said it was prompted by a leftward swing in the state Democratic leadership.

Bliley's support from the Richmond business community virtually assured his election. With a well-funded campaign, he overwhelmed his little-known Democratic opponent and two independent candidates. In 1982, Bliley faced a more aggressive challenger in Henrico County Supervisor John Waldrop. The Democrat criticized Bliley for backing deep cuts in social and educational programs, a charge that played well in mostly black Richmond. Bliley lost the city, but won easily in the white suburbs where most of the votes were.

The Democrats did not field a candidate in 1984, but they ran an ambitious young tax attorney against Bliley two years later. The challenger, Kenneth E. Powell, mounted an extensive grass-roots campaign and labeled Bliley a tool of political action committees (PACs).

But the incumbent flicked aside the criticism, saying, "PACs don't contribute to losers." Bliley touted his congressional work in defense of the tobacco industry, and with a large advantage in money, name identification and big-name support, he swept every jurisdiction, including Democratic Richmond.

After leaving Bliley alone in 1988, the Democrats in 1990 nominated Jay Starke, owner of a plumbing and heating company, who raised little money and attracted slight attention. Bliley won with 65 percent.

Committees

District of Columbia (Ranking)
Fiscal Affairs & Health; Government Operations & Metropolitan Affairs; Judiciary & Education

Energy & Commerce (6th of 16 Republicans)
Oversight & Investigations (ranking); Health & the Environment; Telecommunications & Finance

Elections

1990 General

Thomas J. Bliley Jr. (R)	77,125	(65%)
Jay Starke (D)	36,253	(31%)
Rose L. Simpson (I)	4,317	(4%)

1988 General

Thomas J. Bliley Jr. (R)	187,354	(100%)

Previous Winning Percentages: **1986** (67%) **1984** (86%) **1982** (59%) **1980** (52%)

District Vote For President

	1988	1984	1980	1976
D	86,678 (36%)	83,310 (35%)	80,943 (38%)	79,505 (41%)
R	151,033 (63%)	155,612 (65%)	121,797 (57%)	109,653 (57%)
I			8,596 (4%)	

Campaign Finance

	Receipts	Receipts from PACs		Expend-itures
1990				
Bliley (R)	$632,395	$398,462	(63%)	$710,739
Starke (D)	$57,857	$28,925	(50%)	$57,909
1988				
Bliley (R)	$467,449	$270,550	(58%)	$366,816

Key Votes

1991	
Authorize use of force against Iraq	Y
1990	
Support constitutional amendment on flag desecration	Y
Pass family and medical leave bill over Bush veto	N
Reduce SDI funding	N
Allow abortions in overseas military facilities	N
Approve budget summit plan for spending and taxing	N
Approve civil rights bill	Y
1989	
Halt production of B-2 stealth bomber at 13 planes	N
Oppose capital gains tax cut	N
Approve federal abortion funding in rape or incest cases	N
Approve pay raise and revision of ethics rules	N
Pass Democratic minimum wage plan over Bush veto	N

Voting Studies

	Presidential Support		Party Unity		Conservative Coalition	
Year	**S**	**O**	**S**	**O**	**S**	**O**
1990	66	34	84	13	91	7
1989	80	17	88	9	100	0
1988	61	38	86	11	89	8
1987	70	29	86	12	91	7
1986	69	30	82	16	94	6
1985	74	26	83	15	87	13
1984	74	25	82	14	88	8
1983	85	12	87	10	96	3
1982	86	13	92	5	97	3
1981	75	25	88	11	89	9

Interest Group Ratings

Year	ADA	ACU	AFL-CIO	CCUS
1990	17	83	17	93
1989	0	96	8	100
1988	10	96	21	93
1987	4	96	6	100
1986	5	73	14	88
1985	5	81	24	82
1984	5	83	15	94
1983	5	96	0	84
1982	0	96	5	91
1981	0	93	13	100

4 Norman Sisisky (D)

Of Petersburg — Elected 1982

Born: June 9, 1927, Baltimore, Md.
Education: Virginia Commonwealth U., B.S. 1949.
Military Service: Navy, 1945-46.
Occupation: Beer and soft drink distributor.
Family: Wife, Rhoda Brown; four children.
Religion: Jewish.
Political Career: Va. House, 1974-82.
Capitol Office: 426 Cannon Bldg. 20515; 225-6365.

In Washington: Though not one of the more visible members of the Armed Services Committee, Sisisky has a full load of responsibilities. Along with his four subcommittee assignments, Sisisky is a member of three special panels, one on defense policy, one on nuclear facilities and a third on the North Atlantic Assembly, the legislative affiliate of the North Atlantic Treaty Organization. He also serves on the U.S. delegation to the Assembly.

Much of Sisisky's work is oriented to his southeast Virginia base. Following the release of President Bush's fiscal 1992 budget proposal, Sisisky's office noted that the military construction section contained about $100 million for 4th District projects.

Sisisky is part of Armed Services' "Tidewater Trio." With Sisisky, fellow Democrat Owen B. Pickett and Republican Herbert H. Bateman to look out for the interests of the Norfolk-area naval bases and other local military facilities, few regions are as well defended on Armed Services.

Sisisky has managed to have some influence over broader U.S. defense policy, even as he stands vigil for the 4th's interests. While strongly supportive of the naval forces that form the core of his region's military base, Sisisky has not always been sanguine about Reagan and Bush administration priorities for the Navy.

The issue of "homeporting" is one case in point. During the mid-1980s, when President Reagan's goal of a 600-ship Navy was still current, the Navy's leadership promoted the idea of dispersing the U.S. fleet among several new homeports on the Atlantic, Pacific and Gulf coasts. Advocates said this plan would ease overcrowding at existing ports, such as Norfolk/Newport News, and would provide strategic advantages by placing parts of the fleet nearer to potential trouble spots in Latin America and the Pacific.

However, skeptics viewed the program as a ploy to build political support for Navy expansion by scattering job-producing facilities. Sisisky was one of the more outspoken members of this group.

Although homeporting supporters initially held sway, events began to turn the tide: Fiscal pressures and the thawing of the Cold War scuttled the idea of a 600-ship Navy, and Bush administration officials viewed homeporting as less of a priority. In early 1990, Defense Secretary Dick Cheney imposed a moratorium on homeport building (and on much other military construction), and a Staten Island, N.Y., project was consigned to a study commission.

Sisisky expressed satisfaction in this outcome, and denied that his interest in the issue was strictly parochial. "[Norfolk] would lose some ships, sure, but it really wasn't about that," he said. "They never proved a strategic need [for the new ports]."

A successful businessman before entering politics, Sisisky has made Pentagon fiscal accountability his main cause as a House member. He uses his booming voice to condemn wasteful procurement practices and call for the Defense Department to run like a business.

It was on a defense purchasing issue that Sisisky made a mark as a House freshman. Upon learning of a Pentagon request to build schools for military dependents in Western Europe at a price of $8,500 per pupil, Sisisky headed for a hall telephone and called a contact in Virginia's Department of Education to find out how much schools cost. The figure he came back with was roughly half the requested amount. Sisisky later claimed credit for saving taxpayers some $143 million.

As a member of the Procurement Subcommittee — and a former member of the Investigations Subcommittee — Sisisky employs his business background. He once opposed an inflation allowance for military contracts, citing his experiences in supplying Pepsi-Cola to military bases.

Sisisky did support the effort that began in 1988 to draft a list of obsolete military bases to close, although the forts in his district were possible targets. He approved the process by which Congress would hold a single vote on a list of bases to be closed as "one way to take it

Virginia 4

Southeast — Chesapeake; Portsmouth

With Portsmouth's large black population and blue-collar work force joining diehard rural Democrats, the 4th is a solid Democratic district. When Democrat Charles S. Robb won election to the Senate in 1988, the 4th gave him a larger share of the vote than any other district in the state. Even Michael S. Dukakis managed a respectable 44 percent here in 1988. Black Democratic Lt. Gov. L. Douglas Wilder carried the 4th with 52 percent in his successful 1989 gubernatorial election.

Portsmouth is 45 percent black and casts about one-fifth of the district's vote. The city is oriented toward the naval and shipbuilding economy of Norfolk, Hampton and Newport News. The neighboring city of Chesapeake, slightly larger than Portsmouth, is less black and less industrial. It is home to many who work in Portsmouth's shipyards and factories. In 1988, George Bush won Chesapeake, while Dukakis carried Portsmouth. In 1989, Wilder received 62 percent in Portsmouth and won Chesapeake by 308 votes over Republican J. Marshall Coleman.

There is some industry in the smaller cities of the 4th, which together make up another one-quarter of the district's population. Suffolk processes peanuts, Petersburg makes tobacco products and is home to the Fort Lee military installation, and Hopewell calls itself the chemical capital of the South. Black-majority Petersburg was the only one of the group to go for Dukakis; it gave Wilder 71 percent of its vote.

Peanuts and tobacco are the important crops in the farm lands of the 4th, where roughly one-third of the district's residents live. Democratic ties are still strong there, particularly in a swath of counties that stretch southwestward from the James River to the North Carolina border.

Population: 535,703. White 317,266 (59%), Black 212,598 (40%), Other 3,927 (1%). Spanish origin 5,735 (1%). 18 and over 377,071 (70%), 65 and over 53,225 (10%). Median age: 30.

out of the field of politics ... I think it's the only way we are going to do it."

In the end, Sisisky's homebase interests were not only unharmed — they were enhanced. The presidential commission that developed the base-closing list preserved Sisisky's forts, and added military and civilian positions at Fort Lee as part of a personnel realignment.

Sisisky definitely abhors defense savings from the Navy's budget for warships. He was unhappy when President Reagan's target of 15 aircraft carriers slipped to 14, and unhappier still when President Bush cut the figure to 12 . When Cheney, a former House colleague, testified before Armed Services on the carrier cutback in April 1990, Sisisky grumbled, "If I did not know you, I'd say you were a hanging judge."

As a centrist on the Armed Forces Committee, Sisisky is seen as a reliable ally of Chairman Les Aspin. He often stood by Aspin as more liberal Democrats criticized him in the late 1980s for supporting major weapons systems.

However, in 1989, Sisisky had some cross words for Aspin, when he believed he went too far in supporting Bush adminstration policies. Aspin called Bush's first effort at producing a realistic defense budget a good one, and he urged the Armed Services Subcommittee on Procurement to accept it. The authorization request contained controversial proposals to cut several weapons programs with constituencies on Armed Services. Sisisky said that Aspin was "abrogating the responsibility of the largest subcommittee of Armed Services."

Aspin prevailed in the subcommittee by a 10-9 vote. But the Bush budget suffered setbacks during full committee deliberations. Among the amendments attached to the authorization bill was one by Sisisky and Pennsylvania Republican Curt Weldon restoring funding for the Navy's F-14D fighter jet and for the Osprey, a hybrid helicopter/airplane favored by the Marines.

Outside Armed Services, Sisisky has gone to some length to promote Virginia interests. In March 1987, he was the only Democrat to vote to uphold Reagan's veto of an $88 billion highway-funding bill. Sisisky explained he had done this not for Reagan, but for Virginia's then-Democratic Gov. Gerald L. Baliles, who believed the bill's funding formulas shortchanged the state. The bill also had omitted an improvement project for a hazardous road in Sisisky's district.

Sisisky also applies his business acumen as a member of the Small Business Committee, where he chairs the Subcommittee on Exports, Tax Policy and Special Problems. He held hearings in 1991 to examine how American businesses could play a role in the rebuilding of Kuwait, following the U.S.-led military action to free that nation from occupation by Iraq.

At Home: After a decade of intraparty friction and underfinanced campaigns, Democrats united behind the wealthy Sisisky in 1982. He combined a large campaign treasury and an affable campaign style to oust veteran GOP Rep. Robert W. Daniel Jr. Since then, he has been re-elected four times without a Republican opponent.

The son of Lithuanian immigrants, Sisisky was born in Baltimore. His family moved during the Depression to Richmond, where his father worked in a delicatessen. Sisisky was raised there and attended a local college.

During the 1982 campaign, Sisisky described himself as a self-made businessman. Critics said he married into a wealthy Petersburg family and took over its soft-drink company. But regardless of how he got his start, Sisisky is a natural salesman who turned the operation into one of the most successful Pepsi-Cola distributorships in the country.

After years as a pillar of the business community, Sisisky won a seat in the state House in 1973. With Virginia politics then in a state of flux, he ran as an independent, but caucused with the Democrats and in 1975 sought re-election as a Democrat. In the Legislature he was known as a master compromiser; he was often an intermediary between conservative Southside legislators and their more liberal Northern Virginia counterparts.

Sisisky was widely recognized as his party's strongest potential challenger against Daniel in 1982. But when a black activist announced in early 1982 that he might run as an independent, Sisisky threatened to pull out of the race. Only when the threat of an independent candidacy subsided did Sisisky resume his campaign.

Sisisky charged that Daniel's pro-Reagan record did not represent blacks (who make up 40 percent of the population), farmers or the blue-collar workers of industrial Tidewater. Daniel countered by branding Sisisky a liberal and claiming he was trying to buy the election. In the end, Sisisky carried 15 out of 20 jurisdictions, winning overwhelmingly in Petersburg and in blue-collar Portsmouth.

When the early list of possible 1989 candidates to succeed Gov. Baliles was drawn up, Sisisky, with his strong southern Virginia base, was mentioned. But Lt. Gov. L. Douglas Wilder declared dibs, and Sisisky showed no interest in thwarting Wilder's bid to become the first black elected governor in American history.

Committees

Armed Services (14th of 33 Democrats)
Investigations; Military Installations & Facilities; Procurement & Military Nuclear Systems; Seapower & Strategic & Critical Materials

Select Aging (18th of 42 Democrats)
Health & Long-Term Care; Rural Elderly

Small Business (10th of 27 Democrats)
Exports, Tax Policy & Special Problems (chairman)

Elections

1990 General

Norman Sisisky (D)	71,051	(78%)
Don L. McReynolds (I)	12,295	(14%)
Loretta F. Chandler (I)	7,102	(8%)

1988 General

Norman Sisisky (D)	134,786	(100%)

Previous Winning Percentages: **1986** (100%) **1984** (100%) **1982** (54%)

District Vote For President

	1988	1984	1980	1976
D	89,094 (44%)	91,107 (43%)	91,716 (50%)	96,396 (56%)
R	110,155 (55%)	117,579 (56%)	83,955 (46%)	69,501 (41%)
I			4,589 (3%)	

Campaign Finance

	Receipts	Receipts from PACs	Expend-itures
1990			
Sisisky (D)	$240,553	$158,200 (66%)	$275,502
McReynolds (I)	$19,854	0	$19,883
1988			
Sisisky (D)	$185,555	$102,636 (55%)	$93,232

Key Votes

1991	
Authorize use of force against Iraq	Y
1990	
Support constitutional amendment on flag desecration	Y
Pass family and medical leave bill over Bush veto	N
Reduce SDI funding	N
Allow abortions in overseas military facilities	Y
Approve budget summit plan for spending and taxing	Y
Approve civil rights bill	Y
1989	
Halt production of B-2 stealth bomber at 13 planes	N
Oppose capital gains tax cut	Y
Approve federal abortion funding in rape or incest cases	Y
Approve pay raise and revision of ethics rules	Y
Pass Democratic minimum wage plan over Bush veto	Y

Voting Studies

	Presidential Support		Party Unity		Conservative Coalition	
Year	**S**	**O**	**S**	**O**	**S**	**O**
1990	43 †	57 †	77	22	91	9
1989	51 †	47 †	73 †	25 †	78	20
1988	38	61	77	20	76	21
1987	45	54	74	24	86	9
1986	39	60	75	21	70	30
1985	39 †	58 †	76	22	78	20
1984	54	42	66	32	73	24
1983	43	56	61	32	75	21

† Not eligible for all recorded votes.

Interest Group Ratings

Year	ADA	ACU	AFL-CIO	CCUS
1990	39	42	50	50
1989	55	21	67	60
1988	55	40	86	50
1987	52	39	63	60
1986	45	48	57	56
1985	40	38	47	36
1984	40	38	46	33
1983	65	43	88	30

5 Lewis F. Payne Jr. (D)

Of Nellysford — Elected 1988

Born: July 9, 1945, Amherst, Va.
Education: Virginia Military Institute, B.S. 1967; U. of Virginia, M.B.A. 1973.
Military Service: Army, 1968-70.
Occupation: Developer; businessman.
Family: Wife, Susan King; four children.
Religion: Presbyterian.
Political Career: No previous office.
Capitol Office: 1118 Longworth Bldg. 20515; 225-4711.

In Washington: Payne labeled himself a "progressive conservative" when he entered Congress after a 1988 special election, and he has spent his first three years in the House quietly establishing just that kind of record.

He bolstered his conservative image with votes to support using force against Iraq and by backing a constitutional ban on flag desecration. And his support of President Bush's vetoes of a minimum wage increase and the family and medical leave bill endeared him to the business community.

But Payne complemented those stands with his consistent support of abortion rights, and with his backing of Democratic efforts to pass a civil rights bill, important to the minorities in his district.

Payne's balancing act is evident in the ratings he earned in 1990 from the Chamber of Commerce (64 percent favorable) and the AFL-CIO (50 percent).

Payne also voted for the controversial 1990 budget summit agreement that raised taxes and cut spending, following the Democratic leadership line. Perhaps not coincidentally, he got a seat on the Budget Committee at the start of the 102nd Congress.

Payne was an engineer and businessman who had spent 15 years building the Wintergreen resort in Nelson County and had never run for office before 1988. He first won the 5th in a June special election to fill the unexpired term of 19-year veteran Dan Daniel, who had died in January.

Payne was around for only a few months of the 100th Congress. He did little to attract attention in Washington, concentrating instead on getting better acquainted with his district. He was assigned to the Public Works Committee and to Veterans' Affairs, both solid opportunities to help constituents and both panels on which Virginia had not been represented.

At Home: Republicans targeted the 5th when Daniel in January 1988 announced plans to retire. (He died four days later.) Daniel was a product of the old Harry Byrd machine and a one-time advocate of "massive resistance" to desegregation. Although he stayed in the Democratic Party, he usually voted with Republicans in the House.

The leading Republican candidate was Linda Arey, a 43-year-old attorney who had been a public liaison aide in the Reagan White House. She successfully organized local and county caucuses leading to the district convention, where she defeated a GOP state senator from Danville.

Payne, meanwhile, got a late start but quietly organized key Democrats. The son of a state trooper and a schoolteacher, he had become wealthy enough in his development business to finance 40 percent of his special-election campaign's $500,000 cost out of his own deep pockets.

At the Democrats' district meeting in March he was declared the nominee by acclamation. He was not an accomplished public speaker. But as a self-made success, Army veteran and family man, he seemed to embody many of the virtues Southside Virginians value. He campaigned as a fiscal conservative and managed to alienate neither the blacks who constitute a quarter of the district, nor the bedrock Dixiecrats whose votes decide elections in the 5th.

The national GOP had hopes of prevailing in the district for the first time in a century. In June, Arey broadcast a radio endorsement from President Reagan, and she got a campaign visit from Vice President Bush. But her advertising reach was foreshortened by dwindling campaign funds. Payne prevailed with a solid 59 percent of the vote, and Arey decided against making another bid that November.

In her place, Republicans nominated state Rep. Charles Hawkins. He did not become the party's official nominee until September and could not raise much money. Yet he benefited from the 5th's strong preference for GOP presidential nominee Bush and held Payne to 54 percent of the vote.

But by 1990, Republican interest in the 5th had dissipated. Payne was unopposed for reelection.

Virginia 5

South — Danville

The 5th is in the heart of Virginia's rural "Southside," a largely agricultural region that resembles the Deep South more closely than any other part of the state does. It is relatively poor and has a substantial black population. Tobacco and soybeans are major crops, but this region lacks the rich soil of the Tidewater.

Payne has quickly established a grip on the 5th, but the district has long refused to swallow more liberal Democratic candidates at the state and national levels. Barry Goldwater carried it with 51 percent in 1964; it was one of only two House districts in Virginia to back George C. Wallace in 1968; and it was the only Virginia district in 1988 where every county and independent city supported George Bush for president. The 5th was 1989 Republican gubernatorial nominee J. Marshall Coleman's best district in the state; he got 58 percent against black Democratic Lt. Gov. L. Douglas Wilder.

The district's most famous landmark is Appomattox Court House, where Robert E. Lee surrendered to Ulysses S. Grant to end the Civil War. About 60 miles south is the district's largest city, Danville, a tobacco market and textile center on the North Carolina border that has nearly 45,000 residents. The residents of the city and those of surrounding Pittsylvania County make up one-fifth of the district's population.

Just to the west is Henry County, which surrounds the textile-mill town of Martinsville. With about 56,000 residents, Henry County is the second most populous in the district after Pittsylvania. Traditionally, Henry County has been the best area in the 5th for Democratic candidates; Michael S. Dukakis managed 41 percent there in 1988, as did Wilder in 1989.

The rest of the people are scattered through farming areas and a few factory towns. Most of these areas normally vote Republican at the statewide level.

Blacks comprise about one-quarter of the district population and are most numerous in the eastern counties. Prince Edward and Nelson were the two counties Wilder won in the 5th.

In the western part of the 5th, the terrain becomes more rugged as the Piedmont Plateau yields to the foothills of the Blue Ridge Mountains. The Blue Ridge Parkway runs along the 5th's western flank, roughly separating Southside Virginia from the mountainous western Panhandle.

Population: 531,308. White 398,091 (75%), Black 131,482 (25%). Spanish origin 3,753 (1%). 18 and over 382,312 (72%), 65 and over 63,859 (12%). Median age: 32.

Committees

Budget (22nd of 23 Democrats)
Budget Process, Reconciliation & Enforcement; Community Development & Natural Resources

Public Works & Transportation (20th of 36 Democrats)
Aviation; Surface Transportation; Water Resources

Elections

1990 General		
Lewis F. Payne Jr. (D)	66,532	(99%)
1988 General		
Lewis F. Payne Jr. (D)	97,242	(54%)
Charles Hawkins (R)	78,396	(44%)

Previous Winning Percentage: **1988 *** (59%)

* *Special election.*

District Vote For President

	1988	1984	1980	1976
D	71,107 (37%)	67,480 (34%)	73,569 (42%)	77,138 (48%)
R	119,560 (62%)	131,912 (66%)	97,203 (55%)	78,306 (49%)
I			3,660 (2%)	

Campaign Finance

	Receipts	Receipts from PACs	Expend-itures
1990			
Payne (D)	$317,828	$187,650 (59%)	$317,271
1988			
Payne (D)	$846,908	$199,500 (24%)	$837,864
Hawkins (R)	$105,871	$5,500 (5%)	$150,872

Key Votes

1991	
Authorize use of force against Iraq	Y
1990	
Support constitutional amendment on flag desecration	Y
Pass family and medical leave bill over Bush veto	N
Reduce SDI funding	N
Allow abortions in overseas military facilities	Y
Approve budget summit plan for spending and taxing	Y
Approve civil rights bill	Y
1989	
Halt production of B-2 stealth bomber at 13 planes	N
Oppose capital gains tax cut	N
Approve federal abortion funding in rape or incest cases	Y
Approve pay raise and revision of ethics rules	N
Pass Democratic minimum wage plan over Bush veto	N

Voting Studies

	Presidential Support		Party Unity		Conservative Coalition	
Year	**S**	**O**	**S**	**O**	**S**	**O**
1990	42	58	75	25	83	17
1989	56	43	67	29	88	10
1988	41†	59†	77†	21†	93†	7†

† *Not eligible for all recorded votes.*

Interest Group Ratings

Year	ADA	ACU	AFL-CIO	CCUS
1990	33	33	50	64
1989	35	50	36	90
1988	-	50	83	56

6 Jim Olin (D)

Of Roanoke — Elected 1982

Born: Feb. 28, 1920, Chicago, Ill.
Education: Attended Deep Springs College (Calif.), 1941; Cornell U., B.E.E. 1943.
Military Service: Army, 1943-46.
Occupation: Electronics executive.
Family: Wife, Phyllis Avery; five children.
Religion: Unitarian.
Political Career: Rotterdam (N.Y.) town supervisor, Schenectady County, 1953-55.
Capitol Office: 1410 Longworth Bldg. 20515; 225-5431.

In Washington: A moderate Democrat representing a Republican-leaning district, Olin is careful not to make waves at home. The same cannot always be said of his tactics in Washington, where he has shown that the courage of his convictions can be more important than the approval of his colleagues.

Representing a district that contains Virginia's two largest dairy counties, Olin has focused on dairy issues since his arrival in Washington. Southeastern dairy farmers have a different perspective from other regions' dairy producers. Unlike states in the Midwest and the West and some parts of the Southeast, where more milk is produced than consumed, states such as Virginia produce less milk than their local consumers use. As a result, Olin has opposed other dairy regions' efforts to ensure higher prices by limiting production.

In the 99th Congress, he led an uphill fight against a bipartisan compromise on the dairy section of the 1985 farm bill. Olin was the most active opponent of a controversial proposal to authorize "diversion" payments, partially financed by dairy farmers, to those who cut back on milk production. That brought him into conflict with the leading diversion advocate, Dairy Subcommittee Chairman Tony Coelho of California. Olin frustrated Coelho's efforts to forge a compromise and label the proposal a "dairy unity" bill.

Olin's attempt to kill the diversion program in subcommittee did little to slow it down and much to annoy Coelho. When the bill came to the House floor, Olin joined forces with Minority Leader Robert H. Michel in another attempt to block it. Backed by the Reagan administration and consumer groups, they offered an amendment to tie production more closely to the marketplace by killing the diversion program and steadily reducing price supports.

The amendment failed 166-244, but the diversion program was later stripped from the farm bill in conference. The final bill substituted a new program to reduce milk surpluses by requiring the government to buy up entire herds of dairy cows. Olin was critical of that program as well, but voted for the farm package.

During consideration of the 1990 farm bill, Olin opposed a plan by the Dairy Subcommittee's chairman and ranking Republican, Texan Charles W. Stenholm and Wisconsin's Steve Gunderson, that set a floor under the previously sliding scale of price supports for milk while assessing a penalty on dairy farmers who overproduce milkfat. Olin opposed the plan, arguing that it would penalize Southeastern farmers even though they were not contributing to the national surplus problem.

He offered an amendment to retain most of the dairy provisions from the 1985 law, while raising the surplus level that triggers price-support cuts. It was rejected by the subcommittee, 6-11. Before the bill went to the full committee, however, Olin, Stenholm and Gunderson worked out a compromise on the dairy section that left the Agriculture Department options on how to control overproduction.

Several Civil War battlefields lie in Olin's Shenandoah Valley district. In the 101st Congress, Olin sponsored a bill instructing the Interior secretary to study ways to protect those battlefields, including adding them to the national park system. It became law attached to another wilderness bill.

In 1983, Olin and Virginia Democrat Rick Boucher co-authored a bill that designated as wilderness 56,000 acres of Virginia forests and streams. Olin and Boucher teamed again in the 100th Congress to win passage of a bill preserving some 25,000 more acres from development.

Olin is eager to show that he is a fiscal conservative; he once introduced legislation to repeal a congressional pay raise. That may have hampered his bid at the start of the 101st Congress to join the Budget Committee. But he is no Boll Weevil. In 1989 and 1990, he supported party positions on roll-call votes more often than the average Southern Democrat. He has voted for the Equal Rights Amendment and

Virginia 6

West — Roanoke; Lynchburg

Long before Republicanism was acceptable in other parts of Virginia, it was the preferred political stance in the broad Shenandoah Valley, which runs most of the length of the 6th District. The descendants of the area's 18th-century English, German and Scotch-Irish settlers fought the Tidewater plantation aristocracy and became Republican mavericks in state politics.

But as the Republican Party in Virginia has come to be dominated by suburbanites outside Washington, D.C., and Richmond, and by staunch conservatives who have bailed out of the Democratic Party, the GOP has lost its grip on many voters in the 6th. The brand of Republicanism in the rural valley traditionally has been a moderate one, but there was no moderate on the GOP's statewide ticket in 1985, when Democrats won the three top state offices; all three carried the 6th. In 1989, with a less strident Republican nominee, J. Marshall Coleman, running against a black Democrat, L. Douglas Wilder, the 6th's voters reacquainted themselves with the GOP. Coleman won the 6th with 54 percent.

Roanoke, the major population center in the 6th, has an array of industries that produce textiles, furniture and electrical products. Its sizable black and union elements make it the base of Democratic strength in the district. Michael S. Dukakis' best 1988 margin in the district was from the city. Wilder took 59 percent against Coleman in Roanoke.

Democrats also can succeed in towns to the north, such as Covington and Clifton Forge and the counties surrounding them, Bath and Alleghany. Wilder won these cities but lost the counties to Coleman. There are chemical plants and pulpwood and paper mills in that area.

In national elections, Democratic support in the city of Roanoke is usually surpassed by the Republican vote in Roanoke's suburbs, in Lynchburg and in most of the rural areas. In 1988, George Bush narrowly carried Roanoke, but he did much better in suburban Roanoke County, Lynchburg and the rural counties. The nuclear energy firm of Babcock & Wilcox is one of Lynchburg's major employers, but the city is most famous as the home base of evangelist Jerry Falwell, his huge Thomas Road Baptist Church and Falwell-founded Liberty University (7,500 students). Coleman only received 50 percent in Roanoke County.

Outside metropolitan Roanoke and Lynchburg, the district depends mainly on dairy farming, livestock and poultry. Republican Rockingham County supplies many turkeys for Thanksgiving dinners. Rockingham gave Coleman 69 percent.

Population: 538,360. White 477,114 (89%), Black 58,277 (11%). Spanish origin 3,368 (1%). 18 and over 401,356 (75%), 65 and over 67,927 (13%). Median age: 32.

for a nuclear-weapons freeze, and backed federal funding for abortions for poor women in certain cases. In 1991, he voted against authorizing President Bush to use force in the Persian Gulf.

At Home: There are probably few Democratic congressmen who frustrate Republican campaign strategists more than Olin. Not only does he occupy a historically Republican district in the mountains of western Virginia, but he has gone a long way toward putting his personal stamp on it.

Politically unknown when he launched his first congressional campaign in 1982, Olin drew on his civic ties and business background to put together a winning coalition.

With the support of labor, teachers, black leaders and much of the financial community in the district's population center, Roanoke, Olin edged GOP state Rep. Kevin Miller by 1,655 votes. His victory ended a 30-year Republican grip on the Shenandoah Valley House seat, which was left open by the retirement of M. Caldwell Butler in 1982.

Miller, hampered by a bitterly contested nomination fight, tried to recover by painting Olin as a liberal. But although Olin was a mainstream Democrat on social issues, it was hard to tag a former General Electric vice president as a liberal big spender. On Election Day, Olin's 10,000-vote majority in the Roanoke area barely offset Miller's edge in his home base, the rural northern part of the district.

Republicans were confident they could oust Olin in 1984 with a challenger from the Roanoke area. They selected Ray Garland, a former state senator who was noted for his soaring rhetoric and his identification with the moderate wing of the state GOP.

But Garland was bedeviled by controversy. He created a firestorm of criticism when he called the Democratic Party "a busted-out $2 whore sucking the lifeblood out of this country." And many of Garland's longtime moderate supporters were chagrined by his emergence as a born-again conservative. Olin kept his distance from the national ticket and used his seat on Agriculture to gain an entree to rural Republicans in the Shenandoah Valley.

While Reagan swept all nine counties and 10 independent cities in the district, Garland could carry only two of each. Olin won the pivotal Roanoke area by 15,000 votes.

In 1986, Republicans had trouble finding a candidate. Many felt that if they could not oust Olin in 1984, when Reagan pulled two-thirds of the district vote, 1986 was a lost cause. After numerous potential candidates declined to run, the GOP nomination finally went to Republican national committeewoman Flo Traywick, whose only previous campaign was a losing bid for the state House of Delegates.

Traywick used her party connections to bring in GOP celebrities, including Vice President George Bush. She said the outside help demonstrated her ability to open doors in the White House that Olin could not. And while she sought to depict herself as the true conservative in the race, she also made a pitch for the district's relatively small black vote. She brought in Roy Innis, national chairman of the Congress of Racial Equality, to talk on black capitalism, and former University of Virginia basketball star Ralph Sampson (a Harrisonburg native) to help her deliver an anti-drug message.

But with little money or name identification, the grandmotherly Traywick completely failed in denting either Olin's base in the populous Roanoke area or the ties he had forged to rural Republican voters in the valley. Olin won 70 percent, sweeping every county in the 6th and every city except Staunton.

In 1988, the strong showing of the Republican presidential ticket in the 6th did not impede Olin's progress. He won 64 percent of the vote, slightly better than Bush's tally in the district. In 1990, the GOP gave Olin a free ride; his only opposition came from an independent candidate.

Olin's decision to run for Congress in 1982 followed a long sabbatical from politics. He made his first try for public office during the 1950s when he was elected town supervisor of Rotterdam, N.Y. But his boss at General Electric was upset about the amount of time the job was taking, and he told Olin to choose between the company and politics. Olin chose the company, and went on to complete 35 years before retiring in January 1982.

Committees

Agriculture (14th of 27 Democrats)
Forests, Family Farms & Energy; Livestock, Dairy & Poultry; Wheat, Soybeans & Feed Grains

Small Business (12th of 27 Democrats)
Environment & Employment (chairman); SBA, the General Economy & Minority Enterprise Development

Elections

1990 General

Jim Olin (D)	92,968	(83%)
Gerald E. "Laser" Berg (I)	18,148	(16%)

1988 General

Jim Olin (D)	118,369	(64%)
Charles E. Judd (R)	66,935	(36%)

Previous Winning Percentages: **1986** (70%) **1984** (54%) **1982** (50%)

District Vote For President

	1988	1984	1980	1976
D	74,602 (38%)	68,311 (34%)	82,299 (43%)	82,111 (46%)
R	121,107 (61%)	134,466 (66%)	97,549 (51%)	90,573 (51%)
I			7,368 (4%)	

Campaign Finance

	Receipts	Receipts from PACs		Expenditures
1990				
Olin (D)	$254,058	$153,700	(60%)	$199,904
1988				
Olin (D)	$321,705	$140,400	(44%)	$322,160
Judd (R)	$112,076	$4,150	(4%)	$110,756

Key Votes

1991	
Authorize use of force against Iraq	N
1990	
Support constitutional amendment on flag desecration	Y
Pass family and medical leave bill over Bush veto	N
Reduce SDI funding	Y
Allow abortions in overseas military facilities	Y
Approve budget summit plan for spending and taxing	Y
Approve civil rights bill	Y
1989	
Halt production of B-2 stealth bomber at 13 planes	N
Oppose capital gains tax cut	Y
Approve federal abortion funding in rape or incest cases	Y
Approve pay raise and revision of ethics rules	N
Pass Democratic minimum wage plan over Bush veto	Y

Voting Studies

	Presidential Support		Party Unity		Conservative Coalition	
Year	S	O	S	O	S	O
1990	35	63	76	22	67	30
1989	36	62	84	15	46	51
1988	38	63	82	17	58	42
1987	33	65	77	21	63	37
1986	36	64	71	25	66	30
1985	41	58	72	25	60	36
1984	43	55	65	31	53	42
1983	41	57	64	33	65	34

Interest Group Ratings

Year	ADA	ACU	AFL-CIO	CCUS
1990	50	38	58	43
1989	65	14	67	50
1988	70	28	71	64
1987	64	26	63	47
1986	55	14	57	56
1985	50	38	41	67
1984	55	45	58	46
1983	65	30	53	60

7 D. French Slaughter Jr. (R)

Of Culpeper — Elected 1984

Born: May 20, 1925, Culpeper County, Va.

Education: Attended Virginia Military Institute, 1942-43; U. of Virginia, B.A. 1950, LL.B. 1953.

Military Service: Army, 1943-47.

Occupation: Lawyer.

Family: Widowed; two children.

Religion: Episcopalian.

Political Career: Va. House, 1958-78; sought Democratic nomination for lieutenant governor, 1971.

Capitol Office: 1404 Longworth Bldg. 20515; 225-6561.

In Washington: A cautious conservative with the reserve of an old-fashioned Virginia gentleman, Slaughter has burrowed a quiet niche in the House. Ironically, the biggest publicity splash Slaughter made as an incumbent came in July 1991, when he announced he would leave office mid-term because of a series of mild strokes. His announcement was timed to facilitate a special election in November 1991, when state legislative elections are held.

Slaughter represents a district whose rural character is being changed by growth from metropolitan Washington and Richmond, but he has been reticent to plunge into some of the more contentious issues accompanying urbanization. When developers announced plans in early 1988 to build a shopping mall next to the historic Manassas National Battlefield Park in the 7th, the publicity soon drew the attention of many members. Battle lines were drawn, with local development advocates arrayed against preservationists from Virginia and around the country. Slaughter eventually sided with anti-mall forces who pushed through a "legislative taking" of the proposed development site by the federal government, but he was not conspicuous in the political fray. Subsequently, Slaughter has become more active on the issue of battlefield preservation, offering bills to preserve other threatened battle sites.

If Slaughter steers clear of public debate and is slow to commit to a course of action, he is an experienced student of the legislative process, having served two decades in the Virginia House before coming to Congress. He has been known to spend time in the House chamber observing floor debate, then offering insights to harried colleagues who arrive on the floor needing an update on the matter being considered.

Though he does not speak up on many issues, the fiscally conservative Slaughter follows health care legislation, including group long-term care insurance for some federal workers and a Health Care Savings Account to offer an investment alternative to Medicare.

At Home: Over a long career, Slaughter slowly gravitated from the Democratic Party to the GOP, always maintaining the fiscal conservatism that is the hallmark of Virginia politics.

Elected to the state House in 1957, Slaughter was not an impressive orator or a high-profile politician, but he worked his way onto key legislative committees and was a serious contender for the Democratic nomination for lieutenant governor in 1971.

In 1973, Slaughter sought re-election as an independent. In 1970, Democratic Sen. Harry F. Byrd Jr. had sought and won re-election as an independent, and many thought that a coalition of Republicans, Byrd-allied independents and conservative Democrats could forge a new majority in Virginia politics. But loyalist Democrats prevailed, and Slaughter was relegated to a backbench legislative role. Slaughter began a courtship with Virginia's GOP, and after backing several of its candidates in the mid-1970s, he switched parties.

When GOP Rep. J. Kenneth Robinson retired in 1984, Slaughter easily won the party's nomination. The 7th's Republican complexion made Slaughter the November front-runner. He denounced foe Lewis M. Costello as a "Mondale-O'Neill" Democrat. But even Slaughter's supporters faulted his wooden campaign manner, and Costello scored points by highlighting Slaughter's one-time support for the "massive resistance" plan to defy federal court desegregation rulings. But with the GOP sweeping the 7th for president and Senate, Slaughter won easily. He drew no challengers in 1986 or 1988.

In 1990, Democrats offered David M. Smith, a Methodist minister and son of state Del. Alson H. Smith Jr. The elder Smith was a renowned fundraiser and helped his son amass an impressive sum for a first-time candidate.

Smith badgered Slaughter to debate him. The incumbent would not, so Smith carried a taped radio interview with him and "debated" the recorded Slaughter. But Slaughter was not caught unawares; his fundraising enabled him to buy TV ads in the expensive Washington, D.C., market. He won 58 percent of the vote.

Virginia 7

North — Charlottesville; Winchester

The 7th runs from Richmond's northern suburbs across the Blue Ridge Mountains to Winchester, the center of the state's apple-growing industry and home of Virginia's political dynasty, the Byrd family.

For generations, the district has been rural and conservative. But like former Sen. Harry F. Byrd Jr., who took over his father's Senate seat in 1965 and later became an independent, the 7th has abandoned its Democratic roots. It has emerged as the state's foremost GOP stronghold. In 1988, George Bush carried every Virginia district, but none more decisively than the 7th, where he took two-thirds of the vote. Against black Democratic Lt. Gov. L. Douglas Wilder, white Republican J. Marshall Coleman received 57 percent in the 7th.

In counties along the Blue Ridge Mountains, the agricultural economy is keyed to dairying, livestock and fruit, and there is some manufacturing. In 1988, Bush won 66 percent in the "apple capital" of Winchester, and he did even better in surrounding Frederick County. Coleman won both, though by more modest margins.

Bush's and Coleman's margins were also solid in Spotsylvania and Stafford counties on the eastern flank of the 7th. Those are longtime farming areas that are being taken over by people who drive cars or ride long-distance commuter buses to jobs in metropolitan Washington, D.C.

The few Democratic footholds are in the southern part of the district. Charlottesville, the district's largest city and home of the University of Virginia (17,500 students), was the only jurisdiction in the 7th to vote Democratic in the 1988 presidential race. In 1989, Charlottesville and surrounding Albemarle County were the only 7th District jurisdictions to back Wilder.

Like the areas around Washington and Richmond, Charlottesville, too, has seen much growth in recent years, with a commercial strip spreading ever-northward from town along U.S. 29. But such changes in the district have not erased elements of its old, decidedly Southern, personality. One restaurant owner in the small town of Marshall ran afoul of the law in 1984 for refusing to serve meals to blacks.

Population: 535,147. White 465,497 (87%), Black 65,329 (12%), Other 3,012 (1%). Spanish origin 4,185 (1%). 18 and over 383,878 (72%), 65 and over 53,204 (10%). Median age: 30.

Committees

Judiciary (8th of 13 Republicans)
Economic & Commercial Law

Science, Space & Technology (10th of 19 Republicans)
Science; Space

Small Business (4th of 17 Republicans)
Procurement, Tourism & Rural Development (ranking)

Elections

1990 General		
D. French Slaughter Jr. (R)	81,688	(58%)
David M. Smith (D)	58,684	(42%)
1988 General		
D. French Slaughter Jr. (R)	136,988	(100%)

Previous Winning Percentages: **1986** (98%) **1984** (57%)

District Vote For President

	1988	1984	1980	1976
D	76,202 (33%)	64,593 (31%)	59,092 (32%)	71,046 (44%)
R	149,725 (66%)	142,598 (69%)	112,099 (61%)	86,160 (54%)
I			3,660 (2%)	

Campaign Finance

	Receipts	Receipts from PACs	Expend-itures
1990			
Slaughter (R)	$649,588	$152,865 (24%)	$826,942
Smith (D)	$390,379	$49,250 (13%)	$388,415
1988			
Slaughter (R)	$219,559	$94,496 (43%)	$87,195

Key Votes

1991	
Authorize use of force against Iraq	Y
1990	
Support constitutional amendment on flag desecration	Y
Pass family and medical leave bill over Bush veto	N
Reduce SDI funding	N
Allow abortions in overseas military facilities	N
Approve budget summit plan for spending and taxing	N
Approve civil rights bill	N
1989	
Halt production of B-2 stealth bomber at 13 planes	N
Oppose capital gains tax cut	N
Approve federal abortion funding in rape or incest cases	N
Approve pay raise and revision of ethics rules	N
Pass Democratic minimum wage plan over Bush veto	N

Voting Studies

	Presidential Support		Party Unity		Conservative Coalition	
Year	**S**	**O**	**S**	**O**	**S**	**O**
1990	68	30	87	12	94	6
1989	77	23	93	7	100	0
1988	63	36	86	13	97	3
1987	69	29	86	14	95	5
1986	80	17	86	11	86	12
1985	74	25	90	9	95	5

Interest Group Ratings

Year	ADA	ACU	AFL-CIO	CCUS
1990	6	92	17	86
1989	0	96	0	100
1988	10	92	14	93
1987	4	91	13	93
1986	0	91	21	94
1985	0	86	12	95

8 James P. Moran Jr. (D)

Of Alexandria — Elected 1990

Born: May 16, 1945, Buffalo, N.Y.
Education: College of the Holy Cross, B.A. 1967; U. of Pittsburgh, M.A. 1970.
Occupation: Investment banker.
Family: Wife, Mary Howard; four children.
Religion: Roman Catholic.
Political Career: Alexandria City Council, 1979-84, vice mayor, 1982-84; mayor of Alexandria, 1985-91.
Capitol Office: 1523 Longworth Bldg. 20515; 225-4376.

The Path to Washington: In one of the noisiest House races on the East Coast, Moran ousted GOP Rep. Stan Parris, long one of the scrappiest street fighters of Washington-area politics. Moran, the flamboyant mayor of Alexandria, exchanged blows high and low with Parris in their raucous brawl for a constituency that could be significantly altered after 1991 remapping, as Virginia districts are recast to incorporate an additional seat.

Parris, a twice-failed candidate for the GOP gubernatorial nomination, had garnered regionwide notice for his scorching denunciations of the District of Columbia government of Mayor Marion S. Barry Jr. and for his confrontational conservative rhetoric.

Moran also has a reputation for pugnacity. His service in Alexandria was stormy. First elected to the City Council in 1979, Moran became vice mayor in 1982 as the leading vote-getter in the council election. But his career derailed in 1984 when, after pleading no contest to a misdemeanor conflict of interest charge, he resigned as vice mayor as part of his plea agreement.

A year later, however, Moran resurrected his career. He ran as an independent against the incumbent mayor and defeated him. His continued sensitivity to ethical questions was evident during the 1990 campaign, when he returned a $10,000 check from an Alexandria developer after reporters asked him about it.

Using the results of the 1989 gubernatorial race as a guidepost, Moran banked on voters in the 8th rejecting Parris' conservative social-issue positions. In 1989, Democrat L. Douglas Wilder carried the 8th over Republican J. Marshall Coleman by more than 20,000 votes. One of Wilder's most powerful issues in Northern Virginia was his support for abortion rights; Coleman opposed abortion.

From the day he announced his candidacy, Moran castigated Parris for his longstanding opposition to abortion. Planned Parenthood helped by taking out newspaper ads criticizing Parris' abortion position, and Moran ran TV ads accusing Parris of depriving women of their freedom.

Moran and Parris clearly did not like each other. Parris compared Moran to Iraqi leader Saddam Hussein, and Moran called Parris "a racist" and "a fatuous jerk" and professed a desire to "break his nose."

"I have good reason to punch Stan Parris in the nose, that jerk," Moran said on a local TV station in late October.

Moran's accent betrays his suburban Boston upbringing. He attended Holy Cross on a football scholarship. He spent a decade in Washington specializing in budget analysis for the federal government and serving on the Senate Appropriations Committee staff.

As mayor, Moran stirred some controversy for his forceful approach to drug enforcement. Civil libertarians complained when he ordered eviction of families of suspected drug users from public housing units. He was not averse to the occasional publicity stunt: In December 1989, he challenged Barry to a boxing match to raise funds for antidrug programs.

Moran voices philosophical differences with some establishment Democratic tenets, particularly on the subject of welfare. He says in the past 25 years Democrats have become identified as "ideological elitists who are against people being responsible for their own actions and against family values." He argues that blue-collar white ethnic voters have left the party because they feel threatened by some of the Democrats' policies. "The Founding Fathers never suggested we could make people happy, just enable them to pursue happiness."

Moran favors allowing public housing renters to accrue equity in their homes and limiting the time people may stay in public housing, which he says should be a "way station."

Virginia 8

D.C. Suburbs — Alexandria; Southern Fairfax County

The 8th includes most of the southern portion of Virginia's Washington-area suburbs. Growth there, originally spurred by the rapid expansion of the federal government, now derives from an array of white-collar and service-industry employers.

The district's close-in suburb is Alexandria. This old colonial seaport casts about one-fifth of the district vote, but it is atypical. It is reliable Democratic territory. The revitalized "Old Town" competes fairly with the Georgetown section of Washington, and thousands of Democratic-voting young professionals live there. By the late 1980s, Alexandria, with a per capita income of $22,200, was the second most affluent county or independent city in the country.

On the fringe of Old Town is a black community that comprises one-fifth of the Alexandria population and adds to Democratic strength. In 1988, the city was the only jurisdiction within the 8th to vote for Michael S. Dukakis for president and against GOP Rep. Stan Parris in the House contest. In 1989, it gave black Democratic Lt. Gov. L. Douglas Wilder 68 percent in his successful gubernatorial election. In 1990 Alexandria voters helped boost then-Mayor Moran past Parris; Moran got 64 percent on his home turf.

Beyond Alexandria to the south and southwest, the suburbs are newer, whiter and more Republican. Population in these outlying areas is booming: Fairfax and Prince William counties each grew by more than 30 percent during the 1980s, on the heels of similarly rapid growth in the 1970s.

Once-pastoral Fairfax County is now a suburban colossus with over 747,000 people. More than twice as populous as any other jurisdiction in Virginia, Fairfax County is divided nearly evenly between the 8th and 10th districts. Fairfax residents account for a majority of the population in the 8th. In 1988, Parris took 66 percent of the Fairfax County vote, but in 1990 Moran won Fairfax County by 50 to 47 percent. Much of the 1980s growth in Fairfax County came from minorities. Asians, blacks and Hispanics all saw their numbers increase.

Outside Alexandria and Fairfax, most of the vote is cast in suburban communities near heavily traveled Interstate 95. Prince William County, whose residents make up another fifth of the district's population, has been trending Republican. It voted for Democratic Rep. Herbert E. Harris II in 1980 but by 1988 was giving Parris 58 percent of its vote and George Bush 66 percent. In 1990, Moran edged out Parris in Prince William County by 280 votes.

Farther south along the Interstate 95 corridor is Stafford County, which is split between the 8th and the 7th districts. A longtime farming area, Stafford County is also experiencing suburbanization; its number of motor vehicles has increased fivefold since 1970. In 1990, Parris carried the 8th District portion of Stafford by 332 votes.

Population: 534,366. White 457,482 (86%), Black 54,114 (10%), Other 15,731 (3%). Spanish origin 15,495 (3%). 18 and over 376,074 (70%), 65 and over 23,284 (4%). Median age: 29.

Committees

Banking, Finance & Urban Affairs (27th of 31 Democrats)
Economic Stabilization; Financial Institutions Supervision, Regulation & Insurance; International Development, Finance, Trade & Monetary Policy

Post Office & Civil Service (13th of 15 Democrats)
Civil Service; Human Resources

Campaign Finance

	Receipts	Receipts from PACs		Expend-itures
1990				
Moran (D)	$883,236	$257,821	(29%)	$883,216
Parris (R)	$864,864	$313,852	(36%)	$982,157

Key Vote

1991

Authorize use of force against Iraq	N

Elections

1990 General

James P. Moran Jr. (D)	88,475	(52%)
Stan Parris (R)	76,367	(45%)
Robert T. Murphy (I)	5,958	(3%)

District Vote For President

	1988	1984	1980	1976
D	102,516 (39%)	89,349 (38%)	63,214 (33%)	75,717 (47%)
R	157,228 (60%)	141,992 (61%)	104,891 (55%)	80,978 (51%)
I			18,128 (10%)	

9 Rick Boucher (D)

Of Abingdon — Elected 1982

Born: Aug. 1, 1946, Abingdon, Va.
Education: Roanoke College, B.A. 1968; U. of Virginia, J.D. 1971.
Occupation: Lawyer.
Family: Single.
Religion: Methodist.
Political Career: Va. Senate, 1975-82.
Capitol Office: 405 Cannon Bldg. 20515; 225-3861.

In Washington: A former Wall Street lawyer with a professorial appearance and liberal voting habits, Boucher seems an unlikely fit for his coal-mining district in southwest Virginia. But voters and House colleagues alike seem comfortable around this articulate, low-key legislator.

Boucher does not pursue a broad agenda in Congress, but zeroes in on a few issues of particular concern. That tight focus was evident during the long-running deliberations over reauthorizing the Clean Air Act. Boucher is a member of Energy and Commerce, an assignment he won in the 100th Congress, when Chairman John D. Dingell handpicked him and two other new members who he figured would not champion tougher clean-air standards harmful to auto interests in his Michigan district. Coming from coal country, Boucher also had reason to be wary of clean-air legislation.

In the 100th Congress, Boucher joined with the so-called "group of nine," a caucus of moderate-to-conservative Democrats who tried to end a Clean Air stalemate between Dingell's pro-industry faction and the committee's staunch environmentalists.

Each member saw the complicated issue through the eyes of his constituency, but when the group discussed matters not directly relevant to Virginia, Boucher's attention often strayed. However, throughout the Clean Air debate, ending with passage of a reauthorization in late 1990, Boucher carefully followed developments on acid rain, caused in part by burning high-sulfur coal. He successfully fought for a provision requiring states to help small businesses comply with the new law.

Boucher is one of the most liberal members of his state's delegation; he got a perfect score from the AFL-CIO in 1988. But he has enhanced his appeal in the business community through his work on such issues as Clean Air, and, in the Judiciary Committee, with efforts starting in the 99th Congress to limit liability under the 1970 Racketeer Influenced and Corrupt Organizations Act (RICO).

RICO was originally designed for fighting organized crime, but increasingly it has been used for civil suits against corporations — in part because plaintiffs have the chance to collect triple damages. Business groups saw it as an intrusion on free enterprise, and Boucher agreed. He said the RICO act had been meant solely to help the government seize assets of organized-crime figures and drug dealers, and that it was being abused by greedy litigants.

But law enforcement and consumer groups — and more importantly, Criminal Justice Subcommittee Chairman John Conyers Jr. — feared a change could make it more difficult to attack white-collar crime. Conyers' campaign to stifle the bill forced Boucher to seek the aid of the full committee chairman to move it out of subcommittee. Ultimately, the House passed Boucher's legislation eliminating triple-damage awards in most civil cases, but in the Senate a companion effort by Ohio Democrat Howard M. Metzenbaum was tabled just before Congress adjourned in 1986.

In the 100th Congress, Boucher was back with a modified plan cosponsored by five of the eight subcommittee members. But Conyers complained that the bill favored insurers, accountants and brokers, while hindering the fight against crime. Metzenbaum's companion Senate bill never reached the floor.

The outlook brightened in the 101st Congress, when jurisdiction over RICO moved to the Crime Subcommittee, chaired by William J. Hughes. Boucher and Hughes joined forces on the issue and got a bill, sponsored by Hughes, out of committee. But the legislation eventually died without coming to a floor vote.

Boucher has also taken up the cause of regulating financial planners, a position backed by consumer groups.

On Judiciary, Boucher is known for his opposition to gun control; in 1990, he was the only Democrat on the Crime Subcommittee to reject the ban on semi-automatic rifles.

By the close of the 101st, Boucher had shifted some of his attention to the cable industry. During a debate on a cable regulation bill before Energy and Commerce in summer 1990,

Virginia 9

Southwest — Blacksburg; Bristol

The "Fighting Ninth" earned that name not only because of its tradition of fiercely competitive two-party politics but also because of its ornery isolation from the Virginia political establishment in Richmond.

Southwestern Virginia was settled by Scotch-Irish and German immigrants who had little in common with the English settlers in the Tidewater and Piedmont regions. The Civil War divided the anti-secession mountaineers from slaveholding Confederates elsewhere in the state. In the postwar era, when Democrats routinely dominated Virginia politics, the 9th was the only district in which Republicans were consistently strong.

But as the state GOP has moved into alliance with Richmond's business establishment and Northern Virginia's affluent suburbanites, the party has lost ground in the 9th. Some of the region's burley tobacco growers and other small-scale farmers now are teaming with the traditionally Democratic coal miners.

Democrats are strongest in coal-mining counties along the Kentucky and West Virginia borders. In the 1988 presidential contest, Michael S. Dukakis carried five of the eight border counties, as did L. Douglas Wilder in his successful 1989 gubernatorial bid.

The coal fields region (Buchanan, Dickenson, Lee, Russell, Scott, Tazewell, and Wise counties) have little in common with the rest of Virginia — as many as seven other state capitals are closer than Richmond. While the state prospered during the 1980s, the coal counties suffered from high unemployment.

The United Mine Workers (UMW) still wield political influence here; a UMW-backed candidate crushed a 21-year incumbent for a General Assembly seat in a 1989 write-in campaign.

Republicans normally have an edge in the corridor of counties roughly traced by Interstate 81 as it runs north from Bristol past Blacksburg. Wilder's Republican opponent carried Bristol with 58 percent.

Montgomery County, which contains the district's largest city, Blacksburg (population 35,000), is economically atypical of the 9th. Home to Virginia Tech, the state's largest university (nearly 22,000 students), Blacksburg is a tidy and prosperous-looking city quite unlike the dreary factory and coal towns common throughout the district.

Population: 538,871. White 523,299 (97%), Black 12,920 (2%). Spanish origin 3,045 (1%). 18 and over 388,333 (72%), 65 and over 58,900 (11%). Median age: 29.

Boucher offered an amendment to allow telephone companies to enter the cable TV market. He agreed to withdraw the proposal so as not to jeopardize the broader bill — after extracting a commitment from Edward J. Markey, who chairs the Telecommunications Subcommittee, to hold hearings on the matter in the 102nd.

As a result of committee shufflings at the beginning of the 102nd Congress, Boucher became chairman of the Science Subcommittee of the Science, Space and Technology Committee. It oversees the National Science Foundation.

At Home: The hard work and careful organization that have helped Boucher in the House have also been the secret of his success in the 9th, where voters no longer seem to mind that he lacks a rough-and-tumble air.

Boucher needed all his assets to weather bruising elections in 1982 and 1984. But in 1986, he became the district's first House candidate since 1853 to run unopposed, and again in 1990 he drew no opposition.

Boucher's 1982 victory over veteran GOP Rep. William C. Wampler was the closest race the typically competitive "Fighting Ninth" had seen in nearly three decades, as Boucher won by just 1,123 votes out of more than 150,000 cast. Two years later he expanded his margin, but his was still the closest House race in Virginia.

Despite his scholarly look, Boucher came naturally to politics. Both his grandfather and great-grandfather served in the Virginia state House. His father was commonwealth's attorney in Washington County (Abingdon).

After graduating from the University of Virginia Law School, Boucher joined the Wall Street firm of Milbank, Tweed, Hadley and McCloy. He took time out to work as an advance man for George McGovern's 1972 presidential campaign. The following year he returned to Abingdon to practice law, ultimately joining his family's firm in 1978.

He also began laying the groundwork for his political debut, which he made in a 1975 bid for state Senate. Energetically buttonholing district convention delegates, Boucher defeated a veteran incumbent for the Democratic nomination, then coasted to election.

Democratic Gov. Charles S. Robb and other state party leaders urged Boucher to challenge Wampler in 1982, when high unemployment was plaguing the district's coal fields.

Boucher raised $241,000, less than Wampler, but enough to finance billboards and media advertising on the three TV stations that together cover the district. As Boucher's name identification increased, Wampler began to react. He sought to dismiss Boucher as "a Henry Howell with an Ivy League look," a reference to the controversial Tidewater populist who lost decisively in his last gubernatorial race in 1977.

But Boucher jabbed back, describing the affable Wampler — known to constituents as the "bald eagle of the Cumberland" — as a nice man but ineffective legislator. Boucher termed himself the true fiscal conservative, citing Wampler's support for Reaganomics and its ensuing budget deficits.

The economy was a powerful issue. In some of the coal counties, unemployment neared 20 percent in fall 1982. Turnout there approached the level of the 1980 presidential election, and Boucher, drawing on the active support of the United Mine Workers, ran exceptionally well. Boucher also neutralized Wampler in his home base, the Bristol area just north of Tennessee. Bristol was also part of Boucher's state Senate district; Wampler won it only narrowly.

When Wampler decided against a rematch in 1984, Boucher became a clear favorite. But he did not have an easy race against his well-financed GOP challenger, state Rep. Jefferson Stafford. One of the Legislature's most conservative members, Stafford had been an ardent proponent of reinstituting the death penalty and a zealous foe of financial aid to college students who did not register for the draft. He charged that Boucher was too liberal, tying him to Walter F. Mondale, whose presidential campaign Boucher helped to lead in Virginia.

The incumbent gave Stafford ample chance to make his case — they held about a dozen debates. But Stafford could not put his rival on the defensive. Brandishing endorsements from the National Rifle Association and the Veterans of Foreign Wars, Boucher said he was no flaming liberal. His votes, he added, were dictated by the needs of his low-income constituents, many of them elderly. Boucher emphasized his work for the coal industry and his constituent service, claiming to be an ombudsman for miners, farmers and senior citizens in their battles with federal bureaucrats.

Although Stafford carried most of the 17 counties in the 9th, Boucher survived by taking large majorities in the coal-producing areas.

Committees

Energy & Commerce (17th of 27 Democrats)
Commerce, Consumer Protection & Competitiveness; Telecommunications & Finance; Transportation & Hazardous Materials

Judiciary (13th of 21 Democrats)
Intellectual Property & Judicial Administration

Science, Space & Technology (12th of 32 Democrats)
Science (chairman); Technology & Competitiveness

Elections

1990 General		
Rick Boucher (D)	67,215	(97%)
1988 General		
Rick Boucher (D)	113,309	(63%)
John C. Brown (R)	65,410	(37%)

Previous Winning Percentages: **1986** (99%) **1984** (52%) **1982** (50%)

District Vote For President

	1988	1984	1980	1976
D	82,873 (45%)	82,522 (41%)	84,218 (47%)	87,783 (52%)
R	98,738 (54%)	117,088 (58%)	86,251 (48%)	76,627 (45%)
I			4,573 (3%)	

Campaign Finance

	Receipts	Receipts from PACs		Expenditures
1990				
Boucher (D)	$524,268	$366,584	(70%)	$252,685
1988				
Boucher (D)	$616,821	$367,600	(60%)	$606,420
Brown (R)	$155,094	$3,427	(2%)	$154,515

Key Votes

1991	
Authorize use of force against Iraq	N
1990	
Support constitutional amendment on flag desecration	N
Pass family and medical leave bill over Bush veto	Y
Reduce SDI funding	Y
Allow abortions in overseas military facilities	Y
Approve budget summit plan for spending and taxing	N
Approve civil rights bill	Y
1989	
Halt production of B-2 stealth bomber at 13 planes	Y
Oppose capital gains tax cut	Y
Approve federal abortion funding in rape or incest cases	Y
Approve pay raise and revision of ethics rules	Y
Pass Democratic minimum wage plan over Bush veto	Y

Voting Studies

	Presidential Support		Party Unity		Conservative Coalition	
Year	S	O	S	O	S	O
1990	20	79	90	5	35	57
1989	27 †	67 †	88	6	27	68
1988	19	74	87	5	29	66
1987	22	68	86	7	42	51
1986	23	72	83	6	36	50
1985	29	68	87	7	35	64
1984	35	56	78	12	44	47
1983	22	74	88	7	29	64

† Not eligible for all recorded votes.

Interest Group Ratings

Year	ADA	ACU	AFL-CIO	CCUS
1990	72	13	100	23
1989	80	8	73	30
1988	75	9	100	29
1987	76	0	94	7
1986	65	6	86	20
1985	60	19	65	48
1984	70	29	62	33
1983	80	13	88	35

10 Frank R. Wolf (R)

Of Vienna — Elected 1980

Born: Jan. 30, 1939, Philadelphia, Pa.
Education: Pennsylvania State U., B.A. 1961; Georgetown U., LL.B. 1965.
Military Service: Army, 1962-63; Reserve, 1963-67.
Occupation: Lawyer.
Family: Wife, Carolyn Stover; five children.
Religion: Presbyterian.
Political Career: Sought Republican nomination for U.S. House, 1976; Republican nominee for U.S. House, 1978.
Capitol Office: 104 Cannon Bldg. 20515; 225-5136.

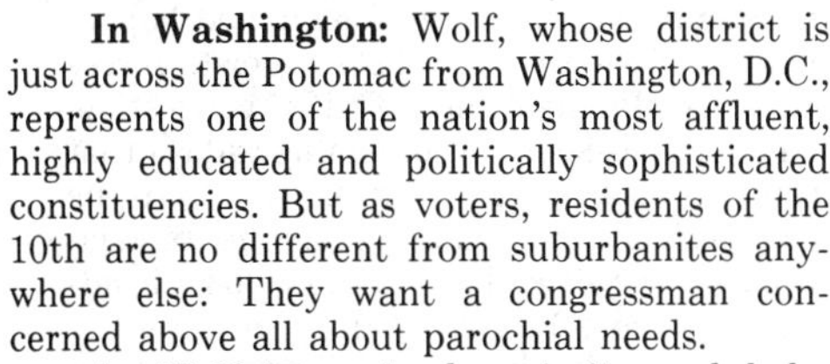

In Washington: Wolf, whose district is just across the Potomac from Washington, D.C., represents one of the nation's most affluent, highly educated and politically sophisticated constituencies. But as voters, residents of the 10th are no different from suburbanites anywhere else: They want a congressman concerned above all about parochial needs.

As Wolf has gained seniority and baby boom suburbanites have gained political clout, some of his parochial concerns have taken on national import. Child care, for instance, has priority for Wolf, because of the many working parents in the 10th.

And while traffic gridlock is technically a local concern, Wolf's work in that area affects the daily lives of some very influential people, including fellow members, key political appointees and media opinion-shapers.

Wolf is well-positioned to practice locally oriented politics. As a member of the Appropriations Subcommittee on Transportation, he meticulously tends to the auto, rail and air traffic problems of concern to Northern Virginia. As a member of the Select Committee on Children, Youth and Families, he has authored legislation directing the federal government (which employs 70,000 of his constituents) to donate space for child care centers.

While these are essentially non-partisan efforts, the GOP can count on Wolf to cast quiet conservative votes on the House floor. In the 101st Congress, for instance, he voted to sustain presidential vetoes of the Family Leave Act and of a Democratic-backed proposal to increase the minimum wage; he voted for a constitutional amendment to ban flag desecration, and against the use of federal funds to pay for abortion in limited circumstances.

Known in the 1980s for his focus on district affairs, Wolf is beginning to broaden his horizons. In the 101st Congress, he was named to the Helsinki human rights commission; and as a member of the Select Committee on Hunger, he traveled to rebel territory in southern Sudan beset by civil war and famine conditions.

For years, Wolf was among the conservatives who decried human rights conditions in Romania. He authored an amendment to the 1988 trade bill to deny the country most-favored-nation trading status. "The Romanian government is bulldozing churches," he said. "They are bulldozing synagogues, they beat a Catholic priest and are persecuting different religious groups." Soon after Romanian citizens overthrew dictator Nicolae Ceausescu in late 1989, Wolf helped Dana Damaceanu, the daughter of a leading dissident, and her husband leave Romania for the United States.

Mostly, however, Wolf still is interested in streets. Every member seeks highway funding for his district, but none plays a more personal role in trying to unravel traffic tie-ups than Wolf. An ombudsman for commuters, he fires off letters to D.C., state and federal transportation officials aimed at easing backups on bridges and at tollgates.

On the Transportation Subcommittee, Wolf generally works well with Democrats. He often joins with Maryland Democrat Steny H. Hoyer to promote funds for Washington's Metro subway system.

During the Reagan era, Wolf was sometimes criticized for his willingness to support domestic budget-cutting efforts, except those that would affect federal workers. When legislation to reform the Hatch Act comes before the House, however, Wolf leads the GOP charge. The legislation, which seeks to roll back the limits on political activity by federal workers, has the strong support of unions representing federal employees. Wolf agrees that the Hatch Act needs revision, but he says the bills that have passed the House in the last two Congresses were badly flawed and would risk politicizing the civil service.

Wolf gained a measure of national publicity for two local issues he has advocated. *People* magazine sung his praises for helping secure a $276,000 federal grant for language immersion

Virginia 10

D.C. Suburbs; Arlington County

The 10th is one of the most affluent districts in any Southern state, but it is hardly fair to identify it with the South. It is basically a set of bedroom communities for civil servants, people who work in the Pentagon, and others whose livelihoods are connected with the federal government. It is one of the most transient areas of the country, with an estimated 20 percent of the registered voters new each year.

Arlington County, just outside Washington, D.C., grew rapidly over the last several decades as the work force of the federal government expanded. Home for more than one out of every four residents in the district, Arlington is the prime source of Democratic votes in the 10th. Ronald Reagan won the county in 1980, but Walter F. Mondale and Michael S. Dukakis took it back for the Democrats. Democratic Lt. Gov. L. Douglas Wilder received 67 percent in Arlington in his successful 1989 gubernatorial race.

Although suburban sprawl has peaked in Arlington, there has been some movement of younger, affluent professionals into condominiums and rental housing. These people tend to be more liberal than the average Virginian, but they are transient and hard to rely on politically.

There are relatively few blacks in Arlington, but the county is becoming a melting pot for other minorities. Asians, Hispanics and other minority groups together make up roughly one-quarter of the population. Arlington has the second-highest concentration of Vietnamese in the country, and it has numerous Vietnamese-owned businesses.

Moving west from Arlington into the northern part of Fairfax County, the GOP vote increases. Like southern Fairfax, which is in the 8th District, this part of the county has in recent years attracted new white-collar industries and expensive new housing developments to accommodate their employees. Soaring property assessments were a top concern of Fairfax residents in the late 1980s, although the current economic slowdown has brought a leveling off in assessments. Still, local government bodies frequently are the stage for pitched battles between pro-growth and slow-growth forces over development and traffic congestion. The latter is such a problem nowadays that some businesses are turning sour on the county. The American Automobile Association, for instance, decided to move its headquarters from Fairfax County to Florida.

George Bush won 60 percent in the Fairfax County portion of the 10th in 1988.

Farther northwest is Loudoun County, home base of long-distance commuters, but also part of Northern Virginia's "hunt" country, a rolling landscape dotted with sprawling country houses, horse farms and an occasional vineyard. Wolf and Bush received solid margins here in 1988, but Wilder narrowly won it in 1989.

Population: 535,125. White 466,595 (87%), Black 35,259 (7%), Other 21,974 (4%). Spanish origin 21,573 (4%). 18 and over 401,286 (75%), 65 and over 40,208 (8%). Median age: 31.

classes in Fairfax County schools. Under the program, three schools teach certain classes in French, Spanish or Japanese.

He was also a prime sponsor of legislation to set a one-year cap on imprisonment for civil contempt. The issue received widespread publicity because of the 22-month incarceration of Dr. Elizabeth Morgan after she defied a court order to disclose the whereabouts of her daughter in a custody case. Dr. Morgan alleged that her former husband had abused the child, a charge he vigorously denied. She was released from jail after Wolf's bill became law.

At Home: Democrats have derisively referred to Wolf as a "pothole" politician. But he has built an increasingly secure political base.

Democratic hopes of ousting Wolf were high in 1986, when the party ran John G. Milliken, a member and past chairman of the Arlington County Board of Supervisors. Unlike previous challengers, who had to fend off either a liberal reputation or a carpetbagger stigma, Milliken had long experience in local government and a reputation as a moderate Democrat in the mold of the state's former governor (and now senator), Charles S. Robb.

As chairman of the Washington Metropolitan Area Transit Authority and the Northern Virginia Transportation Commission, Milliken had dealt with many of the same transportation questions that Wolf had. Milliken said he could match Wolf's expertise on suburban issues yet be more forceful on national ones.

But while Milliken had the image, the roots and money — nearly $750,000 — needed to challenge Wolf, he had trouble making a case for replacing the hard-working, if undynamic, incumbent. Viewed widely as a diligent plodder rather than a conservative ideologue, Wolf had never been a lightning rod for controversy.

Milliken ran TV ads criticizing Wolf's 1984 vote to cut federal aid to schools that barred voluntary prayers, spoken or silent, saying that he would rather fight for better teachers than "to spin my wheels pushing a government-written prayer." Wolf responded with his own ad featuring GOP Sen. John W. Warner saying he had never seen a "worse distortion of the truth" than the Milliken ad.

The episode seemed to slow any momentum Milliken might have had. Wolf swamped Milliken in the populous outer suburbs of Fairfax and Loudoun counties, while running virtually even with his challenger in Democratic Arlington, where Milliken had decisively won re-election to the county board in 1984.

Wolf's impressive victory chilled Democrats' spirits. His 1988 challenger was Bob Weinberg, a prominent Washington attorney with a long history of public service in Arlington. Weinberg ran a heady but severely underfinanced campaign, and Wolf got his biggest share of the vote to date, 68 percent.

In 1990, Wolf won 62 percent against Democrat N. MacKenzie Canter III, who had lost to Weinberg in the 1988 primary, and two independents, including fringe political figure Lyndon H. LaRouche Jr. LaRouche's personal campaigning was hampered by his incarceration in a federal prison in Minnesota.

Wolf's career has been a testament to persistence. Barely a year after Democrat Joseph L. Fisher first won this House seat in 1974, Wolf began campaigning to defeat him. His 1976 effort had the backing of local Reagan activists, but did not survive the primary.

In 1976, with more name recognition and better financing, he won the GOP nomination, but lost to Fisher by almost 9,000 votes. His reward came in 1980. Backed by a huge budget, Wolf ended five years' effort with a narrow win.

Wolf is neither eloquent nor colorful, although he is occasionally accompanied by an aide dressed in a wolf's suit. But he has raised millions of dollars since 1979 and run meticulously organized campaigns. In recognition of the multinational nature of some of his district's less affluent neighborhoods, his direct-mail appeals are written in Spanish and Vietnamese as well as English.

In the early campaigns, Fisher chided Wolf for his lack of government experience. But having been a lobbyist, an aide to GOP Rep. Edward G. Biester of Pennsylvania, and deputy assistant secretary of the interior, Wolf could claim he knew his way around the Capitol.

Committees

Appropriations (15th of 22 Republicans)
Treasury, Postal Service & General Government (ranking); Transportation

Select Children, Youth & Families (Ranking)

Select Hunger (9th of 12 Republicans)
International

Elections

1990 General

Frank R. Wolf (R)	103,761	(62%)
N. MacKenzie Canter III (D)	57,249	(34%)
Barbara S. Minnich (I)	5,273	(3%)
Lyndon H. LaRouche Jr. (I)	2,293	(1%)

1988 General

Frank R. Wolf (R)	188,550	(68%)
Robert L. Weinberg (D)	88,284	(32%)

Previous Winning Percentages: **1986** (60%) **1984** (63%) **1982** (53%) **1980** (51%)

District Vote For President

	1988		1984		1980		1976	
D	121,878	(42%)	106,911	(41%)	76,676	(34%)	95,532	(47%)
R	163,211	(57%)	154,507	(59%)	120,328	(53%)	104,815	(51%)
I					23,999	(11%)		

Campaign Finance

	Receipts	Receipts from PACs		Expend-itures
1990				
Wolf (R)	$514,240	$192,395	(37%)	$511,853
Canter (D)	$97,467	$7,150	(7%)	$93,659
LaRouche (I)	$648,572	0		$647,836
1988				
Wolf (R)	$803,080	$237,490	(30%)	$758,365
Weinberg (D)	$242,787	$34,783	(14%)	$241,445

Key Votes

1991	
Authorize use of force against Iraq	Y
1990	
Support constitutional amendment on flag desecration	Y
Pass family and medical leave bill over Bush veto	N
Reduce SDI funding	N
Allow abortions in overseas military facilities	N
Approve budget summit plan for spending and taxing	Y
Approve civil rights bill	N
1989	
Halt production of B-2 stealth bomber at 13 planes	N
Oppose capital gains tax cut	N
Approve federal abortion funding in rape or incest cases	N
Approve pay raise and revision of ethics rules	Y
Pass Democratic minimum wage plan over Bush veto	N

Voting Studies

	Presidential Support		Party Unity		Conservative Coalition	
Year	**S**	**O**	**S**	**O**	**S**	**O**
1990	71	29	78	21	83	15
1989	81	19	83	16	93	7
1988	59	40	82	17	87	13
1987	65	35	76	23	79	21
1986	67	33	74	25	78	22
1985	70	30	72	25	75	24
1984	64	33	71	27	86	12
1983	77	23	79	19	87	13
1982	56	39	69	28	78	15
1981	76 †	24 †	83	17	88 †	12 †

† Not eligible for all recorded votes.

Interest Group Ratings

Year	ADA	ACU	AFL-CIO	CCUS
1990	6	83	0	71
1989	10	89	17	90
1988	25	88	43	86
1987	16	87	13	73
1986	5	86	21	67
1985	15	71	24	73
1984	10	63	25	63
1983	5	96	6	75
1982	10	67	20	82
1981	10	93	0	100

Washington

U.S. CONGRESS

SENATE 1 D, 1 R
HOUSE 5 D, 3 R

LEGISLATURE

Senate 24 D, 25 R
House 58 D, 40 R

ELECTIONS

1988 Presidential Vote	
Bush	49%
Dukakis	50%
1984 Presidential Vote	
Reagan	56%
Mondale	43%
1980 Presidential Vote	
Reagan	50%
Carter	37%
Anderson	11%
Turnout rate in 1986	39%
Turnout rate in 1988	55%
Turnout rate in 1990	37%

(as percentage of voting age population)

POPULATION AND GROWTH

1980 population	4,132,156
1990 population (18th in the nation)	4,866,692
Percent change 1980-1990	+18%

DEMOGRAPHIC BREAKDOWN

White	89%
Black	3%
Asian or Pacific Islander	4%
(Hispanic origin)	4%
Urban	74%
Rural	26%
Born in state	48%
Foreign-born	6%

MAJOR CITIES

Seattle	516,259
Spokane	177,196
Tacoma	176,664
Bellevue	86,874
Everett	69,961

AREA AND LAND USE

Area	66,511 sq. miles (20th)
Farm	39%
Forest	51%
Federally owned	29%

Gov. Booth Gardner (D)
Of Tacoma — Elected 1984

Born: Aug. 21, 1936, Tacoma, Wash.
Education: U. of Washington, B.A. 1958; Harvard U., M.B.A. 1963.
Occupation: Businessman.
Religion: Protestant.
Political Career: Wash. Senate, 1970-73; Pierce County executive, 1981-85.
Next Election: 1992.

WORK

Occupations	
White-collar	55%
Blue-collar	29%
Service workers	13%
Government Workers	
Federal	64,979
State	110,652
Local	175,833

MONEY

Median family income	$ 21,696	(9th)
Tax burden per capita	$ 1,040	(11th)

EDUCATION

Spending per pupil through grade 12	$ 4,164	(21st)
Persons with college degrees	19%	(11th)

CRIME

Violent crime rate	472 per 100,000 (26th)

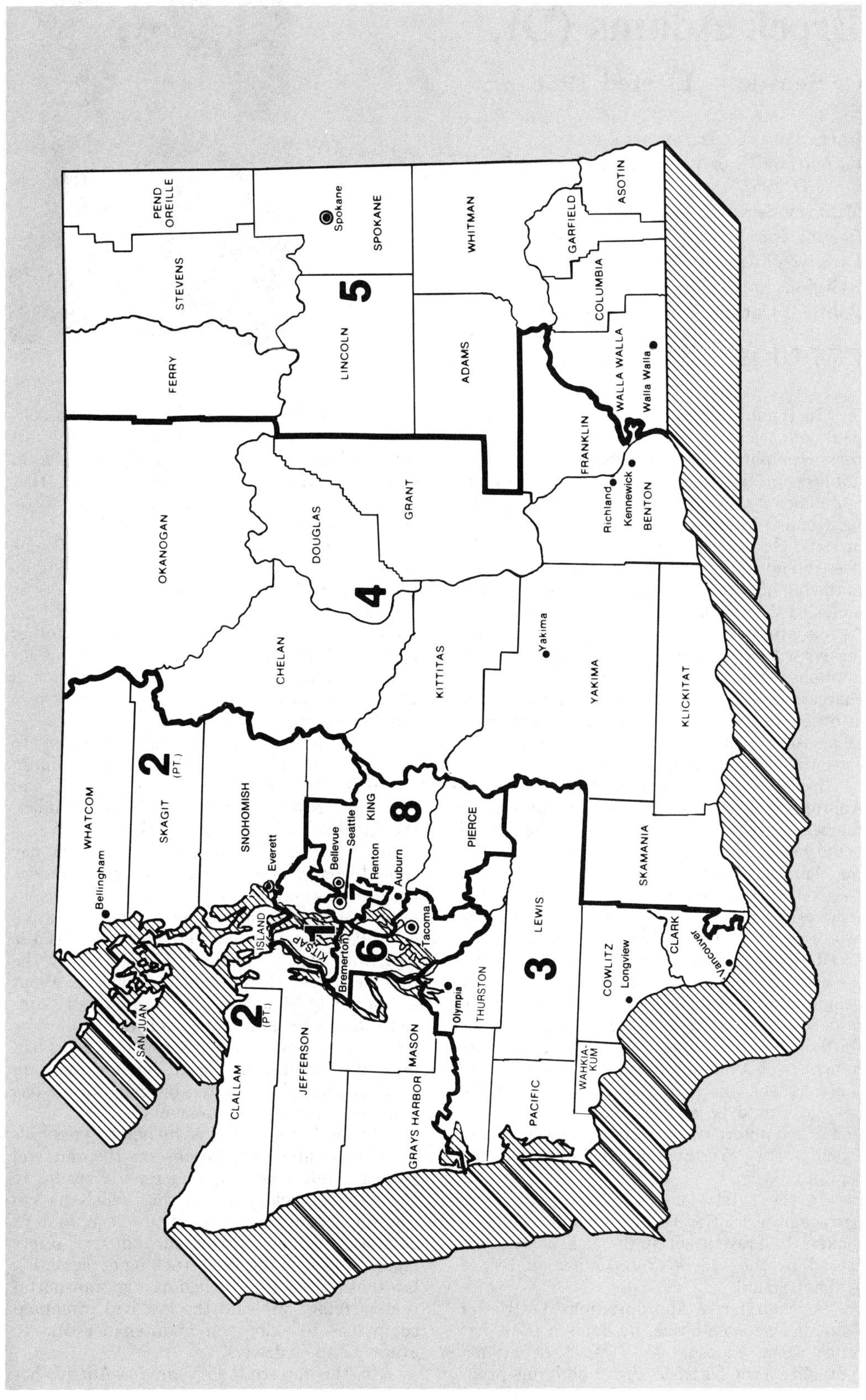
PEND OREILLE
STEVENS
FERRY
Spokane
SPOKANE
5
LINCOLN
WHITMAN
ADAMS
ASOTIN
GARFIELD
COLUMBIA
WALLA WALLA
Walla Walla
FRANKLIN
Richland
Kennewick
BENTON
OKANOGAN
DOUGLAS
GRANT
4
CHELAN
KITTITAS
Yakima
YAKIMA
KLICKITAT
WHATCOM
Bellingham
SKAGIT
2
(PT.)
SNOHOMISH
Everett
KING
Seattle
Bellevue
Renton
Auburn
8
7
1
ISLAND
KITSAP
Bremerton
6
Tacoma
PIERCE
SAN JUAN
2
(PT.)
CLALLAM
JEFFERSON
MASON
Olympia
THURSTON
GRAYS HARBOR
LEWIS
3
SKAMANIA
COWLITZ
Longview
CLARK
Vancouver
WAHKIA-KUM
PACIFIC

Brock Adams (D)

Of Seattle — Elected 1986

Born: Jan. 13, 1927, Atlanta, Ga.
Education: U. of Washington, B.A. 1949; Harvard U., J.D. 1952.
Military Service: Navy, 1944-46.
Occupation: Lawyer.
Family: Wife, Mary Elizabeth Scott; four children.
Religion: Episcopalian.
Political Career: U.S. attorney, 1961-64; U.S. House, 1965-77; U.S. secretary of transportation, 1977-79.
Capitol Office: 513 Hart Bldg. 20510; 224-2621.

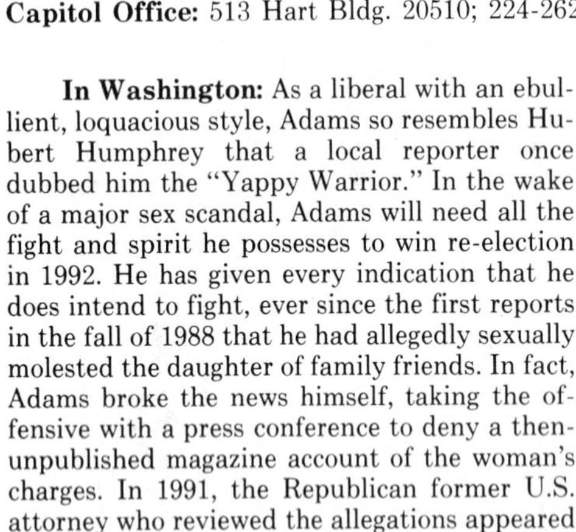

In Washington: As a liberal with an ebullient, loquacious style, Adams so resembles Hubert Humphrey that a local reporter once dubbed him the "Yappy Warrior." In the wake of a major sex scandal, Adams will need all the fight and spirit he possesses to win re-election in 1992. He has given every indication that he does intend to fight, ever since the first reports in the fall of 1988 that he had allegedly sexually molested the daughter of family friends. In fact, Adams broke the news himself, taking the offensive with a press conference to deny a then-unpublished magazine account of the woman's charges. In 1991, the Republican former U.S. attorney who reviewed the allegations appeared at an Adams fundraiser, stating, "To say the case was meritless is an understatement."

Moreover, in 1989 Adams won a seat on the Appropriations Committee, which put him in the best place possible to take home the federal bounty he needs to offset the negative publicity the charges stirred.

Yet, because of the incident, the remaining years of Adams' term have differed from those before it. One of the older and most experienced Democrats in the impressive 1986 class — with House service and a Cabinet post behind him — Adams enjoyed a reservoir of respect that has inevitably eroded somewhat. With his political life endangered, Adams must return to his state often, and tend to its concerns when he is in the capital. Where he had set out to be an influential voice on national and international affairs, now he must attend to two Washingtons: his state and the capital city.

In the 101st Congress, he helped secure passage of legislation requiring double hulls on tankers to prevent oil spills such as the one caused by the 1989 *Exxon Valdez* in Prince William Sound.

As chairman of Appropriations' District of Columbia Subcommittee, he holds a post that brings some exposure — given the national spotlight on the District's drug and crime problems. In his House years, he helped win self-government for District citizens, and that effort was used against him in his 1986 challenge to GOP Sen. Slade Gorton, who charged that Adams had spent too much time as a Seattle congressman working for the capital.

To join Appropriations, Adams left one committee — Commerce, Science and Transportation — that played to his expertise both as a House veteran and as President Jimmy Carter's first transportation secretary, and another panel, Foreign Relations, that reflected his interests abroad. He remains on the Labor and Human Resources Committee, where he is a reliable liberal, pro-labor vote.

Yet Adams has also shown a willingness to stand by principle even if it might hurt him in the polls. In 1990, he reversed himself and opposed further production of the B-2 bomber, though this could put several thousand Washington jobs at risk. Adams said the money should be spent on housing and other domestic programs.

Adams' skepticism about transportation deregulation, which had led Carter to dismiss him, was back in vogue at Commerce by the time he arrived there, thanks to concerns about airline safety, shoddy service and industry concentration after a decade of relaxed regulation. At the Transportation Department, Adams had not only fought with Carter, but also with an auto industry that resisted his calls for air-bag and fuel economy requirements.

In the 100th Congress, he helped pass bills tightening safety regulations on the rail and trucking industries. Arguing for a measure to strengthen trucking standards, which he co-sponsored with Commerce Republican John C. Danforth, Adams attributed industry safety lapses in part to the 1980 trucking deregulation law that passed after he had quit as transportation secretary. He said the law had prompted companies to skimp on maintenance and to overwork their drivers.

In the foreign policy arena, Adams has

repeatedly sought to protect Congress' prerogative in times of war. In 1991, he joined Tom Harkin of Iowa in introducing a resolution demanding that President Bush seek "explicit authorization" from Congress before launching an attack in the Persian Gulf.

Adams was most visible as the chief critic of Reagan's 1987-88 policy of providing Navy escorts to protect Kuwaiti tankers in the Gulf. While members of both parties agreed that the policy was ill-conceived and that Reagan should have sought congressional authorization in keeping with the 1973 War Powers Resolution, most of them were loath to do more than criticize an ongoing operation. Adams' repeated attempts to stop the deployment were either rejected or blocked by GOP filibusters.

Still, Adams showed a doggedness that was impressive — if quixotic and aggravating to senators who did not want to vote on the delicate issue — and a savvy grasp of Senate rules. In late 1987, he won a parliamentarian's ruling that effectively protected his anti-escorts resolutions from further filibusters, which in turn led to a complex compromise that assured him of full debate and a vote in 1988.

At stake, he said, was "the power of the Congress of the United States to determine under the Constitution whether or not a war situation exists and whether or not the nation should be mobilized." Nevertheless, in May 1988 the Senate rebuffed his amendment ending the military escorts, 83-12, and in June voted 54-31 to block another Adams resolution.

Adams' earlier congressional career was a successful one. He was chairman of the House Budget Committee from 1975-77, during the first two years implementing the new congressional fiscal process, and he led efforts to assert congressional authority over the budget. Adams also was a prime mover behind a 1973 bill creating the Conrail freight system.

At Home: The scandal that swirled about Adams in 1988 involved an allegation by Kari Tupper that the senator seduced her at his home in March 1987 while his wife was away. When Adams was informed in September 1988 that a magazine planned to publish an article on the alleged incident, he held a news conference to strongly refute the charges in advance.

The only thing Adams and Tupper agree on is that the woman, then 24, visited his Washington, D.C. home and stayed overnight. Adams, who had helped Tupper obtain a job as a House aide, said he let her sleep on a couch after she complained of illness while seeking job advice. But Tupper, who said she visited Adams to complain about his alleged sexual advances, insisted she passed out after Adams gave her a doctored drink, and later woke up in his bed.

Though hospital tests taken the next day found no signs of assault, Tupper decided in July 1987 to press charges. However, the U.S. Attorney's office turned up no evidence of Tupper's allegations and declined to prosecute. The incident stayed out of the public eye — until Adams learned months later that *Washingtonian* magazine was writing a story on Tupper's version of the incident.

Adams held a news conference and described Tupper's charges as "lies." He accused her of seeking a $400,000 "blackmail" payment.

Adams' denial set off a furor back home; in the middle of the presidential and senatorial races, *The Seattle Times* assigned its entire political staff to the story. Tupper, backed by her parents, responded that her story was true. She also said the payment came up after Adams' lawyer raised the issue of a settlement, and that she would have kept only what was needed to cover her medical and legal expenses, donating the rest to a rape-crisis center.

The *Washingtonian* article, published in November, not only took Tupper's word as fact, but also portrayed Adams as an aging Casanova. A letter in the following month's magazine, from a woman who identified herself as a former Adams aide, may have hurt the senator more than it helped: While defending him against Tupper's charges, the letter indicated that Adams had pursued extramarital affairs.

The damaging contretemps began for Adams just months after the crowning achievement of his political career. In November 1986, he had unseated Gorton in an upset that helped the Democrats regain control of the Senate.

The contest marked Adams' return from self-imposed exile. After more than a decade (1965-77) as a popular House member from Seattle, Adams was considered a likely successor to one of the state's veteran Democratic senators, Warren G. Magnuson and Henry M. Jackson. But Adams left Congress to join Carter's Cabinet, and after leaving that job in 1979, he remained in Washington, D.C. for several years as a lawyer. In the meantime, Gorton defeated Magnuson in 1980, and former Gov. Evans captured the other seat following Jackson's 1983 death.

By the time he returned for his 1986 challenge to Gorton, Adams had no significant political base remaining. He also was slow to organize his campaign, leaving on a trip to the Far East shortly after announcing his candidacy.

But the situation began to change in midsummer, after Gorton voted to confirm Daniel A. Manion, a controversial conservative, as a federal appeals court judge. Gorton's vote was intended as a tradeoff for the approval of Washington state lawyer William L. Dwyer to a separate judgeship, but it sparked an uproar. Gorton caught flak from the right for promoting Dwyer, a liberal Democrat, and from the left for favoring Manion. At the same time, Adams and the media attacked him for making a blatant horse trade that politicized judge selection.

Even with the Manion flap, Adams was not

taken seriously until September, when he did well in the state's open primary, which places candidates of both parties together on the ballot and is thus a "dry run" for the November election. Adams ran virtually even with Gorton.

That showing brought Adams the money and media attention he had sorely lacked, and it forced Gorton, who had ignored Adams' attacks, to change strategies.

Gorton found the change difficult to accomplish. Though widely acknowledged as a competent senator, his cerebral and aloof manner did not generate as warm a response from voters as Adams' more outgoing nature.

Adams took advantage of the Manion vote to harp on Gorton's image as a cold and calculating politician. He also made headway with his criticism of Gorton for allowing the Department of Energy to choose the Hanford Reservation in southeast Washington as one of three possible locations for a high-level nuclear-waste site. Both candidates tried to tie themselves to a referendum on the November ballot opposing the Hanford choice, but Adams compared Gorton with Jackson and Magnuson, who he said would have fought the waste site more effectively.

Meanwhile, Gorton had trouble finding much ammunition in Adams' legislative record, which was more than a decade old. Gorton tried to tie Adams to Carter and the economic problems the state experienced in the late 1970s.

Near the campaign's end, it appeared that Gorton still held an edge. But in the last week he was victimized by an event designed to seal his victory — a visit from President Reagan.

In advance of Reagan's visit, it was widely rumored that the president would make an important announcement about Hanford to blunt Adams' efforts on the issue. But when the president made his appearance, he barely referred to the waste site. The absence of any major new policy put Gorton back on the defensive, as his influence with Reagan was called into question. The momentum shifted to Adams, who won with 51 percent of the vote.

Committees

Appropriations (14th of 16 Democrats)
District of Columbia (chairman); Agriculture, Rural Development & Related Agencies; Commerce, Justice, State & Judiciary; Labor, Health & Human Services, Education; Legislative Branch

Labor & Human Resources (7th of 10 Democrats)
Aging (chairman); Children, Families, Drugs & Alcoholism; Disability Policy; Employment & Productivity

Rules & Administration (9th of 9 Democrats)

Elections

1986 General		
Brock Adams (D)	677,471	(51%)
Slade Gorton (R)	650,931	(49%)
1986 Primary		
Slade Gorton (R)	291,735	(47%)
Brock Adams (D)	287,258	(46%)
Others (D)	26,027	(4%)
Others (R)	22,080	(3%)

† In Washington's "jungle primary," candidates of all parties are listed on one ballot.

Previous Winning Percentages: **1976 *** (73%) **1974 *** (71%) **1972 *** (85%) **1970 *** (67%) **1968 *** (66%) **1966 *** (63%) **1964 *** (56%)

** House elections.*

Campaign Finance

	Receipts	Receipts from PACs		Expenditures
1986				
Adams (D)	$1,793,142	$635,361	(35%)	$1,912,307
Gorton (R)	$3,316,123	$1,192,293	(36%)	$3,290,072

Key Votes

1991	
Authorize use of force against Iraq	N
1990	
Oppose prohibition of certain semiautomatic weapons	N
Support constitutional amendment on flag desecration	N
Oppose requiring parental notice for minors' abortions	Y
Halt production of B-2 stealth bomber at 13 planes	Y
Approve budget that cut spending and raised revenues	N
Pass civil rights bill over Bush veto	Y
1989	
Oppose reduction of SDI funding	N
Oppose barring federal funds for "obscene" art	Y
Allow vote on capital gains tax cut	N

Voting Studies

	Presidential Support		Party Unity		Conservative Coalition	
Year	**S**	**O**	**S**	**O**	**S**	**O**
1990	34	65	93	7	11	89
1989	43	56	94	5	11	87
1988	38	56	82	11	16	73
1987	33	65	88	4	6	81

Interest Group Ratings

Year	ADA	ACU	AFL-CIO	CCUS
1990	94	9	78	8
1989	95	4	100	38
1988	90	0	77	36
1987	95	4	90	38

Slade Gorton (R)

Of Seattle — Elected 1988

Also served 1981-87.

Born: Jan. 8, 1928, Chicago, Ill.
Education: Dartmouth College, A.B. 1950; Columbia U., LL.B. 1953.
Military Service: Army, 1945-46; Air Force, 1953-56; Air Force Reserve, 1956-81.
Occupation: Lawyer.
Family: Wife, Sally Jean Clark; three children.
Religion: Episcopalian.
Political Career: Wash. House, 1959-69, majority leader, 1967-69; Wash. attorney general, 1969-81.
Capitol Office: 730 Hart Bldg. 20510; 224-3441.

In Washington: Gorton was an unnatural fit on the Agriculture Committee, where he was placed for his first two years back in the Senate. But at the start of the 102nd Congress, Gorton traded in his seats on Agriculture and Armed Services for assignments on the Appropriations and Intelligence committees, panels that seem better suited to his interests. He was also put on the Ethics Committee.

Now in his second stint as Washington's freshman senator, Gorton employs the same deliberate style he first brought to Congress in 1981, but he can show a somewhat sharper political edge than he did in his first term. In the 101st Congress, for instance, Gorton prominently allied himself with one side in the Northwest's most turbulent debate — the fight over protecting the northern spotted owl.

The U.S. Fish and Wildlife Service declared the owl a threatened species in 1990, requiring a plan to curtail logging in the ancient "old growth" forests where the owl lives. Gorton staked out an uncompromising position against curbs on logging in old-growth forests.

In visits to timber-dependent communities, Gorton proclaimed solidarity with loggers and millworkers. "Owls are important," he told a group of eastern Washington millworkers. "But people are more important than owls." He introduced a bill to guarantee annual timber harvest levels of 3.5 billion board feet from Northwest forests. The original government study recommended reducing Northwestern timber harvests by 2.4 billion board feet. (The 1990 harvest level was 3.85 billion board feet.)

In April 1991, the Fish and Wildlife Service proposed designating 11.6 million acres of Northwestern forestland as protected habitat needed for the owl's survival. Gorton balked. "If this preliminary proposal is adopted it would mean the loss of more than 30,000 jobs for Northwest working families," he said.

Gorton was comparatively quiet on most other issues during the 101st Congress. On the Commerce Committee, he introduced a bill to impose limits on trucks and rail cars that travel one way with garbage and other hazardous materials, and then return carrying food and drink. A version of his "backhauling" bill became law in 1990.

Gorton joined Nevada Democrat Richard H. Bryan in sponsoring a bill to raise automobile fuel-efficiency standards. Their legislation, dropped from the Clean Air Act rewrite, died in the 101st Congress when the Senate fell three votes short of the 60 votes needed to cut off debate on it. They reintroduced their bill in the 102nd Congress. In March 1991, the Commerce Committee approved a modified version.

During Senate consideration of a legal-immigration bill in 1989, Gorton added an amendment to allow Chinese students to stay in the United States for up to four years and to qualify for legal residency without returning to China, where they faced possible government reprisals. Later that year, President Bush vetoed a bill to allow all Chinese nationals in the country on student visas to remain and work as long as the U.S. government was deferring deportments. Gorton was one of eight Republicans who voted to override the veto.

On the Agriculture Committee, Gorton entered the turf battle that pitted the stock markets against the futures markets, and the Securities and Exchange Commission (SEC) against the Commodity Futures Trading Commission (CFTC). Unlike most committee members, however, Gorton urged that the CFTC's responsibilities be handed over to the SEC. "Why in the world is there any justification for the existence of the CFTC?" he asked CFTC Chairman Wendy Gramm, wife of GOP Sen. Phil Gramm of Texas.

Gorton did not play a major role on the committee's most significant legislation of the 101st Congress, the 1990 farm bill. Washington state does not have much stake in programs covered in the bill. He did attend most of the markup sessions, quietly reading the newspaper while members crafted the five-year reauthorization of farm programs.

During his early years in the Senate, Gorton was generally supportive of President Ronald Reagan's policies, backing his first-term attempts at cutting federal programs and taxes. In supporting Reagan's efforts to increase defense spending, Gorton stood with his Senate colleague, Democratic "hawk" Henry M. Jackson (who died in 1983).

But Gorton maintained a consumerist orientation from his days as state attorney general, and he was a staunch supporter of federal programs for community development and for the homeless. In early 1985, Gorton was a leader among Republicans on the Budget Committee who, under the guidance of then-Majority Leader Bob Dole of Kansas, drafted a plan for a federal budget freeze that included a controversial provision eliminating cost of living allowances (COLAs) for Social Security recipients.

At Home: The 1988 victory that returned Gorton to the Senate capped a most unusual political journey through the 1980s.

Gorton was not among the most ideologically conservative GOP Senate candidates in 1980, but he rode in with the Reagan revolution that gave Republicans Senate control. Six years later, when Republicans of his centrist ilk were winning new Senate terms, Gorton was tossed out. His political career, said then to be finished, was not. The 1988 retirement of GOP Sen. Daniel J. Evans gave him an opening.

Gorton made the most of it, edging Democratic Rep. Mike Lowry to become only the 11th senator in history to be popularly elected, defeated, then returned to the Senate.

His rebound was as unexpected as it was rare. Much of the state media had written him off after his 1986 defeat by Democrat Brock Adams. Even Gorton himself was wary about returning to the fray; Adams' negative campaign in 1986 left voters with deep concerns about the Republican's stands on key state issues, as well as his icy demeanor.

Born to a wealthy Chicago family (whose Yankee ancestors included the founders of the Gorton's of Gloucester fish-processing company), Gorton says Washington state's progressive political legacy led him to settle there. As attorney general, he crafted a pro-consumer record that placed him in the moderate mold of the state's most popular Republicans.

This profile aided Gorton in his 1980 bid against Democratic Sen. Warren G. Magnuson, whose legendary efforts to obtain public works projects for Washington state had earned him six terms in the Senate. Outperforming Reagan in the state, Gorton ousted Magnuson with 54 percent of the vote.

Many of Gorton's constituents, however, were never personally comfortable with him. Averse to the hail-fellow world of personal politics, the brusque, cerebral Gorton was known to cut off political associates and inquisitive constituents in mid-sentence. It was thus easy for state Democrats to convince voters in 1986 that Gorton was "aloof" and "arrogant."

Then came the Manion affair. Reagan had tapped Daniel A. Manion, a conservative Indiana lawyer, to be a federal judge. At the same time, the White House held up the judicial nomination of Seattle lawyer and Gorton ally William L. Dwyer, whose liberal views alienated key Republican conservatives. Gorton let it be known he might line up with Senate Democrats opposing Manion; the Democrats, in fact, thought they had Gorton's crucial vote in the bag, and forced a floor vote in June 1986. But in the midst of the roll call, a White House official called Gorton to tell him that Reagan would proceed with the Dwyer nomination. Gorton then voted for Manion, who was narrowly confirmed. In the aftermath, Gorton claimed he dealt with the White House to protect a home-state interest, but Democrats angrily portrayed him as "Slippery Slade," a craven vote-trader.

In his 1986 re-election bid, Gorton was hurt by this image, by his support for freezing Social Security COLAs, and by the uncertain fate of the Hanford nuclear reservation.

During the 99th Congress, Hanford, in south-central Washington, was named as one of three possible sites for a permanent high-level nuclear waste dump, and Adams argued that Gorton had not done enough to block that eventuality. Also, Adams blasted Gorton for supporting continued plutonium production at Hanford's aging "N Reactor," as well as a plan to produce tritium there.

An overconfident Gorton was slow to respond. Then, in the final week of the campaign, what was expected to be a triumphant moment turned sour for him. Reagan flew to Spokane to appear at a Gorton rally. But when pressed on the Hanford issue by reporters, Reagan showed a lack of familiarity, creating an impression that Gorton had little access to the president.

Adams won with 51 percent and Gorton returned to legal practice in Seattle. In 1987, he worked as a Department of Energy consultant on options for keeping the nuclear industry at Hanford alive.

But late that year, Evans, who had voiced distress at the Senate's lack of legislative productivity, announced he would retire. Unable to persuade GOP Reps. Sid Morrison or Rod Chandler to run, the party leadership turned to Gorton. Hard-line conservatives were uneasy with the choice but could produce only two weak primary challengers, and Gorton breezed into the general election.

He then faced Lowry, who held off House colleague Don Bonker in a more grueling primary. Lowry had succeeded Adams in the 7th

District, and had developed a liberal activist following with his outspoken support for federal social programs and his opposition to Reagan's defense buildup. But with his scraggly beard, rumpled clothes and penchant for arm-waving harangues, Lowry was vulnerable to GOP charges that he was an extremist. This image was part of the reason Lowry had lost to Evans in the 1983 Senate special election to fill Jackson's seat.

The 1988 contest thus matched the losers of the last two Washington Senate races, and both set out to soften the negatives that had previously defeated them. Gorton spent over $1 million during the primary on ads in which he apologized for being arrogant during his previous tenure. Lowry shaved his beard, adopted a neatly pressed appearance, and restrained his rhetoric and temper.

Still, the home-stretch themes were negative. Gorton, pointing to the state's "strong defense" tradition, portrayed Lowry as far out of the mainstream. With drug trafficking a major national concern, Gorton attacked Lowry's House votes against the 1986 and 1988 omnibus drug bills (Lowry, like many liberals, had reservations about the effect on civil liberties of some of the crackdown measures). In turn, Lowry tried to revive the Social Security and Hanford issues Adams had used.

This already unusual campaign was overshadowed by a pair of strange events. In late September, the Washington state media turned its attentions to allegations that Sen. Adams had drugged and seduced a young woman at his Washington, D.C., home. Then, in early October, Lowry collapsed in Chicago while en route to Seattle, and was hospitalized for several days with a bleeding ulcer.

Lowry returned to the campaign trail, though, and Gorton again faced a contest that entered its last week too close to call. But this time Gorton got a last-minute break when Nevada, not Hanford, was designated as the site for the nuclear waste dump and the N Reactor was closed for safety reasons.

Lowry still lashed at Gorton in a TV ad for supporting a tritium "bomb factory," and for receiving $60,000 in consulting fees from the Department of Energy. Unlike 1986, though, Gorton quickly responded with a big gun, the popular incumbent Evans. In an ad run in the campaign's final days, Evans described Lowry's charges as "lies, distortion and garbage."

By getting in the last word, Gorton may have tipped the scales. He won with 51 percent, even as Democrat Michael S. Dukakis carried the state in presidential voting.

Committees

Appropriations (13th of 13 Republicans)
Legislative Branch (ranking); District of Columbia; Interior; Labor, Health & Human Services, Education

Commerce, Science & Transportation (8th of 9 Republicans)
Consumer (ranking); Aviation; Communications; National Ocean Policy Study

Select Ethics (3rd of 3 Republicans)

Select Indian Affairs (4th of 7 Republicans)

Select Intelligence (6th of 7 Republicans)

Elections

1988 General		
Slade Gorton (R)	944,359	(51%)
Mike Lowry (D)	904,183	(49%)
1988 Primary †		
Slade Gorton (R)	335,846	(36%)
Mike Lowry (D)	297,399	(32%)
Don Bonker (D)	241,170	(26%)
Doug Smith (R)	31,512	(3%)
William Goodloe (R)	26,224	(3%)

† In Washington's "jungle primary," candidates of both parties are listed on one ballot.

Previous Winning Percentage: **1980** (54%)

Campaign Finance

	Receipts	Receipts from PACs		Expenditures
1988				
Gorton (R)	$2,736,101	$939,406	(34%)	$2,851,591
Lowry (D)	$2,202,177	$618,074	(28%)	$2,191,187

Key Votes

1991	
Authorize use of force against Iraq	Y
1990	
Oppose prohibition of certain semiautomatic weapons	Y
Support constitutional amendment on flag desecration	Y
Oppose requiring parental notice for minors' abortions	N
Halt production of B-2 stealth bomber at 13 planes	N
Approve budget that cut spending and raised revenues	N
Pass civil rights bill over Bush veto	N
1989	
Oppose reduction of SDI funding	Y
Oppose barring federal funds for "obscene" art	Y
Allow vote on capital gains tax cut	Y

Voting Studies

	Presidential Support		Party Unity		Conservative Coalition	
Year	**S**	**O**	**S**	**O**	**S**	**O**
1990	76	24	81	19	86	14
1989	89	11	80	20	87	13
1986	73	25	74	25	72	26
1985	77	19	79	17	70	27
1984	83	17	83	16	81	19
1983	85	15	76	23	70	30
1982	76	24	78	22	76	24
1981	87	13	86	13	77	21

Interest Group Ratings

Year	ADA	ACU	AFL-CIO	CCUS
1990	17	78	0	92
1989	15	75	20	88
1986	25	19	69	65
1985	35	47	50	41
1984	35	83	18	78
1983	35	65	24	58
1982	45	43	35	62
1981	10	67	6	94

1 John Miller (R)

Of Seattle — Elected 1984

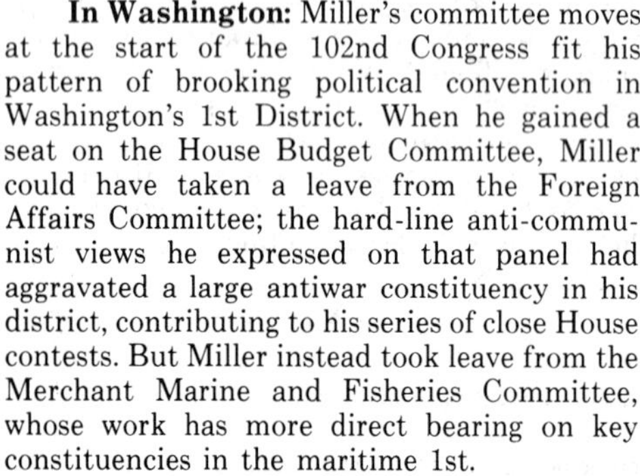

Born: May 23, 1938, New York, N.Y.

Education: Bucknell U., B.A. 1959; Yale U., M.A., LL.B. 1964.

Military Service: Army, 1960-61; Army Reserve, 1961-69.

Occupation: Lawyer.

Family: Wife, June Marion Makar; one child.

Religion: Jewish.

Political Career: Seattle City Council, 1972-80, president, 1978-80; candidate for mayor of Seattle, 1977; independent candidate for Wash. attorney general, 1980.

Capitol Office: 322 Cannon Bldg. 20515; 225-6311.

In Washington: Miller's committee moves at the start of the 102nd Congress fit his pattern of brooking political convention in Washington's 1st District. When he gained a seat on the House Budget Committee, Miller could have taken a leave from the Foreign Affairs Committee; the hard-line anti-communist views he expressed on that panel had aggravated a large antiwar constituency in his district, contributing to his series of close House contests. But Miller instead took leave from the Merchant Marine and Fisheries Committee, whose work has more direct bearing on key constituencies in the maritime 1st.

Yet Miller's decisions to serve on Budget and keep his foreign policy soapbox can be viewed in the broader context in which Miller apparently sees himself. Through mid-1991, Miller was regarded as a likely candidate in 1992 for the Senate seat held by Democrat Brock Adams.

Since his close call in a 1986 House contest, Miller has not been unaware of his tenuous position in the 1st, a mix of liberal Seattle precincts and the suburban areas that sustain him. A New York-born lawyer with an intellectual mien, Miller responded to frequent charges of aloofness by opening more district offices, making more personal appearances and performing a series of "workdays."

Miller also re-emphasized his environmentalist posture — which dates to his political emergence in the 1970s — and moderate views on social policy. During the 101st Congress, he voted to override President Bush's veto of family leave legislation. Overall, he backed Bush on a modest 55 percent of House votes in 1990.

But Miller has not yielded on the priority he gives to foreign affairs — issues that are of great import but do not necessarily touch the soul of the average voter.

During the 1980s, Miller was an outspoken supporter of the contras who were fighting the then-Marxist government of Nicaragua. The fall of the Berlin Wall hardly knocked down Miller's distrust of the Soviet Union's intentions in the Third World.

In late 1990, the House moved to place conditions on U.S. covert aid to the anti-communist insurgent group UNITA, which was fighting the Soviet-backed government of Angola. Miller was able to attach an amendment mandating a "zero-zero" option, under which U.S. aid to the rebels would be cut only after Soviet assistance to the Angolan government was ended. The overall measure was drafted into the fiscal year 1991 intelligence authorization bill, which Bush vetoed over other issues.

Miller's anticommunist views were evident in his work on the Foreign Affairs Subcommittee on Human Rights, where he acted as an advocate for Jewish "refuseniks" seeking to emigrate from the Soviet Union and for the natives of the so-called "captive nations" in the Soviet Baltic region. He is also critical of rightist regimes he sees as violative of human rights: He was a co-founder of the Ad Hoc Group in Support of Democracy in Chile.

Miller supported the January 1991 resolution that authorized Bush to use military force to end Iraq's occupation of Kuwait. "Sometime . . . a dictator will be considering invading his or her neighbor," Miller said. "That dictator will look back on 1991, and [Iraqi dictator] Saddam Hussein, and will ask him or herself . . . [d]id the United States, the leader of the United Nations, stand firm?"

Miller does serve on the Foreign Affairs panel that has a direct impact on the domestic economy, the subcommittee on trade. A member from a district that is dependent on imports as well as exports, Miller takes strong pro-free trade and anti-protectionist stands.

However, Miller did bend on his longtime opposition to restrictions on the export of raw logs. Motivated by worries about the impact of

Washington 1

Northern Seattle and Suburbs

The typical 1st District voter pays very little attention to party label in selecting candidates. Miller has kept the House seat in GOP hands, following in the footsteps of former Republican Rep. Joel Pritchard (now the state's lieutenant governor).

But in 1988, Democrat Michael S. Dukakis carried the district, albeit just barely. He received just over 50 percent of the 1st District vote, beating George Bush by only about 5,000 votes.

As in many districts in the Pacific Northwest, there are strong environmentalist tendencies. There is also a devoted corps of peace activists in Seattle's large liberal community. The mix in the 1st District includes an active Christian fundamentalist community; religious broadcaster Pat Robertson swept the district's delegates in the 1988 Washington state presidential caucuses. But the majority of voters are middle-of-the-road and not partisan-minded.

Shaped like a butterfly hovering over Seattle, the 1st encompasses most of the city's northern suburbs, a collection of largely middle-class communities stretching from northern King County up into Snohomish County, almost to Everett.

Extremes of wealth and poverty are not characteristic of the 1st, but there is some variation. Seattle's northeastern and northwestern corners are part of the 1st, and a few of the neighborhoods there are lower-middle class. The district's ritziest section is the "Gold Coast" — an area on the eastern shore of Lake Washington that includes Hunts Point, Yarrow Point and Medina. Most workers, blue- and white-collar alike, commute to nearby factories or to downtown Seattle offices.

King and Snohomish together account for over 85 percent of the 1st's population. The remainder live across Puget Sound in northern Kitsap County, where several military bases boost the economy. The Navy's Underseas Warfare Engineering Station in Keyport is in the 1st, and just south is Bremerton's Bangor submarine base, home to Trident submarines.

Population: 516,378. White 486,447 (94%), Black 4,632 (1%), Other 19,372 (4%). Spanish origin 8,934 (2%). 18 and over 378,407 (73%), 65 and over 47,894 (9%). Median age: 31.

raw log exports on the sawmills of the Northwest, Miller in May 1990 gained passage of an amendment to the Export Administration Act limiting such exports. That bill was eventually vetoed by Bush, but a separate log-export measure was enacted as part of another bill.

During his tenure on Merchant Marine, Miller looked after the 1st District's shipping and fishing interests. He also showed his environmentalist leanings on a number of oil drilling issues that came under the committee's purview. Miller was not an automatic vote for the environmental movement's viewpoint, though. When an oil-spill liability bill moved through Congress in the wake of the 1989 *Exxon Valdez* oil spill, Miller was for a time the only member of the Washington state delegation opposing a provision to bar federal preemption of state laws with stronger liability requirements. However, Miller eventually signed onto the provision, which was enacted into law.

At Home: After three terms as their representative, Miller has yet to convince a strong majority of 1st District voters that he is the person they want to send to Congress. Miller barely won his first re-election bid in 1986. He earned some breathing room in a 1988 rematch, but two years later squeaked to victory with less than 8,000 votes.

When he launched his first House campaign, Miller was already well-known from his tenure in the 1970s on the Seattle City Council and his unsuccessful runs for Seattle mayor and state attorney general. The New York-born lawyer had kept his profile up as a Seattle TV and radio commentator.

In his 1984 House bid, Miller's anti-communist views appealed to conservative Republicans, while his reputation for support of environmental causes offset the efforts of his Democratic opponent, environmental activist Brock Evans. Miller won with 56 percent of the vote.

That comfortable victory and the 1st District's Republican leanings may have contributed to Miller's complacency about his 1986 election. For whatever reason, Miller was caught off balance by the aggressive campaign of Reese Lindquist, a teacher and former head of the Washington Education Association.

Lindquist launched his House bid late, but raised roughly $400,000. Lindquist focused on the contra-aid issue, saying a majority of district voters opposed the policy and citing Miller's stand as proof of his indifference to constituents' views. Miller just barely hung on, taking 51 percent of the vote.

Lindquist made a second, better-organized attempt in 1988, describing the incumbent as opposed to increased funding for education and seniors' programs. But Miller was not to be blindsided again; he sought media attention for his "workdays" and beefed-up outreach programs, and portrayed Lindquist as a radical who was responsible for a Seattle teachers' strike in 1978.

The campaign evolved into a nasty exchange of TV ads and news coverage focused on misleading claims in both candidates' commercials. But it was Miller's ability to pay for campaign advertising, both positive and negative, that was likely the deciding factor in the contest: He spent nearly $750,000 on TV commercials — close to a third of it a loan to himself — compared with just over $200,000 for Lindquist. Miller won the rematch by a comfortable 55-45 percent margin.

That showing appeared to bode well for Miller's future, particularly when his 1990 opponent, Cynthia Sullivan, got off to a shaky start. Although Democratic leaders were initially enthusiastic about Sullivan, a member of the King County Council, they appeared to lose confidence in her after her campaign suffered early organizational problems. Short of money needed to advertise heavily in the pricey Seattle market, Sullivan struggled to get her anti-incumbent message out to voters. A late challenge for the Democratic nomination also sapped Sullivan's limited resources.

But national disgust over the fall federal budget stalemate provided Sullivan with the incumbent-bashing climate she had not been able to generate alone; she drew close to Miller in the polls, and found party givers at last willing to turn their eyes from the superheated 3rd District race and lend a hand.

Miller, however, did not sit still. Throughout his well-funded campaign, Miller had advertised his political virtues, including endorsements from environmental and business groups alike. In the final weeks, Miller turned his advertising arsenal against Sullivan, airing television attack ads. On Election Day, Miller slipped past Sullivan for his fourth House win.

Committees

Budget (11th of 14 Republicans)
Budget Process, Reconciliation & Enforcement; Defense, Foreign Policy & Space

Foreign Affairs (13th of 18 Republicans)
International Economic Policy & Trade; International Operations

Elections

1990 General		
John Miller (R)	100,339	(52%)
Cynthia Sullivan (D)	92,447	(48%)
1990 Primary †		
John Miller (R)	41,976	(52%)
Cynthia Sullivan (D)	27,410	(34%)
Benny Teal (D)	8,339	(10%)
Kerman Kermoade (R)	2,759	(3%)
1988 General		
John Miller (R)	152,265	(55%)
Reese Lindquist (D)	122,646	(45%)

† In Washington's "jungle primary," candidates of both parties are listed on one ballot.

Previous Winning Percentages: **1986** (51%) **1984** (56%)

District Vote For President

	1988	1984
D	134,311 (50%)	100,102 (42%)
R	129,280 (49%)	134,199 (57%)

Campaign Finance

	Receipts	Receipts from PACs		Expend-itures
1990				
Miller (R)	$913,407	$265,457	(29%)	$912,969
Sullivan (D)	$376,382	$127,537	(34%)	$351,660
1988				
Miller (R)	$1,328,979	$333,860	(25%)	$1,321,021
Lindquist (D)	$625,238	$279,275	(45%)	$625,926

Key Votes

1991	
Authorize use of force against Iraq	Y
1990	
Support constitutional amendment on flag desecration	Y
Pass family and medical leave bill over Bush veto	Y
Reduce SDI funding	N
Allow abortions in overseas military facilities	Y
Approve budget summit plan for spending and taxing	Y
Approve civil rights bill	N
1989	
Halt production of B-2 stealth bomber at 13 planes	N
Oppose capital gains tax cut	N
Approve federal abortion funding in rape or incest cases	Y
Approve pay raise and revision of ethics rules	N
Pass Democratic minimum wage plan over Bush veto	N

Voting Studies

	Presidential Support		Party Unity		Conservative Coalition	
Year	**S**	**O**	**S**	**O**	**S**	**O**
1990	55	43	68	28	57	39
1989	59	36	46	51	63	37
1988	44	51	50	45	66	26
1987	52	48	57	38	63	33
1986	56	43	60	36	58	40
1985	64	36	65	32	62	36

Interest Group Ratings

Year	ADA	ACU	AFL-CIO	CCUS
1990	39	46	17	54
1989	35	68	25	100
1988	60	38	64	79
1987	48	41	44	73
1986	40	55	36	67
1985	25	67	24	86

2 Al Swift (D)

Of Bellingham — Elected 1978

Born: Sept. 12, 1935, Tacoma, Wash.
Education: Attended Whitman College, 1953-55; Central Washington College, B.A. 1957.
Occupation: Broadcaster; congressional aide.
Family: Wife, Paula Jean Jackson; two children.
Religion: Unitarian.
Political Career: No previous office.
Capitol Office: 1502 Longworth Bldg. 20515; 225-2605.

In Washington: Swift's resonant voice is an instant reminder of his days delivering the 11 o'clock news in Bellingham, but it is hard to imagine anyone doing more than Swift to dispel the stereotype of the local TV anchorman as a prisoner of style over substance.

A patient and diligent legislator who often toils outside the spotlight, Swift has thrown himself into some of the more challenging and thankless issues before Congress, such as campaign-finance reform and clean-air legislation.

At the start of the 102nd Congress, Swift became one of the few House members to wield two gavels. He continued as chair of the House Administration Subcommittee on Elections, and he gained the helm of the Transportation and Hazardous Materials Subcommittee on Energy and Commerce. The assignment positioned him to address issues important to his refinery-rich district, such as reauthorization of the Resource Conservation and Recovery Act — which governs hazardous and solid waste — and Amtrak service to the West.

Swift came to his new post well-trained in dealing with hazardous material; in the 101st Congress, he was the key Democratic player in the House on campaign-finance reform, an issue that many colleagues choose to avoid. A chairman of a bipartisan House task force, Swift authored a bill passed by the House that attempted to restructure political action committees and create voluntary spending limits with incentives such as discounted broadcast and postage rates. The bill died in conference, and in the 102nd Congress Swift relinquished the lead role on the issue to a new committee task force headed by Democratic Rep. Sam Gejdenson of Connecticut.

Swift has also been at the center of efforts to prevent the TV networks from projecting presidential election outcomes while polling places are still open. He won pledges from the three major networks in 1985 that they would not forecast results for any state while its polls are open. Since then, he has lobbied persistently for a bill that would close all polls in the continental United States simultaneously at 9 p.m. EST in presidential election years.

Critics have derided the so-called "uniform poll closing" measure as "social tinkering" to satisfy "a few people on the West Coast." But the measure satisfied enough members from other regions to pass the House in the 99th, 100th and 101st Congresses. Each time it died in the Senate.

Swift also gained House passage of the so-called "motor-voter" bill that would have allowed eligible citizens to register to vote when they applied for or renewed their driver's license. That measure also failed in the Senate, but returned as an issue in the 102nd Congress.

Although Swift did not have enough seniority to chair an Energy and Commerce subcommittee until 1991, he earned respect for his legislative activity on the panel. That respect, as well as the personal relationships he has forged, helped him become de facto chairman of a caucus of nine moderate-to-conservative committee Democrats, who organized in the 100th Congress to try to break a long deadlock between environmentalists and an industry-oriented faction who disagreed on reauthorizing the Clean Air Act. Their work on the intractable issue helped create momentum for passage of clean-air legislation in the 101st Congress.

One of Swift's favorite legislative subjects is broadcast deregulation, which emerged as an issue in 1984 after the Federal Communications Commission repealed federal guidelines for TV commercials and public-affairs programming. The battle lines on broadcast deregulation divide mainly between "public interest" forces and those more sympathetic to the broadcast industry. The public-interest side wants strict requirements for news and public-affairs programs, plus a competitive broadcast license-renewal process — resisted by the industry. Swift has favored a middle-ground approach that would require the FCC to set broad categories of public-interest standards but drop competitive license renewals.

Swift is involved in numerous communications issues. Since the court-imposed AT&T breakup, he has worked to see that Congress,

Washington 2

Northwest — Everett; Part of Olympic Peninsula

The geographic and political focal point of the 2nd is blue-collar Everett, a city of 70,000 built by the timber and shipping industries. Labor conflict plagued those industries between the two world wars, and unions became the basis of the local Democratic strength. But the blue-collar tendency to vote Democratic is tempered by the reliance on defense-related industry, which has prospered under GOP White House rule. Everett is the site of a new Navy "homeport"; since the 1960s, it has been closely linked with Boeing's aircraft plants. Electronics and high-technology industries round out Everett's newly diversified economic base.

Everett and surrounding Snohomish County cast about one-third of the district's vote (the populous Seattle suburbs in the southern part of Snohomish are in the neighboring 1st District). The whole county tends to be Republican-leaning, but competitive, in statewide contests. George Bush carried the county with 51 percent in 1988, while GOP Senate winner Slade Gorton took 52 percent.

The second-largest block of 2nd District votes comes from Whatcom County, at the northern edge of the district along the Canadian border. Bellingham (population 52,000), Swift's home base, is dependent on timber, though it also is home to shipping and canning industries. Like most of the northern coast area, it has a large population of Scandinavian descent, especially Norwegian. Michael S. Dukakis took 52 percent of the presidential vote in Whatcom County, breaking a three-election GOP winning streak. Between Snohomish and Whatcom is Skagit County, a more rural and regularly Republican area.

The Olympic Peninsula portion of the 2nd is a lightly populated place of mountains, forests and coastal communities in Clallam, Jefferson and Mason counties. Most of Grays Harbor County is also in the 2nd.

Island County, located between Juan de Fuca Strait and Puget Sound, is still largely a rain-soaked preserve of vegetable farms and forested land. But its position at the edge of the Seattle metropolis has brought it some of that area's rapid growth; population jumped there by 13 percent, to nearly 50,000, between 1980 and 1986. Bush took 60 percent there in 1988.

San Juan County, made up of a chain of islands, has also seen some growth, mostly in the form of retirees. But it remains mostly rural and lightly populated.

Population: 516,568. White 490,840 (95%), Black 2,501 (1%), Other 17,453 (3%). Spanish origin 9,511 (2%). 18 and over 373,304 (72%), 65 and over 62,626 (12%). Median age: 30.

not the courts, sets telecommunications policy. He supported legislation to try to decrease local phone rates by allowing regional phone companies to engage in new businesses and expand their revenue bases.

He has also been the chief opponent of TV Martí, the U.S. government-sponsored attempt to beam independent programming to television sets in Fidel Castro's Cuba. Swift said the project was a waste of money because of Cuban jamming and he warned that it could spur retaliation against U.S. broadcasters.

In the 101st Congress, Swift helped gain a permanent ban on the export of raw logs from federal lands and a restriction on the amount of logs that could be exported from state lands in the Northwest.

Swift started in Congress as a protégé of Sen. Warren G. Magnuson, who pulled levers on the opposite side of the Capitol to help him get on Commerce as a freshman.

Swift was the only legislator from his state on the panel in the 96th Congress as it took up the Northwest power bill. The legislation, designed to allocate scarce power resources in Washington and Oregon, was very controversial in those states, but attracted little attention elsewhere. The committee largely left it to Swift to build a regional consensus behind some sort of bill. The compromise Swift finally got through committee was backed by public and private utilities, but many environmentalists and consumer advocates said it gave too great a role to nuclear power and was too generous to private power companies.

At Home: After a string of easy races, Swift won his 1990 re-election campaign with just over 50 percent of the vote. His GOP opponent, Doug Smith, took 41 percent of the vote while a Libertarian, William L. McCord, took roughly 8 percent.

Smith, a lawyer who had worked as a congressional lobbyist and aide to former President Gerald Ford, had little money and had not been considered a serious threat to Swift. But several factors — low turnout, anti-incumbent feeling and a third name on the ballot — combined to batter Swift at the polls. Swift may also have suffered from a public perception that he has put more energy into national issues than local concerns such as the declining timber industry.

Prior to 1990, Swift had not been in a close congressional race since his first one. Starting out as a disc jockey after graduating from college, Swift spent more than a decade learning the broadcast trade at KVOS-TV in Bellingham, interspersing his progress there with two separate stints as administrative assistant to the local Democratic congressman, Lloyd Meeds.

By the time he decided to try for Congress in 1978, upon Meeds' retirement, Swift had a decade as a TV news director to his credit, and was familiar to viewers along Puget Sound.

But he was considered a long shot, because the Democratic field also included Brian Corcoran, longtime press secretary to Sen. Henry M. Jackson. Corcoran had Jackson's good will and tapped the senator's contributors. He had a weakness, though, in his tepid personal manner and inarticulate speaking style.

Swift, armed with the self-confidence generated by years in front of the camera, was the perfect challenger to take advantage of the problem. Starting from far behind, Swift defeated Corcoran by 3,881 votes.

Swift's next hurdle was Republican John Nance Garner, a namesake and distant relative of Franklin D. Roosevelt's vice president. Garner had nearly ousted Meeds in 1976, mainly because fishermen in the 2nd felt Meeds had not fought enough for them against Indian fishing claims. Garner spent lavishly against Swift in 1978, but no longer had the fishing-rights issue. Swift attacked Garner's heavy spending, turning a supposed advantage into a liability. The outcome was a 51 percent victory for Swift. In the five succeeding elections, Swift took 59 percent of the vote or better.

Committees

Energy & Commerce (6th of 27 Democrats)
Transportation & Hazardous Materials (chairman); Energy & Power

House Administration (5th of 15 Democrats)
Elections (chairman); Accounts

Elections

1990 General		
Al Swift (D)	92,837	(51%)
Doug Smith (R)	75,669	(41%)
William L. McCord (LIBERT)	15,165	(8%)
1990 Primary †		
Al Swift (D)	54,777	(61%)
Doug Smith (R)	25,382	(28%)
L.J. Mansholt (D)	3,288	(4%)
DeMilt Morse (D)	3,205	(4%)
William L. McCord (LIBERT)	3,065	(3%)
1988 General		
Al Swift (D)	175,191	(100%)

† In Washington's "jungle primary," candidates of all parties are listed on one ballot.

Previous Winning Percentages: **1986** (72%) **1984** (59%) **1982** (60%) **1980** (64%) **1978** (51%)

District Vote For President

	1988	1984
D	120,129 (50%)	104,670 (44%)
R	118,711 (50%)	130,640 (55%)

Campaign Finance

	Receipts	Receipts from PACs	Expend-itures
1990			
Swift (D)	$503,123	$272,542 (54%)	$465,249
Smith (R)	$11,408	0	$11,373
1988			
Swift (D)	$376,189	$286,312 (76%)	$301,229

Key Votes

1991	
Authorize use of force against Iraq	N
1990	
Support constitutional amendment on flag desecration	N
Pass family and medical leave bill over Bush veto	Y
Reduce SDI funding	Y
Allow abortions in overseas military facilities	Y
Approve budget summit plan for spending and taxing	Y
Approve civil rights bill	Y
1989	
Halt production of B-2 stealth bomber at 13 planes	N
Oppose capital gains tax cut	Y
Approve federal abortion funding in rape or incest cases	Y
Approve pay raise and revision of ethics rules	Y
Pass Democratic minimum wage plan over Bush veto	Y

Voting Studies

	Presidential Support		Party Unity		Conservative Coalition	
Year	S	O	S	O	S	O
1990	19	80	92	6	15	85
1989	31	65	93	4	27	73
1988	23	72	92	4	16	76
1987	21	78	92	4	21	77
1986	19	78	93	4	22	76
1985	26	73	93	5	29	69
1984	33	65	91 †	7 †	22	78
1983	18	80	91	4	11	89
1982	42	56	90	7	26	73
1981	43	55	86	14	31	69

† Not eligible for all recorded votes.

Interest Group Ratings

Year	ADA	ACU	AFL-CIO	CCUS
1990	89	4	92	21
1989	85	0	92	40
1988	90	0	85	36
1987	92	9	88	23
1986	90	9	79	18
1985	75	14	76	27
1984	80	4	77	33
1983	90	0	100	25
1982	85	14	100	23
1981	85	13	80	21

3 Jolene Unsoeld (D)

Of Olympia — Elected 1988

Born: Dec. 3, 1931, Corvallis, Ore.
Education: Attended Oregon State College, 1949-51.
Occupation: Public official.
Family: Widowed; three children.
Religion: Theist.
Political Career: Democratic National Committee, 1980-88; Wash. House, 1985-89.
Capitol Office: 1508 Longworth Bldg. 20515; 225-3536.

In Washington: A woman of boundless energy, Unsoeld began her second term with far more political security than might have been anticipated. She won re-election with a comfortable 54 percent after cinching her first term by a scant 618 votes.

But to gain that measure of political security, Unsoeld took a few positions that stunned her liberal backers, and she relied heavily on the good will of fellow Washington Democrat Thomas S. Foley. In his first term as Speaker, Foley was not about to lose a seat in his own back yard, and he made re-electing Unsoeld a pet cause. Democratic House members contributed more than $42,000 to her campaign treasury, and Unsoeld was the rare freshman to see more than a dozen bills or amendments with her name on them become law.

Known as a staunch liberal in the state Legislature, Unsoeld repaid Foley with a solidly Democratic voting record, casting more votes against Bush than anyone else in the delegation. But her liberal backers at home were dismayed when she set aside her past support for gun control to champion the National Rifle Association's views on semiautomatic assault weapons. "I don't think we should punish law-abiding citizens just because some law breakers have abused [the right to bear arms]," she said. "For me, it's a civil rights issue."

She authored an amendment to the 1990 crime bill that essentially gutted a prohibition on semiautomatic weapons by banning only firearms assembled with foreign parts. The amendment passed 257-172. In early 1991, she voted against requiring a seven-day waiting period for handgun purchases.

Unsoeld also offered successful legislation to increase funding for Drug Abuse Resistance Education (DARE), and to authorize the restoration of the Chehalis River, and fought for enhanced restrictions on high seas drift nets.

At Home: Unsoeld's hairbreadth election to Congress in 1988 turned her first re-election campaign into a national partisan slugfest. But the hard-hitting, big-spending, much-written-about contest proved to be less of a race than anticipated, with Unsoeld winning re-election by a healthy, if not massive, margin.

Unsoeld was not expected to have such difficulty in her first House campaign, to succeed Democratic Rep. Don Bonker in the reliably Democratic 3rd. But while Bonker had been regarded as a moderate, Unsoeld was seen mainly as a liberal activist.

Unsoeld entered politics as an independent lobbyist in Olympia on "good government" issues such as campaign finance reform. She won her first elective office, a state House seat, in 1984 and was best known in the Legislature for her work on the environment.

In 1988, Unsoeld won the Democratic nomination for the 3rd despite her opponent's claims that she was confrontational and anti-business.

However, Republican nominee Bill Wight used the same tactic to greater effect. While portraying Unsoeld as an extremist, Wight came off as thoughtful and more moderate than previous GOP nominees in the 3rd. A district native who returned in 1988, Wight was a retired Army lieutenant colonel who had worked as a Pentagon and Senate aide. His determination earned him media attention and national GOP money.

Unsoeld held an election night lead of more than 1,800 votes, but absentee ballots sliced into that advantage and a recount put her final victory margin at 618 votes.

That margin — the slimmest of any House victor nationwide — would have been enticement enough for the GOP. But Republicans got further encouragement from controversy over federal efforts to protect the northern spotted owl, which would threaten some logging jobs in districts such as the 3rd.

While Unsoeld tried to stake out a middle ground on the issue, Republican nominee Bob Williams, a former state representative and Weyerhaeuser accountant, took her to task for countenancing any job-threatening owl protections. National GOP leaders helped out with plenty of money and campaign appearances from administration officials.

But Unsoeld had prepared well for such an

Washington 3

Southwest — Olympia; Vancouver

The 3rd, stretching from Puget Sound west to the Pacific and south to the Columbia River border with Oregon, is heavy with maritime and timber interests. With its large number of blue-collar voters, it contains some of the most Democratic territory in the state.

In 1988, Democrat Michael S. Dukakis won in all but one of the eight counties that make up the 3rd. The three counties in the southwest corner — Cowlitz, Pacific and Wahkiakum — voted for Walter F. Mondale for president in 1984.

About two-thirds of the district vote comes from two counties: Thurston (Olympia) in the northern end, and Clark (Vancouver) in the south. Dukakis won each, but with narrow majorities.

Olympia, the state capital, is the largest city in Thurston County, but with only 34,000 people, it has a small-town atmosphere. Olympia's communities of environmental and "good government" activists — from which Unsoeld emerged — give Democrats a leg up in the county.

Clark County has seen its population surge with the growth of its Portland, Ore., suburbs. The aluminum industry is strong along the Columbia River. Vancouver, the district's largest city with 46,000 residents, is an industrial center.

The 3rd has vast stretches of woodland, including the scenic Coastal Range and much of the Cascade Mountains, with Mount Rainier just outside the eastern border. Timber thus dominates the economy of the interior, and in recent years there have been more downs than ups. The area's mills produce paper, timber and cardboard under the state's strict water-pollution standards. Logging is the central activity of Cowlitz County, which includes the cities of Longview and Kelso. Along the coast, fishing and dockwork are predominant, and labor unions are well entrenched among longshoremen.

Rural Lewis County provides the only dependable GOP majorities in the 3rd. George Bush took 62 percent there in 1988.

Population: 516,473. White 495,809 (96%), Black 3,070 (1%), Other 12,496 (2%). Spanish origin 8,264 (2%). 18 and over 360,673 (70%), 65 and over 55,166 (11%). Median age: 30.

onslaught. While bringing in federal flood aid and port dredging projects for the district, Unsoeld also had secured the money needed for a high-power campaign, reaching the half-million mark in contributions by early summer.

Unsoeld outpolled Williams in the September primary, in which all candidates ran on the same ballot. But she fell under attack from the left in October after sponsoring the amendment that aided domestic gun manufacturers, and subsequently accepting a $5,000 contribution from the National Rifle Association. Liberals had no place to go in the conservative Williams, however, and Unsoeld thwarted his challenge.

Committees

Education & Labor (15th of 25 Democrats)
Elementary, Secondary & Vocational Education; Labor-Management Relations; Postsecondary Education

Merchant Marine & Fisheries (23rd of 29 Democrats)
Fisheries & Wildlife Conservation & the Environment; Merchant Marine

Select Aging (32nd of 42 Democrats)
Housing & Consumer Interests

Elections

1990 General		
Jolene Unsoeld (D)	95,645	(54%)
Bob Williams (R)	82,269	(46%)
1990 Primary †		
Jolene Unsoeld (D)	48,891	(52%)
Bob Williams (R)	35,673	(38%)
Ned Norris (D)	5,644	(6%)
Gary L. Snell (R)	3,219	(3%)
1988 General		
Jolene Unsoeld (D)	109,390	(50%)
Bill Wight (R)	108,794	(50%)

† In Washington's "jungle primary," candidates of both parties are listed on one ballot.

District Vote For President

	1988	1984
D	109,731 (52%)	96,470 (45%)
R	108,290 (47%)	113,754 (53%)

Campaign Finance

	Receipts	Receipts from PACs		Expend-itures
1990				
Unsoeld (D)	$1,297,700	$624,498	(48%)	$1,298,593
Williams (R)	$829,603	$204,768	(25%)	$817,944
1988				
Unsoeld (D)	$690,711	$282,082	(41%)	$687,117
Wight (R)	$354,499	$161,379	(46%)	$354,142

Key Votes

1991	
Authorize use of force against Iraq	N
1990	
Support constitutional amendment on flag desecration	N
Pass family and medical leave bill over Bush veto	Y
Reduce SDI funding	+
Allow abortions in overseas military facilities	+
Approve budget summit plan for spending and taxing	N
Approve civil rights bill	Y
1989	
Halt production of B-2 stealth bomber at 13 planes	Y
Oppose capital gains tax cut	Y
Approve federal abortion funding in rape or incest cases	Y
Approve pay raise and revision of ethics rules	N
Pass Democratic minimum wage plan over Bush veto	Y

Voting Studies

	Presidential Support		Party Unity		Conservative Coalition	
Year	**S**	**O**	**S**	**O**	**S**	**O**
1990	15	76	90	4	13	80
1989	27	73	95	3	2	98

Interest Group Ratings

Year	ADA	ACU	AFL-CIO	CCUS
1990	83	9	92	36
1989	100	4	100	40

4 Sid Morrison (R)

Of Zillah — Elected 1980

Born: May 13, 1933, Yakima, Wash.
Education: Washington State U., B.S. 1954.
Military Service: Army, 1954-56.
Occupation: Fruit grower; nurseryman.
Family: Wife, Marcella Britton; four children.
Religion: Methodist.
Political Career: Wash. House, 1967-75; Wash. Senate, 1975-81.
Capitol Office: 1434 Longworth Bldg. 20515; 225-5816.

In Washington: Morrison's sprawling district forces him to focus his attention in a number of very different directions. Many 4th District residents are, like Morrison, fruit growers, and he must watch out for their interests on the Agriculture Committee. A number of his constituents also work in timber-related jobs, a major industry throughout much of the Northwest. And many of his neighbors also depend on nuclear-related jobs for their livelihood, making Morrison one of the industry's big boosters. Working for those tricky constituencies has made him a player in three national issues.

Two unexpected crises emerged during the 101st Congress to occupy much of Morrison's time and energy: the listing of the northern spotted owl as a threatened species and the furor over the use of the chemical Alar in the growing of apples.

In June 1990, the U.S. Fish and Wildlife Service listed the northern spotted owl as "threatened" — a decision that threatened the logging community. While Congress adopted a provision in 1989 trading reduced timber harvests and pledges to protect some owl habitats for a mandate that temporarily freed timber sales from most court-ordered bans, lawmakers such as Morrison prepared for the inevitable clash between environmental and industry forces.

Morrison succeeded in attaching to the 1990 farm bill a provision authorizing the Agriculture secretary to provide assistance — loans, grants, job training and brainpower — to help communities dependent on the timber industry develop and diversify their economies.

When a federal district judge agreed in February 1991 to forbid timbering in areas used by the spotted owl, Morrison teamed up with fellow Washingtonians Al Swift and Jolene Unsoeld, both Democrats, to push a long-term blueprint to protect timbering jobs, retrain workers, and identify "environmentally sustainable yields" of old-growth timber.

The Alar issue, meanwhile, arose after the airing in February 1989 of a segment on CBS' "60 Minutes" that focused on the hesitancy of the Environmental Protection Agency (EPA) to ban Alar, a chemical used to enhance the color, crispness and uniform ripening of apples.

Morrison's district produces more than half of the apples grown in the United States; the area's agricultural economy was jarred by the controversy over the chemical's alleged ill effects. To restore and revitalize the industry, Morrison pushed to get farmers to stop using the product, promoted a major government diversion program to offset the reduction in apple sales and supported more credible federal regulation of the chemical. The EPA announced in September 1989 a plan to phase out permanently the chemical's use; the apple industry bounced back from the scare and enjoyed a significant recovery.

The nuclear industry faced some serious challenges in the 1980s — particularly at the Hanford Nuclear Reservation in the Tri-Cities area of the 4th. Concerns about safety and about job losses have made Hanford a hot political issue in both Washington and Oregon.

The Tri-Cities received a major blow in 1988, when the Department of Energy (DOE) decided to mothball the "N Reactor," which was the centerpiece of the plutonium-production complex. Morrison, ranking Republican on the Science Subcommittee on Energy, had advocated restarting the reactor, but he had to settle for DOE's decision to maintain the reactor for possible future use.

In the 101st Congress, Morrison and the rest of the state delegation managed to fend off an administration attempt to close down the Fast Flux Test Facility (FFTF), a newer and highly advanced experimental reactor, and to secure funding for another year. The DOE in its 1991 budget proposal urged shutting down the reactor after deciding that plutonium-238, used to power space probes, could be produced more cheaply at South Carolina reactors.

Morrison and his Washington colleagues argued that the reactor should stay open if the state could get private and international partners committed to paying part of the FFTF's operating costs. The state launched a marketing

Washington 4

Central — Yakima; Tri-Cities

For nearly four decades, the Hanford Nuclear Reservation — site of much of the nation's nuclear weapons-materials production — was the healthy heart of a booming local economy in the Tri-Cities of Pasco, Kennewick and Richland. But these cities, located in the southeastern part of the 4th District, have been rocked in recent years by news that this economic heart, suffering from severe environment-related problems, needs surgery, if not a transplant.

In 1988, the federal government shut down Hanford's "N Reactor," a plutonium plant likened in design to the reactor in the Soviet city of Chernobyl, site of the world's worst nuclear accident. The shutdown resulted in the loss of 5,000 jobs, a huge setback in a two-county (Benton and Franklin) area of about 150,000 residents.

The Department of Energy then estimated that the cleanup of radioactive and other hazardous wastes that had accumulated at Hanford over the years would cost more than $57 billion to clean up. In February 1989, the state and federal governments reached agreement on a cleanup plan, which would return 2,000 jobs to the Hanford area. The project is expected to take at least 30 years to complete.

Earlier, Hanford was a key issue in the 1986 Senate race. The federal reservation was then being mentioned as a possible site for a permanent nuclear-waste depository, and Republican Sen. Slade Gorton took some blame from state voters for its inclusion on the list. Gorton was defeated that year by Democrat Brock Adams. By the time of Gorton's comeback victory in 1988, though, Hanford had been eliminated as a waste-dump site.

Though Gorton — who, while out of office, acted as a consultant to Hanford on efforts to keep its nuclear industry alive — may have some problems elsewhere in the state, he has solid support in the Tri-Cities. In 1988, he carried Benton and Franklin counties, where Republican tendencies are strong to begin with, with a combined 79 percent of the vote. George Bush won the counties with 64 percent.

The GOP also dominates Yakima County, one of the nation's premier apple-growing areas. The county, which includes the district's largest city, Yakima (population 55,000), gave Bush 56 percent.

The district contains a famous example of man's effort to control nature, and another of his limited ability to do so. On the Columbia River in Grant County is the Grand Coulee Dam, one of the largest construction projects in human history. But in the southwest corner of the district is Mount St. Helens, site of the explosive 1980 volcanic eruption that killed dozens of people and felled thousands of acres of timber.

Population: 516,426. White 463,119 (90%), Black 4,721 (1%), Other 16,897 (3%). Spanish origin 44,562 (9%). 18 and over 359,287 (70%), 65 and over 54,379 (11%). Median age: 29.

effort with the hopes of securing such a contract from the Japanese.

Morrison is also in pursuit of money to clean up the Hanford Reservation, which has now lost thousands of jobs, and says there were great successes in substantially achieving this effort during the 101st Congress. DOE's 1991 budget proposal urged a major emphasis on environmental restoration at Hanford, including increasing total spending at Hanford from $993 million in fiscal 1990 to $1.2 billion in fiscal 1991 and $1.6 billion by fiscal 1995.

In 1982, Morrison surprised many of his colleagues when he authored an amendment to ensure that Hanford would be considered as a possible site for the nation's first high-level nuclear-waste facility. "We don't want to be the nuclear dump for the world, but we are comfortable with nuclear energy," Morrison said.

By 1986, however, Morrison was considerably uneasy with Hanford's selection as one of three possible sites for the proposed nuclear dump. Morrison eventually turned against the plan, and was relieved when 100th Congress legislators picked Nevada for the waste site.

One of Morrison's most significant early legislative accomplishments stemmed from his interest in agriculture, but not farm policy directly. Morrison took a keen interest in immigration legislation that threatened growers' ability to use foreign laborers to harvest crops.

To maintain growers' ready access to "undocumented workers," Morrison joined with California Democrat Leon E. Panetta to express support for the twin goals of reform advocates — gaining control of U.S. borders and preventing the exploitation of illegal aliens. They argued for a flexible "guest worker" program.

Though they were strongly opposed by labor and by Hispanics, the lobbying combination of grower Morrison, a reasonable, moderate-to-conservative Republican, and lawyer Panetta, a Democrat with a reputation for integrity and compassion, was a persuasive one.

They got their plan through to the conference, where the bill died because of a separate controversy. An immigration bill eventually passed in 1986 — with foreign worker provisions.

At Home: Morrison's 1980 victory ended the 10-year reign of Democratic Rep. Mike McCormack, whose survival in the Republican-leaning 4th rested largely on the federal aid that he helped funnel to the area's nuclear industry.

Nuclear power was not at issue in 1980, since both candidates advocated it. Morrison instead chastised McCormack for being too frugal on defense spending. With help from a $400,000 treasury and a GOP surge that brought Washington Republicans the governorship and a U.S. Senate seat, Morrison won 57 percent. He has scored 70 percent or better in his five re-elections bids since.

In late 1987, Republican Sen. Daniel J. Evans announced he would not seek re-election the following year. With former GOP Sen. Slade Gorton, upset by Democrat Brock Adams in 1986, apparently in eclipse, Morrison was urged by party allies to run for the seat.

But Morrison, with his base in Washington's "Eastside," recognized that he was not well-known in the important Seattle media market, and conceded that his close identification with Hanford would likely make his a controversial candidacy. He opted instead for another easy House campaign. Meanwhile, Gorton re-emerged in the Senate contest and staged a successful comeback, defeating Democratic Rep. Mike Lowry.

Morrison's 14 years in the Washington Legislature prepared him for a House career. He forged a reputation in Olympia as an articulate centrist. As chairman of the state Senate Labor Committee, he sought to restrain unemployment compensation costs, but backed state housing subsidies for migrant laborers.

Committees

Agriculture (6th of 18 Republicans)
Forests, Family Farms & Energy (ranking); Department Operations, Research & Foreign Agriculture; Wheat, Soybeans & Feed Grains

Science, Space & Technology (6th of 19 Republicans)
Energy (ranking); Environment

Select Hunger (3rd of 12 Republicans)
Domestic

Elections

1990 General		
Sid Morrison (R)	106,545	(71%)
Ole Hougen (D)	44,241	(29%)
1990 Primary †		
Sid Morrison (R)	71,057	(77%)
Ole Hougen (D)	20,860	(23%)
1988 General		
Sid Morrison (R)	142,938	(75%)
J. Richard Golob (D)	48,850	(25%)

† In Washington's "jungle primary," candidates of both parties are listed on one ballot.

Previous Winning Percentages: **1986** (72%) **1984** (76%) **1982** (70%) **1980** (57%)

District Vote For President

	1988	1984
D	78,620 (42%)	74,423 (35%)
R	108,969 (58%)	134,302 (63%)

Campaign Finance

	Receipts	Receipts from PACs	Expend-itures
1990			
Morrison (R)	$111,371	$42,200 (38%)	$49,935
1988			
Morrison (R)	$202,637	$82,558 (41%)	$194,505
Golob (D)	$58,608	$5,750 (10%)	$58,574

Key Votes

1991	
Authorize use of force against Iraq	Y
1990	
Support constitutional amendment on flag desecration	Y
Pass family and medical leave bill over Bush veto	Y
Reduce SDI funding	N
Allow abortions in overseas military facilities	Y
Approve budget summit plan for spending and taxing	Y
Approve civil rights bill	N
1989	
Halt production of B-2 stealth bomber at 13 planes	N
Oppose capital gains tax cut	N
Approve federal abortion funding in rape or incest cases	Y
Approve pay raise and revision of ethics rules	Y
Pass Democratic minimum wage plan over Bush veto	N

Voting Studies

	Presidential Support		Party Unity		Conservative Coalition	
Year	**S**	**O**	**S**	**O**	**S**	**O**
1990	51	46	49	46	76	24
1989	67	31	51	49	68	32
1988	47	52	59	40	87	13
1987	52	46	52	43	86	12
1986	59	41	56	42	80	18
1985	59	40	72	25	84	15
1984	60	38	63	35	85	14
1983	68	28	67	26	79	19
1982	70	29	78	22	89	11
1981	74	26	83	17	92	8

Interest Group Ratings

Year	ADA	ACU	AFL-CIO	CCUS
1990	22	50	17	64
1989	20	68	17	100
1988	55	64	36	93
1987	40	52	25	67
1986	20	73	38	67
1985	25	71	29	82
1984	40	46	38	75
1983	20	57	13	80
1982	10	62	25	73
1981	5	93	7	100

5 Thomas S. Foley (D)

Of Spokane — Elected 1964

Born: March 6, 1929, Spokane, Wash.
Education: U. of Washington, B.A. 1951, LL.B. 1957.
Occupation: Lawyer.
Family: Wife, Heather Strachan.
Religion: Roman Catholic.
Political Career: No previous office.
Capitol Office: 1201 Longworth Bldg. 20515; 225-2006.

In Washington: In his first two years as Speaker, Foley neither disappointed his admirers nor confounded his critics. He has brought the judicious sort of presence to the job that had been expected — for better or for worse — presiding over the House as a kind of paterfamilias. While intensely political, he has generally defined his politics more in terms of the institution than in terms of its two parties. He is the leader of the House first, the leading figure among Democrats second.

"Above everything else, I am concerned about protecting the reputation and position of the House as an institution," Foley told *The Wall Street Journal* in May 1991. "It happens to be one of the foundations of Democratic Party influence in the country. That is not lost on me."

Indeed, Foley has moments of more partisan mien. He fought against the capital gains cut that emerged from Ways and Means in 1989. He took a prominent role in opposing the use of military force in the Persian Gulf early in 1991. But in neither case did he employ the pressure or parliamentary maneuvering he might have. Despite the knowledge that his side would not prevail, his central concern seemed to be allowing the House to work its will.

And, in the case of the Persian Gulf debate, he served both his overarching goals by positioning both the House and its majority to support the troops once the decision had been made.

More typically, Foley has sought to efface himself altogether, even on issues of longstanding interest to himself or his district. When the House was convulsed in debate over the seven-day waiting period for handgun purchases (the "Brady Bill") in May 1991, Foley seemed devoted to nothing so much as a fair shot for both sides. As he stood aside while the historic measure passed, one might not have known he had opposed gun control throughout his career.

"I want this to be decided by the members of the House without the imposition of any effort on my part to sway their decision," Foley said before the crucial vote on Brady and on a de facto substitute.

It is hard to imagine such a statement by Foley's predecessor as Speaker, Jim Wright of Texas. Wright played to win, assuming that the more power one had the more one was expected to use it. Before his resignation in June 1989 (under attack for alleged violations of House ethics standards), Wright had used every weapon a Speaker could wield in pursuit of policy objectives.

Because Wright pressed so hard, Foley's above-the-fray approach seems almost ethereal by contrast. Refreshing for most, it exasperates those who, on a given issue, view the Democrats as relatively rudderless.

Of course, both Wright and his predecessor, Thomas P. O'Neill Jr. of Massachusetts, held the top House job under different circumstances. When Ronald Reagan was president, his ideological administration seemed to call forth a like response from the House, the last citadel of Democratic hegemony (especially during the six years the GOP controlled the Senate).

The current relationship between Congress and the chief executive has been far more conciliatory on issues from Central America to the Clean Air Act. George Bush's less confrontational persona has allowed Foley to restore a more traditional aura to the Speakership. But while scholars may applaud, many members in both parties find this problematic.

Exhibit A for critics is the fiscal 1991 budget summit compromise, achieved after more than four months of talks. Bush's Republicans rankled at the deal's tax increases, and Foley found his troops unhappy about the tilt of the tax package and the depth of cuts in safety-net programs. When the deal reached the House floor in October, it was roundly rejected by majorities in both parties.

"We will stand our ground when that is the only way to stand for you," Foley had promised in giving the Democratic response to Bush's first State of the Union speech in January 1989. With their vote against the budget in 1990, House Democrats in effect reminded Foley of this pledge.

Washington 5

East — Spokane

The dominance of Democrat Foley in heavily rural eastern Washington is a bit of an anomaly. Though Democrats running for higher office can compete here, the 5th has a definite Republican tilt in contests for president and senator.

In 1984, Ronald Reagan took the 5th District with 60 percent of the vote. Democrat Michael S. Dukakis put up a battle four years later, but George Bush held the district with 51 percent. That year's Republican Senate victor, Slade Gorton, did even better, taking the 5th with 53 percent. Democratic Gov. Booth Gardner won here, as he did throughout the state, but with a margin that fell short of his landslide advantages elsewhere.

The candidate who wins Spokane is almost certain to carry the district. The city of 177,000 is Washington's second largest. Spokane County, one of 11 counties in the district, contributes two-thirds of the district vote. Bush won the county in 1988, but just barely: His margin was 267 votes out of over 137,000 cast.

Spokane is the banking and marketing center of the "Inland Empire," which encompasses wheat- and vegetable-farming counties in Washington, Oregon, Idaho and Montana. The city's sizable aluminum industry takes advantage of the low-cost hydroelectric power that comes from New Deal dams along the Columbia River. Comparatively isolated and marked by a stable, non-transient population, Spokane is one of the most conservative of America's large cities.

Walla Walla County, dominated for generations by a small group of farming families, bolsters Republican chances in the district. Bush got 57 percent in the county in 1988; Reagan took 65 percent in 1984. The district's third-largest county, Whitman, is the site of Washington State University (17,000 students) in Pullman. Republicans usually win Whitman, but do not necessarily dominate; Bush carried the county with 51 percent.

The rest of the district is mainly rural, sparsely populated and generally Republican. But Ferry County, in the district's northwest corner, could not have been more evenly split in 1988; Bush and Dukakis each received 972 votes.

Population: 516,719. White 489,609 (95%), Black 5,705 (1%), Other 13,486 (3%). Spanish origin 11,700 (2%). 18 and over 373,789 (72%), 65 and over 59,889 (12%). Median age: 29.

Foley had known other frustrations in the 101st Congress. He could not stop the House from passing a cut in the capital gains tax because he could not stop 64 Democrats from voting with the GOP. Before the vote there had been whispers of ominous threats from leadership. After the vote, Foley said, "I don't work that way." The next question was: Why not? Said one Democratic defector, "The strongest words I heard from Tom were, 'I'm really disappointed you are doing this.' "

But however strong the Democrats' desire for fiery torch-bearing and imposed discipline may become, it is unlikely either will ever come from Foley. His moderate, understated style has changed little, if at all, through a House career now nearing the end of its third decade.

He has risen to be second in line to the presidency (after the vice president) without having once displayed the kind of vaunting ambition usually associated with such success. Even his first candidacy for Congress in 1964 was reluctantly undertaken at the urging of others.

For years, his admirers — Democratic and Republican, academic and journalistic — have called him uniquely qualified to be Speaker of the House. A cerebral man with a sense of detachment rare among politicians, Foley is perfectly matched to a job meant to be above partisanship.

Most observers had expected Wright to serve multiple terms as Speaker, leaving little if any time for Foley to hold the job. Instead, the Texan became the first Speaker ever forced from office in disgrace. His departure left the House boiling with the bitterest interparty resentments in many years.

Foley was then in his third year as majority leader and naturally in line to succeed Wright. No Democrat contested the succession, and the gavel was passed to him on a party-line vote of 251-164 on June 9, 1989.

Foley had been following Wright in the Democrats' batting order since 1981, when O'Neill had chosen him as majority whip (with Wright's assent). There is no evidence that Foley actively sought the whip job at that time. Nor has he been perceived as pursuing any of the other posts he has won before or since.

He became a subcommittee chairman on the Agriculture Committee, then chairman of the Democratic Study Group, chairman of the full Agriculture Committee and chairman of the House Democratic Caucus before becoming whip.

Throughout his rise, Foley has been on good terms with nearly all Democrats and a remarkable number of Republicans, who typically referred to him as their party's favorite Democrat. But at the time of his election as Speaker, the House was a cauldron of unusually hot and personal emotions.

Besides Wright, the Democratic leadership had just lost the man below Foley on the ladder, Majority Whip Tony Coelho of California. A hard-driven fundraiser who had propelled the party's congressional electoral successes, Coelho had announced in May that he would resign to avoid an inquiry into his personal finances.

For Democrats in that season, Foley held out a hope of healing. To Republicans, he offered his reputation for rising above partisanship. In his first remarks as Speaker, he called for debate "with reason and without rancor."

But even in the first hours of his Speakership he was confronted with a partisan assault. A memo circulated by the Republican National Committee's (RNC) press office referred to Foley as "coming out of the liberal closet." It also compared him to Barney Frank of Massachusetts, a liberal who has publicly declared himself a homosexual.

President Bush pronounced the memo "disgusting," and its author promptly resigned. Foley, in a characteristic response, calmly denied the memo's implication and accepted the apologies of embarrassed Republicans. "A very cheap smear," he said. "I think the issue is closed."

It may be that the personal attack, and the ensuing outrage and shame, released some of the pressure that had built in the House during Wright's yearlong ethics trauma. Foley himself had survived those months of limbo with both his loyalty to Wright and his personal integrity intact.

Foley's principal reputation has been that of a parliamentarian and negotiator. He grew up wanting to be a judge, and it shows: "Heightening tension is just another technique," Foley says, "and it is not one I find particularly congenial."

He does not like to commit himself early on controversial issues, and he can be as skillful at making the case for the opposing side as for his own. "I think I am a little cursed," he once said, "with seeing the other point of view and trying to understand it."

Foley is also a gradualist, skeptical of grand schemes and inclined at times to ask whether difficult problems can be solved legislatively at all. As he said of the 1985 farm bill he helped craft: "There is only so much that government policy can do. An agriculture bill can't turn around world economic decisions."

Although a Westerner by birth and bidding (the first Speaker from west of the Rocky Mountains), Foley is a notably formal man who prefers to campaign in a suit and wing-tip shoes, even in the rural stretches of his mammoth district. For many years, Foley's distinguishing personal characteristic was the contrast between his imposing size (more than 6 foot 3 inches and well over 200 pounds) and his disarming affability. But in 1990 and 1991 he adopted a rigorous regimen of diet and exercise. The ensuing weight loss (more than 80 pounds) slimmed him enough to narrow his face and give new emphasis to his ears.

Foley is admired not only for his temperament but for the superior quality of his mind. Staff members say he can leave a meeting and repeat almost verbatim what each participant said. Even rarer than such intelligence, in the House, is Foley's intellectuality. He has an interest in ideas and a taste for the arts. His conversation is rich with select words and historical allusions. An audiophile, his expensive equipment is primarily devoted to classical fare.

Foley won the Agriculture chairmanship in 1975 in unusual circumstances that prefigured those that would make him Speaker 14 years later. The huge bloc of "Watergate baby" Democrats that year was determined to unseat some of the aging, conservative House chairmen. One of these was W. R. Poage of Texas, who, while popular within his Agriculture Committee, was 75 years old and highly conservative. The caucus unseated Poage by a vote of 152-133. Foley opposed the move and stood by the incumbent. He even gave Poage's nominating speech. But when Poage was beaten, the insurgents promoted Foley over several more senior members of the panel.

Foley was a strong Agriculture chairman — one of his best arguments against critics who said he would be indecisive in the leadership — but he operated almost entirely through conciliation. When circumstances seemed to require confrontation, he was less effective. Chairing a committee meeting, he was sometimes reluctant to bang the gavel even against a member who seemed to be asking for it.

Foley has risen slowly and cautiously in Democratic ranks, taking advantage of his reputation as a good legislative manager. In 1974 he chaired the Democratic Study Group, the strategy and research arm of liberal and moderate Democrats. In 1977 the chairmanship of the Democratic Caucus was open, and as a veteran of numerous reform battles against secrecy and seniority in the committee system, he was a logical choice. He defeated Shirley Chisholm of New York by a vote of 194-96. His four years as chairman were not particularly lively; few important decisions were made and Foley chose not to be an activist.

In 1980 the defeat of John Brademas of Indiana forced Speaker O'Neill to choose a new whip. Chief Deputy Whip Dan Rostenkowski of Illinois, first in line for promotion, decided instead to take over the Ways and Means Committee. Some Democrats urged O'Neill to select a whip from among the 1970s Democratic generation, but O'Neill was looking for parliamentary skill in the coming arguments with House Republicans. Foley was a parliamentary expert, and he got the job.

In 1982, President Reagan had been persuaded to support $98 billion worth of tax increases over a three-year period as a means of bringing down the federal deficit. Speaker O'Neill favored the plan and asked Foley to make the case for it on national television, hoping to create a climate in which wavering Democrats might go along with the legislation.

Foley responded with a masterly television speech, quietly urging members of both parties to summon up "political courage" and cast a vote in favor of "economic reality." He seemed far more comfortable delivering that speech than he had seemed offering more partisan rhetoric in other settings. Afterward, other Democrats speculated that he might have influenced 60 votes on their side of the aisle. Said O'Neill at the time: "A star is born."

Once firmly established on the leadership ladder, he solidified his support with deft handling of several major legislative issues in the 99th Congress. He played a crucial role in drafting the 1985 farm bill and was active in House Democrats' fight against providing military aid to the Nicaraguan contras.

His consensus-building skills proved essential to the House leadership's strategy for handling the Gramm-Rudman-Hollings budget-cutting measure after it was passed by the Senate. Some House Democrats wished simply to oppose the measure and wanted no part of making it more palatable. But Foley's head counts showed that Gramm-Rudman could not be defeated outright.

He coaxed a consensus out of liberal and conservative Democrats about what changes should be made in the law — such as protections for certain antipoverty programs — and the House alternative won the support of all but two Democrats.

When Speaker O'Neill first announced his plan to retire at the end of the 99th Congress, Foley did not seem to be guaranteed the No. 2 job in the ensuing leadership shake-up. Some members initially expressed a desire for a more partisan figure, but no challenger emerged. Foley was elected majority leader by acclamation.

As the 100th Congress began, Foley sometimes seemed uncomfortable as he sought to define a role for himself alongside Wright, who appeared reluctant to give up all the duties of majority leader upon his accession to the speakership. At times, Foley seemed to be trying out a more confrontational style, as when he concluded debate on aid to the Nicaraguan contras with a speech delivered at a decibel level unusual for him.

Sometimes, as floor leader, Foley appeared to be carrying out a strategy he personally questioned. He himself allows that the notorious "overtime" vote on the reconciliation bill of 1987 (which included a tax increase) had been a mistake. The leadership kept open the vote long enough for one Democrat to switch his "no" vote and pass the bill. Republicans cried foul, but Wright was not about to be denied passage of legislation he considered critical.

At Home: In the course of little more than a decade, Foley took over a Republican district, made himself invincible in it and then almost let it slip out of his hands. It took years of political repair work for him to get it under control again.

Foley wanted to be a judge, as his father was. He spent two years as deputy prosecutor in Spokane County and a year as assistant state attorney general. In 1961 he moved to Washington, D.C., to work for Sen. Henry M. Jackson as counsel to the Senate Interior Committee.

Three years later he was a reluctant congressional candidate, persuaded to run by the favorable political climate for Democrats, by Jackson's encouragement and by a Spokane politico who taunted him about the race on the day before the filing deadline. Foley managed to file with minutes to spare. He had no primary competition because no other Democrats wanted to challenge Republican Walt Horan, who had held the seat since 1942. But Horan was ailing at 66, and Foley had fundraising help from Jackson and Sen. Warren Magnuson, as well as the advantage of the Johnson presidential landslide. He upset the incumbent in November by 12,000 votes.

After 1964, Foley worked hard to keep his district, and by 1970 Republicans had stopped running strong candidates against him.

But in 1976 he made a political mistake. Republican nominee Charles Kimball was killed in an airplane crash the month before the election, and Foley essentially stopped campaigning. That allowed Duane Alton, a politically unknown tire dealer from Spokane, to hold him under 60 percent of the vote.

The 1976 result convinced Republicans that Foley was vulnerable, and Alton ran again in 1978. As Agriculture chairman, Foley had become a target for resentment over farm issues among his wheat-growing constituents, and his low profile in the district gave Alton another issue. Even worse for the incumbent, Indian tribal official Mel Tonasket ran as an independent and took away Democratic votes.

Alton was an inarticulate candidate, and his militant conservatism was too much for many moderate Republican voters. Yet Foley scraped by with just 48 percent to 43 percent for Alton.

Again in 1980, Republicans had high

hopes. Foley's opponent this time was John Sonneland, a Spokane surgeon who had once served as state co-chairman of Common Cause. Sonneland moved to the right, calling Foley a fiscally irresponsible liberal and airing television ads accusing the incumbent of having voted to allow experimentation on fetuses.

The incumbent campaigned hard, stressing his more conservative ideas, such as a tax cut and congressional veto of federal regulations produced by the executive branch. Foley recaptured most of the vote he had lost to Tonasket in 1978, but the GOP tide left him with a career-low margin of scarcely 7,000 votes.

Sonneland was back in 1982, replacing the more strident personal attacks with attempts to convince voters that Foley had placed national interests above local concerns. "Do voters want to push someone who is ascending the political ladder," Sonneland asked during a debate, "or someone who will go to the mat?"

Such charges might have succeeded a few years earlier. But Sonneland's 1980 failure in a statewide GOP sweep marked him as a loser to national Republicans, hurting him financially. Meanwhile Foley, chastened by a pair of close calls, paid renewed attention to the district. He not only trounced Sonneland by nearly 2 to 1 in their mutual home base of Spokane County, but also carried most of the 5th District's rural counties for the first time in several elections.

Thereafter, the respect Foley accrued, both nationally and locally, as an honest and temperate Democratic leader became his political armor. By 1984 he was up to 70 percent against Spokane City Councilman Jack Hebner.

In 1990, even amid public grouchiness toward congressional incumbents, Foley got 69 percent.

Despite his rising prominence, Foley exhibited no more interest in running for statewide office than he did in suggestions from some quarters in 1988 that he would be an ideal vice presidential choice for Michael S. Dukakis. That same year, GOP Sen. Daniel J. Evans announced his retirement, but early on Foley made it clear that he would not be a candidate in the Senate contest.

Speaker of the House

Elections

1990 General		
Thomas S. Foley (D)	110,234	(69%)
Marlyn A. Derby (R)	49,965	(31%)
1988 General		
Thomas S. Foley (D)	160,654	(76%)
Marlyn A. Derby (R)	49,657	(24%)

Previous Winning Percentages: **1986** (75%) **1984** (70%) **1982** (64%) **1980** (52%) **1978** (48%) **1976** (58%) **1974** (64%) **1972** (81%) **1970** (67%) **1968** (57%) **1966** (57%) **1964** (53%)

District Vote For President

	1988	1984
D	98,331 (48%)	85,833 (39%)
R	103,841 (51%)	133,109 (60%)

Campaign Finance

	Receipts	Receipts from PACs		Expend-itures
1990				
Foley (D)	$467,084	$326,337	(70%)	$457,754
Derby (R)	$7,154	$375	(5%)	$5,006
1988				
Foley (D)	$968,013	$555,140	(57%)	$663,278
Derby (R)	$13,833	0		$13,534

Key Votes

1991	
Authorize use of force against Iraq	N
1990	
Support constitutional amendment on flag desecration	N
Approve budget summit plan for spending and taxing	Y
1989	
Approve pay raise and revision of ethics rules	Y

Voting Studies

	Presidential Support		Party Unity		Conservative Coalition	
Year	**S**	**O**	**S**	**O**	**S**	**O**
1990	40	60	100	0	0	100
1989	27	73	97	0	17	83
1988	23	67	91	4	21	76
1987	25	71	90	4	30	58
1986	23	73	91	4	40	54
1985	29	71	90	3	29	69
1984	38	57	81	12	32	56
1983	29	59	83	8	25	55
1982	39	51	83	12	40	55
1981	54	45	80	17	51	45

Interest Group Ratings

Year	ADA	ACU	AFL-CIO	CCUS
1990	-	0	-	-
1989	-	0	100	-
1988	85	4	86	38
1987	80	9	87	27
1986	75	14	86	33
1985	75	10	76	27
1984	80	26	54	56
1983	85	13	81	32
1982	65	27	79	33
1981	55	13	73	32

6 Norm Dicks (D)

Of Bremerton — Elected 1976

Born: Dec. 16, 1940, Bremerton, Wash.
Education: U. of Washington, B.A. 1963, J.D. 1968.
Occupation: Congressional aide.
Family: Wife, Suzanne Callison; two children.
Religion: Lutheran.
Political Career: No previous office.
Capitol Office: 2429 Rayburn Bldg. 20515; 225-5916.

In Washington: On Appropriations, Dicks is something like a bull let loose in an exclusive china shop. And in recent years, he has been known as a prize bull, a point man for his fellow Washingtonian, Speaker Thomas S. Foley.

Dicks found his way to Appropriations early in his House career as the protégé of Sen. Warren G. Magnuson, once an Appropriations giant. While the younger man mirrors the wheeling and dealing that made Magnuson famous, Dicks adds an aggressive style. Even Magnuson used to say that the problem with his smart, headstrong aide, a former Rose Bowl linebacker, was that he was always five yards offside.

Indeed, there is nothing subtle about Dicks. On the normally collegial Appropriations panel, he is intense and full of bluster. On the floor, with handshakes, pats on the back and even bear hugs, he makes his case bluntly and repeatedly, annoying his opponents but frequently wearing them down nonetheless.

Dicks relishes the game itself. His field is defense policy, and he has been involved in nearly every major debate in recent years. Knowledgeable about weapons systems and strategies, Dicks has emerged as a moderate on defense spending. While he stakes his case on national security concerns, Dicks is plainly parochial. He keeps an eye on the interests of Boeing Co., a crucial employer in Washington state, and on funds for naval installations and shipbuilding facilities on Puget Sound.

Dicks' reputation as an opponent of deep defense cuts helped exempt him from criticism that Foley had stacked the Intelligence Committee with liberals at the start of the 102nd Congress. Dicks, one of several new additions to Intelligence, was quickly identified as "the Speaker's man" on the panel.

In many ways, he is well suited for the role. Dicks aspires to be a part of the inside maneuverings that enable the leadership to advance its agenda, and that dominate life in the Appropriations netherworld. He cracked an important inner circle in 1985 when he complained that junior members were being left out of House-Senate appropriations conferences. The so-called "College of Cardinals," the 13 Appropriations subcommittee chairmen, gave new slots at the conferences to Dicks and others. Today, Dicks is not far in seniority from becoming a "Cardinal" himself.

In December 1990, as the nation appeared headed toward war with Iraq, Dicks played a pivotal role in moderating the response of House Democrats. The caucus met to approve a non-binding resolution stating that the president should seek congressional authorization before launching a military strike. But Dicks, together with Louisianian W. J. "Billy" Tauzin, won caucus approval for language stipulating that the president could move immediately if American lives were in danger, asserting Democratic support for the U.S. defense of Saudi Arabia and demanding Iraq's immediate withdrawal from Kuwait.

Dicks acknowledged that a poll showing lopsided public support for war with Iraq influenced his decision. "Frankly, a lot of people were a little surprised about the ... poll, and that tempered some views," he said.

On controversial weapons systems, Dicks' record appears carefully crafted. He is a leading congressional supporter of the B-2 bomber, and a supporter of Democratic efforts to substantially pare funding for the strategic defense initiative. On the MX missile, Dicks is among the centrists, who in recent years have sought to ensure that the Midgetman missile is not jettisoned once the rail-MX is in place.

Dicks arrived at the middle ground on MX the hard way. When President Ronald Reagan said he needed the MX in order to negotiate with the Soviet Union from a position of strength, Dicks chose to accept the premise that the administration would negotiate seriously. Readying a fight with his party's left, he wrote a letter to Reagan in 1983 asking for assurances that MX development would be part of an arms control negotiating strategy, not an alternative to it. Reagan's "Dear Norm" letter giving those assurances led the Defense Appropriations Subcommittee to approve the MX by a 9-3 vote.

Washington 6

Puget Sound — Bremerton; Tacoma

Maritime interests dominate the 6th, which surrounds the sinuous waterways of the Puget Sound and the Hood Canal. Docks, naval installations and shipbuilding centers maintain the peninsula's historic links with the sea.

With 177,000 residents, industrial Tacoma (Washington's third-largest city) is the district's population center; the city's 12 percent growth in the 1980s left it just 600 people shy of Spokane.

Like much of the Seattle region, Tacoma's fortunes tend to follow the cycles of Boeing's aircraft business. But the city is less dependent on the huge aerospace firm than is Seattle. Commerce at the dockyards of Tacoma's deepwater port has enjoyed brisk growth. The wood-products and metal-smelting industries are also vital elements in the city's economy.

Tacoma's blue-collar, heavily unionized electorate generally tilts Pierce County to Democrats with moderate profiles. Dicks has dominated here, as has Democratic Gov. Booth Gardner, who served as county executive before his first election as governor in 1984.

But for liberal candidates, the county can be dicey. Michael S. Dukakis hung on there with 51 percent in 1988, but the Democratic Senate candidate, Rep. Mike Lowry from Seattle's 7th District, lost by a narrow margin.

Much of the Republican strength in the district has to do with its large military contingent. With its numerous defense facilities, the area was under the microscope when a federal commission studied possible closures and realignments of military bases in late 1988. In the end, though, the 6th wound up a gainer. McChord Air Force Base and the Army's Fort Lewis, both in Tacoma, gained 900 military and civilian positions under the plan.

Low housing prices and a high quality of life led to a number one ranking for Bremerton (population 36,000) on *Money* magazine's 1990 list of "Best places to live."

The city, located on the Kitsap Peninsula, has a strong labor vote, but surrounding Kitsap County (much of which is in the 1st District) leans Republican; George Bush carried Kitsap in 1988 by just under 1,000 votes.

Population: 516,561. White 451,581 (87%), Black 31,675 (6%), Other 23,224 (5%). Spanish origin 14,660 (3%). 18 and over 374,063 (72%), 65 and over 50,932 (10%). Median age: 28.

Then, forming an alliance with Democrats Les Aspin of Wisconsin and Al Gore of Tennessee, Dicks helped fend off anti-MX amendments on the floor in the remaining months of the 98th Congress and in early 1985, when money for 21 missiles finally cleared.

Dicks traveled to Geneva in March 1985 to watch Reagan's negotiators follow through on his promise to try harder for an agreement with the Soviets. But the Geneva sessions yielded little. In June, the House again faced the MX question, and this time Dicks joined a coalition of MX opponents who won a permanent limit on the number of missiles deployed.

Early in the Reagan years, when the issue was a nuclear-weapons freeze, Dicks acted as a conciliator. He was not among the early activists. But by the time the House finally endorsed the concept in May 1983, after more than 40 hours of debate, Dicks had made himself a force in the negotiations. By offering an amendment that allowed the freeze to lapse if no actual progress was made in reducing nuclear weapons, Dicks cleared the way for a final vote on the proposal.

Earlier in his career, Dicks maneuvered his way through several major controversies affecting his state's aircraft industry. In 1981, he engineered a reversal of a House vote, winning back money for the Export-Import Bank, which channels business to Boeing. The next year Dicks argued unsuccessfully but vehemently for use by the military of Boeing 747 planes, instead of Lockheed's C-5, for transport purposes.

From his seat on the Interior Subcommittee, Dicks has monitored the Department of Energy's share of SDI funding. He is in a fulcrum position on the emerging issue of cleaning up waste that has accumulated for decades at the nation's nuclear-weapons plants. A near neighbor of the nation's largest such facility at Hanford, Wash., he has strong environmental concerns about such waste. On forestry questions that come before the Interior Subcommittee, Dicks tends to side with industry forces seeking more development. In the 101st Congress, he helped negotiate the temporary compromise on the spotted owl.

At Home: After three years as administrative assistant to Magnuson, Dicks decided to go home in 1976 and run for Congress. He had been planning a campaign in the 6th District whenever incumbent Democrat Floyd Hicks chose to retire, and when Hicks was named to the state Supreme Court in 1976, Dicks began running with his usual intensity.

He had to compete with three major candidates for the nomination: a young activist state representative, a former president of Pacific Lutheran University and the mayor of Tacoma. But Dicks' ability to tap the resources of labor and other interest groups helped him put together a winning coalition. He won the primary with 36 percent of the vote.

Dicks had no trouble against a weak Republican that fall, but he went on a slide in the next two elections, pestered by Republican James Beaver, a conservative law professor from Tacoma. Dicks managed to clear 60 percent in 1978, but in 1980, Beaver was buoyed by financial support from the New Right, and held Dicks to 54 percent.

After that narrow escape, Dicks took steps to ensure that his 1982 race would not be so close. He took out full-page newspaper ads to tell voters that "Stormin' Norman" was as effective in the House as he had been on the college gridiron.

While Beaver had attacked the incumbent from the right, Dicks' 1982 challenger, GOP state Sen. Ted Haley, was more liberal. Haley painted the incumbent as a profligate spender too friendly with military contractors. But that charge just gave Dicks an excuse to talk about the pork he had brought home. He claimed credit for the completion of the Tacoma Spur Highway and numerous Navy ship overhauls at Bremerton. Dicks' 63 percent tally indicated he was moving toward security, and he has since won decisive re-election victories.

Republican Sen. Daniel J. Evans' decision to retire in 1988 at first piqued Dicks' interest. But two of his Democratic House colleagues, Mike Lowry and Don Bonker, jumped into the Senate contest, and Dicks recognized he faced an uncertain future as the most conservative candidate in a primary dominated by liberal voters. He stayed put in the 6th.

Committees

Appropriations (14th of 37 Democrats)
Defense; Interior; Military Construction

Select Intelligence (8th of 12 Democrats)
Legislation; Program & Budget Authorization

Elections

1990 General		
Norm Dicks (D)	79,079	(61%)
Norbert Mueller (R)	49,786	(39%)
1990 Primary †		
Norm Dicks (D)	38,346	(58%)
Mike Collier (D)	14,772	(22%)
Norbert Mueller (R)	13,117	(20%)
1988 General		
Norm Dicks (D)	125,904	(68%)
Kevin P. Cook (R)	60,346	(32%)

† In Washington's "jungle primary," candidates of all parties are listed on one ballot.

Previous Winning Percentages: **1986** (71%) **1984** (66%) **1982** (63%) **1980** (54%) **1978** (61%) **1976** (74%)

District Vote For President

	1988	1984
D	98,904 (51%)	82,214 (42%)
R	93,952 (48%)	111,116 (57%)

Campaign Finance

	Receipts	Receipts from PACs		Expend-itures
1990				
Dicks (D)	$392,043	$240,055	(61%)	$565,257
Mueller (R)	$8,048	0		$7,598
1988				
Dicks (D)	$366,934	$213,239	(58%)	$288,168
Cook (R)	$38,551	$1,922	(5%)	$35,445

Key Votes

1991	
Authorize use of force against Iraq	N
1990	
Support constitutional amendment on flag desecration	N
Pass family and medical leave bill over Bush veto	Y
Reduce SDI funding	Y
Allow abortions in overseas military facilities	Y
Approve budget summit plan for spending and taxing	Y
Approve civil rights bill	Y
1989	
Halt production of B-2 stealth bomber at 13 planes	N
Oppose capital gains tax cut	Y
Approve federal abortion funding in rape or incest cases	Y
Approve pay raise and revision of ethics rules	Y
Pass Democratic minimum wage plan over Bush veto	Y

Voting Studies

	Presidential Support		Party Unity		Conservative Coalition	
Year	**S**	**O**	**S**	**O**	**S**	**O**
1990	28	70	91	8	37	63
1989	38	57	91	7	41	59
1988	29	68	90	7	53	47
1987	28	71	87	5	42	51
1986	27	73	90	7	46	54
1985	35	61	85	9	44	53
1984	43	49	79	15	54	42
1983	38	61	83	11	34	60
1982	40	53	89	8	36	63
1981	50	42	68	24	60	35

Interest Group Ratings

Year	ADA	ACU	AFL-CIO	CCUS
1990	83	4	92	21
1989	75	7	91	40
1988	85	9	86	36
1987	76	9	88	13
1986	70	23	79	28
1985	70	24	88	38
1984	70	13	62	38
1983	75	13	94	32
1982	65	10	90	23
1981	50	27	80	42

7 Jim McDermott (D)

Of Seattle — Elected 1988

Born: Dec. 28, 1936, Chicago, Ill.

Education: Wheaton College, B.S. 1958; U. of Illinois, M.D. 1963.

Military Service: Navy Medical Corps, 1968-70.

Occupation: Psychiatrist.

Family: Divorced; two children.

Religion: Episcopalian.

Political Career: Wash. House, 1971-73; Wash. Senate, 1975-87; sought Democratic nomination for governor, 1972, 1984; Democratic nominee for governor, 1980.

Capitol Office: 1707 Longworth Bldg. 20515; 225-3106.

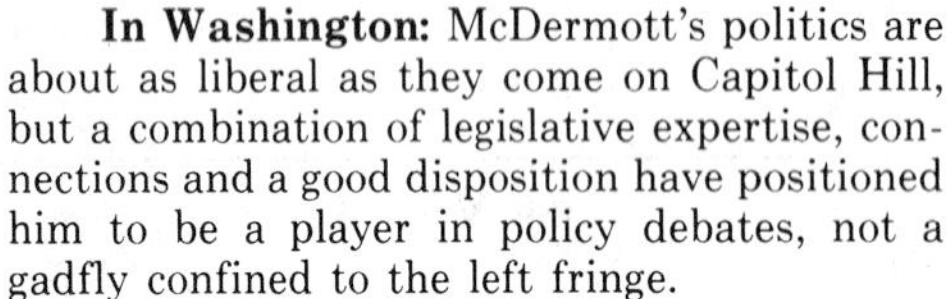

In Washington: McDermott's politics are about as liberal as they come on Capitol Hill, but a combination of legislative expertise, connections and a good disposition have positioned him to be a player in policy debates, not a gadfly confined to the left fringe.

As early as fall 1989, McDermott was talked up for a vacancy on Ways and Means by virtue of his expertise on health issues and his home-state ties to Speaker Thomas S. Foley. McDermott was passed over that time, but he made the panel in the 102nd Congress.

McDermott, who is one of just two physicians in the House, wanted the seat to pursue his goal of national health insurance. While a Washington state legislator, he wrote legislation creating state-sponsored health coverage for the unemployed and uninsured working poor. As a House freshman, he sponsored a bill to help states plan health care initiatives that could later serve as models for a national program.

One of McDermott's first-term committee assignments was Banking, and there too he pursued a health-related concern: housing for AIDS victims. Despite strong opposition from Republicans, McDermott was instrumental in winning a $156 million authorization for housing assistance for people with AIDS.

He also spoke for AIDS victims during debate on the Americans with Disabilities Act, opposing an amendment to allow restaurants to transfer workers with contagious diseases out of food-handling jobs. Alluding to medical evidence that AIDS cannot be spread through food, McDermott said, "This amendment asks us to make policy in spite of the facts we know, in deliberate deference to the fears and prejudices of others." The amendment passed.

McDermott, who sports a full silver beard and a ready sense of humor, is well-liked by colleagues. His personality, his choice of issues and a pragmatic attitude about how legislatures work have helped him build influence, even as he has taken some positions that are clearly outside his party's mainstream. In the early stages of the Persian Gulf War, for example, McDermott was among 42 legislators who wrote to President Bush urging against further military escalation such as a ground offensive.

At Home: Even from a continent away, the 1988 open-seat race for the 7th caught McDermott's eye. The former state senator left his job in Africa to stage a political comeback.

McDermott's earlier political career included more than 14 years in the state Legislature, and three unsuccessful campaigns for governor. But in 1987 McDermott quit the state Senate to take a three-year job in Zaire as a Foreign Service psychiatrist.

When 7th District Democrat Mike Lowry tried for the Senate in 1988, replacement talk centered on Democrats closer to home, such as Seattle City Councilman Norm Rice and King County Assessor Ruthe Ridder. Then, in February McDermott sent word from Zaire that he had gotten a release from his Foreign Service commitment and would seek Lowry's seat.

With his record as a legislative leader and visibility from statewide campaigns, he soon became the front-runner. He got endorsements from the state labor council and most local party organizations. He had more money, and won the primary after a late media blitz. In the strongly Democratic 7th, McDermott's November win was a given, as was his 1990 re-election.

Born in Chicago, McDermott moved to Seattle in 1966 to set up a practice, then left for a stint as a Navy psychiatrist in Long Beach, Calif. In 1970 he came back and won a state House race. In 1972 he ran third in the Democratic gubernatorial primary. After winning state Senate elections in 1974 and 1978, he challenged Democratic Gov. Dixy Lee Ray in the 1980 primary. He beat the conservative Ray, but then lost to Republican John Spellman. His third try for governor flopped, as he lost by nearly 2-to-1 in a 1984 primary against Booth Gardner (who unseated Spellman).

Washington 7

Seattle and Suburbs

Clear-blue Puget Sound, Mount Rainier looming to the east — these images identify Seattle to most people. The city's pleasant aura, combined with its thriving economy rooted in the aerospace industry and Pacific trade, have drawn thousands of newcomers to the Seattle area in recent years.

However, the downside of that growth — gridlocked streets and highways, a skyline crowded with office towers — has sparked widespread concern that Seattle is becoming a less livable place. A burgeoning slow-growth movement scored a big victory in May 1989, with the passage of an initiative placing strict limits on downtown Seattle development.

The downtown growth in recent years has been commercial only; the residential boom is in the suburbs. Seattle's population (about 516,000) actually slipped slightly in the early 1980s, before rebounding to post a 5 percent increase for the decade.

The core of that population is in South Seattle, which has a working-class profile. It is one of the few sizable ethnic enclaves in the Northwest; its varied blue-collar population includes well-defined Scandinavian and Italian communities.

In geographic and economic terms, the Boeing aircraft company is at the center of the 7th. Interstate 5 heading into Seattle parallels the runway of Boeing Field. The district's economic health depends greatly on that of Boeing's, and as the defense boom of the Reagan years evolves into the more austere 1990s, aerospace workers watch warily. But concern over the aging of the nation's passenger airline fleet has helped sustain orders for Boeing commercial aircraft.

The strength of organized labor in this industrial area, a minority population that is the largest among Washington House districts, and a substantial bloc of liberal urbanites make the 7th the most dependably Democratic district in the state. In 1988, Michael S. Dukakis' 67 percent showing here was crucial to his statewide victory.

Population: 516,531. White 412,772 (80%), Black 48,051 (9%), Asian and Pacific Islander 36,744 (7%), Other 7,003 (1%). Spanish origin 13,669 (3%). 18 and over 414,472 (80%), 65 and over 68,925 (13%). Median age: 31.

Committees

District of Columbia (6th of 8 Democrats)
Fiscal Affairs & Health

Standards of Official Conduct (7th of 7 Democrats)

Ways & Means (23rd of 23 Democrats)
Human Resources; Social Security

Elections

1990 General		
Jim McDermott (D)	106,761	(72%)
Larry Penberthy (R)	35,511	(24%)
Robbie Scherr (SW)	5,370	(4%)
1990 Primary †		
Jim McDermott (D)	47,306	(73%)
Larry Penberthy (R)	12,681	(20%)
Patrick Ruckert (D)	3,909	(6%)
Robbie Scherr (SW)	1,125	(2%)
1988 General		
Jim McDermott (D)	173,809	(76%)
Robert Edwards (R)	53,902	(24%)

† In Washington's "jungle primary," candidates of all parties are listed on one ballot.

District Vote For President

	1988		1984	
D	144,221	(67%)	132,482	(60%)
R	67,318	(31%)	86,754	(39%)

Campaign Finance

	Receipts	Receipts from PACs		Expend-itures
1990				
McDermott (D)	$230,973	$196,253	(85%)	$204,296
1988				
McDermott (D)	$373,258	$233,226	(62%)	$354,530
Edwards (R)	$5,921	0		$5,265

Key Votes

1991	
Authorize use of force against Iraq	N
1990	
Support constitutional amendment on flag desecration	N
Pass family and medical leave bill over Bush veto	Y
Reduce SDI funding	Y
Allow abortions in overseas military facilities	Y
Approve budget summit plan for spending and taxing	Y
Approve civil rights bill	Y
1989	
Halt production of B-2 stealth bomber at 13 planes	N
Oppose capital gains tax cut	Y
Approve federal abortion funding in rape or incest cases	Y
Approve pay raise and revision of ethics rules	Y
Pass Democratic minimum wage plan over Bush veto	Y

Voting Studies

	Presidential Support		Party Unity		Conservative Coalition	
Year	S	O	S	O	S	O
1990	20	79	92	5	7	93
1989	29	67	94	2	10	85

Interest Group Ratings

Year	ADA	ACU	AFL-CIO	CCUS
1990	94	0	92	21
1989	95	4	100	20

8 Rod Chandler (R)

Of Bellevue — Elected 1982

Born: July 13, 1942, La Grande, Ore.
Education: Attended Eastern Oregon State College, 1961-62; Oregon State U., B.S. 1968.
Military Service: Ore. National Guard, 1959-64.
Occupation: Public relations consultant; banker; television newscaster.
Family: Wife, Joyce Elaine Laremore; two children.
Religion: Protestant.
Political Career: Wash. House, 1975-83.
Capitol Office: 223 Cannon Bldg. 20515; 225-7761.

In Washington: A party moderate with a former PR man's gift for a quote, Chandler placed himself in the thick of the House GOP's intraparty squabbling in the 101st Congress. He first voted to shake things up, supporting combative conservative Newt Gingrich for minority whip, then later openly voiced the ambivalence felt by many moderates about the change. Chandler's pronouncements raised his visibility, although he is still known within the institution primarily for his interest in pension reforms and his parochial interests on the Ways and Means Committee.

In early 1989, Gingrich persuaded Chandler to abandon his natural political inclinations and support the Georgian's bid for whip. Gingrich's promise of a more aggressive party held considerable appeal for ambitious Republican moderates frustrated by decades of minority status. Their support was essential to Gingrich's victory.

But when Gingrich broke with President Bush and contributed to the collapse of the 1990 budget summit agreement, Chandler cried foul. "I voted for a guy who promised to bring the party together," he said. "If you can't be there [for the president], then as a leader you either resign or keep your mouth shut."

The following day, Chandler was one of just 71 Republicans to vote for the budget summit agreement, which lost 179-254. In the wake of that defeat for the president, Chandler met with a group of 20-odd House Republicans — mostly moderates — who considered but then dropped the idea of mounting a challenge to Gingrich. "I think we learned — or should have learned — what happens when we divide rather than unite," he said.

Chandler also made headlines during the fall 1990 budget contretemps when his work for a district trucking interest helped score a temporary coup for the industry. At the request of Paccar, maker of Peterbilt trucks and a company Chandler calls "my Boeing," he offered an amendment at a Ways and Means markup to impose a 9 cent diesel fuel tax on railroads, which traditionally paid no fuel taxes, since they are dedicated to road repair. The $200 million-a-year tax hike was virtually the only one proposed by a Republican, and the committee jumped on it.

In less than 24 hours, railroads responded to Chandler's move by sending a delegation of Washington state railroad employers and union representatives to visit him. Democratic Sen. Brock Adams, a former Transportation secretary, took the Senate floor to criticize Chandler's amendment as unfair (Chandler's interest in a 1992 Senate bid against Adams is well-known). The tax was ultimately reduced to 2.5 cents per gallon, a sum roughly paralleling the share of truck fuel dedicated to debt reduction.

The episode pitting district and state interests against each other was something of an anomaly for Chandler, who has made a point of watching out for home-state interests well beyond the boundaries of his suburban Seattle district. He has worked to restore the tax-exempt status of the Farm Credit Association of Spokane; helped secure funding for additional Customs Service agents at Seattle-Tacoma International Airport and on the Canadian border; and, after visiting hospitals across the state in 1989, worked to enact legislation increasing Medicare reimbursements for hospitals with a disproportionate number of low-income patients.

On broader policy matters, Chandler is known as an expert on pension and insurance issues — an expertise he honed as chairman of the Washington state House Ways and Means panel. During his years in Congress, he has introduced a number of bills to expand the post-retirement health care and long-term care provided by pension plans, and to simplify laws affecting benefit plans. He was also an early foe of the ill-fated catastrophic health care plan, which was enacted in 1988, then repealed less than a year later.

Chandler's work on these issues typically has not generated much publicity. "It's a problem becoming known. Pensions, employee bene-

Washington 8

Seattle Suburbs — Bellevue

The 8th includes some of Seattle's most prosperous suburbs as well as the landmark that affords the city unique allure — snow-capped, 14,410 foot Mount Rainier.

Encompassing the mainly affluent suburbs and exurbs east, south and west of Seattle, the 8th was drawn to be Republican. Though George Bush lost the state in 1988, he won comfortably here, taking 55 percent of the vote.

For the past 20 years, the suburban area covered by the 8th enjoyed its position as a beneficiary of Seattle's economic boom. But while the boom has brought benefits, it has also brought the traffic jams and rising housing costs that are the downside of growth. While not as obvious as the "no-growth" movement in Seattle — where an initiative to restrict downtown development won approval in 1989 — there is a "slow-down" constituency in the 8th. In 1988, the city of Bellevue instituted a moratorium on high-rise development; concerns over rapid growth in the southern King County region led several communities to incorporate in 1990, including Federal Way.

With almost 87,000 residents, Bellevue is the population center of the King County suburbs that make up the bulk of the 8th. Separating Seattle and Bellevue is Lake Washington, and in the middle of the lake is the exclusive community of Mercer Island. The other notable island in the 8th is Vashon Island, at the district's western end. Though accessible only by Puget Sound ferry or aircraft, its rural character is giving way to housing tracts and light manufacturing.

On the mainland, the 8th takes in such burgeoning suburbs as Des Moines and affluent Normandy Park. South on Interstate 5 is Federal Way, site of the Weyerhaeuser Co.'s headquarters. Also to the south are Auburn and Kent, middle-class suburbs where many residents work for the Boeing Co.

Population: 516,500. White 488,993 (95%), Black 5,219 (1%), Other 16,666 (3%). Spanish origin 8,716 (2%). 18 and over 358,801 (70%), 65 and over 31,751 (6%). Median age: 29.

fits and insurance ... those are not very often front-page, 30-minute newscast stories," said Chandler, a former TV newsman.

Over his years in Congress he has introduced a variety of bills to simplify reporting requirements for employers with pension plans, and to enhance the security of retiree health benefits. In the 101st Congress, he and Arkansas Sen. David Pryor offered legislation to provide favorable tax treatment for employers who set aside funds to pay for retiree health or long-term care benefits.

Chandler (along with Nancy L. Johnson of Connecticut) also co-chairs a House GOP task force on health care. In 1991, the two introduced legislation to broaden the availability of health insurance to the uninsured.

Throughout the 100th and 101st Congresses, Chandler participated in efforts to make across-the-board reductions on a variety of appropriations bills, though there was some risk of cutting federal spending in his district. "When I get up in front of the Rotary Club and say, 'I'm against deficits,' I want to have something on the record to show I mean it," Chandler told a local newspaper.

While Chandler has no committee assignment to give him a role in foreign policy legislation, he sought to find a centrist approach to the polarizing debate on Central America. He was appointed to the bipartisan Presidential Monitoring Committee to observe the 1990 Nicaraguan election, and in 1989, he contributed to a successful amendment to the foreign aid authorization bill establishing criteria for Nicaraguan compliance with the peace accords. In 1988, Chandler joined with Florida Democratic Rep. Buddy MacKay to offer a compromise plan on aid to the contras, though it was later displaced by a cease-fire agreement that spring. In 1989, Chandler voted for a "humanitarian" contra-aid package worked out by President Bush and congressional leaders.

Chandler's overall voting record is that of a moderate, but he gets somewhat higher ratings from conservative and business groups than his GOP colleagues Sid Morrison and John Miller. Like them, he supports abortion rights and opposed a constitutional amendment to ban flag burning. But he was the only one of the three opposing the 1990 civil rights bill and voting to uphold the president's veto of the Family and Medical Leave Act. He dismissed critics of the President's Persian Gulf policy as "shrill and whiney."

At Home: With Chandler openly eyeing a 1992 Senate race, more was riding on Chandler's 1990 showing than simply re-election. The results were solid, but not stunning: Facing the same Democrat who ran against him in 1986, Chandler won decisively, but by a smaller margin than in their first meeting.

Before that, Chandler first had to fend off a primary challenge from Ken Thomasson, a former California police officer and political unknown who was angered by Chandler's vote against a constitutional amendment to ban flag desecration. Chandler won the GOP nomination with little difficulty, then headed into a fall race against Democrat David E. Giles.

Giles, a businessman and anti-nuclear activist, had challenged Chandler in 1986. Despite beginning early and raising more than $100,000, that year Giles won only 35 percent of the vote.

In 1990, Giles started later and with less cash, campaigning mainly on nuclear issues, and the need for arms control. Giles was not considered a serious threat, but the budget squabble kept Chandler in Washington, D.C., into late October and generated voter frustration toward all incumbents. Chandler won with 56 percent of the vote, down from 65 percent in his first race against Giles.

In Chandler's initial House campaign in 1982, his most serious obstacle was getting past a primary in which the GOP electorate was more conservative than he was. Though Chandler endorsed a balanced-budget constitutional amendment, his Republican opponents charged that he was a liberal, citing his opposition to a school prayer amendment and his support for a nuclear freeze and legalized abortion.

The early favorite was state Rep. Bob Eberle, for whom legislative colleagues during redistricting had tailored the newly created 8th. Eberle's association with the national New Right movement gave him a spending advantage, but conservatives split between Eberle and King County Councilman Paul Barden, a born-again Christian stressing social issues. Chandler won nomination.

In November, Democrats offered Mercer Island Mayor Beth Bland. Though intelligent and capable, Bland had a strident manner that contrasted unfavorably with Chandler's "nice guy" image. He won by a solid margin, and has scored comfortable re-election victories.

When Chandler made his first bid for the state Legislature in 1974, he sought treatment for a drinking problem. Chandler has talked openly about his recovery and has volunteered to help others with drinking difficulties.

Committees

Post Office & Civil Service (8th of 8 Republicans)
Investigations (ranking); Census & Population

Ways & Means (8th of 13 Republicans)
Health; Human Resources; Select Revenue Measures

Elections

1990 General		
Rod Chandler (R)	96,323	(56%)
David E. Giles (D)	75,031	(44%)
1990 Primary †		
Rod Chandler (R)	36,551	(58%)
David E. Giles (D)	19,461	(31%)
Kenneth R. Thomasson (R)	6,700	(11%)
1988 General		
Rod Chandler (R)	174,942	(71%)
Jim Kean (D)	71,920	(29%)

† In Washington's "jungle primary," candidates of both parties are listed on one ballot.

Previous Winning Percentages: **1986** (65%) **1984** (62%) **1982** (57%)

District Vote For President

	1988	1984
D	99,728 (44%)	79,915 (36%)
R	125,807 (55%)	138,778 (63%)

Campaign Finance

	Receipts	Receipts from PACs		Expend-itures
1990				
Chandler (R)	$472,433	$300,815	(64%)	$451,296
Giles (D)	$33,866	$300	(1%)	$33,817
1988				
Chandler (R)	$333,019	$191,478	(57%)	$300,048
Kean (D)	$14,822	$5,550	(37%)	$14,820

Key Votes

1991	
Authorize use of force against Iraq	Y
1990	
Support constitutional amendment on flag desecration	N
Pass family and medical leave bill over Bush veto	N
Reduce SDI funding	Y
Allow abortions in overseas military facilities	Y
Approve budget summit plan for spending and taxing	Y
Approve civil rights bill	N
1989	
Halt production of B-2 stealth bomber at 13 planes	N
Oppose capital gains tax cut	N
Approve federal abortion funding in rape or incest cases	Y
Approve pay raise and revision of ethics rules	Y
Pass Democratic minimum wage plan over Bush veto	N

Voting Studies

	Presidential Support		Party Unity		Conservative Coalition	
Year	S	O	S	O	S	O
1990	59	37	71	25	74	20
1989	62	34	71	27	76	22
1988	52	47	72	24	82	16
1987	57	42	77	19	88	9
1986	56	37	66	25	74	26
1985	61	35	72	22	76	22
1984	62	36	63	32	80	17
1983	66	33	67	28	78	22

Interest Group Ratings

Year	ADA	ACU	AFL-CIO	CCUS
1990	28	50	8	85
1989	15	70	9	100
1988	45	56	29	93
1987	36	61	13	93
1986	20	71	21	71
1985	15	67	18	95
1984	45	42	31	88
1983	25	43	6	95

West Virginia

U.S. CONGRESS

SENATE 2 D
HOUSE 4 D

LEGISLATURE

Senate 33 D, 1 R
House 74 D, 26 R

ELECTIONS

1988 Presidential Vote	
Bush	48%
Dukakis	52%
1984 Presidential Vote	
Reagan	55%
Mondale	45%
1980 Presidential Vote	
Reagan	45%
Carter	50%
Anderson	4%
Turnout rate in 1986	28%
Turnout rate in 1988	47%
Turnout rate in 1990	27%

(as percentage of voting age population)

POPULATION AND GROWTH

1980 population	1,949,644
1990 population (34th in the nation)	1,793,477
Percent change 1980-1990	−8%

DEMOGRAPHIC BREAKDOWN

White	96%
Black	3%
Asian or Pacific Islander	0.4%
(Hispanic origin)	1%
Urban	36%
Rural	64%
Born in state	79%
Foreign-born	1%

MAJOR CITIES

Charleston	57,287
Huntington	54,844
Wheeling	34,882
Parkersburg	33,862
Morgantown	25,879

AREA AND LAND USE

Area	24,119 sq. miles (41st)
Farm	23%
Forest	78%
Federally owned	8%

Gov. Gaston Caperton (D)
Of Charleston — Elected 1988

Born: Feb. 21, 1940, Charleston, W.Va.
Education: U. of North Carolina, B.A. 1963.
Occupation: Insurance executive.
Religion: Episcopalian.
Political Career: No previous office.
Next Election: 1992.

WORK

Occupations	
White-collar	45%
Blue-collar	41%
Service workers	13%
Government Workers	
Federal	15,521
State	38,292
Local	65,734

MONEY

Median family income	$ 17,308	(38th)
Tax burden per capita	$ 958	(17th)

EDUCATION

Spending per pupil through grade 12	$ 3,858	(29th)
Persons with college degrees	10%	(50th)

CRIME

Violent crime rate	147 per 100,000 (45th)

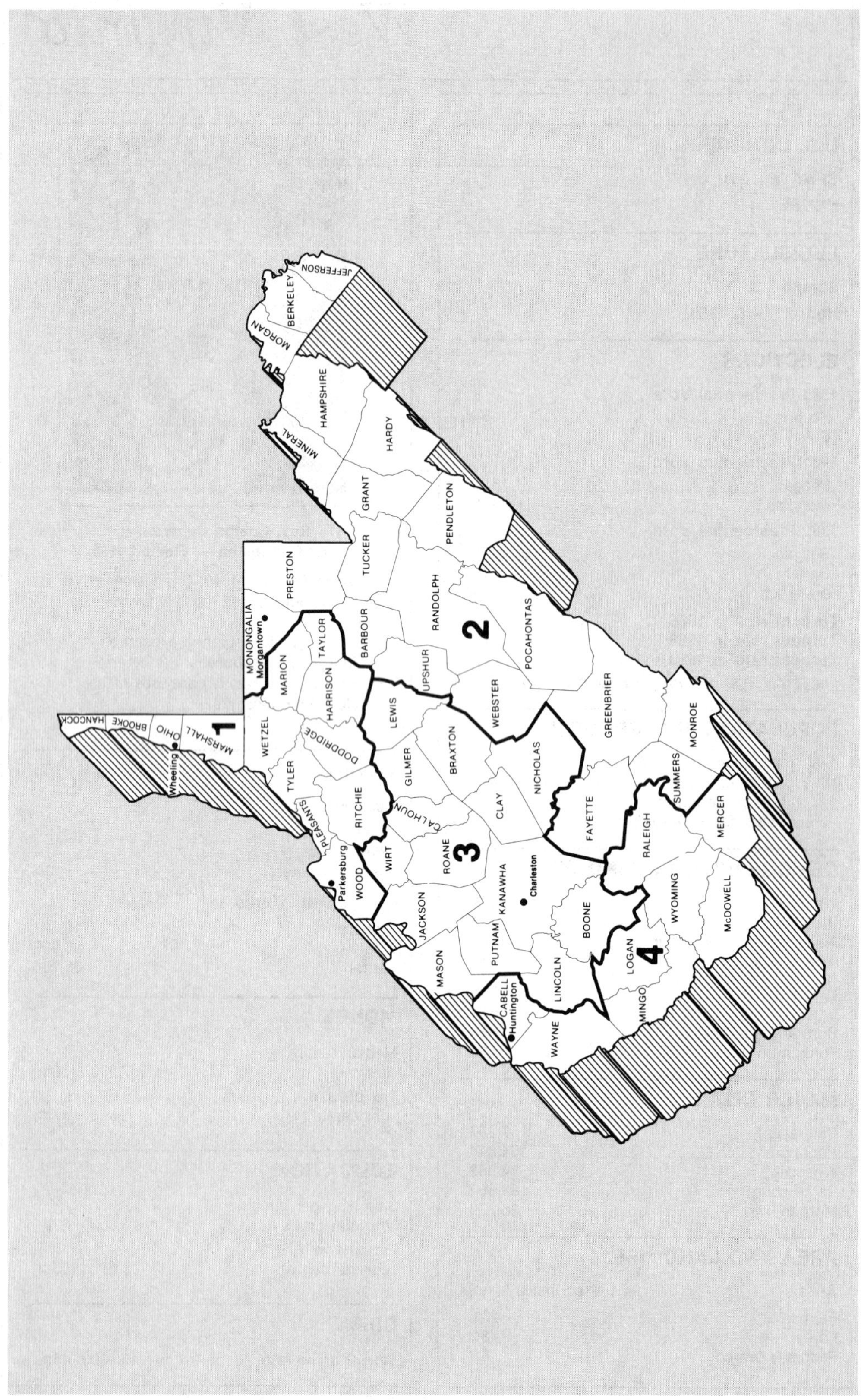
1
2
3
4
HANCOCK
BROOKE
OHIO
Wheeling
MARSHALL
WETZEL
TYLER
PLEASANTS
Parkersburg
WOOD
RITCHIE
DODDRIDGE
MONONGALIA
Morgantown
MARION
TAYLOR
HARRISON
PRESTON
BARBOUR
TUCKER
LEWIS
UPSHUR
RANDOLPH
GILMER
CALHOUN
WIRT
JACKSON
ROANE
BRAXTON
WEBSTER
POCAHONTAS
CLAY
NICHOLAS
GREENBRIER
KANAWHA
Charleston
MASON
PUTNAM
CABELL
Huntington
WAYNE
LINCOLN
BOONE
LOGAN
MINGO
FAYETTE
RALEIGH
WYOMING
McDOWELL
MERCER
SUMMERS
MONROE
PENDLETON
GRANT
HARDY
MINERAL
HAMPSHIRE
MORGAN
BERKELEY
JEFFERSON

Robert C. Byrd (D)

Of Sophia — Elected 1958

Born: Nov. 20, 1917, North Wilkesboro, N.C.
Education: Attended Beckley College; Concord College; Morris Harvey College, 1950-51; Marshall College, 1951-52; American U., J.D. 1963.
Occupation: Lawyer.
Family: Wife, Erma Ora James; two children.
Religion: Baptist.
Political Career: W.Va. House, 1947-51; W.Va. Senate, 1951-53; U.S. House, 1953-59.
Capitol Office: 311 Hart Bldg. 20510; 224-3954.

In Washington: Few took Byrd seriously in 1988 when he said he was forgoing another bid for majority leader because he could do more for West Virginia as Appropriations chairman. But he has converted skeptics into believers by making himself the most powerful chairman in a generation and funneling more than $1 billion to his home state in less than two years.

" 'Whatsoever thy hand findeth to do, do it with thy might,' " he said in 1989, quoting Ecclesiastes. "I have that sense of duty. I follow it meticulously."

Byrd's didactic fascination with the Bible and ancient history suggests that he wants to leave as enduring a mark on the mores of his beloved Senate as he is leaving on the hills of West Virginia. But the changing times that ushered him out as Democratic leader may make that task impossible; with his quirky ways and focus on carrying home federal largess, Byrd seems more a symbol of a bygone Senate than a force that will shape the chamber's future.

Emblematic of Byrd's love of tradition is the seriousness with which he approaches his role as Senate president pro tempore, a job he inherited in 1989 as the most senior member of the Senate majority. The ritualistic position entitles Byrd to preside over the Senate whenever he chooses, and he has done so more than any predecessor in memory. He has also put more money into the office, doubling its budget in his first year.

An intensely private man, Byrd was often criticized during his 12-year tenure as Democratic leader for being too stilted and old fashioned to represent his party in the television age. He has a strong drive for self-improvement; it propelled him from the coal patch to the top levels of U.S. politics, and it motivates him to study and absorb the words of history's great men. But when he muses on the Senate floor about the thoughts of Shakespeare and Socrates, of Machiavelli and Thucydides, Byrd can come across as oddly formal and rhetorically overblown.

However, the insiders' world of Appropriations is ideal for Byrd. Here, he is judged by his devotion to institutional and legislative detail, a realm in which he has no equal. He presides as a sort of benevolent dictator, calling to mind some of the 1950s-era chairmen Byrd watched as a young senator.

As majority leader, Byrd controlled the chamber with his legendary parliamentary skill. As chairman, with the sharp crack of his gavel, he starts hearings on time and tolerates no digression. The Appropriations subcommittees that were once the fiefdoms of their chairmen are now beholden to Byrd.

Byrd is not an omnipotent force, as his successor as leader, George J. Mitchell of Maine, proved in 1990 when he narrowly won a pivotal battle against Byrd on the clean air bill. But as a man with a vest pocket full of IOUs and the power to grant future funding favors, Byrd must be reckoned with. "A lot of people are deathly afraid of Byrd," said Utah Republican Orrin G. Hatch, after Byrd gutted an agreement he had spent months negotiating.

Many have suggested that senators follow Byrd not because they like him, but because they fear him. He has been known to admonish colleagues in public session, or summarily gavel their requests out of order. He has a long memory, and does not hesitate to punish those who cross him. In 1990, after Oklahoma Republican Don Nickles tried in the Budget Committee to cap spending limits, Byrd deleted funds to help restart Amtrak service in Oklahoma.

As the Senate was preparing to vote on the final 1990 budget agreement, Byrd spent hours on the floor turning back questions from senators who were wary of budget-process changes that were part of the agreement. When Republican John H. Chafee of Rhode Island rose, Byrd quickly interjected, "I thank you for your nice card that I received today, your very nice card about the item that I helped you with in the Interior appropriations bill."

That comment drew laughter, which Byrd joined, but his handling of the budget contretemps in 1990 was a serious matter. Through months of budget-summit negotiations between the White House and congressional leaders, Byrd steadfastly demanded that the package include an increase in funding for domestic programs. He was determined to halt the pattern established in the 1980s: As the deficit grew, funds used for education and other domestic programs had been scaled back with approval from the Budget committees. Byrd and his House Appropriations counterpart, Jamie L. Whitten of Mississippi, took this as a direct assault on their authority as appropriators, and they dug in to change it in 1990.

Because no budget plan would pass without Byrd's support, Richard G. Darman, director of the Office of Management and Budget (OMB), often dealt directly with Byrd. Darman eventually agreed to let domestic funding rise with inflation, and he allowed for an extra $20.7 billion in domestic spending over the first three years covered by the budget agreement. In exchange, Byrd agreed to let OMB determine which pieces of supplemental spending bills constitute emergency spending exempt from caps, and he allowed OMB to determine whether expenditures meet budget guidelines or trigger an automatic cut in a related program.

Byrd had won his battle. Spending levels were set through 1995 (usurping the power of the Budget Committee), and he got more money from the White House for his New Deal agenda. When the summit agreement was rejected by a coalition of conservatives (who objected to its tax increases) and liberals (who wanted more for domestic programs), Byrd became a leading advocate for a new package that closely resembled the summit agreement.

But some senators were concerned that Byrd had traded away too much congressional authority to OMB in exchange for the additional domestic funding. Answering question after question from senators concerned about the changes in the budget process, Byrd relied on his reputation as a guardian of Senate prerogatives. "May I say to my friends, there is no need to worry about Robert Byrd giving away the power . . . of this body," he said. "I am as loyal to the Senate . . . as any other senator here in this chamber now, any who has ever sat in the chamber, or any who will ever grace this chamber."

Byrd was thus decisive in securing Senate passage of the deal, but some of his colleagues saw ominous signs in the first test of the new process. Early in 1991, during consideration of a supplemental spending bill, Democratic Sen. Patrick J. Leahy of Vermont won Senate approval of an amendment raising dairy price supports. Byrd reversed field and opposed Leahy's measure, citing Darman's threat that it would trigger automatic spending cuts. Several liberals complained that this amounted to giving OMB a line-item veto.

In the clean air debate during the 101st Congress, Byrd turned his formidable powers toward an effort to protect the jobs of West Virginians. Since 1982, he had stalled efforts to impose stricter standards on urban smog and acid rain. Much of his state's coal is high in sulfur, a key ingredient in acid rain, and Byrd feared that tougher environmental regulations would further depress West Virginia's economy.

Mitchell comes from Maine, a state scarred by acid rain. The 1990 debate pitted the Senate's two most powerful Democrats against one another. At issue was Byrd's amendment to provide $500 million in job-loss benefits to coal miners displaced by the bill. Byrd had twice scaled back his amendment, but refused to accept any compromise that did not provide special benefits for coal miners.

When he refused an offer from Mitchell that would have aided all workers displaced by the bill, the battle line was drawn. "Sen. Mitchell is fighting for what he believes in," Byrd said. "And I'm fighting for what I believe in."

Byrd went door-to-door to meet with Republicans and Democrats alike, and penned and typed many notes. On the day of the vote, Hawaii Democrat Spark M. Matsunaga, suffering from cancer, was transported in a special van and rolled into the chamber in a wheelchair to cast his vote for Byrd.

During the vote, Byrd's confident smile contrasted with Mitchell's pained expression, but the Senate's undisputed champion of nose-counting was off. The vote was 50-49 for Mitchell. Byrd lost one vote because a senator was stranded at an airport, and he lost others thanks to strong-arm tactics from the White House.

This blow to Byrd's pride seemed to strengthen his resolve to deliver almost unprecedented federal largess to West Virginia. He said his goal as Appropriations chairman was to bring $1 billion to the state in five years, but he did it in less than two. Among the plums he picked off is a $185 million FBI fingerprint lab that employees 2,600 and is being transferred from Washington, D.C., to West Virginia.

Byrd's show of power in the 101st Congress followed what was perhaps his most successful term as Senate leader. The 100th Congress marked Byrd's return to majority leader after three terms in the minority. Republicans met Byrd's return with some dread, complaining that he had used his parliamentary skills to override their legitimate minority rights during his first stint as majority leader in the 1970s. Some Democrats, too, were a bit apprehensive, but Byrd rallied them behind an ambitious agenda, and helped make the 100th Congress one of the most productive in more than 20 years.

Byrd's emphasis on procedure and prerogatives over policy helps explain the ease with which he has moved from his party's right toward its left. Few would have forecast a leadership role for Byrd when he arrived in the Senate in 1959. He was parochial and far to the right of most Democrats. He filibustered the 1964 Civil Rights Act, at one point holding the floor with a 14-hour speech that is among the longest on Senate record — something he now says he deeply regrets.

But by 1967, he had a toehold on the Senate leadership ladder, after defeating veteran liberal Joseph Clark of Pennsylvania to become secretary of the Democratic Conference. Byrd catered to his colleagues, scheduling routine business for their convenience. Four years later he ousted a stunned Edward M. Kennedy from the No. 2 leadership job, majority whip. Shaken by the 1969 Chappaquiddick tragedy, Kennedy had been neither an active nor effective whip.

For six years Byrd was a loyal lieutenant to Majority Leader Mike Mansfield of Montana, sitting through long days of floor work while deferring to Mansfield as party spokesman. When Mansfield retired, some liberals wanted Hubert H. Humphrey of Minnesota to succeed him, believing he would be a more eloquent spokesman. But Byrd once again had a long column of accounts receivable. Humphrey, already seriously ill, withdrew. Byrd was elected by acclamation.

Byrd became majority leader as Jimmy Carter became president, and the two had an uneasy relationship. Byrd seemed to regard Carter as an amateur at the exercise of power, and made sure the president knew where the credit belonged when Byrd rescued the administration's legislation. He was instrumental in saving the Panama Canal treaties through nonstop negotiations with wavering senators and Panamanian officials in 1978.

Many Democrats' lingering unease about Byrd crystallized after the 1980 elections cost the party the White House and plunged Senate Democrats into the minority. Byrd's style seemed less appropriate for a party out of power, and his resistance to the Reagan administration was not a sure thing at the start. He voted for President Ronald Reagan's 1981 tax and budget-cut bills. But he became a strong foe after the administration proposed cuts in Social Security.

The feeling that the party needed a more aggressive, telegenic public symbol, however, never went away, and led to an open campaign against Byrd after the 1984 elections. By the time challenger Lawton Chiles of Florida began his campaign, Byrd already had commitments from more than half his colleagues, but the final vote, 36-11 for Byrd, indicated he had some vulnerabilities.

He moved to shore up his strength in the 99th Congress, working to put more verve into his formal oratory and giving the Democratic response to some of Reagan's televised speeches. The unexpectedly large Democratic gains in the 1986 Senate elections ensured that Byrd would remain secure for at least another two years. J. Bennett Johnston of Louisiana had prepared for a face-off with Byrd, but dropped his bid when it became clear the new Democratic majority was in no mood to dump its leader in the midst of triumph. Two years later, Byrd stepped down on his own.

At Home: Since Byrd was elected to the Senate in 1958, he has held the seat with ease — a tribute both to the respect he has engendered at home and the long-running impotence of the state's Republican Party. In five reelections, Byrd's lowest vote share has been 65 percent.

That came in 1988, against freshman GOP state Sen. M. Jay Wolfe. Wolfe campaigned gamely on a conservative platform that combined right-to-work with right-to-life, and enlisted religious broadcaster Pat Robertson to visit West Virginia on his behalf. But he was outspent nearly 10-to-1, and he could not refute Byrd's argument that as Appropriations chairman, he could steer federal money West Virginia's way.

Wolfe had no trouble getting the GOP nomination to meet Byrd, largely because the memory of the incumbent's decisive 1982 victory was vivid in Republicans' minds. Taking advantage of a beleaguered economy and a badly mismanaged GOP effort that year, Byrd drew nearly 70 percent of the vote, humiliating Republican Cleve Benedict, an heir to the Procter & Gamble fortune, who gave up a House seat to run.

The senator was born Cornelius Calvin Sale Jr. When he was 1, his mother died and his father gave him to an aunt and uncle, Vlurma and Titus Byrd; they raised him in the hardscrabble coal country of southern West Virginia.

Byrd graduated first in his high school class, but it took him 12 more years before he could afford to start college. He worked as a gas station attendant, grocery store clerk, shipyard welder and butcher before his talents as a fiddle player helped win him a seat in the state Legislature in 1946.

Friends drove Byrd around the hills and hollows, where he brought the voters out by playing "Cripple Creek" and "Rye Whiskey." From then on, he never lost an election. As he himself once put it, "There are four things people believe in in West Virginia — God Almighty; Sears, Roebuck; Carters Little Liver Pills; and Robert C. Byrd."

When Democrat Erland Hedrick retired from the old 6th District in 1952, Byrd was an obvious contender. But he had to surmount his past membership in the Ku Klux Klan. He had joined the Klan at age 24 and as late as 1946 wrote a letter to the imperial grand wizard urging a Klan rebirth "in every state of the Union."

When this came up publicly in 1952, his opponents and Democratic Gov. Okey L. Patteson called on him to drop out. He refused, explaining his Klan membership as a youthful indiscretion committed because of his alarm over communism. He won the election.

After three House terms, he ran for the Senate in 1958 with AFL-CIO and United Mine Workers support. He crushed his primary opposition and unseated Republican Chapman Revercomb, a veteran who had been in and out of the Senate in the 1940s and won a two-year term in a 1956 comeback. Revercomb was a weak incumbent before the campaign even began, and the 1958 recession hurt the state badly, driving many voters closer to their New Deal Democratic roots.

For the next two decades, West Virginians returned Byrd to the Senate without fuss. In 1964, he trounced Cooper Benedict, a former deputy assistant secretary of Defense and the father of Cleve Benedict. In 1970, the GOP victim was Charleston Mayor Elmer H. Dodson. In 1976, no one at all filed against Byrd.

Committees

Appropriations (Chairman)
Defense; Energy & Water Development; Interior (chairman); Labor, Health & Human Services, Education; Transportation

Armed Services (11th of 11 Democrats)
Conventional Forces & Alliance Defense; Defense Industry & Technology; Manpower & Personnel

Rules & Administration (3rd of 9 Democrats)

Elections

1988 General		
Robert C. Bryd (D)	410,983	(65%)
M. Jay Wolfe (R)	223,564	(35%)
1988 Primary		
Robert C. Byrd (D)	252,767	(81%)

Previous Winning Percentages: **1982** (69%) **1976** (100%) **1970** (78%) **1964** (68%) **1958** (59%) **1956 *** (57%) **1954 *** (63%) **1952 *** (56%)

** House elections.*

Campaign Finance

	Receipts	Receipts from PACs		Expend-itures
1988				
Byrd (D)	$1,407,167	$938,720	(67%)	$1,099,709
Wolfe (R)	$115,314	$23,103	(20%)	$115,284

Key Votes

1991	
Authorize use of force against Iraq	N
1990	
Oppose prohibition of certain semiautomatic weapons	N
Support constitutional amendment on flag desecration	Y
Oppose requiring parental notice for minors' abortions	N
Halt production of B-2 stealth bomber at 13 planes	Y
Approve budget that cut spending and raised revenues	Y
Pass civil rights bill over Bush veto	Y
1989	
Oppose reduction of SDI funding	Y
Oppose barring federal funds for "obscene" art	N
Allow vote on capital gains tax cut	N

Voting Studies

	Presidential Support		Party Unity		Conservative Coalition	
Year	S	O	S	O	S	O
1990	42	58	74	26	62	38
1989	54	46	83	17	50	50
1988	56	44	81	19	49	51
1987	40	60	85	15	44	56
1986	36	64	84	16	30	70
1985	37	63	81	19	55	45
1984	53	45	77	22	45	55
1983	48	51	81	19	36	61
1982	40	60	81	19	56	44
1981	47	48	78	14	43	53

Interest Group Ratings

Year	ADA	ACU	AFL-CIO	CCUS
1990	56	26	89	25
1989	60	14	100	38
1988	55	36	86	29
1987	70	23	100	28
1986	75	26	93	16
1985	65	43	90	21
1984	75	50	73	37
1983	65	16	94	37
1982	60	55	92	48
1981	70	86	89	39

John D. Rockefeller IV (D)

Of Charleston — Elected 1984

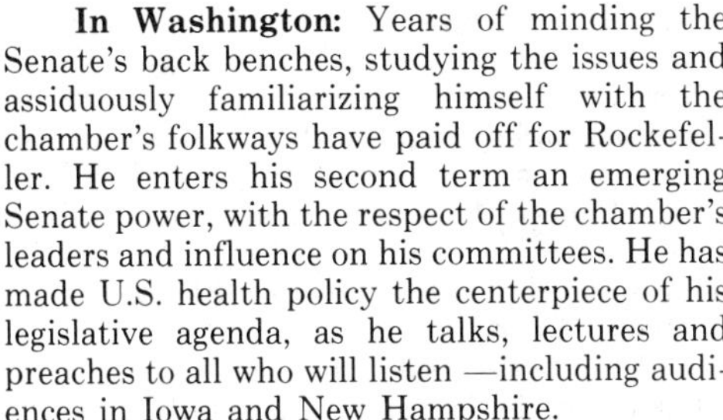

Born: June 18, 1937, New York, N.Y.

Education: Attended International Christian U., Tokyo, Japan, 1957-60; Harvard U., A.B. 1961.

Occupation: Public official.

Family: Wife, Sharon Percy; four children.

Religion: Presbyterian.

Political Career: W.Va. House, 1967-69; W.Va. secretary of state, 1969-73; governor, 1977-85; Democratic nominee for governor, 1972.

Capitol Office: 109 Hart Bldg. 20510; 224-6472.

In Washington: Years of minding the Senate's back benches, studying the issues and assiduously familiarizing himself with the chamber's folkways have paid off for Rockefeller. He enters his second term an emerging Senate power, with the respect of the chamber's leaders and influence on his committees. He has made U.S. health policy the centerpiece of his legislative agenda, as he talks, lectures and preaches to all who will listen —including audiences in Iowa and New Hampshire.

Rockefeller coyly denied White House ambitions until mid-1991, when he said he was thinking of seeking the Democratic nomination for 1992. Such talk — which began in 1968 when he was nominated to be West Virginia's secretary of state and continued during his less-than-awe-inspiring gubernatorial tenure — was finally being treated seriously.

Rockefeller is an old hand at winning over those who think a man born into wealth and power must be spoiled and aloof. More than 20 years ago, he impressed the people of Emmons, W.Va., as a sincere, idealistic VISTA volunteer. During his first term in Washington, he reassured the U.S. Senate. He often impresses observers as personable and unpretentious, according courteous treatment to staff and witnesses at hearings. In his early years in the Senate he was often found writing quietly in the chamber, his six-foot-six-inch frame folded into one of the spartan desks. His behavior is the perfect antidote to the expectation of arrogance.

Generally expected to address international issues, his one-time academic specialty, Rockefeller initially focused on West Virginia concerns — the cost of shipping coal by rail, the job prospects of miners, steelmakers and other workers in Rust Belt industries. In the 101st Congress, events thrust him to the forefront on health care, another likely topic of interest given his state's large population of elderly and of black-lung disease victims.

In many ways, political necessity shaped his parochial agenda. A senator elected with a disappointing 52 percent of the vote after two terms as governor and a $12 million campaign could not afford to range too far afield.

But Rockefeller also seems to delight in disappointing those who expected him to grab headlines in preparation for a leap onto the national stage. "I've done my homework," Rockefeller told a West Virginia newspaper in 1989. "I've started out in a low-profile way but I've gained the respect of my colleagues." He also won over more home-state voters, as he won re-election in 1990 with 68 percent.

At the start of the 101st Congress, Rockefeller was named chairman of a new Finance Subcommittee on Medicare and Long-Term Care. In June 1989, following the death of Rep. Claude Pepper, Rockefeller was chosen to chair the bipartisan Pepper Commission on health policy.

Rockefeller is credited in 1989 with pushing to fruition a far-reaching overhaul of Medicare's physician-payment system. He set out with Republican Dave Durenberger of Minnesota to forge a compromise between the two chambers' bills even after Senate leaders told him that the issue was dead. Rockefeller persevered; over the course of a few days he hammered out a compromise. "He wouldn't take 'no' for an answer," said Durenberger.

In 1990, Rockefeller was one of the leaders on Finance who successfully pushed for the enactment of new Medigap rules to regulate more directly private insurance plans to supplement Medicare. He was also successful in getting, as part of the Medicare provisions of the budget-reconciliation bill, $580 million over five years for home care for frail elderly people.

But it was Rockefeller's work on the Pepper Commission that thrust him most prominently into the spotlight. A politically and philosophically divided commission in March 1990 proposed the creation of two programs: one to provide basic health insurance to those lacking it and a second to underwrite long-term care. The estimated price tag for the two programs was $66.2 billion annually over five years, though the commission did not specify where the revenues should come from.

While Rockefeller often strives hard to reach a middle ground, some find him too accommodating. "Jay doesn't want to offend anybody," said Democratic Rep. Pete Stark of California, a Pepper Commission vice chairman. "But at some point you've got to decide where the winners and losers are," he said.

Despite the lukewarm response to the commission's offerings, Rockefeller hopes to see enactment of some of its recommendations during the 102nd Congress.

A member of both the Finance and Commerce committees, Rockefeller has weighed in on the trade debates of the 100th and 101st Congresses. He had spent several years living in Japan and speaks the language, giving him an understanding of the country that few of his colleagues possess. Yet his state has been badly hurt by competition from Japanese manufacturing. While supporting the aggressive pursuit of reciprocity in trade, Rockefeller has also noted that hard-line protectionism carries risks for West Virginia. Erecting barriers to protect West Virginia steel makers could provoke foreign competitors to stop buying coal from West Virginia mines.

But his empathy with Japan went only so far. Rockefeller joined those senators who unsuccessfully urged the administration to cite Japan for engaging in unfair trade practices and to act to solve the problem or punish Japan through higher tariffs. A reluctant Rockefeller said Japan had to be cited because it needed to accept the fact that economic leadership carried international obligations.

Rockefeller served briefly during the 101st Congress on the Energy and Natural Resources Committee and also has a seat on Veterans' Affairs. Rockefeller has used the position well; he was the sponsor of an amendment shifting $230 million to benefit veterans' programs in the budget resolution for fiscal 1990 passed in 1989.

Yet despite his growing agenda, Rockefeller still looks for the West Virginia angle. When the Senate in mid-1980 considered bills on the status of Puerto Rico, Rockefeller was fearful that the legislation could mean less money for his needy state. "I am unable to separate the representation of my state from the consideration of this amendment," he said in voting against a bill to give the island millions of dollars in special social-program benefits if its citizens chose statehood.

At Home: As the scion of one of the nation's wealthiest families, Rockefeller seems an odd leader for one of the poorest states.

But in a state where money often talks and Democrats nearly always win, he has been a successful politician. He is well-known — newspapers need only refer to him as Jay in the headlines — though his wealth and celebrity engender no small amount of resentment in a state beset with the nation's second-lowest per capita personal income: Past polls have shown him with negative ratings as high as 40 percent.

But Rockefeller has won many friends by patiently working his way up the political ladder over two decades, serving in low-visibility offices before twice winning the governorship and capturing the Senate seat of retiring Democrat Jennings Randolph in 1984.

Rockefeller moved to West Virginia in 1964 as a VISTA volunteer in the Action for Appalachia Youth program, then decided to stay and enter politics, starting near the bottom; he ran for a seat in the state's lower house in 1966. After winning that, he captured the statewide office of secretary of state in 1968.

His political ascent was interrupted in 1972 when he lost the governor's race to Republican Arch A. Moore Jr. Rockefeller was hurt by carpetbagger charges and an environmental platform that opposed strip mining. After the election, he recanted some of his environmental positions and strengthened his ties to the state by serving as president of West Virginia Wesleyan College. Running for governor again in 1976, he won by nearly 2-to-1 over former GOP Gov. Cecil H. Underwood (1957-61). Moore was ineligible to seek re-election.

Despite their differing backgrounds, Rockefeller and the Legislature generally got along well in his first term. Rockefeller, the amateur classical pianist with the Harvard degree, and the pols from West Virginia's grimy courthouses reached an understanding, affording Rockefeller some major legislative successes.

Still, Rockefeller left nothing to chance in 1980, winning re-election after a campaign that bombarded households with direct-mail appeals and TV commercials, even on Pittsburgh and Washington, D.C., stations.

When it was reported he was spending almost $12 million in his re-election campaign against Moore, who was seeking a comeback, bumper stickers appeared with the slogan, "Make Him Spend It All, Arch." But Moore was unable either to drive Rockefeller broke, or out of office. Rockefeller won by 9 points.

Rockefeller's second term was stymied by the state's economic problems. Heavily dependent on the battered coal industry, West Virginia was staggered by high unemployment and sinking revenues. He was the prime target of criticism when taxes were raised, salaries frozen and state spending cut.

With West Virginia's governors restricted to two consecutive terms, it was long apparent that Rockefeller would run for the Senate in 1984, but not who would run against him. Democratic Sen. Jennings Randolph helped him by announcing his retirement plans in early 1983. About a year later, Moore, his strongest potential GOP rival, decided to pass this time, and joined the governor's race.

But Rockefeller was not home free. He was

near the nadir of his popularity when he entered the Senate race. Even many supporters admitted that he had not met the high expectations he had raised as governor; West Virginia struggled toward the end of his second term with the country's highest unemployment rate.

Rockefeller blamed the economic problems on ties to fading industries — steel and glass as well as coal — a global oil glut, and Reagan administration policies. He touted the integrity of his administration and its scattered successes, such as efforts to bolster tourism. "Tough Leadership for Tough Times" became the tag line for his campaign.

Republicans nominated a wealthy young political neophyte, John Raese, who promised to match Rockefeller's spending dollar for dollar. But with Rockefeller mounting another $12 million campaign, that was a pipe dream.

Raese's campaign was further stalled by a series of gaffes. But Rockefeller made him the target of his late media barrage — a tactic widely considered to be a mistake — and the attacks gave Raese publicity he could not afford himself. Aided by Reagan's surge atop the ticket, Raese pulled nearly even with Rockefeller in election-eve polls. But Rockefeller survived, with large majorities in the industrial northern Panhandle and in the southern coal fields.

In his 1990 re-election, Rockefeller spent more than $300,000 in a primary against two challengers who spent less than $1,000 between them, and refused to agree to a $2 million spending limit for the general election. Burned by past charges of attempting to buy public office with his personal fortune, Rockefeller shied away from using his own funds, and instead amassed a war chest from PACs.

Republicans nominated John Yoder, a 39-year-old lawyer from Harpers Ferry. Yoder threw Rockefeller off balance briefly by charging that he was "bought" by special interests. But a lack of funds crippled Yoder's campaign as fall approached. The Rockefeller effort kicked into full gear just as Yoder was being deserted by his national party; Rockefeller won all but three counties.

Committees

Commerce, Science & Transportation (6th of 11 Democrats)
Foreign Commerce & Tourism (chairman); Science, Technology & Space; Surface Transportation

Finance (9th of 11 Democrats)
Medicare & Long Term Care (chairman); Health for Families & the Uninsured; International Trade

Veterans' Affairs (4th of 7 Democrats)

Elections

1990 General		
John D. Rockefeller IV (D)	276,234	(68%)
John Yoder (R)	128,071	(32%)
1990 Primary		
John D. Rockefeller IV (D)	200,161	(85%)
Ken B. Thompson (D)	21,669	(9%)
Paul Nuchims (D)	14,467	(6%)

Previous Winning Percentages: 1984 (52%)

Campaign Finance

	Receipts	Receipts from PACs		Expend-itures
1990				
Rockefeller (D)	$3,479,161	$1,425,405	(41%)	$2,650,320
Yoder (R)	$22,541	0		$22,904

Key Votes

1991	
Authorize use of force against Iraq	N
1990	
Oppose prohibition of certain semiautomatic weapons	N
Support constitutional amendment on flag desecration	Y
Oppose requiring parental notice for minors' abortions	Y
Halt production of B-2 stealth bomber at 13 planes	Y
Approve budget that cut spending and raised revenues	Y
Pass civil rights bill over Bush veto	Y
1989	
Oppose reduction of SDI funding	N
Oppose barring federal funds for "obscene" art	Y
Allow vote on capital gains tax cut	N

Voting Studies

	Presidential Support		Party Unity		Conservative Coalition	
Year	**S**	**O**	**S**	**O**	**S**	**O**
1990	26	73	86	13	41	59
1989	51	49	78	20	50	50
1988	49	50	88	9	30	68
1987	36	60	92	6	28	72
1986	31	69	79	19	18	80
1985	31	61	83	12	47	47

Interest Group Ratings

Year	ADA	ACU	AFL-CIO	CCUS
1990	83	13	78	25
1989	80	14	90	38
1988	70	16	86	36
1987	90	8	100	24
1986	75	13	93	32
1985	60	14	90	36

1 Alan B. Mollohan (D)

Of Fairmont — Elected 1982

Born: May 14, 1943, Fairmont, W.Va.
Education: College of William and Mary, A.B. 1966; West Virginia U., J.D. 1970.
Military Service: Army Reserve, 1970-83.
Occupation: Lawyer.
Family: Wife, Barbara Whiting; five children.
Religion: Baptist.
Political Career: No previous office.
Capitol Office: 229 Cannon Bldg. 20515; 225-4172.

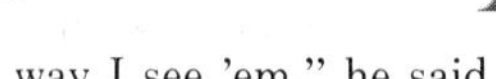

In Washington: Given his focus on obtaining federal programs for West Virginia's economically troubled 1st District, Mollohan benefits from his ties to a pair of senior Democrats: Senate Appropriations Committee Chairman Robert C. Byrd and House Appropriations Defense Subcommittee Chairman John P. Murtha. His alliances with them have helped him push through a number of 1st District projects.

Mollohan remains loyal to the district's bedrock industries, coal and steel. He supports "Buy American" legislation that gives preference to domestic materials in U.S. construction projects. His opposition to what he calls "unsound" acid rain legislation that penalizes coal-burning plants and factories made Mollohan one of only 21 House members in May 1990 to vote against reauthorizing the Clean Air Act.

Yet Mollohan works hard to diminish the district's dependence on these declining industries. He has lobbied the Appalachian Regional Commission and the Economic Development Administration for funds to expand the Mid-Atlantic Aerospace Complex — an avionics and aircraft-repair facility — at Benedum Airport in Harrison County. Mollohan is on the Appropriations subcommittee that oversees the Federal Bureau of Investigation, and acted as a House sponsor of a pet project of Byrd's: the location of an FBI fingerprinting center at Clarksburg in the 1st.

While Byrd has more of a direct interest in West Virginia projects, it was Murtha's personal patronage that helped Mollohan advance in the House. A western Pennsylvania power broker whose sphere includes West Virginia, Murtha sponsored Mollohan's bid for an Appropriations seat.

Mollohan's image as a loyalist got him a seat on the ethics committee, which he held from 1985 to 1991. However, this assignment forced him to pass judgment in 1989 on House Speaker Jim Wright of Texas. He and Pennsylvania Democrat Joseph M. Gaydos, another Murtha ally, voted "no" on most charges against Wright, but Mollohan said his ties to Murtha did not influence him. "I vote 'em the way I see 'em," he said.

Mollohan is a sure vote for the Democratic leadership on labor and trade issues. However, he takes a more conservative line on defense than most House Democrats, and breaks with party orthodoxy on abortion: He is co-chairman of the Congressional Pro-Life Caucus.

At Home: Mollohan followed in the footsteps of his father, Robert Mollohan, who held the 1st District seat for 18 years prior to his 1982 retirement. That year, the father worked hard to transfer political loyalties to his son. But it was not an easy campaign. Though Alan Mollohan was born in Fairmont, for a decade he had been a Washington, D.C., lawyer who counted Pittsburgh-based Consolidation Coal Co. as a major client. Rank-and-file mine workers were leery about a corporate lawyer representing them; many lined up behind Mollohan's pro-labor primary opponent, state Sen. Dan Tonkovich.

The elder Mollohan, however, had close ties to party officials, business and labor leaders in the 1st. Their support proved crucial to his son, who won the primary by 3,137 votes.

In the fall, GOP state Rep. John F. McCuskey also tried to turn Mollohan's corporate law background into a negative, and nearly blocked a United Mine Workers endorsement of the Democrat. But it was a Democratic year, and Mollohan won with 53 percent.

In 1984, Mollohan had to buck a Republican tide and fend off a GOP challenge from Jim Altmeyer. The well-funded Republican had strong credentials: He was a West Point graduate, a Vietnam veteran, a Catholic in an area with a large ethnic Catholic population, and a civic leader in Wheeling, the district's largest city. But Mollohan mounted a late media barrage focusing on Altmeyer's spotty attendance in the Legislature. With large majorities in the northern Panhandle and the coal-mining areas, Mollohan won easily. Republicans have had a hard time mustering opposition since then; Mollohan was unopposed in 1986, and faced a self-employed historian and filling station owner in 1988 and 1990.

West Virginia 1

Northern Panhandle — Wheeling

The 1st is iron and steel in the north and coal farther south, with a largely rural midsection.

The iron and steel area is the Panhandle, a narrow strip between the Pennsylvania border and the Ohio River. Brooke and Hancock counties, steel producers at the Panhandle's northern tip, are the most reliably Democratic counties in the 1st. The Panhandle city of Weirton (Hancock County) is home to Weirton Steel, the country's largest employee-owned company.

Ohio County (Wheeling) is the Panhandle's commercial center, with a significant white-collar population that often produces GOP majorities. Ohio County has voted Republican in the last five presidential elections. The Wheeling-Pittsburgh Steel Corp. moved its corporate headquarters from Pittsburgh to Wheeling in late 1987.

To the southeast, coal is mined in Marion and Harrison counties and shipped up to Pittsburgh along the Monongahela River. Like the Panhandle, the coal region is heavily unionized and populated largely by southern and Eastern European ethnics, descendants of immigrants who were drawn by work in the mines. Together with the Panhandle's millworkers, they usually deliver large enough majorities for a statewide Democratic candidate to carry the 1st.

The other important population center is Wood County (Parkersburg), at the southwestern corner of the district, midway between Wheeling and Huntington on the Ohio River. Like the rural counties that separate it from the district's steel and coal regions, Wood County frequently votes Republican.

Clarksburg (Harrison County) has been designated as the site for a much-publicized, $200 million FBI fingerprinting facility.

Population: 488,568. White 478,672 (98%), Black 7,906 (2%). Spanish origin 3,238 (1%). 18 and over 353,283 (72%), 65 and over 64,928 (13%). Median age: 32.

Committees

Appropriations (29th of 37 Democrats)
Commerce, Justice, State & Judiciary; Veterans Affairs, Housing & Urban Development, & Independent Agencies

Elections

1990 General		
Alan B. Mollohan (D)	72,849	(67%)
Howard K. Tuck (R)	35,657	(33%)
1988 General		
Alan B. Mollohan (D)	119,256	(75%)
Howard Tuck (R)	40,732	(25%)

Previous Winning Percentages: **1986** (100%) **1984** (54%) **1982** (53%)

District Vote For President

	1988	1984	1980	1976
D	89,128 (51%)	84,836 (43%)	93,363 (48%)	111,273 (55%)
R	84,142 (49%)	111,290 (57%)	91,307 (47%)	90,173 (45%)
I			8,711 (5%)	

Campaign Finance

	Receipts	Receipts from PACs	Expend-itures
1990			
Mollohan (D)	$197,997	$131,498 (66%)	$206,688
Tuck (R)	$34,020	0	$34,077
1988			
Mollohan (D)	$168,219	$112,893 (67%)	$103,154
Tuck (R)	$15,350	0	$15,220

Key Votes

1991	
Authorize use of force against Iraq	Y
1990	
Support constitutional amendment on flag desecration	Y
Pass family and medical leave bill over Bush veto	Y
Reduce SDI funding	Y
Allow abortions in overseas military facilities	N
Approve budget summit plan for spending and taxing	Y
Approve civil rights bill	Y
1989	
Halt production of B-2 stealth bomber at 13 planes	N
Oppose capital gains tax cut	Y
Approve federal abortion funding in rape or incest cases	N
Approve pay raise and revision of ethics rules	Y
Pass Democratic minimum wage plan over Bush veto	Y

Voting Studies

	Presidential Support		Party Unity		Conservative Coalition	
Year	**S**	**O**	**S**	**O**	**S**	**O**
1990	31	66	84	11	50	50
1989	55	43	74	25	76	24
1988	36	59	74	19	61	24
1987	40	56	83	12	67	33
1986	36	61	79	15	70	28
1985	40	60	82	17	69	31
1984	49	50	76	22	63	36
1983	34	66	78	21	54	46

Interest Group Ratings

Year	ADA	ACU	AFL-CIO	CCUS
1990	61	21	100	21
1989	55	36	92	40
1988	50	48	100	23
1987	68	17	100	13
1986	50	35	100	24
1985	55	38	82	23
1984	55	33	85	44
1983	65	30	94	20

2 Harley O. Staggers Jr. (D)

Of Keyser — Elected 1982

Born: Feb. 22, 1951, Washington, D.C.
Education: Harvard U., B.A. 1974; West Virginia U., J.D. 1977.
Occupation: Lawyer.
Family: Wife, Leslie Sergy; two children.
Religion: Roman Catholic.
Political Career: Sought Democratic nomination for U.S. House, 1980; W. Va. Senate, 1981-83.
Capitol Office: 1323 Longworth Bldg. 20515; 225-4331.

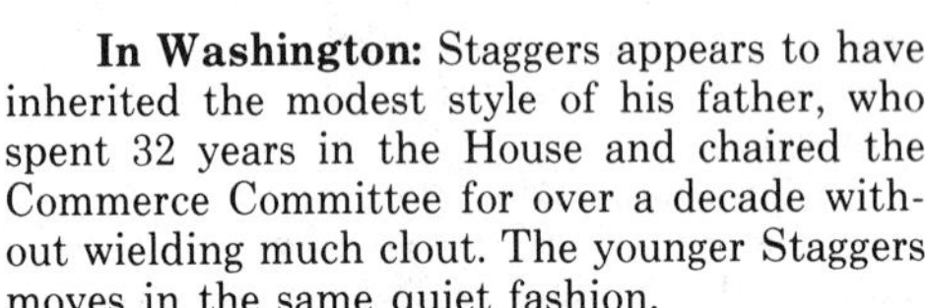

In Washington: Staggers appears to have inherited the modest style of his father, who spent 32 years in the House and chaired the Commerce Committee for over a decade without wielding much clout. The younger Staggers moves in the same quiet fashion.

In the 101st Congress, he got a platform to call his own: the chairmanship of the Veterans' Affairs panel that oversees veterans' housing programs. In 1989, during work on a catchall veterans' benefits bill, the committee attached Staggers' bill requiring recipients of VA-backed loans to pay slightly higher fees to cover the costs of the VA guaranteed home-loan program.

Staggers is also active on the Judiciary Committee. He strongly opposes gun-control legislation. In the 101st and 102nd Congresses, he worked against efforts to enact a seven-day waiting period for people who want to buy handguns — known as the "Brady bill" — as well as a bill to ban U.S.-made assault-style semiautomatic weapons. In 1991, he sponsored the National Rifle Association-backed substitute to thwart the Brady bill. His amendment, to order states to set up an instant check system, lost 193-234. The House passed the Brady bill.

A stalwart opponent of abortion, Staggers also believes capital punishment is immoral. In 1986, he blasted an amendment to the omnibus drug bill to enforce capital punishment for certain illegal drug offenses. "It is ironic," Staggers said, "that the House is attempting to attach a death penalty to a bill that's ultimate purpose is to save lives.... In a civilized society, there is just no place for capital punishment, just as there is no place in a civilized society for abortion. The taking of a life is morally wrong — in every respect."

In 1990, Staggers tried to amend an omnibus anticrime bill so all crimes in the measure would carry only the maximum sentence of life in prison without parole. His amendment lost by voice vote in committee and by 103-322 on the House floor.

Staggers is less visible on the Agriculture Committee, where his subcommittee assignments enable him to fight for food programs for the poor and economic development for his rural district. In the 101st Congress, he added language to rural development legislation to make rural small business "incubators" — umbrella organizations that assist new small businesses — eligible for loans. His amendment was adopted in the House by voice vote.

Likable and low-key, Staggers is a frequent participant in the regular congressional basketball games. He generally tends to issues with a local slant, spending much time on constituent services and local projects.

At Home: Staggers was unopposed in 1986 and won easily in 1988, but the population growth in the eastern Panhandle helped make his re-election margin less comfortable in 1990. Newcomers unfamiliar with the Staggers name gave serious consideration to his high profile GOP challenger. Recruited by the state GOP, Oliver Luck, a former football star at West Virginia University, proved to be a well-financed and effective campaigner.

But his message of jobs and economic development failed to resonate throughout the district, partly because the 2nd had not suffered the same high unemployment rates and population losses as the rest of the state. Staggers drew less than 60 percent in 14 of the 20 counties, but he prevailed with just 56 percent of the vote overall.

The Staggers family wanted an uninterrupted succession in the 2nd, but voters rejected the idea in 1980. The elder Harley announced his departure that year and anointed his son, but the politically inexperienced Harley Jr. did not make it out of the primary.

State party leaders made sure Staggers had a strong base from which to mount his second House campaign. After his 1980 primary loss, he was appointed to a vacancy in the state Senate. Staggers kept a low profile, but worked on his 1982 House effort and was nominated without opposition.

Harley Jr. was far outspent by the GOP nominee, but the elder Staggers rallied his political network behind the scenes. His son swept every county.

West Virginia 2

East — Morgantown; Eastern Panhandle

Much of the 2nd District resembles the other three congressional districts. Its youth are leaving in droves and per capita income is among the lowest in the country. Rural hospitals are financially troubled; in Barbour County, unemployment is almost three times higher than the rest of the state.

Anomalous to the state, however, is the eastern Panhandle. This region is marked by a robust economy, and double-digit growth. Rapid population gains in the three easternmost counties left the 2nd as the only district to gain population in the 1980s; Berkeley registered a 26 percent population gain while Jefferson notched 18 percent.

One of the larger districts east of the Mississippi, the 2nd has no real media markets. Most of it is in the Allegheny Mountains, where the standard of living is the lowest in the state. Politically, the 2nd is marginal. Republican George Bush carried it narrowly in the 1988 presidential election; it was the only district in West Virginia that he won.

Democratic strength is greatest in the few mining and industrial areas along the western fringe. Monongalia County, one of the state's leading coal-producing counties, combines a sizable number of blue-collar voters with the academic community at West Virginia University in Morgantown. Fayette County is the other major Democratic stronghold. It lies at one end of the industrialized Kanawha Valley.

GOP candidates usually run best in the eastern Panhandle including the northern Shenandoah Valley. Pastoral Grant County regularly turns in the highest Republican percentages in the state. It went for Bush by a margin of nearly 4-to-1 in 1988.

Population: 487,438. White 469,213 (96%), Black 15,235 (3%). Spanish origin 3,439 (1%). 18 and over 350,168 (72%), 65 and over 60,621 (12%). Median age: 30.

Committees

Agriculture (13th of 27 Democrats)
Conservation, Credit & Rural Development; Domestic Marketing, Consumer Relations & Nutrition

Judiciary (14th of 21 Democrats)
Administrative Law & Governmental Relations; Economic & Commercial Law

Select Aging (30th of 42 Democrats)
Human Services; Rural Elderly

Veterans' Affairs (6th of 21 Democrats)
Housing & Memorial Affairs (chairman)

Elections

1990 General		
Harley O. Staggers (D)	63,174	(55%)
Oliver Luck (R)	50,708	(45%)
1988 General		
Harley O. Staggers Jr. (D)	118,356	(100%)

Previous Winning Percentages: **1986** (69%) **1984** (56%) **1982** (64%)

District Vote For President

	1988	1984	1980	1976
D	81,178 (48%)	77,702 (42%)	87,423 (48%)	105,527 (57%)
R	86,633 (52%)	107,719 (58%)	86,471 (47%)	79,607 (43%)
I			8,721 (5%)	

Campaign Finance

	Receipts	Receipts from PACs		Expend-itures
1990				
Staggers (D)	$419,859	$302,800	(72%)	$500,133
Luck (R)	$357,109	$57,476	(16%)	$356,282
1988				
Staggers (D)	$146,928	$131,953	(90%)	$90,537

Key Votes

1991	
Authorize use of force against Iraq	N
1990	
Support constitutional amendment on flag desecration	Y
Pass family and medical leave bill over Bush veto	Y
Reduce SDI funding	Y
Allow abortions in overseas military facilities	N
Approve budget summit plan for spending and taxing	N
Approve civil rights bill	Y
1989	
Halt production of B-2 stealth bomber at 13 planes	N
Oppose capital gains tax cut	Y
Approve federal abortion funding in rape or incest cases	N
Approve pay raise and revision of ethics rules	N
Pass Democratic minimum wage plan over Bush veto	Y

Voting Studies

	Presidential Support		Party Unity		Conservative Coalition	
Year	**S**	**O**	**S**	**O**	**S**	**O**
1990	17	80	88	10	28	72
1989	40	59	84	13	39	61
1988	23	77	89	11	47	53
1987	17	81	92	5	28	72
1986	18	82	89	8	32	68
1985	29	70	88	9	33	65
1984	30	70	88	10	29	71
1983	16	84	86	12	30	70

Interest Group Ratings

Year	ADA	ACU	AFL-CIO	CCUS
1990	72	13	83	29
1989	80	18	83	40
1988	80	12	100	21
1987	96	4	100	13
1986	85	5	100	28
1985	70	19	82	38
1984	65	13	85	38
1983	85	13	94	5

3 Bob Wise (D)

Of Clendenin — Elected 1982

Born: Jan. 6, 1948, Washington, D.C.
Education: Duke U., A.B. 1970; Tulane U., J.D. 1975.
Occupation: Lawyer.
Family: Wife, Sandra Casber.
Religion: Episcopalian.
Political Career: W.Va. Senate, 1981-83.
Capitol Office: 1421 Longworth Bldg. 20515; 225-2711.

In Washington: Wise has made great strides in his transition from populist maverick to party insider. He serves on the Budget Committee — a reward for loyal service to the Democratic leadership — and seniority has given him a subcommittee chair on Government Operations. He is an active member of the party's whip organization and chairman of the liberal Democratic Study Group.

All this is a marked change from Wise's profile as a freshman in 1983, when he committed a remarkably rebellious act — taking on his more senior colleagues in the West Virginia delegation by opposing (and temporarily halting) a flood control project they had set in motion for the 3rd District.

Early in his fifth term, a new challenge confronted Wise — the prospect of seeing his district disappear. West Virginia lost a House seat in 1990 reapportionment, setting up a game of redistricting musical chairs involving four incumbents and only three seats. "Things are a little testy in the delegation right now," said Wise in early 1991. "Everyone is looking at one another over their shoulders."

Despite his iconoclastic start in the House, Wise fairly soon began working within the system, applying himself to slicing off pieces of the federal pie for his constituency. The reason was simple: economic necessity. There are so many bad roads, decrepit bridges, unemployed workers and black-lung disease victims in the 3rd that Wise decided he had to get along with those in the congressional appropriations process who can provide federal dollars for relief.

And Wise has gotten along well. An enthusiastic participant in the Democratic whip organization, Wise issues *The Wise Whip Wrapup*, a newsletter that quickly summarizes House Democratic activity (and also includes doodles by Wise). During the 101st Congress, Wise voted with a majority of Democrats more often than his three West Virginia colleagues, and he is the only one of the four to support abortion rights. All this has put Wise in good stead with party leaders.

In 1989, Wise assumed the chairmanship of the Government Operations Subcommittee on Government Information, Justice and Agriculture. He has taken some shots at the Bush administration, citing its lack of openness and the steps it has taken to protect its internal deliberations. "You really have to play hardball to get information from them," he said in early 1990. Just over a year later, Wise was in the congressional forefront when Chief of Staff John H. Sununu came under attack for excessive use of government aircraft. Skilled at getting publicity for his actions, Wise led the call for an independent audit of the situation by the General Accounting Office.

Wise achieved some legislative prominence in 1990 during consideration of the Clean Air Act. The House approved his amendment providing $250 million over five years in transition aid for workers who lost their jobs because of the legislation. While President Bush opposed the amendment, Wise was optimistic about its chances. "I can't believe the president's going to veto the environmental bill of the decade over $50 million a year," said Wise, looking out for his district's coal miners.

Basically, he was correct. The final bill contained a compromise that, while narrower in scope than Wise's amendment, marked the first time since the 1970s that Congress had provided for cash payments to workers dislocated by new legislation.

Wise came to Washington as a self-described populist with a penchant for challenging established power, and he lived up to that reputation early in his first term. He had been in office only a few months when he took on his state's congressional delegation by opposing the Stonewall Jackson Dam, a long-planned flood-control project in the 3rd.

Wise had campaigned on a promise to fight the dam, and when the 1983 water development appropriations bill came up, he attached an amendment eliminating any money for it. The project, he said, was a waste of money. His move angered the state's other Democratic congressmen, including Senate Democratic leader Robert C. Byrd. Still, Wise managed to per-

West Virginia 3

Central — Charleston

The 3rd centers on Charleston, the seat of state government and commerce as well as the most diverse economy in the state. But even Charleston is tied to the up-and-down cycle in the coal industry. As coal struggled in the 1980s so did this area, recording an unemployment rate not far below the state average, which has hovered in or near double digits.

The capital city's large white-collar work force frequently produces GOP majorities. But nearly three out of four voters in Kanawha County live outside Charleston. Many are blue-collar workers employed by the numerous chemical companies that line the Kanawha River. Finding a balance between safety and jobs has been a leading issue in the "Chemical Valley" since late 1984, when poisonous gas leakage from a Union Carbide chemical plant in India killed thousands. Union Carbide has a factory in Institute, less than 10 miles from Charleston.

Most of the blue-collar workers employed in the county vote Democratic. As a result, Kanawha often swings back and forth between the two parties. In 1984, it voted GOP for president, governor and senator, while backing Wise. In 1988, Kanawha voted a Democratic ticket for president, Senate, governor and House.

With 208,000 residents, Kanawha is the most populous county in the state and home for nearly half the 3rd's voters. But in the last decade, its population has decreased by about 25,000, due to declines in the chemical and glass industries and completion of a highway network that has encouraged many residents to move to bedroom communities outside Kanawha.

Democratic candidates usually run ahead in the portion of the district outside Kanawha. But Democratic victories there are not guaranteed. Generally, Republicans can count on a good share of the votes in the terrain north of Interstate 79, the highway that runs northeastward from Charleston toward the Pennsylvania border. Tobacco, corn and livestock provide an agricultural base in these counties in or near the Ohio River Valley. To the south of the Interstate, Democrats dominate. There is some coal and natural gas but little industrialization. Although the coal counties have been particularly hard hit in recent years, the economy has been distressed throughout the district.

Population: 486,112. White 469,089 (97%), Black 14,500 (3%). Spanish origin 2,595 (1%). 18 and over 347,147 (71%), 65 and over 57,194 (12%). Median age: 31.

suade a majority of the House to go his way. Only Senate support for the dam saved it; the House-Senate conference preserved funding.

Before very long, Wise had undergone a remarkable transformation in attitude. By the time he won re-election in 1986, he was extolling the virtues of seniority and comity. "I plan to take a page from Sen. Robert Byrd's book," he said, "by looking to see how I can help colleagues so they will help me."

Since then, Wise has secured funding for such district projects as lock and dam renovation. As co-chair of the Democratic Caucus task force on infrastructure, he has complained that highway trust fund money is piling up instead of being spent on infrastructure improvements.

While Wise is now more loyal to his party and to "the system," he still can go his own way. He opposed the leadership-backed October 1990 budget-summit agreement for its added burden on low- and middle-income taxpayers. "It may meet the Gramm-Rudman-Hollings test," said Wise, referring to mandatory budget cuts, "but it doesn't meet my Trump-Keating-Helmsley test: They're going to make out like bandits, while my people get hit again."

Wise also does not mass-mail newsletters to constituents, and he supports a ban on honoraria. Wise accepts the same salary he received when he first came to Congress; the balance from subsequent raises is donated to scholarship funds at four West Virginia colleges. This does not create much hardship at the Wise household, since his wife Sandra is a high-level Ways and Means staffer.

At Home: While Wise launched his political career as a maverick, he has nurtured it with unabashed displays of state boosterism. He regularly gives district voters what one newspaper described as "an upbeat, feel-good-about-ourselves pitch that sounds like a cross between Norman Vincent Peale ... and President Reagan." And he has gained wide visibility by projects such as "West Virginia First," a TV program designed to encourage high school students to stay in the state.

Critics complain that Wise's real forte is public relations, but there is no doubt he is a rising star in West Virginia politics.

Rather than join an established firm after law school, Wise set up his own practice oriented to low- and moderate-income clients. He then directed a statewide tax reform group that repeatedly took coal companies to court to force them to pay more property tax on their large landholdings.

But legal action had its limits, Wise decided. "Where people lose the battle is when they have to actually go to court," he once said. "It's much better if they win their case in the legislative process."

So in 1980 he capitalized on the resentment of teachers against the small size of a pay raise to upset the conservative state Senate president in the Democratic primary. With a reputation as a giant-killer, he ran for Congress in 1982, benefiting from labor support to swamp a Democratic primary field that included the state House majority leader.

GOP Rep. David Michael Staton had won the seat in 1980 with an extensive grass-roots campaign of his own, but his re-election effort was more aloof. He gave few interviews, relying instead on a heavy media barrage that portrayed him as a religious, family-oriented man who reflected the conservative social values of average West Virginians. If Staton was worried about Wise, he did not show it. "I don't think it will even be close," he said at one point.

It was not close. Wise's small campaign budget and feuds with party leaders masked an effective volunteer network and a knack for drawing enough free media attention to neutralize Staton's ads. Wise ran almost even with Staton in the rural GOP counties north of Charleston, while swamping the incumbent in Kanawha County and the economically distressed coal counties nearby. He won a decisive 58 percent of the vote.

Each election since then, Wise has won more easily. His most spirited re-election contest was in 1986, when Charleston newscaster Tim Sharp left his job in early September to fill the vacancy on the GOP ticket.

Sharp enjoyed instant name identification as a TV news anchorman. Pointing to threatened plant shutdowns in the 3rd, he said it was time to break up West Virginia's all-Democratic congressional delegation and elect a Republican who could work with the Reagan administration and with GOP Gov. Arch A. Moore Jr. to bring in jobs. A born-again Christian, Sharp also stressed his opposition to abortion.

But Sharp drew more ink than votes. Wise swept every county in the district, taking 65 percent overall. After Wise thrashed 1988 GOP nominee Paul W. Hart with 74 percent, Republicans did not field a challenger in 1990.

Committees

Budget (13th of 23 Democrats)
Community Development & Natural Resources; Economic Policy, Projections & Revenues; Human Resources

Government Operations (10th of 25 Democrats)
Government Information, Justice & Agriculture (chairman)

Select Aging (19th of 42 Democrats)
Health & Long-Term Care; Retirement, Income & Employment; Rural Elderly

Elections

1990 General		
Bob Wise (D)	75,327	(100%)
1988 General		
Bob Wise (D)	120,192	(74%)
Paul W. Hart (R)	41,478	(26%)

Previous Winning Percentages: **1986** (65%) **1984** (68%) **1982** (58%)

District Vote For President

	1988	1984	1980	1976
D	90,179 (53%)	84,527 (44%)	93,700 (49%)	113,707 (58%)
R	81,235 (47%)	107,004 (56%)	89,359 (46%)	82,475 (42%)
I			8,959 (5%)	

Campaign Finance

	Receipts	Receipts from PACs		Expend-itures
1990				
Wise (D)	$182,913	$126,118	(69%)	$53,137
1988				
Wise (D)	$173,893	$122,952	(71%)	$165,957
Hart (R)	$2,394	$1,027	(43%)	$4,310

Key Votes

1991	
Authorize use of force against Iraq	N
1990	
Support constitutional amendment on flag desecration	Y
Pass family and medical leave bill over Bush veto	Y
Reduce SDI funding	Y
Allow abortions in overseas military facilities	Y
Approve budget summit plan for spending and taxing	N
Approve civil rights bill	Y
1989	
Halt production of B-2 stealth bomber at 13 planes	N
Oppose capital gains tax cut	Y
Approve federal abortion funding in rape or incest cases	Y
Approve pay raise and revision of ethics rules	N
Pass Democratic minimum wage plan over Bush veto	Y

Voting Studies

	Presidential Support		Party Unity		Conservative Coalition	
Year	**S**	**O**	**S**	**O**	**S**	**O**
1990	19	81	92	6	28	72
1989	31	60	85	7	44	46
1988	21	73	87	9	58	39
1987	17	80	86	5	40	60
1986	23	72	88	8	40	60
1985	26	74	84	9	27	71
1984	33	61	76	17	37	61
1983	13	85	84	13	30	67

Interest Group Ratings

Year	ADA	ACU	AFL-CIO	CCUS
1990	72	13	100	21
1989	75	14	100	30
1988	75	12	100	36
1987	84	0	100	7
1986	75	5	93	22
1985	70	10	82	32
1984	70	18	92	27
1983	90	13	88	10

4 Nick J. Rahall II (D)

Of Beckley — Elected 1976

Born: May 20, 1949, Beckley, W.Va.
Education: Duke U., A.B. 1971; attended George Washington U., 1972.
Occupation: Broadcasting executive; travel agent.
Family: Divorced; three children.
Religion: Presbyterian.
Political Career: No previous office.
Capitol Office: 2104 Rayburn Bldg. 20515; 225-3452.

In Washington: As unhappy as Rahall has been over what he sees as federal inattentiveness to the concerns of his Rust Belt district, Rahall's constituents showed a surprising degree of unhappiness with him in 1990, nearly dumping him for a Republican. For once, all the unfavorable publicity Rahall endured in the 1980s took its toll at the polls.

The 101st Congress got off to a glum start for Rahall because of Speaker Jim Wright's ethics troubles. Rahall, who said Wright had always supported him in committee requests, angrily refused pressure to remove Wright's name from a Rahall birthday fundraiser in May 1989. But within the month, Wright announced he would resign from office.

Rahall is an unabashed special-interest legislator. Representing one of the nation's leading coal-producing districts, he puts coal in the forefront of his congressional concerns.

He has worked himself into several positions of influence over coal-related issues. On Interior, he chairs the Mining Subcommittee. He is a member of a Public Works subcommittee that deals with coal shipping issues, and he chairs the Congressional Coal Group.

But for a pro-coal man, Rahall can some times surprise those who write him off as resolutely pro-industry. On the Interior Committee in the 100th Congress, he advocated a bill extending national park status to parts of three West Virginia rivers. And on many wilderness or historic preservation bills that go through the committee, Rahall votes with conservationists. He has fought strip mining on U.S. forest land, and in 1990 sought to curtail timbering on some federal land in West Virginia.

Deliberations in the 101st Congress on reauthorizing the Clean Air Act caused anxiety in many parts of West Virginia; the bill set up an ambitious program to reduce pollutants that cause acid rain, and high-sulfur Eastern coal, mined in West Virginia, has been tagged as a chief culprit of those pollutants.

In 1989, Rahall told the Virginia Coal Council that the bill could pit low-sulfur coal producers against high-sulfur producers. Rahall exemplified the split: His district produces low-sulfur coal, and, assured that the clean air bill "does no harm to southern West Virginia," Rahall voted for it. "In fact," he added, "in anticipation of this legislation there has been something approaching euphoria in the low-sulfur coalfields of southern West Virginia."

While many members fight to broaden their jurisdiction, one of Rahall's first acts in the 99th Congress as Mining Subcommittee chairman was to give up stewardship over such topics as timber and hydroelectric power. He offered them to another subcommittee so he could stick to coal.

In the 101st Congress, Rahall won House passage of his bill to extend through 2007 the Interior Department's authority to collect fees on coal under a 1977 law. The fees pay for reclamation of coal mine sites abandoned before 1977 where no party has continuing reclamation responsibility under federal or state law. Faced with Bush administration opposition, however, the bill was trimmed: It was stripped of its environmental requirements; authority to collect reclamation fees was extended only through fiscal 1995. It became law as part of the fiscal 1991 deficit-reduction bill.

Though Rahall's coal boosterism benefits mine owners, he is also protective of the interests of coal miners, and votes a pro-labor line in the House. In early 1987, Rahall pledged to use his subcommittee chairmanship to block proposed Reagan administration cutbacks in federal mining health and safety research. He has long supported making it easier for miners with black lung disease to claim benefits.

Rahall calls for a national revival of coal use, but his boosterism fades somewhat when his region's interests are at stake. He has consistently fought plans to build a coal slurry pipeline in the Western United States, which would make Western coal cheaper to transport and more competitive with Eastern coal, including West Virginia's.

In the 98th Congress, Rahall tried and failed to block a slurry plan in the Interior Committee. But he teamed on the House floor

West Virginia 4

South and West — Huntington; Beckley

The Appalachian 4th is the most Democratic district in a Democratic state. It has proved its credentials in the last two presidential elections: Among West Virginia's four districts, only the 4th went for Walter F. Mondale in 1984, and in 1988, it gave Michael S. Dukakis a bigger share of the vote than any of the other districts.

In most years, Republican strength in the 4th is limited to Cabell County (Huntington) and Mercer County (Bluefield) on the fringes of the coal fields at opposite ends of the district. With roughly 20 percent of the district population, Cabell is the most populous county in the 4th. Like other Ohio River counties south of Wheeling, it frequently votes Republican. Huntington grew from a railroad center into the largest city in West Virginia but was overtaken in population by Charleston after losing 14 percent of its residents during the 1980s.

Between Cabell and Mercer is coal country. This is a lucrative area for the mining companies — the district ranks with the Wyoming at-large district and the Kentucky 7th as one of the national leaders in coal production.

The revival of the industry in the 1970s helped reverse decades of population decline here. As the miners returned, all but one of the southern coal counties grew by at least 10 percent over the decade.

But even this population surge left some counties below their levels of 50 years ago — Logan County had more voters in 1928 than in 1980. And the recession of the early 1980s wiped out much of the gain of the previous years. And as the coal mining jobs left, so did the population of McDowell County; the county lost 29 percent of its residents in the 80s.

McDowell is one of the poorest of the coal counties. Blacks make up 13 percent of the population, a higher share than in any other West Virginia county. In recent years, McDowell is the only county that has regularly elected a black representative to the state Legislature.

Population: 487,526. White 457,777 (94%), Black 27,410 (6%). Spanish origin 3,435 (1%). 18 and over 339,410 (70%), 65 and over 55,125 (11%). Median age: 29.

with railroad supporters, who said the slurry would cripple the industry's important coal-hauling business. The bill was defeated decisively. In the 100th Congress, Interior again passed a slurry bill over Rahall's protests. But the bill was also referred to the Public Works Committee, where it died.

Rahall's focus on coal leaves him little time to lead on other issues. On Public Works, he is a member of the pro-development majority, backing dams and other federal largess for his low-income district. When Transportation Secretary Samuel K. Skinner appeared before Public Works' Surface Transportation Subcommittee in early 1990, Rahall criticized the administration for not backing its transportation plans with funds. "Of course we want to get more bang for our buck," Rahall said, "but we need to put more money toward our infrastructure needs."

Later that year, when the House took up an emergency supplemental appropriations bill, Rahall and other Rust Belt lawmakers led an assault on the bill's foreign-aid provisions. Rahall's amendment was unambiguous: It would have struck all the foreign-aid parts of the bill. It was rejected by a 38-379 vote.

Of Lebanese heritage, Rahall has been a vigorous critic of Israel and a supporter of ties to Arab states. As part of a congressional delegation toured Beirut in 1982, he met with Palestine Liberation Organization leader Yasir Arafat. In the 100th Congress, Rahall fought efforts to close the PLO's office at the United Nations, and has sponsored resolutions supporting Palestinians' efforts toward self-determination and statehood. At the outset of the 1991 Persian Gulf War, Rahall denounced FBI interviews of Arab-American business and community leaders aimed at gathering information about possible terrorist activity in the United States.

At Home: In recent years, Rahall has gone from being the strongest vote-getter in his state's delegation to its weakest.

His re-election percentage dropped into the 60s for the first time in 1984, after a Las Vegas gambling casino filed suit against him to collect more than $60,000 in unpaid gambling debts. The suit, which drew headlines a month before the election, was eventually dropped. But coming on the heels of Rahall's separation from his wife, the episode gave his little-known GOP challenger unexpected fodder.

In 1986, a strong Democratic year, Rahall won 71 percent, but in 1988, he dropped to a surprising 61 percent against woefully underfunded GOP challenger Marianne Brewster, the Mercer County GOP chairman.

That anemic showing set the stage for tough primary and general-election campaigns in 1990. In the primary, Rahall faced a comeback attempt from his predecessor in the 4th, Democrat Ken Hechler. Pledging a return to "high moral standards again," Hechler implied that Rahall lacked them, and he criticized the incumbent as too dependent on out-of-state special-interest money. The local media rehashed Rahall's past troubles, including a 1988 guilty plea to alcohol-related reckless driving charges. But Rahall, anticipating a tough fight, worked hard to shore up his base in the party, and prevailed with 57 percent of the vote.

The GOP again nominated Brewster. Economic development themes, lingering voter concerns about Rahall's personal foibles, and the generalized anti-incumbent sentiment of 1990 benefited her. Though heavily outspent, Brewster took 48 percent of the vote, carrying three counties, including Rahall's Raleigh County base. Big margins in the southern coal counties of McDowell, Mingo and Logan saved Rahall.

Rahall was a little-known travel agent and radio sales manager when he entered politics in 1976. His opportunity grew out of then-Rep. Hechler's campaign for governor. Rahall was far from the best-known contender in the Democratic field, but he had family money, and he spent it on a media campaign none of his foes could match, evoking Hechler, Franklin D. Roosevelt and Sen. Robert C. Byrd. Rahall won nomination with 37 percent.

Then, after the primary, Hechler (who did not get the gubernatorial nomination) mounted a write-in drive to keep his House seat. Rahall could never have beaten Hechler in a primary, but the write-in effort was too difficult even for a popular incumbent, especially after Rahall received Democratic organization support. Hechler got nearly 60,000 write-ins, but Rahall won with a 46 percent tally. Hechler immediately announced he would run again in 1978, but he found that incumbency gave Rahall the advantages he once enjoyed. Rahall won renomination with 56 percent.

Committees

Interior & Insular Affairs (5th of 29 Democrats)
Mining & Natural Resources (chairman); National Parks & Public Lands

Public Works & Transportation (6th of 36 Democrats)
Aviation; Surface Transportation; Water Resources

Elections

1990 General		
Nick J. Rahall II (D)	39,948	(52%)
Marianne R. Brewster (R)	36,946	(48%)
1990 Primary		
Nick J. Rahall II (D)	37,581	(57%)
Ken Hechler (D)	28,618	(43%)
1988 General		
Nick J. Rahall II (D)	78,812	(61%)
Marianne R. Brewster (R)	49,753	(39%)

Previous Winning Percentages: **1986** (71%) **1984** (67%) **1982** (81%) **1980** (77%) **1978** (100%) **1976** (46%)

District Vote For President

	1988	1984	1980	1976
D	80,531 (58%)	81,060 (50%)	92,976 (56%)	105,407 (63%)
R	58,055 (42%)	79,470 (49%)	67,069 (40%)	62,505 (37%)
I			5,300 (3%)	

Campaign Finance

	Receipts	Receipts from PACs		Expend-itures
1990				
Rahall (D)	$536,855	$287,250	(54%)	$566,348
Brewster (R)	$66,671	$750	(1%)	$61,471
1988				
Rahall (D)	$333,159	$175,442	(53%)	$152,271
Brewster (R)	$32,041	0		$32,039

Key Votes

1991	
Authorize use of force against Iraq	Y
1990	
Support constitutional amendment on flag desecration	Y
Pass family and medical leave bill over Bush veto	Y
Reduce SDI funding	Y
Allow abortions in overseas military facilities	N
Approve budget summit plan for spending and taxing	N
Approve civil rights bill	Y
1989	
Halt production of B-2 stealth bomber at 13 planes	Y
Oppose capital gains tax cut	Y
Approve federal abortion funding in rape or incest cases	N
Approve pay raise and revision of ethics rules	Y
Pass Democratic minimum wage plan over Bush veto	Y

Voting Studies

	Presidential Support		Party Unity		Conservative Coalition	
Year	S	O	S	O	S	O
1990	14	81	79	16	37	63
1989	40	58	80	15	34	63
1988	25	64	85	11	39	50
1987	24†	71†	87†	10†	35†	65†
1986	21	76	90	6	34	66
1985	20	79	88	6	25	75
1984	32	58	83	9	22	64
1983	15	78	76	16	29	62
1982	29	58	77	10	23	55
1981	37	53	77	17	37	53

† Not eligible for all recorded votes.

Interest Group Ratings

Year	ADA	ACU	AFL-CIO	CCUS
1990	78	13	100	36
1989	85	19	91	40
1988	70	22	100	29
1987	76	4	100	7
1986	90	9	93	17
1985	80	5	88	18
1984	70	4	83	29
1983	85	9	100	25
1982	70	5	89	25
1981	75	14	93	11

Wisconsin

U.S. CONGRESS

SENATE 1 D, 1 R
HOUSE 4 D, 5 R

LEGISLATURE

Senate 19 D, 14 R
House 58 D, 41 R

ELECTIONS

1988 Presidential Vote	
Bush	48%
Dukakis	51%
1984 Presidential Vote	
Reagan	54%
Mondale	45%
1980 Presidential Vote	
Reagan	48%
Carter	43%
Anderson	7%
Turnout rate in 1986	39%
Turnout rate in 1988	62%
Turnout rate in 1990	35%

(as percentage of voting age population)

POPULATION AND GROWTH

1980 population	4,705,767
1990 population (16th in the nation)	4,891,769
Percent change 1980-1990	+4%

DEMOGRAPHIC BREAKDOWN

White	92%
Black	5%
Asian or Pacific Islander	1%
(Hispanic origin)	2%
Urban	64%
Rural	36%
Born in state	77%
Foreign-born	3%

MAJOR CITIES

Milwaukee	628,088
Madison	191,262
Green Bay	96,466
Racine	84,298
Kenosha	80,352

AREA AND LAND USE

Area 54,426 sq. miles (25th)

Farm	50%
Forest	44%
Federally owned	5%

Gov. Tommy G. Thompson (R)
Of Elroy — Elected 1986

Born: Nov. 19, 1941, Elroy, Wis.
Education: U. of Wisconsin, B.S. 1963, J.D. 1966.
Military Service: Army Reserve and National Guard, 1966-76.
Occupation: Lawyer; real estate broker.
Religion: Roman Catholic.
Political Career: Wis. Assembly, 1967-87, Republican floor leader, 1981-87; sought GOP nomination in U.S. House special election, 1979.
Next Election: 1994.

WORK

Occupations	
White-collar	48%
Blue-collar	33%
Service workers	14%
Government Workers	
Federal	27,808
State	88,230
Local	224,984

MONEY

Median family income	$ 20,915	(15th)
Tax burden per capita	$ 1,061	(10th)

EDUCATION

Spending per pupil through grade 12	$ 4,747	(13th)
Persons with college degrees	15%	(30th)

CRIME

Violent crime rate 223 per 100,000 (43rd)

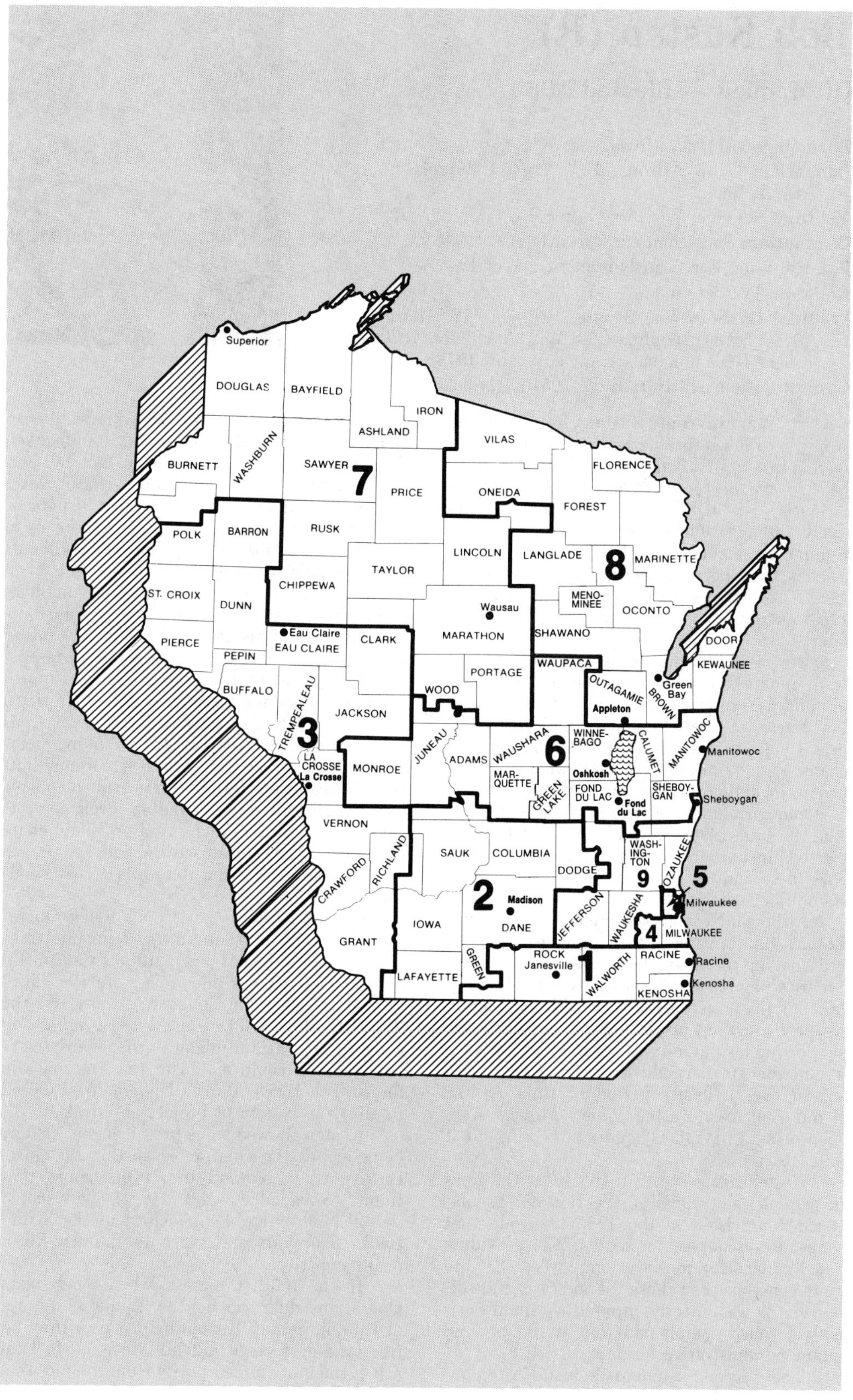
Superior
DOUGLAS
BAYFIELD
IRON
ASHLAND
VILAS
FLORENCE
BURNETT
WASHBURN
SAWYER
7
PRICE
ONEIDA
FOREST
POLK
BARRON
RUSK
LINCOLN
LANGLADE
8
MARINETTE
TAYLOR
CHIPPEWA
ST. CROIX
DUNN
MENO-
MINEE
OCONTO
Wausau
PIERCE
Eau Claire
EAU CLAIRE
CLARK
MARATHON
SHAWANO
DOOR
PEPIN
KEWAUNEE
WAUPACA
PORTAGE
BUFFALO
OUTAGAMIE
Green Bay
BROWN
WOOD
JACKSON
Appleton
TREMPEALEAU
3
WAUSHARA
6
WINNE-
BAGO
CALUMET
MANITOWOC
Manitowoc
JUNEAU
ADAMS
LA CROSSE
La Crosse
MONROE
Oshkosh
MAR-
QUETTE
GREEN LAKE
FOND DU LAC
Fond du Lac
SHEBOY-
GAN
Sheboygan
VERNON
WASH-
ING-
TON
SAUK
COLUMBIA
RICHLAND
DODGE
OZAUKEE
5
9
CRAWFORD
2
Madison
Milwaukee
JEFFERSON
WAUKESHA
IOWA
DANE
4
MILWAUKEE
GRANT
ROCK
Janesville
1
RACINE
Racine
GREEN
LAFAYETTE
WALWORTH
Kenosha
KENOSHA

Bob Kasten (R)

Of Mequon — Elected 1980

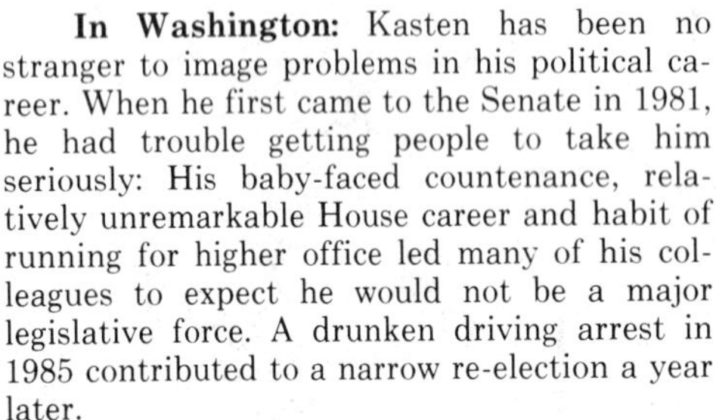

Born: June 19, 1942, Milwaukee, Wis.

Education: U. of Arizona, B.A. 1964; Columbia U., M.B.A. 1966.

Military Service: Wis. Air National Guard, 1967-72.

Occupation: Shoe company executive.

Family: Wife, Eva Jean Nimmons; one child.

Religion: Presbyterian.

Political Career: Wis. Senate, 1973-75; U.S. House, 1975-79; GOP nominee for Wis. Assembly, 1970; sought GOP nomination for governor, 1978.

Capitol Office: 110 Hart Bldg. 20510; 224-5323.

In Washington: Kasten has been no stranger to image problems in his political career. When he first came to the Senate in 1981, he had trouble getting people to take him seriously: His baby-faced countenance, relatively unremarkable House career and habit of running for higher office led many of his colleagues to expect he would not be a major legislative force. A drunken driving arrest in 1985 contributed to a narrow re-election a year later.

But as Kasten heads toward a bid for his third Senate term in 1992, he can give evidence of building a reputation as a productive legislator. As ranking Republican on the Small Business Committee, he has carved a niche as a champion of issues dear to that panel's constituency, including payroll and capital gains tax cuts and curtailment of regulatory bureaucracy. And in late 1990, Kasten's GOP colleagues elected him secretary of the Republican Conference, a second-tier leadership post that helps frame floor-vote strategies.

Although New York Democrat Daniel Patrick Moynihan gained more publicity with his proposal in the 101st Congress to cut Social Security payroll taxes, Kasten was in the forefront of the issue on the GOP side, calling on his party to keep up its lower-taxes image by supporting his payroll tax-cut plan. It included a somewhat smaller reduction than Moynihan's, spread over a longer period of time. In the 102nd Congress, Kasten joined Moynihan in sponsoring a payroll tax reductions bill, but it failed by a 60-38 vote.

Kasten did succeed in the 101st Congress in helping gain repeal of "Section 89" regulations, a provision in the 1986 tax code that sought to discourage employers from providing benefit plans for top-level employees that are more generous than those for the rank and file. Section 89 was bitterly opposed by small businesses, which complained that it imposed an undue administrative burden.

These accomplishments helped Kasten put behind him memories of a nasty 1986 re-election contest in which his arrest for drunken driving was held up as evidence that his personal qualities were unbefitting a senator. After Kasten won that campaign with just 51 percent of the vote, he applied himself more seriously to legislative pursuits, and perhaps more importantly, to showing personal development. When asked about his most significant accomplishments, he pointedly cited his marriage in 1986, and the birth of his daughter in 1987. A "father and legislator," Kasten began calling himself.

Kasten has been very active on the Appropriations Subcommittee on Foreign Operations; he chaired that panel when Republicans controlled the Senate and is now its ranking member, working with Democratic Chairman Patrick J. Leahy of Vermont. The subcommittee has responsibility over funding levels for foreign aid programs, which often provoke Senate strife. But Kasten has used the panel to pursue an environmental issue that cuts across partisan lines.

One of Kasten's goals on Foreign Operations is to get multilateral development banks to put more emphasis on environmental considerations when assessing projects in the Third World. In the 99th Congress, he pressed the World Bank to hold up nearly $500 million in loans for a Brazilian highway that many scientists thought could endanger the Amazon rain forest. The World Bank's leadership promised to alter the system of project approval.

Kasten showed some prescience in 1990 by being among the senators suggesting a comprehensive trade ban on Iraq even before that country invaded Kuwait. He also advocated establishing a new loan facility in the World Bank to provide assistance to Eastern European countries.

In the 100th Congress, when the Foreign Operations chair was held by Daniel K. Inouye of Hawaii, he and Kasten helped pass the first freestanding foreign aid bill since 1981. That achievement stemmed partly from the fact that a budget-summit agreement between the White House and Congress had settled a major issue — how much to spend on foreign aid. With that determined, there was broad support in both chambers for the $14.3 billion bill.

There was still some disagreement, however. For years Kasten, along with Inouye, had pushed to restructure the foreign military aid program, which provides grants and loans to U.S. allies for the purchase of military equipment. Arguing that the loans were adding to the debt burden carried by many poor Third World nations, Kasten has with some success sought to redirect the program toward outright grants.

Kasten's most visible legislative triumph as a senator came early in his first term. Though he was denounced as a tax cheater's champion, a shill for bankers and a proponent of "government by applause meter," Kasten persevered and won in a 1983 crusade to block tax withholding on income from interest and dividends.

Kasten has also been a player in the frustrating effort to rewrite the nation's product liability laws.

In tackling the product liability system in the 99th Congress, Kasten had a popular issue, at least among many businesses and insurance companies. Reeling from the huge awards sometimes given to consumers injured by faulty products — and struggling to comply with the diverse network of state liability laws — business groups strongly supported his proposal to pre-empt state laws with a federal standard governing liability lawsuits. But Kasten's proposals drew criticism from consumer groups and trial lawyers, who feared they would leave consumers defenseless against negligent or unethical manufacturers.

Kasten and his allies sought to improve their chances by dropping a controversial provision that allowed only one victim of a defective product to win punitive damages from its manufacturer. Still, the bill did not get out of the Commerce Committee, failing on an 8-8 tie.

The following year, Kasten offered one of a number of more modest proposals that aimed at setting some limits on damage awards, without confronting the larger issue of pre-empting state liability laws. The committee approved a bill similar to Kasten's, but it fell victim to filibuster threats on the floor.

Kasten's partisan instincts show up in some of his extracurricular activities. In 1988, he served as a co-chairman of the Republican Platform Committee, and he has always taken a strong interest in his colleagues' re-election campaigns. As a House member, his best-known work was political: He was the author of the "Kasten plan," a system of precinct organizing for congressional campaigns.

Kasten considered running for the position of National Republican Senatorial Committee chair in 1982 and again in 1988, but did not. In 1984 he sought the post of majority whip for the 99th Congress, but he lost by a wide margin to the popular Alan K. Simpson of Wyoming.

At Home: As the 1986 election year approached, Democrats were eager for the opportunity to prove their contention that Kasten was too far right and too tainted by questions of personal integrity to win again in a state that had not re-elected a Republican in 30 years. They had been spoiling for Kasten ever since he upset Democratic Sen. Gaylord Nelson in 1980.

And Kasten's detractors had reason to be optimistic. Late in 1985, he was arrested for drunken driving in Washington, D.C. Kasten avoided a criminal record by completing a course in alcohol abuse, but he was still subjected to a barrage of negative media coverage and editorials at home.

That incident also served to reignite other concerns that had troubled him earlier in his term. In 1982 his image was tarnished by publicity about his earlier association with a real estate developer who was accused of theft and fraud and eventually went to jail.

Despite Kasten's potential vulnerability, Democrats failed to pick a candidate strong enough to take advantage of it. Their nominee, former state Deputy Attorney General Ed Garvey, struggled to prove he was not as far to the left of the political consensus as he claimed Kasten was to the right. And in one of the year's most negative contests, Garvey's character became as much of an issue as Kasten's.

Garvey, who was best known for his 13-year tenure outside the state as executive director of the National Football League Players Association, had strong support from organized labor, but he was battered during the primary by an opponent who labeled him a "special-interest puppet."

And though he quickly went on the offensive against Kasten, accusing him of "drinking on the job" and reminding voters that Kasten had once been three years late filing a tax return, Garvey had trouble endearing himself to voters. In September it was reported that a writer hired by Garvey to investigate Kasten had misrepresented himself to gain interviews with several journalists and one Democratic U.S. representative.

Kasten blasted Garvey for his "Watergate tactics" and ran ads citing a report that $750,000 had disappeared from the players' union during Garvey's tenure. Garvey responded by filing a libel suit against Kasten.

The contest left both candidates splattered with mud and made it difficult for Garvey to sell himself as an attractive alternative for voters disenchanted with the incumbent. And Kasten, in addition to having an enormous campaign treasury, capitalized on his growing stature as a legislator and his well-publicized efforts to bring federal funds into the state. In the end, he won 51-47 percent.

Aggressive and determined, Kasten made

it to the Senate in 1981 after a methodical 10-year climb in which he ran for five different offices in six elections and rebounded with surprising agility from his one major defeat.

His early political successes earned him a reputation as the "Golden Boy" of Wisconsin's GOP. He rose quickly from the state Senate in 1973 to Congress in 1975 and became the party's endorsed candidate for governor in 1978.

But his reputation was tarnished that year when he dropped the GOP gubernatorial primary to Lee Sherman Dreyfus, a colorful political novice whose entertaining oratory contrasted with Kasten's more reserved, serious style. In trying to expand his renowned precinct operation to cover the entire state, Kasten spent so much time planning for the general election that he let the primary slip away.

After the unexpected 1978 loss, Kasten knew another failure in 1980 would probably end his political career. But with three unimpressive candidates offering the only opposition for the right to challenge Nelson, he felt it was too good an opportunity to pass up.

Kasten's 1980 campaign showed clearly that he had learned from mistakes made in 1978. Honing his operation for the GOP primary, Kasten focused his efforts in eight key counties — and won all but one. His strength was concentrated in suburban Milwaukee, his old congressional district base.

Still, Kasten entered the 1980 general election as the underdog against Nelson, a two-term governor and three-term senator who had held public office continuously since 1948.

Although Kasten launched his campaign late and trailed significantly in funding, he won narrowly. Many blue-collar Democrats in Milwaukee and the industrial Fox River Valley favored Kasten's calls for less government and lower taxes over Nelson's traditional liberalism.

The nephew of a prominent Milwaukee banker, Kasten worked in a family shoe business before entering politics in the suburbs north and west of the city. After losing a state legislative election at age 28, he defeated a Republican state senator in 1972, then unseated U.S. Rep. Glenn Davis in a 1974 GOP primary.

Committees

Small Business (Ranking)
Rural Economy & Family Farming (ranking); Government Contracting & Paperwork Reduction

Appropriations (5th of 13 Republicans)
Foreign Operations (ranking); Agriculture, Rural Development & Related Agencies; Commerce, Justice, State & Judiciary; Defense; Transportation

Budget (4th of 9 Republicans)

Commerce, Science & Transportation (5th of 9 Republicans)
Surface Transportation (ranking); Aviation; Consumer; Science, Technology & Space; National Ocean Policy Study

Elections

1986 General		
Bob Kasten (R)	754,573	(51%)
Ed Garvey (D)	702,963	(47%)

Previous Winning Percentages: **1980** (50%) **1976 *** (66%) **1974 *** (53%)

* *House elections.*

Campaign Finance

	Receipts	Receipts from PACs		Expenditures
1986				
Kasten (R)	$3,196,093	$1,095,726	(34%)	$3,433,870
Garvey (D)	$1,308,927	$456,082	(35%)	$1,306,702

Key Votes

1991	
Authorize use of force against Iraq	Y
1990	
Oppose prohibition of certain semiautomatic weapons	Y
Support constitutional amendment on flag desecration	Y
Oppose requiring parental notice for minors' abortions	N
Halt production of B-2 stealth bomber at 13 planes	N
Approve budget that cut spending and raised revenues	N
Pass civil rights bill over Bush veto	N
1989	
Oppose reduction of SDI funding	Y
Oppose barring federal funds for "obscene" art	N
Allow vote on capital gains tax cut	Y

Voting Studies

	Presidential Support		Party Unity		Conservative Coalition	
Year	**S**	**O**	**S**	**O**	**S**	**O**
1990	71	29	80	20	81	19
1989	85	15	90	10	84	16
1988	74	19	78	19	84	14
1987	68	31	90	9	91	9
1986	81	19	74	26	87	13
1985	74	26	68	32	75	25
1984	74	21	83	13	87	11
1983	68	32	78	17	93	7
1982	77	22	83	16	88	12
1981	80	20	84	15	88	11

Interest Group Ratings

Year	ADA	ACU	AFL-CIO	CCUS
1990	6	91	44	83
1989	10	89	20	88
1988	10	84	43	71
1987	10	92	30	83
1986	15	83	27	74
1985	10	70	38	72
1984	15	95	18	89
1983	10	76	13	79
1982	5	85	16	70
1981	10	80	16	83

Herb Kohl (D)

Of Milwaukee — Elected 1988

Born: Feb. 7, 1935, Milwaukee, Wis.
Education: U. of Wisconsin, B.A. 1956; Harvard U., M.B.A. 1958.
Military Service: Army Reserve, 1958-64.
Occupation: Businessman; professional basketball team owner.
Family: Single.
Religion: Jewish.
Political Career: Wis. Democratic Party chairman, 1975-77.
Capitol Office: 330 Hart Bldg. 20510; 224-5653.

In Washington: Kohl has found it hard to match the pace of his campaign in the office he now occupies. It took him several months in the 101st Congress to choose his top aide, and his inexperience in government and politics is still evident. Admittedly shy and a loner, the pleasant and wealthy Kohl appears to many to be culturally removed from Congress — the proverbial fish out of water.

Kohl's life had been devoted to running his family's enterprises in food, retailing and real estate. So his adjustment may have fit the pattern of executives who arrive in Congress to find they no longer call the tune, not even for themselves. "I'm always subject to a schedule I don't create," Kohl told a reporter.

Kohl's difficulties started early. Arriving in Washington to vote for party leaders in November 1988, Kohl announced early for George J. Mitchell of Maine as Senate majority leader. Mitchell went on to win, but it did not help Kohl, who asked for seats on Appropriations (where his predecessor, William Proxmire, had sat), Agriculture or even Budget. He got, instead, seats on Governmental Affairs, Judiciary and the Special Committee on Aging — arguably the least impressive assignments meted out to any Senate freshman that term.

Later, at a meeting of the Wisconsin delegation, he suggested that his colleagues had done less than they might have to bring federal spending home. That touchy subject reportedly provoked a rebuke from Wisconsin Democrat David R. Obey, the fifth-ranking Democrat on the House Appropriations Committee.

On Judiciary, Kohl lacks the star quality other Democratic members of the committee have obtained; three of his seven colleagues on the panel have already run for president. During the 101st Congress, Kohl did accomplish his goal of seeing legislation enacted that made it a federal crime to develop, produce, sell or possess a biological weapon. He goes off in a number of directions, but with the exception of chemical warfare, has not become closely identified with any major theme or issue.

Kohl was active during consideration of legislation designed to reduce vertical price fixing; an antitrust bill to prevent manufacturers from fixing prices by their dealers stalled in the Senate at the end of the 101st Congress but passed the chamber in May 1991.

Kohl also has started pushing a privacy measure aimed at regulating telephone "Caller ID" service — by requiring phone companies to give customers the option of blocking the display of their numbers free of charge.

At the start of the 102nd Congress, the Judiciary Committee added a new panel on Juvenile Justice, and made Kohl its chairman. He will oversee such topics as gang violence and youth incarceration.

Kohl generally has shown himself to be sincere and disinclined to follow Proxmire's idiosyncratic patterns. On foreign policy and defense, his positions are predictably liberal. Shortly after his arrival he sided with the majority of his Democratic colleagues in rejecting the nomination of former Sen. John Tower as secretary of defense. And he has consistently been with them on the big votes since: from raising the minimum wage to overriding President Bush's veto of the 1990 civil rights bill to resisting the use of military force in the Persian Gulf in 1991.

A consistent vote to cut weapons systems, Kohl was an early and loud voice opposing President Bush's buildup of U.S. forces in the Persian Gulf. He called the administration's escalating talk of war in December 1990 "deplorable" and criticized Bush for turning the sensitive and multi-faceted Middle East situation into "a game of chicken."

But if Kohl has proven less of a loner than Proxmire, he has also inherited his predecessor's preoccupation with the budget deficit. Kohl's maiden speech was a jeremiad against the deficit, which he said would bring "the economic collapse we all fear."

At Home: Kohl will have to compile a

substantial record of achievement in the Senate before people stop talking about how he got there. Making his first try for public office, Kohl announced about six months before the election yet spent just under $7.5 million, nearly all of it his own. He blew away the best competition in his own party and beat an attractive Republican moderate in November.

Kohl showed some rough edges in the campaign, on one occasion naming Jimmy Carter's secretary of defense when asked who currently held the job. A multimillionaire who owns Milwaukee's professional basketball team, Kohl made a remark about the employment the team had provided for blacks that some found in poor taste.

But Kohl's errors were swept away in a sea of positive images. Mostly, these were communicated by Kohl's saturation TV advertising, which emphasized his private-sector success and commitment to service — beginning with his immigrant parents.

It was a campaign on a scale unlike any the state had seen. Kohl's total outlay doubled the previous state record (he even bought time on Minnesota stations to reach border counties). A Milwaukee columnist suggested that one channel on everyone's TV set simply be rented to Kohl for the duration.

Although his political involvement had been as financier and, briefly, state party chairman, Kohl showed some flair for debate. In the primary, facing former Gov. Anthony S. Earl and 1986 Senate nominee Ed Garvey, Kohl affably deflected their jibes and jabs with personal affability and a simple thematic message: "Nobody's senator but yours."

Kohl's emphasis on his independence played well, especially against efforts to vilify him as a plutocrat. He found the one political positive he could in being one of the state's richest men and used it to strike an improbable, but apparently effective, parallel with Proxmire, the legendary pinchpenny. Proxmire had served three decades without spending much (and sometimes virtually nothing) on his reelection campaigns. He got away with it because he was popular enough to discourage challengers in his weight class. Kohl claimed similar independence based on his ability to self-finance his campaigns.

Some Wisconsin Democrats had been eager to unleash Kohl's assets in the 1986 election against GOP Sen. Bob Kasten. That was the year after Kohl had spent $18.5 million to keep the Milwaukee Bucks franchise in town. But Kohl turned down the overtures then.

When Kohl entered the Democratic primary in late spring 1988, Earl was the front-runner and Rep. Jim Moody of Milwaukee was an apparent second. Moody dropped out, but Earl and Garvey made a bitter fight of it. Earl spent money on negative ads satirizing Kohl's miscues and lack of political sophistication.

Kohl, staying on the high road, posted an easy plurality in the September primary. His November foe was Susan S. Engeleiter, GOP leader in the state Senate and perhaps the most successful woman ever in Wisconsin politics. A decade earlier, when just 26, she had come within a few hundred votes of being nominated to a safe GOP House seat. In the meantime she had finished law school, had a family and worked for a GOP governor.

In the GOP primary, Engeleiter defeated a much more conservative opponent, former state party Chairman Steve King, who challenged her for the nomination when popular Republican Gov. Tommy G. Thompson demurred. King openly questioned whether Engeleiter, with young children at home, should be in public office at all.

Engeleiter was never in danger of losing the nomination, but her winning margin was smaller than expected, and King's attacks highlighted issues on which she differed from much of her party — including her support for limited abortion rights and for the Equal Rights Amendment.

By forcing Engeleiter rightward, albeit briefly, King may have given the unabashedly liberal Kohl running room in the center he otherwise would not have had. Engeleiter tried to compete with the continuing deluge of Kohl ads on TV by portraying herself as more in tune with ordinary people's problems. She downplayed ideology by labeling herself "A Wisconsin Original."

But her financing had never been in a league with Kohl's, so she tried to break out with a dramatic tactic in a debate between the two candidates. She accused a company Kohl's family had owned of selling coffee cakes to the military at inflated prices. Kohl seemed unperturbed. Newspaper reporters subsequently found the difference in price attributable to a difference in size. The issue fizzled.

In the campaign's closing weeks, polls found Engeleiter gaining on Kohl. But time ran out before she could find an issue or other means of closing the last few percentage points of deficit. Shortly after the election, President Bush named her to head the Small Business Administration, a job she held for two years.

Committees

Governmental Affairs (6th of 8 Democrats)
Government Information & Regulation (chairman); Oversight of Government Management; Permanent Subcommittee on Investigations

Judiciary (8th of 8 Democrats)
Juvenile Justice (chairman); Courts & Administrative Practice; Technology & the Law

Special Aging (10th of 11 Democrats)

Elections

1988 General		
Herb Kohl (D)	1,128,625	(52%)
Susan Engeleiter (R)	1,030,440	(48%)
1988 Primary		
Herb Kohl (D)	249,226	(47%)
Anthony S. Earl (D)	203,479	(38%)
Ed Garvey (D)	55,225	(10%)

Campaign Finance

	Receipts	Receipts from PACs		Expend-itures
1988				
Kohl (D)	$7,576,540	0		$7,491,600
Engeleiter (R)	$2,945,328	$993,692	(34%)	$2,908,101

Key Votes

1991	
Authorize use of force against Iraq	N
1990	
Oppose prohibition of certain semiautomatic weapons	N
Support constitutional amendment on flag desecration	N
Oppose requiring parental notice for minors' abortions	Y
Halt production of B-2 stealth bomber at 13 planes	Y
Approve budget that cut spending and raised revenues	Y
Pass civil rights bill over Bush veto	Y
1989	
Oppose reduction of SDI funding	N
Oppose barring federal funds for "obscene" art	Y
Allow vote on capital gains tax cut	N

Voting Studies

	Presidential Support		Party Unity		Conservative Coalition	
Year	**S**	**O**	**S**	**O**	**S**	**O**
1990	25	75	86	12	19	81
1989	47	53	87	13	18	82

Interest Group Ratings

Year	ADA	ACU	AFL-CIO	CCUS
1990	94	9	67	8
1989	95	11	90	25

1 Les Aspin (D)

Of East Troy — Elected 1970

Born: July 21, 1938, Milwaukee, Wis.
Education: Yale U., B.A. 1960; Oxford U., M.A. 1962; Massachusetts Institute of Technology, Ph.D. 1965.
Military Service: Army, 1966-68.
Occupation: Professor of economics.
Family: Divorced.
Religion: Episcopalian.
Political Career: Sought Democratic nomination for Wis. treasurer, 1968.
Capitol Office: 2336 Rayburn Bldg. 20515; 225-3031.

In Washington: The towering intellect of Aspin has long been recognized by his colleagues in Congress and others in the Washington political community. It is acknowledged even by those who have at times bridled at his brash ways as chairman of the Armed Services Committee. But to gain national regard as a political savant — a rank Aspin appeared to achieve early in the 102nd Congress — it takes more than just brainpower: It takes timing.

Aspin earned his exalted status because of his early and outspoken support of using military force to end Iraq's occupation of Kuwait. Aspin stood out not so much for backing the popular hard-line policy of President George Bush — a number of Democrats did that — as for his analytical approach to the conflict. In a series of speeches and "white papers" before and during the war with Iraq, Aspin predicted with stunning accuracy the scenario that unfolded: a massive air assault, followed by a lightning-fast ground offensive with few U.S. casualties.

Aspin's hawkish views on the war did not sit well with many Democrats. Through much of his tenure as Armed Services chairman, centrist Aspin had gotten grief from the liberals who dominate the Democratic Caucus over his willingness to support GOP administrations on certain key defense issues.

In 1987, just two years after he had gained the gavel, Aspin barely held off a coup fueled by liberals angry with his support for the Reagan administration's position on the MX missile. When Aspin in 1989 supported Bush's first defense budget, Democratic critics muttered that he had learned nothing from his earlier close call.

However, Aspin's views on the Persian Gulf War drew no backlash. After the fighting, Democrats who had opposed the early use of military force faced GOP threats that the issue would be used against them at election time. These Democrats much preferred to put the matter behind them than to hold Aspin to some standard of party loyalty.

But Aspin had also helped insulate himself from intraparty attacks by adopting a new approach to the chairmanship during the 101st Congress. Previously known for keeping his own counsel, Aspin consulted more frequently with Democratic colleagues, and brought key members into the process of drawing up sections of the fiscal 1991 defense authorization bill. Moreover, Aspin led the charge in 1990 against several expensive strategic weapons systems — including the B-2 stealth bomber — that had long been opposed by his liberal former critics.

Some in this latter group even saw some benefit in Aspin's strong support for the Persian Gulf War. With Aspin leading the fight against the B-2 and other Bush priorities, he was able to give House Democrats more cover against efforts by Republicans to brand them as "soft on defense."

Aspin did not shock anyone with his views on the crisis that followed Iraq's August 1990 invasion of Kuwait. By early October, he had reached the conclusion that economic sanctions alone would not force Iraqi dictator Saddam Hussein to give up Kuwait.

When Bush doubled the U.S. troop commitment in November and created the possibility of offensive military action, the usually hawkish Senate Armed Services Chairman Sam Nunn turned against him. But Aspin backed Bush. While Nunn's hearings on the crisis featured a parade of witnesses — included former chairmen of the Joint Chiefs of Staff — who warned against a rush to war, Aspin brought in think-tank experts and Defense Department analysts more sanguine about the prospect.

As the Jan. 15, 1991, United Nations-set deadline for Iraqi withdrawal approached, Aspin issued his detailed analyses building a case for force. A former economics professor who is said to regard the think-tank crowd — not his House colleagues — as his peers, Aspin took a typically dry and academic approach to the emotional debate. "I believe prospects are high for a rapid victory with light to moderate American casualties, perhaps three to five thousand

Wisconsin 1

Southeast — Racine; Kenosha

Although it is dominated by four industrialized cities, the 1st is far from a Democratic stronghold.

Until Aspin's election in 1970, Democrats had won this district only twice in the 20th century — in 1958 and 1964. Both incumbents were defeated after serving single terms. The party has not done much better in presidential voting. After Lyndon B. Johnson carried the district in 1964, Democrats endured a long dry spell. Not until 1988 did it return to the Democratic column, and even then Michael S. Dukakis managed just a slim 51 percent victory.

The district's two largest cities are sandwiched between Milwaukee and Chicago on the Lake Michigan shore: Racine, originally settled by Danish immigrants, and Kenosha, home to a sizable Italian community. Kenosha has a branch of the University of Wisconsin and an assembly plant for Jeeps, but its economic base is not as diversified as Racine's. Over 5,000 jobs were lost in Kenosha when the Chrysler Corporation closed the plant that had been a cornerstone of the city's economy for almost nine decades.

But Kenosha has shown a resilient spirit, and within weeks of the plant closing, a waterfront development project was planned. Scores of Chicago commuters, attracted by affordable land prices and quality-of-life concerns, are also moving to the area.

In the west-central part of the district are the smaller industrial cities of Janesville and Beloit, both in politically marginal Rock County. Beloit was settled by a group of immigrants from New Hampshire that founded Beloit College in 1847. Janesville's employers include a General Motors plant.

The strongest Republican vote in the 1st comes from Walworth County, between Janesville and Racine-Kenosha. Resort complexes around Lake Geneva and Lake Delavan cater to wealthy vacationers from Milwaukee and Chicago. Soybeans grow so well in the farming sections of Walworth County that the Japanese Kikkoman soy sauce company built a plant in Walworth to brew and bottle its product.

Population: 522,838. White 491,746 (94%), Black 21,956 (4%), Other 3,054 (1%). Spanish origin 13,173 (3%). 18 and over 366,924 (70%), 65 and over 56,852 (11%). Median age: 29.

including 500 to 1,000 dead," wrote Aspin in a report released four days before Congress authorized Bush to use military force.

This bloodless approach to potential bloodshed enraged those opposed to war, including *Washington Post* columnist Mary McGrory, who called Aspin's definition of light casualties "an obscene utterance" that reflected his "boyish relish in the tough-guy jargon of the military-industrial complex." But Aspin responded that such risk analysis is essential when contemplating war. "People are doing this kind of calculation, implicitly or explicitly," Aspin said. "If you're talking about lives, that's the most important time to do the analysis."

The war unfolded much as Aspin predicted. When Saddam Hussein, on the eve of the U.S.-led ground offensive in February 1991, made several heavily conditioned offers to withdraw from Kuwait, Aspin urged Bush to press for an unconditional surrender. "[The Iraqi army] is on the verge of collapse," Aspin said. "This is not the time to lose our nerve and compromise ... to allow Saddam to 'save face.' "

Thus, on the subject of war, the Aspin of 1991 was a much different person from the Aspin who came to Congress in 1971. An opponent of U.S. involvement in the Vietnam War, Aspin was typecast as a "liberal Pentagon critic" in the 1970s: He led a maverick minority against the conservative "Old Guard" then dominant on Armed Services, and gained attention for his irreverent press releases.

However, both Aspin's allies and adversaries miscast him as a down-the-line liberal. A former Pentagon economist under Defense Secretary Robert S. McNamara, Aspin has always been prone to take a harder line than his fellow liberals. His rebellion against Armed Services' reflexively pro-Pentagon leadership was based more on a desire to re-establish the committee's policy-making role than on zeal to slash the defense budget.

Aspin did in fact support much of the military buildup sponsored by President Ronald Reagan. When liberals in 1983 came close to killing the multi-warhead MX missile, which they opposed for its cost and as a destabilizing element in the U.S.-Soviet arms race, Aspin and other moderates salvaged it in a deal with the Reagan administration. Aspin adopted the view that the missile was a bargaining chip with Moscow, a prod to push Reagan toward arms control talks, and a chance for Democrats to prove their support for defense.

Many of his old liberal allies nonetheless supported Aspin, then seventh in committee seniority, in the 1985 coup that ousted the aged and enfeebled Melvin Price of Illinois as Armed Services chairman. But if they hoped Aspin would move radically to stanch the military buildup, they were to be disappointed.

Calling his victory "a signal that the Democratic Party ought to be doing some serious looking at defense," Aspin insisted that Democrats had to counter voters' image of the party as anti-defense. "If we want to make defense policy in the White House and Pentagon, then we had better stand for something," he said. "The voters are not attracted to national-security naysayers."

Aspin then helped engineer the MX's rescue once again. He negotiated the compromise that capped the number of missiles to be deployed in fixed silos at 50; after the measure was approved, Aspin declared it the last word of Congress on the MX: "It's over. It's done."

That action, along with his 1986 vote to aid the Nicaraguan contras, sparked a "dump Aspin" move at the end of the 99th Congress. Conservative Texas Rep. Marvin Leath formed a coalition of revenge-minded "Old Guard" supporters and angry liberals, who combined to strip Aspin of the chairmanship on a 130-124 vote in January 1987. But Aspin recouped two weeks later: He defeated three challengers, beating Leath on the final ballot, 133-116.

Aspin promised greater consultation. He also provided a stronger committee role for such centrist Democrats as Dave McCurdy of Oklahoma, John M. Spratt Jr. of South Carolina and Richard Ray of Georgia. But other Democrats remained skeptical. In 1989, Aspin — citing the need, driven by budget deficits and thawing U.S.-Soviet relations, to trim the defense budget — urged the committee and House to pass Bush's initial weapons procurement proposal intact. "While the budget may not be perfect, it's a darn good product ... I think [Defense Secretary Dick Cheney] deserves a vote of confidence," Aspin said.

But the Bush plan continued programs, such as the B-2 bomber, MX missile and strategic defense initiative (SDI), that liberals wanted eliminated or reduced. It also cut out such programs as the F-14 fighter and the V-22 Osprey helicopter/airplane, which employed thousands of workers, many in Democratic-held districts. In June 1989, the House voted to restore money to these programs and cut some of Bush's priorities. A dejected Aspin then enraged Democrats again by calling the House bill "a Michael Dukakis defense budget," a reference to the 1988 Democratic presidential nominee's "weak-on-defense" image.

However, Aspin moved soon thereafter to modify what even his ally McCurdy referred to as a "Lone Ranger" style. He revamped the Armed Services staff, bringing on seasoned Hill operatives who improved his liaison with Democratic members. Aspin also established a more adversarial approach toward the Bush administration on defense policy. He chastised Bush and Cheney as reacting too slowly to the reduction in U.S.-Soviet tensions and the fall of communism in Eastern Europe.

Aspin called for a strategy emphasizing conventional weapons and manpower, and lessening dependence on nuclear weapons designed to resist a diminishing Soviet threat. "There are new realities in the world, but no new thinking at home to match them," Aspin said in February 1990, after Bush released his fiscal 1991 defense budget proposal.

In July 1990, Aspin lent his credentials to the effort by a coalition of arms control liberals and fiscally minded conservatives to kill the B-2, a high-tech, radar-evading bomber with an enormous price tag. This move put Aspin on a collision course with Nunn, a fellow intellectual and the dominant force in Senate defense policy, who avidly supported the B-2.

The Senate, with Nunn in the lead, authorized $2.85 billion to complete the 15 already approved B-2s and to buy components for further production; the House voted to cancel the program. A $2.25 billion figure was settled on, but ambiguous language left the question of additional production up in the air. While Nunn argued that the "B-2 is alive and well," Aspin warned the Air Force against using money for any purpose but to complete the authorized 15 planes. "If they jack around, we cut off all B-2 money, and we don't care whether they get 15 operational planes or a lot of boxes of spare parts," he said.

Although Aspin and Nunn are often cast as competitors for the unofficial title of Congress' reigning defense theorist, they have generally worked well together. Both oppose the Reagan/Bush vision of SDI as a space-based antiballistic missile system, and have joined to block administration efforts to reinterpret the 1972 U.S.-Soviet ABM treaty in order to allow airborne testing of SDI technologies.

At Home: When he launched his 1970 congressional campaign, Aspin was a Marquette University economics professor who had just moved into the district. His academic credentials were impressive, and he had been active in statewide politics, but his ties to local politics were not strong.

Two years earlier he had been signed up by the White House to head President Johnson's re-election effort in Wisconsin. When that effort evaporated just before the state's primary, Aspin switched to Robert F. Kennedy's campaign. That September, Aspin was defeated in his first try at elective office, losing the Democratic primary for state treasurer.

Afterward, he moved into the 1st District and became its Democratic chairman. The 1970 House election looked promising for an eager challenger since the incumbent Republican, Henry C. Schadeberg, had won his last two elections with just 51 percent.

To get at Schadeberg, Aspin first had to defeat former Democratic Rep. Gerald T. Flynn and chemistry professor Douglas La Follette in the primary. Flynn posed only a slight problem. But La Follette appealed to the same liberal constituency as Aspin and had a more attractive name — he was a distant relative of the state's legendary governor and U.S. senator, Robert M. La Follette. Aspin appeared to lose the primary but on a recount, won by 20 votes.

The general election offered a clear philosophical choice. Schadeberg emphasized a "return to America's heritage of order, discipline and hard work." Aspin appealed to peace and ecology groups and, when talking with the larger middle-class segment of the electorate, stressed the need to reduce unemployment. With substantial contributions from organized labor and a well-run campaign, Aspin retired Schadeberg with 61 percent.

The 1978 campaign was Aspin's worst political experience of the decade. Some $27,000 in campaign contributions disappeared, stolen by his campaign chairman, who later confessed he took it. And Republican William Petrie, whom Aspin had beaten easily two years before, waged a surprisingly strenuous campaign, holding Aspin to 55 percent, his lowest-ever tally.

In 1980, the GOP line went to surprise primary winner Kathryn H. Canary. For the second consecutive election, Aspin lost the rural areas, but his vote in Racine and Kenosha improved, and he won 56 percent overall.

In 1984, Republicans made one more serious effort behind Pete Jansson, a Racine lawyer armed with a large campaign treasury, backing from the National Republican Congressional Committee and hopes of Reagan coattails. An indication of the seriousness of the challenge was Aspin's acceptance of campaign contributions from the defense contractors he had long criticized. Jansson won conservative Walworth County, but Aspin prevailed in the industrialized areas of Kenosha, Racine and Rock counties, and again won 56 percent. Aspin has won easily since then and in 1990 was re-elected for the first time without Republican opposition.

Committee

Armed Services (Chairman)
Procurement & Military Nuclear Systems (chairman)

Elections

1990 General		
Les Aspin (D)	93,961	(99%)
1990 Primary		
Les Aspin (D)	16,781	(86%)
Charles A. Olson (D)	2,706	(14%)
1988 General		
Les Aspin (D)	158,552	(76%)
Bernie Weaver (R)	49,620	(24%)

Previous Winning Percentages: **1986** (74%) **1984** (56%) **1982** (61%) **1980** (56%) **1978** (55%) **1976** (65%) **1974** (71%) **1972** (64%) **1970** (61%)

District Vote For President

	1988	1984	1980	1976
D	114,078 (51%)	105,412 (45%)	98,916 (42%)	107,718 (48%)
R	107,375 (48%)	126,758 (54%)	117,710 (50%)	108,964 (49%)
I			16,478 (7%)	

Campaign Finance

	Receipts	Receipts from PACs		Expend-itures
1990				
Aspin (D)	$892,153	$322,900	(36%)	$795,806
1988				
Aspin (D)	$618,045	$265,249	(43%)	$631,941
Weaver (R)	$18,626	0		$17,760

Key Votes

1991	
Authorize use of force against Iraq	Y
1990	
Support constitutional amendment on flag desecration	N
Pass family and medical leave bill over Bush veto	N
Reduce SDI funding	Y
Allow abortions in overseas military facilities	Y
Approve budget summit plan for spending and taxing	Y
Approve civil rights bill	Y
1989	
Halt production of B-2 stealth bomber at 13 planes	N
Oppose capital gains tax cut	Y
Approve federal abortion funding in rape or incest cases	?
Approve pay raise and revision of ethics rules	Y
Pass Democratic minimum wage plan over Bush veto	Y

Voting Studies

	Presidential Support		Party Unity		Conservative Coalition	
Year	**S**	**O**	**S**	**O**	**S**	**O**
1990	24	70	83	10	48	46
1989	41	38	70	14	41	51
1988	25	69	78	6	37	50
1987	22	72	81	5	44	51
1986	28	64	83	8	42	48
1985	33	60	82	9	44	49
1984	40	51	73	16	42	54
1983	30	63	84	9	29	67
1982	42	48	77	15	41	53
1981	26	67	80	11	25	68

Interest Group Ratings

Year	ADA	ACU	AFL-CIO	CCUS
1990	61	8	92	38
1989	65	8	82	40
1988	75	4	100	27
1987	76	0	94	8
1986	45	24	80	42
1985	65	19	100	10
1984	75	17	85	36
1983	80	14	94	25
1982	85	10	90	24
1981	75	0	86	7

2 Scott L. Klug (R)

Of Madison — Elected 1990

Born: Jan. 16, 1953, Milwaukee, Wis.

Education: Lawrence U., B.S. 1975; Northwestern U., M.S.J. 1976; U. of Wisconsin, M.B.A. 1990.

Occupation: Television journalist; business development and investment executive.

Family: Wife, Tess Summers; two children.

Religion: Roman Catholic.

Political Career: No previous office.

Capitol Office: 1224 Longworth Bldg. 20515; 225-2906.

The Path to Washington: Less than a month after his upset victory over Democratic Rep. Robert W. Kastenmeier, Klug was one of the featured speakers at a conference in Washington on congressional term limits. It was no accident that Klug was chosen to speak. After unseating a 32-year House incumbent, he is probably more closely identified with the issue than any other member of Congress.

Before term limitation was in vogue nationally, it was a centerpiece of Klug's bid. "The reason I got into this [race], the ideology that really drives me, is the sense that Congress itself is a very troubled institution," said Klug in June. "We need legislation to limit terms in office to 12 years."

As a fundraising device, Klug set up the 32 Club, with contributors paying $32 to join. Those who agreed with the concept of limiting House and Senate members to 12 years in office were asked to give another $12. The club did not collect a lot of money, as Klug raised less than $200,000. But on Election Day, he won with a solid 53 percent.

A former TV journalist, Klug had never held office before, and at the start of the campaign, hardly anyone — from the national GOP to Kastenmeier supporters in Madison — took his chances of winning very seriously.

But Klug had high name familiarity from two years as an investigative reporter and news anchor on WKOW-TV in Madison, and he campaigned effectively against the liberal, antiwar Kastenmeier as an anachronistic part of an ineffective Congress.

Unlike many of Kastenmeier's previous GOP challengers, Klug did not shrilly attack the incumbent. He was frequently complimentary of Kastenmeier, calling him a nice man who had done some good things. But he also criticized him as a career politician who had never made his seniority pay off for the district.

While the Madison-based district has a reputation for knee-jerk liberalism, Klug sought to identify himself with the pocketbook concerns of young families in the growing suburbs of Dane County (Madison). "There are a lot more moderates in this area than there are the politically correct and the terminally hip," Klug said.

He combined a fiscal conservatism — backing both a balanced budget amendment and a line-item veto — with a more libertarian position on social issues. While personally opposed to abortion, he emphasized his support of a woman's right to make the choice herself. And Klug intimated that he would be active on consumer and environmental issues. He produced two documentaries on the topic of farm accidents while at the Madison TV station.

Kastenmeier tried to depict Klug as a carpetbagger. But the challenger was able to deflect the charge by pointing to his Wisconsin roots. The son of an executive with Allis-Chalmers, Klug grew up in the Milwaukee area, graduated from Lawrence University in Appleton, and after a stint as a TV reporter in Seattle and Washington, D.C., returned to the state in 1988 to get a business degree at the University of Wisconsin.

The issue of war and peace came up late in the campaign. On Oct. 1, Kastenmeier was one of just 29 House members — and the only one in the Wisconsin delegation — to vote against the resolution expressing support for President Bush's deployment of troops in the Persian Gulf; Klug backed the deployment.

But Kastenmeier's position failed to rouse the antiwar sentiment that once defined politics in the Madison area. He carried Dane County by less than 4,000 votes, while Klug crushed him by more than 15,000 votes in the rural GOP counties that adjoin Dane.

How partisan will Klug be in Congress? That is an open question. He did not formally join the GOP until a few days before announcing his candidacy in the spring of 1990, and the district he represents has historically supported even the weakest of Democratic presidential candidates.

Wisconsin 2

South — Madison

The 2nd covers a sizable portion of southern Wisconsin's Republican-voting rural areas; its urban centerpiece is the traditionally Democratic city of Madison in Dane County. Madison, the state capital and second largest city in Wisconsin, has its share of industry; meat processor Oscar Mayer, for example, employs nearly 2,500 in its Madison plant. But the city's personality is dominated by its white-collar sector — the bureaucrats who work in local and state government, the 2,300 educators and 41,000 students at the University of Wisconsin, and the large number of insurance company home offices, so many that Madison calls itself a Midwestern Hartford.

Madison boasts a tradition of political liberalism — former GOP Gov. Lee S. Dreyfus once described Madison as "23 square miles surrounded by reality." Since 1924, when Robert M. La Follette carried Dane County as the Progressive Party's presidential candidate, Democrats nearly always win here. Michael S. Dukakis won the county with 60 percent in 1988, and Democratic Senate candidate Herb Kohl polled 58 percent.

But there are signs that Dane County politics is moderating. Longtime Democratic Rep. Robert W. Kastenmeier was upset by Republican Scott L. Klug in 1990 in large part because he could muster only 52 percent of the vote in Dane. Local politicians note that the Madison area is changing, with rapidly growing suburbs such as Middleton and Verona that strike a more conservative tone than the city itself.

Outside the Madison area, agriculture and tourism sustain the district's economy. Dairying is important, and there is some beef production, although many livestock farmers have switched to raising corn as a cash crop.

In New Glarus (Green County), which was founded by the Swiss, the downtown area has been redone to resemble a village in the mother country. Wisconsin Dells (Columbia County) lures big-city tourists to view the garish attractions and natural wonders along the Wisconsin River. Just outside Spring Green (Sauk County) is Frank Lloyd Wright's Taliesin, a studio complex frequently used by the legendary architect that is now a thriving artist colony.

About 50 miles west of Madison is Dodgeville (Iowa County), headquarters to mail order clothier Lands' End. Since the company moved here in 1979, property values have increased and the local economy has blossomed.

The majority of farmers and small-town people in the district are conservative, and they have long chafed at Madison's dominance of district politics. Klug's victory in 1990 showed that the balance of power may be shifting. In 1990, Klug easily offset Kastenmeier's narrow win in Dane County by sweeping every other county in the 2nd.

Population: 523,011. White 509,003 (97%), Black 6,051 (1%), Other 4,986 (1%). Spanish origin 4,233 (1%). 18 and over 383,086 (73%), 65 and over 55,870 (11%). Median age: 29.

Committees

Education & Labor (13th of 14 Republicans)
Elementary, Secondary & Vocational Education; Postsecondary Education; Select Education

Government Operations (15th of 15 Republicans)
Environment, Energy & Natural Resources; Government Activities & Transportation

Select Children, Youth & Families (10th of 14 Republicans)

Campaign Finance

	Receipts	Receipts from PACs		Expend-itures
1990				
Klug (R)	$183,789	$32,800	(18%)	$178,129
Kastenmeier (D)	$358,609	$184,314	(51%)	$371,928

Key Vote

1991

Authorize use of force against Iraq	Y

Elections

1990 General

Scott L. Klug (R)	96,938	(53%)
Robert W. Kastenmeier (D)	85,156	(47%)

District Vote For President

	1988	1984	1980	1976
D	145,141 (55%)	127,626 (50%)	124,236 (47%)	124,106 (51%)
R	114,114 (44%)	124,014 (49%)	106,003 (40%)	109,405 (45%)
I			25,513 (10%)	

3 Steve Gunderson (R)

Of Osseo — Elected 1980

Born: May 10, 1951, Eau Claire, Wis.
Education: U. of Wisconsin, B.A. 1973.; Brown School of Broadcasting, 1974.
Occupation: Public official.
Family: Single.
Religion: Lutheran.
Political Career: Wis. House, 1975-79.
Capitol Office: 2235 Rayburn Bldg. 20515; 225-5506.

In Washington: Few expected Gunderson's support of partisan firebrand Newt Gingrich of Georgia for GOP whip — and his subsequent selection as one of Gingrich's two chief deputy whips — to transform the collegial moderate, long identified with the less doctrinaire faction of House Republicans, into a conservative bomb-thrower. And it has not.

Rather, Gunderson's decision to side with Gingrich over moderate Illinois Republican Edward Madigan in the 1989 whip contest reflected his longstanding desire to reach out to his party's aggressive conservative wing while pursuing an ambitious political agenda.

Gunderson showed interest in a leadership position back in 1987, seeking the chairmanship of the House Republican Research Committee. He served as co-chairman of the moderate GOP '92 Group and took a leading role in party meetings analyzing the 1988 election results.

During all of this, Gunderson was building political relationships with conservatives such as Gingrich, who had made a name with a feisty approach to the Democratic majority. When the party whip job opened up in early 1989, Gunderson worked hard for Gingrich in his contest against Madigan, whose reputation as a low-key insider might have seemed a better fit for the Wisconsin Republican. "Newt adds an element to the leadership team that doesn't exist today," Gunderson said. "He's a ball of energy. He's a visionary and a strategist."

In his new leadership role, Gunderson aims to advance positive GOP alternatives to Democratic programs, rather than simply voicing objections. "We need a governing conservatism that responds to real-life problems, but does so in ways that empower people — not bureaucracies — and maximizes choice rather than federal regulation."

Not long after the new leadership team was in place, a group of Young Turks, led by Texan Steve Bartlett, urged using the movement to repeal a controversial section of the tax code as a test case for a new, more aggressive leadership strategy. Gingrich and Gunderson agreed that repeal of the so-called Section 89 of the 1986 tax-code overhaul was a perfect issue to focus on. The section required employers to prove they were not discriminating among employees on health plans and other benefits.

If nothing else, Gunderson said, an all-out blitz against Section 89 would be "a good learning experience" for the new whip organization. Republicans and supportive Democrats succeeded in publicizing the issue following a close but unsuccessful vote on a procedural measure. The repeal movement gathered steam, and by the end, the House voted 390-36 for repeal.

Gunderson was right behind when Gingrich led a revolt of House Republicans against congressional leaders and President Bush to scuttle the fiscal 1991 budget resolution that had been painstakingly negotiated at a secret bipartisan budget "summit." "We're up in 1990 and he's not," Gunderson said, explaining why Republicans were defecting from their president. He voted against the budget summit agreement, which was soundly rejected, and against the resolution that later prevailed.

Gunderson sheds his partisanship when the subject turns to agriculture. He has been demonstrating his legislative acumen for some time on the Agriculture Committee, where he is ranking Republican on the subcommittee dealing with the dairy programs crucial to Wisconsin. As he has become more politically secure at home, Gunderson also has branched out into other legislative areas, but he is primarily known as "Mr. Dairy," and is second to none in his understanding of dairy-related matters.

When the dairy subcommittee worked on its portion of the 1990 farm bill, Gunderson and Chairman Charles W. Stenholm of Texas produced a plan that set a floor under the previously sliding scale of government price supports for milk. The amendment froze price supports at the existing level of $10.10 per 100 pounds of milk products and barred any decreases for the five-year life of the bill. He argued against attempts to boost the price by 50 cents and by $3 — although he voted for the $3 rise "to protect himself back home," according to an aide. (The amendment was not approved.)

Wisconsin 3

West — Eau Claire; La Crosse

In a state famous for its cows, the 3rd stands at the head of the herd; it has more cows than people and is one of the leading milk-producing districts in the nation. The 3rd hugs western Wisconsin's border with Iowa and Minnesota, and most of its people live on farms or in small crossroads market towns.

In presidential voting, these dairy farmers can be a fickle group. Jimmy Carter carried the district narrowly in 1976, but lost it by 5 points in 1980 as independent candidate John B. Anderson polled 7 percent. Ronald Reagan won the 3rd again in 1984, but four years later it was the Democrats' turn once more, as Michael S. Dukakis beat George Bush 52-47 percent.

There are only two cities of size, roughly equal. Democrats traditionally hold sway in Eau Claire and the counties near it in the northern part of the district. Republicans are dominant in La Crosse and counties south of it along the Mississippi.

Eau Claire was once a wild lumber outpost, cutting logs that floated down the Chippewa River from the northern forests. It still has a paper mill producing disposable diapers and napkins.

La Crosse is Wisconsin's only major Mississippi River city. Two locally owned *Fortune* 500 companies are its mainstays: the Trane Co., manufacturers of heating and air conditioning equipment, employs about 3,000; G. Heileman Brewing Inc. provides about 1,200 jobs.

The rural areas are still heavily Scandinavian. In Osseo, in Trempealeau County, for example, dairy farmers habitually greet the day by trading gossip over coffee and pie at the Norske Nook.

Population: 522,909. White 518,219 (99%), Black 798 (0.2%), Other 2,886 (1%). Spanish origin 1,698 (0.3%). 18 and over 374,265 (72%), 65 and over 68,869 (13%). Median age: 29.

During work on a drought-relief bill in the 100th Congress, Gunderson, working with Minnesota Democrat Timothy J. Penny, came up with an acceptable compromise on an amendment increasing federal price-support payments to dairy farmers. The agreement granted a temporary increase during a three-month period when farmers expected to be hardest hit by drought-related feed costs.

Gunderson also serves on Education and Labor, where he is a team player among the moderate Republicans on the panel who try to work with the Democratic majority when the subject is education. But he can dig his heels in when the order of business is labor legislation.

An active participant in drafting a five-year higher education bill in the 99th Congress, Gunderson focused on expanding aid and services for older, part-time college students — the kind of "non-traditional" students who enroll in large numbers at the many community colleges and technical schools in Gunderson's district. He sponsored, with liberal Democrat Pat Williams of Montana, the overhaul of a near-moribund continuing education program, to focus on such services as mid-career retraining.

In the 101st Congress, Gunderson helped the committee's ranking Republican, Bill Goodling of Pennsylvania, persuade GOP leaders to support a $1 billion omnibus education bill despite a Bush veto threat. But the bill died in the Senate.

Gunderson's philosophy of positive conservatism was tested in 1990 during the divisive debate over a major civil rights bill. The legislation sought to modify or reverse six 1989 Supreme Court decisions that narrowed the scope and reach of laws prohibiting employment discrimination. Republicans and the Bush administration contended that the bill would force employers to use racial quotas in hiring.

Gunderson worked with moderate Democrats and Republicans who tried to broker a compromise bill; Bush had warned that the bill as written by Democrats was unacceptable. But the Democratic sponsors worked to dissuade members from compromising. In the end, they succeeded in passing a bill with few amendments; Bush vetoed it and the Senate sustained the veto. Gunderson began the 102nd Congress setting strategy with administration officials as a member of a Republican "civil rights task force."

During the bill's consideration in the last Congress in the Education and Labor Committee, Gunderson walked out of the committee room when committee Chairman Augustus F. Hawkins tried to limit debate on several GOP-sponsored amendments. "You don't want to discuss these amendments, so why don't you all just go ahead and pass the bill?" Gunderson protested. "This is a civil rights bill, but you don't want to protect the rights of the minority on this committee."

Gunderson was at the center of another roiling debate in the 101st Congress as members sought to restrict the National Endowment for the Arts from funding projects considered obscene. He and E. Thomas Coleman of Missouri, ranking GOP member on the subcommittee with jurisdiction over the NEA, and Michigan Republican Paul B. Henry sought a middle ground between those opposed to any restrictions and those who favored abolishing the NEA. He backed the eventual compromise worked out by Coleman and Williams.

At Home: For a man who insists his real ambition was to become a radio hockey announcer, Gunderson rose in politics quickly. He won his broadcasting license at age 23, and a seat in the Legislature the same year.

As a close associate of GOP Gov. Lee Sherman Dreyfus, Gunderson could have obtained a leadership job in the Legislature. But he quit in mid-1979 to work in Washington as Rep. Toby Roth's legislative director.

In six months, Gunderson was back in Wisconsin, this time to challenge Democratic Rep. Alvin Baldus. Gunderson's job-hopping stirred some complaints that his ambition exceeded his commitment to public service, but 1980 was an excellent Republican year in Wisconsin, and he beat Baldus by demonstrating the same energy that marked his service in the Legislature. Gunderson personally visited thousands of homes in the rural counties of the district, leaving behind his grandmother's recipe for lefse, a Norwegian potato bread.

Gunderson's 1982 Democratic challenger, state Sen. Paul Offner, hoped to unseat him using the Reagan connection. An economist with a Ph.D. from Princeton, Offner presented a detailed plan for economic recovery, including his own federal budget. But Gunderson's tireless campaigning and artful dairy maneuvers won him 57 percent of the vote.

In 1986, Democrats claimed to have a strong candidate in Leland Mulder, a farmer who aimed to tap into rural resentment toward the Reagan administration. Gunderson, however, had no trouble deflecting that strategy. He won 64 percent and has stayed above 60 percent since then, even in 1988 when his district went for Democrat Michael S. Dukakis for president.

Committees

Agriculture (7th of 18 Republicans)
Livestock, Dairy & Poultry (ranking); Conservation, Credit & Rural Development; Department Operations, Research & Foreign Agriculture; Peanuts & Tobacco

Education & Labor (5th of 14 Republicans)
Employment Opportunities (ranking); Elementary, Secondary & Vocational Education; Postsecondary Education

Elections

1990 General		
Steve Gunderson (R)	94,509	(61%)
James L. Ziegeweid (D)	60,409	(39%)
1988 General		
Steve Gunderson (R)	157,513	(68%)
Karl E. Krueger (D)	72,935	(32%)

Previous Winning Percentages: **1986** (64%) **1984** (68%) **1982** (57%) **1980** (51%)

District Vote For President

	1988	1984	1980	1976
D	126,354 (52%)	108,752 (45%)	109,434 (43%)	114,895 (49%)
R	112,830 (47%)	133,386 (55%)	123,312 (48%)	112,422 (48%)
I			18,584 (7%)	

Campaign Finance

	Receipts	Receipts from PACs		Expenditures
1990				
Gunderson (R)	$388,310	$196,595	(51%)	$341,458
Ziegeweid (D)	$57,161	$31,860	(56%)	$57,576
1988				
Gunderson (R)	$404,942	$133,235	(33%)	$359,801
Krueger (D)	$27,156	$6,000	(22%)	$22,626

Key Votes

1991	
Authorize use of force against Iraq	Y
1990	
Support constitutional amendment on flag desecration	Y
Pass family and medical leave bill over Bush veto	N
Reduce SDI funding	N
Allow abortions in overseas military facilities	N
Approve budget summit plan for spending and taxing	N
Approve civil rights bill	N
1989	
Halt production of B-2 stealth bomber at 13 planes	N
Oppose capital gains tax cut	N
Approve federal abortion funding in rape or incest cases	N
Approve pay raise and revision of ethics rules	Y
Pass Democratic minimum wage plan over Bush veto	N

Voting Studies

	Presidential Support		Party Unity		Conservative Coalition	
Year	**S**	**O**	**S**	**O**	**S**	**O**
1990	60	40	67	31	80	19
1989	77	23	66	32	85	15
1988	46	52	58	40	84	13
1987	61	38	68	29	84	12
1986	52	44	66	29	78	20
1985	50	50	74	22	73	25
1984	61	39	74	26	75	25
1983	61	39	70	30	65	35
1982	56	44	74	26	68	32
1981	70	30	75	25	75	25

Interest Group Ratings

Year	ADA	ACU	AFL-CIO	CCUS
1990	33	63	8	77
1989	20	81	17	100
1988	45	54	79	71
1987	20	65	19	86
1986	40	45	67	72
1985	35	43	29	77
1984	20	50	15	75
1983	20	57	12	85
1982	45	50	21	64
1981	30	100	20	84

4 Gerald D. Kleczka (D)

Of Milwaukee — Elected 1984

Born: Nov. 26, 1943, Milwaukee, Wis.
Education: Attended U. of Wisconsin, 1961-62, 1967, 1970.
Military Service: Wis. Air National Guard, 1963-69.
Occupation: Accountant.
Family: Wife, Bonnie L. Scott.
Religion: Roman Catholic.
Political Career: Wis. Assembly, 1969-73; Wis. Senate, 1975-84.
Capitol Office: 226 Cannon Bldg. 20515; 225-4572.

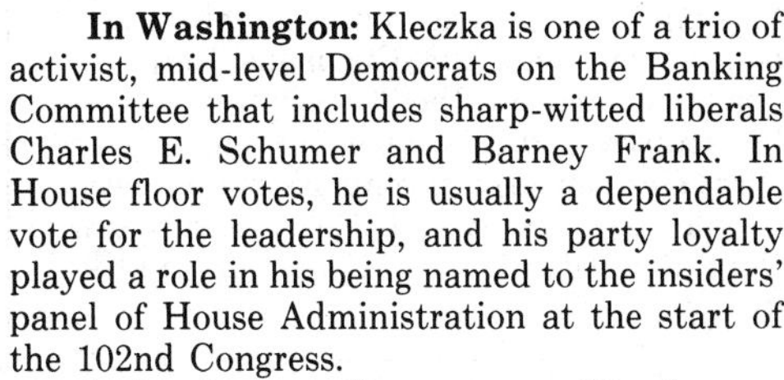

In Washington: Kleczka is one of a trio of activist, mid-level Democrats on the Banking Committee that includes sharp-witted liberals Charles E. Schumer and Barney Frank. In House floor votes, he is usually a dependable vote for the leadership, and his party loyalty played a role in his being named to the insiders' panel of House Administration at the start of the 102nd Congress.

In his first two House terms, Kleczka was more interested in learning the customs and making friends than in trying to impress anyone as a legislative phenom. After he arrived in 1984, he spent much time listening quietly to floor speeches, learning how the oratorical style differed from that of the Wisconsin Senate.

Now that he has the measure of the place, though, Kleczka has shed any bashfulness he might have harbored. He is a street-smart, combative politician who sometimes has to work to keep his temper under control: Early in his state legislative career, he actually came to blows with a lobbyist for a brewery.

As have many Democrats on the Banking Committee, Kleczka has chafed under the leadership of Chairman Henry B. Gonzalez. Kleczka and Georgia Democrat Doug Barnard Jr. led an abortive move early in the 102nd Congress to reallocate some of the committee staff to members who do not have subcommittee chairs.

Kleczka has consistently stood against loosening the federal government's regulatory reins on banks and savings and loan institutions. As the Banking Committee worked on a 1987 bill to bail out the ailing Federal Savings and Loan Insurance Corporation, Kleczka riled the S&L industry by sponsoring an amendment to double the bill's proposed "exit fees" on healthy S&Ls trying to bolt the FSLIC system and convert to commercial banks to receive less costly Federal Deposit Insurance Corporation coverage. But his efforts to amend the bill failed in committee and on the floor.

During the committee's consideration of the 1989 S&L bailout bill, Kleczka won approval of his amendment to require General Accounting Office audits of the Federal National Mortgage Corporation. But an attempt in the Financial Institutions Subcommittee that would have broadened the deposit-insurance system to cover foreign deposits held by U.S. banks was rejected by a 12-34 vote.

The Judiciary Subcommittee on Criminal Justice held hearings on Kleczka's bill to establish a Financial Services Crime Division at the Justice Department. A similar proposal was included in the 1990 crime bill.

Late in the 101st Congress, Kleczka and California Democrat Richard H. Lehman introduced a deposit-insurance reform bill that would limit insurance coverage to 100 percent of the first $50,000 put on deposit by an individual and 90 percent of the next $50,000. They reintroduced their bill in the 102nd Congress.

On the Banking Subcommittee on Housing, Kleczka worked in the 99th and 100th Congresses to end fraud in the Federal Housing Administration's mortgage insurance program. Kleczka said the FHA program was being cheated by real-estate speculators using false income data and inflated property assessments. He introduced legislation providing stiffer penalties for mortgage insurance fraud.

In the 101st Congress, he requested a General Accounting Office study of whether raising the loan limit on FHA single-family home mortgages would increase or decrease risk to the mortgage fund. Kleczka opposed raising the limit during House debate on the fiscal 1990 housing appropriations bill.

"The red flags have been raised on this exact program, the one that we are tampering with today," he said, "and it is really kind of foolhardy for this Congress to raise the limit to provide further exposure for a government program that has lost $4.2 billion this last year." But House members voted overwhelmingly to expand the program.

Kleczka has used his Government Operations Committee seat to try to expand the scope of the Freedom of Information Act. He sponsored a bill in 1988 with Oklahoma Democrat

Wisconsin 4

Southern Milwaukee and Suburbs — Waukesha

Since the turn of the century, Milwaukee's South Side has been the base of the city's huge Polish community. Like many of the Eastern Europeans who migrated to industrial cities, the Poles have been loyal, somewhat conservative Democrats. Their neighborhoods are conspicuously tidy, with immaculate lawns and shrubs.

In the last 20 years, urban flight has influenced a number of Poles, especially younger ones, to leave the South Side and relocate in suburbs such as New Berlin and neighboring Muskego. Some of these migrants have drifted from their political moorings, moving into the Republican column in state and national elections. Waukesha County's strong GOP organization gave Ronald Reagan and George Bush comfortable countywide presidential victories in the 1980s, but districtwide in the 4th, Democrats remain dominant: Michael S. Dukakis carried it easily in 1988 presidential voting.

The departure of some Poles for the suburbs has made room for a greater ethnic mix on the South Side. Though the area remains predominantly Polish, there is a Hispanic community on the near South Side, close to the downtown business district.

Blue-collar voters in Cudahy and South Milwaukee, two cities on the shore of Lake Michigan, strongly support Democratic candidates.

Most residents in the city and the suburbs look to Milwaukee's heavy industries for economic sustenance. Though service industry jobs have increased, many 4th District constituents still make machinery for mining, construction and electronic equipment; the Allis-Chalmers Corp. is headquartered in the 4th, but since its bankruptcy and subsequent purchase by a West German firm, it employs many fewer people than it once did. Delco Electronics Corp. and Allen-Bradley Co. are also in the district.

Population: 522,880. White 506,053 (97%), Black 1,509 (0.3%), Other 5,827 (1%). Spanish origin 20,677 (4%). 18 and over 381,822 (73%), 65 and over 57,760 (11%). Median age: 31.

Glenn English to do just that. In 1986, he offered a floor amendment to speed access to government documents. In the 101st Congress he again introduced legislation to strengthen the act.

Kleczka had been a consistent vote against abortion until the Supreme Court's *Webster* decision. But shortly after the July 1989 ruling, he voted with the majority as the House narrowly agreed with Senate language allowing federal funding of abortions in cases of rape and incest. His vote was part of the 50-vote swing from 1988.

Representing a city with a high number of ethnic Polish, Kleczka pays close attention to developments in Poland. He added an amendment to a refugee bill in the 101st Congress that granted refugee status to Solidarity activists in Europe who would be targets of government persecution if they returned to Poland.

In 1989 he organized a "Polish-American Night" at the National Democratic Club and tried to get Lech Walesa, the leader of the opposition Solidarity trade union, to appear. The event featured kielbasa and polka music, with other Polish-American members of Congress representing the country's major Polish neighborhoods.

At Home: Kleczka represents a secure Democratic district that kept his predecessor in office for 35 years with little challenge.

Before coming to Washington, Kleczka spent virtually his entire adult life in the Wisconsin Legislature. His role and reputation there changed considerably over the 15 years following his first election at age 24.

In his early years in Madison, Kleczka was viewed as being like most of the legislators traditionally sent from Milwaukee's South Side — a neighborhood-minded ethnic Democrat concerned more with local politics than abstract issues. He had a reputation for hard-nosed campaigning and occasional quarrels on the Assembly floor.

But he rose gradually to the chairmanship of the powerful Joint Finance Committee, building a reputation as an effective budget specialist. When Democratic Rep. Clement J. Zablocki, the House Foreign Affairs chairman, died in late 1983, Kleczka quickly became the front-runner for the ensuing special election.

Thanks to his Joint Finance Committee role, Kleczka had no difficulty picking up support from state Senate colleagues and financial help from the economic interests over which his committee held power. He claimed much of Zablocki's backing and was also the choice of the state's Democratic U.S. House delegation.

But while Kleczka's party support was crucial, his advertising stressed a different theme — his roots on the heavily Polish South Side. One TV ad showed an infant in a crib and a grandfather, while a voice-over described Kleczka as "a leader and a neighbor." In another, the camera showed a montage of South Side scenes, while an elderly woman told Kleczka she would vote for him because "you always come back to our neighborhood."

The combination of Kleczka's political status and neighborhood roots brought him 32 percent of the vote — enough to win in a five-way primary that included three other formidable candidates — Milwaukee County District Attorney E. Michael McCann, state Sen. Lynn S. Adelman and Gary Barczak, Milwaukee County circuit court clerk.

By winning big with 44 percent in the city portion of the district, Kleczka overcame his poor showing in affluent suburban precincts and took the nomination decisively over runner-up McCann, who ran respectably everywhere but had no specific base to help him.

Kleczka has had few worries on the home front since then. In 1990 he overwhelmed his Republican foe by a margin of more than 2-to-1; it was his first GOP challenge since 1984.

Committees

Banking, Finance & Urban Affairs (14th of 31 Democrats)
Financial Institutions Supervision, Regulation & Insurance; Housing & Community Development; International Development, Finance, Trade & Monetary Policy

Government Operations (15th of 25 Democrats)
Government Activities & Transportation; Legislation & National Security

House Administration (15th of 15 Democrats)
Campaign Finance Reform; Personnel & Police

Joint Printing

Elections

1990 General		
Gerald D. Kleczka (D)	96,981	(69%)
Joseph L. Cook (R)	43,001	(31%)
1990 Primary		
Gerald D. Kleczka (D)	19,725	(81%)
Daniel Slak (D)	2,955	(12%)
Roman R. Blenski (D)	1,664	(7%)
1988 General		
Gerald D. Kleczka (D)	177,283	(100%)

Previous Winning Percentages: **1986** (100%) **1984** (67%)
1984 * (65%)

* *Special election.*

District Vote For President

	1988	1984	1980	1976
D	142,074 (56%)	125,624 (52%)	118,444 (48%)	129,957 (54%)
R	111,241 (44%)	112,687 (47%)	108,464 (44%)	101,527 (42%)
I			17,338 (7%)	

Campaign Finance

	Receipts	Receipts from PACs		Expend-itures
1990				
Kleczka (D)	$304,440	$186,048	(61%)	$393,562
Cook (R)	$31,850	$2,800	(9%)	$27,986
1988				
Kleczka (D)	$214,093	$129,383	(60%)	$150,270

Key Votes

1991	
Authorize use of force against Iraq	N
1990	
Support constitutional amendment on flag desecration	N
Pass family and medical leave bill over Bush veto	Y
Reduce SDI funding	Y
Allow abortions in overseas military facilities	N
Approve budget summit plan for spending and taxing	N
Approve civil rights bill	Y
1989	
Halt production of B-2 stealth bomber at 13 planes	Y
Oppose capital gains tax cut	Y
Approve federal abortion funding in rape or incest cases	Y
Approve pay raise and revision of ethics rules	Y
Pass Democratic minimum wage plan over Bush veto	Y

Voting Studies

	Presidential Support		Party Unity		Conservative Coalition	
Year	**S**	**O**	**S**	**O**	**S**	**O**
1990	21	78	91	6	17	78
1989	28	66	88	5	17	78
1988	19	73	90	5	16	79
1987	17	81	89	4	28	70
1986	24	76	85	9	28	70
1985	28	71	87	6	24	75
1984	42 †	56 †	84 †	15 †	28 †	72 †

† *Not eligible for all recorded votes.*

Interest Group Ratings

Year	ADA	ACU	AFL-CIO	CCUS
1990	89	17	83	23
1989	95	0	83	40
1988	95	4	93	36
1987	84	5	88	13
1986	75	9	86	25
1985	75	14	82	23
1984	76	9	67	38

5 Jim Moody (D)

Of Shorewood — Elected 1982

Born: Sept. 2, 1935, Richlands, Va.

Education: Haverford College, B.A. 1957; Harvard U., M.P.A. 1967; U. of California, Berkeley, Ph.D. 1973.

Occupation: Economist.

Family: Wife, Janice Boettcher.

Religion: Protestant.

Political Career: Wis. House, 1977-79; Wis. Senate, 1979-83.

Capitol Office: 1019 Longworth Bldg. 20515; 225-3571.

In Washington: Moody has twice begun campaigns for the Senate, pulling back both times when discretion appeared the better part of valor. Undeterred, Moody now seems to think 1992 will be the third time that proves the charm.

After looking at the Senate in 1986, Moody decided instead to concentrate on winning a seat on the Ways and Means Committee, where he is now. In 1988, after running statewide for many months, he admitted he could not compete with the unlimited personal treasury of fellow Democrat and fellow Milwaukeean Herb Kohl, who is now in the Senate.

But 1992 again opens up the seat of GOP Sen. Bob Kasten, who has won his two terms in the Senate with 50 percent and 51 percent of the vote. Moody is building a financial base and adapting his schedule for another statewide campaign. In the early going, at least, few Democrats in the state seemed well-positioned to challenge him for the nomination.

Moody could have a problem with statewide reaction to his record on the Persian Gulf. He was one of the Democrats most in opposition to Bush's handling of the gulf crisis. Not only did he vote against force on Jan. 12, 1991, unlike most of Wisconsin's delegation, he joined with 41 other Democratic members sponsoring a resolution calling on Bush not to escalate the war once the allied bombing had begun.

Meanwhile, Moody has kept busy as an outspoken junior member of Ways and Means. Campaigning for almost two years to get on Ways and Means, he lobbied more than 80 members who were — or might be — on the leadership panel that makes committee assignments. Even more important, Moody had the backing of Ways and Means Chairman Dan Rostenkowski of Illinois. He scored points in the 99th Congress as an informal whip helping Rostenkowski line up votes for his prized legislation overhauling the tax code. Though unpredictable, Moody struck Rostenkowski as a relatively safe Democrat to place on the committee. An individualist, he appeared unlikely to mount the sort of coalitions that could threaten the chairman's control on important issues.

While siding with the chairman on most of the salient issues of the 101st Congress, Moody sometimes exceeded him in zeal. He was part of the hardest core of Democratic opposition to cutting capital gains taxes and joined in proposing that if capital gains got a break, the rate on the highest incomes should be raised.

Moody did risk Rostenkowski's wrath in the 100th Congress by cosponsoring Rep. Claude Pepper's expensive home-health-care bill, which circumvented the Ways and Means Committee but ultimately died.

Despite appearing a team player in the eyes of the Democratic leadership, Moody remains a politician comfortable with ideas and skillful at expressing them, but not a joiner or a foot soldier by instinct. The maverick in Moody still has its moments.

In early 1989, Moody was the only member of the Wisconsin delegation — and one of only 48 members of the House — voting for a 51 percent pay raise for Congress and top federal officials that was eagerly sought by members but vilified by public opinion. "I owe [constituents] my honest assessment of every single issue — even one so subject to political posturing and pandering as this one has been," Moody said.

During a session of the Public Works Committee in 1986, he startled some colleagues by offering an amendment to a highway bill that would have removed more than $1 billion in funding for special "demonstration" projects in members' districts — a futile challenge to the committee's logrolling principle.

One nettled senior Republican told Moody his amendment was as welcome as "an illegitimate child at a family reunion." Another forced a roll-call vote that Moody did not seek and that he lost, 48-2.

Moody also went far afield in the 100th Congress in pursuit of arms control. With two other Democrats (Thomas J. Downey and Bob Carr) he traveled to the Soviet Union in 1987 to visit a Soviet radar station at Krasnoyarsk that had become a key point of contention in debates between President Ronald Reagan

Wisconsin 5

The Menominee River marks the boundary between Milwaukee's North and South sides, and the 5th is the North Side district, taking in the traditional German neighborhoods and other middle-class territory that has become increasingly black in recent years. The district as a whole is now 28 percent black, and reliably Democratic in virtually any election. In 1988, Michael S. Dukakis won 63 percent in the 5th, easily his best showing in any Wisconsin district.

Nearly all of the black population lives in a concentrated area in the central part of the district. The borders of this area have expanded since 1980, as many blacks moved away from the central city in search of newer housing and better quality of life; but as they shifted westward, whites have migrated to the suburbs; one area near Sherman Park saw its racial composition change from 98 percent white to over 80 percent black in just 20 years.

North and west of the black neighborhoods are modest middle-class areas of Milwaukee where despite many German names on the mailboxes there has long since ceased to be much ethnic identification.

Northern Milwaukee and Suburbs — Wauwatosa

The northeastern side of the district, between the Milwaukee River and Lake Michigan, features large, comfortable homes, a gathering of academics who work at Milwaukee's branch of the University of Wisconsin, and white-collar professionals with middle- and upper-management jobs in downtown offices.

To the west of the city is Wauwatosa, a mostly Republican residential area with older housing stock.

The 5th is the focal point of Milwaukee's best-known industry — brewing. Locally owned Schlitz, Pabst and Miller were once the giants, but the structure of the industry has changed in the past decade. In the early 1970s, Miller was bought out by Philip Morris, a New York-based conglomerate. Beset by financial problems, Schlitz closed its Milwaukee brewery in 1981; no longer is "the beer that made Milwaukee famous" brewed anywhere in the city.

Population: 522,854. White 361,847 (69%), Black 147,928 (28%), Other 6,262 (1%). Spanish origin 11,420 (2%). 18 and over 381,248 (73%), 65 and over 67,138 (13%). Median age: 29.

and the Congress over the anti-ballistic missile treaty. The congressional delegation — which included its own independent arms control experts — concluded that the station was a long way from completion and could not control an anti-missile network. Pentagon experts said the members had been victims of "disinformation." Two years later, the Soviets themselves admitted the radar had been a violation of the treaty and began to dismantle it.

At Home: Moody is seen as a liberal in Washington and in many parts of Wisconsin. But when he first ran for his House seat in the 1982 cycle, he stood rather to the right of the 10-candidate field. Moody's is not only the most Democratic district in the state, it is also home to more than 75 percent of the state's blacks. While blacks cast less than a third of the district vote, Moody knows he would be in serious trouble were they to unite behind a primary challenger.

Moody is an economics professor by trade; but his sense of political timing and his luck brought him from academia to the state Legislature to the House in just six years. But both seemed to desert him when he turned his attention to the Senate. In 1986, he had a strong interest in challenging Kasten, and Democrats were eager for a candidate with Moody's abilities. But he chose to remain in the House, even after Kasten's arrest for drunken driving significantly increased his vulnerability. That fall, Kasten barely beat a challenger who had never held elective office.

Two years later, Moody seemed to have a second chance. Thirty-year incumbent Sen. William Proxmire retired, and Moody entered the race to succeed him. Polls showed him a strong second in the Democratic field in the spring of 1988. Then multimillionaire Kohl of Milwaukee entered the contest and not only split Moody's base but bankrolled by far the most extensive TV blitz the state had ever seen. Moody recalculated the odds and, in the nick of time, filed for re-election to the House.

This may have been the prudent move, as Kohl swept on to the nomination and won the seat in November. But Moody's change of heart angered candidates who had spent months vying to succeed him in the House. Other candidates withdrew when Moody got back into the 5th District primary, but former state party Chairman Matthew J. Flynn remained, pressing a bitter fight. In the end, Moody dispatched Flynn rather easily, although his 59 percent share marked him as one of only five House incumbents across the country in 1988 to garner less than 60 percent of the primary vote.

Moody ran much better in 1990. His lone primary opponent was former securities dealer

Peter Y. Taylor Sr., who appeared at news events wearing a heavy chain around his neck to dramatize the debt burden of U.S. citizens.

General elections have never been a problem for Moody. He had no GOP opposition in 1984 and 1986 and when challenged he has never had less than 60 percent of the vote. To win the seat in 1982, Moody had to beat Republican Rod Johnston, a suburban state senator whose slogan was "Vote the man and not the party." Moody took nearly 65 percent of the vote, though hard up for money and tired from his battle for the Democratic nomination.

Moody had won the 1982 primary with a frenetic door-to-door campaign, a two-year effort that took him to 40,000 households. He presented himself as a compassionate liberal with an impressive background in economics, but issues were clearly secondary. It was Moody's smile, reassuring voice and simple stamina that lifted him from a field of 10 Democrats seeking to succeed 14-term veteran Henry S. Reuss.

Moody has a varied professional background. He was a representative of CARE in Yugoslavia, a Peace Corps official in Pakistan, and a loan officer for the Agency for International Development. He worked for the Department of Transportation, helped in Eugene J. McCarthy's 1968 presidential campaign, and eventually became an economics professor at the University of Wisconsin in Milwaukee. He won a term in the Wisconsin House in 1976, and one in the state Senate in 1978.

Committee

Ways & Means (21st of 23 Democrats)
Health; Human Resources

Elections

1990 General		
Jim Moody (D)	77,557	(68%)
Donalda Arnell Hammersmith (R)	31,255	(27%)
Nathaniel J. Stampley (I)	4,968	(4%)
1990 Primary		
Jim Moody (D)	16,995	(79%)
Peter Y. Taylor Sr. (D)	4,585	(21%)
1988 General		
Jim Moody (D)	140,518	(64%)
Helen I. Barnhill (R)	78,307	(36%)

Previous Winning Percentages: **1986** (99%) **1984** (98%) **1982** (64%)

District Vote For President

	1988	1984	1980	1976
D	146,635 (63%)	139,057 (61%)	136,084 (54%)	135,133 (55%)
R	82,606 (36%)	90,027 (39%)	91,520 (37%)	102,120 (42%)
I			19,114 (8%)	

Campaign Finance

	Receipts	Receipts from PACs		Expend-itures
1990				
Moody (D)	$735,212	$450,704	(61%)	$515,159
Hammersmith (R)	$22,508	0		$21,348
1988				
Moody (D)	$1,291,564	$524,503	(41%)	$1,278,526
Barnhill (R)	$209,992	$21,932	(10%)	$197,460

Key Votes

1991	
Authorize use of force against Iraq	N
1990	
Support constitutional amendment on flag desecration	N
Pass family and medical leave bill over Bush veto	Y
Reduce SDI funding	Y
Allow abortions in overseas military facilities	Y
Approve budget summit plan for spending and taxing	N
Approve civil rights bill	Y
1989	
Halt production of B-2 stealth bomber at 13 planes	Y
Oppose capital gains tax cut	Y
Approve federal abortion funding in rape or incest cases	Y
Approve pay raise and revision of ethics rules	Y
Pass Democratic minimum wage plan over Bush veto	Y

Voting Studies

	Presidential Support		Party Unity		Conservative Coalition	
Year	S	O	S	O	S	O
1990	17	78	79	11	15	85
1989	27	73	87	9	20	80
1988	13	58	70	4	8	50
1987	17	77	82	7	12	81
1986	18	82	87	7	16	80
1985	20	79	89	5	11	85
1984	23	68	82	10	12	75
1983	22	73	84	10	15	82

Interest Group Ratings

Year	ADA	ACU	AFL-CIO	CCUS
1990	94	14	83	42
1989	95	11	75	40
1988	80	5	100	23
1987	84	0	93	27
1986	85	5	86	18
1985	80	0	100	18
1984	85	0	83	25
1983	95	0	88	30

6 Tom Petri (R)

Of Fond du Lac — Elected 1979

Born: May 28, 1940, Marinette, Wis.
Education: Harvard U., B.A. 1962, J.D. 1965.
Occupation: Lawyer.
Family: Wife, Anne Neal; one child.
Religion: Lutheran.
Political Career: Wis. Senate, 1973-79; Republican nominee for U.S. Senate, 1974.
Capitol Office: 2245 Rayburn Bldg. 20515; 225-2476.

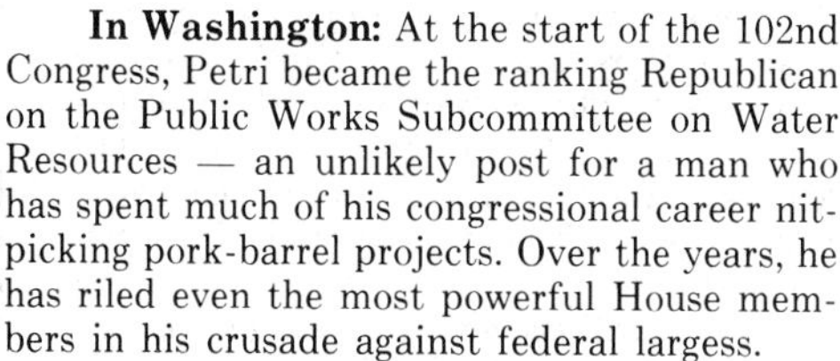

In Washington: At the start of the 102nd Congress, Petri became the ranking Republican on the Public Works Subcommittee on Water Resources — an unlikely post for a man who has spent much of his congressional career nit-picking pork-barrel projects. Over the years, he has riled even the most powerful House members in his crusade against federal largess.

This opposition to business as usual is emblematic of a Wisconsin reformist streak that Petri brought to Congress more than a decade ago — an orientation that helped give him an image as a moderate. But in recent years, opposition to wasteful federal spending has become a conservative mantra. This fact, coupled with Petri's views on social issues — he opposes federal funding of abortion and supported a constitutional amendment to ban flag desecration — makes Petri today look more like a Main Street, upper Midwest conservative.

During the 1988-89 debate on raising the minimum wage, Petri promoted an alternative that focused on expanding a tax break for the working poor known as the earned income tax credit (EITC). He argued that such a break would target aid to those who needed it, while an across-the-board increase in the minimum wage amounted to "trying to achieve a goal with random bombing when a rapier will do."

House Democrats repeatedly blocked Petri's efforts to offer the idea as an amendment to minimum wage legislation, and he ran into the same resistance that meets any revenue-losing idea in the current deficit-conscious climate. Still, House Democrats showed increasing interest in the idea as a way to help the working poor, and even the chairman of the tax-writing Ways and Means Committee, Dan Rostenkowski, came to express the view that an expanded EITC would make more sense than raising the minimum wage.

Later, during 1989 debate on child care legislation, Petri's colleagues on Education and Labor vigorously fought the idea of expanding the EITC to allow parents to pay for day care, and he was denied much of a role in enacting the provisions. It was Rostenkowski and other Ways and Means Democrats who successfully pushed the plan, which helped win White House backing for the bill. Petri complained that their plan was structured to make "welfare more attractive.... One of the reasons we're pushing the EITC is to help make work more attractive than welfare."

Early in his career on Education and Labor, Petri championed the idea of canceling student-loan debts for borrowers who go into the military. He won approval of the concept by taking on senior committee members and beating them on the floor, with help from Armed Services Committee members.

As the 102nd Congress takes up the Higher Education Act, Petri hopes to sell the committee on a new student loan program that would not require federal subsidies after an initial appropriation. Under Petri's plan, the rate at which loans are repaid would be based on one's income. In the 99th Congress, he won funding for a similar demonstration program in which those with high incomes after graduation paid higher interest rates to subsidize lower rates for other borrowers.

When Petri joined the Public Works Committee in 1983, he made no secret of his anti-pork stand — a move akin to joining the Armed Services Committee for the purpose of pushing unilateral disarmament. His most celebrated attack on a pet project came in 1988, when he led a successful fight to kill legislation writing off a federal loan to build a library in honor of former Speaker Thomas P. O'Neill Jr. The move put him at odds with Silvio O. Conte of Massachusetts — a man few wanted to cross because he was ranking Republican on the Appropriations Committee.

In an accomplishment of broader significance, Petri fought to require local beneficiaries of federal water projects to provide a share of the costs "up front," at the start of construction. Petri maintained that requiring a local commitment early on "should clear away projects that are economic pygmies, but political giants." A version of the cost-sharing scheme was enacted in 1986, when it was added

Wisconsin 6

Central — Oshkosh; Fond du Lac; Manitowoc

The 6th reaches west from Lake Michigan across 10 largely rural counties of central Wisconsin, ending about 25 miles from the Minnesota border on the west. It has been closely contested in many state and national elections, but it has sent only one Democrat to Washington since 1938.

The farms and market towns are generally Republican, while Democratic strength is in several small industrialized cities in the eastern part of the 6th — Manitowoc and Two Rivers in Manitowoc County, Oshkosh and Neenah-Menasha in Winnebago County and Fond du Lac in Fond du Lac County.

The most Democratic of the bunch is Manitowoc, a prominent Lake Michigan shipbuilding center in the days when wooden vessels plied the seas. More than half the jobs in Manitowoc County today are involved with manufacturing and processing, and unions are an important force. Goods produced include the Mirro Corporation's aluminum pots and pans, and motel ice-making machines. Manitowoc County went solidly for Jimmy Carter in 1976, narrowly for Ronald Reagan in 1980 and 1984, and then swung to Michael S. Dukakis in 1988.

Though nominal Democrats are numerous in Winnebago and Fond du Lac counties, those who vote Democratic usually find themselves in a minority at election time. GOP Sen. Bob Kasten won both counties in his close 1986 re-election, and Bush carried them both in 1988.

Oshkosh is on the western shore of Lake Winnebago, the state's largest lake. Tourism and a state university branch boost the economy, and factories in Winnebago County turn out auto parts, wood and paper products, and the Oshkosh line of clothing. At the northern end of the lake is Neenah-Menasha, the site of the wood products company of Kimberly Clark, one of the major employers in the district.

At the southern tip of the lake is Fond du Lac County, the home of Mercury outboard motors and Speed Queen laundry equipment. The city of Fond du Lac has strong historical justification for its GOP leanings. About 20 miles west of the city is Ripon, the 1854 birthplace of the Republican Party.

In nearby Sheboygan County is the Kohler Company, the nation's largest producer of plumbing equipment. Besides the industry in the district, farming has a strong presence. After all-important dairying, output from the district's farms is diverse, including corn, peas, beans and cranberries. The peak of Republican strength in the rural part of the 6th is in Green Lake County, a resort area with large summer homes.

Population: 522,477. White 516,637 (99%), Black 1,205 (0.2%), Other 2,988 (1%). Spanish origin 3,385 (1%). 18 and over 370,486 (71%), 65 and over 69,925 (13%). Median age: 30.

to a water projects authorization bill to make it more acceptable to environmentalists and fiscal conservatives, at a time when budget constraints were threatening approval of new water projects. The bill's passage marked the first time in a decade that a new water projects authorization got through Congress.

Petri also has taken on the long-established tobacco price-support system, angering colleagues from tobacco-producing states. He has persisted in this effort — in the 101st Congress he toyed with the idea of joining with Sen. Edward M. Kennedy to offer legislation to eliminate tobacco price supports altogether — despite warnings from some Wisconsin GOP colleagues, who fear that he could provoke retaliation against dairy programs, which Petri's district and much of Wisconsin need.

Petri is one of the few members who volunteered for assignment to the ethics committee, although he did so more out of a sense of duty to the institution than because of active interest. His model was Barber B. Conable Jr., the highly respected New York Republican who served on the ethics committee for a term before the end of his long career in the House.

Petri took that sensitive assignment in the 100th Congress, and sat on the panel through the historic investigation that led to the resignation of Speaker Jim Wright. In the 101st Congress, Petri joined the panel's unanimous decision to recommend a reprimand for Democrat Barney Frank for improperly using his office to help a male prostitute. In the full House, however, he was one of three Republicans on the panel to vote with the GOP majority in an unsuccessful effort to give Frank the harsher punishment of censure.

At Home: Petri built his Wisconsin career out of the moderate Republican politics that worked for his predecessor, William A. Steiger, who died of a heart attack at age 40, one month after winning his seventh House term in 1978.

In the 1979 special election held to choose

Steiger's successor, Petri campaigned on the same reformist issues Steiger had used. His campaign literature boasted of the high ratings he had received in the state Senate from the self-styled citizens' lobby, Common Cause. He noted that he had been a Peace Corps volunteer in Somalia and served as executive director of the Ripon Society, a moderate GOP group.

The campaign reinforced the image Petri had created in 1974, when he was the sacrificial GOP Senate nominee against Democrat Gaylord Nelson. He drew only 35 percent of the vote against Nelson in an awful Republican year, but earned some useful attention.

The Senate effort made Petri the logical Republican contender for Steiger's House seat in 1979. But it did not guarantee him victory against Gary Goyke, a fellow state senator with a more forceful campaign style. Goyke made an issue of Petri's generous campaign financing and implied that the Republican had come out against national health insurance because of a $5,000 contribution he had received from the political action committee of the American Medical Association, a charge Petri denied. For his part, Petri said Goyke had his own source of political funding in organized labor.

Petri won the special election on his strength in rural areas and his ability to cut into Goyke's vote in blue-collar cities, especially Sheboygan, which Petri narrowly carried. His overall margin of victory was barely 1,200 votes.

Eighteen months later there was a rematch. But the 1980 election was a pale shadow of the first contest. Goyke was still in debt from the special election and got a late start. Petri had enhanced his Steiger-like image by hiring some of Steiger's aides and taking his predecessor's place on Education and Labor. With a strong Republican tide at the statewide level, Petri carried every county in the district against Goyke the second time around. In 1982, despite a strong Democratic trend in statewide politics, Petri romped to another term with 65 percent. He has since received three-fourths of the vote (when he has had an opponent at all).

Committees

Education & Labor (3rd of 14 Republicans)
Labor Standards (ranking); Elementary, Secondary & Vocational Education; Labor-Management Relations; Postsecondary Education

Public Works & Transportation (4th of 21 Republicans)
Water Resources (ranking); Aviation; Surface Transportation

Elections

1990 General		
Tom Petri (R)	111,036	(100%)
1988 General		
Tom Petri (R)	165,923	(74%)
Joseph Garrett (D)	57,552	(26%)

Previous Winning Percentages: **1986** (97%) **1984** (76%) **1982** (65%) **1980** (59%) **1979 *** (50%)

** Special election.*

District Vote For President

	1988	1984	1980	1976
D	106,953 (46%)	88,121 (37%)	94,779 (38%)	96,131 (45%)
R	127,820 (53%)	146,167 (62%)	135,709 (54%)	112,146 (53%)
I			14,783 (6%)	

Campaign Finance

	Receipts	Receipts from PACs		Expend-itures
1990				
Petri (R)	$240,501	$98,455	(41%)	$131,156
1988				
Petri (R)	$258,876	$120,980	(47%)	$187,714
Garrett (D)	$19,976	$4,750	(24%)	$19,815

Key Votes

1991	
Authorize use of force against Iraq	Y
1990	
Support constitutional amendment on flag desecration	N
Pass family and medical leave bill over Bush veto	N
Reduce SDI funding	N
Allow abortions in overseas military facilities	N
Approve budget summit plan for spending and taxing	N
Approve civil rights bill	N
1989	
Halt production of B-2 stealth bomber at 13 planes	N
Oppose capital gains tax cut	N
Approve federal abortion funding in rape or incest cases	N
Approve pay raise and revision of ethics rules	N
Pass Democratic minimum wage plan over Bush veto	N

Voting Studies

	Presidential Support		Party Unity		Conservative Coalition	
Year	**S**	**O**	**S**	**O**	**S**	**O**
1990	69	31	78	20	80	19
1989	66	34	67	33	76	24
1988	62	36	66	32	84	13
1987	55	43	70	28	67	30
1986	73	27	74	25	76	24
1985	61	39	60	35	60	40
1984	54	46	76	24	75	25
1983	60	39	76	23	72	28
1982	53	40	71	28	70	30
1981	57	41	71	23	67	32

Interest Group Ratings

Year	ADA	ACU	AFL-CIO	CCUS
1990	22	75	8	86
1989	20	75	17	90
1988	35	75	50	79
1987	16	61	13	80
1986	5	73	0	94
1985	30	62	35	59
1984	20	83	8	63
1983	20	52	24	80
1982	35	64	30	64
1981	40	100	7	83

7 David R. Obey (D)

Of Wausau — Elected 1969

Born: Oct. 3, 1938, Okmulgee, Okla.
Education: U. of Wisconsin, B.S. 1960, M.A. 1962.
Occupation: Real estate broker.
Family: Wife, Joan Lepinski; two children.
Religion: Roman Catholic.
Political Career: Wis. Assembly, 1963-69.
Capitol Office: 2462 Rayburn Bldg. 20515; 225-3365.

In Washington: Since he arrived in the House, Obey has been accurately described as temperamental, impulsive and bullheaded. These traits were once regarded as potential impediments to his advancement. But since seniority brought Obey the chairmanship of the Appropriations Subcommittee on Foreign Operations in 1985, his personality has been central to his effectiveness as a leader who wins through sheer determination and obstinacy.

Obey's strong presence among the "College of Cardinals" (as Appropriations subcommittee chairmen are known) has established him as the dominant voice in the House on foreign aid, and as a key figure in debates on overall spending priorities. Although he waited 15 years to gain a subcommittee gavel, he could end up heading the full Appropriations Committee at an uncommonly early age. In his early 50s, he is fifth in seniority behind three men in their 80s and a fourth who is past 70.

Obey's rise is an example of the seniority system's periodic ability to promote one of the few rebellious sorts on Appropriations, an insular committee that puts a premium on conformity and bipartisan fraternity. He is a loner and a liberal partisan, a complex man of undisputed intelligence, principled independence and a zeal for political combat.

In October 1990, Obey helped organize the rebellion that scuttled the budget summit agreement between Bush administration officials and the congressional leadership. In part, Obey's objections were institutional: The closed-door summit had disrupted the normal budget process and encroached on Appropriations' role and control.

But Obey also objected to the summit on substance. He helped shape the Democratic theme that President Bush was protecting the wealthy and putting the burden of deficit reduction on the less affluent. "It would have hit middle-class taxpayers twice as hard as it hit the wealthiest members of American society," he told a campaign rally in Wisconsin.

He even put some heat on his own party, stating that "after 10 years of wimpy conduct, the Democratic Party finally is back where it ought to be — fighting hard for tax fairness for middle-class working families."

Yet Obey is no fall-on-his-sword liberal. He is a legislator, and that requires compromise. The conflicting facets of Obey's persona were on display during the July 1989 debate to finalize a foreign aid appropriations bill. After negotiations with Foreign Operations' ranking Republican, Mickey Edwards of Oklahoma, Obey worked out a compromise bill that composed partisan differences. Then, when the bill was presented to the subcommittee, he insisted that all GOP members support it intact on the floor.

Republican Rep. Jerry Lewis of California objected to that, saying he wanted to try to reduce funding to the International Development Association, which was lending to China. Obey said he agreed with Lewis in principle, but could not permit changes to the finely tuned bill. Lewis and other Republicans persisted, drawing out Obey's legendary temper; he banged down his gavel, declaring the meeting closed.

Obey then blasted the Bush administration for failing to line up GOP support for the deal. "I am carrying the administration's water on two-thirds of this bill that I think is a pile of junk," he railed. His threat to draw up a Democratic bill drew Bush's attention, and new discussions were opened. Obey's deal-cutting side quickly reappeared, and a foreign aid bill passed the House within a week.

Though often pugnacious, Obey is not reflexively adversarial. In 1989, he played a key role in negotiations between the Bush administration and the congressional leadership on Nicaragua. The talks moved U.S. policy from backing the armed contra insurgents to efforts at reforming the then-Marxist government. Contrasting Bush's flexible approach to President Ronald Reagan's hard-line pro-contra stance, Obey said, "It is nice to sit down with somebody and not be considered an enemy of your own country."

Obey also produced the only concrete legislation enacted in response to the Iran-contra affair. Reacting to evidence that the Reagan administration had elicited support for the

Wisconsin 7

Northwest — Wausau; Superior

The 7th reaches from the center of Wisconsin all the way north to Lake Superior. The southern part of the district is devoted largely to dairy farming; in the north, a booming recreation industry has brought new life to old mining and lumbering areas that were exploited and abandoned earlier in this century.

The southern end of the 7th is anchored by Marathon and Wood counties, politically marginal territory that supported Ronald Reagan in 1984, but was of divided mind four years later. Michael S. Dukakis won Marathon County by just 178 votes in 1988, and George Bush carried Wood County by only 475 votes.

Marathon County's major city is Wausau, which has paper mills, prefabricated-home manufacturers and white-collar employment in the insurance industry. In Wood County, Wisconsin Rapids is a paper mill town and Marshfield has a large medical clinic and research facility. The cities are processing centers for the surrounding dairy lands.

The heaviest Democratic vote in the southern part of the 7th comes out of Portage County. The city of Stevens Point there has a large Polish contingent, a branch of the state university and the headquarters of the Sentry Insurance Co. Walter F. Mondale narrowly carried the county in 1984, and Dukakis won it handily in 1988.

A scattering of streams, rivers, lakes, national forests and state parks covers the northern reaches of the 7th, luring tourists and retirees from urban centers.

The northern sections of the 7th share the same solid Democratic traditions found in Minnesota's Iron Range and the nearby western end of Michigan's Upper Peninsula. The major Democratic bastion is the region's only sizable city, Superior, a working-class town.

The port facilities of Superior and its larger neighbor, Duluth, Minn., are a funnel for soybeans, wheat and a wide range of other commodities raised on the farms of the Midwest. Some ore from the Minnesota Iron Range is still handled here.

Population: 522,623. White 514,200 (98%), Black 483 (0.1%), Other 6,924 (1%). Spanish origin 1,784 (0.3%). 18 and over 366,683 (70%), 65 and over 70,537 (14%). Median age: 30.

contras by promising aid to such nations as Honduras, Obey in 1989 proposed a measure to bar the use of foreign aid "in exchange for" any action that would be in violation of U.S. law if carried out by the U.S. government or its officials. It passed as an amendment to the fiscal 1990 foreign aid appropriations bill.

Still, when the plan was enacted that April, Obey put his own partisan spin on it. While Republicans said the plan would permit aid to the contras to resume, Obey said it "ends the contra war."

During the course of the successful U.S.-led military effort to end Iraq's occupation of Kuwait in early 1991, most members were effusively praising Israel and the Arab nations who backed the campaign. But Obey — who had opposed the January 1991 resolution authorizing Bush to use military force — took another stance: He called for a postwar cutoff of U.S. aid to the Middle East until serious moves were made toward permanent peace in the region.

"The Arab world must recognize Israel and its legitimate security requirements," Obey told a Council on Foreign Relations dinner that February. He added, "We also have a right to demand of Israel one very big thing — a recognition of the right and necessity of the Palestinian people to have their own homeland...." After the war, Obey rejected Bush administration suggestions of renewed military aid to such allies as Egypt, Israel and Turkey. "Reloading everyone's guns is exactly what we should not be doing," he said.

These comments reflected Obey's long-standing effort to change the orientation of U.S. foreign aid. He advocates using American dollars more to advance economic development in the nascent democracies of Eastern Europe and the struggling nations of the Third World, and less to reward and provide military assistance to geopolitical allies.

For example, Obey has tried to end the policy of providing foreign aid in the form of payments to nations for allowing U.S. military bases on their soil. "I don't think we ought to write base agreements with the idea that if we don't pay through the nose we're going to get bounced out," Obey said in January 1990. Citing protests against U.S. naval bases by activists in the Philippines, Obey said, "If the Filipinos don't want our bases there, then I think we ought to pull them out."

His skepticism of many of the programs under his jurisdiction is rather unusual for an Appropriations subcommittee chairman. At least before the 1990 budget agreement placed caps on the various spending categories, many Appropriations subcommittees would come in with "high-ball" proposals in hope of meeting the Republican administrations somewhere in the middle. But Obey's budget proposal for foreign aid frequently fell far below the administration requests.

Obey's perspective reflects his recognition that foreign aid is highly unpopular among the majority of Americans, who view it as taking money away from domestic programs. Also a member of the Appropriations Labor, Health and Human Services Subcommittee (which oversees most social programs), Obey says foreign aid cannot be exempted from the stringency of these lean economic times.

"The Congress, in my judgment, is not going to raise foreign aid in the context of making some of these other very large reductions on the domestic side of the budget," Obey warned Secretary of State James A. Baker III in March 1989. Obey proposed a foreign aid tab that was $1.4 billion less than that proposed by Bush. However, Congress later approved a figure close to Bush's $4.7 billion request.

Outside of his foreign aid bailiwick, Obey shows an aversion to big-ticket projects that he views as draining dollars from other needed programs. In 1989, he tried without success to block the passage of a bill providing the first construction funds for the superconducting super collider (SSC), a giant atom-smasher to be built in Texas. "It's one of the largest public works projects in the history of this country," Obey said. "Absent new revenues, the SSC will destroy the rest of the science budget in this country."

Although Obey's irascibility wears on his colleagues, he does show a rare self-awareness, and is quick to apologize when his anger is misplaced. When his brooding intensity subsides, he is a genial man who picks guitar in a bluegrass band with his sons.

And though Obey is not widely popular, respect for his integrity is widespread. Obey's name was repeatedly invoked in 1989 by Speaker Jim Wright of Texas as he sought unsuccessfully to stave off an ethics committee's investigation.

As the author of the House ethics code, Obey had a stake in its correct interpretation. This provoked him to argue, publicly and in an affidavit, that a rule covering gifts from associates with a legislative interest had been applied too broadly in Wright's case and one dealing with book royalties not broadly enough.

But Obey's influence cut both ways. In early May 1989, it was reported that Obey told some Democrats that Wright deserved a chance to defend himself but was finished politically. The news was one of the clearest signals Wright's fight was lost; he resigned from the speakership and the House soon thereafter.

In early 1989, Obey recognized that congressional pay raises are among the few acts less appreciated by the average voter than foreign aid bills. "I know of no one in this society outside of members of Congress who gets to set their own pay, and I do not believe members of Congress should either," Obey said regarding a planned increase. But Obey later served on a House task force that produced a proposal to raise House members' salaries while tightening ethical standards.

Obey also took on the issue of congressional campaign finance reform. Along with Democratic Rep. Mike Synar of Oklahoma, he proposed limiting political action committee (PAC) contributions to 40 percent of a candidate's take, reducing the maximum individual contribution to $500 and granting up to $100,000 in public funds to candidates.

Briefly in 1990, the Obey-Synar proposal became the campaign finance vehicle for the Democratic leadership. However, the public financing provision — anathema to Republicans and conservative Democrats — threatened the entire bill. That August, Republican House members tried to force Democrats to go on record in favor of public financing, voting "present" en masse on the Obey-Synar amendment. Instead, the leadership pulled back, with even Obey and Synar working against their amendment; it was defeated, 122-128.

Obey's interest in ethics has persisted, despite a cost in career terms. Late in 1980, Obey was a logical successor to the retiring Budget Committee chairman but lost out to Oklahoma Democrat James R. Jones. The national sentiment expressed in the 1980 elections may have helped the more conservative Jones; but Obey also was hurt by some Democrats' lingering resentment over his role in writing a strict ethics code limiting lawmakers' outside income.

As a sort of consolation prize, Obey did chair the Joint Economic Committee in the 99th Congress, which gave him a one-term platform to denounce President Reagan's economic policies. In mid-1987, Obey briefly scouted for support to run for Budget chairman again, but he soon dropped out of the race.

At Home: Twenty years ago, when *The Wall Street Journal* wanted to write about the advantages of incumbency, it sent a reporter to Obey's district, confident of witnessing an expert. The young Democrat had been in office only a few months at the time, but his techniques were already bearing fruit. He was sending out free government publications, writing columns for local newspapers and flooding the district with newsletters, even though he admitted in one that "there hasn't been that much to talk about yet."

Obey knew that unless he made a strong personal impression with the voters, they would return him to his Wausau real-estate business. Chosen in a 1969 special election to succeed

Melvin R. Laird, who was named secretary of Defense, Obey was the first Democrat ever to represent the 7th District.

When Laird's seat had opened up, Obey was beginning his fourth term in the state Assembly, where he had been since age 24. The GOP House candidate, state Sen. Walter Chilsen, was a well-known former newscaster who called himself a "Laird Republican." He tried to make student violence a campaign theme. But Obey deflected that issue. He focused on discontent with the Nixon administration's low milk-support prices and on the unpopular fiscal policies of GOP Gov. Warren Knowles. The changed mood in farming areas turned what was a 44,000-vote Laird win in November 1968 into a 4,055-vote margin for Obey five months later. In 1970, he breezed to re-election.

In 1972, redistricting put Obey in the same district with Alvin E. O'Konski, a 30-year House veteran who was twice his age. The new district was marginally Democratic and had more of Obey's old constituents than O'Konski's. The Republican agonized for months over whether he should retire or fight Obey. When he finally decided to retire, it was too late to have his name removed from the ballot. A few months later, Obey finished the job on O'Konski, winning 63 percent of the vote.

Since then, Obey has met little opposition. In 1986 and 1988, he defeated Kevin Hermening, who had been one of the 52 American hostages held in Iran. Obey won each time with 62 percent.

In early 1990, though, Obey found himself the target of an unusual recall effort by constituents opposed to spearfishing rights for the Chippewa Indians. They accused Obey of not working to rewrite the 19th-century treaties that gave the Indians special fishing and hunting rights off their reservation.

While some scholars expressed doubts about the constitutionality of a congressional recall effort, they were never resolved as the recall proponents failed to file the 43,401 signatures that were required. Obey was easily re-elected in the fall, again with 62 percent of the vote.

Committees

Appropriations (5th of 37 Democrats)
Foreign Operations, Export Financing & Related Programs (chairman); Labor, Health & Human Services, Education & Related Agencies; Rural Development, Agriculture & Related Agencies

Joint Economic

Elections

1990 General		
David R. Obey (D)	100,069	(62%)
John L. McEwen (R)	60,961	(38%)
1988 General		
David R. Obey (D)	142,197	(62%)
Kevin J. Hermening (R)	86,077	(37%)

Previous Winning Percentages: **1986** (62%) **1984** (61%) **1982** (68%) **1980** (65%) **1978** (62%) **1976** (73%) **1974** (71%) **1972** (63%) **1970** (68%) **1969 *** (52%)

* *Special election.*

District Vote For President

	1988	1984	1980	1976
D	128,849 (54%)	115,125 (46%)	118,482 (46%)	128,419 (55%)
R	108,341 (45%)	133,658 (53%)	116,505 (45%)	99,145 (43%)
I			16,153 (6%)	

Campaign Finance

	Receipts	Receipts from PACs	Expend- itures
1990			
Obey (D)	$620,219	$311,550 (50%)	$467,346
McEwen (R)	$10,886	0	$10,683
1988			
Obey (D)	$530,385	$308,399 (58%)	$450,716
Hermening (R)	$201,293	$11,528 (6%)	$203,969

Key Votes

1991	
Authorize use of force against Iraq	N
1990	
Support constitutional amendment on flag desecration	N
Pass family and medical leave bill over Bush veto	Y
Reduce SDI funding	Y
Allow abortions in overseas military facilities	Y
Approve budget summit plan for spending and taxing	N
Approve civil rights bill	Y
1989	
Halt production of B-2 stealth bomber at 13 planes	Y
Oppose capital gains tax cut	Y
Approve federal abortion funding in rape or incest cases	Y
Approve pay raise and revision of ethics rules	Y
Pass Democratic minimum wage plan over Bush veto	Y

Voting Studies

	Presidential Support		Party Unity		Conservative Coalition	
Year	S	O	S	O	S	O
1990	15	83	92	6	15	83
1989	31	67	88	8	17	76
1988	20	76	93	4	8	87
1987	13	87	93	3	7	93
1986	19	79	92	5	20	76
1985	15	84	93	4	7	91
1984	31	68	89	9	17	81
1983	22	77	94	5	11	88
1982	38	57	86	11	18	79
1981	29	70	83	11	13	81

Interest Group Ratings

Year	ADA	ACU	AFL-CIO	CCUS
1990	83	9	91	21
1989	95	0	83	20
1988	90	4	100	9
1987	100	0	94	0
1986	85	10	93	12
1985	90	5	94	18
1984	85	13	69	25
1983	100	0	94	20
1982	100	5	100	9
1981	85	7	87	11

8 Toby Roth (R)

Of Appleton — Elected 1978

Born: Oct. 10, 1938, Strasburg, N.D.
Education: Marquette U., B.A. 1961.
Military Service: Army Reserve, 1962-69.
Occupation: Real estate broker.
Family: Wife, Barbara Fischer; three children.
Religion: Roman Catholic.
Political Career: Wis. Assembly, 1973-79.
Capitol Office: 2352 Rayburn Bldg. 20515; 225-5665.

In Washington: When he addresses issues on the Foreign Affairs and Banking committees or in general debate, Roth leaves no doubt about where he stands. His certitude is a product of supreme confidence: He suggested in the early 1980s that he might have run for the White House if Republican Ronald Reagan had not gotten there first. "I see a lot of people here on the Hill," Roth said. "I don't think any of them could do a better job than I could."

This self-assurance has enabled Roth to play an advocacy role on sundry legislative issues. He is a leading opponent of foreign aid programs and speaks out against infusions of taxpayers' money for the savings and loan bailout. Yet Roth has also developed a reputation as headstrong and prone to bombast.

During the 101st Congress, Roth was an activist in the movement to repeal the catastrophic health-care bill, which had drawn the wrath of Medicare recipients who were expected to pay for the benefits through a tax surcharge. As Congress moved toward passage of a repeal bill, Roth exhibited his proclivity for hyperbolic rhetoric. "This catastrophic bill is the worst legislation Congress ever enacted," Roth told a Capitol Hill rally in September 1989.

Earlier that year, Roth's stubbornness contributed to the removal of his own amendment from the savings and loan bailout bill.

The House Banking Committee had adopted Roth's amendment to require all banks to have annual independent audits of their books. Roth had suggested such audits would be the "first line of defense" against a banking crisis similar to the S&L collapse. However, banking industry officials objected to a clause in the amendment that would have required, in addition to the audits, a "manager's statement" of compliance with federal banking rules; opponents described the requirement as burdensome.

House colleagues, fearing that this would become an outsized issue in the S&L debate, urged Roth to limit his amendment to the audit procedures; Roth refused. House-Senate conferees then voted to eliminate the entire auditing provision. Democratic Rep. Gerald D. Kleczka, a fellow Wisconsinite who had tried to mediate the issue, expressed exasperation at Roth's obstinacy. "He had it right in his hand and it just blew away," Kleczka said.

There are times, though, when Roth's steadfastness protects him politically. During his 1990 House campaign, his Democratic opponent tried to tar Roth, a member of the Banking Subcommittee on Financial Institutions, with some blame for the collapse of the S&L industry. Yet Roth was able to fall back on his opposition to the bailout law.

Later, in March 1991, the Bush administration sought additional funds to fill the depleted coffers of the agency handling the bailout. Roth was one of 37 House members to vote against all six versions of the funding bill, including the final one that passed.

As a member of Foreign Affairs, Roth also beats the drum on another aspect of federal policy — foreign aid — that raises ire in Middle America. He has made a crusade out of limiting aid to the Philippines, citing instability in the government of President Corazon Aquino and the opposition of some Philippine residents to the presence of major U.S. military facilities there.

In February 1990, he launched a broadside against the concept of foreign aid, stating, "It is time that we in this House learn that our foreign aid only wastes taxpayers' money and incurs the contempt of foreign governments."

In terms of legislative responsibility, Roth's main role is as ranking Republican on the Foreign Affairs subcommittee handling trade issues. He is an advocate of the Export Administration Act, which aims to bar the export of computers and other goods that might have military applications to communist nations or those with terrorist associations.

During the 1980s, Roth also supported limits on imports from Marxist-controlled Ethiopia. However, his overall record on economic sanctions is mixed. He has opposed U.S. sanctions against South Africa as an ineffective way to end apartheid. When South African Presi-

Wisconsin 8

Northeast — Green Bay; Appleton

More than half of the 8th District vote is cast in the Fox River Valley counties of Outagamie (Appleton) and Brown (Green Bay). Germans are the most noticeable ethnic group in the industrialized valley. Most of them are Catholic and, even if Democratic, tend to be conservative.

The economy of the valley and the vast wooded area to the north is dependent on trees and paper. The district is an exporter of paper and agricultural products worldwide. Among the economic leaders in Green Bay is the Fort Howard Paper Co. Paper, grain and dairy products go out of Green Bay; fertilizer, cement and coal come in. Green Bay, best known for its football Packers, is the smallest city to host a National Football League club.

Thirty miles southwest is Appleton on the north shore of Lake Winnebago. Here, too, paper manufacturers and paper-making equipment industries are important employers. Appleton also has white-collar jobs at insurance companies and at Lawrence University (1,150 students). It was the hometown of Sen. Joseph R. McCarthy.

Green Bay voted for John F. Kennedy, a Catholic, in the 1960 presidential contest, but it traditionally prefers Republican presidential candidates. Ronald Reagan won Brown County easily in his two White House campaigns, and George Bush edged Michael S. Dukakis there in 1988. Appleton's Outagamie County gave Bush a more comfortable margin, helping him to a 53 percent tally in the district as a whole.

Nature has been generous to the 8th District. The focal points for tourist resorts and vacation homes are Door County, on a peninsula jutting into Lake Michigan, and Vilas County, in a lakes region on the Michigan border. Vilas' population has grown in recent years, as many who had visited there decided to relocate permanently. Both counties are solidly Republican, influenced by the prosperity that has come from serving nature-seekers from all over the Midwest.

The rural counties in the north-central part of the district are mostly Republican, although there are pockets of Democratic strength. Forest County, where lumbering is important, chose Dukakis over Bush in 1988, as did Menominee County, where most of the voters live on the Menominee Indian Reservation.

Population: 523,225. White 509,127 (97%), Black 743 (0.1%), Other 11,938 (2%). Spanish origin 2,302 (0.4%). 18 and over 362,554 (69%), 65 and over 64,184 (12%). Median age: 29.

dent F. W. de Klerk took some steps to ease apartheid in 1990, Roth called for "flexibility" in U.S. policy, including an end to the ban on air flights between the United States and South Africa instituted by a 1986 sanctions bill.

Roth is most wary of sanctions that might disadvantage U.S. exporters — including 8th District farmers — against foreign competitors. This stance provoked Roth in 1988 to oppose a bill to invoke sanctions against Iraq, in response to the Iraqi government's use of poison gas against its Kurdish minority.

Roth called the use of chemical weapons "despicable," but said that by applying unilateral sanctions, "we're not doing anything to Iraq; we're shooting our own exporters in the foot." His was a lonesome position: he was the only member of Foreign Affairs, and one of just 16 House members, to vote against the bill.

Despite his outspokenness, Roth has sparked the greatest controversy with his House office-mailing practices. During the late 1980s, he set up what he called "Project 497," under which he sent out mailings in batches of 497; the maneuver enabled him to get around franking regulations that bar mass mailings (500 pieces or more) within 60 days of an election.

When Roth was accused by some former employees in early 1989 of using his congressional office and staff for re-election purposes, Roth dismissed the claims as sour grapes from disgruntled former staffers.

At Home: In the course of two years, Roth went from being one of the more secure members of the Wisconsin delegation to possibly one of the most vulnerable. His 54 percent vote share in 1990 was the lowest he had attained in any House race.

While Roth's falloff could have been due in part to the anti-Congress mood that swept the country in 1990, it was largely due to an aggressive Democratic challenge from state Sen. Jerome Van Sistine. He had both a base in the district's largest population center (Green Bay) and friends in organized labor.

Van Sistine maintained that the conservative Roth was no friend of the working class and that as a member of the House Banking Subcommittee on Financial Institutions he bore some responsibility for the savings and loan crisis. Roth dismissed both charges.

As evidence of his hands-on concern for job creation in the district, Roth pointed to the annual trade export conference he holds in either Green Bay or his hometown of Appleton. But Van Sistine had the money to get out his message. He carried Brown County (Green Bay) by 8,000 votes, more than matching Roth's 6,000-vote edge in Outagamie County (Appleton). But Roth also carried nine of the other 11 counties partially or entirely within the 8th to hold on to the seat.

Roth initially got to the House the same way he has worked to stay there — by assembling a large and efficient volunteer organization and shaking thousands of hands.

In 1978, when Roth decided to challenge vulnerable Democratic Rep. Robert J. Cornell, many GOP leaders were wary. He was not from Green Bay, the political center of the district. And while Roth's eager-beaver campaign style had worked well in Appleton during his campaigns for the Wisconsin Assembly, party veterans thought he might seem overbearing in a broader campaign against Cornell. They were wrong. Cornell, a Roman Catholic priest, never relished running for office the way Roth does. The incumbent spent his time giving wooden speeches while Roth was out at shopping centers shaking hands. In the last two weeks of the campaign, Roth (by his count) shook 63,000 hands. His volunteer organization and nearly 3-to-1 spending advantage were just as important. Roth won both Brown and Outagamie counties and carried all but four other counties to take 58 percent overall.

Two years later Roth faced former Green Bay Mayor Michael Monfils, used the same approach and won by an even larger margin. His percentage was down significantly in 1982 against Ruth Clusen, former national president of the League of Women Voters, but his 57 percent tally was still comfortable in a year when Democrats were sweeping to victory in statewide contests.

Committees

Banking, Finance & Urban Affairs (7th of 20 Republicans)
Domestic Monetary Policy (ranking); Financial Institutions Supervision, Regulation & Insurance; Policy Research & Insurance

Foreign Affairs (6th of 18 Republicans)
International Economic Policy & Trade (ranking); Africa; Asian & Pacific Affairs

Elections

1990 General		
Toby Roth (R)	95,902	(54%)
Jerome Van Sistine (D)	83,199	(46%)
1990 Primary		
Toby Roth (R)	36,818	(79%)
David J. Hemes (R)	9,935	(21%)
1988 General		
Toby Roth (R)	167,275	(70%)
Robert A. Baron (D)	72,708	(30%)

Previous Winning Percentages: **1986** (67%) **1984** (68%) **1982** (57%) **1980** (68%) **1978** (58%)

District Vote For President

	1988	1984	1980	1976
D	117,217 (47%)	88,922 (36%)	93,714 (37%)	102,935 (46%)
R	132,358 (53%)	154,371 (63%)	139,698 (55%)	115,804 (52%)
I			14,723 (6%)	

Campaign Finance

	Receipts	Receipts from PACs		Expend-itures
1990				
Roth (R)	$390,432	$203,083	(52%)	$499,968
Van Sistine (D)	$284,761	$214,895	(75%)	$274,112
1988				
Roth (R)	$339,852	$180,814	(53%)	$227,823
Baron (D)	$14,571	$10,204	(70%)	$14,421

Key Votes

1991	
Authorize use of force against Iraq	Y
1990	
Support constitutional amendment on flag desecration	Y
Pass family and medical leave bill over Bush veto	N
Reduce SDI funding	N
Allow abortions in overseas military facilities	N
Approve budget summit plan for spending and taxing	N
Approve civil rights bill	N
1989	
Halt production of B-2 stealth bomber at 13 planes	Y
Oppose capital gains tax cut	N
Approve federal abortion funding in rape or incest cases	N
Approve pay raise and revision of ethics rules	N
Pass Democratic minimum wage plan over Bush veto	N

Voting Studies

	Presidential Support		Party Unity		Conservative Coalition	
Year	**S**	**O**	**S**	**O**	**S**	**O**
1990	63	35	77	20	89	7
1989	72	27	81	16	90	10
1988	51	39	78	14	87	0
1987	61	37	79	18	84	14
1986	68	27	79	17	88	8
1985	55	36	76	13	73	24
1984	51	44	61	28	83	14
1983	71	27	84	14	82	18
1982	57	38	73	22	78	18
1981	64	33	77	14	80	12

Interest Group Ratings

Year	ADA	ACU	AFL-CIO	CCUS
1990	6	83	8	93
1989	10	86	9	100
1988	10	83	36	92
1987	4	91	0	100
1986	0	82	8	81
1985	10	80	13	95
1984	15	65	38	63
1983	5	81	7	72
1982	10	86	16	68
1981	10	100	0	88

9 F. James Sensenbrenner Jr. (R)

Of Menomonee Falls — Elected 1978

Born: June 14, 1943, Chicago, Ill.
Education: Stanford U., A.B. 1965; U. of Wisconsin, J.D. 1968.
Occupation: Lawyer.
Family: Wife, Cheryl Warren; two children.
Religion: Episcopalian.
Political Career: Wis. Assembly, 1969-75; Wis. Senate, 1975-79.
Capitol Office: 2444 Rayburn Bldg. 20515; 225-5101.

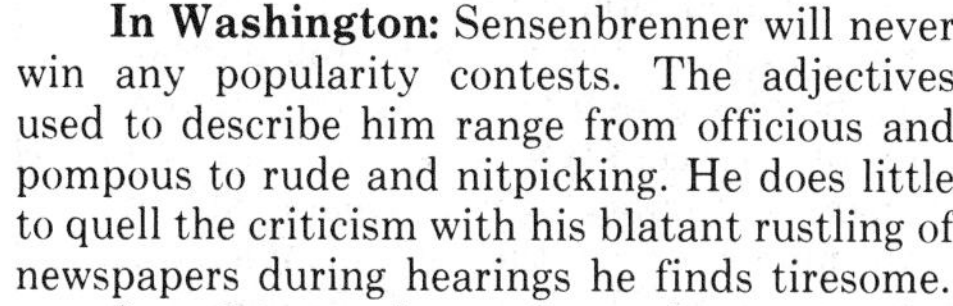

In Washington: Sensenbrenner will never win any popularity contests. The adjectives used to describe him range from officious and pompous to rude and nitpicking. He does little to quell the criticism with his blatant rustling of newspapers during hearings he finds tiresome.

Complaints about Sensenbrenner's demeanor come from partisans ranging the political spectrum. Democrats bristle at his harsh, conservative rhetoric, and even Republicans appreciative of his diligence on the liberal-dominated Judiciary Committee find him tough to take on a personal level.

But the icy regard in which Sensenbrenner is held does not deter him. As ranking Republican on the Civil and Constitutional Rights Subcommittee, he occasionally proved that he could go beyond mere objection to package his views into workable legislation. And he consistently criticizes civil rights legislation. He furiously waved the GOP banner with amendments to the 1990 civil rights bill, the 1988 *Grove City* bill and the 1988 Fair Housing Act.

Sensenbrenner, however, often railed against the subcommittee for its reputation as a "graveyard" for conservative legislation. He called the 1990 debate on a constitutional amendment to ban flag desecration a test "to determine whether we will obfuscate the issues with legal mumble jumble or show leadership in responding to the will of the people."

Sensenbrenner was bumped from that subcommittee's ranking spot in 1991, when Henry J. Hyde's term on the Intelligence Committee expired and seniority allowed him to supersede Sensenbrenner. In turn, Sensenbrenner snagged the ranking seat on the Crime Subcommittee.

His new assignment should give him plenty of opportunity to air his conservative views. But it will also highlight his independence on at least one issue likely to disappoint his ideological brethren: the seven-day waiting period for handgun purchases, the so-called Brady bill. Sensenbrenner supports that bill, noting that Wisconsin's 48-hour waiting period has been effective "in cooling off crimes of passion. If it can work at the state level, it can work at the federal level."

Although not otherwise a gun control advocate, Sensenbrenner has promoted the waiting-period idea since 1988, when he offered it as an amendment to the omnibus drug bill. He is still bitter about what he has called a "scurrilous" letter the National Rifle Association sent to his district criticizing the measure as "back-door registration of American firearms owners."

On most criminal justice issues, however, Sensenbrenner can be expected to take a conservative stand and stick to it. He authored an unsuccessful amendment to the 1990 crime bill to eliminate the racial justice provisions that would have allowed death row inmates to appeal their convictions on the grounds of discrimination.

Sensenbrenner revealed an ability to temper his conservative dogma with compromise during consideration of the Americans with Disabilities Act. Serving as a lead conservative negotiator, he helped work out a compromise that included three amendments important to small businesses. When Democrats accepted those measures, Sensenbrenner in turn fought efforts to dilute the compromise.

Despite his support for the final package, Sensenbrenner persistently pushed an unsuccessful and contentious amendment backed by the administration. It sought to bar punitive-damage awards for victims of intentional discrimination. Sensenbrenner pushed the same issue in consideration of the 1990 civil rights bill with an unsuccessful amendment to strike language expanding damages for intentional discrimination. He offered the amendment again in 1991 without success.

In 1988, Sensenbrenner led the GOP battle against a provision in the fair-housing bill that would have set up a system of administrative-law judges, empowered to rule on discrimination cases and impose financial damages and fines. The final bill contained a compromise

Wisconsin 9

Milwaukee Suburbs; Sheboygan

The 9th is Wisconsin's only full-fledged suburban district. During the 1970s it lured enough people out of Milwaukee's 4th and 5th districts to post a population growth rate of nearly 18 percent, the fastest of any district in the state. Workdays bring a horde of commuters from the 9th to and from Milwaukee's offices and factories.

Not surprisingly, the 9th is also Wisconsin's most staunchly Republican district. In the 1980s, Jimmy Carter, Walter F. Mondale and Michael S. Dukakis all failed to surpass 40 percent of the vote here. The only steady source of Democratic votes comes from heavily unionized, blue-collar Sheboygan.

Republicans generally make their strongest showing in the "Gold Coast" section of the district, a string of exclusive neighborhoods along Lake Michigan north of Milwaukee. In the city's boom days, brewers and other industrial kingpins built mansions on the North Shore; today the property values and the Republican turnouts there are stunning. In some of these affluent communities, such as River Hills, Bush won by margins of more than 2-to-1 in 1988.

The middle-class presence is stronger in the western sections of the 9th. Washington County is a combination of fast-growing bedroom communities and agricultural lands being encroached on by development, with a smattering of industry. The county seat, West Bend, is home to the West Bend Co., whose line of appliances includes the Stir-Crazy Popcorn Popper. Sixty percent of the Washington County vote went for Bush in 1988.

In earlier generations, the lakes of Waukesha County drew Milwaukee's leading families to buy real estate in the county for summer retreats. But in Pewaukee, Hartland and other parts of the county, suburbanization has taken its toll on those large holdings. In 1988, Bush took 65 percent of the county's vote. The areas of Waukesha County where Democrats are most numerous — the city of Waukesha and the southeastern part of the county — were transferred to the 4th District in the last redistricting.

Population: 522,950. White 516,203 (99%), Black 1,919 (0.4%), Other 2,798 (1%). Spanish origin 4,300 (1%). 18 and over 360,879 (69%), 65 and over 53,062 (10%). Median age: 30.

that set up an administrative judge process but gave any party in a discrimination suit the right to request a jury trial.

Sensenbrenner had less success when trying to reshape the 1988 Civil Rights Restoration Act, also known as the *Grove City* bill. The bill was designed to override the Supreme Court decision which said that only the "program or activity" of an institution receiving federal assistance, and not the entire institution, was required to comply with federal anti-discrimination laws. His alternative to the Democrat-backed bill was defeated by the House on a 146-266 vote.

Sensenbrenner was not happy with his setback on the bill. When some Science Committee Democrats opposed a bill, written by Pennsylvania Republican Robert S. Walker, mandating sanctions against federal contractors who do not maintain drug-free work places, Sensenbrenner lashed out. "If you object to using the string of federal funds," he said, "then you should not have supported *Grove City*."

At the start of the 101st Congress, Sensenbrenner took over as ranking Republican on the Science Subcommittee on Space. There, he is part of the panel's bipartisan consensus in favor of U.S. space programs. "Even in times of budget constraints," he says, "the American people want a vibrant space program."

Like others on the panel, Sensenbrenner says he is frustrated by its declining influence in the budgetary process. But he says the fault lies with committee members' unrealistic authorizations and failure to establish priorities. "If we take this bill as it is now written to the floor," he complained in late 1990, "we will be deliberately contributing to our declining relevance. . ."

The Midwesterner is among those interested in capping funding for the superconducting super collider. He authored a successful 1990 amendment axing a provision that would have guaranteed Texas a refund of its $1 billion investment if the project is scrapped before the end of 1995. "Wisconsin residents have already spent $3.5 billion bailing out Texas S&L's without adding the SSC to their tax bill," he said in a press release. "That's more than enough in my opinion."

At Home: Sensenbrenner has held public office practically since his graduation from law school. Despite his reputation for pomposity, his personal resources and conservative views have earned him an undefeated record at the polls.

Sensenbrenner is heir to a paper and cellulose manufacturing fortune, much of which stems from his great-grandfather's invention of the sanitary napkin shortly after World War I. Marketing it under the brand name Kotex, Sensenbrenner's ancestor went on to become chairman of the board of Kimberly-Clark.

To reach Congress in 1978, Sensenbrenner had to dip into family wealth to overcome an unexpectedly strong GOP primary challenge. With Republican Bob Kasten leaving the 9th District to run for governor, Sensenbrenner was viewed as the obvious successor. He had been elected to four terms in the state Assembly before moving in 1975 to the state Senate, where he quickly rose to be assistant minority leader. He had a solid political base in the older, more affluent lakeside suburbs, and his conservative stance reminded voters of the popular Kasten.

But his opponent was Susan Shannon Engeleiter, a state legislator who would later become state Senate GOP leader, the party nominee for the U.S. Senate in 1988 and then director of the Small Business Administration. Just 26 when she challenged Sensenbrenner, Engeleiter put on a strong campaign in the western, more middle-class part of the district, which she represented in the state Assembly. More gregarious than Sensenbrenner, she outpolled him by 5,600 votes in the 9th's four western counties. Only Sensenbrenner's familiarity in the most Republican of Milwaukee's suburbs allowed him to win the primary by 589 votes.

The 1978 Democratic nominee, Milwaukee lawyer Matthew J. Flynn, was also on his way to higher visibility in statewide politics as party chairman and a candidate for the U.S. Senate. But he could not raise enough money to compete with Sensenbrenner, who campaigned on his support for cutting taxes and defeated Flynn by a solid margin. Re-election has come easily since then. In 1982 and 1990 he had no Democratic opposition.

Committees

Judiciary (4th of 13 Republicans)
Crime and Criminal Justice (ranking); Intellectual Property & Judicial Administration

Science, Space & Technology (2nd of 19 Republicans)
Space (ranking); Investigations & Oversight

Select Narcotics Abuse & Control (4th of 14 Republicans)

Elections

1990 General		
F. James Sensenbrenner Jr. (R)	117,967	(100%)
1988 General		
F. James Sensenbrenner Jr. (R)	185,093	(75%)
Thomas J. Hickey (D)	62,003	(25%)

Previous Winning Percentages: **1986** (78%) **1984** (73%) **1982** (100%) **1980** (78%) **1978** (61%)

District Vote For President

	1988	1984	1980	1976
D	99,467 (39%)	97,101 (35%)	87,405 (34%)	100,968 (40%)
R	149,639 (60%)	177,516 (64%)	149,924 (58%)	143,454 (57%)
I			17,971 (7%)	

Campaign Finance

	Receipts	Receipts from PACs	Expend-itures
1990			
Sensenbrenner (R)	$266,285	$98,635 (37%)	$98,609
1988			
Sensenbrenner (R)	$309,612	$109,839 (35%)	$288,505
Hickey (D)	$14,736	0	$14,686

Key Votes

1991	
Authorize use of force against Iraq	Y
1990	
Support constitutional amendment on flag desecration	Y
Pass family and medical leave bill over Bush veto	N
Reduce SDI funding	N
Allow abortions in overseas military facilities	N
Approve budget summit plan for spending and taxing	N
Approve civil rights bill	N
1989	
Halt production of B-2 stealth bomber at 13 planes	Y
Oppose capital gains tax cut	N
Approve federal abortion funding in rape or incest cases	N
Approve pay raise and revision of ethics rules	N
Pass Democratic minimum wage plan over Bush veto	N

Voting Studies

	Presidential Support		Party Unity		Conservative Coalition	
Year	S	O	S	O	S	O
1990	75	25	93	6	80	20
1989	66	34	88	12	78	22
1988	68	30	92	8	87	13
1987	68	31	92	6	77	21
1986	73	27	89	11	80	20
1985	68	33	87	11	69	31
1984	45	20	56	9	44	12
1983	70	30	85	14	74	25
1982	60	36	84	16	70	30
1981	59	41	77	21	75	24

Interest Group Ratings

Year	ADA	ACU	AFL-CIO	CCUS
1990	6	83	0	86
1989	20	71	0	89
1988	15	88	21	100
1987	8	91	0	93
1986	10	77	7	89
1985	20	71	6	86
1984	5	80	11	69
1983	10	83	6	75
1982	25	86	15	73
1981	20	100	13	84

Wyoming

U.S. CONGRESS

SENATE 2 R
HOUSE 1 R

LEGISLATURE

Senate 10 D, 20 R
House 22 D, 42 R

ELECTIONS

1988 Presidential Vote	
Bush	61%
Dukakis	38%
1984 Presidential Vote	
Reagan	71%
Mondale	28%
1980 Presidential Vote	
Reagan	63%
Carter	28%
Anderson	7%
Turnout rate in 1986	44%
Turnout rate in 1988	50%
Turnout rate in 1990	48%

(as percentage of voting age population)

POPULATION AND GROWTH

1980 population	469,557
1990 population (50th in the nation)	453,588
Percent change 1980-1990	−3%

DEMOGRAPHIC BREAKDOWN

White	94%
Black	1%
American Indian, Eskimo, or Aleut	2%
(Hispanic origin)	6%
Urban	63%
Rural	37%
Born in state	39%
Foreign-born	2%

MAJOR CITIES

Cheyenne	50,008
Casper	46,742
Laramie	26,687
Rock Springs	19,050
Gillette	17,635

AREA AND LAND USE

Area 96,989 sq. miles (9th)

Farm	54%
Forest	16%
Federally owned	50%

Gov. Mike Sullivan (D)
Of Casper — Elected 1986

Born: Sept. 22, 1939, Omaha, Neb.
Education: U. of Wyoming, B.S. 1961, J.D. 1964.
Occupation: Lawyer.
Religion: Roman Catholic.
Political Career: No previous office.
Next Election: 1994.

WORK

Occupations	
White-collar	47%
Blue-collar	36%
Service workers	13%
Government Workers	
Federal	6,464
State	12,693
Local	29,702

MONEY

Median family income	$ 22,430	(7th)
Tax burden per capita	$ 1,584	(2nd)

EDUCATION

Spending per pupil through grade 12	$ 5,051	(9th)
Persons with college degrees	17%	(21st)

CRIME

Violent crime rate 258 per 100,000 (41st)

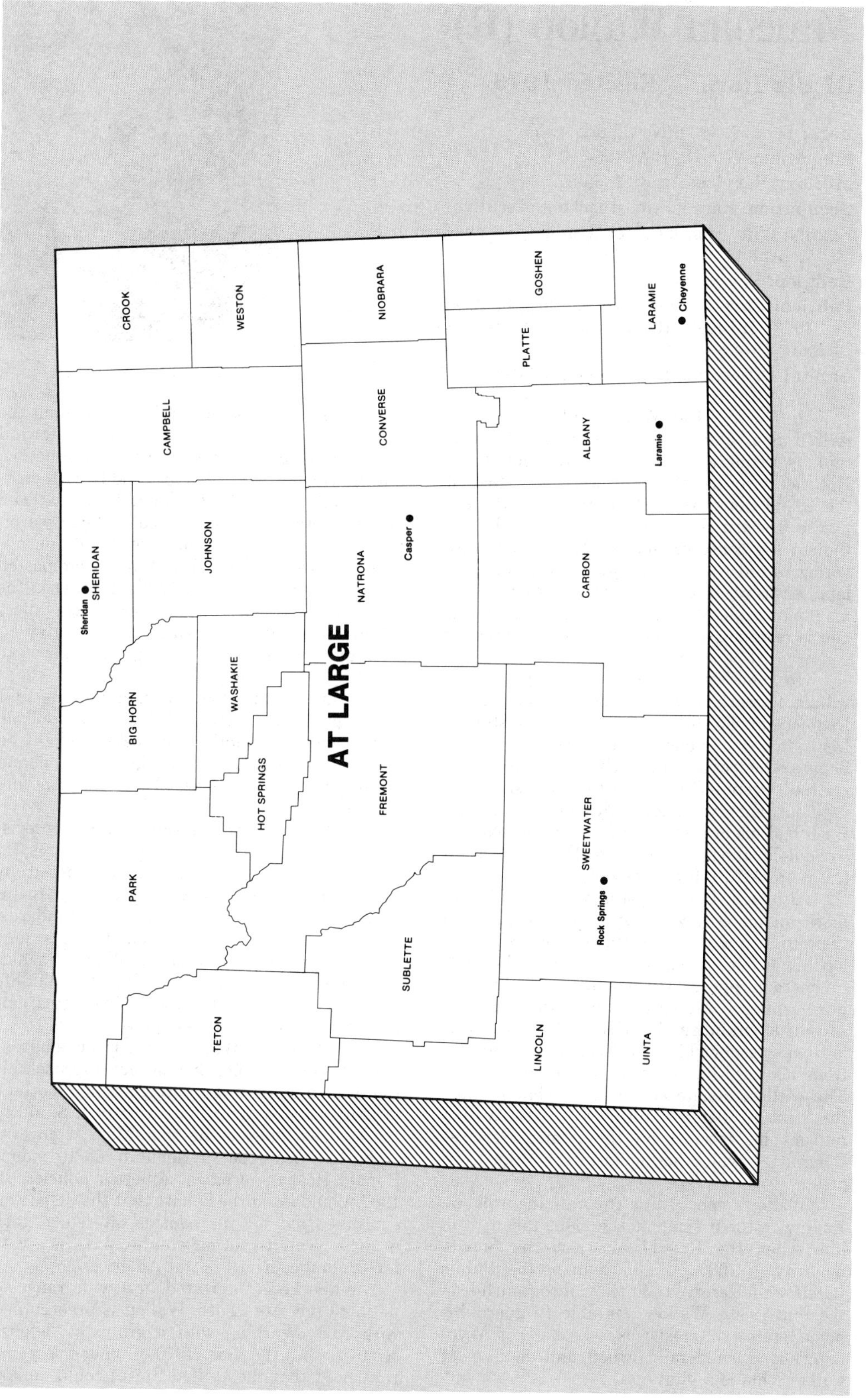
AT LARGE
CROOK
WESTON
NIOBRARA
GOSHEN
LARAMIE
Cheyenne
PLATTE
CAMPBELL
CONVERSE
ALBANY
Laramie
SHERIDAN
Sheridan
JOHNSON
NATRONA
Casper
CARBON
BIG HORN
WASHAKIE
HOT SPRINGS
FREMONT
SWEETWATER
Rock Springs
PARK
SUBLETTE
TETON
LINCOLN
UINTA

Malcolm Wallop (R)

Of Big Horn — Elected 1976

Born: Feb. 27, 1933, New York, N.Y.
Education: Yale U., B.A. 1954.
Military Service: Army, 1955-57.
Occupation: Rancher; meatpacking executive.
Family: Wife, French Carter Gamble; four children, one stepchild.
Religion: Episcopalian.
Political Career: Wyo. House, 1969-73; Wyo. Senate, 1973-77; sought Republican nomination for governor, 1974.
Capitol Office: 237 Russell Bldg. 20510; 224-6441.

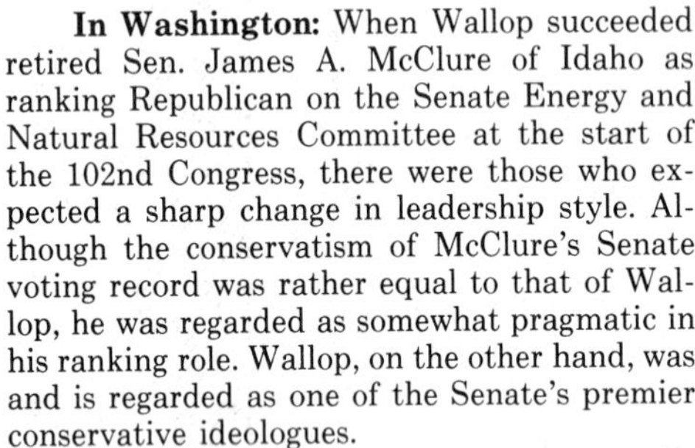

In Washington: When Wallop succeeded retired Sen. James A. McClure of Idaho as ranking Republican on the Senate Energy and Natural Resources Committee at the start of the 102nd Congress, there were those who expected a sharp change in leadership style. Although the conservatism of McClure's Senate voting record was rather equal to that of Wallop, he was regarded as somewhat pragmatic in his ranking role. Wallop, on the other hand, was and is regarded as one of the Senate's premier conservative ideologues.

On some issues, though, Wallop may be willing to work with the Energy Committee's Democratic chairman, J. Bennett Johnston of Louisiana, who is one of the more conservative Senate Democrats. In early 1991, Johnston crafted sweeping legislation to establish a new national energy policy. Although President Bush had his own energy plan, Wallop cosponsored Johnston's bill and helped him keep it on a fast track to full Senate debate.

Although the Johnston-Wallop bill had more mandates for energy conservation than the production-oriented Bush proposal, Wallop's involvement hardly marked a philosophical metamorphosis: He remains an adamantly pro-business conservative and a fierce adversary of environmental activists. Nor has Wallop's new responsibility on Energy diverted him from his hard-line crusade on defense issues. The earliest Senate advocate of what became the strategic defense initiative (SDI), Wallop pursues his interest on the Armed Services Committee, which he joined in the 101st Congress.

Wallop's move into the ranking role on Energy restored some of the clout taken from him when the Republicans lost the Senate majority in 1986. As chairman of the Public Lands and Reserved Water Subcommittee in the mid-1980s, Wallop was able to guard his home state's interests: Nearly half of Wyoming's land is federally owned, and the issue of water rights is a vital one.

In recent years, Wallop's activities on the committee have been largely oriented toward trying to expand domestic energy production, efforts which often put him at odds with environmentalists. In 1990, Colorado Democrat Tim Wirth offered a bill to combat "global warming," to which the burning of fossil fuels is thought to contribute. But Wallop lambasted the lack of any mention of nuclear power in the proposal. Accusing antinuclear forces of a "pack-dog mentality," Wallop said, "Environmentalists need to think things through as to what is best for the globe."

Joining Johnston on the energy bill in 1991 was no great sacrifice for Wallop. Both are from states whose economies are heavily reliant on resource development (Louisiana has oil and natural gas; Wyoming has those, and coal and uranium as well).

To broaden the coalition behind his legislation, Johnston included some measures favored by environmentalists and opposed by Bush: Most prominent was a provision to increase automobile fuel efficiency standards. However, the bill also included items long sought by conservatives such as Wallop, including opening Alaska's Arctic National Wildlife Refuge to oil exploration and easing regulations on the licensing of nuclear power plants.

As strong as Wallop's words on environmental issues can be, they do not approach his rhetoric on defense and foreign policy matters. Wallop was a staunch supporter of U.S. aid to the contras fighting the then-Marxist government of Nicaragua, a linchpin of President Ronald Reagan's Central America policies. In 1987, Wallop told the Senate that the debate on continued aid for the contras offered a stark choice. A vote to cut off aid, he said, "is a vote for communism in Central America."

While he is interested in a wide range of national security issues, Wallop is preoccupied with SDI. Working with a group of defense scientists in the late 1970s, Wallop became convinced that the United States could deploy armed space satellites that could shoot down at least some Soviet missiles at launch — thus throwing a wrench into Soviet planning and making such an attack less likely.

Wallop had difficulty getting his vision taken seriously until 1983, when Reagan unexpectedly unveiled SDI as a program to make nuclear weapons "impotent and obsolete." While Reagan's backing established SDI as a well-funded research program, it was something of a mixed blessing for Wallop: By touting a goal of an impenetrable "peace shield" and targeting research on exotic technologies, Reagan made SDI a target for opponents who described it as infeasible, if not a fantasy.

Wallop advocated a less futuristic system — with potential for near-term deployment — employing thousands of small, orbiting rockets capable of taking out at least some enemy missiles (thus meeting the original goal of disrupting Soviet military planning). This concept, titled "brilliant pebbles," was adopted by Reagan late in his presidency and became the centerpiece of Bush's SDI program.

But efforts to develop such a system have been parried by Armed Services Committee Chairman Sam Nunn of Georgia. Nunn sees any space-based antiballistic missile (ABM) system as violative of the 1972 U.S.-Soviet ABM treaty; he has tried to reorient SDI into research on a more limited ground-based missile system and opposes near-term deployment.

In 1988, Wallop tried a maneuver on the deployment issue by calling for a $100 million program within SDI to build an experimental ground-based system such as the one Nunn favored in principle. But Nunn checked the move, describing it as "premature," because the Defense Department had not established the military- or cost-effectiveness of such a system. Wallop's amendment to the fiscal 1989 defense authorization bill was tabled on a 56-37 vote.

Wallop has continued to pursue his SDI goals as a member of Armed Services. To get that seat, Wallop had to quit the Finance Committee, with its jurisdiction over taxation, entitlement programs and trade. However, Wallop's increased say over Wyoming-related issues on the Energy Committee should temper criticism back home over the move.

Wallop has not abandoned an interest in tax issues. In February 1991, he proposed to link a capital gains tax cut, blasted by many Democrats as a break for the rich, with a 2 percent reduction in Social Security taxes.

Wallop's strongly expressed views have made him a spokesman for the Republican right in Congress. However, his often-acerbic tone can rub even members of his own party the wrong way. In the fall of 1990, Senate Minority Leader Bob Dole was laboring to defend a controversial budget compromise against an onslaught from GOP conservatives. When Wallop persisted, Dole challenged his Wyoming colleague to run against him for leader. "If you feel that way, fine," a senator quoted Dole as saying. "Let's have a ballot right here."

At Home: Although he has won three elections to the Senate, Wallop has never attained the level of statewide popularity enjoyed by GOP colleague Alan K. Simpson and former at-large Rep. Dick Cheney (now secretary of defense). As a result, even with Republicans' 3-to-2 edge in voter registration, Wallop's campaigns are always worth watching.

Ironically, in his first statewide campaign, Wallop found himself at odds with the more conservative wing of the Wyoming GOP. Viewed as a moderate in a four-way gubernatorial primary in 1974 — he drew some of his support from voters sympathetic to environmental causes — Wallop came from far behind to finish a close second. When he did not assist the eventual nominee, conservative rancher Dick Jones, many party loyalists were displeased.

But Wallop solved that problem with remarkable ease in 1976, campaigning from the right against three-term Democratic Sen. Gale W. McGee. Although oil companies and other business interests were somewhat leery about backing him, Wallop got valuable help from national conservative organizations. He depicted McGee as supporting big government and criticized him for infrequent visits to the state. He also maintained that no senator should serve more than 12 years.

The challenger's TV ads were especially effective. Wallop saddled up a horse, donned a cowboy hat and urged voters to join the "Wallop Senate drive." He ridiculed occupational health regulations by portraying a cowboy forced to hitch a portable toilet to his horse.

The ads helped Wallop overcome a personal background that might have been a problem. Although he was a third-generation Wyoming resident and an eight-year state legislator, he was born in New York City, educated at Yale and had a grandfather who once sat in the House of Lords.

By the time of his 1982 election, Wallop found himself under fire from environmentalists, who claimed he had forsaken their cause, and from a Democratic opponent who said he was inaccessible to constituents.

The Democrat was former state Sen. Rodger McDaniel, a 10-year state legislator. McDaniel painted the incumbent as a servant of big-oil interests and an uncritical defender of Reagan's economic policies. But like Wallop in 1974, McDaniel had to be careful not to alienate more conservative members of his own party — some of whom were hesitant to back a man who had been state coordinator for Edward M. Kennedy's 1980 presidential campaign.

Wallop played up his support for the president and promised to work to protect Wyoming water. McDaniel, an energetic campaigner, carried several counties along Wyoming's predominantly Democratic southern tier. But Wallop's $1 million treasury enabled him to nail down a 57 percent victory.

In 1988, Wallop again faced an opponent who accused him of being anti-environment and out of touch with voters. And after six years, Wallop showed that he was even more vulnerable to those charges.

The Democratic nominee, state Sen. John Vinich, did not have the profile of a winner in conservative Wyoming. A liberal, pro-labor senator with longish hair and sideburns, Vinich sponsored programs to benefit the elderly and to tighten regulations on business in his 14 years in the Legislature.

Vinich, whose iconoclasm often placed him at odds with state Democratic leaders, was not the favorite of party insiders. But he outcampaigned his primary opponents.

Vinich did not try to mask his ideology in the Senate race, but he defied classification as an archetypal liberal. He earned the National Rifle Association's top rating for his anti-gun-control record. And he had been regularly reelected from a county with a solid GOP registration advantage.

Vinich accused Wallop of concentrating on a national conservative agenda to the detriment of the state's economic interests. He charged Wallop with hypocrisy for criticizing the National Park Service's "let burn" policy, blamed for prolonging the summer's raging fires in Yellowstone National Park. Vinich said Wallop had ample opportunity to alter the policy when he chaired the subcommittee with jurisdiction over the Park Service.

Wallop had a huge fundraising advantage, and he maintained a comfortable lead in polls for most of the fall. But Vinich was boosted by an intensive eleventh-hour media blitz bankrolled by the national party and labor organizations. He closed a double-digit poll deficit in the last week, but fell 1,322 votes short.

Committees

Energy & Natural Resources (Ranking)

Armed Services (5th of 9 Republicans)
Conventional Forces & Alliance Defense (ranking); Manpower & Personnel; Strategic Forces & Nuclear Deterrence

Small Business (3rd of 8 Republicans)
Export Expansion; Rural Economy & Family Farming

Elections

1988 General		
Malcolm Wallop (R)	91,143	(50%)
John Vinich (D)	89,821	(50%)
1988 Primary		
Malcolm Wallop (R)	55,752	(83%)
Nora Lewis (R)	3,933	(6%)
I. W. Kinney (R)	3,716	(6%)

Previous Winning Percentages: **1982** (57%) **1976** (55%)

Campaign Finance

	Receipts	Receipts from PACs		Expend-itures
1988				
Wallop (R)	$1,492,048	$872,664	(58%)	$1,344,185
Vinich (D)	$491,599	$248,303	(51%)	$490,230

Key Votes

1991	
Authorize use of force against Iraq	Y
1990	
Oppose prohibition of certain semiautomatic weapons	Y
Support constitutional amendment on flag desecration	Y
Oppose requiring parental notice for minors' abortions	N
Halt production of B-2 stealth bomber at 13 planes	N
Approve budget that cut spending and raised revenues	N
Pass civil rights bill over Bush veto	N
1989	
Oppose reduction of SDI funding	Y
Oppose barring federal funds for "obscene" art	N
Allow vote on capital gains tax cut	Y

Voting Studies

	Presidential Support		Party Unity		Conservative Coalition	
Year	**S**	**O**	**S**	**O**	**S**	**O**
1990	76	17	88	6	89	5
1989	78	13	91	4	92	3
1988	72	16	85	1	89	0
1987	74	15	87	6	88	3
1986	93	5	94	3	95	1
1985	73	14	88	5	83	5
1984	86	4	91	1	94	0
1983	72	22	83	9	82	9
1982	71	18	82	10	86	5
1981	85	9	91	3	93	1

Interest Group Ratings

Year	ADA	ACU	AFL-CIO	CCUS
1990	6	95	11	92
1989	0	100	0	100
1988	0	100	11	91
1987	0	96	0	80
1986	0	100	0	95
1985	0	95	5	97
1984	5	91	0	76
1983	5	64	13	83
1982	10	74	8	75
1981	10	71	5	100

Alan K. Simpson (R)

Of Cody — Elected 1978

Born: Sept. 2, 1931, Denver, Colo.
Education: U. of Wyoming, B.S.L. 1954, J.D. 1958.
Military Service: Army, 1954-56.
Occupation: Lawyer.
Family: Wife, Ann Schroll; three children.
Religion: Episcopalian.
Political Career: Cody City attorney, 1959-69; Wyo. House, 1965-77.
Capitol Office: 261 Dirksen Bldg. 20510; 224-3424.

In Washington: Words have often been a tool for Simpson. A raucous sense of humor — much of it self-deprecating — and a Westerner's way with an anecdote helped make him a Senate star and a public personality. A popular figure among his colleagues, Simpson rose to become GOP whip, the party's No. 2 position in the Senate, as a relatively junior member.

But in recent years, Simpson has been using words as a weapon, and he has embroiled himself in a series of controversies in the process. While he has always had a sharp tongue in policy debates, some of Simpson's sallies have been slashingly personal.

In March 1990, Democratic Rep. Richard A. Gephardt criticized President Bush as "without vision" and "without imagination" in his approach to epic political changes in Eastern Europe and the Soviet Union. Simpson responded with a broadside, launched from the Senate floor, in which he described Gephardt — the House majority leader and an unsuccessful candidate for the 1988 Democratic presidential nomination — as a "frustrated font of trivia" with an "obsessive and overweening" ambition to be president.

"It doesn't take any brains to be a critic . . . All you need is a shrill voice and a human target," Simpson railed. "And when the target happens to hold a job that the critic desperately lusts for and has been denied . . . then the frustration levels must be enormous."

Although the incident caused a stir, it paled in comparison to the flareup Simpson provoked with comments during the U.S.-led war against Iraq in early 1991. A number of conservatives had criticized Cable News Network for televising Iraqi-censored reports from Peter Arnett, one of the few Western reporters allowed to remain in Baghdad during the war. However, Simpson went further with his criticisms, and again got personal.

Simpson described Arnett, who had filed reports about U.S. bombing raids that killed Iraqi civilians, as "what we used to call a sympathizer." He also cast doubt on Arnett's loyalty during his prize-winning stint as a Vietnam War correspondent: Simpson said a source had told him that Arnett's Vietnamese-born wife had a brother with ties to the Viet Cong.

Arnett rejected attacks on his reportorial integrity, and said Simpson was rehashing rumors about his family that had been repudiated years before. Many in the media rallied to Arnett, with some reminding Simpson that it was he, not Arnett, who once had kind words for Iraqi dictator Saddam Hussein.

In August 1990, not long after Iraqi troops occupied Kuwait, officials in Iraq leaked a partial transcript of an April 1990 meeting between Saddam Hussein and five U.S. senators, including Simpson. In the quoted remarks, Simpson appeared to blame Saddam's villainous image in the West on unfair media coverage.

"I believe your problems lie with the Western media and not with the U.S. government," Simpson said. "As long as you're isolated from the media, the press — and it is a haughty and pampered press, they all consider themselves political geniuses . . . What I advise is that you invite them to come here and see for themselves."

Simpson never denied making those remarks, but portrayed them as part of a ploy to get Saddam to open his society to outsiders who could expose his repressive regime. He also argued that the Iraqis had left out substantial portions of the interview, in which he and the other senators raised U.S. concerns about the Iraqi regime's use of poison gas against its Kurdish minority, Saddam's belligerent rhetoric against Israel and other issues.

But critics insisted that whatever solace the senators did give Saddam fit a pattern set by the Reagan and Bush administrations of cozying up to the Iraqi strongman before the occupation of Kuwait. "If Peter Arnett had been anywhere near as bootlicky and obsequious with Saddam Hussein as Alan Simpson . . . we could understand why the CNN correspondent was being assaulted for his interviews and coverage," read a *Washington Post* editorial.

There had been previous squalls in Simpson's relationship with the press. Early in 1987, he told reporters the media was doing a "sadistic little disservice" with its investigation of President Ronald Reagan's role in the Iran-contra scandal. "You're asking him things because you know he's off balance," he said. "You'd like to stick it in his gazoo."

But this remark, unlike his comments about Arnett and to Saddam, left no deep scars. It fit into the context of Simpson as a member of the Republican leadership and a conservative partisan. Reporters who followed Simpson — and frequently quoted him — also knew that Simpson was capable of using his lash on colleagues of both parties, and even on himself.

These observers also knew that Simpson, as caustic as he can be in debate and conversation, is an effective and pragmatic legislator. Simpson was widely credited for performing well in the 100th Congress as acting head of the Senate GOP when Minority Leader Bob Dole was busy with his 1988 presidential campaign.

Simpson may speak his piece on the Senate floor, but he has shown time and again his willingness to go behind closed doors to hash out workable, bipartisan legislation. Of liberal Massachusetts Democrat Edward M. Kennedy, with whom he has worked on immigration issues, Simpson once said, "We don't vote together an awful lot, but we legislate together a lot." (Simpson and Kennedy have also done a point-counterpoint syndicated radio show.)

Simpson had exhibited this side of himself in March 1989, after the nomination of former Sen. John G. Tower to be Defense secretary lost on a party-line vote. Simpson staunchly defended Tower and dismissed allegations about his personal life as "absolute garbage." But when the brawl was over, Simpson rejected the idea that it would leave a lasting rift in the Senate. "It won't make a bit of difference," he said. "We'll have lots of fish to fry."

As a member of the Judiciary Committee, Simpson has established himself as the reigning Republican expert on immigration issues. Twice in recent years, he has crossed the partisan divide to craft landmark immigration law with Democratic members.

During the mid-1980s, Simpson and Democratic Rep. Romano L. Mazzoli of Kentucky fought an arduous battle to reform the nation's laws dealing with illegal immigration. Simpson stuck by two ideas that he insisted were crucial to immigration reform. One was that the only effective way to prevent people from coming to America illegally is to deny them the jobs that draw them here by penalizing those who hire them. The other was that many of the millions of illegals who had already been here for years must be offered some way to obtain legal status.

Formidable political obstacles were arrayed against him. Business groups opposed sanctions against employers, and Hispanic leaders warned that the penalties would lead to employment discrimination against Hispanic citizens. Conservatives attacked the notion of amnesty for people who had entered illegally, and state governments worried about the welfare costs of a newly legal population. No group fully backed the bill; each maneuvered and formed new alliances to kill certain sections.

The opposition stymied efforts to enact "Simpson-Mazzoli." In 1982, the bill overwhelmingly passed the Senate, but died in the House. In the next Congress, the bill passed both chambers, but stalled in conference: The House refused to accept a Reagan-backed provision limiting federal aid to states for services provided to aliens granted amnesty.

Undaunted, Simpson came back in 1985, at the start of the 99th Congress, with a modified proposal to delay amnesty until employment of illegal aliens had been reduced. Amended in Judiciary to require amnesty within three years, the bill reached the floor in the closing months of 1985 and passed comfortably.

However, over Simpson's vehement objections, the Senate had approved a new "guest worker" program allowing large numbers of seasonal farm workers to enter the country. That provision reflected the most serious unresolved controversy surrounding the issue — Western growers wanted foreign labor for harvest time while labor unions feared exploitation of workers — and it proved to be the bill's major stumbling block in the House.

Simpson staged intensive negotiations with House members, especially the core group of liberals who supported protections for guest workers. "Every one of us gave up something as painful as hell," Simpson said of the talks, "but we stayed at the table."

Although he was unhappy with some of the final provisions, Simpson expressed deep satisfaction over the product of his handiwork. The bill was "the very absolute quintessential immigration reform," Simpson said, adding that final passage "really tickled my butt."

In the 100th Congress, he turned to the other half of the immigration issue — laws governing the visa-allotment system for legal entry, enacted in 1965 and widely considered outdated. Simpson and Kennedy, the ranking Republican and chairman of Judiciary's Immigration Subcommittee, cosponsored legislation to cap annual admissions and replace the current system's preferences for uniting families with new preferences favoring foreigners with needed skills.

Their bill won the Senate's overwhelming approval, but the House was uninterested. Congress passed only a stripped-down version increasing allowances for the Irish — Kennedy's priority — and for nurses. However, Simpson and Kennedy revived their efforts in the 101st Congress, and achieved final passage just before adjournment in 1990.

The goals of the measure were the same as the one that had passed in 1988. But Simpson was unhappy about some of the baggage it picked up in 1989. Before passing the bill that June, the Senate raised the immigration cap higher than Simpson wanted and eliminated a preference for those competent in English from a special "independent" category aimed at immigrants who have job skills needed in the United States. "You have snorted and rolled and ripped around ... and given birth to a mouse," said Simpson, who nonetheless voted for the bill "with very mixed emotions."

In 1990, the House passed its version of the bill, maintaining the higher cap and adding a provision, sponsored by Rules Committee Chairman Joe Moakley, to provide an 18-month stay of deportation for people from El Salvador living in the United States illegally. While Moakley insisted that most of these Salvadorans were refugees from a civil war, Simpson said many came to the U.S. for economic reasons and were in no immediate danger if returned to their homeland; he also said it was unfair to single out immigrants from a single country for favorable treatment.

With the bill ready for conference in October 1990, Simpson single-handedly held things up to try to eliminate the El Salvador language and tighten penalties against illegal aliens. He settled for a partial victory. The Moakley amendment stayed, but Simpson-backed language was added calling for stepped-up border patrols and deportation procedures, as well as civil penalties for document fraud.

Simpson also pushed for a pilot program to create a forgery-proof driver's license that employers could use to screen out illegal aliens. However, this measure was dropped in the face of a protest by Hispanic legislators, who viewed it as the first step toward a national identification card.

On Judiciary issues that create a more clear-cut partisan divide, Simpson can be found among, or in front, of his fellow Republicans. He favors expanding the federal death penalty, opposes gun control and supports administration drug law enforcement efforts. In 1989, he rejected Democrats' complaints that Bush was not seeking enough money to fight drugs. "Money — that's the real drug around this place," Simpson said.

Simpson's partisan fires burn especially hot when the judicial nominations of GOP presidents are questioned. When Reagan in 1986 picked William H. Rehnquist to be chief justice, Simpson described Rehnquist's critics as a kind of bird: the "bug-eyed zealot." He used the same term for foes of failed Supreme Court nominee Robert H. Bork in 1987.

The one issue on which Simpson deviates greatly from most fellow conservatives is his support for abortion rights. It is this issue above all else that has led many observers to view Simpson, whose overall record is strongly conservative, as a Republican "moderate."

Simpson's pro-business attitude is evident in his work on the Environment and Public Works Committee. When Republicans controlled the Senate in the early 1980s, Simpson gave unenthusiastic support to efforts to revise the Clean Air Act. He used the debate mainly to promote the merits of cleaner-burning Western coal over the high-sulfur coal mined in the eastern United States.

However, President Bush did make the Clean Air Act a priority on taking office. Simpson went along, yet when the bill went to the Senate floor joked that it would be a "riotous occasion" filled with "anguish and horror."

Simpson did play a key role in blocking an effort by Democratic Sen. Robert C. Byrd of West Virginia to provide special benefits to his state's coal miners, who he said could lose their jobs because of the bill. Simpson quipped that he was loath to oppose the Appropriations Committee chairman because of his power over funding for esoteric local projects. Simpson said, "I write him letters all the time, saying, 'How about a little fence around the elk refuge?' " But he warned that Byrd's amendment would cost Republican support, stating, "If you vote for this you're going to lose this bill."

Simpson's other major assignment is the Veterans' Affairs Committee, which he chaired from 1981 to 1985. Here he applies his fiscally conservative principles, and often lacks zeal for what he calls his colleagues' "veteran-o-mania."

A particular proposal that aggravated Simpson was one to provide disability benefits to Vietnam veterans suffering from cancers allegedly connected to their exposure to the herbicide Agent Orange. Simpson argued that there was no definitive proof that the cancers were indeed service-related.

Late in the 101st Congress, supporters of such benefits gained the upper hand, attaching provisions to a veterans' cost of living adjustment (COLA) bill in the House and to a health-care bill in the Senate. Simpson stalled their victory, working with then-ranking Veterans' Affairs Republican Frank H. Murkowski to tie up the Senate bill, while House Veterans' Affairs Chairman G. V. "Sonny" Montgomery, D-Miss., tangled over the COLA.

Yet the opponents, in blocking the Agent Orange measure, also had the effect of sinking the COLA. When supporters of the benefits threatened to tie up the COLA again, Montgomery, Simpson and their allies gave in: the COLA and Agent Orange provisions were enacted early in the 102nd Congress. Simpson is a longtime friend and supporter of George Bush. In 1966, newly elected House member Bush bought a house from Simpson's father, a retiring U.S. Senator.

At Home: If Simpson had not come into his 1990 re-election campaign with a solid base of support, his controversial remarks to Saddam Hussein might have caused him political distress. Had the Democrats fielded a first-rank challenger, the flap might even have jeopardized his re-election.

But neither condition pertained in 1990. Polls continued to show Simpson as one of the most popular public officials in Wyoming. He also benefited from the Democrats' recruiting failure: His opponent, college student Kathy Helling, had emerged from a large field of unknown primary candidates.

Although Helling tried gamely to make an issue of Simpson's meeting with Saddam, she had almost no campaign resources. Also, her best-known political stance — a staunch opposition to abortion — hardly warmed the hearts of state and national Democratic officials.

Nonetheless, Simpson, who was expected to win in a landslide, prevailed with 64 percent of the vote, well below the 78 percent he carried in 1984.

Like his father Milward, a former governor and U.S. senator, Alan Simpson is at his best running an old-fashioned personal campaign, trading ranch talk and old jokes. His friendliness was an enormous asset during his 1978 Senate campaign to succeed retiring Republican Sen. Clifford P. Hansen.

During 12 years as a state legislator, Simpson was active in the drafting of a state land-use planning law. His opponent in the 1978 GOP primary, eccentric oilman Hugh "Bigfoot" Binford, invested in a media campaign charging that Simpson had undermined local control of land decisions. He also said Simpson was shaky in his support of state right-to-work laws.

Simpson fought off Binford's assault, calling it full of distortion. But it was his personal acquaintance with thousands of the state's voters that ensured his nomination. He drew 55 percent in the primary, and coasted against liberal Democrat Raymond B. Whitaker.

By 1984, Democrats had a tough time even finding a credible candidate. Their nominee, chemistry professor Victor A. Ryan, had never been active in state party affairs. He criticized Simpson's stand on immigration, called for more trained scientists in the country and for his efforts received 22 percent of the vote.

Committees

Assistant Minority Leader

Environment & Public Works (2nd of 7 Republicans)
Nuclear Regulation (ranking); Environmental Protection; Superfund, Ocean & Water Protection

Judiciary (3rd of 6 Republicans)
Immigration & Refugee Affairs (ranking); Patents, Copyrights & Trademarks

Special Aging (4th of 10 Republicans)

Veterans' Affairs (3rd of 5 Republicans)

Elections

1990 General		
Alan K. Simpson (R)	100,784	(64%)
Kathy Helling (D)	56,848	(36%)
1990 Primary		
Alan K. Simpson (R)	69,142	(84%)
Nora Marie Lewis (R)	6,577	(8%)
Douglas W. Crook (R)	6,201	(8%)

Previous Winning Percentages: **1984** (78%) **1978** (62%)

Campaign Finance

	Receipts	Receipts from PACs	Expend-itures
1990			
Simpson (R)	$1,253,647	$705,773 (56%)	$1,000,462
Helling (D)	$6,431	$2,500 (39%)	$6,243

Key Votes

1991	
Authorize use of force against Iraq	Y
1990	
Oppose prohibition of certain semiautomatic weapons	Y
Support constitutional amendment on flag desecration	Y
Oppose requiring parental notice for minors' abortions	N
Halt production of B-2 stealth bomber at 13 planes	N
Approve budget that cut spending and raised revenues	Y
Pass civil rights bill over Bush veto	N
1989	
Oppose reduction of SDI funding	Y
Oppose barring federal funds for "obscene" art	Y
Allow vote on capital gains tax cut	Y

Voting Studies

	Presidential Support		Party Unity		Conservative Coalition	
Year	**S**	**O**	**S**	**O**	**S**	**O**
1990	80	17	86	11	97	0
1989	84	10	81	17	87	8
1988	75	25	80	17	86	5
1987	67	24	81	11	78	13
1986	92	8	90	8	92	4
1985	90	10	91	9	85	15
1984	86	9	90	8	89	2
1983	76	20	78	13	75	18
1982	82	14	83	13	91	6
1981	86	11	90	7	89	8

Interest Group Ratings

Year	ADA	ACU	AFL-CIO	CCUS
1990	11	73	11	75
1989	10	70	0	88
1988	15	92	21	86
1987	10	79	11	71
1986	10	86	0	76
1985	10	78	10	90
1984	20	68	0	94
1983	25	61	13	59
1982	15	75	16	76
1981	5	80	0	100

AL Craig Thomas (R)

Of Casper — Elected 1989

Born: Feb. 17, 1933, Cody, Wyo.
Education: U. of Wyoming, B.A. 1955; LaSalle U., LL.B. 1963.
Military Service: Marine Corps, 1955-59.
Occupation: Businessman.
Family: Wife, Susan Roberts; four children.
Religion: Methodist.
Political Career: Sought Republican nomination for Wyo. treasurer, 1978, 1982; Wyo. House, 1985-89.
Capitol Office: 1721 Longworth Bldg. 20515; 225-2311.

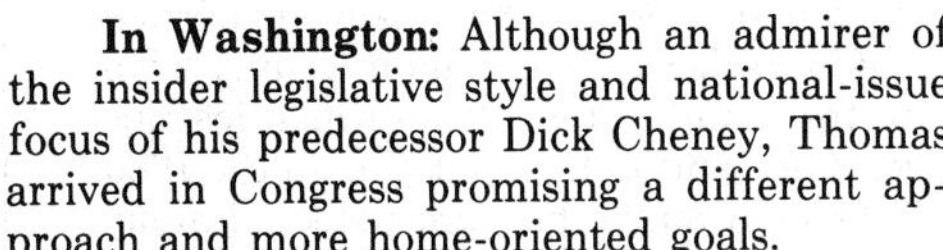

In Washington: Although an admirer of the insider legislative style and national-issue focus of his predecessor Dick Cheney, Thomas arrived in Congress promising a different approach and more home-oriented goals.

"You might see me take a stronger position on a few things," Thomas told the *Casper Star-Tribune* after winning a special election to replace Cheney, who became secretary of Defense in March 1989. "Where Dick would have accomplished something but would have done it through more the insider route, I will probably fuss more."

But in a House with Dornans and Traficants, "fussing" is performance art, and Thomas, with his Western proclivity for a few choice words, does not appear likely to break into that chorus line. A self-described conservative pragmatist, he seems interested in making government work, whether by expanding medical insurance to cover rural Wyoming citizens, by giving the president a line-item veto or by amending the Constitution to require a balanced budget. "I'm not one who thinks efficiency in government is an oxymoron," he said.

On the Interior Committee, Thomas has sought to protect his state's economy by pushing tax incentives for domestic oil exploration and acid rain legislation that would make Wyoming's cleaner-burning, low-sulfur coal more attractive. On Government Operations, Thomas helped agitate for a subcommittee hearing in 1990 on alleged monopolistic practices in the meatpacking industry; Wyoming producers had complained when the Justice Department found no antitrust violations.

Thomas was one of only two members to receive a perfect rating from the U.S. Chamber of Commerce in 1990, and he supports a 12-year term limit for members, saying it would cure the institutional inertia that he blames for continued government overspending.

At Home: Though Thomas fills Cheney's shoes, in personal terms he is closer to GOP Sen. Alan K. Simpson. The two have known each other from childhood: They were high school classmates in Cody and played freshman football together at the University of Wyoming.

Their paths then diverged. Simpson, whose father was a U.S. senator, went into law and politics. Thomas became an executive with the Farm Bureau and then general manager of the Wyoming Rural Electric Association.

When he decided to run for office, Thomas stumbled at first, losing two GOP primaries for state treasurer before winning a state House seat in 1984. In the Legislature, Thomas promoted consolidation of dozens of state agencies into a Cabinet-style government.

With the benefit of Wyoming's Republican tilt, Thomas was a logical favorite after obtaining the GOP nomination to succeed Cheney. But he had to survive a struggle with Democratic state Sen. John Vinich, who had built up high name recognition in a narrow 1988 Senate loss to GOP Sen. Malcolm Wallop.

The National Republican Congressional Committee (NRCC) helped Thomas raise considerable sums of campaign money. But its intervention was a mixed blessing. Embarrassed by special-election defeats in Indiana and Alabama earlier in 1989, NRCC Co-Chairman Edward J. Rollins was quoted as saying he would send two top aides to Wyoming to "take charge" of Thomas' campaign. His remarks played poorly in Wyoming, where people are easily piqued by out-of-state influence.

But Thomas survived his overbearing allies. Vinich helped by making a serious gaffe. Attempting to portray Thomas as soft on crime, he denounced Thomas' vote in the Legislature on a sentencing bill. However, Vinich, who was one of only three state senators taking the opposite view on the bill, was widely condemned for distorting the issue. Thomas gained the initiative and won by 9 points.

In 1990, Thomas fended off a vigorous but underfinanced effort by Democrat Pete Maxfield. Accusing Thomas of failing to boost Wyoming's lagging energy-based economy, Maxfield called for an oil import fee. Thomas won with a not-overwhelming 55 percent.

Wyoming — At Large

In Wyoming, Democrats are competitive in the five counties along the state's southern border — Albany, Carbon, Laramie, Sweetwater and Uinta counties. North of these five they rarely win.

Rarely, but sometimes. Conservative attorney and political neophyte Mike Sullivan succeeded three-term Democratic Gov. Ed Herschler in 1986 by capitalizing on Democratic strength in the southern arc and winning in two normally Republican areas — his hometown of Casper and the agricultural counties of eastern Wyoming. Sullivan won an easy re-election in 1990, but Republicans continue to dominate in the state Legislature and in the congressional delegation.

The Democratic voting tradition in southern Wyoming, where two-fifths of the population lives, dates to the early days of the state. Immigrant laborers, many from Italy, were imported to build the Union Pacific rail line through those southern counties, and coal miners followed. Most of the workingmen were drawn to the Democratic Party, and although their modern-day descendants are conservative on most issues and gave majorities to Ronald Reagan and George Bush in the 1980s, their Democratic sentiments are still evident.

The northern part of the state is the Wyoming of ranch and rock. Its dry plateaus and basins accommodate the cattle ranches that make Wyoming the "Cowboy State." This is conservative country. Ranching interests have traditionally dominated it, although mineral and energy development and the ensuing population growth has shaken up some county power structures. The people in the north are widely scattered; Sheridan and Gillette are the region's only sizable towns.

Wyoming's agriculture, oil and gas and uranium extracting sectors have struggled some in recent years, but with ski resorts and Yellowstone National Park as the lures, the tourist economy has boomed, particularly in Jackson Hole (Teton County). Unlike the state as a whole — which lost just over 3 percent of its population in the 1980s — Teton County has prospered. Summer tourists boost the county's population of 11,000 to almost 10 times that.

Wyoming's two largest cities have about 50,000 people each. Casper (Natrona County), a 1970s energy boom town, has felt more economic hardship of late than the capital city, Cheyenne (Laramie County), which has a more stable employment base thanks to state government and the Francis E. Warren Air Force Base.

Population: 469,557. White 446,488 (95%), Black 3,364 (1%), Other 9,063 (2%). Spanish origin 24,499 (5%). 18 and over 324,004 (69%), 65 and over 37,175 (8%). Median age: 27.

Committees

Banking, Finance & Urban Affairs (19th of 20 Republicans)
Consumer Affairs & Coinage; Economic Stabilization; Housing & Community Development

Government Operations (9th of 15 Republicans)
Human Resources & Intergovernmental Relations (ranking)

Interior & Insular Affairs (10th of 17 Republicans)
Energy & the Environment; Mining & Natural Resources; National Parks & Public Lands

Elections

1990 General		
Craig Thomas (R)	87,078	(55%)
Pete Maxfield (D)	70,977	(45%)
1989 Special		
Craig Thomas (R)	74,384	(52%)
John P. Vinich (D)	60,845	(43%)

District Vote For President

	1988		1984		1980		1976	
D	67,113	(38%)	53,370	(28%)	49,427	(28%)	62,239	(40%)
R	106,867	(61%)	133,241	(71%)	110,700	(63%)	92,717	(59%)
I					12,072	(7%)		

Campaign Finance

	Receipts	Receipts from PACs		Expend-itures
1990				
Thomas (R)	$404,308	$174,996	(43%)	$437,772
Maxfield (D)	$239,474	$33,950	(14%)	$239,116

Key Votes

1991	
Authorize use of force against Iraq	Y
1990	
Support constitutional amendment on flag desecration	Y
Pass family and medical leave bill over Bush veto	N
Reduce SDI funding	N
Allow abortions in overseas military facilities	N
Approve budget summit plan for spending and taxing	N
Approve civil rights bill	N
1989	
Halt production of B-2 stealth bomber at 13 planes	N
Oppose capital gains tax cut	N
Approve federal abortion funding in rape or incest cases	Y
Approve pay raise and revision of ethics rules	N
Pass Democratic minimum wage plan over Bush veto	N

Voting Studies

	Presidential Support		Party Unity		Conservative Coalition	
Year	S	O	S	O	S	O
1990	70	28	86	13	89	9
1989	72 †	25 †	85 †	12 †	95 †	3 †

† Not eligible for all recorded votes.

Interest Group Ratings

Year	ADA	ACU	AFL-CIO	CCUS
1990	11	79	0	100
1989	5	88	0	89

Non-Voting Representatives in the House

They are not exactly members of the House, but they are a part of the legislative process. They make speeches, serve on committees and hold chairmanships, and one of them — Ben Blaz of Guam — was president of the freshman Republican class of 1984. The only thing they are not allowed to do is vote on the House floor.

They are the five people sent to Capitol Hill from American Samoa, the District of Columbia, Guam, Puerto Rico and the Virgin Islands. Four are known officially as "delegates." Puerto Rico sends a "resident commissioner," who, unlike the others, serves a term of four years instead of two.

These positions have existed in some form or other since 1794, when the House received James White as the non-voting delegate from the Territory South of the Ohio River, later to become the state of Tennessee. But most of the current delegates are products of the 1970s.

Because the House Interior Committee has jurisdiction over U.S. territorial affairs, the representatives from Puerto Rico, American Samoa, Guam and the Virgin Islands all serve there.

Ron de Lugo of the Virgin Islands chairs the Insular and International Affairs Subcommittee of Interior. The only newcomer in the 102nd Congress is Eleanor Holmes Norton of the District of Columbia. She replaces Walter E. Fauntroy, who left his seat for an unsuccessful try for the mayoralty of the District of Columbia.

Following are the capsule profiles of those who serve in the House on a non-voting basis.

Ben Blaz (R)

Of Guam — Elected 1984

Born: Feb. 14, 1928, Agana, Guam.
Education: U. of Notre Dame, B.S. 1951; George Washington U., M.A. 1963; attended Naval War College, 1971.
Military Service: Marine Corps, 1951-80.
Occupation: Retired brigadier general.
Family: Wife, Ann Evers; two children.
Religion: Roman Catholic.
Political Career: No previous office.
Capitol Office: 1130 Longworth Bldg. 20515; 225-1188.

Ron de Lugo (D)

Of the Virgin Islands — Elected 1972

Did not serve 1979-81.

Born: Aug. 2, 1930, Englewood, N.J.
Education: Attended Colegio San Jose.
Military Service: Army, 1948-50.
Occupation: Broadcast journalist.
Family: Wife, Sheila Paiewonsky; two children, two stepchildren.
Religion: Roman Catholic.
Political Career: V.I. Senate, 1956-66; Democratic National Committee member, 1959-61; St. Croix administrator, 1961; Washington representative for the Virgin Islands, 1969-73; candidate for governor, 1978.
Capitol Office: 2238 Rayburn Bldg. 20515; 225-1790.

Eni F.H. Faleomavaega (D)

Of American Samoa — Elected 1988

Born: Aug. 15, 1943, Vailoatai, American Samoa.
Education: Brigham Young U., B.A. 1966; U. of Houston, J.D. 1972; U. of California, Berkeley, LL.M. 1973.
Military Service: Army, 1966-69; Army Reserve, 1983-present.
Occupation: Lawyer.
Family: Wife, Hinanui Bambridge Cave; five children.
Religion: Mormon.
Political Career: Lieutenant governor, 1985-89; Democratic candidate for U.S. House delegate, 1984.
Capitol Office: 413 Cannon Bldg. 20515; 225-8577.

Jaime B. Fuster (Pop. Dem.)

Of Puerto Rico — Elected 1984

Resident Commissioner

Born: Jan. 12, 1941, Guayama, Puerto Rico.
Education: U. of Notre Dame, B.A. 1962; U. of Puerto Rico, J.D. 1965; Columbia U., LL.M. 1966; attended Harvard U., 1974.
Occupation: Law professor; university administrator; lawyer.
Family: Wife, Mary Jo Zalduondo; two children.
Religion: Roman Catholic.
Political Career: U.S. deputy assistant attorney general, 1980-81.
Capitol Office: 427 Cannon Bldg. 20515; 225-2615.

Eleanor Holmes Norton (D)

Of Washington — Elected 1990

Born: June 13, 1937, Washington, D.C.
Education: Antioch College, B.A. 1960; Yale U., M.A. 1963, LL.B. 1964.
Occupation: Professor of law; lawyer.
Family: Separated; two children.
Religion: Episcopalian.
Political Career: No previous office.
Capitol Office: 1631 Longworth Bldg. 20515; 225-8050.

Senate Committees and Subcommittees

The standing and select committees of the U.S. Senate are listed below in alphabetical order. The listing includes telephone number, room number, and party ratio for each full committee. Membership is given in order of seniority on the committee.

Subcommittees are listed alphabetically under each committee. Membership is listed in order of seniority on the subcommittee.

Members of the majority party, Democrats, are shown in Roman type; members of the minority party, Republicans, are shown in italic type.

The word "vacancy" indicates that a committee or subcommittee seat had not been filled at press time. Subcommittee vacancies do not necessarily indicate vacancies on full committees, or vice versa.

Asterisks (*) indicate that chairmen and/or ranking minority members are *ex officio* members of all subcommittees of which they are not regular members.

The partisan committees of the Senate begin on page 1664. Members of these committees are listed in alphabetical order, not by seniority.

The telephone area code for Washington, D.C., is 202. Abbreviations for Senate office buildings are: SD — Dirksen Bldg., SH — Hart Bldg., SR — Russell Bldg. The ZIP code for all Senate offices is 20510.

Agriculture, Nutrition and Forestry

224-2035 SR-328A

Party Ratio: D 10 - R 8

Patrick J. Leahy, D-Vt., chairman

David Pryor, Ark.	*Richard G. Lugar, Ind.,*
David L. Boren, Okla.	*Bob Dole, Kan.*
Howell Heflin, Ala.	*Jesse Helms, N.C.*
Tom Harkin, Iowa	*Thad Cochran, Miss.*
Kent Conrad, N.D.	*Mitch McConnell, Ky.*
Wyche Fowler Jr., Ga.	*Larry E. Craig, Idaho*
Tom Daschle, S.D.	*John Seymour, Calif.*
Max Baucus, Mont.	*Charles E. Grassley, Iowa*
Bob Kerrey, Neb.	

Agricultural Credit

224-2035 SR-328A

Conrad – chairman

Boren	*Grassley*
Daschle	*Craig*

Agricultural Production and Stabilization of Prices

224-2035 SR-328A

Pryor – chairman

Baucus	*Helms*
Kerrey	*Dole*
Boren	*Seymour*
Heflin	*Grassley*
Harkin	*Cochran*
Conrad	*McConnell*

Agricultural Research and General Legislation

224-2035 SR-328A

Daschle – chairman

Kerrey	*Seymour*
	Dole

Conservation and Forestry

224-2035 SR-328A

Fowler – chairman

Heflin	*Craig*
Baucus	*Helms*

Domestic and Foreign Marketing and Product Promotion

224-2035 SR-328A

Boren – chairman

Pryor	*Cochran*
Fowler	*Helms*
Baucus	*Seymour*
Harkin	*Grassley*
Conrad	*McConnell*

Nutrition and Investigations

224-2035 SR-328A

Harkin – chairman

Fowler	*McConnell*
Kerrey	*Dole*
Pryor	*Helms*

Rural Development and Rural Electrification

224-2035 SR-328A

Heflin – chairman

Daschle	*Cochran*
Pryor	*Craig*

Appropriations

224-3471 S-128 Capitol

Party Ratio: D 16 - R 13

Robert C. Byrd, D-W.Va., chairman

Daniel K. Inouye, Hawaii	*Mark O. Hatfield, Ore.*
Ernest F. Hollings, S.C.	*Ted Stevens, Alaska*
J. Bennett Johnston, La.	*Jake Garn, Utah*
Quentin N. Burdick, N.D.	*Thad Cochran, Miss.*
Patrick J. Leahy, Vt.	*Bob Kasten, Wis.*
Jim Sasser, Tenn.	*Alfonse M. D'Amato, N.Y.*
Dennis DeConcini, Ariz.	*Warren B. Rudman, N.H.*
Dale Bumpers, Ark.	*Arlen Specter, Pa.*
Frank R. Lautenberg, N.J.	*Pete V. Domenici, N.M.*
Tom Harkin, Iowa	*Don Nickles, Okla.*
Barbara A. Mikulski, Md.	*Phil Gramm, Texas*
Harry Reid, Nev.	*Christopher S. Bond, Mo.*
Brock Adams, Wash.	*Slade Gorton, Wash.*
Wyche Fowler Jr., Ga.	
Bob Kerrey, Neb.	

Agriculture, Rural Development and Related Agencies

224-7240 SD-140

Burdick — chairman

Bumpers	*Cochran*
Harkin	*Kasten*
Adams	*Specter*
Fowler	*Nickles*
Kerrey	*Bond*

Commerce, Justice, State and Judiciary

224-7277 S-146A Capitol

Hollings — chairman

Inouye	*Rudman*
Bumpers	*Stevens*
Lautenberg	*Hatfield*
Sasser	*Kasten*
Adams	*Gramm*

Defense

224-7236 SD-119

Inouye — chairman

Hollings	*Stevens*
Johnston	*Garn*
Byrd	*Kasten*
Leahy	*D'Amato*
Sasser	*Rudman*
DeConcini	*Cochran*
Bumpers	*Specter*
Lautenberg	*Domenici*
Harkin	

District of Columbia

224-7260 S-205 Capitol

Adams — chairman

Fowler	*Bond*
Kerrey	*Gorton*

Energy and Water Development

224-0335 SD-132

Johnston — chairman

Byrd	*Hatfield*
Hollings	*Garn*
Burdick	*Cochran*
Sasser	*Domenici*
DeConcini	*Specter*
Reid	*Nickles*

Foreign Operations

224-7209 SD-136

Leahy — chairman

Inouye	*Kasten*
Johnston	*Hatfield*
DeConcini	*D'Amato*
Lautenberg	*Rudman*
Harkin	*Specter*
Mikulski	*Nickles*

Interior

224-7233 SD-127

Byrd — chairman

Johnston	*Nickles*
Leahy	*Stevens*
DeConcini	*Garn*
Burdick	*Cochran*
Bumpers	*Rudman*
Hollings	*Domenici*
Reid	*Gorton*

Labor, Health and Human Services, Education

224-7283 SD-186

Harkin — chairman

Byrd	*Specter*
Hollings	*Hatfield*
Burdick	*Stevens*
Inouye	*Rudman*
Bumpers	*Cochran*
Reid	*Gramm*
Adams	*Gorton*

Legislative Branch

224-7338 SD-132

Reid — chairman

Mikulski	*Gorton*
Adams	*Bond*

Military Construction

224-7276 SD-131

Sasser — chairman

Inouye	*Gramm*
Reid	*Garn*
Fowler	*Stevens*

Transportation

224-7281 SD-156

Lautenberg — chairman

Byrd	*D'Amato*
Harkin	*Kasten*
Sasser	*Domenici*
Mikulski	*Hatfield*

Treasury, Postal Service and General Government

224-6280 SD-190

DeConcini — chairman

Mikulski	*Domenici*
Kerrey	*D'Amato*

VA, HUD and Independent Agencies

224-7211 SD-142

Mikulski — chairman

Leahy	*Garn*
Johnston	*D'Amato*
Lautenberg	*Nickles*
Fowler	*Gramm*
Kerrey	*Bond*

Armed Services

224-3871 SR-228

Party Ratio: D 11 - R 9

Sam Nunn, D-Ga., chairman

Jim Exon, Neb.	*John W. Warner, Va.*
Carl Levin, Mich.	*Strom Thurmond, S.C.*
Edward M. Kennedy, Mass.	*William S. Cohen, Maine*
Jeff Bingaman, N.M.	*John McCain, Ariz.*
Alan J. Dixon, Ill.	*Malcolm Wallop, Wyo.*
John Glenn, Ohio	*Trent Lott, Miss.*
Al Gore, Tenn.	*Daniel R. Coats, Ind.*
Tim Wirth, Colo.	*Connie Mack, Fla.*
Richard C. Shelby, Ala.	*Robert C. Smith, N.H.*
Robert C. Byrd, W.Va.	

Conventional Forces and Alliance Defense

224-3871 SR-228

Levin — chairman

Dixon	*Wallop*
Glenn	*Thurmond*
Wirth	*Cohen*
Shelby	*McCain*
Byrd	*Coats*

Defense Industry and Technology

224-3871 SR-228

Bingaman — chairman

Gore	*Coats*
Wirth	*Mack*
Byrd	*Smith*

Manpower and Personnel

224-3871 SR-228

Glenn — chairman

Exon	*McCain*
Kennedy	*Wallop*
Byrd	*Smith*

Projection Forces and Regional Defense

224-3871 SR-228

Kennedy — chairman

Exon	*Cohen*
Dixon	*McCain*
Gore	*Lott*
Shelby	*Mack*

Readiness, Sustainability and Support

224-3871 SR-228

Dixon — chairman

Levin	*Lott*
Bingaman	*Thurmond*
Wirth	*Coats*
Shelby	*Mack*

Strategic Forces and Nuclear Deterrence

224-3871 SR-228

Exon — chairman

Levin	*Thurmond*
Kennedy	*Cohen*
Bingaman	*Wallop*
Glenn	*Lott*
Gore	*Smith*

Banking, Housing and Urban Affairs

224-7391 SD-534

Party Ratio: D 12 - R 9

Donald W. Riegle Jr., D-Mich., chairman

Alan Cranston, Calif.	*Jake Garn, Utah*
Paul S. Sarbanes, Md.	*Alfonse M. D'Amato, N.Y.*
Christopher J. Dodd, Conn.	*Phil Gramm, Texas*
Alan J. Dixon, Ill.	*Christopher S. Bond, Mo.*
Jim Sasser, Tenn.	*Connie Mack, Fla.*
Terry Sanford, N.C.	*William V. Roth Jr., Del.*
Richard C. Shelby, Ala.	*Pete V. Domenici, N.M.*
Bob Graham, Fla.	*Nancy Landon Kassebaum, Kan.*
Tim Wirth, Colo.	*Vacancy*
John Kerry, Mass.	
Richard H. Bryan, Nev.	

Consumer and Regulatory Affairs

224-1563 SD-537

Dixon — chairman

Kerry	*Bond*
Bryan	*Vacancy*

Housing and Urban Affairs

224-6348 SD-535

Cranston — chairman

Sasser	*D'Amato*
Sanford	*Gramm*
Graham	*Bond*
Kerry	*Mack*
Bryan	*Roth*
Sarbanes	*Domenici*
Dodd	*Kassebaum*
Shelby	

International Finance and Monetary Policy

224-1564 SD-537

Sarbanes — chairman

Dixon	*Mack*
Graham	*Domenici*
Wirth	*Kassebaum*

Securities

224-9213 SD-541

Dodd — chairman

Shelby	*Gramm*
Wirth	*Roth*
Cranston	*D'Amato*
Sasser	*Bond*
Sanford	*Mack*

Budget

224-0642 SD-621

Party Ratio: D 12 - R 9

Jim Sasser, D-Tenn., chairman

Ernest F. Hollings, S.C.	*Pete V. Domenici, N.M.*
J. Bennett Johnston, La.	*Steve Symms, Idaho*
Donald W. Riegle Jr., Mich.	*Charles E. Grassley, Iowa*
Jim Exon, Neb.	*Bob Kasten, Wis.*
Frank R. Lautenberg, N.J.	*Don Nickles, Okla.*
Paul Simon, Ill.	*Phil Gramm, Texas*
Terry Sanford, N.C.	*Christopher S. Bond, Mo.*
Tim Wirth, Colo.	*Trent Lott, Miss.*
Wyche Fowler Jr., Ga.	*Hank Brown, Colo.*
Kent Conrad, N.D.	
Christopher J. Dodd, Conn.	

Commerce, Science and Transportation

224-5115 SD-508

Party Ratio: D 11 - R 9

Ernest F. Hollings, D-S.C., chairman

Daniel K. Inouye, Hawaii	*John C. Danforth, Mo.*
Wendell H. Ford, Ky.	*Bob Packwood, Ore.*
Jim Exon, Neb.	*Larry Pressler, S.D.*
Al Gore, Tenn.	*Ted Stevens, Alaska*
John D. Rockefeller IV, W.Va.	*Bob Kasten, Wis.*
Lloyd Bentsen, Texas	*John McCain, Ariz.*
John Kerry, Mass.	*Conrad Burns, Mont.*
John B. Breaux, La.	*Slade Gorton, Wash.*
Richard H. Bryan, Nev.	*Trent Lott, Miss.*
Charles S. Robb, Va.	

Aviation

224-9350 SH-428

Ford — chairman

Exon	*McCain*
Inouye	*Stevens*
Kerry	*Kasten*
Bentsen	*Gorton*

Communications

224-9340 SH-227

Inouye — chairman

Hollings	*Packwood*
Ford	*Pressler*
Gore	*Stevens*
Exon	*McCain*
Kerry	*Burns*
Bentsen	*Gorton*
Breaux	

Consumer

224-0415 SH-227

Bryan — chairman

Gore	*Gorton*
Ford	*McCain*
Robb	*Kasten*

Foreign Commerce and Tourism

224-9325 SH-428

Rockefeller — chairman

Hollings	*Burns*
Bryan	*Packwood*

Merchant Marine

224-4914 SH-425

Breaux — chairman

Inouye	*Lott*
Bentsen	*Stevens*

National Ocean Policy Study

224-4912 SH-425

The National Ocean Policy Study is technically not a subcommittee of the Commerce, Science and Transportation Committee; no legislation is referred to it. Numerous *ex officio* members from other Senate committees and from the Senate at large serve on it.

Hollings — chairman

Kerry	*Stevens*
Inouye	*Danforth*
Ford	*Packwood*
Gore	*Kasten*
Bentsen	*Pressler*
Breaux	*Gorton*
Robb	*Lott*

Science, Technology and Space

224-9360 SH-427

Gore — chairman

Rockefeller	*Pressler*
Bentsen	*Stevens*
Kerry	*Kasten*
Bryan	*Lott*
Robb	

Surface Transportation

224-9350 SH-428

Exon — chairman

Rockefeller	*Kasten*
Hollings	*Packwood*
Inouye	*Pressler*
Gore	*Burns*
Breaux	*Lott*
Robb	

Energy and Natural Resources

224-4971 SD-364

Party Ratio: D 11 - R 9

J. Bennett Johnston, D-La., chairman

Dale Bumpers, Ark.	*Malcolm Wallop, Wyo.*
Wendell H. Ford, Ky.	*Mark O. Hatfield, Ore.*
Bill Bradley, N.J.	*Pete V. Domenici, N.M.*
Jeff Bingaman, N.M.	*Frank H. Murkowski, Alaska*
Tim Wirth, Colo.	*Don Nickles, Okla.*
Kent Conrad, N.D.	*Conrad Burns, Mont.*
Daniel K. Akaka, Hawaii	*Larry E. Craig, Idaho*
Wyche Fowler Jr., Ga.	*John Seymour, Calif.*
Richard C. Shelby, Ala.	*Jake Garn, Utah*
Paul Wellstone, Minn.	

Energy Regulation and Conservation

224-4756 SH-212

Wirth — chairman

Akaka	*Nickles*
Bradley	*Domenici*
Fowler	*Murkowski*
Shelby	*Seymour*
Wellstone	*Hatfield*

Energy Research and Development

224-7569 SH-312

Ford — chairman

Shelby	*Domenici*
Bumpers	*Garn*
Bingaman	*Nickles*
Akaka	*Burns*
Fowler	*Craig*
Wellstone	

Mineral Resources Development and Production

224-7568 SD-364

Bingaman — chairman

Bumpers	*Craig*
Ford	*Murkowski*
Conrad	*Nickles*
Shelby	*Garn*

Public Lands, National Parks and Forests

224-7934 SD-308

Bumpers — chairman

Fowler	*Murkowski*
Bradley	*Garn*
Bingaman	*Hatfield*
Wirth	*Domenici*
Conrad	*Burns*
Akaka	*Craig*
Wellstone	*Seymour*

Water and Power

224-6836 SD-306

Bradley — chairman

Conrad	*Burns*
Ford	*Hatfield*
Wirth	*Seymour*

Environment and Public Works

224-6176 SD-458

Party Ratio: D 9 - R 7

Quentin N. Burdick, D-N.D., chairman

Daniel Patrick Moynihan, N.Y.	*John H. Chafee, R.I.*
George J. Mitchell, Maine	*Alan K. Simpson, Wyo.*
Max Baucus, Mont.	*Steve Symms, Idaho*
Frank R. Lautenberg, N.J.	*Dave Durenberger, Minn.*
Harry Reid, Nev.	*John W. Warner, Va.*
Bob Graham, Fla.	*James M. Jeffords, Vt.*
Joseph I. Lieberman, Conn.	*Robert C. Smith, N.H.*
Howard M. Metzenbaum, Ohio	

Environmental Protection

224-6691 SH-408

Baucus — chairman

Moynihan	*Chafee*
Mitchell	*Simpson*
Lautenberg	*Durenberger*
Graham	*Warner*
Lieberman	*Jeffords*
Metzenbaum	*Symms*

Nuclear Regulation

224-5031 SH-415

Graham — chairman

Moynihan	*Simpson*
Reid	*Symms*

Superfund, Ocean and Water Protection

224-5031 SH-415

Lautenberg — chairman

Mitchell	*Durenberger*
Baucus	*Simpson*
Metzenbaum	*Smith*

Toxic Substances, Environmental Oversight, Research and Development

224-3597 SH-508

Reid — chairman

Baucus	*Warner*
Lieberman	*Jeffords*

Water Resources, Transportation and Infrastructure

224-3597 SH-508

Moynihan — chairman

Mitchell	*Symms*
Lautenberg	*Warner*
Reid	*Jeffords*
Graham	*Durenberger*
Lieberman	*Smith*
Metzenbaum	*Chafee*

Finance

224-4515 SD-205

Party Ratio: D 11 - R 9

Lloyd Bentsen, D-Texas, chairman

Daniel Patrick Moynihan, N.Y.	*Bob Packwood, Ore.*
Max Baucus, Mont.	*Bob Dole, Kan.*
David L. Boren, Okla.	*William V. Roth Jr., Del.*
Bill Bradley, N.J.	*John C. Danforth, Mo.*
George J. Mitchell, Maine	*John H. Chafee, R.I.*
David Pryor, Ark.	*Dave Durenberger, Minn.*
Donald W. Riegle Jr., Mich.	*Steve Symms, Idaho*
John D. Rockefeller IV, W.Va.	*Charles E. Grassley, Iowa*
Tom Daschle, S.D.	*Vacancy*
John B. Breaux, La.	

Deficits, Debt Management and International Debt

224-4515 SD-205

Bradley — chairman

Riegle	*Grassley*

Energy and Agricultural Taxation

224-4515 SD-205

Daschle — chairman

Boren	*Symms*
Breaux	*Dole*

Health for Families and the Uninsured

224-4515 SD-205

Riegle — chairman

Bradley	*Chafee*
Mitchell	*Roth*
Rockefeller	*Durenberger*

International Trade

224-4515 SD-205

Baucus — chairman

Bentsen	*Danforth*
Moynihan	*Packwood*
Boren	*Roth*
Bradley	*Chafee*
Mitchell	*Symms*
Riegle	*Grassley*
Rockefeller	*Vacancy*
Daschle	
Breaux	

Medicare and Long-Term Care

224-4515 SD-205

Rockefeller — chairman

Bentsen	*Durenberger*
Baucus	*Packwood*
Mitchell	*Dole*
Pryor	*Chafee*
Daschle	*Danforth*
	Vacancy

Private Retirement Plans and Oversight of the Internal Revenue Service

224-4515 SD-205

Pryor — chairman

Moynihan	*Grassley*
	Vacancy

Social Security and Family Policy

224-4515 SD-205

Moynihan — chairman

Breaux	*Dole*
	Durenberger

Taxation

224-4515 SD-205

Boren — chairman

Bentsen	*Roth*
Baucus	*Packwood*
Pryor	*Danforth*
	Symms

Foreign Relations

224-4651 SD-446

Party Ratio: D 10 - R 8

Claiborne Pell, D-R.I., chairman

Joseph R. Biden Jr., Del.	*Jesse Helms, N.C.*
Paul S. Sarbanes, Md.	*Richard G. Lugar, Ind.*
Alan Cranston, Calif.	*Nancy Landon Kassebaum, Kan.*
Christopher J. Dodd, Conn.	*Larry Pressler, S.D.*
John Kerry, Mass.	*Frank H. Murkowski, Alaska*
Paul Simon, Ill.	*Mitch McConnell, Ky.*
Terry Sanford, N.C.	*Hank Brown, Colo.*
Daniel Patrick Moynihan, N.Y.	*Orrin G. Hatch, Utah*
Charles S. Robb, Va.	

African Affairs

224-4651 SD-446

Simon — chairman

Sanford	*Kassebaum*
Moynihan	*Helms*

East Asian and Pacific Affairs

224-4651 SD-446

Cranston — chairman

Biden	*Murkowski*
Dodd	*Lugar*
Kerry	*McConnell*
Robb	*Brown*

European Affairs

224-4651 SD-446

Biden — chairman

Sarbanes	*Pressler*
Simon	*Brown*

International Economic Policy, Trade, Oceans and Environment

224-4651 SD-446

Sarbanes — chairman

Biden	*McConnell*
Cranston	*Lugar*
Dodd	*Murkowski*
Pell	*Kassebaum*

Near Eastern and South Asian Affairs

224-4651 SD-446

Sanford — chairman

Sarbanes	*Hatch*
Moynihan	*Pressler*
Robb	*Murkowski*

Terrorism, Narcotics and International Operations

224-4651 SD-446

Kerry — chairman

Simon	*Brown*
Moynihan	*McConnell*
Pell	*Hatch*

Western Hemisphere and Peace Corps Affairs

224-4651 SD-446

Dodd — chairman

Cranston	*Lugar*
Kerry	*Kassebaum*
Sanford	*Hatch*
Robb	*Helms*

Governmental Affairs

224-4751 SD-340

Party Ratio: D 8 - R 6

John Glenn, D-Ohio, chairman

Sam Nunn, Ga.	*William V. Roth Jr., Del.*
Carl Levin, Mich.	*Ted Stevens, Alaska*
Jim Sasser, Tenn.	*William S. Cohen, Maine*
David Pryor, Ark.	*Warren B. Rudman, N.H.*
Herb Kohl, Wis.	*John Seymour, Calif.*
Joseph I. Lieberman, Conn.	*Vacancy*
Daniel K. Akaka, Hawaii	

Federal Services, Post Office and Civil Service

224-2254 SH-601

Pryor — chairman

Sasser	*Stevens*
Akaka	*Vacancy*

General Services, Federalism and the District of Columbia

224-4718 SH-432

Sasser — chairman

Lieberman	*Seymour*
Akaka	*Stevens*

Government Information and Regulation

224-9000 SH-605

Kohl — chairman

Nunn	*Rudman*
Levin	*Cohen*
Lieberman	*Seymour*

Oversight of Government Management

224-3682 SH-442

Levin — chairman

Pryor	*Cohen*
Kohl	*Rudman*
Lieberman	*Seymour*
Akaka	*Stevens*
Nunn	*Vacancy*

Permanent Investigations

224-3721 SR-100

Nunn — chairman
Glenn — vice chairman

Levin	*Roth*
Sasser	*Stevens*
Pryor	*Cohen*
Kohl	*Rudman*
Lieberman	*Seymour*

Judiciary

224-5225 SD-224

Party Ratio: D 8 - R 6

Joseph R. Biden Jr., D-Del., chairman

Edward M. Kennedy, Mass.	*Strom Thurmond, S.C.*
Howard M. Metzenbaum, Ohio	*Orrin G. Hatch, Utah*
Dennis DeConcini, Ariz.	*Alan K. Simpson, Wyo.*
Patrick J. Leahy, Vt.	*Charles E. Grassley, Iowa*
Howell Heflin, Ala.	*Arlen Specter, Pa.*
Paul Simon, Ill.	*Hank Brown, Colo.*
Herb Kohl, Wis.	

Antitrust, Monopolies and Business Rights

224-5701 SH-308

Metzenbaum — chairman

DeConcini	*Thurmond*
Heflin	*Specter*
Simon	*Hatch*

Constitution

224-5573 SD-524

Simon — chairman

Metzenbaum	*Specter*
DeConcini	*Hatch*
Kennedy	

Courts and Administrative Practice

224-4022 SH-223

Heflin — chairman

Metzenbaum	*Grassley*
Kohl	*Thurmond*

Immigration and Refugee Affairs

224-7878 SD-520

Kennedy — chairman

Simon	*Simpson*

Juvenile Justice

224-4933 SH-305

Kohl — chairman

Biden	*Brown*

Patents, Copyrights and Trademarks

224-8178 SH-327

DeConcini — chairman

Kennedy	*Hatch*
Leahy	*Simpson*
Heflin	*Grassley*

Technology and the Law

224-3407 SH-815

Leahy — chairman

Kohl	*Brown*

Labor and Human Resources

224-5375 SD-428

Party Ratio: D 10 - R 7

Edward M. Kennedy, D-Mass., chairman

Claiborne Pell, R.I.	*Orrin G. Hatch, Utah*
Howard M. Metzenbaum, Ohio	*Nancy Landon Kassebaum, Kan.*
Christopher J. Dodd, Conn.	*James M. Jeffords, Vt.*
Paul Simon, Ill.	*Daniel R. Coats, Ind.*
Tom Harkin, Iowa	*Strom Thurmond, S.C.*
Brock Adams, Wash.	*Dave Durenberger, Minn.*
Barbara A. Mikulski, Md.	*Thad Cochran, Miss.*
Jeff Bingaman, N.M.	
Paul Wellstone, Minn.	

Aging

224-3239 SH-404

Adams — chairman

Pell	*Cochran*
Metzenbaum	*Durenberger*
Dodd	*Coats*

Children, Family, Drugs and Alcoholism

224-5630 SH-639

Dodd — chairman

Pell	*Coats*
Harkin	*Hatch*
Adams	*Kassebaum*
Mikulski	*Jeffords*
Bingaman	*Thurmond*
Kennedy	*Durenberger*
Wellstone	

Disability Policy

224-6265 SH-113

Harkin — chairman

Metzenbaum	*Durenberger*
Simon	*Hatch*
Adams	*Jeffords*

Education, Arts and Humanities

224-7666 SD-648

Pell — chairman

Metzenbaum	*Kassebaum*
Dodd	*Cochran*
Simon	*Hatch*
Mikulski	*Jeffords*
Bingaman	*Thurmond*
Kennedy	*Coats*
Wellstone	

Employment and Productivity

224-5575 SD-644

Simon — chairman

Harkin	*Thurmond*
Adams	*Durenberger*
Mikulski	*Kassebaum*
Bingaman	*Coats*

Labor

224-5546 SH-608

Metzenbaum — chairman

Harkin	*Jeffords*
Mikulski	*Cochran*
Dodd	*Thurmond*
Kennedy	*Hatch*
Wellstone	

Rules and Administration

224-6352 SR-305

Party Ratio: D 9 - R 7

Wendell H. Ford, D-Ky., chairman

Claiborne Pell, R.I.	*Ted Stevens, Alaska*
Robert C. Byrd, W.Va.	*Mark O. Hatfield, Ore.*
Daniel K. Inouye, Hawaii	*Jesse Helms, N.C.*
Dennis DeConcini, Ariz.	*John W. Warner, Va.*
Al Gore, Tenn.	*Bob Dole, Kan.*
Daniel Patrick Moynihan, N.Y.	*Jake Garn, Utah*
Christopher J. Dodd, Conn.	*Mitch McConnell, Ky.*
Brock Adams, Wash.	

Small Business

224-5175 SR-428A

Party Ratio: D 10 - R 8

Dale Bumpers, D-Ark., chairman

Sam Nunn, Ga.	*Bob Kasten, Wis.*
Max Baucus, Mont.	*Larry Pressler, S.D.*
Carl Levin, Mich.	*Malcolm Wallop, Wyo.*
Alan J. Dixon, Ill.	*Christopher S. Bond, Mo.*
Tom Harkin, Iowa	*Conrad Burns, Mont.*
John Kerry, Mass.	*Ted Stevens, Alaska*
Barbara A. Mikulski, Md.	*Connie Mack, Fla.*
Joseph I. Lieberman, Conn.	*John Seymour, Calif.*
Paul Wellstone, Minn.	

Competitiveness and Economic Opportunity

224-5175 SR-428A

Lieberman — chairman

Harkin	*Mack*

Export Expansion

224-5175 SR-428A

Mikulski — chairman

Harkin	*Pressler*
Lieberman	*Wallop*
Bumpers	*Stevens*

Government Contracting and Paperwork Reduction

224-5175 SR-428A

Dixon — chairman

Lieberman	*Bond*
Nunn	*Kasten*

Innovation, Technology and Productivity

224-5175 SR-428A

Levin — chairman

Baucus	*Stevens*
Kerry	*Seymour*

Rural Economy and Family Farming

224-5175 SR-428A

Baucus — chairman

Nunn	*Kasten*
Levin	*Pressler*
Dixon	*Wallop*
Kerry	*Bond*
Bumpers	*Burns*
Wellstone	*Mack*

Urban and Minority-Owned Business Development

224-5175 SR-428A

Kerry — chairman

Nunn	*Burns*
Mikulski	*Seymour*
Wellstone	*Mack*

Special Aging

224-5364 SD-G31

Party Ratio: D 11 - R 10

David Pryor, D-Ark., chairman

John Glenn, Ohio	*William S. Cohen, Maine*
Bill Bradley, N.J.	*Larry Pressler, S.D.*
Quentin N. Burdick, N.D.	*Charles E. Grassley, Iowa*
J. Bennett Johnston, La.	*Alan K. Simpson, Wyo.*
John B. Breaux, La.	*James M. Jeffords, Vt.*
Richard C. Shelby, Ala.	*John McCain, Ariz.*
Harry Reid, Nev.	*Dave Durenberger, Minn.*
Bob Graham, Fla.	*Larry E. Craig, Idaho*
Herb Kohl, Wis.	*Conrad Burns, Mont.*
Terry Sanford, N.C.	*Vacancy*

Veterans' Affairs

224-9126 SR-414

Party Ratio: D 7 - R 5

Alan Cranston, D-Calif., chairman

Dennis DeConcini, Ariz.
George J. Mitchell, Maine
John D. Rockefeller IV, W.Va.
Bob Graham, Fla.
Daniel K. Akaka, Hawaii
Tom Daschle, S.D.

Arlen Specter, Pa.
Frank H. Murkowski, Alaska
Alan K. Simpson, Wyo.
Strom Thurmond, S.C.
James M. Jeffords, Vt.

Select Ethics

224-2981 SH-220

Party Ratio: D 3 - R 3

Howell Heflin, D-Ala., chairman
Warren B. Rudman, R-N.H., vice chairman

Terry Sanford, N.C.
Jeff Bingaman, N.M.

Trent Lott, Miss.
Slade Gorton, Wash.

Select Indian Affairs

224-2251 SH-838

Party Ratio: D 9 - R 7

Daniel K. Inouye, D-Hawaii, chairman
John McCain, R-Ariz., vice chairman

Dennis DeConcini, Ariz.
Quentin N. Burdick, N.D.
Tom Daschle, S.D.
Kent Conrad, N.D.
Harry Reid, Nev.
Paul Simon, Ill.
Daniel K. Akaka, Hawaii
Paul Wellstone, Minn.

Frank H. Murkowski, Alaska
Thad Cochran, Miss.
Slade Gorton, Wash.
Pete V. Domenici, N.M.
Nancy Landon Kassebaum, Kan.
Don Nickles, Okla.

Select Intelligence

224-1700 SH-211

Party Ratio: D 8 - R 7

David L. Boren, D-Okla., chairman
Frank H. Murkowski, R-Alaska, vice chairman

Sam Nunn, Ga.
Ernest F. Hollings, S.C.
Bill Bradley, N.J.
Alan Cranston, Calif.
Dennis DeConcini, Ariz.
Howard M. Metzenbaum, Ohio
John Glenn, Ohio

John W. Warner, Va.
Alfonse M. D'Amato, N.Y.
John C. Danforth, Mo.
Warren B. Rudman, N.H.
Slade Gorton, Wash.
John H. Chafee, R.I.

Partisan Committees

Democratic Leaders

President Pro Tempore — Robert C. Byrd, W.Va.
Majority Leader — George J. Mitchell, Maine
Majority Whip — Wendell H. Ford, Ky.
Conference Chairman — George J. Mitchell, Maine
Conference Secretary — David Pryor, Ark.
Assistant Floor Leader — Wyche Fowler Jr., Ga.
Chief Deputy Whip — Alan J. Dixon, Ill.

Deputy Whips (listed by region, each with an assistant deputy whip):

East — Patrick J. Leahy, Vt.
Barbara A. Mikulski, Md.

South — Bob Graham, Fla.
Charles S. Robb, Va.

Midwest — Tom Harkin, Iowa
Tom Daschle, S.D.

West — Tim Wirth, Colo.
Brock Adams, Wash.

Policy Committee

224-5551 S-118 Capitol

George J. Mitchell, Maine, chairman

Tom Daschle, S.D., co-chairman

Vice chairmen: Jeff Bingaman, N.M.; John Glenn, Ohio; Terry Sanford, N.C.; Paul S. Sarbanes, Md.

Richard H. Bryan, Nev.
Dale Bumpers, Ark.
Quentin N. Burdick, N.D.
Wendell H. Ford, Ky.
Howell Heflin, Ala.
Ernest F. Hollings, S.C.
Herb Kohl, Wis.
Frank R. Lautenberg, N.J.
Daniel Patrick Moynihan, N.Y.
Claiborne Pell, R.I.
David Pryor, Ark.
Donald W. Riegle Jr., Mich.
Charles S. Robb, Va.
John D. Rockefeller IV, W.Va.
Tim Wirth, Colo.

Steering Committee

224-3735 S-309 Capitol

Daniel K. Inouye, Hawaii, chairman

Brock Adams, Wash.
Max Baucus, Mont.
Lloyd Bentsen, Texas
Joseph R. Biden Jr., Del.
David L. Boren, Okla.
Robert C. Byrd, W.Va.
Kent Conrad, N.D.
Alan Cranston, Calif.
Dennis DeConcini, Ariz.
Christopher J. Dodd, Conn.
Jim Exon, Neb.
Wendell H. Ford, Ky.
Wyche Fowler Jr., Ga.
Bob Graham, Fla.
Tom Harkin, Iowa
Edward M. Kennedy, Mass.
John Kerry, Mass
Patrick J. Leahy, Vt.
Carl Levin, Mich.
Howard M. Metzenbaum, Ohio
George J. Mitchell, Maine
Sam Nunn, Ga.
David Pryor, Ark.
Jim Sasser, Tenn.

Democratic Senatorial Campaign Committee

224-2447 430 S. Capitol St. S.E. 20003
Charles S. Robb, Va., chairman

Republican Leaders

Minority Leader —
Bob Dole, Kan.
Assistant Minority Leader —
Alan K. Simpson, Wyo.
Chairman of the Conference —
Thad Cochran, Miss.
Secretary of the Conference —
Bob Kasten, Wis.

Policy Committee

224-2946 SR-347

Don Nickles, Okla., chairman

John H. Chafee, R.I.
Thad Cochran, Miss.
John C. Danforth, Mo.
Bob Dole, Kan.
Pete V. Domenici, N.M.
Jake Garn, Utah
Phil Gramm, Texas
Orrin G. Hatch, Utah
Mark O. Hatfield, Ore.
Jesse Helms, N.C.
Bob Kasten, Wis.
Trent Lott, Miss.
Richard G. Lugar, Ind.
Frank H. Murkowski, Alaska
Bob Packwood, Ore.
William V. Roth, Del.
Alan K. Simpson, Wyo.
Ted Stevens, Alaska
Strom Thurmond, S.C.
Malcom Wallop, Wyo.
John W. Warner, Va.

Committee on Committees

224-6253 SR-487

Trent Lott, Miss., chairman

Connie Mack, Fla.
Frank H. Murkowski, Alaska
Robert C. Smith, N.H.

National Republican Senatorial Committee

675-6000 425 Second St. N.E. 20002

Phil Gramm, Texas, chairman

Christopher S. Bond, Mo.
Hank Brown, Colo.
Conrad Burns, Mont.
Larry E. Craig, Idaho
Charles E. Grassley, Iowa
Trent Lott, Miss.
Connie Mack, Fla.
Don Nickles, Okla.
Robert C. Smith, N.H.
Steve Symms, Idaho

House Committees and Subcommittees

The standing and select committees of the U.S. House are listed below in alphabetical order. The listing includes the telephone number, room number, and party ratio for each full committee. Membership is given in order of seniority on the committee.

If a non-voting delegate or the resident commissioner is a member of a committee, the party ratio reflects that membership. Non-voting representatives, while they cannot vote on the House floor, enjoy equal status as their voting colleagues on committees.

Subcommittees are listed alphabetically under each committee. Membership is listed in order of seniority on subcommittees.

Members of the majority party, Democrats, are shown in Roman type; members of the minority party, Republicans, are shown in italic type.

The word "vacancy" indicates that a committee or subcommittee seat had not been filled at press time. Subcommittee vacancies do not necessarily indicate vacancies on full committees, or vice versa.

Asterisks (*) indicate that chairmen and/or ranking minority members are also *ex officio* members of all subcommittees of which they are not regular members.

The partisan committees of the House are listed on p. 1687. Members of these committees are listed in alphabetical order, not by seniority.

The telephone area code for Washington, D.C., is 202. Abbreviations for House office buildings are: CHOB — Cannon House Office Bldg., LHOB — Longworth House Office Bldg., RHOB — Rayburn House Office Bldg., HOB Annex #1 and #2 — House Office Bldg. Annex #1 and #2, and Capitol. The ZIP code for all House offices is 20515.

Agriculture

225-2171 1301 LHOB

Party Ratio: D 27 - R 18

E. "Kika" de la Garza, D-Texas, chairman

Walter B. Jones, N.C.
George E. Brown Jr., Calif.
Charlie Rose, N.C.
Glenn English, Okla.
Leon E. Panetta, Calif.
Jerry Huckaby, La.
Dan Glickman, Kan.
Charles W. Stenholm, Texas
Harold L. Volkmer, Mo.
Charles Hatcher, Ga.
Robin Tallon, S.C.
Harley O. Staggers Jr., W.Va.
Jim Olin, Va.
Timothy J. Penny, Minn.
Richard Stallings, Idaho
Dave Nagle, Iowa
Jim Jontz, Ind.
Tim Johnson, S.D.
Ben Nighthorse Campbell, Colo.
Mike Espy, Miss.
Bill Sarpalius, Texas
Jill L. Long, Ind.
Gary Condit, Calif.
Collin C. Peterson, Minn.
Calvin Dooley, Calif.
Mike Kopetski, Ore.

Tom Coleman, Mo.
Ron Marlenee, Mont.
Larry J. Hopkins, Ky.
Pat Roberts, Kan.
Bill Emerson, Mo.
Sid Morrison, Wash.
Steve Gunderson, Wis.
Tom Lewis, Fla.
Bob Smith, Ore.
Larry Combest, Texas
Wally Herger, Calif.
James T. Walsh, N.Y.
Dave Camp, Mich.
Wayne Allard, Colo.
Bill Barrett, Neb.
Jim Nussle, Iowa
John A. Boehner, Ohio
Vacancy

Conservation, Credit and Rural Development

225-0301 1430 LHOB

English — chairman

Staggers
Stallings
Nagle
Sarpalius
Johnson (S.D.)
Huckaby
Glickman
Penny
Espy
Long
Stenholm

Smith
Gunderson
Combest
Allard
Barrett
Nussle
Boehner

Cotton, Rice and Sugar

225-1867 1336 LHOB

Huckaby — chairman

Espy
Peterson (Minn.)
Jones (N.C.)
Condit
Hatcher
Tallon
Stallings
Dooley
Rose
Stenholm

Emerson
Lewis (Fla.)
Combest
Herger
Camp
Nussle
Boehner

Department Operations, Research and Foreign Agriculture

225-8906 1534 LHOB

Rose — chairman

Brown (Calif.)	*Roberts*
Panetta	*Morrison*
Jontz	*Gunderson*
Dooley	*Herger*
Kopetski	*Walsh*
Stenholm	*Allard*
Volkmer	*Barrett*
Hatcher	*Boehner*
Tallon	*Vacancy*
Campbell (Colo.)	
Sarpalius	
Huckaby	
Glickman	

Domestic Marketing, Consumer Relations and Nutrition

225-1496 1301A LHOB

Tallon — chairman

Panetta	*Lewis (Fla.)*
Staggers	*Emerson*
Espy	*Herger*
Hatcher	
Dooley	

Forests, Family Farms and Energy

225-1867 1336 LHOB

Volkmer — chairman

Olin	*Morrison*
Stallings	*Marlenee*
Jontz	*Emerson*
Panetta	*Smith (Ore.)*
Huckaby	*Herger*
Brown (Calif.)	
Kopetski	

Livestock, Dairy and Poultry

225-1496 1301A LHOB

Stenholm — chairman

Olin	*Gunderson*
Campbell (Colo.)	*Hopkins*
Condit	*Roberts*
Peterson (Minn.)	*Lewis (Fla.)*
Dooley	*Smith (Ore.)*
Rose	*Walsh*
Volkmer	*Allard*
Penny	*Boehner*
Nagle	
Johnson (S.D.)	
Sarpalius	
Long	

Peanuts and Tobacco

225-1867 1336 LHOB

Hatcher — chairman

Jones (N.C.)	*Hopkins*
Rose	*Combest*
English	*Gunderson*
Stenholm	

Wheat, Soybeans and Feed Grains

225-0301 1430 LHOB

Glickman — chairman

Penny	*Marlenee*
Long	*Roberts*
English	*Morrison*
Nagle	*Smith (Ore.)*
Johnson (S.D.)	*Camp (Mich.)*
Peterson (Minn.)	*Barrett*
Volkmer	*Nussle*
Sarpalius	
Rose	
Olin	

Appropriations

225-2771 H-218 Capitol

Party Ratio: D 37 - R 22

Jamie L. Whitten, D-Miss., chairman

William H. Natcher, Ky.	*Joseph M. McDade, Pa.*
Neal Smith, Iowa	*John T. Myers, Ind.*
Sidney R. Yates, Ill.	*Clarence E. Miller, Ohio*
David R. Obey, Wis.	*Lawrence Coughlin, Pa.*
Edward R. Roybal, Calif.	*C.W. Bill Young, Fla.*
Louis Stokes, Ohio	*Ralph Regula, Ohio*
Tom Bevill, Ala.	*Carl D. Pursell, Mich.*
Bill Alexander, Ark.	*Mickey Edwards, Okla.*
John P. Murtha, Pa.	*Robert L. Livingston, La.*
Bob Traxler, Mich.	*Bill Green, N.Y.*
Joseph D. Early, Mass.	*Jerry Lewis, Calif.*
Charles Wilson, Texas	*John Porter, Ill.*
Norm Dicks, Wash.	*Harold Rogers, Ky.*
Matthew F. McHugh, N.Y.	*Joe Skeen, N.M.*
William Lehman, Fla.	*Frank R. Wolf, Va.*
Martin Olav Sabo, Minn.	*Bill Lowery, Calif.*
Julian C. Dixon, Calif.	*Vin Weber, Minn.*
Vic Fazio, Calif.	*Tom DeLay, Texas*
W. G. "Bill" Hefner, N.C.	*Jim Kolbe, Ariz.*
Les AuCoin, Ore.	*Dean A. Gallo, N.J.*
William H. Gray III, Pa.	*Barbara F. Vucanovich, Nev.*
Bernard J. Dwyer, N.J.	*Jim Ross Lightfoot, Iowa*
Steny H. Hoyer, Md.	
Bob Carr, Mich.	
Robert J. Mrazek, N.Y.	
Richard J. Durbin, Ill.	
Ronald D. Coleman, Texas	
Alan B. Mollohan, W.Va.	
Lindsay Thomas, Ga.	
Chester G. Atkins, Mass.	
Jim Chapman, Texas	
Marcy Kaptur, Ohio	
Lawrence J. Smith, Fla.	
David E. Skaggs, Colo.	
David Price, N.C.	
Nancy Pelosi, Calif.	

Commerce, Justice, State and Judiciary

225-3351 H-309 Capitol

Smith (Iowa) — chairman

Alexander	*Rogers*
Early	*Regula*
Carr	*Kolbe*
Mollohan	
Pelosi	

Defense

225-2847 H-144 Capitol

Murtha — chairman

Dicks	*McDade*
Wilson	*Young (Fla.)*
Hefner	*Miller (Ohio)*
AuCoin	*Livingston*
Sabo	*Lewis (Calif.)*
Dixon (Calif.)	
Dwyer	

District of Columbia

225-5338 H-302 Capitol

Dixon — chairman

Natcher	*Gallo*
Stokes	*Regula*
Sabo	*DeLay*
AuCoin	
Hoyer	

Energy and Water Development

225-3421 2362 RHOB

Bevill — chairman

Fazio	*Myers*
Thomas (Ga.)	*Pursell*
Chapman	*Gallo*
Skaggs	
Dwyer	

Foreign Operations, Export Financing and Related Programs

225-2041 H-307 Capitol

Obey — chairman

Yates	*Edwards (Okla.)*
McHugh	*Porter*
Lehman (Fla.)	*Green*
Wilson	*Livingston*
Gray	
Coleman (Texas)	
Smith (Fla.)	

Interior

225-3081 B308 RHOB

Yates — chairman

Murtha	*Regula*
Dicks	*McDade*
AuCoin	*Lowery*
Bevill	*Skeen*
Atkins	

Labor, Health and Human Services, and Education

225-3508 2358 RHOB

Natcher — chairman

Smith (Iowa)	*Pursell*
Obey	*Porter*
Roybal	*Young (Fla.)*
Stokes	*Weber*
Early	
Hoyer	
Mrazek	

Legislative

225-5338 H-302 Capitol

Fazio — chairman

Mrazek	*Lewis (Calif.)*
Smith (Fla.)	*Porter*
Alexander	*Vucanovich*
Murtha	
Traxler	

Military Construction

225-3047 B300 RHOB

Hefner — chairman

Alexander	*Lowery*
Thomas (Ga.)	*Edwards (Okla.)*
Coleman (Texas)	*DeLay*
Bevill	*Lightfoot*
Wilson	
Dicks	
Fazio	

Rural Development, Agriculture and Related Agencies

225-2638 2362 RHOB

Whitten — chairman

Traxler	*Skeen*
McHugh	*Myers*
Natcher	*Weber*
Durbin	*Vucanovich*
Kaptur	
Price	
Smith (Iowa)	
Obey	

Transportation

225-2141 2358 RHOB

Lehman (Fla.) — chairman

Gray	*Coughlin*
Carr	*Wolf*
Durbin	*DeLay*
Sabo	
Price	

Treasury, Postal Service and General Government

225-5834 H-164 Capitol

Roybal — chairman

Hoyer	*Wolf*
Skaggs	*Lightfoot*
Pelosi	*Rogers*
Yates	
Early	

Veterans Affairs, Housing and Urban Development, and Independent Agencies

225-3241 H-143 Capitol

Traxler — chairman

Stokes	*Green*
Mollohan	*Coughlin*
Chapman	*Lowery*
Atkins	
Kaptur	

Armed Services

225-4151 2120 RHOB Party Ratio: D 33 - R 22

Les Aspin, D-Wis., chairman

Charles E. Bennett, Fla.	*Bill Dickinson, Ala.*
G. V. "Sonny" Montgomery, Miss.	*Floyd D. Spence, S.C.*
Ronald V. Dellums, Calif.	*Bob Stump, Ariz.*
Patricia Schroeder, Colo.	*Larry J. Hopkins, Ky.*
Beverly B. Byron, Md.	*Robert W. Davis, Mich.*
Nicholas Mavroules, Mass.	*Duncan Hunter, Calif.*
Earl Hutto, Fla.	*David O'B. Martin, N.Y.*
Ike Skelton, Mo.	*John R. Kasich, Ohio*
Dave McCurdy, Okla.	*Herbert H. Bateman, Va.*
Thomas M. Foglietta, Pa.	*Ben Blaz, Guam*
Dennis M. Hertel, Mich.	*Andy Ireland, Fla.*
Marilyn Lloyd, Tenn.	*James V. Hansen, Utah*
Norman Sisisky, Va.	*Curt Weldon, Pa.*
Richard Ray, Ga.	*Jon Kyl, Ariz.*
John M. Spratt Jr., S.C.	*Arthur Ravenel Jr., S.C.*
Frank McCloskey, Ind.	*Robert K. Dornan, Calif.*
Solomon P. Ortiz, Texas	*Joel Hefley, Colo.*
George Darden, Ga.	*Jim McCrery, La.*
Albert G. Bustamante, Texas	*Ronald K. Machtley, R.I.*
Barbara Boxer, Calif.	*H. James Saxton, N.J.*
George J. Hochbrueckner, N.Y.	*Randy "Duke" Cunningham, Calif.*
Owen B. Pickett, Va.	*Gary Franks, Conn.*
H. Martin Lancaster, N.C.	
Lane Evans, Ill.	
James Bilbray, Nev.	
John Tanner, Tenn.	
Michael R. McNulty, N.Y.	
Glen Browder, Ala.	
Gene Taylor, Miss.	
Neil Abercrombie, Hawaii	
Thomas H. Andrews, Maine	
Chet Edwards, Texas	

Investigations

225-2086 2343 RHOB

Mavroules — chairman

Hertel	*Hopkins*
Sisisky	*Stump*
Spratt	*Kyl*
McCloskey	*Ireland*
Darden	*Hefley*
Boxer	*Franks*
Evans	
Tanner	
McNulty	

Military Installations and Facilities

225-7120 2119 RHOB

Schroeder — chairman

Montgomery	*Martin*
McCurdy	*Dickinson*
Foglietta	*Blaz*
Sisisky	*Spence*
Ortiz	*Ravenel*
Bilbray	*Hansen*
Browder	*McCrery*
Abercrombie	*Machtley*
Edwards (Texas)	
Mavroules	
Hutto	

Military Personnel and Compensation

225-7560 2343 RHOB

Byron — chairman

Montgomery	*Bateman*
Skelton	*Ravenel*
Hertel	*Franks*
Lloyd	*Cunningham*
Bustamante	*Saxton*
Boxer	*McCrery*
Hochbrueckner	
Pickett	
Lancaster	

Procurement and Military Nuclear Systems

225-6999 2343 RHOB

Aspin — chairman

Skelton	*Dickinson*
Lloyd	*Hopkins*
Sisisky	*Blaz*
Ray	*Ireland*
Spratt	*Kasich*
McCloskey	*Martin*
Bustamante	*Weldon*
Evans	*Hefley*
Bilbray	*Saxton*
Tanner	
McNulty	
Taylor (Miss.)	

Readiness

225-9644 2339 RHOB

Hutto — chairman

Ray	*Kasich*
Ortiz	*Franks (Conn.)*
Bustamante	*Saxton*
Pickett	*Cunningham*
Lancaster	*Machtley*
Evans	
Abercrombie	
Bennett	

Research and Development

225-5530 2117-A RHOB

Dellums — chairman

McCurdy	*Davis*
Foglietta	*Stump*
Hertel	*Hunter*
Darden	*Kyl*
Boxer	*Dornan*
Hochbrueckner	*Hansen*
Browder	*McCrery*
Andrews (Maine)	*Cunningham*
Edwards (Texas)	*Blaz*
Bennett	
Schroeder	
Byron	

Seapower and Strategic and Critical Materials

225-6704 2343 RHOB

Bennett — chairman

Foglietta	*Spence*
Sisisky	*Hunter*
Ortiz	*Bateman*
Hochbrueckner	*Weldon*
Pickett	*Blaz*
Bilbray	*Dornan*
Taylor (Miss.)	*Machtley*
Andrews (Maine)	
Hutto	

Banking, Finance and Urban Affairs

225-4247 2129 RHOB

Party Ratio: D 31 - R 20

Henry B. Gonzalez, D-Texas, chairman

Frank Annunzio, Ill.	*Chalmers P. Wylie, Ohio*
Stephen L. Neal, N.C.	*Jim Leach, Iowa*
Carroll Hubbard Jr., Ky.	*Bill McCollum, Fla.*
John J. LaFalce, N.Y.	*Marge Roukema, N.J.*
Mary Rose Oakar, Ohio	*Doug Bereuter, Neb.*
Bruce F. Vento, Minn.	*Tom Ridge, Pa.*
Doug Barnard Jr., Ga.	*Toby Roth, Wis.*
Charles E. Schumer, N.Y.	*Al McCandless, Calif.*
Barney Frank, Mass.	*Richard H. Baker, La.*
Ben Erdreich, Ala.	*Cliff Stearns, Fla.*
Thomas R. Carper, Del.	*Paul E. Gillmor, Ohio*
Esteban E. Torres, Calif.	*Bill Paxon, N.Y.*
Gerald D. Kleczka, Wis.	*John J. "Jimmy" Duncan Jr., Tenn.*
Paul E. Kanjorski, Pa.	*Tom Campbell, Calif.*
Liz J. Patterson, S.C.	*Mel Hancock, Mo.*
Joseph P. Kennedy II, Mass.	*Frank Riggs, Calif.*
Floyd H. Flake, N.Y.	*Jim Nussle, Iowa*
Kweisi Mfume, Md.	*Dick Armey, Texas*
Peter Hoagland, Neb.	*Craig Thomas, Wyo.*
Richard E. Neal, Mass.	*Vacancy*
Charles Luken, Ohio	
Maxine Waters, Calif.	
Larry LaRocco, Idaho	
Bill Orton, Utah	
Jim Bacchus, Fla.	**Independent**
James P. Moran Jr., Va.	**Bernard Sanders, Vt.**
John W. Cox Jr., Ill.	
Ted Weiss, N.Y.	
Jim Slattery, Kan.	
Gary L. Ackerman, N.Y.	

Consumer Affairs and Coinage

225-8872 604 OHOB

Torres — chairman

Gonzalez	*McCandless*
Hubbard	*Wylie*
Barnard	*Baker*
Erdreich	*Riggs*
Annunzio	*Armey*
Waters	*Thomas (Wyo.)*
LaRocco	
Weiss	
Vacancy	**Independent**
Vacancy	**Sanders**

Domestic Monetary Policy

226-7315 109 FHOB

Neal (N.C.) — chairman

Barnard	*Roth*
Gonzalez	*Duncan*
Neal (Mass.)	*Campbell (Calif.)*
Vacancy	

Economic Stabilization

226-7511 140 FHOB

Carper — chairman

LaFalce	*Ridge*
Oakar	*Paxon*
Vento	*Hancock*
Kanjorski	*Nussle*
Patterson	*Armey*
Hoagland	*Thomas (Wyo.)*
Luken	
Moran	

Financial Institutions Supervision, Regulation and Insurance

226-3280 212 OHOB

Annunzio — chairman

Hubbard	*Wylie*
Barnard	*Leach*
LaFalce	*McCollum*
Vento	*Roukema*
Schumer	*Bereuter*
Frank (Mass.)	*Roth*
Kanjorski	*Ridge*
Neal (N.C.)	*McCandless*
Kleczka	*Baker*
Patterson	*Stearns*
Kennedy	*Gillmor*
Flake	*Paxon*
Mfume	*Duncan*
Hoagland	*Vacancy*
Neal (Mass.)	
Luken	
LaRocco	
Orton	
Bacchus	
Moran	
Cox	

General Oversight

225-2828 B304 RHOB

Hubbard — chairman

Gonzalez	*McCollum*
Barnard	*McCandless*
Flake	*Hancock*
Annunzio	*Riggs*
Waters	*Nussle*
Ackerman	
Vacancy	

Housing and Community Development

225-7054 B303 RHOB

Gonzalez — chairman

Oakar	*Roukema*
Vento	*Wylie*
Schumer	*Bereuter*
Frank (Mass.)	*Ridge*
Erdreich	*Baker*
Carper	*Paxon*
Torres	*Stearns*
Kleczka	*Gillmor*
Kanjorski	*Campbell (Calif.)*
Neal (N.C.)	*Riggs*
Hubbard	*Armey*
Kennedy	*Thomas (Wyo.)*
Flake	*Vacancy*
Mfume	
LaFalce	
Patterson	**Independent**
Neal (Mass.)	**Sanders**
Waters	
Orton	
Cox	

International Development, Finance, Trade and Monetary Policy

226-7515 2219 RHOB

Oakar — chairman

Neal (N.C.)	*Leach*
LaFalce	*Bereuter*
Torres	*McCandless*
Kleczka	*Stearns*
Kennedy	*McCollum*
Frank (Mass.)	*Roukema*
Flake	*Gillmor*
Neal (Mass.)	*Duncan*
Waters	*Campbell (Calif.)*
LaRocco	*Hancock*
Orton	
Bacchus	
Moran	**Independent**
Cox	**Sanders**

Policy Research and Insurance

225-1271 139 FHOB

Erdreich — chairman

Kanjorski	*Bereuter*
Carper	*Roth*
Gonzalez	*Nussle*
Luken	

Budget

226-7200 214 OHOB

Party Ratio: D 23 - R 14

Leon E. Panetta, D-Calif., chairman

Richard A. Gephardt, Mo.	*Bill Gradison, Ohio*
James L. Oberstar, Minn.	*Alex McMillan, N.C.*
Frank J. Guarini, N.J.	*Bill Thomas, Calif.*
Richard J. Durbin, Ill.	*Harold Rogers, Ky.*
Mike Espy, Miss.	*Dick Armey, Texas*
Dale E. Kildee, Mich.	*Amo Houghton, N.Y.*
Anthony C. Beilenson, Calif.	*Jim McCrery, La.*
	John R. Kasich, Ohio
Jerry Huckaby, La.	*Helen Delich Bentley, Md.*
Martin Olav Sabo, Minn.	*William E. Dannemeyer, Calif.*
Bernard J. Dwyer, N.J.	
Howard L. Berman, Calif.	*John Miller, Wash.*
Bob Wise, W.Va.	*Jim Kolbe, Ariz.*
John Bryant, Texas	*Christopher Shays, Conn.*
John M. Spratt Jr., S.C.	*Rick Santorum, Pa.*
Don J. Pease, Ohio	
Charles W. Stenholm, Texas	
Robert T. Matsui, Calif.	
Barney Frank, Mass.	
Jim Cooper, Tenn.	
Louise M. Slaughter, N.Y.	
Lewis F. Payne Jr., Va.	
Mike Parker, Miss.	

— Task Forces —

Budget Process, Reconciliation and Enforcement

Beilenson — chairman

Espy	*Thomas (Calif.)*
Dwyer	*Rogers*
Sabo	*Armey*
Berman	*Miller (Wash.)*
Spratt	*Houghton*
Stenholm	*Shays*
Frank (Mass.)	
Payne (Va.)	
Parker	

Community Development and Natural Resources

Espy — chairman

Dwyer	*Bentley*
Wise	*Santorum*
Stenholm	
Payne (Va.)	

Defense, Foreign Policy and Space

Durbin — chairman

Guarini	*McCrery*
Beilenson	*Kasich*
Huckaby	*Bentley*
Berman	*Miller (Wash.)*
Bryant	
Spratt	
Pease	
Matsui	
Frank (Mass.)	
Cooper	
Slaughter (N.Y.)	

Economic Policy, Projections and Revenues

Kildee — chairman

Durbin	*Rogers*
Sabo	*Houghton*
Wise	*Kasich*
Pease	*Dannemeyer*
Matsui	*Shays*
Frank (Mass.)	*Santorum*
Parker	

Human Resources

Oberstar — chairman

Durbin	*Kasich*
Kildee	*Bentley*
Wise	*Kolbe*
Bryant	
Matsui	
Cooper	

Urgent Fiscal Issues

Guarini — chairman

Oberstar	*Armey*
Huckaby	*Thomas (Calif.)*
Spratt	*McCrery*
Pease	*Dannemeyer*
Cooper	*Kolbe*
Slaughter (N.Y.)	

District of Columbia

225-4457 1310 LHOB

Party Ratio: D 8 - R 4

Ronald V. Dellums, D-Calif., chairman

Pete Stark, Calif.	*Thomas J. Bliley Jr., Va.*
William H. Gray III, Pa.	*Larry Combest, Texas*
Mervyn M. Dymally, Calif.	*Dana Rohrabacher, Calif.*
Alan Wheat, Mo.	*Bill Lowery, Calif.*
Jim McDermott, Wash.	
Eleanor Holmes Norton, D.C.	
Sander M. Levin, Mich.	

Fiscal Affairs and Health

225-4457 507 OHOB

Stark — chairman

Dellums	*Rohrabacher*
Gray	*Bliley*
McDermott	*Combest*
Norton	

Government Operations and Metropolitan Affairs

225-4457 507 OHOB

Wheat — chairman

Stark	*Combest*
Gray	*Bliley*
Dymally	*Lowery*
Vacancy	

Judiciary and Education

225-4457 441 CHOB

Dymally — chairman

Stark	*Lowery*
Dellums	*Bliley*
Wheat	*Rohrabacher*
Norton	

Education and Labor

225-4527 2181 RHOB

Party Ratio: D 25 - R 14

William D. Ford, D-Mich., chairman

Joseph M. Gaydos, Pa.	*Bill Goodling, Pa.*
William L. Clay, Mo.	*Tom Coleman, Mo.*
George Miller, Calif.	*Tom Petri, Wis.*
Austin J. Murphy, Pa.	*Marge Roukema, N.J.*
Dale E. Kildee, Mich.	*Steve Gunderson, Wis.*
Pat Williams, Mont.	*Dick Armey, Texas*
Matthew G. Martinez, Calif.	*Harris W. Fawell, Ill.*
Major R. Owens, N.Y.	*Paul B. Henry, Mich.*
Charles A. Hayes, Ill.	*Cass Ballenger, N.C.*
Carl C. Perkins, Ky.	*Susan Molinari, N.Y.*
Tom Sawyer, Ohio	*Bill Barrett, Neb.*
Donald M. Payne, N.J.	*John A. Boehner, Ohio*
Nita M. Lowey, N.Y.	*Scott L. Klug, Wis.*
Jolene Unsoeld, Wash.	*Mickey Edwards, Okla.*
Craig Washington, Texas	
Jose E. Serrano, N.Y.	
Patsy T. Mink, Hawaii	
Robert E. Andrews, N.J.	
William J. Jefferson, La.	
John F. Reed, R.I.	
Tim Roemer, Ind.	
Peter J. Visclosky, Ind.	
Ron de Lugo, V.I.	
Jaime B. Fuster, P.R.	

Elementary, Secondary and Vocational Education

225-4368 320 CHOB

Kildee — chairman

Miller (Calif.)	*Goodling*
Williams	*Klug*
Martinez	*Petri*
Perkins	*Roukema*
Hayes (Ill.)	*Gunderson*
Sawyer	*Henry*
Lowey	*Molinari*
Unsoeld	*Boehner*
Jefferson	*Edwards (Okla.)*
Reed	
Roemer	
Washington	
Mink	
Fuster	
Owens (N.Y.)	

Employment Opportunities

225-7594 617 OHOB

Perkins — chairman

Andrews (N.J.)	*Gunderson*
Visclosky	*Molinari*
Vacancy	*Henry*

Health and Safety

225-6876 B345-A RHOB

Gaydos — chairman

Andrews (N.J.)	*Henry*
Murphy	*Ballenger*
Hayes (Ill.)	*Boehner*

Human Resources

225-1850 B346-C RHOB

Martinez — chairman

Kildee	*Fawell*
Lowey	*Coleman (Mo.)*
de Lugo	*Barrett*

Labor-Management Relations

225-5768 112 CHOB

Williams — chairman

Clay	*Roukema*
Kildee	*Armey*
Miller (Calif.)	*Barrett*
Hayes (Ill.)	*Boehner*
Owens (N.Y.)	*Fawell*
Sawyer	*Ballenger*
Murphy	*Petri*
Serrano	*Edwards (Okla.)*
Martinez	
Payne (N.J.)	
Unsoeld	
Washington	
Mink	

Labor Standards

225-1927 B346-A RHOB

Murphy — chairman

Clay	*Petri*
Perkins	*Armey*
Owens (N.Y.)	*Fawell*

Postsecondary Education

226-3681 2451 RHOB

Ford (Mich.) — chairman

Williams	*Coleman (Mo.)*
Hayes (Ill.)	*Molinari*
Gaydos	*Klug*
Miller (Calif.)	*Goodling*
Lowey	*Petri*
Sawyer	*Roukema*
Payne (N.J.)	*Gunderson*
Unsoeld	*Henry*
Washington	*Armey*
Serrano	*Barrett*
Mink	
Andrews (N.J.)	
Jefferson	
Reed	
Roemer	
Kildee	

Select Education

226-7532 518 OHOB

Owens (N.Y.) — chairman

Payne (N.J.)	*Ballenger*
Serrano	*Klug*
Jefferson	*Vacancy*
Williams	

Energy and Commerce

225-2927 2125 RHOB

Party Ratio: D 27 - R 16

John D. Dingell, D-Mich., chairman

James H. Scheuer, N.Y.	*Norman F. Lent, N.Y.*
Henry A. Waxman, Calif.	*Carlos J. Moorhead, Calif.*
Philip R. Sharp, Ind.	*Matthew J. Rinaldo, N.J.*
Edward J. Markey, Mass.	*William E. Dannemeyer, Calif.*
Al Swift, Wash.	*Don Ritter, Pa.*
Cardiss Collins, Ill.	*Thomas J. Bliley Jr., Va.*
Mike Synar, Okla.	*Jack Fields, Texas*
W. J. "Billy" Tauzin, La.	*Michael G. Oxley, Ohio*
Ron Wyden, Ore.	*Michael Bilirakis, Fla.*
Ralph M. Hall, Texas	*Dan Schaefer, Colo.*
Dennis E. Eckart, Ohio	*Joe L. Barton, Texas*
Bill Richardson, N.M.	*Sonny Callahan, Ala.*
Jim Slattery, Kan.	*Alex McMillan, N.C.*
Gerry Sikorski, Minn.	*Dennis Hastert, Ill.*
John Bryant, Texas	*Clyde C. Holloway, La.*
Rick Boucher, Va.	*Fred Upton, Mich.*
Jim Cooper, Tenn.	
Terry L. Bruce, Ill.	
J. Roy Rowland, Ga.	
Thomas J. Manton, N.Y.	
Edolphus Towns, N.Y.	
Tom McMillen, Md.	
Gerry E. Studds, Mass.	
Peter H. Kostmayer, Pa.	
Richard H. Lehman, Calif.	
Claude Harris, Ala.	

Commerce, Consumer Protection and Competitiveness

226-3160 151 FHOB

Collins (Ill.) — chairman

Kostmayer	*McMillan*
Waxman	*Oxley*
Boucher	*Bilirakis*
Cooper	*Barton*
Bruce	*Upton*
Rowland	
Manton	
Towns	
McMillen	

Energy and Power

226-2500 331 FHOB

Sharp — chairman

Tauzin	*Moorhead*
Cooper	*Dannemeyer*
Bruce	*Oxley*
Towns	*Barton*
McMillen	*Callahan*
Studds	*Hastert*
Lehman (Calif.)	*Holloway*
Harris	
Scheuer	
Markey	
Swift	
Synar	

Health and the Environment

225-4952 2415 RHOB

Waxman — chairman

Sikorski	*Dannemeyer*
Bruce	*Bliley*
Rowland	*Fields*
Towns	*Bilirakis*
Studds	*McMillan*
Kostmayer	*Hastert*
Scheuer	*Holloway*
Synar	
Wyden	
Hall (Texas)	
Richardson	
Bryant	

Oversight and Investigations

225-4441 2323 RHOB

Dingell — chairman

Rowland	*Bliley*
Wyden	*Lent*
Eckart	*Schaefer*
Slattery	*Upton*
Sikorski	
Bryant	

Telecommunications and Finance

226-2424 316 FHOB

Markey — chairman

Scheuer	*Rinaldo*
Synar	*Moorhead*
Tauzin	*Ritter*
Hall (Texas)	*Bliley*
Eckart	*Fields*
Richardson	*Oxley*
Slattery	*Bilirakis*
Bryant	*Schaefer*
Boucher	*Barton*
Cooper	
Manton	
McMillen	
Wyden	
Lehman (Calif.)	
Harris	

Transportation and Hazardous Materials

225-9304 324 FHOB

Swift — chairman

Eckart	*Ritter*
Slattery	*Rinaldo*
Sikorski	*Fields*
Boucher	*Schaefer*
Manton	*Callahan*
Sharp	
Collins (Ill.)	
Tauzin	
Richardson	

Foreign Affairs

225-5021 2170 RHOB

Party Ratio: D 28 - R 18

Dante B. Fascell, D-Fla., chairman

Lee H. Hamilton, Ind.	*William S. Broomfield, Mich.*
Gus Yatron, Pa.	*Benjamin A. Gilman, N.Y.*
Stephen J. Solarz, N.Y.	*Robert J. Lagomarsino, Calif.*
Howard Wolpe, Mich.	*Bill Goodling, Pa.*
Sam Gejdenson, Conn.	*Jim Leach, Iowa*
Mervyn M. Dymally, Calif.	*Toby Roth, Wis.*
Tom Lantos, Calif.	*Olympia J. Snowe, Maine*
Robert G. Torricelli, N.J.	*Henry J. Hyde, Ill.*
Howard L. Berman, Calif.	*Doug Bereuter, Neb.*
Mel Levine, Calif.	*Christopher H. Smith, N.J.*
Edward F. Feighan, Ohio	*Dan Burton, Ind.*
Ted Weiss, N.Y.	*Jan Meyers, Kan.*
Gary L. Ackerman, N.Y.	*John Miller, Wash.*
Jaime B. Fuster, P.R.	*Ben Blaz, Guam*
Wayne Owens, Utah	*Elton Gallegly, Calif.*
Harry A. Johnston, Fla.	*Amo Houghton, N.Y.*
Eliot L. Engel, N.Y.	*Porter J. Goss, Fla.*
Eni F.H. Faleomavaega, Am.Samoa	*Ileana Ros-Lehtinen, Fla.*
Gerry E. Studds, Mass.	
Austin J. Murphy, Pa.	
Peter H. Kostmayer, Pa.	
Thomas M. Foglietta, Pa.	
Frank McCloskey, Ind.	
Tom Sawyer, Ohio	
Donald M. Payne, N.J.	
Bill Orton, Utah	
Vacancy	

Africa

226-7807 816 OHOB

Dymally — chairman

Wolpe	*Burton*
Fuster	*Blaz*
Solarz	*Houghton*
Feighan	*Roth*
Payne (N.J.)	

Arms Control, International Security and Science

225-8926 2401-A RHOB

Fascell — chairman

Berman	*Broomfield*
Ackerman	*Hyde*
Faleomavaega	*Snowe*
McCloskey	*Gallegly*
Sawyer	*Goss*
Foglietta	

Asian and Pacific Affairs

226-7801 707 OHOB

Solarz — chairman

Faleomavaega	*Leach*
Lantos	*Blaz*
Torricelli	*Lagomarsino*
Ackerman	*Roth*
Foglietta	

Europe and the Middle East

225-3345 B359 RHOB

Hamilton — chairman

Lantos	*Gilman*
Levine	*Goodling*
Feighan	*Meyers*
Ackerman	*Gallegly*
Owens (Utah)	*Leach*
Johnston	
Engel	

Human Rights and International Organizations

226-7825 B358 RHOB

Yatron — chairman

Owens (Utah)	*Bereuter*
Weiss	*Smith (N.J.)*
Engel	*Hyde*
Studds	*Ros-Lehtinen*
Hamilton	

International Economic Policy and Trade

226-7820 702 OHOB

Gejdenson — chairman

Wolpe	*Roth*
Levine	*Miller (Wash.)*
Feighan	*Houghton*
Johnston	*Bereuter*
Engel	*Blaz*
Murphy	
Orton	

International Narcotics Control

225-5021 2170 RHOB

Feighan — chairman
Ackerman — co-chairman

Johnston	*Gilman*
Yatron	*Meyers*
Payne (N.J.)	*Goss*

International Operations

225-3424 709 OHOB

Berman — chairman

Weiss	*Snowe*
Dymally	*Gilman*
Faleomavaega	*Smith (N.J.)*
Lantos	*Miller (Wash.)*
Levine	

Western Hemisphere Affairs

226-7812 705 OHOB

Torricelli — chairman

Fuster	*Lagomarsino*
Solarz	*Goss*
Gejdenson	*Ros-Lehtinen*
Weiss	*Burton*
Engel	*Meyers*
Studds	
Kostmayer	

Government Operations

225-5051 2157 RHOB

Party Ratio: D 25 - R 15

John Conyers Jr., D-Mich., chairman

Cardiss Collins, Ill.	*Frank Horton, N.Y.*
Glenn English, Okla.	*William F. Clinger, Pa.*
Henry A. Waxman, Calif.	*Al McCandless, Calif.*
Ted Weiss, N.Y.	*Dennis Hastert, Ill.*
Mike Synar, Okla.	*Jon Kyl, Ariz.*
Stephen L. Neal, N.C.	*Christopher Shays, Conn.*
Doug Barnard Jr., Ga.	*Steven H. Schiff, N.M.*
Tom Lantos, Calif.	*C. Christopher Cox, Calif.*
Bob Wise, W.Va.	*Craig Thomas, Wyo.*
Barbara Boxer, Calif.	*Ileana Ros-Lehtinen, Fla.*
Major R. Owens, N.Y.	*Ronald K. Machtley, R.I.*
Edolphus Towns, N.Y.	*Dick Zimmer, N.J.*
Ben Erdreich, Ala.	*Bill Zeliff, N.H.*
Gerald D. Kleczka, Wis.	*David L. Hobson, Ohio*
Albert G. Bustamante, Texas	*Scott L. Klug, Wis.*
Matthew G. Martinez, Calif.	
Donald M. Payne, N.J.	
Gary Condit, Calif.	**Independent**
Patsy T. Mink, Hawaii	**Bernard Sanders, Vt.**
Ray Thornton, Ark.	
Collin C. Peterson, Minn.	
Rosa DeLauro, Conn.	
Charles Luken, Ohio	
John W. Cox Jr., Ill.	

Commerce, Consumer and Monetary Affairs

225-4407 B377 RHOB

Barnard — chairman

Martinez	*Hastert*
Collins (Ill.)	*Machtley*
Waxman	*Zimmer*
Erdreich	*Zeliff*
Bustamante	

Employment and Housing

225-6751 B349-A RHOB

Lantos — chairman

Martinez	*Ros-Lehtinen*
DeLauro	*Kyl*
Luken	*Shays*
Vacancy	

Environment, Energy and Natural Resources

225-6427 B371-B RHOB

Synar — chairman

Towns	*Clinger*
Bustamante	*Hobson*
Erdreich	*Klug*
Luken	
Cox (Ill.)	

Government Activities and Transportation

225-7920 B350-A RHOB

Boxer — chairman

Owens (N.Y.)	*Cox (Calif.)*
English	*Zimmer*
Kleczka	*Klug*
Condit	
Thornton	

Government Information, Justice and Agriculture

225-3741 B349-C RHOB

Wise — chaiman

Condit	*McCandless*
Towns	*Schiff*
Mink	*Machtley*
Peterson (Minn.)	
Cox (Ill.)	

Independent
Sanders

Human Resources and Intergovernmental Relations

225-2548 B372 RHOB

Weiss — chairman

Waxman	*Thomas (Wyo.)*
Payne (N.J.)	*Zeliff*
Mink	*Hobson*
DeLauro	

Independent
Sanders

Legislation and National Security

225-5147 B373 RHOB

Conyers — chairman

English	*Horton*
Neal (N.C.)	*Kyl*
Kleczka	*Shays*
Collins (Ill.)	*Schiff*
Thornton	
Peterson (Minn.)	

House Administration

225-2061 H-326 Capitol

Party Ratio: D 15 - R 9

Charlie Rose, D-N.C., chairman

Frank Annunzio, Ill.	*Bill Thomas, Calif.*
Joseph M. Gaydos, Pa.	*Bill Dickinson, Ala.*
Leon E. Panetta, Calif.	*Newt Gingrich, Ga.*
Al Swift, Wash.	*Pat Roberts, Kan.*
Mary Rose Oakar, Ohio	*Paul E. Gillmor, Ohio*
William L. Clay, Mo.	*James T. Walsh, N.Y.*
Sam Gejdenson, Conn.	*Mickey Edwards, Okla.*
Joe Kolter, Pa.	*Robert L. Livingston, La.*
Martin Frost, Texas	*Bill Barrett, Neb.*
Thomas J. Manton, N.Y.	
Marty Russo, Ill.	
William H. Gray III, Pa.	
Steny H. Hoyer, Md.	
Gerald D. Kleczka, Wis.	

Accounts

226-7540 511 OHOB

Gaydos — chairman

Annunzio	*Gillmor*
Swift	*Gingrich*
Oakar	*Dickinson*
Gejdenson	*Barrett*
Manton	
Russo	

Campaign Finance Reform

225-2870 720 OHOB

Gejdenson — chairman

Panetta	*Thomas (Calif.)*
Frost	*Edwards (Okla.)*
Kleczka	*Walsh*
Gray	

Elections

226-7616 802 OHOB

Swift — chairman

Panetta	*Livingston*
Frost	*Walsh*
Hoyer	*Gillmor*

Libraries and Memorials

226-2307 612 OHOB

Clay — chairman

Kolter	*Barrett*
Frost	*Roberts*
Hoyer	

Office Systems

225-1608 722 OHOB

Gejdenson — chairman

Frost	*Walsh*
Russo	*Dickinson*
Vacancy	

Personnel and Police

226-7614 720 OHOB

Oakar — chairman

Panetta	*Roberts*
Kolter	*Dickinson*
Manton	*Livingston*
Russo	
Kleczka	

Procurement and Printing

225-4658 105 CHOB

Annunzio — chairman

Gaydos	*Edwards (Okla.)*
Gray	*Gingrich*
Hoyer	

Interior and Insular Affairs

225-2761 1324 LHOB

Party Ratio: D 29 - R 17

George Miller, Calif., chairman

Philip R. Sharp, Ind.	*Don Young, Alaska*
Edward J. Markey, Mass.	*Robert J. Lagomarsino, Calif.*
Austin J. Murphy, Pa.	*Ron Marlenee, Mont.*
Nick J. Rahall II, W.Va.	*James V. Hansen, Utah*
Bruce F. Vento, Minn.	*Barbara F. Vucanovich, Nev.*
Pat Williams, Mont.	*Ben Blaz, Guam*
Beverly B. Byron, Md.	*John J. Rhodes III, Ariz.*
Ron de Lugo, V.I.	*Elton Gallegly, Calif.*
Sam Gejdenson, Conn.	*Bob Smith, Ore.*
Peter H. Kostmayer, Pa.	*Craig Thomas, Wyo.*
Richard H. Lehman, Calif.	*John J. "Jimmy" Duncan Jr., Tenn.*
Bill Richardson, N.M.	*Dick Schulze, Pa.*
George "Buddy" Darden, Ga.	*Joel Hefley, Colo.*
Peter J. Visclosky, Ind.	*Charles H. Taylor, N.C.*
Jaime B. Fuster, P.R.	*John T. Doolittle, Calif.*
Mel Levine, Calif.	*Wayne Allard, Colo.*
Wayne Owens, Utah	*Vacancy*
John Lewis, Ga.	
Ben Nighthorse Campbell, Colo.	
Peter A. DeFazio, Ore.	
Eni F. H. Faleomavaega, Amer. Samoa	
Tim Johnson, S.D.	
Charles E. Schumer, N.Y.	
Jim Jontz, Ind.	
Peter Hoagland, Neb.	
Harry A. Johnston, Fla.	
Larry LaRocco, Idaho	
Vacancy	

Energy and the Environment

226-4085 815 OHOB

Kostmayer — chairman

Sharp	*Rhodes*
Markey	*Blaz*
Gejdenson	*Thomas (Wyo.)*
Schumer	*Hefley*
Murphy	*Taylor (N.C.)*
Richardson	*Doolittle*
Darden	*Allard*
Jontz	*Vacancy*
Lehman (Calif.)	
Owens (Utah)	
Vacancy	

General Oversight and California Desert Lands

225-8331 483 FHOB

Lehman (Calif.) — chairman

Kostmayer	*Blaz*
Levine	*Duncan*
Faleomavaega	*Doolittle*

Insular and International Affairs

225-9297 1626 LHOB

de Lugo — chairman

Fuster	*Lagomarsino*
Faleomavaega	*Blaz*
Lewis (Ga.)	*Gallegly*
Darden	
Miller (Calif.)	

Mining and Natural Resources

226-7761 819 OHOB

Rahall — chairman

Campbell (Colo.)	*Vucanovich*
DeFazio	*Thomas (Wyo.)*
Jontz	

National Parks and Public Lands

226-7736 812 OHOB

Vento — chairman

Murphy	*Marlenee*
Williams	*Lagomarsino*
Byron	*Hansen*
Richardson	*Vucanovich*
Darden	*Gallegly*
Visclosky	*Smith (Ore.)*
Levine	*Thomas (Wyo.)*
Owens (Utah)	*Duncan*
Lewis (Ga.)	*Schulze*
Campbell (Colo.)	*Hefley*
DeFazio	*Taylor (N.C.)*
Johnson (S.D.)	*Vacancy*
Jontz	
Hoagland	
Johnston	
LaRocco	
Markey	
Rahall	
de Lugo	
Fuster	
Vacancy	

Water, Power and Offshore Energy Resources

225-6042 1328 LHOB

Miller (Calif.) — chairman

Sharp	*Hansen*
Vento	*Young (Alaska)*
Byron	*Marlenee*
Gejdenson	*Blaz*
Lehman (Calif.)	*Rhodes*
Owens (Utah)	*Smith (Ore.)*
Campbell (Colo.)	*Schulze*
DeFazio	*Taylor (N.C.)*
Johnson (S.D.)	*Doolittle*
Hoagland	*Allard*
Johnston	
LaRocco	
Markey	
Vacancy	

Judiciary

225-3951 2138 RHOB

Party Ratio: D 21 - R 13

Jack Brooks, D-Texas, chairman

Don Edwards, Calif.	*Hamilton Fish Jr., N.Y.*
John Conyers Jr., Mich.	*Carlos J. Moorhead, Calif.*
Romano L. Mazzoli, Ky.	*Henry J. Hyde, Ill.*
William J. Hughes, N.J.	*F. James Sensenbrenner Jr., Wis.*
Mike Synar, Okla.	*Bill McCollum, Fla.*
Patricia Schroeder, Colo.	*George W. Gekas, Pa.*
Dan Glickman, Kan.	*Howard Coble, N.C.*
Barney Frank, Mass.	*D. French Slaughter Jr., Va.*
Charles E. Schumer, N.Y.	*Lamar Smith, Texas*
Edward F. Feighan, Ohio	*Craig T. James, Fla.*
Howard L. Berman, Calif.	*Tom Campbell, Calif.*
Rick Boucher, Va.	*Steven H. Schiff, N.M.*
Harley O. Staggers Jr., W.Va.	*Jim Ramstad, Minn.*
John Bryant, Texas	
Mel Levine, Calif.	
George E. Sangmeister, Ill.	
Craig Washington, Texas	
Peter Hoagland, Neb.	
Mike Kopetski, Ore.	
John F. Reed, R.I.	

Administrative Law and Governmental Relations

225-5741 B351-A RHOB

Frank (Mass.) — chairman

Edwards (Calif.)	*Gekas*
Mazzoli	*Schiff*
Staggers	*Ramstad*
Reed	

Civil and Constitutional Rights

226-7680 806 OHOB

Edwards (Calif.) — chairman

Conyers	*Hyde*
Schroeder	*Coble*
Washington	*McCollum*
Kopetski	

Crime and Criminal Justice

226-2406 362 FHOB

Schumer — chairman

Hughes	*Sensenbrenner*
Feighan	*Schiff*
Bryant	*Ramstad*
Levine	*McCollum*
Sangmeister	*Gekas*
Washington	
Hoagland	

Economic and Commercial Law

225-2825 B353 RHOB

Brooks — chairman

Edwards (Calif.)	*Fish*
Conyers	*Slaughter (Va.)*
Mazzoli	*Smith (Texas)*
Synar	*James*
Glickman	*Campbell (Calif.)*
Feighan	*Moorhead*
Berman	
Staggers	
Bryant	

Intellectual Property and Judicial Administration

225-3926 207 CHOB

Hughes — chairman

Conyers	*Moorhead*
Synar	*Coble*
Schroeder	*Fish*
Glickman	*Sensenbrenner*
Frank (Mass.)	*James*
Schumer	*Campbell (Calif.)*
Boucher	
Levine	
Sangmeister	

International Law, Immigration and Refugees

225-5727 B370-B RHOB

Mazzoli — chairman

Schumer	*McCollum*
Berman	*Smith (Texas)*
Bryant	*James*
Kopetski	

Merchant Marine and Fisheries

225-4047 1334 LHOB

Party Ratio: D 29 - R 17

Walter B. Jones, D-N.C., chairman

Gerry E. Studds, Mass.	*Robert W. Davis, Mich.*
Carroll Hubbard Jr., Ky.	*Don Young, Alaska*
William J. Hughes, N.J.	*Norman F. Lent, N.Y.*
Earl Hutto, Fla.	*Jack Fields, Texas*
W. J. "Billy" Tauzin, La.	*Herbert H. Bateman, Va.*
Thomas M. Foglietta, Pa.	*H. James Saxton, N.J.*
Dennis M. Hertel, Mich.	*Helen Delich Bentley, Md.*
William O. Lipinski, Ill.	*Howard Coble, N.C.*
Robert A. Borski, Pa.	*Curt Weldon, Pa.*
Thomas R. Carper, Del.	*Wally Herger, Calif.*
Robin Tallon, S.C.	*James M. Inhofe, Okla.*
Solomon P. Ortiz, Texas	*Porter J. Goss, Fla.*
Charles E. Bennett, Fla.	*Arthur Ravenel Jr., S.C.*
Thomas J. Manton, N.Y.	*Sonny Callahan, Ala.*
Owen B. Pickett, Va.	*Wayne T. Gilchrest, Md.*
George J. Hochbrueckner, N.Y.	*John T. Doolittle, Calif.*
Bob Clement, Tenn.	*Randy "Duke" Cunningham, Calif.*
Stephen J. Solarz, N.Y.	
Frank Pallone Jr., N.J.	
Greg Laughlin, Texas	
Nita M. Lowey, N.Y.	
Jolene Unsoeld, Wash.	
Gene Taylor, Miss.	
Glenn M. Anderson, Calif.	
Neil Abercrombie, Hawaii	
John F. Reed, R.I.	
William J. Jefferson, La.	
Eni F. H. Faleomavaega, Amer. Samoa	

Coast Guard and Navigation

226-3587 547 FHOB

Tauzin — chairman

Clement	*Fields*
Reed	*Young (Alaska)*
Hughes	*Bateman*
Hutto	*Coble*
Carper	*Inhofe*
Manton	*Goss*
Pickett	*Callahan*
Hochbrueckner	*Gilchrest*
Pallone	
Laughlin	
Lowey	
Taylor (Miss.)	
Anderson	
Studds	
Vacancy	

Fisheries and Wildlife Conservation and the Environment

226-3533 543 FHOB

Studds — chairman

Hughes	*Young (Alaska)*
Hutto	*Saxton*
Carper	*Coble*
Tallon	*Weldon*
Ortiz	*Herger*
Manton	*Goss*
Hochbrueckner	*Ravenel*
Solarz	*Gilchrest*
Pallone	*Doolittle*
Unsoeld	
Laughlin	
Lowey	
Anderson	
Abercrombie	
Reed	
Jefferson	
Faleomavaega	

Merchant Marine

226-2460 575 FHOB

Jones (N.C.) — chairman

Hubbard	*Lent*
Borski	*Fields*
Bennett	*Bateman*
Pickett	*Inhofe*
Taylor (Miss.)	*Ravenel*
Jefferson	*Callahan*
Studds	*Doolittle*
Hertel	*Cunningham*
Tallon	
Ortiz	
Solarz	
Unsoeld	
Abercrombie	
Vacancy	

Oceanography, Great Lakes and Outer Continental Shelf

226-3504 532 FHOB

Hertel — chairman

Tauzin	*Bateman*
Clement	*Saxton*
Hughes	*Weldon*
Pallone	*Herger*
Taylor (Miss.)	
Lipinski	
Vacancy	

Oversight and Investigations

226-3514 579 FHOB

Lipinski — chairman

Borski	*Saxton*
Abercrombie	*Cunningham*

Post Office and Civil Service

225-4054 309 CHOB

Party Ratio: D 15 - R 8

William L. Clay, D-Mo., chairman

Patricia Schroeder, Colo.	*Benjamin A. Gilman, N.Y.*
Gus Yatron, Pa.	*Frank Horton, N.Y.*
Mary Rose Oakar, Ohio	*John T. Myers, Ind.*
Gerry Sikorski, Minn.	*Don Young, Alaska*
Frank McCloskey, Ind.	*Dan Burton, Ind.*
Gary L. Ackerman, N.Y.	*Constance A. Morella, Md.*
Mervyn M. Dymally, Calif.	*Tom Ridge, Pa.*
Tom Sawyer, Ohio	*Rod Chandler, Wash.*
Paul E. Kanjorski, Pa.	
Charles A. Hayes, Ill.	
Michael R. McNulty, N.Y.	
James P. Moran Jr., Va.	
Eleanor Holmes Norton, D.C.	
Vacancy	

Census and Population

226-7523 608 OHOB

Sawyer — chairman

Dymally	*Ridge*
McNulty	*Chandler*

Civil Service

225-4025 122 CHOB

Sikorski — chairman

Moran	*Morella*
Norton	*Ridge*

Compensation and Employee Benefits

226-7546 515 OHOB

Ackerman — chairman

Oakar	*Myers*
Schroeder	*Morella*

Human Resources

225-2821 603 OHOB

Kanjorski — chairman

Yatron	*Burton*
Moran	*Horton*

Investigations

225-6295 219 CHOB

Clay — chairman

McNulty	*Chandler*
McCloskey	*Gilman*

Postal Operations and Services

225-9124 209 CHOB

McCloskey — chairman

Sikorski	*Horton*
Norton	*Young (Alaska)*

Postal Personnel and Modernization

226-7520 406 CHOB

Hayes (Ill.) — chairman

McNulty	*Young (Alaska)*
Yatron	*Myers*

Public Works and Transportation

225-4472 2165 RHOB

Party Ratio: D 36 - R 21

Robert A. Roe, D-N.J., chairman

Glenn M. Anderson, Calif.	*John Paul Hammerschmidt, Ark.*
Norman Y. Mineta, Calif.	*Bud Shuster, Pa.*
James L. Oberstar, Minn.	*William F. Clinger, Pa.*
Henry J. Nowak, N.Y.	*Tom Petri, Wis.*
Nick J. Rahall II, W.Va.	*Ron Packard, Calif.*
Douglas Applegate, Ohio	*Sherwood Boehlert, N.Y.*
Ron de Lugo, V.I.	*Helen Delich Bentley, Md.*
Gus Savage, Ill.	*James M. Inhofe, Okla.*
Robert A. Borski, Pa.	*Cass Ballenger, N.C.*
Joe Kolter, Pa.	*Fred Upton, Mich.*
Tim Valentine, N.C.	*Bill Emerson, Mo.*
William O. Lipinski, Ill.	*John J. "Jimmy" Duncan Jr., Tenn.*
Peter J. Visclosky, Ind.	*Mel Hancock, Mo.*
James A. Traficant Jr., Ohio	*C. Christopher Cox, Calif.*
John Lewis, Ga.	*Susan Molinari, N.Y.*
Peter A. DeFazio, Ore.	*David L. Hobson, Ohio*
Jimmy Hayes, La.	*Frank Riggs, Calif.*
Bob Clement, Tenn.	*Charles H. Taylor, N.C.*
Lewis F. Payne Jr., Va.	*Dick Nichols, Kan.*
Jerry F. Costello, Ill.	*Bill Zeliff, N.H.*
Frank Pallone Jr., N.J.	*Vacancy*
Ben Jones, Ga.	
Mike Parker, Miss.	
Greg Laughlin, Texas	
Pete Geren, Texas	
George E. Sangmeister, Ill.	
Glenn Poshard, Ill.	
Dick Swett, N.H.	
Bill Brewster, Okla.	
Bud Cramer, Ala.	
Rosa DeLauro, Conn.	
Joan Kelly Horn, Mo.	
Barbara-Rose Collins, Mich.	
Pete Peterson, Fla.	
Eleanor Holmes Norton, D.C.	

Aviation

225-9161 2251 RHOB

Oberstar — chairman

Horn	*Clinger*
Collins (Mich.)	*Shuster*
Mineta	*Petri*
Nowak	*Boehlert*
Rahall	*Inhofe*
de Lugo	*Ballenger*
Savage	*Duncan*
Kolter	*Hancock*
Valentine	*Cox (Calif.)*
Lipinski	*Molinari*
Traficant	*Hobson*
Lewis (Ga.)	*Nichols*
DeFazio	*Vacancy*
Hayes (La.)	
Clement	
Payne (Va.)	
Costello	
Parker	
Laughlin	
Geren	
Sangmeister	
Poshard	
Swett	

Economic Development

225-6151 B376 RHOB

Kolter — chairman

Oberstar	*Bentley*
Applegate	*Boehlert*
Savage	*Inhofe*
Swett	*Ballenger*
Cramer	*Upton*
DeLauro	*Emerson*
Horn	
Collins (Mich.)	
Nowak	
Traficant	

Investigations and Oversight

225-3274 586 FHOB

Borski — chairman

DeLauro	*Packard*
Peterson (Fla.)	*Shuster*
Anderson	*Duncan*
Mineta	*Hancock*
Visclosky	*Molinari*
Hayes (La.)	*Hobson*
Laughlin	
Brewster	
Norton	
Oberstar	
Vacancy	

Public Buildings and Grounds

225-9961 B376 RHOB

Savage — chairman

Norton	*Inhofe*
Nowak	*Bentley*
Borski	*Duncan*
Lipinski	*Cox (Calif.)*
Lewis (Ga.)	*Vacancy*
Jones (Ga.)	
Poshard	
Peterson (Fla.)	
Oberstar	
Kolter	

Surface Transportation

225-9989 B376 RHOB

Mineta — chairman

Anderson	*Shuster*
Rahall	*Clinger*
Applegate	*Petri*
de Lugo	*Packard*
Valentine	*Boehlert*
Lipinski	*Upton*
Visclosky	*Emerson*
Traficant	*Cox (Calif.)*
Lewis (Ga.)	*Hobson*
Clement	*Riggs*
Payne (Va.)	*Taylor (N.C.)*
Costello	*Nichols*
Pallone	*Zeliff*
Jones (Ga.)	
Parker	
Laughlin	
Sangmeister	
DeFazio	
Geren	
Poshard	
Swett	
Brewster	
Cramer	
Norton	

Water Resources

225-0060 B370-A RHOB

Nowak — chairman

Hayes (La.)	*Petri*
DeLauro	*Clinger*
Peterson (Fla.)	*Packard*
Anderson	*Bentley*
Oberstar	*Ballenger*
Applegate	*Upton*
Borski	*Emerson*
Visclosky	*Hancock*
Pallone	*Molinari*
Jones (Ga.)	*Riggs*
Brewster	*Taylor (N.C.)*
Cramer	*Zeliff*
Horn	*Vacancy*
Collins (Mich.)	
Rahall	
Kolter	
Clement	
Payne (Va.)	
Costello	
Parker	
Vacancy	

Rules

225-9486 H-312 Capitol

Party Ratio: D 9 - R 4

Joe Moakley, D-Mass., chairman

Butler Derrick, S.C.	*Gerald B.H. Solomon, N.Y.*
Anthony C. Beilenson, Calif.	*James H. Quillen, Tenn.*
	David Dreier, Calif.
Martin Frost, Texas	*Bob McEwen, Ohio*
David E. Bonior, Mich.	
Tony P. Hall, Ohio	
Alan Wheat, Mo.	
Bart Gordon, Tenn.	
Louise M. Slaughter, N.Y.	

Legislative Process

225-1037 1629 LHOB

Derrick — chairman

Frost	*Quillen*
Wheat	*McEwen*
Gordon	
Moakley	

Rules of the House

225-9588 1628 LHOB

Beilenson — chairman

Bonior	*Dreier*
Hall (Ohio)	*Solomon*
Slaughter (N.Y.)	
Moakley	

Science, Space and Technology

Phone: 225-6371

Room: 2321 RHOB

Party Ratio: D 32 - R 19

George E. Brown Jr., D-Calif., chairman

James H. Scheuer, N.Y.	*Robert S. Walker, Pa.*
Marilyn Lloyd, Tenn.	*F. James Sensenbrenner Jr., Wis.*
Dan Glickman, Kan.	*Sherwood Boehlert, N.Y.*
Harold L. Volkmer, Mo.	*Tom Lewis, Fla.*
Howard Wolpe, Mich.	*Don Ritter, Pa.*
Ralph M. Hall, Texas	*Sid Morrison, Wash.*
Dave McCurdy, Okla.	*Ron Packard, Calif.*
Norman Y. Mineta, Calif.	*Paul B. Henry, Mich.*
Tim Valentine, N.C.	*Harris W. Fawell, Ill.*
Robert G. Torricelli, N.J.	*D. French Slaughter Jr., Va.*
Rick Boucher, Va.	*Lamar Smith, Texas*
Terry L. Bruce, Ill.	*Constance A. Morella, Md.*
Richard Stallings, Idaho	*Dana Rohrabacher, Calif.*
James A. Traficant Jr., Ohio	*Steven H. Schiff, N.M.*
Henry J. Nowak, N.Y.	*Tom Campbell, Calif.*
Carl C. Perkins, Ky.	*John J. Rhodes III, Ariz.*
Tom McMillen, Md.	*Joe L. Barton, Texas*
Dave Nagle, Iowa	*Dick Zimmer, N.J.*
Jimmy Hayes, La.	*Wayne T. Gilchrest, Md.*
Jerry F. Costello, Ill.	
John Tanner, Tenn.	
Glen Browder, Ala.	
Pete Geren, Texas	
Ray Thornton, Ark.	
Jim Bacchus, Fla.	
Tim Roemer, Ind.	
Bud Cramer, Ala.	
Dick Swett, N.H.	
Mike Kopetski, Ore.	
Joan Kelly Horn, Mo.	
Barbara-Rose Collins, Mich.	

Energy

225-7858 B374 RHOB

Lloyd — chairman

Costello	*Morrison*
Hall (Texas)	*Fawell*
Bruce	*Smith (Texas)*
Stallings	*Schiff*
Traficant	*Barton*
Cramer	
Wolpe	
Roemer	

Environment

225-6371 2321 RHOB

Scheuer — chairman

Nowak	*Ritter*
Swett	*Morrison*
Wolpe	*Morella*
Kopetski	*Zimmer*
Horn	
Hall (Texas)	
McMillen	

Investigations and Oversight

225-4494 822 OHOB

Wolpe — chairman

Geren	*Boehlert*
Nagle	*Sensenbrenner*
Tanner	
Thornton	

Science

225-7858 2320 RHOB

Boucher — chairman

Bruce	*Packard*
Kopetski	*Boehlert*
Valentine	*Slaughter (Va.)*
Perkins	*Fawell*
Nagle	*Schiff*
Hayes (La.)	*Campbell (Calif.)*
Costello	*Gilchrest*
Browder	
Thornton	
Roemer	
Collins (Mich.)	
Bacchus	

Space

225-8056 B374 RHOB

Hall (Texas) — chairman

Volkmer	*Sensenbrenner*
Stallings	*Lewis (Fla.)*
Traficant	*Packard*
Perkins	*Rhodes*
McMillen	*Henry*
Nagle	*Slaughter (Va.)*
Hayes (La.)	*Smith (Texas)*
Tanner	*Rohrabacher*
Browder	*Zimmer*
Geren	
Bacchus	
Cramer	
Scheuer	
Mineta	
Torricelli	

Technology and Competitiveness

225-9662 B374 RHOB

Valentine — chairman

Glickman	*Lewis (Fla.)*
Mineta	*Ritter*
Torricelli	*Henry*
Thornton	*Rohrabacher*
Roemer	*Campbell (Calif.)*
Horn	*Gilchrest*
Collins (Mich.)	*Morella*
Boucher	
Tanner	
Bacchus	
Swett	
Vacancy	

Small Business

225-5821 2361 RHOB

Party Ratio: D 27 - R 17

John J. LaFalce, D-N.Y., chairman

Neal Smith, Iowa
Ike Skelton, Mo.
Romano L. Mazzoli, Ky.
Nicholas Mavroules, Mass.
Charles Hatcher, Ga.
Ron Wyden, Ore.
Dennis E. Eckart, Ohio
Gus Savage, Ill.
Norman Sisisky, Va.
Esteban E. Torres, Calif.
Jim Olin, Va.
Richard Ray, Ga.
John Conyers Jr., Mich.
James Bilbray, Nev.
Kweisi Mfume, Md.
Floyd H. Flake, N.Y.
H. Martin Lancaster, N.C.
Bill Sarpalius, Texas
Richard E. Neal, Mass.
Glenn Poshard, Ill.
Eliot L. Engel, N.Y.
Jose E. Serrano, N.Y.
Robert E. Andrews, N.J.
Thomas H. Andrews, Maine
Calvin Dooley, Calif.
Bill Orton, Utah

Andy Ireland, Fla.
Joseph M. McDade, Pa.
William S. Broomfield, Mich.
D. French Slaughter Jr., Va.
Jan Meyers, Kan.
Larry Combest, Texas
Richard H. Baker, La.
Joel Hefley, Colo.
Fred Upton, Mich.
Mel Hancock, Mo.
Ronald K. Machtley, R.I.
Jim Ramstad, Minn.
Dave Camp, Mich.
Gary Franks, Conn.
Wayne Allard, Colo.
John A. Boehner, Ohio
Vacancy

Antitrust, Impact of Deregulation and Ecology

225-6026 B363 RHOB

Eckart — chairman

Sarpalius
Serrano
Andrews (N.J.)
Mazzoli

Hefley
Allard
Vacancy

Environment and Employment

225-7673 568-A FHOB

Olin — chairman

Torres
Ray
Poshard

Baker
Upton

Exports, Tax Policy and Special Problems

225-8944 B363 RHOB

Sisisky — chairman

Ray
Lancaster
Hatcher
Andrews (Maine)
Orton
Bilbray

Combest
Ramstad
Franks (Conn.)
Boehner

Procurement, Tourism and Rural Development

225-9368 B363 RHOB

Skelton — chairman

Torres
Bilbray
Poshard
Savage
Lancaster

Slaughter (Va.)
Upton
Hancock
Machtley

Regulation, Business Opportunity and Energy

225-7797 B363 RHOB

Wyden — chairman

Neal (Mass.)
Engel
Flake
Andrews (N.J.)
Dooley
Lancaster

Meyers
Broomfield
Camp (Mich.)
Hancock

SBA, the General Economy and Minority Enterprise Development

225-5821 2361 RHOB

LaFalce — chairman

Smith (Iowa)
Mazzoli
Mavroules
Savage
Conyers
Mfume
Serrano
Olin

Ireland
McDade
Allard
Camp (Mich.)
Franks (Conn.)
Ramstad

Standards of Official Conduct

225-7103 HT-2M Capitol

Party Ratio: D 7 - R 7

Louis Stokes, D-Ohio, chairman

Matthew F. McHugh, N.Y.
Gary L. Ackerman, N.Y.
George Darden, Ga.
Benjamin L. Cardin, Md.
Nancy Pelosi, Calif.
Jim McDermott, Wash.

James V. Hansen, Utah
Fred Grandy, Iowa
Nancy L. Johnson, Conn.
Jim Bunning, Ky.
Jon Kyl, Ariz.
Porter J. Goss, Fla.
David L. Hobson, Ohio

Veterans' Affairs

225-3527 335 CHOB

Party Ratio: D 21 - R 13

G. V. "Sonny" Montgomery, D-Miss., chairman

Don Edwards, Calif.
Douglas Applegate, Ohio
Lane Evans, Ill.
Timothy J. Penny, Minn.
Harley O. Staggers Jr., W.Va.
J. Roy Rowland, Ga.
Jim Slattery, Kan.
Claude Harris, Ala.
Joseph P. Kennedy II, Mass.
Liz J. Patterson, S.C.
George E. Sangmeister, Ill.
Ben Jones, Ga.
Jill L. Long, Ind.
Pete Peterson, Fla.
Chet Edwards, Texas
Maxine Waters, Calif.
Bill Brewster, Okla.
Owen B. Pickett, Va.
Pete Geren, Texas
Vacancy

Bob Stump, Ariz.
John Paul Hammerschmidt, Ark.
Chalmers P. Wylie, Ohio
Christopher H. Smith, N.J.
Dan Burton, Ind.
Michael Bilirakis, Fla.
Tom Ridge, Pa.
Craig T. James, Fla.
Cliff Stearns, Fla.
Bill Paxon, N.Y.
Floyd D. Spence, S.C.
Dick Nichols, Kan.
Rick Santorum, Pa.

Compensation, Pension and Insurance

225-3569 337 CHOB

Applegate — chairman

Evans	*Stump*
Penny	*Wylie*
Rowland	*Spence*
Edwards (Texas)	

Education, Training and Employment

225-9166 337-A CHOB

Penny — chairman

Slattery	*Smith (N.J.)*
Patterson	*Wylie*
Sangmeister	*Santorum*
Geren	*Ridge*
Vacancy	

Hospitals and Health Care

225-9154 338 CHOB

Montgomery — chairman

Rowland	*Hammerschmidt*
Slattery	*Stump*
Harris	*Smith (N.J.)*
Kennedy	*Burton*
Patterson	*Bilirakis*
Sangmeister	*Ridge*
Jones (Ga.)	*James*
Long	
Edwards (Texas)	
Brewster	
Applegate	

Housing and Memorial Affairs

225-9164 337 CHOB

Staggers — chairman

Harris	*Burton*
Jones (Ga.)	*Paxon*
Brewster	*Nichols*
Pickett	*Stearns*
Vacancy	

Oversight and Investigations

225-9044 335 CHOB

Evans — chairman

Edwards (Calif.)	*Bilirakis*
Peterson (Fla.)	*Stearns*
Waters	*James*
Kennedy	*Paxon*
Long	

Ways and Means

225-3625 1102 LHOB

Party Ratio: D 23 - R 13

Dan Rostenkowski, D-Ill., chairman

Sam M. Gibbons, Fla.	*Bill Archer, Texas*
J. J. Pickle, Texas	*Guy Vander Jagt, Mich.*
Charles B. Rangel, N.Y.	*Philip M. Crane, Ill.*
Pete Stark, Calif.	*Dick Schulze, Pa.*
Andrew Jacobs Jr., Ind.	*Bill Gradison, Ohio*
Harold E. Ford, Tenn.	*Bill Thomas, Calif.*
Ed Jenkins, Ga.	*Raymond J. McGrath, N.Y.*
Thomas J. Downey, N.Y.	*Rod Chandler, Wash.*
Frank J. Guarini, N.J.	*E. Clay Shaw Jr., Fla.*
Marty Russo, Ill.	*Don Sundquist, Tenn.*
Don J. Pease, Ohio	*Nancy L. Johnson, Conn.*
Robert T. Matsui, Calif.	*Jim Bunning, Ky.*
Beryl Anthony Jr., Ark.	*Fred Grandy, Iowa*
Byron L. Dorgan, N.D.	
Barbara B. Kennelly, Conn.	
Brian Donnelly, Mass.	
William J. Coyne, Pa.	
Michael A. Andrews, Texas	
Sander M. Levin, Mich.	
Jim Moody, Wis.	
Benjamin L. Cardin, Md.	
Jim McDermott, Wash.	

Health

225-7785 1114 LHOB

Stark — chairman

Russo	*Gradison*
Donnelly	*Chandler*
Coyne	*Johnson (Conn.)*
Levin	*McGrath*
Moody	
Cardin	

Human Resources

225-1025 B317 RHOB

Downey — acting chairman

Ford (Tenn.)	*Shaw*
Kennelly	*Johnson (Conn.)*
Andrews (Texas)	*Grandy*
McDermott	*Chandler*
Levin	
Moody	

Oversight

225-5525 1135 LHOB

Pickle — chairman

Anthony	*Schulze*
Ford (Tenn.)	*Shaw*
Rangel	*Sundquist*
Jacobs	*Bunning*
Jenkins	
Russo	

Select Revenue Measures

225-6649 1105 LHOB

Rangel — chairman

Dorgan	*Vander Jagt*
Kennelly	*Sundquist*
Andrews (Texas)	*Grandy*
Stark	*Chandler*
Donnelly	
Coyne	

Social Security

225-9263 B316 RHOB

Jacobs — chairman

Gibbons	*Bunning*
Cardin	*Crane*
McDermott	*Schulze*
Pickle	

Trade

225-3943 1136 LHOB

Gibbons — chairman

Rostenkowski	*Crane*
Jenkins	*Vander Jagt*
Downey	*Schulze*
Pease	*Thomas (Calif.)*
Guarini	*McGrath*
Matsui	
Anthony	
Dorgan	

Select Aging

226-3375 712 OHOB

Party Ratio: D 42 - R 27

Edward R. Roybal, D-Calif., chairman

Thomas J. Downey, N.Y.	*Matthew J. Rinaldo, N.J.*
Harold E. Ford, Tenn.	*John Paul Hammerschmidt, Ark.*
William J. Hughes, N.J.	*Ralph Regula, Ohio*
Marilyn Lloyd, Tenn.	*Olympia J. Snowe, Maine*
Mary Rose Oakar, Ohio	*Christopher H. Smith, N.J.*
Beverly B. Byron, Md.	*Sherwood Boehlert, N.Y.*
Henry A. Waxman, Calif.	*H. James Saxton, N.J.*
Butler Derrick, S.C.	*Helen Delich Bentley, Md.*
Bruce F. Vento, Minn.	*Harris W. Fawell, Ill.*
Barney Frank, Mass.	*Jan Meyers, Kan.*
Tom Lantos, Calif.	*Ben Blaz, Guam*
Ron Wyden, Ore.	*Paul B. Henry, Mich.*
Ike Skelton, Mo.	*Floyd D. Spence, S.C.*
Dennis M. Hertel, Mich.	*Constance A. Morella, Md.*
Robert A. Borski, Pa.	*John Porter, Ill.*
Ben Erdreich, Ala.	*John J. "Jimmy" Duncan Jr., Tenn.*
Norman Sisisky, Va.	*Cliff Stearns, Fla.*
Bob Wise, W.Va.	*Craig T. James, Fla.*
Bill Richardson, N.M.	*Amo Houghton, N.Y.*
Harold L. Volkmer, Mo.	*Gary Franks, Conn.*
Bart Gordon, Tenn.	*David L. Hobson, Ohio*
Thomas J. Manton, N.Y.	*Charles H. Taylor, N.C.*
Richard Stallings, Idaho	*Wayne T. Gilchrest, Md.*
Joseph P. Kennedy II, Mass.	*Dick Zimmer, N.J.*
Louise M. Slaughter, N.Y.	*Dick Nichols, Kan.*
James Bilbray, Nev.	*Jim Nussle, Iowa*
Jim Jontz, Ind.	*Vacancy*
Jerry F. Costello, Ill.	
Harley O. Staggers Jr., W.Va.	
Frank Pallone Jr., N.J.	
Jolene Unsoeld, Wash.	
Peter A. DeFazio, Ore.	
John Lewis, Ga.	
Wayne Owens, Utah	
Robert A. Roe, N.J.	
Gerry E. Studds, Mass.	
Neil Abercrombie, Hawaii	
Dick Swett, N.H.	
Rosa DeLauro, Conn.	
Vacancy	
Vacancy	

Health and Long-Term Care

226-3381 377 FHOB

Roybal — chairman

Downey	*Regula*
Oakar	*Rinaldo*
Waxman	*Saxton*
Derrick	*Bentley*
Vento	*Henry*
Frank (Mass.)	*Morella*
Wyden	*Stearns*
Skelton	*James*
Hertel	*Hobson*
Borski	*Gilchrest*
Erdreich	*Zimmer*
Sisisky	*Vacancy*
Wise	
Richardson	
Kennedy	
Slaughter (N.Y.)	
Owens (Utah)	

Housing and Consumer Interests

226-3344 717 OHOB

Lloyd — chairman

Ford (Tenn.)	*Smith (N.J.)*
Byron	*Hammerschmidt*
Vento	*Blaz*
Gordon	*Porter*
Manton	*Duncan*
Bilbray	*Taylor (N.C.)*
Costello	*Gilchrest*
Pallone	*Vacancy*
Unsoeld	
Roe	
Abercrombie	

Human Services

226-3348 715 OHOB

Downey — chairman

Richardson	*Snowe*
Slaughter (N.Y.)	*Smith (N.J.)*
Staggers	*Saxton*
Pallone	*Fawell*
DeFazio	*Blaz*
Lewis (Ga.)	*Spence*
Studds	*Duncan*
Abercrombie	*Nussle*
Swett	
DeLauro	

Retirement, Income and Employment

226-3335 714 OHOB

Hughes — chairman

Ford (Tenn.)	*Boehlert*
Oakar	*Meyers*
Lantos	*Spence*
Wise	*Porter*
Volkmer	*Houghton*
Manton	*Franks*
Stallings	*Taylor (N.C.)*
Jontz	*Nichols*
Costello	
DeFazio	
Lewis (Ga.)	

Rural Elderly Task Force

226-3375 712 OHOB

Derrick — chairman

Skelton	*Saxton*
Wise	*Snowe*
Richardson	*Smith (N.J.)*
Volkmer	*Bentley*
Sisisky	*Meyers*
Stallings	*Taylor (N.C.)*
Staggers	
DeFazio	
Lewis (Ga.)	
Swett	

Social Security and Women Task Force

226-3375 712 OHOB

Oakar — chairman

Ford (Tenn.)	*Houghton*
Lloyd	*Hammerschmidt*
Waxman	*Snowe*
Derrick	*Nussle*
Frank	
Manton	
Slaughter (N.Y.)	
Owens (Utah)	
Roe	
Abercrombie	
DeLauro	

Select Children, Youth and Families

226-7660 385 FHOB

Party Ratio: D 22 - R 14

Patricia Schroeder, D-Colo., chairman

George Miller, Calif.	*Frank R. Wolf, Va.*
William Lehman, Fla.	*Dennis Hastert, Ill.*
Matthew F. McHugh, N.Y.	*Clyde C. Holloway, La.*
Ted Weiss, N.Y.	*Curt Weldon, Pa.*
Beryl Anthony Jr., Ark.	*Lamar Smith, Texas*
Barbara Boxer, Calif.	*James T. Walsh, N.Y.*
Sander M. Levin, Mich.	*Ronald K. Machtley, R.I.*
J. Roy Rowland, Ga.	*Bob McEwen, Ohio*
Gerry Sikorski, Minn.	*Michael Bilirakis, Fla.*
Alan Wheat, Mo.	*Scott L. Klug, Wis.*
Matthew G. Martinez, Calif.	*Rick Santorum, Pa.*
Lane Evans, Ill.	*Dave Camp, Mich.*
Richard J. Durbin, Ill.	*Frank Riggs, Calif.*
David E. Skaggs, Colo.	*Bill Barrett, Neb.*
Bill Sarpalius, Texas	
Tim Johnson, S.D.	
Barbara-Rose Collins, Mich.	
Joan Kelly Horn, Mo.	
Jim Bacchus, Fla.	
Pete Peterson, Fla.	
Bud Cramer, Ala.	

Select Hunger

226-5470 505 FHOB

Party Ratio: D 22 - R 12

Tony P. Hall, D-Ohio, chairman

Leon E. Panetta, Calif.	*Bill Emerson, Mo.*
Vic Fazio, Calif.	*Marge Roukema, N.J.*
Peter H. Kostmayer, Pa.	*Sid Morrison, Wash.*
Byron L. Dorgan, N.D.	*Benjamin A. Gilman, N.Y.*
Bob Carr, Mich.	*Bob Smith, Ore.*
Timothy J. Penny, Minn.	*Doug Bereuter, Neb.*
Gary L. Ackerman, N.Y.	*Fred Upton, Mich.*
Mike Espy, Miss.	*Duncan Hunter, Calif.*
Floyd H. Flake, N.Y.	*Frank R. Wolf, Va.*
Liz J. Patterson, S.C.	*Christopher H. Smith, N.J.*
Thomas M. Foglietta, Pa.	*Wayne T. Gilchrest, Md.*
Albert G. Bustamante, Texas	*Frank Riggs, Calif.*
Michael R. McNulty, N.Y.	
Eni F.H. Faleomavaega, Am.Samoa	
Eliot L. Engel, N.Y.	
Les AuCoin, Ore.	
Alan Wheat, Mo.	
Jill L. Long, Ind.	
Mike Synar, Okla.	
Vacancy	
Vacancy	

— Task Forces —

Domestic

Espy — chairman

Panetta	*Roukema*
Ackerman	*Morrison*
Flake	*Upton*
Patterson	*Gilchrest*
Bustamante	
AuCoin	
Engel	
Synar	
Long	

International

Dorgan — chairman

Fazio	*Smith (Ore.)*
Kostmayer	*Bereuter*
Carr	*Gilman*
Penny	*Hunter*
Foglietta	*Wolf*
McNulty	*Smith (N.J.)*
Faleomavaega	
Wheat	

Select Intelligence

225-4121 H-405 Capitol

Party Ratio: D 12 - R 7

Dave McCurdy, D-Okla., chairman

Charles Wilson, Texas	*Bud Shuster, Pa.*
Barbara B. Kennelly, Conn.	*Larry Combest, Texas*
Dan Glickman, Kan.	*Doug Bereuter, Neb.*
Nicholas Mavroules, Mass.	*Robert K. Dornan, Calif.*
Bill Richardson, N.M.	*C.W. Bill Young, Fla.*
Stephen J. Solarz, N.Y.	*David O'B. Martin, N.Y.*
Norm Dicks, Wash.	*George W. Gekas, Pa.*
Ronald V. Dellums, Calif.	
David E. Bonior, Mich.	
Martin Olav Sabo, Minn.	
Wayne Owens, Utah	

Legislation

225-7311 H-405 Capitol

Kennelly — chairman

Solarz	*Gekas*
Dicks	*Bereuter*
Bonior	*Dornan*
Sabo	
Owens (Utah)	

Oversight and Evaluation

225-5658 H-405 Capitol

Wilson — chairman

Mavroules	*Combest*
Bonior	*Dornan*
Kennelly	*Shuster*
Glickman	
Richardson	

Program and Budget Authorization

225-7690 H-405 Capitol

McCurdy — chairman

Glickman	*Shuster*
Richardson	*Bereuter*
Solarz	*Young (Fla.)*
Dicks	*Martin*
Dellums	
Sabo	
Owens (Utah)	

Select Narcotics Abuse and Control

226-3040 234 FHOB

Party Ratio: D 21 - R 14

Charles B. Rangel, D-N.Y., chairman

Jack Brooks, Texas	*Lawrence Coughlin, Pa.*
Pete Stark, Calif.	*Benjamin A. Gilman, N.Y.*
James H. Scheuer, N.Y.	*Michael G. Oxley, Ohio*
Cardiss Collins, Ill.	*F. James Sensenbrenner Jr., Wis.*
Frank J. Guarini, N.J.	*Robert K. Dornan, Calif.*
Dante B. Fascell, Fla.	*Tom Lewis, Fla.*
William J. Hughes, N.J.	*James M. Inhofe, Okla.*
Mel Levine, Calif.	*Wally Herger, Calif.*
Solomon P. Ortiz, Texas	*Christopher Shays, Conn.*
Lawrence J. Smith, Fla.	*Bill Paxon, N.Y.*
Edolphus Towns, N.Y.	*William F. Clinger, Pa.*
James A. Traficant Jr., Ohio	*Howard Coble, N.C.*
Kweisi Mfume, Md.	*Paul E. Gillmor, Ohio*
Nita M. Lowey, N.Y.	*Jim Ramstad, Minn.*
Donald M. Payne, N.J.	
Romano L. Mazzoli, Ky.	
Ron de Lugo, V.I.	
George J. Hochbrueckner, N.Y.	
Craig Washington, Texas	
Robert E. Andrews, N.J.	

Partisan Committees

Democratic Leaders

Speaker of the House — Thomas S. Foley, Wash.
Majority Leader — Richard A. Gephardt, Mo.
Majority Whip — William H. Gray III, Pa.
Chairman of the Caucus — Steny H. Hoyer, Md.
Vice Chairman of the Caucus — Vic Fazio, Calif.
Chief Deputy Whip — David E. Bonior, Mich.

Deputy Whips — Tom Bevill, Ala.; Butler Derrick, S.C.; Dennis E. Eckart, Ohio; Martin Frost, Texas; W. G. "Bill" Hefner, N.C.; Peter H. Kostmayer, Pa.; Norman Y. Mineta, Calif.; Charles B. Rangel, N.Y.; Marty Russo, Ill.; Martin Olav Sabo, Minn.; Patricia Schroeder, Colo.; Lawrence J. Smith, Fla.; Charles W. Stenholm, Texas; Esteban E. Torres, Calif.; Pat Williams, Mont.

Whip Task Force Chairmen — Bart Gordon, Tenn.; David R. Obey, Wis.; Leon E. Panetta, Calif.

At-Large Whips — Les Aspin, Wis.; Chester G. Atkins, Mass.; Les AuCoin, Ore.; Howard L. Berman, Calif.; Rick Boucher, Va.; Barbara Boxer, Calif.; Terry L. Bruce, Ill.; Benjamin L. Cardin, Md.; Bob Carr, Mich.; George "Buddy" Darden, Ga.; Norm Dicks, Wash.; Brian Donnelly, Mass.; Byron L. Dorgan, N.D.; Richard J. Durbin, Ill.; Don Edwards, Calif., Mike Espy, Miss.; Lane Evans, Ill.; William D. Ford, Mich.; Barney Frank, Mass.; Sam Gejdenson, Conn.; Dan Glickman, Kan.; Frank J. Guarini, N.J.; Ed Jenkins, Ga.; Ben Jones, Ga.; Barbara B. Kennelly, Conn.; Dale E. Kildee, Mich.; H. Martin Lancaster, N.C.; Richard H. Lehman, Calif.; Mel Levine, Calif.; John Lewis, Ga.; Robert T. Matsui, Calif.; Dave McCurdy, Okla.; Michael R. McNulty, N.Y.; George Miller, Calif.; James P. Moran Jr., Va.; Robert J. Mrazek, N.Y.; John P. Murtha, Pa.; Mary Rose Oakar, Ohio; James L. Oberstar, Minn.; Timothy J. Penny, Minn.; David Price, N.C.; Bill Richardson, N.M.; Charlie Rose, N.C.; Dan Rostenkowski, Ill.; Charles E. Schumer, N.Y.; Jose E. Serrano, N.Y.; Philip R. Sharp, Ind.; Gerry Sikorski, Minn.; Norman Sisisky, Va.; David E. Skaggs, Colo.; Louise M. Slaughter, N.Y.; John M. Spratt Jr., S.C.; Al Swift, Wash.; Mike Synar, Okla.; W. J. "Billy" Tauzin, La.; Robert G. Torricelli, N.J.; Peter J. Visclosky, Ind.; Harold L. Volkmer, Mo.; Craig Washington, Texas; Bob Wise, W.Va.; Howard Wolpe, Mich.; Ron Wyden, Ore.

Assistant Whips, by zone numbers:

1. Nancy Pelosi, Calif., and Matthew G. Martinez, Calif.
2. Jim McDermott, Wash.
3. Tim Johnson, S.D.
4. Sidney R. Yates, Ill.
5. Jim Slattery, Kan.
6. Ronald D. Coleman, Texas

7. Gerry E. Studds, Mass.

8. Gary L. Ackerman, N.Y., and Thomas J. Downey, N.Y.

9. Paul E. Kanjorski, Pa.

10. Sander M. Levin, Mich.

11. Carroll Hubbard Jr., Ky.

12. Liz J. Patterson, S.C.

13. Bud Cramer, Ala.

14. Harry A. Johnston, Fla.

Steering and Policy Committee

225-8550 H-324 Capitol

Thomas S. Foley, Wash., chairman
Richard A. Gephardt, Mo., vice chairman
Steny H. Hoyer, Md., 2nd vice chairman

David E. Bonior, Mich. †
Albert G. Bustamante, Texas.
Butler Derrick, S.C.
Dennis E. Eckart, Ohio *
Vic Fazio, Calif. †
Martin Frost, Texas
Sam Gejdenson, Conn.
Dan Glickman, Kan.
William H. Gray III, Pa. †
Barbara B. Kennelly, Conn.
Gerald D. Kleczka, Wis.
John Lewis, Ga.
Thomas J. Manton, N.Y.
Robert T. Matsui, Calif.
Romano L. Mazzoli, Ky.
Matthew F. McHugh, N.Y.
Joe Moakley, Mass.
Leon E. Panetta, Calif.
Dan Rostenkowski, Ill.
J. Roy Rowland, Ga.
Marty Russo, Ill.
Norman Sisisky, Va.
Al Swift, Wash.
Mike Synar, Okla.
W. J. "Billy" Tauzin, La.
Ray Thornton, Ark.
Jamie L. Whitten, Miss.
Pat Williams, Mont.

† Member *ex officio* from the leadership.
* Member appointed by the Speaker of the House.

Personnel Committee

225-4068 B343 RHOB

Jack Brooks, Texas, chairman

Democratic Congressional Campaign Committee

863-1500 430 S. Capitol St. S.E. 20003

Vic Fazio, Calif., chairman
Dan Rostenkowski, Ill., vice chairman

Co-Chairmen: Michael A. Andrews, Texas; Richard J. Durbin, Ill.; Dennis E. Eckart, Ohio; Thomas J. Manton, N.Y.; Nancy Pelosi, Calif.; Lawrence J. Smith, Fla.

Neil Abercrombie, Hawaii
Gary L. Ackerman, N.Y.
Bill Alexander, Ark.
Thomas H. Andrews, Maine
Les Aspin, Wis.
Les AuCoin, Ore.
Howard L. Berman, Calif.
Tom Bevill, Ala.
James Bilbray, Nev.
Rick Boucher, Va.
Bill Brewster, Okla.
Terry L. Bruce, Ill.
Beverly B. Byron, Md.
Thomas R. Carper, Del.
Ron de Lugo, Virgin Islands
Norm Dicks, Wash.
John D. Dingell, Mich.
Byron L. Dorgan, N.D.
Mike Espy, Miss.
Eni F. H. Faleomavaega, American Samoa
Edward F. Feighan, Ohio
Jaime B. Fuster, Puerto Rico
Bart Gordon, Tenn.
Frank J. Guarini, N.J.
Lee H. Hamilton, Ind.
Jimmy Hayes, La.
W. G. "Bill" Hefner, N.C.
Peter Hoagland, Neb.
Ed Jenkins, Ga.
Tim Johnson, S.D.
Barbara B. Kennelly, Conn.
H. Martin Lancaster, N.C.
Larry LaRocco, Idaho
Nita M. Lowey, N.Y.
Frank McCloskey, Ind.
Alan B. Mollohan, W.Va.
John P. Murtha, Pa.
Dave Nagle, Iowa
Richard E. Neal, Mass.
Eleanor Holmes Norton, D.C.
Mary Rose Oakar, Ohio
James L. Oberstar, Minn.
David R. Obey, Wis.
Wayne Owens, Utah
Carl C. Perkins, Ky.
Pete Peterson, Fla.
John F. Reed, R.I.
Bill Richardson, N.M.
Martin Olav Sabo, Minn.
Patricia Schroeder, Colo.
Jim Slattery, Kan.
Neal Smith, Iowa
John M. Spratt Jr., S.C.
Charles W. Stenholm, Texas
Dick Swett, N.H.
Mike Synar, Okla.
W. J. "Billy" Tauzin, La.
Esteban E. Torres, Calif.
Harold L. Volkmer, Mo.
Craig Washington, Texas
Maxine Waters, Calif.
Pat Williams, Mont.
Ron Wyden, Ore.

Republican Leaders

Minority Leader — Robert H. Michel, Ill.
Minority Whip — Newt Gingrich, Ga.
Chairman of the Conference — Jerry Lewis, Calif.
Vice Chairman of the Conference — Bill McCollum, Fla.
Secretary of the Conference — Vin Weber, Minn.
Chief Deputy Whips — Steve Gunderson, Wis.; Robert S. Walker, Pa.

Deputy Whips — Joe L. Barton, Texas; Nancy L. Johnson, Conn.; Jon Kyl, Ariz.; Gerald B. H. Solomon, N.Y.; Fred Upton, Mich.

Assistant Deputy Whips — Thomas J. Bliley Jr., Va.; Bill Paxon, N.Y.; Olympia J. Snowe, Maine

Regional Whips — Dean A. Gallo, N.J.; Dennis Hastert, Ill.; Andy Ireland, Fla.; John Miller, Wash.

Committee on Committees

225-0600 H-230 Capitol

Robert H. Michel, Ill., chairman

Wayne Allard, Colo.
Bill Archer, Texas
Rod Chandler, Wash.
Bill Dickinson, Ala.
Mickey Edwards, Okla.
Newt Gingrich, Ga.
Dennis Hastert, Ill.
Frank Horton, N.Y.
Jim McCrery, La.
Joseph M. McDade, Pa.
Ron Packard, Calif.
Tom Petri, Wis.
Carl D. Pursell, Mich.
Ralph Regula, Ohio
Matthew J. Rinaldo, N.J.
Harold Rogers, Ky.
Cliff Stearns, Fla.
Bob Stump, Ariz.
C. W. Bill Young, Fla.
Don Young, Alaska

Policy Committee

225-6168 1616 LHOB

Mickey Edwards, Okla., chairman

Bill Archer, Texas
Doug Bereuter, Neb.
John A. Boehner, Ohio
Tom Campbell, Calif.
William E. Dannemeyer, Calif.
Gary Franks, Conn.
Dean A. Gallo, N.J.
Paul E. Gillmor, Ohio
Newt Gingrich, Ga.
Bill Goodling, Pa.
Bill Gradison, Ohio
Fred Grandy, Iowa
Bill Green, N.Y.
Steve Gunderson, Wis.
Dennis Hastert, Ill.
Paul B. Henry, Mich.
Duncan Hunter, Calif.
Jerry Lewis, Calif.
Bill McCollum, Fla.
Jim McCrery, Fla.
Joseph M. McDade, Pa.
Jan Meyers, Kan.
Robert H. Michel, Ill.
John J. Rhodes III, Ariz.
Ileana Ros-Lehtinen, Fla.
Lamar Smith, Texas
Gerald B. H. Solomon, N.Y.
Floyd D. Spence, S.C.
Craig Thomas, Wyo.
Guy Vander Jagt, Mich.
James T. Walsh, N.Y.
Vin Weber, Minn.

National Republican Congressional Committee

479-7000 320 First St. S.E. 20003

Guy Vander Jagt, Mich., chairman

Bill Barrett, Neb.
Michael Bilirakis, Fla.
Ben Blaz, Guam
Dan Burton, Ind.
Sonny Callahan, Ala.
Dave Camp, Mich.
Lawrence Coughlin, Pa.
David Dreier, Calif.
Mickey Edwards, Okla. †
Bill Emerson, Mo.
Harris W. Fawell, Ill.
Jack Fields, Texas
Gary Franks, Conn.
Paul E. Gillmor, Ohio
Newt Gingrich, Ga. †
John Paul Hammerschmidt, Ark.
James V. Hansen, Utah
Larry J. Hopkins, Ky.
Amo Houghton, N.Y.
Duncan Hunter, Calif. †
James M. Inhofe, Okla.
Scott L. Klug, Wis.
Jim Kolbe, Ariz.
Jerry Lewis, Calif. †
Robert L. Livingston, La.
Ronald K. Machtley, R.I.
Ron Marlenee, Mont.
Bill McCollum, Fla. †
Robert H. Michel, Ill. †
Constance A. Morella, Md.
Sid Morrison, Wash.
Jim Nussle, Iowa
Michael G. Oxley, Ohio
Arthur Ravenel Jr., S.C.
Frank Riggs, Calif.
Pat Roberts, Kan.
Marge Roukema, N.J.
Rick Santorum, Pa.
Dan Schaefer, Colo.
Joe Skeen, N.M.
Bob Smith, Ore.
Olympia J. Snowe, Maine
Don Sundquist, Tenn.
Charles H. Taylor, N.C.
Craig Thomas, Wyo.
Barbara F. Vucanovich, Nev.
Vin Weber, Minn. †
Frank R. Wolf, Va.
Don Young, Alaska
Bill Zeliff, N.H.

† Member *ex officio* from the leadership.

Research Committee

225-0871 1622 LHOB

Duncan Hunter, Calif., chairman

Executive Committee

Doug Bereuter, Neb.
Jim Bunning, Ky.
Larry Combest, Texas
Tom DeLay, Texas
Robert K. Dornan, Calif.
Mickey Edwards, Okla.
Newt Gingrich, Ga.
Porter J. Goss, Fla.
Bill Gradison, Ohio
Steve Gunderson, Wis.
Frank Horton, N.Y.
Henry J. Hyde, Ill.
Jerry Lewis, Calif.
Bill McCollum, Fla.
Robert H. Michel, Ill.
Jim Ramstad, Minn.
John J. Rhodes III, Ariz.
Pat Roberts, Kan.
Vin Weber, Minn.
C. W. Bill Young, Fla.
Bill Zeliff, N.H.

Joint Committee Assignments 102nd Congress

The joint committees of Congress are listed below in alphabetical order. The listing includes the room number, ZIP code and telephone number. The telephone area code for Washington, D.C., is 202.

Membership is drawn from both chambers and both parties. Membership is given in order of seniority on the committees and subcommittees.

In the listing, Democrats are listed on the left in roman type; Republicans are listed on the right in italics. When a senator serves as chairman, the vice chairman is usually a representative, and vice versa. The chairmanship usually rotates from one chamber to the other at the beginning of each Congress.

Economic

224-5171 SD-G01

Sen. Paul S. Sarbanes, D-Md., chairman

Rep. Lee H. Hamilton, D-Ind., vice chairman

Senate Members

Lloyd Bentsen, Texas	*William V. Roth Jr., Del.*
Edward M. Kennedy, Mass.	*Steve Symms, Idaho*
Jeff Bingaman, N.M.	*Connie Mack, Fla.*
Al Gore, Tenn.	*Robert C. Smith, N.H.*
Richard H. Bryan, Nev.	

House Members

David R. Obey, Wis.	*Dick Armey, Texas*
James H. Scheuer, N.Y.	*Chalmers P. Wylie, Ohio*
Pete Stark, Calif.	*Olympia J. Snowe, Maine*
Stephen J. Solarz, N.Y.	*Hamilton Fish Jr., N.Y.*
Kweisi Mfume, Md.	

Economic Goals and Intergovernmental Policy

224-5171 SD-G01

Rep. Hamilton — chairman

Senate Members

Bentsen	*Roth*
Kennedy	

House Members

Mfume	*Wylie*
	Snowe

Economic Growth, Trade and Taxes

224-5171 SD-G01

Sen. Bentsen — chairman

Senate Members

	Roth
	Mack

House Members

Hamilton	*Wylie*
Stark	*Fish*
Solarz	

Economic Resources and Competitiveness

224-5171 SD-G01

Rep. Obey — chairman

Senate Members

Sarbanes	*Symms*
Bingaman	
Gore	
Bryan	

House Members

Solarz	*Armey*

Education and Health

224-5171 SD-G01

Rep. Scheuer — chairman

Senate Members

Bentsen	*Smith*
Bingaman	
Gore	

House Members

	Snowe
	Fish

Fiscal and Monetary Policy

224-5171 SD-G01

Sen. Kennedy — chairman

Senate Members

	Symms
	Smith

House Members

Obey	*Fish*
Stark	

International Economic Policy

224-5171 SD-G01

Sen. Sarbanes — chairman

Senate Members

Kennedy	*Roth*
	Mack

House Members

Hamilton	*Wylie*
Solarz	*Snowe*

Investment, Jobs and Prices

224-5171 SD-G01

Rep. Stark — chairman

Senate Members

Gore	*Symms*
Bryan	

House Members

Scheuer	*Armey*

Technology and National Security

224-5171 SD-G01

Sen. Bingaman — chairman

Senate Members

Sarbanes	*Mack*
Bryan	*Smith*

House Members

Obey	*Armey*
Scheuer	
Mfume	

Library

226-7633 103 HOB Annex #1

Sen. Claiborne Pell, D-R.I., chairman

Rep. Charlie Rose, D-N.C., vice chairman

Senate Members

Dennis DeConcini, Ariz.	*Mark O. Hatfield, Ore.*
Daniel Patrick Moynihan, N.Y.	*Ted Stevens, Alaska*

House Members

Charlie Rose, N.C.,	*Bill Barrett, Neb.*
Joe Kolter, Pa.	*Pat Roberts, Kan.*
Thomas J. Manton, N.Y.	

Printing

224-5241 SH-818

Rep. Charlie Rose, D-N.C., chairman

Sen. Wendell H. Ford, D-Ky., vice chairman

Senate Members

Dennis DeConcini, Ariz.	*Ted Stevens, Alaska*
Al Gore, Tenn.	*Mark O. Hatfield, Ore.*

House Members

Sam Gejdenson, Conn.	*Pat Roberts, Kan.*
Gerald D. Kleczka, Wis.	*Newt Gingrich, Ga.*

Taxation

225-3621 1015 LHOB

Rep. Dan Rostenkowski, D-Ill., chairman

Sen. Lloyd Bentsen, D-Texas, vice chairman

Senate Members

Daniel Patrick Moynihan, N.Y.	*Bob Packwood, Ore.*
Max Baucus, Mont.	*Bob Dole, Kan.*

House Members

Sam Gibbons, Fla.	*Bill Archer, Texas*
J. J. Pickle, Texas	*Guy Vander Jagt, Mich.*

Seniority in the 102nd Congress

Senate Seniority

Senate rank generally is determined according to the official date of the beginning of a member's service, except in the case of new members sworn in at times other than the beginning of a Congress. For those appointed or elected to fill unexpired terms, the date of the appointment, certification or swearing-in determines the senator's rank.

When members are sworn in on the same day, custom decrees that those with prior political experience take precedence. Counted as political experience, in order of importance, is senatorial, House and gubernatorial service. Information on prior experience is given where applicable to seniority ranking. The dates following senators' names refer to the beginning of their present service.

DEMOCRATS

1. Byrd—Jan. 3, 1959
2. Burdick—Aug. 8, 1960
3. Pell—Jan. 3, 1961
4. Kennedy—Nov. 7, 1962
5. Inouye—Jan. 3, 1963
6. Hollings—Nov. 9, 1966
7. Cranston—Jan. 3, 1969
8. Bentsen—Jan. 3, 1971
9. Nunn—Nov. 8, 1972
10. Johnston—Nov. 14, 1972
11. Biden—Jan. 3, 1973
12. Glenn—Dec. 24, 1974
13. Ford—Dec. 28, 1974
14. Bumpers (ex-governor)—Jan. 3, 1975
15. Leahy—Jan. 3, 1975
16. Metzenbaum—Dec. 29, 1976
17. Riegle—Dec. 30, 1976
18. Sarbanes (ex-representative)—Jan. 4, 1977
19. DeConcini—Jan. 4, 1977
    Moynihan—Jan. 4, 1977
    Sasser—Jan. 4, 1977
22. Baucus—Dec. 15, 1978
23. Pryor (ex-representative)—Jan. 15, 1979
24. Boren (ex-governor)—Jan. 15, 1979
    Exon (ex-governor)—Jan. 15, 1979
26. Bradley—Jan. 15, 1979
    Heflin—Jan. 15, 1979
    Levin—Jan. 15, 1979
29. Mitchell—May 19, 1980
30. Dodd (ex-representative)—Jan. 5, 1981
31. Dixon—Jan. 5, 1981
32. Lautenberg—Dec. 27, 1982
33. Bingaman—Jan. 3, 1983
34. Kerry—Jan. 2, 1985
35. Harkin (ex-representative, five House terms)—Jan. 3, 1985
    Simon (ex-representative, five House terms)—Jan. 3, 1985
37. Gore (ex-representative, four House terms)—Jan. 3, 1985
38. Rockefeller—Jan. 15, 1985
39. Sanford—Nov. 5, 1986
40. Breaux (ex-representative, eight House terms)—Jan. 6, 1987
41. Adams (ex-representative, six House terms)—Jan. 6, 1987
    Wirth (ex-representative, six House terms)—Jan. 6, 1987
43. Fowler (ex-representative, five House terms)—Jan. 6, 1987
    Mikulski (ex-representative, five House terms)—Jan. 6, 1987
45. Daschle (ex-representative, four House terms)—Jan. 6, 1987
    Shelby (ex-representative, four House terms)—Jan. 6, 1987
47. Reid (ex-representative, two House terms)—Jan. 6, 1987
48. Graham (ex-governor)—Jan. 6, 1987
49. Conrad—Jan. 6, 1987
50. Bryan (ex-governor)—Jan. 3, 1989
    Kerrey (ex-governor)—Jan. 3, 1989
    Robb (ex-governor)—Jan. 3, 1989
53. Kohl—Jan. 3, 1989
    Lieberman—Jan. 3, 1989
55. Akaka (ex-representative)—April 28, 1990
56. Wellstone—Jan. 3, 1991
57. Wofford—May 9, 1991

REPUBLICANS

1. Thurmond—Nov. 7, 1956*
2. Hatfield—Jan. 10, 1967
3. Stevens—Dec. 24, 1968
4. Dole (ex-representative)—Jan. 3, 1969
5. Packwood—Jan. 3, 1969
6. Roth—Jan. 1, 1971
7. Helms—Jan. 3, 1973
    Domenici—Jan. 3, 1973
9. Garn—Dec. 21, 1974
10. Danforth—Dec. 27, 1976
11. Chafee—Dec. 29, 1976
12. Hatch—Jan. 3, 1977
    Lugar—Jan. 3, 1977
    Wallop—Jan. 3, 1977
15. Durenberger—Nov. 8, 1978
16. Kassebaum—Dec. 23, 1978
17. Cochran—Dec. 27, 1978
18. Simpson—Jan. 1, 1979
19. Warner—Jan. 2, 1979
20. Cohen (ex-representative, three House terms)—Jan. 15, 1979
21. Pressler (ex-representative, two House terms)—Jan. 15, 1979
22. Rudman—Dec. 29, 1980
23. Symms (ex-representative, four House terms)—Jan. 5, 1981

24. Grassley (ex-representative, three House terms)—Jan. 5, 1981
25. Kasten (ex-representative, two House terms)—Jan. 5, 1981
26. D'Amato—Jan. 5, 1981
    Murkowski—Jan. 5, 1981
    Nickles—Jan. 5, 1981
    Specter—Jan. 5, 1981
30. Gramm (ex-representative)—Jan. 3, 1985
31. McConnell—Jan. 3, 1985
32. McCain (ex-representative)—Jan. 6, 1987
33. Bond (ex-governor)—Jan. 6, 1987
34. Gorton (ex-senator)—Jan. 3, 1989
35. Lott (ex-representative, eight House terms)—Jan. 3, 1989
36. Jeffords (ex-representative, seven House terms)—Jan. 3, 1989
37. Coats (ex-representative, four House terms)—Jan. 3, 1989
38. Mack (ex-representative, three House terms)—Jan. 3, 1989
39. Burns—Jan. 3, 1989
40. Smith—Dec. 7, 1990
41. Brown (ex-representative, five House terms)—Jan. 3, 1991
    Craig (ex-representative, five House terms)—Jan. 3, 1991
43. Seymour—Jan. 7, 1991.

* *Thurmond began his Senate service Nov. 7, 1956, as a Democrat. He became a Republican Sept. 16, 1964. The Republican Conference allowed his seniority to count from his 1956 election to the Senate.*

House Seniority

House rank generally is determined according to the official date of the beginning of a member's service, except in the case of members elected to fill vacancies, in which instance the date of election determines rank.

When members enter the House on the same day, those with prior House experience take precedence, starting with those with the longest consecutive service. Experience as a senator or governor is disregarded. Prior experience is given where applicable to seniority ranking. The dates following members' names refer to the beginning of their present service.

DEMOCRATS

1. Whitten (Miss.)—Nov. 4, 1941
2. Bennett (Fla.)—Jan. 3, 1949
3. Brooks (Texas)—Jan. 3, 1953
4. Natcher (Ky.)—Aug. 1, 1953
5. Fascell (Fla.)—Jan. 3, 1955
6. Dingell (Mich.)—Dec. 13, 1955
7. Rostenkowski (Ill.)—Jan. 7, 1959
   Smith (Iowa)—Jan. 7, 1959
9. Gonzalez (Texas)—Nov.4, 1961
10. Edwards (Calif.)—Jan. 9, 1963
    Gibbons (Fla.)—Jan. 9, 1963
    Roybal (Calif.)—Jan. 9, 1963
13. Pickle (Texas)—Dec. 21, 1963
14. Yates (Ill.) (seven terms previously)—Jan. 4, 1965
15. Annunzio (Ill.)—Jan. 4, 1965
    Conyers (Mich.)—Jan. 4, 1965
    de la Garza (Texas)—Jan. 4, 1965
    Foley (Wash.)—Jan. 4, 1965
    Ford (Mich.)—Jan. 4, 1965
    Hamilton (Ind.)—Jan. 4, 1965
21. Jones (N.C.)—Feb. 5, 1966
22. Bevill (Ala.)—Jan. 10, 1967
    Montgomery (Miss.)—Jan. 10, 1967
24. Gaydos (Pa.)—Nov. 5, 1968
25. Alexander (Ark.)—Jan. 3, 1969
    Anderson (Calif.)—Jan. 3, 1969
    Clay (Mo.)—Jan. 3, 1969
    Stokes (Ohio)—Jan. 3, 1969
    Yatron (Pa.)—Jan. 3, 1969
30. Obey (Wis.)—April 1, 1969
31. Roe (N.J.)—Nov. 4, 1969
32. Aspin (Wis.)—Jan. 21, 1971
    Dellums (Calif.)—Jan. 21, 1971
    Mazzoli (Ky.)—Jan. 21, 1971
    Rangel (N.Y.)—Jan. 21, 1971
36. Brown (Calif.) (four terms previously)—Jan. 3, 1973
37. Lehman (Fla.)—Jan. 3, 1973
    Moakley (Mass.)—Jan. 3, 1973
    Rose (N.C.)—Jan. 3, 1973
    Schroeder (Colo.)—Jan. 3, 1973
    Stark (Calif.)—Jan. 3, 1973
    Studds (Mass.)—Jan. 3, 1973
    Wilson (Texas)—Jan. 3, 1973
44. Collins (Ill.)—June 5, 1973
45. Murtha (Pa.)—Feb. 5, 1974
46. Traxler (Mich.)—April 16, 1974
47. Jacobs (Ind.) (four terms previously)—Jan. 14, 1975
    Scheuer (N.Y.) (four terms previously)—Jan. 14, 1975
49. AuCoin (Ore.)—Jan. 14, 1975
    Derrick (S.C.)—Jan. 14, 1975
    Downey (N.Y.)—Jan. 14, 1975
    Early (Mass.)—Jan. 14, 1975
    English (Okla.)—Jan. 14, 1975
    Ford (Tenn.)—Jan. 14, 1975
    Hefner (N.C.)—Jan. 14, 1975
    Hubbard (Ky.)—Jan. 14, 1975
    Hughes (N.J.)—Jan. 14, 1975
    LaFalce (N.Y.)—Jan. 14, 1975
    Lloyd (Tenn.)—Jan. 14, 1975
    McHugh (N.Y.)—Jan. 14, 1975
    Miller (Calif.)—Jan. 14, 1975
    Mineta (Calif.)—Jan. 14, 1975
    Neal (N.C.)—Jan. 14, 1975
    Nowak (N.Y.)—Jan. 14, 1975
    Oberstar (Minn.)—Jan. 14, 1975
    Russo (Ill.)—Jan. 14, 1975
    Sharp (Ind.)—Jan. 14, 1975
    Solarz (N.Y.)—Jan. 14, 1975

Waxman (Calif.)—Jan. 14, 1975
70. Markey (Mass.)—Nov. 2, 1976
71. Applegate (Ohio)—Jan. 4, 1977
Barnard (Ga.)—Jan. 4, 1977
Beilenson (Calif.)—Jan. 4, 1977
Bonior (Mich.)—Jan. 4, 1977
Dicks (Wash.)—Jan. 4, 1977
Gephardt (Mo.)—Jan. 4, 1977
Glickman (Kan.)—Jan. 4, 1977
Huckaby (La.)—Jan. 4, 1977
Jenkins (Ga.)—Jan. 4, 1977
Kildee (Mich.)—Jan. 4, 1977
Murphy (Pa.)—Jan. 4, 1977
Oakar (Ohio)—Jan. 4, 1977
Panetta (Calif.)—Jan. 4, 1977
Pease (Ohio)—Jan. 4, 1977
Rahall (W.Va.)—Jan. 4, 1977
Skelton (Mo.)—Jan. 4, 1977
Vento (Minn.)—Jan. 4, 1977
Volkmer (Mo.)—Jan. 4, 1977
Weiss (N.Y.)—Jan. 4, 1977
90. Anthony (Ark.)—Jan. 15, 1979
Byron (Md.)—Jan. 15, 1979
Dixon (Calif.)—Jan. 15, 1979
Donnelly (Mass.)—Jan. 15, 1979
Fazio (Calif.)—Jan. 15, 1979
Frost (Texas)—Jan. 15, 1979
Gray (Pa.)—Jan. 15, 1979
Guarini (N.J.)—Jan. 15, 1979
Hall (Ohio)—Jan. 15, 1979
Hutto (Fla.)—Jan. 15, 1979
Matsui (Calif.)—Jan. 15, 1979
Mavroules (Mass.)—Jan. 15, 1979
Sabo (Minn.)—Jan. 15, 1979
Stenholm (Texas)—Jan. 15, 1979
Swift (Wash.)—Jan. 15, 1979
Synar (Okla.)—Jan. 15, 1979
Williams (Mont.)—Jan. 15, 1979
Wolpe (Mich.)—Jan. 15, 1979
108. Tauzin (La.)—May 17, 1980
109. Coyne (Pa.)—Jan. 5, 1981
Dorgan (N.D.)—Jan. 5, 1981
Dwyer (N.J.)—Jan. 5, 1981
Dymally (Calif.)—Jan. 5, 1981
Eckart (Ohio)—Jan. 5, 1981
Foglietta (Pa.)—Jan. 5, 1981
Frank (Mass.)—Jan. 5, 1981
Gejdenson (Conn.)—Jan. 5, 1981
Hall (Texas)—Jan. 5, 1981
Hatcher (Ga.)—Jan. 5, 1981
Hertel (Mich.)—Jan. 5, 1981
Lantos (Calif.)—Jan. 5, 1981
McCurdy (Okla.)—Jan. 5, 1981
Savage (Ill.)—Jan. 5, 1981
Schumer (N.Y.)—Jan. 5, 1981
Wyden (Ore.)—Jan. 5, 1981
125. Hoyer (Md.)—May 19, 1981
126. Kennelly (Conn.)—Jan. 12, 1982
127. Martinez (Calif.)—July 13, 1982
128. Carr (Mich.) (three terms previously)—Jan. 3, 1983
129. Kostmayer (Pa.) (two terms previously)—Jan. 3, 1983
130. Andrews (Texas)—Jan. 3, 1983
Berman (Calif.)—Jan. 3, 1983
Borski (Pa.)—Jan. 3, 1983
Boucher (Va.)—Jan. 3, 1983
Boxer (Calif.)—Jan. 3, 1983
Bryant (Texas)—Jan. 3, 1983
Carper (Del.)—Jan. 3, 1983
Coleman (Texas)—Jan. 3, 1983
Cooper (Tenn.)—Jan. 3, 1983
Durbin (Ill.)—Jan. 3, 1983
Erdreich (Ala.)—Jan. 3, 1983
Evans (Ill.)—Jan. 3, 1983
Feighan (Ohio)—Jan. 3, 1983
Kaptur (Ohio)—Jan. 3, 1983
Kolter (Pa.)—Jan. 3, 1983
Lehman (Calif.)—Jan. 3, 1983
Levin (Mich.)—Jan. 3, 1983
Levine (Calif.)—Jan. 3, 1983
Lipinski (Ill.)—Jan. 3, 1983
McCloskey (Ind.)—Jan. 3, 1983
Mollohan (W.Va.)—Jan. 3, 1983
Moody (Wis.)—Jan. 3, 1983
Mrazek (N.Y.)—Jan. 3, 1983
Olin (Va.)—Jan. 3, 1983
Ortiz (Texas)—Jan. 3, 1983
Owens (N.Y.)—Jan. 3, 1983
Penny (Minn.)—Jan. 3, 1983
Ray (Ga.)—Jan. 3, 1983
Richardson (N.M.)—Jan. 3, 1983
Rowland (Ga.)—Jan. 3, 1983
Sikorski (Minn.)—Jan. 3, 1983
Sisisky (Va.)—Jan. 3, 1983
Slattery (Kan.)—Jan. 3, 1983
Smith (Fla.)—Jan. 3, 1983
Spratt (S.C.)—Jan. 3, 1983
Staggers (W.Va.)—Jan. 3, 1983
Tallon (S.C.)—Jan. 3, 1983
Thomas (Ga.)—Jan. 3, 1983
Torres (Calif.)—Jan. 3, 1983
Torricelli (N.J.)—Jan. 3, 1983
Towns (N.Y.)—Jan. 3, 1983
Valentine (N.C.)—Jan. 3, 1983
Wheat (Mo.)—Jan. 3, 1983
Wise (W.Va.)—Jan. 3, 1983
174. Ackerman (N.Y.)—March 1, 1983
175. Hayes (Ill.)—Aug. 23, 1983
176. Darden (Ga.)—Nov. 8, 1983
177. Kleczka (Wis.)—April 3, 1984
178. Perkins (Ky.)—Nov. 6, 1984
179. Atkins (Mass.)—Jan. 3, 1985
Bruce (Ill.)—Jan. 3, 1985
Bustamante (Texas)—Jan. 3, 1985
Gordon (Tenn.)—Jan. 3, 1985
Kanjorski (Pa.)—Jan. 3, 1985
Manton (N.Y.)—Jan. 3, 1985
Stallings (Idaho)—Jan. 3, 1985
Traficant (Ohio)—Jan. 3, 1985
Visclosky (Ind.)—Jan. 3, 1985
188. Chapman (Texas)—Aug. 3, 1985
189. Owens (Utah) (one term previously)—Jan. 6, 1987
190. Bilbray (Nev.)—Jan. 6, 1987
Campbell (Colo.)—Jan. 6, 1987
Cardin (Md.)—Jan. 6, 1987
DeFazio (Ore.)—Jan. 6, 1987

Espy (Miss.)—Jan. 6, 1987
Flake (N.Y.)—Jan. 6, 1987
Harris (Ala.)—Jan. 6, 1987
Hayes (La.)—Jan. 6, 1987
Hochbrueckner (N.Y.)—Jan. 6, 1987
Johnson (S.D.)—Jan. 6, 1987
Jontz (Ind.)—Jan. 6, 1987
Kennedy (Mass.)—Jan. 6, 1987
Lancaster (N.C.)—Jan. 6, 1987
Lewis (Ga.)—Jan. 6, 1987
McMillen (Md.)—Jan. 6, 1987
Mfume (Md.)—Jan. 6, 1987
Nagle (Iowa)—Jan. 6, 1987
Patterson (S.C.)—Jan. 6, 1987
Pickett (Va.)—Jan. 6, 1987
Price (N.C.)—Jan. 6, 1987
Sawyer (Ohio)—Jan. 6, 1987
Skaggs (Colo.)—Jan. 6, 1987
Slaughter (N.Y.)—Jan. 6, 1987
213. Pelosi (Calif.)—June 2, 1987
214. Clement (Tenn.)—Jan. 19, 1988
215. Payne (Va.)—June 14, 1988
216. Costello (Ill.)—Aug. 9, 1988
217. Pallone (N.J.)—Nov. 8, 1988
218. Engel (N.Y.)—Jan. 3, 1989
Hoagland (Neb.)—Jan. 3, 1989
Johnston (Fla.)—Jan. 3, 1989
Jones (Ga.)—Jan. 3, 1989
Laughlin (Texas)—Jan. 3, 1989
Lowey (N.Y.)—Jan. 3, 1989
McDermott (Wash.)—Jan. 3, 1989
McNulty (N.Y.)—Jan. 3, 1989
Neal (Mass.)—Jan. 3, 1989
Parker (Miss.)—Jan. 3, 1989
Payne (N.J.)—Jan. 3, 1989
Poshard (Ill.)—Jan. 3, 1989
Sangmeister (Ill.)—Jan. 3, 1989
Sarpalius (Texas)—Jan. 3, 1989
Tanner (Tenn.)—Jan. 3, 1989
Unsoeld (Wash.)—Jan. 3, 1989
234. Long (Ind.)—March 28, 1989
235. Browder (Ala.)—April 4, 1989
236. Condit (Calif.)—Sept. 12, 1989
Geren (Texas)—Sept. 12, 1989
238. Taylor (Miss.)—Oct. 17, 1989
239. Washington (Texas)—Dec. 9, 1989
240. Serrano (N.Y.)—March 20, 1990
241. Mink (Hawaii)—Sept. 22, 1990
242. Andrews (N.J.)—Nov. 6, 1990
243. Thornton (Ark.) (three terms previously)—Jan. 3, 1991
244. Abercrombie (Hawaii) (one term previously)—Jan. 3, 1991
245. Andrews (Maine)—Jan. 3, 1991
Bacchus (Fla.)—Jan. 3, 1991
Brewster (Okla.)—Jan. 3, 1991
Collins (Mich.)—Jan. 3, 1991
Cox (Ill.)—Jan. 3, 1991
Cramer (Ala.)—Jan. 3, 1991
DeLauro (Conn.)—Jan. 3, 1991
Dooley (Calif.)—Jan. 3, 1991
Edwards (Texas)—Jan. 3, 1991
Horn (Mo.)—Jan. 3, 1991
Jefferson (La.)—Jan. 3, 1991
Kopetski (Ore.)—Jan. 3, 1991
LaRocco (Idaho)—Jan. 3, 1991
Luken (Ohio)—Jan. 3, 1991
Moran (Va.)—Jan. 3, 1991
Orton (Utah)—Jan. 3, 1991
Peterson (Fla.)—Jan. 3, 1991
Peterson (Minn.)—Jan. 3, 1991
Reed (R.I.)—Jan. 3, 1991
Roemer (Ind.)—Jan. 3, 1991
Swett (N.H.)—Jan. 3, 1991
Waters (Calif.)—Jan. 3, 1991
267. Olver (Mass.)

REPUBLICANS

1. Broomfield (Mich.)—Jan. 3, 1957
Michel (Ill.)—Jan. 3, 1957
3. Horton (N.Y.)—Jan. 9, 1963
McDade (Pa.)—Jan. 9, 1963
Quillen (Tenn.)—Jan. 9, 1963
6. Dickinson (Ala.)—Jan. 4, 1965
7. Vander Jagt (Mich.)—Nov. 8, 1966
8. Hammerschmidt (Ark.)—Jan. 10, 1967
Miller (Ohio)—Jan. 10, 1967
Myers (Ind.)—Jan. 10, 1967
Wylie (Ohio)—Jan. 10, 1967
12. Coughlin (Pa.)—Jan. 3, 1969
Fish (N.Y.)—Jan. 3, 1969
14. Crane (Ill.)—Nov. 25, 1969
15. Archer (Texas)—Jan. 21, 1971
Lent (N.Y.)—Jan. 21, 1971
Spence (S.C.)—Jan. 21, 1971
Young (Fla.)—Jan. 21, 1971
19. Gilman (N.Y.)—Jan. 3, 1973
Moorhead (Calif)—Jan. 3, 1973
Regula (Ohio)—Jan. 3, 1973
Rinaldo (N.J.)—Jan. 3, 1973
Shuster (Pa.)—Jan. 3, 1973
24. Young (Alaska)—March 6, 1973
25. Lagomarsino (Calif.)—March 5, 1974
26. Goodling (Pa.)—Jan. 14, 1975
Gradison (Ohio)—Jan. 14, 1975
Hyde (Ill.)—Jan. 14, 1975
Schulze (Pa.)—Jan. 14, 1975
30. Coleman (Mo.)—Nov. 2, 1976
31. Edwards (Okla.)—Jan. 4, 1977
Ireland (Fla.)—Jan. 4, 1977*
Leach (Iowa)—Jan. 4, 1977
Marlenee (Mont.)—Jan. 4, 1977
Pursell (Mich.)—Jan. 4, 1977
Stump (Ariz.)—Jan. 4, 1977*
Walker (Pa.)—Jan. 4, 1977
38. Livingston (La.)—Aug. 27, 1977
39. Green (N.Y.)—Feb. 14, 1978
40. Bereuter (Neb.)—Jan. 15, 1979
Clinger (Pa.)—Jan. 15, 1979
Dannemeyer (Calif.)—Jan. 15, 1979
Davis (Mich.)—Jan. 15, 1979
Gingrich (Ga.)—Jan. 15, 1979
Hopkins (Ky.)—Jan. 15, 1979
Lewis (Calif.)—Jan. 15, 1979
Ritter (Pa.)—Jan. 15, 1979
Roth (Wis.)—Jan. 15, 1979

Sensenbrenner (Wis.)—Jan. 15, 1979
Snowe (Maine)—Jan. 15, 1979
Solomon (N.Y.)—Jan. 15, 1979
Thomas (Calif.)—Jan. 15, 1979
53. Petri (Wis.)—April 3, 1979
54. Porter (Ill.)—Jan. 22, 1980
55. Bliley (Va.)—Jan. 5, 1981
Dreier (Calif.)—Jan. 5, 1981
Emerson (Mo.)—Jan. 5, 1981
Fields (Texas)—Jan. 5, 1981
Gunderson (Wis.)—Jan. 5, 1981
Hansen (Utah)—Jan. 5, 1981
Hunter (Calif.)—Jan. 5, 1981
Lowery (Calif.)—Jan. 5, 1981
Martin (N.Y.)—Jan. 5, 1981
McCollum (Fla.)—Jan. 5, 1981
McEwen (Ohio)—Jan. 5, 1981
McGrath (N.Y.)—Jan. 5, 1981
Morrison (Wash.)—Jan. 5, 1981
Roberts (Kan.)—Jan. 5, 1981
Rogers (Ky.)—Jan. 5, 1981
Roukema (N.J.)—Jan. 5 1981
Shaw (Fla.)—Jan. 5, 1981
Skeen (N.M.)—Jan. 5, 1981
Smith (N.J.) Jan. 5, 1981
Weber (Minn.)—Jan. 5, 1981
Wolf (Va.)—Jan. 5, 1981
76. Oxley (Ohio)—June 25, 1981
Bateman (Va.)—Jan. 3, 1983
Bilirakis (Fla.)—Jan. 3, 1983
Boehlert (N.Y.)—Jan. 3, 1983
Burton (Ind.)—Jan. 3, 1983
Chandler (Wash.)—Jan. 3, 1983
Gekas (Pa.)—Jan. 3, 1983
Johnson (Conn.)—Jan. 3, 1983
Kasich (Ohio)—Jan. 3, 1983
Lewis (Fla.)—Jan. 3, 1983
McCandless (Calif.)—Jan. 3, 1983
Packard (Calif.)—Jan. 3, 1983
Ridge (Pa.)—Jan. 3, 1983
Smith, Robert F. (Ore.)—Jan. 3, 1983
Sundquist (Tenn.)—Jan. 3, 1983
Vucanovich (Nev.)—Jan. 3, 1983
92. Schaefer (Colo.)—March 29, 1983
93. Saxton (N.J.)—Nov. 6, 1984
94. Dornan (Calif.) (three terms previously)—Jan. 3, 1985
95. Armey (Texas)—Jan. 3, 1985
Barton (Texas)—Jan. 3, 1985
Bentley (Md.)—Jan. 3, 1985
Callahan (Ala.)—Jan. 3, 1985
Coble (N.C.)—Jan. 3, 1985
Combest (Texas)—Jan. 3, 1985
DeLay (Texas)—Jan. 3, 1985
Fawell (Ill.)—Jan. 3, 1985
Gallo (N.J.)—Jan. 3, 1985
Henry (Mich.)—Jan. 3, 1985
Kolbe (Ariz.)—Jan. 3, 1985
Lightfoot (Iowa)—Jan. 3, 1985
McMillan (N.C.)—Jan. 3, 1985
Meyers (Kan.)—Jan. 3, 1985
Miller (Wash.)—Jan. 3, 1985
Slaughter (Va.)—Jan. 3, 1985
111. Ballenger (N.C.)—Nov. 4, 1986
112. Baker (La.)—Jan. 6, 1987
Bunning (Ky.)—Jan. 6, 1987
Gallegly (Calif.)—Jan. 6, 1987
Grandy (Iowa)—Jan. 6, 1987
Hastert (Ill.)—Jan. 6, 1987
Hefley (Colo.)—Jan. 6, 1987
Herger (Calif.)—Jan. 6, 1987
Holloway (La.)—Jan. 6, 1987
Houghton (N.Y.)—Jan. 6, 1987
Inhofe (Okla.)—Jan. 6, 1987
Kyl (Ariz.)—Jan. 6, 1987
Morella (Md.)—Jan. 6, 1987
Ravenel (S.C.)—Jan. 6, 1987
Rhodes (Ariz.)—Jan. 6, 1987
Smith (Texas)—Jan. 6, 1987
Upton (Mich.)—Jan. 6, 1987
Weldon (Pa.)—Jan. 6, 1987
129. Shays (Conn.)—Aug. 18, 1987
130. McCrery (La.)—April 16, 1988
131. Duncan (Tenn.)—Nov. 8, 1988
132. Campbell (Calif.)—Jan. 3, 1989
Cox (Calif.)—Jan. 3, 1989
Gillmor (Ohio)—Jan. 3, 1989
Goss (Fla.)—Jan. 3, 1989
Hancock (Mo.)—Jan. 3, 1989
James (Fla.)—Jan. 3, 1989
Machtley (R.I.)—Jan. 3, 1989
Paxon (N.Y.)—Jan. 3, 1989
Rohrabacher (Calif.)—Jan. 3, 1989
Schiff (N.M.)—Jan. 3, 1989
Stearns (Fla.)—Jan. 3, 1989
Walsh (N.Y.)—Jan. 3, 1989
144. Thomas (Wyo.)—April 26, 1989
145. Ros-Lehtinen (Fla.)—Aug. 29, 1989
146. Molinari (N.Y.)—March 20, 1990
147. Allard (Colo.)—Jan. 3, 1991
Barrett (Neb.)—Jan. 3, 1991
Boehner (Ohio)—Jan. 3, 1991
Camp (Mich.)—Jan. 3, 1991
Cunningham (Calif.)—Jan. 3, 1991
Doolittle (Calif.)—Jan. 3, 1991
Franks (Conn.)—Jan. 3, 1991
Gilchrest (Md.)—Jan. 3, 1991
Hobson (Ohio)—Jan. 3, 1991
Klug (Wis.)—Jan. 3, 1991
Nichols (Kan.)—Jan. 3, 1991
Nussle (Iowa)—Jan. 3, 1991
Ramstad (Minn.)—Jan. 3, 1991
Riggs (Calif.)—Jan. 3, 1991
Santorum (Pa.)—Jan. 3, 1991
Taylor (N.C.)—Jan. 3, 1991
Zeliff (N.H.)—Jan. 3, 1991
Zimmer (N.J.)—Jan. 3, 1991
165. Johnson (Texas)—May 22, 1991
166. Ewing (Ill.)—July 2, 1991

** Ireland and Stump began their House service Jan. 3, 1977, as Democrats, but later switched parties. The GOP Conference let their seniority count from 1977.*

Pronunciation Guide for Congress

The following is an informal pronunciation guide for some of the most-often-mispronounced names of members of Congress:

SENATE

Daniel K. Akaka, D-Hawaii (ah KAH ka)
John B. Breaux, D-La. (BRO)
Alfonse M. D'Amato, R-N.Y. (dah MAH toe)
Tom Daschle, D-S.D. (DASH el)
Dennis DeConcini, D-Ariz. (dee con SEE nee)
Pete V. Domenici, R-N.M. (da MEN ah chee)
Wyche Fowler Jr., D-Ga. (WHYch)
Daniel K. Inouye, D-Hawaii (in NO ay)
Joseph I. Lieberman, D-Conn. (LEE ber mun)

HOUSE

Les AuCoin, D-Ore. (oh COIN)
Jim Bacchus, D-Fla. (BACK us)
Anthony C. Beilenson, D-Calif. (BEE lin son)
Doug Bereuter, R-Neb. (BEE right er)
Michael Bilirakis, R-Fla. (bill a RACK us)
Ben Blaz, R-Guam (BLAHS)
Sherwood Boehlert, R-N.Y. (BO lert)
John A. Boehner, R-Ohio (BAY ner)
David E. Bonior, D-Mich. (BON yer)
Rick Boucher, D-Va. (BOUGH cher)
Albert G. Bustamante, D-Texas (BOOST uh MAHN tay)
Lawrence Coughlin, R-Pa. (COFF lin)
Peter A. DeFazio, D-Ore. (da FAH zio)
Rosa DeLauro, D-Conn. (da LAUR oh)
Mervyn M. Dymally, D-Calif. (DIE mal ee)
Ben Erdreich, D-Ala. (ER dritch)
Eni F. H. Faleomavaega, D-Am. Samoa (EN ee FALL eh oh mavah ENGA)
Dante B. Fascell, D-Fla. (DON tay fuh SELL)
Harris W. Fawell, R-Ill. (FAY well)
Vic Fazio, D-Calif. (FAY zee o)
Edward F. Feighan, D-Ohio (FEE an)
Thomas M. Foglietta, D-Pa. (fo lee ET ah)
Jaime B. Fuster, Pop. Dem.-P.R. (HI may foo STAIR)
Elton Gallegly, R-Calif. (GAL uh glee)
Sam Gejdenson, D-Conn. (GAY den son)
Frank J. Guarini, D-N.J. (gwar EE nee)
George J. Hochbrueckner, D-N.Y. (HOCK brewk ner)
Amo Houghton, R-N.Y. (AY mo HO tun)
James M. Inhofe, R-Okla. (IN hoff)
John R. Kasich, R-Ohio (KAY sick)
Barbara B. Kennelly, D-Conn. (ka NEL ly)
Gerald D. Kleczka, D-Wis. (KLETCH ka)
Jim Kolbe, R-Ariz. (COLE bee)
Mike Kopetski, D-Ore. (ka PET skee)
Robert J. Lagomarsino, R-Calif. (LAH go mar SEE no)
Larry LaRocco, D-Idaho (la ROCK oh)
Greg Laughlin, D-Texas (LAWF lin)
Richard H. Lehman, D-Calif. (LEE mun)
William Lehman, D-Fla. (LAY mun)
Mel Levine, D-Calif. (la VINE)
Nita M. Lowey, D-N.Y. (LOW ee)
Ronald K. Machtley, R-R.I. (MAKE lee)
Ron Marlenee, R-Mont. (MAR la nay)
Nicholas Mavroules, D-Mass. (mah VROOL iss)
Bob McEwen, R-Ohio (ma KEW in)
Kweisi Mfume, D-Md. (kwy E say mm FU may)
Robert J. Mrazek, D-N.Y. (ma RAH zik)
David R. Obey, D-Wis. (O bee)
Frank Pallone Jr., D-N.J. (pa LONE)
Nancy Pelosi, D-Calif. (pel LO see)
Thomas E. Petri, R-Wis. (PEE try)
Glenn Poshard, D-Ill. (pa SHARD)
Arthur Ravenel Jr., R-S.C. (RAV nel)
Ralph Regula, R-Ohio (REG you la)
Dana Rohrabacher, R-Calif. (ROAR ah bach er)
Ileana Ros-Lehtinen, R-Fla. (il ee ANNA ross LAY tin nen)
Marge Roukema, R-N.J. (ROCK ah ma)
George E. Sangmeister, D-Ill. (SANG my stir)
Rick Santorum, R-Pa. (san TORE um)
Bill Sarpalius, D-Texas (sar POLL us)
James H. Scheuer, D-N.Y. (SHOY yur)
Steven H. Schiff, R-N.M. (SHIFF)
Patricia Schroeder, D-Colo. (SHRO dur)
Richard T. Schulze, R-Pa. (SHOOLS)
Jose E. Serrano, D-N.Y. (ho ZAY sa RAH no) (rolled 'R')
W. J. "Billy" Tauzin, D-La. (TOE zan)
Robert G. Torricelli, D-N.J. (tor ah SELL ee)
Jolene Unsoeld, D-Wash. (UN sold)
Guy Vander Jagt, R-Mich. (VAN der jack)
Peter J. Visclosky, D-Ind. (vis KLOSS key)
Barbara F. Vucanovich, R-Nev. (voo CAN oh vitch)
Gus Yatron, D-Pa. (YA trin)
Bill Zeliff, R-N.H. (ZELL iff)

Close Calls in 1990 House Elections

There was a marked upsurge in competitive House elections in 1990 after a relative paucity of such contests in the late 1980s. Sixty members (35 Democrats, 25 Republicans) won seats last year with no more than 55 percent of the vote, up from 38 members in 1988. Moreover, 35 of the 1990 crop of "marginal" victors were incumbents, up from 21 in 1988. Of the others who won with 55 percent or less in 1990, 13 were competing for open seats and 12 were challengers.

In the chart below, House incumbents are designated by the letter "I," with the year they were first elected appearing in parentheses. Members who won in 1990 as challengers are designated by the letter "C" and open-seat winners by the designation "OS."

The numbers at right are their percentage shares of the 1990 vote, based on official returns from state election agencies, and are based on total votes cast (not just major-party votes).

Democrats

1) Frank Pallone Jr. (N.J. 3)	I ('88)	49.1
2) Joan Kelly Horn (Mo. 2)	C	50.0
3) Bernard J. Dwyer (N.J. 6)	I ('80)	50.5
Al Swift (Wash. 2)	I ('78)	50.5
5) Carl C. Perkins (Ky. 7)	I ('84)	50.8
6) Tim Roemer (Ind. 3)	C	50.9
7) Charles Luken (Ohio 1)	OS	51.1
8) James P. Moran Jr. (Va. 8)	C	51.7
9) Jim Bacchus (Fla. 11)	OS	51.9
10) Nick J. Rahall II (W.Va. 4)	I ('76)	52.0
11) Rosa DeLauro (Conn. 3)	OS	52.1
12) Chester G. Atkins (Mass. 5)	I ('84)	52.2
Earl Hutto (Fla. 1)	I ('78)	52.2
14) Ben Jones (Ga. 4)	I ('88)	52.4
15) William J. Jefferson (La. 2)	OS	52.5
16) George E. Brown Jr. (Calif. 36)	I ('62)	52.7
Dick Swett (N.H. 2)	C	52.7
18) Larry LaRocco (Idaho 1)	OS	53.0
Marilyn Lloyd (Tenn. 3)	I ('74)	53.0
20) Jim Jontz (Ind. 5)	I ('86)	53.1
21) Robert J. Mrazek (N.Y. 3)	I ('82)	53.3
22) Gerry E. Studds (Mass. 10)	I ('72)	53.4
23) Chet Edwards (Texas 11)	OS	53.5
Collin C. Peterson (Minn. 7)	C	53.5
25) Frank Annunzio (Ill. 11)	I ('64)	53.6
26) Jolene Unsoeld (Wash. 3)	I ('88)	53.8
27) Robert E. Andrews (N.J. 1)	OS	54.3
Greg Laughlin (Texas 14)	I ('88)	54.3
29) Calvin Dooley (Calif. 17)	C	54.5
30) John W. Cox Jr. (Ill. 16)	OS	54.6
31) Vic Fazio (Calif. 4)	I ('78)	54.7
Frank McCloskey (Ind. 8)	I ('82)	54.7
33) John J. LaFalce (N.Y. 32)	I ('74)	55.0
W. G. "Bill" Hefner (N.C. 8)	I ('74)	55.0
Mike Kopetski (Ore. 5)	C	55.0

Republicans

1) Frank Riggs (Calif. 1)	C	43.3
2) Randy "Duke" Cunningham (Calif. 44)	C	46.3
3) Bill Lowery (Calif. 41)	I ('80)	49.2
4) Al McCandless (Calif. 37)	I ('82)	49.7
5) Jim Nussle (Iowa 2)	OS	49.8
6) Newt Gingrich (Ga. 6)	I ('78)	50.3
7) Charles H. Taylor (N.C. 11)	C	50.7
8) Olympia J. Snowe (Maine 2)	I ('78)	51.0
Herbert H. Bateman (Va. 1)	I ('82)	51.0
10) Bill Barrett (Neb. 3)	OS	51.1
11) Bill Dickinson (Ala. 2)	I ('64)	51.3
12) Rick Santorum (Pa. 18)	C	51.4
13) John T. Doolittle (Calif. 14)	OS	51.5
14) Don Young (Alaska AL)	I ('73)	51.7
Gary Franks (Conn. 5)	OS	51.7
16) Tom Coleman (Mo. 6)	I ('76)	51.9
17) John Miller (Wash. 1)	I ('84)	52.0
18) Mel Hancock (Mo. 7)	I ('88)	52.1
James V. Hansen (Utah 1)	I ('80)	52.1
20) Scott L. Klug (Wis. 2)	C	53.2
21) Toby Roth (Wis. 8)	I ('78)	53.5
22) Wayne Allard (Colo. 4)	OS	54.1
23) Robert J. Lagomarsino (Calif. 19)	I ('74)	54.6
Raymond J. McGrath (N.Y. 5)	I ('80)	54.6
25) Guy Vander Jagt (Mich. 9)	I ('66)	54.8

Index

D

E

F

G

H

I, J

K

L

O

P

Q, R

S

T

U, V

W

X, Y, Z